Presented to

_____

_____

By

_____

Date

_____

HOME RELIGIOUS LIBRARY

Containing the

Holy Bible with the Old and New Testament

COMMONLY KNOWN AS THE AUTHORISED OR
KING JAMES VERSION

THE SOUTHWESTERN COMPANY
NASHVILLE, TENNESSEE

TABLE OF CONTENTS

[*Arranged in Sequence as the Features Appear in the Bible*]

* * *

BOOKS OF THE BIBLE

THE BOOKS OF THE OLD TESTAMENT

THE BOOKS OF THE NEW TESTAMENT

ALPHABETICAL INDEX OF THE BOOKS OF THE BIBLE

CONTENTS
OF THE
BOOKS OF THE BIBLE

6

CONTENTS.

CONTENTS.

CONTENTS.

CONTENTS.

CHRISTIAN HOME

The home is God's first institution and today remains central in its importance to the life of a Christian. The mutual nurture and affection of the members of the Christian home and family is a central refuge from the traps and snares of the world. The influence of a strong Christian home does not end. The witness of the family members to the world expands around the lives of its current members. In addition, as each child of a family grows up to begin their family, the blessings pass from generation to generation.

In a like manner, the influence of an evil home life is felt in the lives of its members. Particular forms of sin in ancestors continue in descendants, and qualities in parents are repeated in their children. This may be one reason why, in the Old Testament, children of offenders were slain with their parents, thus preventing the perpetuation of their sin (Num. 16:11; II Sam. 21:1-9). Occasionally, national features are thought of as being hereditary, and are traced back to a single source (Gen. 9:22-27; 21:20,21; 27; 49; Rom. 4:12; 11:26). But there are instances where this law of heredity is reversed for we read of godly fathers having ungodly sons, and of godly children coming from godless parents.

In the giving of the law to His people, God declared that He would visit "the iniquity of the fathers upon the children unto the third and fourth generation of them that hate me" (Exod. 20:5). But children are not condemned and punished for their inherited evil propensities—only for their practiced sinful desires (Ezek. 18:18-32). It is a fact, then, that under God's natural government of the world, the iniquity of parents is visited upon their children. As Ellicott in his comment on this divine law observes,

> Diseases caused by vicious courses are transmitted. The extravagance of parents leave their children beggars. To be the son of a felon is to be heavily handicapped in the race of life . . . We all inherit countless disadvantages on account of our first parents' sin. We each individually inherit special tendencies to this or that form of evil from the misconduct of our several progenitors.

While there are more deeply involved aspects of this law of heredity that we might touch upon, sufficient has been said that this is part of the scheme of divine government by which our world is governed; and that because of this, it is the solemn obligation of parents not to put their children at a disadvantage by not checking in themselves any evil tendency they have inherited. Always aware of the example they set, parents must seek to live sanctified and separated lives so that their children may grow up "dead indeed unto sin, and alive unto God," thereby averting "the law unto sin." The birth of children can become the highest exercise of a faith giving glory to God, and the truest means of advancing the spiritual life of parents and children, as well as the interests of Christ's cause on earth.

The Seal And Promise Of The Covenant. The faith of parents needs just what the faith of every believer does, namely, the willingness to understand, to get an insight into what God has undertaken to be and do. The Bible says "By faith we understand". When faith grasps the truth of divine planning and undertaking then it is a simple exercise to rest and trust, to praise and act. Thus, when believing parents meditate upon the revelation of God as understood and acted upon; and believing, there is the joyous expectation of the fulfillment of the desire to have a home—holy to the Lord. Is this not the testimony of many of the families of ancient Israel; and is it not here that we can appreciate the divine covenant concerning children?

Constitution of the Covenant. Among the several covenants mentioned in Scripture is the prominent one associated with the children of believing parents. In order to comprehend the significance of such a covenant, it is necessary to carry with us an understanding of the nature of a covenant. Some authorities suggest that the word, "covenant," springs from the Assyrian root meaning "fetter" or "to bind," and implies a binding contract between parties, whether between God and man, or between men and men. It is affirmed that there are two shades of meaning, somewhat distinct, of the Hebrew word for

covenant. One is when it is properly a covenant, that is, a solemn mutual agreement.

The other word carries more of a command, that is, instead of an obligation voluntarily assumed, it is an obligation imposed by a superior upon an inferior—which is the nature of all covenants between God and men.

A covenant, then, between contracting parties, is an agreement of a solemn and binding force. Among the early Semites, a covenant was primarily a "blood brotherhood" in which two men became brothers by drinking each other's blood. Such an act not only bound the two together but also brought them into a relationship with the god of the clan who was supposed to govern the community life of the clan. The Old Testament covenant related to children is sometimes expressed in the form of an oath, with promised blessing upon its keeping, or with a curse invoked if the oath or covenant is disregarded.

As used by David, the term is employed in a more general way of an alliance of friendship and confidence between God and those who are His people—"The secret of the Lord is with them that fear him; and he will shew them his covenant" (Ps. 25:14).

Children of the Covenant. When Luke penned the phrase, "the children . . . of the covenant" (Acts 3:25), he traced such a contract back through the ages when God said to Abraham—"He that shall come forth out of thine own bowels shall be thine heir. And he believed in the Lord; and he counted it to him for righteousness" (Gen. 15:4,6). The patriarch had poured out his complaint, "Behold, I go childless," but God made an agreement with Abraham that he would have an heir, whose descendants should be as "the sand of the seashore in multitude." Thus, the natural longing for a child became the channel of the most wonderful fellowship with God, and the natural seed became the heir of God's promise and spiritual blessing.

Although God had begun to acknowledge with Noah the validity of the oneness of parents and children in the dealings of grace—"Come thou and all thy house into the ark" (Gen. 7:1)—there was no previous covenant between God and Noah concerning the latter's children. But with Abraham it was different. From Abraham, in every Hebrew home, the child was to be taken up into the covenant with the promise that from its birth it would be the object of God's care and the parent's faith. In all that is involved in the contract between God and Abraham, concerning children, believing parents are taught that it is not only in their individual capacity, but especially as parents that from the first hope of having children, they are, themselves, in covenant relationship with God, and are called to exercise Abraham's faith.

Thereafter they must receive their children as coming from God's hands, and as being embraced in the covenant between Him and the parents. Being endowed with the wondrous power of bringing children into the world, consecrated parents must fully understand the promises connected with the birth of their offspring, and of how, by faith, they can claim their children for the Lord. Andrew Murray would have us know that this precious truth concentrates on one great lesson, namely—

> The fatherhood and the childhood of this earth hath a Divine and heavenly promise, and everything connected with it must with us be a matter of faith, a religious service holy to the Lord and well-pleasing in His sight.

I must not only believe for myself; if I would fully honour God, my faith must reach forth and embrace my children, grasping the promises of God for them, too. If I would "magnify the riches of God's grace," if I would with my whole nature and all my powers be consecrated to God's service, and if I would accomplish the utmost possible within my reach for the advancement of His Kingdom, it is especially as *parent* that I must believe and labour.

The promise is, "According to your faith be it unto you," and believing parents experience that there is nothing that so mightily quickens the growth of their faith as the reaching out after the divine blessing for their children. There is no limit to what God is able to accomplish through a believing parenthood, as the promise of God is embraced and the power of faith is exercised. It is in this way that "the natural seed becomes the heir of spiritual blessing, and the parental relationship one of the best schools for the life of faith." Our heavenly Father, who has taken into His covenant charge and keeping godly parenthood, has also contracted to sanctify and bless the seed of His people.

Certainty of the Covenant. Another aspect of the covenant God made with Abraham was the assurance that the same promise applied to parents and child alike; and that with the sanctification of the parents, God has a better opportunity of claiming possession of their children before sins get the mastery. Covenant faithfulness is expressed in the phrases—"I will establish my covenant between me and *thee and thy seed* after thee . . . I will be a God unto thee, and to thy seed after thee" (Gen. 17:7).

"A God unto thee, and to thy seed." What a blessed promise, so certain of fulfillment! Because God is true, He cannot go back upon His word, and if the condition of faith is met, He will see to it that the faith of parents for their children will not be disappointed. What must not be forgotten is the fact that God does not hold His promise in abeyance to wait for the child's faith, but the promise is given in response to the faith of the parents with the assurance that the child's faith will follow. Thus, venturing all upon God's faithfulness, and striving after personal holiness, parents, in the training of their children, have the joy of seeing them loving and serving the same Lord. This is the way that children of the covenant become the children of God. Fathers and mothers must believe, not only for themselves, but for the sake of their children.

Command of the Covenant. It is perfectly true, as James reminds us, that, "Faith without works is dead"—a truth that applies to parental faith as well as personal faith. Such parental faith in God's promise concerning children will be manifested by parental faithfulness to God's will in respect to conduct and action. As a parent, Abraham had the reputation of being obedient to the divine command—

> I know him (Abraham), that he will command his children and his household after him, and they shall keep the way of the Lord, to do justice and judgment; that the Lord may bring upon Abraham that which he hath spoken of him (Gen. 18:19).

Faithful parenthood is fully sympathetic with God's plans for the spiritual training of children. Helpless babes are committed into the hands of believing parents for them to influence for God, so that they, too, may become members

of His family on earth. Emphasis in God's conception of Abraham's character is upon the word "command"—"To the end he may *command* his children." It is to be feared that far too many parents do not discern the harmony between authority and love, between obedience and liberty. They forget that as parents they have been clothed by God with a holy authority, to be lovingly exercised in leading their children into paths of righteousness.

There is a sense in which parents are potters, and their children the clay, waiting to be molded according to the divine plan. Their character waits to be influenced by the quiet, tender exercise of authority which, when strengthened by the silent testimony of a living example, never fails in its purpose. Alas! the spirit of modern permissiveness and liberty have penetrated our family life with disastrous results. Command is a missing element in parenthood, and one which children, who have been pampered, and allowed to have their own way, have grown up to scorn. Thomas Carlyle could write, "I acknowledge to all —but omnipotence of early culture and nurture." Would that we had more homes today providing a similar upbringing of children! It was Sir H. Baker who gave us the lines—

> O ye who came that Babe to lay
> Within a Saviour's arms to-day,
> Watch well and guard with careful eye,
> The Heir of Immortality!

Compensation of the Covenant. The promised reward of parental faith and faithfulness is both sure and large. Confident that "Abraham would command his children and his household after him" the divine benediction followed—"That the Lord may bring upon Abraham that which he hath spoken of him." The rich blessings of the covenant came true in the experience of Abraham and Sarah. Linked together in the covenant were their faithfulness and the fulfillment of God's promise. Is it any wonder that because of his performance of the covenant obligation Abraham was rewarded by being called, "the friend of God"?

The prophet Jeremiah would have us know that it is part of God's covenant that He will first teach parents to keep it, and then reward, in His own bountiful way, that keeping. "I will give them one heart, and one way, that they may fear me for ever, for the good of them, and of *their children after them*" (Jer. 32:39). That the psalmist agrees with the prophet as to the blessing accruing from a fulfilled covenant is evident from the words of David that "The mercy of the LORD is from everlasting to everlasting upon them that fear him, and his righteousness unto children's children" (Ps. 103:17). There are two sides to the coin of parental responsibility, namely, to be full of faith, and then to be faithful.

Being full of faith implies implicit trust in the living God, in His covenant for parents and children alike, in His promises for a home ordered after His will, and in His faithfulness to undertake according to His Word.

Being faithful is the other side of the coin. If we are full of faith, then, we shall be faith-full, taking the Bible as the measure of life for the whole family.

Parental faithfulness involves self-discipline and the constant exercise of faith, and results in the blessing of having children like olive plants about the table (Ps. 128). How parents—and all believers—have to pray for that ever-growing faith which is the root of an ever-growing faithfulness! Well might all believing parents pray as Andrew Murray suggests they should—

O my God! hast Thou indeed taken me too into this wonderful covenant, in which Thou art the God of the seed of Thy saints, and makest them the ministers of Thy grace to their children? Open my eyes, I pray Thee, to see the full glory of this Thy covenant, that my faith may know all that Thou hast prepared for me to bestow, and may do all Thou hast prepared for me to perform. O my God! may Thy covenant-keeping faithfulness be the life and strength of my faith. May this faith make me faithful in keeping the covenant.

The Folly of Favoritism. We have already indicated that parents are under the obligation of exercising authority or rule in the home. Some are more naturally rulers than others and command obedience. Reluctance to rule, however, does not take away the responsibility of the parent. Failure to control can result in dire consequences for parent and child alike. One of the saddest rebukes administered to a godly parent for being too indulgent of his children was that which Eli received from God. The aged priest had been unceasingly faithful to God's house and was ready to die for the Ark of God, but he had proved unfaithful as a parent. He loved his sons too much to restrain them. Hophni and Phinehas "made themselves vile, and he (Eli) restrained them not," and such parental weakness brought severe judgment upon the house of Eli (I Sam. 3:13; 4:17).

Tenderhearted, good-natured parents may find it hard to reprove, to thwart, or to punish a child for wrongdoing. But such misnamed kindness is actually unkindness in that it has terrible consequences. When conscience or experience tells parents that they have been too easygoing and guilty of consulting the will and the feelings of their children more than the will and honor of God, they should ponder carefully how Eli and his home came under God's judgment. Parents are destined of God to bear in the home the likeness of His own Fatherly rule, but if they are weak in disciplinary rule, then the character of their children suffer. God-appointed parental rule in the family is the symbol of His own authority, in which parents and children alike are to honor Him: to dishonor Him is to lose His favor and blessing.

Another aspect of parental weakness is that of favoritism in a family; and because "the greatest favorites are in the most danger of falling," as a German proverb puts it, conspicuous preference should be avoided. How apparent this is in the tragic experiences overtaking the home-life of Isaac and Rebekah! While there are those who feel that Rebekah should not be blamed for her partiality, seeing she had a better right to the preference she cultivated than Isaac had to his preference for Esau, the fact remains that the harmony of that ancient home was destroyed through the parents taking sides. "Isaac loved Esau . . . Rebekah loved Jacob." No wonder Esau came to hate Jacob and caused his mother to become weary of her life (Gen. 25:28; 27:41,46). If Esau and Jacob had been equally loved, the friction, jealousy, deception, sorrow, and separation would not have marred their home.

As the two boys grew up, diverse characteristics appeared. Esau became "a cunning hunter, a man of the field," that is, one who loved to roam over the open, uncultivated wilderness in search of game. And Isaac, his father, loved Esau "because he (Isaac) did eat of his venison" which Esau caught. Thus it would seem that Isaac's love for his son originated in a very selfish cause. But with Jacob it was different. He was "a plain man," that is, one of general integrity or uprightness. Esau was more at home

in a tent out in the wide open spaces, but Jacob preferred to stay at home and busy himself with domestic occupations, and, always around his mother, he became her favorite.

Commenting upon the difference of affection on the part of Isaac and Rebekah, Matthew Henry says that "they had but these two children, and, it seems, one was the father's darling and the other the mother's.

(1) Isaac loved to have his son active. Esau knew how to please him, and showed a great respect for him, by treating him often with venison.

(2) Rebekah was mindful of the oracle of God, which had given the preference to Jacob, and therefore she preferred him in her love."

It is quite natural for children to reveal differing temperaments and characteristics as they grow, if all are equally loved then there is unity in the home in spite of diversity. The folly of Isaac and Rebekah was the way they allowed the varying characters of their two children to result in a divergence of feeling toward them. How true it is that as we sow we reap, for when one of the boys became a man and a father of many children, he exhibited the favoritism of his old home, and experienced something of the hatred and agony following in its train. "Israel (Jacob) loved Joseph more than all his children, because he was the son of his old age" (Gen. 37:3). Favoring him above the others, Jacob made him a beautiful coat, with what result? "His brethren saw that their father loved him more than all his brethren, they hated him, and could not speak peaceably unto him." From then on they plotted his death. This demonstrates again the importance of the parent's example and its effect upon their children and children's children.

From the harmful influence of undue favoritism in a home, often causing it to become divided against itself, there is a justifiable favoritism we can heartily recommend. If a child is born mentally or physically deficient, after the initial shock it is often amazing how such an afflicted one becomes the chief one in the family to receive love, patience, care, and sacrifice. What devoted attention this unfortunate child receives from all the rest at home! One has known of homes in which there was a Mongoloid child receiving a wealth of affection that was simply overwhelming to witness. All praise to those parents who are able to favor a stricken child in the family circle!

The Rod of Correction. Among some present-day educators of the young, the abolition of punishment or discipline is stressed. Children must not be repressed or corrected, but given freedom to express themselves as they want to. The Bible, however, thinks differently and has a good deal to say about child correction, as well as God's correction of His children. "Happy is the man whom God correcteth" (Job 5:17; Prov. 3:12; Jer. 2:19; 10:24; 30:11). But think of these exhortations related to child discipline and punishment—

"Correct thy son, and he shall give thee rest; yea, he shall give delight unto thy soul" (Prov. 29:17).

"We have had fathers . . . which corrected us" (Heb. 12:9. See Prov. 3:11,12).

"Foolishness is bound in the heart of a child; but the rod of correction shall drive it far from him" (Prov. 22:15).

"Withhold not correction from the child; for if thou beatest him with the rod, he shall not die" (Prov. 23:13).

"Your children . . . received no correction" (Jer. 2:30; 5:3).

"Train up a child in the way he should go" (Prov. 22:6).

"He that spareth his rod hateth his son" (Prov. 13:24).

Boswell in his monumental *Life of Johnson*, quotes the saying of Samuel Johnson (1709-1784)—"The rod produces an effect which terminates in itself. A child is afraid of being whipped, and gets his task, and there's an end on't." It is from Samuel Butler's *Hudibras* that we have the phrase—"Spare the rod, and spoil the child." There are certainly a good many spoiled "brats" in home and school simply because the rod was spared on them.

Although the education of a Jewish child was stern, paternal and maternal affection for children who were worthy of it was never stinted. We read of Jacob that "All his sons and all his daughters rose up to comfort him" in the hour of his grief (Gen. 37:35). Another touching and vivid example of parental love is heard in Jacob's despairing cry when Benjamin, the child of his old age, was taken from him (Gen. 44:20).

It is to be regretted that we have come to a time when parental authority has become a joke, and discipline is a forgotten word. As for self-restraint, it hardly exists. Too many parents indulge their children in the delusion that they are being good to them, and so we have a young generation possessed by a mania for "a good time." Lord Mountbatten, the renowned British naval hero, had some pertinent things to say to a reporter who interviewed him in his vice-regal home in Hampshire. Talking of his life and times, and of being a stickler for discipline, this famous figure said—

Discipline in general is anathema to youth. It has become a dirty word and youngsters believe it means square-bashing and a half-a-dozen on the backside. But that's not the point of the word. It comes from the Latin and it means teaching, the instruction of disciples . . . I am trying not to be pompous, but being disciplined is being able to control yourself to your best advantage.

Why is the new generation kicking over the traces? Because there has been a lack of discipline, a lack of teaching by their parents . . . and yet youth lacks belief in its parents. Young people should give their parents credit for what they have done.

It is therefore evident that in the purpose of God there must be parental correction as well as parental instruction. God loves children and desires their parents to train them for Himself, just as He wants those whom He loves, and chastizes, for Himself (Rev. 3:19). Parents who are disciplined of God make the best kind of parents, for being subject to divine rule they are fitted to rule their house well. Self-rule is the secret of all rule; as you honor the law yourself in self-command, others learn to honor it too. As God cannot suffer sin to go unpunished in Christian parents, they in turn learn how to administer correction to disobedient children.

Parents, seeking to live under the hand of God, are quick to learn the simplest laws in the art of ruling their children during their growth. All hard, harsh, loveless tones, and punishment beyond what is merited, must be avoided. Parents acting as despotic rulers only add to youthful rebellion. Any necessary rebuke must be given in a quiet deliberate tone with self-control; and if the rod is required it must be held with a hand of tender love. If done this way it will hurt the parent more than the child. It is because weakness can become wickedness,

both in child and parent, that rebuke is necessary. Therefore, not to rule and restrain our children, never to repress them, but always to give them their own way implies that we honor them more than the God who commands parents to exercise authority in the ordering of their home.

The Divine Pattern of Parenthood. Our heavenly Father has not left Himself without witness even in the human parenthood on earth. That the earthly relationship is a reflection of the heavenly is borne by our Lord's question to His own—"If ye then, being evil, know how to give good gifts unto your children, how much more shall your Father which is in heaven give good things to them that ask him?" (Matt. 7:11).

From the fatherliness of God we can learn a great deal about our parental obligations. As He created man in His image and after His likeness, so our children should be, not only objects of our love, but also a reflection of our Godward aspirations. The more the parental heart of God is understood, the truer and more joyful the parenthood on earth. This is one reason why home life is a school as much for training parents as children; the deepest mysteries of God's love are best studied by a parent in his own bosom. The truth Jesus stressed was that if we, who are so imperfect as parents, can do so much for our children, what greater things God the perfect Father, the Fountain of Love, can accomplish for us.

A further lesson to be learned as we compare the fatherhood of heaven with the fatherhood of earth, is that in creating us as parents, God meant us in a real and solemn sense to be His imagebearers, in every way copying Him as our Father so that with Him as our model, the fullest spiritual influence can be exercised upon our children. He educates us as His children into His ways and purposes until they become our own, so we must train our children in the life we seek to live in Christ. It is in this way that children naturally rise from the Christ reflected in the home, to the unseen Christ above, and the home become the gate to the Father's home in heaven. The bright, living, happy piety of the parents, a mingling of holy reverence to God with childlike love, shines on the children from their early youth, so that the name of God as Father will become linked with all that is lovely and holy in the memory of the child.

Alas! the best of us as parents have to confess that we have come far short of such a divine ideal. Having failed in our obligation Godward, we failed to surround our children with those holy influences so necessary as a safeguard as they come to face the temptations in the world.

The Apostle Paul has some pointed things to say to parents, especially if they have any official association with church life and work. Whether elders or deacons, they were under the obligation of "ruling their own children and their own houses well," for unless they ruled well their own home, having "their children in subjection with all gravity," how could they expect to take care of the church of God? (I Tim. 3:4,5,12). Yet many of us have known godly preachers having children who, by lip and life, contradict the solemn truths they were brought up to revere. What a heartbreak it is for a pastor or evangelist to be used in the salvation of others, yet to have those of their own flesh and blood untouched by their influence and ministry! Generally speaking, however, godly homes produce godly heirs.

Example Is Better Than Precept. Both example and precept are necessary in the moral and spiritual culture of children, but the truth lived out day by day in the home gives added force to the truth taught. How apt is the question of Paul as we think of personal, parental self-culture, "Thou therefore which teachest another, teachest thou not thyself?" (Rom. 2:21). The security of children for Christ depends far more upon the life of a parent than upon what he may say. There is no doubt whatever that the atmosphere of a truly Christian, well-regulated home, in which quiet thoughtfulness in speech and act, all unconsciously sets its mark on the children within it.

"Johnny," said a father to his child, who was hesitating about obeying his father's will, "whose will must you do, your own or papa's?"

"Papa's will," was the reluctant answer. But another question followed from child to parent.

"But whose will must papa do, then?"

At once, the father said, "God's will," and went on to explain that His will was a wiser and better will than his own.

To quote Andrew Murray—

> The parent who can appeal to his daily life with his children, that they know how he in all things seeks to do the will of his God, and can in his prayers, in their presence, appeal to his God too, will find in the witness of such a life a mighty power to inculcate obedience in the child.

Parents who desire their children to grow up loving, kind, teachable and obedient, must always be on their guard for little eyes are always watching, and little ears are always listening. What hope have parents of reproving or restraining occasional outbursts of temper in their children if they themselves give way to impulse and anger? Inconsistency nullifies good advice. An old saying has it, "Be what you would make others." It is in the daily life of the parents that the children gain their most indelible impressions. To rightly fill their place as parents, they must daily pray that there may be deeply imprinted on their heart the solemn thought that they can only effectually teach their children as they themselves are taught of God; that the truth influencing their lives will influence those whom God has given them to train.

Parents as Interpreters of Redemption. By a covenant of blood, God promised to be "the God of all the families of Israel." Was this not the message the sacrifice of the Lord's passover conveyed? Instructed of God, Moses exhorted Jewish parents to interpret to their children the origin of the Passover ordinance.

> "It shall come to pass, when your children shall say unto you, What mean ye by this service? That ye shall say, It is the sacrifice of the Lord's passover, who passed over the houses of the children of Israel in Egypt, when he smote the Egyptians, and delivered our houses"
>
> (Exod. 12:26,27).

Can you imagine how the Jewish children would sit open-eyed and enthralled as the story of that great deliverance was repeated? As parents kept the Feast, and observed all its requirements, a twofold aspect would be recognized by those performing the service.

The parents themselves dealt with God on behalf of their children, thus bringing down the blessing of heaven on them. The father of the home, as he sprinkled

the blood of a lamb upon his house, secured God's protection for all beneath its roof.

Then, in dealing with his children for God, the parent sought to lead them up to Him, and by instructing them in what God had done the parent would seek to lead his little ones to accept this mighty Deliverer as their own God. These two parts of parental instruction were closely and inseparably linked to each other, the first being the root and origin of the second—and the second being the full appropriation of the first. Like a *priest,* the parent would sprinkle the blood; and as a *prophet* he would instruct those sheltered by sacrifice.

As Jewish parents were under the obligation of interpreting the holy mystery of the Lord's Passover, so Christian parents have the solemn duty of explaining to their children the message of Christ dying on a cross for the sins of the world. Such interpretation involves the necessity of a personal salvation. The parent must know God, as the God of Redemption, if he is to convince his child of the true significance of the cross. This is the force of the injunction, "Thou shalt shew thy son in that day, saying, This is done because of that which the Lord did *unto me* when I came forth out of Egypt" (Exod. 13:8).

Another thought to contemplate is that when the Jewish father sprinkled the blood upon the door of his house he preserved his child as well as himself from the destroying angel. What the helpless child could not do for himself, his father did for him, and God, who had honored the father so to act in behalf of the child, accepted the deed. Thus, initially the child was made a partaker of the blessing of that sprinkled blood. Thereafter as the father pleaded with God on behalf of his child, he would remind Jehovah of the blood and the oath of the covenant, and claim for his loved one the blessing of redemption. The fervent hope of the parent would be that his child would grow up to personally accept and ratify the covenant.

With the joy of a personal experience of God's redeeming grace in their hearts, and the unceasing guidance of the Holy Spirit to train their children aright, Christian parents, as they testify of a Saviour's love, often have the thrill of seeing their children opening the avenues of their being to Him who died to have them as His children.

Parents and Teachers as Shepherds. While it is perfectly true that our tender heavenly Shepherd carries the lambs in His bosom, He has committed their guardianship to parents, pastors, and Sunday school teachers. These are the undershepherds little eyes can see and come to trust; and who, if they fail in their sacred trust, defeat the will and purpose of the Good Shepherd for His lambs. It is in this connection that we can understand the appeal of Jesus to Peter as He was about to ascend on high, leaving Peter to gather sheep and lambs into His fold. *Feed my lambs!* (John 21:15). What must not be lost sight of is the fact that this was our Lord's commission to His church of all time through Peter, and as such, reveals the place the rearing of little ones has in His loving heart!

Because the children of today will form His church of the morrow, heed must be given to Christ's special charge concerning them. As lambs children are weak and helpless. All who have the care of them must recognize their feebleness and nurture them in every way, seeing they are the hope of the future. Leaving a sheep farm in company with its master one evening, a friend heard him call to a shepherd, "Take great care of the lambs! There is a storm coming." Jesus knew what a terrific storm of persecution would overtake the infant church, and of how Peter himself would be martyred. Therefore we have the moving appeal of one of His last words before His Ascension, "Care for My lambs!"

Peter, as a fisherman, knew a good deal about fish, but *lambs,* well! they were outside his province. When Jesus called Peter to be an apostle, it was that he might become a "fisher of men"—his daily vocation becoming a symbol of his heavenly calling. Now, as the one-time fisherman stands on the threshold of the establishment of the church, his Lord announces that he is no longer a fisherman—catching men—but a shepherd—caring for lambs. Is there not a deep and significant meaning in such a change of occupation? What points of difference are there between fishing and lamb-rearing? Peter as a fisherman knew that what he caught in the sea he neither reared or fed, and once in his net only the full-grown, edible fish were retained, the little ones were cast back into the sea. Further, when caught, the fish were alive but quickly died and became fit for human consumption once dead.

But Peter is now to function as an undershepherd, exercising all possible care for the young and the feeble in Christ's church. If sheep are weak and helpless animals, how much more the little lambs who cannot look after themselves, and on whose growth the hope of the shepherd depends. Like lambs, children are endowed with potential that must be guarded and developed. For these frisky little creatures food is the condition of their growth so they must be fed with the pasture the shepherd provides. Can we imagine how Peter, facing the future as an undershepherd, would weigh the significance of each word of the Great Shepherd of the sheep?

Feed

Lambs cannot seek necessary food for themselves—those responsible for their welfare must supply it, and all they eat comes from without to be assimilated into their bodies. With the feeding of Christ's lambs it is the same. Their small bodies grow and mature by food from the visible world—their minds are nourished by the thoughts entering the mind—their spirits are fed by the precious words of God taught by parent or teacher. So, as a mother studies what her child should eat for its body, so she will strive to feed her lamb with thoughts of divine wisdom and love.

It was to one that had a deep love for Jesus who heard His request, *Feed* My lambs! and only those inspired by the love of, and to, Jesus can truly take charge of the lambs in home and school. It is thus that the food feeding them will have the warmth of a divine love about it. The relationship between parents and children is, or should be, one of love, and where such love is purified and elevated by the love of God, shed abroad in the heart by the Spirit of love, then the tending of the lambs is looked upon as a service of love for Him whose love is ever inspiring.

My

While parents may look upon their children as their own, seeing they are flesh of their flesh, Jesus reminded Peter that they were, primarily, *His* lambs—His property entrusted to parents and undershepherds to care for and

nurture. It is because those He is to use for the spiritual and moral welfare of the next generation are the children of today that those who have their growth in their hand must grasp the possibilities of the future and train them as the coming flock.

Can we say that we look upon children with the eyes of Jesus, and endeavor to catch His spirit as He pleads Feed My lambs? They are His, and He loves them because of their child-like simplicity and heavenliness, and counts them of great worth, not only for what they are, but also for what they are to become. Further, because they are His, we must daily love, feed, and care for them, that they may grow up as the sheep of His pasture. In his pentecostal sermon, Peter reminded the people that the promise of God's salvation was not only for them, but their children as well (Acts 2:39. See Isa. 44:3-5). The daily experience of the heavenly Shepherd's love in his own heart was a daily lesson to Peter on how to feed Christ's little flock of lambs, as well as the grown sheep of His flock.

Lambs

As already indicated, lambs are so dependent upon others. Left to themselves they are weak, feeble, and defenseless; and their very frailty and powerlessness compel shepherds to undertake their safety and provision. In using the figure of lambs, our Lord reminded Peter, and through him, all who have special charge of children, not only of their value but also of their need of all loving care because of their helplessness. It is because "but little children weak, Nor born in any high estate," that we must emulate the example of the divine Shepherd Himself who "gathers the lambs with his arm" (Isa. 40:11). The secret of influence as expressed by F. R. Havergal in the following lines can be adapted and applied to all who have the solemn charge of nourishing and rearing those who are tender in years—

> A Spirit whose power may touch and bind
> With unconscious influence every mind;
> Whose presence brings, like some fabled wand,
> The love which a monarch may not command;—
> As the spring awakens from cold repose
> The bloomless brier, the sweet wild rose—
> Such would I be!

The Necessity and Nature of Child Nurture. In the family of believers, Paul exhorts parents to bring their children up "in the nurture and admonition of the Lord" (Eph. 6:4). There is an inference here that the children of a home belong not only to the parents, but also to the Lord, and that, consequently, undue severity in instruction must not be countenanced. In all Christian education of His little ones there must be gentleness, forbearance and love. Ellicott reminds us that "Christianity gradually softened the stern authority exemplified in the old Roman Law." As to the phrase Paul employs, Ellicott says that it covers the two elements of education—

Nurture is a word signifying generally "the treatment to a child, but by usage appropriated to practical training, or teaching by discipline." This is the same word given as "chastening" in Hebrews 12:4-11.

Admonition implies the "putting children in mind" by word of instruction and is the same word translated "rebuke" in Tit. 3:10, inasmuch as it implies warning, being distinguished from teaching (Co. 3:16).

The principle of all child cultivation and discipline is the development of child faculties, until they reach the perfection of which a child is capable, and the preparation of the child to fulfill its destiny, then the parents' labor will not be in vain if it is *in the Lord*. It is only a full understanding of Solomon's pregnant phrase that is vastly important in all child nurture—"The way in which he should go" (Prov. 22:6), which, if followed, will not be departed from. "When he is old, he will not depart from it." The principle laid down here is universally true. In his exposition of Solomon's dictum, Andrew Murray stresses two points as to failures in the spiritual and moral failures in child-training—

(1) Either the parent did not make "the way in which he should go his one aim in the child's training . . . As to the way in which he should go," we need be in no doubt. "The way of the Lord" God calls it, when He speaks of Abraham training his children. Other designations of "the way in which he should go" come to mind—

"Walking in His ways"
"The way of His footsteps"
"The way of His commandments"
"The way of holiness"
"The way of peace"
"The way of life"
"The new and living way"
"Walk in Him"

Christ, who calls young and old alike to walk in His footsteps, says of Himself, "I am the way." The early, persecuted saints were those whom Saul found and bound of "this way" (Acts 9:2). If parents desire to see their children saved, and growing up in the fear of the Lord, they must from the beginning of their child's understanding guide their thoughts to the way they should go.

(2) Further, they must be "trained up," and the word for "train" is one of deep importance for parents and teachers to understand. Such essential training is not teaching, not commanding, but something beyond these aspects of tuition. What is involved is "not merely telling the child what to do, but showing him how to do it and seeing that it is done, taking care that the advice or the command given is put into practice and adopted as a habit." The illustration is used of the training of a young horse, and of how it is made to yield its will to its master's until at last it is in perfect sympathy with him, and yields to his slightest wish. It is carefully directed and accustomed to do the right thing until it becomes a habit, a second nature. When necessary, its own innate, wild tendencies are checked and restrained; and encouraged thus by a loving master, the young animal is helped to fully exercise its powers in subjection to the master's rule.

As those who train young horses, help with voice and hand and thoughtful care to nurture them, so parents should bestow similar care on the training of their children, seeking by voice and hand to accustom them to do easily and willingly what is asked of them. There are those who were brought up *at* a mother's knee—others were brought up *over* the knee. The habitual effort to bring the developing will of the child to obey the authority of love is a necessary element in training, seeing that success in training depends more on forming habits than inculcating rules. By repetition, a child learns to do certain things until they become so familiar and natural

that it seems strange to him not to do them. Once the habit of obedience is formed, it becomes the root of other habits.

Parents, seeking by faith and prayer to mold, strengthen and guide the will of children in the way of the Lord can count upon His workings in their hearts. They can have the joy of seeing their children not only obeying their commands, but happy in the approval of all that is commanded. Obeying their parents, not because they have to, but because they delight to, knowing that what is asked of them is for their highest welfare. In a summary note at the end of *The Children for Christ,* Andrew Murray extends these points—

(1) Training is more than teaching. Teaching makes a child know what he is to do; training influences him, and sees he does it. The former deals with the mind; the latter with the will.

(2) Prevention is better than cure. Not to watch and correct mistakes, but to watch and *prevent mistakes,* is true training. The highest aim of true training is to lead the child to know he *can* obey and do right, and be happy in obedience.

(3) Habits must precede principles. With a child, the body grows for the first years of life while the mind is to a great extent dormant. Habits prepare the way for obedience from principle, not command.

(4) The cultivation of the feelings precede that of judgment. Early years of childhood are marked by the liveliness of the feelings and the susceptibility of impressions, and these are used by the parent to create feelings favorable to all that is good, making it attractive and desirable.

(5) Example is better than precept. The power of effective training lies, not in that which a parent might say and teach, but in what he *is* and *does.* We cannot teach children ideals we fail to live up to ourselves. When we *live* what we *teach,* we are able to *teach* others to *live.*

(6) Love that draws is more than law that demands. Love never seeks its own, and the love of parents for their children lives and gives itself for their full training. Parental love inspired by divine love exercises a mighty influence in the home and is always the inspiration in the secret of effective nurture.

Handmaids of God's Redeeming Love. The most effective guardians of children are *godly* parents, particularly the mother of the children. For such a task God created wonderful mother-love which, when directed into the right channel transforms a mother into a handmaid of God's redeeming love. When God sought to reveal His love to a lost world He chose a woman to give His eternal Son a human form. As Myers expresses it—

Not to the rich He came and to the ruling
Men full of meat whom wholly He abhors—
Not to the fools grown insolent in fooling
   Most, when the lost are dying at their doors;
Nay, but to her who with a sweet thanksgiving
   Took in tranquility what God might bring
Blessed Him and waited, and within her living
   Felt the arousal of a Holy Thing.

One to whom the phrase of MacDonald applies—"The God-life at thy heart," was the saintly mother of Abraham Lincoln who, until his assassination in 1865, constantly extolled her benign influence over his life. More than once he testified, "All that I am or hope to be, I owe to my angel mother." Countless numbers agree with the sentiment expressed by Strickland Gillilan—

You may have tangible wealth untold;
Caskets of Jewels and coffers of gold;
Richer than I you can never be—
I had a mother who read to me.

A mother is not only a child's first lover and constant babysitter, but a name for God in the lips and hearts of little children as W. M. Thackeray said it. Henry Ward Beecher adds the tribute, "The mother's heart is the child's schoolroom." We can gather many sweet eulogies to the value of mothers from ancient proverbial literature. A Jewish proverb says that, "God could not be everywhere, and so He made mothers." Among Persian proverbs we have, "Heaven is at the feet of mothers." From Spain we have the saying, "An ounce of mother is worth a pound of clergy." A child's first minister of holy things is a Christian mother and because of this, "Men, are what their mothers make them," as Emerson expresses it. No other than Napoleon Bonaparte said, "The future destiny of the child is always the work of the mother."

What a shining light a true mother is to all her loved ones, day and night! She is the only one who can divide her love among several children, and yet each child still has all her love. To a child, the most wonderful face in all the world is that of mother. Does not the Bible give prominence to the sacredness of motherhood? At the opening of New Testament history we read of John the Baptist, "He shall be filled with the Holy Ghost, even from his mother's womb" (Luke 1:15). Thus, a saintly woman's womb was "the work-place of the Holy Spirit." Apart from the divine enduement John received at his birth, he entered the world spiritually fortified because his mother was a Spirit-filled woman before his birth.

What higher commendation could any parents have than that which Luke gives to Elisabeth, and her priestly husband, Zacharias—

"They were both righteous before God, walking in all the commandments and ordinances of the Lord blameless."

Being *"without blame* before him in love," such holy parents could count upon the power of the Holy Spirit in their unborn child, whose conception was miraculous in that Elisabeth being "barren and well stricken in years," was beyond the period of childbearing. With "the sweet omnipotence of Love" at His command God is ready to work any miracle He pleases, but observing His own laws, desiring a holy child as the forerunner of His Son, He sought for holy parents. Thus, "it is the God of Nature, who in the world of cause and effect has ordered that like begets like, who is also the God of Grace."

It is to be feared that the majority of mothers—and fathers, too—do not seek after a life of blamelessness before God, and consequently beget children who are spiritually handicapped from their birth. If only all mothers cherished the highest and the brightest hope of holy motherhood, to have children filled with the Holy Spirit from their birth, what a purer world ours would be! How saintly Elisabeth must have been overawed at the angel's message concerning her unborn child! Luke gives us three aspects of the child born under the covering of the Holy Spirit.

(1) *A favor for John's parents.* "Thou shalt have joy and gladness." Disappointed through many long years

at being childless, how Zacharias and Elisabeth must have been filled with the holy happiness of heaven. How sad that many parents have had reason to sigh in bitter agony, Would God my child had never been born!

(2) *A favor for the world.* "Many shall rejoice at his birth." What mighty things were accomplished through the life and preaching of John the Baptist. Many of the disciples of Jesus, some of whom became apostles, were converted through the revival preaching of John. Blessed are those mothers who live to see their children greatly used for the salvation of lost souls.

(3) *A favor for John himself.* "He shall be great in the sight of the Lord." John bore witness to Jesus, and Jesus said of him that "among them born of woman there hath not risen a greater than John the Baptist," but the crown of all prophecy concerning him was, "He shall be great in the sight of the Lord." So he was a joy to his parents, a blessing to his fellowmen, and an honored man in the sight of God. A man may not be known much among men, yet great in God's sight for He does not see as man sees. How mothers need to be aroused to understand that holy motherhood means in God's sight! If only all of them could live as Elisabeth did—believe and receive what she did, their children would enter the world under the overshadowing of heavenly grace, and prove to be a blessing in it.

Another devout handmaid of the Lord was the Virgin Mary, cousin of Elisabeth, and the one of whom Gabriel could say, "Blessed art thou among women, and blessed is the fruit of the womb, and blessed is she that believed" (Luke 1:42,45). What would you say was the most conspicuous feature, from the human side of Mary's motherhood? Was it not the childlike simplicity of faith manifested in the surrender of herself to the Holy Spirit for the accomplishment of the divine purpose? Doubtless overwhelmed by the heavenly announcement, Mary immediately replied, "Behold the handmaid of the Lord; be it unto me according to thy word" (Luke 1:38). She became the Lord's bondwoman, and in quiet trust and expectancy waited for Him to do what He had said He would. And the miracle happened, for within the womb of the Virgin the Holy Spirit became the love-knot between our Lord's two natures, linking deity and humanity and fusing them into one. He made possible the One who came as God incarnate.

The surrender of Mary teaches every mother to yield herself to God, that through her, His purpose and glory may be made manifest. A truth believing parents must not lose sight of is that each of their children under divine guardianship can be a link in the golden chain of the good pleasure of God's will. Over all the impulses of human love and the instincts of a God-given maternity there hovers a divine purpose using them for the carrying out of His plan. Thus children of a godly home can become as the stones of the great temple of which the holy Child Jesus is the cornerstone.

Twice over it is said of Mary that she "kept all these things, and pondered them in her heart." Such holy quiet of meditation and reflection fitted her for the blessed duties of motherhood. The truths she pondered taught her to regard everything connected with the birth of her Child as being a matter of deepest interest to her heavenly Father, as well as of great importance in His redemptive plan for mankind. Before her Son saw the light of day, Mary claimed all the exceeding great and precious promises on His behalf. No wonder we read of her, *"Blessed* is she that believed."

If only there were more mothers like Mary, there would be more children like her Son, Jesus, His miraculous conception, deity and sinlessness excepted. One of the most remarkable illustrations of unity in the world is the unique oneness of mother and child, not only physically, before the unbilical cord is cut, but in her own life and character she imparts which determines, to a great extent, what her child is to be. When God gave His Son to be born of a woman, this law was not violated, and the mother He chose for His Son was doubtless all that grace could make her to be the fit vessel through whom He should receive His human nature and disposition. How necessary it is for all respective mothers to prepare themselves spiritually, to receive their children according to God's Word. After their birth, the need is to train them in harmony with that Word, so that they can enter into the full enjoyment of all the promises of the Word.

In these days of sexual liberty far too many young women enter into unwanted motherhood, and try to prevent it by abortion. But all God-fearing, rightly married wives, entering motherhood, join in Mary's thanksgiving over her Child, as their children are born—"My soul doth magnify the Lord, and my spirit hath rejoiced in God my Saviour." Birth-pangs give way to exquisite joy as a woman realizes that she has become the living mother of a living child. "She remembereth no more the anguish, for the joy that a man is born into the world." Looking at the precious little treasure God has given her, the mother is stirred to praise Him, and dedicate both herself and her child to Him, so that as an immortal being the child may be fitted to show forth God's salvation among men. With a true and grateful heart she not only rejoices but prays—

> Here am I and this precious child Thou has given me, the witness of Thy power and Thy goodness; may our lives, all our days devoted to Thee, be the sacrifice of thanksgiving we bring Thee.

The Double Surety of Children. The Greek word for "surety" is "bail," that is, one who personally answers for anyone, whether his life or property, and is to be distinguished from a "mediator." As our Surety, Jesus is the personal guarantee of the terms of the new and better covenant secured on the ground of His perfect sacrifice (Heb. 7:22,27). As the context makes clear, His is an abiding and unchanging Priesthood. *Bail,* the person providing security is from the Latin, *bailus,* meaning "burden bearer." When Joseph and Mary brought Jesus to Jerusalem, and in the Temple presented Him to the Lord, although a helpless infant He was yet a pleasing sacrifice, a sweet-smelling savor (Luke 2:22-24).

Jesus was not only Mary's first-born, but also the Father's firstborn among many brethren. He became the Forerunner through whom all little ones can be made acceptable to God. Jesus was made like our children, that they might be made like Him and have Him as their Surety. In respect to His humanity, He was made like us so that through grace we might be made like Him. The object of the presentation in the Temple was an acknowledgement of God's claim upon the children presented, and of the necessity of devoting them to God as His property. Then, as the child can understand it, he must be taught that he was presented with Jesus, like Jesus, to the Father, and of his fellowship in the life and spirit of Him who became the Surety of children. It is in this way that the holy childhood of Jesus overshadows and sanctifies the children of a godly home.

When parents dedicate a child to the Lord in an intelligent, childlike, heartfelt faith, such an act greatly influences the daily treatment of the child because he is thought of as God's devoted and accepted property. As for the parents themselves, they see their responsibility as trustees to whom has been committed the keeping and training of their child; his guardians and guides as they seek to make the holy childhood of Jesus the protection of the childhood of their child. What a wonderful safeguard for children is a sanctified home! Happy is a consecrated home in which all can say, "We will serve the Lord" (Josh. 24:15).

As to the heritage of holiness, is it not another surety for children? Paul gives us the precious, arresting sentence, "Now are they (your children) holy" (I Cor. 7:14), which seems to imply that "God's holiness and our children are meant for each other; as parents we are the God-ordained links for bringing them into perfect union." There has been secured for every child that treasure of sanctification prepared in Christ and which the Spirit of sanctification makes a personal possession as the child is trained in the way of holiness by holy parents.

If "Holiness" is written upon the doorposts of our home, and the home and family are looked upon as God's home, the dwelling place of His holiness, then all that is contrary to holiness will be kept outside the home. Parental holiness is an indispensable condition for educating a holy child and training him to show forth the glory of His holiness. The word holy not only signifies a relation—a destiny—a pledge of divine life-power, it also describes a character, for God is holy, and so urges us to be like Him. It is therefore the solemn task of Christian parents to train their children in such "dispositions and habits, such ways of thinking and feeling and acting, as shall be in harmony with the Faith, that they are holy in Christ and belong to the Spirit, as shall be a preparation for His dwelling in them and using them as His temple." How rewarded are parents who are separated unto God, when they see the young child-life in their home separated from the world, its spirit and its service; and consecrated to God and the fulfillment of His will.

Obligations Of Children Toward Their Parents. Having fully considered parental obligation we now turn to the other side of the coin and discover what the Bible has to say regarding the obligation of children toward their parents—an aspect many present-day children seem to be ignorant of. In ancient times public opinion stoutly upheld respect for, and obedience to, parents. Everywhere in the Bible we have abundant evidence of the bond that bound Jewish families together. In our day the disintegration of family is largely related to Gentile homes. Very few Jewish families, in comparison, fall apart. The characteristic unity of the home circle has been wonderfully maintained through the centuries. Here are a few illustrations of the Biblical affinity between parents and children—

A benediction was pronounced upon those who lovingly honored their parents—a benediction both Jews and Gentiles can enjoy—"That thy days may be long upon the land which the Lord thy God giveth thee" (Exod. 20:12, see Deut. 5:16). Under the same Mosaic Law we have the solemn judgement, "He that smiteth his father, or his mother, shall be surely put to death" (Exod. 21:15).

When King David heard of the tragic death of his son,

Absalom, we read that he was much moved, and retiring to his private chamber, cried, "O my son Absalom, my son, my son Absalom! would God I had died for thee, O Absalom, my son, my son!" (II Sam. 18:33).

Stripped bare of all the comforts and amenities of his large and hitherto happy, holy home Job sighed for the old days, "Oh that I were as in months past . . . When the Almighty was with me, when my children were about me" (Job 29:2,5).

Solomon has much to say about obligations of children toward parents, as well as the parental obligation. Children were taught to hold precious the spiritual instruction received, "My son, keep thy father's commandment, and forsake not the law of thy mother: Bind them continually upon thy heart, and tie them about thy neck. When thou goest, it shall lead thee: when thou sleepest, it shall keep thee; and when thou wakest, it shall talk with thee" (Prov. 6:20-22).

Micah said that one aspect of national apostasy would be, "The son dishonoureth the father, the daughter riseth up against her mother" (7:6). What a tragic situation it is when a man's foes are those of his own household!

When the wife of Zebedee came to worship Jesus she brought her sons with her. (Matt. 20:20).

A father's heartfelt concern for his child, possessed by dumb and dangerous spirit, is expressed in the words, "Straightway the father of the child cried out, and said with tears, Lord, I believe; help thou mine unbelief" (Mark 9:24).

In like manner, the nobleman of Capernaum, distressed over his sick son, besought Jesus, "Sir come down ere my child die" (John 4:49).

Paul wanted young Timothy to know that the reward or recompense of parents by children was "good and acceptable before God" (I Tim. 5:4).

That the home is a closely-knit fellowship is implied in the exclamation, "Behold I and the children which God hath given me" (Heb. 2:13).

While one could gather out further instances of the unity of home life in Israel, and of the concern of one for the other within the home, sufficient has been cited to prove its noble estimation recognized both by parents and children alike. Now let us seek to classify more particularly what the Bible says regarding the accountability of children to parents.

Attendant Upon Parental Instruction. Early education was primarily in the home. We have already seen that it was the parents' responsibility to rear children in the way of the Lord, also the children's responsibility to accept home teaching and obey parents as a preparatory discipline for the higher relationship to God (Gen. 18:19; Deut. 6:7; 11:19). While a boy at twelve years of age became a "son of the law," or became a subject to the law advancing to fuller instruction, at five years of age he was already under his father's tuition. The children grew up more or less under their mother's care, the girl usually continuing with her mother until her marriage (Prov. 6:20; 31:1; II Tim. 1:5; 3:14,15). Sometimes wealthier families employed tutors (I Chron. 27:32). Schools for children are first mentioned by Josephus, the Jewish historian. From The Talmud we learn that the first school for children was instituted about 100 B.C., and by the time of Christ were fairly common.

From early times children were taught to read and write even in the poorer families (Isa. 8:1; 10:19). Solomon, in the Book of Proverbs urges care, even to severity

in the training and teaching of children. (See 3:12; 13:24; 15:5; 22:6; 29:15.) Explicit are the exhortations—"My son, hear the instructions of thy father, and forsake not the law of thy mother" (Prov. 1:8) and "A wise son heareth his father's instruction" (Prov. 13:1).

The significance of religious feasts and ordinances had to be taught the children (Exod. 12:26,27). The acceptance and understanding of the truths taught by parents became as an ornament of grace upon the children's heads and as chains about their necks (Prov. 31:1). Truth lived out in the lives of parents adds reality and power to lip instruction. Too often how they live speaks so loudly that their children cannot hear, or fail to follow, what they say. Timothy became the faithful companion of the greatest of the apostles, because the Scriptural instruction he received from his devoted mother had passed through the crucible of her own heart. Timothy emulated his mother Eunice's unfeigned faith (II Tim. 1:5).

Careful About Honoring Parents. The ancient commandment has never been withdrawn. "Honour thy father and thy mother." No string is attached saying that they should be honored only if they are worthy of it. Parents should always be revered seeing that under God they gave us life. Wise rulers make good subjects, and firm and considerate commanders have faithful soldiers. In like manner, parents honoring God in all their ways make it easy for their children to honor them. The child's fulfillment of this commandment may hinge on the character of the parents.

A young child can only honor what he sees and knows to be worthy of honor, and it is the high calling of parents so to speak and act and live in the presence of children that honor may spontaneously and unconsciously flow out from them to their parents. Kings receive honor, and if parents reign and rule in love and the fear of God, honor will be given them. As a child's first virtue is the honoring and obeying of his parents, how essential it is for them to honor God in the eyes of the child. Andrew Murray observes that—

The sentiment of honour, reverence, is one of the noblest and purest our nature is capable of. The power of perceiving what is worthy of honour, the willingness to acknowledge it, the unselfishness that feels it no degradation, but a pleasure, to render it—all this is itself honourable and ennobling; nothing brings more true honour than giving honour to others. This disposition ought to be cultivated most carefully in the child, as an important part of his education. It is one of the chief elements of a noble character and a preparation for rendering to God the honour due to Him.

Observance of Filial Fear. It is necessary to observe the contrast between reverent awe and slavish terror. The words the Bible uses for "fear" have two principal meanings, as the Zondervan Pictorial Bible Dictionary, points out—

1. That apprehension of evil which normally leads one either to flee or fight.
2. That awe and reverence which a man of sense feels in the presence of God, and to a less extent in the presence of a king or other dread authority.

When the disciples cried out for fear thinking they saw a ghost, they were afraid, terrified (Matt. 14:26); but when Paul speaks to those who have no "fear of God before their eyes" (Rom. 3:18), the second meaning is implied. The word "reverend" occurring only once in the Scripture (Ps. 111:9), means "to be feared," or reverenced. In the Old Testament some fifteen different Hebrew nouns are rendered "fear." The two implications of the word can be found in Psalm 31:13, "Fear was on every side"; and Proverbs 9:10, "The fear of the Lord is the beginning of wisdom."

When Moses explained the earthly relationship and walk of God's earthly people he wrote, "Ye shall fear every man his mother, and his father" (Lev. 19:3), which is equivalent to the exposition on chastening in the epistle to the Hebrews—"We have had fathers of our flesh which corrected us, and we gave them reverence" (12:9). Parents fail in their responsibility when they are cruel, or too demanding, exacting, or inconsiderate in their treatment of the children God gave them. Boys and girls should never be scared, terror stricken, or afraid of their parents. Alas! too many are, and often run away from a house of loveless, harsh atmosphere.

The sort of fear that Moses urges on the part of children for their fathers and mothers is that of loving respect and reverence, because of their godliness, love, sympathy and patience. It was this aspect of fear that Jesus, as a child, manifested toward Mary and Joseph. If "the fear of the Lord" is a definition of piety, then the fear of, or reverence for, parents will enable children to understand more fully what it means for them to look upon the God their parents love and serve as One who is "holy and to be feared" (Ps. 111:9). Such fear is the fundamental principle upon which true religion and a happy home rest (Prov. 29:17). Irreverence on the part of children toward an older person is visited by signal instance of divine judgement (II Kings 2:23,24).

Obedience to Parents. That the Bible has much to say about obedience is evidenced by the fact that the word occurs more than 150 times throughout its pages. God demands obedience from the army of heaven and from the inhabitants of earth, and Jesus is always the model of obedience to God. Then obedience to those who are over us, and to parents by their children, likewise occupies space in Holy Writ. Here are some instances of obedience to parents—

"Jacob obeyed his father, and his mother (Gen. 28:7). "Jacob called his son Joseph . . . thou shalt carry me out of Egypt, and bury me in their buryingplace. And he (Joseph) said, I will do as thou has said" (Gen. 47:29,30).
"Children, obey your parents in the Lord: for this is right" (Eph. 6:1).

Obedience is to be "in the Lord," implying that both parents and children, recognizing the Saviour as Lord of their life, find loving submission pleasant. This is the right and only source of delight. Obedience is never irksome, unpleasant or feigned when it is "in the Lord." What should be the action of a Christian toward obeying the demands of an unchristian parent, especially if they are in conflict with the child's faith in God? The apostolic principle should be observed, "We ought to obey God, rather than men" (Acts 5:29,32).

"Children, obey your parents in all things: for this is well pleasing unto the Lord" (Col. 3:20).

Obedience in some "things" not of the Lord is never well-pleasing to Him. It has been pointed out that the

position of children was one of complete subordination to their parents (Gen. 22; Judg. 11:39), and the sacrifices to Molech of children by parents, indicate that the father had powers of life and death over their children, but these powers were limited (Lev. 18:21; 20:2-5; Deut. 21:18-21; II Kings 23:10; Jer. 32:35). Reverence and obedience on the part of children toward their parents were strongly enjoined (Exod. 20:12; Lev. 19:3; Deut. 17:16).

Christian parents, living in obedience to God's will, are never in danger of repressing the healthy development of a child's moral powers by demanding implicit obedience to their will. Such a child is trained to believe that because of the superior wisdom of his parents, they know what is best for him, and so command him accordingly. When Paul said that children must obey their parents for this is right, it is so, not because the child approves or agrees, but because the command is given by a parent, the one in authority. Children who thus obey, honor their parents.

All parents, who are the Lord's, as well as bishops and deacons, must rule well their own house, having their children in subjection with all gravity (I Tim. 3:4,5-12). This is the "home rule" that magnifies the Lord, and keeps the home as His sacred dwelling place. The lives of obedient children are a hymn of praise to the glory of God, especially if they obey His voice. Obedient children are those who obey the Lord because they love Him—obey Him in all things—find in obedience its own reward. In the keeping of God's commandments, "there is great reward." It was Benjamin Franklin who said, "Let thy child's first lesson be obedience, and the second will be what thou wilt." Further, a truism that must never be lost sight of is that, "a child has to learn obedience in the home or he will never learn obedience to the heavenly Father." Whether young or old, we must walk or learn to walk on the two feet, trust and obey.

Growing Love for Parents. Perhaps the most touching episode in the Bible of a son's love for his father was Joseph's action when he met his father after a long absence. Jacob had mourned his son as being dead. When they ultimately met, Joseph fell on his father's neck, and "wept on his neck a good while" (Gen. 46:29). How Jesus felt toward His mother is seen in the provision of her future as He died upon the cross (John 19:26,27). If heaven gave Him, as the divine Son, a Father's love, earth provided for Him, as the Child Jesus, a mother's love and care so that "in all things he might be made like unto his brethren." How true are the lines of the old melody—

"There is beauty all around, when there's love at home."

Love for God on the part of all the members of the family, and love for each other in the home circle, transforms any home into a palace beautiful. The song of the ideal home goes like this—

"Now abideth love, comfort, sufficiency, these three, but the greatest of these is LOVE."

As the Apostle Paul in his extensive missionary ministry often visited and stayed in homes of believers, one wonders if he had had experience of some of them suffering from a lack of love. Gathering together a few relevant references it would seem as if he warned against three aspects of home education—

1. Children can be often very irksome and provoking.
2. Parents are in danger of allowing themselves to be provoked.
3. The general result is that parents again provoke their children to wrath.

Paul's warning and exhortations open up the vexed question of the difficulty of giving reproof or punishment in the right spirit, or in keeping with one's Christian testimony. It is when a child least deserves love that he needs it more. Certainly the best of parents have need of patience, wisdom and self-control, if the rule of parents is looked upon as a reign of love.

"Love suffereth long, and is kind; . . . seeketh not her own, is not easily provoked" (I Cor. 13:4,5).

"Ye fathers, provoke not your children to wrath" (Eph. 6:4).

"Fathers, provoke not your children to anger, lest they be discouraged" (Col. 3:21).

"Teach the young women . . . to love their children" (Tit. 2:4).

From the above Scriptures we observe that both mothers and fathers share the responsibility of the management of their children. Such a care is not to be thrown upon one or the other but is to be borne together. After a hard and exacting day at work, a father may feel that he cannot be bothered with the children, and their clamor for loving attention may be regarded more as a burden and weariness than as a charge from the Lord to be met in the spirit of love and gladness. It is because "God has joined to the weakness and gentleness of the mother and firmness and strength of the father" that each must take his or her part in the creation of an atmosphere of love in the home. When they are helpers together in such a fruitful task, their little ones grow up loving them, and never fail to show their affection even when the parents are old and gray-headed.

Observation had led the Apostle Paul to exhort fathers, in particular, not to provoke their children to wrath for he knew that a parent giving way to anger or temper slays love in the heart of his child. It is hard for a child to believe in love if it has a scowling face. To inspire a child to love God and his parents it is essential to have a home reflecting the life of love the heavenly Father manifests in the guidance and tuition of His children.

Beloved, let us love: For only Thus
Shall we behold that God Who lovest us.

We readily concede that all children are not alike; that while one in a home may be loving and obedient, another may be the reverse and the constant source of annoyance. But if the child provokes the parents, the latter must be careful how to react to such provocation. Love and patience are necessary to bear with waywardness in children for if the parents are taken up unawares by what is so trying to temper and longsuffering, and give way to angry feelings, the effort to foster love becomes more difficult. A father's hasty temper often inflames a child's passion and he becomes his provocation to wrath. It is because God meant the rule of the family to be like His own—a reign of law inspired by love—that a father needs a love that is not easily provoked, even when there are sudden outbreaks of temper in his children and the little vexations arising from childish mistakes, naughtiness and little quarrels.

In child training, lovingness, tenderness, gentleness and

forbearance are so necessary if a child is to be encouraged into goodness. Parental tranquility and kindness pay rich dividends in the love and confidence children come to manifest, for it will not take them long to reciprocate the love which is a principle of action as well as an evidence of natural instinct. At all times parents must be, by the grace and power of God, models of a holy, patient love, inspiring by it the evergrowing affection of their children. It is only thus that they can be trained after the divine mind and become a joy both to God and their parents.

Filial Care of Parents. While the Bible has much to say about the parental care of children, it speaks with equal voice about the filial care of parents. In so much of our home life today there is little love and long-suffering and children grow up without much respect for their parents, and leave them as soon as they can. What heart-breaks parental negligence produces! Too many forget the sacrifice of those who fed, clothed and educated them. God called upon the heavens and the earth to hear His heart-moan over the cruel treatment He received from the children for whom He had done so much—"I have nourished and brought up children, and they have rebelled against me. The ox knoweth his owner, and the ass his master's crib: but Israel doth not know, my people doth not consider" (Isa. 1:2,3).

Shakespeare, in King Lear, expresses the thought—
How sharper than a serpent's tooth it is to have a thankless child!

The increasing number of lonely old people in a room or two of their home, or in institutions for the aged, testify, in many cases, to thankless, heartless and forgetting children. But divine instructions as to the care of parents are most explicit.

"Thou shalt . . . honour the face of the old man" (Lev. 19:32).

". . . go up to my father, and say unto him, Thus saith thy son Joseph. . . . I will nourish thee" (Gen. 45:9-11; 47:12).

"Whosoever shall say to his father or his mother, It is a gift" (Matt. 15:5).

" (Children) requite (reward) their parents: for that is good and acceptable before God" (I Tim. 5:4).

In writing to the Corinthians, Paul made it clear that "The children ought not to lay up for the parents, but the parents for the children" (II Cor. 12:14).

Then in his first letter to Timothy there was the apostle's declaration that, "If any provide not for his own, and especially for those of his own house, he hath denied the faith, and is worse than an infidel" (I Tim. 5:8).

Strong words these! Would that parents who do not provide for their children, and children who fail to provide for their needy parents in their old age would heed them! Behind the statement—"worse than an infidel"—is the thought that the rules even of the nobler pagan moralist forbid such heartless neglect and selfishness. So, for a professing Christian to deliberately fail in the observance of his plain duties to his nearest relatives, brings shame and disgrace on the cause of the loving Christ who made full provision for His mother before He left her.

We have seen that the primary influence in the home comes from the parents. They have a divine responsibility to set the child upon the path of righteousness and to encourage him in his journey. Likewise, the child has the responsibility to heed those admonitions so that even his actions bring honor to his parents. We can have stronger Christian homes if each of us recognizes and performs his duties. The benefits are inestimable both in this world and the next.

A TABLE OF DAILY BIBLE READINGS

This system of daily Bible reading provides a passage from the Old Testament to be read in the morning, and a passage from the New Testament for the evening reading.

	Old Testament	*New* Testament		*Old* Testament	*New* Testament
January			4	14, 15	13:1-25
1	Gen. 1, 2	Matt. 1	5	16, 17	13:26-52
2	3-5	2	6	18, 19	14
3	6-8:19	3	7	20, 21	15:1-21
4	8:20-11:26	4	8	22-23:26	15:22-35
5	11:27-14	5:1-20	9	23:27-26:51	15:36-16:15
6	15-17	5:21-48	10	26:52-28	16:16-40
7	18, 19	6:1-18	11	29-31	17:1-15
8	20-22	6:19-7:6	12	32, 33	17:16-34
9	23, 24	7:7-29	13	34-36	18:1-23
10	25, 26	8:1-27	14	Deut. 1, 2	18:24-19:20
11	27, 28	8:28-9:17	15	3, 4	19:21-41
12	29, 30	9:18-38	16	5-7:11	20:1-16
13	31-33:17	10:1-23	17	7:12-10:11	20:17-38
14	33:18-35	10:24-11:1	18	10:12-12	21:1-16
15	36, 37	11:2-30	19	13-15	21:17-40
16	38, 39	12:1-21	20	16-18:8	22:1-21
17	40-41:49	12:22-50	21	18:9-21	22:22-23:11
18	41:50-43	13:1-23	22	22-24	23:12-35
19	44, 45	13:24-43	23	25-27	24:1-23
20	46-48	13:44-14:12	24	28	24:24-25:12
21	49, 50	14:13-36	25	29-31:13	25:13-27
22	Exod. 1-3	15:1-28	26	31:14-32	26:1-18
23	4-6:3	15:29-16:12	27	33, 34	26:19-32
24	6:4-7	16:13-17:13	28	Josh. 1, 2	27:1-26
25	8, 9	17:14-18:14	29	3-5:12	27:27-44
26	10-12:20	18:15-35	30	5:13-7	28:1-16
27	12:21-14:4	19:1-15	31	8, 9	28:17-31
28	14:5-15	19:16-20:16	*April*		
29	16, 17	20:17-34	1	Josh. 10-12	Mark 1:1-20
30	18, 19	21:1-32	2	13-15	1:21-45
31	20, 21	21:33-22:14	3	16-19	2:1-22
February			4	20-22	2:23-3:12
1	22, 23	22:15-46	5	23, 24	3:13-35
2	24, 25	23	6	Judg. 1-3:4	4:1-20
3	26-27:19	24:1-28	7	3:5-4	4:21-41
4	27:20-28	24:29-51	8	5, 6	5:1-20
5	29-30:10	25:1-30	9	7, 8	5:21-43
6	30:11-31	25:31-46	10	9	6:1-29
7	32-34:3	26:1-30	11	10-11:28	6:30-56
8	34:4-35	26:31-56	12	11:29-12	7:1-23
9	36, 37	26:57-75	13	13-15	7:24-8:10
10	38, 39	27:1-26	14	16-18	8:11-26
11	40	27:27-44	15	19-21	8:27-9:13
12	Lev. 1-3	27:45-66	16	Ruth 1-4	9:14-32
13	4-5:13	28	17	I Sam. 1-3	9:33-50
14	5:14-7:10	Acts 1	18	4-7	10:1-31
15	7:11-8	2:1-21	19	8-10	10:32-52
16	9, 10	2:22-47	20	11-13	11:1-26
17	11-13:23	3	21	14, 15	11:27-12:17
18	13:24-14:32	4:1-31	22	16-17:31	12:18-44
19	14:33-15	4:32-5:11	23	17:32-19:7	13
20	16-18	5:12-42	24	19:8-22	14:1-26
21	19-21	6	25	23-25	14:27-52
22	22-23:22	7:1-29	26	26-28	14:53-72
23	23:23-24	7:30-8:4	27	29-31	15:1-23
24	25	8:5-40	28	II Sam. 1-3	15:24-47
25	26, 27	9:1-31	29	4-6	16
26	Num. 1, 2	9:32-43	30	7-9	Jude
27	3, 4	10:1-23	*May*		
28	5, 6	10:24-48	1	10-12	I Peter 1
29	John 17	Heb. 13	2	13, 14	2
March			3	15-17	3
1	Num. 7, 8	Acts 11:1-18	4	18, 19	4
2	9-11:3	11:19-30	5	20, 21	5
3	11:4-13	12	6	22	II Peter 1

24

	Old Testament	New Testament		Old Testament	New Testament
7	23, 24	2	17	7-10	9:24-10:13
8	I Kings 1	3	18	11-16	10:14-11:1
9	2, 3	James 1	19	17-18:29	11:2-34
10	4-6	2	20	18:30-19	12
11	7-8:30	3-4:12	21	20-22	13
12	8:31-9	4:13-5	22	23-25	14
13	10-12	Luke 1:1-25	23	26-29	15:1-34
14	13-15	1:26-56	24	30, 31	15:35-58
15	16, 17	1:57-80	25	32-34	16
16	18, 19	2:1-21	26	35-37	II Cor. 1
17	20, 21	2:22-52	27	38-41	2
18	22	3	28	42-44	3-4:6
19	II Kings 1-3	4:1-15	29	45-48	4:7-5:10
20	4, 5	4:16-44	30	49-51	5:11-6:10
21	6, 7	5:1-16	31	52-55	6:11-7
22	8, 9	5:17-39	*August*		
23	10-12	6:1-19	1	56-59	8
24	13-15:31	6:20-49	2	60-63	9
25	15:32-17	7:1-29	3	64-67	10
26	18, 19	7:30-50	4	68, 69	11
27	20-22	8:1-21	5	70-72	12:1-13
28	23-25	8:22-39	6	73-75	12:14-13
29	I Chron. 1-2:49	8:40-56	7	76-78:31	Rom: 1:1-17
30	2:50-3	9:1-17	8	78:32-80	1:18-32
31	4-6:15	9:18-36	9	81-84	2
			10	85-88	3
June			11	89	4:1-22
1	6:16-17	9:37-62	12	90-93	4:23-5:11
2	8-10	10:1-24	13	94-98	5:12-21
3	11-13	10:25-42	14	99-102	6:1-14
4	14-16	11:1-13	15	103, 104	6:15-7:6
5	17-19	11:14-36	16	105, 106	7:7-25
6	20-22	11:37-54	17	107, 108	8:1-17
7	23-25	12:1-21	18	109-112	8:18-39
8	26-29	12:22-40	19	113-117	9:1-29
9	II Chron. 1-4	12:41-59	20	118-119:40	9:30-10
10	5-7	13:1-21	21	119:41-112	11:1-12
11	8-11	13:22-35	22	119:113-176	11:13-36
12	12-15	14:1-24	23	120-127	12
13	16-19	14:25-15:10	24	128-134	13
14	20-22	15:11-32	25	135-138	14:1-18
15	23-25	16	26	139-141	14:19-15:13
16	26-28	17:1-19	27	142-145	15:14-33
17	29, 30	17:20-18:14	28	146-150	16
18	31, 32	18:15-43	29	Prov. 1, 2	Gal. 1
19	33, 34	19:1-28	30	3, 4	2
20	35, 36	19:29-48	31	5-7	3:1-14
21	Ezra 1-4	20:1-19	*September*		
22	5, 6	20:20-21:4	1	8, 9	3:15-29
23	7, 8	21:5-38	2	10, 11	4:1-20
24	9, 10	22:1-30	3	12, 13	4:21-5:9
25	Neh. 1-3	22:31-53	4	14, 15	5:10-26
26	4-6	22:54-23:12	5	16, 17	6
27	7	23:13-46	6	18, 19	Ephes. 1:1-14
28	8-10	23:47-24:12	7	20-22:16	1:15-2:10
29	11-13	24:13-35	8	22:17-23	2:11-22
30	Esther 1, 2	24:36-53	9	24-26:12	3
			10	26:13-28	4:1-16
July			11	29-31	4:17-32
1	3-6	I Thess. 1-2:12	12	Eccles. 1, 2	5:1-21
2	7-10	2:13-3	13	3-5	5:22-6:9
3	Job 1, 2	4	14	6-8	6:10-24
4	3-5	5	15	9-12	Phil. 1:1-20
5	6-8	II Thess. 1	16	Song of Sol. 1, 2	1:21-2:11
6	9-12	2	17	3-5	2:12-30
7	13-15	3	18	6-8	3-4:1
8	16-19	I Cor. 1	19	Obadiah	4:2-23
9	20, 21	2	20	Joel 1-3	Col. 1:1-20
10	22-24	3	21	Jonah 1-4	1:21-2:7
11	25-28	4	22	Amos 1-4	2:8-3:4
12	29-31	5	23	5-9	3:5-4:1
13	32-35	6	24	Hosea 1-3	4:2-18
14	36-39	7	25	4-6	Philemon
15	40-42	8			
16	Psalms 1-6	9:1-23			

A Table of Daily Bible Readings

	Old Testament	New Testament		Old Testament	New Testament
26	7-9	Heb. 1	13	29, 30	10:19-42
27	10-12	2	14	31-32:26	11:1-27
28	Isa. 1, 2	3	15	32:27-33	11:28-54
29	3-5	4:1-13	16	34, 35	11:55-12:19
30	6-8:4	4:14-5:10	17	36, 37	12:20-50
			18	38-40	13:1-30
October			19	41-43	13:31-14:14
1	8:5-10:4	5:11-6	20	44-47	14:15-31
2	10:5-12	7	21	48-50:34	15:1-16
3	13, 14	8	22	50:35-51:58	15:17-16:15
4	15-18	9:1-14	23	51:59-52	16:16-33
5	19-22:14	9:15-28	24	Lam. 1, 2	17
6	22:15-24	10:1-18	25	3-5	18:1-27
7	25, 26	10:19-39	26	Ezek. 1, 2	18:28-19:16
8	27, 28	11:1-16	27	3, 4	19:17-42
9	29, 30	11:17-40	28	5-7	20:1-18
10	31, 32	12:1-17	29	8-10	20:19-31
11	33, 34	12:18-13:6	30	11, 12	21
12	35-37:7	13:7-25			
13	37:8-39	Titus 1-2:8	*December*		
14	40, 41	2:9-3	1	13-15	I John 1-2:11
15	42-44:5	I Tim. 1	2	16	2:12-29
16	44:6-45	2	3	17-19	3
17	46, 47	3	4	20, 21	4
18	48, 49	4	5	22, 23	5
19	50, 51	5	6	24-26	II John
20	52, 53	6	7	27, 28	III John
21	54-56:8	II Tim. 1	8	29, 30	Rev. 1
22	56:9-58	2	9	31, 32	2:1-17
23	59, 60	3	10	33-34	2:18-3:6
24	61-63	4	11	35, 36	3:7-22
25	64-66	John 1:1-18	12	37, 38	4
26	Micah 1-3	1:19-51	13	39, 40	5
27	4, 5	2:1-22	14	41, 42	6
28	6, 7	2:23-3:21	15	43, 44	7
29	Nahum 1-3	3:22-36	16	45, 46	8
30	Hab. 1-3	4:1-30	17	47, 48	9
31	Zeph. 1-3	4:31-54	18	Dan. 1, 2	10
			19	3, 4	11
November			20	5, 6	12
1	Jer. 1-3:5	5:1-23	21	7, 8	13
2	3:6-4	5:24-47	22	9, 10	14
3	5, 6	6:1-21	23	11, 12	15
4	7, 8	6:22-40	24	Haggai 1, 2	16
5	9, 10	6:41-7:1	25	Zech. 1-3	17
6	11, 12	7:2-30	26	4-6	18
7	13, 14	7:31-8:11	27	7, 8	19:1-10
8	15, 16	8:12-30	28	9-11	19:11-20:6
9	17, 18	8:31-59	29	12, 13	20:7-21:8
10	19-22	9:1-17	30	Mal. 1-3:6	21:9-22:5
11	23-25	9:18-41	31	3:7-4	22:6-21
12	26-28	10:1-18			

THE HISTORY OF THE FORMATION AND TRANSLATION OF THE ENGLISH BIBLE

THE CANON OF THE BIBLE

The word "canon" is derived from a Hebrew term meaning "cane" or "reed." Since the reed was one of the first instruments of measurement used by man, the term carries with it the idea of a norm or pattern by which other things are measured. In the Christian church it has been used to refer to that collection of writings which comprises our Bible and which has come to be regarded as the authoritative and inspired word of God. The existence of a definite list of books which were to be considered as final authority was made a necessity by several circumstances. As men began to sense that the authentic voice of God was no longer being heard in religious pronouncements it was inevitable that they should seek to preserve those writings which were acknowledged to bear the stamp of prophetic or apostolic authority. When efforts were made to destroy all extant copies of the writings which Jews and Christians held sacred, it became a matter of no small importance to determine which of these writings were to be singled out as especially precious and worthy of all efforts at protection. In addition, the appearance of fraudulent and heretical documents claiming for themselves divine inspiration called for the formulation of a list of books to which the church could appeal in matters of faith and practice.

The Old Testament Canon

In the first century A.D. there was a body of Jewish sacred literature which bore the general term, "scripture," which believers regarded as inspired of God, but whose limits were not as yet precisely determined. The general Jewish consensus was in favor of the list of books found in the Protestant Bible. In Alexandria, however, there was a tendency to include a larger number of books in the Old Testament canon, the additional writings being those designated by Protestants as the *Apocrypha*. The books of the Apocrypha originated in the "inter-testamental period"—the time between the writing of Malachi (c. 400 B.C.) and the coming of Christ. They include I and II Esdras, Tobit, Judith, the Rest of Esther, the Wisdom of Solomon (similar to Proverbs and Ecclesiastes); Ecclesiasticus, sometimes called the Wisdom of Jesus, the son of Sirach; Baruch, which claims to have been written by the scribe of Jeremiah; three additions to the books of Daniel—the Song of the Three Holy Children, the History of Susanna, and the History of the Destruction of Bel and the Dragon; the Prayer of Manasses, King of Judah; and the historically valuable I and II Maccabees. Since the Reformation, Protestants have rejected the apocryphal books as spurious, but the council of Trent (A.D. 1546), citing Augustine's support of the Alexandrian view, officially included the Apocrypha in the canon recognized by the Catholic church.

The Old Testament scriptures were early divided into the Law, the Prophets, and the Writings. The Law contained the first five books of the Old Testament; this is generally thought to have been the first group of writings to have received canonical standing. It achieved this status at least as early as the end of the third century B.C. and probably much earlier. The Prophets, consisting of the writings of the prophets themselves and the historical books which tell of their times, were regarded as authoritative by the second century B.C. The remaining books of the Old Testament (Psalms, Proverbs, Job, Song of Solomon, Ruth, Lamentations, Ecclesiastes, Esther, Daniel, Ezra, Nehemiah, I and II Chronicles) were known to Jews as the Writings. These received recognition as inspired and authoritative probably about 100 B.C.

Although we give thirty-nine the number of books in the Old Testament, the Jews consider these same books to be only twenty-two. This apparent discrepancy is explained by the fact that the following groups of books are counted as only one book each: Judges-Ruth, I and II Samuel, I and II Kings, I and II Chronicles, Ezra-Nehemiah, Jeremiah-Lamentations, and the twelve minor prophets. Hence, when the Jewish historian, Josephus, writing in the first century A.D., speaks of the Hebrew canon as containing only twenty-two books, he does not reject any of those which comprise our present Old Testament canon.

The New Testament Canon

The development of the New Testament canon was somewhat more complex than that of the Old Testament. A primary reason for this was that while the entire Old Testament was produced within a small geographical area, the various New Testament books had widely divergent origins. This being true, it was only natural that there should be great difference in opinion among the churches as to which books were truly sacred, each church giving preference to those with which it was most familiar. In answer to the need for moral and spiritual support, it became commonplace for the churches to correspond with each other and to exchange the letters which they had received from the apostle or from other outstanding Christian leaders. It is, of course, impossible to trace the exact manner in which this took place, but it is safe to say that a group of writings developed which achieved a place alongside the Old Testament scriptures. Such a collection would ordinarily consist of the Gospel, several of the Pauline letters and several letters bearing the names of apostles or outstanding church leaders such as Peter, John, James, or Jude. To these would be added one or more Apocalypses, usually either that of John, which stands in our canon, or those of Peter and Hermas.

As early as A.D. 95, Clement of Rome wrote a letter to the church in Corinth in which he apparently uses language from Matthew, Luke and several Pauline epistles. Nowhere, however, does he cite these writings as divine. The writings of Ignatius (c. A.D. 115) are also seen to contain considerable Pauline material as well as quotations from the gospel of Matthew, I Peter, and I John. Papias, who wrote in the first half of the second century, quotes from the gospel of John and mentions the writings of Matthew and Mark. *The Teaching of the Twelve Apostles*, or *Didache*, written near the beginning of the second century, either quotes or alludes to Matthew, Luke, John, Acts, Romans, the letters to the Thes-

salonians and the first epistle of Peter. The earliest designation of a passage from the Gospels as scriptures is found in the epistle attributed to Barnabas, which has been dated near A.D. 135. By the time of Justin Martyr (c. A.D. 153), the Gospels were being read in Rome along with the Old Testament books. At about this same time Tatian compiled a harmony of the four Gospels called the *Diatessaron* which is evidence that it was generally agreed upon that only these four Gospels gave an inspired and trustworthy account of the life and teachings of Jesus.

One of the most notable of the heretics who troubled the church in this period was Marcion, a Gnostic teacher. In order to support his views and in an effort to break completely with Judaism, Marcion formed a canon consisting of an expurgation of Luke's gospel and ten of Paul's letters. This is the first clear evidence of the canonization of Pauline writings. As noted above, the struggle with heresy such as that of Marcion forced the church to a decision on which books it was to regard as authoritative and upon which it could rely in its struggle with error. After this period, it is much easier to give an accurate account of the development of the New Testament canon.

Irenaeus, the widely acquainted bishop of Lyons in the latter part of the second century, wrote much in opposition to the heresies which confronted the Christian church. It is significant that in his writings he appealed to the New Testament as scripture, citing the four Gospels, the Acts, the Pauline epistles, the general epistles, and the Apocalypse or Revelation of John. He was explicit in insisting that the number of Gospels be no more nor less than four. Tertullian of Carthage, writing between A.D. 197 and 223, took a position quite similar to that of Irenaeus.

The real landmark of this period is a document known as the Muratorian Fragment, so named after the Italian scholar, Muratori, who discovered it in Milan in 1740. This document dates near the end of the second century and concerns itself with listing those books which were to be considered as canonical. It includes the Gospels, the Acts, the Pauline epistles, the Apocalypse of John, I and II John and Jude. It omits Hebrews, I and II Peter, James, and III John. It also included the Apocalypse of Peter, but admits that it was rejected by some of the churches.

The most outstanding Christian figure of the third century was Origen. The information which he furnishes about the canon is especially valuable because of the wide scope of his learning and his communication with other centers of Christian thought. Of the disputed books, Origen was uncertain concerning James, II Peter, and III John, but he accepted the Revelation of John. In his discussion of Hebrews, Origen made the famous statement that "God alone knows who wrote the epistle to the Hebrews."

For all practical purposes, the fourth century marks the final stages of the development of the New Testament canon. The great church historian of the first quarter of this century, Eusebius of Caesarea, gave a summary of the views on the canon. Eusebius accepted the same books which constitute our New Testament, although he expressed some reservation about Revelation, and acknowledged that the canonicity of several of the books which accepted was disputed by some.

As the church of the fourth century labored to reach a definitive statement of those things which it believed, in its struggle against heresy and in its adjustment to the support of the state, the voice which was clearest in shaping and reflecting orthodox belief was that of Athanasius, bishop of Alexandria. Each year at Easter, Athanasius sent a letter to the churches in his diocese. In the letter of A.D. 367, he included a list of books which were to be recognized as scripture. This list consisted of the twenty-seven books which constitute our New Testament. Athanasius invested these with finality by the statement, "Let no one add to these. Let nothing be taken away."

Just as these men reflected the views of the church as a whole rather than their own opinions, the councils which ultimately fixed the canon were doing little more than putting the official seal of approval on what had already become standard in the churches. Of several councils which spoke on the matter, perhaps the most notable was the council of Carthage of A.D. 397, which ratified the list of books as we now have them. This virtually settled the question of the canon of the Christian Bible, although the Revelation of John was long achieving acceptance in the Eastern churches.

The New Testament "Apocrypha"

Although the term "apocrypha" technically applies only to those books mentioned above which sought a place in the canon of the Old Testament, a number of writings appeared after the close of the period of New Testament literary activity which purported to be inspired of God and worthy of a place in the canon and which may be spoken of as constituting a New Testament "apocrypha." Generally speaking, these were patent forgeries and never received the measure of acceptance which was accorded the Old Testament Apocrypha. They were often attacks on or defenses of some doctrine or heresy, or contained fantastic miracle-stories, which often bordered on the ridiculous, about the life of Jesus. Among these are the Gospels according to Nicodemus, the Hebrews, the Ebionites, the Egyptians, Peter, Pseudo-Matthew, Thomas and Joseph the Carpenter. A good example of how these were used to promulgate private doctrines is seen in the Gospel of the Ebionites. This group, which was vegetarian, pictures John the Baptist as eating wafers instead of locusts and wild honey. In addition to the Gospels there are Acts of Pilate, Paul, Peter, John, Andrew, Philip, and Thomas, the Martyrdom of Matthew, and the Apostolic History of Abdias. In the class of epistles, we find the Letter of Lentulus, the Epistle to the Laodiceans, the Correspondence of Paul and Seneca, and the Epistle of Apostles. Apocalyptic works, characterized by a high degree of symbolism and predictive elements, included the Apocalypses of Peter, Paul, Thomas, and Stephen. With rare exception, there is little difficulty in distinguishing between them and the truly inspired Word.

RECONSTRUCTION OF THE ORIGINAL TEXT

The story of the production and preservation of our Bible is a fascinating and often romantic one. The Old Testament books, of course, had been standardized before the time of Christ and we can be assured that we have texts practically identical to those used by the early church. The case is considerably different with regard to the New Testament. Unfortunately, there are no original manuscripts of the New Testament writings which are known to be in existence. Nevertheless, enough manuscripts of high quality have been found to furnish us with a text which must be quite close to that possessed by the early Christians.

Writing Materials

The writing material which was in current use at the time of the production of the New Testament and for several centuries thereafter was papyrus. This material was produced by taking strips of pith from the papyrus reed and gluing them together in a horizontal and vertical pattern to form a mat.

This was then pounded or pressed and allowed to dry, producing a suitable surface for writing. The width of these pieces might be anywhere from five inches to a foot, depending on their quality. There were recognized grades of this material, used for different purposes, just as we have numerous grades of paper today. These pieces of papyrus were then pasted into scrolls, usually about thirty feet long and occasionally reaching over 100 feet in length. In the second century A.D. the papyrus "codex" came into being. The codex is that form used in our own books; that is, pages were fastened together to form a volume. These could contain a larger amount of writing than a scroll and therefore facilitated the collection of New Testament books into a group. Papyrus was not extremely durable. It rotted easily or became brittle and disintegrated with time. For this reason, there were few fragments of any significance preserved on this material until a large group of extremely valuable papyri dating to the second century A.D. were discovered in this century in Egypt. Before this discovery, all of our ancient manuscripts were written on vellum, which was simply a fine quality of animal skin prepared for writing on both sides.

The Manuscripts

The vellum manuscripts which have been found were made between the fourth and fifteenth centuries. There are two types of these, Uncials and Cursives. The Uncial Manuscripts were written in large capital letters without spaces between them and appeared something like this—PAULANAPOSTLETOTHEGENTILES—though written, of course, in Greek. Although these were more difficult to read than the Cursive, which are written in small connected letters, they are of far greater value because of their age.

There are literally thousands of manuscripts of the Bible or parts of it in existence. The best known of these are three Uncial codices known as the Sinaiticus, Vaticanus and Alexandrinus. The Codex Sinaiticus, so called because it was discovered in the monastery of St. Catharine on Mt. Sinai, is the only extant manuscript which contains the entire New Testament. A German scholar, Constantine Tischendorf, while visiting in the monastery in 1844, recognized the manuscript as it lay in a trash basket, waiting to be burned. The basket contained forty-three leaves of a beautiful copy of the scriptures dating back to the first half of the fourth century. Over a period of fifteen years, Tischendorf carried on an unsuccessful search for the remainder of the manuscripts. Finally, he was able to locate the remainder of the 347-page manuscript. In 1933, the major portion of this same manuscript was sold to the British museum for half a million dollars.

The Codex Vaticanus, so named because it has resided in the Vatican library since 1481, is also dated in the fourth century. This is probably the oldest and best of the Greek manuscripts. It does not, however, contain the entire New Testament, a portion of Hebrews and the Pastoral epistles (I and II Timothy, Titus), Philemon and Revelation being missing. The Codex Alexandrinus was made in the fifth century in Alexandria and contains the entire Bible with some fragments of Matthew, John, and I Corinthians missing. This manuscript is also in the British museum, having been presented to the Royal Library in 1757.

The most noteworthy manuscript in the United States is the fourth century Codex Washingtoniensis, discovered in Egypt in 1906 and presently located in the Smithsonian Library in Washington, D.C. Two other important Uncial manuscripts are the Codex Ephraemi Rescriptus and Codex Bezae. The former of these is what is known as a palimpsest text; that is, the original manuscript was erased and written over, although it is still possible to determine the original text. In this case, the writing was done by Ephraem; hence the designation of the manuscript. A large portion of each of the New Testament books is missing from this manuscript, while two books (II Thessalonians and II John) are missing altogether. Codex Bezae is named for Theodore Beza, who obtained the manuscript from the monastery of St. Irenaeus in Lyons in 1562 and presented it in 1581 to the University of Cambridge where it now resides. This is a text in both Greek and Latin, containing only the Gospels, Acts, and a small section of III John. The most important recent discovery in manuscripts has been the Chester Beatty Papyri, collected in the early years of the twentieth century and dating back into the second century A.D.

Apart from the manuscripts themselves, scholars are able to ascertain the original text by the use of ancient translations from the Greek, from citations of the scriptures by early Christian and Jewish writers and from lectionaries or books containing daily readings for devotional purposes. Through the use of these materials Biblical scholars have been able to reconstruct a text unrivalled for accuracy and integrity by any other ancient writings.

ANCIENT TRANSLATION

The Old Testament which was used by most of the early church was not in its original Hebrew but was a Greek translation of the Hebrew scriptures known as the Septuagint and often designated simply by the Roman numeral LXX. It is so named and abbreviated because of a tradition which asserts that Ptolemy Philadelphius (285-247 B.C.) ordered a Greek version of the scriptures to be completed by about seventy Palestinian elders for use by the Jews in Egypt. It is difficult to determine just how much of the tradition is factual, but the important thing to be noted is that the Jews of the Dispersion were allowing Hebrew to fall into disuse and were in need of a translation into their vernacular. Many of the quotations of the Old Testament which are found in the New Testament are from the Septuagint version.

The need for translations into the languages of the readers resulted in numerous versions. Among the more notable are a second century Syrian version called the Old Syriac, the fourth or fifth century Peshitta ("simple") Syriac which superseded the Old Syriac, the second century translation in Coptic, the vernacular language of Egypt, and the second century Old Latin version. The most important translation before the Reformation was the Latin version commonly referred to as the Vulgate. Just as the settling of the canon was necessitated by the widespread separation of the churches and the rise of heresy, these same factors made a single, authoritative text desirable. The absence of a uniform text to which all Christians could appeal in their encounters with heretical doctrine prompted Damascus, Bishop of Rome, to commission Jerome, the greatest Latin scholar of the latter part of the fourth century, to produce a version which would meet the needs of the church for a standard text. The first installment of this text, a translation of the Gospels, appeared in A.D. 383. Jerome's method in making the translation as to revise the Old Latin versions, aided by the use of Greek manuscripts. His first translation of the Old Testament was made from the Greek Septuagint; however, by A.D. 405, he had completed a translation of the Old Testament from the original Hebrew. It was some time before the new version was able to supersede the Old Latin, but it was destined eventually to become the common Bible of Europe for many centuries. The first English Bible, that of John Wycliffe, was based on this edition. The Vulgate is still the authoritative Bible of the Roman Catholic Church, although it has undergone many revisions.

Translation Into Other European Languages

Prior to and during the period of heaviest activity in English translation of the Bible, with which this review is primarily concerned, there was elsewhere in Europe similar enthusiasm in presenting the Bible to the common people in the vernacular. A Norman-French Bible was in use in Northern France in the middle of the thirteenth century. The fifteenth century brought an Italian and a Dutch version, in addition to various translations in Slavonic and Scandanavian tongues. Many German translations were in existence before the monumental translation of Martin Luther which appeared in the complete Bible in 1534 and which was a chief factor in the standardization of the German language.

THE TRANSLATION OF THE ENGLISH BIBLE

The story of the translation of the Bible into English is one of persecution, courage and intrigue as well as scholarship and spiritual dedication. The clergy and other learned men had always had some access to the Latin Vulgate. Since few of the common people could read and manuscripts were too expensive to buy, this was about all that was required and no complete translation of the Bible or even the New Testament is known to have come from the Anglo-Saxon period. By the middle of the eighth century, however, it is believed that all of the gospels existed in Anglo-Saxon.

John Wycliffe

The first complete English Bible which is known of is that attributed to John Wycliffe (c. 1324-1384). It is difficult to ascertain just what part Wycliffe actually played in the translation. It is often asserted that his colleague, Nicholas of Hereford, was responsible for a great portion of it, especially in the Old Testament. Since the translation was made from the Vulgate edition, it contains the Apocryphal books of the Old Testament. Regardless of his part in the actual translation, Wycliffe was at least the moving spirit behind this version, being motivated by a strong conviction that the laity needed to have an edition of the Bible made available in their common speech. After Wycliffe's death, the work of spreading the copies of his translation was carried on by his followers, known as the "poor priests" or "Lollards." In 1428, forty-four years after his death, the church expressed its disapproval of Wycliffe's labors by ordering his body disinterred, burned, and the ashes cast into the river Swift. Despite the church's efforts to suppress Wycliffe's work, about 170 manuscripts of the Wycliffe Bible are still in existence. This is made even more remarkable when one considers that the printing press had not yet been invented.

William Tyndale

The invention of the printing press loosed a tide of translations that no amount of opposition could stem. A Hebrew Bible appeared in 1488 and the Greek New Testament edited by Erasmus was published in 1516. The first edition of the New Testament to be printed in English was the work of William Tyndale. Tyndale's conviction about the significance of his labors is expressed in his statement that if his life were spared he would enable a common plowhand to know as much of the Bible as the pope. Due to opposition to his work and the lack of funds, Tyndale was forced to pursue his work on the continent, first edition appearing in 1526. In this work he was assisted by John Fryth and William Roye, both of whom later were condemned to death as heretics. In the same year in which the first printing was made, the hierarchy of the English church published a prohibition against the translation. Despite this action, copies continued to make their way into the country. To enforce the prohibitions, the Bishop of London bought up all the copies he could find and burned them. Augustine Packynton, a London merchant who supported Tyndale, raised money for his project by selling Tyndale's Bibles to the Bishop for his bonfire. Through the support of men like Packynton, Tyndale continued his work, beginning work on an English version of the Old Testament and bringing out revisions of the New Testament in 1534 and 1535. In 1530 a royal proclamation was issued, calling for total suppression of the translation of the scriptures "corrupted by William Tyndale." It was stated that the king would provide a translation in the vernacular when such action was deemed expedient. After years of eluding the authorities, Tyndale was finally apprehended and on October 6, 1536, he was strangled and burned at the stake. His dying prayer was "Lord, open the King of England's eyes." It is difficult, if not impossible, to overestimate the value of Tyndale's work in providing us with an English Bible.

Coverdale, Matthew, and Taverner

The first printed edition of the entire Bible into English was that of Miles Coverdale which appeared in 1535. Coverdale, a tactful man, dedicated his translation to King Henry VIII, thus probably sparing his work from some of the difficulties with which it might otherwise have met. The work was substantially based upon that of his friend Tyndale, although there were numerous variations; in addition to the changes in translations, it omitted Tyndale's preface and notes which had been offensive to some. Coverdale included the Apocrypha in his translation, but not without a question as to its validity. The first Bible to obtain official support was probably that published in 1537 under the name of Thomas Matthew. The Taverner Bible of 1539 holds the distinction of being the first Bible printed completely in England. This was a revision of Matthew's and Tyndale's Bible by an English scholar, Richard Taverner, with some individual translation of considerable merit.

The Great Bible

The first "authorized" version was the "Great Bible," so called because of the size of its pages which measured nine by fifteen inches. Oliver Cromwell commissioned Coverdale to serve as editor of this new version. Apart from this, many of the facts involved in the preparation of this Bible are somewhat obscure. Due to superior facilities, the printing was scheduled to have been done in Paris, but difficulties with the authorities forced the work to be completed in London. The Great Bible made its initial appearance in April, 1539. Although the purpose of the translation was to make the scriptures available to the common people, the prologues discouraged public discussion of the Bible by laymen, urging that men of higher learning be consulted on difficult points of interpretation. A second edition of this Bible appeared in 1540 with an introduction by Archbishop Cranmer. Because of this, the Great Bible is often referred to as "Cranmer's Bible."

The Geneva Bible

The next great landmark among English translations was the Geneva Bible of 1558. Such men as Calvin, Knox, and Coverdale were all in touch with this monumental work. The individuals who are usually given credit for the major portion of the actual work are William Whittingham on the New Testament and Anthony Gilby and Thomas Sampson on the Old Testament. These men relied heavily on Tyndale's

work and upon the Great Bible in their translation. Due to the use of the word "breeches" in the translation of Genesis 3:7 ("they sewed fig leaves together and made themselves breeches"), this Bible has often been called the "Breeches Bible." It proved to be the most popular Bible produced in English up to that time. In addition to its translation and annotations, its popularity was enhanced by its use of Roman type and the division of the chapters into verses; this was the first time this had been done in an English Bible. Subsequent versifications of the English Bible owe much to the Geneva Bible.

The second Bible to receive the designation, "authorized," was the Bishops' Bible of 1568, so called because the committee of revisers was composed largely of bishops. A second edition of the Bishops' Bible appeared in 1572.

The Douay-Rheims Catholic Bible

The demand by English-speaking Catholic clergymen for a Bible in their native tongue was met by the efforts of William Cardinal Allen, president and founder of the English college at Douai, France, which was moved to Rheims for a short time. Because of the location of the college, the version which Allen was instrumental in having produced has come to be known as the Douay or Douay-Rheims version. The New Testament in this version was published in 1582 and the Old Testament in 1610. It was made from the Latin Vulgate, in preference to the Hebrew and Greek texts.

The King James Version

The most famous and most durable of all English versions has been the King James Version of 1611. A remark regarding mistranslations in the existing Bibles was made at the Hampton Court Conference on religious grievances in 1604. The idea of a new translation caught the imagination of King James and he determined to have a new version made which might be established as the uniform text of the entire commonwealth. Fifty-four scholars were chosen for the task. These were to be divided into six groups, each being assigned a section of the scripture for translation and revision. Each individual in a group was to make an individual translation of the section assigned to his group. When this was completed, the members of the group were to compare their work and formulate a translation which was acceptable to all. Similarly, each group was to present its product to the entire company for final approval. In addition, all learned individuals in the churches were urged to render any aid which they might in eliminating obscurities in the text. By the time the work was finally begun in 1607, only forty-seven of the original fifty-four were available for work on the project. Ten of these met at Westminster and were assigned the Pentateuch (the first five books of the Old Testament) along with the historical books which follow from Joshua through the two books of Kings. Eight more, at Cambridge, had charge of the rest of the historical books, together with Job, Psalms, Proverbs, Song of Solomon and Ecclesiastes. At Oxford one company of seven had the prophets assigned to them and another company of eight were entrusted with the four Gospels, Acts of Apostles, and the Revelation of John. A second company at Westminster was engaged in translating the remainder of the New Testament while a second company at Cambridge was given the books of the Apocrypha.

The translators received certain general instructions from the king to regulate them in their work. They were required to abide by the translation of the "Bishops' Bible" as much as the original text would allow; to retain proper names in their original form; when several words might fit equally well, to use that which had been preferable to the best ancient writers; to use the current chapter and verse divisions; to use no marginal notes, unless to explain particular Greek or Hebrew words, and to cite references to parallel passages insofar as it seemed desirable. These forty-seven men struggled with the version for over three years, finally bringing it to publication in 1611.

As a result of its arrival on the scene at a propitious time in history, the King James or Authorized Version (although King James did not bear the expenses of the project and there is no record of an official "authorization") has long held the foremost position among English translations insofar as its popularity is concerned. The majesty and beauty of its language, not to mention the familiarity which centuries of use brings, have made this popularity not unjustified. There are, however, certain facts which the serious student should bear in mind. The Authorized Version was based upon the faulty Greek text of Erasmus which was compiled without the benefit of the better manuscripts which have since been discovered. It was never intended to be the final revision of the scriptures "once for all delivered to the saints." In fact, no one today reads the Authorized Version in the English in which it was originally written, as this is so archaic as to sound foreign to modern ears. Yet, this was the language of the common man in the 1600's. An edition was published in 1629 omitting the Apocrypha which had been included in the original version. Extensive revisions of this version appeared in 1762 and 1769. It is also interesting to note that the King James Version aroused the same sort of clamor which has greeted translations of the Bible into modern speech in this century.

Modern Translations of the Bible

With the discovery of better texts and the needs for a Bible in the vernacular—the same need which produced all the great versions—scholars have continued to present the Bible to us in revised forms. The English Revised Version, usually referred to simply as the Revised Version, appeared in the New Testament in 1881 and in the complete Bible in 1885. This version differed from the King James Version in over thirty thousand places in the New Testament alone. In 1901 an American edition known as the American Revised or American Standard Version appeared. This version was similar to the Revised Version although it embodied changes which were preferable to the American Revision committee. In the twentieth century numerous other modern speech translations have occurred, usually the work of one or two individuals. Most notable among these are the versions of Weymouth, Moffatt, Goodspeed, Phillips, and the Riverside New Testament. In 1949, the complete Bible appeared in "Basic English," a simplified form of English based on a 1,000-word vocabulary.

The most widely accepted translation of the twentieth century has been the Revised Standard Version. This work was begun in 1930, the New Testament being complete in 1946 and the Old Testament in 1952. Another well-received translation has been the New English Bible which first appeared in 1961. All of these modern speech translations have met with opposition and cries of corruption of the sacred writing. None, to be sure, is perfect; yet, probably without exception, each has been made with a high regard for the Holy Word and a sincere desire to render more intelligible that which is the true will of God for every man.

Summary of the Translations

John Wycliffe's Bible (c. 1382)
William Tyndale's New Testament (1526)
Miles Coverdale's Bible (1535)
Thomas Matthew's Bible (1537)
Richard Taverner's Bible (1539)
Great Bible—The first "authorized" Bible (1539)
Geneva Bible—The "Breeches Bible" (1558)
Bishop's Bible (1568 and 1572)
Douay-Rheims Catholic Bible (1610)
King James or Authorized Version (1611)
English Revised Version (1881-1885)
American Standard Version (1901)
Revised Standard Version (1946-1952)
The New English Bible (1961)

MODERN DIVISIONS OF THE BIBLE

The original authors of the Bible did not divide their writings into chapters and verses as we have them today; this was a much later development. The Jews had long divided their scriptures into sections for more convenient reference, but the division into chapters as we know them was the work either of Stephen Langton, archbishop of Canterbury in the reigns of John and Henry III, or Cardinal Hugo de St. Caro, the first member of the Dominican order to be raised to the rank of Cardinal. Both of these men were active in the first half of the thirteenth century. It was Hugo who devised the first concordance, which would necessitate some type of versifi-cation in order to prove workable. As stated above, the division of the chapters was identical to our present divisions, but the smaller sub-divisions did not correspond to our system of versification. Instead, the chapters were sub-divided by placing the letters A, B, C, D, E, F, G, in the margin at an equal distance from each other, depending on the length of the chapter. This system of versification was adopted into the Latin Vulgate, which had previously had no sub-divisions at all.

The sub-division of the Old Testament chapters into verses was done by Rabbi Mordecai Nathan, about 1445. This rabbi, in imitation of Hugo, drew up a concordance to the Hebrew scriptures for the use of Jews. Although he followed Hugo in his division of the books into chapters, he improved upon his subdivisions, giving us our present numerical arrangement of verses. This was found to be much more convenient and has been followed since that time. The division of the New Testament chapters into verses first appeared in the Greek text edited by Robert Estienne in 1551. Tradition has it that Estienne devised his system while traveling on horseback from Paris to Lyons.

It ought always to be remembered that the division of the Bible into verses was designed as a reference aid for study of the Bible and was never intended to govern the sense of a passage. A verse or chapter division may often occur in the middle of a narrative or train of thought, thus giving the impression that the discussion of the topic has ended, when such may not be the case. The serious student should be careful not to follow a program of reading which adheres strictly to the humanly-devised divisions of the Bible, but should concern himself with making certain that he has discerned the context in which a verse or chapter is situated.

Bible Stories For Children

THE CREATION

From the very beginning, God has existed. Even before there was a world, or the sky, or animals, or people, He lived, for it was He who made them all.

Because there was darkness everywhere, God first created light. As its brightness shone through the dark, He was pleased and knew that it was good. He called this light Day. But God knew that darkness was needed also, so He allowed some of it to remain and called it Night. These God created on the *first* day.

On the *second* day, God created the air that surrounds us. When we look up as far as we can see, the air appears to be blue, and we call this the sky or Heaven.

Next, God gathered together the waters to form oceans, rivers, and lakes and separated them from the dry land. On the dry land, He caused the grass and trees and plants to grow and make it green and lovely. As the *third* day ended, our earth was beginning to look like it does to us now.

The sun and moon were created on the *fourth* day to brighten the day and the night. Even the twinkling star lights were set in place by God's hand on this day.

The *fifth* day God brought forth living things to fill the water and the air—fish for the seas and birds for the heavens. On the *sixth* day, He continued the creation of living things by making all kinds of animals to live on the earth.

As the last day of the creation was ending, God formed a man. The Bible says that He made this man "in His image." This means that the man was to be higher than the animals and to rule over them. God placed this man in the wonderful home that He had made.

For six days God had worked to make our world —the day with the sun and the night with the moon, the seas filled with fish and the air with birds, the earth covered with plants and animals of every sort, and a man in his own image.

On the *seventh* day, God looked on all that He had made and declared that it was good. He blessed this day on which He rested from His work.

ADAM AND EVE

On the sixth day of the creation, God made a man "from the dust of the ground." This man, called Adam, was different from the rest of the things God had created because he was made in God's own image. This meant that Adam was higher than the animals and able to rule over them. God even let Adam name all the different kinds of animals and birds that were on the earth. Perhaps when Adam saw that all these creatures had others of their own kind to be with, he felt alone and lonesome. We know that God did see that Adam needed a helper, so one day He caused Adam to fall into a deep sleep. While Adam was asleep, God took one of his ribs and from it made a woman to be with Adam. When Adam woke up, he was very happy to find her. He called her Eve.

In a place called Eden, God made an especially beautiful garden to be a home for Adam and Eve. Four rivers flowed through it and caused many different kinds of trees and plants to grow. In the middle of the garden grew two very special trees, the Tree of Life and the Tree of Knowledge of Good and Evil. It was Adam's job to take care of this garden, and in return, he and Eve were free to live there and to eat of the luscious fruits and vegetables that were growing there. God gave them only one rule to follow: they were not to eat from the Tree of Knowledge.

What a happy and simple life this couple had! All that they knew was good. God had given them only one rule to follow. As yet there was no sickness nor wrong nor sadness in the world.

Even as far back as the time of Adam and Eve, the devil was working against God the good that God wanted man to do. Satan tried to figure out a plan that would make Adam and Eve do wrong. One day he appeared in their garden home disguised as a serpent and tried to persuade them to eat from the tree that God had forbidden.

"Did God tell you not to eat of any certain tree in the garden?" he cunningly asked.

Eve answered, "We can eat from every tree here

except the Tree of Knowledge, and God has forbidden us to touch its fruit or we will die."

"Oh, you will not die," said the devil, trying to fool them. "Actually, it will make you as wise as God is and you will be able to understand things as He does."

Foolish Eve believed what the serpent told her and she ate some of the fruit. Then she gave some to Adam and he ate it also. Immediately they knew they had done wrong and began trying to hide from God.

Of course Adam and Eve were not able to hide from God for He always knows about everything we do. Their sin made Him very angry and He sent them away from the garden. He told them that they would have to work very hard, that they would have trouble and sickness, and that one day they would die. If only this first couple had chosen to do right instead of wrong, these terrible things would not have ever entered the world.

Even though God had to punish Adam and Eve, He still loved His creation; and He promised then that some day He would save mankind. We know that He did this when He sent His Son, Jesus Christ, into the world. Through Him, God can forgive men for the wrong they have done.

CAIN AND ABEL

After Adam and Eve had disobeyed and eaten of the forbidden fruit, God sent them away from the Garden of Eden forever. He even sent angels to guard the Tree of Life and to keep them from returning to their first home. Surely Adam and Eve were not as happy away from their home, but one day something wonderful did happen to them —they had a little baby boy. They named him Cain; and later when they had another little boy, they called him Abel. These first babies must have looked beautiful to their mother and father, just as new babies do to us today.

As they were growing up, Cain and Abel were interested in different things. Cain liked to farm and watch things growing in the ground. Abel liked best to be around the animals and to look after the herds of sheep his father kept.

In these early times, people did not worship God by going to church. Instead, they brought something that they had for the Lord and burned it. The offering was called a *sacrifice,* and usually it was burned on a rock or some stones called an *altar.*

One day Cain and Abel brought sacrifices to the Lord. Cain brought some of the fruits and vegetables that he had grown in his garden. Abel brought some of the finest sheep from his flocks. We do not understand exactly why, but God was not pleased with the offering that Cain made, while He thought that Abel's was good. This made Cain very angry, and the Bible tells us that it even showed on his face how displeased he was.

God spoke to Cain and asked him not to look so angry. He told Cain that He would give him another chance to do right and that he could be as pleasing to Him as Abel was.

But Cain kept brooding about the way that God had rejected his offering instead of trying to change and do right. Not only was he angry with God, but he began to blame his brother as well. One day when they were out in a field, Cain got so upset about it that he killed Abel.

Of course, the Lord knew about this terrible thing that Cain had done, but just to test Cain, He asked him where Abel was. Cain puffed up in anger and tried to hide his sin by asking, "Am I my brother's keeper?"

God told Cain that He had known about the murder all along, and because Cain had failed to do right at every chance, He punished him by sending him away from his home. But God put a special mark on Cain so that the strangers whom he met in his wanderings would not harm him. God always loves us even when we do wrong, but He has to punish us to help us remember to obey.

NOAH AND THE ARK

Adam and Eve had other children besides Cain and Abel, and then they had grandchildren. Before many years passed, there were people in great numbers on the earth. Although some of the people, like Abel, tried to obey God, many did not listen to Him. These wicked people got worse and worse, and more of the good people began following their example. As time went on, nearly all the

Loran Raymond Jones

NOAH LEAVING THE ARK ON MOUNT ARARAT

Genesis 8:18; 9:1–17

world was evil. When God looked at men, He was sorry He had ever made them; and He decided to destroy these bad people with a great flood.

The Lord knew, however, that there was one good man living in those days. His name was Noah. Although everyone around him was doing wrong, Noah would have nothing to do with them. He remembered God and taught his three boys, Shem, Ham, and Japheth, to obey Him. The Lord wanted to save Noah, so He told him to build a great ship called an ark. He told Noah the kind of wood to use and the size to make the boat. It was to have a great door and three decks. There were to be rooms inside for the people, pens for the animals, and storerooms of food for all.

For many years, maybe a hundred, Noah worked on the ark, believing that God was going to send the rain some day. While he worked, he tried to tell those that made fun of him that God was going to destroy them unless they quit doing wrong. But no one believed Noah and no one changed.

Finally the ark was finished. God told Noah to go into the ark and to take with him his wife, his sons, and his sons' wives. He also sent Noah a pair of every kind of animal and bird on the earth to put into the ark. When they were all inside, God shut them in. For seven days they waited in suspense, and then it began to rain. It rained as it had never rained before—as though the windows of the sky had opened. The oceans began to rise over the land, and all the rivers and lakes overflowed their banks. Soon all the land was covered, and the people had to run to the mountains for safety; but as the waters rose higher and higher, finally even the mountaintops went out of sight. Everybody had drowned. Only Noah and those with him were safe. The ark floated on waters that had no shore while God Himself watched it and kept it from harm.

For forty days and forty nights it rained without stopping, and then God caused it to stop. The water, however, remained on the earth for many days until He made winds to blow over it and help it dry. Gradually, the water got lower until the ark quit floating and rested on one of the high mountains of Ararat. Then other mountaintops began to appear. One day Noah sent out a raven to see if there was any dry ground, but the raven could fly for a long time and it found dead things to eat, so it never came back. Later he sent out a dove, but the dove likes to rest in the trees and eat their seeds, and he came back when he found no trees. After a week, Noah let the dove fly out again. This time it returned with an olive branch in its beak. Noah knew that the waters had gone down enough for the trees to put on leaves again. When he let the dove go after another week, it never returned. Noah knew then that the time of the flood, which had lasted a whole year, was over. He opened the door of the ark and out poured the eight people and all the animals that God had saved.

What a beautiful sight the fresh, green earth must have been to them after being closed up so long! How grateful they must have been to God for keeping them safe! The first thing they wanted to do was to thank God, so Noah made an altar and burned an animal sacrifice on it as Abel had done.

God was pleased with Noah and his sons, and He made a promise to them that He would never again destroy the earth with such a flood. Until the end of the world, he would keep on sending days and nights, spring, summer, fall, and winter. As a sign of His promise, He set the rainbow in the clouds. It is made when the sunlight shines on the raindrops in the air, and it reminded them of God's pledge. This same promise belongs to us today, and we can remember it and thank God every time we see a rainbow in the sky.

THE TOWER OF BABEL

Noah and his sons had a fresh, new world in which to begin life again. This family was the only one on the earth, as Adam's family once had been. They made new homes, and after a while Shem, Ham, and Japheth each had a big family of his own. These children grew up and had children of their own, and again there were many people on the earth. Before the flood, everyone had lived in the same area, but now they began to scatter and build their homes in different places. God wanted

people to move so that one day people would use all parts of the earth for their homes. That way, people like Noah's family, who wanted to do right, could move away from the wicked people they were living near and either go off by themselves or move near other godly families.

Some of the people moved south from Mount Ararat, where the ark had landed, and lived on a plain in the land of Shinar. This land had the materials for making bricks, and from these bricks the

men were able to make strong houses and walls. When they saw that their city was going to be a strong one, they began to feel very important and said to one another, "Let us also build a great tower that will reach up to the sky. Then we will not be scattered about the earth and separated from one another."

They set about with great energy to build the tower. Some made bricks, some made mortar to put them together, and others laid the bricks, one story above the other. As the tower rose higher and higher, the people felt more and more important and pleased with themselves.

When God saw the city and tower that the men were building, He was not pleased. He saw that the men were beginning to think less of Him and more of their own importance. Soon they might quit thinking of Him at all and worship the things that they were able to make. Besides that, it was not God's plan that all men live close together as they had before the flood. He knew that again the wicked could lead the good away from God, and all the world would become wicked again.

In order to stop the building of the tower, God caused them to speak different languages. Up until this time, everyone had spoken the same language, so that everyone could understand what everyone else said. Now those of one family could not understand what their neighbors of another family were saying. Those working in the city could not understand what people had come to sell or buy. Most important, those building the tower could not understand their fellow workers well enough to continue. They left the tower without finishing it, and it stayed forever that way. As God had planned, gradually families began moving away to other places, where those speaking one language could understand one another.

Afterward, the city was named Babel, which means "confusion." Even later on, it was known as Babylon and was an important city in that part of the world. But those that left went in all directions and settled in other lands as God led them.

HAGAR AND ISHMAEL

Some of the people who moved from Babylon after the languages were confused built a city not too far away to the north. These people called their city Ur, after the moon god idol they worshiped. One good man in the city worshiped the true God, just as Noah had done in his time. God did not want this man's family to grow up in such a wicked place, so He appeared to the man, whose name was Abram. He told Abram to leave Ur and follow Him to a land far away. In this new land, Abram's family would grow in number and become a great people. One day the land would be theirs. God even promised that in the distant future, all the families of the world would be blessed because of Abram's son and his family.

Abram did not understand all that God said to him. Already he was getting old, and he did not have even one child. How could the world be blessed through his family when he had none? He could not realize that the great blessing to the world that God was speaking of was Jesus Christ. Many, many years later, Christ was born into the very family to which Abram had been a father. This way Abram's family gave all the world a blessing by giving them a Savior.

Although Abram did not understand all that God told him, he obeyed through *faith*. This means that he obeyed God and believed what He said even though he could not yet see the new land or his large family or the blessings to come. He just knew that God would keep his promise. So Abram took his wife Sarai, his old father Terah, all his servants, and his cattle and left Ur. When they would come to water on their journeys, they would pitch their tent homes for a while and let the animals enjoy it. At one place called Haran they stayed for a long while, maybe because Terah was too old to go any farther, for we know that he died there.

After a long journey, Abram reached the land of the Canaanites, or Canaan. It was near a great sea and had sloping hills and grass, perfect for cattle and sheep grazing. The Canaanites had built some cities in their land, but Abram continued to live on the open fields in his tent. As he was getting up his tent near an oak tree, God appeared to him again and told him that this was the land that would be his. Believing and trusting in God, Abram built an altar there and worshiped.

Abram and his household continued to live in Canaan except for a time that they spent in Egypt to escape a famine, a time when the land did not produce enough food for the cattle. When they returned, they brought with them an Egyptian girl named Hagar to be Sarai's maid. When years passed and still Abram and Sarai had no child,

Sarai suggested to Abram that Hagar have a child and it could be the child of promise. Later on, however, Hagar displeased Sarai, and Sarai punished her severely. Hagar ran away toward the desert and her home in Egypt, but she stopped to rest by a fountain. Here an angel of the Lord found her and said: "Hagar, where have you come from and where are you going?"

"I am running away from Sarai, my mistress, because I do not want to serve her any longer," replied Hagar.

"Go back to Sarai and obey her," the angel said. "God will be with you and will help you. You will have a son who will grow to be a strong man."

Hagar returned to the house of her mistress and she did have a son. Abram named him Ishmael, which means "God hears." But even though Abram loved Ishmael, he was not the son God had promised. One day Abram and Sarai had a baby boy of their own. This was the one that God promised to bless and make of him a great nation. His name was Isaac. Ishmael was older than Isaac, but he often played with the baby. Sarai did not like the older boy playing with her son, and she asked Abram to send him and his mother away.

Now Abram felt sorry for Hagar and Ishmael, but God told him not to worry about them because He was going to begin a nation with the boy Ishmael too. So Abram sent Hagar and Ishmael off with some food and water for their trip. They traveled toward Egypt again, but on the journey they used up all their food and water. In the hot sun and burning sand, they could go no farther. Hagar laid poor Ishmael down in the shade of a bush because she said, "I cannot bear to see my boy suffer and die."

God heard Hagar in the wilderness a second time, and again He sent an angel to her. The angel told her that God would take care of her and her son. Surely enough, when the angel disappeared, she saw a spring of water bubbling out of the dry ground near her. She filled their empty water bottles and gave Ishmael a drink.

Hagar and Ishmael never returned to Egypt, but made their home in the wilderness, away from other people. Ishmael grew up there to be a strong outdoor man, very skillful with the bow and arrow. His children, like him, grew up in the desert and became a strong, wandering nation.

ABRAHAM'S GREAT TEST

For a long time Abraham did not understand God's promise to him that his family would be great and number as the stars in the sky. It was difficult for him to believe because he did not have a child. He thought that perhaps Ishmael could be the son God promised, but when God sent Ishmael and his mother away, He showed Abram that he was not the one. God wanted Sarai, Abram's wife, to be the child's mother, not an Egyptian servant girl.

God repeated His promise to Abram several times. Sometimes this promise is called the "old covenant" because it was given to Abram. The "new covenant" or promise is the one given in Christ. One time when God was speaking to Abram, He told him He was going to change his name to Abraham, which means the father of many nations. He changed Sarai's name to Sarah, which means a princess.

When Abraham was ninety-nine years old and Sarah was nearly as old, God told them that the time had come for their son to come. Sarah laughed when she heard that she was going to have a baby because she thought that she was too old. But sure enough, God sent them a little baby boy, and they named him Isaac.

Isaac made everyone very happy. Abraham and Sarah were very proud of him; and they gave a great dinner to show him to their friends when he was still a little boy, barely walking about. They took good care of him, and he grew to be a fine boy, obedient to his parents.

One day God gave Abraham a very hard thing to do. He wanted to see if Abraham really believed in Him and loved Him more than anything else in the world, even his son. He asked him to take Isaac and offer him like a sacrifice on an altar.

Of course, this request made Abraham very sad. He loved his boy very much. God had made Abraham the promise that Isaac would be the ancestor of a great nation of people and that they would someday possess the land of Canaan. How could God keep this promise if Isaac were killed? Abraham wondered about this, but he prepared to obey God.

The next morning Abraham and Isaac set off for Mount Moriah to worship God. They took with them two servant men, their donkeys, and wood for the offering. For two days and nights they traveled. On the third day, they saw the mountain in

Loran Raymond Jones

ABRAHAM RESTRAINED FROM SACRIFICING ISAAC

Genesis 22:2–14

the distance. Abraham and Isaac alighted from their donkeys. Abraham said to the servants, "You keep our donkeys here while Isaac and I go up on the mountain and worship. When we have finished, we will come back." He then gave Isaac the wood they had brought for the offering, and he took the vessel with fire in it.

Isaac looked about and asked, "My father! Here you have the fire and I have the wood for our offering. Where is the animal to sacrifice?"

"God Himself will provide a lamb for the offering, my son," Abraham replied.

Together they started up the mountain.

When they reached the place of worship, they set up stones for an altar and lay the wood upon it. Then perhaps Isaac realized that he was the offering God was providing. The Bible tells us that he allowed his father to bind him and lay him across the wood. Sadly and slowly, Abraham raised his knife to kill his only son, the promised one for whom he had waited so many years. Surely the

thoughts of the promises his son was to fulfill crossed his mind at that moment.

But as he lowered the hand that was clutching the knife, an angel of the Lord called out to him, "Abraham! Abraham!"

With relief, Abraham dropped the knife and answered, "Here I am."

"There is no need for you to kill your son, Abraham. God knows now that you trust Him and love Him more than anything—even your own son." This was the message that the angel brought.

Abraham then raised his eyes; and as he did, he spied a ram with its horns caught in a thicket. It was the offering God had provided. He untied Isaac, and they gratefully worshiped God together with the sacrifice that He had given them.

Abraham named the place on Mount Moriah where he and Isaac had built this altar, "The Lord will provide." Surely it was a place that they never forgot, for it was here that Abraham had passed the greatest test of his faith that God ever gave him.

ESAU SELLS HIS BIRTHRIGHT

After Abraham had lived to be an old man and had seen his son Isaac grow up and marry a fine and beautiful young lady, he died. From the years long before when God had called him to leave Ur, he had followed God's every command. He had even been ready to sacrifice his own son, Isaac, when the Lord asked that of him. God had blessed Abraham for his faithfulness, even though some of the promises He made were not to be fulfilled until many more years had passed. Abraham had become the founder of God's specially chosen people, chosen to learn His ways. Into this family one day God planned to have His own Son born. Until this time, He had to watch over and lead His people, the children of Abraham, and to give them the land of Canaan for their home.

Isaac buried his father in a cave that had been bought when Isaac's mother, Sarah, had died. Together Abraham and Sarah were laid in the cave of Machpelah, as the custom was in those days.

Now Isaac and his wife Rebekah were like Abraham and Sarah in that they, too, were married a long time before they had any children. Like Abraham, Isaac wondered how God was going to make theirs a great and wonderful family when there were no children. Rebekah wanted a baby very badly, and Isaac prayed to God that He

would give her one.

God heard Isaac's prayer and He answered it by giving them not one son, but two—twin boys. Some twins are very much alike, but these were different. The first one to be born was a red little boy, covered with soft hair. They named him Esau, which means "hairy." The second baby was smooth-skinned and pink, and they called him Jacob.

Before the babies were born, God had told Rebekah a strange thing about the babies. He had said: "These children are to be two different nations. One people will be stronger than the other; and the elder shall serve the younger." As the twins grew up, it certainly appeared that Esau was the stronger. He was a rugged boy who loved to hunt and stay outdoors. Jacob was no weakling, but he was quieter and more gentle.

It was natural that the boys were rivals from the beginning. Esau, with his red face and thick hair, was Isaac's favorite. After a day of hunting, Esau would bring Isaac some of the deer meat he had gotten and tell him of the adventures of the chase. Isaac loved to eat the meat and listen to Esau. He was proud of Esau's strength, and he loved him best. Jacob, however, was his mother's favorite. Rebekah could see that Jacob had wisdom and a strength of mind that Esau did not have.

After the boys were grown, Esau continued his life of hunting. Jacob was the family shepherd and farmer. One day, probably as he was in the field with the sheep or working with the crops, Jacob stopped to build a fire and fix himself a little pot of stew. As he was cooking it, Esau came in, tired and famished from an unlucky hunt.

When he saw the stew Jacob was cooking, he asked Jacob for some of it. Perhaps there was only enough for one and Jacob argued with him about it. Finally Esau said in desperation, "I would give anything I owned for something to eat!"

"Even your birthright?" asked Jacob.

"What good would a birthright do me if I died of hunger?" answered Esau with a question of his own.

"Promise the birthright shall be mine," said Jacob.

Esau lightly promised and eagerly grabbed the mess of pottage, as stew of this kind was sometimes called. That easily Esau gave up the greatest heritage he had. The birthright usually fell to the oldest son; and it meant that when the father died, he would be the head of the family and take possession of the greatest part of that which the father owned. It meant that he would be the leader of the family, the wisest one, the closest to God. For something just to satisfy himself at the moment, Esau traded these blessings.

Actually, this foolish trade had a place in God's plans although neither Esau nor Jacob nor their parents realized it then. God was preparing to make true his prediction to Rebekah that "the elder shall serve the younger."

JACOB DECEIVES HIS FATHER

The day came when Isaac had grown very old. He had to stay in bed most of the time, and he could hardly see. He knew that he would not live much longer. He called Esau to him and asked, "Take your bow and arrows and go hunt for me. Bring me a deer and cook it the way that I love so well. Perhaps it will make me feel better. We can talk—you can tell me about your hunt and then I will give you the blessing that is your birthright."

Now Rebekah heard Isaac talking with Esau. As Esau hurried out to obey his father's wish, she called to Jacob. Perhaps she knew that Jacob had once bought the birthright from Esau and saw that this was the time to claim it. Together Rebekah and Jacob planned to deceive old Isaac.

Jacob was a little timid about trying to fool his father. He said, "What if he should discover who I am and curse instead of bless me?"

"Let his curse be on me," answered Rebekah. "Now go, and let us hurry with our plan before Esau returns."

So Jacob fetched two kids from his father's flock, as his mother suggested. They killed the kids and skinned them. With the meat Rebekah prepared a stew, seasoning it and cooking it as she would deer meat. She knew that Isaac, old and sick, would probably not be able to tell the difference. Then she took the skin of the goats and wound it around Jacob's hands and the part of his neck that showed. She wanted Isaac to think that he was touching Esau's hairy skin.

At last, Rebekah brought out one of Esau's robes for Jacob to wear. She wanted even the smell of the clothes to lead Isaac to think that this was his favorite, older son. Giving Jacob the stew and some bread, she told him to go to his father. With a little tremble, he went toward his father's room.

"Father?" said Jacob.

"Here I am," said Isaac. "Who are you, my son?" He could scarcely see and Jacob possibly spoke softly so his voice would not be recognized.

"I am Esau, your first-born," lied Jacob. "I have done just as you asked me, Father. Try to sit up and eat some of the venison I have brought you. Then please give me your blessing."

Poor Isaac could not see, but he was not easily deceived. Questions came to his mind. He asked, "How did you find a deer so quickly?"

"God was with me, and I came upon him very soon," said Jacob.

Still Isaac was not satisfied. He asked Jacob to come near so that he might feel him. As he felt the goats' hair that Jacob had on his neck and hands, he was further puzzled. Again he asked if this was really Esau. Then he had Jacob come near so that he could smell of his clothes. As he smelled the outdoor scent that still clung to Esau's robes, he felt satisfied and prepared to give his blessing.

Solemnly he placed his hands on Jacob and said, "God give you the dew of the heaven, the fatness of the earth, and plenty to eat and drink. Let peoples serve you and nations honor you. Let your

mother's children bow down to you. Let him that curses you be cursed, and blessed be he that blesses you."

So Jacob received the blessing.

No sooner had Jacob left Isaac, than Esau came in from the hunt. He hurried to make the deer stew his father was so fond of and brought it to him.

"Who is it now?" asked Isaac.

"Esau, your first-born." This voice could not be mistaken. The smell of the woods and the freshly killed deer still came from Esau's skin and clothes.

Immediately Isaac realized that he had been fooled. Perhaps anger rose within him, but he knew that it was too late. He knew that God could bring good even out of lies and deception. He could make all things work for the best in His plans. He remembered that before the twins were born, God had told Rebekah that the younger would rule.

Esau would not listen to such reasoning. He begged for the blessing, but it was Isaac's to give only once. He had already made Jacob a leader over Esau.

Even a great, fierce man like Esau cried over his lost birthright. He asked, "Have you no blessing for me, Father?"

Isaac gave Esau what blessing he could, but it was not the same one he gave Jacob. Esau was furious and left full of hatred for the brother that had taken his birthright and blessing.

JACOB'S WONDERFUL DREAM

When Esau discovered that Jacob had claimed the blessing that rightly belonged to him, he became so angry that he determined to kill his brother. He planned to wait until their father died. Then when Jacob took over his father's possessions, Esau would slay him and have them for his own.

But Rebekah had the interests of her favorite, Jacob, at heart; and she sent for him when she heard of Esau's evil plans. She warned Jacob to leave at once.

"Go to my brother Laban, who lives at Haran. Stay and visit with him a while, and then perhaps Esau will forget his anger. When he does, I will send for you to come back to us, for I cannot bear to lose both you and your father."

Rebekah did not tell old Isaac about the quarrel between their sons. Instead she told him that Jacob was going to seek a good wife from among their own people. Both Isaac and Rebekah were disappointed in the heathen women that Esau took for his wives, and Isaac agreed that Jacob should find a woman that worshiped the true God. Like most fathers, he forgave Jacob for his deception, and he gave him his parting blessing.

Bidding his mother and father good-by, Jacob set out on the long journey alone. As he traveled slowly on his way, he thought of the trouble that he had brought upon himself. He was afraid that his own brother would kill him, and he did not know if he would ever feel safe to return home. He wondered if he would ever see his old father again. What good was the stolen birthright now that he

might never be able to claim it?

More than the loss of his brother's love and his father's fortunes, Jacob feared that God was not pleased with him. He knew that he had lied, cheated, and stolen something which was not his. Perhaps he repented to God and prayed for forgiveness as he trudged along his lonely path. Whatever his thoughts, we know that God was listening to them.

As the sun went down, Jacob probably felt lonelier than ever. He was very tired, however, and looked for a good place to stop for the night. Finding a smooth stone on which to rest his head, he lay down to sleep.

While he slept, God sent him a wonderful dream. He saw a ladder that reached all the way from earth to heaven. On the ladder were beautiful angels, climbing up and down—from heaven, to earth, and back to their heavenly home. God himself stood at the top of the ladder and spoke to Jacob: "I am the God of your grandfather Abraham and of your father Isaac. This land where you are lying, I will give to you and to your children. Your descendants will be many, as many as the specks of dust on the earth; and through your family, all the peoples of the earth will be blessed. Now, I am with you and will be with you wherever you go, and I will bring you back to this land some day. I will never leave you until I fulfill this promise."

These were familiar words. God had spoken them before to Abraham and to Isaac, and these very words had been the light that led them

throughout their lives. Now they had been repeated to Jacob. What glory he must have felt when he awoke! No longer was he alone. "Surely the Lord is in this place and I knew it not," he whispered to himself. "Why, this is the house of God, the gate of heaven!" he said as he looked about.

Taking the stone that had been his pillow, he set it up as a marker to God, the God of Abraham, of Isaac, and now of Jacob. He named the place Bethel, which means "the house of God," and he made a promise to God that he would give back to Him a tenth of all that God gave him.

After the wonderful dream, Jacob must have felt more light-hearted as he continued on his journey. With God as his companion, the tiresome trip was made easy.

JACOB AND HIS UNCLE LABAN

After many days of travel, Jacob saw that the end of his flight from his brother Esau was in sight. Ahead were some men with three flocks of sheep waiting to be watered. A well was nearby with a large stone covering its mouth.

Jacob wondered what town he was approaching and asked: "Where are you from?"

"From Haran," they replied.

"Do you know a man from Haran named Laban?" asked Jacob.

"Yes, we know him. Look, here comes his daughter Rachel now with his sheep."

Surely enough, his cousin was approaching with her father's sheep, for she was their keeper. It was the time of day that she brought them to be watered. Jacob hurried to meet her and rolled away the stone from the well. As he watered her sheep for her, he told her that he was her kinsman, the son of her father's sister, Rebekah. Probably Rachel had been told of her aunt who had gone long ago to the land of Canaan to become the wife of Abraham's son, Isaac. How warmly the cousins greeted each other! Then in a great hurry, Rachel ran to tell her father of Jacob's arrival.

Laban was glad to have news of his sister Rebekah and he ran out to meet her son, Jacob. He brought him to the house and listened with interest to the tales Jacob had to tell of the land of Canaan, his home. Throughout the evening, however, Jacob's eyes would stray back to the beautiful shepherdess, Rachel. Love for her was blossoming in his heart.

Jacob had been brought up as a shepherd, and he began helping Laban with his flocks. After a month, Laban offered to pay him for his work. "What will you have for your wages?" he asked Jacob.

Without hesitation, Jacob's heart told him what he wanted. "I will work seven years for you if you will give me your daughter Rachel to be my wife."

"You are the kind of husband I would choose for her," said Laban, giving his consent. In those days it was customary for the bridegroom to give some kind of payment like this to the father of the bride, so it did not seem as strange to them as it seems to us.

For seven years Jacob worked to win his lovely Rachel, but he loved her so much that it seemed to him only a few days. When the seven years was ended, Jacob came to Laban to claim his bride. Laban arranged a great wedding feast, and in the evening, he brought in the bride. According to another of their customs, the bride's face was probably covered with a heavy veil. It was not until after the marriage ceremony had ended that Jacob discovered that he had not married Rachel at all! Instead, Laban had brought in Leah, Rachel's older sister, and she had become Jacob's wife.

Leah was not as beautiful as her younger sister, and Jacob did not love her as he did Rachel. Once he had planned a deception himself, but now he was the one deceived, and he realized how it felt to be cheated. He complained to Laban that the father had been unfair. Laban explained that it was customary in their country for the older daughter to marry first. He had another bargain, however. "If you will serve me another seven years, I will give you Rachel for your wife also," he told Jacob. In those days, we know that God allowed men to have more than one wife.

Because Jacob loved Rachel so, he worked another seven years for her father. When those years were over, Jacob wanted to return again to Canaan, but Laban persuaded him to enter into a third bargain. Laban agreed to give Jacob part of his flocks and herds if Jacob would work for him another six years. This way Jacob was able to provide for his own growing family.

During this time, the Lord blessed Jacob bountifully. His herds grew great in number; he acquired a number of servants; his wives gave him a large family. But troubles began to develop between

Loran Raymond Jones

JACOB AND RACHEL AT THE WELL

Genesis 29:9–12

Jacob and Laban. Laban looked at Jacob's good fortune with envy, and he changed Jacob's wages ten times. Disputes and quarrels arose over their property. The Lord appeared to Jacob and told him that the time had come for him to return to Canaan. He promised to guide Jacob on what was to be an eventful journey.

While Laban was away shearing his sheep, Jacob called his two wives to him, gathered up the rest of his family and his flocks, and secretly left Haran. When Laban found that they had gone, three days had already passed. He took with him several men and rode after them, but before he reached Jacob, the Lord appeared to him also. He warned Laban not to harm his son-in-law.

Laban was less angry with Jacob after this warning. He and Jacob were eventually able to settle their disputes. Laban kissed his daughters and grandchildren a warm good-by. He and Jacob set up some stones for a memorial and called the heap of stones Mizpah, or a "watchtower." "The Lord watch over us while we are apart," said Laban, as he turned toward his home in Haran. Jacob's family continued once again on their journey to Canaan.

JACOB'S NAME IS CHANGED

Twenty years had passed since Jacob ran away from his home and the wrath of his brother Esau. He had left as a lonely young man; and now he was returning with two wives, eleven sons and a daughter, many servants, and large flocks and herds. Still he wondered if his brother's anger had died with the years. Had he been forgiven? Was it safe to return?

God sent angels to strengthen Jacob on his trip. When he saw them, he said: "This is God's army!" But still he decided to send some messengers ahead to announce his coming to Esau. The messengers found Esau living in a land southeast of Canaan and returned to Jacob with the message that Esau was coming to meet him. He was bringing with him four hundred men.

This message frightened Jacob. He thought that Esau was coming to kill him. He divided his family and possessions into two groups with the hope that if one was destroyed, the other would be able to escape. Earnestly he prayed that God would spare them, especially for the sake of the mothers and young children. Finally, he chose from his flocks and herds hundreds of animals to send ahead in droves as a present to Esau. The servants leading each drove of animals were to tell Esau when they met him that these were gifts to him from Jacob.

Having sent these rich gifts, Jacob moved his family across a brook in the night; but he stayed on the other side of the bank to pray. As he prayed there in the dark, a strange man came and took hold of him and began to wrestle. All night the two fought; neither of them was able to get the better of the other. Finally as the dawn was breaking, Jacob realized that this was an angel of the Lord that he held.

"Let me go, for day is breaking," said the angel.

Jacob answered, "I will not let you go until you bless me."

"What is your name?" the angel asked.

"Jacob."

"From now on, your name will not be Jacob, but Israel, because you have wrestled with God," was the angel's reply. Israel means "He who strives with God."

The strange contest left Jacob crippled in the thigh, but he was no longer afraid to meet his brother. He rose to see Esau coming in the distance, and he went forward to meet him. When he reached him, he bowed before him in a very humble way seven times. There was no mistake about the way Esau felt now. He rushed to put his arms around Jacob, to kiss him, and to cry tears of joy.

Afterward Esau had questions about the company of women and children with Jacob. Jacob explained how God had blessed him greatly while he was in Haran and given him this fine family. Esau also inquired about the droves of animals that had met him. When he heard that they were gifts for him, he refused them saying that he had great wealth himself. Finally Jacob insisted that he take them, and he accepted.

Esau urged Jacob to return to his home with him, but Jacob wished to continue on toward Canaan. Esau left, and Jacob took his family to Shechem. Later God commanded that he go to Bethel, where he had seen the wonderful dream.

"Go up to Bethel," God told Jacob, "and build there an altar to the God who appeared to you when you were fleeing from your brother Esau." So Jacob gathered his family and his servants to-

Loran Raymond Jones

JACOB WELCOMED BACK TO CANAAN BY ESAU

Genesis 33:1–15

gether and announced to them that they would all go to Bethel, where they would build an altar to God.

Even though they passed among unfriendly tribes of people in Canaan, Jacob and his family reached Bethel unharmed. When he had completed the altar, he named it "El-bethel," which means "God of Bethel." God blessed Jacob and told him once again that his new name was Israel. Then God promised Israel that the land which had been promised to Abraham and Isaac would belong to him and his descendants.

From Bethel, Israel returned to his old home where his father Isaac was still living. On the way, a sad thing happened. His beloved wife Rachel died when a little boy named Benjamin was born to her.

Poor old Isaac was glad to see his son return, but he did not live much longer. Together the reunited brothers, Jacob and Esau, buried their father in the same cave where their mother, Rebekah, and their grandparents, Abraham and Sarah, lay. Many years of struggle for Jacob and Esau finally ended in peace.

JOSEPH, THE DREAMER

Jacob, whose new name was Israel, had a fine, large family of twelve sons; but there was one son he loved better than the others. This was Joseph, the oldest son of Rachel, the wife he had really chosen and cared for the most. Rachel died when her second little boy, Benjamin, was born; and Jacob then gave all his attention to Joseph. He gave to Joseph a beautiful coat of many colors, one that marked Joseph as a son of wealth and his father's heir.

Now all of Joseph's brothers except Benjamin were older than he was, and they disliked having the younger boy singled out by their father. When Jacob gave Joseph the beautiful coat, the envy in their hearts grew to hatred. They never spoke kindly to Joseph. Finally, what made them the most angry was the dreams that Joseph had.

In one dream, he and his brothers were in a field binding sheaves of grain. Joseph's sheaf stood upright, while those of the brothers bowed down to it. In the other dream he saw the sun, moon, and eleven stars bowing down to him. When Joseph told the boys of these dreams they became furious. "Do you think you are going to rule over us?" they asked angrily.

Jacob himself wondered about Joseph's dreams. He wondered if the sun and moon in the dream stood for Joseph's mother and father and the eleven stars for his brothers. Was it right for a father and mother to bow down to their son? He thought over the meaning of these things.

One day when Joseph was seventeen, Jacob called him to do an errand for him: "Your brothers have taken our flocks up to Shechem to find pasture, and they have been gone quite a while now. I would like for you to take a few days and go up there to see how they are doing. You can bring news of them back to me."

It was a long trip for Joseph, and he had trouble finding his brothers, but at last he saw them with their great flocks in the distance. Meanwhile, Joseph's brothers had spotted him, for his bright coat was easy to recognize even far away.

"Here comes the dreamer," said one brother, making fun.

"I have heard enough from him," said another. "Let us get rid of him and then see what comes of his wonderful dreams."

"We can kill him and throw him into a pit."

"People will think that a wild animal got him." The others began to agree.

But Reuben, the oldest son, felt a little more kindly toward Joseph. "Let us not kill him; after all, he is our own brother. We can just put him down in this pit and leave him." In his heart Reuben planned to come back later and rescue him.

So Joseph's own brothers grabbed him roughly, took his beautiful coat from him, and threw him down into an empty pit. Down in the darkness and dampness of the pit, Joseph cried to them to help him; but with no concern for him, the cruel men sat down and ate their lunch. While they were eating, they looked up to see someone else coming across the plain—not just a lonely traveler, but a whole caravan of merchants, traveling to Egypt with spices to sell.

"Here is a way to be rid of our brother and make some money, too," said Judah, one of the brothers. "Let us sell him to these Ishmaelite merchants." The others were willing, so they drew Joseph out of the pit and traded him to the merchants for twenty pieces of silver. As they divided the money among themselves, Joseph was carried

away toward Egypt in the caravan of strangers. He looked back toward his brothers and his homeland, thinking that he would never see them again.

The brothers hoped that this was the last of Joseph. As far as they were concerned, the dreamer was gone forever! Reuben, however, had been gone when Joseph was sold. He was the one who had persuaded the others not to kill Joseph earlier. When he came back, hoping to rescue Joseph from the pit, he was dismayed to find him gone. Crying aloud, he turned to his brothers and asked how he could face their father. When they admitted to having sold Joseph, they made up a story to tell Jacob. Killing a kid from the flock, they dipped Joseph's coat in its blood.

When Jacob saw Joseph's coat, torn and rust-colored from blood, he thought that his son had been killed by some wild animal. He mourned for many days and could not be comforted. "I will go to my grave brokenhearted over my son," he wept. The brothers turned their eyes so their father could not see their guilty expressions, but they never told him the truth about Joseph.

God, however, knew just where Joseph was. It was He Who had sent Joseph his strange dreams, and now He was planning to use Joseph's misfortune to make these very dreams come true.

JOSEPH IN EGYPT

After a long, slow trip with the camel caravan of Ishmaelites, to whom he had been sold by his brothers, Joseph finally arrived in the strange land of Egypt. As he looked about, he saw that the people looked different from his own; they spoke a language he did not understand. He was taken to a crowded market place and thrust upon a slave block. Shoppers stopped to look him over, feel his muscle, and measure his strength. Surely he felt strange and alone. Finally, Potiphar, a captain of the guard and trusted friend of the Egyptian king, bought Joseph and took him to his home.

In this strange land and in a new home, doing the lowly work of a household slave, Joseph never forgot about the God that his father Jacob had served and taught him to love. The thought that God was with him cheered Joseph; and he worked busily, doing all his tasks well. Soon Potiphar noticed what a fine bargain he had gotten when he bought Joseph. He began to assign more important jobs to him and soon Joseph was the manager of all Potiphar's household and his affairs.

Now Potiphar's wife was a wicked woman and she tried to get Joseph to do something wrong. He refused, knowing that Potiphar trusted him and, more important, God was watching over him. Finally, when Potiphar's wife saw that he could not be persuaded, she decided to get even with him. When Potiphar came home, she told him lies about Joseph, lies that made Potiphar so angry that he had Joseph thrown in prison.

It seems unfair that Joseph was made to suffer so badly a second time for the evil of others, but this was God's way of doing something good that eventually would bring honor to Joseph.

Bound in chains in an Egyptian jail, Joseph did not pout and feel sorry for himself, but he made friends with the others in the prison, even the jailkeeper himself. Soon the jailkeeper came to trust him as Potiphar once did, and he put Joseph in charge of all the other prisoners.

One day two new prisoners were entrusted to Joseph's care. Both came from the palace of the king, and the king had them thrown in prison for doing something that made him angry. One had been his chief butler; and the other, the chief baker. After they had been in the ward for a while, Joseph woke one morning to find both of them looking sad. Each had had a dream that left him puzzled.

"Tell me your dreams," said Joseph. "Perhaps my God will help us understand them."

"I dreamed I made wine from a vine that had three branches, and I gave the wine to Pharaoh, the king, in his cup," said the butler.

"This means that in three days you will be pardoned and placed back in Pharaoh's service. When you are set free, please remember me, for I have done nothing that they should put me in this prison."

The butler was happy and promised that he would.

Encouraged by the meaning of the butler's dream, the baker told his to Joseph: "In my dream there were three baskets of food for Pharaoh on my head. Birds came and ate out of the baskets."

"Your dream means that in three days you will be hanged and the birds will eat your flesh," Joseph said sadly.

Within three days all that Joseph had said did come true, but in his happiness at being back in

Loran Raymond Jones

JOSEPH REVEALS HIMSELF TO HIS BRETHREN

Genesis 45:1–15

Pharaoh's service, the butler forgot all about Joseph. For two more years he waited in prison.

Then Pharaoh, the king, began having dreams also. So troubled was he that he called in all his magicians and wise men to try to find their meaning, but no one could give any help.

All of a sudden the chief butler remembered the young Israelite who had helped him when he was in jail. Immediately Joseph was sent for, cleaned up and given a change of clothes, and brought before Pharaoh. When the king asked him if he could tell the meaning of dreams, Joseph answered, "The power is not in me; God will give the answer to you through me."

Pharaoh was not familiar with the God Joseph worshiped, but he was desperate to know the answer to his troubled sleep. "I dream of seven fat cows and of seven poor, lean cows who eat up the fat ones. In my other dream, seven poor, empty ears of corn eat seven full ears that are already on the stalk. What can this mean?" Pharaoh begged of Joseph.

Through God's power, Joseph could see that these dreams had the same meaning. He told Pharaoh that Egypt was going to have seven years of plenty—there would be more food than the people could eat. But after that, there would be seven years of famine when no food would grow. "I suggest that Pharaoh find a wise man and put him in charge of storing food during the years of plenty in order that the people will have something to eat during the years when nothing is growing," Joseph said.

Pharaoh was impressed by Joseph and decided to make him the ruler he had described. From his own hand, the king took a ring and gave it to Joseph; then he gave him a fine robe and put a gold chain around his neck. A new Egyptian name was given him, as well as a lovely Egyptian bride.

What a change came about that day! From a prison cell to second in command to the king of Egypt, he had come. God's plan for his life became more clear to Joseph that day as he left the palace in his new elegant chariot.

JOSEPH REVEALED TO HIS BROTHERS

As second in command to the Egyptian Pharaoh, Joseph had a very important job. He had told the king that there would be seven years of plenty followed by seven years of famine, and it was his duty to buy food and store it for the years of famine. Great storehouses were built and filled with grain as he directed.

Just as God had said, the years of plenty ended and nothing would grow. Then Joseph opened his storehouses and sold the grain that he had been saving. The people of Egypt began to look to him as their savior.

The famine spread to countries around Egypt, and people began coming long distances to buy grain from Joseph. Even the grazing lands of Canaan grew barren and dry. Old Jacob and his eleven sons had practically no food left.

Jacob called his sons in and said, "I hear that there is food in Egypt. Some powerful governor there had stored food and is selling it now. Go down and buy us some grain, only leave Benjamin with me. He is my youngest and I cannot bear to see him go."

In Egypt the ten brothers were led to Joseph to purchase grain. During the years they had been separated from their brother, he had grown from a boy to be an impressive man, dressed in kingly robes; and they did not recognize him. But Joseph recognized them at a glance. However, he pretended not to know them and spoke harshly, accusing them of being spies.

The ten were dismayed at being called spies and tried to convince this mighty lord that they were honest men, trying to purchase food to take back to their old father and a younger brother.

What news this was to Joseph! After twenty years, to find that his father Jacob was still alive! And Benjamin! Joseph began to form a plan in his mind whereby he could see his precious younger brother.

"You still do not convince me that you are not spies," he told them. "In order to prove yourselves, one of you must stay here in prison while the rest go home and bring your younger brother to me." But he could hardly continue talking about his long-lost family, and he had to leave the room so they would not see him cry.

Greatly troubled, the brothers finally decided to let Simeon stay in Egypt while they took the grain home. Then on the way home they found the money they had paid for the grain still in the sacks, as Joseph had secretly instructed the workmen to place it. They could not understand what was happening, but they were afraid that God was

bringing trouble upon them because of the way they had once treated their own brother.

As much as his sons tried to persuade him, Jacob refused to let them take Benjamin back to Egypt. But the sacks of grain did not last forever, and Jacob's house had no food. This time the sons, remembering the strange ruler and their brother Simeon still in prison, refused to go until Jacob gave permission for Benjamin to go also. One of the brothers, Judah, promised to take special care of the younger son.

This time, the Israelite men took a number of gifts with them to Egypt, too. As they bowed low before Joseph again, Joseph could scarcely bear to look at his younger brother without telling them who he was. But instead, he asked that they have dinner with him in his home. Afraid of what this meant, the men approached Joseph's house trying to make explanations for the appearance of the money they had found in their grain sacks on the last trip. Instead of a scolding, they received their brother Simeon.

During the dinner, Joseph tried to remain calm as he inquired about the health of their old father and as he met Benjamin; but once again he had to leave the room to keep them from seeing the tears of excitement in his eyes.

This time when they departed for home, he not only had his servants put their money back in their sacks, but he also had his own silver cup placed in Benjamin's sack. After he had given them time to be on their way, he sent his servants to search them and to find the cup.

The brothers had been convinced that none of them had stolen the cup, and when it was found, they were terrified. Reluctantly, they were led back to Joseph's house. They fell before Joseph with explanations. "Take any of us prisoner except Benjamin. If he does not return, our old father will surely die."

As they told the touching story of the old man's devotion to his son, Joseph could not control himself any longer. He held out his arms to them and cried, "I am Joseph!"

They stared in disbelief, but when they saw that indeed it was so and that he still loved them, they began begging his forgiveness.

"Do not be afraid of me or think that the thing you did was so bad," Joseph reassured them. "It was God's will that I come to Egypt so I could save you from hunger when the famine came. He has guided us all. Now go back to Canaan and bring our father here also."

So Jacob and his sons packed all their belongings and gathered together all their flocks and moved to Egypt, where they could find food until the famine was over. Because he thought so much of Joseph, Pharaoh gave them a special piece of land at Goshen on which to settle. There Joseph was able to visit with his father and brothers often.

Finally old Jacob died; but because he had asked it, his sons took his body back to Canaan and buried it in the cave with Abraham and Sarah, Isaac and Rebekah.

THE YOUNG MOSES

When Jacob moved his family down to Egypt during the famine, they intended to stay only until the grazing lands in Canaan turned green and fruitful again. But the longer they stayed, the larger their families grew and the harder it was to move back. Pharaoh had given them a good place to live in Goshen, and they were soon well settled there. Finally Joseph grew old and died, and the Pharaoh he had served died also. The new Pharaoh had not known Joseph, and he treated Joseph's people unkindly.

By this time many years had passed and there were thousands of people whose ancestors had been one of the twelve sons of Jacob, or Israel. The Egyptians called them Israelites or Hebrews. Because there were so many Israelites, the Egyptians

grew afraid of them—afraid that they might someday turn against them. They were afraid of the powerful God that the Hebrews worshiped. So the new Pharaoh made slaves of the Hebrews. He had them to build great cities of brick for him, and he put officers over them that made them work harder and faster than ever.

Pharaoh's plan was not successful, however, for the harder the Israelites worked, the stronger they became. He had to think of a new way to keep them from growing in number, and the plan he decided upon struck the Hebrew people with horror. Pharaoh command them to drown each baby boy that was born to them!

What a difficult command this was to carry out. During this time, a baby boy was born to one He-

Loran Raymond Jones

FINDING OF MOSES BY THE DAUGHTER OF PHARAOH

Exodus 2:2–10

brew couple who decided that they just could not kill their little boy. He was such a fine little fellow! For three months they did not let anyone know that they had him; they hid him when anyone came to their house. Finally, the mother decided that she could not keep him hidden any longer. He wanted to be awake more now and to play.

So this mother, named Jochebed, made a water-proof basket of reeds and plastered it with pitch. Inside the little ark, she made a soft bed and placed her baby in it. Then she and her little girl carried it to the river Nile, and put it to float among some reeds. It was hard for the mother to leave her baby, but the little boy's sister stayed behind to watch what happened to the baby, afloat on the river.

Miriam, the sister, did not have long to wait before she heard voices approaching. As she peered through the tall reeds, whom should she see coming but the daughter of the wicked Pharaoh. She and her maids were coming down to bathe in the river. As she stood in the water washing herself, the princess spied the floating basket and sent one of her maids to bring it to her. She was curious to know what was in it.

As she turned back the covers in the basket, the baby began to cry. Watching, Miriam held her breath. What would the princess do? The sight of the sweet baby crying touched the heart of the princess. "Why, he is a Hebrew baby whose mother is trying to save it," she cried. "He will come home with me and be my child. I will name him Moses because it means 'drawn out' and I have drawn him out of the water."

Miriam stepped out from behind the reeds and with a bowed head she approached the Egyptian princess. In her mind whirled a bold plan. If only it would work!

"Would you like for me to get a Hebrew nurse for the baby?" Miriam asked the noble lady. "I think I know where I can find one."

The princess was delighted to hire one of the child's own people to nurse him, but little did she know that the nurse Miriam brought to her was the child's own mother! Yes, Moses' mother helped the princess take care of him.

Although Moses was reared as an Egyptian prince and a grandson of the Pharaoh himself, his mother taught him that he was really an Israelite. She taught him the Hebrew language that she spoke, and she told him the stories of his people. He heard about the early fathers of his nation—Abraham, Isaac, Jacob, and Jacob's twelve sons—and he learned of the one true God Whom they had worshiped. Moses' mother told him that some day their God was going to lead them away from Egypt and back to the land that He had promised them, a land where they would be free.

Meanwhile, the princess saw that Moses had every advantage a royal son could have. He lived in the palace, wore royal robes, and studied under special teachers. Until he grew to be a man, this was the only life that he knew. But when he was old enough to leave the palace, Moses began to learn of the way his people were being treated by the Egyptians. As he visited the cities and fields where they were working under the whips of Pharaoh's officers, he saw that their life was little better than that of animals.

One day, Moses saw an Egyptian beating a Hebrew. His eyes clouded over with anger at the unjust treatment his kinsman was receiving, and in haste he killed the Egyptian. Seeing no one around, he hid the body in the sand.

The next day Moses saw two Hebrews fighting with each other, and he stepped in to stop the fight. The guilty man looked at him angrily and said, "Who made you our ruler and judge? Do you intend to kill me as you killed that Egyptian yesterday?"

Moses was stunned at these words. The news of the murder he had committed was known! The Israelites did not understand that he was trying to help them; they thought he was interfering. And Pharaoh—he would hear the news soon! He would have Moses put to death when he heard of it.

So Moses fled from Egypt. Across the desert to the east, he sought refuge in the wilderness of the land of Midian.

MOSES AND THE BURNING BUSH

In the land of Midian, far away from the angry Pharaoh who wanted to take his life, Moses made friends with Jethro, the priest of Midian, and his family. Moses helped Jethro tend his flocks and he made his home with the older man. After some time had passed, he chose one of Jethro's seven daughters to be his wife. Her name was Zipporah.

Moses life in Midian was different from the one

he had lived in the Egyptian palace. He wore the rough robes of an outdoor man, and he grew tanned and tough as he braved the wind and sun, watching Jethro's flocks. On his long, lonely journeys, guiding the sheep to distant pastures, he would remember his people back in Egypt. As he thought of them, he probably prayed to God to relieve their suffering.

Meanwhile, back in Egypt, the king who had sought Moses' life died, and a new Pharaoh took his place. This one was even more cruel than the others, and the Israelites suffered worse than before. As they cried for relief, God heard their prayers. He remembered the covenant He had made with Abraham, Isaac, and Israel; and he determined that now He would take their people, the Israelites, back to the land He had promised them.

One day Moses was alone with his father-in-law's flocks, far away from home, near Mount Horeb. Suddenly, before his eyes he saw a bush bright with flames, yet not burning up. He took a step forward to take a closer look when a voice came to him from the bush: "Moses! Moses! Come no closer! Take off your shoes for you are standing on holy ground."

Moses recognized the voice immediately. This was the same voice that had spoken to Adam and Eve in the garden, to Noah, to Abraham, Isaac, and Jacob; it was the voice of God. Now it was speaking to him!

·"I have heard my people crying in Egypt, and I am going to rescue them from their suffering and take them back to the land I promised them," the Lord said. "Moses, you are the one I have chosen to lead them out of Egypt."

"Oh, Lord," Moses said humbly, "who am I that I could lead them?"

"I will be with you, Moses. I will help you bring them some day to this very mountain to worship me," the voice reassured him.

Then Moses asked, "What if the Hebrews ask me who appointed me their leader; who sent me?"

"Tell them it is I who sent you, the God who has always lived and the One who spoke with their fathers."

"But, Lord, they do not know me. They will never believe me or trust me to lead them."

"What is that in your hand?" God asked Moses.

"A rod, my shepherd's staff," Moses answered.

The Lord commanded Moses to throw it down; and when he did, it became a snake. When Moses ran from it, the Lord told him to reach out and take it by the tail. When he obeyed, he found that he held only the rod in his hand again. Then God had Moses place his hand inside his robe. When he took it out, it was white and covered with the sores of leprosy. But after he laid it inside his robe again, it came out healed, as it was before.

God told Moses that he could use these signs to prove to the children of Israel that he had been chosen by their God to lead them. As a third sign, Moses would have the power to turn water into blood.

Still Moses had an excuse. "O my Lord," he pleaded, "I cannot speak well enough to do this great work. I cannot make my mouth say what I mean to say."

"Did I not make your mouth?" the voice insisted. "I will help you with the things you say."

"Please, Lord, send someone more worthy than I." Moses began again to make excuses, but the Lord was growing impatient. He said, "Your brother Aaron is a fine speaker. I will send him with you. Right now he is coming across the wilderness to meet you."

Sure enough, guided by a message from God, Aaron left Egypt and traveled eastward toward Midian. Satisfied that the Lord would give him strength to perform this mighty task, Moses returned to Jethro and asked for permission to leave him. Granted this leave, Moses and his family set out for Egypt. In his hand, he carried the shepherd's staff through which God had worked miracles. In his heart was the determination to be a leader from God to his people. He was convinced now that God had saved him as a baby that day in the river Nile for just this purpose.

On the journey, Moses met Aaron and they continued toward Egypt together.

THE TEN PLAGUES

The Lord had given Moses a great task—to lead His people, the children of Israel, from the land of Egypt back to Canaan. At first, Moses thought it was an impossible thing for him to do, but the Lord gave him the power to do miraculous things and gave him his brother Aaron to be his helper and speaker. These, together with the knowledge that God was with him, made Moses courageous

enough to return to his people in Egypt. When he showed them the miracles the Lord had shown him and Aaron told them of the Lord's appearing to Moses in the burning bush, the Israelites believed that at last the Lord had heard their prayers and was going to take them away from their life of slavery.

Knowing that the people would follow their leadership now, Moses and Aaron bravely approached the court of the Egyptian king, who was known as Pharaoh. Dressed in their simple, rough robes, they made quite a contrast to the riches and splendor of the palace. On his throne, Pharaoh looked with disgust upon the Hebrew shepherds. At first, they did not ask that Pharaoh let the people leave Egypt forever; instead they said: "Our Lord says that Pharaoh is to let His people go into the wilderness for three days to worship."

Pharaoh's look changed to one of scorn. He was not going to let his army of slaves leave. Where else would he find such able workers to build his great cities? His voice rang out, "I know why the Israelites are eager to go and worship—they do not have enough to keep them busy. I will see to it that they have more to do!"

So Pharaoh gave his officers the command that the Hebrews would not only have to make bricks, but that they would also have to gather their own materials for making them. At the same time, he wanted as many bricks made as before. This was very hard on the Israelites. Often they could not do all that their masters demanded, and they were beaten badly. They became angry at Moses and Aaron and accused them of making their lives worse instead of better.

A second time, the brothers returned to Pharaoh. This time Moses showed Pharaoh the miracles the Lord had shown him in the wilderness. When Aaron threw his shepherd's staff upon the floor, it turned into a writhing snake. Pharaoh merely called in his wise men and magicians, who changed their rods into snakes also. Then, before their eyes, the snake from Aaron's rod swallowed up all the others.

The next morning, the Lord directed Moses and Aaron to show Pharaoh still another sign. As the king was walking out near the water, Aaron held his wonderful rod over the water. When he did, it turned into blood. A terrible smell rose from the brilliant, thick liquid, and the fish began to die. Cries arose from those gathering water to drink. Pharaoh returned with disgust to his house, but he would not change his mind about letting the He-

brews go. For seven days, the Egyptians did without water, then the Lord took away the blood and let the clear water return.

Again Moses stood before Pharaoh. "Will you let my people go now?" he asked. "Our God has more troubles in store for you unless you give us permission to worship Him." But Pharaoh refused and would not let them go.

This time when Aaron stretched out his rod, the Lord sent frogs upon all the land. Millions of frogs came up from the water and went into every house in Egypt. People found them in their ovens, in their dishes, and in their beds. Everywhere they stepped outside, there were frogs.

Pharaoh grew uneasy. He did not like these signs. He called to Moses and said, "If you will remove these frogs, I will let your people go." So Moses prayed to God, and He caused the frogs to die. There were so many that the Egyptians piled them up in great heaps and burned them. When Pharaoh saw that they were gone, he changed his mind and decided not to keep his word after all.

Then the Lord commanded Moses and Aaron to strike the ground with the rod; and when they did, the dust became lice. The little insects covered every man and every animal, but Pharaoh remained stubborn. Next, the Lord sent great swarms of flies, so that they filled the houses and the sky. Where the Israelites lived, in the land of Goshen, however, there were no flies.

At this, Pharaoh began to give in a little. He called Moses and said, "Why can you not worship here in Egypt?"

"It would make the Egyptians angry to see us making our sacrifices here in their land," Moses answered.

"All right. You may go and worship, but you must not go far away and you must come back," said Pharaoh. "Now, pray to your God to take away these terrible flies."

Once more Moses asked God to remove the plague; and when He did, Pharaoh again broke his promise.

Other torments were sent by God upon Pharaoh and the Egyptians—diseases on all their herds and flocks, sore boils on every person, hail that ruined every field, locusts that ate everything the hail had spared, and a thick darkness for three days and nights. Only God's chosen people in the land of Goshen were saved from the plagues.

Finally, after the three days of darkness, Pharaoh became very angry. When Moses came before him again, he could not bear to hear any more about the Hebrews and their God. "Get out of my sight!"

Loran Raymond Jones

THE FIRST FEAST OF THE PASSOVER

Exodus 12:3–17

he shouted to Moses. "If I see you again, I will have you killed!'"

"Very well," said Moses. "You have seen me the last time."

Then God told Moses that there would be only one more plague—a plague so terrible that Pharaoh would change his mind and let the people go. "The time has come," the Lord said, "for the Israelites to prepare to leave Egypt."

THE FIRST PASSOVER

Although the people of the Israelite nation had doubted Moses at first, it soon became clear that God was with him. Whenever Moses and Aaron used their wonderful rod, the Lord sent all kinds of plagues upon the enemies of the Israelites—the Egyptians. And while there was hail in Egypt, the Israelites' homeland had fine weather; when the diseases came, they remained healthy; when the darkness covered Egypt, they worked in bright sunshine.

Now the time had come for them to prepare to leave Egypt. The Lord had told Moses that He was about to send His last plague upon Pharaoh. At midnight he was going to send the angel of death and the oldest son in every house would die. This plague was going to be so terrible that Pharaoh was going to change his mind and send the Israelites away.

In order to escape the angel of death, God gave Moses special instructions to give to His people. Each family was to take a lamb and kill it as they would for a sacrifice. Then they were to take its blood and sprinkle it at the entrance of their house, on the frame over the door and on each side. When the angel came he would pass over the houses where he saw the blood of the lamb. The lamb itself was to be roasted with some vegetables and prepared for a feast. When the family ate the feast, they were to be dressed for their journey, with their shoes and coat on and with their staff in their hand.

Quickly the Israelites set about to obey the commands of God. The lamb was roasted and its blood sprinkled on the door posts. Each family sat down, dressed for traveling, to eat the lamb and little flat wafers, specially prepared for the feast. The feast was known as the first Passover, for it was eaten on the night when the angel *passed over* the Israelites and struck the homes of the Egyptians. It became a great feast for the Hebrew people, and they observed it every year afterward, as they were commanded. It reminded them of the wonderful way God saved them.

Promptly at midnight, death rushed through the land. Not one house of the Egyptians was spared. In every home, from Pharaoh's palace to his least servant's cottage, the oldest boy fell dead. A cry went up from the Egyptians as their children were taken from them. In the middle of the night Pharaoh sent for Moses and Aaron and said, "Take your people and go. Take everything you have and get out of our land. And pray to your God to harm me no more."

Moses and Aaron hurried back to their people. This was the time for which they had been waiting! Four hundred and thirty years had passed since Jacob took his family down into Egypt to be with Joseph during the famine. Now that family of twelve sons had become a nation of more than a million people, divided into twelve tribes, according to the son from which they came.

What a procession the group made! Thousands of people, from babies to grandmothers, many with packs of clothes and household goods upon their backs, marched out of Egypt as God led them. Behind them came cattle, sheep, and goats, braying and bleating in their attempt to follow the crowd. Gone forever were the days of slavery in Egypt, for their God was leading them home to the land He had promised their fathers long before.

CROSSING THE RED SEA

At last the Israelites were on their way from the slavery of Egypt to the promises the land of Canaan held for them. During the four centuries that the family of Jacob and his twelve sons had spent in Egypt, each father had told his children of the blessings that God had given his special people through Abraham, Isaac, and Jacob. Each child wondered if he would be one of those to see

the green grazing lands where Abraham had first heard the promises. Now that time had finally come.

Instead of following the shortest route to Canaan, the Lord told Moses to lead the people toward the Red Sea and the wilderness around it. He did this so that they might escape the warlike Philistines. Moses was familiar with this territory, for it was there he had watched over Jethro's flocks. At the head of the long procession he marched, with the Lord leading the way in a pillar of cloud by day and a pillar of fire at night.

When Pharaoh realized that the Israelites had gone, he was sorry that he had no more slaves to do his hard work. Reports reached him that they had made their way into the wilderness and were hemmed in by the mountains and the Red Sea, and he decided to follow and recapture them. Calling his captains, he instructed them to prepare the war chariots for battle.

In their swift chariots and on trained horses, the army of Pharaoh soon caught up with the Israelites. When the Israelites looked up and saw the dust stirred up by Pharaoh's army in the distance, panic filled their hearts. "Are we any better off now than we were in Egypt?" they cried to Moses. "It would have been better to have remained as slaves there than to come into the wilderness only to be killed."

But Moses remembered the wonders that the Lord had done in Egypt, and he knew that some way the Lord would help them now. "Do not be afraid," he told the people. "The Lord is going to fight for you."

Then as the night fell, the pillar of cloud that had been guiding the Israelites moved between them and the Egyptians so that the Egyptian army could not see ahead. They pitched camp for the night, planning to attack the Israelites in the morning. But in the Israelite camp, no one settled down to rest. By Moses' order they prepared once again to march. Right up to the bank of the Red Sea they went.

Then a marvelous thing happened. Moses held his rod above the waters of the sea, and a strong wind began to blow. It blew so hard that the water parted right down the center, making a path of dry ground walled in on either side by great banks of water. With Moses leading the way, the Israelites walked straight across the Red Sea.

When the Egyptians saw the Israelites marching into the sea, they quickly manned their horses and chariots and followed. But as they entered the path through the sea, the Lord looked down from the pillar of cloud and made it difficult for the Egyptians to make their chariots go. Wheels began to fly off; and as they looked at the mighty walls of water surrounding them, they became afraid. "Let us forget the Israelites!" they cried. "Their God is too powerful and strong for us to fight."

By this time, the last of the Israelites had reached the shores on the other side of the Red Sea and were watching the Egyptian army coming in pursuit. Once more, at God's command, Moses stretched forth his rod over the sea. The walls of water trembled, leaned, and then with a mighty roar they collapsed, swallowing up the Egyptian army with one crushing blow. As the Israelites watched the bodies of the soldiers rising with the waves, they bowed their heads in silence at the great power of their God.

Then Moses began to sing, and all the voices joined in with the words:

"I will sing unto the Lord, for he has triumphed:
The horse and his rider He has thrown into the
  sea.
The Lord is my strength and my song,
And he has saved me."

FOOD FROM HEAVEN

In order to reach the promised land of Canaan, the Israelites had to travel through miles of desert and mountainous country. With so many thousands of people and great herds and flocks, food and water became very scarce. Sometimes the water that they found was not fit for them to drink. One time God had Moses cast a tree into some bitter water, and it became clear and sweet for drinking.

But they had to move on from the good streams, and the paths grew rougher as they approached the great Mount Sinai. Grumbling began to arise from the crowds of people. They complained to Moses and Aaron that their food had been better back in Egypt, even though they had been slaves.

"When you speak like this to us," Moses told them, "you are really speaking against the Lord. Do you not remember that He is leading us and taking care of us? He will not forget us now."

The Lord did not forget them. He said to Moses: "I will send food from heaven to you—bread each morning and quail each evening. Every day you are to gather just enough for one day, for it will not keep without spoiling. On the sixth day of the week, however, I will let you gather enough for two days because I will not send any on the seventh day. It is to be your day of rest."

Just as the Lord said, the next morning when the people woke up, they found little white flakes like frost or snow on the ground. They turned to each other and asked in the Hebrew language, "What is it?" The word for this is "Manhu" and some think that this was the reason they afterward called it "manna."

Moses told them, "This is the bread which the Lord has given for you to eat." Everyone got a basket and began gathering the manna. When they tasted it, they found that it tasted like wafers flavored with honey. It was delicious cooked many different ways; and no matter how much a man gathered, there was plenty for his family. When the sun came up bright and strong, what was left on the ground melted like frost.

Some were greedy and disobeyed God by gathering too much. The next day they found that it was rotten and spoiled and smelled bad. God wanted them to trust in Him to send their food each day.

In the evening, quail came up and covered the camp, so the Lord provided meat for His people also. Six days every week, the Israelites received food from heaven, and on the seventh day they ate the extra that they had gathered the day before. Once a week, God let them keep more than they needed without having it spoil. This way they learned that one day in the week they were to rest as God did on the seventh day of His creation. This day was a holy day to God, and the Israelites called it the Sabbath, which means "day of rest."

The manna continued to fall day by day as long as the Hebrews traveled in the wilderness. Not until they reached the land of Canaan forty years later did it cease.

THE TEN COMMANDMENTS

After three months in the wilderness, camping in several places, the Israelites came to the foot of Mount Sinai. Here they pitched their tents and made preparation for a more permanent camp. Moses looked fondly around the mountain, for it was nearby that he first talked with God in the burning bush. It was nearly impossible to believe that he had really led the Israelites safely out of Egypt since he had last been here.

Then the voice of God spoke to Moses from the mountain: "These people are a treasure to me. I am going to make them a holy nation. Tell them to clean themselves and wash their clothes and prepare their minds, for in three days they are going to see my glory on this mountain. Set a boundary around the mountain so that no person or animal will touch it while I am here."

God's people did as they were told, and they were waiting and praying when the third day arrived. Then suddenly there was lightning and loud thunder from the mountain, a large cloud settled on its heights, smoke began pouring forth as though it were on fire, and the whole mountain trembled. A sound of trumpets came, louder and louder, until the people held one another in fear before their God.

Then out of the cloud came the voice of God, announcing Himself so that all could hear: "I am the Lord thy God, who brought thee out of the land of Egypt, out of the house of bondage." Then He gave them the rules they were to follow as His people. These rules, known as the Ten Commandments, are like this:

I. Thou shalt have no other gods before me; or, I am the one true God, the One you must worship.

II. Thou shalt not make unto thee any graven image; or, you must not worship idols or gods made by men.

III. Thou shalt not take the name of the Lord thy God in vain; or, you must not speak or think lightly of the Lord.

IV. Remember the Sabbath day, to keep it holy; or, you must rest and worship the Lord on the seventh day.

V. Honor thy father and thy mother; or, love and obey your parents.

VI. Thou shalt not kill; or, you must not take the life of any person.

VII. Thou shalt not commit adultery; or, husbands and wives must love and be faithful to one another.

VIII. Thou shalt not steal; or, you must not take things that are not your own.

MOSES AT SINAI

Exodus 32:15–24

IX. Thou shalt not bear false witness against thy neighbor; or, you must not tell a lie about anyone.

X. Thou shalt not covet; or, you must not want something that is not yours.

After God had given these rules and His voice had died away, the people were still afraid. They said to Moses, "Let God speak to you, Moses, and you tell us what He says, for we fear His voice."

"He came to you this way in order for you to know His power and be afraid to disobey Him," Moses explained. Then, taking only Aaron, Aaron's sons, seventy of the wisest and oldest Israelites, and his special helper Joshua, Moses began to climb the mountain. After they got far enough up to see a little of the glory of God, Aaron and his sons and the elders went back down to the camp. Only Joshua and Moses continued climbing higher. At last Moses left Joshua on the side of the mountain and disappeared into the cloud that covered the top. For forty days and nights, he stayed with God alone on Mount Sinai. God gave him many other rules for the Israelites to follow. Most of them told how they should treat one another and how they should worship Him. He also gave Moses two tables of stone on which He had written the Ten Commandments.

The people had not expected Moses to be gone so long, and they began to think that he was not coming back. They begged Aaron to make them a god they could see. So Aaron took gold jewelry that they gave him, melted it, and shaped it into a golden calf. The Israelites were delighted with the idol; and they declared a feast day and began worshiping it with songs and games, the way they had seen the Egyptians do.

While Moses and Joshua were coming down the mountain, they heard the cries of the people, dancing and singing around the golden calf. When they caught sight of the camp, Moses became so angry and discouraged that he threw down the tables of stone; and they broke into little pieces.

The Israelites were severely punished for having disobeyed God's commandment so soon. Those who started the rebellion were killed, and Moses took the calf and broke it to pieces. Then he ground it into a fine powder, mixed it with water, and made the people drink some of it as part of their punishment.

But Moses loved these people that he had brought from Egypt, and he went back up on the mountain to ask God to give them another chance. God did forgive them and wrote the Commandments again on new tables of stone. Moses stayed with Him for another forty days and talked with Him as a friend, closer than any other man ever did. When he came down from the mountain, his face shone from having been so close to God. It was so radiant and bright that he had to put a veil over it when he talked with the people.

THE BUILDING OF THE TABERNACLE

One of the things that God spoke to Moses about when they were on Mount Sinai together was the way He wanted His chosen people to worship Him. All of the people the Israelites had ever seen worshiped carved statues, or idols. But God had told them not to bow down to other gods nor to make graven images. The one true God is a spirit and lives everywhere, so we do not have to have a statue to remind us where He is.

But God knew that it would be a long time before the people could understand this, and He gave them a place of worship that they could see, one that would remind them that He was in their presence at all times. Because the Israelites were camping in the wilderness, travelling from place to place when the pillar of cloud and fire moved, the place of worship was to be something like a tent. It was called a tabernacle. Every part of it was to be made in such a way that it could be quickly taken down, packed up, and carried to a new camping ground.

The directions for making the tabernacle and all that went with it were given to Moses while he was on the mountain; then he told the people exactly what God wanted. He saw that it was going to take much expensive material—gold, silver, bronze, fine linen, goats' skin, wood, oil, spices, and precious stones—so he simply asked the people to give as they felt in their hearts they should. No one was commanded to give any particular amount, but the offering was so great that the builders had to ask Moses to make the people stop bringing them things.

Not only did the people give the materials for making their house of worship, they also gave their time. Those who had the ability built the frames, wove the curtains, molded the metal, or sewed the priestly robes. In charge of it all were two skilled

Loran Raymond Jones

CONSTRUCTING THE ARK OF THE COVENANT

Exodus 37:1–9

craftsmen, Bezalel, of the tribe of Judah, and Oholiab, of the tribe of Dan. These two put on all the finishing touches, did the elaborate weaving, and carved the intricate figures in the wood and metal. For nearly a year the Israelites camped near Sinai, preparing the house of worship.

When all the separate parts of the place of worship were ready, the tabernacle was set into place. This was done on the first day of the first month of the year, the second year after they left Egypt. When it was finished, the tabernacle looked something like this:

Surrounding the tabernacle itself was a courtyard, built exactly in the center of the camp. Outside its entrance was the tent where Moses lived. The courtyard was open, but it had a high curtain around it, hung from bronze poles. The curtain was made of bright colored linen and was higher than a man's head, although there was an opening on the east side where the priests could enter.

Near the entrance, inside the court, stood a large altar. The altar was the place on which the Israelites laid their offering and worshiped God by burning it. It was usually made by piling up stones or by carving a place to build a fire out of a large rock. This altar, however, was built of wood, covered inside and out with bronze so it would not burn. It had no bottom or top, but there was a grating inside on which to build the fire and lay the offering. The ashes would fall on the ground underneath. Rings of metal were fastened on each corner; and when camp was moved, poles were placed through the rings and the priests could carry the altar on their shoulders.

Beyond the altar was a large basin called a laver.

The laver held water with which the priests washed the offerings.

The laver was near the door of the tabernacle itself. The tabernacle looked like a large tent, but its walls were made of board covered with gold and mounted in silver frames. These frames could be taken apart and carried about, but they made the tabernacle sturdy. The boarded walls made up three sides of the tent, but the front was covered only with a curtain. Several curtains made the roof of the tent. The inside one was beautifully woven and decorated; the outside one was of goats' skin to protect the tabernacle from the weather.

The inside of the tabernacle was divided into two rooms. The front one was twice as large as the other and was called the Holy Place. It contained a table covered with gold, on which were placed twelve loaves of bread to represent the twelve tribes; a golden lampstand with seven branches; and an altar of incense, where gum was burned to give off a sweet odor.

The smaller room was called the Holy of Holies, and only the high priest entered this room once a year. It held a wooden chest, covered with gold and intricate carving. Inside the chest lay the tables of stone with the Ten Commandments written upon them. Over the chest two figures called cherubim were carved. This was the place where God Himself was to dwell.

When the tabernacle was in place and the last curtain was hung, the pillar of cloud settled over the tent and the glory of the Lord filled it. Throughout the rest of their journeys, this was where the pillar of cloud by day and of fire by night remained. Whenever it moved, the Israelites knew that they were to leave and follow.

SPYING OUT CANAAN

After the tabernacle, the temporary house of worship, was completed, the pillar of cloud that stayed over it moved one day; and the Israelites knew that the time had come for them to leave Mount Sinai and continue on their journey to the land God had promised them. For several months they would travel for a few days and then camp and rest for a while, gradually coming closer and closer to the border between the desert and the promised land.

At last they pitched camp at Kadesh-barnea, right on the border of Canaan. Now the land was not empty and simply waiting for the Israelites to move in. People were living there who had been

there for many years and had built fine cities. So God suggested that Moses select men to go over into Canaan and inspect it and then return and give a report to the Israelites. This seemed wiser than entering without knowing what to expect.

Moses chose a leader from each of the twelve tribes for this important work. He instructed them to notice the kind of land that was there, the food that could be grown, the kind of people living there, and the cities they had built.

In the fall of the year, just as the grapes were ripening, the men left on their scouting trip. For forty days they walked all over the land, noticing the things that Moses had mentioned. Before they

reached their camp again, they cut a cluster of ripe grapes that was so large it had to be carried between two men on a pole. They also brought back some figs and pomegranates.

When they returned, all the people gathered to hear their report. They said, "This is as fruitful a land as God told us it would be. See these grapes that we gathered in its vineyards? But the people who live there are stronger than we are, and the cities are so protected that we could never capture them."

Caleb, one of the spies, interrupted, "The land is wonderful, as you have said. And with the help of God, I know that we could take it. Let us prepare to go at once."

But all the others except Joshua disagreed. "No," they said, "there is no use to try to make war on those people. They are so big they make us look like grasshoppers."

The people were frightened by this message; and they, too, doubted that they could take the land. They did not believe that God was strong enough to help them overcome any enemy. All night they complained to Moses and Aaron. "Why did we ever leave Egypt?" some asked. "God brought us into the wilderness only to let us die here. Let us choose another leader who will take us back to Egypt."

Joshua and Caleb stood before the people and did everything they could to persuade them to go on into the land. But the people became so angry with them that they wanted to stone them and kill them.

Just then the glory of the Lord, which stayed in the tabernacle within the Holy of Holies, shone from the tabernacle so that everyone could see it. God was so disappointed in the people that He wanted to cut them off and disown them. Only because Moses prayed for them and begged God to forgive them did He change His mind.

But God did not let the people go unpunished. The ten spies who had doubted their strength were killed. All of the other people who were over twenty years old were told that they would never get to see the promised land. They would have to stay in the wilderness another forty years, one year for each day the scouts spent in Canaan, until their children grew up in their place. Of the adults then living, only Joshua and Caleb would live to enter the land of Canaan.

God knew that Moses could teach the children as they grew up to love and trust Him more than their parents had and that he could also train them for war. They would never remember the life of slavery in Egypt that had made their parents so weak and unsure.

Some of the people decided to march upon the land of Canaan anyway; but the Lord did not go with them, and they were killed in battle. The others turned toward the desert again, and there they stayed for forty years.

JOSHUA, A NEW LEADER

After the long journey to the border of the promised land, the Israelites were not able to cross over, but turned back again into the desert and wilderness. For forty years they lived in the Wilderness of Paran, as the Lord had told them they must do as punishment for not trusting Him. During this time Moses continued to be their leader and to settle the problems that arose. Aaron and his sons served as God's priests in the tabernacle. God took care of His people's daily needs by giving them manna and quail to eat, and He made sure that their clothes and shoes never wore out.

Over the years, those who had doubted God's power died; and their children, trained for war, grew up to take their place. As the period of wandering was ending, the cloud moved from the tabernacle and Moses led the people behind it toward Canaan. Instead of entering from Kadesh-barnea, as they had before, they went a long way around the eastern side of the land of the Edomites and the Dead Sea. They did this to avoid fighting with the Edomites, for they were the descendants of Esau, the twin brother of their own family head, Israel, or Jacob.

On the eastern side of the Jordan River, which runs from north to south through the land of Canaan, the Israelites had their first battle with the Amorites. God gave them a great victory; and they destroyed many of the Amorites, including their king, Sihon. At last they camped on the bank of the Jordan River. Behind them was the desert; before them was the rolling river, winding its way through the rich valleys and hills that were to be theirs. In the distance stood the mighty city, Jericho.

Of those who had come out of Egypt as grown men, only three remained—Moses, Joshua, and Caleb. Joshua and Caleb had been the only scouts that had given a good report of the land of Canaan forty years before, and God had promised them then that they would live to enter it. Moses was now one hundred and twenty years old, but he was still a vigorous and strong man. His work was over, for he had led God's people from Egypt to their homeland. Because he had disobeyed in the wilderness by striking a rock to bring forth water instead of speaking to it, God was not going to let him enter Canaan. However, Moses had been faithful over so many things, God did let him see the land.

First, Moses called together the leaders of the twelve tribes and gave them some advice. He told them what God had done for their people; he gave them again the words of the law as God had given it on Mount Sinai. He reminded them that they were not only to keep the law themselves, but to teach it also to their children. Then he laid his hands on Joshua, whom God had chosen to take his place as leader. The power of God's spirit that had been with Moses went to Joshua.

Alone, Moses left the camp and climbed to the top of Mount Nebo. Here he looked at the land of promise—the mountain where Abraham, Isaac, and Jacob were buried, the plains where they had kept their flocks, the city of Jerusalem, and far away, the Great Sea. Then he died, and God Himself buried him in a place that no one knows.

The people were very sad to see Moses leave them, and they mourned for many days. They knew that no other would quite be able to take his place, for the Bible tells us that no other man talked with God so freely, as a friend. But they turned with trust to their new leader, Joshua, for they knew that he, too, would lead them as God led him.

RAHAB AND THE SPIES

It had been forty years since Joshua and Caleb and the other ten scouts had made their trip through the land of Canaan. As the new leader of the Israelites, Joshua knew that changes had probably come about throughout the land. Different people had come in to live; cities had sprung up where none had been before. The Israelites themselves had been blessed with victorious battles and their fame had spread. Joshua wondered just what the Canaanites had heard about them.

Across the Jordan River from the place where the Israelites were camped stood the high-walled city of Jericho. Before they could go beyond and take the rest of the country, Jericho itself had to be captured. Joshua sent two men across the river secretly to find out what they could about the city.

The two spies slipped in through the gates in the great wall of the city among the crowds that went in and out. They found a house inside where they stopped to eat and rest. But they had not been as clever as they thought they had. Someone had spotted them and reported them to the king.

Immediately the king sent messengers to the woman who owned the house where they were staying. Her name was Rahab. When she saw the officers coming, she rushed the Israelites up onto the roof of her house. There stalks of flax, like long reeds, lay spread out to dry, making them ready for her to spin into linen one day. The men lay down on the flat roof and she covered them with the flax. Then she went down to meet the officers.

"Rahab!" the soldiers called out. "The king demands that you turn over to him the two strangers that came into your house. They are known to be spies from Israel."

"Oh, it is true some men were here earlier today," Rahab answered, "but I had no notion that they were spies. They left about dark, so if you intend to catch them, you will have to hurry. They have already had time to get quite a head start."

Hurriedly, the men rode off through the city gates, toward the river where they had seen the Israelites camped. But they never found the men for whom they were searching.

When she knew the messengers had gone, Rahab climbed back onto the roof and told the spies that it was safe to come down.

"Tell us why you hid us and saved our lives," they asked her.

"I know that your God has promised to give you this land. Everyone here in Jericho knows it, and they are afraid. We all heard of the way your God held back the waters of the Red Sea while you crossed over and we heard of the battle you won over the Amorites. We know that He will help you take our city, for the God you worship is truly God in heaven above and on earth beneath.

"Please," she begged, "when you return to take this city, save me and my family. Promise me you will do this."

"Our lives for yours," they promised. "If you will not tell anyone about our being here, we will remember you when we march on the city."

Now Rahab's house was built right into the wall of the city, and it had a window facing outside the wall. Through this window she dropped a strong cord, a brilliant red piece of rope. Before the men slid down the rope to safety, they reminded Rahab, "Gather all your family into your house before we return. That way they will be saved with you."

"How will you remember which house it is?" she asked.

"Keep this red rope hanging from the window,

and we will find you," they answered.

Then she lowered them on the rope and left it tied securely to the window. "Go to the hills and hide for three days until the king stops looking for you," she called softly to them through the darkness of the night.

After three days the king's officers returned to Jericho to report that they had not been successful in capturing the spies. It was safe then for the men to come down from the hills and return to their camp. Excited by their adventure, they hurried to Joshua and gave him this message: "The people of Jericho are afraid of us and will not resist us. It is time to attack!"

CROSSING THE JORDAN

After the spies came back from Jericho and gave the report that the people there were afraid, Joshua gave the command for the Israelites to pack up their camp and move to the banks of the Jordan River. The tents came down; the tabernacle was taken apart. The priests ran poles through the rings in the corners of the ark of the covenant and lifted it to their shoulders. You will remember that the tables of stone on which God had written the Ten Commandments were in the ark, and it was very precious and sacred to the Israelites.

This was during the spring of the year, and the Jordan River was flooded by spring rains. With a powerful current it ran swiftly down to the Dead Sea. It was so broad and moved so fast that only a very strong man could have swum it. The Israelites stood near its banks and looked at it and then at the land of Canaan beyond. How were they going to get across? There were no bridges and they had no boats.

Then Joshua gave commands to his officers and they moved through the crowd, shouting orders. "When you see the priests carrying the ark of the covenant, follow behind at a proper distance."

The priests moved among the people and marched with the ark to the edge of the water. Joshua gave them the command, "Wade into the water!" When the feet of the priests touched the water, God caused a wonderful thing to happen—up the river the water stopped flowing as if an invisible dam held it back. The people saw it rise and pile up without flowing down. Below, the water that was already there flowed

onward toward the Dead Sea until the river bed lay dry and the stones on its bottom were uncovered.

The priests moved out into the very center of the river bed and stood with the ark on their shoulders. Past them marched the entire nation of Israel, following Joshua safely to the other side of the river, exactly as their parents had followed Moses across the Red Sea. God had shown them that His spirit was going to be with Joshua as it once had been with Moses.

When all of Israel had crossed to the other side, Joshua called a man from each of the twelve tribes and said, "Each of you gather a large stone from the river bottom where the priests are standing and pile them in a heap here on the bank. In future years when your children ask you why the stones are here, you can tell them how the Lord made the river dry. They will serve as a monument to you."

Then Joshua himself set up twelve stones in the middle of the river bed. When the two piles were made, one on the bank and one in the river, Joshua gave the command for the priests to join them on the bank. As the feet of the priests touched the shore, the river began suddenly to flow as before, its water tumbling down from the hills, racing for the Dead Sea.

Israel camped that night on the shore of the promised land for the first time since they had left Egypt. The power and glory of the Lord filled their hearts when they looked back at the swift river and thought of having walked through it on dry ground that very day.

The new camp, set up near the heap of stones from the river bed, was named Gilgal. It became the main camp during the time that Israel fought for the land of Canaan. While the Israelites camped here, they ate the Passover feast, as their parents had done for the first time the night before they left Egypt. They made their bread for the feast from grain growing there in the land of Canaan. When they did, the manna that had fallen for forty years fell no more. The days of wandering were over.

THE CAPTURE OF JERICHO

The Israelites camped at Gilgal, on the west side of the Jordan River, waiting for God's commands. One day Joshua, their brave leader, was out walking alone within sight of the great city Jericho. As he walked, he came face to face with an armed man. "Are you a friend or an enemy?" Joshua boldly asked.

"I am neither," the stranger replied. "I have come to you as the commander of the army of the Lord."

When Joshua saw that it was an angel he had approached, he fell to the ground and bowed low before him. "What message do you have from my Lord?" he asked.

Then the angel gave him the plans that God wanted the Israelites to follow when they attacked the city of Jericho. Joshua had never heard such strange plans of war, but he remembered exactly what the angel had said. He returned to camp, determined to do just as he had been told because he felt that the Lord was wiser than he. What the Lord said, he would obey without question.

Now the people of Jericho had become very frightened when they saw the Israelites camped within sight of their city. They closed tight their city gates, and no one came in or went out. Toward this walled city, Joshua commanded the people to march. First, came a special group of armed warriors; then followed seven priests with rams' horns. Behind them came more priests carrying the precious ark of the covenant, covered and borne on their shoulders by poles. Last of all, came the rest of the people, marching in order.

All the way around the walls of the city the Israelites marched. No one talked or shouted. The only noise was the blasts of the rams' horns blown by seven priests. Then they returned to their camp. The next morning they did the same thing. For six days the strange procession made one journey around the city.

Inside the city, the people of Jericho were puzzled. They had expected a brave attack by thousands of armed soldiers. What could this mean? Even the Israelites wondered what was about to happen. But Joshua knew that this was what the Lord had commanded, and he was going to obey.

On the sixth night, he called all the people together. "Tomorrow," he said, "we will march around the city not once, but seven times. Then when the rams' horns give a long blast, everyone is to shout. If we do this, the Lord has promised to give us the city. Remember, however, that God requires that we destroy every living thing in the city except those we find in the house of Rahab, for she saved our spies. Her house will be marked by a red cord hanging from the window. All the gold and silver that is in the city must go into the treasury of the Lord."

The next morning the Israelites rose early and formed their strange procession. Again they marched toward Jericho and around its city walls —once, twice, three times, and up to seven times. Then the marchers stopped still. The priests blew loud and long upon their horns, and then Joshua's voice rang out, "Shout, for the Lord has given you the city!" All the people answered with a great, wild shout; and when they did, the walls of the city began to crack and crumble. They trembled and leaned, and then they fell crashing to the ground.

The Israelite army began climbing over the ruins to fight the people inside the city; but they found them so frightened by the collapse of the walls, that it was an easy victory. The two spies found Rahab's house with all of her family safe inside, and they took them back to the Israelite camp to wait until the battle was over. Rahab remained and made her home with the Israelites, for she had chosen to serve their God. Later on, she married a fine Israelite named Salmon, and she became a great-great-grandmother of David, into whose family Jesus Christ was born.

After the battle of Jericho, the fame of Joshua and the Israelites began to spread throughout the land of Canaan. Others dreaded the day they had to fight against this army whose commander was God.

Loran Raymond Jones

THE FALL OF JERICHO
Joshua 6:1–21

SAMSON AND THE LION

After many years, the Israelites, under the leadership of Joshua, succeeded in conquering all the land of Canaan. At least the people who were still living in Canaan were subdued enough that Joshua could divide up the land among his people.

Because the Israelites were the only people living in that area who did not worship idols, they needed a strong leader to keep reminding them that they were to worship only the one true God. As long as Joshua lived, the people remained faithful; but after everyone died who remembered him, the Israelites turned to the idol gods of the Canaanites. When they forgot God in this way, He would punish them by letting their enemies come in from lands around and conquer them. After suffering under these enemies, the Israelites would begin to think of the help God had been to them in the past and the strength they had had when He was with them. They would turn away from the idols and pray once again to God, and He would hear their prayers. Usually, He would send a great man to lead them in victory against the enemy who was their master.

This leader was usually called a "judge," and as long as the judge lived, the people would serve God and be successful. Then when he died, they would eventually forget God again and fall to another enemy. For several hundred years, this happened over and over.

One of the enemies who conquered the Israelites was the Philistines, a strong nation that lived near the Great Sea. For forty years the Israelites had been serving them, and the Lord had sent no deliverer. Finally, an angel appeared to an Israelite woman and told her that she was going to have a son who would rescue God's people from the Philistines. This boy was to be specially dedicated to God from the time he was born. The woman was not to eat any unclean thing or drink any wine, and the little baby was never to have his hair cut, for he would be a Nazirite. To the Israelites, a Nazirite was one who let his hair grow and drank no wine to show that he belonged to God.

The woman hurried to tell her husband Manoah of the wonderful news, but he could hardly believe it. It was too good to be true! He prayed that God would send the angel again, so they would be sure and understand how they were to treat their special son.

This time the angel appeared to Manoah and his wife while they were out in the fields. Manoah had many questions for the heavenly being, but the angel repeated the same message to them. Manoah was so grateful that he offered a sacrifice to God there. When the flame from the altar rose, the angel ascended to heaven along with the fire.

In time, the promised son came; and the happy parents named him Samson. They took good care of him and saw that he never ate anything unclean and that his hair was never cut. As Samson grew up, his long hair was not the only strange thing people began to notice about him. He was a very strong boy and could do things no one his age, or even those older, could do. But sometimes it seemed that Samson was not serious enough, for he would use his strength just to show off.

When Samson was old enough to get married, he came to his mother and father and told them that he had seen a Philistine woman in the town of Timnath that he wanted to be his wife. Manoah and his wife were very disappointed that Samson had chosen a Philistine instead of one of the Israelite girls. "Is there no young woman among our own people who is appealing to you? Must you choose for your wife a person who is one of the pagan Philistines?" they asked Samson. But Samson's mind was made up. "Please arrange for her to become my wife," he urged his parents, "for she is very pleasing to me." When Samson's parents saw how determined he was, they made a trip with Samson down to Timnath to make arrangements for the marriage.

During the journey, Samson and his parents became separated. Perhaps Samson wandered off alone, away from the road, to explore the wilderness. While he was alone, a lion leaped out at him, ready to attack. In a second, Samson caught the lion and killed him with his bare hands, leaving him in many pieces on the ground. But he never told his parents or anyone else about this.

Arrangements for the marriage were made and Samson and his family went back home. Then at the time planned, he returned to Timnath for the wedding. On the trip, he thought again of the lion he had killed, and he wandered into the brush to look for what was left of it. He found the body of the lion had been eaten by wild beasts and birds,

and only its bones were left. But then he noticed that among the bones some bees had made a honeycomb and left some honey in it. He reached into the honeycomb and took some of the honey to eat. It tasted good to him as he walked along on his long journey. He also took some of the honey home to his father and mother. And though they ate it and enjoyed it, Samson would not tell them where he had found the honeycomb.

After the wedding, it was customary in those days for there to be a long wedding feast or celebration. At Samson's wedding the celebration lasted a whole week. During that time, Samson and the other young men entertained themselves with riddles and guessing games. Samson thought and thought and then he said: "I will give you a riddle. If you can answer it within these seven days, I will give you each a new suit of clothes; but if you cannot answer it, you must give me thirty suits of clothes."

"Fine!" his companions declared. "Now, tell us your riddle."

So he said, "Out of the eater came something to eat. Out of the strong came something sweet."

For three days the men puzzled over Samson's riddle, but they could not find the right answer.

Finally, they came to Samson's bride and told her, "Get Samson to tell you the answer to his riddle. If you cannot find out for us, we will burn your family's house."

So Samson's new wife begged and pleaded with him to tell her the answer to his riddle. Finally she began crying and said, "If you really loved me, you would tell me the answer." She bothered him so much about it that he finally gave in and told her about the lion he had killed and the honey he had found among its bones. Naturally, she gave the answer to the other men.

On the last day of the feast, just as it was ending, the men came confidently to Samson. With a smile they said, "What is sweeter than honey? What is stronger than a lion?"

Samson knew immediately that they had gotten the answer from his wife. He was so angry that he went right out and killed the first Philistines he found and used their clothes to pay his bet. Then, quite angry, he returned to his father's home.

But this was only the beginning of Samson's dealings with the Philistines. The Lord had given him his strength to deliver his people from the Philistines—not with an army, but with his might alone.

SAMSON AND DELILAH

After his adventures with the Philistines, Samson's name became well known throughout Israel. Everyone began looking to him as their leader and judge. They would bring their problems to him, and he would try to advise them the way the Lord would be pleased.

But Samson was restless and could not be still very long. Time and time again he would find opportunity to do some harm to the Philistines. One time he killed a thousand of them in one day with the jawbone of a donkey. Another time, they locked him within a city gate, thinking they had captured him. He not only escaped; he lifted the whole gate with its posts to his shoulders and carried it to a distant hill.

Some of Samson's tricks make us think that he was not as serious about leading his people as he should have been. He seemed to enjoy playing jokes on his enemies more than leading his people to peace. But in all this time, he had obeyed the Nazirite law as the angel had told his mother he must. He had never cut his hair nor eaten anything unclean nor drunk wine.

Then, for the second time, Samson fell in love with a Philistine woman. The Philistine rulers, eager to do away with this fellow who caused them so much trouble, came to the woman with a bargain to make. "Delilah," they said, "if you can find out what makes Samson so strong and how we can overcome him, we will each give you eleven hundred pieces of silver."

It was a great amount of money. Delilah thought about it a bit, and she finally agreed to do as they said.

Now Samson thought that Delilah loved him as much as he loved her, and he never suspected that she would betray him. Still, when she would coax him to tell her the secret of his strength, he would tease her. First, he told her that if he were bound with seven green twigs, he would not be strong any more.

The Philistines secretly brought Delilah the green twigs, and when Samson was asleep, she bound him with them. Then she called out, "Wake up, Samson, the Philistines are coming!" With that, he jumped up, breaking the twigs with ease.

Loran Raymond Jones

THE DEATH OF SAMSON

Judges 16:25–31

She knew that he had not told her the truth.

Samson thought that Delilah was playing some kind of a game; and the next time she begged him to tell her his secret, he told her that he would be weak if he were bound with new ropes. Taking new ropes, she bound him, and again he broke them as though they were threads.

Still playing a game, the next time Samson told her that his strength would leave him if his hair was woven in a loom. Delilah wove his hair into a loom during his sleep and then fastened it tightly with a pin. But this time, when she called out to him, he stood up with the loom still fastened to his hair.

Delilah did not like Samson's game, for she was anxious to get her money from the rulers. She asked him, "How can you say that you love me when you will not tell me the truth?" Every day she would beg and plead with him until he got tired of listening to her. Finally he told her, "My hair has never been cut because I am a Nazirite and belong to the Lord in a special way. If my head were shaved, my strength would be gone."

This time Delilah knew that he had told the truth. She called the rulers to bring her their money. Then she had them wait in another room. When Samson fell asleep, she called in a man with a razor. As the locks fell from the sleeping man's head, his strength began to fail. When Delilah called that the Philistines were upon him, Samson woke and found that the Lord had left him. The rulers drew aside the curtain that hid them and took him their prisoner. They put out his eyes and took him down to a prison. Here, poor, blind Samson pulled a millstone to grind wheat just as a donkey would have done.

But while Samson was in prison his hair began to grow again. And he had a lot of time to think. He probably prayed to God to forgive him for often wasting the marvelous strength that he had been given and then lost.

To celebrate the capture of Samson, the Philistines gave a great festival in the temple of their idol god, Dagon. During the celebration, some began to call for Samson. They wanted him brought out so they could make fun of him. Dragged from the prison, Samson was led between two great pillars so all could see him. What a sight he must have made! Stumbling and ragged, he stood while they laughed at him.

Then Samson asked the boy who was leading him about to show him where the two pillars were so he could rest. With his hands on the pillars Samson began to pray silently: "Lord God, give me my strength just one more time that I may repay the Philistines for the trouble they have caused me."

Then, grasping the two pillars tightly, he began to feel his old strength returning. "Let me die with the Philistines!" he cried; and with one mighty push, he cracked the two pillars and the temple collapsed. All the thousands who had been in the temple, including Samson, were killed. In his brave death, Samson killed more Philistines and did more to set his people free than he did during all his life.

RUTH AND BOAZ

During the time of the judges, a famine came upon the land of the Israelites, as one had in the time of Jacob. Nothing would grow in the fields, and the pastures became dry and barren. When food became scarce, a certain man named Elimelech grew worried about his family. He had two growing boys, as well as a wife, and there simply was not enough food to go around. Finally Elimelech decided to leave his home in Bethlehem and go to the land of Moab to live until the famine was over. There he would be able to find work and food.

So Elimelech and his wife Naomi took their sons to Moab and made a home for them there. Moab is south of Bethlehem and on the opposite side of the Dead Sea. It is one of the countries through which the Israelites had to pass on their journey from Egypt to Canaan.

Poor Elimelech never got to see his home in Bethlehem again, for he died while the family was in Moab. Naomi continued to live there with her sons until they were grown.

The time came for the sons to choose wives, and naturally they each chose one of the Moabite women they knew. Chilion married a woman named Orpah; Mahlon's wife was called Ruth. The lovely brides helped make Naomi's life happier.

Then misfortune struck again. Both of the sons died. All three women were widows. The younger women stayed and continued to make their home with Naomi.

41

One day Naomi received word that the Lord had made the land of Israel green and fruitful once more, and she decided to return to her people. Both Orpah and Ruth made plans to accompany Naomi on her journey, but Naomi would not hear of it. "My daughters," she said, "there is no reason for you to leave your families and your homeland. You are still young, and you have time to find another husband and rear a family. Return to your father's house."

Tearfully Orpah kissed her mother-in-law and said good-by, but Ruth would not leave. "Follow your sister-in-law," Naomi begged. "Return with her to your home."

Ruth had a beautiful reply: "Do not ask me to leave you or to quit following you. I want to go where you go and live where you live. Your people will become my people and your God, my God."

When Naomi saw that Ruth was determined, she said no more. The two made the long trip to Bethlehem together.

News traveled quickly that Naomi was back in town, and many came out to greet her. "Is this Naomi?" they asked.

"Do not call me Naomi any more," she replied. "It means 'pleasant,' and my life has been far from pleasant. A better name for me would be Mara, for it means 'bitter.' I have lost my husband and both my sons while I was away."

Now Naomi and Ruth returned at the time of the barley harvest, and Ruth went out in the fields to gather grain with the other reapers. It was the custom in Israel for the reapers to leave some of the grain for the poor people to gather, and this was what Ruth picked as she followed along.

It so happened that Ruth had chosen to glean in a field which belonged to a rich man of Bethlehem named Boaz. When Boaz came to look over his field, he noticed Ruth among the reapers. He asked the master of the reapers, "Who is the young woman there?"

"She is the Moabite woman who returned to Bethlehem with Naomi," the man replied. "She asked to glean here and has been here since yesterday."

Boaz sought Ruth out and told her, "Stay here in my fields and glean for the rest of the harvest. I will see that everyone is kind to you. When you get thirsty, feel free to take some of our water."

Ruth bowed and thanked Boaz for his kindness to her, especially since she was a stranger in Israel. But Boaz said, "You are really no stranger for I have heard how good and kind you have been to your mother-in-law. I know that you left your home and family to come with her here. May the Lord, in Whom you have come to trust, reward you." Then Boaz invited her to eat with his reapers. When she had finished eating and gone back to work, Boaz asked his reapers to let some of their barley fall on purpose so she could gather it.

That evening Ruth was excited when she returned to Naomi. "Look how much I have gathered today," she said. "I met the owner of the field, and he was the kindest man! He gave me permission to gather there until the end of the harvest."

"Who was this man?" asked Naomi.

"He is called Boaz," Ruth replied.

"Why, he is my husband's near kinsman," Naomi exclaimed. "Stay in his field as he has invited you to do."

By the end of the harvest, Boaz had come to love Ruth; and when he got permission from the elders of the city, he took her to be his wife. Naomi came to make her home with them; and when Ruth had a baby boy, Naomi was its nurse. "Once more," she said to her friends, "my life is pleasant."

The little boy born to Ruth and Boaz was named Obed. His own son was named Jesse, and Jesse was the father of David, the shepherd boy who became king. Thus Ruth, the young Moabitess who followed her mother-in-law to Israel, became the great-great-grandmother of its second king.

SAMUEL HEARS A VOICE

While the judges ruled Israel, the tabernacle was set up at Shiloh, located near the center of the land. The priests who served in the worship in the tabernacle lived in tents near it. All of the Israelites were commanded to come to Shiloh at least once a year and offer sacrifices on the altar that stood before the tabernacle.

There was a man named Elkanah living in the mountains not too far from Shiloh who was always faithful to worship at the tabernacle. Every year he would bring his two wives and all his children with him to the Holy Place to offer sacrifices. Now

all of his children belonged to one of his wives; the other, named Hannah, had none.

One year, while at Shiloh, Hannah prayed earnestly to the Lord to give her a baby boy. She promised God that if He would send her a son, she would dedicate him to the Lord all the days of his life.

While she was praying, Eli, the priest, saw her and promised her that God would answer her prayer. In time, the baby was born and she named him Samuel, which means, "Asked of God."

When Samuel was still a little boy, Hannah brought him to Eli at the tabernacle. "I am the woman you saw praying one day for a son," she said. "This boy is the one the Lord sent me. Just as I promised, I now want to give him back to God to serve Him all his life."

So Samuel came to live with Eli and grow up near the house of God. Every year his mother would make him a little linen coat like the one the priests wore and bring it to him at Shiloh. The Lord blessed Hannah and gave her three more sons and two daughters so she would not get lonesome for Samuel at home.

Eli was growing old and could barely see, so Samuel was a great help to him in the tabernacle worship. Eli needed Samuel all the more because his own sons were very wicked. Even though they were priests of God, they caused the other Israelites to sin when they came to the tabernacle. Eli had not corrected them enough when they were young, and now they had grown too old for him to control.

In those days, God had not spoken to any man, as He had to Abraham and Moses, for a long while. Late one night when the only light still burning was the lamp in the house of the Lord, Samuel woke from his sleep, hearing someone call his name. He thought it was Eli and ran to his bed. "Here I am, for you called me," he said to the old priest.

"No, my son," said Eli, "I have not called you. Go back to your bed."

Back in his bed, Samuel lay, falling asleep, when the voice came again: "Samuel!"

Again he went to Eli, sure that he had been called; but Eli said, "I have not called you, Samuel. Lie down once more."

A third time Samuel heard his name called. This time he said to Eli, "Here I am. I know I heard you calling to me."

Then Eli realized that the Lord had been speaking to Samuel. He told Samuel to go back to bed; and when he heard the voice again, he was to say: "Speak, Lord, for I am listening."

Before long, the voice was heard once more: "Samuel! Samuel!" This time Samuel answered, "Speak, Lord, for I am listening."

Then the Lord told Samuel that he was going to punish Eli's sons for their wickedness.

Samuel lay in his bed until morning. Then he got up and went right to work, opening the doors of the tabernacle. He tried to avoid Eli because he hated to tell him the sad news.

Finally, Eli called to Samuel and asked, "What did the Lord say to you, Samuel?"

Obedient as always, Samuel told Eli all that God had said. The message made Eli very sad, but he said, "Let God do what seems best to him."

It did not take long for word to travel that God had spoken to Samuel. People began to respect him; and when he grew up, they looked to him as a prophet, one through whom God gives messages to His people.

God's promise to punish Eli's sons came true, for both of them were killed in a battle one day with the Philistines. During the battle, the ark of the covenant, which they had taken from the tabernacle, was stolen by the Philistines. When Eli heard this, he, too, died.

Without the ark and the priests, the tabernacle soon became shabby and fell into ruins. Samuel went to his father's home and lived until he grew up. Then he traveled among all the twelve tribes, giving them God's messages. He was the last judge, and he ruled the people in peace instead of leading them into battle.

SAUL, ISRAEL'S FIRST KING

Although Samuel was a good leader and judge over the Israelites, his sons were dishonest, and their decisions were not fair. The elders of the Israelites went to Samuel's house at Ramah and told him that his sons were not fit to rule after his death. "Let us have a king to rule over us like the other nations have," they asked.

Samuel was disappointed at this request. He felt

Loran Raymond Jones

SAMUEL PRESENTING SAUL—FIRST KING OF ISRAEL

I Samuel 10:17–25

that the Lord God should be their only king. God had not meant for His people to be a conquering, fighting nation like the others around them once they had settled in Canaan. Their main interest was supposed to be in serving Him in a quiet, peaceful way; but the people had begun to want power and riches. Samuel prayed to God about this, and God told him: "Go ahead and grant the people a king as they have asked. They are not rejecting you, Samuel; they are turning away from me in wanting another to lead them. But before you appoint the new leader, warn the people of the lives they will lead under a king."

Samuel tried to tell the people that if they had a king, he would take their sons to be his soldiers and their daughters to work in his palace. They would have to pay taxes to him and work for him. "Someday," he warned them, "you will cry to the Lord about your king, but then the Lord will not hear you."

The people would not change their minds. "No, no," they cried, "give us our king! Give us a mighty leader to judge us and lead us in battle!"

So the Lord said to Samuel, "Do as they ask and appoint a king to rule over them." Samuel told the people that their wish would be granted and sent them home.

At this time, there was a powerful man of the tribe of Benjamin named Kish. He had a son named Saul, a noble-looking lad and a very tall one. In a crowd, his head and shoulders showed above everyone else. But although Saul was so manly and fine looking, he still was modest and quiet.

Now Kish was a very rich man and owned many fine animals. One day some of his asses wandered away, and Kish sent Saul and a servant to find them. For several days they searched the countryside, but they found no trace of the lost animals.

"We had better go back home now," Saul told the servant. "My father will have quit worrying about his asses and begun worrying about us."

By this time they had come to Ramah, the city where Samuel lived. The servant had heard of Samuel, and he suggested that they stop and ask the man of God where they could find their asses. It was known that Samuel was a prophet and could tell what was about to happen through God's power.

Now Saul did not know that Samuel had been warned by God to expect him. The day before,

God had told Samuel, "Tomorrow I am going to send a man to you from the tribe of Benjamin. He is the one you are to anoint as king over my people."

When Saul approached Samuel that day, he would hardly have been recognized as a king. He was dirty and tired from his searching, and he only wanted to ask a simple request of the great prophet. But Samuel heard God's voice speaking to him again: "This is the one I was speaking of. This is the future king."

Saul could not understand why he was given special treatment by the prophet. Samuel insisted that Saul come to the feast he was attending and gave him the best food there. Then he invited Saul and the servant to spend the night at his house. That night Saul and Samuel stayed up late to talk of all the things that were going to happen in Israel.

The next morning, Samuel walked with Saul and the servant to the edge of the city. Then he asked the servant to go on ahead while he talked to Saul alone. When no one could see them, Samuel brought out a little bottle filled with oil and poured it on Saul's head. This was called "anointing." Then he announced to Saul, "The Lord has appointed you a prince over His people."

After this, he gave Saul three signs that would happen to him on his way home. First, he would meet two men who would tell him that the asses had been found. Then he would meet three men who would give him some food. Finally, he would meet some prophets; and when God's spirit had come upon him, he would be able to prophesy with them.

All these things happened just as Samuel had said they would.

When Saul finally reached home, an uncle met him and asked where he had been. Saul told him that he had seen Samuel, but he did not tell anyone that he had been anointed Israel's first king.

Then Samuel called all the Israelites together at Mizpah. "You have made God unhappy by asking for a king, but He has heard you and will give you that king. Now, let all the tribes of Israel, family by family, pass in front of me."

One by one, the tribes passed until Samuel chose the smallest and weakest, the tribe of Benjamin. Then of all the families of Benjamin, the family of Kish was singled out. Finally, Saul was called for. But Saul was not with his family! He had hidden from the crowd among the baggage.

Then someone ran and got him, and as he walked toward the people, they all looked eagerly to see what kind of man God had chosen. Everyone was pleased when they saw the tall, handsome young man. "Long live the King!" they shouted as they cheered their approval of the new ruler.

How wonderful it would have been if Saul had remained as pure and good as he was that day.

The Lord blessed Saul as king and made him victorious over many enemies, including the Philistines. But the more successful God made him, the more confident Saul became of himself, and he disobeyed God's laws. Finally, God told Samuel to tell Saul that because of his disobedience the kingdom would be taken from his family and given to one who would obey.

DAVID AND GOLIATH

One of the important enemies that God helped Saul conquer while he was king was the Philistines; but later in his reign, they returned again to attack the Israelites. As the army of the Philistines prepared for battle on one hill, the Israelites pitched camp across from them on another. The fight was to take place in the valley between them.

Before they had begun to fight, a soldier stepped out from among the Philistines, and what a soldier he was! This man, called Goliath, was truly a giant, for he stood nearly twice as tall as a normal man. He wore a bronze helmet and heavy coat of armor, and in his hand he carried an enormous spear. Before him went his shield-bearer. To the armies of Saul, he shouted out a challenge for someone to come and fight him. If Goliath won, the Israelites would serve the Philistines; but if an Israelite conquered Goliath, the Philistines would be servants to the Israelites.

The Israelites were afraid when they heard this challenge, and no one dared to go out and fight with the giant. For forty days, Goliath came out and strutted before the battle lines, but never was an Israelite brave enough to answer his call.

Now, at this time, David was watching his father's sheep at Bethlehem as he was too young to be a soldier; but three of his older brothers were in the army. According to the custom in those days, David's father sent him to the battle lines with food for his brothers; and, in turn, he was to come back and report to his father about them.

When David finally found his brothers among the ranks, he was able to overhear the giant Go-

liath making his mocking challenge. David eagerly begged for a chance to fight the giant himself, but the soldiers made fun of him. He was so anxious, however, that eventually Saul heard of it and sent for him. Saul tried to persuade David that he was too young and inexperienced to meet the giant; but David answered that he had killed a lion and a bear that had attacked his sheep and with God's help, he could conquer the giant, also. When Saul saw that David's mind was made up, he even tried to get him to use his own kingly armor. But David found that he was not used to it and that it only bothered him, so he gave it back to Saul. Instead, all he took with him was his shepherd's staff, his sling, and five smooth stones that he took from a brook and put into his shepherd's bag.

Goliath was angry when he saw the young man coming toward him, for he thought that the Israelites were trying to make fun of him. But David said, "You come to me with a sword and with a spear and with a javelin; but I come to you in the name of the Lord of hosts . . ."

Then, reaching into his bag, he took out one of the stones and placed it in the simple leather sling. With one expert throw, the stone struck the giant in the center of the forehead and he fell to the ground. David rushed up, took the giant's own sword, and cut off Goliath's head.

The Philistines fled in fright while the Israelites began to shout and praise the young hero, David. David himself, though, gave glory to God for the victory, for he knew that he had not won the fight alone. The God that he loved and served had been with him.

DAVID AND JONATHAN

After David killed Goliath, Saul brought him to the palace to live. There, in Saul's house, David

met one of Saul's sons, Jonathan. The two became the closest of friends, and each loved the other

Loran Raymond Jones

DAVID AND GOLIATH

I Samuel 17:1–54

with all of his heart. They promised that they would always love each other; and to seal his promise, Jonathan gave David his robe, his sword, and his bow.

David did everything that Saul asked him to do very well, and it was not long before Saul appointed him to be one of his generals. David was a wonderful fighter, as he had proved when he killed Goliath, and he was very well liked by his men. He was the sort of man who seemed to draw others to him.

On his return from one battle, the people came out to meet David, singing,

"Saul has killed his thousands,
And David his *ten* thousands."

When Saul heard this, he became jealous of David. He already knew that God was not going to allow one of his sons to become king because he had been a disobedient ruler. Perhaps he wondered if the popular young David was going to be the one to take the throne. David had told no one that indeed he was the one God had chosen to be the next king.

Saul's guilt and worrying seemed to drive him nearly mad. A spirit came over him that made him very unhappy, and he would rave like a crazy man. Now David was not only a shepherd and a fighter, he was also a musician. To try to make Saul feel better, he brought in his harp and sang some songs that he had written. But while he was playing, Saul became very angry and threw his spear at David. David jumped aside just in time to miss being hit.

From that time on, Saul was truly afraid of David's power. He knew that the people would not stand for him to kill David, so he sent him on dangerous missions, hoping he would be killed in battle. But David was as successful as before, and performed each duty just as well.

No matter where Saul went, everyone was always speaking of wonderful David. Finally, Saul made no secret of wanting to see David killed, but he called on the wrong person to do it—Jonathan.

Jonathan went straight to David and told David to hide until the danger was over. Then he went to his father and begged for David's life: "Why do you want to kill David, Father? He has never done anything but good for you. Why, he even risked his life to kill Goliath and saved our whole nation. You, too, were proud of him then."

Saul loved his son, and he listened carefully to what he said. "I will not kill David," he promised.

But another battle with the Philistines broke out and David won a great victory. This time, in his jealousy, Saul became sicker than ever. When David came in to play and sing softly to calm him, he became so angry that he tried to pin David to the wall with his spear.

David ran from the palace to his house, but he was not safe there. Saul sent soldiers to find him, and David's wife helped him escape out the window.

This time David ran far away from Saul and came to live at Ramah with the prophet Samuel. Twice Saul sent messengers to find him, and once he went himself, but God protected David each time.

Although David was afraid to be seen near the palace, he and Jonathan planned a secret meeting out in a field. The two friends were glad to see each other after being separated for so long, but their meeting was not a happy one because they had to hide and keep their friendship a secret.

"What have I done?" David asked Jonathan. "Why is your father trying to kill me?"

"He has promised me that he will not hurt you, David," Jonathan said.

"But he knows that we are good friends," David replied. "Because of that, he will keep his plans from you."

"Tell me what I can do to help you," Jonathan asked. "I will try to do anything you ask."

"Go to the feast that the king is giving," said David, "but I will not attend. When King Saul asks for me, make some excuse—say that I had to go to Bethlehem. If he accepts the excuse, I will know it is safe to return; but if he gets angry, I will be certain that my life is indeed in danger."

"Just as you say," Jonathan agreed. Then they arranged a way that Jonathan could signal to David whether or not all was well when he returned.

The first day of the feast, Saul did not mention David's name. But on the second day, the question came, "Where has David been the past two days?"

"He had to make a trip to Bethlehem, Father," Jonathan replied.

Saul's eyes blazed with anger. He lashed out against Jonathan for befriending the very man who was going to succeed to the throne that was Jonathan's own by birth. He swore to find David and kill him. When Jonathan opened his mouth to speak a word for David, Saul became so angry at him that he hurled his spear at his own son.

Jonathan left the banquet and went back to the field where David was hiding. With his bow and arrows he signalled to David that his life was in danger. David came out of hiding and ran to kiss his beloved friend. The two stood and cried, for they did not know if it would ever be safe for them to meet again. They pledged their eternal love.

The Bible never tells us if David and Jonathan met again, for David stayed in hiding from then until both Jonathan and Saul were killed in the same battle. Jonathan died fighting bravely, but Saul tried to take his own life by falling on his sword when he saw that he was losing the battle.

Even though it meant that he would now be king, David was very sad when he heard of the death of Saul and Jonathan. He wrote a beautiful song about them. In the song, he called Jonathan his "brother." In Jonathan's memory he asked that the people be taught the song of the bow, for his friend had been a mighty archer. Years later he was glad when he had a chance to do a favor for Jonathan's son, Mephibosheth, for his love never died for his best friend.

SOLOMON, A WISE KING

David was a good king and reigned over Israel for forty years, but most of his reign was spent fighting first one enemy and then another. Because David was so victorious, however, he left a mighty empire. A time of peace followed his death for the other people were afraid of the strong Israelite nation King David had made.

Young Solomon became the ruler when David died. He took over the throne that his father had built in Jerusalem. Since Samuel's death, the altar of the Lord had been moved from his home in Ramah to Gibeon, a few miles away from Jerusalem. Feeling all the responsibility that he had as leader of God's chosen people, Solomon went out to Gibeon to offer sacrifices and pray. The Lord heard Solomon's prayers, and He appeared to Solomon in a dream, saying, "Ask me for any gift and I will give it to you."

There were so many things that Solomon could have chosen; but he replied, "Lord, I know so little about ruling this wonderful nation. Give me an understanding heart so that I might know how to make the best decisions and be a good leader."

God was pleased with Solomon's request. He answered, "Because you asked for this instead of long life or riches or victory in battle, I am going to grant your wish. You will have a wise mind and be able to tell what is right and what is wrong more than any other man who has ever lived or will live after you. More than that, I am also going to give you the things for which you did not ask. You will have riches and honor; and if you serve me as your father did, I will grant you a long life, too."

It was not long before Solomon had a chance to use the wisdom God gave him. Two women who lived together were brought before him, each claiming that the same baby was her own. One woman's baby had died and she had taken the other woman's child, but no one could tell who the real mother was. They stood before King Solomon arguing. "This child is mine," one would say. "No," the other would reply, "the dead child was yours, and this one is mine."

Solomon looked from one to another, then he finally said, "Bring me a sword!" When the sword was brought, he pointed to the baby. "Cut the child in half and give half of it to each one."

One of the women gave a loud cry and fell to her knees. "Oh, my lord," she begged, "do not cut the baby in half. Give it to her, but let it live."

The other woman stood nodding approval, "That is a good suggestion. Divide it in two, and let us each have half."

"Give the child to the first woman," Solomon said. "She is its true mother for she could not stand to see it killed."

When the people saw how wisely Solomon had made the decision, they knew that indeed God had granted him an understanding heart.

Now David had wanted to move the ark of the covenant and the altar to Jerusalem and build a great temple for worship, but God had not allowed him to do so. David's reign had been a time of war, and God wanted His house of worship built during peace. However, David had collected gold and silver and wood and stone to be used when the great temple was built.

On Mount Moriah in Jerusalem, the Lord permitted Solomon to build the wonderful building that David had planned. Treasures were brought from all over the world to add to those David had gathered to go into the construction. For seven

Loran Raymond Jones

THE QUEEN OF SHEBA MEETS SOLOMON

II Chronicles 9:1–12

years, skilled workmen carefully made each portion of the great house. It was patterned after the tabernacle with a court, containing the altar, and a building, consisting of the Holy Place and the Holy of Holies where the ark was kept. Naturally, it was larger than the tabernacle, large enough for the people to gather in the court, and it was a permanent building of wood and stone rather than a tent.

When it was finished, it was the most splendid building ever seen in those days. Its walls were red cedar wood and its floors shiny marble. Everywhere one looked there was elaborate carving overlaid with gold and inlaid with precious stones. The ark, containing the sacred tablets on which God had written the Ten Commandments, stood behind an ornate scarlet and purple veil that divided the Holy Place from the Holy of Holies.

When the ark was brought from Gibeon to the completed Temple, it was a time of great celebration for the Israelites. They were all gathered to see the cloud of glory that had guided their fathers through the wilderness and had hovered over the tabernacle now fill this magnificent house of worship. Together they prayed with King Solomon for God to bless this house and make it holy by His presence there.

Solomon was not always as true to his desire to serve God faithfully as he was then. As he grew older, he began to listen to some of his foreign wives and he worshiped their idol gods. Because of this, God told him that the kingdom would be taken from his son. Indeed Solomon's reign was the greatest period of glory the Israelites ever knew, but they were never able to reach that point of power again.

ELIJAH'S STRANGE CONTEST

After Solomon's glorious reign, the Israelite nation began to fall. In order to build the Temple and maintain his great kingdom, Solomon had required his people to pay heavy taxes. Unwisely, his son Rehoboam made the burden even heavier. The ten tribes north of Jerusalem drew away under the young soldier Jeroboam and built their own Northern Kingdom. Only the tribes of Judah and Benjamin remained loyal to Rehoboam in Jerusalem.

Soon Jeroboam led his followers away from the worship of God, and they began worshiping idols. The kings who followed him grew worse and worse, and finally the people of the ten tribes of Israel had forgotten all about their heritage as God's chosen people.

Ahab, the sixth king after Jeroboam, was the most evil of all those before him. His wife Jezebel brought to Israel the worship of the gods Baal and Asherah and tried to kill the prophets of the true God. Some fled to caves in the mountains to save their lives.

These things greatly displeased the Lord. One day, without any warning, He sent a prophet, Elijah, right into the presence of King Ahab. Unafraid, Elijah marched up to Ahab and declared to him that the Lord was going to send no rain until he, Elijah, asked for it again. Then he disappeared as strangely as he had come.

Surely enough, no rain nor dew fell for three years. Ahab searched everywhere for Elijah, but he was nowhere to be found. Elijah was living with a widow to whom God had sent him. Miraculously, they always had a supply of food even when the famine came from a lack of rain. By the power of God Elijah was able to bring the widow's son back to life when he fell ill and died while Elijah was there.

Among Ahab's servants was a godly man named Obadiah. Ahab sent Obadiah out one day to search for water, and while he was looking, he met Elijah. Elijah sent Obadiah back to King Ahab to tell him that he was coming back to the palace.

Now King Ahab blamed Elijah for the lack of rain that his country had suffered for three years; and when he saw Elijah, he called him a "troubler of Israel."

"You are the troubler of Israel," Elijah told the king. "You and your wife have brought it upon your people by worshiping Baal."

Then to prove the foolishness of idol gods, Elijah challenged Ahab to a strange contest of prayer. Ahab was to command the people to assemble on Mount Carmel. Then he was to bring the four hundred fifty priests of Baal and four hundred priests of Asherah to meet Elijah there. The king agreed to the meeting.

Several days later, the crowd assembled on

Mount Carmel. Elijah stood before the group and said, "You have wavered back and forth between God and Baal long enough. Today both the prophets of Baal and I will call for fire from our God, and the One who sends it will be Lord indeed, whether He be Baal or our Father in heaven."

The people agreed that it was a fair test. Two oxen were prepared and one placed on the altar to Baal, but no fire was lit. Then the prophets of Baal stood around their altar and called to their god to send fire down upon the altar. "O Baal, answer us," they cried from morning until noon, but there was no reply.

"Cry louder!" Elijah called to them. "Maybe your god is away on a journey, or maybe he is asleep and you will have to wake him."

The prophets of Baal, who were already tired, became furious at this. In desperation they began cutting their bodies with knives until they bled while they chanted their heathen prayers all the louder.

By mid-afternoon their altar stood just as it had at the beginning of the day. The people turned to Elijah. Solemnly he placed twelve stones, one for each tribe, to form an altar. Then he prepared his oxen for the sacrifice and laid it upon wood. Next he called for water and three times drenched the altar, wood, and sacrifice thoroughly. Lifting his eyes toward heaven, he began to pray: "O Lord, God of Abraham, Isaac, and Israel, let it be known today that you are the God of Israel, and that I am your servant and follow your word."

Suddenly the answer came—flames fell from the sky in fiery sheets that burned up the offering and the wood and even the altar and stones on which they were laid. Every drop of water around the altar disappeared in the fierce flames. The people fell on their faces when they saw this terrifying sight. "The Lord, He is God; the Lord, He is God," they cried over and over.

"Take the prophets of Baal; do not let them escape!" Elijah shouted to the people, and the four hundred fifty prophets were killed there at the foot of the mountain.

Then Elijah had one more prayer to make on that memorable day—this time for rain. Before Ahab's chariot reached the palace, the dark clouds had rolled overhead and the huge drops had begun to fall. It had been a victorious day for Elijah and his God.

All of his life Elijah tried to bring the people of Israel back to the worship of the true God. He taught other prophets who helped him in his work. His closest friend and helper was Elisha, who lived with him. One day when Elijah had grown old, he was talking to Elisha about taking his place as a prophet. Suddenly between them came a flurry of hoofbeats and the sound of a great wind. When Elisha looked up, he saw his master Elijah going toward heaven on a fiery chariot, pulled by horses of fire and carried upward in a whirlwind. Only his coat remained where it had fallen at Elisha's feet. Elisha picked it up and looked once more into the sky, but that was the last he ever saw of Elijah. He had gone to heaven to be with his Lord.

THE HEALING OF NAAMAN

In the days of the great prophets Elijah and Elisha, the Syrians and the Israelites of the Northern Kingdom made attacks on one another even when the two were not openly at war. Since the land of the two joined, the towns along the border were often the scenes of these raids. Bands of warriors would destroy the villages, rob the people of grain and cattle, and take away captives to be sold as slaves. During one raid, a little Israelite girl was taken from her family by the Syrian soldiers. She was carried back with them to their homeland, and she became a servant in the house of a great Syrian captain, Naaman. Probably she was sad and lonely away from her family, but God always lets things happen for good, and she was able to do great good in this strange land.

Naaman, the servant girl's master, had won many battles, and he was a favorite of the king of Syria. But this brave and strong soldier became ill with a terrible disease called leprosy. Naaman and his family were distressed and the king was worried because there was no way to cure leprosy. A person who had leprosy would get terrible sores on his body and eventually he would die. No one wanted to come near a leper for fear he would become infected with the disease. Even though Naaman was a great man, he was sure to die.

Loran Raymond Jones

ELISHA REFUSING GIFTS FROM NAAMAN

II Kings 5:15–19

The little Israelite girl that lived in Naaman's house had not forgotten about God and the prophets of her own land. She felt sorry for her master, but she was too timid to go to him. Instead, she went to Naaman's wife, her mistress, and told her that in Israel there was a prophet of God who could cure Naaman.

When Naaman heard of this prophet, he went straight to his king and reported it. The king was interested and gave Naaman a letter to take to the king of Israel, asking that he try to heal the captain. Besides the letter, Naaman took along on his trip many servants and gifts.

When Naaman gave the king of Israel the letter, the king was distressed. He knew that he could not heal the man. He was afraid the king of Syria was only trying to stir up trouble.

Elisha heard that the king of Israel was worried, so he sent word that Naaman was to come to him. When Naaman and his company came to the prophet's house, Elisha did not even come out to greet him. He simply sent word by his servant that Naaman was to wash seven times in the Jordan River and he would be well.

Naaman was very angry when he received this message. He had expected the prophet to come out and do some wonderful thing to heal him. "Why," he said, "the rivers of my own country are better than the Jordan!"

But Naaman's servants were more thoughtful than he was. They asked him, "Master, would you not have done some great thing if he had asked it of you? Why not obey this simple request?"

Naaman listened to his servants and thought it over. Finally he drove down to the Jordan River and stepped out of his chariot. Into the water he went and dipped himself—once, twice, up to seven times. As he came out of the water the last time, every sign of the leprosy was gone. His skin that had been covered with sores was as smooth and clean as a baby's soft skin. God had performed another wonderful miracle through the great prophet Elisha.

When Naaman hurried back to thank Elisha, Elisha refused the rewards and gifts he was offered. He had not healed Naaman for money, but in order to teach him of the wonderful God of the Israelites. Naaman gave him the best gift when he told him that he would never again pray to any god except the true God that had given the waters of the Jordan the power to make him well.

JONAH AND THE BIG FISH

During the time of the prophets Elijah and Elisha, the Syrians were the greatest threat to the Northern Kingdom of Israel, or the Ten Tribes. But as Elisha promised just before his death, the Syrians were finally defeated.

A new power began rising after Syria went down, and this was a nation to the east called Assyria. The Assyrians were spreading to nations around them conquering each one, and those in the land of Israel knew they would have to defend their homeland before long. The Assyrians were noted for their great city, Nineveh, so huge that it would take a man three days to walk around it.

One day the Lord called a new prophet from the Ten Tribes, a man named Jonah. His message to Jonah was an unexpected one: "Go to Nineveh and preach to the people. Warn them of their wicked ways."

"Nineveh?" Jonah asked himself. "Surely the Lord could not have meant for me to go to Nineveh. The Israelites are God's only chosen people; those in Nineveh are idol-worshipers and heathens.

They are not even worth my efforts."

But Jonah was not fully convinced that he should not go. Perhaps he knew that he was doing wrong, because he felt like he wanted to run away and hide. Instead of going to Nineveh, he went the other direction, to the west. Finally he arrived at Joppa, a seaport on the Great Sea. Here he made arrangements to board a trading ship, bound for a faraway port.

No sooner had the ship set sail than a terrible storm arose. The vessel rolled and tossed as great waves broke over the deck. In efforts to save the ship, the sailors threw all the goods overboard so that the load would be as light as possible. Still the boat rocked as though it might go under at any moment. In terror, the sailors fell to their knees and each began praying to his own idol god.

Now all this time Jonah was asleep in his quarters below deck. The captain went down and roused him. "How can you sleep?" he asked. "Begin praying to your God also; perhaps He can save us." But above the sound of the praying, the

Loran Raymond Jones

JONAH IN NINEVEH

Jonah 3:1–10

storm continued. Finally someone decided, "There is a man on this ship who has done wrong and brought this danger upon us. Let us cast lots and find out which of us is guilty."

When the lots were cast, Jonah was the one accused. Immediately the sailors began questioning him. "Who are you? Where are you from? What business do you have here? What have you done to bring about this evil?"

Jonah confessed that he was an Israelite and that he was running away from a mission God had sent him on. Sadly Jonah told them that the only way they could save their ship would be to throw him overboard.

At first the sailors were not willing to sacrifice Jonah's life, and they tried hard to steer the ship to safety themselves. But at last they saw it was no use, and they tossed Jonah over the side of the ship.

When Jonah fell into the sea, the storm immediately grew calm. The sailors, looking on, fell to their knees in worship to the powerful God whom Jonah the Israelite served.

Under the water Jonah's body plunged, but God's mighty hand caused a giant fish to pass that way at that moment. The fish opened its huge mouth and sucked Jonah, alive, right into its stomach. For three days and nights Jonah lived in the slimy darkness of this living death. Most of that time he spent praying to God to forgive him and save him. Then suddenly the fish opened his mouth and threw up Jonah onto a dry beach.

As he stood in the sand, smoothing his ragged clothes and wiping off his skin, he heard the call of the Lord again: "Go to Nineveh and preach." This time he did not hesitate, but hurried as quickly as he could to the great city.

In Nineveh, Jonah told his message to everyone he met. "Unless you turn from evil, the Lord is go-ing to destroy your city," he warned the citizens as he walked up and down each street.

To Jonah's surprise, the people accepted his message. They listened as though they had been just waiting to know how they could save themselves. They grew sorry for their sins, and even their king repented and ordered that everyone pray to the Lord God for forgiveness.

Touched by the effect of Jonah's warning, the Lord forgave the people of Nineveh and decided to save their city. But this made Jonah very angry. He was disappointed that God wanted to save these foreign people. In his heart, he wished that God had gone ahead and destroyed them.

Sulking and stubborn, Jonah marched out of the city. He built himself a little shack on the edge of town and sat down to wait and see whether or not the Lord would destroy the city.

One day God caused a gourd plant to grow up beside Jonah's little shelter. Its big leaves threw shade across Jonah and he rested happily out of the hot sun. Then in the night a worm ate the plant and killed it. As the wind and sun hit Jonah the next day, Jonah wept for his shading vine. He said that he would rather die than suffer in the heat.

Then God spoke to foolish Jonah: "How can you cry over the loss of a little plant that came and went in one day and then show no pity for a great city where thousands of helpless children live?"

Jonah realized then that people are the most precious thing in the world and that God cares for every person, even those who never had a chance to know about Him. Most of the Old Testament tells of God's concern for His chosen people, the Israelites; but the story of Jonah shows us that He is a God of all nations and that everyone falls under the power of His love.

CAPTIVES IN BABYLON

Even though the Lord sent prophets like Elijah, Elisha, and Jonah to the Northern Kingdom of Israel, they were not able to lead the people away from idolatry and back to the worship of the true God. Eventually enemies were able to conquer Israel because it grew weak without God. The mighty Assyrians carried away most of the people to their own land, and in time the ten tribes were lost among the foreigners.

The tribes of Judah and Benjamin, which remained loyal to Rehoboam, Solomon's son and the rightful king, had kings who led them into idolatry, too; but they had some good leaders who served the Lord. They also had had the Temple that Solomon had built in Jerusalem and the Law of Moses which was kept there. These people were the ones God planned to keep separated as His chosen nation, although they were only a small

Loran Raymond Jones

JEREMIAH'S GRIEF AT THE FALL OF JERUSALEM

Jeremiah 39:1–18

part of the original twelve tribes. Usually, this southern kingdom was referred to simply as Judah because Judah was the larger tribe, and the land became known as Judea. It is also from the tribe of Judah that we get the name Jews, which Israelites are often called.

One of the Lord's prophets sent to the Southern Kingdom of Judah was called Jeremiah. Just as the prophets in the Northern Kingdom of Israel had warned their people about the Assyrians, Jeremiah tried to tell the people of Judah that they would be captured by the Babylonians if they continued in sin.

In spite of the warning, the day came when Nebuchadnezzar, mighty king of Babylon, took the city of Jerusalem. The king, noblemen, and many of the best people in the land were carried away to the great Babylonian empire in the east. Most of those taken away were loyal servants of the Lord, and their troubles kept them close to one another and faithful to God.

God told Jeremiah that those taken away to Babylon would be the real blessing to Judah, while those that remained in Judea would eventually be destroyed. Jeremiah sent letters to those in captivity and begged them to be true to their God, for he promised that they would be allowed to return to their own land in seventy years. He chose to remain with the poor people left in Jerusalem, and eventually he was captured and taken to Egypt, where he died.

Jeremiah saw only sadness in his lifetime. He watched the Babylonians capture the city of Jerusalem that had once been so radiant with power and beauty when Solomon reigned. He saw these conquerors tear apart the beautiful Temple of the Lord and gather up the golden bowls used for worship for their treasure. He looked at the ruins of the city, deserted by God's people now having to serve their God as best they could in a strange land. No wonder Jeremiah is known as "the weeping prophet."

DANIEL IN THE LIONS' DEN

Just as the Assyrians had grown in power and finally taken the Ten Tribes or Northern Kingdom of Israel their captives, the Babylonians, or Chaldeans, captured the Southern Kingdom of Judah, as foretold by Jeremiah and other prophets. The people who were taken from Judah to Babylon were among the highest in their nation, some of them princes and noblemen. Nebuchadnezzar, the king of Babylon, was kind to the captives and allowed them to build their own homes and raise their own crops. But these people never forgot their homeland and beloved city of Jerusalem, and they taught their children to worship God as they had once been taught.

Nebuchadnezzar's respect for the Jews grew as he saw the way they prospered in his land, and he gave orders to a prince to choose from among the Jews some young men of noble standing, fine appearance, and brilliance of mind, to come to a special school at the palace. Here the wisest men of Babylon would teach them to be special assistants to the king. Among those chosen for this great honor were Daniel, Shadrach, Meshach, and Abednego. For three years they were in training before they were presented to the king.

In the palace, these four young men were served the same foods and wines that were given to the king; but, according to Jewish law, they could not eat them. They asked to be given only vegetables and bread instead, and in ten days, they looked finer and healthier than all the others who stood before the king. Nebuchadnezzar promoted them to high positions in his court.

After Nebuchadnezzar died, the kingdom of Babylon began to fall. Several other kings reigned, and finally one named Belshazzar came into power. Belshazzar was an unwise ruler and he even served his banquet guests with the golden dishes that had been stolen from the Temple at Jerusalem. During the feast, God's hand wrote a strange message on the wall that only Daniel could interpret. It told that Belshazzar's kingdom was going to be taken from him by the Medes and Persians, and it was that very same night.

The Persian empire that conquered Babylon was greater than that of the Assyrians or Babylonians, for it covered all the Bible lands. Its ruler, Cyrus, sent an old man named Darius to rule over Babylon. Daniel, although now old himself, served Darius as he had other kings.

Again some princes tried to find some fault with the man of God because the king favored him so. They knew that three times every day Daniel opened his window and looked toward Jerusalem

DANIEL IN THE LION'S DEN

Daniel 6:4–23

while he prayed to God. In order to trap him, they asked Darius to make a law that everyone should bow down only to the king for thirty days or be thrown into a den of lions. Darius was foolish and proud, and he agreed to sign the law.

Daniel knew about the law, but still he continued to pray every day to the true God. The princes stood by his window and watched him open it to pray as usual; then they reported it to the king.

Now Darius was sorry that he had signed such a foolish order, and he tried to find some way to save Daniel, but he finally had to send Daniel to the den of lions. In his heart, he hoped that the God Daniel served would save him.

In those days hungry lions were kept in a sealed pit to be used as a special torture. As the soldiers led Daniel toward the pit, the lions' roars could be heard, first clearly, then loudly when the stone covering the den was opened. The guards threw

Daniel in quickly and sealed the opening with the stone again.

All night the king worried about Daniel. He could not even sleep or eat his food. When morning came, he hurried to the lions' den and took away the stone.

"Daniel, was your God able to save you?" he called hopefully.

From deep inside the darkness of the pit, Daniel answered, "My Lord sent an angel who has closed the mouth of the lions, O king, so that you could see that I meant no wrong."

How happy King Darius was! He had Daniel removed from the den, and the jealous princes were thrown in instead. This time, the lions were not guarded by any angel and the men were killed.

Daniel continued to serve in the palace all the days of his life and he continued to make his wonderful prophecies about the kingdom of God which was to come.

QUEEN ESTHER

Cyrus, the Persian king who conquered Babylon, made a law allowing the Jews to go back to their home in the land of Judea and the city of Jerusalem. Many Jews returned, but others had been settled in Babylon for so long that they chose to remain. One of these was a man from the tribe of Benjamin named Mordecai. He lived with his young cousin, Esther, whose own parents were dead, in the new capital city of Persia at Shushan.

By this time, King Darius, who had put Daniel in the den of lions, had died; and in his place, his son Ahasuerus was ruling. During a great feast that Ahasuerus gave for his princes and noblemen, he requested that his beautiful wife Vashti appear before the group. When Vashti refused to come as he had asked, he became very angry. He decided that she would no longer be queen, but that he would have a contest and select the most beautiful girl in his kingdom to take her place.

Among the girls brought to the palace from whom Ahasuerus would select his new queen was the Jewess, Esther. She was as beautiful in heart as she was in body; and when the king saw her, he could not resist her charm. She was the one he claimed to be his bride.

Now Mordecai could no longer visit with Esther after she went to the palace to live, but he kept in touch with her through messengers. Esther had

come to mean as much to him as a daughter, and he missed her very much.

One day Mordecai overheard two men plotting to kill the king, and he reported it to Esther. When she told the king, he immediately took the men and punished them, and he wrote down Mordecai's brave deed in his books of records.

Now the greatest man in the kingdom, next to Ahasuerus, was Haman, chief of all the princes. He thought he was very important and loved to see all the people bow down when he passed by. Mordecai, however, worshiped only God, and he would not bow when he saw Haman. This made Haman very angry. When he found out who Mordecai was and that he was a Jew, he determined to do away with all the Jews.

Haman told the king that the Jews were causing trouble by refusing to obey the laws of the land, and he got permission to kill all of them. The king really did not know anything about the Jews or who they were, and he never dreamed that his own queen was one of them.

The day was set for the slaughter of the Jews, the law was written commanding their death, and copies were sent throughout the kingdom. When Mordecai and the other Jews heard of it, they put on clothes of mourning and roamed about the city, protesting loudly. The report came to Esther of

Loran Raymond Jones

ESTHER EXPOSING HAMAN'S PLOT

Esther 7

Mordecai's strange actions, and she sent a servant to find out what was troubling him. Mordecai told the servant of the terrible command and sent Esther a copy of the law. He asked that she go to the king and ask him to save her people.

When Esther heard of all this, she was greatly distressed also. She sent a message back to Mordecai, saying: "No one in the kingdom may go to the king in his courtroom unless he sends for them. Anyone who tries to do so will be killed unless the king holds out his golden scepter. I, the queen, have not even been called for in thirty days now."

But Mordecai sent word back again, "Do not think that you, as a Jew, will be safe inside the palace. Whether you help us or not, God will find some way to save us; but perhaps this is the very reason He allowed you to come into the kingdom as queen."

This time Esther's reply was for Mordecai and the Jews to pray for her as she and her own maidens would do. Then she would go to the king in three days.

On the third day, Esther dressed in her loveliest robes and walked through the palace halls to the entrance to the throne room. As she stood in the doorway, the king, across the room on his throne, smiled at her and held out his scepter to her. Humbly, she walked across to him and touched the scepter.

"What do you want, Esther?" the king asked. "I shall give you anything, up to half my kingdom."

But Esther did not ask for the wish of her heart at first. Wisely, she asked Haman and the king to come to a dinner she was having for them.

Haman was very pleased that he, alone, was invited to eat with the king and queen. As soon as the dinner was over, he went straight home to tell his wife and friends of the glories of palace life. But on the way he saw the hated Mordecai standing tall as he passed by, and it cast gloom over his happy mood. That day, he ordered the gallows made on which he would hang Mordecai.

On that same night the king was listening to his book of records read and he remembered the time Mordecai had saved his life. The next day he got

Haman to suggest some way to honor a man who had pleased the king very much. Now Haman thought that the king was probably talking about him, and he proudly suggested that the man be dressed finely and then ride on the king's own horse throughout the city with a nobleman walking ahead to announce his good deed.

How astonished Haman was when he learned that the one the king wanted to honor was Mordecai the Jew! He could hardly raise his head as he walked about the city, calling to all of the honor of Mordecai. Here he was, the chief prince, praising the very enemy for whom he had built tall gallows the day before!

Afterward, he hurried to the second dinner Esther had prepared. At the dinner, the king looked at his beautiful wife and was pleased. "Tell me, Esther," he said, "what would you like for me to do for you?"

Solemnly, the queen replied, "My life, O King, and the lives of my people is what I request. We are about to be killed, all of us."

"Who would dare to do such a thing?" Ahasuerus demanded.

Esther turned and looked past the king to the guilty one. "Our enemy—this wicked Haman!" she answered.

Haman at once began begging for his life, but the king was too angry to listen. He ordered Haman to be hanged on the gallows that had been built for Mordecai.

On that day, Mordecai took Haman's place as chief of the princes. The law for killing the Jews could not be changed, but the king made a new law which allowed the Jews to defend themselves against anyone who tried to kill them. Most of the people were too afraid to attack them, but the ones who did were quickly destroyed by the Jews.

So instead of a sorrowful day, the day named for their destruction turned out to be a victorious one. The people celebrated a feast of thanksgiving to God for saving their lives, and the Jews today eat that same feast, the feast of Purim. When they do, they remember the beautiful queen who saved their people.

THE RETURN TO JERUSALEM

When Cyrus, the great Persian king, gave the people of Judea permission to return to Jerusalem,

the prophecy of the weeping prophet, Jeremiah, came true. Freedom was granted after they had

Loran Raymond Jones

NEHEMIAH PLANNING JERUSALEM'S RESTORATION

Nehemiah 2:12–20

spent seventy years in Babylon. During the captivity, those who had made the long journey from Jerusalem remembered their own land, and they told their children how precious it was to them. These children, as they grew up, longed to see the land that was their real home. Some of them, however, had come to think of Babylon as their home, and they decided to stay there.

The Jews who did remain in Babylon wanted to help those who were going to make the long trip to Jerusalem. They gave gifts of gold and silver to help in rebuilding the city. Cyrus returned the golden dishes Nebuchadnezzar had taken from the Temple, so there was quite a treasure to take along.

What a happy group the company returning to Jerusalem made! About forty-two thousand made the journey up the Euphrates River, then down beside the mountains of Lebanon, and through Syria to the land of Judea. But here they met with an unhappy sight. The beautiful city of Jerusalem lay in ruins, the walls crumbled and broken down, and the Temple completely destroyed. It was difficult to believe that it was the same place from which King David and King Solomon had reigned.

Among the ruins, the people found the rock where the altar of the Lord had stood, and they rebuilt the altar and offered sacrifices. Then they prepared homes for themselves, for winter was coming. Early the next year, they began rebuilding the Temple where the altar stood on Mount Moriah.

The ruler that King Cyrus placed over Judea was a prince of the house of David named Zerubbabel. Zerubbabel himself led in the great work of building, and he was helped by the priests and skilled carpenters and bricklayers. Trees were brought down from Lebanon as they had been in Solomon's time. There was a great celebration with music and singing when the first stones were set in place. But some of the old people, who could remember the Temple as Solomon had built it and as it had been before it was destroyed, wept, because they knew it could never be as beautiful again.

Now some of the people of Samaria, to the north of Judea, were from the old Ten Tribes of Israel who had been taken into captivity by the Assyrians. They were jealous of the Jews because God had remained with them. They wrote a letter to the King, Artaxerxes, who became ruler when Cyrus died, and told him that the Jews were trying to rebuild their city and that when it was complete, they were no longer going to serve him.

The king of Persia answered with a letter that commanded that the building stop, so the Temple foundations stood unfinished for many years. Then God sent two prophets, Haggai and Zechariah, who called the people back to work. Permission to continue building was received from the good new King Darius.

Finally Zerubbabel and Joshua, the high priest, finished the house of worship. It was a little larger than the one Solomon had built, but it was not as beautiful and richly decorated. Only a stone block stood where the ark of the covenant had been, as it had been lost and never found.

Many years had now passed since the return to Jerusalem. Although the Temple stood proudly again on Mount Moriah, the rest of the city was still very poor, and the broken walls left it open to attack. Stories of the struggling city were carried back to the Persian kingdom and touched the hearts of God's people still living there. One of these people was Ezra, a prophet in Babylon. Ezra loved God's word, but at that time there were no copies of the Law of Moses as we have now in the Old Testament. All the books had been written by hand and were scattered about in different places. Ezra searched for these books and he copied them; then he put them all together in one book. This Book of the Law contained the writings of Moses, then of the judges down to Samuel, then of the kings through Solomon, and finally of the prophets. Ezra taught the Law to other men called "scribes" because they, too, were "writers" of the Law.

Ezra and these scribes took the books they had collected and copied from Babylon to Jerusalem. Here Ezra opened his scrolls and read from the Law to the people there. Many of them had never heard the word of God read, and they were thankful to Ezra for bringing it to them. They bowed their heads while he read and they listened carefully.

Ezra not only read from the Law, he also taught the people how to live by its teachings. He told them that they were to be God's special people and that they were not to mix with nations around them. Instead, they were to marry only other Jews and try to follow God's law exactly as He gave it. Following God's law as Ezra taught made the people confident that God was with them once more.

The other Jew away from Jerusalem who was moved by stories of the attempt to rebuild the city was Nehemiah, cupbearer to King Artaxerxes in Shushan. He became convinced that it was his duty

to return and help rebuild the broken walls. Arta-xerxes gave Nehemiah permission to make the long journey and even gave him supplies to use in the work.

Nehemiah was looked upon as a fine nobleman when he reached Jerusalem, and the people were eager to follow his leadership in building the walls. Everyone agreed to build some part, whether it was just the portion in front of his own door or a long section. People of every different trade joined happily in the work, and even the women helped.

Again the jealous Samaritans under Sanballat and Tobiah threatened the work, so that the Jews had to work with one hand and carry a weapon in the other. But the Jews stayed busy and refused to be frightened, and within fifty-two days the city was safe within strong, new walls.

After the assistance from Ezra and Nehemiah, the city of Jerusalem began to grow. Other Jews returned from foreign lands to make it their home or to worship God in the Temple. One more prophet, Malachi, came, but with his words our story of the Old Testament ends. He looked toward the future and spoke of the return of the Lord Himself to the Temple. We know that he was speaking of the coming of God's own Son, Jesus Christ. With Him, the next portion of the Bible begins.

THE BIRTH OF JESUS

The Israelites seemed to obey God as He wanted them to when they first returned from their Babylonian captivity; but after a period of time, they returned to their evil ways. As God had done in the past when His people forgot Him, He again allowed their enemies to conquer them. The Israelites were ruled by the Persians, the Greeks, the Syrians, the Egyptians, and the Romans, in turn.

At the time of Christ's coming, four hundred years had passed since the return from Babylon, and the Romans were in power. They had named Herod to be ruler of the land of Judea. He pretended to believe in God and even made Solomon's Temple more beautiful than ever before, but actually he was a mean and cruel ruler.

The Jews felt at this time that their only hope lay in God's sending them the Savior He had promised. First, He had made the promise to Eve when she did wrong; and He told her that some day He would send someone who would bring goodness back to the world. Then He promised to Abraham that this child would be born into his family. Afterward the prophets continued to speak of the coming Savior, telling of the power and mighty kingdom He would possess. The people of Judea thought that if this Savior whom God would send would come, He could save them by over-throwing the Romans and taking Herod's place as king. But God had a wiser plan in mind, and although He did send the One He had promised, He sent Him in such a way that few knew of His coming.

The first to know of Jesus' coming was Mary, the Jewish woman God had chosen to be His Son's mother. Mary was living in the town of Nazareth when God's messenger, the angel Gabriel, announced to her that God had chosen her to be the mother of the Savior of the world. How happy Mary must have been to know that she, among all Israelite women, had been chosen to be the baby's mother! In the book of Luke, a beautiful song is written that she sang to tell of her thankfulness to God.

About the time the baby was ready to be born, the Roman ruler, Caesar Augustus, commanded that a census of the whole world be taken. Mary went with her husband Joseph to Bethlehem to be counted. They went to Bethlehem because they were descendants of David, and Bethlehem was David's home.

The little town was overcrowded with those arriving for the census, and Mary and Joseph could not find a place to stay. When nothing else could be found, they stopped at a stable, where cows and horses were kept, to spend the night. That night the baby Jesus was born, and Mary wrapped Him up warmly and laid Him to sleep in a manger filled with soft hay.

As yet, no one in Bethlehem knew of the birth of the wonderful baby during the night, but God sent an angel to tell the good news to some shepherds watching their sheep on nearby hills. At first, the shepherds were frightened by the angel; but the angel said, "Behold, I bring you tidings of great joy which shall be to all the people: for there is born this day in the city of David, a Savior which is Christ the Lord." The angel also told them that they could find the baby in Bethlehem

Loran Raymond Jones

THE NATIVITY

Luke 2:1–20

in a stable. Then a great chorus of angels appeared, singing praises to God.

The shepherds, filled with wonder by this wonderful message from the angels, hurried to Bethlehem to find the baby. Surely enough, they found Him in the manger, just as they had been told. When they saw Him, they realized that they were looking at the promised Son of God, and they bowed before the little baby. Then they went back to their flocks, praising God and telling everyone they met about the things they had seen and heard.

When the child was eight days old, He was named Jesus, as the angel had said He was to be named before He was born. This name meant "savior."

Then when Jesus was a month old, His parents brought Him to the Temple in Jerusalem in obedience to the Jewish law and made an offering of two pigeons to show that the child would belong to the Lord. There was an old man named Simeon living in Jerusalem at that time who was filled with God's spirit and was anxious for the promised Savior to come. So earnest were his prayers for the child to be born, that God promised him he would not die until he had seen Jesus. On the day that Mary and Joseph came to the Temple to make their sacrifice, the Spirit of God led Simeon there, also. When he saw the baby, his heart told him that this was the one he had been waiting for. He took Jesus from Mary and held Him fondly in his arms while he blessed God. "Now I am ready to die," he said, "for with my own eyes I have seen the one God has sent to be the glory of the Israelites and to save the whole world."

There was also in the Temple an old woman named Anna, who spent most of her time there praying. When she heard Simeon, she gave thanks to God with him and told many in Jerusalem of the coming of the Christ child.

Mary and Joseph looked at each other proudly and stored these sayings in their heart, along with the praise of the shepherds on the night Christ was born. It was a wonderful thing and yet hard for them to realize that this baby God had sent *was* going to save the Israelites from their sins and would be able to permit them and all men who followed Him to live forever with God some day.

THE VISIT OF THE WISEMEN

Far away from Jerusalem and Bethlehem, in a country to the east, there lived some wise men who spent their time studying the stars. They had no modern telescopes, but they were able to learn a great deal by watching the position and movement of the stars. They were so familiar with the stars that they quickly recognized one night that there was a new star in the sky. In some way God sent a message to the hearts of these men, telling them that the new star was heralding the birth of a new king in the country of Judea, the home of the Jews.

The wisemen gathered together precious gifts, suitable for a king, and started on the long journey to Judea. They traveled on camels during the cool of the night when they could follow the star. At last their travels brought them to Jerusalem about the time Jesus was born. They began asking the people they met to show them the way to find the new king. They were dismayed and puzzled when no one seemed to know what they meant.

As you remember, the Roman government, which ruled that part of the world, had appointed a man named Herod to be king over Judea. Word came to Herod that some strange men from the East were in Jerusalem looking for a new king that had been born. This news worried Herod because he was afraid someone might take his position from him. He had heard rumors that the Jewish people were looking for their God to send them a king of their own people, and he called in their priests and scribes to give him some more information. These men spent their time studying the Law of Moses and the prophets, so when Herod asked them where their king was to be born, they knew to answer: "The prophet Micah told us that He was to come from Bethlehem."

Upon finding this out, Herod called for the strangers from the East to visit him in private. He questioned them about the strange star they had followed. Then he suggested that they go to Bethlehem to continue their search, and he asked them to bring word to him if they succeeded in finding the child, for he wanted to go and worship it also. Now Herod really had no intention of worshiping the child, but he was anxious to find if there really was such a person so that he could destroy Him before He had a chance to become king.

On their way to Bethlehem, the wisemen again found the bright star shining in the sky; and they followed its moving path until it stopped over the very place where Baby Jesus lay. The men alighted from their camels and entered the house. There they kneeled before the tiny child who they knew would become a great king. From the treasures they had brought, they took out gold and precious perfumes called frankincense and myrrh, used in offering sacrifices.

Then instead of returning to Jerusalem to tell Herod of the child they had found, the wisemen were warned by God in a dream to return home by another road. Herod waited for them to bring word of what they had found, and he was angry and disappointed when he saw that they had escaped him. He determined to find the child and destroy Him another way.

After the wisemen had gone, God sent Joseph a dream in which He said, "Take Mary and the baby to Egypt until I give you word that it is safe to return. Herod is looking for Jesus and would like to kill Him." Immediately, Joseph got up and awakened Mary, even though it was the middle of the night. He told her to get ready for a journey.

Quietly they gathered up their things, wrapped up the baby, and left for the distant country to the south.

By this time Herod was sure that the wisemen were never going to return to him, and he thought of a wicked plan he would use to be sure the future king was destroyed. He sent soldiers to Bethlehem who killed every baby boy who was under two years old. This way he felt sure that he had rid himself of the child who threatened his kingdom. But God had taken care of His Son, and Jesus was well and safe with His parents down in Egypt.

Wicked Herod did not live long after this. When he died, God told Joseph that it was safe to return to the land of Israel. But before he had reached Judea, Joseph heard that Herod's wicked son was ruling in his place; and he was afraid to settle in Bethlehem, so near to Jerusalem. Instead, he went to the north to a part of the country called Galilee. A more gentle king ruled there. At last the family settled in the little town of Nazareth, where Mary had lived as a girl. There Joseph opened a carpenter's shop and built a home where Jesus lived for many years.

THE BOY JESUS AT THE TEMPLE

As a child, Jesus lived in the little town of Nazareth. His home was probably a very simple, country cottage, and He was taught to work hard and help Joseph in the carpenter shop. Most Jewish boys of that time went to school at the village house of worship, called a "synagogue." Here they were taught from the Law of Moses and the books of the prophets. Since each book had to be copied by hand in those days, the students had none of their own and they had to learn their lessons by heart.

Jesus also went to the synagogue with His family on the Sabbath each week for worship. Again the Old Testament was read and explained, so it is easy to understand how many Jewish boys knew much of the Old Testament by memory.

The biggest occasion of the year was the time of the Passover, when Jews from everywhere went to Jerusalem to celebrate the sacred feast and remember the time when God brought their people out of slavery in the land of Egypt. When Jesus was twelve years old, His parents let Him make the trip to Jerusalem with them for the first time. To-

gether with others from Nazareth, they made the sixty-mile trip in several days, some walking and some riding donkeys in a large caravan. Along the way, others going to worship joined the group.

Finally they saw Jerusalem spread out before them. What an impression the great city and the splendid Temple on Mount Moriah made on the young boy! Already Jesus' heart was full of love for God, His Father, and the desire to do His work. Seeing the house of worship and the priests and observing the solemn feast of the Passover made His desire more intense. He lingered around the Temple, held by His attraction for God's house.

The feast of the Passover lasted for seven days, and then Mary and Joseph prepared to return to Nazareth with the group that had come from there. All one day they traveled without Jesus, but they were not worried because the company was large and they felt sure He was walking along with some of His friends. When evening came and He had not joined them, they began to search for Him among their friends and relatives. No one had seen Jesus all day.

Loran Raymond Jones

THE BOY JESUS IN THE TEMPLE
Luke 2:41–52

There was nothing for the worried parents to do but return to Jerusalem and look for their son. For two days they went every place in Jerusalem they thought Jesus might be. On the third day, the tired couple thought of looking in the Temple. There the boy was found, sitting with some of the smartest students of the Law, completely wrapped up in His conversation with them. They, too, were interested and amazed at this lad who could ask such thoughtful questions and also give answers that showed a deep understanding.

Mary and Joseph were surprised to find their son talking to the brilliant men. Mary had not forgotten the worry He had caused them for three days; and she could not help saying, "Son, why have you done this to us? Your father and I have been searching everywhere and we have been so worried about you."

"Why did you look for me?" Jesus asked. "Do you not realize that I have my Father's work to do?"

Jesus realized that He was old enough now to begin preparing for the great work God had sent Him into the world to do. Mary did not quite understand, but she remembered the words He told her, and she thought about them afterward.

This time Jesus left the city with Mary and Joseph and returned to Nazareth. As years passed by, He grew "in mind and in body, more pleasing to God and to men." He was like other boys around Him, but in one way He was different—He never did wrong. He was not boastful or proud about His goodness, but He prayed often to God and God made His mind and thoughts pure so that He always wanted to do the right thing. This made those around Him love Him, and God saw that His Son was pleasing in every way.

JOHN IN THE WILDERNESS

Until He was about thirty years old, Jesus lived with His family at their home in Nazareth. He was busy working as a carpenter with Joseph, but He never forgot the greater work that God had planned for Him to do.

During this same time, John, the son of Zacharias and Elisabeth, was also busy fulfilling God's plan for his life. As a young man, John had gone out into the wilderness south of the land of Judea. Here he loved to be alone to think about God and the coming Savior God would send. John grew used to desert life, and he was able to live on the dried locusts and wild honey that he found there. He made himself a simple robe of camel's hair and bound it to his waist with a leather belt.

Then one day John heard the call of God to go up to the country near the Jordan River and begin preparing the people for the kingdom of heaven and its mighty King. It did not take long for word to travel that a new prophet was preaching beside the Jordan River. For four hundred years, God had sent no prophets; and the Jews were excited to see this man. In large groups they traveled from Jerusalem and the cities and villages around to hear the message John was preaching. They heard John say that each one had to turn from doing wrong and be baptized to show that his heart was now pure. In this way, they would be ready for the kingdom of heaven, which was soon to come.

The people were touched by these words and they told John, "We want to live better lives and turn away from evil. What can we do?"

"You can share your food and clothes with those who have none," replied John.

Some of the men in the crowd were tax collectors and they wanted to live right before God, also. John told them: "Take no more money from the people than you are commanded by the law to take." To the soldiers he said, "Be gentle to the people and be sure that you are right before you accuse anyone of some wrong. Then, too, you are not to complain about your wages."

When the people accepted the message John taught and promised God that they would try to serve Him more perfectly, John baptized them in the Jordan River as a sign that their sins were washed away. Because of this, he became known as "John the Baptist."

So many people came to John and were impressed with his preaching, that the word began to spread that perhaps he was the coming Christ. When John heard this, he was quick to say, "I am not the promised Savior. He is so much greater than I that I would not even be worthy to stoop down and fasten His sandal. I have baptized you only with water, but He will baptize you with the Holy Spirit."

Crowds upon crowds of people were baptized by John, and among the last to come was Jesus of Nazareth. When John saw Jesus, he knew that this was the one greater and holier than himself. He was timid about baptizing Jesus, for he said, "I should be baptized by you, rather than your coming to me."

Jesus replied kindly that it was God's will for him to do this, as it was for him to do all things that were right. Then Jesus and John walked out into the water, and John baptized Him just as he had all the others. When Jesus came out of the water, He was praying. In that moment, the sky opened and the Holy Spirit flew from heaven in the shape of a dove, alighting on Jesus. Then a voice came out of heaven, saying: "You are my beloved Son, and you have pleased me greatly."

John and those in the crowd could not take their eyes from the man who had come that day to find John beside the Jordan River. They all knew that their search for the coming King was over. He was among them at last.

SATAN TEMPTS JESUS

After Jesus was baptized by John, the Spirit of God led Him into the wilderness, a desert place so barren and lonely that only wild beasts lived there. While he was there, Jesus prayed and talked with God, trying to gain a perfect understanding of the work He had to do on earth. For forty days and nights He stayed, and during all that time He never had anything to eat.

When the forty days had ended, Jesus was hungry to the point of starving. He felt weak and knew that He had to find food immediately. While He felt that way, the devil came to Him, just as he does to us when we are not strong and are not expecting him. The devil knew that Jesus was a man and the son of Mary, but that He was also the Son of God. He wanted to see if he could get Jesus to sin as all men had done since he first persuaded Adam and Eve to disobey God.

Now Satan knew that Jesus was very hungry, so he slyly made this suggestion: "If you are the Son of God, all you have to do is say the words and these stones on the ground would become bread for you to eat."

Jesus knew that indeed He did have the power to turn the stones into bread, but He also knew that His power had not been given to Him to use selfishly, but to serve others. He answered the devil by quoting from the Law of Moses He had learned so well, "Man cannot live on bread alone; he needs the Word of God as well."

But Satan does not give up easily. He tried the weary Savior with something else. This time he took Him to Jerusalem, to the highest point on top of the Temple. "Why do you not jump from here and let the angels save you from harm? I, too, know that your own prophets have said that the angels would bear you up before your foot had touched a stone. If you did this, all could see that you are the Son of God."

Jesus knew that God had not commanded Him to show His power in this way. He was going to show His power through love and good works. This was only putting God to a test; so He answered the devil, "It is also written that 'you shall not try God's power.'"

Still Satan would not go away. He took Jesus with him to the top of a very high mountain. There, in a moment of time, he permitted Jesus to see all the kingdoms of the world and their glory. With the memory of all that splendor on His mind, Jesus was told that He could have these kingdoms if He would only bow before the devil and worship him.

But Jesus had no intention of worshiping Satan, not even for all the glory that was in the world. He had come to earth to conquer the devil, instead. He said, "Leave me, Satan. The Law of Moses commands, 'You shall worship the one true God, and He is the only one you shall serve.'"

Finally the devil was willing to give up for a time. He went away to stay until he could find a better opportunity to attack God's Son.

Jesus was left all alone. He was weary from having faced the devil and starving from having gone without food. But God, in His mercy and kindness, had not forgotten His Son. Angels came from His throne to Jesus, bringing the food and the comfort that He needed.

JESUS CHOOSES HIS DISCIPLES

One day, not too long after the baptism of Jesus, John the Baptist and two of those who believed his message stood talking. When John looked up, he recognized Jesus coming toward them. He turned to the two men with him and said, "Look! Here comes the Son of God now! This is the very one I was speaking of when I said that someone greater than I is coming."

The disciples of John were excited to think that they might get to meet the future King. They left John and ran down the road behind Jesus. When Jesus heard someone following Him, He turned around and asked, "What do you want?"

"Master, we would like to know where you are staying," the two replied.

"Come with me and see," Jesus told them.

Then the men followed Jesus and stayed with Him all day, listening to the wonderful words He had to say. By evening, they were convinced that He was God's own Son, and that He was the Savior the Jews were waiting for.

One of the men who visited with Jesus that day was named Andrew. The other was John. Now Andrew and John lived north of the place where John the Baptist was teaching, up nearer Jesus' home in Nazareth; but perhaps they had come down to hear John and be baptized by him. When Andrew left Jesus, his heart was about to burst with the news that he had discovered the Christ. The first thing he did was to find his brother Simon. "We have found the Anointed King, the Christ!" he told Simon.

Together Andrew and Simon went to find Jesus again. Before Andrew even had time to introduce Simon, Jesus said to him, "You are Simon, and your father is Jona. I am going to call you Peter, which means a 'rock.' " From that time on, Peter and Jesus were fast friends.

The next day Jesus began His journey back to Galilee, the country where Nazareth was. On the way, He saw a man named Philip, whose home was the same town in which Peter and Andrew lived.

Jesus saw immediately that Philip would make a worthy follower, so He called to him, "Follow me." Philip must have already heard something about the Christ, for with only those words, he followed gladly.

Like Andrew, Philip could not keep the new-found treasure to himself. He went to his friend Nathanael and said, "I have found the very one of whom Moses and the prophets told us. He is Jesus, the son of Joseph, from Nazareth."

Now Nathanael himself lived not far from Nazareth, and he knew it to be only a small town. It was hard for him to believe that God's Anointed One had been living there. "Can anyone like this come from Nazareth?" he asked.

"Just come and see," Philip replied.

As the two were approaching, Jesus looked up and saw them. "Here comes an Israelite with a truly pure heart," Jesus said, speaking of Nathanael.

Nathanael blinked with surprise. "How did you know about me?" he questioned.

"Before Philip ever called you, I saw you standing under a fig tree," Jesus replied.

At this Nathanael believed that Jesus was from God, for he knew more than just a man could know. "Master," he said, "You are the Son of God, the King of Israel."

"Do you believe in me just because I saw you under the fig tree?" Jesus asked. "Truly you are going to see greater things than this that will make you know that I am God's Son."

After this, those who followed Jesus did begin to see greater things. They saw Jesus change water into wine at a wedding feast, they saw Him lash out at the money changers who were cheating the people in the Temple, and they watched as He healed a nobleman's son who was very sick. More and more believed when they saw these miracles, and those who followed Jesus were called "disciples."

JESUS CALMS THE STORM

Because of His miracles of healing, more and more people began following Jesus. They would

come to see Him make people well, and then He would have an opportunity to talk with them about

Loran Raymond Jones

"FOLLOW ME"—CALLING OF MATTHEW

Matthew 9:9

the new kingdom He was going to establish. He told them that they would have to make their hearts pure before they could become members of His kingdom. He taught them that He was going to require more of them than simply following the Law of Moses; His new commandment was that they love everyone, both friends and enemies.

Many thought that Jesus' teachings were true and they would invite Him to speak in their synagogues on the Sabbath day when people of the village came to worship. He would read from the Law of Moses and show them how He was making the prophecies of the coming Lord come true. Only in His home in Nazareth did the people get angry at this. Those in Nazareth could remember that He had grown up there as a poor boy and could still see the simple home that had been His. They could not believe that one like that could claim to be a king. When He spoke in the synagogue there, they drove Him out and would have killed Him if He had not slipped away, undiscovered.

After this Jesus spent most of His time in the other cities of Galilee where people were anxious to hear Him. In the middle of the country is the beautiful Sea of Galilee, and many lessons were taught and people healed there on its shore. Day after day Jesus spent, surrounded by crowds, healing those who came or were brought, speaking always of His Father in heaven and the life the Father wanted those on earth to live.

On one instance, after several days of constant teaching, Jesus began to be noticeably tired; but the people gave Him no relief. Wherever He went, they followed close behind, begging for His healing touch or His words of life.

When He saw that there was no other way to rest, Jesus said to His closest disciples, "Let us get in a boat and row to the other side of the lake."

Soon a boat was found and they began rowing across the Sea of Galilee. Exhausted, Jesus went to the front of the boat to rest on a cushion. Within a few moments, He had fallen fast asleep, not noticing the dark clouds swiftly covering the sky.

The disciples began to worry when they saw the darkening sky. Then the wind began to blow and the boat to rock. Still they refused to wake Jesus because they knew how tired He was and how much He needed the rest. But the wind blew strong and stronger, and the waves got higher. They beat against the boat, lifting it high. Some broke over the side of the vessel and filled the floor with water.

No longer were the disciples only worried; now they were terribly frightened. They grabbed Jesus and shook Him to wake Him. "Master, we are about to be drowned!" they cried. "Help us, save us!"

Jesus sat up and looked about at the raging storm. All He had to say was, "Peace, be still." At once, the winds ceased and the water grew calm. The dark clouds passed by, and the little boat rocked gently once again on a calm sea.

"Why were you so afraid?" Jesus asked the disciples. "Why did you become worried when I was here all along? Do you not believe in My power?"

The disciples looked in amazement at the still water, then at Jesus, and finally at one another. They shook their heads as if they could not believe what they had seen. What kind of a man was this who could control even the wind and the water? How could anyone fail to believe that He was the Son of God?

JESUS FEEDS THE FIVE THOUSAND

There were so many people trying to hear Jesus and wanting to be healed by Him, that He could not see them all nor visit all the places where He was wanted. Jesus called His twelve closest disciples, whom He had named to be "apostles," and gave them the power to heal all kinds of sickness. Then He sent them out in pairs to go to different towns and preach to the Jews of the coming kingdom. In every village where good people believed their message, the apostles would stay for a while, talking of Jesus and making sick people well. Some

of the apostles have names with which we are already familiar—Peter, Andrew, John, Philip, and Nathanael or Bartholomew. The other six were Thomas, Matthew, another James who was the son of Alpheus, Thaddeus, Simon the Canaanite, and Judas Iscariot.

After a while the apostles returned to Jesus and told Him of their experiences in the Galilean villages. All of the time they were talking with Jesus, the people pressed closer and closer, each with a request for the amazing healer from Nazareth. Al-

Loran Raymond Jones

THE SERMON ON THE MOUNT

Matthew 5—7

ready tired from their travels, the apostles could not even get through the crowd in order to eat. Jesus saw how weary they were, and He suggested they escape in a boat. They climbed into a nearby vessel and began rowing to a quiet spot across the Sea of Galilee.

The people, however, saw what Jesus and His apostles planned to do, and they went around the lake on foot. When the boat landed, the crowds were already there, waiting for Jesus. When Jesus saw their eagerness, His heart was touched. They wanted and needed Him so badly that He talked to them all afternoon.

As evening came on and the sun was disappearing, the apostles grew concerned. They called Jesus to the side and suggested, "Lord, it is getting late and there is nothing here for the people to eat. In their hurry to follow you, they forgot to bring food. Send them away now, so they will have time to reach a town and buy something to eat."

Jesus knew that the people were tired and hungry. He said to the apostles, "There is no need to send them away. You can feed them."

Now the apostles had had a tiring day themselves, and they were growing a little impatient. Philip answered for them, "Even a great deal of money would not buy enough bread for all these people, and we have no money at all." It was still hard for them to understand that Jesus could do all things.

Jesus had patience with His closest friends. He saw that they needed the lesson He was about to teach as much as the crowd did. He asked them, "Is there anyone here with any food at all?"

Andrew had searched among the people and he answered, "There is a little boy who has brought himself a supper of five barley loaves and two fishes. He is willing to share his small bit."

"That will be plenty," was Jesus' puzzling answer. "Ask the people to sit down in groups of hundreds and fifties upon the grass."

Some of the people were already preparing to leave; but the apostles walked through the multitude, urging all to stay. Soon everyone was seated in orderly groups, waiting to see what Jesus was about to do.

When the crowd grew quiet, Jesus held the loaves and fishes before Him and gave thanks to God. Then He broke the food in pieces, dividing it among the apostles so they could pass it to the people in baskets. At Jesus' touch, the food seemed to multiply. The more He broke it, the more there was. Finally the apostles reported that everyone present—about five thousand—had been fed, and each had eaten enough.

When the meal was finished, the apostles passed again through the crowds with their baskets and picked up all the food that was left over. Even the scraps filled twelve baskets!

The people suddenly began talking among themselves when they realized what a wonderful miracle they had just seen. They stood and began clamoring for Jesus to be their King. They wanted to crown Him a king like David and Solomon were and let Him reign in Jerusalem.

Jesus was their King, but He was not going to be an earthly king. Instead, He was going to rule over the kingdom of heaven, made up of all those everywhere who loved and believed in Him. He was trying to teach this to the people, but He saw that they did not yet understand. He quietly ordered the apostles to sail without Him, and He slipped away into the mountains to pray after He had dismissed the crowd.

JESUS WALKS ON THE WATER

After the feeding of the five thousand, Jesus had ordered the apostles to sail across the Sea of Galilee without Him. He went up into the mountains alone to pray, and He planned to join them later.

The night grew very dark and a stormy wind began to blow on the apostles' boat, now a good distance out from shore. From the mountain, Jesus could see far across the water, and He saw the men battling the waves in their little craft. In the middle of the night He came down to the seashore and began walking toward His friends on the water, walking just as if it were dry ground under His feet.

Through the darkness the apostles saw the strange figure coming toward them on the water. Already frightened by the rocking boat, they began screaming with fear. "It is a ghost!" they cried out. Actually, there are no such things as ghosts, but they did not know how else to explain the weird figure.

Then they heard a familiar voice reassuring

them, "Do not be so afraid. It is I." They knew it was their Lord.

Peter called out to Him, "Lord, if it really is you, let me come to you on the water."

"All right, Peter," Jesus answered. "Come."

Peter climbed over the side of the boat and tried to take a few steps. Surely enough, the water was firm under his feet. With his eyes on Jesus, he began walking toward Him.

But the sound of the wind rushed past Peter's ears, reminding him of the storm. He took his eyes from Jesus and looked at the leaping waves. In that moment, when he forgot Jesus and began to be afraid, Peter started sinking. He called out,

"Master, save me!"

Jesus immediately stretched out His hand and caught Peter's. He pulled him up and helped him to his feet again. Then He said, "Peter, you have so little belief in me. Why did you become afraid when you knew that I was with you?"

Peter had no answer to give. He hung his head in shame.

Once Peter and Jesus reached the boat, the stormy wind stopped as suddenly as it had come. All that were present were made strongly aware of the power of the One they were following. They bowed before Him and confessed again, "Truly You are the Son of God."

THE GOOD SAMARITAN

After Jesus had been teaching and healing for about two years, most of the time in the country of Galilee, He went down to Jerusalem in the fall season to celebrate a Jewish feast day. Afterward He stayed in the country of Judea and taught the people there. Now most of the Jewish scholars, men who studied the Law of Moses, lived in Jerusalem. Word came to them of the teacher from Nazareth who claimed to be the Savior and King of the Jews. They were critical of Jesus and they did not want to believe Him. They thought they knew the Law better than anyone else, and they did not think He was the king of a king God was going to send.

In order to trap Jesus, these experts of the Law would try to think of questions that Jesus could not answer. They wanted to make Him look foolish and themselves appear to be very smart.

In His teaching, Jesus had told the people that the members of His kingdom were going to have eternal life. This meant that when they died and were buried, they would come to heaven and continue living on and on with Him and God, His Father. This idea was a difficult one to understand. Even the lawyers wondered what He meant, and they came to Him, hoping to catch Him in a mistake.

"Master," one of them asked, "what can I do to possess the eternal life you speak of?"

"You know God's Law," replied Jesus. "What does it tell you to do?"

The scholar was surprised at Jesus' question. He answered, "The Law says that I am to love God with all my heart, all my soul, all my strength, and all my mind. And I am to love my neighbor as myself."

"What you have said is right," Jesus said. "If you do that, you will be able to live forever."

This did not satisfy the man. He tried to trap Jesus again by asking, "Just who is my neighbor?"

The best way Jesus knew to explain was to tell a story. This was what He told:

One day a man was taking a trip from Jerusalem to Jericho. The road between these two cities is a dangerous route. The great rocks along the way offer a place for robbers and thieves to hide. Traveling alone, this man was overtaken by a band of robbers. They beat him, stripped off his clothes, took his money, and left him there beside the road, barely alive.

Now that day a priest, one who served in the Temple, was making a trip along the very same road. This priest, who was supposed to be dedicated to God's service, saw the beaten man; but he did not stop to help. He went as far as he could to the other side of the road and passed by.

Later on, a Levite, a member of the Jewish tribe who led in the worship, came by. He, too, merely glanced at the suffering man and continued on his journey as though nothing were unusual.

Finally, a Samaritan came along. Now the Samaritans were hated by the Jews because some of the ancestors of the Samaritans had been members of the ten Jewish tribes who forsook God and turned to idols. The Jews thought that they were much better than the Samaritans and would not even come near to one.

When the Samaritan saw that the sick man was

Loran Raymond Jones

THE PRODIGAL SON

Luke 15:11:32

a Jew, he could have hurried on his journey; but his heart was touched by anyone who was suffering. He took some oil that he had and cleaned off the wounds the man had received in the terrible beating. Then he bound them up with bandages. Finally he lifted him to his own horse and led it until they came to an inn. All night he sat with the wounded man, taking care of him.

The next day he saw that his patient was going to get well. He went to the innkeeper and gave him some money. "Use this to care for the one I brought here. If you have to spend any more, I will repay you when I come back by."

When the story was finished, Jesus turned to the lawyer and asked, "Now which of these three—the priest, the Levite, or the Samaritan—was a neighbor to the man who was robbed?"

"The one who helped him, of course," the lawyer answered.

"Then you go, and help in the same way," Jesus told him. The Lord wanted him to know that he was to help anyone who needed it, regardless of who he was. He was never to think that he was too important to be of service to someone.

THE PRODIGAL SON

The people who came to Jesus loved to hear Him tell stories like the one about the good Samaritan. The messages from God that He taught were so wonderful and so great that the people found they could understand them better if He put them into a simple tale that they could remember. These stories of Jesus that teach great lessons are often called "parables."

Among the crowds of people who loved to hear Jesus were some who had been living sinful lives. His words made them feel sorry for their sins, and they would decide to change and try to be good and kind as He was. They did not like to leave Jesus even for a little while, so they would persuade Him to come home and eat with them at mealtime. This way, Jesus could go right on talking to them.

Now the most particular Jews, some of them scribes and some from a party called the Pharisees, were shocked to see Jesus being friendly with those they knew to be sinners. They thought that a King of God's people should not pay attention to common people. They thought that he would notice only important people, like they thought themselves to be.

Jesus saw that these Jews needed to hear one of His parables, too, so He told them about the adventures of a prodigal son. A prodigal is someone wasteful, one who spends his money on foolish things. This is the way the story went:

Once there lived a man who had two sons. Now this man had worked hard to make a fortune that he could leave for his boys when he died. One day his younger son came to him and said, "Father, I am no longer happy here with you. I want my share of your fortune now so I can spend it as I please." Sadly the father divided up all that he had and gave the son his portion.

Happy with his new wealth, the son did not take long in gathering up his things and leaving home. He traveled to a country far away, sure that his money was going to bring him everything he wanted.

Everywhere he looked in the strange country, there were things to spend his money on. Wicked people taught him to gamble and they cheated him out of great sums. Others pretended to be his good friends and talked him into buying things for them. Every time he turned around he was paying for their rich food and a lot of wine for them to drink.

Before long, the young man found that all his money was gone. Those who had acted as if they were his friends paid no attention to him. He saw that he was going to have to find a job in order to have anything to eat.

Then a famine came upon that country, and food became very scarce. There were no crops to tend, and the man could not find a job. Finally, he found a farmer who agreed to let him feed his pigs. By this time he was so hungry that he would have eaten some of the husks that were fed to the pigs, but no one gave him any.

Among the smelling, grunting pigs, the young man could not help thinking of the clean home he had left. He thought of the servants who worked for his father and how much better off they were than he was. He made up his mind right then:

"Why, I will go back to my father. I will tell him how sinful I have been and that I know I do not deserve to be his son any longer. Maybe, however, he will let me live at home just as a hired servant. That would be enough."

Immediately he set out on the long journey toward home. For many days he traveled. Finally he saw his father's house in the distance. And someone stood there waiting for him—it was his father! The two began running toward each other and fell into each other's arms.

"Father," began the son, "I am not good enough to be your son."

But the father could not stand to hear him speak that way. He turned to a servant and said, "Bring quickly a fine robe for my son, and put a ring on his hand and shoes on his feet. Then we will kill a fatted calf and prepare a great feast. It is time for a celebration!"

Now the older brother had stayed at home all this time, helping his father. He had not asked for his part of the father's fortune nor spent it foolishly. He did not think that his brother deserved to be forgiven by their father, and he refused to come to the feast. The father came outside and found him sulking. He put his arm around his boy and said, "Son, this does not mean that I love you any less. You have been so good to stay with me. But now we should be glad that your brother has come back to us. He that was lost has been found!"

With this story, Jesus showed the important Jews that sinners could become God's children also. God is like the father in the story—He is always ready to welcome those who turn to Him.

JESUS BLESSES THE CHILDREN

All around the countries of Judea, Samaria, and Galilee, the people had come to love Jesus, the Christ. When news came that He was coming to a particular village, everyone in that town would leave whatever they were doing and run to meet Him. Some would help sick friends reach His side so they could be healed. Others would come to listen to His stories and learn the great lessons that helped them become better men and women. The little children loved just to sit around on the ground, as close to His feet as they could get. They could not understand everything He said, but they loved just to hear His kind voice and look into His loving eyes.

Now Jesus talked a great deal about the kingdom over which He was going to reign. His apostles wondered what kind of a kingdom it was going to be. As His closest friends, they wondered what kind of positions they would get to hold in His new kingdom. They began arguing among themselves as to which one would be the greatest, and soon they were engaged in quite a squabble.

Jesus looked sadly at the bickering apostles. It was so hard for Him to show them how His kingdom would be. He needed some way to teach them a great lesson. Then He saw His opportunity:

From the group standing near, He called to a little child, "Come here." Immediately the child ran to His arms. Jesus gave him a squeeze, and then still holding him, He turned to the apostles and said, "This is what my kingdom will be like.

Unless you become like this little child, you cannot be a part of it."

"Doing good for a little child is just like doing good for me," He continued. "But a terrible punishment should go to anyone who teaches a child to do wrong. Why, these little children have angels before God's throne who watch over them."

Later on, the mothers began bringing their children to the One who loved them so. They wanted to be able to tell their little boy or girl that he had been held and blessed by Jesus, the Savior.

The disciples thought that Jesus was too busy to see the great number of little ones. They said to the mothers, "Our Lord is so busy. He cannot possibly see all of you."

But Jesus said, "Do not turn the little children away. Let them come to Me. Remember that the kingdom of heaven belongs to them and those like them."

Then He touched each little child and said a kind word to each one.

The apostles thought and thought about Jesus and the children. It took a long time for them to realize that He meant that their hearts would have to be as pure as a child's in order to be in His kingdom. He wanted them to learn to be as loving, as trusting, and as gentle as the very young. And as children do, He wanted them to put their trust in God as their Father and know that He would care for them.

Loran Raymond Jones

JESUS AND THE LITTLE CHILDREN

Matthew 19:13–15

JESUS ENTERS JERUSALEM AS KING

Although Jesus tried to teach the leaders of the Jews as well as the common people, not many of the leaders would believe His message. For years these scribes and Pharisees had been studying the Law of Moses, and they thought they knew it and obeyed it perfectly. They had read all the prophecies of the Old Testament concerning the coming Savior, and they did not think Jesus acted like the King they pictured. They expected the promised One to pay attention only to important followers of the Law like themselves, not to visit with sinners, poor people, and children. In Jerusalem they told the people who came to worship that they would not be allowed in the synagogues if they listened to Jesus.

When Jesus heard this, He left Jerusalem and went to the surrounding towns. He even crossed the Jordan River and preached to the people on the other side who had only heard of Him, but had never gotten to see Him. In every place, the crowds loved Him and followed Him. He was the King they wanted, even if the Jewish rulers would not approve of Him.

Again and again, Jesus spoke of His kingdom as a heavenly kingdom, not an earthly one. To the apostles He said, "These people are going to try to make Me their King when we go back to Jerusalem. Instead, we have sad things to face there. I am going to be made a prisoner and beaten. Then I shall be killed and rise again in three days."

But the apostles could not understand what Jesus was telling them. They could not believe that He would die.

Now the time had come for the Passover feast, and Jews from all over the world traveled to Jerusalem to celebrate the solemn occasion. Many of them from far away hoped to catch a glimpse of the teacher from Nazareth while they were there. Jesus Himself had not gone into the city yet, as the feast was still nearly a week away. He was staying in a little town named Bethany, a few miles away. Here He visited with Mary, Martha, and their brother Lazarus. Only a short time before, Jesus had raised Lazarus after he was dead.

Word spread in Jerusalem that Jesus had returned from the Jordan country and was in Bethany with Lazarus. Many men, women, and children decide to walk the two miles to Bethany and meet Him there. They also wanted to see the man who had been dead and buried and was now alive.

Jesus decided at the same moment that the time had come for him to enter the city, even though the Jewish priests were so angry with Him and His teaching that they were trying to kill Him. He sent two of His disciples to a nearby village and said, "When you get into the town, you will see a colt tied near its mother. Unfasten the colt and bring him to Me. If anyone asks why you are taking him, just say that the Lord needs him. They will let you have him."

In the village, the disciples found things just as Jesus had said they would. As they were untying the colt, the owner came up and asked, "Why are you taking my donkey?"

"Our Lord needs him," they replied. The owner asked no more questions, but let them lead it away.

When the disciples reached Jesus with the colt, they spread some coats of their own across his back for Jesus to sit upon. As Jesus was riding toward the city, He met the crowd that was coming out to see Him. When they saw Him entering upon a colt as a king might, they grew wild with joy. They thought that He was coming to set up His kingdom in Jerusalem.

Many of the people took off their coats and spread them in the road to make a carpet for Jesus to ride on. Others cut branches from palm trees and spread them on the ground. Then they walked before Him and shouted, "Bless this son of David! Bless this One who comes from God! Bless His great kingdom! God bless our King!"

When the shouting multitude reached the city, people heard the commotion and came out to ask, "Who is coming?"

"It is Jesus from Nazareth," came the answer. . The priests and leading Pharisees tried to get the crowd to quit shouting after Jesus, but Jesus turned to them and said, "You cannot change anything by making the people quiet. If they were still, even the stones would cry out that I am God's Son."

The Pharisees could only step back and let the

Loran Raymond Jones

TRIUMPHAL ENTRY INTO JERUSALEM

Matthew 21:1–11

parade pass on. But they were not ready to give up. If they could not turn the people away from Jesus by persuasion, they were determined to do it another way.

JUDAS BETRAYS JESUS

During the three years that Jesus spent teaching in the villages and cities, twelve men stayed close to His side. Some of the things He told them about His kingdom were hard for them to understand, but they tried their best to learn everything Jesus taught. They loved Him more than anything else in the world, and each one was convinced that He was truly the Son of God. Of course, none of these men were perfect, but each one tried to let Jesus, rather than sin, rule his life. Only one let Satan have control of some of his thoughts, and finally the devil was ruling him completely. This was Judas Iscariot.

Now Judas had wanted to serve Jesus well at first. He was happy when he was given the responsibility of taking care of the money with which the apostles bought food. Gradually, this money became more important to him than the words Jesus was saying. Occasionally he would take some of it without telling any of the others and buy something that he wanted very badly. He grew selfish of the small sum, and was displeased when he saw Lazarus' sister anoint Jesus with some expensive perfume instead of putting the money for it in his bag.

Now the rulers of the Jews had heard as much about Jesus of Nazareth as they could stand. They felt that their explanation of God's Law and prophecy was correct, and that this lowly teacher and healer could not possibly be the Savior for whom they were looking. But they could not persuade the people to turn away from Him. Finally they decided that they would have to kill Him in order to gain control of the people once more.

When Judas learned of the situation, a wicked plan came to his mind. He would sell Jesus to these priests and Pharisees who wanted Him killed. Secretly he went to the chief priests and asked, "What will you give me for turning Jesus over to you?" The priests agreed upon thirty pieces of silver, and Judas was satisfied. "I will let you know when the time is best for you to take Him," Judas told them; and he returned to the other apostles. None of them guessed what he had done; but Jesus, of course, knew.

A few days later, on a Thursday evening, Jesus and all of the twelve ate the Passover feast together in an upper room in Jerusalem. Like all other Jews for many centuries, they did it to remember the time the death angel passed over the Israelites in Egypt. During the meal a sadness seemed to hover over the group, something no one could explain. After eating of the roast lamb, Jesus kneeled and washed the feet of each one there, including Judas. He did this to show them that the one who served others the best would be the greatest in His kingdom.

Later, as they sat about, Jesus looked around the group and made a startling statement: "One of you here with Me is going to betray Me and give Me up to be killed."

A hush fell over the group. Each one turned to Him, hurt at the idea that one of His closest friends would harm Him. "Is it I?" they asked, one after another. No one noticed that Judas remained silent.

"It is one of you eating from this same dish with Me," Jesus replied. "I feel sorry for the one who betrays Me," He added as a warning. "It would have been better if he had never been born."

Finally Judas was able to whisper the words, "Is it I, Lord?" Jesus dipped some bread into the dish of sauce and handed it to Judas, meeting his gaze. "You have said it, Judas. What you must do, do it quickly."

Immediately Judas left the room and went out into the night. The other apostles hardly realized what had happened. They might have thought that Judas was simply going on some errand.

After this, Jesus gave the apostles the bread and the wine that we call the "Lord's Supper." He told them that He wanted them to eat this when they were members of His kingdom; and when they did, they were to remember Him. Then Jesus talked of His leaving them, and they begged Him to stay. Finally, they left the upper room and walked toward a garden on the Mount of Olives, a place they often went together.

When they reached the garden, Jesus' heart was troubled by the suffering He knew He was facing.

He felt that He had to talk with His Father. He asked the disciples to wait, and He went off to pray. Alone with God, He admitted that the grief was almost more than He could bear. But He promised God that He would go through any suffering if it was God's will.

As He finished His agonizing prayer, torches lit the garden. It was Judas, leading a band of armed soldiers. He had known that Jesus would probably be coming in this direction, and he had led the soldiers to Him in order to capture Him. "Stay behind until I show you which one Jesus is," Judas whispered to the officers. "He will be the one that I kiss."

Then he stepped forward and came face to face with Jesus. "Master," he said, as though he were glad to see Jesus. Then he leaned forward and kissed Him.

Jesus gave Judas a long look of pity and said, "Judas, do you mean that you would betray Me with a kiss?" Then He turned to the officers and asked, "Who are you looking for?"

"Jesus of Nazareth," they replied.

"I am He," Jesus said; "you will not need your swords to take Me."

Now Peter could not stand by any longer. He drew out his sword and cut off the ear of the high priest's servant. Jesus turned to Peter and said, "Put your sword away. Do you not realize that My Father could send angels to save Me if I asked Him? But this must be done in order to fulfill God's will." Then He healed the servant's ear.

Finally, He turned to the soldiers and said, "Why did you come to get Me with your swords as though I were a criminal? I have not tried to hide, but I have been teaching openly in the Temple." Then He gave Himself up to them and allowed them to lead Him away.

The disciples were confused and terrified. When they saw that Jesus was not going to let them fight for Him, they ran away in fright, leaving Him to face His betrayers alone.

JESUS ON TRIAL

From the Garden of Gethsemane, Judas and the guards led Jesus to the house of Annas, a very important man among the Jews and once a high priest. Annas was expecting Jesus when He was thrust into the room by the soldiers. At last, Annas had an opportunity to see the man about whom he had heard so much. He questioned Jesus about His disciples and about His teaching.

"Why do you ask Me about My teaching?" Jesus replied. "I have never tried to hide, but I have always spoken openly in the Temple and synagogues. Ask those who heard Me; they know what I said."

When Jesus said this, one of the officers holding Him struck Him with his hand. "How dare you speak this way to a high priest?" he said.

Outside, Peter and John were waiting with a crowd in the courtyard to see what was going to happen to Jesus. While Peter was standing, warming his hands by a fire, one of the maids came up and accused him of being a friend of Jesus. Peter claimed that he did not even know Jesus. Later on another maid saw him and said the same thing, "This man was with Jesus!" Again Peter hotly denied that he knew the Man.

When the third accusation came, Peter got very angry. He began to swear, declaring that he did not know what they were talking about. When he did, he heard a rooster crow, for morning was breaking. He remembered that Jesus had told him, "Before the cock crows, you will deny Me three times." Just a few hours before, Peter had promised that he would go to prison or die before he would deny his Lord. Peter could not stay in the courtyard. He ran outside and fell down, weeping as though his heart would break.

By this time, Annas had all the information from Jesus he cared to hear. He dismissed Him and sent Him, carefully guarded by the soldiers, to the house of Caiaphas, the high priest. Inside with Caiaphas, the respected elders and lawyers who made up the Jewish court were waiting. It was unusual that they had been called to meet in the middle of the night, but they were anxious to find some reason to declare Jesus guilty now that they had Him in their power.

One by one witnesses appeared while the court tried to find some excuse for putting Jesus to death, but no two of the witnesses even agreed. Through it all, Jesus never said a word. Finally the high priest himself stood and faced Jesus. "Are you the Christ, the Son of God?" he asked.

Loran Raymond Jones

JESUS BEARING THE CROSS

John 19:16–42

"I am," Jesus said, finally breaking the silence, "and one day you will see Me sitting on God's own throne and coming in clouds of glory."

Caiaphas turned pale with anger. He faced the rest of the court. "Have you heard what this man said? We need no more witnesses; He has convicted Himself! Do you agree?"

"He is guilty of blasphemy!" came the answer. "Surely this man from Nazareth blasphemes when He claims to be the Son of God. He should be killed!"

The servants holding Jesus turned to Him and began spitting on Him. Some of them blindfolded Him and hit Him. Then they asked Him to prophesy and tell who it was that had done it.

Now Judas had been watching all the things that had been happening to Jesus since He had been brought from the garden. When he heard the high priest accuse Jesus and realized that He would be killed, Judas saw what a terrible thing he had done. He came back to the priests and elders, begging them to take their money. "I have betrayed a man who has done no wrong," he said.

The leaders turned away from him. "That is your business now. You take care of it," they replied, refusing to take the money.

Then Judas threw the money on the floor, and went out and hanged himself. Later the priests took the thirty pieces of silver and bought a field to bury strangers in. It came to be known as the "Field of Blood."

After the Jewish council cast a vote of guilty, Friday morning had begun to dawn. They still had to get permission from the Roman officials before they could kill Jesus. The governor of Judea to whom they went that morning was a man named Pontius Pilate. They told Pilate that Jesus was teaching against the Roman government, teaching that He was the king instead of Caesar.

When Pilate heard this, he took Jesus away privately to question Him, but he could find no fault in Him. He went back out and reported this to the Jews. The Jews were so excited by this time that they were determined to kill Jesus by any means. "He has stirred up the people in Galilee," they reminded Pilate.

"Well, then," Pilate said, "I should not even be judging Him. Herod, governor of Galilee, is in Jerusalem. Take Him to Herod."

But Herod kept Jesus only a short time. Then he sent Him back to Pilate, saying that he could find no reason for Jesus' death.

By this time, Pilate was very concerned about the decision the Jews were pressing him to make. He was convinced that Jesus had done nothing worthy of death; Herod had decided the same thing. Then, too, Pilate's wife had sent a message to him, telling him to free Jesus because she had suffered in a dream about Him.

Desperate now, Pilate thought of one more chance to save Jesus. He came out and said to the people, "It is the custom for us to release one prisoner at your festival time. Let me release Jesus of Nazareth this year."

"No," shouted the people, let us have Barabbas!" Now Barabbas was a wicked prisoner being held at that time, and the priests suggested to the people that they call for him.

"Then what shall I do with Jesus, who is called the Christ?" asked Pilate.

"Crucify him! Crucify him!" chanted the mob.

Pilate was afraid to stand up against them any longer. "Go ahead and crucify Him," he told the Jews. "But I want no part in it. I wash my hands of the whole matter."

"We will take the blame," shouted the angry crowd. So Jesus was led away to be beaten and crucified, and the murderer Barabbas was released in His place.

THE CRUCIFIXION

The enemies of Jesus had finally gotten Pilate, the Roman governor, to consent to Jesus' death. For nearly three years, these Jewish leaders had listened to the carpenter from Nazareth claim to be their promised Savior. From the beginning, they had refused to believe Him; but recently He had been causing such a stir and arousing so many of the people, that they decided they had to kill Him in order to keep control of the Jewish nation.

The order for crucifixion was given by Pilate early on a Friday morning after the night of the Passover supper. Afterward, soldiers took Jesus

away and beat Him. Then they dressed Him up like a king, with a scarlet robe and a crown of thorns. In His hand they placed a reed to serve as His scepter. What fun they made of Him! "Hail, O King," they mocked, and then they spit on Him.

Without a word Jesus stood, calm and serene in the midst of a howling, angry crowd. But the beating had left Him exhausted. When they gave Him His heavy cross to shoulder all the way to the place of crucifixion, He stumbled under its weight. Down the winding little streets of Jerusalem He dragged it, prodded along by the guards on either side of Him. Finally, He dropped to the ground. A guard grabbed a man named Simon from the crowd. Simon was not even from Jerusalem—he had merely come into town from the country—but something about the stranger bowing under the weight of His cross made Simon willing to help. Out of the city and up a hill called Golgotha or Calvary, "Place of the Skull," they marched. Behind them came two criminals who were also being crucified, Roman soldiers, the Jewish leaders, and a crowd of curious onlookers.

By this time, the day's activities were beginning throughout the city, and word was spreading that the Jewish leaders had captured Jesus during the night. Now many of the people in Jerusalem loved Jesus and believed His message. When they heard that He was about to be crucified, they, too, hurried to Calvary. How horrified they were to see three crosses already lying on the ground and soldiers digging the holes to set them in. The disciples looked helplessly from Jesus to one another.

When the holes were dug, the Roman soldiers stretched Jesus out upon His cross and nailed Him to the wooden beams, driving heavy spikes into His hands and feet. Across the top they fastened a sign that read, "Jesus of Nazareth, the King of the Jews." Then they stood the cross upright and dropped it into the hole they had prepared. There Jesus hung, dying just like the thieves on either side of Him. With the blood pouring from the wounds the nails had made, Jesus looked down and said, "Father, forgive them, for they do not realize what they are doing."

Yes, Jesus could still pray for those who had nailed Him to the cross. And all the while, the Roman soldiers stood unconcerned right beneath the dying man, dividing His clothes among themselves. But the disciples who had gathered clung to each other and wept. Among them was Jesus' own mother, Mary, and John, an apostle

whom Jesus dearly loved. When Jesus looked down into their sad faces, He said, "John, take care of My mother for Me." And to Mary He said, "John will be like a son to you in My place."

Some in the crowd curled their lips in disgust when they saw the sorrowful disciples. These were the Jewish scribes and priests, who had paid Judas to bring Jesus to them and voted that He was deserving to die. They were glad to see that He would soon be out of the way. They looked up at Him and mocked, "You saved others. Why don't you save yourself?"

One of the thieves hanging beside Him joined in, "Yes, why don't you save yourself and us, if you are really God's Son?"

But the other thief said to him, "How can you speak this way, knowing that you are about to die? You and I deserve to be here, but this man has done no wrong."

Then he turned to Jesus and said, "Lord, remember me when you come into your kingdom."

With the great love that He still possessed, Jesus answered, "This very day you will be with me in Paradise."

At noon, the sun disappeared from sight and God caused an awful darkness to cover the earth for about three hours. During this time Jesus' pain became more and more dreadful. Although He had done only good all His life, He was having to bear the pain because man was sinful, and God wanted man to be saved. This was the only way it could be done—for God's perfect Son to die for man's sins.

Christ as God had always known that He had to suffer this death, but He was a man, too. As a man, it was almost more than He could bear. At last He could not help sobbing, "My God, my God, why have you forsaken me?"

A little later Jesus took a little drink of vinegar from a sponge that was held up to Him. Then about three o'clock in the afternoon He saw that His work was nearly over. He whispered His last words, "It is finished. Father, into Your hands I give my spirit." After that, He died.

At that moment, the veil of the Temple that separated the Holy Place from the Holy of Holies was torn from top to bottom. The ground shook and trembled as during an earthquake. The Roman captain in charge of Jesus' death looked at his noble prisoner and kneeled before the cross, "Truly this *was* the Son of God," he said.

JESUS RISES FROM THE DEAD

On the same afternoon that Jesus died, one of the Jewish rulers who had believed on Him went to Pilate and asked for Jesus' body so that he mighty bury it. Pilate checked with the captain in charge of the crucifixion; and when he found that Jesus was already dead, he gave this man, named Joseph, permission to take the body away. Joseph wrapped the body with fine linen and with it laid the spices another disciple had given. Then he and the few faithful followers who had remained at the cross took the body to a tomb that Joseph had bought for his own body. It was a tomb common in those days, one carved like a cave out of a ledge of rock. Here they gently laid Jesus to rest and then rolled a stone over the opening of the grave.

The next day was Saturday, the Jewish Sabbath, and the Jewish priests and Pharisees met to celebrate the death of Jesus. One of them said, "I remember Jesus' saying something about rising from the dead in three days. Perhaps we had better seal His tomb carefully or one of His disciples will come and steal the body and say that he has risen." So they went to Pilate, who gave them permission to seal the tomb and also to keep soldiers there on constant guard.

The apostles and the women who had followed Jesus returned to the upper room where Jesus had eaten the Passover and spent a very sad day. For three years they had given their lives to a man and a cause that they loved above everything else. Now there was nothing left of all they believed in except a body in Joseph's tomb. Gone was their future King before He had ever gotten to reign. Gone was His glorious kingdom in which they were to lead. Jesus was dead.

Early the next morning, Mary Magdalene, a woman whom Jesus had healed, and some other women went to the tomb to take more spices to lay with the body. On the way, they wondered how they would move the stone that covered the entrance to the grave. But when they came within sight of the tomb, they saw that the stone was already rolled away. They did not know that earlier that morning the Lord had sent an earthquake, during which an angel came down from heaven and rolled away the stone. When the soldiers on guard saw the dazzling angel, they fell to the ground as if they were dead. Later, when they got up, they ran into the city and told the priests what they had seen. The priests were worried when they heard of it, not because they thought they had done wrong in killing Jesus, but because they did not want the people to know of it. They paid the soldiers to spread the story that the apostles had stolen the body while they were asleep.

When the women reached the tomb, they looked inside. In the place where Jesus' body had lain, two angels in shining white clothes stood. "Do not be afraid," said the angels. "You are looking for Jesus of Nazareth, who was crucified. He is no longer here; He has risen. Go and tell this to the disciples. Tell them that Jesus has gone to Galilee and will meet them there."

The women ran quickly to bring the message to the disciples. When they had delivered it, Peter and John set out running for the tomb. John was younger and could run faster and reached the gravesite first. He went to the tomb itself and found only the linen in which Jesus' body had been wrapped. When Peter arrived, he went inside even farther and found the cloth that had been wrapped around Jesus' face. They left, satisfied that the women had reported the truth.

By this time, Mary Magdalene had returned to the garden alone, this time to look once again for a body that might have been stolen and hidden. She stood by the empty tomb weeping when Jesus Himself stood suddenly beside her. "Mary," He said softly. When she looked and saw that it was He, she could hardly believe it was true. "Master!" she said, her tears becoming ones of joy rather than sadness.

Later all the disciples saw Jesus, talked to Him, and felt the scars in His body that His cruel death had made. For forty days He stayed with them, explaining to them how He had made all the prophecies in the Old Testament come true when He died and rose again. He showed them that this was God's plan to forgive all men who had sinned. He told them of the great work He was leaving for them to do when He went back to heaven.

He said, "You are to go and tell all nations about Me. Those who believe on Me are to be baptized, and their sins will be forgiven. Then you are to teach them to live the life I have shown you."

Loran Raymond Jones

THE RESURRECTION

Matthew 28:1–10

Finally the time came for Jesus to return to His Father. Standing with His disciples on the Mount of Olives, He raised His hand to bless them and began rising into heaven—rising higher and higher until at last a bright cloud hid Him from their sight.

While the disciples were still looking into the sky, two angels appeared beside them. "Why are you looking into the heavens?" the angels asked. "This same Jesus who has just gone to heaven is going to come again to earth in just the way that you saw Him leave."

And indeed He will. When He does, He will take back to heaven with Him all those whose life was changed by the story of the empty tomb.

PETER, A GREAT PREACHER

After Jesus went back to heaven to be with God, His Father, the disciples waited in Jerusalem, just as He had told them to do. They prayed together and worshiped God in the Temple. They also chose a man named Matthias to take Judas' place as an apostle.

On a morning ten days after Jesus' ascension, about one hundred and twenty disciples had met together to worship. Suddenly, there came the sound of a great, rushing wind, and then something looking like a little flame of fire settled above the head of each one there. The Holy Spirit came down upon them, and they felt a new power they had never felt before. They began praising God for His wonderful works.

Now this commotion had aroused interest all about the city, and crowds rushed to see what had happened. In the group were Jews from all over the world who had come to Jerusalem to worship. As they gathered around the disciples, they were surprised to find that each one could hear what was being spoken in his own language.

"What is happening?" some of the foreigners asked. "Are not all these men from Galilee? How is it that we can all understand what they are saying?"

Then Peter stood up, no longer afraid to admit that he was a follower of Jesus. He spoke boldly: "Listen to me, all of you. What you are seeing is the Spirit of God being poured out on us. One of your prophets named Joel told of this day long ago. It is today that you will see the salvation of God.

"You all remember Jesus of Nazareth, the one who did many wonderful miracles by God's power. You put Him to death on a cross, but God raised Him from the dead. All of us know this is true, for we have seen Him. Now He is with God in heaven, for this same Jesus whom you crucified is God's own Son, our Lord and Christ."

When the crowd heard Peter's brave words, they began to see how wrong they had been in killing Jesus. They cried out to Peter and the other apostles, "Men and brethren, what can we do?"

"You can turn from your sins and be baptized, believing that Jesus will forgive you of all that you have done that was wrong. When you do, God will give you His Holy Spirit also."

That day, about three thousand people told the apostles that they believed in Jesus and wanted their sins to be forgiven. They were all baptized, and with great joy they united with the band of disciples there in Jerusalem. Those who were saved from their sins became members of Christ's church, the kingdom over which He rules. All the members of the new kingdom were like one family; they loved one another with a love like Christ had. Others saw their example and came to believe on the same Savior.

This first sermon was one of the greatest that Peter ever preached, but it was only the beginning of his work in Christ's kingdom. Very soon afterward, he and the apostle John healed a lame man in Jesus' name right at the gate of the Temple. When a crowd gathered to see the happy man, Peter used another opportunity to tell them all about Christ, the risen Lord.

The rulers of the Temple, leading Jews, had Peter and John put in prison for this. They had not been among the group who were sorry for killing Jesus. Later they let them go, forbidding them to speak of Jesus again.

But Peter was never silent about Jesus. He continued to tell the good news, or the gospel, about Jesus' power to save man's sins. It was he who first preached the gospel to one outside the Jewish nation and showed that God wanted to save people of all nations who believed in Him and obeyed Him.

Peter remained a great leader in the church at Jerusalem; he helped them decide what was

Loran Raymond Jones

PETER AND THE ROMAN CENTURIAN

Acts 10:1–33

Christ's will for them. Through Peter Christ also worked many miracles of healing and of punishment. Again and again, Peter barely escaped death while he boldly proclaimed Christ. Surely there was no greater witness for Christ than Peter, whose sermon unlocked the gates of Christ's kingdom for all men who believed.

SAUL SEES A VISION

The priests and Pharisees of the Jews thought they had heard the last of Jesus of Nazareth when they had Him killed, but several months passed and His cause grew stronger and stronger. No matter what the Jewish leaders did to them, Christ's disciples went on teaching about their risen Savior. Finally the Jews began entering homes and arresting those who were teaching about Jesus. One man named Stephen was killed because he loved the Christ and would not deny Him.

After Stephen's death, Jerusalem became unsafe for the followers of Christ; and many of them scattered to other places, taking the good news of Jesus with them.

Among the Pharisees who hated Jesus was a man named Saul. Saul had grown up in a distant city named Tarsus, but his parents were devout Jews and sent him to Jerusalem to study under a Jewish teacher. Saul's teacher was one of the greatest students of the Law of Moses, a man named Gamaliel. Under his teaching Saul came to know the Law well, and he tried to keep it in a very strict manner. He felt that the followers of Jesus were disobeying the Law and that it was his duty to do all that he could to stop the spread of the gospel.

At every opportunity, he tried to break up the church, seizing disciples and having them thrown in prison. Not content merely to persecute the church in Jerusalem, when he heard that groups of disciples were in other cities, he determined to go there and do what he could to destroy them.

One city where disciples had fled for safety was Damascus. Knowing this, Saul went to the high priest and obtained permission to go there and search for followers of Christ. Any that he found, he could arrest and bring back to Jerusalem, he was told.

It was just at noon a few days later when Saul saw Damascus at the end of the road ahead. Suddenly a light from heaven, brighter than the sun, flashed about him. It was so blinding that Saul fell to the ground, unable to see. Then he heard a voice calling, "Saul, Saul, why do you persecute Me?"

"Who is speaking?" Saul asked.

"I am Jesus of Nazareth, the one you are fighting," came the answer.

What a surprise this was to Saul! He had thought that Jesus was a false teacher who was dead. But now he knew that He was not dead; He was speaking to Saul from heaven. He really was God's Son.

"What do you want me to do, Lord?" Saul asked humbly.

"Go on into the city and there you will be told what to do," Jesus answered.

Then the light faded and the vision disappeared, but Saul was still blind. The men who had been with him had seen the light and heard the voice, but they had not understood what was said. Their sight was not hurt, so they led Saul into the city.

For three days Saul was in Damascus at the home of a man named Judas. He neither ate nor drank anything; instead, he sat praying to God, concerned over the great wrongs he had done to Christ's church. On the third day, the Lord directed a faithful Christian named Ananias to go to Saul. When Ananias first received the call, he was afraid to go. "Lord," he said, "we have all heard of this Saul. He had done much evil to your followers in Jerusalem, and he has come to Damascus to arrest us."

"Go to him, Ananias," the Lord said. "You have no reason to fear him any longer. I have chosen him to take My name to the Jews, the Gentiles, and even kings. He is going to suffer much for My sake."

So Ananias went to Saul. He came to the blind man and spoke gently, telling Saul that the Lord had sent him. Then he put his hands on Saul's eyes and Saul could see once more. "Now," Ananias said, "why are you waiting? Rise and be baptized in Jesus' name so that your sins may be forgiven."

These were the words Saul had been waiting to hear. How happy he was to know that there was

Loran Raymond Jones

SAUL'S CONVERSION

Acts 9:1–22

some way for him to be forgiven by God for the terrible mistakes he had made. Immediately he was baptized, and he became a member of the very group that he had come to destroy.

After Saul had taken some food, he joined the other disciples in Damascus, eager to tell them of his vision on the road outside the city and the changes in his heart.

PAUL, A GREAT MISSIONARY

Once Saul became a disciple of Christ, he was just as determined to teach others as he had once been to destroy those who taught. He was so enthusiastic, energetic, and courageous that he caused a stir everywhere he went. At first, other disciples were suspicious of him, not knowing what to think of his change of heart; but they came to love and appreciate him when they saw how sincere he was.

When Saul returned to Jerusalem and his old friends among the Jewish rulers heard that he had joined Christ's followers, they tried to take his life. He had to leave and go far away to continue his teaching.

Finally Saul came to a city called Antioch and preached with a good man named Barnabas for the growing church there. Then, after a message was received from the Holy Spirit, Saul and Barnabas left Antioch to travel about and preach the gospel to the Gentiles.

Now the Gentiles were all those who were not Jews. At first the apostles had only tried to teach other Jews, but Jesus wanted everyone to have an opportunity to be saved. Many of the Gentile people had never had anything to worship but idols, and Saul found them anxious to hear about the one true God and the loving Savior. Everywhere Saul and Barnabas went they found people whom they taught to believe in Christ; and when they left a town, they would leave a little church behind.

Paul, as Saul was called after this, and Barnabas had a wonderful trip. They had to suffer many hardships, but they realized that they were doing a wonderful work, taking Christ to places where He had never been heard of before.

Finally they returned to Antioch and told the church there about their journey. They stayed a while, and then Paul became anxious to leave again and visit the little churches that he and Barnabas had established.

This time Paul took a man named Silas with him. Their travels carried them far away to a country in Greece named Macedonia. They came to a Macedonian city named Philippi. Philippi was so far from Judea, the home of the Jews, that there were few, if any, Jews there. At least there were not enough to build a house of worship, so Paul had no place to preach. Finally he found a place down by the riverside where people came to pray. A few women were gathered there, and Paul and Silas talked with them about Jesus.

One of the ladies by the river was a businesswoman named Lydia. When Lydia heard about Christ, her heart was opened to him and she believed in Him. Although she lived in another town, she came to Philippi often to sell her purple dyes, and she had a home there. She invited the preachers to stay with her.

One day, while still in Philippi, Paul and Silas healed a poor little fortuneteller of an evil spirit. When the spirit left her, she would no longer work for her cruel masters; and they became angry because they could make no more money from her fortunetelling. They stirred up a mob against Paul and Silas and had the missionaries beaten and thrown in prison. In the jail, they were locked in wooden stocks which held their arms and legs fast.

You might expect Paul and Silas to complain under those circumstances; but there in the darkness of the prison, they sang hymns and praised God that they were able to suffer for His sake. The other prisoners grew quiet, listening to them.

Suddenly, the ground began to rock with a great earthquake. The foundations of the prison shook, and all the cells flew open. Even the stocks fell apart, setting Paul and Silas free.

When the jailkeeper saw that his prisoners all had a chance to escape, he grabbed a knife to kill himself, for he knew he was responsible for them. But Paul cried out, "Do not kill yourself! No one has escaped—we are all here."

Then the jailer called for a light and rushed to Paul and Silas. He knew that they must be men of God. He begged them, "What must I do to be saved?"

So Paul and Silas told the jailer about Jesus Christ, the one who had died for every man's sins. When the jailer heard, he believed on the Savior

and he was baptized in the middle of the night.

Afterward, he brought Paul and Silas to his home, washed their sore places, and fed them. He and his whole family could not thank the missionaries enough for bringing them the gospel of Christ.

Nearly all of Paul's life was spent on missionary journeys like the one that carried him to Philippi. No one did more to carry Christ to the whole world and to every creature than Paul did. Eventually, he was put in prison in faraway Rome for preaching the gospel, but he continued even there to strengthen the disciples through letters. Our Bible has many of the letters Paul wrote. One is to the Christians at Philippi, the first of whom were probably Lydia, the fortuneteller, and the jailer.

THE SIMPLIFIED TOPICAL INDEX
Based on the Collaboration of Noted Bible Authorities

*New Testament page references appear in italic type.

1

	REFERENCE	PAGE
of Hiram to		
Solomon	1 Ki. 5:1	319
Hoshea to So.	2 Ki. 17:4	362
Jephthah-Ammon	Jdgs. 11:12–28	239
of Moses to Edom	Num. 20:14–19	147
Rabshakah	2 Ki. 19:9	366
Zedekiah to Egypt	Ezek. 17:15	711

Ambassage—*an official group*
seeks peace	Luke 14:32	77

Amber—*a fossil resin* (?)
	Ezek. 1:27	697
	Ezek. 8:2	702

Ambition
Aaron and Miriam	Num. 12:1–11	138
Abimelech	Jdgs. 9:1–6	236
Absalom	2 Sam. 15:1–13	301
Adonijah	1 Ki. 1:5	313
Ahithophel	2 Sam. 17:23	304
among disciples	Mark 9:33–34	*46*
	Mark 10:35–45	*47*
Athaliah	2 Ki. 11:1	356
builders of Babel	Gen. 11:4	9
Diotrephes	3 John 1:9, 10	*240*
does not satisfy	Ps. 49:11, 12	514
Eve's	Gen. 3:1–6	3
Haman	Est. 5:9–13	465
James and John	Mark 10:35–37	*47*
Korah's company	Num. 16:1–35	142
Lucifer	Isa. 14:12–15	600
Moses accused of	Num. 16:12, 13	142
prevents faith	John 5:44	97
in religion	Matt. 23:5–7	27
Sennacherib	2 Ki. 19:23	366
warning against	2 Ki. 14:8–10	359
worldly	1 John 2:16	*236*

Ambush—*concealment for attack*
David-Philistines	2 Sam. 5:23–25	292
Israel against		
Gibeah	Jdgs. 20:29–41	249
by Jehoshaphat	2 Chr. 20:22	419
Jeroboam against		
Judah	2 Chr. 13:13	413
Joshua against Ai	Josh. 8:12	208
men of Shechem	Jdgs. 9:25, 34	237

Amen—("So be it"; "May it be")
an affirmation
to affirm an oath	Num. 5:22	130
	Deut. 27:12–26	192
	Neh. 5:13	451
to affirm a		
statement	1 Ki. 1:36	314
	Jer. 28:6	664
	Rev. 7:12	247
	Rev. 22:20	258
a name for Jesus	Rev. 3:14	245
ratifying God's		
promises	2 Cor. 1:20	*177*
response to prayer	1 Chr. 16:36	390
	Neh. 8:6	454
	Ps. 41:13	511
	Ps. 72:19	524
	Ps. 89:52	532
	Ps. 106:48	540
	Matt. 6:13	8
	1 Cor. 14:16	*173*
	Rev. 5:14	246
	Rev. 19:4	255

Amerce—*to punish by fine*
	Deut. 22:19	188

Amethyst—*a precious stone*
in breastplate of high		
priest	Ex. 28:19	78
	Ex. 39:12	90
in new Jerusalem	Rev. 21:20	*257*

	REFERENCE	PAGE
Ami		
called Amon	Neh. 7:59	453
servant of Solomon	Ezra 2:57	438

Amiable—*lovely*
Lord's house	Ps. 84:1	529

Amittai—*true*
father of Jonah	Jonah 1:1	777

Ammah
hill near Giah in		
Gibeon	2 Sam. 2:24	288

Ammi—*my people*
figurative for Israel	Hosea 2:1, 2	746

Ammiel—*God is kinsman*
father of Bathsheba	1 Chr. 3:5	376
	2 Sam. 11:3	296
father of Machir	2 Sam. 9:4, 5	294
one of twelve spies	Num. 13:12	138
son of Obed-edom	1 Chr. 26:4, 5	398

Ammihud—*kinsman is glory*
father of Elishama	Num. 1:10	123
father of Pedahel	Num. 34:28	163
father of Shemuel	Num. 34:20	163
father of Talmai	2 Sam. 13:37	299
son of Omri	1 Chr. 9:4	383

Amminadab—*kinsman is generous*
1. Father of		
Nashon	Num. 1:7	123
Aaron's		
father-in-law	Ex. 6:23	56
ancestor of David	Ruth 4:19	254
ancestor of Jesus	Luke 3:33	*61*
2. Kohathite Levite	1 Chr. 6:22	379
3. Levite of David	1 Chr. 15:10	389

Ammi-nadib—*meaning uncertain*
	Song 6:12	588

Ammishaddai—*kinsman to shaddai*
father of Ahiezer	Num. 1:12	123

Ammizabad—*kinsman has made a present*
son of Benaiah	1 Chr. 27:6	399

Ammon, Children of
descendants of Lot	Gen. 19:38	16
Israelites delivered		
from	Jdgs. 10:11	238

Ammonites—*descendants of ammon*
allies of Moabites	Jdgs. 3:13	229
	Jdgs. 10:6–9	238
befriended David	2 Sam. 17: 27–29	304
capital taken	2 Sam. 12: 26–31	298
defeated by David	2 Sam. 10:1–19	295
defeated by		
Jehoshaphat	2 Chr. 20:1–25	418
defeated by Jephthah	Jdgs. 11:4, 33	239
defeated by Jotham	2 Chr. 27:5	425
defeated by Saul	1 Sam. 11:11	264
excluded	Deut. 23:3	188
	Neh. 13:1, 2	460
gave gifts to Uzziah	2 Chr. 26:8	424
God's vengeance	Ezek. 25:1–8	720
Jews intermarry with	Neh. 13:23	461
mother of		
Rehoboam	1 Ki. 14:21	333
not to be disturbed	Deut. 2:19, 37	168
opposed Nehemiah	Neh. 2:10–19	448
powerful people	Num. 21:24	148
prophecy against	Amos 1:13–15	771
Solomon takes wives		
from	1 Ki. 11:1	328

	REFERENCE	PAGE
Ammon		
slain by Absalom	2 Sam. 13: 20–29	299
son of David	2 Sam. 3:2	289
son of Shimon	1 Chr. 4:20	377
and Tamar	2 Sam. 13:1–14	298

Amok—*deep*
priest	Neh. 12:7, 20	458

Amon—*skilled workman*
1. Son of Manasseh		
and king of Judah	2 Ki. 21:18, 19	368
	2 Chr. 33:21	432
sacrificed to idols	2 Chr. 33:22	432
slain	2 Ki. 21:23–26	368
2. Governor of		
Samaria	1 Ki. 22:26	343
3. Descendant of Solo-		
mon's servants	Neh. 7:57–59	453
called Ami	Ezra 2:57	438

Amorites—*mountaineers* (?)
conquered by		
Israel	Num. 21:21–30	148
defeated by Joshua	Josh. 10:5, 12	211
defeated by Samuel	1 Sam. 7:14	261
descendants of		
Canaan	Gen. 10:16	8
land given to		
Abraham's		
descendants	Gen. 48:22	48
hornets sent among	Josh. 24:12	225
idol worshipers	Deut. 7:1	173
	Jdgs. 6:10	232
taxed by Solomon	1 Ki. 9:20, 21	326
territory of	Gen. 14:13	12
	Gen. 15:21	13

Amos—*bearer*
ancestor of Christ	Luke 3:25	*60*
herdsman	Amos 7:14	774
vision of	Amos 8:1, 2	775

Amoz—*strong*
father of Isaiah	2 Ki. 19:2	365
	Isa. 1:1	590

Amphipolis
city of Macedonia	Acts 17:1	*136*

Amplias (or Ampliatus)
greeted by Paul	Rom. 16:8	*162*

Amram—*the people is exalted*
1. Father of Moses	Ex. 6:18, 20	55
	Num. 26:58, 59	154
son of Kokath	1 Chr. 6:3, 18	379
2. A son of Dishon	1 Chr. 1:41	374
called Hemdan	Gen. 36:26	35
3. Son of Bani	Ezra 10:34	446

Amraphel
king of Shinar	Gen. 14:1, 9	11

Amusements and Pleasure
abstinence from	1 Pet. 4:3, 4	*232*
bring judgment	Eccl. 11:9	585
cause spiritual		
death	1 Tim. 5:6	*208*
of curiosity	Acts 17:21	*136*
end in sorrow	Prov. 14:13	566
lead to poverty	Prov. 21:17	571
a proof of folly	Eccl. 7:4	582
trait of wicked	2 Tim. 3:4	*211*
wholesome	Eccl. 3:11–13	580
wicked	Eccl. 2:1, 8	579

Amzi
Mararite Levite	1 Chr. 6:46	380
postexilic priest	Neh. 11:10, 12	457

	REFERENCE	PAGE
Aram—*(person)*		
son of Esrom	Matt. 1:3, 4	3
son of Kemuel	Gen. 22:21	19
son of Shamer	1 Chr. 7:34	382
son of Shem	Gen. 10:22, 23	9
Aram—*(place)*		
called Mesopotamia	Gen. 24:10	20
northeast of Palestine	Num. 23:7	150
Aram—*wild goat*		
son of Dishan	Gen. 36:28	35
Ararat		
a kingdom	Jer. 51:27	689
resting place of ark	Gen. 8:4	7
Araunah		
Jebusite	2 Sam. 24:18–25	312
Arba, Arbah—*four*		
father of Anak	Josh. 15:13	216
Arbathite		
man of Beth-Arabah	2 Sam. 23:31	312
	1 Chr. 11:32	386
Arbite		
native of Arab	2 Sam. 23:35	312
Arbitrator—*one with power to decide*		
Paul commends use of	1 Cor. 6:1–8	*166*
Solomon	1 Ki. 3:16–28	318
Archangel—*a chief angel*		
debated with Satan	Jude 1:9	*241*
fought Satan	Rev. 12:7–9	*250*
at second coming	1 Thes. 4:16	*203*
Archelaus		
and Joseph	Matt. 2:22	4
Archer—*a bowman*		
Esau	Gen. 27:3	24
Ishmael	Gen. 21:9–20	17
Jonathan	1 Sam. 20:34–39	276
Saul wounded by	1 Sam. 31:3	286
symbol	Gen. 49: 23	49
	Jer. 50:29	687
Archevites		
lived in Samaria	Ezra 4:9	440
Archi		
called Archite	2 Sam. 15:32	302
town of Canaan	Josh. 16:2	217
Archippus		
minister in Colosse	Col. 4:17	*201*
Paul's fellow soldier	Philem. 2	*215*
Architecture—*part of building*		
Bezaleel	Ex. 31:1–5	81
figurative of God	Ps. 127:1	550
	Heb. 3:4	*217*
	Heb. 11:10	*233*
Hiram of Tyre	1 Ki. 7:13–46	322
in parable of Jesus	Luke 6:48–49	65
requires wisdom	Prov. 24:3	572
Arcturus		
group of stars	Job 9:9	474
Ard—*fugitive*		
Benjamite	Gen. 46:21	46
son of Bela	Num. 26:40	154

	REFERENCE	PAGE
Ardon		
son of Caleb	1 Chr. 2:18	375
Areli		
head of family	Num. 26:17	154
son of Gad	Gen. 46:16	46
Areopagite—*of the Areopagus*		
judge	Acts 17:34	137
Areopagus—*hill of Ares*		
hill in Athens	Acts 17:19	136
Paul at	Acts 17:22	136
Aretas		
king of Syria	2 Cor. 11:32	*183*
Argob		
Gileadite	2 Ki. 15:25	361
region of Bashan	Deut. 3:3	169
Ardai		
son of Haman	Est. 9:8	467
Aridatha		
son of Haman	Est. 9:8	467
Arieh—*lion*		
murdered by Pekah	2 Ki. 15:25	361
Ariel—*lion of God*		
man of Ezra	Ezra 8:16	444
name given Jerusalem	Isa. 29:1, 2	609
Arimathea		
town near Jerusalem	Matt. 27:57–60	*34*
Arioch		
Babylonian officer	Dan. 2:14	747
king of Ellasar	Gen. 14:1	11
Arisai		
son of Haman	Est. 9:9	467
Aristarchus		
with Paul	Acts 19:29	*139*
	Acts 20:4	*139*
	Acts 27:2	*147*
	Col. 4:10	*200*
	Philem. 24	*215*
Aristobulus		
Christian at Rome	Rom. 16:10	*162*
Ark of Bulrushes		
built by faith	Heb. 11:23	*223*
prepared for Moses	Ex. 2:3	51
Ark of the Covenant		
Aaron's rod	Heb. 9:1–5	*221*
abuse of	1 Sam. 6:19	260
book of the law	Deut. 31:26	198
captured by Philistines	1 Sam. 4:10, 11	258
carried around Jericho	Josh. 6:4–13	205
carried by Kohathites	Num. 3:30, 31	126
carried into battle	1 Sam. 4:3–5	258
cause of afflictions	1 Sam. 4:1–12	258
constructed	Ex. 25:10–22	74
	Ex. 37:1–5	88
in heaven	Rev. 11:19	*250*
in house of Abinadab	1 Sam. 7:1, 2	260
moved to Jerusalem	2 Sam. 6:12–17	292
placed in the Holy of Holies	Ex. 26:33	76
	Ex. 40:20	92

	REFERENCE	PAGE
placed in Obededom's home	2 Sam. 6:10, 11	292
	1 Chr. 13:13	388
placed in temple	1 Ki. 8:1–9	323
pot of manna	Ex. 16:33, 34	67
preceded Israel	Josh. 3:3–17	203
removal refused	2 Sam. 15:24, 25	301
returned to Israel	1 Sam. 6:1–18	259
tables of law	Deut. 10:1–5	176
Ark of Noah		
animals placed within	Gen. 6:19–22	6
construction of	Gen. 6:14–16	5
	Matt. 24:38, 39	*29*
figure of baptism	1 Pet. 3:20, 21	*232*
on Mt. Ararat	Gen. 8:1–16	7
testimony to faith	Heb. 11:7	*223*
Arkites		
Canaanite family	Gen. 10:17	8
	1 Chr. 1:15	374
Arm, Arms		
break, figurative of defeat	1 Sam. 2:31	257
	Job. 31:22	486
	Ps. 10:15	498
	Jer. 48:25	683
of Christ	1 Pet. 4:1	*232*
of flesh, figurative of weakness	2 Chr. 32:8	430
of God	Job 40:9	492
	Ps. 44:3	512
	Ps. 77:15	526
	Isa. 51:9	627
	Isa. 53:1	628
	Luke 1:51	*57*
	John 12:38	*106*
lambs in	Isa. 40:11	618
power, figurative of	Ex. 15:16	65
	Deut. 4:34	170
	Jer. 32:17	669
salvation in God's	Isa. 59:16	632
weapons	Num. 31:3	158
Armageddon—*mountain of Megiddo*		
prophetic battlefield	Rev. 16:16	*253*
Armenia		
refuge for Sennacherib's sons	2 Ki. 19:37	367
	Isa. 37:38	616
Armholes		
pillows sewed to	Ezek. 13:18	706
rags under	Jer. 38:12	675
Armoni		
son of Saul	2 Sam. 21:8	309
Armor—*warrior's defensive covering*		
David refused Saul's	1 Sam. 17:38, 39	272
Hezekiah's	2 Ki. 20:13	367
Armor, Figurative		
described	Eph. 6:11–17	*193*
faith, hope, and love	1 Thess. 5:8	*203*
of light	Rom. 13:12	*160*
of righteousness	2 Cor. 6:7	*179*
Armor-Bearers		
David served Saul as	1 Sam. 16:21	270
Goliath's	1 Sam. 17:7	271
Joab's	2 Sam. 18:15	305
Jonathan's	1 Sam. 14:6	267
served kings	Jdgs. 9:54	238

	REFERENCE	PAGE
Bethesda—*house of grace*		
pool at Jerusalem	John 5:2, 4	95
Beth-ezel—*place nearby* (?)		
possibly Azal	Zech. 14:5	799
town of Judah	Micah 1:11	779
Beth-gader—*house of a well*		
possibly Gedor	Josh. 15:58	217
town of Judah	1 Chr. 2:51	376
Beth-gamul		
town of Moab	Jer. 48:23	683
Beth-haccerem—*house of the vineyard*		
place of Judah	Neh. 3:14	449
Beth-haran		
city of Gad	Josh. 13:27	214
same as Beth-aram	Num. 32:36	161
Beth-hogla—*place of a partridge*		
town of Benjamin	Josh. 15:6	215
Beth-horon—*house of a hollow*		
Levites given	Josh. 21:20, 22	222
Solomon builds	1 Ki. 9:17	326
twin towns in Ephraim	2 Chr. 8:5	409
Beth-jeshimoth—*house of the deserts*		
camp of Israel	Num. 33:49	162
city east of Jordan	Josh. 12:3	213
Reuben given	Josh. 13:20	214
Beth-lebaoth—*house of lioness* (?)		
called Lebaoth	Josh. 15:32	216
town of Simeon	Josh. 19:6	219
Beth-lehem—*house of bread*		
birthplace of Jesus	Matt. 2:1	4
built by Salma	1 Chr. 2:51	376
children of	Matt. 2:16	4
home of Boaz	Ruth 2:4	252
home of Jesse	1 Sam. 16:1, 4	270
	1 Sam. 20:6, 28	275, 6
home of Naomi and Ruth	Ruth 1:19	251
prophesied as birth-place of Mesiah	Micah 5:2	781
	Matt. 2:5, 6	4
Rachel died and buried near	Gen. 35:19	34
	Gen. 48:7	48
represented among returning exiles	Ezra 2:21	437
	Neh. 7:26	452
Beth-lehem—(*of Zebulun*)		
town of Ibzan	Jdgs. 12:8	240
village given Zebulun	Josh. 19:15	220
Beth-macchah		
city near Hermon	2 Sam. 20:14	308
Beth-marcaboth—*house of the chariots*		
city of Simeon	Josh. 19:5	219
	1 Chr. 4:31	378
Beth-meon—*house of habitation*		
(See also Beth-baal-meon)		
Moabite town	Jer. 48:23	683
Beth-nimrah—*house of leopard*		
called Nimrah	Num. 32:3	160
city of Gad	Josh. 13:27	214
Beth-palet—*house of escape*		
city of Judah	Josh. 15:27	216

	REFERENCE	PAGE
Beth-pazzez		
city of Issachar	Josh. 19:21	220
Beth-peor—*house of Peor*		
Moses buried near	Deut. 34:6	201
near Mt. Pisgah	Deut. 3:29	169
Reuben given	Josh. 13:15, 20	214
Bethpage—*house of figs*		
village near Bethany	Mark 11:1	48
Beth-rapha—*house of the giant* (?)		
family of Judah	1 Chr. 4:12	377
Beth-rehob—*place of the street* (?)		
town near Dan	Jdgs. 18:28	246
Bethsaida—*house of the fishers*		
blind man healed at	Mark 8:22	44
Christ fed 5,000 at	Luke 9:10–17	69
city of Andrew, Peter	John 1:44	92
city of Galilee	Mark 6:45	42
condemned	Matt. 11:21	13
home of Philip	John 12:21	106
Beth-shean—*house of safety*		
body of Saul shamed in	1 Sam. 31:10, 12	286
city of Manasseh	Josh. 17:11	218
not conquered	Jdgs. 1:27	227
Beth-shemesh—*temple of the sun*		
1. On border of Judah	Josh. 15:10	216
Battle at	2 Ki. 14:11–14	359
men of	1 Sam. 6:19	260
taken by Philistines	2 Chr. 28:18	426
2. City of Egypt	Jer. 43:13	680
3. Town of Issachar	Josh. 19:22	220
4. Town of Naphtali	Josh. 19:38	220
Beth-shittah—*place of Acacia*		
place near Jordan	Jdgs. 7:22	234
Beth-tappuah—*place of apples*		
city of Judah	Josh. 15:53	217
Bethuel—*place of God*		
father of Rebekah	Gen. 24:15	20
town of Simeon	1 Chr. 4:30	378
Beth-zur—*house of the rock*		
city of Judah	Josh. 15:58	217
Betonim—*hallows*		
place on border of Gad	Josh. 13:26	214
Betrayal—*delivery to an enemy*		
of Ahimelech	1 Sam. 22:9–19	277, 8
of Jesus	Matt. 26:14, 16	31
	Luke 22:22, 48	86
of the Messiah foretold	Ps. 41:9	511
predicted	Matt. 10:21	12
	Matt. 24:10	17
of Samson	Jdgs. 16:18–20	244
of the Son of Man, foretold	Matt. 20:18	23
treachery of	Ps. 55:12, 13, 20	516
Betrothal—(See Marriage)		
Betting—(See Gambling)		
Beulah—*married*		
title of restored Palestine	Isa. 62:4	634

	REFERENCE	PAGE
Beware—*be on guard*		
of covetousness	Luke 12:15	74
of evil thoughts	Deut. 15:9	182
of evil workers	Phil. 3:2	196
of false prophets	Matt. 7:15	9
of strong drink	Jdgs. 13:4	241
Bezai		
among returned exiles	Neh. 7:23	452
	Neh. 10:18	456
head of family	Ezra 2:17	437
Bezaleel—*in shadow of God*		
grandson of Hur, built tabernacle	Ex. 31:1–11	81
	Ex. 35:30–35	86
	1 Chr. 2:20	375
took foreign wife	Ezra 10:18, 30	446
Bezek		
city of Judah	Jdgs. 1:4	226
where Saul gathered Israel	1 Sam. 11:8	264
Bezer—*fortress*		
city of Reuben	Deut. 4:43	171
	Josh. 20:8	221
son of Zophah	1 Chr. 7:37	382
Bichri		
father of Sheba	2 Sam. 20:1	307
Bidkar		
Jehu's officer	2 Ki. 9:25	354
Bier—*litter for corpse; coffin*		
Jesus raised body from	Luke 7:14	65
used for Abner	2 Sam. 3:31	290
Bigamy—(See Marriage)		
prohibited	Deut. 17:17	184
Bigotry—*religious intolerance*		
blindness of	John 8:48, 49	101
cure of Peter's	Acts 10:28, 29	128
of Pharisee	Luke 18:9–14	81
regarding other workers	Num. 11:28, 29	137
	Mark 9:38–40	46
Samaritan's error	John 4:9	94
and self-righteous spirit	Isa. 65:5	636
	2 Cor. 10:12	182
unhappiness of	Matt. 21:15	24
(See Intolerance; Persecution)		
Bigtha		
officer of Ahasuerus	Est. 1:10	462
Bigthan		
officer of Ahasuerus	Est. 2:21	463
Bigvai		
founder of postexilic family	Ezra 2:1, 14	437
	Ezra 8:14	444
	Neh. 7:19	452
postexilic leader	Ezra 2:1, 2	437
Bildad—*bel loves* (?)		
friend of Job	Job 2:11	470
Bileam		
called Ibleam (which see)	Josh. 17:11	218
town of Manasseh	1 Chr. 6:70	381

	REFERENCE	PAGE
Cherethites—*tribe of Philistia (?)*		
escorted Solomon	1 Ki. 1:38	314
served David	2 Sam. 8:18	294
Cherith—*brook east of Jordan*		
hiding place of		
Elijah	1 Ki. 17:3–6	336
Cherub—*(place)*		
region of Babylon	Ezra 2:59	438
Cherubim (plural of Cherub)		
on the curtains	Ex. 36:8	87
guards at Eden's		
gate	Gen. 3:24	3
on the mercy seat	Ex. 25:18–22	74
seen by Ezekiel	Ezek. 10:3–22	703
in the temple	1 Ki. 8:6, 7	223
on the vail	Ex. 26:31	76
Chesalon		
town of Judah	Josh. 15:10	216
Chesed		
son of Nahor	Gen. 22:22	19
Chesil		
called Bethul	Josh. 19:4	219
village in Judah	Josh. 15:30	216
Chest—*case or box*		
of cedar	Ezek. 27:24	722
for taking alms	2 Ki. 12:9	357
Chestnut Tree—*plane tree*		
in garden of God	Ezek. 31:8	725
Jacob's use of	Gen. 30:37	28
Chesulloth		
probably same as		
Chisloth-Tabor	Josh. 19:12	219
town of Issachar	Josh. 19:18	220
Chezib		
birthplace of		
Shelah	Gen. 38:5	37
probably same as		
Achzib and		
Chozeba	Josh. 15:44	216
	1 Chr. 4:22	377
Chide—*reprove; rebuke*		
Abimelech and		
Abraham	Gen. 20:9, 10	17
Abimelech and Isaac	Gen. 26:9, 10	23
Cain and God	Gen. 4:13	4
David and Joab	2 Sam. 3:28–31	290
Deborah and Israel	Jdgs. 5:16–23	231
Isaac and Laban	Gen. 31:26–42	29
Israelites and Moses	Ex. 17:7	67
Jacob and Simeon	Gen. 34:30	33
Jesus and disciples		
for forbidding		
children	Matt. 19:14	22
Jesus and disciples		
for sleeping in		
Gethsemane	Matt. 26:40	31
Jesus and disciples		
for slowness of		
understanding	Matt. 15:16	18
	John 14:9	108
Jesus and disciples		
for unbelief	Matt. 8:26	10
	Matt. 14:31	18
	Matt. 16:8–11	19
	Matt. 17:17	20
Joab and David	2 Sam. 19:5–7	306

	REFERENCE	PAGE
Pharaoh and		
Abraham	Gen. 12:18, 19	10
Reuben and his		
brethren	Gen. 42:22	41
Chidon—*(threshing floor)*		
called Nachon	2 Sam. 6:6	292
Uzza's death at	1 Chr. 13:9, 10	388
Child-bearing		
God's command	Gen. 1:28	2
by maidservant	Gen. 30:3–7	27
	Gen. 30:9–11	28
saved in	1 Tim. 2:15	207
Childhood, Characteristics of		
dependence	Num. 11:12	137
humility	Matt. 18:1, 4	21
ignorance	Heb. 5:12, 13	218
need for tutorship	Gal. 4:1, 2	187
unstableness	Eph. 4:14	192
Childlessness—(See Barrenness)		
Childlikeness—*resembling a child*		
in behavior	Ps. 131:1–2	550
in Christian life	Mark 10:15	47
	Luke 18:16	81
in Christian		
motivation	1 Pet. 2:2	230
in following God	Eph. 5:8	192
in obedience	1 Pet. 1:14	230
without malice	1 Cor. 14:20	173
Children		
of Abraham	Gen. 18:17–19	15
blessed by Jesus	Mark 10:13–16	47
the boy Jesus	Luke 2:51	59
burned in sacrifice	2 Ki. 16:2, 3	361
	2 Ki. 17:17, 31	363
	Jer. 32:35	669
	Ezek. 16:20, 21	708
crown of age	Prov. 17:6	568
David	1 Sam. 16:19–23	270
differences	Gen. 25:27	23
disciplined	Prov. 13:24	565
	Prov. 19:18	569
	Prov. 22:15	571
to fear God	Eccl. 12:1	585
the food-bearer	John 6:9	97
forsaken	Ps. 27:10	504
gifts of God	Gen. 33:5	32
	Ruth 4:13	253
	Ps. 127:3–5	550
God's care of	Ps. 27:10	504
haters of Job	Job 19:18	480
imitate parents	1 Ki. 15:11, 26	333
imitated	Matt. 18:3, 4	21
instructed in God's		
word	Deut. 6:4–7	173
Isaac	Gen. 22:7	18
Jephthah's		
daughter	Jdgs. 11:36	240
John the Baptist	Luke 1:80	58
in need	Isa. 40:11	618
to obey parents	Ex. 20:12	70
	Eph. 6:1–3	193
Paul's nephew	Acts 23:16	143
to praise Jesus	Matt. 21:15, 16	24
pride in	Est. 5:10, 11	465
protection of		
orphans	Ex. 22:22	72
to respect old age	1 Pet. 5:5	233
Samuel	1 Sam. 2:26	257
scorners of Elisha	2 Ki. 2:23	346
scornful	Prov. 30:17	577
seeking God	Prov. 8:17	562
show piety	1 Tim. 5:4	208
slain in Egypt	Acts 7:17–19	123
Timothy	2 Tim. 3:15	212
trained	Prov. 22:6	571

	REFERENCE	PAGE
treated with		
kindness	Col. 3:21	200
unhappiness without	1 Sam. 1:5–11	255
Chileab		
called Daniel	1 Chr. 3:1	376
son of David	2 Sam. 3:3	289
Chilion—*wasting away*		
Boaz bought estate		
of	Ruth 4:9	254
son of Elimelech	Ruth 1:2, 4, 5	251
Chilmad—*a place in Assyria (?)*		
traded with Tyre	Ezek. 27:23	722
Chimham		
inn named for	Jer. 41:17	678
son of Barzillai	2 Sam. 19:37–40	307
Chimney		
a latticed opening	Hos. 13:3	766
Chinnereth; Chinneroth; Cinneroth—*harp; lute*		
1. City, and probably		
a district	1 Ki. 15:20	334
	Josh. 19:35	220
2. Sea of Palestine	Josh. 12:3	213
called Gennesaret	Luke 5:1	62
same as Galilee	John 6:1	97
Chios—*(Island of Aegean Sea)*		
Paul at	Acts 20:15	140
Chisleu—*(Also Chislev)*		
ninth month of		
Hebrew calender	Neh. 1:1	447
	Zech. 7:1	795
Chislon—*strength*		
father of Elidad	Num. 34:21	163
Chisloth-tabor—*of Tabor*		
same as Chesulloth	Josh. 19:18	220
town on the border		
of Zebulun	Josh. 19:12	219
Chittim—*(Kittim)* (Sometimes Cyprus)		
commerce of	Ezek. 26:6	720
descendants of		
Javan	Gen. 10:4	8
maritime power	Dan. 11:30	759
port	Isa. 23:1–12	605
prophecy about	Num. 24:24	152
Chiun		
deity made by Israel	Amos 5:26	773
Chloe		
woman of Corinth		
or Ephesus	1 Cor. 1:11	
Choice—*choosing; selection*		
difficult	2 Sam. 24:11–14	312
foolish	Jer. 2:11–13	639
of God	1 Ki. 18:21	337
Israel's	Deut. 26:17, 18	191
Jacob's	Gen. 28:21	26
of life	Deut. 30:19	196
life or death	Num. 21:8, 9	148
Lot's	Gen. 13:10, 11	11
by Mary	Luke 10:42	72
of masters	Josh. 24:15	225
Moses'	Heb. 11:25	223
Naaman's	2 Ki. 5:17	349
rebellious	Jer. 44:15–20	680, 681
of right	Ex. 32:26	83
Ruth's	Ruth 1:16	251
worldly	Matt. 19:21, 22	23

REFERENCE	PAGE

Cleansing, Spiritual
example of...........1 Cor. 6:11 — *166*
God's command.....James 4:8 — *228*
need of...........Jer. 4:14 — *641*
prayer for.........Ps. 51:2, 7 — *515*
promise of........Ezek. 36:25 — *731*
through Christ's
blood...........Heb. 9:14 — *221*
1 John 1:7 — *236*

Clement
companion of
Paul............Phil. 4:3 — *197*

Cleopas—*of a renowned father*
Jesus appeared to...Luke 24:18 — *89*

Cleophas—*of a renowned father*
husband of Mary...John 19:25 — *113*
(See Alphaeus)

Cloak—*loose outer garment*
Paul's............2 Tim. 4:13 — *212*
and sin...........John 15:22 — *109*
1 Pet. 2:16 — *231*
withheld..........Matt. 5:40 — *7*

Closet—*small private chamber*
for secret prayer....Matt. 6:6 — *8*

Clothing—*garments in general*
borrowed from
enemies..........Ex. 12:35 — *62*
of camel's hair.....Matt. 3:4 — *5*
did not grow old...Deut. 8:4 — *175*
disguised by.......Matt. 7:15 — *9*
fine.............2 Sam. 1:24 — *287*
gift of...........1 Sam. 2:18, 19 — *256*
influence of.......James 2:1–4 — *227*
Jesus stripped of...Matt. 27:27, 28 — *33*
kept clean........Num. 19:7 — *146*
of leaves.........Gen. 3:7 — *3*
lots cast for Jesus'...Matt. 27:35 — *33*
modesty in........1 Tim. 2:9 — *207*
new garments torn..1 Ki. 11:29, 30 — *329*
of skins..........Gen. 3:21 — *3*
women forbidden to
wear men's.......Deut. 22:5 — *187*

Cloud—*vapor visible in sky*
covered tabernacle..Ex. 40:34–38 — *92*
filled the temple...2 Chr. 5:13 — *378*
God's handwork....Job 26:8 — *483*
goodness fades like..Hosea 6:4 — *763*
Jesus ascended in...Acts 1:9–11 — *117*
king's favor like a..Prov. 16:15 — *567*
Lord appeared in....Ex. 24:15–18 — *74*
overshadowed
Jesus............Matt. 17:5 — *20*
promises unfulfilled
like...........Prov. 25:14 — *573*
sign to Elijah......1 Ki. 18:44 — *338*
Son of Man shall
appear in........Matt. 24:30 — *28*
Rev. 1:7 — *243*

Cloud, Pillar of
to be given again....Isa. 4:5 — *592*
guided Israel......Ex. 13:21, 22 — *63*

Cnidus—*a city of Asia Minor*
passed by Paul.....Acts 27:7 — *147*

Coal—*charcoal*
for cooking........John 21:9 — *115*
for heating........Isa. 47:14 — *624*
of kindness to
enemy...........Prov. 25:21, 22 — *574*
for offspring.......2 Sam. 14:7 — *300*
for purification....Isa. 6:6, 7 — *594*
used by smiths.....Isa. 44:12 — *622*

Coat—*an outer garment*
of disciples........Matt. 5:40 — *7*
of fine linen.......Ex. 39:27 — *91*
fisher's...........John 21:7 — *115*
giving...........Luke 3:11 — *60*
made by Dorcas....Acts 9:39 — *127*
of mail..........1 Sam. 17:5 — *271*
of many colors.....Gen. 37:3 — *35*
for priests........Ex. 28:4 — *77*
Lev. 8:13 — *99*
Samuel's.........1 Sam. 2:18, 19 — *256*
of skins..........Gen. 3:21 — *3*
without seams.....John 19:23 — *113*

Cockatrice—*serpent*
symbol of violence..Isa. 11:8 — *598*

Cockcrowing
at dawn..........Mark 13:35 — *51*
Peter and.........Matt. 26:34, 74 — *31*

Cockle—*an offensive weed*
with barley........Job 31:40 — *487*

Coffer—*chest; safe; strongbox*
for jewels.........1 Sam. 6:8 — *259*

Coffin—*a chest or case for burying a corpse*
Joseph buried in....Gen. 50:26 — *50*

Col-hozeh—*seeing all*
father of Baruch....Neh. 11:5 — *457*
father of Shallun...Neh. 3:15 — *449*

Collection
more blessed to give
than to receive....Acts 20:35 — *140*
for poor saints.....1 Cor. 16:1 — *175*
required of Israel....2 Chr. 24:6 — *422*
returning God's own..1 Chr. 29:14 — *402*
sent to Jerusalem...Rom. 15:26 — *161*
of tithes.........Mal. 3:10 — *801*
from willing hearts..Ex. 35:5 — *86*
Matt. 10:8 — *12*

College—*second quarter of Jerusalem*
Huldah dwelt in....2 Ki. 22:14 — *369*

Colony—*alien settlement or residence*
aliens in Palestine...Ezra 4:9, 10 — *440*
Israel in Assyria....2 Ki. 17:6, 24 — *362*
Israel in Babylon...2 Ki. 25:8–12 — *372*
Israel in Egypt.....Gen. 46:28 — *46*
Philippi called.....Acts 16:12 — *135*

Colors
black.............Job 3:5 — *470*
Isa. 50:3 — *626*
blue.............Ex. 28:28 — *78*
Est. 8:15 — *467*
coat of man.......Gen. 37:3 — *35*
in decorating......Est. 1:5, 6 — *461*
kinds of..........Ex. 25:4, 5 — *74*
offering of many....Ex. 25:3, 4 — *74*
purple...........Ex. 28:5, 6 — *77*
Jdgs. 8:26 — *235*
red.............Num. 19:2 — *145*
2 Sam. 1:24 — *287*
Isa. 1:18 — *590*
Matt. 27:28 — *33*
Rev. 12:3 — *250*
white............Eccl. 9:8 — *584*

Colosse—*city of Phrygia*
Epaphras and
Archippus at......Col. 1:2, 7 — *198*
Col. 4:17 — *201*
home of Onesimus...Col. 4:9 — *200*

Colt—*young horse or ass*
Jesus asked for.....Matt. 21:2, 5, 7 — *24*

Comfort—*relief of pain or mental distress;
consolation*
administered by
Christians........2 Cor. 2:7 — *177*
1 Thess. 5:11 — *203*
in adversity.......Hab. 3:17–19 — *787*
in affliction.......2 Cor. 1:3–6 — *176*
in Christ's word.....Matt. 9:22 — *11*
dangerous.........Mark 14:54 — *53*
desired by Job.....Job 10:20 — *475*
fraternal.........2 Cor. 7:5–7 — *180*
of the Scriptures....Rom. 15:4 — *161*
short-lived........Jonah 4:6–8 — *779*
for Zion..........Isa. 51:3 — *627*

Comforter—*Holy Ghost*
abides forever......John 14:16 — *108*
aids early
Christians........Acts 9:31 — *127*
guides into all
truth...........John 16:13 — *110*
promised by
Christ..........John 14:26 — *109*
reproves the world..John 16:7, 8 — *110*
testifies of Christ....John 15:26 — *110*
will instruct......Luke 12:12 — *74*

Commandments—*laws; orders*
broad............Ps. 119:96 — *547*
carnal...........Heb. 7:16 — *220*
eleventh
commandment.....John 13:34 — *108*
end of, is charity....1 Tim. 1:5 — *206*
first............Matt. 22:37,38 — *26*
first with promise..Eph. 6:2 — *193*
holy............Rom. 7:12 — *155*
Jesus'...........John 15:12 — *109*
a lamp..........Prov. 6:23 — *561*
new............John 13:34 — *108*
old.............1 John 2:7 — *236*
perfect..........Ps. 19:7 — *501*
second..........Mark 12:31 — *50*
smallest.........Deut. 22:6, 7 — *187*
ten.............Ex. 20:1–17 — *69*
Ex. 32:19 — *83*
Deut. 5:6–21 — *172*
ten, fulfilled by
Christ..........Matt. 5:17 — *6*
ten, renewed......Ex. 34:1–4 — *84*
urgent...........Dan. 3:22 — *749*

Commendation—*approval; approbation*
of faithful labors....Luke 7:28 — *66*
of good work......Mark 14:6 — *52*
of great faith......Matt. 15:28 — *19*
at the judgment....Matt. 25:20, 21 — *29*
letters of.........2 Cor. 3:1 — *177*
of sacrifices......Luke 21:3 — *84*

Commerce—*business intercourse*
in ancient Israel....1 Ki. 5:10, 11 — *319*
in Egypt.........Gen. 47:13, 17 — *47*
wealth from.......Ezek. 28:2–5 — *722*

Commission
of church.........Acts 1:8 — *117*
of evangelists......Luke 10:1–16 — *70*
great...........Matt. 28:19, 20 — *35*
performance of......Acts 26:19, 20 — *146*
of prophets.......Amos 7:15 — *774*
Jonah 1:1, 2 — *777*

Commonwealth—*people of a state*
of Israel..........Eph. 2:12 — *190*

Communion—*fellowship; sympathetic
sharing*
with Christ........Matt. 18:20 — *21*
Acts 4:13 — *120*
1 Cor. 10:16 — *170*
Rev. 3:20 — *245*

	REFERENCE	PAGE
free of offense	Acts 24:16	144
joy-giving	2 Cor. 1:12	177
may be defiled	Titus 1:15	213
may be seared	1 Tim. 4:2	208
of others	1 Cor. 10:28, 29	170
of Paul	Acts 23:1	143
purged	Heb. 9:14	221
witness to evil	Rom. 2:15	151

Conscience Money—*paid in atonement for dishonest action*

	REFERENCE	PAGE
given to priests	2 Ki. 12:16	358
Judas and	Matt. 27:3–5	32
for theft	Jdgs. 17:2	245

Consecration—*dedication for holy purposes*

	REFERENCE	PAGE
of the body	Rom. 12:1	159
of fields, cattle	Lev. 27:28	122
of the first-born	Ex. 13:2, 12	63
	Deut. 15:19	182
of Israel	Ex. 19:6	69
of Jesus	Heb. 7:28	220
of Josiah	2 Ki. 23:2, 3	369
of Levites	Num. 8:5, 6	133
personal	Ex. 32:29	83
of priests	Lev. 8:1–13	99
of Samuel	1 Sam. 1:11	255
of the way by Jesus	Heb. 10:20	222

Conservatism—*moderate; disposition to preserve*

	REFERENCE	PAGE
encouraged	Jer. 6:16	644
evil results	Matt. 15:6	18
parable concerning	Luke 5:36–38	63

Consolation—*solace; comfort*

	REFERENCE	PAGE
God of	Rom. 15:5	161
lacking	Ps. 69:20	522
of the rich	Luke 6:24	64
of Simeon	Luke 2:25	59
spiritual blessings	2 Cor. 1:5	178
in trouble	2 Cor. 1:1–11	176

Conspiracy—*combination for an evil purpose; plot*

	REFERENCE	PAGE
against Christ	Matt. 26:3–5	30
against David	2 Sam. 15:10–13	301
against Moses	Num. 16:1–3	142
against Naboth	1 Ki. 21:8–13	341
against Paul	Acts 23:12–22	143
against Samson	Jdgs. 16:4–21	243
against Stephen	Acts 6:8–15	122
forbidden	Ex. 23:1	72
Joseph's brothers	Gen. 37:18	36

Constancy—*stability; firmness of mind; fidelity*

	REFERENCE	PAGE
in friendship	Prov. 27:10	575
Jonathan	1 Sam. 20:17	275
in obedience	Ps. 119:31, 33	545
in prayer	Luke 18:1	80
	1 Thess. 5:17	203
of Ruth	Ruth 1:16	251
under suffering	Heb. 12:5–6	224
	1 Pet. 4:12–16	232
of women to Jesus	Matt. 27:55	34

Constellations—*groups of stars*

	REFERENCE	PAGE
Arcturus	Job 9:9	474
	Job 38:32	491
Orion	Job 9:9	474
	Amos 5:8	773
Pleiades	Job 38:31	491
the serpent	Job 26:13	483
shall not give light	Isa. 13:10	599

Contempt—*disdain; scorn*

	REFERENCE	PAGE
bigot's	Luke 18:11, 12	81
for Christ	John 9:28, 29	102
critic's	2 Sam. 6:16, 20	120

	REFERENCE	PAGE
disregarded	Neh. 2:17–20	448
enemy's	1 Sam. 17:38–44	272
malicious	Matt. 26:67, 68	32
for Paul's speech	2 Cor. 10:10	182
for the righteous	Ps. 80:6	528
for spiritual things	Matt. 22:2–6	25, 26

Contention—*dispute; contest; strife*

	REFERENCE	PAGE
avoided	Titus 3:9	214
between Paul, Barnabas	Acts 15:36–41	134
in Corinthian church	1 Cor. 1:11	163
destructive	Gal. 5:15	188
fools enter into	Prov. 18:6	568
the gospel with	1 Thess. 2:2	201
left off	Prov. 17:14	568
meddling with	Prov. 26:17	574
pride and	Prov. 13:10	565
removed	Gen. 13:7–12	11
of a wife	Prov. 19:13	569
of a woman	Prov. 27:15	575

Contentment—*satisfaction; freedom from worry*

	REFERENCE	PAGE
better than riches	Eccl. 4:6	580
exhortation to	Heb. 13:5	225
with food, raiment	1 Tim. 6:8	209
with godliness	1 Tim. 6:8	209
with heritage	Ps. 16:6	499
with lot in life	1 Cor. 7:17	167
Paul's	Phil. 4:11	197
with wages	Luke 3:14	60

Contracts—*legally enforceable agreements*

	REFERENCE	PAGE
binding	Gal. 3:15	186
example of	Gen. 23:3–20	19

Contrition—*penitence; a deep sorrow for sin*

	REFERENCE	PAGE
God's promises to contrite	Mal. 3:7	801
of the heart	Ps. 51:17	515
Peter's	Matt. 26:75	32
of the prodigal son	Luke 15:18	78

Controversy—*dispute; debate; quarrel*

	REFERENCE	PAGE
among disciples	Mark 9:34	46
avoided by Jesus	John 4:9–24	94
fatal	Gen. 4:1–8	3
God with nations	Jer. 25:31	661
settle in person	Prov. 25:9	573

Conversation—*conduct; behavior*

	REFERENCE	PAGE
accused falsely	1 Pet. 3:16	232
as becometh gospel	Phil. 1:27	195
without covetousness	Heb. 13:5	225
to be an example	1 Tim. 4:12	208
holy in	1 Pet. 1:15	230
upright brings salvation	Ps. 50:23	515
upright opposed by the wicked	Ps. 37:14	508
used to mean "citizenship"	Phil. 3:20	196
and wisdom	James 3:13	228

Conversation—*speech between two or more people*

	REFERENCE	PAGE
deliberate	Col. 4:6	200
filthy	Col. 3:8	200
integrity in	Matt. 5:37	7
without corruption	Eph. 4:29	192

Conversion—*a turning to religious belief*

	REFERENCE	PAGE
of Cornelius	Acts 10:1–48	127
divine command	Acts 3:19	119
of erring Christians	James 5:19, 20	229
and faithfulness	Matt. 25:19–23	29
of Gentiles	Isa. 60:3	633

	REFERENCE	PAGE
and gentleness	2 Tim. 2:24	211
genuine	Acts 16:25–34	135
God's law perfect in	Ps. 19:7	501
human agents in	Ps. 51:12, 13	515
	Acts 11:19–21	129
and kindness	Col. 3:12	200
and longsuffering	Col. 1:10, 11	198
and love	John 13:34, 35	108
makes new creatures in Christ	2 Cor. 5:17	179
	Eph. 4:23, 24	192
and meekness	Eph. 4:1, 2	191
necessity of	Matt. 18:3	21
and obedience	Phil. 2:12	195
and peacefulness	Rom. 12:18	159
and self-control	1 Cor. 9:25	169
and self-denial	Matt. 16:24	20
and spiritual blindness	Matt. 13:14, 15	16
	John 12:39, 40	106
in spiritual weakness	Luke 22:31, 32	86
superficial	Matt. 13:20, 21	16
turning from sin	1 Ki. 8:35, 36	324
	Acts 11:21	129

Conviction—*forced recognition of truth; firm belief*

	REFERENCE	PAGE
by conscience	John 8:9	100
by Holy Spirit	John 16:8	110
stifling of	Heb. 3:7, 8	217

Convocation—*solemn assembly*

	REFERENCE	PAGE
day of atonement	Lev. 23:28	116
meeting for worship	Lev. 23:2	115
passover feast	Lev. 23:4, 5	116
Pentecost feast	Lev. 23:16	116

Cooking—*preparation for eating by heat*

	REFERENCE	PAGE
baking, boiling	Ezek. 46:20	743
forbidden on Sabbath	Ex. 35:3	86
frying	Lev. 2:7	93
shoulder cut	1 Sam. 9:22–24	262
soup	Jdgs. 6:18–20	232

Co-operation—*mutual help; acting jointly*

	REFERENCE	PAGE
in battle	Jdgs. 20:11	248
foretold	Isa. 41:6	619
God and man	Jdgs. 7:20	234
in prayer	Matt. 18:19	21
in soul-winning	Mark 2:13, 14	37
for success	Neh. 4:16, 17	450
sustains in weakness	Ex. 17:12	67

Coos (or Cos)—*an island*

	REFERENCE	PAGE
visited by Paul	Acts 21:1	140

Copper—(See Brass)

Coppersmith—*a worker in copper*

	REFERENCE	PAGE
	2 Tim. 4:14	212

Coral—*ornamental stone*

	REFERENCE	PAGE
sea stone	Ezek. 27:16	722
wisdom greater than	Job 28:18	484

Corban—*oblation or gift*

	REFERENCE	PAGE
in fulfillment of a vow	Mark 7:11	43

Coriander—*small plant*

	REFERENCE	PAGE
manna like seed of	Ex. 16:31	66

Corinth—*a city of Greece*

	REFERENCE	PAGE
Apollos at	Acts 19:1	138
church at	1 Cor. 1:2	163
home of Erastus	2 Tim. 4:20	212
Paul at	Acts 18:1–4	137

Cormorant—*a bird*

	REFERENCE	PAGE
unclean	Lev. 11:17	102

	REFERENCE	PAGE
Corn—*edible part of cereal plants*		
blasted	2 Ki. 19:26	366
eaten with oil	Lev. 2:14, 15	94
an export	Ezek. 27:17	722
parched	Ruth 2:14	252
plucked by disciples	Matt. 12:1	*14*
vegetable	Gen. 41:49	41
Cornelius—*a roman centurion*		
converted	Acts 10:1–48	*127*
Corner-Stone—*chief stone of building*		
figurative of earth	Job 38:6	491
Jesus	Eph. 2:20	*191*
laid in Zion	Isa. 28:16	608
precious	1 Pet. 2:6	*231*
refused by builders	Ps. 118:22	544
Cornet—*a wind instrument*		
in idol-worship	Dan. 3:7, 10	748
in Jewish rites	1 Chr. 15:28	389
played by David	2 Sam. 6:5	292
in praise	Ps. 98:6	535
Coronation—(See Kings)		
Correction—*discipline; chastening*		
of disobedient		
children	Prov. 13:24	565
	Prov. 23:13	572
by the Lord	Ps. 89:32	532
and Scriptures	2 Tim. 3:16	*212*
of those lacking		
understanding	Prov. 10:13	563
	Prov. 22:15	571
Corruption—*contamination; debasement; impurity*		
from associates	1 Ki. 11:1–11	328
by avarice	Josh. 7:20, 21	207
before the flood	Gen. 6:5	5
of justice	Isa. 59:14	632
moral	Ps. 14:1–3	498
Corruption, Mount of		
altars destroyed	2 Ki. 23:13	370
altars on	1 Ki. 11:7	328
Corruption of Body		
body of Jesus did		
not see	Acts 13:37	*132*
Lazarus	John 11:39	*73*
put off in		
resurrection	1 Cor. 15:42	*174*
result of death	Job 19:26	480
Cosam—*a diviner*		
ancestor of Jesus	Luke 3:28	*60*
Cosmetics—*preparations for altering appearance*		
evil use of	Ezek. 23:40	718
figurative, Judah's		
vain use	Jer. 4:30	642
used by Jezebel	2 Ki. 9:30	354
Council—*Jewish sanhedrin*		
apostles tried by	Acts 4:5–30	*120*
and death penalty	Mark 15:9–14	*54*
	John 18:31	*112*
Jesus' trial before	Matt. 26:57–59	*32*
Paul talks before	Acts 23:1–5	*143*
Stephen accused		
before	Acts 6:12–15	*123*
Counsel—*opinion; advice; mutual advising*		
benefits of	Prov. 11:14	564
brings peace	2 Sam. 20:16–20	308
of the dying	1 Ki. 2:1–10	315
evil	Num. 31:16	159

	REFERENCE	PAGE
of friends	Est. 5:14	465
of God	Josh. 9:14	209
	Jdgs. 20:18	248
to heed	Prov. 12:15	564
rejecting good	Prov. 1:25, 26	558
Counselor—*an adviser*		
of Ahasuerus	Est. 1:14	462
Ahithophel	2 Sam. 16:23	288
Christ	Isa. 9:6	596
Gamaliel	Acts 5:33–40	*122*
Jonathan	1 Chr. 27:32	400
Joseph of		
Arimathea	Mark 15:43	*55*
Countenance—*facial expression; appearance*		
angry	Prov. 25:23	574
	Dan. 3:19	749
beautiful	1 Sam. 16:12	270
Belshazzar's	Dan. 5:9	751
Cain's	Gen. 4:5	4
cheerful	Prov. 15:13	566
	Prov. 17:22	568
fierce	Dan. 8:23	755
heart shows in	Isa. 3:9	592
of Moses	2 Cor. 3:7	*177*
prayer changed	Luke 9:28, 29	*69*
righteousness	Eccl. 8:1	583
	Acts 6:15	*123*
sad	Neh. 2:2, 3	447
sharpened	Prov. 27:17	575
sullen	Gen. 31:1, 2	29
terrifying	Jdgs. 13:6	241
of wicked	Ps. 10:2–4	497
Counterfeit—*imitated; false; spurious*		
apostles	2 Cor. 11:13	*182*
Christians	Gal. 2:3, 4	*185*
Christs	Matt. 24:4, 5, 24	*28*
commandments	Titus 1:13, 14	*213*
doctrines	Heb. 13:9	*225*
gospel	Gal. 1:6–12	*185*
ministers	2 Cor. 11:14, 15	*182*
miracle workers	2 Thess. 2:7–12	*205*
prayers	James 4:3	*228*
prophets	1 John 4:1	*238*
religion	James 1:26	*227*
religious teachers	2 Pet. 2:1	*234*
science	1 Tim. 6:20	*209*
worship	Matt. 15:8, 9	*18*
Country—*land under a particular sovereignty or government; territory of a nation*		
customs of	Gen. 29:26	27
filled with water	2 Ki. 3:20	347
heavenly	Heb. 11:16	*223*
love for	Gen. 30:25	28
	Ps. 137:1–6	552
surrender of	Gen. 12:1–4	10
Courage—*valor; fearlessness in spirit*		
of Daniel	Dan. 6:10–23	753
to face spiritual		
enemies	Dan. 3:17, 18	749
	1 Sam. 17:32	272
	Acts 5:29	*122*
inspired by faith	1 Sam. 17:37, 45	272
loss of	1 Sam. 31:7	286
moral	Acts 21:13, 14	*141*
in old age	Josh. 14:10–12	215
patriotic	Neh. 4:14–18	450
to rebuke	Gal. 2:11–14	*186*
Samson prayed for	Jdgs. 16:28	244
spiritual	Heb. 13:6	*225*
stimulated	Josh. 10:24–26	211
urged for Gideon	Jdgs. 7:11	234
urged for Israel	2 Chr. 32:7, 8	430
urged for Joshua	Josh. 1:5–7	201
urged for leaders	Deut. 31:7	197

	REFERENCE	PAGE
Courses—*regular succession*		
of captains	1 Chr. 27:1–15	399
of earth's		
foundations	Ps. 82:5	529
of Levites	1 Chr. 23:24	396
of porters	1 Chr. 26:1–12	398
of singers	1 Chr. 25:7–31	397
of the stars	Jdgs. 5:20	231
Courtesy—*courtly and genuine politeness*		
corrupted by evil		
talk	1 Cor. 15:33	*174*
examples of	Acts 27:3	*147*
and honor	Prov. 11:16	564
in speech	Prov. 15:1	566
urged	Col. 4:6	*200*
	1 Pet. 3:8	*231*
Courts—*Jewish councils*		
circuit, by Samuel	1 Sam. 7:15–17	261
contempt of	Deut. 17:12	183
for controversies	Deut. 17:9, 11	183
corruption of	Micah 7:3	782
established by		
Moses	Ex. 18:21–26	68
judges of	Deut. 16:18, 19	183
perjury condemned	Zech. 5:4	794
professional lawyers	Acts 24:1	*144*
witnesses	Deut. 19:15	185
Courtship—*act of courting; wooing*		
of Easter	Est. 2:17	463
of Isaac	Gen. 24:1–67	20
of Jacob, Rachel	Gen. 29:9–11	27
of Ruth and Boaz	Ruth 3:4–13	253
of Samson	Jdgs. 14:1–7	242
Courtyard—*enclosed area next to a building*		
a round tabernacle	Ex. 27:9	77
a round temple	1 Ki. 6:36	321
an enclosed area	2 Sam. 17:18	304
gardens in	Est. 1:5	465
Covenant—*an agreement or compact*		
Abrahamic	Gen. 26:3–5	23
	Gen. 28:13–22	26
between Abraham		
and Abimelech	Gen. 21:27–32	18
between Ahab and		
Benhadad	1 Ki. 20:34	340
between David and		
elders	2 Sam. 5:1–3	291
between Jonathan		
and David	1 Sam. 18:3, 4	273
between Judas and		
high priests	Matt. 26:14–16	*31*
between Laban and		
Jacob	Gen. 31:43–55	30
between Solomon		
and Hiram	1 Ki. 5:12	320
in Christ	Heb. 8:6–13	*220*
	Heb. 10:9, 10	*222*
in Christ everlasting	Isa. 55:3	629
in Christ not to be		
despised	Heb. 10:29	*222*
in Christ not		
forgotten by God	Ps. 105:8	538
in Christ sealed by		
blood	Matt. 26:28	*31*
God's, with		
Abraham	Gen. 17:1–14	13
God's, with Adam	Gen. 2:16, 17	2
God's, with David	2 Sam. 7:1–29	293
God's, with Noah	Gen. 9:1–17	7
of the law	Deut. 4:13–23	170
new	Jer. 31:31–34	667
Covenant-Breakers		
cursed by God	Isa. 24:5	606
and unholy		
alliances	Ezek. 44:7	740

	REFERENCE	PAGE
Covenant-Keepers		
blessings on........	Ex. 19:5	69
	Ps. 103:17, 18	538
Covenant of Salt—*purity and perpetuity*		
with David........	2 Chr. 13:5	413
with Levites.......	Num. 18:19	145
Covert—*shelter; shady place; protection*		
Abigail came to....	1 Sam. 25:20	280
destroyed by Ahaz.	2 Ki. 16:18	362
of God's wing......	Ps. 61:4	518
from storm and rain.	Isa. 4:6	592
Covetousness—*inordinately desirous*		
abhorred by the		
Lord.............	Ps. 10:3	497
Abraham free from.	Gen. 14:22, 23	12
Achan.............	Josh. 7:20, 21	207
of an apostle......	Luke 22:3–6	85
aroused...........	Acts 16:19–21	135
begets falsehood....	Acts 5:1–10	121
"the best gifts".....	1 Cor. 12:31	172
consequences of....	1 Tim. 6:9, 10	209
defiling...........	Mark 7:22, 23	43
of evil company....	1 Cor. 5:11	166
forbidden.........	Ex. 20:17	70
	Deut. 5:21	172
idolatry...........	Col. 3:5	199
and Paul..........	Acts 20:33	140
Paul and law against.	Rom. 7:7	155
punishment for....	Eph. 5:5	192
shameless.........	Jer. 8:10, 12	646
warning against....	Luke 12:13–34	74
Cowardice		
cause of failure.....	Prov. 29:25	576
of disciples........	Matt. 26:56	32
fired with fear.....	Lev. 26:17	120
	Isa. 33:14	613
of Israel before		
Goliath..........	1 Sam. 17:24	271
and open confession		
of Christ.........	John 7:13	99
	John 12:42	107
of Peter...........	Mark 14:66–72	53
rebuked...........	Isa. 51:12	627
sent by God.......	Lev. 26:17	120
sets bad example....	Deut. 20:8	186
of ten spies.......	Num. 13:33	139
unnecessary fear....	Ps. 53:5	516
of wicked.........	Prov. 28:1	575
Cows—*females of cattle*		
in Egypt..........	Gen. 41:2	39
milk of...........	2 Sam. 17:29	304
in Palestine.......	1 Sam. 6:7	259
used in offerings....	Lev. 3:1	94
	1 Sam. 6:14	260
Coz—*thorn* (?)		
father of Anub......	1 Chr. 4:8	377
(See also Koz)		
Cozbi—*deceitful*		
a Midianitish		
woman...........	Num. 25:1–18	152
Craft—*a trade or occupation; artifice; guile*		
idol makers........	Deut. 27:15	192
meaning subtlety....	Mark 14:1	52
Paul's, tent making..	Acts 18:1, 3	137
silversmiths........	Acts 19:24–25	138
Craftiness—*skillful in deceiving; cunning*		
of an enemy.......	Prov. 27:6	575
Paul free from......	2 Cor. 4:2	178
perceived by Christ.	Luke 20:23	84
use of............	2 Cor. 12:16	184
warning against.....	Eph. 4:14	192
in words..........	Ps. 55:21	516

	REFERENCE	PAGE
Crane—*large bird*		
chattering.........	Isa. 38:14	617
migratory.........	Jer. 8:7	646
Creation—*the act of causing to exist*		
of animals.........	Gen. 1:21	1
of a clean heart.....	Ps. 51:10	515
by God...........	Ps. 148:5	556
	Heb. 11:3	223
groaneth and		
travaileth........	Rom. 8:22	156
of heaven and earth.	Gen. 1:1–13	1
Jesus Christ in.....	John 1:1–3, 14	91
	Eph. 3:9	121
	Col. 1:16	198
of man...........	Gen. 1:27	2
of stars...........	Isa. 40:26	618
of wind...........	Amos 4:13	773
Creator—*the supreme being*		
Christ also........	John 1:1, 3	91
God called.........	Isa. 40:28	618
remembering......	Eccl. 12:1	585
served............	Rom. 1:25	150
wisdom of.........	Ps. 104:24	538
Creature—*a living being*		
all of God.........	Gen. 1:21	1
new.............	2 Cor. 5:17	179
	Gal. 6:15	189
Creditor—*one to whom something is due*		
children taken away		
by..............	2 Ki. 4:1	347
generosity of......	Deut. 15:1, 2	181
Jews as...........	Neh. 5:1–13	450
lends for gain......	Luke 6:34	64
parable of.........	Matt. 18:23–25	22
	Luke 7:41, 42	66
treated with fairness.	2 Ki. 4:7	347
	Rom. 13:8	160
usury by forbidden..	Ex. 22:25	72
Cremation—*burning of dead*		
of Achan..........	Josh. 7:25	207
of Saul and his sons.	1 Sam. 31:12	286
of Zimri..........	1 Ki. 16:15–19	335
Crescens		
visited Gaul.......	2 Tim. 4:8, 10	212
Crete—*island in Mediterranean Sea*		
Cretians at Pentecost.	Acts 2:1, 11	117
Paul visited.......	Acts 27:7	147
people of, noted for		
lying...........	Titus 1:12	213
Titus sent to......	Titus 1:5	213
Crib—*manger; stall*		
Christ born in.....	Luke 2:7	58
figuratively used....	Isa. 1:3	590
used for grain......	Job 39:9	492
	Prov. 14:4	565
Criminal—*one guilty of crime*		
released at feasts....	Matt. 27:15	33
self-condemned....	Deut. 24:16	190
(See specific crimes		
and punishments of)		
Cripple—*one who is lame*		
healed by Jesus.....	Luke 13:11–12	75
healed by Paul.....	Acts 14:8–10	132
Crisis—*turning point; critical moment*		
encouragement in...	Rom. 8:28	156
example of Jesus in..	Luke 22:41, 42	86
Crispus		
baptized by Paul....	1 Cor. 1:14	163
ruler of synagogue...	Acts 18:8	137

	REFERENCE	PAGE
Crookback		
barred from		
priesthood........	Lev. 21:20, 21	114
Crop		
craw of a bird.....	Lev. 1:16	93
Cross—*an instrument of torture and death*		
borne by Christ's		
followers.........	Matt. 16:24	20
	Luke 14:27	77
compulsory........	Matt. 27:32	33
enemies of Christ's..	Phil. 3:18	196
glorying in........	Gal. 6:14	189
Jesus executed on...	Mark 15:30	54
ordinances nailed to.	Col. 2:14	199
preaching of		
Christ's..........	1 Cor. 1:17	163
shameful death on...	Phil. 2:8	195
symbol of		
redemption.......	Gal. 5:11	188
Crown—*circlet for head*		
cast at Jesus' feet...	Rev. 4:10	245
costly.............	2 Sam. 12:30	298
of glory..........	Isa. 28:5	608
	1 Pet. 5:4	233
of gold...........	Ps. 21:3	501
of high priest.....	Lev. 8:9	99
of a king.........	Est. 6:8	466
of life...........	James 1:12	226
of a queen........	Est. 1:11	462
of righteousness.....	2 Tim. 4:8	212
of thorns.........	Matt. 27:29	33
Crucifixion—*death upon a cross*		
between two thieves.	John 19:18	113
with Christ........	Gal. 2:20	186
Jesus'............	Matt. 27:33, 35	33
of old man........	Rom. 6:6	154
Cruelty—*inhuman or brutal treatment*		
to animals.........	Num. 22:27–35	149
	Prov. 12:10	564
of false witnesses...	Ps. 27:12	504
to persons of faith...	Heb. 11:36	224
of Pharaoh........	Ex. 4:21	54
punishment for.....	Ezek. 18:18	712
Crumbs—*fragments; small bits*		
desired by Lazarus..	Luke 16:20, 21	79
from master's table..	Matt. 15:27	19
Cruse—*small bottle or jug*		
for carrying water...	1 Sam. 26:11	282
for holding oil......	1 Ki. 17:12	336
Crystal—*transparent mineral or stone*		
standard of clarity..	Rev. 21:11	257
	Rev. 22:1	257
in vision of wheels...	Ezek. 1:22	697
wisdom more		
valuable..........	Job 28:17, 20	484
Cubit—*a measure of length*		
measure of forearm..	Deut. 3:11	169
used in measurement		
of ideal temple.....	Ezek. 40:5	735
used in measurement		
of wall of heavenly		
Jerusalem.........	Rev. 21:17	257
Cuckoo—*a bird*		
unclean bird.......	Lev. 11:16	102
Cucumber—*a vegetable*		
eaten by Israelites...	Num. 11:5	136
raised in gardens....	Isa. 1:8	590
Cud—*a portion of food*		
	Lev. 11:3–8	102

	REFERENCE	PAGE
Cummin—*seed used as spice*		
plant	Isa. 28:25, 27	609
tithed by Pharisees	Matt. 23:23	27
Cunning—*crafty; sly*		
of the hand	Ps. 137:5	552
of hired women		
mourners	Jer. 9:17	647
of lewd woman	Prov. 7:6–27	561
of work and		
workman	Ex. 35:35	86
Cup		
of consolation	Jer. 16:7	653
David's	Ps. 23:5	503
of devils	1 Cor. 10:21	170
drinking vessel	2 Sam. 12:3	297
of God's fury	Jer. 25:15	661
of gold	1 Chr. 28:16, 17	401
in the Lord's Supper	Matt. 26:26–28	31
	1 Cor. 10:16	170
of salvation	Ps. 116:13	544
of silver	Gen. 44:2	43
of trembling	Isa. 51:17	627
Cupbearer—*official of kings*		
Nehemiah	Neh. 1:11	447
of Pharoah	Gen. 40:11	38
of Solomon	1 Ki. 10:5	327
Cure—*to heal; to restore to health*		
for all	Luke 4:40	62
of brokenhearted	Ps. 147:3	556
through Christ	Acts 9:34	127
disciples' inability to	Matt. 7:16	9
by faith	Num. 21:8, 9	148
gratitude for	Luke 4:38, 39	62
Jesus performed		
many	Luke 7:21	66
through power of the		
Lord	Luke 5:17	63
progressive	Mark 8:22–25	44
threefold	Matt. 12:22	14
by water	John 5:2–4	95
Curiosity—*prying*		
	1 Sam. 6:19	260
Curiosity Seekers		
Athenians	Acts 17:21	136
certain Greeks	John 12:20–21	106
at the cross	Matt. 27:46–49	34
Eve	Gen. 3:6	3
Herod	Luke 9:9	69
never satisfied	Prov. 27:20	575
Peter	Matt. 26:58	32
visitors to Lazarus	John 12:9	106
Zaccheus	Luke 19:1–6	82
Curse—*invocation of evil; profane oath*		
Barak commanded		
to curse Israel	Num. 22:6	149
	Num. 23:11	150
upon Cain	Gen. 4:11	4
on Canaan	Gen. 9:25	8
Christ redeems from	Gal. 3:13	186
of commandment		
breakers	Lev. 26:14–40	120
	Deut. 28:15–20	193
upon the earth	Gen. 3:17	3
Shimei curses David	2 Sam. 16:5–8	302
of thieves	Zech. 5:1–4	794
Cursing—*act of one who curses*		
Christian response		
to	Matt. 5:4	6
forbidden	Eccl. 10:20	584
	Rom. 12:14	159
of parents	Prov. 30:11	577
	Ex. 21:17	71
of Peter	Matt. 26:74	32

	REFERENCE	PAGE
Curtain—*hanging cover; drape*		
figurative of heaven	Isa. 40:22	618
in palace of		
Ahasuerus	Est. 1:6	461
in tabernacle	Ex. 26:1, 13	75
Cush		
a country	Isa. 11:11	598
name of a		
Benjamite	Ps. 7	496
son of Ham	Gen. 10:6, 8	8
Cushan—*inhabitants of Cush*		
	Hab. 3:7	787
Cushi—*an Ethiopian*		
ancestor of Jehudi	Jer. 36:14	673
father of Zephaniah	Zeph. 1:1	788
servant of David	2 Sam. 18:31	305
Custom—*various meanings*		
attachment to	Acts 6:14	123
clemency at feast	John 18:39	113
duty paid	Rom. 13:6, 7	160
habit of worship	Luke 4:16	61
Matthew, collector		
of	Matt. 9:9	11
observance of	Gen. 29:26	27
Cuthah—*(also Cuth)*		
city of Babylon	2 Ki. 17:24	363
Cymbal—*platelike metallic instrument*		
musical instrument	2 Sam. 6:5	292
used in temple		
services	2 Chr. 5:12	378
words like	1 Cor. 13:1	172
Cypress		
hardwood tree	Isa. 44:14	622
Cyprus—*island of the Mediterranean*		
Barnabas and Mark		
at	Acts 15:39	134
home of Barnabas	Acts 4:36	121
Paul visited	Acts 13:4	131
Cyrene—*city of north Africa*		
converts from	Acts 11:20	129
Simon of	Matt. 27:32	33
Cyrenius		
governor of Syria	Luke 2:1–4	58
Cyrus		
King of Persia	2 Chr. 36:22	436
proclamation of	Ezra 1:1–4	437
prophecy concerning	Isa. 44:28	622

D

	REFERENCE	PAGE
Dabareh (Daberath)		
city in Issachar	Josh. 21:28	222
given to		
Gershonites	1 Chr. 6:71, 72	381
Dabbasheth—*hump*		
town of Zebulun	Josh. 19:11	219
Daberath—*pasture land*		
same as Dabareh	Josh. 19:12	219
Dagger—*short weapon*		
used by Ehud	Jdgs. 3:16–22	229
Dagon—*corn god (?)*		
god of Philistines	Jdgs. 16:23	244
smitten in temple	1 Sam. 5:3, 4	259
Dalaiah—*(See Delaiah)*		

	REFERENCE	PAGE
Dale, The King's—*valley east of Jerusalem*		
Absalom built pillar		
in	2 Sam. 18:18	305
Melchizedek met		
Abraham	Gen. 14:17–20	12
Dalmanutha—*city west of Galilee*		
visited by Jesus	Mark 8:10	44
Dalmatia—*region east of Adriatic Sea*		
Titus sent to	2 Tim. 4:10	212
Dalphon		
son of Haman	Est. 9:7, 10	467
Dam—*bird*		
not to be taken	Deut. 22:6	187
Damages and Compensation		
for causing abortion	Ex. 21:22	71
for embezzlement	Lev. 6:1–7	97
for injury by		
animals	Ex. 21:28–32	71
for injury to stock	Ex. 21:33, 34	71
for personal injury	Ex. 21:18, 19	71
for rape	Deut. 22:28, 29	188
for wife slander	Deut. 22:13–19	188
Damaris—*heifer (?)*		
convert of Paul	Acts 17:34	137
Damascus—*capital of Syria*		
Abraham visited	Gen. 14:15	12
conquered by David	2 Sam. 8:6	294
Elisha's prophecy		
concerning	2 Ki. 8:7–14	352
luxurious, wicked	Amos 3:12	772
Paul baptized at	Acts 9:17–22	126
Paul's journey to	Acts 9:2–16	126
taken by Assyria	2 Ki. 16:9	362
wilderness of	1 Ki. 19:15	339
Damnation—*condemnation to future punishment*		
eternal penalty	Mark 3:29	38
for false religion	Matt. 23:33	27
for hypocrites	Matt. 23:14	27
for renouncing faith	1 Tim. 5:12	208
for unbelief	Mark 16:16	55
	2 Thess. 2:12	205
Damsel—*young unmarried woman; maiden*		
healed by Paul	Acts 16:16–18	135
John's head given to	Matt. 14:10, 11	17
opened gate to Peter	Acts 12:13–19	130
questioned Peter	John 18:17	112
raised from dead	Mark 5:39–42	41
Ruth called	Ruth 2:1–7	252
Dan—*judge*		
1. Son of Jacob	Gen. 30:6	28
2. Town on northern		
boundary of Israel	Jdgs. 20:1	248
	1 Chr. 21:2	393
captured by		
Danites	Josh. 19:2	219
	Jdgs. 18:29	246
center of		
calf-worship	1 Ki. 12:28–30	330
	2 Ki. 10:29	356
destroyed by		
Ben-hadad	1 Ki. 15:20	361
	2 Chr. 16:4	415
3. Tribe of	Num. 1:38	123
Dance—*to jump; to leap; to perform steps to music*		
in celebrating		
military victories	Ex. 15:20	65
	1 Sam. 18:6	273
	Jdgs. 11:34	240

REFERENCE	PAGE
2. In Mesopotamia . . 2 Ki. 19:12	366
3. A son of Joah . . . . 2 Chr. 29:12	427

Edification—*enlightenment; improvement*
of early churches . . . . Acts 9:31	127
and ministry . . . . . . Rom. 14:19	161
Paul's example . . . . . 2 Cor. 12:19	184
through charity . . . . . 1 Cor. 8:1	168

Edom—*red*
1. The Edomites . . . . Num. 20:18	147
Amos 1:6–11	771
Amos 9:12	776
2. Land of Esau . . . . . Gen. 32:3	31
called Idumea . . . . Isa. 34:5	613
fertile land . . . . . . Num. 20:14–21	147
3. Name given Esau . Gen. 25:30	23
judgments against . Jer. 49:7–22	684
sin of . . . . Obad. 1:6–15	776

Edomites—*descendants of Esau*
Amaziah subdued . . . 2 Ki. 14:1, 7	359
David subdued . . . . . 2 Sam. 8:14	294
Esau, father of . . . . . Gen. 36:9	34
governed . . . . Gen. 36:31–39	35
1 Chr. 1:43–51	375
judgments against . . . Ezek. 35:1–15	730
not to be hated . . . . . Deut. 23:7	188
opposed Israelites . . . Num. 20:18–20	147
revolted . . . . 2 Ki. 8:20	353

Edrei
capital of Bashan . . . Deut. 3:10	169
Num. 21:33–35	148
city of Naphtali . . . . . Josh. 19:37	220

Education—*teaching; imparting knowledge*
of children . . . . Prov. 22:6	571
Eph. 6:4	193
of Daniel . . . . Dan. 1:17	746
in Israel . . . . Deut. 11:18–21	178
Deut. 31:11–13	197
lasting value of . . . . . Prov. 22:6	571
by monuments . . . . . . Josh. 4:19–24	204
of Moses . . . . Acts 7:22	123
neglected . . . . Neh. 13:23–30	461
by parables . . . . Matt. 13:34	16
of Paul . . . . Acts 22:3	142

Egg
figurative of riches . Isa. 10:14	597
white of . . . . Job 6:6	472

Eglah—*a heifer*
wife of David . . . . . . 2 Sam. 3:2, 5	289

Eglaim
Moabite town . . . . . . Isa. 15:8	601

Eglon—*circle*
king of Moab . . . . Jdgs. 3:12	229
town of Judah . . . . . . Josh. 15:39	216

Egotism—*excessive love of self; conceit*
of Diotrephes . . . . . . 3 John 1:9, 10	240
of Gentiles . . . . Eph. 4:17	192
of Goliath . . . . 1 Sam. 17:4–11	271
in last days . . . . 2 Tim. 3:1–5	211
of Lucifer . . . . Isa. 14:12, 13	600
of Simon, the	
sorcerer . . . . Acts 8:9–11	125
warnings against . . . . Rom. 12:3, 16	159

Egypt—*country along Nile River*
Abraham in . . . . Gen. 12:10	10
altar to the Lord in . Isa. 19:19	603
army perished . . . . . . Ex. 14:26–28	64
desolation of . . . . Ezek. 32:1–16	726
holy family flees into . Matt. 2:13	4
Jacob and family in . Gen. 46:5, 6	44
Jacob's sons visited . Gen. 42:3	41

REFERENCE	PAGE
Joseph sold into . . . . . Gen. 37:36	37
new king who knew	
not Joseph . . . . Ex. 1:8	51
plagues of . . . . Ex. 7–11	56

Egypt, River of—*(not the Nile)*
probably same as	
Sihor . . . . Josh. 13:3	213
southwest boundary	
of Canaan . . . . Num. 34:5	163

Ehi
same as Ahiram . . . . . Num. 26:38	153
son of Benjamin . . . . Gen. 46:21	46

Ehud—*strong*
son of Bilhan . . . . 1 Chr. 7:10	381
son of Gera . . . . Jdgs. 3:15	229
Jdgs. 3:16–25	229

Eker
son of Ram . . . . 1 Chr. 2:27	375

Ekron
ark at . . . . 1 Sam. 5:10	259
Baal-zebub god of . . . 2 Ki. 1:2	345
city of Philistines . . . Josh. 13:3	213
denounced . . . . Jer. 25:9, 20	660
Amos 1:8	771
given to Dan . . . . Josh. 19:43	220
taken by Judah . . . . . Jdgs. 1:18	227

Eladah
son of Ephraim . . . . . 1 Chr. 7:20	382

Elah—*an oak*
duke of Edom . . . . . . Gen. 36:41	35
father of Hoshea . . . . 2 Ki. 15:30	361
father of Shemei . . . . 1 Ki. 4:18	319
king of Israel . . . . 1 Ki. 16:8	335
son of Caleb . . . . 1 Chr. 4:15	377
son of Uzzi . . . . 1 Chr. 9:8	483
valley of . . . . 1 Sam. 17:2	271

Elam—*highland*
country inhabited by	
Elam . . . . Gen. 14:1	11
Isa. 22:6	604
Jer. 25:25	661
Jer. 49:34, 38	685
a covenant-signer . . . Neh. 10:14	456
Levite porter . . . . 1 Chr. 26:3	398
postexilic family . . . . Ezra 2:7	437
son of Shashak . . . . . 1 Chr. 8:24	383
son of Shem . . . . Gen. 10:22	9

Elasah—*God has made*
son of Pashur . . . . . . Ezra 10:22	446
son of Shaphan . . . . . Jer. 29:3	664
(See also Eleasah)	

Elath, Eloth—*palms or oaks*
built by Azariah . . . . 2 Ki. 14:21, 22	360
held by Syrians . . . . . 2 Ki. 16:6	362
town on Red Sea . . . . 1 Ki. 9:26	327

El-beth-el—*god of Bethel*
altar built by Jacob . Gen. 35:6, 7	33

Eldaah—*God hath called*
son of Midian . . . . . . Gen. 25:4	22

Eldad—*God hath loved*
elder of Moses . . . . . . Num. 11:26, 29	137

Elders—*ruling officers*
accusations against . . 1 Tim. 5:19	209
bound Jesus . . . . Mark 15:1	54
called the presbytery . 1 Tim. 4:14	208
in Christ's day . . . . . Matt. 15:2	18
of Israel . . . . Ex. 3:16, 18	53

REFERENCE	PAGE
in Jerusalem . . . . Acts 11:30	129
of Joshua . . . . Josh. 23:2	224
leaders of nation . . . . Ex. 19:7	69
ministers to sick . . . . James 5:14, 15	229
of Moses . . . . Ex. 24:1	73
not rebuked . . . . 1 Tim. 5:1	208
obeyed . . . . Heb. 13:7, 17	225
opposed Christ . . . . . Matt. 21:23	25
ordained by Paul . . . . Acts 14:19, 23	133
ordained by Titus . . . Titus 1:5	213
Paul's charge to . . . . Acts 20:17–38	140
qualifications of . . . . . 1 Tim. 3:1–7	207
Titus 1:5–14	213
1 Pet. 5:1–4	233
to rule well . . . . 1 Tim. 5:17	209
special consideration	
of . . . . Acts 11:29, 30	129
Acts 15:4, 6, 23	133
and spiritual care	
of church . . . . Acts 20:28	140
Titus 1:5, 9	213

Elead—*God is witness*
son of Ephraim . . . . . 1 Chr. 7:21, 22	382

Eleadah—*(See Eladah)*

Elealeh
Moabite town . . . . . . Isa. 15:1, 4	600
rebuilt by	
Reubenites . . . . Num. 32:37	161

Eleasah—*God hath made*
son of Helez . . . . 1 Chr. 2:39	376
son of Rapha . . . . 1 Chr. 8:37	383

Eleazar—*God has helped*
1. ancestor of Jesus . . Matt. 1:15	3
2. David's captain . . 2 Sam. 23:9	311
3. a Levite . . . . 1 Chr. 23:21	396
4. a musician . . . . . Neh. 12:42	459
5. son of Aaron . . . . Ex. 28:1	77
buried . . . . Josh. 24:33	226
father of Phinehas . Ex. 6:25	56
and Joshua . . . . . . Josh. 14:1	225
made chief Levite . Lev. 10:6–20	101
succeeded Aaron . . Num. 20:25–28	147
6. son of Abinadab . . 1 Sam. 7:1	260
7. son of Parosh . . . . Ezra 10:25	446
8. son of Phinehas . . . Ezra 8:33	443

Elect—*choice; selected*
angels . . . . 1 Tim. 5:21	209
Christians called . . . . 2 Tim. 2:10	211
cornerstone . . . . 1 Pet. 2:6	231
Israel chosen . . . . . . Isa. 45:4	622
lady . . . . 2 John 1:1	240
Messiah called . . . . . Isa. 42:1	619
redeemed . . . . Matt. 24:22–31	128
sister . . . . 2 John 1:13	240

Election—*act of selecting*
blessings of . . . . 2 Pet. 1:5–11	234
through faith . . . . 2 Thess. 2:13	205
few of those called . . . Matt. 20:16	23
of God . . . . 1 Thess. 1:4	201
and God's purpose . . Rom. 9:11	156
Eph. 1:11	190
to good works . . . . . . Eph. 2:10	190
of grace . . . . Rom. 11:5	158
of Paul . . . . Acts 9:15	126
sure . . . . 2 Pet. 1:10	234

El-Elohe-Israel—*God, the God of Israel*
name of altar . . . . . . Gen. 33:20	32

Elements
directed by Moses . . . Ex. 9:33	59
in judgments . . . . Deut. 11:17	178
shall melt . . . . 2 Pet. 3:10	235
under God's control . Job 37:5, 6	490

REFERENCE   PAGE

Eleph
town of Benjamin...Josh. 18:28   219

Elephant—*a huge fourfooted mammal, having tusks and a flexible trunk*
not mentioned in
  text, but in margin.1 Ki. 10:22   327
                2 Chr. 9:21   410
                Job 40:15   492

Elhanan—*God is gracious*
son of Dodo........2 Sam. 23:24   311
            1 Chr. 11:26   386
son of Jair........1 Chr. 20:5   393
            2 Sam. 21:19   309

Eli—*high*
death of..........1 Sam. 4:15–18   258
guardian of Samuel.1 Sam. 1:21–28   255
Hannah blessed by..1 Sam. 1:17   255
High Priest........1 Sam. 1:9   255
            1 Sam. 2:31–35   257
            1 Ki. 2:27   316
rebuked...........1 Sam. 2:22   256
            1 Sam. 3:11–18   257
sons slain.........1 Sam. 4:11   258

Eli—*my God*
            Matt. 27:46   *34*

Eliab—*God is father*
brother of David....1 Sam. 16:6, 7   270
father of Dathan
  and Abiram.......Num. 16:1   142
            Num. 26:9   153
Gadite warrior......1 Chr. 12:9   386
a Levite..........1 Chr. 6:27   380
Levite musician.....1 Chr. 15:20   389
son of Helon.......Num. 1:9   123
            Num. 7:24, 29   131

Eliada, Eliadah—*God knows*
Benjamite warrior...2 Chr. 17:17   416
father of Rezon.....1 Ki. 11:23   328
son of David.......2 Sam. 5:16   291
            1 Chr. 3:8   376
            1 Chr. 14:7   388

Eliah—(See also Elijah)
married foreign wife.Ezra 10:18, 26   446
son of Jeroham.....1 Chr. 8:27   383

Eliahba—*God hides*
hero of David......2 Sam. 23:32   312

Eliakim—*God establishes*
1. Ancestor of Jesus.Matt. 1:13   *3*
2. Ancestor of Jesus.Luke 3:30   *60*
3. Postexilic priest...Neh. 12:41   459
4. Son of Hilkiah....2 Ki. 18:18   364
  and Assyrian army.2 Ki. 18:26–37   365
            Isa. 36:3, 11, 22   614
  brought reply to
    Isaiah.........2 Ki. 19:2   365
            Isa. 37:2   615
  commended......Isa. 22:20–25   605
5. Son of Josiah.....2 Ki. 23:34   371
  placed on throne..2 Chr. 36:4   435
  (See Jehoiakin)

Eliam—*God is kinsman*
father of Bathsheba.2 Sam. 11:3   296
(Called Ammiel)   1 Chr. 3:5   376
son of Ahithophel...2 Sam. 23:34   311

Elias—(Same as Elijah)

Eliasaph—*God has added*
Levite, son of Lael..Num. 3:24   126
prince of Gad......Num. 1:14   123
            Num. 7:42   132

REFERENCE   PAGE

Eliashib—*God will restore*
Davidic priest......1 Chr. 24:12   397
high priest........Neh. 12:10   458
postexilic Levite....Ezra 10:24   446
son of Bani........Ezra 10:34, 36   446
son of Elioenai......1 Chr. 3:24   377
son of Zattu........Ezra 10:27   446

Eliathah—*God hath come*
son of Heman......1 Chr. 25:4   397

Elidad—*God has loved*
prince of Benjamin..Num. 34:21   163

Eliel—*God is God*
ancestor of Samuel.1 Chr. 6:34   380
Gadite warrior......1 Chr. 12:11   387
hero of David......1 Chr. 11:11, 47   385
Mahavite hero.....1 Chr. 11:46   386
Manassite chief.....1 Chr. 5:24   379
overseer of tithes..2 Chr. 31:13   430
son of Hebron.....1 Chr. 15:9, 11   389
son of Shashak.....1 Chr. 8:22   383
son of Shimhi......1 Chr. 8:20   383

Elienai—*my eyes are toward God*
a Benjamite.......1 Chr. 8:20, 21   383

Eliezer—*God is helper*
ancestor of Jesus....Luke 3:29   *60*
married foreign
  wives...........Ezra 10:18   446
            Ezra 10:23, 31   446
priest of David.....1 Chr. 15:24   389
prophet..........2 Chr. 20:37   419
servant of Ezra.....Ezra 8:16   444
son of Beecher.....1 Chr. 7:8   381
son of Moses.......Ex. 18:4   68
son of Zichri.......1 Chr. 27:16   400
steward of
  Abraham.........Gen. 15:2   12

Elihoenai—*my eyes are toward Jehovah*
son of Zerahiah.....Ezra 8:4   443

Elihoreph—*god of autumn*
scribe of Solomon...1 Ki. 4:3   318

Elihu—*my God is he*
ancestor of Samuel.1 Sam. 1:1   255
brother of David....1 Chr. 27:18   400
Manassite captain..1 Chr. 12:20   387
son of Barachel.....Job 32:2   487
temple doorkeeper...1 Chr. 26:7   398

Elijah—*my god is Jehovah*
1. Prophet of Israel..1 Ki. 18:36   338
  and Ahab........1 Ki. 18:17–38   337
            1 Ki. 21:17–21   341
  and Ahaziah......2 Ki. 1:3, 16   344
  called down fire...2 Ki. 1:10–12   345
  divided Jordan....2 Ki. 2:8–22   345
  and Elisha.......1 Ki. 19:16–19   339
            2 Ki. 2:12, 13   345
  hid.............1 Ki. 17:5, 6   336
  and Jesus........Matt. 17:1, 3   *20*
  and Jezebel......1 Ki. 19:1–7   338
  prayed for rain...James 5:17, 18   *229*
  predicted drought.1 Ki. 17:1   336
  prediction fulfilled.1 Ki. 22:37, 38   343
  prophets of Baal..1 Ki. 18:40   338
  translation of....2 Ki. 2:11   345
  and widow's son..1 Ki. 17:17–24   336
2. Son of Harim.....Ezra 10:21   446

Elika—*god of rejection*
warrior of David....2 Sam. 23:25   311

Elim
camp of Israel......Ex. 15: 27   65
palm trees of.......Num. 33:9, 10   161

REFERENCE   PAGE

Elimelech—*God is king*
died..............Ruth 1:3   251
traveled in Moab....Ruth 1:1, 2   251

Elioenai—*my eyes toward Jehovah*
Benjamite.........1 Chr. 7:8   381
Kohrite porter.....1 Chr. 26:1, 3   398
postexilic priest.....Neh. 12:41   458
Simeonite.........1 Chr. 4:36   378
son of Neariah....1 Chr. 3:23, 24   377
son of Zattu.......Ezra 10:27   446

Eliphal—*God hath judged*
warrior of David....1 Chr. 11:35   386

Eliphalet, Eliphelet—*God is deliverance*
Benjamite.........1 Chr. 8:39   383
returned exile......Ezra 8:13   443
son of Ahasbai.....2 Sam. 23:34   312
son of David.......1 Chr. 3:6   376
son of David.......2 Sam. 5:16   291
son of Hashum.....Ezra 10:33   446

Eliphaz—*God is fine gold* (?)
one of Job's friends..Job 2:11   470
            Job 4:1, 5   471
            Job 42:7, 8   494
son of Esau........Gen. 36:2, 4   34

Elipheleh—*God is distinguished*
Levite singer.......1 Chr. 15:18, 21   389

Elisabeth—*God is an oath*
cousin of Mary.....Luke 1:5, 36   *56*
mother of John.....Luke 1:57–60   *57*
promised a son.....Luke 1:13   *56*
salutation to Mary..Luke 1:40–45   *57*

Eliseus
Greek form of
  Elisha...........Luke 4:27   *62*

Elisha—*God is salvation*
anointing of Jehu...2 Ki. 9:1, 2   353
and bad waters.....2 Ki. 2:19–22   346
brings blindness
  upon Syrian army.2 Ki. 6:18   350
called from plow....1 Ki. 19:19   339
caused iron to
  swim...........2 Ki. 6:5, 6   350
and deadly pottage..2 Ki. 4:41   347
death of..........2 Ki. 13:20   359
fed hundred men...2 Ki. 4:42–44   348
healed leprosy.....2 Ki. 5:1–14   349
increased oil.......2 Ki. 4:4–6   347
miracle after death..2 Ki. 13:21   359
mocked by children.2 Ki. 2:23   346
prophesied........2 Ki. 7:1, 2   351
raised dead boy....2 Ki. 4:32–37   348
son of Shaphat.....1 Ki. 19:16   338

Elishah—*God is salvation*
son of Javan.......Gen. 10:4   8

Elishama—*God has heard*
man of Judah......1 Chr. 2:41   376
priest teacher......2 Chr. 17:8   416
prince-scribe......Jer. 36:12   673
son of Ammihud...Num. 1:10   123
            1 Chr. 7:26   382
son of David.......1 Chr. 3:1, 8   376
            2 Sam. 5:15   291
            2 Sam. 5:13, 16   291

Elishaphat—*God hath judged*
a captain who
  helped Jehoiada....2 Chr. 23:1   421

Elisheba—*God is an oath*
wife of Aaron.......Ex. 6:23   56

Elishua—*God is help*
son of David........2 Sam. 5:15   291

	REFERENCE	PAGE
Eliud		
ancestor of Jesus	Matt. 1:14, 15	3
Elizaphan—*God protects*		
1. Son of Parnach	Num. 34:25	163
2. Son of Uzziel	Ex. 6:22	56
chief Kohathite	Num. 3:30	126
family of	2 Chr. 29:12–16	427
Elizur—*God is a rock*		
Reubenite prince	Num. 1:5	123
Elkanah—*God has possessed*		
doorkeeper for ark	1 Chr. 15:23	389
father of Samuel	1 Sam. 1:1, 19	255
Korhite	1 Chr. 12:6	386
Levite	1 Chr. 9:16	383
officer of Ahaz	2 Chr. 28:7	426
son of Joel	1 Chr. 6:36	380
son of Korah	1 Chr. 6:22, 23	379
	Ex. 6:24	56
son of Mahath	1 Chr. 6:35	380
Elkosh		
home of Nahum	Nahum 1:1	783
Ellasar		
place in Babylon	Gen. 14:9	11
Elmodam		
ancestor of Jesus	Luke 3:28	60
Elnaam—*God is pleasantness*		
sons of	1 Chr. 11:46	386
Elnathan—*God has given*		
1. Father,		
Nehushta	2 Ki. 24:8	372
mission to Egypt	Jer. 26:22	662
pleaded with king	Jer. 36:25	673
2. Three Levites	Ezra 8:16	444
Eloi—*My God*—same as Eli		
	Mark 15:34	54
Elon—*oak*		
Hittite	Gen. 26:34	24
judge of Israel	Jdgs. 12:11	241
son of Zebulun	Gen. 46:14	46
village of Dan	Josh. 19:43	220
Elon-beth-hanan		
town in Dan	1 Ki. 4:9	318
Elonites		
descendants of		
Elon	Num. 26:26	153
Eloquent—*expressing oneself with fluency; persuasive*		
Apollos was	Acts 18:24	137
Moses not	Ex. 4:10	53
Paul not	1 Cor. 2:1, 4	164
Eloth—(See Elath)		
Elpaal—*God has done*		
Benjamite	1 Chr. 8:11, 12	382
Elpalet		
son of David	1 Chr. 14:3, 5	388
El-paran		
place near Edom	Gen. 14:6	11
Eltekeh		
city of Dan	Josh. 19:44	220
given to Levites	Josh. 21:23	222
Eltekon		
village in Judah	Josh. 15:59	217

	REFERENCE	PAGE
Eltolad		
called Tolad	1 Chr. 4:29	378
given to Simeon	Josh. 19:4	219
town in Judah	Josh. 15:30	216
Elul		
sixth month	Neh. 6:15	452
Eluzai—*God is my strength*		
hero of David	1 Chr. 12:5	386
Elymas—*a false prophet*		
opposed Paul	Acts 13:6–12	131
Elzabad—*God hath given*		
brave Gadite	1 Chr. 12:12	387
Levite	1 Chr. 26:7, 8	398
Elzaphan—*God protects*		
grandson of Levi	Ex. 6:22	56
prince of Zebulun	Num. 34:25	163
Emancipation—*to set free; to liberate from bondage*		
God source of	Isa. 61:1	663
of Jewish slaves	Jer. 34:9–11	671
truth and	John 8:31, 32	101
Embalming—*preserving a dead body from decay*		
of Jacob and Joseph		
by Egyptians	Gen. 50:2, 3	49
	Gen. 50:26	50
of Jesus	John 19:39, 40	114
Embroidery—*ornamental needlework*		
of Aaron's coat	Ex. 28:38, 39	78
by Bezaleel	Ex. 35:30, 35	86
of garments of		
princes	Ezek. 26:16	721
garments of Sisera	Jdgs. 5:30	232
Emerald—*a precious stone*		
in breastplate of		
high priest	Ex. 28:18	78
	Ex. 39:11	90
foundation stone	Rev. 21:19	257
for ornaments	Ezek. 28:13	723
from Tyre	Ezek. 27:16	722
Emerods—*tumors; boils; plague*		
curse on		
Philistines	1 Sam. 5:6–9	259
threatened by God	Deut. 28:27	193
Emims—*terrible men*		
defeated	Gen. 14:5	11
warlike people	Deut. 2:10	167
Emmanuel—(see also Immanuel)		
Jesus called	Matt. 1:23	4
Emmaus		
town near		
Jerusalem	Luke 24:13–18	89
Emmor—(see Hamor)		
father of Sychem	Acts 7:16	123
Emotion—*strong mental agitation; sentiment*		
agony of Jesus	Luke 22:44	86
of David and people	1 Sam. 30:4	285
of disciples	John 20:1–10, 20	114
fear of God	Ps. 119:120	547
irrepressible	Gen. 43:30, 31	43
in Jewish worship	Neh. 8:6, 9	454
of Joshiah	2 Ki. 22:1, 11	368
mixed	Ezra 3:11–13	439
of a parent	Luke 15:20	78

	REFERENCE	PAGE
Employees—*those who work for wages, salary or other consideration*		
complained of		
inequality	Matt. 20:1–13	23
and employer	1 Tim. 6:1	209
must be paid	Matt. 10:10	12
no work on Sabbath	Ex. 20:10	70
paid daily	Lev. 19:13	112
and pay	Job 7:2	473
treatment of	Luke 15:17	78
Employers—*those who furnish work for others*		
to be considerate	Job 31:13	486
injustice of to be		
punished	James 5:4–5	229
not to oppress	Deut. 24:14	190
to pay fair wages	Mal. 3:5	801
	Col. 4:1	200
Employment—*state of being employed*		
of Adam	Gen. 2:15	1
continual	Ezek. 39:14	734
day and night	1 Chr. 9:33	384
Jesus honored	Mark 6:3	41
Emptiness—*state of containing nothing; vacancy*		
filled by wicked		
spirits	Luke 11:24–26	72
stones of	Isa. 34:11	613
of understanding	Prov. 12:11	564
Enam—*two springs*		
city in Judah	Josh. 15:34	216
Enan—*having eyes; seeing*		
father of Ahira	Num. 1:15	123
Encampment—*pitching of a camp*		
resting place	Num. 33:10	161
Enchantment—*use of charms; spells*		
and divination	2 Ki. 17:17	363
exorcism	Dan. 2:2	746
forbidden	Lev. 19:26	112
	Deut. 18:10, 12	184
magic	Ex. 7:11	56
sorcery	Acts 8:9, 11	125
Encouragement—*incitement or stimulation to courage*		
in affliction	Rom. 8:16–18	155
for Christian		
workers	Matt. 14:27	18
	Acts 23:11	143
example of	Josh. 1:1–9	201
in example	Acts 27:33–36	148
fear and	Isa. 41:13	619
fraternal	Acts 28:12–15	148
given Isaac	Gen. 26:24	24
given Israel	Ex. 14:13	64
in God	1 Sam. 30:6	285
from the past	Ex. 19:3–6	69
Encumbrance—*a burden that impedes action or hinders*		
of Martha	Luke 10:38–42	71
Paul's admonition		
concerning	Heb. 12:1	224
removal of	Luke 13:6–9	75
End—*terminal point; conclusion*		
better than beginning	Eccl. 7:8	582
of earth	Ps. 22:27	502
	Zech. 9:10	796
none, of Jesus'		
kingdom	Luke 1:33	57
of wicked	Ps. 37:38	509
of world	Matt. 13:39–43	16
	Matt. 24:3–44	28

REFERENCE	PAGE

Ephraim—(geographical)
applied to northern
　Kingdom..........Isa. 7:9　594
mount of..........Josh. 17:15–18　218
　　　　　　　　Jdgs. 2:9　228
a wood east of
　Jordan...........2 Sam. 18:6　304

Ephriam—(name for ten tribes)
captivity predicted..Isa. 17:3　601
mercy promised.....Jer. 31:20　667
provoked God.....Hosea 12:7–14　166
separated from
　Judah...........Isa. 7:17　595

Ephraim—(tribe)
against
　Midianites........Jdgs. 7:24, 25　234
defeated by
　Jephthah........Jdgs. 12:1–7　240
greatness of........Deut. 33:17　200
Joshua's tribe......Josh. 19:50　221
quarreled with
　Gideon...........Jdgs. 8:1　234
territory of........Josh. 16:4–10　217

Ephraimites—*of the tribe of Ephraim*
defeated by
　Jephthah.........Jdgs. 12:4–6　240

Ephrain
city near Bethel (?).2 Chr. 13:19　413

Ephratah—(same as Ephrath)
Bethlehem called....Gen. 35:19　34
　　　　　　　　Ruth 4:11　254
land of Ephraim....Ps. 132:6　550
wife of Caleb.......1 Chr. 2:50　376
　　　　　　　　1 Chr. 4:4　377

Ephrathite
inhabitant of
　Ephratah........1 Sam. 17:12　271
member of tribe of
　Ephraim.........1 Sam. 1:1　255
　　　　　　　　1 Ki. 11:26　329

Ephron—*fawn-like*
a mountain........Josh. 15:9　216
son of Zohar.......Gen. 23:8　19

Epicureans—*sect of philosophers*
opposed Paul......Acts 17:18　*136*

Equality
in Christ..........Col. 3:11　*200*
proverbial truth.....Prov. 22:2　571
revealed to Peter....Acts 10:28　*128*
taught by Paul.....Rom. 10:12　*158*
word of Jesus......Matt. 23:8　*27*

Equity—*fairness; impartiality; equal justice*
Lord judges with....Ps. 98:9　535

Er
ancestor of Jesus....Luke 3:28　*60*
son of Judah.......Gen. 38:3　37
son of Shelah.......1 Chr. 4:21　377

Eran
grandson of
　Ephraim.........Num. 26:36　153

Erastus—*amiable*
in Macedonia.......Acts 19:22　*138*
official of Corinth...Rom. 16:23　*162*
　　　　　　　　2 Tim. 4:20　*212*

Erech
city of Nimrod......Gen. 10:10　8

Eri—*watcher*
son of Gad........Gen. 46:16　46

Error—*a mistake; an irregularity*
of Balaam.........Jude 1:11　*242*
in Daniel..........Dan. 6:4　753
in the heart.......Ps. 95:10　534
of Job............Job 19:4　479
recompense of.....Rom. 1:27　*150*
to refuse reproof an..Prov. 10:17　563
sincere............Prov. 14:12　566
spirit of...........1 John 4:6　*238*
sweeping..........Gal. 2:7–16　*186*
Uzzah smitten for...2 Sam. 6:7　292
of wicked.........2 Pet. 3:17　*235*

Esaias—*same as Isaiah*

Esar-haddon—*Asshur has given a brother*
king of Assyria, son
　of Sennacherib.....Isa. 37:37, 38　616

Esau—*Hairy*
anger against
　Jacob............Gen. 27:41　25
appetite of........Gen. 25:32　23
bad bargain of.....Gen. 25:33　23
deprived of
　blessing..........Gen. 27:38　25
married...........Gen. 26:34　24
　　　　　　　　Gen. 36:2, 3　34
reconciliation......Gen. 33:1–15　32
sold birthright.....Gen. 25:29–34　23
son of Isaac.......Gen. 25:21–25　22
unable to repent....Heb. 12:16, 17　*224*
unfit.............Gen. 25:34　23
　(See Edomites)

Escape—*elude; to flee from; successful flight from*
of a few...........Gen. 7:7　6
hasty.............2 Sam.
　　　　　　　　15:14–16　301
of Lot............Gen. 19:15–30　16
by any means.....Acts 27:30–44　*148*
of Moabites.......Jdgs. 3:28, 29　330
narrow...........Job 1:14–19　469
of one............1 Sam.
　　　　　　　　22:18–20　278
of Paul...........Acts 9:24, 25　*126*
from prison........Acts 5:18–20　*121*
with skin of teeth...Job 19:20　480
by strategy........1 Sam.
　　　　　　　　19:10–17　274

Esek—*contention*
well dug by Isaac...Gen. 26:20　23

Esh-baal—*man of baal* (Ish-Bosheth)
son of Saul........1 Chr. 8:33　383

Eshban
son of Dishon......Gen. 36:26　35

Eshcol—*cluster* (of grapes)
an Amorite........Gen. 14:13　12
valley at Hebron....Deut. 1:24　166

Eshean
town in Judah......Josh. 15:52　217

Eshek
descendant of Saul..1 Chr. 8:39　383

Eshkalonites
inhabitants of
　Ashkelon.........Josh. 13:3　213

Eshtaol
given to Danites....Josh. 19:40, 41　220
possessed by Dan...Jdgs. 13:25　242

Samson born and
　buried near......Jdgs. 13:24, 25　242
　　　　　　　　Jdgs. 16:31　244
town of Judah.....Josh. 15:33　216

Eshtaulites
inhabitants of
　Eshtaol..........1 Chr. 2:53　376

Eshtemoa
1. Son of Hodia....1 Chr. 4:19　377
2. Town of Judah...Josh. 15:50　216
given spoils........1 Sam.
　　　　　　　　30:26–28　286
given to priests.....Josh. 21:14　222

Eshton
a Judahite.........1 Chr. 4:11　377

Esli
ancestor of Jesus....Luke 3:25　*60*

Esrom
ancestor of Jesus....Matt. 1:3　*3*
　　　　　　　　Luke 3:33　*61*

Esther—*a star*
beautiful..........Est. 2:7　462
chosen queen......Est. 2:17　463
courageous........Est. 7:1–7　466
patriotic..........Est. 8:1–17　466
queen of Persia....Est. 2:17　463
self-denying.......Est. 4:15, 16　465
tactful...........Est. 5:1–8　465

Estrangement—*condition of being alienated*
of Gentiles........Eph. 2:11, 12　*190*
of the heart.......Matt. 15:8　*18*
idolatry and.......Ezek. 14:5　707
sin and...........Jer. 2:5　639
of wicked.........Ps. 58:3　577

Etam—*lair of birds of prey* (?)
1. Town of Judah...2 Chr. 11:6　412
2. Town of Simeon..1 Chr. 4:32　378
Samson dwelt at....Jdgs. 15:7, 8　243

Eternal—*perpetual; everlasting*
consolation.........2 Thess. 2:16　*202*
damnation.........Mark 3:29　*38*
fire..............Jude 1:7　*241*
glory.............1 Pet. 5:10　*233*
God.............Deut. 33:27　200
house............2 Cor. 5:1　*178*
inheritance........Heb. 9:15　221
judgment..........Heb. 6:2　219
king.............1 Tim. 1:17　*207*
life..............Mark 10:17　*47*
　　　　　　　　John 17:3　*111*
　　　　　　　　Rom. 6:23　*154*
power............Rom. 1:20　*150*
punishment........Matt. 18:8　*21*
purpose of God....Eph. 3:10, 11　*191*
redemption........Heb. 9:12　221
salvation..........Heb. 5:9　218
spirit.............Heb. 9:14　221
things not seen.....2 Cor. 4:18　*178*

Eternity—*infinite duration or existence*
God inhabits.......Isa. 57:15　631
God's existence.....Ps. 90:2　532
kingdom of God....Ps. 145:13　555
reign of the Lord....Ex. 15:18　65

Etham
encampment of
　Israel...........Ex. 13:20　63
　　　　　　　　Num. 33:6　161

Ethan—*enduring*
Gershomite Levite..1 Chr. 6:42, 43　380

REFERENCE	PAGE
for various breaches	
of law..........Gen. 17:14	13
Ex. 12:15	61
Ex.	
30:33, 37, 38	81
Lev. 7:27	98
Lev. 17:8, 9	110
Lev. 19:5–8	112
Lev. 20:18	113
Lev. 22:3	114
Num. 9:13	135
Num. 19:13	146

Excuse—*apology; effort to justify fault*

Aaron's..........Ex. 32:22–24	83
Adam's..........Gen. 3:12	3
false..........1 Sam.	
20:24–29	275
feeble..........Luke 11:5–7	72
Felix's..........Acts 24:25	145
Gideon's..........Jdgs. 6:12–17	232
by gospel rejectors...Luke 14:16–20	76
idler's..........Prov. 22:13	571
Jeremiah's..........Jer. 1:6	638
not acceptable......Rom. 1:20	150
not to follow Jesus...Luke 8:21	67
	Luke 9:59–62	70
Saul's..........1 Sam.	
15:20, 21	269
servant's..........Matt. 25:24, 25	30

Exhortation—*earnest advice; to incite and encourage*

to constancy........Col. 2:1–7	199
to faith..........Heb. 11:1–6	223
to fear God........Prov. 1:7–9	557
to give thanks......Ps. 136:1–26	551
to godliness.......1 Thess. 4:1–6	202
to humility........Phil. 2:3–11	195
to liberality......2 Cor. 8:1–15	180
to love..........Eph. 5:2	192
to obedience......Deut. 4:1–6	170
to patience......Heb. 12:1–13	224
to praise........Ps. 113:1–9	543
to repentance......Acts 2:38	118
to steadfastness....1 Cor. 15:58	175
to unity..........Eph. 4:1–23	191
various, to	
Philippians.......Phil. 4:1–18	197

Exile—*expatriation; banishment*

Absalom..........2 Sam.	
14:13–14, 24	300
of Israel..........2 Ki. 17:23	363
Ittai..........2 Sam. 15:19	301

Exodus—*departure; a going forth*

of Abram from Haran.Gen. 12:4	10
Israel from Egypt...Ex. 12:41	62

Exorcists—*those who cast out evil spirits*

Paul and..........Acts 19:13, 19	138

Expectation—*prospect of good future; anticipation*

of the day of God...2 Pet. 3:12	235
of glory..........Rom. 8:19	156
of lame man......Acts 3:5	119
Paul's..........Phil. 1:20	195
of the righteous....Ps. 62:5	519
	Prov. 24:14	573
of the wicked......Prov. 10:28	563
	Prov. 11:7	564

Expedient—*suitable to the desired end*

Caiaphas..........John 11:50	105
Paul..........1 Cor. 9:22	169
	1 Cor. 10:23	170
	2 Cor. 12:1	183
that Christ go away.John 16:7	110
that one man die....John 18:14	112

REFERENCE	PAGE
Experiment—*test; to search out by trial*	
Elijah's on Mt.	
Carmel..........1 Ki. 18:24	337
meaning to prove...2 Cor. 9:13	181
of Peter..........Matt. 14:28–30	18
in worldly pleasure..Eccl. 1:2	578

Expulsion—*ejection; a driving or forcing out*

of Adam..........Gen. 3:22–24	3
of Jesus from	
Nazareth..........Luke 4:16–29	61
by persecution......Acts 13:50, 51	132
vigorous..........Neh. 13:27, 28	461

Extortion—*unjust gain*

condemned........1 Cor. 5:9, 10	166
no reward in........Ps. 109:11	541
scribes and Pharisees	
guilty of..........Matt. 23:25	27
sin of..........1 Cor. 6:9, 10	166

Eye(s)—*the organs of sight*

and adultery......2 Pet. 2:14	235
affects the heart....Lam. 3:51	694
apple of..........Deut. 32:10	198
to the blind..........Job 29:15	485
of blind, shall see...Isa. 29:18	610
blinded by light.....Acts 22:11	142
consumed by grief...Ps. 6:7	496
dimmed by age.....Gen. 27:1	24
dimmed by sorrow...Job 17:7	479
of a dove..........Song 1:15	586
evil..........Prov. 28:22	576
fountain of tears....Jer. 9:5	646
guide..........Ps. 32:8	506
of Hagar..........Gen. 21:17–19	18
if the right offends..Matt. 5:29	7
importance of......Matt. 6:22	8
of Leah..........Gen. 29:17	27
made red by wine...Gen. 49:12	49
mote in..........Matt. 7:3, 4	8
of needle..........Matt. 19:24	23
never satisfied.....Prov. 27:20	578
	Eccl. 1:8	
opened............Acts 26:18	146
painted............Ezek. 23:40	718
run down with	
tears.............Jer. 14:17	651
of Samson.........Jdgs. 16:20, 21	244
Saul eyed David....1 Sam. 18:9	273
see "eye to eye"....Isa. 52:8	628
symbol of something	
very dear........Matt. 5:29	7
	Gal. 4:15	187
tears from..........Job 16:20	478
temptation	
through..........Gen. 3:6	3
unimpaired by	
age..............Deut. 34:7	201
of wicked..........Job 11:20	475
winking..........Prov. 10:10	563

Eyebrow—*arch over the eye*

lepers shaved off....Lev. 14:2, 9	106

Eyes of the Lord

in every place......Prov. 15:3	566
flame of fire......Rev. 19:11, 12	255
open toward his	
house..........1 Ki. 8:29	324
run to and fro......2 Chr. 16:9	415
upon the	
righteous.........Ps. 34:15	507

Eyesalve

anoint with........Rev. 3:18	245

Eyeservice

censured and	
forbidden........Eph. 6:6	193
	Col. 3:22	200

REFERENCE	PAGE
Ezar—(Ezer)	
son of Seir........Gen. 36:21	35

Ezbai—*Hyssop*

father of one of	
David's men......1 Chr. 11:37	386

Ezbon

a Benjamite........1 Chr. 7:7	381
son of Gad........Gen. 46:16	46

Ezekias

same as Hezekiah...Matt. 1:9	3

Ezekiel—*God strengthens*

adviser of exiled	
Jews..............Ezek. 14:1–11	707
	Ezek. 20:1–44	713
lived with Jewish	
exiles...........Ezek. 3:15	698
prayed for Israel...Ezek. 9:8	703
prophet..........Ezek. 1:3	696
sent to Israel......Ezek. 33:7	727
vision of	
abominations.....Ezek. 8:6	702
vision of dry bones.Ezek. 37:1–14	732
vision of measuring	
temple..........Ezek. 40:1–49	735

Ezel—*departure*

where David meets	
Jonathan..........1 Sam.	
20:18, 19	275

Ezem—(Also Azem)

city of Judah......Josh. 15:29	216
given to Simeon.....Josh. 19:3	219

Ezer (Ezar)—*help*

father of Hushah....1 Chr. 4:4	377
Gadite warrior.....1 Chr. 12:9	386
Horite tribe......1 Chr. 1:38	374
postexilic priest...Neh. 12:42	459
son of Ephraim.....1 Chr. 7:21	382
son of Jeshua......Neh. 3:19	449

Ezion-geber

Israel's	
encampment......Num. 33:35	162
seaport of Israel's	
navy.............1 Ki. 22:48	344
	2 Chr. 8:17	409

Eznite

hero of David......2 Sam. 23:8	311
(See Adina)	

Ezra—*help*

1. A Judahite......1 Chr. 4:17	377
2. Postexilic	
priest..........Neh. 12:1, 33	458
3. Scribe and	
author..........Ezra 7:1, 6	442
appoints fast.....Ezra 8:21	444
charges priests....Ezra 8:29	444
commissioned by	
Artaxerxes.....Ezra 7:8	442
condemns heathen	
wives..........Ezra 9	444
	Ezra 10:1–17	445
dedicates wall of	
Jerusalem......Neh. 12:27–43	459
institutes reforms.Ezra 10:10	446
	Neh. 13:13	460
reads law........Neh. 8:2	454

Ezrahite

descendant of Zerah.1 Ki. 4:31	319

Ezri—*my help*

David's overseer....1 Chr. 27:26	400

	REFERENCE	PAGE
First Fruits—*the first gatherings of a season's produce*		
given to God	Ex. 22:29	72
of resurrection	1 Cor. 15:20	*174*
Fish—*a cold-blooded vertebrate adapted solely for aquatic life*		
created	Gen. 1:20, 21	1
destroyed in Egypt	Ex. 7:20, 21	57
draught of	Luke 5:4–11	*62*
food in Egypt	Num. 11:5	136
food in Palestine	Matt. 4:18	*6*
gate, in Jerusalem	2 Chr. 33:14	432
swallowed Jonah	Jonah 1:17	778
Fishermen—*those who catch fish*		
Simon and Andrew	Mark 1:16, 17	*36*
Fitches—*annual plant of carrot family*		
in Palestine	Isa. 28:25, 27	609
resembled rye	Ezek. 4:9	699
Flag—*a reed*		
water plant	Job 8:11	474
Flagon—*vessel with a handle and narrow mouth*		
vessel for liquids	Isa. 22:24	605
Flattery—*insincere compliment; false praise*		
Absalom and	2 Sam. 15:2–6	301
avoid those given to	Prov. 20:19	570
certain spies and	Luke 20:20, 21	*84*
corrupts good men	Dan. 11:21, 22	759
dangerous	Acts 12:21–23	*130*
deception with	Prov. 29:5	576
of an evil woman	Prov. 6:24	561
Gideon and	Jdgs. 8:1–3	234
Jacob and	Gen. 33:10	32
Mephibosheth and	2 Sam. 9:8	295
not used by apostles	1 Thess. 2:5	*202*
not way to gain favor	Prov. 28:23	576
Paul and	Acts 26:2, 3	*146*
punishment of	Ps. 12:3	498
results in ruin	Prov. 26:28	574
Tertullus and	Acts 24:2–4	*144*
users denounced	Ps. 12:3	498
warnings against	Prov. 20:19	570
widow of Tekoah and	2 Sam. 14:4–20	299
Flax—*obtained from bark of flax plant; fiber used to make linen*		
in Egypt	Ex. 9:31	59
failure of	Hosea 2:9	761
in Palestine	Josh. 2:6	202
smoking	Isa. 42:3	619
	Matt. 12:20	*14*
Flea—*wingless insect; parasite*		
	1 Sam. 26:20	282
Flesh—*various meanings*		
body a member of Christ	1 Cor. 6:15	*166*
body the temple of Holy Ghost	1 Cor. 6:19	*167*
controlled by appetite	Rom. 7:5	*154*
	Rom. 8:4	*155*
husband and wife one	Matt. 19:5	*22*
Jesus was made	John 1:14	*91*
living creatures	Gen. 6:13, 19	*5*
no man hates own	Eph. 5:29	*193*
no profit in	John 6:63	*98*
perishable as grass	Isa. 40:6, 7	618
subdued	Rom. 13:14	*160*
weak	Matt. 26:41	*31*
works of	Gal. 5:19–21	*188*

	REFERENCE	PAGE
Fleshhooks—*forks*		
made of brass	2 Chr. 4:16	405
made of gold	1 Chr. 28:17	401
used in tabernacle	Ex. 27:3	76
	Ex. 38:3	89
Flies—*small winged insects*		
dead	Eccl. 10:1	584
figurative of destruction	Isa. 7:18	595
plagued Egyptians	Ex. 8:21	57
Flint—*a very hard variety of silica*		
forehead harder than	Ezek. 3:9	698
oil out of	Deut. 32:13	198
set face like	Isa. 50:7	626
water out of	Deut. 8:15	175
Flock—*company of people*		
the church	Acts 20:28	*140*
figuratively used	Luke 12:32	*74*
God's people, Israel	Ezek. 34:31	730
he shall feed his	Isa. 40:11	618
Flood—*large flow of water; deluge*		
cannot quench love	Song 8:7	589
figurative references to	Ps. 69:15	522
	Ps. 90:5	532
history of	Gen. 6–8	5
Jesus refers to	Matt. 24:38	*29*
and Noah	Gen. 7:10–12	*6*
	Heb. 11:7	*223*
in parable	Matt. 7:27	*9*
Peter refers to	1 Pet. 3:20	232
	2 Pet. 2:5	234
promise not to destroy earth again	Gen. 9:11	8
Flour—*finely ground substance of cereal plant*		
offered in sacrifice	Lev. 5:11, 13	96
Flowers—*blossoms of a plant*		
beauty of	Luke 12:27	*74*
lilies	Song 5:13	588
	Matt. 6:28	*8*
lily of the valley	Song 2:1	586
rose of Sharon	Song 2:1	586
roses	Isa. 35:1	614
Flute—*a tubular wind instrument*		
musical instrument	Dan. 3:5	748
Folly—*state of being foolish; silliness*		
angels charged with	Job 4:18	471
of Apostle Paul	2 Cor. 11:1	*182*
excelled by wisdom	Eccl. 2:13	579
of fools	Prov. 13:16	565
	Prov. 14:8	566
fool returns to his	Prov. 26:11	574
in Israel	Gen. 34:6–19	32
joy to the ignorant	Prov. 15:21	567
leads astray	Prov. 5:23	560
prophets guilty of	Jer. 23:13	659
set in great dignity	Eccl. 10:6	584
of turning from grace to law	Gal. 3:1, 3	*186*
	Gal. 5:1–6	*188*
Food—*nutriment; sustenance*		
content with	1 Tim. 6:8	*209*
gift of God	Ps. 136:1, 25	551
	Eccl. 3:13	580
given to the hungry	James 2:15, 16	*227*
Jesus tempted with	Matt. 4:1–3	*5*
miraculous supply of	Matt. 14:15–21	*17*
necessity	Acts 27:33–36	*148*

	REFERENCE	PAGE
not to be eaten	Ex. 22:31	72
	Lev. 17:10–16	110
	Lev. 22:8	115
	Deut. 14:10	181
	Ezek. 4:14	699
offered to idols, whether to eat	1 Cor. 8:7–13	*168*
praying for	Matt. 6:9–11	*8*
rules concerning	Lev. 11:1–47	102
and strength	Acts 9:19	*126*
thanks given for	Acts 27:35	*148*
trees planted for	Lev. 19:23	112
Foods of the Bible		
almonds	Gen. 43:11	42
angels' food	Ps. 78:25	526
apples	Prov. 25:11	573
barley cakes	Ezek. 4:12	699
beans	Ezek. 4:9	699
beef	1 Ki. 4:22, 23	319
beetles	Lev. 11:22	102
bread	Gen. 31:54	30
broth	Jdgs. 6:19	232
butter	2 Sam. 17:29	304
cheese	1 Sam. 17:18	271
cucumbers	Num. 11:5	136
dried fruit	1 Sam. 25:18	280
eggs	Luke 11:12	72
figs	Num. 13:23	139
fish	John 21:9–13	*115*
fitches	Ezek. 4:9	699
fowl	1 Ki. 4:23	319
fruit	2 Sam. 16:2	302
garlic	Num. 11:5	136
goat's milk	Prov. 27:27	575
grapes	Deut. 23:24	189
grasshoppers	Lev. 11:22	102
herbs	Prov. 15:17	567
honey	Jdgs. 14:8, 9	242
lamb	Amos 6:4	774
leeks	Num. 11:5	136
lentils	Gen. 25:34	23
locusts	Matt. 3:4	*5*
meal	Gen. 18:6	14
melons	Num. 11:5	136
milk	Ex. 3:8	52
nuts	Gen. 43:11	42
oil	Deut. 12:17	179
olives	Deut. 28:40	194
onions	Num. 11:5	136
parched corn	Josh. 5:10, 11	205
partridge	1 Sam. 26:20	282
pomegranates	Num. 13:23	139
quails	Num. 11:32, 33	137
raisins	2 Sam. 16:1	302
roasting ears	Lev. 2:14	94
salt	Job 6:6	472
sheep's milk	Deut. 32:14	198
spices	Gen. 43:11	42
veal	Gen. 18:7, 8	14
venison	Gen. 25:28	23
vinegar	Ruth 2:14	252
wild honey	Matt. 3:4	*5*
wine	Jdgs. 19:19	247
Food, Spiritual		
Christ the bread of life	John 6:35, 51	*98*
figurative of doctrine	1 Cor. 3:1, 2	*164*
	Heb. 5:12–14	*218*
flesh and blood of Christ	John 6:53–58	*98*
Jews partook of	1 Cor. 10:3, 4	*169*
known to Jesus only	John 4:32	*95*
Foolish—*wanting in judgment; simple; absurd*		
builder on sand	Matt. 7:26	*9*
five virgins	Matt. 25:1–13	*29*
to be forsaken	Prov. 9:6	562
lusts	1 Tim. 6:9	*209*

	REFERENCE	PAGE
Fretting—*complaining; to be vexed or irritated*		
against God	Prov. 19:3	569
forbidden for evil doers	Ps. 37:1	508
	Prov. 24:19	573
God, by man	Ezek. 16:43	709

	REFERENCE	PAGE
Friend—*ally; one attached by love; esteem for another person*		
disciples called	John 15:14	109
genuine	Luke 10:30–35	71
of God	Ex. 33:11	84
	James 2:23	227
Jesus	Matt. 11:19	13
Joseph	John 19:38	114
of mammon	Luke 16:9	110
not to be forsaken	Prov. 27:10	575
qualities of	Prov. 17:17	568
treacherous	Ps. 41:9	511
value of	Prov. 18:24	569
wounded in house of	Zech. 13:6	798

Friends, False

	REFERENCE	PAGE
Ahithophel to David	2 Sam. 15:12	301
butler to Jos. eph	Gen. 40:23	39
David to Joab	1 Ki. 2:5, 6	315
David to Uriah	2 Sam. 11	296
Delilah to Samson	Jdgs. 16:1–20	243
disciples	Matt. 26:56, 58	32
Ephraimite's wife	Jdgs. 19:1–2	246
Joab to Amasa	2 Sam. 20:9, 10	308
Judas	Matt. 26:48, 49	32

Friendless—*forlorn; destitute of friends*

	REFERENCE	PAGE
David	Ps. 142:4	554
the prodigal son	Luke 15:16	78

Friendship—*esteem; amity; friendly attachment*

	REFERENCE	PAGE
ardent	2 Cor. 2:12, 13	177
covenant of	1 Sam. 20:16, 17	275
inseparable	2 Ki. 2:1, 2	345
of Jesus	John 11:5, 7	104
mutual esteem	Prov. 18:24	569
proved by Onesiphorus	2 Tim. 1:16–18	211
test of	John 15:14	109
treacherous	Matt. 26:47–50	32
of the world	James 4:4	228
worldly	2 Chr. 18:1–34	416

Friendship, Instances of

	REFERENCE	PAGE
Abraham and Lot	Gen. 14:14–16	12
Daniel and his three friends	Dan. 2:49	748
David and Abiathar	1 Sam. 22:23	278
David and Hiram	1 Ki. 5:1	319
David and Hushai	2 Sam. 15:32–37	302
David and Ittai	2 Sam. 15:19–21	301
David and Jonathan	1 Sam. 18:1–4	273
	1 Sam. 20	275
	1 Sam. 23:16–18	278
David and Nahash	2 Sam. 10:2	295
Jehu and Jehonadab	2 Ki. 10:15–27	355
Job and his three friends	Job 2:11–13	470
Joram and Ahaziah	2 Ki. 8:28, 29	353
Mary, Martha, and Lazarus	Luke 10:38–42	71
Marys and Joseph of Arimathaea	Matt. 27:55–61	34
Paul and nephew	Acts 23:16	143
Paul, Priscilla and Aquila	Rom. 16:3, 4	162
Paul, Timothy, and Epaphroditus	Phil. 2:19, 20 22, 25	196
Ruth and Naomi	Ruth 1:16, 17	251
Samuel and Saul	1 Sam. 15:35	270

	REFERENCE	PAGE
Frogs—*small tail-less amphibious webfooted animals*		
Egypt smitten with	Ex. 8:1–15	57
figurative of unclean spirits	Rev. 16:13	253

	REFERENCE	PAGE
Frontlets—*a band worn on forehead*		
scriptures written on parchments in	Ex. 13:14–16	63
	Deut. 11:13–21	178
worn by Israelites	Deut. 6:8	173

	REFERENCE	PAGE
Frost—*crystals of ice formed from atmospheric water vapor*		
breath of God	Job 37:10	490
destroyed tree	Ps. 78:47	527
at night	Gen. 31:40	30

	REFERENCE	PAGE
Frowardness—*disobedience; perverseness*		
abominable to God	Prov. 3:32	559
of tongue	Prov. 10:31	563

	REFERENCE	PAGE
Frugality—*strict economy; wise and sparing use*		
of Egyptians against famine	Gen. 41:48, 49 53, 54	41
Jesus encouraged	John 6:11–13	97

	REFERENCE	PAGE
Fruit—*edible product of plant growth*		
for repentance	Matt. 3:8	5
of the righteous	Prov. 11:30	564
of the spirit	Gal. 5:22, 23	188
tree known by	Matt. 12:33	15

Fruit Trees

	REFERENCE	PAGE
preserved by law	Deut. 20:19, 20	186

	REFERENCE	PAGE
Fruitfulness—*fertileness; productiveness*		
faithful and	Deut. 28:4	192
given by God	Acts 14:17	133
in good works	Col. 1:10	198
means of	2 Pet. 1:5–11	233
and prayer	James 5:17, 18	229
source of	John 15:5, 6	109
varied	Matt. 13:23	16
of wife	Ps. 128:3	550

	REFERENCE	PAGE
Fruitless—*barren; without fruit*		
branches cut off	John 15:1–6	109
Christians not to be	Titus 3:14	214
fig tree blighted	Matt. 21:19	25
Israel	Hosea 10:1	765
no fellowship with unfruitful works	Eph. 5:11	192
toil of apostles	John 21:3	115
trees cut down	Matt. 3:10	5
understanding	1 Cor. 14:14	173

	REFERENCE	PAGE
Frying Pan—*shallow pan with long handle*		
use of	Lev. 7:9	98

	REFERENCE	PAGE
Fuel—*material to feed a fire*		
cakes of dung	Ezek. 4:15	699
coal	John 18:18	112
figurative of Israel	Ezek. 21:32	716
for temple	Neh. 10:34	457

	REFERENCE	PAGE
Fugitives—*those who flee*		
Absalom	2 Sam. 13:34–38	299
David	1 Sam. 21:10	277
Moses	Ex. 2:15	52
Onesimus	Philem. 1:15, 16	215
from servitude	Deut. 23:15, 16	189
Shimei's servants	1 Ki. 2:39	317

	REFERENCE	PAGE
Full—*ample; complete*		
of bloody crimes	Ezek. 7:23	702
body, of light	Matt. 6:22	8
of burnt offerings	Isa. 1:11	590
of deadly poison	James 3:8	228

	REFERENCE	PAGE
of dry bones	Ezek. 37:1, 2	732
of eyes	Rev. 4:6	245
of faith	Acts 6:5	122
of good works	Acts 9:36	127
of grace and truth	John 1:14	91
of Holy Ghost	Luke 1:15	56
	Luke 4:1	61
	Acts 6:3	122
	Acts 7:55, 59	124
	Acts 11:22, 24	129
joy may be	1 John 1:4	236
of knowledge	Isa. 11:9	598
woe to those that are	Luke 6:25	64

	REFERENCE	PAGE
Fuller—*one who bleaches cloth*		
in description of transfiguration	Mark 9:3	39
figurative of Lord's messenger	Mal. 3:2	801
fullre's field	2 Ki. 18:17	364
	Isa. 7:3	594

	REFERENCE	PAGE
Funeral—*rites and ceremonies preceding and accompanying burial*		
joyful	Luke 7:11–17	65

	REFERENCE	PAGE
Furlong—*one eighth of a mile*		
a measure	John 6:19	97

	REFERENCE	PAGE
Furnace—*structure or apparatus in which heat is produced*		
of fire	Matt. 13:42	16
an oven	1 Ki. 8:51	325
for punishment	Dan. 3:6, 11	748
for refining gold	Prov. 17:3	568
symbol of bondage in Egypt	Deut. 4:20	170
symbol of trials and chastenings	Ezek. 22:18, 22	716

	REFERENCE	PAGE
Furniture—*movable household articles*		
arranged for Elisha	2 Ki. 4:8–11	347
camel's	Gen. 31:34	30
pleasant	Nahum 2:9	784
of the tabernacle	Ex. 31:7	82

	REFERENCE	PAGE
Fury—*wrath; anger*		
of a brother	Gen. 27:44	25
cup of Lord's	Isa. 51:17	627
of God	Jer. 4:4	641
	Ezek. 20:8	713

	REFERENCE	PAGE
Future—*the time yet to come*		
ignorance of	Luke 19:41–44	83
piety in the	Luke 9:61, 62	70
planning for	James 4:13–15	228
presuming	Luke 12:16–20	74
uncertainty of	Prov. 27:1	574

G

Gaal

	REFERENCE	PAGE
son of Ebed	Jdgs. 9:26	237

Gaash—*quaking*

	REFERENCE	PAGE
brooks of	2 Sam. 23:30	312
hill of Ephraim	Jdgs. 2:9	228
Joshua buried near	Josh. 24:30	226

Gaba—*hill* (also Geba)

	REFERENCE	PAGE
city of Benjamin	Josh. 18:21, 24	219
enemy driven from	2 Sam. 5:25	292
given to Levites	Josh. 21:13, 17	222

Gabbai—*tax gatherer*

	REFERENCE	PAGE
postexilic Benjamite	Neh. 11:7, 8	457

Gabbatha—*pavement*

	REFERENCE	PAGE
Pilate's judgment at	John 19:13	113

Geuel—*majesty of God*
Gadite spy . . . . Num.
      13:15, 16   138

Gezer
allotted to Ephraim . Josh. 16:3, 4   217
Canaanite city . . : . . . Josh. 10:33   211
given to Levites . . . . . Josh. 21:21   222
held by Canaanites . . 1 Ki. 9:16   326

Ghost—*a disembodied spirit; soul*
give up . . . . Gen. 35:29   34
                 Mark 15:37   *133*

Giah
town near Gibeon . . . 2 Sam. 2:24   288

Giants—*any person of great size*
before the flood . . . . . Gen. 6:4   5
destroyed by
   Joshua . . . . Josh. 11:21   212
of Gath, Gaza, and
   Ashdod spared . . . . Josh. 11:22   212
                 Josh. 14:12   215
lived in Canaan . . . . . Deut. 2:10–20   167
many slain . . . . : 2 Sam.
      21:15–22   309
men of great stature . Num.
      13:32, 33   139
men of violence . . . . . Gen. 6:4, 13   5
six-fingered . . . . 2 Sam. 21:20   309
slain by David . . . . . . 1 Sam.
      17:31–58   272
tribe near Jordan . . . Deut. 3:11   169

Gibbar
head of family . . . . . . Ezra 2:20   437

Gibbethon—*mound; height*
assigned to Levites . . Josh. 21:20, 23   222
held by Philistines . . 1 Ki. 16:15, 17   335
Nadab slain at . . . . . . 1 Ki. 15:25–27   334
town of Dan . . . . Josh. 19:44   220

Gibeah—*hill*
"hill of ark" . . . . 2 Sam. 6:3   292
town of Judah . . . . . . Josh. 15:57   217
town near
   Jerusalem . . . . Josh. 18:28   219
                 Jdgs. 19:14   247
                 Jdgs. 19:22, 23   247
                 Jdgs. 20:31–48   249
                 1 Sam. 11:4   264
                 1 Sam. 15:34   270

Gibeath—*probably same as town of Judah,*
   above

Gibeon—*hill city*
Amasa slain at . . . . . . 2 Sam.
      20:8, 10   275
assigned to priests . . . Josh. 21:17   222
city in Benjamin . . . . Josh. 18:25   219
Joab slain at . . . . 1 Ki. 2:28–34   316
pool of . . . . 2 Sam. 2:13   298
                 Jer. 41:12   678
Solomon's dream . . . . 1 Ki. 3:5–15   317
tabernacle of
   Moses at . . . . 1 Chr. 16:39   391
                 2 Chr. 1:1–5   403

Gibeonites—*inhabitants of Gibeon*
deceived Joshua . . . . Josh. 9:3–15   209
laborers . . . . Josh. 9:23–27   210
mistreated by Saul . . 2 Sam. 21:1–5   308
rescued . . . . Josh. 10:1–43   210

Giblites—*people of Gebal*
stone-squarers and
   skilled workmen . . . Josh. 13:5   213
                 1 Ki. 5:18   320

Giddalti—*magnify*
son of Heman . . . . . . 1 Chr. 25:4   397

Giddel—*very great*
head of family of
   Solomon's servants . Ezra 2:55, 56   438
                 Neh. 7:57, 58   453
head of Nethinim
   family . . . . Ezra 2:43, 47   438
                 Neh. 7:46, 49   453

Gideon—*one who cuts down*
army reduced . . . . . . Jdgs. 7:2–7   233
called as deliverer . . . Jdgs. 6:14–40   232
caused Israel to sin . . Jdgs. 8:27   235
died . . . . Jdgs. 8:32   235
father of 71 sons . . . . Jdgs. 8:30, 31   235
made ephod of spoil . . Jdgs. 8:24–27   235
son of Joash . . . . Jdgs. 6:11   232
strategy of . . . . Jdgs. 7:15–23   234
subdued Midianites . Jdgs. 7:19–25   234

Gideoni—*my hewer*
father of Abidan . . . . Num. 1:11   123

Gidom
town of Benjamin . . . Jdgs. 20:12, 45   248

Gier-eagle
unclean bird . . . . Lev. 11:18   102

Gifts—*that which is given; natural endow-*
   ments
as appeasement . . . . . Gen. 20:14–16   17
at betrothal . . . . Gen. 24:50–53   21
between friends . . . . . 1 Ki. 10:10, 13   327
as bribes, forbidden . Ex. 23:8   72
to confirm covenants . Gen. 21:27–32   18
at marriage . . . . Est. 2:15–18   463
to a prophet for aid . . 1 Sam. 9:7, 8   262
in reciprocation . . . . . 1 Sam.
      30:26–31   286
for relief . . . . Luke 10:35   *71*
for reparation . . . . . . Gen. 34:11, 12   33
as rewards . . . . Dan. 5:7   751
as tokens of
   affections . . . . Est. 9:22   468

Gifts from God
ability to earn . . . . . . Deut. 8:18   175
bread from heaven . . John 6:51   *98*
crown of life . . . . Rev. 2:10   *244*
eternal life . . . . John 10:28   *103*
everlasting name . . . Isa. 56:4, 5   630
every blessing . . . . . . James 1:17   *226*
food . . . . Ps. 136:25   552
Holy Spirit . . . . Luke 11:13   *72*
living water . . . . John 4:14   *94*
new heart . . . . Ezek. 11:19   704
of peace . . . . John 14:27   *109*
power over evil . . . . . Luke 10:19   *71*
rains and seasons . . . . Deut. 11:14   178
sleep . . . . Ps. 127:2   550
spiritual knowledge . . Jer. 24:7   660
spiritual rest . . . . Matt. 11:28   *14*
vegetation, fruit . . . . Gen. 1:29   2

Gifts, Spiritual
ability to speak well . Isa. 50:4   626
divine wisdom . . . . . . James 1:5   *226*
from God alone . . . . . John 3:27   *94*
for good of others . . . Rom. 12:6–8   *159*
motivated by love . . . 1 Cor. 13:1–13   *172*
understanding . . . . . . Job 32:8   487
variety of . . . . Matt. 25:15   *29*

Gihon—*bursting forth*
river of Eden . . . . . . Gen. 2:10, 13   2
spring near Jerusalem . 1 Ki. 1:33–45   314
                 2 Chr. 32:30   431
                 2 Chr. 33:14   432

Gilalai
Levite musician . . . . . Neh. 12:36   459

Gilboa
cursed . . . . 2 Sam. 1:21   287
Jonathan and his
   brothers slain at . . . 1 Sam. 31:1, 2   286
                 2 Sam. 1:4   287
mountain near
   Jezreel . . . . 1 Sam. 28:4   283
Saul slain at . . . . 1 Sam. 31:1–7   286

Gilead—*hard; firm (?)*
1. Father of
   Jephthah . . . . Jdgs. 11:1   239
2. A Gadite . . . . 1 Chr. 5:11, 14   378
3. Land east of
   Jordan . . . . Gen. 31:21, 25   29
   balm in . . . . Jer. 8:22   646
   David's refuge . . . . 2 Sam.
      17:26–29   304
   given to Reuben,
   Gad, and
   Manasseh . . . . Deut. 3:12–17   169
                 Josh. 12:2–6   213
   Ishbosheth's
   claim to . . . . 2 Sam. 2:8, 9   288
   land of spices . . . . : Gen. 37:25   36
4. A Manassite . . . . . Num. 26:29   153

Gilgal—*a circle of stone*
1. Town near
   Bethel . . . . 2 Ki. 2:1   345
   home of Elijah . . . . 2 Ki. 4:38   348
2. Town near
   Jericho . . . . Deut. 11:30   178
   David's welcome
   at . . . . 2 Sam.
      19:15, 40   306
   Joshua camped at . Josh. 4:19, 20   204
   Passover kept at . . Josh. 5:10   205
   Saul made king at . 1 Sam. 10:1–25   263
   Saul's rejection at . 1 Sam.
      15:20–23   269
      1 Sam. 16:14   270
   Saul's sacrifices at . 1 Sam. 13:8, 9   266
3. Town near
   Shechem . . . . Josh. 12:23   213
   idolatry of . . . . Hosea 4:15   762
                 Hosea 9:15   765
                 Amos 4:4, 5   772

Giloh
city of Judah . . . . Josh. 15:51   217

Gilonite
inhabitants of
   Gilo . . . . 2 Sam. 15:12   301

Gimzo
village in Judah . . . . . 2 Chr. 28:18   426

Gin—*a trap for game; a snare*
used for catching
   beasts . . . . Job 18:9   479
                 Amos 3:5   772

Ginath
father of Tibni . . . . . . 1 Ki. 16:22   335

Ginnetho
family of priests . . . . Neh. 12:16   458
priest . . . . Neh. 10:6   456

Girdle—*a belt used for girding a loose*
   garment around waist
Jesus used towel
   as . . . . John 13:2, 4   107
symbol of truth . . . . . Eph. 6:14   *193*
worn by John . . . . . . Matt. 3:4   *5*
worn by priests . . . . . Ex. 28:39   78

	REFERENCE	PAGE
Girgashites		
descendants of		
Canaan	Gen. 10:15, 16	8
lived in land of		
Canaan	Deut. 7:1	173
	Josh. 3:10	203
Girl—*a young female*		
playing in streets	Zech. 8:5	795
sold for wine	Joel 3:3	769
Gispa		
postexilic overseer	Neh. 11:21	458
Gittah-hepher—(same as Gath-hepher)		
Gittaim—*two winepresses*		
refuge	2 Sam. 4:3	290
town of Benjamin	Neh. 11:33	458
Gittites—*people of Gath*		
followed David	2 Sam. 15:18–23	301
Gittith		
musical term	Ps. 8	496
Giving to God		
as one is able	Deut. 16:17	183
cheerfully	2 Cor. 8:11, 12	180
example of	2 Chr. 31:5	429
Nahshon	Num. 7:12–17	131
poor widow	Mark 12:41–44	50
regularly	1 Cor. 16:2	175
the tithe	Mal. 3:10	801
Gizonite		
Hashem called	1 Chr. 11:34	386
Gladness—*joyfulness; happiness*		
in the first church	Acts 2:46	119
in Lord's service	2 Chr. 30:21	429
for reward in		
heaven	Matt. 5:11, 12	6
Glass—*mirror*		
a sea of	Rev. 4:6	245
see through, darkly	1 Cor. 13:12	172
taken away	Isa. 3:18–23	592
Gleaning—*picking up, gathering that which remains after a crop is reaped*		
Gideon's proverb	Jdgs. 8:2	234
by Ruth	Ruth 2:5, 7	252
special privilege of		
the poor	Lev. 19:9, 10	112
	Deut. 24:19, 21	190
Glede—*bird of prey*		
unclean	Deut. 14:12, 13	181
Glorified—*praised; elevated in honor*		
Jesus	Acts 3:13	119
prayer of Jesus	John 17:1	111
in the resurrection	Rom. 8:17	155
Glorifying God		
by bearing fruit	John 15:8	109
commanded	1 Chr. 16:28	390
	Ps. 22:23	502
in everything	1 Cor. 10:31	170
by faith, obedience	Acts 4:21	120
in full consecration	1 Cor. 6:20	154
Gentiles, for mercy	Rom. 15:9	161
in good works	Matt. 5:16	121
for holiness	Ps. 99:9	536
for mercy and truth	Ps. 115:1	543
in our bodies	1 Cor. 6:20	167
by praise	Ps. 50:23	515

	REFERENCE	PAGE
punishment for not	Acts 12:23	130
by unity in church	Rom. 15:6	161
Glory—*adoration; praise; honor*		
in the cross	Gal. 6:14	189
from good deeds	John 15:8	109
of man	1 Pet. 1:24	230
of nature	Luke 12:27	74
not in men	1 Cor. 3:21	165
transforming	2 Cor. 3:18	178
in trials	2 Cor. 11:30	183
Glory of Christ		
before creation	John 17:5	111
in heaven	Rev. 5:12	246
at his second		
coming	Matt. 16:27	20
in incarnation	John 1:14	91
shared by believers	Matt. 19:28, 29	23
in transfiguration	Luke 9:28–36	69
Glory of God		
declared by nature	Ps. 19:1	501
filled tabernacle	Ex. 40:34	92
filled temple	1 Ki. 8:11	323
given to martyrs	Acts 7:55	124
at Jesus' birth	Luke 2:8–11	58
on Mt. Sinai	Ex. 24:9–17	74
opened to believers	2 Cor. 3:18	178
Glory of Man		
consumed by death	Ps. 49:17	514
in creation	Heb. 2:6–8	217
increased by trials	2 Cor. 4:16–18	178
lost by sin	Hosea 4:6, 7	762
restored in Christ	Luke 22:28–30	86
transient	1 Pet. 1:24	230
Gluttony—*excessive eating*		
examples of Israel	Num. 11:32, 33	137
Jesus accused of	Matt. 11:19	13
leads to poverty	Prov. 23:21	572
warning against	Prov. 23:1–3	572
Gnashing—*grinding together of teeth; sign of anguish* (See Teeth)		
Gnat—*small two-winged fly*		
blind guides strain		
at	Matt. 23:24	27
Goad—*a point set in the end of a stick*		
mental stimulus	Eccl. 12:11	585
to urge cattle	1 Sam. 13:21	266
as a weapon	Jdgs. 3:31	230
Goat—*a ruminant mammal having hollow horns*		
as food	Deut. 14:4	180
hair made into cloth	Ex. 25:4	74
as sacrifice	Lev. 1:10	93
skins of	Heb. 11:37	224
used figuratively	Matt. 25:33	30
Gob—*pit* (called Gezer)		
Jonathan slew		
Philistine at	2 Sam. 21:18–22	309
	1 Chr. 20:4	393
Goblet—*a drinking vessel with stem and no handle*		
navel like a round	Song 7:2	588
God—*the Supreme Being*		
account to	Rom. 14:12	160
alone is good	Luke 18:19	81
author of		
justification	Rom. 8:33	156

	REFERENCE	PAGE
author of peace	1 Cor. 14:33	173
in the beginning	John 1:1, 2	91
bounties of	Ps. 16:2, 3	499
	Ps. 72:7	523
	2 Cor. 4:15	178
	1 Tim. 1:14	207
called Almighty God	Gen. 17:1	13
called Deliverer	2 Sam. 22:2	309
called Eternal God	Deut. 33:27	200
called Everlasting		
God	Gen. 21:33	18
called Father of		
lights	James 1:17	226
called Fortress	2 Sam. 22:2	309
called God of		
heaven	Jonah 1:9	778
called God of hosts	Ps. 80:7	528
called God of Israel	Num. 16:9	142
called Heavenly		
Father	Matt. 6:26	8
called Holy Lord		
God	1 Sam. 6:20	260
called Holy One of		
Israel	Ps. 71:22	523
called I Am	Ex. 3:14	53
called Jehovah	Ex. 6:3	55
called Judge	Gen. 18:25	15
called King eternal	1 Tim. 1:17	207
called Living God	Deut. 5:26	172
called the Lord God	Ex. 34:6	84
called Lord of Hosts	Isa. 1:24	590
called Lord of		
sabaoth	James 5:4	229
called Mighty God	Isa. 9:6	596
called most high		
God	Gen. 14:18	11
came from Teman	Hab. 3:3	787
can do everything	Job 42:1, 2	493
	Jer. 32:17	669
	Luke 1:37	57
cannot be tempted	James 1:13	226
cannot lie	Heb. 6:18	219
cares for birds and		
animals	Ps. 147:9	556
	Matt. 6:26	8
creator	Gen. 1:1	1
creator of heaven		
and of earth	Gen. 1:1	1
	John 1:1–3	33
	Heb. 11:3	223
creator of man	Gen. 1:26	2
demands our love	Matt. 22:37	26
	Luke 10:27	71
demands our		
worship	Ex. 20:3–5	69
	Matt. 4:10	5
distributes sorrow	Job 21:17	481
does not pity wicked	Ezek. 7:3–9	701
eternity of	Ps. 90:1, 2	532
the father of all	Eph. 4:6	191
father of Christ	2 Cor. 1:3	176
forgives our sins	Eph. 4:32	192
forsook Jesus	Matt. 27:46	34
giver of food	Ps. 136:25	552
gives comfort	2 Cor. 1:3, 4	176
gives eternal life	Rom. 6:23	154
hears prayer	Jer. 29:12	665
holiness of	Lev. 19:2	111
humanity offspring		
of	Acts 17:29	137
immutability of	Heb. 1:12	216
infinity of	Ps. 139:7–12	553
inspired the scrip-		
tures	2 Tim. 3:16	212
is but one	1 Cor. 8:6	168
is a consuming fire	Heb. 12:29	225
is jealous	Nahum 1:2	783
is love	1 John 4:8	238
is not mocked	Gal. 6:7	189
is a spirit	John 4:24	94
judge of all	Heb. 12:23	225

	REFERENCE	PAGE
Guidance—*a leading; direction*		
into all truth	John 16:13	*110*
to the end of life	Ps. 48:14	513
out of uncertainties	Isa. 42:16	620
by spiritual light	Luke 1:79	*58*
in wisdom	Ps. 25:9	503
by wise counsel	Ps. 73:24	524
Guide—*to conduct; to direct in a way*		
divine	Ex. 13:20–22	63
human	Num. 10:29–32	136
spiritual	Acts 8:29–39	*125*
Guni		
Gadite	1 Chr. 5:15	379
son of Naphtali	Gen. 46:24	46
Gur—*dwelling; sojourning*		
Ahaziah died at	2 Ki. 9:27	354
Gur-baal—*dwelling of Baal*		
Arabians dwelt in	2 Chr. 26:7	424

H

	REFERENCE	PAGE
Haahashtari		
descendant of Judah	1 Chr. 4:5, 6	377
Habaiah—*Jehovah hath hidden*		
head of priestly family	Neh. 7:63, 64	453
	Ezra 2:61, 62	438
Habakkuk—*embrace*		
complaint of	Hab. 1:12–17	786
God's answer	Hab. 2:1–20	786
prayer of faith	Hab. 3:1–15	787
the prophet, burden	Hab. 1:1–4	785
Habaziniah		
a Rechabite	Jer. 35:3	672
Habergeon—*a breastplate*		
piece of armor	Neh. 4:16	450
Habit—*a spontaneous action or custom*		
of evil-doing	Jer. 13:23	651
	Jer. 22:21	658
of prayer	Acts 10:1, 2	*127*
of worship	Luke 4:16	*39*
Habor—*a river*		
region of Mesopotamia	2 Ki. 17:6	362
	2 Ki. 18:11	364
	1 Chr. 5:26	379
Hachaliah		
father of Nehemiah	Neh. 1:1	447
Hachilah—*dark*		
hiding place of David	1 Sam. 23:19	278
hills south of Jericho	1 Sam. 26:1–3	282
Hachmoni		
father of Jehiel	1 Chr. 27:32	400
Hadad		
Edomite king	Gen. 36:35, 36	35
	1 Chr. 1:46, 47	375
King of Pai	Gen. 36:39	35
	1 Chr. 1:50	375
prince of Edom	1 Ki. 11:14–22	328
son of Ishmael	Gen. 25:13–15	22
Hadadezer—(also Hadarezer)		
defeated by David	2 Sam. 10:6–19	295
King of Zobah	2 Sam. 8:3–13	294

	REFERENCE	PAGE
Hadadrimmon		
town in Jezreel	Zech. 12:11	798
Hadashah		
town of Judah	Josh. 15:37	216
Hadassah—*Myrtle*		
Jewish name for Esther	Est. 2:7	462
Hadattah		
town of Judah	Josh. 15:25	216
Hades—(See Hell)		
Hadid		
town of Benjamin	Neh. 11:31, 34	458
Hadlai		
an Ephraimite	2 Chr. 28:12	426
Hadoram		
officer of Rehoboam	1 Ki. 4:6	318
(probably Adoniram)	1 Ki. 12:18	330
	2 Chr. 10:18	411
son of Joktan	Gen. 10:26, 27	9
son of Tou	1 Chr. 18:9, 10	392
Hadrach		
place near Damascus	Zech. 9:1	796
Hagab—*grasshopper*		
founder, family of Nethinim	Ezra 2:43, 46	438
Hagaba—*grasshopper*		
founder, family of Nethinim	Ezra 2:43, 45	438
	Neh. 7:46, 48	453
Hagar—*flight*		
allegory of	Gal. 4:22, 26	*187*
comforted by angel	Gen. 16:10, 11	13
mother of Ishmael	Gen. 16:1, 11	13
sent away	Gen. 21:14	17
Hagarenes—*Hagarites*		
hostile tribe	1 Chr. 5:10	378
servant of David	1 Chr. 27:31	400
Haggai—*festal*		
encouraged the people	Haggai 2:1–10	790
the prophet	Ezra 5:1	440
reproved the people	Haggai 1:2–12	790
Haggeri		
father of one of David's heroes	1 Chr. 11:38	386
Haggi—*my feast*		
ancestral head of clan	Num. 26:15	153
son of Gad	Gen. 46:16	46
Haggiah—*feast of Jehovah*		
a Merarite Levite	1 Chr. 6:30	380
Haggith—*festive*		
mother of Adonijah	1 Ki. 1:5	314
wife of David	2 Sam. 3:4	289
Hai—(See Ai)		
Hail—*frozen rain*		
against Israel's foes	Josh. 10:11	210
	Haggai 2:17	791
given for rain	Ps. 105:32	539
plague of Egyptians	Ex. 9:22–25	59
vines destroyed by	Ps. 78:47	527

	REFERENCE	PAGE
Hail—*a greeting; salutation*		
Gabriel to Mary	Luke 1:26–28	*57*
Judas to Christ	Matt. 26:47–49	*32*
soldiers to Christ	Matt. 27:27–29	*33*
Hair(s)—*filaments that grow from the skin of a mammal*		
Absalom's	2 Sam. 14:25, 26	300
braided by women	1 Tim. 2:9	*207*
	1 Pet. 3:3	*231*
gray	1 Sam. 12:2	264
of king	Dan. 4:33	751
long, shame to man	1 Cor. 11:14	*170*
long, woman's glory	1 Cor. 11:15	*170*
Nazarite vow concerning	Num. 6:5	130
	Jdgs. 16:17	244
oil on	Matt. 6:17	*8*
pulled out	Neh. 13:25	461
of saints	Matt. 10:30	*12*
stands up	Job 4:15	471
Hakkatan—*little one; the smallest*		
father of Johanan	Ezra 8:12	443
Hakkoz (also Koz)—*the thorn(?)*		
ancestral head of priestly family	Ezra 2:61, 62	438
	Neh. 7:63, 64	453
descendant of Aaron	1 Chr. 24:1, 10	396
Hakupha		
founder of family of Nethinim	Ezra 2:43, 51	438
	Neh. 7:53	453
Halah		
district of Mesopotamia	2 Ki. 17:6	362
Halak—*the smooth mountain*		
mountain near Seir	Josh. 11:17	212
Halfheartedness—*wanting in sincerity, interest*		
of Amaziah	2 Chr. 25:1, 2	423
of Israelites	2 Chr. 20:33	419
of Jehu	2 Ki. 10:31	356
of Joash	2 Ki. 13:18, 19	358
of Judah	Jer. 3:10	640
of Laodiceans	Rev. 3:16	245
of Northern Kingdom	Hosea 10:1, 2	765
of Solomon	1 Ki. 11:6	328
Halhul		
city of Judah	Josh. 15:58	217
Hali		
village of Asher	Josh. 19:25	220
Hallelujah—(See Alleluia)		
Halohesh—*the speaker of charms*		
covenant signer	Neh. 10:1, 24	456
father of Shallum	Neh. 3:12	449
Ham—*hot(?)*		
Egypt, poetical use	Ps. 78:51	527
place east of Jordan	Gen. 14:5	11
son of Noah	Gen. 5:32	5
	Gen. 9:22–27	8
	Gen. 10:6	8
	1 Chr. 4:39, 40	378
Haman		
angered at Mordecai	Est. 3:5	463
hanged	Est. 7:10	466

	REFERENCE	PAGE
demonstrated by		
throwing stones and		
dirt................2 Sam. 16:13		270
divine............Prov. 6:16–19		560
of Esau for Jacob...Gen. 27:41		25
forbidden.........Lev. 19:17		112
of Herodias for John.Matt. 14:3–12		17
of Jews for Christ....Luke 19:12–14		82
of Jews for Paul.....Acts 23:12		143
of Joseph's brothers.Gen. 37:4		36
of light............John 3:20		93
murderous in spirit..1 John 3:15		238
repay with good....Matt. 5:44		7
sign of darkness.....1 John 2:9		236
of the world for		
Christians........Luke 21:17		85
John 15:18, 19		109

Hattil—*tottering (?)*
ancestral head of
family of Solomon's
servants.........Neh. 7:57, 59 — 453

Hattush
chief of priests.....Neh. 12:1, 2 — 458
descendant of
David............Ezra 8:2 — 443
priest covenant-
signer...........Neh. 10:1, 4 — 456
son of Hashabniah..Neh. 3:10 — 449
son of Shemaiah....1 Chr. 3:22 — 377

Haughtiness—*disdainfulness; arrogance*
condemned........Jer. 48:29 — 683
cruel.............Est. 3:1–6 — 463
in Zion...........Isa. 3:16–26 — 592

Haunt—*a place frequently visited*
place of resort.....1 Sam. 23:22 — 279

Hauran—*hollow land*
region south of
Damascus........Ezek. 47:16 — 743

Haven—*shelter; place of anchorage for ships*
a harbor..........Gen. 49:13 — 49

Havilah
a region, possibly
Arabian..........Gen. 2:11 — 2
son of Cush.......1 Chr. 1:9 — 374
son of Joktan......Gen. 10:29 — 9

Havoth-jair—*villages of Jair*
belonged to Jair....Jdgs. 10:4 — 238
taken by Jair......Num. 32:41 — 161
towns in Bashan....Deut. 3:4, 14 — 169

Hawk—*a bird of prey*
unclean bird.......Lev. 11:13, 16 — 102

Hazael—*whom God beholds*
Elisha's prediction
concerning........2 Ki. 8:7–15 — 352
King of Syria......1 Ki. 19:15 — 339
oppressed Israel....2 Ki. 10:32, 33 — 356
slew Benhadad.....2 Ki. 8:7–15 — 352

Hazaiah—*Jehovah hath seen*
descendant of Judah.Neh. 11:5 — 457

Hazar-addar
place in Canaan.....Num. 34:4 — 163

Hazar-enan
northeast border of
Israel............Num. 34:9 — 163
Ezek. 47:17 — 744

Hazar-gaddah
town in Judah......Josh. 15:21, 27 — 216

	REFERENCE	PAGE
Hazar-hatticon		
town of Hauran.....Ezek. 47:16		743

Hazarmaveth
descendants of
Joktan............Gen. 10:26 — 9
1 Chr. 1:20 — 374

Hazar-shual
given to Simeon.....Josh. 19:1, 3 — 219
town of Judah......Josh. 15:21, 28 — 216

Hazar-susah—*village of horses*
Simeonite village....Josh. 19:1, 5 — 219

Hazelelponi
daughter of Etam...1 Chr. 4:3 — 377

Hazerim—*villages*
region in Canaan....Deut. 2:23 — 168

Hazeroth
camp of Israel......Num. 33:17 — 161
sedition of Miriam
and Aaron at......Num. 11:35 — 138
Num. 12:1–16 — 138

Hazezon-tamar—(also Hazazon-Tamar)
probably same as
Engedi............Gen. 14:7 — 11

Haziel—*vision of God*
a Levite...........1 Chr. 23:9 — 396

Hazo
son of Nahor......Gen. 22:22, 23 — 19

Hazor—*enclosure*
Arabian desert......Jer. 49:28–33 — 685
city of Canaan.....Josh. 11:1–13 — 212
Josh. 12:7, 19 — 213
Josh. 19:32, 36 — 220
2 Ki. 15:29 — 361
town of Benjamin...Neh. 11:31, 33 — 458
town of Judah......Josh. 15:21, 25 — 216

Head—*the part of the body containing the brain and sensory organs; a leader or principal person*
anointed..........Matt. 6:17 — 8
Christ, of church....Col. 1:18 — 199
Christ smote on.....Matt. 27:30 — 33
coals of fire upon....Rom. 12:20 — 159
hallowed..........Num. 6:11 — 130
of John...........Matt. 14:6–11 — 17
not to swear by.....Matt. 5:36 — 7
shaved............Num. 6:9 — 130
Sisera's...........Jdgs. 5:26 — 231
of woman
uncovered.......1 Cor. 11:5 — 170
of woman is man....1 Cor. 11:3 — 170
wounded..........Mark 12:4 — 49

Headband—*a band worn on the head*
article of female
attire............Isa. 3:20 — 592

Heads, Shaven
of Israel..........Amos 8:10 — 775
of Moab..........Isa. 15:2 — 600
of Philistines.......Jer. 47:5 — 683
sign of mourning....Isa. 22:12 — 604
of Tyre...........Ezek. 27:31 — 722

Healing—*restoring to health, soundness*
in answer to
prayer...........James 5:14, 15 — 229
by the apostles.....Acts 5:16 — 121
gift of God........1 Cor. 12:9 — 171
Jesus' ministry of...Matt. 11:5 — 13
Luke 9:6 — 69

	REFERENCE	PAGE
Lord's promise to		
heal.............Ex. 23:25		73
2 Ki. 20:5		367
by Paul..........Acts 19:11, 12		138
by Peter.........Acts 3:6, 7		119
Acts 9:33, 34		127
power given to the		
apostles.........Matt. 10:1		12
Mark 3:13–15		38

Healing, Spiritual
in Christ..........Isa. 53:5 — 628
Luke 4:18 — 61
man's greatest need..Ps. 41:4 — 511
promise of.........Jer. 30:17 — 666
promised to penitent.Jer. 3:22 — 641

Health—*freedom from physical disease*
brotherly concern
about............3 John 1:2 — 240
diet conducive to....Dan. 1:10–16 — 746
food essential to....Acts 27:34 — 148
in God's word......Prov. 4:20–22 — 559
promised to the
obedient.........Ex. 15:26 — 65
Deut. 7:15 — 174
temperance
promotes........Jer. 35:5–8 — 672
wine recommended
for.............1 Tim. 5:23 — 209

Hearer (s)—*those who listen*
disobedient........Ezek. 33:30–32 — 728
Matt. 7:26–27 — 9
divided...........John 10:19–21 — 103
good and bad......Acts 17:32, 34 — 137
Herod............Mark 6:20 — 41
investigating.......Acts 17:11 — 136
and justification....Rom. 2:13 — 151
Mary............Luke 10:38–42 — 71
spellbound........John 7:45, 46 — 100
unwilling..........2 Tim. 4:3, 4 — 212
various...........Matt. 13:3–8 — 15
of the word........James 1:22, 23 — 227

Hearing—*capacity to hear*
precedes believing...Rom. 10:17 — 158
without
understanding.....Matt. 13:13 — 16

Heart—*central organ of the vascular system; seat of affections, feelings, emotions, actions*
applied to wisdom...Ps. 90:12 — 533
as man thinketh in
his.............Prov. 23:7 — 572
Matt. 9:4 — 11
backsliding........Prov. 14:14 — 565
bitter.............Ezek. 27:31 — 722
broken............Ps. 34:18 — 507
burning...........Luke 24:32 — 90
can be stolen......2 Sam. 15:6 — 301
circumcised.......Rom. 2:29 — 151
clean............Ps. 51:10 — 515
communing........Ps. 4:4 — 495
cries out for God....Ps. 84:2 — 530
cut by God's word..Acts 5:29, 33 — 122
deceitful..........Jer. 17:9 — 654
deceived..........Isa. 44:20 — 622
desolate..........Ps. 143:4 — 554
devises man's way..Prov. 16:9 — 567
directed..........2 Thess. 3:5 — 205
divided...........Hosea 10:2 — 765
enlarged..........Ps. 119:32 — 545
errs in unbelief.....Heb. 3:10, 12 — 217
established........Heb. 13:9 — 225
failing............Luke 21:26 — 85
in faith...........Prov. 3:5 — 558
faithful...........Neh. 9:8 — 455
fat...............Isa. 6:10 — 594
fixed.............Ps. 108:1 — 541

	REFERENCE	PAGE
Hoshama—*Jehovah hath heard*		
son of Jeconiah	1 Chr. 3:17, 18	377
Hoshea—*salvation* (Also Oshea)		
covenant-signer	Neh. 10:1, 23	456
Israel's last king	2 Ki. 15:30	361
name of Joshua	Num. 13:8, 16	138
son of Azaziah	1 Chr. 27:20	400
Hospitality—*generous, kind treatment*		
of Abimelech	Gen. 20:14, 15	17
Christian duty	Rom. 12:13	*159*
of David	2 Sam. 9:7, 13	295
to enemies	Rom. 12:20	*159*
forbidden by		
Diotrephes	3 John 1:9, 10	*240*
of Isaac	Gen. 26:26–31	24
of Jethro	Ex. 2:16, 20	52
of Joseph	Gen. 43:30–34	43
joyful	Luke 19:5, 6	*82*
of Laban	Gen. 24:29–33	21
of Lydia	Acts 16:14, 15	*134*
of Melchizedek	Gen. 14:18–20	12
odious	Acts 17:4–9	*136*
of pagans, to Paul	Acts 28:1, 2	*148*
of Pharaoh to Jacob	Gen. 45:16–20	45
to the poor	Luke 14:13	*76*
refused Jesus	Luke 9:51–53	*70*
required of bishops	1 Tim. 3:2	207
of the Shunammite	2 Ki. 4:8	347
sign of goodness	1 Tim. 5:10	208
of sons of Heth	Gen. 23:5, 6	19
to strangers	Heb. 13:2	225
treacherous	Luke 11:53, 54	*73*
ungrudging	1 Pet. 4:9	*232*
wanting	Luke 7:37–46	*66*
Host(s)—*any great multitude, assembly, throng*		
an army	Gen. 21:22	18
heavenly	Luke 2:13	*58*
of heaven, group of		
angels	1 Ki. 22:19	343
of heaven, the		
stars	Deut. 4:19	170
Lord of	Ps. 46:7	513
Hostage—*a person held as a pledge*		
captive for pledge	2 Chr. 25:24	424
Hotham—*seal*		
an Asherite	1 Chr. 7:30, 32	382
father of two of		
David's heroes	1 Chr. 11:26, 44	386
(called Hothan)		
Hothir		
son of Heman	1 Chr. 25:4	397
Hour—*fixed space of time; set, appointed time*		
a definite time	Dan. 3:6, 15	748
divisions of day	Acts 2:15	*118*
eleventh	Matt. 20:6	*23*
ninth	Mark 15:33	*54*
of prayer	Acts 3:1	*119*
sixth	Matt. 27:45	*34*
tenth	John 1:39	*92*
third	Matt. 20:3	*23*
House—*place of abode; edifice*		
ceiled	Haggai 1:4	790
church called	1 Tim. 3:15	208
of David	Luke 2:4	*58*
divided	Mark 3:25	*38*
earthly	2 Cor. 5:1	*178*
a family	Ex. 2:1	51
Father's	John 14:1, 2	*108*
figurative of body	2 Cor. 5:1, 2	*178*
fireplace in	Jer. 36:22	673
of ivory	1 Ki. 22:39	343

	REFERENCE	PAGE
law respecting sale		
of	Lev. 25:29–33	118
mortgaged	Neh. 5:3	450
painted red	Jer. 22:14	658
place of residence	Gen. 19:2, 3	15
prohibited to		
Rechabites	Jer. 35:5–10	672
provide for own	1 Tim. 5:8	208
tapestries in	Est. 1:5, 6	465
on town wall	Josh. 2:15	203
upon a rock	Matt. 7:24, 25	*9*
upon the sand	Matt. 7:26, 27	*9*
House of God		
attendance upon	Deut. 12:5	178
church called	1 Tim. 3:15	208
love for	1 Chr. 29:3	401
manner of worship		
in	Eccl. 5:1	581
place of prayer	Matt. 21:13	*24*
Hukkok—*appointed; decreed*		
place on boundary		
line of Naphtali	Josh. 19:32, 34	220
Hukok—See Helkath		
Hul		
son of Aram	Gen. 10:23	9
Huldah—*weasel* (?)		
foretold destruction		
of Jerusalem	2 Ki. 22:14–20	369
	2 Chr. 34:14–29	433
Humaneness—*compassion; benevolence; sympathy*		
in parable of Jesus	Matt. 18:12	*21*
through precaution	Deut. 22:8	187
toward animals	Ex. 23:5	72
Humanitarianism—*regard for interests of mankind*		
demanded of		
Christian brethren	Eph. 4:32	*192*
	1 Pet. 3:8	*231*
urged by Jesus	Luke 10:30–37	*71*
urged by Paul	Col. 3:14	*200*
Humiliation—*mortification; state of being humiliated*		
confessed by Ezra	Ezra 9:1–10	444
of David's servants	2 Sam. 10:4–5	295
of Job	Job 2:7, 8	470
use of	2 Cor. 12:6–10	*183*
Humility—*deference; courtesy; freedom from pride and arrogance*		
in adversity	2 Chr. 33:11–13	432
afflictions produce	Lev. 26:41	121
Ahab saved by	1 Ki. 21:28, 29	342
before honor	Prov. 18:12	569
benefits of	Luke 18:13, 14	*81*
of the centurion	Matt. 8:8	*10*
childlike	Jer. 1:5–10	638
Christ, our example	Phil. 2:5–8	*195*
divine command	James 4:10	*228*
essential in prayer	2 Chr. 7:14	408
exalted by God	Luke 14:11	*77*
excellency of	Prov. 16:19	567
of Gideon	Jdgs. 6:13–15	232
of Hezekiah	2 Chr. 32:26	431
impulsive	Luke 5:8	*62*
intellectual	Ps. 131:1, 2	550
of Jeremiah	Jer. 1:4–7	638
of Jesus	John 13:3–16	*107*
of Job	Job 42:1–6	493
of John the Baptist	Luke 3:15, 16	*60*
of Josiah	2 Chr. 34:1, 27	433
leads to riches,		
honor	Prov. 22:4	571

	REFERENCE	PAGE
of Manasseh	2 Chr. 33:11–13	432
manifested in		
prayer	Gen. 32:9, 10	**31**
ministerial	1 Cor. 3:4–7	*164*
of Paul and		
Barnabas	Acts 14:11–15	*132*
of Peter	Acts 10:25, 26	*128*
public	Mark 10:17	*47*
required by the Lord	Micah 6:8	782
royal	1 Ki. 3:6–14	317
of Saul	1 Sam. 9:21	262
sign of greatness	Matt. 18:4	*21*
in social life	Luke 14:8–10	*77*
of Solomon	1 Ki. 3:6, 7	317
suitable	Luke 15:17–20	*77*
teachable	Luke 10:39	*72*
in use of gifts	Rom. 12:3–8	*159*
Humtah		
city of Judah	Josh. 15:54	217
Hunger—*craving for food; weakness from lack of food; any strong desire*		
caused murmuring	Ex. 16:2, 3	66
from fasting	Matt. 4:1, 2	*5*
impatience from	Gen. 25:29–34	23
of Jesus	Mark 11:11, 12	*48*
to kill with	Rev. 6:8	*246*
lawful to appease on		
the Sabbath	Matt. 12:1–8	*14*
	Mark 2:23–27	*37*
none in heaven	Rev. 7:14–17	*247*
of Peter	Acts 10:9, 10	*127*
prevented by ravens	1 Ki. 17:1–6	336
spiritual	Luke 6:21	*64*
	John 6:35	*98*
subdued by	Luke 15:11–20	*78*
suffered by Paul	2 Cor. 11:25–27	*183*
Hunters—*those who hunt in any way*		
Esau	Gen. 25:27	23
Ishmael	Gen. 21:20	18
Nimrod	Gen. 10:9	8
Hunting—*chasing, persecuting game*		
animals for food	Gen. 25:27, 28	23
	Gen. 27:3–5	24
with bow and		
arrows	Isa. 7:24	595
with nets and traps	Job 18:10	479
for partridges	1 Sam. 26:20	256
Hupham		
founder of tribal		
family	Num. 26:39	154
son or descendant of		
Benjamin	Gen. 46:21	46
(Huppim)		
Huppah—*canopy; chamber*		
descendant of Aaron	1 Chr. 24:1, 13	396
Huppim—(same as Hupham)		
Hur—*noble* (?)		
father, officer of		
Solomon	1 Ki. 4:7, 8	318
father of Rephaiah	Neh. 3:9	448
Midian prince	Josh. 13:21	214
son of Caleb	Ex. 17:10–12	67
	Ex. 24:14	74
	Ex. 31:1, 2	81
	1 Chr. 2:18–20	375
Hurai		
warrior of David	1 Chr. 11:26, 32	386
Huram		
an artificer of Tyre	2 Chr. 4:11, 16	405
King of Tyre	2 Chr. 2:3	404
son of Bela	1 Chr. 8:3, 5	382

I

	REFERENCE	PAGE
Idolatry—*worship of idols*		
of Ahab	1 Ki. 16:30, 31	335
of Ahaz	2 Chr. 28:1, 2	425
of Amaziah	2 Chr. 25:14	398
of Amon	2 Ki. 21:19–21	368
ancestral worship	Ps. 106:28	539
of Athenians	Acts 17:16	136
of Canaanites	Deut. 29:17	195
degrading	Rom. 1:22, 23	150
during reign of		
Hoshea	2 Ki. 17:12	363
during time of		
Judges	Jdgs. 3:7	229
evidence of		
depravity	Gal. 4:8, 9	187
flee from	1 Cor. 10:14	169
forbidden by the		
Decalogue	Ex. 20:2, 3	69
	Deut. 5:8, 9	172
of Galatians	Gal. 4:8	187
of heathens to be		
destroyed	Num. 33:52	162
	Deut. 7:5	173
helpless	Isa. 45:20	623
of Israelites	Josh. 24:1, 2	225
of Jeroboam	1 Ki. 12:32	330
of Laban's		
household	Gen. 31:30, 32–35	30
of Moabites	Num. 25:1–3	152
New Testament		
warning against	1 John 5:21	96
penalty for enticers	Deut. 13:1–18	180
perishable	Isa. 40:19, 20	618
vigilance against	Deut. 11:16	178
worshiping angels	Col. 2:18	199
worshiping images	Isa. 44:17	622
Idols—*images; representations of a deity*		
large	Dan. 2:31	747
made of gold, silver	Ps. 115:4	543
making of,		
forbidden	Ex. 20:4	69
manufacture of		
described by		
Isaiah	Isa. 44:9–18	622
names of: (See Gods, False)		
small	Gen. 31:34	30
Idumea		
country of Edom	Mark 3:8	38
inhabited by		
Edomites	Isa. 34:5	613
Igal—*(he) redeems (Igeal)*		
one of 12 spies	Num. 13:2, 7	138
son of Shemaiah	1 Chr. 3:22	377
warrior of David	2 Sam. 23:36	312
Igdaliah—*Jehovah is great*		
father of prophet		
Hanan	Jer. 35:4	672
Ignorance—*a lack of knowledge*		
caused by sin	Eph. 4:18	192
concerning God	John 3:19	93
	Acts 17:11, 30	136
conscientious	John 16:1, 2	110
criminal	Acts 3:12–19	119
cure for	2 Tim. 2:15	211
by darkness	1 John 2:11	92
deprecation of	1 Cor. 10:1	169
of a doubter	John 14:5	108
effects of	2 Pet. 3:4–8	235
excusable in part	Luke 12:47, 48	75
loss by	Matt. 13:19	16
of Nicodemus	John 3:9, 10	93
no excuse for sin	Acts 17:30	137
of Pharisees	John 8:13, 19	100

	REFERENCE	PAGE
of Philip	John 14:8, 9	108
of the Sadducees	Matt. 22:23–33	26
of Samaritan		
woman	John 4:9, 10	94
sin offerings for	Num 15:24	141
of sinners	Matt. 13:15	16
of soldiers at the		
cross	Luke 23:34	88
spiritual	Rom. 14:1	160
	Rom. 15:1	161
superstitious	Acts 28:1–6	148
wilful	Zech. 7:11, 12	795
	Matt. 13:15	16
Iim—*ruins*		
town east of Jordan	Num. 33:45	162
town of Judah	Josh. 15:21, 29	216
Ije-abarim		
wilderness camp	Num. 21:11	148
Ijon—*a ruin*		
city of Naphtali	1 Ki 15:20	334
taken by Benhadad	2 Chr. 16:4	390
Ikkesh		
father of Ira, one of		
David's heroes	2 Sam. 23:26	311
Illai		
an Ahohite, warrior		
of David	1 Chr. 11:26, 29	386
Illuminated—*made perceptible; enlightened*		
figurative of		
conversion	Heb. 10:32	222
Illyricum—*Roman province*		
called Dalmatia	2 Tim. 4:10	212
Paul preached at	Rom. 15:19	161
Image—(See Idols)		
Imagination—*formation of mental images*		
evil	Prov. 6:16, 18	560
of heart	Gen. 6:5	5
	Gen. 8:21	7
Lord understands		
all	1 Chr. 28:9	401
vain	Rom. 1:21	150
Imitation—*a likeness; duplication*		
in benevolence	Luke 10:33–37	71
of childhood	Matt. 18:3–6	21
of faithful,		
encouraged	Heb. 6:12	219
of heathen		
neighbors	2 Ki. 17:15	363
unholy	Acts 19:12–17	138
Imlah—*full of*		
called Imla	2 Chr. 18:7, 8	416
father of Micaiah	1 Ki. 22:8, 9	342
Immanuel—*(Emmanuel) God with us*		
name of Jesus	Isa. 7:14	594
	Matt. 1:23	4
Immer—*talkative*		
descendant of		
Aaron	1 Chr. 24:1, 14	396
father of		
Meshillemith	1 Chr. 9:12	383
father of Zadok	Neh. 3:29	449
priest	Jer. 20:1	656
returning exile	Neh. 7:61	453
Immortality—*unending existence; eternal life*		
believers to be		
raised up	John 6:40	98

	REFERENCE	PAGE
brought to light		
through the gospel	2 Tim. 1:10	210
David's faith in	2 Sam. 12:19–23	297
dead shall live	John 5:25, 28–29	96
death swallowed up	Isa. 25:8	660
Elijah and	2 Ki. 2:11	345
Enoch and	Gen. 5:24	5
of God and Christ	1 Tim. 1:17	207
	1 Tim. 6:13–16	209
Jesus and		
requirements for	Matt. 19:16–17, 21	22
lively hope of	1 Pet. 1:3, 4	230
this mortal must put		
on immortality	1 Cor. 15:51–54	175
promised by God	1 John 2:17, 25	93
redemption of the		
soul	Ps. 49:15	514
righteous and		
unrighteous	Matt. 25:46	585
		30
of the spirit of man	Eccl. 12:7	
Imna		
an Asherite chief	1 Chr. 7:35	382
Imnah—*(Jimnah)—right hand*		
a Levite	2 Chr. 31:14	430
son of Asher	Gen. 46:17	46
	Num. 26:44	154
	1 Chr. 7:30	382
Impartiality—*fairness*		
of God	Acts 10:34, 35	128
of God and the		
natural elements	1 Matt. 5:45	7
in judgment	1 Pet. 1:17	230
Impatience—*lack of patience*		
of Christ's disciples	Matt. 15:23	19
folly of human	Prov. 14:29	566
from hunger	Gen. 25:29–34	23
of Israelites	Ex. 32:1	82
of Jesus	Luke 12:50	75
of Job's wife	Job 2:7–9	470
of Jonah	Jonah 4:8, 9	779
of Martha	Luke 10:38–40	71
of Moses	Num. 20:10	147
Impenitence—*hardness of heart; unrepentant*		
in affliction	2 Ki. 1:2	344
of ancient Israel	Jer. 6:15	644
because of delay in		
judgment	Eccl. 8:11	583
	Matt. 11:20	13
certain of punishment	Jer. 7:13–15	645
and eternal death	Luke 13:2, 3	75
invites destruction	Prov. 29:1	576
of Jerusalem	Matt. 23:37, 38	28
resisting Holy Ghost	Acts 7:51	124
unyielding	Luke 16:31	79
warning against	Ps. 95:8	534
Imperfection—*a defect*		
in best of men	Luke 22:24	86
	Gal. 2:9–13	186
of Paul	1 Cor. 9:27	169
universality of	Eccl. 7:20	582
working against	James 3:2	228
Importunity in Prayer		
of the early church	Acts 12:5	130
of Elijah	James 5:17, 18	229
of Jesus	Luke 22:44	87
of Syrophenician		
woman	Mark 7:24–30	43
urged by Christ	Matt. 7:7, 8	8
Impossibilities—*things which cannot exist or be done*		
for certain apostates		
to repent	Heb. 6:4–7	219

	REFERENCE	PAGE
Jehiah—*Jehovah lives*		
Levite doorkeeper	1 Chr. 15:24	389
Jehiel—*God lives*		
father of Gideon	1 Chr. 9:35	384
father of Obadiah	Ezra 8:9	443
Gershonite Levite	1 Chr. 23:8	396
hero of David	1 Chr. 11:44	386
Levite musician	1 Chr. 15:18, 20	389
post exilic priest	Ezra 10:21	446
ruler of the temple	2 Chr. 35:8	434
son of Elam	Ezra 10:2	445
son of Hachmoni	1 Chr. 27:32	399
son of Heman	2 Chr. 29:14	427
son of Jehoshaphat	2 Chr. 21:2	420
Jehieli		
a Gershonite	1 Chr. 26:21	399
Jehizkiah—*Jehovah strengthens*		
son of Shallum	2 Chr. 28:12	426
Jehoadah—*Jehovah hath deposed* (?)		
son of Ahaz	1 Chr. 8:36	383
Jehoaddan—*Jehovah gives delight*		
Amaziah's mother	2 Chr. 25:1	423
Jehoahaz—*Jehovah lays hold*		
1. Same as Ahaziah, king of Judah	2 Chr. 21:17	420
2. Son and successor of Jehu as king of Israel	2 Ki. 10:35	356
	2 Ki. 13:1	358
punished for evil	2 Ki. 13:2–9	358
3. Son of Josiah and successor as king of Judah	2 Ki. 23:30–34	370
	2 Chr. 36:1–4	435
Jehoash—(same as Joash)		
Jehohanan—*Jehovah is gracious*		
father of Ishmael	2 Chr. 23:1	395
Jehoshaphat's captain	2 Chr. 17:10, 15	416
Levite doorkeeper	1 Chr. 26:1, 3	398
postexilic singer	Neh. 12:42	459
priest	Neh. 12:13	458
son of Bebai	Ezra 10:28	446
son of Tobiah	Neh. 6:17, 18	452
Jehoiachin—*Jehovah appoints*		
deported to Babylon	2 Ki. 24:8–16	372
	2 Chr. 36:9, 10	435
released from prison	2 Ki. 25:27–30	373
	1 Jer. 52:31–34	691
son, successor of Jehoiakim as king of Judah	2 Ki. 24:6–8	371
	2 Chr. 36:9, 10	435
(See Jeconiah)		
Jehoiada—*Jehovah knoweth*		
1. David's counselor	1 Chr. 27:34	400
2. a deposed priest	Jer. 29:26	665
3. Father of Benaiah	2 Sam. 23:22	311
warrior of David	1 Ki. 4:4	318
4. High priest	2 Ki. 11:4–16	356
abolished idolatry	2 Chr. 23:16–21	422
aid to Joash	2 Chr. 24:3–15	422
crowned Joash	2 Chr. 23:11	421
repaired the temple	2 Ki. 12:9–16	357
5. Son of Paseah	Neh. 3:6	448
Jehoiakim (Eliakim)—*Jehovah raises up*		
burned manuscript of prophetic book	Jer. 36:1–32	672
death of	2 Ki. 24:6	371

	REFERENCE	PAGE
denounced by prophet	Jer. 22:13–22	658
had Urijah slain	Jer. 26:20–23	662
made vassal king by Nebuchadnezzar	2 Ki. 24:1	371
	Jer. 46:2	681
punished for rebellion by Babylon	2 Ki. 24:1–4	371
	Ezek. 19:8	712
son of Josiah	2 Ki. 23:34–36	371
	2 Chr. 36:4	435
Jehoiarib—*Joseph contendeth*		
descendant of Aaron	1 Chr. 24:1, 7	396
Jehonadab—(See Jonadab)		
Jehonathan—*Jehovah has given*		
Levite teacher	2 Chr. 17:8	416
priest	Neh. 12:1, 18	458
son of Uzziah, one of David's treasurers	1 Chr. 27:25	400
Jehoram—*Jehovah is exalted* (See also Joram)		
priest-teacher	2 Chr. 17:8	416
son and successor of Jehoshaphat	1 Ki. 22:50	344
	2 Ki. 8:16	353
	2 Chr. 21:1–20	419
son of Ahab and successor as king of Israel	2 Ki. 1:17	345
	2 Ki. 3:1–5	346
	2 Ki. 9:24	354
Jehoshabeath—(See Jehosheba)		
Jehoshaphat—*Jehovah has judged*		
called Josaphat, ancestor of Joseph	Matt. 1:8	3
father of Jehu	2 Ki. 9:2	353
priest of David	1 Chr. 15:24	389
purveyor for Solomon	1 Ki. 4:17	319
son of Ahilud	2 Sam. 8:16	294
	2 Sam. 20:24	308
	1 Ki. 4:3	318
son, successor of Asa, king of Judah	1 Ki. 15:24	334
	1 Ki. 22:41–45	343
	2 Chr. 17:1–19	416
	2 Chr. 18:1–34	417
	2 Chr. 19:1–8	418
	2 Chr. 20:1–31	418
	2 Chr. 20:35–37	419
valley of	Joel 3:2	769
Jehosheba, Jehoshabeath—*Jehovah is an oath*		
daughter of Joram	2 Ki. 11:2	356
wife of Jehoida	2 Chr. 22:11	421
Jehoshua, Jehoshuah—*Jehovah saves*		
name of Joshua	Num. 13:16	138
	1 Chr. 7:27	382
Jehovah—*name of God*		
"I am that I am"	Ex. 3:14	53
Jehovah-jireh—*Jehovah will see*		
Isaac brought to, to be sacrificed	Gen. 22:14	19
Jehovah-nissi—*Jehovah is my banner*		
name of altar	Ex. 17:15	67
Jehovah-shalom—*Jehovah is peace*		
name of an altar	Jdgs. 6:24	233

	REFERENCE	PAGE
Jehozabad—*Jehovah hath bestowed*		
a Benjamite chief	2 Chr. 17:18	416
son of a Moabitess	2 Ki. 12:20, 21	358
	2 Chr. 24:26	423
	2 Chr. 25:3	423
son of Obededom	1 Chr. 26:4	398
Jehozadak—*Jehovah is righteous*		
son of Seriah	1 Chr. 6:14	379
(See also Josedech and Jozadak)		
Jehu—*Jehovah is he*		
Benjamite warrior	1 Chr. 12:3	386
grandson of Nimshi	1 Ki. 19:16	339
	2 Ki. 9:2	353
	2 Ki. 10:1	355
	Hosea 1:4	760
son of Hanani and prophet of Judah	1 Ki. 16:1–7	334
	2 Chr. 19:2	418
	2 Chr. 20:34	419
son of Josibiah	1 Chr. 4:35	378
son of Obed	1 Chr. 2:38	376
Jehubbah		
an Ahserite	1 Chr. 7:34	383
Jehucal—*Jehovah is able*		
also called Jucal	Jer. 38:1	675
son of Shelemiah	Jer. 37:3	674
Jehud		
city of Dan	Josh. 19:40, 45	220
Jehudi—*Jew*		
officer of Jehoiakim	Jer. 36:14	673
Jehudijah—*Jewess*		
mother of Jered	1 Chr. 4:18	377
Jehush		
a Benjamite, descendant of Saul	1 Chr. 8:39	383
Jeiel—(Jehiel) *carried away of God*		
a Benjamite	1 Chr. 9:35	384
Levite musician	1 Chr. 16:5	390
Levite of Asaph	2 Chr. 20:14	418
Levite of Josiah	2 Chr. 35:9	434
Levite porter	1 Chr. 15:18	389
one of David's heroes	1 Chr. 11:44	386
priest who had married a foreign wife	Ezra 10:43	446
a returned exile	Ezra 8:13	443
a Reubenite	1 Chr. 5:7	378
scribe of Uzziah	2 Chr. 26:11	425
temple Levite	2 Chr. 29:13	427
Jekabzeel		
village in Judah	Neh. 11:25	458
Jekameam—*may the kinsman establish*		
Kohathite Levite	1 Chr. 24:23	397
son of Hebron	1 Chr. 23:19	396
Jekamiah—*Jehovah establishes*		
son of Jeconiah	1 Chr. 3:17, 18	377
son of Shallum	1 Chr. 2:41	376
Jekuthiel—*obedience of God* (?)		
father of Zanoah	1 Chr. 4:18	377
Jemima—*dove*		
daughter of Job	Job 42:14	494
Jemuel		
called Nemuel	Num. 26:12	153
son of Simeon	Gen. 46:10	46

	REFERENCE	PAGE
Maasiai		
a priest	1 Chr. 9:12	383
Maath		
ancestor of Joseph	Luke 3:26	*60*
Maaz		
son of Ram	1 Chr. 2:27	376
Maaziah		
an Aaronite	1 Chr. 24:1, 18	396
covenant-signer	Neh. 10:1, 8	456
Paul's vision about	Acts 16:9	*135*
Macedonia—*a country north of Greece*		
disciples sent to	Acts 19:22	*138*
liberality of	2 Cor. 8:1–5	*180*
Paul at	Acts 16:12	*135*
	Acts 20:1	*139*
Machbanai		
Gadite warrior	1 Chr. 12:8, 13	386
Machbenah		
son of Sheva	1 Chr. 2:49	376
Machi—*striking (?)*		
father of Geuel	Num. 13:15	138
Machir—*sold*		
son of Ammiel	2 Sam. 9:4	294
	2 Sam. 17:27–29	304
son of Manasseh	Gen. 50:23	50
	Num. 32:39	161
Machnadebai		
son of Bani	Ezra 10:34, 40	446
Machpelah—*double (?)*		
bought by		
Abraham	Gen. 23:7–20	19
patriarchs buried at	Gen. 25:8–10	22
Rebekah and Leah		
buried at	Gen. 49:30, 31	49
Madai		
son of Japheth	Gen. 10:2	8
Madmannah		
town in Judah	Josh. 15:20, 31	216
Madmen		
town in Moab	Jer. 48:2	683
Madmenah		
place in Benjamin,		
north of Jerusalem	Isa. 10:31	598
Madness—*mental disorder; excited beyond self-control*		
feigned by David	1 Sam. 21:12, 13	277
Jesus accused of	John 10:19, 20	*103*
manifest in		
hallucinations,		
ravings, or		
violence	Prov. 26:18	574
	Acts 12:15	*130*
	1 Cor. 14:23	*173*
Paul accused of	Acts 26:24	*146*
sometimes divine		
judgment	Deut. 28:28	193
	1 Sam.	
	16:14–18	270
state of uncontroll-		
able emotion	Jer. 50:38	687
	Ps. 102:8	536
	Luke 6:11	*64*
	Acts 26:9–11	*146*
temporarily produced		
by drunkenness	Jer. 25:16	661
	Jer. 51:7	689

	REFERENCE	PAGE
Madon		
town in Canaan	Josh. 12:19	213
fought Joshua	Josh. 11:1–12	212
Magbish		
exiles of	Ezra 2:30	438
Magdala		
town of Galilee	Matt. 15:39	*19*
Magdalene—(See also under Mary)		
Mary, at		
crucifixion	Matt. 27:56	*34*
Magdiel		
duke of Edom	Gen. 36:43	35
Magi—*wise men*		
worshiped Jesus	Matt. 2:1, 2	*4*
Magician—*one skilled in magic arts; sorcerer; wizard*		
claimed occult		
powers	Ex. 7:11	56
pretended to		
interpret dreams	Dan. 2:10	747
	Gen. 41:8	39
Magistrates—*executive officers*		
apostles before	Luke 12:11	*74*
judges, instructors	Ezra 7:25	443
Laish was without	Jdgs. 18:7	245
obeyed	Titus 3:1	*214*
Paul, Silas before	Acts 16:19, 20	*135*
Roman rulers	Acts 16:36	*135*
Magnanimity—*exhibiting nobleness of soul; generosity towards others*		
of Ahab to		
Benhadad	1 Ki. 20:32–34	340
of apostle Paul	Acts 26:27–29	*146*
to enemies	2 Sam. 19:21–23	306
in forgiveness	1 Sam. 24:4–20	279
fraternal	Gen. 44:32–34	44
gracious	Gen. 13:7–9	11
of Joshua to		
Gibeonites	Josh. 9:3–27	209
Magnificat		
song of Mary	Luke 1:46–55	*57*
Magog		
descendants of		
Japheth	Gen. 10:2	8
enemies of God who		
will be destroyed	Ezek. 38:2–23	733
	Rev. 20:8, 9	*256*
Magor-missabib—*terror on every side*		
name of Pashur	Jer. 20:3	656
Magpiash—*moth slayer*		
covenent-signer	Neh. 10:20	456
Mahalah		
a Manassite	1 Chr. 7:18	382
Mahalaleel—*praise of God*		
a descendant of		
Judah	Neh. 11:4	457
descendant of		
Seth	Gen. 5:12	5
Mahalath—*sickness*		
musical term	Ps. 53:1–6	515
wife of Esau	Gen. 28:9	26
wife of Rehoboam	2 Chr. 11:18	412
Mahali		
son of Merari	Ex. 6:19	55

	REFERENCE	PAGE
Mahanaim—*two camps*		
assigned to Levites	Josh. 21:34, 38	222
David fled to	2 Sam. 17:24	304
given to Gad	Josh. 13:26, 30	214
Ish-bosheth's capital	2 Sam. 2:8	288
Jacob's vision at	Gen. 32:1, 2	31
Mahaneh-dan—*camp of Dan*		
encampment of		
Danites	Jdgs. 18:11, 12	246
Maharai		
one of David's		
heroes	2 Sam. 23:28	311
Mahath		
Kohathite Levite	1 Chr. 6:35	408
a tithe-overseer	2 Chr. 31:13	430
Mahavite		
title of Eliel	1 Chr. 11:46	386
Mahazioth—*visions*		
descendants of		
Heman	1 Chr. 25:4	397
Maher-shalal-hash-baz—*spoil speeds, prey hastens*		
Isaiah's son	Isa. 8:1–4	595
Mahlah—(Mahalah)		
daughter of		
Zelophehad	Num. 26:33	153
Gileadite name	1 Chr. 7:18	382
Mahli—*sick; weak*		
son of Merari	Ex. 6:19	55
	Num. 3:20, 23	126
	Num. 26:58	154
son of Mushi	1 Chr. 6:47	380
	1 Chr. 23:23	396
	1 Chr. 24:30	397
Mahlon—*sickness*		
husband of Ruth	Ruth 4:10	254
son of Naomi	Ruth 1:2–5	251
Mahol		
father of wise men	1 Ki. 4:31	319
Maid—*a young unmarried woman; a female servant*		
fair and beautiful	Est. 2:7	462
ill-treatment of	Ex. 21:20, 21	71
in Namaan's home	2 Ki. 5:1, 2	349
Peter questioned by	Mark 14:66–69	*53*
restored to life	Matt. 9:24, 25	*11*
servant in the home	Luke 12:45	*75*
way of a man with	Prov. 30:19	577
Mail—*communications sent from place to place; armor of chains or scales*		
coat of armor	1 Sam. 17:5	271
sent by post	Est. 3:13	464
Majesty—*exalted dignity; grandeur*		
of Christ	2 Pet. 1:16	*234*
of God	1 Chr. 29:11	402
name of God	Heb. 1:3	*216*
	Heb. 8:1	*220*
Makaz		
town of Judah	1 Ki. 4:9	318
Makheloth		
wilderness camp	Num. 33:25	162
Makkedah—*fold*		
conquered by		
Joshua	Josh. 10:10–27	210
town of Judah	Josh. 15:20, 41	216

	REFERENCE	PAGE
Maoch		
father of Achish	1 Sam. 27:2	283
Maon—*dwelling*		
oppressors of Israel	Jdgs. 10:11, 12	238
son of Shammai	1 Chr. 2:45	376
town in Judah	Josh. 15:55	217
Mara—*bitter*		
name taken by Naomi	Ruth 1:20	252
Marah—*bitterness*		
sweetened	Ex. 15:23–25	65
wilderness station	Num. 33:8, 9	161
Maralah—*earthquake*		
place on boundary of Zebulun	Josh. 19:11	219
Maranatha—*our Lord come* (See Anathema)		
Marble—*compact, granular, partly crystallized limestone*		
grained limestone	Est. 1:6	461
used in temple	1 Chr. 29:1, 2	401
Mareshah		
father of Hebron	1 Chr. 2:42	376
town in Judah	Josh. 15:44	216
Mariners—*sailors; those who navigate ships*		
Hiram had many	1 Ki. 9:27	327
shipwrecked with Paul	Acts 27:1–44	147
some were afraid	Jonah 1:4, 5	777
Mark—(Surname John)		
accompanied Paul	Acts 13:5	131
approved by Paul	2 Tim. 4:11	212
companion of Peter	1 Pet. 5:13	233
contention about him	Acts 15:37–39	134
cousin to Barnabas	Col. 4:10	200
faithful co-worker	2 Tim. 4:11	212
had a godly mother	Acts 12:12	130
left Paul at Perga	Acts 13:13	131
Market—*place of trade*		
children sitting in	Luke 7:32	66
court for trade	Mark 7:4	43
men stood idle in	Matt. 20:3	23
near city gates	2 Ki. 7:17, 18	352
Paul preached in	Acts 17:17	136
seat of court trial	Acts 16:19	135
Maroth		
town of Judah	Micah 1:12	780
Marriage—*state of being married; wedlock*		
binding for life	Rom. 7:2, 3	154
of childless widow to a brother or kinsman	Deut. 25:5, 6	190
	Ruth 3:9	253
	Matt. 22:24	26
Christ's union with his church	2 Cor. 11:2	177
	Eph. 5:23–32	193
	Rev. 19:7	255
commended by Jesus	John 2:1–11	92
continued in perfect felicity	Eccl. 9:9	584
	Prov. 5:18	560
	Eph. 5:22–25	193
daughters given as rewards for valor	Jdgs. 1:12	227
	1 Sam. 17:25	271

	REFERENCE	PAGE
directions for young women	1 Tim. 5:14	208
forbidden by apostates	1 Tim. 4:1–3	208
God's union with his redeemed people	Isa. 54:5	629
	Isa. 62:5	634
	Jer. 3:14	640
of Herod denounced	Mark 6:17, 18	41
honorable	Heb. 13:4	225
instituted by God	Gen. 2:18–24	2
	Mark 10:7–9	46
intermarriage with heathens forbidden	Deut. 7:1–3	173
	Ezra 9:1, 12	444
	2 Cor. 6:14–16	179
in the Lord	1 Cor. 7:39	168
ill-mated one	1 Sam. 25:3	280
may be dissolved only because of adultery	Matt. 19:3–9	22
	Matt. 5:32	7
monogamous under God's appointment	Mark 10:7, 8	46
	Eph. 5:31	193
of Moses criticised	Num. 12:1	138
no marriages in heaven	Matt. 22:30	26
parent's consent required	Gen. 24:50, 51	21
	Ex. 22:17	72
polygamous marriages unlawful	Lev. 18:18	111
	Deut. 17:17	184
preceded by betrothal	Gen. 29:18–20	27
	Luke 1:26, 27	57
rule for widows	1 Cor. 7:8, 9	167
rule of expediency for and against marriage	1 Cor. 7:1–9	167
	1 Cor. 7:25–28	167
	Matt. 19:10–12	22
union of man and woman	Gen. 2:24	3
	Matt. 19:4–6	22
Marsena		
prince of Persia	Est. 1:14	462
Mars Hill—(See Areopagus)		
Martha—*lady*		
instructed by Christ	John 11:20–27	104
reproved by Christ	Luke 10:38–41	71
served at feast given in honor of Jesus	John 12:1–3	105
	Matt. 26:6–13	30
	Mark 14:3–9	52
sister of Lazarus	John 11:39	105
Martyrdom—*affliction; protracted or extreme suffering*		
of Antipas	Rev. 2:13	244
of apostles predicted	John 16:1, 2	110
foretold	Ps. 44:22	512
	Rom. 8:36	156
of James	Acts 12:2	130
of John the Baptist	Mark 6:25, 27	42
no avail without love	1 Cor. 13:3	172
Paul's readiness for	Acts 21:13	141
saints not to fear	Matt. 10:28	12
of Stephen	Acts 7:58, 59	124
of Zachariah	2 Chr. 24:20, 21	423
Mary—*Greek form of Miriam*		
1. Mary Magdalene	Matt. 27:56, 61	34
first to see the risen Saviour	John 20:15–18	114
	Mark 16:9	55

	REFERENCE	PAGE
healed of seven demons	Luke 8:2	67
2. Mary of Bethany	John 11:1	104
anointed Jesus	Mark 14:3–9	52
commended by Jesus	Matt. 26:10–13	31
deeply loved	John 11:5	104
meditative	Luke 10:38–42	71
noted for faith	John 11:28–32	105
3. Mother of Jesus	Luke 2:5–7	58
attended marriage	John 2:1, 5	92
divine conception	Matt. 1:18–23	3
espoused to Joseph	Luke 1:27	57
gave birth, Jesus	Luke 2:1–7	58
had other children	Mark 6:3	41
in John's care	John 19:25–27	113
last mention of	Acts 1:14	117
Magnificat	Luke 1:46–55	57
married to Joseph	Matt. 1:24, 25	4
purification	Luke 2:22–24	59
sought to restrain Jesus in his work	Matt. 12:46–50	15
	Mark 3:31–35	38
	Luke 8:19–21	67
visited by Gabriel	Luke 1:28–38	57
visited Elizabeth	Luke 1:29–41	57
4. Mother of Mark	Acts 12:12	130
5. a Roman disciple	Rom. 16:6	162
6. Wife of Cleophas	John 19:25	113
among women at Jesus' tomb	Matt. 28:1	34
	Luke 24:10	89
mother of James the Less, Joses	Matt. 27:56	34
	Mark 15:40	55
Mash		
son of Aram	Gen. 10:23	9
Mashal—(See also Mishal)		
city of Asher	1 Chr. 6:74	381
Masking—*disguising, veiling*		
Tamar, for deception	Gen. 38:14	37
Mason—*one who builds with stone*		
furnished David by Hiram of Tyre	2 Sam. 5:11	291
	1 Ki. 5:18	320
repaired temple	2 Ki. 12:12	357
Masrekah		
Edomite city	Gen. 36:36	35
Massa—*burden; load*		
Ishmaelite tribe	Gen. 25:12, 14	22
Massacre—*indiscriminate slaughter; killing in great numbers*		
Ahasuerus authorized	Est. 3:8–15	464
Elijah authorized	1 Ki. 18:40	338
God authorized in vision	Ezek. 9:4–9	703
Herod authorized	Matt. 2:16	4
Jehu authorized	2 Ki. 10:20–25	355
Moses authorized	Deut. 20:13	186
Samuel authorized	1 Sam. 15:1–3	268
Massah—*trial; proving*		
name given place where Israel murmured	Ex. 17:7	67
	Ps. 95:8, 9	534
	Deut. 6:16	173
Master—*one who has authority over others; one who has complete knowledge of a subject*		
Christ called	Mark 9:5	45
owner of a slave	Gen. 24:9	20
teacher in Israel	John 3:10	93

	REFERENCE	PAGE

Master-Builder
Paul...............1 Cor. 3:10　*165*

Master-Workmen—*expert craftsmen*
Aquila, Priscilla.....Acts 18:2, 3　*137*
Bezaleel...........Ex. 31:1–5　82
Demetrius.........Acts 19:24　*138*
Hiram............1 Ki. 7:13–50　322
Tubal-cain........Gen. 4:22　4

Materialism—*interest in only the material things of life*
Sadducees were.....Acts 23:8　*143*

Matred—*short spear* (?)
mother-in-law of
Hadar...........Gen. 36:39　35
　　　　　　　　1 Chr. 1:50　375

Matri
Benjamite family...1 Sam. 10:21　263

Mattan—*a gift*
father of Shephatiah.Jer. 38:1　675
priest of Baal.......2 Ki. 11:18　357
　　　　　　　　2 Chr. 23:17　422

Mattanah—*gift*
camp of Israelites...Num. 21:18, 19　148

Mattaniah—*gift of Jehovah*
descendant of Asaph.2 Chr. 20:14　419
father of Zaccur....Neh. 13:13　460
helper of Hezekiah.2 Chr. 29:13　427
Levite musician.....Neh. 11:17　458
name of Zedekiah...2 Ki. 24:17　372
son of Bani.......Ezra 10:37　446
son of Elam.......Ezra 10:26　446
son of Heman......1 Chr. 25:4, 16　397
son of Pahathmoab.Ezra 10:30　446
son of Zattu......Ezra 10:27　446

Mattatha
ancestor of Joseph...Luke 3:31　*61*

Mattathah—*gift of Jehovah*
son of Hashum.....Ezra 10:33　446

Mattathias—*gift of Jehovah*
ancestor of Joseph...Luke 3:25　*60*
another ancestor of
Joseph...........Luke 3:26　*60*

Mattenai
priest of Judah.....Neh. 12:19　459
son of Bani.......Ezra 10:34, 37　446
son of Hashum.....Ezra 10:33　446

Matthan
ancestor of Joseph...Matt. 1:15, 16　*3*

Matthat—*gift*
ancestor of Joseph...Luke 3:24　*60*
another ancestor of
Joseph...........Luke 3:29　*60*

Matthew—*the gift of Jehovah* (Levi)
gave feast to Jesus..Luke 5:29　*63*
at Pentecost.......Acts 1:13　*117*
publican who became
an apostle........Matt. 9:9　*11*
　　　　　　　　Matt. 10:2, 3　*12*
same as Levi......Mark 2:14　*36*

Matthias—*gift of Jehovah*
successor to Judas...Acts 1:23–26　*117*

Mattithiah—*gift of Jehovah*
Levite aid to Ezra...Neh. 8:4　454
a Levite musician...1 Chr. 15:18, 21　389
son of Jeduthun.....1 Chr. 25:3　397

	REFERENCE	PAGE

son of Nebo........Ezra 10:43　446
son of Shallum......1 Chr. 9:31　384

Mattock—*a pickax-like tool*
used in farming.....Isa. 7:25　595

Maul—*a heavy mallet; a war hammer*
weapon of war......Prov. 25:18　574

Maw—*a cavity; the gullet*
inner stomach.......Deut. 18:3　184

Mazzaroth
sign of the heavens..Job 38:32　491

Meadow—*tract of land producing grass for hay*
pasture of Egypt....Gen. 41:2, 18　39

Meah
tower of Jerusalem..Neh. 3:1　448

Meal—*coarsely ground grain; a repast; also its occasion or time*
1. Crushed grain....1 Ki. 17:12　336
used to counteract
poison..........2 Ki. 4:38–41　348
2. A time of eating..Ruth 2:14　252
blessings said and
thanks offered
before.........1 Sam. 9:13　262
　　　　　　　　Matt. 14:19　*17*
　　　　　　　　Matt. 15:36　*19*
　　　　　　　　Acts 27:34, 35　*148*
in the morning and
evening..........Ex. 16:12　66
　　　　　　　　Jdgs. 19:16–21　247
　　　　　　　　1 Ki. 17:6　336
prepared by angel...1 Ki. 19:5–8　338

Mearah—*cave*
place near Sidon....Josh. 13:4　213

Measure—*prescribed limit; extent of dimensions of anything*
of acre—furrow.....1 Sam. 14:14　267
of capacity—
ephah............Ezek. 45:11　741
of length—furlong...Luke 24:13　*89*
(See Jewish Measures)

Meat—*flesh of animals used as food*
clean and unclean...Lev. 11:1–47　102
offered to idols......1 Cor. 8:7–13　*168*

Mebunnai—*built up*
called Sibbecai......1 Chr. 11:29　386
warrior of David....2 Sam. 23:27　311

Mecherathite
native of Mecherah..1 Chr. 11:36　386

Mechanic(s)—*artisans*
Aquila and Priscilla.Acts 18:2, 3　*137*
at Ephesus enraged..Acts 19:24–28　*138*
Hiram.............1 Ki. 7:13, 14　322
Jesus, a divine.....Mark 6:3　*41*
none in Israel.......1 Sam. 13:19, 20　266
one gave opposition..2 Tim. 4:14　*212*
Paul.............2 Thess. 3:7–10　*205*
Sidonians excelled as.1 Ki. 5:6　319
Tubal-cain.........Gen. 4:22　4

Medad
an elder with gift of
prophecy..........Num. 11:26–29　*137*

Medan
son of Abraham and
Keturah..........Gen. 25:1, 2　22
　　　　　　　　1 Chr. 1:32　374

	REFERENCE	PAGE

Meddling—*interfering*
condemned.........1 Pet. 4:15　*232*
with God..........2 Chr. 35:20, 21　435
prohibited..........Deut. 2:4, 5, 19　167

Medeba—*gently flowing waters*
city of Moab.......Num. 21:29, 30　148
given to Reuben....Josh. 13:9, 16　214
reverted to Moab...Isa. 15:2　600

Media
captive Israelites
placed in..........2 Ki. 17:6　363
　　　　　　　　2 Ki. 18:11　364
country in Asia....Dan. 8:20　755
prophecies concerning
captivity by......Isa. 13:17, 18　599
　　　　　　　　Isa. 21:2　603

Mediation—*intercession*
between man and
God..............Num. 16:46–48　143
for transgressors....Ex. 32:30–33　83

Mediator—*a go-between; a reconciler*
Jesus.............1 Tim. 2:5　*207*
　　　　　　　　Heb. 12:24　*225*
Job longed for one..Job 9:33　474
Moses acted as.....Ex. 20:19–21　70
　　　　　　　　Num. 16:48　144

Medicine—*substance with curative or remedial properties*
in Christ's time.....Mark 5:26　*40*
Egyptians noted for.Jer. 46:11　682
figs..............Isa. 38:21　617
merry heart is.....Prov. 17:22　568
oil...............James 5:14　*229*
roots and leaves.....Ezek. 47:12　743
wine.............1 Tim. 5:23　*209*

Meditation—*contemplative thought; devotion*
all the day.........Ps. 119:97　546
divine summons.....Josh. 1:8　202
at eventide.........Gen. 24:63　22
ill-timed...........Luke 12:16–20　*74*
ministerial duty....1 Tim. 4:15　*208*
in nightly quiet.....Ps. 4:4　495
Peter awakened by..Mark 14:72　*53*
prayerful..........Ps. 19:14　501
for the righteous....Ps. 1:1, 2　494
source of strength...Ps. 119:15, 99　545
in time of anxiety...Ps. 39:3　510

Mediterranean Sea
Great Sea.........Num. 34:6　163
the hinder sea......Zech. 14:8　799
Sea of Philistines....Ex. 23:31　73
the utmost sea......Joel 2:20　769
the uttermost sea...Deut. 11:24　178

Meekness—*humility; submissiveness*
in adversity........Isa. 39:5–8　617
of Christ...........Matt. 21:5　*24*
　　　　　　　　Phil. 2:5–8　*215*
with courage......Jer. 26:12–15　662
of David..........2 Sam. 16:5–12　302
divine.............1 Pet. 2:21–23　*231*
essential..........James 1:21　*227*
　　　　　　　　2 Tim. 2:25　*211*
fruit of the Spirit...Gal. 5:22, 23　*188*
glory of...........1 Pet. 2:19, 20　*231*
of Jeremiah.......Jer. 26:12–14　662
of Job............Job 1:20–22　470
meek shall be
exalted...........Ps. 147:6　556
meek shall inherit
the earth.........Ps. 37:11　508
　　　　　　　　Matt. 5:5　*6*
of Moses..........Num. 12:3　138
sought............Zeph. 2:3　788

Metals of the Bible
(See Minerals of the Bible)

Metaphors—*a figure of speech in which one object is likened to another by speaking of it as if it were that other*

Mete—*measure*

Metheg-ammah—*bridle of the mother city* (?)

Methusael—*man of God*

Methuselah—*man of the dart*

Mezahab—*waters of gold*

Miamin—(See Mijamin)

Mibhar

Mibsam

Mibzar—*fortification*

Micah—*who is like Jehovah*
(Micha; Michah)

Micaiah—*who is like Jehovah*

Mice—*small rodents*

Micha—*who is like Jehovah*
(See also Micah)

Michael—*who is like God* (?)

Michael, an Archangel

Michaiah—*who is like Jehovah*

Michal—(abbreviated form of Michael)

Michmash—*hidden away*
(Michmas)

Michmethah

Michri

	REFERENCE	PAGE
death of Nadab and Abihu	Lev. 10:1, 2	101
fire consuming people at Taberah	Num. 11:1–3	136
manna	Ex. 16:14–35	66
plague of boils and blains	Ex. 9:8–11	58
plague of darkness	Ex. 10:21–23	60
plague of death of firstborn	Ex. 12:29, 30	62
plague of flies	Ex. 8:20–24	57
plague of frogs	Ex. 8:5–14	57
plague of lice	Ex. 8:16–18	57
plague of locusts	Ex. 10:12–19	60
plague of murrain	Ex. 9:3–6	58
plague of thunder and hail	Ex. 9:22–26	59
plague of water made blood	Ex. 7:20–25	57
Red Sea divided	Ex. 14:21–31	64
water from rock at Meribah	Num. 20:7–11	147
water from the rock at Rephidim	Ex. 17:5–7	67
waters of Marah sweetened	Ex. 15:23–25	65
under Joshua:		
fall of Jericho	Josh. 6:6–20	205
Jordan stopped	Josh. 3:14–17	203
sun and moon stayed	Josh. 10:12–14	210
under the Kings:		
death of Uzzah	2 Sam. 6:7	292
Jereboam's hand withered and altar destroyed	1 Ki. 13:4–6	331
by Elijah:		
Ahaziah's troops consumed by fire	2 Ki. 1:10–12	345
dividing of Jordan	2 Ki. 2:7, 8	345
Elijah translated to heaven	2 Ki. 2:11	345
sacrifice at Carmel consumed	1 Ki. 18:30–38	337
widow's cruse supplied	1 Ki. 17:14–16	336
widow's son raised	1 Ki. 17:17–24	336
by Elisha:		
axhead floated	2 Ki. 6:5–7	350
deadly pottage corrected	2 Ki. 4:38–41	348
dividing of Jordan	2 Ki. 2:14	346
Jonah's deliverance	Jonah 2:1–10	778
mocking children destroyed by bears	2 Ki. 2:24	346
Naaman's leprosy cured and transferred to Gehazi	2 Ki. 5:10–27	349
100 men fed with 20 loaves	2 Ki. 4:42–44	348
resurrection of a dead man on Elisha's bones	2 Ki. 13:21	359
return of the shadow on sundial of Ahaz	2 Ki. 20:9–11	367
Sennacherib's army destroyed	2 Ki. 19:35	367
Shunammites' son raised	2 Ki. 4:32–37	348
Syrian army smitten and cured	2 Ki. 6:18–20	350
Uzziah smitten with leprosy	2 Chr. 26:16–21	425
water supplied to Jehoshaphat and the allied army	2 Ki. 3:16–20	347
waters of Jericho sweetened	2 Ki. 2:21, 22	346
widow's oil increased	2 Ki. 4:2–7	347

	REFERENCE	PAGE
during the captivity:		
Daniel uninjured in lion's den	Dan. 6:16–23	753
Shadrach, Meshach, and Abednego uninjured in furnace	Dan. 3:19–27	749
in the New Testament:		
blind and dumb demoniac	Matt. 12:22	14
	Luke 11:14	72
blind man healed	Mark 8:22	44
Christ passed unseen through multitude	Luke 4:30	62
curing blind Bartimaeus	Matt. 20:30	24
	Mark 10:46	48
	Luke 18:35	81
curing the demoniac child	Matt. 17:14	20
	Mark 9:17	45
	Luke 9:38	70
cursing the fig tree	Matt. 21:18	24
	Mark 11:12	48
deaf and dumb man healed	Mark 7:31	43
demoniac in synagogue cured	Mark 1:23	36
	Luke 4:33	62
draught of fishes	Luke 5:1	62
	John 21:6	115
dumb demoniac healed	Matt. 9:32	11
feeding the 5,000	Matt. 14:19	17
	Mark 6:35	42
	Luke 9:12	69
	John 6:5	97
feeding the 4,000	Matt. 15:32	19
	Mark 8:1	44
healing centurion's servant	Matt. 8:5	9
	Luke 7:1	65
healing daughter of the Syrophenician	Matt. 15:21	18
	Mark 7:24	43
healing impotent man at Bethesda	John 5:1	95
healing man born blind	John 9:1	102
healing man with dropsy	Luke 14:1	76
healing man with withered hand	Matt. 12:10	14
	Mark 3:1	38
	Luke 6:6	64
healing nobleman's son	John 4:46	95
healing Peter's mother-in-law	Matt. 8:14	10
	Mark 1:30	36
	Luke 4:38	62
healing the ear of Malchus	Luke 22:50	87
healing the crooked woman	Luke 13:11	75
healing the leper	Matt. 8:2	9
	Mark 1:40	36
	Luke 5:12	62
healing the sick man of palsy	Matt. 9:2	10
	Mark 2:3	37
	Luke 5:18	63
healing the ten lepers	Luke 17:11	80
healing woman with issue of blood	Matt. 9:20	11
	Mark 5:25	40
	Luke 8:43	68
legion of devils entering swine	Matt. 8:28	10
	Mark 5:1	40
	Luke 8:27	68

	REFERENCE	PAGE
money in the mouth of fish	Matt. 17:27	21
raising Jairus' daughter	Matt. 9:23	11
	Mark 5:38	41
	Luke 8:49	68
raising of Lazarus	John 11:43	43
raising the widow's son	Luke 7:11	11
stilling the storm	Matt. 8:26	10
	Mark 4:37	40
	Luke 8:22	67
turning water into wine	John 2:1	92
2 blind men healed	Matt. 9:27	11
walking on the sea	Matt. 14:25	18
	Mark 6:48	42
	John 6:19	97
recorded in acts of Apostles:		
apostles freed from prison	Acts 5:21–23	121
blinding of Elymas the sorcerer	Acts 13:11	131
conversion of Paul	Acts 9:1–9	126
cripple at Beautiful Gate cured	Acts 3:1–10	119
death of Ananias and Sapphira	Acts 5:1–11	121
gift of Holy Spirit at Pentecost	Acts 2:1–4	117
many miracles by Paul at Ephesus	Acts 19:11, 12	138
Paul and Silas set free by earthquake	Acts 16:26	135
Paul cures father of Publius and others	Acts 28:7–10	148
Paul cures maid with a spirit of divination at Philippi	Acts 16:16–18	135
Paul heals cripple at Lystra	Acts 14:8–10	132
Paul unhurt by viper's bite	Acts 28:3–6	148
Paul's sight restored by means of Ananias	Acts 9:17–19	126
Peter cures Aenas of palsy	Acts 9:32–35	127
Peter delivered from prison	Acts 12:5–11	130
Peter raises Dorcas to life	Acts 9:36–43	127
Philip's miracles	Acts 8:13	125
raising of Eutychus	Acts 20:9–11	139
Stephen's miracles	Acts 6:8	122
various miracles	Acts 5:12	121
various miracles of Paul and Barnabas at Iconium	Acts 14:3	132

Mire—*marsh; wet, yielding earth*

	REFERENCE	PAGE
figurative; salvation from	Ps. 40:2	510
	Ps. 69:1, 2	521
necessary to growth	Job 8:11	474
sow wallowing in	2 Pet. 2:22	235

Miriam—(Hebrew for Mary)

	REFERENCE	PAGE
1. Another, from Judah	1 Chr. 4:17	377
2. Sister of Aaron and Moses	Micah 6:4	782
	Num. 26:59	154
conspired against Moses; punished	Num. 12:1–16	138
	Deut. 24:8, 9	189
died at Kadesh	Num. 20:1	146
led in victory celebration	Ex. 15:20, 21	65

	REFERENCE	PAGE
Mirma		
Benjamite	1 Chr. 8:10	382
Mirror—*a looking glass; whatever reflects*		
figuratively used	2 Cor. 3:18	*178*
of molten brass	Job 37:18	490
in tabernacle	Ex. 38:8	89
Mirth—*gaiety shown by laughter and jesting*		
divinely commended	Eccl. 8:15	583
end of	Prov. 14:13	566
in festive celebrations of thanks	Neh. 8:12	454
	Jer. 30:19	666
in fruits of work	Eccl. 9:7	584
health producing	Prov. 17:22	568
house of	Eccl. 7:4	582
impossible in Babylon	Ps. 137:1–4	552
Miscegenation—*interbreeding of races; intermarriage*		
forbidden by Abraham	Gen. 24:2, 3	20
reason for	Ex. 34:16	85
results of	Jdgs. 3:6, 7	224
Mischief—*troublesome, annoying action*		
by evildoers, hypocrites	Prov. 4:16	560
Jews, makers of	Acts 17:5–8	*136*
practiced by Saul	1 Sam. 23:9	278
by skeptics	Ps. 36:1, 4	508
Miser—*one who saves and hoards avariciously*		
character of	Eccl. 4:7, 8	581
falls into evil	1 Tim. 6:9	*209*
never satisfied	Eccl. 5:10	581
Misery—*extreme distress; misfortune*		
brutalizing	Acts 7:17–19	*123*
caused by sense of wrongdoing	Job 15:20	478
	Deut. 28:66, 67	195
consequences of sin	Rom. 3:12, 16	*152*
of transgressors	Prov. 13:15	565
Misfortune—*adverse fortune; mischance; calamity*		
for furtherance of gospel	Phil. 1:12	*194*
not understood by Gideon	Jdgs. 6:13	232
of wicked	Prov. 6:12–15	560
Misgab		
city of Moab	Jer. 48:1	683
Mishael—*who is what God is*		
associate of Ezra	Neh. 8:4	454
companion of David	Dan. 1:5, 6	746
Kohathite Levite	Ex. 6:22	56
Mishal—(Misheal; see also Mashal)		
assigned to Levites	Josh. 21:30	222
village of Asher	Josh. 19:24, 26	220
Misham		
a Benjamite	1 Chr. 8:12	382
Mishma		
son of Ishmael	Gen. 25:13, 14	22
son of Mibsam	1 Chr. 4:25	378
Mishmannah		
Gadite warrior	1 Chr. 12:10	387
Mishraites		
Kirjath family	1 Chr. 2:53	376

	REFERENCE	PAGE
Mispereth		
returned exile	Neh. 7:7	452
Misrephoth-maim		
place where Joshua pursued foes	Josh. 11:8	212
	Josh. 13:6	213
Missions—*the act of sending persons on some errand or to accomplish a service*		
among the nations	Luke 24:47	*90*
of Christianity	Isa. 2:2–5	591
	Mal. 1:11	800
divine command	Matt. 24:14	*28*
have Christ's blessing	Matt. 28:18–20	*35*
Old Testament instance	2 Ki. 17:27	363
Missionaries—*those sent to propagate religion*		
Apollos	Acts 18:24	*137*
early church	Acts 8:4	*125*
Jonah	Jonah 3:2, 3	778
Noah	2 Pet. 2:5	*234*
Paul and Barnabas	Acts 13:1–3	*130*
Peter	Acts 15:7	*133*
Philip	Acts 8:5	*125*
Mist—*watery vapor; fog*		
of darkness	2 Pet. 2:17	*235*
fell on Elymas	Acts 13:8–11	*131*
watered the ground	Gen. 2:6	*2*
Misunderstanding—*disagreement; misapprehension*		
among Christians	Acts 6:1	*122*
among Israelites in Egypt	Ps. 106:7	539
of Jesus by heaven	Matt. 13:13	*16*
Mite—*smallest Jewish coin*		
widow	Mark 12:42	*50*
Miter—*headdress worn by high priest*		
inscribed, "holiness to the Lord"	Ex. 28:4, 36–39	77
	Lev. 16:4	109
place on, of Joshua	Zech. 3:5	793
Mithcah		
encampment of Israel	Num. 33:28	162
Mithnite		
Joshaphat one of David's heroes called	1 Chr. 11:43	386
Mithredath—*given by Mithra*		
Persian officer	Ezra 4:7	440
treasurer of Cyrus	Ezra 1:8	437
Mitre—(See Miter)		
Mitylene—*chief city on island of Lesbos*		
Paul visited	Acts 20:13–15	*139*
Mizar—*littleness*		
a hill	Ps. 42:6	511
Mizpah or Mizpeh—*watch-tower*		
near Mt. Hermon	Josh. 11:3	212
place in Moab	1 Sam. 22:3	277
sign of covenant	Gen. 31:4, 49	29
town in Gilead	Jdgs. 10:17	238
town of Benjamin	Josh. 18:21, 26	219
	1 Sam. 7:5–17	260
	1 Sam. 10:17	263
	2 Ki. 25:23–25	373
	Jer. 40:6–16	677
village in Judah	Josh. 15:1, 38	215

	REFERENCE	PAGE
Mizpar—*number*		
(See also Mispereth)		
returned exile	Ezra 2:2	437
Mizraim—*Hebrew of Egypt*		
son of Ham	Gen. 10:6	8
Mizzah		
son of Reuel	Gen. 36:13	34
Mnason		
disciple from Cyprus	Acts 21:16	*141*
Moab—*meaning uncertain*		
country occupied by Moabites	Deut. 29:1	195
	Josh. 13:32	214
son of Lot	Gen. 19:33–37	16
Moabites—*descendants of Moab*		
Balah calls Baalam to curse Israel	Num. 22:24	149
Balah, king of	Num. 22:4	149
conquered by Amorites	Num. 21:26	148
David takes refuge among	1 Sam. 22:3, 4	277
defeated by Judah	2 Chr. 20:20 25	419
excluded from Israel	Deut. 23:3–6	188
invaded ravaged land of Israel	Jdgs. 3:12–30	229
	1 Sam. 12:9	265
Israelites married daughters of	Ezra 9:1–3	444
	Neh. 13:23	461
led Israel to sin	Num. 25:1–5	152
Moses forbidden to oppress	Deut. 2:9	167
	Jdgs. 11:18	239
prophecies concerning judgments upon	Jer. 4:8	641
Ruth	Ruth 2:2	252
Moadiah		
postexilic priest	Neh. 12:1, 17	458
Mob—*a rabble; a turbulent crowd*		
at Ephesus	Acts 19:29	*139*
at Jerusalem	Acts 21:27, 28	*141*
at Thessalonica	Acts 17:5	*136*
Mocking—*mimicking in derision or contempt; jeering*		
Christ	Ps. 22:7, 8	502
	Matt. 27:29, 41	*33*
Elisha	2 Ki. 2:22, 23	346
by fools	Prov. 14:9	566
God	Isa. 57:1–14	630
	Jude 1:18	*242*
God's messengers	2 Chr. 36:15, 16	436
Hezekiah's postmen	2 Chr. 30:10	428
Job, by his friends	Job 12:4	476
Micaiah, by Zedekiah	1 Ki. 22:24	343
Paul	Acts 17:32	*137*
priests of Baal, by Elijah	1 Ki. 18:27	337
saints of God	Heb. 11:36	*224*
Sarah, by Ishmael	Gen. 21:9	17
Modesty—*decorum*		
of John the Baptist	Matt. 3:13–15	*5*
of Saul in early life	1 Sam. 9:21–24	262
in social life	Luke 14:8–10	77
womanly	Est. 1:10–12	462
of women	1 Tim. 2:9	*207*
Moladah—*birth; origin*		
given to Simeonites	Josh. 19:1, 2	219

REFERENCE	PAGE

inhabited after the
captivity..........Neh. 11:26 458
town in Judah......Josh. 15:1, 26 215

Molding—*shaping; fashioning*
of images..........Ex. 32:4–8 82
of mirrors..........Job 37:18 490

Mole—*a small burrowing mammal*
unclean animal.....Lev. 11:29, 30 102

Molech, Moloch—*a deity*
altar of, destroyed...2 Ki. 23:10–14 370
called Milcom....1 Ki. 11:5, 33 328
law against offering
children to.......Lev. 18:21 111
Lev. 20:1–5 113
Ps. 106:38 540
worshiped by
Israelites..........2 Ki. 21:6 368
Jer. 32:35 669
Ezek. 23:37 718
worshiped by
Solomon..........1 Ki. 11:7 328

Molid
man of Judah.......1 Chr. 2:29 376

Molten—*sea*
destroyed by
Nebuchadnezzar...2 Ki. 25:13, 16 373
Jer. 27:19–22 663
great basin in the
inner court of the
temple............1 Ki. 7:23 322
1 Chr. 18:8 392

Monarchy—*government ruled by a monarch*
described..........1 Sam. 8:11–18 261

Money—*a medium of exchange in trade*
answers all things...Eccl. 10:19 584
apostles not to carry.Mark 6:7, 8 41
blood..............Matt. 27:3–8 32
borrowed or lent....Deut. 23:19, 20 189
Ps. 37:21 490
buy without.......Isa. 55:1 629
buys men..........Matt. 28:11–15 35
cannot buy spiritual
power............Acts 8:18–20 36
Zech. 4:6 793
coins inscribed.....Matt. 22:19–21 26
coins used........Ezra 8:26, 27 444
collected for the
Lord's work......Mark 12:41 50
2 Ki. 12:9–12 357
eagerness for.......1 Tim. 6:9 209
flies away.........Prov. 23:5 572
found in a fish.....Matt. 17:27 21
given to Job.......Job 42:11 494
Jesus sold for......Mark 14:10, 11 52
Judas greedy for....Matt. 26:14–16 31
love of............1 Tim. 6:10 209
medium of
trading.........Gen. 23:15, 16 19
monopoly of, in
Egypt...........Gen. 47:14 47
not to glory in......Jer. 9:23 647
often brings misery.Acts 1:16–19 117
priests corrupted by.Micah 3:9–11 780
stolen and hidden...Josh. 7:20, 21 207
taken by fraud......2 Ki. 5:21–27 349
in tithing.........Deut. 14:23–25 181
use and misuse of...Matt. 25:18–30 29
value determined by
weight..........Jer. 32:10 668
Josh. 7:21 207

Money-Changers—*persons who change
money at a prescribed rate*
cast out of temple...Matt. 21:12 24

Monopoly—*exclusive right; exclusive possession or control of anything*
of Pharaoh........Gen. 47:19–26 47
of real estate.......Isa. 5:8 593

Monster—*a fabulous animal*
sea animal........Lam. 4:3 695

Months—*units of time*
(See also Jewish Calendar)
numbered..........Gen. 7:11 6

Moon—*a celestial body*
appointed for
seasons.........Ps. 104:19 538
benefits man.......Deut. 33:14 200
bright as the sun....Isa. 30:26 611
ceased movements...Josh. 10:13 210
has glory of its
own...........1 Cor. 15:41 174
luminary of the
night...........Gen. 1:16 1
new...........Num. 28:11, 16 156
1 Sam. 20:5 275
rule by night......Ps. 136:9 552
shall be turned to
blood...........Joel 2:31 769
Rev. 6:12 247
shall give no light...Matt. 24:29 28
under woman's
feet.............Rev. 12:1 250
worship of.........Deut. 17:3 183
worshiped by
Israelites.........Jer. 8:2 646

Monuments—(See Memorials)

Morality—*moral conduct; ethics*
above ritual........Amos 5:21, 24 773
complete..........Mark 10:17–20 47
false zeal for.......John 8:3–7 100
indispensable......Isa. 1:14–17 590
insufficient........Luke 18:10–14 81

Morasthite
native of Moresheth.Micah 1:1 779

Mordecai—*belonging to Merodach*
returned exile......Ezra 2:2 437
son of Jair........Est. 2:5, 21 462
Est. 3:5 463
Est. 4:1–4 464
Est. 6:1–14 465
Est. 10:1–3 468

Moreh—*soothsayer, teacher*
grove near Shechem.Gen. 12:6 10
hill in Jezreel......Jdgs. 7:1 233

Moresheth-gath
birthplace of Micah..Micah 1:14 780

Moriah
hill of sacrifice of
Abraham's son.....Gen. 22:1–13 18
site of Solomon's
temple...........2 Chr. 3:1 404
site purchased by
David...........2 Sam. 24:18–25 312

Mortar—*a strong vessel in which substances
are ground; a cement-like substance*
binding substance...Gen. 11:3 9
vessel used for
pounding grain....Prov. 27:22 575
Num. 11:8 136

Mortgage—*a lien upon land; a security*
of David's
ambassadors......2 Sam. 10:1–5 295
practiced by Jews...Neh. 5:3 450

Mortification—*act of subduing the passions
and appetites; humiliation*
of members........Col. 3:5 199
through the spirit...Rom. 8:13 155

Mosera, Moseroth
camp of Israel.....Deut. 10:6 177

Moses—*drawn from the water* (?)
adopted by king's
daughter..........Ex. 2:5–10 51
Acts 7:20, 21 123
announced death of
generation........Num. 14:20–39 140
Heb. 3:16–18 217
appointed 70 elders.Num. 11:16, 17 137
arrived at Sinai.....Ex. 19:1, 2 68
beautiful babe......Acts 7:20 123
born in slavery.....Ex. 2:1–10 51
broke law-tables....Ex. 32:15–19 83
brother of Aaron...Ex. 4:14 53
brother of Miriam...Ex. 15:20 65
call renewed.......Ex. 6:1–8 55
called............Ex. 3:9, 10 52
caused ten plagues
on the Egyptians...Ex. 7–12 56
chose Joshua as his
successor.........Deut. 31:7–13 197
Josh. 1:1–9 201
consecrated Aaron..Lev. 8:6–9 99
conspired against...Num. 12:1–11 138
death of Aaron.....Num. 20:22–29 147
death of Miriam....Num. 20:1 146
defeated Amalek....Ex. 17:8–16 67
defeated Balaam...Num. 22:24 149
defended his people..Ex. 2:11, 12 52
delivered farewell
address..........Deut. 32:1–52 198
Deut. 33:1–29 200
delivered Israel by
the Passover lamb..Ex. 12:1–28 61
Heb. 11:28 224
destroyed golden calf.Ex. 32:20–29 83
died..............Deut. 34:5, 6 201
discouraged by
Israel's
murmurings......Num. 11:10–15 137
Deut. 1:9–12 166
divided Red Sea....Ex. 14:13–31 64
divine fellowship...Ex. 33:12–23 84
divinely guided....Num. 10:1–12 135
efforts to aid his
people rejected.....Ex. 2:13, 14 52
Acts 7:26–28 123
erected tabernacle...Ex. 40:1–38 91
face radiant with
glory of God......Ex. 34:29–33 85
2 Cor. 3:13–17 178
faith of...........Heb. 11:24, 28 223
fled into the land of
Midian..........Ex. 2:15 52
Acts 7:29 123
forty days in the
mountain.........Ex. 24:12–18 74
Deut. 9:9 175
gave divers laws....Num. 2–9 124
given Aaron as
helper...........Ex. 4:14–16 53
given highest
learning; royal care.Acts 7:22 123
Heb. 3:2, 3 217
given manna.......Ex. 16:14, 15 66
given tables of law..Ex. 34:1–10 84
God talked with...Ex. 33:1–11 83
God talked with him
at Mt. Sinai......Ex. 19:3–6 69
Acts 7:38 124
guided by pillar of
cloud fire.........Ex. 13:17–22 63
Ps. 78:14 526
healed waters.......Ex. 15:23–25 65

	REFERENCE	PAGE
hidden by river	Ex. 2:3, 4	51
instructed to build tabernacle	Ex. 25–31	75
interceded with God for Israel	Num. 14:1–19	139
	Ps. 106:23	539
intercession of	Ex. 32:30–35	83
invited Hobab's aid	Num. 10:29–32	136
at Jesus' transfiguration	Matt. 17:3	20
	Luke 9:30	69
kept Jethro's sheep	Ex. 3:1	52
led Israel out of Egypt	Ex. 12:31	62
linked self to Israel	Heb. 11:24–26	223
married Ethiopian	Num. 12:1	138
married Zipporah	Ex. 2:21	52
meekness of	Num. 12:3	138
met seditions	Num. 16:1–50	142
mission rejected by king and people	Ex. 5:1–23	54
	Ex. 6:9–13	55
organized nation	Ex. 18:13–26	68
prayed for Israel	Ex. 32:7–14	82
predicted wandering	Num. 14:33, 34	140
promised divine aid and empowerment	Ex. 3:12–14	52
	Ex. 4:2–8	53
provided remedy for bite of serpents	Num. 21:5–9	148
	John 3:14, 15	93
pursued by Pharaoh	Ex. 14:1–12	63
quenched a fire	Num. 11:2, 3	136
received command- ments written by God	Ex. 31:18	82
	Deut 5:22	172
received law of God	Ex. 20:1–26	69
	Deut. 5:1–24	171
repeated divers laws	Num. 15:1–41	141
requested hospitality of Edom	Num. 20:14–21	147
	Deut. 2:1–8	167
roll of Israel	Num. 1:1–54	122
saw promised land	Deut. 34:1–4	201
second 40 days in Sinai	Ex. 34:28	85
sin, struck rock	Num. 20:2–13	146
son of Amram	Ex. 6:20	55
sought excuse	Ex. 3:11	52
spies sent to Canaan	Num. 13:1–33	138
told his mission	Ex. 4:29–31	54
took leave of Jethro	Ex. 4:18–20	54
of tribe of Levi	Ex. 2:1–10	51
two sons born	Acts 7:29	123
visited by Jethro	Ex. 18:1–12	67
wanderings of	Num. 33:1–49	161
water from rock	Ex. 17:1–7	67
wrote victory song	Ex. 15:1–19	65

Most High

name given to God	Gen. 14:18	12

Mote—*minute particle, speck*

symbol of small fault	Matt. 7:3, 5	8

Moth—*nocturnal flying insect some species of which feed on textiles*

destroys clothing	Isa. 50:9	627
figuratively used	Matt. 6:19, 20	8
frailty of	Ps. 39:11	510

Mother—*female parent*

abuse of	Ex. 21:15, 17	71
ambitious	Matt. 20:20, 21	23
Athaliah, a cruel	2 Ki. 11:1	356
brutal	2 Ki. 6:28, 29	351
Deborah	Jdgs. 5:7	231
Eve, "of all living"	Gen. 3:20	3
farewell kiss of	1 Ki. 19:20	339
Hagar, a distressed	Gen. 21:14–16	17

	REFERENCE	PAGE
Hannah, a devout	1 Sam. 1:22–28	255
Herodias, a revengeful	Mark 6:21–24	42
honor, commanded	Ex. 20:12	70
honored	Matt. 15:4	18
indignities toward	Lev. 18:7	111
	Lev. 20:11	113
Jochebed, an ingenious	Ex. 2:1–10	51
law to be kept	Prov. 6:26–23	561
love of	Isa. 49:15	626
	Isa. 66:13	637
Maacah, an idolatrous	1 Ki. 15:13	334
Rebekah, a partial	Gen. 25:28	23
respected in age	Prov. 23:22	572

Mother-in-Law—*mother of one's spouse*

Naomi, a beloved	Ruth 1:16–18	251
of Peter, healed by Jesus	Matt. 8:14, 15	10
	Mark 1:30, 31	36
Rebekah, a vexed	Gen. 26:34, 35	24

Mount, Mountain—*lofty elevation; something of great magnitude*

Abarim	Num. 27:12	155
Ararat	Gen. 8:4	7
Bashan	Ps. 68:15	521
Bethel	1 Sam. 13:2	265
Carmel	1 Ki. 18:19	337
Ebal	Deut. 11:29	178
Ephraim	Josh. 17:15	218
Gerizim	Deut. 11:29	178
Gilboa	1 Sam. 31:1	286
Gilead	Gen. 31:21	29
Hermon	Deut. 3:8	169
Hor	Num. 20:22	147
Horeb	Ex. 3:1	52
Jesus goes up into for prayer	Matt. 14:23	18
Jesus on, after resurrection	Matt. 28:16, 17	35
Jesus tempted upon	Matt. 4:8	5
Jesus transfigured upon	Matt. 17:1–9	20
Lebanon	Deut. 3:25	169
melted	Ps. 97:5	535
	Isa. 64:1–3	635
Mizar	Ps. 42:6	511
Moriah	Gen. 22:2	18
moved by faith	Matt. 21:21	25
Nebo	Deut. 32:49	199
Olives or Olivet	Matt. 21:1	24
Pisgah	Num. 21:20	148
Seir	Gen. 14:6	11
Sephar	Gen. 10:30	9
sermon from	Matt. 5:1	6
Sinai	Num. 3:1	125
Tabor	Jdgs. 4:6	230
Zion, or Sion	Isa. 4:5	592

Mourners—*bereaved ones; those who grieve or sorrow for*

comfort for	1 Thess. 4:13–18	203
genuine, for Dorcas	Acts 9:39	127
good news for	Mark 16:9, 10	55
weeping of	Ps. 137:1–4	552

Mourning—*expressing extreme grief; lamentation*

for Aaron	Num. 20:29	147
Abraham for Sarah	Gen. 23:2	19
David for Abner	2 Sam. 3:31	290
David for Absalom	2 Sam. 18:33	305
for dead wife forbidden	Ezek. 24:15–18	719
by discarding all ornaments	Ex. 33:4	83
	2 Sam. 14:2	299

	REFERENCE	PAGE
by hiring professional mourners	Jer. 9:17, 18	647
	Matt. 9:18, 23	11
for Jacob	Gen. 50:1, 3	49
Jeremiah for Josiah	2 Chr. 35:25	435
Jesus for Lazarus	John 11:33–35	105
for Moses	Deut. 34:8	201
for Saul	1 Sam. 31:11–13	286
by tearing garments	2 Sam. 13:31	299
by wearing sackcloth	Isa. 22:12	604

Mouse—*a small rodent*

destructive	1 Sam. 6:5	259
eaten by Israelites	Isa. 66:17	637
forbidden as food	Lev. 11:29	102

Mouth—*channel of speech*

confession made with	Rom. 10:10	157
of fools	Prov. 15:2	566
in kissing	1 Ki. 19:18	339
noble issues of	Ps. 37:30	509
reveals the heart	Matt. 12:34	15
sinning with	Job 31:30	487

Mower—*one who cuts down, as grass or grain, with a sharp implement*

"Fills not his hands"	Ps. 129:7	550

Moza

son of Caleb	1 Chr. 2:46	376
son of Zimri	1 Chr. 8:36	383

Mozah

town of Benjamin	Josh. 18:21, 26	219

Muffler—*a long veil or scarf*

female dress	Isa. 3:16, 19	592

Mulberry Tree

rustling of leaves a sign for battle	1 Chr. 14:14, 15	388
	2 Sam. 5:23, 24	292

Mule—*hybrid between horse and ass*

in Armenia	Ezek. 27:14	721
has no understanding	Ps. 32:9	506
for riding	2 Sam. 13:29	299

Multitude—*a great number, throng*

fed by Elisha	2 Ki. 4:42–44	348
fed by Jesus	Matt. 14:13–21	17
fed by Moses	Num. 11:30–32	137
followed Jesus	Luke 8:45	68
healed by Jesus	Mark 3:10	38

Munitions—*ammunition; war materials*

kept for war	Nahum 2:1	784

Muppim

called Shuppim	1 Chr. 7:12, 15	381
descendant of Rachel	Gen. 46:21	46

Murder—*to kill a human being with premeditated malice*

atrocious	2 Sam. 4:5–8	290
of David, attempted	1 Sam. 19:10	274
excludes from heaven	Gal. 5:21	188
executed for	Deut. 19:12	185
fair trial for	Num. 35:30	164
for gain	Matt. 21:38	25
hatred called	1 John 3:15	238
indirect	2 Sam. 11:14–17	296
Mosaic law against	Ex. 20:13	70
originates in heart	Matt. 15:19	18

	REFERENCE	PAGE
Nebuzar-adan—*Nebu has given a seed*		
captain of Nebuchad-		
nezzar's army	Jer. 39:9	676
	2 Ki. 25:8	372
deported many		
Jews	Jer. 52:30	691
showed kindness to		
Jeremiah	Jer. 40:1–5	676
	Jer. 39:11–14	676
Necho—(See Pharaoh)		
Neck—*that part of the body that connects the head to the trunk*		
Eli's broken by fall	1 Sam. 4:15–18	258
millstone around	Matt. 18:6	*21*
stiff	Deut. 31:27	198
Necromancer—*inquirer of the dead*		
condemned	Deut. 18:10, 11	184
witch of Endor	1 Sam. 28:7–19	283
Nedabiah—*bounty of Jehovah*		
son of Jeconiah	1 Chr. 3:17, 18	377
Needle—*a small, slender pointed instrument for sewing*		
figuratively used by		
Jesus	Matt. 19:24	*23*
	Mark 10:24–26	*47*
Neesing—*sneezing*		
action of Leviathan	Job 41:1, 18	493
Neginah, Neginoth		
musical term, in title		
of Psalms	Ps. 4	495
	Ps. 54	516
	Ps. 76	525
Neglect—*want of attention or care; carelessness*		
admonition against,		
of gift	1 Tim. 4:14	208
to do good	James 4:17	228
of dress	2 Sam. 19:24	306
excuse for	Matt. 25:24, 25	*30*
folly of	Matt. 25:1–8	*29*
of the gospel	Matt. 22:2–5	*25*
of important		
matters	Matt. 23:23	*27*
of law of God,		
by John	2 Ki. 10:31	356
loss by	Matt. 25:10–12	*29*
parental	1 Sam. 3:12–14	257
of preparation	Matt. 22:11–13	*26*
punished	Matt. 25:27–30	*30*
of salvation	Heb. 2:1–3	216
unfeeling	Luke 10:30–32	*71*
of widows in distri-		
bution of food	Acts 6:1	*122*
Nehelamite		
Shemaiah called	Jer. 29:24	665
Nehemiah		
1. A returned exile	Ezra 2:1, 2	437
2. Son of Azuk	Neh. 3:16	449
3. Son of Hachaliah	Neh. 1:1	447
courageous	Neh. 6:10, 11	451
diligent	Neh. 4:21–23	450
governor of Judea	Neh. 13:1–31	460
grieved for		
Jerusalem	Neh. 1:4–11	447
man of faith	Neh. 4:14	450
patriotic	Neh. 1:1–4	447
persevering	Neh. 13:11–25	460
prayerful	Neh. 1:5–11	447
visit to and rebuild-		
ing of Jerusalem	Neh. 2–6	448
	Neh. 8–10	454

	REFERENCE	PAGE
Nehiloth		
title of Psalm	Ps. 5	495
Nehum—*comfort*		
returned exile	Neh. 7:7	452
Nehushta		
wife of Jehoiakim	2 Ki. 24:6, 8	371
Nehushtan		
brazen serpent		
called	2 Ki. 18:4	364
Neiel		
town on border of		
Asher	Josh. 19:24, 27	220
Neighbor—*a fellow man*		
in bereavement	John 11:19, 31, 33	*104*
be truthful to	Zech. 8:16	796
debate with	Prov. 25:9	573
how to treat	Lev. 19:18	112
love, of, fulfillment		
of law	Gal. 5:14	*188*
	James 2:8	*227*
loved unselfishly	Matt. 19:19	*23*
	Rom. 13:10	*160*
not despised	Prov. 14:21	566
not flattered	Prov. 29:5	576
"Poor is hated of"	Prov. 14:20	566
stealing words from	Jer. 23:30	659
strive to please	Rom. 15:2	*161*
who is my neighbor?	Luke 10:29–37	*71*
Nekeb		
village of Naptali	Josh. 19:32, 33	220
Nekoda—*retreat; departing*		
could not prove		
genealogy	Neh. 7:50	453
	Ezra 2:59, 60	438
head of Nethinim		
family	Ezra 2:48	438
Nemuel		
of a Reubenite	Num. 26:9	153
son of Simeon	Num. 26:12	153
Nepheg		
son of David	2 Sam. 5:13–15	291
son of Izhar	Ex. 6:21	56
Nephishesim		
family of		
Nethinim	Neh. 7:52	453
	Ezra 2:50	438
Nephtoah		
fountain west of		
Jerusalem	Josh. 15:9	216
	Josh. 18:15	219
Ner—*light*		
father of Abner	1 Sam. 14:51	268
grandfather of Saul	1 Chr. 8:33	383
Nereus		
Roman Christian	Rom. 16:15	*161*
Nergal—*hero*		
Babylonian deity	2 Ki. 17:30	363
Nergal-sharezer—*Nergal protect the King*		
Babylonian prince	Jer. 39:3	676
Neri		
ancestor of Joseph	Luke 3:27	*60*
Neriah—*Jehovah is light*		
father of Baruch	Jer. 32:12	668

	REFERENCE	PAGE
Nest—*habitation prepared by a bird for the hatching of its eggs*		
of birds	Matt. 8:20	*10*
birds stir in	Deut. 32:11	198
Net—*snare*		
in fishing	John 21:6	*115*
flattery a	Prov. 29:5	576
in fowling	Prov. 1:17	557
God's kingdom		
likened to	Matt. 13:47, 48	*17*
in hunting	Isa. 51:20	627
a moral snare	Ps. 57:6	517
Nathaneel—*God has given*		
chief of the Levites	2 Chr. 35:9	434
father of Shemaiah	1 Chr. 24:6	397
a Levite teacher	2 Chr. 17:7	416
priest, musician	1 Chr. 15:24	389
priest of Joiakim	Neh. 12:21	459
prince of Issachar	Num. 1:8	123
son of Asaph	Neh. 12:36	459
son of Jesse	1 Chr. 2:13, 14	375
son of Obededom	1 Chr. 26:4	398
son of Pashur	Ezra 10:22	446
Nethaniah—*Jehovah gives*		
father of Ishmael	2 Ki. 25:23, 25	373
father of Jehudi	Jer. 36:14	673
Levite teacher	2 Chr. 17:8	416
son of Asaph	1 Chr. 25:2	397
Nethinim—*the appointed, given*		
among returned		
exiles	Neh. 7:60	453
	Ezra 8:17–20	444
exempt from taxes	Ezra 7:24	443
servants of Levites	Ezra 2:43	438
Nethophah—*dropping*		
occupied by		
postexilic Levites	1 Chr. 9:16	383
	Neh. 12:28	459
town in Judah	1 Chr. 2:54	376
	Neh. 7:26	452
Nethophathite—*inhabitant of Nethophah*		
guardsman of David	2 Sam. 23:28	311
	1 Chr. 27:15	400
Nettles—*prickly herbs*		
refuge for cowards	Job 30:7	485
symbolic of waste		
and desolation	Isa. 34:13	613
	Prov. 24:31	573
New—*recent; recently manifested*		
bottles	Mark 2:22	*37*
cart	1 Sam. 6:7	259
cloth	Matt. 9:16	*11*
commandment	John 13:34	*108*
creature	2 Cor. 5:17	*179*
doctrine	Mark 1:27	*36*
fruit	Ezek. 47:12	743
garment	1 Ki. 11:29, 30	329
gods	Jdgs. 5:8	231
heart	Ezek. 36:26	731
heaven and earth	Rev. 21:1	*256*
king	Ex. 1:8	51
lump	1 Cor. 5:7	*166*
man	Eph. 4:24	*192*
name	Isa. 62:2	634
nothing	Eccl. 1:9	578
sepulcher	John 19:41	*114*
spirit	Ezek. 11:19	704
testament	Heb. 9:15	*221*
thing	Acts 17:21	*136*
timber	Ezra 6:4	441
tomb	Matt. 27:60	*34*
tongues	Mark 16:17	*55*
way	Heb. 10:20	*222*

	REFERENCE	PAGE
Deborah	Gen. 24:59	21
	Gen. 35:8	33
figuratively used	Num. 11:12	137

Nuts—*a fruit consisting of a kernel or seed enclosed in a woody shell*
| grew in garden | Song 6:11 | 588 |
| sent to Pharaoh | Gen. 43:11 | 42 |

Nymphas
| Christian at Laodicea | Col. 4:15 | 200 |

O

Oak—*hardwood tree*
Absalom caught in boughs	2 Sam. 18:9, 14	304
Deborah buried under	Gen. 35:8	33
figurative of strength	Amos 2:9	771
as a landmark	Jdgs. 6:11	232
marked places of important events	Josh. 24:26	226
	Gen. 35:4	33

Oars—*wooden implements for propelling a boat*
| of oak wood | Ezek. 27:6, 29 | 721 |

Oath—*solemn attestation; vow*
by Isaac	Gen. 26:26–31	24
in crowning Joash	2 Ki. 11:2–4	356
enjoined	Ex. 22:11	72
in God's name	Deut. 6:13	173
hand under thigh	Gen. 24:2, 3	20
	Gen. 47:29	47
hands lifted upward in	Gen. 14:21–24	12
	Rev. 10:5, 6	249
by Isaac	Gen. 26:26–31	24
Jacob with Joseph	Gen. 47:29–31	47
Jonathan and David	1 Sam. 20:42	276
Joseph with Israel	Gen. 50:25	50
Judah to Babylon	Ezek. 17:11–13	710
Moses with Caleb	Josh. 14:6–9	215
profane	Lev. 19:12	112
	James 5:12	229
	Josh. 23:7	224
	Matt. 5:33–37	7
rash	Gen. 25:33	23
	Josh. 9:19, 20	210
	Matt. 14:1–7	17
	Acts 23:21	143
Ruth to Naomi	Ruth 1:17	251
in testimony of accused	Num. 5:19	129
	1 Ki. 8:31	324
Zedekiah to Jeremiah	Jer. 38:16	675

Oaths of God
in Abrahamic covenant	Gen. 22:16–29	19
concerning Christ's priesthood	Heb. 7:21–28	220
in Davidic covenant	Ps. 89:34–37	532
in judgment against Israel	Ps. 95:10, 11	534
	Heb. 3:9–11	217
in overthrow of Israel's captivity	Isa. 14:24–32	600
	Isa. 62:8, 9	634
redemption confirmed	Heb. 6:17–19	219

Obadiah—*worshiper of Jehovah*
| covenant signer | Neh. 10:1, 5 | 456 |

	REFERENCE	PAGE
descendant of Jaconiah	1 Chr. 3:21	377
descendant of Joab	Ezra 8:9	443
father of Ishmaiah	1 Chr. 27:19	400
Gadite warrior	1 Chr. 12:8, 9	386
Levite overseer	2 Chr. 34:12	433
Levite porter	Neh. 12:25	459
man of Issachar	1 Chr. 7:1, 3	381
officer of Ahab	1 Ki. 18: 3–16	337
prophet of Judah	Obad. 1:1	776
son of Azel	1 Chr. 8:38	383
teaching prince	2 Chr. 17:7	416

Obal
| descendant: Joktan | Gen. 10:26, 28 | 9 |

Obduracy—*obstinacy; stubbornness; unyielding*
against truth	Acts 19:8, 9	138
defiant	Ex. 5:1, 2	54
foolish	2 Chr. 28:21–25	426
of Israelites	Num. 14:22	140
Jewish	Isa. 48:1–4	624
of Pharaoh	Ex. 7:14, 22	56
of Sodomites	Gen. 19:9, 14	15, 16
unfeeling	Eph. 4:17–19	192

Obed—*worshiper*
father of Azariah	2 Chr. 23:1	421
Levite doorkeeper	1 Chr. 26:1, 7	398
son of Boaz	Ruth 4:17–22	254
son of Ephlal	1 Chr. 2:37	376
warrior of David	1 Chr. 11:47	386

Odeb-edom—*worshiper of Edom*
a Gittite kept ark	2 Sam. 6:10–12	292
	1 Chr. 13:13, 14	388
	1 Chr. 15:25	389
tabernacle porter	1 Chr. 16:37, 38	390
temple treasurer	2 Chr. 25:24	424

Obedience—*submission to command, duty*
assures heaven	Rev. 22:14	258
based on faith	Rom. 1:5	150
better than sacrifice	1 Sam. 15:22	269
	Jer. 7:22, 23	645
to bishops	Heb. 13:7	225
brings blessings	Deut. 11:26–28	178
of children to parents	Eph. 6:1–3	193
complete	Josh. 11:15	212
enjoined	Acts 5:29	122
evidence of Christianity	Matt. 7:21	9
	Luke 8:21	67
to God rather than man	Acts 5:28, 29	122
of gospel necessary	2 Thess. 1:7–9	204
from gratitude	Deut. 7:6–11	174
indispensable	Isa. 1:14–17	590
Jesus delighted in	John 4:32–34	95
key to spiritual knowledge, fellowship	John 7:17	99
	John 14:23	109
lengthens life	1 Ki. 3:14	318
to magistrates	1 Pet. 2:11–25	231
Naaman healed by	2 Ki. 5:1–14	349
Noah saved by	Heb. 11:7	223
and prosperity	Job 36:11	490
success by	Num. 14:24	140
wholehearted	Deut. 32:46	199
of wives to husbands	Titus 2:4, 5	213

Obeisance—*homage; deference; reverence*
| Balaam before the Lord | Num. 22:31 | 150 |
| Bathsheba to David | 1 Ki. 1:16 | 314 |

	REFERENCE	PAGE
David to Saul	1 Sam. 24:8	279
Jairus to Jesus	Luke 8:41	68
Joseph's brothers to Joseph	Gen. 37:7	36
	Gen. 43:28	43
kings before Jesus	Ps. 72:11	523
Moses to Jethro	Ex. 18:7	68
wise men to Jesus	Matt. 2:11	4
woman of Tekoah to David	2 Sam. 14:4	299

Obil
| overseer of David's camels | 1 Chr. 27:30 | 400 |

Oblation—(See Offering)
| bring no vain | Isa. 1:13 | 590 |

Oblivion—*state of being completely forgotten*
fate of those who forsake God	Deut. 32:26	199
	Job 18:17	479
wicked doomed to	Ps. 34:16	507

Oboth—*water skins*
| station in the journeyings of Israel | Num. 21:10 | 148 |

Observation—*act of observing*
| difficult for Zaccheus | Luke 19:1–4 | 82 |
| the kingdom comes without | Luke 17:20 | 80 |

Obstacles—*hindrances*
put by God as judgment	Jer. 6:21	644
to be removed	Isa. 40:4	617
	Isa. 45:2	622
	Isa. 49:9–11	626
removed through prayer	Matt. 21:21	25
riches, to the kingdom	Mark 10:24	47

Obstinacy—*stubborn persistency; adherence to one's own opinion*
of Balaam	Num. 22:21–35	149
provoking	Ex. 32:7–10	82
rebellious	1 Sam. 8:18–20	261

Oded
| father of Azariah | 2 Chr. 15:1 | 414 |
| a prophet | 2 Chr. 28:9–15 | 426 |

Odors, Sweet—*scents*
in acts of devotion	Dan. 2:46	748
	John 12:3	105
symbolic of divine recognition, favor	Ps. 45:8	512
	Song 4:10	587

Offense—*breach of conduct; displeasure*
cannot be avoided	Luke 17:1	79
guarded against	1 Cor. 10:32	170
from prejudice	Mark 6:3	41
remedy	Matt. 18:8, 9	21
woe because of	Matt. 18:7	21

Offering—*a donation, gift, sacrifice*
of first fruits	Deut. 26:1–12	191
humble	1 Sam. 7:9	260
observed	Num. 28:1–31	155
by the princes	Num. 7:10–89	131
withholding	Isa. 43:23, 24	621

Offerings—(Jewish)
| burnt | Ex. 29:18 | 78 |
| drink | Lev. 23:13 | 116 |

	REFERENCE	PAGE
Parched Ground—*glaring sand*		
shall become a pool	Isa. 35:7	614
Parchments—*writing material made from animal skins*		
Paul's request for	2 Tim. 4:13	212
Pardon—(See Forgiveness) *excuse, acquitted*		
through Christ	Acts 13:38	132
completeness of	Isa. 44:22	622
conditional	Mark 11:25, 26	49
God's delight in	Micah 7:18	783
God's willingness to	Isa. 55:7	630
pray for	Ps. 25:11	503
requires confession	1 John 1:9	236
Parents—*fathers or mothers*		
affectionate	2 Sam. 13:39	299
ambitious	Matt. 20:20, 21	23
angry	1 Sam. 20:30, 31	276
to chasten rebellious children	Deut. 21:18–21	187
	Prov. 23:13	572
distressed	Mark 9:17–24	45
of evil influence	1 Ki. 22:51–53	344
examples of, followed	2 Ki. 14:1–3	359
forgiving	Luke 15:17–24	78
good influence of righteousness	2 Chr. 17:3	416
	2 Tim. 1:5	210
governing	Gen. 18:18, 19	15
heedless	Jdgs. 11:30–39	240
honored	Deut. 5:16	172
influential	Jer. 35:5–10	672
injunction to	Prov. 22:6	571
parental indulgence disastrous	Prov. 29:15	576
	1 Sam. 3:13	257
pious	1 Sam. 1:11	255
to provide for children	2 Cor. 12:14	183
	1 Tim. 5:8	208
responsibility of	1 Sam. 3:11–14	257
sons like	2 Chr. 24:7	422
to train their children	Deut. 6:7	173
	Eph. 6:4	193
Parlor—*room for reception of guests*		
Eglon slain in his	Jdgs. 3:17–21	229
sacrificial dining-room	1 Sam. 9:22	262
Parmashta—*chief*		
son of Haman	Est. 9:9, 10	467
Parmenas		
one of 7 deacons	Acts 6:5	122
Parnach		
prince of Zebulun	Num. 34:25	163
Parosh—*flea*		
called Pharosh	Ezra 8:3	443
head of exile family	Ezra 2:3	437
Parricide—*murder of one's father or mother*		
Sennacherib's sons	2 Ki. 19:36, 37	367
Parshandatha—*given by prayer (?)*		
son of Haman	Est. 9:7, 10	445
Parsimony—*stinginess; frugality*		
of disciples	Matt. 26:8, 9	30
in hoarding money	Eccl. 5:13	581
	Prov. 11:24	564
in ignoring the poor	Prov. 21:13	570
	Prov. 28:27	576

	REFERENCE	PAGE
in withholding tithes and offerings	Mal. 3:8	801
	Neh. 13:9, 10	460
Parthians—*inhabitants of Parthia*		
at Pentecost	Acts 2:1, 9	117
Partiality—*favoritism; bias; unfairness*		
complaint against	Acts 6:1–3	122
forbidden in social life	Lev. 19:15	112
	Job 13:10	476
improper	James 2:1–4	227
ministers advised against	1 Tim. 5:21	209
	Acts 10:28, 34	128
not good in judgment	Prov. 24:23	573
	Prov. 18:5	568
not shown by God	Matt. 5:45	7
shown by Jacob	Gen. 37:1, 3	35
surprising	Gen. 43:30–34	43
warning against	Prov. 28:21	576
Partnership—*an association; participation*		
with God	1 Cor. 3:7, 9	164
James, John, Simon	Luke 5:10, 11	62
Partridge—*a small game bird*		
dwelt in mountains	1 Sam. 26:20	282
symbol of fraud	Jer. 17:11	654
Paruah		
father of Jehoshaphat	1 Ki. 4:17	319
Parvaim—*region, unknown*		
gold from	2 Chr. 3:6	405
Pasach		
son of Japhlet	1 Chr. 7:33	382
Pas-dammim		
called Ephes-dammim	1 Sam. 17:1	271
place in Judah	1 Chr. 11:13	385
Paseah—*limping* (Phaseah)		
father of Jehoida	Neh. 3:6	448
head of Nethinim family	Ezra 2:43, 49	438
son of Eshton	1 Chr. 4:12	377
Pashur		
covenant-signer	Neh. 10:1, 3	456
father of Gedaliah	Jer. 38:1	675
head of exile priestly family	Ezra 2:38	438
	Neh. 7:41	453
son of Immer	Jer. 20:1	656
son of Melchiah	Jer. 21:1	657
Passover—*a Jewish feast*		
appointed by God	Ex. 12:3–28	61
Christ observed	Matt. 26:18, 19	31
Christ our	1 Cor. 5:7	166
Ezra observed	Ezra 6:19	442
Joshua observed	Josh. 5:10–12	205
Josiah observed	2 Ki. 23:21–23	368
laws governing	Lev. 23:4	116
	Deut. 16:1–8	182
Moses observed at Sinai	Num. 9:4, 5	134
observed by Jesus	Matt. 26:17–20	31
prisoners released at	Matt. 27:15	33
Passport—*authority to travel; guarantee of citizenship and protection*		
given to Nehemiah	Neh. 2:7–9	448

	REFERENCE	PAGE
Pastors—*shepherds*		
office of divine appointment	Jer. 3:15	640
	Eph. 4:11	192
some were brutish	Jer. 10:21	648
unfaithful punished	Jer. 23:2	658
Pasture—*ground for grazing of domestic animals*		
sought out by Israel	Gen. 47:4	46
	1 Chr. 4:39–41	378
symbolic of God's care	Ps. 23:2	502
	Ps. 79:13	528
Patara—*seaport of Lycia*		
Paul took ship at	Acts 21:1	140
Pathros—*region of upper Egypt*		
baseness of	Ezek. 29:14–16	724
Jews return from	Isa. 11:11	598
Jews scattered to	Jer. 44:1–14	680
Pathrusim		
citizens of Pathros	1 Chr. 1:12	374
descendants of Ham	Gen. 10:14	8
Patience—*ability to wait or endure without complaint; sufferance; composure*		
admonition to	James 5:7, 8	229
brings forth fruit	Luke 8:15	67
of Christ	Heb. 12:1–3	224
Christian virtue	Heb. 10:35, 36	223
	2 Pet. 1:5, 6	234
in Christian work	Heb. 10:36	223
commended	1 Thess. 5:14	203
God of	Rom. 15:5	161
of Job	James 5:11	229
needful	Ps. 37:7–9	508
in old age	Titus 2:2	213
possess soul in	Luke 21:19	85
results of	Heb. 6:12	219
rewarded	Ps. 40:1–3	510
run race with	Heb. 12:1	224
tested	Matt. 18:28–30	22
in tribulation	Rom. 12:12	159
through trying of faith	James 1:3, 4	226
Patmos—*an island in Aegean Sea*		
John an exile on	Rev. 1:9, 10	243
Patriarch—*father and head of a family*		
Abraham	Heb. 7:4	219
David	Acts 2:29	118
sons of Jacob	Acts 7:8, 9	123
Patrimony—*a system of government in which the father or male heir of his choice rules*		
	Deut. 18:8	184
Patriotism—*devotion to one's country*		
enjoined	1 Chr. 19:13	393
extoled by Deborah and Barak	Jdgs. 5:1, 2	231
of Hadad	1 Ki. 11:21	328
of Israelites	Ps. 137:1–6	552
of Nehemiah	Neh. 2:2, 3	447
in tribulation and defeat	Ps. 137:1–6	552
Patrobas		
disciple at Rome	Rom. 16:14	162
Pattern—*example worthy of imitation*		
of altar of the Lord	Josh. 22:28	224
Christians to be	Matt. 5:16	6
	Tit. 2:7	214
in creation of man	Gen. 1:26	2
Jesus a	John 13:15	107
of tabernacle	Heb. 8:5	107

REFERENCE	PAGE

Polytheism—*belief in more than one deity*
ancestors of
  Israelites.........Josh. 24:2, 23   225
of Israelites.........Jdgs. 2:12   228
Jacob's household...Gen. 35:2, 4   33
of Judah.........Jer. 2:28   640
of Laban.........Gen. 31:19   29

Pomegranates—*fruit of a certain tropical tree; also the tree*
ornaments on pillars
  of temple.........1 Ki. 7:20   322
    2 Ki. 25:16, 17   373
in Palestine.......Num. 13:23   139

Pommel—*a knob*
round ornament on
  temple chapiter....2 Chr. 4:12, 13   405
    1 Ki. 7:41, 42   323

Pontus—*district of Asia*
Jews lived in......Acts 2:5, 9   *117*

Pool—*a small pool of fresh water*
Bethesda..........John 5:2   *95*
Gibeon..........2 Sam. 2:13   288
Hebron..........2 Sam. 4:12   291
Samaria..........1 Ki. 22:38   343
Siloam..........John 9:7   *102*
water brought to....2 Ki. 20:20   367

Poor—*those who lack comfortable subsistence; the needy*
always with us......John 12:8   *106*
apostle Peter.......Acts 3:6   *119*
benevolence to.....Luke 19:8   *82*
blessed..........Luke 6:20   *64*
care for..........Prov. 28:27   576
cared for by church..Gal. 2:10   186
causes of poverty....Prov. 10:4–15   563
certain widow.....Mark 12:41–44   50
chosen by God.....James 2:5   227
compassion for.....Lev. 25:35–38   119
extorted by the rich..Amos 8:4–6   775
Gideon..........Jdgs. 6:13, 15   232
gospel preached to...Luke 4:18   *61*
honored by angels...Luke 16:22   *79*
indifference to.....Luke 16:19–23   *79*
Job, a father to.....Job 29:16   485
law for the protection
  and care of.......Ex. 22:25–27   72
    Ex. 23:10, 11   72
    Lev. 19:9–14   112
    Deut. 15:7–11   181
    Deut. 24:10–18   189
Lazarus..........Luke 16:20   *79*
never forgotten by
  God.............Ps. 9:18   497
often very devout...2 Ki. 4:2   347
oppression of......Prov. 22:16   571
to pity............Prov. 19:17   569
sometimes better
  than the rich......Prov. 28:6   575
in spirit...........Matt. 5:3   *6*
treated kindly.....Lev. 19:10   112
widow of Zarephath.1 Ki. 17:10   336

Poplar Tree—*a quick growing tree of the willow family*
Jacob peeled rods of.Gen. 30:37   28
shade of..........Hosea 4:13   762

Popularity—*possessing the favor and confidence of others*
of Absalom.......2 Sam. 15:1–6   301
cause of envy......Acts 13:44, 45   *132*
caution respecting...Col. 3:22   *200*
danger in.........Luke 6:26   *64*
    John 12:43   *107*
of David..........2 Sam. 3:36   290
of a deceiver.......Acts 8:9–11   *125*

REFERENCE	PAGE

honorable..........1 Ki. 4:29–34   319
of Jesus..........Mark 2:2   *37*
    Mark 3:10   *38*
    Luke 5:1   *62*
    Mark 12:37   *50*
sought by acts of
  cruelty to saints....Acts 12:1–3   *130*
    Acts 24:27   *145*
sought by
  hypocrites........John 12:42, 43   *107*

Poratha
son of Haman......Est. 9:8   467

Porch—*covered structure; veranda*
vestibule..........Jdgs. 3:23   229

Porter—*gatekeeper*
Levites acted as.....1 Chr. 23:3, 5   395
in private houses...Mark 13:34   *51*
stationed at gates...2 Sam. 18:26   305
at temple doors.....1 Chr. 9:22   384

Portion—*a part of whole; an allotment*
allowance of food...Gen. 47:22   47
God is the portion
  of saints..........Ps. 73:26   524
    Lam. 3:24   694
one's inheritance....Luke 15:12   *78*
of the wicked, fire
  and brimstone.....Ps. 11:6   498
    Matt. 24:51   *29*

Post—*upright piece of material used for support; a messenger*
messenger.........Est. 3:13   464
    2 Chr. 30:6   428
    Est. 8:10   467
upright side of
  door............1 Ki. 6:33   321

Potentate—*a sovereign*
Christ the only.....1 Tim. 6:15   *209*

Potiphar—*gift of Ra (?)*
imprisoned Joseph...Gen. 39:20   38
officer of Pharaoh...Gen. 39:1   38

Poti-pherah—*he whom Ra gave (?)*
Joseph's
  father-in-law......Gen. 41:45   40

Pots—*vessels of rounded form*
of brass............Ex. 38:3   89
death in..........2 Ki. 4:40, 41   348
used for cooking....2 Chr. 35:13   435
used for refining....Prov. 27:21   575
used for washing....Ps. 60:8   518
used for wine......John 2:6, 7   *92*

Potsherd
fragment of pottery..Job 2:8   470
    Isa. 45:9   623

Pottage—*something boiled; a thick broth or stew*
Esau's birthright....Gen. 25:29–34   23

Potter, Pottery—*one who makes vessels of clay; earthenware vessels*
figurative of God's
  work............Isa. 64:8   635
    Rom. 9:21   *157*
preparation of
  clay............Isa. 41:25   619
work by hand......Jer. 18:4   654

Potter's Field—*burial place for the poor and unknown*
bribe money used to
  buy............Matt. 27:7, 8   *33*

REFERENCE	PAGE

Pound—*unit of weight*
(See also Jewish Measures, Weights,
  and Coins)
parable of.........Luke 19:12–27   *82*
weight for money...Ezra 2:69   439

Poverty—*state of being poor; need; dearth*
(See also Poor)
benevolence in......Mark 12:41–44   *50*
consolation in.....Prov. 19:22   569
from drunkenness...Prov. 23:21   572
from evil
  associations.......Prov. 28:19   576
from famine.......Neh. 5:1–5   450
grave misfortune....Prov. 10:15   563
from indolence......Prov. 6:10, 11   560
leads to temptation..Prov. 30:9   577
from love of pleasure.Prov. 21:17   571
no hindrance to
  David...........1 Sam. 18:22, 23   273
Paul suffered from..2 Cor. 11:25–27   *183*
wealth in..........Prov. 13:7   565

Power of God
creates and controls
  all nature.........Ps. 65:5, 6   519,520
    Job 26:12   483
healed a lame man..Acts 3:11, 12   *119*
infinite.............Matt. 19:26   *23*
provides salvation
  for man...........Isa. 25:9   607
    Zeph. 3:17   789
promised to Joshua..Josh. 1:5–7   201
right hand, glorious..Ex. 15:6   65
in voice............Ps. 29:4   504

Power of Christ—*strength; force*
anointed with, by
  God.............Acts 10:38   *128*
to forgive sin......Matt. 9:6   *11*
to give life........John 17:2   *111*
of his word........Luke 4:32   *62*
infinite...........Matt. 28:18   *35*
over all things......John 3:35   *94*
over demons......Luke 8:2, 36   *67*
over nature........Luke 8:25   *67*

Power, Spiritual
gives men great
  courage..........Micah 3:8   780
    Acts 4:31–33   *120*
and love and sound
  mind.............2 Tim. 1:7   *210*
at Pentecost......Acts 2:1–4   *117*
in preaching......1 Cor. 2:1–4   *164*
superior to physical
  forces............Zech. 4:6   793
    Acts 10:38   *128*
through faith......Matt. 17:20, 21   *20*
through the Holy
  Spirit...........Luke 24:49   *90*
    Acts 1:8   *117*
    1 Thess. 1:5   *201*

Praetorium—*residence of Roman governor*
Christ taken to.....Mark 15:16   *54*

Praise—*laudation to God; honor given*
for deliverance......Ex. 15:1–19   65
given to God by all..Ps. 117:1, 2   544
    Ps. 150:1, 6   556
in heaven.........Rev. 5:11, 12   *246*
with instruments....Ps. 150:3–5   557
irrepressible.......Luke 19:33–38   *82*
love of.............John 12:42, 43   *107*
and Mary.........Luke 1:46   *57*
reasons for........Ps. 147:1–20   555
    1 Pet. 2:9   *231*
received by
  Absalom........2 Sam. 14:25   300
of self.............Prov. 27:2   574

	REFERENCE	PAGE
for the soul	Ps. 31:5	505
	Mark 10:45	48
	Rom. 3:24	152
	Gal. 4:4, 5	187
	1 Pet. 1:18, 19	230

Red Dragon
in John's vision	Rev. 12:3–17	250

Red Heifer
purification offering	Num. 19:2	145

Red Horse
in John's vision	Rev. 6:4	246
in Zechariah's vision	Zech. 1:8	792
	Zech. 6:12	794

Red Sea—*sea of reeds*
boundary of		
promised land	Ex. 23:31	72
Israelites camped by	Num. 33:10, 11	161
Pharaoh perished in	Deut. 11:3, 4	177
Solomon built ships		
on	1 Ki. 9:26	327
waters divided	Ex. 14:26–31	64
wilderness of	Ex. 13:18	63

Reed—*slender, tall grass*
easily broken	2 Ki. 18:21	365
measuring rod	Ezek. 40:5	735
symbol of weakness	Matt. 11:7	13

Reelaiah
called Raamiah	Neh. 7:7	452
returned exile	Ezra 2:2	462

Refining—*purifying*
by afflictions	Isa. 48:10	625
by chastening	John 15:2	109
of gold	1 Chr. 28:18	401
Jesus, our redeemer	Mal. 3:1–3	801
of silver	1 Chr. 29:4	401

Reflection—*contemplation*
acceptable to God	Ps. 19:14	501
desirable subjects of	Phil. 4:8	197
painful	Mark 14:72	53

Reformers—*those who seek improved conditions*
Daniel	Dan. 5:17–22	752
Elijah	1 Ki. 21:17–22	341
John the Baptist	Matt. 14:3–5	17

Reforms, Religious—*changes; righting of evil conditions*
of Asa	1 Ki. 15:9–15	333
of Ezra	Ezra 10:1–3	445
of Hezekiah	2 Chr. 31:10	430
of Jehoiada	2 Ki. 11:17, 18	357
of Jehoshaphat	2 Chr. 19:1–3	418
of Jehu	2 Ki. 10:18–27	355
of Josiah	2 Ki. 23:1–4	369
of Manasseh	2 Chr. 33:10–15	432
of Nehemiah	Neh. 13:19–31	460

Refuge—*shelter; protection*
in Christ	Heb. 6:18	219
from enemies	Ps. 31:20	506
in God	Deut. 33:27	200
in trouble	Ps. 27:5	504

Refuge, Cities of
divinely appointed	Ex. 21:13	70
names given	Josh. 20:7–9	221
for safety of		
innocent	Deut. 4:41, 42	171
six designated	Num. 35:11–14	164

Refugee—*one who flees for safety*
Hadad	1 Ki. 11:14–18	328

	REFERENCE	PAGE
Jesus	Matt. 2:11–15	4
slaves, protection of	Deut. 23:15, 16	189

Regem
son of Jahdai	1 Chr. 2:47	376

Regem-melech—*Regem is king*
sent to Bethel	Zech. 7:2	795

Regeneration—*spiritual renewal*
promise concerning	Matt. 19:28	23
the washing of	Titus 3:5	214
(See Born Again; New Birth)		

Regicide—*killing of a sovereign or king*
of Ahaziah	2 Ki. 9:27	354
of Amaziah	2 Ki. 14:19, 20	359
of Ehud	Jdgs. 3:16–23	229
of Elah	1 Ki. 16:9–11	335
of Ish-bosheth	2 Sam. 4:5–8	290
of Joash	2 Ki. 12:20, 21	358
of Joram	2 Ki. 9:24	354
of Nadab	1 Ki. 15:27–29	361
of Pekah	2 Ki. 15:30	361
of Pekahiah	2 Ki. 15:26	361
of Saul	2 Sam. 1:9–10, 16	287
of Sennacherib	2 Ki. 19:36, 37	367
	Isa. 37:37, 38	616
of Shallum	2 Ki. 15:14	360
of Zechariah	2 Ki. 15:10	360

Register—*genealogical record*
discovered by		
Nehemiah	Neh. 7:5	452
names sought in	Ezra 2:62	438

Rehabiah—*Jehovah has enlarged*
son of Eliezer	1 Chr. 23:17	396

Rehob—*width*
city in northern		
Israel	Num. 13:21	139
	2 Sam. 10:8	295
city of Asher	Josh. 19:24, 28	220
a covenanter	Neh. 10:1, 11	456
father of Hadadezer	2 Sam. 8:3	294

Rehoboam—*the people is enlarged (?)*
badly advised	1 Ki. 12:1–11	329
built many cities	2 Chr. 11:5–12	412
had 18 wives	2 Chr. 11:21	412
and idolatry	2 Chr. 11:13–17	412
kingdom of divided	1 Ki. 12:12–20	330
no war on ten tribes	1 Ki. 12:21–24	330
reigned wickedly	1 Ki. 14:21–31	333
son and successor of		
Solomon	1 Ki. 11:43	329
subjugated by		
Egypt	2 Chr. 12:2–16	412, 413

Rehoboth—*open spaces*
city of Asshur	Gen. 10:11	8
town near		
Euphrates	Gen. 36:37	35
well dug by Isaac	Gen. 26:18–22	23, 24

Rehum—*compassion*
a covenanter	Neh. 10:1, 25	456
Persian officer	Ezra 4:8	464
Postexilic priest	Neh. 12:1, 3	458
returned exile	Ezra 2:1, 2	437
son of Bani	Neh. 3:17	449

Rei—*friend*
loyal to David	1 Ki. 1:8	313

Reins—*word used for kidneys*
searched by God	Rev. 2:23	244
seat of longing	Ps. 26:2	503
vital part of man	Job 16:13	478

	REFERENCE	PAGE
Rejection of Christ—*the forsaking of Christ*		
damning sin	John 3:16–18	93
by his own city	Luke 4:16, 28	61
by his own people	John 1:11	91
from jealousy	Luke 9:50–53	70

Rejection of God and God's Word—*the refusal to accept*
with adamant		
hearts	Zech. 7:12	195
with deafened ears	Jer. 6:10	643
by Israelites	1 Sam. 8:7	261
	1 Sam. 10:19	263
with malice and hate	Jer. 36:23	673
results in ruin	Isa. 5:24	593
wickedness	Ps. 50:16, 17	514

Rejoicing—*feeling joyful; filled with delight*
in afflictions	1 Pet. 4:12, 13	232
of bridegroom	Ps. 19:5	501
of a convert	Acts 16:30–34	135
of the desert	Isa. 35:1	614
duty of Christians	Phil. 4:4	197
duty of Israel	Deut. 12:7	179
in every good thing	Deut. 26:11	191
in famines	Hab. 3:17, 18	787
in gifts	1 Chr. 29:6–9	401
in God's creation	Isa. 65:18	636
great	Luke 19:33–38	82
of heart in God's		
laws	Ps. 19:8	501
in persecution	Acts 5:41	122
in poverty	2 Cor. 6:10	179
in prison	Acts 16:24, 25	135
in reproaches	Luke 6:22, 23	64
in temptation	James 1:2–4	226
wrong kind of	Prov. 24:17	573

Rekem
city of Benjamin	Josh. 18:20, 27	219
Midianite king	Josh. 13:21	214
son of Hebron	1 Chr. 2:43	376

Relatives—*kinsmen or kinswomen*
Gideon feared his	Jdgs. 6:25–27	233
helpful	John 1:40–42	92
hindrance to some	Luke 9:59–62	70
interference of	Num. 12:1, 2	138
of Jesus	Matt. 13:55, 56	17
persecution from	Mark 13:12	51

Relief—*alleviation; comfort; the act of freeing wholly or partly from something oppressive*
aid to poor	Lev. 25:35	119
brings blessing to		
giver	Ps. 41:1	511
by disciples	Acts 11:29	129
from God	Ps. 146:9	555
should be secret	Matt. 6:3	7

Religion, False
abominable to God	Titus 1:16	213
and ceremonialism	Mark 7:3–13	43
and false praying	Matt. 23:14	27
and false		
professions	Ezek. 33:31, 32	728
and flattery of God	Ps. 78:35, 36	527
and formalism	Matt. 23:23	27
and legalism	Luke 13:14–17	76
made easy	1 Ki. 12:27–31	330
and outward show	Matt. 6:5	7
rejected by God	Isa. 29:13–17	609

Religion, True
greatest		
commandment	Mark 12:30, 31	50
knowledge and		
mercy	Hosea 6:6	763
pure and undefiled	James 1:27	227
whole duty of man	Eccl. 12:13	585

	REFERENCE	PAGE
due parents	Deut. 27:16	192
due rulers	Eccl. 10:20	584
of one another	1 Pet. 2:17	231

Respect of Persons—*to show partiality in judgment*

	REFERENCE	PAGE
God does not have	Deut. 10:17	177
	Acts 10:34	128
	Rom. 2:11	151
wrong	Prov. 24:23	573
	James 2:9	227

Responsibility—*duty; accountability*

	REFERENCE	PAGE
assumed by Jews	Matt. 27:24, 25	33
of bishops	Heb. 13:17	225
for carelessness	Ex. 22:6	71
confessed by Jonah	Jonah 1:12	778
disclaimed by Pilate	Matt. 27:24	33
distributed equally	Ex. 32:35	83
evaded on Jericho road	Luke 10:30–32	71
feared by council	Acts 5:27, 28	122
for knowledge	2 Pet. 2:20–22	235
for offenses	Matt. 18:5–7	21
for others	Gen. 4:8–12	4
for our own sins	Ezek. 18:20	712
overwhelmingly to Moses	Num. 11:11–15	137
parental	1 Sam. 3:12–14	257
Paul cleared of	Acts 20:26, 27	140
for personal guilt	Deut. 24:16	190
for spoken words	Matt. 12:36, 37	15

Rest

	REFERENCE	PAGE
commanded as a rebuke	Matt. 26:45	32
enforced	Ex. 10:21–23	60
enjoined by Jesus	Mark 6:31	42
eternal in heaven	Rev. 14:13	245
found in God	Ps. 116:7	544
given by Christ	Matt. 11:28, 29	14
for God's people	Heb. 4:9, 11	218
God's presence gives	Ex. 33:14	84
lost by obstinacy	Isa. 28:12	608
man yearns for	Ps. 55:6	516
one year of	Lev. 25:4, 5	118
received by faith	Heb. 4:3	218
on the Sabbath	Ex. 31:15	82
troubles cease	Job 3:17–20	471

Restitution—*compensation; amends act of restoring something which has been lost or taken away*

	REFERENCE	PAGE
for damaged property	Ex. 22:3–12	71
proof of repentance	Luke 19:8, 9	82
secures forgiveness	Ezek. 33:15, 16	728
seven-fold in theft	Prov. 6:30, 31	561
times of	Acts 3:21	119

Restoration—*renewal*

	REFERENCE	PAGE
based on mercy	Micah 7:18, 19	783
divinely promised	Jer. 30:17	666
a fourfold	Luke 19:8	82
of Israel	Joel 2:28–32	769
	Mal. 3:4	801
prayer for	Ps. 51:11, 12	515
of soul, by God	Ps. 23:3	502

Restraints—*restrictions*

	REFERENCE	PAGE
David's prayer for	Ps. 19:13	501
Jesus' prayer for us	John 17:15	111
necessary for animals	Ps. 32:9	506

Resurrection—*arising again*

	REFERENCE	PAGE
basis of new life	Col. 3:1	199
believed by Isaiah	Isa. 26:19	607
of body, promised	John 5:28, 29	96
Christ's	1 Cor. 15:12–56	174

	REFERENCE	PAGE
a comfort to believers	Rom. 8:23	156
	Phil. 3:8–12	196
Daniel's testimony	Dan. 12:2	760
denied by Sadducees and false teachers	Luke 20:27	84
	1 Cor. 15:12	174
doctrine derided	Acts 17:18, 32	136
of Dorcas	Acts 9:36–40	127
effected by God's power	1 Cor. 6:14	166
	2 Cor. 4:14	178
first	Rev. 20:4–6	256
foretold in vision	Ezek. 37:11–14	732
general	Rev. 20:1–15	256
of Jairus' daughter	Matt. 9:23–25	11
of Lazarus of Bethany	John 11:43, 44	105
of many saints	Matt. 27:52, 53	34
no marriage in	Matt. 22:23–30	26
of only son of a widow	Luke 7:11–15	65
Paul's testimony	Acts 24:10, 15	144
preached by apostles	Acts 4:2	120
proclaimed by Christ	John 6:40	98
saints raised first	1 Thess. 4:16	203
of son of Shunammite	2 Ki. 4:32–35	348
of the son of a widow	1 Ki. 17:17–22	336
symbolized in baptism	Rom. 6:4	154
of an unnamed man	2 Ki. 13:20, 21	358

Resurrection of Christ

	REFERENCE	PAGE
announced by angels	Matt. 28:5, 6	34
basis of future hope	1 Thess. 4:14–18	203
declared by Peter	Acts 10:39–41	128
explained in Pentecostal sermon	Acts 2:22–32	118
foretold	Ps. 16:10, 11	499
foretold by himself	Matt. 16:21	20
gives hope	1 Pet. 1:3	230
for our justification	Rom. 4:25	153
preached by Paul	Acts 26:22, 23	146
witnessed at the ascension	Luke 24:50, 51	90
witnessed by apostles in Galilee	Matt. 28:16, 17	35
witnessed by brother, James	1 Cor. 15:7	174
witnessed by eleven apostles	John 20:26	115
witnessed by five hundred	1 Cor. 15:6	173
witnessed by Mary Magdalene	Mark 16:9	55
witnessed by the other women	Matt. 28:9	34
witnessed by Paul	1 Cor. 15:8	174
witnessed by Peter	Luke 24:34	90
witnessed by sea of Galilee	John 21:1	115
witnessed by ten apostles	John 20:19	115
witnessed by two disciples	Luke 24:13–15	89

Retaliation—*revenge; returning like for like*

	REFERENCE	PAGE
forbidden	Prov. 24:29	573
good for evil	1 Pet. 3:9	231
Paul warns against	Rom. 12:17, 19	159

Retribution—*recompense; punishment*

	REFERENCE	PAGE
backfires on the evil	Ps. 37:14, 15	508
example of David	2 Sam. 12:10	297
fruit of sin	Ps. 7:15, 16	496
inevitable	Heb. 10:30, 31	222
Jezebel's death	2 Ki. 9:30, 37	354

	REFERENCE	PAGE
justice demands	Deut. 7:9, 10	174
justifiable	Est. 7:7–10	466
for sinning angels	2 Pet. 2:4	234

Reu

	REFERENCE	PAGE
called Ragau	Luke 3:35	61
son of Peleg and ancestor of Abraham	Gen. 11:18–26	9, 10

Reuben—*behold a son (?)*

	REFERENCE	PAGE
descendants of	Num. 26:5–9	152
eldest son of Jacob	Gen. 35:22, 23	34
forfeited birthright	Gen. 49:3, 4	48
guilty of gross wrong	Gen. 35:22	34
had four sons	Gen. 46:9	46
not a party to sale of Joseph	Gen. 37:21–29	36
	Gen. 42:22–24	41

Reubenites—*descendants of Reuben, tribe of Reuben*

	REFERENCE	PAGE
aided tribes west of Jordan	Josh. 1:12–18	202
census of its fighting men	Num. 1:18–21	123
	Num. 26:2, 7	152
consisted of four families	Ex. 6:14	55
	Num. 26:5–11	153
defeated the Hagarites	1 Chr. 5:18–22	379
Elizur, wilderness prince of	Num. 1:5	123
	Num. 7:30–35	132
given allotment east of Jordan	Num. 32:1–42	160
	Josh. 18:7	218
honored in future glory of Israel	Ezek. 48:6, 7	744
	Rev. 7:5	247
men who joined Korah's rebellion	Num. 16:1–50	142
	Deut. 11:6	177
reproached by Deborah	Jdgs. 5:15, 16	231
reproached for sin of omission	Jdgs. 5:15, 16	231
taken captive by Assyria	1 Chr. 5:26	379

Reuel—*friend of God*

	REFERENCE	PAGE
descendant of Benjamin	1 Chr. 9:8	383
a Gadite	Num. 2:14	124
Moses' father-in-law	Ex. 2:18	52
	Num. 10:29	136
(See Jethro)		
son of Esau	Gen. 36:2–4	34

Reumah

	REFERENCE	PAGE
Nahor's concubine	Gen. 22:24	19

Revelations of God—*the acts of revealing divine truth*

	REFERENCE	PAGE
by angels	Acts 27:23, 24	147
Christ's incarnation	John 1:14	91
given through nature and visions	Gen. 46:2	45
	Ps. 97:6	535
by the prophets	Heb. 1:1	216
by the spirit	Rev. 1:10	243
in his word	Ps. 119:130	547

Revelries—*noisy, boisterous merrymaking*

	REFERENCE	PAGE
denounced as works of flesh	Gal. 5:21	188
at harvest feasts	1 Sam. 25:36	281
in idol worship	Ex. 32:6	82

	REFERENCE	PAGE
of non-Christians	1 Pet. 4:3	*232*
at social feasts	Jdgs. 16:25	244
in time of great peril	Isa. 22:13	604
in war victories	1 Sam. 30:16	285

Revenge—*retaliation; vindication*

avoided by Jacob	Gen. 27:41–45	25
of a brother	2 Sam. 13:22–29	299
forbidden	Rom. 12:17, 19	*159*
kindness the best	Prov. 25:21, 22	574
punishment for	Ezek. 25:15–17	720
rebuked by Christ	Luke 9:54, 55	*70*
Samson prayed for	Jdgs. 16:28–30	244

Reverence—*veneration; profound respect*

affectionate	Luke 7:36–39	*66*
attitudes of	Neh. 8:4–6	454
of esteem	2 Sam. 9:6	295
to Christ	Phil. 2:9, 11	*195*
to God	Ps. 89:7	531
to God's house	Lev. 19:30	112
to God's name	Deut. 28:58	*194*
to God's word	Rev. 22:18, 19	*258*

Reverend—*worthy of reverence*

God's name holy and	Ps. 111:9	542

Revile(d)—*defamed; abused in act or speech*

blessed to be	Matt. 5:11	*6*
Christ was	Matt. 27:39	*33*
we bless when	1 Cor. 4:12	*165*

Revivals—*occasions of renewed interest in religion*

in Berea	Acts 17:10–13	*136*
in Corinth	Acts 18:1–11	*137*
in Ephesus	Acts 19:1–20	*138*
in Iconium	Acts 14:1	*132*
in Jerusalem	Acts 2:14–47	*118*
prayed for	Ps. 85:6	530
	Hab. 3:2	787
promised	Isa. 35:1–10	614
in Samaria	Acts 8:5–12	*125*
in wilderness of Judea	Matt. 3:1–6	*5*
	Mark 1:2–11	*35*

Rewards

for benevolent acts	Luke 6:35	*64*
for doing good	Rom. 2:10	*151*
earthly	1 Ki. 3:14	318
	Prov. 14:11	566
for martyrdom	Rev. 20:4	*256*
for ministerial aid	Heb. 10:34	*222*
in persecutions	Matt. 5:11, 12	*6*
rejected	Num. 22:7–41	149
	Deut. 16:19	183
	1 Ki. 13:7, 10	331
	Dan. 5:17	752
	Micah 7:3	782
in reproaches	Heb. 11:26	*223*
for stewardship	Matt. 25:23	*30*
for winning souls	Dan. 12:3	760

Rezeph

city conquered by Assyria	Isa. 37:12	615

Rezia

descendant of Asher	1 Chr. 7:39	382

Rezin

head of family of Nethinim	Neh. 7:46, 50	453
king of Syria	2 Ki. 15:37	361
	2 Ki. 16:9	362

Rezon—*prince*

son of Eliada	1 Ki. 11:23–25	228

Rhegium—*a city*

on coast of Italy	Acts 28:13	148

Rhesa

ancestor of Joseph	Luke 3:27	*60*

Rhoda—*rose*

maid in Mary's home	Acts 12:12, 13	*130*

Rhodes—*island southwest of Asia*

visited by Paul	Acts 21:1	*140*

Rib—*one of a series of bones attached to spine*

Eve formed of	Gen. 2:22	2

Ribai

father of Ittai	2 Sam. 23:29	311

Riblah

town in Hamath	2 Ki. 23:33	371
Zedekiah's sons slain at	2 Ki. 25:6, 7	372

Rich—*wealthy persons*

and benevolence	Luke 19:8	*82*
duties of	1 Tim. 6:17–19	*209*
and indifference	Luke 16:19–21	*79*
lose all in death	Ps. 49:16, 17	514
and many friends	Prov. 19:4	569
and oppression	Amos 8:4–6	775
and robbery	2 Sam. 12:1–4	297

Riches, Earthly

of Abraham	Gen. 13:2	11
beget avarice	Ps. 62:10	519
canker the soul	James 5:3	*229*
of David	1 Chr. 29:26–28	402
deceptive	Luke 12:16–21	*74*
do not satisfy	Eccl. 2:26	580
doom of wicked rich	Luke 12:16–21	*74*
endanger integrity	Prov. 28:20	576
given by God	Deut. 8:18	175
	1 Chr. 29:11, 12	402
	Haggai 2:8	791
good name better than	Prov. 22:1	571
hinder conversion	Matt. 19:23	*23*
of Isaac	Gen. 26:12, 14	23
of Jacob	Gen. 30:37–43	28
of Job	Job 1:1, 3	469
of Joseph of Arimathea	Matt. 27:57	*34*
lead to temptation	1 Tim. 6:9	*209*
pass to others	Ps. 49:10	514
result in barrenness	Mark 4:19	*39*
rich young ruler	Mark 10:17–27	*47*
of Solomon	2 Chr. 9:22	410
sometimes inherited	Prov. 19:14	569
take wings	Prov. 23:5	572
transient	Matt. 6:19	*8*
treasurer of vanity	Ps. 39:6	510
turn heart from God	Deut. 8:13, 14	175

Riches, Spiritual

in exchange for possessions	Luke 12:33	*74*
greater than earthly	Heb. 11:26	*223*
Paul as example	2 Cor. 6:10	*179*
of poor	Prov. 13:7	565
promised by God	James 2:5	*227*

Riddle—*a puzzling question; conundrum*

Ezekiel puts forth God's	Ezek. 17:2	710
Samson's	Jdgs. 14:12–19	242
understood by wise	Prov. 1:5, 6	557

Righteous—*virtuous; blameless; upright*

death of	Ps. 116:15	544

objects of God's care	Job 36:7	490
prayers heard	Prov. 15:29	567
shall flourish	Ps. 92:12	533
there is none	Rom. 3:10	*152*

Righteousness—*rectitude; uprightness; justice*

benefits of	Prov. 10:27–32	563
of Christ	Ps. 45:7	512
Christian armor	Eph. 6:14	*193*
evidence of new birth	1 John 2:29	*237*
exalts a nation	Prov. 14:34	566
of God	Ps. 145:17	555
hungering after	Matt. 5:6	*6*
of law and faith	Rom. 10:5, 6	*157*
must be sought	Hosea 10:12	765
robe of	Isa. 61:10	634

Rimmon—*pomegranate*

a Benjamite	2 Sam. 4:2	290
rock near Gibeah	Jdgs. 20:45, 47	249
same as Remmon	Josh. 19:1–7	219
	1 Chr. 6:77	381
Syrian idol	2 Ki. 5:18	349
town of south Judah	Josh. 15:1, 32	215

Rimmon-parez

camp of Israel	Num. 33:19, 20	162

Ring—*circular band worn on finger*

given to prodigal son	Luke 15:22	*78*
mark of wealth	James 2:2	*227*
ornament on finger	Gen. 41:42	40
used as seals	Est. 3:10, 12	464

Rinnah—*shout*

son of Shimon	1 Chr. 4:20	377

Riphath

son of Gomer	Gen. 10:3	8

Rissah

camp of Israel	Num. 33:21, 22	162

Rithmah—*juniper; broom*

station of Israel	Num. 33:18, 19	161

River—*a stream of water larger than a creek*

Abana	2 Ki. 5:12	349
Arnon	Deut. 2:36	168
Chebar	Ezek. 1:1	696
of Egypt, the Nile	Ex. 1:22	51
Euphrates	Gen. 2:14	2
Gihon	Gen. 2:13	2
Gozan	2 Ki. 17:6	362
Jabbok	Deut. 2:37	168
Jesus baptized in	Mark 1:9	*35*
Jordan	Mark 1:5	*35*
Kanah	Josh. 16:8	217
Kishon	Jdgs. 5:21	231
of life	Rev. 22:1	*257*
Nile (Sihor)	Jer. 2:18	639
Pharpar	2 Ki. 5:12	349
Pison	Gen. 2:10, 11	2
Tigris (Hiddekel)	Gen. 2:14	2
turned to blood	Ex. 7:15–18	56
Ulai	Dan. 8:2	755

Rizpah

children of, hanged	2 Sam. 21:8, 9	309
concubine of Saul	2 Sam. 3:7	289

Roads

to Beth-horon	Josh. 10:10	210
to cities of refuge	Deut. 19:3	185
highway	Deut. 2:27	168
to the house of God	Jdgs. 20:31	349

	REFERENCE	PAGE
king's highway	Num. 20:17	147
	Num. 21:22	148
meaning to ride in		
a raid	1 Sam. 27:10	283
to Shechem	Jdgs. 21:19	250

Robbers—*burglars; plunders; those who take away by force*

	REFERENCE	PAGE
den of	Jer. 7:11	645
forbidden	Lev. 19:13	112
on Jericho road	Luke 10:30–37	71
of men	Obad. 1:5	776
men of Shechem	Jdgs. 9:23–25	237
rejectors of Christ	John 10:1, 8	103
sacrilegious	2 Ki. 14:13, 14	359
in tithes, offerings	Mal. 3:8	801
troop of	Hosea 7:1	763

Robe

	REFERENCE	PAGE
of righteousness	Isa. 61:10	634
scarlet, put on Jesus	Matt. 27:28	33
washed in blood of lamb	Rev. 7:14	247
white, for martyrs	Rev. 6:11	247

Rock—*a large mass of stone*

	REFERENCE	PAGE
broken by wind	1 Ki. 19:11	338
"higher than I"	Ps. 61:2	518
of punishment	2 Chr. 25:11, 12	423
rent at Christ's death	Matt. 27:51	34
symbolic of basic truth	Matt. 16:16–18	19
symbolic of God's protection	2 Sam. 22:2, 3	309
symbolic of hard heart	Luke 8:6	67
water brought from	Num. 20:11	147
in a wary land	Isa. 32:2	612

Rod—*a shoot or twig; a scepter; a light pole; a slim piece of wood used to inflict punishment*

	REFERENCE	PAGE
Aaron's budded	Num. 17:8	144
applied to Christ	Isa. 11:1	598
of correction	Prov. 13:24	565
of Moses	Ex. 4:2, 4, 17	53
Paul beaten with	2 Cor. 11:25	183
a scepter	Ezek. 19:14	713
smote rock with	Num. 20:11	147

Roe—*small graceful deer, with slender antlers*

	REFERENCE	PAGE
swift runners	2 Sam. 2:18	288

Roebuck—*a male deer*

	REFERENCE	PAGE
clean animal	Deut. 14:4, 5	180

Rogelim

	REFERENCE	PAGE
home of Barzillai	2 Sam. 17:27	304

Rohgah

	REFERENCE	PAGE
son of Shamer	1 Chr. 7:34	382

Roll—*anything rolled up into cylindrical form*

	REFERENCE	PAGE
parchment writing	Jer. 36:2	673
a volume	Ps. 40:7	510

Romans

	REFERENCE	PAGE
inhabitants of Rome	Acts 2:10	118
representatives of the Roman Government	John 11:48	105
	Acts 25:16	145
	Acts 28:17	149
those possessing rights of citizenship in the Roman Empire	Acts 16:21, 37	135
	Acts 22:25–27	142

Romati-ezer—*whom I exalt, my help* (?)

	REFERENCE	PAGE
son of Heman	1 Chr. 25:4	397

Rome—*strength*

	REFERENCE	PAGE
influential church in	Rom. 1:1–8	150
jews ordered from	Acts 18:2	137
Paul preached in	Acts 28:16–24	149

Root—*any underground growth; an antecedent; an ancestor*

	REFERENCE	PAGE
Christ, of Jesse	Isa. 11:10	598
of evil	1 Tim. 6:10	209
figuratively used	2 Ki. 19:30	366

Rope—*cord made of twisted fiber*

	REFERENCE	PAGE
to find Samson	Jdgs. 16:11, 12	244
in destruction	2 Sam. 17:13	303
sign of servitude	1 Ki. 20:31, 32	340

Rosh—*head*

	REFERENCE	PAGE
northern people	Ezek. 38:2, 3	733
son of Benjamin	Gen. 46:21	46

Rot—*corrupt; decay; decompose*

	REFERENCE	PAGE
names of wicked	Prov. 10:7	563

Rotten Rags—*decomposed; putrid*

	REFERENCE	PAGE
use to rescue Jeremiah	Jer. 38:7–13	675

Rubies—*transparent red gem; stone*

	REFERENCE	PAGE
precious	Prov. 3:15	559
price of wisdom, above	Job 28:18	484
red	Lam. 4:7	695

Rudder—*broader flat device at the stern of a vessel to direct its course*

	REFERENCE	PAGE
bands loosed	Acts 27:40	148

Rue—*a small bushy herb with bitter leaves*

	REFERENCE	PAGE
tithed by Pharisees	Luke 11:42	73

Rufus

	REFERENCE	PAGE
Roman Christian	Rom. 16:13	162
son of Simon	Mark 15:21	54

Ruhamah—*pitted; compassionated*

	REFERENCE	PAGE
symbolical name	Hosea 2:1	761

Ruler—*a sovereign; one in authority*

	REFERENCE	PAGE
Ahab	1 Ki. 21:25, 26	342
chosen by Moses	Ex. 18:25	68
directions for	Ezek. 45:9	741
honored	1 Pet. 2:17	231
of the Jews	John 3:1	93
Saul	1 Sam. 14:24–30	267
selected by God	2 Sam. 7:8	293
of the synagogue	Luke 8:41	68

Rumah

	REFERENCE	PAGE
home of Pedaiah	2 Ki. 23:36	371

Runners—*messengers*

	REFERENCE	PAGE
accompanied king	1 Ki. 14:27, 28	333
king's bodyguard	1 Sam. 22:17	278
stationed at palace	2 Ki. 11:19	357

Rust—*coating caused by corrosive process*

	REFERENCE	PAGE
corrupting	Matt. 6:19	8
of gold and silver	James 5:3	229

Ruth—*companion*

	REFERENCE	PAGE
ancestor of Joseph	Matt. 1:5	3
story of	Ruth 1–4	251

Rye—*edible grain*

	REFERENCE	PAGE
grown in Egypt	Ex. 9:32	59
grown in Palestine	Ezek. 4:9	699

S

Sabachthani—*hast thou forsaken me?*

	REFERENCE	PAGE
spoken by Christ	Matt. 27:46	34

Sabbath—*break off; desist*

	REFERENCE	PAGE
cattle rested on	Ex. 20:10	70
Christ, the lord of	Luke 6:5	64
death penalty for desecration of	Ex. 31:14, 15	82
	Ex. 35:2	86
false zeal for	Luke 13:14–16	76
first mention of its observance	Ex. 16:23–30	66
forbidden to kindle fire on	Ex. 16:23	66
	Ex. 35:3	86
forth commandment of the Decalogue	Ex. 20:8	70
	Deut. 5:12	172
a holy day	Ex. 35:2	86
Jesus attended worship on	Mark 6:2	41
	Luke 4:16	61
lawful to do good deeds on	Matt. 12:10–13	14
	John 7:22, 23	99
made for man	Mark 2:27	37
made known at Sinai	Neh. 9:13, 14	455
man stoned to death	Num. 15:32–36	142
merchandising forbidden on	Neh. 10:31	457
observance of a law to Israelites	Ex. 31:13, 16	82
	Lev. 19:2, 3	111
offerings on	Num. 28:9	155
Paul preached on	Acts 17:2, 3	136
people to remain indoors on	Ex. 16:29	67
polluted by Israelites	Ezek. 20:13	713
sanctified by God	Gen. 2:3	2
the seventh day	Deut. 5:14	172
sign between God and Israelites	Ex. 31:16, 17	82
	Ezek. 20:5, 12	713
from sunset to sunset	Lev. 23:32	116
warnings concerning	Jer. 17:19–27	654
work forbidden on	Lev. 23:3	115
(See First Day of the Week)		

Sabbath Day's Journey

	REFERENCE	PAGE
about ¾ mile	Acts 1:12	117

Sabbatical Year—*every seventh year when Jewish people were required to refrain from tillage*

	REFERENCE	PAGE
every seventh year	Lev. 25:1–7	118
laws regarding	Ex. 23:10–14	72

Sabeans—*men of Sheba*

	REFERENCE	PAGE
descendants of Cush	Gen. 10:7	8
descendants of Joktan	Gen. 10:26, 28	9
"far-off nation"	Joel 3:8	770
noted merchants	Isa. 45:14	623
slew Job's servants	Job 1:14, 15	469

Sabtah, Sabta

	REFERENCE	PAGE
Cushite people	Gen. 10:7	8
third son of Cush	1 Chr. 1:9	374

Sacar—*hire; reward*

	REFERENCE	PAGE
father of Ahiam	1 Chr. 11:35	386
son of Obed-edom	1 Chr. 26:4	398

Sackbut

	REFERENCE	PAGE
stringed musical instrument	Dan. 3:5	748

	REFERENCE	PAGE
imprisoned and abused	Jdgs. 16:21	244
judge of Israel	Jdgs. 16:30, 31	244
married a Philistine	Jdgs. 14:1–11	242
miraculously given	Jdgs. 13:1–5, 24	241
a Nazarite	Jdgs. 16:17	244
physically strong	Jdgs. 14:6	242
	Jdgs. 16:3, 12	243
riddle of	Jdgs. 14:12–14	242
slaughtered many	Jdgs. 15:7, 8	243
slew 1,000 men	Jdgs. 15:15	243
slew 30 Philistines	Jdgs. 14:19	242
son of Manoah	Jdgs. 13:22, 24	241
triumphs in death	Jdgs. 16:23–31	244
wife given to another.	Jdgs. 14:20	242

Samuel—*name of God*

	REFERENCE	PAGE
accepted as leader	1 Sam. 3:20, 21	258
anointed David	1 Sam. 16:1–13	270
anointed Saul	1 Sam. 10:1–13	263
asserted integrity	1 Sam. 12:3–25	265
called in youth	1 Sam. 3:1–19	257
child of prayer	1 Sam. 1:27	256
courageous	1 Sam. 15:15–29	269
death of	1 Sam. 25:1	280
head of school of prophets	1 Sam. 19:18–20	274
inspired prophet	1 Sam. 3:19–21	258
intimate with God	Jer. 15:1	652
judged Israel	1 Sam. 7:15	261
man of faith	Heb. 11:32–34	224
man of prayer	Ps. 99:6	536
old	1 Sam. 12:1, 2	264
pious in childhood	1 Sam. 2:18–26	256
presented to God	1 Sam. 1:19–28	255
rebuked Saul	1 Sam. 13:13	266
served in temple	1 Sam. 2:11, 18	256
son of Elkanah	1 Sam. 1:19, 20	255
sons unfaithful	1 Sam. 8:1–6	261
won battle, prayer	1 Sam. 7:5–14	260

Sanballat—*the moon-god has given life*

	REFERENCE	PAGE
craftiness of	Neh. 6:1–15	451
opposed building walls of Jerusalem	Neh. 4:7, 8	450
Samaritan leader	Neh. 2:10	448

Sanctification—*purification; consecration*

	REFERENCE	PAGE
in Christ	1 Cor. 1:2	163
of Christ	John 17:19	111
by Christ's blood	Heb. 13:12	225
by Christ's body	Heb. 10:10	222
of the church	Eph. 5:25–27	193
of first born	Ex. 13:2	63
by God	Jude 1:1	241
of God, in heart	1 Pet. 3:15	232
by Holy Spirit	Rom. 15:16	161
of the Jewish altar	Ex. 40:10	91
of Jewish priests	2 Chr. 5:11	406
leads to holiness	Rom. 6:22	154
must be wholly	1 Thess. 5:23	204
not self-righteous, boasting	1 John 1:8	236
	1 John 1:10	236
of obedient believers	Heb. 10:10, 14	222
possess vessel in	1 Thess. 4:4	203
by prayer	1 Tim. 4:5	208
qualifies for service	2 Tim. 2:21	211
of the seventh day	Gen. 2:3	2
of the tabernacle	Ex. 29:44	80
by truth	John 17:17	111
of unbelieving husbands	1 Cor. 7:14	167

Sanctuary—(See Tabernacle)

Sand of the Sea

	REFERENCE	PAGE
descendants of Abraham as	Gen. 22:17	19

	REFERENCE	PAGE
figurative of corn stored by Joseph	Gen. 41:49	41
figurative of Israel	Hosea 1:10	761

Sandals—*foot covering*

	REFERENCE	PAGE
angel commands Peter to put on	Acts 12:8	130
worn by apostles	Mark 6:7–9	41

Sanhedrin—*supreme council of Jews*

	REFERENCE	PAGE
conspired against Jesus, apostles	John 11:47–53	105
	Acts 5:21–27	121
Jesus tried before	Matt. 27:1	32
Stephen condemned by	Acts 6:12–15	123

Sanitation—*the removal of elements injurious to health*

	REFERENCE	PAGE
in childbirth	Lev. 12:2–8	103
for contagions, venereal disease	Lev. 13:1–8	103
	Lev. 15:2–18	107
for a dead body	Num. 19:11–22	146
excrement and	Deut. 23:13	189
for menses	Lev. 15:19–31	108
at Passover	Num. 9:6–11	134
in quarantines	Lev. 13:2–46	103
for an unclean beast	Lev. 5:2	96

Sansannah

	REFERENCE	PAGE
town in Judah	Josh. 15:1, 31	215

Sap—*vital fluid of woody plants*

	REFERENCE	PAGE
trees of Lord full of	Ps. 104:16	538

Saph

	REFERENCE	PAGE
Philistine giant	2 Sam. 21:18	309

Saphir

	REFERENCE	PAGE
town of Judah	Micah 1:11	779

Sapphira—*beautiful*

	REFERENCE	PAGE
sin and death of	Acts 5:1–11	121
wife of Ananias	Acts 5:1	121

Sapphire—*hard, transparent, blue gem stone*

	REFERENCE	PAGE
breastplate stone	Ex. 28:18	78
in John's vision	Rev. 21:1, 19	257

Sarah—*princess* (Formerly Sarai)

	REFERENCE	PAGE
1. Daughter of Asher	Num. 26:46	154
2. Wife of Abraham	Gen. 11:29	10
advises concubinage	Gen. 16:2, 3	13
asked Hagar's exile	Gen. 21:9–11	17
childless	Gen. 11:30	10
died	Gen. 23:1, 2	19
gave birth to Isaac	Gen. 21:1–8	17
heroine of faith	Heb. 11:11	223
honored of God	Gen. 17:15, 16	14
noted for beauty	Gen. 12:11	10
skeptical of God's promise of son	Gen. 18:12–15	14

Saraph

	REFERENCE	PAGE
descendant of Shelah	1 Chr. 4:21, 22	377

Sarcasm—*contemptuous, taunting language*

	REFERENCE	PAGE
of Ahad to Ben-hadad	1 Ki. 20:11	339
Cain's answer to God	Gen. 4:9	4
of chief priests, scribes	Mark 15:31, 32	54
of Eliab to David	1 Sam. 17:28	271
of Elijah to Baal	1 Ki. 18:27	337

	REFERENCE	PAGE
of God	Jer. 25:27	661
Israelites reproaching Moses	Ex. 14:11	64
of Jehoash to Amaziah	2 Ki. 14:9	359
of Jesus to Pharisees	Mark 7:6–9	43
Job's answer to his friends	Job 12:2	475
in Jotham's parable	Jdgs. 9:7–15	236
of Paul to Ananias	Acts 23:1–5	143
Sanballat before army of Samaria	Neh. 4:2, 3	449
Sanballat to Jews	Neh. 4:1, 2	449

Sardis—*city of Asia Minor*

	REFERENCE	PAGE
church of	Rev. 1:11	243

Sardites

	REFERENCE	PAGE
descendants of Sered	Num. 26:26	153

Sardius—*stone in the breastplate of a Hebrew high priest*

	REFERENCE	PAGE
in breastplate	Ex. 28:17	78
in John's vision	Rev. 21:1, 20	256
precious stone	Rev. 4:3	245

Sardonyx—*a variety of onyx*

	REFERENCE	PAGE
in John's vision	Rev. 21:1, 20	256

Sargon—*the king is faithful*

	REFERENCE	PAGE
king of Assyria	Isa. 20:1	603

Sarid

	REFERENCE	PAGE
village of Zebulun	Josh. 19:10	219

Sarse-chim

	REFERENCE	PAGE
Babylonian prince	Jer. 39:3	676

Satan—*adversary* (See Devil)

	REFERENCE	PAGE
apostates delivered unto	1 Tim. 1:20	207
appears as an angel	2 Cor. 11:14	182
attends worship	Job 2:1	470
blinds unbelievers	2 Cor. 4:3, 4	178
bound	Rev. 20:2	256
claims authority	Luke 4:5, 6	61
incites men to evil	John 13:2	107
led Ananias astray	Acts 5:3–5	121
a liar	John 8:44	101
loosed	Rev. 20:7–9	256
misuses Scriptures	Matt. 4:6	5
opposes God's people	Zech. 3:1	793
provoked David	1 Chr. 21:1	393
resisted	James 4:7	228
seeks man's ruin	1 Pet. 5:8	233
sinned from beginning	1 John 3:8	236
slanders saints	Job 1:9–11	469
supports the wicked	Ps. 109:6	541
synagogue of	Rev. 2:9	244
tempts man	Gen. 3:4, 5	3
ways known	2 Cor. 2:11	177

Satire—*ridicule*

	REFERENCE	PAGE
of Jesus	Matt. 23:1–33	27

Satisfaction—*complete gratification; that which satisfies*

	REFERENCE	PAGE
complete in heaven	Ps. 17:15	499
fullness of	Luke 2:25–32	59
given by the Lord	Isa. 58:9–14	631
inward	Prov. 14:14	566

Satyr—*he-goat god of Greek mythology*

	REFERENCE	PAGE
dance on ruins of Babylon	Isa. 13:19–21	599

Saul—*asked of Jehovah*

	REFERENCE	PAGE
1. First king of Israel	1 Sam. 10:1–27	263

REFERENCE	PAGE
apostate........1 Sam. 15:11	269
committed suicide.1 Sam. 31:1–6	286
disobedience of...1 Sam. 14:29–48	267
handsome........1 Sam. 9:2	262
humble........1 Sam. 10:21–26	263
inquired of witch..1 Sam. 28:7–25	283
jealous and	
envious........1 Sam. 18:8	273
murderous........1 Sam. 19:1	274
obstinate........1 Sam.	
13:11, 12	266
poised and	
honorable....1 Sam. 11:13	264
rejected by God..1 Sam. 15:1–35	268
sons hanged......2 Sam. 21:3–9	308
sought father's asses,	
found kingdom....1 Sam.	
9:3, 17–20	262
sought to kill	
David...........1 Sam.	
18:10, 11	273
superstitious.......1 Sam. 28:7	283
troubled by an evil	
spirit...........1 Sam.	
16:14–23	270
won favor of people	
by defeat of	
Ammonites......1 Sam. 11:1–15	264
1 Sam. 12:1–25	264
2. A king of Edom....Gen. 36:37, 38	35
3. Saul of Tarsus	
(See Paul)	

Saviour—*deliverer*

applied to God......2 Sam. 22:3	309
applied to Jesus.....Luke 2:11	*58*
one who saves.....2 Ki. 13:5	358

Saviour, Christ as

for all mankind.....Heb. 2:9	*217*
announced at birth..Luke 2:11	*58*
bore sins of men....1 Pet. 2:24	*231*
1 John 3:5	*237*
central gospel truth.John 8:24	*101*
1 Cor. 2:2	*164*
a curse for us......Gal. 3:13	*186*
in death..........Isa. 53:5–12	628
died once for all....1 Pet. 3:18	*232*
exalted by God.....Acts 5:31	*122*
God's purpose in...John 3:16, 17	*241*
his one mission.....Luke 19:10	*82*
for man's sins......Gal. 1:3, 4	*185*
only foundation.....1 Cor. 3:11	*165*
only mediator......1 Tim. 2:5	*207*
only saving message.John 6:67, 68	*99*
only saving name...Acts 4:10, 12	*120*
only spiritual	
nourishment......John 6:35	*98*
for redemption......Titus 2:13, 14	*214*
in sacrificial love....1 John 3:16	*238*

Saw—*a cutting instrument with pointed teeth arranged along the edge of a blade*

for cutting stone....1 Ki. 7:9	321
instrument of	
torture..........2 Sam. 12:31	298

Scab

disease of skin.....Lev. 13:2, 6–8	103
Deut. 28:27	193

Scabbard—*sheath for a weapon*

for sword of God....Jer. 47:6	683

Scales

fell from Paul's eyes.Acts 9:18	*126*
of fish............Lev. 11:9	102
weighing device.....Isa. 40:12	618

Scall

a skin disease......Lev. 13:30	104

REFERENCE	PAGE
Scandal	
involving Eli's sons..1 Sam. 2:22–24	288
public............2 Sam.	
16:21, 22	303

Scant Measure—*just short of measure specified*

an abomination.....Micah 6:10	782

Scapegoat—*goat of departure*

bore sins away......Lev. 16:8–10	109

Scarlet—*brilliant red color*

redemptive sign.....Josh. 2:18	203
symbol of sin.......Isa. 1:18	590
in tabernacle.......Ex. 25:4, 9	74
token of honor.....Dan. 5:29	752
token of riches......2 Sam. 1:24	287

Sceptre—*ornamental staff borne by a sovereign*

of gold............Est. 4:11	464
rod of authority.....Amos 1:5	770
sign of royal	
authority.........Ps. 45:6	512

Sceva—*left-handed*

Jew in Ephesus,	
father of 7	
exorcists.........Acts 19:14–17	*138*

Schism—*division; separation*

in church..........1 Cor. 12:25	*172*

Scholars—*men of learning*

judgments against...Mal. 2:12	801
numbered..........1 Chr. 25:7, 8	397

School—*an education institution*

home instruction....Deut. 6:6–10	173
throughout Judah..2 Chr. 17:7–9	416
singing.............1 Chr. 25:7	397
of Tyrannus........Acts 19:9	*138*

Schoolmaster—*one who teaches school*

the Mosaic law.....Gal. 3:24	*187*

Schools of the Prophets

at Naioth..........1 Sam.	
19:19, 20	274
by Elijah, Elisha....2 Ki. 2:3–7	345

Science—*knowledge; art skill*

Daniel learned in....Dan. 1:3–6	746
false, denies Christ..1 Tim. 6:20, 21	*209*
false, to be rejected..Col. 2:8	*199*

Scoffers—*those who mock, scorn, deride*

of apostles at	
Pentecost........Acts 2:13	*118*
in Acts..........Acts 17:18–21	*136*
denounced by God..Isa. 5:18, 19	593
at God's knowledge..Ps. 73:11	524
of God's messengers.2 Chr. 36:16	436
in last days........2 Pet. 3:3	*235*
Pharisees, of Jesus...Luke 16:14	*79*

Scorners—*those who treat with disdain, flout, taunt*

judgments against...Prov. 19:29	570
lack wisdom........Prov. 14:6	565

Scorpion—*insect of spider specie*

apostles had power	
over.............Luke 10:19	*71*
stings with tail......Rev. 9:10	*248*
symbol of cruelty...1 Ki. 12:11	330
in wilderness.......Deut. 8:15	175

Scourging—*whipping; beating*

authorized by Moses.Deut. 25:1–3	190
Christ victim of.....John 19:1	*113*

REFERENCE	PAGE
inflicted upon Paul..2 Cor. 11:24	*183*
predicted for	
apostles..........Matt. 10:2, 17	*12*
Roman citizens	
exempt from......Acts 22:25–29	*142*

Screech Owl—*a small, nocturnal bird with a shrill cry*

in wilderness.......Isa. 34:14	613

Scribes—*writers*

beware of.........Mark 12:38	*50*
censured by Christ..Matt. 15:1–3	*18*
Christ betrayed	
unto.............Matt. 20:18	*23*
falsely accused	
Christ...........Matt. 9:3	*11*
interpreter of law....Ezra 7:6–10	442
mocked Christ......Matt. 27:41	*34*
opposed Christ......Mark 11:18	*49*
persecuted apostles..Acts 4:5–22	*120*
persecuted Stephen..Acts 6:9–12	*122*
questioned Christ....Mark 12:28	*50*
royal secretary.....2 Sam. 8:17	294
tempted Christ.....John 8:3–11	*100*

Scrip—*bag for carrying food*

apostles not to	
use.............Matt. 10:2–10	*12*
used by	
shepherds........1 Sam. 17:40	272

Scriptures—*sacred writings*

abide forever......1 Pet. 1:25	*230*
Apollos mighty in...Acts 18:24	*137*
basis of gospel	
preaching........1 Cor. 15:1–7	*173*
cannot be broken...John 10:35	*104*
Christ fulfilled......Matt. 26:54, 56	*32*
comfort of.........Rom. 15:4	*161*
confirmed by Christ.Mark 12:10	*49*
explained to	
Ethiopian.........Acts 8:27–35	*125*
expounded by	
Christ...........Luke 24:27	*90*
good for doctrine...2 Tim. 3:16, 17	*212*
how received......James 1:21	*227*
inspired...........2 Tim. 3:16	*212*
to be kept unaltered.Deut. 4:2	170
to be meditated	
upon............Ps. 1:2	494
mighty in power...Heb. 4:12	*218*
misused..........Matt. 4:6	*5*
Matt. 22:23–29	*26*
2 Cor. 2:17	*177*
prove Christ's	
divinity..........Acts 18:28	*138*
to reject..........Heb. 2:1–4	*216*
source of spiritual	
food.............Jer. 15:16	652
1 Pet. 2:2	*230*
source of spiritual	
light.............Ps. 19:8	501
Ps. 119:130	547
source of spiritual	
purification.......John 15:3	*109*
1 Pet. 1:22	*230*
taught diligently....Deut. 6:6, 7	173
testify of Christ.....John 5:39	*96*
Timothy instructed	
in................2 Tim. 3:15	*212*
used by Paul.......Acts 17:2	*136*
wresting of........2 Pet. 3:16	*235*

Scroll—*roll of parchment intended for writing*

heavens departed as.Rev. 6:14	*247*
heavens rolled as....Isa. 34:4	613

Sculpturing—*to carve wood, metal, stone*

certain, forbidden...Ex. 20:4	69
Deut. 4:14–27	170

	REFERENCE	PAGE
Sharon—*a plain*		
pasture east of		
Jordan	1 Chr. 5:16	379
seacoast plains	1 Chr. 27:29	400
	Song 2:1	586
	Isa. 35:2	614
	Isa. 65:10	636
Sharp—*having a keen edge; acute point; quick*		
arrow	Prov. 25:18	574
contention	Acts 15:39	*134*
eyes	Job 16:9	478
knife	Josh. 5:3	205
	Ezek. 5:1	699
razor	Ps. 52:2	515
rock	1 Sam. 14:4	266
sickle	Rev. 14:14	*252*
stone	Ex. 4:25	54
sword	Isa. 21:9	604
threshing		
instrument	Isa. 41:15	619
tongue	Ps. 140:3	553
Sharuhen		
called Shaaraim	1 Chr. 4:31	378
called Shilhim	Josh. 15:32	216
city of Simeon	Josh. 19:1, 6	219
Shashai		
son of Bani	Ezra 10:34, 40	446
Shashak		
a Benjamite	1 Chr. 8:14	383
Shaul—*asked for*		
Edomite king	Gen. 36:37	35
	1 Chr. 1:48	375
a Levite	1 Chr. 6:24	380
son of Simeon	Gen. 46:10	46
Shaveh—*broad open valley*		
meeting place of		
Melchizedek and		
Abraham	Gen. 14:17, 18	12
Shaveh Kiriathaim—*valley of Moab*		
Emims dwelt at	Gen. 14:5	11
Shaving—*making bare or smooth by scraping*		
for ceremonies	Num. 8:7	133
of the face	Gen. 41:14	40
	Lev. 13:33	105
of the head	Job 1:20	470
	Acts 21:24	*141*
partial	2 Sam. 10:4	295
Shavsha (Shisha)		
scribe of David	1 Chr. 18:14, 16	392
served Solomon	1 Ki. 4:1, 3	318
Sheal		
son of Bani	Ezra 10:29	446
Shealtiel—*I have asked God*		
son of King Jeconiah		
and father of		
Zerubbabel	1 Chr. 3:17	377
	Ezra 3:2	439
Sheariah		
son of Azel	1 Chr. 8:38	383
Shearing House		
forty-two men slain		
at	2 Ki. 10:12–14	355
Shear-jashub—*a remnant shall return*		
son of		
Isaiah	Isa. 7:3	594

	REFERENCE	PAGE
Sheba		
Gadite of Bashan	1 Chr. 5:11, 13	378
queen of	1 Ki. 10:1	327
son of Bichri	2 Sam. 20:1, 2	307
	2 Sam. 20:21, 22	308
son of Jokshan	1 Chr. 1:32	374
son of Joktan	1 Chr. 1:20, 22	374
son of Raamah	1 Chr. 1:9	374
town of Simeon	Josh. 19:1, 2	219
Sheba (Same as Beer-sheba)		
Isaac dug well at	Gen. 26:23–33	24
Shebam (See Sibmah)		
town of Moab	Num. 32:3	160
Shebaniah—*Jehovah has brought me back*		
aided Nehemiah	Neh. 9:4, 5	455
head of priest order	Neh. 10:1, 4	456
Levite covenanter	Neh. 10:12	456
Levite trumpeter	1 Chr. 15:24	389
Shebarim—*broken*		
place near Ai	Josh. 7:5	207
Sheber		
son of Caleb	1 Chr. 2:48	376
Shebna		
make treasurer	Isa. 22:15	604
rebuked for graft	Isa. 22:17–25	604
scribe of Hezekiah	2 Ki. 18:18	364
Shebuel		
son of Greshom	1 Chr. 23:16	396
son of Heman	1 Chr. 25:4	397
Shecaniah (Shechaniah)—*Jehovah hath taken up his abode*		
descendant of Aaron	1 Chr. 24:1–11	396
descendant of David	1 Chr. 3:21, 22	377
distributor of tithes	2 Chr. 31:15	430
father of Shemaiah	Neh. 3:29	449
postexilic priest	Neh. 12:3, 7	458
son of Arah	Neh. 6:18	452
son of Jahaziel	Ezra 8:5	443
son of Jehiel	Ezra 10:2, 3	445
Shechem (Sichem, Sychem) *the neck and shoulders*		
1. Son of Gilead	Num. 26:30, 31	153
2. Son of Hamor	Gen. 34:2	32
3. Son of Shemidah	1 Chr. 7:19	382
4. A town		
of Ephraim	Josh. 20:7	221
camp of Abraham	Gen. 12:6	10
Jeroboam's capital	1 Ki. 12:1–20	329
land purchased here		
by Abraham	Gen. 33:18, 19	32
	Josh. 24:32	226
religious center	Josh. 24:1	225
Shedeur—*Shaddai is light*		
father of Elizur	Num. 1:5	123
Sheep—*medium-sized domestic animal*		
early appeared	Gen. 4:2	3
Gentiles called	John 10:16	*103*
God's people called	Heb. 13:20	*225*
herded by Hebrews	Gen. 12:16	10
meek and		
submissive	Isa. 53:7	628
should be fed	John 21:17	*116*
sinners, lost sheep	Matt. 9:36	*11*
Sheepfold, Sheepcote—*small enclosure for sheep*		
built by Israelites	Num. 32:16	160
robbers of	John 10:1	*103*
symbol of		
kingdom	Ezek. 34:10–14	729

	REFERENCE	PAGE
Sheepmaster		
Mesha, king of Moab	2 Ki. 3:4	346
Sheepshearers—*those who shear sheep*		
Nabal employed		
many	1 Sam. 25:11	280
Sheet—*thin, broad-surfaced*		
linen garments	Jdgs. 14:12	242
of Peter's vision	Acts 10:11	*127*
Shehariah—*Jehovah is the dawn*		
a Benjamite	1 Chr. 8:26, 27	383
Shekel—*weight*		
used for metals	Gen. 24:22	20
used in offerings	Ex. 30:13	81
Shekinah		
revealing glory of		
God	Ex. 40:35	92
supernatural light	1 Ki. 8:10	323
Shelah—*request; prayer*		
son of Arphaxad		
(also Salah)	Gen. 10:24	9
	Gen. 11:12–15	9
	1 Chr. 1:18	374
son of Judah	Gen. 38:1–5	37
Shelemiah		
father of Hananiah	Neh. 3:30	449
father of Jucal	Jer. 38:1	675
Jews with alien		
wives	Ezra 10:39, 41	446
priest treasurer	Neh. 13:13	460
son of Abdeel	Jer. 36:26	673
son of Cushi	Jer. 36:14	674
son of Hananiah	Jer. 37:13	674
tabernacle porter	1 Chr. 9:21	384
	1 Chr. 26:14	398
Sheleph		
son of Joktan	Gen. 10:26	9
Shelesh		
an Asherite	1 Chr. 7:35	382
Shelomi		
father of Ahihud	Num. 34:27	163
Shelomith—*peacefulness* (?)		
daughter of Dibri	Lev. 24:11	117
descendant of Moses	1 Chr. 26:25	399
daughter of		
Rehoboam	2 Chr. 11:18, 20	412
daughter of		
Zerubbabel	1 Chr. 3:19	377
son of Izhar	1 Chr. 23:18	396
son of Josiphia	Ezra 8:10	443
son of Shimei	1 Chr. 23:9	396
Shelumiel—*God is conciliated* (?)		
Simeonite prince	Num. 1:6	123
Shem—*renown*		
blessing for	Gen. 9:26, 27	8
respected his father	Gen. 9:23–27	8
saved in the ark	Gen. 7:7	6
son of Noah	Gen. 9:18, 19	8
Shema—*hear thou!*		
assistant to Ezra	Neh. 8:4	454
son of Elpaal	1 Chr. 8:12, 13	382
son of Hebron	1 Chr. 2:43	376
son of Joel	1 Chr. 5:8	378
town in Judah	Josh. 15:1, 26	215
Shemaah		
Benjamite of		
Gibeah	1 Chr. 12:3	386

	REFERENCE	PAGE
Shilshah		
son of Zophah	1 Chr. 7:36, 37	382
Shimea (Shimeah)		
brother of David	1 Chr. 2:13	375
	1 Chr. 20:7	393
Gershomite Levite	1 Chr. 6:39, 44	380
a Merarite Levite	1 Chr. 6:29, 30	380
son of David	2 Sam. 5:14	291
	1 Chr. 3:15	377
son of Mikloth		
(also Shimeam)	1 Chr. 8:32	383
	1 Chr. 9:38	384
Shimeam—(See Shimea)		
Shimeath		
woman of Ammon	2 Chr. 24:26	423
Shimeathites		
family of scribes	1 Chr. 2:55	376
Shimei (Shimi, Shimhi)		
Benjamite (Shimhi)	1 Chr. 8:21	383
Gershomite family	1 Chr. 23:7, 9	396
a Levite	1 Chr. 6:42	380
Levite of Ezra	Ezra 10:23	443
Merarite family	1 Chr. 6:29	380
son of Bani	Ezra 10:34, 38	446
son of Elah	1 Ki. 4:18	319
son of Gera	2 Sam. 16:5	302
son of Gershon	Num. 3:18, 21	126
son of Gog	1 Chr. 5:4	378
son of Hashum	Ezra 10:33	446
son of Heman	2 Chr. 29:14	427
son of Jeduthun	1 Chr. 25:17	398
son of Kish	Est. 2:5	462
son of Zacchur	1 Chr. 4:24–27	378
tithe treasurer	2 Chr. 31:12	430
vine keeper	1 Chr. 27:27	400
Zerubbabel's		
brother	1 Chr. 3:19	377
Shimeon		
son of Harim	Ezra 10:31	446
Shimma—(See Shammah)		
Shimon		
head of a family of		
Judah	1 Chr. 4:1, 20	377
Shimrath		
a descendant of		
Benjamin	1 Chr. 8:21	383
Shimri		
father of Jediael one		
of David's heroes	1 Chr. 11:45	386
Kohathite Levite	2 Chr. 29:13	427
son of Hosah a		
Merarite	1 Chr. 26:10	398
a Simeonite	1 Chr. 4:37	378
Shimrith		
called Shomer	2 Ki. 12:21	358
a Moabitess	2 Chr. 24:26	423
Shimron—*watch-height*		
son of Issachar	Gen. 46:13	46
town of Zebulun	Josh. 19:15	220
Shimron-meron—*watch-height of meron*		
Canaanite town	Josh. 12:20	213
Shimshai—*sunny*		
a scribe, Persian		
official	Ezra 4:8–16	440
Shinab		
King of Admah	Gen. 14:2	11

	REFERENCE	PAGE
Shinar—*plain of Babylonia*		
Jews captives at	Isa. 11:11	598
location of four cities	Gen. 10:10	8
Ships—*large, seagoing vessels*		
foreship	Acts 27:30	*148*
helm	James 3:4	*228*
mast	Ezek. 27:5	721
merchant	Prov. 31:14	578
oars	Ezek. 27:6	721
Paul traveled by	Acts 27:1, 2	*147*
rudder bands	Acts 27:40	*148*
sails	Isa. 33:23	613
stern	Acts 27:29	*148*
tackling	Acts 27:19	*147*
used by apostles	Luke 5:3–7	*62*
used in commerce	Ps. 107:23	540
used in war	Num. 24:24	152
Shiphi		
a Simeonite, father		
of Ziza	1 Chr. 4:37	378
Shiphrah		
Hebrew midwife	Ex. 1:15	51
Shiphtan		
father of Kemuel	Num. 34:24	163
Shipmite—*inhabitant of shephem or shipmoth*		
Zabdi called	1 Chr. 27:27	400
Shipwreck—*partial or total destruction of a vessel at sea*		
figuratively used	1 Tim. 1:19	*207*
suffered three times		
by Paul	Acts 27:41	*148*
	2 Cor. 11:25	183
Shishak—(See Pharaoh)		
Shitrai		
a Sharonite herdman	1 Chr. 27:29	400
Shittim—*Acacias*		
last camp of Israel	Num. 25:1	152
valley north of		
Dead Sea	Joel 3:18	770
Shittim Wood—*wood of shittah tree*		
in altar for burnt		
offerings	Ex. 38:1	89
in altar of incense	Ex. 30:1	80
in ark of covenant	Ex. 25:10, 13	74
boards for		
tabernacle of	Ex. 26:15–37	76
in table of		
shewbread	Ex. 37:10	88
Shiza		
father of Adina a		
Reubenite chief	1 Chr. 11:42	386
Shoa		
name of a people	Ezek. 23:23	718
Shobab—*rebellious*		
son of Caleb	1 Chr. 2:18	375
son of David	2 Sam. 5:13, 14	291
Shobach		
called Shophach	1 Chr. 19:16, 18	393
Syrian captain	2 Sam. 10:16	295
Shobai		
Levite family head	Ezra 2:42	438
Shobal		
a Calebite family	1 Chr. 2:50	376
	1 Chr. 4:1, 2	377

	REFERENCE	PAGE
Shobek		
one who sealed		
the covenant	Neh. 10:1, 24	456
Shobi (an Ammonite)		
son of Nahash, gave		
David food	2 Sam. 17:27–29	304
Shoe—*an outer covering for the foot*		
poor sold for a pair	Amos 2:6	771
removed by servants	Mark 1:7	*35*
removed for meals	Luke 7:37, 38	*66*
removed in reverence	Ex. 3:5	52
removed to seal		
covenant	Ruth 4:7–9	254
same worn 40		
years	Deut. 29:5	195
Shoham—*onyx or beryl*		
a Merarite	1 Chr. 24:27	397
Shomer—*keeper (?)*		
same as Shimrith	2 Ki. 12:21	358
son of Heber	1 Chr. 7:32	382
Shophach—(See also Shobach)		
a Syrian captain	1 Chr. 19:16	393
Shophan		
city in Gad	Num. 32:34, 35	161
Shouting—*sudden outcry*		
form of rejoicing	1 Chr. 15:28	389
by those healed	Luke 17:15	*80*
Shovel—*a flattened scoop with a handle*		
tabernacle utensil	Ex. 27:3	76
winnowing fork	Isa. 30:24	611
Showbread, Shewbread—*unleavened bread*		
eaten by David	Matt. 12:3, 4	*14*
eaten by priests	Lev. 24:5–9	117
forbidden to others	Ex. 29:33	80
given to David	1 Sam. 21:5, 6	276
in holy place	Ex. 25:30	75
Shrine—*sacred place or altar*		
of Diana of Ephesus	Acts 19:24	*138*
Shroud—*a garment for the dead*		
figuratively used	Ezek. 31:3	725
Shuah, Shua		
daughter of Heber	1 Chr. 7:32	382
descendant of Judah	1 Chr. 4:1, 11	377
Judah's		
father-in-law	Gen. 38:2	37
son of Abraham	Gen. 25:1, 2	22
Shual—*fox*		
district north of		
Bethel	1 Sam. 13:17	266
son of Zophah	1 Chr. 7:36	382
Shuham		
son of Dan	Num. 26:42	154
Shuhite—*descendant of Shuah* (Judah's father-in-law)		
Bildad called	Job 2:11	470
Shulamite—*resident of Shunem*		
Solomon's lover	Song 6:13	588
Shumathites		
a Judahite family	1 Chr. 2:53	376
Shunammite—*native of Shunem*		
Abishag called	1 Ki. 1:3	313

	REFERENCE	PAGE
Nabal became as	1 Sam. 25:37	281
names engraved on	Ex. 28:9–12	77
organ of a male	Lev. 21:20	114
Peter called a	John 1:42	92
sealed Jesus' tomb	Matt. 27:66	34
set up by Jacob	Gen. 35:14, 15	34
set up by Samuel	1 Sam. 7:12	261
seventy people slain upon one	Jdgs. 9:5	236
six water-pots of	John 2:6	92
temple built of	1 Ki. 6:7	320
used as a witness	Josh. 24:26, 27	226

Stones, Precious—*gems*

	REFERENCE	PAGE
adamant	Zech. 7:12	795
agate	Isa. 54:12	629
amethyst	Ex. 28:19	78
beryl	Ex. 28:20	78
carbuncle	Ex. 28:17	78
chalcedony	Rev. 21:19	257
chrysolyte	Rev. 21:20	257
chrysoprasus	Rev. 21:20	257
coral	Job 28:18	484
crystal	Job 28:17	484
diamond	Ex. 28:18	78
emerald	Ex. 28:18	78
jacinth	Rev. 21:20	257
jasper	Rev. 21:11	257
ligure	Ex. 39:12	90
onyx	Ex. 28:20	78
pearl	1 Tim. 2:9	207
ruby	Job 28:18	484
sapphire	Ex. 28:18	78
sardius	Ex. 28:17	78
sardonyx	Rev. 21:20	257
topaz	Ex. 28:17	78

Stoning—*hurling stones at; killing by pelting stones*

	REFERENCE	PAGE
of Achan	Josh. 7:20, 25	207
of Adoram	1 Ki. 12:18	330
of David	2 Sam. 16:5, 6	302
of Jesus	John 10:31–33	104
of Naboth	1 Ki. 21:13	341
of Paul	Acts 14:19	133
by the people	Lev. 24:14	117
of Stephen	Acts 7:59	124
of Zechariah	2 Chr. 24:20, 21	423

Store Cities—*for military equipment*

	REFERENCE	PAGE
built by Solomon	1 Ki. 9:16	326

Storehouse—*depository*

	REFERENCE	PAGE
built by Joseph	Gen. 41:56	41
owned by Hezekiah	2 Chr. 32:27, 28	431

Stork—*a long necked, long-legged bird related to heron*

	REFERENCE	PAGE
dwelt in fir trees	Ps. 104:17	538
unclean bird	Lev. 11:13, 19	102

Storm—*atmospheric disturbance*

	REFERENCE	PAGE
an alarming	Ex. 9:23–25	59
destructive	Josh. 10:11	210
on Paul's trip to Rome	Acts 27:14–22	147
prayer in a	Jonah 1:4–14	777
wind	Ps. 55:8	516

Straight—*a direct course; accuracy; honesty*

	REFERENCE	PAGE
figurative of righteousness	Isa. 40:3, 4	617
name of a street	Acts 9:11	126

Strait—*a new pass or passage*

	REFERENCE	PAGE
gate	Matt. 7:13, 14	9

Strangers—*persons who are not acquaintances*

	REFERENCE	PAGE
entertained	Heb. 13:2	225
marriage to	Deut. 25:5	190
not to be king	Deut. 17:14, 15	184
to observe Sabbath	Ex. 20:10	70
taught	Deut. 31:12	197
treated kindly	Lev. 19:34	112
treated with justice	Ex. 22:21	72
usury taken from	Deut. 23:20	189

Strategy—*a maneuver for deceiving the enemy*

	REFERENCE	PAGE
in battle	Josh. 8:1–22	208
success by	2 Sam. 14:28–33	300

Straw—*dry, ripened stalks of grain after threshing*

	REFERENCE	PAGE
food for animals	Jdgs. 19:19	247
mixed with bricks	Ex. 5:7–16	54

Stray Animals—*wanderers*

	REFERENCE	PAGE
instance of	1 Sam. 9	262
to be returned	Ex. 23:4	72

Streets—*public ways in a city or village*

	REFERENCE	PAGE
boys and girls playing in	Zech. 8:5	795
burning of incense	Jer. 44:21	681
called Straight	Acts 9:11	126
children swooning in	Lam. 2:11	693
dwelling place of aged	Zech. 8:4	795
filled with the slain	Ezek. 11:6	704
hypocrites praying in	Matt. 6:5	7
lion in	Prov. 26:13	574
made waste	Zeph. 3:6	789
mourners in	Eccl. 12:5	585
people crying for wine in	Isa. 24:11	606
of pure gold	Rev. 21:21	257
raging chariots in	Nahum 2:4	784
shut doors in	Eccl. 12:4	585
torn carcasses in	Isa. 5:25	593
used by lewd women	Prov. 7:6–23	561
wailing in	Amos 5:16	773
women kneading dough in	Jer. 7:17, 18	645

Strength, Spiritual—*quality of being strong; power*

	REFERENCE	PAGE
found in weakness	2 Cor. 12:9, 10	183
God our	Ps. 46:1	513
of Peter tested	John 18:25–27	112
received by Elijah	1 Ki. 19:2–8	338
secured from God	Eph. 3:16	191

Strife—*contention for superiority; rivalry*

	REFERENCE	PAGE
among apostles	Luke 22:24	86
caused by pride	Prov. 13:10	565
caused by truth	Matt. 10:34–36	13
curse in family	Prov. 18:19	569
dishonor in	Prov. 20:3	570
ended by Abram	Gen. 13:7–11	11
foolish talk causes	1 Tim. 6:4	209
forward soweth	Prov. 16:28	567
great evil in church	2 Cor. 12:20	184
leads to confusion	James 3:16	228
proud heart stirs up	Prov. 28:25	576
stirred by hatred	Prov. 10:12	563
warning against	Phil. 2:3	195
work of the flesh	Gal. 5:19, 20	188

Striker—*a quarrelsome person*

	REFERENCE	PAGE
disqualifies for bishop	1 Tim. 3:3	207
	Titus 1:7	213

Stripes—*blows struck in whipping*

	REFERENCE	PAGE
do not help a fool	Prov. 17:10	568
healed by Christ's	Isa. 53:5	628

	REFERENCE	PAGE
iniquity visited with	Ps. 89:32	532
not to exceed forty	Deut. 25:1–4	190

Strong Drink—*alcoholic beverages*
(See Drunkenness)

Stubbornness—*unyielding; obstinateness*

	REFERENCE	PAGE
brings loss	Prov. 1:24–32	557
example of Israel	Jer. 32:33	669
of Jews in Egypt	Jer. 44:16, 17	680
sin	Isa. 48:4–8	624

Studs—*a detachable button*

	REFERENCE	PAGE
of silver	Song 1:11	586

Study—*learning; education; inquiry*

	REFERENCE	PAGE
approved	2 Tim. 2:15	211
Bereans commended for	Acts 17:10, 11	136
much	Eccl. 12:12	585
quiet	1 Thess. 4:11	203

Stumbling Blocks—*obstacles; hindrances*

	REFERENCE	PAGE
Christ, to the Jews	1 Cor. 1:23	164
hypocrites	Matt. 23:13	27
should be removed	Isa. 57:14	631
spiritual truths	John 6:53–66	98
unfaithful leaders	Mal. 2:7, 8	801
warning against	Rom. 14:13	160

Suah

	REFERENCE	PAGE
descendant of Asher	1 Chr. 7:36	382

Subjection—*being under dominion of another; dependent*

	REFERENCE	PAGE
of Christ to his parents	Luke 2:51	59
of citizens to magistrates	Rom. 13:1–6	159
	Titus 3:1	214
of physical body, to spiritual	Rom. 6:18–22	154
	1 Cor. 9:27	169
of servants to masters	1 Pet. 2:18	231
of wives to husbands	Eph. 5:22–24	193

Submission—*obedience; compliance*

	REFERENCE	PAGE
in bereavement	2 Sam. 12:15–23	297
of Christ	Luke 22:42	86
to civil rulers	Rom. 13:1–7	159
to God's will	James 4:7	228
to punishment	1 Sam. 3:11–18	257
of wives to husbands	Eph. 5:22	193
of young to the older	1 Pet. 5:5	233

Substitute—*one who takes the place of another*

	REFERENCE	PAGE
Christ our	Isa. 53:5	628
Levites for first born of Israelites	Num. 3:12	126

Subtlety—*shrewdness*

	REFERENCE	PAGE
deception by	Gen. 37:29–32	36
of Jonadab	2 Sam. 13:3	298
of the serpent	Gen. 3:1	3

Success—*favorable termination of anything attempted*

	REFERENCE	PAGE
attaining	Josh. 1:7–9	202
dangers of	Jdgs. 7:1–3	233
failure of	Matt. 16:26	20
from God only	1 Cor. 3:4–7	164
humility in	1 Sam. 18:3–16	273
of Jacob	Gen. 30:40, 43	29
piety favors	2 Chr. 27:1–6	425

Succoth—*booths* (place east of Jordan)

	REFERENCE	PAGE
Jacob camped at	Gen. 33:17	32
wilderness camp	Ex. 12:37	62

	REFERENCE	PAGE
Testimony—*affirmation; declaration*		
altar of	Josh. 22:26–28	224
of assurance	Ex. 33:12–17	84
constant duty	Mal. 3:16	802
of deeds	Matt. 11:3–5	13
exalts God's love	Isa. 63:7	635
in the home	Mark 5:18, 19	40
irrepressible	Mark 7:31–36	43
led by the Spirit	Acts 1:8	117
positive	John 9:25	102
unshaken	Acts 12:13–15	130
unwelcome	Acts 16:16–18	135
with readiness	1 Pet. 3:15	232
without shame	2 Tim. 1:8	210
Tetrarch—*ruler of fourth part*		
Roman	Luke 3:1	60
Thaddeus		
one of the twelve	Mark 3:18	38
Thahash		
son of Nahor	Gen. 22:24	19
Thamah—*(same as Tamah)*		
Nethinim family	Ezra 2:53	438
Thamar—*(See also amar)*		
ancestor of Joseph	Matt. 1:3	3
Thankfulness—*expression of gratitude; gratefulness*		
of Daniel	Dan. 2:23	747
expressed	Ps. 100:4	536
for fellow-Christians	2 Thess. 1:3	204
of the healed leper	Luke 17:15, 16	80
for material good	Deut. 8:10	175
of Paul	Acts 28:15	148
for spiritual good	Col. 1:12	198
for victory	1 Cor. 15:57	175
Thanks, Giving—*expressing gratitude*		
in public worship	Ps. 35:18	508
by Jesus	Mark 8:6	44
	John 11:41	105
	Luke 10:17–21	71
	Matt. 26:26, 27	31
at meals	John 6:11	97
for mercies	Isa. 12:1–6	598
in name of Christ	Eph. 5:20	193
in private devotions	Dan. 6:10	753
in public worship	Ps. 35:18	508
Tharshish—*(See Tarshish)*		
Theatre—*a playhouse*		
Paul arraigned in	Acts 19:29	139
Thebez—*brightness (?) (City near Shechem)*		
Abimelech's murder at	2 Sam. 11:21	296
taken by Abimelech	Jdgs. 9:50	238
Theft—*act of stealing; larceny* (See Stealing)		
of a baby	2 Ki. 11:1–3	356
confessed	Jdgs. 17:1–3	245
of the famished	Prov. 6:30	561
improbable	Matt. 28:11–13	35
law concerning kidnapping	Deut. 24:7	189
Thelasar—*hill of Asshur* (See Telassar)		
Theophilus—*loved of God*		
Acts and Gospel of Luke addressed to	Luke 1:3	56
	Acts 1:1	116
Thessalonica—*city of Macedonia*		
Christians of	Acts 20:4	139
	Acts 27:2	147

	REFERENCE	PAGE
epistles to	1 Thess. 1:1	201
	2 Thess. 1:1	204
Paul visited	Acts 17:1–13	136
Theudas		
Jewish insurgent	Acts 5:36	122
Thief—*one who steals; a robber*		
ashamed	Jer. 2:26	639
comes unexpectedly	1 Thess. 5:2	203
conduct of	Luke 10:30	71
enters window	Joel 2:9	768
in the right	Job 24:14	483
in office	John 12:4–6	106
punishment of	Ex. 22:1–4	71
Thimnathan—*(See also Timnah)*		
city in Dan	Josh. 19:43	220
Thirst—*an eager desire especially a desire for liquids*		
famishing	Jdgs. 15:18, 19	243
gracious invitation	Isa. 55:1	629
of Jesus	John 19:28–30	114
relief from	Ex. 17:1–6	67
of the righteous	Ps. 63:1	519
for righteousness	Matt. 5:6	6
satisfaction promised	John 4:14	94
Thistle—*vigorous prickly plant with globular head of tubular flowers*		
origin of	Gen. 3:18	3
parables of	2 Ki. 14:9	359
	2 Chr. 25:18	424
	Matt. 7:16	9
Thomas		
absent when the riven Christ visited the Twelve	John 20:19–24	115
asks questions of Jesus	John 14:5	108
convinced	John 20:27, 28	115
	John 21:1, 2	115
devoted, zealous	John 11:16	104
doubted the resurrection	John 20:25, 26	115
one of the Twelve Apostles, also called Didymus (twin)	Matt. 10:3	12
	Luke 6:13, 15	64
Thongs—*narrow strips of leather*		
Paul bound with	Acts 22:25	142
Thorn—*vexation* (figuratively used)		
in Paul's flesh	2 Cor. 12:1–9	183
Thorns—*thorn-bearing shrubs*		
for fuel	Ps. 58:9	517
	Ps. 118:12	544
hedges of	Hosea 2:6	761
Jesus crowned with	John 19:1–5	113
origin of	Gen. 3:18	3
Thought—*process of using the mind; contemplation*		
of evil	Matt. 15:19	18
of foolishness is sin	Prov. 24:9	572
makes character	Prov. 23:7	572
not all should be spoken	Prov. 29:11	576
to the obedience of Christ	2 Cor. 10:5	182
Spirit, prompter of	Matt. 10:19, 20	12
things to incite	Phil. 4:8	197
Threatenings—*announcements of something to be inflicted*		
against the apostles	Acts 4:17–21	120

	REFERENCE	PAGE
example of Christ	1 Pet. 2:23	231
forborne	Eph. 6:9	193
of Saul, against Christians	Acts 9:1	126
Threshing—*separating grain or seeds from straw or husks*		
with cattle	Deut. 25:4	190
with a flail	Isa. 28:27	609
Throat—*part of the neck*		
David's was dry	Ps. 69:3	521
knife put to	Prov. 23:2	572
an open sepulchre	Ps. 5:9	496
Throne—*royal chair occupied by one with sovereign power*		
of David, declared perpetual	2 Sam. 7:12–16	293
	1 Chr. 29:23	402
of David, given to Jesus Christ	Ps. 132:11	551
	Isa. 9:6, 7	596
	Luke 1:30–33	57
of God	Ps. 45:6	512
	Rev. 20:11	256
	Ps. 103:19	537
	Isa. 66:1	637
	Matt. 5:34	7
of grace	Heb. 4:16	218
	Heb. 10:19–22	222
of ivory and gold	1 Ki. 10:18–20	327
	2 Chr. 9:17–19	410
seat of authority in official acts	1 Ki. 22:10	342
	2 Ki. 11:19	357
	Acts 12:21	130
symbol of sovereignty	2 Sam. 3:10	289
	1 Ki. 2:4	315
	Dan. 7:9	754
	Matt. 19:28	23
Thumb—*short, thick digit on radical side of the human hand*		
of Aaron, anointed	Ex. 29:20	79
of captives, cut off	Jdgs. 1:7	227
of worshiper, anointed	Lev. 14:17	106
Thunder—*sound that accompanies lightning*		
accompanies storms	Ex. 9:23	59
alarming	1 Sam. 12:18, 19	265
James and John, sons of	Mark 3:17	38
symbol of divine wrath	1 Sam. 2:10	256
symbol of God's power	Job 37:2–5	490
Thyatira—*(City of Asia Minor)*		
home of Lydia	Acts 16:14	135
one of 7 churches	Rev. 2:18–24	244
Thyine Wood—*fragrant*		
sold in markets	Rev. 18:12	254
Tiberias		
city of Galilee	John 6:23	97
Sea of Galilee	John 21:1	115
Tiberius Caesar		
Roman emperor	Luke 3:1	60
Tibhath—*level*		
city of Hadadezer, conquered by David	2 Chr. 18:8	417

	REFERENCE	PAGE
Toll—*a fixed compensation*		
tribute money	Ezra 4:13–20	440
Tomb—*a place of internment; grave*		
John laid in	Mark 6:25–29	42
Joseph's	Matt. 27:57–60	34
perfumed	2 Chr. 16:13, 14	415
Tombstone—*a gravestone*		
at Rachel's grave	Gen. 35:20	34
Tongue—*free moving organ of the mouth*		
(See Slander; Talebearers)		
backbiting	Prov. 25:23	574
boasts great things	James 3:5	228
cannot be tamed	James 3:8	228
capable of smiting	Jer. 18:18	655
cloven	Acts 2:3	117
crafty	Job 15:5	477
deceitful	Rom. 3:13	152
of dumb	Isa. 35:6	614
false	Ps. 120:3	548
a fire	James 3:6	228
flattering	Ps. 5:9	496
Hebrew	Acts 21:40	142
just	Prov. 10:20	563
keep from evil	Ps. 34:13	507
like a sharp razor	Ps. 52:2	515
a little member	James 3:5	228
lying	Ps. 78:36	527
mischievous	Ps. 10:7	497
muttering	Isa. 59:3	632
naughty	Prov. 17:4	568
new	Mark 16:17	55
parched in hell	Luke 16:24	79
perverse	Prov. 17:20	568
powerful	Prov. 18:21	569
proper	Acts 1:19	117
scourging	Job 5:21	472
sharpened	Ps. 140:3	553
should be bridled	James 1:26	227
shows the heart	Matt. 12:34	15
singing	Ps. 126:2	549
slow	Ex. 4:10	53
soft	Prov. 25:15	573
stammering	Isa. 32:4	612
swearing	Isa. 45:23	623
walking	Ps. 73:9	324
water lapped with	Jdgs. 7:5, 6	233
whetted	Ps. 64:2, 3	519
wholesome	Prov. 15:4	566
wise	Prov. 15:2	566
Tongues—*languages*		
gift of	1 Cor. 12:4, 10	171
interpreter		
necessary	1 Cor. 14:27, 28	173
language confounded	Gen. 11:1–9	9
Paul spoke with	1 Cor. 14:18	173
sign to unbelievers	1 Cor. 14:22	173
speaking in		
"unknown"	1 Cor. 14:2, 4	172
spoken on Pentecost	Acts 2:1–12	117
they shall cease	1 Cor. 13:8	172
Topaz—*gem stone*		
in breastplate	Ex. 28:17	78
found in Ethiopia	Job 28:19	484
in New Jerusalem	Rev. 21:2, 20	256
Tophel		
wilderness camp	Deut. 1:1	166
Topheth, Tophet		
destroyed by Josiah	2 Ki. 23:10	370
place in Hinnom	Jer. 7:31	645
Torment—*intense bodily pain or anguish; torture*		
of fatal diseases	Matt. 4:24	6
suffered in hell	Luke 16:23	79

	REFERENCE	PAGE
Tormentors—*those who torment, torture*		
tortured prisoners	Matt. 18:34	22
Tortoise—*a turtle*		
unclean animal	Lev. 11:29	102
Towel—*a cloth for drying anything by wiping*		
used by Jesus	John 13:4, 5	107
Towers—*tall structures*		
Babel	Gen. 11:4, 9	9
David	Song 4:4	587
Edar	Gen. 35:21	34
furnaces	Neh. 3:11	449
Hananeel	Neh. 3:1	448
Lebanon	Song 7:4	588
Meah	Neh. 3:1	448
Penuel	Jdgs. 8:17	235
Shechem	Jdgs. 9:46	237
Siloam	Luke 13:4	75
Syene	Ezek. 29:10	724
Town Clerk		
keeper of records	Acts 19:35	139
Trachonitis—*rough, stony region*		
region south of		
Damascus	Luke 3:1	60
Trade—*a business; skilled or specialized handicraft*		
beneficial	Gen. 34:20–23	33
dishonesty in	Amos 8:4–8	775
on Sabbath	Neh. 13:16, 17	460
tricks in,		
forbidden	Deut. 25:13–16	190
Traditions—*knowledge, customs handed down from generation to generation*		
of Jewish elders	Mark 7:5	43
often violate God's		
word	Matt. 15:3	18
Paul once zealous		
for	Gal. 1:14	185
warning against	Col. 2:8	199
Train—*anything drawn out to a length; procession*		
body of attendants	1 Ki. 10:2	327
flowing garments	Isa. 6:1	594
Traitor—*one who betrays a trust; one who commits treason*		
Judas	Luke 6:16	64
wicked person	2 Tim. 3:1–5	211
Trance—*displacement of mind; insensibility to ordinary surroundings*		
of Balaam	Num. 24:4, 16	151
of Paul	Acts 22:17	142
of Peter	Acts 11:4, 5	129
Transfiguration—*to exalt in appearance*		
of Christ	Matt. 17:1–11	20
manifested his		
glory	2 Pet. 1:17, 19	234
Translations		
Elijah	2 Ki. 2:1–11	345
Enoch	Gen. 5:24	5
the saints	1 Thess. 4:16, 17	203
Transportation—*means of travel*		
asses	1 Ki. 13:13	331
camels	1 Ki. 10:1, 2	327
horses	1 Ki. 20:20	340
oxen	1 Sam. 6:7, 8	259
rafts	1 Ki. 5:7–9	319
ships	1 Ki. 22:48	344
wagons	Gen. 46:5	45

	REFERENCE	PAGE
Travail—*labor in childbirth; anguish*		
Christ's death	Isa. 53:11	629
curse placed on Eve	Gen. 3:16	3
pangs of sorrow	Isa. 13:8	599
of Rachel	Gen. 35:16–19	34
spiritual concern	Gal. 4:19	187
Treachery—*perfidy; violation of allegiance; fraud*		
of Absalom	2 Sam. 13:28, 29	299
of David	2 Sam. 11:14, 15	296
of Delilah	Jdgs. 16:18, 19	244
of Haman	Est. 3:8–15	464
of Joab	2 Sam. 3:27	290
of Judas Iscariot	Matt. 26:49	32
of Saul	1 Sam. 18:17–19	273
of Scribes and		
Pharisees	Luke 11:53, 54	73
Treason—*breach of allegiance; betrayal-breach of faith*		
of Absalom	2 Sam. 15:10	301
of Athaliah	2 Chr. 22:10	421
	2 Ki. 11:14	357
of Zimri	1 Ki. 16:15–20	335
Treasure Cities		
for storage of		
royal wealth	Ex. 1:11	51
Treasure-houses		
of heathen god	Dan. 1:2	746
of kings	Ezra 7:20	443
Treasurer—*custodian of monies*		
Judas	John 12:2–6	105
Treasures—*riches, wealth* (See Riches, Earthly)		
do not satisfy	Ps. 39:6	510
insecure	Matt. 6:19	8
realized in heaven	Matt. 6:20	8
of spiritual calling	2 Cor. 4:6, 7	178
uncertain	Prov. 27:24	575
value of spiritual	Luke 12:33	74
Treasury—*depository for monies*		
of the Lord	Josh. 6:19	206
watched by Jesus	Mark 12:41	50
Tree—*a perennial woody plant*		
axe at root of	Matt. 3:10	5
clapped hands	Isa. 55:12	630
cut down	Deut. 19:5	185
full of sap	Ps. 104:16	538
grafted	Rom. 11:24	158
high and low	Ezek. 17:24	711
known by its fruit	Matt. 12:33	15
planted by man	Lev. 19:23	112
stump of	Dan. 4:26	751
Tree of Life		
in Garden of Eden	Gen. 2:8–15	2
man shut out from	Gen. 3:22–24	3
in paradise of God	Rev. 2:7	244
wisdom called	Prov. 3:13, 18	558
Trees of the Bible		
almond	Eccl. 12:5	585
almug	1 Ki. 10:11	327
aloes	Ps. 45:8	512
apple	Song 2:3	586
ash	Isa. 44:14	622
bay	Ps. 37:35	509
box	Isa. 41:19	619
cedar	1 Ki. 4:33	319
cedars of Lebanon	2 Ki. 14:9	359
chestnut	Ezek. 31:8	725

	REFERENCE	PAGE
cypress	Isa. 44:14	622
elm	Hosea 4:13	762
fig	Jdgs. 9:10	236
fir	Isa. 14:8	600
hazel	Gen. 30:37	28
juniper	1 Ki. 19:5	338
lign aloes	Num. 24:6	151
mulberry	2 Sam 5:23	292
myrrh	Song 4:14	587
myrtle	Neh. 8:15	454
oak	Isa. 2:13	591
oil	Isa. 41:19	619
olive	Jdgs. 9:9	236
palm	Ex. 15:27	65
pine	Isa. 41:19	619
pomegranate	1 Sam. 14:2	266
poplar	Hosea 4:13	762
shittah	Isa. 41:19	619
sycamore	1 Ki. 10:27	328
teil	Isa. 6:13	594
willow	Lev. 23:40	117

Trespass Offering—(See Offerings)

Trials—*acts of trying, testing*
of Abram	Gen. 22:1–13	18
after deliverance	Ex. 15:22–24	65
backsliding amid	Num. 11:1–6	136
in business	Gen. 31:36–41	30
encouragement in	2 Cor. 4:17, 18	178
expected	1 Pet. 4:12–14	232
of faith	1 Pet. 1:6–9	230
form character	Ex. 14:27–31	64
hope amid	2 Cor. 4:8–16	178
of Job	Job. 19:1–21	479
often a blessing	Matt. 5:10–12	6
Paul's confidence in	Rom. 8:35–39	156
stubbornness in	2 Chr. 28:21–23	426

Tribes of Israel—*groups of people*
blessed	Gen. 49:1–33	48
numbered	Num. 1:1–54	122
order of	Num. 2:1–34	124

Tribulation—*a condition of affliction and distress*
Christians suffer	John 16:33	111
disciplinary	Rom. 5:3, 4	153
evil effects of	Matt. 13:21	16
God comforts in	2 Cor. 1:3, 4	176
in the last days	Matt. 24:21	28
Paul joyful in	2 Cor. 7:4	180
recompensed	Rev. 7:13–17	247

Tribute—*contribution, tax* (See Taxes)
paid by Christ	Matt. 17:24–27	21
in sheep	2 Ki. 3:4	346
should be paid	Matt. 22:17–21	26
in silver	2 Ki. 15:19, 20	361

Trifles—*things of little importance or value*
Christians to avoid	Titus 3:9	214
magnified	Matt. 23:23	27
Pharisees blinded by	Matt. 23:24, 25	27

Troas—*seaport of Mysia*
cloak left at	2 Tim. 4:13	212
Paul's second visit to	Acts 20:6	139
Paul's vision at	Acts 16:8–11	134

Trogyllium—*seaport of Asia Minor*
Paul passed through	Acts 20:15	140

Trophimus
companion of Paul	Acts 20:4	139
sick at Miletus	2 Tim. 4:20	212
visited Jerusalem	Acts 21:29	141

	REFERENCE	PAGE

Trouble—*state of being distressed; affliction; disturbance; agitation*
Ahaz forsook God in	2 Chr. 28:21–25	426
caused by abundance	Luke 12:16, 17	74
comparison of	Ps. 73:1–5	524
David comforted in	Ps. 142:1–7	554
domestic	Luke 10:38–42	71
dreamer's	Dan. 2:1–6	746
eight years of	Acts 9:32, 33	127
Eli overwhelmed with	1 Sam. 4:15–18	258
explained by Moses	Deut. 8:1–6	174
God, a refuge in	Ps. 46:1	513
idolaters awakened by	Jer. 2:26–30	639
known to God	Acts 7:33, 34	124
man full of	Job 14:1	477
Moses despaired in	Num. 11:10–15	137
patience in	Ps. 40:1–3	510
penitence in	Deut. 4:30–31	171
prayer in	Ps. 31:9–17	505
of Rebekah	Gen. 27:46	26
sinners helpless in	Jdgs. 10:13, 14	238
thirty-eight years of	John 5:5	95
twelve years of	Mark 5:25, 26	40

Truce—*armistice; temporary cessation*
during battle	2 Sam. 2:25–31	289

Trucebreakers
men, in last days	2 Tim. 3:1, 3	211

Trumpet—*a wind musical instrument*
in calling assembly	Num. 10:2	135
for calling off attack	2 Sam. 2:28	289
at final resurrection	1 Cor. 15:52	175
in John's vision	Rev. 8:1, 2	247
for mobilization	Jdgs. 6:34, 35	233
at Mt. Sinai	Ex. 19:16, 19	69
in removal of ark	2 Sam. 6:15	292
to signal an attack	Josh. 6:4	205
in Temple dedication	2 Chr. 5:12	406
at year of jubilee	Lev. 25:9	118

Trumpets, Feast of—(See Feasts)

Trust—*confident reliance*
in God	Ps. 37:3	508
	Ps. 125:1	549
	Isa. 26:3	607
	Heb. 13:6	225
in man	Jer. 17:5	653
	Isa. 31:1	611
in riches	Mark 10:24	47
	1 Tim. 6:9, 17	209

Truth—*justice; fidelity; virtue; veracity*
buy, and sell it not	Prov. 23:23	572
Christians to walk in	2 John 1:4	240
church, pillar of	1 Tim. 3:15	208
God plenteous in	Ps. 86:15	530
God's word is	John 17:17	111
Herod's inquiry	John 18:38	113
Jesus full of	John 1:14	91
Jesus is the	John 14:6	108
leads to light	John 3:21	93
makes men free	John 8:31, 32	101
manifested	2 Cor. 4:2	178
meditate upon	Phil. 4:8	197
none pleaded for	Isa. 59:4	632
purifies	1 Pet. 1:22	230
resisted by some	2 Tim. 3:8	212
rightly divide	2 Tim. 2:15	211
sanctifying agent	John 17:19	111
sent from God	Ps. 57:3	517
serve God in	Josh. 24:14	225
a shield	Ps. 91:4	533

	REFERENCE	PAGE
should be believed	2 Thess. 2:12, 13	205
some did not obey	Rom. 2:8	151
some erred in	2 Tim. 2:18	211
stumbling at	John 8:45, 46	101
wicked turn from	2 Tim. 4:4	212
worship in	John 4:23, 24	94

Tryphena
Christian woman in Rome	Rom. 16:12	162

Tryphosa
Christian woman in Rome	Rom. 16:12	162

Tubal
commerce of	Ezek. 27:12, 13	721
son of Japheth	Gen. 10:2	8
tribe under curse	Ezek. 32:26	727

Tubal-cain
son of Lamech, inventor of edge tools	Gen. 4:19, 22	4

Tumult—*uproar; commotion*
against Christ	Matt. 27:24	33
against Paul	Acts 19:29, 40	139
Christians to avoid	2 Cor. 12:20	184

Turtle—*a reptile with a stout shell*
voice of, heard	Song 2:12	586

Turtle Dove—*old world wild dove*
migratory bird	Jer. 8:7	646
offered by the poor	Luke 2:24	59
symbol of purity	Ps. 74:19	525
used for offerings	Lev. 1:14	93

Tutors—*private teachers; guardians*
overseers of children	Gal. 4:2	187

Twelve
angels	Rev. 21:12	257
apostles	Matt. 10:2–4	12
baskets	Matt. 14:20	18
brazen bulls	Jer. 52:20	691
brethren	Gen. 42:13	41
cakes	Lev. 24:5	117
cities	Josh. 18:24	219
cubits	Jer. 52:21	691
foundations	Rev. 21:14	257
fountains of water	Num. 33:9	161
gates of pearl	Rev. 21:21	257
golden bowls	Num. 7:84	133
golden spoons	Num. 7:86	133
he-goats	Ezra 6:17	442
hours	John 11:9	104
legions of angels	Matt. 26:53	32
lions	2 Chr. 9:19	410
manner of fruits	Rev. 22:2	257
memorial stones	Josh. 4:1–9	204
men	Deut. 1:23	166
months	Est. 2:12	463
officers	1 Ki. 4:7	318
oxen	1 Ki. 7:44	323
patriarchs	Acts 7:8	123
pillars	Ex. 24:4	73
princes	Gen. 17:20	14
rods	Num. 17:2	144
sons of Jacob	Gen. 35:22	34
stars	Rev. 12:1	250
thousand horsemen	1 Ki. 4:26	319
thrones	Matt. 19:28	23
tribes of Israel	Gen. 49:28	49
wells of water	Ex. 15:27	65
years	Gen. 14:4	11

	REFERENCE	PAGE
and nursing	Gen. 35:8	33
and sewing	1 Sam. 2:19	256
and spinning	Ex. 35:25	86
subject to man	Gen. 3:16	3
subtlety of	Eccl. 7:26	582
and teaching	Titus 2:3	213
and tending sheep	Gen. 29:9	27
wise	Prov. 14:1	565

some bad women:

Athaliah	2 Ki. 11:1	356
Delilah	Jdgs. 16:4–19	243
Herodias	Matt. 14:6, 8	17
Jezebel	1 Ki. 18:4	337
Maachah	2 Chr. 15:16	415
Zeresh	Est. 5:14	465

Womanhood—*women collectively*

benevolent	Ex. 35:25	86
chaste	Prov. 11:16	564
chaste in word	1 Pet. 3:1, 2	231
loyal to right	Est. 4:15, 16	465
modest	Gen. 24:65	22
pious, devout	Acts 16:14	135

Woman's Rights—*the rights of woman to enjoy the same privileges with men*

to hold property	Num. 27:6–11	155
to make contracts	Num. 30:3–9	158

Womb—*the uterus*

babe leaped in	Luke 1:41	57
bones grow in	Eccl. 11:5	585
closed by the Lord	Gen. 20:18	17
conception in the	Luke 1:30, 31	57
fashioned in	Job 31:15	486
God opened Rachel's	Gen. 30:22	28
of Hannah	1 Sam. 1:5	255
a miscarrying	Hosea 9:14	765
two nations in Rebekah's	Gen. 25:21–24	22

Wonders of God—*those things which cause astonishment*

disorders in nature	Joel 2:30, 31	769
miracles by Moses	Ex. 4:21	54
performed for Israel	Josh. 3:5	203

Wonders, Lying

spurious miracles	2 Thess. 2:8, 9	205

Wonderful—*marvelous; astonishing*

title of Christ	Isa. 9:6	596

Wood—*the hard, fibrous part of a tree or shrub*

hewers of	Josh. 9:21	210

Woodchoppers—*those who cut wood*

given provisions	2 Chr. 2:3, 10	404

Woof—*the cross threads of fabric*

threads which cross warp	Lev. 13:48	104

Wool—*soft curly hair of sheep*

sins made as	Isa. 1:18	590
used for clothing	Lev. 13:47–59	105

Word—*that which is said*

longest in Bible	Isa. 8:1	595
title of Jesus	John 1:1, 14	91

Word of God

as agent in the new birth	James 1:18	226
	1 Pet. 1:23	230
basis for judgment	John 12:48	107
as begetter of faith	John 20:31	115
	Rom. 10:13–17	158
called faithful word	Titus 1:9	213

	REFERENCE	PAGE
called good word of God	Heb. 6:5	219
called Holy Scriptures	Rom. 1:2	150
called scriptures	John 5:39	96
called the word	2 Tim. 4:2	212
called word of gospel	Acts 15:7	133
called word of life	Phil. 2:16	195
called word of truth	2 Tim. 2:15	211
communicated by the Holy Spirit	Acts 1:16	117
	Acts 28:25–27	149
as crushing hammer	Jer. 23:29	659
as devouring flame	Jer. 5:14	643
diligently read and studied	Deut. 17:18, 19	184
	Isa. 34:16	613
endures forever	1 Pet. 1:25	230
established in heaven	Ps. 119:89, 152	546
faithfully taught to others	Deut. 11:18, 19	178
	2 Chr. 17:9	416
given by inspiration of God	2 Tim. 3:16	212
	2 Pet. 1:21	234
holy and spiritual	Prov. 30:5	577
	Rom. 7:12, 14	155
is not bound	2 Tim. 2:9	211
as life-giving energy	Ezek. 37:7	732
as means of spiritual enlightenment	Ps. 19:8	501
	Ps. 119:105, 130	547
	Prov. 6:23	561
as means of spiritual food and nourishment	Deut. 8:3	174
	Ps. 119:103	547
	Jer. 15:16	652
	1 Pet. 2:2	230
not to be altered, taken from, nor added to	Deut. 4:2	170
	Rev. 22:18, 19	258
not to be handled deceitfully	2 Cor. 2:17	177
	2 Cor. 4:2	178
	2 Tim. 2:15	211
as power unto salvation	Rom. 1:16	150
as purifier of the life	Ps. 119:9	545
	John 15:3	109
	1 Pet. 1:22	230
quick and powerful	Heb. 4:12	218
as quickening instrument	Heb. 4:12	218
as sanctifier of the soul	John 17:17	111
seed of the kingdom	Luke 8:11	67
	Matt. 13:19	16
shall not pass away	Matt. 5:18	6
shall stand forever	Isa. 40:8	618
as source of delight and joy	Ps. 119:47, 97	545
	Matt. 4:4	5
as source of hope	Rom. 15:4	161
as source of spiritual knowledge	1 Cor. 10:11	169
	1 John 5:13	239
a spiritual weapon	2 Cor. 10:4, 5	182
	Eph. 6:17	193
studiously examined	John 5:39	96
	Acts 17:11, 12	136
as weapon against evil and temptation	Ps. 119:11	545
	Eph. 6:17	193
written under direct command of God	Jer. 36:1, 2	672
	Ezek. 1:3	696
	Rev. 14:13	160

Words—*vocal sounds used to signify an idea or thought*

fools known by	Eccl. 5:3	581
give comfort	1 Thess. 4:18	203
idle	Matt. 12:36	15
judged by	Matt. 12:37	15
like apples of gold	Prov. 25:11	573
of perfect man	James 3:2	228
should be few	Prov. 10:19	563
of the wise	Eccl. 12:11	585

Work *exertion or activity directed to some purpose or end*

commanded by God	Gen. 3:19	3
disappointing	Eccl. 2:11	579
Nehemiah's devotion to	Neh. 6:1–4	451
of Paul	Acts 18:1–3	137
prayer in	Neh. 4:6–9	450
required	Eph. 4:28	192

Work, Christian

according to ability	Luke 12:48	75
in Christ's name	Col. 3:17	200
gives great joy	Neh. 12:43	459
important	Titus 3:14	214
influence of	Matt. 5:14–16	6
with others	1 Cor. 3:9	165
requires constancy	1 Cor. 15:58	175
required of all	Mark 13:34	51
wholehearted	Col. 3:23	200

Works, Good—*moral duties; deeds*

Abraham justified by	James 2:21	227
commanded	Heb. 13:16	225
example to others	Titus 2:7	214
exemplifies faith	James 2:17, 18	227
not forgotten by God	Heb. 6:10	219
profitable	Titus 3:8	214
religion is	James 1:27	227

Works of the Flesh

Christians to avoid	Eph. 5:3–5	192
enumerated	Gal. 5:19–21	188

World—*the earth; heavens; universe*

belongs to God	Ps. 24:1	503
to be burned up	2 Pet. 3:10, 11	235
corruption of	Rom. 5:12	153
created	Gen. 1:1	1
end of	Matt. 13:49	17
God's footstool	Isa. 66:1	637
God's love for	John 3:16	93
turned upside down	Acts 17:6	136
will pass away	Rev. 21:1	256

Worldliness—*earthliness; lack of spiritualness*

destroys gospel seed	Matt. 13:22	16
enmity against God	James 4:4	228
entangled by	2 Tim. 2:4	211
guard against	Titus 2:12	214
hinders Christian living	Matt. 13:22	16
leads to apostasy	2 Tim. 4:10	212
offsets faith	John 12:42, 43	107
wars against the soul	1 Pet. 2:11	231

Worm—*a small legless invertebrate crawling animal*

in hell, dies not	Mark 9:43–50	46
Job's mother, sister	Job 17:14	479
man called	Job 25:6	483

Wormwood—*bitter herb*

star called	Rev. 8:11	248
symbol of evil	Deut. 28:18	193
symbol of suffering	Jer. 9:15	647

	REFERENCE	PAGE
Zara		
son of Judas	Matt. 1:3	3
Zarah—(See also Zerah)		
son of Judah	Gen. 38:24–30	37
Zared—(See Zered)		
Zarephath—*a town of Phoenicia (called also Sarepta)*		
place where Elijah raised the dead	1 Ki. 17:8–24	336
	Luke 4:26	62
Zaretan		
called Zartanah	1 Ki. 4:12	318
called Zarthan	1 Ki. 7:46	323
town near Jezreel	Josh. 3:16	204
Zareth-shahar		
Reubenite city	Josh. 13:19	214
Zarhites		
family descending from Zerah	Num. 26:13	153
	1 Chr. 4:24	378
family of Judah descending from Zerah	Josh. 7:17	207
	Num. 26:20	153
Zattu—(Zatthu)		
head of exile family	Ezra 2:8	437
	Neh. 10:14	456
Zavan—(See Zaavan)		
Zaza		
son of Jonathan	1 Chr. 2:33	376
Zeal—*active interest; arbor for a cause; enthusiastic devotion; fervor*		
of Anna	Luke 2:36–38	59
of Apollos	Acts 18:25	138
of Apostle Paul	Acts 20:22–31	140
of Christ	Isa. 59:17	632
	Luke 2:49	59
	John 2:17	93
	John 9:4	102
contagious	2 Cor. 9:1, 2	181
desirable	Gal. 4:18	181
of Epaphras	Col. 4:12, 13	200
of fallen Israel	Micah 7:3	782
for good works	Titus 2:14	214
of healed demoniac	Luke 8:38, 39	68
of the healed leper	Mark 1:41–45	36
of Isaiah	Isa. 62:1	634
lack of	Amos 6:1–6	774
in old age	Josh. 14:10–12	215
an overcoming	Mark 2:1–5	37
a patriotic	Neh. 4:19–23	450
of Paul	Acts 26:9–11	146
of Peter	Mark 14:47	53
of Pharisees, scribes	Matt. 23:15	27
of the Psalmist	Ps. 119:139	547
of Samaritan woman	John 4:27–30	94
for spiritual gifts	1 Cor. 14:12	173
urged by great need	John 4:35	95
without knowledge	Rom. 10:2	157
of Zaccheus	Luke 19:1–4	82
Zebadiah—*Jehovah has given*		
a Benjamite, joined David at Ziklag	1 Chr. 12:7	386
Korhite Levite	1 Chr. 26:1, 2	398
a Levite teacher	2 Chr. 17:8	416
postexilic priest	Ezra 10:20	446
a returned exile	Ezra 8:8	443
son of Asahel	1 Chr. 27:7	399

	REFERENCE	PAGE
son of Ishmael and counselor of the king	2 Chr. 19:11	418
Zebah—*victim*		
king of Midian	Jdgs. 8:4–28	235
Zebaim		
native place of Solomon's servants	Ezra 2:55, 57	438
Zebedee—*Jehovah has given*		
father of James and John	Matt. 4:21	6
	Mark 1:19, 20	36
Zebina		
son of Nebo, divorced alien wife	Ezra 10:18, 19, 43	446
Zeboiim—*hyena (?)*		
warred with Elamites	Gen. 14:8, 9	11
Zeboim—*hyena*		
city of the plains	Gen. 10:19	9
	Deut. 29:23	196
town, postexile	Neh. 11:34	458
valley in Benjamin	1 Sam. 13:16–18	331
Zebudah—*endowed*		
wife of Josiah, king of Judah	2 Ki. 23:28, 36	371
Zebul—*height, high dwelling (?)*		
officer of Abimelech	Jdgs. 9:28	237
Zebulun—*dwelling (Zabulun)*		
head of tribe	Num. 26:26, 27	153
tenth son of Jacob	Gen. 30:19, 20	28
Zebulun, Tribe of		
distinguished in the New Jerusalem	Ezek. 48:33	745
	Rev. 7:8	247
given choice allotment	Josh. 19:10–34	219
joined in making David king	1 Chr. 12:33, 40	387
	1 Chr. 27:19	400
loyal to Judah	2 Chr. 30:10, 11, 18	428
in Messianic blessings	Isa. 9:1, 2	596
	Matt. 4:12–16	5
notable for fighting men	Num. 1:30, 31	123
	Num. 26:27	153
notable in wars	Jdgs. 4:6–10	230
	Jdgs. 5:14, 18	231
	Jdgs. 6:35	233
one of six tribes on Mt. Ebal	Deut. 27:13	192
	Josh. 8:32–35	209
sprang from three sons	Num. 26:26, 27	153
tribal history foretold	Gen. 49:13	49
	Deut. 33:18, 19	200
Zebulunite—(Zebulonite)		
citizen of Zebulun	Num. 26:27	153
Elon called	Jdgs. 12:11, 12	241
Zechariah—*Jehovah remembers*		
aide to Ezra	Neh. 8:4	454
aide to Hezekiah	2 Chr. 29:13	427
aide to Isaiah	Isa. 8:2	595

	REFERENCE	PAGE
aide to Nehemiah	Neh. 12:35, 36	459
chief of Ezra	Ezra 8:16	444
chief of Reuben	1 Chr. 5:7	378
	2 Chr. 29:1	427
father of Iddo	1 Chr. 27:21	400
Judahite exile	Neh. 11:4	457
Kohathite Levite	2 Chr. 34:12	433
Kohathite porter	1 Chr. 9:21	384
Levite musician	1 Chr. 15:18	389
minister of ark	1 Chr. 16:4, 5	390
postexilic leader	Ezra 8:1, 3	443
postexilic priest	Neh. 11:12	457
priest of Iddo line	Neh. 12:16	458
priest trumpeter	1 Chr. 15:24	389
	Neh. 12:41	459
prince teacher	2 Chr. 17:7	416
the prophet	Zech. 1:1	792
prophet adviser	2 Chr. 26:5	424
ruler of temple	2 Chr. 35:8	434
son of Bebai	Ezra 8:11	443
son of Benaiah	2 Chr. 20:14	418
son of Elam	Ezra 10:26	446
son of Hosah	1 Chr. 26:11	398
son of Isshiah	1 Chr. 24:25	397
son of Jehiel	1 Chr. 9:35, 37	384
	1 Chr. 8:31	383
son of Jehoiada	2 Chr. 24:20–22	423
son of Jehoshaphat	2 Chr. 21:2	419
son of Shiloni	Neh. 11:5	457
wise counsellor	1 Chr. 26:14	398
Zedad		
place on northern boundary of Palestine	Ezek. 47:15	743
	Num. 34:8	163
Zedekiah—*righteousness of Jehovah*		
1. A false prophet advised Ahab	2 Chr. 18:10	392
family	1 Ki. 22:11–25	341
2. A lying prophet	Jer. 29:21–23	665
3. Prince of Judah	Jer. 36:12	673
4. Son of Jeconiah	1 Chr. 3:16	377
5. Son of Josiah, last king of Judah	1 Chr. 3:15	377
	2 Ki. 24:17–19	372
double-dealings with Babylonian king	Jer. 27:2–22	663
	Jer. 29:3–7	664
	Jer. 51:59	690
polluted the temple with idolatry	2 Chr. 36:11, 14	436
	Jer. 21:11, 12	657
rebelled against Babylon; captured, his eyes put out and his sons slain; carried to Babylon	2 Ki. 24:17–20	372
	2 Ki. 25:1–7	372
	2 Chr. 36:11–21	436
	Jer. 39:1–14	676
	Jer. 52:11	690
Zeeb—*wolf*		
Midianite prince, slain by Gideon	Jdgs. 7:25	234
Zelah		
Saul buried at	2 Sam. 21:14	309
town of Benjamin	Josh. 18:21, 28	219
Zelak		
an Ammonite, warrior of David	2 Sam. 23:37	312

	REFERENCE	PAGE
Zelophehad		
a Mananssite who had no sons; five daughters received inheritance	Num. 26:33	153
	Num. 27:1–12	154
Zelotes		
surname of Simon	Luke 6:15	*64*
Zelzah		
city of Benjamin	1 Sam. 10:2	263
Zemaraim		
mountain in Ephraim	2 Chr. 13:4	413
town of Benjamin	Josh. 19:21, 22	220
Zemarite		
Canaanite tribe	Gen. 10:18	9
Zemira		
son of Becher	1 Chr. 7:8	381
Zenan		
town in Judah	Josh. 15:37	216
Zenas		
Christian lawyer	Titus 3:13	*214*
Zephaniah—*Jehovah hides*		
father of Josiah	Zech. 6:10, 14	794
a Kohathite	1 Chr. 6:36	380
priest of Zedekiah	Jer. 29:25	665
	Jer. 21:1, 2	657
	2 Ki. 25:18–21	373
the prophet	Zeph. 1:1	788
Zephath		
town in southern Judah	Jdgs. 1:17	227
Zephathah		
valley in Judah	2 Chr. 14:10	414
Zephi—(Zepho)		
duke of Edom	Gen. 36:15	35
son of Eliphaz	1 Chr. 1:36	227
Zephon		
son of Gad	Num. 26:15	153
Zer		
city of Naphtali	Josh. 19:32, 35	220
Zerah—(See also Zarah)		
Ethiopian captain	2 Chr. 14:8–15	414
Gershonite Levite	1 Chr. 6:21	379
son of Judah	Num. 26:20	153
	Josh. 7:1	206
son of Reuel	1 Chr. 1:37	374
	Gen. 36:17	35
son of Simeon	Num. 26:12, 13	153
	Gen. 46:10	46
Zerahiah—*Jehovah has risen*		
son of Pahathmoab	Ezra 8:4	443
son of Uzzi	1 Chr. 6:6	379
Zered—*exuberant growth* (Zared)		
brook or valley of Moab	Num. 21:11–13	148
	Deut. 2:13, 14	168
Zereda		
town in Ephraim	1 Ki. 11:26	329
Zeredathah—(Same as Zereda)		
in plain of Jordan	2 Chr. 4:17	405

	REFERENCE	PAGE
Zereath—(See Zaretan)		
place of uncertain location	Jdgs. 7:22	234
Zeresh		
wife of Haman	Est. 5:10	465
Zereth		
son of Ashur	1 Chr. 4:5–7	377
Zeri—(also Izri)		
son of Jeduthun	1 Chr. 25:3, 11	397
Zeror		
ancestor of Saul	1 Sam. 9:1	262
Zeruah		
Jeroboam's mother	1 Ki. 11:26	329
Zerubbabel—*begotten in Babylon* (Zorobabel)		
ancestor of Joseph	Matt. 1:12, 13	*3*
	Luke 3:27	*60*
called son of Shealtiel	Ezra 3:2, 8	439
	Neh. 12:1	458
	Haggai 2:2, 23	790
	Matt. 1:12	*3*
leader of exiles	Ezra 2:1–70	437
rebuilt the temple in Jerusalem	Ezra 6:14, 15	442
	Haggai 1, 2	790
	Zech. 4:1–14	793
restored worship	Ezra 3:1–6	439
son of Pedaiah	1 Chr. 3:17–19	377
Zeruiah		
sister of David	1 Chr. 2:12–16	375
Zetham		
son of Laadan	1 Chr. 23:8	396
temple treasurer	1 Chr. 26:22	399
Zethan		
a Benjamite	1 Chr. 7:6, 10	381
Zethar		
a chamberlain	Est. 1:10	462
Zia		
Gadite	1 Chr. 5:11, 13	378
Ziba		
Saul's servant	2 Sam. 9:10	306
welcomed David back	2 Sam. 19:17	306
Zibeon—*hyena*		
Hivite chief	Gen. 36:2	34
son of Seir	Gen. 36:20	35
Zibia		
a Benjamite	1 Chr. 8:8, 9	382
Zibiah—*gazelle*		
mother of Jehoash	2 Ki. 12:1	357
Zichri		
descendant: Eliezer	1 Chr. 26:25	399
Ephraimite warrior	2 Chr. 28:7	426
father of Amasiah, and of Elishaphat	2 Chr. 17:16	416
	2 Chr. 23:1	421
father of Joel	Neh. 11:9	457
Levite son of Izhar	Ex. 6:21	56
postexilic priest	Neh. 12:1, 17	458
Reubenite	1 Chr. 27:16	400
son of Asaph	1 Chr. 9:15	383
son of Jeroham	1 Chr. 8:27	383
son of Shashak	1 Chr. 8:23–25	383
son of Shimhi	1 Chr. 8:19–21	383

	REFERENCE	PAGE
Ziddim—*sides*		
city of Naphtali	Josh. 19:35	220
Zidkijah—(Zedekiah)		
covenant-signer	Neh. 10:1	456
Zidon—(Sidon)		
city on Mediterranean	Josh. 11:8	212
Zidonians—*inhabitants of Zidon*		
oppressed Israel	Jdgs. 10:12	238
Zif		
second month of Hebrew year	1 Ki. 6:1	320
Ziha		
head of exile family	Ezra 2:43	438
ruler of Nethinims	Neh. 11:21	458
Ziklag		
burned by Amalekites	1 Sam. 30:1, 3	285
city of Judah	Josh. 15:1, 31	215
given to Simeon	Josh. 19:1, 5	219
held by Philistines	1 Sam. 27:5, 6	283
Ish-bosheth slain at	2 Sam. 4:8, 10	291
occupied after exile	Neh. 11:2	457
occupied by David	1 Chr. 12:1–22	386
Zillah—*shadow*		
wife of Lamech	Gen. 4:19	4
Zilpah		
Leah's maid	Gen. 29:24	27
mother of Gad, Asher	Gen. 30:9–13	28
Zilthai—*shady*		
a Benjamite	1 Chr. 8:20	383
Manassite captain	1 Chr. 12:20	387
Zimmah		
son of Johath and Gershonite Levite	1 Chr. 6:20, 42	379
	2 Chr. 29:12	427
Zimran		
son of Abraham by Keturah	Gen. 25:1, 2	22
	1 Chr. 1:32	374
Zimri—*mountain sheep*		
a Benjamite	1 Chr. 8:36	383
	1 Chr. 9:42	384
king of Israel	1 Ki. 16:9–20	335
prince of Simeon	Num. 25:14	152
son of Zerah	1 Chr. 2:3–6	375
unknown place	Jer. 25:25	661
Zin		
border-line of Edom and Judah	Num. 27:14	155
	Josh. 15:1–3	215
wilderness on border of Moab and Canaan	Num. 13:21	139
	Num. 33:36	162
Zina		
son of Shimei	1 Chr. 23:10	396
Zion—*citadel* (Sion)		
1. Figurative name of Jerusalem and of Israel	Ps. 132:13	551
	Isa. 4:3	592
denounced and left desolate because of sin	Isa. 1:8	590
	Isa. 3:16–26	592
	Lam. 4:1–22	695

THE APOCRYPHAL BOOKS

THE EARLY CHRISTIANS used the Greek Old Testament known as the Septuagint which also included religious writings of highly spiritual value known as the Apocrypha.

These writings were interspersed among the canonical books and used by the Alexandrian Jews as part of their Scriptures.

However, the Palestinian Jew whose Scriptures were in Hebrew would not accept these religious writings as "inspired" and refused to include them as part of their Scriptures.

The word Apocrypha means "secret" or "hidden" and applied to a group of writings relative to portions of the Old Testament, and to similar writings in connection to the New Testament.

What is the Apocrypha? Why has it fallen largely into disuse in Protestantism?

To find the answers to these questions, we need to go back to the three centuries before the birth of Jesus Christ. During that period the civilized world was dominated by Greek culture. Following the conquests of Alexander the Great, including his capture of Palestine, Greek became the language spoken by most educated persons. At Alexandria, Egypt, where a great many Jews lived, seventy scholars translated the Hebrew Scriptures into Greek, so that Greek-speaking Jews might read them. (For many Jews who had been born outside Palestine had not learned Hebrew and Aramaic, the two languages in which the Scriptures were originally written.) This translation was called the Septuagint (meaning "seventy"), referring to the seventy translators. It included fourteen writings now grouped as the Apocrypha. At that time, however, the writings were scattered throughout the Old Testament.

When Christianity spread to the Gentile world of the first century A.D., their Scripture was the Greek version, the Septuagint, for they were Greek-speaking persons. The New Testament was originally written in Greek; and about 80 per cent of the quotations from the Old Testament found in the New Testament were taken from the Septuagint, rather than from the Hebrew edition. Because the Christians thought so highly of the Septuagint, the Jews turned against it. Consequently, those books (now called the Apocrypha) which were written in Alexandria were rejected by the Hebrew-speaking Jews of Palestine. They were preserved by the Christians.

Meanwhile, the Romans overthrew the Greek empire. In the course of a few hundred years, Latin replaced Greek as the common language of the civilized world. In A.D. 383 a great Bible scholar named Jerome was commissioned by the Roman church to translate the Scriptures into Latin. He compared the Hebrew version of the Old Testament and the Septuagint in making his translation of the Bible. Those books which were found in the Septuagint but which were not in the Hebrew Scriptures he called the Apocrypha. Even so, these writings were distributed throughout the Old Testament, just as they appeared in the Greek Bible. Jerome's translation, called the Vulgate (meaning "in the common language"), was the official version of the Bible for a thousand years.

The great Protestant Reformer, Martin Luther, also translated the Bible into the common language of the people of his country (into German). Picking up Jerome's distinction between the Hebrew and Greek versions of the Scriptures, Luther went a step further and in 1534 placed the Apocrypha as a section of the Bible between the Old and New Testaments. Thus the Apocrypha became "a bridge between the Testaments." From this time forward, however, Protestants read these books with less interest than had Christians in earlier centuries.

When the Bible was translated into English, Luther's example was followed and the Apocrypha was printed between the Old and New Testaments. Until the year 1629, all English editions of the Bible, including the King James Version, contained these books. But from 1629 on, these became controversial writings. Many Protestants contended that they should not be printed in the Bible at all. This led, in 1827, to the decision by the British Bible Society and the American Bible Society not to include the Apocrypha in their editions of the Bible.

In modern times, however, the Apocrypha has been "rediscovered." Several translations into English have been made and some versions of the Bible include these books once again. A brief summary of these books is given below.

I ESDRAS

"Esdras" is the Greek form of the name Ezra. This book probably written in Egypt about 150 B.C. Except for the story of the wisdom contest (3:1–5:6) the contents is a version of the history recorded in II Chronicles 35–36:23, Ezra, and Nehemiah 7:73–8:12 covering the period from the Josianic Passover to Ezras reformation. Nothing is known of the author or translator.

II ESDRAS

Some call it Apocalyptic Esdras because the central theme (chapters 3–14) present seven revelations allegedly given to Ezra while in exile. To the original, written by an unknown Jew, at the close of the first century A.D. and later translated into Greek, Christian authors subsequently added Chapters 1, 2, 15 and 16. The Jewish original offers its apocalyptic prospects as an answer to the theodicy problem, acutely posed for Judaism by the fall of Jerusalem in A.D. 70. The Christian addition assigns the casting off of Israel in favor of the Gentiles to Israel's apostacy.

TOBIT

Originally written in Hebrew or Aramaic but known only in Greek of the Septuagint this book was held in high esteem by the Jews. This romantic tale with religious didactic purpose was written at least as early as the second century B.C. Tobiah (Tobit) was departed to Nineveh in 721 B.C. and prospered there. His pious custom of burying the dead brought him disaster; impoverished and blind he asked to be allowed to die. His story becomes entwined with that of his kinswoman Sarah, ex-

iled in Ecbatana. The tragedies of both are remedied through the adventures of Tobit's son Tobias, whom Sarah marries—all under angel Raphael's supervision. The tale is steeped in the piety of Jewish law. The scene of the story is eastern Diaspora.

JUDITH

The name of a pious Jewish widow who is the main personage of this historic Jewish fiction with a religious moral. The story deals with events which are dated to the time of Nebuchadnezzar. The latter's general Holofernes was besieging Bethulia. When the water supply was cut off and the situation in the city became critical Judith went to the enemy's camp. She succeeded in gaining Holofernes' confidence and, at an opportune time, cut off his head. This assassination averted all danger from Bethulia. Judith lived to an age of 105. The book honors her as an example of fidelity to the law of Moses. Some think it was composed to inspire zeal during the Maccabean revolt in the 2nd century B.C.

ADDITIONS TO BOOK OF ESTHER

The canonical Hebrew text of Esther has 163 verses; the Greek version has 270, the additional material being divided into seven sections and distributed at the appropriate points throughout the narrative. Inasmuch as genuine Esther contains explicit references to neither God nor traditional Jewish religious practices other than fasting, it is significant that prayers of Mordecai and Esther are included in the additions and also frequent mention of God. The Greek additions contradict details of canonical Esther and contain other obviously fictional elements added to the original Esther about 100 B.C.

THE WISDOM OF SOLOMON

The author, who identifies himself with the figure of Solomon, apparently was an Alexandrian Jew writing in Greek in the first century B.C. (some judge the book of composite authorship). The influence of Greek philosophy is evidenced by the dependence on logos speculations in the treatment of personified Wisdom and by the acceptance of various pagan teachings: the creation of the world out of pre-existent matter; the pre-existence of souls; the impedimentary character of the body; perhaps too, the doctrine of emanation. The book was written as a warning against the assimilating influence of Hellenism on the Jews of Alexandria. It was apparently known to several New Testament writers including Paul. It contains a beautiful section on immortality beginning with the line: "The souls of the upright are in the hand of God."

ECCLESIASTICUS

This second representative of the wisdom genre of literature is called after its author The Wisdom of Jesus Ben Sira. Written in Hebrew, 180 B.C. or earlier, it was translated into Greek for the Alexandrian Jews by the author's grandson, c. 130 B.C. Ben Sira, apparently a professional scribe and teacher, patterned his *magnum opus* after the style of Proverbs. In it he expounds the nature of Wisdom, applying its counsel to all areas of social and religious life. He contradicts biblical soteriology by teaching that almsgiving makes atonement for sin.

BARUCH

This pseudepigraphic book is evidently composite. The first part (1:1–3:8), dated by some as early as the 3rd century B.C., was probably written in Hebrew, as was possibly also the remainder, which is of later origin. 1:1–3:8, composed in a prophetic prose, purports to have been produced by Jeremiah's helper. It is a confession of national sin petitioning for removal of divine favor. From 3:9 the book is poetry. 3:9–4:4 recalls Israel to wisdom. In 4:5–5:9 Jerusalem laments her exiled children, but assurances of restoration are offered.

THE PRAYER OF AZARIAH AND THE SONG OF THE THREE YOUNG MEN

This is one of three sections added to Daniel in the "Septuagint" translation, probably by the early second century B.C. Between 3:23 and 3:24 of canonical Daniel both Greek and Latin Versions insert: (1) a prayer of national confession with supplication for deliverance which Daniel's friend Azariah (cf. Dan. 1:7) offers while he and his two companions are in the fiery furnace; (2) a psalm of praise (dependent on Pss. 148 and 136), uttered by the three; and (3) a narrative framework, containing details not warranted by the genuine Daniel. This section is itself perhaps of composite authorship and was probably written in Hebrew.

SUSANNA

Susanna follows canonical Daniel as chapter 13; in Greek manuscripts it is prefixed to chapter 1. The story relates how two Israelite elders in Babylon, their salacious advances having been resisted by Susanna, falsely accuse her of adultery. But young Daniel effects Susanna's deliverance and the elders' doom by ensnaring them in contradictory testimony.

BEL AND THE DRAGON

These fables ridiculing heathenism appear as Chapter 13 of Daniel in Greek and as chapter 14 in the Vulgate. They date from the first or second century B.C.; their original language is uncertain. Daniel exposes the fraud of the priests who clandestinely consumed the food-offerings of Bel (Baal, i.e. Marduk). After destroying Bel, Daniel concocts a recipe that explodes a sacred dragon. Consigned to a den of lions Daniel is miraculously fed and delivered.

PRAYER OF MANASSEH

According to II Chronicles 33:11ff, when the wicked king Manasseh had been carried into exile he repented and God restored him to Jerusalem. Verses 18, 19 refer to sources which contained Manasseh's prayer of repentance. The origin of the Apocryphal book which purports to be that prayer is unknown; possibly it was produced in Palestine a century or two before Christ. It contains confession of sin and petition for forgiveness. In Green manuscripts the Prayer appears at the end of the Book of Psalms. In the old Vulgate it came to be placed after II Chronicles.

I MACCABEES

Beginning with the accession of Antiochus IV (Epiphanes) (175 B.C.), the history of the Jewish struggle for religous-political liberation is traced to the death of Simon (135 B.C.). It narrates the exploits of the priest Mattathias and of his sons, Judas, Jonathan, and Simon, who successively led the Hasidim to remarkable victories in their war for independence. To Judas was given the surname "Maccabee," afterwards applied to his brothers and four books (I-IV Maccabees). The author wrote in Hebrew and was a contemporary of John Hyrcanus, son and successor of Simon. Some authorities say that the last three chapters were added and the whole re-edited after the destruction of the Temple.

II MACCABEES

Independent of I Maccabees, this history partly overlaps it, extending from the last year of Seleucus IV (174 B.C.) to the defeat of Nicanor by Judas (161 B.C.). The author states that he has epitomized the (now lost) five-volume history of Jason of Cyrene (2:23). Both Jason and the Epitomist wrote in Greek. Suggested dates for II Maccabees vary from c. 120 B.C. to the early first century A.D. Two introductory letters (1:1–2:18) were perhaps lacking in the first edition. It also inculcates doctrinal errors like the propriety of prayers for the dead.

Bible Lands Visited Today

MODERN TRANSPORTATION and increasing prosperity have made it possible for a growing number of Christians to visit in person many of the places mentioned in the Scriptures. Still, the great majority of people will never have the opportunity to walk through the valleys, villages, and hills so familiar to ancient Bible characters. However, those who are unable to enjoy these scenes in person benefit from the advanced developments in modern color photography. People who view the scenes which follow can capture some of the spirit of awe felt by Christians who have had an opportunity to walk in the same paths followed by well known Bible personages. As he looks at these photographs, the viewer is reminded that the names of these places have been made familiar to hundreds of millions of people down through the centuries and all over the world.

While passing through various areas located in the "cradle of Christianity" the traveler is struck with the vivid contrast between the twentieth century conveniences found in the cities and the ready reminders of an ancient civilization found throughout the countryside. This journey with the photographer through Bible lands begins with a view of the ancient city of Hebron, which was familiar to Abraham, Isaac, and Jacob. As the reader studies the scriptures associated with each photograph, he becomes involved in the unfolding drama of life with the Chosen People. He is reminded of the sojourn into Egypt and return to the Promised Land. Other photographs identify places long associated with dynamic leaders of ancient Israel. Then the reader can accompany the photographer as he visits places prominent in the life of Jesus, such as Bethlehem, Nazareth, Jerusalem, and the Garden of Gethsemane. He travels with Paul to Mars Hill and the Island of Rhodes. His journey is ended with a visit to the Island of Patmos where John wrote the book of Revelation.

Viewing the pictures which follow can give a sense of involvement in the stories associated with each photograph. One is reminded that the story of the Chosen People is an ancient one and yet is very much alive today.

Hebron, Ancient Canaanite City (*Genesis 13:18*)

River Jabbok, Near Place Where Jacob Wrestled the Angel (*Genesis 32:22–32*)

The Nile River in Egypt (*Exodus 1:8–22*)

Wilderness of Sinai Along the Route of the Exodus (*Numbers 33:12,13*)

The Canaanite Fortress of Hazor (*Joshua 11*)

Threshing Wheat as in Bible Times (*Ruth 2–3*)

Valley of Lebonah Near Shiloh (*Judges 21:19*)

Vale of Elah, Battlefield for Israelites and Philistines (*I Samuel 17*)

Egyptian Records Telling About a Campaign in Palestine (*I Kings 14:25–28*)

Elisha's Fountain, Main Water Source for Jericho (*II Kings 2:19–22*)

Sea of Galilee (*Matthew 4:18*)

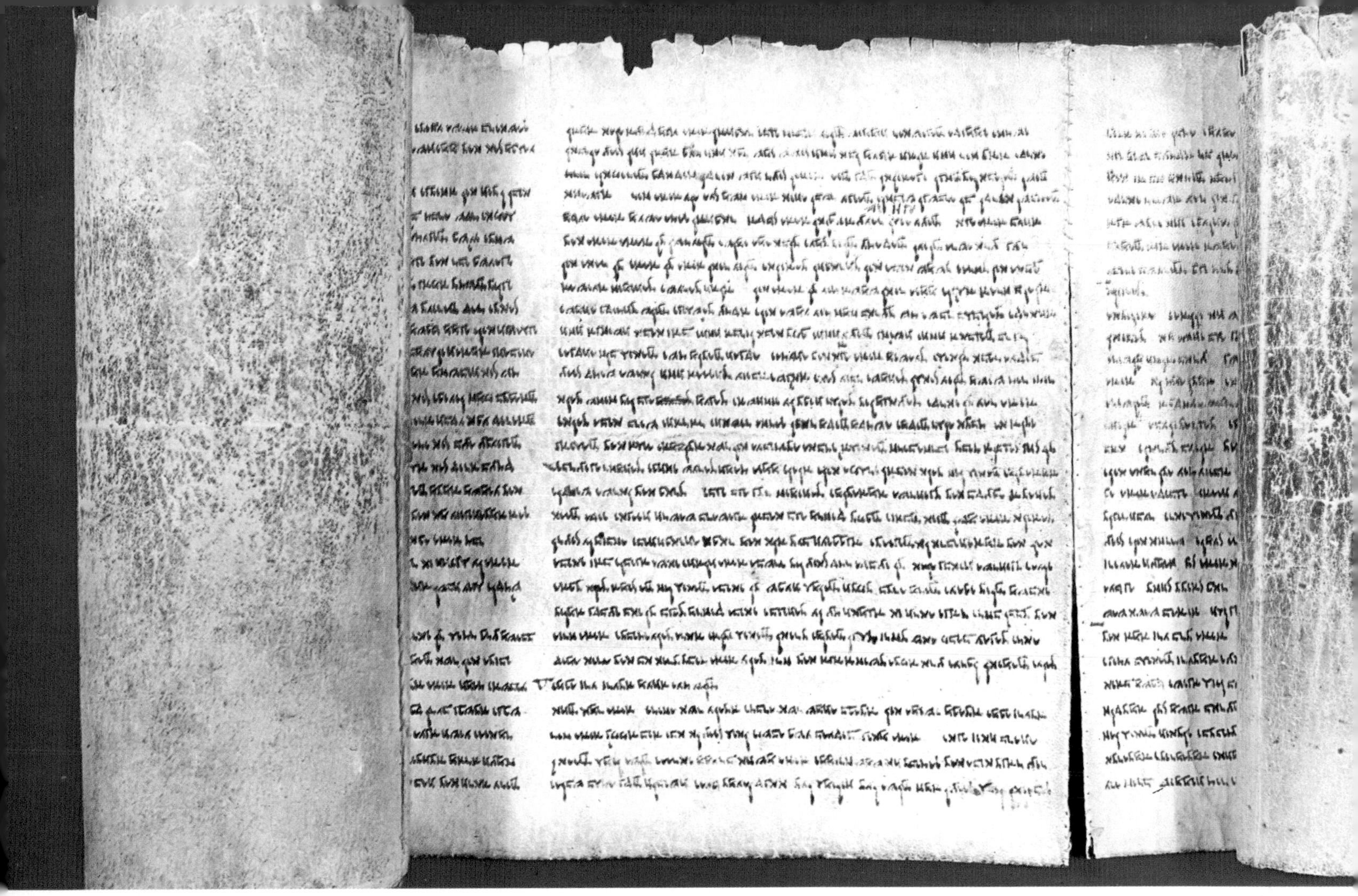

Passage From Isaiah on Dead Sea Scroll (*Isaiah 61:1,2*)

Bethlehem, Birthplace of Jesus (*Matthew 2:1*)

Traditional Birthplace of John the Baptist (*Luke 1:36–80*)

Nazareth, Boyhood Home of Jesus (*Luke 2:39,40*)

The Jordan River, at Traditional Site of Jesus' Baptism (*Mark 1:4–11*)

Capernaum, Where Jesus Taught (*Mark 1:21,22*)

Garden of Gethsemane (*Mark 14:32–50*)

Mars Hill, Where Paul Preached to the Athenians (*Acts 17:22–31*)

Jerusalem (*Acts 1:8*)

Island of Rhodes, Visited by Paul (*Acts 21:1*)

Island of Patmos, Where John Wrote the Book of Revelation (*Revelation 1:9*)

The Old Testament

KING JAMES VERSION

WITH THE HISTORY OF THE
HEBREW PEOPLE IN PICTURES

How to use this
NEW REFERENCE BIBLE

THROUGHOUT the text the reader will find the symbols ᴿ and ᴺ. The symbol ᴿ (for *reference*) indicates that the center column refers to other passages (by book, chapter, and verse) which have further bearing on the word or phrase immediately following the symbol.

The symbol ᴺ (for **note**) before a word indicates that the center column contains an explanatory note on that word.

To find a specific reference or note, simply look in the center column under the chapter and verse in which the ᴿ or ᴺ symbol appears in the text. Verses are shown in boldface numbers under each chapter heading in the center column. Verse numbers relating to the left-hand column of the text will be found on the left of the center column; those referring to the right-hand column of text will be found on the right of the center column.

For example, in the book of Genesis, Chapter 1, verse 1, you will find the symbol ᴿ in the first line before the word *beginning*. Now look in the center reference column under Chapter 1. After the bold 1 on the left, indicating verse 1, you will find John 1:1, 2. This means that in the book of John, Chapter 1, verses 1 and 2, you will find a passage referring to the word *beginning*.

In the same book of Genesis, Chapter 1, verse 6, you will find the symbol ᴺ in the second line before the word *firmament*. Now look in the center reference column under Chapter 1. After the bold 6 on the left, you read "Heb. *expansion.*" This explanatory note calls your attention to the fact that the word "firmament" is actually a rendering of a Hebrew word meaning "expansion."

In the Book of Psalms, an asterisk * in the heading of a psalm indicates that there is a reference or a note in the center column referring to that heading.

A star ★ immediately following a verse in the Old Testament indicate that in the concurrent opinion of many scholars and theologians, the verse embodies a prophetic reference to Christ.

KEY TO PRONUNCIATION

Every reader of the Bible has found the proper names very difficult to pronounce. This difficulty is entirely obviated in this edition of the Holy Scriptures. All the proper names are divided into syllables by a hyphen (-) with the accent (') placed upon the syllable to which it belongs.

In addition to this, the vowels are marked to show what sound they should receive. These and also marks for consonant sounds are shown in the tables below. By attention to this Key the reader can easily pronounce correctly all the proper names in the Bible.

ä	*as in* ah, arm, father.	ị	*as in* peculiar.	āa	= a *of* am.	eů	*as in* neuter.
ă	*as in* abet, hat, dilemma.	ō	*as in* alone.	âa	= a *of* fare.	ēw	*as in* lewd.
ā	*as in* tame.	ŏ	*as in* on, protect.	æ		ôi	*as in* oil.
â	*as in* fare.	ô	*as in* nor.	ae	*as in* mediæval.	ç	*as in* celestial.
ạ	*as in* call.	ǫ	*as in* son.			c͟h	*as in* character.
ĕ	*as in* met, her, second.	ū	*as in* tune.	âi	*as in* aisle.	c̄i	*as in* delicious.
ē	*as in* mete.	û	*as in* rude.	ại	*as in* hail.	ġ	*as in* giant.
ë	= a *in* tame.	ŭ	*as in* us.	āo	= o *of* alone.	ṡ	*as in* his.
ī	*as in* fine.	ụ	*as in* turner.	âu	= o *of* alone.	s̄i	*as in* adhesion.
ĭ	*as in* him, fir, plentiful.	ȳ	*as in* lyre.	êe	*as in* heed.	T͞h	*as in* Thomas.
î	*as in* machine.	ẏ	*as in* typical, fully.	êi	= i *of* fine.	t͞i	*as in* attraction.

THE FIRST BOOK OF MOSES, CALLED

GENESIS

The word "genesis" is derived from a Greek word meaning "generation" or "origin." This is a fitting title for the first book of the Bible, since it records not only the origin of the heavens and the earth, and of plant and animal life, but also the beginning of human institutions and relationships, and specifically presents a survey of the beginnings of Israel's history in the persons of the patriarchs. Genesis forms a preface to the book of Exodus and serves as an introduction to the entire Bible. The first eleven chapters deal with primeval or pre-patriarchal times and present the antecedents of Hebrew history from Adam to Abraham. The remaining chapters center around the persons of the patriarchs, Abraham, Isaac, and Jacob, and of Jacob's son Joseph, all fathers of the people whom God has chosen to carry out His plan and purpose for mankind. The book closes its account with the "chosen people" dwelling in Egypt. The

Patriarchal Period can reasonably be dated ca. 2000–1800 B.C. The authorship of the book of Genesis has traditionally been credited to Moses. The content of Genesis may have come to him through oral tradition, written patriarchal sources, and by divine revelation. Genesis is the first of the five books which comprise the Torah, the law of the Jews.

OUTLINE OF THE BOOK:
I. The account of creation 1:1–2:25
II. Sin and its result 3:1–5:32
III. The flood—God's judgment 6:1–9:29
IV. A new beginning and dispersion 10:1–11:32
V. The life of Abraham 12:1–25:18
VI. Isaac and his sons 25:19–37:1
VII. The migration to Egypt 37:2–50:26

CHAPTER 1

The creation

IN the ᴿbeginning ᴿGod created the heaven and the earth.

2 And the earth was ᴿwithout form, and void; and darkness *was* upon the face of the deep. ᴿAnd the spirit of God moved upon the face of the waters.

3 ᴿAnd God said, ᴿLet there be light: and there was light.

4 And God saw the light, that *it was* good: and God divided ᴺthe light from the darkness.

5 And God called the light ᴿDay, and the darkness he called Night. ᴺAnd the evening and the morning were the first day.

6 And God said, ᴿLet there be a ᴺfirmament in the midst of the waters, and let it divide the waters from the waters.

7 And God made the firmament, ᴿand divided the waters which *were* under the firmament from the waters which *were* ᴿabove the firmament: and it was so.

8 And God called the firmament Heaven. And the evening and the morning were the second day.

9 And God said, ᴿLet the waters under the heaven be gathered together unto one place, and let the dry *land* appear: and it was so.

10 And God called the dry *land* Earth; and the gathering together of the waters called he Seas: and God saw that *it was* good.

11 And God said, Let the earth ᴿbring forth ᴺgrass, the herb yielding seed, *and* the fruit tree yielding ᴿfruit after his kind, whose seed *is* in itself, upon the earth: and it was so.

12 And the earth brought forth grass, *and*

herb yielding seed after his kind, and the tree yielding fruit, whose seed *was* in itself, after his kind: and God saw that *it was* good.

13 And the evening and the morning were the third day.

14 And God said, Let there be lights in the firmament of the heaven to divide ᴺthe day from the night; and let them be for signs, and for seasons, and for days, and years:

15 And let them be for lights in the firmament of the heaven to give light upon the earth: and it was so.

16 And God made two great lights; the ᴿgreater light ᴺto rule the day, and the ᴿlesser light to rule the night: *he made* ᴿthe stars also.

17 And God set them in the firmament of the heaven to give light upon the earth,

18 And to ᴿrule over the day and over the night, and to divide the light from the darkness: and God saw that *it was* good.

19 And the evening and the morning were the fourth day.

20 And God said, Let the waters bring forth abundantly the ᴺmoving creature that hath ᴺlife, and ᴺfowl *that* may fly above the earth in the ᴺopen firmament of heaven.

21 And ᴿGod created great whales, and every living creature that moveth, which the waters brought forth abundantly, after their kind, and every winged fowl after his kind: and God saw that *it was* good.

22 And God blessed them, saying, ᴿBe fruitful, and multiply, and fill the waters in the seas, and let fowl multiply in the earth.

23 And the evening and the morning were the fifth day.

24 And God said, Let the earth bring forth the living creature after his kind, cattle, and

---

Center reference column:

CHAP. 1
BC 4004
1 John 1:1, 2
   Heb. 1:10
1 Ps. 8:3
   Is. 44:24
   Acts 17:24
   Rev. 4:11
2 Jer. 4:23
2 Ps. 33:6
   Is. 40:13, 14
3 Ps. 33:9
3 2 Cor. 4:6
4 Heb. *between the light and between the darkness*
5 Ps. 74:16
5 Heb. *And the evening was, and the morning was*
6 Job 37:18
   Jer. 10:12
6 Heb. *expansion*
7 Prov. 8:28
7 Ps. 148:4
9 Job 26:10
   Prov. 8:29
   Jer. 5:22
   2 Pet. 3:5
11 Heb. 6:7
11 Heb. *tender grass*
11 Luke 6:44

Heb. *between the day and between the night* 14
Ps. 136:8 16
Heb. *for the rule of the day* 16
Ps. 8:3 16
Job 38:7 16
Jer. 31:35 18
Or, *creeping* 20
Heb. *soul* 20
Heb. *let fowl fly* 20
Heb. *face of the firmament of heaven* 20
Ps. 104:26 21
ch. 8:17 22

creeping thing, and beast of the earth after his kind: and it was so.

25 And God made the beast of the earth after his kind, and cattle after their kind, and every thing that creepeth upon the earth after his kind: and God saw that *it was* good.

26 And God said, ᴿLet us make man in our image, after our likeness: and ᴿlet them have dominion over the fish of the sea, and over the fowl of the air, and over the cattle, and over all the earth, and over every creeping thing that creepeth upon the earth.

27 So God created man in his *own* image, ᴿin the image of God created he him; ᴿmale and female created he them.

28 And God blessed them, and God said unto them, ᴿBe fruitful, and multiply, and replenish the earth, and subdue it: and have dominion over the fish of the sea, and over the fowl of the air, and over every living thing that ᴺmoveth upon the earth.

29 And God said, Behold, I have given you every herb ᴺbearing seed, which *is* upon the face of all the earth, and every tree, in the which *is* the fruit of a tree yielding seed; ᴿto you it shall be for meat.

30 And to ᴿevery beast of the earth, and to every ᴿfowl of the air, and to every thing that creepeth upon the earth, wherein *there is* ᴺlife, *I have given* every green herb for meat: and it was so.

31 And ᴿGod saw every thing that he had made, and, behold, *it was* very good. And the evening and the morning were the sixth day.

CHAPTER 2

THUS the heavens and the earth were finished, and ᴿall the host of them.

2 ᴿAnd on the seventh day God ended his work which he had made; and he rested on the seventh day from all his work which he had made.

3 And God ᴿblessed the seventh day, and sanctified it: because that in it he had rested from all his work which God ᴺcreated and made.

4 ᴿThese *are* the generations of the heavens and of the earth when they were created, in the day that the LORD God made the earth and the heavens,

5 And every ᴿplant of the field before it was in the earth, and every herb of the field before it grew: for the LORD God had not ᴿcaused it to rain upon the earth, and *there was* not a man ᴿto till the ground.

6 But ᴺthere went up a mist from the earth, and watered the whole face of the ground.

7 And the LORD God formed man ᴺ*of* the ᴿdust of the ground, and ᴿbreathed into his

ᴿnostrils the breath of life; and ᴿman became a living soul.

The garden of Eden

8 And the LORD God planted ᴿa garden ᴿeastward in ᴿEden; and there he put the man whom he had formed.

9 And out of the ground made the LORD God to grow ᴿevery tree that is pleasant to the sight, and good for food; ᴿthe tree of life also in the midst of the garden, and the tree of knowledge of good and evil.

10 And a river went out of Eden to water the garden; and from thence it was parted, and became into four heads.

11 The name of the first *is* Pī'-sŏn: that *is* it which compasseth ᴿthe whole land of Hăv'-ĭ-läh, where *there is* gold;

12 And the gold of that land *is* good: ᴿthere *is* bdellium and the onyx stone.

13 And the name of the second river *is* Gī'-hŏn: the same *is* it that compasseth the whole land of ᴺĒ-thĭ-ō'-pī-ă.

14 And the name of the third river *is* ᴿHĭd'-dĕ-kĕl: that *is* it which goeth ᴺtoward the east of Assyria. And the fourth river *is* Ēū-phrā'-tēś.

15 And the LORD God took ᴺthe man, and put him into the garden of Eden to dress it and to keep it.

16 And the LORD God commanded the man, saying, Of every tree of the garden ᴺthou mayest freely eat:

17 But of the tree of the knowledge of good and evil, ᴿthou shalt not eat of it: for in the day that thou eatest thereof ᴿthouᴺ shalt surely die.

The creation of woman

18 And the LORD God said, *It is* not good that the man should be alone; ᴿI will make him an help ᴺmeet for him.

19 ᴿAnd out of the ground the LORD God formed every beast of the field, and every fowl of the air; and ᴿbrought *them* unto ᴺAdam to see what he would call them: and whatsoever Adam called every living creature, that *was* the name thereof.

20 And Adam ᴺgave names to all cattle, and to the fowl of the air, and to every beast of the field; but for Adam there was not found an help meet for him.

21 And the LORD God caused a ᴿdeep sleep to fall upon Adam, and he slept: and he took one of his ribs, and closed up the flesh instead thereof;

22 And the rib, which the LORD God had taken from man, ᴺmade he a woman, and ᴿbrought her unto the man.

23 And Adam said, This *is* now ᴿbone of my bones, and flesh of my flesh: she shall be called ᴺWoman, because she was ᴿtaken out of ᴺMan.

24 ᴿTherefore shall a man leave his father and his mother, and shall cleave unto his wife: and they shall be one flesh.

25 ᴿAnd they were both naked, the man and his wife, and were not ᴿashamed.

CHAPTER 3

Temptation and fall

NOW ᴿthe serpent was ᴿmore subtil than any beast of the field which the LORD God had made. And he said unto the woman, ᴺYea, hath God said, Ye shall not eat of every tree of the garden?

2 And the woman said unto the serpent, We may eat of the fruit of the trees of the garden:

3 But of the fruit of the tree which *is* in the midst of the garden, God hath said, Ye shall not eat of it, neither shall ye touch it, lest ye die.

4 ᴿAnd the serpent said unto the woman, Ye shall not surely die:

5 For God doth know that in the day ye eat thereof, then your eyes shall be opened, and ye shall be as gods, knowing good and evil.

6 And when the woman saw that the tree *was* good for food, and that it *was* ᴺpleasant to the eyes, and a tree to be desired to make *one* wise, she took of the fruit thereof, ᴿand did eat, and gave also unto her husband with her; and he did eat.

7 And the eyes of them both were opened, ᴿand they knew that they *were* naked; and they sewed fig leaves together, and made themselves ᴺaprons.

8 And they heard ᴿthe voice of the LORD God walking in the garden in the ᴺcool of the day: and Adam and his wife ᴿhid themselves from the presence of the LORD God amongst the trees of the garden.

9 And the LORD God called unto Adam, and said unto him, Where *art* thou?

10 And he said, I heard thy voice in the garden, ᴿand I was afraid, because I *was* naked; and I hid myself.

11 And he said, Who told thee that thou *wast* naked? Hast thou eaten of the tree, whereof I commanded thee that thou shouldest not eat?

12 And the man said, ᴿThe woman whom thou gavest *to be* with me, she gave me of the tree, and I did eat.

13 And the LORD God said unto the woman, What *is* this *that* thou hast done? And the

woman said, ᴿThe serpent beguiled me, and I did eat.

The curse

14 And the LORD God said unto the serpent, Because thou hast done this, thou *art* cursed above all cattle, and above every beast of the field; upon thy belly shalt thou go, and ᴿdust shalt thou eat all the days of thy life:

15 And I will put enmity between thee and the woman, and between ᴿthy seed and ᴿher seed; ᴿit shall bruise thy head, and thou shalt bruise his heel. ★

16 Unto the woman he said, I will greatly multiply thy sorrow and thy conception; ᴿin sorrow thou shalt bring forth children; ᴿand thy desire *shall be* ᴺto thy husband, and he shall ᴿrule over thee.

17 And unto Adam he said, ᴿBecause thou hast hearkened unto the voice of thy wife, and hast eaten of the tree, ᴿof which I commanded thee, saying, Thou shalt not eat of it: ᴿcursed *is* the ground for thy sake; ᴿin sorrow shalt thou eat *of* it all the days of thy life;

18 Thorns also and thistles shall it ᴺbring forth to thee; and ᴿthou shalt eat the herb of the field;

19 ᴿIn the sweat of thy face shalt thou eat bread, till thou return unto the ground; for out of it wast thou taken: ᴿfor dust thou *art*, and ᴿunto dust shalt thou return.

20 And Adam called his wife's name ᴺEve; because she was the mother of all living.

21 Unto Adam also and to his wife did the LORD God make coats of skins, and clothed them.

Expulsion from the garden

22 And the LORD God said, Behold, the man is become as one of us, to know good and evil: and now, lest he put forth his hand, and take also of the tree of life, and eat, and live for ever:

23 Therefore the LORD God sent him forth from the garden of Eden, ᴿto till the ground from whence he was taken.

24 So he drove out the man; and he placed ᴿat the east of the garden of Eden ᴿChĕr'-ū-bĭms, and a flaming sword which turned every way, to keep the way of the tree of life.

CHAPTER 4

Cain and Abel

AND Adam knew Eve his wife; and she conceived, and bare ᴺCain, and said, I have gotten a man from the LORD.

2 And she again bare his brother ᴺAbel. And Abel was ᴺa keeper of sheep, but Cain was a tiller of the ground.

3 And [N]in process of time it came to pass, that Cain brought [R]of the fruit of the ground an offering unto the LORD.

4 And Abel, he also brought of [R]the firstlings of his [N]flock and of [R]the fat thereof. And the LORD had [R]respect unto Abel and to his offering:

5 But unto Cain and to his offering he had not respect. And Cain was very wroth, [R]and his countenance fell.

6 And the LORD said unto Cain, Why art thou wroth? and why is thy countenance fallen?

7 If thou doest well, shalt thou not [N]be accepted? and if thou doest not well, sin lieth at the door. And [N]unto thee *shall be* his desire, and thou shalt rule over him.

8 And Cain talked with Abel his brother: and it came to pass, when they were in the field, that Cain rose up against Abel his brother, and [R]slew him.

9 And the LORD said unto Cain, Where *is* Abel thy brother? And he said, [R]I know not: *Am* I my brother's keeper?

10 And he said, What hast thou done? the voice of thy brother's [N]blood [R]crieth unto me from the ground.

11 And now *art* thou cursed from the earth, which hath opened her mouth to receive thy brother's blood from thy hand;

12 When thou tillest the ground, it shall not henceforth yield unto thee her strength; a fugitive and a vagabond shalt thou be in the earth.

13 And Cain said unto the LORD, [N]My punishment *is* greater than I can bear.

14 Behold, thou hast driven me out this day from the face of the earth; and [R]from thy face shall I be hid; and I shall be a fugitive and a vagabond in the earth; and it shall come to pass, [R]*that* every one that findeth me shall slay me.

15 And the LORD said unto him, Therefore whosoever slayeth Cain, vengeance shall be taken on him [R]sevenfold. And the LORD set a mark upon Cain, lest any finding him should kill him.

Descendants of Cain

16 And Cain [R]went out from the presence of the LORD, and dwelt in the land of Nod, on the east of Eden.

17 And Cain knew his wife; and she conceived, and bare [N]E'-noch: and he builded a city, [R]and called the name of the city, after the name of his son, E'-noch.

18 And unto E'-noch was born I'-rad: and I'-rad begat Me-hu'-ja-el: and Me-hu'-ja-el

CHAP. 4
BC 4003
3 Heb. *at the end of days*
3 Num. 18:12
4 Num. 18:17
4 Heb. *sheep, or, goats*
4 Lev. 3:16
4 Heb. 11:4
5 ch. 31:2
7 Or, *have the excellency?*
7 Or, *subject unto thee*, ch. 3:16
8 Mat. 23:35
9 John 8:44
10 Heb. *bloods*
10 Heb. 12:24
Rev. 6:10
13 Or, *Mine iniquity is greater than it may be forgiven*
14 Ps. 51:11
14 ch. 9:6
Num. 35:19, 21, 27
15 Ps. 79:12
16 2 Ki. 13:23 & 24:20
Jer. 23:39 & 52:3
17 Heb. *Chanoch*
17 Ps. 49:11

Heb. *Lemech* 18
Heb. *whetter* 22
Or, *I would slay a man in my wound, etc.* 23
Or, *in my hurt* 23
ver. 15 24
ch. 5:3 25
Heb. *Sheth* 25
i.e. *Appointed, or, Put* 25
ch. 5:6 26
Heb. *Enosh* 26
1 Ki. 18:24 26
Ps. 116:17
1 Cor. 1:2
Or, *to call* 26
themselves *by the name of the LORD*

CHAP. 5
BC 4004
ch. 1:26 1
Eph. 4:24 1
Col. 3:10
ch. 1:27 2
ch. 4:25 3
1 Chr. 1:1, *etc.* 4
ch. 1:28 4
ch. 3:19 5
Heb. 9:27
ch. 4:26 6
Heb. *Kenan* 9

begat Me-thu'-sa-el: and Me-thu'-sa-el begat [N]La'-mech.

19 And La'-mech took unto him two wives: the name of the one *was* A'-dah, and the name of the other Zillah.

20 And A'-dah bare Ja'-bal: he was the father of such as dwell in tents, and *of such as have* cattle.

21 And his brother's name *was* Ju'-bal: he was the father of all such as handle the harp and organ.

22 And Zillah, she also bare Tu'-bal-cain, an [N]instructor of every artificer in brass and iron: and the sister of Tu'-bal-cain *was* Na'-a-mah.

23 And La'-mech said unto his wives, A'-dah and Zillah, Hear my voice; ye wives of La'-mech, hearken unto my speech: for [N]I have slain a man to my wounding, and a young man [N]to my hurt.

24 [R]If Cain shall be avenged sevenfold, truly La'-mech seventy and sevenfold.

25 And Adam knew his wife again; and she bare a son, and [R]called his name [N]Seth[N]: For God, *said she*, hath appointed me another seed instead of Abel, whom Cain slew.

26 And to Seth, [R]to him also there was born a son; and he called his name [N]E'-nos: then began men [R]to[N] call upon the name of the LORD.

CHAPTER 5

Descendants of Adam

THIS *is* the book of the generations of Adam. In the day that God created man, in [R]the likeness of God made he him;

2 [R]Male and female created he them; and blessed them, and called their name Adam, in the day when they were created.

3 And Adam lived an hundred and thirty years, and begat *a son* in his own likeness, after his image; and [R]called his name Seth:

4 [R]And the days of Adam after he had begotten Seth were eight hundred years: [R]and he begat sons and daughters:

5 And all the days that Adam lived were nine hundred and thirty years: [R]and he died.

6 And Seth lived an hundred and five years, and [R]begat E'-nos:

7 And Seth lived after he begat E'-nos eight hundred and seven years, and begat sons and daughters:

8 And all the days of Seth were nine hundred and twelve years: and he died.

9 And E'-nos lived ninety years, and begat [N]Ca-i'-nan:

10 And Ē'-nŏs lived after he begat Cā-ī'-năn eight hundred and fifteen years, and begat sons and daughters:

11 And all the days of Ē'-nŏs were nine hundred and five years: and he died.

12 And Cā-ī'-năn lived seventy years, and begat ᴺMă-hăl'-ă-lēĕl:

13 And Cā-ī'-năn lived after he begat Mă-hăl'-ă-lēĕl eight hundred and forty years, and begat sons and daughters:

14 And all the days of Cā-ī'-năn were nine hundred and ten years: and he died.

15 And Mă-hăl'-ă-lēĕl lived sixty and five years, and begat ᴺJâr'-ĕd:

16 And Mă-hăl'-ă-lēĕl lived after he begat Jâr'-ĕd eight hundred and thirty years, and begat sons and daughters:

17 And all the days of Mă-hăl'-ă-lēĕl were eight hundred ninety and five years: and he died.

18 And Jâr'-ĕd lived an hundred sixty and two years, and he begat ᴿĒ'-nŏch:

19 And Jâr'-ĕd lived after he begat Ē'-nŏch eight hundred years, and begat sons and daughters:

20 And all the days of Jâr'-ĕd were nine hundred sixty and two years: and he died.

21 And Ē'-nŏch lived sixty and five years, and begat ᴺMĕ-thū'-sĕ-lăh:

22 And Ē'-nŏch ᴿwalked with God after he begat Mĕ-thū'-sĕ-lăh three hundred years, and begat sons and daughters:

23 And all the days of Ē'-nŏch were three hundred sixty and five years:

24 And ᴿĒ'-nŏch walked with God: and he *was* not; for God took him.

25 And Mĕ-thū'-sĕ-lăh lived an hundred eighty and seven years, and begat ᴺLā'-mĕch:

26 And Mĕ-thū'-sĕ-lăh lived after he begat Lā'-mĕch seven hundred eighty and two years, and begat sons and daughters:

27 And all the days of Mĕ-thū'-sĕ-lăh were nine hundred sixty and nine years: and he died.

Noah born

28 And Lā'-mĕch lived an hundred eighty and two years, and begat a son:

29 And he called his name ᴺᴺNoah, saying, This *same* shall comfort us concerning our work and toil of our hands, because of the ground ᴿwhich the Lᴏʀᴅ hath cursed.

30 And Lā'-mĕch lived after he begat Noah five hundred ninety and five years, and begat sons and daughters:

31 And all the days of Lā'-mĕch were seven hundred seventy and seven years: and he died.

32 And Noah was five hundred years old: and Noah begat ᴿShem, Ham, ᴿand Jā'-phĕth.

CHAPTER 6

Wickedness of man

AND it came to pass, ᴿwhen men began to multiply on the face of the earth, and daughters were born unto them,

2 That the sons of God saw the daughters of men that they *were* fair; and they ᴿtook them wives of all which they chose.

3 And the Lᴏʀᴅ said, ᴿMy spirit shall not always strive with man, ᴿfor that he also *is* flesh: yet his days shall be an hundred and twenty years.

4 There were giants in the earth in those days; and also after that, when the sons of God came in unto the daughters of men, and they bare *children* to them, the same *became* mighty men which *were* of old, men of renown.

5 And God saw that the wickedness of man *was* great in the earth, and *that* ᴺevery ᴿimagination of the thoughts of his heart *was* only evil ᴺcontinually.

6 And ᴿit repented the Lᴏʀᴅ that he had made man on the earth, and it ᴿgrieved him at his heart.

7 And the Lᴏʀᴅ said, I will destroy man whom I have created from the face of the earth; ᴺboth man, and beast, and the creeping thing, and the fowls of the air; for it repenteth me that I have made them.

8 But Noah ᴿfound grace in the eyes of the Lᴏʀᴅ.

9 These *are* the generations of Noah: ᴿNoah was a just man *and* ᴺperfect in his generations, *and* Noah ᴿwalked with God.

10 And Noah begat three sons, ᴿShem, Ham, and Jā'-phĕth.

11 The earth also was corrupt ᴿbefore God, and the earth was ᴿfilled with violence.

12 And God ᴿlooked upon the earth, and, behold, it was corrupt; for all flesh had corrupted his way upon the earth.

13 And God said unto Noah, ᴿThe end of all flesh is come before me; for the earth is filled with violence through them; ᴿand, behold, I will destroy them ᴺwith the earth.

Noah builds the ark

14 Make thee an ark of gō'-phĕr wood; ᴺrooms shalt thou make in the ark, and shalt pitch it within and without with pitch.

15 And this *is the fashion* which thou shalt make it *of:* The length of the ark *shall be* three

hundred cubits, the breadth of it fifty cubits, and the height of it thirty cubits.

16 A window shalt thou make to the ark, and in a cubit shalt thou finish it above; and the door of the ark shalt thou set in the side thereof; *with* lower, second, and third *stories* shalt thou make it.

17 ᴿAnd, behold, I, even I, do bring a flood of waters upon the earth, to destroy all flesh, wherein *is* the breath of life, from under heaven; *and* every thing that *is* in the earth shall die.

18 But with thee will I establish my covenant; and ᴿthou shalt come into the ark, thou, and thy sons, and thy wife, and thy sons' wives with thee.

19 And of every living thing of all flesh, ᴿtwo of every *sort* shalt thou bring into the ark, to keep *them* alive with thee; they shall be male and female.

20 Of fowls after their kind, and of cattle after their kind, of every creeping thing of the earth after his kind, two of every *sort* ᴿshall come unto thee, to keep *them* alive.

21 And take thou unto thee of all food that is eaten, and thou shalt gather *it* to thee; and it shall be for food for thee, and for them.

22 ᴿThus did Noah; ᴿaccording to all that God commanded him, so did he.

CHAPTER 7

Noah fills the ark

AND the Lᴏʀᴅ said unto Noah, ᴿCome thou and all thy house into the ark; for ᴿthee have I seen righteous before me in this generation.

2 Of every ᴿclean beast thou shalt take to thee by ᴺsevens, the male and his female: ᴿand of beasts that *are* not clean by two, the male and his female.

3 Of fowls also of the air by sevens, the male and the female; to keep seed alive upon the face of all the earth.

4 For yet seven days, and I will cause it to rain upon the earth ᴿforty days and forty nights; and every living substance that I have made will I ᴺdestroy from off the face of the earth.

5 ᴿAnd Noah did according unto all that the Lᴏʀᴅ commanded him.

6 And Noah *was* six hundred years old when the flood of waters was upon the earth.

7 ᴿAnd Noah went in, and his sons, and his wife, and his sons' wives with him, into the ark, because of the waters of the flood.

8 Of clean beasts, and of beasts that *are* not

CHAP. 6
BC 2448
17 ch. 7:4, 21-23
2 Pet. 2:5
18 ch. 7:1, 7, 13
1 Pet. 3:20
2 Pet. 2:5
19 ch. 7:8, 9, 15, 16
20 ch. 7:9, 15
22 Heb. 11:7
See Ex. 40:16
22 ch. 7:5, 9, 16

CHAP. 7
BC 2349
1 Mat. 24:38
Luke 17:26
Heb. 11:7
1 Pet. 3:20
2 Pet. 2:5
1 ch. 6:9
Ps. 33:18
Prov. 10:9
2 Pet. 2:9
2 Lev. ch. 11
2 Heb. *seven seven*
2 Lev. 10:10
Ezek. 44:23
4 ver. 12, 17
4 Heb. *blot out*
5 ch. 6:22
7 ver. 1

Or, *on the seventh day*	10
ch. 8:2	11
Prov. 8:28	
Ezek. 26:19	
ch. 8:2	11
Ps. 78:23	
Or, *floodgates*	11
ver. 4, 17	12
ch. 6:19	14
Heb. *wing*	14
ch. 6:20	15
ver. 2, 3	16
ver. 4, 12	17
Ps. 104:26	18
ch. 6:13, 17	21
ch. 2:7	22
Heb. *the breath of the spirit of life*	22
1 Pet. 3:20	23
2 Pet. 2:5	
ch. 8:3 & ch. 8:4 compared with ver. 11 of this chapter	24

clean, and of fowls, and of every thing that creepeth upon the earth,

9 There went in two and two unto Noah into the ark, the male and the female, as God had commanded Noah.

10 And it came to pass ᴺafter seven days, that the waters of the flood were upon the earth.

The flood

11 In the six hundredth year of Noah's life, in the second month, the seventeenth day of the month, the same day were all ᴿthe fountains of the great deep broken up, and the ᴿwindowsᴺ of heaven were opened.

12 ᴿAnd the rain was upon the earth forty days and forty nights.

13 In the selfsame day entered Noah, and Shem, and Ham, and Jā'-phĕth, the sons of Noah, and Noah's wife, and the three wives of his sons with them, into the ark;

14 ᴿThey, and every beast after his kind, and all the cattle after their kind, and every creeping thing that creepeth upon the earth after his kind, and every fowl after his kind, every bird of every ᴺsort.

15 And they ᴿwent in unto Noah into the ark, two and two of all flesh, wherein *is* the breath of life.

16 And they that went in, went in male and female of all flesh, ᴿas God had commanded him: and the Lᴏʀᴅ shut him in.

17 ᴿAnd the flood was forty days upon the earth; and the waters increased, and bare up the ark, and it was lift up above the earth.

18 And the waters prevailed, and were increased greatly upon the earth; ᴿand the ark went upon the face of the waters.

19 And the waters prevailed exceedingly upon the earth; and all the high hills, that *were* under the whole heaven, were covered.

20 Fifteen cubits upward did the waters prevail; and the mountains were covered.

21 ᴿAnd all flesh died that moved upon the earth, both of fowl, and of cattle, and of beast, and of every creeping thing that creepeth upon the earth, and every man:

22 All in ᴿwhose nostrils *was* ᴺthe breath of life, of all that *was* in the dry *land*, died.

23 And every living substance was destroyed which was upon the face of the ground, both man, and cattle, and the creeping things, and the fowl of the heaven; and they were destroyed from the earth: and ᴿNoah only remained *alive*, and they that *were* with him in the ark.

24 ᴿAnd the waters prevailed upon the earth an hundred and fifty days.

CHAPTER 8

The waters subside

AND God ᴿremembered Noah, and every living thing, and all the cattle that *was* with him in the ark: ᴿand God made a wind to pass over the earth, and the waters assuaged;

2 ᴿThe fountains also of the deep and the windows of heaven were stopped, and ᴿthe rain from heaven was restrained;

3 And the waters returned from off the earth ᴺcontinually: and after the end ᴿof the hundred and fifty days the waters were abated.

4 And the ark rested in the seventh month, on the seventeenth day of the month, upon the mountains of Ăr′-ă-răt.

5 And the waters ᴺdecreased continually until the tenth month: in the tenth *month*, on the first *day* of the month, were the tops of the mountains seen.

6 And it came to pass at the end of forty days, that Noah opened ᴿthe window of the ark which he had made:

7 And he sent forth a raven, which went forth ᴺto and fro, until the waters were dried up from off the earth.

8 Also he sent forth a dove from him, to see if the waters were abated from off the face of the ground;

9 But the dove found no rest for the sole of her foot, and she returned unto him into the ark, for the waters *were* on the face of the whole earth: then he put forth his hand, and took her, and ᴺpulled her in unto him into the ark.

10 And he stayed yet other seven days; and again he sent forth the dove out of the ark;

11 And the dove came in to him in the evening; and, lo, in her mouth *was* an olive leaf plucked off: so Noah knew that the waters were abated from off the earth.

12 And he stayed yet other seven days; and sent forth the dove; which returned not again unto him any more.

The earth dries

13 And it came to pass in the six hundredth and first year, in the first *month*, the first *day* of the month, the waters were dried up from off the earth: and Noah removed the covering of the ark, and looked, and, behold, the face of the ground was dry.

14 And in the second month, on the seven and twentieth day of the month, was the earth dried.

15 And God spake unto Noah, saying,

16 Go forth of the ark, ᴿthou, and thy wife, and thy sons, and thy sons' wives with thee.

17 Bring forth with thee every living thing that *is* with thee, of all flesh, *both* of fowl, and of cattle, and of every creeping thing that creepeth upon the earth; that they may breed abundantly in the earth, and ᴿbe fruitful, and multiply upon the earth.

18 And Noah went forth, and his sons, and his wife, and his sons' wives with him:

19 Every beast, every creeping thing, and every fowl, *and* whatsoever creepeth upon the earth, after their ᴺkinds, went forth out of the ark.

Noah builds an altar

20 And Noah builded an altar unto the LORD; and took of ᴿevery clean beast, and of every clean fowl, and offered burnt offerings on the altar.

21 And the LORD smelled ᴿaᴺ sweet savour; and the LORD said in his heart, I will not again ᴿcurse the ground any more for man's sake; ᴺfor the ᴿimagination of man's heart *is* evil from his youth; ᴿneither will I again smite any more every thing living, as I have done.

22 ᴿWhileᴺ the earth remaineth, seedtime and harvest, and cold and heat, and summer and winter, and ᴿday and night shall not cease.

CHAPTER 9

God blesses Noah

AND God blessed Noah and his sons, and said unto them, ᴿBe fruitful, and multiply, and replenish the earth.

2 ᴿAnd the fear of you and the dread of you shall be upon every beast of the earth, and upon every fowl of the air, upon all that moveth *upon* the earth, and upon all the fishes of the sea; into your hand are they delivered.

3 ᴿEvery moving thing that liveth shall be meat for you; even as the ᴿgreen herb have I given you ᴿall things.

4 ᴿBut flesh with the life thereof, *which is* the blood thereof, shall ye not eat.

5 And surely your blood of your lives will I require; ᴿat the hand of every beast will I require it, and ᴿat the hand of man; at the hand of every ᴿman's brother will I require the life of man.

6 ᴿWhoso sheddeth man's blood, by man shall his blood be shed: ᴿfor in the image of God made he man.

7 And you, ᴿbe ye fruitful, and multiply; bring forth abundantly in the earth, and multiply therein.

God's covenant with Noah

8 And God spake unto Noah, and to his sons with him, saying,

9 And I, ᴿbehold, I establish ᴿmy covenant with you, and with your seed after you;

10 ᴿAnd with every living creature that *is* with you, of the fowl, of the cattle, and of every beast of the earth with you; from all that go out of the ark, to every beast of the earth.

11 And ᴿI will establish my covenant with you; neither shall all flesh be cut off any more by the waters of a flood; neither shall there any more be a flood to destroy the earth.

12 And God said, ᴿThis *is* the token of the covenant which I make between me and you and every living creature that *is* with you, for perpetual generations:

13 I do set ᴿmy bow in the cloud, and it shall be for a token of a covenant between me and the earth.

14 And it shall come to pass, when I bring a cloud over the earth, that the bow shall be seen in the cloud:

15 And ᴿI will remember my covenant, which *is* between me and you and every living creature of all flesh; and the waters shall no more become a flood to destroy all flesh.

16 And the bow shall be in the cloud; and I will look upon it, that I may remember ᴿthe everlasting covenant between God and every living creature of all flesh that *is* upon the earth.

17 And God said unto Noah, This *is* the token of the covenant, which I have established between me and all flesh that *is* upon the earth.

Sons of Noah

18 And the sons of Noah, that went forth of the ark, were Shem, and Ham, and Jā'-phĕth: ᴿand Ham *is* the father of ᴺCanaan.

19 ᴿThese *are* the three sons of Noah: ᴿand of them was the whole earth overspread.

20 And Noah began *to be* ᴿan husbandman, and he planted a vineyard:

21 And he drank of the wine, ᴿand was drunken; and he was uncovered within his tent.

22 And Ham, the father of Canaan, saw the nakedness of his father, and told his two brethren without.

23 ᴿAnd Shem and Jā'-phĕth took a garment, and laid *it* upon both their shoulders, and went backward, and covered the nakedness of their father; and their faces *were* backward, and they saw not their father's nakedness.

24 And Noah awoke from his wine, and knew what his younger son had done unto him.

25 And he said, ᴿCursed *be* Canaan; ᴿa

CHAP. 9
BC 2348
9 ch. 6:18
9 Is. 54:9
10 Ps. 145:9
11 Is. 54:9
12 ch. 17:11
13 Rev. 4:3
15 Lev. 26:42, 45
16 ch. 17:13, 19
  Is. 55:3
  Jer. 32:40
  Heb. 13:20
18 ch. 10:6
18 Heb. *Chenaan*
19 ch. 5:32
19 ch. 10:32
  1 Chr. 1:4, etc.
20 ch. 3:19, 23 & 4:2
  Prov. 12:11
21 Prov. 20:1
  1 Cor. 10:12
23 Ex. 20:12
  Gal. 6:1
25 Deut. 27:16
  Josh. 9:23, 27
25 Josh. 9:23
  1 Ki. 9:20, 21

Ps. 144:15   26
Heb. 11:16
Or, *servant to   26
them*
Or, *persuade*   27
Eph. 2:13, 14   27
& 3:6

CHAP. 10
BC 2218
ch. 9:1, 7, 19   1
1 Chr. 1:5, etc.   2
Or, *Rodanim*   4
Ps. 72:10   5
Jer. 2:10 & 25:22
1 Chr. 1:8, etc.   6
Jer. 16:16   9
Mic. 7:2
ch. 6:11   9
Mic. 5:6   10
Gr. *Babylon*   10
Or, *he went out* 11
  into *Assyria*
Or, *the streets of* 11
the city
1 Chr. 1:12   14
Heb. *Tzidon*   15

servant of servants shall he be unto his brethren.

26 And he said, ᴿBlessed *be* the Lᴏʀᴅ God of Shem; and Canaan shall be ᴺhis servant.

27 God shall ᴺenlarge Jā'-phĕth, ᴿand he shall dwell in the tents of Shem; and Canaan shall be his servant.   ★

28 And Noah lived after the flood three hundred and fifty years.

29 And all the days of Noah were nine hundred and fifty years: and he died.

CHAPTER 10

Descendants of Noah

NOW these *are* the generations of the sons of Noah, Shem, Ham, and Jā'-phĕth: ᴿand unto them were sons born after the flood.

2 ᴿThe sons of Jā'-phĕth; Gō'-mĕr, and Mā'-gŏg, and Mā'-dâi, and Jā'-văn, and Tū'-băl, and Mē'-shĕ<u>ch</u>, and Tī'-răs.

3 And the sons of Gō'-mĕr; Ăsh-kē'-năz, and Rī'-phăth, and Tō-gär'-măh.

4 And the sons of Jā'-văn; Ē-lī'-shăh, and Tarshish, Kittim, and ᴺDō'-dă-nīm.

5 By these were ᴿthe isles of the Gentiles divided in their lands; every one after his tongue, after their families, in their nations.

6 ᴿAnd the sons of Ham; Cŭsh, and Mĭz'-rā-ĭm, and Phŭt, and Canaan.

7 And the sons of Cŭsh; Sē'-bă, and Hăv'-ĭ-läh, and Săb'-tăh, and Rā'-ă-măh, and Săb-tē'-<u>ch</u>ă: and the sons of Rā'-ă-măh; Shē'-bă, and Dē'-dăn.

8 And Cŭsh begat Nimrod: he began to be a mighty one in the earth.

9 He was a mighty ᴿhunter ᴿbefore the Lᴏʀᴅ: wherefore it is said, Even as Nimrod the mighty hunter before the Lᴏʀᴅ.

10 ᴿAnd the beginning of his kingdom was ᴺBabel, and ĕr'-ĕ<u>ch</u>, and Ăc'-căd, and Căl'-nĕh, in the land of Shī'-när.

11 Out of that land ᴺwent forth Ăssh'-ur, and builded Nĭn'-ĕ-vēh, and ᴺthe city Rē'-hŏ-bōth, and Cā'-läh,

12 And Rē'-sĕn between Nĭn'-ĕ-vēh and Cā'-läh: the same *is* a great city.

13 And Mĭz'-rā-ĭm begat Lū'-dĭm, and Ăn'-ă-mĭm, and Lĕ-hā'-bĭm, and Năph-tû'-hĭm,

14 And Păth-rû'-sĭm, and Căs-lû'-hĭm, (ᴿout of whom came Philistim,) and Căph'-tō-rĭm.

15 And Canaan begat ᴺsī'-dŏn his firstborn, and Heth,

16 And the Jĕb'-ū-sĭte, and the Amorite, and the Gĭr'-găs-ĭte,

17 And the Hī'-vīte, and the Ăr'-kīte, and the Sī'-nīte,

18 And the Är'-vă-dīte, and the Zĕm'-ă-rīte, and the Hā'-măth-īte: and afterward were the families of the Canaanites spread abroad.

19 [R]And the border of the Canaanites was from Sī'-dŏn, as thou comest to Gē'-rär, unto [N]Gā'-ză; as thou goest, unto Sodom, and Gō-mŏr'-răh, and Ăd'-mäh, and Zē-bō'-ĭm, even unto Lā'-shă.

20 These *are* the sons of Ham, after their families, after their tongues, in their countries, *and* in their nations.

21 Unto Shem also, the father of all the children of Ē'-ber, the brother of Jā'-phĕth the elder, even to him were *children* born.

22 The [R]children of Shem; Ē'-lăm, and Ăssh'-ŭr, and [N]Är-phăx'-ăd, and Lud, and âr'-ăm.

23 And the children of âr'-ăm; Uz, and Hul, and Gē'-thĕr, and Mash.

24 And Är-phăx'-ăd begat [R]Sā'-läh; [N] and Sā'-läh begat Ē'-ber.

25 [R]And unto Ē'-ber were born two sons: the name of one *was* [N]Pē'-lĕg; for in his days was the earth divided; and his brother's name *was* Jŏk'-tăn.

26 And Jŏk'-tăn begat Ăl-mō'-dăd, and Shē'-lĕph, and Hā-zär-mā'-vĕth, and Jē'-räh,

27 And Hă-dôr'-ăm, and Ū'-zăl, and Dĭk'-läh,

28 And ō'-băl, and ă-bĭm'-ā-ĕl, and Shē'-bă,

29 And ō'-phir, and Hăv'-ĭ-läh, and Jō'-băb: all these *were* the sons of Jŏk'-tăn.

30 And their dwelling was from Mē'-shă, as thou goest unto Sē'-phär a mount of the east.

31 These *are* the sons of Shem, after their families, after their tongues, in their lands, after their nations.

32 [R]These *are* the families of the sons of Noah, after their generations, in their nations: [R]and by these were the nations divided in the earth after the flood.

CHAPTER 11

The tower of Babel

AND the whole earth was of one [N]language, and of one [N]speech.

2 And it came to pass, as they journeyed [N]from the east, that they found a plain in the land of Shī'-när; and they dwelt there.

3 And [N]they said one to another, Go to, let us make brick, and [N]burn them throughly. And they had brick for stone, and slime had they for mortar.

4 And they said, Go to, let us build us a city and a tower, [R]whose top *may reach* unto

heaven; and let us make us a name, lest we be scattered abroad upon the face of the whole earth.

5 [R]And the LORD came down to see the city and the tower, which the children of men builded.

6 And the LORD said, Behold, [R]the people *is* one, and they have all [R]one language; and this they begin to do: and now nothing will be restrained from them, which they have [R]imagined to do.

7 Go to, [R]let us go down, and there confound their language, that they may [R]not understand one another's speech.

8 So [R]the LORD scattered them abroad from thence [R]upon the face of all the earth: and they left off to build the city.

9 Therefore is the name of it called [N]Babel; [R]because the LORD did there confound the language of all the earth: and from thence did the LORD scatter them abroad upon the face of all the earth.

Descendants of Shem

10 [R]These *are* the generations of Shem: Shem *was* an hundred years old, and begat Är-phăx'-ăd two years after the flood:

11 And Shem lived after he begat Är-phăx'-ăd five hundred years, and begat sons and daughters.

12 And Är-phăx'-ăd lived five and thirty years, [R]and begat Sā'-läh:

13 And Är-phăx'-ăd lived after he begat Sā'-läh four hundred and three years, and begat sons and daughters.

14 And Sā'-läh lived thirty years, and begat Ē'-ber:

15 And Sā'-läh lived after he begat Ē'-ber four hundred and three years, and begat sons and daughters.

16 [R]And Ē'-ber lived four and thirty years, and begat [R]Pē'-lĕg:

17 And Ē'-ber lived after he begat Pē'-lĕg four hundred and thirty years, and begat sons and daughters.

18 And Pē'-lĕg lived thirty years, and begat Rē'-ū:

19 And Pē'-lĕg lived after he begat Rē'-ū two hundred and nine years, and begat sons and daughters.

20 And Rē'-ū lived two and thirty years, and begat [R]Sē'-rŭg:

21 And Rē'-ū lived after he begat Sē'-rŭg two hundred and seven years, and begat sons and daughters.

22 And Sē'-rŭg lived thirty years, and begat Nahor:

23 And Sē'-rŭg lived after he begat Nahor

two hundred years, and begat sons and daughters.

24 And Nahor lived nine and twenty years, and begat [R]Tē'-räh:

25 And Nahor lived after he begat Tē'-räh an hundred and nineteen years, and begat sons and daughters.

Terah, father of Abram

26 And Tē'-räh lived seventy years, and [R]begat Abram, Nahor, and Hâr'-ăn.

27 Now these *are* the generations of Tē'-räh: Tē'-räh begat Abram, Nahor, and Hâr'-ăn; and Hâr'-ăn begat Lot.

28 And Hâr'-ăn died before his father Tē'-räh in the land of his nativity, in Ur of the Chăl'-dēės.

29 And Abram and Nahor took them wives: the name of Abram's wife *was* [R]Sâr'-ā-ī; and the name of Nahor's wife, [R]Mĭl'-căh, the daughter of Hâr'-ăn, the father of Mĭl'-căh, and the father of Ĭs'-căh.

30 But [R]Sâr'-ā-ī was barren; she *had* no child.

31 And Tē'-räh [R]took Abram his son, and Lot the son of Hâr'-ăn his son's son, and Sâr'-ā-ī his daughter in law, his son Abram's wife; and they went forth with them from [R]Ur of the Chăl'-dēės, to go into [R]the land of Canaan; and they came unto Hâr'-ăn, and dwelt there.

32 And the days of Tē'-räh were two hundred and five years: and Tē'-räh died in Hâr'-ăn.

CHAPTER 12
Abram's call and blessing

NOW the [R]Lord had said unto Abram, Get thee out of thy country, and from thy kindred, and from thy father's house, unto a land that I will shew thee:

2 [R]And I will make of thee a great nation, [R]and I will bless thee, and make thy name great; [R]and thou shalt be a blessing: ★

3 [R]And I will bless them that bless thee, and curse him that curseth thee: [R]and in thee shall all families of the earth be blessed.

4 So Abram departed, as the Lord had spoken unto him; and Lot went with him: and Abram *was* seventy and five years old when he departed out of Hâr'-ăn.

5 And Abram took Sâr'-ā-ī his wife, and Lot his brother's son, and all their substance that they had gathered, and [R]the souls that they had gotten [R]in Hâr'-ăn; and they went forth to go into the land of Canaan; and into the land of Canaan they came.

CHAP. 11
BC c. 2247
24 Luke 3:34, *Thara*
26 Josh. 24:2
1 Chr. 1:26
29 Job 17:15 & 20:12
29 ch. 22:20
30 ch. 16:1, 2
Luke 1:36
31 ch. 12:1
31 Neh. 9:7
Acts 7:4
31 ch. 10:19

CHAP. 12
BC 1921
1 Acts 7:3
Heb. 11:8
2 ch. 17:6 & 18:18
Deut. 26:5
1 Ki. 3:8
2 ch. 24:35
2 ch. 28:4
Gal. 3:14
3 ch. 27:29
Ex. 23:22
Num. 24:9
3 ch. 18:18 & 22:18 & 26:4
Ps. 72:17
Acts 3:25
Gal. 3:8
5 ch. 14:14
5 ch. 11:31

Heb. 11:9   6
Deut. 11:30   6
Judg. 7:1
ch. 10:18, 19   6
ch. 17:1   7
ch. 13:15 & 17:8   7
Ps. 105:9, 11
ch. 13:4   7
ch. 13:4   8
ch. 13:3   9
Heb. *in going and journeying*   9
ch. 26:1   10
Ps. 105:13   10
ch. 43:1   10
ver. 14   11
ch. 26:7
ch. 20:11   12
& 26:7
ch. 20:5, 13   13
ch. 20:14   16
ch. 20:18   17
1 Chr. 16:21
Ps. 105:14
ch. 20:9   18
& 26:10
Prov. 21:1   20

6 And Abram [R]passed through the land unto the place of Sĭ'-chĕm, [R]unto the plain of Mō'-rĕh. [R]And the Canaanite *was* then in the land.

7 [R]And the Lord appeared unto Abram, and said, [R]Unto thy seed will I give this land: and there builded he an [R]altar unto the Lord, who appeared unto him.

8 And he removed from thence unto a mountain on the east of Beth-el, and pitched his tent, *having* Beth-el on the west, and Hā'-ī on the east: and there he builded an altar unto the Lord, and [R]called upon the name of the Lord.

9 And Abram journeyed, [R]going[N] on still toward the south.

Abram goes down to Egypt

10 And there was [R]a famine in the land: and Abram [R]went down into Egypt to sojourn there; for the famine *was* [R]grievous in the land.

11 And it came to pass, when he was come near to enter into Egypt, that he said unto Sâr'-ā-ī his wife, Behold now, I know that thou *art* [R]a fair woman to look upon:

12 Therefore it shall come to pass, when the Egyptians shall see thee, that they shall say, This *is* his wife: and they [R]will kill me, but they will save thee alive.

13 [R]Say, I pray thee, thou *art* my sister: that it may be well with me for thy sake; and my soul shall live because of thee.

14 And it came to pass, that, when Abram was come into Egypt, the Egyptians beheld the woman that she *was* very fair.

15 The princes also of Pharaoh saw her, and commended her before Pharaoh: and the woman was taken into Pharaoh's house.

16 And he [R]entreated Abram well for her sake: and he had sheep, and oxen, and he asses, and menservants, and maidservants, and she asses, and camels.

17 And the Lord [R]plagued Pharaoh and his house with great plagues because of Sâr'-ā-ī Abram's wife.

18 And Pharaoh called Abram, and said, [R]What *is* this *that* thou hast done unto me? why didst thou not tell me that she *was* thy wife?

19 Why saidst thou, She *is* my sister? so I might have taken her to me to wife: now therefore behold thy wife, take *her*, and go thy way.

20 [R]And Pharaoh commanded *his* men concerning him: and they sent him away, and his wife, and all that he had.

CHAPTER 13

Abram and Lot separate

AND Abram went up out of Egypt, he, and his wife, and all that he had, and Lot with him, ᴿinto the south.

2 ᴿAnd Abram *was* very rich in cattle, in silver, and in gold.

3 And he went on his journeys ᴿfrom the south even to Beth-el, unto the place where his tent had been at the beginning, between Beth-el and Hā'-ĭ;

4 Unto the ᴿplace of the altar, which he had made there at the first: and there Abram ᴿcalled on the name of the Lᴏʀᴅ.

5 And Lot also, which went with Abram, had flocks, and herds, and tents.

6 And ᴿthe land was not able to bear them, that they might dwell together: for their substance was great, so that they could not dwell together.

7 And there was ᴿa strife between the herdmen of Abram's cattle and the herdmen of Lot's cattle: ᴿand the Canaanite and the Pĕ-rĭz'-zīte dwelled then in the land.

8 And Abram said unto Lot, ᴿLet there be no strife, I pray thee, between me and thee, and between my herdmen and thy herdmen; for we *be* ᴺbrethren.

9 ᴿ*Is* not the whole land before thee? separate thyself, I pray thee, from me: ᴿif *thou wilt take* the left hand, then I will go to the right; or if *thou depart* to the right hand, then I will go to the left.

10 And Lot lifted up his eyes, and beheld all ᴿthe plain of Jordan, that it *was* well watered every where, before the Lᴏʀᴅ ᴿdestroyed Sodom and Gō-mŏr'-răh, ᴿ*even* as the garden of the Lᴏʀᴅ, like the land of Egypt, as thou comest unto ᴿZō'-är.

11 Then Lot chose him all the plain of Jordan; and Lot journeyed east: and they separated themselves the one from the other.

12 Abram dwelled in the land of Canaan, and Lot ᴿdwelled in the cities of the plain, and ᴿpitched *his* tent toward Sodom.

13 But the men of Sodom ᴿ*were* wicked and ᴿsinners before the Lᴏʀᴅ exceedingly.

Abram moves to Hebron

14 And the Lᴏʀᴅ said unto Abram, after that Lot ᴿwas separated from him, Lift up now thine eyes, and look from the place where thou art ᴿnorthward, and southward, and eastward, and westward:

15 For all the land which thou seest, ᴿto thee will I give it, and ᴿto thy seed for ever.

16 And ᴿI will make thy seed as the dust of the earth: so that if a man can number the dust of the earth, *then* shall thy seed also be numbered.

17 Arise, walk through the land in the length of it and in the breadth of it; for I will give it unto thee.

18 Then Abram removed *his* tent, and came and ᴿdwelt in the ᴺplain of Măm'-rē, ᴿwhich *is* in Hē'-brŏn, and built there an altar unto the Lᴏʀᴅ.

CHAPTER 14

Lot taken captive

AND it came to pass in the days of Ăm-rā'-phĕl king ᴿof Shī'-när, âr'-ĭ-ŏch king of Ĕl-lā'-sär Chĕd-ôr-lā-ō'-mĕr king of ᴿĒ'-lăm, and Tī'-dăl king of nations;

2 *That these* made war with Bē'-ră king of Sodom, and with Bĭr'-shă king of Gō-mŏr'-răh, Shī'-năb king of ᴿĂd'-măh, and Shĕm-ē'-bĕr king of Zĕ-bō'-ĭm, and the king of Bē'-lă, which is ᴿZō'-är.

3 All these were joined together in the vale of Sĭd'-dĭm, ᴿwhich is the salt sea.

4 Twelve years ᴿthey served Chĕd-ôr-lā-ō'-mĕr, and in the thirteenth year they rebelled.

5 And in the fourteenth year came Chĕd-ôr-lā-ō'-mĕr, and the kings that *were* with him, and smote ᴿthe Rĕph'-ā-ĭms in Ăsh'-tĕ-rŏth Kär-nā'-ĭm, and ᴿthe Zū'-zĭms in Ham, ᴿand the Ē'-mĭms in ᴺShā'-vēh Kĭr-ĭ-ă-thā'-ĭm,

6 ᴿAnd the Hôr'-ĭtes in their mount Sē'-ĭr, unto ᴺĔl-pär'-ăn, which *is* by the wilderness.

7 And they returned, and came to Ĕn-mĭsh'-pät, which *is* Kā'-dĕsh, and smote all the country of the Ă-măl'-ĕk-ītes, and also the Amorites, that dwelt ᴿin Hăz'-ĕ-zŏn-tā'-mär.

8 And there went out the king of Sodom, and the king of Gō-mŏr'-răh, and the king of Ăd'-măh, and the king of Zĕ-bō'-ĭm, and the king of Bē'-lă (the same *is* Zō'-är;) and they joined battle with them in the vale of Sĭd'-dĭm;

9 With Chĕd-ôr-lā-ō'-mĕr the king of Ē'-lăm, and with Tī'-dăl king of nations, and Ăm-rā'-phĕl king of Shī'-när, and Ăr'-ĭ-ŏch king of Ĕl-lā'-sär; four kings with five.

10 And the vale of Sĭd'-dĭm *was full of* ᴿslimepits; and the kings of Sodom and Gō-mŏr'-răh fled, and fell there; and they that remained fled ᴿto the mountain.

11 And they took ᴿall the goods of Sodom and Gō-mŏr'-răh, and all their victuals, and went their way.

12 And they took Lot, Abram's ᴿbrother's

son, ᴿwho dwelt in Sodom, and his goods, and departed.

Abram rescues Lot

13 And there came one that had escaped, and told Abram the Hebrew; for ᴿhe dwelt in the plain of Măm'-rē the Amorite, brother of ĕsh'-cŏl, and brother of Aner: ᴿand these *were* confederate with Abram.

14 And when Abram heard that ᴿhis brother was taken captive, he ᴺarmed his ᴺtrained *servants*, ᴿborn in his own house, three hundred and eighteen, and pursued *them* ᴿunto Dan.

15 And he divided himself against them, he and his servants, by night, and ᴿsmote them, and pursued them unto Hō'-băh, which *is* on the left hand of Damascus.

16 And he brought back all the goods, and also brought again his brother Lot, and his goods, and the women also, and the people.

Melchizedek blesses Abram

17 And the king of Sodom ᴿwent out to meet him ᴿafter his return from the slaughter of Chĕd-ôr-lā-ō'-mĕr, and of the kings that *were* with him, at the valley of Shā'-vēh, which *is* the ᴿking's dale.

18 And ᴿMĕl-chĭz'-ĕd-ĕk king of Sā'-lĕm brought forth bread and wine: and he *was* ᴿthe priest of ᴿthe most high God.

19 And he blessed him, and said, ᴿBlessed *be* Abram of the most high God, ᴿpossessor of heaven and earth:

20 And ᴿblessed be the most high God, which hath delivered thine enemies into thy hand. And he gave him tithes ᴿof all.

21 And the king of Sodom said unto Abram, Give me the ᴺpersons, and take the goods to thyself.

22 And Abram said to the king of Sodom, I ᴿhave lift up mine hand unto the LORD, the most high God, ᴿthe possessor of heaven and earth,

23 That ᴿI will not *take* from a thread even to a shoelatchet, and that I will not take any thing that *is* thine, lest thou shouldest say, I have made Abram rich:

24 Save only that which the young men have eaten, and the portion of the men which went with me, Aner, ĕsh'-cŏl, and Măm'-rē; let them take their portion.

CHAPTER 15

Abram's vision

AFTER these things the word of the LORD came unto Abram ᴿin a vision, saying,

CHAP. 14	
BC c. 1913	
12	ch. 13:12
13	ch. 13:18
13	ver. 24
14	ch. 13:8
14	Or, *led forth*
14	Or, *instructed*
14	ch. 15:3
14	Deut. 34:1
15	Is. 41:2, 3
17	1 Sam. 18:6
17	Heb. 7:1
17	2 Sam. 18:18
18	Heb. 7:1
18	Ps. 110:4
	Heb. 5:6
18	Acts 16:17
19	Ruth 3:10
19	ver. 19
	Mat. 11:25
20	ch. 24:27
21	Heb. *souls*
22	Dan. 12:7
22	ver. 19
23	Esth. 9:15, 16

CHAP. 15	
BC 1913	
1	Dan. 10:1

ch. 26:24	1
Dan. 10:12	
Ps. 3:3 & 84:11 & 91:4	1
Prov. 11:18	1
Acts 7:5	2
ch. 14:14	3
2 Sam. 7:12	4
Ps. 147:4	5
Jer. 33:22	5
Ex. 32:13	5
Heb. 11:12	
Rom. 4:3, 9, 22	6
Gal. 3:6	
Ps. 106:31	6
ch. 12:1	7
ch. 11:28, 31	7
Ps. 105:42, 44	7
See ch. 24:13, 14	8
1 Sam. 14:9, 10	
Jer. 34:18	10
Lev. 1:17	10
ch. 2:21	12
Ex. 1:11	13
Acts 7:6	
Ex. 12:40	13
Ex. 6:6	14
Ex. 12:36	14
Job 5:26	15
ch. 25:8	15
Ex. 12:41	16
1 Ki. 21:26	16
Mat. 23:32	16
Heb. *a lamp of fire*	17
ch. 24:7	18
ch. 12:7	18
Ex. 23:31	
Num. 34:3	
Deut. 11:24	
Josh. 1:4	

ᴿFear not, Abram: I *am* thy ᴿshield, *and* thy exceeding ᴿgreat reward.

2 And Abram said, Lord GOD, what wilt thou give me, ᴿseeing I go childless, and the steward of my house *is* this ĕl-ĭ-ē'-zĕr of Damascus?

3 And Abram said, Behold, to me thou hast given no seed: and, lo, ᴿone born in my house is mine heir.

4 And, behold, the word of the LORD *came* unto him, saying, This shall not be thine heir; but he that ᴿshall come forth out of thine own bowels shall be thine heir.

5 And he brought him forth abroad, and said, Look now toward heaven, and ᴿtell the ᴿstars, if thou be able to number them: and he said unto him, ᴿSo shall thy seed be.

6 And he ᴿbelieved in the LORD; and he ᴿcounted it to him for righteousness.

7 And he said unto him, I *am* the LORD that ᴿbrought thee out of ᴿUr of the Chăl'-dēś, ᴿto give thee this land to inherit it.

8 And he said, Lord GOD, ᴿwhereby shall I know that I shall inherit it?

9 And he said unto him, Take me an heifer of three years old, and a she goat of three years old, and a ram of three years old, and a turtledove, and a young pigeon.

10 And he took unto him all these, and ᴿdivided them in the midst, and laid each piece one against another: but ᴿthe birds divided he not.

11 And when the fowls came down upon the carcases, Abram drove them away.

12 And when the sun was going down, ᴿa deep sleep fell upon Abram; and, lo, an horror of great darkness fell upon him.

13 And he said unto Abram, Know of a surety ᴿthat thy seed shall be a stranger in a land *that is* not theirs, and shall serve them; and ᴿthey shall afflict them four hundred years;

14 And also that nation, whom they shall serve, ᴿwill I judge: and afterward ᴿshall they come out with great substance.

15 And ᴿthou shalt go ᴿto thy fathers in peace; ᴿthou shalt be buried in a good old age.

16 But ᴿin the fourth generation they shall come hither again: for the iniquity ᴿof the Amorites ᴿis not yet full.

God's covenant with Abram

17 And it came to pass, that, when the sun went down, and it was dark, behold a smoking furnace, and ᴺa burning lamp that passed between those pieces.

18 In the same day the LORD ᴿmade a covenant with Abram, saying, ᴿUnto thy seed have

I given this land, from the river of Egypt unto the great river, the river, ûu-phrā'-tēś:

19 The Kē'-nītes, and the Kĕ-nĭz'-zītes, and the Kăd'-mō-nītes,

20 And the Hittites, and the Pĕr-rĭz'-zītes, and the Rĕph'-ā-ĭms,

21 And the Amorites, and the Canaanites, and the Gĭr'-gă-shītes, and the Jĕb'-ū-sītes.

CHAPTER 16

Hagar bears Ishmael

NOW Sâr'-ā-ī Abram's wife ᴿbare him no children: and she had an handmaid, ᴿan Egyptian, whose name *was* ᴿHā'-gär.

2 ᴿAnd Sâr'-ā-ī said unto Abram, Behold now, the LORD ᴿhath restrained me from bearing: I pray thee, ᴿgo in unto my maid; it may be that I may ᴺobtain children by her. And Abram ᴿhearkened to the voice of Sâr'-ā-ī.

3 And Sâr'-ā-ī Abram's wife took Hā'-gär her maid the Egyptian, after Abram ᴿhad dwelt ten years in the land of Canaan, and gave her to her husband Abram to be his wife.

4 And he went in unto Hā'-gär, and she conceived: and when she saw that she had conceived, her mistress was ᴿdespised in her eyes.

5 And Sâr'-ā-ī said unto Abram, My wrong *be* upon thee: I have given my maid into thy bosom; and when she saw that she had conceived, I was despised in her eyes: ᴿthe LORD judge between me and thee.

6 ᴿBut Abram said unto Sâr'-ā-ī, Behold, thy maid *is* in thy hand; do to her ᴺas it pleaseth thee. And when Sâr'-ā-ī ᴺdealt hardly with her, ᴿshe fled from her face.

7 And the angel of the LORD found her by a fountain of water in the wilderness, ᴿby the fountain in the way to ᴿShur.

8 And he said, Hā'-gär, Sâr'-ā-ī's maid, whence camest thou? and whither wilt thou go? And she said, I flee from the face of my mistress Sâr'-ā-ī.

9 And the angel of the LORD said unto her, Return to thy mistress, and ᴿsubmit thyself under her hands.

10 And the angel of the LORD said unto her, ᴿI will multiply thy seed exceedingly, that it shall not be numbered for multitude.

11 And the angel of the LORD said unto her, Behold, thou *art* with child, and shalt bear a son, ᴿand shalt call his name ᴺĬsh'-mā-ĕl; because the LORD hath heard thy affliction.

12 ᴿAnd he will be a wild man; his hand *will be* against every man, and every man's

hand against him; ᴿand he shall dwell in the presence of all his brethren.

13 And she called the name of the LORD that spake unto her, Thou God seest me: for she said, Have I also here looked after him ᴿthat seeth me?

14 Wherefore the well was called ᴿBē-ēr-lā'-hāi-rôi;ᴺ behold, *it is* ᴿbetween Kā'-dĕsh and Bē'-rĕd.

15 And ᴿHā'-gär bare Abram a son: and Abram called his son's name, which Hā'-gär bare, Ĭsh'-mā-ĕl.

16 And Abram *was* fourscore and six years old, when Hā'-gär bare Ĭsh'-mā-ĕl to Abram.

CHAPTER 17

The covenant of circumcision

AND when Abram was ninety years old and nine, the LORD appeared to Abram, and said unto him, ᴿI *am* the Almighty God; ᴿwalk before me, and be thou ᴿperfect.ᴺ

2 And I will make my covenant between me and thee, and ᴿwill multiply thee exceedingly.

3 And Abram fell on his face: and God talked with him, saying,

4 As for me, behold, my covenant *is* with thee, and thou shalt be ᴿa father of ᴺmany nations.

5 Neither shall thy name any more be called Abram, but ᴿthy name shall be ᴺAbraham; ᴿfor a father of many nations have I made thee.

6 And I will make thee exceeding fruitful, and I will make ᴿnations of thee, and ᴿkings shall come out of thee.

7 And I will ᴿestablish my covenant between me and thee and thy seed after thee in their generations for an everlasting covenant, ᴿto be a God unto thee, and to ᴿthy seed after thee.

8 And ᴿI will give unto thee, and to thy seed after thee, the land ᴿwhereinᴺ thou art a stranger, all the land of Canaan, for an everlasting possession; and ᴿI will be their God.

9 And God said unto Abraham, Thou shalt keep my covenant therefore, thou, and thy seed after thee in their generations.

10 This *is* my covenant, which ye shall keep, between me and you and thy seed after thee; ᴿEvery man child among you shall be circumcised.

11 And ye shall circumcise the flesh of your foreskin; and it shall be ᴿa token of the covenant betwixt me and you.

12 And ᴺhe that is eight days old ᴿshall be circumcised among you, every man child in

your generations, he that is born in the house, or bought with money of any stranger, which *is* not of thy seed.

13 He that is born in thy house, and he that is bought with thy money, must needs be circumcised: and my covenant shall be in your flesh for an everlasting covenant.

14 And the uncircumcised man child whose flesh of his foreskin is not circumcised, that soul ᴿshall be cut off from his people; he hath broken my covenant.

Sarah promised a son

15 And God said unto Abraham, As for Sâr′-ā-ī thy wife, thou shalt not call her name Sâr′-ā-ī, but ᴺSarah *shall* her name *be*.

16 And I will bless her, ᴿand give thee a son also of her: yea, I will bless her, and ᴺshe shall be *a mother* ᴿof nations; kings of people shall be of her.

17 Then Abraham fell upon his face, ᴿand laughed, and said in his heart, Shall *a child* be born unto him that is an hundred years old? and shall Sarah, that is ninety years old, bear?

18 And Abraham said unto God, O that ĭsh′-mā-ĕl might live before thee!

19 And God said, ᴿSarah thy wife shall bear thee a son indeed; and thou shalt call his name Isaac: and I will establish my covenant with him for an everlasting covenant, *and* with his seed after him. ★

20 And as for ĭsh′-mā-ĕl, I have heard thee: Behold, I have blessed him, and will make him fruitful, and ᴿwill multiply him exceedingly; ᴿtwelve princes shall he beget, ᴿand I will make him a great nation.

21 But my covenant will I establish with Isaac, ᴿwhich Sarah shall bear unto thee at this set time in the next year.

22 And he left off talking with him, and God went up from Abraham.

23 And Abraham took ĭsh′-mā-ĕl his son, and all that were born in his house, and all that were bought with his money, every male among the men of Abraham's house; and circumcised the flesh of their foreskin in the selfsame day, as God had said unto him.

24 And Abraham *was* ninety years old and nine, when he was circumcised in the flesh of his foreskin.

25 And ĭsh′-mā-ĕl his son *was* thirteen years old, when he was circumcised in the flesh of his foreskin.

26 In the selfsame day was Abraham circumcised, and ĭsh′-mā-ĕl his son.

27 And ᴿall the men of his house, born in the house, and bought with money of the stranger, were circumcised with him.

CHAPTER 18

Three men visit Abraham

AND the LORD appeared unto him in the ᴿplains of Măm′-rē: and he sat in the tent door in the heat of the day;

2 ᴿAnd he lift up his eyes and looked, and, lo, three men stood by him: ᴿand when he saw *them*, he ran to meet them from the tent door, and bowed himself toward the ground,

3 And said, My Lord, if now I have found favour in thy sight, pass not away, I pray thee, from thy servant:

4 Let ᴿa little water, I pray you, be fetched, and wash your feet, and rest yourselves under the tree:

5 And ᴿI will fetch a morsel of bread, and ᴿcomfortᴺ ye your hearts; after that ye shall pass on: ᴿfor therefore ᴺare ye come to your servant. And they said, So do, as thou hast said.

6 And Abraham hastened into the tent unto Sarah, and said, ᴺMake ready quickly three measures of fine meal, knead *it*, and make cakes upon the hearth.

7 And Abraham ran unto the herd, and fetched a calf tender and good, and gave *it* unto a young man; and he hasted to dress it.

8 And ᴿhe took butter, and milk, and the calf which he had dressed, and set *it* before them; and he stood by them under the tree, and they did eat.

9 And they said unto him, Where *is* Sarah thy wife? And he said, Behold, ᴿin the tent.

10 And he said, I ᴿwill certainly return unto thee ᴿaccording to the time of life; and, lo, ᴿSarah thy wife shall have a son. And Sarah heard *it* in the tent door, which *was* behind him.

11 Now ᴿAbraham and Sarah *were* old *and* well stricken in age; *and* it ceased to be with Sarah ᴿafter the manner of women.

12 Therefore Sarah ᴿlaughed within herself, saying, ᴿAfter I am waxed old shall I have pleasure, my ᴿlord being old also?

13 And the LORD said unto Abraham, Wherefore did Sarah laugh, saying, Shall I of a surety bear a child, which am old?

14 ᴿIs any thing too hard for the LORD? ᴿAt the time appointed I will return unto thee, according to the time of life, and Sarah shall have a son.

15 Then Sarah denied, saying, I laughed not; for she was afraid. And he said, Nay; but thou didst laugh.

16 And the men rose up from thence, and looked toward Sodom: and Abraham went with them ᴿto bring them on the way.

17 And the LORD said, [R]Shall I hide from Abraham that thing which I do;

18 Seeing that Abraham shall surely become a great and mighty nation, and all the nations of the earth shall be [R]blessed in him? ★

19 For I know him, [R]that he will command his children and his household after him, and they shall keep the way of the LORD, to do justice and judgment; that the LORD may bring upon Abraham that which he hath spoken of him.

20 And the LORD said, Because [R]the cry of Sodom and Gō-mŏr'-răh is great, and because their sin is very grievous;

21 [R]I will go down now, and see whether they have done altogether according to the cry of it, which is come unto me; and if not, [R]I will know.

22 And the men turned their faces from thence, [R]and went toward Sodom: but Abraham [R]stood yet before the LORD.

Abraham bargains for safety of Lot

23 And Abraham [R]drew near, and said, [R]Wilt thou also destroy the righteous with the wicked?

24 [R]Peradventure there be fifty righteous within the city: wilt thou also destroy and not spare the place for the fifty righteous that *are* therein?

25 That be far from thee to do after this manner, to slay the righteous with the wicked: and [R]that the righteous should be as the wicked, that be far from thee: [R]Shall not the Judge of all the earth do right?

26 And the LORD said, [R]If I find in Sodom fifty righteous within the city, then I will spare all the place for their sakes.

27 And Abraham answered and said, [R]Behold now, I have taken upon me to speak unto the Lord, which *am* [R]but dust and ashes:

28 Peradventure there shall lack five of the fifty righteous: wilt thou destroy all the city for *lack of* five? And he said, If I find there forty and five, I will not destroy *it*.

29 And he spake unto him yet again, and said, Peradventure there shall be forty found there. And he said, I will not do *it* for forty's sake.

30 And he said *unto him*, Oh let not the Lord be angry, and I will speak: Peradventure there shall thirty be found there. And he said, I will not do *it*, if I find thirty there.

31 And he said, Behold now, I have taken upon me to speak unto the Lord: Peradventure there shall twenty found there. And he said, I will not destroy *it* for twenty's sake.

32 And he said, [R]Oh let not the Lord be an-

gry, and I will speak yet but this once: Peradventure ten shall be found there. [R]And he said, I will not destroy *it* for ten's sake.

33 And the LORD went his way, as soon as he had left communing with Abraham: and Abraham returned unto his place.

CHAPTER 19

Two angels enter Sodom

AND there [R]came two angels to Sodom at even; and Lot sat in the gate of Sodom: and [R]Lot seeing *them* rose up to meet them; and he bowed himself with his face toward the ground;

2 And he said, Behold now, my lords, [R]turn in, I pray you, into your servant's house, and tarry all night, and [R]wash your feet, and ye shall rise up early, and go on your ways. And they said, [R]Nay; but we will abide in the street all night.

3 And he pressed upon them greatly; and they turned in unto him, and entered into his house; [R]and he made them a feast, and did bake unleavened bread, and they did eat.

4 But before they lay down, the men of the city, *even* the men of Sodom, compassed the house round, both old and young, all the people from every quarter:

5 [R]And they called unto Lot, and said unto him, Where *are* the men which came in to thee this night? [R]bring them out unto us, that we [R]may know them.

6 And [R]Lot went out at the door unto them, and shut the door after him,

7 And said, I pray you, brethren, do not so wickedly.

8 [R]Behold now, I have two daughters which have not known man; let me, I pray you, bring them out unto you, and do ye to them as *is* good in your eyes: only unto these men do nothing; [R]for therefore came they under the shadow of my roof.

9 And they said, Stand back. And they said *again*, This one *fellow* [R]came in to sojourn, [R]and he will needs be a judge: now will we deal worse with thee, than with them. And they pressed sore upon the man, *even* Lot, and came near to break the door.

10 But the men put forth their hand, and pulled Lot into the house to them, and shut to the door.

11 And they smote the men that *were* at the door of the house with blindness, both small and great: so that they wearied themselves to find the door.

12 And the men said unto Lot, Hast thou here any besides? son in law, and thy sons,

and thy daughters, and whatsoever thou hast in the city, ᴿbring *them* out of this place:

13 For we will destroy this place, because the ᴿcry of them is waxen great before the face of the Lᴏʀᴅ; and ᴿthe Lᴏʀᴅ hath sent us to destroy it.

14 And Lot went out, and spake unto his sons in law, ᴿwhich married his daughters, and said, ᴿUp, get you out of this place; for the Lᴏʀᴅ will destroy this city. ᴿBut he seemed as one that mocked unto his sons in law.

Lot's family escapes

15 And when the morning arose, then the angels hastened Lot, saying, ᴿArise, take thy wife, and thy two daughters, which ᴺare here; lest thou be consumed in the ᴺiniquity of the city.

16 And while he lingered, the men laid hold upon his hand, and upon the hand of his wife, and upon the hand of his two daughters; ᴿthe Lᴏʀᴅ being merciful unto him: ᴿand they brought him forth, and set him without the city.

17 And it came to pass, when they had brought them forth abroad, that he said, ᴿEscape for thy life; ᴿlook not behind thee, neither stay thou in all the plain; escape to the mountain, lest thou be consumed.

18 And Lot said unto them, Oh, ᴿnot so, my Lord:

19 Behold now, thy servant hath found grace in thy sight, and thou hast magnified thy mercy, which thou hast shewed unto me in saving my life; and I cannot escape to the mountain, lest some evil take me, and I die:

20 Behold now, this city *is* near to flee unto, and it *is* a little one: Oh, let me escape thither, (*is* it not a little one?) and my soul shall live.

21 And he said unto him, See, ᴿI have accepted ᴺthee concerning this thing also, that I will not overthrow this city, for the which thou hast spoken.

22 Haste thee, escape thither; for ᴿI cannot do any thing till thou be come thither. Therefore ᴿthe name of the city was called ᴺZō'-är.

23 The sun was ᴺrisen upon the earth when Lot entered into Zō'-är.

Sodom and Gomorrah destroyed

24 Then ᴿthe Lᴏʀᴅ rained upon Sodom and upon Gō-môr'-räh brimstone and fire from the Lᴏʀᴅ out of heaven;

25 And he overthrew those cities, and all the plain, and all the inhabitants of the cities, and ᴿthat which grew upon the ground.

26 But his wife looked back from behind him, and she became ᴿa pillar of salt.

27 And Abraham gat up early in the morning to the place where ᴿhe stood before the Lᴏʀᴅ:

28 And he looked toward Sodom and Gō-môr'-räh, and toward all the land of the plain, and beheld, and, lo, ᴿthe smoke of the country went up as the smoke of a furnace.

29 And it came to pass, when God destroyed the cities of the plain, that God ᴿremembered Abraham, and sent Lot out of the midst of the overthrow, when he overthrew the cities in the which Lot dwelt.

Lot's daughters bear sons

30 And Lot went up out of Zō'-är, and ᴿdwelt in the mountain, and his two daughters with him; for he feared to dwell in Zō'-är: and he dwelt in a cave, he and his two daughters.

31 And the firstborn said unto the younger, Our father *is* old, and *there is* not a man in the earth ᴿto come in unto us after the manner of all the earth:

32 Come, let us make our father drink wine, and we will lie with him, that we ᴿmay preserve seed of our father.

33 And they made their father drink wine that night: and the firstborn went in, and lay with her father; and he perceived not when she lay down, nor when she arose.

34 And it came to pass on the morrow, that the firstborn said unto the younger, Behold, I lay yesternight with my father: let us make him drink wine this night also; and go thou in, *and* lie with him, that we may preserve seed of our father.

35 And they made their father drink wine that night also: and the younger arose, and lay with him; and he perceived not when she lay down, nor when she arose.

36 Thus were both the daughters of Lot with child by their father.

37 And the firstborn bare a son, and called his name Moab: ᴿthe same *is* the father of the Moabites unto this day.

38 And the younger, she also bare a son, and called his name Bĕn-ăm'-mī: ᴿthe same *is* the father of the children of Ammon unto this day.

CHAPTER 20

Abraham calls Sarah his sister

AND Abraham journeyed from ᴿthence toward the south country, and dwelled between ᴿKā'-dĕsh and Shur, and ᴿsojourned in Gē'-rär.

2 And Abraham said of Sarah his wife, ᴿShe *is* my sister: and ă-bĭm'-ĕ-lĕ*ch* king of Gē'-rär sent, and ᴿtook Sarah.

3 But ᴿGod came to Ă-bĭm′-ĕ-lĕch ᴿin a dream by night, and said to him, ᴿBehold, thou *art but* a dead man, for the woman which thou hast taken; for she *is* ᴺa man's wife.

4 But Ă-bĭm′-ĕ-lĕch had not come near her: and he said, Lord, ᴿwilt thou slay also a righteous nation?

5 Said he not unto me, She *is* my sister? and she, even she herself said, He *is* my brother: ᴿin the ᴺintegrity of my heart and innocency of my hands have I done this.

6 And God said unto him in a dream, Yea, I know that thou didst this in the integrity of thy heart; for ᴿI also withheld thee from sinning ᴿagainst me: therefore suffered I thee not to touch her.

7 Now therefore restore the man *his* wife; ᴿfor he *is* a prophet, and he shall pray for thee, and thou shalt live: and if thou restore *her* not, ᴿknow thou that thou shalt surely die, thou, ᴿand all that *are* thine.

8 Therefore Ă-bĭm′-ĕ-lĕch rose early in the morning, and called all his servants, and told all these things in their ears: and the men were sore afraid.

9 Then Ă-bĭm′-ĕ-lĕch called Abraham, and said unto him, What hast thou done unto us? and what have I offended thee, ᴿthat thou hast brought on me and on my kingdom a great sin? thou hast done deeds unto me ᴿthat ought not to be done.

10 And Ă-bĭm′-ĕ-lĕch said unto Abraham, What sawest thou, that thou hast done this thing?

11 And Abraham said, Because I thought, Surely ᴿthe fear of God *is* not in this place; and ᴿthey will slay me for my wife's sake.

12 And yet indeed ᴿ*she is* my sister; she *is* the daughter of my father, but not the daughter of my mother; and she became my wife.

13 And it came to pass, when ᴿGod caused me to wander from my father's house, that I said unto her, This *is* thy kindness which thou shalt shew unto me; at every place whither we shall come, ᴿsay of me, He *is* my brother.

Sarah restored to Abraham

14 And Ă-bĭm′-ĕ-lĕch ᴿtook sheep, and oxen, and menservants, and womenservants, and gave *them* unto Abraham, and restored him Sarah his wife.

15 And Ă-bĭm′-ĕ-lĕch said, Behold, ᴿmy land *is* before thee: dwell ᴺwhere it pleaseth thee.

16 And unto Sarah he said, Behold, I have given thy brother a thousand *pieces* of silver: ᴿbehold, he *is* to thee ᴿa covering of the eyes, unto all that *are* with thee, and with all *other:* thus she was reproved.

17 So Abraham ᴿprayed unto God: and

God healed Ă-bĭm′-ĕ-lĕch, and his wife, and his maidservants; and they bare *children.*

18 For the LORD ᴿhad fast closed up all the wombs of the house of Ă-bĭm′-ĕ-lĕch, because of Sarah Abraham's wife.

CHAPTER 21

Sarah bears Isaac

AND the LORD ᴿvisited Sarah as he had said, and the LORD did unto Sarah ᴿas he had spoken.

2 For Sarah ᴿconceived, and bare Abraham a son in his old age, ᴿat the set time of which God had spoken to him.

3 And Abraham called the name of his son that was born unto him, whom Sarah bare to him, ᴿIsaac.

4 And Abraham ᴿcircumcised his son Isaac being eight days old, ᴿas God had commanded him.

5 And ᴿAbraham was an hundred years old, when his son Isaac was born unto him.

6 And Sarah said, ᴿGod hath made me to laugh, *so that* all that hear ᴿwill laugh with me.

7 And she said, Who would have said unto Abraham, that Sarah should have given children suck? ᴿfor I have born *him* a son in his old age.

8 And the child grew, and was weaned: and Abraham made a great feast the *same* day that Isaac was weaned.

Hagar and Ishmael sent away

9 And Sarah saw the son of Hā′-gär ᴿthe Egyptian, ᴿwhich she had born unto Abraham, ᴿmocking.

10 Wherefore she said unto Abraham, ᴿCast out this bondwoman and her son: for the son of this bondwoman shall not be heir with my son, *even* with Isaac.

11 And the thing was very grievous in Abraham's sight ᴿbecause of his son.

12 And God said unto Abraham, Let it not be grievous in thy sight because of the lad, and because of thy bondwoman; in all that Sarah hath said unto thee, hearken unto her voice; for ᴿin Isaac shall thy seed be called. ★

13 And also of the son of the bondwoman will I make ᴿa nation, because he *is* thy seed.

14 And Abraham rose up early in the morning, and took bread, and a bottle of water, and gave *it* unto Hā′-gär, putting *it* on her shoulder, and the child, and ᴿsent her away: and she departed, and wandered in the wilderness of Bēer-shē′-bă.

15 And the water was spent in the bottle, and she cast the child under one of the shrubs.

16 And she went, and sat her down over against *him* a good way off, as it were a bow-shot: for she said, Let me not see the death of the child. And she sat over against *him*, and lift up her voice, and wept.

17 And ᴿGod heard the voice of the lad; and the angel of God called to Hā′-gär out of heaven, and said unto her, What aileth thee, Hā′-gär? fear not; for God hath heard the voice of the lad where he *is*.

18 Arise, lift up the lad, and hold him in thine hand; for ᴿI will make him a great nation.

19 And ᴿGod opened her eyes, and she saw a well of water; and she went, and filled the bottle with water, and gave the lad drink.

20 And God ᴿwas with the lad; and he grew, and dwelt in the wilderness, ᴿand became an archer.

21 And he dwelt in the wilderness of Pâr′-ăn: and his mother ᴿtook him a wife out of the land of Egypt.

Abraham's covenant with Abimelech

22 And it came to pass at that time, that ᴿĂ-bĭm′-ĕ-lĕch and Phĭ′-chŏl the chief captain of his host spake unto Abraham, saying, ᴿGod *is* with thee in all that thou doest:

23 Now therefore ᴿswear unto me here by God ᴺthat thou wilt not deal falsely with me, nor with my son, nor with my son's son: *but* according to the kindness that I have done unto thee, thou shalt do unto me, and to the land wherein thou hast sojourned.

24 And Abraham said, I will swear.

25 And Abraham reproved Ă-bĭm′-ĕ-lĕch because of a well of water, which Ă-bĭm′-ĕ-lĕch's servants ᴿhad violently taken away.

26 And Ă-bĭm′-ĕ-lĕch said, I wot not who hath done this thing: neither didst thou tell me, neither yet heard I *of it*, but to day.

27 And Abraham took sheep and oxen, and gave them unto Ă-bĭm′-ĕ-lĕch; and both of them ᴿmade a covenant.

28 And Abraham set seven ewe lambs of the flock by themselves.

29 And Ă-bĭm′-ĕ-lĕch said unto Abraham, ᴿWhat *mean* these seven ewe lambs which thou hast set by themselves?

30 And he said, For *these* seven ewe lambs shalt thou take of my hand, that ᴿthey may be a witness unto me, that I have digged this well.

31 Wherefore he ᴿcalled that place ᴺBē̂er-shē′-bă; because there they sware both of them.

32 Thus they made a covenant at Bē̂er-shē′-bă: then Ă-bĭm′-ĕ-lĕch rose up, and

CHAP. 21

BC 1892

17 Ex. 3:7
18 ver. 13
19 Num. 22:31
20 ch. 28:15
& 39:2, 3, 21
20 ch. 16:12
21 ch. 24:4
22 ch. 20:2 & 26:26
22 ch. 26:28
23 Josh. 2:12
1 Sam. 24:21
23 Heb. *if thou shalt lie unto me*
25 See ch. 26:15, 18, 20-22
27 ch. 26:31
& 31:44
1 Sam. 18:3
29 ch. 33:8
30 ch. 31:48, 52
31 ch. 26:33
31 i.e. *The well of the oath*

Or, *tree*   33
ch. 4:26   33
Deut. 33:27   33

CHAP. 22

BC 1872

1 Cor. 10:13   1
Heb. 11:17
Jas. 1:12
1 Pet. 1:7
Heb. *Behold me*   1
Heb. 11:17   2
2 Chr. 3:1   2
John 19:17   6
Heb. *Behold me*   7
Or, *kid*   7
Heb. 11:17   9
Jas. 2:21
1 Sam. 15:22   12

Phĭ′-chŏl the chief captain of his host, and they returned into the land of the Philistines.

33 And *Abraham* planted a ᴺgrove in Bē̂er-shē′-bă, and ᴿcalled there on the name of the LORD, ᴿthe everlasting God.

34 And Abraham sojourned in the Philistines' land many days.

CHAPTER 22

God tests Abraham

AND it came to pass after these things, that ᴿGod did tempt Abraham, and said unto him, Abraham: and he said, ᴺBehold, *here* I *am*.

2 And he said, Take now thy son, ᴿthine only *son* Isaac, whom thou lovest, and get thee ᴿinto the land of Mō-rī′-ăh; and offer him there for a burnt offering upon one of the mountains which I will tell thee of.

3 And Abraham rose up early in the morning, and saddled his ass, and took two of his young men with him, and Isaac his son, and clave the wood for the burnt offering, and rose up, and went unto the place of which God had told him.

4 Then on the third day Abraham lifted up his eyes, and saw the place afar off.

5 And Abraham said unto his young men, Abide ye here with the ass; and I and the lad will go yonder and worship, and come again to you.

6 And Abraham took the wood of the burnt offering, and ᴿlaid *it* upon Isaac his son; and he took the fire in his hand, and a knife; and they went both of them together.

7 And Isaac spake unto Abraham his father, and said, My father: and he said, ᴺHere *am I*, my son. And he said, Behold the fire and the wood: but where *is* the ᴺlamb for a burnt offering?

8 And Abraham said, My son, God will provide himself a lamb for a burnt offering: so they went both of them together.

Abraham's sacrifice at Moriah

9 And they came to the place which God had told him of; and Abraham built an altar there, and laid the wood in order, and bound Isaac his son, and ᴿlaid him on the altar upon the wood.

10 And Abraham stretched forth his hand, and took the knife to slay his son.

11 And the angel of the LORD called unto him out of heaven, and said, Abraham, Abraham: and he said, Here *am* I.

12 And he said, ᴿLay not thine hand upon the lad, neither do thou any thing unto him:

for ᴿnow I know that thou fearest God, seeing thou hast not withheld thy son, thine only *son* from me.

13 And Abraham lifted up his eyes, and looked, and behold behind *him* a ram caught in a thickct by his horns: and Abraham went and took the ram, and offered him up for a burnt offering in the stead of his son.

14 And Abraham called the name of that place ᴺJĕ-hō′-văh-jī′-rēh: as it is said *to* this day, In the mount of the Lᴏʀᴅ it shall be seen.

15 And the angel of the Lᴏʀᴅ called unto Abraham out of heaven the second time,

16 And said, ᴿBy myself have I sworn, saith the Lᴏʀᴅ, for because thou hast done this thing, and hast not withheld thy son, thine only *son:*

17 That in blessing I will bless thee, and in multiplying I will multiply thy seed ᴿas the stars of the heaven, ᴿand as the sand which *is* upon the sea ᴺshore; and ᴿthy seed shall possess ᴿthe gate of his enemies;

18 ᴿAnd in thy seed shall all the nations of the earth be blessed; ᴿbecause thou hast obeyed my voice.   ★

19 So Abraham returned unto his young men, and they rose up and went together to ᴿBē-ēr-shē′-bă; and Abraham dwelt at Bē-ēr-shē′-bă.

Abraham's relatives

20 And it came to pass after these things, that it was told Abraham, saying, Behold, ᴿMĭl′-căh, she hath also born children unto thy brother Nahor;

21 ᴿHuz his firstborn, and Buz his brother, and Kĕ-mū′-ĕl the father ᴿof âr′-ăm,

22 And Chĕs′-ĕd, and Hā′-zō, and Pĭl′-dăsh, and Jĭd′-lăph, and Bĕ-thū′-ĕl.

23 And ᴿBĕ-thū′-ĕl begat ᴿRebekah: these eight Mĭl′-căh did bear to Nahor, Abraham's brother.

24 And his concubine, whose name *was* Rĕū′-mäh, she bare also Tē′-bäh, and Gā′-häm, and Thā′-hăsh, and Mā′-ă-chäh.

CHAPTER 23

Death and burial of Sarah

AND Sarah was an hundred and seven and twenty years old: *these were* the years of the life of Sarah.

2 And Sarah died in ᴿKĭr′-jăth-är′-bă; the same *is* ᴿHē′-brŏn in the land of Canaan: and Abraham came to mourn for Sarah, and to weep for her.

3 And Abraham stood up from before his

dead, and spake unto the sons of Heth, saying,

4 ᴿI *am* a stranger and a sojourner with you: ᴿgive me a possession of a buryingplace with you, that I may bury my dead out of my sight.

5 And the children of Heth answered Abraham, saying unto him,

6 Hear us, my lord: thou *art* ᴿaᴺ mighty prince among us: in the choice of our sepulchres bury thy dead; none of us shall withhold from thee his sepulchre, but that thou mayest bury thy dead.

7 And Abraham stood up, and bowed himself to the people of the land, *even* to the children of Heth.

8 And he communed with them, saying, If it be your mind that I should bury my dead out of my sight; hear me, and entreat for me to Ē′-phrŏn the son of Zō′-här,

9 That hc may give me the cave of Măch-pē′-läh, which he hath, which *is* in the end of his field; for ᴺas much money as it is worth he shall give it me for a possession of a buryingplace amongst you.

10 And Ē′-phrŏn dwelt among the children of Heth: and Ē′-phrŏn the Hittite answered Abraham in the ᴺaudience of the children of Heth, *even* of all that ᴿwent in at the gate of his city, saying,

11 ᴿNay, my lord, hear me: the field give I thee, and the cave that *is* therein, I give it thee; in the presence of the sons of my people give I it thee: bury thy dead.

12 And Abraham bowed down himself before the people of the land.

13 And he spake unto Ē′-phrŏn in the audience of the people of the land, saying, But if thou *wilt give it*, I pray thee, hear me: I will give thee money for the field; take *it* of me, and I will bury my dead there.

14 And Ē′-phrŏn answered Abraham, saying unto him,

15 My lord, hearken unto me: the land *is worth* four hundred ᴿshē′-kĕls of silver; what *is* that betwixt me and thee? bury therefore thy dead.

16 And Abraham hearkened unto Ē′-phrŏn; and Abraham ᴿweighed to Ē′-phrŏn the silver, which he had named in the audience of the sons of Heth, four hundred shē′-kĕls of silver, current *money* with the merchant.

17 And ᴿthe field of Ē′-phrŏn, which *was* in Măch-pē′-läh, which *was* before Măm′-rē, the field, and the cave which *was* therein, and all the trees that *were* in the field, that *were* in all the borders round about, were made sure

18 Unto Abraham for a possession in the presence of the children of Heth, before all that went in at the gate of his city.

19 And after this, Abraham buried Sarah his wife in the cave of the field of Măch-pē′-läh before Măm′-rē: the same *is* Hē′-brŏn in the land of Canaan.

20 And the field, and the cave that *is* therein, ᴿwere made sure unto Abraham for a possession of a buryingplace by the sons of Heth.

CHAPTER 24

A wife sought for Isaac

AND Abraham ᴿwas old, *and* ᴺwell stricken in age: and the Lord ᴿhad blessed Abraham in all things.

2 And Abraham said ᴿunto his eldest servant of his house, that ᴿruled over all that he had, ᴿPut, I pray thee, thy hand under my thigh:

3 And I will make thee ᴿswear by the Lord, the God of heaven, and the God of the earth, that ᴿthou shalt not take a wife unto my son of the daughters of the Canaanites, among whom I dwell:

4 ᴿBut thou shalt go ᴿunto my country, and to my kindred, and take a wife unto my son Isaac.

5 And the servant said unto him, Peradventure the woman will not be willing to follow me unto this land: must I needs bring thy son again unto the land from whence thou camest?

6 And Abraham said unto him, Beware thou that thou bring not my son thither again.

7 The Lord God of heaven, which ᴿtook me from my father's house, and from the land of my kindred, and which spake unto me, and that sware unto me, saying, ᴿUnto thy seed will I give this land; ᴿhe shall send his angel before thee, and thou shalt take a wife unto my son from thence.

8 And if the woman will not be willing to follow thee, then ᴿthou shalt be clear from this my oath: only bring not my son thither again.

9 And the servant put his hand under the thigh of Abraham his master, and sware to him concerning that matter.

10 And the servant took ten camels of the camels of his master, and departed; ᴿforᴺ all the goods of his master *were* in his hand: and he arose, and went to Mĕs-ŏ-pŏ-tā′-mĭ-ă, unto ᴿthe city of Nahor.

11 And he made his camels to kneel down without the city by a well of water at the time of the evening, *even* the time ᴿthatᴺ women go out to draw *water.*

12 And he said, ᴿO Lord God of my master Abraham, I pray thee, ᴿsend me good speed this day, and shew kindness unto my master Abraham.

13 Behold, ᴿI stand *here* by the well of wa-

CHAP. 23
BC 1860
20 Jer. 32:10, 11

CHAP. 24
BC 1857
1 ch. 21:5
1 Heb. *gone into days*
1 ver. 35
ch. 13:2
Ps. 112:3
Prov. 10:22
2 ch. 15:2
2 ver. 10
ch. 39:4-6
2 ch. 47:29
1 Chr. 29:24
3 ch. 14:22
Deut. 6:13
Josh. 2:12
3 ch. 26:35
& 28:2
Ex. 34:16
Deut. 7:3
4 ch. 28:2
4 ch. 12:1
7 ch. 12:1
7 ch. 12:7 & 13:15
& 17:8
Ex. 32:13
Deut. 1:8
& 34:4
Acts 7:5
7 Ex. 23:20, 23
& 33:2
Heb. 1:14
8 Josh. 2:17, 20
10 ver. 2
10 Or, *and*
10 ch. 27:43
11 Ex. 2:16
1 Sam. 9:11
11 Heb. *that women which draw* water *go forth*
12 ver. 27
ch. 26:24 & 32:9
Ex. 3:6, 15
12 Neh. 1:11
Ps. 37:5
13 ver. 43

Ex. 2:16	13
See Judg. 6:17, 37	14
1 Sam. 6:7 & 14:10 & 20:7	
ch. 11:29 & 22:23	15
ch. 26:7	16
Heb. *good of countenance*	16
1 Pet. 3:8	18
ver. 12, 56	21
Ex. 32:2, 3	22
Is. 3:19-21	
Or, *jewel for the forehead*	22
ch. 22:23	24
ver. 52	26
Ex. 4:31	
Ex. 18:10	27
Ruth 4:14	
1 Sam. 25:32, 39	
ch. 32:10	27
Ps. 98:3	
ver. 48	27

ter; and ᴿthe daughters of the men of the city come out to draw water:

14 And let it come to pass, that the damsel to whom I shall say, Let down thy pitcher, I pray thee, that I may drink; and she shall say, Drink, and I will give thy camels drink also: *let the same be* she *that* thou hast appointed for thy servant Isaac; and ᴿthereby shall I know that thou hast shewed kindness unto my master.

Rebekah, kinswoman of Abraham

15 And it came to pass, before he had done speaking, that, behold, Rebekah came out, who was born to Bĕ-thū′-ĕl, son of ᴿMĭl′-cäh, the wife of Nahor, Abraham's brother, with her pitcher upon her shoulder.

16 And the damsel ᴿ*was* ᴺvery fair to look upon, a virgin, neither had any man known her: and she went down to the well, and filled her pitcher, and came up.

17 And the servant ran to meet her, and said, Let me, I pray thee, drink a little water of thy pitcher.

18 ᴿAnd she said, Drink, my lord: and she hasted, and let down her pitcher upon her hand, and gave him drink.

19 And when she had done giving him drink, she said, I will draw *water* for thy camels also, until they have done drinking.

20 And she hasted, and emptied her pitcher into the trough, and ran again unto the well to draw *water,* and drew for all his camels.

21 And the man wondering at her held his peace, to wit whether ᴿthe Lord had made his journey prosperous or not.

22 And it came to pass, as the camels had done drinking, that the man took a golden ᴿearringᴺ of half a shē′-kĕl weight, and two bracelets for her hands of ten *shē′-kĕls* weight of gold;

23 And said, Whose daughter *art* thou? tell me, I pray thee: is there room *in* thy father's house for us to lodge in?

24 And she said unto him, ᴿI *am* the daughter of Bĕ-thū′-ĕl the son of Mĭl′-cäh, which she bare unto Nahor.

25 She said moreover unto him, We have both straw and provender enough, and room to lodge in.

26 And the man ᴿbowed down his head, and worshipped the Lord.

27 And he said, ᴿBlessed *be* the Lord God of my master Abraham, who hath not left destitute my master of ᴿhis mercy and his truth: I *being* in the way, the Lord ᴿled me to the house of my master's brethren.

28 And the damsel ran, and told *them of* her mother's house these things.

29 And Rebekah had a brother, and his name *was* ᴿLaban: and Laban ran out unto the man, unto the well.

30 And it came to pass, when he saw the earring and bracelets upon his sister's hands, and when he heard the words of Rebekah his sister, saying, Thus spake the man unto me; that he came unto the man; and, behold, he stood by the camels at the well.

31 And he said, Come in, ᴿthou blessed of the LORD; wherefore standest thou without? for I have prepared the house, and room for the camels.

32 And the man came into the house: and he ungirded his camels, and ᴿgave straw and provender for the camels, and water to wash his feet, and the men's feet that *were* with him.

33 And there was set *meat* before him to eat: but he said, ᴿI will not eat, until I have told mine errand. And he said, Speak on.

Proposal of marriage

34 And he said, I *am* Abraham's servant.

35 And the LORD ᴿhath blessed my master greatly; and he is become great: and he hath given him flocks, and herds, and silver, and gold, and menservants, and maidservants, and camels, and asses.

36 And Sarah my master's wife ᴿbare a son to my master when she was old: and ᴿunto him hath he given all that he hath.

37 And my master ᴿmade me swear, saying, Thou shalt not take a wife to my son of the daughters of the Canaanites, in whose land I dwell:

38 ᴿBut thou shalt go unto my father's house, and to my kindred, and take a wife unto my son.

39 ᴿAnd I said unto my master, Peradventure the woman will not follow me.

40 ᴿAnd he said unto me, The LORD, ᴿbefore whom I walk, will send his angel with thee, and prosper thy way; and thou shalt take a wife for my son of my kindred, and of my father's house:

41 ᴿThen shalt thou be clear from *this* my oath, when thou comest to my kindred; and if they give not thee *one*, thou shalt be clear from my oath.

42 And I came this day unto the well, and said, ᴿO LORD God of my master Abraham, if now thou do prosper my way which I go:

43 ᴿBehold, I stand by the well of water; and it shall come to pass, that when the virgin cometh forth to draw *water*, and I say to her, Give me, I pray thee, a little water of thy pitcher to drink;

44 And she say to me, Both drink thou, and I will also draw for thy camels: *let* the same *be*

the woman whom the LORD hath appointed out for my master's son.

45 ᴿAnd before I had done ᴿspeaking in mine heart, behold, Rebekah came forth with her pitcher on her shoulder; and she went down unto the well, and drew *water:* and I said unto her, Let me drink, I pray thee.

46 And she made haste, and let down her pitcher from her *shoulder*, and said, Drink, and I will give thy camels drink also: so I drank, and she made the camels drink also.

47 And I asked her, and said, Whose daughter *art* thou? And she said, The daughter of Bĕ-thū′-ĕl, Nahor's son, whom Mĭl′-căh bare unto him: and I ᴿput the earring upon her face, and the bracelets upon her hands.

48 ᴿAnd I bowed down my head, and worshipped the LORD, and blessed the LORD God of my master Abraham, which had led me in the right way to take ᴿmy master's brother's daughter unto his son.

49 And now if ye will ᴿdeal kindly and truly with my master, tell me: and if not, tell me; that I may turn to the right hand, or to the left.

Rebekah goes to wed Isaac

50 Then Laban and Bĕ-thū′-ĕl answered and said, ᴿThe thing proceedeth from the LORD: we cannot ᴿspeak unto thee bad or good.

51 Behold, Rebekah ᴿ*is* before thee, take *her*, and go, and let her be thy master's son's wife, as the LORD hath spoken.

52 And it came to pass, that, when Abraham's servant heard their words, he ᴿworshipped the LORD, *bowing himself* to the earth.

53 And the servant brought forth ᴿjewelsᴺ of silver, and jewels of gold, and raiment, and gave *them* to Rebekah: he gave also to her brother and to her mother ᴿprecious things.

54 And they did eat and drink, he and the men that *were* with him, and tarried all night; and they rose up in the morning, and he said, ᴿSend me away unto my master.

55 And her brother and her mother said, Let the damsel abide with us ᴺ*a few* days, at the least ten; after that she shall go.

56 And he said unto them, Hinder me not, seeing the LORD hath prospered my way; send me away that I may go to my master.

57 And they said, We will call the damsel, and inquire at her mouth.

58 And they called Rebekah, and said unto her, Wilt thou go with this man? And she said, I will go.

59 And they sent away Rebekah their sister, and ᴿher nurse, and Abraham's servant, and his men.

60 And they blessed Rebekah, and said unto her, Thou *art* our sister, be thou ᴿ*the mother*

CHAP. **24**
BC 1857
29 ch. 29:5
31 ch. 26:29
Judg. 17:2
Ruth 3:10
Ps. 115:15
32 ch. 43:24
Judg. 19:21
33 Job 23:12
John 4:34
Eph. 6:5-7
35 ver. 1
ch. 13:2
36 ch. 21:2
36 ch. 21:10 & 25:5
37 ver. 3
38 ver. 4
39 ver. 5
40 ver. 7
40 ch. 17:1
41 ver. 8
42 ver. 12
43 ver. 13

ver. 15, etc.   45
1 Sam. 1:13   45
Ezek. 16:11, 12   47
ver. 26   48
ch. 22:23   48
ch. 47:29   49
Josh. 2:14
Ps. 118:23   50
Mat. 21:42
ch. 31:24   50
ch. 20:15   51
ver. 26   52
Ex. 3:22   53
& 11:2
& 12:35
Heb. *vessels*   53
2 Chr. 21:3   53
Ezra 1:6
ver. 56, 59   54
Or, *a full year*,   55
or, *ten* months
ch. 35:8   59
ch. 17:16   60

of thousands of millions, and ᴿlet thy seed possess the gate of those which hate them.

Isaac marries Rebekah

61 And Rebekah arose, and her damsels, and they rode upon the camels, and followed the man: and the servant took Rebekah, and went his way.

62 And Isaac came from the way of the ᴿwell Lā'-hâi-rôi; for he dwelt in the south country.

63 And Isaac went out ᴿtoᴺ meditate in the field at the eventide: and he lifted up his eyes, and saw, and, behold, the camels were coming.

64 And Rebekah lifted up her eyes, and when she saw Isaac, ᴿshe lighted off the camel.

65 For she had said unto the servant, What man is this that walketh in the field to meet us? And the servant had said, It is my master: therefore she took a vail, and covered herself.

66 And the servant told Isaac all things that he had done.

67 And Isaac brought her into his mother Sarah's tent, and took Rebekah, and she became his wife; and he loved her: and Isaac ᴿwas comforted after his mother's death.

CHAPTER 25

Abraham takes another wife

THEN again Abraham took a wife, and her name was Kĕ-tū'-răh.

2 And ᴿshe bare him Zimran, and Jŏk'-shăn, and Mē'-dăn, and Mĭd'-ĭ-ăn, and Ĭsh'-băk, and Shū'-ăh.

3 And Jŏk'-dăn begat Shē'-bă, and Dē'-dăn. And the sons of Dē'-dăn were Ăssh-û'-rĭm, and Lĕ-tû'-shĭm, and Lĕ-ŭm'-mĭm.

4 And the sons of Mĭd'-ĭ-ăn; Ē'-phäh, and Ē'-phĕr, and Hā'-nŏch, and Ă-bī'-dä, and Ĕl-dā'-äh. All these were the children of Kĕ-tū'-răh.

5 And ᴿAbraham gave all that he had unto Isaac.

6 But unto the sons of the concubines, which Abraham had, Abraham gave gifts, and ᴿsent them away from Isaac his son, while he yet lived, eastward, unto ᴿthe east country.

Abraham's death and burial

7 And these are the days of the years of Abraham's life which he lived, an hundred threescore and fifteen years.

8 Then Abraham gave up the ghost, and

CHAP. 24	
BC 1857	
60	ch. 22:17
62	ch. 25:11
63	Josh. 1:8 Ps. 1:2
	& 77:12 & 119:15
	& 143:5
63	Or, *to pray*
64	Josh. 15:18
67	ch. 38:12

CHAP. 25	
BC 1800	
2	1 Chr. 1:32
5	ch. 24:36
6	ch. 21:14
6	Judg. 6:3

ch. 15:15	8
ch. 35:29 & 49:33	8
ch. 35:29 & 50:13	9
ch. 23:16	10
ch. 49:31	10
ch. 16:14	11
ch. 16:15	12
1 Chr. 1:29	13
Or, *Hadad*	15
ch. 17:20	16
ver. 8	17
1 Sam. 15:7	18
Heb. *fell*	18
ch. 16:12	18
Mat. 1:2	19
ch. 22:23	20
ch. 24:29	20
1 Chr. 5:20	21
2 Chr. 33:13	
Ezra 8:23	
Rom. 9:10	21
1 Sam. 9:9	22
& 10:22	
ch. 17:16	23
& 24:60	

ᴿdied in a good old age, an old man, and full of years; and ᴿwas gathered to his people.

9 And ᴿhis sons Isaac and Ĭsh'-mā-ĕl buried him in the cave of Măch-pē'-läh, in the field of Ē'-phrŏn the son of Zō'-här the Hittite, which is before Măm'-rē;

10 ᴿThe field which Abraham purchased of the sons of Heth: ᴿthere was Abraham buried, and Sarah his wife.

11 And it came to pass after the death of Abraham, that God blessed his son Isaac; and Isaac dwelt by the ᴿwell Lā'-hâi-rôi.

Descendants of Ishmael

12 Now these are the generations of Ĭsh'-mā-ĕl, Abraham's son, ᴿwhom Hā'-gär the Egyptian, Sarah's handmaid, bare unto Abraham:

13 And ᴿthese are the names of the sons of Ĭsh'-mā-ĕl, by their names, according to their generations: the firstborn of Ĭsh'-mā-ĕl, Nĕ-bā'-jōth; and Kē'-där, and Ăd'-bĕĕl, and Mĭb'-săm,

14 And Mĭsh'-mă, and Dū'-mäh, and Măs'-să,

15 ᴺHā'-där, and Tē'-mă, Jē'-tŭr, Nā'-phĭsh, and Kē'-dĕ-mäh:

16 These are the sons of Ĭsh'-mā-ĕl, and these are their names, by their towns, and by their castles; ᴿtwelve princes according to their nations.

17 And these are the years of the life of Ĭsh'-mā-ĕl, and hundred and thirty and seven years: and ᴿhe gave up the ghost and died; and was gathered unto his people.

18 ᴿAnd they dwelt from Hăv'-ĭ-läh unto Shur, that is before Egypt, as thou goest toward Assyria: and he ᴺdied ᴿin the presence of all his brethren.

Isaac's twin sons

19 And these are the generations of Isaac, Abraham's son: ᴿAbraham begat Isaac:

20 And Isaac was forty years old when he took Rebekah to wife, ᴿthe daughter of Bĕ-thū'-ĕl the Syrian of Pā'-dăn-âr'-ăm, ᴿthe sister to Laban the Syrian.

21 And Isaac entreated the LORD for his wife, because she was barren: ᴿand the LORD was entreated of him, and ᴿRebekah his wife conceived.

22 And the children struggled together within her; and she said, If it be so, why am I thus? ᴿAnd she went to inquire of the LORD.

23 And the LORD said unto her, ᴿTwo nations are in thy womb, and two manner of people shall be separated from thy bowels; and

ᴿ*the one* people shall be stronger than *the other* people; and ᴿthe elder shall serve the younger.

24 And when her days to be delivered were fulfilled, behold, *there were* twins in her womb.

25 And the first came out red, ᴿall over like an hairy garment; and they called his name Esau.

26 And after that came his brother out, and ᴿhis hand took hold on Esau's heel; and ᴿhis name was called Jacob: and Isaac *was* threescore years old when she bare them.

27 And the boys grew: and Esau was ᴿa cunning hunter, a man of the field; and Jacob *was* ᴿa plain man, ᴿdwelling in tents.

28 And Isaac loved Esau, because ᴺhe did ᴿeat of *his* venison: ᴿbut Rebekah loved Jacob.

Esau sells his birthright

29 And Jacob sod pottage: and Esau came from the field, and he *was* faint:

30 And Esau said to Jacob, Feed me, I pray thee, ᴺwith that same red *pottage;* for I *am* faint: therefore was his name called ᴺĒ'-dom.

31 And Jacob said, Sell me this day thy birthright.

32 And Esau said, Behold, I *am* ᴺat the point to die: and what profit shall this birthright do to me?

33 And Jacob said, Swear to me this day; and he sware unto him: and ᴿhe sold his birthright unto Jacob.

34 Then Jacob gave Esau bread and pottage of lentiles; and ᴿhe did eat and drink, and rose up, and went his way: thus Esau despised *his* birthright.

CHAPTER 26

Isaac dwells in Gerar

Aᴺᴰ there was a famine in the land, beside ᴿthe first famine that was in the days of Abraham. And Isaac went unto ᴿĂ-bīm'-ĕ-lĕch king of the Philistines unto Gē'-rär.

2 And the Lᴏʀᴅ appeared unto him, and said, Go not down into Egypt; dwell in ᴿthe land which I shall tell thee of:

3 ᴿSojourn in this land, and ᴿI will be with thee, and ᴿwill bless thee; for unto thee, and unto thy seed, ᴿI will give all these countries, and I will perform ᴿthe oath which I sware unto Abraham thy father;

4 And ᴿI will make thy seed to multiply as the stars of heaven, and will give unto thy

CHAP. 25
BC 1800
23 2 Sam. 8:14
23 ch. 27:29
Mal. 1:3
Rom. 9:12
25 ch. 27:11, 16, 23
26 Hos. 12:3
26 ch. 27:36
27 ch. 27:3, 5
27 Job 1:1, 8
27 Heb. 11:9
28 Heb.
venison was *in his mouth*
28 ch. 27:19, 25, 31
28 ch. 27:6
30 Heb. *with that red,* with that *red* pottage
30 i.e. *Red*
32 Heb. *going to die*
33 Heb. 12:16
34 Eccl. 8:15 Is. 22:13
1 Cor. 15:32

CHAP. 26
BC 1804
1 ch. 12:10
1 ch. 20:2
2 ch. 12:1
3 ch. 20:1
Ps. 39:12
Heb. 11:9
3 ch. 28:15
3 ch. 12:2
3 ch. 13:15
3 ch. 22:16
Ps. 105:9
4 ch. 15:5 & 22:17

ch. 12:3 & 22:18   4
ch. 22:16, 18   5
ch. 12:13 & 20:2, 13   7
Prov. 29:25   7
ch. 24:16   7
ch. 20:9   10
Ps. 105:15   11
Heb. *found*   12
Mat. 13:8   12
Mark 4:8
ver. 3   12
Job 42:12
ch. 24:35   13
Prov. 10:22
Heb. *went going*   13
Or, *husbandry*   14
ch. 37:11   14
Eccl. 4:4
ch. 21:30   15
Ex. 1:9   16
ch. 21:31   18
Heb. *living*   19
ch. 21:25   20
i.e. *Contention*   20

seed all these countries; ᴿand in thy seed shall all the nations of the earth be blessed;   ★

5 ᴿBecause that Abraham obeyed my voice, and kept my charge, my commandments, my statutes, and my laws.

6 And Isaac dwelt in Gē'-rär:

7 And the men of the place asked *him* of his wife; and ᴿhe said, She *is* my sister: for ᴿhe feared to say, *She is* my wife; lest, *said he,* the men of the place should kill me for Rebekah; because she ᴿwas fair to look upon.

8 And it came to pass, when he had been there a long time, that Ă-bĭm'-ĕ-lĕch king of the Philistines looked out at a window, and saw, and, behold, Isaac *was* sporting with Rebekah his wife.

9 And Ă-bĭm'-ĕ-lĕch called Isaac, and said, Behold, of a surety she *is* thy wife: and how saidst thou, She *is* my sister? And Isaac said unto him, Because I said, Lest I die for her.

10 And Ă-bĭm'-ĕ-lĕch said, What *is* this thou hast done unto us? one of the people might lightly have lien with thy wife, and ᴿthou shouldest have brought guiltiness upon us.

11 And Ă-bĭm'-ĕ-lĕch charged all *his* people, saying, He that ᴿtoucheth this man or his wife shall surely be put to death.

12 Then Isaac sowed in that land, and ᴺreceived in the same year ᴿan hundredfold: and the Lᴏʀᴅ ᴿblessed him.

13 And the man ᴿwaxed great, and ᴺwent forward, and grew until he became very great:

14 For he had possession of flocks, and possession of herds, and great store of ᴺservants: and the Philistines ᴿenvied him.

15 For all the wells ᴿwhich his father's servants had digged in the days of Abraham his father, the Philistines had stopped them, and filled them with earth.

16 And Ă-bĭm'-ĕ-lĕch said unto Isaac, Go from us; for ᴿthou art much mightier than we.

17 And Isaac departed thence, and pitched his tent in the valley of Gē'-rär, and dwelt there.

18 And Isaac digged again the wells of water, which they had digged in the days of Abraham his father; for the Philistines had stopped them after the death of Abraham: ᴿand he called their names after the names by which his father had called them.

19 And Isaac's servants digged in the valley, and found there a well of ᴺspringing water.

20 And the herdmen of Gē'-rär ᴿdid strive with Isaac's herdmen, saying, The water *is* ours: and he called the name of the well ᴺĒ'-sĕk; because they strove with him.

21 And they digged another well, and strove

for that also: and he called the name of it ᴺSĭt'-näh.

22 And he removed from thence, and digged another well; and for that they strove not: and he called the name of it ᴺRē'-hŏ-bōth; and he said, For now the LORD hath made room for us, and we shall ᴿbe fruitful in the land.

Isaac moves to Beer-sheba

23 And he went up from thence to Bēēr-shē'-bă.

24 And the LORD appeared unto him the same night, and said, ᴿI *am* the God of Abraham thy father: ᴿfear not, for ᴿI *am* with thee, and will bless thee, and multiply thy seed for my servant Abraham's sake.

25 And he ᴿbuilded an altar there, and ᴿcalled upon the name of the LORD, and pitched his tent there: and there Isaac's servants digged a well.

26 Then Ă-bĭm'-ĕ-lĕch went to him from Gē'-rär, and Ă-hŭz'-zăth one of his friends, ᴿand Phī'-chŏl the chief captain of his army.

27 And Isaac said unto them, Wherefore come ye to me, seeing ᴿye hate me, and have ᴿsent me away from you?

28 And they said, ᴺWe saw certainly that the LORD ᴿwas with thee: and we said, Let there be now an oath betwixt us, *even* betwixt us and thee, and let us make a covenant with thee;

29 ᴺThat thou wilt do us no hurt, as we have not touched thee, and as we have done unto thee nothing but good, and have sent thee away in peace: ᴿthou *art* now the blessed of the LORD.

30 ᴿAnd he made them a feast, and they did eat and drink.

31 And they rose up betimes in the morning, and ᴿsware one to another: and Isaac sent them away, and they departed from him in peace.

32 And it came to pass the same day, that Isaac's servants came, and told him concerning the well which they had digged, and said unto him, We have found water.

33 And he called it ᴺShē'-băh: ᴿtherefore the name of the city *is* ᴺBēer-shē'-bă unto this day.

Esau's Hittite wives

34 ᴿAnd Esau was forty years old when he took to wife Judith the daughter of Bēēr'-ī the Hittite, and Băsh'-ĕ-măth the daughter of Ē'-lŏn the Hittite:

35 Which ᴿwere ᴺa grief of mind unto Isaac and to Rebekah.

CHAPTER 27

Rebekah and Jacob deceive Isaac

AND it came to pass, that when Isaac was old, and ᴿhis eyes were dim, so that he could not see, he called Esau his eldest son, and said unto him, My son: and he said unto him, Behold, *here am* I.

2 And he said, Behold now, I am old, I ᴿknow not the day of my death:

3 ᴿNow therefore take, I pray thee, thy weapons, thy quiver and thy bow, and go out to the field, and ᴺtake me *some* venison;

4 And make me savoury meat, such as I love, and bring *it* to me, that I may eat; that my soul ᴿmay bless thee before I die.

5 And Rebekah heard when Isaac spake to Esau his son. And Esau went to the field to hunt *for* venison, *and* to bring *it*.

6 And Rebekah spake unto Jacob her son, saying, Behold, I heard thy father speak unto Esau thy brother, saying,

7 Bring me venison, and make me savoury meat, that I may eat, and bless thee before the LORD before my death.

8 Now therefore, my son, ᴿobey my voice according to that which I command thee.

9 Go now to the flock, and fetch me from thence two good kids of the goats; and I will make them ᴿsavoury meat for thy father, such as he loveth:

10 And thou shalt bring *it* to thy father, that he may eat, and that he ᴿmay bless thee before his death.

11 And Jacob said to Rebekah his mother, Behold, ᴿEsau my brother *is* a hairy man, and I *am* a smooth man:

12 My father peradventure will ᴿfeel me, and I shall seem to him as a deceiver; and I shall bring ᴿa curse upon me, and not a blessing.

13 And his mother said unto him, ᴿUpon me *be* thy curse, my son: only obey my voice, and go fetch me *them*.

14 And he went, and fetched, and brought *them* to his mother: and his mother ᴿmade savoury meat, such as his father loved.

15 And Rebekah took ᴿgoodlyᴺ raiment of her eldest son Esau, which *were* with her in the house, and put them upon Jacob her younger son:

16 And she put the skins of the kids of the goats upon his hands, and upon the smooth of his neck:

17 And she gave the savoury meat and the bread, which she had prepared, into the hand of her son Jacob.

Isaac blesses Jacob

18 And he came unto his father, and said, My father: and he said, Here *am* I; who *art* thou, my son?

19 And Jacob said unto his father, I *am* Esau thy firstborn; I have done according as thou badest me: arise, I pray thee, sit and eat of my venison, ᴿthat thy soul may bless me.

20 And Isaac said unto his son, How *is* it that thou hast found *it* so quickly, my son? And he said, Because the LORD thy God brought *it* ᴺto me.

21 And Isaac said unto Jacob, Come near, I pray thee, that I ᴿmay feel thee, my son, whether thou *be* my very son Esau or not.

22 And Jacob went near unto Isaac his father; and he felt him, and said, The voice *is* Jacob's voice, but the hands *are* the hands of Esau.

23 And he discerned him not, because ᴿhis hands were hairy, as his brother Esau's hands: so he blessed him.

24 And he said, *Art* thou my very son Esau? And he said, I *am.*

25 And he said, Bring *it* near to me, and I will eat of my son's venison, ᴿthat my soul may bless thee. And he brought *it* near to him, and he did eat: and he brought him wine, and he drank.

26 And his father Isaac said unto him, Come near now, and kiss me, my son.

27 And he came near, and kissed him: and he smelled the smell of his raiment, and blessed him, and said, See, ᴿthe smell of my son *is* as the smell of a field which the LORD hath blessed:

28 Therefore ᴿGod give thee of ᴿthe dew of heaven, and ᴿthe fatness of the earth, and ᴿplenty of corn and wine:

29 ᴿLet people serve thee, and nations bow down to thee: be lord over thy brethren, and ᴿlet thy mother's sons bow down to thee: ᴿcursed *be* every one that curseth thee, and blessed *be* he that blesseth thee.

Jacob's deception discovered

30 And it came to pass, as soon as Isaac had made an end of blessing Jacob, and Jacob was yet scarce gone out from the presence of Isaac his father, that Esau his brother came in from his hunting.

31 And he also had made savoury meat, and brought it unto his father, and said unto his father, Let my father arise, and ᴿeat of his son's venison, that thy soul may bless me.

32 And Isaac his father said unto him, Who

art thou? And he said, I *am* thy son, thy firstborn Esau.

33 And Isaac ᴺtrembled very exceedingly, and said, Who? where *is* he that hath ᴺtaken venison, and brought *it* me, and I have eaten of all before thou camest, and have blessed him? yea, ᴿ*and* he shall be blessed.

34 And when Esau heard the words of his father, ᴿhe cried with a great and exceeding bitter cry, and said unto his father, Bless me, *even* me also, O my father.

35 And he said, Thy brother came with subtilty, and hath taken away thy blessing.

36 And he said, ᴿIs not he rightly named ᴺJacob? for he hath supplanted me these two times: ᴿhe took away my birthright; and, behold, now he hath taken away my blessing. And he said, Hast thou not reserved a blessing for me?

37 And Isaac answered and said unto Esau, ᴿBehold, I have made him thy lord, and all his brethren have I given to him for servants; and ᴿwith corn and wine have I ᴺsustained him: and what shall I do now unto thee, my son?

38 And Esau said unto his father, Hast thou but one blessing, my father? bless me, *even* me also, O my father. And Esau lifted up his voice, ᴿand wept.

39 And Isaac his father answered and said unto him, Behold, ᴿthy dwelling shall be ᴺthe fatness of the earth, and of the dew of heaven from above;

40 And by thy sword shalt thou live, and ᴿshalt serve thy brother; and ᴿit shall come to pass when thou shalt have the dominion, that thou shalt break his yoke from off thy neck.

41 And Esau ᴿhated Jacob because of the blessing wherewith his father blessed him: and Esau said in his heart, ᴿThe days of mourning for my father are at hand; ᴿthen will I slay my brother Jacob.

42 And these words of Esau her elder son were told to Rebekah: and she sent and called Jacob her younger son, and said unto him, Behold, thy brother Esau, as touching thee, doth ᴿcomfort himself, *purposing* to kill thee.

Jacob sent to Laban

43 Now therefore, my son, obey my voice; and arise, flee thou to Laban my brother ᴿto Hâr′-ăn;

44 And tarry with him a few days, until thy brother's fury turn away;

45 Until thy brother's anger turn away from thee, and he forget *that* which thou hast done to him: then I will send, and fetch thee from

thence: why should I be deprived also of you both in one day?

46 And Rebekah said to Isaac, ᴿI am weary of my life because of the daughters of Heth: ᴿif Jacob take a wife of the daughters of Heth, such as these *which are* of the daughters of the land, what good shall my life do me?

CHAPTER 28

AND Isaac called Jacob, and ᴿblessed him, and charged him, and said unto him, ᴿThou shalt not take a wife of the daughters of Canaan.

2 ᴿArise, go to ᴿPā′-dăn-âr′-ăm, to the house of ᴿBĕ-thū′-ĕl thy mother's father; and take thee a wife from thence of the daughters of ᴿLaban thy mother's brother.

3 ᴿAnd God Almighty bless thee, and make thee fruitful, and multiply thee, that thou mayest be ᴺa multitude of people;

4 And give thee ᴿthe blessing of Abraham, to thee, and to thy seed with thee; that thou mayest inherit the land ᴿwhereinᴺ thou art a stranger, which God gave unto Abraham.   ★

5 And Isaac sent away Jacob: and he went to Pā′-dăn-âr′-ăm unto Laban, son of Bĕ-thū′-ĕl the Syrian, the brother of Rebekah, Jacob's and Esau's mother.

Marriage of Esau

6 When Esau saw that Isaac had blessed Jacob, and sent him away to Pā′-dăn-âr′-ăm, to take him a wife from thence; and that as he blessed him he gave him a charge, saying, Thou shalt not take a wife of the daughters of Canaan;

7 And that Jacob obeyed his father and his mother, and was gone to Pā′-dăn-âr′-ăm;

8 And Esau seeing ᴿthat the daughters of Canaan ᴺpleased not Isaac his father;

9 Then went Esau unto ĭsh′-mā-ĕl, and took unto the wives which he had ᴿMā′-hă-lăth the daughter of ĭsh′-mā-ĕl Abraham's son, ᴿthe sister of Nĕ-bā′-jŏth, to be his wife.

Jacob's dream at Bethel

10 And Jacob ᴿwent out from Bēēr-shē′-bă, and went toward ᴿHâr′-ăn.

11 And he lighted upon a certain place, and tarried there all night, because the sun was set; and he took of the stones of that place, and put *them for* his pillows, and lay down in that place to sleep.

12 And he ᴿdreamed, and behold a ladder set up on the earth, and the top of it reached to heaven: and behold ᴿthe angels of God ascending and descending on it.

13 ᴿAnd, behold, the LORD stood above it, and said, ᴿI *am* the LORD God of Abraham

CHAP. **27**	
BC 1760	
46 ch. 26:35	
& 28:8	
46 ch. 24:3	

CHAP. **28**	
BC 1760	
1 ch. 27:33	
1 ch. 24:3	
2 Hos. 12:12	
2 ch. 25:20	
2 ch. 22:23	
2 ch. 24:29	
3 ch. 17:1, 6	
3 Heb. *an assembly of people*	
4 ch. 12:2	
4 ch. 17:8	
4 Heb. *of thy sojournings*	
8 ch. 24:3 & 26:35	
8 Heb. *were evil in the eyes, etc.*	
9 ch. 36:3, she is called *Bashemath*	
9 ch. 25:13	
10 Hos. 12:12	
10 Called, Acts 7:2, *Charran*	
12 ch. 41:1	
12 John 1:51 Heb. 1:14	
13 ch. 35:1 & 48:3	
13 ch. 26:24	

ch. 13:15 & 35:12	**13**
ch. 13:16	**14**
Heb. *break forth*	**14**
ch. 13:14 Deut. 12:20	**14**
ch. 12:3 & 18:18 & 22:18 & 26:4	**14**
See ver. 20, 21	**15**
ch. 48:16	**15**
ch. 35:6	**15**
Deut. 31:6, 8 Josh. 1:5 1 Ki. 8:57 Heb. 13:5	**15**
Num. 23:19	**15**
Ex. 3:5	**16**
Josh. 5:15 ch. 31:13, 45	**18**
Lev. 8:10-12	**18**
Judg. 1:23, 26 Hos. 4:15	**19**
i.e. *The house of God*	**19**
ch. 31:13 Judg. 11:30 2 Sam. 15:8	**20**
ver. 15	**20**
1 Tim. 6:8	**20**
Judg. 11:31 2 Sam. 19:24, 30 Deut. 26:17	**21**
2 Sam. 15:8 ch. 35:7, 14	**22**
Lev. 27:30	**22**

CHAP. **29**	
BC 1760	
Heb. *lift up his feet*	**1**
Num. 23:7 Hos. 12:12	**1**
Heb. *children*	**1**

thy father, and the God of Isaac: ᴿthe land whereon thou liest, to thee will I give it, and to thy seed;

14 And ᴿthy seed shall be as the dust of the earth, and thou shalt ᴺspread abroad ᴿto the west, and to the east, and to the north, and to the south: and in thee and ᴿin thy seed shall all the families of the earth be blessed.   ★

15 And, behold, ᴿI *am* with thee, and will ᴿkeep thee in all *places* whither thou goest, and will ᴿbring thee again into this land; for ᴿI will not leave thee, ᴿuntil I have done *that* which I have spoken to thee of.

16 And Jacob awaked out of his sleep, and he said, Surely the LORD is in ᴿthis place; and I knew *it* not.

17 And he was afraid, and said, How dreadful *is* this place! this *is* none other but the house of God, and this *is* the gate of heaven.

18 And Jacob rose up early in the morning, and took the stone that he had put *for* his pillows, and ᴿset it up *for* a pillar, ᴿand poured oil upon the top of it.

19 And he called the name of ᴿthat place ᴺBeth-el: but the name of that city *was called* Luz at the first.

20 ᴿAnd Jacob vowed a vow, saying, If ᴿGod will be with me, and will keep me in this way that I go, and will give me ᴿbread to eat, and raiment to put on,

21 So that ᴿI come again to my father's house in peace; ᴿthen shall the LORD be my God:

22 And this stone, which I have set *for* a pillar, ᴿshall be God's house: ᴿand of all that thou shalt give me I will surely give the tenth unto thee.

CHAPTER 29

Jacob meets Rachel

THEN Jacob ᴺwent on his journey, ᴿand came into the land of the ᴺpeople of the east.

2 And he looked, and behold a well in the field, and, lo, there *were* three flocks of sheep lying by it; for out of that well they watered the flocks: and a great stone *was* upon the well's mouth.

3 And thither were all the flocks gathered: and they rolled the stone from the well's mouth, and watered the sheep, and put the stone again upon the well's mouth in his place.

4 And Jacob said unto them, My brethren, whence *be* ye? And they said, Of Hâr′-ăn *are* we.

5 And he said unto them, Know ye Laban the son of Nahor? And they said, We know *him*.

6 And he said unto them, [R]Is[N] he well? And they said, *He is* well: and, behold, Rachel his daughter cometh with the sheep.

7 And he said, Lo, [N]*it is* yet high day, neither *is it* time that the cattle should be gathered together: water ye the sheep, and go *and* feed *them*.

8 And they said, We cannot, until all the flocks be gathered together, and *till* they roll the stone from the well's mouth; then we water the sheep.

9 And while he yet spake with them, [R]Rachel came with her father's sheep: for she kept them.

10 And it came to pass, when Jacob saw Rachel the daughter of Laban his mother's brother, and the sheep of Laban his mother's brother, that Jacob went near, and [R]rolled the stone from the well's mouth, and watered the flock of Laban his mother's brother.

11 And Jacob [R]kissed Rachel, and lifted up his voice, and wept.

12 And Jacob told Rachel that he *was* [R]her father's brother, and that he *was* Rebekah's son: [R]and she ran and told her father.

13 And it came to pass, when Laban heard the [N]tidings of Jacob his sister's son, that [R]he ran to meet him, and embraced him, and kissed him, and brought him to his house. And he told Laban all these things.

14 And Laban said to him, [R]Surely thou *art* my bone and my flesh. And he abode with him [N]the space of a month.

Jacob marries Laban's daughters

15 And Laban said unto Jacob, Because thou *art* my brother, shouldest thou therefore serve me for nought? tell me, what *shall* thy wages *be?*

16 And Laban had two daughters: the name of the elder *was* Leah, and the name of the younger *was* Rachel.

17 Leah *was* tender eyed; but Rachel was beautiful and well favoured.

18 And Jacob loved Rachel; and said, [R]I will serve thee seven years for Rachel thy younger daughter.

19 And Laban said, *It is* better that I give her to thee, than that I should give her to another man: abide with me.

20 And Jacob [R]served seven years for Rachel; and they seemed unto him *but* a few days, for the love he had to her.

21 And Jacob said unto Laban, Give *me* my wife, for my days are fulfilled, that I may [R]go in unto her.

22 And Laban gathered together all the men of the place, and [R]made a feast.

23 And it came to pass in the evening, that

he took Leah his daughter, and brought her to him; and he went in unto her.

24 And Laban gave unto his daughter Leah Zilpah his maid *for* an handmaid.

25 And it came to pass, that in the morning, behold, it *was* Leah: and he said to Laban, What *is* this thou hast done unto me? did not I serve with thee for Rachel? wherefore then hast thou beguiled me?

26 And Laban said, It must not be so done in our [N]country, to give the younger before the firstborn.

27 [R]Fulfil her week, and we will give thee this also for the service which thou shalt serve with me yet seven other years.

28 And Jacob did so, and fulfilled her week: and he gave him Rachel his daughter to wife also.

29 And Laban gave to Rachel his daughter Bĭl'-häh his handmaid to be her maid.

30 And he went in also unto Rachel, and he [R]loved also Rachel more than Leah, and served with him [R]yet seven other years.

Sons of Jacob

31 And when the LORD [R]saw that Leah *was* hated, he [R]opened her womb: but Rachel *was* barren.

32 And Leah conceived, and bare a son, and she called his name [N]Reuben: for she said, Surely the LORD hath [R]looked upon my affliction; now therefore my husband will love me.

33 And she conceived again, and bare a son; and said, Because the LORD hath heard that I *was* hated, he hath therefore given me this *son* also: and she called his name [N]Simeon.

34 And she conceived again, and bare a son; and said, Now this time will my husband be joined unto me, because I have born him three sons: therefore was his name called [N]Levi.

35 And she conceived again, and bare a son: and she said, Now will I praise the LORD: therefore she called his name [R]Judah;[N] and [N]left bearing.

CHAPTER 30

Rivalry between Rachel and Leah

AND when Rachel saw that [R]she bare Jacob no children, Rachel [R]envied her sister; and said unto Jacob, Give me children, [R]or else I die.

2 And Jacob's anger was kindled against Rachel: and he said, [R]*Am* I in God's stead, who hath withheld from thee the fruit of the womb?

3 And she said, Behold [R]my maid Bĭl'-häh, go in unto her; [R]and she shall bear upon my

---

Center reference column:

CHAP. **29**
BC 1760
6 ch. 43:27
6 Heb. *Is there peace to him?*
7 Heb. *yet the day is great*
9 Ex. 2:16
10 Ex. 2:17
11 ch. 33:4 & 45:14, 15
12 ch. 13:8 & 14:14, 16
12 ch. 24:28
13 Heb. *hearing*
13 ch. 24:29
14 ch. 2:23
Judg. 9:2
2 Sam. 5:1 & 19:12, 13
14 Heb. *a month of days*
18 ch. 31:41
2 Sam. 3:14
20 ch. 30:26
Hos. 12:12
21 Judg. 15:1
22 Judg. 14:10
John 2:1, 2

Heb. *place*　　26
Judg. 14:12　　27
Deut. 21:15　　30
ch. 30:26　　30
& 31:41
Hos. 12:12
Ps. 127:3　　31
ch. 30:1　　31
i.e. *See a son*　　32
Ex. 4:31　　32
Deut. 26:7
Ps. 25:18
i.e. *Hearing*　　33
i.e. *Joined*　　34
Mat. 1:2　　35
i.e. *Praise*　　35
Heb. *stood from bearing*　　35

CHAP. **30**
BC 1745
ch. 29:31　　1
ch. 37:11　　1
Job 5:2　　1
ch. 16:2　　2
1 Sam. 1:5
ch. 16:2　　3
ch. 50:23　　3
Job 3:12

knees, [R]that I may also [N]have children by her.

4 And she gave him Bĭl'-häh her handmaid [R]to wife: and Jacob went in unto her.

5 And Bĭl'-häh conceived, and bare Jacob a son.

6 And Rachel said, God hath [R]judged me, and hath also heard my voice, and hath given me a son: therefore called she his name [N]Dan.

7 And Bĭl'-häh Rachel's maid conceived again, and bare Jacob a second son.

8 And Rachel said, With [N]great wrestlings have I wrestled with my sister, and I have prevailed: and she called his name [R]Năph'-tă-lī.[N]

9 When Leah saw that she had left bearing, she took Zilpah her maid, and [R]gave her Jacob to wife.

10 And Zilpah Leah's maid bare Jacob a son.

11 And Leah said, A troop cometh: and she called his name [N]Gad.

12 And Zilpah Leah's maid bare Jacob a second son.

13 And Leah said, [N]Happy am I, for the daughters [R]will call me blessed: and she called his name [N]Asher.

14 And Reuben went in the days of wheat harvest, and found mandrakes in the field, and brought them unto his mother Leah. Then Rachel said to Leah, [R]Give me, I pray thee, of thy son's mandrakes.

15 And she said unto her, [R]Is it a small matter that thou hast taken my husband? and wouldest thou take away my son's mandrakes also? And Rachel said, Therefore he shall lie with thee to night for thy son's mandrakes.

16 And Jacob came out of the field in the evening, and Leah went out to meet him, and said, Thou must come in unto me; for surely I have hired thee with my son's mandrakes. And he lay with her that night.

17 And God hearkened unto Leah, and she conceived, and bare Jacob the fifth son.

18 And Leah said, God hath given me my hire, because I have given my maiden to my husband: and she called his name [N]Ĭs'-să-<u>ch</u>är.

19 And Leah conceived again, and bare Jacob the sixth son.

20 And Leah said, God hath endued me *with* a good dowry; now will my husband dwell with me, because I have born him six sons: and she called his name [R]Zĕ-bū'-lŭn.[N]

21 And afterwards she bare a daughter, and called her name [N]Dinah.

22 And God [R]remembered Rachel, and God hearkened to her, and [R]opened her womb.

23 And she conceived, and bare a son; and said, God hath taken away [R]my reproach:

24 And she called his name [N]Joseph; and said, [R]The LORD shall add to me another son.

Jacob's agreement with Laban

25 And it came to pass, when Rachel had born Joseph, that Jacob said unto Laban, [R]Send me away, that I may go unto [R]mine own place, and to my country.

26 Give *me* my wives and my children, [R]for whom I have served thee, and let me go: for thou knowest my service which I have done thee.

27 And Laban said unto him, I pray thee, if I have found favour in thine eyes, *tarry: for* [R]I have learned by experience that the LORD hath blessed me [R]for thy sake.

28 And he said, [R]Appoint me thy wages, and I will give *it*.

29 And he said unto him, [R]Thou knowest how I have served thee, and how thy cattle was with me.

30 For *it was* little which thou hadst before I *came*, and it is *now* [N]increased unto a multitude; and the LORD hath blessed thee [N]since my coming: and now when shall I [R]provide for mine own house also?

31 And he said, What shall I give thee? And Jacob said, Thou shalt not give me any thing: if thou wilt do this thing for me, I will again feed *and* keep thy flock:

32 I will pass through all thy flock to day, removing from thence all the speckled and spotted cattle, and all the brown cattle among the sheep, and the spotted and speckled among the goats: and [R]of such shall be my hire.

33 So shall my [R]righteousness answer for me [N]in time to come, when it shall come for my hire before thy face: every one that *is* not speckled and spotted among the goats, and brown among the sheep, that shall be counted stolen with me.

34 And Laban said, Behold, I would it might be according to thy word.

35 And he removed that day the he goats that were ringstraked and spotted, and all the she goats that were speckled and spotted, *and* every one that had *some* white in it, and all the brown among the sheep, and gave *them* into the hand of his sons.

36 And he set three days' journey betwixt himself and Jacob: and Jacob fed the rest of Laban's flocks.

Jacob outwits Laban

37 And [R]Jacob took him rods of green poplar, and of the hazel and chesnut tree; and pilled white strakes in them, and made the white appear which *was* in the rods.

38 And he set the rods which he had pilled

before the flocks in the gutters in the watering troughs when the flocks came to drink, that they should conceive when they came to drink.

39 And the flocks conceived before the rods, and brought forth cattle ringstraked, speckled, and spotted.

40 And Jacob did separate the lambs, and set the faces of the flocks toward the ringstraked, and all the brown in the flock of Laban; and he put his own flocks by themselves, and put them not unto Laban's cattle.

41 And it came to pass, whensoever the stronger cattle did conceive, that Jacob laid the rods before the eyes of the cattle in the gutters, that they might conceive among the rods.

42 But when the cattle were feeble, he put *them* not in: so the feebler were Laban's, and the stronger Jacob's.

43 And the man ᴿincreased exceedingly, and ᴿhad much cattle, and maidservants, and menservants, and camels, and asses.

CHAPTER 31

Jacob flees from Laban

AND he heard the words of Laban's sons, saying, Jacob hath taken away all that *was* our father's; and of *that* which *was* our father's hath he gotten all this ᴿglory.

2 And Jacob beheld ᴿthe countenance of Laban, and, behold, it *was* not ᴿtoward him ᴺas before.

3 And the Lᴏʀᴅ said unto Jacob, ᴿReturn unto the land of thy fathers, and to thy kindred; and I will be with thee.

4 And Jacob sent and called Rachel and Leah to the field unto his flock,

5 And said unto them, ᴿI see your father's countenance, that it *is* not toward me as before; but the God of my father ᴿhath been with me.

6 And ᴿye know that with all my power I have served your father.

7 And your father hath deceived me, and ᴿchanged my wages ᴿten times; but God ᴿsuffered him not to hurt me.

8 If he said thus, ᴿThe speckled shall be thy wages; then all the cattle bare speckled: and if he said thus, The ringstraked shall be thy hire; then bare all the cattle ringstraked.

9 Thus God hath ᴿtaken away the cattle of your father, and given *them* to me.

10 And it came to pass at the time that the cattle conceived, that I lifted up mine eyes, and saw in a dream, and, behold, the ᴺrams which leaped upon the cattle *were* ringstraked, speckled, and grisled.

11 And ᴿthe angel of God spake unto me in a dream, *saying*, Jacob: And I said, Here *am* I.

12 And he said, Lift up now thine eyes, and see, all the rams which leap upon the cattle *are* ringstraked, speckled, and grisled: for ᴿI have seen all that Laban doeth unto thee.

13 I *am* the God of Beth-el, ᴿwhere thou anointedst the pillar, *and* where thou vowedst a vow unto me: now ᴿarise, get thee out from this land, and return unto the land of thy kindred.

14 And Rachel and Leah answered and said unto him, ᴿ*Is there* yet any portion or inheritance for us in our father's house?

15 Are we not counted of him strangers? for ᴿhe hath sold us, and hath quite devoured also our money.

16 For all the riches which God hath taken from our father, that *is* ours, and our children's: now then, whatsoever God hath said unto thee, do.

17 Then Jacob rose up, and set his sons and his wives upon camels;

18 And he carried away all his cattle, and all his goods which he had gotten, the cattle of his getting, which he had gotten in Pā'-dăn-âr'-ăm, for to go to Isaac his father in the land of Canaan.

19 And Laban went to shear his sheep: and Rachel had stolen the ᴿimagesᴺ that *were* her father's.

20 And Jacob stole away ᴺunawares to Laban the Syrian, in that he told him not that he fled.

21 So he fled with all that he had; and he rose up, and passed over the river, and ᴿset his face *toward* the mount Gilead.

Laban pursues Jacob

22 And it was told Laban on the third day that Jacob was fled.

23 And he took ᴿhis brethren with him, and pursued after him seven days' journey; and they overtook him in the mount Gilead.

24 And God ᴿcame to Laban the Syrian in a dream by night, and said unto him, Take heed that thou ᴿspeak not to Jacob ᴺeither good or bad.

25 Then Laban overtook Jacob. Now Jacob had pitched his tent in the mount: and Laban with his brethren pitched in the mount of Gilead.

26 And Laban said to Jacob, What hast thou done, that thou hast stolen away unawares to me, and ᴿcarried away my daughters, as captives *taken* with the sword?

27 Wherefore didst thou flee away secretly, and ᴺsteal away from me; and didst not tell me, that I might have sent thee away with

mirth, and with songs, with tabret, and with harp?

28 And hast not suffered me [R]to kiss my sons and my daughters? [R]thou hast now done foolishly in *so* doing.

29 It is in the power of my hand to do you hurt: but the [R]God of your father spake unto me [R]yesternight, saying, Take thou heed that thou speak not to Jacob either good or bad.

30 And now, *though* thou wouldest needs be gone, because thou sore longedst after thy father's house, *yet* wherefore hast thou [R]stolen my gods?

31 And Jacob answered and said to Laban, Because I was afraid: for I said, Peradventure thou wouldest take by force thy daughters from me.

32 With whomsoever thou findest thy gods, [R]let him not live: before our brethren discern thou what *is* thine with me, and take *it* to thee. For Jacob knew not that Rachel had stolen them.

Concealing the household gods

33 And Laban went into Jacob's tent, and into Leah's tent, and into the two maidservants' tents; but he found *them* not. Then went he out of Leah's tent, and entered into Rachel's tent.

34 Now Rachel had taken the images, and put them in the camel's furniture, and sat upon them. And Laban [N]searched all the tent, but found *them* not.

35 And she said to her father, Let it not displease my lord that I cannot [R]rise up before thee; for the custom of women *is* upon me. And he searched, but found not the images.

36 And Jacob was wroth, and chode with Laban: and Jacob answered and said to Laban, What *is* my trespass? what *is* my sin, that thou hast so hotly pursued after me?

37 Whereas thou hast [N]searched all my stuff, what hast thou found of all thy household stuff? set *it* here before my brethren and thy brethren, that they may judge betwixt us both.

38 This twenty years *have* I *been* with thee; thy ewes and thy she goats have not cast their young, and the rams of thy flock have I not eaten.

39 [R]That which was torn *of beasts* I brought not unto thee; I bare the loss of it; of [R]my hand didst thou require it, *whether* stolen by day, or stolen by night.

40 *Thus* I was; in the day the drought consumed me, and the frost by night; and my sleep departed from mine eyes.

41 Thus have I been twenty years in thy

CHAP. **31**

BC 1739

28 ver. 55
Ruth 1:9, 14
1 Ki. 19:20
Acts 20:37
28 1 Sam. 13:13
29 ver. 53
ch. 28:13
29 ver. 24
29 ver. 24
30 ver. 19
Judg. 18:24
32 See ch. 44:9
34 Heb. *felt*
35 Ex. 20:12
Lev. 19:32
37 Heb. *felt*
39 Ex. 22:10, etc.
39 Ex. 22:12

ch. 29:27, 28   41
ver. 7   41
Ps. 124:1, 2   42
ver. 53   42
Is. 8:13
ch. 29:32   42
Ex. 3:7
1 Chr. 12:17   42
ch. 26:28   44
Josh. 24:27   44
ch. 28:18   45
Chald. *The heap of witness*   47
Heb. *The heap of witness*   47
Josh. 24:27   48
Judg. 11:29   49
1 Sam. 7:5
i.e. *A beacon, or, watchtower*   49
ch. 16:5   53
ch. 21:23   53
ver. 42   53
Or, *killed beasts*   54
ch. 28:1   55
ch. 18:33 & 30:25   55
Num. 24:25

house; I [R]served thee fourteen years for thy two daughters, and six years for thy cattle: and [R]thou hast changed my wages ten times.

42 [R]Except the God of my father, the God of Abraham, and [R]the fear of Isaac, had been with me, surely thou hadst sent me away now empty. [R]God hath seen mine affliction and the labour of my hands, and [R]rebuked *thee* yesternight.

Covenant at Mizpah

43 And Laban answered and said unto Jacob, *These* daughters *are* my daughters, and *these* children *are* my children, and *these* cattle *are* my cattle, and all that thou seest *is* mine: and what can I do this day unto these my daughters, or unto their children which they have born?

44 Now therefore come thou, [R]let us make a covenant, I and thou; [R]and let it be for a witness between me and thee.

45 And Jacob [R]took a stone, and set it up *for* a pillar.

46 And Jacob said unto his brethren, Gather stones; and they took stones, and made an heap: and they did eat there upon the heap.

47 And Laban called it [N]Jē'-gär-sā-hă-dū'-thă: but Jacob called it [N]Gā'-lĕĕd.

48 And Laban said, [R]This heap *is* a witness between me and thee this day. Therefore was the name of it called Gā'-lĕĕd;

49 And [R]Mizpah;[N] for he said, The LORD watch between me and thee, when we are absent one from another.

50 If thou shalt afflict my daughters, or if thou shalt take *other* wives beside my daughters, no man *is* with us; see, God *is* witness betwixt me and thee.

51 And Laban said to Jacob, Behold this heap, and behold *this* pillar, which I have cast betwixt me and thee;

52 This heap *be* witness, and *this* pillar *be* witness, that I will not pass over this heap to thee, and that thou shalt not pass over this heap and this pillar unto me, for harm.

53 The God of Abraham, and the God of Nahor, the God of their father, [R]judge betwixt us. And Jacob [R]sware by [R]the fear of his father Isaac.

54 Then Jacob [N]offered sacrifice upon the mount, and called his brethren to eat bread: and they did eat bread, and tarried all night in the mount.

55 And early in the morning Laban rose up, and kissed his sons and his daughters, and [R]blessed them: and Laban departed, and [R]returned unto his place.

CHAPTER 32

Jacob sends messengers to Esau

AND Jacob went on his way, and ᴿthe angels of God met him.

2 And when Jacob saw them, he said, This *is* God's ᴿhost: and he called the name of that place ᴺMā-hă-nā′-ĭm.

3 And Jacob sent messengers before him to Esau his brother ᴿunto the land of Sē′-ĭr, ᴿthe ᴺcountry of Ē′-dǫm.

4 And he commanded them, saying, ᴿThus shall ye speak unto my lord Esau; Thy servant Jacob saith thus, I have sojourned with Laban, and stayed there until now:

5 And ᴿI have oxen, and asses, flocks, and menservants, and womenservants: and I have sent to tell my lord, that ᴿI may find grace in thy sight.

6 And the messengers returned to Jacob, saying, We came to thy brother Esau, and also ᴿhe cometh to meet thee, and four hundred men with him.

7 Then Jacob was greatly afraid and ᴿdistressed: and he divided the people that *was* with him, and the flocks, and herds, and the camels, into two bands;

8 And said, If Esau come to the one company, and smite it, then the other company which is left shall escape.

9 ᴿAnd Jacob said, ᴿO God of my father Abraham, and God of my father Isaac, the Lᴏʀᴅ ᴿwhich saidst unto me, Return unto thy country, and to thy kindred, and I will deal well with thee:

10 ᴺI am not worthy of the least of all the ᴿmercies, and of all the truth, which thou hast shewed unto thy servant; for with ᴿmy staff I passed over this Jordan; and now I am become two bands.

11 ᴿDeliver me, I pray thee, from the hand of my brother, from the hand of Esau: for I fear him, lest he will come and smite me, *and* ᴿthe mother ᴺwith the children.

12 And ᴿthou saidst, I will surely do thee good, and make thy seed as the sand of the sea, which cannot be numbered for multitude.

Jacob appeases Esau

13 And he lodged there that same night; and took of that which came to his hand ᴿa present for Esau his brother;

14 Two hundred she goats, and twenty he goats, two hundred ewes, and twenty rams,

15 Thirty milch camels with their colts, forty kine, and ten bulls, twenty she asses, and ten foals.

CHAP. **32**
BC 1739
1 Ps. 91:11
Heb. 1:14
2 Josh. 5:14
Ps. 103:21
& 148:2
Luke 2:13
2 i.e. *Two hosts,* or, *camps*
3 ch. 33:14, 16
3 ch. 36:6-8
Deut. 2:5
Josh. 24:4
3 Heb. *field*
4 Prov. 15:1
5 ch. 30:43
5 ch. 33:8, 15
6 ch. 33:1·
7 ch. 35:3
9 Ps. 50:15
9 ch. 28:13
9 ch. 31:3, 13
10 Heb. *I am less than all, etc.*
10 ch. 24:27
10 Job 8:7
11 Ps. 59:1, 2
11 Hos. 10:14
11 Heb. *upon*
12 ch. 28:13-15
13 ch. 43:11
Prov. 18:16

Prov. 21:14	**20**
Heb. *my face*	**20**
Deut. 3:16	**22**
Heb. *caused to pass*	**23**
Hos. 12:3, 4	**24**
Heb. *ascending of the morning*	**24**
See Mat. 26:41	
2 Cor. 12:7	**25**
See Luke 24:28	**26**
Hos. 12:4	**26**
ch. 35:10	**28**
2 Ki. 17:34	
i.e. *A prince of God*	**28**
Hos. 12:3, 4	**28**
ch. 25:31	**28**
& 27:33	
Judg. 13:18	**29**
i.e. *The face of God*	**30**
ch. 16:13	**30**
Ex. 24:11	
Deut. 5:24	
Judg. 6:22	
Is. 6:5	

16 And he delivered *them* into the hand of his servants, every drove by themselves; and said unto his servants, Pass over before me, and put a space betwixt drove and drove.

17 And he commanded the foremost, saying, When Esau my brother meeteth thee, and asketh thee, saying, Whose *art* thou? and whither goest thou? and whose *are* these before thee?

18 Then thou shalt say, *They be* thy servant Jacob's; it *is* a present sent unto my lord Esau: and, behold, also he *is* behind us.

19 And so commanded he the second, and the third, and all that followed the droves, saying, On this manner shall ye speak unto Esau, when ye find him.

20 And say ye moreover, Behold, thy servant Jacob *is* behind us. For he said, I will ᴿappease him with the present that goeth before me, and afterward I will see his face; peradventure he will accept ᴺof me.

21 So went the present over before him: and himself lodged that night in the company.

Jacob's name changed

22 And he rose up that night, and took his two wives, and his two womenservants, and his eleven sons, ᴿand passed over the ford Jăb′-bǫk.

23 And he took them, and ᴺsent them over the brook, and sent over that he had.

24 And Jacob was left alone; and there ᴿwrestled a man with him until the ᴺbreaking of the day.

25 And when he saw that he prevailed not against him, he touched the hollow of his thigh; and ᴿthe hollow of Jacob's thigh was out of joint, as he wrestled with him.

26 And ᴿhe said, Let me go, for the day breaketh. And he said, ᴿI will not let thee go, except thou bless me.

27 And he said unto him, What *is* thy name? And he said, Jacob.

28 And he said, ᴿThy name shall be called no more Jacob, but ᴺIsrael: for as a prince hast thou ᴿpower with God and ᴿwith men, and hast prevailed.

29 And Jacob asked *him,* and said, Tell *me,* I pray thee, thy name. And he said, ᴿWherefore *is* it *that* thou dost ask after my name? And he blessed him there.

30 And Jacob called the name of the place ᴺPĕn′-ĭ-ĕl: for ᴿI have seen God face to face, and my life is preserved.

31 And as he passed over Pĕn-ū′-ĕl the sun rose upon him, and he halted upon his thigh.

32 Therefore the children of Israel eat not *of* the sinew which shrank, which *is* upon the

hollow of the thigh, unto this day: because he touched the hollow of Jacob's thigh in the sinew that shrank.

CHAPTER 33

Jacob and Esau meet

AND Jacob lifted up his eyes, and looked, and, behold, ᴿEsau came, and with him four hundred men. And he divided the children unto Leah, and unto Rachel, and unto the two handmaids.

2 And he put the handmaids and their children foremost, and Leah and her children after, and Rachel and Joseph hindermost.

3 And he passed over before them, and ᴿbowed himself to the ground seven times, until he came near to his brother.

4 ᴿAnd Esau ran to meet him, and embraced him, ᴿand fell on his neck, and kissed him: and they wept.

5 And he lifted up his eyes, and saw the women and the children; and said, Who *are* those ᴺwith thee? And he said, The children ᴿwhich God hath graciously given thy servant.

6 Then the handmaidens came near, they and their children, and they bowed themselves.

7 And Leah also with her children came near, and bowed themselves: and after came Joseph near and Rachel, and they bowed themselves.

8 And he said, ᴺWhat *meanest* thou by ᴿall this drove which I met? And he said, *These are* ᴿto find grace in the sight of my lord.

9 And Esau said, I have enough, my brother; ᴺkeep that thou hast unto thyself.

10 And Jacob said, Nay, I pray thee, if now I have found grace in thy sight, then receive my present at my hand: for therefore I ᴿhave seen thy face, as though I had seen the face of God, and thou wast pleased with me.

11 Take, I pray thee, ᴿmy blessing that is brought to thee; because God hath dealt graciously with me, and because I have ᴺenough. ᴿAnd he urged him, and he took *it*.

12 And he said, Let us take our journey, and let us go, and I will go before thee.

13 And he said unto him, My lord knoweth that the children *are* tender, and the flocks and herds with young *are* with me: and if men should overdrive them one day, all the flock will die.

14 Let my lord, I pray thee, pass over before his servant: and I will lead on softly, ᴺaccording as the cattle that goeth before me and the children be able to endure, until I come unto my lord ᴿunto Sē'-ĭr.

15 And Esau said, Let me now ᴺleave with thee *some* of the folk that *are* with me. And he said, ᴺWhat needeth it? ᴿlet me find grace in the sight of my lord.

16 So Esau returned that day on his way unto Sē'-ĭr.

Jacob goes to Shechem

17 And Jacob journeyed to ᴿSŭc'-cōth, and built him an house, and made booths for his cattle: therefore the name of the place is called ᴺSŭc'-cōth.

18 And Jacob came to ᴿShā'-lĕm, a city of ᴿShē'-chĕm,ᴺ which *is* in the land of Canaan, when he came from Pā'-dăn-âr'-ăm; and pitched his tent before the city.

19 And ᴿhe bought a parcel of a field, where he had spread his tent, at the hand of the children of ᴺHā'-môr, Shē'-chĕm's father, for an hundred ᴺpieces of money.

20 And he erected there an altar, and ᴿcalled it ᴺĔl-ĕl'-ō-hē-Ĭś'-rā-ĕl.

CHAPTER 34

Dinah defiled

AND ᴿDinah the daughter of Leah, which she bare unto Jacob, ᴿwent out to see the daughters of the land.

2 And when Shē'-chĕm the son of Hā'-môr the Hī'-vīte, prince of the country, ᴿsaw her, he ᴿtook her, and lay with her, and ᴺdefiled her.

3 And his soul clave unto Dinah the daughter of Jacob, and he loved the damsel, and spake ᴺkindly unto the damsel.

4 And Shē'-chĕm ᴿspake unto his father Hā'-môr, saying, Get me this damsel to wife.

5 And Jacob heard that he had defiled Dinah his daughter: now his sons were with his cattle in the field: and Jacob ᴿheld his peace until they were come.

6 And Hā'-môr the father of Shē'-chĕm went out unto Jacob to commune with him.

7 And the sons of Jacob came out of the field when they heard *it:* and the men were grieved, and they ᴿwere very wroth, because he ᴿhad wrought folly in Israel in lying with Jacob's daughter; ᴿwhich thing ought not to be done.

8 And Hā'-môr communed with them, saying, The soul of my son Shē'-chĕm longeth for your daughter: I pray you give her him to wife.

9 And make ye marriages with us, *and* give your daughters unto us, and take our daughters unto you.

10 And ye shall dwell with us: and ᴿthe land

shall be before you; dwell and ᴿtrade ye therein, and ᴿget you possessions therein.

11 And Shē'-chĕm said unto her father and unto her brethren, Let me find grace in your eyes, and what ye shall say unto me I will give.

12 Ask me never so much ᴿdowry and gift, and I will give according as ye shall say unto me: but give me the damsel to wife.

Deceit of Jacob's sons

13 And the sons of Jacob answered Shē'-chĕm and Hā'-môr his father ᴿdeceitfully, and said, because he had defiled Dinah their sister:

14 And they said unto them, We cannot do this thing, to give our sister to one that is uncircumcised; for ᴿthat *were* a reproach unto us:

15 But in this will we consent unto you: If ye will be as we *be,* that every male of you be circumcised;

16 Then will we give our daughters unto you, and we will take your daughters to us, and we will dwell with you, and we will become one people.

17 But if ye will not hearken unto us, to be circumcised; then will we take our daughter, and we will be gone.

18 And their words pleased Hā'-môr, and Shē'-chĕm Hā'-môr's son.

19 And the young man deferred not to do the thing, because he had delight in Jacob's daughter: and he *was* ᴿmore honorable than all the house of his father.

20 And Hā'-môr and Shē'-chĕm his son came unto the gate of their city, and communed with the men of their city, saying,

21 These men *are* peaceable with us; therefore let them dwell in the land, and trade therein; for the land, behold, *it is* large enough for them; let us take their daughters to us for wives, and let us give them our daughters.

22 Only herein will the men consent unto us for to dwell with us, to be one people, if every male among us be circumcised, as they *are* circumcised.

23 *Shall* not their cattle and their substance and every beast of theirs *be* ours? only let us consent unto them, and they will dwell with us.

24 And unto Hā'-môr and unto Shē'-chĕm his son hearkened all that ᴿwent out of the gate of his city; and every male was circumcised, all that went out of the gate of his city.

Revenge for Dinah

25 And it came to pass on the third day, when they were sore, that two of the sons of

---

Jacob, ᴿSimeon and Levi, Dinah's brethren, took each man his sword, and came upon the city boldly, and slew all the males.

26 And they slew Hā'-môr and Shē'-chĕm his son with the ᴺedge of the sword, and took Dinah out of Shē'-chĕm's house, and went out.

27 The sons of Jacob came upon the slain, and spoiled the city, because they had defiled their sister.

28 They took their sheep, and their oxen, and their asses, and that which *was* in the city, and that which *was* in the field,

29 And all their wealth, and all their little ones, and their wives took they captive, and spoiled even all that *was* in the house.

30 And Jacob said to Simeon and Levi, ᴿYe have ᴿtroubled me ᴿto make me to stink among the inhabitants of the land, among the Canaanites and the Pĕ-rĭz'-zītes: ᴿand I *being* few in number, they shall gather themselves together against me, and slay me; and I shall be destroyed, I and my house.

31 And they said, Should he deal with our sister as with an harlot?

CHAPTER 35

Jacob moves to Bethel

AND God said unto Jacob, Arise, go up to ᴿBeth-el, and dwell there: and make there an altar unto God, ᴿthat appeared unto thee ᴿwhen thou fleddest from the face of Esau thy brother.

2 Then Jacob said unto his ᴿhousehold, and to all that *were* with him, Put away ᴿthe strange gods that *are* among you, and ᴿbe clean, and change your garments:

3 And let us arise, and go up to Beth-el; and I will make there an altar unto God, ᴿwho answered me in the day of my distress, ᴿand was with me in the way which I went.

4 And they gave unto Jacob all the strange gods which *were* in their hand, and *all their* ᴿearrings which *were* in their ears; and Jacob hid them under ᴿthe oak which *was* by Shē'-chĕm.

5 And they journeyed: and ᴿthe terror of God was upon the cities that *were* round about them, and they did not pursue after the sons of Jacob.

6 So Jacob came to ᴿLuz, which *is* in the land of Canaan, that *is,* Beth-el, he and all the people that *were* with him.

7 And he ᴿbuilt there an altar, and called the place ᴺĔl-bĕth'-ĕl: because ᴿthere God appeared unto him, when he fled from the face of his brother.

8 But ᴿDĕb'-ŏ-răh Rebekah's nurse died, and she was buried beneath Beth-el under an oak:

CHAP. 34
BC 1732
10 ch. 42:34
10 ch. 47:27
12 Ex. 22:16, 17
Deut. 22:29
1 Sam. 18:25
13 See 2 Sam. 13:24, etc.
14 Josh. 5:9
19 1 Chr. 4:9
24 ch. 23:10, 18

ch. 49:5-7   25
Heb. *mouth*   26
ch. 49:6   30
Josh. 7:25   30
Ex. 5:21   30
1 Sam. 13:4
Deut. 4:27   30
Ps. 105:12

CHAP. 35
BC 1732
ch. 28:19   1
ch. 28:13   1
ch. 27:43   1
ch. 18:19   2
Josh. 24:15
ch. 31:19, 34   2
Josh. 24:2, 23
1 Sam. 7:3
Ex. 19:10   2
ch. 32:7, 24   3
ch. 28:20   3
& 31:3, 42
Hos. 2:13   4
Josh. 24:26   4
Judg. 9:6
Ex. 15:16   5
Deut. 11:25
Josh. 2:9
1 Sam. 14:15
ch. 28:19, 22   6
Eccl. 5:4   7
i.e. *The God of Beth-el*   7
ch. 28:13   7
ch. 24:59   8

and the name of it was called ᴺĂl′-lŏn-bā-
chûth.

Jacob's new name

9 And ᴿGod appeared unto Jacob again,
when he came out of Pā′-dăn-âr′-ăm, and
blessed him.

10 And God said unto him, Thy name *is*
Jacob: ᴿthy name shall not be called any more
Jacob, ᴿbut Israel shall be thy name: and he
called his name Israel.

11 And God said unto him, ᴿI *am* God Almighty: be fruitful and multiply; ᴿa nation and
a company of nations shall be of thee, and
kings shall come out of thy loins;

12 And the land ᴿwhich I gave Abraham
and Isaac, to thee I will give it, and to thy seed
after thee will I give the land.

13 And God ᴿwent up from him in the place
where he talked with him.

14 And Jacob ᴿset up a pillar in the place
where he talked with him, *even* a pillar of
stone: and he poured a drink offering thereon,
and he poured oil thereon.

15 And Jacob called the name of the place
where God spake with him, ᴿBeth-el.

Rachel dies bearing Benjamin

16 And they journeyed from Beth-el; and
there was but ᴺa little way to come to
Ē′-phrăth: and Rachel travailed, and she had
hard labour.

17 And it came to pass, when she was in
hard labour, that the midwife said unto her,
Fear not; ᴿthou shalt have this son also.

18 And it came to pass, as her soul was in
departing, (for she died) that she called his
name ᴺBĕn-ō′-nī: but his father called him
ᴺBenjamin.

19 And ᴿRachel died, and was buried in the
way to ᴿĒ′-phrăth, which *is* Beth-lehem.

20 And Jacob set a pillar upon her grave:
that *is* the pillar of Rachel's grave ᴿunto this
day.

21 And Israel journeyed, and spread his tent
beyond ᴿthe tower of Ē′-dăr.

22 And it came to pass, when Israel dwelt in
that land, that Reuben went and ᴿlay with Bĭl′-
hăh his father's concubine: and Israel heard
it. Now the sons of Jacob were twelve:

Jacob's twelve sons

23 The sons of Leah; ᴿReuben, Jacob's
firstborn, and Simeon, and Levi, and Judah,
and Ĭs′-să-chăr, and Zĕ-bū′-lŭn:

24 The sons of Rachel; Joseph, and Benjamin:

25 And the sons of Bĭl′-hăh, Rachel's handmaid; Dan, and Năph′-tă-lī:

26 And the sons of Zilpah, Leah's handmaid; Gad, and Asher: these *are* the sons of
Jacob, which were born to him in Pā′-dăn-
âr′-ăm.

Isaac's death and burial

27 And Jacob came unto Isaac his father
unto ᴿMăm′-rē, unto the ᴿcity of Är′-băh,
which *is* Hē′-brŏn, where Abraham and Isaac
sojourned.

28 And the days of Isaac were an hundred
and fourscore years.

29 And Isaac gave up the ghost, and died,
and ᴿwas gathered unto his people, *being* old
and full of days: and ᴿhis sons Esau and Jacob
buried him.

CHAPTER 36

Descendants of Esau

NOW these *are* the generations of Esau,
ᴿwho *is* Ē′-dǫm.

2 ᴿEsau took his wives of the daughters of
Canaan; Ā′-dăh the daughter of Ē′-lŏn the
Hittite, and ᴿĂ-hŏl-ĭ-bā′-măh the daughter of
Ā′-năh the daughter of Zĭb′-ĕ-ǫn the Hī′-vīte;

3 And ᴿBăsh′-ĕ-măth Ĭsh′-mā-ĕl's daughter,
sister of Nĕ-bā′-jōth.

4 And ᴿĀ′-dăh bare to Esau Ĕ-lī′-phăz; and
Băsh′-ĕ-măth bare Reu′-ĕl;

5 And Ă-hŏl-ĭ-bā′-măh bare Jē′-ŭsh, and Jā′-
ă-lăm, and Kôr′-ăh: these *are* the sons of
Esau, which were born unto him in the land of
Canaan.

6 And Esau took his wives, and his sons,
and his daughters, and all the ᴺpersons of his
house, and his cattle, and all his beasts, and all
his substance, which he had got in the land of
Canaan; and went into the country from the
face of his brother Jacob.

7 ᴿFor their riches were more than that they
might dwell together; and ᴿthe land wherein
they were strangers could not bear them because of their cattle.

8 Thus dwelt Esau in ᴿmount Sē′-ĭr: ᴿEsau
is Ē′-dǫm.

9 And these *are* the generations of Esau the
father of ᴺthe Ē′-dǫm-ītes in mount Sē′-ĭr:

10 These *are* the names of Esau's sons; ᴿĔ-
lī′-phăz the son of Ā′-dăh the wife of Esau,
Reu′-ĕl the son of Băsh′-ĕ-măth the wife of
Esau.

11 And the sons of ĕ-lī′-phăz were Tē′-măn,
Omar, ᴺZē′-phō, and Gā′-tăm, and Kē′-năz.

12 And Tĭm′-nă was concubine to ĕ-lī′-phăz
Esau's son; and she bare to ĕ-lī′-phăz
ᴿĂm′-ă-lĕk: these *were* the sons of Ā′-dăh
Esau's wife.

13 And these *are* the sons of Reu′-ĕl; Na-

hath, and Zē'-räh, Shăm'-măh, and Mĭz'-zäh: these were the sons of Băsh'-ĕ-măth Esau's wife.

14 And these were the sons of Ă-hŏl-ĭ-bä'-mäh, the daughter of Ā'-näh the daughter of Zĭb̄'-ĕ-ŏn, Esau's wife: and she bare to Esau Jē'-ŭsh, and Jā'-ă-lăm, and Kôr'-äh.

15 These were dukes of the sons of Esau: the sons of ĕ-lī'-phăz the firstborn son of Esau; duke Tē'-măn, duke Omar, duke Zē'-phō, duke Kē'-năz,

16 Duke Kôr'-äh, duke Gā'-tăm, and duke Ăm'-ă-lĕk: these are the dukes that came of ĕ-lī'-phăz in the land of Ē'-dom; these were the sons of Ā'-däh.

17 And these are the sons of Rĕṵ'-ĕl Esau's son; duke Nahath, duke Zē'-räh, duke Shăm'-măh, duke Mĭz'-zäh: these are the dukes that came of Rĕṵ'-ĕl in the land of Ē'-dom; these are the sons of Băsh'-ĕ-măth Esau's wife.

18 And these are the sons of Ă-hŏl-ĭ-bä'-mäh Esau's wife; duke Jē'-ŭsh, duke Jā'-ă-lăm, duke Kôr'-äh: these were the dukes that came of Ă-hŏl-ĭ-bä'-mäh the daughter of Ā'-näh, Esau's wife.

19 These are the sons of Esau, who is Ē'-dom, and these are their dukes.

Descendants of Seir

20 ᴿThese are the sons of Sē'-ĭr ᴿthe Hôr'-ĭte, who inhabited the land; Lō'-tăn, and Shō'-băl, and Zĭb'-ĕ-ŏn, and Ā'-näh,

21 And Dī'-shŏn, and Ē'-zẽr, and Dī'-shăn: these are the dukes of the Hôr'-ĭtes, the children of Sē'-ĭr in the land of Ē'-dom.

22 And the children of Lō'-tăn were Hôr'-ĭ and ᴺHē'-măm; and Lō'-tăn's sister was Tĭm'-nă.

23 And the children of Shō'-băl were these; ᴺĂl'-văn, and Măn'-ă-hăth, and Ē'-băl, ᴺShē'-phō, and Ō'-năm.

24 And these are the children of Zĭb'-ĕ-ŏn; both Ā'-jäh, and Ā'-näh: this was that Ā'-näh that found ᴿthe mules in the wilderness, as he fed the asses of Zĭb'-ĕ-ŏn his father.

25 And the children of Ā'-näh were these; Dī'-shŏn, and Ă-hŏl-ĭ-bä'-mäh the daughter of Ā'-näh.

26 And these are the children of Dī'-shŏn; ᴺHĕm'-dăn, and ĕsh'-băn, and Ĭth'-răn, and Chē'-răn.

27 The children of Ē'-zẽr are these; Bilhan, and Zā'-ă-văn, and ᴺAkan.

28 The children of Dī'-shăn are these; Uz, and Är'-ăn.

29 These are the dukes that came of the Hôr'-ĭtes; duke Lō'-tăn, duke Shō'-băl, duke Zĭb'-ĕ-ŏn, duke Ā'-näh,

CHAP. **36**
BC 1715
20 1 Chr. 1:38
20 ch. 14:6
Deut. 2:12, 22
22 Or, Homam,
1 Chr. 1:39
23 Or, Alian,
1 Chr. 1:40
23 Or, Shephi,
1 Chr. 1:40
24 See Lev. 19:19
26 Or, Amram,
1 Chr. 1:41
27 Or, Jakan,
1 Chr. 1:42

1 Chr. 1:43   **31**
ch. 10:11   **37**
1 Chr. 1:50,   **39**
Hadad Pai. After his death was an Aristocracy
1 Chr. 1:51   **40**
Or, Aliah   **40**
Heb. Edom   **43**

CHAP. **37**
BC 1729
ch. 17:8   **1**
& 23:4 & 28:4
& 36:7
Heb. 11:9
Heb. of his   **1**
father's sojournings
1 Sam. 2:22-24   **2**
ch. 44:20   **3**

30 Duke Dī'-shŏn, duke Ē'-zẽr, duke Dī'-shăn: these are the dukes that came of Hôr'-ĭ, among their dukes in the land of Sē'-ĭr.

Kings of Edom

31 And ᴿthese are the kings that reigned in the land of Ē'-dom, before there reigned any king over the children of Israel.

32 And Bē'-lă the son of Bē'-ôr reigned in Ē'-dom: and the name of his city was Dĭn'-hă-bäh.

33 And Bē'-lă died, and Jō'-băb the son of Zē'-räh of Bŏz'-räh reigned in his stead.

34 And Jō'-băb died, and Hū'-shăm of the land of Tē'-măn-ĭ reigned in his stead.

35 And Hū'-shăm died, and Hā'-dăd the son of Bē'-dăd, who smote Mĭd'-ĭ-ăn in the field of Moab, reigned in his stead: and the name of his city was Ā'-vĭth.

36 And Hā'-dăd died, and Săm'-läh of Măs-rē'-kăh reigned in his stead.

37 And Săm'-läh died, and Saul of ᴿRē'-hŏ-bŏth by the river reigned in his stead.

38 And Saul died, and Bā'-ăl-hā'-năn the son of Ăch'-bôr reigned in his stead.

39 And Bā'-ăl-hā'-năn the son of Ăch'-bôr died, and ᴿHā'-dăr reigned in his stead: and the name of his city was Pā'-ū; and his wife's name was Mĕ-hĕt'-ă-bĕl, the daughter of Mā'-trĕd, the daughter of Mĕ'-ză-hăb.

Chiefs of Esau

40 And these are the names of ᴿthe dukes that came of Esau, according to their families, after their places, by their names; duke Tĭm'-näh, duke ᴺĂl'-văh, duke Jē'-thĕth,

41 Duke Ă-hŏl-ĭ-bä'-mäh, duke Ē'-läh, duke Pī'-nŏn,

42 Duke Kē'-năz, duke Tē'-măn, duke Mĭb'-zär,

43 Duke Măg'-dĭ-ĕl, duke Ī'-răm: these be the dukes of Ē'-dom, according to their habitations in the land of their possession: he is Esau the father of ᴺthe Ē'-dom-ĭtes.

CHAPTER 37

Joseph's dreams

AND Jacob dwelt in the land ᴿwhereinᴺ his father was a stranger, in the land of Canaan.

2 These are the generations of Jacob. Joseph, being seventeen years old, was feeding the flock with his brethren; and the lad was with the sons of Bĭl'-häh, and with the sons of Zilpah, his father's wives: and Joseph brought unto his father ᴿtheir evil report.

3 Now Israel loved Joseph more than all his children, because he was ᴿthe son of his old

age: and he made him a coat of *many* [N]colours.

4 And when his brethren saw that their father loved him more than all his brethren, they [R]hated him, and could not speak peaceably unto him.

5 And Joseph dreamed a dream, and he told *it* his brethren: and they hated him yet the more.

6 And he said unto them, Hear, I pray you, this dream which I have dreamed:

7 For, [R]behold, we *were* binding sheaves in the field, and, lo, my sheaf arose, and also stood upright; and, behold, your sheaves stood round about, and made obeisance to my sheaf.

8 And his brethren said to him, Shalt thou indeed reign over us? or shalt thou indeed have dominion over us? And they hated him yet the more for his dreams, and for his words.

9 And he dreamed yet another dream, and told it his brethren, and said, Behold, I have dreamed a dream more; and, behold, [R]the sun and the moon and the eleven stars made obeisance to me.

10 And he told *it* to his father, and to his brethren: and his father rebuked him, and said unto him, What *is* this dream that thou hast dreamed? Shall I and thy mother and [R]thy brethren indeed come to bow down ourselves to thee to the earth?

11 And [R]his brethren envied him; but his father [R]observed the saying.

Conspiracy against Joseph

12 And his brethren went to feed their father's flock in [R]Shē'-chĕm.

13 And Israel said unto Joseph, Do not thy brethren feed *the flock* in Shē'-chĕm? come, and I will send thee unto them. And he said to him, Here *am I*.

14 And he said to him, Go, I pray thee, [N]see whether it be well with thy brethren, and well with the flocks; and bring me word again. So he sent him out of the vale of [R]Hē'-brŏn, and he came to Shē'-chĕm.

15 And a certain man found him, and, behold, *he was* wandering in the field: and the man asked him, saying, What seekest thou?

16 And he said, I seek my brethren: [R]tell me, I pray thee, where they feed *their flocks*.

17 And the man said, They are departed hence; for I heard them say, Let us go to Dō'-thăn. And Joseph went after his brethren, and found them in [R]Dō'-thăn.

18 And when they saw him afar off, even before he came near unto them, [R]they conspired against him to slay him.

19 And they said one to another, Behold, this [N]dreamer cometh.

20 [R]Come now therefore, and let us slay him, and cast him into some pit, and we will say, Some evil beast hath devoured him: and we shall see what will become of his dreams.

21 And [R]Reuben heard *it*, and he delivered him out of their hands; and said, Let us not kill him.

22 And Reuben said unto them, Shed no blood, *but* cast him into this pit that *is* in the wilderness, and lay no hand upon him; that he might rid him out of their hands, to deliver him to his father again.

23 And it came to pass, when Joseph was come unto his brethren, that they stript Joseph out of his coat, *his* coat of *many* [N]colours that *was* on him;

24 And they took him, and cast him into a pit: and the pit *was* empty, *there was* no water in it.

Joseph sold into Egypt

25 [R]And they sat down to eat bread: and they lifted up their eyes and looked, and, behold, a company of [R]Ĭsh'-mē̂e-lītes came from Gilead with their camels bearing spicery and [R]balm and myrrh, going to carry *it* down to Egypt.

26 And Judah said unto his brethren, What profit *is it* if we slay our brother, and [R]conceal his blood?

27 Come, and let us sell him to the Ĭsh'-mē̂e-lītes, and [R]let not our hand be upon him; for he *is* [R]our brother *and* [R]our flesh. And his brethren [N]were content.

28 Then there passed by [R]Mĭd'-ĭ-ă-nītes merchantmen; and they drew and lifted up Joseph out of the pit, [R]and sold Joseph to the Ĭsh'-mē̂e-lītes for [R]twenty *pieces* of silver: and they brought Joseph into Egypt.

29 And Reuben returned unto the pit; and, behold, Joseph *was* not in the pit; and he [R]rent his clothes.

30 And he returned unto his brethren, and said, The child [R]*is* not; and I, whither shall I go?

31 And they took [R]Joseph's coat, and killed a kid of the goats, and dipped the coat in the blood;

32 And they sent the coat of *many* colours, and they brought *it* to their father; and said, This have we found: know now whether it *be* thy son's coat or no.

33 And he knew it, and said, *It is* my son's coat; an [R]evil beast hath devoured him; Joseph is without doubt rent in pieces.

34 And Jacob [R]rent his clothes, and put sackcloth upon his loins, and mourned for his son many days.

35 And all his sons and all his daughters

Rrose up to comfort him; but he refused to be comforted; and he said, For RI will go down into the grave unto my son mourning. Thus his father wept for him.

36 And Rthe Mĭd'-ĭ-ă-nītes sold him into Egypt unto Pŏt'-ĭ-phär, an Nofficer of Pharaoh's, and NNcaptain of the guard.

CHAPTER 38

Sons of Judah

AND it came to pass at that time, that Judah went down from his brethren, and Rturned in to a certain Adullamite, whose name was Hī'-räh.

2 And Judah Rsaw there a daughter of a certain Canaanite, whose name was RShû'-äh; and he took her, and went in unto her.

3 And she conceived, and bare a son; and he called his name Er.

4 And she conceived again, and bare a son; and she called his name RŌ'-năn.

5 And she yet again conceived, and bare a son; and called his name RShē'-läh: and he was at Chē'-zĭb, when she bare him.

6 And Judah Rtook a wife for Er his firstborn, whose name was Tā'-mär.

7 And REr, Judah's firstborn, was wicked in the sight of the LORD; Rand the LORD slew him.

8 And Judah said unto ō'-năn, Go in unto Rthy brother's wife, and marry her, and raise up seed to thy brother.

9 And ō'-năn knew that the seed should not be Rhis; and it came to pass, when he went in unto his brother's wife, that he spilled it on the ground, lest that he should give seed to his brother.

10 And the thing which he did Ndispleased the LORD: wherefore he slew Rhim also.

11 Then said Judah to Tā'-mär his daughter in law, RRemain a widow at thy father's house, till Shē'-läh my son be grown: for he said, Lest peradventure he die also, as his brethren did. And Tā'-mär went and dwelt Rin her father's house.

12 And Nin process of time the daughter of Shû'-äh Judah's wife died; and Judah Rwas comforted, and went up unto his sheepshearers to Tĭm'-năth, he and his friend Hī'-räh the Adullamite.

13 And it was told Tā'-mär, saying, Behold thy father in law goeth up Rto Tĭm'-năth to shear his sheep.

14 And she put her widow's garments off from her, and covered her with a vail, and wrapped herself, and Rsat in Nan open place, which is by the way to Tĭm'-năth; for she saw

Rthat Shē'-läh was grown, and she was not given unto him to wife.

15 When Judah saw her, he thought her to be an harlot; because she had covered her face.

16 And he turned unto her by the way, and said, Go to, I pray thee, let me come in unto thee; (for he knew not that she was his daughter in law.) And she said, What wilt thou give me, that thou mayest come in unto me?

17 And he said, RI will send thee Na kid from the flock. And she said, RWilt thou give me a pledge, till thou send it?

18 And he said, What pledge shall I give thee? And she said, RThy signet, and thy bracelets, and thy staff that is in thine hand. And he gave it her, and came in unto her, and she conceived by him.

19 And she arose, and went away, and Rlaid by her vail from her, and put on the garments of her widowhood.

20 And Judah sent the kid by the hand of his friend the Adullamite, to receive his pledge from the woman's hand: but he found her not.

21 Then he asked the men of that place, saying, Where is the harlot, that was Nopenly by the way side? And they said, There was no harlot in this place.

22 And he returned to Judah, and said, I cannot find her; and also the men of the place said, that there was no harlot in this place.

23 And Judah said, Let her take it to her, lest we Nbe shamed: behold, I sent this kid, and thou hast not found her.

24 And it came to pass about three months after, that it was told Judah, saying, Tā'-mär thy daughter in law hath Rplayed the harlot; and also, behold, she is with child by whoredom. And Judah said, Bring her forth, Rand let her be burnt.

25 When she was brought forth, she sent to her father in law, saying, By the man, whose these are, am I with child: and she said, RDiscern, I pray thee, whose are these, Rthe signet, and bracelets, and staff.

26 And Judah Racknowledged them, and said, RShe hath been more righteous than I; because that RI gave her not to Shē'-läh my son. And he knew her again Rno more.

27 And it came to pass in the time of her travail, that, behold, twins were in her womb.

28 And it came to pass, when she travailed, that the one put out his hand: and the midwife took and bound upon his hand a scarlet thread, saying, This came out first.

29 And it came to pass, as he drew back his hand, that, behold, his brother came out: and she said, NHow hast thou broken forth? this

breach *be* upon thee: therefore his name was called ᴿPhâr′-ĕz.ᴺ

30 And afterward came out his brother, that had the scarlet thread upon his hand: and his name was called Zēr′-äh.

CHAPTER 39

Joseph's success as overseer

AND Joseph was brought down to Egypt; and ᴿPŏt′-ĭ-phär, an officer of Pharaoh, captain of the guard, an Egyptian, ᴿbought him of the hands of the ĭsh′-mē-ē-lītes, which had brought him down thither.

2 And ᴿthe LORD was with Joseph, and he was a prosperous man; and he was in the house of his master the Egyptian.

3 And his master saw that the LORD *was* with him, and that the LORD ᴿmade all that he did to prosper in his hand.

4 And Joseph ᴿfound grace in his sight, and he served him: and he made him ᴿoverseer over his house, and all *that* he had he put into his hand.

5 And it came to pass from the time *that* he had made him overseer in his house, and over all that he had, that ᴿthe LORD blessed the Egyptian's house for Joseph's sake; and the blessing of the LORD was upon all that he had in the house, and in the field.

6 And he left all that he had in Joseph's hand; and he knew not aught he had, save the bread which he did eat. And Joseph ᴿwas *a* goodly *person,* and well favoured.

Joseph and Potiphar's wife

7 And it came to pass after these things, that his master's wife cast her eyes upon Joseph; and she said, ᴿLie with me.

8 But he refused, and said unto his master's wife, Behold, my master wotteth not what *is* with me in the house, and he hath committed all that he hath to my hand;

9 *There is* none greater in this house than I; neither hath he kept back any thing from me but thee, because thou *art* his wife: ᴿhow then can I do this great wickedness, and ᴿsin against God?

10 And it came to pass, as she spake to Joseph day by day, that he hearkened not unto her, to lie by her, *or* to be with her.

11 And it came to pass about this time, that *Joseph* went into the house to do his business; and *there was* none of the men of the house there within.

12 And ᴿshe caught him by his garment, saying, Lie with me: and he left his garment in her hand, and fled, and got him out.

13 And it came to pass, when she saw that he had left his garment in her hand, and was fled forth,

14 That she called unto the men of her house, and spake unto them, saying, See, he hath brought in an Hebrew unto us to mock us; he came in unto me to lie with me, and I cried with a ᴺloud voice:

15 And it came to pass, when he heard that I lifted up my voice and cried, that he left his garment with me, and fled, and got him out.

16 And she laid up his garment by her, until his lord came home.

17 And she ᴿspake unto him according to these words, saying, The Hebrew servant, which thou hast brought unto us, came in unto me to mock me:

18 And it came to pass, as I lifted up my voice and cried, that he left his garment with me, and fled out.

19 And it came to pass, when his master heard the words of his wife, which she spake unto him, saying, After this manner did thy servant to me; that his ᴿwrath was kindled.

20 And Joseph's master took him, and ᴿput him into the ᴿprison, a place where the king's prisoners *were* bound: and he was there in the prison.

Joseph prospers in prison

21 But the LORD was with Joseph, and ᴺshewed him mercy, and ᴿgave him favour in the sight of the keeper of the prison.

22 And the keeper of the prison ᴿcommitted to Joseph's hand all the prisoners that *were* in the prison; and whatsoever they did there, he was the doer *of it.*

23 The keeper of the prison looked not to any thing *that was* under his hand; because ᴿthe LORD was with him, and *that* which he did, the LORD made *it* to prosper.

CHAPTER 40

Joseph interprets dreams

AND it came to pass after these things, *that* the ᴿbutler of the king of Egypt and *his* baker had offended their lord the king of Egypt.

2 And Pharaoh was ᴿwroth against two *of* his officers, against the chief of the butlers, and against the chief of the bakers.

3 ᴿAnd he put them in ward in the house of the captain of the guard, into the prison, the place where Joseph *was* bound.

4 And the captain of the guard charged Joseph with them, and he served them: and they continued a season in ward.

CHAP. 38
BC 1729

29	ch. 46:12
	Num. 26:20
	1 Chr. 2:4
	Mat. 1:3
29	i.e. *A breach*

CHAP. 39
BC 1727

1	ch. 37:36
	Ps. 105:17
1	ch. 37:28
2	ver. 21
	ch. 21:22
	& 26:24, 28
	& 28:15
	1 Sam. 16:18
	& 18:14, 28
	Acts 7:9
3	Ps. 1:3
4	ver. 21
4	ch. 24:2
5	ch. 30:27
6	1 Sam. 16:12
7	2 Sam. 13:11
9	Prov. 6:29, 32
9	ch. 20:6
12	Prov. 7:13, etc.

	Heb. *great*	14
	Ex. 23:1	17
	Ps. 120:3	
	Prov. 6:34, 35	19
	Ps. 105:18	20
	1 Pet. 2:19	
	See ch. 40:3, 15 & 41:14	20
	Heb. *extended kindness unto him*	21
	Ex. 3:21	21
	Prov. 16:7	
	Dan. 1:9	
	Acts 7:9, 10	
	ch. 40:3, 4	22
	ver. 2, 3	23

CHAP. 40
BC 1718

	Neh. 1:11	1
	Prov. 16:14	2
	ch. 39:20, 23	3

5 And they dreamed a dream both of them, each man his dream in one night, each man according to the interpretation of his dream, the butler and the baker of the king of Egypt, which *were* bound in the prison.

6 And Joseph came in unto them in the morning, and looked upon them, and, behold, they *were* sad.

7 And he asked Pharaoh's officers that *were* with him in the ward of his lord's house, saying, Wherefore [N]look ye *so* sadly to day?

8 And they said unto him, [R]We have dreamed a dream, and *there is* no interpreter of it. And Joseph said unto them, [R]*Do* not interpretations *belong* to God? tell me *them*, I pray you.

9 And the chief butler told his dream to Joseph, and said to him, In my dream, behold, a vine *was* before me;

10 And in the vine *were* three branches: and it *was* as though it budded, *and* her blossoms shot forth; and the clusters thereof brought forth ripe grapes:

11 And Pharaoh's cup *was* in my hand: and I took the grapes, and pressed them into Pharaoh's cup, and I gave the cup into Paraoh's hand.

12 And Joseph said unto him, [R]This *is* the interpretation of it: The three branches [R]*are* three days:

13 Yet within three days shall Pharaoh [R]lift[N] up thine head, and restore thee unto thy place: and thou shalt deliver Pharaoh's cup into his hand, after the former manner when thou wast his butler.

14 But [R]think[N] on me when it shall be well with thee, and [R]shew kindness, I pray thee, unto me, and make mention of me unto Pharaoh, and bring me out of this house:

15 For indeed I was stolen away out of the land of the Hebrews: [R]and here also have I done nothing that they should put me into the dungeon.

16 When the chief baker saw that the interpretation was good, he said unto Joseph, I also *was* in my dream, and, behold, *I had* three [N]white baskets on my head:

17 And in the uppermost basket *there was* of all manner of [N]bakemeats for Pharaoh; and the birds did eat them out of the basket upon my head.

18 And Joseph answered and said, [R]This *is* the interpretation thereof: The three baskets *are* three days:

19 [R]Yet within three days shall Pharaoh [N]lift up thy head from off thee, and shall hang thee on a tree; and the birds shall eat thy flesh from off thee.

20 And it came to pass the third day, *which was* Pharaoh's [R]birthday, that he [R]made a feast unto all his servants: and he [R]lifted[N] up the head of the chief butler and of the chief baker among his servants.

21 And he [R]restored the chief butler unto his butlership again; and [R]he gave the cup into Pharaoh's hand:

22 But he [R]hanged the chief baker: as Joseph had interpreted to them.

23 Yet did not the chief butler remember Joseph, but [R]forgat him.

CHAPTER 41

Pharaoh's dream

AND it came to pass at the end of two full years, that Pharaoh dreamed: and, behold, he stood by the river.

2 And, behold, there came up out of the river seven well favoured kine and fatfleshed; and they fed in a meadow.

3 And, behold, seven other kine came up after them out of the river, ill favoured and leanfleshed; and stood by the *other* kine upon the brink of the river.

4 And the ill favoured and leanfleshed kine did eat up the seven well favoured and fat kine. So Pharaoh awoke.

5 And he slept and dreamed the second time: and, behold, seven ears of corn came up upon one stalk, [N]rank and good.

6 And, behold, seven thin ears and blasted with the east wind sprung up after them.

7 And the seven thin ears devoured the seven rank and full ears. And Pharaoh awoke, and, behold, *it was* a dream.

8 And it came to pass in the morning [R]that his spirit was troubled; and he sent and called for all [R]the magicians of Egypt, and all the [R]wise men thereof: and Pharaoh told them his dream; but *there was* none that could interpret them unto Pharaoh.

9 Then spake the chief butler unto Pharaoh, saying, I do remember my faults this day:

10 Pharaoh was [R]wroth with his servants, [R]and put me in ward in the captain of the guard's house, *both* me and the chief baker:

11 And [R]we dreamed a dream in one night, I and he; we dreamed each man according to the interpretation of his dream.

12 And *there was* there with us a young man, an Hebrew, [R]servant to the captain of the guard; and we told him, and he [R]interpreted to us our dreams; to each man according to his dream he did interpret.

13 And it came to pass, [R]as he interpreted to

CHAP. 40 — BC 1718; CHAP. 41 — BC 1715; marginal references omitted for brevity

us, so it was; me he restored unto mine office, and him he hanged.

14 [R]Then Pharaoh sent and called Joseph, and they [R]brought[N] him hastily [R]out of the dungeon: and he shaved *himself,* and changed his raiment, and came in unto Pharaoh.

15 And Pharaoh said unto Joseph, I have dreamed a dream, and *there is* none that can interpret it: [R]and I have heard say of thee, *that* [N]thou canst understand a dream to interpret it.

16 And Joseph answered Pharaoh, saying, [R]*It is* not in me: [R]God shall give Pharaoh an answer of peace.

17 And Pharaoh said unto Joseph, [R]In my dream, behold, I stood upon the bank of the river:

18 And, behold, there came up out of the river seven kine, fatfleshed and well favoured; and they fed in a meadow:

19 And, behold, seven other kine came up after them, poor and very ill favoured and leanfleshed, such as I never saw in all the land of Egypt for badness:

20 And the lean and the ill favoured kine did eat up the first seven fat kine:

21 And when they had [N]eaten them up, it could not be known that they had eaten them; but they *were* still ill favoured, as at the beginning. So I awoke.

22 And I saw in my dream, and, behold, seven ears came up in one stalk, full and good:

23 And, behold, seven ears, [N]withered, thin, *and* blasted with the east wind, sprung up after them:

24 And the thin ears devoured the seven good ears: and [R]I told *this* unto the magicians; but *there was* none that could declare *it* to me.

Interpreting Pharaoh's dream

25 And Joseph said unto Pharaoh, The dream of Pharaoh *is* one: [R]God hath shewed Pharaoh what he *is* about to do.

26 The seven good kine *are* seven years; and the seven good ears *are* seven years: the dream *is* one.

27 And the seven thin and ill favoured kine that came up after them *are* seven years; and the seven empty ears blasted with the east wind shall be [R]seven years of famine.

28 [R]This *is* the thing which I have spoken unto Pharaoh: What God *is* about to do he sheweth unto Pharaoh.

29 Behold, there come [R]seven years of great plenty throughout all the land of Egypt:

30 And there shall [R]arise after them seven years of famine; and all the plenty shall be forgotten in the land of Egypt; and the famine [R]shall consume the land;

31 And the plenty shall not be known in the land by reason of that famine following; for it *shall be* very [N]grievous.

32 And for that the dream was doubled unto Pharaoh twice; *it is* because the [R]thing *is* [N]established by God, and God will shortly bring it to pass.

33 Now therefore let Pharaoh look out a man discreet and wise, and set him over the land of Egypt.

34 Let Pharaoh do *this,* and let him appoint [N]officers over the land, and [R]take up the fifth part of the land of Egypt in the seven plenteous years.

35 And [R]let them gather all the food of those good years that come, and lay up corn under the hand of Pharaoh, and let them keep food in the cities.

36 And that food shall be for store to the land against the seven years of famine, which shall be in the land of Egypt; that the land [R]perish[N] not through the famine.

Joseph made ruler in Egypt

37 And [R]the thing was good in the eyes of Pharaoh, and in the eyes of all his servants.

38 And Pharaoh said unto his servants, Can we find *such a one* as this *is,* a man [R]in whom the spirit of God *is?*

39 And Pharaoh said unto Joseph, Forasmuch as God hath shewed thee all this, *there is* none so discreet and wise as thou *art:*

40 [R]Thou shalt be over my house, and according unto thy word shall all my people [N]be ruled: only in the throne will I be greater than thou.

41 And Pharaoh said unto Joseph, See, I have [R]set thee over all the land of Egypt.

42 And Pharaoh [R]took off his ring from his hand, and put it upon Joseph's hand, and [R]arrayed him in vestures of [N]fine linen, [R]and put a gold chain about his neck;

43 And he made him to ride in the second chariot which he had; [R]and they cried before him, [N][N]Bow the knee: and he made him *ruler* [R]over all the land of Egypt.

44 And Pharaoh said unto Joseph, I *am* Pharaoh, and without thee shall no man lift up his hand or foot in all the land of Egypt.

45 And Pharaoh called Joseph's name [N]Zăph′-năth-pā-ā-nē′-ăh; and he gave him to wife Ăs′-ĕ-năth the daughter of Pŏ-tī′-phĕr-ăh [N]priest of On. And Joseph went out over *all* the land of Egypt.

46 And Joseph *was* thirty years old when he [R]stood before Pharaoh king of Egypt. And Joseph went out from the presence of Pharaoh, and went throughout all the land of Egypt.

47 And in the seven plenteous years the earth brought forth by handfuls.

48 And he gathered up all the food of the seven years, which were in the land of Egypt, and laid up the food in the cities: the food of the field, which *was* round about every city, laid he up in the same.

49 And Joseph gathered corn ᴿas the sand of the sea, very much, until he left numbering; for *it was* without number.

Joseph's sons

50 ᴿAnd unto Joseph were born two sons before the years of famine came, which Ăs′-ĕ-năth the daughter of Pŏ-tī′-phĕr-ăh ᴺpriest of On bare unto him.

51 And Joseph called the name of the firstborn ᴺMă-năs′-sēh: For God, *said he,* hath made me forget all my toil, and all my father's house.

52 And the name of the second called he ᴺĒ′-phră-ĭm: For God hath caused me to be ᴿfruitful in the land of my affliction.

Famine averted in Egypt

53 And the seven years of plenteousness, that was in the land of Egypt, were ended.

54 ᴿAnd the seven years of dearth began to come, ᴿaccording as Joseph had said: and the dearth was in all lands; but in all the land of Egypt there was bread.

55 And when all the land of Egypt was famished, the people cried to Pharaoh for bread: and Pharaoh said unto all the Egyptians, Go unto Joseph; what he saith to you, do.

56 And the famine was over all the face of the earth: and Joseph opened ᴺall the storehouses, and ᴿsold unto the Egyptians; and the famine waxed sore in the land of Egypt.

57 ᴿAnd all countries came into Egypt to Joseph for to buy *corn;* because that the famine was *so* sore in all lands.

CHAPTER 42

Jacob's sons sent to Egypt

NOW when ᴿJacob saw that there was corn in Egypt, Jacob said unto his sons, Why do ye look one upon another?

2 And he said, Behold, I have heard that there is corn in Egypt: get you down thither, and buy for us from thence; that we may ᴿlive, and not die.

3 And Joseph's ten brethren went down to buy corn in Egypt.

4 But Benjamin, Joseph's brother, Jacob sent not with his brethren; for he said, ᴿLest peradventure mischief befall him.

CHAP. 41
BC 1715
49 ch. 22:17
Judg. 7:12
1 Sam. 13,5
50 ch. 46:20 & 48:5
50 Or, *prince*
51 i.e. *Forgetting*
52 i.e. *Fruitful*
52 ch. 49:22
54 Ps. 105:16
Acts 7:11
54 ver. 30
56 Heb. *all wherein* was
56 ch. 42:6
57 Deut. 9:28

CHAP. 42
BC 1707
1 Acts 7:12
2 ch. 43:8
Is. 38:1
4 ver. 38

Acts 7:11   5
ch. 41:41   6
ch. 37:7   6
Heb. *hard*
  things with them 7
ch. 37:5, 9   9
ch. 37:30   13
Lam. 5:7
See ch. 44:20
See 1 Sam.   15
1:26 & 17:55
Heb. *bound*   16
Heb. *gathered* 17
Lev. 25:43   18
Neh. 5:15
ver. 34   20
ch. 43:5
  & 44:23
Job 36:8, 9   21
Hos. 5:15
Prov. 21:13   21
Mat. 7:2
ch. 37:21   22

5 And the sons of Israel came to buy *corn* among those that came: for the famine was ᴿin the land of Canaan.

6 And Joseph *was* the governor ᴿover the land, *and* he *it was* that sold to all the people of the land: and Joseph's brethren came, and ᴿbowed down themselves before him *with* their faces to the earth.

7 And Joseph saw his brethren, and he knew them, but made himself strange unto them, and spake ᴺroughly unto them; and he said unto them, Whence come ye? And they said, From the land of Canaan to buy food.

8 And Joseph knew his brethren, but they knew not him.

9 And Joseph ᴿremembered the dreams which he dreamed of them, and said unto them, Ye *are* spies; to see the nakedness of the land ye are come.

10 And they said unto him, Nay, my lord, but to buy food are thy servants come.

11 We *are* all one man's sons; we *are* true *men,* thy servants are no spies.

12 And he said unto them, Nay, but to see the nakedness of the land ye are come.

13 And they said, Thy servants *are* twelve brethren, the sons of one man in the land of Canaan; and, behold, the youngest *is* this day with our father, and one ᴿ*is* not.

14 And Joseph said unto them, That *is it* that I spake unto you, saying, Ye *are* spies:

15 Hereby ye shall be proved: ᴿBy the life of Pharaoh ye shall not go forth hence, except your youngest brother come hither.

16 Send one of you, and let him fetch your brother, and ye shall be ᴺkept in prison, that your words may be proved, whether *there be any* truth in you: or else by the life of Pharaoh surely ye *are* spies.

17 And he ᴺput them all together into ward three days.

Simeon held hostage

18 And Joseph said unto them the third day, This do, and live; ᴿfor I fear God:

19 If ye *be* true *men,* let one of your brethren be bound in the house of your prison: go ye, carry corn for the famine of your houses:

20 But ᴿbring your youngest brother unto me; so shall your words be verified, and ye shall not die. And they did so.

21 And they said one to another, ᴿWe *are* verily guilty concerning our brother, in that we saw the anguish of his soul, when he besought us, and we would not hear; ᴿtherefore is this distress come upon us.

22 And Reuben answered them, saying, ᴿSpake I not unto you, saying, Do not sin

against the child; and ye would not hear? therefore, behold, also his blood is ^Rrequired.

23 And they knew not that Joseph understood *them;* for ^Nhe spake unto them by an interpreter.

24 And he turned himself about from them, and wept; and returned to them again, and communed with them, and took from them Simeon, and bound him before their eyes.

25 Then Joseph commanded to fill their sacks with corn, and to restore every man's money into his sack, and to give them provision for the way: and ^Rthus did he unto them.

26 And they laded their asses with the corn, and departed thence.

27 And as ^Rone of them opened his sack to give his ass provender in the inn, he espied his money; for, behold, it *was* in his sack's mouth.

28 And he said unto his brethren, My money is restored; and, lo, *it is* even in my sack: and their heart ^Nfailed *them,* and they were afraid, saying one to another, What *is* this *that* God hath done unto us?

Nine sons report to Jacob

29 And they came unto Jacob their father unto the land of Canaan, and told him all that befell unto them; saying,

30 The man, *who is* the lord of the land, ^Rspake ^Nroughly to us, and took us for spies of the country.

31 And we said unto him, We *are* true *men;* we are no spies:

32 We *be* twelve brethren, sons of our father; one *is* not, and the youngest *is* this day with our father in the land of Canaan.

33 And the man, the lord of the country, said unto us, ^RHereby shall I know that ye *are* true *men;* leave one of your brethren *here* with me, and take *food for* the famine of your households, and be gone:

34 And bring your youngest brother unto me: then shall I know that ye *are* no spies, but *that* ye *are* true *men: so* will I deliver you your brother, and ye shall ^Rtraffick in the land.

35 And it came to pass as they emptied their sacks, that, behold, ^Revery man's bundle of money *was* in his sack: and when *both* they and their father saw the bundles of money, they were afraid.

36 And Jacob their father said unto them, Me have ye ^Rbereaved *of my children:* Joseph *is* not, and Simeon *is* not, and ye will take Benjamin *away:* all these things are against me.

37 And Reuben spake unto his father, saying, Slay my two sons, if I bring him not to

CHAP. 42
BC 1707
22 ch. 9:5
1 Ki. 2:32
2 Chr. 24:22
Ps. 9:12
Luke 11:50, 51
23 Heb. *an interpreter* was *between them*
25 Mat. 5:44
Rom. 12:17, 20, 21
27 See ch. 43:21
28 Heb. *went forth*
30 ver. 7
30 Heb. *with us hard things*
33 ver. 15, 19, 20
34 ch. 34:10
35 See ch. 43:21
36 ch. 43:14

ver. 13   38
ch. 37:33 & 44:28
ver. 4   38
ch. 44:29
ch. 37:35   38
& 44:31

CHAP. 43
BC 1707
ch. 41:54, 57   1
Heb. *protesting protested*   3
ch. 42:20   3
& 44:23
Heb. *asking asked us*   7
Heb. *mouth*   7
Heb. *knowing could we know*   7
ch. 44:32   9
Philem. 18:19
Or, *twice by this*   10
ch. 32:20   11
Prov. 18:16
ch. 37:25   11
Jer. 8:22
ch. 42:25, 35   12

thee: deliver him into my hand, and I will bring him to thee again.

38 And he said, My son shall not go down with you; for ^Rhis brother is dead, and he is left alone: ^Rif mischief befall him by the way in the which ye go, then shall ye ^Rbring down my gray hairs with sorrow to the grave.

CHAPTER 43

AND the famine *was* ^Rsore in the land.

2 And it came to pass, when they had eaten up the corn which they had brought out of Egypt, their father said unto them, Go again, buy us a little food.

3 And Judah spake unto him, saying, The man ^Ndid solemnly protest unto us, saying, Ye shall not see my face, except your ^Rbrother *be* with you.

4 If thou wilt send our brother with us, we will go down and buy thee food:

5 But if thou wilt not send *him,* we will not go down: for the man said unto us, Ye shall not see my face, except your brother *be* with you.

6 And Israel said, Wherefore dealt ye *so* ill with me, *as* to tell the man whether ye had yet a brother?

7 And they said, The man ^Nasked us straitly of our state, and of our kindred, saying, *Is* your father yet alive? have ye *another* brother? and we told him according to the ^Ntenor of these words: ^Ncould we certainly know that he would say, Bring your brother down?

8 And Judah said unto Israel his father, Send the lad with me, and we will arise and go; that we may live, and not die, both we, and thou, *and* also our little ones.

9 I will be surety for him; of my hand shalt thou require him: ^Rif I bring him not unto thee, and set him before thee, then let me bear the blame for ever:

10 For except we had lingered, surely now we had returned ^Nthis second time.

11 And their father Israel said unto them, If *it must be* so now, do this; take of the best fruits in the land in your vessels, and ^Rcarry down the man a present, a little ^Rbalm, and a little honey, spices, and myrrh, nuts, and almonds:

12 And take double money in your hand; and the money ^Rthat was brought again in the mouth of your sacks, carry *it* again in your hand; peradventure it *was* an oversight:

13 Take also your brother, and arise, go again unto the man:

14 And God Almighty give you mercy before the man, that he may send away your

other brother, and Benjamin. ᴿIfᴺ I be be-reaved *of my children,* I am bereaved.

Sons of Jacob on second journey

15 And the men took that present, and they took double money in their hand, and Benja-min; and rose up, and went down to Egypt, and stood before Joseph.

16 And when Joseph saw Benjamin with them, he said to the ᴿruler of his house, Bring *these* men home, and ᴺslay, and make ready; for *these* men shall ᴺdine with me at noon.

17 And the man did as Joseph bade; and the man brought the men into Joseph's house.

18 And the men were afraid, because they were brought into Joseph's house; and they said, Because of the money that was returned in our sacks at the first time are we brought in; that he may ᴺseek occasion against us, and fall upon us, and take us for bondmen, and our asses.

19 And they came near to the steward of Joseph's house, and they communed with him at the door of the house,

20 And said, O sir, ᴿweᴺ came indeed down at the first time to buy food:

21 And ᴿit came to pass, when we came to the inn, that we opened our sacks, and, be-hold, *every* man's money *was* in the mouth of his sack, our money in full weight: and we have brought it again in our hand.

22 And other money have we brought down in our hands to buy food: we cannot tell who put our money in our sacks.

23 And he said, Peace *be* to you, fear not: your God, and the God of your father, hath given you treasure in your sacks: ᴺI had your money. And he brought Simeon out unto them.

24 And the man brought the men into Jo-seph's house, and ᴿgave *them* water, and they washed their feet; and he gave their asses prov-ender.

25 And they made ready the present against Joseph came at noon: for they heard that they should eat bread there.

Joseph provides a banquet

26 And when Joseph came home, they brought him the present which *was* in their hand into the house, and ᴿbowed themselves to him to the earth.

27 And he asked them of *their* ᴺwelfare, and said, ᴺ*Is* your father well, the old man ᴿof whom ye spake? *Is* he yet alive?

28 And they answered, Thy servant our fa-ther *is* in good health, he *is* yet alive. ᴿAnd

they bowed down their heads, and made obei-sance.

29 And he lifted up his eyes, and saw his brother Benjamin, ᴿhis mother's son, and said, *Is* this your younger brother, ᴿof whom ye spake unto me? And he said, God be gracious unto thee, my son.

30 And Joseph made haste; for ᴿhis bowels did yearn upon his brother: and he sought *where* to weep; and he entered into *his* cham-ber, and ᴿwept there.

31 And he washed his face, and went out, and refrained himself, and said, Set on ᴿbread.

32 And they set on for him by himself, and for them by themselves, and for the Egyptians, which did eat with him, by themselves: be-cause the Egyptians might not eat bread with the Hebrews; for that *is* ᴿan abomination unto the Egyptians.

33 And they sat before him, the firstborn according to his birthright, and the youngest according to his youth: and the men marvelled one at another.

34 And he took *and sent* messes unto them from before him: but Benjamin's mess was ᴿfive times so much as any of theirs. And they drank, and ᴺwere merry with him.

CHAPTER 44

Joseph implicates Benjamin

AND he commanded ᴺthe steward of his house, saying, Fill the men's sacks *with* food, as much as they can carry, and put every man's money in his sack's mouth.

2 And put my cup, the silver cup, in the sack's mouth of the youngest, and his corn money. And he did according to the word that Joseph had spoken.

3 As soon as the morning was light, the men were sent away, they and their asses.

4 *And* when they were gone out of the city, *and* not *yet* far off, Joseph said unto his stew-ard, Up, follow after the men; and when thou dost overtake them, say unto them, Wherefore have ye rewarded evil for good?

5 *Is* not this *it* in which my lord drinketh, and whereby indeed he ᴺdivineth? ye have done evil in so doing.

6 And he overtook them, and he spake unto them these same words.

7 And they said unto him, Wherefore saith my lord these words? God forbid that thy servants should do according to this thing:

8 Behold, ᴿthe money, which we found in our sacks' mouths, we brought again unto thee

CHAP. 43

BC 1707

14 Esth. 4:16
14 Or, *And I, as I have been, etc.*
16 ch. 24:2 & 39:4 & 44:1
16 Heb. *kill a killing*
16 Heb. *eat*
18 Heb. *roll himself upon us*
20 ch. 42:3, 10
20 Heb. *coming down we came down*
21 ch. 42:27, 35
23 Heb. *your money came to me*
24 ch. 18:4 & 24:32
26 ch. 37:7, 10
27 Heb. *peace,* ch. 37:14
27 Heb. *Is there peace to your father?*
27 ch. 42:11, 13
28 ch. 37:7, 10

ch. 35:17, 18   29
ch. 42:13   29
1 Ki. 3:26   30
ch. 42:24   30
ver. 25   31
ch. 46:34   32
Ex. 8:26
ch. 45:22   34
Heb. *drank largely:* See Hag. 1:6 John 2:10

CHAP. 44

BC 1707

Heb. *him that was over his house*   1
Or, *maketh trial?*   5
ch. 43:21   8

out of the land of Canaan: how then should we steal out of thy lord's house silver or gold?

9 With whomsoever of thy servants it be found, ᴿboth let him die, and we also will be my lord's bondmen.

10 And he said, Now also *let it be* according unto your words: he with whom it is found shall be my servant; and ye shall be blameless.

11 Then they speedily took down every man his sack to the ground, and opened every man his sack.

12 And he searched, *and* began at the eldest, and left at the youngest: and the cup was found in Benjamin's sack.

13 Then they ᴿrent their clothes, and laded every man his ass, and returned to the city.

14 And Judah and his brethren came to Joseph's house; for he *was* yet there: and they ᴿfell before him on the ground.

15 And Joseph said unto them, What deed *is* this that ye have done? wot ye not that such a man as I can certainly ᴺdivine?

16 And Judah said, What shall we say unto my lord? what shall we speak? or how shall we clear ourselves? God hath found out the iniquity of thy servants: behold, ᴿwe *are* my lord's servants, both we, and *he* also with whom the cup is found.

17 And he said, ᴿGod forbid that I should do so: *but* the man in whose hand the cup is found, he shall be my servant; and as for you, get you up in peace unto your father.

Judah pleads for Benjamin

18 Then Judah came near unto him, and said, Oh my lord, let thy servant, I pray thee, speak a word in my lord's ears, and ᴿlet not thine anger burn against thy servant: for thou *art* even as Pharaoh.

19 My lord asked his servants, saying, Have ye a father, or a brother?

20 And we said unto my lord, We have a father, an old man, and ᴿa child of his old age, a little one; and his brother is dead, and he alone is left of his mother, and his father loveth him.

21 And thou saidst unto thy servants, ᴿBring him down unto me, that I may set mine eyes upon him.

22 And we said unto my lord, The lad cannot leave his father: for *if* he should leave his father, *his father* would die.

23 And thou saidst unto thy servants, ᴿExcept your youngest brother come down with you, ye shall see my face no more.

24 And it came to pass when we came up unto thy servant my father, we told him the words of my lord.

25 And ᴿour father said, Go again, *and* buy us a little food.

26 And we said, We cannot go down: if our youngest brother be with us, then will we go down: for we may not see the man's face, except our youngest brother *be* with us.

27 And thy servant my father said unto us, Ye know that ᴿmy wife bare me two *sons:*

28 And the one went out from me, and I said, ᴿSurely he is torn in pieces; and I saw him not since:

29 And if ye ᴿtake this also from me, and mischief befall him, ye shall bring down my gray hairs with sorrow to the grave.

30 Now therefore when I come to thy servant my father, and the lad *be* not with us; seeing that ᴿhis life is bound up in the lad's life;

31 It shall come to pass, when he seeth that the lad *is* not *with us,* that he will die: and thy servants shall bring down the gray hairs of thy servant our father with sorrow to the grave.

32 For thy servant became surety for the lad unto my father, saying, ᴿIf I bring him not unto thee, then I shall bear the blame to my father for ever.

33 Now therefore, I pray thee, ᴿlet thy servant abide instead of the lad a bondman to my lord; and let the lad go up with his brethren.

34 For how shall I go up to my father, and the lad *be* not with me? lest peradventure I see the evil that shall ᴺcome on my father.

CHAPTER 45

Joseph makes himself known

THEN Joseph could not refrain himself before all them that stood by him; and he cried, Cause every man to go out from me. And there stood no man with him, while Joseph made himself known unto his brethren.

2 And he ᴺwept aloud: and the Egyptians and the house of Pharaoh heard.

3 And Joseph said unto his brethren, ᴿI *am* Joseph; doth my father yet live? And his brethren could not answer him; for they were ᴺtroubled at his presence.

4 And Joseph said unto his brethren, Come near to me, I pray you. And they came near. And he said, I *am* Joseph your brother, ᴿwhom ye sold into Egypt.

Joseph reveals God's providence

5 Now therefore be not grieved, ᴺnor angry with yourselves, that ye sold me hither: ᴿfor God did send me before you to preserve life.

6 For these two years *hath* the famine *been* in the land: and yet *there are* five years, in the

CHAP. 44

BC 1707

9 ch. 31:32
13 ch. 37:29, 34
 Num. 14:6
 2 Sam. 1:11
14 ch. 37:7
15 Or, *make trial?*
 ver. 5
16 ver. 9
17 Prov. 17:15
18 ch. 18:30, 32
 Ex. 32:22
20 ch. 37:3
21 ch. 42:15, 20
23 ch. 43:3, 5

ch. 43:2   25
ch. 46:19   27
ch. 37:33   28
ch. 42:36, 38   29
1 Sam. 18:1   30
ch. 43:9   32
Ex. 32:32   33
Heb. *find my*   34
 father
 Ex. 18:8
 Job 31:29
 Ps. 116:3
 & 119:143

CHAP. 45

BC 1707

Heb. *gave forth* 2
his voice in
weeping
 Num. 14:1
 Acts 7:13   3
 Or, *terrified*   3
 Job 4:5 & 23:15
 Mat. 14:26
 Mark 6:50
 ch. 37:28   4
 Heb. *neither*   5
let there be anger
in your eyes
 ch. 50:20   5
 Ps. 105:16, 17

which *there shall* neither *be* earing nor harvest.

7 And God sent me before you ᴺto preserve you a posterity in the earth, and to save your lives by a great deliverance.

8 So now *it was* not you *that* sent me hither, but God: and he hath made me ᴿa father to Pharaoh, and lord of all his house, and a ruler throughout all the land of Egypt.

9 Haste ye, and go up to my father, and say unto him, Thus saith thy son Joseph, God hath made me lord of all Egypt: come down unto me, tarry not:

10 And ᴿthou shalt dwell in the land of Gō′-shĕn, and thou shalt be near unto me, thou, and thy children, and thy children's children, and thy flocks, and thy herds, and all that thou hast:

11 And there will I nourish thee; for yet *there are* five years of famine; lest thou, and thy household, and all that thou hast, come to poverty.

12 And, behold, your eyes see, and the eyes of my brother Benjamin, that *it is* ᴿmy mouth that speaketh unto you.

13 And ye shall tell my father of all my glory in Egypt, and of all that ye have seen; and ye shall haste and ᴿbring down my father hither.

14 And he fell upon his brother Benjamin's neck, and wept; and Benjamin wept upon his neck.

15 Moreover he kissed all his brethren, and wept upon them: and after that his brethren talked with him.

Pharaoh invites Joseph's family

16 And the fame thereof was heard in Pharaoh's house, saying, Joseph's brethren are come: and it ᴺpleased Pharaoh well, and his servants.

17 And Pharaoh said unto Joseph, Say unto thy brethren, This do ye; lade your beasts, and go, get you unto the land of Canaan;

18 And take your father and your households, and come unto me: and I will give you the good of the land of Egypt, and ye shall eat ᴿthe fat of the land.

19 Now thou art commanded, this do ye; take you wagons out of the land of Egypt for your little ones, and for your wives, and bring your father, and come.

20 Also ᴺregard not your stuff; for the good of all the land of Egypt *is* yours.

21 And the children of Israel did so: and Joseph gave them wagons, according to the ᴺcommandment of Pharaoh, and gave them provision for the way.

CHAP. 45
BC 1707
7 Heb. *to put for you a remnant*
8 ch. 41:43
Judg. 17:10
10 ch. 47:1
12 ch. 42:23
13 Acts 7:14
16 Heb. *was good in the eyes of Pharaoh*
18 ch. 27:28
Num. 18:12, 29
20 Heb. *let not your eye spare, etc.*
21 Heb. *mouth*

ch. 43:34 — 22
Heb. *carrying* — 23
Job 29:24 — 26
Ps. 126:1
Luke 24:11, 41
Heb. *his* — 26

CHAP. 46
BC 1706
ch. 21:31, 33 & 28:10 — 1
ch. 26:24, 25 & 28:13 & 31:42 — 1
ch. 15:1 — 2
Job 33:14, 15
ch. 28:13 — 3
ch. 12:2 — 3
Deut. 26:5
ch. 28:15 & 48:21 — 4
ch. 15:16 & 50:13, 24, 25 — 4
Ex. 3:8
ch. 50:1 — 4
Acts 7:15 — 5
ch. 45:19, 21 — 5
Deut. 26:5 — 6
Josh. 24:4
Ps. 105:23
Is. 52:4
Ex. 1:1 — 8
Num. 26:5 — 8

22 To all of them he gave each man changes of raiment; but to Benjamin he gave three hundred *pieces* of silver, and ᴿfive changes of raiment.

23 And to his father he sent after this *manner;* ten asses ᴺladen with the good things of Egypt, and ten she asses laden with corn and bread and meat for his father by the way.

24 So he sent his brethren away, and they departed: and he said unto them, See that ye fall not out by the way.

25 And they went up out of Egypt, and came into the land of Canaan unto Jacob their father,

26 And told him, saying, Joseph *is* yet alive, and he *is* governor over all the land of Egypt. ᴿAndᴺ Jacob's heart fainted, for he believed them not.

27 And they told him all the words of Joseph, which he had said unto them: and when he saw the wagons which Joseph had sent to carry him, the spirit of Jacob their father revived:

28 And Israel said, *It is* enough; Joseph my son *is* yet alive: I will go and see him before I die.

CHAPTER 46

Jacob's family moves to Egypt

AND Israel took his journey with all that he had, and came to ᴿBē̆er-shē′-bă, and offered sacrifices ᴿunto the God of his father Isaac.

2 And God spake unto Israel ᴿin the visions of the night, and said, Jacob, Jacob. And he said, Here *am* I.

3 And he said, I *am* God, ᴿthe God of thy father: fear not to go down into Egypt; for I will there ᴿmake of thee a great nation:

4 ᴿI will go down with thee into Egypt; and I will also surely ᴿbring thee up *again:* and ᴿJoseph shall put his hand upon thine eyes.

5 And ᴿJacob rose up from Bē̆er-shē′-bă: and the sons of Israel carried Jacob their father, and their little ones, and their wives, in the wagons ᴿwhich Pharaoh had sent to carry him.

6 And they took their cattle, and their goods, which they had gotten in the land of Canaan, and came into Egypt, ᴿJacob, and all his seed with him:

7 His sons, and his sons' sons with him, his daughters, and his sons' daughters, and all his seed brought he with him into Egypt.

8 And ᴿthese *are* the names of the children of Israel, which came into Egypt, Jacob and his sons: ᴿReuben, Jacob's firstborn.

9 And the sons of Reuben; Hā′-nŏ<u>ch</u>, and Phăl′-lû, and Hĕz′-rŏn, and Cär′-mĭ.

10 And ᴿthe sons of Simeon; ᴺJĕ-mū′-ĕl, and Jā′-mĭn, and ō′-hăd, and ᴺJā′-<u>ch</u>ĭn, and ᴺZō′-här, and Shā′-ŭl the son of a Canaanitish woman.

11 And the sons of ᴿLevi; ᴺGĕr′-shŏn, Kō′-hăth, and Mĕ-râr′-ĭ.

12 And the sons of ᴿJudah; Er, and ō′-năn, and Shē′-läh, and Phâr′-ĕz, and Zĕr′-äh: but ᴿEr and ō′-năn died in the land of Canaan. And ᴿthe sons of Phâr′-ĕz were Hĕz′-rŏn and Hăm′-ŭl.

13 ᴿAnd the sons of ĭs′-să-<u>ch</u>är; Tō′-lă, and ᴺPhū′-väh, and Job, and Shĭm′-rŏn.

14 And the sons of Zĕ-bū′-lŭn; Sē′-rĕd, and ē′-lŏn, and Jäh′-lēĕl.

15 These be the sons of Leah, which she bare unto Jacob in Pā′-dăn-âr′-ăm, with his daughter Dinah: all the souls of his sons and his daughters were thirty and three.

16 And the sons of Gad; ᴿZĭph′-ĭ-ŏn, and Hăg′-gĭ, Shū′-nĭ, and ᴺĕz′-bŏn, ē′-rĭ, and ᴺă-rō′-dĭ, and ă-rē′-lĭ.

17 ᴿAnd the sons of Asher; Jĭm′-năh, and ĭsh′-ū-ăh, and ĭs′-ū-ĭ, and Bĕ-rī′-äh, and Sē′-răh their sister: and the sons of Bĕ-rī′-äh; Hē′-bĕr, and Măl′-<u>ch</u>ĭ-ĕl.

18 ᴿThese are the sons of Zilpah, ᴿwhom Laban gave to Leah his daughter, and these she bare unto Jacob, even sixteen souls.

19 The sons of Rachel ᴿJacob's wife; Joseph, and Benjamin.

20 ᴿAnd unto Joseph in the land of Egypt were born Mă-năs′-sēh and ē′-phră-ĭm, which ăs′-ĕ-năth the daughter of Pŏ-tī′-phĕr-äh ᴺpriest of On bare unto him.

21 ᴿAnd the sons of Benjamin were Bē′-läh, and Bē′-<u>ch</u>er, and ăsh′-bĕl, Gē′-ră, and Nā′-ă-măn, ᴿē′-hĭ, and Rōsh, ᴿMŭp′-pĭm, and ᴺHŭp′-pĭm, and ärd.

22 These are the sons of Rachel, which were born to Jacob: all the souls were fourteen.

23 ᴿAnd the sons of Dan; ᴺHū′-shĭm.

24 ᴿAnd the sons of Năph′-tă-lī; Jäh′-zeĕl, and Gū′-nĭ, and Jē′-zĕr, and Shĭl′-lĕm.

25 ᴿThese are the sons of Bĭl′-häh, ᴿwhich Laban gave unto Rachel his daughter, and she bare these unto Jacob: all the souls were seven.

26 ᴿAll the souls that came with Jacob into Egypt, which came out of his ᴺloins, besides Jacob's sons' wives, all the souls were threescore and six;

27 And the sons of Joseph, which were born him in Egypt, were two souls: ᴿall the souls of

the house of Jacob, which came into Egypt, were threescore and ten.

Joseph welcomes his father

28 And he sent Judah before him unto Joseph, ᴿto direct his face unto Gō′-shĕn; and they came ᴿinto the land of Gō′-shĕn.

29 And Joseph made ready his chariot, and went up to meet Israel his father, to Gō′-shĕn, and presented himself unto him; and he ᴿfell on his neck, and wept on his neck a good while.

30 And Israel said unto Joseph, ᴿNow let me die, since I have seen thy face, because thou art yet alive.

31 And Joseph said unto his brethren, and unto his father's house, ᴿI will go up, and shew Pharaoh, and say unto him, My brethren, and my father's house, which were in the land of Canaan, are come unto me;

32 And the men are shepherds, for ᴺtheir trade hath been to feed cattle; and they have brought their flocks, and their herds, and all that they have.

33 And it shall come to pass, when Pharaoh shall call you, and shall say, ᴿWhat is your occupation?

34 That ye shall say, Thy servants' ᴿtrade hath been about cattle ᴿfrom our youth even until now, both we, and also our fathers: that ye may dwell in the land of Gō′-shĕn; for every shepherd is ᴿan abomination unto the Egyptians.

CHAPTER 47

THEN Joseph ᴿcame and told Pharaoh, and said, My father and my brethren, and their flocks, and their herds, and all that they have, are come out of the land of Canaan; and, behold, they are in ᴿthe land of Gō′-shĕn.

2 And he took some of his brethren, even five men, and ᴿpresented them unto Pharaoh.

3 And Pharaoh said unto his brethren, ᴿWhat is your occupation? And they said unto Pharaoh, ᴿThy servants are shepherds, both we, and also our fathers.

4 They said moreover unto Pharaoh, ᴿFor to sojourn in the land are we come; for thy servants have no pasture for their flocks; ᴿfor the famine is sore in the land of Canaan: now therefore, we pray thee, let thy servants ᴿdwell in the land of Gō′-shĕn.

5 And Pharaoh spake unto Joseph, saying, Thy father and thy brethren are come unto thee:

6 ᴿThe land of Egypt is before thee; in the best of the land make thy father and brethren

CHAP. 46

BC 1706

10 Ex. 6:15
10 Or, Nemuel
10 Or, Jarib
10 Or, Zerah, 1 Chr. 4:24
11 1 Chr. 6:1, 16
11 Or, Gershom
12 1 Chr. 2:3 & 4:21
12 ch. 38:3, 7, 10
12 ch. 38:29
13 1 Chr. 7:1
13 Or, Puah, and Jashub
16 Num. 26:15, etc., Zephon
16 Or, Ozni
16 Or, Arod
17 1 Chr. 7:30
18 ch. 30:10
18 ch. 29:24
19 ch. 44:27
20 ch. 41:50
20 Or, prince
21 1 Chr. 7:6 & 8:1
21 Num. 26:38, Ahiram
21 Num. 26:39, Shupham 1 Chr. 7:12, Shuppim
21 Hupham, Num. 26:39
23 1 Chr. 7:12
23 Or, Shuham, Num. 26:42
24 1 Chr. 7:13
25 ch. 30:5, 7
25 ch. 29:29
26 Ex. 1:5
26 Heb. thigh, ch. 35:11
27 Deut. 10:22
See Acts 7:14

ch. 31:21   28
ch. 47:1   28
ch. 45:14   29
Luke 2:29, 30   30
ch. 47:1   31
Heb. they   32
are men
of cattle
ch. 47:2, 3   33
ver. 32   34
ch. 30:35   34
& 34:5 & 37:12
ch. 43:32   34
Ex. 8:26

CHAP. 47

BC 1706

ch. 46:31   1
ch. 45:10 &   1
46:28
Acts 7:13   2
ch. 46:33   3
ch. 46:34   3
ch. 15:13   4
Deut. 26:5
ch. 43:1   4
Acts 7:11
ch. 46:34   4
ch. 20:15   6

to dwell; ᴿin the land of Gō'-shĕn let them dwell: and if thou knowest *any* men of activity among them, then make them rulers over my cattle.

Jacob blesses Pharaoh

7 And Joseph brought in Jacob his father, and set him before Pharaoh: and Jacob blessed Pharaoh.

8 And Pharaoh said unto Jacob, ᴺHow old *art* thou?

9 And Jacob said unto Pharaoh, ᴿThe days of the years of my pilgrimage *are* an hundred and thirty years: ᴿfew and evil have the days of the years of my life been, and ᴿhave not attained unto the days of the years of the life of my fathers in the days of their pilgrimage.

10 And Jacob ᴿblessed Pharaoh, and went out from before Pharaoh.

11 And Joseph placed his father and his brethren, and gave them a possession in the land of Egypt, in the best of the land, in the land of ᴿRăm'-ĕ-sĕś, ᴿas Pharaoh had commanded.

12 And Joseph nourished his father, and his brethren, and all his father's household, with bread, ᴺᴺaccording to *their* families.

13 And *there was* no bread in all the land; for the famine *was* very sore, ᴿso that the land of Egypt and *all* the land of Canaan fainted by reason of the famine.

14 ᴿAnd Joseph gathered up all the money that was found in the land of Egypt, and in the land of Canaan, for the corn which they bought: and Joseph brought the money into Pharaoh's house.

15 And when money failed in the land of Egypt, and in the land of Canaan, all the Egyptians came unto Joseph, and said, Give us bread: for ᴿwhy should we die in thy presence? for the money faileth.

16 And Joseph said, Give your cattle; and I will give you for your cattle, if money fail.

17 And they brought their cattle unto Joseph: and Joseph gave them bread *in exchange* for horses, and for the flocks, and for the cattle of the herds, and for the asses: and he ᴺfed them with bread for all their cattle for that year.

18 When that year was ended, they came unto him the second year, and said unto him, We will not hide *it* from my lord, how that our money is spent; my lord also hath our herds of cattle; there is not aught left in the sight of my lord, but our bodies, and our lands:

19 Wherefore shall we die before thine eyes, both we and our land? buy us and our land for

CHAP. **47**

BC 1706

6 ver. 4
8 Heb. *How many are the days of the years of thy life?*
9 Ps. 39:12
Heb. 11:9, 13
9 Job 14:1
9 ch. 25:7 & 35:28
10 ver. 7
11 Ex. 1:11
& 12:37
11 ver. 6
12 Or, *as a little child is nourished*
12 Heb. *according to the little ones*
13 ch. 41:30
Acts 7:11
14 ch. 41:56
15 ver. 19
17 Heb. *led them*

Ezra 7:24   **22**
Or, *princes*,   **22**
ch. 41:45
ch. 33:15   **25**
ver. 22   **26**
Or, *princes*,   **26**
ver. 22
ver. 11   **27**
ch. 46:3   **27**
Heb. *the days of the years of his life*   **28**
Deut. 31:14   **29**
1 Ki. 2:1
ch. 24:2   **29**
ch. 24:49   **29**
ch. 50:25   **29**
2 Sam. 19:37   **30**
ch. 49:29   **30**
& 50:5, 13
ch. 48:2   **31**
1 Ki. 1:47
Heb. 11:21

bread, and we and our land will be servants unto Pharaoh: and give *us* seed, that we may live, and not die, that the land be not desolate.

Egyptians sell land to Pharaoh

20 And Joseph bought all the land of Egypt for Pharaoh; for the Egyptians sold every man his field, because the famine prevailed over them: so the land became Pharaoh's.

21 And as for the people, he removed them to cities from *one* end of the borders of Egypt even to the *other* end thereof.

22 ᴿOnly the land of the ᴺpriests bought he not; for the priests had a portion *assigned them* of Pharaoh, and did eat their portion which Pharaoh gave them: wherefore they sold not their lands.

23 Then Joseph said unto the people, Behold, I have bought you this day and your land for Pharaoh: lo, *here is* seed for you, and ye shall sow the land.

24 And it shall come to pass in the increase, that ye shall give the fifth *part* unto Pharaoh, and four parts shall be your own, for seed of the field, and for your food, and for them of your houscholds, and for food for your little ones.

25 And they said, Thou hast saved our lives: ᴿlet us find grace in the sight of my lord, and we will be Pharaoh's servants.

26 And Joseph made it a law over the land of Egypt unto this day, *that* Pharaoh should have the fifth *part;* ᴿexcept the land of the ᴺpriests only, *which* became not Pharaoh's.

Israelites prosper in Egypt

27 And Israel ᴿdwelt in the land of Egypt, in the country of Gō'-shĕn; and they had possessions therein, and ᴿgrew, and multiplied exceedingly.

28 And Jacob lived in the land of Egypt seventeen years; so ᴺthe whole age of Jacob was an hundred forty and seven years.

29 And the time ᴿdrew nigh that Israel must die: and he called his son Joseph, and said unto him, If now I have found grace in thy sight, ᴿput, I pray thee, thy hand under my thigh, and ᴿdeal kindly and truly with me; ᴿbury me not, I pray thee, in Egypt:

30 But ᴿI will lie with my fathers, and thou shalt carry me out of Egypt, and ᴿbury me in their buryingplace. And he said, I will do as thou hast said.

31 And he said, Swear unto me. And he sware unto him. And ᴿIsrael bowed himself upon the bed's head.

CHAPTER 48

Joseph visits Jacob

AND it came to pass after these things, that *one* told Joseph, Behold, thy father *is* sick: and he took with him his two sons, Mă-năs'-sĕh and Ē'-phră-ĭm.

2 And *one* told Jacob, and said, Behold, thy son Joseph cometh unto thee: and Israel strengthened himself, and sat upon the bed.

3 And Jacob said unto Joseph, God Almighty appeared unto me at ᴿLuz in the land of Canaan, and blessed me,

4 And said unto me, Behold, I will make thee fruitful, and multiply thee, and I will make of thee a multitude of people; and will give this land to thy seed after thee ᴿ*for* an everlasting possession.

5 And now thy ᴿtwo sons, Ē'-phră-ĭm and Mă-năs'-sĕh, which were born unto thee in the land of Egypt before I came unto thee into Egypt, *are* mine; as Reuben and Simeon, they shall be mine.

6 And thy issue, which thou begettest after them, shall be thine, *and* shall be called after the name of their brethren in their inheritance.

7 And as for me, when I came from Pā'-dăn, ᴿRachel died by me in the land of Canaan in the way, when yet *there was* but a little way to come unto Ē'-phrăth: and I buried her there in the way of Ē'-phrăth; the same *is* Beth-lehem.

8 And Israel beheld Joseph's sons, and said, Who *are* these?

9 And Joseph said unto his father, ᴿThey *are* my sons, whom God hath given me in this *place*. And he said, Bring them, I pray thee, unto me, and ᴿI will bless them.

10 Now ᴿthe eyes of Israel were ᴺdim for age, *so that* he could not see. And he brought them near unto him; and ᴿhe kissed them, and embraced them.

11 And Israel said unto Joseph, ᴿI had not thought to see thy face: and, lo, God hath shewed me also thy seed.

12 And Joseph brought them out from between his knees, and he bowed himself with his face to the earth.

13 And Joseph took them both, Ē'-phră-ĭm in his right hand toward Israel's left hand, and Mă-năs'-sĕh in his left hand toward Israel's right hand, and brought *them* near unto him.

14 And Israel stretched out his right hand, and laid *it* upon Ē'-phră-ĭm's head, who *was* the younger, and his left hand upon Mă-năs'-sĕh's head, ᴿguiding his hands wittingly; for Mă-năs'-sĕh *was* the firstborn.

15 And ᴿhe blessed Joseph, and said, God, ᴿbefore whom my fathers Abraham and Isaac

did walk, the God which fed me all my life long unto this day,

16 The Angel ᴿwhich redeemed me from all evil, bless the lads; and let ᴿmy name be named on them, and the name of my fathers Abraham and Isaac; and let them ᴺgrow into a multitude in the midst of the earth.

17 And when Joseph saw that his father ᴿlaid his right hand upon the head of Ē'-phră-ĭm, it ᴺdispleased him: and he held up his father's hand, to remove it from Ē'-phră-ĭm's head unto Mă-năs'-sĕh's head.

18 And Joseph said unto his father, Not so, my father: for this *is* the firstborn; put thy right hand upon his head.

19 And his father refused, and said, ᴿI know *it*, my son, I know *it*: he also shall become a people, and he also shall be great: but truly ᴿhis younger brother shall be greater than he, and his seed shall become a ᴺmultitude of nations.

20 And he blessed them that day, saying, ᴿIn thee shall Israel bless, saying, God make thee as Ē'-phră-ĭm and as Mă-năs'-sĕh: and he set Ē'-phră-ĭm before Mă-năs'-sĕh.

21 And Israel said unto Joseph, Behold, I die: but ᴿGod shall be with you, and bring you again unto the land of your fathers.

22 Moreover ᴿI have given to thee one portion above thy brethren, which I took out of the hand ᴿof the Amorite with my sword and with my bow.

CHAPTER 49

Jacob's dying blessing

AND Jacob called unto his sons, and said, Gather yourselves together, that I may ᴿtell you *that* which shall befall you ᴿin the last days.

2 Gather yourselves together, and hear, ye sons of Jacob; and hearken unto Israel your father.

3 Reuben, thou *art* ᴿmy firstborn, my might, and the beginning of my strength, the excellency of dignity, and the excellency of power:

4 Unstable as water, ᴺthou shalt not excel; because thou ᴿwentest up to thy father's bed; then defiledst thou *it*: ᴺhe went up to my couch.

5 ᴿSimeon and Levi *are* brethren; ᴺinstruments of cruelty *are in* their habitations.

6 O my soul, ᴿcome not thou into their secret; ᴿunto their assembly, mine honour, be not thou united: for ᴿin their anger they slew a man, and in their selfwill they ᴺdigged down a wall.

CHAP. 48

BC 1689

3	ch. 28:13, 19 & 35:6, 9, etc.
4	ch. 17:8
5	ch. 41:50 & 46:20 Josh. 13:7 & 14:4
7	ch. 35:9, 16, 19
9	ch. 33:5
9	ch. 27:4
10	ch. 27:1
10	Heb. *heavy*
10	ch. 27:27
11	ch. 45:26
14	ver. 19
15	Heb. 11:21
15	ch. 17:1

ch. 28:15	**16**
Ps. 34:22 & 121:7	
Amos 9:12	**16**
Acts 15:17	
Heb. *as fishes do increase:* See Num. 26:34, 37	**16**
ver. 14	**17**
Heb. *was evil in his eyes*	**17**
ver. 14	**19**
Num. 1:33, 35	**19**
Deut. 33:17	
Heb. *fulness*	**19**
Ruth 4:11, 12	**20**
ch. 46:4	**21**
Josh. 24:32	**22**
John 4:5	
ch. 34:28	**22**

CHAP. 49

BC 1689

Deut. 33:1	**1**
Amos 3:7	
Deut. 4:30	**1**
Is. 39:6	
Jer. 23:20	
Heb. 1:2	
ch. 29:32	**3**
Heb. *do not thou excel*	**4**
ch. 35:22	**4**
Deut. 27:20	
Or, *my couch is gone*	**4**
ch. 29:33, 34	**5**
Or, *their swords are weapons of violence*	**5**
Prov. 1:15, 16	**6**
Ps. 26:9	**6**
Eph. 5:11	
ch. 34:26	**6**
Or, *houghed oxen*	**6**

7 Cursed *be* their anger, for *it was* fierce; and their wrath, for it was cruel: I will divide them in Jacob, and scatter them in Israel.

8 ᴿJudah, thou *art he* whom thy brethren shall praise: ᴿthy hand *shall be* in the neck of thine enemies; ᴿthy father's children shall bow down before thee.

9 Judah *is* ᴿa lion's whelp: from the prey, my son, thou art gone up: ᴿhe stooped down, he couched as a lion, and as an old lion; who shall rouse him up?

10 ᴿThe sceptre shall not depart from Judah, nor ᴿa lawgiver from between his feet, ᴿuntil Shī′-lōh come; ᴿand unto him *shall* the gathering of the people *be*.　★

11 Binding his foal unto the vine, and his ass's colt unto the choice vine; he washed his garments in wine, and his clothes in the blood of grapes:

12 His eyes *shall be* red with wine, and his teeth white with milk.

13 ᴿZĕ-bū′-lŭn shall dwell at the haven of the sea; and he *shall be* for an haven of ships; and his border *shall be* unto Zī′-dŏn.

14 ĭs′-să-chär *is* a strong ass couching down between two burdens:

15 And he saw that rest *was* good, and the land that *it was* pleasant; and bowed ᴿhis shoulder to bear, and became a servant unto tribute.

16 ᴿDan shall judge his people, as one of the tribes of Israel.

17 ᴿDan shall be a serpent by the way, ᴺan adder in the path, that biteth the horse heels, so that his rider shall fall backward.

18 ᴿI have waited for thy salvation, O Lᴏʀᴅ.

19 ᴿGad, a troop shall overcome him: but he shall overcome at the last.

20 ᴿOut of Asher his bread *shall be* fat, and he shall yield royal dainties.

21 ᴿNăph′-tă-lī *is* a hind let loose: he giveth goodly words.

22 Joseph *is* a fruitful bough, *even* a fruitful bough by a well; *whose* ᴺbranches run over the wall:

23 The archers have ᴿsorely grieved him, and shot *at him,* and hated him:

24 But his ᴿbow abode in strength, and the arms of his hands were made strong by the hands of ᴿthe mighty *God* of Jacob; (ᴿfrom thence ᴿ*is* the shepherd, ᴿthe stone of Israel:)

25 ᴿ*Even* by the God of thy father, who shall help thee; ᴿand by the Almighty, ᴿwho shall bless thee with blessings of heaven above, blessings of the deep that lieth under, blessings of the breasts, and of the womb:

26 The blessings of thy father have prevailed above the blessings of my progenitors ᴿunto

the utmost bound of the everlasting hills: ᴿthey shall be on the head of Joseph, and on the crown of the head of him that was separate from his brethren.

27 Benjamin shall ᴿravin *as* a wolf: in the morning he shall devour the prey, ᴿand at night he shall divide the spoil.

Death of Jacob

28 All these *are* the twelve tribes of Israel: and this *is it* that their father spake unto them, and blessed them; every one according to his blessing he blessed them.

29 And he charged them, and said unto them, I ᴿam to be gathered unto my people: ᴿbury me with my fathers ᴿin the cave that *is* in the field of Ē′-phrŏn the Hittite,

30 In the cave that *is* in the field of Măch-pē′-läh, which *is* before Măm′-rē, in the land of Canaan, ᴿwhich Abraham bought with the field of Ē′-phrŏn the Hittite for a possession of a buryingplace.

31 ᴿThere they buried Abraham and Sarah his wife; ᴿthere they buried Isaac and Rebekah his wife; and there I buried Leah.

32 The purchase of the field and of the cave that *is* therein *was* from the children of Heth.

33 And when Jacob had made an end of commanding his sons, he gathered up his feet into the bed, and yielded up the ghost, and ᴿwas gathered unto his people.

CHAPTER 50

AND Joseph ᴿfell upon his father's face, and ᴿwept upon him, and kissed him.

2 And Joseph commanded his servants the physicians to ᴿembalm his father: and the physicians embalmed Israel.

3 And forty days were fulfilled for him; for so are fulfilled the days of those which are embalmed: and the Egyptians ᴿmournedᴺ for him threescore and ten days.

Jacob buried in Canaan

4 And when the days of his mourning were past, Joseph spake unto ᴿthe house of Pharaoh, saying, If now I have found grace in your eyes, speak, I pray you, in the ears of Pharaoh, saying,

5 ᴿMy father made me swear, saying, Lo, I die: in my grave ᴿwhich I have digged for me in the land of Canaan, there shalt thou bury me. Now therefore let me go up, I pray thee, and bury my father, and I will come again.

6 And Pharaoh said, Go up, and bury thy father, according as he made thee swear.

7 And Joseph went up to bury his father:

CHAP. **49**
BC 1689

8	Deut. 33:7
8	Ps. 18:40
8	1 Chr. 5:2
9	Rev. 5:5
9	Num. 23:24
	& 24:9
10	Num. 24:17
	Jer. 30:21
10	Ps. 60:7
10	Is. 11:1
	Mat. 21:9
10	Is. 60:1-5
	Luke 2:30-32
13	Deut. 33:18, 19
	Josh. 19:10, 11
15	1 Sam. 10:9
16	Deut. 33:22
17	Judg. 18:27
17	Heb. *an arrow-snake*
18	Ps. 25:5
	Is. 25:9
19	Deut. 33:20
	1 Chr. 5:18
20	Deut. 33:24
	Josh. 19:24
21	Deut. 33:23
22	Heb. *daughters*
23	ch. 37:4, 24
	Ps. 118:13
24	Job 29:20
	Ps. 37:15
24	Ps. 132:2, 5
24	ch. 45:11
	& 47:12
24	Ps. 80:1
24	Is. 28:16
25	ch. 28:13
	& 35:3 & 43:23
25	ch. 17:1
	& 35:11
25	Deut. 33:13
26	Deut. 33:15
	Hab. 3:6

Deut. 33:16	26
Judg. 20:21, 25	27
Num. 23:24	27
Esth. 8:11	
Ezek. 39:10	
Zech. 14:1	
ch. 15:15 & 25:8	29
ch. 47:30	29
2 Sam. 19:37	
ch. 50:13	29
ch. 23:16	30
ch. 23:19	31
& 25:9	
ch. 35:29	31
ver. 29	33

CHAP. **50**
BC 1689

ch. 46:4	1
2 Ki. 13:14	1
ver. 26	2
2 Chr. 16:14	
Luke 24:1	
John 19:39, 40	
Num. 20:29	3
Deut. 34:8	
Heb. *wept*	3
Esth. 4:2	4
ch. 47:29	5
2 Chr. 16:14	5
Is. 22:16	

and with him went up all the servants of Pharaoh, the elders of his house, and all the elders of the land of Egypt,

8 And all the house of Joseph, and his brethren, and his father's house: only their little ones, and their flocks, and their herds, they left in the land of Gō'-shĕn.

9 And there went up with him both chariots and horsemen: and it was a very great company.

10 And they came to the threshingfloor of Ā'-tăd, which *is* beyond Jordan, and there they ^Rmourned with a great and very sore lamentation: ^Rand he made a mourning for his father seven days.

11 And when the inhabitants of the land, the Canaanites, saw the mourning in the floor of Ā'-tăd, they said, This *is* a grievous mourning to the Egyptians: wherefore the name of it was called ^NĀ'-bĕl-mĭz'-rā-ĭm, which *is* beyond Jordan.

12 And his sons did unto him according as he commanded them:

13 For ^Rhis sons carried him into the land of Canaan, and buried him in the cave of the field of Măch-pē'-läh, which Abraham ^Rbought with the field for a possession of a buryingplace of Ē'-phrŏn the Hittite, before Măm'-rē.

14 And Joseph returned into Egypt, he, and his brethren, and all that went up with him to bury his father, after he had buried his father.

Joseph forgives his brothers

15 And when Joseph's brethren saw that their father was dead, ^Rthey said, Joseph will peradventure hate us, and will certainly requite us all the evil which we did unto him.

16 And they ^Nsent a messenger unto Joseph,

CHAP. **50**
BC 1689
10 Acts 8:2
10 1 Sam. 31:13
Job 2:13
11 i.e. *The mourning of the Egyptians*
13 ch. 49:29
Acts 7:16
13 ch. 23:16
15 Job 15:21
16 Heb. *charged*

Prov. 28:13	**17**
ch. 49:25	**17**
ch. 37:7, 10	**18**
ch. 45:5	**19**
2 Ki. 5:7	**19**
Ps. 56:5	**20**
Acts 3:13-15	**20**
Mat. 5:44	**21**
Heb. *to their hearts*	**21**
Job 42:16	**23**
Num. 32:39	**23**
ch. 30:3	**23**
Heb. *borne*	**23**
ch. 15:14 & 46:4 & 48:21	**24**
Ex. 3:16, 17	
Heb. 11:22	
ch. 26:3 & 35:12 & 46:4	**24**
Ex. 13:19	**25**
Josh. 24:32	
Acts 7:16	

saying, Thy father did command before he died, saying,

17 So shall ye say unto Joseph, Forgive, I pray thee now, the trespass of thy brethren, and their sin; ^Rfor they did unto thee evil: and now, we pray thee, forgive the trespass of the servants of ^Rthe God of thy father. And Joseph wept when they spake unto him.

18 And his brethren also went and ^Rfell down before his face; and they said, Behold, we *be* thy servants.

19 And Joseph said unto them, ^RFear not: ^Rfor *am* I in the place of God?

20 ^RBut as for you, ye thought evil against me; *but* ^RGod meant it unto good, to bring to pass, as *it is* this day, to save much people alive.

21 Now therefore fear ye not: ^RI will nourish you, and your little ones. And he comforted them, and spake ^Nkindly unto them.

Death of Joseph

22 And Joseph dwelt in Egypt, he, and his father's house: and Joseph lived an hundred and ten years.

23 And Joseph saw Ē'-phrā-ĭm's children ^Rof the third *generation:* ^Rthe children also of Mā'-chĭr the son of Mă-năs'-sēh ^Rwere ^Nbrought up upon Joseph's knees.

24 And Joseph said unto his brethren, I die: and ^RGod will surely visit you, and bring you out of this land unto the land ^Rwhich he sware to Abraham, to Isaac, and to Jacob.

25 And ^RJoseph took an oath of the children of Israel, saying, God will surely visit you, and ye shall carry up my bones from hence.

26 So Joseph died, *being* an hundred and ten years old: and they embalmed him, and he was put in a coffin in Egypt.

THE SECOND BOOK OF MOSES, CALLED

EXODUS

"Exodus," meaning "departure," is the name the seventy Elders who translated the Old Testament into Greek gave to the second book of the Old Testament on account of the chief event which it records: the going out or departure of the Israelites from Egypt. It is a continuation of the history given in Genesis. While Genesis is largely biographical, giving an account of individuals and families from which the nation sprang, Exodus is more general in its historical outlook and records the growth and development of Israel as the chosen people of God. Strictly speaking, the title is applicable to the first half of the book only, and takes no account of those chapters which describe the giving of the law, nor of those relating to the tabernacle and the directions concerning the priesthood. The book of Exodus asserts the supremacy of the God of Israel over the heathen gods, demands freedom from Egyptian servitude, and inaugurates a new era for the chosen

people by signs and wonders. In its historical scope the book of Exodus embraces the period from the death of Joseph in Egypt to the building of the tabernacle in the wilderness of Sinai under the direction of Moses. The events and the material in Exodus and in the following three books are closely associated with Moses and were very likely written by him.

OUTLINE OF THE BOOK:
  I. Preparation of Moses 1:1 – 4:31
 II. The contest with Pharaoh 5:1 – 11:10
III. The passover and exodus 12:1 – 15:27
IV. The journey to mount Sinai 16:1 – 18:27
 V. Israel as God's covenant people 19:1 – 31:18
VI. Idolatry and punishment 32:1 – 33:23
VII. Provision for worship 34:1 – 40:38

CHAPTER 1

Growth of Israel

N OW ᴿthese *are* the names of the children of Israel, which came into Egypt; every man and his household came with Jacob.

2 Reuben, Simeon, Levi, and Judah,

3 Ĭs'-să-<u>ch</u>är, Zĕ-bū'-lŭn, and Benjamin,

4 Dan, and Năph'-tă-lī, Gad, and Asher.

5 And all the souls that came out of the ᴺloins of Jacob were ᴿseventy souls: for Joseph was in Egypt *already.*

6 And ᴿJoseph died, and all his brethren, and all that generation.

7 ᴿAnd the children of Israel were fruitful, and increased abundantly, and multiplied, and waxed exceeding mighty; and the land was filled with them.

8 Now there arose up a new king over Egypt, which knew not Joseph.

9 And he said unto his people, Behold, ᴿthe people of the children of Israel *are* more and mightier than we:

10 ᴿCome on, let us ᴿdeal wisely with them; lest they multiply, and it come to pass, that, when there falleth out any war, they join also unto our enemies, and fight against us, and *so* get them up out of the land.

Israelites become slaves

11 Therefore they did set over them taskmasters ᴿto afflict them with their ᴿburdens. And they built for Pharaoh treasure cities, Pī'-thŏm ᴿand Rā-ăm'-sēs.

12 ᴺBut the more they afflicted them, the more they multiplied and grew. And they were grieved because of the children of Israel.

13 And the Egyptians made the children of Israel to serve with rigour:

14 And they ᴿmade their lives bitter with hard bondage, ᴿin mortar, and in brick, and in all manner of service in the field: all their service, wherein they made them serve, *was* with rigour.

Pharaoh instructs the midwives

15 And the king of Egypt spake to the Hebrew midwives, of which the name of the one *was* Shĭph'-răh, and the name of the other Pū'-ăh:

16 And he said, When ye do the office of a midwife to the Hebrew women, and see *them* upon the stools; if it *be* a son, then ye shall kill him: but if it *be* a daughter, then she shall live.

17 But the midwives ᴿfeared God, and did not ᴿas the king of Egypt commanded them, but saved the men children alive.

18 And the king of Egypt called for the midwives, and said unto them, Why have ye done this thing, and have saved the men children alive?

19 And ᴿthe midwives said unto Pharaoh, Because the Hebrew women *are* not as the Egyptian women; for they *are* lively, and are delivered ere the midwives come in unto them.

20 ᴿTherefore God dealt well with the midwives: and the people multiplied, and waxed very mighty.

21 And it came to pass, because the midwives feared God, ᴿthat he made them houses.

22 And Pharaoh charged all his people, saying, ᴿEvery son that is born ye shall cast into the river, and every daughter ye shall save alive.

CHAPTER 2

Birth of Moses

A ND there went ᴿa man of the house of Levi, and took *to wife* a daughter of Levi.

2 And the woman conceived, and bare a son: and ᴿwhen she saw him that he *was a* goodly *child,* she hid him three months.

3 And when she could not longer hide him, she took for him an ark of bulrushes, and daubed it with slime and with pitch, and put the child therein; and she laid *it* in the flags by the river's brink.

4 ᴿAnd his sister stood afar off, to wit what would be done to him.

5 And the ᴿdaughter of Pharaoh came down to wash *herself* at the river; and her maidens walked along by the river's side; and when she saw the ark among the flags, she sent her maid to fetch it.

6 And when she had opened *it,* she saw the child: and, behold, the babe wept. And she had compassion on him, and said, This *is one* of the Hebrews' children.

7 Then said his sister to Pharaoh's daughter, Shall I go and call to thee a nurse of the Hebrew women, that she may nurse the child for thee?

8 And Pharaoh's daughter said to her, Go. And the maid went and called the child's mother.

9 And Pharaoh's daughter said unto her, Take this child away, and nurse it for me, and I will give *thee* thy wages. And the woman took the child, and nursed it.

10 And the child grew, and she brought him unto Pharaoh's daughter, and he became ᴿher son. And she called his name ᴺMoses: and she said, Because I drew him out of the water.

CHAP. 1
BC 1706
1 Gen. 46:8
5 Heb. *thigh*
5 Gen. 46:26, 27
6 Gen. 50:26
Acts 7:15
7 Gen. 46:3
Deut. 26:5
Ps. 105:24
Acts 7:17
9 Ps. 105:24
10 Ps. 83:3, 4
10 Prov. 16:25
Acts 7:19
11 Gen. 15:13
ch. 3:7
Deut. 26:6
11 ch. 5:4, 5
11 Gen. 47:11
12 Heb. *And as they afflicted them, so they multiplied, etc.*
14 ch. 2:23 & 6:9
Num. 20:15
Acts 7:19, 34
14 Ps. 81:6
17 Prov. 16:6
17 Dan. 3:16, 18
Acts 5:29

See Josh. 2:4, etc.   19
2 Sam. 17:19, 20
Prov. 11:18   20
Eccl. 8:12
Is. 3:10
Heb. 6:10
See 1 Sam.   21
2:35
2 Sam. 7:11, 13, 27, 29
1 Ki. 11:38
Ps. 127:1
Acts 7:19   22

CHAP. 2
BC 1571
ch. 6:20   1
Num. 26:59
1 Chr. 23:14
Acts 7:20   2
Heb. 11:23
ch. 15:20   4
Num. 26:59
Acts 7:21   5
Acts 7:21   10
i.e. *Drawn out*   10

Moses slays an Egyptian

11 And it came to pass in those days, [R]when Moses was grown, that he went out unto his brethren, and looked on their [R]burdens: and he spied an Egyptian smiting an Hebrew, one of his brethren.

12 And he looked this way and that way, and when he saw that *there was* no man, he [R]slew the Egyptian, and hid him in the sand.

13 And [R]when he went out the second day, behold, two men of the Hebrews strove together: and he said to him that did the wrong, Wherefore smitest thou thy fellow?

14 And he said, [R]Who made thee [N]a prince and a judge over us? intendest thou to kill me, as thou killedst the Egyptian? And Moses feared, and said, Surely this thing is known.

Moses flees to Midian

15 Now when Pharaoh heard this thing, he sought to slay Moses. But [R]Moses fled from the face of Pharaoh, and dwelt in the land of Mĭd'-ĭ-ăn: and he sat down by [R]a well.

16 [R]Now the [N]priest of Mĭd'-ĭ-ăn had seven daughters: [R]and they came and drew *water,* and filled the troughs to water their father's flock.

17 And the shepherds came and drove them away: but Moses stood up and helped them, and [R]watered their flock.

18 And when they came to [R]Rĕu'-ĕl their father, he said, How *is it that* ye are come so soon to day?

19 And they said, An Egyptian delivered us out of the hand of the shepherds, and also drew *water* enough for us, and watered the flock.

20 And he said unto his daughters, And where *is* he? why *is it that* ye have left the man? call him, that he may [R]eat bread.

21 And Moses was content to dwell with the man: and he gave Moses [R]Zĭp'-pŏ-răh his daughter.

22 And she bare *him* a son, and he called his name [R]Gĕr'-shŏm:[N] for he said, I have been [R]a stranger in a strange land.

23 And it came to pass [R]in process of time, that the king of Egypt died: and the children of Israel [R]sighed by reason of the bondage, and they cried, and [R]their cry came up unto God by reason of the bondage.

24 And God [R]heard their groaning, and God [R]remembered his [R]covenant with Abraham, with Isaac, and with Jacob.

25 And God [R]looked upon the children of Israel, and God [R]had[N] respect unto *them.*

CHAP. 2

BC 1571

11 Acts 7:23, 24
Heb. 11:24-26
11 ch. 1:11
12 Acts 7:24
13 Acts 7:26
14 Acts 7:27, 28
14 Heb. *a man, a prince,* Gen. 13:8
15 Acts 7:29
Heb. 11:27
15 Gen. 24:11
& 29:2
16 ch. 3:1
16 Or, *prince,* as Gen. 41:45
16 Gen. 24:11
1 Sam. 9:11
17 Gen. 29:10
18 Num. 10:29
Called also *Jethro,* or, *Jether,* ch. 3:1 & 4:18
20 Gen. 31:54
21 ch. 18:2
22 ch. 18:3
22 i.e. *A stranger here*
22 Acts 7:29
23 Acts 7:30
23 Deut. 26:7
23 ch. 3:9
Jas. 5:4
24 ch. 6:5
24 ch. 6:5
Ps. 105:8, 42
24 Gen. 15:14
25 ch. 4:31
Luke 1:25
25 ch. 3:7
25 Heb. *knew*

CHAP. 3

BC 1491

ch. 2:16   1
ch. 18:5   1
1 Ki. 19:8
Deut. 33:16   2
Acts 7:30
Acts 7:31   3
Deut. 33:16   4
Josh. 5:15   5
Gen. 28:13   6
ch. 4:5
Mat. 22:32
Acts 7:32
1 Ki. 19:13   6
ch. 2:23-25   7
Ps. 106:44
ch. 1:11   7
Gen. 18:21   7
ch. 2:25
Gen. 50:24   8
ch. 6:6, 8   8
Deut. 1:25   8
& 8:7-9
ver. 17   8
ch. 13:5
Jer. 11:5
Ezek. 20:6
Gen. 15:21   8
ch. 2:23   9
ch. 1:11, 13, 14   9
Mic. 6:4   10
See ch. 6:12   11
1 Sam. 18:18
Gen. 31:3   12
Josh. 1:5
Rom. 8:31

CHAPTER 3

The burning bush

NOW Moses kept the flock of Jĕth'-rō his father in law, [R]the priest of Mĭd'-ĭ-ăn: and he led the flock to the backside of the desert, and came to [R]the mountain of God, *even* to Hôr'-ĕb.

2 And [R]the angel of the LORD appeared unto him in a flame of fire out of the midst of a bush: and he looked, and, behold, the bush burned with fire, and the bush *was* not consumed.

3 And Moses said, I will now turn aside, and see this [R]great sight, why the bush is not burnt.

4 And when the LORD saw that he turned aside to see, God called [R]unto him out of the midst of the bush, and said, Moses, Moses. And he said, Here *am* I.

5 And he said, Draw not nigh hither: [R]put off thy shoes from off thy feet, for the place whereon thou standest *is* holy ground.

6 Moreover he said, [R]I *am* the God of thy father, the God of Abraham, the God of Isaac, and the God of Jacob. And Moses hid his face; for [R]he was afraid to look upon God.

7 And the LORD said, [R]I have surely seen the affliction of my people which *are* in Egypt, and have heard their cry [R]by reason of their taskmasters; for [R]I know their sorrows;

8 And [R]I am come down to [R]deliver them out of the hand of the Egyptians, and to bring them up out of that land [R]unto a good land and a large, unto a land [R]flowing with milk and honey; unto the place of [R]the Canaanites, and the Hittites, and the Amorites, and the Pĕ-rĭz'-zītes, and the Hī'-vītes, and the Jĕb'-ū-śītes.

9 Now therefore, behold, [R]the cry of the children of Israel is come unto me: and I have also seen the [R]oppression wherewith the Egyptians oppress them.

God commissions Moses

10 [R]Come now therefore, and I will send thee unto Pharaoh, that thou mayest bring forth my people the children of Israel out of Egypt.

11 And Moses said unto God, [R]Who *am* I, that I should go unto Pharaoh, and that I should bring forth the children of Israel out of Egypt?

12 And he said, [R]Certainly I will be with thee; and this *shall be* a token unto thee, that I have sent thee: When thou hast brought forth the people out of Egypt, ye shall serve God upon this mountain.

13 And Moses said unto God, Behold, *when* I come unto the children of Israel, and shall say unto them, The God of your fathers hath sent me unto you; and they shall say to me, What *is* his name? what shall I say unto them?

"I AM THAT I AM"

14 And God said unto Moses, I AM THAT I AM: and he said, Thus shalt thou say unto the children of Israel, R I AM hath sent me unto you.

15 And God said moreover unto Moses, Thus shalt thou say unto the children of Israel, The LORD God of your fathers, the God of Abraham, the God of Isaac, and the God of Jacob, hath sent me unto you: this *is* R my name for ever, and this *is* my memorial unto all generations.

16 Go, and K gather the elders of Israel together, and say unto them, The LORD God of your fathers, the God of Abraham, of Isaac, and of Jacob, appeared unto me, saying, R I have surely visited you, and *seen* that which is done to you in Egypt:

17 And I have said, R I will bring you up out of the affliction of Egypt unto the land of the Canaanites, and the Hittites, and the Amorites, and the Pĕ-rĭz'-zītes, and the Hī'-vītes, and the Jĕb'-ū-ŝītes, unto a land flowing with milk and honey.

18 And R they shall hearken to thy voice: and R thou shalt come, thou and the elders of Israel, unto the king of Egypt, and ye shall say unto him, The LORD God of the Hebrews hath R met with us: and now let us go, we beseech thee, three days' journey into the wilderness, that we may sacrifice to the LORD our God.

19 And I am sure that the king of Egypt R will not let you go, N no, not by a mighty hand.

20 And I will R stretch out my hand, and smite Egypt with R all my wonders which I will do in the midst thereof: and R after that he will let you go.

21 And R I will give this people favour in the sight of the Egyptians: and it shall come to pass, that, when ye go, ye shall not go empty:

22 R But every woman shall borrow of her neighbour, and of her that sojourneth in her house, jewels of silver, and jewels of gold, and raiment: and ye shall put *them* upon your sons, and upon your daughters; and R ye shall spoil N the Egyptians.

CHAPTER 4

Two signs given to Moses

AND Moses answered and said, But, behold, they will not believe me, nor

---

CHAP. 3
BC 1491
14 ch. 6:3
John 8:58
Heb. 13:8
15 Ps. 135:13
16 ch. 4:29
16 ch. 2:25
Luke 1:68
17 Gen. 15:14, 16
18 ch. 4:31
18 ch. 5:1, 3
18 Num. 23:3, 4, 15, 16
19 ch. 5:2
19 Or, *but by strong hand*
20 ch. 6:6 & 9:15
20 Deut. 6:22
Neh. 9:10
Acts 7:36
20 ch. 12:31
21 ch. 11:3 & 12:36
Prov. 16:7
22 ch. 11:2
22 Job 27:17
Prov. 13:22
Ezek. 29:10
22 Or, *Egypt*

CHAP. 4	
BC 1491	
ver. 17, 20	**2**
ch. 19:9	**5**
ch. 3:15	**5**
Num. 12:10	**6**
2 Ki. 5:27	
Num. 12:13, 14	**7**
Deut. 32:39	
ch. 7:19	**9**
Heb. *shall be and shall be*	**9**
Heb. *a man of words*	**10**
Heb. *since yesterday, nor since the third day*	**10**
ch. 6:12	**10**
Jer. 1:6	
Ps. 94:9	**11**
Is. 50:4	**12**
Jer. 1:9	
Mat. 10:19	
Mark 13:11	
Luke 12:11, 12 & 21:14, 15	
See Jonah 1:3	**13**
Or, *shouldest*	**13**
ver. 27	**14**
1 Sam. 10:2, 3, 5	
ch. 7:1, 2	**15**
Num. 23:5, 12, 16	**15**

---

hearken unto my voice: for they will say, The LORD hath not appeared unto thee.

2 And the LORD said unto him, What *is* that in thine hand? And he said, R A rod.

3 And he said, Cast it on the ground. And he cast it on the ground, and it became a serpent; and Moses fled from before it.

4 And the LORD said unto Moses, Put forth thine hand, and take it by the tail. And he put forth his hand, and caught it, and it became a rod in his hand:

5 That they may R believe that R the LORD God of their fathers, the God of Abraham, the God of Isaac, and the God of Jacob, hath appeared unto thee.

6 And the LORD said furthermore unto him, Put now thine hand into thy bosom. And he put his hand into his bosom: and when he took it out, behold, his hand *was* leprous R as snow.

7 And he said, Put thine hand into thy bosom again. And he put his hand into his bosom again; and plucked it out of his bosom, and, behold, R it was turned again as his *other* flesh.

8 And it shall come to pass, if they will not believe thee, neither hearken to the voice of the first sign, that they will believe the voice of the latter sign.

9 And it shall come to pass, if they will not believe also these two signs, neither hearken unto thy voice, that thou shalt take of the water of the river, and pour *it* upon the dry *land:* and R the water which thou takest out of the river N shall become blood upon the dry *land.*

Aaron's appointment

10 And Moses said unto the LORD, O my Lord, I *am* not N eloquent, neither N heretofore, nor since thou hast spoken unto thy servant: but R I *am* slow of speech, and of a slow tongue.

11 And the LORD said unto him, R Who hath made man's mouth? or who maketh the dumb, or deaf, or the seeing, or the blind? have not I the LORD?

12 Now therefore go, and I will be R with thy mouth, and teach thee what thou shalt say.

13 And he said, O my Lord, R send, I pray thee, by the hand of *him whom* thou N wilt send.

14 And the anger of the LORD was kindled against Moses, and he said, *Is* not Aaron the Levite thy brother? I know that he can speak well. And also, behold, R he cometh forth to meet thee: and when he seeth thee, he will be glad in his heart.

15 And R thou shalt speak unto him, and R put words in his mouth: and I will be with thy

mouth, and with his mouth, and ᴿwill teach you what ye shall do.

16 And he shall be thy spokesman unto the people: and he shall be, *even* he shall be to thee instead of a mouth, and ᴿthou shalt be to him instead of God.

17 And thou shalt take ᴿthis rod in thine hand, wherewith thou shalt do signs.

18 And Moses went and returned to ᴺJĕth′-rō his father in law, and said unto him, Let me go, I pray thee, and return unto my brethren which *are* in Egypt, and see whether they be yet alive. And Jĕth′-rō said to Moses, Go in peace.

19 And the LORD said unto Moses in Mĭd′-ĭ-ăn, Go, return into Egypt: for ᴿall the men are dead which sought thy life.

20 And Moses took his wife and his sons, and set them upon an ass, and he returned to the land of Egypt: and Moses took ᴿthe rod of God in his hand.

21 And the LORD said unto Moses, When thou goest to return into Egypt, see that thou do all those ᴿwonders before Pharaoh, which I have put in thine hand: but ᴿI will harden his heart, that he shall not let the people go.

22 And thou shalt say unto Pharaoh, Thus saith the LORD, ᴿIsrael *is* my son, ᴿ*even* my firstborn:

23 And I say unto thee, Let my son go, that he may serve me: and if thou refuse to let him go, behold, ᴿI will slay thy son, *even* thy firstborn.

24 And it came to pass by the way in the inn, that the LORD ᴿmet him, and sought to ᴿkill him.

25 Then Zĭp′-pŏ-răh took ᴿa sharp ᴺstone, and cut off the foreskin of her son, and ᴺcast *it* at his feet, and said, Surely a bloody husband *art* thou to me.

26 So he let him go: then she said, A bloody husband *thou art,* because of the circumcision.

27 And the LORD said to Aaron, Go into the wilderness ᴿto meet Moses. And he went, and met him in ᴿthe mount of God, and kissed him.

28 And Moses ᴿtold Aaron all the words of the LORD who had sent him, and all the ᴿsigns which he had commanded him.

29 And Moses and Aaron ᴿwent and gathered together all the elders of the children of Israel:

30 ᴿAnd Aaron spake all the words which the LORD had spoken unto Moses, and did the signs in the sight of the people.

31 And the people ᴿbelieved: and when they heard that the LORD had ᴿvisited the children of Israel, and that he ᴿhad looked upon their

CHAP. **4**
BC 1491
15 Deut. 5:31
16 ch. 7:1
17 ver. 2
18 Heb. *Jether*
19 ch. 2:15, 23
Mat. 2:20
20 Num. 20:8, 9
21 ch. 3:20
21 ch. 7:3, 13 &
9:12, 35
Deut. 2:30
Josh. 11:20
Is. 63:17
John 12:40
22 Hos. 11:1
Rom. 9:4
2 Cor. 6:18
22 Jer. 31:9
Jas. 1:18
23 ch. 11:5
& 12:29
24 Num. 22:22
24 Gen. 17:14
25 Josh. 5:2, 3
25 Or, *knife*
25 Heb. *made it touch*
27 ver. 14
27 ch. 3:1
28 ver. 15, 16
28 ver. 8, 9
29 ch. 3:16
30 ver. 16
31 ver. 8, 9
ch. 3:18
31 ch. 3:16
31 ch. 2:25 & 3:7

Gen. 24:26	**31**
1 Chr. 29:20	

CHAP. **5**
BC 1491

ch. 10:9	**1**
2 Ki. 18:35	**2**
Job 21:15	
ch. 3:19	**2**
ch. 3:18	**3**
ch. 1:11	**4**
ch. 1:7, 9	**5**
ch. 1:11	**6**
Heb. *Let the work be heavy upon the men*	**9**
Heb. *a matter of a day in his day*	**13**

affliction, then ᴿthey bowed their heads and worshipped.

CHAPTER 5

Pharaoh's refusal to free Israel

AND afterward Moses and Aaron went in, and told Pharaoh, Thus saith the LORD God of Israel, Let my people go, that they may hold ᴿa feast unto me in the wilderness.

2 And Pharaoh said, ᴿWho *is* the LORD, that I should obey his voice to let Israel go? I know not the LORD, ᴿneither will I let Israel go.

3 And they said, ᴿThe God of the Hebrews hath met with us: let us go, we pray thee, three days' journey into the desert, and sacrifice unto the LORD our God; lest he fall upon us with pestilence, or with the sword.

4 And the king of Egypt said unto them, Wherefore do ye, Moses and Aaron, let the people from their works? get you unto your ᴿburdens.

5 And Pharaoh said, Behold, the people of the land now *are* ᴿmany, and ye make them rest from their burdens.

6 And Pharaoh commanded the same day the ᴿtaskmasters of the people, and their officers, saying,

7 Ye shall no more give the people straw to make brick, as heretofore: let them go and gather straw for themselves.

8 And the tale of the bricks, which they did make heretofore, ye shall lay upon them; ye shall not diminish *aught* thereof: for they *be* idle; therefore they cry, saying, Let us go *and* sacrifice to our God.

9 ᴺLet there more work be laid upon the men, that they may labour therein; and let them not regard vain words.

The increased burdens

10 And the taskmasters of the people went out, and their officers, and they spake to the people, saying, Thus saith Pharaoh, I will not give you straw.

11 Go ye, get you straw where ye can find it: yet not aught of your work shall be diminished.

12 So the people were scattered abroad throughout all the land of Egypt to gather stubble instead of straw.

13 And the taskmasters hasted *them,* saying, Fulfil your works, ᴺ*your* daily tasks, as when there was straw.

14 And the officers of the children of Israel, which Pharaoh's taskmasters had set over them, were beaten, *and* demanded, Wherefore

have ye not fulfilled your task in making brick both yesterday and to day, as heretofore?

15 Then the officers of the children of Israel came and cried unto Pharaoh, saying, Wherefore dealest thou thus with thy servants?

16 There is no straw given unto thy servants, and they say to us, Make brick: and, behold, thy servants *are* beaten; but the fault *is* in thine own people.

17 But he said, Ye *are* idle, *ye are* idle: therefore ye say, Let us go *and* do sacrifice to the LORD.

18 Go therefore now, *and* work; for there shall no straw be given you, yet shall ye deliver the tale of bricks.

19 And the officers of the children of Israel did see *that* they *were* in evil *case,* after it was said, Ye shall not minish *aught* from your bricks of your daily task.

Murmurings against Moses

20 And they met Moses and Aaron, who stood in the way, as they came forth from Pharaoh:

21 ᴿAnd they said unto them, The LORD look upon you, and judge; because ye have made our savour ᴺto be abhorred in the eyes of Pharaoh, and in the eyes of his servants, to put a sword in their hand to slay us.

22 And Moses returned unto the LORD, and said, Lord, wherefore hast thou *so* evil entreated this people? why *is* it *that* thou hast sent me?

23 For since I came to Pharaoh to speak in thy name, he hath done evil to this people; ᴺneither hast thou delivered thy people at all.

CHAPTER 6

The covenant renewed

THEN the LORD said unto Moses, Now shalt thou see what I will do to Pharaoh: for ᴿwith a strong hand shall he let them go, and with a strong hand ᴿshall he drive them out of his land.

2 And God spake unto Moses, and said unto him, I *am* ᴺthe LORD:

3 And I appeared unto Abraham, unto Isaac, and unto Jacob, by *the name of* ᴿGod Almighty, but by my name ᴿJĕ-HŌ′-VăH was I not known to them.

4 ᴿAnd I have also established my covenant with them, ᴿto give them the land of Canaan, the land of their pilgrimage, wherein they were strangers.

5 And ᴿI have also heard the groaning of the children of Israel, whom the Egyptians keep in

CHAP. 5
BC 1491
21 ch. 6:9
21 Heb. *to stink,*
Gen. 34:30
2 Sam. 10:6
23 Heb. *delivering thou hast not delivered*

CHAP. 6
BC 1619
1 ch. 3:19
1 ch. 12:31, 33, 39
2 Or, *JEHOVAH*
3 Gen. 17:1 & 35:11 & 48:3
3 ch. 3:14
Ps. 83:18
John 8:58
4 Gen. 15:18
4 Gen. 28:4
5 ch. 2:24

ch. 3:17   6
Deut. 26:8
Deut. 7:8   6
1 Chr. 17:21
Deut. 4:20   7
2 Sam. 7:24
ch. 29:45, 46   7
Rev. 21:7
ch. 5:4, 5   7
Gen. 15:18 &   8
26:3
Heb. *lift up*   8
my hand: See
Gen. 14:22
ch. 5:21   9
Heb. *shortness,* 9
or, *straitness*
ver. 30   12
ch. 4:10
Jer. 1:6
Gen. 46:9   14
1 Chr. 5:3
Gen. 46:10   15
1 Chr. 4:24
Gen. 46:11   16
Num. 3:17
1 Chr. 6:17   17
1 Chr. 6:2, 18 18
1 Chr. 6:19   19
& 23:21
ch. 2:1, 2   20

bondage; and I have remembered my covenant.

6 Wherefore say unto the children of Israel, I *am* the LORD, and ᴿI will bring you out from under the burdens of the Egyptians, and I will rid you out of their bondage, and I will ᴿredeem you with a stretched out arm, and with great judgments:

7 And I will ᴿtake you to me for a people, and ᴿI will be to you a God: and ye shall know that I *am* the LORD your God, which bringeth you out ᴿfrom under the burdens of the Egyptians.

8 And I will bring you in unto the land, concerning the which I did ᴿswearᴺ to give it to Abraham, to Isaac, and to Jacob; and I will give it you for an heritage: I *am* the LORD.

9 And Moses spake so unto the children of Israel: ᴿbut they hearkened not unto Moses for ᴺanguish of spirit, and for cruel bondage.

10 And the LORD spake unto Moses, saying,

11 Go in, speak unto Pharaoh king of Egypt, that he let the children of Israel go out of his land.

12 And Moses spake before the LORD, saying, Behold, the children of Israel have not hearkened unto me; how then shall Pharaoh hear me, ᴿwho *am* of uncircumcised lips?

13 And the LORD spake unto Moses and unto Aaron, and gave them a charge unto the children of Israel, and unto Pharaoh king of Egypt, to bring the children of Israel out of the land of Egypt.

The families of Israel

14 These *be* the heads of their fathers' houses: ᴿthe sons of Reuben the firstborn of Israel; Hā′-nŏch, and Păl′-lû, Hĕz′-rŏn, and Cär′-mī: these *be* the families of Reuben.

15 ᴿAnd the sons of Simeon; Jĕ-mū′-ĕl, and Jā′-mīn, and ō′-hăd, and Jā′-chīn, and Zō′-här, and Shā′-ūl the son of a Canaanitish woman: these *are* the families of Simeon.

16 And these *are* the names of ᴿthe sons of Levi according to their generations; Gēr′-shŏn, and Kō′-hăth, and Mĕ-râr′-ī: and the years of the life of Levi *were* an hundred thirty and seven years.

17 ᴿThe sons of Gēr′-shŏn; Lĭb′-nī, and Shĭm′-ī, according to their families.

18 And ᴿthe sons of Kō′-hăth; Amram, and Ĭz′-här, and Hē′-brŏn, and ŭz′-zī-ĕl: and the years of the life of Kō′-hăth *were* an hundred thirty and three years.

19 And ᴿthe sons of Mĕ-râr′-ī; Mā′-hă-lī and Mū′-shī: these *are* the families of Levi according to their generations.

20 And ᴿAmram took him Jŏch′-ĕ-bĕd his

father's sister to wife; and she bare him Aaron and Moses: and the years of the life of Amram *were* an hundred and thirty and seven years.

21 And ᴿthe sons of Ĭz'-här; Kôr'-ăh, and Nĕph'-ĕg, and Zĭch'-rī.

22 And ᴿthe sons of Ŭz'-zī-ĕl; Mĭ'-shā-ĕl, and ĕl-zā'-phăn, and Zĭth'-rī.

23 And Aaron took him Ē-lī'-shĕ-bă, daughter of ᴿĂm-mĭn'-ă-dăb, sister of Nā-ăsh'-ŏn, to wife; and she bare him ᴿNadab, and Ă-bī'-hū, ĕl-ē-ā'-zär, and Ĭth'-ă-mär.

24 And the ᴿsons of Kôr'-ăh; Ăs'-sīr, and ĕl-kā'-năh, and Ă-bī'-ă-săph: these *are* the families of the Kôr'-hītes.

25 And ĕl-ē-ā'-zär Aaron's son took him *one* of the daughters of Pū'-tī-ĕl to wife; and ᴿshe bare him Phĭn'-ĕ-hăs̆: these *are* the heads of the fathers of the Levites according to their families.

26 These *are* that Aaron and Moses, to whom the Lᴏʀᴅ said, Bring out the children of Israel from the land of Egypt according to their ᴿarmies.

27 These *are* they which spake to Pharaoh king of Egypt, ᴿto bring out the children of Israel from Egypt: these *are* that Moses and Aaron.

28 And it came to pass on the day *when* the Lᴏʀᴅ spake unto Moses in the land of Egypt,

29 That the Lᴏʀᴅ spake unto Moses, saying, I *am* the Lᴏʀᴅ: ᴿspeak thou unto Pharaoh king of Egypt all that I say unto thee.

30 And Moses said before the Lᴏʀᴅ, Behold, ᴿI *am* of uncircumcised lips, and how shall Pharaoh hearken unto me?

CHAPTER 7

Moses before Pharaoh

AND the Lᴏʀᴅ said unto Moses, See, I have made thee ᴿa god to Pharaoh: and Aaron thy brother shall be ᴿthy prophet.

2 Thou ᴿshalt speak all that I command thee: and Aaron thy brother shall speak unto Pharaoh, that he send the children of Israel out of his land.

3 And ᴿI will harden Pharaoh's heart, and ᴿmultiply my ᴿsigns and my wonders in the land of Egypt.

4 But Pharaoh shall not hearken unto you, ᴿthat I may lay my hand upon Egypt, and bring forth mine armies, *and* my people the children of Israel, out of the land of Egypt ᴿby great judgments.

5 And the Egyptians ᴿshall know that I *am* the Lᴏʀᴅ, when I ᴿstretch forth mine hand

CHAP. 6	
BC 1619	
21	1 Chr. 6:37, 38
22	Lev. 10:4
23	Ruth 4:19, 20
	Mat. 1:4
23	Lev. 10:1
	Num. 3:2 & 26:60
24	Num. 26:11
25	Num. 25:7, 11
	Josh. 24:33
26	ch. 7:4
	& 12:17, 51
	Num. 33:1
27	ver. 13
	ch. 32:7 & 33:1
	Ps. 77:20
29	ver. 11
	ch. 7:2
30	ver. 12
	ch. 4:10

CHAP. 7	
BC 1491	
1	ch. 4:16
	Jer. 1:10
1	ch. 4:16
2	ch. 4:15
3	ch. 4:21
3	ch. 11:9
3	ch. 4:7
4	ch. 10:1 & 11:9
4	ch. 6:6
5	ver. 17
	ch. 8:22 & 14:4, 18
	Ps. 9:16
5	ch. 3:20

ver. 2	6
Deut. 29:5	7
& 31:2 & 34:7	
Acts 7:23, 30	
Is. 7:11	9
John 2:18 & 6:30	
ch. 4:2, 17	9
ver. 9	10
ch. 4:3	10
Gen. 41:8	11
2 Tim. 3:8	11
ver. 22	11
ch. 8:7, 18	
ch. 8:15 & 10:1,	14
20, 27	
ver. 10	15
ch. 4:2, 3	
ch. 3:18	16
ch. 3:12, 18	16
& 5:1, 3	
ver. 5	17
ch. 5:2	
ch. 4:9	17
Rev. 16:4, 6	17
ch. 8:5, 6, 16	18
ch. 8:5, 6, 16	19
& 9:22 & 10:12, 21	
& 14:21, 26	

upon Egypt, and bring out the children of Israel from among them.

6 And Moses and Aaron ᴿdid as the Lᴏʀᴅ commanded them, so did they.

7 And Moses *was* ᴿfourscore years old, and Aaron fourscore and three years old, when they spake unto Pharaoh.

The rod and serpent

8 And the Lᴏʀᴅ spake unto Moses and unto Aaron, saying,

9 When Pharaoh shall speak unto you, saying, ᴿShew a miracle for you: then thou shalt say unto Aaron, ᴿTake thy rod, and cast *it* before Pharaoh, *and* it shall become a serpent.

10 And Moses and Aaron went in unto Pharaoh, and they did so ᴿas the Lᴏʀᴅ had commanded: and Aaron cast down his rod before Pharaoh, and before his servants, and it ᴿbecame a serpent.

11 Then Pharaoh also ᴿcalled the wise men and ᴿthe sorcerers: now the magicians of Egypt, they also ᴿdid in like manner with their enchantments.

12 For they cast down every man his rod, and they became serpents: but Aaron's rod swallowed up their rods.

13 And he hardened Pharaoh's heart, that he hearkened not unto them; as the Lᴏʀᴅ had said.

14 And the Lᴏʀᴅ said unto Moses, ᴿPharaoh's heart *is* hardened, he refuseth to let the people go.

15 Get thee unto Pharaoh in the morning; lo, he goeth out unto the water; and thou shalt stand by the river's brink against he come; and ᴿthe rod which was turned to a serpent shalt thou take in thine hand.

16 And thou shalt say unto him, ᴿThe Lᴏʀᴅ God of the Hebrews hath sent me unto thee, saying, Let my people go, ᴿthat they may serve me in the wilderness: and, behold, hitherto thou wouldest not hear.

17 Thus saith the Lᴏʀᴅ, In this ᴿthou shalt know that I *am* the Lᴏʀᴅ: behold, I will smite with the rod that *is* in mine hand upon the waters which *are* in the river, and ᴿthey shall be turned ᴿto blood.

18 And the fish that *is* in the river shall die, and the river shall stink; and the Egyptians shall ᴿlothe to drink of the water of the river.

First plague

19 And the Lᴏʀᴅ spake unto Moses, Say unto Aaron, Take thy rod, and ᴿstretch out thine hand upon the waters of Egypt, upon their streams, upon their rivers, and upon their

ponds, and upon all their ᴺpools of water, that they may become blood; and *that* there may be blood throughout all the land of Egypt, both in *vessels of* wood, and in *vessels of* stone.

20 And Moses and Aaron did so, as the LORD commanded; and he ᴿlifted up the rod, and smote the waters that *were* in the river, in the sight of Pharaoh, and in the sight of his servants; and all the ᴿwaters that *were* in the river were turned to blood.

21 And the fish that *was* in the river died; and the river stank, and the Egyptians ᴿcould not drink of the water of the river; and there was blood throughout all the land of Egypt.

22 ᴿAnd the magicians of Egypt did so with their enchantments: and Pharaoh's heart was hardened, neither did he hearken unto them; ᴿas the LORD had said.

23 And Pharaoh turned and went into his house, neither did he set his heart to this also.

24 And all the Egyptians digged round about the river for water to drink; for they could not drink of the water of the river.

25 And seven days were fulfilled, after that the LORD had smitten the river.

CHAPTER 8

The plague of frogs

AND the LORD spake unto Moses, Go unto Pharaoh, and say unto him, Thus saith the LORD, Let my people go, ᴿthat they may serve me.

2 And if thou ᴿrefuse to let *them* go, behold, I will smite all thy borders with ᴿfrogs:

3 And the river shall bring forth frogs abundantly, which shall go up and come into thine house, and into ᴿthy bedchamber, and upon thy bed, and into the house of thy servants, and upon thy people, and into thine ovens, and into thy ᴺkneadingtroughs:

4 And the frogs shall come up both on thee, and upon thy people, and upon all thy servants.

5 And the LORD spake unto Moses, Say unto Aaron, ᴿStretch forth thine hand with thy rod over the streams, over the rivers, and over the ponds, and cause frogs to come up upon the land of Egypt.

6 And Aaron stretched out his hand over the waters of Egypt; and ᴿthe frogs came up, and covered the land of Egypt.

7 ᴿAnd the magicians did so with their enchantments, and brought up frogs upon the land of Egypt.

8 Then Pharaoh called for Moses and Aaron, and said, ᴿEntreat the LORD, that he

may take away the frogs from me, and from my people; and I will let the people go, that they may do sacrifice unto the LORD.

9 And Moses said unto Pharaoh, ᴺGlory over me: ᴺwhen shall I entreat for thee, and for thy servants, and for thy people, ᴺto destroy the frogs from thee and thy houses, *that* they may remain in the river only?

10 And he said, ᴺTo morrow. And he said, *Be it* according to thy word: that thou mayest know that ᴿthere is none like unto the LORD our God.

11 And the frogs shall depart from thee, and from thy houses, and from thy servants, and from thy people; they shall remain in the river only.

12 And Moses and Aaron went out from Pharaoh: and Moses ᴿcried unto the LORD because of the frogs which he had brought against Pharaoh.

13 And the LORD did according to the word of Moses; and the frogs died out of the houses, out of the villages, and out of the fields.

14 And they gathered them together upon heaps: and the land stank.

15 But when Pharaoh saw that there was ᴿrespite, ᴿhe hardened his heart, and hearkened not unto them; as the LORD had said.

The plague of lice

16 And the LORD said unto Moses, Say unto Aaron, Stretch out thy rod, and smite the dust of the land, that it may become lice throughout all the land of Egypt.

17 And they did so; for Aaron stretched out his hand with his rod, and smote the dust of the earth, and ᴿit became lice in man, and in beast; all the dust of the land became lice throughout all the land of Egypt.

18 And ᴿthe magicians did so with their enchantments to bring forth lice, but they ᴿcould not: so there were lice upon man, and upon beast.

19 Then the magicians said unto Pharaoh, This *is* ᴿthe finger of God: and Pharaoh's ᴿheart was hardened, and he hearkened not unto them; as the LORD had said.

Plague of flies

20 And the LORD said unto Moses, ᴿRise up early in the morning, and stand before Pharaoh; lo, he cometh forth to the water; and say unto him, Thus saith the LORD, ᴿLet my people go, that they may serve me.

21 Else, if thou wilt not let my people go, behold, I will send ᴺswarms *of flies* upon thee,

and upon thy servants, and upon thy people, and into thy houses: and the houses of the Egyptians shall be full of swarms *of flies,* and also the ground whereon they *are.*

22 And ᴿI will sever in that day the land of Gŏ′-shĕn, in which my people dwell, that no swarms *of flies* shall be there; to the end thou mayest know that I *am* the Loʀᴅ in the midst of the earth.

23 And I will put ᴺa division between my people and thy people: ᴺto morrow shall this sign be.

24 And the Loʀᴅ did so; and ᴿthere came a grievous swarm *of flies* into the house of Pharaoh, and *into* his servants' houses, and into all the land of Egypt: the land was ᴺcorrupted by reason of the swarm *of flies.*

25 And Pharaoh called for Moses and for Aaron, and said, Go ye, sacrifice to your God in the land.

26 And Moses said, It is not meet so to do; for we shall sacrifice ᴿthe abomination of the Egyptians to the Loʀᴅ our God: lo, shall we sacrifice the abomination of the Egyptians before their eyes, and will they not stone us?

27 We will go ᴿthree days' journey into the wilderness, and sacrifice to the Loʀᴅ our God, as ᴿhe shall command us.

28 And Pharaoh said, I will let you go, that ye may sacrifice to the Loʀᴅ your God in the wilderness; only ye shall not go very far away: ᴿentreat for me.

29 And Moses said, Behold, I go out from thee, and I will entreat the Loʀᴅ that the swarms *of flies* may depart from Pharaoh, from his servants, and from his people, to morrow: but let not Pharaoh ᴿdeal deceitfully any more in not letting the people go to sacrifice to the Loʀᴅ.

30 And Moses went out from Pharaoh, and ᴿentreated the Loʀᴅ.

31 And the Loʀᴅ did according to the word of Moses; and he removed the swarms *of flies* from Pharaoh, from his servants, and from his people; there remained not one.

Pharaoh's heart hardened

32 And Pharaoh ᴿhardened his heart at this time also, neither would he let the people go.

CHAPTER 9

Plague of murrain

THEN the Loʀᴅ said unto Moses, ᴿGo in unto Pharaoh, and tell him, Thus saith the Loʀᴅ God of the Hebrews, Let my people go, that they may serve me.

CHAP. **8**
BC 1491
22 ch. 9:4, 6, 26
& 10:23 & 11:6, 7
& 12:13
23 Heb. *a redemption*
23 Or, *by to morrow*
24 Ps. 78:45
& 105:31
24 Or, *destroyed*
26 Gen. 43:32
& 46:34
Deut. 7:25, 26
& 12:31
27 ch. 3:18
27 ch. 3:12
28 ver. 8
ch. 9:28
1 Ki. 13:6
29 ver. 15
30 ver. 12
32 ver. 15
ch. 4:21

CHAP. **9**
BC 1491
1 ch. 8:1

ch. 8:2   **2**
ch. 7:4   **3**
ch. 8:22   **4**
Ps. 78:50   **6**
ch. 7:14 & 8:32 **7**
Rev. 16:2   **9**
Deut. 28:27   **10**
ch. 8:18, 19   **11**
2 Tim. 3:9
ch. 4:21   **12**
ch. 8:20   **13**
ch. 8:10   **14**
ch. 3:20   **15**

---

2 For if thou ᴿrefuse to let *them* go, and wilt hold them still,

3 Behold, the ᴿhand of the Loʀᴅ is upon thy cattle which *is* in the field, upon the horses, upon the asses, upon the camels, upon the oxen, and upon the sheep: *there shall be* a very grievous murrain.

4 And ᴿthe Loʀᴅ shall sever between the cattle of Israel and the cattle of Egypt: and there shall nothing die of all *that is* the children's of Israel.

5 And the Loʀᴅ appointed a set time, saying, To morrow the Loʀᴅ shall do this thing in the land.

6 And the Loʀᴅ did that thing on the morrow, and ᴿall the cattle of Egypt died: but of the cattle of the children of Israel died not one.

7 And Pharaoh sent, and, behold, there was not one of the cattle of the Israelites dead. And ᴿthe heart of Pharaoh was hardened, and he did not let the people go.

Plague of boils

8 And the Loʀᴅ said unto Moses and unto Aaron, Take to you handfuls of ashes of the furnace, and let Moses sprinkle it toward the heaven in the sight of Pharaoh.

9 And it shall become small dust in all the land of Egypt, and shall be ᴿa boil breaking forth *with* blains upon man, and upon beast, throughout all the land of Egypt.

10 And they took ashes of the furnace, and stood before Pharaoh; and Moses sprinkled it up toward heaven; and it became ᴿa boil breaking forth *with* blains upon man, and upon beast.

11 And the ᴿmagicians could not stand before Moses because of the boils; for the boil was upon the magicians, and upon all the Egyptians.

12 And the Loʀᴅ hardened the heart of Pharaoh, and he hearkened not unto them; ᴿas the Loʀᴅ had spoken unto Moses.

Plague of hail

13 And the Loʀᴅ said unto Moses, ᴿRise up early in the morning, and stand before Pharaoh, and say unto him, Thus saith the Loʀᴅ God of the Hebrews, Let my people go, that they may serve me.

14 For I will at this time send all my plagues upon thine heart, and upon thy servants, and upon thy people; ᴿthat thou mayest know that *there is* none like me in all the earth.

15 For now I will ᴿstretch out my hand, that I may smite thee and thy people with pestilence; and thou shalt be cut off from the earth.

16 And in very deed for ᴿthis *cause* have I ᴺraised thee up, for to shew *in* thee my power; and that my name may be declared throughout all the earth.

17 As yet exaltest thou thyself against my people, that thou wilt not let them go?

18 Behold, to morrow about this time I will cause it to rain a very grievous hail, such as hath not been in Egypt since the foundation thereof even until now.

19 Send therefore now, *and* gather thy cattle, and all that thou hast in the field; *for upon* every man and beast which shall be found in the field, and shall not be brought home, the hail shall come down upon them, and they shall die.

20 He that feared the word of the LORD among the servants of Pharaoh made his servants and his cattle flee into the houses:

21 And he that ᴺregarded not the word of the LORD left his servants and his cattle in the field.

22 And the LORD said unto Moses, Stretch forth thine hand toward heaven, that there may be ᴿhail in all the land of Egypt, upon man, and upon beast, and upon every herb of the field, throughout the land of Egypt.

23 And Moses stretched forth his rod toward heaven: and ᴿthe LORD sent thunder and hail, and the fire ran along upon the ground; and the LORD rained hail upon the land of Egypt.

24 So there was hail, and fire mingled with the hail, very grievous, such as there was none like it in all the land of Egypt since it became a nation.

25 And the hail smote throughout all the land of Egypt all that *was* in the field, both man and beast; and the hail ᴿsmote every herb of the field, and brake every tree of the field.

26 ᴿOnly in the land of Gō'-shĕn, where the children of Israel *were*, was there no hail.

27 And Pharaoh sent, and called for Moses and Aaron, and said unto them, ᴿI have sinned this time: ᴿthe LORD *is* righteous, and I and my people *are* wicked.

28 ᴿEntreat the LORD (for *it is* enough) that there be no *more* ᴺmighty thunderings and hail; and I will let you go, and ye shall stay no longer.

29 And Moses said unto him, As soon as I am gone out of the city, I will ᴿspread abroad my hands unto the LORD; *and* the thunder shall cease, neither shall there be any more hail; that thou mayest know how that the ᴿearth *is* the LORD's.

30 But as for thee and thy servants, ᴿI know that ye will not yet fear the LORD God.

31 And the flax and the barley was smitten: ᴿfor the barley *was* in the ear, and the flax *was* bolled.

32 But the wheat and the rie were not smitten: for they *were* ᴺnot grown up.

33 And Moses went out of the city from Pharaoh, and ᴿspread abroad his hands unto the LORD: and the thunders and hail ceased, and the rain was not poured upon the earth.

34 And when Pharaoh saw that the rain and the hail and the thunders were ceased, he sinned yet more, and hardened his heart, he and his servants.

35 And ᴿthe heart of Pharaoh was hardened, neither would he let the children of Israel go; as the LORD had spoken ᴺby Moses.

CHAPTER 10

Plague of locusts

AND the LORD said unto Moses, Go in unto Pharaoh: ᴿfor I have hardened his heart, and the heart of his servants, ᴿthat I might shew these my signs before him:

2 And that ᴿthou mayest tell in the ears of thy son, and of thy son's son, what things I have wrought in Egypt, and my signs which I have done among them; that ye may know how that I *am* the LORD.

3 And Moses and Aaron came in unto Pharaoh, and said unto him, Thus saith the LORD God of the Hebrews, How long wilt thou refuse to ᴿhumble thyself before me? let my people go, that they may serve me.

4 Else, if thou refuse to let my people go, behold, to morrow will I bring the ᴿlocusts into thy coast:

5 And they shall cover the ᴺface of the earth, that one cannot be able to see the earth: and ᴿthey shall eat the residue of that which is escaped, which remaineth unto you from the hail, and shall eat every tree which groweth for you out of the field:

6 And they shall fill thy houses, and the houses of all thy servants, and the houses of all the Egyptians; which neither thy fathers, nor thy fathers' fathers have seen, since the day that they were upon the earth unto this day. And he turned himself, and went out from Pharaoh.

7 And Pharaoh's servants said unto him, How long shall this man be ᴿa snare unto us? let the men go, that they may serve the LORD their God: knowest thou not yet that Egypt is destroyed?

8 And Moses and Aaron were brought again unto Pharaoh: and he said unto them, Go,

serve the LORD your God: *but* ^Nwho *are* they that shall go?

9 And Moses said, We will go with our young and with our old, with our sons and with our daughters, with our flocks and with our herds will we go; for ^Rwe *must hold* a feast unto the LORD.

10 And he said unto them, Let the LORD be so with you, as I will let you go, and your little ones: look *to it;* for evil *is* before you.

11 Not so: go now ye *that are* men, and serve the LORD; for that ye did desire. And they were driven out from Pharaoh's presence.

12 And the LORD said unto Moses, ^RStretch out thine hand over the land of Egypt for the locusts, that they may come up upon the land of Egypt, and ^Reat every herb of the land, *even* all that the hail hath left.

13 And Moses stretched forth his rod over the land of Egypt, and the LORD brought an east wind upon the land all that day, and all *that* night; *and* when it was morning, the east wind brought the locusts.

14 And ^Rthe locusts went up over all the land of Egypt, and rested in all the coasts of Egypt: very grievous *were they;* ^Rbefore them there were no such locusts as they, neither after them shall be such.

15 For they ^Rcovered the face of the whole earth, so that the land was darkened; and they ^Rdid eat every herb of the land, and all the fruit of the trees which the hail had left: and there remained not any green thing in the trees, or in the herbs of the field, through all the land of Egypt.

16 Then Pharaoh ^Ncalled for Moses and Aaron in haste; and he said, ^RI have sinned against the LORD your God, and against you.

17 Now therefore forgive, I pray thee, my sin only this once, and ^Rentreat the LORD your God, that he may take away from me this death only.

18 And he ^Rwent out from Pharaoh, and entreated the LORD.

19 And the LORD turned a mighty strong west wind, which took away the locusts, and ^Ncast them ^Rinto the Red sea; there remained not one locust in all the coasts of Egypt.

20 But the LORD ^Rhardened Pharaoh's heart, so that he would not let the children of Israel go.

Thick darkness

21 And the LORD said unto Moses, ^RStretch out thine hand toward heaven, that there may be darkness over the land of Egypt, ^Neven darkness *which* may be felt.

22 And Moses stretched forth his hand toward heaven; and there was a ^Rthick darkness in all the land of Egypt three days:

23 They saw not one another, neither rose any from his place for three days: ^Rbut all the children of Israel had light in their dwellings.

24 And Pharaoh called unto Moses, and ^Rsaid, Go ye, serve the LORD; only let your flocks and your herds be stayed: let your ^Rlittle ones also go with you.

25 And Moses said, Thou must give ^Nus also sacrifices and burnt offerings, that we may sacrifice unto the LORD our God.

26 Our cattle also shall go with us; there shall not an hoof be left behind; for thereof must we take to serve the LORD our God; and we know not with what we must serve the LORD, until we come thither.

Pharaoh's heart unchanged

27 But the LORD ^Rhardened Pharaoh's heart, and he would not let them go.

28 And Pharaoh said unto him, Get thee from me, take heed to thyself, see my face no more; for in *that* day thou seest my face thou shalt die.

29 And Moses said, Thou hast spoken well, ^RI will see thy face again no more.

CHAPTER 11

Jewels borrowed

AND the LORD said unto Moses, Yet will I bring one plague *more* upon Pharaoh, and upon Egypt; afterwards he will let you go hence: ^Rwhen he shall let *you* go, he shall surely thrust you out hence altogether.

2 Speak now in the ears of the people, and let every man borrow of his neighbour, and every woman of her neighbour, ^Rjewels of silver, and jewels of gold.

3 ^RAnd the LORD gave the people favour in the sight of the Egyptians. Moreover the man ^RMoses *was* very great in the land of Egypt, in the sight of Pharaoh's servants, and in the sight of the people.

4 And Moses said, Thus saith the LORD, ^RAbout midnight will I go out into the midst of Egypt:

Death of firstborn foretold

5 And ^Rall the firstborn in the land of Egypt shall die, from the firstborn of Pharaoh that sitteth upon his throne, even unto the firstborn of the maidservant that *is* behind the mill; and all the firstborn of beasts.

Center reference column

CHAP. **10**

BC 1491

8 Heb. *who and who, etc.*
9 ch. 5:1
12 ch. 7:19
12 ver. 4, 5
14 Ps. 78:46 &105:34
14 Joel 2:2
15 ver. 5
15 Ps. 105:35
16 Heb. *hastened to call*
16 ch. 9:27
17 ch. 9:28 1 Ki. 13:6
18 ch. 8:30
19 Heb. *fastened*
19 Joel 2:20
20 ch. 4:21 & 11:10
21 ch. 9:22
21 Heb. *that* one *may feel darkness*

Ps. 105:28 — **22**
ch. 8:22 — **23**
ver. 8 — **24**
ver. 10 — **24**
Heb. *into our hands* — **25**
ver. 20 — **27**
ch. 4:21 & 14:4, 8
Heb. 11:27 — **29**

CHAP. **11**

BC 1491

ch. 12:31, 33, 39 — **1**
ch. 3:22 & 12:35 — **2**
ch. 3:21 & 12:36 Ps. 106:46 — **3**
2 Sam. 7:9 Esth. 9:4 — **3**
ch. 12:12, 23, 29 — **4**
ch. 12:12, 29 Amos 4:10 — **5**

6 ᴿAnd there shall be a great cry throughout all the land of Egypt, such as there was none like it, nor shall be like it any more.

7 ᴿBut against any of the children of Israel ᴿshall not a dog move his tongue, against man or beast: that ye may know how that the LORD doth put a difference between the Egyptians and Israel.

8 And ᴿall these thy servants shall come down unto me, and bow down themselves unto me, saying, Get thee out, and all the people ᴺthat follow thee: and after that I will go out. And he went out from Pharaoh in ᴺa great anger.

9 And the LORD said unto Moses, ᴿPharaoh shall not hearken unto you; that ᴿmy wonders may be multiplied in the land of Egypt.

10 And Moses and Aaron did all these wonders before Pharaoh: ᴿand the LORD hardened Pharaoh's heart, so that he would not let the children of Israel go out of his land.

CHAPTER 12

New year begun

AND the LORD spake unto Moses and Aaron in the land of Egypt, saying,

2 ᴿThis month *shall be* unto you the beginning of months: it *shall be* the first month of the year to you.

Passover instituted

3 Speak ye unto all the congregation of Israel, saying, In the tenth *day* of this month they shall take to them every man a ᴺlamb, according to the house of *their* fathers, a lamb for an house:

4 And if the household be too little for the lamb, let him and his neighbour next unto his house take *it* according to the number of the souls; every man according to his eating shall make your count for the lamb.

5 Your lamb shall be ᴿwithout blemish, a male ᴺof the first year: ye shall take *it* out from the sheep, or from the goats:

6 And ye shall keep it up until the ᴿfourteenth day of the same month: and the whole assembly of the congregation of Israel shall kill it ᴺin the evening.

7 And they shall take of the blood, and strike *it* on the two side posts and on the upper door post of the houses, wherein they shall eat it.

8 And they shall eat the flesh in that night, roast with fire, and ᴿunleavened bread; *and* with bitter *herbs* they shall eat it.

9 Eat not of it raw, nor sodden at all with water, but ᴿroast *with* fire; his head with his legs, and with the purtenance thereof.

10 ᴿAnd ye shall let nothing of it remain until the morning; and that which remaineth of it until the morning ye shall burn with fire.

11 And thus shall ye eat it; *with* your loins girded, your shoes on your feet, and your staff in your hand; and ye shall eat it in haste: ᴿit *is* the LORD's passover.

12 For I ᴿwill pass through the land of Egypt this night, and will smite all the firstborn in the land of Egypt, both man and beast; and ᴿagainst all the ᴺgods of Egypt I will execute judgment: ᴿI *am* the LORD.

13 And the blood shall be to you for a token upon the houses where ye *are:* and when I see the blood, I will pass over you, and the plague shall not be upon you ᴺto destroy *you,* when I smite the land of Egypt.

14 And this day shall be unto you ᴿfor a memorial; and ye shall keep it a ᴿfeast to the LORD throughout your generations; ye shall keep it a feast ᴿby an ordinance for ever.

15 ᴿSeven days shall ye eat unleavened bread; even the first day ye shall put away leaven out of your houses: for whosoever eateth leavened bread from the first day until the seventh day, ᴿthat soul shall be cut off from Israel.

16 And in the first day *there shall be* ᴿan holy convocation, and in the seventh day there shall be an holy convocation to you; no manner of work shall be done in them, save *that* which every ᴺman must eat, that only may be done of you.

17 And ye shall observe *the feast of* unleavened bread; for ᴿin this selfsame day have I brought your armies out of the land of Egypt: therefore shall ye observe this day in your generations by an ordinance for ever.

18 ᴿIn the first *month,* on the fourteenth day of the month at even, ye shall eat unleavened bread, until the one and twentieth day of the month at even.

19 ᴿSeven days shall there be no leaven found in your houses: for whosoever eateth that which is leavened, even that soul shall be cut off from the congregation of Israel, whether he be a stranger, or born in the land.

20 Ye shall eat nothing leavened; in all your habitations shall ye eat unleavened bread.

21 Then Moses called for all the elders of Israel, and said unto them, ᴿDraw out and take you a ᴺlamb according to your families, and kill the passover.

22 ᴿAnd ye shall take a bunch of hyssop,

and dip *it* in the blood that *is* in the basin, and [R]strike the lintel and the two side posts with the blood that *is* in the basin; and none of you shall go out at the door of his house until the morning.

23 [R]For the LORD will pass through to smite the Egyptians; and when he seeth the blood upon the lintel, and on the two side posts, the LORD will pass over the door, and [R]will not suffer [R]the destroyer to come in unto your houses to smite *you*.

24 And ye shall observe this thing for an ordinance to thee and to thy sons for ever.

25 And it shall come to pass, when ye be come to the land which the LORD will give you, [R]according as he hath promised, that ye shall keep this service.

26 [R]And it shall come to pass, when your children shall say unto you, What mean ye by this service?

27 That ye shall say, [R]It *is* the sacrifice of the LORD's passover, who passed over the houses of the children of Israel in Egypt, when he smote the Egyptians, and delivered our houses. And the people [R]bowed the head and worshipped.

28 And the children of Israel went away, and [R]did as the LORD had commanded Moses and Aaron, so did they.

Firstborn of Egyptians slain

29 [R]And it came to pass, that at midnight [R]the LORD smote all the firstborn in the land of Egypt, [R]from the firstborn of Pharaoh that sat on his throne unto the firstborn of the captive that *was* in the [N]dungeon; and all the firstborn of cattle.

30 And Pharaoh rose up in the night, he, and all his servants, and all the Egyptians; and there was a [R]great cry in Egypt; for *there was* not a house where *there was* not one dead.

31 And [R]he called for Moses and Aaron by night, and said, Rise up, *and* get you forth from among my people, [R]both ye and the children of Israel; and go, serve the LORD, as ye have said.

32 [R]Also take your flocks and your herds, as ye have said, and be gone; and [R]bless me also.

33 [R]And the Egyptians were urgent upon the people, that they might send them out of the land in haste; for they said, [R]We *be* all dead *men*.

34 And the people took their dough before it was leavened, their [N]kneadingtroughs being bound up in their clothes upon their shoulders.

35 And the children of Israel did according to the word of Moses; and they borrowed of

CHAP. 12	
BC 1491	
22 ver. 7	
23 ver. 12, 13	
23 Ezek. 9:6	
Rev. 7:3	
23 2 Sam. 24:16	
1 Cor. 10:10	
Heb. 11:28	
25 ch. 3:8, 17	
26 ch. 13:8, 14	
Deut. 32:7	
Josh. 4:6	
27 ver. 11	
27 ch. 4:31	
28 Heb. 11:28	
29 ch. 11:4	
29 Num. 8:17	
& 33:4	
Ps. 78:51	
& 105:36	
29 ch. 4:23 & 11:5	
29 Heb. *house of the pit*	
30 ch. 11:6	
Prov. 21:13	
Amos 5:17	
31 ch. 11:1	
Ps. 105:38	
31 ch. 10:9	
32 ch. 10:26	
32 Gen. 27:34	
33 ch. 11:8	
Ps. 105:38	
33 Gen. 20:3	
34 Or, *dough*, ch. 8:3	

ch. 3:22	35
ch. 3:21	36
Gen. 15:14	36
ch. 3:22	
Ps. 105:37	
Num. 33:3, 5	37
Gen. 47:11	37
Gen. 12:2	37
Num. 11:21	
Heb. *a great mixture*	38
ver. 33	39
ch. 6:1	
Gen. 15:13	40
Acts 7:6	
Gal. 3:17	
ch. 7:4	41
See Deut. 16:6	42
Heb. *a night of observations*	
Num. 9:14	43
Gen. 17:12, 13	44
Lev. 22:10	45
Num. 9:12	46
John 19:33, 36	
ver. 6	47
Num. 9:13	
Heb. *do it*	47
Num. 9:14	48
Num. 9:14	49
& 15:15, 16	
Gal. 3:28	

the Egyptians [R]jewels of silver, and jewels of gold, and raiment:

36 [R]And the LORD gave the people favour in the sight of the Egyptians, so that they lent unto them *such things as they required*. And [R]they spoiled the Egyptians.

37 And [R]the children of Israel journeyed from [R]Răm'-ĕ-sēś to Sŭc'-cōth, about [R]six hundred thousand on foot *that were* men, beside children.

38 And [N]a mixed multitude went up also with them; and flocks, and herds, *even* very much cattle.

39 And they baked unleavened cakes of the dough which they brought forth out of Egypt, for it was not leavened; because [R]they were thrust out of Egypt, and could not tarry, neither had they prepared for themselves any victual.

40 Now the sojourning of the children of Israel, who dwelt in Egypt, *was* [R]four hundred and thirty years.

41 And it came to pass at the end of the four hundred and thirty years, even the self-same day it came to pass, that all [R]the hosts of the LORD went out from the land of Egypt.

42 It *is* [R]a night[N] to be much observed unto the LORD for bringing them out from the land of Egypt: this *is* that night of the LORD to be observed of all the children of Israel in their generations.

43 And the LORD said unto Moses and Aaron, This *is* [R]the ordinance of the passover: There shall no stranger eat thereof:

44 But every man's servant that is bought for money, when thou hast [R]circumcised him, then shall he eat thereof.

45 [R]A foreigner and an hired servant shall not eat thereof.

46 In one house shall it be eaten; thou shalt not carry forth aught of the flesh abroad out of the house; [R]neither shall ye break a bone thereof.

47 [R]All the congregation of Israel shall [N]keep it.

48 And [R]when a stranger shall sojourn with thee, and will keep the passover to the LORD, let all his males be circumcised, and then let him come near and keep it; and he shall be as one that is born in the land: for no uncircumcised person shall eat thereof.

49 [R]One law shall be to him that is home-born, and unto the stranger that sojourneth among you.

50 Thus did all the children of Israel; as the LORD commanded Moses and Aaron, so did they.

51 ᴿAnd it came to pass the selfsame day, *that* the LORD did bring the children of Israel out of the land of Egypt ᴿby their armies.

CHAPTER 13

Observance of the passover

AND the LORD spake unto Moses, saying, 2 ᴿSanctify unto me all the firstborn, whatsoever openeth the womb among the children of Israel, *both* of man and of beast: it *is* mine.

3 And Moses said unto the people, ᴿRemember this day, in which ye came out from Egypt, out of the house of ᴺbondage; for ᴿby strength of hand the LORD brought you out from this *place:* ᴿthere shall no leavened bread be eaten.

4 ᴿThis day came ye out in the month Abib.

5 And it shall be when the LORD shall ᴿbring thee into the land of the Canaanites, and the Hittites, and the Amorites, and the Hī'-vītes, and the Jĕb'-ū-ṡītes, which he ᴿsware unto thy fathers to give thee, a land flowing with milk and honey, ᴿthat thou shalt keep this service in this month.

6 ᴿSeven days thou shalt eat unleavened bread, and in the seventh day *shall be* a feast to the LORD.

7 Unleavened bread shall be eaten seven days; and there shall ᴿno leavened bread be seen with thee, neither shall there be leaven seen with thee in all thy quarters.

8 And thou shalt ᴿshew thy son in that day, saying, *This is done* because of that *which* the LORD did unto me when I came forth out of Egypt.

9 And it shall be for ᴿa sign unto thee upon thine hand, and for a memorial between thine eyes, that the LORD's law may be in thy mouth: for with a strong hand hath the LORD brought thee out of Egypt.

10 ᴿThou shalt therefore keep this ordinance in his season from year to year.

11 And it shall be when the LORD shall bring thee into the land of the Canaanites, as he sware unto thee and to thy fathers, and shall give it thee,

12 ᴿThat thou shalt ᴺset apart unto the LORD all that openeth the matrix, and every firstling that cometh of a beast which thou hast; the males *shall be* the LORD's.

13 And ᴿevery firstling of an ass thou shalt redeem with a ᴺlamb; and if thou wilt not redeem it, then thou shalt break his neck: and all the firstborn of man among thy children ᴿshalt thou redeem.

14 ᴿAnd it shall be when thy son asketh thee ᴺin time to come, saying, What *is* this? that thou shalt say unto him, ᴿBy strength of hand the LORD brought us out from Egypt, from the house of bondage:

15 And it came to pass, when Pharaoh would hardly let us go, that ᴿthe LORD slew all the firstborn in the land of Egypt, both the firstborn of man, and the firstborn of beast: therefore I sacrifice to the LORD all that openeth the matrix, being males; but all the firstborn of my children I redeem.

16 And it shall be for ᴿa token upon thine hand, and for frontlets between thine eyes: for by strength of hand the LORD brought us forth out of Egypt.

The exodus begins

17 And it came to pass, when Pharaoh had let the people go, that God led them not *through* the way of the land of the Philistines, although that *was* near; for God said, Lest peradventure the people ᴿrepent when they see war, and ᴿthey return to Egypt:

18 But God ᴿled the people about, *through* the way of the wilderness of the Red sea: and the children of Israel went up ᴺharnessed out of the land of Egypt.

19 And Moses took the bones of Joseph with him: for he had straitly sworn the children of Israel, saying, ᴿGod will surely visit you; and ye shall carry up my bones away hence with you.

20 And ᴿthey took their journey from Sŭc'-cōth, and encamped in Ē'-thăm, in the edge of the wilderness.

Pillars of cloud and fire

21 And ᴿthe LORD went before them by day in a pillar of a cloud, to lead them the way; and by night in a pillar of fire, to give them light; to go by day and night:

22 He took not away the pillar of the cloud by day, nor the pillar of fire by night, *from* before the people.

CHAPTER 14

Israelites receive instructions

AND the LORD spake unto Moses, saying, 2 Speak unto the children of Israel, ᴿthat they turn and encamp before ᴿPī-hă-hī'-rōth, between ᴿMĭg'-dŏl and the sea, over against Bā'-ăl-zē'-phŏn: before it shall ye encamp by the sea.

3 For Pharaoh will say of the children of

CHAP. 12

BC 1491

51 ver. 41
51 ch. 6:26

CHAP. 13

BC 1491

2 ver. 12, 13, 15
ch. 22:29, 30
Num. 3:13
Deut. 15:19
Luke 2:23
3 ch. 12:42
Deut. 16:3
3 Heb. *servants*
3 ch. 6:1
3 ch. 12:8
4 ch. 23:15
& 34:18
Deut. 16:1
5 ch. 3:8
5 ch. 6:8
5 ch. 12:25, 26
6 ch. 12:15, 16
7 ch. 12:19
8 ver. 14
ch. 12:26
9 See ver. 16
Deut. 6:8
Mat. 23:5
10 ch. 12:14, 24
12 ver. 2
Lev. 27:26
12 Heb. *cause to pass over*
13 ch. 34:20
Num. 18:15
13 Or, *kid*
13 Num. 3:46, 47
& 18:15, 16

ch. 12:26 — 14
Deut. 6:20
Josh. 4:6, 21
Heb. *to* — 14
  morrow
ver. 3 — 14
ch. 12:29 — 15
ver. 9 — 16
ch. 14:11 — 17
Num. 14:1-4
Deut. 17:16 — 17
ch. 14:2 — 18
Num. 33:6, etc.
Or, *by five in a rank* — 18
Gen. 50:25 — 19
Josh. 24:32
Num. 33:6 — 20
ch. 14:19, 24 — 21
Num. 9:15
& 14:14
Deut. 1:33
Neh. 9:12
Ps. 78:14
& 99:7
Is. 4:5
1 Cor. 10:1

CHAP. 14

BC 1491

ch. 13:18 — 2
Num. 33:7 — 2
Jer. 44:1 — 2

Israel, [R]They *are* entangled in the land, the wilderness hath shut them in.

4 And [R]I will harden Pharaoh's heart, that he shall follow after them; and I [R]will be honoured upon Pharaoh, and upon all his host; [R]that the Egyptians may know that I *am* the LORD. And they did so.

5 And it was told the king of Egypt that the people fled: and [R]the heart of Pharaoh and of his servants was turned against the people, and they said, Why have we done this, that we have let Israel go from serving us?

6 And he made ready his chariot, and took his people with him:

7 And he took [R]six hundred chosen chariots, and all the chariots of Egypt, and captains over every one of them.

8 And the LORD [R]hardened the heart of Pharaoh king of Egypt, and he pursued after the children of Israel: and [R]the children of Israel went out with an high hand.

9 But the [R]Egyptians pursued after them, all the horses *and* chariots of Pharaoh, and his horsemen, and his army, and overtook them encamping by the sea, beside Pī-hă-hī'-rōth, before Bā'-ăl-zē'-phōn.

10 And when Pharaoh drew nigh, the children of Israel lifted up their eyes, and, behold, the Egyptians marched after them; and they were sore afraid: and the children of Israel [R]cried out unto the LORD.

11 [R]And they said unto Moses, Because *there were* no graves in Egypt, hast thou taken us away to die in the wilderness? wherefore hast thou dealt thus with us, to carry us forth out of Egypt?

12 [R]*Is* not this the word that we did tell thee in Egypt, saying, Let us alone, that we may serve the Egyptians? For *it had been* better for us to serve the Egyptians, than that we should die in the wilderness.

13 And Moses said unto the people, [R]Fear ye not, stand still, and see the salvation of the LORD, which he will shew to you to day: [N]for the Egyptians whom ye have seen to day, ye shall see them again no more for ever.

14 [R]The LORD shall fight for you, and ye shall [R]hold your peace.

15 And the Lord said unto Moses, Wherefore criest thou unto me? speak unto the children of Israel, that they go forward:

16 But [R]lift thou up thy rod, and stretch out thine hand over the sea, and divide it: and the children of Israel shall go on dry *ground* through the midst of the sea.

17 And I, behold, I will [R]harden the hearts of the Egyptians, and they shall follow them:

and I will [R]get me honour upon Pharaoh, and upon all his host, upon his chariots, and upon his horsemen.

18 And the Egyptians [R]shall know that I *am* the LORD, when I have gotten me honour upon Pharaoh, upon his chariots, and upon his horsemen.

19 And the angel of God, [R]which went before the camp of Israel, removed and went behind them; and the pillar of the cloud went from before their face, and stood behind them:

20 And it came between the camp of the Egyptians and the camp of Israel; and [R]it was a cloud and darkness *to them*, but it gave light by night *to these*: so that the one came not near the other all the night.

Israel crosses the Red sea

21 And Moses stretched out his hand over the sea; and the LORD caused the sea to go *back* by a strong east wind all that night, and [R]made the sea dry *land*, and the waters were [R]divided.

22 And [R]the children of Israel went into the midst of the sea upon the dry *ground*: and the waters *were* [R]a wall unto them on their right hand, and on their left.

23 And the Egyptians pursued, and went in after them to the midst of the sea, *even* all Pharaoh's horses, his chariots, and his horsemen.

24 And it came to pass, that in the morning watch [R]the LORD looked unto the host of the Egyptians through the pillar of fire and of the cloud, and troubled the host of the Egyptians,

25 And took off their chariot wheels, [N]that they drave them heavily: so that the Egyptians said, Let us flee from the face of Israel; for the LORD [R]fighteth for them against the Egyptians.

26 And the LORD said unto Moses, Stretch out thine hand over the sea, that the waters may come again upon the Egyptians, upon their chariots, and upon their horsemen.

27 And Moses stretched forth his hand over the sea, and the sea [R]returned to his strength when the morning appeared; and the Egyptians fled against it; and the LORD [R]overthrew[N] the Egyptians in the midst of the sea.

28 And [R]the waters returned, and [R]covered the chariots, and the horsemen, *and* all the host of Pharaoh that came into the sea after them; there remained not so much as one of them.

29 But [R]the children of Israel walked upon dry *land* in the midst of the sea; and the waters *were* a wall unto them on their right hand, and on their left.

30 Thus the Lord ^Rsaved Israel that day out of the hand of the Egyptians; and Israel ^Rsaw the Egyptians dead upon the sea shore.

31 And Israel saw that great ^Nwork which the Lord did upon the Egyptians: and the people feared the Lord, and ^Rbelieved the Lord, and his servant Moses.

CHAPTER 15

Song of Moses

THEN sang ^RMoses and the children of Israel this song unto the Lord, and spake, saying, I will sing unto the Lord, for he hath triumphed gloriously: the horse and his rider hath he thrown into the sea.

2 The Lord *is* my strength and ^Rsong, and he is become my salvation: he *is* my God, and I will prepare him ^Ran habitation; my ^Rfather's God, and I ^Rwill exalt him.

3 The Lord *is* a man of ^Rwar: the Lord *is* his ^Rname.

4 ^RPharaoh's chariots and his host hath he cast into the sea: ^Rhis chosen captains also are drowned in the Red sea.

5 ^RThe depths have covered them: ^Rthey sank into the bottom as a stone.

6 ^RThy right hand, O Lord, is become glorious in power: thy right hand, O Lord, hath dashed in pieces the enemy.

7 And in the greatness of thine ^Rexcellency thou hast overthrown them that rose up against thee: thou sentest forth thy wrath, *which* ^Rconsumed them ^Ras stubble.

8 And ^Rwith the blast of thy nostrils the waters were gathered together, ^Rthe floods stood upright as an heap, *and* the depths were congealed in the heart of the sea.

9 ^RThe enemy said, I will pursue, I will overtake, I will ^Rdivide the spoil; my lust shall be satisfied upon them; I will draw my sword, my hand shall ^Ndestroy them.

10 Thou didst ^Rblow with thy wind, ^Rthe sea covered them: they sank as lead in the mighty waters.

11 ^RWho *is* like unto thee, O Lord, among the ^Ngods? who *is* like thee, ^Rglorious in holiness, fearful *in* praises, ^Rdoing wonders?

12 Thou stretchedst out thy right hand, the earth swallowed them.

13 Thou in thy mercy hast ^Rled forth the people *which* thou hast redeemed: thou hast guided *them* in thy strength unto ^Rthy holy habitation.

14 ^RThe people shall hear, *and* be afraid: ^Rsorrow shall take hold on the inhabitants of Palestina.

15 ^RThen ^Rthe dukes of Ē'-dom shall be amazed; ^Rthe mighty men of Moab, trembling shall take hold upon them; ^Rall the inhabitants of Canaan shall melt away.

16 ^RFear and dread shall fall upon them; by the greatness of thine arm they shall be *as still* ^Ras a stone; till thy people pass over, O Lord, till the people pass over, ^R*which* thou hast purchased.

17 Thou shalt bring them in, and ^Rplant them in the mountain of thine inheritance, *in* the place, O Lord, *which* thou hast made for thee to dwell in, *in* the ^RSanctuary, O Lord, *which* thy hands have established.

18 ^RThe Lord shall reign for ever and ever.

19 For the ^Rhorse of Pharaoh went in with his chariots and with his horsemen into the sea, and ^Rthe Lord brought again the waters of the sea upon them; but the children of Israel went on dry *land* in the midst of the sea.

Miriam's song

20 And Miriam ^Rthe prophetess, ^Rthe sister of Aaron, ^Rtook a timbrel in her hand; and all the women went out after her ^Rwith timbrels and with dances.

21 And Miriam ^Ranswered them, ^RSing ye to the Lord, for he hath triumphed gloriously; the horse and his rider hath he thrown into the sea.

22 So Moses brought Israel from the Red sea, and they went out into the wilderness of ^RShur; and they went three days in the wilderness, and found no water.

Waters of Marah

23 And when they came to ^RMâr'-ăh, they could not drink of the waters of Mâr'-ăh, for they *were* bitter: therefore the name of it was called ^NMâr'-ăh.

24 And the people ^Rmurmured against Moses, saying, What shall we drink?

25 And he cried unto the Lord; and the Lord shewed him a tree, ^R*which* when he had cast into the waters, the waters were made sweet: there he ^Rmade for them a statute and an ordinance, and there ^Rhe proved them,

26 And said, ^RIf thou wilt diligently hearken to the voice of the Lord thy God, and wilt do that which is right in his sight, and wilt give ear to his commandments, and keep all his statutes, I will put none of these ^Rdiseases upon thee, which I have brought upon the Egyptians: for I *am* the Lord ^Rthat healeth thee.

27 ^RAnd they came to Ē'-lĭm, where *were* twelve wells of water, and threescore and ten

palm trees: and they encamped there by the waters.

CHAPTER 16

Wilderness of Sin

AND they [R]took their journey from Ē'-lǐm, and all the congregation of the children of Israel came unto the wilderness of [R]Sin, which *is* between Ē'-lǐm and Sī'-nâi, on the fifteenth day of the second month after their departing out of the land of Egypt.

2 And the whole congregation of the children of Israel [R]murmured against Moses and Aaron in the wilderness:

3 And the children of Israel said unto them, [R]Would to God we had died by the hand of the LORD in the land of Egypt, [R]when we sat by the flesh pots, *and* when we did eat bread to the full; for ye have brought us forth into this wilderness, to kill this whole assembly with hunger.

4 Then said the LORD unto Moses, Behold, I will rain [R]bread from heaven for you; and the people shall go out and gather [N]a certain rate every day, that I may [R]prove them, whether they will walk in my law, or no.

5 And it shall come to pass, that on the sixth day they shall prepare *that* which they bring in; and [R]it shall be twice as much as they gather daily.

6 And Moses and Aaron said unto all the children of Israel, [R]At even, then ye shall know that the LORD hath brought you out from the land of Egypt:

7 And in the morning, then ye shall see [R]the glory of the LORD; for that he heareth your murmurings against the LORD: and [R]what *are* we, that ye murmur against us?

8 And Moses said, *This shall be,* when the LORD shall give you in the evening flesh to eat, and in the morning bread to the full; for that the LORD heareth your murmurings which ye murmur against him: and what *are* we? your murmurings *are* not against us, but [R]against the LORD.

9 And Moses spake unto Aaron, Say unto all the congregation of the children of Israel, [R]Come near before the LORD: for he hath heard your murmurings.

10 And it came to pass, as Aaron spake unto the whole congregation of the children of Israel, that they looked toward the wilderness, and, behold, the glory of the LORD [R]appeared in the cloud.

Sending of quails and manna

11 And the LORD spake unto Moses, saying,

CHAP. **16**
BC 1491
1 Num. 33:10, 11
1 Ezek. 30:15
2 1 Cor. 10:10
3 Lam. 4:9
3 Num. 11:4
4 John 6:31
4 Heb. *the portion of a day in his day*
4 Deut. 8:2, 16
5 See ver. 22
Lev. 25:21
6 See ver. 12, 13 & ch. 6:7
Num. 16:28-30
7 See ver. 10
Is. 35:2 & 40:5
John 11:4, 40
7 Num. 16:11
8 See 1 Sam. 8:7
Luke 10:16
Rom. 13:2
9 Num. 16:16
10 ver. 7
ch. 13:21
Num. 16:19
1 Ki. 8:10, 11

ver. 8	12
ver. 6	12
ver. 7	12
Num. 11:31	13
Ps. 78:27, 28 & 105:40	
Num. 11:9	13
Num. 11:7	14
Deut. 8:3	
Neh. 9:15	
Ps. 78:24 & 105:40	
Or, *What is this?* or, *It is a portion*	15
John 6:31, 49, 58	15
1 Cor. 10:3	
ver. 36	16
Heb. *by the poll,* or, *head*	16
Heb. *souls*	16
2 Cor. 8:15	18
Gen. 2:3	23
ch. 20:8 & 31:15 & 35:3	
Lev. 23:3	
ver. 20	24
ch. 20:9, 10	26

12 [R]I have heard the murmurings of the children of Israel: speak unto them, saying, [R]At even ye shall eat flesh, and [R]in the morning ye shall be filled with bread; and ye shall know that I *am* the LORD your God.

13 And it came to pass, that at even [R]the quails came up, and covered the camp: and in the morning [R]the dew lay round about the host.

14 And when the dew that lay was gone up, behold, upon the face of the wilderness *there lay* [R]a small round thing, *as* small as the hoar frost on the ground.

15 And when the children of Israel saw *it,* they said one to another, [N]It *is* măn'-nă: for they wist not what it *was.* And Moses said unto them, [R]This *is* the bread which the LORD hath given you to eat.

16 This *is* the thing which the LORD hath commanded, Gather of it every man according to his eating, [R]an ō'-měr [N]for every man, *according to* the number of your [N]persons; take ye every man for *them* which *are* in his tents.

17 And the children of Israel did so, and gathered, some more, some less.

18 And when they did mete *it* with an ō'-měr, [R]he that gathered much had nothing over, and he that gathered little had no lack; they gathered every man according to his eating.

19 And Moses said, Let no man leave of it till the morning.

20 Notwithstanding they hearkened not unto Moses; but some of them left of it until the morning, and it bred worms, and stank: and Moses was wroth with them.

21 And they gathered it every morning, every man according to his eating: and when the sun waxed hot, it melted.

22 And it came to pass, *that* on the sixth day they gathered twice as much bread, two ō'-měrs for one *man:* and all the rulers of the congregation came and told Moses.

23 And he said unto them, this *is that* which the LORD hath said, To morrow *is* [R]the rest of the holy sabbath unto the LORD: bake *that* which ye will bake *to day,* and seethe that ye will seethe; and that which remaineth over lay up for you to be kept until the morning.

24 And they laid it up till the morning, as Moses bade: and it did not [R]stink, neither was there any worm therein.

25 And Moses said, Eat that to day; for to day *is* a sabbath unto the LORD: to day ye shall not find it in the field.

26 [R]Six days ye shall gather it; but on the seventh day, *which is* the sabbath, in it there shall be none.

27 And it came to pass, *that* there went out *some* of the people on the seventh day for to gather, and they found none.

28 And the Lord said unto Moses, How long ᴿrefuse ye to keep my commandments and my laws?

29 See, for that the Lord hath given you the sabbath, therefore he giveth you on the sixth day the bread of two days; abide ye every man in his place, let no man go out of his place on the seventh day.

30 So the people rested on the seventh day.

31 And the house of Israel called the name thereof Măn'-nă: and ᴿit *was* like coriander seed, white; and the taste of it *was* like wafers *made* with honey.

32 And Moses said, This *is* the thing which the Lord commandeth, Fill an ō'-mĕr of it to be kept for your generations; that they may see the bread wherewith I have fed you in the wilderness, when I brought you forth from the land of Egypt.

33 And Moses said unto Aaron, Take a pot, and put an ō'-mĕr full of măn'-nă therein, and lay it up before the Lord, to be kept for your generations.

34 As the Lord commanded Moses, so Aaron laid it up ᴿbefore the Testimony, to be kept.

35 And the children of Israel did eat măn'-nă ᴿforty years, ᴿuntil they came to a land inhabited; they did eat măn'-nă, until they came unto the borders of the land of Canaan.

36 Now an ō'-mĕr *is* the tenth *part* of an ē'-phäh.

CHAPTER 17

Water from the rock

AND ᴿall the congregation of the children of Israel journeyed from the wilderness of Sin, after their journeys, according to the commandment of the Lord, and pitched in Rĕph'-ĭ-dĭm: and *there was* no water for the people to drink.

2 ᴿWherefore the people did chide with Moses, and said, Give us water that we may drink. And Moses said unto them, Why chide ye with me? wherefore do ye ᴿtempt the Lord?

3 And the people thirsted there for water; and the people ᴿmurmured against Moses, and said, Wherefore *is* this *that* thou hast brought us up out of Egypt, to kill us and our children and our cattle with thirst?

4 And Moses ᴿcried unto the Lord, saying,

What shall I do unto this people? they be almost ready to ᴿstone me.

5 And the Lord said unto Moses, ᴿGo on before the people, and take with thee of the elders of Israel; and thy rod, wherewith ᴿthou smotest the river, take in thine hand, and go.

6 ᴿBehold, I will stand before thee there upon the rock in Hôr'-ĕb; and thou shalt smite the rock, and there shall come water out of it, that the people may drink. And Moses did so in the sight of the elders of Israel.

7 And he called the name of the place ᴿMăs'-săh,ᴺ and ᴺMĕr'-ĭ-bäh, because of the chiding of the children of Israel, and because they tempted the Lord, saying, Is the Lord among us, or not?

War with Amalek

8 ᴿThen came Ăm'-ă-lĕk, and fought with Israel in Rĕph'-ĭ-dĭm.

9 And Moses said unto ᴿJoshua, Choose us out men, and go out, fight with Ăm'-ă-lĕk: to morrow I will stand on the top of the hill with ᴿthe rod of God in mine hand.

10 So Joshua did as Moses had said to him, and fought with Ăm'-ă-lĕk: and Moses, Aaron, and Hur went up to the top of the hill.

11 And it came to pass, when Moses ᴿheld up his hand, that Israel prevailed: and when he let down his hand, Ăm'-ă-lĕk prevailed.

12 But Moses' hands *were* heavy; and they took a stone, and put *it* under him, and he sat thereon; and Aaron and Hur stayed up his hands, the one on the one side, and the other on the other side; and his hands were steady until the going down of the sun.

13 And Joshua discomfited Ăm'-ă-lĕk and his people with the edge of the sword.

14 And the Lord said unto Moses, ᴿWrite this *for* a memorial in a book, and rehearse *it* in the ears of Joshua: for ᴿI will utterly put out the remembrance of Ăm'-ă-lĕk from under heaven.

Moses builds an altar

15 And Moses built an altar, and called the name of it ᴺJĕ-hō'-văh-nĭs'-sĭ:

16 For he said, ᴺBecause ᴺthe Lord hath sworn *that* the Lord *will have* war with Ăm'-ă-lĕk from generation to generation.

CHAPTER 18

Jethro visits Moses

WHEN ᴿJĕth'-rō, the priest of Mĭd'-ĭ-ăn, Moses' father in law, heard of all that ᴿGod had done for Moses, and for Israel his

people, *and* that the Lord had brought Israel out of Egypt;

2 Then Jĕth′-rō, Moses' father in law, took Zĭp′-pǒ-răh, Moses' wife, ᴿafter he had sent her back,

3 And her ᴿtwo sons; of which the ᴿname of the one *was* ᴺGĕr′-shŏm; for he said, I have been an alien in a strange land:

4 And the name of the other *was* ᴺĔl-ĭ-ē′-zĕr; for the God of my father, *said he, was* mine help, and delivered me from the sword of Pharaoh:

5 And Jĕth′-rō, Moses' father in law, came with his sons and his wife unto Moses into the wilderness, where he encamped at ᴿthe mount of God:

6 And he said unto Moses, I thy father in law Jĕth′-rō am come unto thee, and thy wife, and her two sons with her.

7 And Moses ᴿwent out to meet his father in law, and did obeisance, and ᴿkissed him; and they asked each other of *their* ᴺwelfare; and they came into the tent.

8 And Moses told his father in law all that the Lord had done unto Pharaoh and to the Egyptians for Israel's sake, *and* all the travail that had ᴺcome upon them by the way, and *how* the Lord ᴿdelivered them.

9 And Jĕth′-rō rejoiced for all the goodness which the Lord had done to Israel, whom he had delivered out of the hand of the Egyptians.

10 And Jĕth′-rō said, ᴿBlessed *be* the Lord, who hath delivered you out of the hand of the Egyptians, and out of the hand of Pharaoh, who hath delivered the people from under the hand of the Egyptians.

11 Now I know that the Lord *is* ᴿgreater than all gods: ᴿfor in the thing wherein they dealt ᴿproudly *he was* above them.

12 And Jĕth′-rō, Moses' father in law, took a burnt offering and sacrifices for God: and Aaron came, and all the elders of Israel, to eat bread with Moses' father in law ᴿbefore God.

Jethro's counsel

13 And it came to pass on the morrow, that Moses sat to judge the people: and the people stood by Moses from the morning unto the evening.

14 And when Moses' father in law saw all that he did to the people, he said, What *is* this thing that thou doest to the people? why sittest thou thyself alone, and all the people stand by thee from morning unto even?

15 And Moses said unto his father in law, Because ᴿthe people come unto me to inquire of God:

16 When they have ᴿa matter, they come unto me; and I judge between ᴺone and another, and I do ᴿmake *them* know the statutes of God, and his laws.

17 And Moses' father in law said unto him, The thing that thou doest *is* not good.

18 ᴺThou wilt surely wear away, both thou, and this people that *is* with thee: for this thing *is* too heavy for thee; ᴿthou art not able to perform it thyself alone.

19 Hearken now unto my voice, I will give thee counsel, and ᴿGod shall be with thee: Be thou ᴿfor the people to Godward, that thou mayest ᴿbring the causes unto God:

20 And thou shalt ᴿteach them ordinances and laws, and shalt shew them ᴿthe way wherein they must walk, and ᴿthe work that they must do.

21 Moreover thou shalt provide out of all the people ᴿable men, such as ᴿfear God, ᴿmen of truth, ᴿhating covetousness; and place *such* over them, *to be* rulers of thousands, *and* rulers of hundreds, rulers of fifties, and rulers of tens:

22 And let them judge the people ᴿat all seasons: ᴿand it shall be, *that* every great matter they shall bring unto thee, but every small matter they shall judge: so shall it be easier for thyself, and ᴿthey shall bear *the burden* with thee.

23 If thou shalt do this thing, and God command thee *so,* then thou shalt be ᴿable to endure, and all this people shall also go to ᴿtheir place in peace.

Other judges chosen

24 So Moses hearkened to the voice of his father in law, and did all that he had said.

25 And ᴿMoses chose able men out of all Israel, and made them heads over the people, rulers of thousands, rulers of hundreds, rulers of fifties, and rulers of tens.

26 And they ᴿjudged the people at all seasons: the ᴿhard causes they brought unto Moses, but every small matter they judged themselves.

27 And Moses let his father in law depart; and ᴿhe went his way into his own land.

CHAPTER 19

Encampment at Sinai

IN the third month, when the children of Israel were gone forth out of the land of Egypt, the same day ᴿcame they *into* the wilderness of Sī′-nâi.

2 For they were departed from ᴿRĕph′-ĭ-dĭm, and were come *to* the desert of Sī′-nâi,

and had pitched in the wilderness; and there Israel camped before ᴿthe mount.

Moses on the mount

3 And ᴿMoses went up unto God, and the LORD ᴿcalled unto him out of the mountain, saying, Thus shalt thou say to the house of Jacob, and tell the children of Israel;

4 ᴿYe have seen what I did unto the Egyptians, and *how* ᴿI bare you on eagles' wings, and brought you unto myself.

5 Now ᴿtherefore, if ye will obey my voice indeed, and keep my covenant, then ᴿye shall be a peculiar treasure unto me above all people: for ᴿall the earth *is* mine:

6 And ye shall be unto me a ᴿkingdom of priests, and an ᴿholy nation. These *are* the words which thou shalt speak unto the children of Israel.

7 And Moses came and called for the elders of the people, and laid before their faces all these words which the LORD commanded him.

8 And ᴿall the people answered together, and said, All that the LORD hath spoken we will do. And Moses returned the words of the people unto the LORD.

9 And the LORD said unto Moses, Lo, I come unto thee ᴿin a thick cloud, ᴿthat the people may hear when I speak with thee, and ᴿbelieve thee for ever. And Moses told the words of the people unto the LORD.

10 And the LORD said unto Moses, Go unto the people, and ᴿsanctify them to day and to morrow, and let them ᴿwash their clothes,

11 And be ready against the third day: for the third day the LORD ᴿwill come down in the sight of all the people upon mount Sĭ′-naĭ.

12 And thou shalt set bounds unto the people round about, saying, Take heed to yourselves, *that ye* go *not* up into the mount, or touch the border of it: ᴿwhosoever toucheth the mount shall be surely put to death:

13 There shall not an hand touch it, but he shall surely be stoned, or shot through; whether *it be* beast or man, it shall not live: when the ᴿtrumpetᴺ soundeth long, they shall come up to the mount.

14 And Moses went down from the mount unto the people, and sanctified the people; and they washed their clothes.

15 And he said unto the people, Be ready against the third day: ᴿcome not at *your* wives.

LORD descends upon Sinai

16 And it came to pass on the third day in the morning, that there were ᴿthunders and lightnings, and a ᴿthick cloud upon the mount, and the ᴿvoice of the trumpet exceeding loud;

so that all the people that *was* in the camp ᴿtrembled.

17 And ᴿMoses brought forth the people out of the camp to meet with God; and they stood at the nether part of the mount.

18 And ᴿmount Sĭ′-naĭ was altogether on a smoke, because the LORD descended upon it ᴿin fire: ᴿand the smoke thereof ascended as the smoke of a furnace, and ᴿthe whole mount quaked greatly.

19 And when the voice of the trumpet sounded long, and waxed louder and louder, ᴿMoses spake, and ᴿGod answered him by a voice.

20 And the LORD came down upon mount Sĭ′-naĭ, on the top of the mount: and the LORD called Moses *up* to the top of the mount; and Moses went up.

21 And the LORD said unto Moses, Go down, ᴺcharge the people, lest they break through unto the LORD ᴿto gaze, and many of them perish.

22 And let the priests also, which come near to the LORD, ᴿsanctify themselves, lest the LORD ᴿbreak forth upon them.

23 And Moses said unto the LORD, The people cannot come up to mount Sĭ′-naĭ: for thou chargedst us, saying, ᴿSet bounds about the mount, and sanctify it.

24 And the LORD said unto him, Away, get thee down, and thou shalt come up, thou, and Aaron with thee: but let not the priests and the people break through to come up unto the LORD, lest he break forth upon them.

25 So Moses went down unto the people, and spake unto them.

CHAPTER 20

The commandments given

AND God spake ᴿall these words, saying, 2 ᴿI *am* the LORD thy God, which have brought thee out of the land of Egypt, ᴿout of the house of ᴺbondage.

3 ᴿThou shalt have no other gods before me.

4 ᴿThou shalt not make unto thee any graven image, or any likeness *of any thing* that *is* in heaven above, or that *is* in the earth beneath, or that *is* in the water under the earth:

5 ᴿThou shalt not bow down thyself to them, nor serve them: for I the LORD thy God *am* ᴿa jealous God, ᴿvisiting the iniquity of the fathers upon the children unto the third and fourth *generation* of them that hate me;

6 And ᴿshewing mercy unto thousands of them that love me, and keep my commandments.

7 ᴿThou shalt not take the name of the LORD

CHAP. 19
BC 1491

2 ch. 3:1, 12
3 Acts 7:38
3 ch. 3:4
4 Deut. 29:2
4 Is. 63:9
5 Deut. 5:2
5 Deut. 7:6 & 14:2, 21
1 Ki. 8:53
Ps. 135:4
5 ch. 9:29
Deut. 10:14
Job 41:11
Ps. 24:1
6 Deut. 33:2-4
1 Pet. 2:5, 9
6 Deut. 7:6
Is. 62:12
1 Cor. 3:17
8 Deut. 5:27
9 Mat. 17:5
9 Deut. 4:12, 36
John 12:29, 30
9 ch. 14:31
10 Lev. 11:44, 45
Heb. 10:22
10 ver. 14
11 ver. 16, 18
ch. 34:5
12 Heb. 12:20
13 ver. 16, 19
13 Or, *cornet*
15 1 Cor. 7:5
16 Heb. 12:18, 19
Rev. 8:5
16 ch. 40:34
2 Chr. 5:14
16 Rev. 4:1

Heb. 12:21   16
Deut. 4:10   17
Deut. 4:11   18
& 33:2
Judg. 5:5
Hab. 3:3
ch. 3:2 & 24:17   18
2 Chr. 7:1-3
Gen. 15:17   18
Ps. 144:5
Rev. 15:8
Ps. 68:8   18
Jer. 4:24
Heb. 12:26
Heb. 12:21   19
Neh. 9:13   19
Ps. 81:7
Heb. *contest*   21
See ch. 3:5   21
1 Sam. 6:19
Lev. 10:3   22
2 Sam. 6:7, 8   22
ver. 12   23

CHAP. 20
BC 1491

Deut. 5:22   1
Hos. 13:4   2
ch. 13:3   2
Heb. *servants*   2
Jer. 35:15   3
Deut. 27:15   4
Is. 44:15, 19   5
Deut. 4:24   5
Num. 14:18, 33   5
1 Ki. 21:29
Ps. 79:8
Jer. 32:18
Deut. 7:9   6
Rom. 11:28
Mat. 5:33   7

thy God in vain; for the LORD ^Rwill not hold him guiltless that taketh his name in vain.

8 ^RRemember the sabbath day, to keep it holy.

9 ^RSix days shalt thou labour, and do all thy work:

10 But the ^Rseventh day *is* the sabbath of the LORD thy God: *in it* thou shalt not do any work, thou, nor thy son, nor thy daughter, thy manservant, nor thy maidservant, nor thy cattle, ^Rnor thy stranger that *is* within thy gates:

11 For ^R*in* six days the LORD made heaven and earth, the sea, and all that in them *is,* and rested the seventh day: wherefore the LORD blessed the sabbath day, and hallowed it.

12 ^RHonour thy father and thy mother: that thy days may be long upon the land which the LORD thy God giveth thee.

13 ^RThou shalt not kill.

14 ^RThou shalt not commit adultery.

15 ^RThou shalt not steal.

16 ^RThou shalt not bear false witness against thy neighbour.

17 ^RThou shalt not covet thy neighbour's house, ^Rthou shalt not covet thy neighbour's wife, nor his manservant, nor his maidservant, nor his ox, nor his ass, nor any thing that *is* thy neighbour's.

The people fear God

18 And ^Rall the people ^Rsaw the thunderings, and the lightnings, and the noise of the trumpet, and the mountain ^Rsmoking: and when the people saw *it,* they removed, and stood afar off.

19 And they said unto Moses, ^RSpeak thou with us, and we will hear: but ^Rlet not God speak with us, lest we die.

20 And Moses said unto the people, ^RFear not: ^Rfor God is come to prove you, and ^Rthat his fear may be before your faces, that ye sin not.

21 And the people stood afar off, and Moses drew near unto ^Rthe thick darkness where God *was.*

22 And the LORD said unto Moses, Thus thou shalt say unto the children of Israel, Ye have seen that I have talked with you ^Rfrom heaven.

23 Ye shall not make ^Rwith me gods of silver, neither shall ye make unto you gods of gold.

The altar

24 An altar of earth thou shalt make unto me, and shalt sacrifice thereon thy burnt offerings, and thy peace offerings, ^Rthy sheep, and thine oxen: in all ^Rplaces where I record

---

CHAP. **20**
BC 1491

7 Mic. 6:11
8 Lev. 26:2
9 Ezek. 20:12
Luke 13:14
10 Gen. 2:2, 3
10 Neh. 13:16-19
11 Gen. 2:2
12 Lev. 19:3
Deut. 5:16
Eph. 6:2
13 Rom. 13:9
14 Deut. 5:18
15 Lev. 19:11
16 ch. 23:1
Deut. 5:20
17 Luke 12:15
Eph. 5:3, 5
Heb. 13:5
17 Mat. 5:28
18 Heb. 12:18
18 Rev. 1:10, 12
18 ch. 19:18
19 Gal. 3:19
19 Deut. 5:25
20 Is. 41:10, 13
20 Deut. 13:3
20 Prov. 16:6
Is. 8:13
21 ch. 19:16
22 Deut. 4:36
23 ch. 32:1, 2, 4
24 Lev. 1:2
24 Deut. 16:6, 11
1 Ki. 9:3
2 Chr. 6:6

Gen. 12:2   24
Deut. 27:5   25
Heb. *build them*   25
with *hewing*

CHAP. **21**
BC 1491

Deut. 4:14   1
Jer. 34:14   2
Heb. *with his body* 3
Deut. 15:16, 17   5
Heb. *saying shall   5
say*
ch. 12:12   6
Ps. 40:6   6
Neh. 5:5   7
Heb. *be evil in   8
the eyes of, etc.*
1 Cor. 7:5   10
Gen. 9:6   12
Mat. 26:52
Deut. 19:4, 5   13
1 Sam. 24:4,   13
10, 18
Num. 35:11   13
Deut. 19:3
Josh. 20:2
Deut. 19:11, 12   14
Heb. 10:26
1 Ki. 2:28-34   14

---

my name I will come unto thee, and I will ^Rbless thee.

25 And ^Rif thou wilt make me an altar of stone, thou shalt not ^Nbuild it of hewn stone: for if thou lift up thy tool upon it, thou hast polluted it.

26 Neither shalt thou go up by steps unto mine altar, that thy nakedness be not discovered thereon.

CHAPTER 21

Laws concerning servants

NOW these *are* the judgments which thou shalt ^Rset before them.

2 ^RIf thou buy an Hebrew servant, six years he shall serve: and in the seventh he shall go out free for nothing.

3 If he came in ^Nby himself, he shall go out by himself: if he were married, then his wife shall go out with him.

4 If his master have given him a wife, and she have born him sons or daughters; the wife and her children shall be her master's, and he shall go out by himself.

5 ^RAnd if the servant ^Nshall plainly say, I love my master, my wife, and my children; I will not go out free:

6 Then his master shall bring him unto the ^Rjudges; he shall also bring him to the door, or unto the door post; and his master shall ^Rbore his ear through with an awl; and he shall serve him for ever.

7 And if a man ^Rsell his daughter to be a maidservant, she shall not go out as the menservants do.

8 If she ^Nplease not her master, who hath betrothed her to himself, then shall he let her be redeemed: to sell her unto a strange nation he shall have no power, seeing he hath dealt deceitfully with her.

9 And if he have betrothed her unto his son, he shall deal with her after the manner of daughters.

10 If he take him another *wife;* her food, her raiment, ^Rand her duty of marriage, shall he not diminish.

11 And if he do not these three unto her, then shall she go out free without money.

Crimes with death penalty

12 ^RHe that smiteth a man, so that he die, shall be surely put to death.

13 And ^Rif a man lie not in wait, but God ^Rdeliver *him* into his hand; then ^RI will appoint thee a place whither he shall flee.

14 But if a man come ^Rpresumptuously upon his neighbour, to slay him with guile; ^Rthou

shalt take him from mine altar, that he may die.

15 And he that smiteth his father, or his mother, shall be surely put to death.

16 And ᴿhe that stealeth a man, and ᴿselleth him, or if he be ᴿfound in his hand, he shall surely be put to death.

17 And ᴿhe that ᴺcurseth his father, or his mother, shall be surely put to death.

Personal injury laws

18 And if men strive together, and one smite ᴺanother with a stone, or with *his* fist, and he die not, but keepeth *his* bed:

19 If he rise again, and walk abroad ᴿupon his staff, then shall he that smote *him* be quit: only he shall pay *for* ᴺthe loss of his time, and shall cause *him* to be thoroughly healed.

20 And if a man smite his servant, or his maid, with a rod, and he die under his hand; he shall be surely ᴺpunished.

21 Notwithstanding, if he continue a day or two, he shall not be punished: for he *is* his money.

22 If men strive, and hurt a woman with child, so that her fruit depart *from her,* and yet no mischief follow: he shall be surely punished, according as the woman's husband will lay upon him; and he shall ᴿpay as the judges *determine.*

23 And if *any* mischief follow, then thou shalt give life for life,

24 ᴿEye for eye, tooth for tooth, hand for hand, foot for foot,

25 Burning for burning, wound for wound, stripe for stripe.

26 And if a man smite the eye of his servant, or the eye of his maid, that it perish; he shall let him go free for his eye's sake.

27 And if he smite out his manservant's tooth, or his maidservant's tooth; he shall let him go free for his tooth's sake.

28 If an ox gore a man or a woman, that they die: then ᴿthe ox shall be surely stoned, and his flesh shall not be eaten; but the owner of the ox *shall be* quit.

29 But if the ox were wont to push with his horn in time past, and it hath been testified to his owner, and he hath not kept him in, but that he hath killed a man or a woman; the ox shall be stoned, and his owner also shall be put to death.

30 If there be laid on him a sum of money, then he shall give for ᴿthe ransom of his life whatsoever is laid upon him.

31 Whether he have gored a son, or have gored a daughter, according to this judgment shall it be done unto him.

CHAP. 21
BC 1491
16 Deut. 24:7
16 Gen. 37:28
16 ch. 22:4
17 Mark 7:10
17 Or, *revileth*
18 Or, *his neighbour*
19 2 Sam. 3:29
19 Heb. *his ceasing*
20 Heb. *avenged,* Gen. 4:15, 24
22 ver. 30 Deut. 22:18, 19
24 Lev. 24:20 Deut. 19:21 Mat. 5:38
28 Gen. 9:5
30 ver. 22 Num. 35:31

See Zech.   32
11:12, 13
Mat. 26:15
& 27:3, 9
ver. 28   32

CHAP. 22
BC 1491
Or, *goat*   1
2 Sam. 12:6   1
See Prov. 6:31
Luke 19:8
Mat. 24:43   2
Num. 35:27   2
ch. 21:2   3
ch. 21:16   4
See ver. 1, 7   4
Prov. 6:31
ver. 4   7
ch. 21:6   8
ver. 28
Deut. 25:1   9
2 Chr. 19:10

32 If the ox shall push a manservant or a maidservant; he shall give unto their master ᴿthirty shē'-kĕls of silver, and the ᴿox shall be stoned.

Injury to livestock

33 And if a man shall open a pit, or if a man shall dig a pit, and not cover it, and an ox or an ass fall therein;

34 The owner of the pit shall make *it* good, *and* give money unto the owner of them; and the dead *beast* shall be his.

35 And if one man's ox hurt another's, that he die; then they shall sell the live ox, and divide the money of it; and the dead *ox* also they shall divide.

36 Or if it be known that the ox hath used to push in time past, and his owner hath not kept him in; he shall surely pay ox for ox; and the dead shall be his own.

CHAPTER 22

Judgments for damage

IF a man shall steal an ox, or a ᴺsheep, and kill it, or sell it; he shall restore five oxen for an ox, and ᴿfour sheep for a sheep.

2 If a thief be found ᴿbreaking up, and be smitten that he die, *there shall* ᴿno blood *be shed* for him.

3 If the sun be risen upon him, *there shall be* blood *shed* for him; *for* he should make full restitution; if he have nothing, then he shall be ᴿsold for his theft.

4 If the theft be certainly ᴿfound in his hand alive, whether it be ox, or ass, or sheep; he shall ᴿrestore double.

5 If a man shall cause a field or vineyard to be eaten, and shall put in his beast, and shall feed in another man's field; of the best of his own field, and of the best of his own vineyard, shall he make restitution.

6 If fire break out, and catch in thorns, so that the stacks of corn, or the standing corn, or the field, be consumed *therewith;* he that kindled the fire shall surely make restitution.

7 If a man shall deliver unto his neighbour money or stuff to keep, and it be stolen out of the man's house; ᴿif the thief be found, let him pay double.

8 If the thief be not found, then the master of the house shall be brought unto the ᴿjudges, *to see* whether he have put his hand unto his neighbour's goods.

9 For all manner of trespass, *whether it be* for ox, for ass, for sheep, for raiment, *or* for any manner of lost thing, which *another* challengeth to be his, the ᴿcause of both parties

shall come before the judges; *and* whom the judges shall condemn, he shall pay double unto his neighbour.

10 If a man deliver unto his neighbour an ass, or an ox, or a sheep, or any beast, to keep; and it die, or be hurt, or driven away, no man seeing *it:*

11 *Then* shall an [R]oath of the LORD be between them both, that he hath not put his hand unto his neighbour's goods; and the owner of it shall accept *thereof,* and he shall not make *it* good.

12 And [R]if it be stolen from him, he shall make restitution unto the owner thereof.

13 If it be torn in pieces, *then* let him bring it *for* witness, *and* he shall not make good that which was torn.

14 And if a man borrow *aught* of his neighbour, and it be hurt, or die, the owner thereof *being* not with it, he shall surely make *it* good.

15 *But* if the owner thereof *be* with it, he shall not make *it* good: if it *be* an hired *thing,* it came for his hire.

Laws of human relations

16 And [R]if a man entice a maid that is not betrothed, and lie with her, he shall surely endow her to be his wife.

17 If her father utterly refuse to give her unto him, he shall [N]pay money according to the [R]dowry of virgins.

18 [R]Thou shalt not suffer a witch to live.

19 [R]Whosoever lieth with a beast shall surely be put to death.

20 [R]He that sacrificeth unto *any* god, save unto the LORD only, he shall be utterly destroyed.

21 [R]Thou shalt neither vex a stranger, nor oppress him: for ye were strangers in the land of Egypt.

22 [R]Ye shall not afflict any widow, or fatherless child.

23 If thou afflict them in any wise, and they [R]cry at all unto me, I will surely [R]hear their cry;

24 And my [R]wrath shall wax hot, and I will kill you with the sword; and [R]your wives shall be widows, and your children fatherless.

Laws of usury

25 [R]If thou lend money to *any of* my people *that is* poor by thee, thou shalt not be to him as an usurer, neither shalt thou lay upon him usury.

26 [R]If thou at all take thy neighbour's raiment to pledge, thou shalt deliver it unto him by that the sun goeth down:

27 For that *is* his covering only, it *is* his

CHAP. **22**	
BC 1491	
11 Heb. 6:16	
12 Gen. 31:39	
16 Deut. 22:28, 29	
17 Heb. *weigh,* Gen. 23:16	
17 Gen. 34:12	
18 1 Sam. 28:3	
19 Lev. 18:23	
20 Deut. 17:2, 3, 5	
21 Deut. 10:19	
22 Jas. 1:27	
23 Luke 18:7	
23 Ps. 18:6	
24 Ps. 69:24	
24 Ps. 109:9	
25 Ps. 15:5	
26 Deut. 24:6	

ch. 34:6	27
Eccl. 10:20	28
Or, *judges,* Ps. 82:6	28
ch. 23:16	29
Heb. *thy fulness*	29
Heb. *tear*	29
ch. 13:2, 12	29
Deut. 15:19	30
Lev. 22:27	30
Lev. 19:2	31
Ezek. 4:14	31

CHAP. **23**	
BC 1491	
Ps. 101:5	1
Or, *receive*	1
Acts 6:11	1
Gen. 7:1	2
Lev. 19:15	2
Heb. *answer*	2
Rom. 12:20	4
Deut. 22:4	5
Or, *wilt thou cease to help him?* or, *and wouldest cease to leave* thy business *for him: thou shalt surely leave* it to join *with him*	5
Eccl. 5:8	6
Eph. 4:25	7
Mat. 27:4	7
Rom. 1:18	7
Prov. 15:27	8
Heb. *the seeing*	8
ch. 22:21	9
Heb. *soul*	9
Lev. 25:3, 4	10
Or, *olive trees*	11
Luke 13:14	12

raiment for his skin: wherein shall he sleep? and it shall come to pass, when he crieth unto me, that I will hear; for I *am* [R]gracious.

Duties to God

28 [R]Thou shalt not revile the [N]gods, nor curse the ruler of thy people.

29 Thou shalt not delay *to offer* [R]the[N] first of thy ripe fruits, and of thy [N]liquors: [R]the firstborn of thy sons shalt thou give unto me.

30 [R]Likewise shalt thou do with thine oxen, *and* with thy sheep: [R]seven days it shall be with his dam; on the eighth day thou shalt give it me.

31 And ye shall be [R]holy men unto me: [R]neither shall ye eat *any* flesh *that is* torn of beasts in the field; ye shall cast it to the dogs.

CHAPTER 23

Laws of honesty

THOU [R]shalt not [N]raise a false report: put not thine hand with the wicked to be an [R]unrighteous witness.

2 [R]Thou shalt not follow a multitude to *do* evil; [R]neither shalt thou [N]speak in a cause to decline after many to wrest *judgment:*

3 Neither shalt thou countenance a poor man in his cause.

4 [R]If thou meet thine enemy's ox or his ass going astray, thou shalt surely bring it back to him again.

5 [R]If thou see the ass of him that hateth thee lying under his burden, [N]and wouldest forbear to help him, thou shalt surely help with him.

6 [R]Thou shalt not wrest the judgment of thy poor in his cause.

7 [R]Keep thee far from a false matter; [R]and the innocent and righteous slay thou not: for [R]I will not justify the wicked.

8 And [R]thou shalt take no gift: for the gift blindeth [N]the wise, and perverteth the words of the righteous.

9 Also [R]thou shalt not oppress a stranger: for ye know the [N]heart of a stranger, seeing ye were strangers in the land of Egypt.

Laws of the sabbath

10 And [R]six years thou shalt sow thy land, and shalt gather in the fruits thereof:

11 But the seventh *year* thou shalt let it rest and lie still; that the poor of thy people may eat: and what they leave the beasts of the field shall eat. In like manner thou shalt deal with thy vineyard, *and* with thy [N]oliveyard.

12 [R]Six days thou shalt do thy work, and on the seventh day thou shalt rest: that thine

ox and thine ass may rest, and the son of thy handmaid, and the stranger, may be refreshed.

13 And in all *things* that I have said unto you ᴿbe circumspect: and ᴿmake no mention of the name of other gods, neither let it be heard out of thy mouth.

Three annual feasts

14 ᴿThree times thou shalt keep a feast unto me in the year.

15 ᴿThou shalt keep the feast of unleavened bread: (thou shalt eat unleavened bread seven days, as I commanded thee, in the time appointed of the month Abib; for in it thou camest out from Egypt: ᴿand none shall appear before me empty:)

16 ᴿAnd the feast of harvest, the firstfruits of thy labours, which thou hast sown in the field: and ᴿthe feast of ingathering, *which is* in the end of the year, when thou hast gathered in thy labours out of the field.

17 ᴿThree times in the year all thy males shall appear before the Lord GOD.

18 ᴿThou shalt not offer the blood of my sacrifice with leavened bread; neither shall the fat of my ᴺsacrifice remain until the morning.

19 ᴿThe first of the firstfruits of thy land thou shalt bring into the house of the LORD thy God. ᴿThou shalt not seethe a kid in his mother's milk.

An Angel promised

20 ᴿBehold, I send an Angel before thee, to keep thee in the way, and to bring thee into the place which I have prepared.

21 Beware of him, and obey his voice, ᴿprovoke him not; for he will ᴿnot pardon your transgressions: for ᴿmy name *is* in him.

22 But if thou shalt indeed obey his voice, and do all that I speak; then ᴿI will be an enemy unto thine enemies, and ᴺan adversary unto thine adversaries.

23 ᴿFor mine Angel shall go before thee, and ᴿbring thee in unto the Amorites, and the Hittites, and the Pĕ-rĭz′-zītes, and the Canaanites, the Hī′-vītes, and the Jĕb′-ū-sītes: and I will cut them off.

24 Thou shalt not ᴿbow down to their gods, nor serve them, ᴿnor do after their works: ᴿbut thou shalt utterly overthrow them, and quite break down their images.

25 And ye shall ᴿserve the LORD your God, and ᴿhe shall bless thy bread, and thy water; and ᴿI will take sickness away from the midst of thee.

26 ᴿThere shall nothing cast their young, nor be barren, in thy land: the number of thy days I will ᴿfulfil.

27 I will send ᴿmy fear before thee, and will ᴿdestroy all the people to whom thou shalt come, and I will make all thine enemies turn their ᴺbacks unto thee.

28 And ᴿI will send hornets before thee, which shall drive out the Hī′-vīte, the Canaanite, and the Hittite, from before thee.

29 ᴿI will not drive them out from before thee in one year; lest the land become desolate, and the beast of the field multiply against thee.

30 By little and little I will drive them out from before thee, until thou be increased, and inherit the land.

31 And ᴿI will set thy bounds from the Red sea even unto the sea of the Philistines, and from the desert unto the river: for I will ᴿdeliver the inhabitants of the land into your hand; and thou shalt drive them out before thee.

32 ᴿThou shalt make no covenant with them, nor with their gods.

33 They shall not dwell in thy land, lest they make thee sin against me: for if thou serve their gods, ᴿit will surely be a snare unto thee.

CHAPTER 24

Israel promises obedience

AND he said unto Moses, Come up unto the LORD, thou, and Aaron, ᴿNadab, and Ă-bī′-hū, ᴿand seventy of the elders of Israel; and worship ye afar off.

2 And Moses alone shall come near the LORD: but they shall not come nigh; neither shall the people go up with him.

3 And Moses came and told the people all the words of the LORD, and all the judgments: and all the people answered with one voice, and said, ᴿAll the words which the LORD hath said will we do.

4 And Moses ᴿwrote all the words of the LORD, and rose up early in the morning, and builded an altar under the hill, and twelve ᴿpillars, according to the twelve tribes of Israel.

5 And he sent young men of the children of Israel, which offered burnt offerings, and sacrificed peace offerings of oxen unto the LORD.

6 And Moses ᴿtook half of the blood, and put *it* in basins; and half of the blood he sprinkled on the altar.

7 And he ᴿtook the book of the covenant, and read in the audience of the people: and they said, All that the LORD hath said will we do, and be obedient.

8 And Moses took the blood, and sprinkled *it* on the people, and said, Behold ᴿthe blood

Center reference column

CHAP. **23**
BC 1491
13 1 Tim. 4:16
13 Num. 32:38
14 ch. 34:23
15 ch. 12:15
15 ch. 34:20
16 ch. 34:22
16 Deut. 16:13
17 Deut. 16:16
18 Deut. 16:4
18 Or, *feast*
19 Deut. 26:10
19 Deut. 14:21
20 ch. 14:19
21 Num. 14:11
Ps. 78:40, 56
21 Is. 9:6
Jer. 23:6
22 Deut. 30:7
Jer. 30:20
22 Or, *I will afflict them that afflict thee*
23 ver. 20
23 Josh. 24:8
24 ch. 20:5
24 Deut. 12:30, 31
24 Num. 33:52
24 Deut. 6:13
Mat. 4:10
25 Deut. 28:5
25 ch. 15:26
Deut. 7:15
26 Deut. 7:14 & 28:4
Mal. 3:11
26 1 Chr. 23:1

Deut. 2:25   27
Deut. 7:23   27
Heb. *neck*   27
Josh. 24:12   28
Deut. 7:22   29
Gen. 15:18   31
Deut. 11:24
1 Ki. 4:21, 24
Josh. 21:44   31
ch. 34:12, 15   32
1 Sam. 18:21   33
Ps. 106:36

CHAP. **24**
BC 1491
Lev. 10:1, 2   1
ch. 1:5   1
Num. 11:16
ver. 7   3
ch. 19:8
Deut. 5:27
Gal. 3:19
Deut. 31:9   4
Gen. 28:18   4
Heb. 9:18   6
Heb. 9:19   7
1 Pet. 1:2   8

of the covenant, which the LORD hath made with you concerning all these words.

9 Then went up Moses, and Aaron, Nadab, and Ă-bĭ'-hū, and seventy of the elders of Israel:

10 And they ᴿsaw the God of Israel: and *there was* under his feet as it were a paved work of a ᴿsapphire stone, and as it were the ᴿbody of heaven in *his* clearness.

11 And upon the nobles of the children of Israel he ᴿlaid not his hand: also ᴿthey saw God, and did ᴿeat and drink.

Moses ascends the mount

12 And the LORD said unto Moses, ᴿCome up to me into the mount, and be there: and I will give thee ᴿtables of stone, and a law, and commandments which I have written; that thou mayest teach them.

13 And Moses rose up, and ᴿhis minister Joshua: and Moses went up into the mount of God.

14 And he said unto the elders, Tarry ye here for us, until we come again unto you: and, behold, Aaron and Hur *are* with you: if any man have any matters to do, let him come unto them.

15 And Moses went up into the mount, and ᴿa cloud covered the mount.

16 And ᴿthe glory of the LORD abode upon mount Sī'-nâĭ, and the cloud covered it six days: and the seventh day he called unto Moses out of the midst of the cloud.

17 And the sight of the glory of the LORD *was* like ᴿdevouring fire on the top of the mount in the eyes of the children of Israel.

18 And Moses went into the midst of the cloud, and gat him up into the mount: and ᴿMoses was in the mount forty days and forty nights.

CHAPTER 25

Offering for the tabernacle

AND the LORD spake unto Moses, saying, 2 Speak unto the children of Israel, that they ᴺbring me an ᴺoffering: ᴿof every man that giveth it willingly with his heart ye shall take my offering.

3 And this *is* the offering which ye shall take of them; gold, and silver, and brass,

4 And blue, and purple, and scarlet, and ᴺfine linen, and goats' *hair,*

5 And rams' skins dyed red, and badgers' skins, and shĭt'-tĭm wood,

6 ᴿOil for the light, ᴿspices for anointing oil, and for ᴿsweet incense,

7 Onyx stones, and stones to be set in the

CHAP. **24**
BC 1491
10 John 1:18
1 John 4:12
10 Ezek. 1:26
Rev. 4:3
10 Mat. 17:2
11 ch. 19:21
11 Gen. 32:30
Judg. 13:22
11 1 Cor. 10:18
12 ver. 2, 15
12 ch. 32:15
13 ch. 32:17
15 ch. 19:9
Mat. 17:5
16 ch. 16:10
17 ch. 3:2
Deut. 4:36
Heb. 12:18, 29
18 ch. 34:28
Deut. 9:9

CHAP. **25**
BC 1491
2 Heb. *take for me*
2 Or, *heave offering*
2 ch. 35:5, 21
1 Chr. 29:3, 5, 9, 14
Ezra 2:68
Neh. 11:2
2 Cor. 8:12 & 9:7
4 Or, *silk,*
Gen. 41:42
6 ch. 27:20
6 ch. 30:23
6 ch. 30:34

ch. 28:4, 6	7
ch. 28:15	7
ch. 36:1, 3, 4	8
Lev. 4:6	
& 10:4 & 21:12	
Heb. 9:1, 2	
ch. 29:45	8
1 Ki. 6:13	
2 Cor. 6:16	
Heb. 3:6	
Rev. 21:3	
ver. 40	9
ch. 37:1	10
Deut. 10:3	
Heb. 9:4	
1 Ki. 8:8	15
ch. 16:34	16
& 31:18	
Deut. 31:26	
1 Ki. 8:9	
2 Ki. 11:12	
Heb. 9:4	
ch. 37:6	17
Rom. 3:25	
Heb. 9:5	
Or, *of the matter*	19
of the mercy seat	
1 Ki. 8:7	20
1 Chr. 28:18	
Heb. 9:5	
ch. 26:34	21
ver. 16	21
ch. 29:42, 43	22
Num. 7:89	22
1 Sam. 4:4	
2 Sam. 6:2	
2 Ki. 19:15	
Ps. 80:1	
Is. 37:16	
ch. 37:10	23
1 Ki. 7:48	
2 Chr. 4:8	
Heb. 9:2	

ᴿē'-phŏd, and in the ᴿbreastplate.

8 And let them make me a ᴿsanctuary; that ᴿI may dwell among them.

9 ᴿAccording to all that I shew thee, *after* the pattern of the tabernacle, and the pattern of all the instruments thereof, even so shall ye make *it.*

Furniture of the tabernacle

10 ᴿAnd they shall make an ark *of* shĭt'-tĭm wood: two cubits and a half *shall be* the length thereof, and a cubit and a half the breadth thereof, and a cubit and a half the height thereof.

11 And thou shalt overlay it with pure gold, within and without shalt thou overlay it, and shalt make upon it a crown of gold round about.

12 And thou shalt cast four rings of gold for it, and put *them* in the four corners thereof; and two rings *shall be* in the one side of it, and two rings in the other side of it.

13 And thou shalt make staves *of* shĭt'-tĭm wood, and overlay them with gold.

14 And thou shalt put the staves into the rings by the sides of the ark, that the ark may be borne with them.

15 ᴿThe staves shall be in the rings of the ark: they shall not be taken from it.

16 And thou shalt put into the ark ᴿthe testimony which I shall give thee.

17 And ᴿthou shalt make a mercy seat *of* pure gold: two cubits and a half *shall be* the length thereof, and a cubit and a half the breadth thereof.

18 And thou shalt make two chĕr'-ū-bĭms *of* gold, *of* beaten work shalt thou make them, in the two ends of the mercy seat.

19 And make one cherub on the one end, and the other cherub on the other end: *even* ᴺof the mercy seat shall ye make the chĕr'-ū-bĭms on the two ends thereof.

20 And ᴿthe chĕr'-ū-bĭms shall stretch forth *their* wings on high, covering the mercy seat with their wings, and their faces *shall look* one to another; toward the mercy seat shall the faces of the chĕr'-ū-bĭms be.

21 ᴿAnd thou shalt put the mercy seat above upon the ark; and ᴿin the ark thou shalt put the testimony that I shall give thee.

22 And ᴿthere I will meet with thee, and I will commune with thee from above the mercy seat, from ᴿbetween the two chĕr'-ū-bĭms which *are* upon the ark of the testimony, of all *things* which I will give thee in commandment unto the children of Israel.

23 ᴿThou shalt also make a table *of* shĭt'-tĭm wood: two cubits *shall be* the length thereof,

and a cubit the breadth thereof, and a cubit and a half the height thereof.

24 And thou shalt overlay it with pure gold, and make thereto a crown of gold round about.

25 And thou shalt make unto it a border of an hand breadth round about, and thou shalt make a golden crown to the border thereof round about.

26 And thou shalt make for it four rings of gold, and put the rings in the four corners that *are* on the four feet thereof.

27 Over against the border shall the rings be for places of the staves to bear the table.

28 And thou shalt make the staves *of* shĭt′-tĭm wood, and overlay them with gold, that the table may be borne with them.

29 And thou shalt make ᴿthe dishes thereof, and spoons thereof, and covers thereof, and bowls thereof, ᴺto cover withal: *of* pure gold shalt thou make them.

30 And thou shalt set upon the table ᴿshew-bread before me alway.

31 ᴿAnd thou shalt make a candlestick *of* pure gold: *of* beaten work shall the candlestick be made: his shaft, and his branches, his bowls, his knops, and his flowers, shall be of the same.

32 And six branches shall come out of the sides of it; three branches of the candlestick out of the one side, and three branches of the candlestick out of the other side:

33 ᴿThree bowls made like unto almonds, *with* a knop and a flower in one branch; and three bowls made like almonds in the other branch, *with* a knop and a flower: so in the six branches that come out of the candlestick.

34 And ᴿin the candlestick *shall be* four bowls made like unto almonds, *with* their knops and their flowers.

35 And *there shall be* a knop under two branches of the same, and a knop under two branches of the same, and a knop under two branches of the same, according to the six branches that proceed out of the candlestick.

36 Their knops and their branches shall be of the same: all it *shall be* one beaten work *of* pure gold.

37 And thou shalt make the seven lamps thereof: and ᴿthey shall ᴺlight the lamps thereof, that they may ᴿgive light over against ᴺit.

38 And the tongs thereof, and the snuffdishes thereof, *shall be of* pure gold.

39 *Of* a talent of pure gold shall he make it, with all these vessels.

40 And ᴿlook that thou make *them* after their pattern, ᴺwhich was shewed thee in the mount.

CHAPTER 26

Tabernacle curtains

MOREOVER ᴿthou shalt make the tabernacle *with* ten curtains *of* fine twined linen, and blue, and purple, and scarlet: *with* chĕr′-ū-bĭms ᴺof cunning work shalt thou make them.

2 The length of one curtain *shall be* eight and twenty cubits, and the breadth of one curtain four cubits: and every one of the curtains shall have one measure.

3 The five curtains shall be coupled together one to another; and *other* five curtains *shall be* coupled one to another.

4 And thou shalt make loops of blue upon the edge of the one curtain from the selvedge in the coupling; and likewise shalt thou make in the uttermost edge of *another* curtain, in the coupling of the second.

5 Fifty loops shalt thou make in the one curtain, and fifty loops shalt thou make in the edge of the curtain that *is* in the coupling of the second; that the loops may take hold one of another.

6 And thou shalt make fifty taches of gold, and couple the curtains together with the taches: and it shall be one tabernacle.

7 And ᴿthou shalt make curtains *of* goats' *hair* to be a covering upon the tabernacle: eleven curtains shalt thou make.

8 The length of one curtain *shall be* thirty cubits, and the breadth of one curtain four cubits: and the eleven curtains *shall be all* of one measure.

9 And thou shalt couple five curtains by themselves, and six curtains by themselves, and shalt double the sixth curtain in the forefront of the tabernacle.

10 And thou shalt make fifty loops on the edge of the one curtain *that is* outmost in the coupling, and fifty loops in the edge of the curtain which coupleth the second.

11 And thou shalt make fifty taches of brass, and put the taches into the loops, and couple the ᴺtent together, that it may be one.

12 And the remnant that remaineth of the curtains of the tent, the half curtain that remaineth, shall hang over the backside of the tabernacle.

13 And a cubit on the one side, and a cubit on the other side ᴺof that which remaineth in the length of the curtains of the tent, it shall hang over the sides of the tabernacle on this side and on that side, to cover it.

14 And ᴿthou shalt make a covering for the tent *of* rams' skins dyed red, and a covering above *of* badgers' skins.

Tabernacle frames

15 And thou shalt make boards for the tabernacle *of* shĭt'-tĭm wood standing up.

16 Ten cubits *shall be* the length of a board, and a cubit and a half *shall be* the breadth of one board.

17 Two ᴺtenons *shall there be* in one board, set in order one against another: thus shalt thou make for all the boards of the tabernacle.

18 And thou shalt make the boards for the tabernacle, twenty boards on the south side southward.

19 And thou shalt make forty sockets of silver under the twenty boards; two sockets under one board for his two tenons, and two sockets under another board for his two tenons.

20 And for the second side of the tabernacle on the north side *there shall be* twenty boards:

21 And their forty sockets *of* silver; two sockets under one board, and two sockets under another board.

22 And for the sides of the tabernacle westward thou shalt make six boards.

23 And two boards shalt thou make for the corners of the tabernacle in the two sides.

24 And they shall be ᴺcoupled together beneath, and they shall be coupled together above the head of it unto one ring: thus shall it be for them both; they shall be for the two corners.

25 And they shall be eight boards, and their sockets *of* silver, sixteen sockets; two sockets under one board, and two sockets under another board.

26 And thou shalt make bars *of* shĭt'-tĭm wood; five for the boards of the one side of the tabernacle,

27 And five bars for the boards of the other side of the tabernacle, and five bars for the boards of the side of the tabernacle, for the two sides westward.

28 And the middle bar in the midst of the boards shall reach from end to end.

29 And thou shalt overlay the boards with gold, and make their rings *of* gold *for* places for the bars: and thou shalt overlay the bars with gold.

30 And thou shalt rear up the tabernacle ᴿaccording to the fashion thereof which was shewed thee in the mount.

Vail for the ark

31 And ᴿthou shalt make a vail *of* blue, and purple, and scarlet, and fine twined linen of cunning work: with chĕr'-ū-bĭms shall it be made:

32 And thou shalt hang it upon four pillars of shĭt'-tĭm *wood* overlaid with gold: their hooks *shall be of* gold, upon the four sockets of silver.

33 And thou shalt hang up the vail under the taches, that thou mayest bring in thither within the vail ᴿthe ark of the testimony: and the vail shall divide unto you between ᴿthe holy *place* and the most holy.

34 And ᴿthou shalt put the mercy seat upon the ark of the testimony in the most holy *place*.

35 And ᴿthou shalt set the table without the vail, and ᴿthe candlestick over against the table on the side of the tabernacle toward the south: and thou shalt put the table on the north side.

36 And ᴿthou shalt make an hanging for the door of the tent, *of* blue, and purple, and scarlet, and fine twined linen, wrought with needlework.

37 And thou shalt make for the hanging ᴿfive pillars *of* shĭt'-tĭm *wood*, and overlay them with gold, *and* their hooks *shall be of* gold: and thou shalt cast five sockets of brass for them.

CHAPTER 27

Altar

AND thou shalt make ᴿan altar *of* shĭt'-tĭm wood, five cubits long, and five cubits broad; the altar shall be foursquare: and the height thereof *shall be* three cubits.

2 And thou shalt make the horns of it upon the four corners thereof: his horns shall be of the same: and ᴿthou shalt overlay it with brass.

3 And thou shalt make his pans to receive his ashes, and his shovels, and his basins, and his fleshhooks, and his firepans: all the vessels thereof thou shalt make *of* brass.

4 And thou shalt make for it a grate of network *of* brass; and upon the net shalt thou make four brasen rings in the four corners thereof.

5 And thou shalt put it under the compass of the altar beneath, that the net may be even to the midst of the altar.

6 And thou shalt make staves for the altar, staves *of* shĭt'-tĭm wood, and overlay them with brass.

7 And the staves shall be put into the rings, and the staves shall be upon the two sides of the altar, to bear it.

8 Hollow with boards shalt thou make it: ᴿas ᴺit was shewed thee in the mount, so shall they make *it*.

CHAP. 26
BC 1491
17 Heb. *hands*
24 Heb. *twinned*
30 ch. 25:9, 40
& 27:8
Acts 7:44
Heb. 8:5
31 ch. 36:35
Lev. 16:2
2 Chr. 3:14
Mat. 27:51
Heb. 9:3

ch. 25:16　　　33
& 40:21
Lev. 16:2　　　33
Heb. 9:2, 3
ch. 25:21　　　34
& 40:20
Heb. 9:5
ch. 40:22　　　35
Heb. 9:2
ch. 40:24　　　35
ch. 36:37　　　36
ch. 36:38　　　37

CHAP. 27
BC 1491
ch. 38:1　　　　1
Ezek. 43:13
See Num. 16:38　2
ch. 25:40　　　8
& 26:30
Heb. *he shewed*　8

Court of tabernacle

9 And ᴿthou shalt make the court of the tabernacle: for the south side southward *there shall be* hangings for the court *of* fine twined linen of an hundred cubits long for one side:

10 And the twenty pillars thereof and their twenty sockets *shall be of* brass; the hooks of the pillars and their fillets *shall be of* silver.

11 And likewise for the north side in length *there shall be* hangings of an hundred *cubits* long, and his twenty pillars and their twenty sockets *of* brass; the hooks of the pillars and their fillets *of* silver.

12 And *for* the breadth of the court on the west side *shall be* hangings of fifty cubits: their pillars ten, and their sockets ten.

13 And the breadth of the court on the east side eastward *shall be* fifty cubits.

14 The hangings of one side *of the gate shall be* fifteen cubits: their pillars three, and their sockets three.

15 And on the other side *shall be* hangings fifteen *cubits:* their pillars three, and their sockets three.

16 And for the gate of the court *shall be* an hanging of twenty cubits, *of* blue, and purple, and scarlet, and fine twined linen, wrought with needlework: *and* their pillars *shall be* four, and their sockets four.

17 All the pillars round about the court *shall be* filleted with silver; their hooks *shall be of* silver, and their sockets *of* brass.

18 The length of the court *shall be* an hundred cubits, and the breadth ᴺfifty every where, and the height five cubits *of* fine twined linen, and their sockets *of* brass.

19 All the vessels of the tabernacle in all the service thereof, and all the pins thereof, and all the pins of the court, *shall be of* brass.

Oil for the lamp

20 And ᴿthou shalt command the children of Israel, that they bring thee pure oil olive beaten for the light, to cause the lamp ᴺto burn always.

21 In the tabernacle of the congregation ᴿwithout the vail, which *is* before the testimony, ᴿAaron and his sons shall order it from evening to morning before the LORD: ᴿ*it shall be* a statute for ever unto their generations on the behalf of the children of Israel.

CHAPTER 28

Priesthood established

AND take thou unto thee ᴿAaron thy brother, and his sons with him, from

among the children of Israel, that he may minister unto me in the priest's office, *even* Aaron, Nadab and Ă-bī'-hū, Ĕl-ē-ā'-zär and Ĭth'-ă-mär, Aaron's sons.

2 And ᴿthou shalt make holy garments for Aaron thy brother for glory and for beauty.

3 And ᴿthou shalt speak unto all *that are* wise hearted, ᴿwhom I have filled with the spirit of wisdom, that they may make Aaron's garments to consecrate him, that he may minister unto me in the priest's office.

4 And these *are* the garments which they shall make; ᴿa breastplate, and ᴿan ē'-phŏd, and ᴿa robe, and ᴿa broidered coat, a mitre, and a girdle: and they shall make holy garments for Aaron thy brother, and his sons, that he may minister unto me in the priest's office.

The ephod

5 And they shall take gold, and blue, and purple, and scarlet, and fine linen.

6 ᴿAnd they shall make the ē'-phŏd *of* gold, *of* blue, and *of* purple, *of* scarlet, and fine twined linen, with cunning work.

7 It shall have the two shoulderpieces thereof joined at the two edges thereof; and *so* it shall be joined together.

8 And the ᴺcurious girdle of the ē'-phŏd, which *is* upon it, shall be of the same, according to the work thereof; *even of* gold, *of* blue, and purple, and scarlet, and fine twined linen.

9 And thou shalt take two onyx stones, and grave on them the names of the children of Israel:

10 Six of their names on one stone, and *the other* six names of the rest on the other stone, according to their birth.

11 With the work of an engraver in stone, *like* the engravings of a signet, shalt thou engrave the two stones with the names of the children of Israel: thou shalt make them to be set in ouches of gold.

12 And thou shalt put the two stones upon the shoulders of the ē'-phŏd *for* stones of memorial unto the children of Israel: and ᴿAaron shall bear their names before the LORD upon his two shoulders ᴿfor a memorial.

13 And thou shalt make ouches *of* gold;

14 And two chains *of* pure gold at the ends; *of* wreathen work shalt thou make them, and fasten the wreathen chains to the ouches.

Breastplate of judgment

15 And ᴿthou shalt make the breastplate of judgment with cunning work; after the work of the ē'-phŏd thou shalt make it; *of* gold, *of*

blue, and *of* purple, and *of* scarlet, and *of* fine twined linen, shalt thou make it.

16 Foursquare it shall be *being* doubled; a span *shall be* the length thereof, and a span *shall be* the breadth thereof.

17 ᴿAnd thou shalt ᴺset in it settings of stones, *even* four rows of stones: *the first* row *shall be* a ᴺsardius, a topaz, and a carbuncle: *this shall be* the first row.

18 And the second row *shall be* an emerald, a sapphire, and a diamond.

19 And the third row a ligure, an agate, and an amethyst.

20 And the fourth row a beryl, and an onyx, and a jasper: they shall be set in gold in their ᴺinclosings.

21 And the stones shall be with the names of the children of Israel, twelve, according to their names, *like* the engravings of a signet; every one with his name shall they be according to the twelve tribes.

22 And thou shalt make upon the breastplate chains at the ends *of* wreathen work *of* pure gold.

23 And thou shalt make upon the breastplate two rings of gold, and shalt put the two rings on the two ends of the breastplate.

24 And thou shalt put the two wreathen *chains* of gold in the two rings *which are* on the ends of the breastplate.

25 And *the other* two ends of the two wreathen *chains* thou shalt fasten in the two ouches, and put *them* on the shoulderpieces of the ē'-phŏd before it.

26 And thou shalt make two rings of gold, and thou shalt put them upon the two ends of the breastplate in the border thereof, which *is* in the side of the ē'-phŏd inward.

27 And two *other* rings of gold thou shalt make, and shalt put them on the two sides of the ē'-phŏd underneath, toward the forepart thereof, over against the *other* coupling thereof, above the curious girdle of the ē'-phŏd.

28 And they shall bind the breastplate by the rings thereof unto the rings of the ē'-phŏd with a lace of blue, that *it* may be above the curious girdle of the ē'-phŏd, and that the breastplate be not loosed from the ē'-phŏd.

29 And Aaron shall bear the names of the children of Israel in the breastplate of judgment upon his heart, when he goeth in unto the holy *place,* ᴿfor a memorial before the Lᴏʀᴅ continually.

30 And ᴿthou shalt put in the breastplate of judgment the Ū'-rĭm and the Thŭm'-mĭm; and they shall be upon Aaron's heart, when he goeth in before the Lᴏʀᴅ: and Aaron shall

bear the judgment of the children of Israel upon his heart before the Lᴏʀᴅ continually.

Priests' vestments

31 And ᴿthou shalt make the robe of the ē'-phŏd all *of* blue.

32 And there shall be an hole in the top of it, in the midst thereof: it shall have a binding of woven work round about the hole of it, as it were the hole of an habergeon, that it be not rent.

33 And *beneath* upon the ᴺhem of it thou shalt make pomegranates *of* blue, and *of* purple, and *of* scarlet, round about the hem thereof; and bells of gold between them round about:

34 A golden bell and a pomegranate, a golden bell and a pomegranate, upon the hem of the robe round about.

35 And it shall be upon Aaron to minister: and his sound shall be heard when he goeth in unto the holy *place* before the Lᴏʀᴅ, and when he cometh out, that he die not.

36 And ᴿthou shalt make a plate *of* pure gold, and grave upon it, *like* the engravings of a signet, HOLINESS TO THE LORD.

37 And thou shalt put it on a blue lace, that it may be upon the mitre; upon the forefront of the mitre it shall be.

38 And it shall be upon Aaron's forehead, that Aaron may ᴿbear the iniquity of the holy things, which the children of Israel shall hallow in all their holy gifts; and it shall be always upon his forehead, that they may be ᴿaccepted before the Lᴏʀᴅ.

39 And thou shalt embroider the coat of fine linen, and thou shalt make the mitre *of* fine linen, and thou shalt make the girdle *of* needlework.

40 ᴿAnd for Aaron's sons thou shalt make coats, and thou shalt make for them girdles, and bonnets shalt thou make for them, for glory and for beauty.

41 And thou shalt put them upon Aaron thy brother, and his sons with him; and shalt ᴿannoint them, and ᴿconsecrateᴺthem, and sanctify them, that they may minister unto me in the priest's office.

42 And thou shalt make them ᴿlinen breeches to cover ᴺtheir nakedness; from the loins even unto the thighs they shall ᴺreach:

43 And they shall be upon Aaron, and upon his sons, when they come in unto the tabernacle of the congregation, or when they come near ᴿunto the altar to minister in the holy *place;* that they ᴿbear not iniquity, and die: ᴿit *shall be* a statute for ever unto him and his seed after him.

CHAPTER 29

Consecration of the priests

AND this *is* the thing that thou shalt do unto them to hallow them, to minister unto me in the priest's office: [R]Take one young bullock, and two rams without blemish,

2 And [R]unleavened bread, and cakes unleavened tempered with oil, and wafers unleavened anointed with oil: *of* wheaten flour shalt thou make them.

3 And thou shalt put them into one basket, and bring them in the basket, with the bullock and the two rams.

4 And Aaron and his sons thou shalt bring unto the door of the tabernacle of the congregation, [R]and shalt wash them with water.

5 [R]And thou shalt take the garments, and put upon Aaron the coat, and the robe of the ē′-phŏd, and the ē′-phŏd, and the breastplate, and gird him with [R]the curious girdle of the ē′-phŏd:

6 [R]And thou shalt put the mitre upon his head, and put the holy crown upon the mitre.

7 Then shalt thou take the anointing [R]oil, and pour *it* upon his head, and anoint him.

8 And [R]thou shalt bring his sons, and put coats upon them.

9 And thou shalt gird them with girdles, Aaron and his sons, and [N]put the bonnets on them: and [R]the priest's office shall be theirs for a perpetual statute: and thou shalt [R]consecrate[N] Aaron and his sons.

10 And thou shalt cause a bullock to be brought before the tabernacle of the congregation: and [R]Aaron and his sons shall put their hands upon the head of the bullock.

11 And thou shalt kill the bullock before the LORD, *by* the door of the tabernacle of the congregation.

12 And thou [R]shalt take of the blood of the bullock, and put *it* upon [R]the horns of the altar with thy finger, and pour all the blood beside the bottom of the altar.

13 And [R]thou shalt take all the fat that covereth the inwards, and [N]the caul *that is* above the liver, and the two kidneys, and the fat that *is* upon them, and burn *them* upon the altar.

14 But [R]the flesh of the bullock, and his skin, and his dung, shalt thou burn with fire without the camp: it *is* a sin offering.

15 [R]Thou shalt also take one ram; and Aaron and his sons shall [R]put their hands upon the head of the ram.

16 And thou shalt slay the ram, and thou shalt take his blood, and sprinkle *it* round about upon the altar.

17 And thou shalt cut the ram in pieces, and

CHAP. 29	
BC 1491	
1	Lev. 8:2
2	Lev. 2:4
	& 6:20-22
4	ch. 40:12
	Lev. 8:6
	Heb. 10:22
5	ch. 28:2
	Lev. 8:7
5	ch. 28:8
6	Lev. 8:9
7	ch. 30:25
	Lev. 8:12 & 10:7
	& 21:10
	Num. 35:25
8	Lev. 8:13
9	Heb. *bind*
9	Num. 18:7
9	ch. 28:41
	Lev. 8:22, etc.
	Heb. 7:28
9	Heb. *fill the hand of*
10	Lev. 1:4 & 8:14
12	Lev. 8:15
12	ch. 27:2
13	Lev. 3:3
13	It seemeth by anatomy, and the Hebrew doctors, to be *the midriff*
14	Lev. 4:11, 12, 21
	Heb. 13:11
15	Lev. 8:18
15	Lev. 1:4-9

Or, *upon*	17
Gen. 8:21	18
ver. 3	19
Lev. 8:22	
ch. 30:25, 31	21
ver. 1	21
Heb. 9:22	
Lev. 8:26	23
Lev. 7:30	24
Or, *shake to and fro*	24
Lev. 8:28	25
Lev. 8:29	26
Lev. 7:33	26
Lev. 7:31, 34	27
Num. 18:11, 18	
Deut. 18:3	
Lev. 10:15	28
Lev. 7:34	28

wash the inwards of him, and his legs, and put *them* unto his pieces, and [N]unto his head.

18 And thou shalt burn the whole ram upon the altar: it *is* a burnt offering unto the LORD: it *is* a [R]sweet savour, an offering made by fire unto the LORD.

19 [R]And thou shalt take the other ram; and Aaron and his sons shall put their hands upon the head of the ram.

20 Then shalt thou kill the ram, and take of his blood, and put *it* upon the tip of the right ear of Aaron, and upon the tip of the right ear of his sons, and upon the thumb of their right hand, and upon the great toe of their right foot, and sprinkle the blood upon the altar round about.

21 And thou shalt take of the blood that *is* upon the altar, and of [R]the anointing oil, and sprinkle *it* upon Aaron, and upon his garments, and upon his sons, and upon the garments of his sons with him: and [R]he shall be hallowed, and his garments, and his sons, and his sons' garments with him.

22 Also thou shalt take of the ram the fat and the rump, and the fat that covereth the inwards, and the caul *above* the liver, and the two kidneys, and the fat that *is* upon them, and the right shoulder; for it *is* a ram of consecration:

23 [R]And one loaf of bread, and one cake of oiled bread, and one wafer out of the basket of the unleavened bread that *is* before the LORD:

24 And thou shalt put all in the hands of Aaron, and in the hands of his sons; and shalt [R]wave[N] them *for* a wave offering before the LORD.

25 [R]And thou shalt receive them of their hands, and burn *them* upon the altar for a burnt offering, for a sweet savour before the LORD: it *is* an offering made by fire unto the LORD.

Various offerings

26 And thou shalt take [R]the breast of the ram of Aaron's consecration, and wave it *for* a wave offering before the LORD: and [R]it shall be thy part.

27 And thou shalt sanctify [R]the breast of the wave offering, and the shoulder of the heave offering, which is waved, and which is heaved up, of the ram of the consecration, *even* of *that* which *is* for Aaron, and of *that* which is for his sons:

28 And it shall be Aaron's and his sons' [R]by a statute for ever from the children of Israel: for it *is* an heave offering: and [R]it shall be an heave offering from the children of Israel of

the sacrifice of their peace offerings, *even* their heave offering unto the LORD.

29 And the holy garments of Aaron ᴿshall be his sons' after him, ᴿto be anointed therein, and to be consecrated in them.

30 And ᴿthatᴺ son that is priest in his stead shall put them on ᴿseven days, when he cometh into the tabernacle of the congregation to minister in the holy *place.*

31 And thou shalt take the ram of the consecration, and ᴿseethe his flesh in the holy place.

32 And Aaron and his sons shall eat the flesh of the ram, and the ᴿbread that *is* in the basket, *by* the door of the tabernacle of the congregation.

33 And ᴿthey shall eat those things wherewith the atonement was made, to consecrate *and* to sanctify them: ᴿbut a stranger shall not eat *thereof,* because they *are* holy.

34 And if aught of the flesh of the consecrations, or of the bread, remain unto the morning, then ᴿthou shalt burn the remainder with fire: it shall not be eaten, because it *is* holy.

35 And thus shalt thou do unto Aaron, and to his sons, according to all *things* which I have commanded thee: ᴿseven days shalt thou consecrate them.

36 And thou shalt ᴿoffer every day a bullock *for* a sin offering for atonement: and thou shalt cleanse the altar, when thou hast made an atonement for it, ᴿand thou shalt anoint it, to sanctify it.

37 Seven days thou shalt make an atonement for the altar, and sanctify it; ᴿand it shall be an altar most holy: ᴿwhatsoever toucheth the altar shall be holy.

38 Now this *is that* which thou shalt offer upon the altar; ᴿtwo lambs of the first year ᴿday by day continually.

39 The one lamb thou shalt offer ᴿin the morning; and the other lamb thou shalt offer at even:

40 And with the one lamb a tenth deal of flour mingled with the fourth part of an hĭn of beaten oil; and the fourth part of an hĭn of wine *for* a drink offering.

41 And the other lamb thou shalt ᴿoffer at even, and shalt do thereto according to the meat offering of the morning, and according to the drink offering thereof, for a sweet savour, an offering made by fire unto the LORD.

42 *This shall be* ᴿa continual burnt offering throughout your generations *at* the door of the tabernacle of the congregation before the LORD: ᴿwhere I will meet you, to speak there unto thee.

43 And there I will meet with the children of

Israel, and ᴺ*the tabernacle* ᴿshall be sanctified by my glory.

44 And I will sanctify the tabernacle of the congregation, and the altar: I will ᴿsanctify also both Aaron and his sons, to minister to me in the priest's office.

45 And ᴿI will dwell among the children of Israel, and will be their God.

46 And they shall know that ᴿI *am* the LORD their God, that brought them forth out of the land of Egypt, that I may dwell among them: I *am* the LORD their God.

CHAPTER 30

Altar of burnt incense

AND thou shalt make ᴿan altar ᴿto burn incense upon: *of* shĭt′-tĭm wood shalt thou make it.

2 A cubit *shall be* the length thereof, and a cubit the breadth thereof; foursquare shall it be: and two cubits *shall be* the height thereof: the horns thereof *shall be* of the same.

3 And thou shalt overlay it with pure gold, the ᴺtop thereof, and the ᴺsides thereof round about, and the horns thereof; and thou shalt make unto it a crown of gold round about.

4 And two golden rings shalt thou make to it under the crown of it, by the two ᴺcorners thereof, upon the two sides of it shalt thou make *it;* and they shall be for places for the staves to bear it withal.

5 And thou shalt make the staves *of* shĭt′-tĭm wood, and overlay them with gold.

6 And thou shalt put it before the vail that *is* by the ark of the testimony, before the ᴿmercy seat that *is* over the testimony, where I will meet with thee.

7 And Aaron shall burn thereon ᴿsweetᴺ incense every morning: when ᴿhe dresseth the lamps, he shall burn incense upon it.

8 And when Aaron ᴺlighteth the lamps ᴺat even, he shall burn incense upon it, a perpetual incense before the LORD throughout your generations.

9 Ye shall offer no ᴿstrange incense thereon, nor burnt sacrifice, nor meat offering; neither shall ye pour drink offering thereon.

10 And ᴿAaron shall make an atonement upon the horns of it once in a year with the blood of the sin offering of atonements: once in the year shall he make atonement upon it throughout your generations: it *is* most holy unto the LORD.

Ransom money

11 And the LORD spake unto Moses, saying,

12 ᴿWhen thou takest the sum of the chil-

dren of Israel after ^Ntheir number, then shall they give every man ^Ra ransom for his soul unto the LORD, when thou numberest them; that there be no ^Rplague among them, when *thou* numberest them.

13 ^RThis they shall give, every one that passeth among them that are numbered, half a shē'-kĕl after the shē'-kĕl of the sanctuary: (^Ra shē'-kĕl *is* twenty gē'-răhṡ:) ^Ran half shē'-kĕl *shall be* the offering of the LORD.

14 Evey one that passeth among them that are numbered, from twenty years old above, shall give an offering unto the LORD.

15 The ^Rrich shall not ^Ngive more, and the poor shall not ^Ngive less that half a shē'-kĕl, when *they* give an offering unto the LORD, to make an atonement for your souls.

16 And thou shalt take the atonement money of the children of Israel, and ^Rshalt appoint it for the service of the tabernacle of the congregation; that it may be ^Ra memorial unto the children of Israel before the LORD, to make an atonement for your souls.

Bronze laver

17 And the LORD spake unto Moses, saying,

18 ^RThou shalt also make a laver *of* brass, and his foot *also of* brass, to wash *withal:* and thou shalt ^Rput it between the tabernacle of the congregation and the altar, and thou shalt put water therein.

19 For Aaron and his sons ^Rshall wash their hands and their feet thereat:

20 When they go into the tabernacle of the congregation, thcy shall wash with water, that they die not; or when they come near to the altar to minister, to burn offering made by fire unto the LORD:

21 So they shall wash their hands and their feet, that they die not: and ^Rit shall be a statute for ever to them, *even* to him and to his seed throughout their generations.

The anointing oils

22 Moreover the LORD spake unto Moses, saying,

23 Take thou also unto thcc ^Rprincipal spices, of pure ^Rmyrrh five hundred *shē'-kĕls,* and of sweet cinnamon half so much, *even* two hundred and fifty *shē'-kĕls,* and of sweet ^Rcalamus two hundred and fifty *shē'-kĕls,*

24 And of ^Rcassia five hundred *shē'-kĕls,* after the shē'-kĕl of the sanctuary, and of oil olive an ^Rhĭn:

25 And thou shalt make it an oil of holy ointment, an ointment compound after the art

CHAP. **30**
BC 1491
12 Heb. *them that are to be numbered*
12 See Num. 31:50
Mat. 20:28
1 Pet. 1:18, 19
12 2 Sam. 24:15
13 Mat. 17:24
13 Num. 3:47
13 ch. 38:26
15 Prov. 22:2
Eph. 6:9
15 Heb. *multiply*
15 Heb. *diminish*
16 ch. 38:25
16 Num. 16:40
18 ch. 38:8
1 Ki. 7:38
18 ch. 40:30
19 ch. 40:31, 32
Ps. 26:6
Is. 52:11
John 13:10
Heb. 10:22
21 ch. 28:43
23 S. of S. 4:14
Ezek. 27:22
23 Ps. 45:8
Prov. 7:17
23 S. of S. 4:14
Jer. 6:20
24 Ps. 45:8
24 ch. 29:40

Or, *perfumer*   **25**
ch. 37:29   **25**
   Num. 35:25
   Ps. 89:20
   & 133:2
ch. 40:9   **26**
   Lev. 8:10
   Num. 7:1
ch. 29:37   **29**
ch. 29:7, etc.   **30**
   Lev. 8:12   **30**
ver. 25, 37   **32**
ver. 38   **33**
Gen. 17:14   **33**
   ch. 12:15
   Lev. 7:20, 21
ch. 25:6   **34**
   & 37:29
ver. 25   **35**
Heb. *salted*   **35**
ch. 29:42   **36**
   Lev. 16:2
ver. 32   **36**
   ch. 29:37
Lev. 2:3
ver. 32   **37**
ver. 33   **38**

CHAP. **31**
BC 1491
ch. 35:30   **2**
   & 36:1
1 Chr. 2:20   **2**
ch. 35:31   **3**
1 Ki. 7:14

of the ^Napothecary: it shall be ^Ran holy anointing oil.

26 ^RAnd thou shalt anoint the tabernacle of the congregation therewith, and the ark of the testimony,

27 And the table and all his vessels, and the candlestick and his vessels, and the altar of incense,

28 And the altar of burnt offering with all his vessels, and the laver and his foot.

29 And thou shalt sanctify them, that they may be most holy: ^Rwhatsoever toucheth them shall be holy.

30 ^RAnd thou shalt anoint Aaron and his sons, and consecrate them, that *they* may minister unto me in the priest's office.

31 And thou shalt speak unto the children of Israel, saying, This shall be an holy anointing oil unto me throughout your generations.

32 Upon man's flesh shall it not be poured, neither shall ye make *any other* like it, after the composition of it: ^Rit *is* holy, *and* it shall be holy unto you.

33 ^RWhosoever compoundeth *any* like it, or whosoever putteth *any* of it upon a stranger, ^Rshall even be cut off from his people.

34 And the LORD said unto Moses, ^RTake unto thee sweet spices, stăc'-tē, and ŏn'-ẏ-<u>ch</u>ă, and găl'-bă-nŭm; *these* sweet spices with pure frankincense: of each shall there be a like *weight:*

35 And thou shalt make it a perfume, a confection ^Rafter the art of the apothecary, ^Ntempered together, pure *and* holy:

36 And thou shalt beat *some* of it very small, and put of it before the testimony in the tabernacle of the congregation, ^Rwhere I will meet with thee: ^Rit shall be unto you most holy.

37 And *as for* the perfume which thou shalt make, ^Rye shall not make to yourselves according to the composition thereof: it shall be unto thee holy for the LORD.

38 ^RWhosoever shall make like unto that, to smell thereto, shall even be cut off from his people.

CHAPTER 31

Tabernacle workmen

AND the LORD spake unto Moses, saying, 2 ^RSee, I have called by name Bĕz'-ă-lĕĕl the ^Rson of ū'-rī, the son of Hur, of the tribe of Judah:

3 And I have ^Rfilled him with the spirit of God, in wisdom, and in understanding, and in knowledge, and in all manner of workmanship,

4 To devise cunning works, to work in gold, and in silver, and in brass,

5 And in cutting of stones, to set *them,* and in carving of timber, to work in all manner of workmanship.

6 And I, behold, I have given with him ᴿĂ-hō′-lĭ-ăb, the son of Ă-hĭs′-ă-măch, of the tribe of Dan: and in the hearts of all that are ᴿwise hearted I have put wisdom, that they may make all that I have commanded thee;

7 ᴿThe tabernacle of the congregation, and ᴿthe ark of the testimony, and ᴿthe mercy seat that *is* thereupon, and all the ᴺfurniture of the tabernacle,

8 And ᴿthe table and his furniture, and ᴿthe pure candlestick with all his furniture, and the altar of incense,

9 And ᴿthe altar of burnt offering with all his furniture, and ᴿthe laver and his foot,

10 And ᴿthe cloths of service, and the holy garments for Aaron the priest, and the garments of his sons, to minister in the priest's office,

11 ᴿAnd the anointing oil, and ᴿsweet incense for the holy *place:* according to all that I have commanded thee shall they do.

Law of the sabbath

12 And the LORD spake unto Moses, saying,

13 Speak thou also unto the children of Israel, saying, ᴿVerily my sabbaths ye shall keep: for it *is* a sign between me and you throughout your generations; that *ye* may know that I *am* the LORD that doth sanctify you.

14 ᴿYe shall keep the sabbath therefore; for it *is* holy unto you: every one that defileth it shall surely be put to death: for ᴿwhosoever doeth *any* work therein, that soul shall be cut off from among his people.

15 ᴿSix days may work be done; but in the ᴿseventh *is* the sabbath of rest, ᴺholy to the LORD: whosoever doeth *any* work in the sabbath day, he shall surely be put to death.

16 Wherefore the children of Israel shall keep the sabbath, to observe the sabbath throughout their generations, *for* a perpetual covenant.

17 It *is* ᴿa sign between me and the children of Israel for ever: for ᴿin six days the LORD made heaven and earth, and on the seventh day he rested, and was refreshed.

Two tables of stone

18 And he gave unto Moses, when he had made an end of communing with him upon mount Sī′-nāī, ᴿtwo tables of testimony, tables of stone, written with the finger of God.

CHAPTER 32

The golden calf

AND when the people saw that Moses ᴿdelayed to come down out of the mount, the people gathered themselves together unto Aaron, and said unto him, ᴿUp, make us gods, which shall ᴿgo before us; for *as for* this Moses, the man that brought us up out of the land of Egypt, we wot not what is become of him.

2 And Aaron said unto them, Break off the ᴿgolden earrings, which *are* in the ears of your wives, of your sons, and of your daughters, and bring *them* unto me.

3 And all the people brake off the golden earrings which *were* in their ears, and brought *them* unto Aaron.

4 ᴿAnd he received *them* at their hand, and fashioned it with a graving tool, after he had made it a molten calf: and they said, These *be* thy gods, O Israel, which brought thee up out of the land of Egypt.

5 And when Aaron saw *it,* he built an altar before it; and Aaron made ᴿproclamation, and said, To morrow *is* a feast to the LORD.

6 And they rose up early on the morrow, and offered burnt offerings, and brought peace offerings; and the ᴿpeople sat down to eat and to drink, and rose up to play.

7 And the LORD said unto Moses, ᴿGo, get thee down; for thy people, which thou broughtest out of the land of Egypt, ᴿhave corrupted *themselves:*

8 They have turned aside quickly out of the way which ᴿI commanded them: they have made them a molten calf, and have worshipped it, and have sacrificed thereunto, and said, ᴿThese *be* thy gods, O Israel, which have brought thee up out of the land of Egypt.

9 And the LORD said unto Moses, ᴿI have seen this people, and, behold, it *is* a stiffnecked people:

10 Now therefore ᴿlet me alone, that ᴿmy wrath may wax hot against them, and that I may consume them: and ᴿI will make of thee a great nation.

Moses intercedes

11 ᴿAnd Moses besought ᴺthe LORD his God, and said, LORD, why doth thy wrath wax hot against thy people, which thou hast brought forth out of the land of Egypt with great power, and with a mighty hand?

12 ᴿWherefore should the Egyptians speak, and say, For mischief did he bring them out, to slay them in the mountains, and to consume them from the face of the earth? Turn from

thy fierce wrath, and ᴿrepent of this evil against thy people.

13 Remember Abraham, Isaac, and Israel, thy servants, to whom thou ᴿswarest by thine own self, and saidst unto them, ᴿI will multiply your seed as the stars of heaven, and all this land that I have spoken of will I give unto your seed, and they shall inherit *it* for ever.

14 And the LORD ᴿrepented of the evil which he thought to do unto his people.

15 And ᴿMoses turned, and went down from the mount, and the two tables of the testimony *were* in his hand: the tables *were* written on both their sides; on the one side and on the other *were* they written.

16 And the ᴿtables *were* the work of God, and the writing *was* the writing of God, graven upon the tables.

17 And when Joshua heard the noise of the people as they shouted, he said unto Moses, *There is* a noise of war in the camp.

18 And he said, *It is* not the voice of *them that* shout for mastery, neither *is it* the voice of *them that* cry for ᴺbeing overcome: *but* the noise of *them that* sing do I hear.

Moses breaks the tables

19 And it came to pass, as soon as he came nigh unto the camp, that ᴿhe saw the calf, and the dancing: and Moses' anger waxed hot, and he cast the tables out of his hands, and brake them beneath the mount.

20 ᴿAnd he took the calf which they had made, and burnt *it* in the fire, and ground *it* to powder, and strawed *it* upon the water, and made the children of Israel drink *of it.*

Aaron's excuse

21 And Moses said unto Aaron, ᴿWhat did this people unto thee, that thou hast brought so great a sin upon them?

22 And Aaron said, Let not the anger of my lord wax hot: ᴿthou knowest the people, that they *are set* on mischief.

23 For they said unto me, Make us gods, which shall go before us: for *as for* this Moses, the man that brought us up out of the land of Egypt, we wot not what is become of him.

24 And I said unto them, Whosoever hath any gold, let them break *it* off. So they gave *it* me: then I cast it into the fire, and there came out this calf.

The idolaters slain

25 And when Moses saw that the people *were* ᴿnaked; (for Aaron ᴿhad made them naked unto *their* shame among ᴺtheir enemies:)

CHAP. **32**
BC 1491
12 ver. 14
13 Gen. 22:16
Heb. 6:13
13 Gen. 12:7
& 13:15
& 15:7, 18
& 26:4
& 35:11, 12
14 2 Sam. 24:16
15 Deut. 9:15
16 ch. 31:18
18 Heb. *weakness*
19 Deut. 9:16, 17
20 Deut. 9:21
21 Gen. 26:10
22 ch. 14:11
25 ch. 33:4, 5
25 2 Chr. 28:19
25 Heb. *those that rose up against them*

Num. 25:5   **27**
1 Sam. 15:18, 22   **29**
Prov. 21:3
Zech. 13:3
Or, *And Moses*   **29**
said, Consecrate
yourselves to day
to the LORD
because every
man hath been
against his son,
and against his
brother, etc.
Heb. *Fill your*   **29**
hands
1 Sam. 12:20, 23   **30**
2 Sam. 16:12   **30**
Num. 25:13   **30**
Deut. 9:18   **31**
ch. 20:23   **31**
Ps. 69:28   **32**
Rom. 9:3
Dan. 12:1   **32**
Phil. 4:3
Rev. 3:5
& 21:27
Lev. 23:30   **33**
Ezek. 18:4
ch. 33:2, 14, etc.
Deut. 32:35   **34**
Rom. 2:5, 6
2 Sam. 12:9   **35**

CHAP. **33**
BC 1491
ch. 32:7   **1**
Gen. 12:7   **1**
ch. 32:34   **2**
Josh. 24:11   **2**
ch. 3:8   **3**
ch. 32:9   **3**
Num. 16:21, 45   **3**

---

26 Then Moses stood in the gate of the camp, and said, Who *is* on the LORD's side? *let him come* unto me. And all the sons of Levi gathered themselves together unto him.

27 And he said unto them, Thus saith the LORD God of Israel, Put every man his sword by his side, *and* go in and out from gate to gate throughout the camp, and ᴿslay every man his brother, and every man his companion, and every man his neighbour.

28 And the children of Levi did according to the word of Moses: and there fell of the people that day about three thousand men.

29 ᴿForᴺ Moses had said, ᴺConsecrate yourselves to day to the LORD, even every man upon his son, and upon his brother; that he may bestow upon you a blessing this day.

30 And it came to pass on the morrow, that Moses said unto the people, ᴿYe have sinned a great sin: and now I will go up unto the LORD; ᴿperadventure I shall ᴿmake an atonement for your sin.

31 And Moses ᴿreturned unto the LORD, and said, Oh, this people have sinned a great sin, and have ᴿmade them gods of gold.

32 Yet now, if thou wilt forgive their sin—; and if not, ᴿblot me, I pray thee, ᴿout of thy book which thou hast written.

33 And the LORD said unto Moses, ᴿWhosoever hath sinned against me, him will I blot out of my book.

34 Therefore now go, lead the people unto *the place* of which I have spoken unto thee: ᴿbehold, mine Angel shall go before thee: nevertheless ᴿin the day when I visit I will visit their sin upon them.

35 And the LORD plagued the people, because ᴿthey made the calf, which Aaron made.

CHAPTER 33

Israel's mourning

AND the LORD said unto Moses, Depart, *and* go up hence, thou ᴿand the people which thou hast brought up out of the land of Egypt, unto the land which I sware unto Abraham, to Isaac, and to Jacob, saying, ᴿUnto thy seed will I give it:

2 ᴿAnd I will send an angel before thee; ᴿand I will drive out the Canaanite, the Amorite, and the Hittite, and the Pĕ-rīz'-zīte, the Hī'-vīte, and the Jĕb'-ū-sīte:

3 ᴿUnto a land flowing with milk and honey: for I will not go up in the midst of thee; for thou *art* a ᴿstiffnecked people: lest ᴿI consume thee in the way.

4 And when the people heard these evil ti-

dings, ᴿthey mourned: ᴿand no man did put on him his ornaments.

5 For the LORD had said unto Moses, Say unto the children of Israel, Ye *are* a stiffnecked people: I will come up ᴿinto the midst of thee in a moment, and consume thee: therefore now put off thy ornaments from thee, that I may ᴿknow what to do unto thee.

6 And the children of Israel stripped themselves of their ornaments by the mount Hôr′-ĕb.

The tent of meeting

7 And Moses took the tabernacle, and pitched it without the camp, afar off from the camp, ᴿand called it the Tabernacle of the congregation. And it came to pass, *that* every one which ᴿsought the LORD went out unto the tabernacle of the congregation, which *was* without the camp.

8 And it came to pass, when Moses went out unto the tabernacle, *that* all the people rose up, and stood every man ᴿ*at* his tent door, and looked after Moses, until he was gone into the tabernacle.

9 And it came to pass, as Moses entered into the tabernacle, the cloudy pillar descended, and stood *at* the door of the tabernacle, and *the* LORD ᴿtalked with Moses.

10 And all the people saw the cloudy pillar stand *at* the tabernacle door: and all the people rose up and ᴿworshipped, every man *in* his tent door.

11 And ᴿthe LORD spake unto Moses face to face, as a man speaketh unto his friend. And he turned again into the camp: but ᴿhis servant Joshua, the son of Nun, a young man, departed not out of the tabernacle.

12 And Moses said unto the LORD, See, ᴿthou sayest unto me, Bring up this people: and thou hast not let me know whom thou wilt send with me. Yet thou hast said, ᴿI know thee by name, and thou hast also found grace in my sight.

13 Now therefore, I pray thee, ᴿif I have found grace in thy sight, ᴿshew me now thy way, that I may know thee, that I may find grace in thy sight: and consider that this nation *is* ᴿthy people.

14 And he said, ᴿMy presence shall go *with thee,* and I will give thee ᴿrest.

15 And he said unto him, ᴿIf thy presence go not *with me,* carry us not up hence.

16 For wherein shall it be known here that I and thy people have found grace in thy sight? ᴿ*is it* not in that thou goest with us? so ᴿshall we be separated, I and thy people, from all the people that *are* upon the face of the earth.

17 And the LORD said unto Moses, ᴿI will

do this thing also that thou hast spoken: for ᴿthou hast found grace in my sight, and I know thee by name.

18 And he said, I beseech thee, shew me ᴿthy glory.

19 And he said, I will make all my goodness pass before thee, and I will proclaim the name of the LORD before thee; ᴿand will be ᴿgracious to whom I will be gracious, and will shew mercy on whom I will shew mercy.

20 And he said, Thou canst not see my face: for ᴿthere shall no man see me, and live.

21 And the LORD said, Behold, *there is* a place by me, and thou shalt stand upon a rock:

22 And it shall come to pass, while my glory passeth by, that I will put thee ᴿin a clift of the rock, and will ᴿcover thee with my hand while I pass by:

23 And I will take away mine hand, and thou shalt see my back parts: but my face shall ᴿnot be seen.

CHAPTER 34

God renews the covenant

AND the LORD said unto Moses, ᴿHew thee two tables of stone like unto the first: ᴿand I will write upon *these* tables the words that were in the first tables, which thou brakest.

2 And be ready in the morning, and come up in the morning unto mount Sĭ′-naı̄, and present thyself there to me ᴿin the top of the mount.

3 And no man shall ᴿcome up with thee, neither let any man be seen throughout all the mount; neither let the flocks nor herds feed before that mount.

4 And he hewed two tables of stone like unto the first; and Moses rose up early in the morning, and went up unto mount Sĭ′-naı̄, as the LORD had commanded him, and took in his hand the two tables of stone.

5 And the LORD descended in the cloud, and stood with him there, and ᴿproclaimed the name of the LORD.

6 And the LORD passed by before him, and proclaimed, The LORD, The LORD ᴿGod, merciful and gracious, longsuffering, and abundant in ᴿgoodness and ᴿtruth,

7 ᴿKeeping mercy for thousands, ᴿforgiving iniquity and transgression and sin, and ᴿthat will by no means clear *the guilty;* visiting the iniquity of the fathers upon the children, and upon the children's children, unto the third and to the fourth *generation.*

8 And Moses made haste, and ᴿbowed his head toward the earth, and worshipped.

9 And he said, If now I have found grace in thy sight, O Lord, ᴿlet my Lord, I pray thee,

go among us; for ᴿit *is* a stiffnecked people; and pardon our iniquity and our sin, and take us for ᴿthine inheritance.

10 And he said, Behold, ᴿI make a covenant: before all thy people I will ᴿdo marvels, such as have not been done in all the earth, nor in any nation: and all the people among which thou *art* shall see the work of the LORD: for it *is* ᴿa terrible thing that I will do with thee.

Idolatry prohibited

11 ᴿObserve thou that which I command thee this day: behold, ᴿI drive out before thee the Amorite, and the Canaanite, and the Hittite, and the Pĕ-rĭz'-zīte, and the Hī'-vīte, and the Jĕb'-ū-śīte.

12 ᴿTake heed to thyself, lest thou make a covenant with the inhabitants of the land whither thou goest, lest it be for ᴿa snare in the midst of thee:

13 But ye shall ᴿdestroy their altars, break their ᴺimages, and ᴿcut down their groves:

14 For thou shalt worship ᴿno other god: for the LORD, whose ᴿname *is* Jealous, *is* a ᴿjealous God:

15 ᴿLest thou make a covenant with the inhabitants of the land, and they ᴿgo a whoring after their gods, and do sacrifice unto their gods, and *one* ᴿcall thee, and thou ᴿeat of his sacrifice;

16 And thou take of ᴿtheir daughters unto thy sons, and their daughters ᴿgo a whoring after their gods, and make thy sons go a whoring after their gods.

17 ᴿThou shalt make thee no molten gods.

Three annual feasts

18 The feast of ᴿunleavened bread shalt thou keep. Seven days thou shalt eat unleavened bread, as I commanded thee, in the time of the month Abib: for in the ᴿmonth Abib thou camest out from Egypt.

19 ᴿAll that openeth the matrix *is* mine; and every firstling among thy cattle, *whether* ox or sheep, *that is male.*

20 But ᴿthe firstling of an ass thou shalt redeem with a ᴺlamb: and if thou redeem *him* not, then shalt thou break his neck. All the firstborn of thy sons thou shalt redeem. And none shall appear before me ᴿempty.

21 ᴿSix days thou shalt work, but on the seventh day thou shalt rest: in earing time and in harvest thou shalt rest.

22 ᴿAnd thou shalt observe the feast of weeks, of the firstfruits of wheat harvest, and the feast of ingathering at the ᴺyear's end.

23 ᴿThrice in the year shall all your men children appear before the Lord GOD, the God of Israel.

CHAP. 34	
BC 1491	
9 ch. 33:3	
9 Ps. 33:12	
& 94:14	
10 Deut. 5:2	
10 Deut. 4:32	
Ps. 77:14	
10 Ps. 145:6	
11 Deut. 6:25	
11 ch. 33:2	
12 ch. 23:32	
12 ch. 23:33	
13 Deut. 12:3	
13 Heb. *statues*	
13 2 Ki. 18:4	
2 Chr. 34:3, 4	
14 ch. 20:3, 5	
14 Is. 9:6 & 57:15	
14 ch. 20:5	
15 ver. 12	
15 Judg. 2:17	
15 Num. 25:2	
15 1 Cor. 8:4, 7, 10	
16 Deut. 7:3	
1 Ki. 11:2	
Ezra 9:2	
Neh. 13:25	
16 Num. 25:1, 2	
1 Ki. 11:4	
17 ch. 32:8	
18 ch. 12:15	
18 ch. 13:4	
19 ch. 22:29	
20 ch. 13:13	
20 Or, *kid*	
20 ch. 23:15	
Deut. 16.16	
1 Sam. 9:7, 8	
2 Sam. 24:24	
21 ch. 20:9	
Luke 13:14	
22 ch. 23:16	
22 Heb. *revolution of the year*	
23 ch. 23:14, 17	

ch. 33:2	24
Ps. 78:55	
Deut. 12:20	24
& 19:8	
See Gen. 35:5	24
Acts 18:10	
ch. 23:18	25
ch. 12:10	25
ch. 23:19	26
ch. 23:19	26
Deut. 31:9	27
ch. 24:18	28
ver. 1	28
ch. 31:18	
Deut. 4:13	
& 10:2, 4	
Heb. *words*	28
ch. 32:15	29
Mat. 17:2	29
2 Cor. 3:7, 13	
ch. 24:3	32
2 Cor. 3:13	33
2 Cor. 3:16	34

CHAP. 35	
BC 1491	
ch. 34:32	1

24 For I will ᴿcast out the nations before thee, and ᴿenlarge thy borders: ᴿneither shall any man desire thy land, when thou shalt go up to appear before the LORD thy God thrice in the year.

25 ᴿThou shalt not offer the blood of my sacrifice with leaven; ᴿneither shall the sacrifice of the feast of the passover be left unto the morning.

26 ᴿThe first of the firstfruits of thy land thou shalt bring unto the house of the LORD thy God. ᴿThou shalt not seethe a kid in his mother's milk.

27 And the LORD said unto Moses, Write thou ᴿthese words: for after the tenor of these words I have made a covenant with thee and with Israel.

28 ᴿAnd he was there with the LORD forty days and forty nights; he did neither eat bread, nor drink water. And ᴿhe wrote upon the tables the words of the covenant, the ten ᴺcommandments.

Moses' face shines

29 And it came to pass, when Moses came down from mount Sī'-nāi with the ᴿtwo tables of testimony in Moses' hand, when he came down from the mount, that Moses wist not that ᴿthe skin of his face shone while he talked with him.

30 And when Aaron and all the children of Israel saw Moses, behold, the skin of his face shone; and they were afraid to come nigh him.

31 And Moses called unto them; and Aaron and all the rulers of the congregation returned unto him: and Moses talked with them.

32 And afterward all the children of Israel came nigh: ᴿand he gave them in commandment all that the LORD had spoken with him in mount Sī'-nāi.

33 And *till* Moses had done speaking with them, he put ᴿa vail on his face.

34 But ᴿwhen Moses went in before the LORD to speak with him, he took the vail off, until he came out. And he came out, and spake unto the children of Israel *that* which he was commanded.

35 And the children of Israel saw the face of Moses, that the skin of Moses' face shone: and Moses put the vail upon his face again, until he went in to speak with him.

CHAPTER 35

Moses assembles the people

AND Moses gathered all the congregation of the children of Israel together, and said unto them, ᴿThese *are* the words which

the LORD hath commanded, that *ye* should do them.

2 ᴿSix days shall work be done, but on the seventh day there shall be to you ᴺan holy day, a sabbath of rest to the LORD: whosoever doeth work therein shall be put to death.

3 ᴿYe shall kindle no fire throughout your habitations upon the sabbath day.

4 And Moses spake unto all the congregation of the children of Israel, saying, ᴿThis *is* the thing which the LORD commanded, saying,

5 Take ye from among you an offering unto the LORD: ᴿwhosoever *is* of a willing heart, let him bring it, an offering of the LORD; gold, and silver, and brass,

6 And blue, and purple, and scarlet, and fine linen, and goats' *hair,*

7 And rams' skins dyed red, and badgers' skins, and shĭt'-tĭm wood,

8 And oil for the light, ᴿand spices for anointing oil, and for the sweet incense,

9 And onyx stones, and stones to be set for the ē'-phŏd, and for the breastplate.

10 And ᴿevery wise hearted among you shall come, and make all that the LORD hath commanded;

11 ᴿThe tabernacle, his tent, and his covering, his taches, and his boards, his bars, his pillars, and his sockets,

12 ᴿThe ark, and the staves thereof, *with the* mercy seat, and the vail of the covering,

13 The ᴿtable, and his staves, and all his vessels, ᴿand the shewbread,

14 ᴿThe candlestick also for the light, and his furniture, and his lamps, with the oil for the light,

15 ᴿAnd the incense altar, and his staves, ᴿand the anointing oil, and ᴿthe sweet incense, and the hanging for the door at the entering in of the tabernacle,

16 ᴿThe altar of burnt offering, with his brasen grate, his staves, and all his vessels, the laver and his foot,

17 ᴿThe hangings of the court, his pillars, and their sockets, and the hanging for the door of the court,

18 The pins of the tabernacle, and the pins of the court, and their cords,

19 ᴿThe cloths of service, to do service in the holy *place,* the holy garments for Aaron the priest, and the garments of his sons, to minister in the priest's office.

Offerings for the tabernacle

20 And all the congregation of the children of Israel departed from the presence of Moses.

CHAP. **35**

BC 1491

2 ch. 20:9
Lev. 23:3
2 Heb. *holiness*
3 ch. 16:23
4 ch. 25:1, 2
5 ch. 25:2
8 ch. 25:6
10 ch. 31:6
11 ch. 26:1, 2, etc.
12 ch. 25:10, etc.
13 ch. 25:23
13 ch. 25:30
Lev. 24:5, 6
14 ch. 25:31, etc.
15 ch. 30:1
15 ch. 30:25
15 ch. 30:34
16 ch. 27:1
17 ch. 27:9
19 ch. 31:10
& 39:1, 41
Num. 4:5, 6, etc.

ver. 5, 22, 26, 29 **21**
ch. 36:2
1 Chr. 29:8 **23**
ch. 28:3 **25**
& 31:6
& 36:1
1 Chr. 29:6 **27**
Ezra 2:68
ch. 30:23 **28**
ver. 21 **29**
1 Chr. 29:9
ch. 31:2, etc. **30**
ch. 31:6 **34**
ver. 31 **35**
ch. 31:3, 6
1 Ki. 7:14
2 Chr. 2:14
Is. 28:26

21 And they came, every one ᴿwhose heart stirred him up, and every one whom his spirit made willing, *and* they brought the LORD's offering to the work of the tabernacle of the congregation, and for all his service, and for the holy garments.

22 And they came, both men and women, as many as were willing hearted, *and* brought bracelets, and earrings, and rings, and tablets, all jewels of gold: and every man that offered *offered* an offering of gold unto the LORD.

23 And ᴿevery man, with whom was found blue, and purple, and scarlet, and fine linen, and goats' *hair,* and red skins of rams, and badgers' skins, brought *them.*

24 Every one that did offer an offering of silver and brass brought the LORD's offering: and every man, with whom was found shĭt'-tĭm wood for any work of the service, brought *it.*

25 And all the women that were ᴿwise hearted did spin with their hands, and brought that which they had spun, *both* of blue, and of purple, *and* of scarlet, and of fine linen.

26 And all the women whose heart stirred them up in wisdom spun goats' *hair.*

27 And ᴿthe rulers brought onyx stones, and stones to be set, for the ē'-phŏd, and for the breastplate;

28 And ᴿspice, and oil for the light, and for the anointing oil, and for the sweet incense.

29 The children of Israel brought a ᴿwilling offering unto the LORD, every man and woman, whose heart made them willing to bring for all manner of work, which the LORD had commanded to be made by the hand of Moses.

Workmen instructed

30 And Moses said unto the children of Israel, See, ᴿthe LORD hath called by name Bĕz'-ă-lēel the son of Ū'-rī, the son of Hur, of the tribe of Judah;

31 And he hath filled him with the spirit of God, in wisdom, in understanding, and in knowledge, and in all manner of workmanship;

32 And to devise curious works, to work in gold, and in silver, and in brass,

33 And in the cutting of stones, to set *them,* and in carving of wood, to make any manner of cunning work.

34 And he hath put in his heart that he may teach, *both* he, and ᴿĂ-hō'-lĭ-ăb, the son of Ă-hĭs'-ă-mǎch, of the tribe of Dan.

35 Them hath he ᴿfilled with wisdom of

heart, to work all manner of work, of the engraver, and of the cunning workman, and of the embroiderer, in blue, and in purple, in scarlet, and in fine linen, and of the weaver, *even* of them that do any work, and of those that devise cunning work.

CHAPTER 36

Tabernacle work begun

THEN wrought Bĕz'-ă-lĕel and Ă-hō'-lĭ-ăb, and every ᴿwise hearted man, in whom the LORD put wisdom and understanding to know how to work all manner of work for the service of the ᴿsanctuary, according to all that the LORD had commanded.

2 And Moses called Bĕz'-ă-lĕel and Ă-hō'-lĭ-ăb, and every wise hearted man, in whose heart the LORD had put wisdom, *even* every one ᴿwhose heart stirred him up to come unto the work to do it:

3 And they received of Moses all the offering, which the children of Israel ᴿhad brought for the work of the service of the sanctuary, to make it *withal*. And they brought yet unto him free offerings every morning.

4 And all the wise men, that wrought all the work of the sanctuary, came every man from his work which they made;

5 And they spake unto Moses, saying, ᴿThe people bring much more than enough for the service of the work, which the LORD commanded to make.

6 And Moses gave commandment, and they caused it to be proclaimed throughout the camp, saying, Let neither man nor woman make any more work for the offering of the sanctuary. So the people were restrained from bringing.

7 For the stuff they had was sufficient for all the work to make it, and too much.

8 ᴿAnd every wise hearted man among them that wrought the work of the tabernacle made ten curtains *of* fine twined linen, and blue, and purple, and scarlet: *with* chĕr'-ū-bĭms of cunning work made he them.

9 The length of one curtain *was* twenty and eight cubits, and the breadth of one curtain four cubits: the curtains *were* all of one size.

10 And he coupled the five curtains one unto another: and *the other* five curtains he coupled one unto another.

11 And he made loops of blue on the edge of one curtain from the selvedge in the coupling: likewise he made in the uttermost side of *another* curtain, in the coupling of the second.

CHAP. **36**

BC 1491

1 ch. 28:3
& 31:6
& 35:10, 35
1 ch. 25:8
2 ch. 35:21, 26
1 Chr. 29:5
3 ch. 35:27
5 2 Cor. 8:2, 3
8 ch. 26:1

ch. 26:5   12
ch. 26:7   14
ch. 26:14   19
ch. 26:15   20
Heb. *twinned*   29
Heb. *two sockets, two sockets under one board*
ch. 26:26   31   30

12 ᴿFifty loops made he in one curtain, and fifty loops made he in the edge of the curtain which *was* in the coupling of the second: the loops held one *curtain* to another.

13 And he made fifty taches of gold, and coupled the curtains one unto another with the taches: so it became one tabernacle.

14 ᴿAnd he made curtains *of* goats' *hair* for the tent over the tabernacle: eleven curtains he made them.

15 The length of one curtain *was* thirty cubits, and four cubits *was* the breadth of one curtain: the eleven curtains *were* of one size.

16 And he coupled five curtains by themselves, and six curtains by themselves.

17 And he made fifty loops upon the uttermost edge of the curtain in the coupling, and fifty loops made he upon the edge of the curtain which coupleth the second.

18 And he made fifty taches *of* brass to couple the tent together, that it might be one.

19 ᴿAnd he made a covering for the tent *of* rams' skins dyed red, and a covering *of* badgers' skins above *that*.

20 ᴿAnd he made boards for the tabernacle *of* shĭt'-tĭm wood, standing up.

21 The length of a board *was* ten cubits, and the breadth of a board one cubit and a half.

22 One board had two tenons, equally distant one from another: thus did he make for all the boards of the tabernacle.

23 And he made boards for the tabernacle; twenty boards for the south side southward:

24 And forty sockets of silver he made under the twenty boards; two sockets under one board for his two tenons, and two sockets under another board for his two tenons.

25 And for the other side of the tabernacle, *which is* toward the north corner, he made twenty boards,

26 And their forty sockets of silver; two sockets under one board, and two sockets under another board.

27 And for the sides of the tabernacle westward he made six boards.

28 And two boards made he for the corners of the tabernacle in the two sides.

29 And they were ᴺcoupled beneath, and coupled together at the head thereof, to one ring: thus he did to both of them in both the corners.

30 And there were eight boards; and their sockets *were* sixteen sockets of silver, ᴺunder every board two sockets.

31 And he made ᴿbars of shĭt'-tĭm wood; five for the boards of the one side of the tabernacle,

32 And five bars for the boards of the other side of the tabernacle, and five bars for the boards of the tabernacle for the sides westward.

33 And he made the middle bar to shoot through the boards from the one end to the other.

34 And he overlaid the boards with gold, and made their rings *of* gold *to be* places for the bars, and overlaid the bars with gold.

35 And he made ᴿa vail *of* blue, and purple, and scarlet, and fine twined linen: *with* chĕr'-ū-bĭms made he it of cunning work.

36 And he made thereunto four pillars *of* shĭt'-tĭm *wood,* and overlaid them with gold: their hooks *were of* gold; and he cast for them four sockets of silver.

37 And he made an ᴿhanging for the tabernacle door *of* blue, and purple, and scarlet, and fine twined linen, ᴺof needlework;

38 And the five pillars of it with their hooks: and he overlaid their chapiters and their fillets with gold: but their five sockets *were of* brass.

CHAPTER 37

Furniture of tabernacle

AND Bĕz'-ă-lĕel made ᴿthe ark *of* shĭt'-tĭm wood: two cubits and a half *was* the length of it, and a cubit and a half the breadth of it, and a cubit and a half the height of it:

2 And he overlaid it with pure gold within and without, and made a crown of gold to it round about.

3 And he cast for it four rings of gold, *to be set* by the four corners of it; even two rings upon the one side of it, and two rings upon the other side of it.

4 And he made staves *of* shĭt'-tĭm wood, and overlaid them with gold.

5 And he put the staves into the rings by the sides of the ark, to bear the ark.

6 And he made the ᴿmercy seat *of* pure gold: two cubits and a half *was* the length thereof, and one cubit and a half the breadth thereof.

7 And he made two chĕr'-ū-bĭms *of* gold, beaten out of one piece made he them, on the two ends of the mercy seat;

8 One cherub ᴺon the end on this side, and another cherub ᴺon the *other* end on that side: out of the mercy seat made he the chĕr'-ū-bĭms on the two ends thereof.

9 And the chĕr'-ū-bĭms spread out *their* wings on high, *and* covered with their wings over the mercy seat, with their faces one to another; *even* to the mercy seatward were the faces of the chĕr'-ū-bĭms.

10 And he made ᴿthe table *of* shĭt'-tĭm wood: two cubits *was* the length thereof, and a cubit the breadth thereof, and a cubit and a half the height thereof:

11 And he overlaid it with pure gold, and made thereunto a crown of gold round about.

12 Also he made thereunto a border of an handbreadth round about; and made a crown of gold for the border thereof round about.

13 And he cast for it four rings of gold, and put the rings upon the four corners that *were* in the four feet thereof.

14 Over against the border were the rings, the places for the staves to bear the table.

15 And he made the staves *of* shĭt'-tĭm wood, and overlaid them with gold, to bear the table.

16 And he made the vessels which *were* upon the table, his ᴿdishes, and his spoons, and his bowls, and his covers ᴺto cover withal, *of* pure gold.

17 And he made the ᴿcandlestick *of* pure gold: *of* beaten work made he the candlestick; his shaft, and his branch, his bowls, his knops, and his flowers, were of the same:

18 And six branches going out of the sides thereof; three branches of the candlestick out of the one side thereof, and three branches of the candlestick out of the other side thereof:

19 Three bowls made after the fashion of almonds in one branch, a knop and a flower; and three bowls made like almonds in another branch, a knop and a flower: so throughout the six branches going out of the candlestick.

20 And in the candlestick *were* four bowls made like almonds, his knops, and his flowers:

21 And a knop under two branches of the same, and a knop under two branches of the same, and a knop under two branches of the same, according to the six branches going out of it.

22 Their knops and their branches were of the same: all of it *was* one beaten work *of* pure gold.

23 And he made his seven lamps, and his snuffers, and his snuffdishes, *of* pure gold.

24 *Of* a talent of pure gold made he it, and all the vessels thereof.

25 ᴿAnd he made the incense altar *of* shĭt'-tĭm wood: the length of it *was* a cubit, and the breadth of it a cubit; *it was* foursquare; and two cubits *was* the height of it; the horns thereof were of the same.

26 And he overlaid it with pure gold, *both* the top of it, and the sides thereof round about,

and the horns of it: also he made unto it a crown of gold round about.

27 And he made two rings of gold for it under the crown thereof, by the two corners of it, upon the two sides thereof, to be places for the staves to bear it withal.

28 And he made the staves *of* shĭt′-tĭm wood, and overlaid them with gold.

29 And he made ᴿthe holy anointing oil, and the pure incense of sweet spices, according to the work of the apothecary.

CHAPTER 38

AND ᴿhe made the altar of burnt offering *of* shĭt′-tĭm wood: five cubits *was* the length thereof, and five cubits the breadth thereof; *it was* foursquare; and three cubits the height thereof.

2 And he made the horns thereof on the four corners of it; the horns thereof were of the same: and he overlaid it with brass.

3 And he made all the vessels of the altar, the pots, and the shovels, and the basins, *and* the fleshhooks, and the firepans: all the vessels thereof made he *of* brass.

4 And he made for the altar a brasen grate of network under the compass thereof beneath unto the midst of it.

5 And he cast four rings for the four ends of the grate of brass, *to be* places for the staves.

6 And he made the staves *of* shĭt′-tĭm wood, and overlaid them with brass.

7 And he put the staves into the rings on the sides of the altar, to bear it withal; he made the altar hollow with boards.

8 And he made ᴿthe laver *of* brass, and the foot of it *of* brass, of the ᴺlookingglasses of *the women* ᴺassembling, which assembled *at* the door of the tabernacle of the congregation.

Court of the tabernacle

9 And he made ᴿthe court: on the south side southward the hangings of the court *were of* fine twined linen, an hundred cubits:

10 Their pillars *were* twenty, and their brasen sockets twenty; the hooks of the pillars and their fillets *were of* silver.

11 And for the north side *the hangings were* an hundred cubits, their pillars *were* twenty, and their sockets of brass twenty; the hooks of the pillars and their fillets *of* silver.

12 And for the west side *were* hangings of fifty cubits, their pillars ten, and their sockets ten; the hooks of the pillars and their fillets *of* silver.

13 And for the east side eastward fifty cubits.

14 The hangings of the one side *of the gate were* fifteen cubits; their pillars three, and their sockets three.

15 And for the other side of the court gate, on this hand and that hand, *were* hangings of fifteen cubits; their pillars three, and their sockets three.

16 All the hangings of the court round about *were* of fine twined linen.

17 And the sockets for the pillars *were of* brass; the hooks of the pillars and their fillets *of* silver; and the overlaying of their chapiters *of* silver; and all the pillars of the court *were* filleted with silver.

18 And the hanging for the gate of the court *was* needlework, *of* blue, and purple, and scarlet, and fine twined linen: and twenty cubits *was* the length, and the height in the breadth *was* five cubits, answerable to the hangings of the court.

19 And their pillars *were* four, and their sockets *of* brass four; their hooks *of* silver, and the overlaying of their chapiters and their fillets *of* silver.

20 And all the ᴿpins of the tabernacle, and of the court round about, *were of* brass.

Materials of the tabernacle

21 This is the sum of the tabernacle, *even* of ᴿthe tabernacle of testimony, as it was counted, according to the commandment of Moses, *for* the service of the Levites, ᴿby the hand of ĭth′-ă-mär, son to Aaron the priest.

22 And ᴿBĕz′-ă-lĕel the son of Ū′-rī, the son of Hur, of the tribe of Judah, made all that the Lᴏʀᴅ commanded Moses.

23 And with him *was* Ă-hō′-lĭ-ăb, son of Ă-hĭs′-ă-măch, of the tribe of Dan, an engraver, and a cunning workman, and an embroiderer in blue, and in purple, and in scarlet, and fine linen.

24 All the gold that was occupied for the work in all the work of the holy *place,* even the gold of the offering, was twenty and nine talents, and seven hundred and thirty shē′-kĕls, after ᴿthe shē′-kĕl of the sanctuary.

25 And the silver of them that were numbered of the congregation *was* an hundred talents, and a thousand seven hundred and threescore and fifteen shē′-kĕls, after the shē′-kĕl of the sanctuary:

26 ᴿA bē′-käh for ᴺevery man, *that is,* half a shē′-kĕl, after the shē′-kĕl of the sanctuary, for every one that went to be numbered, from twenty years old and upward, for ᴿsix hundred thousand and three thousand and five hundred and fifty *men.*

CHAP. 37
BC 1491
29 ch. 30:23, 34

CHAP. 38
BC 1491
1 ch. 27:1
8 ch. 30:18
8 Or, *brasen glasses*
8 Heb. *assembling by troops,* as 1 Sam. 2:22
9 ch. 27:9

ch. 27:19   20
Num. 1:50, 53   21
& 9:15
& 10:11
& 17:7, 8
2 Chr. 24:6
Acts 7:44
Num. 4:28, 33   21
ch. 31:2, 6   22
ch. 30:13, 24   24
Lev. 5:15
& 27:3, 25
Num. 3:47
& 18:16
ch. 30:13, 15   26
Heb. *a poll*   26
Num. 1:46   26

27 And of the hundred talents of silver were cast [R]the sockets of the sanctuary, and the sockets of the vail; an hundred sockets of the hundred talents, a talent for a socket.

28 And of the thousand seven hundred seventy and five *shē'-kĕls* he made hooks for the pillars, and overlaid their chapiters, and [R]filleted them.

29 And the brass of the offering *was* seventy talents, and two thousand and four hundred shē'-kĕls.

30 And therewith he made the sockets to the door of the tabernacle of the congregation, and the brasen altar, and the brasen grate for it, and all the vessels of the altar,

31 And the sockets of the court round about, and the sockets of the court gate, and all the pins of the tabernacle, and all the pins of the court round about.

CHAPTER 39

Ephod and breastplate

AND of [R]the blue, and purple, and scarlet, they made [R]cloths of service, to do service in the holy *place,* and made the holy garments for Aaron; [R]as the LORD commanded Moses.

2 [R]And he made the ē'-phŏd *of* gold, blue, and purple, and scarlet, and fine twined linen.

3 And they did beat the gold into thin plates, and cut *it into* wires, to work *it* in the blue, and in the purple, and in the scarlet, and in the fine linen, *with* cunning work.

4 They made shoulderpieces for it, to couple *it* together: by the two edges was it coupled together.

5 And the curious girdle of his ē'-phŏd, that *was* upon it, *was* of the same, according to the work thereof; *of* gold, blue, and purple, and scarlet, and fine twined linen; as the LORD commanded Moses.

6 [R]And they wrought onyx stones inclosed in ouches of gold, graven, as signets are graven, with the names of the children of Israel.

7 And he put them on the shoulders of the ē'-phŏd, *that they should be* stones for a [R]memorial to the children of Israel; as the LORD commanded Moses.

8 [R]And he made the breastplate *of* cunning work, like the work of the ē'-phŏd; *of* gold, blue, and purple, and scarlet, and fine twined linen.

9 It was foursquare; they made the breastplate double: a span *was* the length thereof, and a span the breadth thereof, *being* doubled.

10 [R]And they set in it four rows of stones:

CHAP. 38
BC 1491
27 ch. 26:19, 21, 25, 32
28 ch. 27:17

CHAP. 39
BC 1491
1 ch. 35:23
1 ch. 31:10 & 35:19
1 ch. 28:4
2 ch. 28:6
6 ch. 28:9
7 ch. 28:12
8 ch. 28:15
10 ch. 28:17, etc.

Or, *ruby*   10
Rev. 21:12   14
ch. 28:31   22
ch. 28:33   25

the first row *was* a [N]sardius, a topaz, and a carbuncle: this *was* the first row.

11 And the second row, an emerald, a sapphire, and a diamond.

12 And the third row, a ligure, an agate, and an amethyst.

13 And the fourth row, a beryl, an onyx, and a jasper: *they were* inclosed in ouches of gold in their inclosings.

14 And the stones *were* according to the names of the children of Israel, [R]twelve, according to their names, *like* the engravings of a signet, every one with his name, according to the twelve tribes.

15 And they made upon the breastplate chains at the ends, *of* wreathen work *of* pure gold.

16 And they made two ouches *of* gold, and two gold rings; and put the two rings in the two ends of the breastplate.

17 And they put the two wreathen chains of gold in the two rings on the ends of the breastplate.

18 And the two ends of the two wreathen chains they fastened in the two ouches, and put them on the shoulderpieces of the ē'-phŏd, before it.

19 And they made two rings of gold, and put *them* on the two ends of the breastplate, upon the border of it, which *was* on the side of the ē'-phŏd inward.

20 And they made two *other* golden rings, and put them on the two sides of the ē'-phŏd underneath, toward the forepart of it, over against the *other* coupling thereof, above the curious girdle of the ē'-phŏd.

21 And they did bind the breastplate by his rings unto the rings of the ē'-phŏd with a lace of blue, that it might be above the curious girdle of the ē'-phŏd, and that the breastplate might not be loosed from the ē'-phŏd; as the LORD commanded Moses.

22 [R]And he made the robe of the ē'-phŏd *of* woven work, all *of* blue.

23 And *there was* an hole in the midst of the robe, as the hole of an habergeon, *with* a band round about the hole, that it should not rend.

24 And they made upon the hems of the robe pomegranates *of* blue, and purple, and scarlet, *and* twined *linen.*

25 And they made [R]bells *of* pure gold, and put the bells between the pomegranates upon the hem of the robe, round about between the pomegranates;

26 A bell and a pomegranate, a bell and a pomegranate, round about the hem of the robe to minister *in;* as the LORD commanded Moses.

Other priestly garments

27 ᴿAnd they made coats *of* fine linen *of* woven work for Aaron, and for his sons,

28 ᴿAnd a mitre *of* fine linen, and goodly bonnets *of* fine linen, and ᴿlinen breeches *of* fine twined linen,

29 ᴿAnd a girdle *of* fine twined linen, and blue, and purple, and scarlet, *of* needlework; as the Lᴏʀᴅ commanded Moses.

30 ᴿAnd they made the plate of the holy crown *of* pure gold, and wrote upon it a writing, *like to* the engravings of a signet, HOLINESS TO THE LORD.

31 And they tied unto it a lace of blue, to fasten *it* on high upon the mitre; as the Lᴏʀᴅ commanded Moses.

Moses views and approves

32 Thus was all the work of the tabernacle of the tent of the congregation finished: and the children of Israel did ᴿaccording to all that the Lᴏʀᴅ commanded Moses, so did they.

33 And they brought the tabernacle unto Moses, the tent, and all his furniture, his taches, his boards, his bars, and his pillars, and his sockets,

34 And the covering of rams' skins dyed red, and the covering of badgers' skins, and the vail of the covering,

35 The ark of the testimony, and the staves thereof, and the mercy seat,

36 The table, *and* all the vessels thereof, and the shewbread,

37 The pure candlestick, *with* the lamps thereof, *even with* the lamps to be set in order, and all the vessels thereof, and the oil for light,

38 And the golden altar, and the anointing oil, and ᴺthe sweet incense, and the hanging for the tabernacle door,

39 The brasen altar, and his grate of brass, his staves, and all his vessels, the laver and his foot,

40 The hangings of the court, his pillars, and his sockets, and the hanging for the court gate, his cords, and his pins, and all the vessels of the service of the tabernacle, for the tent of the congregation,

41 The cloths of service to do service in the holy *place,* and the holy garments for Aaron the priest, and his sons' garments, to minister in the priest's office.

42 According to all that the Lᴏʀᴅ commanded Moses, so the children of Israel ᴿmade all the work.

43 And Moses did look upon all the work, and, behold, they had done it as the Lᴏʀᴅ had commanded, even so had they done it: and Moses ᴿblessed them.

CHAPTER 40

Tabernacle erected

Aɴᴅ the Lᴏʀᴅ spake unto Moses, saying, 2 On the first day of the ᴿfirst month shalt thou set up ᴿthe tabernacle of the tent of the congregation.

3 And ᴿthou shalt put therein the ark of the testimony, and cover the ark with the vail.

4 And ᴿthou shalt bring in the table, and ᴿset in order ᴺthe things that are to be set in order upon it; ᴿand thou shalt bring in the candlestick, and light the lamps thereof.

5 ᴿAnd thou shalt set the altar of gold for the incense before the ark of the testimony, and put the hanging of the door to the tabernacle.

6 And thou shalt set the altar of the burnt offering before the door of the tabernacle of the tent of the congregation.

7 And ᴿthou shalt set the laver between the tent of the congregation and the altar, and shalt put water therein.

8 And thou shalt set up the court round about, and hang up the hanging at the court gate.

9 And thou shalt take the anointing oil, and ᴿanoint the tabernacle, and all that *is* therein, and shalt hallow it, and all the vessels thereof: and it shall be holy.

10 And thou shalt anoint the altar of the burnt offering, and all his vessels, and sanctify the altar: and ᴿit shall be an altar ᴺmost holy.

11 And thou shalt anoint the laver and his foot, and sanctify it.

12 ᴿAnd thou shalt bring Aaron and his sons unto the door of the tabernacle of the congregation, and wash them with water.

Anointing of Aaron and his sons

13 And thou shalt put upon Aaron the holy garments, ᴿand anoint him, and sanctify him; that he may minister unto me in the priest's office.

14 And thou shalt bring his sons, and clothe them with coats:

15 And thou shalt anoint them, as thou didst anoint their father, that they may minister unto me in the priest's office: for their anointing shall surely be ᴿan everlasting priesthood throughout their generations.

16 Thus did Moses: according to all that the Lᴏʀᴅ commanded him, so did he.

17 And it came to pass in the first month in the second year, on the first *day* of the month, *that* the ᴿtabernacle was reared up.

18 And Moses reared up the tabernacle, and

fastened his sockets, and set up the boards thereof, and put in the bars thereof, and reared up his pillars.

19 And he spread abroad the tent over the tabernacle, and put the covering of the tent above upon it; as the LORD commanded Moses.

20 And he took and put [R]the testimony into the ark, and set the staves on the ark, and put the mercy seat above upon the ark:

21 And he brought the ark into the tabernacle, and [R]set up the vail of the covering, and covered the ark of the testimony; as the LORD commanded Moses.

22 [R]And he put the table in the tent of the congregation, upon the side of the tabernacle northward, without the vail.

23 [R]And he set the bread in order upon it before the LORD; as the LORD had commanded Moses.

24 [R]And he put the candlestick in the tent of the congregation, over against the table, on the side of the tabernacle southward.

25 And [R]he lighted the lamps before the LORD; as the LORD commanded Moses.

26 [R]And he put the golden altar in the tent of the congregation before the vail:

27 [R]And he burnt sweet incense thereon; as the LORD commanded Moses.

28 [R]And he set up the hanging *at* the door of the tabernacle.

29 [R]And he put the altar of burnt offering *by* the door of the tabernacle of the tent of the congregation, and [R]offered upon it the burnt

CHAP. **40**	
BC 1491	
20 ch. 25:16	
21 ch. 26:33	
22 ch. 26:35	
23 ver. 4	
24 ch. 26:35	
25 ver. 4	
ch. 25:37	
26 ver. 5	
ch. 30:6	
27 ch. 30:7	
28 ver. 5	
ch. 26:36	
29 ver. 6	
29 ch. 29:38, etc.	

ver. 7	**30**
ch. 30:18	
ch. 30:19	**32**
ver. 8	**33**
ch. 27:9, 16	
ch. 29:43	**34**
Lev. 16:2	
Num. 9:15	
2 Chr. 5:13	
Is. 6:4	
Lev. 16:2	**35**
1 Ki. 8:11	
Num. 9:17	**36**
Neh. 9:19	
Heb. *journeyed*	**36**
Num. 9:19-22	**37**
ch. 13:21	**38**
Num. 9:15	

offering and the meat offering; as the LORD commanded Moses.

30 [R]And he set the laver between the tent of the congregation and the altar, and put water there, to wash *withal.*

31 And Moses and Aaron and his sons washed their hands and their feet thereat:

32 When they went into the tent of the congregation, and when they came near unto the altar, they washed; [R]as the LORD commanded Moses.

33 [R]And he reared up the court round about the tabernacle and the altar, and set up the hanging of the court gate. So Moses finished the work.

The glory of the LORD

34 [R]Then a cloud covered the tent of the congregation, and the glory of the LORD filled the tabernacle.

35 And Moses [R]was not able to enter into the tent of the congregation, because the cloud abode thereon, and the glory of the LORD filled the tabernacle.

36 [R]And when the cloud was taken up from over the tabernacle, the children of Israel [N]went onward in all their journeys:

37 But [R]if the cloud were not taken up, then they journeyed not till the day that it was taken up.

38 For [R]the cloud of the LORD *was* upon the tabernacle by day, and fire was on it by night, in the sight of all the house of Israel, throughout all their journeys.

THE THIRD BOOK OF MOSES, CALLED

LEVITICUS

The English title for this third book of the Bible is derived from the Greek name given to it in the Septuagint version: "a book for the Levites." Leviticus records the legislative regulations respecting the offerings of the Aaronic high priesthood and duties and services of the sons of Levi as priests of Israel: laws of ordination, laws of sacrifice, laws of purification, and laws of holiness. These laws and observances were designed to guide Israel in holy living—a pattern of life in contrast to that of the Egyptians and the Canaanites. There are only three historical events which it narrates: the consecration of the priesthood, God's destruction of Nadab and Abihu for profanation, and the magistrates' punishment of Shelomith's son for blasphemy. This book follows in natural order the book of

Exodus, which closes with the erection and completion of the tabernacle: The sanctuary being ready, regulations for sacrifices to be offered are next in order.

OUTLINE OF THE BOOK:
  I. Various sacrifices   1:1 – 7:38
 II. The priesthood consecrated for service   8:1 – 10:20
III. Laws of purification   11:1 – 15:33
 IV. The day of atonement   16:1 – 34
  V. Regulations for holy living   17:1 – 22-33
 VI. Holy convocations and observances   23:1 – 25:55
VII. Conditions for God's favor   26:1 – 27:34

CHAPTER 1

Burnt offerings

AND the LORD ᴿcalled unto Moses, and spake unto him ᴿout of the tabernacle of the congregation, saying,

2 Speak unto the children of Israel, and say unto them, ᴿIf any man of you bring an offering unto the LORD, ye shall bring your offering of the cattle, *even* of the herd, and of the flock.

3 If his offering *be* a burnt sacrifice of the herd, let him offer a male ᴿwithout blemish: he shall offer it of his own voluntary will at the door of the tabernacle of the congregation before the LORD.

4 ᴿAnd he shall put his hand upon the head of the burnt offering; and it shall be ᴿaccepted for him ᴿto make atonement for him.

5 And he shall kill the ᴿbullock before the LORD: ᴿand the priests, Aaron's sons, shall bring the blood, ᴿand sprinkle the blood round about upon the altar that *is* by the door of the tabernacle of the congregation.

6 And he shall flay the burnt offering, and cut it into his pieces.

7 And the sons of Aaron the priest shall put fire upon the altar, and ᴿlay the wood in order upon the fire:

8 And the priests, Aaron's sons, shall lay the parts, the head, and the fat, in order upon the wood that *is* on the fire which *is* upon the altar:

9 But his inwards and his legs shall he wash in water: and the priest shall burn all on the altar, *to be* a burnt sacrifice, an offering made by fire, of a ᴿsweet savour unto the LORD.

10 And if his offering *be* of the flocks, *namely,* of the sheep, or of the goats, for a burnt sacrifice; he shall bring it a male ᴿwithout blemish.

11 ᴿAnd he shall kill it on the side of the altar northward before the LORD: and the priests, Aaron's sons, shall sprinkle his blood round about upon the altar.

12 And he shall cut it into his pieces, with his head and his fat: and the priest shall lay them in order on the wood that *is* on the fire which *is* upon the altar:

13 But he shall wash the inwards and the legs with water: and the priest shall bring *it* all, and burn *it* upon the altar: it *is* a burnt sacrifice, an offering made by fire, of a sweet savour unto the LORD.

14 And if the burnt sacrifice for his offering to the LORD *be* of fowls, then he shall bring his offering of ᴿturtledoves, or of young pigeons.

15 And the priest shall bring it unto the altar, and ᴺwring off his head, and burn *it* on the altar; and the blood thereof shall be wrung out at the side of the altar:

16 And he shall pluck away his crop with ᴺhis feathers, and cast it ᴿbeside the altar on the east part, by the place of the ashes:

17 And he shall cleave it with the wings thereof, *but* ᴿshall not divide *it* asunder: and the priest shall burn it upon the altar, upon the wood that *is* upon the fire: ᴿit *is* a burnt sacrifice, an offering made by fire, of a sweet savour unto the LORD.

CHAPTER 2

Meat offerings

AND when any will offer ᴿa meat offering unto the LORD, his offering shall be *of* fine flour; and he shall pour oil upon it, and put frankincense thereon:

2 And he shall bring it to Aaron's sons the priests: and he shall take thereout his handful of the flour thereof, and of the oil thereof, with all the frankincense thereof; and the priest shall burn ᴿthe memorial of it upon the altar, *to be* an offering made by fire, of a sweet savour unto the LORD:

3 And ᴿthe remnant of the meat offerings *shall be* Aaron's and his sons': ᴿit *is* a thing most holy of the offerings of the LORD made by fire.

4 And if thou bring an oblation of a meat offering baken in the oven, *it shall be* unleavened cakes of fine flour mingled with oil, or unleavened wafers ᴿanointed with oil.

5 And if thy oblation *be* a meat offering baken ᴺin a pan, it shall be *of* fine flour unleavened, mingled with oil.

6 Thou shalt part it in pieces, and pour oil thereon: it *is* a meat offering.

7 And if thy oblation *be* a meat offering baken in the fryingpan, it shall be made *of* fine flour with oil.

8 And thou shalt bring the meat offering that is made of these things unto the LORD: and when it is presented unto the priest, he shall bring it unto the altar.

9 And the priest shall take from the meat offering ᴿa memorial thereof, and shall burn *it* upon the altar: it *is* an ᴿoffering made by fire, of a sweet savour unto the LORD.

10 And ᴿthat which is left of the meat offering *shall be* Aaron's and his sons': it *is* a thing most holy of the offerings of the LORD made by fire.

11 No meat offering, which ye shall bring unto the LORD, shall be made with ᴿleaven:

for ye shall burn no leaven, nor any honey, in any offering of the LORD made by fire.

12 ᴿAs for the oblation of the firstfruits, ye shall offer them unto the LORD: but they shall not ᴺbe burnt on the altar for a sweet savour.

13 And every oblation of thy meat offering ᴿshalt thou season with salt; neither shalt thou suffer ᴿthe salt of the covenant of thy God to be lacking from thy meat offering: ᴿwith all thine offerings thou shalt offer salt.

14 And if thou offer a meat offering of thy firstfruits unto the LORD, ᴿthou shalt offer for the meat offering of thy firstfruits green ears of corn dried by the fire, *even* corn beaten out of ᴿfull ears.

15 And ᴿthou shalt put oil upon it, and lay frankincense thereon: it *is* a meat offering.

16 And the priest shall burn ᴿthe memorial of it, *part* of the beaten corn thereof, and *part* of the oil thereof, with all the frankincense thereof: it *is* an offering made by fire unto the LORD.

CHAPTER 3

Peace offerings

AND if his oblation *be* a ᴿsacrifice of peace offering, if he offer *it* of the herd; whether *it be* a male or female, he shall offer it ᴿwithout blemish before the LORD.

2 And ᴿhe shall lay his hand upon the head of his offering, and kill it *at* the door of the tabernacle of the congregation: and Aaron's sons the priests shall sprinkle the blood upon the altar round about.

3 And he shall offer of the sacrifice of the peace offering an offering made by fire unto the LORD; ᴿtheᴺ fat that covereth the inwards, and all the fat that *is* upon the inwards,

4 And the two kidneys, and the fat that *is* on them, which *is* by the flanks, and the ᴺcaul above the liver, with the kidneys, it shall he take away.

5 And Aaron's sons ᴿshall burn it on the altar upon the burnt sacrifice, which *is* upon the wood that *is* on the fire: it *is* an offering made by fire, of a sweet savour unto the LORD.

6 And if his offering for a sacrifice of peace offering unto the LORD *be* of the flock; male or female, ᴿhe shall offer it without blemish.

7 If he offer a lamb for his offering, then shall he offer it before the LORD.

8 And he shall lay his hand upon the head of his offering, and kill it before the tabernacle of the congregation: and Aaron's sons shall sprinkle the blood thereof round about upon the altar.

9 And he shall offer of the sacrifice of the peace offering an offering made by fire unto the LORD; the fat thereof, *and* the whole rump, it shall he take off hard by the backbone; and the fat that covereth the inwards, and all the fat that *is* upon the inwards,

10 And the two kidneys, and the fat that *is* upon them, which *is* by the flanks, and the caul above the liver, with the kidneys, it shall he take away.

11 And the priest shall burn it upon the altar: *it is* ᴿthe food of the offering made by fire unto the LORD.

12 And if his offering *be* a goat, then ᴿhe shall offer it before the LORD.

13 And he shall lay his hand upon the head of it, and kill it before the tabernacle of the congregation: and the sons of Aaron shall sprinkle the blood thereof upon the altar round about.

14 And he shall offer thereof his offering, *even* an offering made by fire unto the LORD; the fat that covereth the inwards, and all the fat that *is* upon the inwards,

15 And the two kidneys, and the fat that *is* upon them, which *is* by the flanks, and the caul above the liver, with the kidneys, it shall he take away.

16 And the priest shall burn them upon the altar: *it is* the food of the offering made by fire for a sweet savour: ᴿall the fat *is* the LORD's.

17 *It shall be* ᴿperpetual statute for your generations throughout all your dwellings, that ye eat neither ᴿfat nor ᴿblood.

CHAPTER 4

Sin offerings for priests

AND the LORD spake unto Moses, saying, 2 Speak unto the children of Israel, saying, ᴿIf a soul shall sin through ignorance against any of the commandments of the LORD *concerning things* which ought not to be done, and shall do against any of them:

3 ᴿIf the priest that is anointed do sin according to the sin of the people; then let him bring for his sin, which he hath sinned, ᴿa young bullock without blemish unto the LORD for a sin offering.

4 And he shall bring the bullock ᴿunto the door of the tabernacle of the congregation before the LORD; and shall lay his hand upon the bullock's head, and kill the bullock before the LORD.

5 And the priest that is anointed ᴿshall take of the bullock's blood, and bring it to the tabernacle of the congregation:

6 And the priest shall dip his finger in the blood, and sprinkle of the blood seven times

God Chooses a
People to Serve Him

"*For thou art a holy people unto the Lord thy God: the Lord thy God hath chosen thee to be a special people unto himself, above all people that are upon the face of the earth.*"

DEUT. 7:6

Lot and His Daughters

BOUT two thousands years before the birth of Jesus Christ, there lived in the city of Ur in Babylonia a man named Terah. Ur was a city along the banks of the Euphrates River, near the Persian Gulf. Terah became the father of three sons—Abram, Nahor, and Haran; and in due time his son Haran grew up and also had a son whom he named Lot. As the children grew older, Terah became restless. He wanted to move to a new country. Traveling northwest some six hundred miles, Terah and his family established a village which they called Haran.

The spirit of the pioneer was in Terah's descendants. Abram turned his eyes southward and liked what he saw; so he and his nephew Lot and their families moved into Canaan. When a famine descended upon the country, they moved father south and west, into Egypt; but after a few years they returned to Canaan, quite wealthy, and settled at Bethel.

There were so many sheep in Abram's and Lot's flocks that there was not enough grass for all to graze upon. So Abram proposed that they separate their flocks and move away from each other. This was agreeable; so Lot moved east into the Jordan River valley, to the city of Sodom. In a war fought among rival kings, Lot and his family were taken captive and their goods were stolen. But Abram and his tribe rescued Lot and recovered all their possessions.

Now the city of Sodom was an extremely sinful city, so wicked in fact that the Lord proposed to destroy it. But Abram—whose name had been changed to Abraham—pleaded with God to spare the city, if there were fifty righteous persons living there. He kept bargaining, reducing the number until the Lord promised: "I will not destroy it for ten's sake." But even ten righteous persons could not be found in Sodom!

Two angels, who appeared to be men, came to Sodom one evening. Lot saw them and invited them to be guests in his home. While there, the angels revealed that they had been sent to Sodom to destroy the city. So they urged Lot and his family to flee for their lives: "Arise, take thy wife, and thy two daughters, which are here; lest they be consumed in the iniquity of the city." In haste, Lot and his family fled from Sodom and went to a little city called Zoar.

Now the angels had warned them, "Escape for thy life; look not behind thee." Then fire and brimstone fell upon both Sodom and Gomorrah, utterly destroying those cities. Lot's wife, consumed with curiosity about what was happening to the doomed cities, "looked back from behind him, and she became a pillar of salt." In the country around the Dead Sea today, there is a curiously shaped salt formation which is still referred to as "Lot's wife."

Abraham, Lot's uncle, viewed the destruction of Sodom and Gomorrah from a distance. From where he viewed it, "the smoke of the country went up as the smoke of a furnace." Lot was delivered from death in the doomed city of Sodom because of the faith of Abraham.

Lot and his daughters moved from the city of Zoar up into the hill country, for he feared to dwell in Zoar: and he dwelt in a cave, he and his two daughters.

Genesis 11:26–19:30.

The Sacrifice of Isaac

BRAM was becoming a very old man—in fact, he was ninety-nine years old—and he still had no son and heir. One night, in a mood of despair, he complained to God of this fact; and the Lord, causing him to look up at the stars, said: "So shall thy seed be." Could it be true? It was almost beyond belief. But Abram was a man of faith; "he believed in the Lord."

God made a covenant with Abram: His name was changed to Abraham, which means "Father of a multitude." The land of Canaan was given to Abraham and his descendants; and God covenanted to be their God. Further, God promised Abraham: "My covenant will I establish with Isaac, which Sarah shall bear unto thee at this set time in the next year."

Although she too was quite old, Sarah bore Abraham a son, as God had promised. Abraham named his son Isaac, which means "he laughs." As Isaac grew to childhood and youth, we can imagine that Abraham took great pride in his son.

One day, God put Abraham to a severe test: "Take now thy son, thine only son Isaac, whom thou lovest, and get thee into the land of Moriah; and offer him there for a burnt offering upon one of the mountains which I will tell thee of." Abraham must have been stunned, shocked, and almost overcome with anguish. How could God ask this of him? What of the promise God had made, that through Isaac he would have many descendants?

Yet even though many fears and misgivings probably assailed Abraham, he did as he was told. Getting up early the next morning, he took Isaac and two young workmen, saddled his donkey, gathered firewood for the burnt offering, and set off on his heart-breaking mission. For three days they traveled; then Abraham saw the place where the sacrifice was to be made and told the two young men to wait while he and Isaac went to worship God.

Isaac carried the wood, while Abraham carried the knife and the fire. Puzzled, Isaac asked his father: "Where is the lamb for a burnt offering?" Abraham answered him: "My son, God will provide himself a lamb for a burnt offering." But when they had built an altar and laid the wood for the fire, Abraham bound Isaac and laid him on the altar. He must have groaned with anguish as he "took the knife to slay his son."

At that moment, an angel called out to Abraham: "Lay not thine hand upon the lad, neither do thou anything unto him: for now I know that thou fearest God, seeing thou hast not withheld thy son, thine only son from me." And as Abraham looked up in relief and joy, he saw a ram caught in a thicket nearby. So Abraham sacrificed the ram as a burnt offering instead of his son Isaac. The name which Abraham gave to this place of the sacrifice means "The Lord will provide."

Abraham had proved, by his willingness to sacrifice his beloved son, his faith in God and his utter obedience to the divine will. God promised Abraham: "In thy seed shall all the nations of the earth be blessed; because that hast obeyed my voice." So Abraham and Isaac returned with joy to their home at Beersheba.

Genesis 15:3–22:19.

Jacob and Rachel

HEN Jacob had grown to manhood and was ready for marriage, his father Isaac told him: "Thou shalt not take a wife of the daughters of Canaan." Then he directed Jacob to go north to Padan-aram, where Abraham had lived before going down into Canaan, and choose as his wife one of the daughters of Laban.

As Jacob journeyed north, he met some shepherds who were watering their sheep. He fell into conversation with them, and found that they were from Haran, where Jacob's ancestors had lived. And as they talked, a beautiful young shepherdess named Rachel came to water her sheep. This was the daughter of Jacob's kinsman, Laban.

Jacob was moved with emotion when he saw Rachel. First he rolled the large stone from the mouth of the well so that her sheep could get a drink of water, then "Jacob kissed Rachel, and lifted up his voice, and wept." When Rachel learned that Jacob was one of her father's relatives, she ran to tell her father the news, And Laban hurried out to meet Jacob, "and embraced him, and kissed him, and brought him to his house." Jacob was a guest in Laban's home for a month.

One day as Laban talked with Jacob, he asked: "Tell me, what shall thy wages be?" For it was apparent that Jacob was willing to work for Laban. By this time, Jacob had fallen in love with Rachel; so he told Laban: "I will serve thee seven years for Rachel thy younger daughter." Laban agreed. For seven years Jacob helped tend his flocks; and although it was a long time, the time seemed to go quickly.

Finally the day for the wedding arrived. Laban gathered the men of the place and gave a wedding feast. Later that evening, when Jacob was ready to retire, Laban deceived him: instead of sending Rachel to Jacob's tent, he sent his older daughter Leah. When daybreak came, and Jacob could see his bride's face, he was furious. "What is this thou hast done unto me?" he demanded of Laban. "Did not I serve thee for Rachel?"

Laban tried to explain that it was not customary to allow one's younger daughter to get married before the older daughter had a husband. Then Laban made Jacob an offer: for seven more years of service, he could have Rachel for his wife, also. In those days, it was permissible for a man to have more than one wife. So Jacob agreed; and for seven years more he worked for Laban.

Jacob lived with both of his wives, but he loved Rachel more than Leah. This caused some rivalry and jealousy between the two sisters, wives of the same husband. Leah bore Jacob six sons and a daughter; Rachel had two sons— Joseph and Benjamin. Rachel died in giving birth to Benjamin; Jacob, in love and respect, erected a pillar upon her grave which was a revered landmark for the Jews for many years afterward.

Little could Rachel imagine what a great man her son Joseph would become, and what a benefactor of his people he would be in years ahead!

Genesis 27:41–35:20.

TISSOT

Joseph Makes Himself Known

F all his sons, Joseph was Jacob's favorite. This favoritism caused Joseph's brothers to be jealous of him. Therefore, one day when they were out in the fields tending their father's sheep, they plotted to kill Joseph. But even as they planned his death, a caravan of traders bound for Egypt came along and found Joseph in a deep pit where his brothers had placed him. They took him to Egypt and sold him as a slave to a captain of the Pharaoh's guards, a man named Potiphar.

Joseph proved to be a fine worker. Potiphar trusted him completely; so he put Joseph in charge of his house. But Potiphar's wife lied about Joseph, claiming that he had insulted her. In anger, Potiphar threw Joseph into prison.

Even in prison, Joseph made friends and won respect. He became well acquainted with the Pharaoh's butler and banker, who had offended their ruler and thus were in prison. Joseph interpreted their dreams correctly; so later, when the butler had been restored to the Pharaoh's service and his master was troubled by a dream, the butler recalled his fellow-prisoner Joseph, who was still in prison, and told the Pharaoh about him.

Pharaoh had Joseph released from prison and brought to him. When Joseph heard the dream, he interpreted it: Egypt would have seven years of plenty, followed by seven years of famine. Then he advised the Pharaoh to stockpile food during the good years to prevent starvation during the bad years. The Pharaoh was so impressed with Joseph that he made him the ruler of Egypt, second only to the Pharaoh. Joseph proceeded to have food stored against the day of famine.

When the famine struck, it was felt in Canaan where Joseph's father and brothers were living. Hearing of the grain for sale in Egypt, Jacob sent ten of his sons to buy food, but kept his youngest son Benjamin at home. Without revealing who he was, Joseph sold the grain to his brothers and inquired about their father and youngest brother. Pretending to believe that his brothers were spies, Joseph kept them in prison three days, then insisted that they bring their youngest brother to Egypt on their next trip.

When they arrived in Egypt on their next trip, Joseph had a sumptuous feast for his brothers. After dinner, he had their sacks filled with grain and sent them on their way. But he played a trick on them: he put his own silver cup in Benjamin's sack, then had his soldiers to "discover" the "stolen" cup in the sack and bring the brothers back to Egypt. They returned in great fear.

Then Joseph revealed his identity to his brothers: "I am Joseph your brother, whom ye sold into Egypt. Now therefore be not grieved, nor angry with yourselves, that ye sold me hither: for God did send me before you to preserve life."

Joseph sent to Canaan for his father Jacob and for his brothers' wives and children. They would all live in Egypt with the best wishes of the Pharaoh. Jacob was overjoyed when he heard the good news from his sons. "Joseph my son is yet alive," he said, "I will go and see him before I die."

Genesis 37:2–45:28

Moses in the Bulrushes

HEN Joseph invited his brothers and their families to come and live in Egypt to escape the famine in their homeland of Canaan, the Pharaoh had been quite friendly to them. But a new ruler, named Ramses II, came to the throne in 1292 B.C. As he looked around and saw how numerous the Hebrews were, and how much wealth and power they had acquired, the Pharaoh became fearful lest they should ally themselves with Egypt's enemies in the event of war. What should he do?

Ramses had not known Joseph, so he felt no gratitude nor sense of obligation to the Hebrew people. With deliberate cruelty, therefore, he seized the Hebrews and put them to work as slaves. Some of them worked in the fields; others were forced to make mortar and brick. The cities of Pithom and Raamses were built largely with Hebrew slave labor.

Even though they were worked hard and treated shamefully, the Hebrews continued to increase. So Ramses became even harsher in his demands. He ordered the midwives to kill all the boy children born to Hebrew women. But the midwives had too much human kindness and too much fear of God to murder newborn babies as the Pharaoh had ordered. So he next commanded the Hebrews: "Every son that is born ye shall cast into the river."

In such a fearful time, a young couple from the tribe of Levi had their first-born son. As the mother gazed down at her sleeping infant, it was unthinkable that she should throw him into the Nile River! She loved him, and she was resolved to save him from harm.

For three months she hid him at home. Those must have been anxious days, during which the young mother feared every time her baby cried that the Egyptians would hear him and cold-heartedly throw him in the Nile to drown. Finally, she could no longer risk having the baby found in the house. So taking reeds from the edge of the river, she wove a little basket and made it waterproof with pitch and bitumen. Tenderly she put her baby son in the basket and placed it among the bulrushes at the edge of the river.

What would become of her baby boy? She could not bear to leave him alone, yet she dared not stand nearby or her secret would be discovered. So she had her daughter to watch the basket from a short distance away.

A short time later, one of Pharaoh's daughters came down to the river to bathe. Suddenly she noticed the basket and had one of her maids to fetch it for her. How surprised she must have been when she opened the basket and found, not food, but a baby boy! Startled, the baby began to cry; "and she had compassion on him, and said, This is one of the Hebrews' children."

When the sister saw what had happened, she ran up to Pharaoh's daughter and said: "Shall I go and call to thee a nurse of the Hebrew women, that she may nurse the child for thee?" Pharaoh's daughter agreed; so the little girl ran quickly and got the baby's mother. When the young mother arrived, Pharaoh's daughter said: "Take this child away, and nurse it for me, and I will give thee thy wages." And she named the child "Moses," because she "drew him out of the water."

Exodus 1:8–2:10.

Moses Before the Burning Bush

EVEN though Moses had been reared as the son of Pharaoh's daughter, he remembered that the Hebrews were his people. When he saw an Egyptian beating a Hebrew one day, it made him so angry that he killed the Egyptian and buried him in the sand. A short time later, Pharaoh heard of Moses' crime; he sought to kill Moses, so Moses fled as a fugitive from Egypt into the land of Midian.

In Midian, Moses met a priest's daughter named Zipporah whom he married. While living in Midian, Moses worked as a shepherd, tending flocks for his father-in-law. One day, he took his sheep onto the slopes of Mount Horeb, "the mountain of God." Suddenly, Moses noticed a most unusual sight: a bush seemed to be burning, yet it did not burn up! So Moses said to himself, "I will now turn aside, and see this great sight, why the bush is not burnt."

As Moses drew closer to the bush, God spoke out of the burning bush and said: "Put off thy shoes from off thy feet, for the place whereon thou standest is holy ground." Moses must have been startled, awestruck by this encounter with the living God. The voice from the bush continued: "I am the God of thy father, the God of Abraham, the God of Isaac, and the God of Jacob. I have surely seen the affliction of my people which are in Egypt, and have heard their cry. . . . And I am come down to deliver them out of the hand of the Egyptians, and to bring them up out of that land unto a good land. . . . Come now therefore, and I will send thee unto Pharaoh, that thou mayest bring forth my people the children of Israel out of Egypt."

Moses had been afraid when he first heard God's voice; now he must have been even more fearful. Go back to Egypt, where he was wanted for murder? Pharaoh would surely have him killed! So Moses, instead of saying "Yes" to God's call, began first to make excuses. "Who am I," he asked, "that I should go unto Pharaoh, and that I should bring forth the children of Israel out of Egypt?" But God reassured Moses: "Certainly I will be with thee."

But Moses was not yet ready to go to Egypt. How could he convince the Hebrews that God had indeed sent him to lead them out of Egypt? What was God's name? In reply, "God said unto Moses, I AM THAT I AM: and he said, Thus shalt thou say unto the children of Israel, I AM hath sent me unto you." Then God explained to Moses just how he would deal with the Egyptians to make them release the Hebrews from slavery.

Moses continued to make excuses. He was not an effective speaker; but God promised, "I will be with thy mouth, and teach thee what thou shalt say." Still, Moses wanted God to send some other person. These excuses caused the anger of the Lord to be kindled against Moses. But seeing Aaron, Moses' brother, God said: "He shall be thy spokesman unto the people."

So Moses and Aaron went down into Egypt and gathered together all the elders of the Hebrew people. When the Hebrews heard the good news that God intended to deliver them from Egypt, through the leadership of Moses, "the people believed." In profound gratitude, they bowed their heads and worshipped God.

Exodus 2:11–4:31.

FETI

Moses Breaks the Tablets

T HE Hebrews had escaped from Egypt, and now they were at the foot of Mount Sinai, in the wilderness. God called to Moses out of the mountain and commanded him to tell the Hebrew people: "If ye will obey my voice indeed, and keep my covenant, then ye shall be a peculiar treasure unto me above all people: for all the earth is mine: and ye shall be unto me a kingdom of priests, and an holy nation."

After a period of preparation, Moses went up Mount Sinai, while the people stood at the foot of the mountain. Then God gave Moses the Ten Commandments:

1. Thou shalt have no other gods before me.
2. Thou shalt not make unto thee any graven image.
3. Thou shalt not take the name of the Lord thy God in vain.
4. Remember the Sabbath day to keep it holy.
5. Honor thy father and thy mother.
6. Thou shalt not kill.
7. Thou shalt not commit adultery.
8. Thou shalt not steal.
9. Thou shalt not bear false witness against thy neighbor.
10. Thou shalt not covet.

When Moses came down and read the commandments, the basis of God's covenant with the Hebrew people, they all said: "All that the Lord hath said will we do, and be obedient."

Then Moses went up the mountain again, to receive further instructions from the Almighty. He remained there forty days and forty nights. And the Hebrew people became restless, uneasy, and impatient. They told Aaron: "Make us gods, which shall go before us." So Aaron had the people to gather up their golden rings and earrings, and he melted these and made a golden calf. And the people said: "These be thy gods, O Israel, which brought thee up out of the land of Egypt." Aaron announced a feast for the next day.

Everyone got up early the next morning and made sacrifices to the golden calf. "And the people sat down to eat and to drink, and rose up to play." At the height of their celebration, Moses came down the mountain, carrying two stone tablets on which were engraved the commandments which God had given the Hebrew people. When Moses saw the golden calf, and the people dancing around it, he was furious. In tremendous anger, "he cast the tablets out of his hands, and brake them beneath the mount."

Then he called out in a loud voice, "Who is on the Lord's side? Let him come unto me." All the sons of Levi came forward to join Moses. Then he commanded them to take their swords and slay all the others; "and there fell of the people that day about three thousand men."

After this tragic episode, the Lord said to Moses: "Depart, and go hence, thou and the people which thou hast brought up out of the land of Egypt, unto the land which I sware unto Abraham, to Isaac, and to Jacob." God's purposes might be temporarily delayed, but they would be fulfilled.

Exodus 19:1–33:1.

The Ten Commandments

1. Thou shalt have no other gods before me.

2. Thou shalt not make unto thee any graven image.

3. Thou shalt not take the name of the Lord thy God in vain.

4. Remember the Sabbath day, to keep it holy.

5. Honor thy father and thy mother.

6. Thou shalt not kill.

7. Thou shalt not commit adultery.

8. Thou shalt not steal.

9. Thou shalt not bear false witness.

10. Thou shalt not covet.

EXODUS 20:1-17

before the LORD, before the vail of the sanctuary.

7 And the priest shall ^Rput *some* of the blood upon the horns of the altar of sweet incense before the LORD, which *is* in the tabernacle of the congregation; and shall pour ^Rall the blood of the bullock at the bottom of the altar of the burnt offering, which *is at* the door of the tabernacle of the congregation.

8 And he shall take off from it all the fat of the bullock for the sin offering; the fat that covereth the inwards, and all the fat that *is* upon the inwards,

9 And the two kidneys, and the fat that *is* upon them, which *is* by the flanks, and the caul above the liver, with the kidneys, it shall he take away,

10 ^RAs it was taken off from the bullock of the sacrifice of peace offerings: and the priest shall burn them upon the altar of the burnt offering.

11 ^RAnd the skin of the bullock, and all his flesh, with his head, and with his legs, and his inwards, and his dung,

12 Even the whole bullock shall he carry forth ^Nwithout the camp unto a clean place, ^Rwhere the ashes are poured out, and ^Rburn him on the wood with fire: ^Nwhere the ashes are poured out shall he be burnt.

For the congregation

13 And ^Rif the whole congregation of Israel sin through ignorance, ^Rand the thing be hid from the eyes of the assembly, and they have done *somewhat against* any of the commandments of the LORD *concerning things* which should not be done, and are guilty;

14 When the sin, which they have sinned against it, is known, then the congregation shall offer a young bullock for the sin, and bring him before the tabernacle of the congregation.

15 And the elders of the congregation ^Rshall lay their hands upon the head of the bullock before the LORD: and the bullock shall be killed before the LORD.

16 ^RAnd the priest that is anointed shall bring of the bullock's blood to the tabernacle of the congregation:

17 And the priest shall dip his finger *in some* of the blood, and sprinkle *it* seven times before the LORD, *even* before the vail.

18 And he shall put *some* of the blood upon the horns of the altar which *is* before the LORD, that *is* in the tabernacle of the congregation, and shall pour out all the blood at the bottom of the altar of the burnt offering, which *is at* the door of the tabernacle of the congregation.

19 And he shall take all his fat from him, and burn *it* upon the altar.

20 And he shall do with the bullock as he did ^Rwith the bullock for a sin offering, so shall he do with this: ^Rand the priest shall make an atonement for them, and it shall be forgiven them.

21 And he shall carry forth the bullock without the camp, and burn him as he burned the first bullock: it *is* a sin offering for the congregation.

For rulers

22 When a ruler hath sinned, and ^Rdone *somewhat* through ignorance *against* any of the commandments of the LORD his God *concerning things* which should not be done, and is guilty;

23 Or ^Rif his sin, wherein he hath sinned, come to his knowledge; he shall bring his offering, a kid of the goats, a male without blemish:

24 And ^Rhe shall lay his hand upon the head of the goat, and kill it in the place where they kill the burnt offering before the LORD: it *is* a sin offering.

25 ^RAnd the priest shall take of the blood of the sin offering with his finger, and put *it* upon the horns of the altar of burnt offering, and shall pour out his blood at the bottom of the altar of burnt offering.

26 And he shall burn all his fat upon the altar, as ^Rthe fat of the sacrifice of peace offerings: ^Rand the priest shall make an atonement for him as concerning his sin, and it shall be forgiven him.

For common people

27 And ^Rif ^Nany one of the ^Ncommon people sin through ignorance, while he doeth *somewhat against* any of the commandments of the LORD *concerning things* which ought not to be done, and be guilty;

28 Or ^Rif his sin, which he hath sinned, come to his knowledge: then he shall bring his offering, a kid of the goats, a female without blemish, for his sin which he hath sinned.

29 ^RAnd he shall lay his hand upon the head of the sin offering, and slay the sin offering in the place of the burnt offering.

30 And the priest shall take of the blood thereof with his finger, and put *it* upon the horns of the altar of burnt offering, and shall pour out all the blood thereof at the bottom of the altar.

31 And ^Rhe shall take away all the fat thereof, ^Ras the fat is taken away from off the sacrifice of peace offerings; and the priest shall burn *it* upon the altar for a ^Rsweet savour unto

---

CHAP. 4
BC 1490
7 ch. 8:15 & 9:9 & 16:18
7 ch. 5:9
10 ch. 3:3-5
11 Ex. 29:14
Num. 19:5
12 Heb. *to without the camp*
12 ch. 6:11
12 Heb. 13:11
12 Heb. *at the pouring out of the ashes*
13 Num. 15:24
Josh. 7:11
13 ch. 5:2-4, 17
15 ch. 1:4
16 ver. 5
Heb. 9:12-14

ver. 3   20
Num. 19:5   20
ver. 2, 13   22
ver. 14   23
ch. 5:4
ver. 4, etc.   24
Is. 53:6
ver. 30   25
ch. 3:5   26
ver. 20   26
Num. 15:28
ver. 2   27
Num. 15:27
Heb. *any soul* 27
Heb. *people of the land* 27
ver. 23   28
ver. 4, 24   29
ch. 3:14   31
ch. 3:3   31
Gen. 8:21   31
Ex. 29:18
ch. 1:9
Ezra 6:10

the LORD; ^Rand the priest shall make an atonement for him, and it shall be forgiven him.

32 And if he bring a lamb for a sin offering, ^Rhe shall bring it a female without blemish.

33 And he shall lay his hand upon the head of the sin offering, and slay it for a sin offering in the place where they kill the burnt offering.

34 And the priest shall take of the blood of the sin offering with his finger, and put *it* upon the horns of the altar of burnt offering, and shall pour out all the blood thereof at the bottom of the altar:

35 And he shall take away all the fat thereof, as the fat of the lamb is taken away from the sacrifice of the peace offerings; and the priest shall burn them upon the altar, ^Raccording to the offerings made by fire unto the LORD: ^Rand the priest shall make an atonement for his sin that he hath committed, and it shall be forgiven him.

CHAPTER 5

For special cases

AND if a soul sin, ^Rand hear the voice of swearing, and *is* a witness, whether he hath seen or known *of it;* if he do not utter *it,* then he shall ^Rbear his iniquity.

2 Or ^Rif a soul touch any unclean thing, whether *it be* a carcase of an unclean beast, or a carcase of unclean cattle, or the carcase of unclean creeping things, and *if* it be hidden from him; he also shall be unclean, and ^Rguilty.

3 Or if he touch ^Rthe uncleanness of man, whatsoever uncleanness *it be* that a man shall be defiled withal, and it be hid from him; when he knoweth *of it,* then he shall be guilty.

4 Or if a soul swear, pronouncing with *his* lips ^Rto do evil, or ^Rto do good, whatsoever *it be* that a man shall pronounce with an oath, and it be hid from him; when he knoweth *of it,* then he shall be guilty in one of these.

5 And it shall be, when he shall be guilty in one of these *things,* that he shall ^Rconfess that he hath sinned in that *thing:*

6 And he shall bring his trespass offering unto the LORD for his sin which he hath sinned, a female from the flock, a lamb or a kid of the goats, for a sin offering; and the priest shall make an atonement for him concerning his sin.

7 And ^Rif ^Nhe be not able to bring a lamb, then he shall bring for his trespass, which he hath committed, two ^Rturtledoves, or two young pigeons, unto the LORD; one for a sin offering, and the other for a burnt offering.

8 And he shall bring them unto the priest, who shall offer *that* which *is* for the sin offering first, and ^Rwring off his head from his neck, but shall not divide *it* asunder:

9 And he shall sprinkle of the blood of the sin offering upon the side of the altar; and ^Rthe rest of the blood shall be wrung out at the bottom of the altar: it *is* a sin offering.

10 And he shall offer the second *for* a burnt offering, according to the ^Rmanner:^N ^Rand the priest shall make an atonement for him for his sin which he hath sinned, and it shall be forgiven him.

11 But if he be not able to bring two turtledoves, or two young pigeons, then he that sinned shall bring for his offering the tenth part of an e'-phäh of fine flour for a sin offering; ^Rhe shall put no oil upon it, neither shall he put *any* frankincense thereon: for it *is* a sin offering.

12 Then shall he bring it to the priest, and the priest shall take his handful of it, ^R*even* a memorial thereof, and burn *it* on the altar, ^Raccording to the offerings made by fire unto the LORD: it *is* a sin offering.

13 ^RAnd the priest shall make an atonement for him as touching his sin that he hath sinned in one of these, and it shall be forgiven him: and ^R*the remnant* shall be the priest's, as a meat offering.

Guilt offerings

14 And the LORD spake unto Moses, saying,

15 ^RIf a soul commit a trespass, and sin through ignorance, in the holy things of the LORD; then ^Rhe shall bring for his trespass unto the LORD a ram without blemish out of the flocks, with thy estimation by shē'-kĕls of silver, after ^Rthe shē'-kĕl of the sanctuary, for a trespass offering:

16 And he shall make amends for the harm that he hath done in the holy thing, and ^Rshall add the fifth part thereto, and give it unto the priest: ^Rand the priest shall make an atonement for him with the ram of the trespass offering, and it shall be forgiven him.

17 And if a soul sin, and commit any of these things which are forbidden to be done by the commandments of the LORD; ^Rthough he wist *it* not, yet is he ^Rguilty, and shall bear his iniquity.

18 ^RAnd he shall bring a ram without blemish out of the flock, with thy estimation, for a trespass offering, unto the priest: ^Rand the priest shall make an atonement for him concerning his ignorance wherein he erred and wist *it* not, and it shall be forgiven him.

19 It *is* a trespass offering: ^Rhe hath certainly trespassed against the LORD.

CHAPTER 6

AND the LORD spake unto Moses, saying,
2 If a soul sin, and ᴿcommit a trespass against the LORD, and ᴿlie unto his neighbour in that ᴿwhich was delivered him to keep, or in ᴺᴺfellowship, or in a thing taken away by violence, or hath ᴿdeceived his neighbour;

3 Or ᴿhave found that which was lost, and lieth concerning it, and ᴿsweareth falsely; in any of all these that a man doeth, sinning therein:

4 Then it shall be, because he hath sinned, and is guilty, that he shall restore that which he took violently away, or the thing which he hath deceitfully gotten, or that which was delivered him to keep, or the lost thing which he found,

5 Or all that about which he hath sworn falsely; he shall even ᴿrestore it in the principal, and shall add the fifth part more thereto, *and* give it unto him to whom it appertaineth, ᴺᴺin the day of his trespass offering.

6 And he shall bring his trespass offering unto the LORD, ᴿa ram without blemish out of the flock, with thy estimation, for a trespass offering, unto the priest:

7 ᴿAnd the priest shall make an atonement for him before the LORD: and it shall be forgiven him for any thing of all that he hath done in trespassing therein.

Law of the burnt offering

8 And the LORD spake unto Moses, saying,
9 Command Aaron and his sons, saying, This *is* the law of the burnt offering: It *is* the burnt offering, ᴺbecause of the burning upon the altar all night unto the morning, and the fire of the altar shall be burning in it.

10 ᴿAnd the priest shall put on his linen garment, and his linen breeches shall he put upon his flesh, and take up the ashes which the fire hath consumed with the burnt offering on the altar, and he shall put them ᴿbeside the altar.

11 And ᴿhe shall put off his garments, and put on other garments, and carry forth the ashes without the camp ᴿunto a clean place.

12 And the fire upon the altar shall be burning in it; it shall not be put out: and the priest shall burn wood on it every morning, and lay the burnt offering in order upon it; and he shall burn thereon ᴿthe fat of the peace offerings.

13 The fire shall ever be burning upon the altar; it shall never go out.

Law of the meat offering

14 ᴿAnd this *is* the law of the meat offering: the sons of Aaron shall offer it before the LORD, before the altar.

15 And he shall take of it his handful, of the flour of the meat offering, and of the oil thereof, and all the frankincense which *is* upon the meat offering, and shall burn *it* upon the altar *for* a sweet savour, *even* the ᴿmemorial of it, unto the LORD.

16 And ᴿthe remainder thereof shall Aaron and his sons eat: ᴿwith unleavened bread shall it be eaten in the holy place; in the court of the tabernacle of the congregation they shall eat it.

17 ᴿIt shall not be baken with leaven. ᴿI have given it *unto them for* their portion of my offerings made by fire; ᴿit *is* most holy, as *is* the sin offering, and as the trespass offering.

18 ᴿAll the males among the children of Aaron shall eat of it. ᴿIt shall be a statute for ever in your generations concerning the offerings of the LORD made by fire: ᴿevery one that toucheth them shall be holy.

Priestly offerings

19 And the LORD spake unto Moses, saying,
20 ᴿThis *is* the offering of Aaron and of his sons, which they shall offer unto the LORD in the day when he is anointed; the tenth part of an ᴿē´-phäh of fine flour for a meat offering perpetual, half of it in the morning, and half thereof at night.

21 In a pan it shall be made with oil; *and* when it is baken, thou shalt bring it in: *and* the baken pieces of the meat offering shalt thou offer *for* a sweet savour unto the LORD.

22 And the priest of his sons ᴿthat is anointed in his stead shall offer it: *it is* a statute for ever unto the LORD; ᴿit shall be wholly burnt.

23 For every meat offering for the priest shall be wholly burnt: it shall not be eaten.

The sin offering

24 And the LORD spake unto Moses, saying,
25 Speak unto Aaron and to his sons, saying, ᴿThis *is* the law of the sin offering: ᴿIn the place where the burnt offering is killed shall the sin offering be killed before the LORD: ᴿit *is* most holy.

26 ᴿThe priest that offereth it for sin shall eat it: ᴿin the holy place shall it be eaten, in the court of the tabernacle of the congregation.

27 ᴿWhatsoever shall touch the flesh thereof shall be holy: and when there is sprinkled of the blood thereof upon any garment, thou shalt wash that whereon it was sprinkled in the holy place.

28 But the earthen vessel wherein it is sodden ᴿshall be broken: and if it be sodden in a brasen pot, it shall be both scoured, and rinsed in water.

29 ᴿAll the males among the priests shall eat thereof: ᴿit *is* most holy.

CHAP. 6
BC 1490
2 Num. 5:6
2 ch. 19:11
Acts 5:4
Col. 3:9
2 Ex. 22:7, 10
2 Or, *in dealing*
2 Heb. *putting of the hand*
2 Prov. 24:28 & 26:19
3 Deut. 22:1-3
3 Ex. 22:11
ch. 19:12
Jer. 7:9
Zech. 5:4
5 ch. 5:16
Num. 5:7
2 Sam. 12:6
5 Or, *in the day of his being found guilty*
5 Heb. *in the day of his trespass*
6 ch. 5:15
7 ch. 4:26
9 Or, *for the burning*
10 Ex. 28:39-41, 43
ch. 16:4
Ezek. 44:17, 18
10 ch. 1:16
11 Ezek. 44:19
11 ch. 4:12
12 ch. 3:3, 9, 14
14 ch. 2:1
Num. 15:4

ch. 2:2, 9	**15**
ch. 2:3	**16**
Ezek. 44:29	
ver. 26	**16**
ch. 10:12, 13	
Num. 18:10	
ch. 2:11	**17**
Num. 18:9, 10	**17**
ver. 25	**17**
Ex. 29:37	
ch. 2:3 & 7:1	
ver. 29	**18**
Num. 18:10	
ch. 3:17	**18**
Ex. 29:37	**18**
ch. 22:3-7	
Ex. 29:2	**20**
Ex. 16:30	**20**
ch. 4:3	**22**
Ex. 29:25	**22**
ch. 4:2	**25**
ch. 1:3, 5, 11	**25**
ver. 17	**25**
ch. 10:17, 18	**26**
Num. 18:9, 10	
Ezek. 44:28, 29	
ver. 16	**26**
Ex. 29:37	**27**
& 30:29	
ch. 11:33	**28**
& 15:12	
ver. 18	**29**
Num. 18:10	
ver. 25	**29**
ch. 4:7, 11, 12, 18, 21 & 10:18 & 16:27	**30**
Heb. 13:11	

30 ^RAnd no sin offering, whereof *any* of the blood is brought into the tabernacle of the congregation to reconcile *withal* in the holy *place*, shall be eaten: it shall be burnt in the fire.

CHAPTER 7

The guilt offering

LIKEWISE ^Rthis *is* the law of the trespass offering: ^Rit *is* most holy.

2 ^RIn the place where they kill the burnt offering shall they kill the trespass offering: and the blood thereof shall he sprinkle round about upon the altar.

3 And he shall offer of it ^Rall the fat thereof; the rump, and the fat that covereth the inwards,

4 And the two kidneys, and the fat that *is* on them, which *is* by the flanks, and the caul *that is* above the liver, with the kidneys, it shall he take away:

5 And the priest shall burn them upon the altar *for* an offering made by fire unto the Lord: it *is* a trespass offering.

6 ^REvery male among the priests shall eat thereof: it shall be eaten in the holy place: ^Rit *is* most holy.

7 As the sin offering *is,* so *is* ^Rthe trespass offering: *there is* one law for them: the priest that maketh atonement therewith shall have *it.*

8 And the priest that offereth any man's burnt offering, *even* the priest shall have to himself the skin of the burnt offering which he hath offered.

9 And ^Rall the meat offering that is baken in the oven, and all that is dressed in the frying-pan, and ^Nin the pan, shall be the priest's that offereth it.

10 And every meat offering, mingled with oil, and dry, shall all the sons of Aaron have, one *as much* as another.

The peace offerings

11 And ^Rthis *is* the law of the sacrifice of peace offerings, which he shall offer unto the Lord.

12 If he offer it for a thanksgiving, then he shall offer with the sacrifice of thanksgiving unleavened cakes mingled with oil, and unleavened wafers ^Ranointed with oil, and cakes mingled with oil, of fine flour, fried.

13 Besides the cakes, he shall offer *for* his offering ^Rleavened bread with the sacrifice of thanksgiving of his peace offerings.

14 And of it he shall offer one out of the whole oblation *for* an heave offering unto the Lord, ^R*and* it shall be the priest's that sprinkleth the blood of the peace offerings.

15 ^RAnd the flesh of the sacrifice of his peace offerings for thanksgiving shall be eaten the same day that it is offered; he shall not leave any of it until the morning.

16 But ^Rif the sacrifice of his offering *be* a vow, or a voluntary offering, it shall be eaten the same day that he offereth his sacrifice: and on the morrow also the remainder of it shall be eaten:

17 But the remainder of the flesh of the sacrifice on the third day shall be burnt with fire.

18 And if *any* of the flesh of the sacrifice of his peace offerings be eaten at all on the third day, it shall not be accepted, neither shall it be ^Rimputed unto him that offereth it: it shall be an ^Rabomination, and the soul that eateth of it shall bear his iniquity.

19 And the flesh that toucheth any unclean *thing* shall not be eaten; it shall be burnt with fire: and as for the flesh, all that be clean shall eat thereof.

20 But the soul that eateth *of* the flesh of the sacrifice of peace offerings, that *pertain* unto the Lord, ^Rhaving his uncleanness upon him, even that soul ^Rshall be cut off from his people.

21 Moreover the soul that shall touch any unclean *thing, as* ^Rthe uncleanness of man, or *any* ^Runclean beast, or any ^Rabominable unclean *thing,* and eat of the flesh of the sacrifice of peace offerings, which *pertain* unto the Lord, even that soul ^Rshall be cut off from his people.

22 And the Lord spake unto Moses, saying,

23 Speak unto the children of Israel, saying, ^RYe shall eat no manner of fat, of ox, or of sheep, or of goat.

24 And the fat of the ^Nbeast that dieth of itself, and the fat of that which is torn with beasts, may be used in any other use: but ye shall in no wise eat of it.

25 For whosoever eateth the fat of the beast, of which men offer an offering made by fire unto the Lord, even the soul that eateth *it* shall be cut off from his people.

26 ^RMoreover ye shall eat no manner of blood, *whether it be* of fowl or of beast, in any of your dwellings.

27 Whatsoever soul *it be* that eateth any manner of blood, even that soul shall be cut off from his people.

The priests' portion

28 And the Lord spake unto Moses, saying,

29 Speak unto the children of Israel, saying, ^RHe that offereth the sacrifice of his peace offerings unto the Lord shall bring his oblation unto the Lord of the sacrifice of his peace offerings.

30 ᴿHis own hands shall bring the offerings of the Lᴏʀᴅ made by fire, the fat with the breast, it shall he bring, that ᴿthe breast may be waved *for* a wave offering before the Lᴏʀᴅ.

31 ᴿAnd the priest shall burn the fat upon the altar: ᴿbut the breast shall be Aaron's and his sons'.

32 And ᴿthe right shoulder shall ye give unto the priest *for* an heave offering of the sacrifices of your peace offerings.

33 He among the sons of Aaron, that offereth the blood of the peace offerings, and the fat, shall have the right shoulder for *his* part.

34 For ᴿthe wave breast and the heave shoulder have I taken of the children of Israel from off the sacrifices of their peace offerings, and have given them unto Aaron the priest and unto his sons by a statute for ever from among the children of Israel.

35 This *is the portion* of the anointing of Aaron, and of the anointing of his sons, out of the offerings of the Lᴏʀᴅ made by fire, in the day *when* he presented them to minister unto the Lᴏʀᴅ in the priest's office;

36 Which the Lᴏʀᴅ commanded to be given them of the children of Israel, ᴿin the day that he anointed them, *by* a statute for ever throughout their generations.

37 This *is* the law ᴿof the burnt offering, ᴿof the meat offering, ᴿand of the sin offering, ᴿand of the trespass offering, ᴿand of the consecrations, and ᴿof the sacrifice of the peace offerings;

38 Which the Lᴏʀᴅ commanded Moses in mount Sī'-naī, in the day that he commanded the children of Israel ᴿto offer their oblations unto the Lᴏʀᴅ, in the wilderness of Sī'-naī.

CHAPTER 8

Consecration of Aaron and his sons

Aᴺᴰ the Lᴏʀᴅ spake unto Moses, saying, 2 ᴿTake Aaron and his sons with him, and ᴿthe garments, and ᴿthe anointing oil, and a bullock for the sin offering, and two rams, and a basket of unleavened bread;

3 And gather thou all the congregation together unto the door of the tabernacle of the congregation.

4 And Moses did as the Lᴏʀᴅ commanded him; and the assembly was gathered together unto the door of the tabernacle of the congregation.

5 And Moses said unto the congregation, ᴿThis *is* the thing which the Lᴏʀᴅ commanded to be done.

6 And Moses brought Aaron and his sons, ᴿand washed them with water.

7 ᴿAnd he put upon him the ᴿcoat, and

CHAP. 7	
BC 1490	
30	ch. 3:3, 4, 9, 14
30	Ex. 29:24, 27
	ch. 8:27 & 9:21
	Num. 6:20
31	ch. 3:5, 11, 16
31	ver. 34
32	ver. 34
	ch. 9:21
	Num. 6:20
34	Ex. 29:28
	ch. 10:14, 15
	Num. 18:18, 19
	Deut. 18:3
36	Ex. 40:13, 15
	ch. 8:12, 30
37	ch. 6:9
37	ch. 6:14
37	ch. 6:25
37	ver. 1
37	Ex. 29:1
	ch. 6:20
37	ver. 11
38	ch. 1:2

CHAP. 8	
BC 1490	
2	Ex. 29:1-3
2	Ex. 28:2, 4
2	Ex. 30:24, 25
5	Ex. 29:4
6	Ex. 29:4
7	Ex. 29:5
7	Ex. 28:4

Ex. 28:30	8
Ex. 29:6	9
Ex. 28:37, etc.	9
Ex. 30:26-29	10
Ex. 29:7	12
& 30:30	
ch. 21:10, 12	
Ps. 133:2	
Ex. 29:8, 9	13
Heb. *bound*	13
Ex. 29:10	14
Ezek. 43:19	
ch. 4:4	14
Ex. 29:12, 36	15
ch. 4:7	
Ezek. 43:20, 26	
Heb. 9:22	
Ex. 29:13	16
ch. 4:8	
Ex. 29:14	17
ch. 4:11, 12	
Ex. 29:15	18
Ex. 29:18	21
Ex. 29:19, 31	22

girded him with the girdle, and clothed him with the robe, and put the ē'-phŏd upon him, and he girded him with the curious girdle of the ē'-phŏd, and bound *it* unto him therewith.

8 And he put the breastplate upon him: also he ᴿput in the breastplate the Ū'-rĭm and the Thŭm'-mĭm.

9 ᴿAnd he put the mitre upon his head; also upon the mitre, *even* upon his forefront, did he put the golden plate, the holy crown; as the Lᴏʀᴅ ᴿcommanded Moses.

10 ᴿAnd Moses took the anointing oil, and anointed the tabernacle and all that *was* therein, and sanctified them.

11 And he sprinkled thereof upon the altar seven times, and anointed the altar and all his vessels, both the laver and his foot, to sanctify them.

12 And he ᴿpoured of the anointing oil upon Aaron's head, and anointed him, to sanctify him.

13 ᴿAnd Moses brought Aaron's sons, and put coats upon them, and girded them with girdles, and ᴺput bonnets upon them; as the Lᴏʀᴅ commanded Moses.

14 ᴿAnd he brought the bullock for the sin offering: and Aaron and his sons ᴿlaid their hands upon the head of the bullock for the sin offering.

15 And he slew *it;* ᴿand Moses took the blood, and put *it* upon the horns of the altar round about with his finger, and purified the altar, and poured the blood at the bottom of the altar, and sanctified it, to make reconciliation upon it.

16 ᴿAnd he took all the fat that *was* upon the inwards, and the caul *above* the liver, and the two kidneys, and their fat, and Moses burned *it* upon the altar.

17 But the bullock, and his hide, his flesh, and his dung, he burnt with fire without the camp; as the Lᴏʀᴅ ᴿcommanded Moses.

18 ᴿAnd he brought the ram for the burnt offering: and Aaron and his sons laid their hands upon the head of the ram.

19 And he killed *it;* and Moses sprinkled the blood upon the altar round about.

20 And he cut the ram into pieces; and Moses burnt the head, and the pieces, and the fat.

21 And he washed the inwards and the legs in water; and Moses burnt the whole ram upon the altar: it *was* a burnt sacrifice for a sweet savour, *and* an offering made by fire unto the Lᴏʀᴅ; ᴿas the Lᴏʀᴅ commanded Moses.

22 And ᴿhe brought the other ram, the ram of consecration: and Aaron and his sons laid their hands upon the head of the ram.

23 And he slew *it;* and Moses took of the

blood of it, and put *it* upon the tip of Aaron's right ear, and upon the thumb of his right hand, and upon the great toe of his right foot.

24 And he brought Aaron's sons, and Moses put of the blood upon the tip of their right ear, and upon the thumbs of their right hands, and upon the great toes of their right feet: and Moses sprinkled the blood upon the altar round about.

25 ᴿAnd he took the fat, and the rump, and all the fat that *was* upon the inwards, and the caul *above* the liver, and the two kidneys, and their fat, and the right shoulder:

26 ᴿAnd out of the basket of unleavened bread, that *was* before the LORD, he took one unleavened cake, and a cake of oiled bread, and one wafer, and put *them* on the fat, and upon the right shoulder:

27 And he put all ᴿupon Aaron's hands, and upon his sons' hands, and waved them *for a* wave offering before the LORD.

28 ᴿAnd Moses took them from off their hands, and burnt *them* on the altar upon the burnt offering: they *were* consecrations for a sweet savour: it *is* an offering made by fire unto the LORD.

29 And Moses took the breast, and waved it *for* a wave offering before the LORD: *for* of the ram of consecration it was Moses' ᴿpart; as the LORD commanded Moses.

30 And ᴿMoses took of the anointing oil, and of the blood which *was* upon the altar, and sprinkled *it* upon Aaron, *and* upon his garments, and upon his sons, and upon his sons' garments with him; and sanctified Aaron, *and* his garments, and his sons, and his sons' garments with him.

31 And Moses said unto Aaron and to his sons, ᴿBoil the flesh *at* the door of the tabernacle of the congregation: and there eat it with the bread that *is* in the basket of consecrations, as I commanded, saying, Aaron and his sons shall eat it.

32 ᴿAnd that which remaineth of the flesh and of the bread shall ye burn with fire.

33 And ye shall not go out of the door of the tabernacle of the congregation *in* seven days, until the days of your consecration be at an end: for ᴿseven days shall he consecrate you.

34 ᴿAs he hath done this day, *so* the LORD hath commanded to do, to make an atonement for you.

35 Therefore shall ye abide *at* the door of the tabernacle of the congregation day and night seven days, and ᴿkeep the charge of the LORD, that ye die not: for so I am commanded.

36 So Aaron and his sons did all things

which the LORD commanded by the hand of Moses.

CHAPTER 9

Aaron's first sacrifices

AND ᴿit came to pass on the eighth day, *that* Moses called Aaron and his sons, and the elders of Israel;

2 And he said unto Aaron, ᴿTake thee a young calf for a sin offering, ᴿand a ram for a burnt offering, without blemish, and offer *them* before the LORD.

3 And unto the children of Israel thou shalt speak, saying, ᴿTake ye a kid of the goats for a sin offering; and a calf and a lamb, *both* of the first year, without blemish, for a burnt offering;

4 Also a bullock and a ram for peace offerings, to sacrifice before the LORD; and ᴿa meat offering mingled with oil: for ᴿto day the LORD will appear unto you.

5 And they brought *that* which Moses commanded before the tabernacle of the congregation: and all the congregation drew near and stood before the LORD.

6 And Moses said, This *is* the thing which the LORD commanded that ye should do: and ᴿthe glory of the LORD shall appear unto you.

7 And Moses said unto Aaron, Go unto the altar, and ᴿoffer thy sin offering, and thy burnt offering, and make an atonement for thyself, and for the people: and ᴿoffer the offering of the people, and make an atonement for them; as the LORD commanded.

8 Aaron therefore went unto the altar, and slew the calf of the sin offering, which *was* for himself.

9 ᴿAnd the sons of Aaron brought the blood unto him: and he dipped his finger in the blood, and ᴿput *it* upon the horns of the altar, and poured out the blood at the bottom of the altar:

10 ᴿBut the fat, and the kidneys, and the caul above the liver of the sin offering, he burnt upon the altar; ᴿas the LORD commanded Moses.

11 ᴿAnd the flesh and the hide he burnt with fire without the camp.

12 And he slew the burnt offering; and Aaron's sons presented unto him the blood, ᴿwhich he sprinkled round about upon the altar.

13 ᴿAnd they presented the burnt offering unto him, with the pieces thereof, and the head: and he burnt *them* upon the altar.

14 ᴿAnd he did wash the inwards and the

legs, and burnt *them* upon the burnt offering on the altar.

Offering for the people

15 ᴿAnd he brought the people's offering, and took the goat, which *was* the sin offering for the people, and slew it, and offered it for sin, as the first.

16 And he brought the burnt offering, and offered it ᴿaccording to the ᴺmanner.

17 And he brought ᴿthe meat offering, and ᴺtook an handful thereof, and burnt *it* upon the altar, ᴿbeside the burnt sacrifice of the morning.

18 He slew also the bullock and the ram *for* ᴿa sacrifice of peace offerings, which *was* for the people: and Aaron's sons presented unto him the blood, which he sprinkled upon the altar round about,

19 And the fat of the bullock and of the ram, the rump, and that which covereth *the inwards,* and the kidneys, and the caul *above* the liver:

20 And they put the fat upon the breasts, ᴿand he burnt the fat upon the altar:

21 And the breasts and the right shoulder Aaron waved ᴿ*for* a wave offering before the LORD; as Moses commanded.

Glory of the LORD appears

22 And Aaron lifted up his hand toward the people, and ᴿblessed them, and came down from offering of the sin offering, and the burnt offering, and peace offerings.

23 And Moses and Aaron went into the tabernacle of the congregation, and came out, and blessed the people: ᴿand the glory of the LORD appeared unto all the people.

24 And ᴿthere came a fire out from before the LORD, and consumed upon the altar the burnt offering and the fat: *which* when all the people saw, ᴿthey shouted, and fell on their faces.

CHAPTER 10

Nadab and Abihu

AND ᴿNadab and Ă-bī′-hū, the sons of Aaron, ᴿtook either of them his censer, and put fire therein, and put incense thereon, and offered ᴿstrange fire before the LORD, which he commanded them not.

2 And there ᴿwent out fire from the LORD, and devoured them, and they died before the LORD.

3 Then Moses said unto Aaron, This *is it* that the LORD spake, saying, I will be

sanctified in them ᴿthat come nigh me, and before all the people I will be ᴿglorified. ᴿAnd Aaron held his peace.

4 And Moses called Mī′-shā-ĕl and Ĕl-zā′-phăn, the sons of ᴿŬz′-zī-ĕl the uncle of Aaron, and said unto them, Come near, carry your brethren from before the sanctuary out of the camp.

5 So they went near, and carried them in their coats out of the camp; as Moses had said.

Priestly requirements

6 And Moses said unto Aaron, and unto Ĕl-ē-ā′-zär and unto ĭth′-ă-mär, his sons, ᴿUncover not your heads, neither rend your clothes; lest ye die, and lest ᴿwrath come upon all the people: but let your brethren, the whole house of Israel, bewail the burning which the LORD hath kindled.

7 ᴿAnd ye shall not go out from the door of the tabernacle of the congregation, lest ye die: ᴿfor the anointing oil of the LORD *is* upon you. And they did according to the word of Moses.

8 And the LORD spake unto Aaron, saying,

9 ᴿDo not drink wine nor strong drink, thou, nor thy sons with thee, when ye go into the tabernacle of the congregation, lest ye die: *it shall be* a statute for ever throughout your generations:

10 And that ye may ᴿput difference between holy and unholy, and between unclean and clean;

11 ᴿAnd that ye may teach the children of Israel all the statutes which the LORD hath spoken unto them by the hand of Moses.

Priestly dues

12 And Moses spake unto Aaron, and unto Ĕl-ē-ā′-zär and unto ĭth′-ă-mär, his sons that were left, Take ᴿthe meat offering that remaineth of the offerings of the LORD made by fire, and eat it without leaven beside the altar: for ᴿit *is* most holy:

13 And ye shall eat it in the holy place, because it *is* thy due, and thy sons' due, of the sacrifices of the LORD made by fire: for ᴿso I am commanded.

14 And ᴿthe wave breast and heave shoulder shall ye eat in a clean place; thou, and thy sons, and thy daughters with thee: for *they be* thy due, and thy sons' due, *which* are given out of the sacrifices of peace offerings of the children of Israel.

15 ᴿThe heave shoulder and the wave breast shall they bring with the offerings made by fire of the fat, to wave *it for* a wave offering before

the LORD; and it shall be thine, and thy sons' with thee, by a statute for ever; as the LORD hath commanded.

16 And Moses diligently sought ᴿthe goat of the sin offering, and, behold, it was burnt: and he was angry with Ĕl-ē-ā'-zär and ĭth'-ă-mär, the sons of Aaron *which were* left *alive,* saying,

17 ᴿWherefore have ye not eaten the sin offering in the holy place, seeing it *is* most holy, and *God* hath given it you to bear the iniquity of the congregation, to make atonement for them before the LORD?

18 Behold, ᴿthe blood of it was not brought in within the holy *place:* ye should indeed have eaten it in the holy *place,* ᴿas I commanded.

19 And Aaron said unto Moses, Behold, ᴿthis day have they offered their sin offering and their burnt offering before the LORD; and such things have befallen me: and *if* I had eaten the sin offering to day, ᴿshould it have been accepted in the sight of the LORD?

20 And when Moses heard *that,* he was content.

CHAPTER 11

Clean and unclean foods

AND the LORD spake unto Moses and to Aaron, saying unto them,

2 Speak unto the children of Israel, saying, ᴿThese *are* the beasts which ye shall eat among all the beasts that *are* on the earth.

3 Whatsoever parteth the hoof, and is clovenfooted, *and* cheweth the cud, among the beasts, that shall ye eat.

4 Nevertheless these shall ye not eat of them that chew the cud, or of them that divide the hoof: *as* the camel, because he cheweth the cud, but divideth not the hoof; he *is* unclean unto you.

5 And the coney, because he cheweth the cud, but divideth not the hoof; he *is* unclean unto you.

6 And the hare, because he cheweth the cud, but divideth not the hoof; he *is* unclean unto you.

7 And the swine, though he divide the hoof, and be clovenfooted, yet he cheweth not the cud; ᴿhe *is* unclean to you.

8 Of their flesh shall ye not eat, and their carcase shall ye not touch; ᴿthey *are* unclean to you.

9 ᴿThese shall ye eat of all that *are* in the waters: whatsoever hath fins and scales in the waters, in the seas, and in the rivers, them shall ye eat.

10 And all that have not fins and scales in the seas, and in the rivers, of all that move in the waters, and of any living thing which *is* in the waters, they *shall be* an ᴿabomination unto you:

11 They shall be even an abomination unto you; ye shall not eat of their flesh, but ye shall have their carcases in abomination.

12 Whatsoever hath no fins nor scales in the waters, that *shall be* an abomination unto you.

13 ᴿAnd these *are they which* ye shall have in abomination among the fowls; they shall not be eaten, they *are* an abomination: the eagle, and the ossifrage, and the ospray,

14 And the vulture, and the kite after his kind;

15 Every raven after his kind;

16 And the owl, and the night hawk, and the cuckow, and the hawk after his kind,

17 And the little owl, and the cormorant, and the great owl,

18 And the swan, and the pelican, and the gier eagle,

19 And the stork, the heron after her kind, and the lapwing, and the bat.

20 All fowls that creep, going upon *all* four, *shall be* an abomination unto you.

21 Yet these may ye eat of every flying creeping thing that goeth upon *all* four, which have legs above their feet, to leap withal upon the earth;

22 *Even* these of them ye may eat; ᴿthe locust after his kind, and the bald locust after his kind, and the beetle after his kind, and the grasshopper after his kind.

23 But all *other* flying creeping things, which have four feet, *shall be* an abomination unto you.

24 And for these ye shall be unclean: whosoever toucheth the carcase of them shall be unclean until the even.

25 And whosoever beareth *aught* of the carcase of them ᴿshall wash his clothes, and be unclean until the even.

26 *The carcases* of every beast which divideth the hoof, and *is* not clovenfooted, nor cheweth the cud, *are* unclean unto you: every one that toucheth them shall be unclean.

27 And whatsoever goeth upon his paws, among all manner of beasts that go on *all* four, those *are* unclean unto you: whoso toucheth their carcase shall be unclean until the even.

28 And he that beareth the carcase of them shall wash his clothes, and be unclean until the even: they *are* unclean unto you.

29 These also *shall be* unclean unto you among the creeping things that creep upon the earth; the weasel, and ᴿthe mouse, and the tortoise after his kind,

30 And the ferret, and the chameleon, and the lizard, and the snail, and the mole.

31 These *are* unclean to you among all that creep: whosoever doth touch them, when they be dead, shall be unclean until the even.

32 And upon whatsoever *any* of them, when they are dead, doth fall, it shall be unclean; whether *it be* any vessel of wood, or raiment, or skin, or sack, whatsoever vessel *it be*, wherein *any* work is done, ^Rit must be put into water, and it shall be unclean until the even; so it shall be cleansed.

33 And every earthen vessel, whereinto *any* of them falleth, whatsoever *is* in it shall be unclean; and ^Rye shall break it.

34 Of all meat which may be eaten, *that* on which *such* water cometh shall be unclean: and all drink that may be drunk in every *such* vessel shall be unclean.

35 And every *thing* whereupon *any part* of their carcase falleth shall be unclean; *whether it be* oven, or ranges for pots, they shall be broken down: *for* they *are* unclean, and shall be unclean unto you.

36 Nevertheless a fountain or pit, ^N*wherein there is* plenty of water, shall be clean: but that which toucheth their carcase shall be unclean.

37 And if *any part* of their carcase fall upon any sowing seed which is to be sown, it *shall be* clean.

38 But if *any* water be put upon the seed, and *any part* of their carcase fall thereon, it *shall be* unclean unto you.

39 And if any beast, of which ye may eat, die; he that toucheth the carcase thereof shall be unclean until the even.

40 And ^Rhe that eateth of the carcase of it shall wash his clothes, and be unclean until the even: he also that beareth the carcase of it shall wash his clothes, and be unclean until the even.

41 And every creeping thing that creepeth upon the earth *shall be* an abomination; it shall not be eaten.

42 Whatsoever goeth upon the belly, and whatsoever goeth upon *all* four, or whatsoever ^Nhath more feet among all creeping things that creep upon the earth, them ye shall not eat; for they *are* an abomination.

43 ^RYe shall not make your ^Nselves abominable with any creeping thing that creepeth, neither shall ye make yourselves unclean with them, that ye should be defiled thereby.

44 For I *am* the LORD your God: ye shall therefore sanctify yourselves, and ^Rye shall be holy; for I *am* holy: neither shall ye defile yourselves with any manner of creeping thing that creepeth upon the earth.

45 ^RFor I *am* the LORD that bringeth you up out of the land of Egypt, to be your God: ^Rye shall therefore be holy, for I *am* holy.

46 This *is* the law of the beasts, and of the fowl, and of every living creature that moveth in the waters, and of every creature that creepeth upon the earth:

47 ^RTo make a difference between the unclean and the clean, and between the beast that may be eaten and the beast that may not be eaten.

CHAPTER 12

Purification after childbirth

AND the LORD spake unto Moses, saying, 2 Speak unto the children of Israel, saying, If a ^Rwoman have conceived seed, and born a man child: then ^Rshe shall be unclean seven days; ^Raccording to the days of the separation for her infirmity shall she be unclean.

3 And in the ^Reighth day the flesh of his foreskin shall be circumcised.

4 And she shall then continue in the blood of her purifying three and thirty days; she shall touch no hallowed thing, nor come into the sanctuary, until the days of her purifying be fulfilled.

5 But if she bear a maid child, then she shall be unclean two weeks, as in her separation: and she shall continue in the blood of her purifying threescore and six days.

6 And ^Rwhen the days of her purifying are fulfilled, for a son, or for a daughter, she shall bring a lamb ^Nof the first year for a burnt offering, and a young pigeon, or a turtledove, for a sin offering, unto the door of the tabernacle of the congregation, unto the priest:

7 Who shall offer it before the LORD, and make an atonement for her; and she shall be cleansed from the issue of her blood. This *is* the law for her that hath born a male or a female.

8 ^RAnd if ^Nshe be not able to bring a lamb, then she shall bring two turtles, or two young pigeons; the one for the burnt offering, and the other for a sin offering: ^Rand the priest shall make an atonement for her, and she shall be clean.

CHAPTER 13

Tests of leprosy

AND the LORD spake unto Moses and Aaron, saying, 2 When a man shall have in the skin of his flesh a ^Nrising, ^Ra scab, or bright spot, and it be in the skin of his flesh *like* the plague of

leprosy; ᴿthen he shall be brought unto Aaron the priest, or unto one of his sons the priests:

3 And the priest shall look on the plague in the skin of the flesh: and *when* the hair in the plague is turned white, and the plague in sight *be* deeper than the skin of his flesh, it *is* a plague of leprosy: and the priest shall look on him, and pronounce him unclean.

4 If the bright spot *be* white in the skin of his flesh, and in sight *be* not deeper than the skin, and the hair thereof be not turned white; then the priest shall shut up *him that hath* the plague seven days:

5 And the priest shall look on him the seventh day: and, behold, *if* the plague in his sight be at a stay, *and* the plague spread not in the skin; then the priest shall shut him up seven days more:

6 And the priest shall look on him again the seventh day: and, behold, *if* the plague *be* somewhat dark, *and* the plague spread not in the skin, the priest shall pronounce him clean: it *is but* a scab: and he ᴿshall wash his clothes, and be clean.

7 But if the scab spread much abroad in the skin, after that he hath been seen of the priest for his cleansing, he shall be seen of the priest again:

8 And *if* the priest see that, behold, the scab spreadeth in the skin, then the priest shall pronounce him unclean: it *is* a leprosy.

9 When the plague of leprosy is in a man, then he shall be brought unto the priest;

10 ᴿAnd the priest shall see *him*: and, behold, *if* the rising *be* white in the skin, and it have turned the hair white, and *there be* ᴺquick raw flesh in the rising;

11 It *is* an old leprosy in the skin of his flesh, and the priest shall pronounce him unclean, and shall not shut him up: for he *is* unclean.

12 And if a leprosy break out abroad in the skin, and the leprosy cover all the skin of *him that hath* the plague from his head even to his foot, wheresoever the priest looketh;

13 Then the priest shall consider: and, behold, *if* the leprosy have covered all his flesh, he shall pronounce *him* clean *that hath* the plague: it is all turned white: he *is* clean.

14 But when raw flesh appeareth in him, he shall be unclean.

15 And the priest shall see the raw flesh, and pronounce him to be unclean: *for* the raw flesh *is* unclean: it *is* a leprosy.

16 Or if the raw flesh turn again, and be changed unto white, he shall come unto the priest;

17 And the priest shall see him: and, behold, *if* the plague be turned into white; then the

CHAP. 13
BC 1490
2 Deut. 17:8, 9
& 24:8
Mal. 2:7
Luke 17:14
6 ch. 11:25
& 14:8
10 Num. 12:10, 12
2 Ki. 5:27
2 Chr. 26:20
10 Heb. *the quickening of living flesh*

Ex. 9:9   18
& 15:26
Heb. *a burning*   24
of fire

priest shall pronounce *him* clean *that hath* the plague: he *is* clean.

18 The flesh also, in which, *even in the skin* thereof, was a ᴿboil, and is healed,

19 And in the place of the boil there be a white rising, or a bright spot, white, and somewhat reddish, and it be shewed to the priest;

20 And if, when the priest seeth it, behold, it *be* in sight lower than the skin, and the hair thereof be turned white; the priest shall pronounce him unclean: it *is* a plague of leprosy broken out of the boil.

21 But if the priest look on it, and, behold, *there be* no white hairs therein, and *if* it *be* not lower than the skin, but *be* somewhat dark; then the priest shall shut him up seven days:

22 And if it spread much abroad in the skin, then the priest shall pronounce him unclean: it *is* a plague.

23 But if the bright spot stay in his place, *and* spread not, it *is* a burning boil; and the priest shall pronounce him clean.

24 Or if there be *any* flesh, in the skin whereof *there is* ᴺa hot burning, and the quick *flesh* that burneth have a white bright spot, somewhat reddish, or white;

25 Then the priest shall look upon it: and, behold, *if* the hair in the bright spot be turned white, and it *be in* sight deeper than the skin; it *is* a leprosy broken out of the burning: wherefore the priest shall pronounce him unclean: it *is* the plague of leprosy.

26 But if the priest look on it, and, behold, *there be* no white hair in the bright spot, and it *be* no lower than the *other* skin, but *be* somewhat dark; then the priest shall shut him up seven days:

27 And the priest shall look upon him the seventh day: *and* if it be spread much abroad in the skin, then the priest shall pronounce him unclean: it *is* the plague of leprosy.

28 And if the bright spot stay in his place, *and* spread not in the skin, but it *be* somewhat dark; it *is* a rising of the burning, and the priest shall pronounce him clean: for it *is* an inflammation of the burning.

29 If a man or woman have a plague upon the head or the beard;

30 Then the priest shall see the plague: and, behold, if it *be* in sight deeper than the skin; *and there be* in it a yellow thin hair; then the priest shall pronounce him unclean: it *is* a dry scall, *even* a leprosy upon the head or beard.

31 And if the priest look on the plague of the scall, and, behold, it *be* not in sight deeper than the skin, and *that there is* no black hair in

it; then the priest shall shut up *him that hath* the plague of the scall seven days:

32 And in the seventh day the priest shall look on the plague: and, behold, *if* the scall spread not, and there be in it no yellow hair, and the scall *be* not in sight deeper than the skin;

33 He shall be shaven, but the scall shall he not shave; and the priest shall shut up *him that hath* the scall seven days more:

34 And in the seventh day the priest shall look on the scall: and, behold, *if* the scall be not spread in the skin, nor *be* in sight deeper than the skin; then the priest shall pronounce him clean: and he shall wash his clothes, and be clean.

35 But if the scall spread much in the skin after his cleansing;

36 Then the priest shall look on him: and, behold, if the scall be spread in the skin, the priest shall not seek for yellow hair; he *is* unclean.

37 But if the scall be in his sight at a stay, and *that* there is black hair grown up therein; the scall is healed, he *is* clean: and the priest shall pronounce him clean.

38 If a man also or a woman have in the skin of their flesh bright spots, *even* white bright spots;

39 Then the priest shall look: and, behold, *if* the bright spots in the skin of their flesh *be* darkish white; it *is* a freckled spot *that* groweth in the skin; he *is* clean.

40 And the man whose ᴺhair is fallen off his head, he *is* bald; *yet is* he clean.

41 And he that hath his hair fallen off from the part of his head toward his face, he *is* forehead bald: *yet is* he clean.

42 And if there be in the bald head, or bald forehead, a white reddish sore; it *is* a leprosy sprung up in his bald head, or his bald forehead.

43 Then the priest shall look upon it: and, behold, *if* the rising of the sore *be* white reddish in his bald head, or in his bald forehead, as the leprosy appeareth in the skin of the flesh;

44 He is a leprous man, he *is* unclean: the priest shall pronounce him utterly unclean; his plague *is* in his head.

45 And the leper in whom the plague *is*, his clothes shall be rent, and his head bare, and he shall ᴿput a covering upon his upper lip, and shall cry, ᴿUnclean, unclean.

46 All the days wherein the plague *shall be* in him he shall be defiled; he *is* unclean: he shall dwell alone; ᴿwithout the camp *shall* his habitation *be*.

CHAP. **13**

BC 1490
40 Heb. *head is pilled*
45 Ezek. 24:17, 22
Mic. 3:7
45 Lam. 4:15
46 Num. 5:2
& 12:14
2 Ki. 7:3
& 15:5
2 Chr. 26:21
Luke 17:12

Heb. *work of*   **48**
Heb. *vessel*, or,   **49**
instrument
ch. 14:44   **51**
Heb. *whether*   **55**
it be bald in the head thereof, or in the forehead thereof

Leprosy in garments

47 The garment also that the plague of leprosy is in, *whether it be* a woollen garment, or a linen garment;

48 Whether *it be* in the warp, or woof; of linen, or of woollen; whether in a skin, or in any ᴺthing made of skin;

49 And if the plague be greenish or reddish in the garment, or in the skin, either in the warp, or in the woof, or in any ᴺthing of skin; it *is* a plague of leprosy, and shall be shewed unto the priest:

50 And the priest shall look upon the plague, and shut up *it that hath* the plague seven days:

51 And he shall look on the plague on the seventh day: if the plague be spread in the garment, either in the warp, or in the woof, or in a skin, *or* in any work that is made of skin; the plague *is* ᴿa fretting leprosy; it *is* unclean.

52 He shall therefore burn that garment, whether warp or woof, in woollen or in linen, or any thing of skin, wherein the plague is: for it *is* a fretting leprosy; it shall be burnt in the fire.

53 And if the priest shall look, and, behold, the plague be not spread in the garment, either in the warp, or in the woof, or in any thing of skin;

54 Then the priest shall command that they wash *the thing* wherein the plague *is*, and he shall shut it up seven days more:

55 And the priest shall look on the plague, after that it is washed: and, behold, *if* the plague have not changed his colour, and the plague be not spread; it *is* unclean; thou shalt burn it in the fire; it *is* fret inward, ᴺ*whether* it *be* bare within or without.

56 And if the priest look, and, behold, the plague *be* somewhat dark after the washing of it; then he shall rend it out of the garment, or out of the skin, or out of the warp, or out of the woof:

57 And if it appear still in the garment, either in the warp, or in the woof, or in any thing of skin; it *is* a spreading *plague*: thou shalt burn that wherein the plague *is* with fire.

58 And the garment, either warp, or woof, or whatsoever thing of skin *it be*, which thou shalt wash, if the plague be departed from them, then it shall be washed the second time, and shall be clean.

59 This *is* the law of the plague of leprosy in a garment of woollen or linen, either in the warp, or woof, or any thing of skins, to pronounce it clean, or to pronounce it unclean.

CHAPTER 14

Law of cleansing lepers

AND the LORD spake unto Moses, saying,
2 This shall be the law of the leper in the day of his cleansing: He ᴿshall be brought unto the priest:

3 And the priest shall go forth out of the camp; and the priest shall look, and, behold, *if* the plague of leprosy be healed in the leper;

4 Then shall the priest command to take for him that is to be cleansed two ᴺbirds alive *and* clean, and ᴿcedar wood, and ᴿscarlet, and ᴿhyssop:

5 And the priest shall command that one of the birds be killed in an earthen vessel over running water:

6 As for the living bird, he shall take it, and the cedar wood, and the scarlet, and the hyssop, and shall dip them and the living bird in the blood of the bird *that was* killed over the running water:

7 And he shall ᴿsprinkle upon him that is to be cleansed from the leprosy ᴿseven times, and shall pronounce him clean, and shall let the living bird loose ᴺinto the open field.

8 And he that is to be cleansed ᴿshall wash his clothes, and shave off all his hair, ᴿand wash himself in water, that he may be clean: and after that he shall come into the camp, and ᴿshall tarry abroad out of his tent seven days.

9 But it shall be on the seventh day, that he shall shave all his hair off his head and his beard and his eyebrows, even all his hair he shall shave off: and he shall wash his clothes, also he shall wash his flesh in water, and he shall be clean.

10 And on the eighth day ᴿhe shall take two he lambs without blemish, and one ewe lamb ᴺof the first year without blemish, and three tenth deals of fine flour *for* ᴿa meat offering, mingled with oil, and one lŏg of oil.

11 And the priest that maketh *him* clean shall present the man that is to be made clean, and those things, before the LORD, *at* the door of the tabernacle of the congregation:

12 And the priest shall take one he lamb, and ᴿoffer him for a trespass offering, and the lŏg of oil, and ᴿwave them *for* a wave offering before the LORD:

13 And he shall slay the lamb ᴿin the place where he shall kill the sin offering and the burnt offering, in the holy place: for ᴿas the sin offering *is* the priest's, *so is* the trespass offering: ᴿit *is* most holy:

14 And the priest shall take *some* of the blood of the trespass offering, and the priest shall put *it* ᴿupon the tip of the right ear of

CHAP. 14	
BC 1490	
2	Mat. 8:2, 4
	Mark 1:40, 44
	Luke 5:12, 14
	& 17:14
4	Or, *sparrows*
4	Num. 19:6
4	Heb. 9:19
4	Ps. 51:7
7	Num. 19:18, 19
	Is. 52:15
	Heb. 9:13, 21
	& 12:24
7	2 Ki. 5:10, 14
	Ps. 51:2
7	Heb. *upon the face of the field*
8	ch. 13:6
8	ch. 11:25
	Eph. 5:26
	Heb. 10:22
	Rev. 1:5, 6
8	Num. 12:15
10	Mat. 8:4
	Mark 1:44
	Luke 5:14
10	Heb. *the daughter of her year*
10	ch. 2:1
	Num. 15:4
12	ch. 5:2, 18
	& 6:6, 7
12	Ex. 29:24
13	Ex. 29:11
	ch. 1:5
	& 4:4
13	ch. 7:7
13	ch. 2:3
	& 7:6
	& 21:22
14	Ex. 29:20
	ch. 8:23

ch. 4:26	18
& 5:6	
ch. 5:1, 6	19
& 12:7	
ch. 5:7	21
& 12:8	
Heb. *his hand reach not*	21
Heb. *for a waving*	21
ch. 12:8	22
& 5:14, 15	
ver. 10, 11	23
ver. 12	24
ver. 14, 17	25

him that is to be cleansed, and upon the thumb of his right hand, and upon the great toe of his right foot:

15 And the priest shall take *some* of the lŏg of oil, and pour *it* into the palm of his own left hand:

16 And the priest shall dip his right finger in the oil that *is* in his left hand, and shall sprinkle of the oil with his finger seven times before the LORD:

17 And of the rest of the oil that *is* in his hand shall the priest put upon the tip of the right ear of him that is to be cleansed, and upon the thumb of his right hand, and upon the great toe of his right foot, upon the blood of the trespass offering:

18 And the remnant of the oil that *is* in the priest's hand he shall pour upon the head of him that is to be cleansed: ᴿand the priest shall make an atonement for him before the LORD.

19 And the priest shall offer ᴿthe sin offering, and make an atonement for him that is to be cleansed from his uncleanness; and afterward he shall kill the burnt offering:

20 And the priest shall offer the burnt offering and the meat offering upon the altar: and the priest shall make an atonement for him, and he shall be clean.

21 And ᴿif he *be* poor, and ᴺcannot get so much; then he shall take one lamb *for* a trespass offering ᴺto be waved, to make an atonement for him, and one tenth deal of fine flour mingled with oil for a meat offering, and a lŏg of oil;

22 ᴿAnd two turtledoves, or two young pigeons, such as he is able to get; and the one shall be a sin offering, and the other a burnt offering.

23 ᴿAnd he shall bring them on the eighth day for his cleansing unto the priest, unto the door of the tabernacle of the congregation, before the LORD.

24 ᴿAnd the priest shall take the lamb of the trespass offering, and the lŏg of oil, and the priest shall wave them *for* a wave offering before the LORD:

25 And he shall kill the lamb of the trespass offering, ᴿand the priest shall take *some* of the blood of the trespass offering, and put *it* upon the tip of the right ear of him that is to be cleansed, and upon the thumb of his right hand, and upon the great toe of his right foot:

26 And the priest shall pour of the oil into the palm of his own left hand:

27 And the priest shall sprinkle with his right finger *some* of the oil that *is* in his left hand seven times before the LORD:

28 And the priest shall put of the oil that *is* in his hand upon the tip of the right ear of him that is to be cleansed, and upon the thumb of his right hand, and upon the great toe of his right foot, upon the place of the blood of the trespass offering:

29 And the rest of the oil that *is* in the priest's hand he shall put upon the head of him that is to be cleansed, to make an atonement for him before the LORD.

30 And he shall offer the one of ᴿthe turtledoves, or of the young pigeons, such as he can get;

31 *Even* such as he is able to get, the one *for* a sin offering, and the other *for* a burnt offering, with the meat offering: and the priest shall make an atonement for him that is to be cleansed before the LORD.

32 This *is* the law *of him* in whom *is* the plague of leprosy, whose hand is not able to get ᴿ*that which pertaineth* to his cleansing.

Leprosy in houses

33 And the LORD spake unto Moses and unto Aaron, saying,

34 ᴿWhen ye be come into the land of Canaan, which I give to you for a possession, and I put the plague of leprosy in a house of the land of your possession;

35 And he that owneth the house shall come and tell the priest, saying, It seemeth to me *there is* as it were ᴿa plague in the house:

36 Then the priest shall command that they ᴺempty the house, before the priest go *into it* to see the plague, that all that *is* in the house be not made unclean: and afterward the priest shall go in to see the house:

37 And he shall look on the plague, and, behold, *if* the plague *be* in the walls of the house with hollow strakes, greenish or reddish, which in sight *are* lower than the wall;

38 Then the priest shall go out of the house to the door of the house, and shut up the house seven days:

39 And the priest shall come again the seventh day, and shall look: and, behold, *if* the plague be spread in the walls of the house;

40 Then the priest shall command that they take away the stones in which the plague *is,* and they shall cast them into an unclean place without the city:

41 And he shall cause the house to be scraped within round about, and they shall pour out the dust that they scrape off without the city into an unclean place:

42 And they shall take other stones, and put *them* in the place of those stones; and he shall take other mortar, and shall plaster the house.

CHAP. **14**	
BC 1490	
30 ver. 22	
32 ch. 15:14, 15	
32 ver. 10	
34 Gen. 17:8	
Num. 32:22	
Deut. 7:1	
& 32:49	
35 Ps. 91:10	
Prov. 3:33	
Zech. 5:4	
36 Or, *prepare*	

ch. 13:51	44
Zech. 5:4	
Heb. *in*	48
coming in	
shall come	
in, etc.	
ver. 4	49
ver. 20	53
ch. 13:30	54
ch. 13:47	55
ver. 34	55
ch. 13:2	56
Deut. 24:8	57
Ezek. 44:23	
Heb. *in*	57
the day of	
the unclean,	
and in the	
day of the	
clean	

CHAP. **15**	
BC 1490	
ch. 22:4	2
Num. 5:2	
2 Sam. 3:29	
Or, *running*	2
of the reins	

43 And if the plague come again, and break out in the house, after that he hath taken away the stones, and after he hath scraped the house, and after it is plastered;

44 Then the priest shall come and look, and, behold, *if* the plague be spread in the house, it *is* ᴿa fretting leprosy in the house: it *is* unclean.

45 And he shall break down the house, the stones of it, and the timber thereof, and all the mortar of the house; and he shall carry *them* forth out of the city into an unclean place.

46 Moreover he that goeth into the house all the while that it is shut up shall be unclean until the even.

47 And he that lieth in the house shall wash his clothes; and he that eateth in the house shall wash his clothes.

48 And if the priest ᴺshall come in, and look *upon it,* and, behold, the plague hath not spread in the house, after the house was plastered: then the priest shall pronounce the house clean, because the plague is healed.

49 And ᴿhe shall take to cleanse the house two birds, and cedar wood, and scarlet, and hyssop:

50 And he shall kill the one of the birds in an earthen vessel over running water:

51 And he shall take the cedar wood, and the hyssop, and the scarlet, and the living bird, and dip them in the blood of the slain bird, and in the running water, and sprinkle the house seven times:

52 And he shall cleanse the house with the blood of the bird, and with the running water, and with the living bird, and with the cedar wood, and with the hyssop, and with the scarlet:

53 But he shall let go the living bird out of the city into the open fields, and ᴿmake an atonement for the house: and it shall be clean.

54 This *is* the law for all manner of plague of leprosy, and ᴿscall,

55 And for the ᴿleprosy of a garment, ᴿand of a house,

56 And ᴿfor a rising, and for a scab, and for a bright spot:

57 To ᴿteach ᴺwhen *it is* unclean, and when *it is* clean: this *is* the law of leprosy.

CHAPTER 15

Uncleanness of men

AND the LORD spake unto Moses and to Aaron, saying,

2 Speak unto the children of Israel, and say unto them, ᴿWhen any man hath a ᴺrunning issue out of his flesh, *because of* his issue he *is* unclean.

3 And this shall be his uncleanness in his issue: whether his flesh run with his issue, or his flesh be stopped from his issue, it *is* his uncleanness.

4 Every bed, whereon he lieth that hath the issue, is unclean: and every ᴺthing, whereon he sitteth, shall be unclean.

5 And whosoever toucheth his bed shall wash his clothes, ᴿand bathe *himself* in water, and be unclean until the even.

6 And he that sitteth on *any* thing whereon he sat that hath the issue shall wash his clothes, and bathe *himself* in water, and be unclean until the even.

7 And he that toucheth the flesh of him that hath the issue shall wash his clothes, and bathe *himself* in water, and be unclean until the even.

8 And if he that hath the issue spit upon him that is clean; then he shall wash his clothes, and bathe *himself* in water, and be unclean until the even.

9 And what saddle soever he rideth upon that hath the issue shall be unclean.

10 And whosoever toucheth any thing that was under him shall be unclean until the even: and he that beareth *any of* those things shall wash his clothes, and bathe *himself* in water, and be unclean until the even.

11 And whomsoever he toucheth that hath the issue, and hath not rinsed his hands in water, he shall wash his clothes, and bathe *himself* in water, and be unclean until the even.

12 And the ᴿvessel of earth, that he toucheth which hath the issue, shall be broken: and every vessel of wood shall be rinsed in water.

13 And when he that hath an issue is cleansed of his issue; then ᴿhe shall number to himself seven days for his cleansing, and wash his clothes, and bathe his flesh in running water, and shall be clean.

14 And on the eighth day he shall take to him ᴿtwo turtledoves, or two young pigeons, and come before the Lᴏʀᴅ unto the door of the tabernacle of the congregation, and give them unto the priest:

15 And the priest shall offer them, ᴿthe one *for* a sin offering, and the other *for* a burnt offering; ᴿand the priest shall make an atonement for him before the Lᴏʀᴅ for his issue.

16 And ᴿif any man's seed of copulation go out from him, then he shall wash all his flesh in water, and be unclean until the even.

17 And every garment, and every skin, whereon is the seed of copulation, shall be washed with water, and be unclean until the even.

18 The woman also with whom man shall lie

with seed of copulation, they shall *both* bathe *themselves* in water, and ᴿbe unclean until the even.

Uncleanness of women

19 And ᴿif a woman have an issue, *and* her issue in her flesh be blood, she shall be ᴺput apart seven days: and whosoever toucheth her shall be unclean until the even.

20 And every thing that she lieth upon in her separation shall be unclean: every thing also that she sitteth upon shall be unclean.

21 And whosoever toucheth her bed shall wash his clothes, and bathe *himself* in water, and be unclean until the even.

22 And whosoever toucheth any thing that she sat upon shall wash his clothes, and bathe *himself* in water, and be unclean until the even.

23 And if it *be* on *her* bed, or on any thing whereon she sitteth, when he toucheth it, he shall be unclean until the even.

24 And ᴿif any man lie with her at all, and her flowers be upon him, he shall be unclean seven days; and all the bed whereon he lieth shall be unclean.

25 And if ᴿa woman have an issue of her blood many days out of the time of her separation, or if it run beyond the time of her separation; all the days of the issue of her uncleanness shall be as the days of her separation: she *shall be* unclean.

26 Every bed whereon she lieth all the days of her issue shall be unto her as the bed of her separation: and whatsoever she sitteth upon shall be unclean, as the uncleanness of her separation.

27 And whosoever toucheth those things shall be unclean, and shall wash his clothes, and bathe *himself* in water, and be unclean until the even.

28 But ᴿif she be cleansed of her issue, then she shall number to herself seven days, and after that she shall be clean.

29 And on the eighth day she shall take unto her two turtles, or two young pigeons, and bring them unto the priest, to the door of the tabernacle of the congregation.

30 And the priest shall offer the one *for* a sin offering, and the other *for* a burnt offering; and the priest shall make an atonement for her before the Lᴏʀᴅ for the issue of her uncleanness.

31 Thus shall ye ᴿseparate the children of Israel from their uncleanness; that they die not in their uncleanness, when they ᴿdefile my tabernacle that *is* among them.

32 ᴿThis *is* the law of him that hath an issue, ᴿand *of him* whose seed goeth from him, and is defiled therewith;

CHAP. 15

BC 1490

4 Heb. *vessel*
5 ch. 11:25
  & 17:15
12 ch. 6:28
  & 11:32, 33
13 ver. 28
  ch. 14:8
  Num. 19:11, 12
14 ch. 14:22, 23
15 ch. 14:30, 31
15 ch. 14:19, 31
16 ch. 22:4
  Deut. 23:10

Ex. 19:15   18
1 Sam. 21:4
1 Cor. 6:18
ch. 12:2   19
Heb. *in her* 19
  separa-
  tion
See ch. 20:18 24
Mat. 9:20   25
Mark 5:25
Luke 8:43
ver. 13-15   28
ch. 11:47   31
Deut. 24:8
Ezek. 44:23
Heb. 12:15
Num. 5:3   31
  & 19:13, 20
Ezek. 5:11
  & 23:38
ver. 2   32
ver. 16   32

33 ᴿAnd of her that is sick of her flowers, and of him that hath an issue, of the man, ᴿand of the woman, ᴿand of him that lieth with her that is unclean.

CHAPTER 16

Ceremony of atonement

AND the LORD spake unto Moses after ᴿthe death of the two sons of Aaron, when they offered before the LORD, and died;

2 And the LORD said unto Moses, Speak unto Aaron thy brother, that he ᴿcome not at all times into the holy *place* within the vail before the mercy seat, which *is* upon the ark; that he die not: for ᴿI will appear in the cloud upon the mercy seat.

3 Thus shall Aaron ᴿcome into the holy *place:* ᴿwith a young bullock for a sin offering, and a ram for a burnt offering.

4 He shall put on ᴿthe holy linen coat, and he shall have the linen breeches upon his flesh, and shall be girded with a linen girdle, and with the linen mitre shall he be attired: these *are* holy garments; therefore ᴿshall he wash his flesh in water, and *so* put them on.

5 And he shall take of ᴿthe congregation of the children of Israel two kids of the goats for a sin offering, and one ram for a burnt offering.

6 And Aaron shall offer his bullock of the sin offering, which *is* for himself, and ᴿmake an atonement for himself, and for his house.

7 And he shall take the two goats, and present them before the LORD *at* the door of the tabernacle of the congregation.

8 And Aaron shall cast lots upon the two goats; one lot for the LORD, and the other lot for the ᴺscapegoat.

9 And Aaron shall bring the goat upon which the LORD's lot ᴺfell, and offer him *for* a sin offering.

10 But the goat, on which the lot fell to be the scapegoat, shall be presented alive before the LORD, to make ᴿan atonement with him, *and* to let him go for a scapegoat into the wilderness.

11 And Aaron shall bring the bullock of the sin offering, which *is* for himself, and shall make an atonement for himself, and for his house, and shall kill the bullock of the sin offering which *is* for himself:

12 And he shall take ᴿa censer full of burning coals of fire from off the altar before the LORD, and his hands full of ᴿsweet incense beaten small, and bring *it* within the vail:

13 ᴿAnd he shall put the incense upon the fire before the LORD, that the cloud of the in-

cense may cover the ᴿmercy seat that *is* upon the testimony, that he die not:

14 And ᴿhe shall take of the blood of the bullock, and ᴿsprinkle *it* with his finger upon the mercy seat eastward; and before the mercy seat shall he sprinkle of the blood with his finger seven times.

15 ᴿThen shall he kill the goat of the sin offering, that *is* for the people, and bring his blood ᴿwithin the vail, and do with that blood as he did with the blood of the bullock, and sprinkle it upon the mercy seat, and before the mercy seat:

16 And he shall ᴿmake an atonement for the holy *place,* because of the uncleanness of the children of Israel, and because of their transgressions in all their sins: and so shall he do for the tabernacle of the congregation, that ᴺremaineth among them in the midst of their uncleanness.

17 ᴿAnd there shall be no man in the tabernacle of the congregation when he goeth in to make an atonement in the holy *place,* until he come out, and have made an atonement for himself, and for his household, and for all the congregation of Israel.

18 And he shall go out unto the altar that *is* before the LORD, and ᴿmake an atonement for it; and shall take of the blood of the bullock, and of the blood of the goat, and put *it* upon the horns of the altar round about.

19 And he shall sprinkle of the blood upon it with his finger seven times, and cleanse it, and ᴿhallow it from the uncleanness of the children of Israel.

The scapegoat

20 And when he hath made an end of ᴿreconciling the holy *place,* and the tabernacle of the congregation, and the altar, he shall bring the live goat:

21 And Aaron shall lay both his hands upon the head of the live goat, and confess over him all the iniquities of the children of Israel, and all their transgressions in all their sins, ᴿputting them upon the head of the goat, and shall send *him* away by the hand of ᴺa fit man into the wilderness:

22 And the goat shall ᴿbear upon him all their iniquities unto a land ᴺnot inhabited: and he shall let go the goat in the wilderness.

23 And Aaron shall come into the tabernacle of the congregation, ᴿand shall put off the linen garments, which he put on when he went into the holy *place,* and shall leave them there:

24 And he shall wash his flesh with water in the holy place, and put on his garments, and come forth, ᴿand offer his burnt offering, and

the burnt offering of the people, and make an atonement for himself, and for the people.

25 And ᴿthe fat of the sin offering shall he burn upon the altar.

26 And he that let go the goat for the scapegoat shall wash his clothes, ᴿand bathe his flesh in water, and afterward come into the camp.

27 ᴿAnd the bullock *for* the sin offering, and the goat *for* the sin offering, whose blood was brought in to make atonement in the holy *place,* shall *one* carry forth without the camp; and they shall burn in the fire their skins, and their flesh, and their dung.

28 And he that burneth them shall wash his clothes, and bathe his flesh in water, and afterward he shall come into the camp.

Day of atonement

29 And *this* shall be a statute for ever unto you: *that* ᴿin the seventh month, on the tenth *day* of the month, ye shall afflict your souls, and do no work at all, *whether it be* one of your own country, or a stranger that sojourneth among you:

30 For on that day shall *the priest* make an atonement for you, to ᴿcleanse you, *that* ye may be clean from all your sins before the Lord.

31 ᴿIt *shall be* a sabbath of rest unto you, and ye shall afflict your souls, by a statute for ever.

32 ᴿAnd the priest, whom he shall anoint, and whom he shall ᴿconsecrateᴺ to minister in the priest's office in his father's stead, shall make the atonement, and ᴿshall put on the linen clothes, *even* the holy garments:

33 And ᴿhe shall make an atonement for the holy sanctuary, and he shall make an atonement for the tabernacle of the congregation, and for the altar, and he shall make an atonement for the priests, and for all the people of the congregation.

34 ᴿAnd this shall be an everlasting statute unto you, to make an atonement for the children of Israel for all their sins ᴿonce a year. And he did as the Lord commanded Moses.

CHAPTER 17

Blood guiltiness

Aᴺᴰ the Lord spake unto Moses, saying, 2 Speak unto Aaron, and unto his sons, and unto all the children of Israel, and say unto them; This *is* the thing which the Lord hath commanded, saying,

3 What man soever *there be* of the house of Israel, ᴿthat killeth an ox, or lamb, or goat, in the camp, or that killeth *it* out of the camp,

4 ᴿAnd bringeth it not unto the door of the tabernacle of the congregation, to offer an offering unto the Lord before the tabernacle of the Lord; blood shall be ᴿimputed unto that man; he hath shed blood; and that man ᴿshall be cut off from among his people:

5 To the end that the children of Israel may bring their sacrifices, ᴿwhich they offer in the open field, even that they may bring them unto the Lord, unto the door of the tabernacle of the congregation, unto the priest, and offer them *for* peace offerings unto the Lord.

6 And the priest ᴿshall sprinkle the blood upon the altar of the Lord *at* the door of the tabernacle of the congregation, and ᴿburn the fat for a sweet savour unto the Lord.

7 And they shall no more offer their sacrifices ᴿunto devils, after whom they ᴿhave gone a whoring. This shall be a statute for ever unto them throughout their generations.

8 And thou shalt say unto them, Whatsoever man *there be* of the house of Israel, or of the strangers which sojourn among you, ᴿthat offereth a burnt offering or sacrifice,

9 And bringeth it not unto the door of the tabernacle of the congregation, to offer it unto the Lord; even that man shall be cut off from among his people.

Sanctity of blood

10 ᴿAnd whatsoever man *there be* of the house of Israel, or of the strangers that sojourn among you, that eateth any manner of blood; ᴿI will even set my face against that soul that eateth blood, and will cut him off from among his people.

11 For the life of the flesh *is* in the blood: and I have given it to you upon the altar ᴿto make an atonement for your souls: for ᴿit *is* the blood *that* maketh an atonement for the soul.

12 Therefore I said unto the children of Israel, No soul of you shall eat blood, neither shall any stranger that sojourneth among you eat blood.

13 And whatsoever man *there be* of the children of Israel, or of the strangers that sojourn among you, ᴺwhich ᴿhunteth and catcheth any beast or fowl that may be eaten; he shall even ᴿpour out the blood thereof, and ᴿcover it with dust.

14 ᴿFor *it is* the life of all flesh; the blood of it *is* for the life thereof: therefore I said unto the children of Israel, Ye shall eat the blood of no manner of flesh: for the life of all flesh *is* the blood thereof: whosoever eateth it shall be cut off.

15 ᴿAnd every soul that eateth ᴺthat which died *of itself,* or that which was torn *with*

beasts, whether it be one of your own country, or a stranger, [R]he shall both wash his clothes, [R]and bathe *himself* in water, and be unclean until the even: then shall he be clean.

16 But if he wash *them* not, nor bathe his flesh; then [R]he shall bear his iniquity.

CHAPTER 18

Incest forbidden

AND the LORD spake unto Moses, saying, 2 Speak unto the children of Israel, and say unto them, [R]I am the LORD your God.

3 [R]After the doings of the land of Egypt, wherein ye dwelt, shall ye not do: and [R]after the doings of the land of Canaan, whither I bring you, shall ye not do: neither shall ye walk in their ordinances.

4 [R]Ye shall do my judgments, and keep mine ordinances, to walk therein: I *am* the LORD your God.

5 Ye shall therefore keep my statutes, and my judgements: [R]which if a man do, he shall live in them: [R]I *am* the LORD.

6 None of you shall approach to any that is [N]near of kin to him, to uncover *their* nakedness: I *am* the LORD.

7 [R]The nakedness of thy father, or the nakedness of thy mother, shalt thou not uncover: she *is* thy mother; thou shalt not uncover her nakedness.

8 [R]The nakedness of thy father's wife shalt thou not uncover: it *is* thy father's nakedness.

9 [R]The nakedness of thy sister, the daughter of thy father, or daughter of thy mother, *whether she be* born at home, or born abroad, *even* their nakedness thou shalt not uncover.

10 The nakedness of thy son's daughter, or of thy daughter's daughter, *even* their nakedness thou shalt not uncover: for theirs *is* thine own nakedness.

11 The nakedness of thy father's wife's daughter, begotten of thy father, she *is* thy sister, thou shalt not uncover her nakedness.

12 [R]Thou shalt not uncover the nakedness of thy father's sister: she *is* thy father's near kinswoman.

13 Thou shalt not uncover the nakedness of thy mother's sister: for she *is* thy mother's near kinswoman.

14 [R]Thou shalt not uncover the nakedness of thy father's brother, thou shalt not approach to his wife: she *is* thine aunt.

15 [R]Thou shalt not uncover the nakedness of thy daughter in law: she *is* thy son's wife; thou shalt not uncover her nakedness.

16 [R]Thou shalt not uncover the nakedness of thy brother's wife: it *is* thy brother's nakedness.

17 [R]Thou shalt not uncover the nakedness of a woman and her daughter, neither shalt thou take her son's daughter, or her daughter's daughter, to uncover her nakedness; *for* they *are* her near kinswomen: it *is* wickedness.

18 Neither shalt thou take [N]a wife to her sister, [R]to vex *her,* to uncover her nakedness, beside the other in her life *time.*

Defilement and perversion

19 [R]Also thou shalt not approach unto a woman to uncover her nakedness, as long as she is put apart for her uncleanness.

20 Moreover [R]thou shalt not lie carnally with thy neighbour's wife, to defile thyself with her.

21 And thou shalt not let any of thy seed [R]pass through *the fire* to [R]Molech, neither shalt thou [R]profane the name of thy God: I *am* the LORD.

22 [R]Thou shalt not lie with mankind, as with womankind: it *is* abomination.

23 [R]Neither shalt thou lie with any beast to defile thyself therewith: neither shall any woman stand before a beast to lie down thereto: it *is* [R]confusion.

24 [R]Defile not ye yourselves in any of these things: [R]for in all these the nations are defiled which I cast out before you:

25 And [R]the land is defiled: therefore I do [R]visit the iniquity thereof upon it, and the land itself vomiteth out her inhabitants.

26 [R]Ye shall therefore keep my statutes and my judgements, and shall not commit *any* of these abominations; *neither* any of your own nation, nor any stranger that sojourneth among you:

27 (For all these abominations have the men of the land done, which *were* before you, and the land is defiled;)

28 That [R]the land spue not you out also, when ye defile it, as it spued out the nations that *were* before you.

29 For whosoever shall commit any of these abominations, even the souls that commit *them* shall be cut off from among their people.

30 Therefore shall ye keep mine ordinance, [R]that *ye* commit not *any one* of these abominable customs, which were committed before you, and that ye defile not yourselves therein: I *am* the LORD your God.

CHAPTER 19

Rules of conduct

AND the LORD spake unto Moses, saying, 2 Speak unto all the congregation of the children of Israel, and say unto them, [R]Ye

shall be holy: for I the LORD your God *am* holy.

3 [R]Ye shall fear every man his mother, and his father, and [R]keep my sabbaths: I *am* the LORD your God.

4 [R]Turn ye not unto idols, [R]nor make to yourselves molten gods: I *am* the LORD your God.

5 And [R]if ye offer a sacrifice of peace offerings unto the LORD, ye shall offer it at your own will.

6 It shall be eaten the same day ye offer it, and on the morrow: and if aught remain until the third day, it shall be burnt in the fire.

7 And if it be eaten at all on the third day, it *is* abominable; it shall not be accepted.

8 Therefore *every one* that eateth it shall bear his iniquity, because he hath profaned the hallowed thing of the LORD: and that soul shall be cut off from among his people.

9 And [R]when ye reap the harvest of your land, thou shalt not wholly reap the corners of thy field, neither shalt thou gather the gleanings of thy harvest.

10 And thou shalt not glean thy vineyard, neither shalt thou gather *every* grape of thy vineyard; thou shalt leave them for the poor and stranger: I *am* the LORD your God.

11 [R]Ye shall not steal, neither deal falsely, [R]neither lie one to another.

12 And ye shall not [R]swear by my name falsely, [R]neither shalt thou profane the name of thy God: I *am* the LORD.

13 [R]Thou shalt not defraud thy neighbour, neither rob *him*: [R]the wages of him that is hired shall not abide with thee all night until the morning.

14 Thou shalt not curse the deaf, [R]nor put a stumblingblock before the blind, but shalt fear thy God: I *am* the LORD.

15 Ye shall do no unrighteousness in judgment: thou shalt not respect the person of the poor, nor honour the person of the mighty: *but* in righteousness shalt thou judge thy neighbour.

16 [R]Thou shalt not go up and down *as* a talebearer among thy people: neither shalt thou [R]stand against the blood of thy neighbour: I *am* the LORD.

17 [R]Thou shalt not hate thy brother in thine heart: [R]thou shalt in any wise rebuke thy neighbour, [N]and not suffer sin upon him.

18 [R]Thou shalt not avenge, nor bear any grudge against the children of thy people, [R]but thou shalt love thy neighbour as thyself: I *am* the LORD.

19 Ye shall keep my statutes. Thou shalt not let thy cattle gender with a diverse kind: [R]thou shalt not sow thy field with mingled seed:

[R]neither shall a garment mingled of linen and woollen come upon thee.

20 And whosoever lieth carnally with a woman, that *is* a bondmaid, [NN]betrothed to an husband, and not at all redeemed, nor freedom given her; [NN]she shall be scourged; they shall not be put to death, because she was not free.

21 And [R]he shall bring his trespass offering unto the LORD, unto the door of the tabernacle of the congregation, *even* a ram for a trespass offering.

22 And the priest shall make an atonement for him with the ram of the trespass offering before the LORD for his sin which he hath done: and the sin which he hath done shall be forgiven him.

23 And when ye shall come into the land, and shall have planted all manner of trees for food, then ye shall count the fruit thereof as uncircumcised: three years shall it be as uncircumcised unto you: it shall not be eaten of.

24 But in the fourth year all the fruit thereof shall be [N]holy [R]to praise the LORD *withal.*

25 And in the fifth year shall ye eat of the fruit thereof, that it may yield unto you the increase thereof: I *am* the LORD your God.

26 [R]Ye shall not eat *any thing* with the blood: [R]neither shall ye use enchantment, nor observe times.

27 [R]Ye shall not round the corners of your heads, neither shalt thou mar the corners of thy beard.

28 Ye shall not [R]make any cuttings in your flesh for the dead, nor print any marks upon you: I *am* the LORD.

29 [R]Do not [N]prostitute thy daughter, to cause her to be a whore; lest the land fall to whoredom, and the land become full of wickedness.

30 [R]Ye shall keep my sabbaths, and [R]reverence my sanctuary: I *am* the LORD.

31 [R]Regard not them that have familiar spirits, neither seek after wizards, to be defiled by them: I *am* the LORD your God.

32 [R]Thou shalt rise up before the hoary head, and honour the face of the old man, and [R]fear thy God: I *am* the LORD.

33 And [R]if a stranger sojourn with thee in your land, ye shall not [N]vex him.

34 [R]*But* the stranger that dwelleth with you shall be unto you as one born among you, and [R]thou shalt love him as thyself; for ye were strangers in the land of Egypt: I *am* the LORD your God.

Just weights

35 [R]Ye shall do no unrighteousness in judgment, in meteyard, in weight, or in measure.

36 [R]Just balances, just [N]weights, a just

ē'-phäh, and a just hĭn, shall ye have: I *am* the LORD your God, which brought you out of the land of Egypt.

37 ᴿTherefore shall ye observe all my statutes, and all my judgements, and do them: I *am* the LORD.

CHAPTER 20

Various laws and ordinances

AND the LORD spake unto Moses, saying, 2 ᴿAgain, thou shalt say to the children of Israel, ᴿWhosoever *he be* of the children of Israel, or of the strangers that sojourn in Israel, that giveth *any* of his seed unto Molech; he shall surely be put to death: the people of the land shall stone him with stones.

3 And ᴿI will set my face against that man, and will cut him off from among his people; because he hath given of his seed unto Molech, to ᴿdefile my sanctuary, and ᴿto profane my holy name.

4 And if the people of the land do any ways hide their eyes from the man, when he giveth of his seed unto Molech, and ᴿkill him not:

5 Then ᴿI will set my face against that man, and ᴿagainst his family, and will cut him off, and all that ᴿgo a whoring after him, to commit whoredom with Molech, from among their people.

6 And ᴿthe soul that turneth after such as have familiar spirits, and after wizards, to go a whoring after them, I will even set my face against that soul, and will cut him off from among his people.

7 ᴿSanctify yourselves therefore, and be ye holy: for I *am* the LORD your God.

8 ᴿAnd ye shall keep my statutes, and do them: ᴿI *am* the LORD which sanctify you.

9 ᴿFor everyone that curseth his father or his mother shall be surely put to death: he hath cursed his father or his mother; ᴿhis blood *shall be* upon him.

Adultery

10 And ᴿthe man that committeth adultery with *another* man's wife, *even he* that committeth adultery with his neighbour's wife, the adulterer and the adulteress shall surely be put to death.

11 ᴿAnd the man that lieth with his father's wife hath uncovered his father's nakedness: both of them shall surely be put to death; their blood *shall be* upon them.

12 ᴿAnd if a man lie with his daughter in law, both of them shall surely be put to death: ᴿthey have wrought confusion; their blood *shall be* upon them.

CHAP. 19
BC 1490
37 ch. 18:4, 5
Deut. 4:5, 6 & 5:1
& 6:25

CHAP. 20
BC 1490
2 ch. 18:2
2 ch. 18:21
2 Ki. 23:10
2 Chr. 33:6
Jer. 7:31
3 ch. 17:10
3 Ezek. 5:11
& 23:38, 39
3 ch. 18:21
4 Deut. 17:2, 3, 5
5 ch. 17:10
5 Ex. 20:5
5 ch. 17:7
6 ch. 19:31
7 ch. 19:2
8 ch. 19:37
8 Ex. 31:13
9 Ex. 21:17
Deut. 27:16
Prov. 20:20
Mat. 15:4
9 ver. 11, 12, 13, 16, 27
2 Sam. 1:16
10 ch. 18:20
Deut. 22:22
11 ch. 18:8
Deut. 27:23
12 ch. 18:15
12 ch. 18:23
Gen. 19:5

ch. 18:22	13
Deut. 23:17	
Judg. 19:22	
ch. 18:17	14
Deut. 27:23	
ch. 18:23	15
Deut. 27:21	
ch. 18:9	17
Deut. 27:22	
Gen. 20:12	
ch. 15:24	18
Heb.	18
made naked	
ch. 18:12	19
ch. 18:6	19
ch. 18:14	20
ch. 18:16	21
Heb. *a*	21
separation	
ch. 18:26	22
& 19:37	
ch. 18:25	22
ch. 18:3, 24	23
ch. 18:27	23
Deut. 9:5	
Ex. 3:17 & 6:8	24
ver. 26	24
Ex. 19:5 & 33:16	
Deut. 7:6 & 14:2	
1 Ki. 8:53	
ch. 11:47	25
Deut. 14:4	
ch. 11:43	25

13 ᴿIf a man also lie with mankind, as he lieth with a woman, both of them have committed an abomination: they shall surely be put to death; their blood *shall be* upon them.

14 ᴿAnd if a man take a wife and her mother, it *is* wickedness: they shall be burnt with fire, both he and they; that there be no wickedness among you.

15 ᴿAnd if a man lie with a beast, he shall surely be put to death: and ye shall slay the beast.

16 And if a woman approach unto any beast, and lie down thereto, thou shalt kill the woman, and the beast: they shall surely be put to death; their blood *shall be* upon them.

17 ᴿAnd if a man shall take his sister, his father's daughter, or his mother's daughter, and see her nakedness, and she see his nakedness; it *is* a wicked thing; and they shall be cut off in the sight of their people: he hath uncovered his sister's nakedness; he shall bear his iniquity.

18 ᴿAnd if a man shall lie with a woman having her sickness, and shall uncover her nakedness; he hath ᴺdiscovered her fountain, and she hath uncovered the fountain of her blood: and both of them shall be cut off from among their people.

19 ᴿAnd thou shalt not uncover the nakedness of thy mother's sister, nor of thy father's sister: ᴿfor he uncovereth his near kin: they shall bear their iniquity.

20 ᴿAnd if a man shall lie with his uncle's wife, he hath uncovered his uncle's nakedness: they shall bear their sin; they shall die childless.

21 ᴿAnd if a man shall take his brother's wife, it *is* ᴺan unclean thing: he hath uncovered his brother's nakedness; they shall be childless.

Obedience required

22 Ye shall therefore keep all my ᴿstatutes, and all my judgments, and do them: that the land, whither I bring you to dwell therein, ᴿspue you not out.

23 ᴿAnd ye shall not walk in the manners of the nation, which I cast out before you: for they committed all these things, and ᴿtherefore I abhorred them.

24 But ᴿI have said unto you, Ye shall inherit their land, and I will give it unto you to possess it, a land that floweth with milk and honey: I *am* the LORD your God, ᴿwhich have separated you from *other* people.

25 ᴿYe shall therefore put difference between clean beasts and unclean, and between unclean fowls and clean: ᴿand ye shall not make your souls abominable by beast, or by

fowl, or by any manner of living thing that [N]creepeth on the ground, which I have separated from you as unclean.

26 And ye shall be holy unto me: [R]for I the LORD *am* holy, and have severed you from *other* people, that ye should be mine.

27 [R]A man also or woman that hath a familiar spirit, or that is a wizard, shall surely be put to death: they shall stone them with stones: [R]their blood *shall be* upon them.

CHAPTER 21

Sanctity of the priesthood

AND the LORD said unto Moses, Speak unto the priests the sons of Aaron, and say unto them, [R]There shall none be defiled for the dead among his people:

2 But for his kin, that is near unto him, *that is,* for his mother, and for his father, and for his son, and for his daughter, and for his brother,

3 And for his sister a virgin, that is nigh unto him, which hath had no husband; for her may he be defiled.

4 *But* [N]he shall not defile himself, *being* a chief man among his people, to profane himself.

5 [R]They shall not make baldness upon their head, neither shall they shave off the corner of their beard, nor make any cuttings in their flesh.

6 They shall be holy unto their God, and [R]not profane the name of their God: for the offerings of the LORD made by fire, *and* the bread of their God, they do offer: therefore they shall be holy.

7 [R]They shall not take a wife *that is* a whore, or profane; neither shall they take a woman [R]put away from her husband: for he *is* holy unto his God.

8 Thou shalt sanctify him therefore; for he offereth the bread of thy God: he shall be holy unto thee: for I the LORD, which sanctify you, *am* holy.

9 [R]And the daughter of any priest, if she profane herself by playing the whore, she profaneth her father: she shall be burnt with fire.

10 [R]And *he that is* the high priest among his brethren, upon whose head the anointing oil was poured, and [R]that is consecrated to put on the garments, [R]shall not uncover his head, nor rend his clothes;

11 Neither shall he [R]go in to any dead body, nor defile himself for his father, or for his mother;

12 [R]Neither shall he go out of the sanctuary, nor profane the sanctuary of his God; for [R]the

crown of the anointing oil of his God *is* upon him: I *am* the LORD.

13 And [R]he shall take a wife in her virginity.

14 A widow, or a divorced woman, or profane, *or* an harlot, these shall he not take: but he shall take a virgin of his own people to wife.

15 Neither shall he profane his seed among his people: for [R]I the LORD do sanctify him.

Priests with blemishes

16 And the LORD spake unto Moses, saying,

17 Speak unto Aaron, saying, Whosoever *he be* of thy seed in their generations that hath *any* blemish, let him not [R]approach to offer the [N]bread of his God.

18 For whatsoever man *he be* that hath a blemish, he shall not approach: a blind man, or a lame, or he that hath a flat nose, or any thing [R]superfluous,

19 Or a man that is brokenfooted, or brokenhanded,

20 Or crookbacked, or [N]a dwarf, or that hath a blemish in his eye, or be scurvy, or scabbed, or [R]hath his stones broken;

21 No man that hath a blemish of the seed of Aaron the priest shall come nigh to [R]offer the offerings of the LORD made by fire: he hath a blemish; he shall not come nigh to offer the bread of his God.

22 He shall eat the bread of his God, *both* of the [R]most holy, and of the [R]holy.

23 Only he shall not go in unto the vail, nor come nigh unto the altar, because he hath a blemish; that [R]he profane not my sanctuaries: for I the LORD do sanctify them.

24 And Moses told *it* unto Aaron, and to his sons, and unto all the children of Israel.

CHAPTER 22

Priests and holy things

AND the LORD spake unto Moses, saying,

2 Speak unto Aaron and to his sons, that they [R]separate themselves from the holy things of the children of Israel, and that they [R]profane not my holy name *in those things* which they [R]hallow unto me: I *am* the LORD.

3 Say unto them, Whosoever *he be* of all your seed among your generations, that goeth unto the holy things, which the children of Israel hallow unto the LORD, [R]having his uncleanness upon him, that soul shall be cut off from my presence: I *am* the LORD.

4 What man soever of the seed of Aaron *is* a leper, or hath [R]a [N]running issue; he shall not eat of the holy things, [R]until he be clean. And

ʀwhoso toucheth any thing *that is* unclean *by* the dead, or ʀa man whose seed goeth from him;

5 Or ʀwhosoever toucheth any creeping thing, whereby he may be made unclean, or ʀa man of whom he may take uncleanness, whatsoever uncleanness he hath;

6 The soul which hath touched any such shall be unclean until even, and shall not eat of the holy things, unless he ʀwash his flesh with water.

7 And when the sun is down, he shall be clean, and shall afterward eat of the holy things; because ʀit *is* his food.

8 ʀThat which dieth of itself, or is torn *with beasts,* he shall not eat to defile himself therewith: I *am* the Lord.

9 They shall therefore keep mine ordinance, ʀlest they bear sin for it, and die therefore, if they profane it: I the Lord do sanctify them.

10 ʀThere shall no stranger eat *of* the holy thing: a sojourner of the priest, or an hired servant, shall not eat *of* the holy thing.

11 But if the priest buy *any* soul ɴwith his money, he shall eat of it, and he that is born in his house: ʀthey shall eat of his meat.

12 If the priest's daughter also be *married* unto ɴa stranger, she may not eat of an offering of the holy things.

13 But if the priest's daughter be a widow, or divorced, and have no child, and is ʀreturned unto her father's house, ʀas in her youth, she shall eat of her father's meat: but there shall no stranger eat thereof.

14 ʀAnd if a man eat *of* the holy thing unwittingly, then he shall put the fifth *part* thereof unto it, and shall give *it* unto the priest with the holy thing.

15 And ʀthey shall not profane the holy things of the children of Israel, which they offer unto the Lord;

16 Or ɴsuffer them ʀto bear the iniquity of trespass, when they eat their holy things: for I the Lord do sanctify them.

Unacceptable offerings

17 And the Lord spake unto Moses, saying,

18 Speak unto Aaron, and to his sons, and unto all the children of Israel, and say unto them, ʀWhatsoever *he be* of the house of Israel, or of the strangers in Israel, that will offer his oblation for all his vows, and for all his freewill offerings, which they will offer unto the Lord for a burnt offering;

19 ʀ*Ye shall offer* at your own will a male without blemish, of the beeves, of the sheep, or of the goats.

20 ʀ*But* whatsoever hath a blemish, *that*

shall ye not offer: for it shall not be acceptable for you.

21 And ʀwhosoever offereth a sacrifice of peace offerings unto the Lord ʀto accomplish *his* vow, or a freewill offering in beeves or ɴsheep, it shall be perfect to be accepted; there shall be no blemish therein.

22 ʀBlind, or broken, or maimed, or having a wen, or scurvy, or scabbed, ye shall not offer these unto the Lord, nor make ʀan offering by fire of them upon the altar unto the Lord.

23 Either a bullock or a ɴlamb that hath any thing ʀsuperfluous or lacking in his parts, that mayest thou offer *for* a freewill offering; but for a vow it shall not be accepted.

24 Ye shall not offer unto the Lord that which is bruised, or crushed, or broken, or cut; neither shall ye make *any offering thereof* in your land.

25 Neither ʀfrom a stranger's hand shall ye offer ʀthe bread of your God of any of these; because their ʀcorruption *is* in them, *and* blemishes *be* in them: they shall not be accepted for you.

26 And the Lord spake unto Moses, saying,

27 ʀWhen a bullock, or a sheep, or a goat, is brought forth, then it shall be seven days under the dam; and from the eighth day and thenceforth it shall be accepted for an offering made by fire unto the Lord.

28 And *whether it be* cow or ɴewe, ye shall not kill it ʀand her young both in one day.

29 And when ye will ʀoffer a sacrifice of thanksgiving unto the Lord, offer *it* at your own will.

30 On the same day it shall be eaten up; ye shall leave ʀnone of it until the morrow: I *am* the Lord.

31 ʀTherefore shall ye keep my commandments, and do them: I *am* the Lord.

32 ʀNeither shall ye profane my holy name; but ʀI will be hallowed among the children of Israel: I *am* the Lord which ʀhallow you,

33 ʀThat brought you out of the land of Egypt, to be your God: I *am* the Lord.

CHAPTER 23

Appointed feasts: sabbath

A ND the Lord spake unto Moses, saying, 2 Speak unto the children of Israel, and say unto them, *Concerning* ʀthe feasts of the Lord, which ye shall ʀproclaim *to be* holy convocations, *even* these *are* my feasts.

3 ʀSix days shall work be done: but the seventh day *is* the sabbath of rest, an holy convocation; ye shall do no work *therein:* it *is* the sabbath of the Lord in all your dwellings.

Passover

4 ᴿThese *are* the feasts of the LORD, *even* holy convocations, which ye shall proclaim in their seasons.

5 ᴿIn the fourteenth *day* of the first month at even *is* the LORD's passover.

6 And on the fifteenth day of the same month *is* the feast of unleavened bread unto the LORD: seven days ye must eat unleavened bread.

7 ᴿIn the first day ye shall have an holy convocation: ye shall do no servile work therein.

8 But ye shall offer an offering made by fire unto the LORD seven days: in the seventh day *is* an holy convocation: ye shall do no servile work *therein*.

Feast of the firstfruits

9 And the LORD spake unto Moses, saying,

10 Speak unto the children of Israel, and say unto them, ᴿWhen ye be come into the land which I give unto you, and shall reap the harvest thereof, then ye shall bring a ᴺᴺsheaf of ᴿthe firstfruits of your harvest unto the priest:

11 And he shall ᴿwave the sheaf before the LORD, to be accepted for you: on the morrow after the sabbath the priest shall wave it.

12 And ye shall offer that day when ye wave the sheaf an he lamb without blemish of the first year for a burnt offering unto the LORD.

13 ᴿAnd the meat offering thereof *shall be* two tenth deals of fine flour mingled with oil, an offering made by fire unto the LORD *for* a sweet savour: and the drink offering thereof *shall be* of wine, the fourth *part* of an hĭn.

14 And ye shall eat neither bread, nor parched corn, nor green ears, until the selfsame day that ye have brought an offering unto your God: *it shall be* a statute for ever throughout your generations in all your dwellings.

Pentecost

15 And ᴿye shall count unto you from the morrow after the sabbath, from the day that ye brought the sheaf of the wave offering; seven sabbaths shall be complete:

16 Even unto the morrow after the seventh sabbath shall ye number ᴿfifty days; and ye shall offer ᴿa new meat offering unto the LORD.

17 Ye shall bring out of your habitations two wave loaves of two tenth deals: they shall be of fine flour; they shall be baken with leaven; *they are* ᴿthe firstfruits unto the LORD.

18 And ye shall offer with the bread seven lambs without blemish of the first year, and one young bullock, and two rams: they shall be *for* a burnt offering unto the LORD, with

their meat offering, and their drink offerings, *even* an offering made by fire, of sweet savour unto the LORD.

19 Then ye shall sacrifice ᴿone kid of the goats for a sin offering, and two lambs of the first year for a sacrifice of ᴿpeace offerings.

20 And the priest shall wave them with the bread of the firstfruits *for* a wave offering before the LORD, with the two lambs: ᴿthey shall be holy to the LORD for the priest.

21 And ye shall proclaim on the selfsame day, *that* it may be an holy convocation unto you: ye shall do no servile work *therein: it shall be* a statute for ever in all your dwellings throughout your generations.

22 And ᴿwhen ye reap the harvest of your land, thou shalt not make clean riddance of the corners of thy field when thou reapest, neither shalt thou gather any gleaning of thy harvest: thou shalt leave them unto the poor, and to the stranger: I *am* the LORD your God.

Feast of trumpets

23 And the LORD spake unto Moses, saying,

24 Speak unto the children of Israel, saying, In the ᴿseventh month, in the first *day* of the month, shall ye have a sabbath, ᴿa memorial of blowing of trumpets, an holy convocation.

25 Ye shall do no servile work *therein:* but ye shall offer an offering made by fire unto the LORD.

Day of atonement

26 And the LORD spake unto Moses, saying,

27 ᴿAlso on the tenth *day* of this seventh month *there shall be* a day of atonement: it shall be an holy convocation unto you; and ye shall afflict your souls, and offer an offering made by fire unto the LORD.

28 And ye shall do no work in that same day: for it *is* a day of atonement, to make an atonement for you before the LORD your God.

29 For whatsoever soul *it be* that shall not be afflicted in that same day, ᴿhe shall be cut off from among his people.

30 And whatsoever soul *it be* that doeth any work in that same day, ᴿthe same soul will I destroy from among his people.

31 Ye shall do no manner of work: *it shall be* a statute for ever throughout your generations in all your dwellings.

32 It *shall be* unto you a sabbath of rest, and ye shall afflict your souls: in the ninth *day* of the month at even, from even unto even, shall ye ᴺcelebrate your sabbath.

Feasts of tabernacles

33 And the LORD spake unto Moses, saying,

34 Speak unto the children of Israel, saying,

CHAP. 23
BC 1490

4	ver. 37
	Ex. 23:14
5	Ex. 12:6, 14, 18
	& 13:3, 10
	Deut. 16:1-8
7	Ex. 12:16
	Num. 28:18, 25
10	Ex. 34:26
	Deut. 16:9
	Josh. 3:15
10	Or, *handful*
10	Heb. *omer*
10	Rom. 11:16
	Jas. 1:18
	Rev. 14:4
11	Ex. 29:24
13	ch. 2:14-16
15	Ex. 34:22
	ch. 25:8
	Deut. 16:9
16	Acts 2:1
16	Num. 28:26
17	Ex. 23:16, 19
	Num. 15:17-21

ch. 4:23, 28	**19**
Num. 28:30	
ch. 3:1	**19**
Num. 18:12	**20**
Deut. 18:4	
ch. 19:9	**22**
Num. 29:1	**24**
ch. 25:9	**24**
ch. 16:30	**27**
Num. 29:7	
Gen. 17:14	**29**
ch. 20:3, 5, 6	**30**
Heb. *rest*	**32**

RThe fifteenth day of this seventh month *shall be* the feast of tabernacles *for* seven days unto the LORD.

35 On the first day *shall be* an holy convocation: ye shall do no servile work *therein*.

36 Seven days ye shall offer an offering made by fire unto the LORD: Ron the eighth day shall be an holy convocation unto you; and ye shall offer an offering made by fire unto the LORD: it *is* a Rsolemn[N] assembly; *and* ye shall do no servile work *therein*.

37 RThese *are* the feasts of the LORD, which ye shall proclaim *to be* holy convocations, to offer an offering made by fire unto the LORD, a burnt offering, and a meat offering, a sacrifice, and drink offerings, every thing upon his day:

38 RBeside the sabbaths of the LORD, and beside your gifts, and beside all your vows, and beside all your freewill offerings, which ye give unto the LORD.

39 Also in the fifteenth day of the seventh month, when ye have Rgathered in the fruit of the land, ye shall keep a feast unto the LORD seven days: on the first day *shall be* a sabbath, and on the eighth day *shall be* a sabbath.

40 And Rye shall take you on the first day the [N]boughs of goodly trees, branches of palm trees, and the boughs of thick trees, and willows of the brook; Rand ye shall rejoice before the LORD your God seven days.

41 RAnd ye shall keep it a feast unto the LORD seven days in the year. *It shall be* a statute for ever in your generations: ye shall celebrate it in the seventh month.

42 RYe shall dwell in booths seven days; all that are Israelites born shall dwell in booths:

43 RThat your generations may know that I made the children of Israel to dwell in booths, when I brought them out of the land of Egypt: I *am* the LORD your God.

44 And Moses Rdeclared unto the children of Israel the feasts of the LORD.

CHAPTER 24

Ceremonial oil and bread

AND the LORD spake unto Moses, saying, 2 RCommand the children of Israel, that they bring unto thee pure oil olive beaten for the light, [N]to cause the lamps to burn continually.

3 Without the vail of the testimony, in the tabernacle of the congregation, shall Aaron order it from the evening unto the morning before the LORD continually: *it shall be* a statute for ever in your generations.

4 He shall order the lamps upon Rthe pure candlestick before the LORD continually.

5 And thou shalt take fine flour, and bake twelve Rcakes thereof: two tenth deals shall be in one cake.

6 And thou shalt set them in two rows, six on a row, Rupon the pure table before the LORD.

7 And thou shalt put pure frankincense upon *each* row, that it may be on the bread for a memorial, *even* an offering made by fire unto the LORD.

8 REvery sabbath he shall set it in order before the LORD continually, *being taken* from the children of Israel by an everlasting covenant.

9 And Rit shall be Aaron's and his sons'; Rand they shall eat it in the holy place: for it *is* most holy unto him of the offerings of the LORD made by fire by a perpetual statute.

Penalty for blasphemy

10 And the son of an Israelitish woman, whose father *was* an Egyptian, went out among the children of Israel: and this son of the Israelitish *woman* and a man of Israel strove together in the camp;

11 And the Israelitish woman's son blasphemed the name *of the* LORD, and Rcursed. And they Rbrought him unto Moses: (and his mother's name *was* Shĕ-lō'-mith, the daughter of Dĭb'-rī, of the tribe of Dan:)

12 And they Rput him in ward, Rthat[N] the mind of the LORD might be shewed them.

Restitution and retribution

13 And the LORD spake unto Moses, saying,

14 Bring forth him that hath cursed without the camp; and let all that heard *him* Rlay their hands upon his head, and let all the congregation stone him.

15 And thou shalt speak unto the children of Israel, saying, Whosoever curseth his God Rshall bear his sin.

16 And he that Rblasphemeth the name of the LORD, he shall surely be put to death, *and* all the congregation shall certainly stone him: as well the stranger, as he that is born in the land, when he blasphemeth the name *of the* LORD, shall be put to death.

17 RAnd he that [N]killeth any man shall surely be put to death.

18 RAnd he that killeth a beast shall make it good; [N]beast for beast.

19 And if a man cause a blemish in his neighbour; as Rhe hath done, so shall it be done to him;

20 Breach for breach, eye for eye, tooth for tooth: as he hath caused a blemish in a man, so shall it be done to him *again*.

21 RAnd he that killeth a beast, he shall re-

store it: ᴿand he that killeth a man, he shall be put to death.

22 Ye shall have ᴿone manner of law, as well for the stranger, as for one of your own country: for I *am* the Lᴏʀᴅ your God.

23 And Moses spake to the children of Israel, ᴿthat they should bring forth him that had cursed out of the camp, and stone him with stones. And the children of Israel did as the Lᴏʀᴅ commanded Moses.

CHAPTER 25

Sabbath year

AND the Lᴏʀᴅ spake unto Moses in mount Sī′-naī, saying,

2 Speak unto the children of Israel, and say unto them, When ye come into the land which I give you, then shall the land ᴺkeep ᴿa sabbath unto the Lᴏʀᴅ.

3 Six years thou shalt sow thy field, and six years thou shalt prune thy vineyard, and gather in the fruit thereof;

4 But in the seventh year shall be a sabbath of rest unto the land, a sabbath for the Lᴏʀᴅ: thou shalt neither sow thy field, nor prune thy vineyard.

5 ᴿThat which groweth of its own accord of thy harvest thou shalt not reap, neither gather the grapes ᴺof thy vine undressed: *for* it is a year of rest unto the land.

6 And the sabbath of the land shall be meat for you; for thee, and for thy servant, and for thy maid, and for thy hired servant, and for thy stranger that sojourneth with thee,

7 And for thy cattle, and for the beast that *are* in thy land, shall all the increase thereof be meat.

Year of jubilee

8 And thou shalt number seven sabbaths of years unto thee, seven times seven years; and the space of the seven sabbaths of years shall be unto thee forty and nine years.

9 Then shalt thou cause the trumpet ᴺof the jubilee to sound on the tenth *day* of the seventh month, ᴿin the day of atonement shall ye make the trumpet sound throughout all your land.

10 And ye shall hallow the fiftieth year, and ᴿproclaim liberty throughout *all* the land unto all the inhabitants thereof: it shall be a jubilee unto you; ᴿand ye shall return every man unto his possession, and ye shall return every man unto his family.

11 A jubilee shall that fiftieth year be unto you: ᴿye shall not sow, neither reap that which groweth of itself in it, nor gather *the grapes* in it of thy vine undressed.

| CHAP. 24 |
| BC 1490 |
| 21 Ex. 21:33 |
| 21 ver. 17 |
| 22 Ex. 12:49 |
| ch. 19:34 |
| Num. 15:16 |
| 23 ver. 14 |

| CHAP. 25 |
| BC 1491 |
| 2 Heb. *rest* |
| 2 Ex. 23:10 |
| See ch. 26:34, 35 |
| 5 2 Ki. 19:29 |
| 5 Heb. *of thy separation* |
| 9 Heb. *loud of sound* |
| 9 ch. 23:24, 27 |
| 10 Is. 61:2 & 63:4 Jer. 34:8, 15, 17 Luke 4:19 |
| 10 ver. 13 Num. 36:4 |
| 11 ver. 5 |

ver. 6, 7	12
ver. 10	13
ch. 27:24 Num. 36:4	
ch. 27:18	15
ver. 14	17
ver. 43	17
ch. 19:14, 32	
ch. 19:37	18
ch. 26:5 Deut. 12:10 Ps. 4:8	18
ch. 26:5 Ezek. 34:25	19
Mat. 6:25	20
ver. 4, 5	20
See Ex. 16:29	21
2 Ki. 19:29	22
Josh. 5:11	22
Or, *to be quite cut off*	23
Heb. *for cutting off*	23
Deut. 32:43	23
Ps. 39:12	23
Ruth 2:20	25
See Ruth 3:2, 9, 12	25
Heb. *his hand hath attained and found sufficiency*	26
ver. 50-52	27
ver. 13	28

12 For it *is* the jubilee; it shall be holy unto you: ᴿye shall eat the increase thereof out of the field.

13 ᴿIn the year of this jubilee ye shall return every man unto his possession.

14 And if thou sell aught unto they neighbour, or buyest *aught* of thy neighbour's hand, ye shall not oppress one another:

15 ᴿAccording to the number of years after the jubilee thou shalt buy of thy neighbour, *and* according unto the number of years of the fruits he shall sell unto thee:

16 According to the multitude of years thou shalt increase the price thereof, and according to the fewness of years thou shalt diminish the price of it: for *according* to the number *of the years* of the fruits doth he sell unto thee.

17 ᴿYe shall not therefore oppress one another; ᴿbut thou shalt fear thy God: for I *am* the Lᴏʀᴅ your God.

18 ᴿWherefore ye shall do my statutes, and keep my judgments, and do them; ᴿand ye shall dwell in the land in safety.

19 And the land shall yield her fruit, and ᴿye shall eat your fill, and dwell therein in safety.

20 And if ye shall say, ᴿWhat shall we eat the seventh year? behold, ᴿwe shall not sow, nor gather in our increase:

21 Then I will ᴿcommand my blessing upon you in the sixth year, and it shall bring forth fruit for three years.

22 ᴿAnd ye shall sow the eighth year, and eat *yet* of ᴿold fruit until the ninth year; until her fruits come in ye shall eat *of* the old *store.*

Redemption of land

23 The land shall not be sold ᴺᴺfor ever: for ᴿthe land *is* mine; for ye *are* ᴿstrangers and sojourners with me.

24 And in all the land of your possession ye shall grant a redemption for the land.

25 ᴿIf thy brother be waxen poor, and hath sold away *some* of his possession, and if ᴿany of his kin come to redeem it, then shall he redeem that which his brother sold.

26 And if the man have none to redeem it, and ᴺhimself be able to redeem it;

27 Then ᴿlet him count the years of the sale thereof, and restore the overplus unto the man to whom he sold it; that he may return unto his possession.

28 But if he be not able to restore *it* to him, then that which is sold shall remain in the hand of him that hath bought it until the year of jubilee: ᴿand in the jubilee it shall go out, and he shall return unto his possession.

29 And if a man sell a dwelling house in a walled city, then he may redeem it within a

whole year after it is sold; *within* a full year may he redeem it.

30 And if it be not redeemed within the space of a full year, then the house that *is* in the walled city shall be established for ever to him that bought it throughout his generations: it shall not go out in the jubilee.

31 But the houses of the villages which have no wall round about them shall be counted as the fields of the country: [N]they may be redeemed, and they shall go out in the jubilee.

32 Notwithstanding [R]the cities of the Levites, *and* the houses of the cities of their possession, may the Levites redeem at any time.

33 And if [N]a man purchase of the Levites, then the house that was sold, and the city of his possession, shall go out in *the year of* jubilee: for the houses of the cities of the Levites *are* their possession among the children of Israel.

34 But [R]the field of the suburbs of their cities may not be sold; for it *is* their perpetual possession.

Assistance for the poor

35 And if thy brother be waxen poor, and [N]fallen in decay with thee; then thou shalt [R]relieve[N] him: *yea, though he be* a stranger, or a sojourner; that he may live with thee.

36 [R]Take thou no usury of him, or increase: but [R]fear thy God; that thy brother may live with thee.

37 Thou shalt not give him thy money upon usury, nor lend him thy victuals for increase.

38 [R]I *am* the LORD your God, which brought you forth out of the land of Egypt, to give you the land of Canaan, *and* to be your God.

Redemption of slaves

39 And [R]if thy brother *that dwelleth* by thee be waxen poor, and be sold unto thee; thou shalt not [N]compel him to serve as a bondservant:

40 *But* as an hired servant, *and* as a sojourner, he shall be with thee, *and* shall serve thee unto the year of jubilee:

41 And *then* shall he depart from thee, *both* he and his children [R]with him, and shall return unto his own family, and [R]unto the possession of his fathers shall he return.

42 For they *are* [R]my servants, which I brought forth out of the land of Egypt: they shall not be sold [N]as bondmen.

43 [R]Thou shalt not rule over him [R]with rigour; but [R]shalt fear thy God.

44 Both thy bondmen, and thy bondmaids, which thou shalt have, *shall be* of the heathen that are round about you; of them shall ye buy bondmen and bondmaids.

45 Moreover of [R]the children of the strangers that do sojourn among you, of them shall ye buy, and of their families that *are* with you, which they begat in your land: and they shall be your possession.

46 And [R]ye shall take them as an inheritance for your children after you, to inherit *them for* a possession; [N]they shall be your bondmen for ever: but over your brethren the children of Israel, ye shall not rule one over another with rigour.

47 And if a sojourner or stranger [N]wax rich by thee, and [R]thy brother *that dwelleth* by him wax poor, and sell himself unto the stranger *or* sojourner by thee, or to the stock of the stranger's family:

48 After that he is sold he may be redeemed again; one of his brethren may [R]redeem him:

49 Either his uncle, or his uncle's son, may redeem him, or *any* that is nigh of kin unto him of his family may redeem him; or if [R]he be able, he may redeem himself.

50 And he shall reckon with him that bought him from the year that he was sold to him unto the year of jubilee: and the price of his sale shall be according unto the number of years, [R]according to the time of an hired servant shall it be with him.

51 If *there be* yet many years *behind,* according unto them he shall give again the price of his redemption out of the money that he was bought for.

52 And if there remain but few years unto the year of jubilee, then he shall count with him, *and* according unto his years shall he give him again the price of his redemption.

53 *And* as a yearly hired servant shall he be with him: *and the other* shall not rule with rigour over him in thy sight.

54 And if he be not redeemed [N]in these *years,* then he shall go out in the year of jubilee, *both* he, and his children with him.

55 For unto me the children of Israel *are* servants; they *are* my servants whom I brought forth out of the land of Egypt: I *am* the LORD your God.

CHAPTER 26

Blessings of obedience

YE shall make you [R]no idols nor graven image, neither rear you up a [N]standing image, neither shall ye set up *any* [NN]image of stone in your land, to bow down unto it: for I *am* the LORD your God.

2 [R]Ye shall keep my sabbaths, and reverence my sanctuary: I *am* the LORD.

3 [R]If ye walk in my statutes, and keep my commandments, and do them;

4 ᴿThen I will give you rain in due season, ᴿand the land shall yield her increase, and the trees of the field shall yield their fruit.

5 And ᴿyour threshing shall reach unto the vintage, and the vintage shall reach unto the sowing time: and ᴿye shall eat your bread to the full, and ᴿdwell in your land safely.

6 And ᴿI will give peace in the land, and ᴿye shall lie down, and none shall make *you* afraid: and I will ᴺrid ᴿevil beasts out of the land, neither shall ᴿthe sword go through your land.

7 And ye shall chase your enemies, and they shall fall before you by the sword.

8 And ᴿfive of you shall chase an hundred, and an hundred of you shall put ten thousand to flight: and your enemies shall fall before you by the sword.

9 For I will ᴿhave respect unto you, and ᴿmake you fruitful, and multiply you, and establish my covenant with you.

10 And ye shall eat ᴿold store, and bring forth the old because of the new.

11 ᴿAnd I will set my tabernacle among you: and my soul shall not abhor you.

12 ᴿAnd I will walk among you, and will be your God, and ye shall be my people.

13 I *am* the Lᴏʀᴅ your God, which brought you forth out of the land of Egypt, that ye should not be their bondmen; and I have broken the bands of your yoke, and made you go upright.

Chastisement for disobedience

14 ᴿBut if ye will not hearken unto me, and will not do all these commandments;

15 And if ye shall despise my statutes, or if your soul abhor my judgments, so that ye will not do all my commandments, *but* that ye break my covenant:

16 I also will do this unto you; I will even appoint ᴺover you terror, ᴿconsumption, and the burning ague, that shall ᴿconsume the eyes, and cause sorrow of heart: and ᴿye shall sow your seed in vain, for your enemies shall eat it.

17 And ᴿI will set my face against you, and ᴿye shall be slain before your enemies: ᴿthey that hate you shall reign over you; and ᴿye shall flee when none pursueth you.

18 And if ye will not yet for all this hearken unto me, then I will punish you ᴿseven times more for your sins.

19 And I will ᴿbreak the pride of your power; and I ᴿwill make your heaven as iron, and your earth as brass:

20 And your ᴿstrength shall be spent in vain: for ᴿyour land shall not yield her increase, neither shall the trees of the land yield their fruits.

21 And if ye walk ᴺcontrary unto me, and will not hearken unto me; I will bring seven times more plagues upon you according to your sins.

22 ᴿI will also send wild beasts among you, which shall rob you of your children, and destroy your cattle, and make you few in number; and ᴿyour *high* ways shall be desolate.

23 And if ye ᴿwill not be reformed by me by these things, but will walk contrary unto me;

24 ᴿThen will I also walk contrary unto you, and will punish you yet seven times for your sins.

25 And ᴿI will bring a sword upon you, that shall avenge the quarrel of *my* covenant: and when ye are gathered together within your cities, ᴿI will send the pestilence among you; and ye shall be delivered into the hand of the enemy.

26 ᴿ*And* when I have broken the staff of your bread, ten women shall bake your bread in one oven, and they shall deliver *you* your bread again by weight: and ᴿye shall eat, and not be satisfied.

27 And if ye will not for all this hearken unto me, but walk contrary unto me;

28 Then I will walk contrary unto you also ᴿin fury; and I, even I, will chastise you seven times for your sins.

29 ᴿAnd ye shall eat the flesh of your sons, and the flesh of your daughters shall ye eat.

30 And ᴿI will destroy your high places, and cut down your images, and cast your carcases upon the carcases of your idols, and my soul shall abhor you.

31 And I will make your cities waste, and ᴿbring your sanctuaries unto desolation, and I will not smell the savour of your sweet odours.

32 ᴿAnd I will bring the land into desolation: and your enemies which dwell therein shall be astonished at it.

33 And ᴿI will scatter you among the heathen, and will draw out a sword after you: and your land shall be desolate, and your cities waste.

34 ᴿThen shall the land enjoy her sabbaths, as long as it lieth desolate, and ye *be* in your enemies' land; *even* then shall the land rest, and enjoy her sabbaths.

35 As long as it lieth desolate it shall rest; because it did not rest in your ᴿsabbaths, when ye dwelt upon it.

36 And upon them that are left *alive* of you ᴿI will send a faintness into their hearts in the lands of their enemies; and ᴿthe sound of a ᴺshaken leaf shall chase them; and they shall flee, as fleeing from a sword; and they shall fall when none pursueth.

37 And ᴿthey shall fall one upon another, as

CHAP. **26**

BC 1491

4 Is. 30:23
4 Ps. 67:6
Zech. 8:12
5 Amos 9:13
5 ch. 25:19
5 ch. 25:18
6 Is. 45:7
6 Ps. 4:8
Hos. 2:18
Zeph. 3:13
6 Heb. *cause to cease*
6 2 Ki. 17:25
6 Ezek. 14:17
8 Deut. 32:30
9 Ex. 2:25
9 Gen. 17:6, 7
Ps. 107:38
10 ch. 25:22
11 Ex. 25:8
Josh. 22:19
Ps. 76:2
Rev. 21:3
12 2 Cor. 6:16
14 Deut. 28:15
Lam. 2:17
Mal. 2:2
16 Heb. *upon you*
16 Deut. 28:22
16 1 Sam. 2:33
16 Deut. 28:33, 51
Job 31:8
Mic. 6:15
17 ch. 17:10
17 Deut. 28:25
17 Ps. 106:41
17 ver. 36
Ps. 53:5
18 1 Sam. 2:5
19 Is. 25:11
19 Deut. 28:23
20 Ps. 127:1
20 Deut. 11:17
21 Or, *at all adventures with me*, ver. 24

Deut. 32:24	22
2 Chr. 15:5	22
Zech. 7:14	
Jer. 2:30	23
Amos 4:6-12	
Ps. 18:26	24
Ezek. 5:17	25
Deut. 28:21	25
Ps. 105:16	26
Mic. 6:14	26
Jer. 21:5	28
Ezek. 5:13, 15 & 8:18	
Deut. 28:53	29
2 Chr. 34:3	30
Ezek. 6:3-6, 13	
Ps. 74:7	31
Jer. 9:11	32
Deut. 4:27	33
Ezek. 12:15 & 20:23 & 22:15	
Zech. 7:14	
2 Chr. 36:21	34
ch. 25:2	35
Ezek. 21:7, 12, 15	36
ver. 17	36
Prov. 28:1	
Heb. *driven*	36
See Judg. 7:22	37
1 Sam. 14:15, 16	
Is. 10:4	

it were before a sword, when none pursueth: and [R]ye shall have no power to stand before your enemies.

38 And ye shall perish among the heathen, and the land of your enemies shall eat you up.

39 And they that are left of you [R]shall pine away in their iniquity in your enemies' lands; and also in the iniquities of their fathers shall they pine away with them.

God's covenant remembered

40 [R]If they shall confess their iniquity, and the iniquity of their fathers, with their trespass which they trespassed against me, and that also they have walked contrary unto me;

41 And *that* I also have walked contrary unto them, and have brought them into the land of their enemies; if then their [R]uncircumcised hearts be [R]humbled, and they then accept of the punishment of their iniquity:

42 Then will I [R]remember my covenant with Jacob, and also my covenant with Isaac, and also my covenant with Abraham will I remember; and I will [R]remember the land.

43 [R]The land also shall be left of them, and shall enjoy her sabbaths, while she lieth desolate without them: and they shall accept of the punishment of their iniquity: because, even because they [R]despised my judgments, and because their soul abhorred my statutes.

44 And yet for all that, when they be in the land of their enemies, [R]I will not cast them away, neither will I abhor them, to destroy them utterly, and to break my covenant with them: for I *am* the LORD their God.

45 But I will [R]for their sakes remember the covenant of their ancestors, [R]whom I brought forth out of the land of Egypt [R]in the sight of the heathen, that I might be their God: I *am* the LORD.

46 [R]These *are* the statutes and judgments and laws, which the LORD made between him and the children of Israel [R]in mount Sī'-naī by the hand of Moses.

CHAPTER 27

Valuation of votive offerings

AND the LORD spake unto Moses, saying, 2 Speak unto the children of Israel, and say unto them, [R]When a man shall make a singular vow, the persons *shall be* for the LORD by thy estimation.

3 And thy estimation shall be of the male from twenty years old even unto sixty years old, even thy estimation shall be fifty shē'-kĕls of silver, [R]after the shē'-kĕl of the sanctuary.

4 And if it *be* a female, then thy estimation shall be thirty shē'-kĕls.

5 And if *it be* from five years old even unto twenty years old, then thy estimation shall be of the male twenty shē'-kĕls, and for the female ten shē'-kĕls.

6 And if *it be* from a month old even unto five years old, then thy estimation shall be of the male five shē'-kĕls of silver, and for the female thy estimation *shall be* three shē'-kĕls of silver.

7 And if *it be* from sixty years old and above; if *it be* a male, then thy estimation shall be fifteen shē'-kĕls, and for the female ten shē'-kĕls.

8 But if he be poorer than thy estimation, then he shall present himself before the priest, and the priest shall value him; according to his ability that vowed shall the priest value him.

9 And if *it be* a beast, whereof men bring an offering unto the LORD, all that *any man* giveth of such unto the LORD shall be holy.

10 He shall not alter it, nor change it, a good for a bad, or a bad for a good: and if he shall at all change beast for beast, then it and the exchange thereof shall be holy.

11 And if *it be* any unclean beast, of which they do not offer a sacrifice unto the LORD, then he shall present the beast before the priest:

12 And the priest shall value it, whether it be good or bad: [N]as thou valuest it, *who art* the priest, so shall it be.

13 [R]But if he will at all redeem it, then he shall add a fifth *part* thereof unto thy estimation.

14 And when a man shall sanctify his house *to be* holy unto the LORD, then the priest shall estimate it, whether it be good or bad: as the priest shall estimate it, so shall it stand.

15 [R]And if he that sanctified it will redeem his house, then he shall add the fifth *part* of the money of thy estimation unto it, and it shall be his.

16 And if a man shall sanctify unto the LORD *some part* of a field of his possession, then thy estimation shall be according to the seed thereof: [N]an hō'-mĕr of barley seed *shall be valued* at fifty shē'-kĕls of silver.

17 If he sanctify his field from the year of jubilee, according to thy estimation it shall stand.

18 But if he sanctify his field after the jubilee, then the priest shall [R]reckon unto him the money according to the years that remain, even unto the year of the jubilee, and it shall be abated from thy estimation.

19 [R]And if he that sanctified the field will in any wise redeem it, then he shall add the fifth *part* of the money of thy estimation unto it, and it shall be assured to him.

20 And if he will not redeem the field, or if he have sold the field to another man, it shall not be redeemed any more.

21 But the field, ᴿwhen it goeth out in the jubilee, shall be holy unto the LORD, as a field ᴿdevoted; ᴿthe possession thereof shall be the priest's.

22 And if *a man* sanctify unto the LORD a field which he hath bought, which *is* not of the fields of ᴿhis possession;

23 ᴿThen the priest shall reckon unto him the worth of thy estimation, *even* unto the year of the jubilee: and he shall give thine estimation in that day, *as* a holy thing unto the LORD.

24 ᴿIn the year of the jubilee the field shall return unto him of whom it was bought, *even* to him to whom the possession of the land *did belong*.

25 And all thy estimations shall be according to the shē′-kĕl of the sanctuary: ᴿtwenty gē′-rähś shall be the shē′-kĕl.

26 Only the ᴿfirstlingᴺ of the beasts, which should be the LORD's firstling, no man shall sanctify it; whether *it be* ox, or sheep: it *is* the LORD's.

27 And if *it be* of an unclean beast, then he shall redeem *it* according to thine estimation, ᴿand shall add a fifth *part* of it thereto: or if it

be not redeemed, then it shall be sold according to thy estimation.

28 ᴿNotwithstanding no devoted thing, that a man shall devote unto the LORD of all that he hath, *both* of man and beast, and of the field of his possession, shall be sold or redeemed: every devoted thing *is* most holy unto the LORD.

29 ᴿNone devoted, which shall be devoted of men, shall be redeemed; *but* shall surely be put to death.

Redemption and exchange of tithes

30 And ᴿall the tithe of the land, *whether* of the seed of the land, *or* of the fruit of the tree, *is* the LORD's: *it is* holy unto the LORD.

31 ᴿAnd if a man will at all redeem *aught* of his tithes, he shall add thereto the fifth *part* thereof.

32 And concerning the tithe of the herd, or of the flock, *even* of whatsoever ᴿpasseth under the rod, the tenth shall be holy unto the LORD.

33 He shall not search whether it be good or bad, ᴿneither shall he change it: and if he change it at all, then both it and the change thereof shall be holy; it shall not be redeemed.

34 ᴿThese *are* the commandments, which the LORD commanded Moses for the children of Israel in mount Sĭ′-nâi.

CHAP. 27
BC 1491
21 ch. 25:10, 28, 31
21 ver. 28
21 Num. 18:14
  Ezek. 44:29
22 ch. 25:10, 25
23 ver. 18
24 ch. 25:28
25 Ex. 30:13
  Num. 3:47 & 18:16
  Ezek. 45:12
26 Ex. 13:2, 12
  & 22:30
26 Heb. *firstborn*, etc.
27 ver. 11, 12

ver. 21 **28**
Josh. 6:17-19
Num. 21:2 **29**
Gen. 28:22 **30**
  Num. 18:21, 24
  2 Chr. 31:5, 6, 12
  Neh. 13:12
  Mal. 3:8
ver. 13 **31**
Jer. 33:13 **32**
  Ezek. 20:37
  Mic. 7:14
ver. 10 **33**
ch. 26:46 **34**

THE FOURTH BOOK OF MOSES, CALLED

NUMBERS

The title "Numbers" was evidently given to this book because it describes the way in which an elaborate census of Israel was taken on two separate occasions. The name given to the book in Hebrew is "Bomidbar," meaning "in the desert," and is in many respects a more appropriate title than the one given to it in the King James Version.

The narrative core of this book, 10:11-22:1, is an account of the Israelites' thirty-eight years of wandering in their journey from the Sinaitic peninsula to the Plains of Moab. The opening chapters relate in detail the organization and preparation of Israel's advance toward Canaan, while the concluding chapters tell of the Israelites' encounter with the Moabites and record the instructions for the conquest and allotment of the land of Canaan. Certainly not everything that happened in Israel during that extensive period is recorded,

but the chief events of moral and religious importance are given. It appears probable that the incidents given in Chapters 15-19 cover a number of episodes occurring over a long period without regard to chronological order or dates.

OUTLINE OF THE BOOK:
   I. The census and organization of Israel 1:1-4:49
  II. Regulations, vows, and gifts 5:1-7:89
 III. Worship and guidance 8:1-10:10
 IV. From Sinai to Kadesh-barnea 10:11-12:16
  V. Rebellion and years of wandering 13:1-19:22
 VI. From Kadesh-barnea to the plains of Moab 20:1-22:1
 VII. The crisis with Balaam and Balak 22:2-25:18
VIII. Preparation for occupation 26:1-36:13

CHAPTER 1

Census of Israel

Aɴᴅ the LORD spake unto Moses ᴿin the wilderness of Sĭ′-nâi, ᴿin the tabernacle of the congregation, on the first *day* of the second month, in the second year after they

CHAP. 1
BC 1490
1 Ex. 19:1
  ch. 10:11, 12
1 Ex. 25:22

Ex. 30:12 & 38:26 **2**
ch. 26:2, 63, 64
2 Sam. 24:2
1 Chr. 21:2

were come out of the land of Egypt, saying,

2 ᴿTake ye the sum of all the congregation of the children of Israel, after their families, by the house of their fathers, with the number of *their* names, every male by their polls;

3 From twenty years old and upward, all that are able to go forth to war in Israel: thou and

Aaron shall number them by their armies.

4 And with you there shall be a man of every tribe; every one head of the house of his fathers.

5 And these *are* the names of the men that shall stand with you: of *the tribe of* Reuben; Ĕ-lī′-zŭr the son of Shĕd′-ē-ŭr.

6 Of Simeon; Shĕ-lū′-mĭ-ĕl the son of Zū-rĭ-shăd′-dāi.

7 Of Judah; ᴿNăh′-shŏn the son of Ăm-mĭn′-ă-dăb.

8 Of Ĭs′-să-<u>char</u>; Nĕth′-ă-nĕel the son of Zū′-ăr.

9 Of Zĕ-bū′-lŭn; Ē-lī′-ăb the son of Hē′-lŏn.

10 Of the children of Joseph: of Ē′-phră-ĭm; Ē-lī′-shă-mă the son of Ăm′-mĭ-hŭd: of Mă-năs′-sēh; Gă-mā′-lĭ-ĕl the son of Pĕ-dăh′-zŭr.

11 Of Benjamin; Ă-bī′-dăn the son of Gĭd-ĕ-ō′-nī.

12 Of Dan; Ā-hī-ē′-zĕr the son of Ăm-mĭ-shăd′-dāi.

13 Of Asher; Pā′-ġĭ-ĕl the son of Ŏc′-răn.

14 Of Gad; Ē-lī′-ă-săph the son of ᴿDĕu′-ĕl.

15 Of Năph′-tă-lī; Ă-hī′-ră the son of Ē′-năn.

16 ᴿThese *were* the renowned of the congregation, princes of the tribes of their fathers, ᴿheads of thousands in Israel.

17 And Moses and Aaron took these men which are expressed ᴿby *their* names:

18 And they assembled all the congregation together on the first *day* of the second month, and they declared their ᴿpedigrees after their families, by the house of their fathers, according to the number of the names, from twenty years old and upward, by their polls.

Numbering of the tribes

19 As the LORD commanded Moses, so he numbered them in the wilderness of Sĭ′-nāi.

20 And the ᴿchildren of Reuben, Israel's eldest son, by their generations, after their families, by the house of their fathers, according to the number of the names, by their polls, every male from twenty years old and upward, all that were able to go forth to war;

21 Those that were numbered of them, *even* of the tribe of Reuben, *were* forty and six thousand and five hundred.

22 Of the ᴿchildren of Simeon, by their generations, after their families, by the house of their fathers, those that were numbered of them, according to the number of the names, by their polls, every male from twenty years old and upward, all that were able to go forth to war;

23 Those that were numbered of them, *even* of the tribe of Simeon, *were* fifty and nine thousand and three hundred.

CHAP. 1
BC 1490
7 Called *Naasson,* Mat. 1:4
14 ch. 2:14, he is called *Reuel*
16 ch. 7:2
16 1 Chr. 27:16
16 Ex. 18:21, 25
17 Is. 43:1
18 Ezra 2:59
20 ch. 2:10, 11 & 32:6, 15, 21, 29
22 ch. 2:12, 13 & 26:12-14

ch. 2:14, 15 & 26:15-18 & 32:2, 29 & 34:14   24
ch. 2:3, 4 & 26:19-22   26
2 Sam. 24:9
2 Chr. 17:14   27
ch. 2:5, 6   28
ch. 2:7, 8 & 26:26, 27   30
ch. 2:18, 19 & 26:35-37   32
ch. 2:20, 21 & 26:28-34   34
ch. 2:22, 23 & 26:38-41   36
ch. 2:25, 26 & 26:42, 43   38

24 Of the ᴿchildren of Gad, by their generations, after their families, by the house of their fathers, according to the number of the names, from twenty years old and upward, all that were able to go forth to war;

25 Those that were numbered of them, *even* of the tribe of Gad, *were* forty and five thousand six hundred and fifty.

26 Of the ᴿchildren of Judah, by their generations, after their families, by the house of their fathers, according to the number of the names, from twenty years old and upward, all that were able to go forth to war;

27 Those that were numbered of them, *even* of the tribe of Judah, *were* ᴿthreescore and fourteen thousand and six hundred.

28 Of the ᴿchildren of Ĭs′-să-<u>char</u>, by their generations, after their families, by the house of their fathers, according to the number of the names, from twenty years old and upward, all that were able to go forth to war;

29 Those that were numbered of them, *even* of the tribe of Ĭs′-să-<u>char</u>, *were* fifty and four thousand and four hundred.

30 Of the ᴿchildren of Zĕ-bū′-lŭn, by their generations, after their families, by the house of their fathers, according to the number of the names, from twenty years old and upward, all that were able to go forth to war;

31 Those that were numbered of them, *even* of the tribe of Zĕ-bū′-lŭn, *were* fifty and seven thousand and four hundred.

32 Of the children of Joseph, *namely,* of the ᴿchildren of Ē′-phră-ĭm, by their generations, after their families, by the house of their fathers, according to the number of the names, from twenty years old and upward, all that were able to go forth to war;

33 Those that were numbered of them, *even* of the tribe of Ē′-phră-ĭm, *were* forty thousand and five hundred.

34 Of the ᴿchildren of Mă-năs′-sēh, by their generations, after their families, by the house of their fathers, according to the number of the names, from twenty years old and upward, all that were able to go forth to war;

35 Those that were numbered of them, *even* of the tribe of Mă-năs′-sēh, *were* thirty and two thousand and two hundred.

36 Of the ᴿchildren of Benjamin, by their generations, after their families, by the house of their fathers, according to the number of the names, from twenty years old and upward, all that were able to go forth to war;

37 Those that were numbered of them, *even* of the tribe of Benjamin, *were* thirty and five thousand and four hundred.

38 Of the ᴿchildren of Dan, by their generations, after their families, by the house of their

fathers, according to the number of the names, from twenty years old and upward, all that were able to go forth to war;

39 Those that were numbered of them, *even* of the tribe of Dan, *were* threescore and two thousand and seven hundred.

40 Of the ᴿchildren of Asher, by their generations, after their families, by the house of their fathers, according to the number of the names, from twenty years old and upward, all that were able to go forth to war;

41 Those that were numbered of them, *even* of the tribe of Asher, *were* forty and one thousand and five hundred.

42 Of the children of Năph'-tă-lī, throughout their generations, after their families, by the house of their fathers, according to the number of the names, from twenty years old and upward, all that were able to go forth to war;

43 Those that were numbered of them, *even* of the tribe of Năph'-tă-lī, *were* fifty and three thousand and four hundred.

44 ᴿThese *are* those that were numbered, which Moses and Aaron numbered, and the princes of Israel, *being* twelve men: each one was for the house of his fathers.

45 So were all those that were numbered of the children of Israel, by the house of their fathers, from twenty years old and upward, all that were able to go forth to war in Israel;

46 Even all they that were numbered were ᴿsix hundred thousand and three thousand and five hundred and fifty.

Levites not numbered

47 But ᴿthe Levites after the tribe of their fathers were not numbered among them.

48 For the Lᴏʀᴅ had spoken unto Moses, saying,

49 ᴿOnly thou shalt not number the tribe of Levi, neither take the sum of them among the children of Israel:

50 ᴿBut thou shalt appoint the Levites over the tabernacle of testimony, and over all the vessels thereof, and over all things that *belong* to it: they shall bear the tabernacle, and all the vessels thereof; and they shall minister unto it, ᴿand shall encamp round about the tabernacle.

51 ᴿAnd when the tabernacle setteth forward, the Levites shall take it down: and when the tabernacle is to be pitched, the Levites shall set it up: ᴿand the stranger that cometh nigh shall be put to death.

52 And the children of Israel shall pitch their tents, ᴿevery man by his own camp, and every man by his own standard, throughout their hosts.

53 ᴿBut the Levites shall pitch round about

the tabernacle of testimony, that there be no ᴿwrath upon the congregation of the children of Israel: and the Levites shall keep the charge of the tabernacle of testimony.

54 And the children of Israel did according to all that the Lᴏʀᴅ commanded Moses, so did they.

CHAPTER 2

Arrangement of the tribes

AND the Lᴏʀᴅ spake unto Moses and unto Aaron, saying,

2 ᴿEvery man of the children of Israel shall pitch by his own standard, with the ensign of their father's house: ᴿfarᴺ off about the tabernacle of the congregation shall they pitch.

3 And on the east side toward the rising of the sun shall they of the standard of the camp of Judah pitch throughout their armies: and ᴿNäh'-shŏn the son of Ăm-mīn'-ă-dăb *shall be* captain of the children of Judah.

4 And his host, and those that were numbered of them, *were* threescore and fourteen thousand and six hundred.

5 And those that do pitch next unto him *shall be* the tribe of ĭs'-să-chär: and Nĕth'-ă-nĕĕl the son of Zū'-är *shall be* captain of the children of ĭs'-să-chär.

6 And his host, and those that were numbered thereof, *were* fifty and four thousand and four hundred.

7 *Then* the tribe of Zĕ-bū'-lŭn: and Ē-lī'-ăb the son of Hē'-lŏn *shall be* captain of the children of Zĕ-bū'-lŭn.

8 And his host, and those that were numbered thereof, *were* fifty and seven thousand and four hundred.

9 All that were numbered in the camp of Judah *were* an hundred thousand and fourscore thousand and six thousand and four hundred, throughout their armies. ᴿThese shall first set forth.

10 On the south side *shall be* the standard of the camp of Reuben according to their armies: and the captain of the children of Reuben *shall be* Ĕ-lī'-zŭr the son of Shĕd'-ē-ŭr.

11 And his host, and those that were numbered thereof, *were* forty and six thousand and five hundred.

12 And those which pitch by him *shall be* the tribe of Simeon: and the captain of the children of Simeon *shall be* Shĕ-lū'-mĭ-ĕl the son of Zū-rĭ-shăd'-dâi.

13 And his host, and those that were numbered of them, *were* fifty and nine thousand and three hundred.

14 Then the tribe of Gad: and the captain of

the sons of Gad *shall be* Ē-lī′-ă-săph the son of [N]Rĕû′-ĕl.

15 And his host, and those that were numbered of them, *were* forty and five thousand and six hundred and fifty.

16 All that were numbered in the camp of Reuben *were* an hundred thousand and fifty and one thousand and four hundred and fifty, throughout their armies. [R]And they shall set forth in the second rank.

17 [R]Then the tabernacle of the congregation shall set forward with the camp of the Levites in the midst of the camp: as they encamp, so shall they set forward, every man in his place by their standards.

18 On the west side *shall be* the standard of the camp of Ē′-phră-ĭm according to their armies: and the captain of the sons of Ē′-phră-ĭm *shall be* Ē-lī′-shă-mă the son of Ăm′-mĭ hŭd.

19 And his host, and those that were numbered of them, *were* forty thousand and five hundred.

20 And by him *shall be* the tribe of Mă-năs′-sēh: and the captain of the children of Mă-năs′-sēh *shall be* Gă-mā′-lĭ-ĕl the son of Pĕ-dăh′-zŭr.

21 And his host, and those that were numbered of them, *were* thirty and two thousand and two hundred.

22 Then the tribe of Benjamin: and the captain of the sons of Benjamin *shall be* Ă-bī′-dăn the son of Gĭd-ĕ-ō′-nī.

23 And his host, and those that were numbered of them, *were* thirty and five thousand and four hundred.

24 All that were numbered of the camp of Ē′-phră-ĭm *were* an hundred thousand and eight thousand and an hundred, throughout their armies. [R]And they shall go forward in the third rank.

25 The standard of the camp of Dan *shall be* on the north side by their armies: and the captain of the children of Dan *shall be* Ā-hī-ē′-zĕr the son of Ăm-mĭ-shăd′-dâi.

26 And his host, and those that were numbered of them, *were* threescore and two thousand and seven hundred.

27 And those that encamp by him *shall be* the tribe of Asher: and the captain of the children of Asher *shall be* Pā′-ġĭ-ĕl the son of ŏc′-răn.

28 And his host, and those that were numbered of them, *were* forty and one thousand and five hundred.

29 Then the tribe of Năph′-tă-lī: and the captain of the children of Năph′-tă-lī *shall be* Ă-hī′-ră the son of Ē′-năn.

30 And his host, and those that were num-

CHAP. 2	
BC 1490	
14 *Deuel,* ch. 1:14 & 7:42, 47 & 10:20	
16 ch. 10:18	
17 ch. 10:17, 21	
24 ch. 10:22	

ch. 10:25	31
Ex. 38:26	32
ch. 1:46 & 11:21	
ch. 1:47	33
ch. 24:2, 5, 6	34

CHAP. 3	
BC 1490	
Ex. 6:23	2
Ex. 28:41	3
Lev. 8	
Heb. *whose hand he filled*	3
Lev. 10:1	4
ch. 26:61	
1 Chr. 24:2	
ch. 8:6 & 18:2	6
See ch. 1:50	7
& 8:11, 15, 24, 26	
ch. 8:19 & 18:6	9
ch. 18:7	10

bered of them, *were* fifty and three thousand and four hundred.

31 All they that were numbered in the camp of Dan *were* an hundred thousand and fifty and seven thousand and six hundred. [R]They shall go hindmost with their standards.

32 These *are* those which were numbered of the children of Israel by the house of their fathers: [R]all those that were numbered of the camps throughout their hosts *were* six hundred thousand and three thousand and five hundred and fifty.

33 But [R]the Levites were not numbered among the children of Israel; as the LORD commanded Moses.

34 And the children of Israel did according to all that the LORD commanded Moses: [R]so they pitched by their standards, and so they set forward, every one after their families, according to the house of their fathers.

CHAPTER 3

Sons of Aaron

THESE also *are* the generations of Aaron and Moses in the day *that* the LORD spake with Moses in mount Sī′-nâi.

2 And these *are* the names of the sons of Aaron; Nadab the [R]firstborn, and Ă-bī′-hū, Ĕl-ē-ā′-zär, and Ĭth′-ă-mär.

3 These *are* the names of the sons of Aaron, [R]the priests which were anointed, [N]whom he consecrated to minister in the priest's office.

4 [R]And Nadab and Ă-bī′-hū died before the LORD, when they offered strange fire before the LORD, in the wilderness of Sī′-nâi, and they had no children: and ĕl-ē-ā′-zär and ĭth′-ă-mär ministered in the priest's office in the sight of Aaron their father.

Duties of the Levites

5 And the LORD spake unto Moses, saying,

6 [R]Bring the tribe of Levi near, and present them before Aaron the priest, that they may minister unto him.

7 And they shall keep his charge, and the charge of the whole congregation before the tabernacle of the congregation, to do [R]the service of the tabernacle.

8 And they shall keep all the instruments of the tabernacle of the congregation, and the charge of the children of Israel, to do the service of the tabernacle.

9 And [R]thou shalt give the Levites unto Aaron and to his sons: they *are* wholly given unto him out of the children of Israel.

10 And thou shalt appoint Aaron and his sons, [R]and they shall wait on their priest's

office: ᴿand the stranger that cometh nigh shall be put to death.

11 And the LORD spake unto Moses, saying,

12 And I, behold, ᴿI have taken the Levites from among the children of Israel instead of all the firstborn that openeth the matrix among the children of Israel: therefore the Levites shall be mine;

13 Because ᴿall the firstborn *are* mine; ᴿ*for* on the day that I smote all the firstborn in the land of Egypt I hallowed unto me all the firstborn in Israel, both man and beast: mine shall they be: I *am* the LORD.

Levite males numbered

14 And the LORD spake unto Moses in the wilderness of Sī'-nâi, saying,

15 Number the children of Levi after the house of their fathers, by their families: ᴿevery male from a month old and upward shalt thou number them.

16 And Moses numbered them according to the ᴺword of the LORD, as he was commanded.

17 ᴿAnd these were the sons of Levi by their names; Gĕr'-shŏn, and Kō'-hăth, and Mĕ-râr'-ī.

18 And these *are* the names of the sons of Gĕr'-shŏn by their families; ᴿLĭb'-nī, and Shĭm'-ĕ-ī.

19 And the sons of Kō'-hăth by their families; ᴿAmram, and ī'-zĕ-här, Hē'-brŏn, and ŭz'-zī-ĕl.

20 ᴿAnd the sons of Mĕ-râr'-ī by their families; Mäh'-lī, and Mū'-shī. These *are* the families of the Levites according to the house of their fathers.

21 Of Gĕr'-shŏn *was* the family of the Lĭb'-nītes, and the family of the Shĭm'-ītes: these *are* the families of the Gĕr'-shŏn-ītes.

22 Those that were numbered of them, according to the number of all the males, from a month old and upward, *even* those that were numbered of them *were* seven thousand and five hundred.

23 ᴿThe families of the Gĕr'-shŏn-ītes shall pitch behind the tabernacle westward.

24 And the chief of the house of the father of the Gĕr'-shŏn-ītes *shall be* Ē-lī'-ă-săph the son of Lā'-ĕl.

25 And ᴿthe charge of the sons of Gĕr'-shŏn in the tabernacle of the congregation *shall be* ᴿthe tabernacle, and ᴿthe tent, ᴿthe covering thereof, and ᴿthe hanging for the door of the tabernacle of the congregation,

26 And ᴿthe hangings of the court, and ᴿthe curtain for the door of the court, which *is* by the tabernacle, and by the altar round about, and ᴿthe cords of it for all the service thereof.

CHAP. 3
BC 1490
10 ver. 38
ch. 1:51 & 16:40
12 ver. 41
ch. 8:16 & 18:6
13 Ex. 13:2
Lev. 27:26
ch. 8:17
Luke 2:23
13 Ex. 13:12, 15
ch. 8:17
15 ver. 39
ch. 26:62
16 *Heb. mouth*
17 Gen. 46:11
Ex. 6:16
ch. 26:57
1 Chr. 6:1, 16 & 23:6
18 Ex. 6:17
19 Ex. 6:18
20 Ex. 6:19
23 ch. 1:53
25 ch. 4:24-26
25 Ex. 25:9
25 Ex. 26:1
25 Ex. 26:7, 14
25 Ex. 26:36
26 Ex. 27:9
26 Ex. 27:16
26 Ex. 35:18

1 Chr. 26:23   27
ch. 1:53   29
ch. 4:15   31
Ex. 25:10   31
Ex. 25:23   31
Ex. 25:31   31
Ex. 27:1 & 30:1   31
Ex. 26:32   31
ch. 1:53   35
ch. 4:31, 32   36
Heb. the office   36
of the charge
ch. 1:53   38
ch. 18:5   38
ver. 7, 8   38
ver. 10   38
See ch. 26:62   39
ver. 15   40

27 ᴿAnd of Kō'-hăth *was* the family of the Amramites, and the family of the ī'-zĕ-här-ītes, and the family of the Hē'-brŏn-ītes, and the family of the ŭz-zī-ē'-lītes: these *are* the families of the Kō'-hăth-ītes.

28 In the number of all the males, from a month old and upward, *were* eight thousand and six hundred, keeping the charge of the sanctuary.

29 ᴿThe families of the sons of Kō'-hăth shall pitch on the side of the tabernacle southward.

30 And the chief of the house of the father of the families of the Kō'-hăth-ītes *shall be* Ē-lī-zā'-phăn the son of ŭz'-zī-ĕl.

31 And ᴿtheir charge *shall be* ᴿthe ark, and ᴿthe table, and ᴿthe candlestick, and ᴿthe altars, and the vessels of the sanctuary wherewith they minister, and ᴿthe hanging, and all the service thereof.

32 And ĕl-ē-ā'-zär the son of Aaron the priest *shall be* chief over the chief of the Levites, *and have* the oversight of them that keep the charge of the sanctuary.

33 Of Mĕ-râr'-ī *was* the family of the Mäh'-lītes, and the family of the Mū'-shītes: these *are* the families of Mĕ-râr'-ī.

34 And those that were numbered of them, according to the number of all the males, from a month old and upward, *were* six thousand and two hundred.

35 And the chief of the house of the father of the families of Mĕ-râr'-ī *was* Zū'-rĭ-ĕl the son of Ăb'-ī-haịl: ᴿ*these* shall pitch on the side of the tabernacle northward.

36 And ᴿ*under*ᴺ the custody and charge of the sons of Mĕ-râr'-ī *shall be* the boards of the tabernacle, and the bars thereof, and the pillars thereof, and the sockets thereof, and all the vessels thereof, and all that serveth thereto,

37 And the pillars of the court round about, and their sockets, and their pins, and their cords.

38 ᴿBut those that encamp before the tabernacle toward the east, *even* before the tabernacle of the congregation eastward, *shall be* Moses, and Aaron and his sons, ᴿkeeping the charge of the sanctuary ᴿfor the charge of the children of Israel; and ᴿthe stranger that cometh nigh shall be put to death.

39 ᴿAll that were numbered of the Levites, which Moses and Aaron numbered at the commandment of the LORD, throughout their families, all the males from a month old and upward, *were* twenty and two thousand.

Census of the firstborn

40 And the LORD said unto Moses, ᴿNumber all the firstborn of the males of the

children of Israel from a month old and upward, and take the number of their names.

41 ᴿAnd thou shalt take the Levites for me (I *am* the LORD) instead of all the firstborn among the children of Israel; and the cattle of the Levites instead of all the firstlings among the cattle of the children of Israel.

42 And Moses numbered, as the LORD commanded him, all the firstborn among the children of Israel.

43 And all the firstborn males by the number of names, from a month old and upward, of those that were numbered of them, were twenty and two thousand two hundred and threescore and thirteen.

The firstborn redeemed

44 And the LORD spake unto Moses, saying,

45 ᴿTake the Levites instead of all the firstborn among the children of Israel, and the cattle of the Levites instead of their cattle; and the Levites shall be mine: I *am* the LORD.

46 And for those that are to be ᴿredeemed of the two hundred and threescore and thirteen of the firstborn of the children of Israel, ᴿwhich are more than the Levites;

47 Thou shalt even take ᴿfive shē′-kĕls apiece by the poll, after the shē′-kĕl of the sanctuary shalt thou take *them:* (ᴿthe shē′-kĕl *is* twenty gē′-rähś:)

48 And thou shalt give the money, wherewith the odd number of them is to be redeemed, unto Aaron and to his sons.

49 And Moses took the redemption money of them that were over and above them that were redeemed by the Levites:

50 Of the firstborn of the children of Israel took he the money; ᴿa thousand three hundred and threescore and five *shē′-kĕls,* after the shē′-kĕl of the sanctuary:

51 And Moses ᴿgave the money of them that were redeemed unto Aaron and to his sons, according to the word of the LORD, as the LORD commanded Moses.

CHAPTER 4

Duties of the Kohathites

AND the LORD spake unto Moses and unto Aaron, saying,

2 Take the sum of the sons of Kō′-hăth from among the sons of Levi, after their families, by the house of their fathers,

3 ᴿFrom thirty years old and upward even until fifty years old, all that enter into the host, to do the work in the tabernacle of the congregation.

4 ᴿThis *shall be* the service of the sons of

Kō′-hăth in the tabernacle of the congregation, *about* ᴿthe most holy things:

5 And when the camp setteth forward, Aaron shall come, and his sons, and they shall take down ᴿthe covering vail, and cover the ᴿark of testimony with it:

6 And shall put thereon the covering of badgers' skins, and shall spread over *it* a cloth wholly of blue, and shall put in ᴿthe staves thereof.

7 And upon the ᴿtable of shewbread they shall spread a cloth of blue, and put thereon the dishes, and the spoons, and the bowls, and covers to ᴺcover withal: and the continual bread shall be thereon:

8 And they shall spread upon them a cloth of scarlet, and cover the same with a covering of badgers' skins, and shall put in the staves thereof.

9 And they shall take a cloth of blue, and cover the ᴿcandlestick of the light, ᴿand his lamps, and his tongs, and his snuffdishes, and all the oil vessels thereof, wherewith they minister unto it:

10 And they shall put it and all the vessels thereof within a covering of badgers' skins, and shall put *it* upon a bar.

11 And upon ᴿthe golden altar they shall spread a cloth of blue, and cover it with a covering of badgers' skins, and shall put to the staves thereof:

12 And they shall take all the instruments of ministry, wherewith they minister in the sanctuary, and put *them* in a cloth of blue, and cover them with a covering of badgers' skins, and shall put *them* on a bar:

13 And they shall take away the ashes from the altar, and spread a purple cloth thereon:

14 And they shall put upon it all the vessels thereof, wherewith they minister about it, *even* the censers, the fleshhooks, and the shovels, and the ᴺbasins, all the vessels of the altar; and they shall spread upon it a covering of badgers' skins, and put to the staves of it.

15 And when Aaron and his sons have made an end of covering the sanctuary, and all the vessels of the sanctuary, as the camp is to set forward; after that ᴿthe sons of Kō′-hăth shall come to bear *it:* ᴿbut they shall not touch *any* holy thing, lest they die. ᴿThese *things are* the burden of the sons of Kō′-hăth in the tabernacle of the congregation.

The office of Eleazar

16 And to the office of Ĕl-ē-ā′-zär the son of Aaron the priest *pertaineth* ᴿthe oil for the light, and the ᴿsweet incense, and ᴿthe daily meat offering, and the ᴿanointing oil, *and* the oversight of all the tabernacle, and of all that

therein *is,* in the sanctuary, and in the vessels thereof.

17 And the LORD spake unto Moses and unto Aaron, saying,

18 Cut ye not off the tribe of the families of the Kō'-hăth-ītes from among the Levites:

19 But thus do unto them, that they may live, and not die, when they approach unto ᴿthe most holy things: Aaron and his sons shall go in, and appoint them every one to his service and to his burden:

20 ᴿBut they shall not go in to see when the holy things are covered, lest they die.

Duties of the Gershonites

21 And the LORD spake unto Moses, saying,

22 Take also the sum of the sons of Gĕr'-shŏn, throughout the houses of their fathers, by their families;

23 ᴿFrom thirty years old and upward until fifty years old shalt thou number them; all that enter in ᴺto perform the service, to do the work in the tabernacle of the congregation.

24 This *is* the service of the families of the Gĕr'-shŏn-ītes, to serve, and for ᴺburdens:

25 And ᴿthey shall bear the curtains of the tabernacle, and the tabernacle of the congregation, his covering, and the covering of the badgers' skins that *is* above upon it, and the hanging for the door of the tabernacle of the congregation,

26 And the hangings of the court, and the hanging for the door of the gate of the court, which *is* by the tabernacle and by the altar round about, and their cords, and all the instruments of their service, and all that is made for them: so shall they serve.

27 At the ᴺappointment of Aaron and his sons shall be all the service of the sons of the Gĕr'-shŏn-ītes, in all their burdens, and in all their service: and ye shall appoint unto them in charge all their burdens.

28 This *is* the service of the families of the sons of Gĕr'-shŏn in the tabernacle of the congregation: and their charge *shall be* ᴿunder the hand of ĭth'-ă-mär the son of Aaron the priest.

Sons of Merari

29 As for the sons of Mĕ-rär'-ī, thou shalt number them after their families, by the house of their fathers;

30 ᴿFrom thirty years old and upward even unto fifty years old shalt thou number them, every one that entereth into the ᴺservice, to do the work of the tabernacle of the congregation.

31 And ᴿthis *is* the charge of their burden,

CHAP. **4**
BC 1490

19 ver. 4
20 See Ex. 19:21
  1 Sam. 6:19
23 ver. 3
23 Heb. *to war the warfare*
24 Or, *carriage*
25 ch. 3:25, 26
27 Heb. *mouth*
28 ver. 33
30 ver. 3
30 Heb. *warfare*
31 ch. 3:36, 37

Ex. 26:15	**31**
Ex. 38:21	**32**
ver. 2	**34**
ver. 47	**35**
ver. 22	**41**

according to all their service in the tabernacle of the congregation; ᴿthe boards of the tabernacle, and the bars thereof, and the pillars thereof, and sockets thereof,

32 And the pillars of the court round about, and their sockets, and their pins, and their cords, with all their instruments, and with all their service: and by name ye shall ᴿreckon the instruments of the charge of their burden.

33 This *is* the service of the families of the sons of Mĕ-rär'-ī, according to all their service, in the tabernacle of the congregation, under the hand of ĭth'-ă-mär the son of Aaron the priest.

The census

34 ᴿAnd Moses and Aaron and the chief of the congregation numbered the sons of the Kō'-hăth-ītes after their families, and after the house of their fathers,

35 From thirty ᴿyears old and upward even unto fifty years old, every one that entereth into the service, for the work in the tabernacle of the congregation:

36 And those that were numbered of them by their families were two thousand seven hundred and fifty.

37 These *were* they that were numbered of the families of the Kō'-hăth-ītes, all that might do service in the tabernacle of the congregation, which Moses and Aaron did number according to the commandment of the LORD by the hand of Moses.

38 And those that were numbered of the sons of Gĕr'-shŏn, throughout their families, and by the house of their fathers,

39 From thirty years old and upward even unto fifty years old, every one that entereth into the service, for the work in the tabernacle of the congregation,

40 Even those that were numbered of them, throughout their families, by the house of their fathers, were two thousand and six hundred and thirty.

41 ᴿThese *are* they that were numbered of the families of the sons of Gĕr'-shŏn, of all that might do service in the tabernacle of the congregation, whom Moses and Aaron did number according to the commandment of the LORD.

42 And those that were numbered of the families of the sons of Mĕ-rär'-ī, throughout their families, by the house of their fathers,

43 From thirty years old and upward even unto fifty years old, every one that entereth into the service, for the work in the tabernacle of the congregation,

44 Even those that were numbered of them after their families, were three thousand and two hundred.

45 These *be* those that were numbered of the families of the sons of Mĕ-râr'-ĭ, whom Moses and Aaron numbered ᴿaccording to the word of the Lord by the hand of Moses.

46 All those that were numbered of the Levites, whom Moses and Aaron and the chief of Israel numbered, after their families, and after the house of their fathers,

47 ᴿFrom thirty years old and upward even unto fifty years old, every one that came to do the service of the ministry, and the service of the burden in the tabernacle of the congregation,

48 Even those that were numbered of them, were eight thousand and five hundred and fourscore.

49 According to the commandment of the Lord they were numbered by the hand of Moses, ᴿevery one according to his service, and according to his burden: thus were they numbered of him, ᴿas the Lord commanded Moses.

CHAPTER 5

Lepers expelled from the camp

AND the Lord spake unto Moses, saying, 2 Command the children of Israel, that they put out of the camp every ᴿleper, and every one that hath an ᴿissue, and whosoever is defiled by the ᴿdead:

3 Both male and female shall ye put out, without the camp shall ye put them; that they defile not their camps, ᴿin the midst whereof I dwell.

4 And the children of Israel did so, and put them out without the camp: as the Lord spake unto Moses, so did the children of Israel.

Law of restitution

5 And the Lord spake unto Moses, saying,

6 Speak unto the children of Israel, ᴿWhen a man or woman shall commit any sin that men commit, to do a trespass against the Lord, and that person be guilty;

7 ᴿThen they shall confess their sin which they have done: and he shall recompense his trespass ᴿwith the principal thereof, and add unto it the fifth *part* thereof, and give *it* unto *him* against whom he hath trespassed.

8 But if the man have no kinsman to recompense the trespass unto, let the trespass be recompensed unto the Lord, *even* to the priest;

CHAP. 4
BC 1490
45 ver. 29
47 ver. 3, 23, 30
49 ver. 15, 24, 31
49 ver. 1, 21

CHAP. 5
BC 1490
2 Lev. 13:3, 46
2 Lev. 15:2
2 Lev. 21:1
ch. 9:6, 10
& 19:11, 13
& 31:19
3 Lev. 26:11, 12
2 Cor. 6:16
6 Lev. 6:2, 3
7 Lev. 5:5
& 26:40
Josh. 7:19
7 Lev. 6:5

Lev. 6:6, 7 & 7:7 **8**
Ex. 29:28 **9**
Lev. 6:17, 18, 26
& 7:6, 7, 9, 10, 14
Or, *heave offering* **9**
Lev. 10:13 **10**
Lev. 18:20 **13**
Lev. 5:11 **15**
1 Ki. 17:18 **15**
Ezek. 29:16
Or, *being in the* **19**
power of thy
husband
Heb. *under* **19**
thy husband
Josh. 6:26 **21**
1 Sam. 14:24
Neh. 10:29
Jer. 29:22 **21**

---

beside ᴿthe ram of the atonement, whereby an atonement shall be made for him.

9 And every ᴿofferingᴺ of all the holy things of the children of Israel, which they bring unto the priest, shall be his.

10 And every man's hallowed things shall be his: whatsoever any man giveth the priest, it shall be ᴿhis.

Trial of jealousy

11 And the Lord spake unto Moses, saying,

12 Speak unto the children of Israel, and say unto them, If any man's wife go aside, and commit a trespass against him,

13 And a man ᴿlie with her carnally, and it be hid from the eyes of her husband, and be kept close, and she be defiled, and *there be* no witness against her, neither she be taken *with the manner;*

14 And the spirit of jealousy come upon him, and he be jealous of his wife, and she be defiled: or if the spirit of jealousy come upon him, and he be jealous of his wife, and she be not defiled:

15 Then shall the man bring his wife unto the priest, and he shall ᴿbring her offering for her, the tenth *part* of an ē'-phäh of barley meal; he shall pour no oil upon it, nor put frankincense thereon; for it *is* an offering of jealousy, an offering of memorial, ᴿbringing iniquity to remembrance.

16 And the priest shall bring her near, and set her before the Lord :

17 And the priest shall take holy water in an earthen vessel; and of the dust that is in the floor of the tabernacle the priest shall take, and put *it* into the water:

18 And the priest shall set the woman before the Lord, and uncover the woman's head, and put the offering of memorial in her hands, which *is* the jealousy offering: and the priest shall have in his hand the bitter water that causeth the curse:

19 And the priest shall charge her by an oath, and say unto the woman, If no man have lain with thee, and if thou hast not gone aside to uncleanness ᴺᴺ*with another* instead of thy husband, be thou free from this bitter water that causeth the curse:

20 But if thou hast gone aside *to another* instead of thy husband, and if thou be defiled, and some man have lain with thee beside thine husband:

21 Then the priest shall ᴿcharge the woman with an oath of cursing, and the priest shall say unto the woman, ᴿThe Lord make thee a curse and an oath among thy people, when the

LORD doth make thy thigh to ᴺrot, and thy belly to swell;

22 And this water that causeth the curse ᴿshall go into thy bowels, to make *thy* belly to swell, and *thy* thigh to rot: ᴿAnd the woman shall say, Ă'-mĕn, ă'-mĕn.

23 And the priest shall write these curses in a book, and he shall blot *them* out with the bitter water:

24 And he shall cause the woman to drink the bitter water that causeth the curse: and the water that causeth the curse shall enter into her, *and become* bitter.

25 Then the priest shall take the jealousy offering out of the woman's hand, and shall ᴿwave the offering before the LORD, and offer it upon the altar:

26 ᴿAnd the priest shall take an handful of the offering, *even* the memorial thereof, and burn *it* upon the altar, and afterward shall cause the woman to drink the water.

27 And when he hath made her to drink the water, then it shall come to pass, *that,* if she be defiled, and have done trespass against her husband, that the water that causeth the curse shall enter into her, *and become* bitter, and her belly shall swell, and her thigh shall rot: and the woman ᴿshall be a curse among her people.

28 And if the woman be not defiled, but be clean; then she shall be free, and shall conceive seed.

29 This *is* the law of jealousies, when a wife goeth aside *to another* ᴿinstead of her husband, and is defiled;

30 Or when the spirit of jealousy cometh upon him, and he be jealous over his wife, and shall set the woman before the LORD, and the priest shall execute upon her all this law.

31 Then shall the man be guiltless from iniquity, and this woman ᴿshall bear her iniquity.

CHAPTER 6

Law of the Nazarites

AND the LORD spake unto Moses, saying, 2 Speak unto the children of Israel, and say unto them, When either man or woman shall ᴿseparateᴺ *themselves* to vow a vow of a Nazarite, to separate *themselves* unto the LORD:

3 ᴿHe shall separate *himself* from wine and strong drink, and shall drink no vinegar of wine, or vinegar of strong drink, neither shall he drink any liquor of grapes, nor eat moist grapes, or dried.

4 All the days of his ᴺseparation shall he eat

CHAP. **5**
BC 1490
21 Heb. *fall*
22 Ps. 109:18
22 Deut. 27:15
25 Lev. 8:27
26 Lev. 2:2, 9
27 ver. 21
29 ver. 19
31 Lev. 20:17, 19, 20

CHAP. **6**
BC 1490
2 Lev. 27:2
Judg. 13:5
Acts 21:23
Rom. 1:1
2 Or, *make themselves Nazarites*
3 Amos 2:12
Luke 1:15
4 Or, *Nazariteship*

Heb. *vine of the wine*	4
Judg. 13:5 & 16:17	5
1 Sam. 1:11	
Lev. 21:11	6
ch. 19:11, 16	
Lev. 21:1, 2, 11	7
ch. 9:6	
Heb. *separation*	7
2 Cor. 6:17, 18	8
Acts 18:18	9
& 21:24	
Lev. 5:7 & 14:22	10
& 15:14, 29	
Lev. 5:6	12
Heb. *fall*	12
Acts 21:26	13
Lev. 4:2, 27, 32	14
Lev. 3:6	14
Lev. 2:4	15
Ex. 29:2	15
ch. 15:5, 7, 10	15

nothing that is made of the ᴺvine tree, from the kernels even to the husk.

5 All the days of the vow of his separation there shall no ᴿrazor come upon his head: until the days be fulfilled, in the which he separateth *himself* unto the LORD, he shall be holy, *and* shall let the locks of the hair of his head grow.

6 All the days that he separateth *himself* unto the LORD ᴿhe shall come at no dead body.

7 ᴿHe shall not make himself unclean for his father, or for his mother, for his brother, or for his sister, when they die: because the ᴺconsecration of his God *is* upon his head.

8 ᴿAll the days of his separation he *is* holy unto the LORD.

9 And if any man die very suddenly by him, and he hath defiled the head of his consecration; then he shall ᴿshave his head in the day of his cleansing, on the seventh day shall he shave it.

10 And ᴿon the eighth day he shall bring two turtles, or two young pigeons, to the priest, to the door of the tabernacle of the congregation:

11 And the priest shall offer the one for a sin offering, and the other for a burnt offering, and make an atonement for him, for that he sinned by the dead, and shall hallow his head that same day.

12 And he shall consecrate unto the LORD the days of his separation, and shall bring a lamb of the first year ᴿfor a trespass offering: but the days that were before shall ᴺbe lost, because his separation was defiled.

13 And this *is* the law of the Nazarite, ᴿwhen the days of his separation are fulfilled: he shall be brought unto the door of the tabernacle of the congregation:

14 And he shall offer his offering unto the LORD, one he lamb of the first year without blemish for a burnt offering, and one ewe lamb of the first year without blemish ᴿfor a sin offering, and one ram without blemish ᴿfor peace offerings,

15 And a basket of unleavened bread, ᴿcakes of fine flour mingled with oil, and wafers of unleavened bread ᴿanointed with oil, and their meat offering, and their ᴿdrink offerings.

16 And the priest shall bring *them* before the LORD, and shall offer his sin offering, and his burnt offering:

17 And he shall offer the ram *for* a sacrifice of peace offerings unto the LORD, with the basket of unleavened bread: the priest shall offer also his meat offering, and his drink offering.

18 ᴿAnd the Nazarite shall shave the head of his separation *at* the door of the tabernacle of the congregation, and shall take the hair of the head of his separation, and put *it* in the fire which *is* under the sacrifice of the peace offerings.

19 And the priest shall take the ᴿsodden shoulder of the ram, and one unleavened cake out of the basket, and one unleavened wafer, and ᴿshall put *them* upon the hands of the Nazarite, after *the hair of* his separation is shaven:

20 And the priest shall wave them *for a* wave offering before the LORD: ᴿthis *is* holy for the priest, with the wave breast and heave shoulder: and after that the Nazarite may drink wine.

21 This *is* the law of the Nazarite who hath vowed, *and of* his offering unto the LORD for his separation, beside *that* that his hand shall get: according to the vow which he vowed, so he must do after the law of his separation.

Priestly benediction

22 And the LORD spake unto Moses, saying,

23 Speak unto Aaron and unto his sons, saying, On this wise ᴿye shall bless the children of Israel, saying unto them,

24 The LORD bless thee, and ᴿkeep thee:

25 The LORD ᴿmake his face shine upon thee, and ᴿbe gracious unto thee:

26 ᴿThe LORD lift up his countenance upon thee, and ᴿgive thee peace.

27 ᴿAnd they shall put my name upon the children of Israel; and ᴿI will bless them.

CHAPTER 7

Offerings from the tribes

AND it came to pass on the day that Moses had fully ᴿset up the tabernacle, and had anointed it, and sanctified it, and all the instruments thereof, both the altar and all the vessels thereof, and had anointed them, and sanctified them;

2 That ᴿthe princes of Israel, heads of the house of their fathers, who *were* the princes of the tribes, ᴺand were over them that were numbered, offered:

3 And they brought their offering before the LORD, six covered wagons, and twelve oxen; a wagon for two of the princes, and for each one an ox: and they brought them before the tabernacle.

4 And the LORD spake unto Moses, saying,

5 Take *it* of them, that they may be to do the service of the tabernacle of the congregation;

CHAP. 6
BC 1490
18 Acts 21:24
19 1 Sam. 2:15
19 Ex. 29:23, 24
20 Ex. 29:27, 28
23 Lev. 9:22
Deut. 10:8 & 21:5
Josh. 8:33
1 Chr. 23:13
24 Ps. 121:7
John 17:11
25 Ps. 31:16
& 67:1 & 80:3,
7, 19 & 119:135
Dan. 9:17
25 Gen. 43:29
Ex. 33:19
Mal. 1:9
26 Ps. 4:6
26 John 14:27
Phil. 4:7
2 Thes. 3:16
27 Deut. 28:10
2 Chr. 7:14
Is. 43:7
Dan. 9:18, 19
27 ch. 23:20
Ps. 5:12 & 67:7
& 115:12, 13
Eph. 1:3

CHAP. 7
BC 1490
1 Ex. 40:18
Lev. 8:10, 11
2 ch. 1:4, etc.
2 Heb. *who stood*

ch. 4:23	7
ch. 4:33	8
ch. 4:28, 33	8
ch. 4:15	9
ch. 4:6, 8, 10, 12, 14 2 Sam. 6:13	9
See Deut. 20:5 1 Ki. 8:63 2 Chr. 7:5, 9 Ezra 6:16 Neh. 12:27	10
ch. 2:3	12
Ex. 30:13	13
Lev. 2:1	13
Ex. 30:34	14
Lev. 1:2	15
Ex. 12:5	15
Lev. 4:23	16
Lev. 3:1	17

and thou shalt give them unto the Levites, to every man according to his service.

6 And Moses took the wagons and the oxen, and gave them unto the Levites.

7 Two wagons and four oxen ᴿhe gave unto the sons of Gĕr'-shŏn, according to their service:

8 ᴿAnd four wagons and eight oxen he gave unto the sons of Mĕ-râr'-ĭ, according unto their service, ᴿunder the hand of Ĭth'-ă-mär the son of Aaron the priest.

9 But unto the sons of Kō'-hăth he gave none: because ᴿthe service of the sanctuary belonging unto them ᴿ*was that* they should bear upon their shoulders.

10 And the princes offered for ᴿdedicating of the altar in the day that it was anointed, even the princes offered their offering before the altar.

11 And the LORD said unto Moses, They shall offer their offering, each prince on his day, for the dedicating of the altar.

12 And he that offered his offering the first day was ᴿNäh'-shŏn the son of Ăm-mĭn'-ă-dăb, of the tribe of Judah:

13 And his offering *was* one silver charger, the weight thereof *was* an hundred and thirty *shē'-kĕls,* one silver bowl of seventy *shē'-kĕls,* after ᴿthe shē'-kĕl of the sanctuary; both of them *were* full of fine flour mingled with oil for a ᴿmeat offering:

14 One spoon of ten *shē'-kĕls* of gold, full of ᴿincense:

15 ᴿOne young bullock, one ram, one lamb ᴿof the first year, for a burnt offering:

16 One kid of the goats for a ᴿsin offering:

17 And for ᴿa sacrifice of peace offerings, two oxen, five rams, five he goats, five lambs of the first year: this *was* the offering of Näh'-shŏn the son of Ăm-mĭn'-ă-dăb.

18 On the second day Nĕth'-ă-nĕĕl the son of Zū'-är, prince of ĭs'-să-chär, did offer:

19 He offered *for* his offering one silver charger, the weight whereof *was* an hundred and thirty *shē'-kĕls,* one silver bowl of seventy shē'-kĕls, after the shē'-kĕl of the sanctuary; both of them full of fine flour mingled with oil for a meat offering:

20 One spoon of gold of ten *shē'-kĕls,* full of incense:

21 One young bullock, one ram, one lamb of the first year, for a burnt offering:

22 One kid of the goats for a sin offering:

23 And for a sacrifice of peace offerings, two oxen, five rams, five he goats, five lambs of the first year: this *was* the offering of Nĕth'-ă-nĕĕl the son of Zū'-är.

24 On the third day Ē-lī'-ăb the son of

Hē'-lŏn, prince of the children of Zĕ-bū'-lŭn, *did offer:*

25 His offering *was* one silver charger, the weight whereof *was* an hundred and thirty *shē'-kĕls*, one silver bowl of seventy shē'-kĕls, after the shē'-kĕl of the sanctuary; both of them full of fine flour mingled with oil for a meat offering:

26 One golden spoon of ten *shē'-kĕls*, full of incense:

27 One young bullock, one ram, one lamb of the first year, for a burnt offering:

28 One kid of the goats for a sin offering:

29 And for a sacrifice of peace offerings, two oxen, five rams, five he goats, five lambs of the first year: this *was* the offering of Ē-li'-ăb the son of Hē'-lŏn.

30 On the fourth day ᴿĔ-li'-zùr the son of Shĕd'-ē-ùr, prince of the children of Reuben, *did offer:*

31 His offering *was* one silver charger of the weight of an hundred and thirty *shē'-kĕls*, one silver bowl of seventy shē'-kĕls, after the shē'-kĕl of the sanctuary; both of them full of fine flour mingled with oil for a meat offering:

32 One golden spoon of ten *shē'-kĕls*, full of incense:

33 One young bullock, one ram, one lamb of the first year, for a burnt offering:

34 One kid of the goats for a sin offering:

35 And for a sacrifice of peace offerings, two oxen, five rams, five he goats, five lambs of the first year: this *was* the offering of ĕ-li'-zùr the son of Shĕd'-ē-ùr.

36 On the fifth day ᴿShĕ-lû'-mĭ-ĕl the son of Zū-rĭ-shăd'-dâi, prince of the children of Simeon, *did offer:*

37 His offering *was* one silver charger, the weight whereof *was* an hundred and thirty *shē'-kĕls*, one silver bowl of seventy shē'-kĕls, after the shē'-kĕl of the sanctuary; both of them full of fine flour mingled with oil for a meat offering:

38 One golden spoon of ten *shē'-kĕls*, full of incense:

39 One young bullock, one ram, one lamb of the first year, for a burnt offering:

40 One kid of the goats for a sin offering:

41 And for a sacrifice of peace offerings, two oxen, five rams, five he goats, five lambs of the first year: this *was* the offering of Shĕ-lû'-mĭ-ĕl the son of Zū-rĭ-shăd'-dâi.

42 On the sixth day ᴿĒ-li'-ă-săph the son of ᴺDĕû'-ĕl, prince of the children of Gad, *offered:*

43 His offering *was* one silver charger of the weight of an hundred and thirty *shē'-kĕls*, a silver bowl of seventy shē'-kĕls, after the shē'-kĕl of the sanctuary; both of them full

CHAP. 7
BC 1490
30 ch. 1:5 & 2:10
36 ver. 41
 ch. 1:6 & 2:12
42 ch. 1:14 & 2:14
42 Or, *Reuel*

of fine flour mingled with oil for a meat offering:

44 One golden spoon of ten *shē'-kĕls*, full of incense:

45 One young bullock, one ram, one lamb of the first year, for ᴿa burnt offering:

46 One kid of the goats for a sin offering:

47 And for a sacrifice of peace offerings, two oxen, five rams, five he goats, five lambs of the first year: this *was* the offering of Ē-li'-ă-săph the son of Dĕû'-ĕl.

48 On the seventh day ᴿĒ-li'-shă-mă the son of Ăm'-mĭ-hŭd, prince of the children of Ē'-phră-ĭm, *offered:*

49 His offering *was* one silver charger, the weight whereof *was* an hundred and thirty *shē'-kĕls*, one silver bowl of seventy shē'-kĕls, after the shē'-kĕl of the sanctuary; both of them full of fine flour mingled with oil for a meat offering:

50 One golden spoon of ten *shē'-kĕls*, full of incense:

51 One young bullock, one ram, one lamb of the first year, for a burnt offering:

52 One kid of the goats for a sin offering:

53 And for a sacrifice of peace offerings, two oxen, five rams, five he goats, five lambs of the first year: this *was* the offering of Ē-li'-shă-mă the son of Ăm'-mĭ-hŭd.

54 On the eighth day *offered* ᴿGă-mā'-lĭ-ĕl the son of Pĕ-dăh'-zùr, prince of the children of Mă-năs'-sēh:

55 His offering *was* one silver charger of the weight of an hundred and thirty *shē'-kĕls*, one silver bowl of seventy shē'-kĕls, after the shē'-kĕl of the sanctuary; both of them full of fine flour mingled with oil for a meat offering:

56 One golden spoon of ten *shē'-kĕls*, full of incense:

57 One young bullock, one ram, one lamb of the first year, for a burnt offering:

58 One kid of the goats for a sin offering:

59 And for a sacrifice of peace offerings, two oxen, five rams, five he goats, five lambs of the first year: this *was* the offering of Gă-mā'-lĭ-ĕl the son of Pĕ-dăh'-zùr.

60 On the ninth day ᴿĂ-bī'-dăn the son of Gĭd-ĕ-ō'-nĭ, prince of the children of Benjamin, *offered:*

61 His offering *was* one silver charger, the weight whereof *was* an hundred and thirty *shē'-kĕls*, one silver bowl of seventy shē'-kĕls, after the shē'-kĕl of the sanctuary; both of them full of fine flour mingled with oil for a meat offering:

62 One golden spoon of ten *shē'-kĕls*, full of incense:

63 One young bullock, one ram, one lamb of the first year, for a burnt offering:

Ps. 40:6   **45**
ch. 1:10 & 2:18   **48**
ch. 1:10 & 2:20   **54**
ch. 1:11 & 2:22   **60**

64 One kid of the goats for a sin offering:

65 And for a sacrifice of peace offerings, two oxen, five rams, five he goats, five lambs of the first year: this *was* the offering of Ă-bī'-dăn the son of Gĭd-ĕ-ō'-nĭ.

66 On the tenth day [R]Ā-hĭ-ē'-zĕr the son of Ăm-mĭ-shăd'-dâi, prince of the children of Dan, *offered:*

67 His offering *was* one silver charger, the weight whereof *was* an hundred and thirty *shē'-kĕls,* one silver bowl of seventy shē'-kĕls, after the shē'-kĕl of the sanctuary; both of them full of fine flour mingled with oil for a meat offering:

68 One golden spoon of ten *shē'-kĕls,* full of incense:

69 One young bullock, one ram, one lamb of the first year, for a burnt offering:

70 One kid of the goats for a sin offering:

71 And for a sacrifice of peace offerings, two oxen, five rams, five he goats, five lambs of the first year: this *was* the offering of Ā-hĭ-ē'-zĕr the son of Ăm-mĭ-shăd'-dâi.

72 On the eleventh day [R]Pā'-ġĭ-ĕl the son of ŏc'-răn, prince of the children of Asher, *offered:*

73 His offering *was* one silver charger, the weight whereof *was* an hundred and thirty *shē'-kĕls,* one silver bowl of seventy shē'-kĕls, after the shē'-kĕl of the sanctuary; both of them full of fine flour mingled with oil for a meat offering:

74 One golden spoon of ten *shē'-kĕls,* full of incense:

75 One young bullock, one ram, one lamb of the first year, for a burnt offering:

76 One kid of the goats for a sin offering:

77 And for a sacrifice of peace offerings, two oxen, five rams, five he goats, five lambs of the first year: this *was* the offering of Pā'-ġĭ-ĕl the son of ŏc'-răn.

78 On the twelfth day [R]Ă-hĭ'-ră the son of Ē'-năn, prince of the children of Năph'-tă-lī, *offered:*

79 His offering *was* one silver charger, the weight whereof *was* an hundred and thirty *shē'-kĕls,* one silver bowl of seventy shē'-kĕls, after the shē'-kĕl of the sanctuary; both of them full of fine flour mingled with oil for a meat offering:

80 One golden spoon of ten *shē'-kĕls,* full of incense:

81 One young bullock, one ram, one lamb of the first year, for a burnt offering:

82 One kid of the goats for a sin offering:

83 And for a sacrifice of peace offerings, two oxen, five rams, five he goats, five lambs of the first year: this *was* the offering of Ă-hĭ'-ră the son of Ē'-năn.

CHAP. **7**
BC 1490
66 ch. 1:12 & 2:25
72 ch. 1:13 & 2:27
78 ch. 1:15 & 2:29

2 Chr. 7:9 — 84
Judg. 5:9 — 84
ver. 1 — 88
Ex. 33:9, 11 — 89
i.e. *God* — 89
Ex. 25:22 — 89

CHAP. **8**
BC 1490
Ex. 25:37 — 2
& 40:25
Ex. 25:31 — 4
Ex. 25:18 — 4
Ex. 25:40 — 4
ch. 19:9, 17, 18 — 7
Lev. 14:8, 9 — 7
Heb. *let them* — 7
cause a razor to
pass over, etc.

Dedication offering for the altar

84 This *was* [R]the dedication of the altar, in the day when it was anointed, by [R]the princes of Israel: twelve chargers of silver, twelve silver bowls, twelve spoons of gold:

85 Each charger of silver *weighing* an hundred and thirty *shē'-kĕls,* each bowl seventy: all the silver vessels *weighed* two thousand and four hundred *shē'-kĕls,* after the shē'-kĕl of the sanctuary:

86 The golden spoons *were* twelve, full of incense, *weighing* ten *shē'-kĕls* apiece, after the shē'-kĕl of the sanctuary: all the gold of the spoons *was* an hundred and twenty *shē'-kĕls.*

87 All the oxen for the burnt offering *were* twelve bullocks, the rams twelve, the lambs of the first year twelve, with their meat offering: and the kids of the goats for sin offering twelve.

88 And all the oxen for the sacrifice of the peace offerings *were* twenty and four bullocks, the rams sixty, the he goats sixty, the lambs of the first year sixty. This *was* the dedication of the altar, after that it was [R]anointed.

The voice in the tabernacle

89 And when Moses was gone into the tabernacle of the congregation [R]to speak with [N]him, then he heard [R]the voice of one speaking unto him from off the mercy seat that *was* upon the ark of testimony, from between the two chĕr'-ū-bĭms: and he spake unto him.

CHAPTER 8

Lighting of the lamps

AND the LORD spake unto Moses, saying, 2 Speak unto Aaron, and say unto him, When thou [R]lightest the lamps, the seven lamps shall give light over against the candlestick.

3 And Aaron did so; he lighted the lamps thereof over against the candlestick, as the LORD commanded Moses.

4 [R]And this work of the candlestick *was of* beaten gold, unto the shaft thereof, unto the flowers thereof, *was* [R]beaten work: [R]according unto the pattern which the LORD had shewed Moses, so he made the candlestick.

Separation of the Levites

5 And the LORD spake unto Moses, saying, 6 Take the Levites from among the children of Israel, and cleanse them.

7 And thus shalt thou do unto them, to cleanse them: Sprinkle [R]water of purifying upon them, and [R]let[N] them shave all their

flesh, and let them wash their clothes, and *so* make themselves clean.

8 Then let them take a young bullock with ᴿhis meat offering, *even* fine flour mingled with oil, and another young bullock shalt thou take for a sin offering.

9 ᴿAnd thou shalt bring the Levites before the tabernacle of the congregation: ᴿand thou shalt gather the whole assembly of the children of Israel together:

10 And thou shalt bring the Levites before the LORD: and the children of Israel ᴿshall put their hands upon the Levites:

11 And Aaron shall ᴺoffer the Levites before the LORD *for* an ᴺoffering of the children of Israel, that ᴺthey may execute the service of the LORD.

12 ᴿAnd the Levites shall lay their hands upon the heads of the bullocks: and thou shalt offer the one *for* a sin offering, and the other *for* a burnt offering, unto the LORD, to make an atonement for the Levites.

13 And thou shalt set the Levites before Aaron, and before his sons, and offer them *for* an offering unto the LORD.

14 Thus shalt thou separate the Levites from among the children of Israel: and the Levites shall be ᴿmine.

15 And after that shall the Levites go in to do the service of the tabernacle of the congregation: and thou shalt cleanse them, and ᴿoffer them *for* an offering.

16 For they *are* wholly given unto me from among the children of Israel; ᴿinstead of such as open every womb, *even instead of* the firstborn of all the children of Israel, have I taken them unto me.

17 ᴿFor all the firstborn of the children of Israel *are* mine, *both* man and beast: on the day that I smote every firstborn in the land of Egypt I sanctified them for myself.

18 And I have taken the Levites for all the firstborn of the children of Israel.

19 And ᴿI have given the Levites *as* ᴺa gift to Aaron and to his sons from among the children of Israel, to do the service of the children of Israel in the tabernacle of the congregation, and to make an atonement for the children of Israel: ᴿthat there be no plague among the children of Israel, when the children of Israel come nigh unto the sanctuary.

20 And Moses, and Aaron, and all the congregation of the children of Israel, did to the Levites according unto all that the LORD commanded Moses concerning the Levites, so did the children of Israel unto them.

21 ᴿAnd the Levites were purified, and they washed their clothes; and Aaron offered them

as an offering before the LORD; and Aaron made an atonement for them to cleanse them.

22 ᴿAnd after that went the Levites in to do their service in the tabernacle of the congregation before Aaron, and before his sons: ᴿas the LORD had commanded Moses concerning the Levites, so did they unto them.

Term of service

23 And the LORD spake unto Moses, saying,

24 This *is it* that *belongeth* unto the Levites: ᴿfrom twenty and five years old and upward they shall go in ᴺto wait upon the service of the tabernacle of the congregation:

25 And from the age of fifty years they shall ᴺcease waiting upon the service *thereof,* and shall serve no more:

26 But shall minister with their brethren in the tabernacle of the congregation, ᴿto keep the charge, and shall do no service. Thus shalt thou do unto the Levites touching their charge.

CHAPTER 9

The passover

AND the LORD spake unto Moses in the wilderness of Sĭ′-nâi, in the first month of the second year after they were come out of the land of Egypt, saying,

2 Let the children of Israel also keep ᴿthe passover at his appointed season.

3 In the fourteenth day of this month, ᴺat even, ye shall keep it in his appointed season: according to all the rites of it, and according to all the ceremonies thereof, shall ye keep it.

4 And Moses spake unto the children of Israel, that they should keep the passover.

5 And ᴿthey kept the passover on the fourteenth day of the first month at even in the wilderness of Sĭ′-nâi: according to all that the LORD commanded Moses, so did the children of Israel.

6 And there were certain men, who were ᴿdefiled by the dead body of a man, that they could not keep the passover on that day: ᴿand they came before Moses and before Aaron on that day:

7 And those men said unto him, We *are* defiled by the dead body of a man: wherefore are we kept back, that we may not offer an offering of the LORD in his appointed season among the children of Israel?

8 And Moses said unto them, Stand still, and ᴿI will hear what the LORD will command concerning you.

9 And the LORD spake unto Moses, saying,

10 Speak unto the children of Israel, saying, If any man of you or of your posterity shall be

unclean by reason of a dead body, or *be* in a journey afar off, yet he shall keep the passover unto the Lord.

11 ᴿThe fourteenth day of the second month at even they shall keep it, *and* ᴿeat it with unleavened bread and bitter *herbs.*

12 ᴿThey shall leave none of it unto the morning, ᴿnor break any bone of it: ᴿaccording to all the ordinances of the passover they shall keep it.

13 But the man that *is* clean, and is not in a journey, and forbeareth to keep the passover, even the same soul ᴿshall be cut off from among his people: because he ᴿbrought not the offering of the Lord in his appointed season, that man shall ᴿbear his sin.

14 And if a stranger shall sojourn among you, and will keep the passover unto the Lord; according to the ordinance of the passover, and according to the manner thereof, so shall he do: ᴿye shall have one ordinance, both for the stranger, and for him that was born in the land.

The directing cloud

15 And ᴿon the day that the tabernacle was reared up the cloud covered the tabernacle, *namely,* the tent of the testimony: and ᴿat even there was upon the tabernacle as it were the appearance of fire, until the morning.

16 So it was alway: the cloud covered it *by day,* and the appearance of fire by night.

17 And when the cloud ᴿwas taken up from the tabernacle, then after that the children of Israel journeyed: and in the place where the cloud abode, there the children of Israel pitched their tents.

18 At the commandment of the Lord the children of Israel journeyed, and at the commandment of the Lord they pitched: ᴿas long as the cloud abode upon the tabernacle they rested in their tents.

19 And when the cloud ᴺtarried long upon the tabernacle many days, then the children of Israel ᴿkept the charge of the Lord, and journeyed not.

20 And *so* it was, when the cloud was a few days upon the tabernacle; according to the commandment of the Lord they abode in their tents, and according to the commandment of the Lord they journeyed.

21 And *so* it was, when the cloud ᴺabode from even unto the morning, and *that* the cloud was taken up in the morning, then they journeyed: whether *it was* by day or by night that the cloud was taken up, they journeyed.

22 Or *whether it were* two days, or a month, or a year, that the cloud tarried upon the

tabernacle, remaining thereon, the children of Israel ᴿabode in their tents, and journeyed not: but when it was taken up, they journeyed.

23 At the commandment of the Lord they rested in the tents, and at the commandment of the Lord they journeyed: they ᴿkept the charge of the Lord, at the commandment of the Lord by the hand of Moses.

CHAPTER 10

Use of the trumpets

AND the Lord spake unto Moses, saying, 2 Make thee two trumpets of silver; of a whole piece shalt thou make them: that thou mayest use them for the ᴿcalling of the assembly, and for the journeying of the camps.

3 And when ᴿthey shall blow with them, all the assembly shall assemble themselves to thee at the door of the tabernacle of the congregation.

4 And if they blow *but* with one *trumpet,* then the princes, *which are* ᴿheads of the thousands of Israel, shall gather themselves unto thee.

5 When ye blow an alarm, then ᴿthe camps that lie on the east parts shall go forward.

6 When ye blow an alarm the second time, then the camps that lie ᴿon the south side shall take their journey: they shall blow an alarm for their journeys.

7 But when the congregation is to be gathered together, ᴿye shall blow, but ye shall not ᴿsound an alarm.

8 ᴿAnd the sons of Aaron, the priests, shall blow with the trumpets; and they shall be to you for an ordinance for ever throughout your generations.

9 And ᴿif ye go to war in your land against the enemy that ᴿoppresseth you, then ye shall blow an alarm with the trumpets; and ye shall be ᴿremembered before the Lord your God, and ye shall be saved from your enemies.

10 Also ᴿin the day of your gladness, and in your solemn days, and in the beginnings of your months, ye shall blow with the trumpets over your burnt offerings, and over the sacrifices of your peace offerings; that they may be to you ᴿfor a memorial before your God: I *am* the Lord your God.

Departure from Sinai

11 And it came to pass on the twentieth *day* of the second month, in the second year, that the cloud ᴿwas taken up from off the tabernacle of the testimony.

12 And the children of Israel took ᴿtheir

journeys out of the [R]wilderness of Sī'-naï; and the cloud rested in the [R]wilderness of Pâr'-ăn.

13 And they first took their journey [R]according to the commandment of the LORD by the hand of Moses.

14 [R]In the first *place* went the standard of the camp of the children of Judah according to their armies: and over his host *was* [R]Näh'-shŏn the son of Ăm-mĭn-ă-dăb.

15 And over the host of the tribe of the children of ĭs'-să-<u>ch</u>är *was* Nĕth'-ă-nĕel the son of Zū'-är.

16 And over the host of the tribe of the children of Zĕ-bū'-lŭn *was* Ē-lī'-ăb the son of Hē'-lŏn.

17 And [R]the tabernacle was taken down; and the sons of Gēr'-shŏn and the sons of Mĕ-râr'-ĭ set forward, [R]bearing the tabernacle.

18 And [R]the standard of the camp of Reuben set forward according to their armies: and over his host *was* ĕ-lī'-zùr the son of Shĕd'-ē-ùr.

19 And over the host of the tribe of the children of Simeon *was* Shĕ-lû'-mĭ-ĕl the son of Zū-rĭ-shăd'-dâi.

20 And over the host of the tribe of the children of Gad *was* Ē-lī'-ă-săph the son of Dĕû'-ĕl.

21 And the Kō'-häth-ītes set forward, bearing the [R]sanctuary: and [N]*the other* did set up the tabernacle against they came.

22 And [R]the standard of the camp of the children of Ē'-phră-ĭm set forward according to their armies: and over his host *was* Ē-lī'-shă-mă the son of Ăm'-mĭ-hŭd.

23 And over the host of the tribe of the children of Mă-năs'-sēh *was* Gă-mā'-lĭ-ĕl the son of Pĕ-däh'-zùr.

24 And over the host of the tribe of the children of Benjamin *was* Ă-bī'-dăn the son of Gĭd-ĕ-ō'-nĭ.

25 And [R]the standard of the camp of the children of Dan set forward, *which was* the rearward of all the camps throughout their hosts: and over his host *was* Ā-hĭ-ē'-zĕr the son of Ăm-mĭ-shăd'-dâi.

26 And over the host of the tribe of the children of Asher *was* Pā'-gĭ-ĕl the son of ŏc'-răn.

27 And over the host of the tribe of the children of Năph'-tă-lī *was* Ă-hī'-ră the son of Ē'-năn.

28 [R]Thus[N] *were* the journeyings of the children of Israel according to their armies, when they set forward.

29 And Moses said unto Hō'-băb, the son of [R]Ră-gū'-ĕl the Mĭd'-ĭ-ă-nīte, Moses' father in law, We are journeying unto the place of which the LORD said, [R]I will give it you: come

thou with us, and [R]we will do thee good: for [R]the LORD hath spoken good concerning Israel.

30 And he said unto him, I will not go; but I will depart to mine own land, and to my kindred.

31 And he said, Leave us not, I pray thee; forasmuch as thou knowest how we are to encamp in the wilderness, and thou mayest be to us [R]instead of eyes.

32 And it shall be, if thou go with us, yea, it shall be, that [R]what goodness the LORD shall do unto us, the same will we do unto thee.

33 And they departed from [R]the mount of the LORD three days' journey: and the ark of the covenant of the LORD [R]went before them in the three days' journey, to search out a resting place for them.

34 And [R]the cloud of the LORD *was* upon them by day, when they went out of the camp.

35 And it came to pass, when the ark set forward, that Moses said, [R]Rise up, LORD, and let thine enemies be scattered; and let them that hate thee flee before thee.

36 And when it rested, he said, Return, O LORD, unto the [N]many thousands of Israel.

CHAPTER 11

Israel's complaint

AND [R]*when* the people [N]complained, [N]it displeased the LORD: and the LORD heard *it;* [R]and his anger was kindled; and the [R]fire of the LORD burnt among them, and consumed *them that were* in the uttermost parts of the camp.

2 And the people cried unto Moses; and when Moses [R]prayed unto the LORD, the fire [N]was quenched.

3 And he called the name of the place [N]Tăb'-ĕ-räh: because the fire of the LORD burnt among them.

4 And the [R]mixed multitude that *was* among them [N]fell a lusting: and the children of Israel also [N]wept again, and said, [R]Who shall give us flesh to eat?

5 [R]We remember the fish, which we did eat in Egypt freely; the cucumbers, and the melons, and the leeks, and the onions, and the garlick:

6 But now [R]our soul *is* dried away: *there is* nothing at all, beside this măn'-nă, *before* our eyes.

7 And [R]the măn'-nă *was* as coriander seed, and the [N]colour thereof as the colour of bdellium.

8 *And* the people went about, and gathered *it,* and ground *it* in mills, or beat *it* in a mortar,

---

Center reference column:

CHAP. **10**
BC 1490

12	Ex. 19:1
	ch. 1:1 & 9:5
12	Gen. 21:21
	ch. 12:16
	& 13:3, 26
	Deut. 1:1
13	ver. 5, 6
14	ch. 2:3, 9
14	ch. 1:7
17	ch. 1:51
17	ch. 4:24, 31
18	ch. 2:16
21	ch. 4:4, 15
	& 7:9
21	i.e. *the Gershonites and the Merarites:* See ver. 17
	ch. 1:51
22	ch. 2:24
25	ch. 2:31
	Josh. 6:9
28	ch. 2:34
28	Heb. *These*
29	Ex. 2:18
29	Gen. 12:7

Judg. 1:16	29
Gen. 32:12	29
Ex. 3:8	
Job 29:15	31
Judg. 1:16	32
See Ex. 3:1	33
Deut. 1:33	33
Josh. 3:3, 4, 6	
Ezek. 20:6	
Ex. 13:21	34
Neh. 9:12, 19	
Ps. 68:1, 2	35
& 132:8	
Heb. *ten thousand thousands*	36

CHAP. **11**
BC 1490

Deut. 9:22	1
Or, *were as it were complainers*	1
Heb. *it was evil in the ears of, etc.*	1
Ps. 78:21	1
Lev. 10:2	1
2 Ki. 1:12	
Jas. 5:16	2
Heb. *sunk*	2
i.e. *A burning*	3
As Ex. 12:38	4
Heb. *lusted a lust*	4
Heb. *returned and wept*	4
Ps. 78:18	4
1 Cor. 10:6	
Ex. 16:3	5
ch. 21:5	6
Ex. 16:14, 31	7
Heb. *eye of it as the eye of*	7

and baked *it* in pans, and made cakes of it: and [R]the taste of it was as the taste of fresh oil.

9 And [R]when the dew fell upon the camp in the night, the măn'-nă fell upon it.

Moses' heavy burden

10 Then Moses heard the people weep throughout their families, every man in the door of his tent: and [R]the anger of the LORD was kindled greatly; Moses also was displeased.

11 [R]And Moses said unto the LORD, Wherefore hast thou afflicted thy servant? and wherefore have I not found favour in thy sight, that thou layest the burden of all this people upon me?

12 Have I conceived all this people? have I begotten them, that thou shouldest say unto me, [R]Carry them in thy bosom, as a [R]nursing father beareth the sucking child, unto the land which thou [R]swarest unto their fathers?

13 [R]Whence should I have flesh to give unto all this people? for they weep unto me, saying, Give us flesh, that we may eat.

14 [R]I am not able to bear all this people alone, because *it is* too heavy for me.

15 And if thou deal thus with me, [R]kill me, I pray thee, out of hand, if I have found favour in thy sight; and let me not [R]see my wretchedness.

Seventy elders

16 And the LORD said unto Moses, Gather unto me [R]seventy men of the elders of Israel, whom thou knowest to be the elders of the people, and [R]officers over them; and bring them unto the tabernacle of the congregation, that they may stand there with thee.

17 And I will [R]come down and talk with thee there: and [R]I will take of the spirit which *is* upon thee, and will put *it* upon them; and they shall bear the burden of the people with thee, that thou bear *it* not thyself alone.

18 And say thou unto the people, [R]Sanctify yourselves against to morrow, and ye shall eat flesh: for ye have wept [R]in the ears of the LORD, saying, Who shall give us flesh to eat? [R]for *it was* well with us in Egypt: therefore the LORD will give you flesh, and ye shall eat.

19 Ye shall not eat one day, nor two days, nor five days, neither ten days, nor twenty days;

20 [R]*But* even a [N]whole month, until it come out at your nostrils, and it be loathsome unto you: because that ye have despised the LORD which *is* among you, and have wept before him, saying, [R]Why came we forth out of Egypt?

21 And Moses said, [R]The people, among whom I *am, are* six hundred thousand footmen; and thou hast said, I will give them flesh, that they may eat a whole month.

22 [R]Shall the flocks and the herds be slain for them, to suffice them? or shall all the fish of the sea be gathered together for them, to suffice them?

23 And the LORD said unto Moses, [R]Is the LORD's hand waxed short? thou shalt see now whether [R]my word shall come to pass unto thee or not.

24 And Moses went out, and told the people the words of the LORD, and [R]gathered the seventy men of the elders of the people, and set them round about the tabernacle.

25 And the LORD [R]came down in a cloud, and spake unto him, and took of the spirit that *was* upon him, and gave *it* unto the seventy elders: and it came to pass, *that,* [R]when the spirit rested upon them, [R]they prophesied, and did not cease.

26 But there remained two *of the* men in the camp, the name of the one *was* ĕl'-dăd, and the name of the other Mē'-dăd: and the spirit rested upon them; and they *were* of them that were written, but [R]went not out unto the tabernacle: and they prophesied in the camp.

27 And there ran a young man, and told Moses, and said, ĕl'-dăd and Mē'-dăd do prophesy in the camp.

28 And Joshua the son of Nun, the servant of Moses, *one* of his young men, answered and said, My lord Moses, [R]forbid them.

29 And Moses said unto him, Enviest thou for my sake? [R]would God that all the LORD's people were prophets, *and* that the LORD would put his spirit upon them!

30 And Moses gat him into the camp, he and the elders of Israel.

Quail and the plague

31 And there went forth a [R]wind from the LORD, and brought quails from the sea, and let *them* fall by the camp, [N]as it were a day's journey on this side, and as it were a day's journey on the other side, round about the camp, and as it were two cubits *high* upon the face of the earth.

32 And the people stood up all that day, and all *that* night, and all the next day, and they gathered the quails: he that gathered least gathered ten [R]hō'-mĕrs: and they spread *them* all abroad for themselves round about the camp.

33 And while the [R]flesh *was* yet between their teeth, ere it was chewed, the wrath of the LORD was kindled against the people, and the

LORD smote the people with a very great plague.

34 And he called the name of that place ᴺKĭb'-rōth-hăt-tā'-ă-väh: because there they buried the people that lusted.

35 ᴿ*And* the people journeyed from Kĭb'-rōth-hăt-tā'-ă-väh unto Hă-zē'-rōth; and ᴺabode at Hă-zē'-rōth.

CHAPTER 12

Miriam's and Aaron's jealousy

AND Miriam and Aaron spake against Moses because of the ᴺĒ-thĭ-ō'-pĭ-ăn woman whom he had married: for ᴿhe had ᴺmarried an Ē-thĭ-ō'-pĭ-ăn woman.

2 And they said, Hath the LORD indeed spoken only by Moses? ᴿhath he not spoken also by us? And the LORD ᴿheard *it*.

3 (Now the man Moses *was* very meek, above all the men which *were* upon the face of the earth.)

4 ᴿAnd the LORD spake suddenly unto Moses, and unto Aaron, and unto Miriam, Come out ye three unto the tabernacle of the congregation. And they three came out.

5 ᴿAnd the LORD came down in the pillar of the cloud, and stood *in* the door of the tabernacle, and called Aaron and Miriam: and they both came forth.

6 And he said, Hear now my words: If there be a prophet among you, *I* the LORD will make myself known unto him ᴿin a vision, *and* will speak unto him ᴿin a dream.

7 ᴿMy servant Moses *is* not so, ᴿwho *is* faithful in all ᴿmine house.

8 With him will I speak ᴿmouth to mouth, even ᴿapparently, and not in dark speeches; and ᴿthe similitude of the LORD shall he behold: wherefore then ᴿwere ye not afraid to speak against my servant Moses?

Miriam contracts leprosy

9 And the anger of the LORD was kindled against them; and he departed.

10 And the cloud departed from off the tabernacle; and, ᴿbehold, Miriam *became* ᴿleprous, *white* as snow: and Aaron looked upon Miriam, and, behold, *she was* leprous.

11 And Aaron said unto Moses, Alas, my lord, I beseech thee, ᴿlay not the sin upon us, wherein we have done foolishly, and wherein we have sinned.

12 Let her not be ᴿas one dead, of whom the flesh is half consumed when he cometh out of his mother's womb.

13 And Moses cried unto the LORD, saying, Heal her now, O God, I beseech thee.

14 And the LORD said unto Moses, If her

CHAP. 11
BC 1490
34 i.e. *The graves of lust*
35 ch. 33:17
35 Heb. *they were in, etc.*

CHAP. 12
BC 1490
1 Or, *Cushite*
1 Ex. 2:21
1 Heb. *taken*
2 Ex. 15:20
2 Mic. 6:4
2 Gen. 29:33
ch. 11:1
2 Ki. 19:4
Is. 37:4
Ezek. 35:12, 13
4 Ps. 76:9
5 ch. 11:25 & 16:19
6 Gen. 46:2
Job 33:15
Ezek. 1:1
Dan. 8:2
& 10:8, 16
Luke 1:11
Acts 10:11, 17
& 22:17, 18
6 Gen. 31:10
1 Ki. 3:5
Mat. 1:20
7 Ps. 105:26
7 Heb. 3:2, 5
7 1 Tim. 3:11
8 Ex. 33:11
Deut. 34:10
8 1 Cor. 13:12
8 Ex. 33:19
8 2 Pet. 2:10
Jude 8
10 Deut. 24:9
10 2 Ki. 5:27
& 15:5
2 Chr. 26:19, 20
11 2 Sam. 24:10
Prov. 30:32
12 Ps. 88:4

Lev. 13:46   14
ch. 5:2, 3
Deut. 24:9   15
2 Chr. 26:20, 21
ch. 11:35   16
& 33:18

CHAP. 13
BC 1490
ch. 32:8   2
Deut. 1:22
ch. 12:16 & 32:8   3
Deut. 1:19
& 9:23
ch. 34:19   6
1 Chr. 4:15
ver. 30   6
ch. 14:6, 30
Josh. 14:6,
7, 13, 14
Judg. 1:12
ver. 16   8
ver. 8   16
Ex. 17:9
ch. 14:6
ver. 21   17
Judg. 1:9   17

---

father had but spit in her face, should she not be ashamed seven days? let her be ᴿshut out from the camp seven days, and after that let her be received in *again*.

15 ᴿAnd Miriam was shut out from the camp seven days: and the people journeyed not till Miriam was brought in *again*.

16 And afterward the people removed from ᴿHă-zē'-rōth, and pitched in the wilderness of Pâr'-ăn.

CHAPTER 13

Spies sent to Canaan

AND the LORD spake unto Moses, saying, 2 ᴿSend thou men, that they may search the land of Canaan, which I give unto the children of Israel: of every tribe of their fathers shall ye send a man, every one a ruler among them.

3 And Moses by the commandment of the LORD sent them ᴿfrom the wilderness of Pâr'-ăn: all those men *were* heads of the children of Israel.

4 And these *were* their names: of the tribe of Reuben, Shăm'-mū-ă the son of Zăc'-cùr.

5 Of the tribe of Simeon, Shā'-phăt the son of Hôr'-ī.

6 ᴿOf the tribe of Judah, ᴿCaleb the son of Jĕ-phŭn'-nēh.

7 Of the tribe of ĭs'-să-chär, ī'-găl the son of Joseph.

8 Of the tribe of Ē'-phră-ĭm, ᴿŌ-shē'-ă the son of Nun.

9 Of the tribe of Benjamin, Păl'-tī the son of Rā'-phû.

10 Of the tribe of Zĕ-bū'-lŭn, Găd'-dĭ-ĕl the son of Sō'-dī.

11 Of the tribe of Joseph, *namely,* of the tribe of Mă-năs'-sēh, Găd'-dī the son of Sū'-sī.

12 Of the tribe of Dan, ăm'-mĭ-ĕl the son of Gĕ-măl'-lī.

13 Of the tribe of Asher, Sē'-thùr the son of Michael.

14 Of the tribe of Năph'-tă-lī, Năh'-bī the son of Vŏph'-sī.

15 Of the tribe of Gad, Gĕū'-ĕl the son of Mā'-chī.

16 These *are* the names of the men which Moses sent to spy out the land. And Moses called ᴿŌ-shē'-ă the son of Nun Jĕ-hŏsh'-ū-ă.

17 And Moses sent them to spy out the land of Canaan, and said unto them, Get you up this *way* ᴿsouthward, and go up into ᴿthe mountain:

18 And see the land, what it *is;* and the people that dwelleth therein, whether they *be* strong or weak, few or many;

19 And what the land *is* that they dwell in,

whether it *be* good or bad; and what cities *they be* that they dwell in, whether in tents, or in strong holds;

20 And what the land *is,* whether it *be* ᴿfat or lean, whether there be wood therein, or not. And ᴿbe ye of good courage, and bring of the fruit of the land. Now the time *was* the time of the firstripe grapes.

21 So they went up, and searched the land ᴿfrom the wilderness of Zin unto ᴿRē'-hŏb, as men come to Hā'-măth.

22 And they ascended by the south, and came unto Hē'-brŏn; where ᴿĂ-hī'-măn, Shē'-shăi, and Tăl'-măi, ᴿthe children of Anak, *were.* (Now ᴿHē'-brŏn was built seven years before ᴿZō'-ăn in Egypt.)

23 ᴿAnd they came unto the ᴺbrook of ĕsh'-cŏl, and cut down from thence a branch with one cluster of grapes, and they bare it between two upon a staff; and *they brought* of the pomegranates, and of the figs.

24 The place was called the ᴺbrook ᴺĔsh'-cŏl, because of the cluster of grapes which the children of Israel cut down from thence.

Report of the spies

25 And they returned from searching of the land after forty days.

26 And they went and came to Moses, and to Aaron, and to all the congregation of the children of Israel, ᴿunto the wilderness of Pâr'-ăn, to ᴿKā'-dĕsh; and brought back word unto them, and unto all the congregation, and shewed them the fruit of the land.

27 And they told him, and said, We came unto the land whither thou sentest us, and surely it floweth with ᴿmilk and honey; ᴿand this *is* the fruit of it.

28 Nevertheless ᴿthe people *be* strong that dwell in the land, and the cities *are* walled, *and* very great: and moreover we saw ᴿthe children of Anak there.

29 ᴿThe Ă-măl'-ĕk-ītes dwell in the land of the south: and the Hittites, and the Jĕb'-ū-śītes, and the Amorites, dwell in the mountains: and the Canaanites dwell by the sea, and by the coast of Jordan.

Caleb's favourable report

30 And ᴿCaleb stilled the people before Moses, and said, Let us go up at once, and possess it; for we are well able to overcome it.

31 ᴿBut the men that went up with him said, We be not able to go up against the people; for they *are* stronger than we.

32 And they ᴿbrought up an evil report of the land which they had searched unto the children of Israel, saying, The land, through

---

---

which we have gone to search it, *is* a land that eateth up the inhabitants thereof; and ᴿall the people that we saw in it *are* ᴺmen of a great stature.

33 And there we saw the giants, ᴿthe sons of Anak, *which come* of the giants: and we were in our own sight ᴿas grasshoppers, and so we were ᴿin their sight.

CHAPTER 14

Israel's murmuring

AND all the congregation lifted up their voice, and cried; and ᴿthe people wept that night.

2 ᴿAnd all the children of Israel murmured against Moses and against Aaron: and the whole congregation said unto them, Would God that we had died in the land of Egypt! or ᴿwould God we had died in this wilderness!

3 And wherefore hath the LORD brought us unto this land, to fall by the sword, that our wives and our children should be a prey? were it not better for us to return into Egypt?

4 And they said one to another, ᴿLet us make a captain, and ᴿlet us return into Egypt.

5 Then ᴿMoses and Aaron fell on their faces before all the assembly of the congregation of the children of Israel.

6 ᴿAnd Joshua the son of Nun, and Caleb the son of Jĕ-phŭn'-nēh, *which were* of them that searched the land, rent their clothes:

7 And they spake unto all the company of the children of Israel, saying, ᴿThe land, which we passed through to search it, *is* an exceeding good land.

8 If the LORD ᴿdelight in us, then he will bring us into this land, and give it us; ᴿa land which floweth with milk and honey.

9 Only ᴿrebel not ye against the LORD, ᴿneither fear ye the people of the land; for ᴿthey *are* bread for us: their ᴺdefence is departed from them, ᴿand the LORD *is* with us: fear them not.

10 ᴿBut all the congregation bade stone them with stones. And ᴿthe glory of the LORD appeared in the tabernacle of the congregation before all the children of Israel.

11 And the LORD said unto Moses, How long will this people ᴿprovoke me? and how long will it be ere they ᴿbelieve me, for all the signs which I have shewed among them?

12 I will smite them with the pestilence, and disinherit them, and ᴿwill make of thee a greater nation and mightier than they.

Moses intercedes

13 And ᴿMoses said unto the LORD, Then the Egyptians shall hear *it,* (for thou brought-

est up this people in thy might from among them;)

14 And they will tell *it* to the inhabitants of this land: [R]*for* they have heard that thou LORD *art* among this people, that thou LORD art seen face to face, and *that* [R]thy cloud standeth over them, and *that* thou goest before them, by day time in a pillar of a cloud, and in a pillar of fire by night.

15 Now *if* thou shalt kill *all* this people as one man, then the nations which have heard the fame of thee will speak, saying,

16 Because the LORD was not [R]able to bring this people into the land which he sware unto them, therefore he hath slain them in the wilderness.

17 And now, I beseech thee, let the power of my Lord be great, according as thou hast spoken, saying,

18 The LORD *is* [R]longsuffering, and of great mercy, forgiving iniquity and transgression, and by no means clearing *the guilty,* [R]visiting the iniquity of the fathers upon the children unto the third and fourth *generation.*

19 [R]Pardon, I beseech thee, the iniquity of this people [R]according unto the greatness of thy mercy, and [R]as thou hast forgiven this people, from Egypt even [N]until now.

20 And the LORD said, I have pardoned [R]according to thy word:

21 But *as* truly *as* I live, [R]all the earth shall be filled with the glory of the LORD.

22 [R]Because all those men which have seen my glory, and my miracles, which I did in Egypt and in the wilderness, and have tempted me now [R]these ten times, and have not hearkened to my voice;

23 [R]Surely[N] they shall not see the land which I sware unto their fathers, neither shall any of them that provoked me see it:

24 But my servant [R]Caleb, because he had another spirit with him, and [R]hath followed me fully, him will I bring into the land whereinto he went; and his seed shall possess it.

25 (Now the Ă-măl'-ĕk-ites and the Canaanites dwelt in the valley.) To morrow turn you, [R]and get you into the wilderness by the way of the Red sea.

The punishment

26 And the LORD spake unto Moses and unto Aaron, saying,

27 [R]How long *shall I bear with* this evil congregation, which murmur against me? [R]I have heard the murmurings of the children of Israel, which they murmur against me.

28 Say unto them, [R]*As truly as* I live, saith the LORD, [R]as ye have spoken in mine ears, so will I do to you:

29 Your carcases shall fall in this wilderness; and [R]all that were numbered of you, according to your whole number, from twenty years old and upward, which have murmured against me,

30 Doubtless ye shall not come into the land, *concerning* which I [N]sware to make you dwell therein, [R]save Caleb the son of Jĕ-phŭn'-nēh, and Joshua the son of Nun.

31 [R]But your little ones, which ye said should be a prey, them will I bring in, and they shall know the land which [R]ye have despised.

32 But *as for* you, [R]your carcases, they shall fall in this wilderness.

33 And your children shall [R]wander[N] in the wilderness [R]forty years, and [R]bear your whoredoms, until your carcases be wasted in the wilderness.

34 [R]After the number of the days in which ye searched the land, *even* [R]forty days, each day for a year, shall ye bear your iniquities, *even* forty years, [R]and ye shall know my [N]breach of promise.

35 [R]I the LORD have said, I will surely do it unto all [R]this evil congregation, that are gathered together against me: in this wilderness they shall be consumed, and there they shall die.

Fate of the spies

36 [R]And the men, which Moses sent to search the land, who returned, and made all the congregation to murmur against him, by bringing up a slander upon the land,

37 Even those men that did bring up the evil report upon the land, [R]died by the plague before the LORD.

38 [R]But Joshua the son of Nun, and Caleb the son of Jĕ-phŭn'-nēh, *which were* of the men that went to search the land, lived *still.*

Unsuccessful invasion

39 And Moses told these sayings unto all the children of Israel: [R]and the people mourned greatly.

40 And they rose up early in the morning, and gat them up into the top of the mountain, saying, Lo, [R]we *be here,* and will go up unto the place which the LORD hath promised: for we have sinned.

41 And Moses said, Wherefore now do ye transgress [R]the commandment of the LORD? but it shall not prosper.

42 [R]Go not up, for the LORD *is* not among you; that ye be not smitten before your enemies.

43 For the Ă-măl'-ĕk-ites and the Canaanites *are* there before you, and ye shall fall by the

sword: ᴿbecause ye are turned away from the LORD, therefore the LORD will not be with you.

44 ᴿBut they presumed to go up unto the hill top: nevertheless the ark of the covenant of the LORD, and Moses, departed not out of the camp.

45 ᴿThen the Ă-măl'-ĕk-ītes came down, and the Canaanites which dwelt in that hill, and smote them, and discomfited them, *even* unto ᴿHôr'-măh.

CHAPTER 15

Laws concerning offerings

AND the LORD spake unto Moses, saying, 2 ᴿSpeak unto the children of Israel, and say unto them, When ye be come into the land of your habitations, which I give unto you,

3 And ᴿwill make an offering by fire unto the LORD, a burnt offering, or a sacrifice ᴿin ᴺperforming a vow, or in a freewill offering, or ᴿin your solemn feasts, to make a ᴿsweet savour unto the LORD, of the herd, or of the flock:

4 Then ᴿshall he that offereth his offering unto the LORD bring ᴿa meat offering of a tenth deal of flour mingled ᴿwith the fourth *part* of an hïn of oil.

5 ᴿAnd the fourth *part* of an hïn of wine for a drink offering shalt thou prepare with the burnt offering or sacrifice, for one lamb.

6 ᴿOr for a ram, thou shalt prepare *for* a meat offering two tenth deals of flour mingled with the third *part* of an hïn of oil.

7 And for a drink offering thou shalt offer the third *part* of an hïn of wine, *for* a sweet savour unto the LORD.

8 And when thou preparest a bullock *for* a burnt offering, or *for* a sacrifice in performing a vow, or ᴿpeace offerings unto the LORD:

9 Then shall he bring ᴿwith a bullock a meat offering of three tenth deals of flour mingled with half an hïn of oil.

10 And thou shalt bring for a drink offering half an hïn of wine, *for* an offering made by fire, of a sweet savour unto the LORD.

11 ᴿThus shall it be done for one bullock, or for one ram, or for a lamb, or a kid.

12 According to the number that ye shall prepare, so shall ye do to every one according to their number.

13 All that are born of the country shall do these things after this manner, in offering an offering made by fire, of a sweet savour unto the LORD.

14 And if a stranger sojourn with you, or

whosoever *be* among you in your generations, and will offer an offering made by fire, of a sweet savour unto the LORD; as ye do, so he shall do.

15 ᴿOne ordinance *shall be both* for you of the congregation, and also for the stranger that sojourneth *with you,* an ordinance for ever in your generations: as ye *are,* so shall the stranger be before the LORD.

16 One law and one manner shall be for you, and for the stranger that sojourneth with you.

17 And the LORD spake unto Moses, saying,

18 ᴿSpeak unto the children of Israel, and say unto them, When ye come into the land whither I bring you,

19 Then it shall be, that, when ye eat of ᴿthe bread of the land, ye shall offer up an heave offering unto the LORD.

20 ᴿYe shall offer up a cake of the first of your dough *for* an heave offering: as *ye do* ᴿthe heave offering of the threshingfloor, so shall ye heave it.

21 Of the first of your dough ye shall give unto the LORD an heave offering in your generations.

Atonement for errors

22 And ᴿif ye have erred, and not observed all these commandments, which the LORD hath spoken unto Moses,

23 *Even* all that the LORD hath commanded you by the hand of Moses, from the day that the LORD commanded *Moses,* and henceforward among your generations;

24 Then it shall be, ᴿif *aught* be committed by ignorance ᴺwithout the knowledge of the congregation, that all the congregation shall offer one young bullock for a burnt offering, for a sweet savour unto the LORD, ᴿwith his meat offering, and his drink offering, according to the ᴺmanner, and ᴿone kid of the goats for a sin offering.

25 ᴿAnd the priest shall make an atonement for all the congregation of the children of Israel, and it shall be forgiven them; for it *is* ignorance: and they shall bring their offering, a sacrifice made by fire unto the LORD, and their sin offering before the LORD, for their ignorance:

26 And it shall be forgiven all the congregation of the children of Israel, and the stranger that sojourneth among them; seeing all the people *were* in ignorance.

27 And ᴿif any soul sin through ignorance, then he shall bring a she goat of the first year for a sin offering.

28 ᴿAnd the priest shall make an atonement for the soul that sinneth ignorantly, when he

sinneth by ignorance before the LORD, to make an atonement for him; and it shall be forgiven him.

29 ᴿYe shall have one law for him that ᴺsinneth through ignorance, *both for* him that is born among the children of Israel, and for the stranger that sojourneth among them.

30 ᴿBut the soul that doeth *aught* ᴺpresumptuously, *whether he be* born in the land, or a stranger, the same reproacheth the LORD; and that soul shall be cut off from among his people.

31 Because he hath ᴿdespised the word of the LORD, and hath broken his commandment, that soul shall utterly be cut off; ᴿhis iniquity *shall be* upon him.

Sabbath-breakers

32 And while the children of Israel were in the wilderness, ᴿthey found a man that gathered sticks upon the sabbath day.

33 And they that found him gathering sticks brought him unto Moses and Aaron, and unto all the congregation.

34 And they put him ᴿin ward, because it was not declared what should be done to him.

35 And the LORD said unto Moses, ᴿThe man shall be surely put to death: all the congregation shall ᴿstone him with stones without the camp.

36 And all the congregation brought him without the camp, and stoned him with stones, and he died; as the LORD commanded Moses.

Fringes for reminders

37 And the LORD spake unto Moses, saying,

38 Speak unto the children of Israel, and bid ᴿthem that they make them fringes in the borders of their garments throughout their generations, and that they put upon the fringe of the borders a ribband of blue:

39 And it shall be unto you for a fringe, that ye may look upon it, and remember all the commandments of the LORD, and do them; and that ye ᴿseek not after your own heart and your own eyes, after which ye use ᴿto go a whoring:

40 That ye may remember, and do all my commandments, and be ᴿholy unto your God.

41 I *am* the LORD your God, which brought you out of the land of Egypt, to be your God: I *am* the LORD your God.

CHAPTER 16

Korah's rebellion

NOW ᴿKôr'-ăh, the son of ĭz'-hăr, the son of Kō'-hăth, the son of Levi, and Dā'-thăn and Ă-bī'-răm, the sons of Ē-lī'-ăb,

CHAP. 15
BC 1490
29 ver. 15
29 Heb. *doth*
30 Deut. 17:12
Ps. 19:13
Heb. 10:26
30 Heb. *with
an high hand*
31 2 Sam. 12:9
Prov. 13:13
31 Lev. 5:1
Ezek. 18:20
32 Ex. 31:14, 15
& 35:2, 3
34 Lev. 24:12
35 Ex. 31:14, 15
35 Lev. 24:14
1 Ki. 21:13
Acts 7:58
38 Deut. 22:12
Mat. 23:5
39 See Deut. 29:19
39 Ps. 73:27
& 106:39
Jas. 4:4
40 Lev. 11:44, 45
Rom. 12:1
Col. 1:22
1 Pet. 1:15, 16

CHAP. 16
BC 1471
1 Ex. 6:21
ch. 26:9 & 27:3
Jude 11

ch. 26:9   2
Ps. 106:16   3
Heb. It is *much*   3
for you
Ex. 19:6   3
Ex. 29:45   3
ch. 14:14
& 35:34
ch. 14:5   4
& 20:6
ver. 3   5
Lev. 21:6-8, 12, 15
Ex. 28:1   5
ch. 17:5
1 Sam. 2:28
Ezek. 40:46   5
& 44:15, 16
1 Sam. 18:23   9
Is. 7:13
ch. 3:41, 45   9
& 8:14
Deut. 10:8
Ex. 16:8   11
Ex. 2:14   13
Acts 7:27, 35
Ex. 3:8   14
Lev. 20:24
Heb. *bore out*   14
Gen. 4:4, 5   15
1 Sam. 12:3   15
Acts 20:33

and On, the son of Pē'-lĕth, sons of Reuben, took *men:*

2 And they rose up before Moses, with certain of the children of Israel, two hundred and fifty princes of the assembly, ᴿfamous in the congregation, men of renown:

3 And ᴿthey gathered themselves together against Moses and against Aaron, and said unto them, ᴺYe *take* too much upon you, seeing ᴿall the congregation *are* holy, every one of them, ᴿand the LORD *is* among them: wherefore then lift ye up yourselves above the congregation of the LORD?

4 And when Moses heard *it*, ᴿhe fell upon his face:

5 And he spake unto Kôr'-ăh and unto all his company, saying, Even to morrow the LORD will shew who *are* his, and *who is* ᴿholy; and will cause *him* to come near unto him: even *him* whom he hath ᴿchosen will he cause to ᴿcome near unto him.

6 This do; Take you censers, Kôr'-ăh, and all his company;

7 And put fire therein, and put incense in them before the LORD to morrow: and it shall be *that* the man whom the LORD doth choose, he *shall be* holy: *ye take* too much upon you, ye sons of Levi.

8 And Moses said unto Kôr'-ăh, Hear, I pray you, ye sons of Levi:

9 *Seemeth it but* ᴿa small thing unto you, that the God of Israel hath ᴿseparated you from the congregation of Israel, to bring you near to himself to do the service of the tabernacle of the LORD, and to stand before the congregation to minister unto them?

10 And he hath brought thee near *to him,* and all thy brethren the sons of Levi with thee: and seek ye the priesthood also?

11 For which cause *both* thou and all thy company *are* gathered together against the LORD: ᴿand what *is* Aaron, that ye murmur against him?

12 And Moses sent to call Dā'-thăn and Ă-bī'-răm, the sons of Ē-lī'-ăb: which said, We will not come up:

13 *Is it* a small thing that thou hast brought us up out of a land that floweth with milk and honey, to kill us in the wilderness, except thou ᴿmake thyself altogether a prince over us?

14 Moreover thou hast not brought us into ᴿa land that floweth with milk and honey, or given us inheritance of fields and vineyards: wilt thou ᴺput out the eyes of these men? we will not come up.

15 And Moses was very wroth, and said unto the LORD, ᴿRespect not thou their offering: ᴿI have not taken one ass from them, neither have I hurt one of them.

16 And Moses said unto Kôr'-ăh, ᴿBe thou and all thy company ᴿbefore the LORD, thou, and they, and Aaron, to morrow:

17 And take every man his censer, and put incense in them, and bring ye before the LORD every man his censer, two hundred and fifty censers; thou also, and Aaron, each *of you* his censer.

18 And they took every man his censer, and put fire in them, and laid incense thereon, and stood in the door of the tabernacle of the congregation with Moses and Aaron.

19 And Kôr'-ăh gathered all the congregation against them unto the door of the tabernacle of the congregation: and ᴿthe glory of the LORD appeared unto all the congregation.

Moses' intercession

20 And the LORD spake unto Moses and unto Aaron, saying,

21 ᴿSeparate yourselves from among this congregation, that I may ᴿconsume them in a moment.

22 And they ᴿfell upon their faces, and said, O God, ᴿthe God of the spirits of all flesh, shall one man sin, and wilt thou be wroth with all the congregation?

23 And the LORD spake unto Moses, saying,

24 Speak unto the congregation, saying, Get you up from about the tabernacle of Kôr'-ăh, Dā'-thăn, and Ă-bī'-răm.

The punishment

25 And Moses rose up and went unto Dā'-thăn and Ă-bī'-răm; and the elders of Israel followed him.

26 And he spake unto the congregation, saying, ᴿDepart, I pray you, from the tents of these wicked men, and touch nothing of theirs, lest ye be consumed in all their sins.

27 So they gat up from the tabernacle of Kôr'-ăh, Dā'-thăn, and Ă-bī'-răm, on every side: and Dā'-thăn and Ă-bī'-răm came out, and stood in the door of their tents, and their wives, and their sons, and their little children.

28 And Moses said, ᴿHereby ye shall know that the LORD hath sent me to do all these works; for *I have* not *done them* ᴿof mine own mind.

29 If these men die ᴺthe common death of all men, or if they be ᴿvisited after the visitation of all men; *then* the LORD hath not sent me.

30 But if the LORD ᴺmake ᴿa new thing, and the earth open her mouth, and swallow them up, with all that *appertain* unto them, and they ᴿgo down quick into the pit; then ye shall understand that these men have provoked the LORD.

CHAP. 16
BC 1471

16 ver. 6, 7
16 1 Sam. 12:3, 7
19 ver. 42
Ex. 16:7, 10
Lev. 9:6, 23
ch. 14:10
21 ver. 45
See Gen. 19:17, 22
Jer. 51:6
21 ver. 45
Ex. 32:10 & 33:5
22 ver. 45
ch. 14:5
22 ch. 27:16
Job 12:10
Eccl. 12:7
Heb. 12:9
26 Gen. 19:12, 14
28 Ex. 3:12
John 5:36
28 ch. 24:13
Ezek. 13:17
John 5:30 & 6:38
29 Heb. *as every man dieth*
29 Ex. 20:5 & 32:34
Job 35:15
30 Heb. *create a creature*
30 Job 31:3
Is. 28:21
30 ver. 33
Ps. 55:15

ch. 26:10 & 27:3   31
Deut. 11:6
Ps. 106:17
See ver. 17   32
& ch. 26:11
1 Chr. 6:22, 37
Lev. 10:2   35
ch. 11:1
Ps. 106:18
ver. 17   35
See Lev. 27:28   37
Prov. 20:2   38
Hab. 2:10
ch. 17:10   38
& 26:10
Ezek. 14:8
ch. 3:10   40
2 Chr. 26:18
ch. 14:2   41
Ps. 106:25
Ex. 40:34   42
ver. 19   42
ch. 20:6
ver. 21, 24   45
ver. 22   45
ch. 20:6

31 ᴿAnd it came to pass, as he had made an end of speaking all these words, that the ground clave asunder that *was* under them:

32 And the earth opened her mouth, and swallowed them up, and their houses, and ᴿall the men that *appertained* unto Kôr'-ăh, and all *their* goods.

33 They, and all that *appertained* to them, went down alive into the pit, and the earth closed upon them: and they perished from among the congregation.

34 And all Israel that *were* round about them fled at the cry of them: for they said, Lest the earth swallow us up *also*.

35 And there ᴿcame out a fire from the LORD, and consumed ᴿthe two hundred and fifty men that offered incense.

36 And the LORD spake unto Moses, saying,

37 Speak unto Ĕl-ē-ā'-zär the son of Aaron the priest, that he take up the censers out of the burning, and scatter thou the fire yonder; for ᴿthey are hallowed.

38 The censers of these ᴿsinners against their own souls, let them make them broad plates *for* a covering of the altar: for they offered them before the LORD, therefore they are hallowed: ᴿand they shall be a sign unto the children of Israel.

39 And Ĕl-ē-ā'-zär the priest took the brasen censers, wherewith they that were burnt had offered; and they were made broad *plates for* a covering of the altar:

40 *To be* a memorial unto the children of Israel, ᴿthat no stranger, which *is* not of the seed of Aaron, come near to offer incense before the LORD; that he be not as Kôr'-ăh, and as his company: as the LORD said to him by the hand of Moses.

Ravages of the plague

41 But on the morrow ᴿall the congregation of the children of Israel murmured against Moses and against Aaron, saying, Ye have killed the people of the LORD.

42 And it came to pass, when the congregation was gathered against Moses and against Aaron, that they looked toward the tabernacle of the congregation: and, behold, ᴿthe cloud covered it, and ᴿthe glory of the LORD appeared.

43 And Moses and Aaron came before the tabernacle of the congregation.

44 And the LORD spake unto Moses, saying,

45 ᴿGet you up from among this congregation, that I may consume them as in a moment. And ᴿthey fell upon their faces.

46 And Moses said unto Aaron, Take a censer, and put fire therein from off the altar, and put on incense, and go quickly unto the

congregation, and make an atonement for them: ᴿfor there is wrath gone out from the LORD; the plague is begun.

47 And Aaron took as Moses commanded, and ran into the midst of the congregation; and, behold, the plague was begun among the people: and he put on incense, and made an atonement for the people.

48 And he stood between the dead and the living; and ᴿthe plague was stayed.

49 Now they that died in the plague were fourteen thousand and seven hundred, beside them that died about the matter of Kôr′-ăh.

50 And Aaron returned unto Moses unto the door of the tabernacle of the congregation: and the plague was stayed.

CHAPTER 17

Aaron's rod bears almonds

AND the LORD spake unto Moses, saying, 2 Speak unto the children of Israel, and take of every one of them a rod according to the house of *their* fathers, of all their princes according to the house of their fathers twelve rods: write thou every man's name upon his rod.

3 And thou shalt write Aaron's name upon the rod of Levi: for one rod *shall be* for the head of the house of their fathers.

4 And thou shalt lay them up in the tabernacle of the congregation before the testimony, ᴿwhere I will meet with you.

5 And it shall come to pass, *that* the man's rod, ᴿwhom I shall choose, shall blossom: and I will make to cease from me the murmurings of the children of Israel, ᴿwhereby they murmur against you.

6 And Moses spake unto the children of Israel, and every one of their princes gave him ᴺa rod apiece, for each prince one, according to their fathers' houses, *even* twelve rods: and the rod of Aaron *was* among their rods.

7 And Moses laid up the rods before the LORD in ᴿthe tabernacle of witness.

8 And it came to pass, that on the morrow Moses went into the tabernacle of witness; and, behold, the rod of Aaron for the house of Levi was budded, and brought forth buds, and bloomed blossoms, and yielded almonds.

9 And Moses brought out all the rods from before the LORD unto all the children of Israel: and they looked, and took every man his rod.

10 And the LORD said unto Moses, Bring ᴿAaron's rod again before the testimony, to be kept ᴿfor a token against the ᴺrebels; ᴿand thou shalt quite take away their murmurings from me, that they die not.

11 And Moses did *so:* as the LORD commanded him, so did he.

12 And the children of Israel spake unto Moses, saying, Behold, we die, we perish, we all perish.

13 ᴿWhosoever cometh any thing near unto the tabernacle of the LORD shall die: shall we be consumed with dying?

CHAPTER 18

Duties of priests

AND the LORD said unto Aaron, ᴿThou and thy sons and thy father's house with thee shall ᴿbear the iniquity of the sanctuary: and thou and thy sons with thee shall bear the iniquity of your priesthood.

2 And thy brethren also of the tribe of Levi, the tribe of thy father, bring thou with thee, that they may be ᴿjoined unto thee, and ᴿminister unto thee: but ᴿthou and thy sons with thee *shall minister* before the tabernacle of witness.

3 And they shall keep thy charge, and ᴿthe charge of all the tabernacle: ᴿonly they shall not come nigh the vessels of the sanctuary and the altar, ᴿthat neither they, nor ye also, die.

4 And they shall be joined unto thee, and keep the charge of the tabernacle of the congregation, for all the service of the tabernacle: ᴿand a stranger shall not come nigh unto you.

5 And ye shall keep ᴿthe charge of the sanctuary, and the charge of the altar: ᴿthat there be no wrath any more upon the children of Israel.

6 And I, behold, I have ᴿtaken your brethren the Levites from among the children of Israel: ᴿto you *they are* given *as* a gift for the LORD, to do the service of the tabernacle of the congregation.

7 Therefore ᴿthou and thy sons with thee shall keep your priest's office for every thing of the altar, and ᴿwithin the vail; and ye shall serve: I have given your priest's office *unto you as* a service of gift: and the stranger that cometh nigh shall be put to death.

Portion of the priests

8 And the LORD spake unto Aaron, Behold, ᴿI also have given thee the charge of mine heave offerings of all the hallowed things of the children of Israel; unto thee have I given them ᴿby reason of the anointing, and to thy sons, by an ordinance for ever.

9 This shall be thine of the most holy things, *reserved* from the fire: every oblation of theirs, every ᴿmeat offering of theirs, and every ᴿsin

offering of theirs, and every ᴿtrespass offering of theirs, which they shall render unto me, *shall be* most holy for thee and for thy sons.

10 ᴿIn the most holy *place* shalt thou eat it; every male shall eat it: it shall be holy unto thee.

11 And this *is* thine; ᴿthe heave offering of their gift, with all the wave offerings of the children of Israel: I have given them unto thee, and to thy sons and to thy daughters with thee, by a statute for ever: ᴿevery one that is clean in thy house shall eat of it.

12 ᴿAll the ᴺbest of the oil, and all the best of the wine, and of the wheat, ᴿthe firstfruits of them which they shall offer unto the Lord, them have I given thee.

13 *And* whatsoever is first ripe in the land, ᴿwhich they shall bring unto the Lord, shall be thine; every one that is clean in thine house shall eat *of* it.

14 ᴿEvery thing devoted in Israel shall be thine.

15 Every thing that openeth ᴿthe matrix in all flesh, which they bring unto the Lord, *whether it be* of men or beasts, shall be thine: nevertheless ᴿthe firstborn of man shalt thou surely redeem, and the firstling of unclean beasts shalt thou redeem.

16 And those that are to be redeemed from a month old shalt thou redeem, ᴿaccording to thine estimation, for the money of five shē'-kĕls, after the shē'-kĕl of the sanctuary, ᴿwhich *is* twenty gē'-rähś.

17 ᴿBut the firstling of a cow, or the firstling of a sheep, or the firstling of a goat, thou shalt not redeem; they *are* holy: ᴿthou shalt sprinkle their blood upon the altar, and shalt burn their fat *for* an offering made by fire, for a sweet savour unto the Lord.

18 And the flesh of them shall be thine, as the ᴿwave breast and as the right shoulder are thine.

19 All the heave offerings of the holy things, which the children of Israel offer unto the Lord, have I given thee, and thy sons and thy daughters with thee, by a statute for ever: ᴿit *is* a covenant of salt for ever before the Lord unto thee and to thy seed with thee.

20 And the Lord spake unto Aaron, Thou shalt have no inheritance in their land, neither shalt thou have any part among them: ᴿI *am* thy part and thine inheritance among the children of Israel.

Tithe for the Levites

21 And, behold, ᴿI have given the children of Levi all the tenth in Israel for an inheritance, for their service which they serve, *even*

ᴿthe service of the tabernacle of the congregation.

22 ᴿNeither must the children of Israel henceforth come nigh the tabernacle of the congregation, ᴿlest they bear sin, ᴺand die.

23 ᴿBut the Levites shall do the service of the tabernacle of the congregation, and they shall bear their iniquity: *it shall be* a statute for ever throughout your generations, that among the children of Israel they have no inheritance.

24 But the tithes of the children of Israel, which they offer *as* an heave offering unto the Lord, I have given to the Levites to inherit: therefore I have said unto them, Among the children of Israel they shall have no inheritance.

The heave offering

25 And the Lord spake unto Moses, saying,

26 Thus speak unto the Levites, and say unto them, When ye take of the children of Israel the tithes which I have given you from them for your inheritance, then ye shall offer up an heave offering of it for the Lord, *even* ᴿa tenth *part* of the tithe.

27 And *this* your heave offering shall be reckoned unto you, as though *it were* the corn of the threshingfloor, and as the fulness of the winepress.

28 Thus ye also shall offer an heave offering unto the Lord of all your tithes, which ye receive of the children of Israel; and ye shall give thereof the Lord's heave offering to Aaron the priest.

29 Out of all your gifts ye shall offer every heave offering of the Lord, of all the ᴺbest thereof, *even* the hallowed part thereof out of it.

30 Therefore thou shalt say unto them, When ye have heaved the best thereof from it, ᴿthen it shall be counted unto the Levites as the increase of the threshingfloor, and as the increase of the winepress.

31 And ye shall eat it in every place, ye and your households: for it *is* ᴿyour reward for your service in the tabernacle of the congregation.

32 And ye shall ᴿbear no sin by reason of it, when ye have heaved from it the best of it: neither shall ye ᴿpollute the holy things of the children of Israel, lest ye die.

CHAPTER 19

Water of separation

AND the Lord spake unto Moses and unto Aaron, saying,

2 This *is* the ordinance of the law which the

LORD hath commanded, saying, Speak unto the children of Israel, that they bring thee a red heifer without spot, wherein *is* no blemish, ^R*and* upon which never came yoke:

3 And ye shall give her unto ĕl-ē-ā′-zär the priest, that he may bring her ^Rforth without the camp, and *one* shall slay her before his face:

4 And ĕl-ē-ā′-zär the priest shall take of her blood with his finger, and ^Rsprinkle of her blood directly before the tabernacle of the congregation seven times:

5 And *one* shall burn the heifer in his sight; ^Rher skin, and her flesh, and her blood, with her dung, shall he burn:

6 And the priest shall take ^Rcedar wood, and hyssop, and scarlet, and cast *it* into the midst of the burning of the heifer.

7 ^RThen the priest shall wash his clothes, and he shall bathe his flesh in water, and afterward he shall come into the camp, and the priest shall be unclean until the even.

8 And he that burneth her shall wash his clothes in water, and bathe his flesh in water, and shall be unclean until the even.

9 And a man *that is* clean shall gather up ^Rthe ashes of the heifer, and lay *them* up without the camp in a clean place, and it shall be kept for the congregation of the children of Israel ^Rfor a water of separation: it *is* a purification for sin.

10 And he that gathereth the ashes of the heifer shall wash his clothes, and be unclean until the even: and it shall be unto the children of Israel, and unto the stranger that sojourneth among them, for a statute for ever.

Laws for its use

11 ^RHe that toucheth the dead body of any ^Nman shall be unclean seven days.

12 ^RHe shall purify himself with it on the third day, and on the seventh day he shall be clean: but if he purify not himself the third day, then the seventh day he shall not be clean.

13 Whosoever toucheth the dead body of any man that is dead, and purifieth not himself, ^Rdefileth the tabernacle of the LORD; and that soul shall be cut off from Israel: because ^Rthe water of separation was not sprinkled upon him, he shall be unclean; ^Rhis uncleanness *is* yet upon him.

14 This *is* the law, when a man dieth in a tent: all that come into the tent, and all that *is* in the tent, shall be unclean seven days.

15 And every ^Ropen vessel, which hath no covering bound upon it, *is* unclean.

16 And ^Rwhosoever toucheth one that is slain with a sword in the open fields, or a dead

body, or a bone of a man, or a grave, shall be unclean seven days.

17 And for an unclean *person* they shall take of the ^Rashes^N of the burnt heifer of purification for sin, and ^Nrunning water shall be put thereto in a vessel:

18 And a clean person shall take ^Rhyssop, and dip *it* in the water, and sprinkle *it* upon the tent, and upon all the vessels, and upon the persons that were there, and upon him that touched a bone, or one slain, or one dead, or a grave:

19 And the clean *person* shall sprinkle upon the unclean on the third day, and on the seventh day: ^Rand on the seventh day he shall purify himself, and wash his clothes, and bathe himself in water, and shall be clean at even.

20 But the man that shall be unclean, and shall not purify himself, that soul shall be cut off from among the congregation, because he hath ^Rdefiled the sanctuary of the LORD: the water of separation hath not been sprinkled upon him; he *is* unclean.

21 And it shall be a perpetual statute unto them, that he that sprinkleth the water of separation shall wash his clothes; and he that toucheth the water of separation shall be unclean until even.

22 And ^Rwhatsoever the unclean *person* toucheth shall be unclean; and ^Rthe soul that toucheth *it* shall be unclean until even.

CHAPTER 20

Death of Miriam

THEN ^Rcame the children of Israel, *even* the whole congregation, into the desert of Zin in the first month: and the people abode in Kā′-dĕsh; and ^RMiriam died there, and was buried there.

2 ^RAnd there was no water for the congregation: ^Rand they gathered themselves together against Moses and against Aaron.

3 And the people ^Rchode with Moses, and spake, saying, Would God that we had died ^Rwhen our brethren died before the LORD!

4 And ^Rwhy have ye brought up the congregation of the LORD into this wilderness, that we and our cattle should die there?

5 And wherefore have ye made us to come up out of Egypt, to bring us in unto this evil place? it *is* no place of seed, or of figs, or of vines, or of pomegranates; neither *is* there any water to drink.

6 And Moses and Aaron went from the presence of the assembly unto the door of the tabernacle of the congregation, and ^Rthey fell

CHAP. 19

BC 1471

2 Deut. 21:3
1 Sam. 6:7
3 Lev. 4:12, 21
& 16:27
Heb. 13:11
4 Lev. 4:6
& 16:14, 19
Heb. 9:13
5 Ex. 29:14
Lev. 4:11, 12
6 Lev. 14:4, 6, 49
7 Lev. 11:25
& 15:5
9 Heb. 9:13
9 ver. 13, 20, 21
11 ver. 16
Lev. 21:1
ch. 5:2
& 9:6, 10 & 31:19
Lam. 4:14
Hag. 2:13
11 Heb. *soul of man*
12 ch. 31:19
13 Lev. 15:31
13 ver. 9
ch. 8:7
13 Lev. 7:20
& 22:3
15 Lev. 11:32
ch. 31:20
16 ver. 11

ver. 9   17
Heb. *dust*   17
Heb. *living waters shall be given*   17
Ps. 51:7   18
Lev. 14:9   19
ver. 13   20
Hag. 2:13   22
Lev. 15:5   22

CHAP. 20

BC 1471

ch. 33:36   1
Ex. 15:20   1
ch. 26:59
Ex. 17:1   2
ch. 16:19, 42   2
Ex. 17:2   3
ch. 14:2
ch. 11:1, 33   3
& 14:37
& 16:32, 35, 49
Ex. 17:3   4
ch. 14:5   6
& 16:4, 22, 45

upon their faces: and [R]the glory of the LORD appeared unto them.

The waters of Meribah

7 And the LORD spake unto Moses, saying,

8 [R]Take the rod, and gather thou the assembly together, thou, and Aaron thy brother, and speak ye unto the rock before their eyes; and it shall give forth his water, and [R]thou shalt bring forth to them water out of the rock: so thou shalt give the congregation and their beasts drink.

9 And Moses took the rod [R]from before the LORD, as he commanded him.

10 And Moses and Aaron gathered the congregation together before the rock, and he said unto them, [R]Hear now, ye rebels; must we fetch you water out of this rock?

11 And Moses lifted up his hand, and with his rod he smote the rock twice: and [R]the water came out abundantly, and the congregation drank, and their beasts *also*.

12 And the LORD spake unto Moses and Aaron, Because [R]ye believed me not, to [R]sanctify me in the eyes of the children of Israel, therefore ye shall not bring this congregation into the land which I have given them.

13 [R]This *is* the water of [N]Mĕr′-ĭ-bäh; because the children of Israel strove with the LORD, and he was sanctified in them.

14 [R]And Moses sent messengers from Kā′-dĕsh unto the king of Ē′-dom, [R]Thus saith thy brother Israel, Thou knowest all the travail that hath [N]befallen us:

15 [R]How our fathers went down into Egypt, [R]and we have dwelt in Egypt a long time; [R]and the Egyptians vexed us, and our fathers:

16 And [R]when we cried unto the LORD, he heard our voice, and [R]sent an angel, and hath brought us forth out of Egypt: and, behold, we *are* in Kā′-dĕsh, a city in the uttermost of thy border:

17 [R]Let us pass, I pray thee, through thy country: we will not pass through the fields, or through the vineyards, neither will we drink *of* the water of the wells: we will go by the king's *high* way, we will not turn to the right hand nor to the left, until we have passed thy borders.

18 And Ē′-dom said unto him, Thou shalt not pass by me, lest I come out against thee with the sword.

19 And the children of Israel said unto him, We will go by the high way: and if I and my cattle drink of thy water, [R]then I will pay for it: I will only, without *doing* any thing *else*, go through on my feet.

20 And he said, [R]Thou shalt not go through.

And Ē′-dom came out against him with much people, and with a strong hand.

21 Thus Ē′-dom [R]refused to give Israel passage through his border: wherefore Israel [R]turned away from him.

Death of Aaron

22 And the children of Israel, *even* the whole congregation, journeyed from [R]Kā′-dĕsh, [R]and came unto mount Hor.

23 And the LORD spake unto Moses and Aaron in mount Hor, by the coast of the land of Ē′-dom, saying,

24 Aaron shall be [R]gathered unto his people: for he shall not enter into the land which I have given unto the children of Israel, because [R]ye rebelled against my [N]word at the water of Mĕr′-ĭ-bäh.

25 [R]Take Aaron and ĕl-ē-ā′-zär his son, and bring them up unto mount Hor:

26 And strip Aaron of his garments, and put them upon Ĕl-ē-ā′-zär his son: and Aaron shall be gathered *unto his people,* and shall die there.

27 And Moses did as the LORD commanded: and they went up into mount Hor in the sight of all the congregation.

28 [R]And Moses stripped Aaron of his garments, and put them upon ĕl-ē-ā′-zär his son; and [R]Aaron died there in the top of the mount: and Moses and ĕl-ē-ā′-zär came down from the mount.

29 And when all the congregation saw that Aaron was dead, they mourned for Aaron [R]thirty days, *even* all the house of Israel.

CHAPTER 21

Victory over the Canaanites

AND *when* [R]king âr′-ăd the Canaanite, which dwelt in the south, heard tell that Israel came [R]by the way of the spies; then he fought against Israel, and took *some* of them prisoners.

2 [R]And Israel vowed a vow unto the LORD, and said, If thou wilt indeed deliver this people into my hand, then [R]I will utterly destroy their cities.

3 And the LORD hearkened to the voice of Israel, and delivered up the Canaanites; and they utterly destroyed them and their cities: and he called the name of the place [N]Hôr′-măh.

The serpent of brass

4 And [R]they journeyed from mount Hor by the way of the Red sea, to [R]compass the land

of Ē'-dǫm: and the soul of the people was much ᴺᴺdiscouraged because of the way.

5 And the people ᴿspake against God, and against Moses, ᴿWherefore have ye brought us up out of Egypt to die in the wilderness? for *there is* no bread, neither *is there any* water; and ᴿour soul loatheth this light bread.

6 And ᴿthe LORD sent ᴿfiery serpents among the people, and they bit the people; and much people of Israel died.

7 ᴿTherefore the people came to Moses, and said, We have sinned, for ᴿwe have spoken against the LORD, and against thee; ᴿpray unto the LORD, that he take away the serpents from us. And Moses prayed for the people.

8 And the LORD said unto Moses, Make thee a fiery serpent, and set it upon a pole: and it shall come to pass, that every one that is bitten, when he looketh upon it, shall live.

9 And ᴿMoses made a serpent of brass, and put it upon a pole, and it came to pass, that if a serpent had bitten any man, when he beheld the serpent of brass, he lived.

Israel's victories

10 And the children of Israel set forward, and ᴿpitched in ō'-bōth.

11 And they journeyed from ō'-bōth, and ᴿpitched at ᴺĬ'-jĕ-ăb'-ă-rīm, in the wilderness which *is* before Moab, toward the sunrising.

12 ᴿFrom thence they removed, and pitched in the valley of Zâr'-ĕd.

13 From thence they removed, and pitched on the other side of Arnon, which *is* in the wilderness that cometh out of the coasts of the Amorites: for ᴿArnon *is* the border of Moab, between Moab and the Amorites.

14 Wherefore it is said in the book of the wars of the LORD, ᴺWhat he did in the Red sea, and in the brooks of Arnon,

15 And at the stream of the brooks that goeth down to the dwelling of Ar, ᴿand ᴺlieth upon the border of Moab.

16 And from thence *they went* ᴿto Bēẽr: that *is* the well whereof the LORD spake unto Moses, Gather the people together, and I will give them water.

17 ᴿThen Israel sang this song, ᴺSpring up, O well; ᴺsing ye unto it:

18 The princes digged the well, the nobles of the people digged it, by *the direction of* ᴿthe lawgiver, with their staves. And from the wilderness *they went* to Măt-tā'-năh:

19 And from Măt-tā'-năh to Nă-hăl'-ĭ-ĕl: and from Nă-hăl'-ĭ-ĕl to Bā'-mŏth:

20 And from Bā'-mŏth *in* the valley, that *is* in the ᴺcountry of Moab, to the top of ᴺPĭś'-găh, which looketh ᴿtoward ᴺJĕ-shī'-mǫn.

21 And ᴿIsrael sent messengers unto Sī'-hŏn king of the Amorites, saying,

22 ᴿLet me pass through thy land: we will not turn into the fields, or into the vineyards; we will not drink *of* the waters of the well: *but* we will go along by the king's *high* way, until we be past thy borders.

23 ᴿAnd Sī'-hŏn would not suffer Israel to pass through his border: but Sī'-hŏn gathered all his people together, and went out against Israel into the wilderness: ᴿand he came to Jā'-hăz, and fought against Israel.

24 And ᴿIsrael smote him with the edge of the sword, and possessed his land from Arnon unto Jăb'-bǫk, even unto the children of Ammon: for the border of the children of Ammon *was* strong.

25 And Israel took all these cities: and Israel dwelt in all the cities of the Amorites, in Hĕsh'-bŏn, and in all the ᴺvillages thereof.

26 For Hĕsh'-bŏn *was* the city of Sī'-hŏn the king of the Amorites, who had fought against the former king of Moab, and taken all his land out of his hand, even unto Arnon.

27 Wherefore they that speak in proverbs say, Come into Hĕsh'-bŏn, let the city of Sī'-hŏn be built and prepared:

28 For there is ᴿa fire gone out of Hĕsh'-bŏn, a flame from the city of Sī'-hŏn: it hath consumed ᴿAr of Moab, *and* the lords of the high places of Arnon.

29 Woe to thee, Moab! thou art undone, O people of ᴿChē'-mŏsh: he hath given his sons that escaped, and his daughters, into captivity unto Sī'-hŏn king of the Amorites.

30 We have shot at them; Hĕsh'-bŏn is perished even ᴿunto Dī'-bŏn, and we have laid them waste even unto Nō'-phăh, which *reacheth* unto ᴿMē'-dĕ-bă.

Israel defeats Og

31 Thus Israel dwelt in the land of the Amorites.

32 And Moses sent to spy out ᴿJā-ā'-zĕr, and they took the villages thereof, and drove out the Amorites that *were* there.

33 ᴿAnd they turned and went up by the way of Bā'-shăn: and Og the king of Bā'-shăn went out against them, he, and all his people, to the battle ᴿat ĕd'-rĕ-ī.

34 And the LORD said unto Moses, ᴿFear him not: for I have delivered him into thy hand, and all his people, and his land; and ᴿthou shalt do to him as thou didst unto Sī'-hŏn king of the Amorites, which dwelt at Hĕsh'-bŏn.

35 ᴿSo they smote him, and his sons, and all his people, until there was none left him alive: and they possessed his land.

CHAPTER 22

Balak sends for Balaam

AND ᴿthe children of Israel set forward, and pitched in the plains of Moab on this side Jordan *by* Jericho.

2 And ᴿBalak the son of Zĭp'-pôr saw all that Israel had done to the Amorites.

3 And ᴿMoab was sore afraid of the people, because they *were* many: and Moab was distressed because of the children of Israel.

4 And Moab said unto ᴿthe elders of Mĭd'-ĭ-ăn, Now shall this company lick up all *that are* round about us, as the ox licketh up the grass of the field. And Balak the son of Zĭp'-pôr *was* king of the Moabites at that time.

5 ᴿHe sent messengers therefore unto Bā'-lāam the son of Bē'-ôr to ᴿPē'-thôr, which *is* by the river of the land of the children of his people, to call him, saying, Behold, there is a people come out from Egypt: behold, they cover the ᴺface of the earth, and they abide over against me:

6 Come now therefore, I pray thee, ᴿcurse me this people; for they *are* too mighty for me: peradventure I shall prevail, *that* we may smite them, and *that* I may drive them out of the land: for I wot that he whom thou blessest *is* blessed, and he whom thou cursest is cursed.

7 And the elders of Moab and the elders of Mĭd'-ĭ-ăn departed with ᴿthe rewards of divination in their hand; and they came unto Bā'-lāam, and spake unto him the words of Balak.

8 And he said unto them, ᴿLodge here this night, and I will bring you word again, as the LORD shall speak unto me: and the princes of Moab abode with Bā'-lāam.

9 ᴿAnd God came unto Bā'-lāam, and said, What men *are* these with thee?

10 And Bā'-lāam said unto God, Balak the son of Zĭp'-pôr, king of Moab, hath sent unto me, *saying,*

11 Behold, *there is* a people come out of Egypt, which covereth the face of the earth: come now, curse me them; peradventure ᴺI shall be able to overcome them, and drive them out.

12 And God said unto Bā'-lāam, Thou shalt not go with them; thou shalt not curse the people: for ᴿthey *are* blessed.

13 And Bā'-lāam rose up in the morning, and said unto the princes of Balak, Get you into your land: for the LORD refuseth to give me leave to go with you.

14 And the princes of Moab rose up, and they went unto Balak, and said, Bā'-lāam refuseth to come with us.

15 And Balak sent yet again princes, more, and more honourable than they.

16 And they came to Bā'-lāam, and said to him, Thus saith Balak the son of Zĭp'-pôr, ᴺLet nothing, I pray thee, hinder thee from coming unto me:

17 For I will promote thee unto very great honour, and I will do whatsoever thou sayest unto me: ᴿcome therefore, I pray thee, curse me this people.

18 And Bā'-lāam answered and said unto the servants of Balak, ᴿIf Balak would give me his house full of silver and gold, ᴿI cannot go beyond the word of the LORD my God, to do less or more.

19 Now therefore, I pray you, ᴿtarry ye also here this night, that I may know what the LORD will say unto me more.

20 ᴿAnd God came unto Bā'-lāam at night, and said unto him, If the men come to call thee, rise up, *and* go with them; but ᴿyet the word which I shall say unto thee, that shalt thou do.

Balaam's ass speaks

21 And Bā'-lāam rose up in the morning, and saddled his ass, and went with the princes of Moab.

22 And God's anger was kindled because he went: ᴿand the angel of the LORD stood in the way for an adversary against him. Now he was riding upon his ass, and his two servants *were* with him.

23 And ᴿthe ass saw the angel of the LORD standing in the way, and his sword drawn in his hand: and the ass turned aside out of the way, and went into the field: and Bā'-lāam smote the ass, to turn her into the way.

24 But the angel of the LORD stood in a path of the vineyards, a wall *being* on this side, and a wall on that side.

25 And when the ass saw the angel of the LORD, she thrust herself unto the wall, and crushed Bā'-lāam's foot against the wall: and he smote her again.

26 And the angel of the LORD went further, and stood in a narrow place, where *was* no way to turn either to the right hand or to the left.

27 And when the ass saw the angel of the LORD, she fell down under Bā'-lāam: and Bā'-lāam's anger was kindled, and he smote the ass with a staff.

28 And the LORD ᴿopened the mouth of the ass, and she said unto Bā'-lāam, What have I done unto thee, that thou hast smitten me these three times?

29 And Bā'-laăm said unto the ass, Because thou hast mocked me: I would there were a sword in mine hand, ᴿfor now would I kill thee.

30 ᴿAnd the ass said unto Bā'-laăm, *Am* not I thine ass, ᴺupon which thou hast ridden ᴺever since *I was* thine unto this day? was I ever wont to do so unto thee? And he said, Nay.

31 Then the Lᴏʀᴅ ᴿopened the eyes of Bā'-laăm, and he saw the angel of the Lᴏʀᴅ standing in the way, and his sword drawn in his hand: and he ᴿbowed down his head, and ᴺfell flat on his face.

32 And the angel of the Lᴏʀᴅ said unto him, Wherefore hast thou smitten thine ass these three times? behold, I went out ᴺto withstand thee, because *thy* way is ᴿperverse before me:

33 And the ass saw me, and turned from me these three times: unless she had turned from me, surely now also I had slain thee, and saved her alive.

34 And Bā'-laăm said unto the angel of the Lᴏʀᴅ, ᴿI have sinned; for I knew not that thou stoodest in the way against me: now therefore, if it ᴺdisplease thee, I will get me back again.

35 And the angel of the Lᴏʀᴅ said unto Bā'-laăm, Go with the men: ᴿbut only the word that I shall speak unto thee, that thou shalt speak. So Bā'-laăm went with the princes of Balak.

Balak goes to Balaam

36 And when Balak heard that Bā'-laăm was come, ᴿhe went out to meet him unto a city of Moab, ᴿwhich *is* in the border of Arnon, which *is* in the utmost coast.

37 And Balak said unto Bā'-laăm, Did I not earnestly send unto thee to call thee? wherefore camest thou not unto me? am I not able indeed ᴿto promote thee to honour?

38 And Bā'-laăm said unto Balak, Lo, I am come unto thee: have I now any power at all to say any thing? ᴿthe word that God putteth in my mouth, that shall I speak.

39 And Bā'-laăm went with Balak, and they came unto ᴺKīr'-jăth-hū'-zŏth.

40 And Balak offered oxen and sheep, and sent to Bā'-laăm, and to the princes that *were* with him.

Balaam's first oracle

41 And it came to pass on the morrow, that Balak took Bā'-laăm, and brought him up into the ᴿhigh places of Bā'-ăl, that thence he might see the utmost *part* of the people.

CHAPTER 23

AND Bā'-laăm said unto Balak, ᴿBuild me here seven altars, and prepare me here seven oxen and seven rams.

2 And Balak did as Bā'-laăm had spoken; and Balak and Bā'-laăm ᴿoffered on *every* altar a bullock and a ram.

3 And Bā'-laăm said unto Balak, ᴿStand by thy burnt offering, and I will go: peradventure the Lᴏʀᴅ will come ᴿto meet me: and whatsoever he sheweth me I will tell thee. And ᴺhe went to an high place.

4 ᴿAnd God met Bā'-laăm: and he said unto him, I have prepared seven altars, and I have offered upon *every* altar a bullock and a ram.

5 And the Lᴏʀᴅ ᴿput a word in Bā'-laăm's mouth, and said, Return unto Balak, and thus thou shalt speak.

6 And he returned unto him, and, lo, he stood by his burnt sacrifice, he, and all the princes of Moab.

7 And he ᴿtook up his parable, and said, Balak the king of Moab hath brought me from âr'-ăm, out of the mountains of the east, *saying,* ᴿCome, curse me Jacob, and come, ᴿdefy Israel.

8 ᴿHow shall I curse, whom God hath not cursed? or how shall I defy, *whom* the Lᴏʀᴅ hath not defied?

9 For from the top of the rocks I see him, and from the hills I behold him: lo, ᴿthe people shall dwell alone, and ᴿshall not be reckoned among the nations.

10 ᴿWho can count the dust of Jacob, and the number of the fourth *part* of Israel? Let ᴺme die ᴿthe death of the righteous, and let my last end be like his!

11 And Balak said unto Bā'-laăm, What hast thou done unto me? ᴿI took thee to curse mine enemies, and, behold, thou hast blessed *them* altogether.

12 And he answered and said, ᴿMust I not take heed to speak that which the Lᴏʀᴅ hath put in my mouth?

Balaam's second oracle

13 And Balak said unto him, Come, I pray thee, with me unto another place, from whence thou mayest see them: thou shalt see but the utmost part of them, and shalt not see them all: and curse me them from thence.

14 And he brought him into the field of Zŏ'-phĭm, to the top of ᴺPĭś'-găh, ᴿand built seven altars, and offered a bullock and a ram on *every* altar.

15 And he said unto Balak, Stand here by thy burnt offering, while I meet *the* Lᴏʀᴅ yonder.

16 And the LORD met Bā'-lāam, and ᴿput a word in his mouth, and said, Go again unto Balak, and say thus.

17 And when he came to him, behold, he stood by his burnt offering, and the princes of Moab with him. And Balak said unto him, What hath the LORD spoken?

18 And he took up his parable, and said, ᴿRise up, Balak, and hear; hearken unto me, thou son of Zĭp'-pôr:

19 ᴿGod is not a man, that he should lie; neither the son of man, that he should repent: hath he said, and shall he not do it? or hath he spoken, and shall he not make it good?

20 Behold, I have received commandment to bless: and ᴿhe hath blessed; and I cannot reverse it.

21 ᴿHe hath not beheld iniquity in Jacob, neither hath he seen perverseness in Israel: the LORD his God is with him, ᴿand the shout of a king is among them.

22 ᴿGod brought them out of Egypt; he hath as it were ᴿthe strength of an unicorn.

23 Surely there is no enchantment ᴺagainst Jacob, neither is there any divination against Israel: according to this time it shall be said of Jacob and of Israel, ᴿWhat hath God wrought!

24 Behold, the people shall rise up ᴿas a great lion, and lift up himself as a young lion: ᴿhe shall not lie down until he eat of the prey, and drink the blood of the slain.

25 And Balak said unto Bā'-lāam, Neither curse them at all, nor bless them at all.

26 But Bā'-lāam answered and said unto Balak, Told not I thee, saying, ᴿAll that the LORD speaketh, that I must do?

Balaam's third oracle

27 And Balak said unto Bā'-lāam, ᴿCome, I pray thee, I will bring thee unto another place; peradventure it will please God that thou mayest curse me them from thence.

28 And Balak brought Bā'-lāam unto the top of Pē'-ôr, that looketh ᴿtoward Jĕ-shī'-mon.

29 And Bā'-lāam said unto Balak, ᴿBuild me here seven altars, and prepare me here seven bullocks and seven rams.

30 And Balak did as Bā'-lāam had said, and offered a bullock and a ram on every altar.

CHAPTER 24

AND when Bā'-lāam saw that it pleased the LORD to bless Israel, he went not, as at ᴿother times, ᴺto seek for enchantments, but he set his face toward the wilderness.

2 And Bā'-lāam lifted up his eyes, and he saw Israel ᴿabiding in his tents according to

CHAP. 23
BC 1452
16 ver. 5
ch. 22:35
18 Judg. 3:20
19 1 Sam. 15:29
Mal. 3:6
Jas. 1:17
20 Gen. 12:2 & 22:17
ch. 22:12
21 Rom. 4:7, 8
21 Ps. 89:15
22 ch. 24:8
22 Deut. 33:17
Job 39:10
23 Or, in
23 Ps. 31:19 & 44:1
24 Gen. 49:9
24 Gen. 49:27
26 ver. 12
ch. 22:38
27 ver. 13
28 ch. 21:10
29 ver. 1

CHAP. 24
BC 1452
1 ch. 23:3, 15
1 Heb. to the meeting of enchantments
2 ch. 2:2, etc.

ch. 11:25 2
1 Sam. 10:10 & 19:20, 23
2 Chr. 15:1
ch. 23:7, 18 3
Heb. who had his eyes shut, but now opened 3
See 1 Sam. 19:24 4
Ezek. 1:28
Ps. 1:3 6
Jer. 17:8
Ps. 104:16 6
Jer. 51:13 7
Rev. 17:1, 15
1 Sam. 15:9 7
2 Sam. 5:12 7
1 Chr. 14:2
ch. 23:22 8
ch. 14:9 & 23:24 8
Ps. 2:9 8
Jer. 50:17
Ps. 45:5 8
Gen. 49:9 9
Gen. 12:3 9
Ezek. 21:14, 17 10
ch. 23:11 10
Neh. 13:2
ch. 22:17, 37 11
ch. 22:18 13
Mic. 6:5 14
Rev. 2:14
Gen. 49:1 14
Dan. 2:28

their tribes; and ᴿthe spirit of God came upon him.

3 ᴿAnd he took up his parable, and said, Bā'-lāam the son of Bē'-ôr hath said, and the man ᴺwhose eyes are open hath said:

4 He hath said, which heard the words of God, which saw the vision of the Almighty, ᴿfalling *into a trance,* but having his eyes open:

5 How goodly are thy tents, O Jacob, *and* thy tabernacles, O Israel!

6 As the valleys are they spread forth, as gardens by the river's side, ᴿas the trees of lign aloes ᴿwhich the LORD hath planted, *and* as cedar trees beside the waters.

7 He shall pour the water out of his buckets, and his seed *shall be* ᴿin many waters, and his king shall be higher than ᴿAgag, and his ᴿkingdom shall be exalted.

8 ᴿGod brought him forth out of Egypt; he hath as it were the strength of an unicorn: he shall ᴿeat up the nations his enemies, and shall ᴿbreak their bones, and ᴿpierce *them* through with his arrows.

9 ᴿHe couched, he lay down as a lion, and as a great lion: who shall stir him up? ᴿBlessed *is* he that blesseth thee, and cursed *is* he that curseth thee.

Balaam's fourth oracle

10 And Balak's anger was kindled against Bā'-lāam, and he ᴿsmote his hands together: and Balak said unto Bā'-lāam, ᴿI called thee to curse mine enemies, and, behold, thou hast altogether blessed *them* these three times.

11 Therefore now flee thou to thy place: ᴿI thought to promote thee unto great honour; but, lo, the LORD hath kept thee back from honour.

12 And Bā'-lāam said unto Balak, Spake I not also to thy messengers which thou sentest unto me, saying,

13 ᴿIf Balak would give me his house full of silver and gold, I cannot go beyond the commandment of the LORD, to do *either* good or bad of mine own mind; *but* what the LORD saith, that will I speak?

14 And now, behold, I go unto my people: come *therefore, and* ᴿI will advertise thee what this people shall do to thy people ᴿin the latter days.

15 And he took up his parable, and said, Bā'-lāam the son of Bē'-ôr hath said, and the man whose eyes are open hath said:

16 He hath said, which heard the words of God, and knew the knowledge of the most High, *which* saw the vision of the Almighty, falling *into a trance,* but having his eyes open:

17 ᴿI shall see him, but not now: I shall behold him, but not nigh: there shall come ᴿa Star out of Jacob, and ᴿa Sceptre shall rise out of Israel, and shall ᴺsmite the corners of Moab, and destroy all the children of Sheth. ★

18 And ᴿĒ'-dǫm shall be a possession, Sē'-ĭr also shall be a possession for his enemies; and Israel shall do valiantly.

19 ᴿOut of Jacob shall come he that shall have dominion, and shall destroy him that remaineth of the city.   ★

20 And when he looked on Ăm'-ă-lĕk, he took up his parable, and said, Ăm'-ă-lĕk *was* ᴺthe first of the nations; but his latter end ᴺ*shall be* that he perish for ever.

21 And he looked on the Kē'-nĭtes, and took up his parable, and said, Strong is thy dwellingplace, and thou puttest thy nest in a rock.

22 Nevertheless ᴺthe Kē'-nĭte shall be wasted, ᴺuntil Ăssh'-ŭr shall carry thee away captive.

23 And he took up his parable, and said, Alas, who shall live when God doeth this!

24 And ships *shall come* from the coast of ᴿChĭt'-tĭm, and shall afflict Ăssh'-ŭr, and shall afflict ᴿĒ'-bĕr, and he also shall perish for ever.

25 And Bā'-lāam rose up, and went and ᴿreturned to his place: and Balak also went his way.

CHAPTER 25

Worship of Baal

AND Israel abode in ᴿShĭt'-tĭm, and ᴿthe people began to commit whoredom with the daughters of Moab.

2 And ᴿthey called the people unto ᴿthe sacrifices of their gods: and the people did eat, and ᴿbowed down to their gods.

3 And Israel joined himself unto Bā'-ăl-pē'-ôr: and ᴿthe anger of the Lord was kindled against Israel.

4 And the Lord said unto Moses, ᴿTake all the heads of the people, and hang them up before the Lord against the sun, ᴿthat the fierce anger of the Lord may be turned away from Israel.

5 And Moses said unto ᴿthe judges of Israel, ᴿSlay ye every one his men that were joined unto Bā'-ăl-pē'-ôr.

The zeal of Phinehas

6 And, behold, one of the children of Israel çame and brought unto his brethren a Mĭd-ĭ-ă-nī'-tĭsh woman in the sight of Moses, and in the sight of all the congregation of the children

of Israel, ᴿwho *were* weeping *before* the door of the tabernacle of the congregation.

7 And ᴿwhen Phĭn'-ĕ-hăs, ᴿthe son of Ĕl-ē-ā'-zär, the son of Aaron the priest, saw *it,* he rose up from among the congregation, and took a javelin in his hand;

8 And he went after the man of Israel into the tent, and thrust both of them through, the man of Israel, and the woman through her belly. So ᴿthe plague was stayed from the children of Israel.

9 And ᴿthose that died in the plague were twenty and four thousand.

10 And the Lord spake unto Moses, saying,

11 ᴿPhĭn'-ĕ-hăs, the son of Ĕl-ē-ā'-zär, the son of Aaron the priest, hath turned my wrath away from the children of Israel, while he was zealous ᴺfor my sake among them, that I consumed not the children of Israel in ᴿmy jealousy.

12 Wherefore say, ᴿBehold, I give unto him my covenant of peace:

13 And he shall have it, and ᴿhis seed after him, *even* the covenant of ᴿan everlasting priesthood; because he was ᴿzealous for his God, and ᴿmade an atonement for the children of Israel.

14 Now the name of the Israelite that was slain, *even* that was slain with the Mĭd-ĭ-ă-nī'-tĭsh woman, *was* Zimri, the son of Sā'-lû, a prince of a ᴺchief house among the Simeonites.

15 And the name of the Mĭd-ĭ-ă-nī'-tĭsh woman that was slain *was* Cŏz'-bĭ, the daughter of ᴿZur; he *was* head over a people, *and* of a chief house in Mĭd'-ĭ-ăn.

16 And the Lord spake unto Moses, saying,

17 ᴿVex the Mĭd'-ĭ-ă-nĭtes, and smite them:

18 For they vex you with their ᴿwiles, wherewith they have beguiled you in the matter of Pē'-ôr, and in the matter of Cŏz'-bĭ, the daughter of a prince of Mĭd'-ĭ-ăn, their sister, which was slain in the day of the plague for Pē'-ôr's sake.

CHAPTER 26

Israel's second census

AND it came to pass after the plague, that the Lord spake unto Moses and unto Ĕl-ē-ā'-zär the son of Aaron the priest, saying,

2 ᴿTake the sum of all the congregation of the children of Israel, ᴿfrom twenty years old and upward, throughout their fathers' house, all that are able to go to war in Israel.

3 And Moses and Ĕl-ē-ā'-zär the priest spake with them ᴿin the plains of Moab by Jordan *near* Jericho, saying,

4 *Take the sum of the people,* from twenty years old and upward; as the LORD ^Rcommanded Moses and the children of Israel, which went forth out of the land of Egypt.

5 ^RReuben, the eldest son of Israel: the children of Reuben; Hă′-nŏch, *of whom cometh* the family of the Hă′-nŏch-ītes: of Păl′-lû, the family of the Păl′-lū-ītes:

6 Of Hĕz′-rŏn, the family of the Hĕz′-rŏn-ites: of Căr′-mī, the family of the Căr′-mītes.

7 These *are* the families of the Reubenites: and they that were numbered of them were forty and three thousand and seven hundred and thirty.

8 And the sons of Păl′-lû; Ē-lī′-ăb.

9 And the sons of Ē-lī′-ăb; Něm′-ū-ĕl, and Dā′-thăn, and Ă-bī′-răm. This *is that* Dā′-thăn and Ă-bī′-răm, *which were* ^Rfamous in the congregation, who strove against Moses and against Aaron in the company of Kôr′-ăh, when they strove against the LORD:

10 ^RAnd the earth opened her mouth, and swallowed them up together with Kôr′-ăh, when that company died, what time the fire devoured two hundred and fifty men: ^Rand they became a sign.

11 Notwithstanding ^Rthe children of Kôr′-ăh died not.

12 The sons of Simeon after their families: of ^RNěm′-ū-ĕl, the family of the Něm-ū-ē′-lites: of Jā′-mĭn, the family of the Jā′-mĭn-ites: of ^RJā′-chĭn, the family of the Jā′-chĭn-ites:

13 Of ^RZē′-răh, the family of the Zär′-hītes: of Shā′-ŭl, the family of the Shā-ū′-lites.

14 These *are* the families of the Simeonites, twenty and two thousand and two hundred.

15 The children of Gad after their families: of ^RZē′-phŏn, the family of the Zē′-phŏn-ites: of Hăg′-gī, the family of the Hăg′-gītes: of Shû′-nī, the family of the Shû′-nītes:

16 Of ^Nŏz′-nī, the family of the ŏz′-nītes: of Ē′-rī, the family of the Ē′-rītes:

17 Of ^Răr′-ŏd, the family of the âr′-ō-dites: of Ă-rē′-lī, the family of the Ă-rē′-lites.

18 These *are* the families of the children of Gad according to those that were numbered of them, forty thousand and five hundred.

19 ^RThe sons of Judah *were* Er and ō′-năn: and Er and ō′-năn died in the land of Canaan.

20 And ^Rthe sons of Judah after their families were; of Shē′-läh, the family of the Shē-lā′-nites: of Phär′-ĕz, the family of the Phär′-zītes: of Zē′-räh, the family of the Zär′-hites.

21 And the sons of Phär′-ĕz were; of Hĕz′-rŏn, the family of the Hĕz′-rŏn-ites: of Hăm′-ŭl, the family of the Hăm-ū′-lites.

CHAP. **26**
BC 1452
4 ch. 1:1
5 Gen. 46:8
Ex. 6:14
1 Chr. 5:1
9 ch. 16:1, 2
10 ch 16:32, 35
10 ch. 16:38
See 1 Cor. 10:6
2 Pet. 2:6
11 Ex. 6:24
1 Chr. 6:22
12 Gen. 46:10
Ex. 6:15, *Jemuel*
12 1 Chr. 4:24,
Jarib
13 Gen. 46:10,
Zohar
15 Gen. 46:16,
Ziphion
16 Or, *Ezbon*,
Gen. 46:16
17 Gen. 46:16,
Arodi
19 Gen. 38:2, etc.
& 46:12
20 1 Chr. 2:3

Gen. 46:13   **23**
1 Chr. 7:1
Or, *Phuvah*   **23**
Or, *Job*   **24**
Gen. 46:14   **26**
Gen. 46:20   **28**
Josh. 17:1   **29**
1 Chr. 7:14, 15
Called   **30**
Abiezer,
Josh. 17:2
Judg. 6:11, 24, 34
ch. 27:1 & 36:11 **33**
1 Chr. 7:20,   **35**
Bered
Gen. 46:21   **38**
1 Chr. 7:6

22 These *are* the families of Judah according to those that were numbered of them, threescore and sixteen thousand and five hundred.

23 ^R*Of* the sons of ĭs′-să-chär after their families: *of* Tō′-lă, the family of the Tō′-lā-ītes: of ^NPū′-ă, the family of the Pū′-nītes:

24 Of ^NJăsh′-ŭb, the family of the Jăsh′-ū-bites: of Shĭm′-rŏn, the family of the Shĭm′-rŏn-ites.

25 These *are* the families of ĭs′-să-chär according to those that were numbered of them, threescore and four thousand and three hundred.

26 ^R*Of* the sons of Zē-bū′-lŭn after their families: of Sē′-rĕd, the family of the Sär′-dites: of Ē′-lŏn, the family of the Ē′-lŏn-ites: of Jäh′-lĕel, the family of the Jäh′-lĕel-ites.

27 These *are* the families of the Zē-bū′-lŭn-ites according to those that were numbered of them, threescore thousand and five hundred.

28 ^RThe sons of Joseph after their families *were* Mă-năs′-sēh and Ē′-phră-īm.

29 Of the sons of Mă-năs′-sēh: of ^RMā′-chĭr, the family of the Mā′-chĭr-ites: and Mā′-chĭr begat Gilead: of Gilead *come* the family of the Gileadites.

30 These *are* the sons of Gilead: of ^RJē-ē′-zĕr, the family of the Jē-ē′-zĕr-ites: of Hē′-lĕk, the family of the Hē′-lĕk-ites:

31 And *of* Ăś′-rī-ĕl, the family of the Ăś′-rī-ē-lites: and *of* Shē′-chĕm, the family of the Shē′-chĕm-ites:

32 And *of* Shĕ-mī′-dă, the family of the Shĕ-mī′-dā-ites: and *of* Hē′-phĕr, the family of the Hē′-phĕr-ites.

33 And ^RZē-lŏph′-ĕ-hăd the son of Hē′-phĕr had no sons, but daughters: and the names of the daughters of Zē-lŏph′-ĕ-hăd *were* Mäh′-läh, and Noah, Hŏg′-läh, Mĭl′-cäh, and Tĭr′-zäh.

34 These *are* the families of Mă-năs′-sēh, and those that were numbered of them, fifty and two thousand and seven hundred.

35 These *are* the sons of Ē′-phră-īm after their families: of Shû-thē′-läh, the family of the Shû-thăl′-hites: of ^RBē′-chĕr, the family of the Băch′-rites: of Tā′-hăn, the family of the Tā′-hăn-ites.

36 And these *are* the sons of Shû-thē′-läh: of Ē′-răn, the family of the Ē′-răn-ites.

37 These *are* the families of the sons of Ē′-phră-īm according to those that were numbered of them, thirty and two thousand and five hundred. These *are* the sons of Joseph after their families.

38 ^RThe sons of Benjamin after their families: of Bē′-lă, the family of the Bē′-lā-ites: of

Ăsh'-bĕl, the family of the Ăsh'-bĕl-ītes: of ᴿĂ-hī'-răm, the family of the Ă-hī'-răm-ītes:

39 Of ᴿShū'-phăm, the family of the Shū'-phăm-ītes: of Hū'-phăm, the family of the Hū'-phăm-ītes.

40 And the sons of Bē'-lă were ᴿÄrd and Nā'-ă-măn: of Ärd, the family of the Ärd'-ītes: and of Nā'-ă-măn, the family of the Nā'-ă-mītes.

41 These are the sons of Benjamin after their families: and they that were numbered of them were forty and five thousand and six hundred.

42 ᴿThese are the sons of Dan after their families: of ᴺShū'-hăm, the family of the Shū'-hăm-ītes. These are the families of Dan after their families.

43 All the families of the Shū'-hăm-ītes, according to those that were numbered of them, were threescore and four thousand and four hundred.

44 ᴿOf the children of Asher after their families: of Jĭm'-nă, the family of the Jĭm'-nītes: of Jĕs'-ū-ī, the family of the Jĕs'-ū-ītes: of Bĕ-rī'-ăh, the family of the Bĕ-rī'-ītes.

45 Of the sons of Bĕ-rī'-ăh: of Hē'-bĕr, the family of the Hē'-bĕr-ītes: of Măl'-chĭ-ĕl, the family of the Măl-chĭ-ē'-lītes.

46 And the name of the daughter of Asher was Sarah.

47 These are the families of the sons of Asher according to those that were numbered of them; who were fifty and three thousand and four hundred.

48 ᴿOf the sons of Năph'-tă-lī after their families: of Jäh'-zēĕl, the family of the Jäh'-zēĕl-ītes: of Gū'-nī, the family of the Gū'-nītes:

49 Of Jē'-zĕr, the family of the Jē'-zĕr-ītes: of ᴿShĭl'-lĕm, the family of the Shĭl'-lĕm-ītes.

50 These are the families of Năph'-tă-lī according to their families: and they that were numbered of them were forty and five thousand and four hundred.

51 ᴿThese were the numbered of the children of Israel, six hundred thousand and a thousand seven hundred and thirty.

Land inheritance

52 And the LORD spake unto Moses, saying,

53 ᴿUnto these the land shall be divided for an inheritance according to the number of names.

54 ᴿTo many thou shalt ᴺgive the more inheritance, and to few thou shalt ᴺgive the less inheritance: to every one shall his inheritance be given according to those that were numbered of him.

55 Notwithstanding the land shall be ᴿdivided by lot: according to the names of the tribes of their fathers they shall inherit.

56 According to the lot shall the possession thereof be divided between many and few.

Numbering the Levites

57 ᴿAnd these are they that were numbered of the Levites after their families: of Gĕr'-shŏn, the family of the Gĕr'-shŏn-ītes: of Kō'-hăth, the family of the Kō'-hăth-ītes: of Mĕ-râr'-ī, the family of the Mĕ-râr'-ītes.

58 These are the families of the Levites: the family of the Lĭb'-nītes, the family of the Hē'-brŏn-ītes, the family of the Mäh'-lītes, the family of the Mū'-shītes, the family of the Kŏr'-ă-thītes. And Kō'-hăth begat Amram.

59 And the name of Amram's wife was ᴿJŏch'-ĕ-bĕd, the daughter of Levi, whom her mother bare to Levi in Egypt: and she bare unto Amram Aaron and Moses, and Miriam their sister.

60 ᴿAnd unto Aaron was born Nadab, and Ă-bī'-hū, ĕl-ē-ā'-zär, and Ĭth'-ă-mär.

61 And ᴿNadab and Ă-bī'-hū died, when they offered strange fire before the LORD.

62 ᴿAnd those that were numbered of them were twenty and three thousand, all males from a month old and upward: ᴿfor they were not numbered among the children of Israel, because there was ᴿno inheritance given them among the children of Israel.

Moses, Joshua, and Caleb

63 These are they that were numbered by Moses and ĕl-ē-ā'-zär the priest, who numbered the children of Israel ᴿin the plains of Moab by Jordan near Jericho.

64 ᴿBut among these there was not a man of them whom Moses and Aaron the priest numbered, when they numbered the children of Israel in the wilderness of Sī'-nāi.

65 For the LORD had said of them, They ᴿshall surely die in the wilderness. And there was not left a man of them, ᴿsave Caleb the son of Jĕ-phŭn'-nēh, and Joshua the son of Nun.

CHAPTER 27

Law of inheritance

THEN came the daughters of ᴿZĕ-lŏph'-ĕ-hăd, the son of Hē'-phĕr, the son of Gilead, the son of Mā'-chĭr, the son of Mă-năs'-sēh, of the families of Mă-năs'-sēh the son of Joseph: and these are the names of his daughters; Mäh'-läh, Noah, and Hŏg'-läh, and Mĭl'-căh, and Tĭr'-zăh.

CHAP. 26
BC 1452
38 Gen. 46:21, Ehi
1 Chr. 8:1,
Aharah
39 Gen. 46:21
Muppim and
Huppim
40 1 Chr. 8:3,
Addar
42 Gen. 46:23
42 Or, Hushim
44 Gen. 46:17
1 Chr. 7:30
48 Gen. 46:24
1 Chr. 7:13
49 1 Chr. 7:13,
Shallum
51 See ch. 1:46
53 Josh. 11:23
& 14:1
54 ch. 33:54
54 Heb. multiply
his inheritance
54 Heb. diminish
his inheritance

ch. 33:54   55
& 34:13
Josh. 11:23
& 14:2
Gen. 46:11   57
Ex. 6:16-19
1 Chr. 6:1, 16
Ex. 2:1, 2   59
& 6:20
ch. 3:2   60
Lev. 10:1, 2 61
ch. 3:4
1 Chr. 24:2
See ch. 3:39 62
ch. 1:49   62
ch. 18:20, 23, 24 62
Deut. 10:9
Josh. 13:14, 33
ver. 3   63
ch. 1   64
Deut. 2:14, 15
ch. 14:28, 29 65
1 Cor. 10:5, 6
ch. 14:30   65

CHAP. 27
BC 1452
ch. 26:33   1
& 36:1, 11
Josh. 17:3

2 And they stood before Moses, and before Ĕl-ē-ā'-zär the priest, and before the princes and all the congregation, *by* the door of the tabernacle of the congregation, saying,

3 Our father ᴿdied in the wilderness, and he was not in the company of them that gathered themselves together against the LORD ᴿin the company of Kôr'-ăh; but died in his own sin, and had no sons.

4 Why should the name of our father be ᴺdone away from among his family, because he hath no son? ᴿGive unto us *therefore* a possession among the brethren of our father.

5 And Moses ᴿbrought their cause before the LORD.

6 And the LORD spake unto Moses, saying,

7 The daughters of Zē-lŏph'-ĕ-hăd speak right: ᴿthou shalt surely give them a possession of an inheritance among their father's brethren; and thou shalt cause the inheritance of their father to pass unto them.

8 And thou shalt speak unto the children of Israel, saying, If a man die, and have no son, then ye shall cause his inheritance to pass unto his daughter.

9 And if he have no daughter, then ye shall give his inheritance unto his brethren.

10 And if he have no brethren, then ye shall give his inheritance unto his father's brethren.

11 And if his father have no brethren, then ye shall give his inheritance unto his kinsman that is next to him of his family, and he shall possess it: and it shall be unto the children of Israel ᴿa statute of judgment, as the LORD commanded Moses.

Joshua to succeed Moses

12 And the LORD said unto Moses, ᴿGet thee up into this mount Ăb'-ă-rĭm, and see the land which I have given unto the children of Israel.

13 And when thou hast seen it, thou also ᴿshalt be gathered unto thy people, as Aaron thy brother was gathered.

14 For ye ᴿrebelled against my commandment in the desert of Zin, in the strife of the congregation, to sanctify me at the water before their eyes: that *is* the ᴿwater of Mĕr'-ĭ-băh in Kā'-dĕsh in the wilderness of Zin.

15 And Moses spake unto the LORD, saying,

16 Let the LORD, ᴿthe God of the spirits of all flesh, set a man over the congregation,

17 ᴿWhich may go out before them, and which may go in before them, and which may lead them out, and which may bring them in; that the congregation of the LORD be not ᴿas sheep which have no shepherd.

18 And the LORD said unto Moses, Take

thee Joshua the son of Nun, a man ᴿin whom *is* the spirit, and ᴿlay thine hand upon him;

19 And set him before Ĕl-ē-ā'-zär the priest, and before all the congregation; and ᴿgive him a charge in their sight.

20 And ᴿthou shalt put *some* of thine honour upon him, that all the congregation of the children of Israel ᴿmay be obedient.

21 ᴿAnd he shall stand before Ĕl-ē-ā'-zär the priest, who shall ask *counsel* for him ᴿafter the judgment of Ū'-rĭm before the LORD: ᴿat his word shall they go out, and at his word they shall come in, *both* he, and all the children of Israel with him, even all the congregation.

22 And Moses did as the LORD commanded him: and he took Joshua, and set him before Ĕl-ē-ā'-zär the priest, and before all the congregation:

23 And he laid his hands upon him, ᴿand gave him a charge, as the LORD commanded by the hand of Moses.

CHAPTER 28

Daily offerings

AND the LORD spake unto Moses, saying, 2 Command the children of Israel, and say unto them, My offering, *and* ᴿmy bread for my sacrifices made by fire, *for* ᴺa sweet savour unto me, shall ye observe to offer unto me in their due season.

3 And thou shalt say unto them, ᴿThis *is* the offering made by fire which ye shall offer unto the LORD; two lambs of the first year without spot ᴺday by day, *for* a continual burnt offering.

4 The one lamb shalt thou offer in the morning, and the other lamb shalt thou offer ᴺat even;

5 And ᴿa tenth *part* of an ē'-phäh of flour for a ᴿmeat offering, mingled with the fourth *part* of an ᴿhin of beaten oil.

6 *It is* ᴿa continual burnt offering, which was ordained in mount Sī'-nāi for a sweet savour, a sacrifice made by fire unto the LORD.

7 And the drink offering thereof *shall be* the fourth *part* of an hin for the one lamb: ᴿin the holy *place* shalt thou cause the strong wine to be poured unto the LORD *for* a drink offering.

8 And the other lamb shalt thou offer at even: as the meat offering of the morning, and as the drink offering thereof, thou shalt offer *it,* a sacrifice made by fire, of a sweet savour unto the LORD.

Sabbath offerings

9 And on the sabbath day two lambs of the first year without spot, and two tenth deals of

flour *for* a meat offering, mingled with oil, and the drink offering thereof:

10 *This is* ^Rthe burnt offering of every sabbath, beside the continual burnt offering, and his drink offering.

Monthly offerings

11 And ^Rin the beginnings of your months ye shall offer a burnt offering unto the Lord; two young bullocks, and one ram, seven lambs of the first year without spot;

12 And ^Rthree tenth deals of flour *for* a meat offering, mingled with oil, for one bullock; and two tenth deals of flour *for* a meat offering, mingled with oil, for one ram;

13 And a several tenth deal of flour mingled with oil *for* a meat offering unto one lamb; *for* a burnt offering of a sweet savour, a sacrifice made by fire unto the Lord.

14 And their drink offerings shall be half an hīn of wine unto a bullock, and the third *part* of an hīn unto a ram, and a fourth *part* of an hīn unto a lamb: this *is* the burnt offering of every month throughout the months of the year.

15 And ^Rone kid of the goats for a sin offering unto the Lord shall be offered, beside the continual burnt offering, and his drink offering.

Passover offerings

16 ^RAnd in the fourteenth day of the first month *is* the passover of the Lord.

17 ^RAnd in the fifteenth day of this month *is* the feast: seven days shall unleavened bread be eaten.

18 In the ^Rfirst day *shall be* an holy convocation; ye shall do no manner of servile work *therein:*

19 But ye shall offer a sacrifice made by fire *for* a burnt offering unto the Lord; two young bullocks, and one ram, and seven lambs of the first year: ^Rthey shall be unto you without blemish:

20 And their meat offering *shall be of* flour mingled with oil: three tenth deals shall ye offer for a bullock, and two tenth deals for a ram;

21 A several tenth deal shalt thou offer for every lamb, throughout the seven lambs:

22 And ^Rone goat *for* a sin offering, to make an atonement for you.

23 Ye shall offer these beside the burnt offering in the morning, which *is* for a continual burnt offering.

24 After this manner ye shall offer daily, throughout the seven days, the meat of the sacrifice made by fire, of a sweet savour unto

---

CHAP. **28**

BC 1492

10 Ezek. 46:4
11 ch. 10:10
1 Sam. 20:5
1 Chr. 23:31
2 Chr. 2:4
Ezra 3:5
Neh. 10:33
Is. 1:13, 14
Ezek. 45:17
& 46:6
Hos. 2:11
Col. 2:16
12 ch. 15:4-12
15 ver. 22
ch. 15:24
16 Ex. 12:6, 18
Lev. 23:5
ch. 9:3
Deut. 16:1
Ezek. 45:21
17 Lev. 23:6
18 Ex. 12:16
Lev. 23:7
19 ver. 31
Lev. 22:20
ch. 29:8
Deut. 15:21
22 ver. 15

Ex. 13:6   25
Lev. 23:8
Ex. 23:16   26
& 34:22
Lev. 23:10, 15
Deut. 16:10
Acts 2:1
See Lev.   27
23:18, 19
ver. 19   31

CHAP. **29**

BC 1452

Lev. 23:24   1
ch. 28:11   6
ch. 28:3   6
ch. 15:11, 12   6
Lev. 16:29   7
& 23:27
Ps. 35:13   7
Is. 58:5

---

the Lord: it shall be offered beside the continual burnt offering, and his drink offering.

25 And ^Ron the seventh day ye shall have an holy convocation; ye shall do no servile work.

Pentecost offerings

26 Also ^Rin the day of the firstfruits, when ye bring a new meat offering unto the Lord, after your weeks *be out,* ye shall have an holy convocation; ye shall do no servile work:

27 But ye shall offer the burnt offering for a sweet savour unto the Lord; ^Rtwo young bullocks, one ram, seven lambs of the first year;

28 And their meat offering of flour mingled with oil, three tenth deals unto one bullock, two tenth deals unto one ram,

29 A several tenth deal unto one lamb, throughout the seven lambs;

30 *And* one kid of the goats, to make an atonement for you.

31 Ye shall offer *them* beside the continual burnt offering, and his meat offering, (^Rthey shall be unto you without blemish) and their drink offerings.

CHAPTER 29

Feast of trumpets offerings

AND in the seventh month, on the first *day* of the month, ye shall have an holy convocation; ye shall do no servile work: ^Rit is a day of blowing the trumpets unto you.

2 And ye shall offer a burnt offering for a sweet savour unto the Lord; one young bullock, one ram, *and* seven lambs of the first year without blemish:

3 And their meat offering *shall be of* flour mingled with oil, three tenth deals for a bullock, *and* two tenth deals for a ram,

4 And one tenth deal for one lamb, throughout the seven lambs:

5 And one kid of the goats *for* a sin offering, to make an atonement for you:

6 Beside ^Rthe burnt offering of the month, and his meat offering, and ^Rthe daily burnt offering, and his meat offering, and their drink offerings, ^Raccording unto their manner, for a sweet savour, a sacrifice made by fire unto the Lord.

Day of atonement offerings

7 And ^Rye shall have on the tenth *day* of this seventh month an holy convocation; and ye shall ^Rafflict your souls: ye shall not do any work *therein:*

8 But ye shall offer a burnt offering unto the

LORD *for* a sweet savour; one young bullock, one ram, *and* seven lambs of the first year; ^Rthey shall be unto you without blemish:

9 And their meat offering *shall be of* flour mingled with oil, three tenth deals to a bullock, *and* two tenth deals to one ram,

10 A several tenth deal for one lamb, throughout the seven lambs:

11 One kid of the goats *for* a sin offering; beside ^Rthe sin offering of atonement, and the continual burnt offering, and the meat offering of it, and their drink offerings.

Feast of tabernacles offering

12 And ^Ron the fifteenth day of the seventh month ye shall have an holy convocation; ye shall do no servile work, and ye shall keep a feast unto the LORD seven days:

13 And ^Rye shall offer a burnt offering, a sacrifice made by fire, of a sweet savour unto the LORD; thirteen young bullocks, two rams, *and* fourteen lambs of the first year; they shall be without blemish:

14 And their meat offering *shall be of* flour mingled with oil, three tenth deals unto every bullock of the thirteen bullocks, two tenth deals to each ram of the two rams,

15 And a several tenth deal to each lamb of the fourteen lambs:

16 And one kid of the goats *for* a sin offering; beside the continual burnt offering, his meat offering, and his drink offering.

17 And on the second day *ye shall offer* twelve young bullocks, two rams, fourteen lambs of the first year without spot:

18 And their meat offering and their drink offerings for the bullocks, for the rams, and for the lambs, *shall be* according to their number, ^Rafter the manner:

19 And one kid of the goats *for* a sin offering; beside the continual burnt offering, and the meat offering thereof, and their drink offerings.

20 And on the third day eleven bullocks, two rams, fourteen lambs of the first year without blemish;

21 And their meat offering and their drink offerings for the bullocks, for the rams, and for the lambs, *shall be* according to their number, ^Rafter the manner:

22 And one goat *for* a sin offering; beside the continual burnt offering, and his meat offering, and his drink offering.

23 And on the fourth day ten bullocks, two rams, *and* fourteen lambs of the first year without blemish:

24 Their meat offering and their drink offerings for the bullocks, for the rams, and for

the lambs, *shall be* according to their number, after the manner:

25 And one kid of the goats *for* a sin offering; beside the continual burnt offering, his meat offering, and his drink offering.

26 And on the fifth day nine bullocks, two rams, *and* fourteen lambs of the first year without spot:

27 And their meat offering and their drink offerings for the bullocks, for the rams, and for the lambs, *shall be* according to their number, after the manner:

28 And one goat *for* a sin offering; beside the continual burnt offering, and his meat offering, and his drink offering.

29 And on the sixth day eight bullocks, two rams, *and* fourteen lambs of the first year without blemish:

30 And their meat offering and their drink offerings for the bullocks, for the rams, and for the lambs, *shall be* according to their number, after the manner:

31 And one goat *for* a sin offering; beside the continual burnt offering, his meat offering, and his drink offering.

32 And on the seventh day seven bullocks, two rams, *and* fourteen lambs of the first year without blemish:

33 And their meat offering and their drink offerings for the bullocks, for the rams, and for the lambs, *shall be* according to their number, after the manner:

34 And one goat *for* a sin offering; beside the continual burnt offering, his meat offering, and his drink offering.

35 On the eighth day ye shall have a ^Rsolemn assembly: ye shall do no servile work *therein:*

36 But ye shall offer a burnt offering, a sacrifice made by fire, of a sweet savour unto the LORD: one bullock, one ram, seven lambs of the first year without blemish:

37 Their meat offering and their drink offerings for the bullock, for the ram, and for the lambs, *shall be* according to their number, after the manner:

38 And one goat *for* a sin offering; beside the continual burnt offering, and his meat offering, and his drink offering.

39 These *things* ye shall ^Ndo unto the LORD in your ^Rset feasts, beside your ^Rvows, and your freewill offerings, for your burnt offerings, and for your meat offerings, and for your drink offerings, and for your peace offerings.

40 And Moses told the children of Israel according to all that the LORD commanded Moses.

CHAPTER 30

Law of vows and oaths

AND Moses spake unto ᴿthe heads of the tribes concerning the children of Israel, saying, This *is* the thing which the LORD hath commanded.

2 ᴿIf a man vow a vow unto the LORD, or ᴿswear an oath to bind his soul with a bond; he shall not ᴺbreak his word, he shall ᴿdo according to all that proceedeth out of his mouth.

3 If a woman also vow a vow unto the LORD, and bind *herself* by a bond, *being* in her father's house in her youth;

4 And her father hear her vow, and her bond wherewith she hath bound her soul, and her father shall hold his peace at her: then all her vows shall stand, and every bond wherewith she hath bound her soul shall stand.

5 But if her father disallow her in the day that he heareth; not any of her vows, or of her bonds wherewith she hath bound her soul, shall stand: and the LORD shall forgive her, because her father disallowed her.

6 And if she had at all an husband, when ᴺshe vowed, or uttered aught out of her lips, wherewith she bound her soul;

7 And her husband heard *it,* and held his peace at her in the day that he heard *it:* then her vows shall stand, and her bonds wherewith she bound her soul shall stand.

8 But if her husband ᴿdisallowed her on the day that he heard *it;* then he shall make her vow which she vowed, and that which she uttered with her lips, wherewith she bound her soul, of none effect: and the LORD shall forgive her.

9 But every vow of a widow, and of her that is divorced, wherewith they have bound their souls, shall stand against her.

10 And if she vowed in her husband's house, or bound her soul by a bond with an oath;

11 And her husband heard *it,* and held his peace at her, *and* disallowed her not: then all her vows shall stand, and every bond wherewith she bound her soul shall stand.

12 But if her husband hath utterly made them void on the day he heard *them; then* whatsoever proceeded out of her lips concerning her vows, or concerning the bond of her soul, shall not stand: her husband hath made them void; and the LORD shall forgive her.

13 Every vow, and every binding oath to afflict the soul, her husband may establish it, or her husband may make it void.

14 But if her husband altogether hold his peace at her from day to day; then he estab-

lisheth all her vows, or all her bonds, which *are* upon her: he confirmeth them, because he held his peace at her in the day that he heard *them.*

15 But if he shall any ways make them void after that he hath heard *them;* then he shall bear her iniquity.

16 These *are* the statutes, which the LORD commanded Moses, between a man and his wife, between the father and his daughter, *being yet* in her youth in her father's house.

CHAPTER 31

Vengeance on the Midianites

AND the LORD spake unto Moses, saying, 2 ᴿAvenge the children of Israel of the Mĭd′-ĭ-ă-nites: afterward shalt thou ᴿbe gathered unto thy people.

3 And Moses spake unto the people, saying, Arm some of yourselves unto the war, and let them go against the Mĭd′-ĭ-ă-nites, and avenge the LORD of Mĭd′-ĭ-ăn.

4 ᴺOf every tribe a thousand, throughout all the tribes of Israel, shall ye send to the war.

5 So there were delivered out of the thousands of Israel, a thousand of *every* tribe, twelve thousand armed for war.

6 And Moses sent them to the war, a thousand of *every* tribe, them and Phĭn′-ĕ-hăs the son of ĕl-ē-ā′-zär the priest, to the war, with the holy instruments, and ᴿthe trumpets to blow in his hand.

7 And they warred against the Mĭd′-ĭ-ă-nites, as the LORD commanded Moses; and ᴿthey slew all the ᴿmales.

8 And they slew the kings of Mĭd′-ĭ-ăn, beside the rest of them that were slain; *namely,* ᴿĒ′-vī, and Rē′-kĕm, and Zur, and Hur, and Rē′-bă, five kings of Mĭd′-ĭ-ăn: ᴿBā′-lāam also the son of Bē′-ôr they slew with the sword.

9 And the children of Israel took *all* the women of Mĭd′-ĭ-ăn captives, and their little ones, and took the spoil of all their cattle, and all their flocks, and all their goods.

10 And they burnt all their cities wherein they dwelt, and all their goodly castles, with fire.

11 And ᴿthey took all the spoil, and all the prey, *both* of men and of beasts.

12 And they brought the captives, and the prey, and the spoil, unto Moses, and ĕl-ē-ā′-zär the priest, and unto the congregation of the children of Israel, unto the camp at the plains of Moab, which *are* by Jordan *near* Jericho.

13 And Moses, and ĕl-ē-ā′-zär the priest, and all the princes of the congregation, went forth to meet them without the camp.

14 And Moses was wroth with the officers of the host, *with* the captains over thousands, and captains over hundreds, which came from the ᴺbattle.

15 And Moses said unto them, Have ye saved ᴿall the women alive?

16 Behold, ᴿthese caused the children of Israel, through the ᴿcounsel of Bā'-lāam, to commit trespass against the LORD in the matter of Pē'-ôr, and ᴿthere was a plague among the congregation of the LORD.

17 Now therefore ᴿkill every male among the little ones, and kill every woman that hath known man by lying with ᴺhim.

18 But all the women children, that have not known a man by lying with him, keep alive for yourselves.

Purification of the soldiers

19 And ᴿdo ye abide without the camp seven days: whosoever hath killed any person, and ᴿwhosoever hath touched any slain, purify *both* yourselves and your captives on the third day, and on the seventh day.

20 And purify all *your* raiment, and all ᴺthat is made of skins, and all work of goats' *hair,* and all things made of wood.

21 And Ĕl-ē-ā'-zär the priest said unto the men of war which went to the battle, This *is* the ordinance of the law which the LORD commanded Moses;

22 Only the gold, and the silver, the brass, the iron, the tin, and the lead,

23 Every thing that may abide the fire, ye shall make *it* go through the fire, and it shall be clean: nevertheless it shall be purified ᴿwith the water of separation: and all that abideth not the fire ye shall make go through the water.

24 ᴿAnd ye shall wash your clothes on the seventh day, and ye shall be clean, and afterward ye shall come into the camp.

Division of the booty

25 And the LORD spake unto Moses, saying,

26 Take the sum of the prey ᴺthat was taken, *both* of man and of beast, thou, and Ĕl-ē-ā'-zär the priest, and the chief fathers of the congregation:

27 And ᴿdivide the prey into two parts; between them that took the war upon them, who went out to battle, and between all the congregation:

28 And levy a tribute unto the LORD of the men of war which went out to battle: ᴿone soul of five hundred, *both* of the persons, and of the beeves, and of the asses, and of the sheep:

29 Take *it* of their half, and give *it* unto Ĕl-ē-ā'-zär the priest, *for* an heave offering of the LORD.

30 And of the children of Israel's half, thou shalt take ᴿone portion of fifty, of the persons, of the beeves, of the asses, and of the ᴺflocks, of all manner of beasts, and give them unto the Levites, ᴿwhich keep the charge of the tabernacle of the LORD.

31 And Moses and Ĕl-ē-ā'-zär the priest did as the LORD commanded Moses.

32 And the booty, *being* the rest of the prey which the men of war had caught, was six hundred thousand and seventy thousand and five thousand sheep,

33 And threescore and twelve thousand beeves,

34 And threescore and one thousand asses,

35 And thirty and two thousand persons in all, of women that had not known man by lying with him.

36 And the half, *which was* the portion of them that went out to war, was in number three hundred thousand and seven and thirty thousand and five hundred sheep:

37 And the LORD's tribute of the sheep was six hundred and threescore and fifteen.

38 And the beeves *were* thirty and six thousand; of which the LORD's tribute *was* threescore and twelve.

39 And the asses *were* thirty thousand and five hundred; of which the LORD's tribute *was* threescore and one.

40 And the persons *were* sixteen thousand; of which the LORD's tribute *was* thirty and two persons.

41 And Moses gave the tribute, *which was* the LORD's heave offering, unto Ĕl-ē-ā'-zär the priest, ᴿas the LORD commanded Moses.

42 And of the children of Israel's half, which Moses divided from the men that warred,

43 (Now the half *that pertained unto* the congregation was three hundred thousand and thirty thousand *and* seven thousand and five hundred sheep,

44 And thirty and six thousand beeves,

45 And thirty thousand asses and five hundred,

46 And sixteen thousand persons;)

47 Even ᴿof the children of Israel's half, Moses took one portion of fifty, *both* of man and of beast, and gave them unto the Levites, which kept the charge of the tabernacle of the LORD; as the LORD commanded Moses.

The offering of the officers

48 And the officers which *were* over thousands of the host, the captains of thousands,

CHAP. 31
BC 1452
14 Heb. *host of war*
15 See Deut. 20:14
1 Sam. 15:3
16 ch. 25:2
16 ch. 24:14
2 Pet. 2:15
Rev. 2:14
16 ch. 25:9
17 Judg. 21:11
17 Heb. *a male*
19 ch. 5:2
19 ch. 19:11, etc.
20 Heb. *instrument, or, vessel of skins*
23 ch. 19:9, 17
24 Lev. 11:25
26 Heb. *of the captivity*
27 Josh. 22:8
1 Sam. 30:24
28 See ver. 30, 47 & ch. 18:26

See ver. 42-47   30
Or, *goats*   30
ch. 3:7, 8, 25, 31, 30
36 & 18:3, 4
See ch. 18:8, 19   41
ver. 30   47

and captains of hundreds, came near unto Moses:

49 And they said unto Moses, Thy servants have taken the sum of the men of war which *are* under our ᴺcharge, and there lacketh not one man of us.

50 We have therefore brought an oblation for the LORD, what every man hath ᴺgotten, of jewels of gold, chains, and bracelets, rings, earrings, and tablets, ᴿto make an atonement for our souls before the LORD.

51 And Moses and Ĕl-ē-ā'-zär the priest took the gold of them, *even* all wrought jewels.

52 And all the gold of the ᴺoffering that they offered up to the LORD, of the captains of thousands, and of the captains of hundreds, was sixteen thousand seven hundred and fifty shē'-kĕls.

53 (*For* ᴿthe men of war had taken spoil, every man for himself.)

54 And Moses and Ĕl-ē-ā'-zär the priest took the gold of the captains of thousands and of hundreds, and brought it into the tabernacle of the congregation, ᴿ*for* a memorial for the children of Israel before the LORD.

CHAPTER 32

Reuben and Gad settle Gilead

NOW the children of Reuben and the children of Gad had a very great multitude of cattle: and when they saw the land of ᴿJā'-zĕr, and the land of Gilead, that, behold, the place *was* a place for cattle;

2 The children of Gad and the children of Reuben came and spake unto Moses, and to Ĕl-ē-ā'-zär the priest, and unto the princes of the congregation, saying,

3 Ăt'-ă-rŏth, and Dī'-bŏn, and Jā'-zĕr, and ᴿNimrah, and Hĕsh'-bŏn, and Ĕl-ē-ā'-lĕh, and ᴿShē'-băm, and Nē'-bō, and ᴿBē'-ŏn,

4 *Even* the country ᴿwhich the LORD smote before the congregation of Israel, *is* a land for cattle, and thy servants have cattle:

5 Wherefore, said they, if we have found grace in thy sight, let this land be given unto thy servants for a possession, *and* bring us not over Jordan.

6 And Moses said unto the children of Gad and to the children of Reuben, Shall your brethren go to war, and shall ye sit here?

7 And wherefore ᴺdiscourage ye the heart of the children of Israel from going over into the land which the LORD hath given them?

8 Thus did your fathers, ᴿwhen I sent them from Kā'-dĕsh-bär'-nĕ-ă ᴿto see the land.

9 For ᴿwhen they went up unto the valley of Ĕsh'-cŏl, and saw the land, they discouraged the heart of the children of Israel, that they

should not go into the land which the LORD had given them.

10 ᴿAnd the LORD's anger was kindled the same time, and he sware, saying,

11 Surely none of the men that came up out of Egypt, ᴿfrom twenty years old and upward, shall see the land which I sware unto Abraham, unto Isaac, and unto Jacob; because ᴿthey have not ᴺwholly followed me:

12 Save Caleb the son of Jĕ-phŭn'-nēh the Kē'-nĕz-īte, and Joshua the son of Nun: ᴿfor they have wholly followed the LORD.

13 And the LORD's anger was kindled against Israel, and he made them ᴿwander in the wilderness forty years, until ᴿall the generation, that had done evil in the sight of the LORD, was consumed.

14 And, behold, ye are risen up in your father's stead, an increase of sinful men, to augment yet the ᴿfierce anger of the LORD toward Israel.

15 For if ye ᴿturn away from after him, he will yet again leave them in the wilderness; and ye shall destroy all this people.

16 And they came near unto him, and said, We will build sheepfolds here for our cattle, and cities for our little ones:

17 But ᴿwe ourselves will go ready armed before the children of Israel, until we have brought them unto their place: and our little ones shall dwell in the fenced cities because of the inhabitants of the land.

18 ᴿWe will not return unto our houses, until the children of Israel have inherited every man his inheritance.

19 For we will not inherit with them on yonder side Jordan, or forward; ᴿbecause our inheritance is fallen to us on this side Jordan eastward.

Moses' instructions

20 And ᴿMoses said unto them, If ye will do this thing, if ye will go armed before the LORD to war,

21 And will go all of you armed over Jordan before the LORD, until he hath driven out his enemies from before him,

22 And ᴿthe land be subdued before the LORD: then afterward ᴿye shall return, and be guiltless before the LORD, and before Israel; and ᴿthis land shall be your possession before the LORD.

23 But if ye will not do so, behold, ye have sinned against the LORD: and be sure ᴿyour sin will find you out.

24 ᴿBuild you cities for your little ones, and folds for your sheep; and do that which hath proceeded out of your mouth.

25 And the children of Gad and the children

of Reuben spake unto Moses, saying, Thy servants will do as my lord commandeth.

26 ᴿOur little ones, our wives, our flocks, and all our cattle, shall be there in the cities of Gilead:

27 ᴿBut thy servants will pass over, every man armed for war, before the LORD to battle, as my lord saith.

28 So ᴿconcerning them Moses commanded ĕl-ē-ā´-zär the priest, and Joshua the son of Nun, and the chief fathers of the tribes of the children of Israel:

29 And Moses said unto them, If the children of Gad and the children of Reuben will pass with you over Jordan, every man armed to battle, before the LORD, and the land shall be subdued before you; then ye shall give them the land of Gilead for a possession:

30 But if they will not pass over with you armed, they shall have possessions among you in the land of Canaan.

31 And the children of Gad and the children of Reuben answered, saying, As the LORD hath said unto thy servants, so will we do.

32 We will pass over armed before the LORD into the land of Canaan, that the possession of our inheritance on this side Jordan may be ours.

33 And ᴿMoses gave unto them, even to the children of Gad, and to the children of Reuben, and unto half the tribe of Mă-năs´-sĕh the son of Joseph, ᴿthe kingdom of Sĭ´-hŏn king of the Amorites, and the kingdom of Og king of Bā´-shăn, the land, with the cities thereof in the coasts, even the cities of the country round about.

34 And the children of Gad built ᴿDĭ´-bŏn, and Ăt´-ă-rŏth, and ᴿĂ-rō´-ĕr.

35 And Ăt´-rŏth, Shō´-phăn, and ᴿJă-ā´-zĕr, and Jŏg´-bĕ-häh,

36 And ᴿBĕth-nĭm´-räh, and Bĕth-här´-ăn, ᴿfenced cities: and folds for sheep.

37 And the children of Reuben ᴿbuilt Hĕsh´-bŏn, and ĕl-ē-ā´-lĕh, and Kĭr-jă-thā´-ĭm,

38 And ᴿNē´-bo, and ᴿBā´-ăl-mē´-on, (ᴿtheir names being changed,) and Shĭb´-mäh: and ᴺgave other names unto the cities which they builded.

39 And the children of ᴿMā´-chĭr the son of Mă-năs´-sĕh went to Gilead, and took it, and dispossessed the Amorite which was in it.

40 And Moses ᴿgave Gilead unto Mā´-chĭr the son of Mă-năs´-sĕh; and he dwelt therein.

41 And ᴿJā´-ĭr the son of Mă-năs´-sĕh went and took the small towns thereof, and called them ᴿHā´-vŏth-jā´-ĭr.

42 And Nō´-băh went and took Kē´-năth, and the villages thereof, and called it Nō´-băh, after his own name.

CHAPTER 33

The wilderness journey

THESE are the journeys of the children of Israel, which went forth out of the land of Egypt with their armies under the hand of Moses and Aaron.

2 And Moses wrote their goings out according to their journeys by the commandment of the LORD: and these are their journeys according to their goings out.

3 And they ᴿdeparted from Răm´-ĕ-sĕś in ᴿthe first month, on the fifteenth day of the first month; on the morrow after the passover the children of Israel went out ᴿwith an high hand in the sight of all the Egyptians.

4 For the Egyptians buried all their firstborn, ᴿwhich the LORD had smitten among them: ᴿupon their gods also the LORD executed judgments.

5 ᴿAnd the children of Israel removed from Răm´-ĕ-sĕś, and pitched in Sŭc´-cŏth.

6 And they departed from ᴿSŭc´-cŏth, and pitched in Ē´-thăm, which is in the edge of the wilderness.

7 And ᴿthey removed from Ē´-thăm, and turned again unto Pĭ-hă-hī´-rŏth, which is before Bā´-ăl-zē´-phŏn: and they pitched before Mĭg´-dŏl.

8 And they departed from before Pĭ-hă-hī´-rŏth, and ᴿpassed through the midst of the sea into the wilderness, and went three days´ journey in the wilderness of Ē´-thăm, and pitched in Mâr´-äh.

9 And they removed from Mâr´-äh, and ᴿcame unto Ē´-lĭm: and in Ē´-lĭm were twelve fountains of water, and threescore and ten palm trees; and they pitched there.

10 And they removed from Ē´-lĭm, and encamped by the Red sea.

11 And they removed from the Red sea, and encamped in the ᴿwilderness of Sin.

12 And they took their journey out of the wilderness of Sin, and encamped in Dŏph´-kăh.

13 And they departed from Dŏph´-kăh, and encamped in Ā´-lŭsh.

14 And they removed from Ā´-lŭsh, and encamped at ᴿRĕph´-ĭ-dĭm, where was no water for the people to drink.

15 And they departed from Rĕph´-ĭ-dĭm, and pitched in the ᴿwilderness of Sĭ´-nâi.

16 And they removed from the desert of Sĭ´-nâi, and pitched ᴿat ᴺKĭb´-rŏth-hăt-tā´-ă-văh.

17 And they departed from Kĭb´-rŏth-hăt-tā´-ă-văh, and ᴿencamped at Hă-zē´-rŏth.

18 And they departed from Hă-zē´-rŏth, and pitched in ᴿRĭth´-mäh.

19 And they departed from Rĭth′-măh, and pitched at Rĭm′-mŏn-pâr′-ĕz.

20 And they departed from Rĭm′-mŏn-pâr′-ĕz, and pitched in Lĭb′-năh.

21 And they removed from Lĭb′-năh, and pitched at Rĭs′-săh.

22 And they journeyed from Rĭs′-săh, and pitched in Kē-hĕ-lā′-thăh.

23 And they went from Kē-hĕ-lā′-thăh, and pitched in mount Shā′-phĕr.

24 And they removed from mount Shā′-phĕr, and encamped in Hă-rā′-dăh.

25 And they removed from Hă-rā′-dăh, and pitched in Măk-hē′-lŏth.

26 And they removed from Măk-hē′-lŏth, and encamped at Tā′-hăth.

27 And they departed from Tā′-hăth, and pitched at Târ′-ăh.

28 And they removed from Târ′-ăh, and pitched in Mĭth′-căh.

29 And they went from Mĭth′-căh, and pitched in Hăsh-mō′-năh.

30 And they departed from Hăsh-mō′-năh, and ᴿencamped at Mō′-sĕ-rŏth.

31 And they departed from Mō′-sĕ-rŏth, and pitched in Bĕn′-ĕ-jā′-ă-kăn.

32 And they removed from ᴿBĕn′-ĕ-jā′-ă-kăn, and ᴿencamped at Hôr-hă-gĭd′-găd.

33 And they went from Hôr-hă-gĭd′-găd, and pitched in Jŏt′-bă-thăh.

34 And they removed from Jŏt′-bă-thăh, and encamped at Ĕb-rō′-năh.

35 And they departed from Ĕb-rō′-năh, ᴿand encamped at Ē′-zĭ-ŏn-gā′-bĕr.

36 And they removed from Ē′-zĭ-ŏn-gā′-bĕr, and pitched in the ᴿwilderness of Zin, which is Kā′-dĕsh.

37 And they removed from ᴿKā′-dĕsh, and pitched in mount Hor, in the edge of the land of Ē′-dǫm.

38 And ᴿAaron the priest went up into mount Hor at the commandment of the LORD, and died there, in the fortieth year after the children of Israel were come out of the land of Egypt, in the first day of the fifth month.

39 And Aaron was an hundred and twenty and three years old when he died in mount Hor.

40 And ᴿking âr′-ăd the Canaanite, which dwelt in the south in the land of Canaan, heard of the coming of the children of Israel.

41 And they departed from mount ᴿHor, and pitched in Zăl-mō′-năh.

42 And they departed from Zăl-mō′-năh, and pitched in Pū′-nŏn.

43 And they departed from Pū′-nŏn, and ᴿpitched in Ō′-bŏth.

CHAP. **33**

BC 1490

30 Deut. 10:6
32 See Gen. 36:27
Deut. 10:6
1 Chr. 1:42
32 Deut. 10:7
35 Deut. 2:8
1 Ki. 9:26
& 22:48
36 ch. 20:1 & 27:14
37 ch. 20:22, 23
& 21:4
38 ch. 20:25, 28
Deut. 10:6
& 32:50
40 ch. 21:1, etc.
41 ch. 21:4
43 ch. 21:10

ch. 21:11   44
ch. 21:11   44
Or, *Heaps*   44
of Abarim
ch. 32:34   45
Jer. 48:22   46
Ezek. 6:14
ch. 21:20   47
Deut. 32:49
ch. 22:1   48
ch. 25:1   49
Josh. 2:1
Or, *The plains*   49
of Shittim
Deut. 7:1, 2   51
& 9:1
Josh. 3:17
Ex. 23:24, 33   52
& 34:13
Deut. 7:2, 5 & 12:3
Josh. 11:12
Judg. 2:2
ch. 26:53-55   54
Heb. *multiply*   54
his inheritance
Heb. *diminish*   54
his inheritance
Josh. 23:13   55
Judg. 2:3
Ps. 106:34, 36

CHAP. **34**

BC 1452

Gen. 17:8   2
Deut. 1:7
Ps. 78:55
Ezek. 47:14

---

44 And ᴿthey departed from Ō′-bŏth, and pitched in ᴿĬ′-jĕ-ăb′-ă-rĭm,ᴺ in the border of Moab.

45 And they departed from Ĭ′-ĭm, and pitched ᴿin Dī′-bŏn-găd.

46 And they removed from Dī′-bŏn-găd, and encamped in Ăl′-mŏnᴿ–dĭb-lă-thā′-ĭm.

47 And they removed from Ăl′-mŏn–dĭb-lă-thā′-ĭm, ᴿand pitched in the mountains of Ăb′-ă-rĭm, before Nē′-bō.

48 And they departed from the mountains of Ăb′-ă-rĭm, and ᴿpitched in the plains of Moab by Jordan *near* Jericho.

49 And they pitched by Jordan, from Bĕth-jĕs′-ĭ-mŏth *even* unto ᴿĀ′-bĕl-shĭt′-tĭmᴺ in the plains of Moab.

Canaanites to be expelled

50 And the LORD spake unto Moses in the plains of Moab by Jordan *near* Jericho, saying,

51 Speak unto the children of Israel, and say unto them, ᴿWhen ye are passed over Jordan into the land of Canaan;

52 ᴿThen ye shall drive out all the inhabitants of the land from before you, and destroy all their pictures, and destroy all their molten images, and quite pluck down all their high places:

53 And ye shall dispossess *the inhabitants of* the land, and dwell therein: for I have given you the land to possess it.

54 And ᴿye shall divide the land by lot for an inheritance among your families: *and* to the more ye shall ᴺgive the more inheritance, and to the fewer ye shall ᴺgive the less inheritance: every man's *inheritance* shall be in the place where his lot falleth; according to the tribes of your fathers ye shall inherit.

55 But if ye will not drive out the inhabitants of the land from before you; then it shall come to pass, that those which ye let remain of them *shall be* ᴿpricks in your eyes, and thorns in your sides, and shall vex you in the land wherein ye dwell.

56 Moreover it shall come to pass, *that* I shall do unto you, as I thought to do unto them.

CHAPTER 34

Boundaries of Canaan

AND the LORD spake unto Moses, saying, 2 Command the children of Israel, and say unto them, When ye come into ᴿthe land of Canaan; (this *is* the land that shall fall unto you for an inheritance, *even* the land of Canaan with the coasts thereof:)

3 Then ᴿyour south quarter shall be from the wilderness of Zin along by the coast of Ē′-dǫm, and your south border shall be the outmost coast of ᴿthe salt sea eastward:

4 And your border shall turn from the south ᴿto the ascent of Ăk-răb′-bĭm, and pass on to Zin: and the going forth thereof shall be from the south ᴿto Kā′-dĕsh-băr′-nĕ-ă, and shall go on to ᴿHā′-zär-ăd′-där, and pass on to Ăz′-mŏn:

5 And the border shall fetch a compass from Ăz′-mŏn ᴿunto the river of Egypt, and the goings out of it shall be at the sea.

6 And *as for* the western border, ye shall even have the great sea for a border: this shall be your west border.

7 And this shall be your north border: from the great sea ye shall point out for you ᴿmount Hor:

8 From mount Hor ye shall point out *your border* ᴿunto the entrance of Hā′-măth; and the goings forth of the border shall be to ᴿZē′-dăd:

9 And the border shall go on to Zĭph′-rŏn, and the goings out of it shall be at ᴿHā′-zär-ē′-năn: this shall be your north border.

10 And ye shall point out your east border from Hā′-zär-ē′-năn to Shē′-phăm:

11 And the coast shall go down from Shē′-phăm ᴿto Rĭb′-lăh, on the east side of Ā′-ĭn; and the border shall descend, and shall reach unto the ᴺside of the sea ᴿof Chĭn′-nĕ-rĕth eastward:

12 And the border shall go down to Jordan, and the goings out of it shall be at ᴿthe salt sea: this shall be your land with the coasts thereof round about.

13 And Moses commanded the children of Israel, saying, ᴿThis *is* the land which ye shall inherit by lot, which the LORD commanded to give unto the nine tribes, and to the half tribe:

14 ᴿFor the tribe of the children of Reuben according to the house of their fathers, and the tribe of the children of Gad according to the house of their fathers, have received *their inheritance;* and half the tribe of Mă-năs′-sēh have received their inheritance:

15 The two tribes and the half tribe have received their inheritance on this side Jordan *near* Jericho eastward, toward the sunrising.

Princes to partition it

16 And the LORD spake unto Moses, saying,

17 These *are* the names of the men which shall divide the land unto you: ᴿĔl-ē-ā′-zär the priest, and Joshua the son of Nun.

CHAP. 34
BC 1452

3 Josh. 15:1
See Ezek. 47:13, etc.
3 Gen. 14:3
Josh. 15:2
4 Josh. 15:3
4 ch. 13:26 & 32:8
4 See Josh. 15:3, 4
5 Gen. 15:18
Josh. 15:4, 47
1 Ki. 8:65
Is. 27:12
7 ch. 33:37
8 ch. 13:21
2 Ki. 14:25
8 Ezek. 47:15
9 Ezek. 47:17
11 2 Ki. 23:33
Jer. 39:5, 6
11 Heb. *shoulder*
11 Deut. 3:17
Josh. 11:2 & 19:35
Mat. 14:34
Luke 5:1
12 ver. 3
13 ver. 1
Josh. 14:1, 2
14 ch. 32:33
Josh. 14:2
17 Josh. 14:1 & 19:51

ch. 1:4, 16   18

CHAP. 35
BC 1451

See ch. 33:50   1
Josh. 14:3, 4 & 21:2   2
See Ezek. 45:1, etc. & 48:8, etc.
See Lev. 25:34   2

---

18 And ye shall take one ᴿprince of every tribe, to divide the land by inheritance.

19 And the names of the men *are* these: Of the tribe of Judah, Caleb the son of Jĕ-phŭn′-nēh.

20 And of the tribe of the children of Simeon, Shē-mū′-ĕl the son of Ăm′-mĭ-hŭd.

21 Of the tribe of Benjamin, Ē-lī′-dăd the son of Chĭs′-lŏn.

22 And the prince of the tribe of the children of Dan, Bŭk′-kī the son of Jŏg′-lī.

23 The prince of the children of Joseph, for the tribe of the children of Mă-năs′-sēh, Hăn′-nĭ-ĕl the son of Ē′-phŏd.

24 And the prince of the tribe of the children of Ē′-phră-ĭm, Kĕ-mū′-ĕl the son of Shĭph′-tăn.

25 And the prince of the tribe of the children of Zĕ-bū′-lŭn, Ē-lī-zā′-phăn the son of Pär′-năch.

26 And the prince of the tribe of the children of Ĭs′-să-chär, Păl′-tī-ĕl the son of Azzan.

27 And the prince of the tribe of the children of Asher, Ă-hī′-hŭd the son of Shē-lō′-mī.

28 And the prince of the tribe of the children of Năph′-tă-lī, Pĕ-dăh′-ĕl the son of Ăm′-mĭ-hŭd.

29 These *are they* whom the LORD commanded to divide the inheritance unto the children of Israel in the land of Canaan.

CHAPTER 35

Levites' inheritance

AND the LORD spake unto Moses in ᴿthe plains of Moab by Jordan *near* Jericho, saying,

2 ᴿCommand the children of Israel, that they give unto the Levites of the inheritance of their possession cities to dwell in; and ye shall give *also* unto the Levites ᴿsuburbs for the cities round about them.

3 And the cities shall they have to dwell in; and the suburbs of them shall be for their cattle, and for their goods, and for all their beasts.

4 And the suburbs of the cities, which ye shall give unto the Levites, *shall reach* from the wall of the city and outward a thousand cubits round about.

5 And ye shall measure from without the city on the east side two thousand cubits, and on the south side two thousand cubits, and on the west side two thousand cubits, and on the north side two thousand cubits; and the city *shall be* in the midst: this shall be to them the suburbs of the cities.

6 And among the cities which ye shall give unto the Levites *there shall be* [R]six cities for refuge, which ye shall appoint for the manslayer, that he may flee thither: and [N]to them ye shall add forty and two cities.

7 *So* all the cities which ye shall give to the Levites *shall be* [R]forty and eight cities: them *shall ye give* with their suburbs.

8 And the cities which ye shall give *shall be* [R]of the possession of the children of Israel: [R]from *them that have* many ye shall give many; but from *them that have* few ye shall give few: every one shall give of his cities unto the Levites according to his inheritance which [N]he inheriteth.

Cities of refuge

9 And the LORD spake unto Moses, saying,

10 Speak unto the children of Israel, and say unto them, [R]When ye be come over Jordan into the land of Canaan;

11 Then [R]ye shall appoint you cities to be cities of refuge for you; that the slayer may flee thither, which killeth any person [N]at unawares.

12 [R]And they shall be unto you cities for refuge from the avenger; that the manslayer die not, until he stand before the congregation in judgment.

13 And of these cities which ye shall give [R]six cities shall ye have for refuge.

14 [R]Ye shall give three cities on this side Jordan, and three cities shall ye give in the land of Canaan, *which* shall be cities of refuge.

15 These six cities shall be a refuge, *both* for the children of Israel, and [R]for the stranger, and for the sojourner among them: that every one that killeth any person unawares may flee thither.

16 [R]And if he smite him with an instrument of iron, so that he die, he *is* a murderer: the murderer shall surely be put to death.

17 And if he smite him [N]with throwing a stone, wherewith he may die, and he die, he *is* a murderer: the murderer shall surely be put to death.

18 Or *if* he smite him with an hand weapon of wood, wherewith he may die, and he die, he *is* a murderer: the murderer shall surely be put to death.

19 [R]The revenger of blood himself shall slay the murderer: when he meeteth him, he shall slay him.

20 But [R]if he thrust him of hatred, or hurl at him [R]by laying of wait, that he die;

21 Or in enmity smite him with his hand,

that he die: he that smote *him* shall surely be put to death; *for* he *is* a murderer: the revenger of blood shall slay the murderer, when he meeteth him.

22 But if he thrust him suddenly [R]without enmity, or have cast upon him any thing without laying of wait,

23 Or with any stone, wherewith a man may die, seeing *him* not, and cast *it* upon him, that he die, and *was* not his enemy, neither sought his harm:

24 Then [R]the congregation shall judge between the slayer and the revenger of blood according to these judgments:

25 And the congregation shall deliver the slayer out of the hand of the revenger of blood, and the congregation shall restore him to the city of his refuge, whither he was fled: and [R]he shall abide in it unto the death of the high priest, [R]which was anointed with the holy oil.

26 But if the slayer shall at any time come without the border of the city of his refuge, whither he was fled;

27 And the revenger of blood find him without the borders of the city of his refuge, and the revenger of blood kill the slayer; [N]he shall not be guilty of blood:

28 Because he should have remained in the city of his refuge until the death of the high priest: but after the death of the high priest the slayer shall return into the land of his possession.

Laws of murder

29 So these *things* shall be for [R]a statute of judgment unto you throughout your generations in all your dwellings.

30 Whoso killeth any person, the murderer shall be put to death by the [R]mouth of witnesses: but one witness shall not testify against any person *to cause him* to die.

31 Moreover ye shall take no satisfaction for the life of a murderer, which *is* [N]guilty of death: but he shall be surely put to death.

32 And ye shall take no satisfaction for him that is fled to the city of his refuge, that he should come again to dwell in the land, until the death of the priest.

33 So ye shall not pollute the land wherein ye *are*: for blood [R]it defileth the land: and [N]the land cannot be cleansed of the blood that is shed therein, but [R]by the blood of him that shed it.

34 [R]Defile not therefore the land which ye shall inhabit, wherein I dwell: for [R]I the LORD dwell among the children of Israel.

CHAPTER 36

Marriage of heiresses

AND the chief fathers of the families of the ᴿchildren of Gilead, the son of Mā'-chĭr, the son of Mă-năs'-sēh, of the families of the sons of Joseph, came near, and spake before Moses, and before the princes, the chief fathers of the children of Israel:

2 And they said, ᴿThe LORD commanded my lord to give the land for an inheritance by lot to the children of Israel: and ᴿmy lord was commanded by the LORD to give the inheritance of Zē-lŏph'-ĕ-hăd our brother unto his daughters.

3 And if they be married to any of the sons of the *other* tribes of the children of Israel, then shall their inheritance be ᴿtaken from the inheritance of our fathers, and shall be put to the inheritance of the tribe ᴺwhereunto they are received: so shall it be taken from the lot of our inheritance.

4 And when ᴿthe jubilee of the children of Israel shall be, then shall their inheritance be put unto the inheritance of the tribe whereunto they are received: so shall their inheritance be taken away from the inheritance of the tribe of our fathers.

Inter-tribal marriage forbidden

5 And Moses commanded the children of Israel according to the word of the LORD, saying, The tribe of the sons of Joseph ᴿhath said well.

6 This *is* the thing which the LORD doth command concerning the daughters of Zē-lŏph'-ĕ-hăd, saying, Let them ᴺmarry to whom they think best; ᴿonly to the family of the tribe of their father shall they marry.

7 So shall not the inheritance of the children of Israel remove from tribe to tribe: for every one of the children of Israel shall ᴿkeepᴺ himself to the inheritance of the tribe of his fathers.

8 And ᴿevery daughter, that possesseth an inheritance in any tribe of the children of Israel, shall be wife unto one of the family of the tribe of her father, that the children of Israel may enjoy every man the inheritance of his fathers.

9 Neither shall the inheritance remove from *one* tribe to another tribe; but every one of the tribes of the children of Israel shall keep himself to his own inheritance.

10 Even as the LORD commanded Moses, so did the daughters of Zē-lŏph'-ĕ-hăd:

11 ᴿFor Mäh'-läh, Tĭr'-zăh, and Hŏg'-läh, and Mĭl'-cäh, and Noah, the daughters of Zē-lŏph'-ĕ-hăd, were married unto their father's brothers' sons:

12 *And* they were married ᴺinto the families of the sons of Mă-năs'-sēh the son of Joseph, and their inheritance remained in the tribe of the family of their father.

13 These *are* the commandments and the judgments, which the LORD commanded by the hand of Moses unto the children of Israel ᴿin the plains of Moab by Jordan *near* Jericho.

Center reference column

CHAP. **36**
BC 1451
1 ch. 26:29
2 ch. 26:55
 & 33:54
 Josh. 17:4
2 ch. 27:1, 7
 Josh. 17:3, 4
3 ch. 27:4, marg.
3 Heb. *unto whom they shall be*
4 Lev. 25:10
5 ch. 27:7

Heb. *be wives*	6
ver. 11, 12	6
1 Ki. 21:3	7
Heb. *cleave to the, etc.*	7
1 Chr. 23:22	8
ch. 27:1	11
Heb. *to some that were of the families*	12
ch. 26:3 & 33:50	13

THE FIFTH BOOK OF MOSES, CALLED

DEUTERONOMY

"Deuteronomy" is a term derived from the Greek and means "second law" or "the law repeated." Moses completed his ministry giving instructions and delivering several addresses to the whole congregation of Israel. By reviewing their experiences and recounting God's revelation to them, he gave the Israelites practical advice concerning faith and obedience to the law as they conquered and occupied Canaan. The book also contains supplementary instructions regarding the spirit of worship. Moses provided the priests with a written copy of the law, 31:9-13, and commanded them to proclaim it anew to the people every seventh year. In its style the book exhibits remarkable unity throughout and is characterized by a depth of emotion and a peculiar sense of anxiety for the future

of Israel. It is reasonable to ascribe the authorship of these first five books of the Old Testament, the entire Pentateuch, to Moses, and the whole body of this material could have been arranged in its present form as early as the time of Joshua, allowing for some stylistic and linguistic revisions in subsequent periods. Deuteronomy was extensively used by the later prophets and by Our Lord Himself.

OUTLINE OF THE BOOK:
 I. The meaning of Israel's experience 1:1 – 4:43
 II. The significance of the law 4:44 – 28:68
 III. Israel's choice and unique opportunity 29:1 – 34:12

CHAPTER 1

Speech of Moses

THESE *be* the words which Moses spake unto all Israel ᴿon this side Jordan in the wilderness, in the plain over against ᴺthe Red *sea,* between Pâr'-ăn, and Tō'-phĕl, and La-ban, and Hă-zē'-rŏth, and Dī'-ză-hăb.

2 (*There are* eleven days' *journey* from Hôr'-ĕb by the way of mount Sē'-ĭr ᴿunto Kā'-dĕsh-bär'-nĕ-ă.)

3 And it came to pass ᴿin the fortieth year, in the eleventh month, on the first *day* of the month, *that* Moses spake unto the children of Israel, according unto all that the Lᴏʀᴅ had given him in commandment unto them;

4 ᴿAfter he had slain Sī'-hŏn the king of the Amorites, which dwelt in Hĕsh'-bŏn, and Og the king of Bā'-shăn, which dwelt at Ăs'-tă-rŏth ᴿin Ĕd'-rĕ-ī:

5 On this side Jordan, in the land of Moab, began Moses to declare this law, saying,

6 The Lᴏʀᴅ our God spake unto us ᴿin Hôr'-ĕb, saying, Ye have dwelt long ᴿenough in this mount:

7 Turn you, and take your journey, and go to the mount of the Amorites, and unto ᴺall *the places* nigh thereunto, in the plain, in the hills, and in the vale, and in the south, and by the sea side, to the land of the Canaanites, and unto Lĕb'-ă-nᴏn, unto the great river, the river ᴇu-phrā'-tĕś.

8 Behold, I have ᴺset the land before you: go in and possess the land which the Lᴏʀᴅ sware unto your fathers, ᴿAbraham, Isaac, and Ja-cob, to give unto them and to their seed after them.

Choice of leaders

9 And ᴿI spake unto you at that time, say-ing, I am not able to bear you myself alone:

10 The Lᴏʀᴅ your God hath multiplied you, and, behold, ᴿye *are* this day as the stars of heaven for multitude.

11 (ᴿThe Lᴏʀᴅ God of your fathers make you a thousand times so many more as ye *are,* and bless you, ᴿas he hath promised you!)

12 ᴿHow can I myself alone bear your cum-brance, and your burden, and your strife?

13 ᴺTake you wise men, and understanding, and known among your tribes, and I will make them rulers over you.

14 And ye answered me, and said, The thing which thou hast spoken *is* good *for us* to do.

15 So I took ᴿthe chief of your tribes, wise men, and known, ᴿand ᴺmade them heads over you, captains over thousands, and cap-

tains over hundreds, and captains over fifties, and captains over tens, and officers among your tribes.

16 And I charged your judges at that time, saying, Hear *the causes* between your breth-ren, and ᴿjudge righteously between *every* man and his ᴿbrother, and the stranger *that is* with him.

17 ᴿYe shall not ᴺrespect persons in judg-ment; *but* ye shall hear the small as well as the great; ye shall not be afraid of the face of man; for ᴿthe judgment *is* God's: and the cause that is too hard for you, ᴿbring *it* unto me, and I will hear it.

18 And I commanded you at that time all the things which ye should do.

Report of the spies

19 And when we departed from Hôr'-ĕb, ᴿwe went through all that great and terrible wilderness, which ye saw by the way of the mountain of the Amorites, as the Lᴏʀᴅ our God commanded us; and ᴿwe came to Kā'-dĕsh-bär'-nĕ-ă.

20 And I said unto you, Ye are come unto the mountain of the Amorites, which the Lᴏʀᴅ our God doth give unto us.

21 Behold, the Lᴏʀᴅ thy God hath set the land before thee: go up *and* possess *it,* as the Lᴏʀᴅ God of thy fathers hath said unto thee; ᴿfear not, neither be discouraged.

22 And ye came near unto me every one of you, and said, We will send men before us, and they shall search us out the land, and bring us word again by what way we must go up, and into what cities we shall come.

23 And the saying pleased me well: and ᴿI took twelve men of you, one of a tribe:

24 And ᴿthey turned and went up into the mountain, and came unto the valley of Ĕsh'-cŏl, and searched it out.

25 And they took of the fruit of the land in their hands, and brought *it* down unto us, and brought us word again, and said, ᴿIt *is* a good land which the Lᴏʀᴅ our God doth give us.

Rebellion of the people

26 ᴿNotwithstanding ye would not go up, but rebelled against the commandment of the Lᴏʀᴅ your God:

27 And ye murmured in your tents, and said, Because the Lᴏʀᴅ ᴿhated us, he hath brought us forth out of the land of Egypt, to deliver us into the hand of the Amorites, to destroy us.

28 Whither shall we go up? our brethren have ᴺdiscouraged our heart, saying, ᴿThe people *is* greater and taller than we; the cities

are great and walled up to heaven; and moreover we have seen the sons of the [R]Anakims there.

29 Then I said unto you, Dread not, neither be afraid of them.

30 [R]The Lord your God which goeth before you, he shall fight for you, according to all that he did for you in Egypt before your eyes;

31 And in the wilderness, where thou hast seen how that the Lord thy God [R]bare thee, as a man doth bear his son, in all the way that ye went, until ye came into this place.

32 Yet in this thing [R]ye did not believe the Lord your God,

33 [R]Who went in the way before you, [R]to search you out a place to pitch your tents *in,* in fire by night, to shew you by what way ye should go, and in a cloud by day.

34 And the Lord heard the voice of your words, and was wroth, [R]and sware, saying,

35 [R]Surely there shall not one of these men of this evil generation see that good land, which I sware to give unto your fathers,

36 [R]Save Caleb the son of Jĕ-phŭn'-nĕh; he shall see it, and to him will I give the land that he hath trodden upon, and to his children, because [R]he hath [N]wholly followed the Lord.

37 [R]Also the Lord was angry with me for your sakes, saying, Thou also shalt not go in thither.

38 [R]*But* Joshua the son of Nun, [R]which standeth before thee, he shall go in thither: [R]encourage him: for he shall cause Israel to inherit it.

39 [R]Moreover your little ones, which [R]ye said should be a prey, and your children, which in that day [R]had no knowledge between good and evil, they shall go in thither, and unto them will I give it, and they shall possess it.

40 [R]But *as for* you, turn you, and take your journey into the wilderness by the way of the Red sea.

Unsuccessful invasion

41 Then ye answered and said unto me, [R]We have sinned against the Lord, we will go up and fight, according to all that the Lord our God commanded us. And when ye had girded on every man his weapons of war, ye were ready to go up into the hill.

42 And the Lord said unto me, Say unto them, [R]Go not up, neither fight; for I *am* not among you; lest ye be smitten before your enemies.

43 So I spake unto you; and ye would not hear, but rebelled against the commandment of

the Lord, and [R]went[N] presumptuously up into the hill.

44 And the Amorites, which dwelt in that mountain, came out against you, and chased you, [R]as bees do, and destroyed you in Sē'-ĭr, *even* unto Hôr'-măh.

45 And ye returned and wept before the Lord; but the Lord would not hearken to your voice, nor give ear unto you.

46 [R]So ye abode in Kā'-dĕsh many days, according unto the days that ye abode *there.*

CHAPTER 2

Speech of Moses continued

THEN we turned, and took our journey into the wilderness by the way of the Red sea, [R]as the Lord spake unto me: and we compassed mount Sē'-ĭr many days.

2 And the Lord spake unto me, saying,

3 Ye have compassed this mountain [R]long enough: turn you northward.

4 And command thou the people, saying, [R]Ye *are* to pass through the coast of your brethren the children of Esau, which dwell in Sē'-ĭr; and they shall be afraid of you: take ye good heed unto yourselves therefore:

5 Meddle not with them; for I will not give you of their land, [N]no, not so much as a foot breadth; [R]because I have given mount Sē'-ĭr unto Esau *for* a possession.

6 Ye shall buy meat of them for money, that ye may eat; and ye shall also buy water of them for money, that ye may drink.

7 For the Lord thy God hath blessed thee in all the works of thy hand: he knoweth thy walking through this great wilderness: [R]these forty years the Lord thy God *hath been* with thee; thou hast lacked nothing.

8 [R]And when we passed by from our brethren the children of Esau, which dwelt in Sē'-ĭr, through the way of the plain from [R]Ē'-lăth, and from Ē'-zĭ-ŏn-gā'-bĕr, we turned and passed by the way of the wilderness of Moab.

9 And the Lord said unto me, [N]Distress not the Moabites, neither contend with them in battle: for I will not give thee of their land *for* a possession; because I have given [R]Ar unto [R]the children of Lot *for* a possession.

10 [R]The Ē'-mĭmś dwelt therein in times past, a people great, and many, and tall, as [R]the Anakims;

11 Which also were accounted giants, as the Anakims; but the Moabites call them Ē'-mĭmś.

CHAP. 1
BC 1451
28 Num. 13:28
30 Ex. 14:14
Neh. 4:20
31 Ex. 19:4
ch. 32:11, 12
Is. 46:3, 4
& 63:9
Hos. 11:3
See on Acts 13:18
32 Ps. 106:24
Jude 5
33 Ex. 13:21
Ps. 78:14
33 Num. 10:33
Ezek. 20:6
34 ch. 2:14, 15
35 Num. 14:22
Ps. 95:11
36 Num. 14:24
Josh. 14:9
36 Num. 14:24
36 Heb. *fulfilled to go after*
37 Num. 20:12
& 27:14
ch. 3:26 & 4:21
& 34:4
Ps. 106:32
38 Num. 14:30
38 Ex. 24:13
& 33:11
See 1 Sam. 16:22
38 Num. 27:18, 19
ch. 31:7, 23
39 Num. 14:31
39 Num. 14:3
39 Is. 7:15, 16
Rom. 9:11
40 Num. 14:25
41 Num. 14:40
42 Num. 14:42

Num. 14:44   43
Heb. *ye were presumptuous, and went up*   43
Ps. 118:12   44
Num. 13:25   46
& 20:1, 22
Judg. 11:17

CHAP. 2
BC 1453
Num. 14:25   1
ch. 1:40
See ver. 7, 14   3
Num. 20:14   4
Heb. *even to the treading of the sole of the foot*   5
Gen. 36:8   5
Josh. 24:4
ch. 8:2-4   7
Judg. 11:18   8
1 Ki. 9:26   8
Or, *Use no hostility against Moab*   9
Num. 21:28   9
Gen. 19:36, 37   9
Gen. 14:5   10
Num. 13:22, 33   10
ch. 9:2

12 ᴿThe Hôr'-ĭmś also dwelt in Sē'-ĭr beforetime; but the children of Esau ᴺsucceeded them, when they had destroyed them from before them, and dwelt in their ᴺstead; as Israel did unto the land of his possession, which the LORD gave unto them.

13 Now rise up, *said I,* and get you over ᴿthe ᴺbrook Zē'-rĕd. And we went over the brook Zē'-rĕd.

14 And the space in which we came ᴿfrom Kā'-dĕsh-bär'-nĕ-ă, until we were come over the brook Zē'-rĕd, *was* thirty and eight years; ᴿuntil all the generation of the men of war were wasted out from among the host, ᴿas the LORD sware unto them.

15 For indeed the ᴿhand of the LORD was against them, to destroy them from among the host, until they were consumed.

16 So it came to pass, when all the men of war were consumed and dead from among the people,

17 That the LORD spake unto me, saying,

18 Thou art to pass over through Ar, the coast of Moab, this day:

19 And *when* thou comest nigh over against the children of Ammon, distress them not, nor meddle with them: for I will not give thee of the land of the children of Ammon *any* possession; because I have given it unto ᴿthe children of Lot *for* a possession.

20 (That also was accounted a land of giants: giants dwelt therein in old time; and the Ammonites call them ᴿZăm-zŭm'-mĭmś;

21 ᴿA people great, and many, and tall, as the Anakims; but the LORD destroyed them before them; and they succeeded them, and dwelt in their stead:

22 As he did to the children of Esau, ᴿwhich dwelt in Sē'-ĭr, when he destroyed ᴿthe Hôr'-ĭmś from before them; and they succeeded them, and dwelt in their stead even unto this day:

23 And ᴿthe Ā'-vĭmś which dwelt in Hă-zē'-rĭm, *even* unto Azzah, ᴿthe Căph'-tō-rĭmś, which came forth out of Căph'-tôr, destroyed them, and dwelt in their stead.)

24 Rise ye up, take your journey, and ᴿpass over the river Arnon: behold, I have given into thine hand Sī'-hŏn the Amorite, king of Hĕsh'-bŏn, and his land: ᴺbegin to possess *it,* and contend with him in battle.

25 ᴿThis day will I begin to put the dread of thee and the fear of thee upon the nations *that are* under the whole heaven, who shall hear report of thee, and shall tremble, and be in anguish because of thee.

CHAP. 2
BC 1453
12 ver. 22
Gen. 14:6
& 36:20
12 Heb. *inherited them*
12 Or, *room*
13 Num. 21:12
13 Or, *valley,*
Num. 13:23
14 Num. 13:26
14 Num. 14:33
& 26:64
14 Num. 14:35
ch. 1:34, 35
Ezek. 20:15
15 Ps. 78:33
& 106:26
19 Gen. 19:38
20 Gen. 14:5
Zuzims
21 See ver. 10
22 Gen. 36:8
22 Gen. 14:6
& 36:20-30
23 Josh. 13:3
23 Gen. 10:14
Amos 9:7
24 Num. 21:13
Judg. 11:18
24 Heb. *begin, possess*
25 Ex. 15:14, 15

ch. 20:10	26
Num. 21:21, 22	27
Judg. 11:19	
Num. 20:19	28
See Num. 20:18	29
ch. 23:3, 4	
Judg. 11:17	
Num. 21:23	30
Josh. 11:20	30
Ex. 4:21	30
ch. 1:8	31
Num. 21:23	32
ch. 7:2	33
& 20:16	
Num. 21:24	33
ch. 29:7	
Lev. 27:28	34
ch. 7:2, 26	
Heb. *every city of men, and women, and little ones*	34
ch. 3:12	36
& 4:48	
Josh. 13:9	
Ps. 44:3	36
Gen. 32:22	37
Num. 21:24	
ch. 3:16	
ver. 5, 9, 19	37

CHAP. 3
BC 1452
Num. 21:33, etc. 1
ch. 29:7
ch. 1:4 1

Victory over Sihon

26 And I sent messengers out of the wilderness of Kē'-dĕ-mŏth unto Sī'-hŏn king of Hĕsh'-bŏn ᴿwith words of peace, saying,

27 ᴿLet me pass through thy land: I will go along by the high way, I will neither turn unto the right hand nor to the left.

28 Thou shalt sell me meat for money, that I may eat; and give me water for money, that I may drink: ᴿonly I will pass through on my feet;

29 (ᴿAs the children of Esau which dwell in Sē'-ĭr, and the Moabites which dwell in Ar, did unto me;) until I shall pass over Jordan into the land which the LORD our God giveth us.

30 ᴿBut Sī'-hŏn king of Hĕsh'-bŏn would not let us pass by him: for ᴿthe LORD thy God ᴿhardened his spirit, and made his heart obstinate, that he might deliver him into thy hand, as *appeareth* this day.

31 And the LORD said unto me, Behold, I have begun to ᴿgive Sī'-hŏn and his land before thee: begin to possess, that thou mayest inherit his land.

32 ᴿThen Sī'-hŏn came out against us, he and all his people, to fight at Jā'-hăz.

33 And ᴿthe LORD our God delivered him before us; and ᴿwe smote him, and his sons, and all his people.

34 And we took all his cities at that time, and ᴿutterly destroyed ᴺthe men, and the women, and the little ones, of every city, we left none to remain:

35 Only the cattle we took for a prey unto ourselves, and the spoil of the cities which we took.

36 ᴿFrom Ă-rō'-ĕr, which *is* by the brink of the river of Arnon, and *from* the city that *is* by the river, even unto Gilead, there was not one city too strong for us: ᴿthe LORD our God delivered all unto us:

37 Only unto the land of the children of Ammon thou camest not, *nor* unto any place of the river ᴿJăb'-bŏk, nor unto the cities in the mountains, nor unto ᴿwhatsoever the LORD our God forbad us.

CHAPTER 3

Victory over Og

THEN we turned, and went up the way to Bā'-shăn: and ᴿOg the king of Bā'-shăn came out against us, he and all his people, to battle ᴿat Ĕd'-rĕ-ī.

2 And the LORD said unto me, Fear him not: for I will deliver him, and all his people, and his land, into thy hand; and thou shalt do unto him as thou didst unto ᴿSī'-hŏn king of the Amorites, which dwelt at Hĕsh'-bŏn.

3 So the LORD our God delivered into our hands Og also, the king of Bā'-shăn, and all his people: ᴿand we smote him until none was left to him remaining.

4 And we took all his cities at that time, there was not a city which we took not from them, threescore cities, ᴿall the region of Är'-gŏb, the kingdom of Og in Bā'-shăn.

5 All these cities *were* fenced with high walls, gates, and bars; beside unwalled towns a great many.

6 And we utterly destroyed them, as we did unto Sī'-hŏn king ᴿof Hĕsh'-bŏn, utterly destroying the men, women, and children, of every city.

7 But all the cattle, and the spoil of the cities, we took for a prey to ourselves.

8 And we took at that time out of the hand of the two kings of the Amorites the land that *was* on this side Jordan, from the river of Arnon unto mount Hermon;

9 (*Which* ᴿHermon the Ṡi-dō'-nĭ-ăns call Sī'-rĭ-on; and the Amorites call it ᴿShē'-nĭr;)

10 ᴿAll the cities of the plain, and all Gilead, and ᴿall Bā'-shăn, unto Săl'-chăh and Ĕd'-rĕ-ī, cities of the kingdom of Og in Bā'-shăn.

11 ᴿFor only Og king of Bā'-shăn remained of the remnant of ᴿgiants; behold, his bedstead *was* a bedstead of iron; *is* it not in ᴿRăb'-băth of the children of Ammon? nine cubits *was* the length thereof, and four cubits the breadth of it, after the cubit of a man.

Inheritance east of Jordan

12 And this land, *which* we possessed at that time, ᴿfrom Ă-rō'-ĕr, which *is* by the river Arnon, and half mount Gilead, and ᴿthe cities thereof, gave I unto the Reubenites and to the Gadites.

13 ᴿAnd the rest of Gilead, and all Bā'-shăn, *being* the kingdom of Og, gave I unto the half tribe of Mă-năs'-sēh; all the region of Är'-gŏb, with all Bā'-shăn, which was called the land of giants.

14 ᴿJā'-ĭr the son of Mă-năs'-sēh took all the country of Är'-gŏb ᴿunto the coasts of Gĕ-shū'-rī and Mā-ăch'-ā-thī; and ᴿcalled them after his own name, Bā'-shăn-hā'-vŏth-jā'-ĭr, unto this day.

15 ᴿAnd I gave Gilead unto Mā'-chĭr.

16 And unto the Reubenites ᴿand unto the

Gadites I gave from Gilead even unto the river Arnon half the valley, and the border even unto the river Jăb'-bok, ᴿwhich is the border of the children of Ammon;

17 The plain also, and Jordan, and the coast *thereof,* from ᴿChĭn'-nĕ-rĕth ᴿeven unto the sea of the plain, ᴿ*even* the salt sea, ᴺunder Ăsh'-dŏth-pĭs'-găh eastward.

18 And I commanded you at that time, saying, The LORD your God hath given you this land to possess it: ᴿye shall pass over armed before your brethren the children of Israel, all *that are* ᴺmeet for the war.

19 But your wives, and your little ones, and your cattle, (*for* I know that ye have much cattle,) shall abide in your cities which I have given you;

20 Until the LORD have given rest unto your brethren, as well as unto you, and *until* they also possess the land which the LORD your God hath given them beyond Jordan: and *then* shall ye ᴿreturn every man unto his possession, which I have given you.

21 And ᴿI commanded Joshua at that time, saying, Thine eyes have seen all that the LORD your God hath done unto these two kings: so shall the LORD do unto all the kingdoms whither thou passest.

22 Ye shall not fear them: for ᴿthe LORD your God he shall fight for you.

Moses forbidden to cross Jordan

23 And ᴿI besought the LORD at that time, saying,

24 O Lord GOD, thou hast begun to shew thy servant ᴿthy greatness, and thy mighty hand: for ᴿwhat God *is there* in heaven or in earth, that can do according to thy works, and according to thy might?

25 I pray thee, let me go over, and see ᴿthe good land that *is* beyond Jordan, that goodly mountain, and Lĕb'-ă-non.

26 But the LORD ᴿwas wroth with me for your sakes, and would not hear me: and the LORD said unto me, Let it suffice thee; speak no more unto me of this matter.

27 ᴿGet thee up into the top of ᴺPĭs'-găh, and lift up thine eyes westward, and northward, and southward, and eastward, and behold *it* with thine eyes: for thou shalt not go over this Jordan.

28 But ᴿcharge Joshua, and encourage him, and strengthen him: for he shall go over before this people, and he shall cause them to inherit the land which thou shalt see.

29 So we abode in ᴿthe valley over against Bĕth-pē'-ôr.

CHAPTER 4

The command to obedience

NOW therefore hearken, O Israel, unto [R]the statutes and unto the judgments, which I teach you, for to do *them,* that ye may live, and go in and possess the land which the LORD God of your fathers giveth you.

2 [R]Ye shall not add unto the word which I command you, neither shall ye diminish *aught* from it, that ye may keep the commandments of the LORD your God which I command you.

3 Your eyes have seen what the LORD did because of [R]Bā'-ăl-pē'-ôr: for all the men that followed Bā'-ăl-pē'-ôr, the LORD thy God hath destroyed them from among you.

4 But ye that did cleave unto the LORD your God *are* alive every one of you this day.

5 Behold, I have taught you statutes and judgments, even as the LORD my God commanded me, that ye should do so in the land whither ye go to possess it.

6 Keep therefore and do *them;* for this *is* [R]your wisdom and your understanding in the sight of the nations, which shall hear all these statutes, and say, Surely this great nation *is* a wise and understanding people.

7 For [R]what nation *is there so* great, who *hath* [R]God *so* nigh unto them, as the LORD our God *is* in all *things that* we call upon him *for?*

8 And what nation *is there so* great, that hath statutes and judgments *so* righteous as all this law, which I set before you this day?

9 Only take heed to thyself, and [R]keep thy soul diligently, lest thou forget the things which thine eyes have seen, and lest they depart from thy heart all the days of thy life: but [R]teach them thy sons, and thy sons' sons;

10 *Specially* [R]the day that thou stoodest before the LORD thy God in Hôr'-ĕb, when the LORD said unto me, Gather me the people together, and I will make them hear my words, that they may learn to fear me all the days that they shall live upon the earth, and *that* they may teach their children.

11 And ye came near and stood under the mountain; and the [R]mountain burned with fire unto the [N]midst of heaven, with darkness, clouds, and thick darkness.

12 [R]And the LORD spake unto you out of the midst of the fire: ye heard the voice of the words, but saw no similitude; [R]only[N] *ye heard* a voice.

13 [R]And he declared unto you his covenant, which he commanded you to perform, *even* [R]ten commandments; and [R]he wrote them upon two tables of stone.

14 And [R]the LORD commanded me at that time to teach you statutes and judgments, that ye might do them in the land whither ye go over to possess it.

Idolatry forbidden

15 [R]Take ye therefore good heed unto yourselves; for ye saw no manner of [R]similitude on the day *that* the LORD spake unto you in Hôr'-ĕb out of the midst of the fire:

16 Lest ye [R]corrupt *yourselves,* and [R]make you a graven image, the similitude of any figure, [R]the likeness of male or female,

17 The likeness of any beast that *is* on the earth, the likeness of any winged fowl that flieth in the air,

18 The likeness of any thing that creepeth on the ground, the likeness of any fish that *is* in the waters beneath the earth:

19 And lest thou [R]lift up thine eyes unto heaven, and when thou seest the sun, and the moon, and the stars, *even* [R]all the host of heaven, shouldest be driven to [R]worship them, and serve them, which the LORD thy God hath [N]divided unto all nations under the whole heaven.

20 But the LORD hath taken you, and [R]brought you forth out of the iron furnace, *even* out of Egypt, [R]to be unto him a people of inheritance, as *ye are* this day.

21 Furthermore [R]the LORD was angry with me for your sakes, and sware that I should not go over Jordan, and that I should not go in unto that good land, which the LORD thy God giveth thee *for* an inheritance:

22 But [R]I must die in this land, [R]I must not go over Jordan: but ye shall go over, and possess [R]that good land.

23 Take heed unto yourselves, [R]lest ye forget the covenant of the LORD your God, which he made with you, [R]and make you a graven image, *or* the likeness of any *thing,* which the LORD thy God hath forbidden thee.

24 For [R]the LORD thy God *is* a consuming fire, *even* [R]a jealous God.

25 When thou shalt beget children, and children's children, and ye shall have remained long in the land, and shall corrupt *yourselves,* and make a graven image, *or* the likeness of any *thing,* and [R]shall do evil in the sight of the LORD thy God, to provoke him to anger:

26 [R]I call heaven and earth to witness against you this day, that ye shall soon utterly perish from off the land whereunto ye go over Jordan to possess it; ye shall not prolong *your* days upon it, but shall utterly be destroyed.

27 And the LORD [R]shall scatter you among the nations, and ye shall be left few in number

among the heathen, whither the LORD shall lead you.

28 And ᴿthere ye shall serve gods, the work of men's hands, wood and stone, ᴿwhich neither see, nor hear, nor eat, nor smell.

A merciful God

29 ᴿBut if from thence thou shalt seek the LORD thy God, thou shalt find *him,* if thou seek him with all thy heart and with all thy soul.

30 When thou art in tribulation, and all these things ᴺare come upon thee, ᴿ*even* in the latter days, if thou ᴿturn to the LORD thy God, and shalt be obedient unto his voice;

31 (For the LORD thy God *is* ᴿa merciful God;) he will not forsake thee, neither destroy thee, nor forget the covenant of thy fathers which he sware unto them.

God's relation to Israel

32 For ᴿask now of the days that are past, which were before thee, since the day that God created man upon the earth, and *ask* ᴿfrom the one side of heaven unto the other, whether there hath been *any such thing* as this great thing *is,* or hath been heard like it?

33 ᴿDid *ever* people hear the voice of God speaking out of the midst of the fire, as thou hast heard, and live?

34 Or hath God assayed to go *and* take him a nation from the midst of *another* nation, ᴿby temptations, ᴿby signs, and by wonders, and by war, and ᴿby a mighty hand, and ᴿby a stretched out arm, ᴿand by great terrors, according to all that the LORD your God did for you in Egypt before your eyes?

35 Unto thee it was shewed, that thou mightest know that the LORD he *is* God; ᴿ*there is* none else beside him.

36 ᴿOut of heaven he made thee to hear his voice, that he might instruct thee: and upon earth he shewed thee his great fire; and thou heardest his words out of the midst of the fire.

37 And because ᴿhe loved thy fathers, therefore he chose their seed after them, and ᴿbrought thee out in his sight with his mighty power out of Egypt;

38 ᴿTo drive out nations from before thee greater and mightier than thou *art,* to bring thee in, to give thee their land *for* an inheritance, as *it is* this day.

39 Know therefore this day, and consider *it* in thine heart, that ᴿthe LORD he *is* God in heaven above, and upon the earth beneath: *there is* none else.

40 ᴿThou shalt keep therefore his statutes, and his commandments, which I command

thee this day, ᴿthat it may go well with thee, and with thy children after thee, and that thou mayest prolong *thy* days upon the earth, which the LORD thy God giveth thee, for ever.

The cities of refuge

41 Then Moses ᴿsevered three cities on this side Jordan toward the sunrising;

42 ᴿThat the slayer might flee thither, which should kill his neighbour unawares, and hated him not in times past; and that fleeing unto one of these cities he might live:

43 *Namely,* ᴿBē'-zer in the wilderness, in the plain country, of the Reubenites; and Rā'-mŏth in Gilead, of the Gadites; and Gō'-lăn in Bā'-shăn, of the Mă-năs'-sītes.

44 And this *is* the law which Moses set before the children of Israel:

45 These *are* the testimonies, and the statutes, and the judgments, which Moses spake unto the children of Israel, after they came forth out of Egypt,

46 On this side Jordan, ᴿin the valley over against Bĕth-pē'-ôr, in the land of Sī'-hŏn king of the Amorites, who dwelt at Hĕsh'-bŏn, whom Moses and the children of Israel ᴿsmote, after they were come forth out of Egypt:

47 And they possessed his land, and the land ᴿof Og king of Bā'-shăn, two kings of the Amorites, which *were* on this side Jordan toward the sunrising;

48 ᴿFrom Ă-rō'-ĕr, which *is* by the bank of the river Arnon, even unto mount Sī'-ọn, which *is* ᴿHermon,

49 And all the plain on this side Jordan eastward, even unto the sea of the plain, under the ᴿsprings of Pĭś'-găh.

CHAPTER 5

The Ten Commandments

AND Moses called all Israel, and said unto them, Hear, O Israel, the statutes and judgments which I speak in your ears this day, that ye may learn them, and ᴺkeep, and do them.

2 ᴿThe LORD our God made a covenant with us in Hôr'-ĕb.

3 The LORD ᴿmade not this covenant with our fathers, but with us, *even* us, who *are* all of us here alive this day.

4 ᴿThe LORD talked with you face to face in the mount out of the midst of the fire,

5 (ᴿI stood between the LORD and you at that time, to shew you the word of the LORD: for ᴿye were afraid by reason of the fire, and went not up into the mount;) saying,

CHAP. 4	
BC 1451	
28 ch. 28:64	
1 Sam. 26:19	
Jer. 16:13	
28 Ps. 115:4, 5	
& 135:15, 16	
Is. 44:9 & 46:7	
29 Lev. 26:39	
ch. 30:1-3	
2 Chr. 15:4	
Neh. 1:9	
Is. 55:6, 7	
30 Heb. *have found thee,*	
Ex. 18:8	
ch. 31:17	
30 Gen. 49:1	
ch. 31:29	
Jer. 23:20	
Hos. 3:5	
30 Joel 2:12	
31 2 Chr. 30:9	
Neh. 9:31	
Ps. 116:5	
Jonah 4:2	
32 Job 8:8	
32 Mat. 24:31	
33 Ex. 24:11	
& 33:20	
ch. 5:24, 26	
34 ch. 7:19	
34 Ex. 7:3	
34 Ex. 13:3	
34 Ex. 6:6	
34 ch. 26:8 & 34:12	
35 ch. 32:39	
1 Sam. 2:2	
Is. 45:5, 18	
Mark 12:29	
36 Ex. 19:9, 19	
& 20:18, 22	
& 24:16	
Heb. 12:18	
37 ch. 10:15	
37 Ex. 13:3, 9, 14	
38 ch. 7:1	
& 9:1, 4, 5	
39 Josh. 2:11	
40 Lev. 22:31	
ch. 5:16 & 6:3,	40
18 & 12:25, 28	
& 22:7	
Eph. 6:3	
Num. 35:6	41
ch. 19:4	42
Josh. 20:8	43
ch. 3:29	46
Num. 21:24	46
ch. 1:4	
Num. 21:35	47
ch. 3:3, 4	
ch. 2:36 & 3:12	48
ch. 3:9	48
Ps. 133:3	
ch. 3:17	49

CHAP. 5	
BC 1451	
Heb. *keep to do them*	1
Ex. 19:5	2
ch. 4:23	
See Mat. 13:17	3
Heb. 8:9	
Ex. 19:9, 19	4
& 20:22	
ch. 4:33, 36	
& 34:10	
Ex. 20:21	5
Gal. 3:19	
Ex. 19:16	5
& 20:18 & 24:2	

6 ᴿI *am* the Lord thy God, which brought thee out of the land of Egypt, from the house of ᴺbondage.

7 ᴿThou shalt have none other gods before me.

8 ᴿThou shalt not make thee *any* graven image, *or* any likeness *of any thing* that *is* in heaven above, or that *is* in the earth beneath, or that *is* in the waters beneath the earth:

9 Thou shalt not bow down thyself unto them, nor serve them: for I the Lord thy God *am* a jealous God, ᴿvisiting the iniquity of the fathers upon the children unto the third and fourth *generation* of them that hate me,

10 ᴿAnd shewing mercy unto thousands of them that love me and keep my commandments.

11 ᴿThou shalt not take the name of the Lord thy God in vain: for the Lord will not hold *him* guiltless that taketh his name in vain.

12 ᴿKeep the sabbath day to sanctify it, as the Lord thy God hath commanded thee.

13 ᴿSix days thou shalt labour, and do all thy work:

14 But the seventh day *is* the ᴿsabbath of the Lord thy God: *in it* thou shalt not do any work, thou, nor thy son, nor thy daughter, nor thy manservant, nor thy maidservant, nor thine ox, nor thine ass, nor any of thy cattle, nor thy stranger that *is* within thy gates; that thy manservant and thy maidservant may rest as well as thou.

15 ᴿAnd remember that thou wast a servant in the land of Egypt, and *that* the Lord thy God brought thee out hence ᴿthrough a mighty hand and by a stretched out arm: therefore the Lord thy God commanded thee to keep the sabbath day.

16 ᴿHonour thy father and thy mother, as the Lord thy God hath commanded thee; ᴿthat thy days may be prolonged, and that it may go well with thee, in the land which the Lord thy God giveth thee.

17 ᴿThou shalt not kill.

18 ᴿNeither shalt thou commit adultery.

19 ᴿNeither shalt thou steal.

20 ᴿNeither shalt thou bear false witness against thy neighbour.

21 ᴿNeither shalt thou desire thy neighbour's wife, neither shalt thou covet thy neighbour's house, his field, or his manservant, or his maidservant, his ox, or his ass, or any *thing* that *is* thy neighbour's.

Moses as mediator

22 These words the Lord spake unto all your assembly in the mount out of the midst of the fire, of the cloud, and of the thick dark-

ness, with a great voice: and he added no more. And ᴿhe wrote them in two tables of stone, and delivered them unto me.

23 ᴿAnd it came to pass, when ye heard the voice out of the midst of the darkness, (for the mountain did burn with fire,) that ye came near unto me, *even* all the heads of your tribes, and your elders;

24 And ye said, Behold, the Lord our God hath shewed us his glory and his greatness, and ᴿwe have heard his voice out of the midst of the fire: we have seen this day that God doth talk with man, and he ᴿliveth.

25 Now therefore why should we die? for this great fire will consume us: ᴿif we ᴺhear the voice of the Lord our God any more, then we shall die.

26 ᴿFor who *is there of* all flesh, that hath heard the voice of the living God speaking out of the midst of the fire, as we *have*, and lived?

27 Go thou near, and hear all that the Lord our God shall say: and ᴿspeak thou unto us all that the Lord our God shall speak unto thee; and we will hear *it*, and do *it*.

28 And the Lord heard the voice of your words, when ye spake unto me; and the Lord said unto me, I have heard the voice of the words of this people, which they have spoken unto thee: ᴿthey have well said all that they have spoken.

29 ᴿO that there were such an heart in them, that they would fear me, and ᴿkeep all my commandments always, ᴿthat it might be well with them, and with their children for ever!

30 Go say to them, Get you into your tents again.

31 But as for thee, stand thou here by me, ᴿand I will speak unto thee all the commandments, and the statutes, and the judgments, which thou shalt teach them, that they may do *them* in the land which I give them to possess it.

32 Ye shall observe to do therefore as the Lord your God hath commanded you: ᴿye shall not turn aside to the right hand or to the left.

33 Ye shall walk in ᴿall the ways which the Lord your God hath commanded you, that ye may live, ᴿand *that it may be* well with you, and *that* ye may prolong *your* days in the land which ye shall possess.

CHAPTER 6

The great commandment

NOW these *are* ᴿthe commandments, the statutes, and the judgments, which the Lord your God commanded to teach you, that

---

CHAP. 5

BC 1451

6 Ex. 20:2, etc.
6 Heb. *servants*
7 Ex. 20:3
8 Ex. 20:4
9 Ex. 34:7
10 Jer. 32:18
Dan. 9:4
11 Ex. 20:7
Lev. 19:12
Mat. 5:33
12 Ex. 20:8
13 Ex. 23:12
& 35:2
Ezek. 20:12
14 Gen. 2:2
Ex. 16:29
Heb. 4:4
15 ch. 15:15
& 16:12
& 24:18, 22
15 ch. 4:34, 37
16 Ex. 20:12
Lev. 19:3
ch. 27:16
Eph. 6:2, 3
Col. 3:20
16 ch. 4:40
17 Ex. 20:13
Mat. 5:21
18 Ex. 20:14
Luke 18:20
Jas. 2:11
19 Ex. 20:15
Rom. 13:9
20 Ex. 20:16
Mic. 2:2
Hab. 2:9
Luke 12:15
Rom. 7:7

Ex. 24:12   22
& 31:18
ch. 4:13
Ex. 20:18, 19   23
Ex. 19:19   24
ch. 4:33   24
Judg. 13:22
ch. 18:16   25
Heb. *add*   25
to hear
ch. 4:33   26
Ex. 20:19   27
Heb. 12:19
ch. 18:17   28
ch. 32:29   29
Ps. 81:13
Is. 48:18
Mat. 23:37
Luke 19:42
ch. 11:1   29
ch. 4:40   29
Gal. 3:19   31
ch. 17:20   32
& 28:14
Josh. 1:7
Prov. 4:27
ch. 10:12   33
Jer. 7:23
ch. 4:40   33

CHAP. 6

BC 1451

ch. 12:1   1

ye might do *them* in the land whither ye ᴺgo to possess it:

2 ᴿThat thou mightest fear the LORD thy God, to keep all his statutes and his commandments, which I command thee, thou, and thy son, and thy son's son, all the days of thy life; ᴿand that thy days may be prolonged.

3 Hear therefore, O Israel, and observe to do *it;* that it may be well with thee, and that ye may increase mightily, ᴿas the LORD God of thy fathers hath promised thee, in ᴿthe land that floweth with milk and honey.

4 ᴿHear, O Israel: The LORD our God *is* one LORD:

5 And ᴿthou shalt love the LORD thy God ᴿwith all thine heart, and with all thy soul, and with all thy might.

6 And ᴿthese words, which I command thee this day, shall be in thine heart:

7 And ᴿthou shalt ᴺteach them diligently unto thy children, and shalt talk of them when thou sittest in thine house, and when thou walkest by the way, and when thou liest down, and when thou risest up.

8 ᴿAnd thou shalt bind them for a sign upon thine hand, and they shall be as frontlets between thine eyes.

9 ᴿAnd thou shalt write them upon the posts of thy house, and on thy gates.

Rewards of obedience

10 And it shall be, when the LORD thy God shall have brought thee into the land which he sware unto thy fathers, to Abraham, to Isaac, and to Jacob, to give thee great and goodly cities, ᴿwhich thou buildedst not,

11 And houses full of all good *things,* which thou filledst not, and wells digged, which thou diggedst not, vineyards and olive trees, which thou plantedst not; ᴿwhen thou shalt have eaten and be full;

12 *Then* beware lest thou forget the LORD, which brought thee forth out of the land of Egypt, from the house of ᴺbondage.

13 Thou shalt ᴿfear the LORD thy God, and serve him, and ᴿshalt swear by his name.

14 Ye shall not go after other gods, ᴿof the gods of the people which *are* round about you;

15 (For ᴿthe LORD thy God *is* a jealous God among you) ᴿlest the anger of the LORD thy God be kindled against thee, and destroy thee from off the face of the earth.

16 ᴿYe shall not tempt the LORD your God, ᴿas ye tempted *him* in Măs'-săh.

17 Ye shall ᴿdiligently keep the commandments of the LORD your God, and his testimonies, and his statutes, which he hath commanded thee.

18 And thou ᴿshalt do *that which is* right and good in the sight of the LORD: that it may be well with thee, and that thou mayest go in and possess the good land which the LORD sware unto thy fathers,

19 ᴿTo cast out all thine enemies from before thee, as the LORD hath spoken.

Instruction of the children

20 *And* ᴿwhen thy son asketh thee ᴺin time to come, saying, What *mean* the testimonies, and the statutes, and the judgments, which the LORD our God hath commanded you?

21 Then thou shalt say unto thy son, We were Pharaoh's bondmen in Egypt; and the LORD brought us out of Egypt ᴿwith a mighty hand:

22 ᴿAnd the LORD shewed signs and wonders, great and ᴺsore, upon Egypt, upon Pharaoh, and upon all his household, before our eyes:

23 And he brought us out from thence, that he might bring us in, to give us the land which he sware unto our fathers.

24 And the LORD commanded us to do all these statutes, ᴿto fear the LORD our God, ᴿfor our good always, that ᴿhe might preserve us alive, as *it is* at this day.

25 And ᴿit shall be our righteousness, if we observe to do all these commandments before the LORD our God, as he hath commanded us.

CHAPTER 7

Extermination of the Canaanites

WHEN the ᴿLORD thy God shall bring thee into the land whither thou goest to possess it, and hath cast out many nations before thee, ᴿthe Hittites, and the Gĭr'-gă-shītes, and the Amorites, and the Canaanites, and the Pĕ-rĭz'-zītes, and the Hī'-vītes, and the Jĕb'-ū-sītes, seven nations ᴿgreater and mightier than thou;

2 And when the LORD thy God shall ᴿdeliver them before thee; thou shalt smite them, *and* ᴿutterly destroy them; ᴿthou shalt make no covenant with them, nor shew mercy unto them:

3 ᴿNeither shalt thou make marriages with them; thy daughter thou shalt not give unto his son, nor his daughter shalt thou take unto thy son.

4 For they will turn away thy son from following me, that they may serve other gods: ᴿso will the anger of the LORD be kindled against you, and destroy thee suddenly.

5 But thus shall ye deal with them; ye shall ᴿdestroy their altars, and break down their

---

CHAP. 6

BC 1451

1 Heb. *pass over*
2 ch. 10:12, 13
Eccl. 12:13
2 ch. 4:40
Prov. 3:1, 2
3 Gen. 22:17
3 Ex. 3:8
4 John 17:3
1 Cor. 8:4, 6
5 Mat. 22:37
Mark 12:30
5 2 Ki. 23:25
6 ch. 11:18
Ps. 119:11, 98
7 ch. 11:19
Ps. 78:4-6
7 Heb. *whet, or, sharpen*
8 Prov. 6:21
& 7:3
9 ch. 11:20
Is. 57:1
10 Josh. 24:13
Ps. 105:44
11 ch. 8:10
12 Heb. *bondmen, or, servants*
13 Mat. 4:10
Luke 4:8
13 Is. 45:23
& 65:16
Jer. 4:2
14 ch. 13:7
15 Ex. 20:5
ch. 4:24
15 ch. 7:4
& 11:17
16 Mat. 4:7
Luke 4:12
16 1 Cor. 10:9
17 Ps. 119:4

Ex. 15:26 — 18
ch. 12:28
& 13:18
Num. 33:52, 53 — 19
Ex. 13:14 — 20
Heb. *to morrow* — 20
Ex. 13:3 — 21
Ex. 7, & 8, — 22
& 9, & 10
Heb. *evil* — 22
ver. 2 — 24
Job 35:7, 8 — 24
Jer. 32:39
ch. 4:1 — 24
Ps. 41:2
Lev. 18:5 — 25
Rom. 10:3, 5

CHAP. 7

BC 1451

ch. 31:3 — 1
Ex. 33:2 — 1
ch. 4:38 — 1
ch. 23:14 — 2
Josh. 6:17 — 2
& 8:24 & 9:24
Josh. 2:14 — 2
Judg. 1:24 & 2:2
1 Ki. 11:2 — 3
Ezra 9:2
ch. 6:15 — 4
Ex. 23:24 — 5
& 34:13
ch. 12:2, 3

N images, and cut down their groves, and burn their graven images with fire.

A chosen people

6 R For thou *art* an holy people unto the Lord thy God: R the Lord thy God hath chosen thee to be a special people unto himself, above all people that *are* upon the face of the earth.

7 The Lord did not set his love upon you, nor choose you, because ye were more in number than any people; for ye *were* R the fewest of all people:

8 But R because the Lord loved you, and because he would keep R the oath which he had sworn unto your fathers, R hath the Lord brought you out with a mighty hand, and redeemed you out of the house of bondmen, from the hand of Pharaoh king of Egypt.

9 Know therefore that the Lord thy God, he *is* God, R the faithful God, R which keepeth covenant and mercy with them that love him and keep his commandments to a thousand generations;

10 And R repayeth them that hate him to their face, to destroy them: R he will not be slack to him that hateth him, he will repay him to his face.

11 Thou shalt therefore keep the commandments, and the statutes, and the judgments, which I command thee this day, to do them.

Benefits of obedience

12 R Wherefore it shall come to pass, N if ye hearken to these judgments, and keep, and do them, that the Lord thy God shall keep unto thee R the covenant and the mercy which he sware unto thy fathers:

13 And he will R love thee, and bless thee, and multiply thee: R he will also bless the fruit of thy womb, and the fruit of thy land, thy corn, and thy wine, and thine oil, the increase of thy kine, and the flocks of thy sheep, in the land which he sware unto thy fathers to give thee.

14 Thou shalt be blessed above all people: R there shall not be male or female barren among you, or among your cattle.

15 And the Lord will take away from thee all sickness, and will put none of the R evil diseases of Egypt, which thou knowest, upon thee; but will lay them upon all *them* that hate thee.

16 And R thou shalt consume all the people which the Lord thy God shall deliver thee; R thine eye shall have no pity upon them: neither shalt thou serve their gods; for that *will be* R a snare unto thee.

CHAP. 7
BC 1451
5 Heb. *statues, or, pillars*
6 Ps. 50:5
Jer. 2:3
6 Ex. 19:5
Amos 3:2
1 Pet. 2:9
7 ch. 10:22
8 ch. 10:15
8 Luke 1:55, 72, 73
8 Ex. 13:3, 14
9 1 Cor. 1:9
2 Cor. 1:18
2 Thes. 3:3
2 Tim. 2:13
Heb. 11:11
9 Neh. 1:5
Dan. 9:4
10 Is. 59:18
10 ch. 32:35
12 ch. 28:1
12 Heb. *because*
12 Ps. 105:8, 9
13 John 14:21
13 ch. 28:4
14 Ex. 23:26, etc.
15 Ex. 15:26
ch. 28:27, 60
16 ver. 2
16 ch. 19:13, 21
16 Judg. 8:27

Num. 33:53	17
ch. 31:6	18
Ps. 105:5	18
ch. 4:34 & 29:3	19
Josh. 24:12	20
Num. 16:3	21
Josh. 3:10	
Neh. 9:32	21
Ex. 23:29, 30	22
Heb. *pluck off*	22
Heb. *before thy face*	23
Josh. 10:24, 25, 42	24
Ex. 17:14	24
Josh. 23:9	24
Ex. 32:20	25
1 Chr. 14:12	
Josh. 7:1, 21	25
Judg. 8:27	25
Zeph. 1:3	
ch. 17:1	25
Lev. 27:28	26
Josh. 6:17 & 7:1	

CHAP. 8
BC 1451
ch. 4:1 & 5:32, 33 & 6:1-3 ... 1
ch. 1:3 & 2:7 ... 2
Amos 2:10
Ex. 16:4 ... 2
ch. 13:3
John 2:25 ... 2
Ex. 16:2, 3 ... 3
Ex. 16:12, 14, 35 ... 3

---

17 If thou shalt say in thine heart, These nations *are* more than I; how can I R dispossess them?

18 R Thou shalt not be afraid of them: *but* shalt well R remember what the Lord thy God did unto Pharaoh, and unto all Egypt;

19 R The great temptations which thine eyes saw, and the signs, and the wonders, and the mighty hand, and the stretched out arm, whereby the Lord thy God brought thee out: so shall the Lord thy God do unto all the people of whom thou art afraid.

20 R Moreover the Lord thy God will send the hornet among them, until they that are left, and hide themselves from thee, be destroyed.

21 Thou shalt not be affrighted at them: for the Lord thy God *is* R among you, R a mighty God and terrible.

22 R And the Lord thy God will N put out those nations before thee by little and little: thou mayest not consume them at once, lest the beasts of the field increase upon thee.

23 But the Lord thy God shall deliver them N unto thee, and shall destroy them with a mighty destruction, until they be destroyed.

24 And R he shall deliver their kings into thine hand, and thou shalt destroy their name R from under heaven: R there shall no man be able to stand before thee, until thou have destroyed them.

25 The graven images of their gods R shall ye burn with fire: thou R shalt not desire the silver or gold *that is* on them, nor take *it* unto thee, lest thou be R snared therein: for it *is* R an abomination to the Lord thy God.

26 Neither shalt thou bring an abomination into thine house, lest thou be a cursed thing like it: *but* thou shalt utterly detest it, and thou shalt utterly abhor it; R for it *is* a cursed thing.

CHAPTER 8

God's care in the wilderness

ALL the commandments which I command thee this day R shall ye observe to do, that ye may live, and multiply, and go in and possess the land which the Lord sware unto your fathers.

2 And thou shalt remember all the way which the Lord thy God R led thee these forty years in the wilderness, to humble thee, *and* R to prove thee, R to know what *was* in thine heart, whether thou wouldest keep his commandments, or no.

3 And he humbled thee, and R suffered thee to hunger, and R fed thee with măn'-nă, which thou knewest not, neither did thy fathers know; that he might make thee know that man

doth [R]not live by bread only, but by every *word* that proceedeth out of the mouth of the LORD doth man live.

4 [R]Thy raiment waxed not old upon thee, neither did thy foot swell, these forty years.

5 [R]Thou shalt also consider in thine heart, that, as a man chasteneth his son, *so* the LORD thy God chasteneth thee.

6 Therefore thou shalt keep the commandments of the LORD thy God, [R]to walk in his ways, and to fear him.

7 For the LORD thy God bringeth thee into a good land, [R]a land of brooks of water, of fountains and depths that spring out of valleys and hills;

8 A land of wheat, and barley, and vines, and fig trees, and pomegranates; a land [N]of oil olive, and honey;

9 A land wherein thou shalt eat bread without scarceness, thou shalt not lack any *thing* in it; a land [R]whose stones *are* iron, and out of whose hills thou mayest dig brass.

10 [R]When thou hast eaten and art full, then thou shalt bless the LORD thy God for the good land which he hath given thee.

Dangers of wealth

11 Beware that thou forget not the LORD thy God, in not keeping his commandments, and his judgments, and his statutes, which I command thee this day:

12 [R]Lest *when* thou hast eaten and art full, and hast built goodly houses, and dwelt *therein;*

13 And *when* thy herds and thy flocks multiply, and thy silver and thy gold is multiplied, and all that thou hast is multiplied;

14 [R]Then thine heart be lifted up, and thou [R]forget the LORD thy God, which brought thee forth out of the land of Egypt, from the house of bondage;

15 Who [R]led thee through that great and terrible wilderness, [R]*wherein were* fiery serpents, and scorpions, and drought, where *there was* no water; [R]who brought thee forth water out of the rock of flint;

16 Who fed thee in the wilderness with [R]măn'-nă, which thy fathers knew not, that he might humble thee, and that he might prove thee, [R]to do thee good at thy latter end;

17 [R]And thou say in thine heart, My power and the might of *mine* hand hath gotten me this wealth.

18 But thou shalt remember the LORD thy God: [R]for *it is* he that giveth thee power to get wealth, [R]that he may establish his covenant which he sware unto thy fathers, as *it is* this day.

19 And it shall be, if thou do at all forget the LORD thy God, and walk after other gods, and serve them, and worship them, [R]I testify against you this day that ye shall surely perish.

20 As the nations which the LORD destroyeth before your face, [R]so shall ye perish; because ye would not be obedient unto the voice of the LORD your God.

CHAPTER 9

Unmerited success

HEAR, O Israel: Thou *art* to [R]pass over Jordan this day, to go in to possess nations [R]greater and mightier than thyself, cities great and [R]fenced up to heaven,

2 A people great and tall, [R]the children of the Anakims, whom thou knowest, and *of whom* thou hast heard *say,* Who can stand before the children of Anak!

3 Understand therefore this day, that the LORD thy God *is* he which [R]goeth over before thee; *as* a [R]consuming fire [R]he shall destroy them, and he shall bring them down before thy face: [R]so shalt thou drive them out, and destroy them quickly, as the LORD hath said unto thee.

4 [R]Speak not thou in thine heart, after that the LORD thy God hath cast them out from before thee, saying, For my righteousness the LORD hath brought me in to possess this land: but [R]for the wickedness of these nations the LORD doth drive them out from before thee.

5 [R]Not for thy righteousness, or for the uprightness of thine heart, dost thou go to possess their land: but for the wickedness of these nations the LORD thy God doth drive them out from before thee, and that he may perform [R]the word which the LORD sware unto thy fathers, Abraham, Isaac, and Jacob.

Israel's stubbornness

6 Understand therefore, that the LORD thy God giveth thee not this good land to possess it for thy righteousness; for thou *art* [R]a stiffnecked people.

7 Remember, *and* forget not, how thou provokedst the LORD thy God to wrath in the wilderness: [R]from the day that thou didst depart out of the land of Egypt, until ye came unto this place, ye have been rebellious against the LORD.

8 Also [R]in Hôr'-ĕb ye provoked the LORD to wrath, so that the LORD was angry with you to have destroyed you.

9 [R]When I was gone up into the mount to receive the tables of stone, *even* the tables of the covenant which the LORD made with you,

Center reference column

CHAP. 8
BC 1451
3 Mat. 4:4
Luke 4:4
4 ch. 29:5
Neh. 9:21
5 2 Sam. 7:14
Ps. 89:32
Prov. 3:12
Heb. 12:5, 6
Rev. 3:19
6 ch. 5:33
7 ch. 11:10-12
8 Heb. *of olive tree of oil*
9 ch. 33:25
10 ch. 6:11, 12
12 ch. 28:47 & 32:15
Hos. 13:6
14 1 Cor. 4:7
14 Ps. 106:21
15 Is. 63:12-14
Jer. 2:6
15 Num. 21:6
Hos. 13:5
15 Num. 20:11
16 Ex. 16:15
16 Jer. 24:5, 6
Heb. 12:11
17 ch. 9:4
18 Prov. 10:22
Hos. 2:8
18 ch. 7:8, 12

ch. 4:26 & 30:18 19
Dan. 9:11, 12 20

CHAP. 9
BC 1491
ch. 11:31 1
Josh. 3:16 & 4:19
ch. 4:38 & 11:23 1
ch. 1:28 1
Num. 13:22, 28, 32, 33 2
ch. 31:3 3
Josh. 3:11
ch. 4:24 3
Heb. 12:29
ch. 7:23 3
Ex. 23:31 3
ch. 7:24
ch. 8:17 4
Rom. 11:6, 20
1 Cor. 4:4, 7
Gen. 15:16 4
Lev. 18:24
ch. 18:12
Tit. 3:5 5
Gen. 12:7 5
& 13:15 & 15:7 & 17:8 & 26:4
ver. 13 6
Ex. 32:9 & 33:3 & 34:9
Ex. 14:11 7
& 16:2 & 17:2
Num. 11:4 & 20:2 & 25:2
ch. 31:27
Ex. 32:4 8
Ps. 106:19
Ex. 24:12, 15 9

then ^R I abode in the mount forty days and forty nights, I neither did eat bread nor drink water:

10 ^R And the LORD delivered unto me two tables of stone written with the finger of God; and on them *was written* according to all the words, which the LORD spake with you in the mount out of the midst of the fire ^R in the day of the assembly.

11 And it came to pass at the end of forty days and forty nights, *that* the LORD gave me the two tables of stone, *even* the tables of the covenant.

12 And the LORD said unto me, ^R Arise, get thee down quickly from hence; for thy people which thou hast brought forth out of Egypt have corrupted *themselves;* they are ^R quickly turned aside out of the way which I commanded them; they have made them a molten image.

13 Furthermore ^R the LORD spake unto me, saying, I have seen this people, and, behold, ^R it *is* a stiffnecked people:

14 ^R Let me alone, that I may destroy them, and ^R blot out their name from under heaven: ^R and I will make of thee a nation mightier and greater than they.

15 ^R So I turned and came down from the mount, and ^R the mount burned with fire: and the two tables of the covenant *were* in my two hands.

16 And ^R I looked, and, behold, ye had sinned against the LORD your God, *and* had made you a molten calf: ye had turned aside quickly out of the way which the LORD had commanded you.

17 And I took the two tables, and cast them out of my two hands, and brake them before your eyes.

18 And I ^R fell down before the LORD, as at the first, forty days and forty nights: I did neither eat bread, nor drink water, because of all your sins which ye sinned, in doing wickedly in the sight of the LORD, to provoke him to anger.

19 ^R For I was afraid of the anger and hot displeasure, wherewith the LORD was wroth against you to destroy you. ^R But the LORD hearkened unto me at that time also.

20 And the LORD was very angry with Aaron to have destroyed him: and I prayed for Aaron also the same time.

21 And ^R I took your sin, the calf which ye had made, and burnt it with fire, and stamped it, *and* ground *it* very small, *even* until it was as small as dust: and I cast the dust thereof into the brook that descended out of the mount.

CHAP. **9**
BC 1491
9 Ex. 24:18
& 34:28
10 Ex. 31:18
10 Ex. 19:17
& 20:1
ch. 4:10 & 10:4
12 Ex. 32:7
12 ch. 31:29
Judg. 2:17
13 Ex. 32:9
13 ver. 6
ch. 10:16
& 31:27
2 Ki. 17:14
14 Ex. 32:10
14 ch. 29:20
14 Num. 14:12
15 Ex. 32:15
15 Ex. 19:18
ch. 4:11 & 5:23
16 Ex. 32:19
18 Ex. 34:28
19 Ex. 32:10, 11
19 Ex. 32:14
& 33:17
ch. 10:10
Ps. 106:23
21 Ex. 32:20
Is. 31:7

Num. 11:1, 3, 5	22
Ex. 17:7	22
Num. 11:4, 34	22
Num. 13:3	23
& 14:1	
Ps. 106:24, 25	23
ch. 31:27	24
ver. 18	25
Ex. 32:11, etc.	26
Ex. 6:6-8	28
1 Sam. 14:25	
Ex. 32:12	28
Num. 14:16	
ch. 4:20	29
1 Ki. 8:51	
Neh. 1:10	

CHAP. **10**
BC 1491
Ex. 34:1, 2 — 1
Ex. 25:10 — 1
Ex. 25:16, 21 — 2
Ex. 25:5, 10 — 3
Ex. 34:4 — 3
Heb. *words* — 4
Ex. 20:1 — 4
Ex. 34:29 — 5
Ex. 40:20 — 5

22 And at ^R Tăb'-ĕ-räh, and at ^R Măs'-săh, and at ^R Kĭb'-rōth-hăt-tā'-ă-väh, ye provoked the LORD to wrath.

23 Likewise ^R when the LORD sent you from Kā'-dĕsh-bär'-nĕ-ă, saying, Go up and possess the land which I have given you; then ye rebelled against the commandment of the LORD your God, and ^R ye believed him not, nor hearkened to his voice.

24 ^R Ye have been rebellious against the LORD from the day that I knew you.

Moses' intercession

25 ^R Thus I fell down before the LORD forty days and forty nights, as I fell down *at the first;* because the LORD had said he would destroy you.

26 ^R I prayed therefore unto the LORD, and said, O Lord GOD, destroy not thy people and thine inheritance, which thou hast redeemed through thy greatness, which thou hast brought forth out of Egypt with a mighty hand.

27 Remember thy servants, Abraham, Isaac, and Jacob; look not unto the stubbornness of this people, nor to their wickedness, nor to their sin:

28 Lest ^R the land whence thou broughtest us out say, ^R Because the LORD was not able to bring them into the land which he promised them, and because he hated them, he hath brought them out to slay them in the wilderness.

29 ^R Yet they *are* thy people and thine inheritance, which thou broughtest out by thy mighty power and by thy stretched out arm.

CHAPTER 10

The second stone tables

AT that time the LORD said unto me, ^R Hew thee two tables of stone like unto the first, and come up unto me into the mount, and ^R make thee an ark of wood.

2 And I will write on the tables the words that were in the first tables which thou brakest, and ^R thou shalt put them in the ark.

3 And I made an ark of ^R shĭt'-tĭm wood, and ^R hewed two tables of stone like unto the first, and went up into the mount, having the two tables in mine hand.

4 And he wrote on the tables, according to the first writing, the ten ^N commandments, ^R which the LORD spake unto you in the mount out of the midst of the fire in the day of the assembly: and the LORD gave them unto me.

5 And I turned myself and ^R came down from the mount, and ^R put the tables in the ark

which I had made; ᴿand there they be, as the LORD commanded me.

6 And the children of Israel took their journey from Bē͞er'-ōth ᴿof the children of Jā'-ă-kăn to ᴿMō'-sĕ-rā: ᴿthere Aaron died, and there he was buried; and ĕl-ē-ā'-zär his son ministered in the priest's office in his stead.

7 ᴿFrom thence they journeyed unto Gŭd-gō'-dăh; and from Gŭd-gō'-dăh to Jŏt'-băth, a land of rivers of waters.

8 At that time ᴿthe LORD separated the tribe of Levi, ᴿto bear the ark of the covenant of the LORD, ᴿto stand before the LORD to minister unto him, and ᴿto bless in his name, unto this day.

9 ᴿWherefore Levi hath no part nor inheritance with his brethren; the LORD is his inheritance, according as the LORD thy God promised him.

10 And ᴿI stayed in the mount, according to the ᴺfirst time, forty days and forty nights; and ᴿthe LORD hearkened unto me at that time also, and the LORD would not destroy thee.

11 ᴿAnd the LORD said unto me, Arise, ᴺtake thy journey before the people, that they may go in and possess the land, which I sware unto their fathers to give unto them.

God's requirements

12 And now, Israel, ᴿwhat doth the LORD thy God require of thee, but ᴿto fear the LORD thy God, ᴿto walk in all his ways, and ᴿto love him, and to serve the LORD thy God with all thy heart and with all thy soul,

13 To keep the commandments of the LORD, and his statutes, which I command thee this day ᴿfor thy good?

14 Behold, ᴿthe heaven and the heaven of heavens is the LORD's thy God, ᴿthe earth also, with all that therein is.

15 ᴿOnly the LORD had a delight in thy fathers to love them, and he chose their seed after them, even you above all people, as it is this day.

16 Circumcise therefore ᴿthe foreskin of your heart, and be no more ᴿstiffnecked.

17 For the LORD your God is ᴿGod of gods, and ᴿLord of lords, a great God, ᴿa mighty, and a terrible, which ᴿregardeth not persons, nor taketh reward:

18 ᴿHe doth execute the judgment of the fatherless and widow, and loveth the stranger, in giving him food and raiment.

19 ᴿLove ye therefore the stranger: for ye were strangers in the land of Egypt.

20 ᴿThou shalt fear the LORD thy God; him shalt thou serve, and to him shalt thou ᴿcleave, ᴿand swear by his name.

CHAP. 10
BC 1491
5　1 Ki. 8:9
6　Num. 33:31
6　Num. 33:30
6　Num. 20:28
　　& 33:38
7　Num. 33:32, 33
8　Num. 3:6
8　Num. 4:15
8　ch. 18:5
8　Num. 6:23
　　ch. 21:5
9　ch. 18:1, 2
　　Ezek. 44:28
10　Ex. 34:28
　　ch. 9:18, 25
10　Or, former days
10　Ex. 32:14,
　　33, 34 & 33:17
　　ch. 9:19
11　Ex. 33:1
11　Heb. go in
　　journey
12　Mic. 6:8
12　ch. 6:13
12　ch. 5:33
12　ch. 6:5
　　Mat. 22:37
13　ch. 6:24
14　1 Ki. 8:27
14　Ex. 19:5
15　ch. 4:37
16　ch. 30:6
　　Jer. 4:4
　　Rom. 2:28, 29
　　Col. 2:11
16　ch. 9:6, 13
17　Dan. 2:47
17　Rev. 19:16
17　ch. 7:21
17　Acts 10:34
　　Rom. 2:11
　　Eph. 6:9
　　1 Pet. 1:17
18　Ps. 68:5
19　Lev. 19:33, 34
20　Mat. 4:10
20　ch. 11:22
20　Ps. 63:11

Ex. 15:2　　　21
Jer. 17:14
Ps. 106:21, 22　21
Gen. 46:27　　22
Acts 7:14
Gen. 15:5　　　22

CHAP. 11
BC 1491
ch. 10:12　　　1
Zech. 3:7　　　1
ch. 8:5　　　　2
ch. 5:24　　　　2
Ps. 78:12　　　3
& 135:9
Ps. 106:11　　　4
Num. 16:1, 31　6
Or, living
substance which
followed them
Heb. was at
their feet　　　6
ch. 5:3 & 7:19　7
Josh. 1:6, 7　　8
ch. 4:40　　　　9
Prov. 10:27
ch. 9:5　　　　9
Ex. 3:8　　　　9
ch. 8:7　　　11
Heb. seeketh　　12

21 ᴿHe is thy praise, and he is thy God, ᴿthat hath done for thee these great and terrible things, which thine eyes have seen.

22 Thy fathers went down into Egypt ᴿwith threescore and ten persons; and now the LORD thy God hath made thee ᴿas the stars of heaven for multitude.

CHAPTER 11

God's greatness

THEREFORE thou shalt ᴿlove the LORD thy God, and ᴿkeep his charge, and his statutes, and his judgments, and his commandments, alway.

2 And know ye this day: for I speak not with your children which have not known, and which have not seen ᴿthe chastisement of the LORD your God, ᴿhis greatness, his mighty hand, and his stretched out arm,

3 ᴿAnd his miracles, and his acts, which he did in the midst of Egypt unto Pharaoh the king of Egypt, and unto all his land;

4 And what he did unto the army of Egypt, unto their horses, and to their chariots; ᴿhow he made the water of the Red sea to overflow them as they pursued after you, and how the LORD hath destroyed them unto this day;

5 And what he did unto you in the wilderness, until ye came into this place;

6 And ᴿwhat he did unto Dā'-thăn and Ă-bī'-răm, the sons of Ē-lī'-ăb, the son of Reuben: how the earth opened her mouth, and swallowed them up, and their households, and their tents, and all the ᴺsubstance that ᴺwas in their possession, in the midst of all Israel:

7 But ᴿyour eyes have seen all the great acts of the LORD which he did.

Necessity of keeping God's law

8 Therefore shall ye keep all the commandments which I command you this day, that ye may ᴿbe strong, and go in and possess the land, whither ye go to possess it;

9 And ᴿthat ye may prolong your days in the land, ᴿwhich the LORD sware unto your fathers to give unto them and to their seed, ᴿa land that floweth with milk and honey.

10 For the land, whither thou goest in to possess it, is not as the land of Egypt, from whence ye came out, where thou sowedst thy seed, and wateredst it with thy foot, as a garden of herbs:

11 ᴿBut the land, whither ye go to possess it, is a land of hills and valleys, and drinketh water of the rain of heaven:

12 A land which the LORD thy God ᴺcareth

for: ᴿthe eyes of the Lᴏʀᴅ thy God *are* always upon it, from the beginning of the year even unto the end of the year.

Benefits of obedience

13 And it shall come to pass, if ye shall hearken ᴿdiligently unto my commandments which I command you this day, ᴿto love the Lᴏʀᴅ your God, and to serve him with all your heart and with all your soul,

14 That ᴿI will give *you* the rain of your land in his due season, ᴿthe first rain and the latter rain, that thou mayest gather in thy corn, and thy wine, and thine oil.

15 ᴿAnd I will ᴺsend grass in thy fields for thy cattle, that thou mayest ᴿeat and be full.

16 Take heed to yourselves, ᴿthat your heart be not deceived, and ye turn aside, and ᴿserve other gods, and worship them;

17 And *then* ᴿthe Lᴏʀᴅ's wrath be kindled against you, and he ᴿshut up the heaven, that there be no rain, and that the land yield not her fruit; and *lest* ᴿye perish quickly from off the good land which the Lᴏʀᴅ giveth you.

18 Therefore ᴿshall ye lay up these my words in your heart and in your soul, and ᴿbind them for a sign upon your hand, that they may be as frontlets between your eyes.

19 ᴿAnd ye shall teach them your children, speaking of them when thou sittest in thine house, and when thou walkest by the way, when thou liest down, and when thou risest up.

20 ᴿAnd thou shalt write them upon the door posts of thine house, and upon thy gates:

21 That ᴿyour days may be multiplied, and the days of your children, in the land which the Lᴏʀᴅ sware unto your fathers to give them, ᴿas the days of heaven upon the earth.

22 For if ᴿye shall diligently keep all these commandments which I command you, to do them, to love the Lᴏʀᴅ your God, to walk in all his ways, and ᴿto cleave unto him;

23 Then will the Lᴏʀᴅ ᴿdrive out all these nations from before you, and ye shall ᴿpossess greater nations and mightier than yourselves.

24 ᴿEvery place whereon the soles of your feet shall tread shall be yours: ᴿfrom the wilderness and Lĕb'-ȧ-nọn, from the river, the river Ēū-phrā'-tēs, even unto the uttermost sea shall your coast be.

25 ᴿThere shall no man be able to stand before you: *for* the Lᴏʀᴅ your God shall ᴿlay the fear of you and the dread of you upon all the land that ye shall tread upon, ᴿas he hath said unto you.

A blessing and a curse

26 ᴿBehold, I set before you this day a blessing and a curse;

27 ᴿA blessing, if ye obey the commandments of the Lᴏʀᴅ your God, which I command you this day:

28 And a ᴿcurse, if ye will not obey the commandments of the Lᴏʀᴅ your God, but turn aside out of the way which I command you this day, to go after other gods, which ye have not known.

29 And it shall come to pass, when the Lᴏʀᴅ thy God hath brought thee in unto the land whither thou goest to possess it, that thou shalt put ᴿthe blessing upon mount Gĕ-rī'-zĭm, and the curse upon mount Ē'-băl.

30 *Are* they not on the other side Jordan, by the way where the sun goeth down, in the land of the Canaanites, which dwell in the champaign over against Gĭl'-găl, ᴿbeside the plains of Mō'-rēh?

31 ᴿFor ye shall pass over Jordan to go in to possess the land which the Lᴏʀᴅ your God giveth you, and ye shall possess it, and dwell therein.

32 And ye shall observe ᴿto do all the statutes and judgments which I set before you this day.

CHAPTER 12

God will choose his sanctuary

THESE ᴿ*are* the statutes and judgments, which ye shall observe to do in the land, which the Lᴏʀᴅ God of thy fathers giveth thee to possess it, ᴿall the days that ye live upon the earth.

2 ᴿYe shall utterly destroy all the places, wherein the nations which ye shall ᴺpossess served their gods, ᴿupon the high mountains, and upon the hills, and under every green tree:

3 And ᴿye shall ᴺoverthrow their altars, and break their pillars, and burn their groves with fire; and ye shall hew down the graven images of their gods, and destroy the names of them out of that place.

4 ᴿYe shall not do so unto the Lᴏʀᴅ your God.

5 But unto the place which the Lᴏʀᴅ your God shall ᴿchoose out of all your tribes to put his name there, *even* unto his habitation shall ye seek, and thither thou shalt come:

6 And ᴿthither ye shall bring your burnt offerings, and your sacrifices, and your ᴿtithes, and heave offerings of your hand, and your

vows, and your freewill offerings, and the firstlings of your herds and of your flocks:

7 And ᴿthere ye shall eat before the Lᴏʀᴅ your God, and ᴿye shall rejoice in all that ye put your hand unto, ye and your households, wherein the Lᴏʀᴅ thy God hath blessed thee.

8 Ye shall not do after all *the things* that we do here this day, ᴿevery man whatsoever *is* right in his own eyes.

9 For ye are not as yet come to the rest and to the inheritance, which the Lᴏʀᴅ your God giveth you.

10 But *when* ᴿye go over Jordan, and dwell in the land which the Lᴏʀᴅ your God giveth you to inherit, and *when* he giveth you rest from all your enemies round about, so that ye dwell in safety;

11 Then there shall be ᴿa place which the Lᴏʀᴅ your God shall choose to cause his name to dwell there; thither shall ye bring all that I command you; your burnt offerings, and your sacrifices, your tithes, and the heave offering of your hand, and all ᴺyour choice vows which ye vow unto the Lᴏʀᴅ:

12 And ᴿye shall rejoice before the Lᴏʀᴅ your God, ye, and your sons, and your daughters, and your menservants, and your maidservants, and the Levite that *is* within your gates; forasmuch as ᴿhe hath no part nor inheritance with you.

13 ᴿTake heed to thyself that thou offer not thy burnt offerings in every place that thou seest:

14 ᴿBut in the place which the Lᴏʀᴅ shall choose in one of thy tribes, there thou shalt offer thy burnt offerings, and there thou shalt do all that I command thee.

Permission given to eat flesh

15 Notwithstanding ᴿthou mayest kill and eat flesh in all thy gates, whatsoever thy soul lusteth after, according to the blessing of the Lᴏʀᴅ thy God which he hath given thee: ᴿthe unclean and the clean may eat thereof, ᴿas of the roebuck, and as of the hart.

16 ᴿOnly ye shall not eat the blood; ye shall pour it upon the earth as water.

17 Thou mayest not eat within thy gates the tithe of thy corn, or of thy wine, or of thy oil, or the firstlings of thy herds or of thy flock, nor any of thy vows which thou vowest, nor thy freewill offerings, or heave offering of thine hand:

18 ᴿBut thou must eat them before the Lᴏʀᴅ thy God in the place which the Lᴏʀᴅ thy God shall choose, thou, and thy son, and thy daughter, and thy manservant, and thy maid-

servant, and the Levite that *is* within thy gates: and thou shalt rejoice before the Lᴏʀᴅ thy God in all that thou puttest thine hands unto.

19 ᴿTake heed to thyself that thou forsake not the Levite ᴺas long as thou livest upon the earth.

20 When the Lᴏʀᴅ thy God shall enlarge thy border, ᴿas he hath promised thee, and thou shalt say, I will eat flesh, because thy soul longeth to eat flesh; thou mayest eat flesh, whatsoever thy soul lusteth after.

21 If the place which the Lᴏʀᴅ thy God hath chosen to put his name there be too far from thee, then thou shalt kill of thy herd and of thy flock, which the Lᴏʀᴅ hath given thee, as I have commanded thee, and thou shalt eat in thy gates whatsoever thy soul lusteth after.

22 ᴿEven as the roebuck and the hart is eaten, so thou shalt eat them: the unclean and the clean shall eat *of* them alike.

23 ᴿOnly ᴺbe sure that thou eat not the blood: ᴿfor the blood *is* the life; and thou mayest not eat the life with the flesh.

24 Thou shalt not eat it; thou shalt pour it upon the earth as water.

25 Thou shalt not eat it; ᴿthat it may go well with thee, and with thy children after thee, ᴿwhen thou shalt do *that which is* right in the sight of the Lᴏʀᴅ.

26 Only thy ᴿholy things which thou hast, and ᴿthy vows, thou shalt take, and go unto the place which the Lᴏʀᴅ shall choose:

27 And ᴿthou shalt offer thy burnt offerings, the flesh and the blood, upon the altar of the Lᴏʀᴅ thy God: and the blood of thy sacrifices shall be poured out upon the altar of the Lᴏʀᴅ thy God, and thou shalt eat the flesh.

28 Observe and hear all these words which I command thee, ᴿthat it may go well with thee, and with thy children after thee for ever, when thou doest *that which is* good and right in the sight of the Lᴏʀᴅ thy God.

Worship of other gods prohibited

29 When ᴿthe Lᴏʀᴅ thy God shall cut off the nations from before thee, whither thou goest to possess them, and thou ᴺsucceedest them, and dwellest in their land;

30 Take heed to thyself that thou be not snared ᴺby following them, after that they be destroyed from before thee; and that thou inquire not after their gods, saying, How did these nations serve their gods? even so will I do likewise.

31 ᴿThou shalt not do so unto the Lᴏʀᴅ thy God: for every ᴺabomination to the Lᴏʀᴅ,

which he hateth, have they done unto their gods; for ^Reven their sons and their daughters they have burnt in the fire to their gods.

32 What thing soever I command you, observe to do it: ^Rthou shalt not add thereto, nor diminish from it.

CHAPTER 13

Penalties for idolatry

IF there arise among you a prophet, or a ^Rdreamer of dreams, ^Rand giveth thee a sign or a wonder,

2 And ^Rthe sign or the wonder come to pass, whereof he spake unto thee, saying, Let us go after other gods, which thou hast not known, and let us serve them;

3 Thou shalt not hearken unto the words of that prophet, or that dreamer of dreams: for the LORD your God ^Rproveth you, to know whether ye love the LORD your God with all your heart and with all your soul.

4 Ye shall ^Rwalk after the LORD your God, and fear him, and keep his commandments, and obey his voice, and ye shall serve him, and ^Rcleave unto him.

5 And ^Rthat prophet, or that dreamer of dreams, shall be put to death; because he hath ^Nspoken to turn *you* away from the LORD your God, which brought you out of the land of Egypt, and redeemed you out of the house of bondage, to thrust thee out of the way which the LORD thy God commanded thee to walk in. ^RSo shalt thou put the evil away from the midst of thee.

6 ^RIf thy brother, the son of thy mother, or thy son, or thy daughter, or ^Rthe wife of thy bosom, or thy friend, ^Rwhich *is* as thine own soul, entice thee secretly, saying, Let us go and serve other gods, which thou hast not known, thou, nor thy fathers;

7 *Namely,* of the gods of the people which *are* round about you, nigh unto thee, or far off from thee, from the *one* end of the earth even unto the *other* end of the earth;

8 Thou shalt ^Rnot consent unto him, nor hearken unto him; neither shall thine eye pity him, neither shalt thou spare, neither shalt thou conceal him:

9 But ^Rthou shalt surely kill him; ^Rthine hand shall be first upon him to put him to death, and afterwards the hand of all the people.

10 And thou shalt stone him with stones, that he die; because he hath sought to thrust thee away from the LORD thy God, which brought thee out of the land of Egypt, from the house of ^Nbondage.

11 And ^Rall Israel shall hear, and fear, and shall do no more any such wickedness as this is among you.

12 ^RIf thou shalt hear *say* in one of thy cities, which the LORD thy God hath given thee to dwell there, saying,

13 *Certain* men, ^Nthe children of Bē'-lĭ-ăl, ^Rare gone out from among you, and have ^Rwithdrawn the inhabitants of their city, saying, ^RLet us go and serve other gods, which ye have not known;

14 Then shalt thou inquire, and make search, and ask diligently; and, behold, *if it be* truth, *and* the thing certain, *that* such abomination is wrought among you;

15 Thou shalt surely smite the inhabitants of that city with the edge of the sword, ^Rdestroying it utterly, and all that *is* therein, and the cattle thereof, with the edge of the sword.

16 And thou shalt gather all the spoil of it into the midst of the street thereof, and shalt ^Rburn with fire the city, and all the spoil thereof every whit, for the LORD thy God: and it shall be ^Ran heap for ever; it shall not be built again.

17 And ^Rthere shall cleave nought of the ^Ncursed thing to thine hand: that the LORD may ^Rturn from the fierceness of his anger, and shew thee mercy, and have compassion upon thee, and multiply thee, ^R as he hath sworn unto thy fathers;

18 When thou shalt hearken to the voice of the LORD thy God, ^Rto keep all his commandments which I command thee this day, to do *that which is* right in the eyes of the LORD thy God.

CHAPTER 14

A chosen people

YE *are* ^Rthe children of the LORD your God: ^Rye shall not cut yourselves, nor make any baldness between your eyes for the dead.

2 ^RFor thou *art* an holy people unto the LORD thy God, and the LORD hath chosen thee to be a peculiar people unto himself, above all the nations that *are* upon the earth.

Clean and unclean foods

3 ^RThou shalt not eat any abominable thing.

4 ^RThese *are* the beasts which ye shall eat: the ox, the sheep, and the goat,

5 The hart, and the roebuck, and the fallow deer, and the wild goat, and the ^{NN}pygarg, and the wild ox, and the chamois.

6 And every beast that parteth the hoof, and

Center reference column

CHAP. 12
BC 1451

31 ch. 18:10
Jer. 32:35
Ezek. 23:37
32 ch. 4:2
Josh. 1:7
Rev. 22:18

CHAP. 13
BC 1451

1 Zech. 10:2
1 Mat. 24:24
2 Thes. 2:9
2 See ch. 18:22
Mat. 7:22
3 ch. 8:2
See Mat. 24:24
2 Thes. 2:11
4 2 Ki. 23:3
2 Chr. 34:31
4 ch. 30:20
5 Jer. 14:15
Zech. 13:3
5 Heb. *spoken revolt against the LORD*
5 ch. 17:7
1 Cor. 5:13
6 ch. 17:2
6 See Gen. 16:5
ch. 28:54
Prov. 5:20
6 1 Sam. 18:1, 3
& 20:17
8 Prov. 1:10
9 ch. 17:5
9 ch. 17:7
Acts 7:58
10 Heb. *bondmen*

ch. 19:20 — 11
Judg. 20:1, 2 — 12
Or, *naughty men* — 13
1 John 2:19 — 13
Jude 19
2 Ki. 17:21 — 13
ver. 2, 6 — 13
Lev. 27:28 — 15
Josh. 6:17, 21
Josh. 6:24 — 16
Josh. 8:28 — 16
Jer. 49:2
Josh. 6:18 — 17
Or, *devoted* — 17
Josh. 7:26 — 17
Gen. 22:17 — 17
& 26:4, 24,
& 28:14
ch. 12:25, 28, 32 — 18

CHAP. 14
BC 1451

Rom. 8:16 — 1
& 9:8, 26
Gal. 3:26
Lev. 19:28 — 1
& 21:5
Jer. 16:6
& 41:5 & 47:5
1 Thes. 4:13
Lev. 20:26 — 2
ch. 7:6
& 26:18, 19
Ezek. 4:14 — 3
Acts 10:13, 14
Lev. 11:2, etc. — 4
Or, *bison* — 5
Heb. *dishon* — 5

cleaveth the cleft into two claws, *and* cheweth the cud among the beasts, that ye shall eat.

7 Nevertheless these ye shall not eat of them that chew the cud, or of them that divide the cloven hoof; *as* the camel, and the hare, and the coney: for they chew the cud, but divide not the hoof; *therefore* they *are* unclean unto you.

8 And the swine, because it divideth the hoof, yet cheweth not the cud, it *is* unclean unto you: ye shall not eat of their flesh, [R]nor touch their dead carcase.

9 [R]These ye shall eat of all that *are* in the waters: all that have fins and scales shall ye eat:

10 And whatsoever hath not fins and scales ye may not eat; it *is* unclean unto you.

11 *Of* all clean birds ye shall eat.

12 [R]But these *are they* of which ye shall not eat: the eagle, and the ossifrage, and the ospray,

13 And the glede, and the kite, and the vulture after his kind,

14 And every raven after his kind,

15 And the owl, and the night hawk, and the cuckow, and the hawk after his kind,

16 The little owl, and the great owl, and the swan,

17 And the pelican, and the gier eagle, and the cormorant,

18 And the stork, and the heron after her kind, and the lapwing, and the bat.

19 And [R]every creeping thing that flieth *is* unclean unto you: [R]they shall not be eaten.

20 *But of* all clean fowls ye may eat.

21 [R]Ye shall not eat *of* any thing that dieth of itself: thou shalt give it unto the stranger that *is* in thy gates, that he may eat it; or thou mayest sell it unto an alien: [R]for thou *art* an holy people unto the Lord thy God. [R]Thou shalt not seethe a kid in his mother's milk.

The tithe of fruits

22 [R]Thou shalt truly tithe all the increase of thy seed, that the field bringeth forth year by year.

23 [R]And thou shalt eat before the Lord thy God, in the place which he shall choose to place his name there, the tithe of thy corn, of thy wine, and of thine oil, and [R]the firstlings of thy herds and of thy flocks; that thou mayest learn to fear the Lord thy God always.

24 And if the way be too long for thee, so that thou art not able to carry it; *or* [R]if the place be too far from thee, which the Lord thy God shall choose to set his name there, when the Lord thy God hath blessed thee:

25 Then shalt thou turn *it* into money, and

bind up the money in thine hand, and shalt go unto the place which the Lord thy God shall choose:

26 And thou shalt bestow that money for whatsoever thy soul lusteth after, for oxen, or for sheep, or for wine, or for strong drink, or for whatsoever thy soul [N]desireth: [R]and thou shalt eat there before the Lord thy God, and thou shalt rejoice, thou, and thine household,

27 And [R]the Levite that *is* within thy gates; thou shalt not forsake him; for [R]he hath no part nor inheritance with thee.

28 [R]At the end of three years thou shalt bring forth all the tithe of thine increase the same year, and shalt lay *it* up within thy gates:

29 [R]And the Levite, (because [R]he hath no part nor inheritance with thee,) and the stranger, and the fatherless, and the widow, which *are* within thy gates, shall come, and shall eat and be satisfied; that [R]the Lord thy God may bless thee in all the work of thine hand which thou doest.

CHAPTER 15

Cancellation of debts

AT the end of [R]*every* seven years thou shalt make a release.

2 And this is the manner of the release: Every [N]creditor that lendeth *aught* unto his neighbour shall release *it;* he shall not exact *it* of his neighbour, or of his brother; because it is called the Lord's release.

3 [R]Of a foreigner thou mayest exact *it again:* but *that* which is thine with thy brother thine hand shall release;

4 [N]Save when there shall be no poor among you; [R]for the Lord shall greatly bless thee in the land which the Lord thy God giveth thee *for* an inheritance to possess it:

5 Only [R]if thou carefully hearken unto the voice of the Lord thy God, to observe to do all these commandments which I command thee this day.

6 For the Lord thy God blesseth thee, as he promised thee: and [R]thou shalt lend unto many nations, but thou shalt not borrow; and [R]thou shalt reign over many nations, but they shall not reign over thee.

Providing for the poor

7 If there be among you a poor man of one of thy brethren within any of thy gates in thy land which the Lord thy God giveth thee, [R]thou shalt not harden thine heart, nor shut thine hand from thy poor brother:

8 [R]But thou shalt open thine hand wide unto

him, and shalt surely lend him sufficient for his need, *in that* which he wanteth.

9 Beware that there be not a [N]thought in thy [N]wicked heart, saying, The seventh year, the year of release, is at hand; and thine [R]eye be evil against thy poor brother, and thou givest him nought; and [R]he cry unto the Lord against thee, and [R]it be sin unto thee.

10 Thou shalt surely give him, and [R]thine heart shall not be grieved when thou givest unto him: because that [R]for this thing the Lord thy God shall bless thee in all thy works, and in all that thou puttest thine hand unto.

11 For [R]the poor shall never cease out of the land: therefore I command thee, saying, Thou shalt open thine hand wide unto thy brother, to thy poor, and to thy needy, in thy land.

Concerning servants

12 *And* [R]if thy brother, an Hebrew man, or an Hebrew woman, be sold unto thee, and serve thee six years; then in the seventh year thou shalt let him go free from thee.

13 And when thou sendest him out free from thee, thou shalt not let him go away empty:

14 Thou shalt furnish him liberally out of thy flock, and out of thy floor, and out of thy winepress: *of that* wherewith the Lord thy God hath [R]blessed thee thou shalt give unto him.

15 And [R]thou shalt remember that thou wast a bondman in the land of Egypt, and the Lord thy God redeemed thee: therefore I command thee this thing to day.

16 And it shall be, [R]if he say unto thee, I will not go away from thee; because he loveth thee and thine house, because he is well with thee;

17 Then thou shalt take an awl, and thrust *it* through his ear unto the door, and he shall be thy servant for ever. And also unto thy maidservant thou shalt do likewise.

18 It shall not seem hard unto thee, when thou sendest him away free from thee; for he hath been worth [R]a double hired servant *to thee,* in serving thee six years: and the Lord thy God shall bless thee in all that thou doest.

Consecration of firstlings

19 [R]All the firstling males that come of thy herd and of thy flock thou shalt sanctify unto the Lord thy God: thou shalt do no work with the firstling of thy bullock, nor shear the firstling of thy sheep.

20 [R]Thou shalt eat *it* before the Lord thy God year by year in the place which the Lord shall choose, thou and thy household.

CHAP. 15
BC 1451
9 Heb. *word*
9 Heb. *Belial*
9 ch. 28:54, 56
Mat. 20:15
9 ch. 24:15
9 Mat. 25:41, 42
10 2 Cor. 9:5, 7
10 ch. 14:29
& 24:19
11 Mat. 26:11
Mark 14:7
John 12:8
12 Ex. 21:2
Lev. 25:39
Jer. 34:14
14 Prov. 10:22
15 ch. 5:15
& 16:12
16 Ex. 21:5, 6
18 See Is. 16:14
& 21:16
19 Ex. 13:2
& 34:19
Lev. 27:26
Num. 3:13
20 ch. 12:5-7, 17
& 14:23
& 16:11, 14

Lev. 22:20　21
ch. 12:15, 22　22
ch. 12:16, 23　23

CHAP. 16
BC 1451
Ex. 12:2, etc.　1
Ex. 13:4　1
Ex. 12:29, 42　1
Num. 28:19　2
ch. 12:5, 26　2
Ex. 12:15, 19, 39　3
& 13:3, 6, 7
& 34:18
Ex. 13:7　4
Ex. 12:10　4
& 34:25
Or, *kill*　5
Ex. 12:6　6
Ex. 12:8, 9　7
2 Chr. 35:13
2 Ki. 23:23　7
John 2:13 & 11:55
Ex. 12:16　8
& 13:6
Lev. 23:8
Heb. *restraint,*　8
Lev. 23:36
Ex. 23:16　9
& 34:22
Lev. 23:15
Acts 2:1
Or, *sufficiency*　10

21 [R]And if there be *any* blemish therein, *as if it be* lame, or blind, *or have* any ill blemish, thou shalt not sacrifice it unto the Lord thy God.

22 Thou shalt eat it within thy gates: [R]the unclean and the clean *person shall eat it* alike, as the roebuck, and as the hart.

23 [R]Only thou shalt not eat the blood thereof; thou shalt pour it upon the ground as water.

CHAPTER 16

The passover

OBSERVE the [R]month of Abib, and keep the passover unto the Lord thy God: for [R]in the month of Abib the Lord thy God brought thee forth out of Egypt [R]by night.

2 Thou shalt therefore sacrifice the passover unto the Lord thy God, of the flock and [R]the herd, in the [R]place which the Lord shall choose to place his name there.

3 [R]Thou shalt eat no leavened bread with it; seven days shalt thou eat unleavened bread therewith, *even* the bread of affliction; for thou camest forth out of the land of Egypt in haste: that thou mayest remember the day when thou camest forth out of the land of Egypt all the days of thy life.

4 [R]And there shall be no leavened bread seen with thee in all thy coast seven days; [R]neither shall there *any thing* of the flesh, which thou sacrificedst the first day at even, remain all night until the morning.

5 Thou mayest not [N]sacrifice the passover within any of thy gates, which the Lord thy God giveth thee:

6 But at the place which the Lord thy God shall choose to place his name in, there thou shalt sacrifice the passover [R]at even, at the going down of the sun, at the season that thou camest forth out of Egypt.

7 And thou shalt [R]roast and eat *it* [R]in the place which the Lord thy God shall choose: and thou shalt turn in the morning, and go unto thy tents.

8 Six days thou shalt eat unleavened bread: and [R]on the seventh day *shall be* a [N]solemn assembly to the Lord thy God: thou shalt do no work *therein.*

The feast of weeks

9 [R]Seven weeks shalt thou number unto thee: begin to number the seven weeks from *such time as* thou beginnest *to put* the sickle to the corn.

10 And thou shalt keep the feast of weeks unto the Lord thy God with [N]a tribute of a

freewill offering of thine hand, which thou shalt give *unto the* LORD *thy God,* Raccording as the LORD thy God hath blessed thee:

11 And Rthou shalt rejoice before the LORD thy God, thou, and thy son, and thy daughter, and thy manservant, and thy maidservant, and the Levite that *is* within thy gates, and the stranger, and the fatherless, and the widow, that *are* among you, in the place which the LORD thy God hath chosen to place his name there.

12 RAnd thou shalt remember that thou wast a bondman in Egypt: and thou shalt observe and do these statutes.

The feast of tabernacles

13 RThou shalt observe the feast of tabernacles seven days, after that thou hast gathered in thy Ncorn and thy wine:

14 And Rthou shalt rejoice in thy feast, thou, and thy son, and thy daughter, and thy manservant, and thy maidservant, and the Levite, the stranger, and the fatherless, and the widow, that *are* within thy gates.

15 RSeven days shalt thou keep a solemn feast unto the LORD thy God in the place which the LORD shall choose: because the LORD thy God shall bless thee in all thine increase, and in all the works of thine hands, therefore thou shalt surely rejoice.

16 RThree times in a year shall all thy males appear before the LORD thy God in the place which he shall choose; in the feast of unleavened bread, and in the feast of weeks, and in the feast of tabernacles: and Rthey shall not appear before the LORD empty:

17 Every man *shall give* Nas he is able, Raccording to the blessing of the LORD thy God which he hath given thee.

Justice enjoined

18 RJudges and officers shalt thou make thee in all thy gates, which the LORD thy God giveth thee, throughout thy tribes: and they shall judge the people with just judgment.

19 RThou shalt not wrest judgment; Rthou shalt not respect persons, Rneither take a gift: for a gift doth blind the eyes of the wise, and pervert the Nwords of the righteous.

20 NThat which is altogether just shalt thou follow, that thou mayest Rlive, and inherit the land which the LORD thy God giveth thee.

21 RThou shalt not plant thee a grove of any trees near unto the altar of the LORD thy God, which thou shalt make thee.

22 RNeither shalt thou set thee up *any* Nimage; which the LORD thy God hateth.

CHAPTER 17

Penalties for idolatry

THOU Rshalt not sacrifice unto the LORD thy God *any* bullock, or Nsheep, wherein is blemish, *or* any evilfavouredness: for that *is* an abomination unto the LORD thy God.

2 RIf there be found among you, within any of thy gates which the LORD thy God giveth thee, man or woman, that hath wrought wickedness in the sight of the LORD thy God, Rin transgressing his covenant,

3 And hath gone and served other gods, and worshipped them, either Rthe sun, or moon, or any of the host of heaven, Rwhich I have not commanded;

4 RAnd it be told thee, and thou hast heard *of it,* and inquired diligently, and, behold, *it be* true, *and* the thing certain, *that* such abomination is wrought in Israel:

5 Then shalt thou bring forth that man or that woman, which have committed that wicked thing, unto thy gates, *even* that man or that woman, and Rshalt stone them with stones, till they die.

6 RAt the mouth of two witnesses, or three witnesses, shall he that is worthy of death be put to death; *but* at the mouth of one witness he shall not be put to death.

7 RThe hands of the witnesses shall be first upon him to put him to death, and afterward the hands of all the people. So Rthou shalt put the evil away from among you.

8 RIf there arise a matter too hard for thee in judgment, Rbetween blood and blood, between plea and plea, and between stroke and stroke, *being* matters of controversy within thy gates: then shalt thou arise, Rand get thee up into the place which the LORD thy God shall choose;

9 And Rthou shalt come unto the priests the Levites, and Runto the judge that shall be in those days, and inquire; Rand they shall shew thee the sentence of judgment:

10 And thou shalt do according to the sentence, which they of that place which the LORD shall choose shall shew thee; and thou shalt observe to do according to all that they inform thee:

11 According to the sentence of the law which they shall teach thee, and according to the judgment which they shall tell thee, thou shalt do: thou shalt not decline from the sentence which they shall shew thee, *to* the right hand, nor *to* the left.

12 And Rthe man that will do presumptuously, Nand will not hearken unto the priest Rthat standeth to minister there before the LORD thy God, or unto the judge, even that

man shall die: and ᴿthou shalt put away the evil from Israel.

13 ᴿAnd all the people shall hear, and fear, and do no more presumptuously.

Choice of a king

14 When thou art come unto the land which the Lᴏʀᴅ thy God giveth thee, and shalt possess it, and shalt dwell therein, and shalt say, ᴿI will set a king over me, like as all the nations that *are* about me;

15 Thou shalt in any wise set *him* king over thee, ᴿwhom the Lᴏʀᴅ thy God shall choose: *one* ᴿfrom among thy brethren shalt thou set king over thee: thou mayest not set a stranger over thee, which *is* not thy brother.

16 But he shall not multiply ᴿhorses to himself, nor cause the people ᴿto return to Egypt, to the end that he should multiply horses: forasmuch as ᴿthe Lᴏʀᴅ hath said unto you, ᴿYe shall henceforth return no more that way.

17 Neither shall he multiply wives to himself, that ᴿhis heart turn not away: neither shall he greatly multiply to himself silver and gold.

18 ᴿAnd it shall be, when he sitteth upon the throne of his kingdom, that he shall write him a copy of this law in a book out of ᴿ*that which is* before the priests the Levites:

19 And ᴿit shall be with him, and he shall read therein all the days of his life: that he may learn to fear the Lᴏʀᴅ his God, to keep all the words of this law and these statutes, to do them:

20 That his heart be not lifted up above his brethren, and that he ᴿturn not aside from the commandment, *to* the right hand, or *to* the left: to the end that he may prolong *his* days in his kingdom, he, and his children, in the midst of Israel.

CHAPTER 18

Portion of priests and Levites

THE priests the Levites, *and* all the tribe of Levi, ᴿshall have no part nor inheritance with Israel: they ᴿshall eat the offerings of the Lᴏʀᴅ made by fire, and his inheritance.

2 Therefore shall they have no inheritance among their brethren: the Lᴏʀᴅ *is* their inheritance, as he hath said unto them.

3 And this shall be the priest's due from the people, from them that offer a sacrifice, whether *it be* ox or sheep; and ᴿthey shall give unto the priest the shoulder, and the two cheeks, and the maw.

4 ᴿThe firstfruit *also* of thy corn, of thy wine, and of thine oil, and the first of the fleece of thy sheep, shalt thou give him.

5 For ᴿthe Lᴏʀᴅ thy God hath chosen him out of all thy tribes, ᴿto stand to minister in the name of the Lᴏʀᴅ, him and his sons for ever.

6 And if a Levite come from any of thy gates out of all Israel, where he ᴿsojourned, and come with all the desire of his mind ᴿunto the place which the Lᴏʀᴅ shall choose;

7 Then he shall minister in the name of the Lᴏʀᴅ his God, ᴿas all his brethren the Levites *do,* which stand there before the Lᴏʀᴅ.

8 They shall have like ᴿportions to eat, beside ᴺthat which cometh of the sale of his patrimony.

Canaanite practices forbidden

9 When thou art come into the land which the Lᴏʀᴅ thy God giveth thee, ᴿthou shalt not learn to do after the abominations of those nations.

10 There shall not be found among you *any one* that maketh his son or his daughter ᴿto pass through the fire, ᴿ*or* that useth divination, *or* an observer of times, or an enchanter, or a witch,

11 ᴿOr a charmer, or a consulter with familiar spirits, or a wizard, or a ᴿnecromancer.

12 For all that do these things *are* an abomination unto the Lᴏʀᴅ: and ᴿbecause of these abominations the Lᴏʀᴅ thy God doth drive them out from before thee.

13 Thou shalt be ᴺperfect with the Lᴏʀᴅ thy God.

14 For these nations, which thou shalt ᴺpossess, hearkened unto observers of times, and unto diviners: but as for thee, the Lᴏʀᴅ thy God hath not suffered thee so *to do.*

Coming prophet predicted

15 ᴿThe Lᴏʀᴅ thy God will raise up unto thee a Prophet from the midst of thee, of thy brethren, like unto me; unto him ye shall hearken;   ★

16 According to all that thou desiredst of the Lᴏʀᴅ thy God in Hôr'-ĕb ᴿin the day of the assembly, saying, ᴿLet me not hear again the voice of the Lᴏʀᴅ my God, neither let me see this great fire any more, that I die not.

17 And the Lᴏʀᴅ said unto me, ᴿThey have well *spoken that* which they have spoken.

18 ᴿI will raise them up a Prophet from among their brethren, like unto thee, and ᴿwill put my words in his mouth; ᴿand he shall speak unto them all that I shall command him.   ★

19 ᴿAnd it shall come to pass, *that* whosoever will not hearken unto my words which he shall speak in my name, I will require *it* of him.   ★

20 But ᴿthe prophet, which shall presume to

speak a word in my name, which I have not commanded him to speak, or [R]that shall speak in the name of other gods, even that prophet shall die.

21 And if thou say in thine heart, How shall wc know thc word which the LORD hath not spoken?

22 [R]When a prophet speaketh in the name of the LORD, [R]if the thing follow not, nor come to pass, that *is* the thing which the LORD hath not spoken, *but* the prophet hath spoken it [R]presumptuously: thou shalt not be afraid of him.

CHAPTER 19

Cities of refuge

WHEN the LORD thy God [R]hath cut off the nations, whose land the LORD thy God giveth thee, and thou [N]succeedest them, and dwellest in their cities, and in their houses;

2 [R]Thou shalt separate three cities for thee in the midst of thy land, which the LORD thy God giveth thee to possess it.

3 Thou shalt prepare thee a way, and divide the coasts of thy land, which the LORD thy God giveth thee to inherit, into three parts, that every slayer may flee thither.

4 And [R]this *is* the case of the slayer, which shall flee thither, that he may live: Whoso killeth his neighbour ignorantly, whom he hated not [N]in time past;

5 As when a man goeth into the wood with his neighbour to hew wood, and his hand fetcheth a stroke with the axe to cut down the tree, and the [N]head slippeth from the [N]helve, and [N]lighteth upon his neighbour, that he die; he shall flee unto one of those cities, and live:

6 [R]Lest the avenger of the blood pursue the slayer, while his heart is hot, and overtake him, because the way is long, and [N]slay him; whereas he *was* not worthy of death, inasmuch as he hated him not [N]in time past.

7 Wherefore I command thee, saying, Thou shalt separate three cities for thee.

8 And if the LORD thy God [R]enlarge thy coast, as he hath sworn unto thy fathers, and give thee all the land which he promised to give unto thy fathers;

9 If thou shalt keep all these commandments to do them, which I command thee this day, to love the LORD thy God, and to walk ever in his ways; [R]then shalt thou add three cities more for thee, beside these three:

10 That innocent blood be not shed in thy land, which the LORD thy God giveth thee *for* an inheritance, and *so* blood be upon thee.

11 But [R]if any man hate his neighbour, and lie in wait for him, and rise up against him, and smite him [N]mortally that he die, and fleeth into one of these cities:

12 Then the elders of his city shall send and fetch him thence, and deliver him into the hand of the avenger of blood, that he may die.

13 [R]Thine eye shall not pity him, [R]but thou shalt put away *the guilt of* innocent blood from Israel, that it may go well with thee.

Removing landmarks

14 [R]Thou shalt not remove thy neighbour's landmark, which they of old time have set in thine inheritance, which thou shalt inherit in the land that the LORD thy God giveth thee to possess it.

Law of witnesses

15 [R]One witness shall not rise up against a man for any iniquity, or for any sin, in any sin that he sinneth: at the mouth of two witnesses, or at the mouth of three witnesses, shall the matter be established.

16 If a false witness [R]rise up against any man to tcstify against him [N]*that which is* wrong;

17 Then both the men, between whom the controversy *is,* shall stand before the LORD, [R]before the priests and the judges, which shall be in those days;

18 And the judges shall make diligent inquisition: and, behold, *if* the witness *be* a false witness, *and* hath testified falsely against his brother;

19 [R]Then shall ye do unto him, as he had thought to have done unto his brother: so [R]shalt thou put the evil away from among you.

20 [R]And those which remain shall hear, and fear, and shall henceforth commit no more any such evil among you.

21 [R]And thine eye shall not pity; *but* [R]life *shall go* for life, eye for eye, tooth for tooth, hand for hand, foot for foot.

CHAPTER 20

Laws of military service

WHEN thou goest out to battle against thine enemies, and seest [R]horses, and chariots, *and* a people more than thou, be not afraid of them: for the LORD thy God *is* [R]with thee, which brought thee up out of the land of Egypt.

2 And it shall be, when ye are come nigh unto the battle, that the priest shall approach and speak unto the people,

3 And shall say unto them, Hear, O Israel, ye approach this day unto battle against your

---

Center reference column

CHAP. **18**
BC 1451
20 ch. 13:1, 2
Jer. 2:8
22 Jer. 28:9
22 See ch. 13:2
22 ver. 20

CHAP. **19**
BC 1451
1 ch. 12:29
1 Heb. *inheritest, or, possessest*
2 Ex. 21:13
Num. 35:10, 14
Josh. 20:2
4 Num. 35:15
ch. 4:42
4 Heb. *from yesterday the third day*
5 Heb. *iron*
5 Heb. *wood*
5 Heb. *findeth*
6 Num. 35:12
6 Heb. *smite him in life*
6 Heb. *from yesterday the third day*
8 Gen. 15:18
ch. 12:20
9 Josh. 20:7

Num. 35:16, 24   **11**
ch. 27:24
Prov. 28:17
Heb. *in life*   **11**
ch. 13:8   **13**
Num. 35:33, 34   **13**
1 Ki. 2:31
ch. 27:17   **14**
Prov. 22:28
Hos. 5:10
Num. 35:30   **15**
ch. 17:6
Mat. 18:16
John 8:17
2 Cor. 13:1
1 Tim. 5:19
Heb. 10:28
Ps. 27:12   **16**
& 35:11
Or, *falling away*   **16**
ch. 17:9 & 21:5   **17**
Prov. 19:5   **19**
Dan. 6:24
ch. 13:5 & 17:7   **19**
& 21:21 & 22:21
ch. 17:13   **20**
& 21:21
ver. 13   **21**
Ex. 21:23, 24   **21**
Lev. 24:20
Mat. 5:38

CHAP. **20**
BC 1451
See Ps. 20:7   **1**
Is. 31:1
Num 23:21   **1**
ch. 31:6, 8
2 Chr. 13:12
& 32:7, 8

enemies: let not your hearts ᴺfaint, fear not, and do not ᴺtremble, neither be ye terrified because of them;

4 For the LORD your God *is* he that goeth with you, ᴿto fight for you against your enemies, to save you.

5 And the officers shall speak unto the people, saying, What man *is there* that hath built a new house, and hath not ᴿdedicated it? let him go and return to his house, lest he die in the battle, and another man dedicate it.

6 And what man *is he* that hath planted a vineyard, and hath not *yet* ᴺeaten of it? let him *also* go and return unto his house, lest he die in the battle, and another man eat of it.

7 ᴿAnd what man *is there* that hath betrothed a wife, and hath not taken her? let him go and return unto his house, lest he die in the battle, and another man take her.

8 And the officers shall speak further unto the people, and they shall say, ᴿWhat man *is there that is* fearful and fainthearted? let him go and return unto his house, lest his brethren's heart ᴺfaint as well as his heart.

9 And it shall be, when the officers have made an end of speaking unto the people, that they shall make captains of the armies ᴺto lead the people.

Instruction for sieges

10 When thou comest nigh unto a city to fight against it, ᴿthen proclaim peace unto it.

11 And it shall be, if it make thee answer of peace, and open unto thee, then it shall be, *that* all the people *that is* found therein shall be tributaries unto thee, and they shall serve thee.

12 And if it will make no peace with thee, but will make war against thee, then thou shalt besiege it:

13 And when the LORD thy God hath delivered it into thine hands, ᴿthou shalt smite every male thereof with the edge of the sword:

14 But the women, and the little ones, and ᴿthe cattle, and all that is in the city, *even* all the spoil thereof, shalt thou ᴺtake unto thyself; and ᴿthou shalt eat the spoil of thine enemies, which the LORD thy God hath given thee.

15 Thus shalt thou do unto all the cities *which are* very far off from thee, which *are* not of the cities of these nations.

16 But ᴿof the cities of these people, which the LORD thy God doth give thee *for* an inheritance, thou shalt save alive nothing that breatheth:

17 But thou shalt utterly destroy them; *namely,* the Hittites, and the Amorites, the Canaanites, and the Pĕ-rĭz'-zītes, the Hī'-vītes,

and the Jĕb'-ū-śītes; as the LORD thy God hath commanded thee:

18 That ᴿthey teach you not to do after all their abominations, which they have done unto their gods; so should ye ᴿsin against the LORD your God.

19 When thou shalt besiege a city a long time, in making war against it to take it, thou shalt not destroy the trees thereof by forcing an axe against them: for thou mayest eat of them, and thou shalt not cut them down (ᴺfor the tree of the field *is* man's *life*) ᴺto employ *them* in the siege:

20 Only the trees which thou knowest that they *be* not trees for meat, thou shalt destroy and cut them down; and thou shalt build bulwarks against the city that maketh war with thee, until ᴺit be subdued.

CHAPTER 21

Concerning unknown murderer

IF *one* be found slain in the land which the LORD thy God giveth thee to possess it, lying in the field, *and* it be not known who hath slain him:

2 Then thy elders and thy judges shall come forth, and they shall measure unto the cities which *are* round about him that is slain:

3 And it shall be, *that* the city *which is* next unto the slain man, even the elders of that city shall take an heifer, which hath not been wrought with, *and* which hath not drawn in the yoke;

4 And the elders of that city shall bring down the heifer unto a rough valley, which is neither eared nor sown, and shall strike off the heifer's neck there in the valley:

5 And the priests the sons of Levi shall come near; for ᴿthem the LORD thy God hath chosen to minister unto him, and to bless in the name of the LORD; and ᴿby their ᴺword shall every controversy and every stroke be *tried:*

6 And all the elders of that city, *that are* next unto the slain *man,* ᴿshall wash their hands over the heifer that is beheaded in the valley:

7 And they shall answer and say, Our hands have not shed this blood, neither have our eyes seen *it.*

8 Be merciful, O LORD, unto thy people Israel, whom thou hast redeemed, ᴿand lay not innocent blood ᴺunto thy people of Israel's charge. And the blood shall be forgiven them.

9 So ᴿshalt thou put away the *guilt of* innocent blood from among you, when thou shalt do *that which is* right in the sight of the LORD.

Captive women

10 When thou goest forth to war against thine enemies, and the LORD thy God hath delivered them into thine hands, and thou hast taken them captive,

11 And seest among the captives a beautiful woman, and hast a desire unto her, that thou wouldest have her to thy wife;

12 Then thou shalt bring her home to thine house; and she shall shave her head, and NNpare her nails;

13 And she shall put the raiment of her captivity from off her, and shall remain in thine house, and Rbewail her father and her mother a full month: and after that thou shalt go in unto her, and be her husband, and she shall be thy wife.

14 And it shall be, if thou have no delight in her, then thou shalt let her go whither she will; but thou shalt not sell her at all for money, thou shalt not make merchandise of her, because thou hast Rhumbled her.

Law of the firstborn

15 If a man have two wives, one beloved, Rand another hated, and they have born him children, *both* the beloved and the hated; and *if* the firstborn son be hers that was hated:

16 Then it shall be, Rwhen he maketh his sons to inherit *that* which he hath, *that* he may not make the son of the beloved firstborn before the son of the hated, *which is indeed* the firstborn:

17 But he shall acknowledge the son of the hated *for* the firstborn, Rby giving him a double portion of all Nthat he hath: for he *is* Rthe beginning of his strength; Rthe right of the firstborn *is* his.

Stoning of a rebellious son

18 If a man have a stubborn and rebellious son, which will not obey the voice of his father, or the voice of his mother, and *that*, when they have chastened him, will not hearken unto them:

19 Then shall his father and his mother lay hold on him, and bring him out unto the elders of his city, and unto the gate of his place;

20 And they shall say unto the elders of his city, This our son *is* stubborn and rebellious, he will not obey our voice; *he is* a glutton, and a drunkard.

21 And all the men of his city shall stone him with stones, that he die: Rso shalt thou put evil away from among you; Rand all Israel shall hear, and fear.

CHAP. **21**
BC 1451
12 Or, *suffer to grow*
12 Heb. *make, or, dress*
13 See Ps. 45:10
14 Gen. 34.2
ch. 22:29
Judg. 19:24
15 Gen. 29:33
16 1 Chr. 5:2 & 26:10
2 Chr. 11:19, 22
17 See 1 Chr. 5:1
17 Heb. *that is found with him*
17 Gen. 49:3
17 Gen. 25:31, 33
21 ch. 13:5 & 19:19, 20 & 22:21, 24
21 ch. 13:11

ch. 19:6 & 22:26 **22**
Acts 23:29 & 25:11, 25 & 26:31
Josh. 8:29 **23** & 10:26, 27
John 19:31
Gal. 3:13 **23**
Heb. *the curse of God*: See **23**
Num. 25:4
2 Sam. 21:6
Lev. 18:25 **23**
Num. 35:34

CHAP. **22**
BC 1451
Ex. 23:4 **1**
Ex. 23:5 **4**
Lev. 22:28 **6**
ch. 4:40 **7**
Lev. 19:19 **9**
Heb. *fulness of thy seed* **9**
See 2 Cor. **10** 6:14-16
Lev. 19:19 **11**

Punishment by death

22 And if a man have committed a sin Rworthy of death, and he be to be put to death, and thou hang him on a tree:

23 RHis body shall not remain all night upon the tree, but thou shalt in any wise bury him that day; (for Rhe that is hanged *is* Naccursed of God;) that Rthy land be not defiled, which the LORD thy God giveth thee *for* an inheritance.

CHAPTER 22

Various laws

THOU Rshalt not see thy brother's ox or his sheep go astray, and hide thyself from them: thou shalt in any case bring them again unto thy brother.

2 And if thy brother *be* not nigh unto thee, or if thou know him not, then thou shalt bring it unto thine own house, and it shall be with thee until thy brother seek after it, and thou shalt restore it to him again.

3 In like manner shalt thou do with his ass; and so shalt thou do with his raiment; and with all lost thing of thy brother's, which he hath lost, and thou hast found, shalt thou do likewise: thou mayest not hide thyself.

4 RThou shalt not see thy brother's ass or his ox fall down by the way, and hide thyself from them: thou shalt surely help him to lift *them* up again.

5 The woman shall not wear that which pertaineth unto a man, neither shall a man put on a woman's garment: for all that do so *are* abomination unto the LORD thy God.

6 If a bird's nest chance to be before thee in the way in any tree, or on the ground, *whether they be* young ones, or eggs, and the dam sitting upon the young, or upon the eggs, Rthou shalt not take the dam with the young:

7 *But* thou shalt in any wise let the dam go, and take the young to thee; Rthat it may be well with thee, and *that* thou mayest prolong *thy* days.

8 When thou buildest a new house, then thou shalt make a battlement for thy roof, that thou bring not blood upon thine house, if any man fall from thence.

9 RThou shalt not sow thy vineyard with divers seeds: lest the Nfruit of thy seed which thou hast sown, and the fruit of thy vineyard, be defiled.

10 RThou shalt not plow with an ox and an ass together.

11 RThou shalt not wear a garment of divers sorts, *as* of woollen and linen together.

12 Thou shalt make thee ᴿfringes upon the four ᴺquarters of thy vesture, wherewith thou coverest *thyself*.

Laws of morality

13 If any man take a wife, and go in unto her, and hate her,

14 And give occasions of speech against her, and bring up an evil name upon her, and say, I took this woman, and when I came to her, I found her not a maid:

15 Then shall the father of the damsel, and her mother, take and bring forth *the tokens of* the damsel's virginity unto the elders of the city in the gate:

16 And the damsel's father shall say unto the elders, I gave my daughter unto this man to wife, and he hateth her;

17 And, lo, he hath given occasions of speech *against her,* saying, I found not thy daughter a maid; and yet these *are the tokens of* my daughter's virginity. And they shall spread the cloth before the elders of the city.

18 And the elders of that city shall take that man and chastise him;

19 And they shall amerce him in an hundred *shē'-kĕls* of silver, and give *them* unto the father of the damsel, because he hath brought up an evil name upon a virgin of Israel: and she shall be his wife; he may not put her away all his days.

20 But if this thing be true, *and the tokens of* virginity be not found for the damsel:

21 Then they shall bring out the damsel to the door of her father's house, and the men of her city shall stone her with stones that she die: because she hath ᴿwrought folly in Israel, to play the whore in her father's house: ᴿso shalt thou put evil away from among you.

22 ᴿIf a man be found lying with a woman married to an husband, then they shall both of them die, *both* the man that lay with the woman, and the woman: so shalt thou put away evil from Israel.

23 If a damsel *that is* a virgin be ᴿbetrothed unto an husband, and a man find her in the city, and lie with her;

24 Then ye shall bring them both out unto the gate of that city, and ye shall stone them with stones that they die; the damsel, because she cried not, *being* in the city; and the man, because he hath ᴿhumbled his neighbour's wife: ᴿso thou shalt put away evil from among you.

25 But if a man find a betrothed damsel in the field, and the man ᴺforce her, and lie with her: then the man only that lay with her shall die:

26 But unto the damsel thou shalt do nothing; *there is* in the damsel no sin *worthy* of death: for as when a man riseth against his neighbour, and slayeth him, even so *is* this matter:

27 For he found her in the field, *and* the betrothed damsel cried, and *there was* none to save her.

28 ᴿIf a man find a damsel *that is* a virgin, which is not betrothed, and lay hold on her, and lie with her, and they be found;

29 Then the man that lay with her shall give unto the damsel's father fifty *shē'-kĕls* of silver, and she shall be his wife; ᴿbecause he hath humbled her, he may not put her away all his days.

30 ᴿA man shall not take his father's wife, nor ᴿdiscover his father's skirt.

CHAPTER 23

Members of the congregation

HE that is wounded in the stones, or hath his privy member cut off, shall not enter into the congregation of the LORD.

2 A bastard shall not enter into the congregation of the LORD; even to his tenth generation shall he not enter into the congregation of the LORD.

3 ᴿAn Ammonite or Moabite shall not enter into the congregation of the LORD; even to their tenth generation shall they not enter into the congregation of the LORD for ever:

4 ᴿBecause they met you not with bread and with water in the way, when ye came forth out of Egypt; and ᴿbecause they hired against thee Bā'-lāäm the son of Bē'-ôr of Pē'-thôr of Mĕs-ŏ-pŏ-tā'-mĭ-ă, to curse thee.

5 Nevertheless the LORD thy God would not hearken unto Bā'-lāäm; but the LORD thy God turned the curse into a blessing unto thee, because the LORD thy God loved thee.

6 ᴿThou shalt not seek their peace nor their ᴺprosperity all thy days for ever.

7 Thou shalt not abhor an Ē'-dǫm-ĭte; ᴿfor he *is* thy brother: thou shalt not abhor an Egyptian; because ᴿthou wast a stranger in his land.

8 The children that are begotten of them shall enter into the congregation of the LORD in their third generation.

Sanitation in wartime

9 When the host goeth forth against thine enemies, then keep thee from every wicked thing.

10 ᴿIf there be among you any man, that is not clean by reason of uncleanness that chanc-

eth him by night, then shall he go abroad out of the camp, he shall not come within the camp:

11 But it shall be, when evening ᴺcometh on, ᴿhe shall wash *himself* with water: and when the sun is down, he shall come into the camp *again*.

12 Thou shalt have a place also without the camp, whither thou shalt go forth abroad:

13 And thou shalt have a paddle upon thy weapon; and it shall be, when thou ᴺwilt ease thyself abroad, thou shalt dig therewith, and shalt turn back and cover that which cometh from thee:

14 For the LORD thy God ᴿwalketh in the midst of thy camp, to deliver thee, and to give up thine enemies before thee; therefore shall thy camp be holy: that he see no ᴺunclean thing in thee, and turn away from thee.

Incidental laws

15 ᴿThou shalt not deliver unto his master the servant which is escaped from his master unto thee:

16 He shall dwell with thee, *even* among you, in that place which he shall choose in one ·of thy gates, where it ᴺliketh him best: ᴿthou shalt not oppress him.

17 There shall be no ᴺwhore ᴿof the daughters of Israel, nor ᴿa sodomite of the sons of Israel.

18 Thou shalt not bring the hire of a whore, or the price of a dog, into the house of the LORD thy God for any vow: for even both these *are* abomination unto the LORD thy God.

19 ᴿThou shalt not lend upon usury to thy brother; usury of money, usury of victuals, usury of any thing that is lent upon usury:

20 ᴿUnto a stranger thou mayest lend upon usury; but unto thy brother thou shalt not lend upon usury: ᴿthat the LORD thy God may bless thee in all that thou settest thine hand to in the land whether thou goest to possess it.

Integrity of vows

21 ᴿWhen thou shalt vow a vow unto the LORD thy God, thou shalt not slack to pay it: for the LORD thy God will surely require it of thee; and it would be sin in thee.

22 But if thou shalt forbear to vow, it shall be no sin in thee.

23 ᴿThat which is gone out of thy lips thou shalt keep and perform; *even* a freewill offering, according as thou hast vowed unto the LORD thy God, which thou hast promised with thy mouth.

24 When thou comest into thy neighbour's vineyard, then thou mayest eat grapes thy fill

CHAP. 23
BC 1451
11 Heb. *turneth toward*
11 Lev. 15:5
13 Heb. *sittest down*
14 Lev. 26:12
14 Heb. *nakedness of anything*
15 1 Sam. 30:15
16 Heb. *is good for him*
16 Ex. 22:21
17 Or, *sodomitess*
17 Lev. 19:29 See Prov. 2:16
17 Gen. 19:5 2 Ki. 23:7
19 Ex. 22:25 Lev. 25:36, 37
20 See Lev. 19:34 ch. 15:3
20 ch. 15:10
21 Num. 30:2 Eccl. 5:4, 5
23 Num. 30:2 Ps. 66:13, 14

Mat. 12:1   25
Mark 2:23
Luke 6:1

CHAP. 24
BC 1451
Mat. 5:31 & 19:7 1
Mark 10:4
Heb. *matter of nakedness*   1
Heb. *cutting off*   1
Jer. 3:1   4
ch. 20:7   5
Heb. *not any thing shall pass upon him*   5
Prov. 5:18   5
Ex. 21:16   7
ch. 19:19   7
Lev. 13:2 & 14:2   8
See Luke 17:32   9
1 Cor. 10:6
Num. 12:10   9
Heb. *lend the loan of any thing to, etc.*   10

at thine own pleasure; but thou shalt not put *any* in thy vessel.

25 When thou comest into the standing corn of thy neighbour, ᴿthen thou mayest pluck the ears with thine hand; but thou shalt not move a sicklc unto thy neighbour's standing corn.

CHAPTER 24

Law of marriage and divorce

WHEN a ᴿman hath taken a wife, and married her, and it come to pass that she find no favour in his eyes, because he hath found ᴺsome uncleanness in her: then let him write her a bill of ᴺdivorcement, and give *it* in her hand, and send her out of his house.

2 And when she is departed out of his house, she may go and be another man's *wife*.

3 And *if* the latter husband hate her, and write her a bill of divorcement, and giveth *it* in her hand, and sendeth her out of his house; or if the latter husband die, which took her *to be* his wife;

4 ᴿHer former husband, which sent her away, may not take her again to be his wife, after that she is defiled; for that *is* abomination before the LORD: and thou shalt not cause the land to sin, which the LORD thy God giveth thee *for* an inheritance.

5 ᴿWhen a man hath taken a new wife, he shall not go out to war, ᴺneither shall he be charged with any business: *but* he shall be free at home one year, and shall ᴿcheer up his wife which he hath taken.

Laws of human relations

6 No man shall take the nether or the upper millstone to pledge: for he taketh *a man's* life to pledge.

7 ᴿIf a man be found stealing any of his brethren of the children of Israel, and maketh merchandise of him, or selleth him; then that thief shall die; ᴿand thou shalt put evil away from among you.

8 Take heed in ᴿthe plague of leprosy, that thou observe diligently, and do according to all that the priests the Levites shall teach you: as I commanded them, *so* ye shall observe to do.

9 ᴿRemember what the LORD thy God did ᴿunto Miriam by the way, after that ye were come forth out of Egypt.

10 When thou dost ᴺlend thy brother any thing, thou shalt not go into his house to fetch his pledge.

11 Thou shalt stand abroad, and the man to whom thou dost lend shall bring out the pledge abroad unto thee.

12 And if the man *be* poor, thou shalt not sleep with his pledge:

13 [R]In any case thou shalt deliver him the pledge again when the sun goeth down, that he may sleep in his own raiment, and [R]bless thee: and [R]it shall be righteousness unto thee before the Lord thy God.

14 Thou shalt not [R]oppress an hired servant *that is* poor and needy, *whether he be* of thy brethren, or of thy strangers that *are* in thy land within thy gates:

15 At his day [R]thou shalt give *him* his hire, neither shall the sun go down upon it; for he *is* poor, and [N]setteth his heart upon it: [R]lest he cry against thee unto the Lord, and it be sin unto thee.

16 [R]The fathers shall not be put to death for the children, neither shall the children be put to death for the fathers: every man shall be put to death for his own sin.

Consideration for the poor

17 [R]Thou shalt not pervert the judgment of the stranger, *nor* of the fatherless; [R]nor take a widow's raiment to pledge:

18 But [R]thou shalt remember that thou wast a bondman in Egypt, and the Lord thy God redeemed thee thence: therefore I command thee to do this thing.

19 [R]When thou cuttest down thine harvest in thy field, and hast forgot a sheaf in the field, thou shalt not go again to fetch it: it shall be for the stranger, for the fatherless, and for the widow: that the Lord thy God may [R]bless thee in all the work of thine hands.

20 When thou beatest thine olive tree, [N]thou shalt not go over the boughs again: it shall be for the stranger, for the fatherless, and for the widow.

21 When thou gatherest the grapes of thy vineyard, thou shalt not glean *it* [N]afterward: it shall be for the stranger, for the fatherless, and for the widow.

22 And [R]thou shalt remember that thou wast a bondman in the land of Egypt: therefore I command thee to do this thing.

CHAPTER 25

IF there be a [R]controversy between men, and they come unto judgment, that *the judges* may judge them; then they [R]shall justify the righteous, and condemn the wicked.

2 And it shall be, if the wicked man *be* [R]worthy to be beaten, that the judge shall cause him to lie down, [R]and to be beaten before his face, according to his fault, by a certain number.

3 [R]Forty stripes he may give him, *and* not

CHAP. **24**
BC 1451
13 Ex. 22:26
13 Job 29:11
2 Cor. 9:13
2 Tim. 1:18
13 Dan. 4:27
14 Mal. 3:5
15 Lev. 19:13
Jer. 22:13
Jas. 5:4
15 Heb. *lifteth his soul unto it*
15 Jas. 5:4
16 Jer. 31:29
Ezek. 18:20
17 Prov. 22:22
Jer. 5:28
Ezek. 22:29
Zech. 7:10
17 Ex. 22:26
18 ver. 22
ch. 16:12
19 Lev. 19:9 & 23:22
19 Ps. 41:1
Prov. 19:17
20 Heb. *thou shalt not bough it after thee*
21 Heb. *after thee*
22 ver. 18

CHAP. **25**
BC 1451
1 ch. 19:17
Ezek. 44:24
1 See Prov. 17:15
2 Luke 12:48
2 Mat. 10:17
3 2 Cor. 11:24

Job 18:3   **3**
Prov. 12:10   **4**
1 Tim. 5:18
Heb. *thresheth*   **4**
Mat. 22:24   **5**
Luke 20:28
Or, *next kinsman,* **5**
Gen. 38:8
Ruth 1:12, 13 & 3:9
Gen. 38:9   **6**
Ruth 4:10   **6**
Or, *next kinsman's* **7**
wife
Ruth 4:1, 2   **7**
Ruth 4:6   **8**
Ruth 4:7   **9**
Ruth 4:11   **9**
ch. 19:13   **12**
Lev. 19:35, 36   **13**
Prov. 11:1
Ezek. 45:10
Mic. 6:11
Heb. *a stone*   **13**
and a stone
Heb. *an ephah*   **14**
and an ephah
Ex. 20:12   **15**
Prov. 11:1   **16**
1 Thes. 4:6
Ex. 17:8   **17**

exceed: lest, *if* he should exceed, and beat him above these with many stripes, then thy brother should [R]seem vile unto thee.

4 [R]Thou shalt not muzzle the ox when he [N]treadeth out *the corn.*

Duty to brother's wife

5 [R]If brethren dwell together, and one of them die, and have no child, the wife of the dead shall not marry without unto a stranger: her [N]husband's brother shall go in unto her, and take her to him to wife, and perform the duty of an husband's brother unto her.

6 And it shall be, *that* the firstborn which she beareth [R]shall succeed in the name of his brother *which is* dead, that [R]his name be not put out of Israel.

7 And if the man like not to take his [N]brother's wife, then let his brother's wife go up to the [R]gate unto the elders, and say, My husband's brother refuseth to raise up unto his brother a name in Israel, he will not perform the duty of my husband's brother.

8 Then the elders of his city shall call him, and speak unto him: and *if* he stand *to it,* and say, [R]I like not to take her;

9 Then shall his brother's wife come unto him in the presence of the elders, and [R]loose his shoe from off his foot, and spit in his face, and shall answer and say, So shall it be done unto that man that will not [R]build up his brother's house.

10 And his name shall be called in Israel, The house of him that hath his shoe loosed.

11 When men strive together one with another, and the wife of the one draweth near for to deliver her husband out of the hand of him that smiteth him, and putteth forth her hand, and taketh him by the secrets:

12 Then thou shalt cut off her hand, [R]thine eye shall not pity *her.*

Just weights

13 [R]Thou shalt not have in thy bag [N]divers weights, a great and a small.

14 Thou shalt not have in thine house [N]divers measures, a great and a small.

15 *But* thou shalt have a perfect and just weight, a perfect and just measure shalt thou have: [R]that thy days may be lengthened in the land which the Lord thy God giveth thee.

16 For [R]all that do such things, *and* all that do unrighteously, *are* an abomination unto the Lord thy God.

17 [R]Remember what Ăm'-ă-lĕk did unto thee by the way, when ye were come forth out of Egypt;

18 How he met thee by the way, and smote

the hindmost of thee, *even* all *that were* feeble behind thee, when thou *wast* faint and weary; and he ᴿfeared not God.

19 Therefore it shall be, ᴿwhen the Lᴏʀᴅ thy God hath given thee rest from all thine enemies round about, in the land which the Lᴏʀᴅ thy God giveth thee *for* an inheritance to possess it, *that* thou shalt ᴿblot out the remembrance of ăm′-ă-lĕk from under heaven; thou shalt not forget *it*.

CHAPTER 26

Offering of firstfruits

AND it shall be, when thou *art* come in unto the land which the Lᴏʀᴅ thy God giveth thee *for* an inheritance, and possessest it, and dwellest therein;

2 ᴿThat thou shalt take of the first of all the fruit of the earth, which thou shalt bring of thy land that the Lᴏʀᴅ thy God giveth thee, and shalt put *it* in a basket, and shalt ᴿgo unto the place which the Lᴏʀᴅ thy God shall choose to place his name there.

3 And thou shalt go unto the priest that shall be in those days, and say unto him, I profess this day unto the Lᴏʀᴅ thy God, that I am come unto the country which the Lᴏʀᴅ sware unto our fathers for to give us.

4 And the priest shall take the basket out of thine hand, and set it down before the altar of the Lᴏʀᴅ thy God.

5 And thou shalt speak and say before the Lᴏʀᴅ thy God, ᴿA Syrian ᴿready to perish *was* my father, and ᴿhe went down into Egypt, and sojourned there with a ᴿfew, and became there a nation, great, mighty, and populous:

6 And ᴿthe Egyptians evil entreated us, and afflicted us, and laid upon us hard bondage:

7 And ᴿwhen we cried unto the Lᴏʀᴅ God of our fathers, the Lᴏʀᴅ heard our voice, and looked on our affliction, and our labour, and our oppression:

8 And ᴿthe Lᴏʀᴅ brought us forth out of Egypt with a mighty hand, and with an outstretched arm, and ᴿwith great terribleness, and with signs, and with wonders:

9 And he hath brought us into this place, and hath given us this land, *even* ᴿa land that floweth with milk and honey.

10 And now, behold, I have brought the firstfruits of the land, which thou, O Lᴏʀᴅ, hast given me. And thou shalt set it before the Lᴏʀᴅ thy God, and worship before the Lᴏʀᴅ thy God:

11 And ᴿthou shalt rejoice in every good *thing* which the Lᴏʀᴅ thy God hath given

unto thee, and unto thine house, thou, and the Levite, and the stranger that *is* among you.

Third year tithe

12 When thou hast made an end of tithing all the ᴿtithes of thine increase the third year, *which is* ᴿthe year of tithing, and hast given *it* unto the Levite, the stranger, the fatherless, and the widow, that they may eat within thy gates, and be filled;

13 Then thou shalt say before the Lᴏʀᴅ thy God, I have brought away the hallowed things out of *mine* house, and also have given them unto the Levite, and unto the stranger, to the fatherless, and to the widow, according to all thy commandments which thou hast commanded me: I have not transgressed thy commandments, ᴿneither have I forgotten *them*:

14 ᴿI have not eaten thereof in my mourning, neither have I taken away *aught* thereof for *any* unclean *use,* nor given *aught* thereof for the dead: *but* I have hearkened to the voice of the Lᴏʀᴅ my God, *and* have done according to all that thou hast commanded me.

15 ᴿLook down from thy holy habitation, from heaven, and bless thy people Israel, and the land which thou hast given us, as thou swarest unto our fathers, a land that floweth with milk and honey.

16 This day the Lᴏʀᴅ thy God hath commanded thee to do these statutes and judgments: thou shalt therefore keep and do them with all thine heart, and with all thy soul.

17 Thou hast ᴿavouched the Lᴏʀᴅ this day to be thy God, and to walk in his ways, and to keep his statutes, and his commandments, and his judgments, and to hearken unto his voice:

18 And ᴿthe Lᴏʀᴅ hath avouched thee this day to be his peculiar people, as he hath promised thee, and that *thou* shouldest keep all his commandments;

19 And to make thee ᴿhigh above all nations which he hath made, in praise, and in name, and in honour; and that thou mayest be ᴿan holy people unto the Lᴏʀᴅ thy God, as he hath spoken.

CHAPTER 27

Altar at mount Ebal

AND Moses with the elders of Israel commanded the people, saying, Keep all the commandments which I command you this day.

2 And it shall be on the day ᴿwhen ye shall pass over Jordan unto the land which the Lᴏʀᴅ thy God giveth thee, that ᴿthou shalt set

thee up great stones, and plaster them with plaster:

3 And thou shalt write upon them all the words of this law, when thou art passed over, that thou mayest go in unto the land which the Lord thy God giveth thee, a land that floweth with milk and honey; as the Lord God of thy fathers hath promised thee.

4 Therefore it shall be when ye be gone over Jordan, *that* ye shall set up these stones, which I command you this day, R in mount Ē'-băl, and thou shalt plaster them with plaster.

5 And there shalt thou build an altar unto the Lord thy God, an altar of stones: R thou shalt not lift up *any* iron *tool* upon them.

6 Thou shalt build the altar of the Lord thy God of whole stones: and thou shalt offer burnt offerings thereon unto the Lord thy God:

7 And thou shalt offer peace offerings, and shalt eat there, and rejoice before the Lord thy God.

8 And thou shalt write upon the stones all the words of this law very plainly.

9 And Moses and the priests the Levites spake unto all Israel, saying, Take heed, and hearken, O Israel; R this day thou art become the people of the Lord thy God.

10 Thou shalt therefore obey the voice of the Lord thy God, and do his commandments and his statutes, which I command thee this day.

11 And Moses charged the people the same day, saying,

Mount of blessing

12 These shall stand R upon mount Gĕ-rī'-zĭm to bless the people, when ye are come over Jordan; Simeon, and Levi, and Judah, and Ĭs'-să-chär, and Joseph, and Benjamin:

13 And R these shall stand upon mount Ē'-băl N to curse; Reuben, Gad, and Asher, and Zĕ-bū'-lŭn, Dan, and Năph'-tă-lī.

Curses from mount Ebal

14 And R the Levites shall speak, and say unto all the men of Israel with a loud voice,

15 R Cursed *be* the man that maketh *any* graven or molten image, an abomination unto the Lord, the work of the hands of the craftsman, and putteth *it* in *a* secret *place*. R And all the people shall answer and say, Ä'-mĕn.

16 R Cursed *be* he that setteth light by his father or his mother. And all the people shall say, Ä'-mĕn.

17 R Cursed *be* he that removeth his neighbour's landmark. And all the people shall say, Ä'-mĕn.

18 R Cursed *be* he that maketh the blind to wander out of the way. And all the people shall say, Ä'-mĕn.

19 R Cursed *be* he that perverteth the judgment of the stranger, fatherless, and widow. And all the people shall say, Ä'-mĕn.

20 R Cursed *be* he that lieth with his father's wife; because he uncovereth his father's skirt. And all the people shall say, Ä'-mĕn.

21 R Cursed *be* he that lieth with any manner of beast. And all the people shall say, Ä'-mĕn.

22 R Cursed *be* he that lieth with his sister, the daughter of his father, or the daughter of his mother. And all the people shall say, Ä'-mĕn.

23 R Cursed *be* he that lieth with his mother in law. And all the people shall say, Ä'-mĕn.

24 R Cursed *be* he that smiteth his neighbour secretly. And all the people shall say, Ä'-mĕn.

25 R Cursed *be* he that taketh reward to slay an innocent person. And all the people shall say, Ä'-mĕn.

26 R Cursed *be* he that confirmeth not *all* the words of this law to do them. And all the people shall say, Ä'-mĕn.

CHAPTER 28

Blessings of obedience

AND it shall come to pass, R if thou shalt hearken diligently unto the voice of the Lord thy God, to observe *and* to do all his commandments which I command thee this day, that the Lord thy God R will set thee on high above all nations of the earth:

2 And all these blessings shall come on thee, and R overtake thee, if thou shalt hearken unto the voice of the Lord thy God.

3 R Blessed *shalt* thou *be* in the city, and blessed *shalt* thou *be* R in the field.

4 Blessed *shall be* R the fruit of thy body, and the fruit of thy ground, and the fruit of thy cattle, the increase of thy kine, and the flocks of thy sheep.

5 Blessed *shall be* thy basket and thy N store.

6 R Blessed *shalt* thou *be* when thou comest in, and blessed *shalt* thou *be* when thou goest out.

7 The Lord R shall cause thine enemies that rise up against thee to be smitten before thy face: they shall come out against thee one way, and flee before thee seven ways.

8 The Lord shall R command the blessing upon thee in thy N storehouses, and in all that thou R settest thine hand unto; and he shall bless thee in the land which the Lord thy God giveth thee.

CHAP. 27
BC 1451

4 ch. 11:29
Josh. 8:30, 31
5 Ex. 20:25
Josh. 8:31
9 ch. 26:18
12 ch. 11:29
Josh. 8:33
Judg. 9:7
13 ch. 11:29
Josh. 8:33
13 Heb. *for a cursing*
14 ch. 33:10
Josh. 8:33
Dan. 9:11
15 Ex. 20:4, 23 & 34:17
Lev. 19:4 & 26:1
ch. 4:16, 23 & 5:8
Is. 44:9
Hos. 13:2
15 See Num. 5:22
Jer. 11:5
1 Cor. 14:16
16 Ex. 20:12 & 21:17
Lev. 19:3
ch. 21:18
17 ch. 19:14
Prov. 22:28

Lev. 19:14   18
Ex. 22:21, 22   19
ch. 10:18 & 24:17
Mal. 3:5
Lev. 18:8   20
ch. 22:30
Lev. 18:23   21
Lev. 18:9   22
Lev. 18:17   23
Ex. 20:13   24
Lev. 24:17
Num. 35:31
Ex. 23:7, 8   25
ch. 10:17
Ezek. 22:12
Jer. 11:3   26
Gal. 3:10

CHAP. 28
BC 1451

Ex. 15:26   1
Lev. 26:3
Is. 55:2
ch. 26:19   1
Zech. 1:6   2
Ps. 128:1, 4   3
Gen. 39:5   3
Gen. 22:17   4
& 49:25
ch. 7:13
Prov. 10:22
Or, *dough*, or, *kneading-trough*   5
Ps. 121:8   6
Lev. 26:7, 8   7
2 Sam. 22:38, 39, 41
Lev. 25:21   8
Or, *barns*   8
ch. 15:10   8

9 ᴿThe Lᴏʀᴅ shall establish thee an holy people unto himself, as he hath sworn unto thee, if thou shalt keep the commandments of the Lᴏʀᴅ thy God, and walk in his ways.

10 And all people of the earth shall see that thou art ᴿcalled by the name of the Lᴏʀᴅ; and they shall be ᴿafraid of thee.

11 And ᴿthe Lᴏʀᴅ shall make thee plenteous ᴺin goods, in the fruit of thy ᴺbody, and in the fruit of thy cattle, and in the fruit of thy ground, in the land which the Lᴏʀᴅ sware unto thy fathers to give thee.

12 The Lᴏʀᴅ shall open unto thee his good treasure, the heaven ᴿto give the rain unto thy land in his season, and ᴿto bless all the work of thine hand: and ᴿthou shalt lend unto many nations, and thou shalt not borrow.

13 And the Lᴏʀᴅ shall make thee ᴿthe head, and not the tail; and thou shalt be above only, and thou shalt not be beneath; if that thou hearken unto the commandments of the Lᴏʀᴅ thy God, which I command thee this day, to observe and to do *them:*

14 ᴿAnd thou shalt not go aside from any of the words which I command thee this day, *to* the right hand, or *to* the left, to go after other gods to serve them.

Curses for disobedience

15 But it shall come to pass, ᴿif thou wilt not hearken unto the voice of the Lᴏʀᴅ thy God, to observe to do all his commandments and his statutes which I command thee this day; that all these curses shall come upon thee, and overtake thee:

16 Cursed *shalt* thou *be* in the city, and cursed *shalt* thou *be* in the field.

17 Cursed *shall be* thy basket and thy store.

18 Cursed *shall be* the fruit of thy body, and the fruit of thy land, the increase of thy kine, and the flocks of thy sheep.

19 Cursed *shalt* thou *be* when thou comest in, and cursed *shalt* thou *be* when thou goest out.

20 The Lᴏʀᴅ shall send upon thee ᴿcursing, ᴿvexation, and ᴿrebuke, in all that thou settest thine hand unto ᴺfor to do, until thou be destroyed, and until thou perish quickly; because of the wickedness of thy doings, whereby thou hast forsaken me.

21 The Lᴏʀᴅ shall make ᴿthe pestilence cleave unto thee, until he have consumed thee from off the land, whither thou goest to possess it.

22 ᴿThe Lᴏʀᴅ shall smite thee with a consumption, and with a fever, and with an inflammation, and with an extreme burning, and with the ᴺsword, and with ᴿblasting, and

with mildew; and they shall pursue thee until thou perish.

23 And ᴿthy heaven that *is* over thy head shall be brass, and the earth that *is* under thee *shall be* iron.

24 The Lᴏʀᴅ shall make thc rain of thy land powder and dust: from heaven shall it come down upon thee, until thou be destroyed.

25 ᴿThe Lᴏʀᴅ shall cause thee to be smitten before thine enemies: thou shalt go out one way against them, and flee seven ways before them: and ᴿshalt be ᴺremoved into all the kingdoms of the earth.

26 And ᴿthy carcase shall be meat unto all fowls of the air, and unto the beasts of the earth, and no man shall fray *them* away.

27 The Lᴏʀᴅ will smite thee with ᴿthe botch of Egypt, and with ᴿthe emerods, and with the scab, and with the itch, whereof thou canst not be healed.

28 The Lᴏʀᴅ shall smite thee with madness, and blindness, and ᴿastonishment of heart:

29 And thou shalt ᴿgrope at noonday, as the blind gropeth in darkness, and thou shalt not prosper in thy ways: and thou shalt be only oppressed and spoiled evermore, and no man shall save *thee.*

30 ᴿThou shalt betroth a wife, and another man shall lie with her: ᴿthou shalt build an house, and thou shalt not dwell therein: ᴿthou shalt plant a vineyard, and shalt not ᴺgather the grapes thereof.

31 Thine ox *shall be* slain before thine eyes, and thou shalt not eat thereof: thine ass *shall be* violently taken away from before thy face, and ᴺshall not be restored to thee: thy sheep *shall be* given unto thine enemies, and thou shalt have none to rescue *them.*

32 Thy sons and thy daughters *shall be* given unto another people, and thine eyes shall look, and ᴿfail *with longing* for them all the day long: and *there shall be* no might in thine hand.

33 ᴿThe fruit of thy land, and all thy labours, shall a nation which thou knowest not eat up; and thou shalt be only oppressed and crushed alway:

34 So that thou shalt be mad for the sight of thine eyes which thou shalt see.

35 The Lᴏʀᴅ shall smite thee in the knees, and in the legs, with a sore botch that cannot be healed, from the sole of thy foot unto the top of thy head.

36 The Lᴏʀᴅ shall ᴿbring thee, and thy king which thou shalt set over thee, unto a nation which neither thou nor thy fathers have known; and ᴿthere shalt thou serve other gods, wood and stonc.

37 And thou shalt become [R]an astonishment, a proverb, [R]and a byword, among all nations whither the LORD shall lead thee.

38 [R]Thou shalt carry much seed out into the field, and shalt gather *but* little in; for [R]the locust shall consume it.

39 Thou shalt plant vineyards, and dress *them,* but shalt neither drink *of* the wine, nor gather *the grapes;* for the worms shall eat them.

40 Thou shalt have olive trees throughout all thy coasts, but thou shalt not anoint *thyself* with the oil; for thine olive shall cast *his fruit.*

41 Thou shalt beget sons and daughters, but [N]thou shalt not enjoy them; for [R]they shall go into captivity.

42 All thy trees and fruit of thy land shall the locust [N]consume.

43 The stranger that *is* within thee shall get up above thee very high; and thou shalt come down very low.

44 [R]He shall lend to thee, and thou shalt not lend to him: [R]he shall be the head, and thou shalt be the tail.

45 Moreover [R]all these curses shall come upon thee, and shall pursue thee, and overtake thee, till thou be destroyed; because thou hearkenedst not unto the voice of the LORD thy God, to keep his commandments and his statutes which he commanded thee:

46 And they shall be upon thee [R]for a sign and for a wonder, and upon thy seed for ever.

47 [R]Because thou servedst not the LORD thy God with joyfulness, and with gladness of heart, [R]for the abundance of all *things;*

48 Therefore shalt thou serve thine enemies which the LORD shall send against thee, in hunger, and in thirst, and in nakedness, and in want of all *things:* and he [R]shall put a yoke of iron upon thy neck, until he have destroyed thee.

49 [R]The LORD shall bring a nation against thee from far, from the end of the earth, [R]*as swift* as the eagle flieth; a nation whose tongue thou shalt not [N]understand;

50 A nation [N]of fierce countenance, [R]which shall not regard the person of the old, nor shew favour to the young:

51 And he shall [R]eat the fruit of thy cattle, and the fruit of thy land, until thou be destroyed: which *also* shall not leave thee *either* corn, wine, or oil, *or* the increase of thy kine, or flocks of thy sheep, until he have destroyed thee.

52 And he shall [R]besiege thee in all thy gates, until thy high and fenced walls come down, wherein thou trustedst, throughout all

CHAP. **28**
BC 1451
37 Jer. 24:9
Zech. 8:13
37 Ps. 44:14
38 Mic. 6:15
Hag. 1:6
38 Joel 1:4
41 Heb. *they shall not be thine*
41 Lam. 1:5
42 Or, *possess*
44 ver. 12
44 ver. 13
45 ver. 15
46 Is. 8:18
Ezek. 14:8
47 Neh. 9:35-37
47 ch. 32:15
48 Jer. 28:14
49 Jer. 5:15
& 6:22, 23
Luke 19:43
49 Jer. 48:40
& 49:22
Lam. 4:19
Hos. 8:1
49 Heb. *hear*
50 Heb. *strong of face,* Prov. 7:13
Eccl. 8:1
Dan. 8:23
50 2 Chr. 36:17
Is. 47:6
51 ver. 33
Is. 1:7
52 2 Ki. 25:1, 2, 4

Lev. 26:29   53
2 Ki. 6:28, 29
Jer. 19:9
Lam. 2:20 & 4:10
Heb. *belly*   53
ch. 15:9   54
ch. 13:6   54
ver. 54   56
Heb. *afterbirth*   57
Gen. 49:10   57
Ex. 6:3   58
Dan. 9:12   59
ch. 7:15   60
Heb. *cause to*   61
ascend
ch. 4:27   62
ch. 10:22   62
Neh. 9:23
ch. 30:9   63
Jer. 32:41
Prov. 1:26   63
Is. 1:24
Lev. 26:33   64
ch. 4:27, 28
Neh. 1:8
Jer. 16:13

thy land: and he shall besiege thee in all thy gates throughout all thy land, which the LORD thy God hath given thee.

53 And [R]thou shalt eat the fruit of thine own [N]body, the flesh of thy sons and of thy daughters, which the LORD thy God hath given thee, in the siege, and in the straitness, wherewith thine enemies shall distress thee:

54 *So that* the man *that is* tender among you, and very delicate, [R]his eye shall be evil toward his brother, and toward [R]the wife of his bosom, and toward the remnant of his children which he shall leave:

55 So that he will not give to any of them of the flesh of his children whom he shall eat: because he hath nothing left him in the siege, and in the straitness, wherewith thine enemies shall distress thee in all thy gates.

56 The tender and delicate woman among you, which would not adventure to set the sole of her foot upon the ground for delicateness and tenderness, [R]her eye shall be evil toward the husband of her bosom, and toward her son, and toward her daughter,

57 And toward her [N]young one that cometh out [R]from between her feet, and toward her children which she shall bear: for she shall eat them for want of all *things* secretly in the siege and straitness, wherewith thine enemy shall distress thee in thy gates.

58 If thou wilt not observe to do all the words of this law that are written in this book, that thou mayest fear [R]this glorious and fearful name, THE LORD THY GOD;

59 Then the LORD will make thy plagues [R]wonderful, and the plagues of thy seed, *even* great plagues, and of long continuance, and sore sicknesses, and of long continuance.

60 Moreover he will bring upon thee all [R]the diseases of Egypt, which thou wast afraid of; and they shall cleave unto thee.

61 Also every sickness, and every plague, which *is* not written in the book of this law, them will the LORD [N]bring upon thee, until thou be destroyed.

62 And ye [R]shall be left few in number, whereas ye were [R]as the stars of heaven for multitude; because thou wouldest not obey the voice of the LORD thy God.

63 And it shall come to pass, *that* as the LORD [R]rejoiced over you to do you good, and to multiply you; so the LORD [R]will rejoice over you to destroy you, and to bring you to nought; and ye shall be plucked from off the land whither thou goest to possess it.

64 And the LORD [R]shall scatter thee among all people, from the one end of the earth even

unto the other; and ᴿthere thou shalt serve other gods, which neither thou nor thy fathers have known, *even* wood and stone.

65 And ᴿamong these nations shalt thou find no ease, neither shall the sole of thy foot have rest: ᴿbut the Lᴏʀᴅ shall give thee there a trembling heart, and failing of eyes, and ᴿsorrow of mind:

66 And thy life shall hang in doubt before thee; and thou shalt fear day and night, and shalt have none assurance of thy life:

67 ᴿIn the morning thou shalt say, Would God it were even! and at even thou shalt say, Would God it were morning! for the fear of thine heart wherewith thou shalt fear, and ᴿfor the sight of thine eyes which thou shalt see.

68 And the Lᴏʀᴅ ᴿshall bring thee into Egypt again with ships, by the way whereof I spake unto thee, ᴿThou shalt see it no more again: and there ye shall be sold unto your enemies for bondmen and bondwomen, and no man shall buy *you*.

CHAPTER 29

Exhortation to keep the covenant

THESE *are* the words of the covenant, which the Lᴏʀᴅ commanded Moses to make with the children of Israel in the land of Moab, beside ᴿthe covenant which he made with them in Hŏr′-ĕb.

2 And Moses called unto all Israel, and said unto them, ᴿYe have seen all that the Lᴏʀᴅ did before your eyes in the land of Egypt unto Pharaoh, and unto all his servants, and unto all his land;

3 ᴿThe great temptations which thine eyes have seen, the signs, and those great miracles:

4 Yet ᴿthe Lᴏʀᴅ hath not given you an heart to perceive, and eyes to see, and ears to hear, unto this day.

5 ᴿAnd I have led you forty years in the wilderness: ᴿyour clothes are not waxen old upon you, and thy shoe is not waxen old upon thy foot.

6 ᴿYe have not eaten bread, neither have ye drunk wine or strong drink: that ye might know that I *am* the Lᴏʀᴅ your God.

7 And when ye came unto this place, ᴿSī′-hŏn the king of Hĕsh′-bŏn, and Og the king of Bā′-shăn, came out against us unto battle, and we smote them:

8 And we took their land, and ᴿgave it for an inheritance unto the Reubenites, and to the Gadites, and to the half tribe of Mă-năs′-sĕh.

9 ᴿKeep therefore the words of this cove-

nant, and do them, that ye may ᴿprosper in all that ye do.

Covenant entered into

10 Ye stand this day all of you before the Lᴏʀᴅ your God; your captains of your tribes, your elders, and your officers, *with* all the men of Israel,

11 Your little ones, your wives, and thy stranger that *is* in thy camp, from ᴿthe hewer of thy wood unto the drawer of thy water:

12 That thou shouldest ᴺenter into covenant with the Lᴏʀᴅ thy God, and ᴿinto his oath, which the Lᴏʀᴅ thy God maketh with thee this day:

13 That he may ᴿestablish thee to day for a people unto himself, and *that* he may be unto thee a God, ᴿas he hath said unto thee, and ᴿas he hath sworn unto thy fathers, to Abraham, to Isaac, and to Jacob.

14 Neither with you only ᴿdo I make this covenant and this oath;

15 But with *him* that standeth here with us this day before the Lᴏʀᴅ our God, ᴿand also with *him* that *is* not here with us this day:

16 (For ye know how we have dwelt in the land of Egypt; and how we came through the nations which ye passed by;

17 And ye have seen their abominations, and their ᴺidols, wood and stone, silver and gold, which *were* among them:)

18 Lest there should be among you man, or woman, or family, or tribe, ᴿwhose heart turneth away this day from the Lᴏʀᴅ our God, to go *and* serve the gods of these nations; ᴿlest there should be among you a root that beareth ᴺᴺgall and wormwood;

19 And it come to pass, when he heareth the words of this curse, that he bless himself in his heart, saying, I shall have peace, though I walk ᴿin the ᴺimagination of mine heart, ᴿto add ᴺdrunkenness to thirst:

20 ᴿThe Lᴏʀᴅ will not spare him, but then ᴿthe anger of the Lᴏʀᴅ and ᴿhis jealousy shall smoke against that man, and all the curses that are written in this book shall lie upon him, and the Lᴏʀᴅ ᴿshall blot out his name from under heaven.

21 And the Lᴏʀᴅ ᴿshall separate him unto evil out of all the tribes of Israel, according to all the curses of the covenant that ᴺare written in this book of the law:

22 So that the generation to come of your children that shall rise up after you, and the stranger that shall come from a far land, shall say, when they see the plagues of that land,

and the sicknesses ᴺwhich the Lᴏʀᴅ hath laid upon it;

23 *And that* the whole land thereof *is* brimstone, ᴿand salt, *and* burning, *that* it is not sown, nor beareth, nor any grass groweth therein, ᴿlike the overthrow of Sodom, and Gō-mŏr′-răh, ăd′-mäh, and Zĕ-bō′-ĭm, which the Lᴏʀᴅ overthrew in his anger, and in his wrath:

24 Even all nations shall say, ᴿWherefore hath the Lᴏʀᴅ done thus unto this land? what *meaneth* the heat of this great anger?

25 Then men shall say, Because they have forsaken the covenant of the Lᴏʀᴅ God of their fathers, which he made with them when he brought them forth out of the land of Egypt:

26 For they went and served other gods, and worshipped them, gods whom they knew not, and ᴺ*whom* he had not ᴺgiven unto them:

27 And the anger of the Lᴏʀᴅ was kindled against this land, ᴿto bring upon it all the curses that are written in this book:

28 And the Lᴏʀᴅ ᴿrooted them out of their land in anger, and in wrath, and in great indignation, and cast them into another land, as *it is* this day.

Secret things are God's

29 The secret *things belong* unto the Lᴏʀᴅ our God: but those *things which are* revealed *belong* unto us and to our children for ever, that *we* may do all the words of this law.

CHAPTER 30

Rewards of repentance

Aᴺᴰ ᴿit shall come to pass, when ᴿall these things are come upon thee, the blessing and the curse, which I have set before thee, and ᴿthou shalt call *them* to mind among all the nations, whither the Lᴏʀᴅ thy God hath driven thee,

2 And shalt ᴿreturn unto the Lᴏʀᴅ thy God, and shalt obey his voice according to all that I command thee this day, thou and thy children, with all thine heart, and with all thy soul;

3 ᴿThat then the Lᴏʀᴅ thy God will turn thy captivity, and have compassion upon thee, and will return and ᴿgather thee from all the nations, whither the Lᴏʀᴅ thy God hath scattered thee.

4 ᴿIf *any* of thine be driven out unto the outmost *parts* of heaven, from thence will the Lᴏʀᴅ thy God gather thee, and from thence will he fetch thee:

5 And the Lᴏʀᴅ thy God will bring thee into the land which thy fathers possessed, and thou

shalt possess it; and he will do thee good, and multiply thee above thy fathers.

6 And ᴿthe Lᴏʀᴅ thy God will circumcise thine heart, and the heart of thy seed, to love the Lᴏʀᴅ thy God with all thine heart, and with all thy soul, that thou mayest live.

7 And the Lᴏʀᴅ thy God will put all these curses upon thine enemies, and on them that hate thee, which persecuted thee.

8 And thou shalt return and obey the voice of the Lᴏʀᴅ, and do all his commandments which I command thee this day.

9 ᴿAnd the Lᴏʀᴅ thy God will make thee plenteous in every work of thine hand, in the fruit of thy body, and in the fruit of thy cattle, and in the fruit of thy land, for good: for the Lᴏʀᴅ will again ᴿrejoice over thee for good, as he rejoiced over thy fathers:

10 If thou shalt hearken unto the voice of the Lᴏʀᴅ thy God, to keep his commandments and his statutes which are written in this book of the law, *and* if thou turn unto the Lᴏʀᴅ thy God with all thine heart, and with all thy soul.

Nearness of God's word

11 For this commandment which I command thee this day, ᴿit *is* not hidden from thee, neither *is* it far off.

12 ᴿIt *is* not in heaven, that thou shouldest say, Who shall go up for us to heaven, and bring it unto us, that we may hear it, and do it?

13 Neither *is* it beyond the sea, that thou shouldest say, Who shall go over the sea for us, and bring it unto us, that we may hear it, and do it?

14 But the word *is* very nigh unto thee, in thy mouth, and in thy heart, that thou mayest do it.

A choice of life or death

15 See, ᴿI have set before thee this day life and good, and death and evil;

16 In that I command thee this day to love the Lᴏʀᴅ thy God, to walk in his ways, and to keep his commandments and his statutes and his judgments, that thou mayest live and multiply: and the Lᴏʀᴅ thy God shall bless thee in the land whither thou goest to possess it.

17 But if thine heart turn away, so that thou wilt not hear, but shalt be drawn away, and worship other gods, and serve them;

18 ᴿI denounce unto you this day, that ye shall surely perish, *and that* ye shall not prolong *your* days upon the land, whither thou passest over Jordan to go to possess it.

19 ᴿI call heaven and earth to record this day against you, *that* ᴿI have set before you life

CHAP. 29
BC 1451
22 Heb. *wherewith the LORD hath made it sick*
23 Jer. 17:6
Zeph. 2:9
23 Gen. 19:24
Jer. 20:16
24 1 Ki. 9:8, 9
Jer. 22:8, 9
26 Or, *who had not given to them any portion*
26 Heb. *divided*
27 Dan. 9:11, 13, 14
28 1 Ki. 14:15
Ps. 52:5
Prov. 2:22

CHAP. 30
BC 1451
1 Lev. 26:40
1 ch. 28
1 ch. 4:29, 30
1 Ki. 8:47
2 Neh. 1:9
Is. 55:7
Lam. 3:40
Joel 2:12
3 Ps. 106:45
& 126:1, 4
Jer. 29:14
Lam. 3:22, 32
3 Ps. 147:2
Jer. 32:37
Ezek. 34:13
& 36:24
4 ch. 28:64
Neh. 1:9

ch. 10:16   6
Jer. 32:39
Ezek. 11:19
& 36:26
ch. 28:11   9
ch. 28:63   9
Jer. 32:41
Is. 45:19   11
Rom. 10:6, etc.   12
ver. 1, 19   15
ch. 11:26
ch. 4:26 & 8:19   18
ch. 4:26 & 31:28   19
ver. 15   19

and death, blessing and cursing: therefore choose life, that both thou and thy seed may live:

20 That thou mayest love the LORD thy God, *and* that thou mayest obey his voice, and that thou mayest cleave unto him: for he *is* thy ᴿlife, and the length of thy days: that thou mayest dwell in the land which the LORD sware unto thy fathers, to Abraham, to Isaac, and to Jacob, to give them.

CHAPTER 31

The people encouraged

AND Moses went and spake these words unto all Israel.

2 And he said unto them, I ᴿ*am* an hundred and twenty years old this day; I can no more ᴿgo out and come in: also the LORD hath said unto me, ᴿThou shalt not go over this Jordan.

3 The LORD thy God, ᴿhe will go over before thee, *and* he will destroy these nations from before thee, and thou shalt possess them: *and* Joshua, he shall go over before thee, ᴿas the LORD hath said.

4 ᴿAnd the LORD shall do unto them ᴿas he did to Sĭ'-hŏn and to Og, kings of the Amorites, and unto the land of them, whom he destroyed.

5 And ᴿthe LORD shall give them up before your face, that ye may do unto them according unto all the commandments which I have commanded you.

6 ᴿBe strong and of a good courage, ᴿfear not, nor be afraid of them: for the LORD thy God, ᴿhe *it is* that doth go with thee; ᴿhe will not fail thee, nor forsake thee.

Appointment of Joshua

7 And Moses called unto Joshua, and said unto him in the sight of all Israel, ᴿBe strong and of a good courage: for thou must go with this people unto the land which the LORD hath sworn unto their fathers to give them; and thou shalt cause them to inherit it.

8 And the LORD, ᴿhe *it is* that doth go before thee; ᴿhe will be with thee, he will not fail thee, neither forsake thee: fear not, neither be dismayed.

The law to be taught

9 And Moses wrote this law, ᴿand delivered it unto the priests the sons of Levi, ᴿwhich bare the ark of the covenant of the LORD, and unto all the elders of Israel.

10 And Moses commanded them, saying, At the end of *every* seven years, in the solemnity

of the ᴿyear of release, ᴿin the feast of tabernacles,

11 When all Israel is come to ᴿappear before the LORD thy God in the place which he shall choose, ᴿthou shalt read this law before all Israel in their hearing.

12 ᴿGather the people together, men, and women, and children, and thy stranger that *is* within thy gates, that they may hear, and that they may learn, and fear the LORD your God, and observe to do all the words of this law:

13 And *that* their children, ᴿwhich have not known *any thing,* ᴿmay hear, and learn to fear the LORD your God, as long as ye live in the land whither ye go over Jordan to possess it.

God appears to Moses and Joshua

14 And the LORD said unto Moses, ᴿBehold, thy days approach that thou must die: call Joshua, and present yourselves in the tabernacle of the congregation, that ᴿI may give him a charge. And Moses and Joshua went, and presented themselves in the tabernacle of the congregation.

15 And ᴿthe LORD appeared in the tabernacle in a pillar of a cloud: and the pillar of the cloud stood over the door of the tabernacle.

16 And the LORD said unto Moses, Behold, thou shalt ᴺsleep with thy fathers; and this people will ᴿrise up, and ᴿgo a whoring after the gods of the strangers of the land, whither they go *to be* among them, and will ᴿforsake me, and ᴿbreak my covenant which I have made with them.

17 Then my anger shall be kindled against them in that day, and ᴿI will forsake them, and I will ᴿhide my face from them, and they shall be devoured, and many evils and troubles shall ᴺbefall them; so that they will say in that day, ᴿAre not these evils come upon us, because our God *is* ᴿnot among us?

18 And ᴿI will surely hide my face in that day for all the evils which they shall have wrought, in that they are turned unto other gods.

19 Now therefore write ye this song for you, and teach it the children of Israel: put it in their mouths, that this song may be ᴿa witness for me against the children of Israel.

20 For when I shall have brought them into the land which I sware unto their fathers, that floweth with milk and honey; and they shall have eaten and filled themselves, ᴿand waxen fat; ᴿthen will they turn unto other gods, and serve them, and provoke me, and break my covenant.

21 And it shall come to pass, ᴿwhen many

evils and troubles are befallen them, that this song shall testify ᴺagainst them as a witness; for it shall not be forgotten out of the mouths of their seed: for ᴿI know their imagination ᴿwhich they ᴺgo about, even now, before I have brought them into the land which I sware.

22 Moses therefore wrote this song the same day, and taught it the children of Israel.

23 ᴿAnd he gave Joshua the son of Nun a charge, and said, ᴿBe strong and of a good courage: for thou shalt bring the children of Israel into the land which I sware unto them: and I will be with thee.

The law placed in the ark

24 And it came to pass, when Moses had made an end of writing the words of this law in a book, until they were finished,

25 That Moses commanded the Levites, which bare the ark of the covenant of the LORD, saying,

26 Take this book of the law, ᴿand put it in the side of the ark of the covenant of the LORD your God, that it may be there ᴿfor a witness against thee.

27 ᴿFor I know thy rebellion, and thy ᴿstiff neck: behold, while I am yet alive with you this day, ye have been rebellious against the LORD; and how much more after my death?

28 Gather unto me all the elders of your tribes, and your officers, that I may speak these words in their ears, ᴿand call heaven and earth to record against them.

29 For I know that after my death ye will utterly ᴿcorrupt yourselves, and turn aside from the way which I have commanded you; and ᴿevil will befall you ᴿin the latter days; because ye will do evil in the sight of the LORD, to provoke him to anger through the work of your hands.

30 And Moses spake in the ears of all the congregation of Israel the words of this song, until they were ended.

CHAPTER 32

Song of Moses

GIVE ᴿear, O ye heavens, and I will speak; and hear, O earth, the words of my mouth.

2 ᴿMy doctrine shall drop as the rain, my speech shall distil as the dew, ᴿas the small rain upon the tender herb, and as the showers upon the grass:

3 Because I will publish the name of the LORD: ᴿascribe ye greatness unto our God.

CHAP. 31
BC 1451

21 Heb. *before*
21 Hos. 5:3 & 13:5, 6
21 Amos 5:25, 26
21 Heb. *do*
23 ver. 14
23 ver. 7
Josh. 1:6
26 See 2 Ki. 22:8
26 ver. 19
27 ch. 9:24 & 32:20
27 Ex. 32:9
ch. 9:6
28 ch. 30:19 & 32:1
29 ch. 32:5
Judg. 2:19
Hos. 9:9
29 ch. 28:15
29 Gen. 49:1
ch. 4:30

CHAP. 32
BC 1451

1 Is. 1:2
2 1 Cor. 3:6
2 Ps. 72:6
3 1 Chr. 29:11

Ps. 18:2 — 4
2 Sam. 22:31 — 4
Jer. 10:10 — 4
Job 34:10 — 4
ch. 31:29 — 5
Heb. *He hath corrupted to himself* — 5
Or, *that they are not his children, that is their blot* — 5
Phil. 2:15 — 5
Ps. 116:12 — 6
Is. 63:16 — 6
Ps. 74:2 — 6
ver. 15 — 6
Heb. *generation and generation* — 7
Ex. 13:14 — 7
Zech. 9:2 — 8
Gen. 11:8 — 8
Ex. 19:5 — 9
Heb. *cord* — 9
Jer. 2:6 — 10
Or, *compassed him about* — 10
Ps. 17:8 — 10
Is. 31:5 — 11
Is. 58:14 — 13
Ps. 81:16 — 14
Gen. 49:11 — 14
ch. 31:20 — 15
Is. 1:4 — 15
Is. 51:13 — 15
Ps. 95:1 — 15
1 Cor. 10:22 — 16
Rev. 9:20 — 17
Or, *which were not God,* ver. 21 — 17
Is. 17:10 — 18
Jer. 2:32 — 18
Or, *despised* — 19

---

4 *He is* ᴿthe Rock, ᴿhis work *is* perfect: for all his ways *are* judgment: ᴿa God of truth and ᴿwithout iniquity, just and right *is* he.

5 ᴿTheyᴺ have corrupted themselves, ᴺtheir spot *is* not *the spot* of his children: *they are* a ᴿperverse and crooked generation.

6 Do ye thus ᴿrequite the LORD, O foolish people and unwise? *is* not he ᴿthy father *that* hath ᴿbought thee? hath he not ᴿmade thee, and established thee?

7 Remember the days of old, consider the years of ᴺmany generations: ᴿask thy father, and he will shew thee; thy elders, and they will tell thee.

8 When the Most High ᴿdivided to the nations their inheritance, when he ᴿseparated the sons of Adam, he set the bounds of the people according to the number of the children of Israel.

9 For ᴿthe LORD's portion *is* his people; Jacob *is* the ᴺlot of his inheritance.

10 He found him ᴿin a desert land, and in the waste howling wilderness; he ᴺled him about, he instructed him, he ᴿkept him as the apple of his eye.

11 ᴿAs an eagle stirreth up her nest, fluttereth over her young, spreadeth abroad her wings, taketh them, beareth them on her wings:

12 *So* the LORD alone did lead him, and *there was* no strange god with him.

13 ᴿHe made him ride on the high places of the earth, that he might eat the increase of the fields; and he made him to suck honey out of the rock, and oil out of the flinty rock;

14 Butter of kine, and milk of sheep, with fat of lambs, and rams of the breed of Bā'-shăn, and goats, ᴿwith the fat of kidneys of wheat; and thou didst drink the pure ᴿblood of the grape.

15 But Jĕ-shū'-rŭn waxed fat, and kicked: ᴿthou art waxen fat, thou art grown thick, thou art covered *with fatness;* then he ᴿforsook God *which* ᴿmade him, and lightly esteemed the ᴿRock of his salvation.

16 ᴿThey provoked him to jealousy with strange *gods,* with abominations provoked they him to anger.

17 ᴿThey sacrificed unto devils, ᴺnot to God; to gods whom they knew not, to new *gods that* came newly up, whom your fathers feared not.

18 ᴿOf the Rock *that* begat thee thou art unmindful, and hast ᴿforgotten God that formed thee.

19 And when the LORD saw *it,* he ᴺabhorred *them,* because of the provoking of his sons, and of his daughters.

20 And he said, I will hide my face from them, I will see what their end *shall be:* for they *are* a very froward generation, ᴿchildren in whom *is* no faith.

21 ᴿThey have moved me to jealousy with *that which is* not God; they have provoked me to anger ᴿwith their vanities: and ᴿI will move them to jealousy with *those which are* not a people; I will provoke them to anger with a foolish nation.

22 For ᴿa fire is kindled in mine anger, and ᴺshall burn unto the lowest hell, and ᴺshall consume the earth with her increase, and set on fire the foundations of the mountains.

23 I will ᴿheap mischiefs upon them; ᴿI will spend mine arrows upon them.

24 *They shall be* burnt with hunger, and devoured with ᴺburning heat, and with bitter destruction: I will also send the teeth of beasts upon them, with the poison of serpents of the dust.

25 The sword without, and terror ᴺwithin, shall ᴺdestroy both the young man and the virgin, the suckling *also* with the man of gray hairs.

26 I said, I would scatter them into corners, I would make the remembrance of them to cease from among men:

27 Were it not that I feared the wrath of the enemy, lest their adversaries should behave themselves strangely, *and* lest they should say, ᴺOur hand *is* high, and the LORD hath not done all this.

28 For they *are* a nation void of counsel, neither *is there any* understanding in them.

29 ᴿO that they were wise, *that* they understood this, *that* they would consider their latter end!

30 How should one chase a thousand, and two put ten thousand to flight, except their Rock ᴿhad sold them, and the LORD had shut them up?

31 For their rock *is* not as our Rock, ᴿeven our enemies themselves *being* judges.

32 For ᴿtheir vine ᴺ*is* of the vine of Sodom, and of the fields of Gō-mŏr′-răh: their grapes *are* grapes of gall, their clusters *are* bitter:

33 Their wine *is* ᴿthe poison of dragons, and the cruel ᴿvenom of asps.

God will vindicate Israel

34 *Is* not this ᴿlaid up in store with me, *and* sealed up among my treasures?

35 ᴿTo me *belongeth* vengeance, and recompence; their foot shall slide in *due* time: for ᴿthe day of their calamity *is* at hand, and the things that shall come upon them make haste.

36 ᴿFor the LORD shall judge his people,

ᴿand repent himself for his servants, when he seeth that *their* ᴺpower is gone, and ᴿ*there is* none shut up, or left.

37 And he shall say, ᴿWhere *are* their gods, *their* rock in whom they trusted,

38 Which did eat the fat of their sacrifices, *and* drank the wine of their drink offerings? let them rise up and help you, *and* be ᴺyour protection.

39 See now that ᴿI, *even* I, *am* he, and ᴿ*there is* no god with me: ᴿI kill, and I make alive; I wound, and I heal: neither *is there any* that can deliver out of my hand.

40 For I lift up my hand to heaven, and say, I live for ever.

41 ᴿIf I whet my glittering sword, and mine hand take hold on judgment; I will render vengeance to mine enemies, and will reward them that hate me.

42 I will make mine arrows ᴿdrunk with blood, and my sword shall devour flesh; *and that* with the blood of the slain and of the captives, from the beginning of ᴿrevenges upon the enemy.

43 ᴿRejoice, ᴺO ye nations, *with* his people: for he will ᴿavenge the blood of his servants, and will render vengeance to his adversaries, and ᴿwill be merciful unto his land, *and* to his people.

44 And Moses came and spake all the words of this song in the ears of the people, he, and ᴺHō-shē′-ă the son of Nun.

45 And Moses made an end of speaking all these words to all Israel:

46 And he said unto them, ᴿSet your hearts unto all the words which I testify among you this day, which ye shall command your children to observe to do, all the words of this law.

47 For it *is* not a vain thing for you; ᴿbecause it *is* your life: and through this thing ye shall prolong *your* days in the land, whither ye go over Jordan to possess it.

God summons Moses to die

48 ᴿAnd the LORD spake unto Moses that selfsame day, saying,

49 Get thee up into this ᴿmountain Ăb′-ă-rĭm, *unto* mount Nē′-bō, which *is* in the land of Moab, that *is* over against Jericho; and behold the land of Canaan, which I give unto the children of Israel for a possession:

50 And die in the mount whither thou goest up, and be gathered unto thy people; as ᴿAaron thy brother died in mount Hôr, and was gathered unto his people:

51 Because ᴿye trespassed against me among the children of Israel at the waters of

ᴺMĕr'-ĭ-bäh-Kā'-dĕsh, in the wilderness of Zin; because ye ᴿsanctified me not in the midst of the children of Israel.

52 ᴿYet thou shalt see the land before *thee;* but thou shalt not go thither unto the land which I give the children of Israel.

CHAPTER 33

Moses blesses Israel

AND this *is* ᴿthe blessing, wherewith Moses ᴿthe man of God blessed the children of Israel before his death.

2 And he said, ᴿThe Lᴏʀᴅ came from Sī'-naî, and rose up from Sē'-ir unto them; he shined forth from mount Pâr'-ăn, and he came with ᴿten thousands of saints: from his right hand *went* ᴺa fiery law for them.

3 Yea, ᴿhe loved the people; ᴿall his saints *are* in thy hand: and they ᴿsat down at thy feet; *every one* shall ᴿreceive of thy words.

4 ᴿMoses commanded us a law, ᴿ*even* the inheritance of the congregation of Jacob.

5 And he was ᴿking in ᴿJĕ-shū'-rŭn, when the heads of the people *and* the tribes of Israel were gathered together.

6 Let Reuben live, and not die; and let *not* his men be few.

7 And this *is the blessing* of Judah: and he said, Hear, Lᴏʀᴅ, the voice of Judah, and bring him unto his people: ᴿlet his hands be sufficient for him; and be thou ᴿan help *to him* from his enemies.

8 And of Levi he said, ᴿ*Let* thy Thŭm'-mĭm and thy Ū'-rĭm *be* with thy holy one, ᴿwhom thou didst prove at Măs'-săh, *and with* whom thou didst strive at the waters of Mĕr'-ĭ-bäh;

9 Who said unto his father and to his mother, I have not ᴿseen him; ᴿneither did he acknowledge his brethren, nor knew his own children: for ᴿthey have observed thy word, and kept thy covenant.

10 ᴿTheyᴺ shall teach Jacob thy judgments, and Israel thy law: ᴺthey shall put incense ᴺbefore thee, ᴿand whole burnt sacrifice upon thine altar.

11 Bless, Lᴏʀᴅ, his substance, and ᴿaccept the work of his hands: smite through the loins of them that rise against him, and of them that hate him, that they rise not again.

12 *And* of Benjamin he said, The beloved of the Lᴏʀᴅ shall dwell in safety by him; *and the* Lᴏʀᴅ shall cover him all the day long, and he shall dwell between his shoulders.

13 And of Joseph he said, ᴿBlessed of the Lᴏʀᴅ *be* his land, for the precious things of heaven, for ᴿthe dew, and for the deep that coucheth beneath,

14 And for the precious fruits *brought forth* by the sun, and for the precious things ᴺput forth by the ᴺmoon,

15 And for the chief things of ᴿthe ancient mountains, and for the precious things ᴿof the lasting hills,

16 And for the precious things of the earth and fullness thereof, and *for* the good will of ᴿhim that dwelt in the bush: let *the blessing* ᴿcome upon the head of Joseph, and upon the top of the head of him *that was* separated from his brethren.

17 His glory *is like* the ᴿfirstling of his bullock, and his horns *are like* ᴿthe horns of ᴺunicorns: with them ᴿhe shall push the people together to the ends of the earth: and ᴿthey *are* the ten thousands of Ē'-phră-ĭm, and they *are* the thousands of Mă-năs'-sēh.

18 And of Zĕ-bū'-lŭn he said, ᴿRejoice, Zĕ-bū'-lŭn, in thy going out; and, ĭs'-să-<u>ch</u>är, in thy tents.

19 They shall ᴿcall the people unto the mountain; there ᴿthey shall offer sacrifices of righteousness: for they shall suck *of* the abundance of the seas, and *of* treasures hid in the sand.

20 And of Gad he said, Blessed *be* he that ᴿenlargeth Gad: he dwelleth as a lion, and teareth the arm with the crown of the head.

21 And ᴿhe provided the first part for himself, because there, *in* a portion of the lawgiver, *was he* ᴺseated; and ᴿhe came with the heads of the people, he executed the justice of the Lᴏʀᴅ, and his judgments with Israel.

22 And of Dan he said, Dan *is* a lion's whelp: ᴿhe shall leap from Bā'-shăn.

23 And of Năph'-tă-lī he said, O Năph'-tă-lī, ᴿsatisfied with favour, and full with the blessing of the Lᴏʀᴅ: ᴿpossess thou the west and the south.

24 And of Asher he said, ᴿ*Let* Asher *be* blessed with children; let him be acceptable to his brethren, and let him ᴿdip his foot in oil.

25 ᴺThy shoes *shall be* ᴿiron and brass; and as thy days, *so shall* thy strength *be.*

26 *There is* ᴿnone like unto the God of ᴿJĕ-shū'-rŭn, ᴿ*who* rideth upon the heaven in thy help, and in his excellency on the sky.

27 The eternal God *is thy* ᴿrefuge, and underneath *are* the everlasting arms: and ᴿhe shall thrust out the enemy from before thee; and shall say, Destroy *them.*

28 ᴿIsrael then shall dwell in safety alone: ᴿthe fountain of Jacob *shall be* upon a land of corn and wine; also his ᴿheavens shall drop down dew.

29 ᴿHappy *art* thou, O Israel: ᴿwho *is* like unto thee, O people saved by the Lᴏʀᴅ, ᴿthe

shield of thy help, and who *is* the sword of thy excellency! and thine enemies ᴿshallᴺ be found liars unto thee; and ᴿthou shalt tread upon their high places.

CHAPTER 34

Death and burial of Moses

AND Moses went up from the plains of Moab ᴿunto the mountain of Nē′-bō, to the top of ᴺPĭs′-găh, that *is* over against Jericho. And the LORD ᴿshewed him all the land of Gilead, ᴿunto Dan,

2 And all Năph′-tā-lĭ, and the land of Ē′-phră-ĭm, and Mă-năs′-sēh, and all the land of Judah, ᴿunto the utmost sea,

3 And the south, and the plain of the valley of Jericho, ᴿthe city of palm trees, unto Zō′-är.

4 And the LORD said unto him, ᴿThis *is* the land which I sware unto Abraham, unto Isaac, and unto Jacob, saying, I will give it unto thy seed: ᴿI have caused thee to see *it* with thine eyes, but thou shalt not go over thither.

5 ᴿSo Moses the servant of the LORD died there in the land of Moab, according to the word of the LORD.

6 And he buried him in a valley in the land of Moab, over against Bĕth-pē′-ôr: but ᴿno man knoweth of his sepulchre unto this day.

7 ᴿAnd Moses *was* an hundred and twenty years old when he died: ᴿhis eye was not dim, nor his ᴺnatural force ᴺabated.

8 And the children of Israel wept for Moses in the plains of Moab ᴿthirty days: so the days of weeping *and* mourning for Moses were ended.

9 And Joshua the son of Nun was full of the ᴿspirit of wisdom; for ᴿMoses had laid his hands upon him: and the children of Israel hearkened unto him, and did as the LORD commanded Moses.

The greatness of Moses

10 And there ᴿarose not a prophet since in Israel like unto Moses, ᴿwhom the LORD knew face to face,

11 In all ᴿthe signs and the wonders, which the LORD sent him to do in the land of Egypt to Pharaoh, and to all his servants, and to all his land,

12 And in all that mighty hand, and in all the great terror which Moses shewed in the sight of all Israel.

Center reference column

CHAP. 33	
BC 1451	
29 Ps. 18:44	
29 Or, *shall be subdued*	
29 ch. 32:13	
CHAP. 34	
BC 1451	
1 Num. 27:12	
1 Or, *The hill*	
1 ch. 3:27	
1 Gen. 14:14	
2 ch. 11:24	
3 2 Chr. 28:15	
4 Gen. 12:7	
4 ch. 3:27	
5 ch. 32:50	
See Jude 9	6
ch. 31:2	7
Gen. 27:1	7
Heb. *moisture*	7
Heb. *fled*	7
See Gen. 50:3, 10	8
Num. 20:29	
Is. 11:2	9
Dan. 6:3	
Num. 27:18, 23	9
ch. 18:15	10
Ex. 33:11	10
ch. 5.4	
ch. 7:19	11

THE BOOK OF JOSHUA

This book is named for its leading character and is the first book of the Bible to bear the name of an individual. The name "Joshua," spelled "Jesus" in the Greek Septuagint translation, means "the Lord saves," and was the name given our Lord at his birth. Joshua is the first of the twelve historical books of the Old Testament. It is free of legal prescriptions and deals almost exclusively with the conquest of Canaan and the division of the land among the twelve tribes under Joshua's heroic leadership. Joshua forms a natural sequel to the book of Deuteronomy; it continues the story of Israel from the conclusion of that book, and sustains an intimate connection with the history of the nation in the books which follow. We may reasonably assume that Joshua himself provided this account, with possible editorial additions by his contemporaries who outlived him, since he is personally associated with all the major events recorded.

OUTLINE OF THE BOOK:

CHAPTER 1

God instructs Joshua

NOW after the death of Moses the servant of the LORD it came to pass, that the LORD spake unto Joshua the son of Nun, Moses' ᴿminister, saying,

2 ᴿMoses my servant is dead; now therefore arise, go over this Jordan, thou, and all this people, unto the land which I do give to them, *even* to the children of Israel.

3 ᴿEvery place that the sole of your foot shall tread upon, that have I given unto you, as I said unto Moses.

4 ᴿFrom the wilderness and this Lĕb′-ă-nọn even unto the great river, the river Ēu-phrā′-tēs, all the land of the Hittites, and unto the great sea toward the going down of the sun, shall be your coast.

5 ᴿThere shall not any man be able to stand before thee all the days of thy life: ᴿas I was with Moses, *so* ᴿI will be with thee: ᴿI will not fail thee, nor forsake thee.

6 ᴿBe strong and of a good courage: for

Center reference column (Chapter 1)

CHAP. 1	
BC 1451	
1 Ex. 24:13	
Deut. 1:38	
2 Deut. 34:5	
3 Deut. 11:24	
Gen. 15:18	4
Ex. 23:31	
Num. 34:3-12	
Deut. 7:24	5
Ex. 3:12	5
Deut. 31:8, 23	5
ch. 3:7 & 6:27	
Is. 43:2, 5	
Deut. 31:6, 8	5
Deut. 31:7, 23	6

ᴺunto this people shalt thou divide for an inheritance the land, which I sware unto their fathers to give them.

7 Only be thou strong and very courageous, that thou mayest observe to do according to all the law, ᴿwhich Moses my servant commanded thee: ᴿturn not from it *to* the right hand or *to* the left, that thou mayest ᴺprosper whithersoever thou goest.

8 ᴿThis book of the law shall not depart out of thy mouth; but ᴿthou shalt meditate therein day and night, that thou mayest observe to do according to all that is written therein: for then thou shalt make thy way prosperous, and then thou shalt ᴺhave good success.

9 ᴿHave not I commanded thee? Be strong and of a good courage; ᴿbe not afraid, neither be thou dismayed: for the LORD thy God *is* with thee whithersoever thou goest.

Joshua prepares the people

10 Then Joshua commanded the officers of the people, saying,

11 Pass through the host, and command the people, saying, Prepare you victuals; for ᴿwithin three days ye shall pass over this Jordan, to go in to possess the land, which the LORD your God giveth you to possess it.

12 And to the Reubenites, and to the Gadites, and to half the tribe of Mă-năs′-sĕh, spake Joshua, saying,

13 Remember ᴿthe word which Moses the servant of the LORD commanded you, saying, The LORD your God hath given you rest, and hath given you this land.

14 Your wives, your little ones, and your cattle, shall remain in the land which Moses gave you on this side Jordan; but ye shall pass before your brethren ᴺarmed, all the mighty men of valour, and help them;

15 Until the LORD have given your brethren rest, as *he hath given* you, and they also have possessed the land which the LORD your God giveth them: ᴿthen ye shall return unto the land of your possession, and enjoy it, which Moses the LORD's servant gave you on this side Jordan toward the sunrising.

16 And they answered Joshua, saying, All that thou commandest us we will do, and whithersoever thou sendest us, we will go.

17 According as we hearkened unto Moses in all things, so will we hearken unto thee: only the LORD thy God ᴿbe with thee, as he was with Moses.

18 Whosoever *he be* that doth rebel against thy commandment, and will not hearken unto thy words in all that thou commandest him, he shall be put to death: only be strong and of a good courage.

CHAP. **1**
BC 1451
6 Or, *thou shalt cause this people to inherit the land*
7 Num. 27:23
Deut. 31:7
ch. 11:15
7 Deut. 5:32
& 28:14
7 Or, *do wisely*
8 Deut. 17:18, 19
8 Ps. 1:2
8 Or, *do wisely,* ver. 7
9 Deut. 31:7, 8, 23
9 Ps. 27:1
Jer. 1:8
11 Deut. 9:1
& 11:31
13 Num. 32:20-28
ch. 22:2-4
14 Heb. *marshalled by five:* as
Ex. 13:18
15 ch. 22:4, etc.
17 1 Sam. 20:13
1 Ki. 1:37

CHAP. **2**	
BC 1451	
Or, *had sent*	1
Num. 25:1	1
Heb. 11:31	1
Jas. 2:25	
Mat. 1:5	1
Heb. *lay*	1
ver. 22	2
See 2 Sam. 17:19, 20	4
See Ex. 1:17	6
2 Sam. 17:19	
Gen. 35:5	9
Ex. 23:27	
Deut. 2:25	
& 11:25	
Heb. *melt*,	9
Ex. 15:15	
Ex. 14:21	10
ch. 4:23	
Num. 21:24,	10
34, 35	
Ex. 15:14, 15	11
ch. 5:1 & 7:5	11
Is. 13:7	
Heb. *rose up*	11
Deut. 4:39	11
See 1 Sam.	12
20:14, 15, 17	
See 1 Tim. 5:8	12
ver. 18	12
Heb. *instead of you to die*	14

CHAPTER 2

Spies sent to Jericho

AND Joshua the son of Nun ᴺsent ᴿout of Shĭt′-tĭm two men to spy secretly, saying, Go view the land, even Jericho. And they went, and ᴿcame into an harlot's house, named ᴿRahab, and ᴺlodged there.

2 And ᴿit was told the king of Jericho, saying, Behold, there came men in hither to night of the children of Israel to search out the country.

3 And the king of Jericho sent unto Rahab, saying, Bring forth the men that are come to thee, which are entered into thine house: for they be come to search out all the country.

Rahab conceals the spies

4 ᴿAnd the woman took the two men, and hid them, and said thus, There came men unto me, but I wist not whence they *were:*

5 And it came to pass *about the time* of shutting of the gate, when it was dark, that the men went out: whither the men went I wot not: pursue after them quickly; for ye shall overtake them.

6 But ᴿshe had brought them up to the roof of the house, and hid them with the stalks of flax, which she had laid in order upon the roof.

7 And the men pursued after them the way to Jordan unto the fords: and as soon as they which pursued after them were gone out, they shut the gate.

8 And before they were laid down, she came up unto them upon the roof;

9 And she said unto the men, I know that the LORD hath given you the land, and that ᴿyour terror is fallen upon us, and that all the inhabitants of the land ᴺfaint because of you.

10 For we have heard how the LORD ᴿdried up the water of the Red sea for you, when ye came out of Egypt; and ᴿwhat ye did unto the two kings of the Amorites, that *were* on the other side Jordan, Sī′-hŏn and Og, whom ye utterly destroyed.

11 And as soon as we had ᴿheard *these things,* ᴿour hearts did melt, neither ᴺdid there remain any more courage in any man, because of you: for ᴿthe LORD your God, he *is* God in heaven above, and in earth beneath.

12 Now therefore, I pray you, ᴿswear unto me by the LORD, since I have shewed you kindness, that ye will also shew kindness unto ᴿmy father's house, and ᴿgive me a true token:

13 And *that* ye will save alive my father, and my mother, and my brethren, and my sisters, and all that they have, and deliver our lives from death.

14 And the men answered her, Our life ᴺfor

yours, if ye utter not this our business. And it shall be, when the LORD hath given us the land, that ᴿwe will deal kindly and truly with thee.

15 Then she ᴿlet them down by a cord through the window: for her house *was* upon the town wall, and she dwelt upon the wall.

16 And she said unto them, Get you to the mountain, lest the pursuers meet you; and hide yourselves there three days, until the pursuers be returned: and afterward may ye go your way.

17 And the men said unto her, We *will be* ᴿblameless of this thine oath which thou hast made us swear.

18 ᴿBehold, *when* we come into the land, thou shalt bind this line of scarlet thread in the window which thou didst let us down by: ᴿand thou shalt ᴺbring thy father, and thy mother, and thy brethren, and all thy father's household, home unto thee.

19 And it shall be, *that* whosoever shall go out of the doors of thy house into the street, his blood *shall be* upon his head, and we *will be* guiltless: and whosoever shall be with thee in the house, ᴿhis blood *shall be* on our head, if *any* hand be upon him.

20 And if thou utter this our business, then we will be quit of thine oath which thou hast made us to swear.

21 And she said, According unto your words, so *be* it. And she sent them away, and they departed: and she bound the scarlet line in the window.

Report of the spies

22 And they went, and came unto the mountain, and abode there three days, until the pursuers were returned: and the pursuers sought *them* throughout all the way, but found *them* not.

23 So the two men returned, and descended from the mountain, and passed over, and came to Joshua the son of Nun, and told him all *things* that befell them:

24 And they said unto Joshua, Truly ᴿthe LORD hath delivered into our hands all the land; for even all the inhabitants of the country do ᴺfaint because of us.

CHAPTER 3

Final preparations

AND Joshua rose early in the morning; and they removed ᴿfrom Shī́t-tīm, and came to Jordan, he and all the children of Israel, and lodged there before they passed over.

2 And it came to pass ᴿafter three days, that the officers went through the host;

CHAP. 2
BC 1451
14 Judg. 1:24
Mat. 5:7
15 Acts 9:25
17 Ex. 20:7
18 ver. 12
18 ch. 6:23
18 Heb. *gather*
19 1 Ki. 2:32
Mat. 27:25
24 Ex. 23:31
ch. 6:2
& 21:44
24 Heb. *melt*

CHAP. 3
BC 1451
1 ch. 2:1
2 ch. 1:10, 11

See Num. 10:33 **3**
Deut. 31:9, 25 **3**
Ex. 19:12 **4**
Heb. *since yesterday, and the third day* **4**
Ex. 19:10, 14, 15 **5**
Lev. 20:7
Num. 11:18
ch. 7:13
1 Sam. 16:5
Joel 2:16
Num. 4:15 **6**
ch. 4:14 **7**
1 Chr. 29:25
2 Chr. 1:1
ch. 1:5 **7**
ver. 3 **8**
ver. 17 **8**
Deut. 5:26 **10**
1 Sam. 17:26
2 Ki. 19:4
Hos. 1:10
Mat. 16:16
1 Thes. 1:9
Ex. 33:2 **10**
Deut. 7:1
Ps. 44:2
ver. 13 **11**
Mic. 4:13
Zech. 4:14 & 6:5
ch. 4:2 **12**
ver. 15, 16 **13**
ver. 11 **13**
Ps. 78:13 **13**
& 114:3
Acts 7:45 **14**
ver. 13 **15**
1 Chr. 12:15 **15**
Jer. 12:5 & 49:19
ch. 4:18 **15**
& 5:10, 12

---

3 And they commanded the people, saying, ᴿWhen ye see the ark of the covenant of the LORD your God, ᴿand the priests the Levites bearing it, then ye shall remove from your place, and go after it.

4 ᴿYet there shall be a space between you and it, about two thousand cubits by measure: come not near unto it, that ye may know the way by which ye must go: for ye have not passed *this* way ᴺheretofore.

5 And Joshua said unto the people, ᴿSanctify yourselves: for to morrow the LORD will do wonders among you.

6 And Joshua spake unto the priests, saying, ᴿTake up the ark of the covenant, and pass over before the people. And they took up the ark of the covenant, and went before the people.

7 And the LORD said unto Joshua, This day will I begin to ᴿmagnify thee in the sight of all Israel, that they may know that, ᴿas I was with Moses, *so* I will be with thee.

8 And thou shalt command ᴿthe priests that bear the ark of the covenant, saying, When ye are come to the brink of the water of Jordan, ᴿye shall stand still in Jordan.

9 And Joshua said unto the children of Israel, Come hither, and hear the words of the LORD your God.

10 And Joshua said, Hereby ye shall know that ᴿthe living God *is* among you, and *that* he will without fail ᴿdrive out from before you the Canaanites, and the Hittites, and the Hī́-vītes, and the Pĕ-rĭź-zītes, and the Gĭŕ-gă-shītes, and the Amorites, and the Jĕb́-ū-sītes.

11 Behold, the ark of the covenant of ᴿthe Lord of all the earth passeth over before you into Jordan.

12 Now therefore ᴿtake you twelve men out of the tribes of Israel, out of every tribe a man.

13 And it shall come to pass, ᴿas soon as the soles of the feet of the priests that bear the ark of the LORD, ᴿthe Lord of all the earth, shall rest in the waters of Jordan, *that* the waters of Jordan shall be cut off *from* the waters that come down from above; and they ᴿshall stand upon an heap.

Crossing the Jordan

14 And it came to pass, when the people removed from their tents, to pass over Jordan, and the priests bearing the ᴿark of the covenant before the people;

15 And as they that bare the ark were come unto Jordan, and ᴿthe feet of the priests that bare the ark were dipped in the brim of the water, (for ᴿJordan overfloweth all his banks ᴿall the time of harvest,)

16 That the waters which came down from above stood *and* rose up upon an heap very far from the city Adam, that *is* beside ᴿZăr'-ĕ-tăn: and those that came down ᴿtoward the sea of the plain, *even* ᴿthe salt sea, failed, *and* were cut off: and the people passed over right against Jericho.

17 And the priests that bare the ark of the covenant of the Lᴏʀᴅ stood firm on dry ground in the midst of Jordan, ᴿand all the Israelites passed over on dry ground, until all the people were passed clean over Jordan.

CHAPTER 4

Twelve memorial stones

Aᴺᴰ it came to pass, when all the people were clean passed ᴿover Jordan, that the Lᴏʀᴅ spake unto Joshua, saying,

2 ᴿTake you twelve men out of the people, out of every tribe a man,

3 And command ye them, saying, Take you hence out of the midst of Jordan, out of the place where ᴿthe priests' feet stood firm, twelve stones, and ye shall carry them over with you, and leave them in ᴿthe lodging place, where ye shall lodge this night.

4 Then Joshua called the twelve men, whom he had prepared of the children of Israel, out of every tribe a man:

5 And Joshua said unto them, Pass over before the ark of the Lᴏʀᴅ your God into the midst of Jordan, and take ye up every man of you a stone upon his shoulder, according unto the number of the tribes of the children of Israel:

6 That this may be a sign among you, *that* ᴿwhen your children ask *their fathers* ᴺin time to come, saying, What *mean* ye by these stones?

7 Then ye shall answer them, That ᴿthe waters of Jordan were cut off before the ark of the covenant of the Lᴏʀᴅ; when it passed over Jordan, the waters of Jordan were cut off: and these stones shall be for ᴿa memorial unto the children of Israel for ever.

8 And the children of Israel did so as Joshua commanded, and took up twelve stones out of the midst of Jordan, as the Lᴏʀᴅ spake unto Joshua, according to the number of the tribes of the children of Israel, and carried them over with them unto the place where they lodged, and laid them down there.

9 And Joshua set up twelve stones in the midst of Jordan, in the place where the feet of the priests which bare the ark of the covenant stood: and they are there unto this day.

The people cross over

10 For the priests which bare the ark stood in the midst of Jordan, until every thing was finished that the Lᴏʀᴅ commanded Joshua to speak unto the people, according to all that Moses commanded Joshua: and the people hasted and passed over.

11 And it came to pass, when all the people were clean passed over, that the ark of the Lᴏʀᴅ passed over, and the priests, in the presence of the people.

12 And ᴿthe children of Reuben, and the children of Gad, and half the tribe of Mă-năs'-sēh, passed over armed before the children of Israel, as Moses spake unto them:

13 About forty thousand ᴺprepared for war passed over before the Lᴏʀᴅ unto battle, to the plains of Jericho.

14 On that day the Lᴏʀᴅ ᴿmagnified Joshua in the sight of all Israel; and they feared him, as they feared Moses, all the days of his life.

15 And the Lᴏʀᴅ spake unto Joshua, saying,

16 Command the priests that bear ᴿthe ark of the testimony, that they come up out of Jordan.

17 Joshua therefore commanded the priests, saying, Come ye up out of Jordan.

18 And it came to pass, when the priests that bare the ark of the covenant of the Lᴏʀᴅ were come up out of the midst of Jordan, *and* the soles of the priests' feet were ᴺlifted up unto the dry land, that the waters of Jordan returned unto their place, ᴿand ᴺflowed over all his banks, as *they did* before.

Camp at Gilgal

19 And the people came up out of Jordan on the tenth *day* of the first month, and encamped ᴿin Gĭl'-găl, in the east border of Jericho.

20 And ᴿthose twelve stones, which they took out of Jordan, did Joshua pitch in Gĭl'-găl.

21 And he spake unto the children of Israel, saying, ᴿWhen your children shall ask their fathers ᴺin time to come, saying, What *mean* these stones?

22 Then ye shall let your children know, saying, ᴿIsrael came over this Jordan on dry land.

23 For the Lᴏʀᴅ your God dried up the waters of Jordan from before you, until ye were passed over, as the Lᴏʀᴅ your God did to the Red sea, ᴿwhich he dried up from before us, until we were gone over:

24 ᴿThat all the people of the earth might know the hand of the Lᴏʀᴅ, that it *is* ᴿmighty:

that ye might ᴿfear the LORD your God ᴺfor ever.

CHAPTER 5

A second circumcision

AND it came to pass, when all the kings of the Amorites, which *were* on the side of Jordan westward, and all the kings of the Canaanites, ᴿwhich *were* by the sea, ᴿheard that the LORD had dried up the waters of Jordan from before the children of Israel, until we were passed over, that their heart melted, ᴿneither was there spirit in them any more, because of the children of Israel.

2 At that time the LORD said unto Joshua, Make thee ᴿsharpᴺ knives, and circumcise again the children of Israel the second time.

3 And Joshua made him sharp knives, and circumcised the children of Israel at ᴺthe hill of the foreskins.

4 And this *is* the cause why Joshua did circumcise: ᴿAll the people that came out of Egypt, *that were* males, *even* all the men of war, died in the wilderness by the way, after they came out of Egypt.

5 Now all the people that came out were circumcised: but all the people *that were* born in the wilderness by the way as they came forth out of Egypt, *them* they had not circumcised.

6 For the children of Israel walked ᴿforty years in the wilderness, till all the people *that were* men of war, which came out of Egypt, were consumed, because they obeyed not the voice of the LORD: unto whom the LORD sware that ᴿhe would not shew them the land, which the LORD sware unto their fathers that he would give us, ᴿa land that floweth with milk and honey.

7 And ᴿtheir children, *whom* he raised up in their stead, them Joshua circumcised: for they were uncircumcised, because they had not circumcised them by the way.

8 And it came to pass, ᴺwhen they had done circumcising all the people, that they abode in their places in the camp, ᴿtill they were whole.

9 And the LORD said unto Joshua, This day have I rolled away ᴿthe reproach of Egypt from off you. Wherefore the name of the place is called ᴿGĭl′-găl ᴺ unto this day.

The passover observed

10 And the children of Israel encamped in Gĭl′-găl, and kept the passover ᴿon the fourteenth day of the month at even in the plains of Jericho.

CHAP. 4
BC 1451
24 Ex. 14:31
Deut. 6:2
Jer. 10:7
24 Heb. *all days*

CHAP. **5**
BC 1451
1 Num. 13:29
1 Ex. 15:14, 15
1 1 Ki. 10:5
2 Ex. 4:25
2 Or, *knives of flints*
3 Or, *Gibeah-haaraloth*
4 Num. 14:29 & 26:64, 65
Deut. 2:16
6 Num. 14:33
Deut. 1:3
6 Num. 14:23
Heb. 3:11
6 Ex. 3:8
7 Num. 14:31
Deut. 1:39
Heb. *when the people had made an end to be circumcised*
8 See Gen. 34:25
9 Gen. 34:14
9 ch. 4:19
9 i.e. *Rolling*
10 Ex. 12:6
Num. 9:5

Ex. 16:35	12
Gen. 18:2	13
& 32:24	
Ex. 23:23	
Zech. 1:8	
Acts 1:10	
Num. 22:23	13
Or, *prince*,	14
Dan. 10:13, 21	
Gen. 17:3	14
Ex. 3:5	15
Acts 7:33	

CHAP. 6
BC 1451
Heb. *did shut up, and was shut up*   **1**
ch. 2:9, 24 & 8:1   **2**
Deut. 7:24   **2**
See Judg. 7:16, 22   **4**
Num. 10:8   **4**
Heb. *under it*   **5**

11 And they did eat of the old corn of the land on the morrow after the passover, unleavened cakes, and parched *corn* in the selfsame day.

12 And ᴿthe măn′-nă ceased on the morrow after they had eaten of the old corn of the land; neither had the children of Israel măn′-nă any more; but they did eat of the fruit of the land of Canaan that year.

The angel and Joshua

13 And it came to pass, when Joshua was by Jericho, that he lifted up his eyes and looked, and, behold, there stood ᴿa man over against him ᴿwith his sword drawn in his hand: and Joshua went unto him, and said unto him, *Art* thou for us, or for our adversaries?

14 And he said, Nay; but *as* ᴺcaptain of the host of the LORD am I now come. And Joshua ᴿfell on his face to the earth, and did worship, and said unto him, What saith my lord unto his servant?

15 And the captain of the LORD's host said unto Joshua, ᴿLoose thy shoe from off thy foot; for the place whereon thou standest *is* holy. And Joshua did so.

CHAPTER 6

Siege of Jericho

NOW Jericho ᴺwas straitly shut up because of the children of Israel: none went out, and none came in.

2 And the LORD said unto Joshua, See, ᴿI have given into thine hand Jericho, and the ᴿking thereof, *and* the mighty men of valour.

3 And ye shall compass the city, all *ye* men of war, *and* go round about the city once. Thus shalt thou do six days.

4 And seven priests shall bear before the ark seven ᴿtrumpets of rams' horns: and the seventh day ye shall compass the city seven times, and ᴿthe priests shall blow with the trumpets.

5 And it shall come to pass, that when they make a long *blast* with the ram's horn, *and* when ye hear the sound of the trumpet, all the people shall shout with a great shout; and the wall of the city shall fall down ᴺflat, and the people shall ascend up every man straight before him.

6 And Joshua the son of Nun called the priests, and said unto them, Take up the ark of the covenant, and let seven priests bear seven trumpets of rams' horns before the ark of the LORD.

7 And he said unto the people, Pass on, and

compass the city, and let him that is armed pass on before the ark of the LORD.

8 And it came to pass, when Joshua had spoken unto the people, that the seven priests bearing the seven trumpets of rams' horns passed on before the LORD, and blew with the trumpets: and the ark of the covenant of the LORD followed them.

9 And the armed men went before the priests that blew with the trumpets, ᴿand the ᴺrearward came after the ark, *the priests* going on, and blowing with the trumpets.

10 And Joshua had commanded the people, saying, Ye shall not shout, nor ᴺmake any noise with your voice, neither shall *any* word proceed out of your mouth, until the day I bid you shout; then shall ye shout.

11 So the ark of the LORD compassed the city, going about *it* once: and they came into the camp, and lodged in the camp.

12 And Joshua rose early in the morning, ᴿand the priests took up the ark of the LORD.

13 And seven priests bearing seven trumpets of rams' horns before the ark of the LORD went on continually, and blew with the trumpets: and the armed men went before them; but the rearward came after the ark of the LORD, *the priests* going on, and blowing with the trumpets.

14 And the second day they compassed the city once, and returned into the camp: so they did six days.

15 And it came to pass on the seventh day, that they rose early about the dawning of the day, and compassed the city after the same manner seven times: only on that day they compassed the city seven times.

16 And it came to pass at the seventh time, when the priests blew with the trumpets, Joshua said unto the people, Shout; for the LORD hath given you the city.

17 And the city shall be ᴺaccursed, *even* it, and all that *are* therein, to the LORD: only Rahab the harlot shall live, she and all that *are* with her in the house, because ᴿshe hid the messengers that we sent.

18 And ye, ᴿin any wise keep *yourselves* from the accursed thing, lest ye make *yourselves* accursed, when ye take of the accursed thing, and make the camp of Israel a curse, ᴿand trouble it.

19 But all the silver, and gold, and vessels of brass and iron, *are* ᴺconsecrated unto the LORD: they shall come into the treasury of the LORD.

20 So the people shouted when *the priests* blew with the trumpets: and it came to pass, when the people heard the sound of the trum-

CHAP. 6
BC 1451
9 Num. 10:25
9 Heb. *gathering host*
10 Heb. *make your voice to be heard*
12 Deut. 31:25
17 Or, *devoted,* Lev. 27:28
17 ch. 2:4
18 Deut. 7:26 & 13:17 ch. 7:1, 11, 12
18 ch. 7:25 1 Ki. 18:17, 18 Jonah 1:12
19 Heb. *holiness*

ver. 5	20
Heb. 11:30	
Heb. *under it*	20
Deut. 7:2	21
ch. 2:14	22
Heb. 11:31	
ch. 2:13	23
Heb. *families*	23
ver. 19	24
See Mat. 1:5	25
1 Ki. 16:34	26
ch. 1:5	27
ch. 9:1, 3	27

CHAP. 7
BC 1451
ch. 22:20 — 1
1 Chr. 2:7, — 1
Achar Or, *Zimri,* — 1
1 Chr. 2:6

pet, and the people shouted with a great shout, that ᴿthe wall fell down ᴺflat, so that the people went up into the city, every man straight before him, and they took the city.

21 And they ᴿutterly destroyed all that *was* in the city, both man and woman, young and old, and ox, and sheep, and ass, with the edge of the sword.

Rahab saved

22 But Joshua had said unto the two men that had spied out the country, Go into the harlot's house, and bring out thence the woman, and all that she hath, ᴿas ye sware unto her.

23 And the young men that were spies went in, and brought out Rahab, ᴿand her father, and her mother, and her brethren, and all that she had; and they brought out all her ᴺkindred, and left them without the camp of Israel.

24 And they burnt the city with fire, and all that *was* therein: ᴿonly the silver, and the gold, and the vessels of brass and of iron, they put into the treasury of the house of the LORD.

25 And Joshua saved Rahab the harlot alive, and her father's household, and all that she had; and ᴿshe dwelleth in Israel *even* unto this day; because she hid the messengers, which Joshua sent to spy out Jericho.

26 And Joshua adjured *them* at that time, saying, ᴿCursed *be* the man before the LORD, that riseth up and buildeth this city Jericho: he shall lay the foundation thereof in his firstborn, and in his youngest *son* shall he set up the gates of it.

27 ᴿSo the LORD was with Joshua; and ᴿhis fame was *noised* throughout all the country.

CHAPTER 7

The sin of Achan

BUT the children of Israel committed a trespass in the accursed thing: for ᴿᾹ'-chăn,ᴺ the son of Cär'-mĭ, the son of ᴺZăb'-dĭ, the son of Zē'-räh, of the tribe of Judah, took of the accursed thing: and the anger of the LORD was kindled against the children of Israel.

Defeat at Ai

2 And Joshua sent men from Jericho to Ā'-ĭ, which *is* beside Bĕth-ā'-vĕn, on the east side of Beth-el, and spake unto them, saying, Go up and view the country. And the men went up and viewed Ā'-ĭ.

3 And they returned to Joshua, and said unto him, Let not all the people go up; but let ^Nabout two or three thousand men go up and smite A̅'-ī; *and* make not all the people to labour thither; for they *are but* few.

4 So there went up thither of the people about three thousand men: ^Rand they fled before the men of A̅'-ī.

5 And the men of A̅'-ī smote of them about thirty and six men: for they chased them *from* before the gate *even* unto Shĕb'-ă-rĭm, and smote them ^Nin the going down: wherefore ^Rthe hearts of the people melted, and became as water.

6 And Joshua ^Rrent his clothes, and fell to the earth upon his face before the ark of the LORD until the eventide, he and the elders of Israel, and ^Rput dust upon their heads.

7 And Joshua said, Alas, O Lord GOD, ^Rwherefore hast thou at all brought this people over Jordan, to deliver us into the hand of the Amorites, to destroy us? would to God we had been content, and dwelt on the other side Jordan!

8 O Lord, what shall I say, when Israel turneth their ^Nbacks before their enemies!

9 For the Canaanites and all the inhabitants of the land shall hear *of it,* and shall environ us round, and ^Rcut off our name from the earth: and ^Rwhat wilt thou do unto thy great name?

10 And the LORD said unto Joshua, Get thee up; wherefore ^Nliest thou thus upon thy face?

11 ^RIsrael hath sinned, and they have also transgressed my covenant which I commanded them: ^Rfor they have even taken of the accursed thing, and have also stolen, and ^Rdissembled also, and they have put *it* even among their own stuff.

12 ^RTherefore the children of Israel could not stand before their enemies, *but* turned *their* backs before their enemies, because ^Rthey were accursed: neither will I be with you any more, except ye destroy the accursed from among you.

13 Up, ^Rsanctify the people, and say, ^RSanctify yourselves against to morrow: for thus saith the LORD God of Israel, *There is* an accursed thing in the midst of thee, O Israel: thou canst not stand before thine enemies, until ye take away the accursed thing from among you.

14 In the morning therefore ye shall be brought according to your tribes: and it shall be, *that* the tribe which ^Rthe LORD taketh shall come according to the families *thereof;* and the family which the LORD shall take shall come by households; and the household which

the LORD shall take shall come man by man.

15 ^RAnd it shall be, *that* he that is taken with the accursed thing shall be burnt with fire, he and all that he hath: because he hath ^Rtransgressed the covenant of the LORD, and because he ^Rhath wrought ^Nfolly in Israel.

Achan's sin uncovered

16 So Joshua rose up early in the morning, and brought Israel by their tribes; and the tribe of Judah was taken:

17 And he brought the family of Judah; and he took the family of the Zär'-hītes: and he brought the family of the Zär'-hītes man by man; and Zăb'-dī was taken:

18 And he brought his household man by man; and A̅'-chăn, the son of Cär'-mī, the son of Zăb'-dī, the son of Zē'-räh, of the tribe of Judah, ^Rwas taken.

19 And Joshua said unto A̅'-chăn, My son, ^Rgive, I pray thee, glory to the LORD God of Israel, ^Rand make confession unto him; and ^Rtell me now what thou hast done; hide *it* not from me.

20 And A̅'-chăn answered Joshua, and said, Indeed I have sinned against the LORD God of Israel, and thus and thus have I done:

21 When I saw among the spoils a goodly Babylonish garment, and two hundred shē'-kĕls of silver, and a ^Nwedge of gold of fifty shē'-kĕls weight, then I coveted them, and took them; and, behold, they *are* hid in the earth in the midst of my tent, and the silver under it.

22 So Joshua sent messengers, and they ran unto the tent; and, behold, *it was* hid in his tent, and the silver under it.

23 And they took them out of the midst of the tent, and brought them unto Joshua, and unto all the children of Israel, and ^Nlaid them out before the LORD.

24 And Joshua, and all Israel with him, took A̅'-chăn the son of Zē'-räh, and the silver, and the garment, and the wedge of gold, and his sons, and his daughters, and his oxen, and his asses, and his sheep, and his tent, and all that he had: and they brought them unto ^Rthe valley of A̅'-chôr.

25 And Joshua said, ^RWhy hast thou troubled us? the LORD shall trouble thee this day. ^RAnd all Israel stoned him with stones, and burned them with fire, after they had stoned them with stones.

26 And they ^Rraised over him a great heap of stones unto this day. So ^Rthe LORD turned from the fierceness of his anger. Wherefore the name of that place was called, ^RThe valley of ^NA̅'-chôr, unto this day.

CHAPTER 8

Joshua encouraged

AND the LORD said unto Joshua, ᴿFear not, neither be thou dismayed: take all the people of war with thee, and arise, go up to Ā′-ī: see, ᴿI have given into thy hand the king of Ā′-ī, and his people, and his city, and his land:

2 And thou shalt do to Ā′-ī and her king as thou didst unto ᴿJericho and her king: only ᴿthe spoil thereof, and the cattle thereof, shall ye take for a prey unto yourselves: lay thee an ambush for the city behind it.

3 So Joshua arose, and all the people of war, to go up against Ā′-ī: and Joshua chose out thirty thousand mighty men of valour, and sent them away by night.

4 And he commanded them, saying, Behold, ᴿye shall lie in wait against the city, *even* behind the city: go not very far from the city, but be ye all ready:

5 And I, and all the people that *are* with me, will approach unto the city: and it shall come to pass, when they come out against us, as at the first, that ᴿwe will flee before them,

6 (For they will come out after us) till we have ᴺdrawn them from the city; for they will say, They flee before us, as at the first: therefore we will flee before them.

7 Then ye shall rise up from the ambush, and seize upon the city: for the LORD your God will deliver it into your hand.

8 And it shall be, when ye have taken the city, *that* ye shall set the city on fire: according to the commandment of the LORD shall ye do. ᴿSee, I have commanded you.

9 Joshua therefore sent them forth: and they went to lie in ambush, and abode between Beth-el and Ā′-ī, on the west side of Ā′-ī: but Joshua lodged that night among the people.

10 And Joshua rose up early in the morning, and numbered the people, and went up, he and the elders of Israel, before the people to Ā′-ī.

11 ᴿAnd all the people, *even the people* of war that *were* with him, went up, and drew nigh, and came before the city, and pitched on the north side of Ā′-ī: now *there was* a valley between them and Ā′-ī.

12 And he took about five thousand men, and set them to lie in ambush between Beth-el and Ā′-ī, on the west side ᴺof the city.

13 And when they had set the people, *even* all the host that *was* on the north of the city, and ᴺtheir liers in wait on the west of the city, Joshua went that night into the midst of the valley.

14 And it came to pass, when the king of

Ā′-ī saw *it,* that they hasted and rose up early, and the men of the city went out against Israel to battle, he and all his people, at a time appointed, before the plain; but he ᴿwist not that *there were* liers in ambush against him behind the city.

15 And Joshua and all Israel ᴿmade as if they were beaten before them, and fled by the way of the wilderness.

16 And all the people that *were* in Ā′-ī were called together to pursue after them: and they pursued after Joshua, and were drawn away from the city.

17 And there was not a man left in Ā′-ī or Beth-el, that went not out after Israel: and they left the city open, and pursued after Israel.

Victory over Ai

18 And the LORD said unto Joshua, Stretch out the spear that *is* in thy hand toward Ā′-ī; for I will give it into thine hand. And Joshua stretched out the spear that *he had* in his hand toward the city.

19 And the ambush arose quickly out of their place, and they ran as soon as he had stretched out his hand: and they entered into the city, and took it, and hasted and set the city on fire.

20 And when the men of Ā′-ī looked behind them, they saw, and, behold, the smoke of the city ascended up to heaven, and they had no ᴺpower to flee this way or that way: and the people that fled to the wilderness turned back upon the pursuers.

21 And when Joshua and all Israel saw that the ambush had taken the city, and that the smoke of the city ascended, then they turned again, and slew the men of Ā′-ī.

22 And the other issued out of the city against them; so they were in the midst of Israel, some on this side, and some on that side: and they smote them, so that they ᴿlet none of them remain or escape.

23 And the king of Ā′-ī they took alive, and brought him to Joshua.

24 And it came to pass, when Israel had made an end of slaying all the inhabitants of Ā′-ī in the field, in the wilderness wherein they chased them, and when they were all fallen on the edge of the sword, until they were consumed, that all the Israelites returned unto Ā′-ī, and smote it with the edge of the sword.

25 And *so* it was, *that* all that fell that day, both of men and women, *were* twelve thousand, *even* all the men of Ā′-ī.

26 For Joshua drew not his hand back, wherewith he stretched out the spear, until he had utterly destroyed all the inhabitants of Ā′-ī.

27 ᴿOnly the cattle and the spoil of that city Israel took for a prey unto themselves, according unto the word of the Lᴏʀᴅ which he ᴿcommanded Joshua.

28 And Joshua burnt Ā'-ī, and made it ᴿan heap for ever, *even* a desolation unto this day.

29 ᴿAnd the king of Ā'-ī he hanged on a tree until eventide: ᴿand as soon as the sun was down, Joshua commanded that they should take his carcase down from the tree, and cast it at the entering of the gate of the city, and ᴿraise thereon a great heap of stones, *that remaineth* unto this day.

Joshua's altar

30 Then Joshua built an altar unto the Lᴏʀᴅ God of Israel ᴿin mount Ē'-băl,

31 As Moses the servant of the Lᴏʀᴅ commanded the children of Israel, as it is written in the ᴿbook of the law of Moses, an altar of whole stones, over which no man hath lift up *any* iron: and ᴿthey offered thereon burnt offerings unto the Lᴏʀᴅ, and sacrificed peace offerings.

32 And ᴿhe wrote there upon the stones a copy of the law of Moses, which he wrote in the presence of the children of Israel.

33 And all Israel, and their elders, and officers, and their judges, stood on this side the ark and on that side before the priests the Levites, ᴿwhich bare the ark of the covenant of the Lᴏʀᴅ, as well ᴿthe stranger, as he that was born among them; half of them over against mount Gĕ-rī'-zīm, and half of them over against mount Ē'-băl; ᴿas Moses the servant of the Lᴏʀᴅ had commanded before, that they should bless the people of Israel.

Reading of the law

34 And afterward ᴿhe read all the words of the law, ᴿthe blessings and cursings, according to all that is written in the book of the law.

35 There was not a word of all that Moses commanded, which Joshua read not before all the congregation of Israel, ᴿwith the women, and the little ones, and ᴿthe strangers that ᴺwere conversant among them.

CHAPTER 9

Alliance of southern nations

AND it came to pass, when all the kings which *were* on this side Jordan, in the hills, and in the valleys, and in all the coasts of ᴿthe great sea over against Lĕb'-ă-nọn, ᴿthe Hittite, and the Amorite, the Canaanite, the Pĕ-rīz'-zīte, the Hī'-vīte, and the Jĕb'-ū-sīte, heard *thereof;*

2 That they ᴿgathered themselves together, to fight with Joshua and with Israel, with one ᴺaccord.

Treaty with Gibeon

3 And when the inhabitants of ᴿGibeon ᴿheard what Joshua had done unto Jericho and to Ā'-ī,

4 They did work wilily, and went and made as if they had been ambassadors, and took old sacks upon their asses, and wine bottles, old, and rent, and bound up;

5 And old shoes and clouted upon their feet, and old garments upon them; and all the bread of their provision was dry *and* mouldy.

6 And they went to Joshua ᴿunto the camp at Gĭl'-găl, and said unto him, and to the men of Israel, We be come from a far country: now therefore make ye a league with us.

7 And the men of Israel said unto the ᴿHī'-vītes, Peradventure ye dwell among us; and ᴿhow shall we make a league with you?

8 And they said unto Joshua, ᴿWe *are* thy servants. And Joshua said unto them, Who *are* ye? and from whence come ye?

9 And they said unto him, ᴿFrom a very far country thy servants are come because of the name of the Lᴏʀᴅ thy God: for we have ᴿheard the fame of him, and all that he did in Egypt,

10 And ᴿall that he did to the two kings of the Amorites, that *were* beyond Jordan, to Sī'-hŏn king of Hĕsh'-bŏn, and to Og king of Bā'-shăn, which *was* at Ăsh'-tă-rōth.

11 Wherefore our elders and all the inhabitants of our country spake to us, saying, Take victuals ᴺwith you for the journey, and go to meet them, and say unto them, We *are* your servants: therefore now make ye a league with us.

12 This our bread we took hot *for* our provision out of our houses on the day we came forth to go unto you; but now, behold, it is dry, and it is mouldy:

13 And these bottles of wine, which we filled, *were* new; and, behold, they be rent: and these our garments and our shoes are become old by reason of the very long journey.

14 And ᴺthe men took of their victuals, ᴿand asked not *counsel* at the mouth of the Lᴏʀᴅ.

15 And Joshua ᴿmade peace with them, and made a league with them, to let them live: and the princes of the congregation sware unto them.

Gibeonites made slaves

16 And it came to pass at the end of three days after they had made a league with them,

---

that they heard that they *were* their neighbours, and *that* they dwelt among them.

17 And the children of Israel journeyed, and came unto their cities on the third day. Now their cities *were* ᴿGibeon, and C͟hĕ-phī′-răh, and Bḗ͞er′-ōth, and Kĭr′-jăth-jē′-ă-rĭm.

18 And the children of Israel smote them not, ᴿbecause the princes of the congregation had sworn unto them by the Lᴏʀᴅ God of Israel. And all the congregation murmured against the princes.

19 But all the princes said unto all the congregation, We have sworn unto them by the Lᴏʀᴅ God of Israel: now therefore we may not touch them.

20 This we will do to them; we will even let them live, lest ᴿwrath be upon us, because of the oath which we sware unto them.

21 And the princes said unto them, Let them live; but let them be ᴿhewers of wood and drawers of water unto all the congregation; as the princes had ᴿpromised them.

22 And Joshua called for them, and he spake unto them, saying, Wherefore have ye beguiled us, saying, ᴿWe *are* very far from you; when ᴿye dwell among us?

23 Now therefore ye *are* ᴿcursed, and there shall ᴺnone of you be freed from being bondmen, and hewers of wood and drawers of water for the house of my God.

24 And they answered Joshua, and said, Because it was certainly told thy servants, how that the Lᴏʀᴅ thy God ᴿcommanded his servant Moses to give you all the land, and to destroy all the inhabitants of the land from before you, therefore ᴿwe were sore afraid of our lives because of you, and have done this thing.

25 And now, behold, we *are* ᴿin thine hand: as it seemeth good and right unto thee to do unto us, do.

26 And so did he unto them, and delivered them out of the hand of the children of Israel, that they slew them not.

27 And Joshua ᴺmade them that day ᴿhewers of wood and drawers of water for the congregation, and for the altar of the Lᴏʀᴅ, even unto this day, ᴿin the place which he should choose.

CHAPTER 10

Conspiracy against Gibeon

Nᴏᴡ it came to pass, when Ăd′-ō-nī-zē′-dĕc king of Jerusalem had heard how Joshua had taken Ā′-ī, and had utterly destroyed it; ᴿas he had done to Jericho and her king, so he had done to ᴿĀ′-ī and her king; and ᴿhow the inhabitants of Gibeon had made peace with Israel, and were among them;

2 That they ᴿfeared greatly, because Gibeon *was* a great city, as one of the ᴺroyal cities, and because it *was* greater than Ā′-ī, and all the men thereof *were* mighty.

3 Wherefore Ăd′-ō-nī-zē′-dĕc king of Jerusalem sent unto Hō′-hăm king of Hē′-brŏn, and unto Pī′-răm king of Jär′-mûth, and unto Jă-phī′-ă king of Lā′-c͟hĭsh, and unto Dē′-bĭr king of Ĕg′-lŏn, saying,

4 Come up unto me, and help me, that we may smite Gibeon: ᴿfor it hath made peace with Joshua and with the children of Israel.

5 Therefore the five kings of the Amorites, the king of Jerusalem, the king of Hē′-brŏn, the king of Jär′-mûth, the king of Lā′-c͟hĭsh, the king of Ĕg′-lŏn, ᴿgathered themselves together, and went up, they and all their hosts, and encamped before Gibeon, and made war against it.

6 And the men of Gibeon sent unto Joshua ᴿto the camp to Gĭl′-găl, saying, Slack not thy hand from thy servants; come up to us quickly, and save us, and help us: for all the kings of the Amorites that dwell in the mountains are gathered together against us.

7 So Joshua ascended from Gĭl′-găl, he, and ᴿall the people of war with him, and all the mighty men of valour.

8 And the Lᴏʀᴅ said unto Joshua, ᴿFear them not: for I have delivered them into thine hand; ᴿthere shall not a man of them stand before thee.

9 Joshua therefore came unto them suddenly, *and* went up from Gĭl′-găl all night.

10 And the Lᴏʀᴅ ᴿdiscomfited them before Israel, and slew them with a great slaughter at Gibeon, and chased them along the way that goeth up ᴿto Bĕth-hôr′-ŏn, and smote them to ᴿĂ-zē′-kăh, and unto Măk-kē′-däh.

11 And it came to pass, as they fled from before Israel, *and* were in the going down to Bĕth-hôr′-ŏn, ᴿthat the Lᴏʀᴅ cast down great stones from heaven upon them unto Ă-zē′-kăh, and they died: *they were* more which died with hailstones than *they* whom the children of Israel slew with the sword.

The sun stands still

12 Then spake Joshua to the Lᴏʀᴅ in the day when the Lᴏʀᴅ delivered up the Amorites before the children of Israel, and he said in the sight of Israel, ᴿSun, ᴺstand thou still upon Gibeon; and thou, Moon, in the valley of ᴿĂj′-ă-lŏn.

13 And the sun stood still, and the moon stayed, until the people had avenged themselves upon their enemies. ᴿ*Is* not this written in the book of ᴺJăsh′-ĕr? So the sun stood still

in the midst of heaven, and hasted not to go down about a whole day.

14 And there was ᴿno day like that before it or after it, that the LORD hearkened unto the voice of a man: for ᴿthe LORD fought for Israel.

15 ᴿAnd Joshua returned, and all Israel with him, unto the camp to Gĭl'-găl.

Amorite kings slain

16 But these five kings fled, and hid themselves in a cave at Măk-kē'-däh.

17 And it was told Joshua, saying, The five kings are found hid in a cave at Măk-kē'-däh.

18 And Joshua said, Roll great stones upon the mouth of the cave, and set men by it for to keep them:

19 And stay ye not, *but* pursue after your enemies, and ᴺsmite the hindmost of them; suffer them not to enter into their cities: for the LORD your God hath delivered them into your hand.

20 And it came to pass, when Joshua and the children of Israel had made an end of slaying them with a very great slaughter, till they were consumed, that the rest *which* remained of them entered into fenced cities.

21 And all the people returned to the camp to Joshua at Măk-kē'-däh in peace: ᴿnone moved his tongue against any of the children of Israel.

22 Then said Joshua, Open the mouth of the cave, and bring out those five kings unto me out of the cave.

23 And they did so, and brought forth those five kings unto him out of the cave, the king of Jerusalem, the king of Hē'-brŏn, the king of Jär'-mûth, the king of Lā'-chĭsh, *and* the king of Ĕg'-lŏn.

24 And it came to pass, when they brought out those kings unto Joshua, that Joshua called for all the men of Israel, and said unto the captains of the men of war which went with him, Come near, ᴿput your feet upon the necks of these kings. And they came near, and put their feet upon the necks of them.

25 And Joshua said unto them, ᴿFear not, nor be dismayed, be strong and of good courage: for ᴿthus shall the LORD do to all your enemies against whom ye fight.

26 And afterward Joshua smote them, and slew them, and hanged them on five trees: and they ᴿwere hanging upon the trees until the evening.

27 And it came to pass at the time of the going down of the sun, *that* Joshua commanded, and they ᴿtook them down off the trees, and cast them into the cave wherein

they had been hid, and laid great stones in the cave's mouth, *which remain* until this very day.

Further conquests

28 And that day Joshua took Măk-kē'-däh, and smote it with the edge of the sword, and the king thereof he utterly destroyed, them, and all the souls that *were* therein; he let none remain: and he did to the king of Măk-kē'-däh ᴿas he did unto the king of Jericho.

29 Then Joshua passed from Măk-kē'-däh, and all Israel with him, unto Lĭb'-näh, and fought against Lĭb'-näh:

30 And the LORD delivered it also, and the king thereof, into the hand of Israel; and he smote it with the edge of the sword, and all the souls that *were* therein; he let none remain in it; but did unto the king thereof as he did unto the king of Jericho.

31 And Joshua passed from Lĭb'-näh, and all Israel with him, unto Lā'-chĭsh, and encamped against it, and fought against it:

32 And the LORD delivered Lā'-chĭsh into the hand of Israel, which took it on the second day, and smote it with the edge of the sword, and all the souls that *were* therein, according to all that he had done to Lĭb'-näh.

33 Then Hôr'-ăm king of Gē'-zĕr came up to help Lā'-chĭsh; and Joshua smote him and his people, until he had left him none remaining.

34 And from Lā'-chĭsh Joshua passed unto Ĕg'-lŏn, and all Israel with him; and they encamped against it, and fought against it:

35 And they took it on that day, and smote it with the edge of the sword, and all the souls that *were* therein he utterly destroyed that day, according to all that he had done to Lā'-chĭsh.

36 And Joshua went up from Ĕg'-lŏn, and all Israel with him, unto ᴿHē'-brŏn; and they fought against it:

37 And they took it, and smote it with the edge of the sword, and the king thereof, and all the cities thereof, and all the souls that *were* therein; he left none remaining, according to all that he had done to Ĕg'-lŏn; but destroyed it utterly, and all the souls that *were* therein.

38 And Joshua returned, and all Israel with him, to ᴿDē'-bĭr; and fought against it:

39 And he took it, and the king thereof, and all the cities thereof; and they smote them with the edge of the sword, and utterly destroyed all the souls that *were* therein; he left none remaining: as he had done to Hē'-brŏn, so he did to Dē'-bĭr, and to the king thereof; as he had done also to Lĭb'-näh, and to her king.

40 So Joshua smote all the country of the

hills, and of the south, and of the vale, and of the springs, and all their kings: he left none remaining, but utterly destroyed all that breathed, as the LORD God of Israel [R]commanded.

41 And Joshua smote them from Kā′-dĕsh-bär′-nĕ-ă even unto [R]Gā′-ză, [R]and all the country of Gō′-shĕn, even unto Gibeon.

42 And all these kings and their land did Joshua take at one time, [R]because the LORD God of Israel fought for Israel.

43 And Joshua returned, and all Israel with him, unto the camp to Gĭl′-găl.

CHAPTER 11

Alliance of northern nations

AND it came to pass, when Jā′-bĭn king of Hā′-zôr had heard *those things,* that he [R]sent to Jō′-băb king of Mā′-dŏn, and to the king [R]of Shĭm′-rŏn, and to the king of Ăch′-shăph,

2 And to the kings that *were* on the north of the mountains, and of the plains south of [R]Chĭn′-nĕ-rōth, and in the valley, and in the borders [R]of Dor on the west,

3 *And to* the Canaanite on the east and on the west, and *to* the Amorite, and the Hittite, and the Pĕ-rĭz′-zīte, and the Jĕb′-ū-śīte in the mountains, [R]and *to* the Hī′-vīte under [R]Hermon [R]in the land of Mĭz′-pēh.

4 And they went out, they and all their hosts with them, much people, [R]even as the sand that *is* upon the sea shore in multitude, with horses and chariots very many.

5 And when all these kings were [N]met together, they came and pitched together at the waters of Mē′-rŏm, to fight against Israel.

Joshua's victory at Merom

6 And the LORD said unto Joshua, [R]Be not afraid because of them: for to morrow about this time will I deliver them up all slain before Israel: thou shalt [R]hough their horses, and burn their chariots with fire.

7 So Joshua came, and all the people of war with him, against them by the waters of Mē′-rŏm suddenly; and they fell upon them.

8 And the LORD delivered them into the hand of Israel, who smote them, and chased them unto [N]great Zī′-dŏn, and unto [R]Mĭś′-rē-phōth-mā′-ĭm,[NN] and unto the valley of Mĭz′-pēh eastward; and they smote them, until they left them none remaining.

9 And Joshua did unto them as the LORD bade him: he houghed their horses, and burnt their chariots with fire.

Conquest of the north

10 And Joshua at that time turned back, and took Hā′-zôr, and smote the king thereof with the sword: for Hā′-zôr beforetime was the head of all those kingdoms.

11 And they smote all the souls that *were* therein with the edge of the sword, utterly destroying *them;* there was not [N]any left to breathe: and he burnt Hā′-zôr with fire.

12 And all the cities of those kings, and all the kings of them, did Joshua take, and smote them with the edge of the sword, *and* he utterly destroyed them, [R]as Moses the servant of the LORD commanded.

13 But *as for* the cities that stood still [N]in their strength, Israel burned none of them, save Hā′-zôr only; *that* did Joshua burn.

14 And all the spoil of these cities, and the cattle, the children of Israel took for a prey unto themselves; but every man they smote with the edge of the sword, until they had destroyed them, neither left they any to breathe.

15 [R]As the LORD commanded Moses his servant, so [R]did Moses command Joshua, and [R]so did Joshua; [N]he left nothing undone of all that the LORD commanded Moses.

16 So Joshua took all that land, [R]the hills, and all the south country, [R]and all the land of Gō′-shĕn, and the valley, and the plain, and the mountain of Israel, and the valley of the same;

17 [R]*Even* from [N]the mount Hā′-lăk, that goeth up to Sē′-ĭr, even unto Bā′-ăl-găd in the valley of Lĕb′-ă-nŏn under mount Hermon: and [R]all their kings he took, and smote them, and slew them.

18 Joshua made war a long time with all those kings.

19 There was not a city that made peace with the children of Israel, save [R]the Hī′-vītes the inhabitants of Gibeon: all *other* they took in battle.

20 For [R]it was of the LORD to harden their hearts, that they should come against Israel in battle, that he might destroy them utterly, *and* that they might have no favour, but that he might destroy them, [R]as the LORD commanded Moses.

21 And at that time came Joshua, and cut off [R]the Anakims from the mountains, from Hē′-brŏn, from Dē′-bĭr, from Anab, and from all the mountains of Judah, and from all the mountains of Israel: Joshua destroyed them utterly with their cities.

22 There was none of the Anakims left in the land of the children of Israel: only in

Gā'-ză, in ᴿGath, ᴿand in Ăsh'-dŏd, there remained.

23 So Joshua took the whole land, ᴿaccording to all that the Lᴏʀᴅ said unto Moses; and Joshua gave it for an inheritance unto Israel ᴿaccording to their divisions by their tribes. ᴿAnd the land rested from war.

CHAPTER 12

Countries conquered by Moses

Nᴏᴡ these *are* the kings of the land, which the children of Israel smote, and possessed their land on the other side Jordan toward the rising of the sun, ᴿfrom the river Arnon ᴿunto mount Hermon, and all the plain on the east:

2 ᴿSĭ'-hŏn king of the Amorites, who dwelt in Hĕsh'-bŏn, *and* ruled from Ă-rō'-ĕr, which *is* upon the bank of the river Arnon, and from the middle of the river, and from half Gilead, even unto the river Jăb'-bŏk, *which is* the border of the children of Ammon;

3 And ᴿfrom the plain to the sea of Chĭn'-nĕ-rōth on the east, and unto the sea of the plain, *even* the salt sea on the east, ᴿthe way to Bĕth-jĕsh'-ĭ-mōth; and from ᴺthe south, under ᴿĂsh'-dŏth-pĭś'-gäh:ᴺ

4 And ᴿthe coast of Og king of Bā'-shăn, *which was* of ᴿthe remnant of the giants, ᴿthat dwelt at Ăsh'-tă-rōth and at Ĕd'-rĕ-ī,

5 And reigned in ᴿmount Hermon, ᴿand in Săl'-căh, and in all Bā'-shăn, ᴿunto the border of the Gĕ-shū'-rītes and the Mā-ăch'-ă-thītes, and half Gilead, the border of Sĭ'-hŏn king of Hĕsh'-bŏn.

6 ᴿThem did Moses the servant of the Lᴏʀᴅ and the children of Israel smite: and ᴿMoses the servant of the Lᴏʀᴅ gave it *for* a possession unto the Reubenites, and the Gadites, and the half tribe of Mă-năs'-sēh.

Conquests by Joshua

7 And these *are* the kings of the country ᴿwhich Joshua and the children of Israel smote on this side Jordan on the west, from Bā'-ăl-găd in the valley of Lĕb'-ă-nŏn even unto the mount Hā'-lăk, that goeth up to ᴿSē'-ĭr; which Joshua ᴿgave unto the tribes of Israel *for* a possession according to their divisions;

8 ᴿIn the mountains, and in the valleys, and in the plains, and in the springs, and in the wilderness, and in the south country; ᴿthe Hittites, the Amorites, and the Canaanites, the Pĕ-rĭz'-zītes, the Hī'-vītes, and the Jĕb'-ū-sītes:

9 ᴿThe king of Jericho, one; ᴿthe king of Ā'-ī, which *is* beside Beth-el, one;

10 ᴿThe king of Jerusalem, one; the king of Hē'-brŏn, one;

11 The king of Jär'-mŭth, one; the king of Lā'-chĭsh, one;

12 The king of ĕg'-lŏn, one; ᴿthe king of Gē'-zẽr, one;

13 ᴿThe king of Dē'-bĭr, one; the king of Gē'-dĕr, one;

14 The king of Hôr'-măh, one; the king of är'-ăd, one;

15 ᴿThe king of Lĭb'-năh, one; the king of Adullam, one;

16 ᴿThe king of Măk-kē'-däh, one; ᴿthe king of Beth-el, one;

17 The king of Tăp'-pū-ăh, one; ᴿthe king of Hē'-phẽr, one;

18 The king of Ā'-phĕk, one; the king of ᴺLă-shär'-ŏn, one;

19 The king of Mā'-dŏn, one; ᴿthe king of Hā'-zôr, one;

20 The king of ᴿShĭm'-rŏn-mē'-rŏn, one; the king of Ăch'-shăph, one;

21 The king of Tā'-ă-năch, one; the king of Mĕ-gĭd'-dō, one;

22 ᴿThe king of Kē'-dĕsh, one; the king of Jŏk'-nĕ-ăm of Carmel, one;

23 The king of Dor in the ᴿcoast of Dor, one; the king of ᴿthe nations of Gĭl'-găl, one;

24 The king of Tĭr'-zăh, one: all the kings thirty and one.

CHAPTER 13

Land yet unconquered

Nᴏᴡ Joshua ᴿwas old *and* stricken in years; and the Lᴏʀᴅ said unto him, Thou art old *and* stricken in years, and there remaineth yet very much land ᴺto be possessed.

2 ᴿThis *is* the land that yet remaineth: ᴿall the borders of the Philistines, and all ᴿGĕ-shū'-rī,

3 ᴿFrom Sĭ'-hôr, which *is* before Egypt, even unto the borders of Ĕk'-rŏn northward, *which* is counted to the Canaanite: ᴿfive lords of the Philistines; the Gā'-ză-thites, and the Ăsh'-dŏ-thites, the Ĕsh'-kă-lŏn-ites, the Gĭt'-tites, and the Ĕk'-rŏn-ites; also ᴿthe Ā'-vītes:

4 From the south, all the land of the Canaanites, and ᴺMĕ-är'-äh that *is* beside the Śi-dō'-nĭ-ăns, ᴿunto Ā'-phĕk, to the borders of ᴿthe Amorites:

5 And the land of ᴿthe Gĭb'-lītes, and all Lĕb'-ă-nŏn, toward the sunrising, ᴿfrom Bā'-ăl-găd under mount Hermon unto the entering into Hā'-măth.

6 All the inhabitants of the hill country from

Lĕb′-ă-nǫn unto ᴿMĭś′-rĕ-phōth-mā′-ĭm, *and* all the Ṣĭ-dō′-nĭ-ăns, them ᴿwill I drive out from before the children of Israel: only ᴿdivide thou it by lot unto the Israelites for an inheritance, as I have commanded thee.

7 Now therefore divide this land for an inheritance unto the nine tribes, and the half tribe of Mă-năs′-sĕh,

Inheritance east of Jordan

8 With whom the Reubenites and the Gadites have received their inheritance, ᴿwhich Moses gave them, beyond Jordan eastward, *even* as Moses the servant of the LORD gave them;

9 From Ă-rō′-ĕr, that *is* upon the bank of the river Arnon, and the city that *is* in the midst of the river, ᴿand all the plain of Mē′-dĕ-bă unto Dī′-bŏn;

10 And ᴿall the cities of Sī′-hŏn king of the Amorites, which reigned in Hĕsh′-bŏn, unto the border of the children of Ammon;

11 ᴿAnd Gilead, and the border of the Gĕ-shū′-rĭtes and Mā-ăch′-ă-thītes, and all mount Hermon, and all Bā′-shăn unto Săl′-căh;

12 All the kingdom of Og in Bā′-shăn, which reigned in Ăsh′-tă-rōth and in Ĕd′-rĕ-ī, who remained of ᴿthe remnant of the giants: ᴿfor these did Moses smite, and cast them out.

13 Nevertheless the children of Israel expelled ᴿnot the Gĕ-shū′-rĭtes, nor the Mā-ăch′-ă-thītes: but the Gĕ-shū′-rĭtes and the Mā-ăch′-ă-thītes dwell among the Israelites until this day.

14 ᴿOnly unto the tribe of Levi he gave none inheritance; the sacrifices of the LORD God of Israel made by fire *are* their inheritance, ᴿas he said unto them.

Inheritance of the Reubenites

15 And Moses gave unto the tribe of the children of Reuben *inheritance* according to their families.

16 And their coast was ᴿfrom Ă-rō′-ĕr, that *is* on the bank of the river Arnon, ᴿand the city that *is* in the midst of the river, ᴿand all the plain by Mē′-dĕ-bă;

17 Hĕsh′-bŏn, and all her cities that *are* in the plain; Dī′-bŏn, and ᴺBā′-mōth-bā′-ăl, and Bĕth-bā′-ăl-mē′-on,

18 ᴿAnd Jă-hā′-zăh, and Kē′-dĕ-mōth, and Mĕph′-ā-ăth,

19 ᴿAnd Kĭr-jă-thā′-ĭm, and ᴿSĭb′-măh, and Zâr′-ĕth-shā′-här in the mount of the valley,

20 And Bĕth-pē′-ôr, and ᴿĂsh′-dōth-pĭś′-găh,ᴺ and Bĕth-jĕsh′-ĭ-mōth,

21 ᴿAnd all the cities of the plain, and all

the kingdom of Sī′-hŏn king of the Amorites, which reigned in Hĕsh′-bŏn, ᴿwhom Moses smote ᴿwith the princes of Mĭd′-ĭ-ăn, Ē′-vī, and Rē′-kĕm, and Zur, and Hur, and Rē′-bă, *which were* dukes of Sī′-hŏn, dwelling in the country.

22 ᴿBā′-lāăm also the son of Bē′-ôr, the ᴺsoothsayer, did the children of Israel slay with the sword among them that were slain by them.

23 And the border of the children of Reuben was Jordan, and the border *thereof*. This *was* the inheritance of the children of Reuben after their families, the cities and the villages thereof.

Inheritance of the Gadites

24 And Moses gave *inheritance* unto the tribe of Gad, *even* unto the children of Gad according to their families.

25 ᴿAnd their coast was Jā′-zĕr, and all the cities of Gilead, ᴿand half the land of the children of Ammon, unto Ă-rō′-ĕr that *is* before ᴿRăb′-băh;

26 And from Hĕsh′-bŏn unto Rā′-măth-mĭz′-pĕh, and Bĕt′-ō-nĭm; and from Mā-hă-nā′-ĭm unto the border of Dē′-bĭr;

27 And in the valley, ᴿBĕth-âr′-ăm, and Bĕth-nĭm′-răh, ᴿand Sŭc′-cōth, and Zā′-phŏn, the rest of the kingdom of Sī′-hŏn king of Hĕsh′-bŏn, Jordan and *his* border, *even* unto the edge ᴿof the sea of Chĭn′-nĕ-rĕth on the other side Jordan eastward.

28 This *is* the inheritance of the children of Gad after their families, the cities, and their villages.

Inheritance of the half tribe of Manasseh

29 And Moses gave *inheritance* unto the half tribe of Mă-năs′-sĕh: and *this* was *the possession* of the half tribe of the children of Mă-năs′-sĕh by their families.

30 And their coast was from Mā-hă-nā′-ĭm, all Bā′-shăn, all the kingdom of Og king of Bā′-shăn, and ᴿall the towns of Jā′-ĭr, which *are* in Bā′-shăn, threescore cities:

31 And half Gilead, and ᴿĂsh′-tă-rōth, and Ĕd′-rĕ-ī, cities of the kingdom of Og in Bā′-shăn, *were pertaining* unto the children of Mā′-chĭr the son of Mă-năs′-sĕh, *even* to the one half of the ᴿchildren of Mā′-chĭr by their families.

32 These *are the countries* which Moses did distribute for inheritance in the plains of Moab, on the other side Jordan, by Jericho, eastward.

33 ᴿBut unto the tribe of Levi Moses gave

not *any* inheritance: the LORD God of Israel *was* their inheritance, [R]as he said unto them.

CHAPTER 14

Division of the land west of Jordan

AND these *are the countries* which the children of Israel inherited in the land of Canaan, [R]which Ĕl-ē-ā'-zär the priest, and Joshua the son of Nun, and the heads of the fathers of the tribes of the children of Israel, distributed for inheritance to them.

2 [R]By lot *was* their inheritance, as the LORD commanded by the hand of Moses, for the nine tribes, and *for* the half tribe.

3 [R]For Moses had given the inheritance of two tribes and an half tribe on the other side Jordan: but unto the Levites he gave none inheritance among them.

4 For [R]the children of Joseph were two tribes, Mă-năs'-sēh and Ē'-phră-ĭm: therefore they gave no part unto the Levites in the land, save cities to dwell *in,* with their suburbs for their cattle and for their substance.

5 [R]As the LORD commanded Moses, so the children of Israel did, and they divided the land.

Caleb is given Hebron

6 Then the children of Judah came unto Joshua in Gĭl'-găl: and Caleb the son of Jĕ-phŭn'-nēh the [R]Kē'-nĕz-ĭte said unto him, Thou knowest [R]the thing that the LORD said unto Moses the man of God concerning me and thee [R]in Kā'-dĕsh-bär'-nĕ-ă.

7 Forty years old *was* I when Moses the servant of the LORD [R]sent me from Kā'-dĕsh-bär'-nĕ-ă to espy out the land; and I brought him word again as *it was* in mine heart.

8 Nevertheless [R]my brethren that went up with me made the heart of the people melt: but I wholly [R]followed the LORD my God.

9 And Moses sware on that day, saying, [R]Surely the land [R]whereon thy feet have trodden shall be thine inheritance, and thy children's for ever, because thou hast wholly followed the LORD my God.

10 And now, behold, the LORD hath kept me alive, [R]as he said, these forty and five years, even since the LORD spake this word unto Moses, while *the children of* Israel [N]wandered in the wilderness: and now, lo, I *am* this day fourscore and five years old.

11 [R]As yet I *am as* strong this day as *I was* in the day that Moses sent me: as my strength

was then, even so *is* my strength now, for war, both [R]to go out, and to come in.

12 Now therefore give me this mountain, whereof the LORD spake in that day; for thou heardest in that day how [R]the Anakims *were* there, and *that* the cities *were* great *and* fenced: [R]if so be the LORD *will be* with me, then [R]I shall be able to drive them out, as the LORD said.

13 And Joshua [R]blessed him, [R]and gave unto Caleb the son of Jĕ-phŭn'-nēh Hē'-brŏn for an inheritance.

14 [R]Hē'-brŏn therefore became the inheritance of Caleb the son of Jĕ-phŭn'-nēh the Kē'-nĕz-ĭte unto this day, because that he [R]wholly followed the LORD God of Israel.

15 And [R]the name of Hē'-brŏn before *was* Kĭr'-jăth-är'-bă; *which* Är'-bă *was* a great man among the Anakims. [R]And the land had rest from war.

CHAPTER 15

Boundaries of Judah

THIS then was the lot of the tribe of the children of Judah by their families; [R]*even* to the border of Ē'-dŏm the [R]wilderness of Zin southward *was* the uttermost part of the south coast.

2 And their south border was from the shore of the salt sea, from the [N]bay that looketh southward:

3 And it went out to the south side [R]to [N]Mā'-ă-lĕh-ăc-răb'-bĭm, and passed along to Zin, and ascended up on the south side unto Kā'-dĕsh-bär'-nĕ-ă, and passed along to Hĕz'-rŏn, and went up to Ā'-där, and fetched a compass to Kär'-kă-ă:

4 *From thence* it passed [R]toward Ăz'-mŏn, and went out unto the river of Egypt; and the goings out of that coast were at the sea: this shall be your south coast.

5 And the east border *was* the salt sea, *even* unto the end of Jordan. And *their* border in the north quarter *was* from the bay of the sea at the uttermost part of Jordan:

6 And the border went up to [R]Bĕth-hŏg'-lă, and passed along by the north of Bĕth-är'-ă-băh; and the border went up [R]to the stone of Bō'-hăn the son of Reuben:

7 And the border went up toward Dē'-bĭr from [R]the valley of Ā'-chôr, and so northward, looking toward Gĭl'-găl, that *is* before the going up to Ă-dŭm'-mĭm, which *is* on the south side of the river: and the border passed toward the waters of Ĕn-shē'-mĕsh, and the goings out thereof were at [R]Ĕn-rō'-gĕl:

CHAP. 13	
BC 1445	
33	Num. 18:20
	Deut. 10:9
	& 18:1, 2

CHAP. 14	
BC 1444	
1	Num. 34:17, 18
2	Num. 26:55
	& 33:54 & 34:13
3	ch. 13:8, 32, 33
4	Gen. 48:5
	1 Chr. 5:1, 2
5	Num. 35:2
	ch. 21:2
6	Num. 32:12
	& ch. 15:17
6	Num. 14:24, 30
6	Num. 13:26
7	Num. 13:6
	& 14:6
8	Num. 13:31, 32
8	Num. 14:24
	Deut. 1:36
9	Num. 14:23, 24
9	See Num. 13:22
10	Num. 14:30
10	Heb. *walked*
11	See Deut. 34:7

Deut. 31:2	11
Num. 13:28, 33	12
Rom. 8:31	12
ch. 15:14	12
Judg. 1:20	
ch. 22:6	13
ch. 10:37	13
& 15:13	
ch. 21:12	14
ver. 8, 9	14
Gen. 23:2	15
ch. 15:13	
ch. 11:23	15

CHAP. 15	
BC 1444	
Num. 34:3	1
Num. 33:36	1
Heb. *tongue*	2
Num. 34:4	3
Or, *The going up to Acrabbim*	3
Num. 34:5	4
ch. 18:19	6
ch. 18:17	6
ch. 7:26	7
2 Sam. 17:17	7
1 Ki. 1:9	

8 And the border went up ᴿby the valley of the son of Hĭn′-nọm unto the south side of the ᴿJĕb′-ū-śīte; the same *is* Jerusalem: and the border went up to the top of the mountain that *lieth* before the valley of Hĭn′-nọm westward, which *is* at the end ᴿof the valley of the giants northward:

9 And the border was drawn from the top of the hill unto ᴿthe fountain of the water of Nĕph-tō′-ăh, and went out to the cities of mount Ē′-phrŏn; and the border was drawn ᴿto Bā′-ă-läh, which *is* ᴿKĭr′-jăth-jē′-ă-rĭm:

10 And the border compassed from Bā′-ă-läh westward unto mount Sē′-ĭr, and passed along unto the side of mount Jē′-ă-rĭm, which *is* Chĕs′-ă-lŏn, on the north side, and went down to Bĕth-shē′-mĕsh, and passed on to ᴿTĭm′-nȧh:

11 And the border went out unto the side of ᴿĔk′-rŏn northward: and the border was drawn to Shĭc′-rŏn, and passed along to mount Bā′-ă-läh, and went out unto Jăb′-nĕel; and the goings out of the border were at the sea.

12 And the west border *was* ᴿto the great sea, and the coast *thereof*. This *is* the coast of the children of Judah round about according to their families.

13 ᴿAnd unto Caleb the son of Jē-phŭn′-nĕh he gave a part among the children of Judah, according to the commandment of the Lᴏʀᴅ to Joshua, *even* ᴿtheᴺ city of Är′-bȧ the father of Anak, which *city is* Hē′-brŏn.

14 And Caleb drove thence ᴿthe three sons of Anak, ᴿShē′-shâi, and Ă-hī′-măn, and Tăl′-mâi, the children of Anak.

15 And ᴿhe went up thence to the inhabitants of Dē′-bĭr: and the name of Dē′-bĭr before *was* Kĭr′-jăth-sē′-phẽr.

16 ᴿAnd Caleb said, He that smiteth Kĭr′-jăth-sē′-phẽr, and taketh it, to him will I give Ăch′-săh my daughter to wife.

17 And ᴿŎth′-nĭ-ĕl the ᴿson of Kē′-năz, the brother of Caleb, took it: and he gave him Ăch′-săh his daughter to wife.

18 ᴿAnd it came to pass, as she came *unto him,* that she moved him to ask of her father a field: and ᴿshe lighted off *her* ass; and Caleb said unto her, What wouldest thou?

19 Who answered, Give me a ᴿblessing; for thou hast given me a south land; give me also springs of water. And he gave her the upper springs, and the nether springs.

Cities of refuge

20 This *is* the inheritance of the tribe of the children of Judah according to their families.

21 And the uttermost cities of the tribe

of the children of Judah toward the coast of Ē′-dọm southward were Kăb′-zĕel, and Ē′-dẽr, and Jā′-gùr,

22 And Kī′-nȧh, and Dĭ-mō′-năh, and Ă-dā′-dȧh,

23 And Kē′-dĕsh, and Hā′-zôr, and Ĭth′-năn,

24 Ziph, and Tē′-lĕm, and Bē-ā′-lōth,

25 And Hā′-zôr, Hă-dăt′-tȧh, and Kĕr′-ĭ-ōth, *and* Hĕz′-rŏn, which *is* Hā′-zôr,

26 Ā′-măm, and Shē′-mȧ, and Mō-lā′-dȧh,

27 And Hā′-zăr-găd′-dȧh, and Hĕsh′-mŏn, and Bĕth-pā′-lĕt,

28 And Hā′-zăr-shû′-ăl, and Bĕer-shē′-bȧ, and Bĭz-jŏth′-jȧh,

29 Bā′-ă-läh, and Ĭ′-ĭm, and Ā′-zĕm,

30 And Ĕl-tō′-lăd, and Chĕs′-ĭl, and Hôr′-măh,

31 And ᴿZiklag, and Măd-măn′-năh, and Săn-săn′-năh,

32 And Lĕ-bā′-ōth, and Shĭl′-hĭm, and Ā′-ĭn, and Rimmon: all the cities *are* twenty and nine, with their villages:

33 *And* in the valley, ᴿĔsh′-tā-ŏl, and Zôr′-ĕ-ăh, and Ăsh′-năh,

34 And Ză-nō′-ăh, and Ĕn-găn′-nĭm, Tăp′-pū-ăh, and Ē′-năm,

35 Jär′-mûth, and Adullam, Sō′-cōh, and Ă-zē′-kăh,

36 And Shă-rā′-ĭm, and Ăd-ĭ-thā′-ĭm, and Gĕ-dē′-răh, ᴺand Gĕ-dē-rō-thā′-ĭm; fourteen cities with their villages:

37 Zē′-năn, and Hă-dăsh′-ăh, and Mĭg′-dăl-găd,

38 And Dĭ′-lĕ-ăn, and Mĭz′-pēh, ᴿand Jŏk′-thĕel,

39 Lā′-chĭsh, and Bŏz′-kăth, and ĕg′-lŏn,

40 And Căb′-bŏn, and Läh′-măm, and Kĭth′-lĭsh,

41 And Gĕ-dē′-rŏth, Bĕth-dā′-gŏn, and Nā′-ă-măh, and Măk-kē′-dăh; sixteen cities with their villages:

42 Lĭb′-năh, and Ē′-thẽr, and Ăsh′-ăn,

43 And Jĭph′-tăh, and Ăsh′-năh, and Nĕz′-ĭb,

44 And Kē-ĭ′-lăh, and Ăch′-zĭb, and Mă-rē′-shäh; nine cities with their villages:

45 Ĕk′-rŏn, with her towns and her villages:

46 From ĕk′-rŏn even unto the sea, all that *lay* ᴺnear Ăsh′-dŏd, with their villages:

47 Ăsh′-dŏd with her towns and her villages, Gā′-ză with her towns and her villages, unto ᴿthe river of Egypt, and ᴿthe great sea, and the border *thereof:*

48 And in the mountains, Shā′-mĭr, and Jăt′-tĭr, and Sō′-cōh,

49 And Dăn′-năh, and Kĭr′-jăth-săn′-năh, which *is* Dē′-bĭr,

50 And Anab, and Ĕsh′-tĕ-mōh, and Ā′-nĭm,

51 ᴿAnd Gō'-shĕn, and Hō'-lŏn, and Gī'-lōh; eleven cities with their villages:

52 Arab, and Dū'-mäh, and ĕsh'-ĕ-ăn,

53 And ᴺJanum, and Bĕth-tăp'-pū-ăh, and Ă-phē'-käh,

54 And Hŭm'-tăh, and ᴿKĭr'-jăth-är'-bă, which is Hē'-brŏn, and Zī'-ôr; nine cities with their villages:

55 Mā'-ŏn, Carmel, and Ziph, and Jŭt'-tăh,

56 And Jĕz'-rēĕl, and Jŏk'-dĕ-ăm, and Ză-nō'-ăh,

57 Cain, Gĭb'-ĕ-ăh, and Tĭm'-năh; ten cities with their villages:

58 Hăl'-hŭl, Bĕth'-zŭr, and Gē'-dôr,

59 And Mā'-ă-răth, and Bĕth'-ă-nōth, and ĕl'-tĕ-kŏn; six cities with their villages:

60 ᴿKĭr'-jăth-bā'-ăl, which is Kĭr'-jăth-jē'-ă-rĭm, and Răb'-băh; two cities with their villages:

61 In the wilderness, Bĕth-är'-ă-băh, Mĭd'-dĭn, and Sĕ-cā'-căh,

62 And Nĭb'-shăn, and the city of Salt, and ĕn-ġē'-dī; six cities with their villages.

63 As for the Jĕb'-ū-ṡītes the inhabitants of Jerusalem, ᴿthe children of Judah could not drive them out: ᴿbut the Jĕb'-ū-ṡītes dwell with the children of Judah at Jerusalem unto this day.

CHAPTER 16

Inheritance of the tribes of Joseph

AND the lot of the children of Joseph ᴺfell from Jordan by Jericho, unto the water of Jericho on the east, to the wilderness that goeth up from Jericho throughout mount Beth-el,

2 And goeth out from Beth-el to ᴿLuz, and passeth along unto the borders of Är'-chī to Ăt'-ă-rōth,

3 And goeth down westward to the coast of Jăph'-lē-tī, ᴿunto the coast of Bĕth-hôr'-ŏn the nether, and to ᴿGē'-zĕr: and the goings out thereof are at the sea.

4 ᴿSo the children of Joseph, Mă-năs'-sēh and Ē'-phră-ĭm, took their inheritance.

Land of Ephraim

5 And the border of the children of Ē'-phră-ĭm according to their families was thus: even the border of their inheritance on the east side was ᴿĂt'-ă-rōth-ăd'-där, ᴿunto Bĕth-hôr'-ŏn the upper;

6 And the border went out toward the sea to ᴿMĭch-mē'-thăh on the north side; and the border went about eastward unto Tā'-ă-năth-shī'-lōh, and passed by it on the east to Jă-nō'-hăh;

CHAP. 15
BC 1444
51 ch. 10:41 & 11:16
53 Or, Janus
54 ver. 13 ch. 14:15
60 ch. 18:14
63 See Judg. 1:8, 21 2 Sam. 5:6
63 Judg. 1:21

CHAP. 16
BC 1444
1 Heb. went forth
2 ch. 18:13 Judg. 1:26
3 ch. 18:13 2 Chr. 8:5
3 1 Ki. 9:15 1 Chr. 7:28
4 ch. 17:14
5 ch. 18:13
5 2 Chr. 8:5
6 ch. 17:7

1 Chr. 7:28	7
ch. 17:9	8
ch. 17:9	9
Judg. 1:29	10
See 1 Ki. 9:16	

CHAP. 17
BC 1444
Gen. 41:51 & 46:20 & 48:18	1
Gen. 50:23	1
Deut. 3:15	1
Num. 26:29-32	2
1 Chr. 7:18	2
Num. 26:30, Jeezer	2
Num. 26:31	2
Num. 26:32	2
Num. 26:33 & 27:1 & 36:2	
ch. 14:1	4
Num. 27:6, 7	4
ch. 16:6	7

7 And it went down from Jă-nō'-hăh to Ăt'-ă-rŏth, ᴿand to Nā'-ă-răth, and came to Jericho, and went out at Jordan.

8 The border went out from Tăp'-pū-ăh westward unto the ᴿriver Kā'-năh; and the goings out thereof were at the sea. This is the inheritance of the tribe of the children of Ē'-phră-ĭm by their families.

9 And ᴿthe separate cities for the children of Ē'-phră-ĭm were among the inheritance of the children of Mă-năs'-sēh, all the cities with their villages.

10 ᴿAnd they drave not out the Canaanites that dwelt in Gē'-zĕr: but the Canaanites dwell among the Ē'-phră-ĭm-ītes unto this day, and serve under tribute.

CHAPTER 17

Land of Manasseh

THERE was also a lot for the tribe of Mă-năs'-sēh; for he was the ᴿfirstborn of Joseph; to wit, for ᴿMā'-chĭr the firstborn of Mă-năs'-sēh, the father of Gilead: because he was a man of war, therefore he had ᴿGilead and Bā'-shăn.

2 There was also a lot for ᴿthe rest of the children of Mă-năs'-sēh by their families; ᴿfor the children of ᴺĂ-bī-ē'-zĕr, and for the children of Hē'-lĕk, ᴿand for the children of Ăṡ'-rĭ-ĕl, and for the children of Shē'-chĕm, ᴿand for the children of Hē'-phĕr, and for the children of Shĕ-mī'-dă: these were the male children of Mă-năs'-sēh the son of Joseph by their families.

3 But ᴿZē-lŏph'-ĕ-hăd, the son of Hē'-phĕr, the son of Gilead, the son of Mā'-chĭr, the son of Mă-năs'-sēh, had no sons, but daughters: and these are the names of his daughters, Măh'-läh, and Noah, Hŏg'-läh, Mĭl'-cäh, and Tĭr'-zäh.

4 And they came near before ᴿĔl-ē-ā'-zär the priest, and before Joshua the son of Nun, and before the princes, saying, ᴿThe LORD commanded Moses to give us an inheritance among our brethren. Therefore according to the commandment of the LORD he gave them an inheritance among the brethren of their father.

5 And there fell ten portions to Mă-năs'-sēh, beside the land of Gilead and Bā'-shăn, which were on the other side Jordan;

6 Because the daughters of Mă-năs'-sēh had an inheritance among his sons: and the rest of Mă-năs'-sēh's sons had the land of Gilead.

7 And the coast of Mă-năs'-sēh was from Asher to ᴿMĭch-mē'-thăh, that lieth before Shē'-chĕm; and the border went along on the

right hand unto the inhabitants of Ĕn-tăp'-pū-ăh.

8 *Now* Mă-năs'-sēh had the land of Tăp'-pū-ăh: but ᴿTăp'-pū-ăh on the border of Mă-năs'-sēh *belonged* to the children of Ē'-phră-ĭm;

9 And the coast descended unto the ᴺriver Kā'-năh, southward of the river: ᴿthese cities of Ē'-phră-ĭm *are* among the cities of Mă-năs'-sēh: the coast of Mă-năs'-sēh also *was* on the north side of the river, and the outgoings of it were at the sea:

10 Southward *it was* Ē'-phră-ĭm's, and northward *it was* Mă-năs'-sēh's, and the sea is his border; and they met together in Asher on the north, and in ĭs'-să-chär on the east.

11 ᴿAnd Mă-năs'-sēh had in ĭs'-să-chär and in Asher ᴿBĕth-shē'-ăn and her towns, and ĭb'-lĕ-ăm and her towns, and the inhabitants of Dor and her towns, and the inhabitants of En-dor and her towns, and the inhabitants of Tā'-ă-năch and her towns, and the inhabitants of Mĕ-gĭd'-dō and her towns, *even* three countries.

12 Yet ᴿthe children of Mă-năs'-sēh could not drive out *the inhabitants of* those cities; but the Canaanites would dwell in that land.

13 Yet it came to pass, when the children of Israel were waxen strong, that they put the Canaanites to ᴿtribute; but did not utterly drive them out.

Additional land for tribes of Joseph

14 ᴿAnd the children of Joseph spake unto Joshua, saying, Why hast thou given me *but* ᴿone lot and one portion to inherit, seeing I *am* ᴿa great people, forasmuch as the LORD hath blessed me hitherto?

15 And Joshua answered them, If thou *be* a great people, *then* get thee up to the wood *country,* and cut down for thyself there in the land of the Pĕ-rĭz'-zītes and of the ᴺgiants, if mount Ē'-phră-ĭm be too narrow for thee.

16 And the children of Joseph said, The hill is not enough for us: and all the Canaanites that dwell in the land of the valley have ᴿchariots of iron, *both they* who *are* of Bĕth-shē'-ăn and her towns, and *they* who *are* ᴿof the valley of Jĕz'-rĕel.

17 And Joshua spake unto the house of Joseph, *even* to Ē'-phră-ĭm and to Mă-năs'-sēh, saying, Thou *art* a great people, and hast great power: thou shalt not have one lot *only:*

18 But the mountain shall be thine; for it *is* a wood, and thou shalt cut it down: and the outgoings of it shall be thine: for thou shalt drive out the Canaanites, ᴿthough they have iron chariots, *and* though they *be* strong.

CHAP. 17
BC 1444
8 ch. 16:8
9 Or, *brook of reeds*
9 ch. 16:9
11 1 Chr. 7:29
11 1 Sam. 31:10
1 Ki. 4:12
12 Judg. 1:27, 28
13 ch. 16:10
14 ch. 16:4
14 Gen. 48:22
14 Gen. 48:19
Num. 26:34, 37
15 Or, *Rephaims,* Gen. 14:5 & 15:20
16 Judg. 1:19 & 4:3
16 ch. 19:18
1 Ki. 4:12
18 Deut. 20:1

CHAP. 18	
BC 1444	
ch. 19:51 & 21:2 & 22:9	1
Jer. 7:12	
Judg. 18:31	1
1 Sam. 1:3, 24 & 4:3, 4	
Judg. 18:9	3
ch. 15:1	5
ver. 10	6
ch. 14:2	
ch. 13:33	7
ch. 13:8	7

CHAPTER 18

Assembly at Shiloh

AND the whole congregation of the children of Israel assembled together ᴿat Shī'-lōh, and ᴿset up the tabernacle of the congregation there. And the land was subdued before them.

Survey of remaining lands

2 And there remained among the children of Israel seven tribes, which had not yet received their inheritance.

3 And Joshua said unto the children of Israel, ᴿHow long *are* ye slack to go to possess the land, which the LORD God of your fathers hath given you?

4 Give out from among you three men for *each* tribe: and I will send them, and they shall rise, and go through the land, and describe it according to the inheritance of them; and they shall come *again* to me.

5 And they shall divide it into seven parts: ᴿJudah shall abide in their coast on the south, and ᴿthe house of Joseph shall abide in their coasts on the north.

6 Ye shall therefore describe the land *into* seven parts, and bring *the description* hither to me, ᴿthat I may cast lots for you here before the LORD our God.

7 ᴿBut the Levites have no part among you; for the priesthood of the LORD *is* their inheritance: ᴿand Gad, and Reuben, and half the tribe of Mă-năs'-sēh, have received their inheritance beyond Jordan on the east, which Moses the servant of the LORD gave them.

8 And the men arose, and went away: and Joshua charged them that went to describe the land, saying, Go and walk through the land, and describe it, and come again to me, that I may here cast lots for you before the LORD in Shī'-lōh.

9 And the men went and passed through the land, and described it by cities into seven parts in a book, and came *again* to Joshua to the host at Shī'-lōh.

10 And Joshua cast lots for them in Shī'-lōh before the LORD: and there Joshua divided the land unto the children of Israel according to their divisions.

Allotment for Benjamin

11 And the lot of the tribe of the children of Benjamin came up according to their families: and the coast of their lot came forth between the children of Judah and the children of Joseph.

12 ᴿAnd their border on the north side was from Jordan; and the border went up to the side of Jericho on the north side, and went up through the mountains westward; and the goings out thereof were at the wilderness of Bĕth-ā'-ven.

13 And the border went over from thence toward Luz, to the side of Luz, ᴿwhich is Beth-el, southward; and the border descended to Ăt'-ă-rōth-ā'-där, near the hill that lieth on the south side ᴿof the nether Bĕth-hôr'-ŏn.

14 And the border was drawn thence, and compassed the corner of the sea southward, from the hill that lieth before Bĕth-hôr'-ŏn southward; and the goings out thereof were at ᴿKĭr'-jăth-bā'-ăl, which is Kĭr'-jăth-jē'-ă-rĭm, a city of the children of Judah: this was the west quarter.

15 And the south quarter was from the end of Kĭr'-jăth-jē'-ă-rĭm, and the border went out on the west, and went out to ᴿthe well of waters of Nĕph-tō'-ăh:

16 And the border came down to the end of the mountain that lieth before ᴿthe valley of the son of Hĭn'-nŏm, and which is in the valley of the giants on the north, and descended to the valley of Hĭn'-nŏm, to the side of Jĕb'-ū-sĭ on the south, and descended to ᴿĔn-rō'-gĕl,

17 And was drawn from the north, and went forth to Ĕn-shē'-mĕsh, and went forth toward Gĕ-lī'-lŏth, which is over against the going up of Ă-dŭm'-mĭm, and descended to ᴿthe stone of Bō'-hăn the son of Reuben,

18 And passed along toward the side over against ᴿĂr'-ă-băhᴺ northward, and went down unto Ăr'-ă-băh:

19 And the border passed along to the side of Bĕth-hŏg'-lăh northward: and the outgoings of the border were at the north ᴺbay of the salt sea at the south end of Jordan: this was the south coast.

20 And Jordan was the border of it on the east side. This was the inheritance of the children of Benjamin, by the coasts thereof round about, according to their families.

21 Now the cities of the tribe of the children of Benjamin according to their families were Jericho, and Bĕth-hŏg'-lăh, and the valley of Kē'-zĭz,

22 And Bĕth-är'-ă-băh, and Zĕm-ă-rā'-ĭm, and Beth-el,

23 And Ā'-vĭm, and Pär'-ăh, and Ŏph'-răh,

24 And Chē'-phär-hă-ăm'-mō-nâi, and Ŏph'-nī, and Gā'-bă; twelve cities with their villages:

25 Gibeon, and Rā'-măh, and Bēêr'-ōth,

26 And Mĭz'-pĕh, and Chĕ-phī'-răh, and Mō'-zăh,

27 And Rē'-kĕm, and ĭr'-pĕêl, and Tăr'-ă-lăh,

28 And Zē'-lăh, Ē'-lĕph, and ᴿJĕb'-ū-sĭ, which is Jerusalem, Gĭb'-ĕ-ăth, and Kĭr'-jăth; fourteen cities with their villages. This is the inheritance of the children of Benjamin according to their families.

CHAPTER 19

Allotment for Simeon

AND the second lot came forth to Simeon, even for the tribe of the children of Simeon according to their families: ᴿand their inheritance was within the inheritance of the children of Judah.

2 And ᴿthey had in their inheritance Bēêr-shē'-bă, or Shē'-bă, and Mō-lā'-dăh,

3 And Hā'-zär-shû'-ăl, and Bā'-lăh, and Ā'-zĕm,

4 And ĕl-tō'-lăd, and Bĕth'-ŭl, and Hôr'-măh,

5 And Ziklag, and Bĕth-mär'-că-bōth, and Hā'-zär-sû'-săh,

6 And Bĕth-lĕ-bā'-ōth, and Shă-rû'-hĕn; thirteen cities and their villages:

7 Ā'-ĭn, Rĕm'-mŏn, and Ē'-thĕr, and Ăsh'-ăn; four cities and their villages:

8 And all the villages that were round about these cities to Bā'-ă-lăth-bēêr, Rā'-măth of the south. This is the inheritance of the tribe of the children of Simeon according to their families.

9 Out of the portion of the children of Judah was the inheritance of the children of Simeon: for the part of the children of Judah was too much for them: ᴿtherefore the children of Simeon had their inheritance within the inheritance of them.

Allotment for Zebulun

10 And the third lot came up for the children of Zē-bū'-lŭn according to their families: and the border of their inheritance was unto Sär'-ĭd:

11 ᴿAnd their border went up toward the sea, and Măr'-ă-lăh, and reached to Dăb'-bă-shĕth, and reached to the river that is ᴿbefore Jŏk'-nĕ-ăm;

12 And turned from Sär'-ĭd eastward toward the sunrising unto the border of Chĭs'-lōth-tā'-bŏr, and then goeth out to Dăb'-ĕ-răth, and goeth up to Jă-phī'-ă,

13 And from thence passeth on along on the

east to Gĭt'-tăh-hē'-phĕr, to Ĭt'-tăh-kā'-zĭn, and goeth out to Rĕm'-mŏn-ᴺmĕ-thō'-är to Nē'-ăh;

14 And the border compasseth it on the north side to Hăn'-nă-thŏn: and the outgoings thereof are in the valley of Jĭph'-thăh-ĕl:

15 And Kăt'-tăth, and Nă-hăl'-lăl, and Shĭm'-rŏn, and Ĭ'-dă-läh, and Beth-lehem: twelve cities and their villages.

16 This *is* the inheritance of the children of Zĕ-bū'-lŭn according to their families, these cities with their villages.

Allotment for Issachar

17 *And* the fourth lot came out to Ĭs'-să-chär, for the children of Ĭs'-să-chär according to their families.

18 And their border was toward Jĕz'-rēĕl, and Chĕ-sŭl'-lōth, and Shû'-nĕm,

19 And Hăph'-ă-ră-ĭm, and Shĭ'-ŏn, and Ă-nā'-hă-răth,

20 And Răb'-bĭth, and Kĭsh'-ĭŏn, and Abez,

21 And Rĕm'-ĕth, and Ĕn-găn'-nĭm, and Ĕn-hăd'-dăh, and Bĕth-păz'-zĕz;

22 And the coast reacheth to Tā'-bôr, and Shā-hă-zī'-măh, and Bĕth-shē'-mĕsh; and the outgoings of their border were at Jordan: sixteen cities with their villages.

23 This *is* the inheritance of the tribe of the children of Ĭs'-să-chär according to their families, the cities and their villages.

Allotment for Asher

24 And the fifth lot came out for the tribe of the children of Asher according to their families.

25 And their border was Hĕl'-kăth, and Hā'-lī, and Bē'-tĕn, and Ăch'-shăph,

26 And Ă-lăm'-mĕ-lĕch, and Ā'-măd, and Mĭ'-shĕ-ăl; and reacheth to Carmel westward, and to Shĭ'-hôr-lĭb'-năth;

27 And turneth toward the sunrising to Bĕth-dā'-gŏn, and reacheth to Zĕ-bū'-lŭn, and to the valley of Jĭph'-thăh-ĕl toward the north side of Bĕth-ē'-mĕk, and Nĕĭ'-ĕl, and goeth out to Cā'-bŭl on the left hand,

28 And Hē'-brŏn, and Rē'-hŏb, and Hăm'-mŏn, and Kā'-năh, ᴿ*even* unto great Zī'-dŏn;

29 And *then* the coast turneth to Rā'-măh, and to the strong city ᴺTyre; and the coast turneth to Hō'-säh; and the outgoings thereof are at the sea from the coast to ᴿAch'-zĭb:

30 Ŭm'-măh also, and Ā'-phĕk, and Rē'-hŏb: twenty and two cities with their villages.

31 This *is* the inheritance of the tribe of the children of Asher according to their families, these cities with their villages.

CHAP. **19**

BC 1444

13 Or, *which is drawn*
28 ch. 11:8
Judg. 1:31
29 Heb. *Tzor,*
2 Sam. 5:11
29 Judg. 1:31

Deut. 33:23   **34**
Judg. 1:35   **42**
Or, *over against*   **46**
Or, *Joppa,*   **46**
Acts 9:36
See Judg. 18   **47**
Judg. 18:29   **47**

Allotment for Naphtali

32 The sixth lot came out to the children of Năph'-tă-lī, *even* for the children of Năph'-tă-lī according to their families.

33 And their coast was from Hē'-lĕph, from Ăl'-lŏn to Zā-ă-năn'-nĭm, and Ăd'-ă-mī, Nē'-kĕb, and Jăb'-nēĕl, unto Lakum; and the outgoings thereof were at Jordan:

34 And *then* ᴿthe coast turneth westward to Ăz'-nōth-tā'-bôr, and goeth out from thence to Hŭk'-kŏk, and reacheth to Zĕ-bū'-lŭn on the south side, and reacheth to Asher on the west side, and to Judah upon Jordan toward the sunrising.

35 And the fenced cities *are* Zĭd'-dĭm, Zer, and Hăm'-măth, Rakkath, and Chĭn'-nĕ-rĕth,

36 And Ăd'-ă-măh, and Rā'-măh, and Hā'-zôr,

37 And Kē'-dĕsh, and Ĕd'-rĕ-ī, and Ĕn-hā'-zôr,

38 And Ĭ'-rŏn, and Mĭg'-dăl-ĕl, Hôr'-ĕm, and Bĕth'-ă-năth, and Bĕth-shē'-mĕsh; nineteen cities with their villages.

39 This *is* the inheritance of the tribe of the children of Năph'-tă-lī according to their families, the cities and their villages.

Allotment for Dan

40 *And* the seventh lot came out for the tribe of the children of Dan according to their families.

41 And the coast of their inheritance was Zôr'-ăh, and Ĕsh'-tā-ŏl, and Ĭr-shē'-mĕsh,

42 And ᴿShā-ă-lăb'-bĭn, and Ăj'-ă-lŏn, and Jĕth'-läh,

43 And Ē'-lŏn, and Thĭm'-nă-thăh, and Ĕk'-rŏn,

44 And Ĕl'-tĕ-kēh, and Gĭb'-bĕ-thŏn, and Bā'-ă-lăth,

45 And Jehud, and Bĕn'-ĕ-bē'-răk, and Găth-rĭm'-mŏn,

46 And Mĕ-jär'-kŏn, and Rakkon, with the border ᴺbefore ᴺJā'-phō.

47 And ᴿthe coast of the children of Dan went out *too little* for them: therefore the children of Dan went up to fight against Lē'-shĕm, and took it, and smote it with the edge of the sword, and possessed it, and dwelt therein, and called Lē'-shĕm, ᴿDan, after the name of Dan their father.

48 This *is* the inheritance of the tribe of the children of Dan according to their families, these cities with their villages.

Inheritance of Joshua

49 When they had made an end of dividing the land for inheritance by their coasts, the

children of Israel gave an inheritance to Joshua the son of Nun among them:

50 According to the word of the LORD they gave him the city which he asked, *even* ᴿTĭm′-năth-ᴿsē′-răh in mount Ē′-phră-ĭm: and he built the city, and dwelt therein.

51 ᴿThese *are* the inheritances, which ĕl-ē-ā′-zär the priest, and Joshua the son of Nun, and the heads of the fathers of the tribes of the children of Israel, divided for an inheritance by lot ᴿin Shī′-lōh before the LORD, at the door of the tabernacle of the congregation. So they made an end of dividing the country.

CHAPTER 20

Cities of refuge appointed

THE LORD also spake unto Joshua, saying, 2 Speak to the children of Israel, saying, ᴿAppoint out for you cities of refuge, whereof I spake unto you by the hand of Moses:

3 That the slayer that killeth *any* person unawares *and* unwittingly may flee thither: and they shall bc your rcfuge from the avenger of blood.

4 And when he that doth flee unto one of those cities shall stand at the entering of the gate of the city, and shall declare his cause in the ears of the elders of that city, they shall take him into the city unto them, and give him a place, that he may dwell among them.

5 ᴿAnd if the avenger of blood pursue after him, then they shall not deliver the slayer up into his hand; because he smote his neighbour unwittingly, and hated him not beforetime.

6 And he shall dwell in that city, ᴿuntil he stand before the congregation for judgment, *and* until the death of the high priest that shall be in those days: then shall the slayer return, and come unto his own city, and unto his own house, unto the city from whence he fled.

7 And they ᴺappointed ᴿKē′-dĕsh in Galilee in mount Năph′-tă-lī, and ᴿShē′-chĕm in mount Ē′-phră-ĭm, and ᴿKĭr′-jăth-är′-bă, which *is* Hē′-brŏn, in ᴿthe mountain of Judah.

8 And on the other side Jordan by Jericho eastward, they assigned ᴿBē′-zĕr in the wilderness upon the plain out of the tribe of Reuben, and ᴿRā′-mŏth in Gilead out of the tribe of Gad, and ᴿGō′-lăn in Bā′-shăn out of the tribe of Mă-năs′-sĕh.

9 ᴿThese were the cities appointed for all the children of Israel, and for the stranger that sojourneth among them, that whosoever killeth *any* person at unawares might flee thither, and

not die by the hand of the avenger of blood, ᴿuntil he stood before the congregation.

CHAPTER 21

Cities for the Levites

THEN came near the heads of the fathers of the Levites unto ᴿĔl-ē-ā′-zär the priest, and unto Joshua the son of Nun, and unto the heads of the fathers of the tribes of the children of Israel;

2 And they spake unto them at ᴿShī′-lōh in the land of Canaan, saying, ᴿThe LORD commanded by the hand of Moses to give us cities to dwell in, with the suburbs thereof for our cattle.

3 And the children of Israel gave unto the Levites out of their inheritance, at the commandment of the LORD, these cities and their suburbs.

4 And the lot came out for the families of the Kō′-hăth-ītes: and ᴿthe children of Aaron the priest, *which were* of the Levites, ᴿhad by lot out of the tribe of Judah, and out of the tribe of Simeon, and out of the tribe of Benjamin, thirteen cities.

5 And ᴿthe rest of the children of Kō′-hăth *had* by lot out of the families of the tribe of Ē′-phră-ĭm, and out of the tribe of Dan, and out of the half tribe of Mă-năs′-sĕh, ten cities.

6 And ᴿthe children of Gĕr′-shŏn *had* by lot out of the families of the tribe of ĭs′-să-chär, and out of the tribe of Asher, and out of the tribe of Năph′-tă-lī, and out of the half tribe of Mă-năs′-sĕh in Bā′-shăn, thirteen cities.

7 ᴿThe children of Mĕ-râr′-ī by their families *had* out of the tribe of Reuben, and out of the tribe of Gad, and out of the tribe of Zĕ-bū′-lŭn, twelve cities.

8 ᴿAnd the children of Israel gave by lot unto the Levites these cities with their suburbs, ᴿas the LORD commanded by the hand of Moses.

9 And they gave out of the tribe of the children of Judah, and out of the tribe of the children of Simeon, these cities which are *here* ᴺmentioned by name,

10 Which the children of Aaron, *being* of the families of the Kō′-hăth-ītes, *who were* of the children of Levi, had: for their's was the first lot.

11 ᴿAnd they gave them ᴺthe city of Är′-bă the father of ᴿAnak, which *city is* Hē′-brŏn, ᴿin the hill *country* of Judah, with the suburbs thereof round about it.

12 But ᴿthe fields of the city, and the vil-

lages thereof, gave they to Caleb the son of Jĕ-phŭn'-nĕh for his possession.

13 Thus ᴿthey gave to the children of Aaron the priest ᴿHē'-brŏn with her suburbs, *to be* a city of refuge for the slayer; ᴿand Lĭb'-năh with her suburbs,

14 And ᴿJăt'-tĭr with her suburbs, ᴿand Ĕsh-tĕ-mō'-ă with her suburbs,

15 And ᴿHō'-lŏn with her suburbs, ᴿand Dē'-bĭr with her suburbs,

16 And ᴿĀ'-ĭn with her suburbs, ᴿand Jŭt'-tăh with her suburbs, *and* ᴿBĕth-shē'-mĕsh with her suburbs; nine cities out of those two tribes.

17 And out of the tribe of Benjamin, ᴿGib-eon with her suburbs, ᴿGē'-bă was her suburbs,

18 Ăn'-ă-thōth with her suburbs, and ᴿĂl'-mŏn with her suburbs; four cities.

19 All the cities of the children of Aaron, the priests, *were* thirteen cities with their suburbs.

20 ᴿAnd the families of the children of Kō'-hăth, the Levites which remained of the children of Kō'-hăth, even they had the cities of their lot out of the tribe of Ē'-phră-ĭm.

21 For they gave them ᴿShē'-chĕm with her suburbs in mount Ē'-phră-ĭm, *to be* a city of refuge for the slayer; and Gē'-zĕr with her suburbs,

22 And Kĭb'-ză-ĭm with her suburbs, and Bĕth-hôr'-ŏn with her suburbs; four cities.

23 And out of the tribe of Dan, ĕl'-tĕ-kēh with her suburbs, Gĭb'-bĕ-thŏn with her suburbs,

24 Âî'-jă-lŏn with her suburbs, Găth-rĭm'-mŏn with her suburbs; four cities.

25 And out of the half tribe of Mă-năs'-sēh, Tā'-năch with her suburbs, and Găth-rĭm'-mŏn with her suburbs; two cities.

26 All the cities *were* ten with their suburbs for the families of the children of Kō'-hăth that remained.

27 ᴿAnd unto the children of Gĕr'-shŏn, of the families of the Levites, out of the *other* half tribe of Mă-năs'-sēh *they gave* ᴿGō'-lăn in Bā'-shăn with her suburbs, *to be* a city of refuge for the slayer; and Bĕ-ĕsh'-tĕ-răh with her suburbs; two cities.

28 And out of the tribe of Ĭs'-să-chăr, Kĭ'-shŏn with her suburbs, Dăb'-ă-rĕh with her suburbs,

29 Jăr'-mûth with her suburbs, ĕn-găn'-nĭm with her suburbs; four cities.

30 And out of the tribe of Asher, Mĭ'-shăl with her suburbs, Abdon with her suburbs,

31 Hĕl'-kăth with her suburbs, and Rē'-hŏb with her suburbs; four cities.

32 And out of the tribe of Năph'-tă-lĭ, ᴿKē'-

dĕsh in Galilee with her suburbs, *to be* a city of refuge for the slayer; and Hăm'-mōth-dôr with her suburbs, and Kär'-tăn with her suburbs; three cities.

33 All the cities of the Gĕr'-shŏn-ites according to their families *were* thirteen cities with their suburbs.

34 ᴿAnd unto the families of the children of Mĕ-râr'-ĭ, the rest of the Levites, out of the tribe of Zĕ-bū'-lŭn, Jŏk'-nĕ-ăm with her suburbs, and Kär'-tăh with her suburbs,

35 Dĭm'-năh with her suburbs, Nā'-hă-lăl with her suburbs; four cities.

36 And out of the tribe of Reuben, ᴿBē'-zĕr with her suburbs, and Jă-hā'-zăh with her suburbs,

37 Kē'-dĕ-mōth with her suburbs, and Mĕph'-ā-ăth with her suburbs; four cities.

38 And out of the tribe of Gad, ᴿRā'-mōth in Gilead with her suburbs, *to be* a city of refuge for the slayer; and Mā-hă-nā'-ĭm with her suburbs,

39 Hĕsh'-bŏn with her suburbs, Jā'-zĕr with her suburbs; four cities in all.

40 So all the cities for the children of Mĕ-râr'-ĭ by their families, which were remaining of the families of the Levites, were *by* their lot twelve cities.

41 ᴿAll the cities of the Levites within the possession of the children of Israel *were* forty and eight cities with their suburbs.

42 These cities were every one with their suburbs round about them: thus *were* all these cities.

Israel possesses the land

43 And the Lᴏʀᴅ gave unto Israel ᴿall the land which he sware to give unto their fathers; and they possessed it, and dwelt therein.

44 ᴿAnd the Lᴏʀᴅ gave them rest round about, according to all that he sware unto their fathers: and ᴿthere stood not a man of all their enemies before them; the Lᴏʀᴅ delivered all their enemies into their hand.

45 ᴿThere failed not aught of any good thing which the Lᴏʀᴅ had spoken unto the house of Israel; all came to pass.

CHAPTER 22

East Jordan tribes sent home

THEN Joshua called the Reubenites, and the Gadites, and the half tribe of Mă-năs'-sēh,

2 And said unto them, Ye have kept ᴿall that Moses the servant of the Lᴏʀᴅ commanded you, ᴿand have obeyed my voice in all that I commanded you:

3 Ye have not left your brethren these many days unto this day, but have kept the charge of the commandment of the LORD your God.

4 And now the LORD your God hath given rest unto your brethren, as he promised them: therefore now return ye, and get you unto your tents, *and* unto the land of your possession, R which Moses the servant of the LORD gave you on the other side Jordan.

5 But R take diligent heed to do the commandment and the law, which Moses the servant of the LORD charged you, R to love the LORD your God, and to walk in all his ways, and to keep his commandments, and to cleave unto him, and to serve him with all your heart and with all your soul.

6 So Joshua R blessed them, and sent them away: and they went unto their tents.

7 Now to the *one* half of the tribe of Mă-năs'-sĕh Moses had given *possession* in Bā'-shăn: R but unto the *other* half thereof gave Joshua among their brethren on this side Jordan westward. And when Joshua sent them away also unto their tents, then he blessed them,

8 And he spake unto them, saying, Return with much riches unto your tents, and with very much cattle, with silver, and with gold, and with brass, and with iron, and with very much raiment: R divide the spoil of your enemies with your brethren.

9 And the children of Reuben and the children of Gad and the half tribe of Mă-năs'-sĕh returned, and departed from the children of Israel out of Shī'-lōh, which *is* in the land of Canaan, to go unto R the country of Gilead, to the land of their possession, whereof they were possessed, according to the word of the LORD by the hand of Moses.

Their altar

10 And when they came unto the borders of Jordan, that *are* in the land of Canaan, the children of Reuben and the children of Gad and the half tribe of Mă-năs'-sĕh built there an altar by Jordan, a great altar to see to.

11 And the children of Israel R heard say, Behold, the children of Reuben and the children of Gad and the half tribe of Mă-năs'-sĕh have built an altar over against the land of Canaan, in the borders of Jordan, at the passage of the children of Israel.

12 And when the children of Israel heard *of it,* R the whole congregation of the children of Israel gathered themselves together at Shī'-lōh, to go up to war against them.

13 And the children of Israel R sent unto the children of Reuben, and to the children of Gad, and to the half tribe of Mă-năs'-sĕh, into

the land of Gilead, R Phĭn'-ĕ-hăś the son of Ĕl-ē-ā'-zär the priest,

14 And with him ten princes, of each N chief house a prince throughout all the tribes of Israel; and R each one *was* an head of the house of their fathers among the thousands of Israel.

Accusation of the western tribes

15 And they came unto the children of Reuben, and to the children of Gad, and to the half tribe of Mă-năs'-sĕh, unto the land of Gilead, and they spake with them, saying,

16 Thus saith the whole congregation of the LORD, What trespass *is* this that ye have committed against the God of Israel, to turn away this day from following the LORD, in that ye have builded you an altar, R that ye might rebel this day against the LORD?

17 *Is* the iniquity R of Pē'-ôr too little for us, from which we are not cleansed until this day, although there was a plague in the congregation of the LORD,

18 But that ye must turn away this day from following the LORD? and it will be, *seeing* ye rebel to day against the LORD, that to morrow R he will be wroth with the whole congregation of Israel.

19 Notwithstanding, if the land of your possession *be* unclean, *then* pass ye over unto the land of the possession of the LORD, R wherein the LORD's tabernacle dwelleth, and take possession among us: but rebel not against the LORD, nor rebel against us, in building you an altar beside the altar of the LORD our God.

20 R Did not Ā'-chăn the son of Zē'-räh commit a trespass in the accursed thing, and wrath fell on all the congregation of Israel? and that man perished not alone in his iniquity.

Reply of the eastern tribes

21 Then the children of Reuben and the children of Gad and the half tribe of Mă-năs'-sĕh answered, and said unto the heads of the thousands of Israel,

22 The LORD R God of gods, the LORD God of gods, he R knoweth, and Israel he shall know; if *it be* in rebellion, or if in transgression against the LORD, (save us not this day,)

23 That we have built us an altar to turn from following the LORD, or if to offer thereon burnt offering or meat offering, or if to offer peace offerings thereon, let the LORD himself R require *it;*

24 And if we have not *rather* done it for fear of *this* thing, saying, N In time to come your children might speak unto our children, saying, What have ye to do with the LORD God of Israel?

25 For the LORD hath made Jordan a border between us and you, ye children of Reuben and children of Gad; ye have no part in the LORD: so shall your children make our children cease from fearing the LORD.

26 Therefore we said, Let us now prepare to build us an altar, not for burnt offering, nor for sacrifice:

27 But *that* it *may be* ᴿa witness between us, and you, and our generations after us, that we might ᴿdo the service of the LORD before him with our burnt offerings, and with our sacrifices, and with our peace offerings; that your children may not say to our children in time to come, Ye have no part in the LORD.

28 Therefore said we, that it shall be, when they should *so* say to us or to our generations in time to come, that we may say *again,* Behold the pattern of the altar of the LORD, which our fathers made, not for burnt offerings, nor for sacrifices; but it *is* a witness between us and you.

29 God forbid that we should rebel against the LORD, and turn this day from following the LORD, ᴿto build an altar for burnt offerings, for meat offerings, or for sacrifices, beside the altar of the LORD our God that *is* before his tabernacle.

Reconciliation of the tribes

30 And when Phĭn′-ĕ-hăs the priest, and the princes of the congregation and heads of the thousands of Israel which *were* with him, heard the words that the children of Reuben and the children of Gad and the children of Mă-năs′-sēh spake, ᴺit pleased them.

31 And Phĭn′-ĕ-hăs the son of Ĕl-ē-ā′-zär the priest said unto the children of Reuben, and to the children of Gad, and to the children of Mă-năs′-sēh, This day we perceive that the LORD *is* ᴿamong us, because ye have not committed this trespass against the LORD: ᴺnow ye have delivered the children of Israel out of the hand of the LORD.

32 And Phĭn′-ĕ-hăs the son of Ĕl-ē-ā′-zär the priest, and the princes, returned from the children of Reuben, and from the children of Gad, out of the land of Gilead, unto the land of Canaan, to the children of Israel, and brought them word again.

33 And the thing pleased the children of Israel; and the children of Israel ᴿblessed God, and did not intend to go up against them in battle, to destroy the land wherein the children of Reuben and Gad dwelt.

34 And the children of Reuben and the children of Gad called the altar ᴺEd: for it *shall be* a witness between us that the LORD *is* God.

CHAPTER 23

Joshua addresses the people

AND it came to pass a long time after that the LORD ᴿhad given rest unto Israel from all their enemies round about, that Joshua ᴿwaxed old *and* ᴺstricken in age.

2 And Joshua ᴿcalled for all Israel, *and* for their elders, and for their heads, and for their judges, and for their officers, and said unto them, I am old *and* stricken in age:

3 And ye have seen all that the LORD your God hath done unto all these nations because of you; for the ᴿLORD your God *is* he that hath fought for you.

4 Behold, ᴿI have divided unto you by lot these nations that remain, to be an inheritance for your tribes, from Jordan, with all the nations that I have cut off, even unto the great sea ᴺwestward.

5 And the LORD your God, ᴿhe shall expel them from before you, and drive them from out of your sight; and ye shall possess their land, ᴿas the LORD your God hath promised unto you.

6 ᴿBe ye therefore very courageous to keep and to do all that is written in the book of the law of Moses, ᴿthat ye turn not aside therefrom *to* the right hand or *to* the left;

7 That ye ᴿcome not among these nations, these that remain among you; neither ᴿmake mention of the name of their gods, nor cause to swear *by them,* neither serve them, nor bow yourselves unto them:

8 ᴺBut ᴿcleave unto the LORD your God, as ye have done unto this day.

9 ᴿForᴺ the LORD hath driven out from before you great nations and strong: but *as for* you, ᴿno man hath been able to stand before you unto this day.

10 ᴿOne man of you shall chase a thousand: for the LORD your God, he *it is* that fighteth for you, ᴿas he hath promised you.

Against disregarding the covenant

11 ᴿTake good heed therefore unto ᴺyourselves, that ye love the LORD your God.

12 Else if ye do in any wise ᴿgo back, and cleave unto the remnant of these nations, *even* these that remain among you, and shall ᴿmake marriages with them, and go in unto them, and they to you:

13 Know for a certainty that ᴿthe LORD your God will no more drive out *any of* these nations from before you; ᴿbut they shall be snares and traps unto you, and scourges in your sides, and thorns in your eyes, until ye perish from off this good land which the LORD your God hath given you.

14 And, behold, this day [R]I *am* going the way of all the earth: and ye know in all your hearts and in all your souls, that [R]not one thing hath failed of all the good things which the LORD your God spake concerning you; all are come to pass unto you, *and* not one thing hath failed thereof.

15 [R]Therefore it shall come to pass, *that* as all good things are come upon you, which the LORD your God promised you; so shall the LORD bring upon you [R]all evil things, until he have destroyed you from off this good land which the LORD your God hath given you.

16 When ye have transgressed the covenant of the LORD your God, which he commanded you, and have gone and served other gods, and bowed yourselves to them; then shall the anger of the LORD be kindled against you, and ye shall perish quickly from off the good land which he hath given unto you.

CHAPTER 24

Joshua's last address to Israel

AND Joshua gathered all the tribes of Israel to [R]Shē'-chĕm, and [R]called for the elders of Israel, and for their heads, and for their judges, and for their officers; and they [R]presented themselves before God.

2 And Joshua said unto all the people, Thus saith the LORD God of Israel, [R]Your fathers dwelt on the other side of the flood in old time, *even* Tē'-räh, the father of Abraham, and the father of Nā'-chôr: and [R]they served other gods.

3 And [R]I took your father Abraham from the other side of the flood, and led him throughout all the land of Canaan, and multiplied his seed, and [R]gave him Isaac.

4 And I gave unto Isaac [R]Jacob and Esau: and I gave unto [R]Esau mount Sē'-ĭr, to possess it; [R]but Jacob and his children went down into Egypt.

5 [R]I sent Moses also and Aaron, and [R]I plagued Egypt, according to that which I did among them: and afterward I brought you out.

6 And I [R]brought your fathers out of Egypt: and [R]ye came unto the sea; [R]and the Egyptians pursued after your fathers with chariots and horsemen unto the Red sea.

7 And when they cried unto the LORD, [R]he put darkness between you and the Egyptians, [R]and brought the sea upon them, and covered them; and [R]your eyes have seen what I have done in Egypt: and ye dwelt in the wilderness [R]a long season.

8 And I brought you into the land of the Amorites, which dwelt on the other side Jordan; [R]and they fought with you: and I gave

them into your hand, that ye might possess their land; and I destroyed them from before you.

9 Then [R]Balak the son of Zĭp'-pôr, king of Moab, arose and warred against Israel, and [R]sent and called Bā'-lāam the son of Bē'-ôr to curse you:

10 [R]But I would not hearken unto Bā'-lāam; [R]therefore he blessed you still: so I delivered you out of his hand.

11 And [R]ye went over Jordan, and came unto Jericho: and [R]the men of Jericho fought against you, the Amorites, and the Pĕ-rĭz'-zītes, and the Canaanites, and the Hittites, and the Gĭr'-gă-shītes, the Hī'-vītes, and the Jĕb'-ū-śītes; and I delivered them into your hand.

12 And [R]I sent the hornet before you, which drave them out from before you, *even* the two kings of the Amorites; *but* [R]not with thy sword, nor with thy bow.

13 And I have given you a land for which ye did not labour, and [R]cities which ye built not, and ye dwell in them; of the vineyards and oliveyards which ye planted not do ye eat.

14 [R]Now therefore fear the LORD, and serve him in [R]sincerity and in truth: and [R]put away the gods which your fathers served on the other side of the flood, and [R]in Egypt; and serve ye the LORD.

15 And if it seem evil unto you to serve the LORD, [R]choose you this day whom ye will serve; whether [R]the gods which your fathers served that *were* on the other side of the flood, or [R]the gods of the Amorites, in whose land ye dwell: [R]but as for me and my house, we will serve the LORD.

16 And the people answered and said, God forbid that we should forsake the LORD, to serve other gods;

17 For the LORD our God, he *it is* that brought us up and our fathers out of the land of Egypt, from the house of bondage, and which did those great signs in our sight, and preserved us in all the way wherein we went, and among all the people through whom we passed:

18 And the LORD drave out from before us all the people, even the Amorites which dwelt in the land: *therefore* will we also serve the LORD; for he *is* our God.

The covenant renewed

19 And Joshua said unto the people, [R]Ye cannot serve the LORD: for he *is* an [R]holy God; he *is* [R]a jealous God; [R]he will not forgive your transgressions nor your sins.

20 [R]If ye forsake the LORD, and serve strange gods, [R]then he will turn and do you

hurt, and consume you, after that he hath done you good.

21 And the people said unto Joshua, Nay; but we will serve the LORD.

22 And Joshua said unto the people, Ye *are* witnesses against yourselves that ᴿye have chosen you the LORD, to serve him. And they said, *We are* witnesses.

23 Now therefore ᴿput away, *said he,* the strange gods which *are* among you, and incline your heart unto the LORD God of Israel.

24 And the people said unto Joshua, The LORD our God will we serve, and his voice will we obey.

25 So Joshua ᴿmade a covenant with the people that day, and set them a statute and an ordinance ᴿin Shē'-chĕm.

26 And Joshua ᴿwrote these words in the book of the law of God, and took ᴿa great stone, and ᴿset it up there ᴿunder an oak, that *was* by the sanctuary of the LORD.

27 And Joshua said unto all the people, Behold, this stone shall be ᴿa witness unto us; for ᴿit hath heard all the words of the LORD which he spake unto us: it shall be therefore a witness unto you, lest ye deny your God.

28 So ᴿJoshua let the people depart, every man unto his inheritance.

Death and burial of Joshua

29 ᴿAnd it came to pass after these things, that Joshua the son of Nun, the servant of the LORD, died, *being* an hundred and ten years old.

30 And they buried him in the border of his inheritance in ᴿTĭm'-năth-sē'-răh, which *is* in mount Ē'-phrā-ĭm, on the north side of the hill of Gā'-ăsh.

31 And ᴿIsrael served the LORD all the days of Joshua, and all the days of the elders that ᴺoverlived Joshua, and which had ᴿknown all the works of the LORD, that he had done for Israel.

Joseph's bones interred at Shechem

32 And ᴿthe bones of Joseph, which the children of Israel brought up out of Egypt, buried they in Shē'-chĕm, in a parcel of ground ᴿwhich Jacob bought of the sons of Hā'-môr the father of Shē'-chĕm for an hundred ᴺpieces of silver: and it became the inheritance of the children of Joseph.

33 And ĕl-ē-ā'-zär the son of Aaron died; and they buried him in a hill *that pertained to* ᴿPhĭn'-ĕ-hăs his son, which was given him in mount Ē'-phrā-ĭm.

CHAP. 24	
BC 1427	
22 Ps. 119:173	
23 ver. 14	
Gen. 35:2	
25 Ex. 15:25	
2 Ki. 11:17	
25 ver. 1	
26 Deut. 31:24	
26 Judg. 9:6	
26 Gen. 28:18	
ch. 4:3	
26 Gen. 35:4	
27 See Gen. 31:48, 52	
27 Deut. 32:1	
28 Judg. 2:6	
Judg. 2:8	**29**
ch. 19:50	**30**
Judg. 2:7	**31**
Heb. *prolonged their days after Joshua*	**31**
Deut. 11:2	**31**
Gen. 50:25	**32**
Ex. 13:19	
Gen. 33:19	**32**
Or, *lambs*	**32**
Ex. 6:25	**33**
Judg. 20:28	

THE BOOK OF JUDGES

This book constitutes a sequel to the book of Joshua, covering the period between the death of Joshua and the birth of Samuel. It is called "Judges" because it relates the exploits of leaders among the Israelites who were known by this title before the establishment of the monarchy under Saul. The judges provided leadership in delivering Israel from oppressing nations. These judges ruled spasmodically without immediate succession and often were limited to a local area, since there was no national capital nor central government. The years assigned to each judge may overlap. It is therefore impossible to determine with exactness the time covered by this period of Israel's history. In its distinctive character the book of Judges reveals God in His providential dealings with Israel as the Messianic nation. As their covenant God He takes the direction of their history into His own hands, uniformly regards them as a redeemed people, set before them a high ideal of religious character, and provides them with mediators and saviors in every crisis. Throughout the book of Judges, God acknowledges Israel to be His very own despite grievous transgressions. The author of this book is unknown.

OUTLINE OF THE BOOK:
I. General conditions   1:1-3:6
II. Oppressing nations and their defeat   3:7-16:31
III. Idolatry, migration, and crime   17:1-21:25

CHAPTER 1

Conquests by Judah and Simeon

NOW after the death of Joshua it came to pass, that the children of Israel ᴿasked the LORD, saying, Who shall go up for us against the Canaanites first, to fight against them?

2 And the LORD said, ᴿJudah shall go up:

behold, I have delivered the land into his hand.

3 And Judah said unto Simeon his brother, Come up with me into my lot, that we may fight against the Canaanites; and ᴿI likewise will go with thee into thy lot. So Simeon went with him.

4 And Judah went up; and the LORD delivered the Canaanites and the Pĕ-rĭz'-zītes into

CHAP. 1	
BC 1425	
1 Num. 27:21	
ch. 20:18	
2 Gen. 49:8	
ver. 17	**3**

their hand: and they slew of them in ᴿBē'-zĕk ten thousand men.

5 And they found Ăd'-ō-nī-bē'-zĕk in Bē'-zĕk: and they fought against him, and they slew the Canaanites and the Pĕ-rĭz'-zītes.

6 But Ăd'-ō-nī-bē'-zĕk fled; and they pursued after him, and caught him, and cut off his thumbs and his great toes.

7 And Ăd'-ō-nī-bē'-zĕk said, Threescore and ten kings, having ᴺtheir thumbs and their great toes cut off, ᴺgathered *their meat* under my table: ᴿas I have done, so God hath requited me. And they brought him to Jerusalem, and there he died.

8 Now ᴿthe children of Judah had fought against Jerusalem, and had taken it, and smitten it with the edge of the sword, and set the city on fire.

9 ᴿAnd afterward the children of Judah went down to fight against the Canaanites, that dwelt in the mountain, and in the south, and in the ᴺvalley.

10 And Judah went against the Canaanites that dwelt in Hē'-brŏn: (now the name of Hē'-brŏn before *was* ᴿKĭr'-jăth-är'-bă:) and they slew Shē'-shăi, and Ă-hī'-măn, and Tăl'-măi.

11 ᴿAnd from thence he went against the inhabitants of Dē'-bĭr: and the name of Dē'-bĭr before *was* Kĭr'-jăth-sē'-phĕr:

12 ᴿAnd Caleb said, He that smiteth Kĭr'-jăth-sē'-phĕr, and taketh it, to him will I give Ăch'-săh my daughter to wife.

13 And Ŏth'-nĭ-ĕl the son of Kē'-năz, ᴿCaleb's younger brother, took it: and he gave him Ăch'-săh his daughter to wife.

14 ᴿAnd it came to pass, when she came *to him,* that she moved him to ask of her father a field: and she lighted from off *her* ass; and Caleb said unto her, What wilt thou?

15 And she said unto him, ᴿGive me a blessing: for thou hast given me a south land; give me also springs of water. And Caleb gave her the upper springs and the nether springs.

16 ᴿAnd the children of the Kē'-nīte, Moses' father in law, went up out ᴿof the city of palm trees with the children of Judah into the wilderness of Judah, which *lieth* in the south of ᴿĂr'-ăd; ᴿand they went and dwelt among the people.

17 ᴿAnd Judah went with Simeon his brother, and they slew the Canaanites that inhabited Zē'-phăth, and utterly destroyed it. And the name of the city was called ᴿHŏr'-măh.

18 Also Judah took ᴿGā'-ză with the coast thereof, and Ăs'-kĕ-lŏn with the coast thereof, and ĕk'-rŏn with the coast thereof.

19 And ᴿthe LORD was with Judah; and ᴺhe drave out *the inhabitants of* the mountain; but could not drive out the inhabitants of the valley, because they had ᴿchariots of iron.

20 ᴿAnd they gave Hē'-brŏn unto Caleb, as Moses said: and he expelled thence the three sons of Anak.

21 ᴿAnd the children of Benjamin did not drive out the Jĕb'-ū-śītes that inhabited Jerusalem; but the Jĕb'-ū-śītes dwell with the children of Benjamin in Jerusalem unto this day.

Conquest of Beth-el

22 And the house of Joseph, they also went up against Beth-el: ᴿand the LORD *was* with them.

23 And the house of Joseph ᴿsent to descry Beth-el. (Now the name of the city before *was* ᴿLuz.)

24 And the spies saw a man come forth out of the city, and they said unto him, Shew us, we pray thee, the entrance into the city, and ᴿwe will shew thee mercy.

25 And when he shewed them the entrance into the city, they smote the city with the edge of the sword; but they let go the man and all his family.

26 And the man went into the land of the Hittites, and built a city, and called the name thereof Luz: which *is* the name thereof unto this day.

Cities not conquered

27 ᴿNeither did Mă-năs'-sĕh drive out *the inhabitants of* Bĕth-shē'-ăn and her towns, nor Tā'-ă-năch and her towns, nor the inhabitants of Dor and her towns, nor the inhabitants of ĭb'-lĕ-ăm and her towns, nor the inhabitants of Mĕ-gĭd'-dō and her towns: but the Canaanites would dwell in that land.

28 And it came to pass, when Israel was strong, that they put the Canaanites to tribute, and did not utterly drive them out.

29 ᴿNeither did Ē'-phră-ĭm drive out the Canaanites that dwelt in Gē'-zĕr; but the Canaanites dwelt in Gē'-zĕr among them.

30 Neither did Zĕ-bū'-lŭn drive out the inhabitants of Kĭt'-rŏn, nor the ᴿinhabitants of Nā'-hă-lŏl; but the Canaanites dwelt among them, and became tributaries.

31 ᴿNeither did Asher drive out the inhabitants of Ăc'-cho, nor the inhabitants of Zī'-dŏn, nor of Ăh'-lăb, nor of Ăch'-zĭb, nor of Hĕl'-băh, nor of Ă'-phĭk, nor of Rē'-hŏb:

32 But the Asherites ᴿdwelt among the Canaanites, the inhabitants of the land: for they did not drive them out.

33 ᴿNeither did Năph′-tă-lī drive out the inhabitants of Běth-shē′-mĕsh, nor the inhabitants of Běth′-ă-năth; but he ᴿdwelt among the Canaanites, the inhabitants of the land: nevertheless the inhabitants of Běth-shē′-mĕsh and of Běth′-ă-năth ᴿbecame tributaries unto them.

34 And the Amorites forced the children of Dan into the mountain: for they would not suffer them to come down to the valley:

35 But the Amorites would dwell in mount Hē′-rĕś ᴿin Âī′-jă-lŏn, and in Shā-ăl′-bīm: yet the hand of the house of Joseph ᴺprevailed, so that they became tributaries.

36 And the coast of the Amorites *was* ᴿfrom ᴺthe going up to Ăk-răb′-bīm, from the rock, and upward.

CHAPTER 2

An angel of the LORD

AND an ᴺangel of the Lᴏʀᴅ came up from Gĭl′-găl ᴿto Bō′-chĭm, and said, I made you to go up out of Egypt, and have brought you unto the land which I sware unto your fathers; and ᴿI said, I will never break my covenant with you.

2 And ᴿye shall make no league with the inhabitants of this land; ᴿye shall throw down their altars: ᴿbut ye have not obeyed my voice: why have ye done this?

3 Wherefore I also said, I will not drive them out from before you; but they shall be ᴿ*as thorns* in your sides, and ᴿtheir gods shall be a ᴿsnare unto you.

4 And it came to pass, when the angel of the Lᴏʀᴅ spake these words unto all the children of Israel, that the people lifted up their voice, and wept.

5 And they called the name of that place ᴺBō′-chĭm: and they sacrificed there unto the Lᴏʀᴅ.

Death of Joshua

6 And when ᴿJoshua had let the people go, the children of Israel went every man unto his inheritance to possess the land.

7 ᴿAnd the people served the Lᴏʀᴅ all the days of Joshua, and all the days of the elders that ᴺoutlived Joshua, who had seen all the great works of the Lᴏʀᴅ, that he did for Israel.

8 And ᴿJoshua the son of Nun, the servant of the Lᴏʀᴅ, died, *being* an hundred and ten years old.

9 ᴿAnd they buried him in the border of his inheritance in ᴿTĭm′-năth-hē′-rĕś, in the mount of Ē′-phră-ĭm, on the north side of the hill Gā′-ăsh.

10 And also all that generation were gathered unto their fathers: and there arose another

generation after them, which ᴿknew not the Lᴏʀᴅ, nor yet the works which he had done for Israel.

Israel's unfaithfulness

11 And the children of Israel did evil in the sight of the Lᴏʀᴅ, and served Bā′-ă-lĭm:

12 And they ᴿforsook the Lᴏʀᴅ God of their fathers, which brought them out of the land of Egypt, and followed ᴿother gods, of the gods of the people that *were* round about them, and ᴿbowed themselves unto them, and provoked the Lᴏʀᴅ to anger.

13 And they forsook the Lᴏʀᴅ, ᴿand served Bā′-ăl and Ăsh′-tă-rŏth.

14 ᴿAnd the anger of the Lᴏʀᴅ was hot against Israel, and he ᴿdelivered them into the hands of spoilers that spoiled them, and ᴿhe sold them into the hands of their enemies round about, so that they ᴿcould not any longer stand before their enemies.

15 Whithersoever they went out, the hand of the Lᴏʀᴅ was against them for evil, as the Lᴏʀᴅ had said, and ᴿas the Lᴏʀᴅ had sworn unto them: and they were greatly distressed.

Judges defied

16 Nevertheless ᴿthe Lᴏʀᴅ raised up judges, which ᴺdelivered them out of the hand of those that spoiled them.

17 And yet they would not hearken unto their judges, but they ᴿwent a whoring after other gods, and bowed themselves unto them: they turned quickly out of the way which their fathers walked in, obeying the commandments of the Lᴏʀᴅ; *but* they did not so.

18 And when the Lᴏʀᴅ raised them up judges, then ᴿthe Lᴏʀᴅ was with the judge, and delivered them out of the hand of their enemies all the days of the judge: ᴿfor it repented the Lᴏʀᴅ because of their groanings by reason of them that oppressed them and vexed them.

19 And it came to pass, ᴿwhen the judge was dead, *that* they returned, and ᴺcorrupted *themselves* more than their fathers, in following other gods to serve them, and to bow down unto them; ᴺthey ceased not from their own doings, nor from their stubborn way.

20 ᴿAnd the anger of the Lᴏʀᴅ was hot against Israel; and he said, Because that this people hath ᴿtransgressed my covenant which I commanded their fathers, and have not hearkened unto my voice;

21 ᴿI also will not henceforth drive out any from before them of the nations which Joshua left when he died:

22 ᴿThat through them I may ᴿprove Israel, whether they will keep the way of the Lᴏʀᴅ to

walk therein, as their fathers did keep *it,* or not.

23 Therefore the LORD [N]left those nations, without driving them out hastily; neither delivered he them into the hand of Joshua.

CHAPTER 3

Nations left to test Israel

NOW these *are* [R]the nations which the LORD left, to prove Israel by them, *even* as many *of Israel* as had not known all the wars of Canaan;

2 Only that the generations of the children of Israel might know, to teach them war, at the least such as before knew nothing thereof;

3 *Namely,* [R]five lords of the Philistines, and all the Canaanites, and the Sĭ-dō'-nĭ-ăns, and the Hī'-vītes that dwelt in mount Lĕb'-ă-nọn, from mount Bā'-ăl-hĕr'-mọn unto the entering in of Hā'-măth.

4 [R]And they were to prove Israel by them, to know whether they would hearken unto the commandments of the LORD, which he commanded their fathers by the hand of Moses.

5 [R]And the children of Israel dwelt among the Canaanites, Hittites, and Amorites, and Pĕ-rĭz'-zītes, and Hī'-vītes, and Jĕb'-ū-śītes:

6 And [R]they took their daughters to be their wives, and gave their daughters to their sons, and served their gods.

Judgeship of Othniel

7 [R]And the children of Israel did evil in the sight of the LORD, and forgat the LORD their God, [R]and served Bā'-ă-lĭm and [R]the groves.

8 Therefore the anger of the LORD was hot against Israel, and he [R]sold them into the hand of [R]Chû'-shăn-rĭsh-ă-thā'-ĭm king of [N]Mĕs-ŏ-pŏ-tā'-mĭ-ă: and the children of Israel served Chû'-shăn-rĭsh-ă-thā'-ĭm eight years.

9 And when the children of Israel [R]cried unto the LORD, the LORD [R]raised up a [N]deliverer to the children of Israel, who delivered them, *even* [R]Ŏth'-nĭ-ĕl the son of Kē'-năz, Caleb's younger brother.

10 And [R]the spirit of the LORD [N]came upon him, and he judged Israel, and went out to war: and the LORD delivered Chû'-shăn-rĭsh-ă-thā'-ĭm king of [N]Mĕs-ŏ-pŏ-tā'-mĭ-ă into his hand; and his hand prevailed against Chû'-shăn-rĭsh-ă-thā'-ĭm.

11 And the land had rest forty years. And Ŏth'-nĭ-ĕl the son of Kē'-năz died.

Judgeship of Ehud

12 [R]And the children of Israel did evil again in the sight of the LORD: and the LORD strengthened [R]Ĕg'-lŏn the king of Moab

against Israel, because they had done evil in the sight of the LORD.

13 And he gathered unto him the children of Ammon and [R]Ăm'-ă-lĕk, and went and smote Israel, and possessed [R]the city of palm trees.

14 So the children of Israel [R]served Ĕg'-lŏn the king of Moab eighteen years.

15 But when the children of Israel [R]cried unto the LORD, the LORD raised them up a deliverer, Ē'-hŭd the son of Gē'-ră, [N]a Benjamite, a man [N]lefthanded: and by him the children of Israel sent a present unto Ĕg'-lŏn the king of Moab.

16 But Ē'-hŭd made him a dagger which had two edges, of a cubit length; and he did gird it under his raiment upon his right thigh.

17 And he brought the present unto Ĕg'-lŏn king of Moab: and Ĕg'-lŏn *was* a very fat man.

18 And when he had made an end to offer the present, he sent away the people that bare the present.

19 But he himself turned again [R]from the [N]quarries that *were* by Gĭl'-găl, and said, I have a secret errand unto thee, O king: who said, Keep silence. And all that stood by him went out from him.

20 And Ē'-hŭd came unto him; and he was sitting in [N]a summer parlour, which he had for himself alone. And Ē'-hŭd said, I have a message from God unto thee. And he arose out of *his* seat.

21 And Ē'-hŭd put forth his left hand, and took the dagger from his right thigh, and thrust it into his belly:

22 And the haft also went in after the blade; and the fat closed upon the blade, so that he could not draw the dagger out of his belly; and [N]the dirt came out.

23 Then Ē'-hŭd went forth through the porch, and shut the doors of the parlour upon him, and locked them.

24 When he was gone out, his servants came; and when they saw that, behold, the doors of the parlour *were* locked, they said, Surely he [N]covereth his feet in his summer chamber.

25 And they tarried till they were ashamed: and, behold, he opened not the doors of the parlour; therefore they took a key, and opened *them:* and, behold, their lord *was* fallen down dead on the earth.

26 And Ē'-hŭd escaped while they tarried, and passed beyond the quarries, and escaped unto Sē-ĭ'-răth.

27 And it came to pass, when he was come, that [R]he blew a trumpet in the [R]mountain of Ē'-phră-ĭm, and the children of Israel went down with him from the mount, and he before them.

28 And he said unto them, Follow after me: for ᴿthe Lᴏʀᴅ hath delivered your enemies the Moabites into your hand. And they went down after him, and took ᴿthe fords of Jordan toward Moab, and suffered not a man to pass over.

29 And they slew of Moab at that time about ten thousand men, all ᴺlusty, and all men of valour; and there escaped not a man.

30 So Moab was subdued that day under the hand of Israel. And ᴿthe land had rest fourscore years.

Judgeship of Shamgar

31 And after him was ᴿShăm'-gär the son of Ā'-năth, which slew of the Philistines six hundred men ᴿwith an ox goad: ᴿand he also delivered ᴿIsrael.

CHAPTER 4

Judgeship of Deborah

AND ᴿthe children of Israel again did evil in the sight of the Lᴏʀᴅ, when Ē'-hŭd was dead.

2 And the Lᴏʀᴅ ᴿsold them into the hand of Jā'-bĭn king of Canaan, that reigned in ᴿHā'-zôr; the captain of whose host was ᴿSĭs'-ĕ-ră, which dwelt in ᴿHă-rō'-shĕth of the Gentiles.

3 And the children of Israel cried unto the Lᴏʀᴅ: for he had nine hundred ᴿchariots of iron; and twenty years ᴿhe mightily oppressed the children of Israel.

4 And Dĕb'-ŏ-răh, a prophetess, the wife of Lăp'-ĭ-dōth, she judged Israel at that time.

5 ᴿAnd she dwelt under the palm tree of Dĕb'-ŏ-răh between Rā'-măh and Beth-el in mount Ē'-phră-ĭm: and the children of Israel came up to her for judgment.

6 And she sent and called ᴿBâr'-ăk the son of Ă-bĭn'-ŏ-ăm out ᴿof Kē'-dĕsh-năph'-tă-lī, and said unto him, Hath not the Lᴏʀᴅ God of Israel commanded, saying, Go and draw toward mount Tā'-bôr, and take with thee ten thousand men of the children of Năph'-tă-lī and of the children of Zĕ-bū'-lŭn?

7 And ᴿI will draw unto thee to the ᴿriver Kī'-shŏn Sĭs'-ĕ-ră, the captain of Jā'-bĭn's army, with his chariots and his multitude; and I will deliver him into thine hand.

8 And Bâr'-ăk said unto her, If thou wilt go with me, then I will go: but if thou wilt not go with me, then I will not go.

9 And she said, I will surely go with thee: notwithstanding the journey that thou takest shall not be for thine honour; for the Lᴏʀᴅ shall ᴿsell Sĭs'-ĕ-ră into the hand of a woman.

CHAP. 3
BC 1406
28 ch. 7:9, 15
1 Sam. 17:47
28 Josh. 2:7
ch. 12:5
29 Heb. *fat*
30 ver. 11
31 ch. 5:6, 8
1 Sam. 13:19, 22
It seems to concern only the country next to the Philistines
31 1 Sam. 17:47, 50
31 ch. 2:16
31 So part is called Israel, ch. 4:1, 3, etc. & 10:7, 17 & 11:4, etc.
1 Sam. 4:1

CHAP. 4
BC 1316
1 ch. 2:19
2 ch. 2:14
2 Josh. 11:1, 10 & 19:36
2 1 Sam. 12:9
Ps. 83:9
It seems to concern only North Israel
2 ver. 13, 16
3 ch. 1:19
3 ch. 5:8
Ps. 106:42
4 Gen. 35:8
6 Heb. 11:32
6 Josh. 19:37
7 Ex. 14:4
7 ch. 5:21
1 Ki. 18:40
Ps. 83:9, 10
9 ch. 2:14

ch. 5:18	**10**
See Ex. 11:8	**10**
1 Ki. 20:10	
ch. 1:16	**11**
Num. 10:29	**11**
ver. 6	**11**
Heb. *gathered by cry,* or, *proclamation*	**13**
Deut. 9:3	**14**
2 Sam. 5:24	
Ps. 68:7	
Is. 52:12	
Ps. 83:9, 10	**15**
See Josh. 10:10	
Heb. *unto one*	**16**
Or, *rug,* or, *blanket*	**18**
ch. 5:25	**19**
ch. 5:26	**21**

And Dĕb'-ŏ-răh arose, and went with Bâr'-ăk to Kē'-dĕsh.

10 And Bâr'-ăk called ᴿZĕ-bū'-lŭn and Năph'-tă-lī to Kē'-dĕsh; and he went up with ten thousand men ᴿat his feet and Dĕb'-ŏ-răh went up with him.

Deborah and Barak deliver Israel

11 Now Hē'-bĕr ᴿthe Kē'-nīte, which was of the children of ᴿHō'-băb the father in law of Moses, had severed himself from the Kē'-nītes, and pitched his tent unto the plain of Zā-ă-nā'-ĭm, ᴿwhich is by Kē'-dĕsh.

12 And they shewed Sĭs'-ĕ-ră that Bâr'-ăk the son of Ă-bĭn'-ŏ-ăm was gone up to mount Tā'-bôr.

13 And Sĭs'-ĕ-ră ᴺgathered together all his chariots, even nine hundred chariots of iron, and all the people that were with him, from Hă-rō'-shĕth of the Gentiles unto the river of Kī'-shŏn.

14 And Dĕb'-ŏ-răh said unto Bâr'-ăk, Up; for this is the day in which the Lᴏʀᴅ hath delivered Sĭs'-ĕ-ră into thine hand: ᴿis not the Lᴏʀᴅ gone out before thee? So Bâr'-ăk went down from mount Tā'-bôr, and ten thousand men after him.

15 And ᴿthe Lᴏʀᴅ discomfited Sĭs'-ĕ-ră, and all his chariots, and all his host, with the edge of the sword before Bâr'-ăk; so that Sĭs'-ĕ-ră lighted down off his chariot, and fled away on his feet.

16 But Bâr'-ăk pursued after the chariots, and after the host, unto Hă-rō'-shĕth of the Gentiles: and all the host of Sĭs'-ĕ-ră fell upon the edge of the sword; and there was not ᴺa man left.

Death of Sisera

17 Howbeit Sĭs'-ĕ-ră fled away on his feet to the tent of Jā'-ĕl the wife of Hē'-bĕr the Kē'-nīte: for there was peace between Jā'-bĭn the king of Hā'-zôr and the house of Hē'-bĕr the Kē'-nīte.

18 And Jā'-ĕl went out to meet Sĭs'-ĕ-ră, and said unto him, Turn in, my lord, turn in to me; fear not. And when he had turned in unto her into the tent, she covered him with a ᴺmantle.

19 And he said unto her, Give me, I pray thee, a little water to drink; for I am thirsty. And she opened ᴿa bottle of milk, and gave him drink, and covered him.

20 Again he said unto her, Stand in the door of the tent, and it shall be, when any man doth come and inquire of thee, and say, Is there any man here? that thou shalt say, No.

21 Then Jā'-ĕl Hē'-bĕr's wife ᴿtook a nail of

the tent, and [N]took an hammer in her hand, and went softly unto him, and smote the nail into his temples, and fastened it into the ground: for he was fast asleep and weary. So he died.

22 And, behold, as Băr'-ăk pursued Sĭs'-ĕ-ră, Jā'-ĕl came out to meet him, and said unto him, Come, and I will shew thee the man whom thou seekest. And when he came into her *tent,* behold, Sĭs'-ĕ-ră lay dead, and the nail *was* in his temples.

23 So God subdued on that day Jā'-bĭn the king of Canaan before the children of Israel.

24 And the hand of the children of Israel [N]prospered, and prevailed against Jā'-bĭn the king of Canaan, until they had destroyed Jā'-bĭn king of Canaan.

CHAPTER 5

The song of Deborah and Barak

THEN [R]sang Dĕb'-ŏ-răh and Băr'-ăk the son of Ă-bĭn'-ŏ-ăm on that day, saying,

2 Praise ye the LORD for the [R]avenging of Israel, [R]when the people willingly offered themselves.

3 [R]Hear, O ye kings; give ear, O ye princes; I, *even* I, will sing unto the LORD; I will sing *praise* to the LORD God of Israel.

4 LORD, [R]when thou wentest out of Sē'-ĭr, when thou marchedst out of the field of Ē'-dom, [R]the earth trembled, and the heavens dropped, the clouds also dropped water.

5 [R]The mountains [N]melted from before the LORD, *even* [R]that Sĭ'-nāi from before the LORD God of Israel.

6 In the days of Shăm'-gär the son of Anath, in the days of Jā'-ĕl, [R]the highways were unoccupied, and the [N]travellers walked through [N]byways.

7 *The inhabitants of* the villages ceased, they ceased in Israel, until that I Dĕb'-ŏ-răh arose, that I arose [R]a mother in Israel.

8 They [R]chose new gods; then *was* war in the gates: [R]was there a shield or spear seen among forty thousand in Israel?

9 My heart *is* toward the governors of Israel, that offered themselves willingly among the people. Bless ye the LORD.

10 [R]Speak,[N] ye [R]that ride on white asses, [R]ye that sit in judgment, and walk by the way.

11 *They that are delivered* from the noise of archers in the places of drawing water, there shall they rehearse the [R]righteous[N] acts of the LORD, *even* the righteous acts *toward the inhabitants* of his villages in Israel: then shall the people of the LORD go down to the gates.

CHAP. **4**	
BC 1316	
21	Heb. *put*
24	Heb. *going went and was hard*
CHAP. **5**	
BC 1296	
1	See Ex. 15:1
2	Ps. 18:47
2	2 Chr. 17:16
3	Deut. 32:1, 3
4	Deut. 33:2
4	Ps. 68:8
5	Ps. 97:5
5	Heb. *flowed*
5	Ex. 19:18
6	Is. 33:8
6	Heb. *walkers of paths*
6	Heb. *crooked ways*
7	Is. 49:23
8	Deut. 32:16
8	1 Sam. 13:19, 22
10	Ps. 145:5
10	Or, *Meditate*
10	ch. 10:4
10	Ps. 107:32
11	Ps. 145:7
11	Heb. *righteousnesses of the LORD*

Ps. 57:8	12
Ps. 68:18	12
Ps. 49:14	13
Heb. *draw with the pen, etc.*	14
Heb. *his feet*	15
Or, *In the divisions, etc.*	15
Heb. *impressions*	15
Or, *In*	16
See Josh. 13:25, 31	17
Josh. 19:29	17
Or, *port*	17
Or, *creeks*	17
ch. 4:10	18
Heb. *exposed to reproach*	18
Ps. 44:12	19
Ps. 77:17, 18	20
ch. 4:15	20
Heb. *paths*	20
ch. 4:7	21
Or, *tramplings, or, plungings*	22
Neh. 3:5	23
1 Sam. 18:17	23
ch. 4:17	24
Luke 1:28	24
ch. 4:19	25
Heb. *she hammered*	26
Heb. *Between*	27
Heb. *destroyed*	27

12 [R]Awake, awake, Dĕb'-ŏ-răh: awake, awake, utter a song: arise, Băr'-ăk, and [R]lead thy captivity captive, thou son of Ă-bĭn'-ŏ-ăm.

13 Then he made him that remaineth [R]have dominion over the nobles among the people: the LORD made me have dominion over the mighty.

14 Out of Ē'-phră-ĭm *was there* a root of them against Ăm'-ă-lĕk; after thee, Benjamin, among thy people; out of Mā'-chĭr came down governors, and out of Zĕ-bū'-lŭn they that [N]handle the pen of the writer.

15 And the princes of Ĭs'-să-chär *were* with Dĕb'-ŏ-răh; even Ĭs'-să-chär, and also Băr'-ăk: he was sent on [N]foot into the valley. [N]For the divisions of Reuben *there were* great [N]thoughts of heart.

16 Why abodest thou among the sheepfolds, to hear the bleatings of the flocks? [N]For the divisions of Reuben *there were* great searchings of heart.

17 [R]Gilead abode beyond Jordan: and why did Dan remain in ships? [R]Asher continued on the sea [N]shore, and abode in his [N]breaches.

18 [R]Zĕ-bū'-lŭn and Năph'-tă-li *were* a people *that* [N]jeoparded their lives unto the death in the high places of the field.

19 The kings came *and* fought, then fought the kings of Canaan in Tā'-ă-năch by the waters of Mĕ-gĭd'-dō; [R]they took no gain of money.

20 [R]They fought from heaven; [R]the stars in their [N]courses fought against Sĭs'-ĕ-ră.

21 [R]The river of Kĭ'-shŏn swept them away, that ancient river, the river Kĭ'-shŏn. O my soul, thou hast trodden down strength.

22 Then were the horsehoofs broken by the means of the [N]pransings, the pransings of their mighty ones.

23 Curse ye Mĕ'-rŏz, said the angel of the LORD, curse ye bitterly the inhabitants thereof; [R]because they came not to the help [R]of the LORD, to the help of the LORD against the mighty.

24 Blessed above women shall [R]Jā'-ĕl the wife of Hē'-bĕr the Kē'-nīte be, [R]blessed shall she be above women in the tent.

25 [R]He asked water, *and* she gave *him* milk; she brought forth butter in a lordly dish.

26 She put her hand to the nail, and her right hand to the workmen's hammer; and [N]with the hammer she smote Sĭs'-ĕ-ră, she smote off his head, when she had pierced and stricken through his temples.

27 [N]At her feet he bowed, he fell, he lay down: at her feet he bowed, he fell: where he bowed, there he fell down [N]dead.

28 The mother of Sĭs'-ĕ-ră looked out at a

window, and cried through the lattice, Why is his chariot *so* long in coming? why tarry the wheels of his chariots?

29 Her wise ladies answered her, yea, she returned ᴺanswer to herself,

30 ᴿHave they not sped? have they *not* divided the prey; ᴺto every man a damsel *or* two; to Sĭs'-ĕ-rǎ a prey of divers colours, a prey of divers colours of needlework, of divers colours of needlework on both sides, *meet* for the necks of *them that take* the spoil?

31 ᴿSo let all thine enemies perish, O LORD: but *let* them that love him *be* ᴿas the sun ᴿwhen he goeth forth in his might. And the land had rest forty years.

CHAPTER 6

Oppression by the Midianites

AND ᴿthe children of Israel did evil in the sight of the LORD: and the LORD delivered them into the hand ᴿof Mĭd'-ĭ-ăn seven years.

2 And the hand of Mĭd'-ĭ-ăn ᴺprevailed against Israel: *and* because of the Mĭd'-ĭ-ă-nītes the children of Israel made them ᴿthe dens which *are* in the mountains, and caves, and strong holds.

3 And *so* it was, when Israel had sown, that the Mĭd'-ĭ-ă-nītes came up, and ᴿthe Ă-măl'-ĕk-ītes, ᴿand the children of the east, even they came up against them;

4 And they encamped against them, and ᴿdestroyed the increase of the earth, till thou come unto Gā'-zǎ, and left no sustenance for Israel, neither ᴺsheep, nor ox, nor ass.

5 For they came up with their cattle and their tents, and they came ᴿas grasshoppers for multitude; *for* both they and their camels were without number: and they entered into the land to destroy it.

6 And Israel was greatly impoverished because of the Mĭd'-ĭ-ă-nītes; and the children of Israel ᴿcried unto the LORD.

7 And it came to pass, when the children of Israel cried unto the LORD because of the Mĭd'-ĭ-ă-nītes,

8 That the LORD sent ᴺa prophet unto the children of Israel, which said unto them, Thus saith the LORD God of Israel, I brought you up from Egypt, and brought you forth out of the house of bondage;

9 And I delivered you out of the hand of the Egyptians, and out of the hand of all that oppressed you, and ᴿdrave them out from before you, and gave you their land;

10 And I said unto you, I *am* the LORD your God; ᴿfear not the gods of the Amorites, in

whose land ye dwell: but ye have not obeyed my voice.

Gideon and the angel

11 And there came an angel of the LORD, and sat under an oak which *was* in ŏph'-răh, that *pertained* unto Jō'-ăsh ᴿthe Ā'-bĭ-ĕz'-rīte: and his son ᴿGideon threshed wheat by the winepress, ᴺto hide *it* from the Mĭd'-ĭ-ă-nītes.

12 And the ᴿangel of the LORD appeared unto him, and said unto him, The LORD *is* ᴿwith thee, thou mighty man of valour.

13 And Gideon said unto him, Oh my Lord, if the LORD be with us, why then is all this befallen us? and ᴿwhere *be* all his miracles ᴿwhich our fathers told us of, saying, Did not the LORD bring us up from Egypt? but now the LORD hath ᴿforsaken us, and delivered us into the hands of the Mĭd'-ĭ-ă-nītes.

14 And the LORD looked upon him, and said, ᴿGo in this thy might, and thou shalt save Israel from the hand of the Mĭd'-ĭ-ă-nītes: ᴿhave not I sent thee?

15 And he said unto him, Oh my Lord, wherewith shall I save Israel? behold, ᴿmyᴺ family *is* poor in Mă-năs'-sĕh, and I *am* the least in my father's house.

16 And the LORD said unto him, ᴿSurely I will be with thee, and thou shalt smite the Mĭd'-ĭ-ă-nītes as one man.

17 And he said unto him, If now I have found grace in thy sight, then ᴿshew me a sign that thou talkest with me.

18 ᴿDepart not hence, I pray thee, until I come unto thee, and bring forth my ᴺpresent, and set *it* before thee. And he said, I will tarry until thou come again.

19 ᴿAnd Gideon went in, and made ready ᴺa kid, and unleavened cakes of an ē'-phäh of flour: the flesh he put in a basket, and he put the broth in a pot, and brought *it* out unto him under the oak, and presented *it*.

20 And the angel of God said unto him, Take the flesh and the unleavened cakes, and ᴿlay *them* upon this rock, and ᴿpour out the broth. And he did so.

21 Then the angel of the LORD put forth the end of the staff that *was* in his hand, and touched the flesh and the unleavened cakes; and ᴿthere rose up fire out of the rock, and consumed the flesh and the unleavened cakes. Then the angel of the LORD departed out of his sight.

22 And when Gideon ᴿperceived that he *was* an angel of the LORD, Gideon said, Alas, O Lord GOD! ᴿfor because I have seen an angel of the LORD face to face.

23 And the LORD said unto him, ᴿPeace *be* unto thee; fear not: thou shalt not die.

24 Then Gideon built an altar there unto the LORD, and called it [N]Jĕ-hō'-văh-shā'-lŏm: unto this day it *is* yet [R]in ŏph'-răh of the Ā'-bĭ-ĕz'-rītes.

Gideon destroys altar of Baal

25 And it came to pass the same night, that the LORD said unto him, Take thy father's young bullock, [N]even the second bullock of seven years old, and throw down the altar of Bā'-ăl that thy father hath, and [R]cut down the grove that *is* by it:

26 And build an altar unto the LORD thy God upon the top of this [N]rock, [N]in the ordered place, and take the second bullock, and offer a burnt sacrifice with the wood of the grove which thou shalt cut down.

27 Then Gideon took ten men of his servants, and did as the LORD had said unto him: and *so* it was, because he feared his father's household, and the men of the city, that he could not do *it* by day, that he did *it* by night.

28 And when the men of the city arose early in the morning, behold, the altar of Bā'-ăl was cast down, and the grove was cut down that *was* by it, and the second bullock was offered upon the altar *that was* built.

29 And they said one to another, Who hath done this thing? And when they inquired and asked, they said, Gideon the son of Jō'-ăsh hath done this thing.

30 Then the men of the city said unto Jō'-ăsh, Bring out thy son, that he may die: because he hath cast down the altar of Bā'-ăl, and because he hath cut down the grove that *was* by it.

31 And Jō'-ăsh said unto all that stood against him, Will ye plead for Bā'-ăl? will ye save him? he that will plead for him, let him be put to death whilst *it is yet* morning: if he *be* a god, let him plead for himself, because *one* hath cast down his altar.

32 Therefore on that day he called him [R]Jĕr-ŭb-bā'-ăl,[N] saying, Let Bā'-ăl plead against him, because he hath thrown down his altar.

33 Then all [R]the Mĭd'-ĭ-ă-nītes and the Ă-măl'-ĕk-ites and the children of the east were gathered together, and went over, and pitched in [R]the valley of Jĕz'-rêĕl.

34 But [R]the spirit of the LORD [N]came upon Gideon, and he [R]blew a trumpet; and Ā'-bĭ-ē'-zĕr [N]was gathered after him.

35 And he sent messengers throughout all Mă-năs'-sĕh; who also was gathered after him: and he sent messengers unto Asher, and unto Zĕ-bū'-lŭn, and unto Năph'-tă-lī; and they came up to meet them.

CHAP. 6
BC 1249
24 i.e. *The LORD send peace:* See
Gen. 22:14
Ex. 17:15
Jer. 33:16
Ezek. 48:35
24 ch. 8:32
25 Or, *and*
25 Ex. 34:13
Deut. 7:5
26 Heb. *strong place*
26 Or, *in an orderly manner*
32 1 Sam. 12:11
2 Sam. 11:21
Jerubbesheth;
i.e. *Let the shameful thing plead:* See Jer. 11:13
Hos. 9:10
32 i.e. *Let Baal plead*
33 ver. 3
33 Josh. 17:16
34 ch. 3:10
1 Chr. 12:18
2 Chr. 24:20
34 Heb. *clothed*
34 Num. 10:3
ch. 3:27
34 Heb. *was called after him*

See Ex. 4:3-7   37
Gen. 18:32   39

CHAP. 7
BC 1249
ch. 6:32   1
Deut. 8:17   2
1 Cor. 1:29
Deut. 20:8   3

Sign of the fleece

36 And Gideon said unto God, If thou wilt save Israel by mine hand, as thou hast said,

37 [R]Behold, I will put a fleece of wool in the floor; *and* if the dew be on the fleece only, and *it be* dry upon all the earth *beside,* then shall I know that thou wilt save Israel by mine hand, as thou hast said.

38 And it was so: for he rose up early on the morrow, and thrust the fleece together, and wringed the dew out of the fleece, a bowl full of water.

39 And Gideon said unto God, [R]Let not thine anger be hot against me, and I will speak but this once: let me prove, I pray thee, but this once with the fleece; let it now be dry only upon the fleece, and upon all the ground let there be dew.

40 And God did so that night: for it was dry upon the fleece only, and there was dew on all the ground.

CHAPTER 7

Gideon's three hundred

THEN [R]Jĕr-ŭb-bā'-ăl, who *is* Gideon, and all the people that *were* with him, rose up early, and pitched beside the well of Hâr'-ŏd: so that the host of the Mĭd'-ĭ-ă-nītes were on the north side of them, by the hill of Mō'-rēh, in the valley.

2 And the LORD said unto Gideon, The people that *are* with thee *are* too many for me to give the Mĭd'-ĭ-ă-nītes into their hands, lest Israel [R]vaunt themselves against me, saying, Mine own hand hath saved me.

3 Now therefore go to, proclaim in the ears of the people, saying, [R]Whosoever *is* fearful and afraid, let him return and depart early from mount Gilead. And there returned of the people twenty and two thousand; and there remained ten thousand.

4 And the LORD said unto Gideon, The people *are* yet *too* many; bring them down unto the water, and I will try them for thee there: and it shall be, *that* of whom I say unto thee, This shall go with thee, the same shall go with thee; and of whomsoever I say unto thee, This shall not go with thee, the same shall not go.

5 So he brought down the people unto the water: and the LORD said unto Gideon, Every one that lappeth of the water with his tongue, as a dog lappeth, him shalt thou set by himself; likewise every one that boweth down upon his knees to drink.

6 And the number of them that lapped, *put-*

ting their hand to their mouth, were three hundred men: but all the rest of the people bowed down upon their knees to drink water.

7 And the Lord said unto Gideon, ᴿBy the three hundred men that lapped will I save you, and deliver the Mĭd′-ĭ-ă-nītes into thine hand: and let all the *other* people go every man unto his place.

8 So the people took victuals in their hand, and their trumpets: and he sent all *the rest of* Israel every man unto his tent, and retained those three hundred men: and the host of Mĭd′-ĭ-ăn was beneath him in the valley.

Prophecy against Midian

9 And it came to pass the same ᴿnight, that the Lord said unto him, Arise, get thee down unto the host; for I have delivered it into thine hand.

10 But if thou fear to go down, go thou with Phū′-răh thy servant down to the host:

11 And thou shalt ᴿhear what they say; and afterward shall thine hands be strengthened to go down unto the host. Then went he down with Phū′-răh his servant unto the outside of the ᴺarmed men that *were* in the host.

12 And the Mĭd′-ĭ-ă-nītes and the Ă-măl′-ĕk-ītes and ᴿall the children of the east lay along in the valley like grasshoppers for multitude; and their camels *were* without number, as the sand by the sea side for multitude.

13 And when Gideon was come, behold, *there was* a man that told a dream unto his fellow, and said, Behold, I dreamed a dream, and, lo, a cake of barley bread tumbled into the host of Mĭd′-ĭ-ăn, and came unto a tent, and smote it that it fell, and overturned it, that the tent lay along.

14 And his fellow answered and said, This *is* nothing else save the sword of Gideon the son of Jō′-ăsh, a man of Israel: *for* into his hand hath God delivered Mĭd′-ĭ-ăn, and all the host.

15 And it was *so,* when Gideon heard the telling of the dream, and ᴺthe interpretation thereof, that he worshipped, and returned into the host of Israel, and said, Arise; for the Lord hath delivered into your hand the host of Mĭd′-ĭ-ăn.

The lamps and pitchers

16 And he divided the three hundred men *into* three companies, and he put ᴺa trumpet in every man's hand, with empty pitchers, and ᴺlamps within the pitchers.

17 And he said unto them, Look on me, and

CHAP. 7
BC 1249
7 1 Sam. 14:6
9 Gen. 46:2, 3
11 ver. 13-15
See Gen. 24:14
1 Sam. 14:9, 10
11 Or, *ranks by five,* Ex. 13:18
12 ch. 6:5, 33 & 8:10
15 Heb. *the breaking thereof*
16 Heb. *trumpets in the hand of all of them*
16 Or, *firebrands, or, torches*

Ex. 14:13, 14   21
2 Chr. 20:17
2 Ki. 7:7   21
Josh. 6:4, 16, 20 22
See 2 Cor. 4:7
Ps. 83:9   22
Is. 9:4
1 Sam. 14:20   22
2 Chr. 20:23
Or, *toward*   22
Heb. *lip*   22
ch. 3:27   24
ch. 3:28   24
John 1:28   24
ch. 8:3   25
Ps. 83:11
Is. 10:26   25
ch. 8:4   25

CHAP. 8
BC 1249
See ch. 12:1   1
2 Sam. 19:41
Heb. *What thing is this thou hast done unto us* 1
Heb. *strongly*   1

---

do likewise: and, behold, when I come to the outside of the camp, it shall be *that,* as I do, so shall ye do.

18 When I blow with a trumpet, I and all that *are* with me, then blow ye the trumpets also on every side of all the camp, and say, *The sword* of the Lord, and of Gideon.

Midianites routed

19 So Gideon, and the hundred men that *were* with him, came unto the outside of the camp in the beginning of the middle watch; and they had but newly set the watch: and they blew the trumpets, and brake the pitchers that *were* in their hands.

20 And the three companies blew the trumpets, and brake the pitchers, and held the lamps in their left hands, and the trumpets in their right hands to blow *withal:* and they cried, The sword of the Lord, and of Gideon.

21 And they ᴿstood every man in his place round about the camp: ᴿand all the host ran, and cried, and fled.

22 And the three hundred ᴿblew the trumpets, and ᴿthe Lord set ᴿevery man's sword against his fellow, even throughout all the host: and the host fled to Bĕth-shĭt′-tăh ᴺin Zĕr′-ĕ-răth, *and* to the ᴺborder of Ā′-bĕl-mĕ-hō′-läh, unto Tăb′-băth.

23 And the men of Israel gathered themselves together out of Năph′-tă-lī, and out of Asher, and out of all Mă-năs′-sēh, and pursued after the Mĭd′-ĭ-ă-nītes.

24 And Gideon sent messengers throughout all ᴿmount Ē′-phră-ĭm, saying, Come down against the Mĭd′-ĭ-ă-nītes, and take before them the waters unto Bĕth-băr′-äh and Jordan. Then all the men of Ē′-phră-ĭm gathered themselves together, and ᴿtook the waters unto ᴿBĕth-băr′-äh and Jordan.

25 And they took ᴿtwo princes of the Mĭd′-ĭ-ă-nītes, ôr′-ĕb and Zēĕb; and they slew ôr′-ĕb upon ᴿthe rock ôr′-ĕb, and Zēĕb they slew at the winepress of Zēĕb, and pursued Mĭd′-ĭ-ăn, and brought the heads of ôr′-ĕb and Zēĕb to Gideon on the ᴿother side Jordan.

CHAPTER 8

Succoth and Penuel refuse to aid Gideon

AND ᴿthe men of Ē′-phră-ĭm said unto him, ᴺWhy hast thou served us thus, that thou calledst us not, when thou wentest to fight with the Mĭd′-ĭ-ă-nītes? And they did chide with him ᴺsharply.

2 And he said unto them, What have I done

now in comparison of you? *Is* not the gleaning of the grapes of Ē'-phră-ĭm better than the vintage of Ā'-bĭ-ē'-zĕr?

3 ᴿGod hath delivered into your hands the princes of Mĭd'-ĭ-ăn, ŏr'-ĕb and Zēeb: and what was I able to do in comparison of you? Then their ᴿangerᴺ was abated toward him, when he had said that.

4 And Gideon came to Jordan, *and* passed over, he, and the three hundred men that *were* with him, faint, yet pursuing *them.*

5 And he said unto the men of ᴿSŭc'-cŏth, Give, I pray you, loaves of bread unto the people that follow me; for they *be* faint, and I am pursuing after Zē'-bäh and Zăl-mŭn'-nă, kings of Mĭd'-ĭ-ăn.

6 And the princes of Sŭc'-cŏth said, ᴿ*Are* the hands of Zē'-bäh and Zăl-mŭn'-nă now in thine hand, that ᴿwe should give bread unto thine army?

7 And Gideon said, Therefore when the LORD hath delivered Zē'-bäh and Zăl-mŭn'-nă into mine hand, ᴿthen I will ᴺtear your flesh with the thorns of the wilderness and with briers.

8 And he went up thence ᴿto Pĕn'-ū-ĕl, and spake unto them likewise: and the men of Pĕn'-ū-ĕl answered him as the men of Sŭc'-cŏth had answered *him.*

9 And he spake also unto the men of Pĕn'-ū-ĕl, saying, When I ᴿcome again in peace, ᴿI will break down this tower.

Final victory over Midian

10 Now Zē'-bäh and Zăl-mŭn'-nă *were* in Kär'-kôr, and their hosts with them, about fifteen thousand *men,* all that were left of ᴿall the hosts of the children of the east: for there fell ᴺan hundred and twenty thousand men that drew sword.

11 And Gideon went up by the way of them that dwelt in tents on the east of ᴿNō'-bäh and Jŏg'-bĕ-häh, and smote the host: for the host was ᴿsecure.

12 And when Zē'-bäh and Zăl-mŭn'-nă fled, he pursued after them, and ᴿtook the two kings of Mĭd'-ĭ-ăn, Zē'-bäh and Zăl-mŭn'-nă, and ᴺdiscomfited all the host.

13 And Gideon the son of Jō'-ăsh returned from battle before the sun *was up,*

14 And caught a young man of the men of Sŭc'-cŏth, and inquired of him: and he ᴺdescribed unto him the princes of Sŭc'-cŏth, and the elders thereof, *even* three score and seventeen men.

15 And he came unto the men of Sŭc'-cŏth, and said, Behold Zē'-bäh and Zăl-mŭn'-nă,

CHAP. 8	
BC 1249	
3 ch. 7:24, 25	
Phil. 2:3	
3 Prov. 15:1	
3 Heb. *spirit*	
5 Gen. 33:17	
Ps. 60:6	
6 See 1 Ki. 20:11	
6 See 1 Sam. 25:11	
7 ver. 16	
7 Heb. *thresh*	
8 Gen. 32:30	
1 Ki. 12:25	
9 1 Ki. 22:27	
9 ver. 17	
10 ch. 7:12	
10 Or, *an hundred and twenty thousand, every one drawing a sword*	
ch. 20:2, 15, 17, 25	
2 Ki. 3:26	
11 Num. 32:35, 42	
11 ch. 18:27	
1 Thes. 5:3	
12 Ps. 83:11	
12 Heb. *terrified*	
14 Heb. *writ*	

ver. 6	**15**
ver. 7	**16**
Heb. *made to know*	**16**
ver. 9	**17**
1 Ki. 12:25	**17**
ch. 4:6	**18**
Ps. 89:12	
Heb. *according to the form, etc.*	**18**
Ps. 83:11	**21**
Or, *ornaments like the moon*	**21**
1 Sam. 8:7 & 10:19 & 12:12	**23**
Gen. 24:13 & 37:25, 28	**24**
Or, *sweet jewels*	**26**
ch. 17:5	**27**
ch. 6:24	**27**
Ps. 106:39	**27**
Deut. 7:16	**27**

with whom ye did ᴿupbraid me, saying, *Are* the hands of Zē'-bäh and Zăl-mŭn'-nă now in thine hand, that we should give bread unto thy men *that are* weary?

16 ᴿAnd he took the elders of the city, and thorns of the wilderness and briers, and with them he ᴺtaught the men of Sŭc'-cŏth.

17 ᴿAnd he beat down the tower of ᴿPĕn'-ū-ĕl, and slew the men of the city.

18 Then said he unto Zē'-bäh and Zăl-mŭn'-nă, What manner of men *were they* whom ye slew at ᴿTā'-bôr? And they answered, As thou *art,* so *were* they; each one ᴺresembled the children of a king.

19 And he said, They *were* my brethren, *even* the sons of my mother: *as* the LORD liveth, if ye had saved them alive, I would not slay you.

20 And he said unto Jē'-thĕr his firstborn, Up, *and* slay them. But the youth drew not his sword: for he feared, because he *was* yet a youth.

21 Then Zē'-bäh and Zăl-mŭn'-nă said, Rise thou, and fall upon us: for as the man *is,* so is his strength. And Gideon arose, and ᴿslew Zē'-bäh and Zăl-mŭn'-nă, and took away the ᴺornaments that *were* on their camels' necks.

Gideon refuses kingship

22 Then the men of Israel said unto Gideon, Rule thou over us, both thou, and thy son, and thy son's son also: for thou hast delivered us from the hand of Mĭd'-ĭ-ăn.

23 And Gideon said unto them, I will not rule over you, neither shall my son rule over you: ᴿthe LORD shall rule over you.

24 And Gideon said unto them, I would desire a request of you, that ye would give me every man the earrings of his prey. (For they had golden earrings, ᴿbecause they *were* Ĭsh'-mā-ĕ-lītes.)

25 And they answered, We will willingly give *them.* And they spread a garment, and did cast therein every man the earrings of his prey.

26 And the weight of the golden earrings that he requested was a thousand and seven hundred *shē'-kĕls* of gold; beside ornaments, and ᴺcollars, and purple raiment that *was* on the kings of Mĭd'-ĭ-ăn, and beside the chains that *were* about their camels' necks.

27 And Gideon ᴿmade an ē'-phŏd thereof, and put it in his city, *even* ᴿin ŏph'-răh: and all Israel ᴿwent thither a whoring after it: which thing became ᴿa snare unto Gideon, and to his house.

28 Thus was Mĭd'-ĭ-ăn subdued before the children of Israel, so that they lifted up their

heads no more. ᴿAnd the country was in quietness forty years in the days of Gideon.

Death of Gideon

29 And Jĕr-ŭb-bā′-ăl the son of Jō′-ăsh went and dwelt in his own house.

30 And Gideon had ᴿthreescore and ten sons ᴺof his body begotten: for he had many wives.

31 ᴿAnd his concubine that *was* in Shē′-chĕm, she also bare him a son, whose name he ᴺcalled Ă-bĭm′-ĕ-lĕch.

32 And Gideon the son of Jō′-ăsh died ᴿin a good old age, and was buried in the sepulchre of Jō′-ăsh his father, ᴿin ŏph′-răh of the Ā′-bī-ĕz′-rītes.

33 And it came to pass, ᴿas soon as Gideon was dead, that the children of Israel turned again, and ᴿwent a whoring after Bā′-ă-lĭm, ᴿand made Bā′-ăl-bē′-rĭth their God.

34 And the children of Israel ᴿremembered not the Lᴏʀᴅ their God, who had delivered them out of the hands of all their enemies on every side:

35 ᴿNeither shewed they kindness to the house of Jĕr-ŭb-bā′-ăl, *namely,* Gideon, according to all the goodness which he had shewed unto Israel.

CHAPTER 9

Abimelech made king

AND Ă-bĭm′-ĕ-lĕch the son of Jĕr-ŭb-bā′-ăl went to Shē′-chĕm unto ᴿhis mother's brethren, and communed with them, and with all the family of the house of his mother's father, saying,

2 Speak, I pray you, in the ears of all the men of Shē′-chĕm, ᴺWhether *is* better for you, either that all the sons of Jĕr-ŭb-bā′-ăl, *which are* ᴿthreescore and ten persons, reign over you, or that one reign over you? remember also that I *am* ᴿyour bone and your flesh.

3 And his mother's brethren spake of him in the ears of all the men of Shē′-chĕm all these words: and their hearts inclined ᴺto follow Ă-bĭm′-ĕ-lĕch; for they said, He *is* our ᴿbrother.

4 And they gave him threescore and ten *pieces* of silver out of the house of ᴿBā′-ăl-bē′-rĭth, wherewith Ă-bĭm′-ĕ-lĕch hired ᴿvain and light persons, which followed him.

5 And he went unto his father's house ᴿat ŏph′-răh, and ᴿslew his brethren the sons of Jĕr-ŭb-bā′-ăl, *being* threescore and ten persons, upon one stone: notwithstanding yet Jō′-thăm the youngest son of Jĕr-ŭb-bā′-ăl was left; for he hid himself.

6 And all the men of Shē′-chĕm gathered

together, and all the house of Mĭl′-lō, and went, and made Ă-bĭm′-ĕ-lĕch king, ᴺby the plain of the pillar that *was* in Shē′-chĕm.

Jotham's parable

7 And when they told *it* to Jō′-thăm, he went and stood in the top of ᴿmount Gĕ-rī′-zĭm, and lifted up his voice, and cried, and said unto them, Hearken unto me, ye men of Shē′-chĕm, that God may hearken unto you.

8 ᴿThe trees went forth *on a time* to anoint a king over them; and they said unto the olive tree, ᴿReign thou over us.

9 But the olive tree said unto them, Should I leave my fatness, ᴿwherewith by me they honour God and man, and ᴺgo to be promoted over the trees?

10 And the trees said to the fig tree, Come thou, *and* reign over us.

11 But the fig tree said unto them, Should I forsake my sweetness, and my good fruit, and go to be promoted over the trees?

12 Then said the trees unto the vine, Come thou, *and* reign over us.

13 And the vine said unto them, Should I leave my wine, ᴿwhich cheereth God and man, and go to be promoted over the trees?

14 Then said all the trees unto the ᴺbramble, Come thou, *and* reign over us.

15 And the bramble said unto the trees, If in truth ye anoint me king over you, *then* come *and* put your trust in my ᴿshadow: and if not, ᴿlet fire come out of the bramble, and devour the ᴿcedars of Lĕb′-ă-nᴏn.

16 Now therefore, if ye have done truly and sincerely, in that ye have made Ă-bĭm′-ĕ-lĕch king, and if ye have dealt well with Jĕr-ŭb-bā′-ăl and his house, and have done unto him ᴿaccording to the deserving of his hands;

17 (For my father fought for you, and ᴺadventured his life far, and delivered you out of the hand of Mĭd′-ĭ-ăn:

18 ᴿAnd ye are risen up against my father's house this day, and have slain his sons, threescore and ten persons, upon one stone, and have made Ă-bĭm′-ĕ-lĕch, the son of his maidservant, king over the men of Shē′-chĕm, because he *is* your brother;)

19 If ye then have dealt truly and sincerely with Jĕr-ŭb-bā′-ăl and with his house this day, *then* ᴿrejoice ye in Ă-bĭm′-ĕ-lĕch, and let him also rejoice in you:

20 But if not, ᴿlet fire come out from Ă-bĭm′-ĕ-lĕch, and devour the men of Shē′-chĕm, and the house of Mĭl′-lō; and let fire come out from the men of Shē′-chĕm, and

CHAP. 8
BC 1249

28	ch. 5:31
30	ch. 9:2, 5
30	Heb. *going out of his thigh*
31	ch. 9:1
31	Heb. *set*
32	Gen. 25:8
	Job 5:26
32	ver. 27
	ch. 6:24
33	ch. 2:19
33	ch. 2:17
33	ch. 9:4, 46
34	Ps. 78:11, 42 & 106:13, 21
35	ch. 9:16-18
	Eccl. 9:14

CHAP. 9
BC 1209

1	ch. 8:31
2	Heb. *What is good? whether, etc.*
2	ch. 8:30
2	Gen. 29:14
3	Heb. *after*
3	Gen. 29:15
4	ch. 8:33
4	ch. 11:3
	2 Chr. 13:7
	Acts 17:5
5	ch. 6:24
5	2 Ki. 11:1, 2

Or, *by the oak of the pillar:* See Josh. 24:26	6
Deut. 11:29 & 27:12 Josh. 8:33 John 4:20	7
See 2 Ki. 14:9	8
ch. 8:22, 23	8
Ps. 104:15	9
Heb. *go up and down for* other trees	9
Ps. 104:15	13
Or, *thistle*	14
Is. 30:2 Dan. 4:12 Hos. 14:7	15
ver. 20 Num. 21:28 Ezek. 19:14	15
2 Ki. 14:9 Is. 2:13 & 37:34 Ezek. 31:3	15
ch. 8:35	16
Heb. *cast his life*	17
ver. 5, 6	18
Is. 8:6	19
Phil. 3:3	
ver. 15, 56, 57	20

from the house of Mĭl′-lō, and devour Ă-bĭm′-ĕ-lĕch.

21 And Jō′-thăm ran away, and fled, and went to ᴿBēĕr, and dwelt there, for fear of Ă-bĭm′-ĕ-lĕch his brother.

Shechem's rebellion

22 When Ă-bĭm′-ĕ-lĕch had reigned three years over Israel,

23 Then ᴿGod sent an evil spirit between Ă-bĭm′-ĕ-lĕch and the men of Shē′-chĕm; and the men of Shē′-chĕm ᴿdealt treacherously with Ă-bĭm′-ĕ-lĕch:

24 ᴿThat the cruelty *done* to the threescore and ten sons of Jĕr-ŭb-bā′-al might come, and their blood be laid upon Ă-bĭm′-ĕ-lĕch their brother, which slew them; and upon the men of Shē′-chĕm, which ᴺaided him in the killing of his brethren.

25 And the men of Shē′-chĕm set liers in wait for him in the top of the mountains, and they robbed all that came along that way by them: and it was told Ă-bĭm′-ĕ-lĕch.

26 And Gā′-ăl the son of Ē′-bĕd came with his brethren, and went over to Shē′-chĕm: and the men of Shē′-chĕm put their confidence in him.

27 And they went out into the fields, and gathered their vineyards, and trode *the grapes,* and made ᴺmerry, and went into ᴿthe house of their god, and did eat and drink, and cursed Ă-bĭm′-ĕ-lĕch.

28 And Gā′-ăl the son of Ē′-bĕd said, ᴿWho *is* Ă-bĭm′-ĕ-lĕch, and who *is* Shē′-chĕm, that we should serve him? *is* not *he* the son of Jĕr-ŭb-bā′-al? and Zē′-bŭl his officer? serve the men of ᴿHā′-môr the father of Shē′-chĕm: for why should we serve him?

29 And ᴿwould to God this people were under my hand! then would I remove Ă-bĭm′-ĕ-lĕch. And he said to Ă-bĭm′-ĕ-lĕch, Increase thine army, and come out.

30 And when Zē′-bŭl the ruler of the city heard the words of Gā′-ăl the son of Ē′-bĕd, his anger was ᴺkindled.

31 And he sent messengers unto Ă-bĭm′-ĕ-lĕch ᴺprivily, saying, Behold, Gā′-ăl the son of Ē′-bĕd and his brethren be come to Shē′-chĕm; and, behold, they fortify the city against thee.

32 Now therefore up by night, thou and the people that *is* with thee, and lie in wait in the field:

33 And it shall be, *that* in the morning, as soon as the sun is up, thou shalt rise early, and set upon the city: and, behold, *when* he and the people that *is* with him come out against

CHAP. 9
BC 1209
21 2 Sam. 20:14
23 1 Sam. 16:14
& 18:9, 10
See 1 Ki. 22:22
2 Chr. 18:22
Is. 19:14
23 Is. 33:1
24 1 Ki. 2:32
Esth. 9:25
Mat. 23:35, 36
24 Heb. *strengthened his hands to kill*
27 Or, *songs:* See Is. 16:9, 10
Jer. 25:30
27 ver. 4
28 1 Sam. 25:10
1 Ki. 12:16
28 Gen. 34:2, 6
29 2 Sam. 15:4
30 Or, *hot*
31 Heb. *craftily,* or, *to Tormah*

Heb. *as thine hand shall find*   33
Heb. *navel*   37
Or, *The regarders of times,* Deut. 18:14   37
ver. 28, 29   38
ver. 20   45
Deut. 29:23   45
1 Ki. 12:25
2 Ki. 3:25
ch. 8:33   46

thee, then mayest thou do to them ᴺas thou shalt find occasion.

Abimelech quells the revolt

34 And Ă-bĭm′-ĕ-lĕch rose up, and all the people that *were* with him, by night, and they laid wait against Shē′-chĕm in four companies.

35 And Gā′-ăl the son of Ē′-bĕd went out, and stood in the entering of the gate of the city: and Ă-bĭm′-ĕ-lĕch rose up, and the people that *were* with him, from lying in wait.

36 And when Gā′-ăl saw the people, he said to Zē′-bŭl, Behold, there come people down from the top of the mountains. And Zē′-bŭl said unto him, Thou seest the shadow of the mountains as *if they were* men.

37 And Gā′-ăl spake again and said, See there come people down by the ᴺmiddle of the land, and another company come along by the plain of ᴺMē-ō′-nĕ-nĭm.

38 Then said Zē′-bŭl unto him, Where *is* now thy mouth, wherewith thou ᴿsaidst, Who *is* Ă-bĭm′-ĕ-lĕch, that we should serve him? *is* not this the people that thou hast despised? go out, I pray now, and fight with them.

39 And Gā′-ăl went out before the men of Shē′-chĕm, and fought with Ă-bĭm′-ĕ-lĕch.

40 And Ă-bĭm′-ĕ-lĕch chased him, and he fled before him, and many were overthrown *and* wounded, *even* unto the entering of the gate.

41 And Ă-bĭm′-ĕ-lĕch dwelt at Ă-rū′-măh: and Zē′-bŭl thrust out Gā′-ăl and his brethren, that they should not dwell in Shē′-chĕm.

42 And it came to pass on the morrow, that the people went out into the field; and they told Ă-bĭm′-ĕ-lĕch.

43 And he took the people, and divided them into three companies, and laid wait in the field, and looked, and, behold, the people *were* come forth out of the city; and he rose up against them, and smote them.

44 And Ă-bĭm′-ĕ-lĕch, and the company that *was* with him, rushed forward, and stood in the entering of the gate of the city: and the two *other* companies ran upon all *the people* that *were* in the fields, and slew them.

45 And Ă-bĭm′-ĕ-lĕch fought against the city all that day; and ᴿhe took the city, and slew the people that *was* therein, and ᴿbeat down the city, and sowed it with salt.

Tower of Shechem destroyed

46 And when all the men of the tower of Shē′-chĕm heard *that,* they entered into an hold of the house ᴿof the god Bē′-rĭth.

47 And it was told Ă-bĭm′-ĕ-lĕch, that all the

men of the tower of Shē'-chĕm were gathered together.

48 And Ă-bīm'-ĕ-lĕch gat him up to mount ᴿZăl'-mŏn, he and all the people that *were* with him; and Ă-bīm'-ĕ-lĕch took an axe in his hand, and cut down a bough from the trees, and took it, and laid *it* on his shoulder, and said unto the people that *were* with him, What ye have seen ᴺme do, make haste, *and* do as I *have done.*

49 And all the people likewise cut down every man his bough, and followed Ă-bīm'-ĕ-lĕch, and put *them* to the hold, and set the hold on fire upon them; so that all the men of the tower of Shē'-chĕm died also, about a thousand men and women.

Abimelech killed

50 Then went Ă-bīm'-ĕ-lĕch to Thē'-bĕz, and encamped against Thē'-bĕz, and took it.

51 But there was a strong tower within the city, and thither fled all the men and women, and all they of the city, and shut *it* to them, and gat them up to the top of the tower.

52 And Ă-bīm'-ĕ-lĕch came unto the tower, and fought against it, and went hard unto the door of the tower to burn it with fire.

53 And a certain woman ᴿcast a piece of a millstone upon Ă-bīm'-ĕ-lĕch's head, and all to brake his skull.

54 Then ᴿhe called hastily unto the young man his armourbearer, and said unto him, Draw thy sword, and slay me, that men say not of me, A woman slew him. And his young man thrust him through, and he died.

55 And when the men of Israel saw that Ă-bīm'-ĕ-lĕch was dead, they departed every man unto his place.

56 ᴿThus God rendered the wickedness of Ă-bīm'-ĕ-lĕch, which he did unto his father, in slaying his seventy brethren:

57 And all the evil of the men of Shē'-chĕm did God render upon their heads: and upon them came ᴿthe curse of Jō'-thăm the son of Jĕr-ŭb-bā'-ăl.

CHAPTER 10

Judgeship of Tola

AND after Ă-bīm'-ĕ-lĕch there ᴿarose to ᴺᴺdefend Israel Tō'-lă the son of Pū'-ăh, the son of Dodo, a man of Ĭs'-să-chär; and he dwelt in Shā'-mĭr in mount Ē'-phră-ĭm.

2 And he judged Israel twenty and three years, and died, and was buried in Shā'-mĭr.

Judgeship of Jair

3 And after him arose Jā'-ĭr, a Gileadite, and judged Israel twenty and two years.

4 And he had thirty sons that ᴿrode on thirty ass colts, and they had thirty cities, ᴿwhich are called ᴺHā'-vōth-jā'-ĭr unto this day, which *are* in the land of Gilead.

5 And Jā'-ĭr died, and was buried in Cā'-mŏn.

Israel's apostasy and oppression

6 And ᴿthe children of Israel did evil again in the sight of the LORD, and ᴿserved Bā'-ă-lĭm, and Ăsh'-tă-rŏth, and ᴿthe gods of Syria, and the gods of ᴿZĭ'-dŏn, and the gods of Moab, and the gods of the children of Am-mon, and the gods of the Philistines, and for-sook the LORD, and served not him.

7 And the anger of the LORD was hot against Israel, and he ᴿsold them into the hands of the Philistines, and into the hands of the children of Ammon.

8 And that year they vexed and ᴺoppressed the children of Israel: eighteen years, all the children of Israel that *were* on the other side Jordan in the land of the Amorites, which *is* in Gilead.

9 Moreover the children of Ammon passed over Jordan to fight also against Judah, and against Benjamin, and against the house of Ē'-phră-ĭm; so that Israel was sore distressed.

10 ᴿAnd the children of Israel cried unto the LORD, saying, We have sinned against thee, both because we have forsaken our God, and also served Bā'-ă-lĭm.

11 And the LORD said unto the children of Israel, *Did* not *I deliver you* ᴿfrom the Egyptians, and ᴿfrom the Amorites, ᴿfrom the children of Ammon, ᴿand from the Philistines?

12 ᴿThe Zĭ-dō'-nĭ-ăns also, ᴿand the Ă-măl'-ĕk-ītes, and the Mā'-ŏn-ītes, ᴿdid oppress you; and ye cried to me, and I delivered you out of their hand.

13 ᴿYet ye have forsaken me, and served other gods: wherefore I will deliver you no more.

14 Go and ᴿcry unto the gods which ye have chosen; let them deliver you in the time of your tribulation.

15 And the children of Israel said unto the LORD, We have sinned: ᴿdo thou unto us whatsoever ᴺseemeth good unto thee; deliver us only, we pray thee, this day.

16 ᴿAnd they put away the ᴺstrange gods from among them, and served the LORD: and ᴿhis soul ᴺwas grieved for the misery of Is-rael.

17 Then the children of Ammon were ᴺgathered together, and encamped in Gilead. And the children of Israel assembled them-selves together, and encamped in ᴿMĭz'-pĕh.

18 And the people *and* princes of Gilead said one to another, What man *is he* that will begin to fight against the children of Ammon? he shall ᴿbe head over all the inhabitants of Gilead.

CHAPTER 11

Jephthah made judge

NOW ᴿJĕph′-thăh the Gileadite was ᴿa mighty man of valour, and he *was* the son of ᴺan harlot: and Gilead begat Jĕph′-thăh.

2 And Gilead's wife bare him sons; and his wife's sons grew up, and they thrust out Jĕph′-thăh, and said unto him, Thou shalt not inherit in our father's house; for thou *art* the son of a strange woman.

3 Then Jĕph′-thăh fled ᴺfrom his brethren, and dwelt in the land of Tŏb: and there were gathered ᴿvain men to Jĕph′-thăh, and went out with him.

4 And it came to pass ᴺin process of time, that the children of Ammon made war against Israel.

5 And it was so, that when the children of Ammon made war against Israel, the elders of Gilead went to fetch Jĕph′-thăh out of the land of Tŏb:

6 And they said unto Jĕph′-thăh, Come, and be our captain, that we may fight with the children of Ammon.

7 And Jĕph′-thăh said unto the elders of Gilead, ᴿDid not ye hate me, and expel me out of my father's house? and why are ye come unto me now when ye are in distress?

8 ᴿAnd the elders of Gilead said unto Jĕph′-thăh, Therefore we ᴿturn again to thee now, that thou mayest go with us, and fight against the children of Ammon, and be ᴿour head over all the inhabitants of Gilead.

9 And Jĕph′-thăh said unto the elders of Gilead, If ye bring me home again to fight against the children of Ammon, and the LORD deliver them before me, shall I be your head?

10 And the elders of Gilead said unto Jĕph′-thăh, ᴿThe LORD ᴺbe witness between us, if we do not so according to thy words.

11 Then Jĕph′-thăh went with the elders of Gilead, and the people made him ᴿhead and captain over them: and Jĕph′-thăh uttered all his words ᴿbefore the LORD in Mīz′-pēh.

Jephthah's message to the Ammonites

12 And Jĕph′-thăh sent messengers unto the king of the children of Ammon, saying, What hast thou to do with me, that thou art come against me to fight in my land?

13 And the king of the children of Ammon

Center reference column

CHAP. **10**
BC 1206
18 ch. 11:8, 11

CHAP. **11**
BC 1161
1 Heb. 11:32, called *Jephthae*
1 ch. 6:12
2 Ki. 5:1
1 Heb. *a woman an harlot*
3 Heb. *from the face*
3 ch. 9:4
1 Sam. 22:2
4 Heb. *after days*
7 Gen. 26:27
8 ch. 10:18
8 Luke 17:4
8 ch. 10:18
10 Jer. 42:5
10 Heb. *be the hearer between us*
11 ver. 8
11 ch. 10:17 & 20:1
1 Sam. 10:17 & 11:15

Num. 21:24-26	13
Gen. 32:22	13
Deut. 2:9, 19	15
Num. 13:26 & 20:1	16
Deut. 1:46	
Num. 20:14	17
Num. 20:18, 21	17
Num. 20:1	17
Num. 21:4	18
Deut. 2:1-8	
Num. 21:11	18
Num. 21:13 & 22:36	18
Num. 21:21	19
Deut. 2:26	
Num. 21:22	19
Deut. 2:27	
Num. 21:23	20
Deut. 2:32	
Num. 21:24, 25	21
Deut. 2:33, 34	
Deut. 2:36	22
Num. 21:29	24
1 Ki. 11:7	
Jer. 48:7	
Deut. 9:4, 5 & 18:12	24
Josh. 3:10	
Num. 22:2	25
See Josh. 24:9	
Num. 21:25	26
Deut. 2:36	26

answered unto the messengers of Jĕph′-thăh, ᴿBecause Israel took away my land, when they came up out of Egypt, from Arnon even unto ᴿJăb′-bŏk, and unto Jordan: now therefore restore those *lands* again peaceably.

14 And Jĕph′-thăh sent messengers again unto the king of the children of Ammon:

15 And said unto him, Thus saith Jĕph′-thăh, ᴿIsrael took not away the land of Moab, nor the land of the children of Ammon:

16 But when Israel came up from Egypt, and walked through the wilderness unto the Red sea, and ᴿcame to Kā′-dĕsh;

17 Then ᴿIsrael sent messengers unto the king of Ē′-dŏm, saying, Let me, I pray thee, pass through thy land: ᴿbut the king of Ē′-dŏm would not hearken *thereto*. And in like manner they sent unto the king of Moab: but he would not *consent:* and Israel ᴿabode in Kā′-dĕsh.

18 Then they went along through the wilderness, and ᴿcompassed the land of Ē′-dŏm, and the land of Moab, and ᴿcame by the east side of the land of Moab, ᴿand pitched on the other side of Arnon, but came not within the border of Moab: for Arnon *was* the border of Moab.

19 And ᴿIsrael sent messengers unto Sī′-hŏn king of the Amorites, the king of Hĕsh′-bŏn; and Israel said unto him, ᴿLet us pass, we pray thee, through thy land into my place.

20 ᴿBut Sī′-hŏn trusted not Israel to pass through his coast: but Sī′-hŏn gathered all his people together, and pitched in Jā′-hăz, and fought against Israel.

21 And the LORD God of Israel delivered Sī′-hŏn and all his people into the hand of Israel, and they ᴿsmote them: so Israel possessed all the land of the Amorites, the inhabitants of that country.

22 And they possessed ᴿall the coasts of the Amorites, from Arnon even unto Jăb′-bŏk, and from the wilderness even unto Jordan.

23 So now the LORD God of Israel hath dispossessed the Amorites from before his people Israel, and shouldest thou possess it?

24 Wilt not thou possess that which ᴿChĕ′-mŏsh thy god giveth thee to possess? So whomsoever ᴿthe LORD our God shall drive out from before us, them will we possess.

25 And now *art* thou any thing better than ᴿBalak the son of Zĭp′-pôr, king of Moab? did he ever strive against Israel, or did he ever fight against them,

26 While Israel dwelt in ᴿHĕsh′-bŏn and her towns, and in ᴿĂ-rō′-ĕr and her towns, and in all the cities that *be* along by the coasts of Arnon, three hundred years? why therefore did ye not recover *them* within that time?

27 Wherefore I have not sinned against thee, but thou doest me wrong to war against me: the LORD ᴿthe Judge ᴿbe judge this day between the children of Israel and the children of Ammon.

28 Howbeit the king of the children of Ammon hearkened not unto the words of Jĕph′-thăh which he sent him.

Jephthah's vow

29 Then ᴿthe spirit of the LORD came upon ᴺJĕph′-thăh, and he passed over Gilead, and Mă-năs′-sēh, and passed over Mĭz′-pēh of Gilead, and from Mĭz′-pēh of Gilead he passed over *unto* the children of Ammon.

30 And Jĕph′-thăh ᴿvowed a vow unto the LORD, and said, If thou shalt without fail deliver the children of Ammon into mine hands,

31 Then it shall be, that ᴺwhatsoever cometh forth of the doors of my house to meet me, when I return in peace from the children of Ammon, ᴿshall surely be the LORD's, ᴿandᴺ I will offer it up for a burnt offering.

32 So Jĕph′-thăh passed over unto the children of Ammon to fight against them; and the LORD delivered them into his hands.

33 And he smote them from Ă-rō′-ĕr, even till thou come to ᴿMĭn′-nĭth, *even* twenty cities, and unto ᴺthe plain of the vineyards, with a very great slaughter. Thus the children of Ammon were subdued before the children of Israel.

Jephthah's daughter sacrificed

34 And Jĕph′-thăh came to ᴿMĭz′-pēh unto his house, and, behold, ᴿhis daughter came out to meet him with timbrels and with dances: and she *was his* only child; ᴺᴺbeside her he had neither son nor daughter.

35 And it came to pass, when he saw her, that he ᴿrent his clothes, and said, Alas, my daughter! thou hast brought me very low, and thou art one of them that trouble me: for I ᴿhave opened my mouth unto the LORD, and ᴿI cannot go back.

36 And she said unto him, My father, *if* thou hast opened thy mouth unto the LORD, ᴿdo to me according to that which hath proceeded out of thy mouth; forasmuch as ᴿthe LORD hath taken vengeance for thee of thine enemies, *even* of the children of Ammon.

37 And she said unto her father, Let this thing be done for me: let me alone two months, that I may ᴺgo up and down upon the mountains, and bewail my virginity, I and my fellows.

38 And he said, Go. And he sent her away *for* two months: and she went with her com-

panions, and bewailed her virginity upon the mountains.

39 And it came to pass at the end of two months, that she returned unto her father, who ᴿdid with her *according* to his vow which he had vowed: and she knew no man. And it was a ᴺcustom in Israel,

40 *That* the daughters of Israel went ᴺyearly ᴺto lament the daughter of Jĕph′-thăh the Gileadite four days in a year.

CHAPTER 12

Ephraim and Jephthah fight

AND ᴿthe men of Ē′-phră-ĭm ᴺgathered themselves together, and went northward, and said unto Jĕph′-thăh, Wherefore passedst thou over to fight against the children of Ammon, and didst not call us to go with thee? we will burn thine house upon thee with fire.

2 And Jĕph′-thăh said unto them, I and my people were at great strife with the children of Ammon; and when I called you, ye delivered me not out of their hands.

3 And when I saw that ye delivered *me* not, I ᴿput my life in my hands, and passed over against the children of Ammon, and the LORD delivered them into my hand: wherefore then are ye come up unto me this day, to fight against me?

4 Then Jĕph′-thăh gathered together all the men of Gilead, and fought with Ē′-phră-ĭm: and the men of Gilead smote Ē′-phră-ĭm, because they said, Ye Gileadites ᴿ*are* fugitives of Ē′-phră-ĭm among the Ē′-phră-ĭm-ītes, *and* among the Mă-năs′-sītes.

5 And the Gileadites took the ᴿpassages of Jordan before the Ē′-phră-ĭm-ītes: and it was *so,* that when those Ē′-phră-ĭm-ītes which were escaped said, Let me go over; that the men of Gilead said unto him, *Art* thou an Ē′-phră-ĭm-īte? If he said, Nay;

6 Then said they unto him, Say now ᴺShĭb′-bŏ-lĕth: and he said Sĭb′-bŏ-lĕth: for he could not frame to pronounce *it* right. Then they took him, and slew him at the passages of Jordan: and there fell at that time of the Ē′-phră-ĭm-ītes forty and two thousand.

7 And Jĕph′-thăh judged Israel six years. Then died Jĕph′-thăh the Gileadite, and was buried in *one of* the cities of Gilead.

Judgeship of Ibzan

8 And after him ᴺĬb′-zăn of Beth-lehem judged Israel.

9 And he had thirty sons, and thirty daughters, *whom* he sent abroad, and took in thirty

---

CHAP. 11

BC 1161

27 Gen. 18:25
27 Gen. 16:5 & 31:53
1 Sam. 24:12, 15
29 ch. 3:10
29 Jephthah seems to have been Judge only of North-east *Israel*
30 Gen. 28:20
31 Heb. *that which cometh forth, which shall come forth*
31 See 1 Sam. 1:11, 28
31 Ps. 66:13
31 Or, *or I will offer it, etc.*
33 Ezek. 27:17
33 Or, *Abel*
34 ver. 11 ch. 10:17
34 Ex. 15:20 Ps. 68:25 Jer. 31:4
34 Or, *he had not of his own either son or daughter*
34 Heb. *of himself*
35 Gen. 37:29, 34
35 Eccl. 5:2
35 Num. 30:2
36 Num. 30:2
36 2 Sam. 18:19, 31
37 Heb. *go and go down*

ver. 31   39
1 Sam. 1:22, 24
Or, *ordinance*   39
Heb. *from year   40 to year*
Or, *to talk with, 40 ch. 5:11*

CHAP. 12

BC 1143

See ch. 8:1   1
Heb. *were called*   1
1 Sam. 19:5   3
Ps. 119:109
See 1 Sam. 25:10   4
Josh. 22:11   5
ch. 3:28
Which signifieth   6
a stream, or, *flood*
He seems to have   8
been only a civil
Judge to do justice
in North-east
Israel

daughters from abroad for his sons. And he judged Israel seven years.

10 Then died ĭb'-zăn, and was buried at Beth-lehem.

Judgeship of Elon

11 And after him [N]Ē'-lŏn, a Zĕ-bū'-lŏn-ite, judged Israel; and he judged Israel ten years.

12 And Ē'-lŏn the Zĕ-bū'-lŏn-ite died, and was buried in Âi'-jă-lŏn in the country of Zĕ-bū'-lŭn.

Judgeship of Abdon

13 And after him [N]Abdon the son of Hĭl'-lĕl, a Pĭ-rā'-thŏn-ite, judged Israel.

14 And he had forty sons and thirty [N]nephews, that [R]rode on threescore and ten ass colts: and he judged Israel eight years.

15 And Abdon the son of Hĭl'-lĕl the Pĭ-rā'-thŏn-ite died, and was buried in Pĭ-rā'-thŏn in the land of Ē'-phră-ĭm, [R]in the mount of the Ă-măl'-ĕk-ĭtes.

CHAPTER 13

Oppression by the Philistines

AND the children of Israel [R]did[N] evil again in the sight of the LORD; [N]and the LORD delivered them [R]into the hand of the Philistines forty years.

Manoah and his wife promised a son

2 And there was a certain man of [R]Zôr'-ăh, of the family of the Danites, whose name was Mă-nō'-ăh; and his wife was barren, and bare not.

3 And the [R]angel of the LORD appeared unto the woman, and said unto her, Behold now, thou art barren, and bearest not: but thou shalt conceive, and bear a son.

4 Now therefore beware, I pray thee, and [R]drink not wine nor strong drink, and eat not any unclean thing:

5 For, lo, thou shalt conceive, and bear a son; and no [R]razor shall come on his head: for the child shall be [R]a Nazarite unto God from the womb: and he shall [R]begin to deliver Israel out of the hand of the Philistines.

6 Then the woman came and told her husband, saying, [R]A man of God came unto me, and his [R]countenance was like the countenance of an angel of God, very terrible: but I [R]asked him not whence he was, neither told he me his name:

7 But he said unto me, Behold, thou shalt conceive, and bear a son; and now drink no wine nor strong drink, neither eat any unclean thing: for the child shall be a Nazarite to God from the womb to the day of his death.

CHAP. 12
BC 1143
11 A civil Judge in North-east Israel
13 A civil Judge also in North-east Israel
14 Heb. sons' sons
14 ch. 5:10 & 10:4
15 ch. 3:13, 27 & 5:14

CHAP. 13
BC 1161
1 ch. 2:11 & 3:7 & 4:1 & 6:1 & 10:6
1 Heb. added to commit, etc.
1 This seems a partial captivity
1 1 Sam. 12:9
2 Josh. 19:41
3 ch. 6:12
Luke 1:11, 13, 28, 31
4 ver. 14
Num. 6:2, 3
Luke 1:15
5 Num. 6:5
1 Sam. 1:11
5 Num. 6:2
5 See 1 Sam. 7:13
2 Sam. 8:1
1 Chr. 18:1
6 Deut. 33:1
1 Sam. 2:27 & 9:6
6 Mat. 28:3
Luke 9:29
Acts 6:15
6 ver. 17, 18

Heb. What shall 12 be the manner of the, etc.
Or, what 12 shall he do?
Heb. what shall 12 be his work?
ver. 4 14
Gen. 18:5 15
ch. 6:18
Heb. before thee 15
Gen. 32:29 18
Or, wonderful, 18
Is. 9:6
ch. 6:19, 20 19
Lev. 9:24 20
1 Chr. 21:16
Ezek. 1:28
Mat. 17:6
ch. 6:22 21

8 Then Mă-nō'-ăh entreated the LORD, and said, O my Lord, let the man of God which thou didst send come again unto us, and teach us what we shall do unto the child that shall be born.

9 And God hearkened to the voice of Mă-nō'-ăh; and the angel of God came again unto the woman as she sat in the field: but Mă-nō'-ăh her husband was not with her.

10 And the woman made haste, and ran, and shewed her husband, and said unto him, Behold, the man hath appeared unto me, that came unto me the other day.

11 And Mă-nō'-ăh arose, and went after his wife, and came to the man, and said unto him, Art thou the man that spakest unto the woman? And he said, I am.

12 And Mă-nō'-ăh said, Now let thy words come to pass. [N]How shall we order the child, and [NN]how shall we do unto him?

13 And the angel of the LORD said unto Mă-nō'-ăh, Of all that I said unto the woman let her beware.

14 She may not eat of any thing that cometh of the vine, [R]neither let her drink wine or strong drink, nor eat any unclean thing: all that I commanded her let her observe.

Manoah's offering to the LORD

15 And Mă-nō'-ăh said unto the angel of the LORD, I pray thee, [R]let us detain thee, until we shall have made ready a kid [N]for thee.

16 And the angel of the LORD said unto Mă-nō'-ăh, Though thou detain me, I will not eat of thy bread: and if thou wilt offer a burnt offering, thou must offer it unto the LORD. For Mă-nō'-ăh knew not that he was an angel of the LORD.

17 And Mă-nō'-ăh said unto the angel of the LORD, What is thy name, that when thy sayings come to pass we may do thee honour?

18 And the angel of the LORD said unto him, [R]Why askest thou thus after my name, seeing it is [N]secret?

19 So Mă-nō'-ăh took a kid with a meat offering, [R]and offered it upon a rock unto the LORD: and the angel did wondrously; and Mă-nō'-ăh and his wife looked on.

20 For it came to pass, when the flame went up toward heaven from off the altar, that the angel of the LORD ascended in the flame of the altar. And Mă-nō'-ăh and his wife looked on it, and [R]fell on their faces to the ground.

Birth of Samson

21 But the angel of the LORD did no more appear to Mă-nō'-ăh and to his wife. [R]Then Mă-nō'-ăh knew that he was an angel of the LORD.

22 And Mă-nō'-ăh said unto his wife, ᴿWe shall surely die, because we have seen God.

23 But his wife said unto him, If the LORD were pleased to kill us, he would not have received a burnt offering and a meat offering at our hands, neither would he have shewed us all these *things,* nor would as at this time have told us *such things* as these.

24 And the woman bare a son, and called his name ᴿSamson: and ᴿthe child grew, and the LORD blessed him.

25 ᴿAnd the spirit of the LORD began to move him at times in ᴺthe camp of Dan ᴿbetween Zôr'-ăh and ĕsh'-tā-ŏl.

CHAPTER 14

Samson marries a woman of Timnath

AND Samson went down ᴿto Tĭm'-năth, and ᴿsaw a woman in Tĭm'-măth of the daughters of the Philistines.

2 And he came up, and told his father and his mother, and said, I have seen a woman in Tĭm'-năth of the daughters of the Philistines: now therefore ᴿget her for me to wife.

3 Then his father and his mother said unto him, *Is there* never a woman among the daughters of ᴿthy brethren, or among all my people, that thou goest to take a wife of the ᴿuncircumcised Philistines? And Samson said unto his father, Get her for me; for ᴺshe pleaseth me well.

4 But his father and his mother knew not that it *was* ᴿof the LORD, that he sought an occasion against the Philistines: for at that time ᴿthe Philistines had dominion over Israel.

5 Then went Samson down, and his father and his mother, to Tĭm'-năth, and came to the vineyards of Tĭm'-năth: and, behold, a young lion roared ᴺagainst him.

6 And ᴿthe spirit of the LORD came mightily upon him, and he rent him as he would have rent a kid, and *he had* nothing in his hand: but he told not his father or his mother what he had done.

7 And he went down, and talked with the woman; and she pleased Samson well.

8 And after a time he returned to take her, and he turned aside to see the carcase of the lion: and, behold, *there was* a swarm of bees and honey in the carcase of the lion.

9 And he took thereof in his hands, and went on eating, and came to his father and mother, and he gave them, and they did eat: but he told not them that he had taken the honey out of the carcase of the lion.

Samson's riddle

10 So his father went down unto the woman:

CHAP. 13
BC 1161
22 Gen. 32:30
Ex. 33:20
Deut. 5:26
ch. 6:22
24 Heb. 11:32
24 1 Sam. 3:19
Luke 1:80
& 2:52
25 ch. 3:10
1 Sam. 11:6
Mat. 4:1
25 Heb.
Mahanehdan,
as ch. 18:12
25 Josh. 15:33
ch. 18:11

CHAP. 14
BC 1141
1 Gen. 38:13
Josh. 15:10
1 Gen. 34:2
2 Gen. 21:21
& 34:4
3 Gen. 24:3, 4
3 Gen. 34:14
Ex. 34:16
Deut. 7:3
3 Heb. *she is right in mine eyes*
4 Josh. 11:20
1 Ki. 12:15
2 Ki. 6:33
2 Chr. 10:15
& 22:7 & 25:20
4 ch. 13:1
Deut. 28:48
5 Heb. *in meeting him*
6 ch. 3:10
& 13:25
1 Sam. 11:6

1 Ki. 10:1　　12
Ezek. 17:2
Luke 14:7
Gen. 29:27　　12
Or, *shirts*　　12
Gen. 45:22　　12
2 Ki. 5:22
ch. 16:5　　15
ch. 15:6　　15
Heb. *to possess us,* or, *to impoverish us?*　　15
ch. 16:15　　16
Or, *the rest of the seven days, etc.*　　17
ch. 3:10 & 13:25　　19
Or, *apparel*　　19
ch. 15:2　　20
John 3:29　　20

CHAP. 15
BC 1140
ch. 14:20　　2

---

and Samson made there a feast; for so used the young men to do.

11 And it came to pass, when they saw him, that they brought thirty companions to be with him.

12 And Samson said unto them, I will now ᴿput forth a riddle unto you: if ye can certainly declare it me ᴿwithin the seven days of the feast, and find *it* out, then I will give you thirty ᴺsheets and thirty ᴿchange of garments:

13 But if ye cannot declare *it* me, then shall ye give me thirty sheets and thirty change of garments. And they said unto him, Put forth thy riddle, that we may hear it.

14 And he said unto them, Out of the eater came forth meat, and out of the strong came forth sweetness. And they could not in three days expound the riddle.

15 And it came to pass on the seventh day, that they said unto Samson's wife, ᴿEntice thy husband, that he may declare unto us the riddle, ᴿlest we burn thee and thy father's house with fire: have ye called us ᴺto take that we have? *is it* not *so?*

16 And Samson's wife wept before him, and said, ᴿThou dost but hate me, and lovest me not: thou hast put forth a riddle unto the children of my people, and hast not told *it* me. And he said unto her, Behold, I have not told *it* my father nor my mother, and shall I tell *it* thee?

17 And she wept before him ᴺthe seven days, while their feast lasted: and it came to pass on the seventh day, that he told her, because she lay sore upon him: and she told the riddle to the children of her people.

18 And the men of the city said unto him on the seventh day before the sun went down, What *is* sweeter than honey? and what *is* stronger than a lion? And he said unto them, If ye had not plowed with my heifer, ye had not found out my riddle.

19 And ᴿthe spirit of the LORD came upon him, and he went down to Ăsh'-kĕ-lon, and slew thirty men of them, and took their ᴺspoil, and gave change of garments unto them which expounded the riddle. And his anger was kindled, and he went up to his father's house.

20 But Samson's wife ᴿwas *given* to his companion, whom he had used as ᴿhis friend.

CHAPTER 15

Samson burns Philistine fields

BUT it came to pass within a while after, in the time of wheat harvest, that Samson visited his wife with a kid; and he said, I will go in to my wife into the chamber. But her father would not suffer him to go in.

2 And her father said, I verily thought that thou hadst utterly ᴿhated her; therefore I gave

her to thy companion: *is* not her younger sister fairer than she? ᴺtake her, I pray thee, instead of her.

3 And Samson said concerning them, ᴺNow shall I be more blameless than the Philistines, though I do them a displeasure.

4 And Samson went and caught three hundred foxes, and took ᴺfirebrands, and turned tail to tail, and put a firebrand in the midst between two tails.

5 And when he had set the brands on fire, he let *them* go into the standing corn of the Philistines, and burnt up both the shocks, and also the standing corn, with the vineyards *and* olives.

6 Then the Philistines said, Who hath done this? And they answered, Samson, the son in law of the Tĭm'-nĭte, because he had taken his wife, and given her to his companion. ᴿAnd the Philistines came up, and burnt her and her father with fire.

7 And Samson said unto them, Though ye have done this, yet will I be avenged of you, and after that I will cease.

8 And he smote them hip and thigh with a great slaughter: and he went down and dwelt in the top of the rock Ē'-tăm.

Samson slays the Philistines

9 Then the Philistines went up, and pitched in Judah, and spread themselves ᴿin Lē'-hī.

10 And the men of Judah said, Why are ye come up against us? And they answered, To bind Samson are we come up, to do to him as he hath done to us.

11 Then three thousand men of Judah ᴺwent to the top of the rock Ē'-tăm, and said to Samson, Knowest thou not that the Philistines *are* ᴿrulers over us? what *is* this *that* thou hast done unto us? And he said unto them, As they did unto me, so have I done unto them.

12 And they said unto him, We are come down to bind thee, that we may deliver thee into the hand of the Philistines. And Samson said unto them, Swear unto me, that ye will not fall upon me yourselves.

13 And they spake unto him, saying, No; but we will bind thee fast, and deliver thee into their hand: but surely we will not kill thee. And they bound him with two new cords, and brought him up from the rock.

14 *And* when he came unto Lē'-hī, the Philistines shouted against him: and ᴿthe spirit of the Lᴏʀᴅ came mightily upon him, and the cords that *were* upon his arms became as flax that was burnt with fire, and his bands ᴺloosed from off his hands.

15 And he found a ᴺnew jawbone of an ass, and put forth his hand, and took it, and ᴿslew a thousand men therewith.

16 And Samson said, With the jawbone of an ass, ᴺhcaps upon heaps, with the jaw of an ass have I slain a thousand men.

17 And it came to pass, when he had made an end of speaking, that he cast away the jawbone out of his hand, and called that place ᴺRā'-măth-lē'-hī.

18 And he was sore athirst, and called on the Lᴏʀᴅ, and said, ᴿThou hast given this great deliverance into the hand of thy servant: and now shall I die for thirst, and fall into the hand of the uncircumcised?

19 But God clave an hollow place that *was* in ᴺthe jaw, and there came water thereout; and when he had drunk, ᴿhis spirit came again, and he revived: wherefore he called the name thereof ᴺĔn-hăk-kôr'-ē, which *is* in Lē'-hī unto this day.

20 ᴺAnd he judged Israel ᴿin the days of the Philistines twenty years.

CHAPTER 16

Samson at Gaza

THEN went Samson to Gā'-ză, and saw there ᴺan harlot, and went in unto her.

2 *And it was told* the Gā'-zītes, saying, Samson is come hither. And they ᴿcompassed *him* in, and laid wait for him all night in the gate of the city, and were ᴺquiet all the night, saying, In the morning, when it is day, we shall kill him.

3 And Samson lay till midnight, and arose at midnight, and took the doors of the gate of the city, and the two posts, and went away with them, ᴺbar and all, and put *them* upon his shoulders, and carried them up to the top of an hill that *is* before Hē'-brŏn.

Samson and Delilah

4 And it came to pass afterward, that he loved a woman ᴺin the valley of Sôr'-ĕk, whose name *was* Dĕ-lī'-lăh.

5 And the lords of the Philistines came up unto her, and said unto her, ᴿEntice him, and see wherein his great strength *lieth,* and by what *means* we may prevail against him, that we may bind him to ᴺafflict him: and we will give thee every one of us eleven hundred *pieces* of silver.

6 And Dĕ-lī'-lăh said to Samson, Tell me, I pray thee, wherein thy great strength *lieth,* and wherewith thou mightest be bound to afflict thee.

7 And Samson said unto her, If they bind me with seven ᴺᴺgreen withs that were never dried, then shall I be weak, and be as ᴺanother man.

8 Then the lords of the Philistines brought

up to her seven green withs which had not been dried, and she bound him with them.

9 Now *there were* men lying in wait, abiding with her in the chamber. And she said unto him, The Philistines *be* upon thee, Samson. And he brake the withs, as a thread of tow is broken when it ᴺtoucheth the fire. So his strength was not known.

10 And Dĕ-li′-lăh said unto Samson, Behold, thou hast mocked me, and told me lies: now tell me, I pray thee, wherewith thou mightest be bound.

11 And he said unto her, If they bind me fast with new ropes ᴺthat never were occupied, then shall I be weak, and be as another man.

12 Dĕ-li′-lăh therefore took new ropes, and bound him therewith, and said unto him, The Philistines *be* upon thee, Samson. And *there were* liers in wait abiding in the chamber. And he brake them from off his arms like a thread.

13 And Dĕ-li′-lăh said unto Samson, Hitherto thou hast mocked me, and told me lies: tell me wherewith thou mightest be bound. And he said unto her, If thou weavest the seven locks of my head with the web.

14 And she fastened *it* with the pin, and said unto him, The Philistines *be* upon thee, Samson. And he awaked out of his sleep, and went away with the pin of the beam, and with the web.

The secret of Samson's strength

15 And she said unto him, ᴿHow canst thou say, I love thee, when thine heart *is* not with me? thou hast mocked me these three times, and hast not told me wherein thy great strength *lieth*.

16 And it came to pass, when she pressed him daily with her words, and urged him, *so* that his soul was ᴺvexed unto death;

17 That he ᴿtold her all his heart, and said unto her, ᴿThere hath not come a razor upon mine head; for I *have been* a Nazarite unto God from my mother's womb: if I be shaven, then my strength will go from me, and I shall become weak, and be like any *other* man.

Samson betrayed and blinded

18 And when Dĕ-li′-lăh saw that he had told her all his heart, she sent and called for the lords of the Philistines, saying, Come up this once, for he hath shewed me all his heart. Then the lords of the Philistines came up unto her, and brought money in their hand.

19 ᴿAnd she made him sleep upon her knees; and she called for a man, and she caused him to shave off the seven locks of his

CHAP. **16**
BC 1120
9 Heb. *smelleth*
11 Heb. *wherewith work hath not been done*
15 ch. 14:16
16 Heb. *shortened*
17 Mic. 7:5
17 Num. 6:5
ch. 13:5
19 Prov. 7:26, 27

Num. 14:9,   **20**
42, 43
Josh. 7:12
1 Sam. 16:14
& 18:12
& 28:15, 16
2 Chr. 15:2
Heb. *bored out* **21**
Or, *as when he* **22**
was shaven
Dan. 5:4   **24**
Heb. *and who* **24**
multiplied our
slain
ch. 9:27   **25**
Heb. *before them* **25**
Deut. 22:8   **27**
Jer. 15:15   **28**
Or, *he leaned* **29**
on them
Heb. *my soul*   **30**

head; and she began to afflict him, and his strength went from him.

20 And she said, The Philistines *be* upon thee, Samson. And he awoke out of his sleep, and said, I will go out as at other times before, and shake myself. And he wist not that the Lord ᴿwas departed from him.

21 But the Philistines took him, and ᴺput out his eyes, and brought him down to Gā′-ză, and bound him with fetters of brass; and he did grind in the prison house.

22 Howbeit the hair of his head began to grow again ᴺafter he was shaven.

Samson's revenge and death

23 Then the lords of the Philistines gathered them together for to offer a great sacrifice unto Dā′-gŏn their god, and to rejoice: for they said, Our god hath delivered Samson our enemy into our hand.

24 And when the people saw him, they ᴿpraised their god: for they said, Our god hath delivered into our hands our enemy, and the destroyer of our country, ᴺwhich slew many of us.

25 And it came to pass, when their hearts were ᴿmerry, that they said, Call for Samson, that he may make us sport. And they called for Samson out of the prison house; and he made ᴺthem sport: and they set him between the pillars.

26 And Samson said unto the lad that held him by the hand, Suffer me that I may feel the pillars whereupon the house standeth, that I may lean upon them.

27 Now the house was full of men and women; and all the lords of the Philistines *were* there; and *there were* upon the ᴿroof about three thousand men and women, that beheld while Samson made sport.

28 And Samson called unto the Lord, and said, O Lord God, ᴿremember me, I pray thee, and strengthen me, I pray thee, only this once, O God, that I may be at once avenged of the Philistines for my two eyes.

29 And Samson took hold of the two middle pillars upon which the house stood, and ᴺon which it was borne up, of the one with his right hand, and of the other with his left.

30 And Samson said, Let ᴺme die with the Philistines. And he bowed himself with *all his* might; and the house fell upon the lords, and upon all the people that *were* therein. So the dead which he slew at his death were more than *they* which he slew in his life.

31 Then his brethren and all the house of his father came down, and took him, and brought

him up, and ᴿburied him between Zôr'-ăh and Ĕsh'-tā-ŏl in the buryingplace of Mă-nō'-ăh his father. And he judged Israel twenty years.

CHAPTER 17

Micah's idols

AND there was a man of mount Ē'-phră-ĭm, whose name *was* Mī'-căh.

2 And he said unto his mother, The eleven hundred *shē'-kĕls* of silver that were taken from thee, about which thou cursedst, and spakest of also in mine ears, behold, the silver *is* with me; I took it. And his mother said, ᴿBlessed *be thou* of the LORD, my son.

3 And when he had restored the eleven hundred *shē'-kĕls* of silver to his mother, his mother said, I had wholly dedicated the silver unto the LORD from my hand for my son, to ᴿmake a graven image and a molten image: now therefore I will restore it unto thee.

4 Yet he restored the money unto his mother; and his mother ᴿtook two hundred *shē'-kĕls* of silver, and gave them to the founder, who made thereof a graven image and a molten image: and they were in the house of Mī'-căh.

5 And the man Mī'-căh had an house of gods, and made an ᴿē'-phŏd, and ᴿtĕr'-ă-phĭm, and ᴺconsecrated one of his sons, who became his priest.

6 ᴿIn those days *there was* no king in Israel, ᴿbut every man did *that which was* right in his own eyes.

Micah's hired priest

7 And there was a young man out of ᴿBeth-lehem-judah of the family of Judah, who *was* a Levite, and he sojourned there.

8 And the man departed out of the city from Beth-lehem-judah to sojourn where he could find *a place:* and he came to mount Ē'-phră-ĭm to the house of Mī'-căh, ᴺas he journeyed.

9 And Mī'-căh said unto him, Whence comest thou? And he said unto him, I *am* a Levite of Beth-lehem-judah, and I go to sojourn where I may find *a place.*

10 And Mī'-căh said unto him, Dwell with me, ᴿand be unto me a ᴿfather and a priest, and I will give thee ten *shē'-kĕls* of silver by the year, and ᴺᴺa suit of apparel, and thy victuals. So the Levite went in.

11 And the Levite was content to dwell with the man; and the young man was unto him as one of his sons.

12 And Mī'-căh ᴿconsecrated the Levite;

CHAP. 16	
BC 1120	
31	ch. 13:25

CHAP. 17	
BC 1120	
2	Gen. 14:19
3	See Ex. 20:4, 23
	Lev. 19:4
4	Is. 46:6
5	ch. 8:27
5	Gen. 31:19, 30
	Hos. 3:4
5	Heb. *filled the hand,*
	Ex. 29:9
6	ch. 18:1 & 19:1 & 21:25
6	Deut. 12:8
7	See Josh. 19:15
	ch. 19:1
	Ruth 1:1, 2
	Mic. 5:2
	Mat. 2:1, 5, 6
8	Heb. *in making his way*
10	ch. 18:19
10	Gen. 45:8
	Job 29:16
10	Or, *a double suit, etc.*
10	Heb. *an order of garments*
12	ver. 5

ch. 18:30	**12**

CHAP. 18	
BC 1406	
ch. 17:6 & 21:25	**1**
Josh. 19:47	**1**
Heb. *sons*	**2**
ch. 13:25	**2**
Num. 13:17	**2**
Josh. 2:1	
ch. 17:1	**2**
ch. 17:10	**4**
1 Ki. 22:5	**5**
Is. 30:1	
Hos. 4:12	
See ch. 17:5	**5**
ver. 14	
1 Ki. 22:6	**6**
Josh. 19:47,	**7**
Called *Leshem*	
ver. 27, 28	**7**
Heb. *possessor,*	**7**
or, *heir of restraint*	
ver. 2	**8**
Num. 13:30	**9**
Josh. 2:23, 24	
1 Ki. 22:3	**9**
ver. 7, 27	**10**
Deut. 8:9	**10**

and the young man ᴿbecame his priest, and was in the house of Mī'-căh.

13 Then said Mī'-căh, Now know I that the LORD will do me good, seeing I have a Levite to *my* priest.

CHAPTER 18

The Danite spies

IN ᴿthose days *there was* no king in Israel: and in those days ᴿthe tribe of the Danites sought them an inheritance to dwell in; for unto that day *all their* inheritance had not fallen unto them among the tribes of Israel.

2 And the children of Dan sent of their family five men from their coasts, ᴺmen of valour, from ᴿZôr'-ăh, and from Ĕsh'-tā-ŏl, ᴿto spy out the land, and to search it; and they said unto them, Go, search the land: who when they came to mount Ē'-phră-ĭm, to the ᴿhouse of Mī'-căh, they lodged there.

3 When they *were* by the house of Mī'-căh, they knew the voice of the young man the Levite: and they turned in thither, and said unto him, Who brought thee hither? and what makest thou in this *place?* and what hast thou here?

4 And he said unto them, Thus and thus dealeth Mī'-căh with me, and hath ᴿhired me, and I am his priest.

5 And they said unto him, ᴿAsk counsel, we pray thee, ᴿof God, that we may know whether our way which we go shall be prosperous.

6 And the priest said unto them, ᴿGo in peace: before the LORD *is* your way wherein ye go.

7 Then the five men departed, and came to ᴿLā'-ĭsh, and saw the people that *were* therein, ᴿhow they dwelt careless, after the manner of the Zĭ-dō'-nĭ-ăns, quiet and secure; and *there was* no ᴺmagistrate in the land, that might put *them* to shame in *any* thing; and they *were* far from the Zĭ-dō'-nĭ-ăns, and had no business with *any* man.

8 And they came unto their brethren to ᴿZôr'-ăh and Ĕsh'-tā-ŏl: and their brethren said unto them, What *say* ye?

9 And they said, ᴿArise, that we may go up against them: for we have seen the land, and, behold, it *is* very good: and *are* ye ᴿstill? be not slothful to go, *and* to enter to possess the land.

10 When ye go, ye shall come unto a people ᴿsecure, and to a large land: for God hath given it into your hands; ᴿa place where *there is* no want of any thing that *is* in the earth.

11 And there went from thence of the family of the Danites, out of Zôr'-ăh and out of Ēsh'-tā-ŏl, six hundred men ᴺappointed with weapons of war.

12 And they went up, and pitched in ᴿKir'-jăth-jē'-ă-rĭm, in Judah: wherefore they called that place ᴿMā'-hă-nēh-dăn unto this day: behold, it is behind Kĭr'-jăth-jē'-ă-rĭm.

13 And they passed thence unto mount Ē'-phră-ĭm, and came unto ᴿthe house of Mī'-căh.

Idols and priest stolen

14 ᴿThen answered the five men that went to spy out the country of Lā'-ish, and said unto their brethren, Do ye know that ᴿthere is in these houses an ē'-phŏd, and tĕr'-ă-phĭm, and a graven image, and a molten image? now therefore consider what ye have to do.

15 And they turned thitherward, and came to the house of the young man the Levite, even unto the house of Mī'-căh, and ᴺsaluted him.

16 And the ᴿsix hundred men appointed with their weapons of war, which were of the children of Dan, stood by the entering of the gate.

17 And ᴿthe five men that went to spy out the land went up, and came in thither, and took ᴿthe graven image, and the ē'-phŏd, and the tĕr'-ă-phĭm, and the molten image: and the priest stood in the entering of the gate with the six hundred men that were appointed with weapons of war.

18 And these went into Mī'-căh's house, and fetched the carved image, the ē'-phŏd, and the tĕr'-ă-phĭm, and the molten image. Then said the priest unto them, What do ye?

19 And they said unto him, Hold thy peace, ᴿlay thine hand upon thy mouth, and go with us, ᴿand be to us a father and a priest: is it better for thee to be a priest unto the house of one man, or that thou be a priest unto a tribe and a family in Israel?

20 And the priest's heart was glad, and he took the ē'-phŏd, and the tĕr'-ă-phĭm, and the graven image, and went in the midst of the people.

21 So they turned and departed, and put the little ones and the cattle and the carriage before them.

22 And when they were a good way from the house of Mī'-căh, the men that were in the houses near to Mī'-căh's house were gathered together, and overtook the children of Dan.

23 And they cried unto the children of Dan. And they turned their faces, and said unto Mī'-căh, What aileth thee, ᴺthat thou comest with such a company?

24 And he said, Ye have taken away my gods which I made, and the priest, and ye are gone away: and what have I more? and what is this that ye say unto me, What aileth thee?

25 And the children of Dan said unto him, Let not thy voice be heard among us, lest ᴺangry fellows run upon thee, and thou lose thy life, with the lives of thy household.

26 And the children of Dan went their way: and when Mī'-căh saw that they were too strong for him, he turned and went back unto his house.

Idols set up at Dan

27 And they took the things which Mī'-căh had made, and the priest which he had, and came unto Lā'-ish, unto a people that were at quiet and secure: ᴿand they smote them with the edge of the sword, and burnt the city with fire.

28 And there was no deliverer, because it was ᴿfar from Zī'-dŏn, and they had no business with any man; and it was in the valley that lieth ᴿby Bĕth-rē'-hŏb. And they built a city, and dwelt therein.

29 And ᴿthey called the name of the city ᴿDan, after the name of Dan their father, who was born unto Israel: howbeit the name of the city was Lā'-ish at the first.

30 And the children of Dan set up the graven image: and Jonathan, the son of Gĕr'-shŏm, the son of Mă-năs'-sēh, he and his sons were priests to the tribe of Dan ᴿuntil the day of the captivity of the land.

31 And they set them up Mī'-căh's graven image, which he made, ᴿall the time that the house of God was in Shī'-lōh.

CHAPTER 19

A Levite and his concubine

AND it came to pass in those days, ᴿwhen there was no king in Israel, that there was a certain Levite sojourning on the side of mount Ē'-phră-ĭm, who took to him ᴺa concubine out of ᴿBeth-lehem-judah.

2 And his concubine played the whore against him, and went away from him unto her father's house to Beth-lehem-judah, and was there ᴺᴺfour whole months.

3 And her husband arose, and went after her, to speak ᴺfriendly unto her, and to bring her again, having his servant with him, and a couple of asses: and she brought him into her father's house: and when the father of the damsel saw him, he rejoiced to meet him.

4 And his father in law, the damsel's father,

retained him; and he abode with him three days: so they did eat and drink, and lodged there.

5 And it came to pass on the fourth day, when they arose early in the morning, that he rose up to depart: and the damsel's father said unto his son in law, ᴿComfortᴺ thine heart with a morsel of bread, and afterward go your way.

6 And they sat down, and did eat and drink both of them together: for the damsel's father had said unto the man, Be content, I pray thee, and tarry all night, and let thine heart be merry.

7 And when the man rose up to depart, his father in law urged him: therefore he lodged there again.

8 And he arose early in the morning on the fifth day to depart: and the damsel's father said, Comfort thine heart, I pray thee. And they tarried ᴺuntil afternoon, and they did eat both of them.

9 And when the man rose up to depart, he, and his concubine, and his servant, his father in law, the damsel's father, said unto him, Behold, now the day ᴺdraweth toward evening, I pray you tarry all night: behold, ᴺthe day groweth to an end, lodge here, that thine heart may be merry; and to morrow get you early on your way, that thou mayest go ᴺhome.

10 But the man would not tarry that night, but he rose up and departed, and came ᴺover against ᴿJē'-bŭs, which is Jerusalem; and there were with him two asses saddled, his concubine also was with him.

11 And when they were by Jē'-bŭs, the day was far spent; and the servant said unto his master, Come, I pray thee, and let us turn in into this city ᴿof the Jĕb'-ū-sītes, and lodge in it.

12 And his master said unto him, We will not turn aside hither into the city of a stranger, that is not of the children of Israel; we will pass over ᴿto Gĭb'-ĕ-ăh.

13 And he said unto his servant, Come, and let us draw near to one of these places to lodge all night, in Gĭb'-ĕ-ăh, or in ᴿRā'-măh.

14 And they passed on and went their way; and the sun went down upon them when they were by Gĭb'-ĕ-ăh, which belongeth to Benjamin.

15 And they turned aside thither, to go in and to lodge in Gĭb'-ĕ-ăh: and when he went in, he sat him down in a street of the city: for there was no man that ᴿtook them into his house to lodging.

16 And, behold, there came an old man from ᴿhis work out of the field at even, which was also of mount Ē'-phră-ĭm; and he sojourned in

CHAP. **19**
BC 1406
5 Gen. 18:5
5 Heb.
Strengthen
8 Heb. *till the*
day declined
9 Heb. *is weak*
9 Heb. it is *the*
pitching time
of the day
9 Heb. *to thy tent*
10 Heb. *to*
over against
10 Josh. 18:28
11 Josh. 15:8, 63
12 Josh. 18:28
13 Josh. 18:25
15 Mat. 25:43
16 Ps. 104:23

Josh. 18:1 **18**
ch. 18:31 & 20:18
1 Sam. 1:3, 7
Heb. *gathereth,* **18**
ver. 15
Gen. 43:23 **20**
ch. 6:23
Gen. 19:2 **20**
Gen. 24:32 **21**
& 43:24
Gen. 18:4 **21**
John 13:5
Gen. 19:4 **22**
ch. 20:5
Hos. 9:9 & 10:9
Deut. 13:13 **22**
Gen. 19:5 **22**
Rom. 1:26, 27
Gen. 19:6, 7 **23**
2 Sam. 13:12 **23**
Gen. 19:8 **24**
Gen. 34:2 **24**
Deut. 21:14
Heb. *the matter* **24**
of this folly
Gen. 4:1 **25**
ch. 20:5 **28**

Gĭb'-ĕ-ăh: but the men of the place were Benjamites.

17 And when he had lifted up his eyes, he saw a wayfaring man in the street of the city: and the old man said, Whither goest thou? and whence comest thou?

18 And he said unto him, We are passing from Beth-lehem-judah toward the side of mount Ē'-phră-ĭm; from thence am I: and I went to Beth-lehem-judah, but I an now going to ᴿthe house of the Lord; and there is no man that ᴺreceiveth me to house.

19 Yet there is both straw and provender for our asses; and there is bread and wine also for me, and for thy handmaid, and for the young man which is with thy servants: there is no want of any thing.

20 And the old man said, ᴿPeace be with thee; howsoever let all thy wants lie upon me; ᴿonly lodge not in the street.

21 ᴿSo he brought him into his house, and gave provender unto the asses: ᴿand they washed their feet, and did eat and drink.

The concubine abused

22 Now as they were making their hearts merry, behold, ᴿthe men of the city, certain ᴿsons of Bē'-lī-ăl, beset the house round about, and beat at the door, and spake to the master of the house, the old man, saying, ᴿBring forth the man that came into thine house, that we may know him.

23 And ᴿthe man, the master of the house, went out unto them, and said unto them, Nay, my brethren, nay, I pray you, do not so wickedly; seeing that this man is come into mine house, ᴿdo not this folly.

24 ᴿBehold, here is my daughter a maiden, and his concubine; them I will bring out now, and ᴿhumble ye them, and do with them what seemeth good unto you: but unto this man do not ᴺso vile a thing.

25 But the men would not hearken to him: so the man took his concubine, and brought her forth unto them; and they ᴿknew her, and abused her all the night until the morning: and when the day began to spring, they let her go.

26 Then came the woman in the dawning of the day, and fell down at the door of the man's house where her lord was, till it was light.

27 And her lord rose up in the morning, and opened the doors of the house, and went out to go his way: and, behold, the woman his concubine was fallen down at the door of the house, and her hands were upon the threshold.

28 And he said unto her, Up, and let us be going. But ᴿnone answered. Then the man

took her *up* upon an ass, and the man rose up, and gat him unto his place.

29 And when he was come into his house, he took a knife, and laid hold on his concubine, and ᴿdivided her, *together* with her bones, into twelve pieces, and sent her into all the coasts of Israel.

30 And it was so, that all that saw it said, There was no such deed done nor seen from the day that the children of Israel came up out of the land of Egypt unto this day: consider of it, ᴿtake advice, and speak *your minds.*

CHAPTER 20

Report of the crime to Israel

THEN ᴿall the children of Israel went out, and the congregation was gathered together as one man, from ᴿDan even to Bēer-shē′-bă, with the land of Gilead, unto the Lᴏʀᴅ ᴿin Mīz′-pēh.

2 And the chief of all the people, *even* of all the tribes of Israel, presented themselves in the assembly of the people of God, four hundred thousand footmen ᴿthat drew sword.

3 (Now the children of Benjamin heard that the children of Israel were gone up to Mīz′-pēh.) Then said the children of Israel, Tell *us,* how was this wickedness?

4 And ᴺthe Levite, the husband of the woman that was slain, answered and said, ᴿI came into Gīb′-ĕ-ăh that *belongeth* to Benjamin, I and my concubine, to lodge.

5 ᴿAnd the men of Gīb′-ĕ-ăh rose against me, and beset the house round about upon me by night, *and* thought to have slain me: ᴿand my concubine have they ᴺforced, that she is dead.

6 And ᴿI took my concubine, and cut her in pieces, and sent her throughout all the country of the inheritance of Israel: for they ᴿhave committed lewdness and folly in Israel.

7 Behold, ye *are* all children of Israel; ᴿgive here your advice and counsel.

Declaration of war

8 And all the people arose as one man, saying, We will not any *of us* go to his tent, neither will we any *of us* turn into his house.

9 But now this *shall be* the thing which we will do to Gīb′-ĕ-ăh; *we will go up* by lot against it;

10 And we will take ten men of an hundred throughout all the tribes of Israel, and an hundred of a thousand, and a thousand out of ten thousand, to fetch victual for the people, that they may do, when they come to Gīb′-ĕ-ăh of Benjamin, according to all the folly that they have wrought in Israel.

11 So all the men of Israel were gathered against the city, ᴺknit together as one man.

12 ᴿAnd the tribes of Israel sent men through all the tribe of Benjamin, saying, What wickedness *is* this that is done among you?

13 Now therefore deliver *us* the men, ᴿthe children of Bē′-lĭ-ăl, which *are* in Gīb′-ĕ-ăh, that we may put them to death, and ᴿput away evil from Israel. But the children of Benjamin would not hearken to the voice of their brethren the children of Israel:

14 But the children of Benjamin gathered themselves together out of the cities unto Gīb′-ĕ-ăh, to go out to battle against the children of Israel.

15 And the children of Benjamin were numbered at that time out of the cities twenty and six thousand men that drew sword, beside the inhabitants of Gīb′-ĕ-ăh, which were numbered seven hundred chosen men.

16 Among all this people *there were* seven hundred chosen men ᴿlefthanded; every one could sling stones at an hair *breadth,* and not miss.

17 And the men of Israel, beside Benjamin, were numbered four hundred thousand men that drew sword: all these *were* men of war.

War between Benjamin and Israel

18 And the children of Israel arose, and ᴿwent up to the house of God, and ᴿasked counsel of God, and said, Which of us shall go up first to the battle against the children of Benjamin? And the Lᴏʀᴅ said, Judah *shall go up* first.

19 And the children of Israel rose up in the morning, and encamped against Gīb′-ĕ-ăh.

20 And the men of Israel went out to battle against Benjamin; and the men of Israel put themselves in array to fight against them at Gīb′-ĕ-ăh.

21 And ᴿthe children of Benjamin came forth out of Gīb′-ĕ-ăh, and destroyed down to the ground of the Israelites that day twenty and two thousand men.

22 And the people the men of Israel encouraged themselves, and set their battle again in array in the place where they put themselves in array the first day.

23 (ᴿAnd the children of Israel went up and wept before the Lᴏʀᴅ until even, and asked counsel of the Lᴏʀᴅ, saying, Shall I go up again to battle against the children of Benjamin my brother? And the Lᴏʀᴅ said, Go up against him.)

24 And the children of Israel came near against the children of Benjamin the second day.

25 And ᴿBenjamin went forth against them out of Gĭb'-ĕ-ăh the second day, and destroyed down to the ground of the children of Israel again eighteen thousand men; all these drew the sword.

26 Then all the children of Israel, and all the people, ᴿwent up, and came unto the house of God, and wept, and sat there before the LORD, and fasted that day until even, and offered burnt offerings and peace offerings before the LORD.

27 And the children of Israel inquired of the LORD, (for ᴿthe ark of the covenant of God was there in those days,

28 ᴿAnd Phĭn'-ĕ-hăs, the son of ĕl-ē-ā'-zär, the son of Aaron, ᴿstood before it in those days,) saying, Shall I yet again go out to battle against the children of Benjamin my brother, or shall I cease? And the LORD said, Go up; for to morrow I will deliver them into thine hand.

Defeat of Benjamin

29 And Israel ᴿset liers in wait round about Gĭb'-ĕ-ăh.

30 And the children of Israel went up against the children of Benjamin on the third day, and put themselves in array against Gĭb'-ĕ-ăh, as at other times.

31 And the children of Benjamin went out against the people, and were drawn away from the city; and they began ᴺto smite of the people, and kill, as at other times, in the highways, of which one goeth up to ᴺthe house of God, and the other to Gĭb'-ĕ-ăh in the field, about thirty men of Israel.

32 And the children of Benjamin said, They are smitten down before us, as at the first. But the children of Israel said, Let us flee, and draw them from the city unto the highways.

33 And all the men of Israel rose up out of their place, and put themselves in array at Bā'-ăl-tā'-mär: and the liers in wait of Israel came forth out of their places, even out of the meadows of Gĭb'-ĕ-ăh.

34 And there came against Gĭb'-ĕ-ăh ten thousand chosen men out of all Israel, and the battle was sore: ᴿbut they knew not that evil was near them.

35 And the LORD smote Benjamin before Israel: and the children of Israel destroyed of the Benjamites that day twenty and five thousand and an hundred men: all these drew the sword.

36 So the children of Benjamin saw that they were smitten: ᴿfor the men of Israel gave place to the Benjamites, because they trusted unto the liers in wait which they had set beside Gĭb'-ĕ-ăh.

37 ᴿAnd the liers in wait hasted, and rushed upon Gĭb'-ĕ-ăh; and the liers in wait ᴺdrew themselves along, and smote all the city with the edge of the sword.

38 Now there was an appointed ᴺsign between the men of Israel ᴺand the liers in wait, that they should make a great ᴺflame with smoke rise up out of the city.

39 And when the men of Israel retired in the battle, Benjamin began ᴺto smite and kill of the men of Israel about thirty persons: for they said, Surely they are smitten down before us, as in the first battle.

40 But when the flame began to arise up out of the city with a pillar of smoke, the Benjamites ᴿlooked behind them, and, behold, ᴺthe flame of the city ascended up to heaven.

41 And when the men of Israel turned again, the men of Benjamin were amazed: for they saw that evil ᴺwas come upon them.

42 Therefore they turned their backs before the men of Israel unto the way of the wilderness; but the battle overtook them; and them which came out of the cities they destroyed in the midst of them.

43 Thus they inclosed the Benjamites round about, and chased them, and trode them down ᴺwith ease ᴺover against Gĭb'-ĕ-ăh toward the sunrising.

44 And there fell of Benjamin eighteen thousand men; all these were men of valour.

45 And they turned and fled toward the wilderness unto the rock of ᴿRimmon: and they gleaned of them in the highways five thousand men; and pursued hard after them unto Gĭ'-dŏm, and slew two thousand men of them.

46 So that all which fell that day of Benjamin were twenty and five thousand men that drew the sword; all these were men of valour.

47 ᴿBut six hundred men turned and fled to the wilderness unto the rock Rimmon, and abode in the rock Rimmon four months.

48 And the men of Israel turned again upon the children of Benjamin, and smote them with the edge of the sword, as well the men of every city, as the beast, and all that ᴺcame to hand: also they set on fire all the cities that ᴺthey came to.

CHAPTER 21

Oath at Mizpeh

NOW ᴿthe men of Israel had sworn in Mĭz'-pēh, saying, There shall not any of us give his daughter unto Benjamin to wife.

2 And the people came ᴿto the house of God, and abode there till even before God, and lifted up their voices, and wept sore;

CHAP. 20
BC 1406
25 ver. 21
26 ver. 18
27 Josh. 18:1
1 Sam. 4:3, 4
28 Josh. 24:33
28 Deut. 10:8
& 18:5
29 Josh. 8:4
31 Heb. to smite
of the people
wounded as at, etc.
31 Or, Beth-el
34 Josh. 8:14
Is. 47:11
36 Josh. 8:15

Josh. 8:19   37
Or, made a long 37
sound with the
trumpet, Josh. 6:5
Or, time   38
Heb. with   38
Heb. elevation   38
Heb. to smite   39
the wounded
Josh. 8:20   40
Heb. the whole   40
consumption
Heb. touched   41
them
Or, from   43
Menuchah, etc.
Heb. unto   43
over against
Josh. 15:32   45
ch. 21:13   47
Heb. was found 48
Heb. were found 48

CHAP. 21
BC 1406
ch. 20:1   1
ch. 20:18, 26   2

3 And said, O Lord God of Israel, why is this come to pass in Israel, that there should be to day one tribe lacking in Israel?

4 And it came to pass on the morrow, that the people rose early, and Rbuilt there an altar, and offered burnt offerings and peace offerings.

5 And the children of Israel said, Who *is there* among all the tribes of Israel that came not up with the congregation unto the Lord? RFor they had made a great oath concerning him that came not up to the Lord to Mĭz'-pĕh, saying, He shall surely be put to death.

6 And the children of Israel repented them for Benjamin their brother, and said, There is one tribe cut off from Israel this day.

7 How shall we do for wives for them that remain, seeing we have sworn by the Lord that we will not give them of our daughters to wives?

Wives from Jabesh-gilead

8 And they said, What one *is there* of the tribes of Israel that came not up to Mĭz'-pĕh to the Lord? And, behold, there came none to the camp from RJā'-bĕsh-gĭl'-ĕ-ăd to the assembly.

9 For the people were numbered, and, behold, *there were* none of the inhabitants of Jā'-bĕsh-gĭl'-ĕ-ăd there.

10 And the congregation sent thither twelve thousand men of the valiantest, and commanded them, saying, RGo and smite the inhabitants of Jā'-bĕsh-gĭl'-ĕ-ăd with the edge of the sword, with the women and the children.

11 And this *is* the thing that ye shall do, RYe shall utterly destroy every male, and every woman that Nhath lain by man.

12 And they found among the inhabitants of Jā'-bĕsh-gĭl'-ĕ-ăd four hundred Nyoung virgins, that had known no man by lying with any male: and they brought them unto the camp to RShĭ'-lōh, which *is* in the land of Canaan.

Peace with Benjamin established

13 And the whole congregation sent *some* Nto speak to the children of Benjamin Rthat *were* in the rock Rimmon, and to Ncall peaceably unto them.

14 And Benjamin came again at that time; and they gave them wives which they had

saved alive of the women of Jā'-bĕsh-gĭl'-ĕ-ăd: and yet so they sufficed them not.

15 And the people Rrepented them for Benjamin, because that the Lord had made a breach in the tribes of Israel.

Wives for Benjamin from Shiloh

16 Then the elders of the congregation said, How shall we do for wives for them that remain, seeing the women are destroyed out of Benjamin?

17 And they said, *There must be* an inheritance for them that be escaped of Benjamin, that a tribe be not destroyed out of Israel.

18 Howbeit we may not give them wives of our daughters: Rfor the children of Israel have sworn, saying, Cursed *be* he that giveth a wife to Benjamin.

19 Then they said, Behold, *there is* a feast of the Lord in Shĭ'-lōh Nyearly *in a place* which *is* on the north side of Beth-el, Non the east side Nof the highway that goeth up from Beth-el to Shē'-chĕm, and on the south of Lĕ-bō'-năh.

20 Therefore they commanded the children of Benjamin, saying, Go and lie in wait in the vineyards;

21 And see, and, behold, if the daughters of Shĭ'-lōh come out Rto dance in dances, then come ye out of the vineyards, and catch you every man his wife of the daughters of Shĭ'-lōh, and go to the land of Benjamin.

22 And it shall be, when their fathers or their brethren come unto us to complain, that we will say unto them, NBe favourable unto them for our sakes: because we reserved not to each man his wife in the war: for ye did not give unto them at this time, *that* ye should be guilty.

23 And the children of Benjamin did so, and took *them* wives, according to their number, of them that danced, whom they caught: and they went and returned unto their inheritance, and Rrepaired the cities, and dwelt in them.

24 And the children of Israel departed thence at that time, every man to his tribe and to his family, and they went out from thence every man to his inheritance.

25 RIn those days *there was* no king in Israel: Revery man did *that which was* right in his own eyes.

CHAP. 21

BC 1406

4 2 Sam. 24:25
5 ch. 5:23
8 1 Sam. 11:1
& 31:11
10 ver. 5
ch. 5:23
1 Sam. 11:7
11 Num. 31:17
11 Heb. *knoweth the lying* with *man*
12 Heb. *young women virgins*
12 Josh. 18:1
13 Heb. *and spake and called*
13 ch. 20:47
13 Or, *proclaim peace,*
Deut. 20:10

ver. 6   15
ver. 1   18
ch. 11:35
Heb. *from year to year*   19
Or, *toward the sunrising*   19
Or, *on*   19
See Ex. 15:20   21
ch. 11:34
1 Sam. 18:6
Or, *Gratify us in them*   22
See ch. 20:48   23
ch. 17:6 & 18:1   25
& 19:1
Deut. 12:8   25
ch. 17:6

THE BOOK OF RUTH

The book of Ruth is a narrative belonging to the period of the judges in its historical setting. It is named from its central figure. The book forms a natural connecting link between the book of Judges and that of Samuel, and carries the Messianic line into the house of David, establishing the monarchy within the tribe of Judah. By marriage and by choice Ruth the Moabitess comes into the nation of Israel. In its literary character the book of Ruth is a romantic and historical Hebrew idyl, profoundly human, deeply religious, and serenely domestic.

In its fundamental teachings the book dignifies and makes holy the secular things of life and sets forth the power of love to overcome all alienations, hostilities, and prejudices. A member of an alien race is adopted into the household of faith and is exalted because of her simple trust in God. The book of Ruth sheds light upon the Jewish customs of ancient times, such as the joy of the harvest season and the kindly treatment of the poor.

OUTLINE OF THE BOOK:
I. Migration of Elimelech and his family to Moab and the return of Naomi accompanied by Ruth.   Chap. 1
II. The gleaning of Ruth in the field of Boaz.   Chap. 2
III. The rights of mutual conjugal love and family claims presented.   Chap. 3
IV. Vindication of the law of the nearer kinsman and the marriage of Ruth and Boaz.   Chap. 4

CHAPTER 1

Naomi's bereavement in Moab

NOW it came to pass in the days when ᴿthe judges ᴺruled, that there was ᴿa famine in the land. And a certain man of ᴿBeth-lehem-judah went to sojourn in the country of Moab, he, and his wife, and his two sons.

2 And the name of the man *was* Ē-lĭm′-ĕ-lĕch, and the name of his wife Nā′-ō-mī, and the name of his two sons Mäh′-lŏn and Chī′-lĭ-ŏn, ᴿĔph′-ră-thītes of Beth-lehem-judah. And they came ᴿinto the country of Moab, and ᴺcontinued there.

3 And Ē-lĭm′-ĕ-lĕch Nā′-ō-mī's husband died; and she was left, and her two sons.

4 And they took them wives of the women of Moab; the name of the one *was* ôr′-păh, and the name of the other Ruth: and they dwelled there about ten years.

5 And Mäh′-lŏn and Chī′-lĭ-ŏn died also both of them; and the woman was left of her two sons and her husband.

Naomi's daughters in law

6 Then she arose with her daughters in law, that she might return from the country of Moab: for she had heard in the country of Moab how that the LORD had ᴿvisited his people in ᴿgiving them bread.

7 Wherefore she went forth out of the place where she was, and her two daughters in law with her; and they went on the way to return unto the land of Judah.

8 And Nā′-ō-mī said unto her two daughters in law, ᴿGo, return each to her mother's house: ᴿthe LORD deal kindly with you, as ye have dealt with ᴿthe dead, and with me.

9 The LORD grant you that ye may find ᴿrest, each *of you* in the house of her husband.

Then she kissed them; and they lifted up their voice, and wept.

10 And they said unto her, Surely we will return with thee unto thy people.

11 And Nā′-ō-mī said, Turn again, my daughters: why will ye go with me? *are there* yet *any more* sons in my womb, ᴿthat they may be your husbands?

12 Turn again, my daughters, go *your way;* for I am too old to have an husband. If I should say, I have hope, ᴺif I should have an husband also to night, and should also bear sons;

13 Would ye ᴺtarry for them till they were grown? would ye stay for them from having husbands? nay, my daughters; for ᴺit grieveth me much for your sakes that ᴿthe hand of the LORD is gone out against me.

14 And they lifted up their voice, and wept again: and ôr′-păh kissed her mother in law; but Ruth ᴿclave unto her.

Ruth's devotion to Naomi

15 And she said, Behold, thy sister in law is gone back unto her people, and unto ᴿher gods: ᴿreturn thou after thy sister in law.

16 And Ruth said, ᴿEntreatᴺ me not to leave thee, *or* to return from following after thee: for whither thou goest, I will go; and where thou lodgest, I will lodge: ᴿthy people *shall be* my people, and thy God my God:

17 Where thou diest, will I die, and there will I be buried: ᴿthe LORD do so to me, and more also, *if aught* but death part thee and me.

18 ᴿWhen she saw that she ᴺwas stedfastly minded to go with her, then she left speaking unto her.

Return to Beth-lehem

19 So they two went until they came to Beth-lehem. And it came to pass, when they

CHAP. 1
BC 1322
1 Judg. 2:16
1 Heb. *judged*
1 Gen. 12:10 & 26:1
2 Ki. 8:1
1 Judg. 17:8
2 Gen. 35:19
2 Judg. 3:30
2 Heb. *were*
6 Ex. 4:31
Luke 1:68
6 Mat. 6:11
8 See Josh. 24:15
8 2 Tim. 1:16-18
8 ver. 5
ch. 2:20
9 ch. 3:1

Gen. 38:11	11
Deut. 25:5	
Or, if *I were with an husband*	12
Heb. *hope*	13
Heb. *I have much bitterness*	13
Judg. 2:15	13
Job 19:21	
Prov. 17:17 & 18:24	14
Judg. 11:24	15
See Josh. 24:15, 19	15
2 Ki. 2:2	
Luke 24:28	
2 Ki. 2:2, 4, 6	16
Or, *Be not against me*	16
ch. 2:11, 12	16
1 Sam. 3:17 & 25:22	17
2 Sam. 19:13	
2 Ki. 6:31	
Acts 21:14	18
Heb. *strengthened herself*	18

were come to Beth-lehem, that ^Rall the city was moved about them, and they said, ^R*Is* this Nā'-ō-mī?

20 And she said unto them, Call me not ^NNā'-ō-mī, call me ^NMâr'-ă: for the Almighty hath dealt very bitterly with me.

21 I went out full, ^Rand the LORD hath brought me home again empty: why *then* call ye me Nā'-ō-mī, seeing the LORD hath testified against me, and the Almighty hath afflicted me?

22 So Nā'-ō-mī returned, and Ruth the Moabitess, her daughter in law, with her, which returned out of the country of Moab: and they came to Beth-lehem ^Rin the beginning of barley harvest.

CHAPTER 2

Ruth gleans in field of Boaz

AND Nā'-ō-mī had a ^Rkinsman of her husband's, a mighty man of wealth, of the family of Ē-lĭm'-ĕ-lĕ<u>ch</u>; and his name *was* ^RBō'-ăz.^N

2 And Ruth the Moabitess said unto Nā'-ō-mī, Let me now go to the field, and ^Rglean ears of corn after *him* in whose sight I shall find grace. And she said unto her, Go, my daughter.

3 And she went, and came, and gleaned in the field after the reapers: and her ^Nhap was to light on a part of the field *belonging* unto Bō'-ăz, who *was* of the kindred of Ē-lĭm'-ĕ-lĕ<u>ch</u>.

4 And, behold, Bō'-ăz came from Bethlehem, and said unto the reapers, ^RThe LORD *be* with you. And they answered him, The LORD bless thee.

5 Then said Bō'-ăz unto his servant that was set over the reapers, Whose damsel *is* this?

6 And the servant that was set over the reapers answered and said, It *is* the Moabitish damsel ^Rthat came back with Nā'-ō-mī out of the country of Moab:

7 And she said, I pray you, let me glean and gather after the reapers among the sheaves: so she came, and hath continued even from the morning until now, that she tarried a little in the house.

Boaz talks with Ruth

8 Then said Bō'-ăz unto Ruth, Hearest thou not, my daughter? Go not to glean in another field, neither go from hence, but abide here fast by my maidens:

9 *Let* thine eyes *be* on the field that they do reap, and go thou after them: have I not charged the young men that they shall not touch thee? and when thou art athirst, go unto the vessels, and drink of *that* which the young men have drawn.

10 Then she ^Rfell on her face, and bowed herself to the ground, and said unto him, Why have I found grace in thine eyes, that thou shouldest take knowledge of me, seeing I *am* a stranger?

11 And Bō'-ăz answered and said unto her, It hath fully been shewed me, ^Rall that thou hast done unto thy mother in law since the death of thine husband: and *how* thou hast left thy father and thy mother, and the land of thy nativity, and art come unto a people which thou knewest not heretofore.

12 ^RThe LORD recompense thy work, and a full reward be given thee of the LORD God of Israel, ^Runder whose wings thou art come to trust.

13 Then she said, ^RLet^N me find favour in thy sight, my lord; for that thou hast comforted me, and for that thou hast spoken ^Nfriendly unto thine handmaid, ^Rthough I be not like unto one of thine handmaidens.

Boaz provides for Ruth

14 And Bō'-ăz said unto her, At mealtime come thou hither, and eat of the bread, and dip thy morsel in the vinegar. And she sat beside the reapers: and he reached her parched *corn,* and she did eat, and ^Rwas sufficed, and left.

15 And when she was risen up to glean, Bō'-ăz commanded his young men, saying, Let her glean even among the sheaves, and ^Nreproach her not:

16 And let fall also *some* of the handfuls of purpose for her, and leave *them,* that she may glean *them,* and rebuke her not.

17 So she gleaned in the field until even, and beat out that she had gleaned: and it was about an ē'-phäh of barley.

18 And she took *it* up, and went into the city: and her mother in law saw what she had gleaned: and she brought forth, and gave to her ^Rthat she had reserved after she was sufficed.

19 And her mother in law said unto her, Where hast thou gleaned to day? and where wroughtest thou? blessed be he that did ^Rtake knowledge of thee. And she shewed her mother in law with whom she had wrought, and said, The man's name with whom I wrought to day *is* Bō'-ăz.

20 And Nā'-ō-mī said unto her daughter in law, ^RBlessed *be* he of the LORD, who ^Rhath not left off his kindness to the living and to the dead. And Nā'-ō-mī said unto her, The man *is*

CHAP. 1

BC 1322

19 Mat. 21:10
19 See Is. 23:7
Lam. 2:15
20 i.e. *Pleasant*
20 i.e. *Bitter*
21 Job 1:21
22 Ex. 9:31, 32
ch. 2:23
2 Sam. 21:9

CHAP. 2

BC 1312

1 ch. 3:2, 12
1 ch. 4:21
1 Called *Booz,*
Mat. 1:5
2 Lev. 19:9
Deut. 24:19
3 Heb. *hap happened*
4 Luke 1:28
2 Thes. 3:16
6 ch. 1:22

1 Sam. 25:23   10
ch. 1:14, 16, 17   11
1 Sam. 24:19   12
ch. 1:16   12
Ps. 17:8
Gen. 33:15   13
1 Sam. 1:18
Or, *I find favour*   13
Heb. *to the heart,*   13
Gen. 34:3
Judg. 19:3
1 Sam. 25:41   13
ver. 18   14
Heb. *shame her not*   15
ver. 14   18
ver. 10   19
Ps. 41:1
ch. 3:10   20
2 Sam. 2:5
Job 29:13
Prov. 17:17   20

near of kin unto us, ^Rone^N of our next kinsmen.

21 And Ruth the Moabitess said, He said unto me also, Thou shalt keep fast by my young men, until they have ended all my harvest.

22 And Nā'-ō-mī said unto Ruth her daughter in law, *It is* good, my daughter, that thou go out with his maidens, that they ^Nmeet thee not in any other field.

23 So she kept fast by the maidens of Bō'-ăz to glean unto the end of barley harvest and of wheat harvest; and dwelt with her mother in law.

CHAPTER 3

Naomi counsels Ruth

THEN Nā'-ō-mī her mother in law said unto her, My daughter, ^Rshall I not seek ^Rrest for thee, that it may be well with thee?
2 And now *is* not Bō'-ăz of our kindred, ^Rwith whose maidens thou wast? Behold, he winnoweth barley to night in the threshingfloor.

3 Wash thyself therefore, ^Rand anoint thee, and put thy raiment upon thee, and get thee down to the floor: *but* make not thyself known unto the man, until he shall have done eating and drinking.

4 And it shall be, when he lieth down, that thou shalt mark the place where he shall lie, and thou shalt go in, and ^Nuncover his feet, and lay thee down; and he will tell thee what thou shalt do.

5 And she said unto her, All that thou sayest unto me I will do.

Ruth at the threshingfloor

6 And she went down unto the floor, and did according to all that her mother in law bade her.

7 And when Bō'-ăz had eaten and drunk, and ^Rhis heart was merry, he went to lie down at the end of the heap of corn: and she came softly, and uncovered his feet, and laid her down.

8 And it came to pass at midnight, that the man was afraid, and ^Nturned himself: and, behold, a woman lay at his feet.

9 And he said, Who *art* thou? And she answered, I *am* Ruth thine handmaid: ^Rspread therefore thy skirt over thine handmaid; for thou *art* ^Ra^N near kinsman.

10 And he said, ^RBlessed *be* thou of the LORD, my daughter: *for* thou hast shewed more kindness in the latter end than ^Rat the

beginning, inasmuch as thou followedst not young men, whether poor or rich.

11 And now, my daughter, fear not; I will do to thee all that thou requirest: for all the ^Ncity of my people doth know that thou *art* ^Ra virtuous woman.

12 And now it is true that I *am thy* ^Rnear kinsman: howbeit ^Rthere is a kinsman nearer than I.

13 Tarry this night, and it shall be in the morning, *that* if he will ^Rperform unto thee the part of a kinsman, well; let him do the kinsman's part: but if he will not do the part of a kinsman to thee, then will I do the part of a kinsman to thee, ^R*as* the LORD liveth: lie down until the morning.

Ruth reports to Naomi

14 And she lay at his feet until the morning: and she rose up before one could know another. And he said, ^RLet it not be known that a woman came into the floor.

15 Also he said, Bring the ^Nvail that *thou hast* upon thee, and hold it. And when she held it, he measured six *measures* of barley, and laid *it* on her: and she went into the city.

16 And when she came to her mother in law, she said, Who *art* thou, my daughter? And she told her all that the man had done to her.

17 And she said, These six *measures* of barley gave he me; for he said to me, Go not empty unto thy mother in law.

18 Then said she, ^RSit still, my daughter, until thou know how the matter will fall: for the man will not be in rest, until he have finished the thing this day.

CHAPTER 4

Boaz buys Naomi's inheritance

THEN went Bō''-ăz up to the gate, and sat him down there: and, behold, ^Rthe kinsman of whom Bō'-ăz spake came by; unto whom he said, Ho, such a one! turn aside, sit down here. And he turned aside, and sat down.

2 And he took ten men of ^Rthe elders of the city, and said, Sit ye down here. And they sat down.

3 And he said unto the kinsman, Nā'-ō-mī, that is come again out of the country of Moab, selleth a parcel of land, which *was* our brother Ē-lĭm'-ĕ-lĕch's:

4 And ^NI thought to advertise thee, saying, ^RBuy *it* ^Rbefore the inhabitants, and before the elders of my people. If thou wilt redeem *it,* redeem *it:* but if thou wilt not redeem *it, then* tell me, that I may know: ^Rfor *there is* none to

redeem *it* beside thee; and I *am* after thee. And he said, I will redeem *it*.

5 Then said Bō'-ăz, What day thou buyest the field of the hand of Nā'-ō-mī, thou must buy *it* also of Ruth the Moabitess, the wife of the dead, ^Rto raise up the name of the dead upon his inheritance.

6 ^RAnd the kinsman said, I cannot redeem *it* for myself, lest I mar mine own inheritance: redeem thou my right to thyself; for I cannot redeem *it*.

7 ^RNow this *was the manner* in former time in Israel concerning redeeming and concerning changing, for to confirm all things; a man plucked off his shoe, and gave *it* to his neighbour: and this *was* a testimony in Israel.

8 Therefore the kinsman said unto Bō'-ăz, Buy *it* for thee. So he drew off his shoe.

9 And Bō'-ăz said unto the elders, and *unto* all the people, Ye *are* witnesses this day, that I have bought all that *was* Ē-lĭm'-ĕ-lĕch's, and all that *was* Chĭ'-lĭ-ŏn's and Măh'-lŏn's, of the hand of Nā'-ō-mī.

10 Moreover Ruth the Moabitess, the wife of Măh'-lŏn, have I purchased to be my wife, to raise up the name of the dead upon his inheritance, ^Rthat the name of the dead be not cut off from among his brethren, and from the gate of his place: ye *are* witnesses this day.

11 And all the people that *were* in the gate, and the elders, said, *We are* witnesses. ^RThe LORD make the woman that is come into thine house like Rachel and like Leah, which two did ^Rbuild the house of Israel: and ^Ndo thou worthily in ^RĔph'-ră-tăh, and ^Nbe famous in Beth-lehem:

12 And let thy house be like the house of Phâr'-ĕz, ^Rwhom Tā'-mär bare unto Judah, of ^Rthe seed which the LORD shall give thee of this young woman.

Boaz marries Ruth

13 So Bō'-ăz ^Rtook Ruth, and she was his wife: and when he went in unto her, ^Rthe LORD gave her conception, and she bare a son.

14 And ^Rthe women said unto Nā'-ō-mī, Blessed *be* the LORD, which hath not ^Nleft thee this day without a ^Nkinsman, that his name may be famous in Israel.

15 And he shall be unto thee a restorer of *thy* life, and ^Na nourisher of ^Nthine old age: for thy daughter in law, which loveth thee, which is ^Rbetter to thee than seven sons, hath born him.

16 And Nā'-ō-mī took the child, and laid it in her bosom, and became nurse unto it.

The Davidic line

17 ^RAnd the women her neighbours gave it a name, saying, There is a son born to Nā'-ō-mī; and they called his name ō'-bĕd: he *is* the father of Jesse, the father of David.

18 Now these *are* the generations of Phâr'-ĕz: ^RPhâr'-ĕz begat Hĕz'-rŏn,

19 And Hĕz'-rŏn begat Ram, and Ram begat Ăm-mĭn'-ă-dăb,

20 And Ăm-mĭn'-ă-dăb begat ^RNăh'-shŏn, and Năh'-shŏn begat ^RSăl'-mŏn,^N

21 And Săl'-mŏn begat Bō'-ăz, and Bō'-ăz begat ō'-bĕd,

22 And ō'-bĕd begat Jesse, and Jesse begat ^RDavid.

CHAP. 4
BC 1312
5 Gen. 38:8
Deut. 25:5, 6
ch. 3:13
Mat. 22:24
6 ch. 3:12, 13
7 Deut. 25:7, 9
10 Deut. 25:6
11 Ps. 127:3
& 128:3
11 Deut. 25:9
11 Or, *get thee riches*, or, *power*
11 Gen. 35:16
11 Heb. *proclaim thy name*

1 Chr. 2:4	12
Mat. 1:3	
1 Sam. 2:20	12
ch. 3:11	13
Gen. 29:31	13
Luke 1:58	14
Heb. *caused to cease unto thee*	14
Or, *redeemer*	14
Heb. *to nourish*	15
Heb. *thy gray hairs*	15
1 Sam. 1:8	15
Luke 1:58	17
1 Chr. 2:4	18
Num. 1:7	20
Mat. 1:4	20
Or, *Salmah*	20
1 Chr. 2:15	22
Mat. 1:6	

THE
FIRST BOOK OF SAMUEL
OTHERWISE CALLED
THE FIRST BOOK OF THE KINGS

In the ancient manuscripts the two books of Samuel constituted one work. In the Greek Septuagint translation they were grouped with the two books of Kings, the four books being called "The Books of the Kingdom." This arrangement was quite appropriate, since these four books preserve the complete history of the monarchy from its founding under Saul and its development under David as recorded in the two books of Samuel, through the histories of Solomon's reign, the division of the kingdom, and the two separate kingdoms as recorded in the books of Kings.

The First Book of Samuel views the development of Israel during the period of transition from a theocracy to a monarchy.

Samuel, known as a great prophetic and spiritual leader, anointed both Saul and David as kings. While the former forfeited his stewardship as captain over God's people Israel (9:16; 10:1,) the latter emerges as a truly theocratic king. The early chapters of the first book are concerned chiefly with the ministries of Samuel and Saul, including an introduction that sets forth the extraordinary circumstances of Samuel's birth and his childhood call and induction into the prophetic office. A Philistine oppression of twenty years ends with the recognition of Samuel as "Judge." There follows in natural order the account of Samuel's upright and peaceful rule. The narratives continue with Saul occupying the position of central in-

terest. Much of the story is taken up with Saul's unjustifiable hatred of David, and finally the account of the death of Saul and his son Jonathan. The authorship of the book is unknown, although it is probable that it was written during David's reign.

OUTLINE OF THE BOOK:
I. Eli's failure as priest and judge   1:1-4:22
II. Samuel's career and support of Saul   5:1-12:25
III. Saul forfeits the kingdom through disobedience   13:1-15:35
IV. Saul's failure—David's success   16:1-31:13

CHAPTER 1

Hannah's childlessness

NOW there was a certain man of Rā-mă-thā′-ĭm-zō′-phĭm, of mount Ē′-phră-ĭm, and his name *was* ᴿĕl-kā′-năh, the son of Jĕ-rō′-hăm, the son of Ĕ-lī′-hū, the son of Tō′-hū, the son of Zuph, ᴿan ĕph′-ră-thīte:

2 And he had two wives; the name of the one *was* Hannah, and the name of the other Pĕ-nĭn′-năh: and Pĕ-nĭn′-năh had children, but Hannah had no children.

3 And this man went up out of his city ᴿyearlyᴺ ᴿto worship and to sacrifice unto the Lord of hosts in ᴿShī′-lōh. And the two sons of Ē′-lī, Hŏph′-nī and Phĭn′-ĕ-hăś, the priests of the Lord, *were* there.

4 And when the time was that ĕl-kā′-năh ᴿoffered, he gave to Pĕ-nĭn′-năh his wife, and to all her sons and her daughters, portions:

5 But unto Hannah he gave ᴺa worthy portion; for he loved Hannah: ᴿbut the Lord had shut up her womb.

6 And her adversary also ᴿprovokedᴺ her sore, for to make her fret, because the Lord had shut up her womb.

7 And *as* he did so year by year, ᴺᴺwhen she went up to the house of the Lord, so she provoked her; therefore she wept, and did not eat.

8 Then said ĕl-kā′-năh her husband to her, Hannah, why weepest thou? and why eatest thou not? and why is thy heart grieved? *am* not I ᴿbetter to thee than ten sons?

Prayer and vow of Hannah

9 So Hannah rose up after they had eaten in Shī′-lōh, and after they had drunk. Now Ē′-lī the priest sat upon a seat by a post of ᴿthe temple of the Lord.

10 ᴿAnd she *was* ᴺin bitterness of soul, and prayed unto the Lord, and wept sore.

11 And she ᴿvowed a vow, and said, O Lord of hosts, if thou wilt indeed ᴿlook on the affliction of thine handmaid, and ᴿremember me, and not forget thine handmaid, but wilt give unto thine handmaid ᴺa man child, then I will give him unto the Lord all the days of his life, and ᴿthere shall no razor come upon his head.

CHAP. 1
BC 1171
1 1 Chr. 6:27, 34
1 Ruth 1:2
3 Ex. 23:14
Luke 2:41
3 Heb. *from year to year*
3 Deut. 12:5
3 Josh. 18:1
4 Deut. 12:17
5 Or, *a double portion*
5 Gen. 30:2
6 Job 24:21
6 Heb. *angered her*
7 Or, *from the time that she*
7 Heb. *from her going up*
8 Ruth 4:15
9 ch. 3:3
10 Job 7:11
10 Heb. *bitter of soul*
11 Gen. 28:20
11 Ps. 25:18
11 Gen. 8:1
11 Heb. *seed of men*
11 Num. 6:5
Heb. *multiplied to pray* 12
Heb. *hard of spirit* 15
Ps. 62:8 15
Deut. 13:13 16
Or, *meditation* 16
Judg. 18:6 17
Mark 5:34
Ps. 20:4, 5 17
Ruth 2:13 18
Eccl. 9:7 18
Gen. 4:1 19
Gen. 30:22 19
Heb. *in revolution of days* 20
i.e. *Asked of God* 20
ver. 3 21
Luke 2:22 22
ver. 11, 28 22
Ex. 21:6 22
Num. 30:7 23
2 Sam. 7:25 23

12 And it came to pass, as she ᴺcontinued praying before the Lord, that Ē′-lī marked her mouth.

13 Now Hannah, she spake in her heart; only her lips moved, but her voice was not heard: therefore Ē′-lī thought she had been drunken.

14 And Ē′-lī said unto her, How long wilt thou be drunken? put away thy wine from thee.

15 And Hannah answered and said, No, my lord, I *am* a woman ᴺof a sorrowful spirit: I have drunk neither wine nor strong drink, but have ᴿpoured out my soul before the Lord.

16 Count not thine handmaid for a daughter of ᴿBē′-lĭ-ăl: for out of the abundance of my ᴺcomplaint and grief have I spoken hitherto.

17 Then Ē′-lī answered and said, ᴿGo in peace: and ᴿthe God of Israel grant *thee* thy petition that thou hast asked of him.

18 And she said, ᴿLet thine handmaid find grace in thy sight. So the woman ᴿwent her way, and did eat, and her countenance was no more *sad*.

Birth of Samuel

19 And they rose up in the morning early, and worshipped before the Lord, and returned, and came to their house to Rā′-măh: and ĕl-kā′-năh ᴿknew Hannah his wife; and ᴿthe Lord remembered her.

20 Wherefore it came to pass, ᴺwhen the time was come about after Hannah had conceived, that she bare a son, and called his name ᴺSamuel, *saying*, Because I have asked him of the Lord.

21 And the man ĕl-kā′-năh, and all his house, ᴿwent up to offer unto the Lord the yearly sacrifice, and his vow.

22 But Hannah went not up; for she said unto her husband, *I will not go up* until the child be weaned, and *then* I will ᴿbring him, that he may appear before the Lord, and there ᴿabide ᴿfor ever.

23 And ᴿĕl-kā′-năh her husband said unto her, Do what seemeth thee good; tarry until thou have weaned him; ᴿonly the Lord establish his word. So the woman abode, and gave her son suck until she weaned him.

24 And when she had weaned him, she

Rtook him up with her, with three bullocks, and one ē'-phäh of flour, and a bottle of wine, and brought him unto Rthe house of the LORD in Shī'-lōh: and the child *was* young.

25 And they slew a bullock, and Rbrought the child to Ē'-lī.

26 And she said, Oh my lord, R*as* thy soul liveth, my lord, I *am* the woman that stood by thee here, praying unto the LORD.

27 RFor this child I prayed; and the LORD hath given me my petition which I asked of him:

28 Therefore also I have Nlent him to the LORD; as long as he liveth Nhe shall be lent to the LORD. And he Rworshipped the LORD there.

CHAPTER 2

Hannah's song

AND Hannah Rprayed, and said, RMy heart rejoiceth in the LORD, Rmine horn is exalted in the LORD: my mouth is enlarged over mine enemies; because I Rrejoice in thy salvation.

2 R*There is* none holy as the LORD: for *there is* Rnone beside thee: neither *is there* any rock like our God.

3 Talk no more so exceeding proudly; Rlet *not* Narrogancy come out of your mouth: for the LORD *is* a God of knowledge, and by him actions are weighed.

4 RThe bows of the mighty men *are* broken, and they that stumbled are girded with strength.

5 *They that were* full have hired out themselves for bread; and *they that were* hungry ceased: so that Rthe barren hath born seven; and Rshe that hath many children is waxed feeble.

6 RThe LORD killeth, and maketh alive: he bringeth down to the grave, and bringeth up.

7 The LORD Rmaketh poor, and maketh rich: Rhe bringeth low, and lifteth up.

8 RHe raiseth up the poor out of the dust, *and* lifteth up the beggar from the dunghill, Rto set *them* among princes, and to make them inherit the throne of glory: for Rthe pillars of the earth *are* the LORD's, and he hath set the world upon them.

9 RHe will keep the feet of his saints, and the wicked shall be silent in darkness; for by strength shall no man prevail.

10 The adversaries of the LORD shall be Rbroken to pieces; Rout of heaven shall he thunder upon them: Rthe LORD shall judge the ends of the earth; and he shall give strength

unto his king, and Rexalt the horn of his anointed.   ★

The sons of Eli

11 And ĕl-kā'-näh went to Rā'-mäh to his house. RAnd the child did minister unto the LORD before Ē'-lī the priest.

12 Now the sons of Ē'-lī *were* Rsons of Bē'-lī-ăl; Rthey knew not the LORD.

13 And the priests' custom with the people *was, that,* when any man offered sacrifice, the priest's servant came, while the flesh was in seething, with a fleshhook of three teeth in his hand;

14 And he struck *it* into the pan, or kettle, or caldron, or pot; all that the fleshhook brought up the priest took for himself. So they did in Shī'-lōh unto all the Israelites that came thither.

15 Also before they Rburnt the fat, the priest's servant came, and said to the man that sacrificed, Give flesh to roast for the priest; for he will not have sodden flesh of thee, but raw.

16 And *if* any man said unto him, Let them not fail to burn the fat Npresently, and *then* take *as much* as thy soul desireth; then he would answer him, *Nay;* but thou shalt give *it me* now: and if not, I will take *it* by force.

17 Wherefore the sin of the young men was very great Rbefore the LORD: for men Rabhorred the offering of the LORD.

18 RBut Samuel ministered before the LORD, *being* a child, Rgirded with a linen ē'-phŏd.

19 Moreover his mother made him a little coat, and brought *it* to him from year to year, when she Rcame up with her husband to offer the yearly sacrifice.

20 And Ē'-lī Rblessed ĕl-kā'-näh and his wife, and said, The LORD give thee seed of this woman for the Nloan which is Rlent to the LORD. And they went unto their own home.

21 And the LORD Rvisited Hannah, so that she conceived, and bare three sons and two daughters. And the child Samuel Rgrew before the LORD.

22 Now Ē'-lī was very old, and heard all that his sons did unto all Israel; and how they lay with Rthe women that Nassembled *at* the door of the tabernacle of the congregation.

23 And he said unto them, Why do ye such things? for NI hear of your evil dealings by all this people.

24 Nay, my sons; for *it is* no good report that I hear: ye make the LORD's people Nto transgress.

25 If one man sin against another, the judge shall judge him: but if a man Rsin against the

---

CHAP. 1
BC 1171

24 Deut. 12:5, 6, 11
24 Josh. 18:1
25 Luke 2:22
26 2 Ki. 2:2, 4, 6
27 Mat. 7:7
28 Or, *returned him, whom I have obtained by petition, to the LORD*
28 Or, *he whom I have obtained by petition shall be returned*
28 Gen. 24:26, 52

CHAP. 2
BC 1165

1 Phil. 4:6
1 See Luke 1:46, etc.
1 Ps. 92:10
1 Ps. 9:14
2 Ex. 15:11
2 Deut. 4:35
3 Ps. 94:4 Jude 15
3 Heb. *hard*
4 Ps. 37:15
5 Ps. 113:9
5 Is. 54:1
6 Job 5:18 Hos. 6:1
7 Job 1:21
7 Ps. 75:7
8 Luke 1:52
8 Job 36:7
8 Job 38:4-6
9 Ps. 91:11
10 Ps. 2:9
10 Ps. 18:13
10 Ps. 96:13

Ps. 89:24   10
ver. 18   11
ch. 3:1
Deut. 13:13   12
Judg. 2:10   12
Rom. 1:28
Lev. 3:3, 4, 5, 16   15
Heb. *as on the day*   16
Gen. 6:11   17
Mal. 2:8   17
ver. 11   18
Ex. 28:4   18
ch. 1:3   19
Gen. 14:19   20
Or, *petition which she asked, etc.*   20
ch. 1:28   20
Gen. 21:1   21
ver. 26   21
Judg. 13:24
Ex. 38:8   22
Heb. *assembled by troops*   22
Or, *I hear evil words of you*   23
Or, *to cry out*   24
Num. 15:30   25

LORD, who shall entreat for him? Notwithstanding they hearkened not unto the voice of their father, ᴿbecause the LORD would slay them.

Samuel's favour with God

26 And the child Samuel ᴿgrew on, and was ᴿin favour both with the LORD, and also with men.

Prophecy against Eli's house

27 ᴿAnd there came a man of God unto Ē'-lī, and said unto him, Thus saith the LORD, ᴿDid I plainly appear unto the house of thy father, when they were in Egypt in Pharaoh's house?

28 And did I ᴿchoose him out of all the tribes of Israel *to be* my priest, to offer upon mine altar, to burn incense, to wear an ē'-phŏd before me? and ᴿdid I give unto the house of thy father all the offerings made by fire of the children of Israel?

29 Wherefore ᴿkick ye at my sacrifice and at mine offering, which I have commanded *in my* ᴿhabitation; and honourest thy sons above me, to make yourselves fat with the chiefest of all the offerings of Israel my people?

30 Wherefore the LORD God of Israel saith, ᴿI said indeed *that* thy house, and the house of thy father, should walk before me for ever: but now the LORD saith, ᴿBe it far from me; for them that honour me ᴿI will honour, and ᴿthey that despise me shall be lightly esteemed.

31 Behold, ᴿthe days come, that I will cut off thine arm, and the arm of thy father's house, that there shall not be an old man in thine house.

32 And thou shalt see ᴺan enemy *in my* habitation, in all *the wealth* which *God* shall give Israel: and there shall not be ᴿan old man in thine house for ever.

33 And the man of thine, *whom* I shall not cut off from mine altar, *shall be* to consume thine eyes, and to grieve thine heart: and all the increase of thine house shall die ᴺin the flower of their age.

34 And this *shall be* ᴿa sign unto thee, that shall come upon thy two sons, on Hŏph'-nī and Phĭn'-ĕ-hăs; ᴿin one day they shall die both of them.

35 And ᴿI will raise me up a faithful priest, *that* shall do according to *that* which *is* in mine heart and in my mind: and ᴿI will build him a sure house; and he shall walk before ᴿmine anointed for ever.   ★

36 ᴿAnd it shall come to pass, *that* every one that is left in thine house shall come *and*

crouch to him for a piece of silver and a morsel of bread, and shall say, ᴺPut me, I pray thee, into ᴺone of the priests' offices, that I may eat a piece of bread.

CHAPTER 3

The call of Samuel

AND ᴿthe child Samuel ministered unto the LORD before Ē'-lī. And ᴿthe word of the LORD was precious in those days; *there was* no open vision.

2 And it came to pass at that time, when Ē'-lī *was* laid down in his place, and his eyes began to wax dim, *that* he could not see;

3 And ere ᴿthe lamp of God went out ᴿin the temple of the LORD, where the ark of God *was*, and Samuel was laid down *to sleep;*

4 That the LORD called Samuel: and he answered, Here *am* I.

5 And he ran unto Ē'-lī, and said, Here *am* I; for thou calledst me. And he said, I called not; lie down again. And he went and lay down.

6 And the LORD called yet again, Samuel. And Samuel arose and went to Ē'-lī, and said, Here *am* I; for thou didst call me. And he answered, I called not, my son; lie down again.

7 ᴺNow Samuel ᴿdid not yet know the LORD, neither was the word of the LORD yet revealed unto him.

8 And the LORD called Samuel again the third time. And he arose and went to Ē'-lī, and said, Here *am* I; for thou didst call me. And Ē'-lī perceived that the LORD had called the child.

9 Therefore Ē'-lī said unto Samuel, Go, lie down: and it shall be, if he call thee, that thou shalt say, Speak, LORD; for thy servant heareth. So Samuel went and lay down in his place.

10 And the LORD came, and stood, and called as at other times, Samuel, Samuel. Then Samuel answered, Speak; for thy servant heareth.

11 And the LORD said to Samuel, Behold, I will do a thing in Israel, ᴿat which both the ears of every one that heareth it shall tingle.

12 In that day I will perform against Ē'-lī ᴿall *things* which I have spoken concerning his house: ᴺwhen I begin, I will also make an end.

13 ᴿFor ᴺI have told him that I will ᴿjudge his house for ever for the iniquity which he knoweth; because ᴿhis sons made themselves ᴺvile, and he ᴿrestrainedᴺ them not.

14 And therefore I have sworn unto the house of Ē'-lī, that the iniquity of Ē'-lī's house

R shall not be purged with sacrifice nor offering for ever.

15 And Samuel lay until the morning, and opened the doors of the house of the LORD. And Samuel feared to shew E′-li the vision.

16 Then E′-li called Samuel, and said, Samuel, my son. And he answered, Here *am* I.

17 And he said, What *is* the thing that *the* LORD hath said unto thee? I pray thee hide *it* not from me: R God do so to thee, and N more also, if thou hide *any* N thing from me of all the things that he said unto thee.

18 And Samuel told him N every whit, and hid nothing from him. And he said, R It *is* the LORD: let him do what seemeth him good.

Samuel established as a prophet

19 And Samuel R grew, and R the LORD was with him, R and did let none of his words fall to the ground.

20 And all Israel R from Dan even to Beer-shē′-bă knew that Samuel *was* N established *to be* a prophet of the LORD.

21 And the LORD appeared again in Shī′-lōh: for the LORD revealed himself to Samuel in Shī′-lōh by R the word of the LORD.

CHAPTER 4

The ark captured

AND the word of Samuel NN came to all Israel. Now Israel went out against the Philistines to battle, and pitched beside R Ĕb′-ĕn-ē′-zĕr: and the Philistines pitched in Ā′-phĕk.

2 And the Philistines put themselves in array against Israel: and when N they joined battle, Israel was smitten before the Philistines: and they slew of N the army in the field about four thousand men.

3 And when the people were come into the camp, the elders of Israel said, Wherefore hath the LORD smitten us to day before the Philistines? Let us N fetch the ark of the covenant of the LORD out of Shī′-lōh unto us, that, when it cometh among us, it may save us out of the hand of our enemies.

4 So the people sent to Shī′-lōh, that they might bring from thence the ark of the covenant of the LORD of hosts, R which dwelleth *between* R the chĕr′-ū-bĭms: and the two sons of E′-li, Hŏph′-nĭ and Phīn′-ĕ-hăs̀, *were* there with the ark of the covenant of God.

5 And when the ark of the covenant of the LORD came into the camp, all Israel shouted with a great shout, so that the earth rang again.

6 And when the Philistines heard the noise of the shout, they said, What *meaneth* the

noise of this great shout in the camp of the Hebrews? And they understood that the ark of the LORD was come into the camp.

7 And the Philistines were afraid, for they said, God is come into the camp. And they said, Woe unto us! for there hath not been such a thing N heretofore.

8 Woe unto us! who shall deliver us out of the hand of these mighty Gods? these *are* the Gods that smote the Egyptians with all the plagues in the wilderness.

9 R Be strong, and quit yourselves like men, O ye Philistines, that ye be not servants unto the Hebrews, R as they have been to you: N quit yourselves like men, and fight.

10 And the Philistines fought, and R Israel was smitten, and they fled every man into his tent: and there was a very great slaughter; for there fell of Israel thirty thousand footmen.

11 And R the ark of God was taken; and R the two sons of E′-li, Hŏph′-nĭ and Phīn′-ĕ-hăs̀, N were slain.

Death of Eli

12 And there ran a man of Benjamin out of the army, and R came to Shī′-lōh the same day with his clothes rent, and R with earth upon his head.

13 And when he came, lo, E′-li sat upon R a seat by the wayside watching: for his heart trembled for the ark of God. And when the man came into the city, and told *it*, all the city cried out.

14 And when E′-li heard the noise of the crying, he said, What *meaneth* the noise of this tumult? And the man came in hastily, and told E′-li.

15 Now E′-li was ninety and eight years old; and R his eyes N were dim, that he could not see.

16 And the man said unto E′-li, I *am* he that came out of the army, and I fled to day out of the army. And he said, R What N is there done, my son?

17 And the messenger answered and said, Israel is fled before the Philistines, and there hath been also a great slaughter among the people, and thy two sons also, Hŏph′-nĭ and Phīn′-ĕ-hăs̀, are dead, and the ark of God is taken.

18 And it came to pass, when he made mention of the ark of God, that he fell from off the seat backward by the side of the gate, and his neck brake, and he died: for he was an old man, and heavy. N And he had judged Israel forty years.

19 And his daughter in law, Phīn′-ĕ-hăs̀′ wife, was with child, *near* N to be delivered:

and when she heard the tidings that the ark of God was taken, and that her father in law and her husband were dead, she bowed herself and travailed; for her pains ᴺcame upon her.

20 And about the time of her death ᴿthe women that stood by her said unto her, Fear not; for thou hast borne a son. But she answered not, ᴺneither did she regard *it*.

21 And she named the child ᴿĪ′-chă-bŏd,ᴺ saying, ᴿThe glory is departed from Israel: because the ark of God was taken, and because of her father in law and her husband.

22 And she said, The glory is departed from Israel: for the ark of God is taken.

CHAPTER 5

The ark taken to Ashdod

AND the Philistines took the ark of God, and brought it ᴿfrom ĕb′-ĕn-ē′-zer unto Ăsh′-dŏd.

2 When the Philistines took the ark of God, they brought it into the house of ᴿDā′-gŏn, and set it by Dā′-gŏn.

3 And when they of Ăsh′-dŏd arose early on the morrow, behold, Dā′-gŏn *was* ᴿfallen upon his face to the earth before the ark of the Lord. And they took Dā′-gŏn, and ᴿset him in his place again.

4 And when they arose early on the morrow morning, behold, Dā′-gŏn *was* fallen upon his face to the ground before the ark of the Lord; and ᴿthe head of Dā′-gŏn and both the palms of his hands *were* cut off upon the threshold; only ᴺ*the stump of* Dā′-gŏn was left to him.

5 Therefore neither the priests of Dā′-gŏn, nor any that come into Dā′-gŏn's house, ᴿtread on the threshold of Dā′-gŏn in Ăsh′-dŏd unto this day.

6 But ᴿthe hand of the Lord was heavy upon them of Ăsh′-dŏd, and he ᴿdestroyed them, and smote them with ᴿemerods, *even* Ăsh′-dŏd and the coasts thereof.

7 And when the men of Ăsh′-dŏd saw that *it was* so, they said, The ark of the God of Israel shall not abide with us: for his hand is sore upon us, and upon Dā′-gŏn our god.

8 They sent therefore and gathered all the lords of the Philistines unto them, and said, What shall we do with the ark of the God of Israel? And they answered, Let the ark of the God of Israel be carried about unto Gath. And they carried the ark of the God of Israel about *thither*.

9 And it was *so,* that, after they had carried it about, ᴿthe hand of the Lord was against the city ᴿwith a very great destruction: and ᴿhe smote the men of the city, both small and

great, and they had emerods in their secret parts.

10 Therefore they sent the ark of God to Ĕk′-rŏn. And it came to pass, as the ark of God came to Ĕk′-rŏn, that the Ĕk′-rŏn-ītes cried out, saying, They have brought about the ark of the God of Israel to ᴺus, to slay us and our people.

11 So they sent and gathered together all the lords of the Philistines, and said, Send away the ark of the God of Israel, and let it go again to his own place, that it slay ᴺus not, and our people: for there was a deadly destruction throughout all the city; ᴿthe hand of God was very heavy there.

12 And the men that died not were smitten with the emerods: and the cry of the city went up to heaven.

CHAPTER 6

Return of the ark

AND the ark of the Lord was in the country of the Philistines seven months.

2 And the Philistines ᴿcalled for the priests and the diviners, saying, What shall we do to the ark of the Lord? tell us wherewith we shall send it to his place.

3 And they said, If ye send away the ark of the God of Israel, send it not ᴿempty; but in any wise return him ᴿa trespass offering: then ye shall be healed, and it shall ᴿbe known to you why his hand is not removed from you.

4 Then said they, What *shall be* the trespass offering which we shall return to him? They answered, Five golden emerods, and five golden mice, ᴿ*according to* the number of the lords of the Philistines: for one plague *was* on ᴺyou all, and on your lords.

5 Wherefore ye shall make images of your emerods, and images of your mice that ᴿmar the land; and ye shall ᴿgive glory unto the God of Israel: peradventure he will ᴿlighten his hand from off you, and from off ᴿyour gods, and from off your land.

6 Wherefore then do ye harden your hearts, ᴿas the Egyptians and Pharaoh hardened their hearts? when he had wrought ᴺwonderfully among them, ᴿdid they not let ᴺthe people go, and they departed?

7 Now therefore make ᴿa new cart, and take two milch kine, ᴿon which there hath come no yoke, and tie the kine to the cart, and bring their calves home from them:

8 And take the ark of the Lord, and lay it upon the cart; and put ᴿthe jewels of gold, which ye return him *for* a trespass offering, in

CHAP. 4

BC 1141

19 Heb. *were turned*
20 Gen. 35:17
20 Heb. *set not her heart*
21 ch. 14:3
21 i.e. *Where is the glory?* or, There is *no glory*
21 Ps. 26:8 & 78:61

CHAP. 5

BC 1141

1 ch. 4:1 & 7:12
2 Judg. 16:23
3 Is. 19:1 & 46:1, 2
3 Is. 46:7
4 Jer. 50:2 Ezek. 6:4, 6 Mic. 1:7
4 Or, *the fishy part*
5 Zeph. 1:9
6 ver. 7, 11 Ex. 9:3 Ps. 32:4 Acts 13:11
6 ch. 6:5
6 Deut. 28:27 Ps. 78:66
9 Deut. 2:15 ch. 7:13 & 12:15
9 ver. 11
9 ver. 6 Ps. 78:66

Heb. *me, to slay me and my*　10
Heb. *me not, and my*　11
ver. 6, 9　11

CHAP. 6

BC 1140

Gen. 41:8　2
Ex. 7:11
Dan. 2:2 & 5:7
Mat. 2:4
Ex. 23:15　3
Deut. 16:16
Lev. 5:15, 16　3
ver. 9　3
See ver. 17, 18　4
Josh. 13:3
Judg. 3:3
Heb. *them*　4
ch. 5:6　5
Josh. 7:19　5
Is. 42:12
Mal. 2:2
John 9:24
See ch. 5:6, 11　5
Ps. 39:10
ch. 5:3, 4, 7　5
Ex. 7:13　6 & 8:15 & 14:17
Or, *reproachfully*　6
Ex. 12:31　6
Heb. *them*　6
2 Sam. 6:3　7
Num. 19:2　7
ver. 4, 5　8

a coffer by the side thereof; and send it away, that it may go.

9 And see, if it goeth up by the way of his own coast to ᴿBĕth-shē´-mĕsh, *then* ᴺhe hath done us this great evil: but if not, then ᴿwe shall know that *it is* not his hand *that* smote us; it *was* a chance *that* happened to us.

Offerings of the Philistines

10 And the men did so; and took two milch kine, and tied them to the cart, and shut up their calves at home:

11 And they laid the ark of the LORD upon the cart, and the coffer with the mice of gold and the images of their emerods.

12 And the kine took the straight way to the way of Bĕth-shē´-mĕsh, *and* went along the highway, lowing as they went, and turned not aside *to* the right hand or *to* the left; and the lords of the Philistines went after them unto the border of Bĕth-shē´-mĕsh.

13 And *they of* Bĕth-shē´-mĕsh *were* reaping their wheat harvest in the valley: and they lifted up their eyes, and saw the ark, and rejoiced to see *it.*

14 And the cart came into the field of Joshua, a Bĕth-shē´-mīte, and stood there, where *there was* a great stone: and they clave the wood of the cart, and offered the kine a burnt offering unto the LORD.

15 And the Levites took down the ark of the LORD, and the coffer that *was* with it, wherein the jewels of gold *were,* and put *them* on the great stone: and the men of Bĕth-shē´-mĕsh offered burnt offerings and sacrificed sacrifices the same day unto the LORD.

16 And when ᴿthe five lords of the Philistines had seen *it,* they returned to Ĕk´-rŏn the same day.

17 ᴿAnd these *are* the golden emerods which the Philistines returned *for* a trespass offering unto the LORD; for ăsh´-dŏd one, for Gā´-ză one, for Ăs´-kĕ-lon one, for Gath one, for Ĕk´-rŏn one;

18 And the golden mice, *according to* the number of all the cities of the Philistines *belonging* to the five lords, *both* of fenced cities, and of country villages, even unto the ᴺgreat *stone of* Abel, whereon they set down the ark of the LORD: *which stone remaineth* unto this day in the field of Joshua, the Bĕth-shē´-mīte.

19 And ᴿhe smote the men of Bĕth-shē´-mĕsh, because they had looked into the ark of the LORD, even he smote of the people fifty thousand and threescore and ten men: and the people lamented, because the LORD had smitten *many* of the people with a great slaughter.

20 And the men of Bĕth-shē´-mĕsh said,

ᴿWho is able to stand before this holy LORD God? and to whom shall he go up from us?

21 And they sent messengers to the inhabitants of ᴿKĭr´-jăth-jē´-ă-rĭm, saying, The Philistines have brought again the ark of the LORD; come ye down, *and* fetch it up to you.

CHAPTER 7

AND the men of ᴿKĭr´-jăth-jē´-ă-rĭm came, and fetched up the ark of the LORD, and brought it into the house of ᴿĂ-bĭn´-ă-dăb in the hill, and sanctified ĕl-ē-ā´-zär his son to keep the ark of the LORD.

2 And it came to pass, while the ark abode in Kĭr´-jăth-jē´-ă-rĭm, that the time was long; for it was twenty years: and all the house of Israel lamented after the LORD.

Samuel calls for repentance

3 And Samuel spake unto all the house of Israel, saying, If ye do ᴿreturn unto the LORD with all your hearts, *then* ᴿput away the strange gods and ᴿĂsh´-tă-rōth from among you, and ᴿprepare your hearts unto the LORD, and ᴿserve him only: and he will deliver you out of the hand of the Philistines.

4 Then the children of Israel did put away ᴿBā´-ă-lĭm and Ăsh´-tă-rōth, and served the LORD only.

Israel's victory at Mizpeh

5 And Samuel said, ᴿGather all Israel to Mĭz´-pēh, and I will pray for you unto the LORD.

6 And they gathered together to Mĭz´-pēh, ᴿand drew water, and poured *it* out before the LORD, and ᴿfasted on that day, and said there, ᴿWe have sinned against the LORD. And Samuel judged the children of Israel in Mĭz´-pēh.

7 And when the Philistines heard that the children of Israel were gathered together to Mĭz´-pēh, the lords of the Philistines went up against Israel. And when the children of Israel heard *it,* they were afraid of the Philistines.

8 And the children of Israel said to Samuel, ᴿCease ᴺnot to cry unto the LORD our God for us, that he will save us out of the hand of the Philistines.

9 And Samuel took a sucking lamb, and offered *it for* a burnt offering wholly unto the LORD: and ᴿSamuel cried unto the LORD for Israel; and the LORD ᴺheard him.

10 And as Samuel was offering up the burnt offering, the Philistines drew near to battle against Israel: ᴿbut the LORD thundered with a great thunder on that day upon the Philistines, and discomfited them; and they were smitten before Israel.

11 And the men of Israel went out of Mĭz′-pĕh, and pursued the Philistines, and smote them, until *they came* under Bĕth′-cär.

12 Then Samuel ᴿtook a stone, and set *it* between Mĭz′-pĕh and Shen, and called the name of it ᴺĔb′-ĕn-ē′-zĕr, saying, Hitherto hath the LORD helped us.

13 ᴿSo the Philistines were subdued, and they ᴿcame no more into the coast of Israel: and the hand of the LORD was against the Philistines all the days of Samuel.

14 And the cities which the Philistines had taken from Israel were restored to Israel, from ĕk′-rŏn even unto Gath; and the coasts thereof did Israel deliver out of the hands of the Philistines. And there was peace between Israel and the Amorites.

Samuel a judge in Israel

15 And Samuel ᴿjudged Israel all the days of his life.

16 And he went from year to year ᴺin circuit to Beth-el, and Gĭl′-găl, and Mĭz′-pĕh, and judged Israel in all those places.

17 And ᴿhis return *was* to Rā′-măh; for there *was* his house; and there he judged Israel; and there he ᴿbuilt an altar unto the LORD.

CHAPTER 8

Sons of Samuel

AND it came to pass, when Samuel was old, that he ᴿmade his ᴿsons judges over Israel.

2 Now the name of his firstborn was ᴺJō′-ĕl; and the name of his second, Ă-bī′-ăh: *they were* judges in Bē͡er-shē′-bă.

3 And his sons ᴿwalked not in his ways, but turned aside ᴿafter lucre, and ᴿtook bribes, and perverted judgment.

Israel asks for a king

4 Then all the elders of Israel gathered themselves together, and came to Samuel unto Rā′-măh,

5 And said unto him, Behold, thou art old, and thy sons walk not in thy ways: now ᴿmake us a king to judge us like all the nations.

6 But the thing ᴺdispleased Samuel, when they said, Give us a king to judge us. And Samuel prayed unto the LORD.

7 And the LORD said unto Samuel, Hearken unto the voice of the people in all that they say unto thee: for ᴿthey have not rejected thee, but ᴿthey have rejected me, that I should not reign over them.

8 According to all the works which they have done since the day that I brought them up out of Egypt even unto this day, wherewith they have forsaken me, and served other gods, so do they also unto thee.

9 Now therefore ᴺhearken unto their voice: ᴺhowbeit yet protest solemnly unto them, and ᴿshew them the manner of the king that shall reign over them.

Advice of Samuel

10 And Samuel told all the words of the LORD unto the people that asked of him a king.

11 And he said, ᴿThis will be the manner of the king that shall reign over you: ᴿHe will take your sons, and appoint *them* for himself, for his chariots, and *to be* his horsemen; and *some* shall run before his chariots.

12 And he will appoint him captains over thousands, and captains over fifties; and *will set them* to ear his ground, and to reap his harvest, and to make his instruments of war, and instruments of his chariots.

13 And he will take your daughters *to be* confectionaries, and *to be* cooks, and *to be* bakers.

14 And ᴿhe will take your fields, and your vineyards, and your oliveyards, *even* the best *of them,* and give *them* to his servants.

15 And he will take the tenth of your seed, and of your vineyards, and give to his ᴺofficers, and to his servants.

16 And he will take your menservants, and your maidservants, and your goodliest young men, and your asses, and put *them* to his work.

17 He will take the tenth of your sheep: and ye shall be his servants.

18 And ye shall cry out in that day because of your king which ye shall have chosen you; and the LORD ᴿwill not hear you in that day.

Israel's insistence

19 Nevertheless the people ᴿrefused to obey the voice of Samuel; and they said, Nay; but we will have a king over us;

20 That we also may be ᴿlike all the nations; and that our king may judge us, and go out before us, and fight our battles.

21 And Samuel heard all the words of the people, and he rehearsed them in the ears of the LORD.

22 And the LORD said to Samuel, ᴿHearken unto their voice, and make them a king. And Samuel said unto the men of Israel, Go ye every man unto his city.

CHAP. 7
BC 1112
12 Gen. 28:18
Josh. 4:9
12 i.e. *The stone of help*, ch. 4:1
13 Judg. 13:1
13 ch. 13:5
15 ch. 12:11
Judg. 2:16
16 Heb. *and he circuited*
17 ch. 8:4
17 Judg. 21:4

CHAP. 8
BC 1112
1 Deut. 16:18
2 Chr. 19:5
1 Judg. 10:4
& 12:14
compared with
Judg. 5:10
2 *Vashni,*
1 Chr. 6:28
3 Jer. 22:15-17
3 Ex. 18:21
1 Tim. 3:3
& 6:10
3 Deut. 16:19
Ps. 15:5
5 ver. 19, 20
Deut. 17:14
Hos. 13:10
Acts 13:21
6 Heb. *was evil in the eyes of Samuel*
7 See Ex. 16:8
7 ch. 10:19
& 12:17, 19
Hos. 13:10, 11

Or, *obey*   9
Or, *notwithstanding when thou hast solemnly protested against them, then thou shalt shew, etc.*
ver. 11   9
See Deut. 17:16, 11 etc.
ch. 10:25
ch. 14:52   11
1 Ki. 21:7   14
See Ezek. 46:18
Heb. *eunuchs,*   15
Gen. 37:36
Is. 1:15   18
Mic. 3:4
Jer. 44:16   19
ver. 5   20
ver. 7   22
Hos. 13:11

CHAPTER 9

Saul comes to Samuel

NOW there was a man of Benjamin, whose name *was* [R]Kish, the son of Ă-bī′-ĕl, the son of Zē′-rôr, the son of Bĕ-chō′-răth, the son of Ă-phī′-ăh, [N]a Benjamite, a mighty man of [N]power.

2 And he had a son, whose name *was* Saul, a choice young man, and a goodly: and *there was* not among the children of Israel a goodlier person than he: [R]from his shoulders and upward *he was* higher than any of the people.

3 And the asses of Kish Saul's father were lost. And Kish said to Saul his son, Take now one of the servants with thee, and arise, go seek the asses.

4 And he passed through mount Ē′-phră-ĭm, and passed through the land of [R]Shăl′-ĭ-sha, but they found *them* not: then they passed through the land of Shā′-lĭm, and *there they were* not: and he passed through the land of the Benjamites, but they found *them* not.

5 *And* when they were come to the land of Zuph, Saul said to his servant that *was* with him, Come, and let us return; lest my father leave *caring* for the asses, and take thought for us.

6 And he said unto him, Behold now, *there is* in this city [R]a man of God, and *he is* an honourable man; [R]all that he saith cometh surely to pass: now let us go thither; peradventure he can shew us our way that we should go.

7 Then said Saul to his servant, But, behold, *if* we go, [R]what shall we bring the man? for the bread [N]is spent in our vessels, and *there is* not a present to bring to the man of God: what [N]have we?

8 And the servant answered Saul again, and said, Behold, [N]I have here at hand the fourth part of a shĕ′-kĕl of silver: *that* will I give to the man of God, to tell us our way.

9 (Beforetime in Israel, when a man [R]went to inquire of God, thus he spake, Come, and let us go to the seer: for *he that is* now *called* a Prophet was beforetime called [R]a Seer.)

10 Then said Saul to his servant, [N]Well said; come, let us go. So they went unto the city where the man of God *was*.

11 *And* as they went up [N]the hill to the city, [R]they found young maidens going out to draw water, and said unto them, Is the seer here?

12 And they answered them, and said, He is; behold, *he is* before you: make haste now, for he came to day to the city; for [R]there is a [N]sacrifice of the people to day [R]in the high place:

13 As soon as ye be come into the city, ye shall straightway find him, before he go up to

CHAP. **9**
BC 1095
1 ch. 14:51
1 Chr. 8:33
& 9:39
1 Or, *the son of a man of Jemini*
1 Or, *substance*
2 ch. 10:23
4 2 Ki. 4:42
6 Deut. 33:1
1 Ki. 13:1
6 ch. 3:19
7 See Judg. 6:18
& 13:17
1 Ki. 14:3
2 Ki. 4:42
& 8:8
7 Heb. *is gone out of, etc.*
7 Heb. *is with us*
8 Heb. *there is found in my hand*
9 Gen. 25:22
9 2 Sam. 24:11
2 Ki. 17:13
1 Chr. 26:28
& 29:29
2 Chr. 16:7, 10
Is. 30:10
Amos 7:12
10 Heb. *Thy word is good*
11 Heb. *in the ascent of the city*
11 Gen. 24:11
12 Gen. 31:54
ch. 16:2
12 Or, *feast*
12 1 Ki. 3:2

Heb. *to day*　　13
ch. 15:1　　　　15
Acts 13:21
Heb. *revealed*　15
the ear of Samuel,
ch. 20:2
ch. 10:1　　　　16
Ex. 2:25　　　　16
& 3:7, 9
ch. 16:12　　　17
Hos. 13:11
Heb. *restrain in*　17
ver. 3
Heb. *to day*　　20
three days
ch. 8:5, 19　　　20
& 12:13
ch. 15:17　　　21
Judg. 20:46-48　21
See Judg. 6:15　21
Heb. *according*　21
to this word?
Lev. 7:32, 33　　24
Ezek. 24:4
Or, *reserved*　　24

the high place to eat: for the people will not eat until he come, because he doth bless the sacrifice; *and* afterwards they eat that be bidden. Now therefore get you up; for about [N]this time ye shall find him.

14 And they went up into the city: *and* when they were come into the city, behold, Samuel came out against them, for to go up to the high place.

God reveals his choice

15 [R]Now the LORD had [N]told Samuel in his ear a day before Saul came, saying,

16 To morrow about this time I will send thee a man out of the land of Benjamin, [R]and thou shalt anoint him *to be* captain over my people Israel, that he may save my people out of the hand of the Philistines: for I have [R]looked upon my people, because their cry is come unto me.

17 And when Samuel saw Saul, the LORD said unto him, [R]Behold the man whom I spake to thee of! this same shall [N]reign over my people.

18 Then Saul drew near to Samuel in the gate, and said, Tell me, I pray thee, where the seer's house *is*.

19 And Samuel answered Saul, and said, I *am* the seer: go up before me unto the high place; for ye shall eat with me to day, and to morrow I will let thee go, and will tell thee all that *is* in thine heart.

20 And as for [R]thine asses that were lost [N]three days ago, set not thy mind on them; for they are found. And on whom [R]*is* all the desire of Israel? *Is it* not on thee, and on all thy father's house?

21 And Saul answered and said, [R]*Am* not I a Benjamite, of the [R]smallest of the tribes of Israel? and [R]my family the least of all the families of the tribe of Benjamin? wherefore then speakest thou [N]so to me?

Saul entertained

22 And Samuel took Saul and his servant, and brought them into the parlour, and made them sit in the chiefest place among them that were bidden, which *were* about thirty persons.

23 And Samuel said unto the cook, Bring the portion which I gave thee, of which I said unto thee, Set it by thee.

24 And the cook took up [R]the shoulder, and *that* which *was* upon it, and set *it* before Saul. And *Samuel* said, Behold that which is [N]left! set *it* before thee, *and* eat: for unto this time hath it been kept for thee since I said, I have invited the people. So Saul did eat with Samuel that day.

25 And when they were come down from the high place into the city, *Samuel* communed with Saul upon [R]the top of the house.

26 And they arose early: and it came to pass about the spring of the day, that Samuel called Saul to the top of the house, saying, Up, that I may send thee away. And Saul arose, and they went out both of them, he and Samuel, abroad.

27 *And* as they were going down to the end of the city, Samuel said to Saul, Bid the servant pass on before us, (and he passed on,) but stand thou still [N]a while, that I may shew thee the word of God.

CHAPTER 10

Saul anointed prince over Israel

THEN [R]Samuel took a vial of oil, and poured *it* upon his head, [R]and kissed him, and said, *Is it* not because [R]the LORD hath anointed thee *to be* captain over [R]his inheritance?

2 When thou art departed from me to day, then thou shalt find two men by [R]Rachel's sepulchre in the border of Benjamin [R]at Zĕl'-zăh; and they will say unto thee, The asses which thou wentest to seek are found: and, lo, thy father hath left [N]the care of the asses, and sorroweth for you, saying, What shall I do for my son?

3 Then shalt thou go on forward from thence, and thou shalt come to the plain of Tā'-bôr, and there shall meet thee three men going up [R]to God to Beth-el, one carrying three kids, and another carrying three loaves of bread, and another carrying a bottle of wine:

4 And they will [N]salute thee, and give thee two *loaves* of bread; which thou shalt receive of their hands.

5 After that thou shalt come to the hill of God, [R]where *is* the garrison of the Philistines: and it shall come to pass, when thou art come thither to the city, that thou shalt meet a company of prophets coming down [R]from the high place with a psaltery, and a tabret, and a pipe, and a harp, before them; [R]and they shall prophesy:

6 And [R]the spirit of the LORD will come upon thee, and [R]thou shalt prophesy with them, and shalt be turned into another man.

7 And [N]let it be, when these [R]signs are come unto thee, [N]*that* thou do as occasion serve thee; for [R]God *is* with thee.

8 And thou shalt go down before me [R]to Gĭl'-găl; and, behold, I will come down unto thee, to offer burnt offerings, *and* to sacrifice sacrifices of peace offerings: [R]seven days shalt

thou tarry, till I come to thee, and shew thee what thou shalt do.

Saul among the prophets

9 And it was *so,* that when he had turned his [N]back to go from Samuel, God [N]gave him another heart: and all those signs came to pass that day.

10 And [R]when they came thither to the hill, behold, [R]a company of prophets met him; and the spirit of God came upon him, and he prophesied among them.

11 And it came to pass, when all that knew him beforetime saw that, behold, he prophesied among the prophets, then the people said [N]one to another, What *is* this *that* is come unto the son of Kish? [R]*Is* Saul also among the prophets?

12 And one [N]of the same place answered and said, But [R]who *is* their father? Therefore it became a proverb, *Is* Saul also among the prophets?

13 And when he had made an end of prophesying, he came to the high place.

14 And Saul's uncle said unto him and to his servant, Whither went ye? And he said, To seek the asses: and when we saw that *they* were no where, we came to Samuel.

15 And Saul's uncle said, Tell me, I pray thee, what Samuel said unto you.

16 And Saul said unto his uncle, He told us plainly that the asses were found. But of the matter of the kingdom, whereof Samuel spake, he told him not.

Saul proclaimed king at Mizpeh

17 And Samuel called the people together [R]unto the LORD [R]to Mĭz'-pēh;

18 And said unto the children of Israel, [R]Thus saith the LORD God of Israel, I brought up Israel out of Egypt, and delivered you out of the hand of the Egyptians, and out of the hand of all kingdoms, *and* of them that oppressed you:

19 [R]And ye have this day rejected your God, who himself saved you out of all your adversities and your tribulations; and ye have said unto him, *Nay,* but set a king over us. Now therefore present yourselves before the LORD by your tribes, and by your thousands.

20 And when Samuel had [R]caused all the tribes of Israel to come near, the tribe of Benjamin was taken.

21 When he had caused the tribe of Benjamin to come near by their families, the family of Mā'-trī was taken, and Saul the son of Kish was taken: and when they sought him, he could not be found.

22 Therefore they ᴿinquired of the Lᴏʀᴅ further, if the man should yet come thither. And the Lᴏʀᴅ answered, Behold, he hath hid himself among the stuff.

23 And they ran and fetched him thence: and when he stood among the people, ᴿhe was higher than any of the people from his shoulders and upward.

24 And Samuel said to all the people, See ye him ᴿwhom the Lᴏʀᴅ hath chosen, that *there is* none like him among all the people? And all the people shouted, and said, ᴿGodᴺ save the king.

Rights and duties of kingship

25 Then Samuel told the people ᴿthe manner of the kingdom, and wrote *it* in a book, and laid *it* up before the Lᴏʀᴅ. And Samuel sent all the people away, every man to his house.

26 And Saul also went home ᴿto Gĭb′-ĕ-ăh; and there went with him a band of men, whose hearts God had touched.

27 ᴿBut the ᴿchildren of Bē′-lĭ-ăl said, How shall this man save us? And they despised him, ᴿand brought him no presents. But ᴺhe held his peace.

CHAPTER 11

Saul defeats the Ammonites

THEN ᴿNahash the Ammonite came up, and encamped against ᴿJā′-bĕsh-gĭl′-ĕ-ăd: and all the men of Jā′-bĕsh said unto Nahash, ᴿMake a covenant with us, and we will serve thee.

2 And Nahash the Ammonite answered them, On this *condition* will I make *a covenant* with you, that I may thrust out all your right eyes, and lay it *for* ᴿa reproach upon all Israel.

3 And the elders of Jā′-bĕsh said unto him, ᴺGive us seven days′ respite, that we may send messengers unto all the coasts of Israel: and then, if *there be* no man to save us, we will come out to thee.

4 Then came the messengers ᴿto Gĭb′-ĕ-ăh of Saul, and told the tidings in the ears of the people: and ᴿall the people lifted up their voices, and wept.

5 And, behold, Saul came after the herd out of the field; and Saul said, What *aileth* the people that they weep? And they told him the tidings of the men of Jā′-bĕsh.

6 ᴿAnd the spirit of God came upon Saul when he heard those tidings, and his anger was kindled greatly.

7 And he took a yoke of oxen, and ᴿhewed them in pieces, and sent *them* throughout all

CHAP. 10
BC 1095
22 ch. 23:2, 4, 10, 11
23 ch. 9:2
24 2 Sam. 21:6
24 1 Ki. 1:25, 39
24 Heb. *Let the king live*
25 ch. 8:11
26 Judg. 20:14
ch. 11:4
27 ch. 11:12
27 Deut. 13:13
27 2 Sam. 8:2
1 Ki. 4:21
Mat. 2:11
27 Or, *he was as though he had been deaf*

CHAP. 11
BC 1095
1 ch. 12:12
1 Judg. 21:8
1 Gen. 26:28
1 Ki. 20:34
2 Gen. 34:14
ch. 17:26
3 Heb. *Forbear us*
4 ch. 10:26 & 15:34
2 Sam. 21:6
4 Judg. 2:4
6 Judg. 3:10 & 6:34
ch. 10:10
7 Judg. 19:29

Judg. 21:5, 8, 10	7
Heb. *as one man,*	7
Judg. 20:1	
Judg. 1:5	8
2 Sam. 24:9	8
Or, *deliverance*	9
ver. 3	10
See ch. 31:11	11
Judg. 7:16	11
ch. 10:27	
See Luke 19:27	12
2 Sam. 19:22	13
Ex. 14:13, 30	13
ch. 19:5	
ch. 10:8	14
ch. 10:17	15
ch. 10:8	15

CHAP. 12
BC 1095
ch. 8:5, 19, 20 ... 1
ch. 10:24 ... 1
Num. 27:17 ... 2
ch. 8:20	
ch. 8:1, 5 ... 2

the coasts of Israel by the hands of messengers, saying, ᴿWhosoever cometh not forth after Saul and after Samuel, so shall it be done unto his oxen. And the fear of the Lᴏʀᴅ fell on the people, and they came out ᴺwith one consent.

8 And when he numbered them in ᴿBē′-zĕk, the children ᴿof Israel were three hundred thousand, and the men of Judah thirty thousand.

9 And they said unto the messengers that came, Thus shall ye say unto the men of Jā′-bĕsh-gĭl′-ĕ-ăd, To morrow, by *that time* the sun be hot, ye shall have ᴺhelp. And the messengers came and shewed *it* to the men of Jā′-bĕsh; and they were glad.

10 Therefore the men of Jā′-bĕsh said, To morrow ᴿwe will come out unto you, and ye shall do with us all that seemeth good unto you.

11 And it was *so* on the morrow, that ᴿSaul put the people ᴿin three companies; and they came into the midst of the host in the morning watch, and slew the Ammonites until the heat of the day: and it came to pass, that they which remained were scattered, so that two of them were not left together.

Saul proclaimed king in Gilgal

12 And the people said unto Samuel, ᴿWho *is* he that said, Shall Saul reign over us? ᴿbring the men, that we may put them to death.

13 And Saul said, ᴿThere shall not a man be put to death this day: for to day ᴿthe Lᴏʀᴅ hath wrought salvation in Israel.

14 Then said Samuel to the people, Come, and let us go ᴿto Gĭl′-găl, and renew the kingdom there.

15 And all the people went to Gĭl′-găl; and there they made Saul king ᴿbefore the Lᴏʀᴅ in Gĭl′-găl; and ᴿthere they sacrificed sacrifices of peace offerings before the Lᴏʀᴅ; and there Saul and all the men of Israel rejoiced greatly.

CHAPTER 12

Samuel's address to Israel

AND Samuel said unto all Israel, Behold, I have hearkened unto ᴿyour voice in all that ye said unto me, and ᴿhave made a king over you.

2 And now, behold, the king ᴿwalketh before you: ᴿand I am old and grayheaded; and, behold, my sons *are* with you: and I have walked before you from my childhood unto this day.

3 Behold, here I *am:* witness against me before the LORD, and before [R]his anointed: [R]whose ox have I taken? or whose ass have I taken? or whom have I defrauded? whom have I oppressed? or of whose hand have I received *any* [N]bribe to [R]blind mine eyes therewith? and I will restore it you.

4 And they said, Thou hast not defrauded us, nor oppressed us, neither hast thou taken aught of any man's hand.

5 And he said unto them, The LORD *is* witness against you, and his anointed *is* witness this day, [R]that ye have not found aught [R]in my hand. And they answered, *He is* witness.

6 And Samuel said unto the people, [R]*It is* the LORD that [N]advanced Moses and Aaron, and that brought your fathers up out of the land of Egypt.

7 Now therefore stand still, that I may [R]reason with you before the LORD of all the [N]righteous acts of the LORD, which he did [N]to you and to your fathers.

8 [R]When Jacob was come into Egypt, and your fathers [R]cried unto the LORD, then the LORD [R]sent Moses and Aaron, which brought forth your fathers out of Egypt, and made them dwell in this place.

9 And when they [R]forgat the LORD their God, [R]he sold them into the hand of Sĭs'-ĕ-rä, captain of the host of Hā'-zôr, and into the hand of [R]the Philistines, and into the hand of the king [R]of Moab, and they fought against them.

10 And they cried unto the LORD, and said, [R]We have sinned, because we have forsaken the LORD, [R]and have served Bā'-ă-lĭm and Ăsh'-tă-rŏth: but now [R]deliver us out of the hand of our enemies, and we will serve thee.

11 And the LORD sent [R]Jĕr-ŭb-bā'-ăl, and Bē'-dăn, and [R]Jĕph'-thăh, and [R]Samuel, and delivered you out of the hand of your enemies on every side, and ye dwelled safe.

12 And when ye saw that [R]Nahash the king of the children of Ammon came against you, [R]ye said unto me, Nay; but a king shall reign over us: when [R]the LORD your God *was* your king.

13 Now therefore [R]behold the king [R]whom ye have chosen, *and* whom ye have desired! and, behold, [R]the LORD hath set a king over you.

14 If ye will [R]fear the LORD, and serve him, and obey his voice, and not rebel against the [N]commandment of the LORD, then shall both ye and also the king that reigneth over you [N]continue following the LORD your God:

15 But if ye will [R]not obey the voice of the LORD, but rebel against the commandment of

the LORD, then shall the hand of the LORD be against you, [R]as *it was* against your fathers.

16 Now therefore [R]stand and see this great thing, which the LORD will do before your eyes.

17 *Is it* not [R]wheat harvest to day? [R]I will call unto the LORD, and he shall send thunder and rain; that ye may perceive and see that [R]your wickedness *is* great, which ye have done in the sight of the LORD, in asking you a king.

18 So Samuel called unto the LORD; and the LORD sent thunder and rain that day: and [R]all the people greatly feared the LORD and Samuel.

19 And all the people said unto Samuel, [R]Pray for thy servants unto the LORD thy God, that we die not: for we have added unto all our sins *this* evil, to ask us a king.

20 And Samuel said unto the people, Fear not: ye have done all this wickedness: yet turn not aside from following the LORD, but serve the LORD with all your heart;

21 And [R]turn ye not aside: [R]for *then should ye go* after vain *things,* which cannot profit nor deliver; for they *are* vain.

22 For [R]the LORD will not forsake his people [R]for his great name's sake: because [R]it hath pleased the LORD to make you his people.

23 Moreover as for me, God forbid that I should sin against the LORD [R]in[N] ceasing to pray for you: but [R]I will teach you the [R]good and the right way:

24 [R]Only fear the LORD, and serve him in truth with all your heart: for [R]consider·[N]how [R]great *things* he hath done for you.

25 But if ye shall still do wickedly, [R]ye shall be consumed, [R]both ye and your king.

CHAPTER 13

War with the Philistines

SAUL [N]reigned one year; and when he had reigned two years over Israel,

2 Saul chose him three thousand *men* of Israel; *whereof* two thousand were with Saul in Mĭch'-măsh and in mount Beth-el, and a thousand were with Jonathan in [R]Gĭb'-ĕ-ăh of Benjamin: and the rest of the people he sent every man to his tent.

3 And Jonathan smote [R]the garrison of the Philistines that *was* in [N]Gē'-bă, and the Philistines heard *of it.* And Saul blew the trumpet throughout all the land, saying, Let the Hebrews hear.

4 And all Israel heard say *that* Saul had smitten a garrison of the Philistines, and *that*

Israel also [N]was had in abomination with the Philistines. And the people were called together after Saul to Gĭl'-găl.

5 And the Philistines gathered themselves together to fight with Israel, thirty thousand chariots, and six thousand horsemen, and people as the sand which *is* on the sea shore in multitude: and they came up, and pitched in Mĭch'-măsh, eastward from Bĕth-ā'-vĕn.

6 When the men of Israel saw that they were in a strait, (for the people were distressed,) then the people [R]did hide themselves in caves, and in thickets, and in rocks, and in high places, and in pits.

7 And *some of* the Hebrews went over Jordan to the land of Gad and Gilead. As for Saul, he *was* yet in Gĭl'-găl, and all the people [N]followed him trembling.

Saul's foolish offering

8 [R]And he tarried seven days, according to the set time that Samuel *had appointed:* but Samuel came not to Gĭl'-găl; and the people were scattered from him.

9 And Saul said, Bring hither a burnt offering to me, and peace offerings. And he offered the burnt offering.

10 And it came to pass, that as soon as he had made an end of offering the burnt offering, behold, Samuel came; and Saul went out to meet him, that he might [N]salute him.

11 And Samuel said, What hast thou done? And Saul said, Because I saw that the people were scattered from me, and *that* thou camest not within the days appointed, and *that* the Philistines gathered themselves together at Mĭch'-măsh;

12 Therefore said I, The Philistines will come down now upon me to Gĭl'-găl, and I have not [N]made supplication unto the LORD: I forced myself therefore, and offered a burnt offering.

13 And Samuel said to Saul, [R]Thou hast done foolishly: [R]thou hast not kept the commandment of the LORD thy God, which he commanded thee: for now would the LORD have established thy kingdom upon Israel for ever.

14 [R]But now thy kingdom shall not continue: [R]the LORD hath sought him a man after his own heart, and the LORD hath commanded him *to be* captain over his people, because thou hast not kept *that* which the LORD commanded thee.

Saul's army

15 And Samuel arose, and gat him up from Gĭl'-găl unto Gĭb'-ĕ-äh of Benjamin. And Saul

numbered the people *that were* [N]present with him, [R]about six hundred men.

16 And Saul, and Jonathan his son, and the people *that were* present with them, abode in [N]Gĭb'-ĕ-äh of Benjamin: but the Philistines encamped in Mĭch'-măsh.

17 And the spoilers came out of the camp of the Philistines in three companies: one company turned unto the way *that leadeth to* [R]Ŏph'-räh, unto the land of Shū'-ăl:

18 And another company turned the way *to* [R]Bĕth-hôr'-ŏn: and another company turned *to* the way of the border that looketh to the valley of [R]Zĕ-bō'-ĭm toward the wilderness.

19 Now [R]there was no smith found throughout all the land of Israel: for the Philistines said, Lest the Hebrews make *them* swords or spears:

20 But all the Israelites went down to the Philistines, to sharpen every man his share, and his coulter, and his axe, and his mattock.

21 Yet they had [N]a file for the mattocks, and for the coulters, and for the forks, and for the axes, and [N]to sharpen the goads.

22 So it came to pass in the day of battle, that [R]there was neither sword nor spear found in the hand of any of the people that *were* with Saul and Jonathan: but with Saul and with Jonathan his son was there found.

23 [R]And the [N]garrison of the Philistines went out to the passage of Mĭch'-măsh.

CHAPTER 14

Victory of Jonathan at Michmash

NOW [N]it came to pass upon a day, that Jonathan the son of Saul said unto the young man that bare his armour, Come, and let us go over to the Philistines' garrison, that *is* on the other side. But he told not his father.

2 And Saul tarried in the uttermost part of Gĭb'-ĕ-äh under a pomegranate tree which *is* in Mĭg'-rŏn: and the people that *were* with him *were* [R]about six hundred men;

3 And [R]Ă-hī'-äh, the son of Ă-hī'-tŭb, [R]Ī'-chȧ-bŏd's brother, the son of Phĭn'-ĕ-hăs, the son of Ē'-lī, the LORD's priest in Shī'-lōh, [R]wearing an ē'-phŏd. And the people knew not that Jonathan was gone.

4 And between the passages, by which Jonathan sought to go over [R]unto the Philistines' garrison, *there was* a sharp rock on the one side, and a sharp rock on the other side: and the name of the one *was* Bō'-zĕz, and the name of the other Sĕn'-ĕh.

5 The [N]forefront of the one *was* situate northward over against Mĭch'-măsh, and the other southward over against Gĭb'-ĕ-äh.

6 And Jonathan said to the young man that bare his armour, Come, and let us go over unto the garrison of these uncircumcised: it may be that the LORD will work for us: for *there is* no restraint to the LORD [R]to save by many or by few.

7 And his armourbearer said unto him, Do all that *is* in thine heart: turn thee; behold, I *am* with thee according to thy heart.

8 Then said Jonathan, Behold, we will pass over unto *these* men, and we will discover ourselves unto them.

9 If they say thus unto us, [N]Tarry until we come to you; then we will stand still in our place, and will not go up unto them.

10 But if they say thus, Come up unto us; then we will go up: for the LORD hath delivered them into our hand: and [R]this *shall be* a sign unto us.

11 And both of them discovered themselves unto the garrison of the Philistines: and the Philistines said, Behold, the Hebrews come forth out of the holes where they had hid themselves.

12 And the men of the garrison answered Jonathan and his armourbearer, and said, Come up to us, and we will shew you a thing. And Jonathan said unto his armourbearer, Come up after me: for the LORD hath delivered them into the hand of Israel.

13 And Jonathan climbed up upon his hands and upon his feet, and his armourbearer after him: and they fell before Jonathan; and his armourbearer slew after him.

14 And that first slaughter, which Jonathan and his armourbearer made, was about twenty men, within as it were [N]an half acre of land, *which* a yoke *of oxen might plow.*

15 And [R]there was trembling in the host, in the field, and among all the people: the garrison, and [R]the spoilers, they also trembled, and the earth quaked: so it was [R]a[N] very great trembling.

16 And the watchmen of Saul in Gĭb'-ĕ-ăh of Benjamin looked; and, behold, the multitude melted away, and they [R]went on beating down *one another.*

17 Then said Saul unto the people that *were* with him, Number now, and see who is gone from us. And when they had numbered, behold, Jonathan and his armourbearer *were* not *there.*

18 And Saul said unto Ă-hī'-ăh, Bring hither the ark of God. For the ark of God was at that time with the children of Israel.

19 And it came to pass, while Saul [R]talked unto the priest, that the [N]noise that *was* in the host of the Philistines went on and increased:

CHAP. **14**
BC 1087
6 Judg. 7:4, 7
2 Chr. 14:11
9 Heb. *Be still*
10 See Gen. 24:14
Judg. 7:11
14 Or, *half a furrow of an acre of land,*
Judg. 7:21
15 2 Ki. 7:7
Job 18:11
15 ch. 13:17
15 Gen. 35:5
15 Heb. *a trembling of God*
16 ver. 20
19 Num. 27:21
19 Or, *tumult*

Heb. *were cried together* 20
Judg. 7:22 20
2 Chr. 20:23
ch. 13:6 22
Ex. 14:30 23
Hos. 1:7
ch. 13:5 23
Josh. 6:26 24
Deut. 9:28 25
Mat. 3:5
Ex. 3:8 25
Num. 13:27
Mat. 3:4
Or, *weary* 28

and Saul said unto the priest, Withdraw thine hand.

20 And Saul and all the people that *were* with him [N]assembled themselves, and they came to the battle: and, behold, [R]every man's sword was against his fellow, *and there was* a very great discomfiture.

21 Moreover the Hebrews *that* were with the Philistines before that time, which went up with them into the camp *from the country* round about, even they also *turned* to be with the Israelites that *were* with Saul and Jonathan.

22 Likewise all the men of Israel which [R]had hid themselves in mount Ē'-phră-ĭm, *when* they heard that the Philistines fled, even they also followed hard after them in the battle.

23 [R]So the LORD saved Israel that day: and the battle passed over [R]unto Bĕth-ā'-vĕn.

Jonathan transgresses Saul's oath

24 And the men of Israel were distressed that day: for Saul had [R]adjured the people, saying, Cursed *be* the man that eateth *any* food until evening, that I may be avenged on mine enemies. So none of the people tasted *any* food.

25 [R]And all *they of* the land came to a wood; and there was [R]honey upon the ground.

26 And when the people were come into the wood, behold, the honey dropped; but no man put his hand to his mouth: for the people feared the oath.

27 But Jonathan heard not when his father charged the people with the oath: wherefore he put forth the end of the rod that *was* in his hand, and dipped it in an honeycomb, and put his hand to his mouth; and his eyes were enlightened.

28 Then answered one of the people, and said, Thy father straitly charged the people with an oath, saying, Cursed *be* the man that eateth *any* food this day. And the people were [N]faint.

29 Then said Jonathan, My father hath troubled the land: see, I pray you, how mine eyes have been enlightened, because I tasted a little of this honey.

30 How much more, if haply the people had eaten freely to day of the spoil of their enemies which they found? for had there not been now a much greater slaughter among the Philistines?

31 And they smote the Philistines that day from Mĭch'-măsh to Ăĭ'-jă-lŏn: and the people were very faint.

32 And the people flew upon the spoil, and

took sheep, and oxen, and calves, and slew *them* on the ground: and the people did eat *them* ᴿwith the blood.

33 Then they told Saul, saying, Behold, the people sin against the Lᴏʀᴅ, in that they eat with the blood. And he said, Ye have ᴺtransgressed: roll a great stone unto me this day.

34 And Saul said, Disperse yourselves among the people, and say unto them, Bring me hither every man his ox, and every man his sheep, and slay *them* here, and eat; and sin not against the Lᴏʀᴅ in eating with the blood. And all the people brought every man his ox ᴺwith him that night, and slew *them* there.

35 And Saul ᴿbuilt an altar unto the Lᴏʀᴅ: ᴺthe same was the first altar that he built unto the Lᴏʀᴅ.

36 And Saul said, Let us go down after the Philistines by night, and spoil them until the morning light, and let us not leave a man of them. And they said, Do whatsoever seemeth good unto thee. Then said the priest, Let us draw near hither unto God.

37 And Saul asked counsel of God, Shall I go down after the Philistines? wilt thou deliver them into the hand of Israel? But ᴿhe answered him not that day.

38 And Saul said, ᴿDraw ye near hither, all the ᴺchief of the people: and know and see wherein this sin hath been this day.

39 For, ᴿas the Lᴏʀᴅ liveth, which saveth Israel, though it be in Jonathan my son, he shall surely die. But *there was* not a man among all the people *that* answered him.

40 Then said he unto all Israel, Be ye on one side, and I and Jonathan my son will be on the other side. And the people said unto Saul, Do what seemeth good unto thee.

41 Therefore Saul said unto the Lᴏʀᴅ God of Israel, ᴿGiveᴺ a perfect *lot*. ᴿAnd Saul and Jonathan were taken: but the people ᴺescaped.

42 And Saul said, Cast *lots* between me and Jonathan my son. And Jonathan was taken.

The people save Jonathan

43 Then Saul said to Jonathan, ᴿTell me what thou hast done. And Jonathan told him, and said, ᴿI did but taste a little honey with the end of the rod that *was* in mine hand, *and*, lo, I must die.

44 And Saul answered, ᴿGod do so and more also: ᴿfor thou shalt surely die, Jonathan.

45 And the people said unto Saul, Shall Jonathan die, who hath wrought this great salvation in Israel? God forbid: ᴿas the Lᴏʀᴅ liveth, there shall not one hair of his head fall

to the ground; for he hath wrought with God this day. So the people rescued Jonathan, that he died not.

46 Then Saul went up from following the Philistines: and the Philistines went to their own place.

Other wars

47 So Saul took the kingdom over Israel, and fought against all his enemies on every side, against Moab, and against the children of ᴿAmmon, and against Ē'-dom, and against the kings of ᴿZō'-bah, and against the Philistines: and whithersoever he turned himself, he vexed *them*.

48 And he ᴺgathered an host, and ᴿsmote the Ă-măl'-ĕk-ītes, and delivered Israel out of the hands of them that spoiled them.

Saul's family

49 Now ᴿthe sons of Saul were Jonathan, and ĭsh'-ū-ī, and Măl'-chī-shû'-ă: and the names of his two daughters *were these;* the name of the firstborn Mē'-răb, and the name of the younger Michal:

50 And the name of Saul's wife *was* Ă-hĭn'-ŏ-ăm, the daughter of Ă-hī'-mă-ăz: and the name of the captain of his host *was* ᴺAbner, the son of Ner, Saul's uncle.

51 ᴿAnd Kish *was* the father of Saul; and Ner the father of Abner *was* the son of Ă-bī'-ĕl.

52 And there was sore war against the Philistines all the days of Saul: and when Saul saw any strong man, or any valiant man, ᴿhe took him unto him.

CHAPTER 15

Israel's revenge upon the Amalekites

SAMUEL also said unto Saul, ᴿThe Lᴏʀᴅ sent me to anoint thee *to be* king over his people, over Israel: now therefore hearken thou unto the voice of the words of the Lᴏʀᴅ.

2 Thus saith the Lᴏʀᴅ of hosts, I remember *that* which Ăm'-ă-lĕk did to Israel, ᴿhow he laid *wait* for him in the way, when he came up from Egypt.

3 Now go and smite Ăm'-ă-lĕk, and ᴿutterly destroy all that they have, and spare them not; but slay both man and woman, infant and suckling, ox and sheep, camel and ass.

Disobedience of Saul

4 And Saul gathered the people together, and numbered them in Tĕ-lā'-ĭm, two hundred

---

CHAP. **14**
BC 1087

32 Lev. 3:17
& 7:26
& 17:10
& 19:26
Deut. 12:16, 23, 24
33 Or, *dealt treacherously*
34 Heb. *in his hand*
35 ch. 7:17
35 Heb. *that altar he began to build unto the LORD*
37 ch. 28:6
38 Josh. 7:14
ch. 10:19
38 Heb. *corners,* Judg. 20:2
39 2 Sam. 12:5
41 Prov. 16:33
Acts 1:24
41 Or, *Shew the innocent*
41 Josh. 7:16
ch. 10:20, 21
41 Heb. *went forth*
43 Josh. 7:19
43 ver. 27
44 Ruth 1:17
44 ver. 39
45 2 Sam. 14:11
1 Ki. 1:52
Luke 21:18

ch. 11:11 — 47
2 Sam. 10:6 — 47
Or, *wrought mightily* — 48
ch. 15:3, 7 — 48
ch. 31:2 — 49
1 Chr. 8:33
Heb. *Abiner* — 50
ch. 9:1 — 51
ch. 8:11 — 52

CHAP. **15**
BC 1079

ch. 9:16 — 1
Ex. 17:8, 14 — 2
Num. 24:20
Deut. 25:17-19
Lev. 27:28, 29 — 3
Josh. 6:17, 21

thousand footmen, and ten thousand men of Judah.

5 And Saul came to a city of Ăm'-ă-lĕk, and [N]laid wait in the valley.

6 And Saul said unto [R]the Kē'-nītes, [R]Go, depart, get you down from among the Ă-măl'-ĕk-ītes, lest I destroy you with them: for [R]ye shewed kindness to all the children of Israel, when they came up out of Egypt. So the Kē'-nītes departed from among the Ă-măl'-ĕk-ītes.

7 [R]And Saul smote the Ă-măl'-ĕk-ītes from [R]Hăv'-ī-lăh *until* thou comest to [R]Shur, that *is* over against Egypt.

8 And [R]he took Agag the king of the Ă-măl'-ĕk-ītes alive, and [R]utterly destroyed all the people with the edge of the sword.

9 But Saul and the people [R]spared Agag, and the best of the sheep, and of the oxen, and [N]of the fatlings, and the lambs, and all *that was* good, and would not utterly destroy them: but every thing *that was* vile and refuse, that they destroyed utterly.

Samuel rebukes Saul

10 Then came the word of the LORD unto Samuel saying,

11 [R]It repenteth me that I have set up Saul *to be* king: for he is [R]turned back from following me, [R]and hath not performed my commandments. And it [R]grieved Samuel; and he cried unto the LORD all night.

12 And when Samuel rose early to meet Saul in the morning, it was told Samuel, saying, Saul came to [R]Carmel, and, behold, he set him up a place, and is gone about, and passed on, and gone down to Gĭl'-găl.

13 And Samuel came to Saul: and Saul said unto him, [R]Blessed *be* thou of the LORD: I have performed the commandment of the LORD.

14 And Samuel said, What *meaneth* then this bleating of the sheep in mine ears, and the lowing of the oxen which I hear?

15 And Saul said, They have brought them from the Ă-măl'-ĕk-ītes: [R]for the people spared the best of the sheep and of the oxen, to sacrifice unto the LORD thy God; and the rest we have utterly destroyed.

16 Then Samuel said unto Saul, Stay, and I will tell thee what the LORD hath said to me this night. And he said unto him, Say on.

17 And Samuel said, [R]When thou *wast* little in thine own sight, *wast* thou not *made* the head of the tribes of Israel, and the LORD anointed thee king over Israel?

18 And the LORD sent thee on a journey,

and said, Go and utterly destroy the sinners the Ă-măl'-ĕk-ītes, and fight against them until [N]they be consumed.

19 Wherefore then didst thou not obey the voice of the LORD, but didst fly upon the spoil, and didst evil in the sight of the LORD?

20 And Saul said unto Samuel, Yea, [R]I have obeyed the voice of the LORD, and have gone the way which the LORD sent me, and have brought Agag the king of Ăm'-ă-lĕk, and have utterly destroyed the Ă-măl'-ĕk-ītes.

21 [R]But the people took of the spoil, sheep and oxen, the chief of the things which should have been utterly destroyed, to sacrifice unto the LORD thy God in Gĭl'-găl.

22 And Samuel said, [R]Hath the LORD *as great* delight in burnt offerings and sacrifices, as in obeying the voice of the LORD? Behold, [R]to obey *is* better than sacrifice, *and* to hearken than the fat of rams.

23 For rebellion *is as* the sin of [N]witchcraft, and stubbornness *is as* iniquity and idolatry. Because thou hast rejected the word of the LORD, [R]he hath also rejected thee from *being* king.

Saul repents

24 [R]And Saul said unto Samuel, I have sinned: for I have transgressed the commandment of the LORD, and thy words: because I [R]feared the people, and obeyed their voice.

25 Now therefore, I pray thee, pardon my sin, and turn again with me, that I may worship the LORD.

26 And Samuel said unto Saul, I will not return with thee: [R]for thou hast rejected the word of the LORD, and the LORD hath rejected thee from being king over Israel.

27 And as Samuel turned about to go away, [R]he laid hold upon the skirt of his mantle, and it rent.

28 And Samuel said unto him, [R]The LORD hath rent the kingdom of Israel from thee this day, and hath given it to a neighbour of thine, *that is* better than thou.

29 And also the [N]Strength of Israel [R]will not lie nor repent: for he *is* not a man, that he should repent.

30 Then he said, I have sinned: *yet* [R]honour me now, I pray thee, before the elders of my people, and before Israel, and turn again with me, that I may worship the LORD thy God.

31 So Samuel turned again after Saul; and Saul worshipped the LORD.

32 Then said Samuel, Bring ye hither to me Agag the king of the Ă-măl'-ĕk-ītes. And Agag

came unto him delicately. And Agag said, Surely the bitterness of death is past.

33 And Samuel said, [R]As thy sword hath made women childless, so shall thy mother be childless among women. And Samuel hewed Agag in pieces before the LORD in Gĭl'-găl.

34 Then Samuel went to Rā'-măh; and Saul went up to his house to [R]Gĭb'-ĕ-ăh of Saul.

35 And [R]Samuel came no more to see Saul until the day of his death: nevertheless Samuel [R]mourned for Saul: and the LORD [R]repented that he had made Saul king over Israel.

CHAPTER 16

Samuel sent to the house of Jesse

AND the LORD said unto Samuel, [R]How long wilt thou mourn for Saul, seeing [R]I have rejected him from reigning over Israel? [R]fill thine horn with oil, and go, I will send thee to Jesse the Beth-lehemite: for [R]I have provided me a king among his sons.

2 And Samuel said, How can I go? if Saul hear *it*, he will kill me. And the LORD said, Take an heifer [N]with thee, and say, [R]I am come to sacrifice to the LORD.

3 And call Jesse to the sacrifice, and [R]I will shew thee what thou shalt do: and [R]thou shalt anoint unto me *him* whom I name unto thee.

4 And Samuel did that which the LORD spake, and came to Beth-lehem. And the elders of the town [R]trembled at his [N]coming, and said, [R]Comest thou peaceably?

5 And he said, Peaceably: I am come to sacrifice unto the LORD: [R]sanctify yourselves, and come with me to the sacrifice. And he sanctified Jesse and his sons, and called them to the sacrifice.

Samuel anoints David

6 And it came to pass, when they were come, that he looked on [R]Ē-lī'-ăb, and [R]said, Surely the LORD's anointed *is* before him.

7 But the LORD said unto Samuel, Look not on [R]his countenance, or on the height of his stature; because I have refused him: [R]for *the LORD seeth* not as man seeth; for man [R]looketh on the [N]outward appearance, but the LORD looketh on the [R]heart.

8 Then Jesse called [R]Ă-bĭn'-ă-dăb, and made him pass before Samuel. And he said, Neither hath the LORD chosen this.

9 Then Jesse made [R]Shăm'-măh[N] to pass by. And he said, Neither hath the LORD chosen this.

10 Again, Jesse made seven of his sons to pass before Samuel. And Samuel said unto Jesse, The LORD hath not chosen these.

11 And Samuel said unto Jesse, Are here all *thy* children? And he said, [R]There remaineth yet the youngest, and, behold, he keepeth the sheep. And Samuel said unto Jesse, [R]Send and fetch him: for we will not sit [N]down till he come hither.

12 And he sent, and brought him in. Now he *was* [R]ruddy, *and* withal [N]of a beautiful countenance, and goodly to look to. [R]And the LORD said, Arise, anoint him: for this *is* he.

13 Then Samuel took the horn of oil, and [R]anointed him in the midst of his brethren: and [R]the spirit of the LORD came upon David from that day forward. So Samuel rose up, and went to Rā'-măh.

Saul sends for David

14 [R]But the spirit of the LORD departed from Saul, and [R]an evil spirit from the LORD [N]troubled him.

15 And Saul's servants said unto him, Behold now, an evil spirit from God troubleth thee.

16 Let our lord now command thy servants, *which are* [R]before thee, to seek out a man, *who is* a cunning player on an harp: and it shall come to pass, when the evil spirit from God is upon thee, that he shall [R]play with his hand, and thou shalt be well.

17 And Saul said unto his servants, Provide me now a man that can play well, and bring *him* to me.

18 Then answered one of the servants, and said, Behold, I have seen a son of Jesse the Beth-lehemite, *that is* cunning in playing, and [R]a mighty valiant man, and a man of war, and prudent in [N]matters, and a comely person, and [R]the LORD *is* with him.

19 Wherefore Saul sent messengers unto Jesse, and said, Send me David thy son, [R]which *is* with the sheep.

20 And Jesse [R]took an ass *laden* with bread, and a bottle of wine, and a kid, and sent *them* by David his son unto Saul.

21 And David came to Saul, and [R]stood before him: and he loved him greatly; and he became his armourbearer.

22 And Saul sent to Jesse, saying, Let David, I pray thee, stand before me; for he hath found favour in my sight.

23 And it came to pass, when [R]the *evil* spirit from God was upon Saul, that David took an harp, and played with his hand: so Saul was refreshed, and was well, and the evil spirit departed from him.

Center column references

CHAP. 15
BC 1079
33 Ex. 17:11
Num. 14:45
See Judg. 1:7
34 ch. 11:4
35 See ch. 19:24
35 ver. 11
ch. 16:1
35 ver. 11

CHAP. 16
BC 1063
1 ch. 15:35
1 ch. 15:23
1 ch. 9:16
2 Ki. 9:1
1 Ps. 78:70
Acts 13:22
2 Heb. *in thine hand*
2 ch. 9:12 & 20:29
3 Ex. 4:15
3 ch. 9:16
4 ch. 21:1
4 Heb. *meeting*
4 1 Ki. 2:13
2 Ki. 9:22
5 Ex. 19:10
6 ch. 17:13
Called Elihu, 1 Chr. 27:18
6 1 Ki. 12:26
7 Ps. 147:10
7 Is. 55:8
7 2 Cor. 10:7
7 Heb. *eyes*
7 1 Ki. 8:39
8 ch. 17:13
9 ch. 17:13
9 *Shimeah,* 2 Sam. 13:3 *Shimma,* 1 Chr. 2:13

ch. 17:12   11
2 Sam. 7:8   11
Heb. *round*   11
ch. 17:42   12
Heb. *fair of eyes*   12
ch. 9:17   12
ch. 10:1   13
Num. 27:18   13
Judg. 11:29 & 13:25
ch. 10:6, 10
Judg. 16:20   14
Judg. 9:23   14
Or, *terrified*   14
ver. 21, 22   16
Gen. 41:46
ver. 23   16
2 Ki. 3:15
ch. 17:32, 34-36
Or, *speech*   18
ch. 3:19   18
& 18:12, 14
ver. 11   19
ch. 17:15
ch. 10:27   20
& 17:18
Gen. 41:46   21
ver. 14, 16   23

CHAPTER 17

Challenge of Goliath

NOW the Philistines gathered together their armies to battle, and were gathered together at ᴿShō′-chōh, which *belongeth* to Judah, and pitched between Shō′-chōh and Ă-zē′-kăh, in ᴺĒ′-phĕś-dăm′-mĭm.

2 And Saul and the men of Israel were gathered together, and pitched by the valley of Ē′-läh, and ᴺset the battle in array against the Philistines.

3 And the Philistines stood on a mountain on the one side, and Israel stood on a mountain on the other side: and *there was* a valley between them.

4 And there went out a champion out of the camp of the Philistines, named ᴿGō-lī′-ăth, of ᴿGath, whose height *was* six cubits and a span.

5 And *he had* an helmet of brass upon his head, and he *was* ᴺarmed with a coat of mail; and the weight of the coat *was* five thousand shē′-kĕls of brass.

6 And *he had* greaves of brass upon his legs, and a ᴺtarget of brass between his shoulders.

7 And the staff of his spear *was* like a weaver's beam; and his spear's head *weighed* six hundred shē′-kĕls of iron: and one bearing a shield went before him.

8 And he stood and cried unto the armies of Israel, and said unto them, Why are ye come out to set *your* battle in array? *am* not I a Philistine, and ye ᴿservants to Saul? choose you a man for you, and let him come down to me.

9 If he be able to fight with me, and to kill me, then will we be your servants: but if I prevail against him, and kill him, then shall ye be our servants, and ᴿserve us.

10 And the Philistine said, I ᴿdefy the armies of Israel this day; give me a man, that we may fight together.

11 When Saul and all Israel heard those words of the Philistine, they were dismayed, and greatly afraid.

David accepts the challenge

12 Now David *was* ᴿthe son of that ᴿĔph′-rȧ-thīte of Beth-lehem-judah, whose name *was* Jesse; and he had ᴿeight sons: and the man went among men *for* an old man in the days of Saul.

13 And the three eldest sons of Jesse went *and* followed Saul to the battle: and the ᴿnames of his three sons that went to the battle *were* Ē-lī′-ăb the firstborn, and next unto him Ă-bĭn′-ȧ-dăb, and the third Shăm′-măh.

CHAP. **17**
BC 1063
1 Josh. 15:35
1 Or, *The coast of Dammim,* called *Pas-dammim,* 1 Chr. 11:13
2 Heb. *ranged the battle*
4 2 Sam. 21:19
4 Josh. 11:22
5 Heb. *clothed*
6 Or, *gorget*
8 ch. 8:17
9 ch. 11:1
10 ver. 26 2 Sam. 21:21
12 ver. 58 Ruth 4:22 ch. 16:1, 18
12 Gen. 35:19
12 ch. 16:10, 11 See 1 Chr. 2:13-15
13 ch. 16:6, 8, 9
ch. 16:19   15
Heb. *cheeses of milk*   18
Heb. *captain of a thousand*   18
Gen. 37:14   18
Or, *place of the carriage,* ch. 26:5   20
Or, *battle array,* or, *place of fight*   20
Heb. *the vessels from upon him*   22
Heb. *asked his brethren of peace,* as Judg. 18:15   22
ver. 8   23
Heb. *from his face*   24
Josh. 15:16   25
ch. 11:2   26
ch. 14:6   26
ver. 10   26
Deut. 5:26   26
ver. 25   27
Gen. 37:4, 8, 11   28 Mat. 10:36

14 And David *was* the youngest: and the three eldest followed Saul.

15 But David went and returned from Saul ᴿto feed his father's sheep at Beth-lehem.

16 And the Philistine drew near morning and evening, and presented himself forty days.

17 And Jesse said unto David his son, Take now for thy brethren an ē′-phäh of this parched *corn,* and these ten loaves, and run to the camp to thy brethren;

18 And carry these ten ᴺcheeses unto the ᴺcaptain of *their* thousand, and ᴿlook how thy brethren fare, and take their pledge.

19 Now Saul, and they, and all the men of Israel, *were* in the valley of Ē′-läh, fighting with the Philistines.

20 And David rose up early in the morning, and left the sheep with a keeper, and took, and went, as Jesse had commanded him; and he came to the ᴺtrench, as the host was going forth to the ᴺfight, and shouted for the battle.

21 For Israel and the Philistines had put the battle in array, army against army.

22 And David left ᴺhis carriage in the hand of the keeper of the carriage, and ran into the army, and came and ᴺsaluted his brethren.

23 And as he talked with them, behold, there came up the champion, the Philistine of Gath, Gō-lī′-ăth by name, out of the armies of the Philistines, and spake ᴿaccording to the same words: and David heard *them.*

24 And all the men of Israel, when they saw the man, fled ᴺfrom him, and were sore afraid.

25 And the men of Israel said, Have ye seen this man that is come up? surely to defy Israel is he come up: and it shall be, *that* the man who killeth him, the king will enrich him with great riches, and ᴿwill give him his daughter, and make his father's house free in Israel.

26 And David spake to the men that stood by him, saying, What shall be done to the man that killeth this Philistine, and taketh away ᴿthe reproach from Israel? for who *is* this ᴿuncircumcised Philistine, that he should ᴿdefy the armies of ᴿthe living God?

27 And the people answered him after this manner, saying, ᴿSo shall it be done to the man that killeth him.

28 And Ē-lī′-ăb his eldest brother heard when he spake unto the men; and Ē-lī′-ăb's ᴿanger was kindled against David, and he said, Why camest thou down hither? and with whom hast thou left those few sheep in the wilderness? I know thy pride, and the naughtiness of thine heart; for thou are come down that thou mightest see the battle.

29 And David said, What have I now done? [R]*Is there* not a cause?

30 And he turned from him toward another, and [R]spake after the same [N]manner: and the people answered him again after the former manner.

31 And when the words were heard which David spake, they rehearsed *them* before Saul: and he [N]sent for him.

32 And David said to Saul, [R]Let no man's heart fail because of him; [R]thy servant will go and fight with this Philistine.

33 And Saul said to David, [R]Thou art not able to go against this Philistine to fight with him: for thou *art but* a youth, and he a man of war from his youth.

34 And David said unto Saul, Thy servant kept his father's sheep, and there came a lion, and a bear, and took a [N]lamb out of the flock:

35 And I went out after him, and smote him, and delivered *it* out of his mouth: and when he arose against me, I caught *him* by his beard, and smote him, and slew him.

36 Thy servant slew both the lion and the bear: and this uncircumcised Philistine shall be as one of them, seeing he hath defied the armies of the living God.

37 David said moreover, [R]The LORD that delivered me out of the paw of the lion, and out of the paw of the bear, he will deliver me out of the hand of this Philistine. And Saul said unto David, Go, and [R]the LORD be with thee.

38 And Saul [N]armed David with his armour, and he put an helmet of brass upon his head; also he armed him with a coat of mail.

39 And David girded his sword upon his armour, and he assayed to go; for he had not proved *it*. And David said unto Saul, I cannot go with these; for I have not proved *them*. And David put them off him.

40 And he took his staff in his hand, and chose him five smooth stones out of the [N]brook, and put them in a shepherd's [N]bag which he had, even in a scrip; and his sling *was* in his hand: and he drew near to the Philistine.

David slays Goliath

41 And the Philistine came on and drew near unto David; and the man that bare the shield *went* before him.

42 And when the Philistine looked about, and saw David, he [R]disdained him: for he was *but* a youth, and [R]ruddy, and of a fair countenance.

43 And the Philistine said unto David, [R]*Am* I a dog, that thou comest to me with

---

CHAP. 17
BC 1063

29 ver. 17
30 ver. 26, 27
30 Heb. *word*
31 Heb. *took him*
32 Deut. 20:1, 3
32 ch. 16:18
33 See Num. 13:31
Deut. 9:2
34 Or, *kid*
37 2 Cor. 1:10
2 Tim. 4:17, 18
37 ch. 20:13
1 Chr. 22:11, 16
38 Heb. *clothed David with his clothes*
40 Or, *valley*
40 Heb. *vessel*
42 1 Cor. 1:27, 28
42 ch. 16:12
43 ch. 24:14
2 Sam. 3:8 & 9:8 & 16:9
2 Ki. 8:13

1 Ki. 20:10, 11 **44**
2 Sam. 22:33, 35 **45**
2 Cor. 10:4
Heb. 11:33, 34
ver. 10 **45**
Heb. *shut thee up* **46**
Deut. 28:26 **46**
Josh. 4:24 **46**
1 Ki. 8:43 & 18:36
2 Ki. 19:19
Is. 52:10
Hos. 1:7 **47**
Zech. 4:6
2 Chr. 20:15 **47**
ch. 21:9 **50**
See Judg. 3:31 & 15:15
2 Sam. 23:21
Heb. 11:34 **51**
Josh. 15:36 **52**
See ch. 16:21, 22 **55**

---

staves? And the Philistine cursed David by his gods.

44 And the Philistine [R]said to David, Come to me, and I will give thy flesh unto the fowls of the air, and to the beasts of the field.

45 Then said David to the Philistine, Thou comest to me with a sword, and with a spear, and with a shield: [R]but I come to thee in the name of the LORD of hosts, the God of the armies of Israel, whom thou hast [R]defied.

46 This day will the LORD [N]deliver thee into mine hand; and I will smite thee, and take thine head from thee; and I will give [R]the carcases of the host of the Philistines this day unto the fowls of the air, and to the wild beasts of the earth; [R]that all the earth may know that there is a God in Israel.

47 And all this assembly shall know that the LORD [R]saveth not with sword and spear: for [R]the battle *is* the LORD's, and he will give you into our hands.

48 And it came to pass, when the Philistine arose, and came and drew nigh to meet David, that David hasted, and ran toward the army to meet the Philistine.

49 And David put his hand in his bag, and took thence a stone, and slang *it*, and smote the Philistine in his forehead, that the stone sunk into his forehead; and he fell upon his face to the earth.

50 So [R]David prevailed over the Philistine with a sling and with a stone, and smote the Philistine, and slew him; but *there was* no sword in the hand of David.

51 Therefore David ran, and stood upon the Philistine, and took his sword, and drew it out of the sheath thereof, and slew him, and cut off his head therewith. And when the Philistines saw their champion was dead, [R]they fled.

52 And the men of Israel and of Judah arose, and shouted, and pursued the Philistines, until thou come to the valley, and to the gates of ĕk'-rŏn. And the wounded of the Philistines fell down by the way to [R]Shā-ă-rā'-ĭm, even unto Gath, and unto ĕk'-rŏn.

53 And the children of Israel returned from chasing after the Philistines, and they spoiled their tents.

54 And David took the head of the Philistine, and brought it to Jerusalem; but he put his armour in his tent.

55 And when Saul saw David go forth against the Philistine, he said unto Abner, the captain of the host, Abner, [R]whose son *is* this youth? And Abner said, *As* thy soul liveth, O king, I cannot tell.

56 And the king said, Inquire thou whose son the stripling *is*.

57 And as David returned from the slaughter of the Philistine, Abner took him, and brought him before Saul ᴿwith the head of the Philistine in his hand.

58 And Saul said to him, Whose son *art* thou, *thou* young man? And David answered, ᴿI *am* the son of thy servant Jesse the Bethlehemite.

CHAPTER 18

Jonathan befriends David

AND it came to pass, when he had made an end of speaking unto Saul, that ᴿthe soul of Jonathan was knit with the soul of David, ᴿand Jonathan loved him as his own soul.

2 And Saul took him that day, ᴿand would let him go no more home to his father's house.

3 Then Jonathan and David made a covenant, because he loved him as his own soul.

4 And Jonathan stripped himself of the robe that *was* upon him, and gave it to David, and his garments, even to his sword, and to his bow, and to his girdle.

5 And David went out whithersoever Saul sent him, *and* ᴺbehaved himself wisely: and Saul set him over the men of war, and he was accepted in the sight of all the people, and also in the sight of Saul's servants.

Saul's anger against David

6 And it came to pass as they came, when David was returned from the slaughter of the ᴺPhilistine, that ᴿthe women came out of all cities of Israel, singing and dancing, to meet king Saul, with tabrets, with joy, and with ᴺinstruments of musick.

7 And the women ᴿanswered *one another* as they played, and said, ᴿSaul hath slain his thousands, and David his ten thousands.

8 And Saul was very wroth, and the saying ᴿdispleasedᴺ him; and he said, They have ascribed unto David ten thousands, and to me they have ascribed *but* thousands: and *what* can he have more but ᴿthe kingdom?

9 And Saul eyed David from that day and forward.

10 And it came to pass on the morrow, that ᴿthe evil spirit from God came upon Saul, ᴿand he prophesied in the midst of the house: and David played with his hand, as at other times: ᴿand *there was* a javelin in Saul's hand.

11 And Saul ᴿcast the javelin; for he said, I will smite David even to the wall *with it*. And David avoided out of his presence twice.

12 And Saul was ᴿafraid of David, because ᴿthe LORD was with him, and was ᴿdeparted from Saul.

13 Therefore Saul removed him from him, and made him his captain over a thousand; and ᴿhe went out and came in before the people.

14 And David ᴺbehaved himself wisely in all his ways; and ᴿthe LORD *was* with him.

15 Wherefore when Saul saw that he behaved himself very wisely, he was afraid of him.

16 But ᴿall Israel and Judah loved David, because he went out and came in before them.

17 And Saul said to David, Behold my elder daughter Mē'-răb, ᴿher will I give thee to wife: only be thou ᴺvaliant for me, and fight ᴿthe LORD's battles. For Saul said, ᴿLet not mine hand be upon him, but let the hand of the Philistines be upon him.

18 And David said unto Saul, ᴿWho *am* I? and what *is* my life, *or* my father's family in Israel, that I should be son in law to the king?

19 But it came to pass at the time when Mē'-răb Saul's daughter should have been given to David, that she was given unto ᴿĀ'-drĭ-ĕl the ᴿMĕ-hō'-lă-thīte to wife.

David marries Saul's daughter

20 ᴿAnd Michal Saul's daughter loved David: and they told Saul, and the thing ᴺpleased him.

21 And Saul said, I will give him her, that she may be a snare to him, and that ᴿthe hand of the Philistines may be against him. Wherefore Saul said to David, Thou shalt ᴿthis day be my son in law in *the one of* the twain.

22 And Saul commanded his servants, *saying*, Commune with David secretly, and say, Behold, the king hath delight in thee, and all his servants love thee: now therefore be the king's son in law.

23 And Saul's servants spake those words in the ears of David. And David said, Seemeth it to you *a light thing* to be a king's son in law, seeing that I *am* a poor man, and lightly esteemed?

24 And the servants of Saul told him, saying, ᴺOn this manner spake David.

25 And Saul said, Thus shall ye say to David, The king desireth not any ᴿdowry, but an hundred foreskins of the Philistines, to be ᴿavenged of the king's enemies. But Saul ᴿthought to make David fall by the hand of the Philistines.

26 And when his servants told David these words, it pleased David well to be the king's son in law: and ᴿthe days were not ᴺexpired.

27 Wherefore David arose and went, he and

^Rhis men, and slew of the Philistines two hundred men; and ^RDavid brought their foreskins, and they gave them in full tale to the king, that he might be the king's son in law. And Saul gave him Michal his daughter to wife.

28 And Saul saw and knew that the LORD *was* with David, and *that* Michal Saul's daughter loved him.

29 And Saul was yet the more afraid of David; and Saul became David's enemy continually.

30 Then the princes of the Philistines ^Rwent forth: and it came to pass, after they went forth, *that* David ^Rbehaved himself more wisely than all the servants of Saul; so that his name was much ^Nset by.

CHAPTER 19

Jonathan intercedes for David

AND Saul spake to Jonathan his son, and to all his servants, that they should kill David.

2 But Jonathan Saul's son ^Rdelighted much in David: and Jonathan told David, saying, Saul my father seeketh to kill thee: now therefore, I pray thee, take heed to thyself until the morning, and abide in a secret *place,* and hide thyself:

3 And I will go out and stand beside my father in the field where thou *art,* and I will commune with my father of thee; and what I see, that I will tell thee.

4 And Jonathan ^Rspake good of David unto Saul his father, and said unto him, Let not the king ^Rsin against his servant, against David; because he hath not sinned against thee, and because his works *have been* to thee-ward very good:

5 For he did put his ^Rlife in his hand, and ^Rslew the Philistine, and ^Rthe LORD wrought a great salvation for all Israel: thou sawest *it,* and didst rejoice: ^Rwherefore then wilt thou ^Rsin against innocent blood, to slay David without a cause?

6 And Saul hearkened unto the voice of Jonathan: and Saul sware, *As* the LORD liveth, he shall not be slain.

7 And Jonathan called David, and Jonathan shewed him all those things. And Jonathan brought David to Saul, and he was in his presence, ^Ras ^Nin times past.

Saul attempts to kill David

8 And there was war again: and David went out, and fought with the Philistines, and slew

---

---

them with a great slaughter; and they fled from ^Nhim.

9 And ^Rthe evil spirit from the LORD was upon Saul, as he sat in his house with his javelin in his hand: and David played with *his* hand.

10 And Saul sought to smite David even to the wall with the javelin; but he slipped away out of Saul's presence, and he smote the javelin into the wall: and David fled, and escaped that night.

Michal saves David's life

11 ^RSaul also sent messengers unto David's house, to watch him, and to slay him in the morning: and Michal David's wife told him, saying, If thou save not thy life to night, to morrow thou shalt be slain.

12 So Michal ^Rlet David down through a window: and he went, and fled, and escaped.

13 And Michal took an ^Nimage, and laid *it* in the bed, and put a pillow of goats' *hair* for his bolster, and covered *it* with a cloth.

14 And when Saul sent messengers to take David, she said, He *is* sick.

15 And Saul sent the messengers *again* to see David, saying, Bring him up to me in the bed, that I may slay him.

16 And when the messengers were come in, behold, *there was* an image in the bed, with a pillow of goats' *hair* for his bolster.

17 And Saul said unto Michal, Why hast thou deceived me so, and sent away mine enemy, that he is escaped? And Michal answered Saul, He said unto me, Let me go; ^Rwhy should I kill thee?

Saul prophesies at Naioth

18 So David fled, and escaped, and came to Samuel to Rā'-mäh, and told him all that Saul had done to him. And he and Samuel went and dwelt in Nái'-ōth.

19 And it was told Saul, saying, Behold, David *is* at Nái'-ōth in Rā'-mäh.

20 And ^RSaul sent messengers to take David: ^Rand when they saw the company of the prophets prophesying, and Samuel standing *as* appointed over them, the spirit of God was upon the messengers of Saul, and they also ^Rprophesied.

21 And when it was told Saul, he sent other messengers, and they prophesied likewise. And Saul sent messengers again the third time, and they prophesied also.

22 Then went he also to Rā'-mäh, and came to a great well that *is* in Sē'-chû: and he asked and said, Where *are* Samuel and David? And

one said, Behold, *they be* at Năĭ'-ŏth in Ră'-măh.

23 And he went thither to Năĭ'-ŏth in Ră'-măh: and ᴿthe spirit of God was upon him also, and he went on, and prophesied, until he came to Năĭ'-ŏth in Ră'-măh.

24 ᴿAnd he stripped off his clothes also, and prophesied before Samuel in like manner, and ᴺlay down ᴿnaked all that day and all that night. Wherefore they say, ᴿ*Is* Saul also among the prophets?

CHAPTER 20

Jonathan's covenant with David

AND David fled from Năĭ'-ŏth in Ră'-măh, and came and said before Jonathan, What have I done? what *is* mine iniquity? and what *is* my sin before thy father, that he seeketh my life?

2 And he said unto him, God forbid; thou shalt not die: behold, my father will do nothing either great or small, but that he will ᴺshew it me: and why should my father hide this thing from me? it *is* not *so.*

3 And David sware moreover, and said, Thy father certainly knoweth that I have found grace in thine eyes; and he saith, Let not Jonathan know this, lest he be grieved: but truly *as* the LORD liveth, and *as* thy soul liveth, *there is* but a step between me and death.

4 Then said Jonathan unto David, ᴺWhatsoever thy soul ᴺdesireth, I will even do *it* for thee.

5 And David said unto Jonathan, Behold, to morrow *is* the ᴿnew moon, and I should not fail to sit with the king at meat: but let me go, that I may ᴿhide myself in the field unto the third *day* at even.

6 If thy father at all miss me, then say, David earnestly asked *leave* of me that he might run ᴿto Beth-lehem his city: for *there is* a yearly ᴺsacrifice there for all the family.

7 ᴿIf he say thus, *It is* well; thy servant shall have peace: but if he be very wroth, *then* be sure that ᴿevil is determined by him.

8 Therefore thou shalt ᴿdeal kindly with thy servant; for ᴿthou hast brought thy servant into a covenant of the LORD with thee: notwithstanding, ᴿif there be in me iniquity, slay me thyself; for why shouldest thou bring me to thy father?

9 And Jonathan said, Far be it from thee: for if I knew certainly that evil were determined by my father to come upon thee, then would not I tell it thee?

CHAP. 19
BC 1062
23 ch. 10:10
24 Is. 20:2
24 Heb. *fell,* Num. 24:4
24 Mic. 1:8 See 2 Sam. 6:14, 20
24 ch. 10:11

CHAP. 20
BC 1062
2 Heb. *uncover mine ear,* ver. 12 ch. 9:15
4 Or, *Say what is thy mind, and I will do, etc.*
4 Heb. *speaketh,* or, *thinketh*
5 Num. 10:10 & 28:11
5 ch. 19:2
6 ch. 16:4
6 Or, *feast,* ch. 9:12
7 See Deut. 1:23 2 Sam. 17:4
7 ch. 25:17 Esth. 7:7
8 Josh. 2:14
8 ver. 16 ch. 18:3 & 23:18
8 2 Sam. 14:32

Heb. *searched*	12
Heb. *uncover thine ear*	12
Ruth 1:17	13
Josh. 1:5	13
ch. 17:37 1 Chr. 22:11, 16	
2 Sam. 9:1, 3, 7 & 21:7	15
Heb. *cut*	16
ch. 25:22	16
See ch. 31:2 2 Sam. 4:7 & 21:8	
Or, *by his love toward him*	17
ch. 18:1	17
ver. 5	18
Heb. *missed*	18
Or, *diligently*	19
Heb. *greatly*	19
ch. 19:2	19
Heb. *in the day of the business*	19
Or, *that sheweth the way*	19
Heb. *not any thing*	21
Jer. 4:2	21
ver. 14, 15	23
See ver. 42	

10 Then said David to Jonathan, Who shall tell me? or what *if* thy father answer thee roughly?

11 And Jonathan said unto David, Come, and let us go out into the field. And they went out both of them into the field.

12 And Jonathan said unto David, O LORD God of Israel, when I have ᴺsounded my father about to morrow any time, *or* the third *day,* and, behold, *if there be* good toward David, and I then send not unto thee, and ᴺshew it thee;

13 ᴿThe LORD do so and much more to Jonathan: but if it please my father *to do* thee evil, then I will shew it thee, and send thee away, that thou mayest go in peace: and ᴿthe LORD be with thee, as he hath been with my father.

14 And thou shalt not only while yet I live shew me the kindness of the LORD, that I die not:

15 But *also* ᴿthou shalt not cut off thy kindness from my house for ever: no, not when the LORD hath cut off the enemies of David every one from the face of the earth.

16 So Jonathan ᴺmade *a covenant* with the house of David, *saying,* ᴿLet the LORD even require *it* at the hand of David's enemies.

17 And Jonathan caused David to swear again, ᴺbecause he loved him: ᴿfor he loved him as he loved his own soul.

Jonathan arranges signals

18 Then Jonathan said to David, ᴿTo morrow *is* the new moon: and thou shalt be missed, because thy seat will be ᴺempty.

19 And *when* thou hast stayed three days, *then* thou shalt go down ᴺᴺquickly, and come to ᴿthe place where thou didst hide thyself ᴺwhen the business was *in hand,* and shalt remain by the stone ᴺĒ'-zĕl.

20 And I will shoot three arrows on the side *thereof,* as though I shot at a mark.

21 And, behold, I will send a lad, *saying,* Go, find out the arrows. If I expressly say unto the lad, Behold, the arrows *are* on this side of thee, take them; then come thou: for *there is* peace to thee, and ᴺno hurt; ᴿas the LORD liveth.

22 But if I say thus unto the young man, Behold, the arrows *are* beyond thee; go thy way: for the LORD hath sent thee away.

23 And *as touching* ᴿthe matter which thou and I have spoken of, behold, the LORD *be* between thee and me for ever.

David missed at court

24 So David hid himself in the field: and

when the new moon was come, the king sat him down to eat meat.

25 And the king sat upon his seat, as at other times, *even* upon a seat by the wall: and Jonathan arose, and Abner sat by Saul's side, and David's place was empty.

26 Nevertheless Saul spake not any thing that day: for he thought, Something hath befallen him, he *is* ^Rnot clean; surely he *is* not clean.

27 And it came to pass on the morrow, *which was* the second *day* of the month, that David's place was empty: and Saul said unto Jonathan his son, Wherefore cometh not the son of Jesse to meat, neither yesterday, nor to day?

28 And Jonathan ^Ranswered Saul, David earnestly asked *leave* of me *to go* to Beth-le-hem:

29 And he said, Let me go, I pray thee; for our family hath a sacrifice in the city; and my brother, he hath commanded me *to be there:* and now, if I have found favour in thine eyes, let me get away, I pray thee, and see my brethren. Therefore he cometh not unto the king's table.

Saul's anger at Jonathan

30 Then Saul's anger was kindled against Jonathan, and he said unto him, ^{NN}Thou son of the perverse rebellious *woman,* do not I know that thou hast chosen the son of Jesse to thine own confusion, and unto the confusion of thy mother's nakedness?

31 For as long as the son of Jesse liveth upon the ground, thou shalt not be established, nor thy kingdom. Wherefore now send and fetch him unto me, for he ^Nshall surely die.

32 And Jonathan answered Saul his father, and said unto him, ^RWherefore shall he be slain? what hath he done?

33 And Saul ^Rcast a javelin at him to smite him: ^Rwhereby Jonathan knew that it was determined of his father to slay David.

34 So Jonathan arose from the table in fierce anger, and did eat no meat the second day of the month: for he was grieved for David, because his father had done him shame.

Jonathan warns David

35 And it came to pass in the morning, that Jonathan went out into the field at the time appointed with David, and a little lad with him.

36 And he said unto his lad, Run, find out now the arrows which I shoot. *And* as the lad ran, he shot an arrow ^Nbeyond him.

37 And when the lad was come to the

CHAP. 20

BC 1062

26 Lev. 7:21
& 15:5, etc.
28 ver. 6
30 Or, *Thou perverse rebel*
30 Heb. *Son of perverse rebellion*
31 Heb. is *the son of death*
32 ch. 19:5
Mat. 27:23
Luke 23:22
33 ch. 18:11
33 ver. 7
36 Heb. *to pass over him*

Heb. *instruments* 40
Heb. *that was his* 40
ch. 1:17   42
Or, the LORD   42
be witness of that which, etc., see ver. 23

CHAP. 21

BC 1062

ch. 14:3, called   1
Ahiah, Called also *Abiathar,* Mark 2:26
ch. 16:4   1
Heb. *found*   3
Ex. 25:30   4
Lev. 24:5
Mat. 12:4
Ex. 19:15   4
Zech. 7:3
1 Thes. 4:4   5
Or, *especially when this day there is* other *sanctified in the vessel*
Lev. 8:26   5
Mat. 12:3, 4   6
Mark 2:25, 26
Luke 6:3, 4
Lev. 24:8, 9   6

---

place of the arrow which Jonathan had shot, Jonathan cried after the lad, and said, *Is* not the arrow beyond thee?

38 And Jonathan cried after the lad, Make speed, haste, stay not. And Jonathan's lad gathered up the arrows, and came to his master.

39 But the lad knew not any thing: only Jonathan and David knew the matter.

40 And Jonathan gave his ^Nartillery unto ^Nhis lad, and said unto him, Go, carry *them* to the city.

41 *And* as soon as the lad was gone, David arose out of *a place* toward the south, and fell on his face to the ground, and bowed himself three times: and they kissed one another, and wept one with another, until David exceeded.

42 And Jonathan said to David, ^RGo in peace, ^Nforasmuch as we have sworn both of us in the name of the LORD, saying, The LORD be between me and thee, and between my seed and thy seed for ever. And he arose and departed: and Jonathan went into the city.

CHAPTER 21

David aided by Ahimelech

THEN came David to Nob to ^RĂ-hĭm′-ĕ-lĕch the priest: and Ă-hĭm′-ĕ-lĕch was ^Rafraid at the meeting of David, and said unto him, Why *art* thou alone, and no man with thee?

2 And David said unto Ă-hĭm′-ĕ-lĕch the priest, The king hath commanded me a business, and hath said unto me, Let no man know any thing of the business whereabout I send thee, and what I have commanded thee: and I have appointed *my* servants to such and such a place.

3 Now therefore what is under thine hand? give *me* five *loaves of* bread in mine hand, or what there is ^Npresent.

4 And the priest answered David, and said, *There is* no common bread under mine hand, but there is ^Rhallowed bread; ^Rif the young men have kept themselves at least from women.

5 And David answered the priest, and said unto him, Of a truth women *have been* kept from us about these three days, since I came out, and the ^Rvessels of the young men are holy, and *the bread is* in a manner common, ^Nyea, though it were sanctified this day ^Rin the vessel.

6 So the priest ^Rgave him hallowed *bread:* for there was no bread there but the shewbread, ^Rthat was taken from before the LORD, to put hot bread in the day when it was taken away.

7 Now a certain man of the servants of Saul *was* there that day, detained before the LORD; and his name *was* [R]Dō'-ĕg, an Ē'-dom-īte, the chiefest of the herdmen that *belonged* to Saul.

8 And David said unto Ă-hĭm'-ĕ-lĕch, And is there not here under thine hand spear or sword? for I have neither brought my sword nor my weapons with me, because the king's business required haste.

9 And the priest said, The sword of Gō-lī'-ăth the Philistine, whom thou slewest in [R]the valley of Ē'-lăh, [R]behold, it *is here* wrapped in a cloth behind the ē'-phŏd: if thou wilt take that, take *it:* for *there is* no other save that here. And David said, *There is* none like that; give it me.

10 And David arose, and fled that day for fear of Saul, and went to [N]Ā'-chĭsh the king of Gath.

11 And [R]the servants of Ā'-chĭsh said unto him, *Is* not this David the king of the land? did they not sing one to another of him in dances, saying, [R]Saul hath slain his thousands, and David his ten thousands?

David feigns madness

12 And David [R]laid up these words in his heart, and was sore afraid of Ā'-chĭsh the king of Gath.

13 And [R]he changed his behavior before them, and feigned himself mad in their hands, and [N]scrabbled on the doors of the gate, and let his spittle fall down upon his beard.

14 Then said Ā'-chĭsh unto his servants, Lo, ye see the man [N]is mad: wherefore *then* have ye brought him to me?

15 Have I need of mad men, that ye have brought this *fellow* to play the mad man in my presence? shall this *fellow* come into my house?

CHAPTER 22

David's escape to Adullam

DAVID therefore departed thence, and [R]escaped [R]to the cave Adullam: and when his brethren and all his father's house heard *it,* they went down thither to him.

2 [R]And every one *that was* in distress, and every one that [N]*was* in debt, and every one *that was* [N]discontented, gathered themselves unto him; and he became a captain over them: and there were with him about four hundred men.

3 And David went thence to Mĭz'-pēh of Moab: and he said unto the king of Moab, Let my father and my mother, I pray thee, come

---

---

forth, *and be* with you, till I know what God will do for me.

4 And he brought them before the king of Moab: and they dwelt with him all the while that David was in the hold.

5 And the prophet [R]Gad said unto David, Abide not in the hold; depart, and get thee into the land of Judah. Then David departed, and came into the forest of Hâr'-ĕth.

6 When Saul heard that David was discovered, and the men that *were* with him, (now Saul abode in Gĭb'-ĕ-ăh under a [N]tree in Rā'-măh, having his spear in his hand, and all his servants *were* standing about him;)

7 Then Saul said unto his servants that stood about him, Hear now, ye Benjamites; will the son of Jesse [R]give every one of you fields and vineyards, *and* make you all captains of thousands, and captains of hundreds;

8 That all of you have conspired against me, and *there is* none that [N]sheweth me that [R]my son hath made a league with the son of Jesse, and *there is* none of you that is sorry for me, or sheweth unto me that my son hath stirred up my servant against me, to lie in wait, as at this day?

9 Then answered [R]Dō'-ĕg the Ē'-dom-īte, which was set over the servants of Saul, and said, I saw the son of Jesse coming to Nob, to [R]Ă-hĭm'-ĕ-lĕch the son of [R]Ă-hī'-tŭb.

10 [R]And he inquired of the LORD for him, and [R]gave him victuals, and gave him the sword of Gō-lī'-ăth the Philistine.

Saul destroys the city of Nob

11 Then the king sent to call Ă-hĭm'-ĕ-lĕch the priest, the son of Ă-hī'-tŭb, and all his father's house, the priests that *were* in Nob: and they came all of them to the king.

12 And Saul said, Hear now, thou son of Ă-hī'-tŭb. And he answered, [N]Here I *am,* my lord.

13 And Saul said unto him, Why have ye conspired against me, thou and the son of Jesse, in that thou hast given him bread, and a sword, and hast inquired of God for him, that he should rise against me, to lie in wait, as at this day?

14 Then Ă-hĭm'-ĕ-lĕch answered the king, and said, And who *is so* faithful among all thy servants as David, which is the king's son in law, and goeth at thy bidding, and is honourable in thine house?

15 Did I then begin to inquire of God for him? be it far from me: let not the king impute *any* thing unto his servant, *nor* to all the house of my father: for thy servant knew nothing of all this, [N]less or more.

16 And the king said, Thou shalt surely die, Ă-hĭm'-ĕ-lĕ<u>ch</u>, thou, and all thy father's house.

17 And the king said unto the ᴺᴺfootmen that stood about him, Turn, and slay the priests of the LORD; because their hand also *is* with David, and because they knew when he fled, and did not shew it to me. But the servants of the king ᴿwould not put forth their hand to fall upon the priests of the LORD.

18 And the king said to Dō'-ĕg, Turn thou, and fall upon the priests. And Dō'-ĕg the Ē'-dŏm-īte turned, and he fell upon the priests, and ᴿslew on that day fourscore and five persons that did wear a linen ē'-phŏd.

19 ᴿAnd Nob, the city of the priests, smote he with the edge of the sword, both men and women, children and sucklings, and oxen, and asses, and sheep, with the edge of the sword.

Abiathar escapes to David

20 ᴿAnd one of the sons of Ă-hĭm'-ĕ-lĕ<u>ch</u> the son of Ă-hī'-tŭb, named Ă-bī'-ă-thär, ᴿescaped, and fled after David.

21 And Ă-bī'-ă-thär shewed David that Saul had slain the LORD's priests.

22 And David said unto Ă-bī'-ă-thär, I knew *it* that day, when Dō'-ĕg the Ē'-dŏm-īte *was* there, that he would surely tell Saul: I have occasioned *the death* of all the persons of thy father's house.

23 Abide thou with me, fear not: ᴿfor he that seeketh my life seeketh thy life: but with me thou *shalt be* in safeguard.

CHAPTER 23

David saves Keilah

THEN they told David, saying, Behold, the Philistines fight against ᴿKē-ī'-läh, and they rob the threshingfloors.

2 Therefore David ᴿinquired of the LORD, saying, Shall I go and smite these Philistines? And the LORD said unto David, Go, and smite the Philistines, and save Kē-ī'-läh.

3 And David's men said unto him, Behold, we be afraid here in Judah: how much more then if we come to Kē-ī'-läh against the armies of the Philistines?

4 Then David inquired of the LORD yet again. And the LORD answered him and said, Arise, go down to Kē-ī'-läh; for I will deliver the Philistines into thine hand.

5 So David and his men went to Kē-ī'-läh, and fought with the Philistines, and brought away their cattle, and smote them with a great slaughter. So David saved the inhabitants of Kē-ī'-läh.

6 And it came to pass, when Ă-bī'-ă-thär the

CHAP. **22**
BC 1062
17 Or, *guard*
17 Heb. *runners*
17 See Ex. 1:17
18 See ch. 2:31
19 ver. 9, 11
20 ch. 23:6
20 ch. 2:33
23 1 Ki. 2:26

CHAP. **23**
BC 1061
1 Josh. 15:44
2 ver. 4, 6, 9
ch. 30:8
2 Sam. 5:19, 23

ch. 22:20	**6**
Num. 27:21	**9**
ch. 30:7	
ch. 22:19	**10**
Heb. *shut up*	**12**
ch. 22:2 & 25:13	**13**
Ps. 11:1	**14**
Josh. 15:55	**14**
Ps. 54:3,4	**14**
ch. 24:20	**17**
ch. 18:3	**18**
& 20:16, 42	
2 Sam. 21:7	
See ch. 26:1	
Ps. 54, title	**19**

son of Ă-hĭm'-ĕ-lĕ<u>ch</u> ᴿfled to David to Kē-ī'-läh, *that* he came down *with* an ē'-phŏd in his hand.

7 And it was told Saul that David was come to Kē-ī'-läh. And Saul said, God hath delivered him into mine hand; for he is shut in, by entering into a town that hath gates and bars.

8 And Saul called all the people together to war, to go down to Kē-ī'-läh, to besiege David and his men.

9 And David knew that Saul secretly practised mischief against him; and ᴿhe said to Ă-bī'-ă-thär the priest, Bring hither the ē'-phŏd.

10 Then said David, O LORD God of Israel, thy servant hath certainly heard that Saul seeketh to come to Kē-ī'-läh, ᴿto destroy the city for my sake.

11 Will the men of Kē-ī'-läh deliver me up into his hand? will Saul come down, as thy servant hath heard? O LORD God of Israel, I beseech thee, tell thy servant. And the LORD said, He will come down.

12 Then said David, Will the men of Kē-ī'-läh ᴺdeliver me and my men into the hand of Saul? And the LORD said, They will deliver *thee* up.

13 Then David and his men, ᴿ*which were* about six hundred, arose and departed out of Kē-ī'-läh, and went whithersoever they could go. And it was told Saul that David was escaped from Kē-ī'-läh; and he forbare to go forth.

14 And David abode in the wilderness in strong holds, and remained in ᴿa mountain in the wilderness of ᴿZiph. And Saul ᴿsought him every day, but God delivered him not into his hand.

Jonathan encourages David

15 And David saw that Saul was come out to seek his life: and David *was* in the wilderness of Ziph in a wood.

16 And Jonathan Saul's son arose, and went to David into the wood, and strengthened his hand in God.

17 And he said unto him, Fear not: for the hand of Saul my father shall not find thee; and thou shalt be king over Israel, and I shall be next unto thee; and ᴿthat also Saul my father knoweth.

18 And they two ᴿmade a covenant before the LORD: and David abode in the wood, and Jonathan went to his house.

David in the wilderness of Ziph

19 Then ᴿcame up the Ziphites to Saul to Gĭb'-ĕ-äh, saying, Doth not David hide himself with us in strong holds in the wood, in the

hill of Hă-<u>chi</u>′-lăh, which *is* ^Non the south of ^NJĕ-shĭ′-m<u>o</u>n?

20 Now therefore, O king, come down according to all the desire of thy soul to come down; and ^Rour part *shall be* to deliver him into thc king's hand.

21 And Saul said, Blessed *be* ye of the LORD; for ye have compassion on me.

22 Go, I pray you, prepare yet, and know and see his place where his ^Nhaunt is, *and* who hath seen him there: for it is told me *that* he dealeth very subtilly.

23 See therefore, and take knowledge of all the lurking places where he hideth himself, and come ye again to me with the certainty, and I will go with you: and it shall come to pass, if he be in the land, that I will search him out throughout all the thousands of Judah.

24 And they arose, and went to Ziph before Saul: but David and his men *were* in the wilderness ^Rof Mā′-ŏn, in the plain on the south of Jĕ-shĭ′-m<u>o</u>n.

25 Saul also and his men went to seek *him.* And they told David: wherefore he came down ^Ninto a rock, and abode in the wilderness of Mā′-ŏn. And when Saul heard *that,* he pursued after David in the wilderness of Mā′-ŏn.

26 And Saul went on this side of the mountain, and David and his men on that side of the mountain: ^Rand David made haste to get away for fear of Saul; for Saul and his men ^Rcompassed David and his men round about to take them.

27 ^RBut there came a messenger unto Saul, saying, Haste thee, and come; for the Philistines have ^Ninvaded the land.

28 Wherefore Saul returned from pursuing after David, and went against the Philistines: therefore they called that place ^NSē′-lä-hăm-mäh′-lĕ-k<u>o</u>th.

29 And David went up from thence, and dwelt in strong holds at ^RĔn-ġē′-dĭ.

CHAPTER 24

David spares Saul's life

AND it came to pass, ^Rwhen Saul was returned from ^Nfollowing the Philistines, that it was told him, saying, Behold, David *is* in the wilderness of Ĕn-ġē′-dĭ.

2 Then Saul took three thousand chosen men out of all Israel, and ^Rwent to seek David and his men upon the rocks of the wild goats.

3 And he came to the sheepcotes by the way, where *was* a cave; and ^RSaul went in to ^Rcover his feet: and ^RDavid and his men remained in the sides of the cave.

CHAP. 23

BC 1061

19 Heb. *on the right hand*
19 Or, *the wilderness?*
20 Ps. 54:3
22 Heb. *foot shall be*
24 Josh. 15:55
  ch. 25:2
25 Or, *from the rock*
26 Ps. 31:22
26 Ps. 17:9
27 See 2 Ki. 19:9
27 Heb. *spread themselves upon, etc.*
28 i.e. *The rock of divisions*
29 2 Chr. 20:2

CHAP. 24

BC 1061

1 ch. 23:28
1 Heb. *after*
2 Ps. 38:12
3 ver. 10
3 Judg. 3:24
3 Ps. 57, title & 142, title

ch. 26:8   4
Heb. *the robe which* was *Saul's*   4
2 Sam. 24:10   5
ch. 26:11   6
Ps. 7:4   7
  Mat. 5:44
  Rom. 12:17, 19
Heb. *cut off*   7
Ps. 141:6   9
Prov. 16:28 & 17:9
Ps. 7:3 & 35:7   11
ch. 26:20   11
Gen. 16:5   12
  Judg. 11:27
  ch. 26:10
  Job 5:8
ch. 17:43   14
  2 Sam. 9:8
ch. 26:20   14
ver. 12   15
2 Chr. 24:22   15
Ps. 35:1 & 43:1   15
  Mic. 7:9
Heb. *judge*   15
ch. 26:17   16

4 ^RAnd the men of David said unto him, Behold the day of which the LORD said unto thee, Behold, I will deliver thine enemy into thine hand, that thou mayest do to him as it shall seem good unto thee. Then David arose, and cut off the skirt of ^NSaul's robe privily.

5 And it came to pass afterward, that ^RDavid's heart smote him, because he had cut off Saul's skirt.

6 And he said unto his men, ^RThe LORD forbid that I should do this thing unto my master, the LORD's anointed, to stretch forth mine hand against him, seeing he *is* the anointed of the LORD.

7 So David ^Rstayed^N his servants with these words, and suffered them not to rise against Saul. But Saul rose up out of the cave, and went on *his* way.

8 David also arose afterward, and went out of the cave, and cried after Saul, saying, My lord the king. And when Saul looked behind him, David stooped with his face to the earth, and bowed himself.

9 And David said to Saul, ^RWherefore hearest thou men's words, saying, Behold, David seeketh thy hurt?

10 Behold, this day thine eyes have seen how that the LORD had delivered thee to day into mine hand in the cave: and *some* bade *me* kill thee: but *mine eye* spared thee; and I said, I will not put forth mine hand against my lord; for he *is* the LORD's anointed.

11 Moreover, my father, see, yea, see the skirt of thy robe in my hand: for in that I cut off the skirt of thy robe, and killed thee not, know thou and see that *there is* ^Rneither evil nor transgression in mine hand, and I have not sinned against thee; yet thou ^Rhuntest my soul to take it.

12 ^RThe LORD judge between me and thee, and the LORD avenge me of thee: but mine hand shall not be upon thee.

13 As saith the proverb of the ancients, Wickedness proceedeth from the wicked: but mine hand shall not be upon thee.

14 After whom is the king of Israel come out? after whom dost thou pursue? ^Rafter a dead dog, after ^Ra flea.

15 ^RThe LORD therefore be judge, and judge between me and thee, and ^Rsee, and ^Rplead my cause, and ^Ndeliver me out of thine hand.

Saul seeks David's favour

16 And it came to pass, when David had made an end of speaking these words unto Saul, that Saul said, ^R*Is* this thy voice, my son David? And Saul lifted up his voice, and wept.

17 [R]And he said to David, Thou *art* [R]more righteous than I: for [R]thou hast rewarded me good, whereas I have rewarded thee evil.

18 And thou hast shewed this day how that thou hast dealt well with me: forasmuch as when [R]the LORD had [N]delivered me into thine hand, thou killedst me not.

19 For if a man find his enemy, will he let him go well away? wherefore the LORD reward thee good for that thou hast done unto me this day.

20 And now, behold, [R]I know well that thou shalt surely be king, and that the kingdom of Israel shall be established in thine hand.

21 [R]Swear now therefore unto me by the LORD, [R]that thou wilt not cut off my seed after me, and that thou wilt not destroy my name out of my father's house.

22 And David sware unto Saul. And Saul went home; but David and his men gat them up unto [R]the hold.

CHAPTER 25

Death of Samuel

AND [R]Samuel died; and all the Israelites were gathered together, and [R]lamented him, and buried him in his house at Rā'-măh. And David arose, and went down [R]to the wilderness of Pâr'-ăn.

Nabal refuses David provisions

2 And *there was* a man [R]in Mā'-ŏn, whose [N]possessions *were* in [R]Carmel; and the man *was* very great, and he had three thousand sheep, and a thousand goats: and he was shearing his sheep in Carmel.

3 Now the name of the man *was* Nā'-băl; and the name of his wife Ăb'-ĭ-gail: and *she was* a woman of good understanding, and of a beautiful countenance: but the man *was* churlish and evil in his doings; and he *was* of the house of Caleb.

4 And David heard in the wilderness that Nā'-băl did [R]shear his sheep.

5 And David sent out ten young men, and David said unto the young men, Get you up to Carmel, and go to Nā'-băl, and [N]greet him in my name:

6 And thus shall ye say to him that liveth *in prosperity,* [R]Peace *be* both to thee, and peace *be* to thine house, and peace *be* unto all that thou hast.

7 And now I have heard that thou hast shearers: now thy shepherds which were with us, we [N]hurt them not, [R]neither was there

CHAP. 24
BC 1061
17 ch. 26:21
17 Gen. 38:26
17 Mat. 5:44
18 Heb. *shut up,* ch. 23:12 & 26:8
20 ch. 23:17
21 Gen. 21:23
21 2 Sam. 21:6, 8
22 ch. 23:29

CHAP. 25
BC 1060
1 ch. 28:3
1 Num. 20:29 Deut. 34:8
1 Gen. 21:21 Ps. 120:5
2 ch. 23:24
2 Or, *business*
2 Josh. 15:55
4 Gen. 38:13 2 Sam. 13:23
5 Heb. *ask him in my name of peace,* ch. 17:22
6 1 Chr. 12:18 Luke 10:5
7 Heb. *shamed*
7 ver. 15, 21

Neh. 8:10   8
Esth. 9:19
Heb. *rested*   9
Judg. 9:28   10
Judg. 8:6   11
Heb. *slaughter*   11
ch. 30:24   13
Heb. *flew*   14
upon them
ver. 7   15
Heb. *shamed*   15
Ex. 14:22   16
Job 1:10
ch. 20:7   17
Deut. 13:13   17
Judg. 19:22
Gen. 32:13   18
Prov. 18:16
& 21:14
Or, *lumps*   18
Gen. 32:16, 20   19

aught missing unto them, all the while they were in Carmel.

8 Ask thy young men, and they will shew thee. Wherefore let the young men find favour in thine eyes: for we come in [R]a good day: give, I pray thee, whatsoever cometh to thine hand unto thy servants, and to thy son David.

9 And when David's young men came, they spake to Nā'-băl according to all those words in the name of David, and [N]ceased.

10 And Nā'-băl answered David's servants, and said, [R]Who *is* David? and who *is* the son of Jesse? there be many servants now a days that break away every man from his master.

11 [R]Shall I then take my bread, and my water, and my [N]flesh that I have killed for my shearers, and give *it* unto men, whom I know not whence they *be?*

12 So David's young men turned their way, and went again, and came and told him all those sayings.

13 And David said unto his men, Gird ye on every man his sword. And they girded on every man his sword; and David also girded on his sword: and there went up after David about four hundred men; and two hundred [R]abode by the stuff.

14 But one of the young men told Ăb'-ĭ-gail, Nā'-băl's wife, saying, Behold, David sent messengers out of the wilderness to salute our master; and he [N]railed on them.

15 But the men *were* very good unto us, and [R]we were not [N]hurt, neither missed we any thing, as long as we were conversant with them, when we were in the fields:

16 They were [R]a wall unto us both by night and day, all the while we were with them keeping the sheep.

17 Now therefore know and consider what thou wilt do; for [R]evil is determined against our master, and against all his household: for he *is* such a son of [R]Bē'-lĭ-ăl, that *a man* cannot speak to him.

Abigail pacifies David

18 Then Ăb'-ĭ-gail made haste, and [R]took two hundred loaves, and two bottles of wine, and five sheep ready dressed, and five measures of parched *corn,* and an hundred [N]clusters of raisins, and two hundred cakes of figs, and laid *them* on asses.

19 And she said unto her servants, [R]Go on before me; behold, I come after you. But she told not her husband Nā'-băl.

20 And it was *so, as* she rode on the ass, that she came down by the covert of the hill, and,

behold, David and his men came down against her; and she met them.

21 Now David had said, Surely in vain have I kept all that this *fellow* hath in the wilderness, so that nothing was missed of all that *pertained* unto him: and he hath ᴿrequited me evil for good.

22 ᴿSo and more also do God unto the enemies of David, if I ᴿleave of all that *pertain* to him by the morning light ᴿany that pisseth against the wall.

23 And when Ăb'-ĭ-gail saw David, she hasted, and ᴿlighted off the ass, and fell before David on her face, and bowed herself to the ground,

24 And fell at his feet, and said, Upon me, my lord, *upon* me *let this* iniquity *be:* and let thine handmaid, I pray thee, speak in thine ᴺaudience, and hear the words of thine handmaid.

25 Let not my lord, I pray thee, ᴺregard this man of Bē'-lĭ-ăl, *even* Nā'-băl: for as his name *is,* so *is* he; ᴺNā'-băl *is* his name, and folly *is* with him: but I thine handmaid saw not the young men of my lord, whom thou didst send.

26 Now therefore, my lord, ᴿas the Lᴏʀᴅ liveth, and *as* thy soul liveth, seeing the Lᴏʀᴅ hath ᴿwithholden thee from coming to *shed* blood, and from ᴿavengingᴺ thyself with thine own hand, now ᴿlet thine enemies, and they that seek evil to my lord, be as Nā'-băl.

27 And now ᴿthis ᴺblessing which thine handmaid hath brought unto my lord, let it even be given unto the young men that ᴺfollow my lord.

28 I pray thee, forgive the trespass of thine handmaid: for ᴿthe Lᴏʀᴅ will certainly make my lord a sure house; because my lord ᴿfighteth the battles of the Lᴏʀᴅ, and ᴿevil hath not been found in thee *all* thy days.

29 Yet a man is risen to pursue thee, and to seek thy soul: but the soul of my lord shall be bound in the bundle of life with the Lᴏʀᴅ thy God; and the souls of thine enemies, them shall he ᴿsling out, ᴺas out of the middle of a sling.

30 And it shall come to pass, when the Lᴏʀᴅ shall have done to my lord according to all the good that he hath spoken concerning thee, and shall have appointed thee ruler over Israel;

31 That this shall be ᴺno grief unto thee, nor offence of heart unto my lord, either that thou hast shed blood causeless, or that my lord hath avenged himself: but when the Lᴏʀᴅ shall have dealt well with my lord, then remember thine handmaid.

CHAP. **25**
BC 1060
21 Ps. 109:5
22 Ruth 1:17
ch. 3:17
& 20:13, 16
22 ver. 34
22 1 Ki. 14:10
& 21:21
2 Ki. 9:8
23 Josh. 15:18
Judg. 1:14
24 Heb. *ears*
25 Heb. *lay it to his heart*
25 i.e. *Fool*
26 2 Ki. 2:2
26 ver. 33
Gen. 20:6
26 Rom. 12:19
26 Heb. *saving thyself*
26 2 Sam. 18:32
27 Gen. 33:11
ch. 30:26
2 Ki. 5:15
27 Or, *present*
27 Heb. *walk at the feet of, etc.,* ver. 42
Judg. 4:10
28 2 Sam. 7:11, 27
1 Ki. 9:5
1 Chr. 17:10, 25
28 ch. 18:17
28 ch. 24:11
29 Jer. 10:18
29 Heb. *In the midst of the bought of a sling*
31 Heb. *no staggering, or, stumbling*

Gen. 24:27　**32**
Ex. 18:10
Luke 1:68
ver. 26　**33**
ver. 26　**34**
ver. 22　**34**
ch. 20:42　**35**
2 Sam. 15:9
2 Ki. 5:19
Luke 7:50 & 8:48
Gen. 19:21　**35**
2 Sam. 13:23　**36**
ver. 32　**39**
Prov. 22:23　**39**
ver. 26, 34　**39**
1 Ki. 2:44　**39**
Heb. *at her feet,*　**42**
ver. 27
Josh. 15:56　**43**
ch. 27:3 & 30:5　**43**
2 Sam. 3:14　**44**

32 And David said to Ăb'-ĭ-gail, ᴿBlessed *be* the Lᴏʀᴅ God of Israel, which sent thee this day to meet me:

33 And blessed *be* thy advice, and blessed *be* thou, which hast ᴿkept me this day from coming to *shed* blood, and from avenging myself with mine own hand.

34 For in very deed, *as* the Lᴏʀᴅ God of Israel liveth, which hath ᴿkept me back from hurting thee, except thou hadst hasted and come to meet me, surely there had ᴿnot been left unto Nā'-băl by the morning light any that pisseth against the wall.

35 So David received of her hand *that* which she had brought him, and said unto her, ᴿGo up in peace to thine house; see, I have hearkened to thy voice, and have ᴿaccepted thy person.

Death of Nabal

36 And Ăb'-ĭ-gail came to Nā'-băl; and, behold, ᴿhe held a feast in his house, like the feast of a king; and Nā'-băl's heart *was* merry within him, for he *was* very drunken: wherefore she told him nothing, less or more, until the morning light.

37 But it came to pass in the morning, when the wine was gone out of Nā'-băl, and his wife had told him these things, that his heart died within him, and he became *as* a stone.

38 And it came to pass about ten days *after,* that the Lᴏʀᴅ smote Nā'-băl, that he died.

David marries Abigail and Ahinoam

39 And when David heard that Nā'-băl was dead, he said, ᴿBlessed *be* the Lᴏʀᴅ, that hath ᴿpleaded the cause of my reproach from the hand of Nā'-băl, and hath ᴿkept his servant from evil: for the Lᴏʀᴅ hath ᴿreturned the wickedness of Nā'-băl upon his own head. And David sent and communed with Ăb'-ĭ-gail, to take her to him to wife.

40 And when the servants of David were come to Ăb'-ĭ-gail to Carmel, they spake unto her, saying, David sent us unto thee, to take thee to him to wife.

41 And she arose, and bowed herself on *her* face to the earth, and said, Behold, *let* thine handmaid *be* a servant to wash the feet of the servants of my lord.

42 And Ăb'-ĭ-gail hasted, and arose, and rode upon an ass, with five damsels of her's that went ᴺafter her; and she went after the messengers of David, and became his wife.

43 David also took Ă-hĭn'-ŏ-ăm ᴿof Jĕz'-rēĕl; ᴿand they were also both of them his wives.

44 But Saul had given ᴿMichal his daughter,

David's wife, to ᴺPhăl'-tĭ the son of Lā'-ĭsh, which *was* of ᴿGăl'-lĭm.

CHAPTER 26

Ziphites betray David

AND the Ziphites came unto Saul to Gĭb'-ĕ-ăh, saying, ᴿDoth not David hide himself in the hill of Hă-chĭ'-läh, *which is* before Jĕ-shĭ'-mon?

2 Then Saul arose, and went down to the wilderness of Ziph, having three thousand chosen men of Israel with him, to seek David in the wilderness of Ziph.

3 And Saul pitched in the hill of Hă-chĭ'-läh, which *is* before Jĕ-shĭ'-mon, by the way. But David abode in the wilderness, and he saw that Saul came after him into the wilderness.

4 David therefore sent out spies, and understood that Saul was come in very deed.

5 And David arose, and came to the place where Saul had pitched: and David beheld the place where Saul lay, and ᴿAbner the son of Ner, the captain of his host: and Saul lay in the ᴺtrench, and the people pitched round about him.

David spares Saul's life again

6 Then answered David and said to Ă-hĭm'-ĕ-lĕch the Hittite, and to Ăb'-ĭ-shâi ᴿthe son of Zĕr-ū-ĭ'-ăh, brother to Jō'-ăb, saying, Who will ᴿgo down with me to Saul to the camp? And Ăb'-ĭ-shâi said, I will go down with thee.

7 So David and Ăb'-ĭ-shâi came to the people by night: and, behold, Saul lay sleeping within the trench, and his spear stuck in the ground at his bolster: but Abner and the people lay round about him.

8 Then said Ăb'-ĭ-shâi to David, God hath ᴺdelivered thine enemy into thine hand this day: now therefore let me smite him, I pray thee, with the spear even to the earth at once, and I will not *smite* him the second time.

9 And David said to Ăb'-ĭ-shâi, Destroy him not: ᴿfor who can stretch forth his hand against the Lᴏʀᴅ's anointed, and be guiltless?

10 David said furthermore, *As* the Lᴏʀᴅ liveth, ᴿthe Lᴏʀᴅ shall smite him; or ᴿhis day shall come to die; or he shall ᴿdescend into battle, and perish.

11 ᴿThe Lᴏʀᴅ forbid that I should stretch forth mine hand against the Lᴏʀᴅ's anointed: but, I pray thee, take thou now the spear that *is* at his bolster, and the cruse of water, and let us go.

12 So David took the spear and the cruse of water from Saul's bolster; and they gat them

away, and no man saw *it,* nor knew *it,* neither awaked: for they *were* all asleep; because ᴿa deep sleep from the Lᴏʀᴅ was fallen upon them.

13 Then David went over to the other side, and stood on the top of an hill afar off; a great space *being* between them:

14 And David cried to the people, and to Abner the son of Ner, saying, Answerest thou not, Abner? Then Abner answered and said, Who *art* thou *that* criest to the king?

15 And David said to Abner, *Art* not thou a *valiant* man? and who *is* like to thee in Israel? wherefore then hast thou not kept thy lord the king? for there came one of the people in to destroy the king thy lord.

16 This thing *is* not good that thou hast done. *As* the Lᴏʀᴅ liveth, ye *are* ᴺworthy to die, because ye have not kept your master, the Lᴏʀᴅ's anointed. And now see where the king's spear *is,* and the cruse of water that *was* at his bolster.

17 And Saul knew David's voice, and said, ᴿ*Is* this thy voice, my son David? And David said, *It is* my voice, my lord, O king.

18 And he said, ᴿWherefore doth my lord thus pursue after his servant? for what have I done? or what evil *is* in mine hand?

19 Now therefore, I pray thee, let my lord the king hear the words of his servant. If the Lᴏʀᴅ have ᴿstirred thee up against me, let him ᴺaccept an offering: but if *they be* the children of men, cursed *be* they before the Lᴏʀᴅ; ᴿfor they have driven me out this day from ᴺabiding in the ᴿinheritance of the Lᴏʀᴅ, saying, Go, serve other gods.

20 Now therefore, let not my blood fall to the earth before the face of the Lᴏʀᴅ: for the king of Israel is come out to seek ᴿa flea, as when one doth hunt a partridge in the mountains.

Saul returns home

21 Then said Saul, ᴿI have sinned: return, my son David: for I will no more do thee harm, because my soul was ᴿprecious in thine eyes this day: behold, I have played the fool, and have erred exceedingly.

22 And David answered and said, Behold the king's spear! and let one of the young men come over and fetch it.

23 ᴿThe Lᴏʀᴅ render to every man his righteousness and his faithfulness: for the Lᴏʀᴅ delivered thee into *my* hand to day, but I would not stretch forth mine hand against the Lᴏʀᴅ's anointed.

24 And, behold, as thy life was much set by this day in mine eyes, so let my life be much

set by in the eyes of the LORD, and let him deliver me out of all tribulation.

25 Then Saul said to David, Blessed *be* thou, my son David: thou shalt both do great *things,* and also shalt still ᴿprevail. So David went on his way, and Saul returned to his place.

CHAPTER 27

David lives with the Philistines

AND David said in his heart, I shall now ᴺperish one day by the hand of Saul: *there is* nothing better for me than that I should speedily escape into the land of the Philistines; and Saul shall despair of me, to seek me any more in any coast of Israel: so shall I escape out of his hand.

2 And David arose, ᴿand he passed over with the six hundred men that *were* with him ᴿunto Ā'-chĭsh, the son of Mā'-ŏch, king of Gath.

3 And David dwelt with Ā'-chĭsh at Gath, he and his men, every man with his household, *even* David ᴿwith his two wives, ă-hĭn'-ŏ-ăm the Jĕz-rĕ͞el-ĭ'-tĕss, and Ăb'-ĭ-gail the Carmeli-tess, Nā'-băl's wife.

4 And it was told Saul that David was fled to Gath: and he sought no more again for him.

5 And David said unto Ā'-chĭsh, If I have now found grace in thine eyes, let them give me a place in some town in the country, that I may dwell there: for why should thy servant dwell in the royal city with thee?

6 Then Ā'-chĭsh gave him Ziklag that day: wherefore ᴿZiklag pertaineth unto the kings of Judah unto this day.

7 And ᴺthe time that David dwelt in the country of the Philistines was ᴺa full year and four months.

Raids of David

8 And David and his men went up, and invaded ᴿthe Gĕ-shū'-rītes, ᴿand the ᴺGĕz'-rītes, and the ᴿĂ-măl'-ĕk-ītes: for those *nations were* of old the inhabitants of the land, ᴿas thou goest to Shur, even unto the land of Egypt.

9 And David smote the land, and left neither man nor woman alive, and took away the sheep, and the oxen, and the asses, and the camels, and the apparel, and returned, and came to Ā'-chĭsh.

10 And Ā'-chĭsh said, ᴺWhither have ye made a road to day? And David said, Against the south of Judah, and against the south of ᴿthe Jĕ-răh'-mĕ͞el-ītes, and against the south of ᴿthe Kē'-nītes.

11 And David saved neither man nor woman

alive, to bring *tidings* to Gath, saying, Lest they should tell on us, saying, So did David, and so *will be* his manner all the while he dwelleth in the country of the Philistines.

12 And Ā'-chĭsh believed David, saying, He hath made his people Israel ᴺutterly to abhor him; therefore he shall be my servant for ever.

CHAPTER 28

Philistines make war against Israel

AND ᴿit came to pass in those days, that the Philistines gathered their armies together for warfare, to fight with Israel. And Ā'-chĭsh said unto David, Know thou assured-ly, that thou shalt go out with me to battle, thou and thy men.

2 And David said to Ā'-chĭsh, Surely thou shalt know what thy servant can do. And Ā'-chĭsh said to David, Therefore will I make thee keeper of mine head for ever.

3 Now ᴿSamuel was dead, and all Israel had lamented him, and buried him in ᴿRā'-măh, even in his own city. And Saul had put away ᴿthose that had familiar spirits, and the wiz-ards, out of the land.

4 And the Philistines gathered themselves together, and came and pitched in ᴿShû'-nĕm: and Saul gathered all Israel together, and they pitched in ᴿGĭl-bō'-ă.

5 And when Saul saw the host of the Philis-tines, he was ᴿafraid, and his heart greatly trembled.

6 And when Saul inquired of the LORD, ᴿthe LORD answered him not, neither by ᴿdreams, nor ᴿby Ū'-rĭm, nor by prophets.

7 Then said Saul unto his servants, Seek me a woman that hath a familiar spirit, that I may go to her, and inquire of her. And his servants said to him, Behold, *there is* a woman that hath a familiar spirit at En-dor.

Saul and the medium of En-dor

8 And Saul disguised himself, and put on other raiment, and he went, and two men with him, and they came to the woman by night: and ᴿhe said, I pray thee, divine unto me by the familiar spirit, and bring me *him* up, whom I shall name unto thee.

9 And the woman said unto him, Behold, thou knowest what Saul hath done, how he hath ᴿcut off those that have familiar spirits, and the wizards, out of the land: wherefore then layest thou a snare for my life, to cause me to die?

10 And Saul sware to her by the LORD, say-ing, *As* the LORD liveth, there shall no pun-ishment happen to thee for this thing.

11 Then said the woman, Whom shall I bring up unto thee? And he said, Bring me up Samuel.

12 And when the woman saw Samuel, she cried with a loud voice: and the woman spake to Saul, saying, Why hast thou deceived me? for thou *art* Saul.

13 And the king said unto her, Be not afraid: for what sawest thou? And the woman said unto Saul, I saw ^Rgods ascending out of the earth.

14 And he said unto her, ^NWhat form *is* he of? And she said, An old man cometh up; and he *is* covered with ^Ra mantle. And Saul perceived that it *was* Samuel, and he stooped with *his* face to the ground, and bowed himself.

Samuel appears

15 And Samuel said to Saul, Why hast thou disquieted me, to bring me up? And Saul answered, ^RI am sore distressed; for the Philistines make war against me, and ^RGod is departed from me, and ^Ranswereth me no more, neither ^Nby prophets, nor by dreams: therefore I have called thee, that thou mayest make known unto me what I shall do.

16 Then said Samuel, Wherefore then dost thou ask of me, seeing the LORD is departed from thee, and is become thine enemy?

17 And the LORD hath done ^Nto him, ^Ras he spake by ^Nme: for the LORD hath rent the kingdom out of thine hand, and given it to thy neighbour, *even* to David:

18 ^RBecause thou obeyedst not the voice of the LORD, nor executedst his fierce wrath upon Ăm′-ă-lĕk, therefore hath the LORD done this thing unto thee this day.

19 Moreover the LORD will also deliver Israel with thee into the hand of the Philistines: and to morrow *shalt* thou and thy sons *be* with me: the LORD also shall deliver the host of Israel into the hand of the Philistines.

20 Then Saul ^Nfell straightway all along on the earth, and was sore afraid, because of the words of Samuel: and there was no strength in him; for he had eaten no bread all the day, nor all the night.

21 And the woman came unto Saul, and saw that he was sore troubled, and said unto him, Behold, thine handmaid hath obeyed thy voice, and I have ^Rput my life in my hand, and have hearkened unto thy words which thou spakest unto me.

22 Now therefore, I pray thee, hearken thou also unto the voice of thine handmaid, and let me set a morsel of bread before thee; and eat, that thou mayest have strength, when thou goest on thy way.

CHAP. 28
BC 1056
13 Ex. 22:28
14 Heb. *What is his form?*
14 ch. 15:27
2 Ki. 2:8, 13
15 Prov. 5:11-13
& 14:14
15 ch. 18:12
15 ver. 6
15 Heb. *by the hand of prophets*
17 Or, *for himself*
17 ch. 15:28
17 Heb. *mine hand*
18 ch. 15:9
1 Ki. 20:42
1 Chr. 10:13
Jer. 48:10
20 Heb. *made haste, and fell with the fullness of his stature*
21 Judg. 12:3
ch. 19:5
Job 13:14

CHAP. 29
BC 1056
ch. 28:1   1
ch. 4:1   1
ch. 28:1, 2   2
See ch. 27:7   3
Dan. 6:5   3
1 Chr. 12:19   4
As ch. 15:21   4
ch. 18:7   5
& 21:11
2 Sam. 3:25   6
2 Ki. 19:27
ver. 3   6
Heb. *thou* art 6
not good in the eyes of the lords
Heb. *do not evil* 7
in the eyes of the lords
Heb. *before*   8
thee

23 But he refused, and said, I will not eat. But his servants, together with the woman, compelled him; and he hearkened unto their voice. So he arose from the earth, and sat upon the bed.

24 And the woman had a fat calf in the house; and she hasted, and killed it, and took flour, and kneaded *it,* and did bake unleavened bread thereof:

25 And she brought *it* before Saul, and before his servants; and they did eat. Then they rose up, and went away that night.

CHAPTER 29

Philistines dismiss David

NOW ^Rthe Philistines gathered together all their armies ^Rto Ā′-phĕk: and the Israelites pitched by a fountain which *is* in Jĕz′-rĕĕl.

2 And the lords of the Philistines passed on by hundreds, and by thousands: but David and his men passed on in the rearward ^Rwith Ā′-chĭsh.

3 Then said the princes of the Philistines, What *do* these Hebrews *here?* And Ā′-chĭsh said unto the princes of the Philistines, *Is* not this David, the servant of Saul the king of Israel, which hath been with me ^Rthese days, or these years, and I have ^Rfound no fault in him since he fell *unto me* unto this day?

4 And the princes of the Philistines were wroth with him; and the princes of the Philistines said unto him, ^RMake this fellow return, that he may go again to his place which thou hast appointed him, and let him not go down with us to battle, lest ^Rin the battle he be an adversary to us: for wherewith should he reconcile himself unto his master? *should it* not *be* with the heads of these men?

5 *Is* not this David, of whom they sang one to another in dances, saying, ^RSaul slew his thousands, and David his ten thousands?

6 Then Ā′-chĭsh called David, and said unto him, Surely, *as* the LORD liveth, thou hast been upright, and ^Rthy going out and thy coming in with me in the host *is* good in my sight: for ^RI have not found evil in thee since the day of thy coming unto me unto this day: nevertheless ^Nthe lords favour thee not.

7 Wherefore now return, and go in peace, that thou ^Ndisplease not the lords of the Philistines.

8 And David said unto Ā′-chĭsh, But what have I done? and what hast thou found in thy servant so long as I have been ^Nwith thee unto this day, that I may not go fight against the enemies of my lord the king?

9 And Ā′-chĭsh answered and said to David,

I know that thou *art* good in my sight, [R]as an angel of God: notwithstanding [R]the princes of the Philistines have said, He shall not go up with us to the battle.

10 Wherefore now rise up early in the morning with thy master's servants that are come with thee: and as soon as ye be up early in the morning, and have light, depart.

11 So David and his men rose up early to depart in the morning, to return into the land of the Philistines. [R]And the Philistines went up to Jĕz'-reĕl.

CHAPTER 30

Amalekites raid David's home

AND it came to pass, when David and his men were come to Ziklag on the third day, that the [R]Ă-măl'-ĕk-ītes had invaded the south, and Ziklag, and smitten Ziklag, and burned it with fire;

2 And had taken the women captives, that *were* therein: they slew not any, either great or small, but carried *them* away, and went on their way.

3 So David and his men came to the city, and, behold, *it was* burned with fire; and their wives, and their sons, and their daughters, were taken captives.

4 Then David and the people that *were* with him lifted up their voice and wept, until they had no more power to weep.

5 And David's [R]two wives were taken captives, Ă-hĭn'-ō-ăm the Jĕz-reĕl-ī'-tĕss, and ăb'-ĭ-gail the wife of Nā'-băl the Carmelite.

6 And David was greatly distressed; [R]for the people spake of stoning him, because the soul of all the people was [N]grieved, every man for his sons and for his daughters: [R]but David encouraged himself in the LORD his God.

7 [R]And David said to Ă-bī'-ă-thär the priest, Ă-hĭm'-ĕ-lĕch's son, I pray thee, bring me hither the ē'-phŏd. And Ă-bī'-ă-thär brought thither the ē'-phŏd to David.

8 [R]And David inquired at the LORD, saying, Shall I pursue after this troop? shall I overtake them? And he answered him, Pursue: for thou shalt surely overtake *them,* and without fail recover *all.*

9 So David went, he and the six hundred men that *were* with him, and came to the brook Bē'-sôr, where those that were left behind stayed.

10 But David pursued, he and four hundred men: [R]for two hundred abode behind, which were so faint that they could not go over the brook Bē'-sôr.

The Amalekite servant

11 And they found an Egyptian in the field, and brought him to David, and gave him bread, and he did eat; and they made him drink water;

12 And they gave him a piece of [R]a cake of figs, and two clusters of raisins: and [R]when he had eaten, his spirit came again to him: for he had eaten no bread, nor drunk *any* water, three days and three nights.

13 And David said unto him, To whom *belongest* thou? and whence *art* thou? And he said, I *am* a young man of Egypt, servant to an Ă-măl'-ĕk-īte; and my master left me, because three days agone I fell sick.

14 We made an invasion *upon* the south of [R]the Chĕr'-ĕ-thītes, and upon *the coast* which *belongeth* to Judah, and upon the south of [R]Caleb; and we burned Ziklag with fire.

15 And David said to him, Canst thou bring me down to this company? And he said, Swear unto me by God, that thou wilt neither kill me, nor deliver me into the hands of my master, and I will bring thee down to this company.

David defeats the Amalekites

16 And when he had brought him down, behold, *they were* spread abroad upon all the earth, [R]eating and drinking, and dancing, because of all the great spoil that they had taken out of the land of the Philistines, and out of the land of Judah.

17 And David smote them from the twilight even unto the evening of [N]the next day: and there escaped not a man of them, save four hundred young men, which rode upon camels, and fled.

18 And David recovered all that the Ă-măl'-ĕk-ītes had carried away: and David rescued his two wives.

19 And there was nothing lacking to them, neither small nor great, neither sons nor daughters, neither spoil, nor any *thing* that they had taken to them: [R]David recovered all.

20 And David took all the flocks and the herds, *which* they drave before those *other* cattle, and said, This *is* David's spoil.

21 And David came to the [R]two hundred men, which were so faint that they could not follow David, whom they had made also to abide at the brook Bē'-sôr: and they went forth to meet David, and to meet the people that *were* with him: and when David came near to the people, he [N]saluted them.

22 Then answered all the wicked men and *men* [R]of Bē'-lĭ-ăl, of [N]those that went with

David, and said, Because they went not with us, we will not give them *aught* of the spoil that we have recovered, save to every man his wife and his children, that they may lead *them* away, and depart.

23 Then said David, Ye shall not do so, my brethren, with that which the Lᴏʀᴅ hath given us, who hath preserved us, and delivered the company that came against us into our hand.

24 For who will hearken unto you in this matter? but ᴿas his part *is* that goeth down to the battle, so *shall* his part *be* that tarrieth by the stuff: they shall part alike.

25 And it was *so* from that day ᴺforward, that he made it a statute and an ordinance for Israel unto this day.

26 And when David came to Ziklag, he sent of the spoil unto the elders of Judah, *even* to his friends, saying, Behold a ᴺpresent for you of the spoil of the enemies of the Lᴏʀᴅ;

27 To *them* which *were* in Beth-el, and to *them* which *were* in ᴿsouth Rā′-mŏth, and to *them* which *were* in ᴿJăt′-tĭr,

28 And to *them* which *were* in ᴿĂ-rō′-ĕr, and to *them* which *were* in Sĭph′-mŏth, and to *them* which *were* in ᴿĔsh-tĕ-mō′-ă,

29 And to *them* which *were* in Rā′-chăl, and to *them* which *were* in the cities of ᴿthe Jĕ-răh′-mēel-ītes, and to *them* which *were* in the cities of the ᴿKē′-nītes,

30 And to *them* which *were* in ᴿHôr′-măh, and to *them* which *were* in Chŏr-ăsh′-ăn, and to *them* which *were* in Ā′-thăch,

31 And to *them* which *were* in ᴿHē′-brŏn, and to all the places where David himself and his men were wont to haunt.

CHAPTER 31

Death of Saul and his sons

NOW ᴿthe Philistines fought against Israel: and the men of Israel fled from before the Philistines, and fell down ᴺslain in mount ᴿGĭl-bō′-ă.

2 And the Philistines followed hard upon Saul and upon his sons; and the Philistines slew ᴿJonathan, and Ă-bĭn′-ă-dăb, and Măl′-chĭ-shû′-ă, Saul's sons.

3 And ᴿthe battle went sore against Saul, and the ᴺarchers ᴺhit him; and he was sore wounded of the archers.

4 ᴿThen said Saul unto his armourbearer, Draw thy sword, and thrust me through therewith; lest ᴿthese uncircumcised come and thrust me through, and ᴺabuse me. But his armourbearer would not; ᴿfor he was sore afraid. Therefore Saul took a sword, and ᴿfell upon it.

5 And when his armourbearer saw that Saul was dead, he fell likewise upon his sword, and died with him.

6 So Saul died, and his three sons, and his armourbearer, and all his men, that same day together.

7 And when the men of Israel that *were* on the other side of the valley, and *they* that *were* on the other side Jordan, saw that the men of Israel fled, and that Saul and his sons were dead, they forsook the cities, and fled; and the Philistines came and dwelt in them.

8 And it came to pass on the morrow, when the Philistines came to strip the slain, that they found Saul and his three sons fallen in mount Gĭl-bō′-ă.

9 And they cut off his head, and stripped off his armour, and sent into the land of the Philistines round about, to ᴿpublish *it in* the house of their idols, and among the people.

10 ᴿAnd they put his armour in the house of ᴿĂsh′-tă-rŏth: and ᴿthey fastened his body to the wall of ᴿBĕth′-shăn.

11 ᴿAnd when the inhabitants of Jā′-bĕsh-gĭl′-ĕ-ăd heard ᴺof that which the Philistines had done to Saul;

12 ᴿAll the valiant men arose, and went all night, and took the body of Saul and the bodies of his sons from the wall of Bĕth′-shăn, and came to Jā′-bĕsh, and ᴿburnt them there.

13 And they took their bones, and ᴿburied *them* under a tree at Jā′-bĕsh, ᴿand fasted seven days.

THE
SECOND BOOK OF SAMUEL
OTHERWISE CALLED
THE SECOND BOOK OF THE KINGS

The entire book of Second Samuel is devoted to the history of David's reign over Israel. Stories of his gradual progress to the summit of power, of his capture of Jerusalem and its establishment as his capital city, of his removal of the ark from Gilboah to Jerusalem, of his resolution and preparation for the building of the temple, and of his extension of the borders of

God's People and the Promised Land

"Be strong and of a good courage: for
unto this people shalt thou divide for an
inheritance the land, which I sware
unto their fathers to give them."

JOSHUA 1:6

Balaam and His Donkey

THE people of Israel had reached the plains of Moab, just across the Jordan River from Jericho. When the king, whose name was Balak, saw how many Israelites were camped there, he became fearful. Now, the people of that day believed that a prophet could pronounce a curse on a group and bring harm upon them. So Balak sent for a prophet named Balaam to come pronounce a curse on the Israelites.

When Balak's messengers arrived at Balaam's home, he urged them to spend the night while he sought God's will in the matter. And God said to Balaam: "Thou shalt not go with them; thou shalt not curse the people: for they are blessed." So Balaam refused to go with Balak's messengers.

When Balak heard what had happened, he sent even more messengers with greater promises of wealth and honor, if Balaam would only come and curse the Israelites. Once more, Balaam asked that they spend the night at his house; and during the night God told him to go with them, but to be sure to do and say only what God desired of him.

The next morning Balaam saddled his donkey and set out on his journey to the land of Moab, where Balak was king. But as he rode along, the donkey saw the angel of the Lord standing in the way, a drawn sword in his hand. So the donkey walked off the road into a field, and for this Balaam beat her. A second time the angel stood in the way, and the donkey scraped against a wall, hurting Balaam's foot; and again he beat her. When the angel appeared the third time, the donkey lay down; and Balaam began to beat her again.

At this, the donkey began to speak to Balaam: "What have I done unto thee, that thou hast smitten me these three times?" Balaam's anger apparently was greater than his surprise, for he replied: "Because thou hast mocked me: I would there were a sword in mine hand, for now would I kill thee." But the donkey reminded Balaam of all her years of faithful service to him.

"Then the Lord opened the eyes of Balaam, and he saw the angel of the Lord standing in the way, and his sword drawn in his hand: and he bowed down his head, and fell flat on his face." Balaam promised the angel that, if God wanted him to do so, he would turn around and go back home. But the angel told him to go ahead to Balak's land, but to be sure to speak only those words which the angel would tell him to speak.

When Balaam and the messengers arrived in Moab, Balak took Balaam up onto a high mountain and showed him the Israelites camped nearby. In preparation for his utterance, Balaam had seven altars built, and on each altar had a bull and a ram sacrificed. Then he said: "How shall I curse, whom God hath not cursed?" Balak was angry; he shouted out that he had hired Balaam to curse the Israelites, but that instead he had blessed them. But Balaam replied that he could only speak whatever God put into his mouth to speak.

Three times this happened: the altars were built, sacrifices were made, and Balaam blessed the Israelites rather than cursing them. No harm that Balak could threaten, and no reward that he could offer, would make Balaam curse the Israelites. So the two men went their separate ways.

Numbers 22:1–24:25.

Jephthah's Daughter

N the days when the Israelites were often at war with other tribes, some men became famous as warriors. One such person was Jephthah, "a mighty man of valour," who was an illegitimate son of Gilead. Gilead's other sons drove Jephthah away from home; so he went to live in the land of Tob.

After a time the Ammonites made war against Israel, and the Israelites were desperate for a powerful military leader. So they sent some of their elders to plead with Jephthah to return to Gilead and help them fight the Ammonites. They were willing to promise almost anything to get Jephthah to help them in their life-and-death struggle. In fact, they promised that if he were victorious over the Ammonites they would make him the ruler of Gilead!

First, Jephthah tried to negotiate with the king of Ammon; but neither side would back down. So Jephthah saw that the war must be won on the battlefield. He wanted God's help in achieving a victory; therefore, he made a vow to God: "If thou shalt without fail deliver the children of Ammon into mine hands, then it shall be, that whatsoever cometh forth of the doors of my house to meet me, when I return in peace from the children of Ammon, shall surely be the Lord's, and I will offer it up for a burnt offering."

With that, Jephthah and his soldiers attacked the Ammonites and won victory after victory, until the Ammonites made peace with Israel. When Jephthah returned home in triumph, his daughter came out to meet him. How happy she was over her father's victory! She came out playing the timbrel and dancing with joy. Now, she was Jephthah's only child, and ordinarily he would have been most happy to see her. But with dismay and anguish of heart, Jephthah recalled his vow to God.

Heartbroken, Jephthah tore his clothes and cried out: "Alas, my daughter! thou hast brought me very low, and thou art one of them that trouble me: for I have opened my mouth unto the Lord, and I cannot go back."

Jephthah's daughter must have been filled with despair. She was young and unmarried; before her life was half over it must be cut short. But she believed in keeping vows that had been made to God. So she told her father: "My father, if thou hast opened thy mouth unto the Lord, do to me according to that which hath proceeded out of thy mouth; forasmuch as the Lord hath taken vengeance for thee for thine enemies, even of the children of Ammon."

One thing only she asked of her father: that she and her friends might have two months to grieve, before she was sacrificed. Jephthah agreed to her request; so she and her companions went up into the mountains for two months. At the end of that time, she returned to her home. And with profound sorrow, Jephthah sacrificed his daughter to keep his vow to God.

In the years that followed, it became a custom for young women in Israel to mourn for Jephthah's daughter four days every year.

Judges 11:1-40.

TISSOT

Samson and Delilah

MONG the bitterest enemies of the Israelites were the Philistines. At the height of the rivalry beween these nations, a remarkably strong young man named Samson came on the scene. He was fearless, as well as strong. For example, one day as he was walking through a vineyard at Timnah, a lion roared fiercely at him. But instead of running, Samson grabbed the lion and with his bare hands literally tore him apart. Samson had a weakness for women. His first wife was a Philistine who betrayed him to her people. In anger, Samson killed thirty men of the town and returned to his own father's house.

Sometime later, Samson fell in love with a woman who lived in the valley of Sorek, a beautiful young woman named Delilah. After she and Samson were married, some Philistine leaders came to her and promised her a great amount of silver money if she would find out the secret of Samson's great strength and tell them what it was.

The lure of money was too much for Delilah. So she began to try to wheedle Samson's secret from him. He must have been suspicious, for he did not immediately tell her his secret. First, he told her that, if he were bound with seven fresh bowstrings he could not escape. So Delilah tied him up with the bowstrings while he slept; several Philistines were waiting in the next room. Then she cried out: "The Philistines be upon thee, Samson." Awakening, Samson snapped the bowstrings as if they were nothing.

Later, Delilah chided Samson for not telling her the truth, and begged him to tell her the secret of his strength. So he told her that if he were bound with new ropes that had not been used, he could not escape. Waiting until he fell asleep, Delilah bound him with new ropes. Then she called out: "The Philistines be upon thee, Samson." Once again, Samson snapped the ropes as if they were thread.

Delilah accused Samson of lying to her, and once again begged him to tell her the secret of his strength. This time, Samson told her that if his hair were woven tightly into a loom, he could not escape. After he had fallen asleep, Delilah wove his hair into the web of a loom, then cried out that the Philistines were about to seize Samson. A third time, Samson tore himself loose easily.

Using woman's wiles, Delilah pouted: "How canst thou say, I love thee, when thine heart is not with me? Thou hast mocked me these three times, and hast not told me wherein thy great strengh lieth." Delilah's constant nagging wore Samson down, so finally he told her that if his hair were shaved off, he would lose his great strength. This time, Delilah was convinced that Samson was telling her the truth. So she sent word to the Philistines to come and bring the money which they had promised her. And while Samson slept, a Philistine shaved off his hair.

A fourth time, then, Delilah called out: "The Philistines be upon thee Samson." When he woke up, Samson found that his great strength was gone. So the Philistines were able to take him captive. Cruelly, they gouged out his eyes, and took him as a prisoner to Gaza.

Judges 14:1–16:22.

TISSOT

Samson at the Treadmill

T HE last chapter in Samson's life opens upon a pitiful sight. Samson is blind, a prisoner of the Philistines in Gaza, and forced to work at hard labor grinding grain with a hand mill. But this is not to be the last word in the story of a man of tremendous strength and violent emotions. For as Samson's hair began to grow out, after having been shaved off by the Philistines, Samson regained his strength.

As he walked about day after day at the treadmill, Samson must have recalled many incidents from his youth and young adulthood. Perhaps he chuckled as he remembered how he had once tied burning sticks to foxes' tails and chased them into the Philistines' grain fields, so that their crops were burned up. He must have felt bitterness, however, as he realized that he was no longer able to fight the Philistines—that he was, in fact, their prisoner.

It was time for the Philistines to make a sacrifice to their pagan god Dagon, who had been worshipped by persons in Mesopotamia since about 2400 B.C. As the people gathered in the temple for the feast and sacrifice, they gloated over the capture of their former enemy—now their slave—Samson. "Our god hath delivered Samson our enemy into our hand," they said.

As they drank wine the Philistines swaggered with self-satisfaction. They yelled to the jailors: "Call for Samson, that he may make us sport." They intended to have some fun by mocking the blind man who had once struck such terror to their hearts.

Samson was led in by his jailor. In a low voice, Samson made a request: "Let me feel the pillars whereupon the house standeth, that I may lean upon them." Perhaps the guard thought merely that Samson was weary from walking hours upon end at the treadmill, and that he therefore wanted to rest by leaning against the columns that supported the temple. So he led Samson over to the pillars.

The temple was filled with Philistines upon this festival occasion. In all, there were more than three thousand persons present, jeering at Samson, drinking and laughing as they feasted in honor of their god Dagon. As the rumble of many voices filled Samson's ears, he could imagine how they looked. He began to feel a surge of anger at his enemies, as he had in the old days. Intensely he prayed: "O Lord God, remember me, I pray thee, and strengthen me, I pray thee, only this once, O God, that I may be at once avenged of the Philistines for my two eyes."

Then Samson grasped the two central columns of the temple with his powerful hands and pushed with all his might. "Let me die with the Philistines!" he cried out. "And the house fell upon the lords and upon all the people that were therein. So the dead which he slew at his death were more than they which he slew in his life."

After Samson's death, his brothers and relatives came to claim his body and buried him in the burying place of Manoah his father.

Judges 16:21–31.

Ruth and Boaz

NE year when a terrible famine struck Judah, Elimelech took his wife Naomi and their two sons to the land of Moab, which was south and east of their home town of Bethlehem. But after a time Elimelech died, leaving his widow and two sons. When the sons were grown, they married two young Moabite women, named Orpah and Ruth. After only ten years, both sons died. Naomi and her daughters-in-law were all widows, in an alien land. What should they do?

Naomi decided to return to Bethlehem. But she did not want to force her two daughters-in-law to leave their home country and friends merely out of loyalty to her. So in a spirit of love and good will, Naomi told them: "Go return each to her mother's house: the Lord deal kindly with you, as ye have dealt with the dead, and with me." Then she kissed them a tearful good-bye. Orpah and Ruth protested that they would go to Judah with their mother-in-law; but she insisted that they stay among their own people. At this, Orpah kissed Naomi good-bye and returned to live with her relatives. But Ruth was determined to stay with her mother-in-law; she voiced her loyalty in these beautiful words: "Intreat me not to leave thee, or to return from following after thee: for whither thou goest, I will go; and where thou lodgest, I will lodge: thy people shall be my people, and thy God my God: where thou diest, will I die, and there will I be buried: the Lord do so to me, and more also, if ought but death part thee and me."

So Naomi and her daughter-in-law Ruth returned to Bethlehem. When they arrived, the farmers were just beginning to harvest their crops of grain. Now, it was customary for landowners to leave a small amount of grain behind in the fields, which the very poor people could gather or "glean" and thus have some feed to eat. So Ruth went out in the fields to glean some grain for Naomi and herself. She worked hard; and when Boaz, the owner of the fields, came by he was attracted to her.

Boaz instructed his workmen to leave behind even more grain than usual, so that Ruth could gather enough to feed herself and her mother-in-law. When Ruth got home that night and told Naomi all that had happened to her, Naomi was very pleased. She recognized Boaz as a kinsman, as well as a fine man, so she urged Ruth to continue working in his fields.

Naomi was eager to find a suitable husband for Ruth. Was not Boaz just the kind of man to whom Ruth should be married? Naomi believed in direct action: she had Ruth to go to the threshing floor where Boaz was sleeping and propose marriage to him. Boaz was very pleased. "I will do to thee all that thou requirest," he told Ruth, "for all the city of my people doth know that thou art a virtuous woman." So Boaz married Ruth.

In due time, Ruth and Boaz had their first child, a son whom they named Obed. No one was happier than Naomi, who was the little boy's nurse. When he grew up, this boy became the father of Jesse, and the grandfather of the great king David.

Ruth 1:1–4:17.

Hannah Brings Samuel Before Eli

N the hill country of Ephraim, north of Judah, there lived a man named Elkanah who had two wives. One, named Peninnah, had several children; but the other, whose name was Hannah, had none at all. This was a source of great unhappiness to Hannah. Often, she wept because she was so unhappy.

Elkanah took his wives and children to Shiloh each year, to sacrifice at the temple where Eli was priest. After the family had eaten, Hannah went into the temple to pray. She was very unhappy about the fact that she had no children, and she wept bitterly. Then she made a vow to God: "O Lord of hosts," she promised, "if thou wilt indeed look on the affliction of thine handmaid, and remember me, and not forget thine handmaid, but wilt give unto thine handmaid a man child, then I will give him unto the Lord all the days of his life, and there shall no razor come upon his head." In other words, Hannah promised God that if she should have a son, he would be dedicated to religious leadership of the Jewish people.

Hannah was praying with great earnestness, but silently. Eli saw her lips moving, but heard no words; therefore, he thought she was drunk and rebuked her. But Hannah explained that she was not drunk: "I have drunk neither wine nor strong drink, but have poured out my soul before the Lord." At this, Eli blessed her: "Go in peace: and the God of Israel grant thee thy petition that thou hast asked of him."

After Hannah had returned home, she and her husband had their first child, a son, whom they named Samuel. She remembered her vow to God; and when Samuel was a little boy Hannah took him to the temple at Shiloh, to live with Eli. She also brought along animals, flour, and wine to sacrifice.

When Hannah and her little boy Samuel entered the temple, they went up to the priest Eli and Hannah told him: "Oh my lord, as thy soul liveth, my lord, I am the woman that stood by thee here, praying unto the Lord. For this child I prayed; and the Lord hath given me my petition which I asked of him: therefore also I have lent him to the Lord; as long as he liveth he shall be lent to the Lord." Eli must have been moved as he gazed down at the little boy Samuel, and as he remembered the earnest prayer of Hannah in the temple several years before. Here was a fine child, Hannah's only son, dedicated to the service of God in the temple!

Hannah felt exultant at this moment. Her prayer as she brought her son Samuel to the temple at Shiloh was a mighty outpouring of praise to God:

"My heart rejoiceth in the Lord, mine horn is exalted in the Lord: my mouth is enlarged over mine enemies; because I rejoice in thy salvation.

"There is none holy as the Lord: for there is none beside thee: neither is there any rock like our God."

Here, then, was a boy dedicated to God's service; and, as the future would reveal, he was a person marked for greatness.

1 Samuel 1:1-28.

Samuel and Saul

 AMUEL grew in stature and in favor with God and with men. He served God in the temple at Shiloh as Eli's helper. One night, as he lay sleeping, he thought he heard Eli calling him. So he ran into Eli's room and said: "Here am I; for thou calledst me." But Eli replied: "I called not; lie down again." This happened three times; then Eli realized that it was God seeking to speak to the boy Samuel. He instructed Samuel to say, if he heard God's voice again: "Speak, Lord; for thy servant heareth."

Once again God called Samuel. This time, he responded: "Speak; for thy servant heareth." Then God revealed to Samuel that he would destroy Eli's sons for their wickedness. How painful it must have been for Samuel to tell Eli what God had revealed to him! But Eli received the bad news with resignation: "It is the Lord," he said. "Let him do what seemeth him good." Meanwhile, Samuel's reputation as a prophet of the Lord spread throughout Israel.

At this time, the Philistines became powerful and defeated the Israelites in battle after battle. In one such battle, thirty thousand soldiers of Israel were slaughtered! Worst of all, the ark of God was seized by the Philistines in 1050 B.C. and put in a pagan temple in which the god Dagon was worshipped. Eli's sons were killed in battle; upon receiving this sad news, Eli fell over in a faint, accidentally breaking his neck so that he died.

Samuel was now leader of Israel. He called the people to repentance and dedication to God: "Prepare your hearts unto the Lord, and serve him only: and he will deliver you out of the hand of the Philistines." Samuel's prophecy came true: the Israelites overcame the Philistines.

It must have been a bitter disappointment to Samuel that his sons, like Eli's sons, were not fit leaders for the Israelites: they "turned aside after lucre, and took bribes, and perverted judgment." The citizens therefore came to Samuel and requested that he appoint a man to serve as king of Israel. This displeased Samuel; but as he prayed he discovered that God was willing for the Israelites to have a king.

Samuel set out to find a suitable man to rule the Israelites. One day he met Saul, a handsome young man from the tribe of Benjamin, who was a head taller than any of his fellow men. The Lord told Samuel: "Behold the man whom I spake to thee of! this same shall reign over my people." So Samuel talked with Saul, and made him the guest of honor at a feast. The next day, Samuel took a vial of oil and poured it upon Saul's head. This was a symbolic act, known as "anointing," and was used for the consecration of kings. For centuries after this, the kings of Israel would be called "the Lord's anointed."

Then Samuel called all the Israelites together at the town of Mizpah. He called for Saul, but Saul had hidden himself. When he was found, Samuel said to all the people: "See ye him whom the Lord hath chosen, that there is none like him among all the people?" At that, all the people shouted out: "God save the king!"

1 Samuel 2:11–10:26.

TISSOT

The Lord is my shepherd; I shall not want.

He maketh me to lie down in green pastures:
he leadeth me beside the still waters.

He restoreth my soul: he leadeth me in the
paths of righteousness for his name's sake.

Yea, though I walk through the valley of
the shadow of death, I will fear no evil: for
thou art with me; thy rod and thy staff
they comfort me.

Thou preparest a table before me in the
presence of mine enemies: thou anointest my
head with oil; my cup runneth over.

Surely goodness and mercy shall follow me
all the days of my life: and I will dwell in
the house of the Lord forever."

PSALM 23

Israel are all told in vivid detail and beauty. The essential facts of his various wars and successes are given with graphic clarity. While First Chronicles also covers the period of David's reign, this book provides a frank and unreserved account of sin in the royal family. The inspired historian made no attempt to conceal the evil of David's life, relating with all honesty the king's equivocation to Achish, his adultery with Bath-sheba culminating in the shameful slaying of her husband Uriah in battle, and the haughtiness he displayed in his numbering of the people. The evils which accrued to the monarchy through the unnatural rebellion of Absalom are preserved in striking colorings. The book is easily understood and reveals the workings of Providence in the history of Israel. The closing events of David's reign are recorded in the First Book of Kings.

OUTLINE OF THE BOOK:
  I. David established as king of Israel   1:1-7:29
  II. Expansion of the kingdom   8:1-10:19
  III. Sin and its consequences   11:1-20:26
  IV. David's final years   21:1-24:25

CHAPTER 1

News of Saul's death reaches David

NOW it came to pass after the death of Saul, when David was returned from ᴿthe slaughter of the Ă-măl′-ĕk-ītes, and David had abode two days in Ziklag;

2 It came even to pass on the third day, that, behold, ᴿa man came out of the camp from Saul ᴿwith his clothes rent, and earth upon his head: and *so* it was, when he came to David, that he fell to the earth, and did obeisance.

3 And David said unto him, From whence comest thou? And he said unto him, Out of the camp of Israel am I escaped.

4 And David said unto him, ᴺHow went the matter? I pray thee, tell me. And he answered, That the people are fled from the battle, and many of the people also are fallen and dead; and Saul and Jonathan his son are dead also.

5 And David said unto the young man that told him, How knowest thou that Saul and Jonathan his son be dead?

6 And the young man that told him said, As I happened by chance upon ᴿmount Gĭl-bō′-ă, behold, ᴿSaul leaned upon his spear; and, lo, the chariots and horsemen followed hard after him.

7 And when he looked behind him, he saw me, and called unto me. And I answered, ᴺHere *am* I.

8 And he said unto me, Who *art* thou? And I answered him, I *am* an Ă-măl′-ĕk-īte.

9 He said unto me again, Stand, I pray thee, upon me, and slay me: for ᴺanguish is come upon me, because my life *is* yet whole in me.

10 So I stood upon him, and ᴿslew him, because I was sure that he could not live after that he was fallen: and I took the crown that *was* upon his head, and the bracelet that *was* on his arm, and have brought them hither unto my lord.

11 Then David took hold on his clothes, and ᴿrent them; and likewise all the men that *were* with him:

12 And they mourned, and wept, and fasted until even, for Saul, and for Jonathan his son,

CHAP. **1**	
BC 1056	
1 1 Sam. 30:17, 26	
2 ch. 4:10	
2 1 Sam. 4:12	
4 Heb. *What was, etc.,*	
1 Sam. 4:16	
6 1 Sam. 31:1	
6 See 1 Sam. 31:2-4	
7 Heb. *Behold me*	
9 Or, *my coat of mail,* or, *my embroidered coat hindereth me, that my, etc.*	
10 Judg. 9:54	
11 ch. 3:31 & 13:31	
Num. 12:8	**14**
1 Sam. 31:4	**14**
1 Sam. 24:6 & 26:9	**14**
Ps. 105:15	
ch. 4:10, 12	**15**
1 Sam. 26:9	**16**
1 Ki. 2:32, 33, 37	
ver. 10 Luke 19:22	**16**
1 Sam. 31:3	**18**
Josh. 10:13	**18**
Or, *of the upright*	**18**
ver. 27	**19**
1 Sam. 31:9 Mic. 1:10	**20**
See Judg. 16:23	
See Ex. 15:20 Judg. 11:34 1 Sam. 18:6	**20**
1 Sam. 31:4	**20**
1 Sam. 31:1	**21**
Judg. 5:23	**21**
Job 3:3, 4 Jer. 20:14	
1 Sam. 10:1	**21**
1 Sam. 18:4	**22**
Or, *sweet*	**23**
Judg. 14:18	**23**

and for the people of the LORD, and for the house of Israel; because they were fallen by the sword.

13 And David said unto the young man that told him, Whence *art* thou? And he answered, I *am* the son of a stranger, an Ă-măl′-ĕk-īte.

14 And David said unto him, ᴿHow wast thou not ᴿafraid to ᴿstretch forth thine hand to destroy the LORD's anointed?

15 And ᴿDavid called one of the young men, and said, Go near, *and* fall upon him. And he smote him that he died.

16 And David said unto him, ᴿThy blood *be* upon thy head; for ᴿthy mouth hath testified against thee, saying, I have slain the LORD's anointed.

David's lament for Saul and Jonathan

17 And David lamented with this lamentation over Saul and over Jonathan his son:

18 (ᴿAlso he bade them teach the children of Judah *the use of* the bow: behold, *it is* written ᴿin the book ᴺof Jăsh′-ĕr.)

19 The beauty of Israel is slain upon thy high places: ᴿhow are the mighty fallen!

20 ᴿTell *it* not in Gath, publish *it* not in the streets of Ăs′-kĕ-lŏn; lest ᴿthe daughters of the Philistines rejoice, lest the daughters of ᴿthe uncircumcised triumph.

21 Ye ᴿmountains of Gĭl-bō′-ă, ᴿ*let there be* no dew, neither *let there be* rain, upon you, nor fields of offerings: for there the shield of the mighty is vilely cast away, the shield of Saul, *as though he had* not *been* ᴿanointed with oil.

22 From the blood of the slain, from the fat of the mighty, ᴿthe bow of Jonathan turned not back, and the sword of Saul returned not empty.

23 Saul and Jonathan *were* lovely and ᴺpleasant in their lives, and in their death they were not divided: they were swifter than eagles, they were ᴿstronger than lions.

24 Ye daughters of Israel, weep over Saul, who clothed you in scarlet, with *other* delights, who put on ornaments of gold upon your apparel.

25 How are the mighty fallen in the midst of

the battle! O Jonathan, *thou wast* slain in thine high places.

26 I am distressed for thee, my brother Jonathan: very pleasant hast thou been unto me: ᴿthy love to me was wonderful, passing the love of women.

27 ᴿHow are the mighty fallen, and the weapons of war perished!

CHAPTER 2

David anointed king of Judah

AND it came to pass after this, that David ᴿinquired of the Lord, saying, Shall I go up into any of the cities of Judah? And the Lord said unto him, Go up. And David said, Whither shall I go up? And he said, Unto ᴿHē′-brŏn.

2 So David went up thither, and his ᴿtwo wives also, Ă-hĭn′-ŏ-ăm the Jĕz-rēĕl-ī′-tĕss, and Ăb′-ĭ-gail Nā′-băl's wife the Carmelite.

3 And ᴿhis men that *were* with him did David bring up, every man with his household: and they dwelt in the cities of Hē′-brŏn.

4 ᴿAnd the men of Judah came, and there they anointed David king over the house of Judah. And they told David, saying, *That* ᴿthe men of Jā′-bĕsh-gĭl′-ĕ-ăd *were they* that buried Saul.

5 And David sent messengers unto the men of Jā′-bĕsh-gĭl′-ĕ-ăd, and said unto them, ᴿBlessed *be* ye of the Lord, that ye have shewed this kindness unto your lord, *even* unto Saul, and have buried him.

6 And now ᴿthe Lord shew kindness and truth unto you: and I also will requite you this kindness, because ye have done this thing.

7 Therefore now let your hands be strengthened, and ᴺbe ye valiant: for your master Saul is dead, and also the house of Judah have anointed me king over them.

Ish-bosheth made king of Israel

8 But ᴿAbner the son of Ner, captain of ᴺSaul's host, took ᴺĬsh-bŏsh′-ĕth the son of Saul, and brought him over to Mā-hă-nā′-ĭm;

9 And made him king over Gilead, and over the Ăsh′-ū-rītes, and over Jĕz′-rēĕl, and over Ē′-phră-ĭm, and over Benjamin, and over all Israel.

10 Ĭsh-bŏsh′-ĕth Saul's son *was* forty years old when he began to reign over Israel, and reigned two years. But the house of Judah followed David.

11 And ᴿthe ᴺtime that David was king in Hē′-brŏn over the house of Judah was seven years and six months.

Abner defeated

12 And Abner the son of Ner, and the servants of Ĭsh-bŏsh′-ĕth the son of Saul, went out from Mā-hă-nā′-ĭm to ᴿGibeon.

13 And Jŏ′-ăb the son of Zĕr-ū-ī′-ăh, and the servants of David, went out, and met ᴺtogether by ᴿthe pool of Gibeon: and they sat down, the one on the one side of the pool, and the other on the other side of the pool.

14 And Abner said to Jŏ′-ăb, Let the young men now arise, and play before us. And Jŏ′-ăb said, Let them arise.

15 Then there arose and went over by number twelve of Benjamin, which *pertained* to Ĭsh-bŏsh′-ĕth the son of Saul, and twelve of the servants of David.

16 And they caught every one his fellow by the head, and *thrust* his sword in his fellow's side; so they fell down together: wherefore that place was called ᴺHĕl′-kăth-hăz-zū′-rĭm, which *is* in Gibeon.

17 And there was a very sore battle that day; and Abner was beaten, and the men of Israel, before the servants of David.

Abner slays Asahel

18 And there were ᴿthree sons of Zĕr-ū-ī′-ăh there, Jŏ′-ăb, and Ăb′-ĭ-shâi, and Ăs′-ă-hĕl: and Ăs′-ă-hĕl *was* ᴿ*as* light ᴺof foot ᴿasᴺ a wild roe.

19 And Ăs′-ă-hĕl pursued after Abner; and in going he turned not to the right hand nor to the left ᴺfrom following Abner.

20 Then Abner looked behind him, and said, *Art* thou Ăs′-ă-hĕl? And he answered, I *am*.

21 And Abner said to him, Turn thee aside to thy right hand or to thy left, and lay thee hold on one of the young men, and take thee his ᴺarmour. But Ăs′-ă-hĕl would not turn aside from following of him.

22 And Abner said again to Ăs′-ă-hĕl, Turn thee aside from following me: wherefore should I smite thee to the ground? how then should I hold up my face to Jŏ′-ăb thy brother?

23 Howbeit he refused to turn aside: wherefore Abner with the hinder end of the spear smote him ᴿunder the fifth *rib,* that the spear came out behind him; and he fell down there, and died in the same place: and it came to pass, *that* as many as came to the place where Ăs′-ă-hĕl fell down and died stood still.

Truce between Abner and Joab

24 Jŏ′-ăb also and Ăb′-ĭ-shâi pursued after Abner: and the sun went down when they were come to the hill of Ăm′-măh, that *lieth*

before Gī'-ăh by the way of the wilderness of Gibeon.

25 And the children of Benjamin gathered themselves together after Abner, and became one troop, and stood on the top of an hill.

26 Then Abner called to Jō'-ăb, and said, Shall the sword devour for ever? knowest thou not that it will be bitterness in the latter end? how long shall it be then, ere thou bid the people return from following their brethren?

27 And Jō'-ăb said, As God liveth, unless [R]thou hadst spoken, surely then [N]in the morning the people had [N]gone up every one from following his brother.

28 So Jō'-ăb blew a trumpet, and all the people stood still, and pursued after Israel no more, neither fought they any more.

29 And Abner and his men walked all that night through the plain, and passed over Jordan, and went through all Bīth'-rŏn, and they came to Mā-hă-nā'-ĭm.

30 And Jō'-ăb returned from following Abner: and when he had gathered all the people together, there lacked of David's servants nineteen men and Ăs'-ă-hĕl.

31 But the servants of David had smitten of Benjamin, and of Abner's men, so that three hundred and threescore men died.

32 And they took up Ăs'-ă-hĕl, and buried him in the sepulchre of his father, which was in Beth-lehem. And Jō'-ăb and his men went all night, and they came to Hē'-brŏn at break of day.

CHAPTER 3

Sons of David

NOW there was long war between the house of Saul and the house of David: but David waxed stronger and stronger, and the house of Saul waxed weaker and weaker.

2 And [R]unto David were sons born in Hē'-brŏn: and his firstborn was Amnon, [R]of Ă-hīn'-ŏ-ăm the Jĕz-rēel-ī'-tĕss;

3 And his second, [N]Chī'-lĕ-ăb, of Ăb'-ĭ-gail the wife of Nā'-băl the Carmelite; and the third, Ăb'-să-lŏm the son of Mā'-ă-căh the daughter of Tăl'-maī king [R]of Gē'-shŭr;

4 And the fourth, [R]Ăd-ō-nī'-jăh the son of Hăg'-gĭth; and the fifth, Shĕph-ă-tī'-ăh the son of Ă-bī'-tăl;

5 And the sixth, Ĭth'-rĕ-ăm, by ĕg'-lăh David's wife. These were born to David in Hē'-brŏn.

Abner quarrels with Ish-bosheth

6 And it came to pass, while there was war between the house of Saul and the house of

CHAP. **2**
BC 1056
27 ver. 14
Prov. 17:14
27 Heb. *from the morning*
27 Or, *gone away*

CHAP. **3**
BC 1048
2 1 Chr. 3:1-4
2 1 Sam. 25:43
3 Or, *Daniel*, 1 Chr. 3:1
3 1 Sam. 27:8
ch. 13:37
4 1 Ki. 1:5

ch. 21:8, 10   7
ch. 16:21   7
Deut. 23:18   8
1 Sam. 24:14
ch. 9:8 & 16:9
Ruth 1:17   9
1 Ki. 19:2
1 Sam. 15:28   9
& 16:1, 12 & 28:17
1 Chr. 12:23
Judg. 20:1   10
ch. 17:11
1 Ki. 4:25
Heb. *saying*   13
Gen. 43:3   13
1 Sam. 18:20   13
1 Sam. 18:25, 27 14
1 Sam. 25:44,   15
Phalti
Heb. *going   16
and weeping*
ch. 19:16   16
Heb. *both   17
yesterday and the
third day*
ver. 9   18
1 Chr. 12:29   19

David, that Abner made himself strong for the house of Saul.

7 And Saul had a concubine, whose name was [R]Rīz'-păh, the daughter of Āī'-ăh: and Ĭsh-bŏsh'-ĕth said to Abner, Wherefore hast thou [R]gone in unto my father's concubine?

8 Then was Abner very wroth for the words of ĭsh-bŏsh'-ĕth, and said, Am I [R]a dog's head, which against Judah do shew kindness this day unto the house of Saul thy father, to his brethren, and to his friends, and have not delivered thee into the hand of David, that thou chargest me to day with a fault concerning this woman?

9 [R]So do God to Abner, and more also, except, [R]as the LORD hath sworn to David, even so I do to him;

10 To translate the kingdom from the house of Saul, and to set up the throne of David over Israel and over Judah, [R]from Dan even to Bēer-shē'-bă.

11 And he could not answer Abner a word again, because he feared him.

12 And Abner sent messengers to David on his behalf, saying, Whose is the land? saying also, Make thy league with me, and, behold, my hand shall be with thee, to bring about all Israel unto thee.

13 And he said, Well; I will make a league with thee: but one thing I require of thee, [N]that is, [R]Thou shalt not see my face, except thou first bring [R]Michal Saul's daughter, when thou comest to see my face.

14 And David sent messengers to ĭsh-bŏsh'-ĕth Saul's son, saying, Deliver me my wife Michal, which I espoused to me [R]for an hundred foreskins of the Philistines.

15 And ĭsh-bŏsh'-ĕth sent, and took her from her husband, even from [R]Phăl'-tī-ĕl the son of Lā'-ĭsh.

16 And her husband went with her [N]along weeping behind her to [R]Bă-hū'-rĭm. Then said Abner unto him, Go, return. And he returned.

Abner revolts to David

17 And Abner had communication with the elders of Israel, saying, Ye sought for David [N]in times past to be king over you:

18 Now then do it: [R]for the LORD hath spoken of David, saying, By the hand of my servant David I will save my people Israel out of the hand of the Philistines, and out of the hand of all their enemies.

19 And Abner also spake in the ears of [R]Benjamin: and Abner went also to speak in the ears of David in Hē'-brŏn all that seemed good to Israel, and that seemed good to the whole house of Benjamin.

20 So Abner came to David to Hḗ'-brŏn, and twenty men with him. And David made Abner and the men that *were* with him a feast.

21 And Abner said unto David, I will arise and go, and ᴿwill gather all Israel unto my lord the king, that they may make a league with thee, and that thou mayest ᴿreign over all that thine heart desireth. And David sent Abner away; and he went in peace.

Abner killed by Joab

22 And, behold, the servants of David and Jō'-ăb came from *pursuing* a troop, and brought in a great spoil with them: but Abner *was* not with David in Hḗ'-brŏn; for he had sent him away, and he was gone in peace.

23 When Jō'-ăb and all the host that *was* with him were come, they told Jō'-ăb, saying, Abner the son of Ner came to the king, and he hath sent him away, and he is gone in peace.

24 Then Jō'-ăb came to the king, and said, What hast thou done? behold, Abner came unto thee; why *is* it *that* thou hast sent him away, and he is quite gone?

25 Thou knowest Abner the son of Ner, that he came to deceive thee, and to know ᴿthy going out and thy coming in, and to know all that thou doest.

26 And when Jō'-ăb was come out from David, he sent messengers after Abner, which brought him again from the well of Sī'-răh: but David knew *it* not.

27 And when Abner was returned to Hḗ'-brŏn, Jō'-ăb ᴿtook him aside in the gate to speak with him ᴺquietly, and smote him there ᴿunder the fifth *rib,* that he died, for the blood of ᴿǍs'-ă-hĕl his brother.

28 And afterward when David heard *it,* he said, I and my kingdom *are* guiltless before the LORD for ever from the ᴺblood of Abner the son of Ner:

29 ᴿLet it rest on the head of Jō'-ăb, and on all his father's house; and let there not ᴺfail from the house of Jō'-ăb one ᴿthat hath an issue, or that is a leper, or that leaneth on a staff, or that falleth on the sword, or that lacketh bread.

30 So Jō'-ăb and Ǎb'-ĭ-shâi his brother slew Abner, because he had slain their brother ᴿǍs'-ă-hĕl at Gibeon in the battle.

David's lament for Abner

31 And David said to Jō'-ăb, and to all the people that *were* with him, ᴿRend your clothes, and ᴿgird you with sackcloth, and mourn before Abner. And king David *himself* followed the ᴺbier.

32 And they buried Abner in Hḗ'-brŏn: and the king lifted up his voice, and wept at the grave of Abner; and all the people wept.

33 And the king lamented over Abner, and said, Died Abner as a ᴿfool dieth?

34 Thy hands *were* not bound, nor thy feet put into fetters: as a man falleth before ᴺwicked men, *so* fellest thou. And all the people wept again over him.

35 And when all the people came ᴿto cause David to eat meat while it was yet day, David sware, saying, ᴿSo do God to me, and more also, if I taste bread, or aught else, ᴿtill the sun be down.

36 And all the people took notice *of it,* and it ᴺpleased them: as whatsoever the king did pleased all the people.

37 For all the people and all Israel understood that day that it was not of the king to slay Abner the son of Ner.

38 And the king said unto his servants, Know ye not that there is a prince and a great man fallen this day in Israel?

39 And I *am* this day ᴺweak, though anointed king; and these men the sons of Zĕr-ū-ī'-ăh ᴿbe too hard for me: ᴿthe LORD shall reward the doer of evil according to his wickedness.

CHAPTER 4

Ish-bosheth murdered

AND when Saul's son heard that Abner was dead in Hḗ'-brŏn, ᴿhis hands were feeble, and all the Israelites were ᴿtroubled.

2 And Saul's son had two men *that were* captains of bands: the name of the one *was* Bā'-ă-năh, and the name of the ᴺother Rḗ'-chăb, the sons of Rimmon a Bēēr'-ŏ-thīte, of the children of Benjamin: (for ᴿBēēr'-ŏth also was reckoned to Benjamin:

3 And the Bēēr'-ŏ-thītes fled to ᴿGĭt-tā'-ĭm, and were sojourners there until this day.)

4 And ᴿJonathan, Saul's son, had a son *that was* lame of *his* feet. He was five years old when the tidings came of Saul and Jonathan ᴿout of Jĕz'-rēēl, and his nurse took him up, and fled: and it came to pass, as she made haste to flee, that he fell, and became lame. And his name *was* ᴺMĕ-phīb'-ŏ-shĕth.

5 And the sons of Rimmon the Bēēr'-ŏ-thīte, Rḗ'-chăb and Bā'-ă-năh, went, and came about the heat of the day to the house of ĭsh-bŏsh'-ĕth, who lay on a bed at noon.

6 And they came thither into the midst of the house, *as though* they would have fetched wheat; and they smote him ᴿunder the fifth

rib: and Rē'-chab and Bā'-a-nah his brother escaped.

7 For when they came into the house, he lay on his bed in his bedchamber, and they smote him, and slew him, and beheaded him, and took his head, and gat them away through the plain all night.

8 And they brought the head of ĭsh-bŏsh'-ĕth unto David to Hē'-brŏn, and said to the king, Behold the head of ĭsh-bŏsh'-ĕth the son of Saul thine enemy, ᴿwhich sought thy life; and the Lᴏʀᴅ hath avenged my lord the king this day of Saul, and of his seed.

9 And David answered Rē'-chab and Bā'-a-nah his brother, the sons of Rimmon the Bēēr'-ō-thīte, and said unto them, *As* the Lᴏʀᴅ liveth, ᴿwho hath redeemed my soul out of all adversity,

10 When ᴿone told me, saying, Behold, Saul is dead, ᴺthinking to have brought good tidings, I took hold of him, and slew him in Ziklag, ᴺwho *thought* that I would have given him a reward for his tidings:

11 How much more, when wicked men have slain a righteous person in his own house upon his bed? shall I not therefore now ᴿrequire his blood of your hand, and take you away from the earth?

12 And David ᴿcommanded his young men, and they slew them, and cut off their hands and their feet, and hanged *them* up over the pool in Hē'-brŏn. But they took the head of ĭsh-bŏsh'-ĕth, and buried *it* in the ᴿsepulchre of Abner in Hē'-brŏn.

CHAPTER 5

David anointed king of Israel

THEN ᴿcame all the tribes of Israel to David unto Hē'-brŏn, and spake, saying, Behold, ᴿwe *are* thy bone and thy flesh.

2 Also in time past, when Saul was king over us, ᴿthou wast he that leddest out and broughtest in Israel: and the Lᴏʀᴅ said to thee, ᴿThou shalt feed my people Israel, and thou shalt be a captain over Israel.

3 ᴿSo all the elders of Israel came to the king to Hē'-brŏn; ᴿand king David made a league with them in Hē'-brŏn ᴿbefore the Lᴏʀᴅ: and they anointed David king over Israel.

4 David *was* thirty years old when he began to reign, ᴿ*and* he reigned forty years.

5 In Hē'-brŏn he reigned over Judah ᴿseven years and six months: and in Jerusalem he reigned thirty and three years over all Israel and Judah.

CHAP. **4**
BC 1048
8 1 Sam. 19:2, 10, 11
9 Gen. 48:16
1 Ki. 1:29
10 ch. 1:2, 4, 15
10 Heb. *he was in his own eyes as a bringer, etc.*
10 Or, *which was the reward I gave him for his tidings*
11 Gen. 9:5, 6
12 ch. 1:15
12 ch. 3:32

CHAP. **5**
BC 1048
1 1 Chr. 11:1
1 Gen. 29:14
2 1 Sam. 18:13
2 1 Sam. 16:1
3 1 Chr. 11:3
3 2 Ki. 11:17
3 Judg. 11:11
1 Sam. 23:18
4 1 Chr. 26:31 & 29:27
5 ch. 2:11
1 Chr. 3:4

Judg. 1:21   6
Josh. 15:63   6
Judg. 1:8 & 19:11, 12
Or, *saying, David shall not, etc.*   6
1 Ki. 2:10 & 8:1   7
1 Chr. 11:6-9   8
Or, *Because they had said, even the blind and the lame, He shall not come into the house* ver. 7   8
Heb. *went going and growing*   9, 10
1 Ki. 5:2   11
Heb. *hewers of the stone of the wall*   11
Deut. 17:17   13
1 Chr. 3:9
1 Chr. 3:5   14
Or, *Shimea,* 1 Chr. 3:5   14
Or, *Elishama,* 1 Chr. 3:6   15
Or, *Beeliada,* 1 Chr. 14:7   16
1 Chr. 11:16   17
ch. 23:14   17
Josh. 15:8   18
Is. 17:5
1 Sam. 23:2, 4   19
Is. 28:21   20

David captures Zion

6 And the king and his men went ᴿto Jerusalem unto ᴿthe Jĕb'-ū-sĭtes, the inhabitants of the land: which spake unto David, saying, Except thou take away the blind and the lame, thou shalt not come in hither: ᴺthinking, David cannot come in hither.

7 Nevertheless David took the strong hold of Zion: ᴿthe same *is* the city of David.

8 And David said on that day, Whosoever getteth up to the gutter, and smiteth the Jĕb'-ū-sĭtes, and the lame and the blind, *that are* hated of David's soul, ᴿ*he shall be chief and captain.* ᴺWherefore they said, The blind and the lame shall not come into the house.

9 So David dwelt in the fort, and called it ᴿthe city of David. And David built round about from Mĭl'-lō and inward.

10 And David ᴺwent on, and grew great, and the Lᴏʀᴅ God of hosts *was* with him.

David's house

11 And ᴿHiram king of Tyre sent messengers to David, and cedar trees, and carpenters, and ᴺmasons: and they built David an house.

12 And David perceived that the Lᴏʀᴅ had established him king over Israel, and that he had exalted his kingdom for his people Israel's sake.

13 And ᴿDavid took *him* more concubines and wives out of Jerusalem, after he was come from Hē'-brŏn: and there were yet sons and daughters born to David.

14 And ᴿthese *be* the names of those that were born unto him in Jerusalem; ᴺShăm'-mū-ă, and Shō'-băb, and Nathan, and Solomon,

15 Ĭb'-här also, and ᴺE-lī'-shû-ă, and Nĕph'-ĕg, and Jă-phī'-ă,

16 And E-lī'-shă-mă, and ᴺE-lī'-ă-dă, and E-lĭph'-ă-lĕt.

David defeats the Philistines

17 ᴿBut when the Philistines heard that they had anointed David king over Israel, all the Philistines came up to seek David; and David heard *of it,* ᴿand went down to the hold.

18 The Philistines also came and spread themselves in ᴿthe valley of Rĕph'-ā-ĭm.

19 And David ᴿinquired of the Lᴏʀᴅ, saying, Shall I go up to the Philistines? wilt thou deliver them into mine hand? And the Lᴏʀᴅ said unto David, Go up: for I will doubtless deliver the Philistines into thine hand.

20 And David came to ᴿBā'-ăl-pĕ-rā'-zĭm, and David smote them there, and said, The

LORD hath broken forth upon mine enemies before me, as the breach of waters. Therefore he called the name of that place [N]Bā'-ăl-pĕ-rā'-zĭm.

21 And there they left their images, and David and his men [R]burned[N] them.

22 [R]And the Philistines came up yet again, and spread themselves in the valley of Rĕph'-ā-ĭm.

23 And when [R]David inquired of the LORD, he said, Thou shalt not go up; *but* fetch a compass behind them, and come upon them over against the mulberry trees.

24 And let it be, when thou [R]hearest the sound of a going in the tops of the mulberry trees, that then thou shalt bestir thyself: for then [R]shall the LORD go out before thee, to smite the host of the Philistines.

25 And David did so, as the LORD had commanded him; and smote the Philistines from [R]Gē'-bă until thou come to [R]Gā'-zĕr.

CHAPTER 6

Death of Uzzah

AGAIN, David gathered together all *the* chosen *men* of Israel, thirty thousand.

2 And [R]David arose, and went with all the people that *were* with him from [N]Bā'-ă-lē of Judah, to bring up from thence the ark of God, [N]whose name is called by the name of the LORD of hosts [R]that dwelleth *between* the chĕr'-ū-bĭms.

3 And they [N]set the ark of God upon a new cart, and brought it out of the house of Ă-bĭn'-ă-dăb that *was* in [N]Gĭb'-ĕ-ăh: and ŭz'-zăh and Ă-hī'-ō, the sons of Ă-bĭn'-ă-dăb, drave the new cart.

4 And they brought it out of [R]the house of Ă-bĭn'-ă-dăb which *was* at Gĭb'-ĕ-ăh, [N]accompanying the ark of God: and Ă-hī'-ō went before the ark.

5 And David and all the house of Israel played before the LORD on all manner of *instruments made of* fir wood, even on harps, and on psalteries, and on timbrels, and on cornets, and on cymbals.

6 And when they came to [R]Nā'-chŏn's threshingfloor, ŭz'-zăh put forth *his hand* to the ark of God, and took hold of it; for the oxen [N]shook *it.*

7 And the anger of the LORD was kindled against ŭz'-zăh; and [R]God smote him there for *his* [N]error; and there he died by the ark of God.

8 And David was displeased, because the LORD had [N]made a breach upon ŭz'-zăh: and

he called the name of the place [N]Pĕ'-rĕz-ŭz'-zăh to this day.

9 And [R]David was afraid of the LORD that day, and said, How shall the ark of the LORD come to me?

10 So David would not remove the ark of the LORD unto him into the city of David: but David carried it aside into the house of ō'-bĕd-ē'-dǫm [R]the Gĭt'-tīte.

11 [R]And the ark of the LORD continued in the house of ō'-bĕd-ē'-dǫm the Gĭt'-tīte three months: and the LORD [R]blessed ō'-bĕd-ē'-dǫm, and all his household.

The ark brought to Jerusalem

12 And it was told king David, saying, The LORD hath blessed the house of ō'-bĕd-ē'-dǫm, and all that *pertaineth* unto him, because of the ark of God. [R]So David went and brought up the ark of God from the house of ō'-bĕd-ē'-dǫm into the city of David with gladness.

13 And it was *so,* that when [R]they that bare the ark of the LORD had gone six paces, he sacrificed [R]oxen and fatlings.

14 And David [R]danced before the LORD with all *his* might; and David *was* girded [R]with a linen ē'-phǒd.

15 [R]So David and all the house of Israel brought up the ark of the LORD with shouting, and with the sound of the trumpet.

16 And as the ark of the LORD came into the city of David, Michal Saul's daughter looked through a window, and saw king David leaping and dancing before the LORD; and she despised him in her heart.

17 And [R]they brought in the ark of the LORD, and set it in [R]his place, in the midst of the tabernacle that David had [N]pitched for it: and David [R]offered burnt offerings and peace offerings before the LORD.

18 And as soon as David had made an end of offering burnt offerings and peace offerings, [R]he blessed the people in the name of the LORD of hosts.

19 [R]And he dealt among all the people, *even* among the whole multitude of Israel, as well to the women as men, to every one a cake of bread, and a good piece *of flesh,* and a flagon *of wine.* So all the people departed every one to his house.

The sin of Michal

20 [R]Then David returned to bless his household. And Michal the daughter of Saul came out to meet David, and said, How glorious was the king of Israel to day, who [R]uncovered himself to day in the eyes of the handmaids of

his servants, as one of the [R]vain fellows [N]shamelessly uncovereth himself!

21 And David said unto Michal, *It was* before the LORD, [R]which chose me before thy father, and before all his house, to appoint me ruler over the people of the LORD, over Israel: therefore will I play before the LORD.

22 And I will yet be more vile than thus, and will be base in mine own sight: and [N]of the maidservants which thou hast spoken of, of them shall I be had in honour.

23 Therefore Michal the daughter of Saul had no child [R]unto the day of her death.

CHAPTER 7

Nathan's prophecy

AND it came to pass, [R]when the king sat in his house, and the LORD had given him rest round about from all his enemies;

2 That the king said unto Nathan the prophet, See now, I dwell in [R]an house of cedar, [R]but the ark of God dwelleth within [R]curtains.

3 And Nathan said to the king, Go, do all that *is* in thine heart; for the LORD *is* with thee.

4 And it came to pass that night, that the word of the LORD came unto Nathan, saying,

5 Go and tell [N]my servant David, Thus saith the LORD, [R]Shalt thou build me an house for me to dwell in?

6 Whereas I have not dwelt in *any* house [R]since the time that I brought up the children of Israel out of Egypt, even to this day, but have walked in [R]a tent and in a tabernacle.

7 In all *the places* wherein I have [R]walked with all the children of Israel spake I a word with [N]any of the tribes of Israel, whom I commanded [R]to feed my people Israel, saying, Why build ye not me an house of cedar?

8 Now therefore so shalt thou say unto my servant David, Thus saith the LORD of hosts, [R]I took thee from the sheepcote, [N]from following the sheep, to be ruler over my people, over Israel:

9 And [R]I was with thee whithersoever thou wentest, [R]and have cut off all thine enemies [N]out of thy sight, and have made thee a great name, like unto the name of the great *men* that *are* in the earth.

10 Moreover I will appoint a place for my people Israel, and will [R]plant them, that they may dwell in a place of their own, and move no more; [R]neither shall the children of wickedness afflict them any more, as beforetime,

11 And as [R]since the time that I commanded judges *to be* over my people Israel, and have caused thee to rest from all thine enemies. Also the LORD telleth thee [R]that he will make thee an house.

12 And [R]when thy days be fulfilled, and thou [R]shalt sleep with thy fathers, [R]I will set up thy seed after thee, which shall proceed out of thy bowels, and I will establish his kingdom.

13 [R]He shall build an house for my name, and I will [R]stablish the throne of his kingdom for ever. ★

14 [R]I will be his father, and he shall be my son. [R]If he commit iniquity, I will chasten him with the rod of men, and with the stripes of the children of men:

15 But my mercy shall not depart away from him, [R]as I took *it* from Saul, whom I put away before thee.

16 And [R]thine house and thy kingdom shall be established for ever before thee: thy throne shall be established for ever. ★

17 According to all these words, and according to all this vision, so did Nathan speak unto David.

Prayer of David

18 Then went king David in, and sat before the LORD, and he said, [R]Who *am* I, O Lord GOD? and what *is* my house, that thou hast brought me hitherto?

19 And this was yet a small thing in thy sight, O Lord GOD; but thou hast spoken also of thy servant's house for a great while to come. [R]And *is* this the [N]manner of man, O Lord GOD?

20 And what can David say more unto thee? for thou, Lord GOD, [R]knowest thy servant.

21 For thy word's sake, and according to thine own heart, hast thou done all these great things, to make thy servant know *them*.

22 Wherefore [R]thou art great, O LORD God: for [R]*there is* none like thee, neither *is there any* God beside thee, according to all that we have heard with our ears.

23 And [R]what one nation in the earth *is* like thy people, *even* like Israel, whom God went to redeem for a people to himself, and to make him a name, and to do for you great things and terrible, for thy land, before [R]thy people, which thou redeemedst to thee from Egypt, *from* the nations and their gods?

24 For [R]thou hast confirmed to thyself thy people Israel *to be* a people unto thee for ever: [R]and thou, LORD, art become their God.

25 And now, O LORD God, the word that thou hast spoken concerning thy servant, and

CHAP. **6**
BC 1042
20 Judg. 9:4
20 Or, *openly*
21 1 Sam. 13:14
22 Or, *of the handmaids* of my servants
23 See 1 Sam. 15:35
Is. 22:14

CHAP. **7**
BC 1042
1 1 Chr. 17:1
2 ch. 5:11
2 See Acts 7:46
2 Ex. 26:1
5 Heb. *to my servant, to David*
5 1 Ki. 5:3 & 8:19
1 Chr. 22:8
6 1 Ki. 8:16
6 Ex. 40:18, 19, 34
7 Lev. 26:11
Deut. 23:14
any of the judges,
1 Chr. 17:6
7 Mat. 2:6
Acts 20:28
8 1 Sam. 16:11, 12
8 Heb. *from after*
9 1 Sam. 18:14
ch. 5:10
9 1 Sam. 31:6
9 Heb. *from thy face*
10 Ps. 44:2 & 80:8
Jer. 24:6
10 Ps. 89:22

Judg. 2:14   **11**
1 Sam. 12:9
ver. 27   **11**
Ex. 1:21
1 Ki. 2:1   **12**
Deut. 31:16   **12**
Ps. 132:11   **12**
1 Ki. 5:5 & 8:19   **13**
ver. 16   **13**
Heb. 1:5   **14**
Ps. 89:30   **14**
1 Sam. 15:23, 28   **15**
& 16:14
ver. 13   **16**
John 12:34
Gen. 32:10   **18**
Is. 55:8   **19**
Heb. *law*   **19**
Ps. 139:1   **20**
1 Chr. 16:25   **22**
2 Chr. 2:5
Jer. 10:6
Deut. 3:24   **22**
& 4:35 & 32:39
Ps. 147:20   **23**
Deut. 9:26   **23**
Deut. 26:18   **24**
Ps. 48:14   **24**

concerning his house, establish *it* for ever, and
do as thou hast said.
26 And let thy name be magnified for ever,
saying, The LORD of hosts *is* the God over
Israel: and let the house of thy servant David
be established before thee.
27 For thou, O LORD of hosts, God of Israel, hast [N]revealed to thy servant, saying, I
will build thee an house: therefore hath thy
servant found in his heart to pray this prayer
unto thee.
28 And now, O Lord GOD, thou *art* that
God, and [R]thy words be true, and thou hast
promised this goodness unto thy servant:
29 Therefore now [N]let it please thee to bless
the house of thy servant, that it may continue
for ever before thee: for thou, O Lord GOD,
hast spoken *it:* and with thy blessing let the
house of thy servant be blessed [R]for ever.

CHAPTER 8

David extends his kingdom

AND after this it came to pass, that David
smote the Philistines, and subdued
them: and David took [N]Mĕth′-ĕg-ăm′-măh out
of the hand of the Philistines.
2 And [R]he smote Moab, and measured them
with a line, casting them down to the ground;
even with two lines measured he to put to
death, and with one full line to keep alive.
And *so* the Moabites became David's servants, *and* [R]brought gifts.
3 David smote also [N]Hăd-ă-dē′-zĕr, the son
of Rē′-hŏb, king of [R]Zō′-băh, as he went to
recover [R]his border at the river Eū-phrā′-tēs.
4 And David took [N]from him a thousand
[N]*chariots,* and seven hundred horsemen, and
twenty thousand footmen: and David [R]houghed
all the chariot *horses,* but reserved of them *for*
an hundred chariots.
5 [R]And when the Syrians of Damascus came
to succour Hăd-ă-dē′-zĕr king of Zō′-băh, David slew of the Syrians two and twenty thousand men.
6 Then David put garrisons in Syria of Damascus: and the Syrians became servants to
David, *and* brought gifts. [R]And the LORD
preserved David whithersoever he went.
7 And David took [R]the shields of gold that
were on the servants of Hăd-ă-dē′-zĕr, and
brought them to Jerusalem.
8 And from [N]Bē′-tăh, and from [N]Bĕ-rō′-thâi,
cities of Hăd-ă-dē′-zĕr, king David took exceeding much brass.
9 When [N]Tō′-ī king of Hā′-măth heard
that David had smitten all the host of
Hăd-ă-dē′-zĕr,
10 Then Tō′-ī sent [R]Joram his son unto king
David, to [N]salute him, and to bless him, because he had fought against Hăd-ă-dē′-zĕr, and
smitten him: for Hăd-ă-dē′-zĕr [N]had wars with
Tō′-ī. And *Joram* [N]brought with him vessels
of silver, and vessels of gold, and vessels of
brass:
11 Which also king David [R]did dedicate
unto the LORD, with the silver and gold that he
had dedicated of all nations which he subdued;
12 Of Syria, and of Moab, and of the children of Ammon, and of the Philistines, and of
Ăm′-ă-lĕk, and of the spoil of Hăd-ă-dē′-zĕr,
son of Rē′-hŏb, king of Zō′-băh.
13 And David gat *him* a name when he returned from [N]smiting of the Syrians in [R]the
valley of salt, [R]*being*[N] eighteen thousand *men.*
14 And he put garrisons in Ē′-dọm; throughout all Ē′-dọm put he garrisons, and [R]all they
of Ē′-dọm became David's servants. And the
LORD preserved David whithersoever he
went.
15 And David reigned over all Israel; and
David executed judgment and justice unto all
his people.
16 [R]And Jō′-ăb the son of Zĕr-ū-ī′-ăh *was*
over the host; and [R]Jĕ-hŏsh′-ă-phăt the son of
Ă-hī′-lŭd *was* [N]recorder;
17 And [R]Zā′-dŏk the son of Ă-hī′-tŭb, and
Ă-hĭm′-ĕ-lĕch the son of Ă-bī′-ă-thăr, *were* the
priests; and Sĕ-râi′-ăh *was* the [N]scribe;
18 [R]And Bĕ-nâi′-ăh the son of Jĕ-hôi′-
ă-dă *was over* both the [R]Chĕ′-ĕ-thītes and the
Pĕl′-ĕ-thītes; and David's sons were [N]chief
rulers.

CHAPTER 9

Mephibosheth joins David's household

AND David said, Is there yet any that is left
of the house of Saul, that I may [R]shew
him kindness for Jonathan's sake?
2 And *there was* of the house of Saul a
servant whose name *was* [R]Zī′-bă. And when
they had called him unto David, the king said
unto him, *Art* thou Zī′-bă? And he said, Thy
servant *is he.*
3 And the king said, *Is* there not yet any of
the house of Saul, that I may shew [R]the kindness of God unto him? And Zī′-bă said unto
the king, Jonathan hath yet a son, *which is*
[R]lame on *his* feet.
4 And the king said unto him, Where *is* he?
And Zī′-bă said unto the king, Behold, he *is* in
the house of [R]Mā′-chĭr, the son of Ăm′-mĭ-ĕl,
in Lō′-dĕ-băr.
5 Then king David sent, and fetched him out

CHAP. 7
BC 1042
27 Heb. *opened the ear,* 1 Sam. 9:15
28 John 17:17
29 Heb. *be thou pleased and bless*
29 ch. 22:51

CHAP. 8
BC 1040
1 Or, *The Bridle of Ammah*
2 Num. 24:17
2 See 1 Sam. 10:27
3 Or, *Hadarezer,* 1 Chr. 18:3
3 ch. 10:6 Ps. 60, title
3 See Gen. 15:18
4 Or, *of his*
4 As 1 Chr. 18:4
4 Josh. 11:6, 9
5 1 Ki. 11:23
6 ver. 14 ch. 7:9
7 See 1 Ki. 10:16
8 Or, *Tibhath*
8 Or, *Chun,* 1 Chr. 18:8
9 *Tou,* 1 Chr. 18:9

1 Chr. 18:10, *Hadoram* 10
Heb. *ask him of peace* 10
Heb. *was a man of wars with* 10
Heb. *in his hand were* 10
1 Ki. 7:51 11
Heb. *his smiting* 13
2 Ki. 14:7 13
See 1 Chr. 18:12 Ps. 60, title 13
Or, *slaying* 13
Gen. 27:29, 37, 40 Num. 24:18 14
ch. 19:13 & 20:23 1 Chr. 11:6 16
1 Ki. 4:3 16
Or, *remembrancer,* or, *writer of chronicles* 16
1 Chr. 24:3 17
Or, *secretary* 17
1 Chr. 18:17 18
1 Sam. 30:14 18
Or, *princes* 18

CHAP. 9
BC 1040
1 Sam. 18:3 Prov. 27:10 1
ch. 16:1 & 19:17, 29 2
1 Sam. 20:14 3
ch. 4:4 3
ch. 17:27 4

of the house of Mā'-chīr, the son of Ăm'-mĭ-ĕl, from Lō'-dĕ-bär.

6 Now when ᴺMĕ-phĭb'-ŏ-shĕth, the son of Jonathan, the son of Saul, was come unto David, he fell on his face, and did reverence. And David said, Mĕ-phĭb'-ŏ-shĕth. And he answered, Behold thy servant!

7 And David said unto him, Fear not: for I will surely shew thee kindness for Jonathan thy father's sake, and will restore thee all the land of Saul thy father; and thou shalt eat bread at my table continually.

8 And he bowed himself, and said, What is thy servant, that thou shouldest look upon such ᴿa dead dog as I am?

9 Then the king called to Zī'-bă, Saul's servant, and said unto him, ᴿI have given unto thy master's son all that pertained to Saul and to all his house.

10 Thou therefore, and thy sons, and thy servants, shall till the land for him, and thou shalt bring in the fruits, that thy master's son may have food to eat: but Mĕ-phĭb'-ŏ-shĕth thy master's son ᴿshall eat bread alway at my table. Now Zī'-bă had ᴿfifteen sons and twenty servants.

11 Then said Zī'-bă unto the king, According to all that my lord the king hath commanded his servant, so shall thy servant do. As for Mĕ-phĭb'-ŏ-shĕth, said the king, he shall eat at my table, as one of the king's sons.

12 And Mĕ-phĭb'-ŏ-shĕth had a young son, ᴿwhose name was Mī'-chă. And all that dwelt in the house of Zī'-bă were servants unto Mĕ-phĭb'-ŏ-shĕth.

13 So Mĕ-phĭb'-ŏ-shĕth dwelt in Jerusalem: ᴿfor he did eat continually at the king's table; and ᴿwas lame on both his feet.

CHAPTER 10

David's ambassadors mistreated

AND it came to pass after this, that the ᴿking of the children of Ammon died, and Hā'-nŭn his son reigned in his stead.

2 Then said David, I will shew kindness unto Hā'-nŭn the son of Nahash, as his father shewed kindness unto me. And David sent to comfort him by the hand of his servants for his father. And David's servants came into the land of the children of Ammon.

3 And the princes of the children of Ammon said unto Hā'-nŭn their lord, ᴺThinkest thou that David doth honour thy father, that he hath sent comforters unto thee? hath not David rather sent his servants unto thee, to search the city, and to spy it out, and to overthrow it?

4 Wherefore Hā'-nŭn took David's servants,

and shaved off the one half of their beards, and cut off their garments in the middle, ᴿeven to their buttocks, and sent them away.

5 When they told it unto David, he sent to meet them, because the men were greatly ashamed: and the king said, Tarry at Jericho until your beards be grown, and then return.

6 And when the children of Ammon saw that they ᴿstank before David, the children of Ammon sent and hired ᴿthe Syrians of Bĕth-rē'-hŏb, and the Syrians of Zō'-bă, twenty thousand footmen, and of king Mā'-ă-căh a thousand men, and of ᴺĬsh'-tŏb twelve thousand men.

7 And when David heard of it, he sent Jō'-ăb, and all the host of ᴿthe mighty men.

8 And the children of Ammon came out, and put the battle in array at the entering in of the gate: and ᴿthe Syrians of Zō'-bă, and of Rē'-hŏb, and ĭsh'-tŏb, and Mā'-ă-căh, were by themselves in the field.

Defeat of the Ammonites and Syrians

9 When Jō'-ăb saw that the front of the battle was against him before and behind, he chose of all the choice men of Israel, and put them in array against the Syrians:

10 And the rest of the people he delivered into the hand of Ăb'-ĭ-shaī his brother, that he might put them in array against the children of Ammon.

11 And he said, If the Syrians be too strong for me, then thou shalt help me: but if the children of Ammon be too strong for thee, then I will come and help thee.

12 ᴿBe of good courage, and let us ᴿplay the men for our people, and for the cities of our God: and ᴿthe LORD do that which seemeth him good.

13 And Jō'-ăb drew nigh, and the people that were with him, unto the battle against the Syrians: and they fled before him.

14 And when the children of Ammon saw that the Syrians were fled, then fled they also before Ăb'-ĭ-shaī, and entered into the city. So Jō'-ăb returned from the children of Ammon, and came to Jerusalem.

15 And when the Syrians saw that they were smitten before Israel, they gathered themselves together.

16 And Hăd-ă-rē'-zĕr sent, and brought out the Syrians that were beyond ᴺthe river: and they came to Hē'-lăm; and ᴺShō'-băch the captain of the host of Hăd-ă-rē'-zĕr went before them.

17 And when it was told David, he gathered all Israel together, and passed over Jordan, and came to Hē'-lăm. And the Syrians set them-

selves in array against David, and fought with him.

18 And the Syrians fled before Israel; and David slew *the men of* seven hundred chariots of the Syrians, and forty thousand [R]horsemen, and smote Shō'-băch the captain of their host, who died there.

19 And when all the kings *that were* servants to Hăd-ă-rē'-zĕr saw that they were smitten before Israel, they made peace with Israel, and [R]served them. So the Syrians feared to help the children of Ammon any more.

CHAPTER 11

David's adultery with Bath-sheba

AND it came to pass, [N]after the year was expired, at the time when kings go forth *to battle,* that [R]David sent Jō'-ăb, and his servants with him, and all Israel; and they destroyed the children of Ammon, and besieged Răb'-băh. But David tarried still at Jerusalem.

2 And it came to pass in an eveningtide, that David arose from off his bed, [R]and walked upon the roof of the king's house: and from the roof he [R]saw a woman washing herself; and the woman *was* very beautiful to look upon.

3 And David sent and inquired after the woman. And *one* said, *Is* not this [N]Băth'-shĕ-bă, the daughter of [N]Ē-li'-ăm, the wife [R]of Ū-rī'-ăh the Hittite?

4 And David sent messengers, and took her; and she came in unto him, and [R]he lay with her; [N]for she was [R]purified from her uncleanness: and she returned unto her house.

5 And the woman conceived, and sent and told David, and said, I *am* with child.

David sends for Uriah

6 And David sent to Jō'-ăb, *saying,* Send me Ū-rī'-ăh the Hittite. And Jō'-ăb sent Ū-rī'-ăh to David.

7 And when Ū-rī'-ăh was come unto him, David demanded *of him* [N]how Jō'-ăb did, and how the people did, and how the war prospered.

8 And David said to Ū-rī'-ăh, Go down to thy house, and [R]wash thy feet. And Ū-rī'-ăh departed out of the king's house, and there [N]followed him a mess *of meat* from the king.

9 But Ū-rī'-ăh slept at the door of the king's house with all the servants of his lord, and went not down to his house.

10 And when they had told David, saying, Ū-rī'-ăh went not down unto his house, David said unto Ū-rī'-ăh, Camest thou not from *thy* journey? why *then* didst thou not go down unto thine house?

CHAP. 10
BC 1037
18 1 Chr. 19:18, *footmen*
19 ch. 8:6

CHAP. 11
BC 1035
1 Heb. *at the return of the year*
1 1 Chr. 20:1
2 Deut. 22:8
2 Gen. 34:2
Job 31:1
Mat. 5:28
3 Or, *Bathshuah,* 1 Chr. 3:5
3 Or, *Ammiel*
3 ch. 23:39
4 Ps. 51, title
Jas. 1:14
4 Or, *and when she had purified herself, etc., she returned*
4 Lev. 15:19, 28 & 18:19
7 Heb. *of the peace of, etc.*
8 Gen. 18:4 & 19:2
8 Heb. *went out after him*

ch. 7:2, 6   11
ch. 20:6   11
Gen. 19:33, 35   13
ver. 9   13
See 1 Ki. 21:8, 9 14
Heb. *strong*   15
Heb. *from after him* 15
ch. 12:9   15
Judg. 9:53   21
Judg. 6:32,   21
Jerubbaal

11 And Ū-rī'-ăh said unto David, [R]The ark, and Israel, and Judah, abide in tents; and [R]my lord Jō'-ăb, and the servants of my lord, are encamped in the open fields; shall I then go into mine house, to eat and to drink, and to lie with my wife? *as* thou livest, and *as* thy soul liveth, I will not do this thing.

12 And David said to Ū-rī'-ăh, Tarry here to day also, and to morrow I will let thee depart. So Ū-rī'-ăh abode in Jerusalem that day, and the morrow.

13 And when David had called him, he did eat and drink before him; and he made him [R]drunk: and at even he went out to lie on his bed [R]with the servants of his lord, but went not down to his house.

David has Uriah killed

14 And it came to pass in the morning, that David [R]wrote a letter to Jō'-ăb, and sent *it* by the hand of Ū-rī'-ăh.

15 And he wrote in the letter, saying, Set ye Ū-rī'-ăh in the forefront of the [N]hottest battle, and retire ye [N]from him, that he may [R]be smitten, and die.

16 And it came to pass, when Jō'-ăb observed the city, that he assigned Ū-rī'-ăh unto a place where he knew that valiant men *were.*

17 And the men of the city went out, and fought with Jō'-ăb: and there fell *some* of the people of the servants of David; and Ū-rī'-ăh the Hittite died also.

18 Then Jō'-ăb sent and told David all the things concerning the war;

19 And charged the messenger, saying, When thou hast made an end of telling the matters of the war unto the king,

20 And if so be that the king's wrath arise, and he say unto thee, Wherefore approached ye so nigh unto the city when ye did fight? knew ye not that they would shoot from the wall?

21 Who smote [R]Ă-bĭm'-ĕ-lĕch the son of [R]Jĕ-rŭb'-bĕ-shĕth? did not a woman cast a piece of a millstone upon him from the wall, that he died in Thē'-bĕz? why went ye nigh the wall? then say thou, Thy servant Ū-rī'-ăh the Hittite is dead also.

22 So the messenger went, and came and shewed David all that Jō'-ăb had sent him for.

23 And the messenger said unto David, Surely the men prevailed against us, and came out unto us into the field, and we were upon them even unto the entering of the gate.

24 And the shooters shot from off the wall upon thy servants; and *some* of the king's servants be dead, and thy servant Ū-rī'-ăh the Hittite is dead also.

25 Then David said unto the messenger,

Thus shalt thou say unto Jō'-ăb, Let not this thing ᴺdispleasethee, for the sword devoureth ᴺone as well as another: make thy battle more strong against the city, and overthrow it: and encourage thou him.

David marries Bath-sheba

26 And when the wife of Ū-rī'-ăh heard that Ū-rī'-ăh her husband was dead, she mourned for her husband.

27 And when the mourning was past, David sent and fetched her to his house, and she ᴿbecame his wife, and bare him a son. But the thing that David had done ᴺdispleased the Lᴏʀᴅ.

CHAPTER 12

Parable of Nathan

AND the Lᴏʀᴅ sent Nathan unto David. And ᴿhe came unto him, and ᴿsaid unto him, There were two men in one city; the one rich, and the other poor.

2 The rich *man* had exceeding many flocks and herds:

3 But the poor *man* had nothing, save one little ewe lamb, which he had bought and nourished up: and it grew up together with him, and with his children; it did eat of his own ᴺmeat, and drank of his own cup, and lay in his bosom, and was unto him as a daughter.

4 And there came a traveller unto the rich man, and he spared to take of his own flock and of his own herd, to dress for the wayfaring man that was come unto him; but took the poor man's lamb, and dressed it for the man that was come to him.

5 And David's anger was greatly kindled against the man; and he said to Nathan, *As* the Lᴏʀᴅ liveth, the man that hath done this *thing* ᴺshall surely die:

6 And he shall restore the lamb ᴿfourfold, because he did this thing, and because he had no pity.

Nathan rebukes David

7 And Nathan said to David, Thou *art* the man. Thus saith the Lᴏʀᴅ God of Israel, I ᴿanointed thee king over Israel, and I delivered thee out of the hand of Saul;

8 And I gave thee thy master's house, and thy master's wives into thy bosom, and gave thee the house of Israel and of Judah; and if *that had been* too little, I would moreover have given unto thee such and such things.

9 ᴿWherefore hast thou ᴿdespised the commandment of the Lᴏʀᴅ, to do evil in his sight? ᴿthou hast killed Ū-rī'-ăh the Hittite with the sword, and hast taken his wife *to be* thy wife,

CHAP. **11**
BC 1035
25 Heb. *be evil in thine eyes*
25 Heb. *so and such*
27 ch. 12:9
27 Heb. *was evil in the eyes of*

CHAP. **12**
BC 1035
1 Ps. 51, title
1 See ch. 14:5, etc.
1 Ki. 20:35-41
1 Is. 5:3
3 Heb. *morsel*
5 Or, *is worthy to die*, or, *is a son of death*, 1 Sam. 26:16
6 Ex. 22:1 Luke 19:8
7 1 Sam. 16:13
9 See 1 Sam. 15:19
9 Num. 15:31
9 ch. 11:15-17, 27

Amos 7:9	**10**
Deut. 28:30	**11**
ch. 16:22	
ch. 16:22	**12**
See 1 Sam. 15:24	**13**
ch. 24:10	**13**
Job 7:20	
Prov. 28:13	
ch. 24:10	**13**
Job 7:21	
Mic. 7:18	
Zech. 3:4	
Is. 52:5	**14**
Ezek. 36:20, 23	
Rom. 2:24	
Heb. *fasted a fast*	**16**
ch. 13:31	**16**
Heb. *do hurt*	**18**
Job 1:20	**20**
See Is. 38:1, 5	**22**
Jonah 3:9	

and hast slain him with the sword of the children of Ammon.

10 Now therefore ᴿthe sword shall never depart from thine house; because thou hast despised me, and hast taken the wife of Ū-rī'-ăh the Hittite to be thy wife.

11 Thus saith the Lᴏʀᴅ, Behold, I will raise up evil against thee out of thine own house, and I will ᴿtake thy wives before thine eyes, and give *them* unto thy neighbour, and he shall lie with thy wives in the sight of this sun.

12 For thou didst *it* secretly: ᴿbut I will do this thing before all Israel, and before the sun.

13 ᴿAnd David said unto Nathan, ᴿI have sinned against the Lᴏʀᴅ. And Nathan said unto David, The Lᴏʀᴅ also hath ᴿput away thy sin; thou shalt not die.

14 Howbeit, because by this deed thou hast given great occasion to the enemies of the Lᴏʀᴅ ᴿto blaspheme, the child also *that is* born unto thee shall surely die.

15 And Nathan departed unto his house.

David's son dies

And the Lᴏʀᴅ struck the child that Ū-rī'-ăh's wife bare unto David, and it was very sick.

16 David therefore besought God for the child; and David ᴺfasted, and went in, and ᴿlay all night upon the earth.

17 And the elders of his house arose, *and went* to him, to raise him up from the earth: but he would not, neither did he eat bread with them.

18 And it came to pass on the seventh day, that the child died. And the servants of David feared to tell him that the child was dead: for they said, Behold, while the child was yet alive, we spake unto him, and he would not hearken unto our voice: how will he then ᴺvex himself, if we tell him that the child is dead?

19 But when David saw that his servants whispered, David perceived that the child was dead: therefore David said unto his servants, Is the child dead? And they said, He is dead.

20 Then David arose from the earth, and washed, and anointed *himself,* and changed his apparel, and came into the house of the Lᴏʀᴅ, and ᴿworshipped: then he came to his own house; and when he required, they set bread before him, and he did eat.

21 Then said his servants unto him, What thing *is* this that thou hast done? thou didst fast and weep for the child, *while it was* alive; but when the child was dead, thou didst rise and eat bread.

22 And he said, While the child was yet alive, I fasted and wept: ᴿfor I said, Who can tell *whether* Gᴏᴅ will be gracious to me, that the child may live?

23 But now he is dead, wherefore should I fast? can I bring him back again? I shall go to him, but [R]he shall not return to me.

Birth of Solomon

24 And David comforted Băth'-shĕ-bă his wife, and went in unto her, and lay with her: and [R]she bare a son, and [R]he called his name Solomon: and the LORD loved him.

25 And he sent by the hand of Nathan the prophet; and he called his name [N]Jĕd-ĭ-dī'-ăh, because of the LORD.

Rabbah conquered

26 And [R]Jō'-ăb fought against [R]Răb'-băh of the children of Ammon, and took the royal city.

27 And Jō'-ăb sent messengers to David, and said, I have fought against Răb'-băh, and have taken the city of waters.

28 Now therefore gather the rest of the people together, and encamp against the city, and take it: lest I take the city, and [N]it be called after my name.

29 And David gathered all the people together, and went to Răb'-băh, and fought against it, and took it.

30 [R]And he took their king's crown from off his head, the weight whereof was a talent of gold with the precious stones: and it was set on David's head. And he brought forth the spoil of the city [N]in great abundance.

31 And he brought forth the people that were therein, and put them under saws, and under harrows of iron, and under axes of iron, and made them pass through the brickkiln: and thus did he unto all the cities of the children of Ammon. So David and all the people returned unto Jerusalem.

CHAPTER 13

Amnon commits incest

AND it came to pass after this, [R]that Ăb'-să-lǫm the son of David had a fair sister, whose name was [R]Tā'-mär; and Amnon the son of David loved her.

2 And Amnon was so vexed, that he fell sick for his sister Tā'-mär; for she was a virgin; and [N]Amnon thought it hard for him to do any thing to her.

3 But Amnon had a friend, whose name was Jŏn'-ă-dăb, [R]the son of Shĭm'-ĕ-ă David's brother: and Jŏn'-ă-dăb was a very subtil man.

4 And he said unto him, Why art thou, being the king's son, [N]lean [N]from day to day? wilt thou not tell me? And Amnon said unto him, I love Tā'-mär, my brother Ăb'-să-lǫm's sister.

CHAP. 12
BC 1035
23 Job 7:8-10
24 Mat. 1:6
24 1 Chr. 22:9
25 i.e. *Beloved of the LORD*
26 1 Chr. 20:1
26 Deut. 3:11
28 Heb. *my name be called upon it*
30 1 Chr. 20:2
30 Heb. *very great*

CHAP. 13
BC 1032
1 ch. 3:2, 3
1 1 Chr. 3:9
2 Heb. *it was marvellous,* or, *hidden in the eyes of Amnon*
3 See 1 Sam. 16:9
4 Heb. *thin*
4 Heb. *morning by morning*

Gen. 18:6	6
Or, *paste*	8
Gen. 45:1	9
Gen. 39:12	11
Heb. *humble me,*	12
Gen. 34:2	
Lev. 18:9, 11	12
& 20:17	
Heb. *it ought not so to be done*	12
Gen. 34:7	12
Judg. 19:23 & 20:6	
See Lev. 18:9, 11	13
Deut. 22:25	14
See ch. 12:11	
Heb. *with great hatred greatly*	15
Gen. 37:3	18
Judg. 5:30	

5 And Jŏn'-ă-dăb said unto him, Lay thee down on thy bed, and make thyself sick: and when thy father cometh to see thee, say unto him, I pray thee, let my sister Tā'-mär come, and give me meat, and dress the meat in my sight, that I may see it, and eat it at her hand.

6 So Amnon lay down, and made himself sick: and when the king was come to see him, Amnon said unto the king, I pray thee, let Tā'-mär my sister come, and [R]make me a couple of cakes in my sight, that I may eat at her hand.

7 Then David sent home to Tā'-mär, saying, Go now to thy brother Amnon's house, and dress him meat.

8 So Tā'-mär went to her brother Amnon's house; and he was laid down. And she took [N]flour, and kneaded it, and made cakes in his sight, and did bake the cakes.

9 And she took a pan, and poured them out before him; but he refused to eat. And Amnon said, [R]Have out all men from me. And they went out every man from him.

10 And Amnon said unto Tā'-mär, Bring the meat into the chamber, that I may eat of thine hand. And Tā'-mär took the cakes which she had made, and brought them into the chamber to Amnon her brother.

11 And when she had brought them unto him to eat, he [R]took hold of her, and said unto her, Come lie with me, my sister.

12 And she answered him, Nay, my brother, do not [N]force me; for [R]no[N] such thing ought to be done in Israel: do not thou this [R]folly.

13 And I, whither shall I cause my shame to go? and as for thee, thou shalt be as one of the fools in Israel. Now therefore, I pray thee, speak unto the king; [R]for he will not withhold me from thee.

14 Howbeit he would not hearken unto her voice: but, being stronger than she, [R]forced her, and lay with her.

Mourning of Tamar

15 Then Amnon hated her [N]exceedingly; so that the hatred wherewith he hated her was greater than the love wherewith he had loved her. And Amnon said unto her, Arise, be gone.

16 And she said unto him, *There is* no cause: this evil in sending me away is greater than the other that thou didst unto me. But he would not hearken unto her.

17 Then he called his servant that ministered unto him, and said, Put now this woman out from me, and bolt the door after her.

18 And she had [R]a garment of divers colours upon her: for with such robes were the king's

daughters *that were* virgins apparelled. Then his servant brought her out, and bolted the door after her.

19 And Tā′-mär put ᴿashes on her head, and rent her garment of divers colours that *was* on her, and ᴿlaid her hand on her head, and went on crying.

Absalom murders Amnon

20 And Ăb′-să-lǫm her brother said unto her, Hath ᴺAmnon thy brother been with thee? but hold now thy peace, my sister: he *is* thy brother; ᴺregard not this thing. So Tā′-mär remained ᴺdesolate in her brother Ăb′-să-lǫm′s house.

21 But when king David heard of all these things, he was very wroth.

22 And Ăb′-să-lǫm spake unto his brother Amnon ᴿneither good nor bad: for Ăb′-să-lǫm ᴿhated Amnon, because he had forced his sister Tā′-mär.

23 And it came to pass after two full years, that Ăb′-să-lǫm ᴿhad sheepshearers in Bā′-ăl-hā′-zôr, which *is* beside Ē′-phră-ĭm: and Ăb′-să-lǫm invited all the king's sons.

24 And Ăb′-să-lǫm came to the king, and said, Behold now, thy servant hath sheepshearers; let the king, I beseech thee, and his servants go with thy servant.

25 And the king said to Ăb′-să-lǫm, Nay, my son, let us not all now go, lest we be chargeable unto thee. And he pressed him: howbeit he would not go, but blessed him.

26 Then said Ăb′-să-lǫm, If not, I pray thee, let my brother Amnon go with us. And the king said unto him, Why should he go with thee?

27 But Ăb′-să-lǫm pressed him, that he let Amnon and all the king's sons go with him.

28 Now Ăb′-să-lǫm had commanded his servants, saying, Mark ye now when Amnon's ᴿheart is merry with wine, and when I say unto you, Smite Amnon; then kill him, fear not: ᴺhave not I commanded you? be courageous, and be ᴺvaliant.

29 And the servants of Ăb′-să-lǫm did unto Amnon as Ăb′-să-lǫm had commanded. Then all the king's sons arose, and every man ᴺgat him up upon his mule, and fled.

30 And it came to pass, while they were in the way, that tidings came to David, saying, Ăb′-să-lǫm hath slain all the king's sons, and there is not one of them left.

31 Then the king arose, and ᴿtare his garments, and ᴿlay on the earth; and all his servants stood by with their clothes rent.

32 Anh ᴿJŏn′-ă-dăb, the son of Shĭm′-ĕ-ă David's brother, answered and said, Let not

my lord suppose *that* they have slain all the young men the king's sons; for Amnon only is dead: for by the ᴺappointment of Ăb′-să-lǫm this hath been ᴺdetermined from the day that he forced his sister Tā′-mär.

33 Now therefore ᴿlet not my lord the king take the thing to his heart, to think that all the king's sons are dead: for Amnon only is dead.

Absalom flees

34 ᴿBut Ăb′-să-lǫm fled. And the young man that kept the watch lifted up his eyes, and looked, and, behold, there came much people by the way of the hill side behind him.

35 And Jŏn′-ă-dăb said unto the king, Behold, the king's sons come: ᴺas thy servant said, so it is.

36 And it came to pass, as soon as he had made an end of speaking, that, behold, the king's sons came, and lifted up their voice and wept: and the king also and all his servants wept ᴺvery sore.

37 But Ăb′-să-lǫm fled, and went to ᴿTăl′-mâi, the son of ᴺĂm′-mĭ-hŭd, king of Gē′-shùr. And *David* mourned for his son every day.

38 So Ăb′-să-lǫm fled, and went to ᴿGē′-shùr, and was there three years.

39 And *the soul of* king David ᴺlonged to go forth unto Ăb′-să-lǫm: for he was ᴿcomforted concerning Amnon, seeing he was dead.

CHAPTER 14

The wise woman of Tekoah

NOW Jō′-ăb the son of Zĕr-ū-ī′-ăh perceived that the king's heart *was* ᴿtoward Ăb′-să-lǫm.

2 And Jō′-ăb sent to ᴿTĕ-kō′-ăh, and fetched thence a wise woman, and said unto her, I pray thee, feign thyself to be a mourner, ᴿand put on now mourning apparel, and anoint not thyself with oil, but be as a woman that had a long time mourned for the dead:

3 And come to the king, and speak on this manner unto him. So Jō′-ăb ᴿput the words in her mouth.

4 And when the woman of Tĕ-kō′-ăh spake to the king, she ᴿfell on her face to the ground, and did obeisance, and said, ᴿHelp,ᴺ O king.

5 And the king said unto her, What aileth thee? And she answered, ᴿI *am* indeed a widow woman, and mine husband is dead.

6 And thy handmaid had two sons, and they two strove together in the field, and *there was* ᴺnone to part them, but the one smote the other, and slew him.

7 And, behold, the whole family is risen against thine handmaid, and they said, Deliver him that smote his brother, that we may kill him, for the life of his brother whom he slew; and we will destroy the heir also: and so they shall quench my coal which is left, and shall not leave to my husband *neither* name nor remainder ᴺupon the earth.

8 And the king said unto the woman, Go to thine house, and I will give charge concerning thee.

9 And the woman of Tĕ-kō'-ăh said unto the king, My lord, O king, ᴿthe iniquity *be* on me, and on my father's house: ᴿand the king and his throne *be* guiltless.

10 And the king said, Whosoever saith *aught* unto thee, bring him to me, and he shall not touch thee any more.

11 Then said she, I pray thee, let the king remember the LORD thy God, ᴺthat thou wouldest not suffer ᴿthe revengers of blood to destroy any more, lest they destroy my son. And he said, ᴿAs the LORD liveth, there shall not one hair of thy son fall to the earth.

12 Then the woman said, Let thine handmaid, I pray thee, speak *one* word unto my lord the king. And he said, Say on.

13 And the woman said, Wherefore then hast thou thought such a thing against ᴿthe people of God? for the king doth speak this thing as one which is faulty, in that the king doth not fetch home again ᴿhis banished.

14 For we ᴿmust needs die, and *are* as water spilt on the ground, which cannot be gathered up again; ᴺneither doth God respect *any* person: yet doth he ᴿdevise means, that his banished be not expelled from him.

15 Now therefore that I am come to speak of this thing unto my lord the king, *it is* because the people have made me afraid: and thy handmaid said, I will now speak unto the king; it may be that the king will perform the request of his handmaid.

16 For the king will hear, to deliver his handmaid out of the hand of the man *that would* destroy me and my son together out of the inheritance of God.

17 Then thine handmaid said, The word of my lord the king shall now be ᴺcomfortable: for ᴿas an angel of God, so *is* my lord the king ᴺto discern good and bad: therefore the LORD thy God will be with thee.

18 Then the king answered and said unto the woman, Hide not from me, I pray thee, the thing that I shall ask thee. And the woman said, Let my lord the king now speak.

19 And the king said, *Is not* the hand of Jō'-ăb with thee in all this? And the woman

CHAP. 14
BC 1027
7 Heb. *upon the face of the earth*
9 Gen. 27:13
1 Sam. 25:24
Mat. 27:25
9 ch. 3:28, 29
1 Ki. 2:33
11 Heb. *That the revenger of blood do not multiply to destroy*
11 Num. 35:19
11 1 Sam. 14:45
Acts 27:34
13 Judg. 20:2
13 ch. 13:37, 38
14 Job 34:15
Heb. 9:27
14 Or, *because God hath not taken away his life, he hath also devised means, etc.*
14 Num. 35:15, 25, 28
17 Heb. *for rest*
17 ver. 20
ch. 19:27
17 Heb. *to hear*

ver. 3   19
ver. 17   20
ch. 19:27
Heb. *blessed*   22
Or, *thy*   22
ch. 13:37   23
Gen. 43:3   24
ch. 3:13
Heb. *And as Absalom there was not a beautiful man in all Israel to praise greatly* 25
Is. 1:6   25
See ch. 18:18   27
ver. 24   28
Heb. *near my place* 30

answered and said, As thy soul liveth, my lord the king, none can turn to the right hand or to the left from aught that my lord the king hath spoken: for thy servant Jō'-ăb, he bade me, and ᴿhe put all these words in the mouth of thine handmaid:

20 To fetch about this form of speech hath thy servant Jō'-ăb done this thing: and my lord *is* wise, ᴿaccording to the wisdom of an angel of God, to know all *things* that *are* in the earth.

Absalom returns to Jerusalem

21 And the king said unto Jō'-ăb, Behold now, I have done this thing: go therefore, bring the young man Ăb'-să-lŏm again.

22 And Jō'-ăb fell to the ground on his face, and bowed himself, and ᴺthanked the king: and Jō'-ăb said, To day thy servant knoweth that I have found grace in thy sight, my lord, O king, in that the king hath fulfilled the request of ᴺhis servant.

23 So Jō'-ăb arose ᴿand went to Gē'-shŭr, and brought Ăb'-să-lŏm to Jerusalem.

24 And the king said, Let him turn to his own house, and let him ᴿnot see my face. So Ăb'-să-lŏm returned to his own house, and saw not the king's face.

25 ᴺBut in all Israel there was none to be so much praised as Ăb'-să-lŏm for his beauty: ᴿfrom the sole of his foot even to the crown of his head there was no blemish in him.

26 And when he polled his head, (for it was at every year's end that he polled *it:* because *the hair* was heavy on him, therefore he polled it:) he weighed the hair of his head at two hundred shē'-kĕls after the king's weight.

27 And ᴿunto Ăb'-să-lŏm there were born three sons, and one daughter, whose name *was* Tā'-mär: she was a woman of a fair countenance.

28 So Ăb'-să-lŏm dwelt two full years in Jerusalem, ᴿand saw not the king's face.

29 Therefore Ăb'-să-lŏm sent for Jō'-ăb, to have sent him to the king; but he would not come to him: and when he sent again the second time, he would not come.

30 Therefore he said unto his servants, See, Jō'-ăb's field is ᴺnear mine, and he hath barley there; go and set it on fire. And Ăb'-să-lŏm's servants set the field on fire.

31. Then Jō'-ăb arose, and came to Ăb'-să-lŏm unto *his* house, and said unto him, Wherefore have thy servants set my field on fire?

32 And Ăb'-să-lŏm answered Jō'-ăb, Behold, I sent unto thee, saying, Come hither, that I may send thee to the king, to say, Wherefore

am I come from Gē′-shŭr? *it had been* good for me *to have been* there still: now therefore let me see the king's face; and if there be *any* iniquity in me, let him kill me.

33 So Jō′-ăb came to the king, and told him: and when he had called for Ăb′-să-lŏm, he came to the king, and bowed himself on his face to the ground before the king: and the king ᴿkissed Ăb′-să-lŏm.

CHAPTER 15

Absalom's conspiracy

AND ᴿit came to pass after this, that Ăb′-să-lŏm ᴿprepared him chariots and horses, and fifty men to run before him.

2 And Ăb′-să-lŏm rose up early, and stood beside the way of the gate: and it was *so,* that when any man that had a controversy ᴺcame to the king for judgment, then Ăb′-să-lŏm called unto him, and said, Of what city *art* thou? And he said, Thy servant *is* of one of the tribes of Israel.

3 And Ăb′-să-lŏm said unto him, See, thy matters *are* good and right; but ᴺ*there is* no man *deputed* of the king to hear thee.

4 Ăb′-să-lŏm said moreover, ᴿOh that I were made judge in the land, that every man which hath any suit or cause might come unto me, and I would do him justice!

5 And it was *so,* that when any man came nigh *to him* to do him obeisance, he put forth his hand, and took him, and kissed him.

6 And on this manner did Ăb′-să-lŏm to all Israel that came to the king for judgment: ᴿso Ăb′-să-lŏm stole the hearts of the men of Israel.

7 And it came to pass ᴿafter forty years, that Ăb′-să-lŏm said unto the king, I pray thee, let me go and pay my vow, which I have vowed unto the LORD, in Hē′-brŏn.

8 ᴿFor thy servant ᴿvowed a vow ᴿwhile I abode at Gē′-shŭr in Syria, saying, If the LORD shall bring me again indeed to Jerusalem, then I will serve the LORD.

9 And the king said unto him, Go in peace. So he arose, and went to Hē′-brŏn.

10 But Ăb′-să-lŏm sent spies throughout all the tribes of Israel, saying, As soon as ye hear the sound of the trumpet, then ye shall say, Ăb′-să-lŏm reigneth in Hē′-brŏn.

11 And with Ăb′-să-lŏm went two hundred men out of Jerusalem, *that were* ᴿcalled; and they went ᴿin their simplicity, and they knew not any thing.

12 And Ăb′-să-lŏm sent for Ă-hĭth′-ŏ-phĕl the Gī′-lō-nīte, ᴿDavid's counsellor, from

his city, *even* from ᴿGī′-lōh, while he offered sacrifices. And the conspiracy was strong; for the people ᴿincreased continually with Ăb′-să-lŏm.

David flees

13 And there came a messenger to David, saying, ᴿThe hearts of the men of Israel are after Ăb′-să-lŏm.

14 And David said unto all his servants that *were* with him at Jerusalem, Arise, and let us ᴿflee; for we shall not *else* escape from Ăb′-să-lŏm: make speed to depart, lest he overtake us suddenly, and ᴺbring evil upon us, and smite the city with the edge of the sword.

15 And the king's servants said unto the king, Behold, thy servants *are ready to do* whatsoever my lord the king shall ᴺappoint.

16 And ᴿthe king went forth, and all his household ᴺafter him. And the king left ᴿten women, *which were* concubines, to keep the house.

17 And the king went forth, and all the people after him, and tarried in a place that was far off.

18 And all his servants passed on beside him; ᴿand all the Chĕr′-ĕ-thītes, and all the Pĕl′-ĕ-thītes, and all the Gĭt′-tītes, six hundred men which came after him from Gath, passed on before the king.

19 Then said the king to ᴿĬt-tā′-ī the Gĭt′-tīte, Wherefore goest thou also with us? return to thy place, and abide with the king: for thou *art* a stranger, and also an exile.

20 Whereas thou camest *but* yesterday, should I this day ᴺmake thee go up and down with us? seeing I go ᴿwhither I may, return thou, and take back thy brethren: mercy and truth *be* with thee.

21 And Ĭt-tā′-ī answered the king, and said, ᴿ*As* the LORD liveth, and *as* my lord the king liveth, surely in what place my lord the king shall be, whether in death or life, even there also will thy servant be.

22 And David said to Ĭt-tā′-ī, Go and pass over. And Ĭt-tā′-ī the Gĭt′-tīte passed over, and all his men, and all the little ones that *were* with him.

23 And all the country wept with a loud voice, and all the people passed over: the king also himself passed over the brook ᴺKĭ′-drŏn, and all the people passed over, toward the way of the ᴿwilderness.

The ark returned to Jerusalem

24 And lo Zā′-dŏk also, and all the Levites *were* with him, bearing the ark of the covenant of God: and they set down the ark of God; and

Ă-bĭ′-ă-thär went up, until all the people had done passing out of the city.

25 And the king said unto Zā′-dŏk, Carry back the ark of God into the city: if I shall find favour in the eyes of the LORD, he ᴿwill bring me again, and shew me *both* it, and his habitation:

26 But if he thus say, I have no ᴿdelight in thee; behold, *here am* I, ᴿlet him do to me as seemeth good unto him.

27 The king said also unto Zā′-dŏk the priest, *Art not* thou a ᴿseer? return into the city in peace, and ᴿyour two sons with you, Ă-hĭ′-mă-ăz thy son, and Jonathan the son of Ă-bĭ′-ă-thär.

28 See, ᴿI will tarry in the plain of the wilderness, until there come word from you to certify me.

29 Zā′-dŏk therefore and Ă-bĭ′-ă-thär carried the ark of God again to Jerusalem: and they tarried there.

30 And David went up by the ascent of *mount* Olivet, ᴺand wept as he went up, and ᴿhad his head covered, and he went ᴿbarefoot: and all the people that *was* with him ᴿcovered every man his head, and they went up, ᴿweeping as they went up.

31 And *one* told David, saying, ᴿĂ-hĭth′-ŏ-phĕl *is* among the conspirators with Ăb′-să-lŏm. And David said, O LORD, I pray thee, ᴿturn the counsel of Ă-hĭth′-ŏ-phĕl into foolishness.

Hushai sent to spy on Absalom

32 And it came to pass, that *when* David was come to the top *of the mount,* where he worshipped God, behold, Hū′-shāi the ᴿĂr′-chite came to meet him ᴿwith his coat rent, and earth upon his head:

33 Unto whom David said, If thou passest on with me, then thou shalt be ᴿa burden unto me:

34 But if thou return to the city, and say unto Ăb′-să-lŏm, ᴿI will be thy servant, O king; *as I have been* thy father's servant hitherto, so *will* I now also *be* thy servant: then mayest thou for me defeat the counsel of Ă-hĭth′-ŏ-phĕl.

35 And *hast thou* not there with thee Zā′-dŏk and Ă-bĭ′-ă-thär the priests? therefore it shall be, *that* what thing soever thou shalt hear out of the king's house, ᴿthou shalt tell *it* to Zā′-dŏk and Ă-bĭ′-ă-thär the priests.

36 Behold, *they have* there ᴿwith them their two sons, Ă-hĭ′-mă-ăz Zā′-dŏk's *son,* and Jonathan Ă-bĭ′-ă-thär's *son;* and by them ye shall send unto me every thing that ye can hear.

37 So Hū′-shāi ᴿDavid's friend came into the city, ᴿand Ăb′-să-lŏm came into Jerusalem.

CHAPTER 16

Deceit of Ziba

AND ᴿwhen David was a little past the top *of the hill,* behold, ᴿZī′-bă the servant of Mĕ-phĭb′-ŏ-shĕth met him, with a couple of asses saddled, and upon them two hundred *loaves* of bread, and an hundred bunches of raisins, and an hundred of summer fruits, and a bottle of wine.

2 And the king said unto Zī′-bă, What meanest thou by these? And Zī′-bă said, The asses *be* for the king's household to ride on; and the bread and summer fruit for the young men to eat; and the wine, ᴿthat such as be faint in the wilderness may drink.

3 And the king said, And where *is* thy master's son? ᴿAnd Zī′-bă said unto the king, Behold, he abideth at Jerusalem: for he said, To day shall the house of Israel restore me the kingdom of my father.

4 Then said the king to Zī′-bă, Behold, thine *are* all that *pertained* unto Mĕ-phĭb′-ŏ-shĕth. And Zī′-bă said, ᴺI humbly beseech thee *that* I may find grace in thy sight, my lord, O king.

Shimei curses David

5 And when king David came to Bă-hū′-rĭm, behold, thence came out a man of the family of the house of Saul, whose name *was* ᴿShĭm′-ĕ-ī, the son of Gē′-ră: ᴺhe came forth, and cursed still as he came.

6 And he cast stones at David, and at all the servants of king David: and all the people and all the mighty men *were* on his right hand and on his left.

7 And thus said Shĭm′-ĕ-ī when he cursed, Come out, come out, thou ᴺbloody man, and thou ᴿman of Bē′-lĭ-ăl:

8 The LORD hath ᴿreturned upon thee all ᴿthe blood of the house of Saul, in whose stead thou hast reigned; and the LORD hath delivered the kingdom into the hand of Ăb′-să-lŏm thy son: and, ᴺbehold, thou *art taken* in thy mischief, because thou *art* a bloody man.

9 Then said Ăb′-ī-shāi the son of Zĕr-ū-ī′-ăh unto the king, Why should this ᴿdead dog ᴿcurse my lord the king? let me go over, I pray thee, and take off his head.

10 And the king said, ᴿWhat have I to do with you, ye sons of Zĕr-ū-ī′-ăh? so let him curse, because ᴿthe LORD hath said unto him, Curse David. ᴿWho shall then say, Wherefore hast thou done so?

11 And David said to Ăb′-ī-shāi, and to all his servants, Behold, ᴿmy son, which ᴿcame forth of my bowels, seeketh my life: how

much more now *may this* Benjamite *do it?* let him alone, and let him curse; for the LORD hath bidden him.

12 It may be that the LORD will look on mine [NN]affliction, and that the LORD will [R]requite me good for his cursing this day.

13 And as David and his men went by the way, Shĭm'-ĕ-ī went along on the hill's side over against him, and cursed as he went, and threw stones at him, and [N]cast dust.

14 And the king, and all the people that *were* with him, came weary, and refreshed themselves there.

15 And [R]Ăb'-să-lom, and all the people the men of Israel, came to Jerusalem, and Ă-hĭth'-ŏ-phĕl with him.

Absalom enters Jerusalem

16 And it came to pass, when Hū'-shaï the Är'-chïte, [R]David's friend, was come unto Ăb'-să-lom, that Hū'-shaï said unto Ăb'-să-lom, [N]God save the king, God save the king.

17 And Ăb'-să-lom said to Hū'-shaï, *Is this* thy kindness to thy friend? [R]why wentest thou not with thy friend?

18 And Hū'-shaï said unto Ăb'-să-lom, Nay; but whom the LORD, and this people, and all the men of Israel, choose, his will I be, and with him will I abide.

19 And again, [R]whom should I serve? *should I* not *serve* in the presence of his son? as I have served in thy father's presence, so will I be in thy presence.

20 Then said Ăb'-să-lom to Ă-hĭth'-ŏ-phĕl, Give counsel among you what we shall do.

21 And Ă-hĭth'-ŏ-phĕl said unto Ăb'-să-lom, Go in unto thy father's [R]concubines, which he hath left to keep the house; and all Israel shall hear that thou [R]art abhorred of thy father: then shall [R]the hands of all that *are* with thee be strong.

22 So they spread Ăb'-să-lom a tent upon the top of the house; and Ăb'-să-lom went in unto his father's concubines [R]in the sight of all Israel.

23 And the counsel of Ă-hĭth'-ŏ-phĕl, which he counselled in those days, *was* as if a man had inquired at the [N]oracle of God: so *was* all the counsel of Ă-hĭth'-ŏ-phĕl [R]both with David and with Ăb'-să-lom.

CHAPTER 17

Hushai's counsel taken

MOREOVER Ă-hĭth'-ŏ-phĕl said unto Ăb'-să-lom, Let me now choose out twelve thousand men, and I will arise and pursue after David this night:

CHAP. 16
BC 1023
12 Or, *tears*
12 Heb. *eye,* Gen. 29:32
1 Sam. 1:11
12 Rom. 8:28
13 Heb. *dusted him with dust*
15 ch. 15:37
16 ch. 15:37
16 Heb. *Let the king live*
17 ch. 19:25
Prov. 17:17
19 ch. 15:34
21 ch. 15:16 & 20:3
21 Gen. 34:30
1 Sam. 13:4
21 ch. 2:7
Zech. 8:13
22 ch. 12:11, 12
23 Heb. *word*
23 ch. 15:12

CHAP. 17	
BC 1023	
See Deut. 25:18	2
ch. 16:14	
Zech. 13:7	2
Heb. *was right in the eyes of, etc.,*	4
1 Sam. 18:20	
Heb. *what is in his mouth*	5
Heb. *word?*	6
Heb. *counselled*	7
Heb. *bitter of soul*	8
Hos. 13:8	8
Heb. *fallen*	9
Josh. 2:11	10
Judg. 20:1	11
Gen. 22:17	11
Heb. *that thy face,* or, *presence go, etc.*	11
ch. 15:31, 34	14
Heb. *commanded*	14

2 And I will come upon him while he *is* [R]weary and weak handed, and will make him afraid: and all the people that *are* with him shall flee; and I will [R]smite the king only:

3 And I will bring back all the people unto thee: the man whom thou seekest *is* as if all returned: *so* all the people shall be in peace.

4 And the saying [N]pleased Ăb'-să-lom well, and all the elders of Israel.

5 Then said Ăb'-să-lom, Call now Hū'-shaï the Är'-chïte also, and let us hear likewise [N]what he saith.

6 And when Hū'-shaï was come to Ăb'-să-lom, Ăb'-să-lom spake unto him, saying, Ă-hĭth'-ŏ-phĕl hath spoken after this manner: shall we do *after* his [N]saying? if not; speak thou.

7 And Hū'-shaï said unto Ăb'-să-lom, The counsel that Ă-hĭth'-ŏ-phĕl hath [N]given *is* not good at this time.

8 For, said Hū'-shaï, thou knowest thy father and his men, that they *be* mighty men, and they *be* [N]chafed in their minds, as [R]a bear robbed of her whelps in the field: and thy father *is* a man of war, and will not lodge with the people.

9 Behold, he is hid now in some pit, or in some *other* place: and it will come to pass, when some of them be [N]overthrown at the first, that whosoever heareth it will say, There is a slaughter among the people that follow Ăb'-să-lom.

10 And he also *that is* valiant, whose heart *is* as the heart of a lion, shall utterly [R]melt: for all Israel knoweth that thy father *is* a mighty man, and *they* which *be* with him *are* valiant men.

11 Therefore I counsel that all Israel be generally gathered unto thee, [R]from Dan even to Bēēr-shē'-bă, [R]as the sand that *is* by the sea for multitude; and [N]that thou go to battle in thine own person.

12 So shall we come upon him in some place where he shall be found, and we will light upon him as the dew falleth on the ground: and of him and of all the men that *are* with him there shall not be left so much as one.

13 Moreover, if he be gotten into a city, then shall all Israel bring ropes to that city, and we will draw it into the river, until there be not one small stone found there.

14 And Ăb'-să-lom and all the men of Israel said, The counsel of Hū'-shaï the Är'-chïte *is* better than the counsel of Ă-hĭth'-ŏ-phĕl. For [R]the LORD had [N]appointed to defeat the good counsel of Ă-hĭth'-ŏ-phĕl, to the intent that the LORD might bring evil upon Ăb'-să-lom.

Hushai sends word to David

15 ᴿThen said Hū′-shaï unto Zā′-dŏk and to
Ă-bī′-ă-thär the priests, Thus and thus did Ă-
hĭth′-ŏ-phĕl counsel Ăb′-să-lŏm and the elders
of Israel; and thus and thus have I counselled.

16 Now therefore send quickly and tell David, saying, Lodge not this night ᴿin the plains
of the wilderness, but speedily pass over; lest
the king be swallowed up, and all the people
that *are* with him.

17 ᴿNow Jonathan and Ă-hī′-mă-ăz ᴿstayed
by ᴿĔn-rō′-gĕl; for they might not be seen to
come into the city: and a wench went and told
them; and they went and told king David.

18 Nevertheless a lad saw them, and told
Ăb′-să-lŏm: but they went both of them away
quickly, and came to a man's house ᴿin
Bă-hū′-rĭm, which had a well in his court;
whither they went down.

19 And ᴿthe woman took and spread a
covering over the well's mouth, and spread
ground corn thereon; and the thing was not
known.

20 And when Ăb′-să-lŏm's servants came to
the woman to the house, they said, Where *is*
Ă-hī′-mă-ăz and Jonathan? And ᴿthe woman
said unto them, They be gone over the brook
of water. And when they had sought and could
not find *them,* they returned to Jerusalem.

David crosses the Jordan

21 And it came to pass, after they were departed, that they came up out of the well, and
went and told king David, and said unto David, ᴿArise, and pass quickly over the water:
for thus hath Ă-hĭth′-ŏ-phĕl counselled against
you.

22 Then David arose, and all the people that
were with him, and they passed over Jordan:
by the morning light there lacked not one of
them that was not gone over Jordan.

23 And when Ă-hĭth′-ŏ-phĕl saw that his
counsel was not ᴺfollowed, he saddled *his* ass,
and arose, and gat him home to his house, to
ᴿhis city, and ᴺput his household in order, and
ᴿhanged himself, and died, and was buried in
the sepulchre of his father.

24 Then David came to ᴿMā-hă-nā′-ĭm. And
Ăb′-să-lŏm passed over Jordan, he and all the
men of Israel with him.

25 And Ăb′-să-lŏm made Ă-mā′-să captain of
the host instead of Jō′-ăb: which Ă-mā′-să *was*
a man's son, whose name *was* ᴺĬth′-ră an Israelite, that went in to ᴿĂb′-ĭ-gail ᴺ the daughter of ᴺNahash, sister to Zĕr-ū-ī′-ăh Jō′-ăb's
mother.

CHAP. 17
BC 1023
15 ch. 15:35
16 ch. 15:28
17 ch. 15:27, 36
17 Josh. 2:4, etc.
17 Josh. 15:7
& 18:16
18 ch. 16:5
19 See Josh. 2:6
20 See Ex. 1:19
Josh. 2:4, 5
21 ver. 15, 16
23 Heb. *done*
23 ch. 15:12
23 Heb. *gave
charge concerning
his house,*
2 Ki. 20:1
23 Mat. 27:5
24 Gen. 32:2
Josh. 13:26
ch. 2:8
25 Or, *Jether an
Ishmaelite*
25 1 Chr. 2:16, 17
25 Heb. *Abigal*
25 Or, *Jesse,*
See 1 Chr. 2:13, 16

See ch. 10:1   27
& 12:29
ch. 9:4   27
ch. 19:31, 32   27
1 Ki. 2:7
Or, *cups*   28
ch. 16:2   29

CHAP. 18
BC 1023
ch. 15:19   2
ch. 21:17   3
Heb. *set their
heart on us*
Heb. *as ten
thousand of us*
Heb. *be to
succour*
ver. 12   5
Josh. 17:15, 18   6
Heb. *multiplied
to devour*   8

26 So Israel and Ăb′-să-lŏm pitched in the
land of Gilead.

27 And it came to pass, when David was
come to Mā-hă-nā′-ĭm, that ᴿShō′-bī the son
of Nahash of Răb′-băh of the children of Ammon, and ᴿMā′-chĭr the son of Ăm′-mĭ-ĕl of
Lō′-dĕ-bär, and ᴿBär-zĭl-lā′-ī the Gileadite of
Rō′-gĕ-lĭm,

28 Brought beds, and ᴺbasins, and earthen
vessels, and wheat, and barley, and flour, and
parched *corn,* and beans, and lentiles, and
parched *pulse,*

29 And honey, and butter, and sheep, and
cheese of kine, for David, and for the people
that *were* with him, to eat: for they said, The
people *is* hungry, and weary, and thirsty, ᴿin
the wilderness.

CHAPTER 18

David's army dispatched

AND David numbered the people that *were*
with him, and set captains of thousands
and captains of hundreds over them.

2 And David sent forth a third part of the
people under the hand of Jō′-ăb, and a third
part under the hand of Ăb′-ĭ-shaï the son of
Zĕr-ū-ī′-ăh, Jō′-ăb's brother, ᴿand a third part
under the hand of Ĭt-tā′-ī the Gĭt′-tīte. And the
king said unto the people, I will surely go
forth with you myself also.

3 ᴿBut the people answered, Thou shalt not
go forth: for if we flee away, they will not
ᴺcare for us; neither if half of us die, will they
care for us: but now *thou art* ᴺworth ten thousand of us: therefore now *it is* better that thou
ᴺsuccour us out of the city.

4 And the king said unto them, What seemeth you best I will do. And the king stood by
the gate side, and all the people came out by
hundreds and by thousands.

5 And the king commanded Jō′-ăb and Ăb′-
ĭ-shaï and Ĭt-tā′-ī, saying, *Deal* gently for my
sake with the young man, *even* with Ăb′-să-lŏm.
ᴿAnd all the people heard when the king gave
all the captains charge concerning Ăb′-să-lŏm.

Absalom defeated and killed

6 So the people went out into the field
against Israel: and the battle was in the ᴿwood
of Ē′-phră-ĭm;

7 Where the people of Israel were slain before the servants of David, and there was there
a great slaughter that day of twenty thousand
men.

8 For the battle was there scattered over the
face of all the country: and the wood ᴺde-

voured more people that day than the sword devoured.

9 And Ăb'-să-lŏm met the servants of David. And Ăb'-să-lŏm rode upon a mule, and the mule went under the thick boughs of a great oak, and his head caught hold of the oak, and he was taken up between the heaven and the earth; and the mule that *was* under him went away.

10 And a certain man saw *it*, and told Jō'-ăb, and said, Behold, I saw Ăb'-să-lŏm hanged in an oak.

11 And Jō'-ăb said unto the man that told him, And, behold, thou sawest *him*, and why didst thou not smite him there to the ground? and I would have given thee ten *shē'-kĕls* of silver, and a girdle.

12 And the man said unto Jō'-ăb, Though I should ᴺreceive a thousand *shē'-kĕls* of silver in mine hand, *yet* would I not put forth mine hand against the king's son: ᴿfor in our hearing the king charged thee and Ăb'-ī-shâi and Ĭt-tā'-ī, saying, ᴺBeware that none *touch* the young man Ăb'-să-lŏm.

13 Otherwise I should have wrought falsehood against mine own life: for there is no matter hid from the king, and thou thyself wouldest have set thyself against *me*.

14 Then said Jō'-ăb, I may not tarry thus ᴺwith thee. And he took three darts in his hand, and thrust them through the heart of Ăb'-să-lŏm, while he *was* yet alive in the ᴺmidst of the oak.

15 And ten young men that bare Jō'-ăb's armour compassed about and smote Ăb'-să-lŏm, and slew him.

16 And Jō'-ăb blew the trumpet, and the people returned from pursuing after Israel: for Jō'-ăb held back the people.

17 And they took Ăb'-să-lŏm, and cast him into a great pit in the wood, and ᴿlaid a very great heap of stones upon him: and all Israel fled every one to his tent.

18 Now Ăb'-să-lŏm in his lifetime had taken and reared up for himself a pillar, which *is* in ᴿthe king's dale: for he said, ᴿI have no son to keep my name in remembrance: and he called the pillar after his own name: and it is called unto this day, Ăb'-să-lŏm's place.

19 Then said Ă-hī'-mă-ăz the son of Zā'-dŏk, Let me now run, and bear the king tidings, how that the LORD hath ᴺavenged him of his enemies.

20 And Jō'-ăb said unto him, Thou shalt not ᴺbear tidings this day, but thou shalt bear tidings another day: but this day thou shalt bear no tidings, because the king's son is dead.

CHAP. **18**
BC 1023
12 Heb. *weigh upon mine hand*
12 ver. 5
12 Heb. *Beware whosoever ye be of, etc.*
14 Heb. *before thee*
14 Heb. *heart*
17 Josh. 7:26
18 Gen. 14:17
18 See ch. 14:27
19 Heb. *judged him from the hand, etc.*
20 Heb. *be a man of tidings*

Heb. *be what* may   **22**
Or, *convenient*   **22**
2 Ki. 9:17   **24**
Heb. *I see the running* **27**
Or, *Peace be to thee* **28**
Heb. *Peace*   **28**
Heb. *shut up*   **28**
Heb. *Is there peace?* **29**
Heb. *Tidings is brought* **31**
ch. 19:4   **33**

21 Then said Jō'-ăb to Cū'-shī, Go tell the king what thou hast seen. And Cū'-shī bowed himself unto Jō'-ăb, and ran.

22 Then said Ă-hī'-mă-ăz the son of Zā'-dŏk yet again to Jō'-ăb, But ᴺhowsoever, let me, I pray thee, also run after Cū'-shī. And Jō'-ăb said, Wherefore wilt thou run, my son, seeing that thou hast no tidings ᴺready?

23 But howsoever, *said he,* let me run. And he said unto him, Run. Then Ă-hī'-mă-ăz ran by the way of the plain, and overran Cū'-shī.

David mourns Absalom's death

24 And David sat between the two gates: and ᴿthe watchman went up to the roof over the gate unto the wall, and lifted up his eyes, and looked, and behold a man running alone.

25 And the watchman cried, and told the king. And the king said, If he *be* alone, *there is* tidings in his mouth. And he came apace, and drew near.

26 And the watchman saw another man running: and the watchman called unto the porter, and said, Behold *another* man running alone. And the king said, He also bringeth tidings.

27 And the watchman said, ᴺMe thinketh the running of the foremost is like the running of Ă-hī'-mă-ăz the son of Zā'-dŏk. And the king said, He *is* a good man, and cometh with good tidings.

28 And Ă-hī'-mă-ăz called, and said unto the king, ᴺᴺAll is well. And he fell down to the earth upon his face before the king, and said, Blessed *be* the LORD thy God, which hath ᴺdelivered up the men that lifted up their hand against my lord the king.

29 And the king said, ᴺIs the young man Ăb'-să-lŏm safe? And Ă-hī'-mă-ăz answered, When Jō'-ăb sent the king's servant, and *me* thy servant, I saw a great tumult, but I knew not what *it was*.

30 And the king said *unto him,* Turn aside, *and* stand here. And he turned aside, and stood still.

31 And, behold, Cū'-shī came; and Cū'-shī said, ᴺTidings, my lord the king: for the LORD hath avenged thee this day of all them that rose up against thee.

32 And the king said unto Cū'-shī, Is the young man Ăb'-să-lŏm safe? And Cū'-shī answered, The enemies of my lord the king, and all that rise against thee to do *thee* hurt, be as *that* young man *is*.

33 And the king was much moved, and went up to the chamber over the gate, and wept: and as he went, thus he said, ᴿO my son Ăb'-să-lŏm, my son, my son Ăb'-să-lŏm! would

God I had died for thee, O Ăb′-sá-lŏm, my son, my son!

CHAPTER 19

All the people mourn

AND it was told Jō′-ăb, Behold, the king weepeth and mourneth for Ăb′-sá-lŏm.

2 And the ᴺvictory that day was *turned* into mourning unto all the people: for the people heard say that day how the king was grieved for his son.

3 And the people gat them by stealth that day ᴿinto the city, as people being ashamed steal away when they flee in battle.

4 But the king ᴿcovered his face, and the king cried with a loud voice, ᴿO my son Ăb′-sá-lŏm, O Ăb′-sá-lŏm, my son, my son!

5 And Jō′-ăb came into the house to the king, and said, Thou hast shamed this day the faces of all thy servants, which this day have saved thy life, and the lives of thy sons and of thy daughters, and the lives of thy wives, and the lives of thy concubines;

6 ᴺIn that thou lovest thine enemies, and hatest thy friends. For thou hast declared this day, ᴺthat thou regardest neither princes nor servants: for this day I perceive, that if Ăb′-sá-lŏm had lived, and all we had died this day, then it had pleased thee well.

7 Now therefore arise, go forth, and speak ᴺcomfortably unto thy servants: for I swear by the LORD, if thou go not forth, there will not tarry one with thee this night: and that will be worse unto thee than all the evil that befell thee from thy youth until now.

8 Then the king arose, and sat in the gate. And they told unto all the people, saying, Behold, the king doth sit in the gate. And all the people came before the king: for Israel had fled every man to his tent.

9 And all the people were at strife throughout all the tribes of Israel, saying, The king saved us out of the hand of our enemies, and he delivered us out of the hand of the Philistines; and now he is ᴿfled out of the land for Ăb′-sá-lŏm.

10 And Ăb′-sá-lŏm, whom we anointed over us, is dead in battle. Now therefore why ᴺspeak ye not a word of bringing the king back?

Joab replaced

11 And king David sent to Zā′-dŏk and to Ă-bī′-á-thär the priests, saying, Speak unto the elders of Judah, saying, Why are ye the last to bring the king back to his house? seeing the speech of all Israel is come to the king, *even* to his house.

CHAP. 19
BC 1023

2 Heb. *salvation,* or, *deliverance*
3 ver. 32
4 ch. 15:30
4 ch. 18:33
6 Heb. *By loving,* etc.
6 Heb. *that princes or servants* are *not to thee*
7 Heb. *to the heart of thy servants,* Gen. 34:3
9 ch. 15:14
10 Heb. *are ye silent?*

ch. 5:1   12
ch. 17:25   13
Ruth 1:17   13
Judg. 20:1   14
Josh. 5:9   15
ch. 16:5   16
   1 Ki. 2:8
ch. 9:2, 10   17
   & 16:1, 2
Heb. *the good*   18
   in his eyes
1 Sam. 22:15   19
ch. 16:5, 6, etc.   19
ch. 13:33   19
See ch. 16:5   20
Ex. 22:28   21
   1 Sam. 26:9
ch. 16:10   22
1 Sam. 11:13   22
1 Ki. 2:8,   23
   9, 37, 46
ch. 9:6   24

---

12 Ye *are* my brethren, ye *are* ᴿmy bones and my flesh: wherefore then are ye the last to bring back the king?

13 ᴿAnd say ye to Ă-mā′-sá, *Art* thou not of my bone, and of my flesh? ᴿGod do so to me, and more also, if thou be not captain of the host before me continually in the room of Jō′-ăb.

14 And he bowed the heart of all the men of Judah, ᴿeven as *the heart of* one man; so that they sent *this word* unto the king, Return thou, and all thy servants.

15 So the king returned, and came to Jordan. And Judah came to ᴿGĭl′-găl, to go to meet the king, to conduct the king over Jordan.

Shimei forgiven

16 And ᴿShĭm′-ĕ-ī the son of Gē′-rá, a Benjamite, which *was* of Bă-hū′-rĭm, hasted and came down with the men of Judah to meet king David.

17 And *there were* a thousand men of Benjamin with him, and ᴿZī′-bă the servant of the house of Saul, and his fifteen sons and his twenty servants with him; and they went over Jordan before the king.

18 And there went over a ferry boat to carry over the king's household, and to do ᴺwhat he thought good. And Shĭm′-ĕ-ī the son of Gē′-rá fell down before the king, as he was come over Jordan;

19 And said unto the king, ᴿLet not my lord impute iniquity unto me, neither do thou remember ᴿthat which thy servant did perversely the day that my lord the king went out of Jerusalem, that the king should ᴿtake it to his heart.

20 For thy servant doth know that I have sinned: therefore, behold, I am come the first this day of all ᴿthe house of Joseph to go down to meet my lord the king.

21 But Ăb′-ĭ-shâi the son of Zĕr-ū-ī′-áh answered and said, Shall not Shĭm′-ĕ-ī be put to death for this, because he ᴿcursed the LORD's anointed?

22 And David said, ᴿWhat have I to do with you, ye sons of Zĕr-ū-ī′-áh, that ye should this day be adversaries unto me? ᴿshall there any man be put to death this day in Israel? for do not I know that I *am* this day king over Israel?

23 Therefore ᴿthe king said unto Shĭm′-ĕ-ī, Thou shalt not die. And the king sware unto him.

Mephibosheth's explanation

24 And ᴿMĕ-phĭb′-ŏ-shĕth the son of Saul came down to meet the king, and had neither dressed his feet, nor trimmed his beard, nor washed his clothes, from the day the king de-

parted until the day he came *again* in peace.

25 And it came to pass, when he was come to Jerusalem to meet the king, that the king said unto him, ᴿWherefore wentest not thou with me, Mĕ-phĭb'-ŏ-shĕth?

26 And he answered, My lord, O king, my servant deceived me: for thy servant said, I will saddle me an ass, that I may ride thereon, and go to the king; because thy servant *is* lame.

27 And ᴿhe hath slandered thy servant unto my lord the king; ᴿbut my lord the king *is* as an angel of God: do therefore *what is* good in thine eyes.

28 For all *of* my father's house were but ᴺdead men before my lord the king: ᴿyet didst thou set thy servant among them that did eat at thine own table. What right therefore have I yet to cry any more unto the king?

29 And the king said unto him, Why speakest thou any more of thy matters? I have said, Thou and Zĭ'-bă divide the land.

30 And Mĕ-phĭb'-ŏ-shĕth said unto the king, Yea, let him take all, forasmuch as my lord the king is come again in peace unto his own house.

Barzillai blessed by David

31 And ᴿBär-zĭl-lā'-ĭ the Gileadite came down from Rō'-gĕ-lĭm, and went over Jordan with the king, to conduct him over Jordan.

32 Now Bär-zĭl-lā'-ĭ was a very aged man, *even* fourscore years old: and ᴿhe had provided the king of sustenance while he lay at Mā-hă-nā'-ĭm; for he *was* a very great man.

33 And the king said unto Bär-zĭl-lā'-ĭ, Come thou over with me, and I will feed thee with me in Jerusalem.

34 And Bär-zĭl-lā'-ĭ said unto the king, ᴺHow long have I to live, that I should go up with the king unto Jerusalem?

35 I *am* this day ᴿfourscore years old: *and* can I discern between good and evil? can thy servant taste what I eat or what I drink? can I hear any more the voice of singing men and singing women? wherefore then should thy servant be yet a burden unto my lord the king?

36 Thy servant will go a little way over Jordan with the king: and why should the king recompense it me with such a reward?

37 Let thy servant, I pray thee, turn back again, that I may die in mine own city, *and be buried* by the grave of my father and of my mother. But behold thy servant ᴿChĭm'-hăm; let him go over with my lord the king; and do to him what shall seem good unto thee.

38 And the king answered, Chĭm'-hăm shall go over with me, and I will do to him that which shall seem good unto thee: and what-

soever thou shalt ᴺrequire of me, *that* will I do for thee.

39 And all the people went over Jordan. And when the king was come over, the king ᴿkissed Bär-zĭl-lā'-ĭ, and blessed him; and he returned unto his own place.

40 Then the king went on to Gĭl'-găl, and ᴺChĭm'-hăm went on with him: and all the people of Judah conducted the king, and also half the people of Israel.

Israel's jealousy of Judah

41 And, behold, all the men of Israel came to the king, and said unto the king, Why have our brethren the men of Judah stolen thee away, and ᴿhave brought the king, and his household, and all David's men with him, over Jordan?

42 And all the men of Judah answered the men of Israel, Because the king *is* ᴿnear of kin to us: wherefore then be ye angry for this matter? have we eaten at all of the king's *cost?* or hath he given us any gift?

43 And the men of Israel answered the men of Judah, and said, We have ten parts in the king, and we have also more *right* in David than ye: why then did ye ᴺdespise us, that our advice should not be first had in bringing back our king? And ᴿthe words of the men of Judah were fiercer than the words of the men of Israel.

CHAPTER 20

Rebellion of Sheba

AND there happened to be there a man of Bē'-lĭ-ăl, whose name *was* Shē'-bă, the son of Bĭch'-rĭ, a Benjamite: and he blew a trumpet, and said, ᴿWe have no part in David, neither have we inheritance in the son of Jesse: ᴿevery man to his tents, O Israel.

2 So every man of Israel went up from after David, *and* followed Shē'-bă the son of Bĭch'-rĭ: but the men of Judah clave unto their king, from Jordan even to Jerusalem.

3 And David came to his house at Jerusalem; and the king took the ten women *his* ᴿconcubines, whom he had left to keep the house, and put them in ᴺward, and fed them, but went not in unto them. So they were ᴺshut up unto the day of their death, ᴺliving in widowhood.

4 Then said the king to Ă-mā'-să, ᴿAssembleᴺ me the men of Judah within three days, and be thou here present.

5 So Ă-mā'-să went to assemble *the men of* Judah: but he tarried longer than the set time which he had appointed him.

6 And David said to Ăb'-ĭ-shāi, Now shall

Shē'-bă the son of Bĭch'-rĭ do us more harm than *did* Ăb'-să-lom: take thou ᴿthy lord's servants, and pursue after him, lest he get him fenced cities, and ᴺescape us.

7 And there went out after him Jō'-ăb's men, and the ᴿChĕr'-e-thītes, and the Pĕl'-e-thītes, and all the mighty men: and they went out of Jerusalem, to pursue after Shē'-bă the son of Bĭch'-rĭ.

8 When they *were* at the great stone which *is* in Gibeon, Ă-mā'-să went before them. And Jō'-ăb's garment that he had put on was girded unto him, and upon it a girdle *with* a sword fastened upon his loins in the sheath thereof; and as he went forth it fell out.

9 And Jō'-ăb said to Ă-mā'-să, *Art* thou in health, my brother? ᴿAnd Jō'-ăb took Ă-mā'-să by the beard with the right hand to kiss him.

10 But Ă-mā'-să took no heed to the sword that *was* in Jō'-ăb's hand: so ᴿhe smote him therewith ᴿin the fifth *rib,* and shed out his bowels to the ground, and ᴺstruck him not again; and he died. So Jō'-ăb and Ăb'-ĭ-shăĭ his brother pursued after Shē'-bă the son of Bĭch'-rĭ.

11 And one of Jō'-ăb's men stood by him, and said, He that favoureth Jō'-ăb, and he that *is* for David, *let him go* after Jō'-ăb.

12 And Ă-mā'-să wallowed in blood in the midst of the highway. And when the man saw that all the people stood still, he removed Ă-mā'-să out of the highway into the field, and cast a cloth upon him, when he saw that every one that came by him stood still.

13 When he was removed out of the highway, all the people went on after Jō'-ăb, to pursue after Shē'-bă the son of Bĭch'-rĭ.

The rebellion quelled

14 And he went through all the tribes of Israel unto ᴿAbel, and to Bĕth-mā'-ă-chăh, and all the Bē'-rĭtes: and they were gathered together, and went also after him.

15 And they came and besieged him in Abel of Bĕth-mā'-ă-chăh, and they ᴿcast up a bank against the city, and ᴺit stood in the trench: and all the people that *were* with Jō'-ăb ᴺbattered the wall, to throw it down.

16 Then cried a wise woman out of the city, Hear, hear; say, I pray you, unto Jō'-ăb, Come near hither, that I may speak with thee.

17 And when he was come near unto her, the woman said, *Art* thou Jō'-ăb? And he answered, I *am he.* Then she said unto him, Hear the words of thine handmaid. And he answered, I do hear.

18 Then she spake, saying, ᴺThey were wont to speak in old time, saying, They shall

surely ask *counsel* at Abel: and so they ended *the matter.*

19 I *am one of them that are* peaceable *and* faithful in Israel: thou seekest to destroy a city and a mother in Israel: why wilt thou swallow up ᴿthe inheritance of the Lᴏʀᴅ?

20 And Jō'-ăb answered and said, Far be it, far be it from me, that I should swallow up or destroy.

21 The matter *is* not so: but a man of mount Ē'-phră-ĭm, Shē'-bă the son of Bĭch'-rĭ ᴺby name, hath lifted up his hand against the king, *even* against David: deliver him only, and I will depart from the city. And the woman said unto Jō'-ăb, Behold, his head shall be thrown to thee over the wall.

22 Then the woman went unto all the people ᴿin her wisdom. And they cut off the head of Shē'-bă the son of Bĭch'-rĭ, and cast *it* out to Jō'-ăb. And he blew a trumpet, and they ᴺretired from the city, every man to his tent. And Jō'-ăb returned to Jerusalem unto the king.

23 Now ᴿJō'-ăb *was* over all the host of Israel: and Bĕ-nāĭ'-ăh the son of Jĕ-hoĭ'-ă-dă *was* over the Chĕr'-e-thītes and over the Pĕl'-e-thītes:

24 And Ă-dôr'-ăm *was* ᴿover the tribute: and ᴿJĕ-hŏsh'-ă-phăt the son of Ă-hī'-lŭd *was* ᴺrecorder:

25 And Shē'-vă *was* scribe: and ᴿZā'-dŏk and Ă-bī'-ă-thär *were* the priests:

26 ᴿAnd ī'-ră also the Jā'-ĭr-ĭte was ᴺa chief ruler about David.

CHAPTER 21

David makes expiation for Saul's sin

THEN there was a famine in the days of David three years, year after year; and David ᴺinquired of the Lᴏʀᴅ. And the Lᴏʀᴅ answered, It is for Saul, and for *his* bloody house, because he slew the Gibeonites.

2 And the king called the Gibeonites, and said unto them; (now the Gibeonites *were* not of the children of Israel, but ᴿof the remnant of the Amorites; and the children of Israel had sworn unto them: and Saul sought to slay them in his zeal to the children of Israel and Judah.)

3 Wherefore David said unto the Gibeonites, What shall I do for you? and wherewith shall I make the atonement, that ye may bless ᴿthe inheritance of the Lᴏʀᴅ?

4 And the Gibeonites said unto him, ᴺWe will have no silver nor gold of Saul, nor of his house; neither for us shalt thou kill any man in Israel. And he said, What ye shall say, *that* will I do for you.

5 And they answered the king, The man that

consumed us, and that ᴺdevised against us *that* we should be destroyed from remaining in any of the coasts of Israel,

6 Let seven men of his sons be delivered unto us, and we will hang them up unto the LORD ᴿin Gĭb′-ĕ-ăh of Saul, ᴿ*whom*ᴺ the LORD did choose. And the king said, I will give *them.*

7 But the king spared Mĕ-phĭb′-ŏ-shĕth, the son of Jonathan the son of Saul, because of ᴿthe LORD's oath that *was* between them, between David and Jonathan the son of Saul.

8 But the king took the two sons of ᴿRĭz′-păh the daughter of Aî′-ăh, whom she bare unto Saul, Ăr-mō′-nī and Mĕ-phĭb′-ŏ-shĕth; and the five sons of ᴺMichal the daughter of Saul, whom she ᴺbrought up for Ā′-drĭ-ĕl the son of Bär-zĭl-lā′-ĭ the Mĕ-hō′-lă-thīte:

9 And he delivered them into the hands of the Gibeonites, and they hanged them in the hill ᴿbefore the LORD: and they fell *all* seven together, and were put to death in the days of harvest, in the first *days,* in the beginning of barley harvest.

Burial of Saul and Jonathan

10 And ᴿRĭz′-păh the daughter of Aî′-ăh took sackcloth, and spread it for her upon the rock, ᴿfrom the beginning of harvest until water dropped upon them out of heaven, and suffered neither the birds of the air to rest on them by day, nor the beasts of the field by night.

11 And it was told David what Rĭz′-păh the daughter of Aî′-ăh, the concubine of Saul, had done.

12 And David went and took the bones of Saul and the bones of Jonathan his son from the men of ᴿJā′-bĕsh-gĭl′-ĕ-ăd, which had stolen them from the street of Bĕth′-shăn, where the Philistines had hanged them, when the Philistines had slain Saul in Gĭl-bō′-ă:

13 And he brought up from thence the bones of Saul and the bones of Jonathan his son; and they gathered the bones of them that were hanged.

14 And the bones of Saul and Jonathan his son buried they in the country of Benjamin in ᴿZē′-lăh, in the sepulchre of Kish his father: and they performed all that the king commanded. And after that ᴿGod was entreated for the land.

Victory over the Philistines

15 Moreover the Philistines had yet war again with Israel; and David went down, and his servants with him, and fought against the Philistines: and David waxed faint.

16 And Ĭsh′-bī-bē′-nŏb, which *was* of the sons of ᴺthe giant, the weight of whose ᴺspear *weighed* three hundred *shē′-kĕls* of brass in weight, he being girded with a new *sword,* thought to have slain David.

17 But Ăb′-ĭ-shaî the son of Zĕr-ū-ī′-ăh succoured him, and smote the Philistine, and killed him. Then the men of David sware unto him, saying, ᴿThou shalt go no more out with us to battle, that thou quench not the ᴿlightᴺ of Israel.

18 ᴿAnd it came to pass after this, that there was again a battle with the Philistines at Gob: then ᴿSĭb′-bĕ-chaî the Hū′-shă-thīte slew ᴺSăph, which *was* of the sons of ᴺthe giant.

19 And there was again a battle in Gob with the Philistines, where ĕl-hā′-năn the son of ᴺJā′-ă-rĕ-ôr′-ĕ-gĭm, a Beth-lehemite, slew ᴿ*the brother of* Gō-lī′-ăth the Gĭt′-tīte, the staff of whose spear *was* like a weaver's beam.

20 And ᴿthere was yet a battle in Gath, where was a man of *great* stature, that had on every hand six fingers, and on every foot six toes, four and twenty in number; and he also was born to ᴺthe giant.

21 And when he ᴺdefied Israel, Jonathan the son of ᴿShĭm′-ĕ-ă the brother of David slew him.

22 ᴿThese four were born to the giant in Gath, and fell by the hand of David, and by the hand of his servants.

CHAPTER 22

David's song of deliverance

AND David ᴿspake unto the LORD the words of this song in the day *that* the LORD had ᴿdelivered him out of the hand of all his enemies, and out of the hand of Saul:

2 And he said, ᴿThe LORD *is* my rock, and my fortress, and my deliverer;

3 The God of my rock; ᴿin him will I trust: *he is* my ᴿshield, and the ᴿhorn of my salvation, my high ᴿtower, and my ᴿrefuge, my saviour; thou savest me from violence.

4 I will call on the LORD, *who is* worthy to be praised: so shall I be saved from mine enemies.

5 When the ᴺwaves of death compassed me, the floods of ᴺungodly men made me afraid;

6 The ᴿsorrowsᴺ of hell compassed me about; the snares of death prevented me;

7 In my distress ᴿI called upon the LORD, and cried to my God: and he did ᴿhear my voice out of his temple, and my cry *did enter* into his ears.

8 Then ᴿthe earth shook and trembled; ᴿthe

foundations of heaven moved and shook, because he was wroth.

9 There went up a smoke Nout of his nostrils, and Rfire out of his mouth devoured: coals were kindled by it.

10 He Rbowed the heavens also, and came down; and Rdarkness was under his feet.

11 And he rode upon a cherub, and did fly: and he was seen Rupon the wings of the wind.

12 And he made Rdarkness pavilions round about him, Ndark waters, and thick clouds of the skies.

13 Through the brightness before him were Rcoals of fire kindled.

14 The LORD Rthundered from heaven, and the most High uttered his voice.

15 And he sent out Rarrows, and scattered them; lightning, and discomfited them.

16 And the channels of the sea appeared, the foundations of the world were discovered, at the Rrebuking of the LORD, at the blast of the breath of his nostrils.

17 RHe sent from above, he took me; he drew me out of Nmany waters;

18 RHe delivered me from my strong enemy, and from them that hated me: for they were too strong for me.

19 They prevented me in the day of my calamity: but the LORD was my stay.

20 RHe brought me forth also into a large place: he delivered me, because he Rdelighted in me.

21 RThe LORD rewarded me according to my righteousness: according to the Rcleanness of my hands hath he recompensed me.

22 For I have Rkept the ways of the LORD, and have not wickedly departed from my God.

23 For all his Rjudgments were before me: and as for his statutes, I did not depart from them.

24 I was also Rupright Nbefore him, and have kept myself from mine iniquity.

25 Therefore Rthe LORD hath recompensed me according to my righteousness; according to my cleanness Nin his eye sight.

26 With Rthe merciful thou wilt shew thyself merciful, and with the upright man thou wilt shew thyself upright.

27 With the pure thou wilt shew thyself pure; and Rwith the froward thou wilt Nshew thyself unsavoury.

28 And the Rafflicted people thou wilt save: but thine eyes are upon Rthe haughty, that thou mayest bring them down.

29 For thou art my Nlamp, O LORD: and the LORD will lighten my darkness.

30 For by thee I have Nrun through a troop: by my God have I leaped over a wall.

31 As for God, Rhis way is perfect; Rthe word of the LORD is Ntried: he is a buckler to all them that trust in him.

32 For Rwho is God, save the LORD? and who is a rock, save our God?

33 God is my Rstrength and power: and he RmakethN my way Rperfect.

34 He Nmaketh my feet Rlike hinds' feet: and Rsetteth me upon my high places.

35 RHe teacheth my hands Nto war; so that a bow of steel is broken by mine arms.

36 Thou hast also given me the shield of thy salvation: and thy gentleness hath Nmade me great.

37 Thou hast Renlarged my steps under me; so that my Nfeet did not slip.

38 I have pursued mine enemies, and destroyed them; and turned not again until I had consumed them.

39 And I have consumed them, and wounded them, that they could not arise: yea, they are fallen Runder my feet.

40 For thou hast Rgirded me with strength to battle: Rthem that rose up against me hast thou Nsubdued under me.

41 Thou hast also given me the Rnecks of mine enemies, that I might destroy them that hate me.

42 They looked, but there was none to save; even Runto the LORD, but he answered them not.

43 Then did I beat them as small Ras the dust of the earth, I did stamp them Ras the mire of the street, and did spread them abroad.

44 RThou also hast delivered me from the strivings of my people, thou hast kept me to be Rhead of the heathen: Ra people which I knew not shall serve me.

45 NStrangers shall NNsubmit themselves unto me: as soon as they hear, they shall be obedient unto me.

46 Strangers shall fade away, and they shall be afraid Rout of their close places.

47 The LORD liveth; and blessed be my rock; and exalted be the God of the Rrock of my salvation.

48 It is God that Navengeth me, and that Rbringeth down the people under me,

49 And that bringeth me forth from mine enemies: thou also hast lifted me up on high above them that rose up against me: thou hast delivered me from the Rviolent man.

50 Therefore I will give thanks unto thee, O LORD, among Rthe heathen, and I will sing praises unto thy name.

51 RHe is the tower of salvation for his king: and sheweth mercy to his Ranointed, unto David, and Rto his seed for evermore.

CHAPTER 23

Final words of David

NOW these *be* the last words of David. David the son of Jesse said, ^Rand the man *who was* raised up on high, ^Rthe anointed of the God of Jacob, and the sweet psalmist of Israel, said,

2 ^RThe spirit of the LORD spake by me, and his word *was* in my tongue.

3 The God of Israel said, ^Rthe Rock of Israel spake to me, ^NHe that ruleth over men *must be* just, ruling ^Rin the fear of God. ★

4 And ^R*he shall be* as the light of the morning, *when* the sun riseth, *even* a morning without clouds; *as* the tender grass *springing* out of the earth by clear shining after rain. ★

5 Although my house *be* not so with God; ^Ryet he hath made with me an everlasting covenant, ordered in all *things,* and sure: for *this is* all my salvation, and all *my* desire, although he make *it* not to grow.

6 But *the sons* of Bē′-lĭ-ăl *shall be* all of them as thorns thrust away, because they cannot be taken with hands:

7 But the man *that* shall touch them must be ^Nfenced with iron and the staff of a spear; and they shall be utterly burned with fire in the *same* place.

David's mighty men

8 These *be* the names of the mighty men whom David had: ^NThe Tăch′-mō-nīte that sat in the seat, chief among the captains; the same *was* Ăd′-ĭ-nō the Ĕz′-nīte: ^N*he lift up his spear* against eight hundred, ^Nwhom he slew at one time.

9 And after him *was* ^RĔl-ē-ā′-zär the son of Dodo the Ă-hō′-hīte, *one* of the three mighty men with David, when they defied the Philistines *that* were there gathered together to battle, and the men of Israel were gone away:

10 He arose, and smote the Philistines until his hand was weary, and his hand clave unto the sword: and the LORD wrought a great victory that day; and the people returned after him only to spoil.

11 And after him *was* ^RShăm′-măh the son of Ā′-ġeē the Hâr′-a-rīte. ^RAnd the Philistines were gathered together ^Ninto a troop, where was a piece of ground full of lentiles: and the people fled from the Philistines.

12 But he stood in the midst of the ground, and defended it, and slew the Philistines: and the LORD wrought a great victory.

13 And ^Rthree^N of the thirty chief went down, and came to David in the harvest time

unto ^Rthe cave of Adullam: and the troop of the Philistines pitched in ^Rthe valley of Rĕph′-ā-ĭm.

14 And David *was* then in ^Ran hold, and the garrison of the Philistines *was* then *in* Beth-lehem.

15 And David longed, and said, Oh that one would give me drink of the water of the well of Beth-lehem, which *is* by the gate!

16 And the three mighty men brake through the host of the Philistines, and drew water out of the well of Beth-lehem, that *was* by the gate, and took *it,* and brought *it* to David: nevertheless he would not drink thereof, but poured it out unto the LORD.

17 And he said, Be it far from me, O LORD, that I should do this: *is not this* ^Rthe blood of the men that went in jeopardy of their lives? therefore he would not drink it. These things did these three mighty men.

18 And ^RĂb′-ĭ-shâi, the brother of Jō′-ăb, the son of Zĕr-ū-ĭ′-ăh, was chief among three. And he lifted up his spear against three hundred, ^N*and* slew *them,* and had the name among three.

19 Was he not most honourable of three? therefore he was their captain: howbeit he attained not unto the *first* three.

20 And Bĕ-nāi′-ăh the son of Jĕ-hoi′-ă-dă, the son of a valiant man, of ^RKăb′-zĕēl, ^Nwho had done many acts, ^Rhe slew two ^Nlionlike men of Moab: he went down also and slew a lion in the midst of a pit in time of snow:

21 And he slew an Egyptian, ^Na goodly man: and the Egyptian had a spear in his hand; but he went down to him with a staff, and plucked the spear out of the Egyptian's hand, and slew him with his own spear.

22 These *things* did Bĕ-nāi′-ăh the son of Jĕ-hoi′-ă-dă, and had the name among three mighty men.

23 He was ^Nmore honourable than the thirty, but he attained not to the *first* three. And David set him ^Rover his ^{NN}guard.

24 ^RĂs′-ă-hĕl the brother of Jō′-ăb *was* one of the thirty; ĕl-hā′-năn the son of Dodo of Beth-lehem,

25 ^RShăm′-măh the Hâr′-ŏd-īte, Ē-lĭ′-kă the Hâr′-ŏd-īte,

26 Hē′-lĕz the Păl′-tīte, ĭ′-ră the son of ĭk′-kĕsh the Tĕ-kō′-īte,

27 Ă-bĭ-ē′-zĕr the Ăn-ĕ-thō′-thīte, Mĕ-bŭn′-nāi the Hū′-shă-thīte,

28 Zăl′-mŏn the Ă-hō′-hīte, Mā′-hă-rāi the Nĕ-tŏph′-ă-thīte,

29 Hē′-lĕb the son of Bā′-ă-năh, a Nĕ-tŏph′-ă-thīte, ĭt-tā′-ī the son of Rĭ-bā′-ī out of Gĭb′-ĕ-ăh of the children of Benjamin,

30 Bĕ-naī'-ăh the Pī-rā'-thŏn-īte, Hĭd-dā'-ī of the ᴺbrooks of ᴿGā'-ăsh,

31 Ā'-bī-ăl'-bŏn the Ăr'-bă-thīte, Ăz-mā'-vĕth the Băr-hū'-mīte,

32 Ē-lī-ăh'-bă the Shā-ăl-bō'-nīte, of the sons of Jăsh'-ĕn, Jonathan,

33 Shăm'-măh the Hâr'-ă-rīte, Ā-hī'-ăm the son of Shâr'-är the Hâr'-ă-rīte,

34 Ē-lĭph'-ĕ-lĕt the son of Ă-hăś'-baī, the son of the Mā-ăch'-ă-thīte, Ē-lī'-ăm the son of Ă-hĭth'-ŏ-phĕl the Gī'-lō-nīte,

35 Hĕz'-rā-ī the Carmelite, Pā'-ă-raī the Är'-bīte,

36 Ī'-găl the son of Nathan of Zō'-băh, Bā'-nī the Gadite,

37 Zē'-lĕk the Ammonite, Nā'-hă-raī the Bēer'-ō-thīte, armourbearer to Jō'-ăb the son of Zĕr-ū-ī'-ăh,

38 ᴿĪ'-ră an ĭth'-rīte, Gâr'-ĕb an ĭth'-rīte,

39 ᴿŪ-rī'-ăh the Hittite: thirty and seven in all.

CHAPTER 24

Census of the kingdom

AND ᴿagain the anger of the Lᴏʀᴅ was kindled against Israel, and ᴺhe moved David against them to say, ᴿGo, number Israel and Judah.

2 For the king said to Jō'-ăb the captain of the host, which *was* with him, ᴺGo now through all the tribes of Israel, ᴿfrom Dan even to Bēer-shē'-bă, and number ye the people, that ᴿI may know the number of the people.

3 And Jō'-ăb said unto the king, Now the Lᴏʀᴅ thy God add unto the people, how many soever they be, an hundredfold, and that the eyes of my lord the king may see *it:* but why doth my lord the king delight in this thing?

4 Notwithstanding the king's word prevailed against Jō'-ăb, and against the captains of the host. And Jō'-ăb and the captains of the host went out from the presence of the king, to number the people of Israel.

5 And they passed over Jordan, and pitched in ᴿĂ-rō'-ĕr, on the right side of the city that *lieth* in the midst of the ᴺriver of Gad, and toward ᴿJā'-zĕr:

6 Then they came to Gilead, and to the ᴺland of Tăh'-tīm-hŏd'-shī; and they came to ᴿDăn-jā'-ăn, and about to ᴿZī'-dŏn,

7 And came to the strong hold of Tyre, and to all the cities of the Hī'-vītes, and of the Canaanites: and they went out to the south of Judah, *even* to Bēer-shē'-bă.

8 So when they had gone through all the

land, they came to Jerusalem at the end of nine months and twenty days.

9 And Jō'-ăb gave up the sum of the number of the people unto the king: ᴿand there were in Israel eight hundred thousand valiant men that drew the sword; and the men of Judah *were* five hundred thousand men.

Choice of David

10 And ᴿDavid's heart smote him after that he had numbered the people. And David said unto the Lᴏʀᴅ, ᴿI have sinned greatly in that I have done: and now, I beseech thee, O Lᴏʀᴅ, take away the iniquity of thy servant; for I have ᴿdone very foolishly.

11 For when David was up in the morning, the word of the Lᴏʀᴅ came unto the prophet ᴿGad, David's ᴿseer, saying,

12 Go and say unto David, Thus saith the Lᴏʀᴅ, I offer thee three *things;* choose thee one of them, that I may *do it* unto thee.

13 So Gad came to David, and told him, and said unto him, Shall ᴿseven years of famine come unto thee in thy land? or wilt thou flee three months before thine enemies, while they pursue thee? or that there be three days' pestilence in thy land? now advise, and see what answer I shall return to him that sent me.

14 And David said unto Gad, I am in a great strait: let us fall now into the hand of the Lᴏʀᴅ; ᴿfor his mercies *are* ᴺgreat: and ᴿlet me not fall into the hand of man.

15 So ᴿthe Lᴏʀᴅ sent a pestilence upon Israel from the morning even to the time appointed: and there died of the people from Dan even to Bēer-shē'-bă seventy thousand men.

16 ᴿAnd when the angel stretched out his hand upon Jerusalem to destroy it, ᴿthe Lᴏʀᴅ repented him of the evil, and said to the angel that destroyed the people, It is enough: stay now thine hand. And the angel of the Lᴏʀᴅ was by the threshingplace of ᴿĂ-raū'-năh the Jĕb'-ū-śīte.

17 And David spake unto the Lᴏʀᴅ when he saw the angel that smote the people, and said, Lo, ᴿI have sinned, and I have done wickedly: but these sheep, what have they done? let thine hand, I pray thee, be against me, and against my father's house.

18 And Gad came that day to David, and said unto him, ᴿGo up, rear an altar unto the Lᴏʀᴅ in the threshingfloor of ᴺĂ-raū'-năh the Jĕb'-ū-śīte.

19 And David, according to the saying of Gad, went up as the Lᴏʀᴅ commanded.

20 And Ă-raū'-năh looked, and saw the king and his servants coming on toward him: and

Ă-raŭ'-năh went out, and bowed himself before the king on his face upon the ground.

21 And Ă-raŭ'-năh said, Wherefore is my lord the king come to his servant? [R]And David said, To buy the threshingfloor of thee, to build an altar unto the LORD, that [R]the plague may be stayed from the people.

22 And Ă-raŭ'-năh said unto David, Let my lord the king take and offer up what *seemeth* good unto him: [R]behold, *here be* oxen for burnt sacrifice, and threshing instruments and *other* instruments of the oxen for wood.

23 All these *things* did Ă-raŭ'-năh, *as* a king,

give unto the king. And Ă-raŭ'-năh said unto the king, The LORD thy God [R]accept thee.

24 And the king said unto Ă-raŭ'-năh, Nay; but I will surely buy *it* of thee at a price: neither will I offer burnt offerings unto the LORD my God of that which doth cost me nothing. So [R]David bought the threshingfloor and the oxen for fifty shē'-kĕls of silver.

25 And David built there an altar unto the LORD, and offered burnt offerings and peace offerings. [R]So the LORD was entreated for the land, and [R]the plague was stayed from Israel.

CHAP. 24	
BC 1017	
21 See Gen. 23:8-16	
21 Num. 16:48, 50	
22 1 Ki. 19:21	
Ezek. 20:40, 41	23
See 1 Chr.	24
21:24, 25	
ch. 21:14	25
ver. 21	25

THE FIRST
BOOK OF THE KINGS

COMMONLY CALLED

THE THIRD BOOK OF THE KINGS

The two books of Kings originally constituted one work and were classified in the ancient Hebrew text as the "Earlier and Former Prophets." First and Second Kings continue the history of Israel and its monarchy and disclose a religious character rather than a mere political record. The period begins with the reign of Solomon, ca. 971, and continues through the destruction of the northern kingdom of Israel, 721 B.C., and the fall of the southern kingdom of Judah, 586 B.C., and ends with the release of Jehoiachin from a Babylonian prison in 562 B.C.

The First Book of Kings records the reign of Solomon and approximately eight decades of the history of the divided kingdom through the reigns of Ahab of Israel and of Jehoshophat of Judah. Various prophets may have provided the records used for the final edition of these books.

OUTLINE OF THE BOOK:
I. The reign of Solomon 1:1-11:43
II. Warfare between the North and the South 12:1-16:20
III. Alliance between Judah and Israel 16:21-22:50

CHAPTER 1

Adonijah usurps the throne

NOW king David was old *and* [N]stricken in years; and they covered him with clothes, but he gat no heat.

2 Wherefore his servants said unto him, [N]Let there be sought for my lord the king [N]a young virgin: and let her stand before the king, and let her [N]cherish him, and let her lie in thy bosom, that my lord the king may get heat.

3 So they sought for a fair damsel throughout all the coasts of Israel, and found Ăb'-ĭ-shăg a [R]Shû-năm'-mīte, and brought her to the king.

4 And the damsel *was* very fair, and cherished the king, and ministered to him: but the king knew her not.

5 Then [R]Ăd-ō-nī'-jăh the son of Hăg'-gīth exalted himself, saying, I will [N]be king: and he prepared him chariots and horsemen, and fifty men to run before him.

6 And his father had not displeased him [N]at

CHAP. 1	
BC 1015	
1 Heb. *entered into days*	
2 Heb. *Let them seek*	
2 Heb. *a damsel, a virgin*	
2 Heb. *be a cherisher unto him*	
3 Josh. 19:18	
5 2 Sam. 3:4	
5 Heb. *reign*	
6 Heb. *from his days*	
2 Sam. 3:3	6
1 Chr. 3:2	
Heb. *his words were with Joab*	7
2 Sam. 20:25	7
ch. 2:22, 28	7
Heb. *helped after Adonijah*	7
ch. 4:18	8
2 Sam. 23:3	8
Or, *The well Rogel,*	9
2 Sam. 17:17	

any time in saying, Why hast thou done so? and he also *was a* very goodly *man;* [R]and *his mother* bare him after Ăb'-să-lŏm.

7 And [N]he conferred with Jō'-ăb the son of Zĕr-ū-ī'-ăh, and with [R]Ă-bī'-ă-thär the priest: and [R]they [N]following Ăd-ō-nī'-jăh helped *him.*

8 But Zā'-dŏk the priest, and Bĕ-nāī'-ăh the son of Jĕ-hoī'-ă-dă, and Nathan the prophet, and [R]Shĭm'-ĕ-ī, and Rē'-ī, and [R]the mighty men which *belonged* to David, were not with Ăd-ō-nī'-jăh.

9 And Ăd-ō-nī'-jăh slew sheep and oxen and fat cattle by the stone of Zō'-hĕ-lĕth, which *is* by [N]Ĕn-rō'-gĕl, and called all his brethren the king's sons, and all the men of Judah the king's servants:

10 But Nathan the prophet, and Bĕ-nāī'-ăh, and the mighty men, and Solomon his brother, he called not.

Nathan and Bath-sheba

11 Wherefore Nathan spake unto Băth'-shĕ-bă the mother of Solomon, saying,

Hast thou not heard that Ăd-o-nī'-jăh the son of ᴿHăg'-gĭth doth reign, and David our lord knoweth *it* not?

12 Now therefore come, let me, I pray thee, give thee counsel, that thou mayest save thine own life, and the life of thy son Solomon.

13 Go and get thee in unto king David, and say unto him, Didst not thou, my lord, O king, swear unto thine handmaid, saying, ᴿAssuredly Solomon thy son shall reign after me, and he shall sit upon my throne? why then doth Ăd-o-nī'-jăh reign?

14 Behold, while thou yet talkest there with the king, I also will come in after thee, and ᴺconfirm thy words.

15 And Băth'-she-bă went in unto the king into the chamber: and the king was very old; and Ăb'-ĭ-shăg the Shû-năm'-mĭte ministered unto the king.

16 And Băth'-she-bă bowed, and did o-beisance unto the king. And the king said, ᴺWhat wouldest thou?

17 And she said unto him, My lord, ᴿthou swarest by the Lᴏʀᴅ thy God unto thine handmaid, *saying,* Assuredly Solomon thy son shall reign after me, and he shall sit upon my throne.

18 And now, behold, Ăd-o-nī'-jăh reigneth; and now, my lord the king, thou knowest *it* not:

19 ᴿAnd he hath slain oxen and fat cattle and sheep in abundance, and hath called all the sons of the king, and Ă-bī'-ă-thär the priest, and Jō'-ăb the captain of the host: but Solomon thy servant hath he not called.

20 And thou, my lord, O king, the eyes of all Israel *are* upon thee, that thou shouldest tell them who shall sit on the throne of my lord the king after him.

21 Otherwise it shall come to pass, when my lord the king shall ᴿsleep with his fathers, that I and my son Solomon shall be counted ᴺoffenders.

22 And, lo, while she yet talked with the king, Nathan the prophet also came in.

23 And they told the king, saying, Behold Nathan the prophet. And when he was come in before the king, he bowed himself before the king with his face to the ground.

24 And Nathan said, My lord, O king, hast thou said, Ăd-o-nī'-jăh shall reign after me, and he shall sit upon my throne?

25 ᴿFor he is gone down this day, and hath slain oxen and fat cattle and sheep in abundance, and hath called all the king's sons, and the captains of the host, and Ă-bī'-ă-thär the priest; and, behold, they eat and drink before

CHAP. 1
BC 1015
11 2 Sam. 3:4
13 1 Chr. 22:9
14 Heb. *fill up*
16 Heb. *What to thee?*
17 ver. 13, 30
19 ver. 7-9, 25
21 Deut. 31:16
ch. 2:10
21 Heb. *sinners*
25 ver. 19

1 Sam. 10:24　25
Heb. *Let king Adonijah live*　25
Heb. *before the king*　28
2 Sam. 4:9　29
ver. 17　30
Neh. 2:3　31
Dan. 2:4
2 Sam. 20:6　33
Heb. *which belongeth to me*: See Esth. 6:8　33
2 Chr. 32:30　33
1 Sam. 10:1 & 16:3, 12　34
2 Sam. 2:4 & 5:3
ch. 19:16
2 Ki. 9:3 & 11:12
2 Sam. 15:10　34
2 Ki. 9:13 & 11:14
Josh. 1:5, 17　37
1 Sam. 20:13
ver. 47　37
2 Sam. 8:18 & 23:20-23　38

him, and say, ᴿGodᴺ save king Ăd-o-nī'-jăh.

26 But me, *even* me thy servant, and Ză'-dŏk the priest, and Bĕ-nāi-ăh the son of Jĕ-hoi'-ă-dă, and thy servant Solomon, hath he not called.

27 Is this thing done by my lord the king, and thou hast not shewed *it* unto thy servant, who should sit on the throne of my lord the king after him?

Solomon appointed king by David

28 Then king David answered and said, Call me Băth'-she-bă. And she came ᴺinto the king's presence, and stood before the king.

29 And the king sware, and said, ᴿ*As* the Lᴏʀᴅ liveth, that hath redeemed my soul out of all distress,

30 ᴿEven as I sware unto thee by the Lᴏʀᴅ God of Israel, saying, Assuredly Solomon thy son shall reign after me, and he shall sit upon my throne in my stead; even so will I certainly do this day.

31 Then Băth'-she-bă bowed with *her* face to the earth, and did reverence to the king, and said, ᴿLet my lord king David live for ever.

32 And king David said, Call me Ză'-dŏk the priest, and Nathan the prophet, and Bĕ-nāi'-ăh the son of Jĕ-hoi'-ă-dă. And they came before the king.

33 The king also said unto them, ᴿTake with you the servants of your lord, and cause Solomon my son to ride upon ᴺmine own mule, and bring him down to ᴿGī'-hŏn:

34 And let Ză'-dŏk the priest and Nathan the prophet ᴿanoint him there king over Israel: and ᴿblow ye with the trumpet, and say, God save king Solomon.

35 Then ye shall come up after him, that he may come and sit upon my throne; for he shall be king in my stead: and I have appointed him to be ruler over Israel and over Judah.

36 And Bĕ-nāi'-ăh the son of Jĕ-hoi'-ă-dă answered the king, and said, Ā'-mĕn: the Lᴏʀᴅ God of my lord the king say so *too.*

37 ᴿAs the Lᴏʀᴅ hath been with my lord the king, even so be he with Solomon, and ᴿmake his throne greater than the throne of my lord king David.

Solomon anointed king at Gihon

38 So Ză'-dŏk the priest, and Nathan the prophet, ᴿand Bĕ-nāi'-ăh the son of Jĕ-hoi'-ă-dă, and the Chĕr'-e-thītes, and the Pĕl'-e-thītes, went down, and caused Solomon to ride upon king David's mule, and brought him to Gī'-hŏn.

39 And Zā'-dŏk the priest took an horn of ᴿoil out of the tabernacle, and ᴿanointed Solomon. And they blew the trumpet; ᴿand all the people said, God save king Solomon.

40 And all the people came up after him, and the people piped with ᴺpipes, and rejoiced with great joy, so that the earth rent with the sound of them.

Adonijah submits

41 And Ăd-ō-nī'-jäh and all the guests that *were* with him heard *it* as they had made an end of eating. And when Jō'-ăb heard the sound of the trumpet, he said, Wherefore *is this* noise of the city being in an uproar?

42 And while he yet spake, behold, Jonathan the son of Ă-bī'-ă-thär the priest came: and Ăd-ō-nī'-jäh said unto him, Come in; for ᴿthou *art* a valiant man, and bringest good tidings.

43 And Jonathan answered and said to Ăd-ō-nī'-jäh, Verily our lord king David hath made Solomon king.

44 And the king hath sent with him Zā'-dŏk the priest, and Nathan the prophet, and Bĕ-nāî'-äh the son of Jĕ-hōî'-ă-dă, and the Chĕr'-ĕ-thītes, and the Pĕl'-ĕ-thītes, and they have caused him to ride upon the king's mule:

45 And Zā'-dŏk the priest and Nathan the prophet have anointed him king in Gī'-hŏn: and they are come up from thence rejoicing, so that the city rang again. This *is* the noise that ye have heard.

46 And also Solomon ᴿsitteth on the throne of the kingdom.

47 And moreover the king's servants came to bless our lord king David, saying, ᴿGod make the name of Solomon better than thy name, and make his throne greater than thy throne. ᴿAnd the king bowed himself upon the bed.

48 And also thus said the king, Blessed *be* the LORD God of Israel, which hath ᴿgiven *one* to sit on my throne this day, mine eyes even seeing *it*.

49 And all the guests that *were* with Ăd-ō-nī'-jäh were afraid, and rose up, and went every man his way.

50 And Ăd-ō-nī'-jäh feared because of Solomon, and arose, and went, and ᴿcaught hold on the horns of the altar.

51 And it was told Solomon, saying, Behold, Ăd-ō-nī'-jäh feareth king Solomon: for, lo, he hath caught hold on the horns of the altar, saying, Let king Solomon swear unto me to day that he will not slay his servant with the sword.

52 And Solomon said, If he will shew him-

self a worthy man, ᴿthere shall not an hair of him fall to the earth: but if wickedness shall be found in him, he shall die.

53 So king Solomon sent, and they brought him down from the altar. And he came and bowed himself to king Solomon: and Solomon said unto him, Go to thine house.

CHAPTER 2

David's advice to Solomon

NOW ᴿthe days of David drew nigh that he should die; and he charged Solomon his son, saying,

2 ᴿI go the way of all the earth: ᴿbe thou strong therefore, and shew thyself a man;

3 And keep the charge of the LORD thy God, to walk in his ways, to keep his statutes, and his commandments, and his judgments, and his testimonies, as it is written in the law of Moses, that thou mayest ᴿprosperᴺ in all that thou doest, and whithersoever thou turnest thyself:

4 That the LORD may ᴿcontinue his word which he spake concerning me, saying, ᴿIf thy children take heed to their way, to ᴿwalk before me in truth with all their heart and with all their soul, ᴿthere shall not ᴺfail thee (said he) a man on the throne of Israel.

5 Moreover thou knowest also what Jō'-ăb the son of Zĕr-ū-ī'-äh ᴿdid to me, *and* what he did to the two captains of the hosts of Israel, unto ᴿAbner the son of Ner, and unto ᴿĂ-mā'-sä the son of Jĕ'-thĕr, whom he slew, and ᴺshed the blood of war in peace, and put the blood of war upon his girdle that *was* about his loins, and in his shoes that *were* on his feet.

6 Do therefore ᴿaccording to thy wisdom, and let not his hoar head go down to the grave in peace.

7 But shew kindness unto the sons of ᴿBär-zĭl-lā'-ī the Gileadite, and let them be of those that ᴿeat at thy table: for so ᴿthey came to me when I fled because of Ăb'-să-lŏm thy brother.

8 And, behold, *thou hast* with thee ᴿShĭm'-ĕ-ī the son of Gē'-rä, a Benjamite of Bă-hū'-rĭm, which cursed me with a ᴺgrievous curse in the day when I went to Mā-hă-nā'-ĭm: but ᴿhe came down to meet me at Jordan, and ᴿI sware to him by the LORD, saying, I will not put thee to death with the sword.

9 Now therefore ᴿhold him not guiltless: for thou *art* a wise man, and knowest what thou oughtest to do unto him; but his hoar head ᴿbring thou down to the grave with blood.

Death of David

10 So ᴿDavid slept with his fathers, and was buried in ᴿthe city of David.

11 And the days that David ᴿreigned over Israel *were* forty years: seven years reigned he in Hē′-brŏn, and thirty and three years reigned he in Jerusalem.

12 ᴿThen sat Solomon upon the throne of David his father; and his kingdom was established greatly.

Adonijah put to death

13 And Ăd-ō-nī′-jăh the son of Hăg′-gĭth came to Băth′-shĕ-bă the mother of Solomon. And she said, ᴿComest thou peaceably? And he said, Peaceably.

14 He said moreover, I have somewhat to say unto thee. And she said, Say on.

15 And he said, Thou knowest that the kingdom was mine, and *that* all Israel set their faces on me, that I should reign: howbeit the kingdom is turned about, and is become my brother's: for ᴿit was his from the LORD.

16 And now I ask one petition of thee, ᴺdeny me not. And she said unto him, Say on.

17 And he said, Speak, I pray thee, unto Solomon the king, (for he will not say thee nay,) that he give me ᴿĂb′-ĭ-shăg the Shū-năm′-mīte to wife.

18 And Băth′-shĕ-bă said, Well; I will speak for thee unto the king.

19 Băth′-shĕ-bă therefore went unto king Solomon, to speak unto him for Ăd-ō-nī′-jăh. And the king rose up to meet her, and ᴿbowed himself unto her, and sat down on his throne, and caused a seat to be set for the king's mother; ᴿand she sat on his right hand.

20 Then she said, I desire one small petition of thee; *I pray thee,* say me not nay. And the king said unto her, Ask on, my mother: for I will not say thee nay.

21 And she said, Let Ăb′-ĭ-shăg the Shū-năm′-mīte be given to Ăd-ō-nī′-jăh thy brother to wife.

22 And king Solomon answered and said unto his mother, And why dost thou ask Ăb′-ĭ-shăg the Shū-năm′-mīte for Ăd-ō-nī′-jăh? ask for him the kingdom also; for he *is* mine elder brother; even for him, and for ᴿĂ-bī′-ă-thär the priest, and for Jō′-ăb the son of Zĕr-ū-ī′-ăh.

23 Then king Solomon sware by the LORD, saying, ᴿGod do so to me, and more also, if Ăd-ō-nī′-jăh have not spoken this word against his own life.

24 Now therefore, *as* the LORD liveth, which

CHAP. 2
BC 1014
10 ch. 1:21
Acts 2:29
& 13:36
10 2 Sam. 5:7
11 2 Sam. 5:4
1 Chr. 29:26, 27
12 1 Chr. 29:23
2 Chr. 1:1
13 1 Sam. 16:4, 5
15 1 Chr. 22:9, 10
& 28:5-7
Dan. 2:21
16 Heb. *turn not away my face*
17 ch. 1:3, 4
19 Ex. 20:12
19 See Ps. 45:9
22 ch. 1:7
23 Ruth 1:17

2 Sam. 7:11, 13   **24**
1 Chr. 22:10
Josh. 21:18   **26**
Heb. *a man of death*   **26**
1 Sam. 23:6   **26**
2 Sam. 15:24, 29
1 Sam. 22:20, 23   **26**
2 Sam. 15:24
1 Sam. 2:31-35   **27**
ch. 1:7   **28**
ch. 1:50   **28**
Ex. 21:14   **31**
Num. 35:33   **31**
Deut. 19:13
& 21:8, 9
Judg. 9:24, 57   **32**
2 Chr. 21:13   **32**
2 Sam. 3:27   **32**
2 Sam. 20:10   **32**
2 Sam. 3:29   **33**
Prov. 25:5   **33**

hath established me, and set me on the throne of David my father, and who hath made me an house, as he ᴿpromised, Ăd-ō-nī′-jăh shall be put to death this day.

25 And king Solomon sent by the hand of Bĕ-nāī′-ăh the son of Jĕ-hoī′-ă-dă; and he fell upon him that he died.

Abiathar expelled from Jerusalem

26 And unto Ă-bī′-ă-thär the priest said the king, Get thee to ᴿĂn′-ă-thŏth, unto thine own fields; for thou *art* ᴺworthy of death: but I will not at this time put thee to death, ᴿbecause thou barest the ark of the Lord GOD before David my father, and because ᴿthou hast been afflicted in all wherein my father was afflicted.

27 So Solomon thrust out Ă-bī′-ă-thär from being priest unto the LORD; that he might ᴿfulfil the word of the LORD, which he spake concerning the house of Ē′-lī in Shī′-lōh.

Joab slain

28 Then tidings came to Jō′-ăb: for Jō′-ăb ᴿhad turned after Ăd-ō-nī′-jăh, though he turned not after Ăb′-să-lǫm. And Jō′-ăb fled unto the tabernacle of the LORD, and ᴿcaught hold on the horns of the altar.

29 And it was told king Solomon that Jō′-ăb was fled unto the tabernacle of the LORD; and, behold, *he is* by the altar. Then Solomon sent Bĕ-nāī′-ăh the son of Jĕ-hoī′-ă-dă, saying, Go, fall upon him.

30 And Bĕ-nāī′-ăh came to the tabernacle of the LORD, and said unto him, Thus saith the king, Come forth. And he said, Nay; but I will die here. And Bĕ-nāī′-ăh brought the king word again, saying, Thus said Jō′-ăb, and thus he answered me.

31 And the king said unto him, ᴿDo as he hath said, and fall upon him, and bury him; ᴿthat thou mayest take away the innocent blood, which Jō′-ăb shed, from me, and from the house of my father.

32 And the LORD ᴿshall return his blood upon his own head, who fell upon two men more righteous ᴿand better than he, and slew them with the sword, my father David not knowing *thereof, to wit,* ᴿAbner the son of Ner, captain of the host of Israel, and ᴿĂ-mā′-să the son of Jē′-thĕr, captain of the host of Judah.

33 Their blood shall therefore return upon the head of Jō′-ăb, and ᴿupon the head of his seed for ever: ᴿbut upon David, and upon his seed, and upon his house, and upon his throne, shall there be peace for ever from the LORD.

34 So Bĕ-nāi'-ăh the son of Jĕ-hói'-ă-dă went up, and fell upon him, and slew him: and he was buried in his own house in the wilderness.

35 And the king put Bĕ-nāi'-ăh the son of Jĕ-hói'-ă-dă in his room over the host: and ᴿZā'-dŏk the priest did the king put in the room of ᴿĂ-bĭ'-ă-thăr.

Death of Shimei

36 And the king sent and called for ᴿShĭm'-ĕ-ī, and said unto him, Build thee an house in Jerusalem, and dwell there, and go not forth thence any whither.

37 For it shall be, *that* on the day thou goest out, and passest over ᴿthe brook Kī'-drŏn, thou shalt know for certain that thou shalt surely die: ᴿthy blood shall be upon thine own head.

38 And Shĭm'-ĕ-ī said unto the king, The saying *is* good: as my lord the king hath said, so will thy servant do. And Shĭm'-ĕ-ī dwelt in Jerusalem many days.

39 And it came to pass at the end of three years, that two of the servants of Shĭm'-ĕ-ī ran away unto ᴿĀ'-chĭsh son of Mā'-ă-chăh king of Gath. And they told Shĭm'-ĕ-ī, saying, Behold, thy servants *be* in Gath.

40 And Shĭm'-ĕ-ī arose, and saddled his ass, and went to Gath to Ā'-chĭsh to seek his servants: and Shĭm'-ĕ-ī went, and brought his servants from Gath.

41 And it was told Solomon that Shĭm'-ĕ-ī had gone from Jerusalem to Gath, and was come again.

42 And the king sent and called for Shĭm'-ĕ-ī, and said unto him, Did I not make thee to swear by the LORD, and protested unto thee, saying, Know for a certain, on the day thou goest out, and walkest abroad any whither, that thou shalt surely die? and thou saidst unto me, The word *that* I have heard *is* good.

43 Why then hast thou not kept the oath of the LORD, and the commandment that I have charged thee with?

44 The king said moreover to Shĭm'-ĕ-ī, Thou knowest ᴿall the wickedness which thine heart is privy to, that thou didst to David my father: therefore the LORD shall ᴿreturn thy wickedness upon thine own head;

45 And king Solomon *shall be* blessed, and ᴿthe throne of David shall be established before the LORD for ever.

46 So the king commanded Bĕ-nāi'-ăh the son of Jĕ-hói'-ă-dă; which went out, and fell upon him, that he died. And the ᴿkingdom was established in the hand of Solomon.

CHAPTER 3

Solomon's marriage alliance

AND ᴿSolomon made affinity with Pharaoh king of Egypt, and took Pharaoh's daughter, and brought her into the ᴿcity of David, until he had made an end of building his ᴿown house, and ᴿthe house of the LORD, and ᴿthe wall of Jerusalem round about.

2 ᴿOnly the people sacrificed in high places, because there was no house built unto the name of the LORD, until those days.

Solomon's prayer for wisdom

3 And Solomon ᴿloved the LORD, ᴿwalking in the statutes of David his father: only he sacrificed and burnt incense in high places.

4 And ᴿthe king went to Gibeon to sacrifice there; ᴿfor that *was* the great high place: a thousand burnt offerings did Solomon offer upon that altar.

5 ᴿIn Gibeon the LORD appeared to Solomon ᴿin a dream by night: and God said, Ask what I shall give thee.

6 ᴿAnd Solomon said, Thou hast shewed unto thy servant David my father great ᴺmercy, according as he ᴿwalked before thee in truth, and in righteousness, and in uprightness of heart with thee; and thou hast kept for him this great kindness, that thou ᴿhast given him a son to sit on his throne, as *it is* this day.

7 And now, O LORD my God, thou hast made thy servant king instead of David my father: and I *am but* a little child: I know not *how* ᴿto go out or come in.

8 And thy servant *is* in the midst of thy people which thou ᴿhast chosen, a great people, ᴿthat cannot be numbered nor counted for multitude.

9 ᴿGive therefore thy servant an ᴺunderstanding heart ᴿto judge thy people, that I may ᴿdiscern between good and bad: for who is able to judge this thy so great a people?

10 And the speech pleased the LORD, that Solomon had asked this thing.

11 And God said unto him, Because thou hast asked this thing, and hast ᴿnot asked for thyself ᴺlong life; neither hast asked riches for thyself, nor hast asked the life of thine enemies; but hast asked for thyself understanding ᴺto discern judgment;

12 ᴿBehold, I have done according to thy words: ᴿlo, I have given thee a wise and an understanding heart; so that there was none like thee before thee, neither after thee shall any arise like unto thee.

13 And I have also ᴿgiven thee that which

thou hast not asked, both ᴿriches, and honour: so that there ᴺshall not be any among the kings like unto thee all thy days.

14 And if thou wilt walk in my ways, to keep my statutes and my commandments, ᴿas thy father David did walk, then I will ᴿlengthen thy days.

15 And Solomon ᴿawoke; and, behold, *it was* a dream. And he came to Jerusalem, and stood before the ark of the covenant of the LORD, and offered up burnt offerings, and offered peace offerings, and ᴿmade a feast to all his servants.

Solomon's wise judgment

16 Then came there two women, *that were* harlots, unto the king, and ᴿstood before him.

17 And the one woman said, O my lord, I and this woman dwell in one house; and I was delivered of a child with her in the house.

18 And it came to pass the third day after that I was delivered, that this woman was delivered also: and we *were* together; *there was* no stranger with us in the house, save we two in the house.

19 And this woman's child died in the night; because she overlaid it.

20 And she arose at midnight, and took my son from beside me, while thine handmaid slept, and laid it in her bosom, and laid her dead child in my bosom.

21 And when I rose in the morning to give my child suck, behold, it was dead: but when I had considered it in the morning, behold, it was not my son, which I did bear.

22 And the other woman said, Nay; but the living *is* my son, and the dead *is* thy son. And this said, No; but the dead *is* thy son, and the living *is* my son. Thus they spake before the king.

23 Then said the king, The one saith, This *is* my son that liveth, and thy son *is* the dead: and the other saith, Nay; but thy son *is* the dead, and my son *is* the living.

24 And the king said, Bring me a sword. And they brought a sword before the king.

25 And the king said, Divide the living child in two, and give half to the one, and half to the other.

26 Then spake the woman whose the living child *was* unto the king, for ᴿher bowels ᴺyearned upon her son, and she said, O my lord, give her the living child, and in no wise slay it. But the other said, Let it be neither mine nor thine, *but* divide *it*.

27 Then the king answered and said, Give her the living child, and in no wise slay it: she *is* the mother thereof.

28 And all Israel heard of the judgment

which the king had judged; and they feared the king: for they saw that the ᴿwisdom of God *was* ᴺin him, to do judgment.

CHAPTER 4
Solomon's high officials

SO king Solomon was king over all Israel. 2 And these *were* the princes which he had; Ăz-ă-rī'-ăh the son of Zā'-dŏk ᴺthe priest,

3 Ē-li-hôr'-ĕph and Ă-hī'-ăh, the sons of Shī'-shă, ᴺscribes; ᴿJĕ-hŏsh'-ă-phăt the son of Ă-hī'-lŭd, the ᴺrecorder.

4 And ᴿBĕ-naī'-ăh the son of Jĕ-hoī'-ă-dă *was* over the host: and Zā'-dŏk and ᴿĂ-bī'-ă-thär *were* the priests:

5 And Ăz-ă-rī'-ăh the son of Nathan *was* over ᴿthe officers: and Zā'-bŭd the son of Nathan *was* ᴿprincipal officer, *and* ᴿthe king's friend:

6 And Ă-hī'-shär *was* over the household: and ᴿĂd-ō-nī'-răm the son of Abda *was* over the ᴺtribute.

Maintenance of Solomon's government

7 And Solomon had twelve officers over all Israel, which provided victuals for the king and his household: each man his month in a year made provision.

8 And these *are* their names: ᴺThe son of Hur, in mount Ē'-phră-ĭm:

9 ᴺThe son of Dē'-kär, in Mā'-kăz, and in Shă-ăl'-bĭm, and Bĕth-shē'-mĕsh, and Ē'-lŏn-bĕth-hā'-năn:

10 ᴺThe son of Hē'-sĕd, in Ă-rū'-bōth; to him *pertained* Sō'-chōh, and all the land of Hē'-phĕr:

11 ᴺThe son of Ă-bĭn'-ă-dăb, in all the region of Dor; which had Tā'-phăth the daughter of Solomon to wife:

12 Bā'-ă-nă the son of Ă-hī'-lŭd; *to him pertained* Tā'-ă-năch and Mĕ-gĭd'-dō, and all Bĕth-shē'-ăn, which *is* by Zăr-tā'-năh beneath Jĕz'-rĕĕl, from Bĕth-shē'-ăn to Ā'-bĕl-mĕ-hō'-lăh, *even* unto *the place that is* beyond Jŏk'-nĕ-ăm:

13 ᴺThe son of Gē'-bĕr, in Rā'-mŏth-gĭl'-ĕ-ăd; to him *pertained* ᴿthe towns of Jā'-ĭr the son of Mă-năs'-sĕh, which *are* in Gilead; to him *also pertained* ᴿthe region of Är'-gŏb, which *is* in Bā'-shăn, threescore great cities with walls and brasen bars:

14 Ă-hĭn'-ă-dăb the son of Ĭd'-dō had ᴺMă-hă-nā'-ĭm:

15 Ă-hī'-mă-ăz *was* in Năph'-tă-lī; he also took Băs'-măth the daughter of Solomon to wife:

16 Bā'-ă-năh the son of Hū'-shaī *was* in Asher and in Ā'-lŏth:

17 Jĕ-hŏsh′-ă-phăt the son of Pä′-rû-ăh, in Ĭs′-să-<u>char</u>:

18 Shĭm′-ĕ-ī the son of Ē′-läh, in Benjamin:

19 Gē′-bĕr the son of Ū′-rī *was* in the country of Gilead, *in* ᴿthe country of Sī′-hŏn king of the Amorites, and of Og king of Bā′-shăn; and *he was* the only officer which *was* in the land.

20 Judah and Israel *were* many, ᴿas the sand which *is* by the sea in multitude, ᴿeating and drinking, and making merry.

21 And ᴿSolomon reigned over all kingdoms from ᴿthe river unto the land of the Philistines, and unto the border of Egypt: ᴿthey brought presents, and served Solomon all the days of his life.

22 And Solomon's ᴺprovision for one day was thirty ᴺmeasures of fine flour, and threescore measures of meal,

23 Ten fat oxen, and twenty oxen out of the pastures, and an hundred sheep, beside harts, and roebucks, and fallowdeer, and fatted fowl.

24 For he had dominion over all *the region* on this side the river, from Tĭph′-săh even to Azzah, over ᴿall the kings on this side the river: and ᴿhe had peace on all sides round about him.

25 And Judah and Israel ᴿdwelt ᴺsafely, ᴿevery man under his vine and under his fig tree, ᴿfrom Dan even to Bēēr-shē′-bă, all the days of Solomon.

26 And ᴿSolomon had forty thousand stalls of ᴿhorses for his chariots, and twelve thousand horsemen.

27 And ᴿthose officers provided victual for king Solomon, and for all that came unto king Solomon's table, every man in his month: they lacked nothing.

28 Barley also and straw for the horses and ᴺdromedaries brought they unto the place where *the officers* were, every man according to his charge.

Solomon's unsurpassed wisdom

29 And ᴿGod gave Solomon wisdom and understanding exceeding much, and largeness of heart, even as the sand that *is* on the sea shore.

30 And Solomon's wisdom excelled the wisdom of all the children ᴿof the east country, and all ᴿthe wisdom of Egypt.

31 For he was ᴿwiser than all men; ᴿthan Ē′-thăn the Ĕz′-ră-hīte, ᴿand Hē′-măn, and <u>Ch</u>ăl′-cŏl, and Där′-dă, the sons of Mā′-hŏl: and his fame was in all nations round about.

32 And ᴿhe spake three thousand proverbs: and his ᴿsongs were a thousand and five.

33 And he spake of trees, from the cedar tree that *is* in Lĕb′-ă-non even unto the hyssop

CHAP. **4**

BC 1014

19 Deut. 3:8
20 Gen. 22:17
ch. 3:8
Prov. 14:28
20 Ps. 72:3, 7
Mic. 4:4
21 2 Chr. 9:26
Ps. 72:8
21 Gen. 15:18
Josh. 1:4
21 Ps. 68:29
& 72:10, 11
22 Heb. *bread*
22 Heb. *cors*
24 Ps. 72:11
24 1 Chr. 22:9
25 See Jer. 23:6
25 Heb. *confidently*
25 Mic. 4:4
Zech. 3:10
25 Judg. 20:1
26 ch. 10:26
2 Chr. 1:14
26 See Deut. 17:16
27 ver. 7
28 Or, *mules,*
or, *swift beasts,*
Esth. 8:14
Mic. 1:13
29 ch. 3:12
30 Gen. 25:6
30 See Acts 7:22
31 ch. 3:12
31 1 Chr. 15:19
Ps. 89, title
31 See 1 Chr. 2:6
& 6:33 & 15:19
Ps. 88, title
32 Prov. 1:1
Eccl. 12:9
32 S. of S. 1:1

ch. 10:1   **34**
2 Chr. 9:1, 23

CHAP. **5**

BC 1014

ver. 10, 18   **1**
2 Chr. 2:3, *Huram*
2 Sam. 5:11   **1**
1 Chr. 14:1
Amos 1:9
2 Chr. 2:3   **2**
1 Chr. 22:8   **3**
& 28:3
ch. 4:24   **4**
1 Chr. 22:9
2 Chr. 2:4   **5**
Heb. *say*   **5**
2 Sam. 7:13   **5**
1 Chr. 17:12
2 Chr. 2:8, 10   **6**
Heb. *say*   **6**
Heb. *heard*   **8**
Heb. *send*   **9**
See Ezra 3:7
Ezek. 27:17   **9**
Acts 12:20
See 2 Chr. 2:10   **11**
Heb. *cors*   **11**

that springeth out of the wall: he spake also of beasts, and of fowl, and of creeping things, and of fishes.

34 And ᴿthere came of all people to hear the wisdom of Solomon, from all kings of the earth, which had heard of his wisdom.

CHAPTER 5

Solomon's agreement with king Hiram

AND ᴿHiram king of Tyre sent his servants unto Solomon; for he had heard that they had anointed him king in the room of his father: ᴿfor Hiram was ever a lover of David.

2 And ᴿSolomon sent to Hiram, saying,

3 Thou knowest how that David my father could not build an house unto the name of the Lᴏʀᴅ his God ᴿfor the wars which were about him on every side, until the Lᴏʀᴅ put them under the soles of his feet.

4 But now the Lᴏʀᴅ my God hath given me ᴿrest on every side, *so that there is* neither adversary nor evil occurrent.

5 ᴿAnd, behold, I ᴺpurpose to build an house unto the name of the Lᴏʀᴅ my God, ᴿas the Lᴏʀᴅ spake unto David my father, saying, Thy son, whom I will set upon thy throne in thy room, he shall build an house unto my name.

6 Now therefore command thou that they hew me ᴿcedar trees out of Lĕb′-ă-non; and my servants shall be with thy servants: and unto thee will I give hire for thy servants according to all that thou shalt ᴺappoint: for thou knowest that *there is* not among us any that can skill to hew timber like unto the Sī-dō′-nī-ăns.

7 And it came to pass, when Hiram heard the words of Solomon, that he rejoiced greatly, and said, Blessed *be* the Lᴏʀᴅ this day, which hath given unto David a wise son over this great people.

8 And Hiram sent to Solomon, saying, I have ᴺconsidered the things which thou sentest to me for: *and* I will do all thy desire concerning timber of cedar, and concerning timber of fir.

9 My servants shall bring *them* down from Lĕb′-ă-non unto the sea: and I will convey them by sea in floats unto the place that thou shalt ᴺappoint me, and will cause them to be discharged there, and thou shalt receive *them:* and thou shalt accomplish my desire, ᴿin giving food for my household.

10 So Hiram gave Solomon cedar trees and fir trees *according to* all his desire.

11 ᴿAnd Solomon gave Hiram twenty thousand ᴺmeasures of wheat *for* food to his

household, and twenty measures of pure oil: thus gave Solomon to Hiram year by year.

12 And the LORD gave Solomon wisdom, [R]as he promised him: and there was peace between Hiram and Solomon; and they two made a league together.

Labour force of Solomon

13 And king Solomon raised a [N]levy out of all Israel; and the levy was thirty thousand men.

14 And he sent them to Lĕb′-ă-nǫn, ten thousand a month by courses: a month they were in Lĕb′-ă-nǫn, *and* two months at home: and [R]Ăd-ō-nī′-răm *was* over the levy.

15 [R]And Solomon had threescore and ten thousand that bare burdens, and fourscore thousand hewers in the mountains;

16 Beside the chief of Solomon's officers which *were* over the work, three thousand and three hundred, which ruled over the people that wrought in the work.

17 And the king commanded, and they brought great stones, costly stones, *and* [R]hewed stones, to lay the foundation of the house.

18 And Solomon's builders and Hiram's builders did hew *them,* and the [N]stonesquarers: so they prepared timber and stones to build the house.

CHAPTER 6

Description of the temple

AND [R]it came to pass in the four hundred and eightieth year after the children of Israel were come out of the land of Egypt, in the fourth year of Solomon's reign over Israel, in the month Zif, which *is* the second month, that [R]he [N]began to build the house of the LORD.

2 And [R]the house which king Solomon built for the LORD, the length thereof *was* threescore cubits, and the breadth thereof twenty *cubits,* and the height thereof thirty cubits.

3 And the porch before the temple of the house, twenty cubits *was* the length thereof, according to the breadth of the house; *and* ten cubits *was* the breadth thereof before the house.

4 And for the house he made [R]windows[N] of narrow lights.

5 And [N]against the wall of the house he built [R]chambers[N] round about, *against* the walls of the house round about, *both* of the temple [R]and of the oracle: and he made [N]chambers round about:

6 The nethermost chamber *was* five cubits broad, and the middle *was* six cubits broad, and the third *was* seven cubits broad: for without *in the wall* of the house he made [N]narrowed rests round about, that *the beams* should not be fastened in the walls of the house.

7 And [R]the house, when it was in building, was built of stone made ready before it was brought thither: so that there was neither hammer nor axe *nor* any tool of iron heard in the house, while it was in building.

8 The door for the middle chamber *was* in the right [N]side of the house: and they went up with winding stairs into the middle *chamber,* and out of the middle into the third.

9 [R]So he built the house, and finished it; and covered the house [N]with beams and boards of cedar.

10 And *then* he built chambers against all the house, five cubits high: and they rested on the house with timber of cedar.

The temple completed

11 And the word of the LORD came to Solomon, saying,

12 *Concerning* this house which thou art in building, [R]if thou wilt walk in my statutes, and execute my judgments, and keep all my commandments to walk in them; then will I perform my word with thee, [R]which I spake unto David thy father:

13 And [R]I will dwell among the children of Israel, and will not [R]forsake my people Israel.

14 So Solomon built the house, and finished it.

15 And he built the walls of the house within with boards of cedar, [N]both the floor of the house, and the walls of the ceiling: *and* he covered *them* on the inside with wood, and covered the floor of the house with planks of fir.

16 And he built twenty cubits on the sides of the house, both the floor and the walls with boards of cedar: he even built *them* for it within, *even* for the oracle, *even* for the [R]most holy *place.*

17 And the house, that *is,* the temple before it, was forty cubits *long.*

18 And the cedar of the house within *was* carved with [N]knops and [N]open flowers: all *was* cedar; there was no stone seen.

19 And the oracle he prepared in the house within, to set there the ark of the covenant of the LORD.

20 And the oracle in the forepart *was* twenty cubits in length, and twenty cubits in breadth, and twenty cubits in the height thereof: and he

overlaid it with ᴺpure gold; and *so* covered the altar *which was of* cedar.

21 So Solomon overlaid the house within with pure gold: and he made a partition by the chains of gold before the oracle; and he overlaid it with gold.

22 And the whole house he overlaid with gold, until he had finished all the house: also ᴿthe whole altar that *was* by the oracle he overlaid with gold.

23 And within the oracle ᴿhe made two chĕr'-ū-bĭms *of* ᴺᴺolive tree, *each* ten cubits high.

24 And five cubits *was* the one wing of the cherub, and five cubits the other wing of the cherub: from the uttermost part of the one wing unto the uttermost part of the other *were* ten cubits.

25 And the other cherub *was* ten cubits: both the chĕr'-ū-bĭms *were* of one measure and one size.

26 The height of the one cherub *was* ten cubits, and so *was it* of the other cherub.

27 And he set the chĕr'-ū-bĭms within the inner house: and ᴿthey ᴺ stretched forth the wings of the chĕr'-ū-bĭms, so that the wing of the one touched the *one* wall, and the wing of the other cherub touched the other wall; and their wings touched one another in the midst of the house.

28 And he overlaid the chĕr'-ū-bĭms with gold.

29 And he carved all the walls of the house round about with carved figures of chĕr'-ū-bĭms and palm trees and ᴺopen flowers, within and without.

30 And the floor of the house he overlaid with gold, within and without.

31 And for the entering of the oracle he made doors *of* olive tree: the lintel *and* side posts *were* ᴺa fifth part *of the wall.*

32 The ᴺtwo doors also *were of* olive tree; and he carved upon them carvings of chĕr'-ū-bĭms and palm trees and ᴺopen flowers, and overlaid *them* with gold, and spread gold upon the chĕr'-ū-bĭms, and upon the palm trees.

33 So also made he for the door of the temple posts *of* olive tree, ᴺa fourth part *of the wall.*

34 And the two doors *were of* fir tree: the ᴿtwo leaves of the one door *were* folding, and the two leaves of the other door *were* folding.

35 And he carved *thereon* chĕr'-ū-bĭms and palm trees and open flowers: and covered *them* with gold fitted upon the carved work.

36 And he built the inner court with three

rows of hewed stone, and a row of cedar beams.

37 ᴿIn the fourth year was the foundation of the house of the Lᴏʀᴅ laid, in the month Zif:

38 And in the eleventh year, in the month Bul, which *is* the eighth month, was the house finished ᴺthroughout all the parts thereof, and according to all the fashion of it. So was he ᴿseven years in building it.

CHAPTER 7

Solomon's house

BUT Solomon was building his own house ᴿthirteen years, and he finished all his house.

2 He built also the house of the forest of Lĕb'-ă-non; the length thereof *was* an hundred cubits, and the breadth thereof fifty cubits, and the height thereof thirty cubits, upon four rows of cedar pillars, with cedar beams upon the pillars.

3 And *it was* covered with cedar above upon the ᴺbeams, that *lay* on forty five pillars, fifteen *in* a row.

4 And *there were* windows *in* three rows, and ᴺlight *was* against light *in* three ranks.

5 And all the ᴺdoors and posts *were* square, with the windows: and light *was* against light *in* three ranks.

6 And he made a porch of pillars; the length thereof *was* fifty cubits, and the breadth thereof thirty cubits: and the porch *was* ᴺbefore them: and the *other* pillars and the thick beam *were* ᴺbefore them.

7 Then he made a porch for the throne where he might judge, *even* the porch of judgment: and *it was* covered with cedar ᴺfrom one side of the floor to the other.

8 And his house where he dwelt *had* another court within the porch, *which* was of the like work. Solomon made also an house for Pharaoh's daughter, ᴿwhom he had taken *to wife,* like unto this porch.

9 All these *were of* costly stones, according to the measures of hewed stones, sawed with saws, within and without, even from the foundation unto the coping, and *so* on the outside toward the great court.

10 And the foundation *was of* costly stones, even great stones, stones of ten cubits, and stones of eight cubits.

11 And above *were* costly stones, after the measures of hewed stones, and cedars.

12 And the great court round about *was* with three rows of hewed stones, and a row of cedar beams, both for the inner court of the

house of the LORD, [R]and for the porch of the house.

Bronzework of the temple

13 And king Solomon sent and fetched [R]Hiram out of Tyre.

14 [R]He *was* [N]a widow's son of the tribe of Năph'-tă-lī, and [R]his father *was* a man of Tyre, a worker in brass: and [R]he was filled with wisdom, and understanding, and cunning to work all works in brass. And he came to king Solomon, and wrought all his work.

15 For he [N]cast [R]two pillars of brass, of eighteen cubits high apiece: and a line of twelve cubits did compass either of them about.

16 And he made two chapiters *of* molten brass, to set upon the tops of the pillars: the height of the one chapiter *was* five cubits, and the height of the other chapiter *was* five cubits:

17 *And* nets of checker work, and wreaths of chain work, for the chapiters which *were* upon the top of the pillars; seven for the one chapiter, and seven for the other chapiter.

18 And he made the pillars, and two rows round about upon the one network, to cover the chapiters that *were* upon the top, with pomegranates: and so did he for the other chapiter.

19 And the chapiters that *were* upon the top of the pillars *were* of lily work in the porch, four cubits.

20 And the chapiters upon the two pillars *had pomegranates* also above, over against the belly which *was* by the network: and the pomegranates *were* [R]two hundred in rows round about upon the other chapiter.

21 [R]And he set up the pillars in the porch of the temple: and he set up the right pillar, and called the name thereof [N]Jā'-<u>ch</u>ĭn: and he set up the left pillar, and called the name thereof [N]Bō'-ăz.

22 And upon the top of the pillars *was* lily work: so was the work of the pillars finished.

23 And he made [R]a molten sea, ten cubits [N]from the one brim to the other: *it was* round all about, and his height *was* five cubits: and a line of thirty cubits did compass it round about.

24 And under the brim of it round about *there were* knops compassing it, ten in a cubit, [R]compassing the sea round about: the knops *were* cast in two rows, when it was cast.

25 It stood upon [R]twelve oxen, three looking toward the north, and three looking toward the west, and three looking toward the south, and three looking toward the east: and the sea *was set* above upon them, and all their hinder parts *were* inward.

CHAP. 7
BC 1005-992
12 John 10:23
Acts 3:11
13 2 Chr. 4:11,
Huram:
See ver. 40
14 2 Chr. 2:14
14 Heb. *the son of a widow woman*
14 2 Chr. 4:16
15 Heb. *fashioned*
15 2 Ki. 25:17
2 Chr. 3:15 & 4:12
Jer. 52:21
20 See 2 Chr. 3:16 & 4:13
Jer. 52:23
21 2 Chr. 3:17
21 i.e. *He shall establish*
21 i.e. *In it is strength*
23 2 Ki. 25:13
2 Chr. 4:2
Jer. 52:17
23 Heb. *from his brim to his brim*
24 2 Chr. 4:3
25 2 Chr. 4:4, 5
Jer. 52:20

See 2 Chr. 4:5   26
Heb. *in the base* 32
Heb. *nakedness* 36
2 Chr. 4:6   38
Heb. *shoulder* 39
Heb. *Hirom:*   40
See ver. 13

26 And it *was* an hand breadth thick, and the brim thereof was wrought like the brim of a cup, with flowers of lilies: it contained [R]two thousand băths.

27 And he made ten bases of brass; four cubits *was* the length of one base, and four cubits the breadth thereof, and three cubits the height of it.

28 And the work of the bases *was* on this manner: they had borders, and the borders *were* between the ledges:

29 And on the borders that *were* between the ledges *were* lions, oxen, and chĕr'-ū-bĭms: and upon the ledges *there was* a base above: and beneath the lions and oxen *were* certain additions made of thin work.

30 And every base had four brasen wheels, and plates of brass: and the four corners thereof had undersetters: under the laver *were* undersetters molten, at the side of every addition.

31 And the mouth of it within the chapiter and above *was* a cubit: but the mouth thereof *was* round *after* the work of the base, a cubit and a half: and also upon the mouth of it *were* gravings with their borders, foursquare, not round.

32 And under the borders *were* four wheels; and the axletrees of the wheels *were* [N]joined to the base: and the height of a wheel *was* a cubit and half a cubit.

33 And the work of the wheels *was* like the work of a chariot wheel: their axletrees, and their naves, and their felloes, and their spokes, *were* all molten.

34 And *there were* four undersetters to the four corners of one base: *and* the undersetters *were* of the very base itself.

35 And in the top of the base *was there* a round compass of half a cubit high: and on the top of the base the ledges thereof and the borders thereof *were* of the same.

36 For on the plates of the ledges thereof, and on the borders thereof, he graved chĕr'-ū-bĭms, lions, and palm trees, according to the [N]proportion of every one, and additions round about.

37 After this *manner* he made the ten bases: all of them had one casting, one measure, *and* one size.

38 Then [R]made he ten lavers of brass: one laver contained forty băths: *and* every laver was four cubits: *and* upon every one of the ten bases one laver.

39 And he put five bases on the right [N]side of the house, and five on the left side of the house: and he set the sea on the right side of the house eastward over against the south.

40 And [N]Hiram made the lavers, and the

shovels, and the basins. So Hiram made an end of doing all the work that he made king Solomon for the house of the LORD:

41 The two pillars, and the *two* bowls of the chapiters that *were* on the top of the two pillars; and the two ᴿnetworks, to cover the two bowls of the chapiters which *were* upon the top of the pillars;

42 And four hundred pomegranates for the two networks, *even* two rows of pomegranates for one network, to cover the two bowls of the chapiters that *were* ᴺupon the pillars;

43 And the ten bases, and ten lavers on the bases;

44 And one sea, and twelve oxen under the sea;

45 ᴿAnd the pots, and the shovels, and the basins: and all these vessels, which Hiram made to king Solomon for the house of the LORD, *were of* ᴺbright brass.

46 ᴿIn the plain of Jordan did the king cast them, ᴺin the clay ground between ᴿSŭc'-cōth and ᴿZăr'-thăn.

47 And Solomon left all the vessels *unweighed,* ᴺbecause they were exceeding many: neither was the weight of the brass ᴺfound out.

48 And Solomon made all the vessels that *pertained* unto the house of the LORD: ᴿthe altar of gold, and ᴿthe table of gold, whereupon ᴿthe shewbread *was,*

49 And the candlesticks of pure gold, five on the right *side,* and five on the left, before the oracle, with the flowers, and the lamps, and the tongs *of* gold,

50 And the bowls, and the snuffers, and the basins, and the spoons, and the ᴺcensers *of* pure gold; and the hinges *of* gold, *both* for the doors of the inner house, the most holy *place, and* for the doors of the house, *to wit,* of the temple.

51 So was ended all the work that king Solomon made for the house of the LORD. And Solomon brought in the ᴺthings ᴿwhich David his father had dedicated; *even* the silver, and the gold, and the vessels, did he put among the treasures of the house of the LORD.

CHAPTER 8

The ark brought into the temple

THEN ᴿSolomon assembled the elders of Israel, and all the heads of the tribes, the ᴺchief of the fathers of the children of Israel, unto king Solomon in Jerusalem, ᴿthat they might bring up the ark of the covenant of the LORD ᴿout of the city of David, which *is* Zion.

2 And all the men of Israel assembled themselves unto king Solomon at the ᴿfeast in the

---

CHAP. 7
BC 1005-992
41 ver. 17, 18
42 Heb. *upon the face of the pillars*
45 Ex. 27:3
2 Chr. 4:16
45 Heb. *made bright,* or, *scoured*
46 2 Chr. 4:17
46 Heb. *in the thickness of the ground*
46 Gen. 33:17
46 Josh. 3:16
47 Heb. *for the exceeding multitude*
47 Heb. *searched,* 1 Chr. 22:14
48 Ex. 37:25, etc.
48 Ex. 37:10, etc.
48 Lev. 24:5-8
50 Heb. *ash pans*
51 Heb. *holy things of David*
51 2 Sam. 8:11

CHAP. 8
BC 1004
1 2 Chr. 5:2, etc.
1 Heb. *princes*
1 2 Sam. 6:17
1 2 Sam. 5:7 & 6:12, 16
2 Lev. 23:34
2 Chr. 7:8

Num. 4:15   3
2 Chr. 1:3   4
2 Sam. 6:13   5
2 Sam. 6:17   6
Ex. 26:33, 34   6
ch. 6:19
ch. 6:27   6
Ex. 25:14   8
Heb. *heads*   8
Or, *ark:* as   8
2 Chr. 5:9
Ex. 25:21   9
Deut. 10:2
Deut. 10:5   9
Heb. 9:4
Ex. 40:20   9
Ex. 34:27, 28   9
Or, *where*   9
Ex. 40:34   10
2 Chr. 6:1, etc.   12
Ps. 18:11   12
2 Sam. 7:13   13
Ps. 132:14   13
2 Sam. 6:18   14
Luke 1:68   15
2 Sam. 7:5, 25   15
ver. 29   16
1 Sam. 16:1   16
2 Sam. 7:8
1 Chr. 28:4
2 Sam. 7:2   17

---

month Ĕ-th'-ă-nĭm, which *is* the seventh month.

3 And all the elders of Israel came, ᴿand the priests took up the ark.

4 And they brought up the ark of the LORD, ᴿand the tabernacle of the congregation, and all the holy vessels that *were* in the tabernacle, even those did the priests and the Levites bring up.

5 And king Solomon, and all the congregation of Israel, that were assembled unto him, *were* with him before the ark, ᴿsacrificing sheep and oxen, that could not be told nor numbered for multitude.

6 And the priests ᴿbrought in the ark of the covenant of the LORD unto ᴿhis place, into the oracle of the house, to the most holy *place, even* ᴿunder the wings of the chĕr'-ū-bĭms.

7 For the chĕr'-ū-bĭms spread forth *their* two wings over the place of the ark, and the chĕr'-ū-bĭms covered the ark and the staves thereof above.

8 And they ᴿdrew out the staves, that the ᴺends of the staves were seen out in the ᴺholy *place* before the oracle, and they were not seen without: and there they are unto this day.

9 ᴿ*There was* nothing in the ark ᴿsave the two tables of stone, which Moses ᴿput there at Hôr'-ĕb, ᴿwhenᴺ the LORD made *a covenant* with the children of Israel, when they came out of the land of Egypt.

10 And it came to pass, when the priests were come out of the holy *place,* that the cloud ᴿfilled the house of the LORD,

11 So that the priests could not stand to minister because of the cloud: for the glory of the LORD had filled the house of the LORD.

12 ᴿThen spake Solomon, The LORD said that he would dwell ᴿin the thick darkness.

13 ᴿI have surely built thee an house to dwell in, ᴿa settled place for thee to abide in for ever.

Solomon's address to the people

14 And the king turned his face about, and ᴿblessed all the congregation of Israel: (and all the congregation of Israel stood;)

15 And he said, ᴿBlessed *be* the LORD God of Israel, which ᴿspake with his mouth unto David my father, and hath with his hand fulfilled *it,* saying,

16 Since the day that I brought forth my people Israel out of Egypt, I chose no city out of all the tribes of Israel to build an house, that ᴿmy name might be therein; but I chose ᴿDavid to be over my people Israel.

17 And ᴿit was in the heart of David my father to build an house for the name of the LORD God of Israel.

18 ᴿAnd the LORD said unto David my father, Whereas it was in thine heart to build an house unto my name, thou didst well that it was in thine heart.

19 Nevertheless ᴿthou shalt not build the house; but thy son that shall come forth out of thy loins, he shall build the house unto my name.

20 And the LORD hath performed his word that he spake, and I am risen up in the room of David my father, and sit on the throne of Israel, ᴿas the LORD promised, and have built an house for the name of the LORD God of Israel.

21 And I have set there a place for the ark, wherein is ᴿthe covenant of the LORD, which he made with our fathers, when he brought them out of the land of Egypt.

Solomon's prayer of dedication

22 And Solomon stood before ᴿthe altar of the LORD in the presence of all the congregation of Israel, and ᴿspread forth his hands toward heaven:

23 And he said, LORD God of Israel, ᴿthere is no God like thee, in heaven above, or on earth beneath, ᴿwho keepest covenant and mercy with thy servants that ᴿwalk before thee with all their heart:

24 Who hast kept with thy servant David my father that thou promisedst him: thou spakest also with thy mouth, and hast fulfilled it with thine hand, as it is this day.

25 Therefore now, LORD God of Israel, keep with thy servant David my father that thou promisedst him, saying, ᴿThereᴺ shall not fail thee a man in my sight to sit on the throne of Israel; ᴺso that thy children take heed to their way, that they walk before me as thou hast walked before me.

26 ᴿAnd now, O God of Israel, let thy word, I pray thee, be verified, which thou spakest unto thy servant David my father.

27 But ᴿwill God indeed dwell on the earth? behold, the heaven and ᴿheaven of heavens cannot contain thee; how much less this house that I have builded?

28 Yet have thou respect unto the prayer of thy servant, and to his supplication, O LORD my God, to hearken unto the cry and to the prayer, which thy servant prayeth before thee to day:

29 That thine eyes may be open toward this house night and day, even toward the place of which thou hast said, ᴿMy name shall be there: that thou mayest hearken unto the prayer which thy servant shall make ᴿtowardᴺ this place.

30 ᴿAnd hearken thou to the supplication of

thy servant, and of thy people Israel, when they shall pray ᴺtoward this place: and hear thou in heaven thy dwelling place: and when thou hearest, forgive.

31 If any man trespass against his neighbour, ᴺand ᴿan oath be laid upon him to cause him to swear, and the oath come before thine altar in this house:

32 Then hear thou in heaven, and do, and judge thy servants, ᴿcondemning the wicked, to bring his way upon his head; and justifying the righteous, to give him according to his righteousness.

33 ᴿWhen thy people Israel be smitten down before the enemy, because they have sinned against thee, and ᴿshall turn again to thee, and confess thy name, and pray, and make supplication unto thee ᴺin this house:

34 Then hear thou in heaven, and forgive the sin of thy people Israel, and bring them again unto the land which thou gavest unto their fathers.

35 ᴿWhen heaven is shut up, and there is no rain, because they have sinned against thee; if they pray toward this place, and confess thy name, and turn from their sin, when thou afflictest them:

36 Then hear thou in heaven, and forgive the sin of thy servants, and of thy people Israel, that thou ᴿteach them ᴿthe good way wherein they should walk, and give rain upon thy land, which thou hast given to thy people for an inheritance.

37 ᴿIf there be in the land famine, if there be pestilence, blasting, mildew, locust, or if there be caterpiller; if their enemy besiege them in the land of their ᴺcities; whatsoever plague, whatsoever sickness there be;

38 What prayer and supplication soever be made by any man, or by all thy people Israel, which shall know every man the plague of his own heart, and spread forth his hands toward this house:

39 Then hear thou in heaven thy dwelling place, and forgive, and do, and give to every man according to his ways, whose heart thou knowest; (for thou, even thou only, ᴿknowest the hearts of all the children of men;)

40 ᴿThat they may fear thee all the days that they live in the land which thou gavest unto our fathers.

41 Moreover concerning a stranger, that is not of thy people Israel, but cometh out of a far country for thy name's sake;

42 (For they shall hear of thy great name, and of thy ᴿstrong hand, and of thy stretched out arm;) when he shall come and pray toward this house;

43 Hear thou in heaven thy dwelling place, and do according to all that the stranger calleth to thee for: ᴿthat all people of the earth may know thy name, to ᴿfear thee, as *do* thy people Israel; and that they may know that ᴺthis house, which I have builded, is called by thy name.

44 If thy people go out to battle against their enemy, whithersoever thou shalt send them, and shall pray unto the Lᴏʀᴅ ᴺtoward the city which thou hast chosen, and *toward* the house that I have built for thy name:

45 Then hear thou in heaven their prayer and their supplication, and maintain their ᴺcause.

46 If they sin against thee, (ᴿfor *there is* no man that sinneth not,) and thou be angry with them, and deliver them to the enemy, so that they carry them away captives ᴿunto the land of the enemy, far or near;

47 ᴿ*Yet* if they shall ᴺbethink themselves in the land whither they were carried captives, and repent, and make supplication unto thee in the land of them that carried them captives, ᴿsaying, We have sinned, and have done perversely, we have committed wickedness;

48 And *so* ᴿreturn unto thee with all their heart, and with all their soul, in the land of their enemies, which led them away captive, and ᴿpray unto thee toward their land, which thou gavest unto their fathers, the city which thou hast chosen, and the house which I have built for thy name:

49 Then hear thou their prayer and their supplication in heaven thy dwelling place, and maintain their ᴺcause,

50 And forgive thy people that have sinned against thee, and all their transgressions wherein they have transgressed against thee, and ᴿgive them compassion before them who carried them captive, that they may have compassion on them:

51 For ᴿthey *be* thy people, and thine inheritance, which thou broughtest forth out of Egypt, ᴿfrom the midst of the furnace of iron:

52 That thine eyes may be open unto the supplication of thy servant, and unto the supplication of thy people Israel, to hearken unto them in all that they call for unto thee.

53 For thou didst separate them from among all the people of the earth, *to be* thine inheritance, ᴿas thou spakest by the hand of Moses thy servant, when thou broughtest our fathers out of Egypt, O Lord Gᴏᴅ.

Solomon blesses the people

54 And it was *so,* that when Solomon had made an end of praying all this prayer and

supplication unto the Lᴏʀᴅ, he arose from before the altar of the Lᴏʀᴅ, from kneeling on his knees with his hands spread up to heaven.

55 And he stood, ᴿand blessed all the congregation of Israel with a loud voice, saying,

56 Blessed *be* the Lᴏʀᴅ, that hath given rest unto his people Israel, according to all that he promised: ᴿthere hath not ᴺfailed one word of all his good promise, which he promised by the hand of Moses his servant.

57 The Lᴏʀᴅ our God be with us, as he was with our fathers: ᴿlet him not leave us, nor forsake us:

58 That he may ᴿincline our hearts unto him, to walk in all his ways, and to keep his commandments, and his statutes, and his judgments, which he commanded our fathers.

59 And let these my words, wherewith I have made supplication before the Lᴏʀᴅ, be nigh unto the Lᴏʀᴅ our God day and night, that he maintain the cause of his servant, and the cause of his people Israel ᴺat all times, as the matter shall require:

60 ᴿThat all the people of the earth may know that ᴿthe Lᴏʀᴅ *is* God, *and that there is* none else.

61 Let your ᴿheart therefore be perfect with the Lᴏʀᴅ our God, to walk in his statutes, and to keep his commandments, as at this day.

Solomon's sacrifice

62 And ᴿthe king, and all Israel with him, offered sacrifice before the Lᴏʀᴅ.

63 And Solomon offered a sacrifice of peace offerings, which he offered unto the Lᴏʀᴅ, two and twenty thousand oxen, and an hundred and twenty thousand sheep. So the king and all the children of Israel dedicated the house of the Lᴏʀᴅ.

64 ᴿThe same day did the king hallow the middle of the court that *was* before the house of the Lᴏʀᴅ: for there he offered burnt offerings, and meat offerings, and the fat of the peace offerings: because ᴿthe brasen altar that *was* before the Lᴏʀᴅ *was* too little to receive the burnt offerings, and meat offerings, and the fat of the peace offerings.

65 And at that time Solomon held ᴿa feast, and all Israel with him, a great congregation, from ᴿthe entering in of Hā′-măth unto ᴿthe river of Egypt, before the Lᴏʀᴅ our God, ᴿseven days and seven days, *even* fourteen days.

66 ᴿOn the eighth day he sent the people away: and they ᴺblessed the king, and went unto their tents joyful and glad of heart for all

the goodness that the LORD had done for David his servant, and for Israel his people.

CHAPTER 9

God's covenant with Solomon

AND ᴿit came to pass, when Solomon had finished the building of the house of the LORD, ᴿand the king's house, and ᴿall Solomon's desire which he was pleased to do,

2 That the LORD appeared to Solomon the second time, ᴿas he had appeared unto him at Gibeon.

3 And the LORD said unto him, ᴿI have heard thy prayer and thy supplication, that thou hast made before me: I have hallowed this house, which thou hast built, ᴿto put my name there for ever; ᴿand mine eyes and mine heart shall be there perpetually.

4 And if thou wilt ᴿwalk before me, ᴿas David thy father walked, in integrity of heart, and in uprightness, to do according to all that I have commanded thee, and wilt keep my statutes and my judgments:

5 Then I will establish the throne of thy kingdom upon Israel for ever, ᴿas I promised to David thy father, saying, There shall not fail thee a man upon the throne of Israel.

6 ᴿBut if ye shall at all turn from following me, ye or your children, and will not keep my commandments and my statutes which I have set before you, but go and serve other gods, and worship them:

7 ᴿThen will I cut off Israel out of the land which I have given them; and this house, which I have hallowed ᴿfor my name, will I cast out of my sight; ᴿand Israel shall be a proverb and a byword among all people:

8 And ᴿat this house, which is high, every one that passeth by it shall be astonished, and shall hiss; and they shall say, ᴿWhy hath the LORD done thus unto this land, and to this house?

9 And they shall answer, Because they forsook the LORD their God, who brought forth their fathers out of the land of Egypt, and have taken hold upon other gods, and have worshipped them, and served them: therefore hath the LORD brought upon them all this evil.

Hiram's disappointment

10 And ᴿit came to pass at the end of twenty years, when Solomon had built the two houses, the house of the LORD, and the king's house,

11 ᴿ(Now Hiram the king of Tyre had furnished Solomon with cedar trees and fir trees, and with gold, according to all his desire,) that

then king Solomon gave Hiram twenty cities in the land of Galilee.

12 And Hiram came out from Tyre to see the cities which Solomon had given him; and they ᴺpleased him not.

13 And he said, What cities are these which thou hast given me, my brother? ᴿAnd he called them the land of ᴺCā'-bûl unto this day.

14 And Hiram sent to the king sixscore talents of gold.

Solomon's forced labour

15 And this is the reason of ᴿthe levy which king Solomon raised; for to build the house of the LORD, and his own house, and ᴿMĭl'-lō, and the wall of Jerusalem, and ᴿHā'-zôr, and ᴿMĕ-gĭd'-dō, and ᴿGē'-zĕr.

16 For Pharaoh king of Egypt had gone up, and taken Gē'-zĕr, and burnt it with fire, ᴿand slain the Canaanites that dwelt in the city, and given it for a present unto his daughter, Solomon's wife.

17 And Solomon built Gē'-zĕr, and ᴿBĕth-hôr'-ŏn the nether,

18 And ᴿBā'-ă-lăth, and Tăd'-môr in the wilderness, in the land,

19 And all the cities of store that Solomon had, and cities for ᴿhis chariots, and cities for his horsemen, and ᴺthat which Solomon ᴿdesired to build in Jerusalem, and in Lĕb'-ă-nọn, and in all the land of his dominion.

20 ᴿAnd all the people that were left of the Amorites, Hittites, Pĕ-rĭz'-zītes, Hī'-vītes, and Jĕb'-ū-śītes, which were not of the children of Israel,

21 Their children ᴿthat were left after them in the land, ᴿwhom the children of Israel also were not able utterly to destroy, ᴿupon those did Solomon levy a tribute of ᴿbondservice unto this day.

22 But of the children of Israel did Solomon ᴿmake no bondmen: but they were men of war, and his servants, and his princes, and his captains, and rulers of his chariots, and his horsemen.

23 These were the chief of the officers that were over Solomon's work, ᴿfive hundred and fifty, which bare rule over the people that wrought in the work.

24 But ᴿPharaoh's daughter came up out of the city of David unto ᴿher house which Solomon had built for her: ᴿthen did he build Mĭl'-lō.

25 ᴿAnd three times in a year did Solomon offer burnt offerings and peace offerings upon the altar which he built unto the LORD, and he burnt incense ᴺupon the altar that was before the LORD. So he finished the house.

Fleet of Solomon

26 And ᴿking Solomon made a navy of ships in ᴿE̅'-zĭ-ŏn-ge̅'-bĕr, which *is* beside E̅'-lŏth, on the ᴺshore of the Red sea, in the land of E̅'-dǫm.

27 ᴿAnd Hiram sent in the navy his servants, shipmen that had knowledge of the sea, with the servants of Solomon.

28 And they came to ᴿO̅'-phĭr, and fetched from thence gold, four hundred and twenty talents, and brought *it* to king Solomon.

CHAPTER 10

Visit of queen of Sheba

AND when the ᴿqueen of She̅'-bă heard of the fame of Solomon concerning the name of the Lᴏʀᴅ, she came ᴿto prove him with hard questions.

2 And she came to Jerusalem with a very great train, with camels that bare spices, and very much gold, and precious stones: and when she was come to Solomon, she communed with him of all that was in her heart.

3 And Solomon told her all her ᴺquestions: there was not *any* thing hid from the king, which he told her not.

4 And when the queen of She̅'-bă had seen all Solomon's wisdom, and the house that he had built,

5 And the meat of his table, and the sitting of his servants, and the ᴺattendance of his ministers, and their apparel, and his ᴺcup-bearers, ᴿand his ascent by which he went up unto the house of the Lᴏʀᴅ; there was no more spirit in her.

6 And she said to the king, It was a true ᴺreport that I heard in mine own land of thy ᴺacts and of thy wisdom.

7 Howbeit I believed not the words, until I came, and mine eyes had seen *it:* and, behold, the half was not told me: ᴺthy wisdom and prosperity exceedeth the fame which I heard.

8 ᴿHappy *are* thy men, happy *are* these thy servants, which stand continually before thee, *and* that hear thy wisdom.

9 ᴿBlessed be the Lᴏʀᴅ thy God, which delighted in thee, to set thee on the throne of Israel: because the Lᴏʀᴅ loved Israel for ever, therefore made he thee king, ᴿto do judgment and justice.

10 And she ᴿgave the king an hundred and twenty talents of gold, and of spices very great store, and precious stones: there came no more such abundance of spices as these which the queen of She̅'-bă gave to king Solomon.

11 ᴿAnd the navy also of Hiram, that

brought gold from O̅'-phĭr, brought in from O̅'-phĭr great plenty of ᴺăl'-mŭg trees, and precious stones.

12 ᴿAnd the king made of the ăl'-mŭg trees ᴺᴺpillars for the house of the Lᴏʀᴅ, and for the king's house, harps also and psalteries for singers: there came no such ᴿăl'-mŭg trees, nor were seen unto this day.

13 And king Solomon gave unto the queen of She̅'-bă all her desire, whatsoever she asked, beside *that* which Solomon gave her ᴺof his royal bounty. So she turned and went to her own country, she and her servants.

Wealth of Solomon

14 Now the weight of gold that came to Solomon in one year was six hundred three-score and six talents of gold,

15 Beside *that he had* of the merchantmen, and of the traffick of the spice merchants, and ᴿof all the kings of Arabia, and of the ᴺgovernors of the country.

16 And king Solomon made two hundred targets *of* beaten gold: six hundred *she̅'-kĕls* of gold went to one target.

17 And *he made* ᴿthree hundred shields *of* beaten gold; three pound of gold went to one shield: and the king put them in the ᴿhouse of the forest of Lĕb'-ă-nǫn.

18 ᴿMoreover the king made a great throne of ivory, and overlaid it with the best gold.

19 The throne had six steps, and the top of the throne *was* round ᴺbehind: and *there were* ᴺstays on either side on the place of the seat, and two lions stood beside the stays.

20 And twelve lions stood there on the one side and on the other upon the six steps: there was not ᴺthe like made in any kingdom.

21 ᴿAnd all king Solomon's drinking vessels *were of* gold, and all the vessels of the house of the forest of Lĕb'-ă-nǫn *were of* pure gold; ᴺnone *were of* silver: it was nothing accounted of in the days of Solomon.

22 For the king had at sea a navy of ᴿThär'-shĭsh with the navy of Hiram: once in three years came the navy of Thär'-shĭsh, bringing gold, and silver, ᴺivory, and apes, and peacocks.

23 So ᴿking Solomon exceeded all the kings of the earth for riches and for wisdom.

24 And all the earth ᴺsought to Solomon, to hear his wisdom, which God had put in his heart.

25 And they brought every man his present, vessels of silver, and vessels of gold, and garments, and armour, and spices, horses, and mules, a rate year by year.

26 ᴿAnd Solomon ᴿgathered together char-

iots and horsemen: and he had a thousand and four hundred chariots, and twelve thousand horsemen, whom he bestowed in the cities for chariots, and with the king at Jerusalem.

27 ᴿAnd the king ᴺmade silver *to be* in Jerusalem as stones, and cedars made he *to be* as the sycomore trees that *are* in the vale, for abundance.

28 ᴿAndᴺ Solomon had horses brought out of Egypt, and linen yarn: the king's merchants received the linen yarn at a price.

29 And a chariot came up ·and went out of Egypt for six hundred *shḗ'-kĕls* of silver, and an horse for an hundred and fifty: ᴿand so for all the kings of the Hittites, and for the kings of Syria, did they bring *them* out ᴺby their means.

CHAPTER 11

Solomon's foreign wives

BUT ᴿking Solomon loved ᴿmany strange women, ᴺtogether with the daughter of Pharaoh, women of the Moabites, Ammonites, Ē'-dŏm-ītes, Zĭ-dō'-nĭ-ăns, *and* Hittites;

2 Of the nations *concerning* which the LORD said unto the children of Israel, ᴿYe shall not go in to them, neither shall they come in unto you: *for* surely they will turn away your heart after their gods: Solomon clave unto these in love.

3 And he had seven hundred wives, princesses, and three hundred concubines: and his wives turned away his heart.

4 For it came to pass, when Solomon was old, ᴿ*that* his wives turned away his heart after other gods: and his ᴿheart was not perfect with the LORD his God, ᴿas *was* the heart of David his father.

5 For Solomon went after ᴿĂsh'-tō-rĕth the goddess of the Zĭ-dō'-nĭ-ăns, and after ᴺMĭl'-cŏm the abomination of the Ammonites.

6 And Solomon did evil in the sight of the LORD, and ᴺwent not fully after the LORD, as *did* David his father.

7 ᴿThen did Solomon build an high place for ᴿChē'-mŏsh, the abomination of Moab, in ᴿthe hill that *is* before Jerusalem, and for Molech, the abomination of the children of Ammon.

8 And likewise did he for all his strange wives, which burnt incense and sacrificed unto their gods.

Disobedience of Solomon

9 And the LORD was angry with Solomon, because his heart was turned from the LORD God of Israel, ᴿwhich had appeared unto him twice,

CHAP. **10**
BC 992
27 2 Chr. 1:15-17
27 Heb. *gave*
28 Deut. 17:16
2 Chr. 1:16
& 9:28
28 Heb. *And the going forth of the horses which* was *Solomon's*
29 Josh. 1:4
2 Ki. 7:6
29 Heb. *by their hand*

CHAP. **11**
BC 984
1 Neh. 13:26
1 Deut. 17:17
1 Or, *beside*
2 Ex. 34:16
Deut. 7:3, 4
4 Deut. 17:17
Neh. 13:26
4 ch. 8:61
4 ch. 9:4
5 ver. 33
Judg. 2:13
2 Ki. 23:13
5 Called *Molech*, ver. 7
6 Heb. *fulfilled not after*, Num. 14:24
7 Num. 33:52
7 Num. 21:29
Judg. 11:24
7 2 Ki. 23:13
9 ch. 3:5 & 9:2

ch. 6:12 & 9:6　**10**
Heb. *is with thee*　**11**
ver. 31　**11**
ch. 12:15, 16
2 Sam. 7:15　**13**
ch. 12:20　**13**
Deut. 12:11　**13**
1 Chr. 5:26　**14**
2 Sam. 8:14　**15**
1 Chr. 18:12
Num. 24:19　**15**
Deut. 20:13
ch. 2:10, 34　**21**
Heb. *Send me away*　**21**
Heb. *Not*　**22**

10 And ᴿhad commanded him concerning this thing, that he should not go after other gods: but he kept not that which the LORD commanded.

11 Wherefore the LORD said unto Solomon, Forasmuch as this ᴺis done of thee, and thou hast not kept my covenant and my statutes, which I have commanded thee, ᴿI will surely rend the kingdom from thee, and will give it to thy servant.

12 Notwithstanding in thy days I will not do it for David thy father's sake: *but* I will rend it out of the hand of thy son.

13 ᴿHowbeit I will not rend away all the kingdom; *but* will give ᴿone tribe to thy son for David my servant's sake, and for Jerusalem's sake ᴿwhich I have chosen.

Adversaries of Solomon

14 And the LORD ᴿstirred up an adversary unto Solomon, Hā'-dăd the Ē'-dŏm-īte: he *was* of the king's seed in Ē'-dŏm.

15 ᴿFor it came to pass, when David was in Ē'-dŏm, and Jō'-ăb the captain of the host was gone up to bury the slain, ᴿafter he had smitten every male in Ē'-dŏm;

16 (For six months did Jō'-ăb remain there with all Israel, until he had cut off every male in Ē'-dŏm:)

17 That Hā'-dăd fled, he and certain Ē'-dŏm-ītes of his father's servants with him, to go into Egypt; Hā'-dăd *being* yet a little child.

18 And they arose out of Mĭd'-ĭ-ăn, and came to Pâr'-ăn: and they took men with them out of Pâr'-ăn, and they came to Egypt, unto Pharaoh king of Egypt; which gave him an house, and appointed him victuals, and gave him land.

19 And Hā'-dăd found great favour in the sight of Pharaoh, so that he gave him to wife the sister of his own wife, the sister of Täh'-pĕn-ēś the queen.

20 And the sister of Täh'-pĕn-ēś bare him Gĕ-nū'-băth his son, whom Täh'-pĕn-ēś weaned in Pharaoh's house: and Gĕ-nū'-băth was in Pharaoh's household among the sons of Pharaoh.

21 ᴿAnd when Hā'-dăd heard in Egypt that David slept with his fathers, and that Jō'-ăb the captain of the host was dead, Hā'-dăd said to Pharaoh, ᴺLet me depart, that I may go to mine own country.

22 Then Pharaoh said unto him, But what hast thou lacked with me, that, behold, thou seekest to go to thine own country? And he answered, ᴺNothing: howbeit let me go in any wise.

23 And God stirred him up *another* adver-

sary, Rē′-zŏn the son of Ē-lī′-ă-dăh, which fled from his lord ᴿHăd-ă-dē′-zĕr king of Zō′-băh:

24 And he gathered men unto him, and became captain over a band, ᴿwhen David slew them *of Zō′-băh:* and they went to Damascus, and dwelt therein, and reigned in Damascus.

25 And he was an adversary to Israel all the days of Solomon, beside the mischief that Hā′-dăd *did:* and he abhorred Israel, and reigned over Syria.

Prophecy of Ahijah

26 And ᴿJĕr-ŏ-bō′-ăm the son of Nē′-băt, an ĕph′-ră-thīte of Zĕr′-ĕ-dă, Solomon's servant, whose mother's name *was* Zĕ-rû′-ăh, a widow woman, even he ᴿlifted up *his* hand against the king.

27 And this *was* the cause that he lifted up *his* hand against the king: ᴿSolomon built Mĭl′-lō, *and* ᴺrepaired the breaches of the city of David his father.

28 And the man Jĕr-ŏ-bō′-ăm *was* a mighty man of valour: and Solomon seeing the young man that he ᴺwas industrious, he made him ruler over all the ᴺcharge of the house of Joseph.

29 And it came to pass at that time when Jĕr-ŏ-bō′-ăm went out of Jerusalem, that the prophet ᴿĂ-hī′-jăh the Shī′-lō-nīte found him in the way; and he had clad himself with a new garment; and they two *were* alone in the field:

30 And Ă-hī′-jăh caught the new garment that *was* on him, and ᴿrent it *in* twelve pieces:

31 And he said to Jĕr-ŏ-bō′-ăm, Take thee ten pieces: for ᴿthus saith the Lᴏʀᴅ, the God of Israel, Behold, I will rend the kingdom out of the hand of Solomon, and will give ten tribes to thee:

32 (But he shall have one tribe for my servant David's sake, and for Jerusalem's sake, the city which I have chosen out of all the tribes of Israel:)

33 ᴿBecause that they have forsaken me, and have worshipped Ăsh′-tō-rĕth the goddess of the Zī-dō′-nĭ-ăns, Chē′-mŏsh the god of the Moabites, and Mĭl′-cŏm the god of the children of Ammon, and have not walked in my ways, to do *that which is* right in mine eyes, and *to keep* my statutes and my judgments, as *did* David his father.

34 Howbeit I will not take the whole kingdom out of his hand: but I will make him prince all the days of his life for David my servant's sake, whom I chose, because he kept my commandments and my statutes:

35 But ᴿI will take the kingdom out of his son's hand, and will give it unto thee, *even* ten tribes.

36 And unto his son will I give one tribe,

that ᴿDavid my servant may have a ᴺlight alway before me in Jerusalem, the city which I have chosen me to put my name there.

37 And I will take thee, and thou shalt reign according to all that thy soul desireth, and shalt be king over Israel.

38 And it shall be, if thou wilt hearken unto all that I command thee, and wilt walk in my ways, and do *that is* right in my sight, to keep my statutes and my commandments, as David my servant did; that ᴿI will be with thee, and ᴿbuild thee a sure house, as I built for David, and will give Israel unto thee.

39 And I will for this afflict the seed of David, but not for ever.

40 Solomon sought therefore to kill Jĕr-ŏ-bō′-ăm. And Jĕr-ŏ-bō′-ăm arose, and fled into Egypt, unto Shī′-shăk king of Egypt, and was in Egypt until the death of Solomon.

Death of Solomon

41 And ᴿthe rest of the ᴺacts of Solomon, and all that he did, and his wisdom, *are* they not written in the book of the acts of Solomon?

42 ᴿAnd the ᴺtime that Solomon reigned in Jerusalem over all Israel *was* forty years.

43 ᴿAnd Solomon slept with his fathers, and was buried in the city of David his father: and ᴿRē-hŏ-bō′-ăm his son reigned in his stead.

CHAPTER 12

Rehoboam succeeds Solomon

AND ᴿRē-hŏ-bō′-ăm went to Shē′-chĕm: for all Israel were come to Shē′-chĕm to make him king.

2 And it came to pass, when ᴿJĕr-ŏ-bō′-ăm the son of Nē′-băt, who was yet in ᴿEgypt, heard *of it,* (for he was fled from the presence of king Solomon, and Jĕr-ŏ-bō′-ăm dwelt in Egypt;)

3 That they sent and called him. And Jĕr-ŏ-bō′-ăm and all the congregation of Israel came, and spake unto Rē-hŏ-bō′-ăm, saying,

4 Thy father made our ᴿyoke grievous: now therefore make thou the grievous service of thy father, and his heavy yoke which he put upon us, lighter, and we will serve thee.

5 And he said unto them, Depart yet *for* three days, then come again to me. And the people departed.

6 And king Rē-hŏ-bō′-ăm consulted with the old men, that stood before Solomon his father while he yet lived, and said, How do ye advise that I may answer this people?

7 And they spake unto him, saying, ᴿIf thou wilt be a servant unto this people this day, and wilt serve them, and answer them, and speak

good words to them, then they will be thy servants for ever.

8 But he forsook the counsel of the old men, which they had given him, and consulted with the young men that were grown up with him, *and* which stood before him:

9 And he said unto them, What counsel give ye that we may answer this people, who have spoken to me, saying, Make the yoke which thy father did put upon us lighter?

10 And the young men that were grown up with him spake unto him, saying, Thus shalt thou speak unto this people that spake unto thee, saying, Thy father made our yoke heavy, but make thou *it* lighter unto us; thus shalt thou say unto them, My little *finger* shall be thicker than my father's loins.

11 And now whereas my father did lade you with a heavy yoke, I will add to your yoke: my father hath chastised you with whips, but I will chastise you with scorpions.

12 So Jĕr-ŏ-bō′-ăm and all the people came to Rē-hŏ-bō′-ăm the third day, as the king had appointed, saying, Come to me again the third day.

13 And the king answered the people ᴺroughly, and forsook the old men's counsel that they gave him;

14 And spake to them after the counsel of the young men, saying, My father made your yoke heavy, and I will add to your yoke: my father *also* chastised you with whips, but I will chastise you with scorpions.

15 Wherefore the king hearkened not unto the people; for ᴿthe cause was from the LORD, that he might perform his saying, which the LORD ᴿspake by Ă-hī′-jăh the Shī′-lō-nīte unto Jĕr-ŏ-bō′-ăm the son of Nē′-băt.

Jeroboam, king of the ten tribes

16 So when all Israel saw that the king hearkened not unto them, the people answered the king, saying, ᴿWhat portion have we in David? neither *have we* inheritance in the son of Jesse: to your tents, O Israel: now see to thine own house, David. So Israel departed unto their tents.

17 But ᴿas for the children of Israel which dwelt in the cities of Judah, Rē-hŏ-bō′-ăm reigned over them.

18 Then king Rē-hŏ-bō′-ăm ᴿsent Ă-dôr′-ăm, who *was* over the tribute; and all Israel stoned him with stones, that he died. Therefore king Rē-hŏ-bō′-ăm ᴺmade speed to get him up to his chariot, to flee to Jerusalem.

19 So ᴿIsrael ᴺrebelled against the house of David unto this day.

20 And it came to pass, when all Israel heard that Jĕr-ŏ-bō′-ăm was come again, that they sent and called him unto the congregation, and made him king over all Israel: there was none that followed the house of David, but the tribe of Judah ᴿonly.

21 And when ᴿRē-hŏ-bō′-ăm was come to Jerusalem, he assembled all the house of Judah, with the tribe of Benjamin, an hundred and fourscore thousand chosen men, which were warriors, to fight against the house of Israel, to bring the kingdom again to Rē-hŏ-bō′-ăm the son of Solomon.

22 But ᴿthe word of God came unto Shĕm-ā′-ăh the man of God, saying,

23 Speak unto Rē-hŏ-bō′-ăm, the son of Solomon, king of Judah, and unto all the house of Judah and Benjamin, and to the remnant of the people, saying,

24 Thus saith the LORD, Ye shall not go up, nor fight against your brethren the children of Israel: return every man to his house; ᴿfor this thing is from me. They hearkened therefore to the word of the LORD, and returned to depart, according to the word of the LORD.

Golden calves of Jeroboam

25 Then Jĕr-ŏ-bō′-ăm ᴿbuilt Shē′-chĕm in mount Ē′-phră-ĭm, and dwelt therein; and went out from thence, and built ᴿPĕn′-ū-ĕl.

26 And Jĕr-ŏ-bō′-ăm said in his heart, Now shall the kingdom return to the house of David:

27 If this people ᴿgo up to do sacrifice in the house of the LORD at Jerusalem, then shall the heart of this people turn again unto their lord, *even* unto Rē-hŏ-bō′-ăm king of Judah, and they shall kill me, and go again to Rē-hŏ-bō′-ăm king of Judah.

28 Whereupon the king took counsel, and ᴿmade two calves *of* gold, and said unto them, It is too much for you to go up to Jerusalem: ᴿbehold thy gods, O Israel, which brought thee up out of the land of Egypt.

29 And he set the one in ᴿBeth-el, and the other put he in ᴿDan.

30 And this thing became ᴿa sin: for the people went *to worship* before the one, *even* unto Dan.

31 And he made an ᴿhouse of high places, ᴿand made priests of the lowest of the people, which were not of the sons of Levi.

32 And Jĕr-ŏ-bō′-ăm ordained a feast in the eighth month, on the fifteenth day of the month, like unto ᴿthe feast that *is* in Judah, and he ᴺoffered upon the altar. So did he in Beth-el, ᴺsacrificing unto the calves that he

had made: ᴿand he placed in Beth-el the priests of the high places which he had made.

33 So he ᴺoffered upon the altar which he had made in Beth-el the fifteenth day of the eighth month, *even* in the month which he had ᴿdevised of his own heart; and ordained a feast unto the children of Israel: and he offered upon the altar, ᴺand ᴿburnt incense.

CHAPTER 13

Jeroboam warned

AND, behold, there ᴿcame a man of God out of Judah by the word of the LORD unto Beth-el: ᴿand Jĕr-ŏ-bō′-ăm stood by the altar ᴺto burn incense.

2 And he cried against the altar in the word of the LORD, and said, O altar, altar, thus saith the LORD; Behold, a child shall be born unto the house of David, ᴿJō-sī′-ăh by name; and upon thee shall he offer the priests of the high places that burn incense upon thee, and men's bones shall be burnt upon thee.

3 And he gave ᴿa sign the same day, saying, This *is* the sign which the LORD hath spoken; Behold, the altar shall be rent, and the ashes that *are* upon it shall be poured out.

4 And it came to pass, when king Jĕr-ŏ-bō′-ăm heard the saying of the man of God, which had cried against the altar in Beth-el, that he put forth his hand from the altar, saying, Lay hold on him. And his hand, which he put forth against him, dried up, so that he could not pull it in again to him.

5 The altar also was rent, and the ashes poured out from the altar, according to the sign which the man of God had given by the word of the LORD.

6 And the king answered and said unto the man of God, ᴿEntreat now the face of the LORD thy God, and pray for me, that my hand may be restored me again. And the man of God besought ᴺthe LORD, and the king's hand was restored him again, and became as *it was* before.

7 And the king said unto the man of God, Come home with me, and refresh thyself, and ᴿI will give thee a reward.

8 And the man of God said unto the king, ᴿIf thou wilt give me half thine house, I will not go in with thee, neither will I eat bread nor drink water in this place:

9 For so was it charged me by the word of the LORD, saying, ᴿEat no bread, nor drink water, nor turn again by the same way that thou camest.

CHAP. 12
BC 975
32 Amos 7:13
33 Or, *went up to the altar, etc.*
33 Num. 15:39
33 Heb. *to burn incense*
33 ch. 13:1

CHAP. 13
BC 975
1 2 Ki. 23:17
1 ch. 12:32, 33
1 Or, *to offer*
2 2 Ki. 23:15, 16
3 Is. 7:14
John 2:18
1 Cor. 1:22
6 Ex. 8:8 & 9:28 & 10:17
Num. 21:7
Acts 8:24
Jas. 5:16
6 Heb. *the face of the LORD*
7 1 Sam. 9:7
2 Ki. 5:15
8 Num. 22:18 & 24:13
9 1 Cor. 5:11

Heb. *son*   **11**
ver. 8, 9   **16**
Heb. *a word was* **17**
ch. 20:35   **17**
1 Thes. 4:15
ch. 20:36   **24**

10 So he went another way, and returned not by the way that he came to Beth-el.

The prophet's lie

11 Now there dwelt an old prophet in Beth-el; and his ᴺsons came and told him all the works that the man of God had done that day in Beth-el: the words which he had spoken unto the king, them they told also to their father.

12 And their father said unto them, What way went he? For his sons had seen what way the man of God went, which came from Judah.

13 And he said unto his sons, Saddle me the ass. So they saddled him the ass: and he rode thereon,

14 And went after the man of God, and found him sitting under an oak: and he said unto him, *Art* thou the man of God that camest from Judah? And he said, I *am*.

15 Then he said unto him, Come home with me, and eat bread.

16 And he said, ᴿI may not return with thee, nor go in with thee: neither will I eat bread nor drink water with thee in this place:

17 For ᴺit was said to me ᴿby the word of the LORD, Thou shalt eat no bread nor drink water there, nor turn again to go by the way that thou camest.

18 He said unto him, I *am* a prophet also as thou *art;* and an angel spake unto me by the word of the LORD, saying, Bring him back with thee into thine house, that he may eat bread and drink water. *But* he lied unto him.

19 So he went back with him, and did eat bread in his house, and drank water.

Disobedient prophet killed

20 And it came to pass, as they sat at the table, that the word of the LORD came unto the prophet that brought him back:

21 And he cried unto the man of God that came from Judah, saying, Thus saith the LORD, Forasmuch as thou hast disobeyed the mouth of the LORD, and hast not kept the commandment which the LORD thy God commanded thee,

22 But camest back, and hast eaten bread and drunk water in the place, of the which *the LORD* did say to thee, Eat no bread, and drink no water; thy carcase shall not come unto the sepulchre of thy fathers.

23 And it came to pass, after he had eaten bread, and after he had drunk, that he saddled for him the ass, *to wit,* for the prophet whom he had brought back.

24 And when he was gone, ᴿa lion met him

by the way, and slew him: and his carcase was
cast in the way, and the ass stood by it, the
lion also stood by the carcase.
25 And, behold, men passed by, and saw the
carcase cast in the way, and the lion standing
by the carcase: and they came and told *it* in
the city where the old prophet dwelt.
26 And when the prophet that brought him
back from the way heard *thereof,* he said, It *is*
the man of God, who was disobedient unto the
word of the LORD: therefore the LORD hath
delivered him unto the lion, which hath [N]torn
him, and slain him, according to the word of
the LORD, which he spake unto him.
27 And he spake to his sons, saying, Saddle
me the ass. And they saddled *him.*
28 And he went and found his carcase cast
in the way, and the ass and the lion standing
by the carcase: the lion had not eaten the carcase, nor [N]torn the ass.
29 And the prophet took up the carcase of
the man of God, and laid it upon the ass, and
brought it back: and the old prophet came to
the city, to mourn and to bury him.
30 And he laid his carcase in his own grave;
and they mourned over him, *saying,* [R]Alas,
my brother!
31 And it came to pass, after he had buried
him, that he spake to his sons, saying, When I
am dead, then bury me in the sepulchre
wherein the man of God *is* buried; [R]lay my
bones beside his bones:
32 [R]For the saying which he cried by the
word of the LORD against the altar in Beth-el,
and against all the houses of the high places
which *are* in the cities of [R]Să-mâr′-ĭ-ă, shall
surely come to pass.
33 [R]After this thing Jĕr-ŏ-bō′-ăm returned
not from his evil way, but [N]made again of the
lowest of the people priests of the high places:
whosoever would, he [N]consecrated him, and
he became *one* of the priests of the high
places.
34 [R]And this thing became sin unto the
house of Jĕr-ŏ-bō′-ăm, even [R]to cut *it* off, and
to destroy *it* from off the face of the earth.

CHAPTER 14

Ahijah prophesies Jeroboam's fall

AT that time Ă-bī′-jăh the son of Jĕr-ŏ-bō′-
ăm fell sick.
2 And Jĕr-ŏ-bō′-ăm said to his wife, Arise, I
pray thee, and disguise thyself, that thou be
not known to be the wife of Jĕr-ŏ-bō′-ăm; and
get thee to Shī′-lōh: behold, there *is* Ă-hī′-jăh
the prophet, which told me that [R]*I should be*
king over this people.
3 [R]And take [N]with thee ten loaves, and
[N]cracknels, and a [N]cruse of honey, and go to
him: he shall tell thee what shall become of
the child.
4 And Jĕr-ŏ-bō′-ăm's wife did so, and arose,
[R]and went to Shī′-lōh, and came to the house
of Ă-hī′-jăh. But Ă-hī′-jăh could not see; for his
eyes [N]were set by reason of his age.
5 And the LORD said unto Ă-hī′-jăh, Behold,
the wife of Jĕr-ŏ-bō′-ăm cometh to ask a thing
of thee for her son; for he *is* sick: thus and
thus shalt thou say unto her: for it shall be,
when she cometh in, that she shall feign herself *to be* another *woman.*
6 And it was *so,* when Ă-hī′-jăh heard the
sound of her feet, as she came in at the door,
that he said, Come in, thou wife of Jĕr-ŏ-bō′-
ăm; why feignest thou thyself *to be* another?
for I *am* sent to thee *with* [N]heavy *tidings.*
7 Go, tell Jĕr-ŏ-bō′-ăm, Thus saith the LORD
God of Israel, [R]Forasmuch as I exalted thee
from among the people, and made thee prince
over my people Israel,
8 And [R]rent the kingdom away from the
house of David, and gave it thee: and *yet* thou
hast not been as my servant David, [R]who kept
my commandments, and who followed me
with all his heart, to do *that* only *which was*
right in mine eyes;
9 But hast done evil above all that were before thee: [R]for thou hast gone and made thee
other gods, and molten images, to provoke me
to anger, and [R]hast cast me behind thy back:
10 Therefore, behold, [R]I will bring evil upon
the house of Jĕr-ŏ-bō′-ăm, and [R]will cut off
from Jĕr-ŏ-bō′-ăm him that pisseth against the
wall, [R]*and* him that is shut up and left in Israel, and will take away the remnant of the
house of Jĕr-ŏ-bō′-ăm, as a man taketh away
dung, till it be all gone.
11 [R]Him that dieth of Jĕr-ŏ-bō′-ăm in the city
shall the dogs eat; and him that dieth in the
field shall the fowls of the air eat: for the
LORD hath spoken *it.*
12 Arise thou therefore, get thee to thine
own house: *and* [R]when thy feet enter into the
city, the child shall die.
13 And all Israel shall mourn for him, and
bury him: for he only of Jĕr-ŏ-bō′-ăm shall
come to the grave, because in him [R]there is
found *some* good thing toward the LORD God
of Israel in the house of Jĕr-ŏ-bō′-ăm.
14 [R]Moreover the LORD shall raise him up a
king over Israel, who shall cut off the house of
Jĕr-ŏ-bō′-ăm that day: but what? even now.
15 For the LORD shall smite Israel, as a reed
is shaken in the water, and he shall [R]root up
Israel out of this [R]good land, which he gave to

CHAP. 13
BC 975
26 Heb. *broken*
28 Heb. *broken*
30 Jer. 22:18
31 2 Ki. 23:17, 18
32 ver. 2
2 Ki. 23:16, 19
32 See ch. 16:24
33 ch. 12:31, 32
2 Chr. 11:15
& 13:9
33 Heb. *returned and made*
33 Heb. *filled his hand,*
Judg. 17:12
34 ch. 12:30
34 ch. 14:10

CHAP. 14
BC 956
2 ch. 11:31
See 1 Sam. 9:7, 8 **3**
Heb. *in thine hand* **3**
Or, *cakes* **3**
Or, *bottle* **3**
ch. 11:29 **4**
Heb. *stood for his hoariness* **4**
Heb. *hard* **6**
See 2 Sam. 12:7, 8 **7**
ch. 11:31 **8**
ch. 11:33, 38 & 15:5 **8**
ch. 12:28 **9**
2 Chr. 11:15
Neh. 9:26 **9**
Ps. 50:17
ch. 15:29 **10**
ch. 21:21 **10**
2 Ki. 9:8
Deut. 32:36 **10**
2 Ki. 14:26
ch. 16:4 **11**
& 21:24
ver. 17 **12**
2 Chr. 12:12 **13**
& 19:3
ch. 15:27-29 **14**
2 Ki. 17:6 **15**
Ps. 52:5

their fathers, and shall scatter them [R]beyond the river, [R]because they have made their groves, provoking the LORD to anger.

16 And he shall give Israel up because of the sins of Jĕr-ŏ-bō′-ăm, [R]who did sin, and who made Israel to sin.

Death of Jeroboam

17 And Jĕr-ŏ-bō′-ăm's wife arose, and departed, and came to [R]Tîr′-zăh: *and* [R]when she came to the threshold of the door, the child died;

18 And they buried him; and all Israel mourned for him, [R]according to the word of the LORD, which he spake by the hand of his servant Ă-hī′-jăh the prophet.

19 And the rest of the acts of Jĕr-ŏ-bō′-ăm, how he [R]warred, and how he reigned, behold, they *are* written in the book of the chronicles of the kings of Israel.

20 And the days which Jĕr-ŏ-bō′-ăm reigned *were* two and twenty years: and he [N]slept with his fathers, and Nadab his son reigned in his stead.

Rehoboam's reign in Judah

21 And Rē-hŏ-bō′-ăm the son of Solomon reigned in Judah. [R]Rē-hŏ-bō′-ăm *was* forty and one years old when he began to reign, and he reigned seventeen years in Jerusalem, the city [R]which the LORD did choose out of all the tribes of Israel, to put his name there. [R]And his mother's name *was* Nā′-ă-măh an Ammonitess.

22 [R]And Judah did evil in the sight of the LORD, and they [R]provoked him to jealousy with their sins which they had committed, above all that their fathers had done.

23 For they also built them [R]high places, and [N]images, [R]and groves, on every high hill, and [R]under every green tree.

24 [R]And there were also sodomites in the land: *and* they did according to all the abominations of the nations which the LORD cast out before the children of Israel.

25 [R]And it came to pass in the fifth year of king Rē-hŏ-bō′-ăm, *that* Shī′-shăk king of Egypt came up against Jerusalem:

26 [R]And he took away the treasures of the house of the LORD, and the treasures of the king's house; he even took away all: and he took away all the shields of gold [R]which Solomon had made.

27 And king Rē-hŏ-bō′-ăm made in their stead brasen shields, and committed *them* unto the hands of the chief of the [N]guard, which kept the door of the king's house.

28 And it was *so,* when the king went into

the house of the LORD, that the guard bare them, and brought them back into the guard chamber.

29 [R]Now the rest of the acts of Rē-hŏ-bō′-ăm, and all that he did, *are* they not written in the book of the chronicles of the kings of Judah?

30 And there was [R]war between Rē-hŏ-bō′-ăm and Jĕr-ŏ-bō′-ăm all *their* days.

31 [R]And Rē-hŏ-bō′-ăm slept with his fathers, and was buried with his fathers in the city of David. [R]And his mother's name *was* Nā′-ă-măh an Ammonitess. And [R]Ă-bī′-jăm his son reigned in his stead.

CHAPTER 15

Abijam's reign in Judah

NOW [R]in the eighteenth year of king Jĕr-ŏ-bō′-ăm the son of Nē′-băt reigned Ă-bī′-jăm over Judah.

2 Three years reigned he in Jerusalem. [R]And his mother's name *was* [R]Mā′-ă-<u>ch</u>äh, the daughter of [R]Ă-bī′-shă-lŏm.

3 And he walked in all the sins of his father, which he had done before him: and [R]his heart was not perfect with the LORD his God, as the heart of David his father.

4 Nevertheless [R]for David's sake did the LORD his God give him a [N]lamp in Jerusalem, to set up his son after him, and to establish Jerusalem:

5 Because David [R]did *that which was* right in the eyes of the LORD, and turned not aside from any *thing* that he commanded him all the days of his life, [R]save only in the matter of Ū-rī′-ăh the Hittite.

6 [R]And there was war between Rē-hŏ-bō′-ăm and Jĕr-ŏ-bō′-ăm all the days of his life.

7 [R]Now the rest of the acts of Ă-bī′-jăm, and all that he did, *are* they not written in the book of the chronicles of the kings of Judah? And there was war between Ă-bī′-jăm and Jĕr-ŏ-bō′-ăm.

8 [R]And Ă-bī′-jăm slept with his fathers; and they buried him in the city of David: and Ā′-să his son reigned in his stead.

Asa's reign in Judah

9 And in the twentieth year of Jĕr-ŏ-bō′-ăm king of Israel reigned Ā′-să over Judah.

10 And forty and one years reigned he in Jerusalem. And his [N]mother's name *was* Mā′-ă-<u>ch</u>äh, the daughter of Ă-bī′-shă-lŏm.

11 [R]And Ā′-să did *that which was* right in the eyes of the LORD, as *did* David his father.

12 [R]And he took away the sodomites out of

the land, and removed all the idols that his fathers had made.

13 And also ^RMā′-ȧ-<u>ch</u>äh his mother, even her he removed from *being* queen, because she had made an idol in a grove; and Ā′-sä ^Ndestroyed her idol, and ^Rburnt *it* by the brook Kī′-drŏn.

14 ^RBut the high places were not removed: nevertheless Ā′-sä's ^Rheart was perfect with the LORD all his days.

15 And he brought in the ^Nthings which his father had dedicated, and the things which himself had dedicated, into the house of the LORD, silver, and gold, and vessels.

16 And there was war between Ā′-sä and Bā-ăsh′-ȧ king of Israel all their days.

17 And ^RBā-ăsh′-ȧ king of Israel went up against Judah, and built ^RRā′-mäh, ^Rthat he might not suffer any to go out or come in to Ā′-sä king of Judah.

18 Then Ā′-sä took all the silver and the gold *that were* left in the treasures of the house of the LORD, and the treasures of the king's house, and delivered them into the hand of his servants: and king Ā′-sä sent them to ^RBĕn-hā′-dăd, the son of Tăb-rĭm′-ŏn, the son of Hē′-zĭ-ŏn, king of Syria, that dwelt at ^RDamascus, saying,

19 *There is* a league between me and thee, *and* between my father and thy father: behold, I have sent unto thee a present of silver and gold; come and break thy league with Bā-ăsh′-ȧ king of Israel, that he may ^Ndepart from me.

20 So Bĕn-hā′-dăd hearkened unto king Ā′-sä, and sent the captains of the hosts which he had against the cities of Israel, and smote ^RĪ′-jŏn, and ^RDan, and ^RĀ′-bĕl-bĕth-mā′-ȧ-<u>ch</u>äh, and all Cĭn′-nĕ-rŏth, with all the land of Năph′-tȧ-lī.

21 And it came to pass, when Bā-ăsh′-ȧ heard *thereof,* that he left off building of Rā′-mäh, and dwelt in Tīr′-zäh.

22 ^RThen king Ā′-sä made a proclamation throughout all Judah; none *was* ^Nexempted: and they took away the stones of Rā′-mäh, and the timber thereof, wherewith Bā-ăsh′-ȧ had builded; and king Ā′-sä built with them ^RGē′-bä of Benjamin, and ^RMizpah.

23 The rest of all the acts of Ā′-sä, and all his might, and all that he did, and the cities which he built, *are* they not written in the book of the chronicles of the kings of Judah? Nevertheless ^Rin the time of his old age he was diseased in his feet.

24 And Ā′-sä slept with his fathers, and was buried with his fathers in the city of David his father: ^Rand ^RJĕ-hŏsh′-ȧ-phăt his son reigned in his stead.

Heirs of Jeroboam destroyed

25 And Nadab the son of Jĕr-ŏ-bō′-ăm ^Nbegan to reign over Israel in the second year of Ā′-sä king of Judah, and reigned over Israel two years.

26 And he did evil in the sight of the LORD, and walked in the way of his father, and in ^Rhis sin wherewith he made Israel to sin.

27 ^RAnd Bā-ăsh′-ȧ the son of Ă-hī′-jäh, of the house of Ĭs′-sȧ-<u>ch</u>är, conspired against him; and Bā-ăsh′-ȧ smote him at ^RGĭb′-bĕ-thŏn, which *belonged* to the Philistines; for Nadab and all Israel laid siege to Gĭb′-bĕ-thŏn.

28 Even in the third year of Ā′-sä king of Judah did Bā-ăsh′-ȧ slay him, and reigned in his stead.

29 And it came to pass, when he reigned, *that* he smote all the house of Jĕr-ŏ-bō′-ăm; he left not to Jĕr-ŏ-bō′-ăm any that breathed, until he had destroyed him, according unto ^Rthe saying of the LORD, which he spake by his servant Ă-hī′-jäh the Shī′-lō-nīte:

30 ^RBecause of the sins of Jĕr-ŏ-bō′-ăm which he sinned, and which he made Israel sin, by his provocation wherewith he provoked the LORD God of Israel to anger.

31 Now the rest of the acts of Nadab, and all that he did, *are* they not written in the book of the chronicles of the kings of Israel?

32 ^RAnd there was war between Ā′-sä and Bā-ăsh′-ȧ king of Israel all their days.

Baasha's reign in Israel

33 In the third year of Ā′-sä king of Judah began Bā-ăsh′-ȧ the son of Ă-hī′-jäh to reign over all Israel in Tīr′-zäh, twenty and four years.

34 And he did evil in the sight of the LORD, and walked in ^Rthe way of Jĕr-ŏ-bō′-ăm, and in his sin wherewith he made Israel to sin.

CHAPTER 16

THEN the word of the LORD came to ^RJehu the son of Hȧ-nā′-nī against Bā-ăsh′-ȧ, saying,

2 ^RForasmuch as I exalted thee out of the dust, and made thee prince over my people Israel; and ^Rthou hast walked in the way of Jĕr-ŏ-bō′-ăm, and hast made my people Israel to sin, to provoke me to anger with their sins;

3 Behold, I will ^Rtake away the posterity of Bā-ăsh′-ȧ, and the posterity of his house; and will make thy house like ^Rthe house of Jĕr-ŏ-bō′-ăm the son of Nē′-băt.

4 ^RHim that dieth of Bā-ăsh′-ȧ in the city shall the dogs eat; and him that dieth of his in the fields shall the fowls of the air eat.

5 Now the rest of the acts of Bā-ăsh′-ȧ, and

what he did, and his might, ᴿ*are* they not written in the book of the chronicles of the kings of Israel?

6 So Bā-ăsh′-ă slept with his fathers, and was buried in ᴿTĭr′-zăh: and Ē′-lăh his son reigned in his stead.

7 And also by the hand of the prophet ᴿJehu the son of Hă-nā′-nī came the word of the LORD against Bā-ăsh′-ă, and against his house, even for all the evil that he did in the sight of the LORD, in provoking him to anger with the work of his hands, in being like the house of Jĕr-ŏ-bō′-ăm; and because ᴿhe killed him.

Elah's reign in Israel

8 In the twenty and sixth year of Ā′-să king of Judah began Ē′-lăh the son of Bā-ăsh′-ă to reign over Israel in Tĭr′-zăh, two years.

9 ᴿAnd his servant Zimri, captain of half *his* chariots, conspired against him, as he was in Tĭr′-zăh, drinking himself drunk in the house of Arza ᴺsteward of *his* house in Tĭr′-zăh.

10 And Zimri went in and smote him, and killed him, in the twenty and seventh year of Ā′-să king of Judah, and reigned in his stead.

Zimri's reign in Israel

11 And it came to pass, when he began to reign, as soon as he sat on his throne, *that* he slew all the house of Bā-ăsh′-ă: he left him ᴿnot one that pisseth against a wall, ᴺneither of his kinsfolks, nor of his friends.

12 Thus did Zimri destroy all the house of Bā-ăsh′-ă, ᴿaccording to the word of the LORD, which he spake against Bā-ăsh′-ă ᴿbyᴺ Jehu the prophet,

13 For all the sins of Bā-ăsh′-ă, and the sins of Ē′-lăh his son, by which they sinned, and by which they made Israel to sin, in provoking the LORD God of Israel to anger ᴿwith their vanities.

14 Now the rest of the acts of Ē′-lăh, and all that he did, *are* they not written in the book of the chronicles of the kings of Israel?

Omri's reign in Israel

15 In the twenty and seventh year of Ā′-să king of Judah did Zimri reign seven days in Tĭr′-zăh. And the people *were* encamped ᴿagainst Gĭb′-bĕ-thŏn, which *belonged* to the Philistines.

16 And the people *that were* encamped heard say, Zimri hath conspired, and hath also slain the king: wherefore all Israel made Omri, the captain of the host, king over Israel that day in the camp.

17 And Omri went up from Gĭb′-bĕ-thŏn, and all Israel with him, and they beseiged Tĭr′-zăh.

18 And it came to pass, when Zimri saw that the city was taken, that he went into the palace of the king's house, and burnt the king's house over him with fire, and died,

19 For his sins which he sinned in doing evil in the sight of the LORD, ᴿin walking in the way of Jĕr-ŏ-bō′-ăm, and in his sin which he did, to make Israel to sin.

20 Now the rest of the acts of Zimri, and his treason that he wrought, *are* they not written in the book of the chronicles of the kings of Israel?

21 Then were the people of Israel divided into two parts: half of the people followed Tĭb′-nī the son of Gī′-năth, to make him king; and half followed Omri.

22 But the people that followed Omri prevailed against the people that followed Tĭb′-nī the son of Gī′-năth: so Tĭb′-nī died, and Omri reigned.

23 In the thirty and first year of Ā′-să king of Judah began Omri to reign over Israel, twelve years: six years reigned he in Tĭr′-zăh.

24 And he bought the hill Să-mâr′-ĭ-ă of Shē′-mĕr for two talents of silver, and built on the hill, and called the name of the city which he built, after the name of Shē′-mĕr, owner of the hill, ᴿSă-mâr′-ĭ-ă.ᴺ

25 But ᴿOmri wrought evil in the eyes of the LORD, and did worse than all that *were* before him.

26 For he ᴿwalked in all the way of Jĕr-ŏ-bō′-ăm the son of Nē′-băt, and in his sin wherewith he made Israel to sin, to provoke the LORD God of Israel to anger with their ᴿvanities.

27 Now the rest of the acts of Omri which he did, and his might that he shewed, *are* they not written in the book of the chronicles of the kings of Israel?

28 So Omri slept with his fathers, and was buried in Să-mâr′-ĭ-ă: and Ahab his son reigned in his stead.

Ahab's reign begins in Israel

29 And in the thirty and eighth year of Ā′-să king of Judah began Ahab the son of Omri to reign over Israel: and Ahab the son of Omri reigned over Israel in Să-mâr′-ĭ-ă twenty and two years.

30 And Ahab the son of Omri did evil in the sight of the LORD above all that *were* before him.

31 And it came to pass, ᴺas if it had been a light thing for him to walk in the sins of Jĕr-ŏ-bō′-ăm the son of Nē′-băt, ᴿthat he took to wife Jĕz′-ĕ-bĕl the daughter of Ĕth-bā′-ăl king of the ᴿZī-dō′-nī-ăns, ᴿand went and served Bā′-ăl, and worshipped him.

CHAP. 16
BC 930
5 2 Chr. 16:1
6 ch. 14:17 & 15:21
7 ver. 1
7 ch. 15:27, 29 See Hos. 1:4
9 2 Ki. 9:31
9 Heb. *which was over*
11 1 Sam. 25:22
11 Or, *both his kinsmen and his friends*
12 ver. 3
12 ver. 1
12 Heb. *by the hand of*
13 Deut. 32:21
1 Sam. 12:21
Is. 41:29
Jonah 2:8
1 Cor. 8:4 & 10:19
15 ch. 15:27

ch. 12:28 & 15:26, 34 — 19
See ch. 13:32 — 24
2 Ki. 17:24
John 4:4
Heb. *Shomeron* — 24
Mic. 6:16 — 25
ver. 19 — 26
ver. 13 — 26
Heb. *was it a light thing, etc.* — 31
Deut. 7:3 — 31
Judg. 18:7 — 31
ch. 21:25, 26 — 31
2 Ki. 10:18 & 17:16

32 And he reared up an altar for Bā′-ăl in
ᴿthe house of Bā′-ăl, which he had built in
Să-mâr′-ĭ-ă.

33 ᴿAnd Ahab made a grove; and Ahab
ᴿdid more to provoke the Lᴏʀᴅ God of Israel
to anger than all the kings of Israel that were
before him.

34 In his days did Hī′-ĕl the Beth-elite build
Jericho: he laid the foundation thereof in
Ă-bī′-răm his firstborn, and set up the gates
thereof in his youngest *son* Sē′-gŭb, ᴿaccording to the word of the Lᴏʀᴅ, which he spake
by Joshua the son of Nun.

CHAPTER 17

Elijah at Cherith

AND ᴺĒ-lī′-jăh the Tĭsh′-bĭte, *who was* of
the inhabitants of Gilead, said unto
Ahab, ᴿAs the Lᴏʀᴅ God of Israel liveth,
ᴿbefore whom I stand, ᴿthere shall not be dew
nor rain ᴿthese years, but according to my
word.

2 And the word of the Lᴏʀᴅ came unto him,
saying,

3 Get thee hence, and turn thee eastward,
and hide thyself by the brook Chē′-rĭth, that *is*
before Jordan.

4 And it shall be, *that* thou shalt drink of the
brook; and I have commanded the ravens to
feed thee there.

5 So he went and did according unto the
word of the Lᴏʀᴅ: for he went and dwelt by
the brook Chē′-rĭth, that *is* before Jordan.

6 And the ravens brought him bread and
flesh in the morning, and bread and flesh in the
evening; and he drank of the brook.

7 And it came to pass ᴺafter a while, that the
brook dried up, because there had been no rain
in the land.

Elijah and the widow of Zarephath

8 And the word of the Lᴏʀᴅ came unto him,
saying,

9 Arise, get thee to ᴿZăr′-ĕ-phăth, which
belongeth to Zī′-dŏn, and dwell there: behold,
I have commanded a widow woman there to
sustain thee.

10 So he arose and went to Zăr′-ĕ-phăth.
And when he came to the gate of the city, behold, the widow woman *was* there gathering
of sticks: and he called to her, and said, Fetch
me, I pray thee, a little water in a vessel, that I
may drink.

11 And as she was going to fetch *it,* he
called to her, and said, Bring me, I pray thee,
a morsel of bread in thine hand.

12 And she said, As the Lᴏʀᴅ thy God liveth, I have not a cake, but an handful of meal

in a barrel, and a little oil in a cruse: and, behold, I *am* gathering two sticks, that I may go
in and dress it for me and my son, that we
may eat it, and die.

13 And Ē-lī′-jăh said unto her, Fear not; go
and do as thou hast said: but make me thereof
a little cake first, and bring *it* unto me, and
after make for thee and for thy son.

14 For thus saith the Lᴏʀᴅ God of Israel,
The barrel of meal shall not waste, neither
shall the cruse of oil fail, until the day *that* the
Lᴏʀᴅ ᴺsendeth rain upon the earth.

15 And she went and did according to the
saying of Ē-lī′-jăh: and she, and he, and her
house, did eat ᴺmany days.

16 *And* the barrel of meal wasted not, neither did the cruse of oil fail, according to the
word of the Lᴏʀᴅ, which he spake ᴺby Ē-lī′-
jăh.

Elijah heals the widow's son

17 And it came to pass after these things,
that the son of the woman, the mistress of the
house, fell sick; and his sickness was so sore,
that there was no breath left in him.

18 And she said unto Ē-lī′-jăh, ᴿWhat have I
to do with thee, O thou man of God? art thou
come unto me to call my sin to remembrance,
and to slay my son?

19 And he said unto her, Give me thy son.
And he took him out of her bosom, and carried him up into a loft, where he abode, and
laid him upon his own bed.

20 And he cried unto the Lᴏʀᴅ, and said, O
Lᴏʀᴅ my God, hast thou also brought evil
upon the widow with whom I sojourn, by
slaying her son?

21 ᴿAnd he ᴺstretched himself upon the
child three times, and cried unto the Lᴏʀᴅ,
and said, O Lᴏʀᴅ my God, I pray thee, let
this child's soul come ᴺinto him again.

22 And the Lᴏʀᴅ heard the voice of Ē-lī′-
jăh; and the soul of the child came into him
again, and he ᴿrevived.

23 And Ē-lī′-jăh took the child, and brought
him down out of the chamber into the house,
and delivered him unto his mother: and Ē-lī′-
jăh said, See, thy son liveth.

24 And the woman said to Ē-lī′-jăh, Now by
this ᴿI know that thou *art* a man of God, *and*
that the word of the Lᴏʀᴅ in thy mouth *is*
truth.

CHAPTER 18

Elijah returns to Israel

AND it came to pass *after* ᴿmany days, that
the word of the Lᴏʀᴅ came to Ē-lī′-jăh
in the third year, saying, Go, shew thyself

CHAP. **16**
BC 930
32 2 Ki. 10:21, 26, 27
33 2 Ki. 13:6 & 17:10 & 21:3
Jer. 17:2
33 ver. 30
ch. 21:25
34 Josh. 6:26

CHAP. **17**
BC 910
1 Heb. *Elijahu,* Luke 1:17 & 4:25, he is called *Elias*
1 2 Ki. 3:14
1 Deut. 10:8
1 Jas. 5:17
1 Luke 4:25
7 Heb. *at the end of days*
9 Obad. 20
Luke 4:26, called *Sarepta*

Heb. *giveth*   14
Or, *a full year*   15
Heb. *by the*   16
  hand of
See Luke 5:8   18
2 Ki. 4:34, 35   21
Heb.   21
  measured
Heb. *into his*   21
  inward parts
Heb. 11:35   22
John 3:2   24
  & 16:30

CHAP. **18**
BC 906
Luke 4:25
Jas. 5:17   **1**

unto Ahab; and [R]I will send rain upon the earth.

2 And Ē-lī'-jäh went to shew himself unto Ahab. And *there was* a sore famine in Să-mâr'-ĭ-ă.

3 And Ahab called [N]Ō-bă-dī'-ăh, which *was* [N]the governor of *his* house. (Now ō-bă-dī'-ăh feared the LORD greatly:

4 For it was *so,* when [N]Jĕz'-ĕ-bĕl cut off the prophets of the LORD, that ō-bă-dī'-ăh took an hundred prophets, and hid them by fifty in a cave, and fed them with bread and water.)

5 And Ahab said unto ō-bă-dī'-ăh, Go into the land, unto all fountains of water, and unto all brooks: peradventure we may find grass to save the horses and mules alive, [N]that we lose not all the beasts.

6 So they divided the land between them to pass throughout it: Ahab went one way by himself, and ō-bă-dī'-ăh went another way by himself.

7 And as ō-bă-dī'-ăh was in the way, behold, Ē-lī'-jäh met him: and he knew him, and fell on his face, and said, *Art* thou that my lord Ē-lī'-jäh?

8 And he answered him, I *am:* go, tell thy lord, Behold, Ē-lī'-jäh *is here.*

9 And he said, What have I sinned, that thou wouldest deliver thy servant into the hand of Ahab, to slay me?

10 *As* the LORD thy God liveth, there is no nation or kingdom, whither my lord hath not sent to seek thee: and when they said, *He is* not *there;* he took an oath of the kingdom and nation, that they found thee not.

11 And now thou sayest, Go, tell thy lord, Behold, Ē-lī'-jäh *is here.*

12 And it shall come to pass, *as soon as* I am gone from thee, that [R]the spirit of the LORD shall carry thee whither I know not; and *so* when I come and tell Ahab, and he cannot find thee, he shall slay me: but I thy servant fear the LORD from my youth.

13 Was it not told my lord what I did when Jĕz'-ĕ-bĕl slew the prophets of the LORD, how I hid an hundred men of the LORD's prophets by fifty in a cave, and fed them with bread and water?

14 And now thou sayest, Go, tell thy lord, Behold, Ē-lī'-jäh *is here:* and he shall slay me.

15 And Ē-lī'-jäh said, *As* the LORD of hosts liveth, before whom I stand, I will surely shew myself unto him to day.

16 So ō-bă-dī'-ăh went to meet Ahab, and told him: and Ahab went to meet Ē-lī'-jäh.

17 And it came to pass, when Ahab saw Ē-lī'-jäh, that Ahab said unto him, [R]*Art* thou he that [R]troubleth Israel?

18 And he answered, I have not troubled

Israel; but thou, and thy father's house, [R]in that ye have forsaken the commandments of the LORD, and thou hast followed Bā'-ă-lĭm.

19 Now therefore send, *and* gather to me all Israel unto mount [R]Carmel, and the prophets of Bā'-ăl four hundred and fifty, [R]and the prophets of the groves four hundred, which eat at Jĕz'-ĕ-bĕl's table.

Contest on mount Carmel

20 So Ahab sent unto all the children of Israel, and [R]gathered the prophets together unto mount Carmel.

21 And Ē-lī'-jäh came unto all the people, and said, [R]How long halt ye between two [N]opinions? if the LORD *be* God, follow him: but if Bā'-ăl, [R]*then* follow him. And the people answered him not a word.

22 Then said Ē-lī'-jäh unto the people, [R]I, *even* I only, remain a prophet of the LORD; [R]but Bā'-ăl's prophets *are* four hundred and fifty men.

23 Let them therefore give us two bullocks; and let them choose one bullock for themselves, and cut it in pieces, and lay *it* on wood, and put no fire *under:* and I will dress the other bullock, and lay *it* on wood, and put no fire *under:*

24 And call ye on the name of your gods, and I will call on the name of the LORD: and the God that [R]answereth by fire, let him be God. And all the people answered and said, [N]It is well spoken.

25 And Ē-lī'-jäh said unto the prophets of Bā'-ăl, Choose you one bullock for yourselves, and dress *it* first; for ye *are* many; and call on the name of your gods, but put no fire *under.*

26 And they took the bullock which was given them, and they dressed *it,* and called on the name of Bā'-ăl from morning even until noon, saying, O Bā'-ăl, [N]hear us. But *there was* [R]no voice, nor any that [N]answered. And they [N]leaped upon the altar which was made.

27 And it came to pass at noon, that Ē-lī'-jäh mocked them, and said, Cry [N]aloud: for he *is* a god; either [N]he is talking, or he [N]is pursuing, or he is in a journey, *or* peradventure he sleepeth, and must be awaked.

28 And they cried aloud, and [R]cut themselves after their manner with knives and lancets, till [N]the blood gushed out upon them.

29 And it came to pass, when midday was past, [R]and they prophesied until the *time* of the [N]offering of the *evening* sacrifice, that *there was* [R]neither voice, nor any to answer, nor any [N]that regarded.

30 And Ē-lī'-jäh said unto all the people, Come near unto me. And all the people came

near unto him. ᴿAnd he repaired the altar of the Lᴏʀᴅ *that was* broken down.

31 And Ē-lī′-jăh took twelve stones, according to the number of the tribes of the sons of Jacob, unto whom the word of the Lᴏʀᴅ came, saying, ᴿIsrael shall be thy name:

32 And with the stones he built an altar ᴿin the name of the Lᴏʀᴅ: and he made a trench about the altar, as great as would contain two measures of seed.

33 And he ᴿput the wood in order, and cut the bullock in pieces, and laid *him* on the wood, and said, Fill four barrels with water, and ᴿpour *it* on the burnt sacrifice, and on the wood.

34 And he said, Do *it* the second time. And they did *it* the second time. And he said, Do *it* the third time. And they did *it* the third time.

35 And the water ᴺran round about the altar; and he filled ᴿthe trench also with water.

Fire consumes Elijah's offering

36 And it came to pass at *the time of* the offering of the *evening* sacrifice, that Ē-lī′-jăh the prophet came near, and said, Lᴏʀᴅ ᴿGod of Abraham, Isaac, and of Israel, ᴿlet it be known this day that thou *art* God in Israel, and *that* I *am* thy servant, and *that* ᴿI have done all these things at thy word.

37 Hear me, O Lᴏʀᴅ, hear me, that this people may know that thou *art* the Lᴏʀᴅ God, and *that* thou hast turned their heart back again.

38 Then ᴿthe fire of the Lᴏʀᴅ fell, and consumed the burnt sacrifice, and the wood, and the stones, and the dust, and licked up the water that *was* in the trench.

39 And when all the people saw *it*, they fell on their faces: and they said, ᴿThe Lᴏʀᴅ, he *is* the God; the Lᴏʀᴅ, he *is* the God.

40 And Ē-lī′-jăh said unto them, ᴿTakeᴺ the prophets of Bā′-ăl; let not one of them escape. And they took them: and Ē-lī′-jăh brought them down to the brook Kī′-shŏn, and ᴿslew them there.

41 And Ē-lī′-jăh said unto Ahab, Get thee up, eat and drink; for *there is* ᴺa sound of abundance of rain.

42 So Ahab went up to eat and to drink. And Ē-lī′-jăh went up to the top of Carmel; ᴿand he cast himself down upon the earth, and put his face between his knees,

43 And said to his servant, Go up now, look toward the sea. And he went up, and looked, and said, *There is* nothing. And he said, Go again seven times.

44 And it came to pass at the seventh time, that he said, Behold, there ariseth a little cloud out of the sea, like a man's hand. And he said,

Go up, say unto Ahab, ᴺPrepare *thy chariot*, and get thee down, that the rain stop thee not.

45 And it came to pass in the mean while, that the heaven was black with clouds and wind, and there was a great rain. And Ahab rode, and went to Jĕz′-rēĕl.

46 And the hand of the Lᴏʀᴅ was on Ē-lī′-jăh; and he ᴿgirded up his loins, and ran before Ahab ᴺto the entrance of Jĕz′-rēĕl.

CHAPTER 19

Elijah flees from Jezebel

AND Ahab told Jĕz′-ĕ-bĕl all that Ē-lī′-jăh had done, and withal how he had ᴿslain all the prophets with the sword.

2 Then Jĕz′-ĕ-bĕl sent a messenger unto Ē-lī′-jăh, saying, ᴿSo let the gods do *to me*, and more also, if I make not thy life as the life of one of them by to morrow about this time.

3 And when he saw *that*, he arose, and went for his life, and came to Bēĕr-shē′-bă, which *belongeth* to Judah, and left his servant there.

4 But he himself went a day's journey into the wilderness, and came and sat down under a juniper tree: and he ᴿrequested ᴺfor himself that he might die; and said, It is enough; now, O Lᴏʀᴅ, take away my life; for I *am* not better than my fathers.

5 And as he lay and slept under a juniper tree, behold, then an angel touched him, and said unto him, Arise *and* eat.

6 And he looked, and, behold, *there was* a cake baken on the coals, and a cruse of water at his ᴺhead. And he did eat and drink, and laid him down again.

7 And the angel of the Lᴏʀᴅ came again the second time, and touched him, and said, Arise *and* eat; because the journey *is* too great for thee.

8 And he arose, and did eat and drink, and went in the strength of that meat ᴿforty days and forty nights unto ᴿHôr′-ĕb the mount of God.

"A still small voice"

9 And he came thither unto a cave, and lodged there; and, behold, the word of the Lᴏʀᴅ *came* to him, and he said unto him, What doest thou here, Ē-lī′-jăh?

10 And he said, ᴿI have been very ᴿjealous for the Lᴏʀᴅ God of hosts: for the children of Israel have forsaken thy covenant, thrown down thine altars, and ᴿslain thy prophets with the sword; and ᴿI, *even* I only, am left; and they seek my life, to take it away.

11 And he said, Go forth, and stand ᴿupon the mount before the Lᴏʀᴅ. And, behold, the Lᴏʀᴅ passed by, and ᴿa great and strong wind

rent the mountains, and brake in pieces the rocks before the LORD; *but* the LORD *was* not in the wind: and after the wind an earthquake; *but* the LORD *was* not in the earthquake:

12 And after the earthquake a fire; *but* the LORD *was* not in the fire: and after the fire a still small voice.

13 And it was *so,* when Ē-lī′-jăh heard *it,* that ᴿhe wrapped his face in his mantle, and went out, and stood in the entering in of the cave. ᴿAnd, behold, *there came* a voice unto him, and said, What doest thou here, Ē-lī′-jăh?

14 ᴿAnd he said, I have been very jealous for the LORD God of hosts: because the children of Israel have forsaken thy covenant, thrown down thine altars, and slain thy prophets with the sword; and I, *even* I only, am left; and they seek my life, to take it away.

15 And the LORD said unto him, Go, return on thy way to the wilderness of Damascus: ᴿand when thou comest, anoint Hă-zā′-ĕl *to be* king over Syria:

16 And ᴿJehu the son of Nimshi shalt thou anoint *to be* king over Israel: and ᴿĒ-lī′-shă the son of Shā′-phăt of Ā′-bĕl-mĕ-hō′-lăh shalt thou anoint *to be* prophet in thy room.

17 And ᴿit shall come to pass, *that* him that escapeth the sword of Hă-zā′-ĕl shall Jehu slay: and him that escapeth from the sword of Jehu ᴿshall Ē-lī′-shă slay.

18 ᴿYet ᴺI have left *me* seven thousand in Israel, all the knees which have not bowed unto Bā′-ăl, ᴿand every mouth which hath not kissed him.

Elijah finds Elisha

19 So he departed thence, and found Ē-lī′-shă the son of Shā′-phăt, who *was* plowing *with* twelve yoke *of oxen* before him, and he with the twelfth: and Ē-lī′-jăh passed by him, and cast his mantle upon him.

20 And he left the oxen, and ran after Ē-lī′-jăh, and said, ᴿLet me, I pray thee, kiss my father and my mother, and *then* I will follow thee. And he said unto him, ᴺGo back again: for what have I done to thee?

21 And he returned back from him, and took a yoke of oxen, and slew them, and ᴿboiled their flesh with the instruments of the oxen, and gave unto the people, and they did eat. Then he arose, and went after Ē-lī′-jăh, and ministered unto him.

CHAPTER 20

Samaria beseiged

AND Bĕn-hā′-dăd the king of Syria gathered all his host together: and *there were* thirty and two kings with him, and horses, and

CHAP. 19
BC 906
13 Ex. 3:6
Is. 6:2
13 ver. 9
14 ver. 10
15 2 Ki. 8:12, 13
16 2 Ki. 9:1-3
16 Luke 4:27, called *Eliseus*
17 2 Ki. 8:12 & 9:14, etc. & 10:6, etc. & 13:3
17 See Hos. 6:5
18 Rom. 11:4
18 Or, *I will leave*
18 See Hos. 13:2
20 Mat. 8:21, 22 Luke 9:61, 62
20 Heb. *Go return*
21 2 Sam. 24:22

CHAP. 20
BC 901
Heb. *desirable* 6
Heb. *I kept not back from him* 7
ch. 19:2 10
Heb. *are at my feet* 10
Ex. 11:8
Judg. 4:10
Heb. *word* 12
ver. 16 12
Or, *tents* 12
Or, *Place the engines: And they placed* engines 12
Heb. *approached* 13
ver. 28 13
Or, *servants* 14

chariots: and he went up and besieged Să-mâr′-ĭ-ă, and warred against it.

2 And he sent messengers to Ahab king of Israel into the city, and said unto him, Thus saith Bĕn-hā′-dăd,

3 Thy silver and thy gold *is* mine; thy wives also and thy children, *even* the goodliest, *are* mine.

4 And the king of Israel answered and said, My lord, O king, according to thy saying, I *am* thine, and all that I have.

5 And the messengers came again, and said, Thus speaketh Bĕn-hā′-dăd, saying, Although I have sent unto thee, saying, Thou shalt deliver me thy silver, and thy gold, and thy wives, and thy children;

6 Yet I will send my servants unto thee to morrow about this time, and they shall search thine house, and the houses of thy servants; and it shall be, *that* whatsoever is ᴺpleasant in thine eyes, they shall put *it* in their hand, and take *it* away.

7 Then the king of Israel called all the elders of the land, and said, Mark, I pray you, and see how this *man* seeketh mischief: for he sent unto me for my wives, and for my children, and for my silver, and for my gold; and ᴺI denied him not.

8 And all the elders and all the people said unto him, Hearken not *unto him,* nor consent.

9 Wherefore he said unto the messengers of Bĕn-hā′-dăd, Tell my lord the king, All that thou didst send for to thy servant at the first I will do: but this thing I may not do. And the messengers departed, and brought him word again.

10 And Bĕn-hā′-dăd sent unto him, and said, ᴿThe gods do so unto me, and more also, if the dust of Să-mâr′-ĭ-ă shall suffice for handfuls for all the people that ᴺfollow me.

11 And the king of Israel answered and said, Tell *him,* Let not him that girdeth on *his harness* boast himself as he that putteth it off.

12 And it came to pass, when *Bĕn-hā′-dăd* heard this ᴺmessage, as he *was* ᴿdrinking, he and the kings in the ᴺpavilions, that he said unto his servants, ᴺSet *yourselves in array.* And they set *themselves in array* against the city.

Ahab routs the Syrians

13 And, behold, there ᴺcame a prophet unto Ahab king of Israel, saying, Thus saith the LORD, Hast thou seen all this great multitude? behold, ᴿI will deliver it into thine hand this day; and thou shalt know that I *am* the LORD.

14 And Ahab said, By whom? And he said, Thus saith the LORD, *Even* by the ᴺyoung men of the princes of the provinces. Then he said,

Who shall ᴺorder the battle? And he answered, Thou.

15 Then he numbered the young men of the princes of the provinces, and they were two hundred and thirty two: and after them he numbered all the people, *even* all the children of Israel, *being* seven thousand.

16 And they went out at noon. But Bĕn-hā′-dăd *was* ᴿdrinking himself drunk in the pavilions, he and the kings, the thirty and two kings that helped him.

17 And the young men of the princes of the provinces went out first; and Bĕn-hā′-dăd sent out, and they told him, saying, There are men come out of Să-mâr′-ĭ-ă.

18 And he said, Whether they be come out for peace, take them alive; or whether they be come out for war, take them alive.

19 So these young men of the princes of the provinces came out of the city, and the army which followed them.

20 And they slew every one his man: and the Syrians fled; and Israel pursued them: and Bĕn-hā′-dăd the king of Syria escaped on an horse with the horsemen.

21 And the king of Israel went out, and smote the horses and chariots, and slew the Syrians with a great slaughter.

22 And the prophet came to the king of Israel, and said unto him, Go, strengthen thyself, and mark, and see what thou doest: ᴿfor at the return of the year the king of Syria will come up against thee.

Ben-hadad defeated at Aphek

23 And the servants of the king of Syria said unto him, Their gods *are* gods of the hills; therefore they were stronger than we; but let us fight against them in the plain, and surely we shall be stronger than they.

24 And do this thing, Take the kings away, every man out of his place, and put captains in their rooms:

25 And number thee an army, like the army ᴺthat thou hast lost, horse for horse, and chariot for chariot: and we will fight against them in the plain, *and* surely we shall be stronger than they. And he hearkened unto their voice, and did so.

26 And it came to pass at the return of the year, that Bĕn-hā′-dăd numbered the Syrians, and went up to ᴿĀ′-phĕk, ᴺto fight against Israel.

27 And the children of Israel were numbered, and ᴺwere all present, and went against them: and the children of Israel pitched before them like two little flocks of kids; but the Syrians filled the country.

CHAP. **20**
BC 901

14 Heb. *bind,* or, *tie*
16 ver. 12
ch. 16:9
22 2 Sam. 11:1
25 Heb. *that was fallen*
26 Josh. 13:4
26 Heb. *to the war with Israel*
27 Or, *were victualled*

ver. 13   **28**
Or, *from   **30** chamber to chamber*
Heb. *into a   **30** chamber within a chamber*
Gen. 37:34   **31**
ch. 15:20   **34**
2 Ki. 2:3, 5, 7, 15
ch. 13:17, 18   **35**
ch. 13:24   **36**
Heb. *smiting   **37** and wounding*

28 And there came a man of God, and spake unto the king of Israel, and said, Thus saith the Lᴏʀᴅ, Because the Syrians have said, The Lᴏʀᴅ *is* God of the hills, but he *is* not God of the valleys, therefore ᴿwill I deliver all this great multitude into thine hand, and ye shall know that I *am* the Lᴏʀᴅ.

29 And they pitched one over against the other seven days. And *so* it was, that in the seventh day the battle was joined: and the children of Israel slew of the Syrians an hundred thousand footmen in one day.

30 But the rest fled to Ā′-phĕk, into the city; and *there* a wall fell upon twenty and seven thousand of the men *that were* left.

Ahab spares Ben-hadad's life

And Bĕn-hā′-dăd fled, and came into the city, ᴺᴺinto an inner chamber.

31 And his servants said unto him, Behold now, we have heard that the kings of the house of Israel *are* merciful kings: let us, I pray thee, ᴿput sackcloth on our loins, and ropes upon our heads, and go out to the king of Israel: peradventure he will save thy life.

32 So they girded sackcloth on their loins, and *put* ropes on their heads, and came to the king of Israel, and said, Thy servant Bĕn-hā′-dăd saith, I pray thee, let me live. And he said, *Is* he yet alive? he *is* my brother.

33 Now the men did diligently observe whether *any thing would come* from him, and did hastily catch *it:* and they said, Thy brother Bĕn-hā′-dăd. Then he said, Go ye, bring him. Then Bĕn-hā′-dăd came forth to him; and he caused him to come up into the chariot.

34 And *Bĕn-hā′-dăd* said unto him, ᴿThe cities, which my father took from thy father, I will restore; and thou shalt make streets for thee in Damascus, as my father made in Să-mâr′-ĭ-ă. Then *said Ahab,* I will send thee away with this covenant. So he made a covenant with him, and sent him away.

The prophet's reproof of Ahab

35 And a certain man of ᴿthe sons of the prophets said unto his neighbour ᴿin the word of the Lᴏʀᴅ, Smite me, I pray thee. And the man refused to smite him.

36 Then said he unto him, Because thou hast not obeyed the voice of the Lᴏʀᴅ, behold, as soon as thou art departed from me, a lion shall slay thee. And as soon as he was departed from him, ᴿa lion found him, and slew him.

37 Then he found another man, and said, Smite me, I pray thee. And the man smote him, ᴺso that in smiting he wounded *him.*

38 So the prophet departed, and waited for

the king by the way, and disguised himself with ashes upon his face.

39 And ᴿas the king passed by, he cried unto the king: and he said, Thy servant went out into the midst of the battle; and, behold, a man turned aside, and brought a man unto me, and said, Keep this man: if by any means he be missing, then ᴿshall thy life be for his life, or else thou shalt ᴺpay a talent of silver.

40 And as thy servant was busy here and there, ᴺhe was gone. And the king of Israel said unto him, So *shall* thy judgment *be;* thyself hast decided *it.*

41 And he hasted, and took the ashes away from his face; and the king of Israel discerned him that he *was* of the prophets.

42 And he said unto him, Thus saith the LORD, ᴿBecause thou hast let go out of *thy* hand a man whom I appointed to utter destruction, therefore thy life shall go for his life, and thy people for his people.

43 And the king of Israel ᴿwent to his house heavy and displeased, and came to Să-mâr′-ĭ-ă.

CHAPTER 21

Ahab covets Naboth's vineyard

AND it came to pass after these things, *that* Naboth the Jĕz′-rĕel-īte had a vineyard, which *was* in Jĕz′-rĕel, hard by the palace of Ahab king of Să-mâr′-ĭ-ă.

2 And Ahab spake unto Naboth, saying, Give me thy ᴿvineyard, that I may have it for a garden of herbs, because it *is* near unto my house: and I will give thee for it a better vineyard than it; *or,* if it ᴺseem good to thee, I will give thee the worth of it in money.

3 And Naboth said to Ahab, The LORD forbid it me, ᴿthat I should give the inheritance of my fathers unto thee.

4 And Ahab came into his house heavy and displeased because of the word which Naboth the Jĕz′-rĕel-īte had spoken to him: for he had said, I will not give thee the inheritance of my fathers. And he laid him down upon his bed, and turned away his face, and would eat no bread.

5 But Jĕz′-ĕ-bĕl his wife came to him, and said unto him, Why is thy spirit so sad, that thou eatest no bread?

6 And he said unto her, Because I spake unto Naboth the Jĕz′-rĕel-īte, and said unto him, Give me thy vineyard for money; or else, if it please thee, I will give thee *another* vineyard for it: and he answered, I will not give thee my vineyard.

7 And Jĕz′-ĕ-bĕl his wife said unto him, Dost thou now govern the kingdom of Israel?

CHAP. **20**
BC 901
39 See 2 Sam. 12:1, etc.
39 2 Ki. 10:24
39 Heb. *weigh*
40 Heb. *he was not*
42 ch. 22:31-37
43 ch. 21:4

CHAP. **21**
BC 899
2 1 Sam. 8:14
2 Heb. be *good in thine eyes*
3 Lev. 25:23
Num. 36:7
Ezek. 46:18

Heb. *in the*	9
top of the people	
Ex. 22:28	10
Lev. 24:15, 16	
Acts 6:11	
Lev. 24:14	10
Is. 58:4	12
See 2 Ki. 9:26	13
Ps. 9:12	17
ch. 13:32	18
2 Chr. 22:9	
ch. 22:38	19
ch. 18:17	20

arise, *and* eat bread, and let thine heart be merry: I will give thee the vineyard of Naboth the Jĕz′-rĕel-īte.

Jezebel orders Naboth killed

8 So she wrote letters in Ahab's name, and sealed *them* with his seal, and sent the letters unto the elders and to the nobles that *were* in his city, dwelling with Naboth.

9 And she wrote in the letters, saying, Proclaim a fast, and set Naboth ᴺon high among the people:

10 And set two men, sons of Bē′-lĭ-ăl, before him, to bear witness against him, saying, Thou didst ᴿblaspheme God and the king. And *then* carry him out, and ᴿstone him, that he may die.

11 And the men of his city, *even* the elders and the nobles who were the inhabitants in his city, did as Jĕz′-ĕ-bĕl had sent unto them, *and* as it *was* written in the letters which she had sent unto them.

12 ᴿThey proclaimed a fast, and set Naboth on high among the people.

13 And there came in two men, children of Bē′-lĭ-ăl, and sat before him: and the men of Bē′-lĭ-ăl witnessed against him, *even* against Naboth, in the presence of the people, saying, Naboth did blaspheme God and the king. ᴿThen they carried him forth out of the city, and stoned him with stones, that he died.

14 Then they sent to Jĕz′-ĕ-bĕl, saying, Naboth is stoned, and is dead.

15 And it came to pass, when Jĕz′-ĕ-bĕl heard that Naboth was stoned, and was dead, that Jĕz′-ĕ-bĕl said to Ahab, Arise, take possession of the vineyard of Naboth the Jĕz′-rĕel-īte, which he refused to give thee for money: for Naboth is not alive, but dead.

16 And it came to pass, when Ahab heard that Naboth was dead, that Ahab rose up to go down to the vineyard of Naboth the Jĕz′-rĕel-īte, to take possession of it.

Elijah prophesies doom

17 ᴿAnd the word of the LORD came to Ē-lī′-jăh the Tĭsh′-bīte, saying,

18 Arise, go down to meet Ahab king of Israel, ᴿwhich *is* in Să-mâr′-ĭ-ă: behold, *he is* in the vineyard of Naboth, whither he is gone down to possess it.

19 And thou shalt speak unto him, saying, Thus saith the LORD, Hast thou killed, and also taken possession? And thou shalt speak unto him, saying, Thus saith the LORD, ᴿIn the place where dogs licked the blood of Naboth shall dogs lick thy blood, even thine.

20 And Ahab said to Ē-lī′-jăh, ᴿHast thou

found me, O mine enemy? And he answered,
I have found *thee:* because [R]thou hast sold
thyself to work evil in the sight of the LORD.

21 Behold, [R]I will bring evil upon thee, and
will take away thy posterity, and will cut off
from Ahab [R]him that pisseth against the wall,
and [R]him that is shut up and left in Israel,

22 And will make thine house like the house
of [R]Jĕr-ŏ-bō'-ăm the son of Nē'-băt, and like
the house of [R]Bā-ăsh'-ă the son of Ă-hī'-jăh,
for the provocation wherewith thou hast provoked *me* to anger, and made Israel to sin.

23 And [R]of Jĕz'-ĕ-bĕl also spake the LORD,
saying, The dogs shall eat Jĕz'-ĕ-bĕl by the
[N]wall of Jĕz'-rĕĕl.

24 [R]Him that dieth of Ahab in the city the
dogs shall eat; and him that dieth in the field
shall the fowls of the air eat.

25 But [R]there was none like unto Ahab,
which did sell himself to work wickedness in
the sight of the LORD, [R]whom Jĕz'-ĕ-bĕl his
wife [N]stirred up.

26 And he did very abominably in following
idols, according to all *things* [R]as did the
Amorites, whom the LORD cast out before the
children of Israel.

27 And it came to pass, when Ahab heard
those words, that he rent his clothes, and [R]put
sackcloth upon his flesh, and fasted, and lay in
sackcloth, and went softly.

28 And the word of the LORD came to
Ē-lī'-jăh the Tīsh'-bīte, saying,

29 Seest thou how Ahab humbleth himself
before me? because he humbleth himself before me, I will not bring the evil in his days:
but [R]in his son's days will I bring the evil
upon his house.

CHAPTER 22

Ahab's false prophets

AND they continued three years without
war between Syria and Israel.

2 And it came to pass in the third year, that
[R]Jĕ-hŏsh'-ă-phăt the king of Judah came down
to the king of Israel.

3 And the king of Israel said unto his servants, Know ye that [R]Rā'-mŏth in Gilead *is*
ours, and we *be* [N]still, *and* take it not out of
the hand of the king of Syria?

4 And he said unto Jĕ-hŏsh'-ă-phăt, Wilt
thou go with me to battle to Rā'-mŏth-gĭl'-
ĕ-ăd? And Jĕ-hŏsh'-ă-phăt said to the king of
Israel, [R]I *am* as thou *art,* my people as thy
people, my horses as thy horses.

5 And Jĕ-hŏsh'-ă-phăt said unto the king of
Israel, Inquire, I pray thee, at the word of the
LORD to day.

6 Then the king of Israel [R]gathered the

prophets together, about four hundred men,
and said unto them, Shall I go against Rā'-
mŏth-gĭl'-ĕ-ăd to battle, or shall I forbear?
And they said, Go up; for the Lord shall deliver *it* into the hand of the king.

7 And [R]Jĕ-hŏsh'-ă-phăt said, *Is there* not
here a prophet of the LORD besides, that we
might inquire of him?

8 And the king of Israel said unto Jĕ-hŏsh'-
ă-phăt, *There is* yet one man, Mī-cāi-ăh the
son of Ĭm'-lăh, by whom we may inquire
of the LORD: but I hate him; for he doth not
prophesy good concerning me, but evil. And
Jĕ-hŏsh'-ă-phăt said, Let not the king say so.

9 Then the king of Israel called an [N]officer,
and said, Hasten *hither* Mī-cāi'-ăh the son of
Ĭm'-lăh.

10 And the king of Israel and Jĕ-hŏsh'-ă-phăt
the king of Judah sat each on his throne, having put on their robes, in a [N]void place in the
entrance of the gate of Să-mâr'-ĭ-ă; and all the
prophets prophesied before them.

11 And Zĕd-ē-kī'-ăh the son of Chĕ-nā'-
ă-năh made him horns of iron: and he said,
Thus saith the LORD, With these shalt thou
push the Syrians, until thou have consumed
them.

12 And all the prophets prophesied so, saying, Go up to Rā'-mŏth-gĭl'-ĕ-ăd, and prosper:
for the LORD shall deliver *it* into the king's
hand.

Micaiah prophesies the truth

13 And the messenger that was gone to call
Mī-cāi'-ăh spake unto him, saying, Behold
now, the words of the prophets *declare* good
unto the king with one mouth: let thy word, I
pray thee, be like the word of one of them,
and speak *that which is* good.

14 And Mī-cāi'-ăh said, *As* the LORD liveth,
[R]what the LORD saith unto me, that will I
speak.

15 So he came to the king. And the king
said unto him, Mī-cāi'-ăh, shall we go against
Rā'-mŏth-gĭl'-ĕ-ăd to battle, or shall we forbear? And he answered him, Go, and prosper:
for the LORD shall deliver *it* into the hand of
the king.

16 And the king said unto him, How many
times shall I adjure thee that thou tell me
nothing but *that which is* true in the name of
the LORD?

17 And he said, I saw all Israel [R]scattered
upon the hills, as sheep that have not a shepherd: and the LORD said, These have no
master: let them return every man to his house
in peace.

18 And the king of Israel said unto
Jĕ-hŏsh'-ă-phăt, Did I not tell thee that he

CHAP. **21**	
BC 899	
20 2 Ki. 17:17	
Rom. 7:14	
21 ch. 14:10	
2 Ki. 9:8	
21 1 Sam. 25:22	
21 ch. 14:10	
22 ch. 15:29	
22 ch. 16:3, 11	
23 2 Ki. 9:36	
23 Or, *ditch*	
24 ch. 14:11	
& 16:4	
25 ch. 16:30, etc.	
25 ch. 16:31	
25 Or, *incited*	
26 Gen. 15:16	
2 Ki. 21:11	
27 Gen. 37:34	
29 2 Ki. 9:25	

CHAP. **22**	
BC 897	
2 2 Chr. 18:2, etc.	
3 Deut. 4:43	
3 Heb. *silent from taking it*	
4 2 Ki. 3:7	

ch. 18:19	**6**
2 Ki. 3:11	**7**
Or, *eunuch*	**9**
Heb. *floor*	**10**
Num. 22:38	**14**
Mat. 9:36	**17**

would prophesy no good concerning me, but evil?

19 And he said, Hear thou therefore the word of the LORD: ᴿI saw the LORD sitting on his throne, ᴿand all the host of heaven standing by him on his right hand and on his left.

20 And the LORD said, Who shall ᴺpersuade Ahab, that he may go up and fall at Rā′-mŏth-gĭl′-ĕ-ăd? And one said on this manner, and another said on that manner.

21 And there came forth a spirit, and stood before the LORD, and said, I will persuade him.

22 And the LORD said unto him, Wherewith? And he said, I will go forth, and I will be a lying spirit in the mouth of all his prophets. And he said, ᴿThou shalt persuade him, and prevail also: go forth, and do so.

23 ᴿNow therefore, behold, the LORD hath put a lying spirit in the mouth of all these thy prophets, and the LORD hath spoken evil concerning thee.

Micaiah imprisoned

24 But Zĕd-ē-kī′-ah the son of Chĕ-nā′-ă-năh went near, and smote Mī-cāī′-ah on the cheek, and said, ᴿWhich way went the spirit of the LORD from me to speak unto thee?

25 And Mī-cāī′-ah said, Behold, thou shalt see in that day, when thou shalt go ᴺinto ᴺan inner chamber to hide thyself.

26 And the king of Israel said, Take Mī-cāī′-ah, and carry him back unto Amon the governor of the city, and to Jō′-ăsh the king's son;

27 And say, Thus saith the king, Put this *fellow* in the prison, and feed him with bread of affliction and with water of affliction, until I come in peace.

28 And Mī-cāī′-ah said, If thou return at all in peace, ᴿthe LORD hath not spoken by me. And he said, Hearken, O people, every one of you.

Ahab killed in battle

29 So the king of Israel and Jĕ-hŏsh′-ă-phăt the king of Judah went up to Rā′-mŏth-gĭl′-ĕ-ăd.

30 And the king of Israel said unto Jĕ-hŏsh′-ă-phăt, ᴺI will disguise myself, and enter into the battle; but put thou on thy robes. And the king of Israel ᴿdisguised himself, and went into the battle.

31 But the king of Syria commanded his thirty and two captains that had rule over his chariots, saying, Fight neither with small nor great, save only with the king of Israel.

32 And it came to pass, when the captains of the chariots saw Jĕ-hŏsh′-ă-phăt, that they

---

CHAP. 22
BC 897

19 Is. 6:1
Dan. 7:9
19 Job 1:6
& 2:1
Dan. 7:10
Zech. 1:10
Mat. 18:10
Heb. 1:7, 14
20 Or, *deceive*
22 Judg. 9:23
Job 12:16
Ezek. 14:9
2 Thes. 2:11
23 Ezek. 14:9
24 2 Chr. 18:23
25 Or, *from chamber to chamber*
25 Heb. *a chamber in a chamber,* ch. 20:30
28 Num. 16:29
Deut. 18:20-22
30 Or, *when he was to disguise himself, and enter into the battle*
30 2 Chr. 35:22

2 Chr. 18:31 — **32**
Prov. 13:20
Heb. *in his simplicity,* — **34**
2 Sam. 15:11
Heb. *joints and the breastplate* — **34**
Heb. *made sick* — **34**
Heb. *ascended* — **35**
Heb. *bosom* — **35**
Heb. *came* — **37**
ch. 21:19 — **38**
Amos 3:15 — **39**
2 Chr. 20:31 — **41**
2 Chr. 17:3 — **43**
ch. 14:23 & 15:14 — **43**
2 Ki. 12:3
2 Chr. 19:2 — **44**
2 Cor. 6:14
ch. 14:24 — **46**
& 15:12

---

said, Surely it *is* the king of Israel. And they turned aside to fight against him: and Jĕ-hŏsh′-ă-phăt ᴿcried out.

33 And it came to pass, when the captains of the chariots perceived that it *was* not the king of Israel, that they turned back from pursuing him.

34 And a *certain* man drew a bow ᴺat a venture, and smote the king of Israel between the ᴺjoints of the harness: wherefore he said unto the driver of his chariot, Turn thine hand, and carry me out of the host; for I am ᴺwounded.

35 And the battle ᴺincreased that day: and the king was stayed up in his chariot against the Syrians, and died at even: and the blood ran out of the wound into the ᴺmidst of the chariot.

36 And there went a proclamation throughout the host about the going down of the sun, saying, Every man to his city, and every man to his own country.

37 So the king died, and ᴺwas brought to Să-mâr′-ĭ-ă; and they buried the king in Să-mâr′-ĭ-ă.

38 And *one* washed the chariot in the pool of Să-mâr′-ĭ-ă; and the dogs licked up his blood; and they washed his armour; according ᴿunto the word of the LORD which he spake.

39 Now the rest of the acts of Ahab, and all that he did, and ᴿthe ivory house which he made, and all the cities that he built, *are* they not written in the book of the chronicles of the kings of Israel?

40 So Ahab slept with his fathers; and Ā-hă-zī′-ăh his son reigned in his stead.

Jehoshaphat's reign in Judah

41 And ᴿJĕ-hŏsh′-ă-phăt the son of Ā′-să began to reign over Judah in the fourth year of Ahab king of Israel.

42 Jĕ-hŏsh′-ă-phăt *was* thirty and five years old when he began to reign; and he reigned twenty and five years in Jerusalem. And his mother's name *was* Ă-zū′-băh the daughter of Shĭl′-hī.

43 And ᴿhe walked in all the ways of Ā′-să his father; he turned not aside from it, doing *that which was* right in the eyes of the LORD: nevertheless ᴿthe high places were not taken away; *for* the people offered and burnt incense yet in the high places.

44 And ᴿJĕ-hŏsh′-ă-phăt made peace with the king of Israel.

45 Now the rest of the acts of Jĕ-hŏsh′-ă-phăt, and his might that he shewed, and how he warred, *are* they not written in the book of the chronicles of the kings of Judah?

46 ᴿAnd the remnant of the sodomites,

which remained in the days of his father Ā'-să, he took out of the land.

47 ᴿThere was then no king in Ē'-dǫm: a deputy was king.

48 ᴿJĕ-hŏsh'-ă-phăt ᴿmadeᴺ ships of Thär'-shĭsh to go to Ō'-phĭr for gold: ᴿbut they went not; for the ships were broken at ᴿĒ'-zĭ-ŏn-gē'-bĕr.

49 Then said Ā-hă-zī'-ăh the son of Ahab unto Jĕ-hŏsh'-ă-phăt, Let my servants go with thy servants in the ships. But Jĕ-hŏsh'-ă-phăt would not.

50 And ᴿJĕ-hŏsh'-ă-phăt slept with his fathers, and was buried with his fathers in the city of David his father: and Jĕ-hôr'-ăm his son reigned in his stead.

CHAP. 22
BC 897
47 Gen. 25:23
2 Sam. 8:14
2 Ki. 3:9 & 8:20
48 2 Chr. 20:35, etc.
48 ch. 10:22
48 Or, had ten ships
48 2 Chr. 20:37
48 ch. 9:26
50 2 Chr. 21:1

ver. 40	51
ch. 15:26	52
Judg. 2:11	53
ch. 16:31	

Ahaziah's reign in Israel

51 ᴿĀ-hă-zī'-ăh the son of Ahab began to reign over Israel in Să-mâr'-ĭ-ă the seventeenth year of Jĕ-hŏsh'-ă-phăt king of Judah, and reigned two years over Israel.

52 And he did evil in the sight of the LORD, and ᴿwalked in the way of his father, and in the way of his mother, and in the way of Jĕr-ŏ-bō'-ăm the son of Nē'-băt, who made Israel to sin:

53 For ᴿhe served Bā'-ăl, and worshipped him, and provoked to anger the LORD God of Israel, according to all that his father had done.

THE SECOND
BOOK OF THE KINGS

COMMONLY CALLED
THE FOURTH BOOK OF THE KINGS

Second Kings continues the history of the two monarchies of Israel and Judah and gives an account of their decline and termination. The destruction of both kingdoms is attributed to their unfaithfulness to God. A period of nearly three centuries is covered by these accounts, ca. 850-562 B.C. The first part (Chapters 1-17) continues the history of the two Hebrew kingdoms to the destruction of the northern kingdom of Israel by the Assyrians in 722 B.C. The second part (Chapters 18-25) records the history of the surviving southern kingdom of Judah to its destruction by the Babylonians in 586 B.C. The books of Kings cannot be credited to one particular author, although it is quite probable that they were brought to their present form by one editor during the last half of the Babylonian exile. Many competent scholars have thought that Jeremiah may have been the editor.

OUTLINE OF THE BOOK:
  I. Omride dynasty influence terminated   1:1-11:21
  II. Prosperity and fall of Israel—Judah survives   12:1-17:41
  III. Judah outlasts Assyria   18:1-23:30
  IV. Decline and fall of Judah   23:31-25:30

CHAPTER 1

Elijah prophesies Ahaziah's death

THEN Moab ᴿrebelled against Israel ᴿafter the death of Ahab.

2 And Ā-hă-zī'-ăh fell down through a lattice in his upper chamber that was in Să-mâr'-ĭ-ă, and was sick: and he sent messengers, and said unto them, Go, inquire of Bā'-ăl-zē'-bŭb the god of ᴿĔk'-rŏn whether I shall recover of this disease.

3 But the angel of the LORD said to Ē-lī'-jäh the Tĭsh'-bĭte, Arise, go up to meet the messengers of the king of Să-mâr'-ĭ-ă, and say unto them, Is it not because there is not a God in Israel, that ye go to inquire of Bā'-ăl-zē'-bŭb the god of ĕk'-rŏn?

4 Now therefore thus saith the LORD, ᴺThou shalt not come down from that bed on which

CHAP. 1
BC 896
1 2 Sam. 8:2
1 ch. 3:5
2 1 Sam. 5:10
4 Heb. The bed whither thou art gone up, thou shalt not come down from it

Heb. What was the manner of the man?	7
See Zech. 13:4	8
Mat. 3:4	

thou art gone up, but shalt surely die. And Ē-lī'-jäh departed.

5 And when the messengers turned back unto him, he said unto them, Why are ye now turned back?

6 And they said unto him, There came a man up to meet us, and said unto us, Go, turn again unto the king that sent you, and say unto him, Thus saith the LORD, Is it not because there is not a God in Israel, that thou sendest to inquire of Bā'-ăl-zē'-bŭb the god of ĕk'-rŏn? therefore thou shalt not come down from that bed on which thou art gone up, but shalt surely die.

7 And he said unto them, ᴺWhat manner of man was he which came up to meet you, and told you these words?

8 And they answered him, He was ᴿan hairy man, and girt with a girdle of leather about his loins. And he said, It is Ē-lī'-jäh the Tĭsh'-bĭte.

Attempts to seize Elijah

9 Then the king sent unto him a captain of fifty with his fifty. And he went up to him: and, behold, he sat on the top of an hill. And he spake unto him, Thou man of God, the king hath said, Come down.

10 And Ē-lī'-jăh answered and said to the captain of fifty, If I *be* a man of God, then ^Rlet fire come down from heaven, and consume thee and thy fifty. And there came down fire from heaven, and consumed him and his fifty.

11 Again also he sent unto him another captain of fifty with his fifty. And he answered and said unto him, O man of God, thus hath the king said, Come down quickly.

12 And Ē-lī'-jăh answered and said unto them, If I *be* a man of God, let fire come down from heaven, and consume thee and thy fifty. And the fire of God came down from heaven, and consumed him and his fifty.

13 And he sent again a captain of the third fifty with his fifty. And the third captain of fifty went up, and came and ^Nfell on his knees before Ē-lī'-jăh, and besought him, and said unto him, O man of God, I pray thee, let my life, and the life of these fifty thy servants, ^Rbe precious in thy sight.

14 Behold, there came fire down from heaven, and burnt up the two captains of the former fifties with their fifties: therefore let my life now be precious in thy sight.

15 And the angel of the LORD said unto Ē-lī'-jăh, Go down with him: be not afraid of him. And he arose, and went down with him unto the king.

16 And he said unto him, Thus saith the LORD, Forasmuch as thou hast sent messengers to inquire of Bā'-ăl-zē'-bŭb the god of Ĕk'-rŏn, *is it* not because *there is* no God in Israel to inquire of his word? therefore thou shalt not come down off that bed on which thou art gone up, but shalt surely die.

17 So he died according to the word of the LORD which Ē-lī'-jăh had spoken. And ^NJĕ-hôr'-ăm reigned in his stead in the second year of Jĕ-hôr'-ăm the son of Jĕ-hŏsh'-ă-phăt king of Judah; because he had no son.

18 Now the rest of the acts of Ā-hă-zī'-ăh which he did, *are* they not written in the book of the chronicles of the kings of Israel?

CHAPTER 2

Elijah taken up to heaven

AND it came to pass, when the LORD would ^Rtake up Ē-lī'-jăh into heaven by a

whirlwind, that Ē-lī'-jăh went with ^RĒ-lī'-shă from Gĭl'-găl.

2 And Ē-lī'-jăh said unto Ē-lī'-shă, ^RTarry here, I pray thee; for the LORD hath sent me to Beth-el. And Ē-lī'-shă said *unto him,* As the LORD liveth, and ^R*as* thy soul liveth, I will not leave thee. So they went down to Beth-el.

3 And ^Rthe sons of the prophets that *were* at Beth-el came forth to Ē-lī'-shă, and said unto him, Knowest thou that the LORD will take away thy master from thy head to day? And he said, Yea, I know *it;* hold ye your peace.

4 And Ē-lī'-jăh said unto him, Ē-lī'-shă, tarry here, I pray thee; for the LORD hath sent me to Jericho. And he said, *As* the LORD liveth, and *as* thy soul liveth, I will not leave thee. So they came to Jericho.

5 And the sons of the prophets that *were* at Jericho came to Ē-lī'-shă, and said unto him, Knowest thou that the LORD will take away thy master from thy head to day? And he answered, Yea, I know *it;* hold ye your peace.

6 And Ē-lī'-jăh said unto him, Tarry, I pray thee, here; for the LORD hath sent me to Jordan. And he said, *As* the LORD liveth, and *as* thy soul liveth, I will not leave thee. And they two went on.

7 And fifty men of the sons of the prophets went, and stood ^Nto view afar off: and they two stood by Jordan.

8 And Ē-lī'-jăh took his mantle, and wrapped *it* together, and smote the waters, and ^Rthey were divided hither and thither, so that they two went over on dry ground.

9 And it came to pass, when they were gone over, that Ē-lī'-jăh said unto Ē-lī'-shă, Ask what I shall do for thee, before I be taken away from thee. And Ē-lī'-shă said, I pray thee, let a double portion of thy spirit be upon me.

10 And he said, ^NThou hast asked a hard thing: *nevertheless,* if thou see me *when I am* taken from thee, it shall be so unto thee; but if not, it shall not be *so.*

11 And it came to pass, as they still went on, and talked, that, behold, *there appeared* ^Ra chariot of fire, and horses of fire, and parted them both asunder; and Ē-lī'-jăh went up by a whirlwind into heaven.

12 And Ē-lī'-shă saw *it,* and he cried, ^RMy father, my father, the chariot of Israel, and the horsemen thereof. And he saw him no more: and he took hold of his own clothes, and rent them in two pieces.

Elisha takes up Elijah's mantle

13 He took up also the mantle of Ē-lī'-jăh that fell from him, and went back, and stood by the ^Nbank of Jordan;

14 And he took the mantle of Ē-lī'-jăh that fell from him, and smote the waters, and said, Where *is* the LORD God of Ē-lī'-jăh? and when he also had smitten the waters, [R]they parted hither and thither: and Ē-lī'-shă went over.

15 And when the sons of the prophets which *were* [R]to view at Jericho saw him, they said, The spirit of Ē-lī'-jăh doth rest on Ē-lī'-shă. And they came to meet him, and bowed themselves to the ground before him.

16 And they said unto him, Behold now, there be with thy servants fifty [N]strong men; let them go, we pray thee, and seek thy master: [R]lest peradventure the spirit of the LORD hath taken him up, and cast him upon [N]some mountain, or into some valley. And he said, Ye shall not send.

17 And when they urged him till he was ashamed, he said, Send. They sent therefore fifty men; and they sought three days, but found him not.

18 And when they came again to him, (for he tarried at Jericho,) he said unto them, Did I not say unto you, Go not?

Elisha sweetens water of Jericho

19 And the men of the city said unto Ē-lī'-shă, Behold, I pray thee, the situation of this city *is* pleasant, as my lord seeth: but the water *is* naught, and the ground [N]barren.

20 And he said, Bring me a new cruse, and put salt therein. And they brought *it* to him.

21 And he went forth unto the spring of the waters, and [R]cast the salt in there, and said, Thus saith the LORD, I have healed these waters; there shall not be from thence any more death or barren *land.*

22 So the waters were healed unto this day, according to the saying of Ē-lī'-shă which he spake.

23 And he went up from thence unto Bethel: and as he was going up by the way, there came forth little children out of the city, and mocked him, and said unto him, Go up, thou bald head; go up, thou bald head.

24 And he turned back, and looked on them, and cursed them in the name of the LORD. And there came forth two she bears out of the wood, and tare forty and two children of them.

25 And he went from thence to mount Carmel, and from thence he returned to Să-mâr'-ĭ-ă.

CHAPTER 3

Jehoram's reign in Israel

NOW [R]Jĕ-hôr'-ăm the son of Ahab began to reign over Israel in Să-mâr'-ĭ-ă the eighteenth year of Jĕ-hŏsh'-ă-phăt king of Judah, and reigned twelve years.

2 And he wrought evil in the sight of the LORD; but not like his father, and like his mother: for he put away the [N]image of Bā'-ăl [R]that his father had made.

3 Nevertheless he cleaved unto [R]the sins of Jĕr-ŏ-bō'-ăm the son of Nē'-băt, which made Israel to sin; he departed not therefrom.

Moab's rebellion

4 And Mē'-shă king of Moab was a sheepmaster, and rendered unto the king of Israel an hundred thousand [R]lambs, and an hundred thousand rams, with the wool.

5 But it came to pass, when [R]Ahab was dead, that the king of Moab rebelled against the king of Israel.

6 And king Jĕ-hôr'-ăm went out of Să-mâr'-ĭ-ă the same time, and numbered all Israel.

7 And he went and sent to Jĕ-hŏsh'-ă-phăt the king of Judah, saying, The king of Moab hath rebelled against me: wilt thou go with me against Moab to battle? And he said, I will go up: [R]I *am* as thou *art,* my people as thy people, *and* my horses as thy horses.

8 And he said, Which way shall we go up? And he answered, The way through the wilderness of Ē'-dŏm.

9 So the king of Israel went, and the king of Judah, and the king of Ē'-dŏm: and they fetched a compass of seven days' journey: and there was no water for the host, and for the cattle [N]that followed them.

10 And the king of Israel said, Alas! that the LORD hath called these three kings together, to deliver them into the hand of Moab!

11 But [R]Jĕ-hŏsh'-ă-phăt said, *Is there* not here a prophet of the LORD, that we may inquire of the LORD by him? And one of the king of Israel's servants answered and said, Here *is* Ē-lī'-shă the son of Shā'-phăt, which poured water on the hands of Ē-lī'-jăh.

12 And Jĕ-hŏsh'-ă-phăt said, The word of the LORD is with him. So the king of Israel and Jĕ-hŏsh'-ă-phăt and the king of Ē'-dŏm [R]went down to him.

Elisha predicts victory over Moab

13 And Ē-lī'-shă said unto the king of Israel, [R]What have I to do with thee? [R]get thee to [R]the prophets of thy father, and to the prophets of thy mother. And the king of Israel said unto him, Nay: for the LORD hath called these three kings together, to deliver them into the hand of Moab.

14 And Ē-lī'-shă said, [R]*As* the LORD of hosts

Center reference column:

CHAP. 2
BC 896
14 ver. 8
15 ver. 7
16 Heb. *sons of strength*
16 See 1 Ki. 18:12
Ezek. 8:3
Acts 8:39
16 Heb. *one of the mountains*
19 Heb. *causing to miscarry*
21 See Ex. 15:25
ch. 4:41 & 6:6
John 9:6

CHAP. 3
BC 895
1 ch. 1:17

Heb. *statue*　2
1 Ki. 16:31, 32　2
1 Ki. 12:28, 31, 32　3
See Is. 16:1　4
ch. 1:1　5
1 Ki. 22:4　7
Heb. *at their feet:*　9
See Ex. 11:8
1 Ki. 22:7　11
ch. 2:25　12
Ezek. 14:3　13
Judg. 10:14　13
Ruth 1:15
1 Ki. 18:19　13
1 Ki. 17:1　14
ch. 5:16

liveth, before whom I stand, surely, were it not that I regard the presence of Jĕ-hŏsh′-ă-phăt the king of Judah, I would not look toward thee, nor see thee.

15 But now bring me ᴿa minstrel. And it came to pass, when the minstrel played, that ᴿthe hand of the LORD came upon him.

16 And he said, Thus saith the LORD, ᴿMake this valley full of ditches.

17 For thus saith the LORD, Ye shall not see wind, neither shall ye see rain; yet that valley shall be filled with water, that ye may drink, both ye, and your cattle, and your beasts.

18 And this is *but* a light thing in the sight of the LORD: he will deliver the Moabites also into your hand.

19 And ye shall smite every fenced city, and every choice city, and shall fell every good tree, and stop all wells of water, and ᴺmar every good piece of land with stones.

20 And it came to pass in the morning, when ᴿthe meat offering was offered, that, behold, there came water by the way of Ē′-dom, and the country was filled with water.

Defeat of Moab

21 And when all the Moabites heard that the kings were come up to fight against them, they ᴺgathered all that were able to ᴺput on armour, and upward, and stood in the border.

22 And they rose up early in the morning, and the sun shone upon the water, and the Moabites saw the water on the other side *as* red as blood:

23 And they said, This *is* blood: the kings are surely ᴺslain, and they have smitten one another: now therefore, Moab, to the spoil.

24 And when they came to the camp of Israel, the Israelites rose up and smote the Moabites, so that they fled before them: but ᴺthey went forward smiting the Moabites, even in *their* country.

25 And they beat down the cities, and on every good piece of land cast every man his stone, and filled it; and they stopped all the wells of water, and felled all the good trees: ᴺonly in ᴿKĭr-hăr′-ă-sĕth left they the stones thereof; howbeit the slingers went about *it*, and smote it.

26 And when the king of Moab saw that the battle was too sore for him, he took with him seven hundred men that drew swords, to break through *even* unto the king of Ē′-dom: but they could not.

27 Then ᴿhe took his eldest son that should have reigned in his stead, and offered him *for* a burnt offering upon the wall. And there was great indignation against Israel: ᴿand they de-

CHAP. 3

BC 895

15 See 1 Sam. 10:5
15 Ezek. 1:3
& 3:14, 22 & 8:1
16 ch. 4:3
19 Heb. *grieve*
20 Ex. 29:39, 40
21 Heb. *were cried together*
21 Heb. *gird himself with a girdle*
23 Heb. *destroyed*
24 Or, *they smote in it even smiting*
25 Heb. *until he left the stones thereof in Kirharaseth*
25 Is. 16:7, 11
27 Amos 2:1
27 ch. 8:20

parted from him, and returned to *their own* land.

CHAPTER 4

The widow's oil

NOW there cried a certain woman of the wives of ᴿthe sons of the prophets unto Ē-lī′-shă, saying, Thy servant my husband is dead; and thou knowest that thy servant did fear the LORD: and the creditor is come ᴿto take unto him my two sons to be bondmen.

2 And Ē-lī′-shă said unto her, What shall I do for thee? tell me, what hast thou in the house? And she said, Thine handmaid hath not any thing in the house, save a pot of oil.

3 Then he said, Go, borrow thee vessels abroad of all thy neighbours, *even* empty vessels; ᴿborrow ᴺnot a few.

4 And when thou art come in, thou shalt shut the door upon thee and upon thy sons, and shalt pour out into all those vessels, and thou shalt set aside that which is full.

5 So she went from him, and shut the door upon her and upon her sons, who brought *the vessels* to her; and she poured out.

6 And it came to pass, when the vessels were full, that she said unto her son, Bring me yet a vessel. And he said unto her, *There is* not a vessel more. And the oil stayed.

7 Then she came and told the man of God. And he said, Go, sell the oil, and pay thy ᴺdebt, and live thou and thy children of the rest.

The Shunammite woman promised a son

8 And ᴺit fell on a day, that Ē-lī′-shă passed to ᴿShû′-nĕm, where *was* a great woman; and she ᴺconstrained him to eat bread. And *so* it was, *that* as oft as he passed by, he turned in thither to eat bread.

9 And she said unto her husband, Behold now, I perceive that this *is* an holy man of God, which passeth by us continually.

10 Let us make a little chamber, I pray thee, on the wall; and let us set for him there a bed, and a table, and a stool, and a candlestick: and it shall be, when he cometh to us, that he shall turn in thither.

11 And it fell on a day, that he came thither, and he turned into the chamber, and lay there.

12 And he said to Gĕ-hā′-zī his servant, Call this Shû-năm′-mīte. And when he had called her, she stood before him.

13 And he said unto him, Say now unto her, Behold, thou hast been careful for us with all this care; what *is* to be done for thee? wouldest thou be spoken for to the king, or to the

CHAP. 4

BC 895

1 Ki. 20:35 — 1
See Lev. 25:39 — 1
Mat. 18:25
See ch. 3:16 — 3
Or, *scant not* — 3
Or, *creditor* — 7
Heb. *there was a day* — 8
Josh. 19:18 — 8
Heb. *laid hold on him* — 8

captain of the host? And she answered, I dwell among mine own people.

14 And he said, What then *is* to be done for her? And Gĕ-hā′-zī answered, Verily she hath no child, and her husband is old.

15 And he said, Call her. And when he had called her, she stood in the door.

16 And he said, ᴿAbout this ᴺseason, according to the time of life, thou shalt embrace a son. And she said, Nay, my lord, *thou* man of God, ᴿdo not lie unto thine handmaid.

17 And the woman conceived, and bare a son at that season that Ē-lī′-shă had said unto her, according to the time of life.

Elisha restores the child's life

18 And when the child was grown, it fell on a day, that he went out to his father to the reapers.

19 And he said unto his father, My head, my head. And he said to a lad, Carry him to his mother.

20 And when he had taken him, and brought him to his mother, he sat on her knees till noon, and *then* died.

21 And she went up, and laid him on the bed of the man of God, and shut *the door* upon him, and went out.

22 And she called unto her husband, and said, Send me, I pray thee, one of the young men, and one of the asses, that I may run to the man of God, and come again.

23 And he said, Wherefore wilt thou go to him to day? *it is* neither new moon, nor sabbath. And she said, *It shall be* ᴺwell.

24 Then she saddled an ass, and said to her servant, Drive, and go forward; ᴺslack not *thy* riding for me, except I bid thee.

25 So she went and came unto the man of God ᴿto mount Carmel. And it came to pass, when the man of God saw her afar off, that he said to Gĕ-hā′-zī his servant, Behold, *yonder is* that Shû-năm′-mīte:

26 Run now, I pray thee, to meet her, and say unto her, *Is it* well with thee? *is it* well with thy husband? *is it* well with the child? And she answered, *It is* well.

27 And when she came to the man of God to the hill, she caught ᴺhim by the feet: but Gĕ-hā′-zī came near to thrust her away. And the man of God said, Let her alone; for her soul *is* ᴺvexed within her: and the LORD hath hid *it* from me, and hath not told me.

28 Then she said, Did I desire a son of my lord? ᴿdid I not say, Do not deceive me?

29 Then he said to Gĕ-hā′-zī, ᴿGird up thy loins, and take my staff in thine hand, and go thy way: if thou meet any man, ᴿsalute him

not; and if any salute thee, answer him not again: and ᴿlay my staff upon the face of the child.

30 And the mother of the child said, ᴿ*As* the LORD liveth, and *as* thy soul liveth, I will not leave thee. And he arose, and followed her.

31 And Gĕ-hā′-zī passed on before them, and laid the staff upon the face of the child; but *there was* neither voice, nor ᴺhearing. Wherefore he went again to meet him, and told him, saying, The child is ᴿnot awaked.

32 And when Ē-lī′-shă was come into the house, behold, the child was dead, *and* laid upon his bed.

33 He ᴿwent in therefore, and shut the door upon them twain, ᴿand prayed unto the LORD.

34 And he went up, and lay upon the child, and put his mouth upon his mouth, and his eyes upon his eyes, and his hands upon his hands: and ᴿhe stretched himself upon the child; and the flesh of the child waxed warm.

35 Then he returned, and walked in the house ᴺto and fro; and went up, ᴿand stretched himself upon him: and ᴿthe child sneezed seven times, and the child opened his eyes.

36 And he called Gĕ-hā′-zī, and said, Call this Shû-năm′-mīte. So he called her. And when she was come in unto him, he said, Take up thy son.

37 Then she went in, and fell at his feet, and bowed herself to the ground, and ᴿtook up her son, and went out.

Elisha makes poisoned food harmless

38 And Ē-lī′-shă came again to ᴿGĭl′-găl: and *there was* a ᴿdearth in the land; and the sons of the prophets *were* ᴿsitting before him: and he said unto his servant, Set on the great pot, and seethe pottage for the sons of the prophets.

39 And one went out into the field to gather herbs, and found a wild vine, and gathered thereof wild gourds his lap full, and came and shred *them* into the pot of pottage: for they knew *them* not.

40 So they poured out for the men to eat. And it came to pass, as they were eating of the pottage, that they cried out, and said, O *thou* man of God, *there is* ᴿdeath in the pot. And they could not eat *thereof.*

41 But he said, Then bring meal. And ᴿhe cast *it* into the pot; and he said, Pour out for the people, that they may eat. And there was no ᴺharm in the pot.

42 And there came a man from ᴿBā′-ăl-shăl′-ĭ-shă, ᴿand brought the man of God bread of the firstfruits, twenty loaves of barley, and full ears of corn ᴺin the husk thereof. And

CHAP. **4**

BC 895

16 Gen. 18:10, 14
16 Heb. *set time*
16 ver. 28
23 Heb. *peace*
24 Heb. *restrain not for me to ride*
25 ch. 2:25
27 Heb. *by his feet,* Mat. 28:9
27 Heb. *bitter,* 1 Sam. 1:10
28 ver. 16
29 1 Ki. 18:46 ch. 9:1
29 Luke 10:4

See Ex. 7:19 & 14:16 — 29
Acts 19:12
ch. 2:8, 14
ch. 2:2 — 30
Heb. *attention* — 31
John 11:11 — 31
ver. 4 — 33
Mat. 6:6
1 Ki. 17:20 — 33
1 Ki. 17:21 — 34
Acts 20:10
Heb. *once hither, and once thither* — 35
1 Ki. 17:21 — 35
ch. 8:1, 5 — 35
1 Ki. 17:23 — 37
Heb. 11:35
ch. 2:1 — 38
ch. 8:1 — 38
ch. 2:3 — 38
Luke 10:39
Acts 22:3
Ex. 10:17 — 40
See Ex. 15:25 — 41
ch. 2:21 & 5:10
John 9:6
Heb. *evil thing* — 41
1 Sam. 9:4 — 42
1 Sam. 9:7 — 42
1 Cor. 9:11
Gal. 6:6
Or, *in his scrip, or, garment* — 42

he said, Give unto the people, that they may eat.

43 And his servitor said, ^RWhat, should I set this before an hundred men? He said again, Give the people, that they may eat: for thus saith the LORD, ^RThey shall eat, and shall leave *thereof.*

44 So he set *it* before them, and they did eat, ^Rand left *thereof,* according to the word of the LORD.

CHAPTER 5

Naaman's leprosy cured

NOW ^RNā'-ă-măn, captain of the host of the king of Syria, was ^Ra great man ^Nwith his master, and ^{NN}honourable, because by him the LORD had given ^Ndeliverance unto Syria: he was also a mighty man in valour, *but he was* a leper.

2 And the Syrians had gone out by companies, and had brought away captive out of the land of Israel a little maid; and she ^Nwaited on Nā'-ă-măn's wife.

3 And she said unto her mistress, Would God my lord *were* ^Nwith the prophet that *is* in Să-mâr'-ĭ-ă! for he would ^Nrecover him of his leprosy.

4 And *one* went in, and told his lord, saying, Thus and thus said the maid that *is* of the land of Israel.

5 And the king of Syria said, Go to, go, and I will send a letter unto the king of Israel. And he departed, and ^Rtook ^Nwith him ten talents of silver, and six thousand *pieces* of gold, and ten changes of raiment.

6 And he brought the letter to the king of Israel, saying, Now when this letter is come unto thee, behold, I have *therewith* sent Nā'-ă-măn my servant to thee, that thou mayest recover him of his leprosy.

7 And it came to pass, when the king of Israel had read the letter, that he rent his clothes, and said, *Am* I ^RGod, to kill and to make alive, that this man doth send unto me to recover a man of his leprosy? wherefore consider, I pray you, and see how he seeketh a quarrel against me.

8 And it was *so,* when Ē-lī'-shă the man of God had heard that the king of Israel had rent his clothes, that he sent to the king, saying, Wherefore hast thou rent thy clothes? let him come now to me, and he shall know that there is a prophet in Israel.

9 So Nā'-ă-măn came with his horses and with his chariot, and stood at the door of the house of Ē-lī'-shă.

CHAP. 4
BC 895
43 Luke 9:13
John 6:9
43 Luke 9:17
John 6:11
44 Mat. 14:20
& 15:37
John 6:13

CHAP. 5
BC 894
1 Luke 4:27
1 Ex. 11:3
1 Heb. *before*
1 Or, *gracious*
1 Heb. *lifted up,* or, *accepted in countenance*
1 Or, *victory*
2 Heb. *was before*
3 Heb. *before*
3 Heb. *gather in*
5 1 Sam. 9:8
ch. 8:8, 9
5 Heb. *in his hand*
7 Gen. 30:2
Deut. 32:39
1 Sam. 2:6

See ch. 4:41	10
John 9:7	
Heb. *I said*	11
Or, *I said with myself, He will surely come out, etc.*	11
Heb. *move up and down*	11
Or, *Amana*	12
Job 33:25	14
Luke 4:27	14
Dan. 2:47	15
& 3:29 & 6:26, 27	
Gen. 33:11	15
ch. 3:14	16
Gen. 14:23	16
See Mat. 10:8	
Acts 8:18, 20	
ch. 7:2, 17	18
Heb. *a little piece of ground, as* Gen. 35:16	19

10 And Ē-lī'-shă sent a messenger unto him, saying, Go and ^Rwash in Jordan seven times, and thy flesh shall come again to thee, and thou shalt be clean.

11 But Nā'-ă-măn was wroth, and went away, and said, Behold, ^{NN}I thought, He will surely come out to me, and stand, and call on the name of the LORD his God, and ^Nstrike his hand over the place, and recover the leper.

12 *Are* not ^NĂb'-ă-nă and Phär'-pär, rivers of Damascus, better than all the waters of Israel? may I not wash in them, and be clean? So he turned and went away in a rage.

13 And his servants came near, and spake unto him, and said, My father, *if* the prophet had bid thee *do some* great thing, wouldest thou not have done *it?* how much rather then, when he saith to thee, Wash, and be clean?

14 Then went he down, and dipped himself seven times in Jordan, according to the saying of the man of God: and ^Rhis flesh came again like unto the flesh of a little child, and ^Rhe was clean.

Elisha refuses payment

15 And he returned to the man of God, he and all his company, and came, and stood before him: and he said, Behold, now I know that *there is* ^Rno God in all the earth, but in Israel: now therefore, I pray thee, take ^Ra blessing of thy servant.

16 But he said, ^RAs the LORD liveth, before whom I stand, ^RI will receive none. And he urged him to take *it;* but he refused.

17 And Nā'-ă-măn said, Shall there not then, I pray thee, be given to thy servant two mules' burden of earth? for thy servant will henceforth offer neither burnt offering nor sacrifice unto other gods, but unto the LORD.

18 In this thing the LORD pardon thy servant, *that* when my master goeth into the house of Rimmon to worship there, and ^Rhe leaneth on my hand, and I bow myself in the house of Rimmon: when I bow down myself in the house of Rimmon, the LORD pardon thy servant in this thing.

Gehazi contracts leprosy

19 And he said unto him, Go in peace. So he departed from him ^Na little way.

20 But Gĕ-hā'-zī, the servant of Ē-lī'-shă the man of God, said, Behold, my master hath spared Nā'-ă-măn this Syrian, in not receiving at his hands that which he brought: but, *as* the LORD liveth, I will run after him, and take somewhat of him.

21 So Gĕ-hā'-zī followed after Nā'-ă-măn. And when Nā'-ă-măn saw *him* running after

him, he lighted down from the chariot to meet him, and said, ^N*Is* all well?

22 And he said, All *is* well. My master hath sent me, saying, Behold, even now there be come to me from mount Ē'-phră-ĭm two young men of the sons of the prophets: give them, I pray thee, a talent of silver, and two changes of garments.

23 And Nā'-ă-măn said, Be content, take two talents. And he urged him, and bound two talents of silver in two bags, with two changes of garments, and laid *them* upon two of his servants; and they bare *them* before him.

24 And when he came to the ^Ntower, he took *them* from their hand, and bestowed *them* in the house: and he let the men go, and they departed.

25 But he went in, and stood before his master. And Ē-lī'-shă said unto him, Whence *comest thou,* Gĕ-hā'-zī? And he said, Thy servant went ^Nno whither.

26 And he said unto him, Went not mine heart *with thee,* when the man turned again from his chariot to meet thee? *Is it* a time to receive money, and to receive garments, and oliveyards, and vineyards, and sheep, and oxen, and menservants, and maidservants?

27 The leprosy therefore of Nā'-ă-măn ^Rshall cleave unto thee, and unto thy seed for ever. And he went out from his presence ^Ra leper *as white* as snow.

CHAPTER 6

The axe head floats

AND ^Rthe sons of the prophets said unto Ē-lī'-shă, Behold now, the place where we dwell with thee is too strait for us.

2 Let us go, we pray thee, unto Jordan, and take thence every man a beam, and let us make us a place there, where we may dwell. And he answered, Go ye.

3 And one said, Be content, I pray thee, and go with thy servants. And he answered, I will go.

4 So he went with them. And when they came to Jordan, they cut down wood.

5 But as one was felling a beam, the ^Naxe head fell into the water: and he cried, and said, Alas, master! for it was borrowed.

6 And the man of God said, Where fell it? And he shewed him the place. And ^Rhe cut down a stick, and cast *it* in thither; and the iron did swim.

7 Therefore said he, Take *it* up to thee. And he put out his hand, and took it.

Elisha and the Syrians

8 Then the king of Syria warred against Israel, and took counsel with his servants, saying, In such and such a place *shall be* my ^Ncamp.

9 And the man of God sent unto the king of Israel, saying, Beware that thou pass not such a place; for thither the Syrians are come down.

10 And the king of Israel sent to the place which the man of God told him and warned him of, and saved himself there, not once nor twice.

11 Therefore the heart of the king of Syria was sore troubled for this thing; and he called his servants, and said unto them, Will ye not shew me which of us *is* for the king of Israel?

12 And one of his servants said, ^NNone, my lord, O king: but Ē-lī'-shă, the prophet that *is* in Israel, telleth the king of Israel the words that thou speakest in thy bedchamber.

13 And he said, Go and spy where he *is,* that I may send and fetch him. And it was told him, saying, Behold, *he is* in ^RDō'-thăn.

14 Therefore sent he thither horses, and chariots, and a ^Ngreat host: and they came by night, and compassed the city about.

15 And when the ^Nservant of the man of God was risen early, and gone forth, behold, an host compassed the city both with horses and chariots. And his servants said unto him, Alas, my master! how shall we do?

16 And he answered, Fear not: for ^Rthey that *be* with us *are* more than they that *be* with them.

17 And Ē-lī'-shă prayed, and said, Lord, I pray thee, open his eyes, that he may see. And the Lord opened the eyes of the young man; and he saw: and, behold, the mountain *was* full of ^Rhorses and chariots of fire round about Ē-lī'-shă.

18 And when they came down to him, Ē-lī'-shă prayed unto the Lord, and said, Smite this people, I pray thee, with blindness. And ^Rhe smote them with blindness according to the word of Ē-lī'-shă.

19 And Ē-lī'-shă said unto them, This *is* not the way, neither *is* this the city: ^Nfollow me, and I will bring you to the man whom ye seek. But he led them to Să-mâr'-ĭ-ă.

20 And it came to pass, when they were come into Să-mâr'-ĭ-ă, that Ē-lī'-shă said, Lord, open the eyes of these *men,* that they may see. And the Lord opened their eyes, and they saw; and, behold, *they were* in the midst of Să-mâr'-ĭ-ă.

21 And the king of Israel said unto Ē-lī'-shă,

when he saw them, My father, shall I smite *them?* shall I smite *them?*

22 And he answered, Thou shalt not smite *them:* wouldest thou smite those whom thou hast taken captive with thy sword and with thy bow? ᴿset bread and water before them, that they may eat and drink, and go to their master.

23 And he prepared great provision for them: and when they had eaten and drunk, he sent them away, and they went to their master. So ᴿthe bands of Syria came no more into the land of Israel.

Ben-hadad besieges Samaria

24 And it came to pass after this, that Bĕn-hā'-dăd king of Syria gathered all his host, and went up, and besieged Să-mâr'-ĭ-ă.

25 And there was a great famine in Să-mâr'-ĭ-ă: and, behold, they besieged it, until an ass's head was *sold* for fourscore *pieces* of silver, and the fourth part of a căb of dove's dung for five *pieces* of silver.

26 And as the king of Israel was passing by upon the wall, there cried a woman unto him, saying, Help, my lord, O king.

27 And he said, ᴺIf the Lᴏʀᴅ do not help thee, whence shall I help thee? out of the barnfloor, or out of the winepress?

28 And the king said unto her, What aileth thee? And she answered, This woman said unto me, Give thy son, that we may eat him to day, and we will eat my son to morrow.

29 So ᴿwe boiled my son, and did eat him: and I said unto her on the ᴺnext day, Give thy son, that we may eat him: and she hath hid her son.

30 And it came to pass, when the king heard the words of the woman, that he ᴿrent his clothes; and he passed by upon the wall, and the people looked, and, behold, *he had* sackcloth within upon his flesh.

31 Then he said, ᴿGod do so and more also to me, if the head of Ē-lī'-shă the son of Shā'-phăt shall stand on him this day.

Prophecy of Elisha

32 But Ē-lī'-shă sat in his house, and ᴿthe elders sat with him; and *the king* sent a man from before him: but ere the messenger came to him, he said to the elders, ᴿSee ye how this son of ᴿa murderer hath sent to take away mine head? look, when the messenger cometh, shut the door, and hold him fast at the door: *is* not the sound of his master's feet behind him?

33 And while he yet talked with them, behold, the messenger came down unto him: and

CHAP. 6
BC 893
22 Rom. 12:20
23 ver. 8, 9
ch. 5:2
27 Or, *Let not the LORD save thee*
29 Lev. 26:29
Deut. 28:53, 57
29 Heb. *other*
30 1 Ki. 21:27
31 Heb. 1:17
1 Ki. 19:2
32 Ezek. 8:1 & 20:1
32 Luke 13:32
32 1 Ki. 18:4

Job 2:9   33

CHAP. 7
BC 892
ver. 18, 19   1
ver. 17, 19, 20   2
Heb. *a lord*   2
which belonged *to the king leaning upon his hand,*
ch. 5:18
Mal. 3:10   2
Lev. 13:46   3
2 Sam. 5:24   6
ch. 19:7
Job 15:21
1 Ki. 10:29   6
Ps. 48:4-6   7
Prov. 28:1
Heb. *we shall find punishment*   9

he said, Behold, this evil *is* of the Lᴏʀᴅ; ᴿwhat should I wait for the Lᴏʀᴅ any longer?

CHAPTER 7

THEN Ē-lī'-shă said, Hear ye the word of the Lᴏʀᴅ; Thus saith the Lᴏʀᴅ, ᴿTo morrow about this time *shall* a measure of fine flour *be sold* for a shē'-kĕl, and two measures of barley for a shē'-kĕl, in the gate of Să-mâr'-ĭ-ă.

2 ᴿThen ᴺa lord on whose hand the king leaned answered the man of God, and said, Behold, ᴿ*if* the Lᴏʀᴅ would make windows in heaven, might this thing be? And he said, Behold, thou shalt see *it* with thine eyes, but shalt not eat thereof.

The Syrians flee

3 And there were four leprous men ᴿat the entering in of the gate: and they said one to another, Why sit we here until we die?

4 If we say, We will enter into the city, then the famine *is* in the city, and we shall die there: and if we sit still here, we die also. Now therefore come, and let us fall unto the host of the Syrians: if they save us alive, we shall live; and if they kill us, we shall but die.

5 And they rose up in the twilight, to go unto the camp of the Syrians: and when they were come to the uttermost part of the camp of Syria, behold, *there was* no man there.

6 For the Lord had made the host of the Syrians ᴿto hear a noise of chariots, and a noise of horses, *even* the noise of a great host: and they said one to another, Lo, the king of Israel hath hired against us ᴿthe kings of the Hittites, and the kings of the Egyptians, to come upon us.

7 Wherefore they ᴿarose and fled in the twilight, and left their tents, and their horses, and their asses, even the camp as it *was,* and fled for their life.

8 And when these lepers came to the uttermost part of the camp, they went into one tent, and did eat and drink, and carried thence silver, and gold, and raiment, and went and hid *it;* and came again, and entered into another tent, and carried thence *also,* and went and hid *it.*

9 Then they said one to another, We do not well: this day *is* a day of good tidings, and we hold our peace: if we tarry till the morning light, ᴺsome mischief will come upon us: now therefore come, that we may go and tell the king's household.

10 So they came and called unto the porter of the city: and they told them, saying, We

came to the camp of the Syrians, and, behold, *there was* no man there, neither voice of man, but horses tied, and asses tied, and the tents as they *were*.

11 And he called the porters; and they told *it* to the king's house within.

12 And the king arose in the night, and said unto his servants, I will now shew you what the Syrians have done to us. They know that we *be* hungry; therefore are they gone out of the camp to hide themselves in the field, saying, When they come out of the city, we shall catch them alive, and get into the city.

13 And one of his servants answered and said, Let *some* take, I pray thee, five of the horses that remain, which are left ᴺin the city, (behold, they *are* as all the multitude of Israel that are left in it: behold, *I say,* they *are* even as all the multitude of the Israelites that are consumed:) and let us send and see.

14 They took therefore two chariot horses; and the king sent after the host of the Syrians, saying, Go and see.

15 And they went after them unto Jordan: and, lo, all the way *was* full of garments and vessels, which the Syrians had cast away in their haste. And the messengers returned, and told the king.

Israel plunders the Syrian camp

16 And the people went out, and spoiled the tents of the Syrians. So a measure of fine flour was *sold* for a shē′-kĕl, and two measures of barley for a shē′-kĕl, ᴿaccording to the word of the Lᴏʀᴅ.

17 And the king appointed the lord on whose hand he leaned to have the charge of the gate: and the people trode upon him in the gate, and he died, ᴿas the man of God had said, who spake when the king came down to him.

18 And it came to pass as the man of God had spoken to the king, saying, ᴿTwo measures of barley for a shē′-kĕl, and a measure of fine flour for a shē′-kĕl, shall be to morrow about this time in the gate of Să-mâr′-ĭ-ă:

19 And that lord answered the man of God, and said, Now, behold, *if* the Lᴏʀᴅ should make windows in heaven, might such a thing be? And he said, Behold, thou shalt see it with thine eyes, but shalt not eat thereof.

20 And so it fell out unto him: for the people trode upon him in the gate, and he died.

CHAPTER 8

Return of the Shunammite

THEN spake Ē-lī′-shă unto the woman, ᴿwhose son he had restored to life, say-

ing, Arise, and go thou and thine household, and sojourn wheresoever thou canst sojourn: for the Lᴏʀᴅ ᴿhath called for a famine; and it shall also come upon the land seven years.

2 And the woman arose, and did after the saying of the man of God: and she went with her household, and sojourned in the land of the Philistines seven years.

3 And it came to pass at the seven years' end, that the woman returned out of the land of the Philistines: and she went forth to cry unto the king for her house and for her land.

4 And the king talked with ᴿGĕ-hā′-zī the servant of the man of God, saying, Tell me, I pray thee, all the great things that Ē-lī′-shă hath done.

5 And it came to pass, as he was telling the king how he had ᴿrestored a dead body to life, that, behold, the woman, whose son he had restored to life, cried to the king for her house and for her land. And Gĕ-hā′-zī said, My lord, O king, this *is* the woman, and this *is* her son, whom Ē-lī′-shă restored to life.

6 And when the king asked the woman, she told him. So the king appointed unto her a certain ᴺofficer, saying, Restore all that *was* hers, and all the fruits of the field since the day that she left the land, even until now.

Hazael becomes king of Syria

7 And Ē-lī′-shă came to Damascus; and Bĕn-hā′-dăd the king of Syria was sick; and it was told him, saying, The man of God is come hither.

8 And the king said unto ᴿHă-zā′-ĕl, ᴿTake a present in thine hand, and go, meet the man of God, and ᴿinquire of the Lᴏʀᴅ by him, saying, Shall I recover of this disease?

9 So Hă-zā′-ĕl went to meet him, and took a present ᴺwith him, even of every good thing of Damascus, forty camels' burden, and came and stood before him, and said, Thy son Bĕn-hā′-dăd king of Syria hath sent me to thee, saying, Shall I recover of this disease?

10 And Ē-lī′-shă said unto him, Go, say unto him, Thou mayest certainly recover: howbeit the Lᴏʀᴅ hath shewed me that ᴿhe shall surely die.

11 And he settled his countenance ᴺstedfastly, until he was ashamed: and the man of God ᴿwept.

12 And Hă-zā′-ĕl said, Why weepeth my lord? And he answered, Because I know ᴿthe evil that thou wilt do unto the children of Israel: their strong holds wilt thou set on fire, and their young men wilt thou slay with the sword, and ᴿwilt dash their children, and rip up their women with child.

13 And Hă-zā′-ĕl said, But what, ᴿ*is* thy

servant a dog, that he should do this great thing? And Ē-lī'-shă answered, [R]The LORD hath shewed me that thou *shalt be* king over Syria.

14 So he departed from Ē-lī'-shă, and came to his master; who said to him, What said Ē-lī'-shă to thee? And he answered, He told me *that* thou shouldest surely recover.

15 And it came to pass on the morrow, that he took a thick cloth, and dipped *it* in water, and spread *it* on his face, so that he died: and Hă-zā'-ĕl reigned in his stead.

Jehoram's reign in Judah

16 And in the fifth year of Joram the son of Ahab king of Israel, Jĕ-hŏsh'-ă-phăt *being* then king of Judah, [R]Jĕ-hôr'-ăm the son of Jĕ-hŏsh'-ă-phăt king of Judah [N]began to reign.

17 [R]Thirty and two years old was he when he began to reign; and he reigned eight years in Jerusalem.

18 And he walked in the way of the kings of Israel, as did the house of Ahab: for [R]the daughter of Ahab was his wife: and he did evil in the sight of the LORD.

19 Yet the LORD would not destroy Judah for David his servant's sake, [R]as he promised him to give him alway a [N]light, *and* to his children.

20 In his days [R]Ē'-dom revolted from under the hand of Judah, [R]and made a king over themselves.

21 So Joram went over to Zā'-ĭr, and all the chariots with him: and he rose by night, and smote the Ē'-dom-ītes which compassed him about, and the captains of the chariots: and the people fled into their tents.

22 [N]Yet Ē'-dom revolted from under the hand of Judah unto this day. [R]Then Lĭb'-năh revolted at the same time.

23 And the rest of the acts of Joram, and all that he did, *are* they not written in the book of the chronicles of the kings of Judah?

24 And Joram slept with his fathers, and was buried with his fathers in the city of David: and [R]Ā-hă-zī'-ăh[N] his son reigned in his stead.

Ahaziah's reign in Judah

25 In the twelfth year of Joram the son of Ahab king of Israel did Ā-hă-zī'-ăh the son of Jĕ-hôr'-ăm king of Judah begin to reign.

26 [R]Two and twenty years old *was* Ā-hă-zī'-ăh when he began to reign; and he reigned one year in Jerusalem. And his mother's name *was* Ăth-ă-lī'-ăh, the [N]daughter of Omri king of Israel.

27 [R]And he walked in the way of the house of Ahab, and did evil in the sight of the LORD,

as *did* the house of Ahab: for he *was* the son in law of the house of Ahab.

28 And he went [R]with Joram the son of Ahab to the war against Hă-zā'-ĕl king of Syria in Rā'-mŏth-gĭl'-ĕ-ăd; and the Syrians wounded Joram.

29 And [R]king Joram went back to be healed in Jĕz'-rĕel of the wounds [N]which the Syrians had given him at [N]Rā'-măh, when he fought against Hă-zā'-ĕl king of Syria. [R]And Ā-hă-zī'-ăh the son of Jĕ-hôr'-ăm king of Judah went down to see Joram the son of Ahab in Jĕz'-rĕel, because he was [N]sick.

CHAPTER 9

Jehu anointed king of Israel

AND Ē-lī'-shă the prophet called one of [R]the children of the prophets, and said unto him, [R]Gird up thy loins, and take this box of oil in thine hand, [R]and go to Rā'-mŏth-gĭl'-ĕ-ăd:

2 And when thou comest thither, look out there Jehu the son of Jĕ-hŏsh'-ă-phăt the son of Nimshi, and go in, and make him arise up from among [R]his brethren, and carry him to an [N]inner chamber;

3 Then [R]take the box of oil, and pour *it* on his head, and say, Thus saith the LORD, I have anointed thee king over Israel. Then open the door, and flee, and tarry not.

4 So the young man, *even* the young man the prophet, went to Rā'-mŏth-gĭl'-ĕ-ăd.

5 And when he came, behold, the captains of the host *were* sitting; and he said, I have an errand to thee, O captain. And Jehu said, Unto which of all us? And he said, To thee, O captain.

6 And he arose, and went into the house; and he poured the oil on his head, and said unto him, [R]Thus saith the LORD God of Israel, I have anointed thee king over the people of the LORD, *even* over Israel.

7 And thou shalt smite the house of Ahab thy master, that I may avenge the blood of my servants the prophets, and the blood of all the servants of the LORD, [R]at the hand of Jĕz'-ĕ-bĕl.

8 For the whole house of Ahab shall perish: and [R]I will cut off from Ahab [R]him that pisseth against the wall, and [R]him that is shut up and left in Israel:

9 And I will make the house of Ahab like the house of [R]Jĕr-ŏ-bō'-ăm the son of Nē'-băt, and like the house of [R]Bā-ăsh'-ă the son of Ă-hī'-jăh:

10 [R]And the dogs shall eat Jĕz'-ĕ-bĕl in the portion of Jĕz'-rĕel, and *there shall be* none to bury *her*. And he opened the door, and fled.

11 Then Jehu came forth to the servants of his lord: and *one* said unto him, *Is* all well? wherefore came ᴿthis mad *fellow* to thee? And he said unto them, Ye know the man, and his communication.

12 And they said, *It is* false; tell us now. And he said, Thus and thus spake he to me, saying, Thus saith the LORD, I have anointed thee king over Israel.

13 Then they hasted, and ᴿtook every man his garment, and put *it* under him on the top of the stairs, and blew with trumpets, saying, Jehu ᴺis king.

14 So Jehu the son of Jĕ-hŏsh'-ă-phăt the son of Nimshi conspired against Joram. (Now Joram had kept Rā'-mŏth-gĭl'-ĕ-ăd, he and all Israel, because of Hă-zā'-ĕl king of Syria.

15 But ᴿking ᴺJoram was returned to be healed in Jĕz'-rĕĕl of the wounds which the Syrians ᴺhad given him, when he fought with Hă-zā'-ĕl king of Syria.) And Jehu said, If it be your minds, *then* ᴺlet none go forth *nor* escape out of the city to go to tell *it* in Jĕz'-rĕĕl.

16 So Jehu rode in a chariot, and went to Jĕz'-rĕĕl; for Joram lay there. ᴿAnd Ā-hă-zī'-ăh king of Judah was come down to see Joram.

17 And there stood a watchman on the tower in Jĕz'-rĕĕl, and he spied the company of Jehu as he came, and said, I see a company. And Joram said, Take an horseman, and send to meet them, and let him say, *Is it* peace?

18 So there went one on horseback to meet him, and said, Thus saith the king, *Is it* peace? And Jehu said, What hast thou to do with peace? turn thee behind me. And the watchman told, saying, The messenger came to them, but he cometh not again.

19 Then he sent out a second on horseback, which came to them, and said, Thus saith the king, *Is it* peace? And Jehu answered, What hast thou to do with peace? turn thee behind me.

20 And the watchman told, saying, He came even unto them, and cometh not again: and the ᴺdriving *is* like the driving of Jehu the son of Nimshi; for he driveth ᴺfuriously.

21 And Joram said, ᴺMake ready. And his chariot was made ready. And ᴿJoram king of Israel and Ā-hă-zī'-ăh king of Judah went out, each in his chariot, and they went out against Jehu, and ᴺmet him in the portion of Naboth the Jĕz'-rĕĕl-īte.

22 And it came to pass, when Joram saw Jehu, that he said, *Is it* peace, Jehu? And he answered, What peace, so long as the whoredoms of thy mother Jĕz'-ĕ-bĕl and her witchcrafts *are so* many?

CHAP. **9**

BC 884

11 Jer. 29:26
John 10:20
Acts 26:24
1 Cor. 4:10
13 Mat. 21:7
13 Heb. *reigneth*
15 ch. 8:29
15 Heb. *Jehoram*
15 Heb. *smote*
15 Heb. *let no escaper go, etc.*
16 ch. 8:29
20 Or, *marching*
20 Heb. *in madness*
21 Heb. *Bind*
21 2 Chr. 22:7
21 Heb. *found*

Heb. *filled his his hand with a bow* 24
Heb. *bowed* 24
1 Ki. 21:29 25
Heb. *bloods* 26
Or, *portion* 26
In the kingdom 27
of *Samaria*, 2 Chr. 22:9
Ezek. 23:40 30
Heb. *put her eyes in painting* 30
1 Ki. 16:9-20 31
Or, *chamberlains* 32
1 Ki. 16:31 34
Heb. *by the hand of* 36
1 Ki. 21:23 36

Jehu slays Joram and Ahaziah

23 And Joram turned his hands, and fled, and said to Ā-hă-zī'-ăh, *There is* treachery, O Ā-hă-zī'-ăh.

24 And Jehu ᴺdrew a bow with his full strength, and smote Jĕ-hôr'-ăm between his arms, and the arrow went out at his heart, and he ᴺsunk down in his chariot.

25 Then said *Jehu* to Bĭd'-kär his captain, Take up, *and* cast him in the portion of the field of Naboth the Jĕz'-rĕĕl-īte: for remember how that, when I and thou rode together after Ahab his father, ᴿthe LORD laid this burden upon him;

26 Surely I have seen yesterday the ᴺblood of Naboth, and the blood of his sons, saith the LORD; and I will requite thee in this ᴺplat, saith the LORD. Now therefore take *and* cast him into the plat *of ground,* according to the word of the LORD.

27 But when Ā-hă-zī'-ăh the king of Judah saw *this,* he fled by the way of the garden house. And Jehu followed after him, and said, Smite him also in the chariot. *And they did so* at the going up to Gŭr, which *is* by Ĭb'-lĕ-ăm. And he fled to ᴿMĕ-gĭd'-dō, and died there.

28 And his servants carried him in a chariot to Jerusalem, and buried him in his sepulchre with his fathers in the city of David.

29 And in the eleventh year of Joram the son of Ahab began Ā-hă-zī'-ăh to reign over Judah.

Jezebel is killed

30 And when Jehu was come to Jĕz'-rĕĕl, Jĕz'-ĕ-bĕl heard *of it;* ᴿand she ᴺpainted her face, and tired her head, and looked out at a window.

31 And as Jehu entered in at the gate, she said, ᴿ*Had* Zimri peace, who slew his master?

32 And he lifted up his face to the window, and said, Who *is* on my side? who? And there looked out to him two *or* three ᴺeunuchs.

33 And he said, Throw her down. So they threw her down: and *some* of her blood was sprinkled on the wall, and on the horses: and he trode her under foot.

34 And when he was come in, he did eat and drink, and said, Go, see now this cursed *woman,* and bury her: for ᴿshe *is* a king's daughter.

35 And they went to bury her: but they found no more of her than the skull, and the feet, and the palms of *her* hands.

36 Wherefore they came again, and told him. And he said, This *is* the word of the LORD, which he spake ᴺby his servant Ē-lī'-jăh the Tīsh'-bīte, saying, ᴿIn the portion of

Jĕz'-rĕel shall dogs eat the flesh of Jĕz'-ĕ-bĕl:

37 And the carcase of Jĕz'-ĕ-bĕl shall be ᴿas dung upon the face of the field in the portion of Jĕz'-rĕel; *so* that they shall not say, This *is* Jĕz'-ĕ-bĕl.

CHAPTER 10

Ahab's house extinguished

AND Ahab had seventy sons in Să-mâr'-ĭ-ă. And Jehu wrote letters, and sent to Să-mâr'-ĭ-ă, unto the rulers of Jĕz'-rĕel, to the elders, and to ᴺthem that brought up Ahab's *children*, saying,

2 Now as soon as this letter cometh to you, seeing your master's sons *are* with you, and *there are* with you chariots and horses, a fenced city also, and armour;

3 Look even out the best and meetest of your master's sons, and set *him* on his father's throne, and fight for your master's house.

4 But they were exceedingly afraid, and said, Behold, two kings stood not before him: how then shall we stand?

5 And he that *was* over the house, and he that *was* over the city, the elders also, and the bringers up *of the children,* sent to Jehu, saying, We *are* thy servants, and will do all that thou shalt bid us; we will not make any king: do thou *that which is* good in thine eyes.

6 Then he wrote a letter the second time to them, saying, If ye *be* ᴺmine, and *if* ye will hearken unto my voice, take ye the heads of the men your master's sons, and come to me to Jĕz'-rĕel by to morrow this time. Now the king's sons, *being* seventy persons, *were* with the great men of the city, which brought them up.

7 And it came to pass, when the letter came to them, that they took the king's sons, and ᴿslew seventy persons, and put their heads in baskets, and sent him *them* to Jĕz'-rĕel.

8 And there came a messenger, and told him, saying, They have brought the heads of the king's sons. And he said, Lay ye them in two heaps at the entering in of the gate until the morning.

9 And it came to pass in the morning, that he went out, and stood, and said to all the people, Ye *be* righteous: behold, ᴿI conspired against my master, and slew him: but who slew all these?

10 Know now that there shall ᴿfall unto the earth nothing of the word of the LORD, which the LORD spake concerning the house of Ahab: for the LORD hath done *that* which he spake ᴿbyᴺ his servant Ē-lī'-jäh.

CHAP. 9
BC 884
37 Ps. 83:10

CHAP. 10
BC 884
1 Heb. *nourishers*
6 Heb. *for me*
7 1 Ki. 21:21
9 ch. 9:14, 24
10 1 Sam. 3:19
Jer. 44:28
10 1 Ki. 21:19, 21, 29
10 Heb. *by the hand of*

Or, *acquaintance* 11
Heb. *house of shepherds binding sheep* 12
ch. 8:29 13
2 Chr. 22:8
Heb. *found* 13
Heb. *to the peace of, etc.* 13
Heb. *house* 15
Jer. 35:6, etc. 15
1 Chr. 2:55 15
Heb. *blessed* 15
Ezra 10:19 15
1 Ki. 19:10 16
ch. 9:8 17
2 Chr. 22:8
1 Ki. 21:21 17
1 Ki. 16:31, 32 18
1 Ki. 22:6 19
Heb. *Sanctify* 20
1 Ki. 16:32 21
Or, *so full, that they stood mouth to mouth* 21

11 So Jehu slew all that remained of the house of Ahab in Jĕz'-rĕel, and all his great men, and his ᴺkinsfolks, and his priests, until he left him none remaining.

Ahaziah's brethren slain

12 And he arose and departed, and came to Să-mâr'-ĭ-ă. *And* as he *was* at the ᴺshearing house in the way,

13 ᴿJehuᴺ met with the brethren of Ā-hă-zī'-ăh king of Judah, and said, Who *are* ye? And they answered, We *are* the brethren of Ā-hă-zī'-ăh; and we go down ᴺto salute the children of the king and the children of the queen.

14 And he said, Take them alive. And they took them alive, and slew them at the pit of the shearing house, *even* two and forty men; neither left he any of them.

15 And when he was departed thence, he ᴺlighted on ᴿJĕ-hŏn'-ă-dăb the son of ᴿRĕ'-chăb *coming* to meet him: and he ᴺsaluted him, and said to him, Is thine heart right, as my heart *is* with thy heart? And Jĕ-hŏn'-ă-dăb answered, It is. If it be, ᴿgive *me* thine hand. And he gave *him* his hand; and he took him up to him into the chariot.

16 And he said, Come with me, and see my ᴿzeal for the LORD. So they made him ride in his chariot.

17 And when he came to Să-mâr'-ĭ-ă, ᴿhe slew all that remained unto Ahab in Să-mâr'-ĭ-ă, till hc had destroyed him, according to the saying of the LORD, ᴿwhich he spake to Ē-lī'-jäh.

Country purged of Baal worship

18 And Jehu gathered all the people together, and said unto them, ᴿAhab served Bā'-ăl a little; *but* Jehu shall serve him much.

19 Now therefore call unto me all the ᴿprophets of Bā'-ăl, all his servants, and all his priests; let none be wanting: for I have a great sacrifice *to do* to Bā'-ăl; whosoever shall be wanting, he shall not live. But Jehu did *it* in subtilty, to the intent that he might destroy the worshippers of Bā'-ăl.

20 And Jehu said, ᴺProclaim a solemn assembly for Bā'-ăl. And they proclaimed *it*.

21 And Jehu sent through all Israel: and all the worshippers of Bā'-ăl came, so that there was not a man left that came not. And they came into the ᴿhouse of Bā'-ăl; and the house of Bā'-ăl was ᴺfull from one end to another.

22 And he said unto him that *was* over the vestry, Bring forth vestments for all the worshippers of Bā'-ăl. And he brought them forth vestments.

23 And Jehu went, and Jĕ-hŏn'-ă-dăb the son of Rē'-chăb, into the house of Bā'-ăl, and said unto the worshippers of Bā'-ăl, Search, and look that there be here with you none of the servants of the LORD, but the worshippers of Bā'-ăl only.

24 And when they went in to offer sacrifices and burnt offerings, Jehu appointed fourscore men without, and said, *If* any of the men whom I have brought into your hands escape, *he that letteth him go,* Rhis life *shall be* for the life of him.

25 And it came to pass, as soon as he had made an end of offering the burnt offering, that Jehu said to the guard and to the captains, Go in, *and* slay them; let none come forth. And they smote them with Nthe edge of the sword; and the guard and the captains cast *them* out, and went to the city of the house of Bā'-ăl.

26 And they brought forth the Rimages N out of the house of Bā'-ăl, and burned them.

27 And they brake down the image of Bā'-ăl, and brake down the house of Bā'-ăl, Rand made it a draught house unto this day.

28 Thus Jehu destroyed Bā'-ăl out of Israel.

29 Howbeit *from* the sins of Jĕr-ŏ-bō'-ăm the son of Nē'-băt, who made Israel to sin, Jehu departed not from after them, *to wit,* Rthe golden calves that *were* in Beth-el, and that *were* in Dan.

30 And the LORD said unto Jehu, Because thou hast done well in executing *that which is* right in mine eyes, *and* hast done unto the house of Ahab according to all that *was* in mine heart, Rthy children of the fourth *generation* shall sit on the throne of Israel.

31 But Jehu Ntook no heed to walk in the law of the LORD God of Israel with all his heart: for he departed not from Rthe sins of Jĕr-ŏ-bō'-ăm, which made Israel to sin.

Oppression of Israel

32 In those days the LORD began Nto cut Israel short: and RHă-zā'-ĕl smote them in all the coasts of Israel;

33 From Jordan Neastward, all the land of Gilead, the Gadites, and the Reubenites, and the Mă-năs'-sītes, from Ă-rō'-ĕr, which *is* by the river Arnon, Neven RGilead and Bā'-shăn.

34 Now the rest of the acts of Jehu, and all that he did, and all his might, *are* they not written in the book of the chronicles of the kings of Israel?

35 And Jehu slept with his fathers: and they buried him in Să-mâr'-ĭ-ă. And Jĕ-hō'-ă-hăz his son reigned in his stead.

36 And Nthe time that Jehu reigned over Israel in Să-mâr'-ĭ-ă *was* twenty and eight years.

CHAPTER 11

Joash saved from the slaughter

AND when RĂth-ă-lī'-ăh Rthe mother of Ā-hă-zī'-ăh saw that her son was dead, she arose and destroyed all the Nseed royal.

2 But NJĕ-hōsh'-ĕ-bă, the daughter of king Joram, sister of Ā-hă-zī'-ăh, took NJō'-ăsh the son of Ā-hă-zī'-ăh, and stole him from among the king's sons *which were* slain; and they hid him, *even* him and his nurse, in the bedchamber from Ăth-ă-lī'-ăh, so that he was not slain.

3 And he was with her hid in the house of the LORD six years. And Ăth-ă-lī'-ăh did reign over the land.

Joash made king of Judah

4 And Rthe seventh year Jĕ-hoī'-ă-dă sent and fetched the rulers over hundreds, with the captains and the guard, and brought them to him into the house of the LORD, and made a covenant with them, and took an oath of them in the house of the LORD, and shewed them the king's son.

5 And he commanded them, saying, This *is* the thing that ye shall do; A third part of you that enter in Ron the sabbath shall even be keepers of the watch of the king's house;

6 And a third part *shall be* at the gate of Sùr; and a third part at the gate behind the guard: so shall ye keep the watch of the house, Nthat it be not broken down.

7 And two NNparts of all you that go forth on the sabbath, even they shall keep the watch of the house of the LORD about the king.

8 And ye shall compass the king round about, every man with his weapons in his hand: and he that cometh within the ranges, let him be slain: and be ye with the king as he goeth out and as he cometh in.

9 RAnd the captains over the hundreds did according to all *things* that Jĕ-hoī'-ă-dă the priest commanded: and they took every man his men that were to come in on the sabbath, with them that should go out on the sabbath, and came to Jĕ-hoī'-ă-dă the priest.

10 And to the captains over hundreds did the priest give king David's spears and shields, Rthat *were* in the temple of the LORD.

11 And the guard stood, every man with his weapons in his hand, round about the king, from the right Ncorner of the temple to the left corner of the temple, *along* by the altar and the temple.

12 And he brought forth the king's son, and put the crown upon him, and *gave him* the testimony; and they made him king, and

anointed him; and they clapped their hands, and said, ^RGod^N save the king.

Athaliah slain

13 ^RAnd when Ăth-ă-lī'-ăh heard the noise of the guard *and* of the people, she came to the people into the temple of the LORD.

14 And when she looked, behold, the king stood by ^Ra pillar, as the manner *was,* and the princes and the trumpeters by the king, and all the people of the land rejoiced, and blew with trumpets: and Ăth-ă-lī'-ăh rent her clothes, and cried, Treason, Treason.

15 But Jĕ-hoi'-ă-dă the priest commanded the captains of the hundreds, the officers of the host, and said unto them, Have her forth without the ranges: and him that followeth her kill with the sword. For the priest had said, Let her not be slain in the house of the LORD.

16 And they laid hands on her; and she went by the way by the which the horses came into the king's house: and there was she slain.

Jehoiada makes a covenant

17 ^RAnd Jĕ-hoi'-ă-dă made a covenant between the LORD and the king and the people, that they should be the LORD'S people; ^Rbetween the king also and the people.

18 And all the people of the land went into the ^Rhouse of Bā'-ăl, and brake it down; his altars and his images ^Rbrake they in pieces thoroughly, and slew Măt'-tăn the priest of Bā'-ăl before the altars. And ^Rthe priest appointed ^Nofficers over the house of the LORD.

19 And he took the rulers over hundreds, and the captains, and the guard, and all the people of the land; and they brought down the king from the house of the LORD, and came by the way of the gate of the guard to the king's house. And he sat on the throne of the kings.

20 And all the people of the land rejoiced, and the city was in quiet: and they slew Ăth-ă-lī'-ăh with the sword *beside* the king's house.

21 ^RSeven years old *was* Jĕ-hō'-ăsh when he began to reign.

CHAPTER 12

Jehoash begins to reign

IN the seventh year of Jehu ^RJĕ-hō'-ăsh began to reign; and forty years reigned he in Jerusalem. And his mother's name *was* Zĭ'-bĭ-ăh of Bēer-shē'-bă.

2 And Jĕ-hō'-ăsh did *that which was* right in the sight of the LORD all his days wherein Jĕ-hoi'-ă-dă the priest instructed him.

3 But ^Rthe high places were not taken away:

the people still sacrificed and burnt incense in the high places.

Jehoash repairs the temple

4 And Jĕ-hō'-ăsh said to the priests, ^RAll the money of the ^{NN}dedicated things that is brought into the house of the LORD, *even* ^Rthe money of every one that passeth *the account,* ^Nthe money that every man is set at, *and* all the money that ^Rcometh ^Ninto any man's heart to bring into the house of the LORD,

5 Let the priests take *it* to them, every man of his acquaintance: and let them repair the breaches of the house, wheresoever any breach shall be found.

6 But it was *so, that* ^Nin the three and twentieth year of king Jĕ-hō'-ăsh ^Rthe priests had not repaired the breaches of the house.

7 ^RThen king Jĕ-hō'-ăsh called for Jĕ-hoi'-ă-dă the priest, and the *other* priests, and said unto them, Why repair ye not the breaches of the house? now therefore receive no *more* money of your acquaintance, but deliver it for the breaches of the house.

8 And the priests consented to receive no *more* money of the people, neither to repair the breaches of the house.

9 But Jĕ-hoi'-ă-dă the priest took ^Ra chest, and bored a hole in the lid of it, and set it beside the altar, on the right side as one cometh into the house of the LORD: and the priests that kept the ^Ndoor put therein all the money *that was* brought into the house of the LORD.

10 And it was *so,* when they saw that *there was* much money in the chest, that the king's ^Nscribe and the high priest came up, and they ^Nput up in bags, and told the money that was found in the house of the LORD.

11 And they gave the money, being told, into the hands of them that did the work, that had the oversight of the house of the LORD: and they ^Nlaid it out to the carpenters and builders, that wrought upon the house of the LORD,

12 And to masons, and hewers of stone, and to buy timber and hewed stone to repair the breaches of the house of the LORD, and for all that ^Nwas laid out for the house to repair *it.*

Jehoahaz reigns in Israel

13 Howbeit ^Rthere were not made for the house of the LORD bowls of silver, snuffers, basins, trumpets, any vessels of gold, or vessels of silver, of the money *that was* brought into the house of the LORD:

14 But they gave that to the workmen, and repaired therewith the house of the LORD.

15 Moreover ^Rthey reckoned not with the

CHAP. **11**
BC 878
12 1 Sam. 10:24
12 Heb. *Let the king live*
13 2 Chr. 23:12, etc.
14 ch. 23:3
2 Chr. 34:31
17 2 Chr. 23:16
17 2 Sam. 5:3
18 ch. 10:26
18 Deut. 12:3
2 Chr. 23:17
18 2 Chr. 23:18, etc.
18 Heb. *offices*
21 2 Chr. 24:1

CHAP. **12**
BC 878
1 2 Chr. 24:1
3 1 Ki. 15:14 & 22:43
ch. 14:4

ch. 22:4	4
Or, *holy things*	4
Heb. *holinesses*	4
Ex. 30:13	4
Heb. *the money of the souls of his estimation*	4
Ex. 35:5	4
1 Chr. 29:9	
Heb. *ascendeth upon the heart of a man*	4
Heb. *in the twentieth year and third year*	6
2 Chr. 24:5	6
2 Chr. 24:6	7
2 Chr. 24:8, etc.	9
Heb. *threshold*	9
Or, *secretary*	10
Heb. *bound up*	10
Heb. *brought it forth*	11
Heb. *went forth*	12
See 2 Chr. 24:14	13
ch. 22:7	15

men, into whose hand they delivered the money to be bestowed on workmen: for they dealt faithfully.

16 ^RThe trespass money and sin money was not brought into the house of the LORD: ^Rit was the priests'.

Jehoash pacifies Hazael

17 Then ^RHă-zā'-ĕl king of Syria went up, and fought against Gath, and took it: and ^RHă-zā'-ĕl set his face to go up to Jerusalem.

18 And Jĕ-hō'-ăsh king of Judah ^Rtook all the hallowed things that Jĕ-hŏsh'-ă-phăt, and Jĕ-hôr'-ăm, and Ā-hă-zī'-ăh, his fathers, kings of Judah, had dedicated, and his own hallowed things, and all the gold *that was* found in the treasures of the house of the LORD, and in the king's house, and sent *it* to Hă-zā'-ĕl king of Syria: and he ^Nwent away from Jerusalem.

19 And the rest of the acts of Jō'-ăsh, and all that he did, *are* they not written in the book of the chronicles of the kings of Judah?

20 And ^Rhis servants arose, and made a conspiracy, and slew Jō'-ăsh in ^Nthe house of Mĭl'-lō, which goeth down to Sĭl'-lă.

21 For ^RJō'-ză-<u>ch</u>är the son of Shĭm'-ĕ-ăth, and Jĕ-hō'-ză-băd the son of ^NShō'-mĕr, his servants, smote him, and he died; and they buried him with his fathers in the city of Da-vid: and ^RĂm-ă-zī'-ăh his son reigned in his stead.

CHAPTER 13

IN ^Nthe three and twentieth year of Jō'-ăsh the son of Ā-hă-zī'-ăh king of Judah Jĕ-hō'-ă-hăz the son of Jehu began to reign over Israel in Să-mâr'-ĭ-ă, *and reigned* seventeen years.

2 And he did *that which was* evil in the sight of the LORD, and ^Nfollowed the sins of Jĕr-ŏ-bō'-ăm the son of Nē'-băt, which made Israel to sin; he departed not therefrom.

3 And ^Rthe anger of the LORD was kindled against Israel, and he delivered them into the hand of ^RHă-zā'-ĕl king of Syria, and into the hand of Bĕn-hā'-dăd the son of Hă-zā'-ĕl, all *their* days.

4 And Jĕ-hō'-ă-hăz ^Rbesought the LORD, and the LORD hearkened unto him: for ^Rhe saw the oppression of Israel, because the king of Syria oppressed them.

5 (^RAnd the LORD gave Israel a saviour, so that they went out from under the hand of the Syrians: and the children of Israel dwelt in their tents, ^Nas beforetime.

6 Nevertheless they departed not from the sins of the house of Jĕr-ŏ-bō'-ăm, who made Israel sin, *but* ^Nwalked therein: ^Rand there ^Nremained the grove also in Să-mâr'-ĭ-ă.)

CHAP. **12**	
BC 878	
16	Lev. 5:15, 18
16	Lev. 7:7
	Num. 18:9
17	ch. 8:12
17	See 2 Chr. 24:23
18	1 Ki. 15:18
	ch. 18:15, 16
18	Heb. *went up*
20	ch. 14:5
	2 Chr. 24:25
20	Or, *Bethmillo*
21	2 Chr. 24:26, *Zabad*
21	Or, *Shimrith*
21	2 Chr. 24:27

CHAP. **13**	
BC 856	
1	Heb. *the twentieth year and third year*
2	Heb. *walked after*
3	Judg. 2:14
3	ch. 8:12
4	Ps. 78:34
4	Ex. 3:7
	ch. 14:26
5	See ver. 25 & ch. 14:25, 27
5	Heb. *as yesterday,* and *third day*
6	Heb. *he walked*
6	1 Ki. 16:33
6	Heb. *stood*

Amos 1:3	7
ver. 10, *Jehoash*	9
Alone	9
In consort with his father,	10
ch. 14:1	
ch. 14:15	12
See ver. 14, 25	12
ch. 14:9, etc.	12
2 Chr. 25:17, etc.	
ch. 2:12	14
Heb. *Make thine hand to ride*	16
1 Ki. 20:26	17

7 Neither did he leave of the people to Jĕ-hō'-ă-hăz but fifty horsemen, and ten chariots, and ten thousand footmen; for the king of Syria had destroyed them, ^Rand had made them like the dust by threshing.

8 Now the rest of the acts of Jĕ-hō'-ă-hăz, and all that he did, and his might, *are* they not written in the book of the chronicles of the kings of Israel?

9 And Jĕ-hō'-ă-hăz slept with his fathers; and they buried him in Să-mâr'-ĭ-ă: and ^NJō'-ăsh his son reigned in his stead. ^N

Jehoash reigns in Israel

10 In the thirty and seventh year of Jō'-ăsh king of Judah began ^NJĕ-hō'-ăsh the son of Jĕ-hō'-ă-hăz to reign over Israel in Să-mâr'-ĭ-ă, *and reigned* sixteen years.

11 And he did *that which was* evil in the sight of the LORD; he departed not from all the sins of Jĕr-ŏ-bō'-ăm the son of Nē'-băt, who made Israel sin: *but* he walked therein.

12 ^RAnd the rest of the acts of Jō'-ăsh, and ^Rall that he did, and ^Rhis might wherewith he fought against Ăm-ă-zī'-ăh king of Judah, *are* they not written in the book of the chronicles of the kings of Israel?

13 And Jō'-ăsh slept with his fathers; and Jĕr-ŏ-bō'-ăm sat upon his throne: and Jō'-ăsh was buried in Să-mâr'-ĭ-ă with the kings of Israel.

Death of Elisha

14 Now Ē-lī'-shă was fallen sick of his sickness whereof he died. And Jō'-ăsh the king of Israel came down unto him, and wept over his face, and said, O my father, my father, ^Rthe chariot of Israel, and the horsemen thereof.

15 And Ē-lī'-shă said unto him, Take bow and arrows. And he took unto him bow and arrows.

16 And he said to the king of Israel, ^NPut thine hand upon the bow. And he put his hand *upon it:* and Ē-lī'-shă put his hands upon the king's hands.

17 And he said, Open the window eastward. And he opened *it.* Then Ē-lī'-shă said, Shoot. And he shot. And he said, The arrow of the LORD's deliverance, and the arrow of deliverance from Syria: for thou shalt smite the Syrians in ^RĀ'-phĕk, till thou have consumed *them.*

18 And he said, Take the arrows. And he took *them.* And he said unto the king of Israel, Smite upon the ground. And he smote thrice, and stayed.

19 And the man of God was wroth with him, and said, Thou shouldest have smitten five or six times; then hadst thou smitten Syria

till thou hadst consumed *it:* ᴿwhereas now thou shalt smite Syria *but* thrice.

20 And Ē-lī′-shā died, and they buried him. And the bands of the Moabites invaded the land at the coming in of the year.

21 And it came to pass, as they were burying a man, that, behold, they spied a band *of men;* and they cast the man into the sepulchre of Ē-lī′-shā: and when the man ᴺwas let down, and touched the bones of Ē-lī′-shā, he revived, and stood up on his feet.

22 But ᴿHă-zā′-ĕl king of Syria oppressed Israel all the days of Jĕ-hō′-ă-hăz.

23 And the LORD was gracious unto them, and had compassion on them, and ᴿhad respect unto them, ᴿbecause of his covenant with Abraham, Isaac, and Jacob, and would not destroy them, neither cast he them from his ᴺpresence as yet.

24 So Hă-zā′-ĕl king of Syria died; and Bĕn-hā′-dăd his son reigned in his stead.

25 And Jē-hō′-ăsh the son of Jĕ-hō′-ă-hăz ᴺtook again out of the hand of Bĕn-hā′-dăd the son of Hă-zā′-ĕl the cities, which he had taken out of the hand of Jĕ-hō′-ă-hăz his father by war. ᴿThree times did Jō′-ăsh beat him, and recovered the cities of Israel.

CHAPTER 14

Amaziah's reign in Judah

IN ᴿthe second year of Jō′-ăsh son of Jĕ-hō′-ă-hăz king of Israel reigned ᴿĂm-ă-zī′-ăh the son of Jō′-ăsh king of Judah.

2 He was twenty and five years old when he began to reign, and reigned twenty and nine years in Jerusalem. And his mother's name *was* Jĕ-hō-ăd′-dăn of Jerusalem.

3 And he did *that which was* right in the sight of the LORD, yet not like David his father: he did according to all things as Jō′-ăsh his father did.

4 ᴿHowbeit the high places were not taken away: as yet the people did sacrifice and burnt incense on the high places.

5 And it came to pass, as soon as the kingdom was confirmed in his hand, that he slew his servants ᴿwhich had slain the king his father.

6 But the children of the murderers he slew not: according unto that which is written in the book of the law of Moses, wherein the LORD commanded, saying, ᴿThe fathers shall not be put to death for the children, nor the children be put to death for the fathers; but every man shall be put to death for his own sin.

7 ᴿHe slew of Ē′-dom in ᴿthe valley of salt ten thousand, and took ᴺSē′-läh by war,

ᴿand called the name of it Jŏk′-thĕĕl unto this day.

Judah defeated by Israel

8 ᴿThen Ăm-ă-zī′-ăh sent messengers to Jĕ-hō′-ăsh, the son of Jĕ-hō′-ă-hăz son of Jehu, king of Israel, saying, Come, let us look one another in the face.

9 And Jĕ-hō′-ăsh the king of Israel sent to Ăm-ă-zī′-ăh king of Judah, saying, ᴿThe thistle that *was* in Lĕb′-ă-nọn sent to the ᴿcedar that *was* in Lĕb′-ă-nọn, saying, Give thy daughter to my son to wife: and there passed by a wild beast that *was* in Lĕb′-ă-nọn, and trode down the thistle.

10 Thou hast indeed smitten Ē′-dom, and ᴿthine heart hath lifted thee up: glory *of this,* and tarry ᴺat home: for why shouldest thou meddle to *thy* hurt, that thou shouldest fall, *even* thou, and Judah with thee?

11 But Ăm-ă-zī′-ăh would not hear. Therefore Jĕ-hō′-ăsh king of Israel went up; and he and Ăm-ă-zī′-ăh king of Judah looked one another in the face at ᴿBĕth-shē′-mĕsh, which *belongeth* to Judah.

12 And Judah ᴺwas put to the worse before Israel; and they fled every man to their tents.

13 And Jĕ-hō′-ăsh king of Israel took Ăm-ă-zī′-ăh king of Judah, the son of Jĕ-hō′-ăsh the son of Ā-hă-zī′-ăh, at Bĕth-shē′-mĕsh, and came to Jerusalem, and brake down the wall of Jerusalem from ᴿthe gate of Ē′-phră-ĭm unto ᴿthe corner gate, four hundred cubits.

14 And he took all ᴿthe gold and silver, and all the vessels that were found in the house of the LORD, and in the treasures of the king's house, and hostages, and returned to Să-mâr′-ĭ-ă.

Death of Jehoash

15 ᴿNow the rest of the acts of Jĕ-hō′-ăsh which he did, and his might, and how he fought with Ăm-ă-zī′-ăh king of Judah, *are* they not written in the book of the chronicles of the kings of Israel?

16 And Jĕ-hō′-ăsh slept with his fathers, and was buried in Să-mâr′-ĭ-ă with the kings of Israel; and Jĕr-ŏ-bō′-ăm his son reigned in his stead.

Amaziah's death

17 ᴿAnd Ăm-ă-zī′-ăh the son of Jō′-ăsh king of Judah lived after the death of Jĕ-hō′-ăsh son of Jĕ-hō′-ă-hăz king of Israel fifteen years.

18 And the rest of the acts of Ăm-ă-zī′-ăh, *are* they not written in the book of the chronicles of the kings of Judah?

19 Now ᴿthey made a conspiracy against him in Jerusalem: and he fled to ᴿLā′-chĭsh;

CHAP. 13
BC 856

19	ver. 25
21	Heb. *went* down
22	ch. 8:12
23	Ex. 2:24, 25
23	Ex. 32:13
23	Heb. *face*
25	Heb. *returned and took*
25	ver. 18, 19

CHAP. 14
BC 839

1	ch. 13:10
1	2 Chr. 25:1
4	ch. 12:3
5	ch. 12:20
6	Deut. 24:16
	Ezek. 18:4, 20
7	2 Chr. 25:11
7	2 Sam. 8:13
	Ps. 60, title
7	Or, *The rock*

Josh. 15:38	**7**
2 Chr. 25:17, 18, etc.	**8**
See Judg. 9:8	**9**
1 Ki. 4:33	**9**
Deut. 8:14	**10**
2 Chr. 32:25	
Ezek. 28:2, 5, 17	
Hab. 2:4	
Heb. *at thy house*	**10**
Josh. 19:38 & 21:16	**11**
Heb. *was smitten*	**12**
Neh. 8:16 & 12:39	**13**
Jer. 31:38	**13**
Zech. 14:10	
1 Ki. 7:51	**14**
ch. 13:12	**15**
2 Chr. 25:25, etc.	**17**
2 Chr. 25:27	**19**
Josh. 10:31	**19**

but they sent after him to Lā′-chīsh, and slew him there.

20 And they brought him on horses: and he was buried at Jerusalem with his fathers in the city of David.

21 And all the people of Judah took [R]Ăz-ă-rī′-ăh, which *was* sixteen years old, and made him king instead of his father Ăm-ă-zī′-ăh.

22 He built [R]Ē′-lăth, and restored it to Judah, after that the king slept with his fathers.

Jeroboam reigns in Israel

23 In the fifteenth year of Ăm-ă-zī′-ăh the son of Jō′-ăsh king of Judah Jĕr-ŏ-bō′-ăm the son of Jō′-ăsh king of Israel began to reign in Să-mâr′-ĭ-ă, *and reigned* forty and one years.

24 And he did *that which was* evil in the sight of the LORD: he departed not from all the sins of Jĕr-ŏ-bō′-ăm the son of Nē′-băt, who made Israel to sin.

25 He restored the coast of Israel [R]from the entering of Hā′-măth unto [R]the sea of the plain, according to the word of the LORD God of Israel, which he spake by the hand of his servant [R]Jonah, the son of Ă-mĭt′-tâi, the prophet, which *was* of [R]Găth-hē′-phĕr.

26 For the LORD [R]saw the affliction of Israel, *that it was* very bitter: for [R]*there was* not any shut up, nor any left, nor any helper for Israel.

27 [R]And the LORD said not that he would blot out the name of Israel from under heaven: but he saved them by the hand of Jĕr-ŏ-bō′-ăm the son of Jō′-ăsh.

28 Now the rest of the acts of Jĕr-ŏ-bō′-ăm, and all that he did, and his might, how he warred, and how he recovered Damascus, and Hā′-măth, [R]*which belonged* to Judah, for Israel, *are* they not written in the book of the chronicles of the kings of Israel?

29 And Jĕr-ŏ-bō′-ăm slept with his fathers, *even* with the kings of Israel; and [R]Zăch-ă-rī′-ăh his son reigned in his stead.

CHAPTER 15

Azariah's reign in Judah

IN the twenty and seventh year of Jĕr-ŏ-bō′-ăm king of Israel [R]began [R]Ăz-ă-rī′-ăh son of Ăm-ă-zī′-ăh king of Judah to reign.

2 Sixteen years old was he when he began to reign, and he reigned two and fifty years in Jerusalem. And his mother's name *was* Jĕch-ŏ-lī′-ăh of Jerusalem.

3 And he did *that which was* right in the sight of the LORD, according to all that his father Ăm-ă-zī′-ăh had done;

4 [R]Save that the high places were not removed: the people sacrificed and burnt incense still on the high places.

5 And the LORD [R]smote the king, so that he was a leper unto the day of his death, and [R]dwelt in a several house. And Jō′-thăm the king's son *was* over the house, judging the people of the land.

6 And the rest of the acts of Ăz-ă-rī′-ăh, and all that he did, *are* they not written in the book of the chronicles of the kings of Judah?

7 So Ăz-ă-rī′-ăh slept with his fathers; and [R]they buried him with his fathers in the city of David: and Jō′-thăm his son reigned in his stead.

Zechariah's reign in Israel

8 In the thirty and eighth year of Ăz-ă-rī′-ăh king of Judah did Zăch-ă-rī′-ăh the son of Jĕr-ŏ-bō′-ăm reign over Israel in Să-mâr′-ĭ-ă six months.

9 And he did *that which was* evil in the sight of the LORD, as his fathers had done: he departed not from the sins of Jĕr-ŏ-bō′-ăm the son of Nē′-băt, who made Israel to sin.

10 And Shăl′-lŭm the son of Jā′-bĕsh conspired against him, and [R]smote him before the people, and slew him, and reigned in his stead.

11 And the rest of the acts of Zăch-ă-rī′-ăh, behold, they *are* written in the book of the chronicles of the kings of Israel.

12 This *was* [R]the word of the LORD which he spake unto Jehu, saying, Thy sons shall sit on the throne of Israel unto the fourth *generation.* And so it came to pass.

Shallum's reign in Israel

13 Shăl′-lŭm the son of Jā′-bĕsh began to reign in the nine and thirtieth year of [R]Ŭz-zī′-ăh king of Judah; and he reigned [N]a full month in Să-mâr′-ĭ-ă.

14 For Mĕn′-ă-hĕm the son of Gā′-dī went up from [R]Tĭr′-zăh, and came to Să-mâr′-ĭ-ă, and smote Shăl′-lŭm the son of Jā′-bĕsh in Să-mâr′-ĭ-ă, and slew him, and reigned in his stead.

15 And the rest of the acts of Shăl′-lŭm, and his conspiracy which he made, behold, they *are* written in the book of the chronicles of the kings of Israel.

16 Then Mĕn′-ă-hĕm smote [R]Tĭph′-săh, and all that *were* therein, and the coasts thereof from Tĭr′-zăh: because they opened not *to him,* therefore he smote *it; and* all [R]the women therein that were with child he ripped up.

Menahem's reign in Israel

17 In the nine and thirtieth year of Ăz-ă-rī′-ăh king of Judah began Mĕn′-ă-hĕm the son of

CHAP. 14
BC 839
21 ch. 15:13 & 2 Chr. 26:1, he is called *Uzziah*
22 ch. 16:6 2 Chr. 26:2
25 Num. 13:21 & 34:8
25 Deut. 3:17
25 Jonah 1:1 Mat. 12:39, 40, called *Jonas*
25 Josh. 19:13
26 ch. 13:4
26 Deut. 32:36
27 ch. 13:5
28 2 Sam. 8:6 1 Ki. 11:24 2 Chr. 8:3
29 After an interregnum of 11 years, ch. 15:8

CHAP. 15
BC 772
1 ch. 14:21 2 Chr. 26:1, 3, 4
1 Called *Uzziah,* ver. 13, 30, etc. & 2 Chr. 26:1
4 ver. 35 ch. 12:3 & 14:4

2 Chr. 26:19-21 5
Lev. 13:46 5
2 Chr. 26:23 7
As prophesied, Amos 7:9 10
ch. 10:30 12
Mat. 1:8, 9, called *Ozias* and ver. 1, *Azariah* 13
Heb. *a month of days* 13
1 Ki. 14:17 14
1 Ki. 4:24 16
ch. 8:12 16

Gā'-dī to reign over Israel, *and reigned* ten years in Să-mâr'-ĭ-ă.

18 And he did *that which was* evil in the sight of the LORD: he departed not all his days from the sins of Jẽr-ŏ-bō'-ăm the son of Nē'-băt, who made Israel to sin.

19 *And* ᴿPŭl the king of Assyria came against the land: and Mĕn'-ă-hĕm gave Pŭl a thousand talents of silver, that his hand might be with him to ᴿconfirm the kingdom in his hand.

20 And Mĕn'-ă-hĕm ᴺexacted the money of Israel, *even* of all the mighty men of wealth, of each man fifty shē'-kĕls of silver, to give to the king of Assyria. So the king of Assyria turned back, and stayed not there in the land.

21 And the rest of the acts of Mĕn'-ă-hĕm, and all that he did, *are* they not written in the book of the chronicles of the kings of Israel?

22 And Mĕn'-ă-hĕm slept with his fathers; and Pĕk-ă-hī'-ăh his son reigned in his stead.

Pekahiah's reign in Israel

23 In the fiftieth year of Ăz-ă-rī'-ăh king of Judah Pĕk-ă-hī'-ăh the son of Mĕn'-ă-hĕm began to reign over Israel in Să-mâr'-ĭ-ă, *and reigned* two years.

24 And he did *that which was* evil in the sight of the LORD: he departed not from the sins of Jẽr-ŏ-bō'-ăm the son of Nē'-băt, who made Israel to sin.

25 But Pē'-käh the son of Rĕm-ă-lī'-ăh, a captain of his, conspired against him, and smote him in Să-mâr'-ĭ-ă, in the palace of the king's house, with Är'-gŏb and Är'-ĭ-ēh, and with him fifty men of the Gileadites: and he killed him, and reigned in his room.

26 And the rest of the acts of Pĕk-ă-hī'-ăh, and all that he did, behold, they *are* written in the book of the chronicles of the kings of Israel.

Pekah's reign in Israel

27 In the two and fiftieth year of Ăz-ă-rī'-ăh king of Judah ᴿPē'-käh the son of Rĕm-ă-lī'-ăh began to reign over Israel in Să-mâr'-ĭ-ă, *and reigned* twenty years.

28 And he did *that which was* evil in the sight of the LORD: he departed not from the sins of Jẽr-ŏ-bō'-ăm the son of Nē'-băt, who made Israel to sin.

29 In the days of Pē'-käh king of Israel ᴿcame Tĭg'-lăth-pĭ-lē'-sẽr king of Assyria, and took ᴿĬ'-jŏn, and Ā'-bĕl-bĕth-mā'-ă-<u>ch</u>äh, and Jă-nō'-ăh, and Kē'-dĕsh, and Hā'-zôr, and Gilead, and Galilee, all the land of Năph'-tă-lī, and carried them captive to Assyria.

30 And Hō-shē'-ă the son of Ē'-lăh made a conspiracy against Pē'-käh the son of Rĕm-ă-lī'-ăh, and smote him, and slew him, and ᴿreigned in his stead, ᴿin the twentieth year of Jō'-thăm the son of Ŭz-zī'-ăh.

31 And the rest of the acts of Pē'-käh, and all that he did, behold, they *are* written in the book of the chronicles of the kings of Israel.

Jotham's reign in Judah

32 In the second year of Pē'-käh the son of Rĕm-ă-lī'-ăh king of Israel began ᴿJō'-thăm the son of Ŭz-zī'-ăh king of Judah to reign.

33 Five and twenty years old was he when he began to reign, and he reigned sixteen years in Jerusalem. And his mother's name *was* Jĕ-rû'-shă, the daughter of Zā'-dŏk.

34 And he did *that which was* right in the sight of the LORD: he did ᴿaccording to all that his father Ŭz-zī'-ăh had done.

35 ᴿHowbeit the high places were not removed: the people sacrificed and burned incense still in the high places. ᴿHe built the higher gate of the house of the LORD.

36 Now the rest of the acts of Jō'-thăm, and all that he did, *are* they not written in the book of the chronicles of the kings of Judah?

37 In those days the LORD began to send against Judah ᴿRē'-zĭn the king of Syria, and ᴿPē'-käh the son of Rĕm-ă-lī'-ăh.

38 And Jō'-thăm slept with his fathers, and was buried with his fathers in the city of David his father: and Ahaz his son reigned in his stead.

CHAPTER 16

Ahaz reigns in Judah

IN the seventeenth year of Pē'-käh the son of Rĕm-ă-lī'-ăh ᴿAhaz the son of Jō'-thăm king of Judah began to reign.

2 Twenty years old *was* Ahaz when he began to reign, and reigned sixteen years in Jerusalem, and did not *that which was* right in the sight of the LORD his God, like David his father.

3 But he walked in the way of the kings of Israel, yea, ᴿand made his son to pass through the fire, according to the ᴿabominations of the heathen, whom the LORD cast out from before the children of Israel.

4 And he sacrificed and burnt incense in the high places, and ᴿon the hills, and under every green tree.

5 ᴿThen Rē'-zĭn king of Syria and Pē'-käh son of Rĕm-ă-lī'-ăh king of Israel came up to

---

CHAP. 15

BC 772

19	1 Chr. 5:26
	Is. 66:19
	Hos. 8:9
19	ch. 14:5
20	Heb. *caused to come forth*
27	Is. 7:1
29	1 Chr. 5:26
	Is. 9:1
29	1 Ki. 15:20

After an anarchy for some years, ch. 17:1 Hos. 10:3, 7, 15	30
In the fourth year of Ahaz, in the twentieth year after Jotham had begun to reign: *Ush*	30
2 Chr. 27:1	32
ver. 3	34
ver. 4	35
2 Chr. 27:3, etc.	35
ch. 16:5	37
Is. 7:1	
ver. 27	37

CHAP. 16

BC 740

2 Chr. 28:1, etc.	1
Lev. 18:21	3
2 Chr. 28:3 Ps. 106:37, 38	
Deut. 12:31	3
Deut. 12:2 1 Ki. 14:23	4
Is. 7:1, 4, etc.	5

Jerusalem to war: and they besieged Ahaz, but could not overcome *him*.

6 At that time Rē'-zĭn king of Syria [R]recovered Ē'-lăth to Syria, and drave the Jews from [N]Ē'-lăth: and the Syrians came to Ē'-lăth, and dwelt there unto this day.

7 So Ahaz sent messengers [R]to [N]Tĭg'-lăth-pĭ-lē'-sĕr king of Assyria, saying, I *am* thy servant and thy son: come up, and save me out of the hand of the king of Syria, and out of the hand of the king of Israel, which rise up against me.

8 And Ahaz [R]took the silver and gold that was found in the house of the Lord, and in the treasures of the king's house, and sent *it for* a present to the king of Assyria.

9 And the king of Assyria hearkened unto him: for the king of Assyria went up against [N]Damascus, and [R]took it, and carried *the people of* it captive to Kĭr, and slew Rē'-zĭn.

Apostasy of Ahaz

10 And king Ahaz went to Damascus to meet Tĭg'-lăth-pĭ-lē'-sĕr king of Assyria, and saw an altar that *was* at Damascus: and king Ahaz sent to Ū-rī'-jăh the priest the fashion of the altar, and the pattern of it, according to all the workmanship thereof.

11 And Ū-rī'-jăh the priest built an altar according to all that king Ahaz had sent from Damascus: so Ū-rī'-jăh the priest made *it* against king Ahaz came from Damascus.

12 And when the king was come from Damascus, the king saw the altar: and [R]the king approached to the altar, and offered thereon.

13 And he burnt his burnt offering and his meat offering, and poured his drink offering, and sprinkled the blood of [N]his peace offerings, upon the altar.

14 And he brought also [R]the brasen altar, which *was* before the Lord, from the forefront of the house, from between the altar and the house of the Lord, and put it on the north side of the altar.

15 And king Ahaz commanded Ū-rī'-jăh the priest, saying, Upon the great altar burn [R]the morning burnt offering, and the evening meat offering, and the king's burnt sacrifice, and his meat offering, with the burnt offering of all the people of the land, and their meat offering, and their drink offerings; and sprinkle upon it all the blood of the burnt offering, and all the blood of the sacrifice: and the brasen altar shall be for me to inquire *by*.

16 Thus did Ū-rī'-jăh the priest, according to all that king Ahaz commanded.

17 [R]And king Ahaz cut off [R]the borders of the bases, and removed the laver from off them; and took down [R]the sea from off the

brasen oxen that *were* under it, and put it upon a pavement of stones.

18 And the covert for the sabbath that they had built in the house, and the king's entry without, turned he from the house of the Lord for the king of Assyria.

19 Now the rest of the acts of Ahaz which he did, *are* they not written in the book of the chronicles of the kings of Judah?

20 And Ahaz slept with his fathers, and [R]was buried with his fathers in the city of David: and Hĕz-ē-kī'-ăh his son reigned in his stead.

CHAPTER 17

Hoshea's reign in Israel

IN the twelfth year of Ahaz king of Judah began [R]Hō-shē'-ă the son of Ē'-lăh to reign in Să-mâr'-ĭ-ă over Israel nine years.

2 And he did *that which was* evil in the sight of the Lord, but not as the kings of Israel that were before him.

3 Against him came up [R]Shăl-măn-ē'-sĕr king of Assyria; and Hō-shē'-ă became his servant, and [N]gave him [N]presents.

4 And the king of Assyria found conspiracy in Hō-shē'-ă: for he had sent messengers to So king of Egypt, and brought no present to the king of Assyria, as *he had done* year by year: therefore the king of Assyria shut him up, and bound him in prison.

Assyria conquers Israel

5 Then [R]the king of Assyria came up throughout all the land, and went up to Să-mâr'-ĭ-ă, and besieged it three years.

6 [R]In the ninth year of Hō-shē'-ă the king of Assyria took Să-mâr'-ĭ-ă, and [R]carried Israel away into Assyria, [R]and placed them in Hā'-lăh and in Hā'-bôr *by* the river of Gō'-zăn, and in the cities of the Mēdeś.

Israel's history of apostasy

7 For *so* it was, that the children of Israel had sinned against the Lord their God, which had brought them up out of the land of Egypt, from under the hand of Pharaoh king of Egypt, and had feared other gods.

8 And [R]walked in the statutes of the heathen, whom the Lord cast out from before the children of Israel, and of the kings of Israel, which they had made.

9 And the children of Israel did secretly *those* things that *were* not right against the Lord their God, and they built them high places in all their cities, [R]from the tower of the watchmen to the fenced city.

10 [R]And they set them up [N]images and

R groves R in every high hill, and under every green tree:

11 And there they burnt incense in all the high places, as *did* the heathen whom the LORD carried away before them; and wrought wicked things to provoke the LORD to anger:

12 For they served idols, R whereof the LORD had said unto them, R Ye shall not do this thing.

13 Yet the LORD testified against Israel, and against Judah, N by all the prophets, *and by* all R the seers, saying, R Turn ye from your evil ways, and keep my commandments *and* my statutes, according to all the law which I commanded your fathers, and which I sent to you by my servants the prophets.

14 Notwithstanding they would not hear, but R hardened their necks, like to the neck of their fathers, that did not believe in the LORD their God.

15 And they rejected his statutes, R and his covenant that he made with their fathers, and his testimonies which he testified against them; and they followed R vanity, and R became vain, and went after the heathen that *were* round about them, *concerning* whom the LORD had charged them, that they should R not do like them.

16 And they left all the commandments of the LORD their God, and R made them molten images, *even* two calves, R and made a grove, and worshipped all the host of heaven, R and served Bā′-ăl.

17 R And they caused their sons and their daughters to pass through the fire, and R used divination and enchantments, and R sold themselves to do evil in the sight of the LORD, to provoke him to anger.

18 Therefore the LORD was very angry with Israel, and removed them out of his sight: there was none left R but the tribe of Judah only.

19 Also R Judah kept not the commandments of the LORD their God, but walked in the statutes of Israel which they made.

20 And the LORD rejected all the seed of Israel, and afflicted them, and R delivered them into the hand of spoilers, until he had cast them out of his sight.

21 For R he rent Israel from the house of David; and R they made Jĕr-ŏ-bō′-ăm the son of Nē′-băt king: and Jĕr-ŏ-bō′-ăm drave Israel from following the LORD, and made them sin a great sin.

22 For the children of Israel walked in all the sins of Jĕr-ŏ-bō′-ăm which he did; they departed not from them;

23 Until the LORD removed Israel out of his

sight, R as he had said by all his servants the prophets. R So was Israel carried away out of their own land to Assyria unto this day.

Samaria's population mixed

24 R And the king of Assyria brought *men* from Babylon, and from Cū′-thăh, and from R Ā′-vă, and from Hā′-măth, and from Sē-phar-vā′-ĭm, and placed *them* in the cities of Să-mâr′-ĭ-ă instead of the children of Israel: and they possessed Să-mâr′-ĭ-ă, and dwelt in the cities thereof.

25 And *so* it was at the beginning of their dwelling there, *that* they feared not the LORD: therefore the LORD sent lions among them, which slew *some* of them.

26 Wherefore they spake to the king of Assyria, saying, The nations which thou hast removed, and placed in the cities of Să-mâr′-ĭ-ă, know not the manner of the God of the land: therefore he hath sent lions among them, and, behold, they slay them, because they know not the manner of the God of the land.

27 Then the king of Assyria commanded, saying, Carry thither one of the priests whom ye brought from thence; and let them go and dwell there, and let him teach them the manner of the God of the land.

28 Then one of the priests whom they had carried away from Să-mâr′-ĭ-ă came and dwelt in Beth-el, and taught them how they should fear the LORD.

29 Howbeit every nation made gods of their own, and put *them* in the houses of the high places which the Să-mâr′-ĭ-tăns had made, every nation in their cities wherein they dwelt.

30 And the men of R Babylon made Sŭc′-cōth-bē′-nōth, and the men of Cŭth made Nēr′-găl, and the men of Hā′-măth made Ă-shī′-mă,

31 R And the Ā′-vītes made Nĭb′-hăz and Tartak, and the Sē-phar′-vītes R burnt their children in fire to Ă-drăm′-mĕ-lĕch and Ă-năm′-mĕ-lĕch, the gods of Sē-phar-vā′-ĭm.

32 So they feared the LORD, R and made unto themselves of the lowest of them priests of the high places, which sacrificed for them in the houses of the high places.

33 R They feared the LORD, and served their own gods, after the manner of the nations N whom they carried away from thence.

34 Unto this day they do after the former manners: they fear not the LORD, neither do they after their statutes, or after their ordinances, or after the law and commandment which the LORD commanded the children of Jacob, R whom he named Israel;

35 With whom the LORD had made a cove-

CHAP. **17**

BC 721

10 Ex. 34:13
Deut. 16:21
Mic. 5:14
10 Deut. 12:2
ch. 16:4
12 Ex. 20:3, 4
Lev. 26:1
Deut. 5:7, 8
12 Deut. 4:19
13 Heb. *by the hand of all*
13 1 Sam. 9:9
13 Jer. 18:11 & 25:5 & 35:15
14 Deut. 31:27
Prov. 29:1
15 Deut. 29:25
15 Deut. 32:21
1 Ki. 16:13
1 Cor. 8:4
15 Ps. 115:8
Rom. 1:21
15 Deut. 12:30, 31
16 Ex. 32:8
1 Ki. 12:28
16 1 Ki. 14:15
16 1 Ki. 16:31 & 22:53
ch. 11:18
17 Lev. 18:21
ch. 16:3
Ezek. 23:37
17 Deut. 18:10
17 1 Ki. 21:20
18 1 Ki. 11:13, 32
19 Jer. 3:8
20 ch. 13:3 & 15:29
21 1 Ki. 11:11, 31
21 1 Ki. 12:20, 28

1 Ki. 14:16 **23**
ver. 6 **23**
Ezra 4:2, 10 **24**
ch. 18:34, *Ivah* **24**
ver. 24 **30**
Ezra 4:9 **31**
Lev. 18:21 **31**
Deut. 12:31
1 Ki. 12:31 **32**
Zeph. 1:5 **33**
Or, *who carried them away from thence* **33**
Gen. 32:28 & 35:10 **34**
1 Ki. 18:31

nant, and charged them, saying, ᴿYe shall not fear other gods, nor ᴿbow yourselves to them, nor serve them, nor sacrifice to them:

36 But the LORD, who brought you up out of the land of Egypt with great power and ᴿa stretched out arm, ᴿhim shall ye fear, and him shall ye worship, and to him shall ye do sacrifice.

37 And the statutes, and the ordinances, and the law, and the commandment, which he wrote for you, ᴿye shall observe to do for evermore; and ye shall not fear other gods.

38 And the covenant that I have made with you ᴿye shall not forget; neither shall ye fear other gods.

39 But the LORD your God ye shall fear; and he shall deliver you out of the hand of all your enemies.

40 Howbeit they did not hearken, but they did after their former manner.

41 ᴿSo these nations feared the LORD, and served their graven images, both their children, and their children's children: as did their fathers, so do they unto this day.

CHAPTER 18

Hezekiah's reign in Judah

NOW it came to pass in the third year of Hō-shē′-ă son of Ē′-lăh king of Israel, *that* ᴿHĕz-ē-kī′-ăh the son of Ahaz king of Judah began to reign.

2 Twenty and five years old was he when he began to reign; and he reigned twenty and nine years in Jerusalem. His mother's name also *was* ᴿAbi, the daughter of Zăch-ă-rī′-ăh.

3 And he did *that which was* right in the sight of the LORD, according to all that David his father did.

4 ᴿHe removed the high places, and brake the ᴺimages, and cut down the groves, and brake in pieces the ᴿbrasen serpent that Moses had made: for unto those days the children of Israel did burn incense to it: and he called it ᴺNĕ-hŭsh′-tăn.

5 He ᴿtrusted in the LORD God of Israel; ᴿso that after him was none like him among all the kings of Judah, nor *any* that were before him.

6 For he ᴿclave to the LORD, *and* departed not ᴺfrom following him, but kept his commandments, which the LORD commanded Moses.

7 And the LORD ᴿwas with him; *and* he ᴿprospered whithersoever he went forth: and he ᴿrebelled against the king of Assyria, and served him not.

8 ᴿHe smote the Philistines, *even* unto ᴺGaza, and the borders thereof, ᴿfrom the tower of the watchmen to the fenced city.

9 And ᴿit came to pass in the fourth year of king Hĕz-ē-kī′-ăh, which *was* the seventh year of Hō-shē′-ă son of Ē′-lăh king of Israel, *that* Shăl-măn-ē′-şĕr king of Assyria came up against Să-mâr′-ĭ-ă, and besieged it.

10 And at the end of three years they took it: *even* in the sixth year of Hĕz-ē-kī′-ăh, that *is* ᴿthe ninth year of Hō-shē′-ă king of Israel, Să-mâr′-ĭ-ă was taken.

11 ᴿAnd the king of Assyria did carry away Israel unto Assyria, and put them ᴿin Hā′-lăh and in Hā′-bôr *by* the river of Gō′-zăn, and in the cities of the Mēdeṡ:

12 Because they obeyed not the voice of the LORD their God, but transgressed his covenant, *and* all that Moses the servant of the LORD commanded, and would not hear *them,* nor do *them.*

Assyria invades Judah

13 Now ᴿin the fourteenth year of king Hĕz-ē-kī′-ăh did ᴺSĕn-năch′-ĕr-ĭb king of Assyria come up against all the fenced cities of Judah, and took them.

14 And Hĕz-ē-kī′-ăh king of Judah sent to the king of Assyria to Lā′-chĭsh, saying, I have offended; return from me: that which thou puttest on me will I bear. And the king of Assyria appointed unto Hĕz-ē-kī′-ăh king of Judah three hundred talents of silver and thirty talents of gold.

15 And Hĕz-ē-kī′-ăh ᴿgave *him* all the silver that was found in the house of the LORD, and in the treasures of the king's house.

16 At that time did Hĕz-ē-kī′-ăh cut off *the gold from* the doors of the temple of the LORD, and *from* the pillars which Hĕz-ē-kī′-ăh king of Judah had overlaid, and gave ᴺit to the king of Assyria.

17 And the king of Assyria sent Tartan and Răb′-să-rĭs and Răb′-shă-kēh from Lā′-chĭsh to king Hĕz-ē-kī′-ăh with a ᴺgreat host against Jerusalem. And they went up and came to Jerusalem. And when they were come up, they came and stood by the conduit of the upper pool, ᴿwhich *is* in the highway of the fuller's field.

18 And when they had called to the king, there came out to them Ē-lī′-ă-kĭm the son of Hĭl-kī′-ăh, which *was* over the household, and Shĕb′-nă the ᴺscribe, and Jō′-ăh the son of Ā′-săph the recorder.

Messengers of Sennacherib

19 And Răb′-shă-kēh said unto them, Speak ye now to Hĕz-ē-kī′-ăh, Thus saith the great king, the king of Assyria, ᴿWhat confidence *is* this wherein thou trustest?

20 Thou ᴺsayest, (but *they are but* ᴺvain

words,) ᴺ*I have* counsel and strength for the war. Now on whom dost thou trust, that thou rebellest against me?

21 ᴿNow, behold, thou ᴺtrustest upon the staff of this bruised reed, *even* upon Egypt, on which if a man lean, it will go into his hand, and pierce it: so *is* Pharaoh king of Egypt unto all that trust on him.

22 But if ye say unto me, We trust in the Lᴏʀᴅ our God: *is* not that he, ᴿwhose high places and whose altars Hĕz-ē-kī′-ăh hath taken away, and hath said to Judah and Jerusalem, Ye shall worship before this altar in Jerusalem?

23 Now therefore, I pray thee, give ᴺpledges to my lord the king of Assyria, and I will deliver thee two thousand horses, if thou be able on thy part to set riders upon them.

24 How then wilt thou turn away the face of one captain of the least of my master's servants, and put thy trust on Egypt for chariots and for horsemen?

25 Am I now come up without the Lᴏʀᴅ against this place to destroy it? The Lᴏʀᴅ said to me, Go up against this land, and destroy it.

26 Then said Ē-lī′-ă-kĭm the son of Hĭl-kī′-ăh, and Shĕb′-nă, and Jō′-ăh, unto Răb′-shă-kēh, Speak, I pray thee, to thy servants in the Syrian language; for we understand *it:* and talk not with us in the Jews' language in the ears of the people that *are* on the wall.

27 But Răb′-shă-kēh said unto them, Hath my master sent me to thy master, and to thee, to speak these words? *hath he* not *sent me* to the men which sit on the wall, that they may eat their own dung, and drink ᴺtheir own piss with you?

28 Then Răb′-shă-kēh stood and cried with a loud voice in the Jews' language, and spake, saying, Hear the word of the great king, the king of Assyria:

29 Thus saith the king, ᴿLet not Hĕz-ē-kī′-ăh deceive you: for he shall not be able to deliver you out of his hand:

30 Neither let Hĕz-ē-kī′-ăh make you trust in the Lᴏʀᴅ, saying, The Lᴏʀᴅ will surely deliver us, and this city shall not be delivered into the hand of the king of Assyria.

31 Hearken not to Hĕz-ē-kī′-ăh: for thus saith the king of Assyria, ᴺᴺMake *an agreement* with me by a present, and come out to me, and *then* eat ye every man of his own vine, and every one of his fig tree, and drink ye every one of the waters of his ᴺcistern:

32 Until I come and take you away to a land like your own land, ᴿa land of corn and wine, a land of bread and vineyards, a land of oil olive and of honey, that ye may live, and not die: and hearken not unto Hĕz-ē-kī′-ăh, when

CHAP. 18	
BC 710	
20 Or, *But counsel and strength* are *for the war*	
21 Ezek. 29:6, 7	
21 Heb. *trustest thee*	
22 ver. 4	
2 Chr. 31:1	
& 32:12	
23 Or, *hostages*	
27 Heb. *the water of their feet*	
29 2 Chr. 32:15	
31 Or, *Seek my favour*	
31 Heb. *Make with me a blessing*	
31 Or, *pit*	
32 Deut. 8:7, 8	

Or, *deceiveth*	32
ch. 19:12	33
2 Chr. 32:14	
Is. 10:10, 11	
ch. 19:13	34
ch. 17:24, *Ava?*	34
Dan. 3:15	35
Is. 33:7	37

CHAP. 19	
BC 710	
Is. 37:1, etc.	1
Luke 3:4, called *Esaias*	2
Or, *provocation*	3
2 Sam. 16:12	4
ch. 18:35	4
Ps. 50:21	4
Heb. *found*	4
Is. 37:6, etc.	6
ch. 18:17	6
ver. 35-37	7
Jer. 51:1	

he ᴺpersuadeth you, saying, The Lᴏʀᴅ will deliver us.

33 ᴿHath any of the gods of the nations delivered at all his land out of the hand of the king of Assyria?

34 ᴿWhere *are* the gods of Hā′-măth, and of Arpad? where *are* the gods of Sē-phär-vā′-ĭm, Hē′-nă, and ᴿĪ′-văh? have they delivered Să-mâr′-ī-ă out of mine hand?

35 Who *are* they among all the gods of the countries, that have delivered their country out of mine hand, ᴿthat the Lᴏʀᴅ should deliver Jerusalem out of mine hand?

36 But the people held their peace, and answered him not a word: for the king's commandment was, saying, Answer him not.

37 Then came Ē-lī′-ă-kĭm the son of Hĭl-kī′-ăh, which *was* over the household, and Shĕb′-nă the scribe, and Jō′-ăh the son of Ā′-săph the recorder, to Hĕz-ē-kī′-ăh ᴿwith *their* clothes rent, and told him the words of Răb′-shă-kēh.

CHAPTER 19

Hezekiah sends for Isaiah

ᴀᴺᴅ ᴿit came to pass, when king Hĕz-ē-kī′-ăh heard *it,* that he rent his clothes, and covered himself with sackcloth, and went into the house of the Lᴏʀᴅ.

2 And he sent Ē-lī′-ă-kĭm, which *was* over the household, and Shĕb′-nă the scribe, and the elders of the priests, covered with sackcloth, to ᴿIsaiah the prophet the son of Amoz.

3 And they said unto him, Thus saith Hĕz-ē-kī′-ăh, This day *is* a day of trouble, and of rebuke, and ᴺblasphemy: for the children are come to the birth, and *there is* not strength to bring forth.

4 ᴿIt may be the Lᴏʀᴅ thy God will hear all the words of Răb′-shă-kēh, ᴿwhom the king of Assyria his master hath sent to reproach the living God; and will ᴿreprove the words which the Lᴏʀᴅ thy God hath heard: wherefore lift up *thy* prayer for the remnant that are ᴺleft.

5 So the servants of king Hĕz-ē-kī′-ăh came to Isaiah.

6 ᴿAnd Isaiah said unto them, Thus shall ye say to your master, Thus saith the Lᴏʀᴅ, Be not afraid of the words which thou hast heard, with which the ᴿservants of the king of Assyria have blasphemed me.

7 Behold, I will send ᴿa blast upon him, and he shall hear a rumour, and shall return to his own land; and I will cause him to fall by the sword in his own land.

8 So Răb′-shă-kēh returned, and found the

king of Assyria warring against Lĭb′-năh: for he had heard that he was departed ᴿfrom Lā′-chĭsh.

9 And ᴿwhen he heard say of Tĭr-hā′-kăh king of Ē-thĭ-ō′-pĭ-ă, Behold, he is come out to fight against thee: he sent messengers again unto Hĕz-ē-kĭ′-ăh, saying,

10 Thus shall ye speak to Hĕz-ē-kĭ′-ăh king of Judah, saying, Let not thy God ᴿin whom thou trustest deceive thee, saying, Jerusalem shall not be delivered into the hand of the king of Assyria.

11 Behold, thou hast heard what the kings of Assyria have done to all lands, by destroying them utterly: and shalt thou be delivered?

12 ᴿHave the gods of the nations delivered them which my fathers have destroyed; as Gō′-zăn, and Hâr′-ăn, and Rĕ′-zĕph, and the children of ᴿEden which were in Thĕl′-ă-sär?

13 ᴿWhere is the king of Hā′-măth, and the king of Arpad, and the king of the city of Sē-phär-vā′-ĭm, of Hē′-nă, and Ĭ′-văh?

Hezekiah's prayer

14 ᴿAnd Hĕz-ē-kĭ′-ăh received the letter of the hand of the messengers, and read it: and Hĕz-ē-kĭ′-ăh went up into the house of the Lᴏʀᴅ, and spread it before the Lᴏʀᴅ.

15 And Hĕz-ē-kĭ′-ăh prayed before the Lᴏʀᴅ, and said, O Lᴏʀᴅ God of Israel, ᴿwhich dwellest *between* the chĕr′-ū-bĭms, ᴿthou art the God, *even* thou alone, of all the kingdoms of the earth; thou hast made heaven and earth.

16 Lᴏʀᴅ, ᴿbow down thine ear, and hear: ᴿopen, Lᴏʀᴅ, thine eyes, and see: and hear the words of Sĕn-năch′-ĕr-ĭb, ᴿwhich hath sent him to reproach the living God.

17 Of a truth, Lᴏʀᴅ, the kings of Assyria have destroyed the nations and their lands,

18 And have ᴺcast their gods into the fire: for they *were* no gods, but ᴿthe work of men's hands, wood and stone: therefore they have destroyed them.

19 Now therefore, O Lᴏʀᴅ our God, I beseech thee, save thou us out of his hand, ᴿthat all the kingdoms of the earth may know that thou *art* the Lᴏʀᴅ God, *even* thou only.

Isaiah's prophecy

20 Then Isaiah the son of Amoz sent to Hĕz-ē-kĭ′-ăh, saying, Thus saith the Lᴏʀᴅ God of Israel, ᴿ*That* which thou hast prayed to me against Sĕn-năch′-ĕr-ĭb king of Assyria ᴿI have heard.

21 This *is* the word that the Lᴏʀᴅ hath spoken concerning him; The virgin ᴿthe daughter

of Zion hath despised thee, *and* laughed thee to scorn; the daughter of Jerusalem ᴿhath shaken her head at thee.

22 Whom hast thou reproached and blasphemed? and against whom hast thou exalted *thy* voice, and lifted up thine eyes on high? *even* against ᴿthe Holy *One* of Israel.

23 ᴿBy ᴺ thy messengers thou hast reproached the Lᴏʀᴅ, and hast said, ᴿWith the multitude of my chariots I am come up to the height of the mountains, to the sides of Lĕb′-ă-nᴏn, and will cut down ᴺthe tall cedar trees thereof, *and* the choice fir trees thereof: and I will enter into the lodgings of his borders, *and into* ᴺthe forest of his Carmel.

24 I have digged and drunk strange waters, and with the sole of my feet have I dried up all the rivers of ᴺbesieged places.

25 ᴺHast thou not heard long ago *how* ᴿI have done it, *and* of ancient times that I have formed it? now have I brought it to pass, that ᴿthou shouldest be to lay waste fenced cities *into* ruinous heaps.

26 Therefore their inhabitants were ᴺof small power, they were dismayed and confounded; they were *as* the grass of the field, and *as* the green herb, *as* ᴿthe grass on the housetops, and *as corn* blasted before it be grown up.

27 But ᴿI know thy ᴺabode, and thy going out, and thy coming in, and thy rage against me.

28 Because thy rage against me and thy tumult is come up into mine ears, therefore ᴿI will put my hook in thy nose, and my bridle in thy lips, and I will turn thee back ᴿby the way by which thou camest.

29 And this *shall be* a sign unto thee, Ye shall eat this year such things as grow of themselves, and in the second year that which springeth of the same; and in the third year sow ye, and reap, and plant vineyards, and eat the fruits thereof.

30 ᴿAnd ᴺthe remnant that is escaped of the house of Judah shall yet again take root downward, and bear fruit upward.

31 For out of Jerusalem shall go forth a remnant, and ᴺthey that escape out of mount Zion: ᴿthe zeal of the Lᴏʀᴅ *of hosts* shall do this.

32 Therefore thus saith the Lᴏʀᴅ concerning the king of Assyria, He shall not come into this city, nor shoot an arrow there, nor come before it with shield, nor cast a bank against it.

33 By the way that he came, by the same shall he return, and shall not come into this city, saith the Lᴏʀᴅ.

34 For ᴿI will defend this city, to save it, for

mine own sake, and ᴿfor my servant David's sake.

Sennacherib's army slain

35 And ᴿit came to pass that night, that the angel of the LORD went out, and smote in the camp of the Assyrians an hundred fourscore and five thousand: and when they arose early in the morning, behold, they *were* all dead corpses.

36 So Sĕn-năch'-ĕr-ĭb king of Assyria departed, and went and returned, and dwelt at ᴿNĭn'-ĕ-vĕh.

37 And it came to pass, as he was worshipping in the house of Nĭs'-rŏch his god, that ᴿĂ-drăm'-mĕ-lĕch and Shă-rē'-zĕr his sons ᴿsmote him with the sword: and they escaped into the land of ᴺÄr-mē'-nĭ-ă. And ᴿE-sär-hăd'-dǫn his son reigned in his stead.

CHAPTER 20

Hezekiah's sickness

IN ᴿthose days was Hĕz-ē-kī'-ăh sick unto death. And the prophet Isaiah the son of Amoz came to him, and said unto him, Thus saith the LORD, ᴺSet thine house in order; for thou shalt die, and not live.

2 Then he turned his face to the wall, and prayed unto the LORD, saying,

3 I beseech thee, O LORD, ᴿremember now how I have walked before thee in truth and with a perfect heart, and have done *that which is* good in thy sight. And Hĕz-ē-kī'-ăh wept ᴺsore.

4 And it came to pass, afore Isaiah was gone out into the middle ᴺcourt, that the word of the LORD came to him, saying,

5 Turn again, and tell Hĕz-ē-kī'-ăh ᴿthe captain of my people, Thus saith the LORD, the God of David thy father, ᴿI have heard thy prayer, I have seen ᴿthy tears: behold, I will heal thee: on the third day thou shalt go up unto the house of the LORD.

6 And I will add unto thy days fifteen years; and I will deliver thee and this city out of the hand of the king of Assyria; and ᴿI will defend this city for mine own sake, and for my servant David's sake.

7 And ᴿIsaiah said, Take a lump of figs. And they took and laid *it* on the boil, and he recovered.

8 And Hĕz-ē-kī'-ăh said unto Isaiah, ᴿWhat *shall be* the sign that the LORD will heal me, and that I shall go up into the house of the LORD the third day?

9 And Isaiah said, ᴿThis sign shalt thou

have of the LORD, that the LORD will do the thing that he hath spoken: shall the shadow go forward ten degrees, or go back ten degrees?

10 And Hĕz-ē-kī'-ăh answered, It is a light thing for the shadow to go down ten degrees: nay, but let the shadow return backward ten degrees.

11 And Isaiah the prophet cried unto the LORD: and ᴿhe brought the shadow ten degrees backward, by which it had gone down in the ᴺdial of Ahaz.

Babylonian captivity foretold

12 ᴿAt that time ᴺBĕr-ō'-dăch-băl'-ă-dăn, the son of Băl'-ă-dăn, king of Babylon, sent letters and a present unto Hĕz-ē-kī'-ăh: for he had heard that Hĕz-ē-kī'-ăh had been sick.

13 And ᴿHĕz-ē-kī'-ăh hearkened unto them, and shewed them all the house of his ᴺprecious things, the silver, and the gold, and the spices, and the precious ointment, and *all* the house of his ᴺ ᴺarmour, and all that was found in his treasures: there was nothing in his house, nor in all his dominion, that Hĕz-ē-kī'-ăh shewed them not.

14 Then came Isaiah the prophet unto king Hĕz-ē-kī'-ăh, and said unto him, What said these men? and from whence came they unto thee? And Hĕz-ē-kī'-ăh said, They are come from a far country, *even* from Babylon.

15 And he said, What have they seen in thine house? And Hĕz-ē-kī'-ăh answered, ᴿAll *the things* that *are* in mine house have they seen: there is nothing among my treasures that I have not shewed them.

16 And Isaiah said unto Hĕz-ē-kī'-ăh, Hear the word of the LORD.

17 Behold, the days come, that all that *is* in thine house, and that which thy fathers have laid up in store unto this day, ᴿshall be carried into Babylon: nothing shall be left, saith the LORD.

18 And of thy sons that shall issue from thee, which thou shalt beget, ᴿshall they take away; and they shall be eunuchs in the palace of the king of Babylon.

19 Then said Hĕz-ē-kī'-ăh unto Isaiah, ᴿGood *is* the word of the LORD which thou hast spoken. And he said, ᴺ*Is it* not *good,* if peace and truth be in my days?

20 ᴿAnd the rest of the acts of Hĕz-ē-kī'-ăh, and all his might, and how he ᴿmade a pool, and a conduit, and ᴿbrought water into the city, *are* they not written in the book of the chronicles of the kings of Judah?

21 And ᴿHĕz-ē-kī'-ăh slept with his fathers: and Mă-năs'-sēh his son reigned in his stead.

CHAPTER 21

Manasseh's reign in Jerusalem

M̆Ă-N̆ĂS'-SĒH ᴿ*was* twelve years old when he began to reign, and reigned fifty and five years in Jerusalem. And his mother's name *was* H̆ĕph'-zĭ-băh.

2 And he did *that which was* evil in the sight of the Lᴏʀᴅ, ᴿafter the abominations of the heathen, whom the Lᴏʀᴅ cast out before the children of Israel.

3 For he built up again the high places ᴿwhich H̆ĕz-ē-kĭ'-ăh his father had destroyed; and he reared up altars for Bā'-ăl, and made a grove, ᴿas did Ahab king of Israel; and ᴿworshipped all the host of heaven, and served them.

4 And ᴿhe built altars in the house of the Lᴏʀᴅ, of which the Lᴏʀᴅ said, ᴿIn Jerusalem will I put my name.

5 And he built altars for all the host of heaven in the two courts of the house of the Lᴏʀᴅ.

6 ᴿAnd he made his son pass through the fire, and observed ᴿtimes, and used enchantments, and dealt with familiar spirits and wizards: he wrought much wickedness in the sight of the Lᴏʀᴅ, to provoke *him* to anger.

7 And he set a graven image of the grove that he had made in the house, of which the Lᴏʀᴅ said to David, and to Solomon his son, ᴿIn this house, and in Jerusalem, which I have chosen out of all tribes of Israel, will I put my name for ever:

8 ᴿNeither will I make the feet of Israel move any more out of the land which I gave their fathers; only if they will observe to do according to all that I have commanded them, and according to all the law that my servant Moses commanded them.

9 But they hearkened not: and M̆ă-năs'-sēh ᴿseduced them to do more evil than did the nations whom the Lᴏʀᴅ destroyed before the children of Israel.

Prophetic judgment of Jerusalem

10 And the Lᴏʀᴅ spake by his servants the prophets, saying,

11 ᴿBecause M̆ă-năs'-sēh king of Judah hath done these abominations, ᴿ*and* hath done wickedly above all that the Amorites did, which *were* before him, and ᴿhath made Judah also to sin with his idols:

12 Therefore thus saith the Lᴏʀᴅ God of Israel, Behold, I *am* bringing *such* evil upon Jerusalem and Judah, that whosoever heareth of it, both ᴿhis ears shall tingle.

13 And I will stretch over Jerusalem ᴿthe line of S̆ă-mâr'-ĭ-ă, and the plummet of the

house of Ahab: and I will wipe Jerusalem as *a man* wipeth a dish, ᴺwiping *it,* and turning *it* upside down.

14 And I will forsake the remnant of mine inheritance, and deliver them into the hand of their enemies; and they shall become a prey and a spoil to all their enemies;

15 Because they have done *that which was* evil in my sight, and have provoked me to anger, since the day their fathers came forth out of Egypt, even unto this day.

16 ᴿMoreover M̆ă-năs'-sēh shed innocent blood very much, till he had filled Jerusalem ᴺfrom one end to another; beside his sin wherewith he made Judah to sin, in doing *that which was* evil in the sight of the Lᴏʀᴅ.

17 Now ᴿthe rest of the acts of M̆ă-năs'-sēh, and all that he did, and his sin that he sinned, *are* they not written in the book of the chronicles of the kings of Judah?

18 And ᴿM̆ă-năs'-sēh slept with his fathers, and was buried in the garden of his own house, in the garden of ŭz'-ză: and Amon his son reigned in his stead.

Amon's reign in Jerusalem

19 ᴿAmon *was* twenty and two years old when he began to reign, and he reigned two years in Jerusalem. And his mother's name *was* M̆ĕ-shŭl'-lĕ-mĕth, the daughter of Hâr'-ŭz of Jŏt'-băh.

20 And he did *that which was* evil in the sight of the Lᴏʀᴅ, ᴿas his father M̆ă-năs'-sēh did.

21 And he walked in all the way that his father walked in, and served the idols that his father served, and worshipped them:

22 And he ᴿforsook the Lᴏʀᴅ God of his fathers, and walked not in the way of the Lᴏʀᴅ.

23 ᴿAnd the servants of Amon conspired against him, and slew the king in his own house.

24 And the people of the land slew all them that had conspired against king Amon; and the people of the land made Jō-sī'-ăh his son king in his stead.

25 Now the rest of the acts of Amon which he did, *are* they not written in the book of the chronicles of the kings of Judah?

26 And he was buried in his sepulchre in the garden of ŭz'-ză: and ᴿJō-sī'-ăh his son reigned in his stead.

CHAPTER 22

Josiah's reign in Jerusalem

Jō-Sī'-Ăʜ ᴿ*was* eight years old when he began to reign, and he reigned thirty and one

---

CHAP. **21**
BC 698
1 2 Chr. 33:1, etc.
2 ch. 16:3
3 ch. 18:4
3 1 Ki. 16:32
3 Deut. 4:19
& 17:3
ch. 17:16
4 Jer. 32:34
4 2 Sam. 7:13
1 Ki. 8:29
& 9:3
6 Lev. 18:21
& 20:2
ch. 16:3 & 17:17
6 Lev. 19:26, 31
Deut. 18:10, 11
ch. 17:17
7 2 Sam. 7:13
1 Ki. 8:29 & 9:3
ch. 23:27
Jer. 32:34
8 2 Sam. 7:10
9 Prov. 29:12
11 ch. 23:26, 27
& 24:3, 4
Jer. 15:4
11 1 Ki. 21:26
11 ver. 9
12 1 Sam. 3:11
Jer. 19:3
13 See Is. 34:11
Lam. 2:8
Amos 7:7, 8

Heb. *he wipeth* 13
and turneth it
upon the face
thereof
ch. 24:4   16
Heb. *from mouth* 16
to mouth
2 Chr. 33:11-19 17
2 Chr. 33:20   18
2 Chr. 33:21-23 19
ver. 2, etc.   20
1 Ki. 11:33   22
2 Chr. 33:24, 25 23
Mat. 1:10, called 26
Josias

CHAP. **22**
BC 641
2 Chr. 34:1   1

years in Jerusalem. And his mother's name *was* Jĕ-dī′-dăh, the daughter of Ă-daī′-ăh of ᴿBŏs′-căth.

2 And he did *that which was* right in the sight of the LORD, and walked in all the way of David his father, and ᴿturned not aside to the right hand or to the left.

The temple repaired

3 ᴿAnd it came to pass in the eighteenth year of king Jō-sī′-ăh, *that* the king sent Shā′-phăn the son of Ăz-ă-lī′-ăh, the son of Mĕ-shŭl′-lăm, the scribe, to the house of the LORD, saying,

4 Go up to Hīl-kī′-ăh the high priest, that he may sum the silver which is ᴿbrought into the house of the LORD, which ᴿthe keepers of the ᴺdoor have gathered of the people:

5 And let them ᴿdeliver it into the hand of the doers of the work, that have the oversight of the house of the LORD: and let them give it to the doers of the work which *is* in the house of the LORD, to repair the breaches of the house,

6 Unto carpenters, and builders, and masons, and to buy timber and hewn stone to repair the house.

7 Howbeit ᴿthere was no reckoning made with them of the money that was delivered into their hand, because they dealt faithfully.

Book of the law found

8 And Hīl-kī′-ăh the high priest said unto Shā′-phăn the scribe, ᴿI have found the book of the law in the house of the LORD. And Hīl-kī′-ăh gave the book to Shā′-phăn, and he read it.

9 And Shā′-phăn the scribe came to the king, and brought the king word again, and said, Thy servants have ᴺgathered the money that was found in the house, and have delivered it into the hand of them that do the work, that have the oversight of the house of the LORD.

10 And Shā′-phăn the scribe shewed the king, saying, Hīl-kī′-ăh the priest hath delivered me a book. And Shā′-phăn read it before the king.

11 And it came to pass, when the king had heard the words of the book of the law, that he rent his clothes.

12 And the king commanded Hīl-kī′-ăh the priest, and Ă-hī′-kăm the son of Shā′-phăn, and ᴿĂch′-bôr the son of ᴺMī-chaī′-ăh, and Shā′-phăn the scribe, and Ăs-ă-hī′-ăh a servant of the king's, saying,

13 Go ye, inquire of the LORD for me, and for the people, and for all Judah, concerning the words of this book that is found: for great

is ᴿthe wrath of the LORD that is kindled against us, because our fathers have not hearkened unto the words of this book, to do according unto all that which is written concerning us.

Huldah's prophecy

14 So Hīl-kī′-ăh the priest, and Ă-hī′-kăm, and Ăch′-bôr, and Shā′-phăn, and Ăs-ă-hī′-ăh, went unto Hŭl′-dăh the prophetess, the wife of Shăl′-lŭm the son of ᴿTĭk′-văh, the son of ᴺHär′-hăs, keeper of the ᴺwardrobe; (now she dwelt in Jerusalem ᴺin the college;) and they communed with her.

15 And she said unto them, Thus saith the LORD God of Israel, Tell the man that sent you to me,

16 Thus saith the LORD, Behold, ᴿI will bring evil upon this place, and upon the inhabitants thereof, *even* all the words of the book which the king of Judah hath read:

17 ᴿBecause they have forsaken me, and have burned incense unto other gods, that they might provoke me to anger with all the works of their hands; therefore my wrath shall be kindled against this place, and shall not be quenched.

18 But to ᴿthe king of Judah which sent you to inquire of the LORD, thus shall ye say to him, Thus saith the LORD God of Israel, *As touching* the words which thou hast heard;

19 Because thine ᴿheart was tender, and thou hast ᴿhumbled thyself before the LORD, when thou heardest what I spake against this place, and against the inhabitants thereof, that they should become ᴿa desolation and ᴿa curse, and hast rent thy clothes, and wept before me; I also have heard *thee,* saith the LORD.

20 Behold therefore, I will gather thee unto thy fathers, and thou ᴿshalt be gathered into thy grave in peace; and thine eyes shall not see all the evil which I will bring upon this place. And they brought the king word again.

CHAPTER 23

Josiah renews the covenant

AND ᴿthe king sent, and they gathered unto him all the elders of Judah and of Jerusalem.

2 And the king went up into the house of the LORD, and all the men of Judah and all the inhabitants of Jerusalem with him, and the priests, and the prophets, and all the people, ᴺboth small and great: and he read in their ears all the words of the book of the covenant ᴿwhich was found in the house of the LORD.

3 And the king ᴿstood by a pillar, and made

a covenant before the LORD, to walk after the LORD, and to keep his commandments and his testimonies and his statutes with all *their* heart and all *their* soul, to perform the words of this covenant that were written in this book. And all the people stood to the covenant.

Reforms instituted

4 And the king commanded Hĭl-kī′-ăh the high priest, and the priests of the second order, and the keepers of the door, to bring forth out of the temple of the LORD all the vessels that were made for Bā′-ăl, and for ᴿthe grove, and for all the host of heaven: and he burned them without Jerusalem in the fields of Kĭ′-drŏn, and carried the ashes of them unto Beth-el.

5 And he ᴺput down the ᴺidolatrous priests, whom the kings of Judah had ordained to burn incense in the high places in the cities of Judah, and in the places round about Jerusalem; them also that burned incense unto Bā′-ăl, to the sun, and to the moon, and to the ᴺplanets, and to ᴿall the host of heaven.

6 And he brought out the ᴿgrove from the house of the LORD, without Jerusalem, unto the brook Kĭ′-drŏn, and burned it at the brook Kĭ′-drŏn, and stamped *it* small to powder, and cast the powder thereof upon ᴿthe graves of the children of the people.

7 And he brake down the houses ᴿof the sodomites, that *were* by the house of the LORD, ᴿwhere the women wove ᴺhangings for the grove.

8 And he brought all the priests out of the cities of Judah, and defiled the high places where the priests had burned incense, from ᴿGē′-bă to Bēẽr-shē′-bă, and brake down the high places of the gates that *were* in the entering in of the gate of Joshua the governor of the city, which *were* on a man's left hand at the gate of the city.

9 ᴿNevertheless the priests of the high places came not up to the altar of the LORD in Jerusalem, ᴿbut they did eat of the unleavened bread among their brethren.

10 And he defiled ᴿTō′-phĕth, which *is* in ᴿthe valley of the children of Hĭn′-nom, ᴿthat no man might make his son or his daughter to pass through the fire to Molech.

11 And he took away the horses that the kings of Judah had given to the sun, at the entering in of the house of the LORD, by the chamber of Nā′-thăn-mē′-lĕch the ᴺchamberlain, which *was* in the suburbs, and burned the chariots of the sun with fire.

12 And the altars that *were* ᴿon the top of the upper chamber of Ahaz, which the kings

of Judah had made, and the altars which ᴿMă-năs′-sĕh had made in the two courts of the house of the LORD, did the king beat down, and ᴺbrake *them* down from thence, and cast the dust of them into the brook Kĭ′-drŏn.

13 And the high places that *were* before Jerusalem, which *were* on the right hand of ᴺthe mount of corruption, which ᴿSolomon the king of Israel had builded for Ăsh′-tō-rĕth the abomination of the Zĭ-dō′-nĭ-ăns, and for Chē′-mŏsh the abomination of the Moabites, and for Mĭl′-cŏm the abomination of the children of Ammon, did the king defile.

14 And he ᴿbrake in pieces the ᴺimages, and cut down the groves, and filled their places with the bones of men.

15 Moreover the altar that *was* at Beth-el, *and* the high place ᴿwhich Jĕr-ŏ-bō′-ăm the son of Nē′-băt, who made Israel to sin, had made, both that altar and the high place he brake down, and burned the high place, *and* stamped *it* small to powder, and burned the grove.

16 And as Jō-sī′-ăh turned himself, he spied the sepulchres that *were* there in the mount, and sent, and took the bones out of the sepulchres, and burned *them* upon the altar, and polluted it, according to the ᴿword of the LORD which the man of God proclaimed, who proclaimed these words.

17 Then he said, What title *is* that that I see? And the men of the city told him, *It is* ᴿthe sepulchre of the man of God, which came from Judah, and proclaimed these things that thou hast done against the altar of Beth-el.

18 And he said, Let him alone; let no man move his bones. So they let his bones ᴺalone, with the bones of ᴿthe prophet that came out of Să-mâr′-ĭ-ă.

19 And all the houses also of the high places that *were* ᴿin the cities of Să-mâr′-ĭ-ă, which the kings of Israel had made to provoke *the* LORD to anger, Jō-sī′-ăh took away, and did to them according to all the acts that he had done in Beth-el.

20 And ᴿhe ᴿslewᴺ all the priests of the high places that *were* there upon the altars, and ᴿburned men's bones upon them, and returned to Jerusalem.

Passover kept

21 And the king commanded all the people, saying, ᴿKeep the passover unto the LORD your God, ᴿas *it is* written in the book of this covenant.

22 Surely ᴿthere was not holden such a

passover from the days of the judges that judged Israel, nor in all the days of the kings of Israel, nor of the kings of Judah;

23 But in the eighteenth year of king Jō-sī'-ăh, *wherein* this passover was holden to the LORD in Jerusalem.

24 Moreover the *workers with* familiar spirits, and the wizards, and the ᴺimages, and the idols, and all the abominations that were spied in the land of Judah and in Jerusalem, did Jō-sī'-ăh put away, that he might perform the words of ᴿthe law which were written in the book that Hĭl-kī'-ăh the priest found in the house of the LORD.

25 ᴿAnd like unto him was there no king before him, that turned to the LORD with all his heart, and with all his soul, and with all his might, according to all the law of Moses; neither after him arose there *any* like him.

26 Notwithstanding the LORD turned not from the fierceness of his great wrath, wherewith his anger was kindled against Judah, ᴿbecause of all the ᴺprovocations that Mă-năs'-sĕh had provoked him withal.

27 And the LORD said, I will remove Judah also out of my sight, as ᴿI have removed Israel, and will cast off this city Jerusalem which I have chosen, and the house of which I said, ᴿMy name shall be there.

Josiah slain by Pharaoh-nechoh

28 Now the rest of the acts of Jō-sī'-ăh, and all that he did, *are* they not written in the book of the chronicles of the kings of Judah?

29 ᴿIn his days Phâr'-aōh-nē'-choh king of Egypt went up against the king of Assyria to the river Ȇu-phrā'-tĕś: and king Jō-sī'-ăh went against him; and he slew him at ᴿMĕ-gĭd'-dō, when he ᴿhad seen him.

30 ᴿAnd his servants carried him in a chariot dead from Mĕ-gĭd'-dō, and brought him to Jerusalem, and buried him in his own sepulchre. And ᴿthe people of the land took Jĕ-hō'-ă-hăz the son of Jō-sī'-ăh, and anointed him, and made him king in his father's stead.

Jehoahaz's reign and captivity

31 ᴺJĕ-hō'-ă-hăz *was* twenty and three years old when he began to reign; and he reigned three months in Jerusalem. And his mother's name *was* ᴿHă-mū'-tăl, the daughter of Jeremiah of Lĭb'-năh.

32 And he did *that which was* evil in the sight of the LORD, according to all that his fathers had done.

33 And Phâr'-aōh-nē'-choh put him in bands

ᴿat Rĭb'-lăh in the land of Hā'-măth, ᴺthat he might not reign in Jerusalem; and ᴺput the land to a tribute of an hundred talents of silver, and a talent of gold.

Eliakim made king of Judah

34 And ᴿPhâr'-aōh-nē'-choh made Ē-lī'-ă-kĭm the son of Jō-sī'-ăh king in the room of Jō-sī'-ăh his father, and ᴿturned his name to ᴿJĕ-hoī'-ă-kĭm, and took Jĕ-hō'-ă-hăz away: ᴿand he came to Egypt, and died there.

35 And Jĕ-hoī'-ă-kĭm gave ᴿthe silver and the gold to Pharaoh; but he taxed the land to give the money according to the commandment of Pharaoh: he exacted the silver and the gold of the people of the land, of every one according to his taxation, to give *it* unto Phâr'-aōh-nē'-choh.

36 ᴿJĕ-hoī'-ă-kĭm *was* twenty and five years old when he began to reign; and he reigned eleven years in Jerusalem. And his mother's name *was* Zĕ-bū'-dăh, the daughter of Pĕ-daī'-ăh of Rû'-măh.

37 And he did *that which was* evil in the sight of the LORD, according to all that his fathers had done.

CHAPTER 24

IN ᴿhis days Nĕb-ū-chăd-nĕz'-zär king of Babylon came up, and Jĕ-hoī'-ă-kĭm became his servant three years: then he turned and rebelled against him.

2 ᴿAnd the LORD sent against him bands of the Chăl'-dēéś, and bands of the Syrians, and bands of the Moabites, and bands of the children of Ammon, and sent them against Judah to destroy it, ᴿaccording to the word of the LORD, which he spake ᴺby his servants the prophets.

3 Surely at the commandment of the LORD came *this* upon Judah, to remove *them* out of his sight, ᴿfor the sins of Mă-năs'-sĕh, according to all that he did;

4 ᴿAnd also for the innocent blood that he shed: for he filled Jerusalem with innocent blood; which the LORD would not pardon.

5 Now the rest of the acts of Jĕ-hoī'-ă-kĭm, and all that he did, *are* they not written in the book of the chronicles of the kings of Judah?

6 ᴿSo Jĕ-hoī'-ă-kĭm slept with his fathers: and Jĕ-hoī'-ă-chĭn his son reigned in his stead.

7 And ᴿthe king of Egypt came not again any more out of his land: for ᴿthe king of Babylon had taken from the river of Egypt unto the river Ȇu-phrā'-tĕś all that pertained to the king of Egypt.

Jehoiachin's brief reign

8 ᴿJĕ-hoĭ'-ă-chĭnᴺ *was* eighteen years old when he began to reign, and he reigned in Jerusalem three months. And his mother's name *was* Nĕ-hŭsh'-tă, the daughter of ĕl-nā'-thăn of Jerusalem.

9 And he did *that which was* evil in the sight of the LORD, according to all that his father had done.

Judah carried into captivity

10 ᴿAt that time the servants of Nĕb-ū-chăd-nĕz'-zär king of Babylon came up against Jerusalem, and the city ᴺwas besieged.

11 And Nĕb-ū-chăd-nĕz'-zär king of Babylon came against the city, and his servants did besiege it.

12 ᴿAnd Jĕ-hoĭ'-ă-chĭn the king of Judah went out to the king of Babylon, he, and his mother, and his servants, and his princes, and his ᴺofficers: ᴿand the king of Babylon ᴿtook him ᴿin the eighth year of his reign.

13 ᴿAnd he carried out thence all the treasures of the house of the LORD, and the treasures of the king's house, and ᴿcut in pieces all the vessels of gold which Solomon king of Israel had made in the temple of the LORD, ᴿas the LORD had said.

14 And ᴿhe carried away all Jerusalem, and all the princes, and all the mighty men of valour, ᴿ*even* ten thousand captives, and ᴿall the craftsmen and smiths: none remained, save ᴿthe poorest sort of the people of the land.

15 And ᴿhe carried away Jĕ-hoĭ'-ă-chĭn to Babylon, and the king's mother, and the king's wives, and his ᴺofficers, and the mighty of the land, *those* carried he into captivity from Jerusalem to Babylon.

16 And ᴿall the men of might, *even* seven thousand, and craftsmen and smiths a thousand, all *that were* strong *and* apt for war, even them the king of Babylon brought captive to Babylon.

17 And ᴿthe king of Babylon made Măt-tă-nī'-ăh ᴿhis father's brother king in his stead, and ᴿchanged his name to Zĕd-ē-kī'-ăh.

Zedekiah's reign and rebellion

18 ᴿZĕd-ē-kī'-ăh *was* twenty and one years old when he began to reign, and he reigned eleven years in Jerusalem. And his mother's name *was* ᴿHă-mū'-tăl, the daughter of Jeremiah of Lĭb'-năh.

19 ᴿAnd he did *that which was* evil in the sight of the LORD, according to all that Jĕ-hoĭ'-ă-kĭm had done.

20 For through the anger of the LORD it

came to pass in Jerusalem and Judah, until he had cast them out from his presence, ᴿthat Zĕd-ē-kī'-ăh rebelled against the king of Babylon.

CHAPTER 25

AND it came to pass ᴿin the ninth year of his reign, in the tenth month, in the tenth *day* of the month, *that* Nĕb-ū-chăd-nĕz'-zär king of Babylon came, he, and all his host, against Jerusalem, and pitched against it; and they built forts against it round about.

2 And the city was besieged unto the eleventh year of king Zĕd-ē-kī'-ăh.

3 And on the ninth *day* of the ᴿ*fourth* month the famine prevailed in the city, and there was no bread for the people of the land.

4 And ᴿthe city was broken up, and all the men of war *fled* by night by the way of the gate between two walls, which *is* by the king's garden: (now the Chăl'-dēēś *were* against the city round about:) and ᴿ*the king* went the way toward the plain.

5 And the army of the Chăl'-dēēś pursued after the king, and overtook him in the plains of Jericho: and all his army were scattered from him.

6 So they took the king, and brought him up to the king of Babylon ᴿto Rĭb'-lăh; and they ᴺgave judgment upon him.

7 And they slew the sons of Zĕd-ē-kī'-ăh before his eyes, and ᴿputᴺ out the eyes of Zĕd-ē-kī'-ăh, and bound him with fetters of brass, and carried him to Babylon.

Jerusalem burned

8 And in the fifth month, ᴿon the seventh *day* of the month, which *is* ᴿthe nineteenth year of king Nĕb-ū-chăd-nĕz'-zär king of Babylon, ᴿcame Nĕb-ū'-zär-ăd'-ăn, ᴺcaptain of the guard, a servant of the king of Babylon, unto Jerusalem:

9 ᴿAnd he burnt the house of the LORD, ᴿand the king's house, and all the houses of Jerusalem, and every great *man's* house burnt he with fire.

10 And all the army of the Chăl'-dēēś, that *were with* the captain of the guard, ᴿbrake down the walls of Jerusalem round about.

11 ᴿNow the rest of the people *that were* left in the city, and the ᴺfugitives that fell away to the king of Babylon, with the remnant of the multitude, did Nĕb-ū'-zär-ăd'-ăn the captain of the guard carry away.

12 But the captain of the guard ᴿleft of the poor of the land *to be* vinedressers and husbandmen.

13 And ᴿthe ᴿpillars of brass that *were* in the house of the Lᴏʀᴅ, and ᴿthe bases, and ᴿthe brasen sea that *was* in the house of the Lᴏʀᴅ, did the Chăl'-dēēś break in pieces, and carried the brass of them to Babylon.

14 And ᴿthe pots, and the shovels, and the snuffers, and the spoons, and all the vessels of brass wherewith they ministered, took they away.

15 And the firepans, and the bowls, *and* such things as *were* of gold, *in* gold, and of silver, *in* silver, the captain of the guard took away.

16 The two pillars, ᴺone sea, and the bases which Solomon had made for the house of the Lᴏʀᴅ; ᴿthe brass of all these vessels was without weight.

17 ᴿThe height of the one pillar *was* eighteen cubits, and the chapiter upon it *was* brass: and the height of the chapiter three cubits; and the wreathen work, and pomegranates upon the chapiter round about, all of brass: and like unto these had the second pillar with wreathen work.

18 ᴿAnd the captain of the guard took ᴿSĕ-raî'-ăh the chief priest, and ᴿZĕph-ă-nī'-ăh the second priest, and the three keepers of the ᴺdoor:

19 And out of the city he took an ᴺofficer that was set over the men of war, and ᴿfive men of them that ᴺwere in the king's presence, which were found in the city, and the ᴺprincipal scribe of the host, which mustered the people of the land, and threescore men of the people of the land *that were* found in the city:

20 And Nĕb-ū'-zär-ăd'-ăn captain of the guard took these, and brought them to the king of Babylon to Rĭb'-lăh:

21 And the king of Babylon smote them, and slew them at Rĭb'-lăh in the land of Hā'-măth. ᴿSo Judah was carried away out of their land.

Gedaliah murdered

22 ᴿAnd *as for* the people that remained in the land of Judah, whom Nĕb-ū-chăd-nĕz'-zär king of Babylon had left, even over them he

made Gĕd-ă-lī'-ăh the son of Ă-hī'-kăm, the son of Shā'-phăn, ruler.

23 And when all the ᴿcaptains of the armies, they and their men, heard that the king of Babylon had made Gĕd-ă-lī'-ăh governor, there came to Gĕd-ă-lī'-ăh to Mizpah, even ĭsh'-mā-ĕl the son of Nĕth-ă-nī'-ăh, and Jō-hā'-năn the son of Că-rē'-ăh, and Sĕ-raî'-ăh the son of Tăn-hū'-mĕth the Nĕ-tŏph'-ă-thīte, and Jā-ăz-ă-nī'-ăh the son of a Mā-ăch'-ă-thīte, they and their men.

24 And Gĕd-ă-lī'-ăh sware to them, and to their men, and said unto them, Fear not to be the servants of the Chăl'-dēēś: dwell in the land, and serve the king of Babylon; and it shall be well with you.

25 But ᴿit came to pass in the seventh month, that ĭsh'-mā-ĕl the son of Nĕth-ă-nī'-ăh, the son of Ē-lī'-shă-mă, of the seed ᴺroyal, came, and ten men with him, and smote Gĕd-ă-lī'-ăh, that he died, and the Jews and the Chăl'-dēēś that were with him at Mizpah.

26 And all the people, both small and great, and the captains of the armies, arose, ᴿand came to Egypt: for they were afraid of the Chăl'-dēēś.

Jehoiachin freed from prison

27 ᴿAnd it came to pass in the seven and thirtieth year of the captivity of Jĕ-hoî'-ă-chĭn king of Judah, in the twelfth month, on the seven and twentieth *day* of the month, *that* Ē'-vĭl-mĕr'-ō-dăch king of Babylon in the year that he began to reign ᴿdid lift up the head of Jĕ-hoî'-ă-chĭn king of Judah out of prison;

28 And he spake ᴺkindly to him, and set his throne above the throne of the kings that *were* with him in Babylon;

29 And changed his prison garments: and he did ᴿeat bread continually before him all the days of his life.

30 And his allowance *was* a continual allowance given him of the king, a daily rate for every day, all the days of his life.

Center column references:

CHAP. 25
BC 588
13 Jer. 27:19 & 52:17
13 1 Ki. 7:15
13 1 Ki. 7:27
13 1 Ki. 7:23
14 Ex. 27:3
1 Ki. 7:45
16 Heb. *the one sea*
16 1 Ki. 7:47
17 1 Ki. 7:15
Jer. 52:21
18 Jer. 52:24
18 1 Chr. 6:14
Ezra 7:1
18 Jer. 21:1
18 Heb. *threshold*
19 Or, *eunuch*
19 Jer. 52:25
19 Heb. *saw the king's face*
19 Or, *scribe of the captain of the host*
21 Lev. 26:33
Deut. 28:36, 64
ch. 23:27
22 Jer. 40:5

Jer. 40:7-9   23
Jer. 41:1, 2   25
Heb. *of the kingdom*   25
Jer. 43:4, 7   26
Jer. 52:31, etc.   27
See Gen. 40:13, 20   27
Heb. *good things with him*   28
2 Sam. 9:7   29

THE FIRST BOOK OF THE
CHRONICLES

The two books of Chronicles were originally one book in the Hebrew text and were called "Words of the Days." The Septuagint translators gave them a title meaning "things left over, or omitted," implying their use as a supplement to Samuel and Kings. Jerome (340-420) called them "a chronicle of the whole sacred history," hence the English title "Chronicles."

First and Second Chronicles provide a panoramic perspective of the history of Israel up to the Babylonian captivity in 586 B.C. and the edict of restoration issued by Cyrus in 539 B.C.

The first book of Chronicles supplements the account of David's reign which is given in Second Samuel. The first nine chapters present a whole series of genealogies in which it is

made clear that the writer is recording the history of a chosen people. Genealogically David's line is traced back to Adam. The major part of the book (10-29) is an account of David as a great king and the real founder of the temple and its services. Great interest is shown in the services of the priests, Levites, musicians, and others who were associated with the temple.

OUTLINE OF THE BOOK:
  I. Genealogical background 1:1-9:44
  II. David established as king 10:1-12:40
  III. Success and prosperity 13:1-21:27
  IV. Preparation for worship 22:1-29:30

CHAPTER 1

Patriarchal genealogy

ADAM, ᴿSheth, Ē'-nŏsh,
2 Kē'-năn, Mă-hăl'-ă-lĕĕl, Jē'-rĕd,
3 Hē'-nŏch, Mĕ-thū'-sĕ-lăh, Lā'-mĕch,
4 Noah, Shem, Ham, and Jā'-phĕth.
5 ᴿThe sons of Jā'-phĕth; Gō'-mĕr, and Mā'-gŏg, and Mā'-dăi, and Jā'-văn, and Tū'-băl, and Mē'-shĕch, and Tī'-răs.
6 And the sons of Gō'-mĕr; Ăsh-chē'-năz, and ᴺRĭ'-phăth, and Tō-găr'-măh.
7 And the sons of Jā'-văn; Ē-lĭ'-shăh, and Tarshish, Kittim, and ᴺDō'-dă-nĭm.
8 ᴿThe sons of Ham; Cŭsh, and Mĭz'-rā-ĭm, Pŭt, and Canaan.
9 And the sons of Cŭsh; Sē'-bă, and Hăv'-ĭ-lăh, and Săb'-tă, and Rā'-ă-măh, and Săb-tē'-chă. And the sons of Rā'-ă-măh; Shē'-bă, and Dē'-dăn.
10 And Cŭsh ᴿbegat Nimrod: he began to be mighty upon the earth.
11 And Mĭz'-rā-ĭm begat Lū'-dĭm, and Ăn'-ă-mĭm, and Lĕ-hā'-bĭm, and Năph-tû'-hĭm,
12 And Păth-rû'-sĭm, and Căs-lû'-hĭm, (of whom came the Philistines,) and ᴿCăph'-thō-rĭm.
13 And ᴿCanaan begat Zī'-dŏn his firstborn, and Heth,
14 The Jĕb'-ū-sīte also, and the Amorite, and the Gĭr'-gă-shīte,
15 And the Hī'-vīte, and the Ăr'-kīte, and the Sī'-nīte,
16 And the Ăr'-vă-dīte, and the Zĕm'-ă-rīte, and the Hā'-măth-īte.
17 The sons of ᴿShem; Ē'-lăm, and Ăssh'-ŭr, and Ăr-phăx'-ăd, and Lud, and âr'-ăm, and Uz, and Hul, and Gē'-thĕr, and ᴺMē'-shĕch.
18 And Ăr-phăx'-ăd begat Shē'-lăh, and Shē'-lăh begat Ē'-bĕr.
19 And unto Ē'-bĕr were born two sons: the name of the one was ᴺPē'-lĕg; because in his days the earth was divided: and his brother's name was Jŏk'-tăn.
20 And ᴿJŏk'-tăn begat Ăl-mō'-dăd, and Shē'-lĕph, and Hā-zăr-mā'-vĕth, and Jē'-răh,
21 Hă-dôr'-ăm also, and Ū'-zăl, and Dĭk'-lăh,
22 And Ē'-băl, and Ă-bĭm'-ā-ĕl, and Shē'-bă,

CHAP. 1
BC 4004
1 Gen. 4:25, 26 & 5:3, 9
5 Gen. 10:2, etc.
6 Or, *Diphath,* as it is in some copies
7 Or, *Rodanim,* according to some copies
8 Gen. 10:6, etc.
10 Gen. 10:8, 13, etc.
12 Deut. 2:23
13 Gen. 10:15, etc.
17 Gen. 10:22 & 11:10
17 Or, *Mash,* Gen. 10:23
19 i.e. *Division,* Gen. 10:25
20 Gen. 10:26

Gen. 11:10 | 24
Luke 3:36 |
Gen. 11:15 | 25
Gen. 17:5 | 27
Gen. 21:2 | 28
Gen. 16:11, 15 | 28
Gen. 25:13-16 | 29
Or, *Hadar,* Gen. 25:15 | 30
Gen. 25:1 | 32
Gen. 21:2 | 34
Gen. 25:25, 26 | 34
Gen. 36:9, 10 | 35
Or, *Zepho,* Gen. 36:11 | 36
Gen. 36:20 | 38
Or, *Hemam,* Gen. 36:22 | 39
Or, *Alvan,* Gen. 36:23 | 40
Or, *Shepho,* Gen. 36:23 | 40
Gen. 36:25 | 41
Or, *Hemdan,* Gen. 36:26 | 41
Or, *Akan,* Gen. 36:27 | 42

23 And Ō'-phĭr, and Hăv'-ĭ-lăh, and Jō'-băb. All these were the sons of Jŏk'-tăn.
24 ᴿShem, Ăr-phăx'-ăd, Shē'-lăh,
25 ᴿĒ'-bĕr, Pē'-lĕg, Rē'-ū,
26 Sē'-rŭg, Nahor, Tē'-răh,
27 ᴿAbram; the same is Abraham.

Line of Abraham

28 The sons of Abraham; ᴿIsaac, and ᴿĬsh'-mā-ĕl.
29 These are their generations: The ᴿfirstborn of Ĭsh'-mā-ĕl, Nĕ-bāi'-ōth; then Kē'-där, and Ăd'-bĕĕl, and Mĭb'-săm,
30 Mĭsh'-mă, and Dū'-măh, Măs'-să, ᴺHā'-dăd, and Tē'-mă,
31 Jē'-tŭr, Nā'-phĭsh, and Kē'-dĕ-măh. These are the sons of Ĭsh'-mā-ĕl.
32 Now ᴿthe sons of Kĕ-tū'-răh, Abraham's concubine: she bare Zimran, and Jŏk'-shăn, and Mē'-dăn, and Mĭd'-ĭ-ăn, and Ĭsh'-băk, and Shû'-äh. And the sons of Jŏk'-shăn; Shē'-bă, and Dē'-dăn.
33 And the sons of Mĭd'-ĭ-ăn; Ē'-phăh, and Ē'-phĕr, and Hē'-nŏch, and Ă-bī'-dă, and Ĕl-dā'-äh. All these are the sons of Kĕ-tū'-răh.
34 And ᴿAbraham begat Isaac. ᴿThe sons of Isaac; Esau and Israel.
35 The sons of ᴿEsau; Ĕ-lĭ'-phăz, Rĕû'-ĕl, and Jē'-ŭsh, and Jā'-ă-lăm, and Kôr'-ăh.
36 The sons of Ĕ-lĭ'-phăz; Tē'-măn, and Omar, ᴺZē'-phī, and Gā'-tăm, Kē'-năz, and Tĭm'-nă, and Ăm'-ă-lĕk.
37 The sons of Rĕû'-ĕl; Nahath, Zē'-răh, Shăm'-măh, and Mĭz'-zäh.
38 And ᴿthe sons of Sē'-ĭr; Lō'-tăn, and Shō'-băl, and Zĭb'-ĕ-ŏn, and Ā'-năh, and Dī'-shŏn, and Ē'-zĕr, and Dī'-shăn.
39 And the sons of Lō'-tăn; Hôr'-ĭ, and ᴺHō'-măm: and Tĭm'-nă was Lō'-tăn's sister.
40 The sons of Shō'-băl; ᴺĂl'-ĭ-ăn, and Măn'-ă-hăth, and Ē'-băl, ᴺShē'-phī, and Ō'-năm. And the sons of Zĭb'-ĕ-ŏn; Āi'-ăh, and Ā'-năh.
41 The sons of Ā'-năh; ᴿDī'-shŏn. And the sons of Dī'-shŏn; ᴺAmram, and Ĕsh'-băn, and Ĭth'-răn, and Chē'-răn.
42 The sons of Ē'-zĕr; Bilhan, and Zā'-văn, and ᴺJakan. The sons of Dī'-shăn; Uz, and Âr'-ăn.

43 Now these *are* the ᴿkings that reigned in the land of Ē'-dom before *any* king reigned over the children of Israel; Bē'-lä the son of Bē'-ôr: and the name of his city *was* Dĭn'-hä-bäh.

44 And when Bē'-lä was dead, Jō'-băb the son of Zē'-räh of Bŏz'-räh reigned in his stead.

45 And when Jō'-băb was dead, Hū'-shăm of the land of the Tē'-măn-ītes reigned in his stead.

46 And when Hū'-shăm was dead, Hā'-dăd the son of Bē'-dăd, which smote Mĭd'-ĭ-ăn in the field of Moab, reigned in his stead: and the name of his city *was* Ā'-vĭth.

47 And when Hā'-dăd was dead, Săm'-läh of Măs-rē'-käh reigned in his stead.

48 ᴿAnd when Săm'-läh was dead, Shā'-ŭl of Rē'-hŏ-bŏth by the river reigned in his stead.

49 And when Shā'-ŭl was dead, Bā'-ăl-hā'-năn the son of Ăch'-bôr reigned in his stead.

50 And when Bā'-ăl-hā'-năn was dead, ᴺHā'-dăd reigned in his stead: and the name of his city *was* ᴺPā'-ī; and his wife's name *was* Mĕ-hĕt'-ă-bĕl, the daughter of Mā'-trĕd, the daughter of Mē'-ză-häb.

51 Hā'-dăd died also. And the ᴿdukes of Ē'-dom were; duke Tĭm'-näh, duke ᴺĂl'-ĭ-äh, duke Jē'-thĕth,

52 Duke Ă-hŏl-ĭ-bä'-mäh, duke Ē'-läh, duke Pī'-nŏn,

53 Duke Kē'-năz, duke Tē'-măn, duke Mĭb'-zär,

54 Duke Măg'-dĭ-ĕl, duke Ĭ'-răm. These *are* the dukes of Ē'-dom.

CHAPTER 2

Descendants of Israel and Judah

THESE *are* the sons of ᴺIsrael; ᴿReuben, Simeon, Levi, and Judah, Ĭs'-să-chär, and Zē-bū'-lŭn,

2 Dan, Joseph, and Benjamin, Năph'-tă-lī, Gad, and Asher.

3 The sons of ᴿJudah; Er, and Ō'-năn, and Shē'-läh: *which* three were born unto him of the daughter of ᴿShû'-ă the Canaanitess. And ᴿEr, the firstborn of Judah, was evil in the sight of the LORD; and he slew him.

4 And ᴿTā'-mär his daughter in law bare him Phâr'-ĕz and Zē'-räh. All the sons of Judah *were* five.

5 The sons of ᴿPhâr'-ĕz; Hĕz'-rŏn, and Hăm'-ŭl.

6 And the sons of Zē'-räh; ᴺZimri, ᴿand Ē'-thăn, and Hē'-măn, and Căl'-cŏl, and ᴺDâr'-ă: five of them in all.

7 And the sons of ᴿCär'-mī; ᴺĀ'-chär, the troubler of Israel, who transgressed in the thing ᴿaccursed.

8 And the sons of Ē'-thăn; Ăz-ă-rī'-äh.

9 The sons also of Hĕz'-rŏn, that were born unto him; Jĕ-räh'-mēĕl, and ᴺRam, and ᴺChĕ-lū'-bâi.

10 And Ram ᴿbegat Ăm-mĭn'-ă-dăb; and Ăm-mĭn'-ă-dăb begat Näh'-shŏn, ᴿprince of the children of Judah;

11 And Näh'-shŏn begat ᴺSăl'-mä, and Săl'-mä begat Bō'-ăz,

12 And Bō'-ăz begat Ō'-bĕd, and Ō'-bĕd begat Jesse,

13 ᴿAnd Jesse begat his firstborn Ē-lī'-ăb, and Ă-bĭn'-ă-dăb the second, and ᴺShĭm'-mä the third,

14 Nĕth'-ă-nēĕl the fourth, Răd'-dā-ī the fifth.

15 Ō'-zĕm the sixth, David the seventh:

16 Whose sisters *were* Zĕr-ū-ī'-äh, and Ăb'-ĭ-gail. ᴿAnd the sons of Zĕr-ū-ī'-äh; Ăb'-ĭ-shâi, and Jō'-ăb, and Ăs'-ă-hĕl, three.

17 And ᴿĂb'-ĭ-gail bare Ă-mā'-să: and the father of Ă-mā'-să *was* ᴺJē'-thĕr the Ĭsh'-mēĕl-īte.

18 And Caleb the son of Hĕz'-rŏn begat *children* of Ă-zū'-băh *his* wife, and of Jĕr'-ĭ-ŏth: her sons *are* these; Jē'-shĕr, and Shō'-băb, and Ardon.

19 And when Ă-zū'-băh was dead, Caleb took unto him ᴿĒ'-phräth, which bare him Hur.

20 And Hur begat Ū'-rī, and Ū'-rī begat ᴿBĕz'-ă-lēĕl.

21 And afterward Hĕz'-rŏn went in to the daughter of ᴿMā'-chĭr the father of Gilead, whom he ᴺmarried when he *was* threescore years old; and she bare him Sē'-gŭb.

22 And Sē'-gŭb begat Jā'-ĭr, who had three and twenty cities in the land of Gilead.

23 ᴿAnd he took Gē'-shŭr, and âr'-ăm, with the towns of Jā'-ĭr, from them, with Kē'-năth, and the towns thereof, *even* threescore cities. All these *belonged to* the sons of Mā'-chĭr the father of Gilead.

24 And after that Hĕz'-rŏn was dead in Cā'-lĕb-ĕph'-ră-täh, then Ă-bī'-äh Hĕz'-rŏn's wife bare him ᴿAshur the father of Tĕ-kō'-ă.

25 And the sons of Jĕ-räh'-mēĕl the firstborn of Hĕz'-rŏn were, Ram the firstborn, and Bū'-näh, and Ô'-rĕn, and Ō'-zĕm, *and* Ă-hī'-jäh.

26 Jĕ-räh'-mēĕl had also another wife, whose name *was* Ăt'-ă-räh; she *was* the mother of Ō'-năm.

27 And the sons of Ram the firstborn of Jĕ-räh'-mēĕl were, Mā'-ăz, and Jā'-mĭn, and Ē'-kĕr.

28 And the sons of Ō'-năm were, Shăm'-mā-ī, and Jā'-dă. And the sons of Shăm'-mā-ī; Nadab, and Ă-bī'-shùr.

29 And the name of the wife of Ă-bī'-shùr *was* Ăb'-ĭ-haïl, and she bare him Ăh'-băn, and Mō'-lĭd.

30 And the sons of Nadab; Sē'-lĕd, and Ăp'-pā-ĭm: but Sē'-lĕd died without children.

31 And the sons of Ăp'-pā-ĭm; Ĭsh'-ī. And the sons of Ĭsh'-ī; Shē'-shăn. And ᴿthe children of Shē'-shăn; Ăh'-lā-ī.

32 And the sons of Jā'-dă the brother of Shăm'-mā-ī; Jē'-thĕr, and Jonathan: and Jē'-thĕr died without children.

33 And the sons of Jonathan; Pē'-lĕth, and Ză'-ză. These were the sons of Jĕ-răh'-mēĕl.

34 Now Shē'-shăn had no sons, but daughters. And Shē'-shăn had a servant, an Egyptian, whose name *was* Jär'-hă.

35 And Shē'-shăn gave his daughter to Jär'-hă his servant to wife; and she bare him Ăt'-tā-ī.

36 And Ăt'-tā-ī begat Nathan, and Nathan begat ᴿZā'-băd,

37 And Zā'-băd begat ĕph'-lăl, and ĕph'-lăl begat ō'-bĕd,

38 And ō'-bĕd begat Jehu, and Jehu begat Ăz-ă-rī'-ăh,

39 And Ăz-ă-rī'-ăh begat Hē'-lĕz, and Hē'-lĕz begat ĕl-ē-ā'-săh,

40 And ĕl-ē-ā'-săh begat Sĭs'-ă-mâī, and Sĭs'-ă-mâī begat Shăl'-lŭm,

41 And Shăl'-lŭm begat Jĕk-ă-mī'-ăh, and Jĕk-ă-mī'-ăh begat Ē-lī'-shă-mă.

42 Now the sons of Caleb the brother of Jĕ-răh'-mēĕl *were*, Mē'-shă his firstborn, which *was* the father of Ziph; and the sons of Mă-rē'-shăh the father of Hē'-brŏn.

43 And the sons of Hē'-brŏn; Kôr'-ăh, and Tăp'-pū-ăh, and Rē'-kĕm, and Shē'-mă.

44 And Shē'-mă begat Raham, the father of Jôr'-kō-ăm: and Rē'-kĕm begat Shăm'-mā-ī.

45 And the son of Shăm'-mā-ī *was* Mā'-ŏn: and Mā'-ŏn *was* the father of Bĕth'-zûr.

46 And Ē'-phăh, Caleb's concubine, bare Hâr'-ăn, and Mō'-ză, and Gā'-zĕz: and Hâr'-ăn begat Gā'-zĕz.

47 And the sons of Jăh'-dā-ī; Rē'-gĕm, and Jō'-thăm, and Gē'-shăn, and Pē'-lĕt, and Ē'-phăh, and Shā'-ăph.

48 Mā'-ă-chăh, Caleb's concubine, bare Shē'-bĕr, and Tîr-hă'-năh.

49 She bare also Shā'-ăph the father of Măd-măn'-năh, Shē'-vă the father of Măch-bē'-năh, and the father of Gĭb'-ĕ-ă: and the daughter of Caleb *was* ᴿĂch'-săh.

50 These were the sons of Caleb the son of

Hur, the firstborn of ᴺĕph'-ră-tăh; Shō'-băl the father of Kĭr'-jăth-jē'-ă-rĭm,

51 Săl'-mă the father of Beth-lehem, Hâr'-ĕph the father of Bĕth-gā'-dĕr.

52 And Shō'-băl the father of Kĭr'-jăth-jē'-ă-rĭm had sons; ᴺHă-rō'-ĕh, *and* ᴺhalf of the Măn-ă-hē'-thĭtes.

53 And the families of Kĭr'-jăth-jē'-ă-rĭm; the Ĭth'-rĭtes, and the Pū'-hĭtes, and the Shū'-mă-thĭtes, and the Mĭsh'-rā-ĭtes; of them came the Ză-rē'-ă-thĭtes, and the Ĕsh-tā-ū'-lĭtes.

54 The sons of Săl'-mă; Beth-lehem, and the Nĕ-tŏph'-ă-thĭtes, ᴺĂt'-ă-rōth, the house of Jō'-ăb, and half of the Măn-ă-hē'-thĭtes, the Zôr'-ĭtes.

55 And the families of the scribes which dwelt at Jā'-bĕz; the Tī'-ră-thĭtes, the Shĭm'-ĕ-ă-thĭtes, *and* Sū'-chă-thĭtes. These *are* the ᴿKē'-nĭtes that came of Hē'-măth, the father of the house of ᴿRē'-chăb.

CHAPTER 3

Descendants of David

NOW these were the sons of David, which were born unto him in Hē'-brŏn; the firstborn ᴿAmnon, of Ă-hĭn'-ŏ-ăm the ᴿJĕz-rēĕl-ī'-tĕss; the second ᴺDaniel, of Ăb'-ĭ-gail the Carmelitess:

2 The third, Ăb'-să-lŏm the son of Mā'-ă-chăh the daughter of Tăl'-mâī king of Gē'-shùr: the fourth, Ăd-ō-nī'-jăh the son of Hăg'-gĭth:

3 The fifth, Shĕph-ă-tī'-ăh of Ă-bī'-tăl: the sixth, Ĭth'-rĕ-ăm by ᴿĔg'-lăh his wife.

4 *These* six were born unto him in Hē'-brŏn; and ᴿthere he reigned seven years and six months: and ᴿin Jerusalem he reigned thirty and three years.

5 ᴿAnd these were born unto him in Jerusalem; ᴺShĭm'-ĕ-ă, and Shō'-băb, and Nathan, and ᴿSolomon, four, of ᴺBăth'-shū-ă the daughter of ᴺĂm'-mĭ-ĕl:

6 Ĭb'-hăr also, and ᴺĒ-lī'-shă-mă, and Ē-lĭph'-ĕ-lĕt,

7 And Nō'-găh, and Nĕph'-ĕg, and Jă-phī'-ă,

8 And Ē-lī'-shă-mă, and ᴺĒ-lī'-ă-dă, and Ē-lĭph'-ĕ-lĕt, ᴿnine.

9 *These were* all the sons of David, beside the sons of the concubines, and ᴿTā'-mär their sister.

10 And Solomon's son *was* ᴿRĕ-hŏ-bō'-ăm, ᴺĂ-bī'-ă his son, Ā'-să his son, Jĕ-hŏsh'-ă-phăt his son,

11 Joram his son, ᴺĀ-hă-zī'-ăh his son, Jō'-ăsh his son,

12 Ăm-ă-zī'-ăh his son, ᴺĂz-ă-rī'-ăh his son, Jō'-thăm his son,

13 Ahaz his son, Hĕz-ē-kī'-ăh his son, Mă-năs'-sĕh his son,

14 Amon his son, Jō-sī'-ăh his son.

15 And the sons of Jō-sī'-ăh were, the firstborn ᴺJō-hā'-năn, the second ᴺJĕ-hoī'-ă-kĭm, the third ᴺZĕd-ē-kī'-ăh, the fourth Shăl'-lŭm.

16 And the sons of ᴿJĕ-hoī'-ă-kĭm: ᴺJĕc-ō-nī'-ăh his son, Zĕd-ē-kī'-ăh ᴿhis son,

17 And the sons of Jĕc-ō-nī'-ăh; Ăs'-sīr, ᴺSă-lā'-thī-ĕl ᴿhis son,

18 Măl-chī'-răm also, and Pĕ-dāi'-ăh, and Shĕn-ā'-zăr, Jĕc-ă-mī'-ăh, Hō'-shă-mă, and Nĕd-ă-bī'-ăh.

19 And the sons of Pĕ-dāi'-ăh were, Zĕ-rŭb'-bă-bĕl, and Shĭm'-ĕ-ī: and the sons of Zĕ-rŭb'-bă-bĕl; Mĕ-shŭl'-lăm, and Hăn-ă-nī'-ăh, and Shĕ-lō'-mĭth their sister:

20 And Hă-shŭ'-băh, and ō'-hĕl, and Bĕr-ē-chī'-ăh, and Hăs-ă-dī'-ăh, Jŭ'-shăb-hĕs'-ĕd, five.

21 And the sons of Hăn-ă-nī'-ăh; Pĕl-ă-tī'-ăh, and Jĕ-sāi'-ăh: the sons of Rĕ-phāi'-ăh, the sons of Arnan, the sons of ō-bă-dī'-ăh, the sons of Shĕch-ă-nī'-ăh.

22 And the sons of Shĕch-ă-nī'-ăh; Shĕm-āi'-ăh: and the sons of Shĕm-āi'-ăh; ᴿHăt'-tŭsh, and ī'-gĕ-ăl, and Bă-rī'-ăh, and Nē-ă-rī'-ăh, and Shā'-phăt, six.

23 And the sons of Nē-ă-rī'-ăh; ĕl-ĭ-ō-ē'-nāi, and ᴺHĕz-ē-kī'-ăh, and Ăz-rī'-kăm, three.

24 And the sons of ĕl-ĭ-ō-ē'-nāi were, Hō-dāi'-ăh, and ē-lī-ăsh'-ĭb, and Pĕ-lāi'-ăh, and Ăk'-kŭb, and Jō-hā'-năn, and Dă-lāi'-ăh, and Ă-nā'-nī, seven.

CHAPTER 4

Descendants of Judah

THE sons of Judah; ᴿPhâr'-ĕz, Hĕz'-rŏn, and ᴺCăr'-mī, and Hur, and Shō'-băl.

2 And ᴺRē-āi'-ăh the son of Shō'-băl begat Jā'-hăth; and Jā'-hăth begat Ă-hū'-māi, and Lā'-hăd. These are the families of the Zôr'-ă-thītes.

3 And these were of the father of ē'-tăm; Jĕz'-rēĕl, and ĭsh'-mă, and ĭd'-băsh: and the name of their sister was Hăz-ĕl-ĕl-pō'-nī:

4 And Pĕn'-ū-ĕl the father of Gē'-dôr, and ē'-zĕr the father of Hū'-shăh. These are the sons of ᴿHur, the firstborn of ĕph'-ră-tăh, the father of Beth-lehem.

5 And ᴿAshur the father of Tĕ-kō'-ă had two wives, Hē'-lăh and Nā'-ă-răh.

6 And Nā'-ă-răh bare him Ă-hū'-zăm, and

Hē'-phĕr, and Tē'-mĕ-nī, and Hā-ă-hăsh'-tă-rī. These were the sons of Nā'-ă-răh.

7 And the sons of Hē'-lăh were, Zē'-rĕth, and Jĕ-zō'-ăr, and ĕth'-năn.

8 And Cŏz begat Anub, and Zō-bē'-băh, and the families of Ă-hăr'-hĕl the son of Hâr'-ŭm.

9 And Jā'-bĕz was ᴿmore honourable than his brethren: and his mother called his name ᴺJā'-bĕz, saying, Because I bare him with sorrow.

10 And Jā'-bĕz called on the God of Israel, saying, ᴺOh that thou wouldest bless me indeed, and enlarge my coast, and that thine hand might be with me, and that thou wouldest ᴺkeep me from evil, that it may not grieve me! And God granted him that which he requested.

11 And Chē'-lŭb the brother of Shû'-ăh begat Mē'-hīr, which was the father of ĕsh'-tŏn.

12 And ĕsh'-tŏn begat Bĕth-rā'-phă, and Pă-sē'-ăh, and Tĕ-hĭn'-năh the father of ᴺĭr-nā'-hăsh. These are the men of Rē'-chăh.

13 And the sons of Kē'-năz; ᴿŏth'-nĭ-ĕl, and Sĕ-rāi'-ăh: and the sons of ŏth'-nĭ-ĕl; ᴺHā'-thăth.

14 And Mē-ō'-nō-thāi begat ŏph'-răh: and Sĕ-rāi'-ăh begat Jō'-ăb, the father of ᴿthe ᴺvalley of ᴺChă-rā'-shīm; for they were craftsmen.

15 And the sons of Caleb the son of Jĕ-phŭn'-nēh; ī'-rû, ē'-lăh, and Nā'-ăm: and the sons of ē'-lăh, ᴺeven Kē'-năz.

16 And the sons of Jĕ-hăl'-ĕ-lēĕl; Ziph, and Zī'-phăh, Tī'-rī-ă, and Ăs'-ă-rēĕl.

17 And the sons of Ezra were, Jē'-thĕr, and Mē'-rĕd, and ē'-phĕr, and Jalon: and she bare Miriam, and Shăm'-mā-ī, and ĭsh'-băh the father of ĕsh-tĕ-mō'-ă.

18 And his wife ᴺJĕ-hū-dī'-jăh bare Jē'-rĕd the father of Gē'-dôr, and Hē'-bĕr the father of Sō'-chō, and Jĕ-kū'-thī-ĕl the father of Ză-nō'-ăh. And these are the sons of Bĭth'-ĭ-ăh the daughter of Pharaoh, which Mē'-rĕd took.

19 And the sons of his wife ᴺHō-dī'-ăh the sister of Naham, the father of Kē-ī'-lăh the Gär'-mīte, and ĕsh-tĕ-mō'-ă the Mā-ăch'-ă-thīte.

20 And the sons of Shī'-mŏn were, Amnon, and Rĭn'-năh, Bĕn-hā'-năn, and Tī'-lŏn. And the sons of ĭsh'-ī were, Zō'-hĕth, and Bĕn-zō'-hĕth.

21 The sons of Shē'-läh ᴿthe son of Judah were, Er the father of Lē'-căh, and Lā'-ă-dăh the father of Mă-rē'-shăh, and the families of the house of them that wrought fine linen, of the house of Ăsh-bē'-ă,

22 And Jō'-kĭm, and the men of Chō-zē'-bă,

and Jō'-ăsh, and Sâr'-ăph, who had the dominion in Moab, and Jă-shū'-bĭ-lē'-hĕm. And *these are* ancient things.

23 These *were* the potters, and those that dwelt among plants and hedges: there they dwelt with the king for his work.

Descendants of Simeon

24 The sons of Simeon *were,* NNĕm'-ū-ĕl, and Jā'-mĭn, NJâr'-ĭb, Zē'-răh, *and* Shā'-ŭl:

25 Shăl'-lŭm his son, Mĭb'-săm his son, Mĭsh'-mă his son.

26 And the sons of Mĭsh'-mă; Hăm'-ū-ĕl his son, Zăc'-chŭr his son, Shĭm'-ĕ-ĭ his son.

27 And Shĭm'-ĕ-ĭ had sixteen sons and six daughters; but his brethren had not many children, neither did all their family multiply, Nlike to the children of Judah.

28 And they dwelt at RBē̂r-shē'-bă, and Mō-lā'-dăh, and Hā'-zär-shû'-ăl,

29 And at NBĭl'-hăh, and at Ē'-zĕm, and at NTō'-lăd,

30 And at Bĕ-thū'-ĕl, and at Hôr'-măh, and at Ziklag,

31 And at Bĕth-măr'-că-bŏth, and NHā'-zär-sû'-sĭm, and at Bĕth-bĭr'-ĕ-ĭ, and at Shā-ă-rā'-ĭm. These *were* their cities unto the reign of David.

32 And their villages *were,* NĒ'-tăm, and Ā'-ĭn, Rimmon, and Tō'-chĕn, and Ăsh'-ăn, five cities:

33 And all their villages that *were* round about the same cities, unto NBā'-ăl. These *were* their habitations, and Ntheir genealogy.

34 And Mĕ-shō'-băb, and Jăm'-lĕch, and Jō'-shäh the son of Ăm-ă-zī'-ăh,

35 And Jō'-ĕl, and Jehu the son of Jŏs-ĭ-bī'-äh, the son of Sĕ-rā'-ĭ-ĕl, the son of Ăs'-ĭ-ĕl,

36 And ĕl-ĭ-ō-ē'-nāi, and Jā-ă-kō'-băh, and Jĕsh-ō-hāi'-ăh, and Ă-sāi'-ăh, and Ăd'-ĭ-ĕl, and Jĕ-sĭm'-ĭ-ĕl, and Bĕ-nāi'-ăh,

37 And Zī'-ză the son of Shī'-phĭ, the son of Ăl'-lŏn, the son of Jĕ-dāi'-ăh, the son of Shĭm'-rĭ, the son of Shĕm-āi'-ăh;

38 These Nmentioned by *their* names *were* princes in their families: and the house of their fathers increased greatly.

39 And they went to the entrance of Gē'-dôr, *even* unto the east side of the valley, to seek pasture for their flocks.

40 And they found fat pasture and good, and the land *was* wide, and quiet, and peaceable; for *they* of Ham had dwelt there of old.

41 And these written by name came in the days of Hĕz-ē-kī'-ăh king of Judah, and Rsmote their tents, and the habitations that were found there, and destroyed them utterly

unto this day, and dwelt in their rooms: because *there was* pasture there for their flocks.

42 And *some* of them, *even* of the sons of Simeon, five hundred men, went to mount Sē'-ĭr, having for their captains Pĕl-ă-tī'-ăh, and Nĕ-ă-rī'-ăh, and Rĕ-phāi'-ăh, and ŭz'-zĭ-ĕl, the sons of ĭsh'-ĭ.

43 And they smote Rthe rest of the Ă-măl'-ĕk-ītes that were escaped, and dwelt there unto this day.

CHAPTER 5

Descendants of Reuben

NOW the sons of Reuben the firstborn of Israel, (for Rhe *was* the firstborn; but, forasmuch as he Rdefiled his father's bed, Rhis birthright was given unto the sons of Joseph the son of Israel: and the genealogy is not to be reckoned after the birthright.

2 For RJudah prevailed above his brethren, and of him *came* the Rchief Nruler; but the birthright *was* Joseph's:)

3 The sons, *I say,* of RReuben the firstborn of Israel *were,* Hā'-nŏch, and Păl'-lû, Hĕz'-rŏn, and Cär'-mĭ.

4 The sons of Jō'-ĕl; Shĕm-āi'-ăh his son, Gog his son, Shĭm'-ĕ-ĭ his son,

5 Mī'-căh his son, Rĕ-āi'-ă his son, Bā'-ăl his son,

6 Bē̂r'-ăh his son, whom NTĭl'-găth-pĭl-nē'-sĕr king of Assyria carried away *captive:* he *was* prince of the Reubenites.

7 And his brethren by their families, Rwhen the genealogy of their generations was reckoned, *were* the chief, Jē-ĭ'-ĕl, and Zĕch-ă-rī'-äh,

8 And Bē'-lă the son of Ā'-zăz, the son of NShē'-mă, the son of Jō'-ĕl, who dwelt in RĂ-rō'-ĕr, even unto Nē'-bō and Bā'-ăl-mē'-on:

9 And eastward he inhabited unto the entering in of the wilderness from the river ēu-phrā'-tēs: because their cattle were multiplied Rin the land of Gilead.

10 And in the days of Saul they made war Rwith the Hăg'-ă-rītes, who fell by their hand: and they dwelt in their tents Nthroughout all the east *land* of Gilead.

Descendants of Gad

11 And the children of Gad dwelt over against them, in the land of RBā'-shăn unto Săl'-chăh:

12 Jō'-ĕl the chief, and Shā'-phăm the next, and Jā'-ă-nāi, and Shā'-phăt in Bā'-shăn.

13 And their brethren of the house of their

fathers *were*, Michael, and Mĕ-shŭl'-lăm, and Shē'-bă, and Jō'-rā-ī, and Jā'-chăn, and Zī'-ă, and Hē'-bĕr, seven.

14 These *are* the children of Ăb'-ĭ-haïl the son of Hū'-rī, the son of Jă-rō'-ăh, the son of Gilead, the son of Michael, the son of Jĕ-shĭsh'-aï, the son of Jăh'-dō, the son of Buz;

15 Ā'-hī the son of Ăb'-dĭ-ĕl, the son of Gū'-nī, chief of the house of their fathers.

16 And they dwelt in Gilead in Bā'-shăn, and in her towns, and in all the suburbs of [R]Shär'-ọn, upon [N]their borders.

17 All these were reckoned by genealogies in the days of [R]Jō'-thăm king of Judah, and in the days of [R]Jĕr-ŏ-bō'-ăm king of Israel.

18 The sons of Reuben, and the Gadites, and half the tribe of Mă-năs'-sēh, [N]of valiant men, men able to bear buckler and sword, and to shoot with bow, and skilful in war, *were* four and forty thousand seven hundred and threescore, that went out to the war.

19 And they made war with the Hăg'-ă-rītes, with [R]Jĕ'-tŭr, and Nĕph'-ĭsh, and Nō'-dăb.

20 And [R]they were helped against them, and the Hăg'-ă-rītes were delivered into their hand, and all that *were* with them: for they cried to God in the battle, and he was entreated of them; because they [R]put their trust in him.

21 And they [N]took away their cattle; of their camels fifty thousand, and of sheep two hundred and fifty thousand, and of asses two thousand, and of [N]men an hundred thousand.

22 For there fell down many slain, because the war *was* of God. And they dwelt in their steads until [R]the captivity.

The half tribe of Manasseh

23 And the children of the half tribe of Mă-năs'-sēh dwelt in the land: they increased from Bā'-shăn unto Bā'-ăl-hĕr'-mọn and Sē'-nïr, and unto mount Hĕr'-mọn.

24 And these *were* the heads of the house of their fathers, even Ē'-phĕr, and ĭsh'-ī, and Ē-lī'-ĕl, and Ăz'-rī-ĕl, and Jeremiah, and Hō-dă-vī'-ăh, and Jăh'-dĭ-ĕl, mighty men of valour, [N]famous men, *and* heads of the house of their fathers.

25 And they transgressed against the God of their fathers, and went a [R]whoring after the gods of the people of the land, whom God destroyed before them.

26 And the God of Israel stirred up the spirit of [R]Pŭl king of Assyria, and the spirit of [R]Tĭl'-găth-pĭl-nē'-sĕr king of Assyria, and he carried them away, even the Reubenites, and the Gadites, and the half tribe of Mă-năs'-sēh, and brought them unto [R]Hā'-lăh, and Hā'-bôr,

---

CHAP. **5**

BC 1300

16 ch. 27:29
16 Heb. *their goings forth*
17 2 Ki. 15:5, 32
17 2 Ki. 14:16, 28
18 Heb. *sons of valour*
19 Gen. 25:15 ch. 1:31
20 See ver. 22
20 Ps. 22:4, 5
21 Heb. *led captive*
21 Heb. *souls of men: as* Num. 31:35
22 2 Ki. 15:29 & 17:6
24 Heb. *men of names*
25 2 Ki. 17:7
26 2 Ki. 15:19
26 2 Ki. 15:29
26 2 Ki. 17:6 & 18:11

CHAP. **6**

BC 1280

Gen. 46:11	1
Ex. 6:16	
Num. 26:57	
ch. 23:6	
Or, *Gershom*, ver. 16	1
See ver. 22	2
Lev. 10:1	3
2 Sam. 8:17	8
2 Sam. 15:27	8
See 2 Chr. 26:17, 18	10
Heb. *in the house*	10
1 Ki. 6	10
2 Chr. 3	
See Ezra 7:3	11
Or, *Meshullam*, ch. 9:11	12
Neh. 11:11	14
2 Ki. 25:18	15
Ex. 6:16	16
Or, *Gershon*, ver. 1	16
ver. 42	20
Or, *Ethan*, ver. 42	21
Or, *Adaiah*, ver. 41	21
Or, *Ethni*, ver. 41	21
Or, *Izhar*, ver. 2, 18	22

---

and Hăr'-ă, and to the river Gō'-zăn, unto this day.

CHAPTER 6

Descendants of Levi

THE sons of Levi; [R]Gĕr'-shŏn, [N]Kō'-hăth, and Mĕ-râr'-ī.

2 And the sons of Kō'-hăth; Amram, [R]Ĭz'-här, and Hē'-brŏn, and ŭz'-zī-ĕl.

3 And the children of Amram; Aaron, and Moses, and Miriam. The sons also of Aaron; [R]Nadab, and Ă-bī'-hū, ĕl-ē-ā'-zär, and ĭth'-ă-mär.

4 ĕl-ē-ā'-zär begat Phĭn'-ĕ-hăś, Phĭn'-ĕ-hăś begat Ă-bī'-shū-ă,

5 And Ă-bī'-shū-ă begat Bŭk'-kī, and Bŭk'-kī begat ŭz'-zī,

6 And ŭz'-zī begat Zĕr-ă-hī'-ăh, and Zĕr-ă-hī'-ăh begat Mĕ-râī'-ōth,

7 Mĕ-râī'-ōth begat Ăm-ă-rī'-ăh, and Ăm-ă-rī'-ăh begat Ă-hī'-tŭb,

8 And [R]Ă-hī'-tŭb begat Zā'-dŏk, and [R]Zā'-dŏk begat Ă-hī'-mă-ăz,

9 And Ă-hī'-mă-ăz begat Ăz-ă-rī'-ăh, and Ăz-ă-rī'-ăh begat Jō-hā'-năn,

10 And Jō-hā'-năn begat Ăz-ă-rī'-ăh, (he *it is* [R]that executed the priest's office [N]in the [R]temple that Solomon built in Jerusalem:)

11 And [R]Ăz-ă-rī'-ăh begat Ăm-ă-rī'-ăh, and Ăm-ă-rī'-ăh begat Ă-hī'-tŭb,

12 And Ă-hī'-tŭb begat Zā'-dŏk, and Zā'-dŏk begat [N]Shăl'-lŭm,

13 And Shăl'-lŭm begat Hĭl-kī'-ăh, and Hĭl-kī'-ăh begat Ăz-ă-rī'-ăh,

14 And Ăz-ă-rī'-ăh begat [R]Sĕ-râī'-ăh, and Sĕ-râī'-ăh begat Jĕ-hō'-ză-dăk,

15 And Jĕ-hō'-ză-dăk went *into captivity,* [R]when the LORD carried away Judah and Jerusalem by the hand of Nĕb-ū-chăd-nĕz'-zär.

16 The sons of Levi; [R]Gĕr'-shŏm, [N]Kō'-hăth, and Mĕ-râr'-ī.

17 And these *be* the names of the sons of Gĕr'-shŏm; Lĭb'-nī, and Shĭm'-ĕ-ī.

18 And the sons of Kō'-hăth *were*, Amram, and ĭz'-här, and Hē'-brŏn, and ŭz'-zī-ĕl.

19 The sons of Mĕ-râr'-ī; Mäh'-lī, and Mū'-shī. And these *are* the families of the Levites according to their fathers.

20 Of Gĕr'-shŏm; Lĭb'-nī his son, Jā'-hăth his son, [R]Zimmah his son,

21 [N]Jō'-ăh his son, [N]ĭd'-dō his son, Zē'-räh his son, [N]Jĕ-ăt'-ĕ-râī his son.

22 The sons of Kō'-hăth; [N]Ăm-mĭn'-ă-dăb his son, Kôr'-ăh his son, Ăs'-sīr his son,

23 ĕl-kā'-năh his son, and Ē-bī'-ă-săph his son, and Ăs'-sīr his son,

24 Tā′-hăth his son, ᴺŪ′-rĭ-ĕl his son, ŭz-zī′-ăh his son, and Shā′-ŭl his son.

25 And the sons of Ĕl-kā′-năh; ᴿĂ-mā′-săi, and Ă-hī′-mōth.

26 As for Ĕl-kā′-năh: the sons of Ĕl-kā′-năh; ᴺZō′-phăi his son, and ᴿNahath his son,

27 ᴿĒ-lī′-ăb his son, Jĕ-rō′-hăm his son, Ĕl-kā′-năh his son.

28 And the sons of Samuel; the firstborn ᴺVăsh′-nī, and Ă-bī′-ăh.

29 The sons of Mĕ-rār′-ī; Măh′-lī, Lĭb′-nī his son, Shĭm′-ĕ-ī his son, ŭz′-ză his son,

30 Shĭm′-ĕ-ă his son, Hăg-gī′-ăh his son, Ă-săi′-ăh his son.

31 And these are they whom David set over the service of song in the house of the Lᴏʀᴅ, after that the ᴿark had rest.

32 And they ministered before the dwelling place of the tabernacle of the congregation with singing, until Solomon had built the house of the Lᴏʀᴅ in Jerusalem: and then they waited on their office according to their order.

33 And these are they that ᴺwaited with their children. Of the sons of the Kō′-hăth-ites: Hē′-măn a singer, the son of Jō′-ĕl, the son of Shĕ-mū′-ĕl,

34 The son of Ĕl-kā′-năh, the son of Jĕ-rō′-hăm, the son of Ē-lī′-ĕl, the son of ᴺTō′-ăh,

35 The son of ᴺZuph, the son of Ĕl-kā′-năh, the son of Mā′-hăth, the son of Ă-mā′-săi,

36 The son of Ĕl-kā′-năh, the son of ᴺJō′-ĕl, the son of Ăz-ă-rī′-ăh, the son of Zĕph-ă-nī′-ăh,

37 The son of Tā′-hăth, the son of Ăs′-sīr, the son of ᴿĒ-bī′-ă-săph, the son of Kôr′-ăh,

38 The son of Ĭz′-hăr, the son of Kō′-hăth, the son of Levi, the son of Israel.

39 And his brother Ā′-săph, who stood on his right hand, even Ā′-săph the son of Bĕr-ă-chī′-ăh, the son of Shĭm′-ĕ-ă,

40 The son of Michael, the son of Bā-ă-sēi′-ăh, the son of Măl-chī′-ăh,

41 The son of ᴿĔth′-nī, the son of Zē′-răh, the son of Ă-dāi′-ăh,

42 The son of Ē′-thăn, the son of Zimmah, the son of Shĭm′-ĕ-ī,

43 The son of Jā′-hăth, the son of Gĕr′-shŏm, the son of Levi.

44 And their brethren the sons of Mĕ-rār′-ī stood on the left hand: ᴺĒ′-thăn the son of ᴺKĭsh′-ī, the son of Abdi, the son of Măl′-lŭch,

45 The son of Hăsh-ă-bī′-ăh, the son of Ăm-ă-zī′-ăh, the son of Hĭl-kī′-ăh,

46 The son of Amzi, the son of Bā′-nī, the son of Shā′-mĕr,

47 The son of Măh′-lī, the son of Mū′-shī, the son of Mĕ-rār′-ī, the son of Levi.

48 Their brethren also the Levites were ap-

CHAP. 6
BC 1280
24 Or, Zephaniah, Azariah, Joel, ver. 36
25 See ver. 35, 36
26 Or, Zuph, ver. 35
1 Sam. 1:1
26 ver. 34, Toah
27 ver. 34, Eliel
28 Called also Joel, ver. 33
1 Sam. 8:2
31 ch. 16:1
33 Heb. stood
34 ver. 26, Nahath
35 Or, Zophai
36 ver. 24, Shaul, Uzziah, Uriel
37 Ex. 6:24
41 See ver. 21
44 Called Jeduthun, ch. 9:16 & 25:1, 3, 6
44 Or, Kushaiah, ch. 15:17

Lev. 1:9   49
Ex. 30:7   49
Josh. 21   54
Josh. 21:11, 12   55
Josh. 14:13 & 15:13   56
Josh. 21:13   57
Or, Holon, Josh. 21:15   58
Or, Ain, Josh. 21:16   59
Or, Almon, Josh. 21:18   60
ver. 66   61
Josh. 21:5   61
Josh. 21:7, 34   63

pointed unto all manner of service of the tabernacle of the house of God.

Descendants of Aaron

49 But Aaron and his sons offered ᴿupon the altar of the burnt offering, and ᴿon the altar of incense, and were appointed for all the work of the place most holy, and to make an atonement for Israel, according to all that Moses the servant of God had commanded.

50 And these are the sons of Aaron; Ĕl-ē-ā′-zär his son, Phĭn′-ĕ-hăs his son, Ă-bĭ′-shû-ă his son,

51 Bŭk′-kī his son, ŭz′-zī his son, Zĕr-ă-hī′-ăh his son,

52 Mĕ-rāi′-ōth his son, Ăm-ă-rī′-ăh his son, Ă-hī′-tŭb his son,

53 Zā′-dŏk his son, Ă-hī′-mă-ăz his son.

54 ᴿNow these are their dwelling places throughout their castles in their coasts, of the sons of Aaron, of the families of the Kō′-hăth-ītes: for theirs was the lot.

55 ᴿAnd they gave them Hē′-brŏn in the land of Judah, and the suburbs thereof round about it.

56 ᴿBut the fields of the city, and the villages thereof, they gave to Caleb the son of Jĕ-phŭn′-nĕh.

57 And ᴿto the sons of Aaron they gave the cities of Judah, namely, Hē′-brŏn, the city of refuge, and Lĭb′-năh with her suburbs, and Jăt′-tīr, and Ĕsh-tĕ-mō′-ă, with their suburbs,

58 And ᴺHĭ′-lĕn with her suburbs, Dē′-bĭr with her suburbs,

59 And ᴺĂsh′-ăn with her suburbs, and Bĕth-shē′-mĕsh with her suburbs:

60 And out of the tribe of Benjamin; Gē′-bă with her suburbs, and ᴺĂl′-ĕ-mĕth with her suburbs, and Ăn′-ă-thŏth with her suburbs. All their cities throughout their families were thirteen cities.

61 And unto the sons of Kō′-hăth, ᴿwhich were left of the family of that tribe, were cities given out of the half tribe, namely, out of the half tribe of Mă-năs′-sēh, ᴿby lot, ten cities.

62 And to the sons of Gĕr′-shŏm throughout their families out of the tribe of Ĭs′-să-chär, and out of the tribe of Asher, and out of the tribe of Năph′-tă-lī, and out of the tribe of Mă-năs′-sēh in Bā′-shăn, thirteen cities.

63 Unto the sons of Mĕ-rār′-ī were given by lot, throughout their families, out of the tribe of Reuben, and out of the tribe of Gad, and out of the tribe of Zĕ-bū′-lŭn, ᴿtwelve cities.

64 And the children of Israel gave to the Levites these cities with their suburbs.

65 And they gave by lot out of the tribe of the children of Judah, and out of the tribe of the children of Simeon, and out of

the tribe of the children of Benjamin, these cities, which are called by *their* names.

66 And ᴿ*the residue* of the families of the sons of Kō'-hăth had cities of their coasts out of the tribe of Ē'-phrä-ĭm.

67 ᴿAnd they gave unto them, *of* the cities of refuge, Shē'-chĕm in mount Ē'-phrä-ĭm with her suburbs; *they gave* also Gē'-zer with her suburbs,

68 And ᴿJŏk'-mĕ-ăm with her suburbs, and Bĕth-hôr'-ŏn with her suburbs,

69 And Âĭ'-jä-lŏn with her suburbs, and Găth-rĭm'-mon with her suburbs:

70 And out of the half tribe of Mă-năs'-sĕh; Aner with her suburbs, and Bĭ'-lĕ-ăm with her suburbs, for the family of the remnant of the sons of Kō'-hăth.

71 Unto the sons of Gĕr'-shŏm *were given* out of the family of the half tribe of Mă-năs'-sĕh, Gō'-lăn in Bā'-shăn with her suburbs, and Ăsh'-tă-rōth with her suburbs:

72 And out of the tribe of ĭs'-să-chär; Kē'-dĕsh with her suburbs, Dăb'-ĕ-răth with her suburbs,

73 And Rā'-mŏth with her suburbs, and Anem with her suburbs:

74 And out of the tribe of Asher; Mā'-shăl with her suburbs, and Abdon with her suburbs,

75 And Hū'-kŏk with her suburbs, and Rē'-hŏb with her suburbs:

76 And out of the tribe of Năph'-tă-lĭ; Kē'-dĕsh in Galilee with her suburbs, and Hăm'-mŏn with her suburbs, and Kĭr-ja-thā'-ĭm with her suburbs.

77 Unto the rest of the children of Mĕ-râr'-ĭ *were given* out of the tribe of Zē-bū'-lŭn, Rimmon with her suburbs, Tā'-bôr with her suburbs:

78 And on the other side Jordan by Jericho, on the east side of Jordan, *were given them* out of the tribe of Reuben, Bē'-zer in the wilderness with her suburbs, and Jăh'-zăh with her suburbs,

79 Kē'-dĕ-mŏth also with her suburbs, and Mĕph'-ā-ăth with her suburbs:

80 And out of the tribe of Gad; Rā'-mŏth in Gilead with her suburbs, and Mā-hă-nā'-ĭm with her suburbs,

81 And Hĕsh'-bŏn with her suburbs, and Jā'-zer with her suburbs.

CHAPTER 7

Descendants of Issachar

Now the sons of ĭs'-să-chär *were*, ᴿTō'-lä, and ᴺPū'-äh, Jăsh'-ŭb, and Shĭm'-rŏn, four.

CHAP. 6
BC 1280
66 ver. 61
67 Josh. 21:21
68 See Josh. 21:22-35 where many of these cities have other names

CHAP. 7
BC 1400
1 Gen. 46:13
Num. 26:23
1 *Phuvah, Job*

2 Sam. 24:1, 2   **2**
ch. 27:1
Gen. 46:21   **6**
Num. 26:38
ch. 8:1, etc.
Num. 26:39,   **12**
Shupham, and
Hupham
Or, *Iri,*   **12**
ver. 7
Or, *Ahiram,*   **12**
Num. 26:38
Gen. 46:24,   **13**
Shillem

---

2 And the sons of Tō'-lä; ŭz'-zī, and Rĕ-phâi'-ăh, and Jĕr'-ĭ-ĕl, and Jăh'-ma-ĭ, and Jĭb'-săm, and Shĕ-mū'-ĕl, heads of their father's house, *to wit,* of Tō'-lä: *they were* valiant men of might in their generations; ᴿwhose number *was* in the days of David two and twenty thousand and six hundred.

3 And the sons of ŭz'-zī; ĭz-ră-hī'-ăh: and the sons of ĭz-ră-hī'-ăh; Michael, and ō-bă-dī'-ăh, and Jō'-ĕl, ĭsh-ĭ'-ăh, five: all of them chief men.

4 And with them, by their generations, after the house of their fathers, *were* bands of soldiers for war, six and thirty thousand *men:* for they had many wives and sons.

5 And their brethren among all the families of ĭs'-să-chär *were* valiant men of might, reckoned in all by their genealogies fourscore and seven thousand.

Descendants of Benjamin

6 *The sons* of ᴿBenjamin; Bē'-lä, and Bē'-chĕr, and Jĕd-ĭ-ā'-ĕl, three.

7 And the sons of Bē'-lä; ĕz'-bŏn, and ŭz'-zī, and ŭz'-zī-ĕl, and Jĕr'-ĭ-mŏth, and ĭ'-rĭ, five; heads of the house of *their* fathers, mighty men of valour; and were reckoned by their genealogies twenty and two thousand and thirty and four.

8 And the sons of Bē'-chĕr; Zē-mī'-rä, and Jō'-ăsh, and ĕl-ĭ-ē'-zer, and ĕl-ĭ-ō-ē'-nâĭ, and Omri, and Jĕr'-ĭ-mŏth, and Ă-bī'-ăh, and Ăn'-ă-thōth, and Ăl'-ă-mĕth. All these *are* the sons of Bē'-chĕr.

9 And the number of them, after their genealogy by their generations, heads of the house of their fathers, mighty men of valour, *was* twenty thousand and two hundred.

10 The sons also of Jĕd-ĭ-ā'-ĕl; Bilhan: and the sons of Bilhan; Jē'-ŭsh, and Benjamin, and Ē'-hŭd, and Chĕ-nā'-ă-năh, and Zē'-thăn, and Thăr'-shĭsh, and Ă-hī'-shā-hăr.

11 All these the sons of Jĕd-ĭ-ā'-ĕl, by the heads of their fathers, mighty men of valour, *were* seventeen thousand and two hundred *soldiers,* fit to go out for war *and* battle.

12 ᴿShŭp'-pĭm also, and Hŭp'-pĭm, the children of ᴺIr, *and* Hū'-shĭm, the sons of ᴺĀ'-hĕr.

Descendants of Naphtali

13 The sons of Năph'-tă-lĭ; Jăh'-zĭ-ĕl, and Gū'-nĭ, and Jē'-zer, and ᴿShăl'-lŭm, the sons of Bĭl'-häh.

14 The sons of Mă-năs'-sĕh; Ăsh'-rĭ-ĕl, whom she bare: (*but* his concubine the Ăr-ăm-ĭ'-tĕss bare Mā'-chĭr the father of Gĭl'-ĕ-ăd:

15 And Mā'-chĭr took to wife *the sister* of Hŭp'-pĭm and Shŭp'-pĭm, whose sister's name *was* Mā'-ă-chäh;) and the name of the second

was Zē-lŏph'-ĕ-hăd: and Zē-lŏph'-ĕ-hăd had daughters.

16 And Mā'-ă-chāh the wife of Mā'-chĭr bare a son, and she called his name Pē'-rĕsh; and the name of his brother *was* Shē'-rĕsh; and his sons *were* Ū'-lăm and Rā'-kĕm.

17 And the sons of Ū'-lăm; ᴿBē'-dăn. These *were* the sons of Gĭl'-ĕ-ăd, the son of Mā'-chĭr, the son of Mă-năs'-sēh.

18 And his sister Hăm-mō'-lĕ-kĕth bare Ī'-shŏd, and ᴿĀ-bĭ-ē'-zer, and Mă-hā'-lăh.

19 And the sons of Shĕm-ĭ'-dă were, Ă-hī'-ăn, and Shē'-chĕm, and Lĭk'-hī, and Ă-nī'-ăm.

Descendants of Ephraim

20 And ᴿthe sons of Ē'-phră-ĭm; Shû-thē'-lăh, and Bē'-rĕd his son, and Tā'-hăth his son, and Ĕl'-ă-dăh his son, and Tā'-hăth his son,

21 And Zā'-băd his son, and Shû-thē'-lăh his son, and Ē'-zer, and Ĕl'-ĕ-ăd, whom the men of Gath *that were* born in *that* land slew, because they came down to take away their cattle.

22 And Ē'-phră-ĭm their father mourned many days, and his brethren came to comfort him.

23 And when he went in to his wife, she conceived, and bare a son, and he called his name Bĕ-rī'-ăh, because it went evil with his house.

24 (And his daughter *was* Shē'-răh, who built Bĕth-hôr'-ŏn the nether, and the upper, and ŭz'-zĕn-shē'-răh.)

25 And Rē'-phăh *was* his son, also Rē'-shĕph, and Tē'-lăh his son, and Tā'-hăn his son,

26 Lā'-ă-dăn his son, Ăm'-mī-hŭd his son, Ē-lī'-shă-mă his son,

27 ᴺNon his son, Jē-hŏsh'-ū-ă his son.

28 And their possessions and habitations *were,* Beth-el and the towns thereof, and eastward ᴿNā'-ă-răn, and westward Gē'-zer, with the ᴺtowns thereof; Shē'-chĕm also and the towns thereof, unto Gā'-ză and the towns thereof:

29 And by the borders of the children of ᴿMă-năs'-sēh, Bĕth-shē'-ăn and her towns, Tā'-ă-năch and her towns, ᴿMĕ-gĭd'-dō and her towns, Dor and her towns. In these dwelt the children of Joseph the son of Israel.

Descendants of Asher

30 ᴿThe sons of Asher; Ĭm'-năh, and Ĭs'-ū-ăh, and Ĭsh'-ū-aî, and Bĕ-rī'-ăh, and Sē'-răh their sister.

31 And the sons of Bĕ-rī'-ăh; Hē'-ber, and Măl'-chī-ĕl, who *is* the father of Bĭr-zā'-vĭth.

32 And Hē'-ber begat Jăph'-lĕt, and ᴿShō'-

| CHAP. 7 |
| BC 1400 |
| 17 1 Sam. 12:11 |
| 18 Num. 26:30, *Jeezer* |
| 20 Num. 26:35 |
| 27 Or, *Nun,* Num. 13:8, 16 |
| 28 Josh. 16:7, *Naarath* |
| 28 Heb. *daughters* |
| 29 Josh. 17:7 |
| 29 Josh. 17:11 |
| 30 Gen. 46:17 Num. 26:44 |
| 32 ver. 34, *Shamer* |

ver. 32, *Shomer* 34

| CHAP. 8 |
| BC 1400 |
| Gen. 46:21 Num. 26:38 ch. 7:6 1 |
| Or, *Ard,* Gen. 46:21 3 |
| Or, *Shupham,* Num. 26:39 See ch. 7:12 5 |
| ch. 2:52 6 |

mer, and Hō'-thăm, and Shû'-ă their sister.

33 And the sons of Jăph'-lĕt; Pā'-săch, and Bimhal, and Ăsh'-văth. These *are* the children of Jăph'-lĕt.

34 And the sons of ᴿShā'-mer; Ā'-hī, and Rōh'-găh, Jĕ-hŭb'-băh, and Ăr'-ăm.

35 And the sons of his brother Hē'-lĕm; Zō'-phăh, and Ĭm'-nă, and Shē'-lĕsh, and Ā'-măl.

36 The sons of Zō'-phăh; Sū'-ăh, and Hăr'-nĕ-pher, and Shû'-ăl, and Bē'-rī, and Ĭm'-răh,

37 Bē'-zer, and Hod, and Shăm'-mă, and Shĭl'-shăh, and Ĭth'-răn, and Bēêr'-ă.

38 And the sons of Jē'-ther; Jĕ-phŭn'-nēh, and Pĭs'-păh, and Âr'-ă.

39 And the sons of ŭl'-lă; Âr'-ăh, and Hăn'-ĭ-ĕl, and Rē'-zĭ-ă.

40 All these *were* the children of Asher, heads of *their* father's house, choice *and* mighty men of valour, chief of the princes. And the number throughout the genealogy of them that were apt to the war *and* to battle *was* twenty and six thousand men.

CHAPTER 8

Descendants of Benjamin

NOW Benjamin begat ᴿBē'-lă his firstborn, Ăsh'-bĕl the second, and Ă-hâr'-ăh the third,

2 Nō'-hăh the fourth, and Rā'-phă the fifth.

3 And the sons of Bē'-lă were, ᴺĂd'-där, and Gē'-ră, and Ă-bī'-hŭd,

4 And Ă-bī'-shû-ă, and Nā'-ă-măn, and Ă-hō'-ăh,

5 And Gē'-ră, and ᴺShĕ-phū'-phăn, and Hū'-răm.

6 And these *are* the sons of Ē'-hŭd: these are the heads of the fathers of the inhabitants of Gē'-bă, and they removed them to ᴿMăn'-ă-hăth:

7 And Nā'-ă-măn, and Ă-hī'-ăh, and Gē'-ră, he removed them, and begat ūz'-ză, and Ă-hī'-hŭd.

8 And Shā-hă-rā'-ĭm begat *children* in the country of Moab, after he had sent them away; Hū'-shĭm and Bā'-ă-ră *were* his wives.

9 And he begat of Hō'-dĕsh his wife, Jō'-băb, and Zĭ'-bĭ-ă, and Mē'-shă, and Măl'-chăm,

10 And Jē'-ūz, and Shă-chī'-ă, and Mĭr'-mă. These *were* his sons, heads of the fathers.

11 And of Hū'-shĭm he begat Ă-bī'-tŭb, and Ĕl-pā'-ăl.

12 The sons of Ĕl-pā'-ăl; Ē'-ber, and Mĭ'-shăm, and Shā'-mĕd, who built Ō'-nō, and Lod, with the towns thereof:

13 Bĕ-rī′-ăh also, and ᴿShē′-mă, who *were* heads of the fathers of the inhabitants of Âī′-jă-lŏn, who drove away the inhabitants of Gath:

14 And Ă-hī′-ō, Shā′-shăk, and Jĕr′-ĕ-mŏth,

15 And Zĕb-ă-dī′-ăh, and âr′-ăd, and Ā′-dĕr,

16 And Michael, and ĭs′-păh, and Jō′-hă, the sons of Bĕ-rī′-ăh;

17 And Zĕb-ă-dī′-ăh, and Mĕ-shŭl′-lăm, and Hĕz′-ĕ-kī, and Hē′-bĕr,

18 ĭsh′-mĕ-rāī also, and Jĕz-lī′-ăh, and Jō′-băb, the sons of ĕl-pā′-ăl;

19 And Jakim, and Zĭch′-rī, and Zăb′-dī,

20 And ĕl-ĭ-ē′-nāī, and Zĭl′-thāī, and Ē-lī′-ĕl,

21 And Ă-dāī′-ăh, and Bĕ-rāī′-ăh, and Shĭm′-răth, the sons of ᴺShĭm′-hī;

22 And ĭsh′-păn, and Hē′-bĕr, and Ē-lī′-ĕl,

23 And Abdon, and Zĭch′-rī, and Hā′-năn,

24 And Hăn-ă-nī′-ăh, and Ē′-lăm, and Ăn-tō-thī′-jăh,

25 And ĭph-ĕ-dēī′-ăh, and Pĕn′-ū-ĕl, the sons of Shā′-shăk;

26 And Shăm′-shĕ-rāī, and Shē-hă-rī′-ăh, and Ăth-ă-lī′-ăh,

27 And Jăr-ĕ-sī′-ăh, and Ē-lī′-ăh, and Zĭch′-rī, the sons of Jĕ-rō′-hăm.

28 These *were* heads of the fathers, by their generations, chief *men*. These dwelt in Jerusalem.

29 And at Gibeon dwelt the ᴺfather of Gibeon; whose ᴿwife′s name *was* Mā′-ă-chăh:

30 And his firstborn son Abdon, and Zur, and Kish, and Bā′-ăl, and Nadab,

31 And Gē′-dôr, and Ă-hī′-ō, and ᴺZā′-chĕr.

32 And Mĭk′-lōth begat ᴺShĭm′-ĕ-ăh. And these also dwelt with their brethren in Jerusalem, over against them.

33 And ᴿNer begat Kish, and Kish begat Saul, and Saul begat Jonathan, and Măl′-chĭ-shû′-ă, and ᴿĂ-bĭn′-ă-dăb, and ᴺĔsh-bā′-ăl.

34 And the son of Jonathan *was* ᴺMĕr′-ĭb-bā′-ăl; and Mĕr′-ĭb-bā′-ăl begat ᴿMī′-căh.

35 And the sons of Mī′-căh *were,* Pī′-thŏn, and Mē′-lĕch, and ᴺTâr′-ĕ-ă, and Ahaz.

36 And Ahaz begat ᴿJĕ-hō′-ă-dăh; and Jĕ-hō′-ă-dăh begat Ăl′-ĕ-mĕth, and Ăz-mā′-vĕth, and Zimri; and Zimri begat Mō′-ză,

37 And Mō′-ză begat Bī′-nĕ-ă: ᴿRā′-phă *was* his son, ĕl-ĕ-ā′-săh his son, Ā′-zĕl his son:

38 And Ā′-zĕl had six sons, whose names *are* these, Ăz-rī′-kăm, Bō′-chĕ-rû, and ĭsh′-mā-ĕl, and Shē-ă-rī′-ăh, and ō-bă-dī′-ăh, and Hā′-năn. All these *were* the sons of Ā′-zĕl.

39 And the sons of Ē′-shĕk his brother *were,* ū′-lăm his firstborn, Jē′-hŭsh the second, and Ē-lĭph′-ĕ-lĕt the third.

40 And the sons of ū′-lăm were mighty men of valour, archers, and had many sons, and

sons′ sons, an hundred and fifty. All these *are* of the sons of Benjamin.

CHAPTER 9

Book of Israel′s genealogies

SO ᴿall Israel were reckoned by genealogies; and, behold, they *were* written in the book of the kings of Israel and Judah, *who* were carried away to Babylon for their transgression.

2 ᴿNow the first inhabitants that *dwelt* in their possessions in their cities *were,* the Israelites, the priests, Levites, and ᴿthe Nĕth′-ĭ-nĭmś.

3 And in ᴿJerusalem dwelt of the children of Judah, and of the children of Benjamin, and of the children of Ē′-phră-ĭm, and Mă-năs′-sēh;

4 ū′-thāī the son of Ăm′-mĭ-hŭd, the son of Omri, the son of Imri, the son of Bā′-nī, of the children of Phâr′-ĕz the son of Judah.

5 And of the Shī′-lō-nītes; Ă-sāī′-ăh the firstborn, and his sons.

6 And of the sons of Zē′-răh; Jĕū′-ĕl, and their brethren, six hundred and ninety.

7 And of the sons of Benjamin; Săl′-lû the son of Mĕ-shŭl′-lăm, the son of Hŏ-dă-vī′-ăh, the son of Hăs-ĕ-nū′-ăh,

8 And ĭb-nēī′-ăh the son of Jĕ-rō′-hăm, and Ē′-lăh the son of ŭz′-zī, the son of Mĭch′-rī, and Mĕ-shŭl′-lăm the son of Shĕph-ă-thī′-ăh, the son of Rĕū′-ĕl, the son of ĭb-nī′-jăh;

9 And their brethren, according to their generations, nine hundred and fifty and six. All these men *were* chief of the fathers in the house of their fathers.

10 ᴿAnd of the priests; Jĕ-dāī′-ăh, and Jĕ-hŏī′-ă-rĭb, and Jā′-chĭn,

11 And ᴺĂz-ă-rī′-ăh the son of Hĭl-kī′-ăh, the son of Mĕ-shŭl′-lăm, the son of Zā′-dŏk, the son of Mĕ-rāī′-ōth, the son of Ă-hī′-tŭb, the ruler of the house of God;

12 And Ă-dāī′-ăh the son of Jĕ-rō′-hăm, the son of Păsh′-ùr, the son of Măl-chī′-jăh, and Mā-ăs-ĭ-ā′-ī the son of Ăd′-ĭ-ĕl, the son of Jäh′-zĕ-răh, the son of Mĕ-shŭl′-lăm, the son of Mĕ-shĭl′-lĕ-mĭth, the son of ĭm′-mĕr;

13 And their brethren, heads of the house of their fathers, a thousand and seven hundred and threescore; ᴺvery able men for the work of the service of the house of God.

14 And of the Levites; Shĕm-āī′-ăh the son of Hăs′-shŭb, the son of Ăz-rī′-kăm, the son of Hăsh-ă-bī′-ăh, of the sons of Mĕ-râr′-ī;

15 And Băk-băk′-kär, Hē′-rĕsh, and Gā′-lăl, and Măt-tă-nī′-ăh the son of Mī′-căh, the son of Zĭch′-rī, the son of Ā′-săph;

16 And ō-bă-dī′-ăh the son of Shĕm-āī′-ăh,

the son of Gā′-lăl, the son of Jĕ-dū′-thŭn, and Bĕr-ē-<u>ch</u>ī′-ăh the son of Ā′-să, the son of ĕl-kā′-năh, that dwelt in the villages of the Nĕ-tŏph′-ă-thītes.

17 And the porters *were*, Shăl′-lŭm, and Ăk′-kŭb, and Tăl′-mŏn, and Ă-hī′-măn, and their brethren: Shăl′-lŭm *was* the chief;

18 Who hitherto *waited* in the king's gate eastward: they *were* porters in the companies of the children of Levi.

19 And Shăl′-lŭm the son of Kôr′-ē, the son of Ē-bī′-ă-săph, the son of Kôr′-ăh, and his brethren, of the house of his father, the Kôr′-ă-hītes, *were* over the work of the service, keepers of the ᴺgates of the tabernacle: and their fathers, *being* over the host of the LORD, *were* keepers of the entry.

20 And ᴿPhĭn′-ĕ-hăś the son of ĕl-ē-ā′-zär was the ruler over them in time past, *and* the LORD *was* with him.

21 *And* Zĕ<u>ch</u>-ă-rī′-ăh the son of Mĕ-shĕl-ĕ-mī′-ăh *was* porter of the door of the tabernacle of the congregation.

22 All these *which were* chosen to be porters in the gates *were* two hundred and twelve. These were reckoned by their genealogy in their villages, whom ᴿDavid and Samuel ᴿthe seer ᴺdid ordain in their ᴺset office.

23 So they and their children *had* the oversight of the gates of the house of the LORD, *namely*, the house of the tabernacle, by wards.

24 In four quarters were the porters, toward the east, west, north, and south.

25 And their brethren, *which were* in their villages, *were* to come ᴿafter seven days from time to time with them.

26 For these Levites, the four chief porters, were in *their* ᴺset office, and were over the ᴺchambers and treasuries of the house of God.

27 And they lodged round about the house of God, because the charge *was* upon them, and the opening thereof every morning *pertained* to them.

28 And *certain* of them had the charge of the ministering vessels, that they should ᴺbring them in and out by tale.

29 *Some* of them also *were* appointed to oversee the vessels, and all the ᴺinstruments of the sanctuary, and the fine flour, and the wine, and the oil, and the frankincense, and the spices.

30 And *some* of the sons of the priests made ᴿthe ointment of the spices.

31 And Măt-tĭ-thī′-ăh, *one* of the Levites, who *was* the firstborn of Shăl′-lŭm the Kôr′-ă-hīte, had the ᴺset office ᴿover the things that were made ᴺin the pans.

32 And *other* of their brethren, of the sons

of the Kō′-hăth-ītes, ᴿwere over the ᴺshewbread, to prepare *it* every sabbath.

33 And these *are* ᴿthe singers, chief of the fathers of the Levites, *who remaining* in the chambers *were* free: for ᴺthey were employed in *that* work day and night.

34 These chief fathers of the Levites *were* chief throughout their generations; these dwelt at Jerusalem.

Family of Saul

35 And in Gibeon dwelt the father of Gibeon, Jĕ-hī′-ĕl, whose wife's name *was* ᴿMā′-ă-<u>ch</u>ăh:

36 And his firstborn son Abdon, then Zur, and Kish, and Bā′-ăl, and Ner, and Nadab,

37 And Gē′-dôr, and Ă-hī′-ō, and Zĕ<u>ch</u>-ă-rī′-ăh, and Mĭk′-lōth.

38 And Mĭk′-lōth begat Shĭm′-ĕ-ăm. And they also dwelt with their brethren at Jerusalem, over against their brethren.

39 ᴿAnd Ner begat Kish; and Kish begat Saul; and Saul begat Jonathan, and Măl′-<u>ch</u>ī-shū′-ă, and Ă-bĭn′-ă-dăb, and ĕsh-bā′-ăl.

40 And the son of Jonathan *was* Mĕr′-ĭb-bā′-ăl: and Mĕr′-ĭb-bā′-ăl begat Mī′-căh.

41 And the sons of Mī′-căh *were*, Pī′-thŏn, and Mē′-lĕ<u>ch</u>, and Tăh′-rĕ-ă, ᴿand Ahaz.

42 And Ahaz begat Jâr′-ăh; and Jâr′-ăh begat Ăl′-ĕ-mĕth, and Ăz-mā′-vĕth, and Zimri; and Zimri begat Mō′-ză;

43 And Mō′-ză begat Bĭ′-nĕ-ă; and Rĕ-phā′-ăh his son, ĕl-ē-ā′-săh his son, Ā′-zĕl his son.

44 And Ā′-zĕl had six sons, whose names *are* these, Ăz-rī′-kăm, Bō′-<u>ch</u>ĕ-rû, and ĭsh′-mā-ĕl, and Shē-ă-rī′-ăh, and ō-bă-dī′-ăh, and Hā′-năn: these *were* the sons of Ā′-zĕl.

CHAPTER 10

Death of Saul and his sons

NOW ᴿthe Philistines fought against Israel; and the men of Israel fled from before the Philistines, and fell down ᴺslain in mount Gĭl-bō′-ă.

2 And the Philistines followed hard after Saul, and after his sons; and the Philistines slew Jonathan, and ᴺĂ-bĭn′-ă-dăb, and Măl′-<u>ch</u>ī-shū′-ă, the sons of Saul.

3 And the battle went sore against Saul, and the ᴺarchers ᴺhit him, and he was wounded of the archers.

4 Then said Saul to his armourbearer, Draw thy sword, and thrust me through therewith; lest these uncircumcised come and ᴺabuse me. But his armourbearer would not; for he was

sore afraid. So Saul took a sword, and fell upon it.

5 And when his armourbearer saw that Saul was dead, he fell likewise on the sword, and died.

6 So Saul died, and his three sons, and all his house died together.

7 And when all the men of Israel that *were* in the valley saw that they fled, and that Saul and his sons were dead, then they forsook their cities, and fled: and the Philistines came and dwelt in them.

8 And it came to pass on the morrow, when the Philistines came to strip the slain, that they found Saul and his sons fallen in mount Gĭl-bō′-ă.

9 And when they had stripped him, they took his head, and his armour, and sent into the land of the Philistines round about, to carry tidings unto their idols, and to the people.

10 ᴿAnd they put his armour in the house of their gods, and fastened his head in the temple of Dā′-gŏn.

11 And when all Jā′-bĕsh-gĭl′-ĕ-ăd heard all that the Philistines had done to Saul,

12 They arose, all the valiant men, and took away the body of Saul, and the bodies of his sons, and brought them to Jā′-bĕsh, and buried their bones under the oak in Jā′-bĕsh, and fasted seven days.

13 So Saul died for his transgression which he ᴺcommitted against the LORD, ᴿ*even* against the word of the LORD, which he kept not, and also for asking *counsel* of *one that had* a familiar spirit, ᴿto inquire *of it;*

14 And inquired not of the LORD: therefore he slew him, and ᴿturned the kingdom unto David the son of ᴺJesse.

CHAPTER 11

David anointed king of all Israel

THEN ᴿall Israel gathered themselves to David unto Hē′-brŏn, saying, Behold, we *are* thy bone and thy flesh.

2 And moreover ᴺin time past, even when Saul was king, thou *wast* he that leddest out and broughtest in Israel: and the LORD thy God said unto thee, Thou shalt ᴿfeedᴺ my people Israel, and thou shalt be ruler over my people Israel.

3 Therefore came all the elders of Israel to the king to Hē′-brŏn; and David made a covenant with them in Hē′-brŏn before the LORD; and ᴿthey anointed David king over Israel, according to the word of the LORD ᴺby ᴿSamuel.

CHAP. **10**
BC 1056
10 1 Sam. 31:10
13 Heb. *transgressed*
13 1 Sam. 13:13 & 15:23
13 1 Sam. 28:7
14 1 Sam. 15:28 2 Sam. 3:9, 10 & 5:3
14 Heb. *Isai*

CHAP. **11**
BC 1047
1 2 Sam. 5:1
2 Heb. *both yesterday and the third day*
2 Ps. 78:71
2 Or, *rule*
3 2 Sam. 5:3
3 Heb. *by the hand of*
3 1 Sam. 16:1, 12, 13

2 Sam. 5:6	4
Judg. 1:21 & 19:10	4
Heb. *head*	6
i.e. *Zion,* 2 Sam. 5:7	7
Heb. *revived*	8
Heb. *went in going and increasing*	9
2 Sam. 23:8	10
Or, *held strongly with him*	10
1 Sam. 16:1, 12	10
Or, *son of Hachmoni*	11
Or, *Ephes-dammim,* 1 Sam. 17:1	13
Or, *stood*	14
Or, *salvation*	14
Or, *three captains over the thirty*	15
2 Sam. 23:13	15
ch. 14:9	15

---

4 And David and all Israel ᴿwent to Jerusalem, which *is* Jē′-bŭs; ᴿwhere the Jĕb′-ū-śītes *were,* the inhabitants of the land.

5 And the inhabitants of Jē′-bŭs said to David, Thou shalt not come hither. Nevertheless David took the castle of Zion, which *is* the city of David.

6 And David said, Whosoever smiteth the Jĕb′-ū-śītes first shall be ᴺchief and captain. So Jō′-ăb the son of Zĕr-ū-ī′-ăh went first up, and was chief.

7 And David dwelt in the castle; therefore they called ᴺit the city of David.

8 And he built the city round about, even from Mĭl′-lō round about: and Jō′-ăb ᴺrepaired the rest of the city.

9 So David ᴺwaxed greater and greater: for the LORD of hosts *was* with him.

David's mighty men

10 ᴿThese also *are* the chief of the mighty men whom David had, who ᴺstrengthened themselves with him in his kingdom, *and* with all Israel, to make him king, according to ᴿthe word of the LORD concerning Israel.

11 And this *is* the number of the mighty men whom David had; Jă-shŏb′-ĕ-ăm, ᴺan Hăch′-mō-nīte, the chief of the captains: he lifted up his spear against three hundred slain *by him* at one time.

12 And after him *was* Ĕl-ē-ā′-zär the son of Dodo, the Ă-hō′-hīte, who *was* one of the three mighties.

13 He was with David at ᴺPăs-dăm′-mĭm, and there the Philistines were gathered together to battle, where was a parcel of ground full of barley; and the people fled from before the Philistines.

14 And they ᴺset themselves in the midst of *that* parcel, and delivered it, and slew the Philistines; and the LORD saved *them* by a great ᴺdeliverance.

15 Now ᴺthree of the thirty captains ᴿwent down to the rock to David, into the cave of Adullam; and the host of the Philistines encamped ᴿin the valley of Rĕph′-ā-ĭm.

16 And David *was* then in the hold, and the Philistines' garrison *was* then at Beth-lehem.

17 And David longed, and said, Oh that one would give me drink of the water of the well of Beth-lehem, that *is* at the gate!

18 And the three brake through the host of the Philistines, and drew water out of the well of Beth-lehem, that *was* by the gate, and took *it,* and brought *it* to David: but David would not drink *of* it, but poured it out to the LORD,

19 And said, My God forbid it me, that I should do this thing: shall I drink the blood of

these men ᴺthat have put their lives in jeopardy? for with *the jeopardy of* their lives they brought it. Therefore he would not drink it. These things did these three mightiest.

20 ᴿAnd Ăb'-ĭ-shâi the brother of Jō'-ăb, he was chief of the three: for lifting up his spear against three hundred, he slew *them,* and had a name among the three.

21 ᴿOf the three, he was more honourable than the two; for he was their captain: howbeit he attained not to the *first* three.

22 Bĕ-nâi'-ăh the son of Jĕ-hŏi'-ă-dă, the son of a valiant man of Kăb'-zeĕl, ᴺwho had done many acts; ᴿhe slew two lionlike men of Moab: also he went down and slew a lion in a pit in a snowy day.

23 And he slew an Egyptian, ᴺa man of *great* stature, five cubits high; and in the Egyptian's hand *was* a spear like a weaver's beam; and he went down to him with a staff, and plucked the spear out of the Egyptian's hand, and slew him with his own spear.

24 These *things* did Bĕ-nâi'-ăh the son of Jĕ-hŏi'-ă-dă, and had the name among the three mighties.

25 Behold, he was honourable among the thirty, but attained not to the *first* three: and David set him over his guard.

26 Also the valiant men of the armies *were,* ᴿĂs'-ă-hĕl the brother of Jō'-ăb, Ĕl-hā'-năn the son of Dodo of Beth-lehem,

27 ᴺShăm'-mōth the ᴺHâr'-ō-rīte, Hē'-lĕz the ᴺPē'-lō-nīte,

28 ĭ'-ră the son of ĭk'-kĕsh the Tĕ-kō'-īte, Ā'-bĭ-ē'-zĕr the Ăn'-tō-thīte,

29 ᴺSĭb'-bĕ-câi the Hū'-shă-thīte, ᴺĭ'-lā-i the Ă-hō'-hīte,

30 Mā'-hă-râi the Nĕ-tŏph'-ă-thīte, ᴺHē'-lĕd the son of Bā'-ă-năh the Nĕ-tŏph'-ă-thīte,

31 ĭ-thā'-i the son of Rĭ-bā'-i of Gĭb'-ĕ-ăh, *that pertained* to the children of Benjamin, Bĕ-nâi'-ăh the Pĭ-rā'-thŏn-īte,

32 ᴺHū-rā'-i of the brooks of Gā'-ăsh, ᴺĂ-bĭ'-ĕl the Är'-bă-thīte,

33 Ăz-mā'-vĕth the Bā-hă-rû'-mīte, Ē-lĭ-ăh'-bă the Shā-ăl-bō'-nīte,

34 The sons of ᴺHăsh'-ĕm the Gĭ'-zŏn-īte, Jonathan the son of Shā'-gē the Hâr'-ă-rīte,

35 Ă-hī'-ăm the son of ᴺSā'-cär the Hâr'-ă-rīte, ᴺĒ-lĭ'-phăl the son of ᴺUr,

36 Hē'-phĕr the Mĕ-chē'-ră-thīte, Ă-hī'-jăh the Pē'-lō-nīte,

37 ᴺHĕz'-rō the Carmelite, ᴺNā'-ă-râi the son of ĕz'-bâi,

38 Jō'-ĕl the brother of Nathan, Mĭb'-här ᴺthe son of Hăg-gē'-rī,

39 Zē'-lĕk the Ammonite, Nā'-hă-râi the

Bē'-rō-thīte, the armourbearer of Jō'-ăb the son of Zĕr-ū-ĭ'-ăh,

40 ĭ'-ră the ĭth'-rīte, Gâr'-ĕb the ĭth'-rīte,

41 Ū-rī'-ăh the Hittite, Zā'-băd the son of Äh'-lā-i,

42 Ăd'-ĭ-nă the son of Shī'-ză the Reubenite, a captain of the Reubenites, and thirty with him,

43 Hā'-năn the son of Mā'-ă-chăh, and Jōsh'-ă-phăt the Mĭth'-nīte,

44 Ŭz-zī'-ă the Ăsh-tē'-ră-thīte, Shā'-mă and Jĕ-hī'-ĕl the sons of Hō'-thăn the Ă-rō'-ĕr-īte,

45 Jĕd-ĭ-ā'-ĕl the ᴺson of Shĭm'-rī, and Jō'-hă his brother, the Tī'-zīte,

46 Ē-lī'-ĕl the Mă-hā'-vīte, and Jĕr-ĭ-bā'-i, and Jōsh-ă-vī'-ăh, the sons of Ĕl-nā'-ăm, and ĭth'-măh the Moabite,

47 Ē-lī'-ĕl, and ō'-bĕd, and Jăs'-ĭ-ĕl the Mĕ-sŏb'-ā-īte.

CHAPTER 12

David's followers

NOW ᴿthese *are* they that came to David to ᴿZiklag, ᴺwhile he yet kept himself close because of Saul the son of Kish: and they *were* among the mighty men, helpers of the war.

2 *They were* armed with bows, and could use both the right hand and ᴿthe left in *hurling* stones and *shooting* arrows out of a bow, *even* of Saul's brethren of Benjamin.

3 The chief *was* Ā-hī-ē'-zĕr, then Jō'-ăsh, the sons of ᴺShĕm'-ă-ăh the Gĭb'-ĕ-ă-thīte; and Jē'-zĭ-ĕl, and Pē'-lĕt, the sons of Ăz-mā'-vĕth; and Bĕ-rā'-chăh, and Jehu the Ăn'-tō-thīte,

4 And ĭs-mâi'-ăh the Gibeonite, a mighty man among the thirty, and over the thirty; and Jeremiah, and Jă-hā'-zĭ-ĕl, and Jō-hā'-năn, and Jōs'-ă-băd the Gĕ-dē'-ră-thīte,

5 Ē-lū'-zâi, and Jĕr'-ĭ-mōth, and Bē-ă-lī'-ăh, and Shĕm-ă-rī'-ăh, and Shĕph-ă-tī'-ăh the Hă-rū'-phīte,

6 Ĕl-kā'-năh, and Jĕ-sī'-ăh, and Ăz'-ă-reĕl, and Jō-ē'-zĕr, and Jă-shŏb'-ĕ-ăm, the Kôr'-hītes,

7 And Jō-ē'-lăh, and Zĕb-ă-dī'-ăh, the sons of Jĕ-rō'-hăm of Gē'-dôr.

8 And of the Gadites there separated themselves unto David into the hold to the wilderness men of might, *and* men ᴺof war *fit* for the battle, that could handle shield and buckler, whose faces *were like* the faces of lions, and *were* ᴿasᴺ swift as the roes upon the mountains;

9 Ē'-zĕr the first, ō-bă-dī'-ăh the second, Ē-lī'-ăb the third,

10 Mĭsh-măn'-năh the fourth, Jeremiah the fifth,

11 Ăt-tā'-ĭ the sixth, Ē-lī'-ĕl the seventh,

12 Jō-hā'-năn the eighth, ĕl-zā'-băd the ninth,

13 Jeremiah the tenth, Mặch-bā'-naĭ the eleventh.

14 These *were* of the sons of Gad, captains of the host: ᴺone of the least *was* over an hundred, and the greatest over a thousand.

15 These *are* they that went over Jordan in the first month, when it had ᴺoverflown all his ᴿbanks; and they put to flight all *them* of the valleys, *both* toward the east, and toward the west.

16 And there came of the children of Benjamin and Judah to the hold unto David.

17 And David went out ᴺto meet them, and answered and said unto them, If ye be come peaceably unto me to help me, mine heart shall ᴺbe knit unto you: but if *ye be come* to betray me to mine enemies, seeing *there is* no ᴺwrong in mine hands, the God of our fathers look *thereon,* and rebuke *it.*

18 Then ᴺthe spirit came upon ᴿĂ-mā'-saĭ, *who was* chief of the captains, *and he said,* Thine *are* we, David, and on thy side, thou son of Jesse: peace, peace *be* unto thee, and peace *be* to thine helpers; for thy God helpeth thee. Then David received them, and made them captains of the band.

19 And there fell *some* of Mă-năs'-sĕh to David, ᴿwhen he came with the Philistines against Saul to battle: but they helped them not: for the lords of the Philistines upon advisement sent him away, saying, ᴿHe will fall to his master Saul ᴺto *the jeopardy of* our heads.

20 As he went to Ziklag, there fell to him of Mă-năs'-sĕh, Ăd'-năh, and Jō'-ză-băd, and Jĕd-ĭ-ā'-ĕl, and Michael, and Jō'-ză-băd, and Ĕ-lī'-hū, and Zĭl'-thaĭ, captains of the thousands that *were* of Mă-năs'-sĕh.

21 And they helped David ᴺagainst ᴿthe band *of the rovers:* for they *were* all mighty men of valour, and were captains in the host.

22 For at *that* time day by day there came to David to help him, until *it was* a great host, like the host of God.

David's troops at Hebron

23 And these *are* the numbers of the ᴺᴺbands *that were* ready armed to the war, *and* ᴿcame to David to Hē'-bron, to ᴿturn the kingdom of Saul to him, ᴿaccording to the word of the LORD.

24 The children of Judah that bare shield

CHAP. 12
BC 1058
14 Or, *one that was least could resist an hundred, and the greatest a thousand*
15 Heb. *filled over*
15 Josh. 3:15
17 Heb. *before them*
17 Heb. *be one*
17 Or, *violence*
18 Heb. *the spirit clothed Amasai:* Judg. 6:34
18 2 Sam. 17:25
19 1 Sam. 29:2
19 1 Sam. 29:4
19 Or, *on our heads*
21 Or, *with a band*
21 1 Sam. 30:1, 9, 10
23 Or, *captains, or, men*
23 Heb. *heads*
23 2 Sam. 2:3
23 ch. 10:14
23 1 Sam. 16:1

Or, *prepared* 24
2 Sam. 8:17 28
Heb. *brethren,* 29 Gen. 31:23
2 Sam. 2:8, 9 29
Heb. *a multitude* 29 *of them*
Heb. *men* 30 *of names*
Esth. 1:13 32
Or, *rangers of* 33 *battle, or, ranged in battle*
Or, *set the* 33 *battle in array*
Heb. *without a* 33 *heart and a heart,* Ps. 12:2
Or, *keeping* 36 *their rank*
Or, *victual* 40 *of meal*

and spear *were* six thousand and eight hundred, ready ᴺarmed to the war.

25 Of the children of Simeon, mighty men of valour for the war, seven thousand and one hundred.

26 Of the children of Levi four thousand and six hundred.

27 And Jĕ-hoĭ'-ă-dă *was* the leader of the Aaronites, and with him *were* three thousand and seven hundred;

28 And ᴿZā'-dŏk, a young man mighty of valour, and of his father's house twenty and two captains.

29 And of the children of Benjamin, the ᴺkindred of Saul, three thousand: for hitherto ᴿtheᴺ greatest part of them had kept the ward of the house of Saul.

30 And of the children of Ē'-phră-ĭm twenty thousand and eight hundred, mighty men of valour, ᴺfamous throughout the house of their fathers.

31 And of the half tribe of Mă-năs'-sĕh eighteen thousand, which were expressed by name, to come and make David king.

32 And of the children of ĭs'-să-chär, ᴿwhich were men* that had understanding of the times, to know what Israel ought to do; the heads of them *were* two hundred; and all their brethren *were* at their commandment.

33 Of Zĕ-bū'-lŭn, such as went forth to battle, ᴺexpert in war, with all instruments of war, fifty thousand, which could ᴺkeep rank: *they were* ᴺnot of double heart.

34 And of Năph'-tă-lī a thousand captains, and with them with shield and spear thirty and seven thousand.

35 And of the Danites expert in war twenty and eight thousand and six hundred.

36 And of Asher, such as went forth to battle, ᴺexpert in war, forty thousand.

37 And on the other side of Jordan, of the Reubenites, and the Gadites, and of the half tribe of Mă-năs'-sĕh, with all manner of instruments of war for the battle, an hundred and twenty thousand.

38 All these men of war, that could keep rank, came with a perfect heart to Hē'-bron, to make David king over all Israel: and all the rest also of Israel *were* of one heart to make David king.

39 And there they were with David three days, eating and drinking: for their brethren had prepared for them.

40 Moreover they that were nigh them, *even* unto ĭs'-să-chär and Zĕ-bū'-lŭn and Năph'-tă-lī, brought bread on asses, and on camels, and on mules, and on oxen, *and* ᴺmeat, meal,

cakes of figs, and bunches of raisins, and wine, and oil, and oxen, and sheep abundantly: for *there was* joy in Israel.

CHAPTER 13

The removal of the ark

AND David consulted with the captains of thousands and hundreds, *and* with every leader.

2 And David said unto all the congregation of Israel, If *it seem* good unto you, and *that it be* of the LORD our God, N let us send abroad unto our brethren every where, *that are* R left in all the land of Israel, and with them *also* to the priests and Levites *which are* N in their cities *and* suburbs, that they may gather themselves unto us:

3 And let us N bring again the ark of our God to us: R for we inquired not at it in the days of Saul.

4 And all the congregation said that they would do so: for the thing was right in the eyes of all the people.

5 So R David gathered all Israel together, from R Shī'-hôr of Egypt even unto the entering of Hē'-măth, to bring the ark of God R from Kĭr'-jăth-jē'-ă-rĭm.

6 And David went up, and all Israel, to R Bā'-ă-lăh, *that is,* to Kĭr'-jăth-jē'-ă-rĭm, which *belonged* to Judah, to bring up thence the ark of God the LORD, R that dwelleth *between* the chĕr'-ū-bĭms, whose name is called *on it.*

7 And they N carried the ark of God R in a new cart R out of the house of Ă-bĭn'-ă-dăb: and ŭz'-ză and Ă-hī'-ō drave the cart.

8 R And David and all Israel played before God with all *their* might, and with N singing, and with harps, and with psalteries, and with timbrels, and with cymbals, and with trumpets.

Death of Uzza

9 And when they came unto the threshing-floor of N Chī'-dŏn, ŭz'-ză put forth his hand to hold the ark; for the oxen N stumbled.

10 And the anger of the LORD was kindled against ŭz'-ză, and he smote him, R because he put his hand to the ark: and there he R died before God.

11 And David was displeased, because the LORD had made a breach upon ŭz'-ză: wherefore that place is called N Pē'-rĕz-ŭz'-ză to this day.

12 And David was afraid of God that day, saying, How shall I bring the ark of God *home* to me?

13 So David N brought not the ark *home* to himself to the city of David, but carried it

aside into the house of ō'-bĕd-ē'-dŏm the Gĭt'-tĭte.

14 R And the ark of God remained with the family of ō'-bĕd-ē'-dŏm in his house three months. And the LORD blessed R the house of ō'-bĕd-ē'-dŏm, and all that he had.

CHAPTER 14

Hiram assists David

NOW R Hiram king of Tyre sent messengers to David, and timber of cedars, with masons and carpenters, to build him an house.

2 And David perceived that the LORD had confirmed him king over Israel, for his kingdom was lifted up on high, because of his people Israel.

David's wives and children

3 And David took N more wives at Jerusalem: and David begat more sons and daughters.

4 Now R these *are* the names of *his* children which he had in Jerusalem; Shăm'-mū-ă, and Shō'-băb, Nathan, and Solomon,

5 And ĭb'-hăr, and Ē-lī'-shû-ă, and ĕl'-pă-lĕt,

6 And Nō'-găh, and Nĕph'-ĕg, and Jă-phī'-ă,

7 And Ē-lī'-shă-mă, and N Bēē-lī'-ă-dă, and Ē-lĭph'-ă-lĕt.

Wars with the Philistines

8 And when the Philistines heard that R David was anointed king over all Israel, all the Philistines went up to seek David. And David heard *of it,* and went out against them.

9 And the Philistines came and spread themselves R in the valley of Rĕph'-ā-ĭm.

10 And David inquired of God, saying, Shall I go up against the Philistines? and wilt thou deliver them into mine hand? And the LORD said unto him, Go up; for I will deliver them into thine hand.

11 So they came up to Bā'-ăl-pĕ-rā'-zĭm; and David smote them there. Then David said, God hath broken in upon mine enemies by mine hand like the breaking forth of waters: therefore they called the name of that place N Bā'-ăl-pĕ-rā'-zĭm.

12 And when they had left their gods there, David gave a commandment, and they were burned with fire.

13 R And the Philistines yet again spread themselves abroad in the valley.

14 Therefore David inquired again of God; and God said unto him, Go not up after them; turn away from them, R and come upon them over against the mulberry trees.

15 And it shall be, when thou shalt hear a sound of going in the tops of the mulberry trees, *that* then thou shalt go out to battle: for God is gone forth before thee to smite the host of the Philistines.

16 David therefore did as God commanded him: and they smote the host of the Philistines from ᴿGibeon even to Gā'-zĕr.

17 And ᴿthe fame of David went out into all lands; and the Lord ᴿbrought the fear of him upon all nations.

CHAPTER 15

The ark brought to Jerusalem

AND *David* made him houses in the city of David, and prepared a place for the ark of God, ᴿand pitched for it a tent.

2 Then David said, ᴺNone ought to carry the ᴿark of God but the Levites: for them hath the Lord chosen to carry the ark of God, and to minister unto him for ever.

3 And David ᴿgathered all Israel together to Jerusalem, to bring up the ark of the Lord unto his place, which he had prepared for it.

4 And David assembled the children of Aaron, and the Levites:

5 Of the sons of Kō'-hăth; Ū'-rĭ-ĕl the chief, and his ᴺbrethren an hundred and twenty:

6 Of the sons of Mĕ-râr'-ĭ; Ă-sāi'-ăh the chief, and his brethren two hundred and twenty:

7 Of the sons of Gĕr'-shŏm; Jō'-ĕl the chief, and his brethren an hundred and thirty:

8 Of the sons of ᴿE-lĭ-zā'-phăn; Shĕm-āi'-ăh the chief, and his brethren two hundred:

9 Of the sons of ᴿHē'-brŏn; E-lĭ'-ĕl the chief, and his brethren fourscore:

10 Of the sons of ŭz'-zĭ-ĕl; Ăm-mĭn'-ă-dăb the chief, and his brethren an hundred and twelve.

11 And David called for Zā'-dŏk and Ă-bī'-ă-thär the priests, and for the Levites, for Ū'-rĭ-ĕl, Ă-sāi'-ăh, and Jō'-ĕl, Shĕm-āi'-ăh, and E-lĭ'-ĕl, and Ăm-mĭn'-ă-dăb,

12 And said unto them, Ye *are* the chief of the fathers of the Levites: sanctify yourselves, *both* ye and your brethren, that ye may bring up the ark of the Lord God of Israel unto *the place that* I have prepared for it.

13 For ᴿbecause ye *did it* not at the first, ᴿthe Lord our God made a breach upon us, for that we sought him not after the due order.

14 So the priests and the Levites sanctified themselves to bring up the ark of the Lord God of Israel.

15 And the children of the Levites bare the ark of God upon their shoulders with the staves thereon, as ᴿMoses commanded according to the word of the Lord.

Festivities in Jerusalem

16 And David spake to the chief of the Levites to appoint their brethren *to be* the singers with instruments of musick, psalteries and harps and cymbals, sounding, by lifting up the voice with joy.

17 So the Levites appointed ᴿHē'-măn the son of Jō'-ĕl; and of his brethren, ᴿĀ'-săph the son of Bĕr-e-chī'-ăh; and of the sons of Mĕ-râr'-ĭ their brethren, ᴿE'-thăn the son of Kū-shāi'-ăh;

18 And with them their brethren of the second *degree,* Zĕch-ă-rī'-ăh, Ben, and Jā-ā'-zĭ-ĕl, and Shĕ-mī'-ră-mŏth, and Jĕ-hī'-ĕl, and ŭn'-nĭ, E-lī'-ăb, and Bĕ-nāi'-ăh, and Mā-ă-sēi'-ăh, and Măt-tī-thī'-ăh, and E-lĭph'-ĕ-lēh, and Mĭk-nēi'-ăh, and ō'-bĕd-ē'-dŏm, and Jĕ-ī'-ĕl, the porters.

19 So the singers, Hē'-măn, Ā'-săph, and E'-thăn, *were appointed* to sound with cymbals of brass;

20 And Zĕch-ă-rī'-ăh, and ᴺĀ'-zĭ-ĕl, and Shĕ-mī'-ră-mŏth, and Jĕ-hī'-ĕl, and ŭn'-nĭ, and E-lī'-ăb, and Mā-ă-sēi'-ăh, and Bĕ-nāi'-ăh, with psalteries ᴿon Ăl'-ă-mŏth;

21 And Măt-tī-thī'-ăh, and E-lĭph'-ĕ-lēh, and Mĭk-nēi'-ăh, and ō'-bĕd-ē'-dŏm, and Jĕ-ī'-ĕl, and Ăz-ă-zī'-ăh, with harps ᴺon the Shĕm'-ĭn-ĭth to excel.

22 And Chĕn-ă-nī'-ăh, chief of the Levites, ᴺwas for ᴺsong: he instructed about the song, because he *was* skilful.

23 And Bĕr-e-chī'-ăh and ĕl-kā'-năh *were* doorkeepers for the ark.

24 And Shĕb-ă-nī'-ăh, and Jĕ-hŏsh'-ă-phăt, and Nĕth'-ă-nēĕl, and Ă-mā'-săi, and Zĕch-ă-rī'-ăh, and Bĕ-nāi'-ăh, and ĕl-ĭ-ē'-zĕr, the priests, ᴿdid blow with the trumpets before the ark of God: and ō'-bĕd-ē'-dŏm and Jĕ-hī'-ăh *were* doorkeepers for the ark.

25 So ᴿDavid, and the elders of Israel, and the captains over thousands, went to bring up the ark of the covenant of the Lord out of the house of ō'-bĕd-ē'-dŏm with joy.

26 And it came to pass, when God helped the Levites that bare the ark of the covenant of the Lord, that they offered seven bullocks and seven rams.

27 And David *was* clothed with a robe of fine linen, and all the Levites that bare the ark, and the singers, and Chĕn-ă-nī'-ăh the master of the ᴺsong with the singers: David also *had* upon him an ē'-phŏd of linen.

28 ᴿThus all Israel brought up the ark of the covenant of the Lord with shouting, and with

Cross-references (center column)

CHAP. 14
BC 1043
16 2 Sam. 5:25, Geba
17 Josh. 6:27
2 Chr. 26:8
17 Deut. 2:25 & 11:25

CHAP. 15
BC 1042
1 ch. 16:1
2 Heb. It is *not to carry the ark of God, but for the Levites*
2 Num. 4:2, 15
Deut. 10:8 & 31:9
3 1 Ki. 8:1
ch. 13:5
5 Or, *kinsmen*
8 Ex. 6:22
9 Ex. 6:18
13 2 Sam. 6:3
ch. 13:7
13 ch. 13:10, 11

Ex. 25:14   15
Num. 4:15 & 7:9
ch. 6:33   17
ch. 6:39   17
ch. 6:44   17
ver. 18, *Jaaziel*   20
Ps. 46, title   20
Or, *on the eighth to oversee,* Ps. 6, title   21
Or, was *for the carriage: he instructed about the carriage* 22
Heb. *lifting up*   22
Num. 10:8   24
Ps. 81:3
2 Sam. 6:12, 13, etc. 25
1 Ki. 8:1
Or, *carriage*   27
ch. 13:8   28

sound of the cornet, and with trumpets, and with cymbals, making a noise with psalteries and harps.

29 And it came to pass, ᴿas the ark of the covenant of the LORD came to the city of David, that Michal the daughter of Saul looking out at a window saw king David dancing and playing: and she despised him in her heart.

CHAPTER 16

The ark placed in the tent

SO ᴿthey brought the ark of God, and set it in the midst of the tent that David had pitched for it: and they offered burnt sacrifices and peace offerings before God.

2 And when David had made an end of offering the burnt offerings and the peace offerings, he blessed the people in the name of the LORD.

3 And he dealt to every one of Israel, both man and woman, to every one a loaf of bread, and a good piece of flesh, and a flagon *of wine*.

4 And he appointed *certain* of the Levites to minister before the ark of the LORD, and to ᴿrecord, and to thank and praise the LORD God of Israel:

5 Ā′-săph the chief, and next to him Zĕch-ă-rī′-ăh, Jĕ-ī′-ĕl, and Shĕ-mī′-ră-mŏth, and Jĕ-hī′-ĕl, and Măt-tī-thī′-ăh, and Ē-lī′-ăb, and Bĕ-nā̄i′-ăh, and Ō′-bĕd-ē′-dom: and Jĕ-ī′-ĕl ᴺwith psalteries and with harps; but Ā′-săph made a sound with cymbals;

6 Bĕ-nā̄i′-ăh also and Jă-hā′-zī-ĕl the priests with trumpets continually before the ark of the covenant of God.

Psalm of thanksgiving

7 Then on that day David delivered ᴿfirst *this psalm* to thank the LORD into the hand of Ā′-săph and his brethren.

8 ᴿGive thanks unto the LORD, call upon his name, make known his deeds among the people.

9 Sing unto him, sing psalms unto him, talk ye of all his wondrous works.

10 Glory ye in his holy name: let the heart of them rejoice that seek the LORD.

11 Seek the LORD and his strength, seek his face continually.

12 Remember his marvellous works that he hath done, his wonders, and the judgments of his mouth;

13 O ye seed of Israel his servant, ye children of Jacob, his chosen ones.

14 He *is* the LORD our God; his judgments *are* in all the earth.

15 Be ye mindful always of his covenant;

the word *which* he commanded to a thousand generations;

16 *Even of the* ᴿcovenant which he made with Abraham, and of his oath unto Isaac;

17 And hath confirmed the same to Jacob for a law, *and* to Israel *for* an everlasting covenant,

18 Saying, Unto thee will I give the land of Canaan, ᴺthe lot of your inheritance;

19 When ye were but ᴺfew, ᴿeven a few, and strangers in it.

20 And *when* they went from nation to nation, and from *one* kingdom to another people;

21 He suffered no man to do them wrong: yea, he ᴿreproved kings for their sakes,

22 *Saying,* ᴿTouch not mine anointed, and do my prophets no harm.

23 ᴿSing unto the LORD, all the earth; shew forth from day to day his salvation.

24 Declare his glory among the heathen; his marvellous works among all nations.

25 For great *is* the LORD, and greatly to be praised: he also *is* to be feared above all gods.

26 For all the gods ᴿof the people *are* idols: but the LORD made the heavens.

27 Glory and honour *are* in his presence; strength and gladness *are* in his place.

28 Give unto the LORD, ye kindreds of the people, give unto the LORD glory and strength.

29 Give unto the LORD the glory *due* unto his name: bring an offering, and come before him: worship the LORD in the beauty of holiness.

30 Fear before him, all the earth: the world also shall be stable, that it be not moved.

31 Let the heavens be glad, and let the earth rejoice: and let *men* say among the nations, The LORD reigneth.

32 Let the sea roar, and the fulness thereof: let the fields rejoice, and all that *is* therein.

33 Then shall the trees of the wood sing out at the presence of the LORD, because he cometh to judge the earth.

34 ᴿO give thanks unto the LORD; for *he is* good; for his mercy *endureth* for ever.

35 ᴿAnd say ye, Save us, O God of our salvation, and gather us together, and deliver us from the heathen, that we may give thanks to thy holy name, *and* glory in thy praise.

36 ᴿBlessed *be* the LORD God of Israel for ever and ever. And all ᴿthe people said, Ä′-mĕn, and praised the LORD.

Ministers for the ark

37 So he left there before the ark of the covenant of the LORD Ā′-săph and his brethren, to minister before the ark continually, as every day's work required:

38 And ō'-bĕd-ē'-dǫm with their brethren, threescore and eight; ō'-bĕd-ē'-dǫm also the son of Jĕ-dū'-thŭn and Hō'-sặh *to be* porters:

39 And Zā'-dŏk the priest, and his brethren the priests, ^Rbeforc the tabernacle of the LORD ^Rin the high place that *was* at Gibeon,

40 To offer burnt offerings unto the LORD upon the altar of the burnt offering continually ^Rmorning^N and evening, and *to do* according to all that is written in the law of the LORD, which he commanded Israel;

41 And with them Hē'-mặn and Jĕ-dū'-thŭn, and the rest that were chosen, who were expressed by name, to give thanks to the LORD, ^Rbecause his mercy *endureth* for ever;

42 And with them Hē'-mặn and Jĕ-dū'-thŭn with trumpets and cymbals for those that should make a sound, and with musical instruments of God. And the sons of Jĕ-dū'-thŭn *were* ^Nporters.

43 ^RAnd all the people departed every man to his house: and David returned to bless his house.

CHAPTER 17

A house for the LORD

NOW ^Rit came to pass, as David sat in his house, that David said to Nathan thc prophet, Lo, I dwell in an house of cedars, but the ark of the covenant of the LORD *remaineth* under curtains.

2 Then Nathan said unto David, Do all that *is* in thine heart; for God *is* with thee.

Nathan's prophecy

3 And it came to pass the same night, that the word of God came to Nathan, saying,

4 Go and tell David my servant, Thus saith the LORD, Thou shalt not build me an house to dwell in:

5 For I have not dwelt in an house since the day that I brought up Israel unto this day; but ^Nhave gone from tent to tent, and from *one* tabernacle *to another.*

6 Wheresoever I have walked with all Israel, spake I a word to any of the judges of Israel, whom I commanded to feed my people, saying, Why have ye not built me an house of cedars?

7 Now therefore thus shalt thou say unto my servant David, Thus saith the LORD of hosts, I took thee from the sheepcote, *even* ^Nfrom following the sheep, that thou shouldest be ruler over my people Israel:

8 And I have been with the whithersoever thou hast walked, and have cut off all thine

CHAP. **16**
BC 1042
39 ch. 21:29
2 Chr. 1:3
39 1 Ki. 3:4
40 Ex. 29:38
Num. 28:3
40 Heb. *in the morning, and in the evening*
41 ver. 34
2 Chr. 5:13 & 7:3
Ezra 3:11
Jer. 33:11
42 Heb. *for the gate*
43 2 Sam. 6:19, 20

CHAP. **17**
BC 1042
1 2 Sam. 7:1, etc.
5 Heb. *have been*
7 Heb. *from after*

2 Sam. 7:14, 15	**13**
Luke 1:33	**14**
2 Sam. 7:18	**16**
Heb. *greatnesses*	**19**

enemies from before thee, and have made thee a name like the name of the great men that *are* in the earth.

9 Also I will ordain a place for my people Israel, and will plant them, and they shall dwell in their place, and shall be moved no more; neither shall the children of wickcdness waste them any more, as at the beginning,

10 And since the time that I commanded judges *to be* over my people Israel. Moreover I will subdue all thine enemies. Furthermore I tell thee that the LORD will build thee an house.

11 And it shall come to pass, when thy days be expired that thou must go *to be* with thy fathers, that I will raise up thy seed after thee, which shall be of thy sons; and I will establish his kingdom.

12 He shall build me an house, and I will stablish his throne for ever.   ★

13 ^RI will be his father, and he shall be my son: and I will not take my mercy away from him, as I took *it* from *him* that was before thee:

14 But ^RI will settle him in mine house and in my kingdom for ever: and his throne shall be established for evermore.   ★

15 According to all these words, and according to all this vision, so did Nathan speak unto David.

David's prayer

16 ^RAnd David the king came and sat before the LORD, and said, Who *am* I, O LORD God, and what *is* mine house, that thou hast brought me hitherto?

17 And *yet* this was a small thing in thine eyes, O God; for thou hast *also* spoken of thy servant's house for a great while to come, and hast regarded me according to the estate of a man of high degree, O LORD God.

18 What can David *speak* more to thee for the honour of thy servant? for thou knowest thy servant.

19 O LORD, for thy servant's sake, and according to thine own heart, hast thou done all this greatness, in making known all *these* ^Ngreat things.

20 O LORD, *there is* none like thee, neither *is there any* God beside thee, according to all that we have heard with our ears.

21 And what one nation in the earth *is* like thy people Israel, whom God went to redeem *to be* his own people, to make thee a name of greatness and terribleness, by driving out nations from before thy people, whom thou hast redeemed out of Egypt?

22 For thy people Israel didst thou make

thine own people for ever; and thou, LORD, becamest their God.

23 Therefore now, LORD, let the thing that thou hast spoken concerning thy servant and concerning his house be established for ever, and do as thou hast said.

24 Let it even be established, that thy name may be magnified for ever, saying, The LORD of hosts *is* the God of Israel, *even* a God to Israel: and *let* the house of David thy servant *be* established before thee.

25 For thou, O my God, ᴺhast told thy servant that thou wilt build him an house: therefore thy servant hath found *in his heart* to pray before thee.

26 And now, LORD, thou art God, and hast promised this goodness unto thy servant:

27 Now therefore ᴺlet it please thee to bless the house of thy servant, that it may be before thee for ever: for thou blessest, O LORD, and *it shall be* blessed for ever.

CHAPTER 18

David extends his kingdom

NOW after this ᴿit came to pass, that David smote the Philistines, and subdued them, and took Gath and her towns out of the hands of the Philistines.

2 And he smote Moab; and the Moabites became David's servants, *and* brought gifts.

3 And David smote ᴺHăd-ă-rē'-zĕr king of Zō'-băh unto Hā'-măth, as he went to stablish his dominion by the river ᴱu-phrā'-tĕś.

4 And David took from him a thousand chariots, and ᴿseven thousand horsemen, and twenty thousand footmen: David also houghed all the chariot *horses,* but reserved of them an hundred chariots.

5 And when the Syrians of ᴺDamascus came to help Hăd-ă-rē'-zĕr king of Zō'-băh, David slew of the Syrians two and twenty thousand men.

6 Then David put *garrisons* in Syria-damascus; and the Syrians became David's servants, *and* brought gifts. Thus the LORD preserved David whithersoever he went.

7 And David took the shields of gold that were on the servants of Hăd-ă-rē'-zĕr, and brought them to Jerusalem.

8 Likewise from ᴺTĭb'-hăth, and from Chŭn, cities of Hăd-ă-rē'-zĕr, brought David very much brass, wherewith ᴿSolomon made the brasen sea, and the pillars, and the vessels of brass.

9 Now when ᴺTō'-ū king of Hā'-măth heard how David had smitten all the host of Hăd-ă-rē'-zĕr king of Zō'-băh;

10 He sent ᴺHă-dôr'-ăm his son to king Da-

CHAP. 17
BC 1042
25 Heb. *hast revealed the ear of thy servant*
27 Or, *it hath pleased thee*

CHAP. 18
BC 1040
1 2 Sam. 8:1, etc.
3 Or, *Hadadezer,* 2 Sam. 8:3
4 2 Sam. 8:4, *seven hundred*
5 Heb. *Darmesek*
8 Called in the book of Samuel *Betah, and Berothai*
8 1 Ki. 7:15, 23 2 Chr. 4:12, 15, 16
9 Or, *Toi,* 2 Sam. 8:9
10 Or, *Joram,* 2 Sam. 8:10

Or, *to salute*	10
Heb. *to bless*	10
Heb. *was the man of wars*	10
Heb. *Abshai*	12
2 Sam. 8:13	12
2 Sam. 8:14, etc.	13
Or, *remembrancer*	15
Called *Ahimelech,* 2 Sam. 8:17	16
Called *Seraiah,* 2 Sam. 8:17 *and Shisha,* 1 Ki. 4:3	16
2 Sam. 8:18	17
Heb. *at the hand of the king*	17

CHAP. 19
BC 1037
2 Sam. 10:1, etc.   1
Heb. *In thine eyes doth David, etc.*   3

vid, ᴺto inquire of his welfare, and ᴺto congratulate him, because he had fought against Hăd-ă-rē'-zĕr, and smitten him; (for Hăd-ă-rē'-zĕr ᴺhad war with Tō'-ū;) and *with him* all manner of vessels of gold and silver and brass.

11 Them also king David dedicated unto the LORD, with the silver and the gold that he brought from all *these* nations; from ᴱ'-dŏm, and from Moab, and from the children of Ammon, and from the Philistines, and from Ăm'-ă-lĕk.

12 Moreover ᴺĂb'-ĭ-shâi the son of Zĕr-ū-ĭ'-ăh slew of the ᴱ'-dŏm-ītes in the valley of salt ᴿeighteen thousand.

13 ᴿAnd he put garrisons in ᴱ'-dŏm; and all the ᴱ'-dŏm-ītes became David's servants. Thus the LORD preserved David whithersoever he went.

14 So David reigned over all Israel, and executed judgment and justice among all his people.

15 And Jō'-ăb the son of Zĕr-ū-ĭ'-ăh *was* over the host; and Jĕ-hŏsh'-ă-phăt the son of Ă-hĭ'-lŭd, ᴺrecorder.

16 And Zā'-dŏk the son of Ă-hĭ'-tŭb, and ᴺĂ-bĭm'-ĕ-lĕch the son of Ă-bĭ'-ă-thär, *were* the priests; and ᴺShăv'-shă was scribe;

17 ᴿAnd Bĕ-nâi'-ăh the son of Jĕ-hŏi'-ă-dä *was* over the Chĕr'-ĕ-thītes and the Pĕl'-ĕ-thītes; and the sons of David *were* chief ᴺabout the king.

CHAPTER 19

David's ambassadors humiliated

NOW ᴿit came to pass after this, that Nahash the king of the children of Ammon died, and his son reigned in his stead.

2 And David said, I will shew kindness unto Hā'-nŭn the son of Nahash, because his father shewed kindness to me. And David sent messengers to comfort him concerning his father. So the servants of David came into the land of the children of Ammon to Hā'-nŭn, to comfort him.

3 But the princes of the children of Ammon said to Hā'-nŭn, ᴺThinkest thou that David doth honour thy father, that he hath sent comforters unto thee? are not his servants come unto thee for to search, and to overthrow, and to spy out the land?

4 Wherefore Hā'-nŭn took David's servants, and shaved them, and cut off their garments in the midst hard by their buttocks, and sent them away.

5 Then there went *certain,* and told David how the men were served. And he sent to meet them: for the men were greatly ashamed.

And the king said, Tarry at Jericho until your beards be grown, and *then* return.

6 And when the children of Ammon saw that they had made themselves ᴺodious to David, Hā'-nŭn and the children of Ammon sent a thousand talents of silver to hire them chariots and horsemen out of Mĕs-ŏ-pŏ-tā'-mĭ-ă, and out of Sўr'-ĭ-ă-mā'-ă-<u>ch</u>ăh, ᴿand out of Zō'-băh.

7 So they hired thirty and two thousand chariots, and the king of Mā'-ă-<u>ch</u>ăh and his people; who came and pitched before Mē'-dĕ-bă. And the children of Ammon gathered themselves together from their cities, and came to battle.

8 And when David heard *of it,* he sent Jō'-ăb, and all the host of the mighty men.

9 And the children of Ammon came out, and put the battle in array before the gate of the city: and the kings that were come *were* by themselves in the field.

Syria and Ammon defeated

10 Now when Jō'-ăb saw that ᴺthe battle was set against him before and behind, he chose out of all the ᴺchoice of Israel, and put *them* in array against the Syrians.

11 And the rest of the people he delivered unto the hand of ᴺĂb'-ĭ-shâi his brother, and they set *themselves* in array against the children of Ammon.

12 And he said, If the Syrians be too strong for me, then thou shalt help me: but if the children of Ammon be too strong for thee, then I will help thee.

13 Be of good courage, and let us behave ourselves valiantly for our people, and for the cities of our God: and let the Lᴏʀᴅ do *that which is* good in his sight.

14 So Jō'-ăb and the people that *were* with him drew nigh before the Syrians unto the battle; and they fled before him.

15 And when the children of Ammon saw that the Syrians were fled, they likewise fled before Ăb'-ĭ-shâi his brother, and entered into the city. Then Jō'-ăb came to Jerusalem.

16 And when the Syrians saw that they were put to the worse before Israel, they sent messengers, and drew forth the Syrians that *were* beyond the ᴺriver: and ᴺShō'-phăch the captain of the host of Hăd-ă-rē'-zĕr *went* before them.

17 And it was told David; and he gathered all Israel, and passed over Jordan, and came upon them, and set *the battle* in array against them. So when David had put the battle in array against the Syrians, they fought with him.

18 But the Syrians fled before Israel; and

David slew of the Syrians seven thousand *men which fought in* chariots, and forty thousand footmen, and killed Shō'-phăch the captain of the host.

19 And when the servants of Hăd-ă-rē'-zĕr saw that they were put to the worse before Israel, they made peace with David, and became his servants: neither would the Syrians help the children of Ammon any more.

CHAPTER 20

AND ᴿit came to pass, that ᴺafter the year was expired, at the time that kings go out *to battle,* Jō'-ăb led forth the power of the army, and wasted the country of the children of Ammon, and came and besieged Răb'-băh. But David tarried at Jerusalem. And ᴿJō'-ăb smote Răb'-băh, and destroyed it.

2 And David ᴿtook the crown of their king from off his head, and found it ᴺto weigh a talent of gold, and *there were* precious stones in it; and it was set upon David's head: and he brought also exceeding much spoil out of the city.

3 And he brought out the people that *were* in it, and cut *them* with saws, and with harrows of iron, and with axes. Even so dealt David with all the cities of the children of Ammon. And David and all the people returned to Jerusalem.

Wars with the Philistines

4 And it came to pass after this, ᴿthat there ᴺᴺarose war at ᴺGē'-zĕr with the Philistines; at which time ᴿSĭb'-bĕ-<u>ch</u>âi the Hū'-shă-thīte slew ᴺSĭp'-pā-ĭ, *that was* of the children of ᴺthe giant: and they were subdued.

5 And there was war again with the Philistines; and ĕl-hā'-năn the son of ᴺJā'-ĭr slew Lăh'-mī the brother of Gō-lĭ'-ăth the Gĭt'-tīte, whose spear staff *was* like a weaver's beam.

6 And yet again ᴿthere was war at Gath, where was ᴺa man of *great* stature, whose fingers and toes *were* four and twenty, six *on each hand,* and six *on each foot:* and he also was ᴺthe son of the giant.

7 But when he ᴺdefied Israel, Jonathan the son of ᴺShĭm'-ĕ-ă David's brother slew him.

8 These were born unto the giant in Gath; and they fell by the hand of David, and by the hand of his servants.

CHAPTER 21

Census of Israel

AND ᴿSatan stood up against Israel, and provoked David to number Israel.

2 And David said to Jō'-ăb and to the rulers of the people, Go, number Israel from

CHAP. 19
BC 1037
6 Heb. *to stink*
6 ch. 18:5, 9
10 Heb. *the face of the battle was*
10 Or, *young men*
11 Heb. *Abshai*
16 i.e. *Euphrates*
16 Or, *Shobach,* 2 Sam. 10:16

CHAP. 20
BC 1017
2 Sam. 11:1   1
Heb. *at the return of the year*   1
2 Sam. 12:26   1
2 Sam. 12:30, 31   2
Heb. *the weight of*   2
2 Sam. 21:18   4
Or, *continued*   4
Heb. *stood*   4
Or, *Gob*   4
ch. 11:29   4
Or, *Saph,* 2 Sam. 21:18   4
Or, *Rapha*   4
Called also *Jaareoregim,* 2 Sam. 21:19   5
2 Sam. 21:20   6
Heb. *a man of measure*   6
Heb. *born to the giant,* or, *Rapha*   6
Or, *reproached*   7
Called *Shammah,* 1 Sam. 16:9   7

CHAP. 21
BC 1017
2 Sam. 24:1, etc.   1

Beer-she'-ba even to Dan; ^Rand bring the number of them to me, that I may know *it*.

3 And Jo'-ab answered, The LORD make his people an hundred times so many more as they *be*: but, my lord the king, *are* they not all my lord's servants? why then doth my lord require this thing? why will he be a cause of trespass to Israel?

4 Nevertheless the king's word prevailed against Jo'-ab. Wherefore Jo'-ab departed, and went throughout all Israel, and came to Jerusalem.

5 And Jo'-ab gave the sum of the number of the people unto David. And all *they of* Israel were a thousand thousand and an hundred thousand men that drew sword: and Judah *was* four hundred threescore and ten thousand men that drew sword.

6 ^RBut Levi and Benjamin counted he not among them: for the king's word was abominable to Jo'-ab.

David's choice

7 ^NAnd God was displeased with this thing; therefore he smote Israel.

8 And David said unto God, ^RI have sinned greatly, because I have done this thing: ^Rbut now, I beseech thee, do away the iniquity of thy servant; for I have done very foolishly.

9 And the LORD spake unto Gad, David's ^Rseer, saying,

10 Go and tell David, saying, Thus saith the LORD, I ^Noffer thee three *things:* choose thee one of them, that I may do *it* unto thee.

11 So Gad came to David, and said unto him, Thus saith the LORD, ^NChoose thee

12 ^REither three years' famine; or three months to be destroyed before thy foes, while that the sword of thine enemies overtaketh *thee;* or else three days the sword of the LORD, even the pestilence, in the land, and the angel of the LORD destroying throughout all the coasts of Israel. Now therefore advise thyself what word I shall bring again to him that sent me.

13 And David said unto Gad, I am in a great strait: let me fall now into the hand of the LORD; for very ^Ngreat *are* his mercies: but let me not fall into the hand of man.

Pestilence in Israel

14 So the LORD sent pestilence upon Israel: and there fell of Israel seventy thousand men.

15 And God sent an ^Rangel unto Jerusalem to destroy it: and as he was destroying, the LORD beheld, and ^Rhe repented him of the evil, and said to the angel that destroyed, It is enough, stay now thine hand. And the angel of

the LORD stood by the threshingfloor of ^NOr'-nan the Jeb'-u-site.

16 And David lifted up his eyes, and ^Rsaw the angel of the LORD stand between the earth and the heaven, having a drawn sword in his hand stretched out over Jerusalem. Then David and the elders *of Israel, who were* clothed in sackcloth, fell upon their faces.

17 And David said unto God, *Is it* not I *that* commanded the people to be numbered? even I it is that have sinned and done evil indeed; but *as for* these sheep, what have they done? let thine hand, I pray thee, O LORD my God, be on me, and on my father's house; but not on thy people, that they should be plagued.

Ornan's threshingfloor

18 Then the ^Rangel of the LORD commanded Gad to say to David, that David should go up, and set up an altar unto the LORD in the threshingfloor of Or'-nan the Jeb'-u-site.

19 And David went up at the saying of Gad, which he spake in the name of the LORD.

20 ^NAnd Or'-nan turned back, and saw the angel; and his four sons with him hid themselves. Now Or'-nan was threshing wheat.

21 And as David came to Or'-nan, Or'-nan looked and saw David, and went out of the threshingfloor, and bowed himself to David with *his* face to the ground.

22 Then David said to Or'-nan, ^NGrant me the place of *this* threshingfloor, that I may build an altar therein unto the LORD: thou shalt grant it me for the full price: that the plague may be stayed from the people.

23 And Or'-nan said unto David, Take *it* to thee, and let my lord the king do *that which is* good in his eyes: lo, I give *thee* the oxen *also* for burnt offerings, and the threshing instruments for wood, and the wheat for the meat offering; I give it all.

24 And king David said to Or'-nan, Nay; but I will verily buy it for the full price: for I will not take *that* which *is* thine for the LORD, nor offer burnt offerings without cost.

25 So ^RDavid gave to Or'-nan for the place six hundred she'-kels of gold by weight.

26 And David built there an altar unto the LORD, and offered burnt offerings and peace offerings, and called upon the LORD; and ^Rhe answered him from heaven by fire upon the altar of burnt offering.

27 And the LORD commanded the angel; and he put up his sword again into the sheath thereof.

28 At that time when David saw that the LORD had answered him in the threshingfloor

of ôr′-năn the Jĕb′-ū-sĭte, then he sacrificed there.

29 ᴿFor the tabernacle of the LORD, which Moses made in the wilderness, and the altar of the burnt offering, *were* at that season in the high place at ᴿGibeon.

30 But David could not go before it to inquire of God: for he was afraid because of the sword of the angel of the LORD.

CHAPTER 22

THEN David said, ᴿThis *is* the house of the LORD God, and this *is* the altar of the burnt offering for Israel.

David provides for the temple

2 And David commanded to gather together ᴿthe strangers that *were* in the land of Israel; and he set masons to hew wrought stones to build the house of God.

3 And David prepared iron in abundance for the nails for the doors of the gates, and for the joinings; and brass in abundance ᴿwithout weight;

4 Also cedar trees in abundance: for the ᴿZĭ-dō′-nĭ-ăns and they of Tyre brought much cedar wood to David.

5 And David said, ᴿSolomon my son *is* young and tender, and the house *that is* to be builded for the LORD *must be* exceeding magnifical, of fame and of glory throughout all countries: I will *therefore* now make preparation for it. So David prepared abundantly before his death.

David's charge to Solomon

6 Then he called for Solomon his son, and charged him to build an house for the LORD God of Israel.

7 And David said to Solomon, My son, as for me, ᴿit was in my mind to build an house ᴿunto the name of the LORD my God:

8 But the word of the LORD came to me, saying, ᴿThou hast shed blood abundantly, and hast made great wars: thou shalt not build an house unto my name, because thou hast shed much blood upon the earth in my sight.

9 ᴿBehold, a son shall be born to thee, who shall be a man of rest; and I will give him ᴿrest from all his enemies round about: for his name shall be ᴺSolomon, and I will give peace and quietness unto Israel in his days.

10 ᴿHe shall build an house for my name; and ᴿhe shall be my son, and I *will be* his father; and I will establish the throne of his kingdom over Israel for ever.

11 Now, my son, ᴿthe LORD be with thee;

and prosper thou, and build the house of the LORD thy God, as he hath said of thee.

12 Only the LORD ᴿgive thee wisdom and understanding, and give thee charge concerning Israel, that thou mayest keep the law of the LORD thy God.

13 ᴿThen shalt thou prosper, if thou takest heed to fulfil the statutes and judgments which the LORD charged Moses with concerning Israel: ᴿbe strong, and of good courage; dread not, nor be dismayed.

14 Now, behold, ᴺin my trouble I have prepared for the house of the LORD an hundred thousand talents of gold, and a thousand thousand talents of silver; and of brass and iron ᴿwithout weight; for it is in abundance: timber also and stone have I prepared; and thou mayest add thereto.

15 Moreover *there are* workmen with thee in abundance, hewers and ᴺworkers of stone and timber, and all manner of cunning men for every manner of work.

16 Of the gold, the silver, and the brass, and the iron, *there is* no number. Arise *therefore*, and be doing, and ᴿthe LORD be with thee.

17 David also commanded all the princes of Israel to help Solomon his son, *saying*,

18 *Is* not the LORD your God with you? ᴿand hath he *not* given you rest on every side? for he hath given the inhabitants of the land into mine hand; and the land is subdued before the LORD, and before his people.

19 Now set your heart and your soul to seek the LORD your God; arise therefore, and build ye the sanctuary of the LORD God, to ᴿbring the ark of the covenant of the LORD, and the holy vessels of God, into the house that is to be built ᴿto the name of the LORD.

CHAPTER 23

David makes Solomon king

SO when David was old and full of days, he made ᴿSolomon his son king over Israel.

Levites organized

2 And he gathered together all the princes of Israel, with the priests and the Levites.

3 Now the Levites were numbered from the age of ᴿthirty years and upward: and their number by their polls, man by man, was thirty and eight thousand.

4 Of which, twenty and four thousand *were* ᴺto set forward the work of the house of the LORD; and six thousand *were* ᴿofficers and judges:

5 Moreover four thousand *were* porters; and four thousand praised the LORD with the in-

struments ᴿwhich I made, *said David,* to praise *therewith.*

6 And ᴿDavid divided them into ᴺcourses among the sons of Levi, *namely,* Gĕr'-shŏn, Kō'-hăth, and Mĕ-râr'-ĭ.

7 Of the ᴿGĕr'-shŏn-ītes *were,* ᴺLā'-ă-dăn, and Shĭm'-ĕ-ĭ.

8 The sons of Lā'-ă-dăn; the chief *was* Jĕ-hī'-ĕl, and Zē'-thăm, and Jō'-ĕl, three.

9 The sons of Shĭm'-ĕ-ĭ; Shĕ-lō'-mĭth, and Hā'-zĭ-ĕl, and Hâr'-ăn, three. These *were* the chief of the fathers of Lā'-ă-dăn.

10 And the sons of Shĭm'-ĕ-ĭ *were,* Jā'-hăth, ᴺZī'-nă, and Jē'-ŭsh, and Bĕ-rī'-ăh. These four *were* the sons of Shĭm'-ĕ-ĭ.

11 And Jā'-hăth was the chief, and Zī'-zăh the second: but Jē'-ŭsh and Bĕ-rī'-ăh ᴺhad not many sons; therefore they were in one reckoning, according to *their* father's house.

12 ᴿThe sons of Kō'-hăth; Amram, ĭz'-här, Hē'-brŏn, and ŭz'-zĭ-ĕl, four.

13 The sons of ᴿAmram; Aaron and Moses: and ᴿAaron was separated, that he should sanctify the most holy things, he and his sons for ever, ᴿto burn incense before the Lᴏʀᴅ, ᴿto minister unto him, and ᴿto bless in his name for ever.

14 Now *concerning* Moses the man of God, ᴿhis sons were named of the tribe of Levi.

15 ᴿThe sons of Moses *were,* Gĕr'-shŏm, and ĕl-ĭ-ē'-zĕr.

16 Of the sons of Gĕr'-shŏm, ᴿShĕ-bū'-ĕlᴺ *was* the chief.

17 And the sons of ĕl-ĭ-ē'-zĕr *were,* ᴿRē-hă-bī'-ăh ᴺthe chief. And ĕl-ĭ-ē'-zĕr had none other sons; but the sons of Rē-hă-bī'-ăh ᴺwere very many.

18 Of the sons of ĭz'-här; ᴺShĕ-lō'-mĭth the chief.

19 ᴿOf the sons of Hē'-brŏn; Jĕ-rī'-ăh the first, Ăm-ă-rī'-ăh the second, Jă-hā'-zĭ-ĕl the third, and Jĕ-kăm'-ĕ-ăm the fourth.

20 Of the sons of ŭz'-zĭ-ĕl; Mī'-chăh the first, and Jĕ-sī'-ăh the second.

21 ᴿThe sons of Mĕ-râr'-ĭ; Măh'-lĭ, and Mū'-shī. The sons of Măh'-lĭ; ĕl-ē-ā'-zär, and ᴿKish.

22 And ĕl-ē-ā'-zär died, and ᴿhad no sons, but daughters: and their ᴺbrethren the sons of Kish ᴿtook them.

23 ᴿThe sons of Mū'-shī; Măh'-lĭ, and Ē'-dĕr, and Jĕr'-ĕ-mōth, three.

Duties of Levites

24 These *were* the sons of ᴿLevi after the house of their fathers; *even* the chief of the fathers, as they were counted by number of names by their polls, that did the work for the service of the house of the Lᴏʀᴅ, from the age of ᴿtwenty years and upward.

25 For David said, The Lᴏʀᴅ God of Israel ᴿhath given rest unto his people, ᴺthat they may dwell in Jerusalem for ever:

26 And also unto the Levites; they shall no *more* ᴿcarry the tabernacle, nor any vessels of it for the service thereof.

27 For by the last words of David the Levites *were* ᴺnumbered from twenty years old and above:

28 Because ᴺtheir office *was* to wait on the sons of Aaron for the service of the house of the Lᴏʀᴅ, in the courts, and in the chambers, and in the purifying of all holy things, and the work of the service of the house of God;

29 Both for ᴿthe shewbread, and for ᴿthe fine flour for meat offering, and for ᴿthe unleavened cakes, and for ᴿthat which is baked in the ᴺpan, and for that which is fried, and for all manner of ᴿmeasure and size;

30 And to stand every morning to thank and praise the Lᴏʀᴅ, and likewise at even;

31 And to offer all burnt sacrifices unto the Lᴏʀᴅ ᴿin the sabbaths, in the new moons, and on the ᴿset feasts, by number, according to the order commanded unto them, continually before the Lᴏʀᴅ:

32 And that they should ᴿkeep the charge of the tabernacle of the congregation, and the charge of the holy *place,* and ᴿthe charge of the sons of Aaron their brethren, in the service of the house of the Lᴏʀᴅ.

CHAPTER 24

Organization of the priests

NOW *these are* the divisions of the sons of Aaron. ᴿThe sons of Aaron; Nadab, and Ă-bī'-hū, ĕl-ē-ā'-zär, and ĭth'-ă-mär.

2 But ᴿNadab and Ă-bī'-hū died before their father, and had no children: therefore ĕl-ē-ā'-zär and ĭth'-ă-mär executed the priest's office.

3 And David distributed them, both Zā'-dŏk of the sons of ĕl-ē-ā'-zär, and Ă-hīm'-ĕ-lĕch of the sons of ĭth'-ă-mär, according to their offices in their service.

4 And there were more chief men found of the sons of ĕl-ē-ā'-zär than of the sons of ĭth'-ă-mär, and *thus* they were divided. Among the sons of ĕl-ē-ā'-zär *there were* sixteen chief men of the house of *their* fathers, and eight among the sons of ĭth'-ă-mär according to the house of their fathers.

5 Thus were they divided by lot, one sort with another; for the governors of the sanctu-

ary, and governors *of the house* of God, were of the sons of Ĕl-ē-ā'-zär, and of the sons of Ĭth'-ă-mär.

6 And Shĕm-āī'-äh the son of Nĕth'-ă-nĕĕl the scribe, *one* of the Levites, wrote them before the king, and the princes, and Zā'-dŏk the priest, and Ă-hĭm'-ĕ-lĕch the son of Ă-bī'-ă-thär, and *before* the chief of the fathers of the priests and Levites: one ᴺprincipal household being taken for ĕl-ē-ā'-zär, and *one* taken for Ĭth'-ă-mär.

7 Now the first lot came forth to Jĕ-hŏī'-ă-rĭb, the second to Jĕ-dāī'-äh,

8 The third to Hâr'-ĭm, the fourth to Sē-ôr'-ĭm,

9 The fifth to Măl-chī'-jäh, the sixth to Mĭ'-jă-mĭn,

10 The seventh to Hăk'-kŏz, the eighth to ᴿĂ-bī'-jäh,

11 The ninth to Jĕsh'-ū-ă, the tenth to Shĕc-ă-nī'-äh,

12 The eleventh to Ē-lĭ-ăsh'-ĭb, the twelfth to Jakim,

13 The thirteenth to Hŭp'-päh, the fourteenth to Jĕ-shĕb'-ĕ-äb,

14 The fifteenth to Bĭl'-gäh, the sixteenth to Ĭm'-mĕr,

15 The seventeenth to Hē'-zĭr, the eighteenth to ăph'-sĕś,

16 The nineteenth to Pĕth-ă-hī'-äh, the twentieth to Jĕ-hĕz'-ĕk-ĕl,

17 The one and twentieth to Jā'-chĭn, the two and twentieth to Găm'-ŭl,

18 The three and twentieth to Dĕl-āī'-äh, the four and twentieth to Mā-ă-zī'-äh.

19 These *were* the orderings of them in their service ᴿto come into the house of the LORD, according to their manner, under Aaron their father, as the LORD God of Israel had commanded him.

Other sons of Levi

20 And the rest of the sons of Levi *were these:* Of the sons of Amram; ᴿShû'-bā-ĕl: of the sons of Shû'-bā-ĕl; Jĕh-dāī'-äh.

21 Concerning ᴿRē-hă-bī'-äh: of the sons of Rē-hă-bī'-äh, the first *was* Ĭs-shī'-äh.

22 Of the Ĭz-här'-ītes; ᴿShē-lō'-mŏth: of the sons of Shē-lō'-mŏth; Jā'-hăth.

23 And the sons *of* ᴿHēbrŏn; Jĕ-rī'-äh *the first,* Ăm-ă-rī'-äh the second, Jă-hā'-zī-ĕl the third, Jĕ-kăm'-ĕ-ăm the fourth.

24 *Of* the sons of ŭz'-zī-ĕl; Mī'-chăh: of the sons of Mī'-chăh; Shā'-mĭr.

25 The brother of Mī'-chăh *was* Ĭs-shī'-äh: of the sons of Ĭs-shī'-äh; Zĕch-ă-rī'-äh.

26 ᴿThe sons of Mĕ-râr'-ī *were* Mäh'-lī and Mū'-shī: the sons of Jā-ă-zī'-äh; Bē'-nō.

27 The sons of Mĕ-râr'-ī by Jā-ă-zī'-äh; Bē'-nō, and Shō'-häm, and Zăc'-cùr, and Ĭb'-rī.

28 Of Mäh'-lī *came* Ĕl-ē-ā'-zär, ᴿwho had no sons.

29 Concerning Kish: the son of Kish *was* Jĕ-räh'-mĕĕl.

30 ᴿThe sons also of Mū'-shī; Mäh'-lī, and Ē'-dĕr, and Jĕr'-ĭ-mŏth. These *were* the sons of the Levites after the house of their fathers.

31 These likewise cast lots over against their brethren the sons of Aaron in the presence of David the king, and Zā'-dŏk, and Ă-hĭm'-ĕ-lĕch, and the chief of the fathers of the priests and Levites, even the principal fathers over against their younger brethren.

CHAPTER 25

Organization of the musicians

MOREOVER David and the captains of the host separated to the service of the sons of ᴿĀ'-săph, and of Hē'-măn, and of Jĕ-dū'-thŭn, who should prophesy with harps, with psalteries, and with cymbals: and the number of the workmen according to their service was:

2 Of the sons of Ā'-săph; Zăc'-cùr, and Joseph, and Nĕth-ă-nī'-äh, and ᴺĂs-ă-rē'-läh, the sons of Ā'-săph under the hands of Ā'-săph, which prophesied ᴺaccording to the order of the king.

3 Of Jĕ-dū'-thŭn: the sons of Jĕ-dū'-thŭn; Gĕd-ă-lī'-äh, and ᴺZē'-rī, and Jĕ-shāī'-äh, Hăsh-ă-bī'-äh, and Măt-tĭ-thī'-äh, ᴺsix, under the hands of their father Jĕ-dū'thŭn, who prophesied with a harp, to give thanks and to praise the LORD.

4 Of Hē'-măn: the sons of Hē'-măn; Bŭk-kī'-äh, Măt-tă-nī'-äh, ᴺŬz'-zī-ĕl, ᴺShĕ-bū'-ĕl, and Jĕr'-ĭ-mŏth, Hăn-ă-nī'-äh, Hă-nā'-nī, Ē-lī'-ă-thäh, Gĭd-dăl'-tī, and Rō-măm'-tī-ē'-zĕr, Jŏsh-bĕ-kăsh'-äh, Măl-lō'-thī, Hō'-thĭr, *and* Mă-hā'-zī-ōth:

5 All these .were the sons of Hē'-măn the king's seer in the ᴺwords of God, to lift up the horn. And God gave to Hē'-măn fourteen sons and three daughters.

6 All these *were* under the hands of their father for song *in* the house of the LORD, with cymbals, psalteries, and harps, for the service of the house of God, ᴿaccordingᴺ to the king's order to Ā'-săph, Jĕ-dū'-thŭn, and Hē'-măn.

7 So the number of them, with their brethren that were instructed in the songs of the LORD, *even* all that were cunning, was two hundred fourscore and eight.

8 And they cast lots, ward against *ward,* as

well the small as the great, [R]the teacher as the scholar.

9 Now the first lot came forth for Ā'-săph to Joseph: the second to Gĕd-a-lī'-ăh, who with his brethren and sons *were* twelve:

10 The third to Zăc'-cŭr, *he*, his sons, and his brethren, *were* twelve:

11 The fourth to ĭz'-rī, *he*, his sons, and his brethren, *were* twelve:

12 The fifth to Nĕth-a-nī'-ăh, *he*, his sons, and his brethren, *were* twelve:

13 The sixth to Bŭk-kī'-ăh, *he*, his sons, and his brethren, *were* twelve:

14 The seventh to Jĕsh-a-rē'-lăh, *he*, his sons, and his brethren, *were* twelve:

15 The eighth to Jĕ-shaī'-ăh, *he*, his sons, and his brethren, *were* twelve:

16 The ninth to Măt-ta-nī'-ăh, *he*, his sons, and his brethren, *were* twelve:

17 The tenth to Shĭm'-ĕ-ī, *he*, his sons, and his brethren, *were* twelve:

18 The eleventh to Ăz'-a-rēĕl, *he*, his sons, and his brethren, *were* twelve:

19 The twelfth to Hăsh-a-bī'-ăh, *he*, his sons, and his brethren, *were* twelve:

20 The thirteenth to Shū'-ba-ēl, *he*, his sons, and his brethren, *were* twelve:

21 The fourteenth to Măt-tĭ-thī'-ăh, *he*, his sons, and his brethren, *were* twelve:

22 The fifteenth to Jĕr'-e-mōth, *he*, his sons, and his brethren, *were* twelve:

23 The sixteenth to Hăn-a-nī'-ăh, *he*, his sons, and his brethren, *were* twelve:

24 The seventeenth to Jŏsh-bĕ-kăsh'-ăh, *he*, his sons, and his brethren, *were* twelve:

25 The eighteenth to Hă-nā'-nī, *he*, his sons, and his brethren, *were* twelve:

26 The nineteenth to Măl-lō'-thī, *he*, his sons, and his brethren, *were* twelve:

27 The twentieth to Ē-lī'-a-thăh, *he*, his sons, and his brethren, *were* twelve:

28 The one and twentieth to Hō'-thĭr, *he*, his sons, and his brethren, *were* twelve:

29 The two and twentieth to Gĭd-dăl'-tī, *he*, his sons, and his brethren, *were* twelve:

30 The three and twentieth to Mă-hā'-zĭ-ōth, *he*, his sons, and his brethren, *were* twelve:

31 The four and twentieth to Rō-măm'-tĭ-ē'-zĕr, *he*, his sons, and his brethren, *were* twelve:

CHAPTER 26

Organization of the gatekeepers

CONCERNING the divisions of the porters: Of the Kôr'-hītes *was* [N]Mĕ-shĕl-ĕ-mī'-ăh the son of Kôr'-ē, of the sons of [N]Ā'-săph.

CHAP. 25
BC 1015
8 2 Chr. 23:13

CHAP. 26
BC 1015
1 Or, *Shelemiah*, ver. 14
1 Or, *Ebiasaph*, ch. 6:37 & 9:19

i.e. Obed-dedom, 5 as ch. 13:14
ch. 16:38　　　10
Or, *as well for* 13 *the small as for the great*
Called　　　　14 *Meshelemiah*, ver. 1
Heb. *Gatherings* 15
See 1 Ki. 10:5　16
2 Chr. 9:4

---

2 And the sons of Mĕ-shĕl-ĕ-mī'-ăh *were*, Zĕch-a-rī'-ăh the firstborn, Jĕd-ĭ-ā'-ĕl the second, Zĕb-a-dī'-ăh the third, Jăth'-nĭ-ĕl the fourth,

3 Ē'-lăm the fifth, Jĕ-hō-hā'-năn the sixth, Ĕl-ĭ-ō-ē'-naī the seventh.

4 Moreover the sons of ō'-bĕd-ē'-dom *were*, Shĕm-aī'-ăh the firstborn, Jĕ-hō'-za-băd the second, Jō'-ăh the third, and Sā'-căr the fourth, and Nĕth'-a-nēĕl the fifth,

5 Ăm'-mĭ-ĕl the sixth, ĭs'-să-chär the seventh, Pē-ŭl'-thaī the eighth: for God blessed [N]him.

6 Also unto Shĕm-aī'-ăh his son were sons born, that ruled throughout the house of their father: for they *were* mighty men of valour.

7 The sons of Shĕm-aī'-ăh; ŏth'-nī, and Rĕph'-ā-ĕl, and ō'-bĕd, ĕl-zā'-băd, whose brethren *were* strong men, Ĕ-lī'-hū, and Sĕm-a-chī'-ăh.

8 All these of the sons of ō'-bĕd-ē'-dom: they and their sons and their brethren, able men for strength for the service, *were* threescore and two of ō'-bĕd-ē'-dom.

9 And Mĕ-shĕl-ĕ-mī'-ăh had sons and brethren, strong men, eighteen.

10 Also [R]Hō'-săh, of the children of Mĕ-râr'-ī, had sons; Simri the chief, (for *though* he was not the firstborn, yet his father made him the chief;)

11 Hĭl-kī'-ăh the second, Tĕb-a-lī'-ăh the third, Zĕch-a-rī'-ăh the fourth: all the sons and brethren of Hō'-săh *were* thirteen.

12 Among these *were* the divisions of the porters, *even* among the chief men, *having* wards one against another, to minister in the house of the LORD.

13 And they cast lots, [N]as well the small as the great, according to the house of their fathers, for every gate.

14 And the lot eastward fell to [N]Shĕl-ĕ-mī'-ăh. Then for Zĕch-a-rī'-ăh his son, a wise counsellor, they cast lots; and his lot came out northward.

15 To ō'-bĕd-ē'-dom southward; and to his sons the house of [N]Ă-sŭp'-pīm.

16 To Shŭp'-pīm and Hō'-săh *the lot came forth* westward, with the gate Shăl'-lĕ-chĕth, by the causeway of the going [N]up, ward against ward.

17 Eastward *were* six Levites, northward four a day, southward four a day, and toward Ă-sŭp'-pīm two *and* two.

18 At Pär'-bär westward, four at the causeway, *and* two at Pär'-bär.

19 These *are* the divisions of the porters among the sons of Kôr'-ē, and among the sons of Mĕ-râr'-ī.

Keepers of the treasures

20 And of the Levites, Ă-hī'-jăh *was* ᴿover the treasures of the house of God, and over the treasures of the ᴺdedicated things.

21 *As concerning* the sons of ᴺLā'-ă-dăn; the sons of the Gĕr'-shŏn-īte Lā'-ă-dăn, chief fathers, *even* of Lā'-ă-dăn the Gĕr'-shŏn-īte, *were* ᴺJĕ-hī-ē'-lī.

22 The sons of Jĕ-hī-ē'-lī; Zē'-thăm, and Jō'-ĕl his brother, *which were* over the treasures of the house of the LORD.

23 Of the Amramites, *and* the ĭz-här'-ītes, the Hē'-brŏn-ītes, *and* the ŭz-zī-ē'-lītes:

24 And ᴿShĕ-bū'-ĕl the son of Gĕr'-shŏm, the son of Moses, *was* ruler of the treasures.

25 And his brethren by Ĕl-ĭ-ē'-zĕr; Rē-hă-bī'-ăh his son, and Jĕ-shāi'-ăh his son, and Joram his son, and Zĭch'-rī his son, and ᴿShĕ-lō'-mĭth his son.

26 Which Shĕ-lō'-mĭth and his brethren *were* over all the treasures of the dedicated things, which David the king, and the chief fathers, the captains over thousands and hundreds, and the captains of the host, had dedicated.

27 ᴺOut of the spoils won in battles did they dedicate to maintain the house of the LORD.

28 And all that Samuel ᴿthe seer, and Saul the son of Kish, and Abner the son of Ner, and Jō'-ăb the son of Zĕr-ū-ī'-ăh, had dedicated; *and* whosoever had dedicated *any thing, it was* under the hand of Shĕ-lō'-mĭth, and of his brethren.

Officers and judges appointed

29 Of the ĭz-här'-ītes, Chĕn-ă-nī'-ăh and his sons *were* for the outward business over Israel, for ᴿofficers and judges.

30 *And* of the Hē'-brŏn-ītes, Hăsh-ă-bī'-ăh and his brethren, men of valour, a thousand and seven hundred, *were* ᴺofficers among them of Israel on this side Jordan westward in all the business of the LORD, and in the service of the king.

31 Among the Hē'-brŏn-ītes *was* ᴿJĕ-rī'-jăh the chief, *even* among the Hē'-brŏn-ītes, according to the generations of his fathers. In the fortieth year of the reign of David they were sought for, and there were found among them mighty men of valour ᴿat Jā'-zĕr of Gilead.

32 And his brethren, men of valour, *were* two thousand and seven hundred chief fathers, whom king David made rulers over the Reubenites, the Gadites, and the half tribe of Mă-năs'-sēh, for every matter pertaining to God, and ᴿaffairsᴺ of the king.

CHAP. 26
BC 1015
20 ch. 28:12
Mal. 3:10
20 Heb. *holy things*
21 Or, *Libni,*
ch. 6:17
21 Or, *Jehiel,*
ch. 23:8 & 29:8
24 ch. 23:16
25 ch. 23:18
27 Heb. *Out of the battles and spoils*
28 1 Sam. 9:9
29 ch. 23:4
30 Heb. *over the charge*
31 ch. 23:19
31 See Josh. 21:39
32 2 Chr. 19:11
32 Heb. *thing*

CHAP. 27	
BC 1015	
2 Sam. 23:8	**2**
ch. 11:11	
Or, *Dodo,*	**4**
2 Sam. 23:9	
Or, *principal officer,*	**5**
1 Ki. 4:5	
2 Sam. 23:20, 22, 23	**6**
ch. 11:22, etc.	
2 Sam. 23:24	**7**
ch. 11:26	
ch. 11:28	**9**
ch. 11:27	**10**
2 Sam. 21:18	**11**
ch. 11:28	**12**
2 Sam. 23:28	**13**
ch. 11:30	
ch. 11:31	**14**

CHAPTER 27

Officers and counsellors

NOW the children of Israel after their number, *to wit,* the chief fathers and captains of thousands and hundreds, and their officers that served the king in any matter of the courses, which came in and went out month by month throughout all the months of the year, of every course *were* twenty and four thousand.

2 Over the first course for the first month *was* ᴿJă-shŏb'-ĕ-ăm the son of Zăb'-dĭ-ĕl: and in his course *were* twenty and four thousand.

3 Of the children of Pē'-rĕz *was* the chief of all the captains of the host for the first month.

4 And over the course of the second month *was* ᴺDō'-dāi an Ă-hō'-hīte, and of his course *was* Mĭk'-lŏth also the ruler: in his course likewise *were* twenty and four thousand.

5 The third captain of the host for the third month *was* Bĕ-nāi'-ăh the son of Jĕ-hoi'-ă-dă, a ᴺchief priest: and in his course *were* twenty and four thousand.

6 This *is that* Bĕ-nāi'-ăh, *who was* ᴿmighty among the thirty, and above the thirty: and in his course *was* Ăm-mī'-ză-băd his son.

7 The fourth *captain* for the fourth month *was* ᴿĂs'-ă-hĕl the brother of Jō'-ăb, and Zĕb-ă-dī'-ăh his son after him: and in his course *were* twenty and four thousand.

8 The fifth captain for the fifth month *was* Shăm'-hŭth the ĭz'-ră-hīte: and in his course *were* twenty and four thousand.

9 The sixth *captain* for the sixth month *was* ᴿĪ'-ră the son of ĭk'-kĕsh the Tĕ-kō'-īte: and in his course *were* twenty and four thousand.

10 The seventh *captain* for the seventh month *was* ᴿHē'-lĕz the Pē'-lō-nīte, of the children of Ē'-phrā-ĭm: and in his course *were* twenty and four thousand.

11 The eighth *captain* for the eighth month *was* ᴿSĭb'-bĕ-cāi the Hū'-shă-thīte, of the Zăr'-hītes: and in his course *were* twenty and four thousand.

12 The ninth *captain* for the ninth month *was* ᴿĀ-bī-ē'-zĕr the Ăn-ĕ-tō'-thīte, of the Benjamites: and in his course *were* twenty and four thousand.

13 The tenth *captain* for the tenth month *was* ᴿMā'-hă-rāi the Nĕ-tŏph'-ă-thīte, of the Zăr'-hītes: and in his course *were* twenty and four thousand.

14 The eleventh *captain* for the eleventh month *was* ᴿBĕ-nāi'-ăh the Pī-rā'-thŏn-īte, of the children of Ē'-phră-ĭm: and in his course *were* twenty and four thousand.

15 The twelfth *captain* for the twelfth month was ^NHĕl′-dai the Nĕ-tŏph′-ă-thīte, of ŏth′-nĭ-ĕl: and in his course *were* twenty and four thousand.

16 Furthermore over the tribes of Israel: the ruler of the Reubenites *was* Ĕl-ĭ-ē′-zĕr the son of Zĭch′-rī: of the Simeonites, Shĕph-ă-tī′-ăh the son of Mā′-ă-chăh:

17 Of the Levites, ^RHăsh-ă-bī′-ah the son of Kĕ-mū′-ĕl: of the Aaronites, Zā′-dŏk:

18 Of Judah, ^RĔ-lī′-hū, *one* of the brethren of David: of Ĭs′-să-chär, Omri the son of Michael:

19 Of Zĕ-bū′-lŭn, Ĭsh-mai′-ăh the son of Ō-bă-dī′-ăh: of Năph′-tă-lī, Jĕr′-ĭ-mōth the son of Ăz′-rĭ-ĕl:

20 Of the children of Ē′-phră-ĭm, Hō-shē′-ă the son of Ăz-ă-zī′-ăh: of the half tribe of Mă-năs′-sĕh, Jō′-ĕl the son of Pĕ-dai′-ăh:

21 Of the half *tribe* of Mă-năs′-sĕh in Gilead, Ĭd′-dō the son of Zĕch-ă-rī′-ăh: of Benjamin, Jā-ăs′-ĭ-ĕl the son of Abner:

22 Of Dan, Ăz′-ă-rĕĕl the son of Jĕ-rō′-hăm. These *were* the princes of the tribes of Israel.

23 But David took not the number of them from twenty years old and under: because ^Rthe Lord had said he would increase Israel like to the stars of the heavens.

24 Jō′-ăb the son of Zĕr-ū-ī′-ăh began to number, but he finished not, because ^Rthere fell wrath for it against Israel; neither ^Nwas the number put in the account of the chronicles of king David.

25 And over the king's treasures *was* Ăz-mā′-vĕth the son of Ăd′-ĭ-ĕl: and over the storehouses in the fields, in the cities, and in the villages, and in the castles, *was* Jĕ-hŏn′-ă-thăn the son of Ŭz-zī′-ăh:

26 And over them that did the work of the field for tillage of the ground *was* Ĕz′-rī the son of Chē′-lŭb:

27 And over the vineyards *was* Shĭm′-ĕ-ī the Rā′-măth-īte: ^Nover the increase of the vineyards for the wine cellars *was* Zăb′-dī the Shĭph′-mīte:

28 And over the olive trees and the sycomore trees that *were* in the low plains *was* Bā′-ăl-hā′-năn the Gĕ-dē′-rīte: and over the cellars of oil *was* Jō′-ăsh:

29 And over the herds that fed in Shär′-on *was* Shĭt-rā′-ī the Shär′-on-īte: and over the herds *that were* in the valleys *was* Shā′-phăt the son of Ăd-lā′-ī:

30 Over the camels also *was* Ō′-bĭl the Ĭsh′-mā-ĕl-īte: and over the asses *was* Jĕh-dĕi′-ăh the Mĕ-rō′-nō-thīte:

31 And over the flocks *was* Jā′-zīz the

Hă-gē′-rīte. All these *were* the rulers of the substance which *was* king David's.

32 Also Jonathan David's uncle was a counsellor, a wise man, and a ^Nscribe: and Jĕ-hī′-ĕl the ^Nson of Hăch-mō′-nī *was* with the king's sons:

33 And ^RĂ-hĭth′-ŏ-phĕl *was* the king's counsellor: and ^RHū′-shai the Är′-chīte *was* the king's companion:

34 And after Ă-hĭth′-ŏ-phĕl *was* Jĕ-hoi′-ă-dă the son of Bĕ-nai′-ăh, and ^RĂ-bī′-ă-thär: and the general of the king's army *was* ^RJō′-ăb.

CHAPTER 28

David's address to his officers

AND David assembled all the princes of Israel, ^Rthe princes of the tribes, and ^Rthe captains of the companies that ministered to the king by course, and the captains over the thousands, and captains over the hundreds, and ^Rthe stewards over all the substance and ^Npossession of the king, ^Nand of his sons, with the ^Nofficers, and with ^Rthe mighty men, and with all the valiant men, unto Jerusalem.

2 Then David the king stood up upon his feet, and said, Hear me, my brethren, and my people: *As for me,* ^RI *had* in mine heart to build an house of rest for the ark of the covenant of the Lord, and for ^Rthe footstool of our God, and had made ready for the building:

3 But God said unto me, ^RThou shalt not build an house for my name, because thou *hast been* a man of war, and hast shed ^Nblood.

4 Howbeit the Lord God of Israel ^Rchose me before all the house of my father to be king over Israel for ever: for he hath chosen ^RJudah *to be* the ruler; and of the house of Judah, ^Rthe house of my father; and ^Ramong the sons of my father he liked me to make *me* king over all Israel:

5 ^RAnd of all my sons, (for the Lord hath given me many sons,) ^Rhe hath chosen Solomon my son to sit upon the throne of the kingdom of the Lord over Israel.

6 And he said unto me, ^RSolomon thy son, he shall build my house and my courts: for I have chosen him *to be* my son, and I will be his father.

7 Moreover I will establish his kingdom for ever, ^Rif he be ^Nconstant to do my commandments and my judgments, as at this day.

David's instructions to Solomon

8 Now therefore in the sight of all Israel the congregation of the Lord, and in the audience of our God, keep and seek for all the com-

mandments of the LORD your God: that ye may possess this good land, and leave *it* for an inheritance for your children after you for ever.

9 And thou, Solomon my son, ᴿknow thou the God of thy father, and serve him ᴿwith a perfect heart and with a willing mind: for ᴿthe LORD searcheth all hearts, and understandeth all the imaginations of the thoughts: ᴿif thou seek him, he will be found of thee; but if thou forsake him, he will cast thee off for ever.

10 Take heed now; ᴿfor the LORD hath chosen thee to build an house for the sanctuary: be strong, and do *it*.

11 Then David gave to Solomon his son ᴿthe pattern of the porch, and of the houses thereof, and of the treasuries thereof, and of the upper chambers thereof, and of the inner parlours thereof, and of the place of the mercy seat,

12 And the pattern ᴺof all that he had by the spirit, of the courts of the house of the LORD, and of all the chambers round about, ᴿof the treasuries of the house of God, and of the treasuries of the dedicated things:

13 Also for the courses of the priests and the Levites, and for all the work of the service of the house of the LORD, and for all the vessels of service in the house of the LORD.

14 *He gave* of gold by weight for *things* of gold, for all instruments of all manner of service; *silver also* for all instruments of silver by weight, for all instruments of every kind of service:

15 Even the weight for the candlesticks of gold, and for their lamps of gold, by weight for every candlestick, and for the lamps thereof: and for the candlesticks of silver by weight, *both* for the candlestick, and *also* for the lamps thereof, according to the use of every candlestick.

16 And by weight *he gave* gold for the tables of shewbread, for every table; and *likewise* silver for the tables of silver:

17 Also pure gold for the fleshhooks, and the bowls, and the cups: and for the golden basins *he gave gold* by weight for every basin; and *likewise silver* by weight for every basin of silver:

18 And for the altar of incense refined gold by weight; and gold for the pattern of the chariot of the ᴿchĕr′-ū-bĭms, that spread out *their wings,* and covered the ark of the covenant of the LORD.

19 All *this, said David,* ᴿthe LORD made me understand in writing by *his* hand upon me, *even* all the works of this pattern.

CHAP. 28
BC 1015
9 Jer. 9:24
Hos. 4:1
John 17:3
9 2 Ki. 20:3
9 1 Sam. 16:7
1 Ki. 8:39
ch. 29:17
Jer. 11:20
& 17:10 & 20:12
Rev. 2:23
9 2 Chr. 15:2
10 ver. 6
11 ver. 19
See Ex. 25:40
12 Heb. *of all that was with him*
12 ch. 26:20
18 Ex. 25:18-22
1 Sam. 4:4
1 Ki. 6:23, etc.
19 ver. 11, 12
See Ex. 25:40

Deut. 31:7, 8   **20**
Josh. 1:6, 7, 9
ch. 22:13
Josh. 1:5   **20**
ch. 24, & 25,   **21**
& 26
Ex. 35:25, 26   **21**

CHAP. 29
BC 1015
1 Ki. 3:7   **1**
ch. 22:5
Prov. 4:3
See Is. 54:11, 12   **2**
Rev. 21:18, etc.
1 Ki. 9:28   **4**
Heb. *to*   **5**
fill his hand
ch. 27:1   **6**
ch. 27:25, etc.   **6**

20 And David said to Solomon his son, ᴿBe strong and of good courage, and do *it:* fear not, nor be dismayed: for the LORD God, *even* my God, *will be* with thee; ᴿhe will not fail thee, nor forsake thee, until thou hast finished all the work for the service of the house of the LORD.

21 And, behold, ᴿthe courses of the priests and the Levites, *even they shall be with thee* for all the service of the house of God: and *there shall be* with thee for all manner of workmanship ᴿevery willing skilful man, for any manner of service: also the princes and all the people *will be* wholly at thy commandment.

CHAPTER 29

Offerings for the temple

FURTHERMORE David the king said unto all the congregation, Solomon my son, whom alone God hath chosen, *is yet* ᴿyoung and tender, and the work *is* great: for the palace *is* not for man, but for the LORD God.

2 Now I have prepared with all my might for the house of my God the gold for *things to be made* of gold, and the silver for *things* of silver, and the brass for *things* of brass, the iron for *things* of iron, and wood for *things* of wood; ᴿonyx stones, and *stones* to be set, glistering stones, and of divers colours, and all manner of precious stones, and marble stones in abundance.

3 Moreover, because I have set my affection to the house of my God, I have of mine own proper good, of gold and silver, *which* I have given to the house of my God, over and above all that I have prepared for the holy house,

4 *Even* three thousand talents of gold, of the gold of ᴿō′-phĭr, and seven thousand talents of refined silver, to overlay the walls of the houses *withal:*

5 The gold for *things* of gold, and the silver for *things* of silver, and for all manner of work *to be made* by the hands of artificers. And who *then* is willing ᴺto consecrate his service this day unto the LORD?

6 Then ᴿthe chief of the fathers and princes of the tribes of Israel, and the captains of thousands and of hundreds, with ᴿthe rulers of the king's work, offered willingly,

7 And gave for the service of the house of God of gold five thousand talents and ten thousand drams, and of silver ten thousand talents, and of brass eighteen thousand talents, and one hundred thousand talents of iron.

8 And they with whom *precious* stones were found gave *them* to the treasure of the house of the Lord, by the hand of [R]Jĕ-hī'-ĕl the Gĕr'-shŏn-īte.

9 Then the people rejoiced, for that they offered willingly, because with perfect heart they [R]offered willingly to the Lord: and David the king also rejoiced with great joy.

David's prayer

10 Wherefore David blessed the Lord before all the congregation: and David said, Blessed *be* thou, Lord God of Israel our father, for ever and ever.

11 [R]Thine, O Lord, *is* the greatness, and the power, and the glory, and the victory, and the majesty: for all *that is* in the heaven and in the earth *is thine;* thine *is* the kingdom, O Lord, and thou art exalted as head above all.

12 [R]Both riches and honour *come* of thee, and thou reignest over all; and in thine hand *is* power and might; and in thine hand *it is* to make great, and to give strength unto all.

13 Now therefore, our God, we thank thee, and praise thy glorious name.

14 But who *am* I, and what *is* my people, that we should [N]be able to offer so willingly after this sort? for all things *come* of thee, and [N]of thine own have we given thee.

15 For [R]we *are* strangers before thee, and sojourners, as *were* all our fathers: [R]our days on the earth *are* as a shadow, and *there is* none [N]abiding.

16 O Lord our God, all this store that we have prepared to build thee an house for thine holy name *cometh* of thine hand, and *is* all thine own.

17 I know also, my God, that thou [R]triest the heart, and [R]hast pleasure in uprightness. As for me, in the uprightness of mine heart I have willingly offered all these things: and now have I seen with joy thy people, which are [N]present here, to offer willingly unto thee.

18 O Lord God of Abraham, Isaac, and of Israel, our fathers, keep this for ever in the imagination of the thoughts of the heart of thy people, and [N]prepare their heart unto thee:

19 And [R]give unto Solomon my son a perfect heart, to keep thy commandments, thy testimonies, and thy statutes, and to do all

CHAP. **29**
BC 1015
8 ch. 26:21
9 2 Cor. 9:7
11 Mat. 6:13
1 Tim. 1:17
Rev. 5:13
12 Rom. 11:36
14 Heb. *retain,* or, *obtain strength*
14 Heb. *of thine hand*
15 Ps. 39:12
Heb. 11:13
1 Pet. 2:11
15 Job 14:2
Ps. 90:9
15 Heb. *expectation*
17 1 Sam. 16:7
ch. 28:9
17 Prov. 11:20
17 Or, *found*
18 Or, *stablish*
19 Ps. 72:1

ver. 2	**19**
ch. 22:14	
1 Ki. 1:35, 39	**22**
Eccl. 8:2	**24**
Heb. *gave the hand under Solomon:* See	**24**
Gen. 24:2 & 47:29	
2 Chr. 30:8	
Ezek. 17:18	
1 Ki. 3:13	**25**
2 Chr. 1:12	
Eccl. 2:9	
2 Sam. 5:4	**27**
1 Ki. 2:11	
2 Sam. 5:5	**27**
Gen. 25:8	**28**
ch. 23:1	**28**
Or, *history*	**29**
Heb. *words*	**29**
Dan. 2:21	**30**

these things, and to build the palace, *for* the which [R]I have made provision.

Solomon made king

20 And David said to all the congregation, Now bless the Lord your God. And all the congregation blessed the Lord God of their fathers, and bowed down their heads, and worshipped the Lord, and the king.

21 And they sacrificed sacrifices unto the Lord, and offered burnt offerings unto the Lord, on the morrow after that day, *even* a thousand bullocks, a thousand rams, *and* a thousand lambs, with their drink offerings, and sacrifices in abundance for all Israel:

22 And did eat and drink before the Lord on that day with great gladness. And they made Solomon the son of David king the second time, and [R]anointed *him* unto the Lord *to be* the chief governor, and Zā'-dŏk *to be* priest.

23 Then Solomon sat on the throne of the Lord as king instead of David his father, and prospered; and all Israel obeyed him.

24 And all the princes, and the mighty men, and all the sons likewise of king David, [R]submitted[N] themselves unto Solomon the king.

25 And the Lord magnified Solomon exceedingly in the sight of all Israel, and [R]bestowed upon him *such* royal majesty as had not been on any king before him in Israel.

Death of David

26 Thus David the son of Jesse reigned over all Israel.

27 [R]And the time that he reigned over Israel *was* forty years; [R]seven years reigned he in Hē'-brŏn, and thirty and three *years* reigned he in Jerusalem.

28 And he [R]died in a good old age, [R]full of days, riches, and honour: and Solomon his son reigned in his stead.

29 Now the acts of David the king, first and last, behold, they *are* written in the [N]book[N] of Samuel the seer, and in the book of Nathan the prophet, and in the book of Gad the seer,

30 With all his reign and his might, [R]and the times that went over him, and over Israel, and over all the kingdoms of the countries.

THE SECOND BOOK OF THE
CHRONICLES

The general character of the Second Book of Chronicles is indicated in the introduction to the first book, in which it is stated that the two books of Chronicles were originally one volume, and that they collectively present a perspective of Israel's history from Adam to the Babylonian captivity.

Second Chronicles takes up the story immediately after the death of David and presents in the first nine chapters an account of the reign of Solomon. The major part of the book is devoted to the history of the divided kingdoms, and in particular to the history of the southern kingdom of Judah. Chronologically, this book parallels the period of time covered in First and Second Kings. Whereas the latter account for both kingdoms, the Second Chronicles is limited primarily to the royal line of David and the southern kingdom, and is concerned with the northern kingdom of Israel only when events in that kingdom have a bearing on events in Judah. It begins in the reign of Solomon in 971 B.C. and ends with the release from captivity by the decree of Cyrus in 539 B.C.

OUTLINE OF THE BOOK:

CHAPTER 1

Solomon's offering at Gibeon

AND ᴿSolomon the son of David was strengthened in his kingdom, and ᴿthe LORD his God *was* with him, and ᴿmagnified him exceedingly.

2 Then Solomon spake unto all Israel, to ᴿthe captains of thousands and of hundreds, and to the judges, and to every governor in all Israel, the chief of the fathers.

3 So Solomon, and all the congregation with him, went to the high place that *was* at ᴿGibeon; for there was the tabernacle of the congregation of God, which Moses the servant of the LORD had made in the wilderness.

4 ᴿBut the ark of God had David brought up from Kĭr'-jăth-jē'-ă-rĭm to *the place which* David had prepared for it: for he had pitched a tent for it at Jerusalem.

5 Moreover ᴿthe brasen altar, that ᴿBĕz'-ă-lĕel the son of Ū'-rī, the son of Hur, had made, ᴺhe put before the tabernacle of the LORD: and Solomon and the congregation sought unto it.

6 And Solomon went up thither to the brasen altar before the LORD, which *was* at the tabernacle of the congregation, and ᴿoffered a thousand burnt offerings upon it.

Solomon's prayer for wisdom

7 ᴿIn that night did God appear unto Solomon, and said unto him, Ask what I shall give thee.

8 And Solomon said unto God, Thou hast shewed great mercy unto David my father, and hast made me ᴿto reign in his stead.

9 Now, O LORD God, let thy promise unto David my father be established: ᴿfor thou hast made me king over a people ᴺlike the dust of the earth in multitude.

10 ᴿGive me now wisdom and knowledge, that I may ᴿgo out and come in before this people: for who can judge this thy people, *that is so* great?

11 ᴿAnd God said to Solomon, Because this was in thine heart, and thou hast not asked riches, wealth, or honour, nor the life of thine enemies, neither yet hast asked long life; but hast asked wisdom and knowledge for thyself, that thou mayest judge my people, over whom I have made thee king:

12 Wisdom and knowledge *is* granted unto thee; and I will give thee riches, and wealth, and honour, such as ᴿnone of the kings have had that *have been* before thee, neither shall there any after thee have the like.

13 Then Solomon came *from his journey* to the high place that *was* at Gibeon to Jerusalem, from before the tabernacle of the congregation, and reigned over Israel.

Solomon's wealth

14 ᴿAnd Solomon gathered chariots and horsemen: and he had a thousand and four hundred chariots, and twelve thousand horsemen, which he placed in the chariot cities, and with the king at Jerusalem.

15 ᴿAnd the king ᴺmade silver and gold at Jerusalem *as plenteous* as stones, and cedar trees made he as the sycomore trees that *are* in the vale for abundance.

16 ᴿAnd ᴺSolomon had horses brought out of Egypt, and linen yarn: the king's merchants received the linen yarn at a price.

17 And they fetched up, and brought forth out of Egypt a chariot for six hundred shē'-kĕls of silver, and an horse for an hundred and fifty: and so brought they out *horses* for all the kings of the Hittites, and for the kings of Syria, ᴺby their means.

Center reference column

CHAP. 1
BC 1015
1 1 Ki. 2:46
1 Gen. 39:2
1 1 Chr. 29:25
2 1 Chr. 27:1
3 1 Ki. 3:4
   1 Chr. 16:39
   & 21:29
4 2 Sam. 6:2, 17
   1 Chr. 15:1
5 Ex. 27:1, 2
   & 38:1, 2
5 Ex. 31:2
5 Or, was *there*
6 1 Ki. 3:4
7 1 Ki. 3:5
8 1 Chr. 28:5
9 1 Ki. 3:7, 8
9 Heb. *much as the dust of the earth*

1 Ki. 3:9   10
Num. 27:17   10
Deut. 31:2
1 Ki. 3:11-13   11
1 Chr. 29:25   12
Eccl. 2:9
1 Ki. 4:26   14
& 10:26, etc.
ch. 9:25
1 Ki. 10:27   15
ch. 9:27
Job 22:24
Heb. *gave*   15
1 Ki. 10:28   16
ch. 9:28
Heb. *the going   16
forth of the horses
which was
Solomon's*
Heb. *by   17
their hand*

CHAPTER 2

Solomon's agreement with Huram

AND Solomon [R]determined to build an house for the name of the LORD, and an house for his kingdom.

2 And [R]Solomon told out threescore and ten thousand men to bear burdens, and fourscore thousand to hew in the mountain, and three thousand and six hundred to oversee them.

3 And Solomon sent to [N]Hū′-răm the king of Tyre, saying, [R]As thou didst deal with David my father, and didst send him cedars to build him an house to dwell therein, *even so deal with me.*

4 Behold, [R]I build an house to the name of the LORD my God, to dedicate *it* to him, *and* [R]to burn before him [N]sweet incense, and for [R]the continual shewbread, and for [R]the burnt offerings morning and evening, on the sabbaths, and on the new moons, and on the solemn feasts of the LORD our God. This *is an ordinance* for ever to Israel.

5 And the house which I build *is* great: for [R]great *is* our God above all gods.

6 [R]But who [N]is able to build him an house, seeing the heaven and heaven of heavens cannot contain him? who *am* I then, that I should build him an house, save only to burn sacrifice before him?

7 Send me now therefore a man cunning to work in gold, and in silver, and in brass, and in iron, and in purple, and crimson, and blue, and that can skill [N]to grave with the cunning men that *are* with me in Judah and in Jerusalem, [R]whom David my father did provide.

8 [R]Send me also cedar trees, fir trees, and [N]ăl′-gŭm trees, out of Lĕb′-ă-nọn: for I know that thy servants can skill to cut timber in Lĕb′-ă-nọn; and, behold, my servants *shall be* with thy servants,

9 Even to prepare me timber in abundance: for the house which I am about to build *shall be* [N]wonderful great.

10 [R]And, behold, I will give to thy servants, the hewers that cut timber, twenty thousand measures of beaten wheat, and twenty thousand measures of barley, and twenty thousand bāths of wine, and twenty thousand bāths of oil.

11 Then Hū′-răm the king of Tyre answered in writing, which he sent to Solomon, [R]Because the LORD hath loved his people, he hath made thee king over them.

12 Hū′-răm said moreover, [R]Blessed *be* the LORD God of Israel, [R]that made heaven and earth, who hath given to David the king a wise son, [N]endued with prudence and understand-

ing, that might build an house for the LORD, and an house for his kingdom.

13 And now I have sent a cunning man, endued with understanding, of Hū′-răm my father's,

14 [R]The son of a woman of the daughters of Dan, and his father *was* a man of Tyre, skilful to work in gold, and in silver, in brass, in iron, in stone, and in timber, in purple, in blue, and in fine linen, and in crimson; also to grave any manner of graving, and to find out every device which shall be put to him, with thy cunning men, and with the cunning men of my lord David thy father.

15 Now therefore the wheat, and the barley, the oil, and the wine, which [R]my lord hath spoken of, let him send unto his servants:

16 [R]And we will cut wood out of Lĕb′-ă-nọn, [N]as much as thou shalt need: and we will bring it to thee in floats by sea to [N]Joppa; and thou shalt carry it up to Jerusalem.

Solomon's forced labour

17 [R]And Solomon numbered all [N]the strangers that *were* in the land of Israel, after the numbering wherewith [R]David his father had numbered them; and they were found an hundred and fifty thousand and three thousand and six hundred.

18 And he set [R]threescore and ten thousand of them *to be* bearers of burdens, and fourscore thousand *to be* hewers in the mountain, and three thousand and six hundred overseers to set the people a work.

CHAPTER 3

Building the temple

THEN [R]Solomon began to build the house of the LORD at [R]Jerusalem in mount Mō-rī′-ăh, [N]where *the LORD* appeared unto David his father, in the place that David had prepared in the threshingfloor of [R]Ôr′-năn [N] the Jĕb′-ū-śīte.

2 And he began to build in the second *day* of the second month, in the fourth year of his reign.

3 Now these *are* the things [R]wherein Solomon was [N]instructed for the building of the house of God. The length by cubits after the first measure *was* threescore cubits, and the breadth twenty cubits.

4 And the [R]porch that *was* in the front *of the house,* the length *of it was* according to the breadth of the house, twenty cubits, and the height *was* an hundred and twenty: and he overlaid it within with pure gold.

5 And [R]the greater house he ceiled with fir

CHAP. 2
BC 1015

1 1 Ki. 5:5
2 ver. 18
1 Ki. 5:15
3 Or, *Hiram*
3 1 Chr. 14:1
4 ver. 1
4 Ex. 30:7
4 Heb. *incense of spices* .
4 Ex. 25:30
Lev. 24:8
4 Num. 28:3, 9, 11
5 Ps. 135:5
6 1 Ki. 8:27
Is. 66:1
6 Heb. *hath retained,* or, *obtained strength*
7 Heb. *to grave gravings*
7 1 Chr. 22:15
8 1 Ki. 5:6
8 Or, *almuggim,* 1 Ki. 10:11
9 Heb. *great and wonderful*
10 1 Ki. 5:11
11 1 Ki. 10:9
ch. 9:8
12 1 Ki. 5:7
12 Gen. 1, & 2
Acts 4:24
& 14:15
Rev. 10:6
12 Heb. *knowing prudence and understanding*

1 Ki. 7:13   14
ver. 10   15
1 Ki. 5:8, 9   16
Heb. *according to all thy need*   16
Heb. *Japho,*   16
Josh. 19:46
Acts 9:36
As ver. 2   17
1 Ki. 5:13
ch. 8:7, 8
Heb. *the men the strangers*   17
1 Chr. 22:2   17
As it is ver. 2   18

CHAP. 3
BC 1012

1 Ki. 6:1   1
Gen. 22:2   1
Or, *which was seen of David his father*   1
1 Chr. 21:18   1
& 22:1
Or, *Araunah,*   1
2 Sam. 24:18
1 Ki. 6:2   3
Heb. *founded*   3
1 Ki. 6:3   4
1 Ki. 6:15   5

tree, which he overlaid with fine gold, and set thereon palm trees and chains.

6 And he [N]garnished the house with precious stones for beauty: and the gold *was* gold of Pär-vā'-ĭm.

7 He overlaid also the house, the beams, the posts, and the walls thereof, and the doors thereof, with gold; and graved chĕr'-ū-bĭms on the walls.

8 And he made the most holy house, the length whereof *was* according to the breadth of the house, twenty cubits, and the breadth thereof twenty cubits: and he overlaid it with fine gold, *amounting* to six hundred talents.

9 And the weight of the nails *was* fifty shē'-kĕls of gold. And he overlaid the upper chambers with gold.

10 [R]And in the most holy house he made two chĕr'-ū-bĭms [N]of image work, and overlaid them with gold.

11 And the wings of the chĕr'-ū-bĭms *were* twenty cubits long: one wing *of the one cherub was* five cubits, reaching to the wall of the house: and the other wing *was likewise* five cubits, reaching to the wing of the other cherub.

12 And *one* wing of the other cherub *was* five cubits, reaching to the wall of the house: and the other wing *was* five cubits *also,* joining to the wing of the other cherub.

13 The wings of these chĕr'-ū-bĭms spread themselves forth twenty cubits: and they stood on their feet, and their faces *were* [N]inward.

14 And he made the [R]vail *of* blue, and purple, and crimson, and fine linen, and [N]wrought chĕr'-ū-bĭms thereon.

15 Also he made before the house [R]two pillars of thirty and five cubits [N]high, and the chapiter that *was* on the top of each of them *was* five cubits.

16 And he made chains, *as* in the oracle, and put *them* on the heads of the pillars; and made [R]an hundred pomegranates, and put *them* on the chains.

17 And he [R]reared up the pillars before the temple, one on the right hand, and the other on the left; and called the name of that on the right hand [N]Jā'-chĭn, and the name of that on the left [N]Bō'-ăz.

CHAPTER 4

Temple furnishings

MOREOVER he made [R]an altar of brass, twenty cubits the length thereof, and twenty cubits the breadth thereof, and ten cubits the height thereof.

CHAP. 3
BC 1012
6 Heb. *covered*
10 1 Ki. 6:23
10 Or (as some think), *of moveable work*
13 Or, *toward the house*
14 Ex. 26:31
   Mat. 27:51
   Heb. 9:3
14 Heb. *caused to ascend*
15 1 Ki. 7:15
   Jer. 52:21
15 Heb. *long*
16 1 Ki. 7:20
17 1 Ki. 7:21
17 i.e. *He shall establish*
17 i.e. *In it is strength*

CHAP. 4
BC 1012
1 Ex. 27:1, 2
2 Ki. 16:14
  Ezek. 43:13, 16

1 Ki. 7:23   2
Heb. *from his brim to his brim*   2
1 Ki. 7:24-26   3
Or, *like a lilyflower*   5
See 1 Ki. 7:26   5
1 Ki. 7:38   6
Heb. *the work of burnt offering*   6
1 Ki. 7:49   7
Ex. 25:31   7
1 Chr. 28:12, 19
1 Ki. 7:48   8
Or, *bowls*   8
1 Ki. 6:36   9
1 Ki. 7:39   10
See 1 Ki. 7:40   11
Or, *bowls*   11
Heb. *finished to make*   11
1 Ki. 7:41   12
See 1 Ki. 7:20   13
Heb. *upon the face*   13
1 Ki. 7:27, 43   14
Or, *caldrons*   14
1 Ki. 7:14, 45   16
Heb. *made bright, or, scoured*   16
1 Ki. 7:46   17

2 [R]Also he made a molten sea of ten cubits [N]from brim to brim, round in compass, and five cubits the height thereof; and a line of thirty cubits did compass it round about.

3 [R]And under it *was* the similitude of oxen, which did compass it round about: ten in a cubit, compassing the sea round about. Two rows of oxen *were* cast, when it was cast.

4 It stood upon twelve oxen, three looking toward the north, and three looking toward the west, and three looking toward the south, and three looking toward the east: and the sea *was set* above upon them, and all their hinder parts *were* inward.

5 And the thickness of it *was* an handbreadth, and the brim of it like the work of the brim of a cup, [N]with flowers of lilies; *and* it received and held [R]three thousand bäths.

6 He made also [R]ten lavers, and put five on the right hand, and five on the left, to wash in them: [N]such things as they offered for the burnt offering they washed in them; but the sea *was* for the priests to wash in.

7 [R]And he made ten candlesticks of gold [R]according to their form, and set *them* in the temple, five on the right hand, and five on the left.

8 [R]He made also ten tables, and placed *them* in the temple, five on the right side, and five on the left. And he made an hundred [N]basins of gold.

9 Furthermore [R]he made the court of the priests, and the great court, and doors for the court, and overlaid the doors of them with brass.

10 And [R]he set the sea on the right side of the east end, over against the south.

11 And [R]Hū'-răm made the pots and the shovels, and the [N]basins. And Hū'-răm [N]finished the work that he was to make for king Solomon for the house of God;

12 *To wit,* the two pillars, and [R]the pommels, and the chapiters *which were* on the top of the two pillars, and the two wreaths to cover the two pommels of the chapiters which *were* on the top of the pillars;

13 And [R]four hundred pomegranates on the two wreaths; two rows of pomegranates on each wreath, to cover the two pommels of the chapiters which *were* [N]upon the pillars.

14 He made also [R]bases, and [N]lavers made he upon the bases;

15 One sea, and twelve oxen under it.

16 The pots also, and the shovels, and the fleshhooks, and all their instruments, did [R]Hū'-răm his father make to king Solomon for the house of the LORD of [N]bright brass.

17 [R]In the plain of Jordan did the king cast

them, in the ᴺclay ground between Sŭc'-cōth and Zĕr-ĕ-dā'-thăh.

18 ᴿThus Solomon made all these vessels in great abundance: for the weight of the brass could not be found out.

19 And ᴿSolomon made all the vessels that *were for* the house of God, the golden altar also, and the tables whereon ᴿthe shewbread *was set;*

20 Moreover the candlesticks with their lamps, that they should burn ᴿafter the manner before the oracle, of pure gold;

21 And ᴿthe flowers, and the lamps, and the tongs, *made he of* gold, *and* that ᴺperfect gold;

22 And the snuffers, and the ᴺbasins, and the spoons, and the censers, *of* pure gold: and the entry of the house, the inner doors thereof for the most holy *place,* and the doors of the house of the temple, *were of* gold.

CHAPTER 5

The ark placed in the temple

THUS ᴿall the work that Solomon made for the house of the LORD was finished: and Solomon brought in *all* the things that David his father had dedicated; and the silver, and the gold, and all the instruments, put he among the treasures of the house of God.

2 ᴿThen Solomon assembled the elders of Israel, and all the heads of the tribes, the chief of the fathers of the children of Israel, unto Jerusalem, to bring up the ark of the covenant of the LORD ᴿout of the city of David, which *is* Zion.

3 ᴿWherefore all the men of Israel assembled themselves unto the king ᴿin the feast which *was* in the seventh month.

4 And all the elders of Israel came; and the Levites took up the ark.

5 And they brought up the ark, and the tabernacle of the congregation, and all the holy vessels that *were* in the tabernacle, these did the priests *and* the Levites bring up.

6 Also king Solomon, and all the congregation of Israel that were assembled unto him before the ark, sacrificed sheep and oxen, which could not be told nor numbered for multitude.

7 And the priests brought in the ark of the covenant of the LORD unto his place, to the oracle of the house, into the most holy *place,* *even* under the wings of the chĕr'-ū-bĭms:

8 For the chĕr'-ū-bĭms spread forth *their* wings over the place of the ark, and the chĕr'-ū-bĭms covered the ark and the staves thereof above.

9 And they drew out the staves *of the ark,* that the ends of the staves were seen from the

ark before the oracle; but they were not seen without. And ᴺthere it is unto this day.

10 *There was* nothing in the ark save the two tables which Moses ᴿput *therein* at Hôr'-ĕb, ᴺwhen the LORD made *a covenant* with the children of Israel, when they came out of Egypt.

11 And it came to pass, when the priests were come out of the holy *place:* (for all the priests *that were* ᴺpresent were sanctified, *and* did not *then* wait by course:

12 ᴿAlso the Levites *which were* the singers, all of them of Ā'-săph, of Hē'-măn, of Jĕ-dū'-thŭn, with their sons and their brethren, *being* arrayed in white linen, having cymbals and psalteries and harps, stood at the east end of the altar, ᴿand with them an hundred and twenty priests sounding with trumpets:)

13 It came even to pass, as the trumpeters and singers *were* as one, to make one sound to be heard in praising and thanking the LORD; and when they lifted up *their* voice with the trumpets and cymbals and instruments of musick, and praised the LORD, *saying,* ᴿFor *he is* good; for his mercy *endureth* for ever: that *then* the house was filled with a cloud, *even* the house of the LORD;

14 So that the priests could not stand to minister by reason of the cloud: ᴿfor the glory of the LORD had filled the house of God.

CHAPTER 6

Solomon's address to the people

THEN ᴿsaid Solomon, The LORD hath said that he would dwell in the ᴿthick darkness.

2 But I have built an house of habitation for thee, and a place for thy dwelling for ever.

3 And the king turned his face, and blessed the whole congregation of Israel: and all the congregation of Israel stood.

4 And he said, Blessed *be* the LORD God of Israel, who hath with his hands fulfilled *that* which he spake with his mouth to my father David, saying,

5 Since the day that I brought forth my people out of the land of Egypt I chose no city among all the tribes of Israel to build an house in, that my name might be there; neither chose I any man to be a ruler over my people Israel:

6 ᴿBut I have chosen Jerusalem, that my name might be there; and ᴿhave chosen David to be over my people Israel.

7 Now ᴿit was in the heart of David my father to build an house for the name of the LORD God of Israel.

8 But the LORD said to David my father, Forasmuch as it was in thine heart to build an

---

CHAP. 4

BC 1012

17 Heb. *thicknesses of the ground*
18 1 Ki. 7:47
19 1 Ki. 7:48-50
20 Ex. 25:30
21 Ex. 27:20, 21
21 Ex. 25:31, etc.
21 Heb. *perfections of gold*
22 Or, *bowls*

CHAP. 5

BC 1005

1 1 Ki. 7:51
2 1 Ki. 8:1, etc.
2 2 Sam. 6:12
3 1 Ki. 8:2
3 See ch. 7:8-10

Or, *they are there,* 9
as 1 Ki. 8:8
Deut. 10:2, 5 10
ch. 6:11
Or, *where* 10
Heb. *found* 11
1 Chr. 25:1 12
1 Chr. 15:24 12
Ps. 136 13
See 1 Chr. 16:34, 41
Ex. 40:35 14
ch. 7:2

CHAP. 6

BC 1004

1 Ki. 8:12, etc. 1
Lev. 16:2 1
ch. 12:13 6
1 Chr. 28:4 6
2 Sam. 7:2 7
1 Chr. 17:1 & 28:2

house for my name, thou didst well in that it was in thine heart:

9 Notwithstanding thou shalt not build the house; but thy son which shall come forth out of thy loins, he shall build the house for my name.

10 The LORD therefore hath performed his word that he hath spoken: for I am risen up in the room of David my father, and am set on the throne of Israel, as the LORD promised, and have built the house for the name of the LORD God of Israel.

11 And in it have I put the ark, ᴿwherein *is* the covenant of the LORD, that he made with the children of Israel.

Solomon's prayer of dedication

12 ᴿAnd he stood before the altar of the LORD in the presence of all the congregation of Israel, and spread forth his hands:

13 For Solomon had made a brasen scaffold, of five cubits ᴺlong, and five cubits broad, and three cubits high, and had set it in the midst of the court: and upon it he stood, and kneeled down upon his knees before all the congregation of Israel, and spread forth his hands toward heaven,

14 And said, O LORD God of Israel, ᴿ*there is* no God like thee in the heaven, nor in the earth; which keepest covenant, and *shewest* mercy unto thy servants, that walk before thee with all their hearts:

15 ᴿThou which hast kept with thy servant David my father that which thou hast promised him; and spakest with thy mouth, and hast fulfilled *it* with thine hand, as *it is* this day.

16 Now therefore, O LORD God of Israel, keep with thy servant David my father that which thou hast promised him, saying, ᴿThereᴺ shall not fail thee a man in my sight to sit upon the throne of Israel; ᴿyet so that thy children take heed to their way to walk in my law, as thou hast walked before me.

17 Now then, O LORD God of Israel, let thy word be verified, which thou hast spoken unto thy servant David.

18 But will God in very deed dwell with men on the earth? ᴿbehold, heaven and the heaven of heavens cannot contain thee; how much less this house which I have built!

19 Have respect therefore to the prayer of thy servant, and to his supplication, O LORD my God, to hearken unto the cry and the prayer which thy servant prayeth before thee:

20 That thine eyes may be open upon this house day and night, upon the place whereof thou hast said that thou wouldest put thy name there; to hearken unto the prayer which thy servant prayeth ᴺtoward this place.

21 Hearken therefore unto the supplications of thy servant, and of thy people Israel, which they shall ᴺmake toward this place: hear thou from thy dwelling place, *even* from heaven; and when thou hearest, forgive.

22 If a man sin against his neighbour, ᴺand an oath be laid upon him to make him swear, and the oath come before thine altar in this house;

23 Then hear thou from heaven, and do, and judge thy servants, by requiting the wicked, by recompensing his way upon his own head; and by justifying the righteous, by giving him according to his righteousness.

24 And if thy people Israel ᴺbe put to the worse before the enemy, because they have sinned against thee; and shall return and confess thy name, and pray and make supplication before thee ᴺin this house;

25 Then hear thou from the heavens, and forgive the sin of thy people Israel, and bring them again unto the land which thou gavest to them and to their fathers.

26 When the ᴿheaven is shut up, and there is no rain, because they have sinned against thee; *yet* if they pray toward this place, and confess thy name, and turn from their sin, when thou dost afflict them;

27 Then hear thou from heaven, and forgive the sin of thy servants, and of thy people Israel, when thou hast taught them the good way, wherein they should walk; and send rain upon thy land, which thou hast given unto thy people for an inheritance.

28 If there ᴿbe dearth in the land, if there be pestilence, if there be blasting, or mildew, locusts, or caterpillers; if their enemies besiege them ᴺin the cities of their land; whatsoever sore or whatsoever sickness *there be*:

29 *Then* what prayer *or* what supplication soever shall be made of any man, or of all thy people Israel, when every one shall know his own sore and his own grief, and shall spread forth his hands ᴺin this house:

30 Then hear thou from heaven thy dwelling place, and forgive, and render unto every man according unto all his ways, whose heart thou knowest; (for thou only ᴿknowest the hearts of the children of men:)

31 That they may fear thee, to walk in thy ways, ᴺso long as they live ᴺin the land which thou gavest unto our fathers.

32 Moreover concerning the stranger, ᴿwhich is not of thy people Israel, but is come from a far country for thy great name's sake, and thy mighty hand, and thy stretched out arm; if they come and pray in this house;

33 Then hear thou from the heavens, *even* from thy dwelling place, and do according to

all that the stranger calleth to thee for; that all people of the earth may know thy name, and fear thee, as *doth* thy people Israel, and may know that ᴺthis house which I have built is called by thy name.

34 If thy people go out to war against their enemies by the way that thou shalt send them, and they pray unto thee toward this city which thou hast chosen, and the house which I have built for thy name;

35 Then hear thou from the heavens their prayer and their supplication, and maintain their ᴺcause.

36 If they sin against thee, (for *there is* ᴿno man which sinneth not,) and thou be angry with them, and deliver them over before *their* enemies, and ᴺthey carry them away captives unto a land far off or near;

37 Yet *if* they ᴺbethink themselves in the land whither they are carried captive, and turn and pray unto thee in the land of their captivity, saying, We have sinned, we have done amiss, and have dealt wickedly;

38 If they return to thee with all their heart and with all their soul in the land of their captivity, whither they have carried them captives, and pray toward their land, which thou gavest unto their fathers, and *toward* the city which thou hast chosen, and toward the house which I have built for thy name:

39 Then hear thou from the heavens, *even* from thy dwelling place, their prayer and their supplications, and maintain their ᴺcause, and forgive thy people which have sinned against thee.

40 Now, my God, let, I beseech thee, thine eyes be open, and *let* thine ears *be* attent ᴺunto the prayer *that is made* in this place.

41 Now ᴿtherefore arise, O Lᴏʀᴅ God, into thy ᴿresting place, thou, and the ark of thy strength: let thy priests, O Lᴏʀᴅ God, be clothed with salvation, and let thy saints ᴿrejoice in goodness.

42 O Lᴏʀᴅ God, turn not away the face of thine anointed: ᴿremember the mercies of David thy servant.

CHAPTER 7

Fire consumes the offerings

Nᴼᵂ ᴿwhen Solomon had made an end of praying, the ᴿfire came down from heaven, and consumed the burnt offering and the sacrifices; and ᴿthe glory of the Lᴏʀᴅ filled the house.

2 ᴿAnd the priests could not enter into the house of the Lᴏʀᴅ, because the glory of the Lᴏʀᴅ had filled the Lᴏʀᴅ's house.

CHAP. **6**
BC 1004
33 Heb. *thy name is called upon this house*
35 Or, *right*
36 Prov. 20:9
Eccl. 7:20
Jas. 3:2
1 John 1:8
36 Heb. *they that take them captives carry them away*
37 Heb. *bring back to their heart*
39 Or, *right*
40 Heb. *to the prayer of this place*
41 Ps. 132:8-10, 16
41 1 Chr. 28:2
41 Neh. 9:25
42 Ps. 132:1
Is. 55:3

CHAP. **7**
BC 1004
1 1 Ki. 8:54
1 Lev. 9:24
Judg. 6:21
1 Ki. 18:38
1 Chr. 21:26
1 1 Ki. 8:10, 11
2 ch. 5:41

---

ch. 5:13		**3**
Ps. 136:1
1 Chr. 16:41		**3**
ch. 20:21
1 Ki. 8:62, 63		**4**
1 Chr. 15:16		**6**
Heb. *by their hand* **6**
ch. 5:12		**6**
1 Ki. 8:64		**7**
1 Ki. 8:65		**8**
Josh. 13:3		**8**
Heb. *a restraint*		**9**
1 Ki. 8:66		**10**
1 Ki. 9:1, etc.		**11**
Deut. 12:5		**12**
ch. 6:26, 28		**13**
Heb. *upon whom my name is called* **14**
Jas. 4:10		**14**

---

3 And when all the children of Israel saw how the fire came down, and the glory of the Lᴏʀᴅ upon the house, they bowed themselves with their faces to the ground upon the pavement, and worshipped, and praised the Lᴏʀᴅ, ᴿ*saying,* For *he is* good; ᴿfor his mercy *endureth* for ever.

Other sacrifices

4 ᴿThen the king and all the people offered sacrifices before the Lᴏʀᴅ.

5 And king Solomon offered a sacrifice of twenty and two thousand oxen, and an hundred and twenty thousand sheep: so the king and all the people dedicated the house of God.

6 ᴿAnd the priests waited on their offices: the Levites also with instruments of musick of the Lᴏʀᴅ, which David the king had made to praise the Lᴏʀᴅ, because his mercy *endureth* for ever, when David praised ᴺby their ministry; and ᴿthe priests sounded trumpets before them, and all Israel stood.

7 Moreover ᴿSolomon hallowed the middle of the court that *was* before the house of the Lᴏʀᴅ: for there he offered burnt offerings, and the fat of the peace offerings, because the brasen altar which Solomon had made was not able to receive the burnt offerings, and the meat offerings, and the fat.

8 ᴿAlso at the same time Solomon kept the feast seven days, and all Israel with him, a very great congregation, from the entering in of Hā′-măth unto ᴿthe river of Egypt.

9 And in the eighth day they made ᴺa solemn assembly: for they kept the dedication of the altar seven days, and the feast seven days.

10 And ᴿon the three and twentieth day of the seventh month he sent the people away into their tents, glad and merry in heart for the goodness that the Lᴏʀᴅ had shewed unto David, and to Solomon, and to Israel his people.

The LORD'S promise to Solomon

11 Thus ᴿSolomon finished the house of the Lᴏʀᴅ, and the king's house: and all that came into Solomon's heart to make in the house of the Lᴏʀᴅ, and in his own house, he prosperously effected.

12 And the Lᴏʀᴅ appeared to Solomon by night, and said unto him, I have heard thy prayer, ᴿand have chosen this place to myself for an house of sacrifice.

13 ᴿIf I shut up heaven that there be no rain, or if I command the locusts to devour the land, or if I send pestilence among my people;

14 If my people, ᴺwhich are called by my name, shall ᴿhumble themselves, and pray, and seek my face, and turn from their wicked

ways; ^Rthen will I hear from heaven, and will forgive their sin, and will heal their land.

15 Now ^Rmine eyes shall be open, and mine ears attent ^Nunto the prayer *that is made* in this place.

16 For now have ^RI chosen and sanctified this house, that my name may be there for ever: and mine eyes and mine heart shall be there perpetually.

17 ^RAnd as for thee, if thou wilt walk before me, as David thy father walked, and do according to all that I have commanded thee, and shalt observe my statutes and my judgments;

18 Then will I stablish the throne of thy kingdom, according as I have covenanted with David thy father, saying, ^RThere^N shall not fail thee a man *to be* ruler in Israel.

19 ^RBut if ye turn away, and forsake my statutes and my commandments, which I have set before you, and shall go and serve other gods, and worship them;

20 Then will I pluck them up by the roots out of my land which I have given them; and this house, which I have sanctified for my name, will I cast out of my sight, and will make it *to be* a proverb and a byword among all nations.

21 And this house, which is high, shall be an astonishment to every one that passeth by it; so that he shall say, ^RWhy hath the LORD done thus unto this land, and unto this house?

22 And it shall be answered, Because they forsook the LORD God of their fathers, which brought them forth out of the land of Egypt, and laid hold on other gods, and worshipped them, and served them: therefore hath he brought all this evil upon them.

CHAPTER 8

Solomon uses forced labour

A**ND** ^Rit came to pass at the end of twenty years, wherein Solomon had built the house of the LORD, and his own house,

2 That the cities which Hū'-răm had restored to Solomon, Solomon built them, and caused the children of Israel to dwell there.

3 And Solomon went to Hā'-măth-zō'-băh, and prevailed against it.

4 ^RAnd he built Tăd'-môr in the wilderness, and all the store cities, which he built in Hā'-măth.

5 Also he built Bĕth-hôr'-ŏn the upper, and Bĕth-hôr'-ŏn the nether, fenced cities, with walls, gates, and bars;

6 And Bā'-ă-lăth, and all the store cities that Solomon had, and all the chariot cities, and the cities of the horsemen, and ^Nall that Solo-

CHAP. 7
BC 1004
14 ch. 6:27, 30
15 ch. 6:40
15 Heb. *to the prayer of this place*
16 1 Ki. 9:3
ch. 6:6
17 1 Ki. 9:4, etc.
18 ch. 6:16
18 Heb. *There shall not be cut off to thee*
19 Lev. 26:14, 33
Deut. 28:15, 36, 37
21 Deut. 29:24

CHAP. 8
BC 992
1 1 Ki. 9:10, etc.
4 1 Ki. 9:17, etc.
6 Heb. *all the desire of Solomon which he desired to build*

1 Ki. 9:20, etc.   7
See 1 Ki. 9:23   10
1 Ki. 3:1   11
  & 7:8 & 9:24
Heb. *holiness*   11
Ex. 29:38   13
Num. 28:3, 9,
  11, 26
  & 29:1, etc.
Ex. 23:14   13
Deut. 16:16
1 Chr. 24:3   14
1 Chr. 25:1   14
1 Chr. 9:17   14
  & 26:1
Heb. *so was the*   14
commandment of David the man of God
1 Ki. 9:26   17
Or, *Elath*,   17
Deut. 2:8
2 Ki. 14:22
1 Ki. 9:27   18
ch. 9:10, 13

mon desired to build in Jerusalem, and in Lĕb'-ă-nŏn, and throughout all the land of his dominion.

7 ^R*As for* all the people *that were* left of the Hittites, and the Amorites, and the Pĕ-rĭz'-zītes, and the Hī'-vītes, and the Jĕb'-ū-šītes, which *were* not of Israel,

8 *But* of their children, who were left after them in the land, whom the children of Israel consumed not, them did Solomon make to pay tribute until this day.

9 But of the children of Israel did Solomon make no servants for his work; but they *were* men of war, and chief of his captains, and captains of his chariots and horsemen.

10 And these *were* the chief of king Solomon's officers, *even* ^Rtwo hundred and fifty, that bare rule over the people.

11 And Solomon ^Rbrought up the daughter of Pharaoh out of the city of David unto the house that he had built for her: for he said, My wife shall not dwell in the house of David king of Israel, because *the places are* ^Nholy, whereunto the ark of the LORD hath come.

Burnt offerings

12 Then Solomon offered burnt offerings unto the LORD on the altar of the LORD, which he had built before the porch,

13 Even after a certain rate ^Revery day, offering according to the commandment of Moses, on the sabbaths, and on the new moons, and on the solemn feasts, ^Rthree times in the year, *even* in the feast of unleavened bread, and in the feast of weeks, and in the feast of tabernacles.

14 And he appointed, according to the order of David his father, the ^Rcourses of the priests to their service, and ^Rthe Levites to their charges, to praise and minister before the priests, as the duty of every day required: the ^Rporters also by their courses at every gate: for ^Nso had David the man of God commanded.

15 And they departed not from the commandment of the king unto the priests and Levites concerning any matter, or concerning the treasures.

16 Now all the work of Solomon was prepared unto the day of the foundation of the house of the LORD, and until it was finished. *So* the house of the LORD was perfected.

Solomon's fleet

17 Then went Solomon to ^RĒ'-zī-ŏn-gē'-bĕr, and to ^NĒ'-lōth, at the sea side in the land of Ē'-dom.

18 ^RAnd Hū'-răm sent him by the hands of his servants ships, and servants that had knowledge of the sea; and they went with the

servants of Solomon to ō'-phĭr, and took thence four hundred and fifty talents of gold, and brought *them* to king Solomon.

CHAPTER 9

Queen of Sheba's visit

AND ᴿwhen the queen of Shē'-bă heard of the fame of Solomon, she came to prove Solomon with hard questions at Jerusalem, with a very great company, and camels that bare spices, and gold in abundance, and precious stones: and when she was come to Solomon, she communed with him of all that was in her heart.

2 And Solomon told her all her questions: and there was nothing hid from Solomon which he told her not.

3 And when the queen of Shē'-bă had seen the wisdom of Solomon, and the house that he had built,

4 And the meat of his table, and the sitting of his servants, and the attendance of his ministers, and their apparel; his ᴺcupbearers also, and their apparel; and his ascent by which he went up into the house of the LORD; there was no more spirit in her.

5 And she said to the king, *It was* a true ᴺreport which I heard in mine own land of thine ᴺacts, and of thy wisdom:

6 Howbeit I believed not their words, until I came, and mine eyes had seen *it:* and, behold, the one half of the greatness of thy wisdom was not told me: *for* thou exceedest the fame that I heard.

7 Happy *are* thy men, and happy *are* these thy servants, which stand continually before thee, and hear thy wisdom.

8 Blessed be the LORD thy God, which delighted in thee to set thee on his throne, *to be* king for the LORD thy God: because thy God loved Israel, to establish them for ever, therefore made he thee king over them, to do judgment and justice.

9 And she gave the king an hundred and twenty talents of gold, and of spices great abundance, and precious stones: neither was there any such spice as the queen of Shē'-bă gave king Solomon.

10 And the servants also of Hū'-răm, and the servants of Solomon, ᴿwhich brought gold from ō'-phĭr, brought ᴿăl'-gŭm trees and precious stones.

11 And the king made *of* the ăl'-gŭm trees ᴺᴺterraces to the house of the LORD, and to the king's palace, and harps and psalteries for singers: and there were none such seen before in the land of Judah.

Center column references

CHAP. **9**

BC 992

1 1 Ki. 10:1, etc.
Mat. 12:42
Luke 11:31
4 Or, *butlers*
5 Heb. *word*
5 Or, *sayings*
10 ch. 8:18
10 1 Ki. 10:11,
almug trees
11 Or, *stairs*
11 Heb. *highways*

Or, *captains*   **14**
Heb. *hands*   **18**
Heb. *shut up*   **20**
Or, there was   **20**
no silver in them
Or, *elephants'*   **21**
teeth
1 Ki. 4:26   **25**
& 10:26
ch. 1:14
1 Ki. 4:21   **26**
Gen. 15:18   **26**
Ps. 72:8
i.e. *Euphrates*   **26**

12 And king Solomon gave to the queen of Shē'-bă all her desire, whatsoever she asked, beside *that* which she had brought unto the king. So she turned, and went away to her own land, she and her servants.

Solomon's unsurpassed wealth

13 Now the weight of gold that came to Solomon in one year was six hundred and threescore and six talents of gold;

14 Beside *that which* chapmen and merchants brought. And all the kings of Arabia and ᴺgovernors of the country brought gold and silver to Solomon.

15 And king Solomon made two hundred targets *of* beaten gold: six hundred shē'-kĕls of beaten gold went to one target.

16 And three hundred shields *made he of* beaten gold: three hundred shē'-kĕls of gold went to one shield. And the king put them in the house of the forest of Lĕb'-ă-nọn.

17 Moreover the king made a great throne of ivory, and overlaid it with pure gold.

18 And *there were* six steps to the throne, with a footstool of gold, *which were* fastened to the throne, and ᴺstays on each side of the sitting place, and two lions standing by the stays:

19 And twelve lions stood there on the one side and on the other upon the six steps. There was not the like made in any kingdom.

20 And all the drinking vessels of king Solomon *were of* gold, and all the vessels of the house of the forest of Lĕb'-ă-nọn *were of* ᴺpure gold: ᴺnone *were of* silver; it was *not* any thing accounted of in the days of Solomon.

21 For the king's ships went to Tarshish with the servants of Hū'-răm: every three years once came the ships of Tarshish bringing gold, and silver, ᴺivory, and apes, and peacocks.

22 And king Solomon passed all the kings of the earth in riches and wisdom.

23 And all the kings of the earth sought the presence of Solomon, to hear his wisdom, that God had put in his heart.

24 And they brought every man his present, vessels of silver, and vessels of gold, and raiment, harness, and spices, horses, and mules, a rate year by year.

25 And Solomon ᴿhad four thousand stalls for horses and chariots, and twelve thousand horsemen; whom he bestowed in the chariot cities, and with the king at Jerusalem.

26 ᴿAnd he reigned over all the kings ᴿfrom the ᴺriver even unto the land of the Philistines, and to the border of Egypt.

27 [R]And the king [N]made silver in Jerusalem as stones, and cedar trees made he as the sycomore trees that *are* in the low plains in abundance.

28 [R]And they brought unto Solomon horses out of Egypt, and out of all lands.

Death of Solomon

29 [R]Now the rest of the acts of Solomon, first and last, *are* they not written in the [N]book of Nathan the prophet, and in the prophecy of [R]Ă-hī'-jăh the Shī'-lō-nīte, and in the visions of [R]Ĭd'-dō the seer against Jĕr-ŏ-bō'-ăm the son of Nē'-băt?

30 [R]And Solomon reigned in Jerusalem over all Israel forty years.

31 And Solomon slept with his fathers, and he was buried in the city of David his father: and Rē-hŏ-bō'-ăm his son reigned in his stead.

CHAPTER 10

Rehoboam forsakes good counsel

AND [R]Rē-hŏ-bō'-ăm went to Shē'-chem: for to Shē'-chem were all Israel come to make him king.

2 And it came to pass, when Jĕr-ŏ-bō'-ăm the son of Nē'-băt, who *was* in Egypt, [R]whither he had fled from the presence of Solomon the king, heard *it*, that Jĕr-ŏ-bō'-ăm returned out of Egypt.

3 And they sent and called him. So Jĕr-ŏ-bō'-ăm and all Israel came and spake to Rē-hŏ-bō'-ăm, saying,

4 Thy father made our yoke grievous: now therefore ease thou somewhat the grievous servitude of thy father, and his heavy yoke that he put upon us, and we will serve thee.

5 And he said unto them, Come again unto me after three days. And the people departed.

6 And king Rē-hŏ-bō'-ăm took counsel with the old men that had stood before Solomon his father while he yet lived, saying, What counsel give ye *me* to return answer to this people?

7 And they spake unto him, saying, If thou be kind to this people, and please them, and speak good words to them, they will be thy servants for ever.

8 But he forsook the counsel which the old men gave him, and took counsel with the young men that were brought up with him, that stood before him.

9 And he said unto them, What advice give ye that we may return answer to this people, which have spoken to me, saying, Ease somewhat the yoke that thy father did put upon us?

10 And the young men that were brought up with him spake unto him, saying, Thus shalt

thou answer the people that spake unto thee, saying, Thy father made our yoke heavy, but make thou *it* somewhat lighter for us; thus shalt thou say unto them, My little *finger* shall be thicker than my father's loins.

11 For whereas my father [N]put a heavy yoke upon you, I will put more to your yoke: my father chastised you with whips, but I *will chastise you* with scorpions.

Revolt of the ten tribes

12 So Jĕr-ŏ-bō'-ăm and all the people came to Rē-hŏ-bō'-ăm on the third day, as the king bade, saying, Come again to me on the third day.

13 And the king answered them roughly; and king Rē-hŏ-bō'-ăm forsook the counsel of the old men,

14 And answered them after the advice of the young men, saying, My father made your yoke heavy, but I will add thereto: my father chastised you with whips, but I *will chastise you* with scorpions.

15 So the king hearkened not unto the people: [R]for the cause was of God, that the LORD might perform his word, which he spake by the [R]hand of Ă-hī'-jăh the Shī'-lō-nīte to Jĕr-ŏ-bō'-ăm the son of Nē'-băt.

16 And when all Israel *saw* that the king would not hearken unto them, the people answered the king, saying, What portion have we in David? and *we have* none inheritance in the son of Jesse: every man to your tents, O Israel: *and* now, David, see to thine own house. So all Israel went to their tents.

17 But *as for* the children of Israel that dwelt in the cities of Judah, Rē-hŏ-bō'-ăm reigned over them.

18 Then king Rē-hŏ-bō'-ăm sent Hă-dôr'-ăm that *was* over the tribute; and the children of Israel stoned him with stones, that he died. But king Rē-hō-bō'-ăm [N]made speed to get him up to *his* chariot, to flee to Jerusalem.

19 [R]And Israel rebelled against the house of David unto this day.

CHAPTER 11

Reign of Rehoboam

AND [R]when Rē-hŏ-bō'-ăm was come to Jerusalem, he gathered of the house of Judah and Benjamin an hundred and fourscore thousand chosen *men*, which were warriors, to fight against Israel, that he might bring the kingdom again to Rē-hŏ-bō'-ăm.

2 But the word of the LORD came [R]to Shĕm-aī'-ăh the man of God, saying,

3 Speak unto Rē-hŏ-bō'-ăm the son of Solo-

CHAP. 9
BC 992
27 1 Ki. 10:27
ch. 1:15
27 Heb. *gave*
28 1 Ki. 10:28
ch. 1:16
29 1 Ki. 11:41
29 Heb. *words*
29 1 Ki. 11:29
29 ch. 12:15
& 13:22
30 1 Ki. 11:42, 43

CHAP. 10
BC 975
1 1 Ki. 12:1, etc.
2 1 Ki. 11:40

Heb. *laded* 11
1 Sam. 2:25 15
1 Ki. 12:15, 24
1 Ki. 11:29 15
Heb. 18
strengthened himself
1 Ki. 12:19 19

CHAP. 11
BC 974
1 Ki. 12:21, etc.
ch. 12:15 2

mon, king of Judah, and to all Israel in Judah and Benjamin, saying,

4 Thus saith the LORD, Ye shall not go up, nor fight against your brethren: return every man to his house: for this thing is done of me. And they obeyed the words of the LORD, and returned from going against Jĕr-ŏ-bō′-ăm.

5 And Rē-hŏ-bō′-ăm dwelt in Jerusalem, and built cities for defence in Judah.

6 He built even Beth-lehem, and Ē′-tăm, and Tĕ-kō′-ă,

7 And Bĕth′-zŭr, and Shō′-cō, and Adullam,

8 And Gath, and Mă-rē′-shäh, and Ziph,

9 And Ăd-ō-rā′-ĭm, and Lā′-chĭsh, and Ă-zē′-käh,

10 And Zôr′-ăh, and Âī′-jă-lŏn, and Hē′-brŏn, which are in Judah and in Benjamin fenced cities.

11 And he fortified the strong holds, and put captains in them, and store of victual, and of oil and wine.

12 And in every several city he put shields and spears, and made them exceeding strong, having Judah and Benjamin on his side.

13 And the priests and the Levites that were in all Israel ᴺresorted to him out of all their coasts.

14 For the Levites left ᴿtheir suburbs and their possession, and came to Judah and Jerusalem: for ᴿJĕr-ŏ-bō′-ăm and his sons had cast them off from executing the priest's office unto the LORD:

15 ᴿAnd he ordained him priests for the high places, and for ᴿthe devils, and for ᴿthe calves which he had made.

16 ᴿAnd after them out of all the tribes of Israel such as set their hearts to seek the LORD God of Israel came to Jerusalem, to sacrifice unto the LORD God of their fathers.

17 So they ᴿstrengthened the kingdom of Judah, and made Rē-hŏ-bō′-ăm the son of Solomon strong, three years: for three years they walked in the way of David and Solomon.

18 And Rē-hŏ-bō′-ăm took him Mā′-hă-lăth the daughter of Jĕr′-ĭ-mōth the son of David to wife, and Ăb′-ĭ-hail the daughter of Ē-lī′-ăb the son of Jesse;

19 Which bare him children; Jē′-ŭsh, and Shăm-ă-rī′-ăh, and Zā′-hăm.

20 And after her he took ᴿMā′-ă-chäh the daughter of Ăb′-să-lŏm; which bare him Ă-bī′-jäh, and Ăt-tā′-ī, and Zī′-ză, and Shĕ-lō′-mĭth.

21 And Rē-hŏ-bō′-ăm loved Mā′-ă-chäh the daughter of Ăb′-să-lŏm above all his wives and his concubines: (for he took eighteen wives, and threescore concubines; and begat twenty and eight sons, and threescore daughters.)

22 And Rē-hŏ-bō′-ăm ᴿmade Ă-bī′-jäh the son of Mā′-ă-chäh the chief, to be ruler among his brethren: for he thought to make him king.

23 And he dealt wisely, and dispersed of all his children throughout all the countries of Judah and Benjamin, unto every fenced city: and he gave them victual in abundance. And he desired ᴺmany wives.

CHAPTER 12

Rehoboam forsakes the law

AND ᴿit came to pass, when Rē-hŏ-bō′-ăm had established the kingdom, and had strengthened himself, ᴿhe forsook the law of the LORD, and all Israel with him.

2 ᴿAnd it came to pass, that in the fifth year of king Rē-hŏ-bō′-ăm Shī′-shăk king of Egypt came up against Jerusalem, because they had transgressed against the LORD,

3 With twelve hundred chariots, and threescore thousand horsemen: and the people were without number that came with him out of Egypt; ᴿthe Lū′-bĭms, the Sŭk′-kĭ-ĭms, and the Ē-thĭ-ō′-pĭ-ăns.

4 And he took the fenced cities which pertained to Judah, and came to Jerusalem.

5 Then came ᴿShĕm-âī′-ăh the prophet to Rē-hŏ-bō′-ăm, and to the princes of Judah, that were gathered together to Jerusalem because of Shī′-shăk, and said unto them, Thus saith the LORD, Ye have forsaken me, and therefore have I also left you in the hand of Shī′-shăk.

6 Whereupon the princes of Israel and the king ᴿhumbled themselves; and they said, ᴿThe LORD is righteous.

7 And when the LORD saw that they humbled themselves, ᴿthe word of the LORD came to Shĕm-âī′-ăh, saying, They have humbled themselves; therefore I will not destroy them, but I will grant them ᴺsome deliverance; and my wrath shall not be poured out upon Jerusalem by the hand of Shī′-shăk.

8 Nevertheless ᴿthey shall be his servants; that they may know ᴿmy service, and the service of the kingdoms of the countries.

9 ᴿSo Shī′-shăk king of Egypt came up against Jerusalem, and took away the treasures of the house of the LORD, and the treasures of the king's house; he took all: he carried away also the shields of gold which Solomon had ᴿmade.

10 Instead of which king Rē-hŏ-bō′-ăm made shields of brass, and committed them ᴿto the hands of the chief of the guard, that kept the entrance of the king's house.

11 And when the king entered into the house

of the LORD, the guard came and fetched them, and brought them again into the guard chamber.

12 And when he humbled himself, the wrath of the LORD turned from him, that he would not destroy *him* altogether: ᴺand also in Judah things went well.

13 So king Rē-hŏ-bō'-ăm strengthened himself in Jerusalem, and reigned: for ᴿRē-hŏ-bō'-ăm *was* one and forty years old when he began to reign, and he reigned seventeen years in Jerusalem, ᴿthe city which the LORD had chosen out of all the tribes of Israel, to put his name there. And his mother's name *was* Nā'-ă-măh an Ammonitess.

14 And he did evil, because he ᴺprepared not his heart to seek the LORD.

15 Now the acts of Rē-hŏ-bō'-ăm, first and last, *are* they not written in the ᴺbook of Shĕm-âi'-ăh the prophet, ᴿand of ĭd'-dō the seer concerning genealogies? ᴿAnd *there were* wars between Rē-hŏ-bō'-ăm and Jĕr-ŏ-bō'-ăm continually.

16 And Rē-hŏ-bō'-ăm slept with his fathers, and was buried in the city of David: and ᴿĂ-bī'-jăh his son reigned in his stead.

CHAPTER 13

Reign of Abijah

NOW ᴿin the eighteenth year of king Jĕr-ŏ-bō'-ăm began Ă-bī'-jăh to reign over Judah.

2 He reigned three years in Jerusalem. His mother's name also *was* ᴿMī-châi'-ăh the daughter of Ū'-rĭ-ĕl of Gĭb'-ĕ-ăh. And there was war between Ă-bī'-jăh and Jĕr-ŏ-bō'-ăm.

3 And Ă-bī'-jăh ᴺset the battle in array with an army of valiant men of war, *even* four hundred thousand chosen men: Jĕr-ŏ-bō'-ăm also set the battle in array against him with eight hundred thousand chosen men, *being* mighty men of valour.

4 And Ă-bī'-jăh stood up upon mount ᴿZĕm-ă-rā'-ĭm, which *is* in mount Ē'-phră-ĭm, and said, Hear me, thou Jĕr-ŏ-bō'-ăm, and all Israel;

5 Ought ye not to know that the LORD God of Israel ᴿgave the kingdom over Israel to David for ever, *even* to him and to his sons ᴿby a covenant of salt?

6 Yet Jĕr-ŏ-bō'-ăm the son of Nē'-băt, the servant of Solomon the son of David, is risen up, and hath ᴿrebelled against his lord.

7 And there are gathered unto him ᴿvain men, the children of Bē'-lĭ-ăl, and have strengthened themselves against Rē-hŏ-bō'-ăm

the son of Solomon, when Rē-hŏ-bō'-ăm was young and tenderhearted, and could not withstand them.

Judah defeats Israel

8 And now ye think to withstand the kingdom of the LORD in the hand of the sons of David; and ye *be* a great multitude, and *there are* with you golden calves, which Jĕr-ŏ-bō'-ăm ᴿmade you for gods.

9 ᴿHave ye not cast out the priests of the LORD, the sons of Aaron, and the Levites, and have made you priests after the manner of the nations of *other* lands? ᴿso that whosoever cometh ᴺto consecrate himself with a young bullock and seven rams, *the same* may be a priest of *them that are* no gods.

10 But as for us, the LORD *is* our God, and we have not forsaken him; and the priests, which minister unto the LORD, *are* the sons of Aaron, and the Levites *wait* upon *their* business:

11 ᴿAnd they burn unto the LORD every morning and every evening burnt sacrifices and sweet incense: the ᴿshewbread also *set they in order* upon the pure table; and the candlestick of gold with the lamps thereof, ᴿto burn every evening: for we keep the charge of the LORD our God; but ye have forsaken him.

12 And, behold, God himself *is* with us for *our* captain, ᴿand his priests with sounding trumpets to cry alarm against you. O children of Israel, fight ye not against the LORD God of your fathers; for ye shall not prosper.

13 But Jĕr-ŏ-bō'-ăm caused an ambushment to come about behind them: so they were before Judah, and the ambushment *was* behind them.

14 And when Judah looked back, behold, the battle *was* before and behind: and they cried unto the LORD, and the priests sounded with the trumpets.

15 Then the men of Judah gave a shout: and as the men of Judah shouted, it came to pass, that God ᴿsmote Jĕr-ŏ-bō'-ăm and all Israel before Ă-bī'-jăh and Judah.

16 And the children of Israel fled before Judah: and God delivered them into their hand.

17 And Ă-bī'-jăh and his people slew them with a great slaughter: so there fell down slain of Israel five hundred thousand chosen men.

18 Thus the children of Israel were brought under at that time, and the children of Judah prevailed, ᴿbecause they relied upon the LORD God of their fathers.

19 And Ă-bī'-jăh pursued after Jĕr-ŏ-bō'-ăm, and took cities from him, Beth-el with the towns thereof, and Jĕ-shā'-năh with the towns

---

Center column references:

CHAP. 12
BC 972
12 Or, *and yet in Judah there were good things:*
See Gen. 18:24
1 Ki. 14:13
ch. 19:3
13 1 Ki. 14:21
13 ch. 6:6
14 Or, *fixed*
15 Heb. *words*
15 ch. 9:29 & 13:22
15 1 Ki. 14:30
16 1 Ki. 14:31, *Abijam*

CHAP. 13
BC 957
1 1 Ki. 15:1, etc.
2 See ch. 11:20
3 Heb. *bound together*
4 Josh. 18:22
5 2 Sam. 7:12, 13, 16
5 Num. 18:19
6 1 Ki. 11:26 & 12:20
7 Judg. 9:4

1 Ki. 12:28 8
& 14:9
Hos. 8:6
ch. 11:14, 15 9
Ex. 29:35 9
Heb. *to fill his hand:*
See Ex. 29:1
Lev. 8:2
ch. 2:4 11
Lev. 24:6 11
Ex. 27:20, 21 11
Lev. 24:2, 3
Num. 10:8 12
ch. 14:12 15
1 Chr. 5:20 18
Ps. 22:5

thereof, and ^RĒ'-phră-ĭn with the towns thereof.

20 Neither did Jĕr-ŏ-bō'-ăm recover strength again in the days of Ă-bī'-jăh: and the LORD ^Rstruck him, and ^Rhe died.

21 But Ă-bī'-jăh waxed mighty, and married fourteen wives, and begat twenty and two sons, and sixteen daughters.

22 And the rest of the acts of Ă-bī'-jăh, and his ways, and his sayings, *are* written in the ^Nstory of the prophet ^Rĭd'-dō.

CHAPTER 14

Reign of Asa

SO Ă-bī'-jăh slept with his fathers, and they buried him in the city of David: and ^RĀ'-să his son reigned in his stead. In his days the land was quiet ten years.

2 And Ā'-să did *that which was* good and right in the eyes of the LORD his God:

3 For he took away the altars of the strange *gods,* and ^Rthe high places, and ^Rbrake down the ^Nimages, ^Rand cut down the groves:

4 And commanded Judah to seek the LORD God of their fathers, and to do the law and the commandment.

5 Also he took away out of all the cities of Judah the high places and the ^Nimages: and the kingdom was quiet before him.

6 And he built fenced cities in Judah: for the land had rest, and he had no war in those years; because the LORD had given him rest.

7 Therefore he said unto Judah, Let us build these cities, and make about *them* walls, and towers, gates, and bars, *while* the land *is* yet before us; because we have sought the LORD our God, we have sought *him,* and he hath given us rest on every side. So they built and prospered.

8 And Ā'-să had an army *of men* that bare targets and spears, out of Judah three hundred thousand; and out of Benjamin, that bare shields and drew bows, two hundred and fourscore thousand: all these *were* mighty men of valour.

Asa defeats the Ethiopians

9 ^RAnd there came out against them Zē'-răh the Ē-thĭ-ō'-pĭ-ăn with an host of a thousand thousand, and three hundred chariots; and came unto ^RMă-rē'-shăh.

10 Then Ā'-să went out against him, and they set the battle in array in the valley of Zĕph'-ă-thăh at Mă-rē'-shăh.

11 And Ā'-să ^Rcried unto the LORD his God, and said, LORD, *it is* ^Rnothing with thee to

help, whether with many, or with them that have no power: help us, O LORD our God; for we rest on thee, and ^Rin thy name we go against this multitude. O LORD, thou *art* our God; let not ^Nman prevail against thee.

12 So the LORD ^Rsmote the Ē-thĭ-ō'-pĭ-ăns before Ā'-să, and before Judah; and the Ē-thĭ-ō'-pĭ-ăns fled.

13 And Ā'-să and the people that *were* with him pursued them unto ^RGē'-răr: and the Ē-thĭ-ō'-pĭ-ăns were overthrown, that they could not recover themselves; for they were ^Ndestroyed before the LORD, and before his host; and they carried away very much spoil.

14 And they smote all the cities round about Gē'-răr; for ^Rthe fear of the LORD came upon them: and they spoiled all the cities; for there was exceeding much spoil in them.

15 They smote also the tents of cattle, and carried away sheep and camels in abundance, and returned to Jerusalem.

CHAPTER 15

Azariah prophesies

AND ^Rthe spirit of God came upon Ăz-ă-rī'-ăh the son of ō'-dĕd:

2 And he went out ^Nto meet Ā'-să, and said unto him, Hear ye me, Ā'-să, and all Judah and Benjamin; ^RThe LORD *is* with you, while ye be with him; and ^Rif ye seek him, he will be found of you; but ^Rif ye forsake him, he will forsake you.

3 Now ^Rfor a long season Israel *hath been* without the true God, and without ^Ra teaching priest, and without law.

4 But ^Rwhen they in their trouble did turn unto the LORD God of Israel, and sought him, he was found of them.

5 And in those times *there was* no peace to him that went out, nor to him that came in, but great vexations *were* upon all the inhabitants of the countries.

6 ^RAnd nation was ^Ndestroyed of nation, and city of city: for God did vex them with all adversity.

7 Be ye strong therefore, and let not your hands be weak: for your work shall be rewarded.

Asa's religious reforms

8 And when Ā'-să heard these words, and the prophecy of ō'-dĕd the prophet, he took courage, and put away the ^Nabominable idols out of all the land of Judah and Benjamin, and out of the cities ^Rwhich he had taken from mount Ē'-phră-ĭm, and renewed the altar of the LORD, that *was* before the porch of the LORD.

9 And he gathered all Judah and Benjamin, and [R]the strangers with them out of Ē'-phră-ĭm and Mă-năs'-sĕh, and out of Simeon: for they fell to him out of Israel in abundance, when they saw that the LORD his God *was* with him.

10 So they gathered themselves together at Jerusalem in the third month, in the fifteenth year of the reign of Ā'-să.

11 [R]And they offered unto the LORD [N]the same time, of [R]the spoil *which* they had brought, seven hundred oxen and seven thousand sheep.

12 And they [R]entered into a covenant to seek the LORD God of their fathers with all their heart and with all their soul;

13 [R]That whosoever would not seek the LORD God of Israel [R]should be put to death, whether small or great, whether man or woman.

14 And they sware unto the LORD with a loud voice, and with shouting, and with trumpets, and with cornets.

15 And all Judah rejoiced at the oath: for they had sworn with all their heart, and [R]sought him with their whole desire; and he was found of them: and the LORD gave them rest round about.

16 And also *concerning* [R]Mā'-ă-<u>ch</u>äh the [N]mother of Ā'-să the king, he removed her from *being* queen, because she had made an [N]idol in a grove: and Ā'-să cut down her idol, and stamped *it*, and burnt *it* at the brook Kĭ'-drŏn.

17 But [R]the high places were not taken away out of Israel: nevertheless the heart of Ā'-să was perfect all his days.

18 And he brought into the house of God the things that his father had dedicated, and that he himself had dedicated, silver, and gold, and vessels.

19 And there was no *more* war unto the five and thirtieth year of the reign of Ā'-să.

CHAPTER 16

Asa's alliance with Syria

IN the six and thirtieth year of the reign of Ā'-să [R]Bā-ăsh'-ă king of Israel came up against Judah, and built Rā'-măh, [R]to the intent that he might let none go out or come in to Ā'-să king of Judah.

2 Then Ā'-să brought out silver and gold out of the treasures of the house of the LORD and of the king's house, and sent to Bĕn-hā'-dăd king of Syria, that dwelt at [N]Damascus, saying,

3 *There is* a league between me and thee, as

there was between my father and thy father: behold, I have sent thee silver and gold; go, break thy league with Bā-ăsh'-ă king of Israel, that he may depart from me.

4 And Bĕn-hā'-dăd hearkened unto king Ā'-să, and sent the captains of [N]his armies against the cities of Israel; and they smote Ĭ'-jŏn, and Dan, and Ā'-bĕl-mā'-ĭm, and all the store cities of Năph'-tă-lĭ.

5 And it came to pass, when Bā-ăsh'-ă heard *it*, that he left off building of Rā'-măh, and let his work cease.

6 Then Ā'-să the king took all Judah; and they carried away the stones of Rā'-măh, and the timber thereof, wherewith Bā-ăsh'-ă was building; and he built therewith Gē'-bă and Mizpah.

Hanani denounces the alliance

7 And at that time [R]Hă-nā'-nĭ the seer came to Ā'-să king of Judah, and said unto him, [R]Because thou hast relied on the king of Syria, and not relied on the LORD thy God, therefore is the host of the king of Syria escaped out of thine hand.

8 Were not [R]the Ē-thĭ-ō'-pĭ-ăns and [R]the Lū'-bĭms [N]a huge host, with very many chariots and horsemen? yet, because thou didst rely on the LORD, he delivered them into thine hand.

9 [R]For the eyes of the LORD run to and fro throughout the whole earth, [N]to shew himself strong in the behalf of *them* whose heart *is* perfect toward him. Herein [R]thou hast done foolishly: therefore from henceforth [R]thou shalt have wars.

10 Then Ā'-să was wroth with the seer, and [R]put him in a prison house; for *he was* in a rage with him because of this *thing*. And Ā'-să [N]oppressed *some* of the people the same time.

Asa's death

11 [R]And, behold, the acts of Ā'-să, first and last, lo, they *are* written in the book of the kings of Judah and Israel.

12 And Ā'-să in the thirty and ninth year of his reign was diseased in his feet, until his disease *was* exceeding *great:* yet in his disease he [R]sought not to the LORD, but to the physicians.

13 [R]And Ā'-să slept with his fathers, and died in the one and fortieth year of his reign.

14 And they buried him in his own sepulchres, which he had [N]made for himself in the city of David, and laid him in the bed which was filled [R]with sweet odours and divers kinds *of spices* prepared by the apothecaries' art: and they made [R]a very great burning for him.

CHAPTER 17

Reign of Jehoshaphat

AND ᴿJĕ-hŏsh′-ă-phăt his son reigned in his stead, and strengthened himself against Israel.

2 And he placed forces in all the fenced cities of Judah, and set garrisons in the land of Judah, and in the cities of Ē′-phră-ĭm, ᴿwhich Ā′-să his father had taken.

3 And the LORD was with Jĕ-hŏsh′-ă-phăt, because he walked in the first ways ᴺof his father David, and sought not unto Bā′-ă-lĭm;

4 But sought to the *LORD* God of his father, and walked in his commandments, and not after ᴿthe doings of Israel.

5 Therefore the LORD stablished the kingdom in his hand; and all Judah ᴿbrought ᴺto Jĕ-hŏsh′-ă-phăt presents; ᴿand he had riches and honour in abundance.

6 And his heart ᴺwas lifted up in the ways of the LORD: moreover ᴿhe took away the high places and groves out of Judah.

7 Also in the third year of his reign he sent to his princes, *even* to Bĕn′-hail, and to Ō-bă-dī′-ăh, and to Zĕch-ă-rī′-ăh, and to Nĕth′-ă-nēĕl, and to Mī-chāi′-ăh, ᴿto teach in the cities of Judah.

8 And with them *he sent* Levites, *even* Shĕm-āi′-ăh, and Nĕth-ă-nī′-ăh, and Zĕb-ă-dī′-ăh, and Ăs′-ă-hĕl, and Shĕ-mī′-ră-mōth, and Jĕ-hŏn′-ă-thăn, and Ăd-ō-nī′-jăh, and Tō-bī′-jăh, and Tŏb-ăd-ō-nī′-jăh, Levites; and with them Ē-lī′-shă-mă and Jĕ-hôr′-ăm, priests.

9 ᴿAnd they taught in Judah, and *had* the book of the law of the LORD with them, and went about throughout all the cities of Judah, and taught the people.

10 And ᴿthe fear of the LORD ᴺfell upon all the kingdoms of the lands that *were* round about Judah, so that they made no war against Jĕ-hŏsh′-ă-phăt.

11 Also *some* of the Philistines ᴿbrought Jĕ-hŏsh′-ă-phăt presents, and tribute silver; and the Arabians brought him flocks, seven thousand and seven hundred rams, and seven thousand and seven hundred he goats.

12 And Jĕ-hŏsh′-ă-phăt waxed great exceedingly; and he built in Judah ᴺcastles, and cities of store.

13 And he had much business in the cities of Judah: and the men of war, mighty men of valour, *were* in Jerusalem.

14 And these *are* the numbers of them according to the house of their fathers: Of Judah, the captains of thousands; Ăd′-năh the chief, and with him mighty men of valour three hundred thousand.

15 And ᴺnext to him *was* Jē-hō-hā′-năn the captain, and with him two hundred and fourscore thousand.

16 And next him *was* Ăm-ă-sī′-ăh the son of Zĭch′-rī, ᴿwho willingly offered himself unto the LORD; and with him two hundred thousand mighty men of valour.

17 And of Benjamin; Ē-lī′-ă-dă a mighty man of valour, and with him armed men with bow and shield two hundred thousand.

18 And next him *was* Jĕ-hō′-ză-băd, and with him an hundred and fourscore thousand ready prepared for the war.

19 These waited on the king, beside ᴿ*those* whom the king put in the fenced cities throughout all Judah.

CHAPTER 18

Jehoshaphat's alliance with Ahab

NOW Jĕ-hŏsh′-ă-phăt ᴿhad riches and honour in abundance, and ᴿjoined affinity with Ahab.

2 ᴿAnd ᴺafter *certain* years he went down to Ahab to Să-mâr′-ĭ-ă. And Ahab killed sheep and oxen for him in abundance, and for the people that *he had* with him, and persuaded him to go up *with him* to Rā′-mŏth-gĭl′-ĕ-ăd.

3 And Ahab king of Israel said unto Jĕ-hŏsh′-ă-phăt king of Judah, Wilt thou go with me to Rā′-mŏth-gĭl′-ĕ-ăd? And he answered him, I *am* as thou *art,* and my people as thy people; and *we will be* with thee in the war.

False prophets

4 And Jĕ-hŏsh′-ă-phăt said unto the king of Israel, ᴿInquire, I pray thee, at the word of the LORD to day.

5 Therefore the king of Israel gathered together of prophets four hundred men, and said unto them, Shall we go to Rā′-mŏth-gĭl′-ĕ-ăd to battle, or shall I forbear? And they said, Go up; for God will deliver *it* into the king's hand.

6 But Jĕ-hŏsh′-ă-phăt said, *Is there* not here a prophet of the LORD ᴺbesides, that we might inquire of him?

7 And the king of Israel said unto Jĕ-hŏsh′-ă-phăt, *There is* yet one man, by whom we may inquire of the LORD: but I hate him; for he never prophesied good unto me, but always evil: the same *is* Mī-cāi′-ăh the son of Ĭm′-lă. And Jĕ-hŏsh′-ă-phăt said, Let not the king say so.

8 And the king of Israel called for one *of his* ᴺofficers, and said, ᴺFetch quickly Mī-cāi′-ăh the son of Ĭm′-lă.

CHAP. 17
BC 912
1 1 Ki. 15:24
2 ch. 15:8
3 Or, *of his father, and of David*
4 1 Ki. 12:28
5 1 Sam. 10:27
   1 Ki. 10:25
5 Heb. *gave*
5 1 Ki. 10:27
   ch. 18:1
6 i.e. *was encouraged*
6 1 Ki. 22:43
   ch. 15:17 & 19:3 & 20:33
7 ch. 15:3
9 ch. 35:3
   Neh. 8:7
10 Gen. 35:5
10 Heb. *was*
11 2 Sam. 8:2
12 Or, *palaces*

Heb. *at his hand* 15
Judg. 5:2, 9 16
ver. 2 19

CHAP. 18
BC 897
ch. 17:5 1
2 Ki. 8:18 1
1 Ki. 22:2, etc. 2
Heb. *at the end of years* 2
1 Sam. 23:2, 4, 9 4
2 Sam. 2:1
Heb. *yet, or, more* 6
Or, *eunuchs* 8
Heb. *Hasten* 8

9 And the king of Israel and Jĕ-hŏsh′-ă-phăt king of Judah sat either of them on his throne, clothed in *their* robes, and they sat in a ᴺvoid place at the entering in of the gate of Să-mâr′-ĭ-ă; and all the prophets prophesied before them.

10 And Zĕd-ē-kī′-ăh the son of Chĕ-nā′-ă-năh had made him horns of iron, and said, Thus saith the LORD, With these thou shalt push Syria until ᴺthey be consumed.

11 And all the prophets prophesied so, saying, Go up to Rā′-mŏth-gĭl′-ĕ-ăd, and prosper: for the LORD shall deliver *it* into the hand of the king.

Micaiah's true prophecy

12 And the messenger that went to call Mī-cāī′-ăh spake to him, saying, Behold, the words of the prophets *declare* good to the king ᴺwith one assent; let thy word therefore, I pray thee, be like one of theirs, and speak thou good.

13 And Mī-cāī′-ăh said, *As* the LORD liveth, ᴿeven what my God saith, that will I speak.

14 And when he was come to the king, the king said unto him, Mī-cāī′-ăh, shall we go to Rā′-mŏth-gĭl′-ĕ-ăd to battle, or shall I forbear? And he said, Go ye up, and prosper, and they shall be delivered into your hand.

15 And the king said to him, How many times shall I adjure thee that thou say nothing but the truth to me in the name of the LORD?

16 Then he said, I did see all Israel scattered upon the mountains, as sheep that have no shepherd: and the LORD said, These have no master; let them return *therefore* every man to his house in peace.

17 And the king of Israel said to Jĕ-hŏsh′-ă-phăt, Did I not tell thee *that* he would not prophesy good unto me, ᴺbut evil?

18 Again he said, Therefore hear the word of the LORD; I saw the LORD sitting upon his throne, and all the host of heaven standing on his right hand and *on* his left.

19 And the LORD said, Who shall entice Ahab king of Israel, that he may go up and fall at Rā′-mŏth-gĭl′-ĕ-ăd? And one spake saying after this manner, and another saying after that manner.

20 Then there came out a ᴿspirit, and stood before the LORD, and said, I will entice him. And the LORD said unto him, Wherewith?

21 And he said, I will go out, and be a lying spirit in the mouth of all his prophets. And *the* LORD said, Thou shalt entice *him,* and thou shalt also prevail: go out, and do *even* so.

22 Now therefore, behold, ᴿthe LORD hath

CHAP. **18**
BC 897
9 Or, *floor*
10 Heb. *thou consume them*
12 Heb. *with one mouth*
13 Num. 22:18, 20, 35 & 23:12, 26 & 24:13
1 Ki. 22:14
17 Or, *but for evil?*
20 Job 1:6
22 Job 12:16
Is. 19:14
Ezek. 14:9

Jer. 20:2 23
Mark 14:65
Acts 23:2
Or, *from chamber to chamber* 24
Heb. *a chamber in a chamber* 24
ch. 16:10 26
Heb. *from after him* 32
Heb. *in his simplicity* 33
Heb. *between the joints and between the breastplate* 33
Heb. *made sick* 33

put a lying spirit in the mouth of these thy prophets, and the LORD hath spoken evil against thee.

23 Then Zĕd-ē-kī′-ăh the son of Chĕ-nā′-ă-năh came near, and ᴿsmote Mī-cāī′-ăh upon the cheek, and said, Which way went the spirit of the LORD from me to speak unto thee?

24 And Mī-cāī′-ăh said, Behold, thou shalt see on that day when thou shalt go ᴺinto ᴺan inner chamber to hide thyself.

25 Then the king of Israel said, Take ye Mī-cāī′-ăh, and carry him back to Amon the governor of the city, and to Jō′-ăsh the king's son;

26 And say, Thus saith the king, ᴿPut this *fellow* in the prison, and feed him with bread of affliction and with water of affliction, until I return in peace.

27 And Mī-cāī′-ăh said, If thou certainly return in peace, *then* hath not the LORD spoken by me. And he said, Hearken, all ye people.

Ahab killed in battle

28 So the king of Israel and Jĕ-hŏsh′-ă-phăt the king of Judah went up to Rā′-mŏth-gĭl′-ĕ-ăd.

29 And the king of Israel said unto Jĕ-hŏsh′-ă-phăt, I will disguise myself, and will go to the battle; but put thou on thy robes. So the king of Israel disguised himself; and they went to the battle.

30 Now the king of Syria had commanded the captains of the chariots that *were* with him, saying, Fight ye not with small or great, save only with the king of Israel.

31 And it came to pass, when the captains of the chariots saw Jĕ-hŏsh′-ă-phăt, that they said, It *is* the king of Israel. Therefore they compassed about him to fight: but Jĕ-hŏsh′-ă-phăt cried out, and the LORD helped him; and God moved them *to depart* from him.

32 For it came to pass, that, when the captains of the chariots perceived that it was not the king of Israel, they turned back again ᴺfrom pursuing him.

33 And a *certain* man drew a bow ᴺat a venture, and smote the king of Israel ᴺbetween the joints of the harness: therefore he said to his chariot man, Turn thine hand, that thou mayest carry me out of the host; for I am ᴺwounded.

34 And the battle increased that day: howbeit the king of Israel stayed *himself* up in *his* chariot against the Syrians until the even: and about the time of the sun going down he died.

CHAPTER 19

Jehoshaphat's judicial reforms

AND Jĕ-hŏsh′-ă-phăt the king of Judah returned to his house in peace to Jerusalem.

2 And Jehu the son of Hă-nā′-nī ᴿthe seer went out to meet him, and said to king Jĕ-hŏsh′-ă-phăt, Shouldest thou help the ungodly, and ᴿlove them that hate the LORD? therefore *is* ᴿwrath upon thee from before the LORD.

3 Nevertheless there are ᴿgood things found in thee, in that thou hast taken away the groves out of the land, and hast ᴿprepared thine heart to seek God.

4 And Jĕ-hŏsh′-ă-phăt dwelt at Jerusalem: and ᴺhe went out again through the people from Bēˉer-shē′-bă to mount Ē′-phră-ĭm, and brought them back unto the LORD God of their fathers.

5 And he set judges in the land throughout all the fenced cities of Judah, city by city,

6 And said to the judges, Take heed what ye do: for ᴿye judge not for man, but for the LORD, ᴿwho *is* with you ᴺin the judgment.

7 Wherefore now let the fear of the LORD be upon you; take heed and do *it:* for ᴿ*there is* no iniquity with the LORD our God, nor ᴿrespect of persons, nor taking of gifts.

8 Moreover in Jerusalem did Jĕ-hŏsh′-ă-phăt ᴿset of the Levites, and *of* the priests, and of the chief of the fathers of Israel, for the judgment of the LORD, and for controversies, when they returned to Jerusalem.

9 And he charged them, saying, Thus shall ye do ᴿin the fear of the LORD, faithfully, and with a perfect heart.

10 ᴿAnd what cause soever shall come to you of your brethren that dwell in their cities, between blood and blood, between law and commandment, statutes and judgments, ye shall even warn them that they trespass not against the LORD, and *so* ᴿwrath come upon ᴿyou, and upon your brethren: this do, and ye shall not trespass.

11 And, behold, Ăm-ă-rī′-ăh the chief priest *is* over you ᴿin all matters of the LORD; and Zĕb-ă-dī′-ăh the son of Ĭsh′-mā-ĕl, the ruler of the house of Judah, for all the king's matters: also the Levites *shall be* officers before you. ᴺDeal courageously, and the LORD shall be ᴿwith the good.

CHAPTER 20

Jehoshaphat's fast and prayer

IT came to pass after this also, *that* the children of Moab, and the children of

Ammon, and with them *other* beside the Ammonites, came against Jĕ-hŏsh′-ă-phăt to battle.

2 Then there came some that told Jĕ-hŏsh′-ă-phăt, saying, There cometh a great multitude against thee from beyond the sea on this side Syria; and, behold, they *be* ᴿin Hăz′-ă-zŏn-tā′-măr, which *is* ᴿĔn-ġē′-dī.

3 And Jĕ-hŏsh′-ă-phăt feared, and set ᴺhimself to ᴿseek the LORD, and ᴿproclaimed a fast throughout all Judah.

4 And Judah gathered themselves together, to ask *help* of the LORD: even out of all the cities of Judah they came to seek the LORD.

5 And Jĕ-hŏsh′-ă-phăt stood in the congregation of Judah and Jerusalem, in the house of the LORD, before the new court,

6 And said, O LORD God of our fathers, *art* not thou ᴿGod in heaven? and ᴿrulest *not* thou over all the kingdoms of the heathen? and ᴿin thine hand *is there not* power and might, so that none is able to withstand thee?

7 *Art* not thou ᴿour God, ᴺ*who* ᴿdidst drive out the inhabitants of this land before thy people Israel, and gavest it to the seed of Abraham ᴿthy friend for ever?

8 And they dwelt therein, and have built thee a sanctuary therein for thy name, saying,

9 ᴿIf, *when* evil cometh upon us, *as* the sword, judgment, or pestilence, or famine, we stand before this house, and in thy presence, (for thy ᴿname *is* in this house,) and cry unto thee in our affliction, then thou wilt hear and help.

10 And now, behold, the children of Ammon and Moab and mount Sē′-ĭr, whom thou ᴿwouldest not let Israel invade, when they came out of the land of Egypt, but ᴿthey turned from them, and destroyed them not;

11 Behold, *I say, how* they reward us, ᴿto come to cast us out of thy possession, which thou hast given us to inherit.

12 O our God, wilt thou not ᴿjudge them? for we have no might against this great company that cometh against us; neither know we what to do: but ᴿour eyes *are* upon thee.

Jahaziel's prophecy

13 And all Judah stood before the LORD, with their little ones, their wives, and their children.

14 Then upon Jă-hā′-zī-ĕl the son of Zĕch-ă-rī′-ăh, the son of Bĕ-nā′-ăh, the son of Jē-ĭ′-ĕl, the son of Măt-tă-nī′-ăh, a Levite of the sons of Ā′-săph, ᴿcame the spirit of the LORD in the midst of the congregation;

15 And he said, Hearken ye, all Judah, and ye inhabitants of Jerusalem, and thou king Jĕ-hŏsh′-ă-phăt, Thus saith the LORD unto

CHAP. 19
BC 896
2 1 Sam. 9:9
2 Ps. 139:21
2 ch. 32:25
3 ch. 17:4, 6
3 ch. 30:19
Ezra 7:10
4 Heb. *he returned and went out*
6 Deut. 1:17
6 Ps. 82:1
Eccl. 5:8
6 Heb. *in the matter of judgment*
7 Deut. 32:4
Rom. 9:14
7 Deut. 10:17
Job 34:19
Acts 10:34
Rom. 2:11
Gal. 2:6
Eph. 6:9
Col. 3:25
8 Deut. 16:18
ch. 17:8
9 2 Sam. 23:3
10 Deut. 17:8
10 Num. 16:46
10 Ezek. 3:18
11 1 Chr. 26:30
11 Heb. *Take courage and do*
11 ch. 15:2

CHAP. 20
BC 896
Gen. 14:7   2
Josh. 15:62   2
Heb. *his face*   3
ch. 19:3   3
Ezra 8:21   3
Jer. 36:9
Jonah 3:5
Deut. 4:39   6
Josh. 2:11
1 Ki. 8:23
Mat. 6:9
Ps. 47:2, 8   6
Dan. 4:17
1 Chr. 29:12   6
Ps. 62:11
Mat. 6:13
Gen. 17:7   7
Ex. 6:7
Heb. *thou*   7
Ps. 44:2   7
Is. 41:8   7
Jas. 2:23
1 Ki. 8:33, 37   9
ch. 6:28-30
ch. 6:20   9
Deut. 2:4, 9, 19   10
Num. 20:21   10
Ps. 83:12   11
1 Sam. 3:13   12
Ps. 25:15   12
& 121:1, 2
& 123:1, 2
& 141:8
Num. 11:25, 26   14
& 24:2
ch. 15:1

you, ^RBe not afraid nor dismayed by reason of this great multitude; for the battle *is* not yours, but God's.

16 To morrow go ye down against them: behold, they come up by the ^Ncliff of Zĭz; and ye shall find them at the end of the ^Nbrook, before the wilderness of Jĕ-rû'ĕl.

17 ^RYe shall not *need* to fight in this *battle:* set yourselves, stand ye *still,* and see the salvation of the LORD with you, O Judah and Jerusalem: fear not, nor be dismayed; to morrow go out against them: ^Rfor the LORD *will be* with you.

18 And Jĕ-hŏsh'-ă-phăt ^Rbowed his head with *his* face to the ground: and all Judah and the inhabitants of Jerusalem fell before the LORD, worshipping the LORD.

19 And the Levites, of the children of the Kō'-hăth-ītes, and of the children of the Kôr'-hītes, stood up to praise the LORD God of Israel with a loud voice on high.

Deliverance from Moab and Ammon

20 And they rose early in the morning, and went forth into the wilderness of Tĕ-kō'-ă: and as they went forth, Jĕ-hŏsh'-ă-phăt stood and said, Hear me, O Judah, and ye inhabitants of Jerusalem; ^RBelieve in the LORD your God, so shall ye be established; believe his prophets, so shall ye prosper.

21 And when he had consulted with the people, he appointed singers unto the LORD, ^Rand ^Nthat should praise the beauty of holiness, as they went out before the army, and to say, ^RPraise the LORD; ^Rfor his mercy *endureth* for ever.

22 ^NAnd when they began ^Nto sing and to praise, ^Rthe LORD set ambushments against the children of Ammon, Moab, and mount Sē'-ĭr, which were come against Judah; and ^Nthey were smitten.

23 For the children of Ammon and Moab stood up against the inhabitants of mount Sē'-ĭr, utterly to slay and destroy *them:* and when they had made an end of the inhabitants of Sē'-ĭr, every one helped ^Nto destroy another.

24 And when Judah came toward the watch tower in the wilderness, they looked unto the multitude, and, behold, they *were* dead bodies fallen to the earth, and ^Nnone escaped.

25 And when Jĕ-hŏsh'-ă-phăt and his people came to take away the spoil of them, they found among them in abundance both riches with the dead bodies, and precious jewels, which they stripped off for themselves, more than they could carry away: and they were three days in gathering of the spoil, it was so much.

CHAP. 20	
BC 896	
15	Ex. 14:13, 14
	Deut. 1:29, 30
	& 31:6, 8
	ch. 32:7
16	Heb. *ascent*
16	Or, *valley*
17	Ex. 14:13, 14
17	Num. 14:9
	ch. 15:2
	& 32:8
18	Ex. 4:31
20	Is. 7:9
21	1 Chr. 16:29
21	Heb. *praisers*
21	1 Chr. 16:34
	Ps. 136:1
21	1 Chr. 16:41
	ch. 5:13
22	Heb. *And in the time that they, etc.*
22	Heb. *in singing and praise*
22	Judg. 7:22
	1 Sam. 14:20
22	Or, *they smote one another*
23	Heb. *for the destruction*
24	Heb. *there was not an escaping*
i.e. *Blessing*	26
Heb. *head*	27
Neh. 12:43	27
ch. 17:10	29
ch. 15:15	30
Job 34:29	
1 Ki. 22:41, etc.	31
See ch. 17:6	33
ch. 12:14	33
& 19:3	
Heb. *words*	34
1 Ki. 16:1, 7	34
Heb. *was made to ascend*	34
1 Ki. 22:48, 49	35
At first Jehoshaphat was unwilling, 1 Ki. 22:49	36
1 Ki. 22:48	37
ch. 9:21	37
CHAP. 21	
BC 896	
1 Ki. 22:50	1
Alone	1

26 And on the fourth day they assembled themselves in the valley of ^NBĕ-rā'-chăh; for there they blessed the LORD: therefore the name of the same place was called, The valley of Bĕ-rā'-chăh, unto this day.

27 Then they returned, every man of Judah and Jerusalem, and Jĕ-hŏsh'-ă-phăt in the ^Nforefront of them, to go again to Jerusalem with joy; for the LORD had ^Rmade them to rejoice over their enemies.

28 And they came to Jerusalem with psalteries and harps and trumpets unto the house of the LORD.

29 And ^Rthe fear of God was on all the kingdoms of *those* countries, when they had heard that the LORD fought against the enemies of Israel.

30 So the realm of Jĕ-hŏsh'-ă-phăt was quiet: for his ^RGod gave him rest round about.

Death of Jehoshaphat

31 ^RAnd Jĕ-hŏsh'-ă-phăt reigned over Judah: *he was* thirty and five years old when he began to reign, and he reigned twenty and five years in Jerusalem. And his mother's name *was* Ă-zū'-băh the daughter of Shĭl'-hī.

32 And he walked in the way of Ā'-să his father, and departed not from it, doing *that which was* right in the sight of the LORD.

33 Howbeit ^Rthe high places were not taken away: for as yet the people had not ^Rprepared their hearts unto the God of their fathers.

34 Now the rest of the acts of Jĕ-hŏsh'-ă-phăt, first and last, behold, they *are* written in the ^Nbook of Jehu the son of Hă-nā'-nī, ^Rwho ^N*is* mentioned in the book of the kings of Israel.

35 And after this ^Rdid Jĕ-hŏsh'-ă-phăt king of Judah join himself with Ā-hă-zī'-ăh king of Israel, who did very wickedly:

36 ^NAnd he joined himself with him to make ships to go to Tarshish: and they made the ships in Ē'-zĭ-ŏn-gē'-bĕr.

37 Then ĕl-ĭ-ē'-zĕr the son of Dō'-dă-văh of Mă-rē'-shăh prophesied against Jĕ-hŏsh'-ă-phăt, saying, Because thou hast joined thyself with Ā-hă-zī'-ăh, the LORD hath broken thy works. ^RAnd the ships were broken, that they were not able to go ^Rto Tarshish.

CHAPTER 21

Reign of Jehoram

NOW ^RJĕ-hŏsh'-ă-phăt slept with his fathers, and was buried with his fathers in the city of David. And Jĕ-hôr'-ăm his son ^Nreigned in his stead.

2 And he had brethren the sons of Jĕ-

hŏsh'-ă-phăt, Ăz-ă-rī'-ăh, and Jĕ-hī'-ĕl, and Zĕch-ă-rī'-ăh, and Ăz-ă-rī'-ăh, and Michael, and Shĕph-ă-tī'-ăh: all these *were* the sons of Jĕ-hŏsh'-ă-phăt king of Israel.

3 And their father gave them great gifts of silver, and of gold, and of precious things, with fenced cities in Judah: but the kingdom gave he to ᴺJĕ-hôr'-ăm; because he *was* the firstborn.

4 Now when Jĕ-hôr'-ăm was risen up to the kingdom of his father, he strengthened himself, and slew all his brethren with the sword, and *divers* also of the princes of Israel.

5 ᴿJĕ-hôr'-ăm *was* thirty and two years old when he began to reign, and he reigned eight years in Jerusalem.

6 And he walked in the way of the kings of Israel, like as did the house of Ahab: for he had the daughter of ᴿAhab to wife: and he wrought *that which was* evil in the eyes of the LORD.

7 Howbeit the LORD would not destroy the house of David, because of the covenant that he had made with David, and as he promised to give a ᴺlight to him and to his ᴿsons for ever.

8 ᴿIn his days the Ē'-dŏm-ītes revolted from under the ᴺdominion of Judah, and made themselves a king.

9 Then Jĕ-hôr'-ăm went forth with his princes, and all his chariots with him: and he rose up by night, and smote the Ē'-dŏm-ītes which compassed him in, and the captains of the chariots.

10 So the Ē'-dŏm-ītes revolted from under the hand of Judah unto this day. The same time *also* did Lĭb'-năh revolt from under his hand; because he had forsaken the LORD God of his fathers.

11 Moreover he made high places in the mountains of Judah, and caused the inhabitants of Jerusalem to ᴿcommit fornication, and compelled Judah *thereto*.

12 And there came a ᴺwriting to him from Ē-lī'-jăh the prophet, saying, Thus saith the LORD God of David thy father, Because thou hast not walked in the ways of Jĕ-hŏsh'-ă-phăt thy father, nor in the ways of Ā'-să king of Judah,

13 But hast walked in the way of the kings of Israel, and hast ᴿmade Judah and the inhabitants of Jerusalem to ᴿgo a whoring, like to the ᴿwhoredoms of the house of Ahab, and also hast ᴿslain thy brethren of thy father's house, *which were* better than thyself:

14 Behold, with ᴺa great plague will the LORD smite thy people, and thy children, and thy wives, and all thy goods:

CHAP. 21
BC 896
3 Jehoram made partner of the kingdom with his father,
2 Ki. 8:16
5 In consort,
2 Ki. 8:17
6 ch. 22:2
7 Heb. *lamp,* or, *candle*
7 2 Sam. 7:12, 13
1 Ki. 11:36
2 Ki. 8:19
Ps. 132:11
8 2 Ki. 8:20
8 Heb. *hand*
11 Lev. 20:5
12 Which was writ before his death,
2 Ki. 2:1
13 ver. 11
13 Ex. 34:15
Deut. 31:16
13 1 Ki. 16:31-33
2 Ki. 9:22
13 ver. 4
14 Heb. *a great stroke*

ver. 18, 19   15
Heb. *carried*   17
captive:
See ch. 22:1
ch. 24:7   17
Or, *Ahaziah,*   17
ch. 22:1, or,
Azariah,
ch. 22:6
His son   18
Ahaziah Prorex,
2 Ki. 9:29
soon after
ver. 15   18
ch. 16:14   19
Heb. *without*   20
desire,
Jer. 22:18

CHAP. 22
BC 885
ver. 6   1
ch. 21:17
ch. 21:17   1
2 Ki. 8:26   2
ch. 21:6   2
2 Ki. 8:28, etc.   5
2 Ki. 9:15   6
Heb. *wherewith*
they wounded him
Otherwise called   6
Ahaziah,
ver. 1 and
Jehoahaz,
ch. 21:17

---

15 And thou *shalt have* great sickness by ᴿdisease of thy bowels, until thy bowels fall out by reason of the sickness day by day.

16 Moreover the LORD stirred up against Jĕ-hôr'-ăm the spirit of the Philistines, and of the Arabians, that *were* near the Ē-thĭ-ō'-pĭ-ăns:

17 And they came up into Judah, and brake into it, and ᴺcarried away all the substance that was found in the king's house, and ᴿhis sons also, and his wives; so that there was never a son left him, save ᴺJĕ-hō'-ă-hăz, the youngest of his sons.

18 ᴺAnd after all this the LORD smote him ᴿin his bowels with an incurable disease.

19 And it came to pass, that in process of time, after the end of two years, his bowels fell out by reason of his sickness: so he died of sore diseases. And his people made no burning for him, like ᴿthe burning of his fathers.

20 Thirty and two years old was he when he began to reign, and he reigned in Jerusalem eight years, and departed ᴺwithout being desired. Howbeit they buried him in the city of David, but not in the sepulchres of the kings.

CHAPTER 22

Reign of Ahaziah

AND the inhabitants of Jerusalem made ᴿĀ-hă-zī'-ăh his youngest son king in his stead: for the band of men that came with the Arabians to the camp had slain all the ᴿeldest. So Ā-hă-zī'-ăh the son of Jĕ-hôr'-ăm king of Judah reigned.

2 ᴿForty and two years old *was* Ā-hă-zī'-ăh when he began to reign, and he reigned one year in Jerusalem. His mother's name also *was* ᴿĂth-ă-lī'-ăh the daughter of Omri.

3 He also walked in the ways of the house of Ahab: for his mother was his counsellor to do wickedly.

4 Wherefore he did evil in the sight of the LORD like the house of Ahab: for they were his counsellors after the death of his father to his destruction.

5 He walked also after their counsel, and ᴿwent with Jĕ-hôr'-ăm the son of Ahab king of Israel to war against Hă-zā'-ĕl king of Syria at Rā'-mŏth-gĭl'-ĕ-ăd: and the Syrians smote Joram.

6 ᴿAnd he returned to be healed in Jĕz'-rēĕl because of the wounds ᴺwhich were given him at Rā'-măh, when he fought with Hă-zā'-ĕl king of Syria. And ᴺĂz-ă-rī'-ăh the son of Jĕ-hôr'-ăm king of Judah went down to see Jĕ-hôr'-ăm the son of Ahab at Jĕz'-rēĕl, because he was sick.

7 And the ᴺdestruction of Ā-hă-zī′-ăh ᴿwas of God by coming to Joram: for when he was come, he ᴿwent out with Jĕ-hôr′-ăm against Jehu the son of Nimshi, ᴿwhom the Lord had anointed to cut off the house of Ahab.

8 And it came to pass, that, when Jehu was ᴿexecuting judgment upon the house of Ahab, and ᴿfound the princes of Judah, and the sons of the brethren of Ā-hă-zī′-ăh, that ministered to Ā-hă-zī′-ăh, he slew them.

9 ᴿAnd he sought Ā-hă-zī′-ăh: and they caught him, (for he was hid in Să-mâr′-ĭ-ă,) and brought him to Jehu: and when they had slain him, they buried him: Because, said they, he *is* the son of Jĕ-hŏsh′-ă-phăt, who ᴿsought the Lord with all his heart. So the house of Ā-hă-zī′-ăh had no power to keep still the kingdom.

Joash saved from slaughter

10 ᴿBut when Ăth-ă-lī′-ăh the mother of Ā-hă-zī′-ăh saw that her son was dead, she arose and destroyed all the seed royal of the house of Judah.

11 But ᴿJĕ-hō-shăb′-ĕ-ăth, the daughter of the king, took Jō′-ăsh the son of Ā-hă-zī′-ăh, and stole him from among the king's sons that were slain, and put him and his nurse in a bedchamber. So Jĕ-hō-shăb′-ĕ-ăth, the daughter of king Jĕ-hôr′-ăm, the wife of Jĕ-hoi′-ă-dă the priest, (for she was the sister of Ā-hă-zī′-ăh,) hid him from Ăth-ă-lī′-ăh, so that she slew him not.

12 And he was with them hid in the house of God six years: and Ăth-ă-lī′-ăh reigned over the land.

CHAPTER 23

Joash made king

AND ᴿin the seventh year Jĕ-hoi′-ă-dă strengthened himself, and took the captains of hundreds, Ăz-ă-rī′-ăh the son of Jĕ-rō′-hăm, and ĭsh′-mā-ĕl the son of Jĕ-hō-hā′-năn, and Ăz-ă-rī′-ăh the son of Ō′-bĕd, and Mā-ă-sei′-ăh the son of Ă-dai′-ăh, and Ē-lī-shā′-phăt the son of Zĭch′-rī, into covenant with him.

2 And they went about in Judah, and gathered the Levites out of all the cities of Judah, and the chief of the fathers of Israel, and they came to Jerusalem.

3 And all the congregation made a covenant with the king in the house of God. And he said unto them, Behold, the king's son shall reign, as the Lord hath ᴿsaid of the sons of David.

4 This *is* the thing that ye shall do; A third

part of you ᴿentering on the sabbath, of the priests and of the Levites, *shall be* porters of the ᴺdoors;

5 And a third part *shall be* at the king's house; and a third part at the gate of the foundation: and all the people *shall be* in the courts of the house of the Lord.

6 But let none come into the house of the Lord, save the priests, and ᴿthey that minister of the Levites; they shall go in, for they *are* holy: but all the people shall keep the watch of the Lord.

7 And the Levites shall compass the king round about, every man with his weapons in his hand; and whosoever *else* cometh into the house, he shall be put to death: but be ye with the king when he cometh in, and when he goeth out.

8 So the Levites and all Judah did according to all things that Jĕ-hoi′-ă-dă the priest had commanded, and took every man his men that were to come in on the sabbath, with them that were to go *out* on the sabbath: for Jĕ-hoi′-ă-dă the priest dismissed not ᴿthe courses.

9 Moreover Jĕ-hoi′-ă-dă the priest delivered to the captains of hundreds spears, and bucklers, and shields, that *had been* king David's, which *were* in the house of God.

10 And he set all the people, every man having his weapon in his hand, from the right ᴺside of the ᴺtemple to the left side of the temple, along by the altar and the temple, by the king round about.

11 Then they brought out the king's son, and put upon him the crown, and ᴿ*gave him* the testimony, and made him king. And Jĕ-hoi′-ă-dă and his sons anointed him, and said, ᴺGod save the king.

Athaliah's death

12 Now when Ăth-ă-lī′-ăh heard the noise of the people running and praising the king, she came to the people into the house of the Lord:

13 And she looked, and, behold, the king stood at his pillar at the entering in, and the princes and the trumpets by the king: and all the people of the land rejoiced, and sounded with trumpets, also the singers with instruments of musick, and ᴿsuch as taught to sing praise. Then Ăth-ă-lī′-ăh rent her clothes, and said, ᴺTreason, Treason.

14 Then Jĕ-hoi′-ă-dă the priest brought out the captains of hundreds that were set over the host, and said unto them, Have her forth of the ranges: and whoso followeth her, let him be slain with the sword. For the priest said, Slay her not in the house of the Lord.

Center reference column

CHAP. **22**
BC 885
7 Heb. *treading down*
7 Judg. 14:4
1 Ki. 12:15
ch. 10:15
7 2 Ki. 9:21
7 2 Ki. 9:6, 7
8 2 Ki. 10:10, 11
8 2 Ki. 10:13, 14
9 2 Ki. 9:27, at *Megiddo* in the kingdom of *Samaria*
9 ch. 17:4
10 2 Ki. 11:1, etc.
11 2 Ki. 11:2, *Jehosheba*

CHAP. **23**
BC 878
1 2 Ki. 11:4, etc.
3 2 Sam. 7:12
1 Ki. 2:4
& 9:5
ch. 6:16
& 7:18
& 21:7

1 Chr. 9:25   **4**
Heb. *thresholds*   **4**
1 Chr. 23:28, 29   **6**
See 1 Chr. 24   **8**
& 25
Heb. *shoulder*   **10**
Heb. *house*   **10**
Deut. 17:18   **11**
Heb. *Let the king live*   **11**
1 Chr. 25:8   **13**
Heb. *Conspiracy*   **13**

15 So they laid hands on her; and when she was come to the entering ^Rof the horse gate by the king's house, they slew her there.

16 And Jĕ-hoi'-ă-dă made a covenant between him, and between all the people, and between the king, that they should be the Lord's people.

17 Then all the people went to the house of Bā'-ăl, and brake it down, and brake his altars and his images in pieces, and ^Rslew Măt'-tăn the priest of Bā'-ăl before the altars.

18 Also Jĕ-hoi'-ă-dă appointed the offices of the house of the Lord by the hand of the priests the Levites, whom David had ^Rdistributed in the house of the Lord, to offer the burnt offerings of the Lord, as *it is* written in the ^Rlaw of Moses, with rejoicing and with singing, *as it was ordained* ^Nby David.

19 And he set the ^Rporters at the gates of the house of the Lord, that none *which was* unclean in any thing should enter in.

20 ^RAnd he took the captains of hundreds, and the nobles, and the governors of the people, and all the people of the land, and brought down the king from the house of the Lord: and they came through the high gate into the king's house, and set the king upon the throne of the kingdom.

21 And all the people of the land rejoiced: and the city was quiet, after that they had slain Ăth-ă-lī'-ăh with the sword.

CHAPTER 24

Reign of Joash

Jō'-ĂSH ^R*was* seven years old when he began to reign, and he reigned forty years in Jerusalem. His mother's name also *was* Zī'-bī-ăh of Beer-shē'-bă.

2 And Jō'-ăsh ^Rdid *that which was* right in the sight of the Lord all the days of Jĕ-hoi'-ă-dă the priest.

3 And Jĕ-hoi'-ă-dă took for him two wives; and he begat sons and daughters.

Joash repairs the temple

4 And it came to pass after this, *that* Jō'-ăsh was minded ^Nto repair the house of the Lord.

5 And he gathered together the priests and the Levites, and said to them, Go out unto the cities of Judah, and ^Rgather of all Israel money to repair the house of your God from year to year, and see that ye hasten the matter. Howbeit the Levites hastened *it* not.

6 ^RAnd the king called for Jĕ-hoi'-ă-dă the chief, and said unto him, Why hast thou not required of the Levites to bring in out of Judah

and out of Jerusalem the collection, *according to the commandment* of ^RMoses the servant of the Lord, and of the congregation of Israel, for the ^Rtabernacle of witness?

7 For ^Rthe sons of Ăth-ă-lī'-ăh, that wicked woman, had broken up the house of God; and also all the ^Rdedicated things of the house of the Lord did they bestow upon Bā'-ă-lĭm.

8 And at the king's commandment ^Rthey made a chest, and set it without at the gate of the house of the Lord.

9 And they made ^Na proclamation through Judah and Jerusalem, to bring in to the Lord ^Rthe collection *that* Moses the servant of God *laid* upon Israel in the wilderness.

10 And all the princes and all the people rejoiced, and brought in, and cast into the chest, until they had made an end.

11 Now it came to pass, that at what time the chest was brought unto the king's office by the hand of the Levites, and ^Rwhen they saw that *there was* much money, the king's scribe and the high priest's officer came and emptied the chest, and took it, and carried it to his place again. Thus they did day by day, and gathered money in abundance.

12 And the king and Jĕ-hoi'-ă-dă gave it to such as did the work of the service of the house of the Lord, and hired masons and carpenters to repair the house of the Lord, and also such as wrought iron and brass to mend the house of the Lord.

13 So the workmen wrought, and ^Nthe work was perfected by them, and they set the house of God in his state, and strengthened it.

14 And when they had finished *it,* they brought the rest of the money before the king and Jĕ-hoi'-ă-dă, ^Rwhereof were made vessels for the house of the Lord, *even* vessels to minister, and ^Nto offer *withal,* and spoons, and vessels of gold and silver. And they offered burnt offerings in the house of the Lord continually all the days of Jĕ-hoi'-ă-dă.

Death of Jehoiada

15 But Jĕ-hoi'-ă-dă waxed old, and was full of days when he died; an hundred and thirty years old *was he* when he died.

16 And they buried him in the city of David among the kings, because he had done good in Israel, both toward God, and toward his house.

17 Now after the death of Jĕ-hoi'-ă-dă came the princes of Judah, and made obeisance to the king. Then the king hearkened unto them.

18 And they left the house of the Lord God of their fathers, and served ^Rgroves and idols:

and ᴿwrath came upon Judah and Jerusalem for this their trespass.

19 Yet he ᴿsent prophets to them, to bring them again unto the LORD; and they testified against them: but they would not give ear.

20 And the spirit of God ᴺcame upon Zĕch-a-rī'-ăh the son of Jĕ-hoi'-a-dă the priest, which stood above the people, and said unto them, Thus saith God, ᴿWhy transgress ye the commandments of the LORD, that ye cannot prosper? ᴿbecause ye have forsaken the LORD, he hath also forsaken you.

21 And they conspired against him, and ᴿstoned him with stones at the commandment of the king in the court of the house of the LORD.

22 Thus Jō'-ăsh the king remembered not the kindness which Jĕ-hoi'-a-dă his father had done to him, but slew his son. And when he died, he said, The LORD look upon *it,* and require *it.*

Joash defeated and slain

23 And it came to pass ᴺat the end of the year, *that* ᴿthe host of Syria came up against him: and they came to Judah and Jerusalem, and destroyed all the princes of the people from among the people, and sent all the spoil of them unto the king of ᴺDamascus.

24 For the army of the Syrians ᴿcame with a small company of men, and the LORD ᴿdelivered a very great host into their hand, because they had forsaken the LORD God of their fathers. So they ᴿexecuted judgment against Jō'-ăsh.

25 And when they were departed from him, (for they left him in great diseases,) ᴿhis own servants conspired against him for the blood of the ᴿsons of Jĕ-hoi'-a-dă the priest, and slew him on his bed, and he died: and they buried him in the city of David, but they buried him not in the sepulchres of the kings.

26 And these are they that conspired against him; ᴺZā'-băd the son of Shĭm'-ĕ-ăth an Ammonitess, and Jĕ-hō'-ză-băd the son of ᴺShĭm'-rĭth a Moabitess.

27 Now *concerning* his sons, and the greatness of ᴿthe burdens *laid* upon him, and the ᴺrepairing of the house of God, behold, they *are* written in the ᴺstory of the book of the kings. ᴿAnd Ăm-a-zī'-ăh his son reigned in his stead.

CHAPTER 25

Reign of Amaziah

ĂM-Ă-ZĪ'-ĂH ᴿwas twenty and five years old *when* he began to reign, and he reigned

---

CHAP. **24**

BC 878

18 Judg. 5:8
ch. 19:2 & 28:13
& 29:8 & 32:25
19 ch. 36:15
Jer. 7:25, 26
& 25:4
20 Heb. *clothed,* as
Judg. 6:34
20 Num. 14:41
20 ch. 15:2
21 Mat. 23:35
Acts 7:58, 59
23 Heb. *in the
revolution of
the year*
23 2 Ki. 12:17
23 Heb. *Darmesek*
24 Lev. 26:8
Deut. 32:30
Is. 30:17
24 Lev. 26:25
Deut. 28:25
24 ch. 22:8
Is. 10:5
25 2 Ki. 12:20
25 ver. 21
26 Or, *Jozachar,*
2 Ki. 12:21
26 Or, *Shomer*
27 2 Ki. 12:18
27 Heb. *founding*
27 Or, *commentary*
27 2 Ki. 12:21

CHAP. **25**

BC 827

1 2 Ki. 14:1, etc.

ver. 14　　　**2**
See 2 Ki. 14:4
2 Ki. 14:5, etc.　**3**
Heb. *confirmed*　**3**
upon him
Deut. 24:16　　**4**
2 Ki. 14:6
Jer. 31:30
Ezek. 18:20
Num. 1:3　　　**5**
ch. 20:6　　　**8**
Heb. *band*　　**9**
Prov. 10:22　　**9**
Heb. *to*　　　**10**
their place
Heb. *in heat*　**10**
of anger
2 Ki. 14:7　　**11**
Heb. *the sons*　**13**
of the band

---

twenty and nine years in Jerusalem. And his mother's name *was* Jĕ-hō-ăd'-dăn of Jerusalem.

2 And he did *that which was* right in the sight of the LORD, ᴿbut not with a perfect heart.

3 ᴿNow it came to pass, when the kingdom was ᴺestablished to him, that he slew his servants that had killed the king his father.

4 But he slew not their children, but *did* as *it is* written in the law in the book of Moses, where the LORD commanded, saying, ᴿThe father shall not die for the children, neither shall the children die for the fathers, but every man shall die for his own sin.

5 Moreover Ăm-a-zī'-ăh gathered Judah together, and made them captains over thousands, and captains over hundreds, according to the houses of *their* fathers, throughout all Judah and Benjamin: and he numbered them ᴿfrom twenty years old and above, and found them three hundred thousand choice *men, able* to go forth to war, that could handle spear and shield.

6 He hired also an hundred thousand mighty men of valour out of Israel for an hundred talents of silver.

7 But there came a man of God to him, saying, O king, let not the army of Israel go with thee; for the LORD *is* not with Israel, *to wit, with* all the children of Ē'-phră-ĭm.

8 But if thou wilt go, do *it,* be strong for the battle: God shall make thee fall before the enemy: for God hath ᴿpower to help, and to cast down.

9 And Ăm-a-zī'-ăh said to the man of God, But what shall we do for the hundred talents which I have given to the ᴺarmy of Israel? And the man of God answered, ᴿThe LORD is able to give thee much more than this.

10 Then Ăm-a-zī'-ăh separated them, *to wit,* the army that was come to him out of Ē'-phră-ĭm, to go ᴺhome again: wherefore their anger was greatly kindled against Judah, and they returned home ᴺin great anger.

11 And Ăm-a-zī'-ăh strengthened himself, and led forth his people, and went to ᴿthe valley of salt, and smote of the children of Sē'-ĭr ten thousand.

12 And *other* ten thousand *left* alive did the children of Judah carry away captive, and brought them unto the top of the rock, and cast them down from the top of the rock, that they all were broken in pieces.

13 But ᴺthe soldiers of the army which Ăm-a-zī'-ăh sent back, that they should not go with him to battle, fell upon the cities of Ju-

dah, from Să-mâr'-ĭ-ă even unto Běth-hôr'-ŏn, and smote three thousand of them, and took much spoil.

14 Now it came to pass, after that Ăm-ă-zī'-ăh was come from the slaughter of the Ē'-dom-ītes, that ᴿhe brought the gods of the children of Sē'-ĭr, and set them up *to be* ᴿhis gods, and bowed down himself before them, and burned incense unto them.

15 Wherefore the anger of the LORD was kindled against Ăm-ă-zī'-ăh, and he sent unto him a prophet, which said unto him, Why hast thou sought after ᴿthe gods of the people, which ᴿcould not deliver their own people out of thine hand?

16 And it came to pass, as he talked with him, that *the king* said unto him, Art thou made of the king's counsel? forbear; why shouldest thou be smitten? Then the prophet forbare, and said, I know that God hath ᴿdeterminedᴺ to destroy thee, because thou hast done this, and hast not hearkened unto my counsel.

Judah defeated by Israel

17 Then ᴿĂm-ă-zī'-ăh king of Judah took advice, and sent to Jō'-ăsh, the son of Jĕ-hō'-ă-hăz, the son of Jehu, king of Israel, saying, Come, let us see one another in the face.

18 And Jō'-ăsh king of Israel sent to Ăm-ă-zī'-ăh king of Judah, saying, The ᴺthistle that *was* in Lĕb'-ă-non sent to the cedar that *was* in Lĕb'-ă-non, saying, Give thy daughter to my son to wife: and there passed by ᴺa wild beast that *was* in Lĕb'-ă-non, and trode down the thistle.

19 Thou sayest, Lo, thou hast smitten the Ē'-dom-ītes; and thine heart lifteth thee up to boast: abide now at home; why shouldest thou meddle to *thine* hurt, that thou shouldest fall, *even* thou, and Judah with thee?

20 But Ăm-ă-zī'-ăh would not hear; for ᴿit came of God, that he might deliver them into the hand *of their enemies*, because they ᴿsought after the gods of Ē'-dom.

21 So Jō'-ăsh the king of Israel went up; and they saw one another in the face, *both* he and Ăm-ă-zī'-ăh king of Judah, at Běth-shē'-měsh, which *belongeth* to Judah.

22 And Judah was ᴺput to the worse before Israel, and they fled every man to his tent.

23 And Jō'-ăsh the king of Israel took Ăm-ă-zī'-ăh king of Judah, the son of Jō'-ăsh, the son of ᴿJĕ-hō'-ă-hăz, at Běth-shē'-měsh, and brought him to Jerusalem, and brake down the wall of Jerusalem from the gate of Ē'-phră-ĭm to ᴺthe corner gate, four hundred cubits.

24 And *he took* all the gold and the silver,

CHAP. 25
BC 827
14 See ch. 28:23
14 Ex. 20:3, 5
15 Ps. 96:5
15 ver. 11
16 1 Sam. 2:25
16 Heb. *counselled*
17 2 Ki. 14:8, 9, etc.
18 Or, *furze bush,* or, *thorn*
18 Heb. *a beast of the field*
20 1 Ki. 12:15 ch. 22:7
20 ver. 14
22 Heb. *smitten*
23 See ch. 21:17 & 22:1, 6
23 Heb. *the gate of it that looketh*

2 Ki. 14:17	25
Heb. *from after*	27
Heb. *conspired a conspiracy*	27
i.e. *The city of David,* as it is 2 Ki. 14:20	28

CHAP. 26
BC 810
2 Ki. 14:21, 22 & 15:1, etc.   **1**
Or, *Azariah*   **1**
See ch. 24:2   **5**
Gen. 41:15   **5**
Dan. 1:17 & 10:1
Heb. *in the seeing of God*   **5**
Is. 14:29   **6**
Or, *in the country of Ashdod*   **6**
ch. 21:16   **7**
2 Sam. 8:2   **8**
ch. 17:11
2 Ki. 14:13   **8**
Neh. 3:13, 19, 32   **9**
Zech. 14:10
Or, *repaired*   **9**

and all the vessels that were found in the house of God with Ō'-bĕd-ē'-dom, and the treasures of the king's house, the hostages also, and returned to Să-mâr'-ĭ-ă.

25 ᴿAnd Ăm-ă-zī'-ăh the son of Jō'-ăsh king of Judah lived after the death of Jō'-ăsh son of Jĕ-hō'-ă-hăz king of Israel fifteen years.

26 Now the rest of the acts of Ăm-ă-zī'-ăh, first and last, behold, *are* they not written in the book of the kings of Judah and Israel?

27 Now after the time that Ăm-ă-zī'-ăh did turn away ᴺfrom following the LORD they ᴺmade a conspiracy against him in Jerusalem; and he fled to Lā'-chĭsh: but they sent to Lā'-chĭsh after him, and slew him there.

28 And they brought him upon horses, and buried him with his fathers in the city of ᴺJudah.

CHAPTER 26

Reign of Uzziah

THEN all the people of Judah took ᴿŬz-zī'-ăh,ᴺ who *was* sixteen years old, and made him king in the room of his father Ăm-ă-zī'-ăh.

2 He built Ē'-lōth, and restored it to Judah, after that the king slept with his fathers.

3 Sixteen years old *was* ŭz-zī'-ăh when he began to reign, and he reigned fifty and two years in Jerusalem. His mother's name also *was* Jěc-ŏ-lī'-ăh of Jerusalem.

4 And he did *that which was* right in the sight of the LORD, according to all that his father Ăm-ă-zī'-ăh did.

5 And ᴿhe sought God in the days of Zěch-ă-rī'-ăh, who ᴿhad understanding ᴺin the visions of God: and as long as he sought the LORD, God made him to prosper.

Military feats of Uzziah

6 And he went forth and ᴿwarred against the Philistines, and brake down the wall of Gath, and the wall of Jăb'-nĕh, and the wall of Ăsh'-dŏd, and built cities ᴺabout Ăsh'-dŏd, and among the Philistines.

7 And God helped him against ᴿthe Philistines, and against the Arabians that dwelt in Gûr-bā'-ăl, and the Mě-hū'-nĭms.

8 And the Ammonites ᴿgave gifts to ŭz-zī'-ăh: and his name ᴺspread abroad *even* to the entering in of Egypt; for he strengthened *himself* exceedingly.

9 Moreover ŭz-zī'-ăh built towers in Jerusalem at the ᴿcorner gate, and at the valley gate, and at the turning *of the wall,* and ᴺfortified them.

10 Also he built towers in the desert, and
^Ndigged many wells: for he had much cattle,
both in the low country, and in the plains:
husbandmen *also,* and vine dressers in the
mountains, and in ^NCarmel: for he loved
^Nhusbandry.

11 Moreover ŭz-zī'-ăh had an host of
fighting men, that went out to war by bands,
according to the number of their account by
the hand of Jē-ī'-ĕl the scribe and Mā-ă-sĕī'-ăh
the ruler, under the hand of Hăn-ă-nī'-ăh, *one*
of the king's captains.

12 The whole number of the chief of the
fathers of the mighty men of valour *were*
two thousand and six hundred.

13 And under their hand *was* ^Nan army,
three hundred thousand and seven thousand
and five hundred, that made war with mighty
power, to help the king against the enemy.

14 And ŭz-zī'-ăh prepared for them
throughout all the host shields, and spears, and
helmets, and habergeons, and bows, and
^Nslings *to cast* stones.

15 And he made in Jerusalem engines, invented by cunning men, to be on the towers
and upon the bulwarks, to shoot arrows and
great stones withal. And his name ^Nspread
far abroad; for he was marvellously helped,
till he was strong.

Uzziah's sin and leprosy

16 But ^Rwhen he was strong, his heart was
^Rlifted up to *his* destruction: for he trans-
gressed against the LORD his God, and ^Rwent
into the temple of the LORD to burn incense
upon the altar of incense.

17 And ^RĂz-ă-rī'-ăh the priest went in after
him, and with him fourscore priests of the
LORD, *that were* valiant men:

18 And they withstood ŭz-zī'-ăh the king,
and said unto him, It ^Rappertaineth not unto
thee, ŭz-zī'-ăh, to burn incense unto the LORD,
but to the ^Rpriests the sons of Aaron, that are
consecrated to burn incense: go out of the
sanctuary; for thou hast trespassed; neither
shall it be for thine honour from the LORD
God.

19 Then ŭz-zī'-ăh was wroth, and *had* a
censer in his hand to burn incense: and while
he was wroth with the priests, ^Rthe leprosy
even rose up in his forehead before the priests
in the house of the LORD, from beside the
incense altar.

20 And Ăz-ă-rī'-ăh the chief priest, and all
the priests, looked upon him, and, behold, he
was leprous in his forehead, and they thrust
him out from thence; yea, himself ^Rhasted also
to go out, because the LORD had smitten him.

21 ^RAnd ŭz-zī'-ăh the king was a leper unto
the day of his death, and dwelt in a ^Rseveral^N
house, *being* a leper; for he was cut off from
the house of the LORD: and Jō'-thăm his son
was over the king's house, judging the people
of the land.

22 Now the rest of the acts of ŭz-zī'-ăh, first
and last, did ^RIsaiah the prophet, the son of
Amoz, write.

23 ^RSo ŭz-zī'-ăh slept with his fathers, and
they buried him with his fathers in the field of
the burial which *belonged* to the kings; for
they said, He *is* a leper: and Jō'-thăm his son
reigned in his stead.

CHAPTER 27

Reign of Jotham

JŌ'THĂM ^R*was* twenty and five years old
when he began to reign, and he reigned
sixteen years in Jerusalem. His mother's name
also *was* Jĕ-rû'-shäh, the daughter of Zā'-dŏk.

2 And he did *that which was* right in the
sight of the LORD, according to all that his
father ŭz-zī'-ăh did: howbeit he entered not
into the temple of the LORD. And ^Rthe people
did yet corruptly.

3 He built the high gate of the house of the
LORD, and on the wall of ^NŌ'-phĕl he built
much.

4 Moreover he built cities in the mountains
of Judah, and in the forests he built castles and
towers.

5 He fought also with the king of the Ammonites, and prevailed against them. And the
children of Ammon gave him the same year
an hundred talents of silver, and ten thousand
measures of wheat, and ten thousand of barley. ^NSo much did the children of Ammon pay
unto him, both the second year, and the third.

6 So Jō'-thăm became mighty, because he
^Nprepared his ways before the LORD his God.

7 Now the rest of the acts of Jō'-thăm, and
all his wars, and his ways, lo, they *are* written
in the book of the kings of Israel and Judah.

8 He was five and twenty years old when he
began to reign, and reigned sixteen years in
Jerusalem.

9 ^RAnd Jō'-thăm slept with his fathers, and
they buried him in the city of David: and
Ahaz his son reigned in his stead.

CHAPTER 28

Reign of Ahaz

AHAZ ^R*was* twenty years old when he began to reign, and he reigned sixteen
years in Jerusalem: but he did not *that which*

was right in the sight of the LORD, like David his father:

2 For he walked in the ways of the kings of Israel, and made also ᴿmolten images for ᴿBā'-ă-lĭm.

3 Moreover he ᴺburnt incense in ᴿthe valley of the son of Hĭn'-nọm, and burnt ᴿhis children in the fire, after the abominations of the heathen whom the LORD had cast out before the children of Israel.

4 He sacrificed also and burnt incense in the high places, and on the hills, and under every green tree.

Defeat of Judah

5 Wherefore ᴿthe LORD his God delivered him into the hand of the king of Syria; and they ᴿsmote him, and carried away a great multitude of them captives, and brought *them* to ᴺDamascus. And he was also delivered into the hand of the king of Israel, who smote him with a great slaughter.

6 For ᴿPē'-kăh the son of Rĕm-ă-lī'-ăh slew in Judah an hundred and twenty thousand in one day, *which were* all ᴺvaliant men; because they had forsaken the LORD God of their fathers.

7 And Zĭch'-rī, a mighty man of Ē'-phră-ĭm, slew Mā-ă-sêi'-ăh the king's son, and Ăz-rī'-kăm the governor of the house, and Ĕl-kā'-năh *that was* ᴺnext to the king.

8 And the children of Israel carried away captive of their ᴿbrethren two hundred thousand, women, sons, and daughters, and took also away much spoil from them, and brought the spoil to Să-mâr'-ĭ-ă.

9 But a prophet of the LORD was there, whose name *was* ō'-dĕd: and he went out before the host that came to Să-mâr'-ĭ-ă, and said unto them, Behold, ᴿbecause the LORD God of your fathers was wroth with Judah, he hath delivered them into your hand, and ye have slain them in a rage *that* ᴿreacheth up unto heaven.

10 And now ye purpose to keep under the children of Judah and Jerusalem for ᴿbondmen and bondwomen unto you: *but are there* not with you, even with you, sins against the LORD your God?

11 Now hear me therefore, and deliver the captives again, which ye have taken captive of your brethren: ᴿfor the fierce wrath of the LORD *is* upon you.

12 Then certain of the heads of the children of Ē'-phră-ĭm, Ăz-ă-rī'-ăh the son of Jō-hā'-năn, Bĕr-ē-chī'-ăh the son of Mĕ-shĭl'-lĕ-mŏth, and Jĕ-hĭz-kī'-ăh the son of Shăl'-lŭm, and Ă-mā'-să the son of Hăd-lā'-ī, stood up against them that came from the war,

CHAP. **28**

BC 741

2 Ex. 34:17
Lev. 19:4
2 Judg. 2:11
3 Or, *offered sacrifice*
3 2 Ki. 23:10
3 Lev. 18:21
2 Ki. 16:3
ch. 33:6
5 Is. 7:1
5 2 Ki. 16:5, 6
5 Heb. *Darmesek*
6 2 Ki. 15:27
6 Heb. *sons of valour*
7 Heb. *the second to the king*
8 ch. 11:4
9 Is. 10:5 & 47:6
Ezek. 25:12, 15 & 26:2
Obad. 10, etc.
Zech. 1:15
9 Ezra 9:6
Rev. 18:5
10 Lev. 25:39, 42, 43, 46
11 Jas. 2:13

ver. 12   **15**
2 Ki. 6:22   **15**
Luke 6:27
Rom. 12:20
Deut. 34:3   **15**
Judg. 1:16
2 Ki. 16:7   **16**
Heb. *a captivity* **17**
Ezek. 16:27, 57 **18**
ch. 21:2   **19**
Ex. 32:25   **19**
2 Ki. 15:29   **20**
& 16:7-9
See ch. 25:14 **23**
Heb. *Darmesek* **23**
Jer. 44:17, 18 **23**
See ch. 29:3, 7 **24**

13 And said unto them, Ye shall not bring in the captives hither: for whereas we have offended against the LORD *already,* ye intend to add *more* to our sins and to our trespass: for our trespass is great, and *there is* fierce wrath against Israel.

14 So the armed men left the captives and the spoil before the princes and all the congregation.

15 And the men ᴿwhich were expressed by name rose up, and took the captives, and with the spoil clothed all that were naked among them, and arrayed them, and shod them, and ᴿgave them to eat and to drink, and anointed them, and carried all the feeble of them upon asses, and brought them to Jericho, ᴿthe city of palm trees, to their brethren: then they returned to Să-mâr'-ĭ-ă.

Ahaz appeals to Assyria

16 ᴿAt that time did king Ahaz send unto the kings of Assyria to help him.

17 For again the Ē'-dọm-ītes had come and smitten Judah, and carried away ᴺcaptives.

18 ᴿThe Philistines also had invaded the cities of the low country, and of the south of Judah, and had taken Bĕth-shē'-mĕsh, and Ăj'-ă-lŏn, and Gĕ-dē'-rŏth, and Shō'-chō with the villages thereof, and Tĭm'-năh with the villages thereof, Gĭm'-zō also and the villages thereof: and they dwelt there.

19 For the LORD brought Judah low because of Ahaz king of ᴿIsrael; for he ᴿmade Judah naked, and transgressed sore against the LORD.

20 And ᴿTĭl'-găth-pĭl-nē'-sĕr king of Assyria came unto him, and distressed him, but strengthened him not.

21 For Ahaz took away a portion *out* of the house of the LORD, and *out* of the house of the king, and of the princes, and gave *it* unto the king of Assyria: but he helped him not.

Ahaz practices idolatry

22 And in the time of his distress did he trespass yet more against the LORD: this *is that* king Ahaz.

23 For ᴿhe sacrificed unto the gods of ᴺDamascus, which smote him: and he said, Because the gods of the kings of Syria help them, *therefore* will I sacrifice to them, that ᴿthey may help me. But they were the ruin of him, and of all Israel.

24 And Ahaz gathered together the vessels of the house of God, and cut in pieces the vessels of the house of God, ᴿand shut up the doors of the house of the LORD, and he made him altars in every corner of Jerusalem.

25 And in every several city of Judah he

made high places Nto burn incense unto other gods, and provoked to anger the LORD God of his fathers.

26 RNow the rest of his acts and of all his ways, first and last, behold, they *are* written in the book of the kings of Judah and Israel.

27 And Ahaz slept with his fathers, and they buried him in the city, *even* in Jerusalem: but they brought him not into the sepulchres of the kings of Israel: and Hĕz-ē-kī'-ăh his son reigned in his stead.

CHAPTER 29

Reign of Hezekiah

HĕZ-Ē-KĪ'-ĂH Rbegan to reign *when he was* five and twenty years old, and he reigned nine and twenty years in Jerusalem. And his mother's name *was* Ă-bī'-jäh, the daughter Rof Zĕch-ă-rī'-ăh.

2 And he did *that which was* right in the sight of the LORD, according to all that David his father had done.

Hezekiah cleanses the temple

3 He in the first year of his reign, in the first month, Ropened the doors of the house of the LORD, and repaired them.

4 And he brought in the priests and the Levites, and gathered them together into the east street,

5 And said unto them, Hear me, ye Levites, Rsanctify now yourselves, and sanctify the house of the LORD God of your fathers, and carry forth the filthiness out of the holy *place.*

6 For our fathers have trespassed, and done *that which was* evil in the eyes of the LORD our God, and have forsaken him, and have Rturned away their faces from the habitation of the LORD, and Nturned *their* backs.

7 RAlso they have shut up the doors of the porch, and put out the lamps, and have not burned incense nor offered burnt offerings in the holy *place* unto the God of Israel.

8 Wherefore the Rwrath of the LORD was upon Judah and Jerusalem, and he hath delivered them to Ntrouble, to astonishment, and to Rhissing, as ye see with your eyes.

9 For, lo, Rour fathers have fallen by the sword, and our sons and our daughters and our wives *are* in captivity for this.

10 Now *it is* in mine heart to make Ra covenant with the LORD God of Israel, that his fierce wrath may turn away from us.

11 My sons, Nbe not now negligent: for the LORD hath Rchosen you to stand before him, to serve him, and that ye should minister unto him, and Nburn incense.

12 Then the Levites arose, Mā'-hăth the son of Ă-mā'-săi, and Jō'-ĕl the son of Ăz-ă-rī'-ăh, of the sons of the Kō'-hăth-ītes: and of the sons of Mĕ-râr'-ī, Kish the son of Abdi, and Ăz-ă-rī'-ăh the son of Jĕ-hăl'-ĕ-lĕl: and of the Gĕr'-shŏn-ītes; Jō'-äh the son of Zimmah, and Eden the son of Jō'-äh:

13 And of the sons of Ē-lĭ-zā'-phăn; Shĭm'-rī, and Jē-ĭ'-ĕl: and of the sons of Ā'-săph; Zĕch-ă-rī'-ăh, and Măt-tă-nī'-ăh:

14 And of the sons of Hē'-măn; Jĕ-hī'-ĕl, and Shĭm'-ĕ-ī: and of the sons of Jĕ-dū'-thŭn; Shĕm-aī'-äh, and Ŭz'-zī-ĕl.

15 And they gathered their brethren, and Rsanctified themselves, and came, according to the commandment of the king, Nby the words of the LORD, Rto cleanse the house of the LORD.

16 And the priests went into the inner part of the house of the LORD, to cleanse *it,* and brought out all the uncleanness that they found in the temple of the LORD into the court of the house of the LORD. And the Levites took *it,* to carry *it* out abroad into the brook Kī'-drŏn.

17 Now they began on the first *day* of the first month to sanctify, and on the eighth day of the month came they to the porch of the LORD: so they sanctified the house of the LORD in eight days; and in the sixteenth day of the first month they made an end.

18 Then they went in to Hĕz-ē-kī'-ăh the king, and said, We have cleansed all the house of the LORD, and the altar of burnt offering, with all the vessels thereof, and the shewbread table, with all the vessels thereof.

19 Moreover all the vessels, which king Ahaz in his reign did Rcast away in his transgression, have we prepared and sanctified, and, behold, they *are* before the altar of the LORD.

The temple consecrated

20 Then Hĕz-ē-kī'-ăh the king rose early, and gathered the rulers of the city, and went up to the house of the LORD.

21 And they brought seven bullocks, and seven rams, and seven lambs, and seven he goats, for a Rsin offering for the kingdom, and for the sanctuary, and for Judah. And he commanded the priests the sons of Aaron to offer *them* on the altar of the LORD.

22 So they killed the bullocks, and the priests received the blood, and Rsprinkled *it* on the altar: likewise, when they had killed the rams, they sprinkled the blood upon the altar: they killed also the lambs, and they sprinkled the blood upon the altar.

23 And they brought Nforth the he goats *for* the sin offering before the king and the con-

gregation; and they laid their ᴿhands upon them:

24 And the priests killed them, and they made reconciliation with their blood upon the altar, ᴿto make an atonement for all Israel: for the king commanded *that* the burnt offering and the sin offering *should be made* for all Israel.

25 ᴿAnd he set the Levites in the house of the LORD with cymbals, with psalteries, and with harps, ᴿaccording to the commandment of David, and of ᴿGad the king's seer, and Nathan the prophet: ᴿfor *so was* the commandment ᴺof the LORD ᴺby his prophets.

26 And the Levites stood with the instruments ᴿof David, and the priests with ᴿthe trumpets.

27 And Hĕz-ē-kī'-ăh commanded to offer the burnt offering upon the altar. And ᴺwhen the burnt offering began, ᴿthe song of the LORD began *also* with the trumpets, and with the ᴺinstruments *ordained* by David king of Israel.

28 And all the congregation worshipped, and the ᴺsingers sang, and the trumpeters sounded: *and all this continued* until the burnt offering was finished.

29 And when they had made an end of offering, ᴿthe king and all that were ᴺpresent with him bowed themselves, and worshipped.

30 Moreover Hĕz-ē-kī'-ăh the king and the princes commanded the Levites to sing praise unto the LORD with the words of David, and of Ā'-săph the seer. And they sang praises with gladness, and they bowed their heads and worshipped.

31 Then Hĕz-ē-kī'-ăh answered and said, Now ye have ᴺconsecrated yourselves unto the LORD, come near and bring sacrifices and ᴿthank offerings into the house of the LORD. And the congregation brought in sacrifices and thank offerings; and as many as were of a free heart burnt offerings.

32 And the number of the burnt offerings, which the congregation brought, was threescore and ten bullocks, an hundred rams, *and* two hundred lambs: all these *were* for a burnt offering to the LORD.

33 And the consecrated things *were* six hundred oxen and three thousand sheep.

34 But the priests were too few, so that they could not flay all the burnt offerings: wherefore ᴿtheir brethren the Levites ᴺdid help them, till the work was ended, and until the *other* priests had sanctified themselves: ᴿfor the Levites *were* more ᴿupright in heart to sanctify themselves than the priests.

35 And also the burnt offerings *were* in

abundance, with ᴿthe fat of the peace offerings, and ᴿthe drink offerings for *every* burnt offering. So the service of the house of the LORD was set in order.

36 And Hĕz-ē-kī'-ăh rejoiced, and all the people, that God had prepared the people: for the thing was *done* suddenly.

CHAPTER 30

Call to keep the passover

AND Hĕz-ē-kī'-ăh sent to all Israel and Judah, and wrote letters also to Ē'-phră-ĭm and Mă-năs'-sēh, that they should come to the house of the LORD at Jerusalem, to keep the passover unto the LORD God of Israel.

2 For the king had taken counsel, and his princes, and all the congregation in Jerusalem, to keep the passover in the second ᴿmonth.

3 For they could not keep it ᴿat that time, ᴿbecause the priests had not sanctified themselves sufficiently, neither had the people gathered themselves together to Jerusalem.

4 And the thing ᴺpleased the king and all the congregation.

5 So they established a decree to make proclamation throughout all Israel, from Bē'ĕr-shē'-bă even to Dan, that they should come to keep the passover unto the LORD God of Israel at Jerusalem: for they had not done *it* of a long *time in such sort* as it was written.

6 So the posts went with the letters ᴺfrom the king and his princes throughout all Israel and Judah, and according to the commandment of the king, saying, Ye children of Israel, ᴿturn again unto the LORD God of Abraham, Isaac, and Israel, and he will return to the remnant of you, that are escaped out of the hand of ᴿthe kings of Assyria.

7 And be not ye ᴿlike your fathers, and like your brethren, which trespassed against the LORD God of their fathers, *who* therefore ᴿgave them up to desolation, as ye see.

8 Now ᴺbe ye not ᴿstiffnecked, as your fathers *were, but* ᴺyield yourselves unto the LORD, and enter into his sanctuary, which he hath sanctified for ever: and serve the LORD your God, ᴿthat the fierceness of his wrath may turn away from you.

9 For if ye turn again unto the LORD, your brethren and your children *shall find* ᴿcompassion before them that lead them captive, so that they shall come again into this land: for the LORD your God *is* ᴿgracious and merciful, and will not turn away *his* face from you, if ye ᴿreturn unto him.

10 So the posts passed from city to city through the country of Ē'-phră-ĭm and

Mă-năs′-sēh even unto Zĕ-bū′-lŭn: but ᴿthey laughed them to scorn, and mocked them.

11 Nevertheless ᴿdivers of Asher and Mă-năs′-sēh and of Zĕ-bū′-lŭn humbled themselves, and came to Jerusalem.

12 Also in Judah ᴿthe hand of God was to give them one heart to do the commandment of the king and of the princes, ᴿby the word of the LORD.

The passover kept

13 And there assembled at Jerusalem much people to keep the feast of unleavened bread in the second month, a very great congregation.

14 And they arose and took away the ᴿaltars that *were* in Jerusalem, and all the altars for incense took they away, and cast *them* into the brook Kĭ′-drŏn.

15 Then they killed the passover on the fourteenth *day* of the second month: and the priests and the Levites were ᴿashamed, and sanctified themselves, and brought in the burnt offerings into the house of the LORD.

16 And they stood in ᴺtheir place after their manner, according to the law of Moses the man of God: the priests sprinkled the blood, *which they received* of the hand of the Levites.

17 For *there were* many in the congregation that were not sanctified: ᴿtherefore the Levites had the charge of the killing of the passovers for every one *that was* not clean, to sanctify *them* unto the LORD.

18 For a multitude of the people, *even* ᴿmany of Ē′-phră-ĭm, and Mă-năs′-sēh, ĭs′-să-<u>chär</u>, and Zĕ-bū′-lŭn, had not cleansed themselves, ᴿyet did they eat the passover otherwise than it was written. But Hĕz-ē-kī′-ăh prayed for them, saying, The good LORD pardon every one

19 That ᴿprepareth his heart to seek God, the LORD God of his fathers, though *he be* not *cleansed* according to the purification of the sanctuary.

20 And the LORD hearkened to Hĕz-ē-kī′-ăh, and healed the people.

21 And the children of Israel that were ᴺpresent at Jerusalem kept ᴿthe feast of unleavened bread seven days with great gladness: and the Levites and the priests praised the LORD day by day, *singing* with ᴺloud instruments unto the LORD.

22 And Hĕz-ē-kī′-ăh spake ᴺcomfortably unto all the Levites ᴿthat taught the good knowledge of the LORD: and they did eat throughout the feast seven days, offering peace offerings, and ᴿmaking confession to the LORD God of their fathers.

23 And the whole assembly took counsel to keep ᴿother seven days: and they kept *other* seven days with gladness.

24 For Hĕz-ē-kī′-ăh king of Judah ᴿdidᴺ give to the congregation a thousand bullocks and seven thousand sheep; and the princes gave to the congregation a thousand bullocks and ten thousand sheep: and a great number of priests ᴿsanctified themselves.

25 And all the congregation of Judah, with the priests and the Levites, and all the congregation ᴿthat came out of Israel, and the strangers that came out of the land of Israel, and that dwelt in Judah, rejoiced.

26 So there was great joy in Jerusalem: for since the time of Solomon the son of David king of Israel *there was* not the like in Jerusalem.

27 Then the priests the Levites arose and ᴿblessed the people: and their voice was heard, and their prayer came *up* to ᴺhis holy dwelling place, *even* unto heaven.

CHAPTER 31

High places destroyed

NOW when all this was finished, all Israel that were ᴺpresent went out to the cities of Judah, and ᴿbrake the ᴺimages in pieces, and cut down the groves, and threw down the high places and the altars out of all Judah and Benjamin, in Ē′-phră-ĭm also and Mă-năs′-sēh, ᴺuntil they had utterly destroyed them all. Then all the children of Israel returned, every man to his possession, into their own cities.

Appointment of priests and Levites

2 And Hĕz-ē-kī′-ăh appointed ᴿthe courses of the priests and the Levites after their courses, every man according to his service, the priests and Levites ᴿfor burnt offerings and for peace offerings, to minister, and to give thanks, and to praise in the gates of the tents of the LORD.

3 *He appointed* also the king's portion of his substance for the burnt offerings, *to wit,* for the morning and evening burnt offerings, and the burnt offerings for the sabbaths, and for the new moons, and for the set feasts, as *it is* written in the ᴿlaw of the LORD.

4 Moreover he commanded the people that dwelt in Jerusalem to give the ᴿportion of the priests and the Levites, that they might be encouraged in ᴿthe law of the LORD.

5 And as soon as the commandment ᴺcame abroad, the children of Israel brought in abundance ᴿthe firstfruits of corn, wine, and oil,

and ᴺhoney, and of all the increase of the field; and the tithe of all *things* brought they in abundantly.

6 And *concerning* the children of Israel and Judah, that dwelt in the cities of Judah, they also brought in the tithe of oxen and sheep, and the ᴿtithe of holy things which were consecrated unto the Lᴏʀᴅ their God, and laid *them* ᴺby heaps.

7 In the third month they began to lay the foundation of the heaps, and finished *them* in the seventh month.

8 And when Hĕz-ē-kī′-ăh and the princes came and saw the heaps, they blessed the Lᴏʀᴅ, and his people Israel.

9 Then Hĕz-ē-kī′-ăh questioned with the priests and the Levites concerning the heaps.

10 And Ăz-à-rī′-ăh the chief priest of the house of Zā′-dŏk answered him, and said, ᴿSince *the people* began to bring the offerings into the house of the Lᴏʀᴅ, we have had enough to eat, and have left plenty: for the Lᴏʀᴅ hath blessed his people; and that which is left *is* this great store.

11 Then Hĕz-ē-kī′-ăh commanded to prepare ᴺchambers in the house of the Lᴏʀᴅ; and they prepared *them,*

12 And brought in the offerings and the tithes and the dedicated *things* faithfully: ᴿover which Cō-nō-nī′-ăh the Levite *was* ruler, and Shĭm′-ĕ-ī his brother *was* the next.

13 And Jĕ-hī′-ĕl, and Ăz-à-zī′-ăh, and Na-hath, and Ăs′-à-hĕl, and Jĕr′-ī-mōth, and Jō′-zà-băd, and Ē-lī′-ĕl, and Ĭs-mà-chī′-ăh, and Mā′-hăth, and Bĕ-nāī′-ăh, *were* overseers ᴺunder the hand of Cō-nō-nī′-ăh and Shĭm′-ĕ-ī his brother, at the commandment of Hĕz-ē-kī′-ăh the king, and Ăz-à-rī′-ăh the ruler of the house of God.

14 And Kôr′-ē the son of Ĭm′-năh the Levite, the porter toward the east, *was* over the free-will offerings of God, to distribute the oblations of the Lᴏʀᴅ, and the most holy things.

15 And ᴺnext him *were* Eden, and Mĭn-ī′-à-mĭn, and Jĕsh′-ū-à, and Shĕm-āī′-ăh, Ăm-à-rī′-ăh, and Shĕc-à-nī′-ăh, in ᴿthe cities of the priests, in *their* ᴺset office, to give to their brethren by courses, as well to the great as to the small:

16 Beside their genealogy of males, from three years old and upward, *even* unto every one that entereth into the house of the Lᴏʀᴅ, his daily portion for their service in their charges according to their courses;

17 Both to the genealogy of the priests by the house of their fathers, and the Levites ᴿfrom twenty years old and upward, in their charges by their courses;

18 And to the genealogy of all their little ones, their wives, and their sons, and their daughters, through all the congregation: for in their ᴺset office they sanctified themselves in holiness:

19 Also of the sons of Aaron the priests, *which were* in ᴿthe fields of the suburbs of their cities, in every several city, the men that were ᴿexpressed by name, to give portions to all the males among the priests, and to all that were reckoned by genealogies among the Levites.

20 And thus did Hĕz-ē-kī′-ăh throughout all Judah, and ᴿwrought *that which was* good and right and truth before the Lᴏʀᴅ his God.

21 And in every work that he began in the service of the house of God, and in the law, and in the commandments, to seek his God, he did *it* with all his heart, and prospered.

CHAPTER 32

Assyria's invasion

AFTER ᴿthese things, and the establishment thereof, Sĕn-năch′-ĕr-ĭb king of Assyria came, and entered into Judah, and encamped against the fenced cities, and thought ᴺto win them for himself.

2 And when Hĕz-ē-kī′-ăh saw that Sĕn-năch′-ĕr-ĭb was come, and that ᴺhe was purposed to fight against Jerusalem,

3 He took counsel with his princes and his mighty men to stop the waters of the fountains which *were* without the city: and they did help him.

4 So there was gathered much people together, who stopped all the fountains, and the brook that ᴺran through the midst of the land, saying, Why should the kings of Assyria come, and find much water?

5 Also ᴿhe strengthened himself, ᴿand built up all the wall that was broken, and raised *it* up to the towers, and another wall without, and repaired ᴿMĭl′-lō *in* the city of David, and made ᴺdarts and shields in abundance.

6 And he set captains of war over the people, and gathered them together to him in the street of the gate of the city and ᴺspake comfortably to them, saying,

7 ᴿBe strong and courageous, ᴿbe not afraid nor dismayed for the king of Assyria, nor for all the multitude that *is* with him: for ᴿthere be more with us than with him:

8 With him *is* an ᴿarm of flesh; but ᴿwith us *is* the Lᴏʀᴅ our God to help us, and to fight our battles. And the people ᴺrested themselves upon the words of Hĕz-ē-kī′-ăh king of Judah.

Sennacherib's messengers

9 ᴿAfter this did Sĕn-năch'-ĕr-ĭb king of Assyria send his servants to Jerusalem, (but he *himself laid siege* against Lā'-chĭsh, and all his ᴺpower with him,) unto Hĕz-ē-kī'-ăh king of Judah, and unto all Judah that *were* at Jerusalem, saying,

10 ᴿThus saith Sĕn-năch'-ĕr-ĭb king of Assyria, Whereon do ye trust, that ye abide ᴺin the siege in Jerusalem?

11 Doth not Hĕz-ē-kī'-ăh persuade you to give over yourselves to die by famine and by thirst, saying, ᴿThe LORD our God shall deliver us out of the hand of the king of Assyria?

12 ᴿHath not the same Hĕz-ē-kī'-ăh taken away his high places and his altars, and commanded Judah and Jerusalem, saying, Ye shall worship before one altar, and burn incense upon it?

13 Know ye not what I and my fathers have done unto all the people of *other* lands? ᴿwere the gods of the nations of those lands any ways able to deliver their lands out of mine hand?

14 Who *was there* among all the gods of those nations that my fathers utterly destroyed, that could deliver his people out of mine hand, that your God should be able to deliver you out of mine hand?

15 Now therefore ᴿlet not Hĕz-ē-kī'-ăh deceive you, nor persuade you on this manner, neither yet believe him: for no god of any nation or kingdom was able to deliver his people out of mine hand, and out of the hand of my fathers: how much less shall your God deliver you out of mine hand?

16 And his servants spake yet *more* against the LORD God, and against his servant Hĕz-ē-kī'-ăh.

17 ᴿHe wrote also letters to rail on the LORD God of Israel, and to speak against him, saying, ᴿAs the gods of the nations of *other* lands have not delivered their people out of mine hand, so shall not the God of Hĕz-ē-kī'-ăh deliver his people out of mine hand.

18 ᴿThen they cried with a loud voice in the Jews' speech unto the people of Jerusalem that *were* on the wall, to affright them, and to trouble them; that they might take the city.

19 And they spake against the God of Jerusalem, as against the gods of the people of the earth, *which were* ᴿthe work of the hands of man.

Sennacherib's army destroyed

20 ᴿAnd for this *cause* Hĕz-ē-kī'-ăh the king, and ᴿthe prophet Isaiah the son of Amoz, prayed and cried to heaven.

21 ᴿAnd the LORD sent an angel, which cut off all the mighty men of valour, and the leaders and captains in the camp of the king of Assyria. So he returned with shame of face to his own land. And when he was come into the house of his god, they that came forth of his own bowels ᴺslew him there with the sword.

22 Thus the LORD saved Hĕz-ē-kī'-ăh and the inhabitants of Jerusalem from the hand of Sĕn-năch'-ĕr-ĭb the king of Assyria, and from the hand of all *other,* and guided them on every side.

23 And many brought gifts unto the LORD to Jerusalem, and ᴿpresentsᴺ to Hĕz-ē-kī'-ăh king of Judah: so that he was ᴿmagnified in the sight of all nations from thenceforth.

Hezekiah's honour and wealth

24 ᴿIn those days Hĕz-ē-kī'-ăh was sick to the death, and prayed unto the LORD: and he spake unto him, and he ᴺgave him a sign.

25 But Hĕz-ē-kī'-ăh ᴿrendered not again according to the benefit *done* unto him; for ᴿhis heart was lifted up: ᴿtherefore there was wrath upon him, and upon Judah and Jerusalem.

26 ᴿNotwithstanding Hĕz-ē-kī'-ăh humbled himself for ᴺthe pride of his heart, *both* he and the inhabitants of Jerusalem, so that the wrath of the LORD came not upon them ᴿin the days of Hĕz-ē-kī'-ăh.

27 And Hĕz-ē-kī'-ăh had exceeding much riches and honour: and he made himself treasuries for silver, and for gold, and for precious stones, and for spices, and for shields, and for all manner of ᴺpleasant jewels;

28 Storehouses also for the increase of corn, and wine, and oil; and stalls for all manner of beasts, and cotes for flocks.

29 Moreover he provided him cities, and possessions of flocks and herds in abundance: for ᴿGod had given him substance very much.

30 ᴿThis same Hĕz-ē-kī'-ăh also stopped the upper watercourse of Gī'-hŏn, and brought it straight down to the west side of the city of David. And Hĕz-ē-kī'-ăh prospered in all his works.

31 Howbeit in *the business of* the ᴺambassadors of the princes of Babylon, who ᴿsent unto him to inquire of the wonder that was *done* in the land, God left him, to ᴿtry him, that he might know all *that was* in his heart.

32 Now the rest of the acts of Hĕz-ē-kī'-ăh, and his ᴺgoodness, behold, they *are* written in ᴿthe vision of Isaiah the prophet, the son of Amoz, *and* in the ᴿbook of the kings of Judah and Israel.

33 ᴿAnd Hĕz-ē-kī'-ăh slept with his fathers, and they buried him in the ᴺchiefest of the

sepulchres of the sons of David: and all Judah and the inhabitants of Jerusalem did him [R]honour at his death. And Mă-nas'-sĕh his son reigned in his stead.

CHAPTER 33

Reign of Manasseh

Mă-NăS'-SĔH [R]*was* twelve years old when he began to reign, and he reigned fifty and five years in Jerusalem:

2 But did *that which was* evil in the sight of the LORD, like unto the [R]abominations of the heathen, whom the LORD had cast out before the children of Israel.

3 For [N]he built again the high places which Hĕz-ē-kī'-ăh his father had [R]broken down, and he reared up altars for Bā'-ă-lĭm, and [R]made groves, and worshipped [R]all the host of heaven, and served them.

4 Also he built altars in the house of the LORD, whereof the LORD had said, [R]In Jerusalem shall my name be for ever.

5 And he built altars for all the host of heaven [R]in the two courts of the house of the LORD.

6 [R]And he caused his children to pass through the fire in the valley of the son of Hĭn'-nŏm: also he observed times, and used enchantments, and used witchcraft, and [R]dealt with a familiar spirit, and with wizards: he wrought much evil in the sight of the LORD, to provoke him to anger.

7 And [R]he set a carved image, the idol which he had made, in the house of God, of which God had said to David and to Solomon his son, In this house, and in Jerusalem, which I have chosen before all the tribes of Israel, will I put my name for ever:

8 [R]Neither will I any more remove the foot of Israel from out of the land which I have appointed for your fathers; so that they will take heed to do all that I have commanded them, according to the whole law and the statutes and the ordinances by the hand of Moses.

9 So Mă-nas'-sĕh made Judah and the inhabitants of Jerusalem to err, *and* to do worse than the heathen, whom the LORD had destroyed before the children of Israel.

Manasseh's capture and restoration

10 And the LORD spake to Mă-nas'-sĕh, and to his people: but they would not hearken.

11 [R]Wherefore the LORD brought upon them the captains of the host [N]of the king of Assyria, which took Mă-nas'-sĕh among the thorns, and [R]bound him with [N]fetters, and carried him to Babylon.

| CHAP. **32** |
| BC 710 |
| 33 Prov. 10:7 |

| CHAP. **33** |
| BC 698 |
| 1 2 Ki. 21:1, etc. |
| 2 Deut. 18:9 |
| 2 Chr. 28:3 |
| 3 Heb. *he returned and built* |
| 3 2 Ki. 18:4 |
| ch. 30:14 |
| & 31:1 |
| 3 Deut. 16:21 |
| 3 Deut. 17:3 |
| 4 Deut. 12:11 |
| 1 Ki. 8:29 |
| & 9:3 |
| ch. 6:6 |
| & 7:16 |
| 5 ch. 4:9 |
| 6 Lev. 18:21 |
| Deut. 18:10 |
| 2 Ki. 23:10 |
| ch. 28:3 |
| Ezek. 23:37, 39 |
| 6 2 Ki. 21:6 |
| 7 2 Ki. 21:7 |
| 8 2 Sam. 7:10 |
| 11 Deut. 28:36 |
| 11 Heb. *which were the king's* |
| 11 Job 36:8 |
| Ps. 107:10, 11 |
| 11 Or, *chains* |

1 Pet. 5:6	12
1 Chr. 5:20	13
Ezra 8:23	
Ps. 9:16	13
Dan. 4:25	
1 Ki. 1:33	14
ch. 27:3	14
Or, *The tower*	14
ver. 3, 5, 7	15
Lev. 7:12	16
ch. 32:12	17
1 Sam. 9:9	18
Or, *Hosai*	19
2 Ki. 21:18	20
2 Ki. 21:19, etc.	21
ver. 12	23
Heb. *multiplied trespass*	23
2 Ki. 21:23, 24	24

12 And when he was in affliction, he besought the LORD his God, and [R]humbled himself greatly before the God of his fathers,

13 And prayed unto him: and he was [R]entreated of him, and heard his supplication, and brought him again to Jerusalem into his kingdom. Then Mă-nas'-sĕh [R]knew that the LORD he *was* God.

14 Now after this he built a wall without the city of David, on the west side of [R]Gī'-hŏn, in the valley, even to the entering in at the fish gate, and compassed [R]about [N]Ō'-phĕl, and raised it up a very great height, and put captains of war in all the fenced cities of Judah.

15 And he took away [R]the strange gods, and the idol out of the house of the LORD, and all the altars that he had built in the mount of the house of the LORD, and in Jerusalem, and cast *them* out of the city.

16 And he repaired the altar of the LORD, and sacrificed thereon peace offerings and [R]thank offerings, and commanded Judah to serve the LORD God of Israel.

17 [R]Nevertheless the people did sacrifice still in the high places, *yet* unto the LORD their God only.

18 Now the rest of the acts of Mă-nas'-sĕh, and his prayer unto his God, and the words of [R]the seers that spake to him in the name of the LORD God of Israel, behold, they *are written* in the book of the kings of Israel.

19 His prayer also, and *how God* was entreated of him, and all his sin, and his trespass, and the places wherein he built high places, and set up groves and graven images, before he was humbled: behold, they *are* written among the sayings of [N]the seers.

20 [R]So Mă-nas'-sĕh slept with his fathers, and they buried him in his own house: and Amon his son reigned in his stead.

Reign of Amon

21 [R]Amon *was* two and twenty years old when he began to reign, and reigned two years in Jerusalem.

22 But he did *that which was* evil in the sight of the LORD, as did Mă-nas'-sĕh his father: for Amon sacrificed unto all the carved images which Mă-nas'-sĕh his father had made, and served them;

23 And humbled not himself before the LORD, [R]as Mă-nas'-sĕh his father had humbled himself; but Amon [N]trespassed more and more.

24 [R]And his servants conspired against him, and slew him in his own house.

25 But the people of the land slew all them that had conspired against king Amon; and the people of the land made Jō-sī'-ăh his son king in his stead.

CHAPTER 34

Reign of Josiah

JŌ-SĪ'-ĂH ᴿ*was* eight years old when he began to reign, and he reigned in Jerusalem one and thirty years.

2 And he did *that which was* right in the sight of the LORD, and walked in the ways of David his father, and declined *neither* to the right hand, nor to the left.

3 For in the eighth year of his reign, while he was yet young, he began to ᴿseek after the God of David his father: and in the twelfth year he began ᴿto purge Judah and Jerusalem ᴿfrom the high places, and the groves, and the carved images, and the molten images.

4 ᴿAnd they brake down the altars of Bā'-ă-lĭm in his presence; and the ᴺimages, that *were* on high above them, he cut down; and the groves, and the carved images, and the molten images, he brake in pieces, and made dust *of them,* ᴿand strowed *it* upon the ᴺgraves of them that had sacrificed unto them.

5 And he ᴿburnt the bones of the priests upon their altars, and cleansed Judah and Jerusalem.

6 And *so did he* in the cities of Mă-năs'-sēh, and Ē'-phră-ĭm, and Simeon, even unto Năph'-tă-lī, with their ᴺmattocks round about.

7 And when he had broken down the altars and the groves, and had ᴿbeaten the graven images ᴺinto powder, and cut down all the idols throughout all the land of Israel, he returned to Jerusalem.

The temple to be repaired

8 Now ᴿin the eighteenth year of his reign, when he had purged the land, and the house, he sent Shā'-phăn the son of ăz-ă-lī'-ăh, and Mā-ă-sēī'-ăh the governor of the city, and Jō'-ăh the son of Jō'-ă-hăz the recorder, to repair the house of the LORD his God.

9 And when they came to Hĭl-kī'-ăh the high priest, they delivered ᴿthe money that was brought into the house of God, which the Levites that kept the doors had gathered of the hand of Mă-năs'-sēh and Ē'-phră-ĭm, and of all the remnant of Israel, and of all Judah and Benjamin; and they returned to Jerusalem.

10 And they put *it* in the hand of the workmen that had the oversight of the house of the LORD, and they gave it to the workmen that wrought in the house of the LORD, to repair and amend the house:

11 Even to the artificers and builders gave they *it,* to buy hewn stone, and timber for couplings, and ᴺto floor the houses which the kings of Judah had destroyed.

12 And the men did the work faithfully: and

the overseers of them *were* Jā'-hăth and Ō-bă-dī'-ăh, the Levites, of the sons of Mĕ-râr'-ī; and Zĕch-ă-rī'-ăh and Mĕ-shŭl'-lăm, of the sons of the Kō'-hăth-ĭtes, to set *it* forward; and *other of* the Levites, all that could skill of instruments of musick.

13 Also *they were* over the bearers of burdens, and *were* overseers of all that wrought the work in any manner of service: ᴿand of the Levites *there were* scribes, and officers, and porters.

The book of the law found

14 And when they brought out the money that was brought into the house of the LORD, Hĭl-kī'-ăh the priest ᴿfound a book of the law of the LORD *given* ᴺby Moses.

15 And Hĭl-kī'-ăh answered and said to Shā'-phăn the scribe, I have found the book of the law in the house of the LORD. And Hĭl-kī'-ăh delivered the book to Shā'-phăn.

16 And Shā'-phăn carried the book to the king, and brought the king word back again, saying, All that was committed ᴺto thy servants, they do *it.*

17 And they have ᴺgathered together the money that was found in the house of the LORD, and have delivered it into the hand of the overseers, and to the hand of the workmen.

18 Then Shā'-phăn the scribe told the king, saying, Hĭl-kī'-ăh the priest hath given me a book. And Shā'-phăn read ᴺit before the king.

19 And it came to pass, when the king had heard the words of the law, that he rent his clothes.

20 And the king commanded Hĭl-kī'-ăh, and Ă-hī'-kăm the son of Shā'-phăn, and ᴺAbdon the son of Mī'-căh, and Shā'-phăn the scribe, and Ă-sāī'-ăh a servant of the king's, saying,

21 Go, inquire of the LORD for me, and for them that are left in Israel and in Judah, concerning the words of the book that is found: for great *is* the wrath of the LORD that is poured out upon us, because our fathers have not kept the word of the LORD, to do after all that is written in this book.

Huldah consulted

22 And Hĭl-kī'-ăh, and *they* that the king *had appointed,* went to Hŭl'-dăh the prophetess, the wife of Shăl'-lŭm the son of ᴿTĭk'-văth, the son of ᴺHăs'-răh, keeper of the ᴺwardrobe; (now she dwelt in Jerusalem ᴺin the college:) and they spake to her to that *effect.*

23 And she answered them, Thus saith the LORD God of Israel, Tell ye the man that sent you to me,

24 Thus saith the LORD, Behold, I will bring

evil upon this place, and upon the inhabitants thereof, *even* all the curses that are written in the book which they have read before the king of Judah:

25 Because they have forsaken me, and have burned incense unto other gods, that they might provoke me to anger with all the works of their hands; therefore my wrath shall be poured out upon this place, and shall not be quenched.

26 And as for the king of Judah, who sent you to inquire of the LORD, so shall ye say unto him, Thus saith the LORD God of Israel *concerning* the words which thou hast heard;

27 Because thine heart was tender, and thou didst humble thyself before God, when thou heardest his words against this place, and against the inhabitants thereof, and humbledst thyself before me, and didst rend thy clothes, and weep before me; I have even heard *thee* also, saith the LORD.

28 Behold, I will gather thee to thy fathers, and thou shalt be gathered to thy grave in peace, neither shall thine eyes see all the evil that I will bring upon this place, and upon the inhabitants of the same. So they brought the king word again.

The covenant renewed

29 ᴿThen the king sent and gathered together all the elders of Judah and Jerusalem.

30 And the king went up into the house of the LORD, and all the men of Judah, and the inhabitants of Jerusalem, and the priests, and the Levites, and all the people, ᴺgreat and small: and he read in their ears all the words of the book of the covenant that was found in the house of the LORD.

31 And the king stood in ᴿhis place, and made a covenant before the LORD, to walk after the LORD, and to keep his commandments, and his testimonies, and his statutes, with all his heart, and with all his soul, to perform the words of the covenant which are written in this book.

32 And he caused all that were ᴺpresent in Jerusalem and Benjamin to stand *to it*. And the inhabitants of Jerusalem did according to the covenant of God, the God of their fathers.

33 And Jō-sī'-ăh took away all the ᴿabominations out of all the countries that *pertained* to the children of Israel, and made all that were present in Israel to serve, *even* to serve the LORD their God. ᴿAnd all his days they departed not ᴺfrom following the LORD, the God of their fathers.

CHAPTER 35

Passover celebrated

MOREOVER ᴿJō-sī'-ăh kept a passover unto the LORD in Jerusalem: and they killed the passover on the ᴿfourteenth *day* of the first month.

2 And he set the priests in their ᴿcharges, and ᴿencouraged them to the service of the house of the LORD,

3 And said unto the Levites ᴿthat taught all Israel, which were holy unto the LORD, ᴿPut the holy ark ᴿin the house which Solomon the son of David king of Israel did build; ᴿ*it shall not be* a burden upon *your* shoulders: serve now the LORD your God, and his people Israel,

4 And prepare *yourselves* ᴿby the houses of your fathers, after your courses, according to the ᴿwriting of David king of Israel, and according to the ᴿwriting of Solomon his son.

5 And ᴿstand in the holy *place* according to the divisions of ᴺthe families of the fathers of your brethren ᴺthe people, and *after* the division of the families of the Levites.

6 So kill the passover, and ᴿsanctify yourselves, and prepare your brethren, that *they* may do according to the word of the LORD by the hand of Moses.

7 And Jō-sī'-ăh ᴿgaveᴺ to the people, of the flock, lambs and kids, all for the passover offerings, for all that were present, to the number of thirty thousand, and three thousand bullocks: these *were* of the king's substance.

8 And his princes ᴺgave willingly unto the people, to the priests, and to the Levites: Hĭl-kī'-ăh and Zĕch-ă-rī'-ăh and Jĕ-hī'-ĕl, rulers of the house of God, gave unto the priests for the passover offerings two thousand and six hundred *small cattle,* and three hundred oxen.

9 Cō-nă-nī'-ăh also, and Shĕm-aī'-ăh and Nĕth'-ă-nĕĕl, his brethren, and Hăsh-ă-bī'-ăh and Jĕ-ī'-ĕl and Jō'-ză-băd, chief of the Levites, ᴺgave unto the Levites for passover offerings five thousand *small cattle,* and five hundred oxen.

10 So the service was prepared, and the priests ᴿstood in their place, and the Levites in their courses, according to the king's commandment.

11 And they killed the passover, and the priests ᴿsprinkled *the blood* from their hands, and the Levites ᴿflayed *them.*

12 And they removed the burnt offerings, that they might give according to the divisions

of the families of the people, to offer unto the LORD, as *it is* written [R]in the book of Moses. And so *did they* with the oxen.

13 And they [R]roasted the passover with fire according to the ordinance: but the *other* holy *offerings* [R]sod they in pots, and in caldrons, and in pans, and [N]divided *them* speedily among all the people.

14 And afterward they made ready for themselves, and for the priests: because the priests the sons of Aaron *were busied* in offering of burnt offerings and the fat until night; therefore the Levites prepared for themselves, and for the priests the sons of Aaron.

15 And the singers the sons of Ā'-săph *were* in their [N]place, according to the [R]commandment of David, and Ā'-săph, and Hē'-măn, and Jĕ-dū'-thŭn the king's seer; and the porters [R]waited at every gate; they might not depart from their service; for their brethren the Levites prepared for them.

16 So all the service of the LORD was prepared the same day, to keep the passover, and to offer burnt offerings upon the altar of the LORD, according to the commandment of king Jō-sī'-ăh.

17 And the children of Israel that were [N]present kept the passover at that time, and the feast of [R]unleavened bread seven days.

18 And [R]there was no passover like to that kept in Israel from the days of Samuel the prophet; neither did all the kings of Israel keep such a passover as Jō-sī'-ăh kept, and the priests, and the Levites, and all Judah and Israel that were present, and the inhabitants of Jerusalem.

19 In the eighteenth year of the reign of Jō-sī'-ăh was this passover kept.

Death of Josiah

20 [R]After all this, when Jō-sī'-ăh had prepared the [N]temple, Nē'-chō king of Egypt came up to fight against Cär-chē'-mĭsh by Ēu-phrā'-tēś: and Jō-sī'-ăh went out against him.

21 But he sent ambassadors to him, saying, What have I to do with thee, thou king of Judah? *I come* not against thee this day, but against [N]the house wherewith I have war: for God commanded me to make haste: forbear thee from *meddling with* God, who *is* with me, that he destroy thee not.

22 Nevertheless Jō-sī'-ăh would not turn his face from him, but disguised himself, that he might fight with him, and hearkened not unto the words of Nē'-chō from the mouth of God, and came to fight in the valley of Mĕ-gĭd'-dō.

23 And the archers shot at king Jō-sī'-ăh; and the king said to his servants, Have me away; for I am sore [N]wounded.

24 [R]His servants therefore took him out of that chariot, and put him in the second chariot that he had; and they brought him to Jerusalem, and he died, and was buried [N]in *one of* the sepulchres of his fathers. And [R]all Judah and Jerusalem mourned for Jō-sī'-ăh.

25 And Jeremiah [R]lamented for Jō-sī'-ăh: and [R]all the singing men and the singing women spake of Jō-sī'-ăh in their lamentations to this day, [R]and made them an ordinance in Israel: and, behold, they *are* written in the lamentations.

26 Now the rest of the acts of Jō-sī'-ăh, and his [N]goodness, according to *that which was* written in the law of the LORD,

27 And his deeds, first and last, behold, they *are* written in the book of the kings of Israel and Judah.

CHAPTER 36

Jehoahaz captive in Egypt

THEN [R]the people of the land took Jĕ-hō'-ă-hăz the son of Jō-sī'-ăh, and made him king in his father's stead in Jerusalem.

2 Jĕ-hō'-ă-hăz *was* twenty and three years old when he began to reign, and he reigned three months in Jerusalem.

3 And the king of Egypt [N]put him down at Jerusalem, and [N]condemned the land in an hundred talents of silver and a talent of gold.

4 And the king of Egypt made Ē-lī'-ă-kĭm his brother king over Judah and Jerusalem, and turned his name to Jĕ-hōi'-ă-kĭm. And Nē'-chō took Jĕ-hō'-ă-hăz his brother, and carried him to Egypt.

Jehoiakim's captivity

5 [R]Jĕ-hōi'-ă-kĭm *was* twenty and five years old when he began to reign, and he reigned eleven years in Jerusalem: and he did *that which was* evil in the sight of the LORD his God.

6 [R]Against him came up Nĕb-ū-chăd-nĕz'-zär king of Babylon, and bound him in [N]fetters, to [R]carry him to Babylon.

7 [R]Nĕb-ū-chăd-nĕz'-zär also carried of the vessels of the house of the LORD to Babylon, and put them in his temple at Babylon.

8 Now the rest of the acts of Jĕ-hōi'-ă-kĭm, and his abominations which he did, and that which was found in him, behold, they *are* written in the book of the kings of Israel and

Judah: and ᴺJĕ-hoĭ′-ă-c̲h̲ĭn his son reigned in his stead.

Jehoiachin's exile

9 ᴿJĕ-hoĭ′-ă-c̲h̲ĭn *was* eight years old when he began to reign, and he reigned three months and ten days in Jerusalem: and he did *that which was* evil in the sight of the LORD.

10 And ᴺwhen the year was expired, ᴿking Nĕb-ū-c̲h̲ăd-nĕz′-zär sent, and brought him to Babylon, ᴿwith the ᴺgoodly vessels of the house of the LORD, and made ᴿZĕd-ē-kī′-ăhᴺ his brother king over Judah and Jerusalem.

Zedekiah's reign

11 ᴿZĕd-ē-kī′-ăh *was* one and twenty years old when he began to reign, and reigned eleven years in Jerusalem.

12 And he did *that which was* evil in the sight of the LORD his God, *and* humbled not himself before Jeremiah the prophet *speaking* from the mouth of the LORD.

13 And he also rebelled against king Nĕb-ū-c̲h̲ăd-nĕz′-zär, who had made him swear by God: but he ᴿstiffened his neck, and hardened his heart from turning unto the LORD God of Israel.

14 Moreover all the chief of the priests, and the people, transgressed very much after all the abominations of the heathen; and polluted the house of the LORD which he had hallowed in Jerusalem.

15 ᴿAnd the LORD God of their fathers sent to them ᴺby his messengers, rising up ᴺbetimes, and sending; because he had compassion on his people, and on his dwelling place:

16 But ᴿthey mocked the messengers of God, and ᴿdespised his words, and ᴿmisused his prophets, until the ᴿwrath of the LORD arose against his people, till *there was* no ᴺremedy.

CHAP. 36
BC 593
8 Or, *Jeconiah,*
1 Chr. 3:16, or,
Coniah,
Jer. 22:24
9 2 Ki. 24:8
10 Heb. *at the return of the year*
10 2 Ki. 24:10-17
10 Dan. 1:1, 2
10 Heb. *vessels of desire*
10 Jer. 37:1
10 Or, *Mattaniah, his father's brother,* 2 Ki. 24:17
11 2 Ki. 24:18
Jer. 52:1
13 2 Ki. 17:14
15 Jer. 25:3, 4
15 Heb. *by the hand of his messengers*
15 i.e. *continually and carefully*
16 Jer. 5:12
16 Prov. 1:25
16 Jer. 38:6
Mat. 23:34
16 Ps. 79:5
16 Heb. *healing*

Deut. 28:49   17
2 Ki. 25:1
Ezra 9:7
Ps. 74:20   17
2 Ki. 25:13, etc. 18
2 Ki. 25:9   19
Ps. 79:1, 7
2 Ki. 25:11   20
Heb. *the   20
remainder
from the sword*
Jer. 27:7   20
Jer. 26:6, 7   21
Lev. 26:34   21
Dan. 9:2
Lev. 25:4, 5   21
Ezra 1:1   22
Jer. 29:10   22
Is. 44:28   22
Ezra 1:2, 3   23

Jerusalem burned

17 ᴿTherefore he brought upon them the king of the C̲h̲ăl′-dēês̲, who ᴿslew their young men with the sword in the house of their sanctuary, and had no compassion upon young man or maiden, old man, or him that stooped for age: he gave *them* all into his hand.

18 ᴿAnd all the vessels of the house of God, great and small, and the treasures of the house of the LORD, and the treasures of the king, and of his princes; all *these* he brought to Babylon.

19 ᴿAnd they burnt the house of God, and brake down the wall of Jerusalem, and burnt all the palaces thereof with fire, and destroyed all the goodly vessels thereof.

Exile in Babylon

20 And ᴿthemᴺ that had escaped from the sword carried he away to Babylon; ᴿwhere they were servants to him and his sons until the reign of the kingdom of Persia:

21 To fulfil the word of the LORD by the mouth of ᴿJeremiah, until the land ᴿhad enjoyed her sabbaths: *for* as long as she lay desolate ᴿshe kept sabbath, to fulfil threescore and ten years.

Proclamation of Cyrus

22 ᴿNow in the first year of Cyrus king of Persia, that the word of the LORD *spoken* by the mouth of ᴿJeremiah might be accomplished, the LORD stirred up the spirit of ᴿCyrus king of Persia, that he made a proclamation throughout all his kingdom, and *put it* also in writing, saying,

23 ᴿThus saith Cyrus king of Persia, All the kingdoms of the earth hath the LORD God of heaven given me; and he hath charged me to build him an house in Jerusalem, which *is* in Judah. Who *is there* among you of all his people? The LORD his God *be* with him, and let him go up.

EZRA

The books of Ezra and Nehemiah were regarded as a single book by the Jews, according to Josephus. They were subsequently divided under separate titles as we have them today. The book of Ezra gives an account of the decree by Cyrus in 539 B.C. which permitted the Jews to return to Palestine; the organization of the expedition under Zerubbabel; the arrival of the expedition in Jerusalem and the setting up of an altar for worship; the celebration of the feast of tabernacles; the rebuilding and dedication of the temple during the years 520-515 B.C.; and the ministry of Ezra himself ca. 457 B.C., the account of which is given in the last four chapters. Ezra who exercised a profound influence upon this era is usually regarded as the author.

There appears to have been several stages in the return from captivity: the initial return following the decree of Cyrus; the return of a group led by Ezra, (457 B.C.); and finally the return of a group led by Nehemiah, (444 B.C.).

OUTLINE OF THE BOOK:
   I. The first return of the exiles   1:1 – 2:70
  II. The Jewish settlement at Jerusalem   3:1 – 4:23
 III. The building of the temple   5:1 – 6:22
 IV. Ezra's return and reformation   7:1 – 10:44

CHAPTER 1

Edict of Cyrus

NOW in the first year of Cyrus king of Persia, that the word of the LORD ^Rby the mouth of Jeremiah might be fulfilled, the LORD stirred up the spirit of Cyrus king of Persia, ^Rthat he ^Nmade a proclamation throughout all his kingdom, and *put it* also in writing, saying,

2 Thus saith Cyrus king of Persia, The LORD God of heaven hath given me all the kingdoms of the earth; and he hath ^Rcharged me to build him an house at Jerusalem, which *is* in Judah.

3 Who *is there* among you of all his people? his God be with him, and let him go up to Jerusalem, which *is* in Judah, and build the house of the LORD God of Israel, (^Rhe *is* the God,) which *is* in Jerusalem.

4 And whosoever remaineth in any place where he sojourneth, let the men of his place ^Nhelp him with silver, and with gold, and with goods, and with beasts, beside the freewill offering for the house of God that *is* in Jerusalem.

Temple vessels returned

5 Then rose up the chief of the fathers of Judah and Benjamin, and the priests, and the Levites, with all *them* whose spirit ^RGod had raised, to go up to build the house of the LORD which *is* in Jerusalem.

6 And all they that *were* about them ^Nstrengthened their hands with vessels of silver, with gold, with goods, and with beasts, and with precious things, beside all *that* was willingly offered.

7 ^RAlso Cyrus the king brought forth the vessels of the house of the LORD, ^Rwhich Nĕb-ū-chăd-nĕz′-zär had brought forth out of Jerusalem, and had put them in the house of his gods;

8 Even those did Cyrus king of Persia bring forth by the hand of Mĭth′-rĕ-dăth the treasurer, and numbered them unto ^RShĕsh-băz′-zär, the prince of Judah.

9 And this *is* the number of them: thirty chargers of gold, a thousand chargers of silver, nine and twenty knives,

10 Thirty basins of gold, silver basins of a second *sort* four hundred and ten, *and* other vessels a thousand.

11 All the vessels of gold and of silver *were* five thousand and four hundred. All *these* did Shĕsh-băz′-zär bring up with *them of* ^Nthe captivity that were brought up from Babylon unto Jerusalem.

CHAP. 1
BC 536
1 2 Chr. 36:22, 23
1 ch. 5:13, 14
1 Heb. *caused a voice to pass*
2 Is. 44:28 & 45:1, 13
3 Dan. 6:26
4 Heb. *lift him up*
5 Phil. 2:13
6 i.e. *helped them*
7 ch. 5:14 & 6:5
7 2 Ki. 24:13 2 Chr. 36:7
8 See ch. 5:14
11 Heb. *the transportation*

CHAP. 2
BC 536
Neh. 7:6, etc. 1
2 Ki. 24:14-16 1 & 25:11 2 Chr. 36:20
Or, *Azariah,* 2 Neh. 7:7
Or, *Raamiah* 2
Or, *Mispereth* 2
Or, *Nehum* 2
See Neh. 7:10 5
Neh. 7:11 6
Or, *Binnui,* 10 Neh. 7:15
Or, *Hariph,* 18 Neh. 7:24
Or, *Gibeon,* 20 Neh. 7:25
Or, *Beth-* 24 *azmaveth,* Neh. 7:28

CHAPTER 2

Return of the exiles

NOW ^Rthese *are* the children of the province that went up out of the captivity, of those which had been carried away, ^Rwhom Nĕb-ū-chăd-nĕz′-zär the king of Babylon had carried away unto Babylon, and came again unto Jerusalem and Judah, every one unto his city;

2 Which came with Zĕ-rŭb′-bă-bĕl: Jĕsh′-ū-ă, Nē-hĕm-ī′-ăh, ^NSĕ-raī′-ăh, ^NRē-ĕl-aī′-ăh, Môr-dĕ-cā′-ī, Bilshan, ^NMispar, Bĭg-vā′-ī, ^NRē′-hŭm, Bā′-ă-năh. The number of the men of the people of Israel:

3 The children of Pâr′-ŏsh, two thousand an hundred seventy and two.

4 The children of Shĕph-ă-tī′-ăh, three hundred seventy and two.

5 The children of Âr′-ăh, ^Rseven hundred seventy and five.

6 The children of ^RPā′-hăth-mō′-ăb, of the children of Jĕsh′-ū-ă *and* Jō′-ăb, two thousand eight hundred and twelve.

7 The children of Ē′-lăm, a thousand two hundred fifty and four.

8 The children of Zăt′-tû, nine hundred forty and five.

9 The children of Zăc-cā′-ī, seven hundred and threescore.

10 The children of ^NBā′-nī, six hundred forty and two.

11 The children of Bē-bā′-ī, six hundred twenty and three.

12 The children of Azgad, a thousand two hundred twenty and two.

13 The children of Ăd-ō-nī′-kăm, six hundred sixty and six.

14 The children of Bĭg-vā′-ī, two thousand fifty and six.

15 The children of Ā′-dĭn, four hundred fifty and four.

16 The children of Ā′-tĕr of Hĕz-ē-kī′-ăh, ninety and eight.

17 The children of Bē-zā′-ī, three hundred twenty and three.

18 The children of ^NJôr′-ăh, an hundred and twelve.

19 The children of Hăsh′-ŭm, two hundred twenty and three.

20 The children of ^NGĭb′-băr, ninety and five.

21 The children of Beth-lehem, an hundred twenty and three.

22 The men of Nē-tō′-phăh, fifty and six.

23 The men of Ăn′-ă-thŏth, an hundred twenty and eight.

24 The children of ^NĂz-mā′-vĕth, forty and two.

25 The children of Kĭr′-jăth-âr′-ĭm, Chĕ-phĭ′-răh, and Bēêr′-ōth, seven hundred and forty and three.

26 The children of Rā′-măh and Gā′-bă, six hundred twenty and one.

27 The men of Mĭch′-măs, an hundred twenty and two.

28 The men of Beth-el and Ā′-ī, two hundred twenty and three.

29 The children of Nē′-bō, fifty and two.

30 The children of Măg′-bĭsh, an hundred fifty and six.

31 The children of the other ᴿE′-lăm, a thousand two hundred fifty and four.

32 The children of Hâr′-ĭm, three hundred and twenty.

33 The children of Lod, ᴺHā′-dĭd, and ō′-nō, seven hundred twenty and five.

34 The children of Jericho, three hundred forty and five.

35 The children of Sĕn′-ă-ah, three thousand and six hundred and thirty.

36 The priests: the children of ᴿJĕ-dăī′-ăh, of the house of Jĕsh′-ū-ă, nine hundred seventy and three.

37 The children of ᴿĬm′-mĕr, a thousand fifty and two.

38 The children of ᴿPăsh′-ŭr, a thousand two hundred forty and seven.

39 The children of ᴿHâr′-ĭm, a thousand and seventeen.

40 The Levites: the children of Jĕsh′-ū-ă and Kăd′-mĭ-ĕl, of the children of ᴺHō-dă-vī′-ăh, seventy and four.

41 The singers: the children of Ā′-săph, an hundred twenty and eight.

42 The children of the porters: the children of Shăl′-lŭm, the children of Ā′-tĕr, the children of Tăl′-mŏn, the children of Ăk′-kŭb, the children of Hă-tī′-tă, the children of Shō-bā′-ī, in all an hundred thirty and nine.

43 ᴿThe Nĕth′-ĭ-nĭmś: the children of Zī′-hă, the children of Hă-sū′-phă, the children of Tăb-bā′-ōth,

44 The children of Kē′-rŏs, the children of ᴺSī′-ă-hă, the children of Pā′-dŏn,

45 The children of Lĕ-bā′-năh, the children of Hăg′-ă-băh, the children of Ăk′-kŭb,

46 The children of Hā′-găb, the children of ᴺShăl′-maī, the children of Hā′-năn,

47 The children of Gĭd′-dĕl, the children of Gā′-hăr, the children of Rē-āī′-ăh,

48 The children of Rē′-zĭn, the children of Nĕ-kō′-dă, the children of Găz′-zăm,

49 The children of ŭz′-ză, the children of Pă-sē′-ăh, the children of Bē′-saī,

50 The children of Ăs′-năh, the children of Mĕ-hū′-nĭm, the children of ᴺNĕ-phū′-sĭm,

51 The children of Băk′-bŭk, the children of Hă-kū′-phă, the children of Här′-hŭr,

52 The children of ᴺBăz′-lŭth, the children of Mĕ-hī′-dă, the children of Här′-shă,

53 The children of Bär′-kŏs, the children of Sĭs′-ĕ-ră, the children of Thā′-măh,

54 The children of Nĕ-zī′-ăh, the children of Hă-tī′-phă.

55 The children of ᴿSolomon's servants: the children of Sō-tā′-ī, the children of Sō′-phĕ-rĕth, the children of ᴺPĕ-rû′-dă,

56 The children of Jā′-ă-lăh, the children of Där′-kŏn, the children of Gĭd′-dĕl,

57 The children of Shĕph-ă-tī′-ăh, the children of Hăt′-tĭl, the children of Pō′-chĕ-rĕth of Zĕ-bā′-ĭm, the children of ᴺĀ′-mī.

58 All the ᴿNĕth′-ĭ-nĭmś, and the children of ᴿSolomon's servants, were three hundred ninety and two.

59 And these were they which went up from Tĕl-mē′-lăh, Tĕl-här′-să, Cherub, ᴺĂd′-dăn, and ĭm′-mĕr: but they could not shew their father's house, and their ᴺseed, whether they were of Israel:

60 The children of Dĕl-āī′-ăh, the children of Tō-bī′-ăh, the children of Nĕ-kō′-dă, six hundred fifty and two.

61 And of the children of the priests: the children of Hă-bāī′-ăh, the children of Kŏz, the children of Bär-zĭl-lā′-ī; which took a wife of the daughters of ᴿBär-zĭl-lā′-ī the Gileadite, and was called after their name:

62 These sought their register among those that were reckoned by genealogy, but they were not found: ᴿtherefore ᴺwere they, as polluted, put from the priesthood.

63 And the ᴺTĭr′-shă-thă said unto them, that they ᴿshould not eat of the most holy things, till there stood up a priest with ᴿŪ′-rĭm and with Thŭm′-mĭm.

64 ᴿThe whole congregation together was forty and two thousand three hundred and threescore,

65 Beside their servants and their maids, of whom there were seven thousand three hundred thirty and seven: and there were among them two hundred singing men and singing women.

66 Their horses were seven hundred thirty and six; their mules, two hundred forty and five;

67 Their camels, four hundred thirty and five; their asses, six thousand seven hundred and twenty.

68 ᴿAnd some of the chief of the fathers, when they came to the house of the LORD which is at Jerusalem, offered freely for the house of God to set it up in his place:

CHAP. 2
BC 536
31 See ver. 7
33 Or, Harid, as it is in some copies
36 1 Chr. 24:7
37 1 Chr. 24:14
38 1 Chr. 9:12
39 1 Chr. 24:8
40 Or, Judah, ch. 3:9 Called also Hodevah, Neh. 7:43
43 1 Chr. 9:2
44 Or, Sia
46 Or, Shamlai
50 Or, Nephishesim

Or, Bazlith, Neh. 7:54 — 52
1 Ki. 9:21 — 55
Or, Perida, Neh. 7:57 — 55
Or, Amon, Neh. 7:59 — 57
Josh. 9:21, 27 — 58
1 Chr. 9:2 — 58
1 Ki. 9:21 — 58
Or, Addon, Neh. 7:61 — 59
Or, pedigree — 59
2 Sam. 17:27 — 61
Num. 3:10 — 62
Heb. they were polluted from the priesthood — 62
Or, governor: See Neh. 8:9 — 63
Lev. 22:2, 10, 15, 16 — 63
Ex. 28:30 — 63
Num. 27:21 — 63
Neh. 7:66, etc. — 64
Neh. 7:70 — 68

69 They gave after their ability unto the ᴿtreasure of the work threescore and one thousand drams of gold, and five thousand pound of silver, and one hundred priests' garments.

70 ᴿSo the priests, and the Levites, and *some* of the people, and the singers, and the porters, and the Něth'-ĭ-nĭmś, dwelt in their cities, and all Israel in their cities.

CHAPTER 3

Altar rebuilt in Jerusalem

AND when the seventh month was come, and the children of Israel *were* in the cities, the people gathered themselves together as one man to Jerusalem.

2 Then stood up ᴺJěsh'-ū-ă the son of Jō'-ză-dăk, and his brethren the priests, and ᴺZĕ-rŭb'-bă-bĕl the son of ᴿShē-ăl'-tĭ-ĕl, and his brethren, and builded the altar of the God of Israel, to offer burnt offerings thereon, as *it is* ᴿwritten in the law of Moses the man of God

3 And they set the altar upon his bases; for fear *was* upon them because of the people of those countries: and they offered burnt offerings thereon unto the LORD, *even* ᴿburnt offerings morning and evening.

4 ᴿThey kept also the feast of tabernacles, ᴿas *it is* written, and ᴿ*offered* the daily burnt offerings by number, according to the custom, ᴺas the duty of every day required;

5 And afterward *offered* the ᴿcontinual burnt offering, both of the new moons, and of all the set feasts of the LORD that were consecrated, and of every one that willingly offered a freewill offering unto the LORD.

6 From the first day of the seventh month began they to offer burnt offerings unto the LORD. But ᴺthe foundation of the temple of the LORD was not *yet* laid.

7 They gave money also unto the masons, and to the ᴺcarpenters; and ᴿmeat, and drink, and oil, unto them of Zī'-dŏn, and to them of Tyre, to bring cedar trees from Lĕb'-ă-nǫn to the sea of ᴿJŏp'-pă, ᴿaccording to the grant that they had of Cyrus king of Persia.

Temple rebuilding begins

8 Now in the second year of their coming unto the house of God at Jerusalem, in the second month, began Zĕ-rŭb'-bă-bĕl the son of Shē-ăl'-tĭ-ĕl, and Jěsh'-ū-ă the son of Jō'-ză-dăk, and the remnant of their brethren the priests and the Levites, and all they that were come out of the captivity unto Jerusalem; ᴿand appointed the Levites, from twenty years old and

upward, to set forward the work of the house of the LORD.

9 Then stood ᴿJěsh'-ū-ă *with* his sons and his brethren, Kăd'-mĭ-ĕl and his sons, the sons of ᴺJudah, ᴺtogether, to set forward the workmen in the house of God: the sons of Hěn-ā'-dăd, *with* their sons and their brethren the Levites.

10 And when the builders laid the foundation of the temple of the LORD, ᴿthey set the priests in their apparel with trumpets, and the Levites the sons of Ā'-săph with cymbals, to praise the LORD, after the ᴿordinance of David king of Israel.

11 ᴿAnd they sang together by course in praising and giving thanks unto the LORD; ᴿbecause *he is* good, ᴿfor his mercy *endureth* for ever toward Israel. And all the people shouted with a great shout, when they praised the LORD, because the foundation of the house of the LORD was laid.

12 But many of the priests and Levites and chief of the fathers, *who were* ancient men, that had seen the first house, when the foundation of this house was laid before their eyes, wept with a loud voice; and many shouted aloud for joy:

13 So that the people could not discern the noise of the shout of joy from the noise of the weeping of the people: for the people shouted with a loud shout, and the noise was heard afar off.

CHAPTER 4

Building stopped

NOW when ᴿthe adversaries of Judah and Benjamin heard that ᴺthe children of the captivity builded the temple unto the LORD God of Israel;

2 Then they came to Zĕ-rŭb'-bă-bĕl, and to the chief of the fathers, and said unto them, Let us build with you: for we seek your God, as ye *do;* and we do sacrifice unto him ᴿsince the days of Ē'-sär-hăd'-dǫn king of Assur, which brought us up hither.

3 But Zĕ-rŭb'-bă-bĕl, and Jěsh'-ū-ă, and the rest of the chief of the fathers of Israel, said unto them, ᴿYe have nothing to do with us to build an house unto our God; but we ourselves together will build unto the LORD God of Israel, as ᴿking Cyrus the king of Persia hath commanded us.

4 Then ᴿthe people of the land weakened the hands of the people of Judah, and troubled them in building,

5 And hired counsellors against them, to frustrate their purpose, all the days of Cyrus

---

CHAP. 2
BC 536
69 1 Chr. 26:20
70 ch. 6:16, 17
Neh. 7:73

CHAP. 3
BC 536
2 Or, *Joshua,*
Hag. 1:1
& 2:2
Zech. 3:1
2 Called
Zorobabel,
Mat. 1:12
Luke 3:27
2 Mat. 1:12
& Luke 3:27,
called *Salathiel*
2 Deut. 12:5
3 Num. 28:3
4 Neh. 8:14
Zech. 14:16
4 Ex. 23:16
4 Num. 29:12
4 Heb. *the matter of the day in his day*
5 Ex. 29:38
Num. 28:3, 11, 19, 26
6 Heb. *the temple of the LORD was not yet founded*
7 Or, *workmen*
7 1 Ki. 5:6, 9
2 Chr. 2:10
Acts 12:20
7 2 Chr. 2:16
Acts 9:36
7 ch. 6:3
8 1 Chr. 23:24, 27

ch. 2:40   9
Or, *Hodaviah,*
ch. 2:40   9
Heb. *as one*   9
1 Chr. 16:5   10
1 Chr. 6:31   10
& 16:4
& 25:1
Ex. 15:21   11
2 Chr. 7:3
Neh. 12:24
1 Chr. 16:34   11
Ps. 136:1
1 Chr. 16:41   11
Jer. 33:11

CHAP. 4
BC 535
See ver. 7-9   1
Heb. *the sons of the transportation*
ver. 10   2
2 Ki. 17:24, 32, 33
& 19:37
Neh. 2:20   3
ch. 1:1-3   3
ch. 3:3   4

king of Persia, even until the reign of Dă-rī′-ŭs king of Persia.

Zerubbabel's men accused

6 And in the reign of ᴺĂ-hăś-ū-ē′-rŭs, in the beginning of his reign, wrote they *unto him* an accusation against the inhabitants of Judah and Jerusalem.

7 And in the days of Är-tă-xĕrx′-ēś wrote ᴺBĭsh′-lăm, Mĭth′-rĕ-dăth, Tăb′-ēĕl, and the rest of their ᴺcompanions, unto Är-tă-xĕrx′-ēś king of Persia; and the writing of the letter *was* written in the Syrian tongue, and interpreted in the Syrian tongue.

8 Rē′-hŭm the chancellor and Shĭm′-shâi the ᴺscribe wrote a letter against Jerusalem to Är-tă-xĕrx′-ēś the king in this sort:

9 Then *wrote* Rē′-hŭm the chancellor, and Shĭm′-shâi the scribe, and the rest of their ᴺcompanions; ᴿthe Dī′-nā-ītes, the Ă-phär-săth′-chītes, the Tär′-pē-lītes, the Ă-phär′-sītes, the Är′-chĕ-vītes, the Babylonians, the Sû-săn′-chītes, the Dĕ-hā′-vītes, *and* the Ē′-lăm-ītes,

10 ᴿAnd the rest of the nations whom the great and noble Ăs-năp′-pär brought over, and set in the cities of Să-mâr′-ĭ-ă, and the rest *that are* on this side the river, ᴿand ᴺat such a time.

11 This *is* the copy of the letter that they sent unto him, *even* unto Är-tă-xĕrx′-ēś the king; Thy servants the men on this side the river, and at such a time.

12 Be it known unto the king, that the Jews which came up from thee to us are come unto Jerusalem, building the rebellious and the bad city, and have ᴺset up the walls *thereof,* and ᴺjoined the foundations.

13 Be it known now unto the king, that, if this city be builded, and the walls set up *again,* *then* will they not ᴺpay ᴿtoll, tribute, and custom, and *so* thou shalt endamage the ᴺrevenue of the kings.

14 Now because ᴺwe have maintenance from *the king's* palace, and it was not meet for us to see the king's dishonour, therefore have we sent and certified the king;

15 That search may be made in the book of the records of thy fathers: so shalt thou find in the book of the records, and know that this city *is* a rebellious city, and hurtful unto kings and provinces, and that they have ᴺmoved sedition ᴺwithin the same of old time: for which cause was this city destroyed.

16 We certify the king that, if this city be builded *again,* and the walls thereof set up, by this means thou shalt have no portion on this side the river.

CHAP. 4

BC 535

6 Heb. *Ahashverosh*
7 Or, *in peace*
7 Heb. *societies*
8 Or, *secretary*
9 Chald. *societies*
9 2 Ki. 17:30, 31
10 ver. 1
10 ver. 11, 17
ch. 7:12
10 Chald. *Cheeneth*
12 Or, *finished*
12 Chald. *sewed together*
13 Chald. *give*
13 ch. 7:24
13 Or, *strength*
14 Chald. *we are salted with the salt of the palace*
15 Chald. *made*
15 Chald. *in the midst thereof*

Chald. *societies* 17
Chald. *by me* 19
  a decree is set
Chald. *lifted* 19
  up itself
1 Ki. 4:21 20
Ps. 72:8
Gen. 15:18 20
Josh. 1:4
Chald. *Make* 21
  a decree
Chald. *by* 23
  arm and power

CHAP. 5

BC 520

Hag. 1:1 1
Zech. 1:1 1
  ch. 3:2
  ver. 6 3
  ch. 6:6
  ver. 9 3
  ver. 10 4

Decree of Artaxerxes

17 *Then* sent the king an answer unto Rē′-hŭm the chancellor, and *to* Shĭm′-shâi the scribe, and *to* the rest of their ᴺcompanions that dwell in Să-mâr′-ĭ-ă, and *unto* the rest beyond the river, Peace, and at such a time.

18 The letter which ye sent unto us hath been plainly read before me.

19 And ᴺI commanded, and search hath been made, and it is found that this city of old time hath ᴺmade insurrection against kings, and *that* rebellion and sedition have been made therein.

20 There have been mighty kings also over Jerusalem, which have ᴿruled over all *countries* ᴿbeyond the river; and toll, tribute, and custom, was paid unto them.

21 ᴺGive ye now commandment to cause these men to cease, and that this city be not builded, until *another* commandment shall be given from me.

22 Take heed now that ye fail not to do this: why should damage grow to the hurt of the kings?

23 Now when the copy of king Är-tă-xĕrx′-ēś′ letter *was* read before Rē′-hŭm, and Shĭm′-shâi the scribe, and their companions, they went up in haste to Jerusalem unto the Jews, and made them to cease ᴺby force and power.

24 Then ceased the work of the house of God which *is* at Jerusalem. So it ceased unto the second year of the reign of Dă-rī′-ŭs king of Persia.

CHAPTER 5

Haggai and Zechariah prophesy

THEN the prophets, ᴿHăg′-gâi the prophet, and ᴿZĕch-ă-rī′-ăh the son of Ĭd′-dō, prophesied unto the Jews that *were* in Judah and Jerusalem in the name of the God of Israel, *even* unto them.

2 Then rose up ᴿZĕ-rŭb′-bă-bĕl the son of Shē-ăl′-tī-ĕl, and Jĕsh′-ū-ă the son of Jō′-ză-dăk, and began to build the house of God which *is* at Jerusalem: and with them *were* the prophets of God helping them.

3 At the same time came to them ᴿTăt′-nâi, governor on this side the river, and Shē′-thär-bŏz′-nâi, and their companions, and said thus unto them, ᴿWho hath commanded you to build this house, and to make up this wall?

4 ᴿThen said we unto them after this man-

ner, What are the names of the men ^Nthat make this building?

5 But ^Rthe eye of their God was upon the elders of the Jews, that they could not cause them to cease, till the matter came to Dă-rī′-ŭs: and then they returned ^Ranswer by letter concerning this *matter*.

Adversaries write Darius

6 The copy of the letter that Tăt′-nâi, governor on this side the river, and Shē′-thär-bŏz′-nâi, ^Rand his companions the Ă-phär′-să-<u>ch</u>ites, which *were* on this side the river, sent unto Dă-rī′-ŭs the king:

7 They sent a letter unto him, ^Nwherein was written thus; Unto Dă-rī′-ŭs the king, all peace.

8 Be it known unto the king, that we went into the province of Judea, to the house of the great God, which is builded with ^Ngreat stones, and timber is laid in the walls, and this work goeth fast on, and prospereth in their hands.

9 Then asked we those elders, *and* said unto them thus, ^RWho commanded you to build this house, and to make up these walls?

10 We asked their names also, to certify thee, that we might write the names of the men that *were* the chief of them.

11 And thus they returned us answer, saying, We are the servants of the God of heaven and earth, and build the house that was builded these many years ago, which a great king of Israel builded ^Rand set up.

12 But ^Rafter that our fathers had provoked the God of heaven unto wrath, he gave them into the hand of ^RNĕb-ū-<u>ch</u>ăd-nĕz′-zär the king of Babylon, the <u>Ch</u>ăl-dē′-ăn, who destroyed this house, and carried the people away into Babylon.

13 But in the first year of ^RCyrus the king of Babylon *the same* king Cyrus made a decree to build this house of God.

14 And ^Rthe vessels also of gold and silver of the house of God, which Nĕb-ū-<u>ch</u>ăd-nĕz′-zär took out of the temple that *was* in Jerusalem, and brought them into the temple of Babylon, those did Cyrus the king take out of the temple of Babylon, and they were delivered unto *one,* ^Rwhose name *was* Shĕsh-băz′-zär, whom he had made ^Ngovernor;

15 And said unto him, Take these vessels, go, carry them into the temple that *is* in Jerusalem, and let the house of God be builded in his place.

16 Then came the same Shĕsh-băz′-zär, *and* ^Rlaid the foundation of the house of God

---

CHAP. 5
BC 520
4 Chald. *that build this building?*
5 See ch. 7:6, 28
  Ps. 33:18
5 ch. 6:6
6 ch. 4:9
7 Chald. *in the midst whereof*
8 Chald. *stones of rolling*
9 ver. 3, 4
11 1 Ki. 6:1
12 2 Chr. 36:16, 17
12 2 Ki. 24:2
  & 25:8, 9, 11
13 ch. 1:1
14 ch. 1:7, 8 & 6:5
14 Hag. 1:14
  & 2:2, 21
14 Or, *deputy*
16 ch. 3:8, 10

ch. 6:15   16
ch. 6:1, 2   17

CHAP. 6
BC 515
ch. 5:17   1
Chald. *books*   1
Chald. *made to descend* 1
Or, *Ecbatana,* or, *in a coffer* 2
1 Ki. 6:36   4
ch. 1:7, 8   5
  & 5:14
Chald. *go*   5
ch. 5:3   6
Chald. *their societies* 6
Chald. *by me a decree is made* 8
Chald. *made to cease* 8

---

which *is* in Jerusalem: and since that time even until now hath it been in building, and ^Ryet it is not finished.

17 Now therefore, if *it seem* good to the king, ^Rlet there be search made in the king's treasure house, which *is* there at Babylon, whether it be *so,* that a decree was made of Cyrus the king to build this house of God at Jerusalem, and let the king send his pleasure to us concerning this matter.

CHAPTER 6

Darius finds decree of Cyrus

THEN Dă-rī′-ŭs the king made a decree, ^Rand search was made in the house of the ^Nrolls, where the treasures were ^Nlaid up in Babylon.

2 And there was found at ^NĂch-mē′-thă, in the palace that *is* in the province of the Mēdeś, a roll, and therein *was* a record thus written:

3 In the first year of Cyrus the king *the same* Cyrus the king made a decree *concerning* the house of God at Jerusalem, Let the house be builded, the place where they offered sacrifices, and let the foundations thereof be strongly laid; the height thereof threescore cubits, *and* the breadth thereof threescore cubits;

4 ^R*With* three rows of great stones, and a row of new timber: and let the expenses be given out of the king's house:

5 And also let ^Rthe golden and silver vessels of the house of God, which Nĕb-ū-<u>ch</u>ăd-nĕz′-zär took forth out of the temple which *is* at Jerusalem, and brought unto Babylon, be restored, and ^Nbrought again unto the temple which *is* at Jerusalem, *every one* to his place, and place *them* in the house of God.

6 ^RNow *therefore,* Tăt′-nâi, governor beyond the river, Shē′-thär-bŏz′-nâi, and ^Nyour companions the Ă-phär′-să-<u>ch</u>ites, which *are* beyond the river, be ye far from thence:

7 Let the work of this house of God alone; let the governor of the Jews and the elders of the Jews build this house of God in his place.

8 Moreover ^NI make a decree what ye shall do to the elders of these Jews for the building of this house of God: that of the king's goods, *even* of the tribute beyond the river, forthwith expenses be given unto these men, that they be not ^Nhindered.

9 And that which they have need of, both young bullocks, and rams, and lambs, for the burnt offerings of the God of heaven, wheat, salt, wine, and oil, according to the appoint-

ment of the priests which *are* at Jerusalem, let it be given them day by day without fail:

10 [R]That they may offer sacrifices [N]of sweet savours unto the God of heaven, and pray for the life of the king, and of his sons.

11 Also I have made a decree, that whosoever shall alter this word, let timber be pulled down from his house, and being set up, [N]let him be hanged thereon; [R]and let his house be made a dunghill for this.

12 And the God that hath caused his [R]name to dwell there destroy all kings and people, that shall put to their hand to alter *and* to destroy this house of God which *is* at Jerusalem. I Dă-rī'-ŭs have made a decree; let it be done with speed.

Temple completed and dedicated

13 Then Tăt'-naĭ, governor on this side the river, Shē'-thär-bŏz'-naĭ, and their companions, according to that which Dă-rī'-ŭs the king had sent, so they did speedily.

14 [R]And the elders of the Jews builded, and they prospered through the prophesying of Hăg'-gaĭ the prophet and Zĕch-ă-rī'-ăh the son of ĭd'-dō. And they builded, and finished *it,* according to the commandment of the God of Israel, and according to the [N]commandment of [R]Cyrus, and [R]Dă-rī'-ŭs, and [R]Är-tă-xĕrx'-ēś king of Persia.

15 And this house was finished on the third day of the month Ā'-där, which was in the sixth year of the reign of Dă-rī'-ŭs the king.

16 And the children of Israel, the priests, and the Levites, and the rest of [N]the children of the captivity, kept [R]the dedication of this house of God with joy,

17 And [R]offered at the dedication of this house of God an hundred bullocks, two hundred rams, four hundred lambs; and for a sin offering for all Israel, twelve he goats, according to the number of the tribes of Israel.

18 And they set the priests in their [R]divisions, and the Levites in their [R]courses, for the service of God, which *is* at Jerusalem; [R]as[N] it is written in the book of Moses.

Passover celebrated

19 And the children of the captivity kept the passover [R]upon the fourteenth *day* of the first month.

20 For the priests and the Levites were [R]purified together, all of them *were* pure, and [R]killed the passover for all the children of the captivity, and for their brethren the priests, and for themselves.

21 And the children of Israel, which were come again out of captivity, and all such as

had separated themselves unto them from the [R]filthiness of the heathen of the land, to seek the LORD God of Israel, did eat,

22 And kept the [R]feast of unleavened bread seven days with joy: for the LORD had made them joyful, and [R]turned the heart [R]of the king of Assyria unto them, to strengthen their hands in the work of the house of God, the God of Israel.

CHAPTER 7

Ezra's grant from Artaxerxes

NOW after these things, in the reign of [R]Är-tă-xĕrx'-ēś king of Persia, Ezra [R]the son of Sĕ-raĭ'-ăh, the son of Ăz-ă-rī'-ăh, the son of Hĭl-kī'-ăh,

2 The son of Shăl'-lŭm, the son of Zā'-dŏk, the son of Ă-hī'-tŭb,

3 The son of Ăm-ă-rī'-ăh, the son of Ăz-ă-rī' ăh, the son of Mĕ-raĭ'-ōth,

4 The son of Zĕr-ă-hī'-ăh, the son of ŭz'-zī, the son of Bŭk'-kī,

5 The son of Ă-bī'-shû-ă, the son of Phĭn'-ĕ-hăś, the son of ĕl-ē-ā'-zär, the son of Aaron the chief priest:

6 This Ezra went up from Babylon; and he *was* [R]a ready scribe in the law of Moses, which the LORD God of Israel had given: and the king granted him all his request, [R]according to the hand of the LORD his God upon him.

7 [R]And there went up *some* of the children of Israel, and of the priests, and [R]the Levites, and the singers, and the porters, and [R]the Nĕth'-ī-nĭmś, unto Jerusalem, in the seventh year of Är-tă-xĕrx'-ēś the king.

8 And he came to Jerusalem in the fifth month, which *was* in the seventh year of the king.

9 For upon the first *day* of the first month [N]began he to go up from Babylon, and on the first *day* of the fifth month came he to Jerusalem, [R]according to the good hand of his God upon him.

10 For Ezra had prepared his heart to [R]seek the law of the LORD, and to do *it,* and to [R]teach in Israel statutes and judgments.

11 Now this *is* the copy of the letter that the king Är-tă-xĕrx'-ēś gave unto Ezra the priest, the scribe, *even* a scribe of the words of the commandments of the LORD, and of his statutes to Israel.

12 Är-tă-xĕrx'-ēś, [R]king of kings, [N]unto Ezra the priest, a scribe of the law of the God of heaven, perfect *peace,* [R]and at such a time.

13 I make a decree, that all they of the people of Israel, and *of* his priests and Levites, in

my realm, which are minded of their own freewill to go up to Jerusalem, go with thee.

14 Forasmuch as thou art sent ᴺof the king, and of his ᴿseven counsellors, to inquire concerning Judah and Jerusalem, according to the law of thy God which *is* in thine hand;

15 And to carry the silver and gold, which the king and his counsellors have freely offered unto the God of Israel, ᴿwhose habitation *is* in Jerusalem,

16 ᴿAnd all the silver and gold that thou canst find in all the province of Babylon, with the freewill offering of the people, and of the priests, ᴿoffering willingly for the house of their God which *is* in Jerusalem:

17 That thou mayest buy speedily with this money bullocks, rams, lambs, with their ᴿmeat offerings and their drink offerings, and ᴿoffer them upon the altar of the house of your God which *is* in Jerusalem.

18 And whatsoever shall seem good to thee, and to thy brethren, to do with the rest of the silver and the gold, that do after the will of your God.

19 The vessels also that are given thee for the service of the house of thy God, *those* deliver thou before the God of Jerusalem.

20 And whatsoever more shall be needful for the house of thy God, which thou shalt have occasion to bestow, bestow *it* out of the king's treasure house.

21 And I, *even* I Är-tă-xĕrx'-ēś the king, do make a decree to all the treasurers which *are* beyond the river, that whatsoever Ezra the priest, the scribe of the law of the God of heaven, shall require of you, it be done speedily,

22 Unto an hundred talents of silver, and to an hundred ᴺmeasures of wheat, and to an hundred băths of wine, and to an hundred băths of oil, and salt without prescribing *how much.*

23 ᴺWhatsoever is commanded by the God of heaven, let it be diligently done for the house of the God of heaven: for why should there be wrath against the realm of the king and his sons?

24 Also we certify you, that touching any of the priests and Levites, singers, porters, Nĕth'-ĭ-nĭmś, or ministers of this house of God, it shall not be lawful to impose toll, tribute, or custom, upon them.

25 And thou, Ezra, after the wisdom of thy God, that *is* in thine hand, ᴿset magistrates and judges, which may judge all the people that *are* beyond the river, all such as know the laws of thy God; and ᴿteach ye them that know *them* not.

26 And whosoever will not do the law of thy God, and the law of the king, let judgment be executed speedily upon him, whether *it be* unto death, or ᴺto banishment, or to confiscation of goods, or to imprisonment.

27 ᴿBlessed *be* the LORD God of our fathers, ᴿwhich hath put *such a thing* as this in the king's heart, to beautify the house of the LORD which *is* in Jerusalem:

28 And ᴿhath extended mercy unto me before the king, and his counsellors, and before all the king's mighty princes. And I was strengthened as ᴿthe hand of the LORD my God *was* upon me, and I gathered together out of Israel chief men to go up with me.

CHAPTER 8

People returning with Ezra

THESE *are* now the chief of their fathers, and *this is* the genealogy of them that went up with me from Babylon, in the reign of Är-tă-xĕrx'-ēś the king.

2 Of the sons of Phĭn'-ĕ-hăś; Gĕr'-shŏm: of the sons of ĭth'-ă-mär; Daniel: of the sons of David; ᴿHăt'-tŭsh.

3 Of the sons of Shĕch-ă-nī'-ăh, of the sons of ᴿPhâr'-ŏsh; Zĕch-ă-rī'-ăh: and with him were reckoned by genealogy of the males an hundred and fifty.

4 Of the sons of Pā'-hăth-mō'-ăb; Ĕl-ĭ-hō-ē'-nâi the son of Zĕr-ă-hī'-ăh, and with him two hundred males.

5 Of the sons of Shĕch-ă-nī'-ăh; the son of Jă-hā'-zī-ĕl, and with him three hundred males.

6 Of the sons also of Ā'-dĭn; Ē'-bĕd the son of Jonathan, and with him fifty males.

7 And of the sons of Ē'-lăm; Jĕ-shâi'-ăh the son of Ăth-ă-lī'-ăh, and with him seventy males.

8 And of the sons of Shĕph-ă-tī'-ăh; Zĕb-ă-dī'-ăh the son of Michael, and with him fourscore males.

9 Of the sons of Jō'-ăb; Ō-bă-dī'-ăh the son of Jĕ-hī'-ĕl, and with him two hundred and eighteen males.

10 And of the sons of Shĕ-lō'-mĭth; the son of Jŏs-ĭ-phī'-ăh, and with him an hundred and threescore males.

11 And of the sons of Bē-bā'-ĭ; Zĕch-ă-rī'-ăh the son of Bē-bā'-ĭ, and with him twenty and eight males.

12 And of the sons of Azgad; Jō-hā'-năn ᴺthe son of Hăk'-kă-tăn, and with him an hundred and ten males.

13 And of the last sons of Ăd-ō-nī'-kăm, whose names *are* these, Ē-lĭph'-ĕ-lĕt, Jĕ-ĭ'-ĕl,

and Shĕm-aî'-ăh, and with them threescore males.

14 Of the sons also of Bĭg-vā'-ī; Ū'-thaî, and ᴺZăb'-bŭd, and with them seventy males.

15 And I gathered them together to the river that runneth to ă-hā'-vă; and there ᴺabode we in tents three days: and I viewed the people, and the priests, and found there none of the ᴿsons of Levi.

16 Then sent I for Ĕl-ĭ-ē'-zĕr, for Âr'-ĭ-ĕl, for Shĕm-aî'-ăh, and for ĕl-nā'-thăn, and for Jâr'-ĭb, and for ĕl-nā'-thăn, and for Nathan, and for Zĕch-ȧ-rī'-ăh, and for Mĕ-shŭl'-lăm, chief men; also for Joî'-ȧ-rĭb, and for Ĕl-nā'-thăn, men of understanding.

17 And I sent them with commandment unto ĭd'-dō the chief at the place Căs-ĭ-phī'-ă, and ᴺI told them what they should say unto ĭd'-dō, and to his brethren the Nĕth'-ĭ-nĭmś, at the place Căs-ĭ-phī'-ă, that they should bring unto us ministers for the house of our God.

18 And by the good hand of our God upon us they ᴿbrought us a man of understanding, of the sons of Măh'-lī, the son of Levi, the son of Israel; and Shĕr-ē-bī'-ăh, with his sons and his brethren, eighteen;

19 And Hăsh-ȧ-bī'-ăh, and with him Jĕ-shaî'-ăh of the sons of Mĕ-râr'-ī, his brethren and their sons, twenty;

20 ᴿAlso of the Nĕth'-ĭ-nĭmś, whom David and the princes had appointed for the service of the Levites, two hundred and twenty Nĕth'-ĭ-nĭmś: all of them were expressed by name.

A fast proclaimed

21 Then I ᴿproclaimed a fast there, at the river of ă-hā'-vă, that we might ᴿafflict ourselves before our God, to seek of him a ᴿright way for us, and for our little ones, and for all our substance.

22 For ᴿI was ashamed to require of the king a band of soldiers and horsemen to help us against the enemy in the way: because we had spoken unto the king, saying, ᴿThe hand of our God is upon all them for ᴿgood that seek him; but his power and his wrath is ᴿagainst all them that ᴿforsake him.

23 So we fasted and besought our God for this: and he was ᴿentreated of us.

24 Then I separated twelve of the chief of the priests, Shĕr-ē-bī'-ăh, Hăsh-ȧ-bī'-ăh, and ten of their brethren with them,

25 And weighed unto them ᴿthe silver, and the gold, and the vessels, even the offering of the house of our God, which the king, and his counsellors, and his lords, and all Israel there present, had offered:

26 I even weighed unto their hand six hun-

dred and fifty talents of silver, and silver vessels an hundred talents, and of gold an hundred talents;

27 Also twenty basins of gold, of a thousand drams; and two vessels of ᴺfine copper, ᴺprecious as gold.

28 And I said unto them, Ye are ᴿholy unto the Lᴏʀᴅ; the vessels are ᴿholy also; and the silver and the gold are a freewill offering unto the Lᴏʀᴅ God of your fathers.

29 Watch ye, and keep them, until ye weigh them before the chief of the priests and the Levites, and chief of the fathers of Israel, at Jerusalem, in the chambers of the house of the Lᴏʀᴅ.

30 So took the priests and the Levites the weight of the silver, and the gold, and the vessels, to bring them to Jerusalem unto the house of our God.

Arrival in Jerusalem

31 Then we departed from the river of Ă-hā'-vă on the twelfth day of the first month, to go unto Jerusalem: and ᴿthe hand of our God was upon us, and he delivered us from the hand of the enemy, and of such as lay in wait by the way.

32 And we ᴿcame to Jerusalem, and abode there three days.

33 Now on the fourth day was the silver and the gold and the vessels ᴿweighed in the house of our God by the hand of Mĕr'-ĕ-mōth the son of Ū-rī'-ăh the priest; and with him was Ĕl-ē-ā'-zär the son of Phĭn'-ĕ-hăś; and with them was Jō'-ză-băd the son of Jĕsh'-ū-ă, and Nō-ă-dī'-ăh the son of Bĭn'-nū-ī, Levites;

34 By number and by weight of every one: and all the weight was written at that time.

35 Also the children of those that had been carried away, which were come out of the captivity, ᴿoffered burnt offerings unto the God of Israel, twelve bullocks for all Israel, ninety and six rams, seventy and seven lambs, twelve he goats for a sin offering: all this was a burnt offering unto the Lᴏʀᴅ.

36 And they delivered the king's ᴿcommissions unto the king's lieutenants, and to the governors on this side the river: and they furthered the people, and the house of God.

CHAPTER 9

Report about mixed marriages

Nᴏᴡ when these things were done, the princes came to me, saying, The people of Israel, and the priests, and the Levites, have not ᴿseparated themselves from the people of the lands, ᴿdoing according to their abomina-

tions, *even* of the Canaanites, the Hittites, the Pĕ-rĭz'-zītes, the Jĕb'-ū-sītes, the Ammonites, the Moabites, the Egyptians, and the Amorites.

2 For they have ᴿtaken of their daughters for themselves, and for their sons: so that the ᴿholy seed have ᴿmingled themselves with the people of *those* lands: yea, the hand of the princes and rulers hath been chief in this trespass.

3 And when I heard this thing, ᴿI rent my garment and my mantle, and plucked off the hair of my head and of my beard, and sat down ᴿastonied.

4 Then were assembled unto me every one that ᴿtrembled at the words of the God of Israel, because of the transgression of those that had been carried away; and I sat astonied until the ᴿevening sacrifice.

Ezra's prayer

5 And at the evening sacrifice I arose up from my ᴺheaviness; and having rent my garment and my mantle, I fell upon my knees, and ᴿspread out my hands unto the Lᴏʀᴅ my God,

6 And said, O my God, I am ᴿashamed and blush to lift up my face to thee, my God: for ᴿour iniquities are increased over *our* head, and our ᴺtrespass is ᴿgrown up unto the heavens.

7 Since the days of our fathers *have* ᴿwe *been* in a great trespass unto this day; and for our iniquities ᴿhave we, our kings, *and* our priests, been delivered into the hand of the kings of the lands, to the sword, to captivity, and to a spoil, and to ᴿconfusion of face, as *it is* this day.

8 And now for a ᴺlittle space grace hath been *shewed* from the Lᴏʀᴅ our God, to leave us a remnant to escape, and to give us ᴺa nail in his holy place, that our God may ᴿlighten our eyes, and give us a little reviving in our bondage.

9 ᴿFor we *were* bondmen; ᴿyet our God hath not forsaken us in our bondage, but ᴿhath extended mercy unto us in the sight of the kings of Persia, to give us a reviving, to set up the house of our God, and ᴺto repair the desolations thereof, and to give us ᴿa wall in Judah and in Jerusalem.

10 And now, O our God, what shall we say after this? for we have forsaken thy commandments,

11 Which thou hast commanded ᴺby thy servants the prophets, saying, The land, unto which ye go to possess it, is an unclean land with the filthiness of the people of the lands, with their abominations, which have filled it

ᴺfrom one end to another with their uncleanness.

12 Now therefore ᴿgive not your daughters unto their sons, neither take their daughters unto your sons, ᴿnor seek their peace or their wealth for ever: that ye may be strong, and eat the good of the land, and ᴿleave *it* for an inheritance to your children for ever.

13 And after all that is come upon us for our evil deeds, and for our great trespass, seeing that thou our God ᴿhastᴺ punished us less than our iniquities *deserve,* and hast given us *such* deliverance as this;

14 Should we ᴿagain break thy commandments, and ᴿjoin in affinity with the people of these abominations? wouldest not thou be ᴿangry with us till thou hadst consumed *us,* so that *there should be* no remnant nor escaping?

15 O Lᴏʀᴅ God of Israel, ᴿthou *art* righteous: for we remain yet escaped, as *it is* this day: behold, we *are* ᴿbefore thee ᴿin our trespasses: for we cannot stand before thee because of this.

CHAPTER 10

Mixed marriages abandoned

NOW ᴿwhen Ezra had prayed, and when he had confessed, weeping and casting himself down ᴿbefore the house of God, there assembled unto him out of Israel a very great congregation of men and women and children: for the people ᴺwept very sore.

2 And Shĕch-ă-nī'-ăh the son of Jĕ-hī'-ĕl, *one* of the sons of Ē'-lăm, answered and said unto Ezra, We have ᴿtrespassed against our God, and have taken strange wives of the people of the land: yet now there is hope in Israel concerning this thing.

3 Now therefore let us make ᴿa covenant with our God ᴺto put away all the wives, and such as are born of them, according to the counsel of my lord, and of those that ᴿtremble at ᴿthe commandment of our God; and let it be done according to the law.

4 Arise; for *this* matter *belongeth* unto thee: we also *will be* with thee: ᴿbe of good courage, and do *it.*

5 Then arose Ezra, and made the chief priests, the Levites, and all Israel, ᴿto swear that they should do according to this word. And they sware.

6 Then Ezra rose up from before the house of God, and went into the chamber of Jō-hā'-năn the son of Ē-lī-ăsh'-ĭb: and *when* he came thither, he ᴿdid eat no bread, nor drink water: for he mourned because of the transgression of them that had been carried away.

7 And they made proclamation throughout Judah and Jerusalem unto all the children of the captivity, that they should gather themselves together unto Jerusalem;

8 And that whosoever would not come within three days, according to the counsel of the princes and the elders, all his substance should be ᴺforfeited, and himself separated from the congreagation of those that had been carried away.

9 Then all the men of Judah and Benjamin gathered themselves together unto Jerusalem within three days. It *was* the ninth month, on the twentieth *day* of the month; and ᴿall the people sat in the street of the house of God, trembling because of *this* matter, and for ᴺthe great rain.

10 And Ezra the priest stood up, and said unto them, Ye have transgressed, and ᴺhave taken strange wives, to increase the trespass of Israel.

11 Now therefore ᴿmake confession unto the Lord God of your fathers, and do his pleas ure: and ᴿseparate yourselves from the people of the land, and from the strange wives.

12 Then all the congregation answered and said with a loud voice, As thou hast said, so must we do.

13 But the people *are* many, and *it is* a time of much rain, and we are not able to stand without, neither *is this* a work of one day or two: for ᴺwe are many that have transgressed in this thing.

14 Let now our rulers of all the congregation stand, and let all them which have taken strange wives in our cities come at appointed times, and with them the elders of every city, and the judges thereof, until ᴿthe fierce wrath of our God ᴺfor this matter be turned from us.

15 Only Jonathan the son of Ăs'-ă-hĕl and Jā-hă-zī'-ăh the son of Tĭk'-văh ᴺwere employed about this *matter:* and Mĕ-shŭl'-lăm and Shăb'-bĕ-thaî the Levite helped them.

16 And the children of the captivity did so. And Ezra the priest, *with* certain chief of the fathers, after the house of their fathers, and all of them by *their* names, were separated, and sat down in the first day of the tenth month to examine the matter.

17 And they made an end with all the men that had taken strange wives by the first day of the first month.

18 And among the sons of the priests there were found that had taken strange wives: *namely,* of the sons of Jĕsh'-ū-ă the son of Jō'-ză-dăk, and his brethren; Mā-ă-seî'-ăh, and ĕl-ĭ-ē'-zĕr, and Jâr'-ĭb, and Gĕd-ă-lī'-ăh.

19 And they ᴿgave their hands that they would put away their wives; and *being*

CHAP. 10
BC 457
8 Heb. *devoted*
9 See 1 Sam. 12:18
9 Heb. *the showers*
10 Heb. *have caused to dwell, or, have brought back*
11 Josh. 7:19
Prov. 28:13
11 ver. 3
13 Or, *we have greatly offended in this thing*
14 2 Chr. 30:8
14 Or, *till this matter be* dispatched
15 Heb. *stood*
19 2 Ki. 10:15
1 Chr. 29:24
2 Chr. 30:8

Lev. 6:4, 6   19
Or, *Mabnadebai,* 40
according to some copies

ᴿguilty, *they offered* a ram of the flock for their trespass.

20 And of the sons of ĭm'-mĕr; Hă-nā'-nī, and Zĕb-ă-dī'-ăh.

21 And of the sons of Hâr'-ĭm; Mā-ă-seî'-ăh, and Ē-lī'-jăh, and Shĕm-aî'-ăh, and Jĕ-hī'-ĕl, and ŭz-zī'-ăh.

22 And of the sons of Păsh'-ŭr; ĕl-ĭ-ō-ē'-naî, Mā-ă-seî'-ăh, ĭsh'-mā-ĕl, Nĕth'-ă-neĕl, Jō'-ză-băd, and ĕl-ā'-săh.

23 Also of the Levites; Jō'-ză-băd, and Shĭm'-ĕ-ī, and Kĕ-laî'-ăh, (the same *is* Kĕ-lī'-tă,) Pĕth-ă-hī'-ăh, Judah, and ĕl-ĭ-ē'-zĕr.

24 Of the singers also; Ē-lī-ăsh'-ĭb: and of the porters; Shăl'-lŭm, and Tē'-lĕm, and Ū'-rī.

25 Moreover of Israel: of the sons of Pâr'-ŏsh; Ră-mī'-ăh, and Jĕ-zī'-ăh, and Măl-chī'-ăh, and Mĭ'-ă-mĭn, and ĕl-ē-ā'-zär, and Măl-chī'-jăh, and Bĕ-naî'-ăh.

26 And of the sons of Ē'-lăm; Măt-tă-nī'-ăh, Zĕch-ă-rī'-ăh, and Jĕ-hī'-ĕl, and Abdi, and Jĕr'-ĕ-mŏth, and Ē-lī'-ăh.

27 And of the sons of Zăt'-tû; ĕl-ĭ-ō-ē'-naî, Ē-lī-ăsh'-ĭb, Măt-tă-nī'-ăh, and Jĕr'-ĕ-mŏth, and Zā'-băd, and Ă-zī'-ză.

28 Of the sons also of Bē-bā'-ī; Jĕ-hō-hā'-năn, Hăn-ă-nī'-ăh, Zăb-bā'-ī, *and* Ăth-lā'-ī.

29 And of the sons of Bā'-nī; Mĕ-shŭl'-lăm, Măl'-lŭch, and Ă-daî'-ăh, Jăsh'-ŭb, and Shē'-ăl, and Rā'-mŏth.

30 And of the sons of Pā'-hăth-mō'-ăb; Adna, and Chē'-lăl, Bĕ-naî'-ăh, Mā-ă-seî'-ăh, Măt-tă-nī'-ăh, Bĕz'-ă-leĕl, and Bĭn'-nū-ī, and Mă-năs'-sĕh.

31 And *of* the sons of Hâr'-ĭm; ĕl-ĭ-ē'-zĕr, ĭsh-ī'-jăh, Măl-chī'-ăh, Shĕm-aî'-ăh, Shĭm'-ĕ-on,

32 Benjamin, Măl'-lŭch, *and* Shĕm-ă-rī'-ăh.

33 Of the sons of Hăsh'-ŭm; Măt-tē'-naî, Măt'-tă-thăh, Zā'-băd, Ē-lĭph'-ĕ-lĕt, Jĕr-ĕ-mā'-ī, Mă-năs'-sĕh, *and* Shĭm'-ĕ-ī.

34 Of the sons of Bā'-nī; Mā-ă-dā'-ī, Amram, and Ū'-ĕl,

35 Bĕ-naî'-ăh, Bĕ-deî'-ăh, Chĕl'-lûh,

36 Vă-nī'-ăh, Mĕr'-ĕ-mŏth, Ē-lī-ăsh'-ĭb,

37 Măt-tă-nī'-ăh, Măt-tē'-naî, and Jā'-ă-saû,

38 And Bā'-nī, and Bĭn'-nū-ī, Shĭm'-ĕ-ī,

39 And Shĕl-ē-mī'-ăh, and Nathan, and Ă-daî'-ăh,

40 ᴺMăch-năd'-ĕ-baî, Shā'-shaî, Shâr-ā'-ī,

41 Ăz'-ă-reĕl, and Shĕl-ē-mī'-ăh, Shĕm-ă-rī'-ăh,

42 Shăl'-lŭm, ăm-ă-rī'-ăh, *and* Joseph.

43 Of the sons of Nē'-bo; Jĕ-ī'-ĕl, Măt-tĭ-thī'-ăh, Zā'-băd, Zĕ-bī'-nă, Jā'-daû, and Jō'-ĕl, Bĕ-naî'-ăh.

44 All these had taken strange wives: and *some* of them had wives by whom they had children.

THE
BOOK OF NEHEMIAH

The book of Nehemiah takes its name from the leading character whose work and activities it narrates. Originally, the memoirs of Nehemiah were very likely incorporated by Ezra into his own accounts to make one volume, the form in which it appeared in the Jewish canon. The present book gives an account of the return of Nehemiah to Jerusalem in 444 B.C. It provides a record of his appointment by the king of Persia as governor over the province of Judah and outlines his work and achievements during his administration. Nehemiah provided security for the returned exiles while rebuilding the walls of Jerusalem, and the aggressive and dedicated leadership of both Nehemiah and Ezra inspired the religious and moral regeneration of the people. Chapters 1 – 6 provide an interesting narrative of Nehemiah's work in rebuilding the walls and the restoration of order. Chapters 7 – 12 record the work of Ezra and Nehemiah in moral and spiritual reformation of the people and give an account of the dedication of the rebuilt walls. The last chapter concerns Nehemiah's second visit to Palestine.

OUTLINE OF THE BOOK:
- I. Nehemiah the cupbearer 1:1 – 2:8
- II. Rebuilding the walls 3:1 – 6:19
- III. The reform movement 7:1 – 10:39
- IV. Program and policies for Judah 11:1 – 13:31

CHAPTER 1

Nehemiah's prayer

THE words of ᴿNĕ-hĕm-ĭ′-ăh the son of Hăch-ă-lī′-ăh. And it came to pass in the month Chĭs′-lĕŭ, in the twentieth year, as I was in Shū′-shăn the palace,

2 That Hă-nā′-nī, one of my brethren, came, he and *certain* men of Judah; and I asked them concerning the Jews that had escaped, which were left of the captivity, and concerning Jerusalem.

3 And they said unto me, The remnant that are left of the captivity there in the province *are* in great affliction and reproach: ᴿthe wall of Jerusalem also ᴿ*is* broken down, and the gates thereof are burned with fire.

4 And it came to pass, when I heard these words, that I sat down and wept, and mourned *certain* days, and fasted, and prayed before the God of heaven,

5 And said, I beseech thee, ᴿO Lᴏʀᴅ God of heaven, the great and terrible God, ᴿthat keepeth covenant and mercy for them that love him and observe his commandments:

6 Let thine ear now be attentive, and ᴿthine eyes open, that thou mayest hear the prayer of thy servant, which I pray before thee now, day and night, for the children of Israel thy servants, and ᴿconfess the sins of the children of Israel, which we have sinned against thee: both I and my father's house have sinned.

7 ᴿWe have dealt very corruptly against thee, and have ᴿnot kept the commandments, nor the statutes, nor the judgments, which thou commandedst thy servant Moses.

8 Remember, I beseech thee, the word that thou commandedst thy servant Moses, saying, ᴿ*If* ye transgress, I will scatter you abroad among the nations:

9 ᴿBut *if* ye turn unto me, and keep my commandments, and do them; ᴿthough there were of you cast out unto the uttermost part of the heaven, *yet* will I gather them from thence, and will bring them unto the place that I have chosen to set my name there.

10 ᴿNow these *are* thy servants and thy people, whom thou hast redeemed by thy great power, and by thy strong hand.

11 O Lᴏʀᴅ, I beseech thee, ᴿlet now thine ear be attentive to the prayer of thy servant, and to the prayer of thy servants, who ᴿdesire to fear thy name: and prosper, I pray thee, thy servant this day, and grant him mercy in the sight of this man. For I was the king's ᴿcupbearer.

CHAPTER 2

Nehemiah's request of the king

AND it came to pass in the month Nī′-săn, in the twentieth year of ᴿÄr-tă-xĕrx′-ēś the king, *that* wine *was* before him: and ᴿI took up the wine, and gave *it* unto the king. Now I had not been *beforetime* sad in his presence.

2 Wherefore the king said unto me, Why *is* thy countenance sad, seeing thou *art* not sick? this *is* nothing *else* but ᴿsorrow of heart. Then I was very sore afraid,

3 And said unto the king, ᴿLet the king live for ever: why should not my countenance be sad, when ᴿthe city, the place of my fathers' sepulchres, *lieth* waste, and the gates thereof are consumed with fire?

4 Then the king said unto me, For what dost thou make request? So I prayed to the God of heaven.

5 And I said unto the king, If it please the king, and if thy servant have found favour in thy sight, that thou wouldest send me unto

Judah, unto the city of my fathers' sepulchres, that I may build it.

6 And the king said unto me, (the ᴺqueen also sitting by him,) For how long shall thy journey be? and when wilt thou return? So it pleased the king to send me; and I set him ᴿa time.

7 Moreover I said unto the king, If it please the king, let letters be given me to the governors beyond the river, that they may convey me over till I come into Judah;

8 And a letter unto Ā'-săph the keeper of the king's forest, that he may give me timber to make beams for the gates of the palace which *appertained* ᴿto the house, and for the wall of the city, and for the house that I shall enter into. And the king granted me, ᴿaccording to the good hand of my God upon me.

9 Then I came to the governors beyond the river, and gave them the king's letters. Now the king had sent captains of the army and horsemen with me.

10 When Săn-băl'-lăt the Hôr'-ŏn-īte, and Tō-bī'-ăh the servant, the Ammonite, heard *of it,* it grieved them exceedingly that there was come a man to seek the welfare of the children of Israel.

Nehemiah inspects the walls

11 So I ᴿcame to Jerusalem, and was there three days.

12 And I arose in the night, I and some few men with me; neither told I *any* man what my God had put in my heart to do at Jerusalem: neither *was there any* beast with me, save the beast that I rode upon.

13 And I went out by night ᴿby the gate of the valley, even before the dragon well, and to the dung port, and viewed the walls of Jerusalem, which were ᴿbroken down, and the gates thereof were consumed with fire.

14 Then I went on to the ᴿgate of the fountain, and to the king's pool: but *there was* no place for the beast *that was* under me to pass.

15 Then went I up in the night by the ᴿbrook, and viewed the wall, and turned back, and entered by the gate of the valley, and *so* returned.

16 And the rulers knew not whither I went, or what I did; neither had I as yet told *it* to the Jews, nor to the priests, nor to the nobles, nor to the rulers, nor to the rest that did the work.

17 Then said I unto them, Ye see the distress that we *are* in, how Jerusalem *lieth* waste, and the gates thereof are burned with fire: come, and let us build up the wall of Jerusalem, that we be no more ᴿa reproach.

18 Then I told them of ᴿthe hand of my God

CHAP. **2**

BC 445

6 Heb. *wife*
6 ch. 5:14 & 13:6
8 ch. 3:7
8 ver. 18
Ezra 5:5
& 7:6, 9, 28
11 Ezra 8:32
13 2 Chr. 26:9
ch. 3:13
13 ver. 17
ch. 1:3
14 ch. 3:15
15 2 Sam. 15:23
Jer. 31:40
17 ch. 1:3
Ps. 44:13
& 79:4
Jer. 24:9
Ezek. 5:14, 15
& 22:4
18 ver. 8

2 Sam. 2:7   **18**
ch. 6:6   **19**
Ezra 4:3   **20**

CHAP. **3**

BC 445

ch. 12:10   **1**
John 5:2   **1**
ch. 12:39   **1**
Jer. 31:38   **1**
Zech. 14:10
Heb. *at his hand*   **2**
Ezra 2:34   **2**
2 Chr. 33:14   **3**
ch. 12:39
Zeph. 1:10
See ch. 6:1   **3**
& 7:1
Judg. 5:23   **5**
ch. 12:39   **6**
ch. 2:8   **7**
Or, *left Jerusalem unto the broad wall*   **8**
ch. 12:38   **8**

which was good upon me; as also the king's words that he had spoken unto me. And they said, Let us rise up and build. So they ᴿstrengthened their hands for *this* good *work.*

19 But when Săn-băl'-lăt the Hôr'-ŏn-īte, and Tō-bī'-ăh the servant, the Ammonite, and Gē'-shĕm the Arabian, heard *it,* they laughed us to scorn, and despised us, and said, What *is* this thing that ye do? ᴿwill ye rebel against the king?

20 Then answered I them, and said unto them, The God of heaven, he will prosper us; therefore we his servants will arise and build: ᴿbut ye have no portion, nor right, nor memorial, in Jerusalem.

CHAPTER 3

Assignments for building

THEN ᴿE-lī-ăsh'-ĭb the high priest rose up with his brethren the priests, ᴿand they builded the sheep gate; they sanctified it, and set up the doors of it; ᴿeven unto the tower of Mē'-ăh they sanctified it, unto the tower of ᴿHăn'-ă-nĕel.

2 And ᴺnext unto him builded ᴿthe men of Jericho. And next to them builded Zăc'-cùr the son of Imri.

3 ᴿBut the fish gate did the sons of Hăs-sĕ-nā'-ăh build, who *also* laid the beams thereof, and ᴿset up the doors thereof, the locks thereof, and the bars thereof.

4 And next unto them repaired Mĕr'-ĕ-mŏth the son of Ū-rī'-jăh, the son of Kŏz. And next unto them repaired Mĕ-shŭl'-lăm the son of Bĕr-ē-chī'-ăh, the son of Mĕ-shĕz'-ă-bĕel. And next unto them repaired Zā'-dŏk the son of Bā'-ă-nă.

5 And next unto them the Tĕ-kō'-ītes repaired; but their nobles put not their necks to ᴿthe work of their Lord.

6 Moreover ᴿthe old gate repaired Jĕ-hŏi'-ă-dă the son of Pă-sē'-ăh, and Mĕ-shŭl'-lăm the son of Bĕs-ō-dĕi'-ăh; they laid the beams thereof, and set up the doors thereof, and the locks thereof, and the bars thereof.

7 And next unto them repaired Mĕl-ă-tī'-ăh the Gibeonite, and Jā'-dŏn the Mĕ-rō'-nō-thīte, the men of Gibeon, and of Mizpah, unto the ᴿthrone of the governor on this side the river.

8 Next unto him repaired Ŭz'-zī-ĕl the son of Här-hāi'-ăh, of the goldsmiths. Next unto him also repaired Hăn-ă-nī'-ăh the son of *one of* the apothecaries, and they ᴺfortified Jerusalem unto the ᴿbroad wall.

9 And next unto them repaired Rĕ-phāi'-ăh

the son of Hur, the ruler of the half part of Jerusalem.

10 And next unto them repaired Jĕ-dā́ʹ-ăh the son of Hă-rū́ʹ-măph, even over against his house. And next unto him repaired Hăt́ʹ-tŭsh the son of Hăsh-ăb-nī́ʹ-ăh.

11 Măl-chī́ʹ-jah the son of Hâŕʹ-ĭm, and Hăsh́ʹ-ŭb the son of Pā́ʹ-hăth-mṓʹ-ăb, repaired the ᴺother piece, ᴿand the tower of the furnaces.

12 And next unto him repaired Shăĺʹ-lŭm the son of Hă-lṓʹ-hĕsh, the ruler of the half part of Jerusalem, he and his daughters.

13 ᴿThe valley gate repaired Hā́ʹ-nŭn, and the inhabitants of Ză-nṓʹ-ăh; they built it, and set up the doors thereof, the locks thereof, and the bars thereof, and a thousand cubits on the wall unto ᴿthe dung gate.

14 But the dung gate repaired Măl-chī́ʹ-ăh the son of Rḗʹ-chăb, the ruler of part of Bĕth-hăćʹ-cĕ-rĕm; he built it, and set up the doors thereof, the locks thereof, and the bars thereof.

15 But ᴿthe gate of the fountain repaired Shăĺʹ-lŭn the son of Cŏl-hṓʹ-zĕh, the ruler of part of Mizpah; he built it, and covered it, and set up the doors thereof, the locks thereof, and the bars thereof, and the wall of the pool of ᴿSĭ-lṓʹ-ăh by the king's garden, and unto the stairs that go down from the city of David.

16 After him repaired Nē-hĕm-ī́ʹ-ăh the son of Ăźʹ-bŭk, the ruler of the half part of Bĕth́ʹ-zùr, unto *the place* over against the sepulchres of David, and to the ᴿpool that was made, and unto the house of the mighty.

17 After him repaired the Levites, Rḗʹ-hŭm the son of Bā́ʹ-nī. Next unto him repaired Hăsh-ă-bī́ʹ-ăh, the ruler of the half part of Kē-ī́ʹ-lăh, in his part.

18 After him repaired their brethren, Bā-vā́ʹ-ī the son of Hĕn-ā́ʹ-dăd, the ruler of the half part of Kē-ī́ʹ-lăh.

19 And next to him repaired Ḗʹ-zĕr the son of Jĕsh́ʹ-ū-ă, the ruler of Mizpah, another piece over against the going up to the armoury at the ᴿturning *of the wall.*

20 After him Bâŕʹ-ŭch the son of ᴺZăb-bā́ʹ-ī earnestly repaired the other piece, from the turning *of the wall* unto the door of the house of Ē-lĭ-ăsh́ʹ-ĭb the high priest.

21 After him repaired Mĕŕʹ-ĕ-mŏth the son of Ū-rī́ʹ-jăh the son of Kŏz another piece, from the door of the house of Ē-lĭ-ăsh́ʹ-ĭb even to the end of the house of Ē-lĭ-ăsh́ʹ-ĭb.

22 And after him repaired the priests, the men of the plain.

23 After him repaired Benjamin and Hăsh́ʹ-ŭb over against their house. After him

repaired Ăz-ă-rī́ʹ-ăh the son of Mā-ă-sēī́ʹ-ăh the son of Ăn-ă-nī́ʹ-ăh by his house.

24 After him repaired Bĭńʹ-nū-ī the son of Hĕn-ā́ʹ-dăd another piece, from the house of Ăz-ă-rī́ʹ-ăh unto ᴿthe turning *of the wall,* even unto the corner.

25 Pā́ʹ-lăl the son of Ū́ʹ-zăī, over against the turning *of the wall,* and the tower which lieth out from the king's high house, that *was* by the ᴿcourt of the prison. After him Pĕ-dāī́ʹ-ăh the son of Pâŕʹ-ŏsh.

26 Moreover ᴿthe Nĕth́ʹ-ĭ-nĭmś ᴺdwelt in ᴿṒʹ-phĕl,ᴺ unto *the place* over against ᴿthe water gate toward the east, and the tower that lieth out.

27 After them the Tĕ-kṓʹ-ītes repaired another piece, over against the great tower that lieth out, even unto the wall of Ṓʹ-phĕl.

28 From above the ᴿhorse gate repaired the priests, every one over against his house.

29 After them repaired Zā́ʹ-dŏk the son of ĭḿʹ-mĕr over against his house. After him repaired also Shĕm-āī́ʹ-ăh the son of Shĕch-ă-nī́ʹ-ăh, the keeper of the east gate.

30 After him repaired Hăn-ă-nī́ʹ-ăh the son of Shĕl-ē-mī́ʹ-ăh, and Hā́ʹ-nŭn the sixth son of Zā́ʹ-lăph, another piece. After him repaired Mĕ-shŭĺʹ-lăm the son of Bĕr-ē-chī́ʹ-ăh over against his chamber.

31 After him repaired Măl-chī́ʹ-ăh the goldsmith's son unto the place of the Nĕth́ʹ-ĭ-nĭmś, and of the merchants, over against the gate Mĭph́ʹ-kăd, and to the ᴺgoing up of the corner.

32 And between the going up of the corner unto the sheep gate repaired the goldsmiths and the merchants.

CHAPTER 4

Opposition of Sanballat

BUT it came to pass, ᴿthat when Săn-băĺʹ-lăt heard that we builded the wall, he was wroth, and took great indignation, and mocked the Jews.

2 And he spake before his brethren and the army of Să-mâŕʹ-ĭ-ă, and said, What do these feeble Jews? will they ᴺfortify themselves? will they sacrifice? will they make an end in a day? will they revive the stones out of the heaps of the rubbish which are burned?

3 Now ᴿTō-bī́ʹ-ăh the Ammonite *was* by him, and he said, Even that which they build, if a fox go up, he shall even break down their stone wall.

4 ᴿHear, O our God; for we are ᴺdespised: and ᴿturn their reproach upon their own head, and give them for a prey in the land of captivity:

CHAP. 3

BC 445

11 Heb. *second measure*
11 ch. 12:38
13 ch. 2:13
13 ch. 2:13
15 ch. 2:14
15 John 9:7
16 2 Ki. 20:20
   Is. 22:11
19 2 Chr. 26:9
20 Or, *Zaccai*

ver. 19   24
Jer. 32:2   25
  & 33:1
  & 37:21
Ezra 2:43   26
  ch. 11:21
Or, which   26
dwelt in Ophel,
repaired unto
2 Chr. 27:3   26
Or, *The tower*   26
ch. 8:1, 3   26
  & 12:37
2 Ki. 11:16   28
  2 Chr. 23:15
Jer. 31:40
Or, *corner*   31
chamber

CHAP. 4

BC 445

ch. 2:10, 19   1
Heb. *leave to*   2
themselves
ch. 2:10, 19   3
Ps. 123:3, 4   4
Heb. *despite*   4
Ps. 79:12   4
Prov. 3:34

5 And [R]cover not their iniquity, and let not their sin be blotted out from before thee: for they have provoked *thee* to anger before the builders.

6 So built we the wall; and all the wall was joined together unto the half thereof: for the people had a mind to work.

7 But it came to pass, *that* [R]when Săn-băl'-lăt, and Tō-bī'-ăh, and the Arabians, and the Ammonites, and the Ăsh'-dō-dītes, heard that the walls of Jerusalem [N]were made up, *and* that the breaches began to be stopped, then they were very wroth,

8 And [R]conspired all of them together to come *and* to fight against Jerusalem, and [N]to hinder it.

9 Nevertheless [R]we made our prayer unto our God, and set a watch against them day and night, because of them.

Guards posted

10 And Judah said, The strength of the bearers of burdens is decayed, and *there is* much rubbish; so that we are not able to build the wall.

11 And our adversaries said, They shall not know, neither see, till we come in the midst among them, and slay them, and cause the work to cease.

12 And it came to pass, that when the Jews which dwelt by them came, they said unto us ten times, [N]From all places whence ye shall return unto us *they will be upon you.*

13 Therefore set I [N]in the lower places behind the wall, *and* on the higher places, I even set the people after their families with their swords, their spears, and their bows.

14 And I looked, and rose up, and said unto the nobles, and to the rulers, and to the rest of the people, [R]Be not ye afraid of them: remember the LORD, *which is* [R]great and terrible, and [R]fight for your brethren, your sons, and your daughters, your wives, and your houses.

15 And it came to pass, when our enemies heard that it was known unto us, [R]and God had brought their counsel to nought, that we returned all of us to the wall, every one unto his work.

16 And it came to pass from that time forth, *that* the half of my servants wrought in the work, and the other half of them held both the spears, the shields, and the bows, and the habergeons; and the rulers *were* behind all the house of Judah.

17 They which builded on the wall, and they that bare burdens, with those that laded, *every one* with one of his hands wrought in the

work, and with the other *hand* held a weapon.

18 For the builders, every one had his sword girded [N]by his side, and *so* builded. And he that sounded the trumpet *was* by me.

19 And I said unto the nobles, and to the rulers, and to the rest of the people, The work *is* great and large, and we are separated upon the wall, one far from another.

20 In what place *therefore* ye hear the sound of the trumpet, resort ye thither unto us: [R]our God shall fight for us.

21 So we laboured in the work: and half of them held the spears from the rising of the morning till the stars appeared.

22 Likewise at the same time said I unto the people, Let every one with his servant lodge within Jerusalem, that in the night they may be a guard to us, and labour on the day.

23 So neither I, nor my brethren, nor my servants, nor the men of the guard which followed me, none of us put off our clothes, [N]*saving that* every one put them off for washing.

CHAPTER 5

Interest charges cancelled

AND there was a great [R]cry of the people and of their wives against their [R]brethren the Jews.

2 For there were that said, We, our sons, and our daughters, *are* many: therefore we take up corn *for them,* that we may eat, and live.

3 *Some* also there were that said, We have mortgaged our lands, vineyards, and houses, that we might buy corn, because of the dearth.

4 There were also that said, We have borrowed money for the king's tribute, *and that upon* our lands and vineyards.

5 Yet now [R]our flesh *is* as the flesh of our brethren, our children as their children: and, lo, we [R]bring into bondage our sons and our daughters to be servants, and *some* of our daughters are brought unto bondage *already:* neither *is it* in our power *to redeem them;* for other men have our lands and vineyards.

6 And I was very angry when I heard their cry and these words.

7 Then [N]I consulted with myself, and I rebuked the nobles, and the rulers, and said unto them, [R]Ye exact usury, every one of his brother. And I set a great assembly against them.

8 And I said unto them, We after our ability have [R]redeemed our brethren the Jews, which were sold unto the heathen; and will ye even

sell your brethren? or shall they be sold unto us? Then held they their peace, and found nothing *to answer.*

9 Also I said, It *is* not good that ye do: ought ye not to walk ᴿin the fear of our God ᴿbecause of the reproach of the heathen our enemies?

10 I likewise, *and* my brethren, and my servants, might exact of them money and corn: I pray you, let us leave off this usury.

11 Restore, I pray you, to them, even this day, their lands, their vineyards, their oliveyards, and their houses, also the hundredth *part* of the money, and of the corn, the wine, and the oil, that ye exact of them.

12 Then said they, We will restore *them,* and will require nothing of them; so will we do as thou sayest. Then I called the priests, ᴿand took an oath of them, that they should do according to this promise.

13 Also ᴿI shook my lap, and said, So God shake out every man from his house, and from his labour, that performeth not this promise, even thus be he shaken out, and ᴺemptied. And all the congregation said, Ä'-mĕn, and praised the LORD. ᴿAnd the people did according to this promise.

Nehemiah's benevolent rule

14 Moreover from the time that I was appointed to be their governor in the land of Judah, from the twentieth year ᴿeven unto the two and thirtieth year of Är-tă-xĕrx'-ēś the king, *that is,* twelve years, I and my brethren have not ᴿeaten the bread of the governor.

15 But the former governors that *had been* before me were chargeable unto the people, and had taken of them bread and wine, beside forty shē'-kĕls of silver; yea, even their servants bare rule over the people: but ᴿso did not I, because of the ᴿfear of God.

16 Yea, also I continued in the work of this wall, neither bought we any land: and all my servants *were* gathered thither unto the work.

17 Moreover *there were* ᴿat my table an hundred and fifty of the Jews and rulers, beside those that came unto us from among the heathen that *are* about us.

18 Now *that* ᴿwhich was prepared *for me* daily *was* one ox *and* six choice sheep; also fowls were prepared for me, and once in ten days store of all sorts of wine: yet for all this ᴿrequired not I the bread of the governor, because the bondage was heavy upon this people.

19 ᴿThink upon me, my God, for good, *according* to all that I have done for this people.

CHAPTER 6

Sanballat's plot

NOW it came to pass, ᴿwhen Săn-băl'-lăt, and Tō-bī'-ăh, and ᴺGē'-shĕm the Arabian, and the rest of our enemies, heard that I had builded the wall, and *that* there was no breach left therein; (ᴿthough at that time I had not set up the doors upon the gates;)

2 That Săn-băl'-lăt and Gē'-shĕm ᴿsent unto me, saying, Come, let us meet together in *some one of* the villages in the plain of ᴿŌ'-nō. But they ᴿthought to do me mischief.

3 And I sent messengers unto them, saying, I *am* doing a great work, so that I cannot come down: why should the work cease, whilst I leave it, and come down to you?

4 Yet they sent unto me four times after this sort; and I answered them after the same manner.

5 Then sent Săn-băl'-lăt his servant unto me in like manner the fifth time with an open letter in his hand;

6 Wherein *was* written, It is reported among the heathen, and ᴺGăsh'-mû saith *it,* ᴿthat thou and the Jews think to rebel: for which cause thou buildest the wall, that thou mayest be their king, according to these words.

7 And thou hast also appointed prophets to preach of thee at Jerusalem, saying, *There is* a king in Judah: and now shall it be reported to the king according to these words. Come now therefore, and let us take counsel together.

8 Then I sent unto him, saying, There are no such things done as thou sayest, but thou feignest them out of thine own heart.

9 For they all made us afraid, saying, Their hands shall be weakened from the work, that it be not done. Now therefore, *O God,* strengthen my hands.

10 Afterward I came unto the house of Shĕm-aī'-ăh the son of Dĕl-aī'-ăh the son of Mĕ-hĕt'-ă-bĕel, who *was* shut up; and he said, Let us meet together in the house of God, within the temple, and let us shut the doors of the temple: for they will come to slay thee; yea, in the night will they come to slay thee.

11 And I said, Should such a man as I flee? and who *is there,* that, *being* as I *am,* would go into the temple to save his life? I will not go in.

12 And, lo, I perceived that God had not sent him; but that ᴿhe pronounced this prophecy against me: for Tō-bī'-ăh and Săn-băl'-lăt had hired him.

13 Therefore *was* he hired, that I should be afraid, and do so, and sin, and *that* they might

have *matter* for an evil report, that they might reproach me.

14 ᴿMy God, think thou upon Tō-bī′-ăh and Săn-băl′-lăt according to these their works, and on the ᴿprophetess Nō-ă-dī′-ăh, and the rest of the prophets, that would have put me in fear.

The wall completed

15 So the wall was finished in the twenty and fifth *day* of *the month* Ē′-lŭl, in fifty and two days.

16 And it came to pass, that ᴿwhen all our enemies heard *thereof,* and all the heathen that *were* about us saw *these things,* they were much cast down in their own eyes: for ᴿthey perceived that this work was wrought of our God.

17 Moreover in those days the nobles of Judah ᴺsent many letters unto Tō-bī′-ăh, and *the letters* of Tō-bī′-ăh came unto them.

18 For *there were* many in Judah sworn unto him, because he *was* the son in law of Shĕch-ă-nī′-ăh the son of âr′-ăh; and his son Jō-hā′-năn had taken the daughter of Mĕ-shŭl′-lăm the son of Bĕr-ē-chī′-ăh.

19 Also they reported his good deeds before me, and uttered my ᴺwords to him. *And* Tō-bī′-ăh sent letters to put me in fear.

CHAPTER 7

City officials appointed

NOW it came to pass, when the wall was built, and I had ᴿset up the doors, and the porters and the singers and the Levites were appointed,

2 That I gave my brother Hă-nā′-nī, and Hăn-ă-nī′-ăh the ruler ᴿof the palace, charge over Jerusalem: for he *was* a faithful man, and ᴿfeared God above many.

3 And I said unto them, Let not the gates of Jerusalem be opened until the sun be hot; and while they stand by, let them shut the doors, and bar *them:* and appoint watches of the inhabitants of Jerusalem, every one in his watch, and every one *to be* over against his house.

4 Now the city *was* ᴺlarge and great: but the people *were* few therein, and the houses *were* not builded.

Census by families

5 And my God put into mine heart to gather together the nobles, and the rulers, and the people, that they might be reckoned by genealogy. And I found a register of the genealogy of them which came up at the first, and found written therein,

6 ᴿThese *are* the children of the province, that went up out of the captivity, of those that had been carried away, whom Nĕb-ū-chăd-nĕz′-zär the king of Babylon had carried away, and came again to Jerusalem and to Judah, every one unto his city;

7 Who came with Zĕ-rŭb′-bă-bĕl, Jĕsh′-ū-ă, Nē-hĕm-ī′-ăh, ᴺĂz-ă-rī′-ăh, Rā-ă-mī′-ăh, Nā-hă-mā′-nī, Môr-dĕ-cā′-ī, Bilshan, Mĭs′-pĕ-rĕth, Bĭg-vā′-ī, Nē′-hŭm, Bā′-ă-năh. The number, *I say,* of the men of the people of Israel *was this;*

8 The children of Pär′-ŏsh, two thousand an hundred seventy and two.

9 The children of Shĕph-ă-tī′-ăh, three hundred seventy and two.

10 The children of âr′-ăh, six hundred fifty and two.

11 The children of Pā′-hăth-mō′-ăb, of the children of Jĕsh′-ū-ă and Jō′-ăb, two thousand and eight hundred *and* eighteen.

12 The children of Ē′-lăm, a thousand two hundred fifty and four.

13 The children of Zăt′-tû, eight hundred forty and five.

14 The children of Zăc-cā′-ī, seven hundred and threescore.

15 The children of ᴺBĭn′-nū-ī, six hundred forty and eight.

16 The children of Bē-bā′-ī, six hundred twenty and eight.

17 The children of Azgad, two thousand three hundred twenty and two.

18 The children of Ăd-ō-nī′-kăm, six hundred threescore and seven.

19 The children of Bĭg-vā′-ī, two thousand threescore and seven.

20 The children of Ā′-dĭn, six hundred fifty and five.

21 The children of Ā′-tĕr of Hĕz-ē-kī′-ăh, ninety and eight.

22 The children of Hăsh′-ŭm, three hundred twenty and eight.

23 The children of Bē-zā′-ī, three hundred twenty and four.

24 The children of ᴺHâr′-ĭph, an hundred and twelve.

25 The children of ᴺGibeon, ninety and five.

26 The men of Beth-lehem and Nĕ-tō′-phăh, an hundred fourscore and eight.

27 The men of Ăn′-ă-thŏth, an hundred twenty and eight.

28 The men of ᴺBĕth-ăz-mā′-vĕth, forty and two.

29 The men of ᴺKĭr′-jăth-jē′-ă-rĭm, Chĕ-phī′-răh, and Bēĕr′-ōth, seven hundred forty and three.

30 The men of Rā′-măh and Gā′-bă, six hundred twenty and one.

31 The men of Mĭch'-măs, an hundred and twenty and two.

32 The men of Beth-el and Ā'-ī, an hundred twenty and three.

33 The men of the other Nē'-bō, fifty and two.

34 The children of the other ᴿĒ'-lăm, a thousand two hundred fifty and four.

35 The children of Hăr'-ĭm, three hundred and twenty.

36 The children of Jericho, three hundred forty and five.

37 The children of Lod, Hā'-dĭd, and Ō'-nō, seven hundred twenty and one.

38 The children of Sĕn'-ă-ăh, three thousand nine hundred and thirty.

39 The priests: the children of ᴿJĕ-dāi'-ăh, of the house of Jĕsh'-ū-ă, nine hundred seventy and three.

40 The children of ᴿĬm'-mĕr, a thousand fifty and two.

41 The children of ᴿPăsh'-ŭr, a thousand two hundred forty and seven.

42 The children of ᴿHăr'-ĭm, a thousand and seventeen.

43 The Levites: the children of Jĕsh'-ū-ă, of Kăd'-mĭ-ĕl, and of the children of ᴺHō'-dĕ-văh, seventy and four.

44 The singers: the children of Ā'-săph, an hundred forty and eight.

45 The porters: the children of Shăl'-lŭm, the children of Ā'-tĕr, the children of Tăl'-mŏn, the children of Ăk'-kŭb, the children of Hă-tī'-tă, the children of Shō-bā'-ī, an hundred thirty and eight.

46 The Nĕth'-ĭ-nĭmś: the children of Zī'-hă, the children of Hă-shū'-phă, the children of Tăb-bā'-ōth,

47 The children of Kē'-rŏs, the children of ᴺSī'-ă, the children of Pā'-dŏn,

48 The children of Lĕ-bā'-nă, the children of Hăg'-ă-bă, the children of ᴺShăl'-māi,

49 The children of Hā'-năn, the children of Gĭd'-dĕl, the children of Gā'-hăr,

50 The children of Rĕ-āi'-ăh, the children of Rē'-zĭn, the children of Nĕ-kō'-dă,

51 The children of Găz'-zăm, the children of Ŭz'-ză, the children of Phă-sē'-ăh,

52 The children of Bē'-sāi, the children of Mĕ-ū'-nĭm, the children of ᴺNĕ-phĭsh'-ĕ-sĭm,

53 The children of Băk'-bŭk, the children of Hă-kū'-phă, the children of Hăr'-hŭr,

54 The children of ᴺBăz'-lĭth, the children of Mĕ-hī'-dă, the children of Hăr'-shă,

55 The children of Băr'-kŏs, the children of Sĭs'-ĕ-ră, the children of Tā'-măh,

56 The children of Nĕ-zī'-ăh, the children of Hă-tī'-phă.

57 The children of Solomon's servants: the children of Sō-tā'-ī, the children of Sō'-phĕ-rĕth, the children of ᴺPĕ-rī'-dă,

58 The children of Jā'-ă-lă, the children of Dăr'-kŏn, the children of Gĭd'-dĕl,

59 The children of Shĕph-ă-tī'-ăh, the children of Hăt'-tĭl, the children of Pō'-chĕ-rĕth of Zĕ-bā'-ĭm, the children of ᴺAmon.

60 All the Nĕth'-ĭ-nĭmś, and the children of Solomon's servants, were three hundred ninety and two.

61 ᴿAnd these were they which went up also from Tĕl-mē'-lăh, Tĕl-hă-rē'-shă, Cherub, ᴺĂd'-dŏn, and Ĭm'-mĕr: but they could not shew their father's house, nor their ᴺseed, whether they were of Israel.

62 The children of Dĕl-āi'-ăh, the children of Tō-bī'-ăh, the children of Nĕ-kō'-dă, six hundred forty and two.

63 And of the priests: the children of Hă-bāi'-ăh, the children of Kŏz, the children of Bär-zĭl-lā'-ī, which took one of the daughters of Bär-zĭl-lā'-ī the Gileadite to wife, and was called after their name.

64 These sought their register among those that were reckoned by genealogy, but it was not found: therefore were they, as polluted, put from the priesthood.

65 And ᴺthe Tĭr'-shă-thă said unto them, that they should not eat of the most holy things, till there stood up a priest with Ū'-rĭm and Thŭm'-mĭm.

66 The whole congregation together was forty and two thousand three hundred and threescore,

67 Beside their manservants and their maidservants, of whom there were seven thousand three hundred thirty and seven: and they had two hundred forty and five singing men and singing women.

68 Their horses, seven hundred thirty and six: their mules, two hundred forty and five:

69 Their camels, four hundred thirty and five: six thousand seven hundred and twenty asses.

Gifts to the treasury

70 And ᴺsome of the chief of the fathers gave unto the work. ᴿThe Tĭr'-shă-thă gave to the treasure a thousand drams of gold, fifty basins, five hundred and thirty priests' garments.

71 And some of the chief of the fathers gave to the treasure of the work ᴿtwenty thousand drams of gold, and two thousand and two hundred pound of silver.

72 And that which the rest of the people gave was twenty thousand drams of gold, and two thousand pound of silver, and threescore and seven priests' garments.

CHAP. **7**
BC 445
34 See ver. 12
39 1 Chr. 24:7
40 1 Chr. 24:14
41 See 1 Chr. 9:12 & 24:9
42 1 Chr. 24:8
43 Or, *Hodaviah*, Ezra 2:40, or, *Judah*, Ezra 3:9
47 Or, *Siaha*
48 Or, *Shamlai*
52 Or, *Nephusim*
54 Or, *Bazluth*

Or, *Peruda*   57
Or, *Ami*   59
Ezra 2:59   61
Or, *Addan*   61
Or, *pedigree*   61
Or, *the governor*, 65 ch. 8:9
Heb. *part*   70
ch. 8:9   70
Ezra 2:59   71

73 So the priests, and the Levites, and the porters, and the singers, and *some* of the people, and the Něth′-ĭ-nĭmś, and all Israel, dwelt in their cities; ᴿand when the seventh month came, the children of Israel *were* in their cities.

CHAPTER 8

Ezra's explanation of the law

AND all ᴿthe people gathered themselves together as one man into the street that *was* ᴿbefore the water gate; and they spake unto Ezra the ᴿscribe to bring the book of the ᶜlaw of Moses, which the LORD had commanded to Israel.

2 And Ezra the priest brought ᴿthe law before the congregation both of men and women, and all ᴺthat could hear with understanding, ᴿupon the first day of the seventh month.

3 And he read therein before the street that *was* before the water gate ᴺfrom the morning until midday, before the men and the women, and those that could understand; and the ears of all the people *were attentive* unto the book of the law.

4 And Ezra the scribe stood upon a ᴺpulpit of wood, which they had made for the purpose; and beside him stood Măt-tĭ-thī′-ăh, and Shē′-mă, and Ă-naī′-ăh, and Ū-rī′-jăh, and Hĭl-kī′-ăh, and Mā-ă-sēī′-ăh, on his right hand; and on his left hand, Pĕ-daī′-ăh, and Mĭ′-shā-ĕl, and Măl-chī′-ăh, and Hăsh′-ŭm, and Hăsh-bă-dā′-nă, Zĕch-ă-rī′-ăh, *and* Mĕ-shŭl′-lăm.

5 And Ezra opened the book in the ᴺsight of all the people; (for he was above all the people;) and when he opened it, all the people ᴿstood up:

6 And Ezra blessed the LORD, the great God. And all the people ᴿanswered, Ä′-mĕn, Ä′-mĕn, with ᴿlifting up their hands: and they ᴿbowed their heads, and worshipped the LORD with *their* faces to the ground.

7 Also Jĕsh′-ū-ă, and Bā′-nĭ, and Shĕr-ē-dī′-jăh, Mā-ă-sēī′-ăh, Kĕ-lī′-tă, Ăz-ă-rī′-ăh, Jŏ′-ză-băd, Hā′-năn, Pĕ-laī′-ăh, and the Levites, ᴿcaused the people to understand the law: and the people *stood* in their place.

8 So they read in the book in the law of God distinctly, and gave the sense, and caused *them* to understand the reading.

9 ᴿAnd Nē-hĕm-ĭ′-ăh, which *is* ᴺthe Tĭr′-shă-thă, and Ezra the priest the scribe, and the Levites that taught the people, said unto all the people, ᴿThis day *is* holy unto the LORD your God; ᴿmourn not, nor weep. For all the

people wept, when they heard the words of the law.

10 Then he said unto them, Go your way, eat the fat, and drink the sweet, ᴿand send portions unto them for whom nothing is prepared: for *this* day *is* holy unto our LORD: neither be ye sorry; for the joy of the LORD is your strength.

11 So the Levites stilled all the people, saying, Hold your peace, for the day *is* holy; neither be ye grieved.

12 And all the people went their way to eat, and to drink, and to ᴿsend portions, and to make great mirth, because they had ᴿunderstood the words that were declared unto them.

Feast of tabernacles celebrated

13 And on the second day were gathered together the chief of the fathers of all the people, the priests, and the Levites, unto Ezra the scribe, even ᴺto understand the words of the law.

14 And they found written in the law which the LORD had commanded ᴺby Moses, that the children of Israel should dwell in ᴿbooths in the feast of the seventh month:

15 And ᴿthat they should publish and proclaim in all their cities, and ᴿin Jerusalem, saying, Go forth unto the mount, and ᴿfetch olive branches, and pine branches, and myrtle branches, and palm branches, and branches of thick trees, to make booths, as *it is* written.

16 So the people went forth, and brought *them,* and made themselves booths, every one upon the ᴿroof of his house, and in their courts, and in the courts of the house of God, and in the street of the ᴿwater gate, ᴿand in the street of the gate of Ē′-phră-ĭm.

17 And all the congregation of them that were come again out of the captivity made booths, and sat under the booths: for since the days of Jĕsh′-ū-ă the son of Nun unto that day had not the children of Israel done so. And there was very ᴿgreat gladness.

18 Also ᴿday by day, from the first day unto the last day, he read in the book of the law of God. And they kept the feast seven days; and on the eighth day *was* ᴺa solemn assembly, ᴿaccording unto the manner.

CHAPTER 9

Public confession of sin

NOW in the twenty and fourth day of ᴿthis month the children of Israel were assembled with fasting, and with sackclothes, ᴿand earth upon them.

CHAP. 7

BC 445

73 Ezra 3:1

CHAP. 8

BC 445

1 Ezra 3:1
1 ch. 3:26
1 Ezra 7:6
2 Deut. 31:11, 12
2 Heb. *that understood in hearing*
2 Lev. 23:24
3 Heb. *from the light*
4 Heb. *tower of wood*
5 Heb. *eyes*
5 Judg. 3:20
6 1 Cor. 14:16
6 Lam. 3:41
1 Tim. 2:8
6 Ex. 4:31 & 12:27
2 Chr. 20:18
7 Lev. 10:11
Deut. 33:10
2 Chr. 17:7
Mal. 2:7
9 Ezra 2:63
ch. 7:65 & 10:1
9 Or, *the governor*
9 Lev. 23:24
Num. 29:1
9 Deut. 16:14
Eccl. 3:4

Esth. 9:19   10
Rev. 11:10
ver. 10   12
ver. 7, 8   12
Or, *that they might instruct in the words of the law*   13
Heb. *by the hand of*   14
Lev. 23:34, 42   14
Deut. 16:13
Lev. 23:4   15
Deut. 16:16   15
Lev. 23:40   15
Deut. 22:8   16
ch. 12:37   16
2 Ki. 14:13   16
ch. 12:39
2 Chr. 30:21   17
Deut. 31:10, etc.   18
Heb. *a restraint*   18
Lev. 23:36   18
Num. 29:35

CHAP. 9

BC 445

ch. 8:2   1
Josh. 7:6   1
1 Sam. 4:12
2 Sam. 1:2
Job 2:12

2 And ^Rthe seed of Israel separated themselves from all ^Nstrangers, and stood and confessed their sins, and the iniquities of their fathers.

3 And they stood up in their place, and ^Rread in the book of the law of the LORD their God *one* fourth part of the day; and *another* fourth part they confessed, and worshipped the LORD their God.

4 Then stood up upon the ^Nstairs, of the Levites, Jĕsh'-ū-ă, and Bā'-nī, Kăd'-mĭ-ĕl, Shĕb-ă-nī'-ăh, Bŭn'-nī, Shĕr-ē-bī'-ăh, Bā'-nī, *and* Chĕ-nā'-nī, and cried with a loud voice unto the LORD their God.

5 Then the Levites, Jĕsh'-ū-ă, and Kăd'-mĭ-ĕl, Bā'-nī, Hăsh-ăb-nī'-ăh, Shĕr-ē-bī'-ăh, Hō-dī'-jăh, Shĕb-ă-nī'-ăh, *and* Pĕth-ă-hī'-ăh, said, Stand up *and* bless the LORD your God for ever and ever: and blessed be ^Rthy glorious name, which is exalted above all blessing and praise.

Ezra's prayer

6 ^RThou, *even* thou, *art* LORD alone; ^Rthou hast made heaven, ^Rthe heaven of heavens, with ^Rall their host, the earth, and all *things* that *are* therein, ·the seas, and all that *is* therein, and thou ^Rpreservest them all; and the host of heaven worshippeth thee.

7 Thou *art* the LORD the God, who didst choose ^RAbram, and broughtest him forth out of Ur of the Chăl'-dēĕś, and gavest him the name of ^RAbraham;

8 And foundest his heart ^Rfaithful before thee, and madest a ^Rcovenant with him to give the land of the Canaanites, the Hittites, the Amorites, and the Pĕ-rĭz'-zītes, and the Jĕb'-ū-śītes, and the Gĭr'-gă-shītes, to give *it*, I say, to his seed, and ^Rhast performed thy words; for thou *art* righteous:

9 ^RAnd didst see the affliction of our fathers in Egypt, and ^Rheardest their cry by the Red sea;

10 And ^Rshewedst signs and wonders upon Pharaoh, and on all his servants, and on all the people of his land: for thou knewest that they ^Rdealt proudly against them. So didst thou ^Rget thee a name, as *it is* this day.

11 ^RAnd thou didst divide the sea before them, so that they went through the midst of the sea on the dry land; and their persecutors thou threwest into the deeps, ^Ras a stone into the mighty waters.

12 Moreover thou ^Rleddest them in the day by a cloudy pillar; and in the night by a pillar of fire, to give them light in the way wherein they should go.

CHAP. **9**

BC 445

2 Ezra 10:11
ch. 13:3, 30
2 Heb. *strange children*
3 ch. 8:7, 8
4 Or, *scaffold*
5 1 Chr. 29:13
6 2 Ki. 19:15, 19
Ps. 86:10
Is. 37:16, 20
6 Gen. 1:1
Ex. 20:11
Rev. 14:7
6 Deut. 10:14
1 Ki. 8:27
6 Gen. 2:1
6 Ps. 36:6
7 Gen. 11:31
7 Gen. 17:5
8 Gen. 15:6
8 Gen. 15:18
8 Josh. 23:14
9 Ex. 2:25
9 Ex. 14:10
10 Ex. 7-10, & 12, & 14
10 Ex. 18:11
10 Jer. 32:20
11 Ex. 14:21
Ps. 78:13
11 Ex. 15:5
12 Ex. 13:21

Ex. 20:1   13
Rom. 7:12   13
Heb. *laws of*   13
truth
Gen. 2:3   14
Ex. 20:8
Ex. 16:14   15
John 6:31
Ex. 17:6   15
Deut. 1:8   15
Heb. *which thou* 15
hadst lift up thine
hand to give them,
Num. 14:30
Ps. 106:6   16
Deut. 31:27   16
Ps. 78:11   17
Num. 14:4   17
Heb. *a God*   17
of pardons
Joel 2:13   17
Ex. 32:4   18
Ps. 106:45   19
1 Cor. 10:1   19
Num. 11:17   20
Is. 63:11
Ex. 16:15   20
Josh. 5:12
Ex. 17:6   20
Deut. 2:7   21
Deut. 8:4 & 29:5 21
Num. 21:21   22
Gen. 22:17   23
Josh. 1:2   24
Ps. 44:2, 3   24

13 ^RThou camest down also upon mount Sĭ'-nâi, and spakest with them from heaven, and gavest them ^Rright judgments, and ^Ntrue laws, good statutes and commandments:

14 And madest known unto them thy ^Rholy sabbath, and commandedst them precepts, statutes, and laws, by the hand of Moses thy servant:

15 And ^Rgavest them bread from heaven for their hunger, and ^Rbroughtest forth water for them out of the rock for their thirst, and promisedst them that they should ^Rgo in to possess the land ^Nwhich thou hadst sworn to give them.

16 ^RBut they and our fathers dealt proudly, and ^Rhardened their necks, and hearkened not to thy commandments,

17 And refused to obey, ^Rneither were mindful of thy wonders that thou didst among them; but hardened their necks, and in their rebellion appointed ^Ra captain to return to their bondage: but thou *art* ^Na God ready to pardon, ^Rgracious and merciful, slow to anger, and of great kindness, and forsookest them not.

18 Yea, ^Rwhen they had made them a molten calf, and said, This *is* thy God that brought thee up out of Egypt, and had wrought great provocations;

19 Yet thou in thy ^Rmanifold mercies forsookest them not in the wilderness: the ^Rpillar of the cloud departed not from them by day, to lead them in the way; neither the pillar of fire by night, to shew them light, and the way wherein they should go.

20 Thou gavest also thy ^Rgood spirit to instruct them, and withheldest not thy ^Rmăn'-nă from their mouth, and gavest them ^Rwater for their thirst.

21 Yea, ^Rforty years didst thou sustain them in the wilderness, *so that* they lacked nothing; their ^Rclothes waxed not old, and their feet swelled not.

22 Moreover thou gavest them kingdoms and nations, and didst divide them into corners: so they possessed the land of ^RSĭ'-hŏn, and the land of the king of Hĕsh'-bŏn, and the land of Og king of Bā'-shăn.

23 ^RTheir children also multipliedst thou as the stars of heaven, and broughtest them into the land, concerning which thou hadst promised to their fathers, that they should go in to possess *it*.

24 So ^Rthe children went in and possessed the land, and ^Rthou subduedst before them the inhabitants of the land, the Canaanites, and gavest them into their hands, with their kings,

and the people of the land, that they might do with them ᴺas they would.

25 And they took strong cities, and a ᴿfat land, and possessed ᴿhouses full of all goods, ᴺwells digged, vineyards, and oliveyards, and ᴺfruit trees in abundance: so they did eat, and were filled, and ᴿbecame fat, and delighted themselves in thy great ᴿgoodness.

26 Nevertheless they ᴿwere disobedient, and rebelled against thee, and ᴿcast thy law behind their backs, and slew thy ᴿprophets which testified against them to turn them to thee, and they wrought great provocations.

27 ᴿTherefore thou deliveredst them into the hand of their enemies, who vexed them: and in the time of their trouble, when they cried unto thee, thou ᴿheardest *them* from heaven; and according to thy manifold mercies ᴿthou gavest them saviours, who saved them out of the hand of their enemies.

28 But after they had rest, ᴿthey ᴺ did evil again before thee: therefore leftest thou them in the hand of their enemies, so that they had the dominion over them: yet when they returned, and cried unto thee, thou heardest *them* from heaven; and ᴿmany times didst thou deliver them according to thy mercies;

29 And testifiedst against them, that thou mightest bring them again unto thy law: yet they dealt proudly, and hearkened not unto thy commandments, but sinned against thy judgments, (ᴿwhich if a man do, he shall live in them;) and ᴺwithdrew the shoulder, and hardened their neck, and would not hear.

30 Yet many years didst thou ᴺforbear them, and testifiedst ᴿagainst them by thy spirit ᴿin ᴺthy prophets: yet would they not give ear: ᴿtherefore gavest thou them into the hand of the people of the lands.

31 Nevertheless for thy great mercies' sake ᴿthou didst not utterly consume them, nor forsake them; for thou *art* a gracious and merciful God.

32 Now therefore, our God, the great, the ᴿmighty, and the terrible God, who keepest covenant and mercy, let not all the ᴺtrouble seem little before thee, ᴺthat hath come upon us, on our kings, on our princes, and on our priests, and on our prophets, and on our fathers, and on all thy people, ᴿsince the time of the kings of Assyria unto this day.

33 Howbeit ᴿthou *art* just in all that is brought upon us; for thou hast done right, but ᴿwe have done wickedly:

34 Neither have our kings, our princes, our priests, nor our fathers, kept thy law, nor hearkened unto thy commandments and thy testimonies, wherewith thou didst testify against them.

35 For they have ᴿnot served thee in their kingdom, and in thy great goodness that thou gavest them, and in the large and fat land which thou gavest before them, neither turned they from their wicked works.

36 Behold, ᴿwe *are* servants this day, and *for* the land that thou gavest unto our fathers to eat the fruit thereof and the good thereof, behold, we *are* servants in it:

37 And ᴿit yieldeth much increase unto the kings whom thou hast set over us because of our sins: also they have ᴿdominion over our bodies, and over our cattle, at their pleasure, and we *are* in great distress.

Covenant signed

38 And because of all this we ᴿmake a sure *covenant,* and write *it;* and our princes, Levites, *and* priests, ᴺseal *unto it.·*

CHAPTER 10

NOW ᴺthose that sealed *were* Nē-hĕm-ī'-ăh, ᴺthe Tĩr'-shă-thā, ᴿthe son of Hăch-ă-lī'-ăh, and Zĭd-kī'-jăh,

2 ᴿSĕ-raī'-ăh, Ăz-ă-rī'-ăh, Jeremiah,

3 Păsh'-ùr, Ăm-ă-rī'-ăh, Măl-chī'-jăh,

4 Hăt'-tūsh, Shĕb-ă-nī'-ăh, Măl'-lŭch,

5 Hâr'-ĭm, Mĕr'-ĕ-mŏth, ō-bă-dī'-ăh,

6 Daniel, Gĭn'-nĕ-thŏn, Bâr'-ŭch,

7 Mĕ-shŭl'-lăm, Ă-bī'-jăh, Mī'-jă-mĭn,

8 Mā-ă-zī'-ăh, Bĭl-gā'-ĭ, Shĕm-aī'-ăh: these *were* the priests.

9 And the Levites: both Jĕsh'-ū-ă the son of Ăz-ă-nī'-ăh, Bĭn'-nū-ĭ of the sons of Hĕn-ā'-dăd, Kăd'-mĭ-ĕl;

10 And their brethren, Shĕb-ă-nī'-ăh, Hō-dī'-jăh, Kĕ-lī'-tă, Pĕ-laī'-ăh, Hā'-năn,

11 Mī'-chă, Rē'-hŏb, Hăsh-ă-bī'-ăh,

12 Zăc'-cùr, Shĕr-ē-bī'-ăh, Shĕb-ă-nī'-ăh,

13 Hō-dī'-jăh, Bā'-nī, Bĕ-nī'-nû.

14 The chief of the people; ᴿPâr'-ŏsh, Pā'-hăth-mō'-ăb, Ē'-lăm, Zăt'-thû, Bā'-nī,

15 Bŭn'-nī, Azgad, Bē-bā'-ĭ,

16 Ăd-ō-nī'-jăh, Bĭg-vā'-ĭ, Ā'-dĭn,

17 Ā'-tĕr, Hĭz-kī'-jăh, Azzur,

18 Hō-dī'-jăh, Hăsh'-ŭm, Bē-zā'-ĭ,

19 Hâr'-ĭph, Ăn'-ă-thŏth, Nē-bā'-ĭ,

20 Măg'-pī-ăsh, Mĕ-shŭl'-lăm, Hē'-zĭr,

21 Mĕ-shĕz'-ă-bēĕl, Zā'-dŏk, Jăd'-dū-ă,

22 Pĕl-ă-tī'-ăh, Hā'-năn, Ă-naī'-ăh,

23 Hō-shē'-ă, Hăn-ă-nī'-ăh, Hăsh'-ŭb,

24 Hăl-lō'-hĕsh, Pī'-lĕ-hă, Shō'-bĕk,

25 Rē'-hŭm, Hă-shăb'-năh, Mā-ă-seī'-ăh,

26 And Ă-hī'-jăh, Hā'-năn, Anan,

27 Măl'-lŭch, Hâr'-ĭm, Bā'-ă-năh.

Oaths taken

28 ᴿAnd the rest of the people, the priests, the Levites, the porters, the singers, the Nĕth'-

ĭ-nĭmś, ᴿand all they that had separated them-selves from the people of the lands unto the law of God, their wives, their sons, and their daughters, every one having knowledge, and having understanding;

29 They clave to their brethren, their nobles, ᴿand entered into a curse, and into an oath, ᴿto walk in God's law, which was given ᴺby Moses the servant of God, and to observe and do all the commandments of the LORD our Lord, and his judgments and his statutes;

30 And that we would not give ᴿour daugh-ters unto the people of the land, nor take their daughters for our sons:

31 ᴿAnd if the people of the land bring ware or any victuals on the sabbath day to sell, that we would not buy it of them on the sabbath, or on the holy day: and that we would leave the ᴿseventh year, and the ᴿexaction of ᴺevery debt.

32 Also we made ordinances for us, to charge ourselves yearly with the third part of a shē'-kĕl for the service of the house of our God;

33 For ᴿthe shewbread, and for the ᴿcon-tinual meat offering, and for the continual burnt offering, of the sabbaths, of the new moons, for the set feasts, and for the holy things, and for the sin offerings to make an atonement for Israel, and for all the work of the house of our God.

34 And we cast the lots among the priests, the Levites, and the people, ᴿfor the wood offering, to bring it into the house of our God, after the houses of our fathers, at times ap-pointed year by year, to burn upon the altar of the LORD our God, ᴿas it is written in the law:

35 And ᴿto bring the firstfruits of our ground, and the firstfruits of all fruit of all trees, year by year, unto the house of the LORD:

36 Also the firstborn of our sons, and of our cattle, as it is written ᴿin the law, and the firstlings of our herds and of our flocks, to bring to the house of our God, unto the priests that minister in the house of our God:

37 ᴿAnd that we should bring the firstfruits of our dough, and our offerings, and the fruit of all manner of trees, of wine and of oil, unto the priests, to the chambers of the house of our God; and ᴿthe tithes of our ground unto the Levites, that the same Levites might have the tithes in all the cities of our tillage.

38 And the priest the son of Aaron shall be with the Levites, ᴿwhen the Levites take tithes: and the Levites shall bring up the tithe of the tithes unto the house of our God, to ᴿthe chambers, into the treasure house.

39 For the children of Israel and the children

of Levi ᴿshall bring the offering of the corn, of the new wine, and the oil, unto the chambers, where are the vessels of the sanctuary, and the priests that minister, and the porters, and the singers: ᴿand we will not forsake the house of our God.

CHAPTER 11

Inhabitants of Jerusalem

AND the rulers of the people dwelt at Jeru-salem: the rest of the people also cast lots, to bring one of ten to dwell in Jerusalem ᴿthe holy city, and nine parts to dwell in other cities.

2 And the people blessed all the men, that ᴿwillingly offered themselves to dwell at Jeru-salem.

3 ᴿNow these are the chief of the province that dwelt in Jerusalem: but in the cities of Judah dwelt every one in his possession in their cities, to wit, Israel, the priests, and the Levites, and ᴿthe Nĕth'-ĭ-nĭmś, and ᴿthe chil-dren of Solomon's servants.

4 And ᴿat Jerusalem dwelt certain of the children of Judah, and of the children of Ben-jamin. Of the children of Judah; Ă-thâi'-ăh the son of ŭz-zī'-ăh, the son of Zĕch-ă-rī'-ăh, the son of Ăm-ă-rī'-ăh, the son of Shĕph-ă-tī'-ăh, the son of Mă-hăl'-ă-lĕĕl, of the children of ᴿPē'-rĕz;

5 And Mā-ă-sēi'-ăh the son of Bâr'-ŭch, the son of Cŏl-hō'-zĕh, the son of Hă-zā'ī-ăh, the son of Ă-dā'-ăh, the son of Jôi'-ă-rĭb, the son of Zĕch-ă-rī'-ăh, the son of Shī-lō'-nī.

6 All the sons of Pē'-rĕz that dwelt at Jeru-salem were four hundred threescore and eight valiant men.

7 And these are the sons of Benjamin; Săl'-lû the son of Mĕ-shŭl'-lăm, the son of Jō'-ĕd, the son of Pĕ-dâi'-ăh, the son of Kō-lâi'-ăh, the son of Mā-ă-sēi'-ăh, the son of ĭ'-thī-ĕl, the son of Jĕ-sâi'-ăh.

8 And after him Găb-bā'-ī, Săl-lā'-ī, nine hundred twenty and eight.

9 And Jō'-ĕl the son of Zĭch'-rī was their overseer: and Judah the son of Sĕn'-ū-ăh was second over the city.

10 ᴿOf the priests: Jĕ-dâi'-ăh the son of Jôi'-ă-rĭb, Jā'-chĭn.

11 Sĕ-râi'-ăh the son of Hĭl-kī'-ăh, the son of Mĕ-shŭl'-lăm, the son of Zā'-dŏk, the son of Mĕ-râi'-ōth, the son of Ă-hī'-tŭb, was the ruler of the house of God.

12 And their brethren that did the work of the house were eight hundred twenty and two: and Ă-dā'-ăh the son of Jĕ-rō'-hăm, the son of Pĕl-ă-lī'-ăh, the son of Amzi, the son of

Zĕch-a-rī'-ăh, the son of Păsh'-ùr, the son of Măl-chī'-ăh,

13 And his brethren, chief of the fathers, two hundred forty and two: and Ă-măsh'-ăĭ the son of Ăz'-a-rĕĕl, the son of Ă-hā'-săĭ, the son of Mĕ-shĭl'-lĕ-mōth, the son of Ĭm'-mĕr,

14 And their brethren, mighty men of valour, an hundred twenty and eight: and their overseer was Zăb'-dĭ-ĕl, ᴺthe son of one of the great men.

15 Also of the Levites: Shĕm-ăĭ'-ăh the son of Hăsh'-ŭb, the son of Ăz-rī'-kăm, the son of Hăsh-a-bī'-ăh, the son of Bŭn'-nī;

16 And Shăb'-bĕ-thăĭ and Jō'-za-băd, of the chief of the Levites, ᴺhad the oversight of ᴿthe outward business of the house of God.

17 And Măt-ta-nī'-ăh the son of Mī'-cha, the son of Zăb'-dī, the son of Ā'-săph, was the principal to begin the thanksgiving in prayer: and Băk-bū-kī'-ăh the second among his brethren, and Abda the son of Shăm'-mū-ă, the son of Gā'-lăl, the son of Jĕ-dū'-thŭn.

18 All the Levites in ᴿthe holy city were two hundred fourscore and four.

19 Moreover the porters, Ăk'-kŭb, Tăl'-mŏn, and their brethren that kept ᴺthe gates, were an hundred seventy and two.

20 And the residue of Israel, of the priests, and the Levites, were in all the cities of Judah, every one in his inheritance.

21 ᴿBut the Nĕth'-ĭ-nĭmś dwelt in ᴺŌ'-phĕl: and Zī'-hă and Gĭs'-pă were over the Nĕth'-ĭ-nĭmś.

22 The overseer also of the Levites at Jerusalem was ŭz'-zī the son of Bā'-nī, the son of Hăsh-a-bī'-ăh, the son of Măt-ta-nī'-ăh, the son of Mī'-cha. Of the sons of Ā'-săph, the singers were over the business of the house of God.

23 For ᴿit was the king's commandment concerning them, that ᴺa certain portion should be for the singers, due for every day.

24 And Pĕth-a-hī'-ăh the son of Mĕ-shĕz'-a-bĕĕl, of the children of ᴿZē'-räh the son of Judah, was ᴿat the king's hand in all matters concerning the people.

Cities of Judah and Benjamin

25 And for the villages, with their fields, some of the children of Judah dwelt at ᴿKĭr'-jăth-är'-bă, and in the villages thereof, and at Dī'-bŏn, and in the villages thereof, and at Jĕ-kăb'-zĕĕl, and in the villages thereof,

26 And at Jĕsh'-ū-ă, and at Mō-lā'-dăh, and at Bĕth'-phĕ-lĕt,

27 And at Hā'-zăr-shû'-ăl, and at Bĕĕr-shē'-bă, and in the villages thereof,

28 And at Ziklag, and at Mĕ-kō'-năh, and in the villages thereof,

29 And at Ĕn-rĭm'-mọn, and at Ză-rē'-ăh, and at Jär'-mŭth,

30 Ză-nō'-ăh, Adullam, and in their villages, at Lā'-chĭsh, and the fields thereof, at Ă-zē'-kăh, and in the villages thereof. And they dwelt from Bĕĕr-shē'-bă unto the valley of Hĭn'-nọm.

31 The children also of Benjamin ᴺfrom Gē'-bă dwelt ᴺat Mĭch'-măsh, and Ăĭ'-jă, and Beth-el, and in their villages,

32 And at Ăn'-a-thŏth, Nob, ăn-a-nī'-ăh,

33 Hā'-zôr, Rā'-măh, Gĭt-tā'-ĭm,

34 Hā'-dĭd, Zĕ-bō'-ĭm, Nĕ-băl'-lăt,

35 Lod, and Ō'-nō, ᴿthe valley of craftsmen.

36 And of the Levites were divisions in Judah, and in Benjamin.

CHAPTER 12

Priests and Levites

NOW these are the ᴿpriests and the Levites that went up with Zĕ-rŭb'-ba-bĕl the son of Shē-ăl'-tĭ-ĕl, and Jĕsh'-ū-ă: ᴿSĕ-răĭ'-ăh, Jeremiah, Ezra,

2 Ăm-a-rī'-ăh, ᴺMăl'-lŭch, Hăt'-tŭsh,

3 ᴺShĕch-a-nī'-ăh, ᴺRē'-hŭm, ᴺMĕr'-ĕ-mōth,

4 Ĭd'-dō, ᴺGĭn'-nĕ-thō, ᴿĂ-bī'-jăh,

5 ᴺMĭ'-a-mĭn, ᴺMā-a-dī'-ăh, Bĭl'-găh,

6 Shĕm-ăĭ'-ăh, and Jŏĭ'-a-rĭb, Jĕ-dăĭ'-ăh,

7 ᴺSăl'-lū, Ā'-mŏk, Hĭl-kī'-ăh, Jĕ-dăĭ'-ăh. These were the chief of the priests and of their brethren in the days of ᴿJĕsh'-ū-ă.

8 Moreover the Levites: Jĕsh'-ū-ă, Bĭn'-nū-ī, Kăd'-mĭ-ĕl, Shĕr-ē-bī'-ăh, Judah, and Măt-ta-nī'-ăh, ᴿwhich was over ᴺthe thanksgiving, he and his brethren.

9 Also Băk-bū-kī'-ăh and ŭn'-nī, their brethren, were over against them in the watches.

10 And Jĕsh'-ū-ă begat Jŏĭ'-a-kĭm, Jŏĭ'-a-kĭm also begat Ē-lī-ăsh'-ĭb, and Ē-lī-ăsh'-ĭb begat Jŏĭ'-a-dă,

11 And Jŏĭ'-a-dă begat Jonathan, and Jonathan begat Jăd'-dū-ă.

12 And in the days of Jŏĭ'-a-kĭm were priests, the chief of the fathers: of Sĕ-răĭ'-ăh, Mĕ-răĭ'-ăh; of Jeremiah, Hăn-a-nī'-ăh;

13 Of Ezra, Mĕ-shŭl'-lăm; of Ăm-a-rī'-ăh, Jĕ-hō-hā'-năn;

14 Of Mĕl'-ĭ-cû, Jonathan; of Shĕb-a-nī'-ăh, Joseph;

15 Of Hăr'-ĭm, Adna; of Mĕ-răĭ'-ōth, Hĕl-kā'-ĭ;

16 Of Ĭd'-dō, Zĕch-a-rī'-ăh; of Gĭn'-nĕ-thŏn, Mĕ-shŭl'-lăm;

17 Of Ă-bī'-jăh, Zĭch'-rī; of Mĭn-ĭ-a-mĭn, of Mō-a-dī'-ăh, Pĭl-tā'-ĭ;

18 Of Bĭl'-găh, Shăm'-mū-ă; of Shĕm-ăĭ'-ăh, Jĕ-hŏn'-a-thăn;

19 And of Jŏı̄'-ă-rı̆b, Măt-tē'-naı̄; of Jĕ-daı̄'-ăh, ŭz'-zı̄;

20 Of Săl-laı̄'-ı̄, Kăl-laı̄'-ı̄; of aı̄'-mŏk, ē'-bĕr;

21 Of Hı̆l-kı̄'-ăh, Hăsh-ă-bı̄'-ăh of Jĕ-daı̄'-ăh, Nĕth'-ă-nĕ̄el.

22 The Levites in the days of ē-lı̄-ăsh'-ı̆b, Jŏı̄'-ă-dă, and Jō-hā'-năn, and Jăd'-dū-ă, *were* recorded chief of the fathers: also the priests, to the reign of Dă-rı̄'-ŭs the Persian.

23 The sons of Levi, the chief of the fathers, *were* written in the book of the ᴿchronicles, even until the days of Jō-hā'-năn the son of ē-lı̆-ăsh'-ı̆b.

24 And the chief of the Levites: Hăsh-ă-bı̄'-ăh, Shĕr-ē-bı̄'-ăh, and Jĕsh'-ū-ă the son of Kăd'-mı̄-ĕl, with their brethren over against them, to praise *and* to give thanks, ᴿaccording to the commandment of David the man of God, ᴿward over against ward.

25 Măt-tă-nı̄'-ăh, and Băk-bū-kı̄'-ăh, ō-bă-dı̄'-ăh, Mĕ-shŭl'-lăm, Tăl'-mŏn, Ăk'-kŭb, *were* porters keeping the ward at the ᴺthresholds of the gates.

26 These *were* in the days of Jŏı̄'-ă-kı̄m the son of Jĕsh'-ū-ă, the son of Jō'-ză-dăk, and in the days of Nē-hĕm-ı̄'-ăh ᴿthe governor, and of Ezra the priest, ᴿthe scribe.

The wall dedicated

27 And at ᴿthe dedication of the wall of Jerusalem they sought the Levites out of all their places, to bring them to Jerusalem, to keep the dedication with gladness, ᴿboth with thanksgivings, and with singing, *with* cymbals, psalteries, and with harps.

28 And the sons of the singers gathered themselves together, both out of the plain country round about Jerusalem, and from the villages of Nē-tŏph'-ă-thı̄;

29 Also from the house of Gı̆l'-găl, and out of the fields of Gē'-bă and Ăz-mā'-vĕth: for the singers had builded them villages round about Jerusalem.

30 And the priests and the Levites purified themselves, and purified the people, and the gates, and the wall.

31 Then I brought up the princes of Judah upon the wall, and appointed two great *companies of them that gave* thanks, *whereof* ᴿone went on the right hand upon the wall ᴿtoward the dung gate:

32 And after them went Hō-shaı̄'-ăh, and half of the princes of Judah,

33 And Ăz-ă-rı̄'-ăh, Ezra, and Mĕ-shŭl'-lăm,

34 Judah, and Benjamin, and Shĕm-aı̄'-ăh, and Jeremiah,

35 And *certain* of the priests' sons ᴿwith trumpets; *namely*, Zĕch-ă-rı̄'-ăh the son of

CHAP. 12
BC 536
23 1 Chr. 9:14, etc.
24 1 Chr. 23, & 25, & 26
24 Ezra 3:11
25 Or, *treasuries, or, assemblies*
26 ch. 8:9
26 Ezra 7:6, 11
27 Deut. 20:5
Ps. 30, title
27 1 Chr. 25:6
2 Chr. 5:13 & 7:6
31 See ver. 38
31 ch. 2:13 & 3:13
35 Num. 10:2, 8

1 Chr. 23:5   36
ch. 2:14   37
& 3:15
ch. 3:15   37
ch. 3:26   37
& 8:1, 3, 16
See ver. 31   38
ch. 3:11   38
ch. 3:8   38
2 Ki. 14:13   39
ch. 8:16
ch. 3:6   39
ch. 3:3   39
ch. 3:1   39
ch. 3:32   39
Jer. 32:2   39
Heb. *made their voice to be heard*   42
2 Chr. 31:11, 12   44
ch. 13:5, 12, 13
i.e. *appointed by the law*   44
Heb. *for the joy of Judah*   44
Heb. *that stood*   44
1 Chr. 25, & 26   45
1 Chr. 25:1, etc.   46

Jonathan, the son of Shĕm-aı̄'-ăh, the son of Măt-tă-nı̄'-ăh, the son of Mı̄-chaı̄'-ăh, the son of Zăc'-cŭr, the son of aı̄'-săph:

36 And his brethren, Shĕm-aı̄'-ăh, and Ăz-ă-rā'-ĕl, Mı̆l'-ă-laı̄, Gı̆l'-ă-laı̄, Mā-ā'-ı̄, Nĕth'-ă-nĕ̄el, and Judah, Hă-nā'-nı̄, with ᴿthe musical instruments of David the man of God, and Ezra the scribe before them.

37 ᴿAnd at the fountain gate, which was over against them, they went up by ᴿthe stairs of the city of David, at the going up of the wall, above the house of David, even unto ᴿthe water gate eastward.

38 ᴿAnd the other *company of them that gave* thanks went over against *them,* and I after them, and the half of the people upon the wall, from beyond ᴿthe tower of the furnaces even unto ᴿthe broad wall;

39 ᴿAnd from above the gate of ē'-phră-ı̆m, and above ᴿthe old gate, and above ᴿthe fish gate, ᴿand the tower of Hăn'-ă-nĕ̄el, and the tower of Mē'-ăh, even unto ᴿthe sheep gate: and they stood still in ᴿthe prison gate.

40 So stood the two *companies of them that gave* thanks in the house of God, and I, and the half of the rulers with me:

41 And the priests; ē-lı̄'-ă-kı̄m, Mā-ă-sĕı̄'-ăh, Mı̄n-ı̄'-ă-mı̄n, Mı̄-chaı̄'-ăh, ĕl-ı̄-ō-ē'-naı̄, Zĕch-ă-rı̄'-ăh, *and* Hăn-ă-nı̄'-ăh, with trumpets;

42 And Mā-ă-sĕı̄'-ăh, and Shĕm-aı̄'-ăh, and ĕl-ē-ā'-zär, and ŭz'-zı̄, and Jē-hō-hā'-năn, and Măl-chı̄'-jăh, and ē'-lăm, and ē'-zĕr. And the singers ᴺsang loud, with Jĕz-ră-hı̄'-ăh *their* overseer.

43 Also that day they offered great sacrifices, and rejoiced: for God had made them rejoice with great joy: the wives also and the children rejoiced: so that the joy of Jerusalem was heard even afar off.

Provisions for the tithes

44 ᴿAnd at that time were some appointed over the chambers for the treasures, for the offerings, for the firstfruits, and for the tithes, to gather into them out of the fields of the cities the portions ᴺof the law for the priests and Levites: ᴺfor Judah rejoiced for the priests and for the Levites ᴺthat waited.

45 And both the singers and the porters kept the ward of their God, and the ward of the purification, ᴿaccording to the commandment of David, *and* of Solomon his son.

46 For in the days of David ᴿand aı̄'-săph of old *there were* chief of the singers, and songs of praise and thanksgiving unto God.

47 And all Israel in the days of Zĕ-rŭb'-bă-bĕl, and in the days of Nē-hĕm-ı̄'-ăh, gave the portions of the singers and the

porters, every day his portion: ᴿand they ᴺsanctified *holy things* unto the Levites; ᴿand the Levites sanctified *them* unto the children of Aaron.

CHAPTER 13

Separation from foreigners

ON that day ᴿthey ᴺ read in the book of Moses in the ᴺaudience of the people; and therein was found written, ᴿthat the Ammonite and the Moabite should not come into the congregation of God for ever;

2 Because they met not the children of Israel with bread and with water, but ᴿhired Balaam against them, that he should curse them: ᴿhowbeit our God turned the curse into a blessing.

3 Now it came to pass, when they had heard the law, ᴿthat they separated from Israel all the mixed multitude.

Temple chambers cleansed

4 And before this, Ē-lī-ăsh′-ĭb the priest, ᴺhaving the oversight of the chamber of the house of our God, *was* allied unto Tō-bī′-ăh:

5 And he had prepared for him a great chamber, ᴿwhere aforetime they laid the meat offerings, the frankincense, and the vessels, and the tithes of the corn, the new wine, and the oil, ᴿwhichᴺ was commanded *to be given* to the Levites, and the singers, and the porters; and the offerings of the priests.

6 But in all this *time* was not I at Jerusalem: ᴿfor in the two and thirtieth year of Ăr-tă-xĕrx′-ēś king of Babylon came I unto the king, and ᴺafter certain days ᴺobtained I leave of the king:

7 And I came to Jerusalem, and understood of the evil that Ē-lī-ăsh′-ĭb did for Tō-bī′-ăh, in ᴿpreparing him a chamber in the courts of the house of God.

8 And it grieved me sore: therefore I cast forth all the household stuff of Tō-bī′-ăh out of the chamber.

9 Then I commanded, and they ᴿcleansed the chambers: and thither brought I again the vessels of the house of God, with the meat offering and the frankincense.

Tithing begun

10 And I perceived that the portions of the Levites had ᴿnot been given *them:* for the Levites and the singers, that did the work, were fled every one to ᴿhis field.

11 Then ᴿcontended I with the rulers, and said, ᴿWhy is the house of God forsaken?

CHAP. 12
BC 536
47 Num. 18:21, 24
47 i.e. *set apart*
47 Num. 18:26

CHAP. 13
BC 445
1 Deut. 31:11, 12
2 Ki. 23:2
ch. 8:3, 8
& 9:3
Is. 34:16
1 Heb. *there was read*
1 Heb. *ears*
1 Deut. 23:3, 4
2 Num. 22:5
Josh. 24:9, 10
2 Num. 23:11
& 24:10
Deut. 23:5
3 ch. 9:2
& 10:28
4 Heb. *being set over,*
ch. 12:44
5 ch. 12:44
5 Num. 18:21, 24
5 Heb. *the commandment of the Levites*
6 ch. 5:14
6 Heb. *at the end of days*
6 Or, *I earnestly requested*
7 ver. 1, 5
9 2 Chr. 29:5
10 Mal. 3:8
10 Num. 35:2
11 ver. 17, 25
11 ch. 10:39

Heb. *standing*	11
ch. 10:38	12
Or, *storehouses*	12
2 Chr. 31:12	13
Heb. *at their hand*	13
1 Cor. 4:2	13
Heb. *it was upon them*	13
ch. 5:19	14
Heb. *kindnesses*	14
Or, *observations*	14
Ex. 20:10	15
ch. 10:31	15
Jer. 17:21	
Jer. 17:21	18
Lev. 23:32	19
Jer. 17:21	19
Heb. *before the wall?*	21
ch. 12:30	22
Or, *multitude*	22

And I gathered them together, and set them in their ᴺplace.

12 ᴿThen brought all Judah the tithe of the corn and the new wine and the oil unto the ᴺtreasuries.

13 ᴿAnd I made treasurers over the treasuries, Shĕl-ē-mī′-ăh the priest, and Zā′-dŏk the scribe, and of the Levites, Pĕ-dā′-ăh: and ᴺnext to them *was* Hā′-năn the son of Zăc′-cùr, the son of Măt-tă-nī′-ăh: for they were counted ᴿfaithful, and ᴺtheir office *was* to distribute unto their brethren.

14 ᴿRemember me, O my God, concerning this, and wipe not out my ᴺgood deeds that I have done for the house of my God, and for the ᴺoffices thereof.

Sabbath reforms

15 In those days saw I in Judah *some* treading wine presses ᴿon the sabbath, and bringing in sheaves, and lading asses; as also wine, grapes, and figs, and all *manner of* burdens, ᴿwhich they brought into Jerusalem on the sabbath day: and I testified *against them* in the day wherein they sold victuals.

16 There dwelt men of Tyre also therein, which brought fish, and all manner of ware, and sold on the sabbath unto the children of Judah, and in Jerusalem.

17 Then I contended with the nobles of Judah, and said unto them, What evil thing *is* this that ye do, and profane the sabbath day?

18 ᴿDid not your fathers thus, and did not our God bring all this evil upon us, and upon this city? yet ye bring more wrath upon Israel by profaning the sabbath.

19 And it came to pass, that when the gates of Jerusalem ᴿbegan to be dark before the sabbath, I commanded that the gates should be shut, and charged that they should not be opened till after the sabbath: ᴿand *some* of my servants set I at the gates, *that* there should no burden be brought in on the sabbath day.

20 So the merchants and sellers of all kind of ware lodged without Jerusalem once or twice.

21 Then I testified against them, and said unto them, Why lodge ye ᴺabout the wall? if ye do *so* again, I will lay hands on you. From that time forth came they no *more* on the sabbath.

22 And I commanded the Levites that ᴿthey should cleanse themselves, and *that* they should come *and* keep the gates, to sanctify the sabbath day. Remember me, O my God, *concerning* this also, and spare me according to the ᴺgreatness of thy mercy.

Mixed marriages condemned

23 In those days also saw I Jews *that* [R]had[N] married wives of Ăsh′-dŏd, of Ammon, *and* of Moab:

24 And their children spake half in the speech of Ăsh′-dŏd, and [N]could not speak in the Jews' language, but according to the language [N]of each people.

25 And I [R]contended with them, and [N]cursed them, and smote certain of them, and plucked off their hair, and made them [R]swear by God, *saying,* Ye shall not give your daughters unto their sons, nor take their daughters unto your sons, or for yourselves.

26 [R]Did not Solomon king of Israel sin by these things? yet among many nations was there no king like him, [R]who was beloved of his God, and God made him king over all Is-

rael: [R]nevertheless even him did outlandish women cause to sin.

27 Shall we then hearken unto you to do all this great evil, to [R]transgress against our God in marrying strange wives?

28 And *one* of the sons [R]of Jŏi′-ă-dă, the son of E-lī-ăsh′-ĭb the high priest, *was* son in law to Săn-băl′-lăt the Hôr′-ŏn-īte: therefore I chased him from me.

29 [R]Remember them, O my God, [N]because they have defiled the priesthood, and [R]the covenant of the priesthood, and of the Levites.

30 [R]Thus cleansed I them from all strangers, and [R]appointed the wards of the priests and the Levites, every one in his business;

31 And for [R]the wood offering, at times appointed, and for the firstfruits. [R]Remember me, O my God, for good.

CHAP. 13
BC 445
23 Ezra 9:2
23 Heb. *had made to dwell* with them
24 Heb. *they discerned not to speak*
24 Heb. *of people and people*
25 Prov. 28:4
25 Or, *reviled them*
25 Ezra 10:5
ch. 10:29
26 1 Ki. 11:1
26 2 Sam. 12:24

1 Ki. 11:4	26
Ezra 10:2	27
ch. 12:10, 22	28
ch. 6:14	29
Heb. *for the defilings*	29
Mal. 2:4, 11, 12	29
ch. 10:30	30
ch. 12:1	30
ch. 10:34	31
ver. 14, 22	31

THE
BOOK OF ESTHER

The book of Esther is the story of a Jewish maiden who became queen of Persia and has its setting in the palace of Shushan, or Susa, one of the three capitals of the Persian Empire. Historically, the story of Esther is identified with the reign of Ahasuerus or Xerxes, (485-465 B.C.). It gives us some insight into the experiences of the Jews in exile, of the hostility of their non-Jewish enemies in Persia, and of how Esther became queen, subsequently risking her life to save her people, the Jews, from total destruction. God's providential care is emphasized throughout the account. The commemoration of this daring and heroic deed on the part of Esther is called Purim and is celebrated annually throughout Judaism.

OUTLINE OF THE BOOK:
    I. Jews at the Persian court 1:1 – 2:23
   II. The Jewish people threatened 3:1 – 5:14
  III. Triumph of the Jews 6:1 – 10:3

CHAPTER 1

The royal banquet

NOW it came to pass in the days of [R]Ă-hăś-ū-ē′-rŭs, (this *is* Ă-hăś-ū-ē′-rŭs which reigned, [R]from India even unto E-thĭ-ō′-pĭ-ă, [R]*over* an hundred and seven and twenty provinces:)

2 *That* in those days, when the king Ă-hăś-ū-ē′-rŭs [R]sat on the throne of his kingdom, which *was* in [R]Shû′-shăn the palace,

3 In the third year of his reign, he [R]made a feast unto all his princes and his servants; the power of Persia and Mē′-dĭ-ă, the nobles and princes of the provinces, *being* before him:

4 When he shewed the riches of his glorious kingdom and the honour of his excellent majesty many days, *even* an hundred and fourscore days.

5 And when these days were expired, the

king made a feast unto all the people that were [N]present in Shû′-shăn the palace, both unto great and small, seven days, in the court of the garden of the king's palace;

6 *Where were* white, green, and [N]blue, *hangings,* fastened with cords of fine linen and purple to silver rings and pillars of marble: [R]the beds *were of* gold and silver, upon a pavement [N]of red, and blue, and white, and black, marble.

7 And they gave *them* drink in vessels of gold, (the vessels being diverse one from another,) and [N]royal wine in abundance, [N]according to the state of the king.

8 And the drinking *was* according to the law; none did compel: for so the king had appointed to all the officers of his house, that they should do according to every man's pleasure.

9 Also Vashti the queen made a feast for the

CHAP. 1
BC 521
1 Ezra 4:6
Dan. 9:1
1 ch. 8:9
1 Dan. 6:1
2 1 Ki. 1:46
2 Neh. 1:1
3 Gen. 40:20
ch. 2:18

Heb. *found*	5
Or, *violet*	6
ch. 7:8	6
Amos 2:8 & 6:4	6
Or, *of porphyre, and marble, and alabaster, and stone of blue colour*	6
Heb. *wine of the kingdom*	7
Heb. *according to the hand of the king*	7

women *in* the royal house which *belonged* to king Ă-hăś-ū-ē′-rŭs.

10 On the seventh day, when the heart of the king was merry with wine, he commanded Mĕ-hū′-măn, Bĭz′-thă, [R]Här-bō′-nă, Bĭg′-thă, and Ă-băg′-thă, Zē′-thär, and Cär′-căs, the seven [N]chamberlains that served in the presence of Ă-hăś-ū-ē′-rŭs the king,

11 To bring Vashti the queen before the king with the crown royal, to shew the people and the princes her beauty: for she *was* [N]fair to look on.

12 But the queen Vashti refused to come at the king's commandment [N]by *his* chamberlains: therefore was the king very wroth, and his anger burned in him.

Queen Vashti deposed

13 Then the king said to the [R]wise men, [R]which knew the times, (for so *was* the king's manner toward all that knew law and judgment:

14 And the next unto him *was* Cär-shē′-nă, Shē′-thär, Ăd-mā′-thă, Tarshish, Mē′-rĕś, Mär-sē′-nă, *and* Mĕ-mū′-căn, the [R]seven princes of Persia and Mē′-dĭ-ă, [R]which saw the king's face, *and* which sat the first in the kingdom;)

15 [N]What shall we do unto the queen Vashti according to law, because she hath not performed the commandment of the king Ă-hăś-ū-ē′-rŭs by the chamberlains?

16 And Mĕ-mū′-căn answered before the king and the princes, Vashti the queen hath not done wrong to the king only, but also to all the princes, and to all the people that *are* in all the provinces of the king Ă-hăś-ū-ē′-rŭs.

17 For *this* deed of the queen shall come abroad unto all women, so that they shall [R]despise their husbands in their eyes, when it shall be reported, The king Ă-hăś-ū-ē′-rŭs commanded Vashti the queen to be brought in before him, but she came not.

18 *Likewise* shall the ladies of Persia and Mē′-dĭ-ă say this day unto all the king's princes, which have heard of the deed of the queen. Thus *shall there arise* too much contempt and wrath.

19 [N]If it please the king, let there go a royal commandment [N]from him, and let it be written among the laws of the Persians and the Mēdeś, [N]that it be not altered, That Vashti come no more before king Ă-hăś-ū-ē′-rŭs; and let the king give her royal estate [N]unto another that is better than she.

20 And when the king's decree which he shall make shall be published throughout all

his empire, (for it is great,) all the wives shall [R]give to their husbands honour, both to great and small.

21 And the saying [N]pleased the king and the princes; and the king did according to the word of Mĕ-mū′-căn:

22 For he sent letters into all the king's provinces, [R]into every province according to the writing thereof, and to every people after their language, that every man should [R]bear rule in his own house, and [N]that *it* should be published according to the language of every people.

CHAPTER 2

Esther joins the king's house

AFTER these things, when the wrath of king Ă-hăś-ū-ē′-rŭs was appeased, he remembered Vashti, and what she had done, and [R]what was decreed against her.

2 Then said the king's servants that ministered unto him, Let there be fair young virgins sought for the king:

3 And let the king appoint officers in all the provinces of his kingdom, that they may gather together all the fair young virgins unto Shû′-shăn the palace, to the house of the women, [N]unto the custody of [N]Hē′-gē the king's chamberlain, keeper of the women; and let their things for purification be given *them*:

4 And let the maiden which pleaseth the king be queen instead of Vashti. And the thing pleased the king; and he did so.

5 *Now* in Shû′-shăn the palace there was a certain Jew, whose name *was* Môr-dĕ-cā′-ĭ, the son of Jā′-ĭr, the son of Shĭm′-ĕ-ĭ, the son of Kish, a Benjamite;

6 [R]Who had been carried away from Jerusalem with the captivity which had been carried away with [N]Jĕc-ō-nĭ′-ăh king of Judah, whom Nĕb-ū-chăd-nĕz′-zär the king of Babylon had carried away.

7 And he [N]brought up Hă-dăs′-săh, that *is,* Esther, [R]his uncle's daughter: for she had neither father nor mother, and the maid *was* [N]fair and beautiful; whom Môr-dĕ-cā′-ĭ, when her father and mother were dead, took for his own daughter.

8 So it came to pass, when the king's commandment and his decree was heard, and when many maidens were [R]gathered together unto Shû′-shăn the palace, to the custody of Hē′-gāi, that Esther was brought also unto the king's house, to the custody of Hē′-gāi, keeper of the women.

9 And the maiden pleased him, and she ob-

tained kindness of him; and he speedily gave her her Rthings for purification, with Nsuch things as belonged to her, and seven maidens, *which were* meet to be given her, out of the king's house: and Nhe preferred her and her maids unto the best *place* of the house of the women.

10 REsther had not shewed her people nor her kindred: for Môr-dĕ-cā′-ī had charged her that she should not shew *it*.

11 And Môr-dĕ-cā′-ī walked every day before the court of the women's house, Nto know how Esther did, and what should become of her.

12 Now when every maid's turn was come to go in to king Ă-hăs-ū-ē′-rŭs, after that she had been twelve months, according to the manner of the women, (for so were the days of their purifications accomplished, *to wit*, six months with oil of myrrh, and six months with sweet odours, and with *other* things for the purifying of the women;)

13 Then thus came *every* maiden unto the king; whatsoever she desired was given her to go with her out of the house of the women unto the king's house.

14 In the evening she went, and on the morrow she returned into the second house of the women, to the custody of Shā-ăsh′-găz, the king's chamberlain, which kept the concubines: she came in unto the king no more, except the king delighted in her, and that she were called by name.

Esther becomes queen

15 Now when the turn of Esther, Rthe daughter of Ăb′-ĭ-hạil the uncle of Môr-dĕ-cā′-ī, who had taken her for his daughter, was come to go in unto the king, she required nothing but what Hē′-gai the king's chamberlain, the keeper of the women, appointed. And Esther obtained favour in the sight of all them that looked upon her.

16 So Esther was taken unto king Ă-hăs-ū-ē′-rŭs into his house royal in the tenth month, which *is* the month Tē′-bĕth, in the seventh year of his reign.

17 And the king loved Esther above all the women, and she obtained grace and Nfavour Nin his sight more than all the virgins; so that he set the royal crown upon her head, and made her queen instead of Vashti.

18 Then the king Rmade a great feast unto all his princes and his servants, *even* Esther's feast; and he made a Nrelease to the provinces, and gave gifts, according to the state of the king.

CHAP. 2
BC 518
9 ver. 3, 12
9 Heb. *her portions*
9 Heb. *he changed her*
10 ver. 20
11 Heb. *to know the peace*
15 ver. 7
17 Or, *kindness*
17 Heb. *before him*
18 ch. 1:3
18 Heb. *rest*

ver. 21	19
ch. 3:2	
ver. 10	20
Or, *Bigthana*,	21
ch. 6:2	
Heb. *the threshold*	21
ch. 6:2	22
ch. 6:1	23

CHAP. 3
BC 510
Num. 24:7 — 1
1 Sam. 15:8	
ch. 2:19 — 2
ver. 5 — 2
Ps. 15:4	
ver. 2 — 3
ver. 2 — 5
ch. 5:9	
Dan. 3:19 — 5
Ps. 83:4 — 6

Mordecai saves the king's life

19 And when the virgins were gathered together the second time, then Môr-dĕ-cā′-ī sat Rin the king's gate.

20 REsther had not *yet* shewed her kindred nor her people; as Môr-dĕ-cā′-ī had charged her: for Esther did the commandment of Môr-dĕ-cā′-ī, like as when she was brought up with him.

21 In those days, while Môr-dĕ-cā′-ī sat in the king's gate, two of the king's chamberlains, NBĭg′-thăn and Tē′-rĕsh, of those which kept Nthe door, were wroth, and sought to lay hand on the king Ă-hăs-ū-ē′-rŭs.

22 And the thing was known to Môr-dĕ-cā′-ī, Rwho told *it* unto Esther the queen; and Esther certified the king *thereof* in Môr-dĕ-cā′-ī's name.

23 And when inquisition was made of the matter, it was found out; therefore they were both hanged on a tree: and it was written in Rthe book of the chronicles before the king.

CHAPTER 3

Mordecai refuses to bow

AFTER these things did king Ă-hăs-ū-ē′-rŭs promote Hā′-măn the son of Hăm-mĕ-dā′-thă the RĂg′-ă-gīte, and advanced him, and set his seat above all the princes that *were* with him.

2 And all the king's servants, that *were* Rin the king's gate, bowed, and reverenced Hā′-măn: for the king had so commanded concerning him. But Môr-dĕ-cā′-ī Rbowed not, nor did *him* reverence.

3 Then the king's servants, which *were* in the king's gate, said unto Môr-dĕ-cā′-ī, Why transgressest thou the Rking's commandment?

4 Now it came to pass, when they spake daily unto him, and he hearkened not unto them, that they told Hā′-măn, to see whether Môr-dĕ-cā′-ī's matters would stand: for he had told them that he *was* a Jew.

5 And when Hā′-măn saw that Môr-dĕ-cā′-ī Rbowed not, nor did him reverence, then was Hā′-măn Rfull of wrath.

6 And he thought scorn to lay hands on Môr-dĕ-cā′-ī alone; for they had shewed him the people of Môr-dĕ-cā′-ī: wherefore Hā′-măn Rsought to destroy all the Jews that *were* throughout the whole kingdom of Ă-hăs-ū-ē′-rŭs, *even* the people of Môr-dĕ-cā′-ī.

Haman's plot to destroy the Jews

7 In the first month, that *is*, the month Nī′-săn, in the twelfth year of king Ă-hăs-ū-ē′-

rŭs, ᴿthey cast Pur, that *is,* the lot, before Hā′-măn from day to day, and from month to month, *to* the twelfth *month, that is,* the month ā′-där.

8 And Hā′-măn said unto king ă-hăs-ū-ē′-rŭs, There is a certain people scattered abroad and dispersed among the people in all the provinces of thy kingdom; and ᴿtheir laws *are* diverse from all people; neither keep they the king's laws: therefore it *is* not ᴺfor the king's profit to suffer them.

9 If it please the king, let it be written ᴺthat they may be destroyed: and I will ᴺpay ten thousand talents of silver to the hands of those that have the charge of the business, to bring *it* into the king's treasuries.

10 And the king ᴿtook ᴿhis ring from his hand, and gave it unto Hā′-măn the son of Hăm-mĕ-dā′-thă the Ăg′-ă-gīte, the Jews' ᴺenemy.

11 And the king said unto Hā′-măn, The silver *is* given to thee, the people also, to do with them as it seemeth good to thee.

Haman's proclamation

12 ᴿThen were the king's ᴺscribes called on the thirteenth day of the first month, and there was written according to all that Hā′-măn had commanded unto the king's lieutenants, and to the governors that *were* over every province, and to the rulers of every people of every province ᴿaccording to the writing thereof, and *to* every people after their language; ᴿin the name of king ă-hăs-ū-ē′-rŭs was it written, and sealed with the king's ring.

13 And the letters were ᴿsent by posts into all the king's provinces, to destroy, to kill, and to cause to perish, all Jews, both young and old, little children and women, ᴿin one day, *even* upon the thirteenth *day* of the twelfth month, which *is* the month ā′-där, and ᴿ*to take* the spoil of them for a prey.

14 ᴿThe copy of the writing for a commandment to be given in every province was published unto all people, that they should be ready against that day.

15 The posts went out, being hastened by the king's commandment, and the decree was given in Shū′-shăn the palace. And the king and Hā′-măn sat down to drink; but ᴿthe city Shū′-shăn was perplexed.

CHAPTER 4

WHEN Môr-dĕ-cā′-ī perceived all that was done, Môr-dĕ-cā′-ī ᴿrent his clothes, and put on sackcloth ᴿwith ashes, and went out into the midst of the city, and ᴿcried with a loud and a bitter cry;

CHAP. 3
BC 510
7 ch. 9:24
8 Ezra 4:13
  Acts 16:20
8 Heb. *meet,*
  or, *equal*
9 Heb. *to destroy
  them*
9 Heb. *weigh*
10 Gen. 41:42
10 ch. 8:2, 8
10 Or, *oppressor,*
  ch. 7:6
12 ch. 8:9
12 Or, *secretaries*
12 ch. 1:22
12 1 Ki. 21:8
  ch. 8:8, 10
13 ch. 8:10
13 ch. 8:12, etc.
13 ch. 8:11
14 ch. 8:13, 14
15 See ch. 8:15
  Prov. 29:2

CHAP. 4
BC 510
1 2 Sam. 1:11
1 Josh. 7:6
  Ezek. 27:30
1 Gen. 27:34

Heb. *sackcloth*   3
*and ashes were
laid under many*
Heb. *eunuchs*   4
Heb. *whom he
had set before her*
ch. 3:9   7
ch. 3:14, 15   8
ch. 5:1   11
Dan. 2:9   11
ch. 5:2   11
& 8:4
Heb. *respiration,*   14
Job 9:18

2 And came even before the king's gate: for none *might* enter into the king's gate clothed with sackcloth.

3 And in every province, whithersoever the king's commandment and his decree came, *there was* great mourning among the Jews, and fasting, and weeping, and wailing; and ᴺmany lay in sackcloth and ashes.

Esther promises help

4 So Esther's maids and her ᴺchamberlains came and told *it* her. Then was the queen exceedingly grieved; and she sent raiment to clothe Môr-dĕ-cā′-ī, and to take away his sackcloth from him: but he received *it* not.

5 Then called Esther for Hā′-tăch, *one* of the king's chamberlains, ᴺwhom he had appointed to attend upon her, and gave him a commandment to Môr-dĕ-cā′-ī, to know what it *was,* and why it *was.*

6 So Hā′-tăch went forth to Môr-dĕ-cā′-ī unto the street of the city, which *was* before the king's gate.

7 And Môr-dĕ-cā′-ī told him of all that had happened unto him, and of ᴿthe sum of the money that Hā′-măn had promised to pay to the king's treasuries for the Jews, to destroy them.

8 Also he gave him ᴿthe copy of the writing of the decree that was given at Shū′-shăn to destroy them, to shew *it* unto Esther, and to declare *it* unto her, and to charge her that she should go in unto the king, to make supplication unto him, and to make request before him for her people.

9 And Hā′-tăch came and told Esther the words of Môr-dĕ-cā′-ī.

10 Again Esther spake unto Hā′-tăch, and gave him commandment unto Môr-dĕ-cā′-ī;

11 All the king's servants, and the people of the king's provinces, do know, that whosoever, whether man or woman, shall come unto the king into ᴿthe inner court, who is not called, ᴿ*there is* one law of his to put *him* to death, except such ᴿto whom the king shall hold out the golden sceptre, that he may live: but I have not been called to come in unto the king these thirty days.

12 And they told to Môr-dĕ-cā′-ī Esther's words.

13 Then Môr-dĕ-cā′-ī commanded to answer Esther, Think not with thyself that thou shalt escape in the king's house, more than all the Jews.

14 For if thou altogether holdest thy peace at this time, *then* shall there ᴺenlargement and deliverance arise to the Jews from another place; but thou and thy father's house shall be

destroyed: and who knoweth whether thou art come to the kingdom for *such* a time as this?

15 Then Esther bade *them* return Môr-dĕ-cā′-ĭ *this answer,*

16 Go, gather together all the Jews that are ᴺpresent in Shû′-shăn, and fast ye for me, and neither eat nor drink ᴿthree days, night or day: I also and my maidens will fast likewise; and so will I go in unto the king, which *is* not according to the law: ᴿand if I perish, I perish.

17 So Môr-dĕ-cā′-ĭ ᴺwent his way, and did according to all that Esther had commanded him.

CHAPTER 5

Esther's banquet

N̲OW it came to pass ᴿon the third day, that Esther put on *her* royal *apparel,* and stood in ᴿthe inner court of the king's house, over against the king's house: and the king sat upon his royal throne in the royal house, over against the gate of the house.

2 And it was so, when the king saw Esther the queen standing in the court, *that* ᴿshe obtained favour in his sight: and ᴿthe king held out to Esther the golden sceptre that *was* in his hand. So Esther drew near, and touched the top of the sceptre.

3 Then said the king unto her, What wilt thou, queen Esther? and what *is* thy request? ᴿit shall be even given thee to the half of the kingdom.

4 And Esther answered, If *it seem* good unto the king, let the king and Hā′-măn come this day unto the banquet that I have prepared for him.

5 Then the king said, Cause Hā′-măn to make haste, that he may do as Esther hath said. So the king and Hā′-măn came to the banquet that Esther had prepared.

6 ᴿAnd the king said unto Esther at the banquet of wine, ᴿWhat *is* thy petition? and it shall be granted thee: and what *is* thy request? even to the half of the kingdom it shall be performed.

7 Then answered Esther, and said, My petition and my request *is;*

8 If I have found favour in the sight of the king, and if it please the king to grant my petition, and ᴺto perform my request, let the king and Hā′-măn come to the banquet that I shall prepare for them, and I will do to morrow as the king hath said.

Haman's wrath against Mordecai

9 Then went Hā′-măn forth that day joyful and with a glad heart: but when Hā′-măn saw

Môr-dĕ-cā′-ĭ in the king's gate, ᴿthat he stood not up, nor moved for him, he was full of indignation against Môr-dĕ-cā′-ĭ.

10 Nevertheless Hā′-măn ᴿrefrained himself: and when he came home, he sent and ᴺcalled for his friends, and Zē′-rĕsh his wife.

11 And Hā′-măn told them of the glory of his riches, and ᴿthe multitude of his children, and all *the things* wherein the king had promoted him, and how he had advanced him above the princes and servants of the king.

12 Hā′-măn said moreover, Yea, Esther the queen did let no man come in with the king unto the banquet that she had prepared but myself; and to morrow am I invited unto her also with the king.

13 Yet all this availeth me nothing, so long as I see Môr-dĕ-cā′-ĭ the Jew sitting at the king's gate.

14 Then said Zē′-rĕsh his wife and all his friends unto him, Let a ᴿgallowsᴺ be made of fifty cubits high, and to morrow ᴿspeak thou unto the king that Môr-dĕ-cā′-ĭ may be hanged thereon: then go thou in merrily with the king unto the banquet. And the thing pleased Hā′-măn; and he caused ᴿthe gallows to be made.

CHAPTER 6

Haman's plot fails

O̲N that night ᴺcould not the king sleep, and he commanded to bring ᴿthe book of records of the chronicles; and they were read before the king.

2 And it was found written, that Môr-dĕ-cā′-ĭ had told of ᴺBĭg-thā′-nă and Tē′-rĕsh, two of the king's chamberlains, the keepers of the ᴺdoor, who sought to lay hand on the king Ă-hăś-ū-ē′-rŭs.

3 And the king said, What honour and dignity hath been done to Môr-dĕ-cā′-ĭ for this? Then said the king's servants that ministered unto him, There is nothing done for him.

4 And the king said, Who *is* in the court? Now Hā′-măn was come into ᴿthe outward court of the king's house, ᴿto speak unto the king to hang Môr-dĕ-cā′-ĭ on the gallows that he had prepared for him.

5 And the king's servants said unto him, Behold, Hā′-măn standeth in the court. And the king said, Let him come in.

6 So Hā′-măn came in. And the king said unto him, What shall be done unto the man ᴺwhom the king delighteth to honour? Now Hā′-măn thought in his heart, To whom would the king delight to do honour more than to myself?

CHAP. 4
BC 510
15 Heb. *found*
16 See ch. 5:1
16 See Gen. 43:14
17 Heb. *passed*

CHAP. 5
BC 510
1 See ch. 4:16
1 See ch. 4:11
  & 6:4
2 Prov. 21:1
2 ch. 4:11
  & 8:4
3 Mark 6:23
6 ch. 7:2
6 ch. 9:12
8 Heb. *to do*

ch. 3:5   9
2 Sam. 13:22   10
Heb. *caused to come*   10
ch. 9:7, etc.   11
ch. 7:9   14
Heb. *tree*   14
ch. 6:4   14
ch. 7:10   14

CHAP. 6
BC 510
Heb. *the king's sleep fled away*   1
ch. 2:23   1
Or, *Bigthan,*   2
  ch. 2:21
Heb. *threshold*   2
See ch. 5:1   4
ch. 5:14   4
Heb. *in whose honour the king delighteth*   6

7 And Hā'-măn answered the king, For the man ᴺwhom the king delighteth to honour,

8 ᴺLet the royal apparel be brought ᴺwhich the king *useth* to wear, and ᴿthe horse that the king rideth upon, and the crown royal which is set upon his head:

9 And let this apparel and horse be delivered to the hand of one of the king's most noble princes, that they may array the man *withal* whom the king delighteth to honour, and ᴺbring him on horseback through the street of the city, ᴿand proclaim before him, Thus shall it be done to the man whom the king delighteth to honour.

10 Then the king said to Hā'-măn, Make haste, *and* take the apparel and the horse, as thou hast said, and do even so to Môr-dĕ-cā'-ī the Jew, that sitteth at the king's gate: ᴺlet nothing fail of all that thou hast spoken.

11 Then took Hā'-măn the apparel and the horse, and arrayed Môr-dĕ-cā'-ī, and brought him on horseback through the street of the city, and proclaimed before him, Thus shall it be done unto the man whom the king delighteth to honour.

12 And Môr-dĕ-cā'-ī came again to the king's gate. But Hā'-măn ᴿhasted to his house mourning, ᴿand having his head covered.

13 And Hā'-măn told Zē'-rĕsh his wife and all his friends every *thing* that had befallen him. Then said his wise men and Zē'-rĕsh his wife unto him, If Môr-dĕ-cā'-ī *be* of the seed of the Jews, before whom thou hast begun to fall, thou shalt not prevail against him, but shalt surely fall before him.

14 And while they *were* yet talking with him, came the king's chamberlains, and hasted to bring Hā'-măn unto ᴿthe banquet that Esther had prepared.

CHAPTER 7

Esther's petition

SO the king and Hā'-măn came ᴺto banquet with Esther the queen.

2 And the king said again unto Esther on the second day ᴿat the banquet of wine, What *is* thy petition, queen Esther? and it shall be granted thee: and what *is* thy request? and it shall be performed, *even* to the half of the kingdom.

3 Then Esther the queen answered and said, If I have found favour in thy sight, O king, and if it please the king, let my life be given me at my petition, and my people at my request:

4 For we are ᴿsold, I and my people, ᴺto be destroyed, to be slain, and to perish. But if we

---

---

had been sold for bondmen and bondwomen, I had held my tongue, although the enemy could not countervail the king's damage.

5 Then the king Ă-hăś-ū-ē'-rŭs answered and said unto Esther the queen, Who is he, and where is he, ᴺthat durst presume in his heart to do so?

6 And Esther said, ᴺThe adversary and enemy *is* this wicked Hā'-măn. Then Hā'-măn was afraid ᴺbefore the king and the queen.

7 And the king arising from the banquet of wine in his wrath *went* into the palace garden: and Hā'-măn stood up to make request for his life to Esther the queen; for he saw that there was evil determined against him by the king.

8 Then the king returned out of the palace garden into the place of the banquet of wine; and Hā'-măn was fallen upon ᴿthe bed whereon Esther *was*. Then said the king, Will he force the queen also ᴺbefore me in the house? As the word went out of the king's mouth, they ᴿcovered Hā'-măn's face.

Haman hanged

9 And ᴿHär-bō'-năh, one of the chamberlains, said before the king, Behold also, ᴿthe ᴺgallows fifty cubits high, which Hā'-măn had made for Môr-dĕ-cā'-ī, who had spoken good for the king, standeth in the house of Hā'-măn. Then the king said, Hang him thereon.

10 So ᴿthey hanged Hā'-măn on the gallows that he had prepared for Môr-dĕ-cā'-ī. Then was the king's wrath pacified.

CHAPTER 8

Mordecai promoted

ON that day did the king Ă-hăś-ū-ē'-rŭs give the house of Hā'-măn the Jews' enemy unto Esther the queen. And Môr-dĕ-cā'-ī came before the king; for Esther had told ᴿwhat he *was* unto her.

2 And the king took off ᴿhis ring, which he had taken from Hā'-măn, and gave it unto Môr-dĕ-cā'-ī. And Esther set Môr-dĕ-cā'-ī over the house of Hā'-măn.

Esther's petition granted

3 And Esther spake yet again before the king, and fell down at his feet, ᴺand besought him with tears to put away the mischief of Hā'-măn the Ăg'-ă-gīte, and his device that he had devised against the Jews.

4 Then ᴿthe king held out the golden sceptre toward Esther. So Esther arose, and stood before the king,

5 And said, If it please the king, and if I have found favour in his sight, and the thing

seem right before the king, and I *be* pleasing in his eyes, let it be written to reverse ᴺthe letters devised by Hā'-măn the son of Hăm-mĕ-dā'-thă the Ăg'-ă-gīte, ᴺwhich he wrote to destroy the Jews which *are* in all the king's provinces:

6 For how can I ᴺendure to see ᴿthe evil that shall come unto my people? or how can I endure to see the destruction of my kindred?

7 Then the king Ă-hăś-ū-ē'-rŭs said unto Esther the queen and to Môr-dĕ-cā'-ī the Jew, Behold, ᴿI have given Esther the house of Hā'-măn, and him they have hanged upon the gallows, because he laid his hand upon the Jews.

8 Write ye also for the Jews, as it liketh you, in the king's name, and seal *it* with the king's ring: for the writing which is written in the king's name, and sealed with the king's ring, ᴿmay no man reverse.

The new proclamation

9 ᴿThen were the king's scribes called at that time in the third month, that *is*, the month Sī'-văn, on the three and twentieth *day* thereof; and it was written according to all that Môr-dĕ-cā'-ī commanded unto the Jews, and to the lieutenants, and the deputies and rulers of the provinces which *are* ᴿfrom India unto Ē-thī-ō'-pī-ă, an hundred twenty and seven provinces, unto every province ᴿaccording to the writing thereof, and unto every people after their language, and to the Jews according to their writing, and according to their language.

10 ᴿAnd he wrote in the king Ă-hăś-ū-ē'-rŭs' name, and sealed *it* with the king's ring, and sent letters by posts on horseback, *and* riders on mules, camels, *and* young dromedaries:

11 Wherein the king granted the Jews which *were* in every city to gather themselves together, and to stand for their life, to destroy, to slay, and to cause to perish, all the power of the people and province that would assault them, *both* little ones and women, and ᴿto take the spoil of them for a prey,

12 ᴿUpon one day in all the provinces of king Ă-hăś-ū-ē'-rŭs, *namely,* upon the thirteenth *day* of the twelfth month, which *is* the month Ā'-där.

13 ᴿThe copy of the writing for a commandment to be given in every province *was* ᴺpublished unto all people, and that the Jews should be ready against that day to avenge themselves on their enemies.

14 *So* the posts that rode upon mules *and* camels went out, being hastened and pressed on by the king's commandment. And the decree was given at Shû'-shăn the palace.

15 And Môr-dĕ-cā'-ī went out from the presence of the king in royal apparel of ᴺblue and white, and with a great crown of gold, and with a garment of fine linen and purple: and ᴿthe city of Shû'-shăn rejoiced and was glad.

16 The Jews had ᴿlight, and gladness, and joy, and honour.

17 And in every province, and in every city, whithersoever the king's commandment and his decree came, the Jews had joy and gladness, a feast ᴿand a good day. And many of the people of the land ᴿbecame Jews; for ᴿthe fear of the Jews fell upon them.

CHAPTER 9

The Jews destroy their enemies

NOW ᴿin the twelfth month, that *is*, the month Ā'-där, on the thirteenth day of the same, ᴿwhen the king's commandment and his decree drew near to be put in execution, in the day that the enemies of the Jews hoped to have power over them, (though it was turned to the contrary, that the Jews ᴿhad rule over them that hated them;)

2 The Jews ᴿgathered themselves together in their cities throughout all the provinces of the king Ă-hăś-ū-ē'-rŭs, to lay hand on such as ᴿsought their hurt: and no man could withstand them; for ᴿthe fear of them fell upon all people.

3 And all the rulers of the provinces, and the lieutenants, and the deputies, and ᴺofficers of the king, helped the Jews; because the fear of Môr-dĕ-cā'-ī fell upon them.

4 For Môr-dĕ-cā'-ī *was* great in the king's house, and his fame went out throughout all the provinces: for this man Môr-dĕ-cā'-ī ᴿwaxed greater and greater.

5 Thus the Jews smote all their enemies with the stroke of the sword, and slaughter, and destruction, and did ᴺwhat they would unto those that hated them.

6 And in Shû'-shăn the palace the Jews slew and destroyed five hundred men.

7 And Pär-shăn-dā'-thă, and Dăl'-phŏn, and Ăs-pā'-thă,

8 And Pôr-ā'-thă, and Ă-dā'-lī-ă, and Ăr-ī-dā'-thă,

9 And Pär-măsh'-tă, and Ăr'-ī-săi, and Ăr-ī-dăi, and Vă-jĕz'-ă-thă,

10 ᴿThe ten sons of Hā'-măn the son of Hăm-mĕ-dā'-thă, the enemy of the Jews, slew they; ᴿbut on the spoil laid they not their hand.

11 On that day the number of those that were slain in Shû'-shăn the palace ᴺwas brought before the king.

12 And the king said unto Esther the queen, The Jews have slain and destroyed five hundred men in Shû'-shăn the palace, and the ten sons of Hā'-măn; what have they done in the rest of the king's provinces? now [R]what *is* thy petition? and it shall be granted thee: or what *is* thy request further? and it shall be done.

13 Then said Esther, If it please the king, let it be granted to the Jews which *are* in Shû'-shăn to do to morrow also [R]according unto this day's decree, and [N]let Hā'-măn's ten sons [R]be hanged upon the gallows.

14 And the king commanded it so to be done: and the decree was given at Shû'-shăn; and they hanged Hā'-măn's ten sons.

15 For the Jews that *were* in Shû'-shăn [R]gathered themselves together on the fourteenth day also of the month Ā'-där, and slew three hundred men at Shû'-shăn; [R]but on the prey they laid not their hand.

16 But the other Jews that *were* in the king's provinces [R]gathered themselves together, and stood for their lives, and had rest from their enemies, and slew of their foes seventy and five thousand, [R]but they laid not their hands on the prey,

17 On the thirteenth day of the month Ā'-där; and on the fourteenth day [N]of the same rested they, and made it a day of feasting and gladness.

18 But the Jews that *were* at Shû'-shăn assembled together [R]on the thirteenth *day* thereof, and on the fourteenth thereof; and on the fifteenth *day* of the same they rested, and made it a day of feasting and gladness.

19 Therefore the Jews of the villages, that dwelt in the unwalled towns, made the fourteenth day of the month Ā'-där [R]*a day of* gladness and feasting, [R]and a good day, and of [R]sending portions one to another.

Feast of Purim instituted

20 And Môr-dĕ-cā'-ī wrote these things, and sent letters unto all the Jews that *were* in all the provinces of the king Ă-hăś-ū-ē'-rŭs, *both* nigh and far,

21 To stablish *this* among them, that they should keep the fourteenth day of the month Ā'-där, and the fifteenth day of the same, yearly,

22 As the days wherein the Jews rested from their enemies, and the month which was turned unto them from sorrow to joy, and from mourning into a good day: that they should make them days of feasting and joy, and of [R]sending portions one to another, and gifts to the poor.

CHAP. 9	
BC 510	
12 ch. 5:6	
& 7:2	
13 ch. 8:11	
13 Heb. *let men*	
hang	
13 2 Sam. 21:6, 9	
15 ver. 2	
ch. 8:11	
15 ver. 10	
16 ver. 2	
ch. 8:11	
16 See ch. 8:11	
17 Heb. *in it*	
18 ver. 11, 15	
19 Deut. 16:11, 14	
19 ch. 8:17	
19 ver. 22	
Neh. 8:10, 12	
22 ver. 19	
Neh. 8:10	

ch. 3:6, 7	24
Heb. *crush*	24
ver. 13, 14	25
ch. 7:5, etc.	
& 8:3, etc.	
Heb. *when she*	25
came	
ch. 7:10	25
Ps. 7:16	
i.e. *Lot*	26
ver. 20	26
ch. 8:17	27
Is. 56:3, 6	
Zech. 2:11	
Heb. *pass*	27
Heb. *pass*	28
Heb. *be ended*	28
ch. 2:15	29
Heb. *all*	29
strength	
See ch. 8:10	29
& ver. 20	
ch. 1:1	30
Heb. *for*	31
their souls	
ch. 4:3, 16	31

CHAP. 10	
BC 509	
Gen. 10:5	1
Ps. 72:10	
Is. 24:15	
ch. 8:15	2
& 9:4	
Heb. *made*	2
him great	

23 And the Jews undertook to do as they had begun, and as Môr-dĕ-cā'-ī had written unto them;

24 Because Hā'-măn the son of Hăm-mĕ-dā'-thă, the Ăg'-ă-gīte, the enemy of all the Jews, [R]had devised against the Jews to destroy them, and had cast Pur, that *is*, the lot, to [N]consume them, and to destroy them;

25 But [R]when[N] *Esther* came before the king, he commanded by letters that his wicked device, which he devised against the Jews, should [R]return upon his own head, and that he and his sons should be hanged on the gallows.

26 Wherefore they called these days Pū'-rĭm after the name of [N]Pur. Therefore for all the words of [R]this letter, and *of that* which they had seen concerning this matter, and which had come unto them,

27 The Jews ordained, and took upon them, and upon their seed, and upon all such as [R]joined themselves unto them, so as it should not [N]fail, that they would keep these two days according to their writing, and according to their *appointed* time every year;

28 And *that* these days *should be* remembered and kept throughout every generation, every family, every province, and every city; and *that* these days of Pū'-rĭm should not [N]fail from among the Jews, nor the memorial of them [N]perish from their seed.

29 Then Esther the queen, [R]the daughter of Ăb'-ĭ-haïl, and Môr-dĕ-cā'-ī the Jew, wrote with [N]all authority, to confirm this [R]second letter of Pū'-rĭm.

30 And he sent the letters unto all the Jews, to [R]the hundred twenty and seven provinces of the kingdom of Ă-hăś-ū-ē'-rŭs, *with* words of peace and truth,

31 To confirm these days of Pū'-rĭm in their times *appointed,* according as Môr-dĕ-cā'-ī the Jew and Esther the queen had enjoined them, and as they had decreed [N]for themselves and for their seed, the matters of [R]the fastings and their cry.

32 And the decree of Esther confirmed these matters of Pū'-rĭm; and it was written in the book.

CHAPTER 10

Mordecai's greatness

AND the king Ă-hăś-ū-ē'-rŭs laid a tribute upon the land, and *upon* [R]the isles of the sea.

2 And all the acts of his power and of his might, and the declaration of the greatness of Môr-dĕ-cā'-ī, [R]whereunto the king [N]advanced

him, *are* they not written in the book of the chronicles of the kings of Mḗ'-dĭ-ă and Persia?

3 For Môr-dĕ-cā'-ī the Jew *was* ᴿnext unto king Ă-hăś-ū-ē'-rŭs, and great among the Jews,

and accepted of the multitude of his brethren, ᴿseeking the wealth of his people, and speaking peace to all his seed.

CHAP. 10
BC 509
3 Gen. 41:40
2 Chr. 28:7
Neh. 2:10   **3**

THE BOOK OF JOB

The book of Job, so named from its chief character, deals with the ageless question—the problem of suffering, particularly the suffering of the righteous as exemplified in the affliction of Job. Recognized as one of the greatest literary productions of all times, this book has been appropriately designated an epic-drama.

The book is divided into three parts, namely, a prologue, a poem, and an epilogue. The prologue consists of the first two chapters which introduce the characters and tell how they came together; the poem is in the form of a dialogue between Job and his friends Eliphaz, Bildad, and Zophar probing the reasons for Job's affliction. Job seeks to answer their questions by appealing to the sovereign and incomprehensible wisdom of God. The dialogue ends with the problem unresolved. The epilogue describes the joyous restoration of Job's wealth and family. This sequel was in accord with the prevalent religious

ideas of that era. The book's principal aim was to refute the popular view that all suffering is the result of wrongdoing on the part of the sufferer. Both the date and author are uncertain. It may be the oldest composition in the Bible, possibly belonging to the patriarchal era.

OUTLINE OF THE BOOK:
I. The historical setting   1:1 – 3:26
II. Dialogue—Job and his three friends   4:1 – 31:40
                God and human suffering   4:1 – 14:22
                Suffering and sin   15:1 – 21:34
                Job defies accusation   22:1 – 31:40
III. Elihu's analysis   32:1 – 37:24
IV. The Almighty speaks   38:1 – 41:34
V. The conclusion   42:1 – 17

CHAPTER 1

Job and his family

THERE was a man ᴿin the land of Uz, whose name *was* ᴿJob; and that man was ᴿperfect and upright, and one that ᴿfeared God, and eschewed evil.

2 And there were born unto him seven sons and three daughters.

3 His ᴺsubstance also was seven thousand sheep, and three thousand camels, and five hundred yoke of oxen, and five hundred she asses, and a very great ᴺhousehold; so that this man was the greatest of all the ᴺmen of the east.

4 And his sons went and feasted *in their* houses, every one his day; and sent and called for their three sisters to eat and to drink with them.

5 And it was so, when the days of *their* feasting were gone about, that Job sent and sanctified them, and rose up early in the morning, ᴿand offered burnt offerings *according* to the number of them all: for Job said, It may be that my sons have sinned, and ᴿcursed God in their hearts. Thus did Job ᴺcontinually.

Satan permitted to test Job

6 Now ᴿthere was a day when the sons of God came to present themselves before the LORD, and ᴺSatan came also ᴺamong them.

CHAP. 1
BC 1520
1 1 Chr. 1:17
1 Ezek. 14:14
Jas. 5:11
1 Gen. 17:1
1 Prov. 16:6
3 Or, *cattle*
3 Or, *husbandry*
3 Heb. *sons of the east*
5 ch. 42:8
5 1 Ki. 21:10
5 Heb. *all the days*
6 ch. 2:1
6 Heb. *the Adversary*
6 Heb. *in the midst of them*
1 Pet. 5:8   **7**
Heb. *Hast thou*   **8** *set thy heart on*
Ps. 34:7   **10**
Is. 5:2
Ps. 128:1, 2   **10**
Prov. 10:22
Or, *cattle*   **10**
ch. 2:5   **11**
& 19:21
Heb. *if he curse* **11** *thee not to thy face*
Is. 8:21   **11**
Mal. 3:13, 14
Heb. *hand*,   **12** Gen. 16:6
Eccl. 9:12   **13**

7 And the LORD said unto Satan, Whence comest thou? Then Satan answered the LORD, and said, From ᴿgoing to and fro in the earth, and from walking up and down in it.

8 And the LORD said unto Satan, ᴺHast thou considered my servant Job, that *there is* none like him in the earth, a perfect and an upright man, one that feareth God, and escheweth evil?

9 Then Satan answered the LORD, and said, Doth Job fear God for nought?

10 ᴿHast not thou made an hedge about him, and about his house, and about all that he hath on every side? ᴿthou hast blessed the work of his hands, and his ᴺsubstance is increased in the land.

11 ᴿBut put forth thine hand now, and touch all that he hath, ᴺand he will ᴿcurse thee to thy face.

12 And the LORD said unto Satan, Behold, all that he hath *is* in thy ᴺpower; only upon himself put not forth thine hand. So Satan went forth from the presence of the LORD.

The first test

13 And there was a day ᴿwhen his sons and his daughters *were* eating and drinking wine in their eldest brother's house:

14 And there came a messenger unto Job, and said, The oxen were plowing, and the asses feeding beside them:

15 And the Să-bē'-ănś fell *upon them,* and took them away; yea, they have slain the servants with the edge of the sword; and I only am escaped alone to tell thee.

16 While he *was* yet speaking, there came also another, and said, ^NThe fire of God is fallen from heaven, and hath burned up the sheep, and the servants, and consumed them; and I only am escaped alone to tell thee.

17 While he *was* yet speaking, there came also another, and said, The Chăl-dē'-ăns made out three bands, and ^Nfell upon the camels, and have carried them away, yea, and slain the servants with the edge of the sword; and I only am escaped alone to tell thee.

18 While he *was* yet speaking, there came also another, and said, ^RThy sons and thy daughters *were* eating and drinking wine in their eldest brother's house:

19 And, behold, there came a great wind ^Nfrom the wilderness, and smote the four corners of the house, and it fell upon the young men, and they are dead; and I only am escaped alone to tell thee.

20 Then Job arose, ^Rand rent his ^Nmantle, and shaved his head, and ^Rfell down upon the ground, and worshipped,

21 And said, ^RNaked came I out of my mother's womb, and naked shall I return thither: the Lord ^Rgave, and the Lord hath ^Rtaken away; ^Rblessed be the name of the Lord.

22 ^RIn all this Job sinned not, nor ^Ncharged God foolishly.

CHAPTER 2

The second test

AGAIN ^Rthere was a day when the sons of God came to present themselves before the Lord, and Satan came also among them to present himself before the Lord.

2 And the Lord said unto Satan, From whence comest thou? And ^RSatan answered the Lord, and said, From going to and fro in the earth, and from walking up and down in it.

3 And the Lord said unto Satan, Hast thou considered my servant Job, that *there is* none like him in the earth, ^Ra perfect and an upright man, one that feareth God, and escheweth evil? and still he ^Rholdeth fast his integrity, although thou movedst me against him, ^Rto^N destroy him without cause.

4 And Satan answered the Lord, and said, Skin for skin, yea, all that a man hath will he give for his life.

5 ^RBut put forth thine hand now, and touch

his ^Rbone and his flesh, and he will curse thee to thy face.

6 ^RAnd the Lord said unto Satan, Behold, he *is* in thine hand; ^Nbut save his life.

7 So went Satan forth from the presence of the Lord, and smote Job with sore boils ^Rfrom the sole of his foot unto his crown.

8 And he took him a potsherd to scrape himself withal; ^Rand he sat down among the ashes.

9 Then said his wife unto him, Dost thou still retain thine integrity? curse God, and die.

10 But he said unto her, Thou speakest as one of the foolish women speaketh. What? ^Rshall we receive good at the hand of God, and shall we not receive evil? ^RIn all this did not Job ^Rsin with his lips.

Job's three friends

11 Now when Job's three friends heard of all this evil that was come upon him, they came every one from his own place; Ĕ-lī'-phăz the ^RTē'-măn-ite, and Bildad the ^RShû'-hite, and Zō'-phăr the Nā-ăm'-ă-thīte: for they had made an appointment together to come ^Rto mourn with him and to comfort him.

12 And when they lifted up their eyes afar off, and knew him not, they lifted up their voice, and wept; and they rent every one his mantle, and ^Rsprinkled dust upon their heads toward heaven.

13 So they sat down with him upon the ground ^Rseven days and seven nights, and none spake a word unto him: for they saw that *his* grief was very great.

CHAPTER 3

Job bewails his birth

AFTER this opened Job his mouth, and cursed his day.

2 And Job ^Nspake, and said,

3 ^RLet the day perish wherein I was born, and the night *in which* it was said, There is a man child conceived.

4 Let that day be darkness; let not God regard it from above, neither let the light shine upon it.

5 Let darkness and ^Rthe shadow of death ^Nstain it; let a cloud dwell upon it; ^Nlet the blackness of the day terrify it.

6 *As for* that night, let darkness seize upon it; ^Nlet it not be joined unto the days of the year, let it not come into the number of the months.

7 Lo, let that night be solitary, let no joyful voice come therein.

8 Let them curse it that curse the day, [R]who are ready to raise up [N]their mourning.

9 Let the stars of the twilight thereof be dark; let it look for light, but *have* none; neither let it see [N]the dawning of the day:

10 Because it shut not up the doors of my *mother's* womb, nor hid sorrow from mine eyes.

11 [R]Why died I not from the womb? *why did I not* give up the ghost when I came out of the belly?

12 [R]Why did the knees prevent me? or why the breasts that I should suck?

13 For now should I have lain still and been quiet, I should have slept: then had I been at rest,

14 With kings and counsellors of the earth, which [R]built desolate places for themselves;

15 Or with princes that had gold, who filled their houses with silver:

16 Or [R]as an hidden untimely birth I had not been; as infants *which* never saw light.

17 There the wicked cease *from* troubling; and there the [N]weary be at rest.

18 *There* the prisoners rest together; [R]they hear not the voice of the oppressor.

19 The small and great are there; and the servant *is* free from his master.

20 [R]Wherefore is light given to him that is in misery, and life unto the [R]bitter *in* soul;

21 Which [R]long[N] for death, but it *cometh* not; and dig for it more than [R]for hid treasures;

22 Which rejoice exceedingly, *and* are glad, when they can find the grave?

23 *Why is light given* to a man whose way is hid, [R]and whom God hath hedged in?

24 For my sighing cometh [N]before I eat, and my roarings are poured out like the waters.

25 For [N]the thing which I greatly feared is come upon me, and that which I was afraid of is come unto me.

26 I was not in safety, neither had I rest, neither was I quiet; yet trouble came.

CHAPTER 4

First speech of Eliphaz

THEN ĕ-lĭ'-phăz the Tē'-măn-īte answered and said,

2 *If* we assay [N]to commune with thee, wilt thou be grieved? but [N]who can withhold himself from speaking?

3 Behold, thou hast instructed many, and thou [R]hast strengthened the weak hands.

4 Thy words have upholden him that was

CHAP. 3

BC 1520

8 Jer. 9:17
8 Or, *a leviathan*
9 Heb. *the eyelids of the morning,* ch. 41:18
11 ch. 10:18
12 Gen. 30:3
14 ch. 15:28
16 Ps. 58:8
17 Heb. *wearied in strength*
18 ch. 39:7
20 Jer. 20:18
20 2 Ki. 4:27
21 Rev. 9:6
21 Heb. *wait*
21 Prov. 2:4
23 Lam. 3:7
24 Heb. *before my meat*
25 Heb. *I feared a fear, and it came upon me*

CHAP. 4

BC 1520

2 Heb. *a word*
2 Heb. *who can refrain from words?*
3 Is. 35:3

Is. 35:3	4
Heb. *the bowing knees,* Heb. 12:12	4
ch. 1:1	6
Prov. 3:26	6
Ps. 37:25	7
Prov. 22:8	8
i.e. *by his anger:* as Is. 30:33	9
Ps. 58:6	10
Ps. 34:10	11
Heb. *by stealth*	12
ch. 33:15	13
Heb. *met me*	14
Hab. 3:16	14
Heb. *the multitude of my bones*	14
Or, *I heard a still voice*	16
ch. 15:15	18
Or, *nor in his angels, in whom he put light*	18
Ps. 90:5, 6	20
Heb. *beaten in pieces*	20

CHAP. 5

BC 1520

Or, *look?*	1
Or, *indignation*	2
Jer. 12:2, 3	3

---

falling, and thou [R]hast strengthened [N]the feeble knees.

5 But now it is come upon thee, and thou faintest; it toucheth thee, and thou art troubled.

6 *Is* not *this* [R]thy fear, [R]thy confidence, thy hope, and the uprightness of thy ways?

7 Remember, I pray thee, [R]who *ever* perished, being innocent? or where were the righteous cut off?

8 Even as I have seen, [R]they that plow iniquity, and sow wickedness, reap the same.

9 By the blast of God they perish, and [N]by the breath of his nostrils are they consumed.

10 The roaring of the lion, and the voice of the fierce lion, and [R]the teeth of the young lions, are broken.

11 [R]The old lion perisheth for lack of prey, and the stout lion's whelps are scattered abroad.

12 Now a thing was [N]secretly brought to me, and mine ear received a little thereof.

13 [R]In thoughts from the visions of the night, when deep sleep falleth on men,

14 Fear [N]came upon me, and [R]trembling, which made [N]all my bones to shake.

15 Then a spirit passed before my face; the hair of my flesh stood up:

16 It stood still, but I could not discern the form thereof: an image *was* before mine eyes, [N]*there was* silence, and I heard a voice, *saying,*

17 Shall mortal man be more just than God? shall a man be more pure than his maker?

18 Behold, he [R]put no trust in his servants; [N]and his angels he charged with folly:

19 How much less *in* them that dwell in houses of clay, whose foundation *is* in the dust, *which* are crushed before the moth?

20 [R]They are [N]destroyed from morning to evening: they perish for ever without any regarding *it.*

21 Doth not their excellency *which is* in them go away? they die, even without wisdom.

CHAPTER 5

"Man is born unto trouble"

CALL now, if there be any that will answer thee; and to which of the saints wilt thou [N]turn?

2 For wrath killeth the foolish man, and [N]envy slayeth the silly one.

3 [R]I have seen the foolish taking root: but suddenly I cursed his habitation.

4 His children are far from safety, and they

are crushed in the gate, neither *is there* any to deliver *them*.

5 Whose harvest the hungry eateth up, and taketh it even out of the thorns, and the robber swalloweth up their substance.

6 Although ᴺaffliction cometh not forth of the dust, neither doth trouble spring out of the ground;

7 Yet man is born unto ᴺtrouble, as ᴺthe sparks fly upward.

8 I would seek unto God, and unto God would I commit my cause:

9 Which doeth great things ᴺand unsearchable; marvellous things ᴺwithout number:

10 Who giveth rain upon the earth, and sendeth waters upon the ᴺfields:

11 ᴿTo set up on high those that be low; that those which mourn may be exalted to safety.

12 ᴿHe disappointeth the devices of the crafty, so that their hands ᴺcannot perform *their* enterprise.

13 He taketh the wise in their own craftiness: and the counsel of the froward is carried headlong.

14 They ᴺmeet with darkness in the daytime, and grope in the noonday as in the night.

15 But ᴿhe saveth the poor from the sword, from their mouth, and from the hand of the mighty.

16 ᴿSo the poor hath hope, and iniquity stoppeth her mouth.

"Despise not thou the chastening"

17 ᴿBehold, happy *is* the man whom God correcteth: therefore despise not thou the chastening of the Almighty:

18 ᴿFor he maketh sore, and bindeth up: he woundeth, and his hands make whole.

19 ᴿHe shall deliver thee in six troubles: yea, in seven ᴿthere shall no evil touch thee.

20 ᴿIn famine he shall redeem thee from death: and in war ᴺfrom the power of the sword.

21 ᴿThou shalt be hid ᴺfrom the scourge of the tongue: neither shalt thou be afraid of destruction when it cometh.

22 At destruction and famine thou shalt laugh: ᴿneither shalt thou be afraid of the beasts of the earth.

23 ᴿFor thou shalt be in league with the stones of the field: and the beasts of the field shall be at peace with thee.

24 And thou shalt know ᴺthat thy tabernacle *shall be* in peace; and thou shalt visit thy habitation, and shalt not ᴺsin.

25 Thou shalt know also that ᴿthy seed *shall be* ᴺgreat, and thine offspring ᴿas the grass of the earth.

26 ᴿThou shalt come to *thy* grave in a full age, like as a shock of corn ᴺcometh in in his season.

27 Lo this, we have ᴿsearched it, so it *is;* hear it, and know thou *it* ᴺfor thy good.

CHAPTER 6

Job's answer

BUT Job answered and said,

2 Oh that my grief were throughly weighed, and my calamity ᴺlaid in the balances together!

3 For now it would be heavier than the sand of the sea: therefore ᴺmy words are swallowed up.

4 ᴿFor the arrows of the Almighty *are* within me, the poison whereof drinketh up my spirit: ᴿthe terrors of God do set themselves in array against me.

5 Doth the wild ass bray ᴺwhen he hath grass? or loweth the ox over his fodder?

6 Can that which is unsavoury be eaten withou salt? or is there *any* taste in the white of an egg?

7 The things *that* my soul refused to touch *are* as my sorrowful meat.

8 Oh that I might have my request; and that God would grant *me* ᴺthe thing that I long for!

9 Even that it would please God to destroy me; that he would let loose his hand, and cut me off!

10 Then should I yet have comfort; yea, I would harden myself in sorrow: let him not spare; for ᴿI have not concealed the words of ᴿthe Holy One.

11 What *is* my strength, that I should hope? and what *is* mine end, that I should prolong my life?

12 *Is* my strength the strength of stones? or *is* my flesh ᴺof brass?

13 *Is* not my help in me? and is wisdom driven quite from me?

Job reproaches his friends

14 ᴿToᴺ him that is afflicted pity *should be shewed* from his friend; but he forsaketh the fear of the Almighty.

15 ᴿMy brethren have dealt deceitfully as a brook, *and* ᴿas the stream of brooks they pass away;

16 Which are blackish by reason of the ice, *and* wherein the snow is hid:

17 What time they wax warm, ᴺthey vanish: ᴺwhen it is hot, they are ᴺconsumed out of their place.

18 The paths of their way are turned aside; they go to nothing, and perish.

19 The troops of ᴿTē'-mă looked, the companies of ᴿShē'-bă waited for them.

20 They were ᴿconfounded because they had hoped; they came thither, and were ashamed.

21 ᴺFor now ᴿye are ᴺnothing; ye see *my* casting down, and ᴿare afraid.

22 Did I say, Bring unto me? or, Give a reward for me of your substance?

23 Or, Deliver me from the enemy's hand? or, Redeem me from the hand of the mighty?

24 Teach me, and I will hold my tongue: and cause me to understand wherein I have erred.

25 How forcible are right words! but what doth your arguing reprove?

26 Do ye imagine to reprove words, and the speeches of one that is desperate, *which are* as wind?

27 Yea, ᴺye overwhelm the fatherless, and ye ᴿdig *a pit* for your friend.

28 Now therefore be content, look upon me; for *it is* ᴺevident unto you if I lie.

29 ᴿReturn, I pray you, let it not be iniquity; yea, return again, my righteousness *is* ᴺin it.

30 Is there iniquity in my tongue? cannot ᴺmy taste discern perverse things?

CHAPTER 7

IS there not ᴿanᴺ appointed time to man upon earth? *are not* his days also like the days of an hireling?

2 As a servant ᴺearnestly desireth the shadow, and as an hireling looketh for *the reward of* his work:

3 So am I made to possess ᴿmonths of vanity, and wearisome nights are appointed to me.

4 ᴿWhen I lie down, I say, When shall I arise, and ᴺthe night be gone? and I am full of tossings to and fro unto the dawning of the day.

5 My flesh is ᴿclothed with worms and clods of dust; my skin is broken, and become loathsome.

6 ᴿMy days are swifter than a weaver's shuttle, and are spent without hope.

Job remonstrates with God

7 O remember that ᴿmy life *is* wind: mine eye ᴺshall no more ᴺsee good.

8 ᴿThe eye of him that hath seen me shall see me no *more:* thine eyes *are* upon me, and ᴺI *am* not.

9 *As* the cloud is consumed and vanisheth away: so ᴿhe that goeth down to the grave shall come up no *more.*

10 He shall return no more to his house, ᴿneither shall his place know him any more.

11 Therefore I will ᴿnot refrain my mouth; I

CHAP. **6**
BC 1520
19 Gen. 25:15
19 Ps. 72:10
20 Jer. 14:3
21 Or, *For now ye are like to them,* Heb. *to it*
21 ch. 13:4
21 Heb. *not*
21 Ps. 38:11
27 Heb. *ye cause to fall upon*
27 Ps. 57:6
28 Heb. *before your face*
29 ch. 17:10
29 i.e. *in this matter*
30 Heb. *my palate*

CHAP. **7**
BC 1520
1 ch. 14:5
1 Or, *a warfare*
2 Heb. *gapeth after*
3 ch. 29:2
4 Deut. 28:67
4 Heb. *the evening be measured?*
5 Is. 14:11
6 ch. 9:25
7 Ps. 78:39
7 Heb. *shall not return*
7 to see, i.e. *to enjoy*
8 ch. 20:9
8 i.e. *I can live no longer*
9 2 Sam. 12:23
10 ch. 8:18
11 Ps. 39:1, 9

1 Sam. 1:10   11
ch. 9:27   13
Heb. *than my bones*   15
ch. 10:1   16
ch. 14:6   16
Ps. 62:9   16
Ps. 8:4   17
Ps. 36:6   20
Ps. 21:12   20
Lam. 3:12

CHAP. **8**
BC 1520
Gen. 18:25   3
ch. 1:5, 18   4
Heb. *in the hand of their transgression*
ch. 11:13   5
Deut. 4:32   8
Gen. 47:9   9
1 Chr. 29:15
ch. 7:6
Heb. *not*   9

will speak in the anguish of my spirit; I will ᴿcomplain in the bitterness of my soul.

12 *Am* I a sea, or a whale, that thou settest a watch over me?

13 ᴿWhen I say, My bed shall comfort me, my couch shall ease my complaint;

14 Then thou scarest me with dreams, and terrifiest me through visions:

15 So that my soul chooseth strangling, *and* death rather ᴺthan my life.

16 ᴿI loathe *it;* I would not live alway: ᴿlet me alone; for ᴿmy days *are* vanity.

17 ᴿWhat *is* man, that thou shouldest magnify him? and that thou shouldest set thine heart upon him?

18 And *that* thou shouldest visit him every morning, *and* try him every moment?

19 How long wilt thou not depart from me, nor let me alone till I swallow down my spittle?

20 I have sinned; what shall I do unto thee, ᴿO thou preserver of men? why ᴿhast thou set me as a mark against thee, so that I am a burden to myself?

21 And why dost thou not pardon my transgression, and take away mine iniquity? for now shall I sleep in the dust; and thou shalt seek me in the morning, but I *shall* not *be.*

CHAPTER 8

Bildad's first speech

THEN answered Bildad the Shû'-hite, and said,

2 How long wilt thou speak these *things?* and *how long shall* the words of thy mouth *be like* a strong wind?

3 ᴿDoth God pervert judgment? or doth the Almighty pervert justice?

4 If ᴿthy children have sinned against him, and he have cast them away ᴺfor their transgression;

5 ᴿIf thou wouldest seek unto God betimes, and make thy supplication to the Almighty;

6 If thou *wert* pure and upright; surely now he would awake for thee, and make the habitation of thy righteousness prosperous.

7 Though thy beginning was small, yet thy latter end should greatly increase.

8 ᴿFor inquire, I pray thee, of the former age, and prepare thyself to the search of their fathers:

9 (For ᴿwe *are but of* yesterday, and know ᴺnothing, because our days upon earth *are* a shadow:)

10 Shall not they teach thee, *and* tell thee, and utter words out of their heart?

11 Can the rush grow up without mire? can the flag grow without water?

12 ᴿWhilst it *is* yet in his greenness, *and* not cut down, it withereth before any *other* herb.

13 So *are* the paths of all that forget God; and the ᴿhypocrite's hope shall perish:

14 Whose hope shall be cut off, and whose trust *shall be* ᴺa spider's web.

15 ᴿHe shall lean upon his house, but it shall not stand: he shall hold it fast, but it shall not endure.

16 He *is* green before the sun, and his branch shooteth forth in his garden.

17 His roots are wrapped about the heap, *and* seeth the place of stones.

18 ᴿIf he destroy him from his place, then *it* shall deny him, *saying,* I have not seen thee.

19 Behold, this *is* the joy of his way, and ᴿout of the earth shall others grow.

20 Behold, God will not cast away a perfect *man,* neither will he ᴺhelp the evil doers:

21 Till he fill thy mouth with laughing, and thy lips with ᴺrejoicing.

22 They that hate thee shall be ᴿclothed with shame; and the dwelling place of the wicked ᴺshall come to nought.

CHAPTER 9

Job's answer

THEN Job answered and said,

2 I know *it is* so of a truth: but how should ᴿman be just ᴺwith God?

3 If he will contend with him, he cannot answer him one of a thousand.

4 ᴿ*He is* wise in heart, and mighty in strength: who hath hardened *himself* against him, and hath prospered?

5 Which removeth the mountains, and they know not: which overturneth them in his anger.

6 Which ᴿshaketh the earth out of her place, and ᴿthe pillars thereof tremble.

7 Which commandeth the sun, and it riseth not; and sealeth up the stars.

8 ᴿWhich alone spreadeth out the heavens, and treadeth upon the ᴺwaves of the sea.

9 ᴿWhich maketh ᴺĂrc-tū'-rŭs, ō-rī'-ọn, and Plēī'-ă-dēṣ, and the chambers of the south.

10 ᴿWhich doeth great things past finding out; yea, and wonders without number.

11 ᴿLo, he goeth by me, and I see *him* not: he passeth on also, but I perceive him not.

12 ᴿBehold, he taketh away, ᴺwho can hinder him? who will say unto him, What doest thou?

13 *If* God will not withdraw his anger, ᴿthe ᴺproud helpers do stoop under him.

14 How much less shall I answer him, *and* choose out my words *to reason* with him?

15 ᴿWhom, though I were righteous, *yet* would I not answer, *but* I would make supplication to my judge.

16 If I had called, and he had answered me; *yet* would I not believe that he had hearkened unto my voice.

17 For he breaketh me with a tempest, and multiplieth my wounds ᴿwithout cause.

18 He will not suffer me to take my breath, but filleth me with bitterness.

19 If *I speak* of strength, lo, *he is* strong: and if of judgment, who shall set me a time *to plead?*

20 If I justify myself, mine own mouth shall condemn me: *if I say,* I *am* perfect, it shall also prove me perverse.

21 *Though* I *were* perfect, *yet* would I not know my soul: I would despise my life.

22 This *is* one *thing,* therefore I said *it,* ᴿHe destroyeth the perfect and the wicked.

23 If the scourge slay suddenly, he will laugh at the trial of the innocent.

24 The earth is given into the hand of the wicked: he covereth the faces of the judges thereof; if not, where, *and* who *is* he?

25 Now ᴿmy days are swifter than a post: they flee away, they see no good.

26 They are passed away as the ᴺᴺswift ships: ᴿas the eagle *that* hasteth to the prey.

27 ᴿIf I say, I will forget my complaint, I will leave off my heaviness, and comfort *myself:*

28 ᴿI am afraid of all my sorrows, I know that thou ᴿwilt not hold me innocent.

29 *If* I be wicked, why then labour I in vain?

30 ᴿIf I wash myself with snow water, and make my hands never so clean;

31 Yet shalt thou plunge me in the ditch, and mine own clothes shall ᴺabhor me.

32 For ᴿhe *is* not a man, as I *am, that* I should answer him, *and* we should come together in judgment.

33 ᴿNeither is there ᴺany ᴺdaysman betwixt us, *that* might lay his hand upon us both.

34 ᴿLet him take his rod away from me, and let not his fear terrify me:

35 *Then* would I speak, and not fear him; ᴺbut *it is* not so with me.

CHAPTER 10

Job complains to God

MY ᴿsoul is ᴺweary of my life; I will leave my complaint upon myself; ᴿI will speak in the bitterness of my soul.

2 I will say unto God, Do not condemn me; shew me wherefore thou contendest with me.

3 *Is it* good unto thee that thou shouldest oppress, that thou shouldest despise ᴺthe work of thine hands, and shine upon the counsel of the wicked?

4 Hast thou eyes of flesh? or ᴿseest thou as man seeth?

5 *Are* thy days as the days of man? *are* thy years as man's days,

6 That thou inquirest after mine iniquity, and searchest after my sin?

7 ᴺThou knowest that I am not wicked; and *there is* none that can deliver out of thine hand.

8 ᴿThine hands ᴺhave made me and fashioned me together round about; yet thou dost destroy me.

9 Remember, I beseech thee, that ᴿthou hast made me as the clay; and wilt thou bring me into dust again?

10 ᴿHast thou not poured me out as milk, and curdled me like cheese?

11 Thou hast clothed me with skin and flesh, and hast ᴺfenced me with bones and sinews.

12 Thou hast granted me life and favour, and thy visitation hath preserved my spirit.

13 And these *things* hast thou hid in thine heart: I know that this *is* with thee.

14 If I sin, then ᴿthou markest me, and thou wilt not acquit me from mine iniquity.

15 If I be wicked, ᴿwoe unto me; ᴿand *if* I be righteous, *yet* will I not lift up my head. *I am* full of confusion; therefore ᴿsee thou mine affliction;

16 For it increaseth. ᴿThou huntest me as a fierce lion: and again thou shewest thyself marvellous upon me.

17 Thou renewest ᴺthy witnesses against me, and increasest thine indignation upon me; changes and war *are* against me.

18 ᴿWherefore then hast thou brought me forth out of the womb? Oh that I had given up the ghost, and no eye had seen me!

19 I should have been as though I had not been; I should have been carried from the womb to the grave.

20 ᴿ*Are* not my days few? cease *then, and* ᴿlet me alone, that I may take comfort a little,

21 Before I go *whence* I shall not return, ᴿ*even* to the land of darkness ᴿand the shadow of death;

22 A land of darkness, as darkness *itself; and* of the shadow of death, without any order, and *where* the light *is* as darkness.

CHAPTER 11

Zophar's first speech

THEN answered Zō'-phär the Nā-ăm'-ă-thīte, and said,

CHAP. 10
BC 1520
3 Heb. *the labour of thine hands*
4 1 Sam. 16:7
7 Heb. It is *upon thy knowledge*
8 Ps. 119:73
8 Heb. *took pains about me*
9 Gen. 2:7
Is. 64:8
10 Ps. 139:14-16
11 Heb. *hedged*
14 Ps. 139:1
15 Is. 3:11
15 ch. 9:12, 15
15 Ps. 25:18
16 Is. 38:13
Lam. 3:10
17 i.e. *thy plagues,* Ruth 1:21
18 ch. 3:11
20 Ps. 39:5
20 ch. 7:16, 19
21 Ps. 88:12
21 Ps. 23:4

CHAP. 11
BC 1520
Heb. *a man of lips* 2
Or, *devices* 3
ch. 6:30 4
Ezra 9:13 6
Eccl. 3:11 7
Heb. *the heights of heaven* 8
ch. 9:12 10
Rev. 3:7
Or, *make a change* 10
Heb. *who can turn him away?* 10
Ps. 10:14 11
Rom. 1:22 12
Heb. *empty* 12
1 Sam. 7:3 13
Ps. 88:9 13
Ps. 101:3 14
ch. 22:26 15
Ps. 119:6
1 John 3:21
Is. 65:16 16
Ps. 37:6 17
Prov. 4:18
Is. 58:8, 10
Heb. *shall arise* 17
above the noonday
Lev. 26:5, 6 18
Ps. 3:5
Prov. 3:24
Heb. *entreat thy* 19
face, Ps. 45:12
Lev. 26:16 20
Deut. 28:65
Heb. *flight shall* 20
perish from them
ch. 18:14 20
Prov. 11:7
Or, *a puff of breath* 20

CHAP. 12
BC 1520
Heb. *an heart* 3

2 Should not the multitude of words be answered? and should ᴺa man full of talk be justified?

3 Should thy ᴺlies make men hold their peace? and when thou mockest, shall no man make thee ashamed?

4 For ᴿthou hast said, My doctrine *is* pure, and I am clean in thine eyes.

5 But oh that God would speak, and open his lips against thee;

6 And that he would shew thee the secrets of wisdom, that *they are* double to that which is! Know therefore that ᴿGod exacteth of thee *less* than thine iniquity *deserveth.*

7 ᴿCanst thou by searching find out God? canst thou find out the Almighty unto perfection?

8 *It is* ᴺas high as heaven; what canst thou do? deeper than hell; what canst thou know?

9 The measure thereof *is* longer than the earth, and broader than the sea.

10 ᴿIf he ᴺcut off, and shut up, or gather together, then ᴺwho can hinder him?

11 For ᴿhe knoweth vain men: he seeth wickedness also; will he not then consider *it?*

12 For ᴿvainᴺ man would be wise, though man be born *like* a wild ass's colt.

God is the source of wisdom

13 If thou ᴿprepare thine heart, and ᴿstretch out thine hands toward him;

14 If iniquity *be* in thine hand, put it far away, and ᴿlet not wickedness dwell in thy tabernacles.

15 ᴿFor then shalt thou lift up thy face without spot; yea, thou shalt be stedfast, and shalt not fear:

16 Because thou shalt ᴿforget *thy* misery, *and* remember *it* as waters *that* pass away:

17 And *thine* age ᴿshallᴺ be clearer than the noonday; thou shalt shine forth, thou shalt be as the morning.

18 And thou shalt be secure, because there is hope; yea, thou shalt dig *about thee, and* ᴿthou shalt take thy rest in safety.

19 Also thou shalt lie down, and none shall make *thee* afraid; yea, many shall ᴺmake suit unto thee.

20 But ᴿthe eyes of the wicked shall fail, and ᴺthey shall not escape, and ᴿtheir hope *shall be as* ᴺthe giving up of the ghost.

CHAPTER 12

Job's answer

AND Job answered and said,

2 No doubt but ye *are* the people, and wisdom shall die with you.

3 But I have ᴺunderstanding as well as you;

^NI *am* not inferior to you: yea, ^Nwho knoweth not such things as these?

4 ^RI am *as* one mocked of his neighbour, who ^Rcalleth upon God, and he answereth him: the just upright *man is* laughed to scorn.

5 ^RHe that is ready to slip with *his* feet *is as* a lamp despised in the thought of him that is at ease.

6 ^RThe tabernacles of robbers prosper, and they that provoke God are secure; into whose hand God bringeth *abundantly*.

7 But ask now the beasts, and they shall teach thee; and the fowls of the air, and they shall tell thee:

8 Or speak to the earth, and it shall teach thee: and the fishes of the sea shall declare unto thee.

9 Who knoweth not in all these that the hand of the LORD hath wrought this?

10 In whose hand *is* the ^Nsoul of every living thing, and the breath of ^Nall mankind.

11 Doth not the ear try words? and the ^Nmouth taste his meat?

12 With the ancient *is* wisdom; and in length of days understanding.

13 ^NWith him *is* wisdom and strength, he hath counsel and understanding.

14 Behold, he breaketh down, and it cannot be built again: he shutteth ^Nup a man, and there can be no opening.

15 Behold, he ^Rwithholdeth the waters, and they dry up: also he ^Rsendeth them out, and they overturn the earth.

16 With him *is* strength and wisdom: the deceived and the deceiver *are* his.

17 He leadeth counsellors away spoiled, and maketh the judges fools.

18 He looseth the bond of kings, and girdeth their loins with a girdle.

19 He leadeth princes away spoiled, and overthroweth the mighty.

20 ^RHe removeth away ^Nthe speech of the trusty, and taketh away the understanding of the aged.

21 ^RHe poureth contempt upon princes, and ^Nweakeneth the strength of the mighty.

22 He discovereth deep things out of darkness, and bringeth out to light the shadow of death.

23 ^RHe increaseth the nations, and destroyeth them: he enlargeth the nations, and ^Nstraiteneth them *again*.

24 He taketh away the heart of the chief of the people of the earth, and ^Rcauseth them to wander in a wilderness *where there is* no way.

25 ^RThey grope in the dark without light, and he maketh them to ^Rstagger^N like *a* drunken *man*.

CHAPTER 13

Job's estimate of his friends

LO, mine eye hath seen all *this,* mine ear hath heard and understood it.

2 ^RWhat ye know, *the same* do I know also: I *am* not inferior unto you.

3 ^RSurely I would speak to the Almighty, and I desire to reason with God.

4 But ye *are* forgers of lies, ^Rye *are.* all physicians of no value.

5 O that ye would altogether hold your peace! and ^Rit should be your wisdom.

6 Hear now my reasoning, and hearken to the pleadings of my lips.

7 ^RWill ye speak wickedly for God? and talk deceitfully for him?

8 Will ye accept his person? will ye contend for God?

9 Is it good that he should search you out? or as one man mocketh another, do ye *so* mock him?

10 He will surely reprove you, if ye do secretly accept persons.

11 Shall not his excellency make you afraid? and his dread fall upon you?

12 Your remembrances *are* like unto ashes, your bodies to bodies of clay.

Job's defence of his integrity

13 ^NHold your peace, let me alone, that I may speak, and let come on me what *will.*

14 Wherefore ^Rdo I take my flesh in my teeth, and put my life in mine hand?

15 ^RThough he slay me, yet will I trust in him: ^Rbut I will ^Nmaintain mine own ways before him.

16 He also *shall be* my salvation: for an hypocrite shall not come before him.

17 Hear diligently my speech, and my declaration with your ears.

18 Behold now, I have ordered *my* cause; I know that I shall be justified.

19 ^RWho *is* he *that* will plead with me? for now, if I hold my tongue, I shall give up the ghost.

20 ^ROnly do not two *things* unto me: then will I not hide myself from thee.

21 ^RWithdraw thine hand far from me: and let not thy dread make me afraid.

22 Then call thou, and I will answer: or let me speak, and answer thou me.

23 How many *are* mine iniquities and sins? make me to know my transgression and my sin.

24 ^RWherefore hidest thou thy face, and ^Rholdest me for thine enemy?

25 ᴿWilt thou break a leaf driven to and fro? and wilt thou pursue the dry stubble?

26 For thou writest bitter things against me, and ᴿmakest me to possess the iniquities of my youth.

27 ᴿThou puttest my feet also in the stocks, and ᴺlookest narrowly unto all my paths; thou settest a print upon the ᴺheels of my feet.

28 And he, as a rotten thing, consumeth, as a garment that is moth eaten.

CHAPTER 14

The frailty of man

MAN *that is* born of a woman *is* ᴺof few days, and ᴿfull of trouble.

2 ᴿHe cometh forth like a flower, and is cut down: he fleeth also as a shadow, and continueth not.

3 And ᴿdost thou open thine eyes upon such an one, and ᴿbringest me into judgment with thee?

4 ᴺWho ᴿcan bring a clean *thing* out of an unclean? not one.

5 ᴿSeeing his days *are* determined, the number of his months *are* with thee, thou hast appointed his bounds that he cannot pass;

6 ᴿTurn from him, that he may ᴺrest, till he shall accomplish, ᴿas an hireling, his day.

"If a man die, shall he live again?"

7 For there is hope of a tree, if it be cut down, that it will sprout again, and that the tender branch thereof will not cease.

8 Though the root thereof wax old in the earth, and the stock thereof die in the ground;

9 *Yet* through the scent of water it will bud, and bring forth boughs like a plant.

10 But man dieth, and ᴺwasteth away: yea, man giveth up the ghost, and where *is* he?

11 *As* the waters fail from the sea, and the flood decayeth and drieth up:

12 So man lieth down, and riseth not: ᴿtill the heavens *be* no more, they shall not awake, nor be raised out of their sleep.

13 O that thou wouldest hide me in the grave, that thou wouldest keep me secret, until thy wrath be past, that thou wouldest appoint me a set time, and remember me!

14 If a man die, shall he live *again?* all the days of my appointed time ᴿwill I wait, till my change come.

15 ᴿThou shalt call, and I will answer thee: thou wilt have a desire to the work of thine hands.

16 ᴿFor now thou numberest my steps: dost thou not watch over my sin?

17 ᴿMy transgression *is* sealed up in a bag, and thou sewest up mine iniquity.

18 And surely the mountain falling ᴺcometh to nought, and the rock is removed out of his place.

19 The waters wear the stones: thou ᴺwashest away the things which grow *out* of the dust of the earth; and thou destroyest the hope of man.

20 Thou prevailest for ever against him, and he passeth: thou changest his countenance, and sendest him away.

21 His sons come to honour, and ᴿhe knoweth *it* not; and they are brought low, but he perceiveth *it* not of them.

22 But his flesh upon him shall have pain, and his soul within him shall mourn.

CHAPTER 15

Second speech of Eliphaz

THEN answered Ĕ-lī′-phăz the Tē′-măn-īte, and said,

2 Should a wise man utter ᴺvain knowledge, and fill his belly with the east wind?

3 Should he reason with unprofitable talk? or with speeches wherewith he can do no good?

4 Yea, ᴺthou castest off fear, and restrainest ᴺprayer before God.

5 For thy mouth ᴺuttereth thine iniquity, and thou choosest the tongue of the crafty.

6 ᴿThine own mouth condemneth thee, and not I: yea, thine own lips testify against thee.

7 *Art* thou the first man *that* was born? ᴿor wast thou made before the hills?

8 ᴿHast thou heard the secret of God? and dost thou restrain wisdom to thyself?

9 ᴿWhat knowest thou, that we know not? *what* understandest thou, which *is* not in us?

10 ᴿWith us *are* both the grayheaded and very aged men, much elder than thy father.

11 *Are* the consolations of God small with thee? is there any secret thing with thee?

12 Why doth thine heart carry thee away? and what do thy eyes wink at,

13 That thou turnest thy spirit against God, and lettest *such* words go out of thy mouth?

14 ᴿWhat *is* man, that he should be clean? and *he which is* born of a woman, that he should be righteous?

15 ᴿBehold, he putteth no trust in his saints; yea, the heavens are not clean in his sight.

16 ᴿHow much more abominable and filthy *is* man, ᴿwhich drinketh iniquity like water?

The end of a wicked man

17 I will shew thee, hear me; and that *which* I have seen I will declare;

18 Which wise men have told ᴿfrom their fathers, and have not hid *it:*

19 Unto whom alone the earth was given, and ᴿno stranger passed among them.

20 The wicked man travaileth with pain all *his* days, ᴿand the number of years is hidden to the oppressor.

21 ᴺA dreadful sound *is* in his ears: ᴿin prosperity the destroyer shall come upon him.

22 He believeth not that he shall return out of darkness, and he is waited for of the sword.

23 He ᴿwandereth abroad for bread, *saying,* Where *is it?* he knoweth that ᴿthe day of darkness is ready at his hand.

24 Trouble and anguish shall make him afraid; they shall prevail against him, as a king ready to the battle.

25 For he stretcheth out his hand against God, and strengtheneth himself against the Almighty.

26 He runneth upon him, *even* on *his* neck, upon the thick bosses of his bucklers:

27 ᴿBecause he covereth his face with his fatness, and maketh collops of fat on *his* flanks.

28 And he dwelleth in desolate cities, *and* in houses which no man inhabiteth, which are ready to become heaps.

29 He shall not be rich, neither shall his substance continue, neither shall he prolong the perfection thereof upon the earth.

30 He shall not depart out of darkness; the flame shall dry up his branches, and by the breath of his mouth shall he go away.

31 Let not him that is deceived ᴿtrust in vanity: for vanity shall be his recompence.

32 It shall be ᴺaccomplished ᴿbefore his time, and his branch shall not be green.

33 He shall shake off his unripe grape as the vine, and shall cast off his flower as the olive.

34 For the congregation of hypocrites *shall be* desolate, and fire shall consume the tabernacles of bribery.

35 ᴿThey conceive mischief, and bring forth ᴺvanity, and their belly prepareth deceit.

CHAPTER 16

Job's answer

THEN Job answered and said,

2 I have heard many such things: ᴿmiserableᴺ comforters *are* ye all.

3 Shall ᴺvain words have an end? or what emboldeneth thee that thou answerest?

4 I also could speak as ye *do:* if your soul were in my soul's stead, I could heap up words against you, and ᴿshake mine head at you.

5 *But* I would strengthen you with my

mouth, and the moving of my lips should assuage *your* grief.

6 Though I speak, my grief is not assuaged: and *though* I forbear, ᴺwhat am I eased?

7 But now he hath made me weary: thou hast made desolate all my company.

8 And thou hast filled me with wrinkles, *which* is a witness *against me:* and my leanness rising up in me beareth witness to my face.

9 ᴿHe teareth *me* in his wrath, who hateth me: he gnasheth upon me with his teeth; ᴿmine enemy sharpeneth his eyes upon me.

10 They have ᴿgaped upon me with their mouth; they ᴿhave smitten me upon the cheek reproachfully; they have gathered themselves together against me.

11 God ᴿhathᴺ delivered me to the ungodly, and turned me over into the hands of the wicked.

12 I was at ease, but he hath broken me asunder: he hath also taken *me* by my neck, and shaken me to pieces, and ᴿset me up for his mark.

13 His archers compass me round about, he cleaveth my reins asunder, and doth not spare; he poureth out my gall upon the ground.

14 He breaketh me with breach upon breach, he runneth upon me like a giant.

15 I have sewed sackcloth upon my skin, and ᴿdefiled my horn in the dust.

16 My face is foul with weeping, and on my eyelids *is* the shadow of death;

17 Not for *any* injustice in mine hands: also my prayer *is* pure.

18 O earth, cover not thou my blood, and ᴿlet my cry have no place.

"My witness is in heaven"

19 Also now, behold, ᴿmy witness *is* in heaven, and my record *is* ᴺon high.

20 My friends ᴺscorn me: *but* mine eye poureth out *tears* unto God.

21 ᴿO that one might plead for a man with God, as a man *pleadeth* for his ᴺneighbour!

22 When ᴺa few years are come, then I shall ᴿgo the way *whence* I shall not return.

CHAPTER 17

MY ᴺbreath is corrupt, my days are extinct, ᴿthe graves *are ready* for me.

2 *Are there* not mockers with me? and doth not mine eye ᴺcontinue in their ᴿprovocation?

3 Lay down now, put me in a surety with thee; who *is* he *that* ᴿwill strike hands with me?

4 For thou hast hid their heart from understanding: therefore shalt thou not exalt *them.*

5 He that speaketh flattery to *his* friends, even the eyes of his children shall fail.

6 He hath made me also ^Ra byword of the people; and ^Naforetime I was as a tabret.

7 ^RMine eye also is dim by reason of sorrow, and all ^Nmy members *are* as a shadow.

8 Upright *men* shall be astonied at this, and the innocent shall stir up himself against the hypocrite.

9 The righteous also shall hold on his way, and he that hath ^Rclean hands ^Nshall be stronger and stronger.

10 But as for you all, ^Rdo ye return, and come now: for I cannot find *one* wise *man* among you.

11 ^RMy days are past, my purposes are broken off, *even* ^Nthe thoughts of my heart.

12 They change the night into day: the light *is* ^Nshort because of darkness.

13 If I wait, the grave *is* mine house: I have made my bed in the darkness.

14 I have ^Nsaid to corruption, Thou *art* my father: to the worm, *Thou art* my mother, and my sister.

15 And where *is* now my hope? as for my hope, who shall see it?

16 They shall go down ^Rto the bars of the pit, when our ^Rrest together *is* in the dust.

CHAPTER 18

Bildad's second speech

THEN answered Bildad the Shû'-hīte, and said,

2 How long *will it be ere* ye make an end of words? mark, and afterwards we will speak.

3 Wherefore are we counted ^Ras beasts, *and* reputed vile in your sight?

4 ^RHe teareth ^Nhimself in his anger: shall the earth be forsaken for thee? and shall the rock be removed out of his place?

The lot of the wicked man

5 Yea, ^Rthe light of the wicked shall be put out, and the spark of his fire shall not shine.

6 The light shall be dark in his tabernacle, ^Rand his ^Ncandle shall be put out with him.

7 The steps of his strength shall be straitened, and ^Rhis own counsel shall cast him down.

8 For ^Rhe is cast into a net by his own feet, and he walketh upon a snare.

9 The gin shall take *him* by the heel, *and* ^Rthe robber shall prevail against him.

10 The snare *is* ^Nlaid for him in the ground, and a trap for him in the way.

11 ^RTerrors shall make him afraid on every side, and shall ^Ndrive him to his feet.

12 His strength shall be hungerbitten, and ^Rdestruction *shall be* ready at his side.

13 It shall devour the ^Nstrength of his skin: *even* the firstborn of death shall devour his strength.

14 ^RHis confidence shall be rooted out of his tabernacle, and it shall bring him to the king of terrors.

15 It shall dwell in his tabernacle, because *it is* none of his: brimstone shall be scattered upon his habitation.

16 ^RHis roots shall be dried up beneath, and above shall his branch be cut off.

17 ^RHis remembrance shall perish from the earth, and he shall have no name in the street.

18 ^NHe shall be driven from light into darkness, and chased out of the world.

19 ^RHe shall neither have son nor nephew among his people, nor any remaining in his dwellings.

20 They that come after *him* shall be astonied at his day, as they that ^Nwent before ^Nwere affrighted.

21 Surely such *are* the dwellings of the wicked, and this *is* the place *of him that* ^Rknoweth not God.

CHAPTER 19

Job's answer

THEN Job answered and said,

2 How long will ye vex my soul, and break me in pieces with words?

3 These ten times have ye reproached me: ye are not ashamed *that* ye ^Nmake yourselves strange to me.

4 And be it indeed *that* I have erred, mine error remaineth with myself.

5 If indeed ye will ^Rmagnify *yourselves* against me, and plead against me my reproach:

6 Know now that God hath overthrown me, and hath compassed me with his net.

7 Behold, I cry out of ^Nwrong, but I am not heard: I cry aloud, but *there is* no judgment.

8 He hath fenced up my way that I cannot pass, and he hath set darkness in my paths.

9 He hath stripped me of my glory, and taken the crown *from* my head.

10 He hath destroyed me on every side, and I am gone: and mine hope hath he removed like a tree.

11 He hath also kindled his wrath against me, and ^Rhe counteth me unto him as *one of* his enemies.

12 His troops come together, and raise up

CHAP. 17
BC 1520

6 Ps. 30:9
6 Or, *before them*
7 Ps. 6:7
& 31:9
7 Or, *my thoughts*
9 Ps. 24:4
9 Heb. *shall add strength*
10 ch. 6:29
11 ch. 7:6
11 Heb. *the possessions*
12 Heb. *near*
14 Heb. *cried,* or, *called*
16 Jonah 2:6
16 ch. 3:17-19

CHAP. 18
BC 1520

3 Ps. 73:22
4 ch. 13:14
4 Heb. *his soul*
5 Prov. 13:9
6 ch. 21:17
Ps. 18:28
6 Or, *lamp*
7 ch. 5:13
8 ch. 22:10
Ps. 9:15
& 35:8
9 ch. 5:5
10 Heb. *hidden*

ch. 20:25	11
Jer. 6:25	
& 20:3, 4	
Heb. *scatter him*	11
ch. 15:23	12
Heb. *bars*	13
ch. 11:20	14
Ps. 112:10	
Prov. 10:28	
ch. 29:19	16
Is. 5:24	
Amos 2:9	
Mal. 4:1	
Ps. 34:16	17
& 109:13	
Prov. 2:22	
& 10:7	
Heb. *They shall drive him*	18
Is. 14:22	19
Jer. 22:30	
Or, *lived with him*	20
Heb. *laid hold on horror*	20
Jer. 9:3	21
1 Thes. 4:5	

CHAP. 19
BC 1520

Or, *harden yourselves against me*	3
Ps. 38:16	5
Or, *violence*	7
ch. 13:24	11

their way against me, and encamp round about my tabernacle.

13 He hath put my brethren far from me, and mine acquaintance are verily estranged from me.

"Friends have forgotten me"

14 My kinsfolk have failed, and my familiar friends have forgotten me.

15 They that dwell in mine house, and my maids, count me for a stranger: I am an alien in their sight.

16 I called my servant, and he gave me no answer; I entreated him with my mouth.

17 My breath is strange to my wife, though I entreated for the children's sake of ᴺmine own body.

18 Yea, ᴿyoungᴺ children despised me; I arose, and they spake against me.

19 ᴿAll ᴺmy inward friends abhorred me: and they whom I loved are turned against me.

20 ᴿMy bone cleaveth to my skin ᴺand to my flesh, and I am escaped with the skin of my teeth.

21 Have pity upon me, have pity upon me, O ye my friends; for the hand of God hath touched me.

22 Why do ye ᴿpersecute me as God, and are not satisfied with my flesh?

23 ᴺOh that my words were now written! oh that they were printed in a book!

24 That they were graven with an iron pen and lead in the rock for ever!

"I know that my redeemer liveth"

25 For I know that my redeemer liveth, and that he shall stand at the latter day upon the earth:

26 ᴺAnd though after my skin worms destroy this body, yet ᴿin my flesh shall I see God:

27 Whom I shall see for myself, and mine eyes shall behold, and not ᴺanother; ᴺthough my reins be consumed ᴺwithin me.

28 But ye should say, Why persecute we him, ᴺseeing the root of the matter is found in me?

29 Be ye afraid of the sword: for wrath bringeth the punishments of the sword, that ye may know there is a judgment.

CHAPTER 20

Zophar's second speech

THEN answered Zō'-phär the Nā-ăm'-ă-thīte, and said,

2 Therefore do my thoughts cause me to answer, and for this ᴺI make haste.

3 I have heard the check of my reproach,

CHAP. 19

BC 1520

17 Heb. my belly
18 2 Ki. 2:23
18 Or, the wicked
19 Ps. 55:13
19 Heb. the men of my secret
20 Ps. 102:5
20 Or, as
22 Ps. 69:26
23 Heb. Who will give, etc.
26 Or, After I shall awake, though this body be destroyed, yet out of my flesh shall I see God
26 Ps. 17:15
1 Cor. 13:12
27 Heb. a stranger
27 Or, my reins within me are consumed with earnest desire [for that day]
27 Heb. in my bosom
28 Or, and what root of matter is found in me?

CHAP. 20

BC 1520

2 Heb. my haste is in me

Ps. 37:35   5
Heb. from near   5
Is. 14:13, 14   6
Obad. 3, 4
Heb. cloud   6
Ps. 73:20   8
Or, The poor shall oppress his children   10
ch. 13:26   11
ch. 21:26   11
Heb. in the midst of his palate   13
Ps. 36:8   17
Jer. 17:8
Or, streaming brooks   17
Heb. according to the substance of his exchange   18
Heb. crushed   19
Eccl. 5:13   20
Heb. know   20
Or, There shall be none left for his meat   21
Or, troublesome 22
Is. 24:18   24
Amos 5:19

---

and the spirit of my understanding causeth me to answer.

4 Knowest thou not this of old, since man was placed upon earth,

5 ᴿThat the triumphing of the wicked is ᴺshort, and the joy of the hypocrite but for a moment?

6 ᴿThough his excellency mount up to the heavens, and his head reach unto the ᴺclouds;

7 Yet he shall perish for ever like his own dung: they which have seen him shall say, Where is he?

8 He shall fly away ᴿas a dream, and shall not be found: yea, he shall be chased away as a vision of the night.

9 The eye also which saw him shall see him no more; neither shall his place any more behold him.

10 ᴺHis children shall seek to please the poor, and his hands shall restore their goods.

11 His bones are full of ᴿthe sin of his youth, ᴿwhich shall lie down with him in the dust.

God's dealing with the wicked

12 Though wickedness be sweet in his mouth, though he hide it under his tongue;

13 Though he spare it, and forsake it not; but keep it still ᴺwithin his mouth:

14 Yet his meat in his bowels is turned, it is the gall of asps within him.

15 He hath swallowed down riches, and he shall vomit them up again: God shall cast them out of his belly.

16 He shall suck the poison of asps: the viper's tongue shall slay him.

17 He shall not see ᴿthe rivers, ᴺthe floods, the brooks of honey and butter.

18 That which he laboured for shall he restore, and shall not swallow it down: ᴺaccording to his substance shall the restitution be, and he shall not rejoice therein.

19 Because he hath ᴺoppressed and hath forsaken the poor; because he hath violently taken away an house which he builded not;

20 ᴿSurely he shall not ᴺfeel quietness in his belly, he shall not save of that which he desired.

21 ᴺThere shall none of his meat be left; therefore shall no man look for his goods.

22 In the fulness of his sufficiency he shall be in straits: every hand of the ᴺwicked shall come upon him.

23 When he is about to fill his belly, God shall cast the fury of his wrath upon him, and shall rain it upon him while he is eating.

24 ᴿHe shall flee from the iron weapon, and the bow of steel shall strike him through.

25 It is drawn, and cometh out of the body;

yea, ^Rthe glittering sword cometh out of his gall: ^Rterrors *are* upon him.

26 All darkness *shall be* hid in his secret places: ^Ra fire not blown shall consume him; it shall go ill with him that is left in his tabernacle.

27 The heaven shall reveal his iniquity; and the earth shall rise up against him.

28 The increase of his house shall depart, *and his goods* shall flow away in the day of his wrath.

29 ^RThis *is* the portion of a wicked man from God, and the heritage ^Nappointed unto him by God.

CHAPTER 21

Job's answer

B UT Job answered and said,
2 Hear diligently my speech, and let this be your consolations.

3 Suffer me that I may speak; and after that I have spoken, ^Rmock on.

4 As for me, *is* my complaint to man? and if *it were so,* why should not my spirit be ^Ntroubled?

5 ^NMark me, and be astonished, ^Rand lay *your* hand upon *your* mouth.

6 Even when I remember I am afraid, and trembling taketh hold on my flesh.

Prosperity of the wicked

7 ^RWherefore do the wicked live, become old, yea, are mighty in power?

8 Their seed is established in their sight with them, and their offspring before their eyes.

9 Their houses ^Nare safe from fear, ^Rneither *is* the rod of God upon them.

10 Their bull gendereth, and faileth not; their cow calveth, and ^Rcasteth not her calf.

11 They send forth their little ones like a flock, and their children dance.

12 They take the timbrel and harp, and rejoice at the sound of the organ.

13 They ^Rspend their days ^Nin wealth, and in a moment go down to the grave.

14 ^RTherefore they say unto God, Depart from us; for we desire not the knowledge of thy ways.

15 ^RWhat *is* the Almighty, that we should serve him? and ^Rwhat profit should we have, if we pray unto him?

16 Lo, their good *is* not in their hand: ^Rthe counsel of the wicked is far from me.

Death of the wicked

17 How oft is the ^Ncandle of the wicked put out! and *how oft* cometh their destruction

upon them! *God* ^Rdistributeth sorrows in his anger.

18 ^RThey are as stubble before the wind, and as chaff that the storm ^Ncarrieth away.

19 God layeth up ^Nhis iniquity ^Rfor his children: he rewardeth him, and he shall know *it.*

20 His eyes shall see his destruction, and ^Rhe shall drink of the wrath of the Almighty.

21 For what pleasure *hath* he in his house after him, when the number of his months is cut off in the midst?

22 ^RShall *any* teach God knowledge? seeing he judgeth those that are high.

23 One dieth ^Nin his full strength, being wholly at ease and quiet.

24 His ^Nbreasts are full of milk, and his bones are moistened with marrow.

25 And another dieth in the bitterness of his soul, and never eateth with pleasure.

26 They shall ^Rlie down alike in the dust, and the worms shall cover them.

27 Behold, I know your thoughts, and the devices *which* ye wrongfully imagine against me.

28 For ye say, Where *is* the house of the prince? and where *are* ^Nthe dwelling places of the wicked?

29 Have ye not asked them that go by the way? and do ye not know their tokens,

30 ^RThat the wicked is reserved to the day of destruction? they shall be brought forth to ^Nthe day of wrath.

31 Who shall declare his way to his face? and who shall repay him *what* he hath done?

32 Yet shall he be brought to the ^Ngrave, and shall ^Nremain in the tomb.

33 The clods of the valley shall be sweet unto him, and ^Revery man shall draw after him, as *there are* innumerable before him.

34 How then comfort ye me in vain, seeing in your answers there remaineth ^Nfalsehood?

CHAPTER 22

Third speech of Eliphaz

T HEN ĕ-lī'-phăz the Tē'-măn-īte answered and said,
2 ^RCan a man be profitable unto God, ^Nas he that is wise may be profitable unto himself?

3 *Is it* any pleasure to the Almighty, that thou art righteous? or *is it* gain *to him,* that thou makest thy ways perfect?

4 Will he reprove thee for fear of thee? will he enter with thee into judgment?

5 *Is* not thy wickedness great? and thine iniquities infinite?

6 For thou hast ^Rtaken a pledge from thy

brother for nought, and ᴺstripped the naked of their clothing.

7 Thou hast not given water to the weary to drink, and thou ᴿhast withholden bread from the hungry.

8 But *as for* ᴺthe mighty man, he had the earth; and the ᴺhonourable man dwelt in it.

9 Thou hast sent widows away empty, and the arms of the fatherless have been broken.

10 Therefore snares *are* round about thee, and sudden fear troubleth thee;

11 Or darkness, *that* thou canst not see; and abundance of ᴿwaters cover thee.

12 *Is* not God in the height of heaven? and behold ᴺthe height of the stars, how high they are!

13 And thou sayest, ᴿHowᴺ doth God know? can he judge through the dark cloud?

14 Thick clouds *are* a covering to him, that he seeth not; and he walketh in the circuit of heaven.

15 Hast thou marked the old way which wicked men have trodden?

16 Which ᴿwere cut down out of time, ᴺwhose foundation was overflown with a flood:

17 ᴿWhich said unto God, Depart from us: and what can the Almighty do ᴺfor them?

18 Yet he filled their houses with good *things:* but the counsel of the wicked is far from me.

19 ᴿThe righteous see *it,* and are glad: and the innocent laugh them to scorn.

20 Whereas our ᴺsubstance is not cut down, but ᴺthe remnant of them the fire consumeth.

21 Acquaint now thyself ᴺwith him, and ᴿbe at peace: thereby good shall come unto thee.

22 Receive, I pray thee, the law from his mouth, and ᴿlay up his words in thine heart.

23 If thou return to the Almighty, thou shalt be built up, thou shalt put away iniquity far from thy tabernacles.

24 Then shalt thou ᴿlay up gold ᴺas dust, and the *gold* of ō'-phir as the stones of the brooks.

25 Yea, the Almighty shall be thy ᴺdefence, and thou shalt have ᴺplenty of silver.

26 For then shalt thou have thy ᴿdelight in the Almighty, and shalt lift up thy face unto God.

27 ᴿThou shalt make thy prayer unto him, and he shall hear thee, and thou shalt pay thy vows.

28 Thou shalt also decree a thing, and it shall be established unto thee: and the light shall shine upon thy ways.

29 When *men* are cast down, then thou shalt say, *There is* lifting up; and ᴿhe shall save ᴺthe humble person.

30 ᴺHe shall deliver the island of the innocent: and it is delivered by the pureness of thine hands.

CHAPTER 23

"Oh that I knew where I might find him!"

THEN Job answered and said,

2 Even to day *is* my complaint bitter: ᴺmy stroke is heavier than my groaning.

3 Oh that I knew where I might find him! *that* I might come *even* to his seat!

4 I would order *my* cause before him, and fill my mouth with arguments.

5 I would know the words *which* he would answer me, and understand what he would say unto me.

6 ᴿWill he plead against me with *his* great power? No; but he would put *strength* in me.

7 There the righteous might dispute with him; so should I be delivered for ever from my judge.

8 ᴿBehold, I go forward, but he *is* not *there;* and backward, but I cannot perceive him:

9 On the left hand, where he doth work, but I cannot behold *him:* he hideth himself on the right hand, that I cannot see *him:*

10 But he ᴿknoweth ᴺthe way that I take: when ᴿhe hath tried me, I shall come forth as gold.

11 ᴿMy foot hath held his steps, his way have I kept, and not declined.

12 Neither have I gone back from the commandment of his lips; ᴿIᴺ have esteemed the words of his mouth more than ᴺmy necessary *food.*

13 But he *is* in one *mind,* and who can turn him? and *what* ᴿhis soul desireth, even *that* he doeth.

14 For he performeth *the thing that is* ᴿappointed for me: and many such *things are* with him.

15 Therefore am I troubled at his presence: when I consider, I am afraid of him.

16 For God ᴿmaketh my heart soft, and the Almighty troubleth me:

17 Because I was not cut off before the darkness, *neither* hath he covered the darkness from my face.

CHAPTER 24

The wicked prosper

WHY, seeing ᴿtimes are not hidden from the Almighty, do they that know him not see his days?

2 *Some* remove the ᴿlandmarks; they violently take away flocks, and ᴺfeed *thereof.*

3 They drive away the ass of the fatherless, they ^Rtake the widow's ox for a pledge.

4 They turn the needy out of the way: ^Rthe poor of the earth hide themselves together.

5 Behold, *as* wild asses in the desert, go they forth to their work; rising betimes for a prey: the wilderness *yieldeth* food for them *and* for *their* children.

6 They reap *every one* his ^Ncorn in the field: and ^Nthey gather the vintage of the wicked.

7 They ^Rcause the naked to lodge without clothing, that *they have* no covering in the cold.

8 They are wet with the showers of the mountains, and ^Rembrace the rock for want of a shelter.

9 They pluck the fatherless from the breast, and take a pledge of the poor.

10 They cause *him* to go naked without clothing, and they take away the sheaf *from* the hungry;

11 *Which* make oil within their walls, *and* tread *their* winepresses, and suffer thirst.

12 Men groan from out of the city, and the soul of the wounded crieth out: yet God layeth not folly *to them.*

13 They are of those that rebel against the light; they know not the ways thereof, nor abide in the paths thereof.

14 ^RThe murderer rising with the light killeth the poor and needy, and in the night is as a thief.

15 ^RThe eye also of the adulterer waiteth for the twilight, ^Rsaying, No eye shall see me: and ^Ndisguiseth *his* face.

16 In the dark they dig through houses, *which* they had marked for themselves in the daytime: ^Rthey know not the light.

17 For the morning *is* to them even as the shadow of death: if *one* know *them, they are* in the terrors of the shadow of death.

18 He *is* swift as the waters; their portion is cursed in the earth: he beholdeth not the way of the vineyards.

19 Drought and heat ^Nconsume the snow waters: *so doth* the grave *those which* have sinned.

20 The womb shall forget him; the worm shall feed sweetly on him; ^Rhe shall be no more remembered; and wickedness shall be broken as a tree.

21 He evil entreateth the barren *that* beareth not: and doeth not good to the widow.

22 He draweth also the mighty with his power: he riseth up, ^Nand no *man* is sure of life.

23 *Though* it be given him *to be* in safety, whereon he resteth; yet ^Rhis eyes *are* upon their ways.

24 They are exalted for a little while, but ^Nare gone and brought low; they are ^Ntaken out of the way as all *other,* and cut off as the tops of the ears of corn.

25 And if *it be* not *so* now, who will make me a liar, and make my speech nothing worth?

CHAPTER 25

Bildad's third speech

THEN answered Bildad the Shû'-hīte, and said,

2 Dominion and fear *are* with him, he maketh peace in his high places.

3 Is there any number of his armies? and upon whom doth not ^Rhis light arise?

4 ^RHow then can man be justified with God? or how can he be clean *that is* born of a woman?

5 Behold even to the moon, and it shineth not; yea, the stars are not pure in his sight.

6 How much less man, *that is* ^Ra worm? and the son of man, *which is* a worm?

CHAPTER 26

Job's answer

BUT Job answered and said,

2 How hast thou helped *him that is* without power? *how* savest thou the arm *that hath* no strength?

3 How hast thou counselled *him that hath* no wisdom? and *how* hast thou plentifully declared the thing as it is?

4 To whom hast thou uttered words? and whose spirit came from thee?

5 Dead *things* are formed from under the waters, ^Nand the inhabitants thereof.

6 ^RHell *is* naked before him, and destruction hath no covering.

7 ^RHe stretcheth out the north over the empty place, *and* hangeth the earth upon nothing.

8 ^RHe bindeth up the waters in his thick clouds; and the cloud is not rent under them.

9 He holdeth back the face of his throne, *and* spreadeth his cloud upon it.

10 ^RHe hath compassed the waters with bounds, ^Nuntil the day and night come to an end.

11 The pillars of heaven tremble and are astonished at his reproof.

12 ^RHe divideth the sea with his power, and by his understanding he smiteth through ^Nthe proud.

13 ^RBy his spirit he hath garnished the heavens; his hand hath formed ^Rthe crooked serpent.

CHAP. 24

BC 1520

3 Deut. 24:6; 10, 12, 17 ch. 22:6
4 Prov. 28:28
6 Heb. *mingled corn,* or, *dredge*
6 Heb. *the wicked gather the vintage*
7 Ex. 22:26 Deut. 24:12, 13 ch. 22:6
8 Lam. 4:5
14 Ps. 10:8
15 Prov. 7:9
15 Ps. 10:11
15 Heb. *setteth his face in secret*
16 John 3:20
19 Heb. *violently take*
20 Prov. 10:7
22 Or, *he trusteth not* his own *life*
23 Ps. 11:4 Prov. 15:3

Heb. *are not* 24
Heb. *closed up* 24

CHAP. 25

BC 1520

Jas. 1:17 3
ch. 4:17, etc. 4
& 15:14, etc.
Ps. 22:6 6

CHAP. 26

BC 1520

Or, *with the inhabitants* 5
Ps. 139:8 6
Prov. 15:11
Heb. 4:13
ch. 9:8 7
Ps. 24:2
& 104:2, etc.
Prov. 30:4 8
ch. 38:8 10
Ps. 33:7
& 104:9
Heb. *until the end of light with darkness* 10
Ex. 14:21 12
Is. 51:15
Jer. 31:35
Heb. *pride* 12
Ps. 33:6 13
Is. 27:1 13

14 Lo, these *are* parts of his ways: but how little a portion is heard of him? but the thunder of his power who can understand?

CHAPTER 27

"My righteousness I hold fast"

MOREOVER Job [N]continued his parable, and said,

2 *As* God liveth, [R]*who* hath taken away my judgment; and the Almighty, *who* hath [N]vexed my soul;

3 All the while my breath *is* in me, and [N]the spirit of God *is* in my nostrils;

4 My lips shall not speak wickedness, nor my tongue utter deceit.

5 God forbid that I should justify you: till I die [R]I will not remove mine integrity from me.

6 My righteousness I [R]hold fast, and will not let it go: [R]my heart shall not reproach *me* [N]so long as I live.

7 Let mine enemy be as the wicked, and he that riseth up against me as the unrighteous.

8 [R]For what *is* the hope of the hypocrite, though he hath gained, when God taketh away his soul?

9 [R]Will God hear his cry when trouble cometh upon him?

10 [R]Will he delight himself in the Almighty? will he always call upon God?

11 I will teach you [N]by the hand of God: *that* which *is* with the Almighty will I not conceal.

12 Behold, all ye yourselves have seen *it;* why then are ye thus altogether vain?

The portion of the wicked man

13 [R]This *is* the portion of a wicked man with God, and the heritage of oppressors, *which* they shall receive of the Almighty.

14 [R]If his children be multiplied, *it is* for the sword: and his offspring shall not be satisfied with bread.

15 Those that remain of him shall be buried in death: and [R]his widows shall not weep.

16 Though he heap up silver as the dust, and prepare raiment as the clay;

17 He may prepare *it,* but [R]the just shall put *it* on, and the innocent shall divide the silver.

18 He buildeth his house as a moth, and [R]as a booth *that* the keeper maketh.

19 The rich man shall lie down, but he shall not be gathered: he openeth his eyes, and he *is* not.

20 [R]Terrors take hold on him as waters, a tempest stealeth him away in the night.

21 The east wind carrieth him away, and he

departeth: and as a storm hurleth him out of his place.

22 For *God* shall cast upon him, and not spare: [N]he would fain flee out of his hand.

23 *Men* shall clap their hands at him, and shall hiss him out of his place.

CHAPTER 28

Search for wisdom

SURELY there is [N]a vein for the silver, and a place for gold *where* they fine *it.*

2 Iron is taken out of the [N]earth, and brass *is* molten *out of* the stone.

3 He setteth an end to darkness, and searcheth out all perfection: the stones of darkness, and the shadow of death.

4 The flood breaketh out from the inhabitant; *even the waters* forgotten of the foot: they are dried up, they are gone away from men.

5 *As for* the earth, out of it cometh bread: and under it is turned up as it were fire.

6 The stones of it *are* the place of sapphires: and it hath [N]dust of gold.

7 *There is* a path which no fowl knoweth, and which the vulture's eye hath not seen:

8 The lion's whelps have not trodden it, nor the fierce lion passed by it.

9 He putteth forth his hand upon the [N]rock; he overturneth the mountains by the roots.

10 He cutteth out rivers among the rocks; and his eye seeth every precious thing.

11 He bindeth the floods [N]from overflowing; and *the thing that is* hid bringeth he forth to light.

12 [R]But where shall wisdom be found? and where *is* the place of understanding?

13 Man knoweth not the [R]price thereof; neither is it found in the land of the living.

14 [R]The depth saith, It *is* not in me: and the sea saith, *It is* not with me.

15 [N]It [R]cannot be gotten for gold, neither shall silver be weighed *for* the price thereof.

16 It cannot be valued with the gold of ō´-phĭr, with the precious onyx, or the sapphire.

17 The gold and the crystal cannot equal it: and the exchange of it *shall not be for* [N]jewels of fine gold.

18 No mention shall be made of [N]coral, or of pearls: for the price of wisdom *is* above rubies.

19 The topaz of Ē-thĭ-ō´-pĭ-ă shall not equal it, neither shall it be valued with pure gold.

20 [R]Whence then cometh wisdom? and where *is* the place of understanding?

21 Seeing it is hid from the eyes of all living, and kept close from the fowls of the ᴺair.

22 ᴿDestruction and death say, We have heard the fame thereof with our ears.

Fear of the Lord is wisdom

23 God understandeth the way thereof, and he knoweth the place thereof.

24 For he looketh to the ends of the earth, *and* ᴿseeth under the whole heaven;

25 ᴿTo make the weight for the winds; and he weigheth the waters by measure.

26 When he ᴿmade a decree for the rain, and a way for the lightning of the thunder:

27 Then did he see it, and ᴺdeclare it; he prepared it, yea, and searched it out.

28 And unto man he said, Behold, ᴿthe fear of the Lord, that *is* wisdom; and to depart from evil *is* understanding.

CHAPTER 29

Job's former prosperity

MOREOVER Job ᴺcontinued his parable, and said,

2 Oh that I were as *in* months past, as *in* the days *when* God preserved me;

3 ᴿWhen his ᴺcandle shined upon my head, *and when* by his light I walked *through* darkness;

4 As I was in the days of my youth, when ᴿthe secret of God *was* upon my tabernacle;

5 When the Almighty *was* yet with me, *when* my children *were* about me;

6 When ᴿI washed my steps with butter, and ᴿthe rock poured ᴺme out rivers of oil;

7 When I went out to the gate through the city, *when* I prepared my seat in the street!

8 The young men saw me, and hid themselves: and the aged arose, *and* stood up.

9 The princes refrained talking, and ᴿlaid *their* hand on their mouth.

10 ᴺThe nobles held their peace, and their ᴿtongue cleaved to the roof of their mouth.

11 When the ear heard *me,* then it blessed me; and when the eye saw *me,* it gave witness to me:

12 Because ᴿI delivered the poor that cried, and the fatherless, and *him that had* none to help him.

13 The blessing of him that was ready to perish came upon me: and I caused the widow's heart to sing for joy.

14 ᴿI put on righteousness, and it clothed me: my judgment *was* as a robe and a diadem.

15 I was ᴿeyes to the blind, and feet *was* I to the lame.

16 I *was* a father to the poor: and ᴿthe cause *which* I knew not I searched out.

17 And I brake ᴿthe ᴺjaws of the wicked, and ᴺplucked the spoil out of his teeth.

18 Then I said, ᴿI shall die in my nest, and I shall multiply *my* days as the sand.

19 ᴿMy root *was* ᴺspread out ᴿby the waters, and the dew lay all night upon my branch.

20 My glory *was* ᴺfresh in me, and my ᴿbow was ᴺrenewed in my hand.

21 Unto me *men* gave ear, and waited, and kept silence at my counsel.

22 After my words they spake not again; and my speech dropped upon them.

23 And they waited for me as for the rain; and they opened their mouth wide *as* for ᴿthe latter rain.

24 *If* I laughed on them, they believed *it* not; and the light of my countenance they cast not down.

25 I chose out their way, and sat chief, and dwelt as a king in the army, as one *that* comforteth the mourners.

CHAPTER 30

BUT now *they that are* ᴺyounger than I have me in derision, whose fathers I would have disdained to have set with the dogs of my flock.

2 Yea, whereto *might* the strength of their hands *profit* me, in whom old age was perished?

3 For want and famine *they were* ᴺsolitary; fleeing into the wilderness ᴺin former time desolate and waste.

4 Who cut up mallows by the bushes, and juniper roots *for* their meat.

5 They were driven forth from among *men,* (they cried after them as *after* a thief;)

6 To dwell in the cliffs of the valleys, *in* ᴺcaves of the earth, and *in* the rocks.

7 Among the bushes they brayed; under the nettles they were gathered together.

8 *They were* children of fools, yea, children of ᴺbase men: they were viler than the earth.

9 ᴿAnd now am I their song, yea, I am their byword.

10 They abhor me, they flee far from me, ᴺand spare not ᴿto spit in my face.

11 Because he ᴿhath loosed my cord, and afflicted me, they have also let loose the bridle before me.

12 Upon *my* right *hand* rise the youth; they push away my feet, and ᴿthey raise up against me the ways of their destruction.

---

13 They mar my path, they set forward my calamity, they have no helper.

14 They came *upon me* as a wide breaking in *of waters:* in the desolation they rolled themselves *upon me.*

15 Terrors are turned upon me: they pursue ^N my soul as the wind: and my welfare passeth away as a cloud.

Job laments his affliction

16 ^R And now my soul is poured out upon me; the days of affliction have taken hold upon me.

17 My bones are pierced in me in the night season: and my sinews take no rest.

18 By the great force *of my disease* is my garment changed: it bindeth me about as the collar of my coat.

19 He hath cast me into the mire, and I am become like dust and ashes.

20 I cry unto thee, and thou dost not hear me: I stand up, and thou regardest me *not.*

21 Thou art ^N become cruel to me: with ^N thy strong hand thou opposest thyself against me.

22 Thou liftest me up to the wind; thou causest me to ride *upon it,* and dissolvest my ^N substance.

23 For I know *that* thou wilt bring me *to* death, and *to* the house ^R appointed for all living.

24 Howbeit he will not stretch out *his* hand to the ^N grave, though they cry in his destruction.

25 ^R Did not I weep ^N for him that was in trouble? was *not* my soul grieved for the poor?

26 ^R When I looked for good, then evil came *unto me:* and when I waited for light, there came darkness.

27 My bowels boiled, and rested not: the days of affliction prevented me.

28 ^R I went mourning without the sun: I stood up, *and* I cried in the congregation.

29 ^R I am a brother to dragons, and a companion to ^N owls.

30 ^R My skin is black upon me, and ^R my bones are burned with heat.

31 My harp also is *turned* to mourning, and my organ into the voice of them that weep.

CHAPTER 31

Summation of Job's integrity

I MADE a covenant with mine ^R eyes; why then should I think upon a maid?

2 For what ^R portion of God *is there* from above? and *what* inheritance of the Almighty from on high?

CHAP. 30

BC 1520

15 Heb. *my principal one*
16 Ps. 42:4
21 Heb. *turned to be cruel*
21 Heb. *the strength of thy hand*
22 Or, *wisdom*
23 Heb. 9:27
24 Heb. *heap*
25 Ps. 35:13
Rom. 12:15
25 Heb. *for him that was hard of day?*
26 Jer. 8:15
28 Ps. 42:9
29 Ps. 102:6
Mic. 1:8
29 Or, *ostriches*
30 Ps. 119:83
Lam. 4:8
30 Ps. 102:3

CHAP. 31

BC 1520

1 Mat. 5:28
2 ch. 20:29

2 Chr. 16:9   4
Prov. 5:21
Jer. 32:19
Heb. *Let him weigh me in balances of justice*   6
See Num. 15:39   7
Eccl. 11:9
Ezek. 6:9
Mat. 5:29
Lev. 26:16   8
Deut. 28:30, 38, etc.
2 Sam. 12:11   10
Jer. 8:10
Gen. 38:24   11
Lev. 20:10
See ver. 28
Ps. 44:21   14
ch. 34:19   15
Or, *did he not fashion us in one womb?*   15
i.e. *the widow*   18
Deut. 24:13   20
ch. 22:9   21
Or, *the chanelbone*   22
Is. 13:6   23
Mark 10:24   24
Ps. 62:10   25
Heb. *found much*   25

---

3 *Is* not destruction to the wicked? and a strange *punishment* to the workers of iniquity?

4 ^R Doth not he see my ways, and count all my steps?

5 If I have walked with vanity, or if my foot hath hasted to deceit;

6 ^N Let me be weighed in an even balance, that God may know mine integrity.

7 If my step hath turned out of the way, and ^R mine heart walked after mine eyes, and if any blot hath cleaved to mine hands;

8 *Then* ^R let me sow, and let another eat; yea, let my offspring be rooted out.

9 If mine heart have been deceived by a woman, or *if* I have laid wait at my neighbour's door;

10 *Then* let my wife grind unto ^R another, and let others bow down upon her.

11 For this *is* an heinous crime; yea, ^R it *is* an iniquity *to be punished by* the judges.

12 For it *is* a fire *that* consumeth to destruction, and would root out all mine increase.

13 If I did despise the cause of my manservant or of my maidservant, when they contended with me;

14 What then shall I do when ^R God riseth up? and when he visiteth, what shall I answer him?

15 ^R Did not he that made me in the womb make him? and ^N did not one fashion us in the womb?

16 If I have withheld the poor from *their* desire, or have caused the eyes of the widow to fail;

17 Or have eaten my morsel myself alone, and the fatherless hath not eaten thereof;

18 (For from my youth he was brought up with me, as *with* a father, and I have guided ^N her from my mother's womb;)

19 If I have seen any perish for want of clothing, or any poor without covering;

20 If his loins have not ^R blessed me, and *if* he were *not* warmed with the fleece of my sheep;

21 If I have lifted up my hand ^R against the fatherless, when I saw my help in the gate:

22 *Then* let mine arm fall from my shoulder blade, and mine arm be broken from ^N the bone.

23 For ^R destruction *from* God *was* a terror to me, and by reason of his highness I could not endure.

24 ^R If I have made gold my hope, or have said to the fine gold, *Thou art* my confidence;

25 ^R If I rejoiced because my wealth *was* great, and because mine hand had ^N gotten much;

26 ᴿIf I beheld ᴺthe sun when it shined, or the moon walking ᴺin brightness;

27 And my heart hath been secretly enticed, or ᴺmy mouth hath kissed my hand:

28 This also *were* an iniquity *to be punished by* the judge: for I should have denied the God *that is* above.

29 ᴿIf I rejoiced at the destruction of him that hated me, or lifted up myself when evil found him:

30 ᴿNeither have I suffered ᴺmy mouth to sin by wishing a curse to his soul.

31 If the men of my tabernacle said not, Oh that we had of his flesh! we cannot be satisfied.

32 ᴿThe stranger did not lodge in the street: *but* I opened my doors ᴺto the traveller.

33 If I covered my transgressions ᴿasᴺ Adam, by hiding mine iniquity in my bosom:

34 Did I fear a great ᴿmultitude, or did the contempt of families terrify me, that I kept silence, *and* went not out of the door?

35 Oh that one would hear me! ᴺbehold, my desire *is,* ᴿ*that* the Almighty would answer me, and *that* mine adversary had written a book.

36 Surely I would take it upon my shoulder, *and* bind it *as* a crown to me.

37 I would declare unto him the number of my steps; as a prince would I go near unto him.

38 If my land cry against me, or that the furrows likewise thereof ᴺcomplain;

39 If ᴿI have eaten ᴺthe fruits thereof without money, or ᴿhave ᴺcaused the owners thereof to lose their life:

40 Let ᴿthistles grow instead of wheat, and ᴺcockle instead of barley. The words of Job are ended.

CHAPTER 32

Elihu's speech

So these three men ceased ᴺto answer Job, because he *was* ᴿrighteous in his own eyes.

2 Then was kindled the wrath of Ĕ-lī′-hū the son of Bă-rā′-chĕl the Bū′-zīte, of the kindred of Ram: against Job was his wrath kindled, because he justified ᴺhimself rather than God.

3 Also against his three friends was his wrath kindled, because they had found no answer, and *yet* had condemned Job.

4 Now Ĕ-lī′-hū had ᴺwaited till Job had spoken, because they *were* ᴺelder than he.

5 When Ĕ-lī′-hū saw that *there was* no an-

swer in the mouth of *these* three men, then his wrath was kindled.

Wisdom comes not from age

6 And Ĕ-lī′-hū the son of Bă-rā′-chĕl the Bū′-zīte answered and said, I *am* ᴺyoung, and ye *are* very old; wherefore I was afraid, and ᴺdurst not shew you mine opinion.

7 I said, Days should speak, and multitude of years should teach wisdom.

8 But *there is* a spirit in man: and ᴿthe inspiration of the Almighty giveth them understanding.

9 ᴿGreat men are not *always* wise: neither do the aged understand judgment.

10 Therefore I said, Hearken to me; I also will shew mine opinion.

11 Behold, I waited for your words; I gave ear to your ᴺreasons, whilst ye searched out ᴺwhat to say.

12 Yea, I attended unto you, and, behold, *there was* none of you that convinced Job, *or* that answered his words:

13 ᴿLest ye should say, We have found out wisdom: God thrusteth him down, not man.

14 Now he hath not ᴺdirected *his* words against me: neither will I answer him with your speeches.

15 They were amazed, they answered no more: ᴺthey left off speaking.

16 When I had waited, (for they spake not, but stood still, *and* answered no more;)

17 *I said,* I will answer also my part, I also will shew mine opinion.

18 For I am full of ᴺmatter, ᴺthe spirit within me constraineth me.

19 Behold, my belly *is* as wine *which* ᴺhath no vent; it is ready to burst like new bottles.

20 I will speak, ᴺthat I may be refreshed: I will open my lips and answer.

21 Let me not, I pray you, accept any man's person, neither let me give flattering titles unto man.

22 For I know not to give flattering titles; *in so doing* my maker would soon take me away.

CHAPTER 33

Elihu challenges Job

Wherefore, Job, I pray thee, hear my speeches, and hearken to all my words.

2 Behold, now I have opened my mouth, my tongue hath spoken ᴺin my mouth.

3 My words *shall be of* the uprightness of my heart: and my lips shall utter knowledge clearly.

4 ᴿThe spirit of God hath made me, and the breath of the Almighty hath given me life.

5 If thou canst answer me, set *thy words* in order before me, stand up.

6 ᴿBehold, I *am* ᴺaccording to thy wish in God's stead: I also am ᴺformed out of the clay.

7 ᴿBehold, my terror shall not make thee afraid, neither shall my hand be heavy upon thee.

8 Surely thou hast spoken ᴺin mine hearing, and I have heard the voice of *thy* words, *saying,*

9 ᴿI am clean without transgression, I *am* innocent; neither *is there* iniquity in me.

10 Behold, he findeth occasions against me, ᴿhe counteth me for his enemy,

11 ᴿHe putteth my feet in the stocks, he marketh all my paths.

12 Behold, *in* this thou art not just: I will answer thee, that God is greater than man.

13 Why dost thou ᴿstrive against him? for ᴺhe giveth not account of any of his matters.

14 ᴿFor God speaketh once, yea twice, *yet man* perceiveth it not.

15 ᴿIn a dream, in a vision of the night, when deep sleep falleth upon men, in slumberings upon the bed;

16 ᴿThen ᴺhe openeth the ears of men, and sealeth their instruction,

17 That he may withdraw man *from his* ᴺpurpose, and hide pride from man.

18 He keepeth back his soul from the pit, and his life ᴺfrom perishing by the sword.

19 He is chastened also with pain upon his bed, and the multitude of his bones with strong *pain:*

20 ᴿSo that his life abhorreth bread, and his soul ᴺdainty meat.

21 His flesh is consumed away, that it cannot be seen; and his bones *that* were not seen stick out.

22 Yea, his soul draweth near unto the grave, and his life to the destroyers.

23 If there be a messenger with him, an interpreter, one among a thousand, to shew unto man his uprightness: ★

24 Then he is gracious unto him, and saith, Deliver him from going down to the pit: I have found ᴺa ransom.   ★

25 His flesh shall be fresher ᴺthan a child's: he shall return to the days of his youth:

26 He shall pray unto God, and he will be favourable unto him: and he shall see his face with joy: for he will render unto man his righteousness.

27 ᴺHe looketh upon men, and *if any* ᴿsay, I have sinned, and perverted *that which was* right, and it ᴿprofited me not;

---

28 ᴺHe will ᴿdeliver his soul from going into the pit, and his life shall see the light.

29 Lo, all these *things* worketh God ᴺoftentimes with man,

30 ᴿTo bring back his soul from the pit, to be enlightened with the light of the living.

31 Mark well, O Job, hearken unto me: hold thy peace, and I will speak.

32 If thou hast any thing to say, answer me: speak, for I desire to justify thee.

33 If not, ᴿhearken unto me: hold thy peace, and I shall teach thee wisdom.

CHAPTER 34

Elihu challenges Job's friends

FURTHERMORE Ĕ-li′-hū answered and said,

2 Hear my words, O ye wise *men;* and give ear unto me, ye that have knowledge.

3 ᴿFor the ear trieth words, as the ᴺmouth tasteth meat.

4 Let us choose to us judgment: let us know among ourselves what *is* good.

5 For Job hath said, ᴿI am righteous: and ᴿGod hath taken away my judgment.

6 ᴿShould I lie against my right? ᴺmy wound *is* incurable without transgression.

7 What man *is* like Job, ᴿ*who* drinketh up scorning like water?

8 Which goeth in company with the workers of iniquity, and walketh with wicked men.

9 For ᴿhe hath said, It profiteth a man nothing that he should delight himself with God.

Elihu justifies God

10 Therefore hearken unto me, ye ᴺmen of understanding: ᴿfar be it from God, *that he should do* wickedness; and *from* the Almighty, *that he should commit* iniquity.

11 ᴿFor the work of a man shall he render unto him, and cause every man to find according to *his* ways.

12 Yea, surely God will not do wickedly, neither will the Almighty ᴿpervert judgment.

13 Who hath given him a charge over the earth? or who hath disposed ᴺthe whole world?

14 If he set his heart ᴺupon man, *if* he ᴿgather unto himself his spirit and his breath;

15 ᴿAll flesh shall perish together, and man shall turn again unto dust.

16 If now *thou hast* understanding, hear this: hearken to the voice of my words.

17 ᴿShall even he that hateth right ᴺgovern? and wilt thou condemn him that is most just?

18 ᴿ*Is it* fit to say to a king, *Thou art* wicked? *and* to princes, *Ye are* ungodly?

19 *How much less to him* that ᴿaccepteth not

the persons of princes, nor regardeth the rich more than the poor? for [R]they all *are* the work of his hands.

20 In a moment shall they die, and the people shall be troubled [R]at midnight, and pass away: and [N]the mighty shall be taken away without hand.

21 [R]For his eyes *are* upon the ways of man, and he seeth all his goings.

22 [R]*There is* no darkness, nor shadow of death, where the workers of iniquity may hide themselves.

23 For he will not lay upon man more *than right;* that he should [N]enter into judgment with God.

24 [R]He shall break in pieces mighty men [N]without number, and set others in their stead.

25 Therefore he knoweth their works, and he overturneth *them* in the night, so that they are [N]destroyed.

26 He striketh them as wicked men [N]in the open sight of others;

27 Because they [R]turned back [N]from him, and [R]would not consider any of his ways:

28 So that they [R]cause the cry of the poor to come unto him, and he [R]heareth the cry of the afflicted.

29 When he giveth quietness, who then can make trouble? and when he hideth *his* face, who then can behold him? whether *it be done* against a nation, or against a man only:

30 That the hypocrite reign not, lest [R]the people be ensnared.

31 Surely it is meet to be said unto God, I have borne *chastisement,* I will not offend *any more:*

32 *That which* I see not teach thou me: if I have done iniquity, I will do no more.

33 [N]*Should it be* according to thy mind? he will recompense it, whether thou refuse, or whether thou choose; and not I: therefore speak what thou knowest.

34 Let men [N]of understanding tell me, and let a wise man hearken unto me.

35 [R]Job hath spoken without knowledge, and his words *were* without wisdom.

36 [N]My desire *is that* Job may be tried unto the end because of *his* answers for wicked men.

37 For he addeth rebellion unto his sin, he clappeth *his* hands among us, and multiplieth his words against God.

CHAPTER 35

Comparison not to be made with God

E-Lī'-HŪ spake moreover, and said,
2 Thinkest thou this to be right, *that*

CHAP. 34
BC 1520
19 ch. 31:15
20 Ex. 12:29
20 Heb. *they shall take away the mighty*
21 ch. 31:4
22 Ps. 139:12
Amos 9:2, 3
23 Heb. *go*
24 Dan. 2:21
24 Heb. *without searching out*
25 Heb. *crushed*
26 Heb. *in the place of beholders*
27 1 Sam. 15:11
27 Heb. *from after him*
27 Ps. 28:5
Is. 5:12
28 Jas. 5:4
28 Ex. 22:23
30 1 Ki. 12:28, 30
33 Heb. Should it be *from with thee?*
34 Heb. *of heart*
35 ch. 35:16
36 Or, *My father, let Job be tried*

CHAP. 35	
BC 1520	
ch. 21:15	3
Or, *by it more than by my sin?*	3
Heb. *I will return to thee words*	4
ch. 34:8	4
ch. 22:12	5
Prov. 8:36	6
Jer. 7:19	
Ps. 16:2	7
Prov. 9:12	
ch. 34:28	9
Is. 51:13	10
Ps. 42:8	10
Acts 16:25	
Ps. 94:12	11
Prov. 1:28	12
Is. 1:15	13
Jer. 11:11	
ch. 9:11	14
Ps. 37:5, 6	14
i.e. *God*	15
Ps. 89:32	15
i.e. *Job*	15
ch. 34:35	16

CHAP. 36	
BC 1520	
Heb. *that there are yet words for God*	2
ch. 9:4	5
Heb. *heart*	5
Or, *afflicted*	6
Ps. 33:18	7
Ps. 113:8	7
Ps. 107:10	8

---

thou saidst, My righteousness *is* more than God's?

3 For [R]thou saidst, What advantage will it be unto thee? *and,* What profit shall I have, [N]*if I be cleansed* from my sin?

4 [N]I will answer thee, and [R]thy companions with thee.

5 [R]Look unto the heavens, and see; and behold the clouds *which* are higher than thou.

6 If thou sinnest, what doest thou [R]against him? or *if* thy transgressions be multipled, what doest thou unto him?

7 [R]If thou be righteous, what givest thou him? or what receiveth he of thine hand?

8 Thy wickedness *may hurt* a man as thou *art;* and thy righteousness *may profit* the son of man.

9 [R]By reason of the multitude of oppressions they make *the oppressed* to cry: they cry out by reason of the arm of the mighty.

10 But none saith, [R]Where *is* God my maker, [R]who giveth songs in the night;

11 Who [R]teacheth us more than the beasts of the earth, and maketh us wiser than the fowls of heaven?

12 [R]There they cry, but none giveth answer, because of the pride of evil men.

13 [R]Surely God will not hear vanity, neither will the Almighty regard it.

14 [R]Although thou sayest thou shalt not see him, *yet* judgment *is* before him; therefore [R]trust thou in him.

15 But now, because *it is* not *so,* [N]he hath [R]visited in his anger; yet [N]he knoweth *it* not in great extremity:

16 [R]Therefore doth Job open his mouth in vain; he multiplieth words without knowledge.

CHAPTER 36

God's ways are just

E-Lī'-HŪ also proceeded, and said,
2 Suffer me a little, and I will shew thee [N]that *I have* yet to speak on God's behalf.

3 I will fetch my knowledge from afar, and will ascribe righteousness to my Maker.

4 For truly my words *shall* not *be* false: he that is perfect in knowledge *is* with thee.

5 Behold, God *is* mighty, and despiseth not *any:* [R]he is mighty in strength *and* [N]wisdom.

6 He preserveth not the life of the wicked: but giveth right to the [N]poor.

7 [R]He withdraweth not his eyes from the righteous: but [R]with kings *are they* on the throne; yea, he doth establish them for ever, and they are exalted.

8 And [R]if *they be* bound in fetters, *and* be holden in cords of affliction;

9 Then he sheweth them their work, and

their transgressions that they have exceeded.

10 ᴿHe openeth also their ear to discipline, and commandeth that they return from iniquity.

11 If they obey and serve *him,* they shall ᴿspend their days in prosperity, and their years in pleasures.

12 But if they obey not, ᴺthey shall perish by the sword, and they shall die without knowledge.

13 But the hypocrites in heart ᴿheap up wrath: they cry not when he bindeth them.

14 ᴿThey ᴺdie in youth, and their life *is* among the ᴺunclean.

15 He delivereth the poor in his affliction, and openeth their ears in oppression.

16 Even so would he have removed thee out of the strait ᴿ*into* a broad place, where *there is* no straitness; and ᴿthatᴺ which should be set on thy table *should be* full of ᴿfatness.

17 But thou hast fulfilled the judgment of the wicked: ᴺjudgment and justice take hold *on thee.*

18 Because *there is* wrath, *beware* lest he take thee away with *his* stroke: then ᴿa great ransom cannot ᴺdeliver thee.

19 ᴿWill he esteem thy riches? *no,* not gold, nor all the forces of strength.

20 Desire not the night, when people are cut off in their place.

21 Take heed, ᴿregard not iniquity: for ᴿthis hast thou chosen rather than affliction.

22 Behold, God exalteth by his power: who teacheth like him?

23 ᴿWho hath enjoined him his way? or who can say, Thou hast wrought iniquity?

Praise of God's work

24 Remember that thou ᴿmagnify his work, which men behold.

25 Every man may see it; man may behold *it* afar off.

26 Behold, God *is* great, and we ᴿknow *him* not, ᴿneither can the number of his years be searched out.

27 For he ᴿmaketh small the drops of water: they pour down rain according to the vapour thereof:

28 ᴿWhich the clouds do drop *and* distil upon man abundantly.

29 Also can *any* understand the spreadings of the clouds, *or* the noise of his tabernacle?

30 Behold, he ᴿspreadeth his light upon it, and covereth ᴺthe bottom of the sea.

31 For ᴿby them judgeth he the people; he ᴿgiveth meat in abundance.

32 ᴿWith clouds he covereth the light; and commandeth it *not to shine* by *the cloud* that cometh betwixt.

CHAP. **36**
BC 1520
10 ch. 33:16
11 ch. 21:13
Is. 1:19, 20
12 Heb. *they shall pass away by the sword*
13 Rom. 2:5
14 Ps. 55:23
14 Heb. *Their soul dieth*
14 Or, *Sodomites,* Deut. 23:17
16 Ps. 18:19
16 Ps. 23:5
16 Heb. *the rest of thy table*
16 Ps. 36:8
17 Or, *judgment and justice should uphold* thee
18 Ps. 49:7
18 Heb. *turn thee aside*
19 Prov. 11:4
21 Ps. 66:18
21 Heb. 11:25
22 Is. 40:13
1 Cor. 2:16
23 ch. 34:13
24 Ps. 92:5
Rev. 15:3
26 1 Cor. 13:12
26 Ps. 90:2
Heb. 1:12
27 Ps. 147:8
28 Prov. 3:20
30 ch. 37:3
30 Heb. *roots*
31 ch. 37:13
31 Acts 14:17
32 Ps. 147:8
1 Ki. 18:41 **33**
Heb. *that* **33** *which goeth up*

CHAP. **37**
BC 1520
Heb. *Hear* **2** *in hearing*
Heb. *light* **3**
Heb. *wings* **3** *of the earth*
Ps. 29:3 **4**
ch. 5:9 **5**
Ps. 147:16 **6**
Heb. *and to* **6** *the showers of rain of his strength*
Ps. 109:27 **7**
Ps. 104:22 **8**
Heb. *Out of the* **9** *chamber*
Heb. *scattering* **9** *winds*
Ps. 147:17 **10**
Heb. *the cloud* **11** *of his light*
Ps. 148:8 **12**
Ex. 9:18 **13**
Heb. *a rod* **13**
ch. 38:26 **13**
2 Sam. 21:10 **13**
1 Ki. 18:45
Ps. 111:2 **14**
ch. 36:29 **16**
ch. 36:4 **16**
Gen. 1:6 **18**
Is. 44:24

33 ᴿThe noise thereof sheweth concerning it, the cattle also concerning ᴺthe vapour.

CHAPTER 37

AT this also my heart trembleth, and is moved out of his place.

2 ᴺHear attentively the noise of his voice, and the sound *that* goeth out of his mouth.

3 He directeth it under the whole heaven, and his ᴺlightning unto the ᴺends of the earth.

4 After it ᴿa voice roareth: he thundereth with the voice of his excellency; and he will not stay them when his voice is heard.

5 God thundereth marvellously with his voice; ᴿgreat things doeth he, which we cannot comprehend.

6 For ᴿhe saith to the snow, Be thou *on* the earth; ᴺlikewise to the small rain, and to the great rain of his strength.

7 He sealeth up the hand of every man; ᴿthat all men may know his work.

8 Then the beasts ᴿgo into dens, and remain in their places.

9 ᴺOut of the south cometh the whirlwind: and cold out of the ᴺnorth.

10 ᴿBy the breath of God frost is given: and the breadth of the waters is straitened.

11 Also by watering he wearieth the thick cloud: he scattereth ᴺhis bright cloud:

12 And it is turned round about by his counsels: that they may ᴿdo whatsoever he commandeth them upon the face of the world in the earth.

13 ᴿHe causeth it to come, whether for ᴺcorrection, or ᴿfor his land, or ᴿfor mercy.

Elihu challenges Job

14 Hearken unto this, O Job: stand still, and ᴿconsider the wondrous works of God.

15 Dost thou know when God disposed them, and caused the light of his cloud to shine?

16 ᴿDost thou know the balancings of the clouds, the wondrous works of ᴿhim which is perfect in knowledge?

17 How thy garments *are* warm, when he quieteth the earth by the south *wind?*

18 Hast thou with him ᴿspread out the sky, *which is* strong, *and* as a molten looking glass?

19 Teach us what we shall say unto him; *for* we cannot order *our speech* by reason of darkness.

20 Shall it be told him that I speak? if a man speak, surely he shall be swallowed up.

21 And now *men* see not the bright light which *is* in the clouds: but the wind passeth, and cleanseth them.

22 ᴺFair weather cometh out of the north: with God *is* terrible majesty.

23 *Touching* the Almighty, ᴿwe cannot find him out: ᴿ*he is* excellent in power, and in judgment, and in plenty of justice: he will not afflict.

24 Men do therefore ᴿfear him: he respecteth not any *that are* ᴿwise of heart.

CHAPTER 38

God challenges Job to answer

Tʜᴇɴ the Lᴏʀᴅ answered Job ᴿout of the whirlwind, and said,

2 ᴿWho *is* this that darkeneth counsel by ᴿwords without knowledge?

3 ᴿGird up now thy loins like a man; for I will demand of thee, and ᴺanswer thou me.

4 ᴿWhere wast thou when I laid the foundations of the earth? declare, ᴺif thou hast understanding.

5 Who hath laid the measures thereof, if thou knowest? or who hath stretched the line upon it?

6 Whereupon are the ᴺfoundations thereof ᴺfastened? or who laid the corner stone thereof;

7 When the morning stars sang together, and all ᴿthe sons of God shouted for joy?

8 ᴿOr *who* shut up the sea with doors, when it brake forth, *as if* it had issued out of the womb?

9 When I made the cloud the garment thereof, and thick darkness a swaddlingband for it,

10 And ᴿbrakeᴺ up for it my decreed *place,* and set bars and doors,

11 And said, Hitherto shalt thou come, but no further: and here shall ᴺthy proud waves ᴿbe stayed?

12 Hast thou ᴿcommanded the morning since thy days; *and* caused the dayspring to know his place;

13 That it might take hold of the ᴺends of the earth, that ᴿthe wicked might be shaken out of it?

14 It is turned as clay *to* the seal; and they stand as a garment.

15 And from the wicked their ᴿlight is withholden, and ᴿthe high arm shall be broken.

16 Hast thou ᴿentered into the springs of the sea? or hast thou walked in the search of the depth?

17 Have ᴿthe gates of death been opened unto thee? or hast thou seen the doors of the shadow of death?

18 Hast thou perceived the breadth of the earth? declare if thou knowest it all.

19 Where *is* the way *where* light dwelleth? and *as for* darkness, where *is* the place thereof,

20 That thou shouldest take it ᴺto the bound thereof, and that thou shouldest know the paths *to* the house thereof?

21 Knowest thou *it,* because thou wast then born? or *because* the number of thy days *is* great?

22 Hast thou entered into ᴿthe treasures of the snow? or hast thou seen the treasures of the hail,

23 ᴿWhich I have reserved against the time of trouble, against the day of battle and war?

24 By what way is the light parted, *which* scattereth the east wind upon the earth?

25 Who ᴿhath divided a watercourse for the overflowing of waters, or a way for the lightning of thunder;

26 To cause it to rain on the earth, *where* no man *is; on* the wilderness, wherein *there is* no man;

27 ᴿTo satisfy the desolate and waste *ground;* and to cause the bud of the tender herb to spring forth?

28 ᴿHath the rain a father? or who hath begotten the drops of dew?

29 Out of whose womb came the ice? and the ᴿhoary frost of heaven, who hath gendered it?

30 The waters are hid as *with* a stone, and the face of the deep ᴺis ᴿfrozen.

31 Canst thou bind the sweet influences of ᴿPlēi′-ă-dēś,ᴺᴺ or loose the bands of ᴺŌ-rī′-on?

32 Canst thou bring forth ᴺMăzz′-ă-rōth in his season? or canst thou ᴺguide Ärc-tū′-rŭs with his sons?

33 Knowest thou ᴿthe ordinances of heaven? canst thou set the dominion thereof in the earth?

34 Canst thou lift up thy voice to the clouds, that abundance of waters may cover thee?

35 Canst thou send lightnings, that they may go, and say unto thee, ᴺHere we *are?*

36 ᴿWho hath put wisdom in the inward parts? or who hath given understanding to the heart?

37 Who can number the clouds in wisdom? or ᴺwho can stay the bottles of heaven,

38 ᴺWhen the dust ᴺgroweth into hardness, and the clods cleave fast together?

39 ᴿWilt thou hunt the prey for the lion? or fill ᴺthe appetite of the young lions,

40 When they couch in *their* dens, *and* abide in the covert to lie in wait?

41 ᴿWho provideth for the raven his food? when his young ones cry unto God, they wander for lack of meat.

CHAP. 37
BC 1520
22 Heb. *Gold*
23 1 Tim. 6:16
23 ch. 36:5
24 Mat. 10:28
24 Mat. 11:25

CHAP. 38
BC 1520
1 Ex. 19:16
2 ch. 34:35
2 1 Tim. 1:7
3 ch. 40:7
3 Heb. *make me know*
4 Ps. 104:5
 Prov. 8:29
4 Heb. *if thou knowest understanding*
6 Heb. *sockets*
6 Heb. *made to sink?*
7 ch. 1:6
8 Gen. 1:9
10 ch. 26:10
10 Or, *established my decree upon it*
11 Heb. *the pride of thy waves*
11 Ps. 89:9
12 Ps. 148:5
13 Heb. *wings*
13 Ps. 104:35
15 ch. 18:5
15 Ps. 10:15
16 Ps. 77:19
17 Ps. 9:13

Or, *at*   20
Ps. 135:7   22
Ex. 9:18   23
 Josh. 10:11
 Is. 30:30
 Ezek. 13:11, 13
 Rev. 16:21
ch. 28:26   25
Ps. 107:35   27
Ps. 147:8   28
 Jer. 14:22
Ps. 147:16   29
Heb. *is taken*   30
ch. 37:10   30
ch. 9:9   31
 Amos 5:8
Or, *The seven*   31
 stars
Heb. *Cimah*   31
Heb. *Cesil?*   31
Or, *The twelve signs* 32
Heb. *guide them*   32
 Jer. 31:35
Heb. *Behold us?*   35
ch. 32:8   36
 Ps. 51:6
 Eccl. 2:26
Heb. *who can cause to lie down* 37
Or, *When the dust is turned into mire* 38
Heb. *is poured*   38
Ps. 104:21   39
 & 145:15
Heb. *the life*   39
Ps. 147:9   41
 Mat. 6:26

CHAPTER 39

God continues his challenge

KNOWEST thou the time when the wild goats of the rock bring forth? *or* canst thou mark when ᴿthe hinds do calve?

2 Canst thou number the months *that* they fulfil? or knowest thou the time when they bring forth?

3 They bow themselves, they bring forth their young ones, they cast out their sorrows.

4 Their young ones are in good liking, they grow up with corn; they go forth, and return not unto them.

5 Who hath sent out the wild ass free? or who hath loosed the bands of the wild ass?

6 ᴿWhose house I have made the wilderness, and the ᴺbarren land his dwellings.

7 He scorneth the multitude of the city, neither regardeth he the crying ᴺof the driver.

8 The range of the mountains *is* his pasture, and he searcheth after every green thing.

9 Will the ᴿunicorn be willing to serve thee, or abide by thy crib?

10 Canst thou bind the unicorn with his band in the furrow? or will he harrow the valleys after thee?

11 Wilt thou trust him, because his strength *is* great? or wilt thou leave thy labour to him?

12 Wilt thou believe him, that he will bring home thy seed, and gather *it into* thy barn?

13 *Gavest thou* the goodly wings unto the peacocks? or ᴺwings and feathers unto the ostrich?

14 Which leaveth her eggs in the earth, and warmeth them in dust,

15 And forgetteth that the foot may crush them, or that the wild beast may break them.

16 She is ᴿhardened against her young ones, as though *they were* not her's: her labour is in vain without fear;

17 Because God hath deprived her of wisdom, neither hath he ᴿimparted to her understanding.

18 What time she lifteth up herself on high, she scorneth the horse and his rider.

19 Hast thou given the horse strength? hast thou clothed his neck with thunder?

20 Canst thou make him afraid as a grasshopper? the glory of his nostrils *is* ᴺterrible.

21 ᴺHe paweth in the valley, and rejoiceth in *his* strength: ᴿhe goeth on to meet ᴺthe armed men.

22 He mocketh at fear, and is not affrighted; neither turneth he back from the sword.

23 The quiver rattleth against him, the glittering spear and the shield.

24 He swalloweth the ground with fierceness and rage: neither believeth he that *it is* the sound of the trumpet.

25 He saith among the trumpets, Ha, ha; and he smelleth the battle afar off, the thunder of the captains, and the shouting.

26 Doth the hawk fly by thy wisdom, *and* stretch her wings toward the south?

27 Doth the eagle mount up ᴺat thy command, and ᴿmake her nest on high?

28 She dwelleth and abideth on the rock, upon the crag of the rock, and the strong place.

29 From thence she seeketh the prey, *and* her eyes behold afar off.

30 Her young ones also suck up blood: and ᴿwhere the slain *are,* there *is* she.

CHAPTER 40

Job humbles himself

MOREOVER the Lᴏʀᴅ answered Job, and said,

2 Shall he that ᴿcontendeth with the Almighty instruct *him?* he that reproveth God, let him answer it.

3 Then Job answered the Lᴏʀᴅ, and said,

4 ᴿBehold, I am vile; what shall I answer thee? ᴿI will lay mine hand upon my mouth.

5 Once have I spoken; but I will not answer: yea, twice; but I will proceed no further.

God's power and wisdom

6 ᴿThen answered the Lᴏʀᴅ unto Job out of the whirlwind, and said,

7 ᴿGird up thy loins now like a man: ᴿI will demand of thee, and declare thou unto me.

8 ᴿWilt thou also disannul my judgment? wilt thou condemn me, that thou mayest be righteous?

9 Hast thou an arm like God? or canst thou thunder with ᴿa voice like him?

10 ᴿDeck thyself now *with* majesty and excellency; and array thyself with glory and beauty.

11 Cast abroad the rage of thy wrath: and behold every one *that is* proud, and abase him.

12 Look on every one *that is* ᴿproud, *and* bring him low; and tread down the wicked in their place.

13 Hide them in the dust together; *and* bind their faces in secret.

14 Then will I also confess unto thee that thine own right hand can save thee.

15 Behold now ᴺbē′-hĕ-mōth, which I made with thee; he eateth grass as an ox.

16 Lo now, his strength *is* in his loins, and his force *is* in the navel of his belly.

17 ᴺHe moveth his tail like a cedar: the sinews of his stones are wrapped together.

18 His bones *are as* strong pieces of brass; his bones *are* like bars of iron.

19 He *is* the chief of the ways of God: he that made him can make his sword to approach *unto him.*

20 Surely the mountains ᴿbring him forth food, where all the beasts of the field play.

21 He lieth under the shady trees, in the covert of the reed, and fens.

22 The shady trees cover him *with* their shadow; the willows of the brook compass him about.

23 Behold, ᴺhe drinketh up a river, *and* hasteth not: he trusteth that he can draw up Jordan into his mouth.

24 ᴺHe taketh it with his eyes: *his* nose pierceth through snares.

CHAPTER 41

The power of God in the leviathan

CANST thou draw out ᴿlē-vī′ ă-thăn ᴺ with an hook? or his tongue with a cord ᴺ*which* thou lettest down?

2 Canst thou ᴿput an hook into his nose? or bore his jaw through with a thorn?

3 Will he make many supplications unto thee? will he speak soft *words* unto thee?

4 Will he make a covenant with thee? wilt thou take him for a servant for ever?

5 Wilt thou play with him as *with* a bird? or wilt thou bind him for thy maidens?

6 Shall the companions make a banquet of him? shall they part him among the merchants?

7 Canst thou fill his skin with barbed irons? or his head with fish spears?

8 Lay thine hand upon him, remember the battle, do no more.

9 Behold, the hope of him is in vain: shall not *one* be cast down even at the sight of him?

10 None *is* so fierce that dare stir him up: who then is able to stand before me?

11 ᴿWho hath prevented me, that I should repay *him?* ᴿwhatsoever *is* under the whole heaven is mine.

12 I will not conceal his parts, nor his power, nor his comely proportion.

13 Who can discover the face of his garment? *or* who can come *to him* ᴺwith his double bridle?

14 Who can open the doors of his face? his teeth *are* terrible round about.

Center column notes

CHAP. 40
BC 1520
17 Or, *He setteth up*
20 Ps. 104:14
23 Heb. *he oppresseth*
24 Or, *Will* any take him in his sight, or, *bore his nose with a gin?,* ch. 41:1, 2

CHAP. 41
BC 1520
1 Ps. 104:26
1 Is. 27:1
1 i.e. *a whale,* or, *a whirlpool*
1 Heb. which *thou drownest?*
2 Is. 37:29
11 Rom. 11:35
11 Ex. 19:5
Deut. 10:14
Ps. 24:1 & 50:12
1 Cor. 10:26, 28
13 Or, *within*

Heb. *strong pieces of shields* 15
Heb. *sorrow rejoiceth* 22
Heb. *The fallings* 23
Or, *breastplate* 26
Heb. *Sharp pieces of potsherd* 30
Or, *who behave themselves without fear* 33

CHAP. 42
BC 1520
Gen. 18:14 2
Mat. 19:26
Mark 10:27
& 14:36
Luke 18:27
Or, *no thought of thine can be hindered* 2
ch. 38:2 3
Ps. 40:5 3
& 131:1 & 139:6
ch. 38:3 & 40:7 4

---

15 *His* ᴺscales *are his* pride, shut up together *as with* a close seal.

16 One is so near to another, that no air can come between them.

17 They are joined one to another, they stick together, that they cannot be sundered.

18 By his neesings a light doth shine, and his eyes *are* like the eyelids of the morning.

19 Out of his mouth go burning lamps, *and* sparks of fire leap out.

20 Out of his nostrils goeth smoke, as *out* of a seething pot or caldron.

21 His breath kindleth coals, and a flame goeth out of his mouth.

22 In his neck remaineth strength, and ᴺsorrow is turned into joy before him.

23 ᴺThe flakes of his flesh are joined together: they are firm in themselves; they cannot be moved.

24 His heart is as firm as a stone; yea, as hard as a peice of the nether *millstone.*

25 When he raiseth up himself, the mighty are afraid: by reason of breakings they purify themselves.

26 The sword of him that layeth at him cannot hold: the spear, the dart, nor the ᴺhabergeon.

27 He esteemeth iron as straw, *and* brass as rotten wood.

28 The arrow cannot make him flee: slingstones are turned with him into stubble.

29 Darts are counted as stubble: he laugheth at the shaking of a spear.

30 ᴺSharp stones *are* under him: he spreadeth sharp pointed things upon the mire.

31 He maketh the deep to boil like a pot: he maketh the sea like a pot of ointment.

32 He maketh a path to shine after him; *one* would think the deep *to be* hoary.

33 Upon earth there is not his like, ᴺwho is made without fear.

34 He beholdeth all high *things:* he *is* a king over all the children of pride.

CHAPTER 42

Job's repentance

THEN Job answered the Lord, and said,

2 I know that thou ᴿcanst do every *thing,* and *that* ᴺno thought can be withholden from thee.

3 ᴿWho *is* he that hideth counsel without knowledge? therefore have I uttered that I understood not; ᴿthings too wonderful for me, which I knew not.

4 Hear, I beseech thee, and I will speak: ᴿI will demand of thee, and declare thou unto me.

5 I have heard of thee by the hearing of the ear: but now mine eye seeth thee.

6 Wherefore I Rabhor *myself,* and repent in dust and ashes.

God reproves Job's three friends

7 And it was *so,* that after the LORD had spoken these words unto Job, the LORD said to Ĕ-lĭ'-phăz the Tē'-măn-īte, My wrath is kindled against thee, and against thy two friends: for ye have not spoken of me *the thing that is* right, as my servant Job *hath.*

8 Therefore take unto you now Rseven bullocks and seven rams, and Rgo to my servant Job, and offer up for yourselves a burnt offering; and my servant Job shall Rpray for you: for Nhim will I accept: lest I deal with you *after your* folly, in that ye have not spoken of me *the thing which is* right, like my servant Job.

9 So Ĕ-lĭ'-phăz the Tē'-măn-īte and Bildad the Shû'-hīte *and* Zō'-phär the Nā-ăm'-ă-thīte went, and did according as the LORD commanded them: the LORD also accepted NJob.

Job's fortunes restored

10 RAnd the LORD turned the captivity of Job, when he prayed for his friends: also the

LORD Ngave Job Rtwice as much as he had before.

11 Then came there unto him Rall his brethren, and all his sisters, and all they that had been of his acquaintance before, and did eat bread with him in his house: and they bemoaned him, and comforted him over all the evil that the LORD had brought upon him: every man also gave him a piece of money, and every one an earring of gold.

12 So the LORD blessed Rthe latter end of Job more than his beginning: for he had Rfourteen thousand sheep, and six thousand camels, and a thousand yoke of oxen, and a thousand she asses.

13 RHe had also seven sons and three daughters.

14 And he called the name of the first, Jĕ-mī'-mă; and the name of the second, Kĕ-zī'-ă; and the name of the third, Kĕr'-ĕn-hăp'-pŭch.

15 And in all the land were no women found *so* fair as the daughters of Job: and their father gave them inheritance among their brethren.

16 After this Rlived Job an hundred and forty years, and saw his sons, and his sons' sons, *even* four generations.

17 So Job died, *being* old and Rfull of days.

CHAP. 42	
BC 1520	
6 Ezra 9:6	
ch. 40:4	
8 Num. 23:1	
8 Mat. 5:24	
8 Gen. 20:17	
Jas. 5:15, 16	
1 John 5:16	
8 Heb. *his face,* or, *person,* 1 Sam. 25:35	
Mal. 1:8	
9 Heb. *the face of Job*	
10 Ps. 14:7 & 126:1	
Heb. *added all that* had been *to Job unto the double*	10
Is. 40:2	10
See ch. 19:13	11
ch. 8:7	12
Jas. 5:11	
See ch. 1:3	12
ch. 1:2	13
ch. 5:26	16
Prov. 3:16	
Gen. 25:8	17

THE
BOOK OF PSALMS

The word "psalm" comes to us from the Greek word "psalmos", meaning "a song to be sung to the accompaniment of the harp". The book of Psalms, called "Praises" in Hebrew, is a collection of one hundred and fifty sacred songs, poems, and odes written over an extended period by numerous authors: David, the most celebrated psalmist and major contributor, Asaph, the sons of Korah, and others. The collection of these psalms may have been unified under Ezra's supervision at the time of the restoration of worship at Jerusalem.

As early as Davidic times the Israelites sang psalms, called "graduals" while journeying to worship on Mt. Zion. Incorporation of the Psalms in the liturgy of the Christian church indicates the deep reverence accorded this book. It has come to be termed the "official" prayer book of Christianity.

The Psalms reflect the complete scope of experience common to the human race; emotions and personal feelings, ranging from imprecatory prayers to thanksgiving and praise. Penitential psalms such as 32, 51, and others manifest the author's profoundly sorrowful confession of sin with a plea for forgiveness. Messianic psalms such as 16, 22, and others portray the future suffering, death, resurrection, and the spiritual kingdom of the Messiah. Psalms 120 – 134 reflect the joys of pilgrimages to worship in Jerusalem, while historical psalms such as 78, 135, and others recount the mercies of God evident in Israel's past. A division of the Psalms preserved in the Hebrew text is as follows: I (Psalms 1 – 41), II (42 – 72), III (73 – 89), IV (90 – 106), V (107 – 150).

PSALM 1

The righteous and the wicked

BLESSED Ris the man that walketh not in the counsel of the Nungodly, nor standeth in the way of sinners, Rnor sitteth in the seat of the scornful.

2 But Rhis delight *is* in the law of the LORD;

Rand in his law doth he meditate day and night.

3 And he shall be like a tree Rplanted by the rivers of water, that bringeth forth his fruit in his season; his leaf also shall not Nwither; and whatsoever he doeth shall Rprosper.

4 The ungodly *are* not so: but *are* Rlike the chaff which the wind driveth away.

5 Therefore the ungodly shall not stand in

PSALM 1	
1 Prov. 4:14	
1 Or, *wicked*	
1 Ps. 26:4	
2 Ps. 119:35	
Josh. 1:8	2
Ps. 119:1	
Jer. 17:8	3
Ezek. 47:12	
Heb. *fade*	3
Gen. 39:3	3
Job 21:18	4
Is. 17:13	

the judgment, nor sinners in the congregation of the righteous.

6 For ᴿthe Lᴏʀᴅ knoweth the way of the righteous: but the way of the ungodly shall perish.

PSALM 2

The kingdom of the Son

WᴴYᴿ do the heathen ᴺrage, and the people ᴺimagine a vain thing?   ★

2 The kings of the earth set themselves, and the rulers take counsel together, against the Lᴏʀᴅ, and against his ᴿanointed, *saying,*   ★

3 ᴿLet us break their bands asunder, and cast away their cords from us.   ★

4 He that sitteth in the heavens ᴿshall laugh: the Lord shall have them in derision.   ★

5 Then shall he speak unto them in his wrath, and ᴺvex them in his sore displeasure.★

6 Yet have I ᴺset my king ᴿuponᴺ my holy hill of Zion.   ★

7 I will declare ᴺthe decree: the Lᴏʀᴅ hath said unto me, ᴿThou *art* my Son; this day have I begotten thee.   ★

8 ᴿAsk of me, and I shall give *thee* the heathen *for* thine inheritance, and the uttermost parts of the earth *for* thy possession.   ★

9 ᴿThou shalt break them with a rod of iron; thou shalt dash them in pieces like a potter's vessel.   ★

10 Be wise now therefore, O ye kings: be instructed, ye judges of the earth.   ★

11 ᴿServe the Lᴏʀᴅ with fear, and rejoice ᴿwith trembling.   ★

12 ᴿKiss the Son, lest he be angry, and ye perish *from* the way, when ᴿhis wrath is kindled but a little. ᴿBlessed *are* all they that put their trust in him.   ★

PSALM 3

A prayer of trust in God

A Psalm of David, *when he fled from Ăb′-să-lọm his son.

Lᴏʀᴅ, ᴿhow are they increased that trouble me! many *are* they that rise up against me.

2 Many *there be* which say of my soul, ᴿ*There is* no help for him in God. Sē′-läh.

3 But thou, O Lᴏʀᴅ, *art* ᴿa shield ᴺfor me; my glory, and ᴿthe lifter up of mine head.

4 I cried unto the Lᴏʀᴅ with my voice, and ᴿhe heard me out of his ᴿholy hill. Sē′-läh.

5 ᴿI laid me down and slept; I awaked; for the Lᴏʀᴅ sustained me.

6 ᴿI will not be afraid of ten thousands of people, that have set *themselves* against me round about.

7 Arise, O Lᴏʀᴅ; save me, O my God: ᴿfor

PSALM 1	
6 Ps. 37:18	
2 Tim. 2:19	

PSALM 2	
1 Acts 4:25	
1 Or, *tumultuously assemble*	
1 Heb. *meditate*	
2 John 1:41	
3 Luke 19:14	
4 Ps. 37:13	
Prov. 1:26	
5 Or, *trouble*	
6 Heb. *anointed*	
6 2 Sam. 5:7	
6 Heb. *upon Zion, the hill of my holiness*	
7 Or, *for a decree*	
7 Acts 13:33	
8 Ps. 22:27	
9 Ps. 89:23	
Rev. 2:27	
11 Heb. 12:28	
11 Phil. 2:12	
12 John 5:23	
12 Rev. 6:16	
12 Ps. 34:8	
Is. 30:18	
Rom. 9:33	

PSALM 3	
* 2 Sam. 15-18	
1 2 Sam. 15:12	
2 Ps. 71;11	
3 Ps. 28:7	
3 Or, *about*	
3 Ps. 27:6	
4 Ps. 34:4	
4 Ps. 2:6	
5 Lev. 26:6	
Prov. 3:24	
6 Ps. 27:3	
7 Job 16:10	
Lam. 3:30	
Is. 43:11	8

PSALM 4	
Or, *overseer*	*
Or, *be gracious unto me*	1
2 Tim. 2:19	3
2 Pet. 2:9	
Eph. 4:26	4
Ps. 77:6	4
Deut. 33:19	5
Ps. 50:14	
Ps. 37:3	5
Num. 6:26	6
Is. 9:3	7
Ps. 3:5	8
Lev. 25:18	8

PSALM 5	
Ps. 3:4	2
Ps. 80:5	3
Heb. *before thine eyes*	5
Rev. 21:8	6
Ps. 55:23	6
Heb. *the man of bloods and deceit*	6
Heb. *the temple of thy holiness*	7
Ps. 25:5	8

thou hast smitten all mine enemies *upon* the cheek bone; thou hast broken the teeth of the ungodly.

8 ᴿSalvation *belongeth* unto the Lᴏʀᴅ: thy blessing *is* upon thy people. Sē′-läh.

PSALM 4

An evening prayer of trust

To the *chief Musician on Nĕ-gĭ′-nŏth, A Psalm of David.

Hᴇᴀʀ me when I call, O God of my righteousness: thou hast enlarged me *when I was* in distress; ᴺhave mercy upon me, and hear my prayer.

2 O ye sons of men, how long *will ye turn* my glory into shame? *how long* will ye love vanity, *and* seek after leasing? Sē′-läh.

3 But know that ᴿthe Lᴏʀᴅ hath set apart him that is godly for himself: the Lᴏʀᴅ will hear when I call unto him.

4 ᴿStand in awe, and sin not: ᴿcommune with your own heart upon your bed, and be still. Sē′-läh.

5 Offer ᴿthe sacrifices of righteousness, and ᴿput your trust in the Lᴏʀᴅ.

6 *There be* many that say, Who will shew us *any* good? ᴿLᴏʀᴅ, lift thou up the light of thy countenance upon us.

7 Thou hast put ᴿgladness in my heart, more than in the time *that* their corn and their wine increased.

8 ᴿI will both lay me down in peace, and sleep: ᴿfor thou, Lᴏʀᴅ, only makest me dwell in safety.

PSALM 5

A morning prayer of trust

To the chief Musician upon Nĕ-hĭl′-ŏth, A Psalm of David.

Gɪᴠᴇ ear to my words, O Lᴏʀᴅ, consider my meditation.

2 Hearken unto the ᴿvoice of my cry, my King, and my God: for unto thee will I pray.

3 ᴿMy voice shalt thou hear in the morning, O Lᴏʀᴅ; in the morning will I direct *my prayer* unto thee, and will look up.

4 For thou *art* not a God that hath pleasure in wickedness: neither shall evil dwell with thee.

5 The foolish shall not stand ᴺin thy sight: thou hatest all workers of iniquity.

6 ᴿThou shalt destroy them that speak leasing: ᴿthe Lᴏʀᴅ will abhor ᴺthe bloody and deceitful man.

7 But as for me, I will come *into* thy house in the multitude of thy mercy: *and* in thy fear will I worship toward ᴺthy holy temple.

8 ᴿLead me, O Lᴏʀᴅ, in thy righteousness

because of [N]mine enemies; make thy way straight before my face.

9 For *there is* no [N]faithfulness [N]in their mouth; their inward part *is* [N]very wickedness; [R]their throat *is* an open sepulchre; [R]they flatter with their tongue.

10 [N]Destroy thou them, O God; let them fall [N]by their own counsels; cast them out in the multitude of their transgressions; for they have rebelled against thee.

11 But let all those that put their trust in thee [R]rejoice: let them ever shout for joy, because [N]thou defendest them: let them also that love thy name be joyful in thee.

12 For thou, LORD, wilt bless the righteous; with favour wilt thou [N]compass him as *with a* shield.

PSALM 6

A prayer in time of trouble

To the chief Musician on Nĕ-gî′-nōth *upon
*Shĕm′-ĭn-ĭth, A Psalm of David.

O LORD, rebuke me not in thine anger, neither chasten me in thy hot displeasure.

2 Have mercy upon me, O LORD; for I *am* weak: O LORD, [R]heal me; for my bones are vexed.

3 My soul is also sore vexed: but thou, O LORD, how long?

4 Return, O LORD, deliver my soul: oh save me for thy mercies' sake.

5 [R]For in death *there is* no remembrance of thee: in the grave who shall give thee thanks?

6 I am weary with my groaning; [N]all the night make I my bed to swim; I water my couch with my tears.

7 [R]Mine eye is consumed because of grief; it waxeth old because of all mine enemies.

8 [R]Depart from me, all ye workers of iniquity; for the LORD hath [R]heard the voice of my weeping.

9 The LORD hath heard my supplication; the LORD will receive my prayer.

10 Let all mine enemies be ashamed and sore vexed: let them return *and* be ashamed suddenly.

PSALM 7

A prayer for righteous judgment

*Shĭg-gâī′-ŏn of David, which he sang unto the LORD, *concerning the *words of Cŭsh the Benjamite.

O LORD my God, in thee do I put my trust: [R]save me from all them that persecute me, and deliver me:

PSALM 5

8 Heb. *those which observe me*
9 Or, *stedfastness*
9 Heb. *in his mouth,* i.e. *in the mouth of any of them*
9 Heb. *wickednesses*
9 Luke 11:44 Rom. 3:13
9 Ps. 62:4
10 Or, *Make them guilty*
10 Or, *from their counsels*
11 Is. 65:13
11 Heb. *thou coverest over,* or, *protectest them*
12 Heb. *crown him*

PSALM 6

* Ps. 12, title Or, *upon the eighth:*
* 1 Chr. 15:21
2 Hos. 6:1
5 Ps. 30:9
6 Or, *every night*
7 Job 17:7
8 Mat. 25:41
8 Ps. 3:4

PSALM 7

* Hab. 3:1
* 2 Sam. 16
* Or, *business*
1 Ps. 31:15

Is. 38:13	2
Ps. 50:22	2
Heb. *not a deliverer*	2
2 Sam. 16:7	3
1 Sam. 24:11	3
1 Sam. 24:7	4
Ps. 94:2	6
Ps. 44:23	6
Ps. 18:20	8
1 Sam. 16:7	9
Heb. *My buckler is* upon *God*	10
Ps. 125:4	10
Or, *God is a righteous judge*	11
Deut. 32:41	12
Job 15:35	14
Heb. *He hath digged a pit*	15
Job 4:8	15
Esth. 9:25	16

PSALM 8

Ps. 81, & 84, title	*
Ps. 148:13	1
Ps. 113:4	1
1 Cor. 1:27	2
Heb. *founded*	2
Ps. 44:16	2
Ps. 111:2	3

---

2 [R]Lest he tear my soul like a lion, [R]rending *it* in pieces, while *there is* [N]none to deliver.

3 O LORD my God, [R]if I have done this; if there be [R]iniquity in my hands;

4 If I have rewarded evil unto him that was at peace with me; (yea, [R]I have delivered him that without cause is mine enemy:)

5 Let the enemy persecute my soul, and take *it;* yea, let him tread down my life upon the earth, and lay mine honour in the dust. Sĕ′-läh.

6 Arise, O LORD, in thine anger, [R]lift up thyself because of the rage of mine enemies: and [R]awake for me *to* the judgment *that* thou hast commanded.

7 So shall the congregation of the people compass thee about: for their sakes therefore return thou on high.

8 The LORD shall judge the people: judge me, O LORD, [R]according to my righteousness, and according to mine integrity *that is* in me.

9 Oh let the wickedness of the wicked come to an end; but establish the just: [R]for the righteous God trieth the hearts and reins.

10 [N]My defence *is* of God, which saveth the [R]upright in heart.

11 [N]God judgeth the righteous, and God is angry *with the wicked* every day.

12 If he turn not, he will [R]whet his sword; he hath bent his bow, and made it ready.

13 He hath also prepared for him the instruments of death; he ordaineth his arrows against the persecutors.

14 [R]Behold, he travaileth with iniquity, and hath conceived mischief, and brought forth falsehood.

15 [N]He made a pit, and digged it, [R]and is fallen into the ditch *which* he made.

16 [R]His mischief shall return upon his own head, and his violent dealing shall come down upon his own pate.

17 I will praise the LORD according to his righteousness: and will sing praise to the name of the LORD most high.

PSALM 8

The incomparable majesty of God

To the chief Musician *upon Gĭt′-tĭth,
A Psalm of David.

O LORD our Lord, how [R]excellent *is* thy name in all the earth! who [R]hast set thy glory above the heavens.

2 [R]Out of the mouth of babes and sucklings hast thou [N]ordained strength because of thine enemies, that thou mightest still [R]the enemy and the avenger.

3 When I [R]consider thy heavens, the work of

thy fingers, the moon and the stars, which thou hast ordained;

4 [R]What is man, that thou art mindful of him? and the son of man, that thou visitest him?

5 For thou hast made him a little lower than the angels, and hast crowned him with glory and honour.

6 [R]Thou madest him to have dominion over the works of thy hands; [R]thou hast put all *things* under his feet:

7 [N]All sheep and oxen, yea, and the beasts of the field;

8 The fowl of the air, and the fish of the sea, *and whatsoever* passeth through the paths of the seas.

9 [R]O L ORD our Lord, how excellent *is* thy name in all the earth!

PSALM 9

Thanksgiving for God's justice

To the chief Musician upon Mŭth-lăb'-bĕn, A Psalm of David.

I WILL praise *thee,* O L ORD, with my whole heart; I will shew forth all thy marvellous works.

2 I will be glad and [R]rejoice in thee: I will sing praise to thy name, O [R]thou most High.

3 When mine enemies are turned back, they shall fall and perish at thy presence.

4 For [N]thou hast maintained my right and my cause; thou satest in the throne judging [N]right.

5 Thou hast rebuked the heathen, thou hast destroyed the wicked, thou hast [R]put out their name for ever and ever.

6 [N]O thou enemy, destructions are come to a perpetual end: and thou hast destroyed cities; their memorial is perished with them.

7 [R]But the L ORD shall endure for ever: he hath prepared his throne for judgment.

8 And [R]he shall judge the world in righteousness, he shall minister judgment to the people in uprightness.

9 [R]The L ORD also will be [N]a refuge for the oppressed, a refuge in times of trouble.

10 And they that [R]know thy name will put their trust in thee: for thou, L ORD, hast not forsaken them that seek thee.

11 Sing praises to the L ORD, which dwelleth in Zion: [R]declare among the people his doings.

12 [R]When he maketh inquisition for blood, he remembereth them: he forgetteth not the cry of the [N]humble.

13 Have mercy upon me, O L ORD; consider my trouble *which I suffer* of them that hate

PSALM 8	
4	Job 7:17
6	Gen. 1:26
6	Heb. 2:8
7	Heb. *Flocks and oxen all of them*
9	ver. 1

PSALM 9	
2	Ps. 5:11
2	Ps. 83:18
4	Heb. *thou hast made my judgment*
4	Heb. *in righteousness*
5	Prov. 10:7
6	Or, *The destructions of the enemy are come to a perpetual end: and* their *cities hast thou destroyed, etc.*
7	Heb. 1:11
8	Ps. 96:13
9	Ps. 32:7
9	Heb. *an high place*
10	Ps. 91:14
11	Ps. 107:22
12	Gen. 9:5
12	Or, *afflicted*

Ps. 13:5	14
Ps. 7:15, 16	15
Ex. 7:5	16
Ps. 92:3	16
i.e. *Meditation*	16
Job 8:13	17
Ps. 12:5	18
Prov. 23:18	18

PSALM 10	
Heb. *In the pride of the wicked he doth persecute*	2
Ps. 7:16	2
Ps. 94:4	3
Heb. *soul's*	3
Prov. 28:4	3
Or, *the covetous blesseth* himself, *he abhorreth the* LORD	3
Or, *all his thoughts* are, There is *no God*	4
Ps. 14:1	4
Eccl. 8:11	6
Is. 56:12	
Rev. 18:7	6
Heb. *unto generation and generation*	6
Rom. 3:14	7
Heb. *deceits*	7
Or, *iniquity*	7
Heb. *hide themselves*	8
Heb. *in the secret places*	9
Heb. *He breaketh himself*	10
Or, *into his strong parts*	10
Job 22:13	11

me, thou that liftest me up from the gates of death:

14 That I may shew forth all thy praise in the gates of the daughter of Zion: I will [R]rejoice in thy salvation.

15 [R]The heathen are sunk down in the pit *that* they made: in the net which they hid is their own foot taken.

16 The L ORD is [R]known *by* the judgment *which* he executeth: the wicked is snared in the work of his own hands. [R]Hĭg-gā́-ŏn.[N] Sē'-läh.

17 The wicked shall be turned into hell, *and* all the nations [R]that forget God.

18 [R]For the needy shall not alway be forgotten: [R]the expectation of the poor shall *not* perish for ever.

19 Arise, O L ORD; let not man prevail: let the heathen be judged in thy sight.

20 Put them in fear, O L ORD: *that* the nations may know themselves *to be but* men. Sē'-läh.

PSALM 10

Prayer for judgment of the wicked

W HY standest thou afar off, O L ORD? *why* hidest thou *thyself* in times of trouble?

2 [N]The wicked in *his* pride doth persecute the poor: [R]let them be taken in the devices that they have imagined.

3 For the wicked [R]boasteth of his [N]heart's desire, and [R]blesseth[N] the covetous, *whom* the L ORD abhorreth.

4 The wicked, through the pride of his countenance, will not seek *after God:* [N]God *is* not in all his [R]thoughts.

5 His ways are always grievous; thy judgments *are* far above out of his sight: *as for* all his enemies, he puffeth at them.

6 [R]He hath said in his heart, I shall not be moved: [R]for *I shall* [N]never *be* in adversity.

7 [R]His mouth is full of cursing and [N]deceit and fraud: under his tongue *is* mischief and [N]vanity.

8 He sitteth in the lurking places of the villages: in the secret places doth he murder the innocent: his eyes [N]are privily set against the poor.

9 He lieth in wait [N]secretly as a lion in his den: he lieth in wait to catch the poor: he doth catch the poor, when he draweth him into his net.

10 [N]He croucheth, *and* humbleth himself, that the poor may fall [N]by his strong ones.

11 He hath said in his heart, God hath forgotten: [R]he hideth his face; he will never see *it.*

12 Arise, O Lord; O God, ᴿlift up thine hand: forget not the ᴺhumble.

13 Wherefore doth the wicked contemn God? he hath said in his heart, Thou wilt not require *it*.

14 Thou hast seen *it;* for thou beholdest mischief and spite, to requite *it* with thy hand: the poor ᴿcommitteth ᴺ himself unto thee; ᴿthou art the helper of the fatherless.

15 Break thou the arm of the wicked and the evil *man:* seek out his wickedness *till* thou find none.

16 ᴿThe Lord *is* King for ever and ever: the heathen are perished out of his land.

17 Lord, thou hast heard the desire of the humble: thou wilt ᴺprepare their heart, thou wilt cause thine ear to hear:

18 To ᴿjudge the fatherless and the oppressed, that the man of the earth may no more ᴺoppress.

PSALM 11

The righteous find refuge in God

To the chief Musician,
A Psalm of David.

Iᴺᴿ the Lord put I my trust: how say ye to my soul, Flee *as* a bird to your mountain?

2 For, lo, ᴿthe wicked bend *their* bow, they make ready their arrow upon the string, that they may ᴺprivily shoot at the upright in heart.

3 ᴿIf the foundations be destroyed, what can the righteous do?

4 The Lord *is* in his holy temple, the Lord's throne *is* in heaven: ᴿhis eyes behold, his eyelids try, the children of men.

5 The Lord ᴿtrieth the righteous: but the wicked and him that loveth violence his soul hateth.

6 Upon the wicked he shall rain ᴺsnares, fire and brimstone, and ᴺan horrible tempest: ᴿ*this shall be* the portion of their cup.

7 For the righteous Lord ᴿloveth righteousness; his countenance doth behold the upright.

PSALM 12

God's pure promises

To the chief Musician *upon* Shĕm′-ĭn-ĭth, A Psalm of David.

HᴺELP, Lord; for the godly man ceaseth; for the faithful fail from among the children of men.

2 ᴿThey speak vanity every one with his neighbour: *with* flattering lips *and* with ᴺa double heart do they speak.

3 The Lord shall cut off all flattering lips, *and* the tongue that speaketh ᴺproud things:

4 Who have said, With our tongue will we

prevail; our lips ᴺ*are* our own: who *is* lord over us?

5 For the oppression of the poor, for the sighing of the needy, now will I arise, saith the Lord; I will set *him* in safety *from him that* ᴺpuffeth at him.

6 The words of the Lord *are* ᴿpure words: *as* silver tried in a furnace of earth, purified seven times.

7 Thou shalt keep them, O Lord, thou shalt preserve ᴺthem from this generation for ever.

8 The wicked walk on every side, when ᴺthe vilest men are exalted.

PSALM 13

Trust in time of doubt

To the *chief Musician, A Psalm of David.

HOW long wilt thou forget me, O Lord? for ever? ᴿhow long wilt thou hide thy face from me?

2 How long shall I take counsel in my soul, *having* sorrow in my heart daily? how long shall mine enemy be exalted over me?

3 Consider *and* hear me, O Lord my God: ᴿlighten mine eyes, ᴿlest I sleep the *sleep of* death;

4 Lest mine enemy say, I have prevailed against him; *and* those that trouble me rejoice when I am moved.

5 But I have trusted in thy mercy; my heart shall rejoice in thy salvation.

6 I will sing unto the Lord, because he hath dealt bountifully with me.

PSALM 14

Foolishness of men

To the chief Musician, *A Psalm* of David.

THE ᴿfool hath said in his heart, *There is* no God. They are corrupt, they have done abominable works, *there is* none that doeth good.

2 ᴿThe Lord looked down from heaven upon the children of men, to see if there were any that did understand, *and* seek God.

3 They are all gone aside, they are *all* together become ᴺfilthy: *there is* none that doeth good, no, not one.

4 Have all the workers of iniquity no knowledge? who eat up my people *as* they eat bread, and ᴿcall not upon the Lord.

5 There ᴺwere they in great fear: for God *is* in the generation of the righteous.

6 Ye have shamed the counsel of the poor, because the Lord *is* his ᴿrefuge.

7 ᴿOhᴺ that the salvation of Israel *were come* out of Zion! ᴿwhen the Lord bringeth

---

back the captivity of his people, Jacob shall rejoice, *and* Israel shall be glad.

PSALM 15

Members of God's household

A Psalm of David.

LORD, ᴿwho shall ᴺabide in thy tabernacle? who shall dwell in thy holy hill?

2 He that walketh uprightly, and worketh righteousness, and speaketh the truth in his heart.

3 *He that* backbiteth not with his tongue, nor doeth evil to his neighbour, ᴿnor ᴺtaketh up a reproach against his neighbour.

4 ᴿIn whose eyes a vile person is contemned; but he honoureth them that fear the LORD. *He that* sweareth to *his own* hurt, and changeth not.

5 *He that* putteth not out his money to usury, nor taketh reward against the innocent. He that doeth these *things* ᴿshall never be moved.

PSALM 16

God, source of goodness

Mĭch′-tăm of David.

PRESERVE me, O God: for in thee do I put my trust.

2 *O my soul,* thou hast said unto the LORD, Thou *art* my Lord: ᴿmy goodness *extendeth* not to thee;

3 *But* to the saints that *are* in the earth, and *to* the excellent, in whom *is* all my delight.

4 Their sorrows shall be multiplied *that* ᴺhasten *after* another *god:* their drink offerings of blood will I not offer, ᴿnor take up their names into my lips.

5 The LORD *is* the portion ᴺof mine inheritance and of my cup: thou maintainest my lot.

6 The lines are fallen unto me in pleasant *places;* yea, I have a goodly heritage.

7 I will bless the LORD, who hath given me counsel: my reins also instruct me in the night seasons.

8 I have set the LORD always before me: because *he is* at my right hand, I shall not be moved. ★

9 Therefore my heart is glad, and my glory rejoiceth: my flesh also shall ᴺrest in hope. ★

10 ᴿFor thou wilt not leave my soul in hell; neither wilt thou suffer thine Holy One to see corruption. ★

11 Thou wilt shew me the ᴿpath of life: in thy presence *is* fulness of joy; at thy right hand *there are* pleasures for evermore.

PSALM 15	
1	Ps. 24:3, *etc.*
1	Heb. *sojourn*
3	Ex. 23:1
3	Or, *receiveth, or, endureth*
4	Esth. 3:2
5	2 Pet 1:10

PSALM 16	
*	Ps. 56–60
*	Or, *A golden Psalm of David*
2	Job 35:7
4	Or, *give gifts to another*
4	Ex. 23:13
5	Heb. *of my part*
9	Heb. *dwell confidently*
10	Ps. 49:15
11	Mat. 7:14

PSALM 17	
Heb. *justice*	1
Heb. *without lips of deceit*	1
Job 23:10	3
Ps. 119:133	5
Heb. *be not moved*	5
Ps. 116:2	6
Or, *that savest them which trust* in thee *from those that rise up against thy right hand*	7
Heb. *that waste me*	9
Heb. *my enemies against the soul*	9
1 Sam. 2:3	10
Heb. *The likeness of him (i.e. of every one of them) is as a lion that desireth to ravin*	12
Heb. *sitting*	12
Heb. *prevent his face*	13
Or, *by thy sword*	13
Or, *by thine hand*	14
Or, *their children are full*	14
1 John 3:2	15
Ps. 4:6, 7 & 16:11	15

PSALM 18	
Ps. 36, title	*
2 Sam. 22	*

PSALM 17

Cry for God's protection

A Prayer of David.

HEAR ᴺthe right, O LORD, attend unto my cry, give ear unto my prayer, *that goeth* ᴺnot out of feigned lips.

2 Let my sentence come forth from thy presence; let thine eyes behold the things that are equal.

3 Thou hast proved mine heart; thou hast visited *me* in the night; ᴿthou hast tried me, *and* shalt find nothing; I am purposed *that* my mouth shall not transgress.

4 Concerning the works of men, by the word of thy lips I have kept *me from* the paths of the destroyer.

5 ᴿHold up my goings in thy paths, *that* my footsteps ᴺslip not.

6 ᴿI have called upon thee, for thou wilt hear me, O God: incline thine ear unto me, *and hear* my speech.

7 Shew thy marvellous lovingkindness, O thou ᴺthat savest by thy right hand them which put their trust *in thee* from those that rise up *against them.*

8 Keep me as the apple of the eye, hide me under the shadow of thy wings,

9 From the wicked ᴺthat oppress me, *from* ᴺmy deadly enemies, *who* compass me about.

10 They are inclosed in their own fat: with their mouth they ᴿspeak proudly.

11 They have now compassed us in our steps: they have set their eyes bowing down to the earth;

12 ᴺLike as a lion *that* is greedy of his prey, and as it were a young lion ᴺlurking in secret places.

13 Arise, O LORD, ᴺdisappoint him, cast him down: deliver my soul from the wicked, ᴺ*which is* thy sword:

14 From men ᴺ*which are* thy hand, O LORD, from men of the world, *which have* their portion in *this* life, and whose belly thou fillest with thy hid *treasure:* ᴺthey are full of children, and leave the rest of their *substance* to their babes.

15 As for me, ᴿI will behold thy face in righteousness: ᴿI shall be satisfied, when I awake, with thy likeness.

PSALM 18

God's perfect way

To the chief Musician, *A Psalm* of David, *the servant of the LORD, who spake unto the LORD the words of *this song in the day *that* the LORD delivered him from the hand of all his enemies, and from the hand of Saul: And he said,

I [R]WILL love thee, O Lord, my strength.

2 The Lord is my rock, and my fortress, and my deliverer; my God, [N]my strength, [R]in whom I will trust; my buckler, and the horn of my salvation, and my high tower.

3 I will call upon the Lord, [R]who is worthy to be praised: so shall I be saved from mine enemies.

4 [R]The sorrows of death compassed me, and the floods of [N]ungodly men made me afraid.

5 The [N]sorrows of hell compassed me about: the snares of death prevented me.

6 In my distress I called upon the Lord, and cried unto my God: he heard my voice out of his temple, and my cry came before him, even into his ears.

7 [R]Then the earth shook and trembled; the foundations also of the hills moved and were shaken, because he was wroth.

8 There went up a smoke [N]out of his nostrils, and fire out of his mouth devoured: coals were kindled by it.

9 [R]He bowed the heavens also, and came down: and darkness was under his feet.

10 [R]And he rode upon a cherub, and did fly: yea, [R]he did fly upon the wings of the wind.

11 He made darkness his secret place; [R]his pavilion round about him were dark waters and thick clouds of the skies.

12 [R]At the brightness that was before him his thick clouds passed, hail stones and coals of fire.

13 The Lord also thundered in the heavens, and the Highest gave [R]his voice; hail stones and coals of fire.

14 [R]Yea, he sent out his arrows, and scattered them; and he shot out lightnings, and discomfited them.

15 Then the channels of water were seen, and the foundations of the world were discovered at thy rebuke, O Lord, at the blast of the breath of thy nostrils.

16 [R]He sent from above, he took me, he drew me out of [N]many waters.

17 He delivered me from my strong enemy, and from them which hated me: for they were too strong for me.

18 They prevented me in the day of my calamity: but the Lord was my stay.

19 [R]He brought me forth also into a large place; he delivered me, because he delighted in me.

20 [R]The Lord rewarded me according to my righteousness; according to the cleanness of my hands hath he recompensed me.

21 For I have kept the ways of the Lord, and have not wickedly departed from my God.

22 For all his judgments were before me,

and I did not put away his statutes from me.

23 I was also upright [N]before him, and I kept myself from mine iniquity.

24 [R]Therefore hath the Lord recompensed me according to my righteousness, according to the cleanness of my hands in his eyesight.

25 [R]With the merciful thou wilt shew thyself merciful; with an upright man thou wilt shew thyself upright;

26 With the pure thou wilt shew thyself pure; and [R]with the froward thou wilt [N]shew thyself froward.

27 For thou wilt save the afflicted people; but wilt bring down [R]high looks.

28 [R]For thou wilt light my [N]candle: the Lord my God will enlighten my darkness.

29 For by thee I have [N]run through a troop; and by my God have I leaped over a wall.

30 As for God, [R]his way is perfect: [R]the word of the Lord is [N]tried: he is a buckler [R]to all those that trust in him.

31 [R]For who is God save the Lord? or who is a rock save our God?

32 It is God that [R]girdeth me with strength, and maketh my way perfect.

33 [R]He maketh my feet like hinds' feet, and [R]setteth me upon my high places.

34 [R]He teacheth my hands to war, so that a bow of steel is broken by mine arms.

35 Thou hast also given me the shield of thy salvation: and thy right hand hath holden me up, and [N]thy gentleness hath made me great.

36 Thou hast enlarged my steps under me, [R]that [N]my feet did not slip.

37 I have pursued mine enemies, and overtaken them: neither did I turn again till they were consumed.

38 I have wounded them that they were not able to rise: they are fallen under my feet.

39 For thou hast girded me with strength unto the battle: thou hast [N]subdued under me those that rose up against me.

40 Thou hast also given me the necks of mine enemies; that I might destroy them that hate me.

41 They cried, but there was none to save them: [R]even unto the Lord, but he answered them not.

42 Then did I beat them small as the dust before the wind: I did [R]cast them out as the dirt in the streets.

43 Thou hast delivered me from the strivings of the people; and [R]thou hast made me the head of the heathen: [R]a people whom I have not known shall serve me.

44 [N]As soon as they hear of me, they shall obey me: [N]the strangers shall [N]submit themselves unto me.

45 ᴿThe strangers shall fade away, and be afraid out of their close places.

46 The LORD liveth; and blessed *be* my rock; and let the God of my salvation be exalted.

47 *It is* God that ᴺavengeth me, ᴿand ᴺsubdueth the people under me.

48 He delivereth me from mine enemies: yea, ᴿthou liftest me up above those that rise up against me: thou hast delivered me from the ᴺviolent man.

49 ᴿTherefore will I ᴺgive thanks unto thee, O LORD, among the heathen, and sing praises unto thy name.

50 ᴿGreat deliverance giveth he to his king; and sheweth mercy to his anointed, to David, and to his seed for evermore.

PSALM 19

God's glory in works and word

To the chief Musician, A Psalm of David.

THE ᴿheavens declare the glory of God; and the firmament sheweth his handywork.

2 Day unto day uttereth speech, and night unto night sheweth knowledge.

3 *There is* no speech nor language, ᴺᴺ*where* their voice is not heard.

4 ᴿTheirᴺ line is gone out through all the earth, and their words to the end of the world. In them hath he set a tabernacle for the sun,

5 Which *is* as a bridegroom coming out of his chamber, ᴿ*and* rejoiceth as a strong man to run a race.

6 His going forth *is* from the end of the heaven, and his circuit unto the ends of it: and there is nothing hid from the heat thereof.

7 ᴿThe ᴺlaw of the LORD *is* perfect, ᴺconverting the soul: the testimony of the LORD *is* sure, making wise the simple.

8 The statutes of the LORD *are* right, rejoicing the heart: the commandment of the LORD *is* pure, enlightening the eyes.

9 The fear of the LORD *is* clean, enduring for ever: the judgments of the LORD *are* ᴺtrue *and* righteous altogether.

10 More to be desired *are they* than gold, yea, than much fine gold: sweeter also than honey and ᴺthe honeycomb.

11 Moreover by them is thy servant warned: *and* in keeping of them *there is* great reward.

12 Who can understand *his* errors? cleanse thou me from secret *faults.*

13 Keep back thy servant also from presumptuous *sins;* let them not have dominion over me: then shall I be upright, and I shall

be innocent from ᴺthe great transgression.

14 Let the words of my mouth, and the meditation of my heart, be acceptable in thy sight, O LORD, ᴺmy strength, and my ᴿredeemer.

PSALM 20

Prayer for victory

To the chief Musician, A Psalm of David.

THE LORD hear thee in the day of trouble; the name of the God of Jacob ᴺdefend thee;

2 Send ᴺthee help from the sanctuary, and ᴺstrengthen thee out of Zion;

3 Remember all thy offerings, and ᴺaccept thy burnt sacrifice; Sē'-läh.

4 Grant thee according to thine own heart, and fulfil all thy counsel.

5 We will rejoice in thy salvation, and in the name of our God we will set up *our* banners: the LORD fulfil all thy petitions.

6 Now know I that the LORD saveth his anointed; he will hear him ᴺfrom his holy heaven ᴺwith the saving strength of his right hand.

7 Some *trust* in chariots, and some in horses: but we will remember the name of the LORD our God.

8 They are brought down and fallen: but we are risen, and stand upright.

9 Save, LORD: let the king hear us when we call.

PSALM 21

Rewards of trust

To the chief Musician, A Psalm of David.

THE king shall joy in thy strength, O LORD; and in thy salvation how greatly shall he rejoice!

2 Thou hast given him his heart's desire, and hast not withholden the request of his lips. Sē'-läh.

3 For thou preventest him with the blessings of goodness: thou settest a crown of pure gold on his head.

4 ᴿHe asked life of thee, *and* thou gavest *it* him, *even* length of days for ever and ever.

5 His glory *is* great in thy salvation: honour and majesty hast thou laid upon him.

6 For thou hast ᴺmade him most blessed for ever: thou hast ᴺmade him exceeding glad with thy countenance.

7 For the king trusteth in the LORD, and through the mercy of the most High he shall not be moved.

8 Thine hand shall find out all thine enemies:

PSALM 18

45 Mic. 7:17
47 Heb. *giveth avengements for me*
47 Ps. 47:3
47 Or, *destroyeth*
48 Ps. 59:1
48 Heb. *man of violence*
49 Rom. 15:9
49 Or, *confess*
50 Ps. 144:10

PSALM 19

1 Is. 40:22
3 Or, *without these their voice is heard*
3 Heb. *without their voice heard*
4 Rom. 10:18
4 Or, *Their rule,* or, *direction*
5 Eccl. 1:5
7 Ps. 111:7
7 Or, *doctrine*
7 Or, *restoring*
9 Heb. *truth*
10 Heb. *the dropping of honeycombs*

Or, *much*   13
Heb. *my rock*   14
Is. 47:4   14

PSALM 20

Heb. *set thee on an high place*   1
Heb. *thy place*   2
Heb. *support thee* 2
Heb. *turn to ashes:* or, *make fat* 3
Heb. *from the heaven of his holiness* 6
Heb. *by the strength of the salvation of his right hand* 6

PSALM 21

Ps. 61:5, 6   4
Heb. *set him to be blessings,* Ps. 72:17 6
Heb. *gladded him with joy* 6

thy right hand shall find out those that hate thee.

9 Thou shalt make them as a fiery oven in the time of thine anger: the LORD shall swallow them up in his wrath, and the fire shall devour them.

10 Their fruit shalt thou destroy from the earth, and their seed from among the children of men.

11 For they intended evil against thee: they imagined a mischievous device, *which* they are not able *to perform*.

12 Therefore [N]shalt thou make them turn their [N]back, *when* thou shalt make ready *thine arrows* upon thy strings against the face of them.

13 Be thou exalted, LORD, in thine own strength: *so* will we sing and praise thy power.

PSALM 22

Cry of the forsaken

To the chief Musician upon *Âi′-jĕ-lĕth Shā′-här, A Psalm of David.

MY [R]God, my God, why hast thou forsaken me? *why art thou so* far [N]from helping me, *and from* the words of my roaring? ★

2 O my God, I cry in the daytime, but thou hearest not; and in the night season, and [N]am not silent.

3 But thou *art* holy, *O thou* that inhabitest the [R]praises of Israel.

4 Our fathers trusted in thee: they trusted, and thou didst deliver them.

5 They cried unto thee, and were delivered: [R]they trusted in thee, and were not confounded.

6 But I *am* [R]a worm, and no man; [R]a reproach of men, and despised of the people. ★

7 [R]All they that see me laugh me to scorn: they [N]shoot out the lip, [R]they shake the head, *saying*, ★

8 [R]He[N] trusted on the LORD *that* he would deliver him: [R]let him deliver him, [N]seeing he delighted in him. ★

9 [R]But thou *art* he that took me out of the womb: thou [N]didst make me hope *when I was* upon my mother's breasts.

10 I was cast upon thee from the womb: [R]thou *art* my God from my mother's belly.

11 Be not far from me; for trouble *is* near; for *there is* [N]none to help.

12 [R]Many bulls have compassed me: strong *bulls* of Bā′-shan have beset me round.

13 [R]They [N]gaped upon me *with* their mouths, *as* a ravening and a roaring lion. ★

14 I am poured out like water, [R]and all my

bones are [N]out of joint: my heart is like wax; it is melted in the midst of my bowels.

15 [R]My strength is dried up like a potsherd; and [R]my tongue cleaveth to my jaws; and thou hast brought me into the dust of death.

16 For dogs have compassed me: the assembly of the wicked have inclosed me: [R]they pierced my hands and my feet. ★

17 I may tell all my bones: [R]they look *and* stare upon me. ★

18 [R]They part my garments among them, and cast lots upon my vesture. ★

19 But be not thou far from me, O LORD: O my strength, haste thee to help me.

20 Deliver my soul from the sword; [R]my[N] darling [N]from the power of the dog.

21 [R]Save me from the lion's mouth: [R]for thou hast heard me from the horns of the unicorns.

22 [R]I will declare thy name unto [R]my brethren: in the midst of the congregation will I praise thee. ★

23 [R]Ye that fear the LORD, praise him; all ye the seed of Jacob, glorify him; and fear him, all ye the seed of Israel.

24 For he hath not despised nor abhorred the affliction of the afflicted; neither hath he hid his face from him; but [R]when he cried unto him, he heard.

25 [R]My praise *shall be* of thee in the great congregation: [R]I will pay my vows before them that fear him.

26 The meek shall eat and be satisfied: they shall praise the LORD that seek him: your heart shall live for ever.

27 All the ends of the world shall remember and turn unto the LORD: and all the kindreds of the nations shall worship before thee.

28 [R]For the kingdom *is* the LORD'S: and he *is* the governor among the nations.

29 [R]All *they that be* fat upon earth shall eat and worship: [R]all they that go down to the dust shall bow before him: and none can keep alive his own soul.

30 A seed shall serve him; [R]it shall be accounted to the LORD for a generation.

31 [R]They shall come, and shall declare his righteousness unto a people that shall be born, that he hath done *this*. ★

PSALM 23

The Shepherd Psalm

A Psalm of David.

THE LORD *is* [R]my shepherd; [R]I shall not want.

2 [R]He maketh me to lie down in [N]green pastures: [R]he leadeth me beside the [N]still waters.

3 He restoreth my soul: [R]he leadeth me in

Center reference column

PSALM 21

12 Or, *thou shalt set them* as *a butt:* See Job 7:20
12 Heb. *shoulder*

PSALM 22

* Or, *the hind of the morning*
1 Mark 15:34
1 Heb. *from my salvation*
2 Heb. *there is no silence to me*
3 Deut. 10:21
5 Is. 49:23
6 Job 25:6
6 Is. 53:3
7 Mat. 27:39
7 Heb. *open*
7 Job 16:4
8 Mat. 27:43
8 Heb. *He rolled himself on the LORD*
8 Ps. 91:14
8 Or, *if he delight in him*
9 Ps. 71:6
9 Or, *keptest me in safety*
10 Is. 46:3
11 Heb. *not a helper*
12 Ps. 68:30
13 Lam. 2:16
13 Heb. *opened their mouths against me*
14 Dan. 5:6

Or, *sundered*	14
Prov. 17:22	15
John 19:28	15
Mat. 27:35	16
Luke 23:27, 35	17
Luke 23:34	18
Ps. 35:17	20
Heb. *my only one*	20
Heb. *from the hand*	20
2 Tim. 4:17	21
Is. 34:7	21
Heb. 2:12	22
Rom. 8:29	22
Ps. 135:19	23
Heb. 5:7	24
Ps. 35:18	25
Eccl. 5:4	25
Mat. 6:13	28
Ps. 45:12	29
Is. 26:19	29
Ps. 87:6	30
Ps. 78:6	31

PSALM 23

Is. 40:11	1
John 10:11	1
Phil. 4:19	1
Ezek. 34:14	2
Heb. *pastures of tender grass*	2
Rev. 7:17	2
Heb. *waters of quietness*	2
Ps. 5:8	3

the paths of righteousness for his name's sake.

4 Yea, though I walk through the valley of [R]the shadow of death, [R]I will fear no evil: [R]for thou *art* with me; thy rod and thy staff they comfort me.

5 Thou preparest a table before me in the presence of mine enemies: thou [R]anointest[N] my head with oil; my cup runneth over.

6 Surely goodness and mercy shall follow me all the days of my life: and I will dwell in the house of the LORD [N]for ever.

PSALM 24

The King of glory

A Psalm of David.

THE [R]earth *is* the LORD's, and the fulness thereof; the world, and they that dwell therein.

2 For he hath founded it upon the seas, and established it upon the floods.

3 [R]Who shall ascend into the hill of the LORD? or who shall stand in his holy place?

4 [N]He that hath [R]clean hands, and [R]a pure heart; who hath not lifted up his soul unto vanity, nor [R]sworn deceitfully.

5 He shall receive the blessing from the LORD, and righteousness from the God of his salvation.

6 This *is* the generation of them that seek him, that [R]seek thy face, [N]O Jacob. Sē′-läh.

7 [R]Lift up your heads, O ye gates; and be ye lift up, ye everlasting doors; [R]and the King of glory shall come in.

8 Who *is* this King of glory? The LORD strong and mighty, the LORD mighty in battle.

9 Lift up your heads, O ye gates; even lift *them* up, ye everlasting doors; and the King of glory shall come in.

10 Who is this King of glory? The LORD of hosts, he *is* the King of glory. Sē′-läh.

PSALM 25

Prayer for guidance and help

A *Psalm* of David.

UNTO [R]thee, O LORD, do I lift up my soul.

2 O my God, I [R]trust in thee: let me not be ashamed, [R]let not mine enemies triumph over me.

3 Yea, let none that wait on thee be ashamed: let them be ashamed which transgress without cause.

4 [R]Shew me thy ways, O LORD; teach me thy paths.

5 Lead me in thy truth, and teach me: for thou *art* the God of my salvation; on thee do I wait all the day.

PSALM 23	
4	Job 10:21, 22
	Ps. 44:19
4	Ps. 3:6
4	Is. 43:2
5	Ps. 92:10
5	Heb. *makest fat*
6	Heb. *to length of days*
PSALM 24	
1	Ex. 9:29
	Job 41:11
3	Ps. 15:1
4	Heb. *The clean of hands*
4	Job 17:9
	1 Tim. 2:8
4	Mat. 5:8
4	Ps. 15:4
6	Ps. 27:8
6	Or, O God of *Jacob*
7	Is. 26:2
7	Ps. 97:6
	Hag. 2:7
	Mal. 3:1
PSALM 25	
1	Ps. 86:4
2	Ps. 34:8
	Is. 28:16
2	Ps. 13:4
4	Ex. 33:13
	Ps. 5:8

Ps. 103:17	6
Is. 63:15	
Heb. *thy bowels*	6
Job 13:26	7
Jer. 3:25	
Ps. 51:1	7
Ps. 31:3 & 79:9	11
Rom. 5:20	11
Ps. 37:23	12
Prov. 19:23	13
Heb. *shall lodge in goodness*	13
Ps. 37:11	13
Prov. 3:32	14
John 7:17	
Or, *and his covenant to make them know* it	14
Ps. 141:8	15
Heb. *bring forth*	15
Ps. 69:16	16
2 Sam. 16:12	18
Heb. *hatred of violence*	19
Ps. 130:8	22
PSALM 26	
Ps. 7:8	1
2 Ki. 20:3	1
Ps. 28:7	1
Prov. 29:25	
Ps. 17:3	2
2 Ki. 20:3	3
Ps. 1:1	4
Ps. 31:6	5
Ps. 1:1	5
Ps. 73:13	6

6 Remember, O LORD, [R]thy[N] tender mercies and thy lovingkindnesses; for they *have been* ever of old.

7 Remember not [R]the sins of my youth, nor my transgressions: [R]according to thy mercy remember thou me for thy goodness' sake, O LORD.

8 Good and upright *is* the LORD: therefore will he teach sinners in the way.

9 The meek will he guide in judgment: and the meek will he teach his way.

10 All the paths of the LORD *are* mercy and truth unto such as keep his covenant and his testimonies.

11 [R]For thy name's sake, O LORD, pardon mine iniquity; [R]for it *is* great.

12 What man *is* he that feareth the LORD? [R]him shall he teach in the way *that* he shall choose.

13 [R]His soul [N]shall dwell at ease; and [R]his seed shall inherit the earth.

14 [R]The secret of the LORD *is* with them that fear him; [N]and he will shew them his covenant.

15 [R]Mine eyes *are* ever toward the LORD; for he shall [N]pluck my feet out of the net.

16 [R]Turn thee unto me, and have mercy upon me; for I *am* desolate and afflicted.

17 The troubles of my heart are enlarged: *O* bring thou me out of my distresses.

18 [R]Look upon mine affliction and my pain; and forgive all my sins.

19 Consider mine enemies; for they are many; and they hate me with [N]cruel hatred.

20 O keep my soul, and deliver me: let me not be ashamed; for I put my trust in thee.

21 Let integrity and uprightness preserve me; for I wait on thee.

22 [R]Redeem Israel, O God, out of all his troubles.

PSALM 26

Plea for vindication

A *Psalm* of David.

JUDGE [R]me, O LORD; for I have [R]walked in mine integrity: [R]I have trusted also in the LORD; *therefore* I shall not slide.

2 [R]Examine me, O LORD, and prove me; try my reins and my heart.

3 For thy lovingkindness *is* before mine eyes: and [R]I have walked in thy truth.

4 [R]I have not sat with vain persons, neither will I go in with dissemblers.

5 I have [R]hated the congregation of evil doers; [R]and will not sit with the wicked.

6 [R]I will wash mine hands in innocency: so will I compass thine altar, O LORD:

7 That I may publish with the voice of

thanksgiving, and tell of all thy wondrous works.

8 LORD, ᴿI have loved the habitation of thy house, and the place ᴺwhere thine honour dwelleth.

9 ᴿGatherᴺ not my soul with sinners, nor my life with ᴺbloody men:

10 In whose hands *is* mischief, and their right hand is ᴺfull of ᴿbribes.

11 But as for me, I will walk in mine integrity: redeem me, and be merciful unto me.

12 ᴿMy foot standeth in an ᴿeven place: ᴿin the congregations will I bless the LORD.

PSALM 27

The strength of life

A Psalm of David.

THE LORD *is* ᴿmy light and ᴿmy salvation; whom shall I fear? ᴿthe LORD *is* the strength of my life; of whom shall I be afraid?

2 When the wicked, *even* mine enemies and my foes, ᴺcame upon me to ᴿeat up my flesh, they stumbled and fell.

3 ᴿThough an host should encamp against me, my heart shall not fear: though war should rise against me, in this *will* I *be* confident.

4 ᴿOne *thing* have I desired of the LORD, that will I seek after; that I may ᴿdwell in the house of the LORD all the days of my life, to behold ᴿtheᴺ beauty of the LORD, and to inquire in his temple.

5 For ᴿin the time of trouble he shall hide me in his pavilion: in the secret of his tabernacle shall he hide me; he shall ᴿset me up upon a rock.

6 And now shall ᴿmine head be lifted up above mine enemies round about me: therefore will I offer in his tabernacle sacrifices ᴺof joy; I will sing, yea, I will sing praises unto the LORD.

7 Hear, O LORD, *when* I cry with my voice: have mercy also upon me, and answer me.

8 ᴺ*When thou saidst,* Seek ye my face; my heart said unto thee, Thy face, LORD, will I seek.

9 ᴿHide not thy face *far* from me; put not thy servant away in anger: thou hast been my help; leave me not, neither forsake me, O God of my salvation.

10 ᴿWhen my father and my mother forsake me, then the LORD ᴺwill take me up.

11 ᴿTeach me thy way, O LORD, and lead me in ᴺa plain path, because of ᴺmine enemies.

12 Deliver me not over unto the will of mine

enemies: for false witnesses are risen up against me, and such as breathe out cruelty.

13 *I had fainted,* unless I had believed to see the goodness of the LORD ᴿin the land of the living.

14 Wait on the LORD: be of good courage, and he shall strengthen thine heart: wait, I say, on the LORD.

PSALM 28

A cry for help

A *Psalm* of David.

UNTO thee will I cry, O LORD my rock; ᴿbe not silent ᴺto me: ᴿlest, *if* thou be silent to me, I become like them that go down into the pit.

2 Hear the voice of my supplications, when I cry unto thee, ᴿwhen I lift up my hands ᴿtowardᴺ thy holy oracle.

3 Draw me not away with the wicked, and with the workers of iniquity, ᴿwhich speak peace to their neighbours, but mischief *is* in their hearts.

4 ᴿGive them according to their deeds, and according to the wickedness of their endeavours: give them after the work of their hands; render to them their desert.

5 Because ᴿthey regard not the works of the LORD, nor the operation of his hands, he shall destroy them, and not build them up.

6 Blessed *be* the LORD, because he hath heard the voice of my supplications.

7 The LORD *is* ᴿmy strength and my shield; my heart ᴿtrusted in him, and I am helped: therefore my heart greatly rejoiceth; and with my song will I praise him.

8 The LORD *is* ᴺtheir strength, and he *is* the ᴿsavingᴺ strength of his anointed.

9 Save thy people, and bless ᴿthine inheritance: ᴺfeed them also, ᴿand lift them up for ever.

PSALM 29

The voice of the LORD

A Psalm of David.

GIVEᴿ unto the LORD, O ᴺye mighty, give unto the LORD glory and strength.

2 Give unto the LORD ᴺthe glory due unto his name; worship the LORD ᴺin ᴿthe beauty of holiness.

3 The voice of the LORD *is* upon the waters: ᴿthe God of glory thundereth: the LORD *is* upon ᴺmany waters.

4 The voice of the LORD *is* ᴺpowerful; the voice of the LORD *is* ᴺfull of majesty.

5 The voice of the LORD breaketh the cedars; yea, the LORD breaketh ᴿthe cedars of Lĕb′-ă-nọn.

6 ᴿHe maketh them also to skip like a calf; Lĕb′-ă-nọn and ᴿSĩr′-ĭ-ọn like a young unicorn.

7 The voice of the LORD ᴺdivideth the flames of fire.

8 The voice of the LORD shaketh the wilderness; the LORD shaketh the wilderness of ᴿKā′-dĕsh.

9 The voice of the LORD maketh the hinds ᴺto calve, and discovereth the forests: and in his temple ᴺdoth every one speak of *his* glory.

10 The LORD sitteth upon the flood; yea, ᴿthe LORD sitteth King for ever.

11 ᴿThe LORD will give strength unto his people; the LORD will bless his people with peace.

PSALM 30

Thanksgiving for God's mercy

A Psalm *and* Song *at the dedication of the house of David.

I WILL extol thee, O LORD; for thou hast ᴿlifted me up, and hast not made my foes to ᴿrejoice over me.

2 O LORD my God, I cried unto thee, and thou hast healed me.

3 O LORD, ᴿthou hast brought up my soul from the grave: thou hast kept me alive, that I should not go down to the pit.

4 Sing unto the LORD, O ye saints of his, and give thanks ᴺat the remembrance of his holiness.

5 For ᴿhisᴺ anger *endureth but* a moment; ᴿin his favour *is* life: weeping may endure ᴺfor a night, but ᴺjoy *cometh* in the morning.

6 And in my prosperity I said, I shall never be moved.

7 LORD, by thy favour thou hast ᴺmade my mountain to stand strong: ᴿthou didst hide thy face, *and* I was troubled.

8 I cried to thee, O LORD; and unto the LORD I made supplication.

9 What profit *is there* in my blood, when I go down to the pit? ᴿShall the dust praise thee? shall it declare thy truth?

10 Hear, O LORD, and have mercy upon me: LORD, be thou my helper.

11 Thou hast turned for me my mourning into dancing: thou hast put off my sackcloth, and girded me with gladness;

12 To the end that ᴺmy glory may sing praise to thee, and not be silent. O LORD my God, I will give thanks unto thee for ever.

PSALM 29

5 Is. 2:13
6 Ps. 114:4
6 Deut. 3:9
7 Heb. *cutteth out*
8 Num. 13:26
9 Or, *to be in pain*
9 Or, *every whit of it uttereth, etc.*
10 Ps. 10:16
11 Ps. 28:8

PSALM 30

* Deut. 20:5
1 Ps. 28:9
1 Ps. 25:2
3 Ps. 86:13
4 Or, *to the memorial*
5 Ps. 103:9
5 Heb. *there is but a moment in his anger*
5 Ps. 63:3
5 Heb. *in the evening*
5 Heb. *singing*
7 Heb. *settled strength for my mountain*
7 Ps. 104:29
9 Ps. 6:5
12 i.e. my *tongue,* or, my *soul:* See Ps. 57:8

PSALM 31

Ps. 22:5   1
Ps. 71:2   2
Heb. *to me for a rock of strength*   2
Ps. 18:2   3
Ps. 23:3   3
Luke 23:46   5
Jonah 2:8   6
John 10:27   7
Deut. 32:30   8
Ps. 6:7   9
Is. 53:4   11
Job 19:13   11
Ps. 64:8   11
Ps. 88:4, 5   12
Heb. *a vessel that perisheth* 12
Jer. 20:10   13
Lam. 2:22   13
Mat. 27:1   13
Ps. 4:6   16
Ps. 25:2   17
Ps. 115:17   17
Or, *let them be cut off for the grave* 17
Ps. 120:2   18
Ps. 94:4   18
Heb. *a hard thing* 18
Is. 64:4   19

PSALM 31

A prayer of trust

To the chief Musician, A Psalm of David.

I Nᴿ thee, O LORD, do I put my trust; let me never be ashamed: deliver me in thy righteousness.

2 ᴿBow down thine ear to me; deliver me speedily: be thou ᴺmy strong rock, for an house of defence to save me.

3 ᴿFor thou *art* my rock and my fortress; therefore ᴿfor thy name's sake lead me, and guide me.

4 Pull me out of the net that they have laid privily for me: for thou *art* my strength.

5 ᴿInto thine hand I commit my spirit: thou hast redeemed me, O LORD God of truth.

6 I have hated them ᴿthat regard lying vanities: but I trust in the LORD.

7 I will be glad and rejoice in thy mercy: for thou hast considered my trouble; thou hast ᴿknown my soul in adversities;

8 And hast not ᴿshut me up into the hand of the enemy: thou hast set my feet in a large room.

9 Have mercy upon me, O LORD, for I am in trouble: ᴿmine eye is consumed with grief, *yea,* my soul and my belly.

10 For my life is spent with grief, and my years with sighing: my strength faileth because of mine iniquity, and my bones are consumed.

11 ᴿI was a reproach among all mine enemies, but ᴿespecially among my neighbours, and a fear to mine acquaintance: ᴿthey that did see me without fled from me.

12 ᴿI am forgotten as a dead man out of mind: I am like ᴺa broken vessel.

13 ᴿFor I have heard the slander of many: ᴿfear *was* on every side: while they ᴿtook counsel together against me, they devised to take away my life.

14 But I trusted in thee, O LORD: I said, Thou *art* my God.

15 My times *are* in thy hand: deliver me from the hand of mine enemies, and from them that persecute me.

16 ᴿMake thy face to shine upon thy servant: save me for thy mercies' sake.

17 ᴿLet me not be ashamed, O LORD; for I have called upon thee: let the wicked be ashamed, *and* ᴿletᴺ them be silent in the grave.

18 ᴿLet the lying lips be put to silence; which ᴿspeak ᴺgrievous things proudly and contemptuously against the righteous.

19 ᴿOh how great *is* thy goodness, which thou hast laid up for them that fear thee; *which*

thou hast wrought for them that trust in thee before the sons of men!

20 [R]Thou shalt hide them in the secret of thy presence from the pride of man: [R]thou shalt keep them secretly in a pavilion from the strife of tongues.

21 Blessed *be* the LORD: for [R]he hath shewed me his marvellous kindness [R]in a [N]strong city.

22 For [R]I said in my haste, [R]I am cut off from before thine eyes: nevertheless thou heardest the voice of my supplications when I cried unto thee.

23 [R]O love the LORD, all ye his saints: *for* the LORD preserveth the faithful, and plentifully rewardeth the proud doer.

24 [R]Be of good courage, and he shall strengthen your heart, all ye that hope in the LORD.

PSALM 32

Song of the forgiven man

A Psalm of David, Măs′-chîl.

B LESSED *is he whose* [R]transgression *is* forgiven, *whose* sin *is* covered.

2 Blessed *is* the man unto whom the LORD [R]imputeth not iniquity, and [R]in whose spirit *there is* no guile.

3 When I kept silence, my bones waxed old through my roaring all the day long.

4 For day and night thy [R]hand was heavy upon me: my moisture is turned into the drought of summer. Sē′-läh.

5 I acknowledged my sin unto thee, and mine iniquity have I not hid. [R]I said, I will confess my transgressions unto the LORD; and thou forgavest the iniquity of my sin. Sē′-läh.

6 [R]For this shall every one that is godly [R]pray unto thee [N]in a time when thou mayest be found: surely in the floods of great waters they shall not come nigh unto him.

7 [R]Thou *art* my hiding place; thou shalt preserve me from trouble; thou shalt compass me about with [R]songs of deliverance. Sē′-läh.

8 I will instruct thee and teach thee in the way which thou shalt go: [N]I will guide thee with mine eye.

9 [R]Be ye not as the horse, *or* as the mule, *which* have [R]no understanding: whose mouth must be held in with bit and bridle, lest they come near unto thee.

10 [R]Many sorrows *shall be* to the wicked: but [R]he that trusteth in the LORD, mercy shall compass him about.

11 [R]Be glad in the LORD, and rejoice, ye

righteous: and shout for joy, all *ye that are* upright in heart.

PSALM 33

Praise to the Creator and Preserver

R EJOICE [R]in the LORD, O ye righteous: *for* [R]praise is comely for the upright.

2 Praise the LORD with harp: sing unto him with the psaltery [R]*and* an instrument of ten strings.

3 [R]Sing unto him a new song; play skilfully with a loud noise.

4 For the word of the LORD *is* right; and all his works *are done* in truth.

5 [R]He loveth righteousness and judgment: [R]the earth is full of the [N]goodness of the LORD.

6 [R]By the word of the LORD were the heavens made; and all the host of them [R]by the breath of his mouth.

7 [R]He gathereth the waters of the sea together as an heap: he layeth up the depth in storehouses.

8 Let all the earth fear the LORD: let all the inhabitants of the world stand in awe of him.

9 For [R]he spake, and it was *done;* he commanded, and it stood fast.

10 [R]The LORD [N]bringeth the counsel of the heathen to nought: he maketh the devices of the people of none effect.

11 [R]The counsel of the LORD standeth for ever, the thoughts of his heart [N]to all generations.

12 Blessed *is* the nation whose God *is* the LORD; *and* the people *whom* he hath [R]chosen for his own inheritance.

13 [R]The LORD looketh from heaven; he beholdeth all the sons of men.

14 From the place of his habitation he looketh upon all the inhabitants of the earth.

15 He fashioneth their hearts alike; [R]he considereth all their works.

16 [R]There is no king saved by the multitude of an host: a mighty man is not delivered by much strength.

17 [R]An horse *is* a vain thing for safety: neither shall he deliver *any* by his great strength.

18 [R]Behold, the eye of the LORD *is* [R]upon them that fear him, upon them that hope in his mercy;

19 To deliver their soul from death, and [R]to keep them alive in famine.

20 [R]Our soul waiteth for the LORD: he *is* our help and our shield.

21 For our [R]heart shall rejoice in him, because we have trusted in his holy name.

22 Let thy mercy, O LORD, be upon us, according as we hope in thee.

PSALM 34

Praise for God's salvation

A *Psalm* of David, when he changed his behavior before *Ă-bĭm′-ĕ-lĕch; who drove him away, and he departed.

I WILL ᴿbless the LORD at all times: his praise *shall* continually *be* in my mouth.

2 My soul shall make her ᴿboast in the LORD: ᴿthe humble shall hear *thereof*, and be glad.

3 O ᴿmagnify the LORD with me, and let us exalt his name together.

4 I ᴿsought the LORD, and he heard me, and delivered me from all my fears.

5 ᴺThey looked unto him, and were lightened: and their faces were not ashamed.

6 ᴿThis poor man cried, and the LORD heard *him,* and ᴿsaved him out of all his troubles.

7 ᴿThe angel of the LORD ᴿencampeth round about them that fear him, and delivereth them.

8 O ᴿtaste and see that the LORD *is* good: ᴿblessed *is* the man *that* trusteth in him.

9 O fear the LORD, ye his saints: for *there is* no want to them that fear him.

10 The young lions do lack, and suffer hunger: ᴿbut they that seek the LORD shall not want any good *thing.*

11 Come, ye children, hearken unto me: ᴿI will teach you the fear of the LORD.

12 ᴿWhat man *is he that* desireth life, *and* loveth *many* days, that he may see good?

13 Keep thy tongue from evil, and thy lips from speaking guile.

14 ᴿDepart from evil, and do good; ᴿseek peace, and pursue it.

15 ᴿThe eyes of the LORD *are* upon the righteous, and his ears *are open* unto their cry.

16 ᴿThe face of the LORD *is* against them that do evil, ᴿto cut off the remembrance of them from the earth.

17 *The righteous* cry, and ᴿthe LORD heareth, and delivereth them out of all their troubles.

18 ᴿThe LORD *is* nigh ᴿuntoᴺ them that are of a broken heart; and saveth such as be ᴺof a contrite spirit.

19 ᴿMany *are* the afflictions of the righteous: ᴿbut the LORD delivereth him out of them all.

20 He keepeth all his bones: ᴿnot one of them is broken.   ★

21 ᴿEvil shall slay the wicked: and they that hate the righteous ᴺshall be desolate.

22 The LORD ᴿredeemeth the soul of his servants: and none of them that trust in him shall be desolate.

PSALM 35

Prayer for divine defence

A *Psalm* of David.

PLEAD ᴿ*my cause,* O LORD, with them that strive with me: ᴿfight against them that fight against me.

2 ᴿTake hold of shield and buckler, and stand up for mine help.

3 Draw out also the spear, and stop *the way* against them that persecute me: say unto my soul, I *am* thy salvation.

4 ᴿLet them be confounded and put to shame that seek after my soul: let them be turned back and brought to confusion that devise my hurt.

5 ᴿLet them be as chaff before the wind: and let the angel of the LORD chase *them.*

6 Let their way be ᴿdarkᴺ and slippery: and let the angel of the LORD persecute them.

7 For without cause have they ᴿhid for me their net *in* a pit, *which* without cause they have digged for my soul.

8 Let ᴿdestruction come upon him ᴺat unawares; and let his net that he hath hid catch himself: into that very destruction let him fall.

9 And my soul shall be joyful in the LORD: it shall rejoice in his salvation.

10 All my bones shall say, LORD, ᴿwho *is* like unto thee, which deliverest the poor from him that is too strong for him, yea, the poor and the needy from him that spoileth him?

11 ᴺFalse witnesses did rise up; ᴺthey laid to my charge *things* that I knew not.

12 ᴿThey rewarded me evil for good *to* the ᴺspoiling of my soul.

13 But as for me, ᴿwhen they were sick, my clothing *was* sackcloth: I ᴺhumbled my soul with fasting; and my prayer returned into mine own bosom.

14 I ᴺbehaved myself ᴺas though *he had been* my friend *or* brother: I bowed down heavily, as one that mourneth *for his* mother.

15 But in mine ᴺadversity they rejoiced, and gathered themselves together: *yea,* ᴿthe abjects gathered themselves together against me, and I knew *it* not; they did ᴿtear *me,* and ceased not:

16 With hypocritical mockers in feasts, ᴿthey gnashed upon me with their teeth.

17 Lord, how long wilt thou ᴿlook on? rescue my soul from their destructions, ᴿmyᴺ darling from the lions.

PSALM 34
* Or, *Achish,*
1 Sam. 21:13
1 Eph. 5:20
2 Jer. 9:24
2 Ps. 119:74
3 Luke 1:46
4 Mat. 7:7
5 Or, *They flowed* unto him
6 Ps. 3:4
6 ver. 17, 19
7 Dan. 6:22
7 2 Ki. 6:17
8 1 Pet. 2:3
8 Ps. 2:12
10 Ps. 84:11
11 Ps. 32:8
12 1 Pet. 3:10
14 Ps. 37:27
14 Heb. 12:14
15 Job 36:7
16 Lev. 17:10
16 Prov. 10:7
17 Ps. 145:19
18 Ps. 145:18
18 Is. 57:15
18 Heb. *to the broken of heart*
18 Heb. *contrite of spirit*
19 Prov. 24:16
19 ver. 6, 17
20 John 19:36
21 Ps. 94:23
21 Or, *shall be guilty*

1 Ki. 1:29   22
Ps. 71:23

PSALM 35
Ps. 43:1   1
Ex. 14:25   1
Is. 42:13   2
Ps. 70:2, 3   4
Job 21:18   5
Ps. 1:4   6
Ps. 73:18   6
Heb. *darkness and slipperiness*
Ps. 9:15   7
1 Thes. 5:3   8
Heb. *which he knoweth not of* 8
Ex. 15:11   10
Heb. *Witnesses of wrong* 11
Heb. *they asked me* 11
John 10:32   12
Heb. *depriving* 12
Job 30:25   13
Or, *afflicted* 13
Heb. *walked*   14
Heb. *as a friend, as a brother to me* 14
Heb. *halting* 15
Job 30:1, 8   15
Job 16:9   15
Job 16:9   16
Lam. 2:16
Hab. 1:13   17
Ps. 22:20   17
Heb. *my only one* 17

18 I will give thee thanks in the great congregation: I will praise thee among ᴺmuch people.

19 ᴿLet not them that are mine enemies ᴺwrongfully rejoice over me: *neither* ᴿlet them wink with the eye ᴿthat hate me without a cause.

20 For they speak not peace: but they devise deceitful matters against *them that are* quiet in the land.

21 Yea, they ᴿopened their mouth wide against me, *and* said, ᴿAha, aha, our eye hath seen *it*.

22 *This* thou hast ᴿseen, O Lᴏʀᴅ: ᴿkeep not silence: O Lord, be not ᴿfar from me.

23 ᴿStir up thyself, and awake to my judgment, *even* unto my cause, my God and my Lord.

24 Judge me, O Lᴏʀᴅ my God, ᴿaccording to thy righteousness; and let them not rejoice over me.

25 Let them not say in their hearts, ᴺAh, so would we have it: let them not say, ᴿWe have swallowed him up.

26 Let them be ashamed and brought to confusion together that rejoice at mine hurt: let them be ᴿclothed with shame and dishonour that magnify *themselves* against me.

27 ᴿLet them shout for joy, and be glad, that favour ᴺmy righteous cause: yea, let them say continually, Let the Lᴏʀᴅ be magnified, which hath pleasure in the prosperity of his servant.

28 And my tongue shall speak of thy righteousness *and* of thy praise all the day long.

PSALM 36

God's faithfulness

To the chief Musician, *A Psalm* of David the servant of the Lᴏʀᴅ.

THE transgression of the wicked saith within my heart, *that* ᴿthere is no fear of God before his eyes.

2 For he flattereth himself in his own eyes, ᴺuntil his iniquity be found to be hateful.

3 The words of his mouth *are* iniquity and deceit: ᴿhe hath left off to be wise, *and* to do good.

4 ᴿHe deviseth ᴺmischief upon his bed; he setteth himself ᴿin a way *that is* not good; he abhorreth not evil.

5 Thy mercy, O Lᴏʀᴅ, *is* in the heavens; *and* thy faithfulness *reacheth* unto the clouds.

6 Thy righteousness *is* like ᴺthe great mountains; ᴿthy judgments *are* a great deep: O Lᴏʀᴅ, thou preservest man and beast.

7 How ᴺexcellent *is* thy lovingkindness, O

God! therefore the children of men ᴿput their trust under the shadow of thy wings.

8 ᴿThey shall be ᴺabundantly satisfied with the fatness of thy house; and thou shalt make them drink of ᴿthe river of thy pleasures.

9 ᴿFor with thee *is* the fountain of life: ᴿin thy light shall we see light.

10 O ᴺcontinue thy lovingkindness unto them that know thee; and thy righteousness to the upright in heart.

11 Let not the foot of pride come against me, and let not the hand of the wicked remove me.

12 There are the workers of iniquity fallen: they are cast down, and shall not be able to rise.

PSALM 37

God's care of the righteous

A Psalm of David.

FRET ᴿnot thyself because of evildoers, neither be thou envious against the workers of iniquity.

2 For they shall soon be cut down ᴿlike the grass, and wither as the green herb.

3 Trust in the Lᴏʀᴅ, and do good; *so* shalt thou dwell in the land, and ᴺverily thou shalt be fed.

4 ᴿDelight thyself also in the Lᴏʀᴅ; and he shall give thee the desires of thine heart.

5 ᴿCommitᴺ thy way unto the Lᴏʀᴅ; trust also in him; and he shall bring *it* to pass.

6 ᴿAnd he shall bring forth thy righteousness as the light, and thy judgment as the noonday.

7 ᴺRest in the Lᴏʀᴅ, ᴿand wait patiently for him: fret not thyself because of him who prospereth in his way, because of the man who bringeth wicked devices to pass.

8 Cease from anger, and forsake wrath: ᴿfret not thyself in any wise to do evil.

9 For evildoers shall be cut off: but those that wait upon the Lᴏʀᴅ, they shall ᴿinherit the earth.

10 For ᴿyet a little while, and the wicked *shall* not *be:* yea, ᴿthou shalt diligently consider his place, and it *shall* not *be*.

11 ᴿBut the meek shall inherit the earth; and shall delight themselves in the abundance of peace.

12 The wicked ᴺplotteth against the just, ᴿand gnasheth upon him with his teeth.

13 ᴿThe Lord shall laugh at him: for he seeth that ᴿhis day is coming.

14 The wicked have drawn out the sword, and have bent their bow, to cast down the poor

---

PSALM 35

18 Heb. *strong*
19 Ps. 13:4
19 Heb. *falsely,*
  Ps. 38:19
19 Job 15:12
19 Ps. 69:4
21 Ps. 22:13
21 Ps. 40:15
22 Ex. 3:7
22 Ps. 28:1
22 Ps. 10:1
23 Ps. 44:23
24 2 Thes. 1:6
25 Heb. *Ah, ah, our soul*
25 Lam. 2:16
26 Ps. 109:29
27 Rom. 12:15
27 Heb. *my righteousness*

PSALM 36

1 Rom. 3:18
2 Heb. *to find his iniquity to hate*
3 Jer. 4:22
4 Prov. 4:16
4 Or, *vanity*
4 Is. 65:2
6 Heb. *the mountains of God*
6 Rom. 11:33
7 Heb. *precious*

Ps. 17:8   7
Ps. 65:4   8
Heb. *watered*   8
Job 20:17   8
  Rev. 22:1
Jer. 2:13   9
1 Pet. 2:9   9
Heb. *draw out at length*   10

PSALM 37

Ps. 73:3   1
  Prov. 23:17
Ps. 90:5, 6   2
Heb. *in truth, or, stableness*   3
Is. 58:14   4
Ps. 55:22   5
  Mat. 6:25
Heb. *Roll thy way upon the LORD*   5
Job 11:17   6
Heb. *Be silent to the LORD*   7
Lam. 3:26   7
Ps. 73:3   8
  Eph. 4:26
Is. 57:13   9
Heb. 10:36   10
Job 7:10   10
Mat. 5:5   11
Or, *practiseth*   12
Ps. 35:16   12
Ps. 2:4   13
1 Sam. 26:10   13

and needy, *and* to slay [N]such as be of upright conversation.

15 [R]Their sword shall enter into their own heart, and their bows shall be broken.

16 [R]A little that a righteous man hath *is* better than the riches of many wicked.

17 For [R]the arms of the wicked shall be broken: but the LORD upholdeth the righteous.

18 The LORD [R]knoweth the days of the upright: and their inheritance shall be [R]for ever.

19 They shall not be ashamed in the evil time: and [R]in the days of famine they shall be satisfied.

20 But the wicked shall perish, and the enemies of the LORD *shall be* as [N]the fat of lambs: they shall consume; [R]into smoke shall they consume away.

21 The wicked borroweth, and payeth not again: but [R]the righteous sheweth mercy, and giveth.

22 [R]For *such as be* blessed of him shall inherit the earth; and *they that be* cursed of him shall be cut off.

23 [R]The steps of a *good* man are [N]ordered by the LORD: and he delighteth in his way.

24 [R]Though he fall, he shall not be utterly cast down: for the LORD upholdeth *him with* his hand.

25 I have been young, and *now* am old; yet have I not seen the righteous forsaken, nor his seed [R]begging bread.

26 [R]*He is* [N]ever merciful, and lendeth; and his seed *is* blessed.

27 [R]Depart from evil, and do good; and dwell for evermore.

28 For the LORD [R]loveth judgment, and forsaketh not his saints; they are preserved for ever: [R]but the seed of the wicked shall be cut off.

29 [R]The righteous shall inherit the land, and dwell therein for ever.

30 [R]The mouth of the righteous speaketh wisdom, and his tongue talketh of judgment.

31 [R]The law of his God *is* in his heart; none of his [N]steps shall slide.

32 The wicked [R]watcheth the righteous, and seeketh to slay him.

33 The LORD [R]will not leave him in his hand, nor [R]condemn him when he is judged.

34 [R]Wait on the LORD, and keep his way, and he shall exalt thee to inherit the land: [R]when the wicked are cut off, thou shalt see *it*.

35 [R]I have seen the wicked in great power, and spreading himself like [N]a green bay tree.

36 Yet he [R]passed away, and, lo, he *was* not: yea, I sought him, but he could not be found.

37 Mark the perfect *man*, and behold the upright: for [R]the end of *that* man *is* peace.

38 [R]But the transgressors shall be destroyed together: the end of the wicked shall be cut off.

39 But [R]the salvation of the righteous *is* of the LORD: he *is* their strength [R]in the time of trouble.

40 And [R]the LORD shall help them, and deliver them: he shall deliver them from the wicked, and save them, [R]because they trust in him.

PSALM 38

Prayer of confession

A Psalm of David, *to bring to remembrance.

O LORD, rebuke me not in thy wrath: neither chasten me in thy hot displeasure.

2 For [R]thine arrows stick fast in me, and [R]thy hand presseth me sore.

3 *There is* no soundness in my flesh because of thine anger; [R]neither *is there any* [N]rest in my bones because of my sin.

4 For [R]mine iniquities are gone over mine head: as an heavy burden they are too [R]heavy for me.

5 My wounds stink *and* are corrupt because of my foolishness.

6 I am [N]troubled; [R]I am bowed down greatly; [R]I go mourning all the day long.

7 For my loins are filled with a [R]loathsome *disease:* and *there is* no soundness in my flesh.

8 I am feeble and sore broken: [R]I have roared by reason of the disquietness of my heart.

9 Lord, all my desire *is* before thee; and my groaning is not hid from thee.

10 My heart panteth, my strength faileth me: as for [R]the light of mine eyes, it also [N]is gone from me.

11 [R]My lovers and my friends [R]stand aloof from my [N]sore; and [N]my kinsmen [R]stand afar off.

12 They also that seek after my life [R]lay snares *for me:* and they that seek my hurt [R]speak mischievous things, and imagine deceits all the day long.

13 But [R]I, as a deaf *man*, heard not; [R]and *I was* as a dumb man *that* openeth not his mouth.

14 Thus I was as a man that heareth not, and in whose mouth *are* no reproofs.

15 For [N]in thee, O LORD, [R]do I hope: thou wilt [N]hear, O Lord my God.

16 For I said, *Hear me,* ^Rlest *otherwise* they should rejoice over me: when my foot slippeth, they ^Rmagnify *themselves* against me.

17 For I *am* ready ^Nto halt, and my sorrow *is* continually before me.

18 For I will ^Rdeclare mine iniquity; I will be ^Rsorry for my sin.

19 But mine enemies ^N*are* lively, *and* they are strong: and they that hate me wrongfully are multiplied.

20 They also ^Rthat render evil for good are mine adversaries; because I follow *the thing that* good *is.*

21 Forsake me not, O LORD: O my God, ^Rbe not far from me.

22 Make haste ^Nto help me, O Lord my salvation.

PSALM 39

God is our hope

To the chief Musician, *even to* *Jĕ-dū′-thŭn, A Psalm of David.

I SAID, I will ^Rtake heed to my ways, that I sin not with my tongue: I will keep ^Nmy mouth with a bridle, while the wicked is before me.

2 ^RI was dumb with silence, I held my peace, *even* from good; and my sorrow was ^Nstirred.

3 My heart was hot within me, while I was musing the fire burned: *then* spake I with my tongue,

4 LORD, make me to know mine end, and the measure of my days, what it *is; that* I may know ^Nhow frail I *am.*

5 Behold, thou hast made my days *as* an handbreadth; and mine age *is* as nothing before thee: verily every man ^Nat his best state *is* altogether vanity. Sē′-läh.

6 Surely every man walketh in ^Na vain shew: surely they are disquieted in vain: ^Rhe heapeth up *riches,* and knoweth not who shall gather them.

7 And now, Lord, what wait I for? my hope *is* in thee.

8 Deliver me from all my transgressions: make me not ^Rthe reproach of the foolish.

9 ^RI was dumb, I opened not my mouth; because ^Rthou didst *it.*

10 Remove thy stroke away from me: I am consumed by the ^Nblow of thine hand.

11 When thou with rebukes dost correct man for iniquity, thou makest ^Nhis beauty ^Rto consume away like a moth: surely every man *is* vanity. Sē′-läh.

12 Hear my prayer, O LORD, and give ear unto my cry; hold not thy peace at my tears:

for I *am* a stranger with thee, *and* a sojourner, ^Ras all my fathers *were.*

13 ^RO spare me, that I may recover strength, before I go hence, and ^Rbe no more.

PSALM 40

Praise for God's help

To the chief Musician, A Psalm of David.

I ^RWAITED^N patiently for the LORD; and he inclined unto me, and heard my cry.

2 He brought me up also out of ^Nan horrible pit, out of ^Rthe miry clay, and ^Rset my feet upon a rock, *and* established my goings.

3 ^RAnd he hath put a new song in my mouth, *even* praise unto our God: many shall see *it,* and fear, and shall trust in the LORD.

4 ^RBlessed *is* that man that maketh the LORD his trust, and respecteth not the proud, nor such as turn aside to lies.

5 ^RMany, O LORD my God, *are* thy wonderful works *which* thou hast done, ^Rand thy thoughts *which are* to us-ward: ^Nthey cannot be reckoned up in order unto thee: *if* I would declare and speak *of them,* they are more than can be numbered.

6 Sacrifice and offering thou didst not desire; mine ears hast thou ^Nopened: burnt offering and sin offering hast thou not required. ★

7 Then said I, Lo, I come: in the volume of the book *it is* written of me, ★

8 ^RI delight to do thy will, O my God: yea, thy law *is* ^Rwithin^N my heart. ★

9 ^RI have preached righteousness in the great congregation: lo, ^RI have not refrained my lips, O LORD, thou knowest.

10 ^RI have not hid thy righteousness within my heart; I have declared thy faithfulness and thy salvation: I have not concealed thy lovingkindness and thy truth from the great congregation.

11 Withhold not thou thy tender mercies from me, O LORD: ^Rlet thy lovingkindness and thy truth continually preserve me.

12 For innumerable evils have compassed me about: ^Rmine iniquities have taken hold upon me, so that I am not able to look up; they are more than the hairs of mine head: therefore my heart ^Nfaileth me.

13 ^RBe pleased, O LORD, to deliver me: O LORD, make haste to help me.

14 ^RLet them be ashamed and confounded together that seek after my soul to destroy it; let them be driven backward and put to shame that wish me evil.

15 Let them be ^Rdesolate for a reward of their shame that say unto me, Aha, aha.

16 ᴿLet all those that seek thee rejoice and be glad in thee: let such as love thy salvation ᴿsay continually, The LORD be magnified.

17 ᴿBut I *am* poor and needy; *yet* the Lord thinketh upon me: thou *art* my help and my deliverer; make no tarrying, O my God.

PSALM 41

God sustains his own

To the chief Musician, A Psalm of David.

BLESSED *is* he that considereth ᴺthe poor: the LORD will deliver him ᴺin time of trouble.

2 The LORD will preserve him, and keep him alive; *and* he shall be blessed upon the earth: ᴿand ᴺthou wilt not deliver him unto the will of his enemies.

3 The LORD will strengthen him upon the bed of languishing: thou wilt ᴺmake all his bed in his sickness.

4 I said, LORD, be merciful unto me: heal my soul; for I have sinned against thee.

5 Mine enemies speak evil of me, When shall he die, and his name perish?

6 And if he come to see *me,* he speaketh vanity: his heart gathereth iniquity to itself; *when* he goeth abroad, he telleth *it.*

7 All that hate me whisper together against me: against me do they devise ᴺmy hurt.

8 ᴺAn evil disease, *say they,* cleaveth fast unto him: and *now* that he lieth he shall rise up no more.

9 ᴿYea, ᴺmine own familiar friend, in whom I trusted, ᴿwhich did eat of my bread, hath ᴺlifted up *his* heel against me.

10 But thou, O LORD, be merciful unto me, and raise me up, that I may requite them.

11 By this I know that thou favourest me, because mine enemy doth not triumph over me.

12 And as for me, thou upholdest me in mine integrity, and ᴿsettest me before thy face for ever.

13 ᴿBlessed *be* the LORD God of Israel from everlasting, and to everlasting. Ä'-mĕn, and Ä'-mĕn.

PSALM 42

Hope in God

To the chief Musician, *Mäs'-chil,* for the sons of Kôr'-ăh.

AS the hart ᴺpanteth after the water brooks, so panteth my soul after thee, O God.

Center references

PSALM 40
16 Ps. 70:4
16 Ps. 35:27
17 Ps. 70:5

PSALM 41
1 Or, *the weak, or, sick*
1 Heb. *in the day of evil*
2 Ps. 27:12
2 Or, *do not thou deliver*
3 Heb. *turn*
7 Heb. *evil to me*
8 Heb. *A thing of Belial*
9 2 Sam. 15:12
Job 19:19
Ps. 55:12
9 Heb. *the man of my peace*
9 Obad. 7
John 13:18
9 Heb. *magnified*
12 Job 36:7
Ps. 34:15
13 Ps. 106:48

PSALM 42
* Or, A Psalm *giving instruction of the sons, etc.:* See 1 Chr. 6:33
1 Heb. *brayeth*

Ps. 63:1	2
Ps. 80:5	3
Job 30:16	4
Is. 30:29	4
ver. 11	5
Heb. *bowed down*	5
Lam. 3:24	5
Or, *give thanks*	5
Or, *his presence is salvation*	5
Or, *the little hill,* Ps. 133:3	6
Ps. 88:7	7
Job 35:10	8
Ps. 38:6	9
Or, *killing*	10
Joel 2:17	10
Mic. 7:10	10
Ps. 43:5	11

PSALM 43
Ps. 26:1	1
Ps. 35:1	1
Or, *unmerciful*	1
Heb. *from a man of deceit and iniquity*	1
Ps. 42:9	2
Ps. 40:11 & 57:3	3
Ps. 3:4	3
Heb. *the gladness of my joy*	4
Ps. 42:5, 11	5

2 ᴿMy soul thirsteth for God, for the living God: when shall I come and appear before God?

3 ᴿMy tears have been my meat day and night, while they continually say unto me, Where *is* thy God?

4 When I remember these *things,* ᴿI pour out my soul in me: for I had gone with the multitude, ᴿI went with them to the house of God, with the voice of joy and praise, with a multitude that kept holyday.

5 ᴿWhy art thou ᴺcast down, O my soul? and *why* art thou disquieted in me? ᴿhope thou in God: for I shall yet ᴺpraise him ᴺ*for* the help of his countenance.

6 O my God, my soul is cast down within me: therefore will I remember thee from the land of Jordan, and of the Hĕr'-mō-nītes, from ᴺthe hill Mĭ'-zär.

7 Deep calleth unto deep at the noise of thy waterspouts: ᴿall thy waves and thy billows are gone over me.

8 *Yet* the LORD will command his lovingkindness in the daytime, and ᴿin the night his song *shall be* with me, *and* my prayer unto the God of my life.

9 I will say unto God my rock, Why hast thou forgotten me? ᴿwhy go I mourning because of the oppression of the enemy?

10 *As* with a ᴺsword in my bones, mine enemies reproach me; ᴿwhile they say daily unto me, Where *is* thy God?

11 ᴿWhy art thou cast down, O my soul? and why art thou disquieted within me? hope thou in God: for I shall yet praise him, *who is* the health of my countenance, and my God.

PSALM 43

Hope in God

JUDGE ᴿme, O God, and ᴿplead my cause against an ᴺungodly nation: O deliver me ᴺfrom the deceitful and unjust man.

2 For thou *art* the God of my strength: why dost thou cast me off? ᴿwhy go I mourning because of the oppression of the enemy?

3 ᴿO send out thy light and thy truth: let them lead me; let them bring me unto ᴿthy holy hill, and to thy tabernacles.

4 Then will I go unto the altar of God, unto God ᴺmy exceeding joy: yea, upon the harp will I praise thee, O God my God.

5 ᴿWhy art thou cast down, O my soul? and why art thou disquieted within me? hope in God: for I shall yet praise him, *who is* the health of my countenance, and my God.

PSALM 44

Plea for deliverance

To the chief Musician for the sons
of Kŏr′-ăh, Măs′-chĭl.

WE have heard with our ears, O God,
ᴿour fathers have told us, *what* work
thou didst in their days, in the times of old.

2 *How* ᴿthou didst drive out the heathen
with thy hand, and plantedst them; *how* thou
didst afflict the people, and cast them out.

3 For ᴿthey got not the land in possession by
their own sword, neither did their own arm
save them: but thy right hand, and thine arm,
and the light of thy countenance, ᴿbecause
thou hadst a favour unto them.

4 ᴿThou art my King, O God: command
deliverances for Jacob.

5 Through thee ᴿwill we push down our enemies: through thy name will we tread them
under that rise up against us.

6 For ᴿI will not trust in my bow, neither
shall my sword save me.

7 But thou hast saved us from our enemies,
and hast ᴿput them to shame that hated us.

8 ᴿIn God we boast all the day long, and
praise thy name for ever. Sē′-läh.

9 But ᴿthou hast cast off, and put us to
shame; and goest not forth with our armies.

10 Thou makest us to ᴿturn back from the
enemy: and they which hate us spoil for themselves.

11 ᴿThou hast given us ᴺlike sheep *appointed* for meat; and hast ᴿscattered us
among the heathen.

12 ᴿThou sellest thy people ᴺfor nought, and
dost not increase *thy wealth* by their price.

13 ᴿThou makest us a reproach to our
neighbours, a scorn and a derision to them that
are round about us.

14 ᴿThou makest us a byword among the
heathen, ᴿa shaking of the head among the
people.

15 My confusion *is* continually before me,
and the shame of my face hath covered me,

16 For the voice of him that reproacheth and
blasphemeth; ᴿby reason of the enemy and
avenger.

17 ᴿAll this is come upon us; yet have we
not forgotten thee, neither have we dealt
falsely in thy covenant.

18 Our heart is not turned back, ᴿneither
have our ᴺsteps declined from thy way;

19 Though thou hast sore broken us in ᴿthe
place of dragons, and covered us ᴿwith the
shadow of death.

20 If we have forgotten the name of our

God, or ᴿstretched out our hands to a strange
god;

21 ᴿShall not God search this out? for he
knoweth the secrets of the heart.

22 ᴿYea, for thy sake are we killed all the
day long; we are counted as sheep for the
slaughter.

23 ᴿAwake, why sleepest thou, O Lord?
arise, cast *us* not off for ever.

24 ᴿWherefore hidest thou thy face, *and*
forgettest our affliction and our oppression?

25 For ᴿour soul is bowed down to the dust:
our belly cleaveth unto the earth.

26 Arise ᴺfor our help, and redeem us for
thy mercies' sake.

PSALM 45

Song for the royal wedding

To the chief Musician *upon Shō-shănn′-ĭm, for the sons of
Kŏr′-ăh, *Măs′-chĭl, A Song of loves.

MY heart ᴺis inditing a good matter: I
speak of the things which I have made
touching the king: my tongue *is* the pen of a
ready writer.

2 Thou art fairer than the children of men:
ᴿgrace is poured into thy lips: therefore God
hath blessed thee for ever.   ★

3 Gird thy ᴿsword upon *thy* thigh, ᴿO *most*
mighty, with thy glory and thy majesty.

4 ᴿAnd in thy majesty ᴺride prosperously
because of truth and meekness *and* righteousness; and thy right hand shall teach thee terrible things.

5 Thine arrows *are* sharp in the heart of the
king's enemies; *whereby* the people fall under
thee.

6 ᴿThy throne, O God, *is* for ever and ever:
the sceptre of thy kingdom *is* a right sceptre. ★

7 ᴿThou lovest righteousness, and hatest
wickedness: therefore ᴿGod,ᴺ thy God, ᴿhath
anointed thee with the oil ᴿof gladness above
thy fellows.   ★

8 ᴿAll thy garments *smell* of myrrh, and
aloes, *and* cassia, out of the ivory palaces,
whereby they have made thee glad.

9 Kings' daughters *were* among thy honourable women: ᴿupon thy right hand did
stand the queen in gold of ō′-phĭr.

10 Hearken, O daughter, and consider, and
incline thine ear; ᴿforget also thine own people, and thy father's house;

11 So shall the king greatly desire thy
beauty: ᴿfor he *is* thy Lord; and worship thou
him.

12 And the daughter of Tyre *shall be there*
with a gift; *even* ᴿthe rich among the people
shall entreat ᴺthy favour.

PSALM 44

1 Ex. 12:26
Ps. 78:3
2 Ex. 15:17
Deut. 7:1
Ps. 80:8
3 Deut. 8:17
Josh. 24:12
3 Deut. 7:7, 8
4 Ps. 74:12
5 Dan. 8:4
6 Ps. 33:16
7 Ps. 40:14
8 Ps. 34:2
Jer. 9:24
9 Ps. 60:1
10 Lev. 26:17
Deut. 28:25
11 Rom. 8:36
11 Heb. *as
sheep of meat*
11 Deut. 28:64
Ps. 60:1
12 Is. 52:3, 4
Jer. 15:13
12 Heb. *without
riches*
13 Deut. 28:37
14 Jer. 24:9
14 Job 16:4
Ps. 22:7
16 Ps. 8:2
17 Dan. 9:13
18 Job 23:11
18 Or, *goings*
19 Is. 34:13
19 Ps. 23:4

Deut. 6:14   20
Ps. 88:9
Job 31:14   21
Ps. 139:1
Rom. 8:36   22
Ps. 7:6   23
Job 13:24   24
Ps. 13:1
Ps. 119:25   25
Heb. *a   26
help for us*

PSALM 45

Ps. 69, & 80, title *
Or, *of instruction* *
Heb. *boileth*, or,   1
bubbleth up
Luke 4:22   2
Is. 49:2   3
Heb. 4:12
Rev. 1:16
Is. 9:6   3
Rev. 6:2   4
Heb. *prosper thou,* 4
ride thou
Ps. 93:2   6
Heb. 1:8
Ps. 33:5   7
Is. 61:1   7
Or, *O God*   7
1 Ki. 1:39   7
Ps. 79:4
Ps. 21:6   7
S. of S. 1:3   8
1 Ki. 2:19   9
See Deut. 21:13   10
Ps. 95:6   11
Is. 54:5
Is. 49:23   12
Heb. *thy face*   12

13 ᴿThe king's daughter *is* all glorious within: her clothing *is* of wrought gold.

14 ᴿShe shall be brought unto the king in raiment of needlework: the virgins her companions that follow her shall be brought unto thee.

15 With gladness and rejoicing shall they be brought: they shall enter into the king's palace.

16 Instead of thy fathers shall be thy children, ᴿwhom thou mayest make princes in all the earth.

17 I will make thy name to be remembered in all generations: therefore shall the people praise thee for ever and ever.   ★

PSALM 46

God our refuge and strength

To the chief Musician *for the sons of Kôr'-ăh, *A Song upon *ăl'-ă-mōth.

GOD *is* our refuge and strength, ᴿa very present help in trouble.

2 Therefore will not we fear, though the earth be removed, and though the mountains be carried into ᴺthe midst of the sea;

3 ᴿ*Though* the waters thereof roar *and* be troubled, *though* the mountains shake with the swelling thereof. Sē'-läh.

4 *There is* ᴿa river, the streams whereof shall make glad ᴿthe city of God, the holy *place* of the tabernacles of the most High.

5 God *is* ᴿin the midst of her; she shall not be moved: God shall help her, ᴺ*and that* right early.

6 ᴿThe heathen raged, the kingdoms were moved: he uttered his voice, ᴿthe earth melted.

7 The LORD of hosts *is* with us; the God of Jacob *is* ᴺour refuge. Sē'-läh.

8 ᴿCome, behold the works of the LORD, what desolations he hath made in the earth.

9 ᴿHe maketh wars to cease unto the end of the earth; ᴿhe breaketh the bow, and cutteth the spear in sunder; ᴿhe burneth the chariot in the fire.

10 Be still, and know that I *am* God: ᴿI will be exalted among the heathen, I will be exalted in the earth.

11 The LORD of hosts *is* with us; the God of Jacob *is* our refuge. Sē'-läh.

PSALM 47

God's world-wide reign

To the chief Musician, A Psalm *for the sons of Kôr'-ăh.

OʳCLAP your hands, all ye people; shout unto God with the voice of triumph.

PSALM 45

13 Is. 61:10
14 S. of S. 1:4
16 1 Pet. 2:9
   Rev. 1:6 & 20:6

PSALM 46

* Or, *of*
* Ps. 48, & 66
* 1 Chr. 15:20
1 Deut. 4:7
2 Heb. *the heart of the seas*
3 Ps. 93:3, 4
4 See Is. 8:7
4 Ps. 48:1, 8
   Is. 60:14
5 Is. 12:6
   Ezek. 43:7
5 Heb. *when the morning appeareth*
6 Ps. 2:1
6 Josh. 2:9
7 Heb. *an high place for us,* Ps. 9:9
8 Ps. 66:5
9 Is. 2:4
9 Ps. 76:3
9 Ezek. 39:9
10 Is. 2:11, 17

PSALM 47

* Or, *of*
1 Is. 55:12

Deut. 7:21   2
Ps. 76:12
Mal. 1:14   2
Ps. 18:47   3
1 Pet. 1:4   4
Ps. 68:33   5
Zech. 14:9   7
1 Cor. 14:15 7
Or, *every one that hath understanding*   7
1 Chr. 16:31 8
Ps. 93:1
Rev. 19:6
Or, *The voluntary of the people are gathered* unto *the people of the God of Abraham*   9
Ps. 89:18   9

PSALM 48

Or, *of*   *
Ps. 46:4   1
Is. 2:2, 3   1
Mic. 4:1
Zech. 8:3
Ps. 50:2   2
Jer. 3:19
Is. 14:13   2
Mat. 5:35   2
2 Sam. 10:6,   4
   14, 16, 18, 19
Ex. 15:15   6
Ezek. 27:26   7
Jer. 18:17   7
Ps. 26:3   9
Deut. 28:58   10
Heb. *Set your heart to her bulwarks*   13
Or, *raise up* 13

---

2 For the LORD most high *is* ᴿterrible; ᴿ*he is* a great King over all the earth.

3 ᴿHe shall subdue the people under us, and the nations under our feet.

4 He shall choose our ᴿinheritance for us, the excellency of Jacob whom he loved. Sē'-läh.

5 ᴿGod is gone up with a shout, the LORD with the sound of a trumpet.

6 Sing praises to God, sing praises: sing praises unto our King, sing praises.

7 ᴿFor God *is* the King of all the earth: ᴿsing ye praises ᴺwith understanding.

8 ᴿGod reigneth over the heathen: God sitteth upon the throne of his holiness.

9 ᴺThe princes of the people are gathered together, *even* the people of the God of Abraham: ᴿfor the shields of the earth *belong* unto God: he is greatly exalted.

PSALM 48

God's greatness

A Song *and* Psalm *for the sons of Kôr'-ăh.

GREAT *is* the LORD, and greatly to be praised ᴿin the city of our God, *in* the ᴿmountain of his holiness.

2 ᴿBeautiful for situation, the joy of the whole earth, *is* mount Zion, ᴿ*on* the sides of the north, ᴿthe city of the great King.

3 God is known in her palaces for a refuge.

4 For, lo, ᴿthe kings were assembled, they passed by together.

5 They saw *it, and* so they marvelled; they were troubled, *and* hasted away.

6 Fear ᴿtook hold upon them there, *and* pain, as of a woman in travail.

7 Thou ᴿbreakest the ships of Tarshish ᴿwith an east wind.

8 As we have heard, so have we seen in the city of the LORD of hosts, in the city of our God: God will establish it for ever. Sē'-läh.

9 We have thought of ᴿthy lovingkindness, O God, in the midst of thy temple.

10 According to ᴿthy name, O God, so *is* thy praise unto the ends of the earth: thy right hand is full of righteousness.

11 Let mount Zion rejoice, let the daughters of Judah be glad, because of thy judgments.

12 Walk about Zion, and go round about her: tell the towers thereof.

13 ᴺMark ye well her bulwarks, ᴺconsider her palaces; that ye may tell *it* to the generation following.

14 For this God *is* our God for ever and ever: he will be our guide *even* unto death.

PSALM 49

God alone ransoms the soul

To the chief Musician, A Psalm *for
the sons of Kôr'-ăh.

HEAR this, all *ye* people; give ear, all *ye*
inhabitants of the world:

2 Both low and high, rich and poor, together.

3 My mouth shall speak of wisdom; and the meditation of my heart *shall be* of understanding.

4 [R]I will incline mine ear to a parable: I will open my dark saying upon the harp.

5 Wherefore should I fear in the days of evil, *when* the iniquity of my heels shall compass me about?

6 They that [R]trust in their wealth, and boast themselves in the multitude of their riches;

7 None *of them* can by any means redeem his brother, nor [R]give to God a ransom for him:

8 (For [R]the redemption of their soul *is* precious, and it ceaseth for ever:)

9 That he should still live for ever, *and* [R]not see corruption.

10 For he seeth *that* [R]wise men die, likewise the fool and the brutish person perish, [R]and leave their wealth to others.

11 Their inward thought *is, that* their houses *shall continue* for ever, *and* their dwelling places [N]to all generations; they [R]call *their* lands after their own names.

12 Nevertheless man *being* in honour abideth not: he is like the beasts *that* perish.

13 This their way *is* their [R]folly: yet their posterity [N]approve their sayings. Sē'-läh.

14 Like sheep they are laid in the grave; death shall feed on them; and [R]the upright shall have dominion over them in the morning; [R]and their [N]beauty shall consume [N]in the grave from their dwelling.

15 But God [R]will redeem my soul [N]from the power of [N]the grave: for he shall receive me. Sē'-läh.

16 Be not thou afraid when one is made rich, when the glory of his house is increased;

17 For when he dieth he shall carry nothing away: his glory shall not descend after him.

18 Though [N]while he lived [R]he blessed his soul: and *men* will praise thee, when thou doest well to thyself.

19 [N]He shall go to the generation of his fathers; they shall never see [R]light.

20 Man *that is* in honour, and understandeth not, [R]is like the beasts *that* perish.

PSALM 50

The judgment of God

A Psalm *of* ā'-săph.

THE [R]mighty God, *even* the LORD, hath spoken, and called the earth from the rising of the sun unto the going down thereof.

2 Out of Zion, the perfection of beauty, [R]God hath shined.

3 Our God shall come, and shall not keep silence: [R]a fire shall devour before him, and it shall be very tempestuous round about him.

4 [R]He shall call to the heavens from above, and to the earth, that he may judge his people.

5 Gather [R]my saints together unto me; [R]those that have made a covenant with me by sacrifice.

6 And the heavens shall declare his righteousness: for [R]God *is* judge himself. Sē'-läh.

7 Hear, O my people, and I will speak; O Israel, and I will testify against thee: [R]I *am* God, *even* thy God.

8 [R]I will not reprove thee [R]for thy sacrifices or thy burnt offerings, *to have been* continually before me.

9 [R]I will take no bullock out of thy house, *nor* he goats out of thy folds.

10 For every beast of the forest *is* mine, *and* the cattle upon a thousand hills.

11 I know all the fowls of the mountains: and the wild beasts of the field *are* [N]mine.

12 If I were hungry, I would not tell thee: [R]for the world *is* mine, and the fulness thereof.

13 Will I eat the flesh of bulls, or drink the blood of goats?

14 [R]Offer unto God thanksgiving; and [R]pay thy vows unto the most High:

15 And [R]call upon me in the day of trouble: I will deliver thee, and thou shalt [R]glorify me.

16 But unto the wicked God saith, What hast thou to do to declare my statutes, or *that* thou shouldest take my covenant in thy mouth?

17 [R]Seeing thou hatest instruction, and [R]castest my words behind thee.

18 When thou sawest a thief, then thou [R]consentedst with him, and [N]hast been [R]partaker with adulterers.

19 [N]Thou givest thy mouth to evil, and [R]thy tongue frameth deceit.

20 Thou sittest *and* speakest against thy brother; thou slanderest thine own mother's son.

21 These *things* hast thou done, [R]and I kept silence; [R]thou thoughtest that I was altogether

such an one as thyself: *but* [R]I will reprove thee, and set *them* in order before thine eyes.

22 Now consider this, ye that [R]forget God, lest I tear *you* in pieces, and *there be* none to deliver.

23 [R]Whoso offereth praise glorifieth me: and [R]to him [N]that ordereth *his* conversation *aright* will I shew the salvation of God.

PSALM 51

The prayer of a penitent soul

To the chief Musician, A Psalm of David, *when Nathan the prophet came unto him, after he had gone in to Băth′-shĕ-bă.

HAVE mercy upon me, O God, according to thy lovingkindness: according unto the multitude of thy tender mercies [R]blot out my transgressions.

2 [R]Wash me throughly from mine iniquity, and cleanse me from my sin.

3 For I acknowledge my transgressions: and my sin *is* ever before me.

4 [R]Against thee, thee only, have I sinned, and done *this* evil [R]in thy sight: [R]that thou mightest be justified when thou speakest, *and* be clear when thou judgest.

5 [R]Behold, I was shapen in iniquity; [R]and in sin did my mother [N]conceive me.

6 Behold, thou desirest truth in the inward parts: and in the hidden *part* thou shalt make me to know wisdom.

7 [R]Purge me with hyssop, and I shall be clean: wash me, and I shall be [R]whiter than snow.

8 Make me to hear joy and gladness; *that* the bones *which* thou hast broken [R]may rejoice.

9 [R]Hide thy face from my sins, and blot out all mine iniquities.

10 [R]Create in me a clean heart, O God; and renew [N]a right spirit within me.

11 Cast me not away [R]from thy presence; and take not thy [R]holy spirit from me.

12 Restore unto me the joy of thy salvation; and uphold me *with thy* [R]free spirit.

13 *Then* will I teach transgressors thy ways; and sinners shall be converted unto thee.

14 Deliver me from [R]bloodguiltiness,[N] O God, thou God of my salvation: *and* [R]my tongue shall sing aloud of thy righteousness.

15 O Lord, open thou my lips; and my mouth shall shew forth thy praise.

16 For [R]thou desirest not sacrifice; [N]else would I give *it*: thou delightest not in burnt offering.

17 [R]The sacrifices of God *are* a broken spirit: a broken and a contrite heart, O God, thou wilt not despise.

18 Do good in thy good pleasure unto Zion: build thou the walls of Jerusalem.

19 Then shalt thou be pleased with [R]the sacrifices of righteousness, with burnt offering and whole burnt offering: then shall they offer bullocks upon thine altar.

PSALM 52

Confidence in God

To the chief Musician, Măs′-chîl, *A Psalm* of David, *when Dō′-ĕg the Ē′-dom-ite came and *told Saul, and said unto him, David is come to the house of Ă-hĭm′-ē-ĕch.

WHY boastest thou thyself in mischief, O [R]mighty man? the goodness of God *endureth* continually.

2 [R]Thy tongue deviseth mischiefs; [R]like a sharp razor, working deceitfully.

3 Thou lovest evil more than good; *and* [R]lying rather than to speak righteousness. Sē′-läh.

4 Thou lovest all devouring words, [N]O *thou* deceitful tongue.

5 God shall likewise [N]destroy thee for ever, he shall take thee away, and pluck thee out of *thy* dwelling place, and [R]root thee out of the land of the living. Sē′-läh.

6 [R]The righteous also shall see, and fear, [R]and shall laugh at him:

7 Lo, *this is* the man *that* made not God his strength; but [R]trusted in the abundance of his riches, *and* strengthened himself in his [N]wickedness.

8 But I *am* [R]like a green olive tree in the house of God: I trust in the mercy of God for ever and ever.

9 I will praise thee for ever, because thou hast done *it:* and I will wait on thy name; [R]for *it is* good before thy saints.

PSALM 53

The folly of denying God

To the chief Musician upon Mā′-hă-lăth, Măs′-chîl, *A Psalm* of David.

THE [R]fool hath said in his heart, *There is* no God. Corrupt are they, and have done abominable iniquity: [R]*there is* none that doeth good.

2 God [R]looked down from heaven upon the children of men, to see if there were *any* that did understand, that did [R]seek God.

3 Every one of them is gone back: they are altogether become filthy; *there is* none that doeth good, no, not one.

4 Have the workers of iniquity [R]no knowl-

Center reference column

PSALM 50

21	Ps. 90:8
22	Job 8:13
	Ps. 9:17
	Is. 51:13
23	Ps. 27:6
23	Gal. 6:16
23	Heb. *that disposeth* his *way*

PSALM 51

*	2 Sam. 12:1
&	11:2, 4
1	Is. 43:25
	Col. 2:14
2	Heb. 9:14
	1 John 1:7
4	2 Sam. 12:13
4	Luke 15:21
4	Rom. 3:4
4	Job 14:4
5	Job 14:4
5	Heb. *warm me*
7	Lev. 14:4
	Heb. 9:19
7	Is. 1:18
8	Mat. 5:4
9	Jer. 16:17
10	Ezek. 18:31
	Acts 15:19
10	Or, *a constant spirit*
11	Gen. 4:14
11	Luke 11:13
	Eph. 4:30
12	2 Cor. 3:17
14	2 Sam. 12:9
14	Heb. *bloods*
14	Ps. 35:28
16	1 Sam. 15:22
	Ps. 40:6
	Is. 1:11
	Jer. 7:22
16	Or, *that I should give it*
17	Ps. 34:18
	Is. 57:15

Ps. 4:5	19
Mal. 3:3	

PSALM 52

1 Sam. 22:9	*
Ezek. 22:9	*
1 Sam. 21:7	1
Ps. 50:19	2
Ps. 57:4	2
Jer. 9:4, 5	3
Or, *and the deceitful tongue*	4
Heb. *beat thee down*	5
Prov. 2:22	5
Job 22:19	6
Ps. 37:34	
Mal. 1:5	
Ps. 58:10	6
Ps. 49:6	7
Or, *substance*	7
Jer. 11:16	8
Hos. 14:6	
Ps. 54:6	9

PSALM 53

Ps. 10:4	1
Rom. 3:10	1
Ps. 33:13	2
2 Chr. 15:2	2
Jer. 4:22	4

edge? who eat up my people *as* they eat bread: they have not called upon God.

5 ^RThere ^Nwere they in great fear, *where* no fear was: for God hath ^Rscattered the bones of him that encampeth *against* thee: thou hast put *them* to shame, because God hath despised them.

6 ^ROh^N that the salvation of Israel *were* come out of Zion! When God bringeth back the captivity of his people, Jacob shall rejoice, *and* Israel shall be glad.

PSALM 54

A prayer for vindication

To the chief Musician on Nĕ-gî′-nŏth, Măs′-chîl, *A Psalm* of David, *when the Ziphims came and said to Saul, Doth not David hide himself with us?

SAVE me, O God, by thy name, and judge me by thy strength.

2 Hear my prayer, O God; give ear to the words of my mouth.

3 For ^Rstrangers are risen up against me, and oppressors seek after my soul: they have not set God before them. Sē′-läh.

4 Behold, God *is* mine helper: ^Rthe Lord *is* with them that uphold my soul.

5 He shall reward evil unto ^Nmine enemies: cut them off ^Rin thy truth.

6 I will freely sacrifice unto thee: I will praise thy name, O LORD; ^Rfor *it is* good.

7 For he hath delivered me out of all trouble: ^Rand mine eye hath seen *his desire* upon mine enemies.

PSALM 55

Anguish over treachery of a friend

To the chief Musician on Nĕ-gî′-nŏth, Măs′-chîl, *A Psalm* of David.

GIVE ear to my prayer, O God; and hide not thyself from my supplication.

2 Attend unto me, and hear me: I ^Rmourn in my complaint, and make a noise;

3 Because of the voice of the enemy, because of the oppression of the wicked: ^Rfor they cast iniquity upon me, and in wrath they hate me.

4 ^RMy heart is sore pained within me: and the terrors of death are fallen upon me.

5 Fearfulness and trembling are come upon me, and horror hath ^Noverwhelmed me.

6 And I said, Oh that I had wings like a dove! *for then* would I fly away, and be at rest.

7 Lo, *then* would I wander far off, *and* remain in the wilderness. Sē′-läh.

8 I would hasten my escape from the windy storm *and* tempest.

9 Destroy, O Lord, *and* divide their tongues: for I have seen ^Rviolence and strife in the city.

10 Day and night they go about it upon the walls thereof: mischief also and sorrow *are* in the midst of it.

11 Wickedness *is* in the midst thereof: deceit and guile depart not from her streets.

12 ^RFor *it was* not an enemy *that* reproached me; then I could have borne *it:* neither *was it* he that hated me *that* did ^Rmagnify *himself* against me; then I would have hid myself from him:

13 But *it was* thou, ^Na man mine equal, ^Rmy guide, and mine acquaintance.

14 ^NWe took sweet counsel together, *and* ^Rwalked unto the house of God in company.

15 Let death seize upon them, *and* let them ^Rgo down quick into ^Nhell: for wickedness *is* in their dwellings, *and* among them.

16 As for me, I will call upon God; and the LORD shall save me.

17 ^REvening, and morning, and at noon, will I pray, and cry aloud: and he shall hear my voice.

18 He hath delivered my soul in peace from the battle *that was* against me: for ^Rthere were many with me.

19 God shall hear, and afflict them, ^Reven he that abideth of old. Sē′-läh. ^NBecause they have no changes, therefore they fear not God.

20 He hath ^Rput forth his hands against such as ^Rbe at peace with him: ^Nhe hath broken his covenant.

21 ^R*The words* of his mouth were smoother than butter, but war *was* in his heart: his words were softer than oil, yet *were* they drawn swords.

22 ^RCast thy ^Nburden upon the LORD, and he shall sustain thee: ^Rhe shall never suffer the righteous to be moved.

23 But thou, O God, shalt bring them down into the pit of destruction: ^Rbloody^N and deceitful men ^Rshall^N not live out half their days; but I will trust in thee.

PSALM 56

Remedy for fear

To the chief Musician upon Jō′-năth-ē′-lĕm-rĕ-chō′-kĭm, *Mĭch′-tăm of David, when the *Philistines took him in Gath.

BE ^Rmerciful unto me, O God: for man would swallow me up; he fighting daily oppresseth me.

2 ^NMine enemies would daily ^Rswallow *me*

Center reference column

PSALM 53
5 Lev. 26:17
5 Heb. *they feared a fear*
5 Ezek. 6:5
6 Ps. 14:7
6 Heb. *Who will give salvations, etc.*

PSALM 54
* 1 Sam. 23:19
3 Ps. 86:14
4 Ps. 118:7
5 Heb. *those that observe me,* Ps. 5:8
5 Ps. 89:49
6 Ps. 52:9
7 Ps. 59:10

PSALM 55
2 Is. 38:14
3 2 Sam. 16:7, 8
4 Ps. 116:3
5 Heb. *covered me*

Jer. 6:7 — 9
Ps. 41:9 — 12
Ps. 35:26 — 12
Heb. *a man according to my rank* — 13
2 Sam. 15:12 — 13
Ps. 41:9
Jer. 9:4
Heb. *Who sweetened counsel* — 14
Ps. 42:4 — 14
Num. 16:30 — 15
Or, *the grave* — 15
Luke 18:1 — 17
2 Chr. 32:7, 8 — 18
Deut. 33:27 — 19
Or, *With whom also there be no changes, yet they fear not God* — 19
Acts 12:1 — 20
Ps. 7:4 — 20
Heb. *he hath profaned* — 20
Ps. 28:3 — 21
Ps. 37:5 — 22
Mat. 6:25
Or, *gift* — 22
Ps. 37:24 — 22
Ps. 5:6 — 23
Heb. *men of bloods and deceit* — 23
Job 15:32 — 23
Prov. 10:27
Eccl. 7:17
Heb. *shall not half their days* — 23

PSALM 56
Or, *A golden Psalm of David,* Ps. 16 — *
1 Sam. 21:11 — *
Ps. 57:1 — 1
Heb. *Mine observers,* Ps. 54:5 — 2
Ps. 57:3 — 2

up: for *they be* many that fight against me, O thou most High.

3 What time I am afraid, I will trust in thee.

4 In God I will praise his word, in God I have put my trust; [R]I will not fear what flesh can do unto me.

5 Every day they wrest my words: all their thoughts *are* against me for evil.

6 [R]They gather themselves together, they hide themselves, they mark my steps, [R]when they wait for my soul.

7 Shall they escape by iniquity? in *thine* anger cast down the people, O God.

8 Thou tellest my wanderings: put thou my tears into thy bottle: *are they* not in thy book?

9 When I cry *unto thee,* then shall mine enemies turn back: this I know; for [R]God *is* for me.

10 In God will I praise *his* word: in the LORD will I praise *his* word.

11 In God have I put my trust: I will not be afraid what man can do unto me.

12 Thy vows *are* upon me, O God: I will render praises unto thee.

13 For [R]thou hast delivered my soul from death: *wilt* not *thou deliver* my feet from falling, that I may walk before God in [R]the light of the living?

PSALM 57

A prayer of confidence

To the chief Musician, *Ăl-tăs′-<u>ch</u>îth, Mĭ<u>ch</u>′-tăm of David, *when he fled from Saul in the cave.

BE merciful unto me, O God, be merciful unto me: for my soul trusteth in thee: [R]yea, in the shadow of thy wings will I make my refuge, [R]until *these* calamities be overpast.

2 I will cry unto God most high; unto God [R]that performeth *all things* for me.

3 He shall send from heaven, and save me [N]*from* the reproach of him that would swallow me up. Sē′-läh. God [R]shall send forth his mercy and his truth.

4 My soul *is* among lions: *and* I lie *even* among them that are set on fire, *even* the sons of men, [R]whose teeth *are* spears and arrows, and their tongue a sharp sword.

5 [R]Be thou exalted, O God, above the heavens; *let* thy glory *be* above all the earth.

6 [R]They have prepared a net for my steps; my soul is bowed down: they have digged a pit before me, into the midst whereof they are fallen *themselves.* Sē′-läh.

7 [R]My heart is [N]fixed, O God, my heart is fixed: I will sing and give praise.

8 Awake up, [R]my glory; awake, psaltery and harp: I *myself* will awake early.

PSALM 56
4 Ps. 118:6
Is. 31:3
5 Ps. 59:3
6 Ps. 71:10
9 Rom. 8:31
13 Ps. 116:8
13 Job 33:30

PSALM 57
* Or, *Destroy not, A golden* Psalm
* 1 Sam. 22:1
Ps. 142, title
1 Ps. 17:8
1 Is. 26:20
2 Ps. 138:8
3 Or, *he reproacheth him that would swallow me up*
3 Ps. 43:3
4 Prov. 30:14
5 Ps. 108:5
6 Ps. 9:15
7 Ps. 108:1
7 Or, *prepared*
8 Ps. 16:9

Ps. 108:3   9
Ps. 103:11   10
ver. 5   11

PSALM 58
Ps. 57, title   *
Or, *Destroy not,*   *
A golden Psalm *of David*
Is. 48:8   3
Heb. *from the belly*   3
Eccl. 10:11   4
Heb. *according to the likeness*   4
Or, *asp*   4
Or, *be the charmer never so cunning*   5
Job 4:10   6
Job 3:16   8
Prov. 10:25   9
Heb. *as living as wrath*   9
Ps. 68:23   10
Ps. 92:15   11
Heb. *fruit of the, etc.*   11

PSALM 59
Ps. 57, title   *
Or, *Destroy not,*   *
A golden Psalm *of David*
1 Sam. 19:11   *
Heb. *set me on high*   1
Ps. 56:6   3

9 [R]I will praise thee, O Lord, among the people: I will sing unto thee among the nations.

10 [R]For thy mercy *is* great unto the heavens, and thy truth unto the clouds.

11 [R]Be thou exalted, O God, above the heavens: *let* thy glory *be* above all the earth.

PSALM 58

Futility of perverted justice

To the chief Musician, *Ăl-tăs′-<u>ch</u>îth,* Mĭ<u>ch</u>′-tăm of David.

DO ye indeed speak righteousness, O congregation? do ye judge uprightly, O ye sons of men?

2 Yea, in heart ye work wickedness; ye weigh the violence of your hands in the earth.

3 [R]The wicked are estranged from the womb: they go astray [N]as soon as they be born, speaking lies.

4 [R]Their poison *is* [N]like the poison of a serpent: *they are* like the deaf [N]adder *that* stoppeth her ear;

5 Which will not hearken to the voice of charmers, [N]charming never so wisely.

6 [R]Break their teeth, O God, in their mouth: break out the great teeth of the young lions, O LORD.

7 Let them melt away as waters *which* run continually: *when* he bendeth *his bow to shoot* his arrows, let them be as cut in pieces.

8 As a snail *which* melteth, let *every one of them* pass away: [R]*like* the untimely birth of a woman, *that* they may not see the sun.

9 Before your pots can feel the thorns, he shall take them away [R]as with a whirlwind, [N]both living, and in *his* wrath.

10 The righteous shall rejoice when he seeth the vengeance: [R]he shall wash his feet in the blood of the wicked.

11 [R]So that a man shall say, Verily *there is* [N]a reward for the righteous: verily he is a God that judgeth in the earth.

PSALM 59

Prayer for deliverance from enemies

To the chief Musician, *Ăl-tăs′-<u>ch</u>îth,* Mĭ<u>ch</u>′-tăm of David; *when Saul sent, and they watched the house to kill him.

DELIVER me from mine enemies, O my God: [N]defend me from them that rise up against me.

2 Deliver me from the workers of iniquity, and save me from bloody men.

3 For, lo, they lie in wait for my soul: [R]the mighty are gathered against me; not *for* my transgression, nor *for* my sin, O LORD.

4 They run and prepare themselves without *my* fault: ^Rawake ^Nto help me, and behold.

5 Thou therefore, O LORD God of hosts, the God of Israel, awake to visit all the heathen: be not merciful to any wicked transgressors. Sē'-läh.

6 ^RThey return at evening: they make a noise like a dog, and go round about the city.

7 Behold, they belch out with their mouth: ^Rswords *are* in their lips: for ^Rwho, *say they,* doth hear?

8 But ^Rthou, O LORD, shalt laugh at them; thou shalt have all the heathen in derision.

9 *Because of* his strength will I wait upon thee: ^Rfor God *is* ^Nmy defence.

10 The God of my mercy shall ^Rprevent me: God shall let ^Rme see *my desire* upon ^Nmine enemies.

11 Slay them not, lest my people forget: scatter them by thy power; and bring them down, O Lord our shield.

12 ^R*For* the sin of their mouth *and* the words of their lips let them even be taken in their pride: and for cursing and lying *which* they speak.

13 Consume *them* in wrath, consume *them,* that they *may* not *be:* and let them know that God ruleth in Jacob unto the ends of the earth. Sē'-läh.

14 And ^Rat evening let them return; *and* let them make a noise like a dog, and go round about the city.

15 Let them ^Rwander up and down ^Nfor meat, ^Nand grudge if they be not satisfied.

16 But I will sing of thy power; yea, I will sing aloud of thy mercy in the morning: for thou hast been my defence and refuge in the day of my trouble.

17 Unto thee, ^RO my strength, will I sing: for God *is* my defence, *and* the God of my mercy.

PSALM 60

Prayer after defeat in battle

To the chief Musician *upon Shŭ'-shăn-ē'-dûth, *Mĭch'-tăm of David, to teach; *when he strove with âr'-ăm-nā-hā-rā'-ĭm and with âr'-ăm-zō'-băh, when Jō'-ăb returned, and smote of Ē'-dŏm in the valley of salt twelve thousand.

O GOD, ^Rthou hast cast us off, thou hast ^Nscattered us, thou hast been displeased; O turn thyself to us again.

2 Thou hast made the earth to tremble; thou hast broken it: ^Rheal the breaches thereof; for it shaketh.

3 ^RThou hast shewed thy people hard things: ^Rthou hast made us to drink the wine of astonishment.

Center reference column:

	PSALM 59
4	Ps. 35:23
4	Heb. *to meet me*
6	ver. 14
7	Ps. 57:4
	Prov. 12:18
7	Ps. 10:11
8	Prov. 1:26
9	Ps. 62:2
9	Heb. *my high place*
10	Ps. 21:3
10	Ps. 54:7
10	Heb. *mine observers*
12	Prov. 12:13
14	ver. 6
15	Job 15:23
15	Heb. *to eat*
15	Or, *if they be not satisfied, then they will stay all night*
17	Ps. 18:1

	PSALM 60
*	Ps. 80
*	Or, *A golden Psalm*
*	2 Sam. 8:3
	1 Chr. 18:3
1	Ps. 44:9
1	Heb. *broken*
2	2 Chr. 7:14
3	Ps. 71:20
3	Jer. 25:15

Ps. 20:5	4
Ps. 108:6	5
Ps. 89:35	6
Josh. 1:6	6
Gen. 12:6	6
Josh. 13:27	6
Deut. 33:17	7
Gen. 49:10	7
2 Sam. 8:1	8
Or, *triumph thou over me:* (by an irony)	8
Heb. *city of strength?*	9
2 Sam. 11:1	
Ps. 108:11	10
Josh. 7:12	10
Heb. *salvation*	11
Num. 24:18	12

	PSALM 61
Prov. 18:10	3
Ps. 91:4	4
Or, *make my refuge*	4
Heb. *Thou shalt add days to the days of the king*	6
Heb. *as generation and generation*	6
Ps. 40:11	7

	PSALM 62
1 Chr. 25:1	*
Or, *Only*	1
Ps. 33:20	1
Heb. *is silent*	1
Heb. *high place,* Ps. 59:9, 17	2

---

4 ^RThou hast given a banner to them that fear thee, that it may be displayed because of the truth. Sē'-läh.

5 ^RThat thy beloved may be delivered; save *with* thy right hand, and hear me.

6 God hath ^Rspoken in his holiness; I will rejoice, I will ^Rdivide ^RShē'-chĕm, and mete out ^Rthe valley of Sŭc'-cōth.

7 Gilead *is* mine, and Mă-năs'-sēh *is* mine; ^RĒ'-phră-ĭm also *is* the strength of mine head; ^RJudah *is* my lawgiver;

8 Moab *is* my washpot; over Ē'-dŏm will I cast out my shoe: ^RPhilistia, ^Ntriumph thou because of me.

9 Who will bring me *into* the ^Nstrong city? who will lead me into Ē'-dŏm?

10 *Wilt* not thou, O God, *which* ^Rhadst cast us off? and *thou,* O God, *which* didst ^Rnot go out with our armies?

11 Give us help from trouble: for vain *is* the ^Nhelp of man.

12 Through God ^Rwe shall do valiantly: for he *it is that* shall tread down our enemies.

PSALM 61

"The rock that is higher than I"

To the chief Musician upon Nĕ-gî'-näh, *A Psalm* of David.

HEAR my cry, O God; attend unto my prayer.

2 From the end of the earth will I cry unto thee, when my heart is overwhelmed: lead me to the rock *that* is higher than I.

3 For thou hast been a shelter for me, *and* ^Ra strong tower from the enemy.

4 I will abide in thy tabernacle for ever: ^RI will ^Ntrust in the covert of thy wings. Sē'-läh.

5 For thou, O God, hast heard my vows: thou hast given *me* the heritage of those that fear thy name.

6 ^NThou wilt prolong the king's life: *and* his years ^Nas many generations.

7 He shall abide before God for ever: O prepare mercy ^Rand truth, *which* may preserve him.

8 So will I sing praise unto thy name for ever, that I may daily perform my vows.

PSALM 62

Patient trust in God

To the chief Musician, to *Jĕ-dū'-thŭn, *A Psalm* of David.

TRULY^N ^Rmy soul ^Nwaiteth upon God: from him *cometh* my salvation.

2 He only *is* my rock and my salvation; *he is* my ^Ndefence; I shall not be greatly moved.

3 How long will ye imagine mischief against a man? ye shall be slain all of you: ᴿas a bowing wall *shall ye be, and as* a tottering fence.

4 They only consult to cast *him* down from his excellency: they delight in lies: ᴿthey bless with their mouth, but they curse ᴺinwardly. Sē'-läh.

5 My soul, wait thou only upon God; for my expectation *is* from him.

6 He only *is* my rock and my salvation: *he is* my defence; I shall not be moved.

7 ᴿIn God *is* my salvation and my glory: the rock of my strength, *and* my refuge, *is* in God.

8 Trust in him at all times; ye people, ᴿpour out your heart before him: God *is* a refuge for us. Sē'-läh.

9 ᴿSurely men of low degree *are* vanity, *and* men of high degree *are* a lie: to be laid in the balance, they *are* ᴺaltogether *lighter* than vanity.

10 Trust not in oppression, and become not vain in robbery: ᴿif riches increase, set not your heart *upon them.*

11 God hath spoken ᴿonce; twice have I heard this; that ᴺpower *belongeth* unto God.

12 Also unto thee, O Lord, *belongeth* mercy: for ᴿthou renderest to every man according to his work.

PSALM 63

The soul thirsts for God

A Psalm of David, *when he was in the wilderness of Judah.*

O GOD, thou *art* my God; early will I seek thee: ᴿmy soul thirsteth for thee, my flesh longeth for thee in a dry and ᴺthirsty land, ᴺwhere no water is;

2 To see ᴿthy power and thy glory, so *as* I have seen thee in the sanctuary.

3 Because thy lovingkindness *is* better than life, my lips shall praise thee.

4 Thus will I bless thee while I live: I will lift up my hands in thy name.

5 My soul shall be satisfied as *with* ᴺmarrow and fatness; and my mouth shall praise *thee* with joyful lips:

6 When ᴿI remember thee upon my bed, *and* meditate on thee in the *night* watches.

7 Because thou hast been my help, therefore in the shadow of thy wings will I rejoice.

8 My soul followeth hard after thee: thy right hand upholdeth me.

9 But those *that* seek my soul, to destroy *it,* shall go into the lower parts of the earth.

10 ᴺThey shall fall by the sword: they shall be a portion for foxes.

11 But the king shall rejoice in God; ᴿevery one that sweareth by him shall glory: but the mouth of them that speak lies shall be stopped.

PSALM 64

Prayer for God's protection

To the chief Musician, A Psalm of David.

HEAR my voice, O God, in my prayer: preserve my life from fear of the enemy.

2 Hide me from the secret counsel of the wicked; from the insurrection of the workers of iniquity:

3 Who whet their tongue like a sword, ᴿ*and* bend *their bows to shoot* their arrows, *even* bitter words:

4 That they may shoot in secret at the perfect: suddenly do they shoot at him, and fear not.

5 They encourage themselves *in* an evil ᴺmatter: they commune ᴺof laying snares privily; ᴿthey say, Who shall see them?

6 They search out iniquities; ᴺthey accomplish ᴺa diligent search: both the inward *thought* of every one *of them,* and the heart, *is* deep.

7 But God shall shoot at them *with* an arrow; suddenly ᴺshall they be wounded.

8 So they shall make their own tongue to fall upon themselves: ᴿall that see them shall flee away.

9 And all men shall fear, and shall ᴿdeclare the work of God; for they shall wisely consider of his doing.

10 The righteous shall be glad in the LORD, and shall trust in him; and all the upright in heart shall glory.

PSALM 65

Praise of God's grace and providence

To the chief Musician, A Psalm *and* Song of David.

PRAISE ᴺwaiteth for thee, O God, in Sī'-on: and unto thee shall the vow be performed.

2 O thou that hearest prayer, ᴿunto thee shall all flesh come.

3 ᴺIniquities prevail against me: *as for* our transgressions, thou shalt ᴿpurge them away.

4 ᴿBlessed *is* the man *whom* thou ᴿchoosest, and causest to approach *unto thee, that* he may dwell in thy courts: ᴿwe shall be satisfied with the goodness of thy house, *even* of thy holy temple.

5 *By* terrible things in righteousness wilt thou answer us, O God of our salvation; *who*

Center reference column

PSALM 62

3 Is. 30:13
4 Ps. 28:3
4 Heb. *in their inward parts*
7 Jer. 3:23
8 1 Sam. 1:15
   Lam. 2:19
9 Ps. 39:5
   Is. 40:17
9 Or, *alike*
10 Luke 12:15
11 Job 33:14
11 Or, *strength*
12 Mat. 16:27

PSALM 63

* 1 Sam. 22:5
1 Ps. 42:2
1 Heb. *weary*
1 Heb. *without water*
2 Ps. 27:4
5 Heb. *fatness*
6 Ps. 42:8
10 Heb. *They shall make him run* like water *by the hands of the sword*

Deut. 6:13   11

PSALM 64

Ps. 58:7   3
Or, *speech*   5
Heb. *to hide snares*   5
Ps. 10:11   5
Or, *we are consumed by that which they have throughly searched*   6
Heb. *a search searched*   6
Heb. *their wound shall be*   7
Ps. 31:11   8
Jer. 50:28 & 51:10   9

PSALM 65

Heb. *is silent,* Ps. 62:1   1
Is. 66:23   2
Heb. *Words,* or, *Matters of iniquities*   3
Heb. 9:14   3
Ps. 33:12   4
Ps. 4:3   4
Ps. 36:8   4

art the confidence of all the ends of the earth, and of them that are afar off *upon* the sea:

6 Which by his strength setteth fast the mountains; [R]*being* girded with power:

7 [R]Which stilleth the noise of the seas, the noise of their waves, [R]and the tumult of the people.

8 They also that dwell in the uttermost parts are afraid at thy tokens: thou makest the outgoings of the morning and evening [N]to rejoice.

9 Thou visitest the earth, and [R]waterest[N] it: thou greatly enrichest it [R]with the river of God, *which* is full of water: thou preparest them corn, when thou hast so provided for it.

10 Thou waterest the ridges thereof abundantly: [N]thou settlest the furrows thereof: [N]thou makest it soft with showers: thou blessest the springing thereof.

11 Thou crownest [N]the year with thy goodness; and thy paths drop fatness.

12 They drop *upon* the pastures of the wilderness: and the little hills [N]rejoice on every side.

13 The pastures are clothed with flocks; [R]the valleys also are covered over with corn; they shout for joy, they also sing.

PSALM 66

Praise of God's deeds

To the chief Musician,
A Song *or* Psalm.

MAKE[R] a joyful noise unto God, [N]all ye lands:

2 Sing forth the honour of his name: make his praise glorious.

3 Say unto God, How [R]terrible *art thou in* thy works! through the greatness of thy power shall thine enemies [NN]submit themselves unto thee.

4 [R]All the earth shall worship thee, and shall sing unto thee; they shall sing *to* thy name. Sē′-läh.

5 Come and see the works of God: *he is* terrible *in his* doing toward the children of men.

6 [R]He turned the sea into dry *land:* they went through the flood on foot: there did we rejoice in him.

7 He ruleth by his power for ever; his eyes behold the nations: let not the rebellious exalt themselves. Sē′-läh.

8 O bless our God, ye people, and make the voice of his praise to be heard:

9 Which [N]holdeth our soul in life, and suffereth not our feet to be moved.

PSALM 65

6 Ps. 93:1
7 Mat. 8:26
7 Is. 17:13
8 Or, *to sing*
9 Jer. 5:24
9 Or, *after thou hadst made it to desire* rain
9 Ps. 46:4
10 Or, *thou causest* rain *to descend into the furrows thereof*
10 Heb. *thou dissolvest it*
11 Heb. *the year of thy goodness*
12 Heb. *are girded with joy*
13 Is. 55:12

PSALM 66

1 Ps. 100:1
1 Heb. *all the earth*
3 Ps. 65:5
3 Or, *yield feigned obedience,* Ps. 18:44
3 Heb. *lie*
4 Ps. 117:1
6 Ex. 14:21
9 Heb. *putteth*

Ps. 17:3   10
Is. 48:10
Zech. 13:9   10
1 Pet. 1:7
Lam. 1:13   11
Is. 51:23   12
Is. 43:2   12
Heb. *moist*   12
Eccl. 5:4   13
Heb. *opened*   14
Heb. *marrow*   15
Is. 1:15   18
John 9:31
Jas. 4:3
Ps. 116:1, 2   19

PSALM 67

Num. 6:25   1
Ps. 4:6
Heb. *with us*   1
Acts 18:25   2
Is. 52:10   2
Tit. 2:11
Ps. 96:10   4
Heb. *lead*   4
Lev. 26:4   6
Ps. 85:12
Ezek. 34:27

PSALM 68

Num. 10:35   1
Is. 33:3
Heb. *from his face* 1
Is. 9:18   2
Hos. 13:3

10 For [R]thou, O God, hast proved us: [R]thou hast tried us, as silver is tried.

11 [R]Thou broughtest us into the net; thou laidst affliction upon our loins.

12 [R]Thou hast caused men to ride over our heads; [R]we went through fire and through water: but thou broughtest us out into a [N]wealthy *place.*

13 I will go into thy house with burnt offerings: [R]I will pay thee my vows,

14 Which my lips have [N]uttered, and my mouth hath spoken, when I was in trouble.

15 I will offer unto thee burnt sacrifices of [N]fatlings, with the incense of rams; I will offer bullocks with goats. Sē′-läh.

16 Come *and* hear, all ye that fear God, and I will declare what he hath done for my soul.

17 I cried unto him with my mouth, and he was extolled with my tongue.

18 [R]If I regard iniquity in my heart, the Lord will not hear *me:*

19 *But* verily God [R]hath heard *me;* he hath attended to the voice of my prayer.

20 Blessed *be* God, which hath not turned away my prayer, nor his mercy from me.

PSALM 67

Doxology for God's guidance

To the chief Musician on Nĕ-gî′-nŏth,
A Psalm *or* Song.

GOD be merciful unto us, and bless us; *and* [R]cause his face to shine [N]upon us; Sē′-läh.

2 That [R]thy way may be known upon earth, [R]thy saving health among all nations.

3 Let the people praise thee, O God; let all the people praise thee.

4 O let the nations be glad and sing for joy: for [R]thou shalt judge the people righteously, and [N]govern the nations upon earth. Sē′-läh.

5 Let the people praise thee, O God; let all the people praise thee.

6 [R]*Then* shall the earth yield her increase; *and* God, *even* our own God, shall bless us.

7 God shall bless us; and all the ends of the earth shall fear him.

PSALM 68

Israel's God in the wilderness

To the chief Musician, A Psalm
or Song of David.

LET [R]God arise, let his enemies be scattered: let them also that hate him flee [N]before him.

2 [R]As smoke is driven away, *so* drive *them*

away: ᴿas wax meltcth before the fire, *so* let the wicked perish at the presence of God.

3 But ᴿlet the righteous be glad; let them rejoice before God: yea, let them ᴺexceedingly rejoice.

4 Sing unto God, sing praises to his name: ᴿextol him that rideth upon the heavens ᴿby his name JAH, and rejoice before him.

5 ᴿA father of the fatherless, and a judge of the widows, *is* God in his holy habitation.

6 ᴿGod setteth the solitary ᴺin families: ᴿhe bringeth out those which are bound with chains: but ᴿthe rebellious dwell in a dry *land.*

7 O God, ᴿwhen thou wentest forth before thy people, when thou didst march through the wilderness; Sĕ′-läh:

8 The earth shook, the heavens also dropped at the presence of God: *even* Sī′-nâi itself *was moved* at the presence of God, the God of Israel.

9 ᴿThou, O God, didst ᴺsend a plentiful rain, whereby thou didst ᴺconfirm thine inheritance, when it was weary.

10 Thy congregation hath dwelt therein: ᴿthou, O God, hast prepared of thy goodness for the poor.

11 The Lord gave the word: great *was* the ᴺcompany of those that published *it.*

12 ᴿKings of armies ᴺdid flee apace: and she that tarried at home divided the spoil.

13 ᴿThough ye have lien among the pots, ᴿ*yet shall ye be as* the wings of a dove covered with silver, and her feathers with yellow gold.

14 ᴿWhen the Almighty scattered kings ᴺin it, it was *white* as snow in Săl′-mŏn.

15 The hill of God *is as* the hill of Bā′-shăn; an high hill *as* the hill of Bā′-shăn.

16 Why leap ye, ye high hills? ᴿ*this is* the hill *which* God desireth to dwell in; yea, the Lᴏʀᴅ will dwell *in it* for ever.

17 ᴿThe chariots of God *are* twenty thousand, ᴺ*even* thousands of angels: the Lord *is* among them, *as in* Sī′-nâi, in the holy *place.*

18 ᴿThou hast ascended on high, ᴿthou hast led captivity captive: ᴿthou hast received gifts ᴺfor men; yea, *for* ᴿthe rebellious also, ᴿthat the Lᴏʀᴅ God might dwell *among them.* ★

19 Blessed *be* the Lord, *who* daily loadeth us *with benefits, even* the God of our salvation. Sĕ′-läh.

20 *He that is* our God *is* the God of salvation; and ᴿunto Gᴏᴅ the Lord *belong* the issues from death.

21 But ᴿGod shall wound the head of his enemies, ᴿ*and* the hairy scalp of such an one as goeth on still in his trespasses.

PSALM **68**	
2 Mic. 1:4	
3 Ps. 32:11	
3 Heb. *rejoice with gladness*	
4 Deut. 33:26	
4 Ex. 6:3	
5 Ps. 10:14	
6 1 Sam. 2:5	
Ps. 107:4-7	
6 Heb. *in a house*	
6 Acts 12:6	
6 Ps. 107:34	
7 Ex. 13:21	
Judg. 4:14	
9 Deut. 11:11	
9 Heb. *shake out*	
9 Heb. *confirm it*	
10 Deut. 26:5	
Ps. 74:19	
11 Heb. *army*	
12 Num. 31:8	
Josh. 10:16	
12 Heb. *did flee, did flee*	
13 Ps. 81:6	
13 Ps. 105:37	
14 Josh. 10:10	
14 Or, *for her, she was*	
16 Deut. 12:5	
17 Deut. 33:2	
17 Or, *even many thousands*	
18 Eph. 4:8	
18 Judg. 5:12	
18 Acts 2:4, 33	
18 Heb. *in the man*	
18 1 Tim. 1:13	
18 Ps. 78:60	
20 Deut. 32:39	
21 Hab. 3:13	
21 Ps. 55:23	
Num. 21:33	**22**
Ex. 14:22	**22**
Ps. 58:10	**23**
Or, *red*	**23**
1 Ki. 21:19	**23**
1 Chr. 13:8	**25**
Or, ye that are *of the fountain of Israel*	**26**
Deut. 33:28	**26**
Is. 48:1	
1 Sam. 9:21	**27**
Or, *with their company*	**27**
Ps. 42:8	**28**
Ps. 72:10	**29**
Or, *the beasts of the reeds,*	**30**
Jer. 51:32	
Ps. 22:12	**30**
2 Sam. 8:2	**30**
Or, *he scattereth*	**30**
Is. 19:21	**31**
Is. 45:14	**31**
Ps. 44:20	**31**
Ps. 18:10	**33**
Heb. *give*	**33**
Ps. 29:1	**34**
Or, *heavens*	**34**
Ps. 76:12	**35**

PSALM **69**	
Ps. 45, title	＊
Jonah 2:5	**1**
Ps. 40:2	**2**
Heb. *the mire of depth*	**2**
Heb. *depth of waters*	**2**
Ps. 6:6	**3**
Ps. 119:82	**3**

22 The Lᴏʀᴅ said, I will bring ᴿagain from Bā′-shăn, I will bring *my people* again ᴿfrom the depths of the sea:

23 ᴿThat thy foot may be ᴺdipped in the blood of *thine* enemies, ᴿ*and* the tongue of thy dogs in the same.

24 They have seen thy goings, O God; *even* the goings of my God, my King, in the sanctuary.

25 ᴿThe singers went before, the players on instruments *followed* after; among *them were* the damsels playing with timbrels.

26 Bless ye God in the congregations, *even* the Lord, ᴺfrom ᴿthe fountain of Israel.

27 There *is* ᴿlittle Benjamin *with* their ruler, the princes of Judah ᴺ*and* their council, the princes of Zĕ-bū′-lŭn, *and* the princes of Năph′-tă-lī.

28 Thy God hath ᴿcommanded thy strength: strengthen, O God, that which thou hast wrought for us.

29 Because of thy temple at Jerusalem ᴿshall kings bring presents unto thee.

30 Rebuke ᴺthe company of spearmen, ᴿthe multitude of the bulls, with the calves of the people, *till every one* ᴿsubmit himself with pieces of silver: ᴺscatter thou the people *that* delight in war.

31 ᴿPrinces shall come out of Egypt; ᴿĒ-thĭ-ō′-pĭ-ă shall soon ᴿstretch out her hands unto God.

32 Sing unto God, ye kingdoms of the earth; O sing praises unto the Lord; Sĕ′-läh:

33 To him ᴿthat rideth upon the heavens of heavens, *which were* of old; lo, he doth ᴺsend out his voice, *and that* a mighty voice.

34 ᴿAscribe ye strength unto God: his excellency *is* over Israel, and his strength *is* in the ᴺclouds.

35 O God, ᴿ*thou art* terrible out of thy holy places: the God of Israel *is* he that giveth strength and power unto *his* people. Blessed *be* God.

PSALM 69

Cry of distress

To the chief Musician ＊upon Shō-shănn′-īm, *A Psalm* of David.

Sᴀᴠᴇ me, O God; for ᴿthe waters are come in unto *my* soul.

2 ᴿI sink in ᴺdeep mire, where *there is* no standing: I am come into ᴺdeep waters, where the floods overflow me.

3 ᴿI am weary of my crying: my throat is dried: ᴿmine eyes fail while I wait for my God.

4 They that ᴿhate me without a cause are more than the hairs of mine head: they that would destroy me, *being* mine enemies wrongfully, are mighty: then I restored *that* which I took not away.

5 O God, thou knowest my foolishness; and my ᴺsins are not hid from thee.

6 Let not them that wait on thee, O Lord GOD of hosts, be ashamed for my sake: let not those that seek thee be confounded for my sake, O God of Israel.

7 Because for thy sake I have borne reproach; shame hath covered my face.

8 ᴿI am become a stranger unto my brethren, and an alien unto my mother's children.

9 ᴿFor the zeal of thine house hath eaten me up; ᴿand the reproaches of them that reproached thee are fallen upon me.   ★

10 ᴿWhen I wept, *and chastened* my soul with fasting, that was to my reproach.

11 I made sackcloth also my garment; ᴿand I became a proverb to them.

12 They that sit in the gate speak against me; and ᴿI *was* the song of the ᴺdrunkards.

13 But as for me, my prayer *is* unto thee, O LORD, ᴿ*in* an acceptable time: O God, in the multitude of thy mercy hear me, in the truth of thy salvation.

14 Deliver me out of the mire, and let me not sink: ᴿlet me be delivered from them that hate me, and out of ᴿthe deep waters.

15 Let not the waterflood overflow me, neither let the deep swallow me up, and let not the pit ᴿshut her mouth upon me.

16 Hear me, O LORD; for thy lovingkindness *is* good: ᴿturn unto me according to the multitude of thy tender mercies.

17 And ᴿhide not thy face from thy servant; for I am in trouble: ᴺhear me speedily.

18 Draw nigh unto my soul, *and* redeem it: deliver me because of mine enemies.

19 Thou hast known ᴿmy reproach, and my shame, and my dishonour: mine adversaries *are* all before thee.

20 Reproach hath broken my heart; and I am full of heaviness: and ᴿI looked *for some* ᴺto take pity, but *there was* none; and for ᴿcomforters, but I found none.

21 They gave me also gall for my meat; ᴿand in my thirst they gave me vinegar to drink.   ★

22 ᴿLet their table become a snare before them: and *that which should have been* for *their* welfare, *let it become* a trap.

23 ᴿLet their eyes be darkened, that they see not; and make their loins continually to shake.

24 ᴿPour out thine indignation upon them, and let thy wrathful anger take hold of them.

25 ᴿLet ᴺtheir habitation be desolate; *and* ᴺlet none dwell in their tents.

26 For they persecute ᴿhim whom thou hast smitten; and they talk to the grief of ᴺthose whom thou hast wounded.

27 ᴿAdd ᴺiniquity unto their iniquity: ᴿand let them not come into thy righteousness.

28 Let them ᴿbe blotted out of the book of the living, ᴿand not be written with the righteous.

29 But I *am* poor and sorrowful: let thy salvation, O God, set me up on high.

30 ᴿI will praise the name of God with a song, and will magnify him with thanksgiving.

31 ᴿ*This* also shall please the LORD better than an ox *or* bullock that hath horns and hoofs.

32 ᴿThe ᴺhumble shall see *this, and* be glad: and ᴿyour heart shall live that seek God.

33 For the LORD heareth the poor, and despiseth not ᴿhis prisoners.

34 ᴿLet the heaven and earth praise him, the seas, ᴿand every thing that ᴺmoveth therein.

35 ᴿFor God will save Zion, and will build the cities of Judah: that they may dwell there, and have it in possession.

36 ᴿThe seed also of his servants shall inherit it: and they that love his name shall dwell therein.

PSALM 70

Prayer for deliverance

To the chief Musician, *A Psalm* of David,
*to bring to remembrance.

MAKE haste, ᴿO God, to deliver me; make haste ᴺto help me, O LORD.

2 ᴿLet them be ashamed and confounded that seek after my soul: let them be turned backward, and put to confusion, that desire my hurt.

3 ᴿLet them be turned back for a reward of their shame that say, Aha, aha.

4 Let all those that seek thee rejoice and be glad in thee: and let such as love thy salvation say continually, Let God be magnified.

5 ᴿBut I *am* poor and needy: ᴿmake haste unto me, O God: thou *art* my help and my deliverer; O LORD, make no tarrying.

PSALM 71

Prayer of an aged man

IN ᴿthee, O LORD, do I put my trust: let me never be put to confusion.

2 ᴿDeliver me in thy righteousness, and cause me to escape: ᴿincline thine ear unto me, and save me.

Center reference column

PSALM 69

4 Ps. 35:19
 John 15:25
5 Heb. *guiltiness*
8 Is. 53:3
9 John 2:17
9 Rom. 15:3
10 Ps. 35:13
11 Jer. 24:9
12 Job 30:9
12 Heb. *drinkers of strong drink*
13 Is. 49:8
14 Ps. 144:7
14 ver. 1, 2, 15
15 Num. 16:33
16 Ps. 25:16
17 Ps. 27:9
17 Heb. *make haste to hear me*
19 Ps. 22:6, 7
 Is. 53:3
20 Is. 63:5
20 Heb. *to lament with me*
20 Job 16:2
21 Mat. 27:34
 Mark 15:23
 John 19:29
22 Rom. 11:9
23 Is. 6:9, 10
 Rom. 11:10
24 1 Thes. 2:16

Mat. 23:38   25
Heb. *their palace* 25
Heb. *let there*   25
 not be a dweller
Is. 53:4   26
Heb. *thy*   26
 wounded
Rom. 1:28   27
Or, *punishment* 27
 of iniquity
Is. 26:10   27
Ex. 32:32   28
 Phil. 4:3
Ezek. 13:9   28
Ps. 28:7   30
Ps. 50:13   31
Ps. 34:2   32
Or, *meek*   32
Ps. 22:26   32
Eph. 3:1   33
Ps. 96:11   34
 & 148:1
 Is. 44:23
Is. 55:12   34
Heb. *creepeth*   34
Ps. 51:18   35
 Is. 44:26
Ps. 102:28   36

PSALM 70

Ps. 38, title   *
Ps. 40:13   1
Heb. *to my help*   1
Ps. 35:4, 26   2
Ps. 40:15   3
Ps. 40:17   5
Ps. 141:1   5

PSALM 71

Ps. 25:2, 3   1
Ps. 31:1   2
Ps. 17:6   2

3 ᴿBeᴺ thou my strong habitation, whereunto I may continually resort: thou hast given ᴿcommandment to save me; for thou *art* my rock and my fortress.

4 ᴿDeliver me, O my God, out of the hand of the wicked, out of the hand of the unrighteous and cruel man.

5 For thou *art* ᴿmy hope, O Lord GOD: *thou art* my trust from my youth.

6 ᴿBy thee have I been holden up from the womb: thou art he that took me out of my mother's bowels: my praise *shall be* continually of thee.

7 ᴿI am as a wonder unto many; but thou *art* my strong refuge.

8 Let ᴿmy mouth be filled *with* thy praise *and with* thy honour all the day.

9 ᴿCast me not off in the time of old age; forsake me not when my strength faileth.

10 For mine enemies speak against me; and they that ᴺlay wait for my soul ᴿtake counsel together,

11 Saying, God hath forsaken him: persecute and take him; for *there is* none to deliver *him*.

12 ᴿO God, be not far from me: O my God, ᴿmake haste for my help.

13 ᴿLet them be confounded *and* consumed that are adversaries to my soul; let them be covered *with* reproach and dishonour that seek my hurt.

14 But I will hope continually, and will yet praise thee more and more.

15 ᴿMy mouth shall shew forth thy righteousness *and* thy salvation all the day; for ᴿI know not the numbers *thereof*.

16 I will go in the strength of the Lord GOD: I will make mention of thy righeousness, *even* of thine only.

17 O God, thou hast taught me from my youth: and hitherto have I declared thy wondrous works.

18 ᴿNow also ᴺwhen I am old and grayheaded, O God, forsake me not; until I have shewed ᴺthy strength unto *this* generation, *and* thy power to every one *that* is to come.

19 ᴿThy righteousness also, O God, *is* very high, who hast done great things: ᴿO God, who *is* like unto thee!

20 ᴿ*Thou,* which hast shewed me great and sore troubles, ᴿshalt quicken me again, and shalt bring me up again from the depths of the earth.

21 Thou shalt increase my greatness, and comfort me on every side.

22 I will also praise thee ᴿwithᴺ the psaltery, *even* thy truth, O my God: unto thee will I sing with the harp, O thou ᴿHoly One of Israel.

PSALM **71**

3 Ps. 31:2, 3
3 Heb. *Be thou to me for a rock of habitation*
3 Ps. 44:4
4 Ps. 140:1, 4
5 Jer. 17:7
6 Ps. 22:9, 10　Is. 46:3
7 Is. 8:18
8 Ps. 35:28
9 ver. 18
10 Heb. *watch,* or, *observe*
10 2 Sam. 17:1　Mat. 27:1
12 Ps. 35:22
12 Ps. 70:1
13 ver. 24
15 Ps. 35:28
15 Ps. 40:5
18 ver. 9
18 Heb. *unto old age and gray hairs*
18 Heb. *thine arm*
19 Ps. 57:10
19 Ps. 35:10
20 Ps. 60:3
20 Hos. 6:1, 2
22 Ps. 92:1-3
22 Heb. *with the instrument of psaltery*
22 2 Ki. 19:22　Is. 60:9

Ps. 103:4　23

PSALM **72**

Ps. 127, title　*
Or, *of*　*
Is. 32:1　2
Ps. 85:10　3
Is. 32:17
Is. 11:4　4
ver. 7, 17　5
Hos. 6:3　6
Is. 2:4　7
Jer. 33:6
Luke 1:33
Heb. *till there be no moon*　7
Ex. 23:31　8
Zech. 9:10
Ps. 74:14　9
Is. 49:23　9
2 Chr. 9:21　10
Is. 49:23　11
Job 29:12　12
Ps. 116:15　14
Heb. *one shall give*　15
1 Ki. 4:20　16
Ps. 89:36　17
Heb. *shall be*　17
Heb. *shall be as a son to continue his father's name for ever*　17
Gen. 12:3　17
Jer. 4:2
Luke 1:48　17

23 My lips shall greatly rejoice when I sing unto thee; and ᴿmy soul, which thou hast redeemed.

24 My tongue also shall talk of thy righteousness all the day long: for they are confounded, for they are brought unto shame, that seek my hurt.

PSALM 72

Prayer for wisdom in judgment

A Psalm *for* Solomon.

GIVE the king thy judgments, O God, and thy righteousness unto the king's son. ★

2 ᴿHe shall judge thy people with righteousness, and thy poor with judgment. ★

3 ᴿThe mountains shall bring peace to the people, and the little hills, by righteousness. ★

4 ᴿHe shall judge the poor of the people, he shall save the children of the needy, and shall break in pieces the oppressor. ★

5 They shall fear thee ᴿas long as the sun and moon endure, throughout all generations. ★

6 ᴿHe shall come down like rain upon the mown grass: as showers *that* water the earth. ★

7 In his days shall the righteous flourish; ᴿand abundance of peace ᴺso long as the moon endureth. ★

8 ᴿHe shall have dominion also from sea to sea, and from the river unto the ends of the earth. ★

9 ᴿThey that dwell in the wilderness shall bow before him; ᴿand his enemies shall lick the dust. ★

10 ᴿThe kings of Tarshish and of the isles shall bring presents: the kings of Shē'-bă and Sē'-bă shall offer gifts. ★

11 ᴿYea, all kings shall fall down before him: all nations shall serve him.

12 For he ᴿshall deliver the needy when he crieth; the poor also, and *him* that hath no helper. ★

13 He shall spare the poor and needy, and shall save the souls of the needy. ★

14 He shall redeem their soul from deceit and violence: and ᴿprecious shall their blood be in his sight. ★

15 And he shall live, and to him ᴺshall be given of the gold of Shē'-bă: prayer also shall be made for him continually; *and* daily shall he be praised. ★

16 There shall be an handful of corn in the earth upon the top of the mountains; the fruit thereof shall shake like Lĕb'-ă-nŏn: ᴿand *they* of the city shall flourish like grass of the earth. ★

17 ᴿHis name ᴺshall endure for ever: ᴺhis name shall be continued as long as the sun:

and ᴿmen shall be blessed in him: ᴿall nations shall call him blessed.   ★

18 ᴿBlessed *be* the Lᴏʀᴅ God, the God of Israel, ᴿwho only doeth wondrous things.

19 And ᴿblessed *be* his glorious name for ever: ᴿand let the whole earth be filled *with* his glory; Ä′-mĕn, and Ä′-mĕn.

20 The prayers of David the son of Jesse are ended.

PSALM 73

Envy not the wicked

*A Psalm of *Ä′-săph.

Tʀᴜʟʏᴺ God *is* good to Israel, *even* to such as are ᴺof a clean heart.

2 But as for me, my feet were almost gone; my steps had well nigh slipped.

3 ᴿFor I was envious at the foolish, *when I* saw the prosperity of the wicked.

4 For *there are* no bands in their death: but their strength *is* ᴺfirm.

5 ᴿThey *are* not ᴺin trouble *as other* men; neither are they plagued ᴺlike *other* men.

6 Therefore pride compasseth them about as a chain; violence covereth them ᴿ*as* a garment.

7 ᴿTheir eyes stand out with fatness: ᴺthey have more than heart could wish.

8 ᴿThey are corrupt, and speak wickedly *concerning* oppression: they ᴿspeak loftily.

9 They set their mouth ᴿagainst the heavens, and their tongue walketh through the earth.

10 Therefore his people return hither: ᴿand waters of a full *cup* are wrung out to them.

11 And they say, ᴿHow doth God know? and is there knowledge in the most High?

12 Behold, these *are* the ungodly, who prosper in the world; they increase *in* riches.

13 ᴿVerily I have cleansed my heart *in* vain, and ᴿwashed my hands in innocency.

14 For all the day long have I been plagued, and ᴺchastened every morning.

15 If I say, I will speak thus; behold, I should offend *against* the generation of thy children.

16 ᴿWhen I thought to know this, ᴺit *was* too painful for me;

17 Until ᴿI went into the sanctuary of God; *then* understood I ᴿtheir end.

18 Surely ᴿthou didst set them in slippery places: thou castedst them down into destruction.

19 How are they *brought* into desolation, as in a moment! they are utterly consumed with terrors.

20 ᴿAs a dream when *one* awaketh; *so,* O

PSALM 72	
17 Gen. 12:3	
Jer. 4:2	
17 Luke 1:48	
18 1 Chr. 29:10	
18 Ex. 15:11	
19 Neh. 9:5	
19 Num. 14:21	
Hab. 2:14	

PSALM 73	
* Or, *A Psalm for Asaph*	
* Ps. 50, title	
1 Or, *Yet*	
1 Heb. *clean of heart*	
3 Job 21:7	
Ps. 37:1	
4 Heb. *fat*	
5 Job 21:9	
5 Heb. *in the trouble of* other *men*	
5 Heb. *with*	
6 Ps. 109:18	
7 Jer. 5:28	
7 Heb. *they pass the thoughts of the heart*	
8 Ps. 53:1	
8 Jude 16	
9 Rev. 13:6	
10 Ps. 75:8	
11 Job 22:13	
13 Job 34:9	
Mal. 3:14	
13 Ps. 26:6	
14 Heb. *my chastisement* was	
16 Eccl. 8:17	
16 Heb. *it was labour in mine eyes*	
17 Ps. 77:13	
17 Ps. 37:38	
18 Ps. 35:6	
20 Job 20:8	
Ps. 90:5	

Ps. 92:6	22
Prov. 30:2	
Heb. *I knew not*	22
Heb. *with thee*	22
Ps. 32:8 & 48:14	24
Phil. 3:8	25
Ps. 84:2 & 119:81	26
Heb. *rock*	26
Ps. 119:155	27
Heb. 10:22	28

PSALM 74	
Or, *A Psalm for Asaph to give instruction*	*
Ps. 44:9, 23	1
Jer. 31:37	
Deut. 29:20	1
Ps. 95:7	1
Or, *tribe*	2
Dan. 6:27	4
Heb. *They have sent thy sanctuary into the fire*	7
Ps. 83:4	8
Heb. *break*	8
Amos 8:11	9

Lord, when thou awakest, thou shalt despise their image.

21 Thus my heart was grieved, and I was pricked in my reins.

22 ᴿSo foolish *was* I, and ᴺignorant: I was *as* a beast ᴺbefore thee.

23 Nevertheless I *am* continually with thee: thou hast holden *me* by my right hand.

24 ᴿThou shalt guide me with thy counsel, and afterward receive me *to* glory.

25 ᴿWhom have I in heaven *but thee?* and *there is* none upon earth *that* I desire beside thee.

26 ᴿMy flesh and my heart faileth: *but* God *is* the ᴺstrength of my heart, and my portion for ever.

27 For, lo, ᴿthey that are far from thee shall perish: thou hast destroyed all them that go a whoring from thee.

28 But *it is* good for me to ᴿdraw near to God: I have put my trust in the Lord Gᴏᴅ, that I may declare all thy works.

PSALM 74

Plea for help against scoffers

*Măs′-chĭl of Ä′-săph.

O GOD, why hast thou ᴿcast *us* off for ever? *why* doth thine anger ᴿsmoke against ᴿthe sheep of thy pasture?

2 Remember thy congregation, *which* thou hast purchased of old; the ᴺrod of thine inheritance, *which* thou hast redeemed; this mount Zion, wherein thou hast dwelt.

3 Lift up thy feet unto the perpetual desolations; *even* all *that* the enemy hath done wickedly in the sanctuary.

4 Thine enemies roar in the midst of thy congregations; ᴿthey set up their ensigns *for* signs.

5 *A man* was famous according as he had lifted up axes upon the thick trees.

6 But now they break down the carved work thereof at once with axes and hammers.

7 ᴺThey have cast fire into thy sanctuary, they have defiled *by casting down* the dwelling place of thy name to the ground.

8 ᴿThey said in their hearts, Let us ᴺdestroy them together: they have burned up all the synagogues of God in the land.

9 We see not our signs: ᴿ*there is* no more any prophet: neither *is there* among us any that knoweth how long.

10 O God, how long shall the adversary reproach? shall the enemy blaspheme thy name for ever?

11 ᴿWhy withdrawest thou thy hand, even thy right hand? pluck *it* out of thy bosom.

12 For ᴿGod *is* my King of old, working salvation in the midst of the earth.

13 ᴿThou didst ᴺdivide the sea by thy strength: ᴿthou brakest the heads of the ᴺdragons in the waters.

14 Thou brakest the heads of lē-vī'-ă-thăn in pieces, *and* gavest him ᴿto be meat to the people inhabiting the wilderness.

15 ᴿThou didst cleave the fountain and the flood: ᴿthou driedst up ᴺmighty rivers.

16 The day *is* thine, the night also *is* thine: thou hast prepared the light and the sun.

17 Thou hast set all the borders of the earth: ᴿthou hast ᴺmade summer and winter.

18 ᴿRemember this, *that* the enemy hath reproached, O Lord, and *that* ᴿthe foolish people have blasphemed thy name.

19 O deliver not the soul ᴿof thy turtledove unto the multitude *of the wicked:* ᴿforget not the congregation of thy poor for ever.

20 ᴿHave respect unto the covenant: for the dark places of the earth are full of the habitations of cruelty.

21 O let not the oppressed return ashamed: let the poor and needy praise thy name.

22 Arise, O God, plead thine own cause: ᴿremember how the foolish man reproacheth thee daily.

23 Forget not the voice of thine enemies: the tumult of those that rise up against thee ᴺincreaseth continually.

PSALM 75

Thanksgiving for God's judgment

To the chief Musician, *ăl-tăs'-chĭth,*
A Psalm *or* Song *of ā'-săph.

UNTO thee, O God, do we give thanks, *unto thee* do we give thanks: for *that* thy name is near thy wondrous works declare.

2 ᴺWhen I shall receive the congregation I will judge uprightly.

3 The earth and all the inhabitants thereof are dissolved: I bear up the pillars of it. Sē'-läh.

4 I said unto the fools, Deal not foolishly: and to the wicked, ᴿLift not up the horn:

5 Lift not up your horn on high: speak *not with* a stiff neck.

6 For promotion *cometh* neither from the east, nor from the west, nor from the ᴺsouth.

7 But ᴿGod *is* the judge: ᴿhe putteth down one, and setteth up another.

8 For ᴿin the hand of the Lord *there is* a cup, and the wine is red; it is ᴿfull of mixture; and he poureth out of the same: ᴿbut the dregs

thereof, all the wicked of the earth shall wring *them* out, *and* drink *them.*

9 But I will declare for ever; I will sing praises to the God of Jacob.

10 ᴿAll the horns of the wicked also will I cut off; *but* ᴿthe horns of the righteous shall be exalted.

PSALM 76

Victorious power of God

To the chief Musician on Nĕ-gĭ'-nŏth,
A Psalm *or* Song *of ā'-săph.

IN ᴿJudah *is* God known: his name *is* great in Israel.

2 In Sā'-lĕm also is his tabernacle, and his dwelling place in Zion.

3 ᴿThere brake he the arrows of the bow, the shield, and the sword, and the battle. Sē'-läh.

4 Thou *art* more glorious *and* excellent ᴿthan the mountains of prey.

5 ᴿThe stouthearted are spoiled, ᴿthey have slept their sleep: and none of the men of might have found their hands.

6 ᴿAt thy rebuke, O God of Jacob, both the chariot and horse are cast into a dead sleep.

7 Thou, *even* thou, *art* to be feared: and ᴿwho may stand in thy sight when once thou art angry?

8 ᴿThou didst cause judgment to be heard from heaven; ᴿthe earth feared, and was still,

9 When God ᴿarose to judgment, to save all the meek of the earth. Sē'-läh.

10 ᴿSurely the wrath of man shall praise thee: the remainder of wrath shalt thou restrain.

11 ᴿVow, and pay unto the Lord your God: ᴿlet all that be round about him bring presents ᴺunto him that ought to be feared.

12 He shall cut off the spirit of princes: ᴿhe *is* terrible to the kings of the earth.

PSALM 77

Prayer of recollection

To the chief Musician, *to Jĕ-dū'-thŭn,
A Psalm *of ā'-săph.

I ᴿCRIED unto God with my voice, *even* unto God with my voice; and he gave ear unto me.

2 ᴿIn the day of my trouble I ᴿsought the Lord: ᴺmy sore ran in the night, and ceased not: my soul refused to be comforted.

3 I remembered God, and was troubled: I complained, and ᴿmy spirit was overwhelmed. Sē'-läh.

4 Thou holdest mine eyes waking: I am so troubled that I cannot speak.

5 ᴿI have considered the days of old, the years of ancient times.

6 I call to remembrance ᴿmy song in the night: ᴿI commune with mine own heart: and my spirit made diligent search.

7 ᴿWill the Lord cast off for ever? and will he ᴿbe favourable no more?

8 Is his mercy clean gone for ever? doth ᴿhis promise fail ᴺfor evermore?

9 Hath God ᴿforgotten to be gracious? hath he in anger shut up his tender mercies? Sē'-läh.

10 And I said, This *is* ᴿmy infirmity: *but I will remember* the years of the right hand of the most High.

11 ᴿI will remember the works of the Lᴏʀᴅ: surely I will remember thy wonders of old.

12 I will meditate also of all thy work, and talk of thy doings.

13 ᴿThy way, O God, *is* in the sanctuary: ᴿwho *is so* great a God as *our* God?

14 Thou *art* the God that doest wonders: thou hast declared thy strength among the people.

15 ᴿThou hast with *thine* arm redeemed thy people, the sons of Jacob and Joseph. Sē'-läh.

16 ᴿThe waters saw thee, O God, the waters saw thee; they were afraid: the depths also were troubled.

17 ᴺThe clouds poured out water: the skies sent out a sound: ᴿthine arrows also went abroad.

18 The voice of thy thunder *was* in the heaven: the lightnings lightened the world: ᴿthe earth trembled and shook.

19 ᴿThy way *is* in the sea, and thy path in the great waters, ᴿand thy footsteps are not known.

20 ᴿThou leddest thy people like a flock by the hand of Moses and Aaron.

PSALM 78

God's guidance of Israel

Măs'-chĭl of Ā'-săph.

GIVEᴿ ear, O my people, *to* my law: incline your ears to the words of my mouth.

2 ᴿI will open my mouth in a parable: I will utter dark sayings of old:

3 ᴿWhich we have heard and known, and our fathers have told us.

4 ᴿWe will not hide *them* from their children, ᴿshewing to the generation to come the praises of the Lᴏʀᴅ, and his strength, and his wonderful works that he hath done.

PSALM **77**
5 Deut. 32:7
Ps. 143:5
Is. 51:9
6 Ps. 42:8
6 Ps. 4:4
7 Ps. 74:1
7 Ps. 85:1
8 Rom. 9:6
8 Heb. *to genera-tion and gen-eration?*
9 Is. 49:15
10 Ps. 31:22
11 Ps. 143:5
13 Ps. 73:17
13 Ex. 15:11
15 Ex. 6:6
Deut. 9:29
16 Ex. 14:21
17 Heb. *The clouds were poured forth with water*
17 2 Sam. 22:15
18 2 Sam. 22:8
19 Hab. 3:15
19 Ex. 14:28
20 Ex. 13:21
Is. 63:11, 12

PSALM **78**
* Ps. 74, title
* Or, A Psalm *for Asaph to give instruction*
1 Is. 51:4
2 Mat. 13:35
3 Ps. 44:1
4 Deut. 6:7
Joel 1:3
4 Ex. 13:8, 14

Ps. 147:19   5
Deut. 4:9   5
Ps. 102:18   6
2 Ki. 17:14   8
Ex. 32:9   8
ver. 37   8
Heb. *that prepared not their heart*
Heb. *throwing forth*   9
2 Ki. 17:15   10
Ps. 106:13   11
Ex. 7, & 8, & 9, 12
  & 10, & 11, & 12
Num. 13:22   12
Ex. 14:21   13
Ex. 15:8   13
Ex. 13:21   14
Num. 20:11   15
Deut. 9:21   16
Heb. 3:16   17
Ex. 16:2   18
Num. 11:4   19
Heb. *order*   19
Num. 20:11   20
Num. 11:1   21
Heb. 3:18   22
Mal. 3:10   23
John 6:31   24
Or, *Every one did eat the bread of the mighty* 25
Num. 11:31   26
Heb. *to go*   26

---

5 For ᴿhe established a testimony in Jacob, and appointed a law in Israel, which he commanded our fathers, ᴿthat they should make them known to their children:

6 ᴿThat the generation to come might know *them, even* the children *which* should be born; *who* should arise and declare *them* to their children:

7 That they might set their hope in God, and not forget the works of God, but keep his commandments:

8 And ᴿmight not be as their fathers, ᴿa stubborn and rebellious generation; a generation ᴿ*that*ᴺ set not their heart aright, and whose spirit was not stedfast with God.

9 The children of Ē'-phră-ĭm, *being* armed, *and* ᴺcarrying bows, turned back in the day of battle.

10 ᴿThey kept not the covenant of God, and refused to walk in his law;

11 And ᴿforgat his works, and his wonders that he had shewed them.

12 ᴿMarvellous things did he in the sight of their fathers, in the land of Egypt, ᴿ*in* the field of Zō'-ăn.

13 ᴿHe divided the sea, and caused them to pass through; and ᴿhe made the waters to stand as an heap.

14 ᴿIn the daytime also he led them with a cloud, and all the night with a light of fire.

15 ᴿHe clave the rocks in the wilderness, and gave *them* drink as *out of* the great depths.

16 He brought ᴿstreams also out of the rock, and caused waters to run down like rivers.

17 And they sinned yet more against him by ᴿprovoking the most High in the wilderness.

18 And ᴿthey tempted God in their heart by asking meat for their lust.

19 ᴿYea, they spake against God; they said, Can God ᴺfurnish a table in the wilderness?

20 ᴿBehold, he smote the rock, that the waters gushed out, and the streams overflowed; can he give bread also? can he provide flesh for his people?

21 Therefore the Lᴏʀᴅ heard *this,* and ᴿwas wroth: so a fire was kindled against Jacob, and anger also came up against Israel;

22 Because they ᴿbelieved not in God, and trusted not in his salvation:

23 Though he had commanded the clouds from above, ᴿand opened the doors of heaven,

24 ᴿAnd had rained down măn'-nă upon them to eat, and had given them of the corn of heaven.

25 ᴺMan did eat angels' food: he sent them meat to the full.

26 ᴿHe caused an east wind ᴺto blow in the

heaven: and by his power he brought in the south wind.

27 He rained flesh also upon them as dust, and ᴺfeathered fowls like as the sand of the sea:

28 And he let *it* fall in the midst of their camp, round about their habitations.

29 ᴿSo they did eat, and were well filled: for he gave them their own desire;

30 They were not estranged from their lust. But ᴿwhile their meat *was* yet in their mouths,

31 The wrath of God came upon them, and slew the fattest of them, and ᴺsmote down the ᴺchosen *men* of Israel.

32 For all this ᴿthey sinned still, and ᴿbelieved not for his wondrous works.

33 ᴿTherefore their days did he consume in vanity, and their years in trouble.

34 ᴿWhen he slew them, then they sought him: and they returned and inquired early after God.

35 And they remembered that ᴿGod *was* their rock, and the high God ᴿtheir redeemer.

36 Nevertheless they did ᴿflatter him with their mouth, and they lied unto him with their tongues.

37 For their heart was not right with him, neither were they stedfast in his covenant.

38 ᴿBut he, *being* full of compassion, forgave *their* iniquity, and destroyed *them* not: yea, many a time ᴿturned he his anger away, ᴿand did not stir up all his wrath.

39 For ᴿhe remembered ᴿthat they *were but* flesh; ᴿa wind that passeth away, and cometh not again.

40 How oft did they ᴿprovokeᴺ him in the wilderness, *and* grieve him in the desert!

41 Yea, ᴿthey turned back and tempted God, and limited the Holy One of Israel.

42 They remembered not his hand, *nor* the day when he delivered them ᴺfrom the enemy.

43 How he had ᴺwrought his signs in Egypt, and his wonders in the field of Zō'-ăn:

44 ᴿAnd had turned their rivers into blood; and their floods, that they could not drink.

45 ᴿHe sent divers sorts of flies among them, which devoured them; and ᴿfrogs, which destroyed them.

46 He gave also their increase unto the caterpiller, and their labour unto the locust.

47 ᴿHe ᴺdestroyed their vines with hail, and their sycomore trees with ᴺfrost.

48 ᴿHeᴺ gave up their cattle also to the hail, and their flocks to ᴺhot thunderbolts.

49 He cast upon them the fierceness of his anger, wrath, and indignation, and trouble, by sending evil angels *among them.*

50 ᴺHe made a way to his anger; he spared

PSALM **78**
27 Heb. *fowl of wing*
29 Num. 11:20
30 Num. 11:33
31 Heb. *made to bow*
31 Or, *young men*
32 Num. 14, & 16, & 17
32 ver. 22
33 Num. 14:29
34 Hos. 5:15
35 Deut. 32:4, 15, 31
35 Is. 41:14 & 63:9
36 Ezek. 33:31
38 Num. 14:18, 20
38 Is. 48:9
38 1 Ki. 21:29
39 Ps. 103:14
39 John 3:6
39 Job 7:7, 16
40 Ps. 95:8-10 Heb. 3:16
40 Or, *rebel against him*
41 Num. 14:22 Deut. 6:16
42 Or, *from affliction*
43 Heb. *set*
44 Ex. 7:20 Ps. 105:29
45 Ex. 8:24 Ps. 105:31
45 Ex. 8:6
47 Ex. 9:23, 25 Ps. 105:33
47 Heb. *killed*
47 Or, *great hailstones*
48 Ex. 9:23-25
48 Heb. *He shut up*
48 Or, *lightnings*
50 Heb. *He weighed a path*

Or, *their beasts to the murrain*	50
Ex. 12:29	51
Ps. 106:22	51
Ps. 77:20	52
Ex. 14:19	53
Ex. 14:27	53
Heb. *covered*	53
Ex. 15:17	54
Ps. 44:3	54
Ps. 44:2	55
Josh. 13:7	55
Judg. 2:11	56
Ezek. 20:27	57
Hos. 7:16	57
Deut. 32:16, 21	58
Judg. 2:12	
Deut. 12:2	58
Judg. 18:30	61
1 Sam. 4:10	62
Jer. 7:34	63
Heb. *praised*	63
1 Sam. 22:18	64
Job 27:15	64
Is. 42:13	65
1 Sam. 5:6	66
Ps. 87:2	68
Heb. *founded*	69
1 Sam. 16:11, 12	70
Heb. *From after*	71
Is. 40:11	71
2 Sam. 5:2	71
1 Ki. 9:4	72

not their soul from death, but gave ᴺtheir life over to the pestilence;

51 ᴿAnd smote all the firstborn in Egypt; the chief of *their* strength in ᴿthe tabernacles of Ham:

52 But ᴿmade his own people to go forth like sheep, and guided them in the wilderness like a flock.

53 And he ᴿled them on safely, so that they feared not: but the sea ᴿoverwhelmedᴺ their enemies.

54 And he brought them to the border of his ᴿsanctuary, *even to* this mountain, ᴿ*which* his right hand had purchased.

55 ᴿHe cast out the heathen also before them, and ᴿdivided them an inheritance by line, and made the tribes of Israel to dwell in their tents.

56 ᴿYet they tempted and provoked the most high God, and kept not his testimonies:

57 But ᴿturned back, and dealt unfaithfully like their fathers: they were turned aside ᴿlike a deceitful bow.

58 ᴿFor they provoked him to anger with their ᴿhigh places, and moved him to jealousy with their graven images.

59 When God heard *this,* he was wroth, and greatly abhorred Israel:

60 So that he forsook the tabernacle of Shī'-lōh, the tent *which* he placed among men;

61 ᴿAnd delivered his strength into captivity, and his glory into the enemy's hand.

62 ᴿHe gave his people over also unto the sword; and was wroth with his inheritance.

63 The fire consumed their young men; and ᴿtheir maidens were not ᴺgiven to marriage.

64 ᴿTheir priests fell by the sword; and ᴿtheir widows made no lamentation.

65 Then the Lord awaked as one out of sleep, *and* ᴿlike a mighty man that shouteth by reason of wine.

66 And ᴿhe smote his enemies in the hinder parts: he put them to a perpetual reproach.

67 Moreover he refused the tabernacle of Joseph, and chose not the tribe of Ē'-phrā-ĭm:

68 But chose the tribe of Judah, the mount Zion ᴿwhich he loved.

69 And he built his sanctuary like high *palaces,* like the earth which he hath ᴺestablished for ever.

70 ᴿHe chose David also his servant, and took him from the sheepfolds:

71 ᴺFrom following ᴿthe ewes great with young he brought him ᴿto feed Jacob his people, and Israel his inheritance.

72 So he fed them according to the ᴿintegrity of his heart; and guided them by the skilfulness of his hands.

PSALM 79

Lament over the fall of Jerusalem

A Psalm *of Ā'-sāph.

O GOD, the heathen are come into ^Rthine inheritance; thy holy temple have they defiled; ^Rthey have laid Jerusalem on heaps.

2 ^RThe dead bodies of thy servants have they given *to be* meat unto the fowls of the heaven, the flesh of thy saints unto the beasts of the earth.

3 Their blood have they shed like water round about Jerusalem; and *there was* none to bury *them*.

4 We are become a reproach to our neighbours, a scorn and derision to them that are round about us.

5 ^RHow long, LORD? wilt thou be angry for ever? shall thy ^Rjealousy burn like fire?

6 ^RPour out thy wrath upon the heathen that have ^Rnot known thee, and upon the kingdoms that have ^Rnot called upon thy name.

7 For they have devoured Jacob, and laid waste his dwelling place.

8 ^RO remember not against us ^Nformer iniquities: let thy tender mercies speedily prevent us: for we are brought very low.

9 Help us, O God of our salvation, for the glory of thy name: and deliver us, and purge away our sins, ^Rfor thy name's sake.

10 ^RWherefore should the heathen say, Where *is* their God? let him be known among the heathen in our sight *by* the ^Nrevenging of the blood of thy servants *which is* shed.

11 Let ^Rthe sighing of the prisoner come before thee; according to the greatness of ^Nthy power ^Npreserve thou those that are appointed to die;

12 And render unto our neighbours ^Rsevenfold into their bosom ^Rtheir reproach, wherewith they have reproached thee, O Lord.

13 So ^Rwe thy people and sheep of thy pasture will give thee thanks for ever: ^Rwe will shew forth thy praise ^Nto all generations.

PSALM 80

Appeal for restoration

To the chief Musician *upon Shō-shănn'-im-Ē'-dŭth, A Psalm *of Ā'-sāph.

G IVE ear, O Shepherd of Israel, thou that leadest Joseph ^Rlike a flock; thou that dwellest *between* the chĕr'-ū-bĭms, ^Rshine forth.

2 Before Ē'-phră-ĭm and Benjamin and

Mă-năs'-sēh stir up thy strength, and ^Ncome *and* save us.

3 ^RTurn us again, O God, ^Rand cause thy face to shine; and we shall be saved.

4 O LORD God of hosts, how long ^Nwilt thou be angry against the prayer of thy people?

5 ^RThou feedest them with the bread of tears; and givest them tears to drink in great measure.

6 Thou makest us a strife unto our neighbours: and our enemies laugh among themselves.

7 Turn us again, O God of hosts, and cause thy face to shine; and we shall be saved.

8 Thou hast brought ^Ra vine out of Egypt: ^Rthou hast cast out the heathen, and planted it.

9 Thou preparedst *room* before it, and didst cause it to take deep root, and it filled the land.

10 The hills were covered with the shadow of it, and the boughs thereof *were like* ^Nthe goodly cedars.

11 She sent out her boughs unto the sea, and her branches unto the river.

12 Why hast thou *then* ^Rbroken down her hedges, so that all they which pass by the way do pluck her?

13 The boar out of the wood doth waste it, and the wild beast of the field doth devour it.

14 Return, we beseech thee, O God of hosts: ^Rlook down from heaven, and behold, and visit this vine;

15 And the vineyard which thy right hand hath planted, and the branch *that* thou madest strong for thyself.

16 *It is* burned with fire, *it is* cut down: ^Rthey perish at the rebuke of thy countenance.

17 ^RLet thy hand be upon the man of thy right hand, upon the son of man *whom* thou madest strong for thyself.

18 So will not we go back from thee: quicken us, and we will call upon thy name.

19 Turn us again, O LORD God of hosts, cause thy face to shine; and we shall be saved.

PSALM 81

Israel's infidelity

To the chief Musician *upon Gĭt'-tĭth, A Psalm *of Ā'-sāph.

S ING aloud unto God our strength: make a joyful noise unto the God of Jacob.

2 Take a psalm, and bring hither the timbrel, the pleasant harp with the psaltery.

3 Blow up the trumpet in the new moon, in the time appointed, on our solemn feast day.

PSALM 79

* Or, *for Asaph*
1 Ps. 74:2
1 Mic. 3:12
2 Jer. 7:33
5 Ps. 74:1, 9
5 Zeph. 3:8
6 Jer. 10:25
Rev. 16:1
6 Is. 45:4, 5
2 Thes. 1:8
8 Ps. 53:4
8 Is. 64:9
8 Or, *the iniquities of them that were before us*
9 Jer. 14:7
10 Ps. 42:10
10 Heb. *vengeance*
11 Ps. 102:20
11 Heb. *thine arm*
11 Heb. *reserve the children of death*
12 Gen. 4:15
Is. 65:6, 7
Jer. 32:18
Luke 6:38
12 Ps. 74:18
13 Ps. 74:1 & 95:7
13 Is. 43:21
13 Heb. *to generation and generation*

PSALM 80

* Ps. 45, & 69, title
* Or, *for Asaph*
1 Ps. 77:20
1 Deut. 33:2
Ps. 50:2

Heb. *come for salvation to us* 2
Lam. 5:21 3
Num. 6:25 3
Ps. 4:6
Heb. *wilt thou smoke* 4
Ps. 42:3 5
Is. 30:20
Is. 5:1, 7 8
Jer. 2:21
Ezek. 15:6
Ps. 44:2 8
Heb. *the cedars of God* 10
Is. 5:5 12
Nah. 2:2
Is. 63:15 14
Ps. 39:11 & 76:7 16
Ps. 89:21 17

PSALM 81

Ps. 8, title *
Or, *for Asaph* *

4 For this *was* a statute for Israel, *and* a law of the God of Jacob.

5 This he ordained in Joseph *for* a testimony, when he went out ᴺthrough the land of Egypt: ᴿ*where* I heard a language *that* I understood not.

6 I removed his shoulder from the burden: his hands ᴺwere delivered from the pots.

7 ᴿThou calledst in trouble, and I delivered thee; ᴿI answered thee in the secret place of thunder: I ᴿproved thee at the waters of ᴺMĕr'-ĭ-bäh. Sē'-läh.

8 ᴿHear, O my people, and I will testify unto thee: O Israel, if thou wilt hearken unto me;

9 There shall no ᴿstrange god be in thee; neither shalt thou worship any strange god.

10 ᴿI *am* the Lᴏʀᴅ thy God, which brought thee out of the land of Egypt: ᴿopen thy mouth wide, and I will fill it.

11 But my people would not hearken to my voice; and Israel would ᴿnone of me.

12 ᴿSo I gave them up ᴺunto their own hearts' lust: *and* they walked in their own counsels.

13 ᴿOh that my people had hearkened unto me, *and* Israel had walked in my ways!

14 I should soon have subdued their enemies, and turned my hand against their adversaries.

15 ᴿThe haters of the Lᴏʀᴅ should have ᴺᴺsubmitted themselves unto him: but their time should have endured for ever.

16 He should ᴿhave fed them also ᴺwith the finest of the wheat: and with honey ᴿout of the rock should I have satisfied thee.

PSALM 82

Plea for justice for the needy

A Psalm *of Ā'-săph.

GOD ᴿstandeth in the congregation of the mighty; he judgeth among ᴿthe gods.

2 How long will ye judge unjustly, and ᴿaccept the persons of the wicked? Sē'-läh.

3 ᴺDefend the poor and fatherless: ᴿdo justice to the afflicted and needy.

4 ᴿDeliver the poor and needy: rid *them* out of the hand of the wicked.

5 They ᴿknow not, neither will they understand; they walk on in darkness: ᴿall the foundations of the earth are ᴺout of course.

6 ᴿI have said, Ye *are* gods; and all of you *are* children of the most High.

7 But ᴿye shall die like men, and fall like one of the princes.

8 ᴿArise, O God, judge the earth: ᴿfor thou shalt inherit all nations.

PSALM 83

Appeal for victory over enemies

A Song *or* Psalm *of Ā'-săph.

KEEP ᴿnot thou silence, O God: hold not thy peace, and be not still, O God.

2 For, lo, ᴿthine enemies make a tumult: and they that ᴿhate thee have lifted up the head.

3 They have taken crafty counsel against thy people, and consulted ᴿagainst thy hidden ones.

4 They have said, Come, and ᴿlet us cut them off from *being* a nation; that the name of Israel may be no more in remembrance.

5 For they have consulted together with one ᴺconsent: they are confederate against thee:

6 ᴿThe tabernacles of Ē'-dǫm, and the ĭsh'-mā-ē-lites; of Moab, and the Hăg'-ā-rēnes;

7 Gē'-băl, and Ammon, and Ăm'-ā-lĕk; the Philistines with the inhabitants of Tyre;

8 Assur also is joined with them: ᴺthey have holpen the children of Lot. Sē'-läh.

9 Do unto them as *unto* the Mĭd'-ĭ-ā-nītes; as *to* ᴿSĭs'-ĕ-rā, as *to* Jā'-bĭn, at the brook of Kī'-sǫn:

10 *Which* perished at En-dor: ᴿthey became *as* dung for the earth.

11 Make their nobles like ôr'-ĕb, and like Zēĕb: yea, all their princes as ᴿZē'-bäh, and as Zăl-mŭn'-nä:

12 Who said, Let us take to ourselves the houses of God in possession.

13 ᴿO my God, make them like a wheel; ᴿas the stubble before the wind.

14 As the fire burneth a wood, and as the flame ᴿsetteth the mountains on fire;

15 So persecute them with thy tempest, and make them afraid with thy storm.

16 Fill their faces with shame; that they may seek thy name, O Lᴏʀᴅ.

17 Let them be confounded and troubled for ever; yea, let them be put to shame, and perish:

18 ᴿThat *men* may know that thou, whose ᴿname alone *is* Jĕ-Hō'-VᴀH, *art* ᴿthe most high over all the earth.

PSALM 84

Delight in God's house

To the chief Musician *upon Gĭt'-tĭth, A Psalm *for the sons of Kôr'-ăh.

HOW ᴿamiable *are* thy tabernacles, O Lᴏʀᴅ of hosts!

2 ᴿMy soul longeth, yea, even fainteth for the courts of the LORD: my heart and my flesh crieth out for the living God.

3 Yea, the sparrow hath found an house, and the swallow a nest for herself, where she may lay her young, *even* thine altars, O LORD of hosts, my King, and my God.

4 Blessed *are* they that dwell in thy house: they will be still praising thee. Sē'-läh.

5 Blessed *is* the man whose strength *is* in thee; in whose heart *are* the ways *of them.*

6 *Who* passing through the valley ᴿofᴺ Bā'-că make it a well; the rain also ᴺfilleth the pools.

7 They go ᴿfromᴺ strength to strength, *every one of them* in Zion ᴿappeareth before God.

8 O LORD God of hosts, hear my prayer: give ear, O God of Jacob. Sē'-läh.

9 Behold, ᴿO God our shield, and look upon the face of thine anointed.

10 For a day in thy courts *is* better than a thousand. ᴺI had rather be a doorkeeper in the house of my God, than to dwell in the tents of wickedness.

11 For the LORD God *is* ᴿa sun and ᴿshield: the LORD will give grace and glory: ᴿno good *thing* will he withhold from them that walk uprightly.

12 O LORD of hosts, ᴿblessed *is* the man that trusteth in thee.

PSALM 85

Prayer for restoration

To the chief Musician, A Psalm *for* the sons of Kôr'-ăh.

LORD, thou hast been ᴺfavourable unto thy land: thou hast ᴿbrought back the captivity of Jacob.

2 Thou hast forgiven the iniquity of thy people, thou hast covered all their sin. Sē'-läh.

3 Thou hast taken away all thy wrath: ᴺthou hast turned *thyself* from the fierceness of thine anger.

4 ᴿTurn us, O God of our salvation, and cause thine anger toward us to cease.

5 ᴿWilt thou be angry with us for ever? wilt thou draw out thine anger to all generations?

6 Wilt thou not ᴿrevive us again: that thy people may rejoice in thee?

7 Shew us thy mercy, O LORD, and grant us thy salvation.

8 ᴿI will hear what God the LORD will speak: for ᴿhe will speak peace unto his people, and to his saints: but let them not ᴿturn again to folly.

9 Surely ᴿhis salvation *is* nigh them that fear him; ᴿthat glory may dwell in our land.

10 Mercy and truth are met together;

PSALM 84	
2	Ps. 42:1, 2
6	2 Sam. 5:23
6	Or, *of mulberry trees make him a well, etc.*
6	Heb. *covereth*
7	Prov. 4:18
7	Or, *from company to company*
7	Deut. 16:16
9	ver. 11
10	Heb. *I would choose rather to sit at the threshold*
11	Is. 60:19
11	Gen. 15:1
	Ps. 115:9
	Prov. 2:7
11	Ps. 34:9
12	Ps. 2:12

PSALM 85	
*	Ps. 42, title
*	Or, *of*
1	Or, *well pleased,* Ps. 77:7
1	Ezra 1:11
	Jer. 30:18
	Ezek. 39:25
	Joel 3:1
3	Or, *thou hast turned thine anger from waxing hot,* Deut. 13:17
4	Ps. 80:7
5	Ps. 79:5
6	Hab. 3:2
8	Hab. 2:1
8	Zech. 9:10
8	2 Pet. 2:20
9	Is. 46:13
9	Zech. 2:5
Ps. 72:3	10
Is. 32:17	
Luke 2:14	
Ps. 84:11	12
Jas. 1:17	
Ps. 89:14	13

PSALM 86	
Or, *A Prayer, being a Psalm of David*	*
Or, *one whom thou favourest*	2
Ps. 56:1 & 57:1	3
Or, *all the day*	3
Ps. 25:1 & 143:8	4
Ps. 130:7 & 145:9	5
Joel 2:13	
Ex. 15:11	8
Ps. 89:6	
Deut. 3:24	8
Ps. 22:31	9
Is. 43:7	
Rev. 15:4	
Ex. 15:11	10
Ps. 72:18	
Deut. 6:4	10
Mark 12:29	
Ps. 25:4	11
Or, *grave*	13
Heb. *terrible*	14
Ex. 34:6	15
Neh. 9:17	
Ps. 103:8	
Joel 2:13	

ᴿrighteousness and peace have kissed *each other.*

11 Truth shall spring out of the earth; and righteousness shall look down from heaven.

12 ᴿYea, the LORD shall give *that which is* good; and our land shall yield her increase.

13 ᴿRighteousness shall go before him; and shall set *us* in the way of his steps.

PSALM 86

Prayer in a day of trouble

*A Prayer of David.

BOW down thine ear, O LORD, hear me: for I *am* poor and needy.

2 Preserve my soul; for I *am* ᴺholy: O thou my God, save thy servant that trusteth in thee.

3 ᴿBe merciful unto me, O Lord: for I cry unto thee ᴺdaily.

4 Rejoice the soul of thy servant: ᴿfor unto thee, O Lord, do I lift up my soul.

5 ᴿFor thou, Lord, *art* good, and ready to forgive; and plenteous in mercy unto all them that call upon thee.

6 Give ear, O LORD, unto my prayer; and attend to the voice of my supplications.

7 In the day of my trouble I will call upon thee: for thou wilt answer me.

8 ᴿAmong the gods *there is* none like unto thee, O Lord; ᴿneither *are there any works* like unto thy works.

9 ᴿAll nations whom thou hast made shall come and worship before thee, O Lord; and shall glorify thy name.

10 For thou *art* great, and ᴿdoest wondrous things: ᴿthou *art* God alone.

11 ᴿTeach me thy way, O LORD; I will walk in thy truth: unite my heart to fear thy name.

12 I will praise thee, O Lord my God, with all my heart: and I will glorify thy name for evermore.

13 For great *is* thy mercy toward me: and thou hast delivered my soul from the lowest ᴺhell.

14 O God, the proud are risen against me, and the assemblies of ᴺviolent *men* have sought after my soul; and have not set thee before them.

15 ᴿBut thou, O Lord, *art* a God full of compassion, and gracious, longsuffering, and plenteous in mercy and truth.

16 O turn unto me, and have mercy upon me; give thy strength unto thy servant, and save the son of thine handmaid.

17 Shew me a token for good; that they which hate me may see *it,* and be ashamed: because thou, LORD, hast holpen me, and comforted me.

PSALM 87

Praise of Zion

A Psalm *or* Song *for the sons of
Kôr′-ăh.

HIS foundation *is* in the holy mountains.
2 ᴿThe LORD loveth the gates of Zion more than all the dwellings of Jacob.

3 ᴿGlorious things are spoken of thee, O city of God. Sē′-läh.

4 I will make mention of Rahab and Babylon to them that know me: behold Philistia, and Tyre, with Ē-thĭ-ō′-pĭ-ă; this *man* was born there.

5 And of Zion it shall be said, This and that man was born in her: and the highest himself shall establish her.

6 The LORD shall count, when he ᴿwriteth up the people, *that* this *man* was born there. Sē′-läh.

7 As well the singers as the players on instruments *shall be there:* all my springs *are* in thee.

PSALM 88

Prayer to be spared from death

A Song *or* Psalm *for the sons of Kôr′-ăh, to the chief Musician upon Mā′-hă-lăth Lē-ăn′-nōth, *Măs′-chîl of *Hē′-măn the ĕz′-ră-hīte.

O LORD ᴿGod of my salvation, I have cried day *and* night before thee:
2 Let my prayer come before thee: incline thine ear unto my cry;

3 For my soul is full of troubles: and my life ᴿdraweth nigh unto the grave.

4 ᴿI am counted with them that go down into the pit: I am as a man *that hath* no strength:

5 Free among the dead, like the slain that lie in the grave, whom thou rememberest no more: and they are ᴿcut off ᴺfrom thy hand.

6 Thou hast laid me in the lowest pit, in darkness, in the deeps.

7 Thy wrath lieth hard upon me, and ᴿthou hast afflicted *me* with all thy waves. Sē′-läh.

8 ᴿThou hast put away mine acquaintance far from me; thou hast made me an abomination unto them: ᴿ*I am* shut up, and I cannot come forth.

9 ᴿMine eye mourneth by reason of affliction: LORD, ᴿI have called daily upon thee, ᴿI have stretched out my hands unto thee.

10 ᴿWilt thou shew wonders to the dead? shall the dead arise *and* praise thee? Sē′-läh.

11 Shall thy lovingkindness be declared in the grave? *or* thy faithfulness in destruction?

12 ᴿShall thy wonders be known in the dark? and thy righteousness in the land of forgetfulness?

13 But unto thee have I cried, O LORD; and ᴿin the morning shall my prayer prevent thee.

14 LORD, why castest thou off my soul? *why* ᴿhidest thou thy face from me?

15 I *am* afflicted and ready to die from *my* youth up: *while* ᴿI suffer thy terrors I am distracted.

16 Thy fierce wrath goeth over me; thy terrors have cut me off.

17 They came round about me ᴺdaily like water; they ᴿcompassed me about together.

18 ᴿLover and friend hast thou put far from me, *and* mine acquaintance into darkness.

PSALM 89

God's covenant with David

*Măs′-chîl of *Ē′-thăn the ĕz′-ră-hīte.

I ᴿWILL sing of the mercies of the LORD for ever: with my mouth will I make known thy faithfulness ᴺto all generations.

2 For I have said, Mercy shall be built up for ever: ᴿthy faithfulness shalt thou establish in the very heavens.

3 ᴿI have made a covenant with my chosen, I have ᴿsworn unto David my servant,

4 Thy seed will I establish for ever, and build up thy throne ᴿto all generations. Sē′-läh.   ★

5 And ᴿthe heavens shall praise thy wonders, O LORD: thy faithfulness also in the congregation of the saints.

6 For who in the heaven can be compared unto the LORD? *who* among the sons of the mighty can be likened unto the LORD?

7 ᴿGod is greatly to be feared in the assembly of the saints, and to be had in reverence of all *them that are* about him.

8 O LORD God of hosts, who *is* a strong LORD like unto thee? or to thy faithfulness round about thee?

9 ᴿThou rulest the raging of the sea: when the waves thereof arise, thou stillest them.

10 ᴿThou hast broken ᴺRahab in pieces, as one that is slain; thou hast scattered thine enemies ᴺwith thy strong arm.

11 ᴿThe heavens *are* thine, the earth also *is* thine: *as for* the world and the fulness thereof, thou hast founded them.

12 The north and the south thou hast created them: ᴿTā′-bôr and ᴿHĕr′-mon shall rejoice in thy name.

13 Thou hast ᴺa mighty arm: strong is thy hand, *and* high is thy right hand.

14 Justice and judgment *are* the ᴺhabitation of thy throne: mercy and truth shall go before thy face.

15 Blessed *is* the people that know the ᴿjoy-

ful sound: they shall walk, O Lord, in the light of thy countenance.

16 In thy name shall they rejoice all the day: and in thy righteousness shall they be exalted.

17 For thou *art* the glory of their strength: and in thy favour our horn shall be exalted.

18 For ᴺthe Lord *is* our defence; and the Holy One of Israel *is* our king.

19 Then thou spakest in vision to thy holy one, and saidst, I have laid help upon *one that is* mighty; I have exalted *one* ᴿchosen out of the people. ★

20 ᴿI have found David my servant; with my holy oil have I anointed him:

21 ᴿWith whom my hand shall be established: mine arm also shall strengthen him.

22 ᴿThe enemy shall not exact upon him; nor the son of wickedness afflict him.

23 ᴿAnd I will beat down his foes before his face, and plague them that hate him.

24 But ᴿmy faithfulness and my mercy *shall be* with him: and in my name shall his horn be exalted.

25 I will set his hand also in the sea, and his right hand in the rivers.

26 He shall cry unto me, Thou *art* ᴿmy father, my God, and ᴿthe rock of my salvation.

27 Also I will make him ᴿ*my* firstborn, ᴿhigher than the kings of the earth. ★

28 ᴿMy mercy will I keep for him for evermore, and my covenant shall stand fast with him.

29 His seed also will I make *to endure* for ever, ᴿand his throne ᴿas the days of heaven. ★

30 ᴿIf his children ᴿforsake my law, and walk not in my judgments;

31 If they ᴺbreak my statutes, and keep not my commandments;

32 Then ᴿwill I visit their transgression with the rod, and their iniquity with stripes.

33 ᴿNevertheless my lovingkindness ᴺwill I not utterly take from him, nor suffer my faithfulness ᴺto fail.

34 My covenant will I not break, nor alter the thing that is gone out of my lips.

35 Once have I sworn ᴿby my holiness ᴺthat I will not lie unto David.

36 ᴿHis seed shall endure for ever, and his throne ᴿas the sun before me. ★

37 It shall be established for ever as the moon, and *as* a faithful witness in heaven. Sē′-läh. ★

38 But thou hast ᴿcast off and ᴿabhorred, thou hast been wroth with thine anointed.

39 Thou hast made void the covenant of thy servant: ᴿthou hast profaned his crown *by casting it* to the ground.

40 Thou hast broken down all his hedges; thou hast brought his strong holds to ruin.

41 All that pass by the way spoil him: he is ᴿa reproach to his neighbours.

42 Thou hast set up the right hand of his adversaries; thou hast made all his enemies to rejoice.

43 Thou hast also turned the edge of his sword, and hast not made him to stand in the battle.

44 Thou hast made his ᴺglory to cease, and cast his throne down to the ground.

45 The days of his youth hast thou shortened: thou hast covered him with shame. Sē′-läh.

46 ᴿHow long, Lord? wilt thou hide thyself for ever? shall thy wrath burn like fire?

47 ᴿRemember how short my time is: wherefore hast thou made all men in vain?

48 ᴿWhat man *is he that* liveth, and shall not ᴿsee death? shall he deliver his soul from the hand of the grave? Sē′-läh.

49 Lord, where *are* thy former lovingkindnesses, *which* thou ᴿswarest unto David ᴿin thy truth?

50 Remember, Lord, the reproach of thy servants; ᴿ*how* I do bear in my bosom *the reproach of* all the mighty people;

51 ᴿWherewith thine enemies have reproached, O Lord; wherewith they have reproached the footsteps of thine anointed.

52 ᴿBlessed *be* the Lord for evermore. Ä′-mĕn, and Ä′-mĕn.

PSALM 90

God our dwelling place

*A Prayer *of Moses the man of God.

LORD, ᴿthou hast been our dwelling place ᴺin all generations.

2 ᴿBefore the mountains were brought forth, or ever thou hadst formed the earth and the world, even from everlasting to everlasting, thou *art* God.

3 Thou turnest man to destruction; and sayest, ᴿReturn, ye children of men.

4 ᴿFor a thousand years in thy sight *are but* as yesterday ᴺwhen it is past, and *as* a watch in the night.

5 Thou carriest them away as with a flood; ᴿthey are *as* a sleep: in the morning ᴿ*they are* like grass which ᴺgroweth up.

6 In the morning it flourisheth, and groweth up; in the evening it is cut down, and withereth.

7 For we are consumed by thine anger, and by thy wrath are we troubled.

PSALM 89
18 Or, *our shield is of the LORD, and our king is of the Holy One of Israel,* Ps. 47:9
19 1 Ki. 11:34
20 1 Sam. 16:1
21 Ps. 80:17
22 2 Sam. 7:10
23 2 Sam. 7:9
24 2 Sam. 7:15
26 1 Chr. 22:10
26 2 Sam. 22:47
27 Col. 1:15
27 Num. 24:7
28 Is. 55:3
29 Jer. 33:17
29 Deut. 11:21
30 2 Sam. 7:14
30 Ps. 119:53
Jer. 9:13
31 Heb. *profane my statutes*
32 2 Sam. 7:14
33 2 Sam. 7:15
33 Heb. *I will not make void from him*
33 Heb. *to lie*
35 Amos 4:2
35 Heb. *if I lie*
36 Luke 1:33
36 Ps. 72:17
38 1 Chr. 28:9
38 Deut. 32:19
39 Lam. 5:16

Ps. 44:13 — 41
Heb. *brightness* — 44
Ps. 79:5 — 46
Job 7:7 — 47
Ps. 49:9 — 48
Heb. 11:5 — 48
2 Sam. 7:15 — 49
Ps. 54:5 — 49
Ps. 69:9, 19 — 50
Ps. 74:22 — 51
Ps. 41:13 — 52

PSALM 90
Or, *A Prayer, being a Psalm of Moses* *
Deut. 33:1 *
Ezek. 11:16 1
Heb. *in generation and generation* 1
Prov. 8:25 2
Gen. 3:19 3
2 Pet. 3:8 4
Or, *when he hath passed* them 4
Ps. 73:20 5
Is. 40:6 5
Or, *is changed* 5

8 ᴿThou hast set our iniquities before thee, our ᴿsecret *sins* in the light of thy countenance.

9 For all our days are ᴺpassed away in thy wrath: we spend our years ᴺas a tale *that is told.*

10 ᴺThe days of our years *are* threescore years and ten; and if by reason of strength *they be* fourscore years, yet *is* their strength labour and sorrow; for it is soon cut off, and we fly away.

11 Who knoweth the power of thine anger? even according to thy fear, *so is* thy wrath.

12 ᴿSo teach *us* to number our days, that we may ᴺapply *our* hearts unto wisdom.

13 Return, O Lᴏʀᴅ, how long? and let it ᴿrepent thee concerning thy servants.

14 O satisfy us early with thy mercy; ᴿthat we may rejoice and be glad all our days.

15 Make us glad according to the days *wherein* thou hast afflicted us, *and* the years *wherein* we have seen evil.

16 Let ᴿthy work appear unto thy servants, and thy glory unto their children.

17 ᴿAnd let the beauty of the Lᴏʀᴅ our God be upon us: and ᴿestablish thou the work of our hands upon us; yea, the work of our hands establish thou it.

PSALM 91

Security of God's protection

HE ᴿthat dwelleth in the secret place of the most High shall ᴺabide ᴿunder the shadow of the Almighty.

2 ᴿI will say of the Lᴏʀᴅ, *He is* my refuge and my fortress: my God; in him will I trust.

3 Surely ᴿhe shall deliver thee from the snare of the fowler, *and* from the noisome pestilence.

4 ᴿHe shall cover thee with his feathers, and under his wings shalt thou trust: his truth *shall be thy* shield and buckler.

5 ᴿThou shalt not be afraid for the terror by night; *nor* for the arrow *that* flieth by day;

6 *Nor* for the pestilence *that* walketh in darkness; *nor* for the destruction *that* wasteth at noonday.

7 A thousand shall fall at thy side, and ten thousand at thy right hand; *but* it shall not come nigh thee.

8 Only ᴿwith thine eyes shalt thou behold and see the reward of the wicked.

9 Because thou hast made the Lᴏʀᴅ, *which is* ᴿmy refuge, *even* the most High, ᴿthy habitation;

10 ᴿThere shall no evil befall thee, neither shall any plague come nigh thy dwelling.

11 ᴿFor he shall give his angels charge over thee, to keep thee in all thy ways.

12 They shall bear thee up in *their* hands, ᴿlest thou dash thy foot against a stone.

13 Thou shalt tread upon the lion and ᴺadder: the young lion and the dragon shalt thou trample under feet.

14 Because he hath set his love upon me, therefore will I deliver him: I will set him on high, because he hath ᴿknown my name.

15 ᴿHe shall call upon me, and I will answer him: ᴿI *will be* with him in trouble; I will deliver him, and honour him.

16 With ᴺlong life will I satisfy him, and shew him my salvation.

PSALM 92

Singing God's praises

A Psalm *or* Song for the sabbath day.

IT is a ᴿgood *thing* to give thanks unto the Lᴏʀᴅ, and to sing praises unto thy name, O most High:

2 To ᴿshew forth thy lovingkindness in the morning, and thy faithfulness ᴺevery night,

3 ᴿUpon an instrument of ten strings, and upon the psaltery; ᴺupon the harp with ᴺa solemn sound.

4 For thou, Lᴏʀᴅ, hast made me glad through thy work: I will triumph in the works of thy hands.

5 ᴿO Lᴏʀᴅ, how great are thy works! *and* ᴿthy thoughts are very deep.

6 ᴿA brutish man knoweth not; neither doth a fool understand this.

7 When ᴿthe wicked spring as the grass, and when all the workers of iniquity do flourish; *it is* that they shall be destroyed for ever:

8 ᴿBut thou, Lᴏʀᴅ, *art most* high for evermore.

9 For, lo, thine enemies, O Lᴏʀᴅ, for, lo, thine enemies shall perish; all the workers of iniquity shall ᴿbe scattered.

10 But ᴿmy horn shalt thou exalt like *the horn of* an unicorn: I shall be ᴿanointed with fresh oil.

11 ᴿMine eye also shall see *my desire* on mine enemies, *and* mine ears shall hear *my desire* of the wicked that rise up against me.

12 ᴿThe righteous shall flourish like the palm tree: he shall grow like a cedar in Lĕb′-ă-nọn.

13 Those that be planted in the house of the Lᴏʀᴅ shall flourish ᴿin the courts of our God.

Center column references

PSALM 90
8 Ps. 50:21
8 Ps. 19:12
9 Heb. *turned away*
9 Or, *as a meditation*
10 Heb. As for *the days of our years, in them are seventy years*
12 Ps. 39:4
12 Heb. *cause to come*
13 Deut. 32:36
  Ps. 135:14
14 Ps. 85:6
16 Hab. 3:2
17 Ps. 27:4
17 Is. 26:12

PSALM 91
1 Ps. 31:20
1 Heb. *lodge*
1 Ps. 17:8
2 Ps. 142:5
3 Ps. 124:7
4 Ps. 17:8
5 Job 5:19
  Ps. 112:7
  Prov. 3:23
  Is. 43:2
8 Mal. 1:5
9 ver. 2
9 Ps. 90:1

Prov. 12:21   10
Ps. 34:7 & 71:3   11
Mat. 4:6
Luke 4:10
Heb. 1:14
Job 5:23   12
Ps. 37:24
Or, *asp*   13
Ps. 9:10   14
Ps. 50:15   15
Is. 43:2   15
Heb. *length of*   16
days, Prov. 3:2

PSALM 92
Ps. 147:1   1
Ps. 89:1   2
Heb. *in the*   2
nights
1 Chr. 23:5   3
Ps. 33:2
Or, *upon the*   3
solemn sound with the harp
Heb. *Higgaion,*   3
Ps. 9:16
Ps. 40:5   5
Is. 28:29   5
Rom. 11:33
Ps. 73:22   6
Job 12:6   7
Ps. 37:1, 2
Jer. 12:1, 2
Mal. 3:15
Ps. 83:18   8
Ps. 68:1   9
Ps. 89:17   10
Ps. 23:5   10
Ps. 54:7   11
& 59:10
Ps. 52:8   12
Is. 65:22
Hos. 14:5, 6
Ps. 100:4   13

14 They shall still bring forth fruit in old age; they shall be fat and ^Nflourishing;

15 To shew that the LORD *is* upright: ^R*he is* my rock, and ^R*there is* no unrighteousness in him.

PSALM 93

The sure decrees of God

THE ^RLORD reigneth, ^Rhe is clothed with majesty; the LORD is clothed with strength, ^R*wherewith* he hath girded himself: the world also is stablished, that it cannot be moved.

2 ^RThy throne *is* established ^Nof old: thou *art* from everlasting.

3 The floods have lifted up, O LORD, the floods have lifted up their voice; the floods lift up their waves.

4 ^RThe LORD on high *is* mightier than the noise of many waters, *yea, than* the mighty waves of the sea.

5 Thy testimonies are very sure: holiness becometh thine house, O LORD, ^Nfor ever.

PSALM 94

Plea for God's vengeance

O LORD ^NGod, ^Rto whom vengeance belongeth; O God, to whom vengeance belongeth, ^Nshew thyself.

2 ^RLift up thyself, thou ^Rjudge of the earth: render a reward to the proud.

3 LORD, ^Rhow long shall the wicked, how long shall the wicked triumph?

4 *How long* shall they ^Rutter *and* speak hard things? *and* all the workers of iniquity boast themselves?

5 They break in pieces thy people, O LORD, and afflict thine heritage.

6 They slay the widow and the stranger, and murder the fatherless.

7 ^RYet they say, The LORD shall not see, neither shall the God of Jacob regard *it*.

8 ^RUnderstand, ye brutish among the people: and ye fools, when will ye be wise?

9 ^RHe that planted the ear, shall he not hear? he that formed the eye, shall he not see?

10 He that chastiseth the heathen, shall not he correct? he that ^Rteacheth man knowledge, *shall not he know?*

11 ^RThe LORD knoweth the thoughts of man, that they *are* vanity.

12 ^RBlessed *is* the man whom thou chastenest, O LORD, and teachest him out of thy law;

13 That thou mayest give him rest from the days of adversity, until the pit be digged for the wicked.

14 ^RFor the LORD will not cast off his people, neither will he forsake his inheritance.

15 But judgment shall return unto righteousness: and all the upright in heart ^Nshall follow it.

16 Who will rise up for me against the evil-doers? *or* who will stand up for me against the workers of iniquity?

17 ^RUnless the LORD *had been* my help, my soul had ^Nalmost dwelt in silence.

18 When I said, ^RMy foot slippeth; thy mercy, O LORD, held me up.

19 In the multitude of my thoughts within me thy comforts delight my soul.

20 Shall ^Rthe throne of iniquity have fellowship with thee, which ^Rframeth mischief by a law?

21 ^RThey gather themselves together against the soul of the righteous, and ^Rcondemn the innocent blood.

22 But the LORD is ^Rmy defence; and my God *is* the rock of my refuge.

23 And ^Rhe shall bring upon them their own iniquity, and shall cut them off in their own wickedness; *yea,* the LORD our God shall cut them off.

PSALM 95

Song of thanksgiving

O COME, let us sing unto the LORD: ^Rlet us make a joyful noise to ^Rthe rock of our salvation.

2 Let us ^Ncome before his presence with thanksgiving, and make a joyful noise unto him with psalms.

3 For ^Rthe LORD *is* a great God, and a great King above all gods.

4 ^NIn his hand *are* the deep places of the earth: ^Nthe strength of the hills *is* his also.

5 ^RThe^N sea *is* his, and he made it: and his hands formed the dry *land.*

6 O come, let us worship and bow down: let ^Rus kneel before the LORD our maker.

7 For he *is* our God; and ^Rwe *are* the people of his pasture, and the sheep of his hand. ^RTo day if ye will hear his voice,

8 Harden not your heart, ^Ras in the ^Nprovocation, *and* as *in* the day of temptation in the wilderness:

9 When ^Ryour fathers tempted me, proved me, and ^Rsaw my work.

10 ^RForty years long was I grieved with *this* generation, and said, It *is* a people that do err in their heart, and they have not known my ways:

11 Unto whom ^RI sware in my wrath ^Nthat they should not enter into my rest.

Center reference column

PSALM 92
14 Heb. *green*
15 Deut. 32:4
15 Rom. 9:14

PSALM 93
1 Ps. 96:10 & 97:1
Is. 52:7
Rev. 19:6
1 Ps. 104:1
1 Ps. 65:6
2 Ps. 45:6
Prov. 8:22
2 Heb. *from then*
4 Ps. 65:7 & 89:9
5 Heb. *to length of days*

PSALM 94
1 Heb. *God of revenges*
1 Nah. 1:2
1 Heb. *shine forth,* Ps. 80:1
2 Ps. 7:6
2 Gen. 18:25
3 Job 20:5
4 Ps. 31:18
Jude 15
7 Ps. 10:11
8 Ps. 73:22 & 92:6
9 Ex. 4:11
10 Job 35:11
Is. 28:26
11 1 Cor. 3:20
12 Job 5:17
Heb. 12:5

1 Sam. 12:22	14
Rom. 11:1	
Heb. *shall be after it*	15
Ps. 124:1, 2	17
Or, *quickly*	17
Ps. 38:16	18
Amos 6:3	20
Is. 10:1	20
Mat. 27:1	21
Prov. 17:15	21
Ps. 59:9	22
Ps. 7:16	23
Prov. 2:22	

PSALM 95
Ps. 100:1	1
Deut. 32:15	1
2 Sam. 22:47	
Heb. *prevent his face*	2
Ps. 96:4	3
Heb. *In whose*	4
Or, *the heights of the hills* are *his*	4
Gen. 1:9, 10	5
Heb. *Whose the sea* is	5
Phil. 2:10	6
Ps. 79:13 & 100:3	7
Heb. 3:7	7
Ex. 17:2, 7	8
Heb. *contention*	8
Ps. 78:18	9
1 Cor. 10:9	
Num. 14:22	9
Heb. 3:10	10
Heb. 4:3, 5	11
Heb. *if they enter into my rest*	11

PSALM 96

A new song to the LORD

O [R]SING unto the LORD a new song: sing unto the LORD, all the earth.

2 Sing unto the LORD, bless his name; shew forth his salvation from day to day.

3 Declare his glory among the heathen, his wonders among all people.

4 For [R]the LORD *is* great, and [R]greatly to be praised: [R]he *is* to be feared above all gods.

5 For [R]all the gods of the nations *are* idols: [R]but the LORD made the heavens.

6 Honour and majesty *are* before him: strength and [R]beauty *are* in his sanctuary.

7 [R]Give unto the LORD, O ye kindreds of the people, give unto the LORD glory and strength.

8 Give unto the LORD the glory [N]*due unto* his name: bring an offering, and come into his courts.

9 O worship the LORD [R]in[N] the beauty of holiness: fear before him, all the earth.

10 Say among the heathen *that* [R]the LORD reigneth: the world also shall be established that it shall not be moved: [R]he shall judge the people righteously.

11 [R]Let the heavens rejoice, and let the earth be glad; [R]let the sea roar, and the fulness thereof.

12 Let the field be joyful, and all that *is* therein: then shall all the trees of the wood rejoice

13 Before the LORD: for he cometh, for he cometh to judge the earth: [R]he shall judge the world with righteousness, and the people with his truth.

PSALM 97

The LORD reigneth

THE [R]LORD reigneth; let the earth rejoice; let the [N]multitude of [R]isles be glad *thereof.*

2 [R]Clouds and darkness *are* round about him: [R]righteousness and judgment *are* the [N]habitation of his throne.

3 [R]A fire goeth before him, and burneth up his enemies round about.

4 [R]His lightnings enlightened the world: the earth saw, and trembled.

5 [R]The hills melted like wax at the presence of the LORD, at the presence of the Lord of the whole earth.

6 [R]The heavens declare his righteousness, and all the people see his glory.

7 [R]Confounded be all they that serve graven

images, that boast themselves of idols: [R]worship him, all *ye* gods.

8 Zion heard, and was glad; and the daughters of Judah rejoiced because of thy judgments, O LORD.

9 For thou, LORD, *art* [R]high above all the earth: [R]thou art exalted far above all gods.

10 Ye that love the LORD, [R]hate evil: [R]he preserveth the souls of his saints; [R]he delivereth them out of the hand of the wicked.

11 [R]Light is sown for the righteous, and gladness for the upright in heart.

12 [R]Rejoice in the LORD, ye righteous; [R]and give thanks [N]at the remembrance of his holiness.

PSALM 98

Song of God's marvellous deeds

A Psalm.

O [R]SING unto the LORD a new song; for [R]he hath done marvellous things: [R]his right hand, and his holy arm, hath gotten him the victory.

2 [R]The LORD hath made known his salvation: [R]his righteousness hath he [N]openly shewed in the sight of the heathen.

3 He hath [R]remembered his mercy and his truth toward the house of Israel: [R]all the ends of the earth have seen the salvation of our God.

4 [R]Make a joyful noise unto the LORD, all the earth: make a loud noise, and rejoice, and sing praise.

5 Sing unto the LORD with the harp; with the harp, and the voice of a psalm.

6 [R]With trumpets and sound of cornet make a joyful noise before the LORD, the King.

7 Let the sea roar, and the fulness thereof; the world, and they that dwell therein.

8 Let the floods [R]clap *their* hands: let the hills be joyful together

9 Before the LORD; [R]for he cometh to judge the earth: with righteousness shall he judge the world, and the people with equity.

PSALM 99

Worship our Holy God

THE LORD reigneth; let the people tremble: [R]he sitteth *between* the chĕr'-ū-bīms; let the earth [N]be moved.

2 The LORD *is* great in Zion; and he *is* [R]high above all the people.

3 Let them praise thy great and terrible name; *for* it *is* holy.

4 [R]The king's strength also loveth judgment;

Center reference column

PSALM 96

1	1 Chr. 16:23-33
4	Ps. 145:3
4	Ps. 18:3
4	Ps. 95:3
5	Jer. 10:11
5	Ps. 115:15
	Is. 42:5
6	Ps. 29:2
7	Ps. 29:1, 2
8	Heb. *of his name*
9	Ps. 29:2
9	Or, *in the glorious sanctuary*
10	Ps. 97:1
10	Ps. 67:4
11	Ps. 69:34
11	Ps. 98:7
13	Rev. 19:11

PSALM 97

1	Ps. 96:10
1	Heb. *many, or, great isles*
1	Is. 60:9
2	Ps. 18:11
2	Ps. 89:14
2	Or, *establishment*
3	Ps. 18:8
4	Ex. 19:18
5	Mic. 1:4
6	Ps. 19:1
7	Ex. 20:4
	Lev. 26:1

Heb. 1:6	7
Ps. 83:18	9
Ex. 18:11	9
Ps. 95:3	
Ps. 34:14	10
Amos 5:15	
Prov. 2:8	10
Ps. 37:39	10
Dan. 3:28	
Job 22:28	11
Prov. 4:18	
Ps. 33:1	12
Ps. 30:4	12
Or, *to the memorial*	12

PSALM 98

Ps. 96:1	1
Is. 42:10	
Ex. 15:11	1
Ps. 77:14	
Ex. 15:6	1
Is. 63:5	
Is. 52:10	2
Luke 2:30	
Is. 62:2	2
Or, *revealed*	2
Luke 1:54	3
Is. 49:6	3
Ps. 95:1	4
Num. 10:10	6
Is. 55:12	8
Ps. 96:10	9

PSALM 99

Ex. 25:22	1
Heb. *stagger*	1
Ps. 97:9	2
Job 36:5-7	4

thou dost establish equity, thou executest judgment and righteousness in Jacob.

5 Exalt ye the LORD our God, and worship at [R]his footstool; *for* [R]he[N] *is* holy.

6 [R]Moses and Aaron among his priests, and Samuel among them that call upon his name; they [R]called upon the LORD, and he answered them.

7 [R]He spake unto them in the cloudy pillar: they kept his testimonies, and the ordinance *that* he gave them.

8 Thou answeredst them, O LORD our God: [R]thou wast a God that forgavest them, though [R]thou tookest vengeance of their inventions.

9 [R]Exalt the LORD our God, and worship at his holy hill; for the LORD our God *is* holy.

PSALM 100

Song of praise and thanksgiving

*A Psalm of *praise.

MAKE [R]a joyful noise unto the LORD, [N]all ye lands.

2 Serve the LORD with gladness: come before his presence with singing.

3 Know ye that the LORD he *is* God: [R]*it is* he *that* hath made us, [N]and not we ourselves; [R]*we are* his people, and the sheep of his pasture.

4 [R]Enter into his gates with thanksgiving, *and* into his courts with praise: be thankful unto him, *and* bless his name.

5 For the LORD *is* good; [R]his mercy *is* everlasting; and his truth *endureth* [N]to all generations.

PSALM 101

Purity in God's city

A Psalm of David.

I WILL sing of mercy and judgment: unto thee, O LORD, will I sing.

2 I will [R]behave myself wisely in a perfect way. O when wilt thou come unto me? I will [R]walk within my house with a perfect heart.

3 I will set no [N]wicked thing before mine eyes: [R]I hate the work of them [R]that turn aside; *it* shall not cleave to me.

4 A froward heart shall depart from me: I will not [R]know a wicked *person.*

5 Whoso privily slandereth his neighbour, him will I cut off: [R]him that hath an high look and a proud heart will not I suffer.

6 Mine eyes *shall be* upon the faithful of the land, that they may dwell with me: he that walketh [N]in a perfect way, he shall serve me.

7 He that worketh deceit shall not dwell within my house: he that telleth lies [N]shall not tarry in my sight.

8 I will [R]early destroy all the wicked of the land; that I may cut off all wicked doers [R]from the city of the LORD.

PSALM 102

In time of distress

A Prayer *of the afflicted, *when he is overwhelmed, and poureth out his complaint before the LORD.

HEAR my prayer, O LORD, and let my cry [R]come unto thee.

2 [R]Hide not thy face from me in the day *when* I am in trouble; [R]incline thine ear unto me: in the day *when* I call answer me speedily.

3 [R]For my days are consumed [N]like smoke, and [R]my bones are burned as an hearth.

4 My heart is smitten, and [R]withered like grass; so that I forget to eat my bread.

5 By reason of the voice of my groaning [R]my bones cleave to my [N]skin.

6 [R]I am like [R]a pelican of the wilderness: I am like an owl of the desert.

7 I [R]watch, and am as a sparrow [R]alone upon the house top.

8 Mine enemies reproach me all the day; *and* they that are [R]mad against me are [R]sworn against me.

9 For I have eaten ashes like bread, and [R]mingled my drink with weeping,

10 Because of thine indignation and thy wrath: for [R]thou hast lifted me up, and cast me down.

11 [R]My days *are* like a shadow that declineth; and [R]I am withered like grass.

12 But [R]thou, O LORD, shalt endure for ever; and [R]thy remembrance unto all generations.

13 Thou shalt arise, *and* [R]have mercy upon Zion: for the time to favour her, yea, the [R]set time, is come.

14 For thy servants take pleasure in [R]her stones, and favour the dust thereof.

15 So the heathen shall [R]fear the name of the LORD, and all the kings of the earth thy glory.

16 When the LORD shall build up Zion, [R]he shall appear in his glory.

17 [R]He will regard the prayer of the destitute, and not despise their prayer.

18 This shall be [R]written for the generation to come: and [R]the people which shall be created shall praise the LORD.

19 For he hath [R]looked down from the height of his sanctuary; from heaven did the LORD behold the earth;

20 [R]To hear the groaning of the prisoner; to loose [N]those that are appointed to death;

PSALM 99

5 Ps. 132:7
5 Lev. 19:2
5 Or, *it* is *holy*
6 Jer. 15:1
6 Ex. 14:15
1 Sam. 7:9
7 Ex. 33:9
8 Num. 14:20
8 Deut. 9:20
9 Ps. 34:3

PSALM 100

* Ps. 145, title
* Or, *thanksgiving*
1 Ps. 95:1
1 Heb. *all the earth*
3 Eph. 2:10
3 Or, *and his we* are
3 Ezek. 34:31
4 Ps. 116:17
5 Ps. 136:1
5 Heb. *to generation and generation,* Ps. 89:1

PSALM 101

2 1 Sam. 18:14
2 1 Ki. 11:4
3 Heb. *thing of Belial*
3 Ps. 97:10
3 Josh. 23:6
4 Ps. 119:115
5 Prov. 6:17
6 Or, *perfect in the way*
Heb. *shall not be established* 7
Ps. 75:10 8
Jer. 21:12
Ps. 48:2, 8 8

PSALM 102

Or, *for* *
Ps. 61:2 *
Ps. 18:6 1
Ps. 69:17 2
Ps. 71:2 2
Jas. 4:14 3
Or, (as some read) *into smoke* 3
Job 30:30 3
Ps. 31:10
Ps. 37:2 4
Job 19:20 5
Or, *flesh* 5
Job 30:29 6
Is. 34:11 6
Ps. 77:4 7
Ps. 38:11 7
Acts 26:11 8
Acts 23:12 8
Ps. 42:3 9
Ps. 30:7 10
Eccl. 6:12 11
Is. 40:6-8 11
Jas. 1:10
Ps. 9:7 12
Ps. 135:13 12
Is. 60:10 13
Is. 40:2 13
Ps. 79:1 14
1 Ki. 8:43 15
Is. 60:1, 2 16
Neh. 1:6 17
Rom. 15:4 18
Ps. 22:31 18
Deut. 26:15 19
Ps. 79:11 20
Heb. *the children of death* 20

21 To ᴿdeclare the name of the LORD in Zion, and his praise in Jerusalem;

22 When the people are gathered together, and the kingdoms, to serve the LORD.

23 He ᴺweakened my strength in the way; he ᴿshortened my days.

24 ᴿI said, O my God, take me not away in the midst of my days: ᴿthy years are throughout all generations.

25 ᴿOf old hast thou laid the foundation of the earth: and the heavens are the work of thy hands.

26 ᴿThey shall perish, but thou shalt ᴺendure: yea, all of them shall wax old like a garment; as a vesture shalt thou change them, and they shall be changed:

27 But ᴿthou art the same, and thy years shall have no end.

28 ᴿThe children of thy servants shall continue, and their seed shall be established before thee.

PSALM 103

Praise of God's works to men

A Psalm of David.

BLESS ᴿthe LORD, O my soul: and all that is within me, *bless* his holy name.

2 Bless the LORD, O my soul, and forget not all his benefits:

3 ᴿWho forgiveth all thine iniquities; who ᴿhealeth all thy diseases;

4 Who redeemeth thy life from destruction; ᴿwho crowneth thee with lovingkindness and tender mercies;

5 Who satisfieth thy mouth with good *things;* so that ᴿthy youth is renewed like the eagle's.

6 The LORD executeth righteousness and judgment for all that are oppressed.

7 ᴿHe made known his ways unto Moses, his acts unto the children of Israel.

8 ᴿThe LORD is merciful and gracious, slow to anger, and ᴺplenteous in mercy.

9 ᴿHe will not always chide: neither will he keep *his anger* for ever.

10 ᴿHe hath not dealt with us after our sins; nor rewarded us according to our iniquities.

11 For ᴺas the heaven is high above the earth, *so* great is his mercy toward them that fear him.

12 As far as the east is from the west, *so* far hath he ᴿremoved our transgressions from us.

13 ᴿLike as a father pitieth *his* children, *so* the LORD pitieth them that fear him.

14 For he knoweth our frame; he remembereth that we are ᴿdust.

15 *As for* man, ᴿhis days *are* as grass: ᴿas a flower of the field, so he flourisheth.

16 For the wind passeth over it, and ᴺit is gone; and ᴿthe place thereof shall know it no more.

17 But the mercy of the LORD *is* from everlasting to everlasting upon them that fear him, and his righteousness unto children's children;

18 ᴿTo such as keep his covenant, and to those that remember his commandments to do them.

19 The LORD hath prepared his throne in the heavens; and ᴿhis kingdom ruleth over all.

20 ᴿBless the LORD, ye his angels, ᴺthat excel in strength, that ᴿdo his commandments, hearkening unto the voice of his word.

21 Bless ye the LORD, all *ye* ᴿhis hosts; ᴿ*ye* ministers of his, that do his pleasure.

22 Bless the LORD, all his works in all places of his dominion: bless the LORD, O my soul.

PSALM 104

Praise of God's works of nature

BLESS ᴿthe LORD, O my soul. O LORD my God, thou art very great; thou art clothed with honour and majesty.

2 ᴿWho coverest *thyself* with light as *with* a garment: ᴿwho stretchest out the heavens like a curtain:

3 ᴿWho layeth the beams of his chambers in the waters: ᴿwho maketh the clouds his chariot: ᴿwho walketh upon the wings of the wind:

4 ᴿWho maketh his angels spirits; his ministers a flaming fire:

5 ᴿ*Who*ᴺ laid the foundations of the earth, *that* it should not be removed for ever.

6 ᴿThou coveredst it with the deep as *with* a garment: the waters stood above the mountains.

7 At thy rebuke they fled; at the voice of thy thunder they hasted away.

8 ᴿTheyᴺ go up by the mountains; they go down by the valleys unto the place which thou hast founded for them.

9 ᴿThou hast set a bound that they may not pass over; ᴿthat they turn not again to cover the earth.

10 ᴺHe sendeth the springs into the valleys, *which* ᴺrun among the hills.

11 They give drink to every beast of the field: the wild asses ᴺquench their thirst.

12 By them shall the fowls of the heaven have their habitation, *which* ᴺsing among the branches.

13 ᴿHe watereth the hills from his chambers: the earth is satisfied with ᴿthe fruit of thy works.

14 ᴿHe causeth the grass to grow for the cattle, and herb for the service of man: that he may bring forth ᴿfood out of the earth;

15 And ᴿwine *that* maketh glad the heart of man, *and* ᴺoil to make *his* face to shine, and bread *which* strengtheneth man's heart.

16 The trees of the LORD are full *of sap;* the cedars of Lĕb′-ă-nọn, which he hath planted;

17 Where the birds make their nests: *as for* the stork, the fir trees *are* her house.

18 The high hills *are* a refuge for the wild goats; *and* the rocks for the conies.

19 ᴿHe appointed the moon for seasons: the sun knoweth his going down.

20 ᴿThou makest darkness, and it is night: wherein ᴺall the beasts of the forest do creep *forth.*

21 ᴿThe young lions roar after their prey, and seek their meat from God.

22 The sun ariseth, they gather themselves together, and lay them down in their dens.

23 Man goeth forth unto ᴿhis work and to his labour until the evening.

24 ᴿO LORD, how manifold are thy works! in wisdom hast thou made them all: the earth is full of thy riches.

25 *So is* this great and wide sea, wherein *are* things creeping innumerable, both small and great beasts.

26 There go the ships: *there is* that ᴿlē-vī′-ă-thăn, *whom* thou hast ᴺmade to play therein.

27 ᴿThese wait all upon thee; that thou mayest give *them* their meat in due season.

28 *That* thou givest them they gather: thou openest thine hand, they are filled with good.

29 Thou hidest thy face, they are troubled: ᴿthou takest away their breath, they die, and return to their dust.

30 ᴿThou sendest forth thy spirit, they are created: and thou renewest the face of the earth.

31 The glory of the LORD ᴺshall endure for ever: the LORD ᴿshall rejoice in his works.

32 He looketh on the earth, and it ᴿtrembleth: ᴿhe toucheth the hills, and they smoke.

33 ᴿI will sing unto the LORD as long as I live: I will sing praise to my God while I have my being.

34 My meditation of him shall be sweet: I will be glad in the LORD.

35 Let ᴿthe sinners be consumed out of the earth, and let the wicked be no more. Bless thou the LORD, O my soul. Praise ye the LORD.

PSALM 105

God's guidance of Israel

O GIVE thanks unto the LORD; call upon his name: ᴿmake known his deeds among the people.

2 Sing unto him, sing psalms unto him: ᴿtalk ye of all his wondrous works.

3 Glory ye in his holy name: let the heart of them rejoice that seek the LORD.

4 Seek the LORD, and his strength: ᴿseek his face evermore.

5 ᴿRemember his marvellous works that he hath done; his wonders, and the judgments of his mouth;

6 O ye seed of Abraham his servant, ye children of Jacob his chosen.

7 He *is* the LORD our God: ᴿhis judgments *are* in all the earth.

8 He hath ᴿremembered his covenant for ever, the word *which* he commanded to a thousand generations.

9 ᴿWhich *covenant* he made with Abraham, and his oath unto Isaac;

10 And confirmed the same unto Jacob for a law, *and* to Israel *for* an everlasting covenant:

11 Saying, ᴿUnto thee will I give the land of Canaan, ᴺthe lot of your inheritance:

12 ᴿWhen they were *but* a few men in number; yea, very few, ᴿand strangers in it.

13 When they went from one nation to another, from *one* kingdom to another people;

14 ᴿHe suffered no man to do them wrong: yea, ᴿhe reproved kings for their sakes;

15 *Saying,* Touch not mine anointed, and do my prophets no harm.

16 Moreover ᴿhe called for a famine upon the land: he brake the whole ᴿstaff of bread.

17 ᴿHe sent a man before them, *even* Joseph, *who* ᴿwas sold for a servant:

18 ᴿWhose feet they hurt with fetters: ᴺhe was laid in iron:

19 Until the time that his word came: ᴿthe word of the LORD tried him.

20 ᴿThe king sent and loosed him; *even* the ruler of the people, and let him go free.

21 ᴿHe made him lord of his house, and ruler of all his ᴺsubstance:

22 To bind his princes at his pleasure; and teach his senators wisdom.

23 ᴿIsrael also came into Egypt; and Jacob sojourned ᴿin the land of Ham.

24 And ᴿhe increased his people greatly; and made them stronger than their enemies.

25 ᴿHe turned their heart to hate his people, to deal subtilly with his servants.

26 ᴿHe sent Moses his servant; *and* Aaron whom he had chosen.

27 ᴿThey shewed ᴺhis signs among them, ᴿand wonders in the land of Ham.

28 ᴿHe sent darkness, and made it dark; and ᴿthey rebelled not against his word.

29 ᴿHe turned their waters into blood, and slew their fish.

30 ᴿTheir land brought forth frogs in abundance, in the chambers of their kings.

31 ᴿHe spake, and there came divers sorts of flies, *and* lice in all their coasts.

32 ᴿHeᴺ gave them hail for rain, *and* flaming fire in their land.

33 ᴿHe smote their vines also and their fig trees; and brake the trees of their coasts.

34 ᴿHe spake, and the locusts came, and caterpillers, and that without number,

35 And did eat up all the herbs in their land, and devoured the fruit of their ground.

36 ᴿHe smote also all the firstborn in their land, ᴿthe chief of all their strength.

37 ᴿHe brought them forth also with silver and gold: and *there was* not one feeble *person* among their tribes.

38 ᴿEgypt was glad when they departed: for the fear of them fell upon them.

39 ᴿHe spread a cloud for a covering; and fire to give light in the night.

40 ᴿ*The people* asked, and he brought quails, and ᴿsatisfied them with the bread of heaven.

41 ᴿHe opened the rock, and the waters gushed out; they ran in the dry places *like* a river.

42 For he remembered ᴿhis holy promise, *and* Abraham his servant.

43 And he brought forth his people with joy, *and* his chosen with ᴺgladness:

44 ᴿAnd gave them the lands of the heathen: and they inherited the labour of the people;

45 ᴿThat they might observe his statutes, and keep his laws. ᴺPraise ye the Lᴏʀᴅ.

PSALM 106

God's mercy and Israel's rebellions

Pᴿᴀɪꜱᴱᴺ ye the Lᴏʀᴅ. ᴿO give thanks unto the Lᴏʀᴅ; for *he is* good: for his mercy *endureth* for ever.

2 Who can utter the mighty acts of the Lᴏʀᴅ? *who* can shew forth all his praise?

3 Blessed *are* they that keep judgment, *and* he that ᴿdoeth righteousness at ᴿall times.

4 ᴿRemember me, O Lᴏʀᴅ, with the favour *that thou bearest unto* thy people: O visit me with thy salvation;

PSALM 105	
26	Ex. 3:10
27	Ex. 7-12
27	Heb. *words of his signs*
27	Ps. 106:22
28	Ex. 10:22
28	Ps. 99:7
29	Ex. 7:20
	Ps. 78:44
30	Ex. 8:6
	Ps. 78:45
31	Ex. 8:17
	Ps. 78:45
32	Ex. 9:23
	Ps. 78:48
32	Heb. *He gave their rain hail*
33	Ps. 78:47
34	Ex. 10:4
	Ps. 78:46
36	Ex. 12:29
	Ps. 78:51
36	Gen. 49:3
37	Ex. 12:35
38	Ex. 12:33
39	Ex. 13:21
40	Ex. 16:12
	Ps. 78:18
40	Ps. 78:24
41	Ex. 17:6
	Ps. 78:15
42	Gen. 15:14
43	Heb. *singing*
44	Josh. 13:7
45	Deut. 4:1 & 6:21-25
25	Heb. *Hallelujah*

PSALM 106	
1	Heb. *Hallelujah*
1	1 Chr. 16:34
3	Ps. 15:2
3	Gal. 6:9
4	Ps. 119:132
Dan. 9:5	6
Ex. 14:11	7
Ex. 9:16	8
Ex. 14:21	9
Ps. 18:15	
Is. 63:11	9
Ex. 14:30	10
Ex. 14:27	11
Ex. 15:1	12
Ex. 15:24	13
Heb. *They made haste, they forgat*	13
1 Cor. 10:6	14
Heb. *lusted a lust*	14
Num. 11:31	15
Is. 10:16	15
Num. 16:1	16
Deut. 11:6	17
Num. 16:35, 46	18
Ex. 32:4	19
Jer. 2:11	20
Ps. 78:11	21
Ps. 78:51	22
Ex. 32:10	23
Deut. 9:19	
Ezek. 22:30	23
Deut. 8:7	24
Heb. *a land of desire*	24
Heb. 3:18	24
Num. 14:2	25
Ezek. 20:15	26
Num. 14:29	26
Lev. 26:33	27
Heb. *To make them fall*	27
Hos. 9:10	28

5 That I may see the good of thy chosen, that I may rejoice in the gladness of thy nation, that I may glory with thine inheritance.

6 ᴿWe have sinned with our fathers, we have comitted iniquity, we have done wickedly.

7 Our fathers understood not thy wonders in Egypt; they remembered not the multitude of thy mercies; ᴿbut provoked *him* at the sea, *even* at the Red sea.

8 Nevertheless he saved them for his name's sake, ᴿthat he might make his mighty power to be known.

9 ᴿHe rebuked the Red sea also, and it was dried up: so ᴿhe led them through the depths, as through the wilderness.

10 And he ᴿsaved them from the hand of him that hated *them,* and redeemed them from the hand of the enemy.

11 ᴿAnd the waters covered their enemies: there was not one of them left.

12 ᴿThen believed they his words; they sang his praise.

13 ᴿTheyᴺ soon forgat his works; they waited not for his counsel:

14 ᴿBut ᴺlusted exceedingly in the wilderness, and tempted God in the desert.

15 ᴿAnd he gave them their request; but ᴿsent leanness into their soul.

16 ᴿThey envied Moses also in the camp, *and* Aaron the saint of the Lᴏʀᴅ.

17 ᴿThe earth opened and swallowed up Dā′-thăn, and covered the company of Ă-bī′-răm.

18 ᴿAnd a fire was kindled in their company; the flame burned up the wicked.

19 ᴿThey made a calf in Hôr′-ĕb, and worshipped the molten image.

20 Thus ᴿthey changed their glory into the similitude of an ox that eateth grass.

21 They ᴿforgat God their saviour, which had done great things in Egypt;

22 Wondrous works in ᴿthe land of Ham, *and* terrible things by the Red sea.

23 ᴿTherefore he said that he would destroy them, had not Moses his chosen ᴿstood before him in the breach, to turn away his wrath, lest he should destroy *them.*

24 Yea, they despised ᴿtheᴺ pleasant land, they ᴿbelieved not his word:

25 ᴿBut murmured in their tents, *and* hearkened not unto the voice of the Lᴏʀᴅ.

26 ᴿTherefore he lifted up his hand against them, ᴿto overthrow them in the wilderness:

27 ᴿToᴺ overthrow their seed also among the nations, and to scatter them in the lands.

28 ᴿThey joined themselves also unto Bā′-ăl-pē′-ôr, and ate the sacrifices of the dead.

29 Thus they provoked *him* to anger with their inventions: and the plague brake in upon them.

30 ᴿThen stood up Phĭn′-ĕ-hăs̓, and executed judgment: and *so* the plague was stayed.

31 And that was counted unto him ᴿfor righteousness unto all generations for evermore.

32 ᴿThey angered *him* also at the waters of strife, so that it went ill with Moses for their sakes:

33 ᴿBecause they provoked his spirit, so that he spake unadvisedly with his lips.

34 ᴿThey did not destroy the nations, ᴿconcerning whom the LORD commanded them:

35 ᴿBut were mingled among the heathen, and learned their works.

36 And ᴿthey served their idols: ᴿwhich were a snare unto them.

37 Yea, ᴿthey sacrificed their sons and their daughters unto ᴿdevils,

38 And shed innocent blood, *even* the blood of their sons and of their daughters, whom they sacrificed unto the idols of Canaan: and ᴿthe land was polluted with blood.

39 Thus were they ᴿdefiled with their own works, and ᴿwent a whoring with their own inventions.

40 Therefore ᴿwas the wrath of the LORD kindled against his people, insomuch that he abhorred ᴿhis own inheritance.

41 And ᴿhe gave them into the hand of the heathen; and they that hated them ruled over them.

42 Their enemies also oppressed them, and they were brought into subjection under their hand.

43 ᴿMany times did he deliver them; but they provoked *him* with their counsel, and were ᴺbrought low for their iniquity.

44 Nevertheless he regarded their affliction, when ᴿhe heard their cry:

45 ᴿAnd he remembered for them his covenant, and ᴿrepented ᴿaccording to the multitude of his mercies.

46 ᴿHe made them also to be pitied of all those that carried them captives.

47 ᴿSave us, O LORD our God, and gather us from among the heathen, to give thanks unto thy holy name, *and* to triumph in thy praise.

48 ᴿBlessed *be* the LORD God of Israel from everlasting to everlasting: and let all the people say, Ā′-mĕn. ᴺPraise ye the LORD.

PSALM 107

God's enduring mercy

O ᴿGIVE thanks unto the LORD, for ᴿ*he is* good: for his mercy *endureth* for ever.

2 Let the redeemed of the LORD say *so*, ᴿwhom he hath redeemed from the hand of the enemy;

3 And ᴿgathered them out of the lands, from the east, and from the west, from the north, and ᴺfrom the south.

4 They wandered in ᴿthe wilderness in a solitary way; they found no city to dwell in.

5 Hungry and thirsty, their soul fainted in them.

6 ᴿThen they cried unto the LORD in their trouble, *and* he delivered them out of their distresses.

7 And he led them forth by the ᴿright way, that they might go to a city of habitation.

8 ᴿOh that *men* would praise the LORD *for* his goodness, and *for* his wonderful works to the children of men!

9 For ᴿhe satisfieth the longing soul, and filleth the hungry soul with goodness.

10 Such as ᴿsit in darkness and in the shadow of death, *being* ᴿbound in affliction and iron;

11 Because they ᴿrebelled against the words of God, and contemned ᴿthe counsel of the most High:

12 Therefore he brought down their heart with labour; they fell down, and *there was* ᴿnone to help.

13 Then they cried unto the LORD in their trouble, *and* he saved them out of their distresses.

14 ᴿHe brought them out of darkness and the shadow of death, and brake their bands in sunder.

15 ᴿOh that *men* would praise the LORD *for* his goodness, and *for* his wonderful works to the children of men!

16 For he hath ᴿbroken the gates of brass, and cut the bars of iron in sunder.

17 Fools ᴿbecause of their transgression, and because of their iniquities, are afflicted.

18 ᴿTheir soul abhorreth all manner of meat; and they ᴿdraw near unto the gates of death.

19 Then they cry unto the LORD in their trouble, *and* he saveth them out of their distresses.

20 ᴿHe sent his word, and ᴿhealed them, and ᴿdelivered *them* from their destructions.

21 Oh that *men* would praise the LORD *for* his goodness, and *for* his wonderful works to the children of men!

22 And ᴿlet them sacrifice the sacrifices of thanksgiving, and ᴿdeclare his works with ᴺrejoicing.

23 They that go down to the sea in ships, that do business in great waters;

24 These see the works of the LORD, and his wonders in the deep.

PSALM 106

30 Num. 25:7
31 Num. 25:11
32 Num. 20:3
Ps. 81:7
33 Num. 20:10
34 Judg. 1:21
34 Deut. 7:2
Judg. 2:2
35 Judg. 3:5, 6
Is. 2:6
36 Judg. 2:12
36 Deut. 7:16
37 2 Ki. 16:3
37 Lev. 17:7
38 Num. 35:33
39 Ezek. 20:18
39 Lev. 17:7
Num. 15:39
Ezek. 20:30
40 Judg. 2:14
40 Deut. 9:29
41 Judg. 2:14
Neh. 9:27
43 Judg. 2:16
Neh. 9:27
43 Or, *impoverished*, or, *weakened*
44 Judg. 10:10
45 Lev. 26:41
45 Judg. 2:18
45 Ps. 69:16
46 Ezra 9:9
Jer. 42:12
47 1 Chr. 16:35
48 Ps. 41:13
48 Heb. *Hallelujah*

PSALM 107

1 Ps. 106:1
1 Ps. 119:68

Ps. 106:10 — 2
Ps. 106:47 — 3
Heb. *from the sea* — 3
Deut. 32:10 — 4
Ps. 50:15 — 6
Hos. 5:15
Ezra 8:21 — 7
ver. 15, 21 — 8
Ps. 34:10 — 9
Luke 1:53
Luke 1:79 — 10
Job 36:8 — 10
Lam. 3:42 — 11
Ps. 73:24 — 11
Luke 7:30
Acts 20:27
Ps. 22:11 — 12
Is. 63:5
Ps. 68:6 — 14
Acts 12:7
ver. 8, 21, 31 — 15
Is. 45:2 — 16
Lam. 3:39 — 17
Job 33:20 — 18
Job 33:22 — 18
Ps. 9:13
Mat. 8:8 — 20
Ps. 30:2 — 20
& 103:3
Job 33:28 — 20
Ps. 30:3
& 49:15
Lev. 7:12 — 22
Ps. 116:17
Heb. 13:15
Ps. 9:11 — 22
& 73:28
& 118:17
Heb. *singing* — 22

25 For he commandeth, and [R]raiseth[N] the stormy wind, which lifteth up the waves thereof.

26 They mount up to the heaven, they go down again to the depths: [R]their soul is melted because of trouble.

27 They reel to and fro, and stagger like a drunken man, and [N]are at their wit's end.

28 [R]Then they cry unto the LORD in their trouble, and he bringeth them out of their distresses.

29 [R]He maketh the storm a calm, so that the waves thereof are still.

30 Then are they glad because they be quiet; so he bringeth them unto their desired haven.

31 [R]Oh that *men* would praise the LORD *for* his goodness, and *for* his wonderful works to the children of men!

32 Let them exalt him also [R]in the congregation of the people, and praise him in the assembly of the elders.

33 He [R]turneth rivers into a wilderness, and the watersprings into dry ground;

34 A [R]fruitful land into [N]barrenness, for the wickedness of them that dwell therein.

35 [R]He turneth the wilderness into a standing water, and dry ground into watersprings.

36 And there he maketh the hungry to dwell, that they may prepare a city for habitation;

37 And sow the fields, and plant vineyards, which may yield fruits of increase.

38 [R]He blesseth them also, so that they [R]are multiplied greatly; and suffereth not their cattle to decrease.

39 Again, they are [R]minished and brought low through oppression, affliction, and sorrow.

40 [R]He poureth contempt upon princes, and causeth them to wander in the [N]wilderness, *where there is* no way.

41 [R]Yet setteth he the poor on high [N]from affliction, and [R]maketh *him* families like a flock.

42 [R]The righteous shall see *it,* and rejoice: and all [R]iniquity shall stop her mouth.

43 [R]Whoso *is* wise, and will observe these *things,* even they shall understand the lovingkindness of the LORD.

PSALM 108

Prayer for God's assistance

A Song *or* Psalm of David.

O[R] GOD, my heart is fixed; I will sing and give praise, even with my glory.

2 [R]Awake, psaltery and harp: I *myself* will awake early.

3 I will praise thee, O LORD, among the people: and I will sing praises unto thee among the nations.

4 For thy mercy *is* great above the heavens: and thy truth *reacheth* unto the [N]clouds.

5 [R]Be thou exalted, O God, above the heavens: and thy glory above all the earth;

6 [R]That thy beloved may be delivered: save *with* thy right hand, and answer me.

7 God hath spoken in his holiness; I will rejoice, I will divide Shē'-chĕm, and mete out the valley of Sŭc'-cōth.

8 Gilead *is* mine; Mă-năs'-sēh *is* mine; Ē'-phră-ĭm also *is* the strength of mine head; [R]Judah *is* my lawgiver;

9 Moab *is* my washpot; over Ē'-dom will I cast out my shoe; over Philistia will I triumph.

10 [R]Who will bring me into the strong city? who will lead me into Ē'-dom?

11 *Wilt* not *thou,* O God, *who* hast cast us off? and wilt not thou, O God, go forth with our hosts?

12 Give us help from trouble: for vain *is* the help of man.

13 [R]Through God we shall do valiantly: for he *it is that* shall tread down our enemies.

PSALM 109

Cry for vengeance

To the chief Musician, A Psalm of David.

H OLD [R]not thy peace, O God of my praise;

2 For the mouth of the wicked and the [N]mouth of the deceitful [N]are opened against me: they have spoken against me with a lying tongue.

3 They compassed me about also with words of hatred; and fought against me [R]without a cause.

4 For my love they are my adversaries: but I *give myself unto* prayer.

5 And [R]they have rewarded me evil for good, and hatred for my love.

6 Set thou a wicked man over him: and let [R]Satan[N] stand at his right hand.

7 When he shall be judged, let him [N]be condemned: and [R]let his prayer become sin.

8 Let his days be few; *and* [R]let another take his [N]office.

9 [R]Let his children be fatherless, and his wife a widow.

10 Let his children be continually vagabonds, and beg: let them seek *their bread* also out of their desolate places.

11 [R]Let the extortioner catch all that he hath; and let the strangers spoil his labour.

12 Let there be none to extend mercy unto him: neither let there be any to favour his fatherless children.

13 [R]Let his posterity be cut off; *and* in the

PSALM 107
25 Jonah 1:4
25 Heb. *maketh to stand*
26 Ps. 22:14
27 Heb. *all their wisdom is swallowed up*
28 ver. 6, 13, 19
29 Ps. 89:9
Mat. 8:26
31 ver. 8, 15, 21
32 Ps. 22:22, 25
33 1 Ki. 17:1, 7
34 Gen. 13:10
& 14:3
& 19:25
34 Heb. *saltness*
35 Ps. 114:8
Is. 41:18
38 Gen. 12:2
& 17:16, 20
38 Ex. 1:7
39 2 Ki. 10:32
40 Job 12:21, 24
40 Or, *void place*
41 1 Sam. 2:8
Ps. 113:7, 8
41 Or, *after*
41 Ps. 78:52
42 Job 5:15, 16
42 Job 5:16
Ps. 63:11
Prov. 10:11
Rom. 3:19
43 Ps. 64:9
Jer. 9:12
Hos. 14:9

PSALM 108
1 Ps. 57:7
2 Ps. 57:8-11

Or, *skies* 4
Ps. 57:5, 11 5
Ps. 60:5, etc. 6
Gen. 49:10 8
Ps. 60:9 10
Ps. 60:12 13

PSALM 109
Ps. 83:1 1
Heb. *mouth of deceit* 2
Heb. *have opened themselves* 2
Ps. 35:7 3
& 69:4
John 15:25
Ps. 35:7, 12 5
& 38:20
Zech. 3:1 6
Or, *an adversary* 6
Heb. *go out guilty,* or, *wicked* 7
Prov. 28:9 7
Acts 1:20 8
Or, *charge* 8
Ex. 22:24 9
Job 5:5 11
& 18:9
Job 18:19 13
Ps. 37:28

generation following let their ᴿname be blotted out.

14 ᴿLet the iniquity of his fathers be remembered with the LORD; and let not the sin of his mother ᴿbe blotted out.

15 Let them be before the LORD continually, that he may ᴿcut off the memory of them from the earth.

16 Because that he remembered not to shew mercy, but persecuted the poor and needy man, that he might even slay the ᴿbroken in heart.

17 ᴿAs he loved cursing, so let it come unto him: as he delighted not in blessing, so let it be far from him.

18 As he clothed himself with cursing like as with his garment, so let it ᴿcome ᴺinto his bowels like water, and like oil into his bones.

19 Let it be unto him as the garment *which* covereth him, and for a girdle wherewith he is girded continually.

20 *Let* this *be* the reward of mine adversaries from the LORD, and of them that speak evil against my soul.

21 But do thou for me, O GOD the Lord, for thy name's sake: because thy mercy *is* good, deliver thou me.

22 For I *am* poor and needy, and my heart is wounded within me.

23 I am gone ᴿlike the shadow when it declineth: I am tossed up and down as the locust.

24 My ᴿknees are weak through fasting; and my flesh faileth of fatness.

25 I became also ᴿa reproach unto them: *when* they looked upon me ᴿthey shaked their heads.

26 Help me, O LORD my God: O save me according to thy mercy:

27 ᴿThat they may know that this *is* thy hand; *that* thou, LORD, hast done it.

28 ᴿLet them curse, but bless thou: when they arise, let them be ashamed; but let ᴿthy servant rejoice.

29 ᴿLet mine adversaries be clothed with shame, and let them cover themselves with their own confusion, as with a mantle.

30 I will greatly praise the LORD with my mouth; yea, ᴿI will praise him among the multitude.

31 For ᴿhe shall stand at the right hand of the poor, to save *him* ᴺfrom those that condemn his soul.

PSALM 110

God's reign over the nations

A Psalm of David.

THE ᴿLORD said unto my Lord, Sit thou at my right hand, until I make thine enemies thy footstool.   ★

2 The LORD shall send the rod of thy strength out of Zion: rule thou in the midst of thine enemies.   ★

3 ᴿThy people *shall be* willing in the day of thy power, ᴿin the beauties of holiness ᴺfrom the womb of the morning: thou hast the dew of thy youth.   ★

4 The LORD hath sworn, and ᴿwill not repent, Thou *art* a priest for ever after the order of Mĕl-<u>chīz</u>′-ĕd-ĕk.   ★

5 The Lord ᴿat thy right hand shall strike through kings ᴿin the day of his wrath.   ★

6 He shall judge among the heathen, he shall fill *the places* with the dead bodies; ᴿhe shall wound the heads over ᴺmany countries.   ★

7 He shall drink of the brook in the way: ᴿtherefore shall he lift up the head.   ★

PSALM 111

The beginning of wisdom

PRAISEᴺ ye the LORD. ᴿI will praise the LORD with *my* whole heart, in the assembly of the upright, and *in* the congregation.

2 ᴿThe works of the LORD *are* great, ᴿsought out of all them that have pleasure therein.

3 His work *is* ᴿhonourable and glorious: and his righteousness endureth for ever.

4 He hath made his wonderful works to be remembered: ᴿthe LORD *is* gracious and full of compassion.

5 He hath given ᴿmeatᴺ unto them that fear him: he will ever be mindful of his covenant.

6 He hath shewed his people the power of his works, that he may give them the heritage of the heathen.

7 The works of his hands *are* ᴿverity and judgment; ᴿall his commandments *are* sure.

8 ᴿThey ᴺstand fast for ever and ever, *and are* ᴿdone in truth and uprightness.

9 ᴿHe sent redemption unto his people: he hath commanded his covenant for ever: ᴿholy and reverend *is* his name.

10 ᴿThe fear of the LORD *is* the beginning of wisdom: ᴺa good understanding have all they ᴺthat do *his commandments*: his praise endureth for ever.

PSALM 112

Security of the righteous

PRAISE ye the LORD. Blessed *is* the man *that* feareth the LORD, *that* ᴿdelighteth greatly in his commandments.

2 ᴿHis seed shall be mighty upon earth: the generation of the upright shall be blessed.

3 ᴿWealth and riches *shall be* in his house: and his righteousness endureth for ever.

Center reference column

PSALM 109

13	Prov. 10:7
14	Ex. 20:5
14	Neh. 4:5
	Jer. 18:23
15	Job 18:17
	Ps. 34:16
16	Ps. 34:18
17	Prov. 14:14
	Ezek. 35:6
18	Num. 5:22
18	Heb. *within him*
23	Ps. 102:11
24	Heb. 12:12
25	Ps. 22:6, 7
25	Mat. 27:39
27	Job 37:7
28	2 Sam. 16:11
28	Is. 65:14
29	Ps. 35:26
	& 132:18
30	Ps. 35:18
	& 111:1
31	Ps. 16:8
	& 73:23
31	Heb. *from the judges of his soul*

PSALM 110

1	Mat. 22:44
	Mark 12:36
	Luke 20:42
	Acts 2:34
	1 Cor. 15:25
Judg. 5:2	3
Ps. 96:9	3
Or, *more than the womb of the morning: thou shalt have, etc.*	3
Num. 23:19	4
Ps. 16:8	5
Ps. 2:5, 12	5
Rom. 2:5	6
Ps. 68:21	
Hab. 3:13	
Or, *great*	6
Is. 53:12	7

PSALM 111

Heb. *Hallelujah*	1
Ps. 35:18	1
& 89:5	
& 107:32	
Job 38-41	2
Ps. 143:5	2
Ps. 145:4	3
Ps. 86:5	4
Mat. 6:26	5
Heb. *prey*	5
Rev. 15:3	7
Ps. 19:7	7
Is. 40:8	8
Heb. are *established*	8
Rev. 15:3	8
Luke 1:68	9
Luke 1:49	9
Eccl. 12:13	10
Or, *good success*	10
Heb. *that do them*	10

PSALM 112

Ps. 119:16	1
Ps. 102:28	2
Mat. 6:33	3

4 ᴿUnto the upright there ariseth light in the darkness: *he is* gracious, and full of compassion, and righteous.

5 ᴿA good man sheweth favour, and lendeth: he will guide his affairs ᴿwith ᴺdiscretion.

6 Surely he shall not be moved for ever: ᴿthe righteous shall be in everlasting remembrance.

7 ᴿHe shall not be afraid of evil tidings: his ᴿheart is fixed, ᴿtrusting in the LORD.

8 His heart *is* established, ᴿhe shall not be afraid, until he ᴿsee *his desire* upon his enemies.

9 ᴿHe hath dispersed, he hath given to the poor; his righteousness endureth for ever; ᴿhis horn shall be exalted with honour.

10 ᴿThe wicked shall see *it,* and be grieved; ᴿhe shall gnash with his teeth, and ᴿmelt away: ᴿthe desire of the wicked shall perish.

PSALM 113

Who is like God?

PRAISE ye the LORD. ᴿPraise, O ye servants of the LORD, praise the name of the LORD.

2 ᴿBlessed be the name of the LORD from this time forth and for evermore.

3 ᴿFrom the rising of the sun unto the going down of the same the LORD's name *is* to be praised.

4 The LORD *is* ᴿhigh above all nations, *and* ᴿhis glory above the heavens.

5 ᴿWho *is* like unto the LORD our God, who ᴺdwelleth on high,

6 ᴿWho humbleth *himself* to behold *the things that are* in heaven, and in the earth!

7 ᴿHe raiseth up the poor out of the dust, *and* lifteth the needy out of the dunghill;

8 That he may ᴿset *him* with princes, *even* with the princes of his people.

9 ᴿHe maketh the barren woman to keep house, *and to be* a joyful mother of children. Praise ye the LORD.

PSALM 114

God's guidance in the exodus

WHEN ᴿIsrael went out of Egypt, the house of Jacob ᴿfrom a people of strange language;

2 ᴿJudah was his sanctuary, *and* Israel his dominion.

3 ᴿThe sea saw *it,* and fled: ᴿJordan was driven back.

4 ᴿThe mountains skipped like rams, *and* the little hills like lambs.

5 ᴿWhat *ailed* thee, O thou sea, that thou fleddest? thou Jordan, *that* thou wast driven back?

PSALM 112	
4 Job 11:17	
Ps. 97:11	
5 Ps. 37:26	
5 Eph. 5:15	
Col. 4:5	
5 Heb. *judgment*	
6 Prov. 10:7	
7 Prov. 1:33	
7 Ps. 57:7	
7 Ps. 64:10	
8 Prov. 1:33	
8 Ps. 59:10	
9 2 Cor. 9:9	
9 Ps. 75:10	
10 Luke 13:28	
10 Ps. 37:12	
10 Ps. 58:7, 8	
10 Prov 11:7	

PSALM 113	
1 Ps. 135:1	
2 Dan. 2:20	
3 Is. 59:19	
Mal. 1:11	
4 Ps. 97:9	
& 99:2	
4 Ps. 8:1	
5 Ps. 89:6	
5 Heb. *exalteth himself to dwell*	
6 Ps. 11:4	
Is. 57:15	
7 1 Sam. 2:8	
Ps. 107:41	
8 Job 36:7	
9 1 Sam. 2:5	
Is. 54:1	
Gal. 4:27	

PSALM 114	
1 Ex. 13:3	
1 Ps. 81:5	
2 Ex. 6:7	
Deut. 27:9	
3 Ex. 14:21	
3 Josh. 3:13	
4 Ps. 29:6	
5 Hab. 3:8	
Ex. 17:6	8
Num. 20:11	
Ps. 107:35	

PSALM 115	
Is. 48:11	1
Ezek. 36:32	
Ps. 42:3, 10	2
& 79:10	
Joel 2:17	
1 Chr. 16:26	3
Ps. 135:6	
Dan. 4:35	
Deut. 4:28	4
Ps. 135:15	
Jer. 10:3	
Ps. 135:18	8
Is. 44:9-11	
Ps. 118:2, 3	9
Ps. 33:20	9
Ps. 128:1	13
Heb. *with*	13
Gen. 14:19	15
Gen. 1:1	15
Ps. 96:5	
Ps. 6:5	17
& 88:10-12	
Is. 38:18	
Ps. 113:2	18
Dan. 2:20	

PSALM 116	
Ps. 18:1	1
Heb. *in my days*	2

6 Ye mountains, *that* ye skipped like rams; *and* ye little hills, like lambs?

7 Tremble, thou earth, at the presence of the Lord, at the presence of the God of Jacob;

8 ᴿWhich turned the rock *into* a standing water, the flint into a fountain of waters.

PSALM 115

God's superiority to idols

NOT ᴿunto us, O LORD, not unto us, but unto thy name give glory, for thy mercy, *and* for thy truth's sake.

2 Wherefore should the heathen say, ᴿWhere *is* now their God?

3 ᴿBut our God *is* in the heavens: he hath done whatsoever he hath pleased.

4 ᴿTheir idols *are* silver and gold, the work of men's hands.

5 They have mouths, but they speak not: eyes have they, but they see not:

6 They have ears, but they hear not: noses have they, but they smell not:

7 They have hands, but they handle not: feet have they, but they walk not: neither speak they through their throat.

8 ᴿThey that make them are like unto them; *so is* every one that trusteth in them.

9 ᴿO Israel, trust thou in the LORD: ᴿhe *is* their help and their shield.

10 O house of Aaron, trust in the LORD: he *is* their help and their shield.

11 Ye that fear the LORD, trust in the LORD: he *is* their help and their shield.

12 The LORD hath been mindful of us: he will bless *us;* he will bless the house of Israel; he will bless the house of Aaron.

13 ᴿHe will bless them that fear the LORD, *both* small ᴺand great.

14 The LORD shall increase you more and more, you and your children.

15 Ye *are* ᴿblessed of the LORD ᴿwhich made heaven and earth.

16 The heaven, *even* the heavens, *are* the LORD's: but the earth hath he given to the children of men.

17 ᴿThe dead praise not the LORD, neither any that go down into silence.

18 ᴿBut we will bless the LORD from this time forth and for evermore. Praise the LORD.

PSALM 116

Fulfillment of faith

I ᴿLOVE the LORD, because he hath heard my voice *and* my supplications.

2 Because he hath inclined his ear unto me, therefore will I call upon *him* ᴺas long as I live.

3 ᴿThe sorrows of death compassed me, and the pains of hell ᴺgat hold upon me: I found trouble and sorrow.

4 Then called I upon the name of the LORD; O LORD, I beseech thee, deliver my soul.

5 ᴿGracious *is* the LORD, and ᴿrighteous; yea, our God *is* merciful.

6 The LORD preserveth the simple: I was brought low, and he helped me.

7 Return unto thy ᴿrest, O my soul; for ᴿthe LORD hath dealt bountifully with thee.

8 ᴿFor thou hast delivered my soul from death, mine eyes from tears, *and* my feet from falling.

9 I will walk before the LORD ᴿin the land of the living.

10 ᴿI believed, therefore have I spoken: I was greatly afflicted:

11 ᴿI said in my haste, ᴿAll men *are* liars.

12 What shall I render unto the LORD *for* all his benefits toward me?

13 I will take the cup of salvation, and call upon the name of the LORD.

14 ᴿI will pay my vows unto the LORD now in the presence of all his people.

15 ᴿPrecious in the sight of the LORD *is* the death of his saints.

16 O LORD, truly ᴿI *am* thy servant; I *am* thy servant, *and* ᴿthe son of thine handmaid: thou hast loosed my bonds.

17 I will offer to thee ᴿthe sacrifice of thanksgiving, and will call upon the name of the LORD.

18 I will pay my vows unto the LORD now in the presence of all his people,

19 In the ᴿcourts of the LORD's house, in the midst of thee, O Jerusalem. Praise ye the LORD.

PSALM 117

God's enduring faithfulness

Oᴿ PRAISE the LORD, all ye nations: praise him, all ye people.

2 For his merciful kindness is great toward us: and ᴿthe truth of the LORD *endureth* for ever. Praise ye the LORD.

PSALM 118

God's enduring love

Oᴿ GIVE thanks unto the LORD; for *he is* good: because his mercy *endureth* for ever.

2 ᴿLet Israel now say, that his mercy *endureth* for ever.

3 Let the house of Aaron now say, that his mercy *endureth* for ever.

4 Let them now that fear the LORD say, that his mercy *endureth* for ever.

5 ᴿI called upon the LORD ᴺin distress: the LORD answered me, *and* ᴿset *me* in a large place.

6 ᴿThe LORD *is* ᴺon my side; I will not fear: what can man do unto me?

7 ᴿThe LORD taketh my part with them that help me: therefore shall ᴿI see *my desire* upon them that hate me.

8 ᴿ*It is* better to trust in the LORD than to put confidence in man.

9 ᴿ*It is* better to trust in the LORD than to put confidence in princes.

10 All nations compassed me about: but in the name of the LORD will I ᴺdestroy them.

11 They ᴿcompassed me about; yea, they compassed me about: but in the name of the LORD I will destroy them.

12 They compassed me about ᴿlike bees; they are quenched ᴿas the fire of thorns: for in the name of the LORD I will ᴺdestroy them.

13 Thou hast thrust sore at me that I might fall: but the LORD helped me.

14 ᴿThe LORD *is* my strength and song, and is become my salvation.

15 The voice of rejoicing and salvation *is* in the tabernacles of the righteous: the right hand of the LORD doeth valiantly.

16 ᴿThe right hand of the LORD is exalted: the right hand of the LORD doeth valiantly.

17 ᴿI shall not die, but live, and ᴿdeclare the works of the LORD.

18 The LORD hath ᴿchastened me sore: but he hath not given me over unto death.

19 ᴿOpen to me the gates of righteousness: I will go into them, *and* I will praise the LORD:

20 ᴿThis gate of the LORD, ᴿinto which the righteous shall enter.

21 I will praise thee: for thou hast ᴿheard me, and ᴿart become my salvation.

22 ᴿThe stone *which* the builders refused is become the head *stone* of the corner.   ★

23 ᴺThis is the LORD's doing; it *is* marvellous in our eyes.

24 This *is* the day *which* the LORD hath made; we will rejoice and be glad in it.

25 Save now, I beseech thee, O LORD: O LORD, I beseech thee, send now prosperity.

26 ᴿBlessed *be* he that cometh in the name of the LORD: we have blessed you out of the house of the LORD.   ★

27 God *is* the LORD, which hath shewed us ᴿlight: bind the sacrifice with cords, *even* unto the horns of the altar.

28 Thou *art* my God, and I will praise thee: ᴿ*thou art* my God, I will exalt thee.

29 ᴿO give thanks unto the LORD; for *he is* good: for his mercy *endureth* for ever.

PSALM 119

Meditation on God's law

א Ä'-LĔPH.

BLESSED *are* the [N]undefiled in the way, [R]who walk in the law of the LORD.

2 Blessed *are* they that keep his testimonies, *and that* seek him with the whole heart.

3 [R]They also do no iniquity: they walk in his ways.

4 Thou hast commanded *us* to keep thy precepts diligently.

5 O that my ways were directed to keep thy statutes!

6 [R]Then shall I not be ashamed, when I have respect unto all thy commandments.

7 [R]I will praise thee with uprightness of heart, when I shall have learned [N]thy righteous judgments.

8 I will keep thy statutes: O forsake me not utterly.

ב BĔTH.

9 Wherewithal shall a young man cleanse his way? by taking heed *thereto* according to thy word.

10 With my whole heart have I [R]sought thee: O let me not [R]wander from thy commandments.

11 [R]Thy word have I hid in mine heart, that I might not sin against thee.

12 Blessed *art* thou, O LORD: [R]teach me thy statutes.

13 With my lips have I [R]declared all the judgments of thy mouth.

14 I have rejoiced in the way of thy testimonies, as *much as* in all riches.

15 I will [R]meditate in thy precepts, and have respect unto thy ways.

16 I will [R]delight myself in thy statutes: I will not forget thy word.

ג GÎ'-MĔL.

17 [R]Deal bountifully with thy servant, *that* I may live, and keep thy word.

18 [N]Open thou mine eyes, that I may behold wondrous things out of thy law.

19 [R]I *am* a stranger in the earth: hide not thy commandments from me.

20 [R]My soul breaketh for the longing *that it hath* unto thy judgments at all times.

21 Thou hast rebuked the proud *that are* cursed, which do [R]err from thy commandments.

22 [R]Remove from me reproach and contempt; for I have kept thy testimonies.

23 Princes also did sit *and* speak against me: *but* thy servant did [R]meditate in thy statutes.

24 [R]Thy testimonies also *are* my delight *and* [N]my counsellors.

ד DÄ'-LĔTH.

25 [R]My soul cleaveth unto the dust: [R]quicken thou me according to thy word.

26 I have declared my ways, and thou heardest me: [R]teach me thy statutes.

27 Make me to understand the way of thy precepts: so [R]shall I talk of thy wondrous works.

28 [R]My soul [N]melteth for heaviness: strengthen thou me according unto thy word.

29 Remove from me the way of lying: and grant me thy law graciously.

30 I have chosen the way of truth: thy judgments have I laid *before me.*

31 I have stuck unto thy testimonies: O LORD, put me not to shame.

32 I will run the way of thy commandments, when thou shalt [R]enlarge my heart.

ה HĔ.

33 [R]Teach me, O LORD, the way of thy statutes; and I shall keep it [R]*unto* the end.

34 Give me understanding, and I shall keep thy law; yea, I shall observe it with *my* whole heart.

35 Make me to go in the path of thy commandments; for therein do I [R]delight.

36 Incline my heart unto thy testimonies, and not to [R]covetousness.

37 [R]Turn[N] away mine eyes from [R]beholding vanity; *and* quicken thou me in thy way.

38 [R]Stablish thy word unto thy servant, who *is devoted* to thy fear.

39 Turn away my reproach which I fear: for thy judgments *are* good.

40 Behold, I have [R]longed after thy precepts: [R]quicken me in thy righteousness.

ו VÂU.

41 [R]Let thy mercies come also unto me, O LORD, *even* thy salvation, according to thy word.

42 [N]So shall I have wherewith to answer him that reproacheth me: for I trust in thy word.

43 And take not the word of truth utterly out of my mouth; for I have hoped in thy judgments.

44 So shall I keep thy law continually for ever and ever.

45 And I will walk [N]at liberty: for I seek thy precepts.

46 [R]I will speak of thy testimonies also before kings, and will not be ashamed.

47 And I will [R]delight myself in thy commandments, which I have loved.

48 My hands also will I lift up unto thy commandments, which I have loved; and I will [R]meditate in thy statutes.

ז ZAÏN.

49 Remember the word unto thy servant, upon which thou hast caused me to ᴿhope.

50 This *is* my ᴿcomfort in my affliction: for thy word hath quickened me.

51 The proud have had me greatly ᴿin derision: *yet* have I not ᴿdeclined from thy law.

52 I remembered thy judgments of old, O Lᴏʀᴅ; and have comforted myself.

53 ᴿHorror hath taken hold upon me because of the wicked that forsake thy law.

54 Thy statutes have been my songs in the house of my pilgrimage.

55 ᴿI have remembered thy name, O Lᴏʀᴅ, in the night, and have kept thy law.

56 This I had, because I kept thy precepts.

ח CHÊTH.

57 ᴿ*Thou art* my portion, O Lᴏʀᴅ: I have said that I would keep thy words.

58 I entreated thy ᴺfavour with *my* whole heart: be merciful unto me ᴿaccording to thy word.

59 I ᴿthought on my ways, and turned my feet unto thy testimonies.

60 I made haste, and delayed not to keep thy commandments.

61 The ᴺbands of the wicked have robbed me: *but* I have not forgotten thy law.

62 ᴿAt midnight I will rise to give thanks unto thee because of thy righteous judgments.

63 I *am* a companion of all *them* that fear thee, and of them that keep thy precepts.

64 ᴿThe earth, O Lᴏʀᴅ, is full of thy mercy: ᴿteach me thy statutes.

ט TÊTH.

65 Thou hast dealt well with thy servant, O Lᴏʀᴅ, according unto thy word.

66 Teach me good judgment and knowledge: for I have believed thy commandments.

67 ᴿBefore I was afflicted I went astray: but now have I kept thy word.

68 Thou *art* ᴿgood, and doest good; ᴿteach me thy statutes.

69 The proud have ᴿforged a lie against me: *but* I will keep thy precepts with *my* whole heart.

70 ᴿTheir heart is as fat as grease; *but* I ᴿdelight in thy law.

71 ᴿ*It is* good for me that I have been afflicted; that I might learn thy statutes.

72 ᴿThe law of thy mouth *is* better unto me than thousands of gold and silver.

י JÔD.

73 ᴿThy hands have made me and fashioned me: ᴿgive me understanding, that I may learn thy commandments.

74 ᴿThey that fear thee will be glad when they see me; because ᴿI have hoped in thy word.

75 I know, O Lᴏʀᴅ, that thy judgments *are* ᴺright, and ᴿ*that* thou in faithfulness hast afflicted me.

76 Let, I pray thee, thy merciful kindness be ᴺfor my comfort, according to thy word unto thy servant.

77 ᴿLet thy tender mercies come unto me, that I may live: for ᴿthy law *is* my delight.

78 Let the proud ᴿbe ashamed; ᴿfor they dealt perversely with me without a cause: *but* I will ᴿmeditate in thy precepts.

79 Let those that fear thee turn unto me, and those that have known thy testimonies.

80 Let my heart be sound in thy statutes; that I be not ashamed.

כ CÂPH.

81 ᴿMy soul fainteth for thy salvation: *but* ᴿI hope in thy word.

82 ᴿMine eyes fail for thy word, saying, When wilt thou comfort me?

83 For ᴿI am become like a bottle in the smoke; *yet* do I not forget thy statutes.

84 ᴿHow many *are* the days of thy servant? ᴿwhen wilt thou execute judgment on them that persecute me?

85 ᴿThe proud have digged pits for me, which *are* not after thy law.

86 All thy commandments *are* ᴺfaithful: ᴿthey persecute me ᴿwrongfully; help thou me.

87 They had almost consumed me upon earth; but I forsook not thy precepts.

88 ᴿQuicken me after thy lovingkindness; so shall I keep the testimony of thy mouth.

ל LÄ'-MĔD.

89 ᴿFor ever, O Lᴏʀᴅ, thy word is settled in heaven.

90 Thy faithfulness *is* ᴺunto all generations: thou hast established the earth, and it ᴺabideth.

91 They continue this day according to ᴿthine ordinances: for all *are* thy servants.

92 Unless ᴿthy law *had been* my delights, I should then have perished in mine affliction.

93 I will never forget thy precepts: for with them thou hast quickened me.

94 I *am* thine, save me; for I have sought thy precepts.

95 The wicked have waited for me to destroy me: *but* I will consider thy testimonies.

96 ᴿI have seen an end of all perfection: *but* thy commandment *is* exceeding broad.

מ MĔM.

97 O how love I thy law! ᴿit *is* my meditation all the day.

98 Thou through thy commandments hast made me ^Rwiser than mine enemies: for ^Nthey *are* ever with me.

99 I have more understanding than all my teachers: ^Rfor thy testimonies *are* my meditation.

100 ^RI understand more than the ancients, because I keep thy precepts.

101 I have ^Rrefrained my feet from every evil way, that I might keep thy word.

102 I have not departed from thy judgments: for thou hast taught me.

103 ^RHow sweet are thy words unto my ^Ntaste! *yea, sweeter* than honey to my mouth!

104 Through thy precepts I get understanding: therefore ^RI hate every false way.

נ NŪN.

105 ^RThy word *is* a ^Nlamp unto my feet, and a light unto my path.

106 ^RI have sworn, and I will perform *it,* that I will keep thy righteous judgments.

107 I am afflicted very much: ^Rquicken me, O LORD, according unto thy word.

108 Accept, I beseech thee, ^Rthe freewill offerings of my mouth, O LORD, and ^Rteach me thy judgments.

109 ^RMy soul *is* continually in my hand: yet do I not forget thy law.

110 ^RThe wicked have laid a snare for me: yet I ^Rerred not from thy precepts.

111 ^RThy testimonies have I taken as an heritage for ever: for ^Rthey *are* the rejoicing of my heart.

112 I have inclined mine heart ^Nto perform thy statutes alway, ^R*even unto* the end.

ס SÄ'-MĔCH.

113 I hate *vain* thoughts: but thy law do I love.

114 ^RThou *art* my hiding place and my shield: ^RI hope in thy word.

115 ^RDepart from me, ye evildoers: for I will keep the commandments of my God.

116 Uphold me according unto thy word, that I may live: and let me not ^Rbe ashamed of my hope.

117 Hold thou me up, and I shall be safe: and I will have respect unto thy statutes continually.

118 Thou hast trodden down all them that ^Rerr from thy statutes: for their deceit *is* falsehood.

119 Thou ^Nputtest away all the wicked of the earth ^R*like* dross: therefore I love thy testimonies.

120 ^RMy flesh trembleth for fear of thee; and I am afraid of thy judgments.

PSALM 119	
98	Deut. 4:6
98	Heb. *it is ever with me*
99	2 Tim. 3:15
100	Job 32:7-9
101	Prov. 1:15
103	Ps. 19:10
	Prov. 8:11
103	Heb. *palate*
104	ver. 128
105	Prov. 6:23
105	Or, *candle*
106	Neh. 10:29
107	ver. 88
108	Hos. 14:2
	Heb. 13:15
108	ver. 12, 26
109	Job 13:14
110	Ps. 140:5
110	ver. 10, 21
111	Deut. 33:4
111	ver. 77, 92
112	Heb. *to do*
112	ver. 33
114	Ps. 32:7
114	ver. 81
115	Ps. 6:8
	Mat. 7:23
116	Ps. 25:2
	Rom. 5:5
118	ver. 21
119	Heb. *causest to cease*
119	Ezek. 22:18
120	Hab. 3:16

Heb. 7:22	122
ver. 81, 82	123
ver. 12	124
Ps. 116:16	125
Ps. 19:10	127
ver. 104	128
Ps. 19:7	130
ver. 20	131
Ps. 106:4	132
2 Thes. 1:6	132
Heb. *according to the custom towards those, etc.*	132
Ps. 17:5	133
Ps. 19:13	133
Rom. 6:12	
Luke 1:74	134
Ps. 4:6	135
ver. 12, 26	135
Jer. 9:1	136
Ezek. 9:4	
Neh. 9:33	137
Ps. 19:7-9	138
Heb. *righteousness*	138
Heb. *faithfulness*	138
Ps. 69:9	139
John 2:17	
Heb. *cut me off*	139
Ps. 12:6	140
Heb. *tried,* or, *refined*	140
Ps. 19:9	142
Heb. *found me*	143
ver. 77	143
ver. 34, 73	144

ע AIN.

121 I have done judgment and justice: leave me not to mine oppressors.

122 Be ^Rsurety for thy servant for good: let not the proud oppress me.

123 ^RMine eyes fail for thy salvation, and for the word of thy righteousness.

124 Deal with thy servant according unto thy mercy, and ^Rteach me thy statutes.

125 ^RI *am* thy servant; give me understanding, that I may know thy testimonies.

126 *It is* time for *thee,* LORD, to work: *for* they have made void thy law.

127 ^RTherefore I love thy commandments above gold; yea, above fine gold.

128 Therefore I esteem all *thy* precepts *concerning* all *things to be* right; *and* I ^Rhate every false way.

פ PĚ.

129 Thy testimonies *are* wonderful: therefore doth my soul keep them.

130 The entrance of thy words giveth light; ^Rit giveth understanding unto the simple.

131 I opened my mouth, and panted: for I ^Rlonged for thy commandments.

132 ^RLook thou upon me, and be merciful unto me, ^Ras^N thou usest to do unto those that love thy name.

133 ^ROrder my steps in thy word: and ^Rlet not any iniquity have dominion over me.

134 ^RDeliver me from the oppression of man: so will I keep thy precepts.

135 ^RMake thy face to shine upon thy servant; and ^Rteach me thy statutes.

136 ^RRivers of waters run down mine eyes, because they keep not thy law.

צ TZĂD'-DÎ.

137 ^RRighteous *art* thou, O LORD, and upright *are* thy judgments.

138 ^RThy testimonies *that* thou hast commanded *are* ^Nrighteous and very ^Nfaithful.

139 ^RMy zeal hath ^Nconsumed me, because mine enemies have forgotten thy words.

140 ^RThy word *is* very ^Npure: therefore thy servant loveth it.

141 I *am* small and despised: *yet* do not I forget thy precepts.

142 Thy righteousness *is* an everlasting righteousness, and thy law *is* ^Rthe truth.

143 Trouble and anguish have ^Ntaken hold on me: *yet* thy commandments *are* ^Rmy delights.

144 The righteousness of thy testimonies *is* everlasting: ^Rgive me understanding, and I shall live.

ק KŌPH.

145 I cried with *my* whole heart; hear me, O LORD: I will keep thy statutes.

146 I cried unto thee; save me, ᴺand I shall keep thy testimonies.

147 ᴿI prevented the dawning of the morning, and cried: ᴿI hoped in thy word.

148 ᴿMine eyes prevent the *night* watches, that I might meditate in thy word.

149 Hear my voice according unto thy lovingkindness: O LORD, ᴿquicken me according to thy judgment.

150 They draw nigh that follow after mischief: they are far from thy law.

151 Thou *art* ᴿnear, O LORD; ᴿand all thy commandments *are* truth.

152 Concerning thy testimonies, I have known of old that thou hast founded them ᴿfor ever.

ר RĒSH.

153 ᴿConsider mine affliction, and deliver me: for I do not forget thy law.

154 ᴿPlead my cause, and deliver me: ᴿquicken me according to thy word.

155 ᴿSalvation *is* far from the wicked: for they seek not thy statutes.

156 ᴺGreat *are* thy tender mercies, O LORD: ᴿquicken me according to thy judgments.

157 Many *are* my persecutors and mine enemies; *yet* do I not ᴿdecline from thy testimonies.

158 I beheld the transgressors, and ᴿwas grieved; because they kept not thy word.

159 Consider how I love thy precepts: ᴿquicken me, O LORD, according to thy lovingkindness.

160 ᴺThy word *is* true *from* the beginning: and every one of thy righteous judgments *endureth* for ever.

ש SCHĪN.

161 ᴿPrinces have persecuted me without a cause: but my heart standeth in awe of thy word.

162 I rejoice at thy word, as one that findeth great spoil.

163 I hate and abhor lying: *but* thy law do I love.

164 Seven times a day do I praise thee because of thy righteous judgments.

165 ᴿGreat peace have they which love thy law: and ᴺnothing shall offend them.

166 ᴿLORD, I have hoped for thy salvation, and done thy commandments.

167 My soul hath kept thy testimonies; and I love them exceedingly.

PSALM 119	
146 Or, *that I may keep*	
147 Ps. 5:3	
147 ver. 74	
148 Ps. 63:1, 6	
149 ver. 40	
151 Ps. 145:18	
151 ver. 142	
152 Luke 21:33	
153 Lam. 5:1	
154 1 Sam. 24:15	
154 ver. 40	
155 Job 5:4	
156 Or, *Many*	
156 ver. 149	
157 Ps. 44:18	
158 Ezek. 9:4	
159 ver. 88	
160 Heb. *The beginning of thy word is true*	
161 1 Sam. 24:11	
165 Prov. 3:2	
Is. 32:17	
165 Heb. *they shall have no stumblingblock*	
166 Gen. 49:18	

Prov. 5:21	168
ver. 144	169
ver. 7	171
Josh. 24:22	173
ver. 166	174
ver. 16, 24	174
Is. 53:6	176

PSALM 120	
Jonah 2:2	1
Or, *What shall the deceitful tongue give unto thee? or, What shall it profit thee*	3
Heb. *added*	3
Or, It is as *the sharp arrows of the mighty* man, *with coals of juniper*	4
Gen. 10:2	5
Ezek. 27:13	
Gen. 25:13	5
1 Sam. 25:1	
Jer. 49:28	
Or, a man *of peace*	7

PSALM 121	
Or, *Shall I lift up mine eyes to the hills? whence should my help come?*	1
Jer. 3:23	
Ps. 124:8	2
1 Sam. 2:9	3
Ps. 127:1	3
Is. 27:3	
Is. 25:4	5
Ps. 16:8	5

---

168 I have kept thy precepts and thy testimonies: ᴿfor all my ways *are* before thee.

ת TĀU.

169 Let my cry come near before thee, O LORD: ᴿgive me understanding according to thy word.

170 Let my supplication come before thee: deliver me according to thy word.

171 ᴿMy lips shall utter praise, when thou hast taught me thy statutes.

172 My tongue shall speak of thy word: for all thy commandments *are* righteousness.

173 Let thine hand help me; for ᴿI have chosen thy precepts.

174 ᴿI have longed for thy salvation, O LORD; and ᴿthy law *is* my delight.

175 Let my soul live, and it shall praise thee; and let thy judgments help me.

176 ᴿI have gone astray like a lost sheep; seek thy servant; for I do not forget thy commandments.

PSALM 120

A cry of distress

A Song of degrees.

IN ᴿmy distress I cried unto the LORD, and he heard me.

2 Deliver my soul, O LORD, from lying lips, *and* from a deceitful tongue.

3 ᴺWhat shall be given unto thee? or what shall be ᴺdone unto thee, thou false tongue?

4 ᴺSharp arrows of the mighty, with coals of juniper.

5 Woe is me, that I sojourn in ᴿMē'-sĕch, ᴿ*that* I dwell in the tents of Kē'-där!

6 My soul hath long dwelt with him that hateth peace.

7 I *am* ᴺ*for* peace: but when I speak, they *are* for war.

PSALM 121

"The LORD is thy keeper"

A Song of degrees.

I ᴺWILL lift up mine eyes unto the hills, from whence cometh my help.

2 ᴿMy help *cometh* from the LORD, which made heaven and earth.

3 ᴿHe will not suffer thy foot to be moved: ᴿhe that keepeth thee will not slumber.

4 Behold, he that keepeth Israel shall neither slumber nor sleep.

5 The LORD *is* thy keeper: the LORD *is* ᴿthy shade ᴿupon thy right hand.

6 ᴿThe sun shall not smite thee by day, nor the moon by night.

7 The LORD shall preserve thee from all evil: he shall ᴿpreserve thy soul.

8 The LORD shall ᴿpreserve thy going out and thy coming in from this time forth, and even for evermore.

PSALM 122

The house of the LORD

A Song of degrees of David.

I WAS glad when they said unto me, ᴿLet us go into the house of the LORD.

2 Our feet shall stand within thy gates, O Jerusalem.

3 Jerusalem is builded as a city that is ᴿcompact together:

4 ᴿWhither the tribes go up, the tribes of the LORD, unto ᴿthe testimony of Israel, to give thanks unto the name of the LORD.

5 ᴿFor there ᴺare set thrones of judgment, the thrones of the house of David.

6 ᴿPray for the peace of Jerusalem: they shall prosper that love thee.

7 Peace be within thy walls, *and* prosperity within thy palaces.

8 For my brethren and companions' sakes, I will now say, Peace *be* within thee.

9 Because of the house of the LORD our God I will ᴿseek thy good.

PSALM 123

Prayer for mercy

A Song of degrees.

U NTO thee ᴿlift I up mine eyes, O thou ᴿthat dwellest in the heavens.

2 Behold, as the eyes of servants *look* unto the hand of their masters, *and* as the eyes of a maiden unto the hand of her mistress; so our eyes *wait* upon the LORD our God, until that he have mercy upon us.

3 Have mercy upon us, O LORD, have mercy upon us: for we are exceedingly filled with contempt.

4 Our soul is exceedingly filled with the scorning of those that are at ease, *and* with the contempt of the proud.

PSALM 124

Praise to the deliverer

A Song of degrees of David.

I F *it had not been* the LORD who was on our side, ᴿnow may Israel say;

2 If *it had not been* the LORD who was on our side, when men rose up against us:

3 Then they had ᴿswallowed us up quick, when their wrath was kindled against us:

4 Then the waters had overwhelmed us, the stream had gone over our soul:

5 Then the proud waters had gone over our soul.

6 Blessed *be* the LORD, who hath not given us *as* a prey to their teeth.

7 Our soul is escaped ᴿas a bird out of the snare of the fowlers: the snare is broken, and we are escaped.

8 ᴿOur help *is* in the name of the LORD, ᴿwho made heaven and earth.

PSALM 125

The security of the faithful

A Song of degrees.

T HEY that trust in the LORD *shall be* as mount Zion, *which* cannot be removed, *but* abideth for ever.

2 *As* the mountains *are* round about Jerusalem, so the LORD *is* round about his people from henceforth even for ever.

3 For ᴿthe rod of ᴺthe wicked shall not rest upon the lot of the righteous; lest the righteous put forth their hands unto iniquity.

4 Do good, O LORD, unto *those that be* good, and to *them that are* upright in their hearts.

5 As for such as turn aside unto their ᴿcrooked ways, the LORD shall lead them forth with the workers of iniquity: *but* ᴿpeace *shall be* upon Israel.

PSALM 126

The joy of restoration

A Song of degrees.

W HEN the LORD ᴺturned again the captivity of Zion, ᴿwe were like them that dream.

2 Then ᴿwas our mouth filled with laughter, and our tongue with singing: then said they among the heathen, The LORD ᴺhath done great things for them.

3 The LORD hath done great things for us; *whereof* we are glad.

4 Turn again our captivity, O LORD, as the streams in the south.

5 ᴿThey that sow in tears shall reap in ᴺjoy.

6 He that goeth forth and weepeth, bearing ᴺprecious seed, shall doubtless come again with rejoicing, bringing his sheaves *with him*.

PSALM 121
6 Ps. 91:5
Is. 49:10
7 Ps. 41:2
8 Deut. 28:6

PSALM 122
1 Is. 2:3
Zech. 8:21
3 See 2 Sam. 5:9
4 Ex. 23:17
Deut. 16:16
4 Ex. 16:34
5 Deut. 17:8
2 Chr. 19:8
5 Heb. *do sit*
6 Ps. 51:18
9 Neh. 2:10

PSALM 123
1 Ps. 121:1 & 141:8
1 Ps. 2:4 & 11:4 & 115:3

PSALM 124
1 Ps. 129:1

Ps. 56:1, 2 & 57:3 3
Prov. 1:12
Ps. 91:3   7
Prov. 6:5
Ps. 121:2   8
Gen. 1:1   8
Ps. 134:3

PSALM 125
Prov. 22:8   3
Is. 14:5
Heb. *wickedness*   3
Prov. 2:15   5
Ps. 128:6   5

PSALM 126
Heb. *returned the* 1
returning of Zion,
Ps. 53:6 & 85:1
Hos. 6:11
Joel 3:1
Acts 12:9   1
Job 8:21   2
Heb. *hath*   2
magnified to
do with them
See Jer. 31:9,   5
etc.
Or, *singing*   5
Or, *seed basket*   6

PSALM 127

God's protection and providence

A Song of degrees *for Solomon.

EXCEPT the LORD build the house, they labour in vain ᴺthat build it: except ᴿthe LORD keep the city, the watchman waketh *but* in vain.

2 *It is* vain for you to rise up early, to sit up late, to ᴿeat the bread of sorrows: *for* so he giveth his beloved sleep.

3 Lo, ᴿchildren *are* an heritage of the LORD: *and* ᴿthe fruit of the womb *is his* reward.

4 As arrows *are* in the hand of a mighty man; so *are* children of the youth.

5 Happy *is* the man that ᴺhath his quiver full of them: ᴿthey shall not be ashamed, but they ᴺshall speak with the enemies in the gate.

PSALM 128

Rewards of the faithful

A Song of degrees.

BLESSED ᴿ*is* every one that feareth the LORD; that walketh in his ways.

2 ᴿFor thou shalt eat the labour of thine hands: happy *shalt* thou *be,* and *it shall be* well with thee.

3 Thy wife *shall be* ᴿas a fruitful vine by the sides of thine house: thy children ᴿlike olive plants round about thy table.

4 Behold, that thus shall the man be blessed that feareth the LORD.

5 ᴿThe LORD shall bless thee out of Zion: and thou shalt see the good of Jerusalem all the days of thy life.

6 Yea, thou shalt ᴿsee thy children's children, *and* ᴿpeace upon Israel.

PSALM 129

God's mercy to Israel

A Song of degrees.

MANYᴺ a time have they afflicted me from ᴿmy youth, ᴿmay Israel now say:

2 Many a time have they afflicted me from my youth: yet they have not prevailed against me.

3 The plowers plowed upon my back: they made long their furrows.

4 The LORD *is* righteous: he hath cut asunder the cords of the wicked.

5 Let them all be confounded and turned back that hate Zion.

6 Let them be as ᴿthe grass *upon* the housetops, which withereth afore it groweth up:

7 Wherewith the mower filleth not his hand; nor he that bindeth sheaves his bosom.

8 Neither do they which go by say, ᴿThe

PSALM 127
* Or, *of Solomon,* Ps. 72, title
1 Heb. *that are builders of it in it*
1 Ps. 121:3-5
2 Gen. 3:17, 19
3 Gen. 33:5 & 48:4 Josh. 24:3, 4
3 Deut. 28:4
5 Heb. *hath filled his quiver with them*
5 Job 5:4 Prov. 27:11
5 Or, *shall subdue,* as Ps. 18:47, or, *destroy*

PSALM 128
1 Ps. 119:1
2 Is. 3:10
3 Ezek. 19:10
3 Ps. 52:8 & 144:12
5 Ps. 134:3
6 Gen. 50:23 Job 42:16
6 Ps. 125:5

PSALM 129
1 Or, *Much*
1 Ezek. 23:3 Hos. 2:15
1 Ps. 124:1
6 Ps. 37:2
8 Ruth 2:4 Ps. 118:26

PSALM 130
Lam. 3:55   1
Jonah 2:2
Ps. 143:2   3
Rom. 3:20
Ex. 34:7   4
1 Ki. 8:40   4
Ps. 2:11
Jer. 33:8
Ps. 27:14   5
Is. 8:17
Ps. 119:81   5
Ps. 119:147   6
Or, *which watch*   6
unto the morning
Ps. 131:3   7
Ps. 86:5   7
Is. 55:7
Ps. 103:3, 4   8
Mat. 1:21

PSALM 131
Rom. 12:16   1
Heb. *walk*   1
Heb. *wonderful,*   1
Job 42:3
Ps. 139:6
Heb. *my soul*   2
Mat. 18:3   2
1 Cor. 14:20
Ps. 130:7   3
Heb. *from now*   3

PSALM 132
Ps. 65:1   2
Gen. 49:24   2
Prov. 6:4   4
Acts 7:46   5
Heb. *habitations*   5
1 Sam. 17:12   6
1 Sam. 7:1   6
1 Chr. 13:5   6
Ps. 5:7 & 99:5   7
Num. 10:35   8
2 Chr. 6:41
Ps. 78:61   8

---

blessing of the LORD *be* upon you: we bless you in the name of the LORD.

PSALM 130

"Out of the depths"

A Song of degrees.

OUT ᴿof the depths have I cried unto thee, O LORD.

2 Lord, hear my voice: let thine ears be attentive to the voice of my supplications.

3 ᴿIf thou, LORD, shouldest mark iniquities, O Lord, who shall stand?

4 But *there is* ᴿforgiveness with thee, that ᴿthou mayest be feared.

5 ᴿI wait for the LORD, my soul doth wait, and ᴿin his word do I hope.

6 ᴿMy soul *waiteth* for the Lord more than they that watch for the morning: ᴺ*I say, more than* they that watch for the morning.

7 ᴿLet Israel hope in the LORD: for ᴿwith the LORD *there is* mercy, and with him *is* plenteous redemption.

8 And ᴿhe shall redeem Israel from all his iniquities.

PSALM 131

Humble trust in God

A Song of degrees of David.

LORD, my heart is not haughty, nor mine eyes lofty: ᴿneither do I ᴺexercise myself in great matters, or in things too ᴺhigh for me.

2 Surely I have behaved and quieted ᴺmyself, ᴿas a child that is weaned of his mother: my soul *is* even as a weaned child.

3 ᴿLet Israel hope in the LORD ᴺfrom henceforth and for ever.

PSALM 132

Prayer for God's sanctuary

A Song of degrees.

LORD, remember David, *and* all his afflictions:

2 How he sware unto the LORD, ᴿ*and* vowed unto ᴿthe mighty *God* of Jacob;

3 Surely I will not come into the tabernacle of my house, nor go up into my bed;

4 I will ᴿnot give sleep to mine eyes, *or* slumber to mine eyelids,

5 Until I ᴿfind out a place for the LORD, ᴺan habitation for the mighty *God* of Jacob.

6 Lo, we heard of it ᴿat Ĕph'-ră-tăh: ᴿwe found it ᴿin the fields of the wood.

7 We will go into his tabernacles: ᴿwe will worship at his footstool.

8 ᴿArise, O LORD, into thy rest; thou, and ᴿthe ark of thy strength.

9 Let thy priests ᴿbe clothed with righteousness; and let thy saints shout for joy.

10 For thy servant David's sake turn not away the face of thine anointed.

11 ᴿThe LORD hath sworn *in* truth unto David; he will not turn from it; ᴿOf the fruit of ᴺthy body will I set upon thy throne.

12 If thy children will keep my covenant and my testimony that I shall teach them, their children shall also sit upon thy throne for evermore.

13 ᴿFor the LORD hath chosen Zion; he hath desired *it* for his habitation.

14 ᴿThis *is* my rest for ever: here will I dwell; for I have desired it.

15 ᴿI will ᴺabundantly bless her provision: I will satisfy her poor with bread.

16 ᴿI will also clothe her priests with salvation: ᴿand her saints shall shout aloud for joy.

17 ᴿThere will I make the horn of David to bud: ᴿI have ordained a ᴺlamp for mine anointed.

18 His enemies will I ᴿclothe with shame: but upon himself shall his crown flourish.

PSALM 133

Blessings of brotherhood

A Song of degrees of David.

BEHOLD, how good and how pleasant *it is* for ᴿbrethren to dwell ᴺtogether in unity!

2 *It is* like ᴿthe precious ointment upon the head, that ran down upon the beard, *even* Aaron's beard: that went down to the skirts of his garments;

3 As the dew of ᴿHĕr'-mon, *and as the dew* that descended upon the mountains of Zion: for ᴿthere the LORD commanded the blessing, *even* life for evermore.

PSALM 134

Call to worship God

A Song of degrees.

BEHOLD, bless ye the LORD, ᴿall *ye* servants of the LORD, ᴿwhich by night stand in the house of the LORD.

2 ᴿLift up your hands ᴺ*in* the sanctuary, and bless the LORD.

3 ᴿThe LORD that made heaven and earth ᴿbless thee out of Zion.

PSALM 135

Praise God for His greatness

PRAISE ye the LORD. Praise ye the name of the LORD; ᴿpraise *him,* O ye servants of the LORD.

2 ᴿYe that stand in the house of the LORD, in ᴿthe courts of the house of our God,

3 Praise the LORD; for ᴿthe LORD *is* good: sing praises unto his name; ᴿfor *it is* pleasant.

4 For ᴿthe LORD hath chosen Jacob unto himself, *and* Israel for his peculiar treasure.

5 For I know that ᴷthe LORD *is* great, and *that* our Lord *is* above all gods.

6 ᴿWhatsoever the LORD pleased, *that* did he in heaven, and in earth, in the seas, and all deep places.

7 ᴿHe causeth the vapours to ascend from the ends of the earth; ᴿhe maketh lightnings for the rain; he bringeth the wind out of his ᴿtreasuries.

8 ᴿWho smote the firstborn of Egypt, ᴺboth of man and beast.

9 ᴿ*Who* sent tokens and wonders into the midst of thee, O Egypt, ᴿupon Pharaoh, and upon all his servants.

10 ᴿWho smote great nations, and slew mighty kings;

11 Sī'-hŏn king of the Amorites, and Og king of Bā'-shăn, and ᴿall the kingdoms of Canaan:

12 ᴿAnd gave their land *for* an heritage, an heritage unto Israel his people.

13 ᴿThy name, O LORD, *endureth* for ever; *and* thy memorial, O LORD, ᴺthroughout all generations.

14 ᴿFor the LORD will judge his people, and he will repent himself concerning his servants.

15 ᴿThe idols of the heathen *are* silver and gold, the work of men's hands.

16 They have mouths, but they speak not; eyes have they, but they see not;

17 They have ears, but they hear not; neither is there *any* breath in their mouths.

18 They that make them are like unto them: *so is* every one that trusteth in them.

19 ᴿBless the LORD, O house of Israel: bless the LORD, O house of Aaron:

20 Bless the LORD, O house of Levi: ye that fear the LORD, bless the LORD.

21 Blessed be the LORD ᴿout of Zion, which dwelleth at Jerusalem. Praise ye the LORD.

PSALM 136

Prayer of thanksgiving

OᴿGIVE thanks unto the LORD; for *he is* good: ᴿfor his mercy *endureth* for ever.

2 O give thanks unto ᴿthe God of gods: for his mercy *endureth* for ever.

3 O give thanks to the Lord of lords: for his mercy *endureth* for ever.

4 To him ᴿwho alone doeth great wonders: for his mercy *endureth* for ever.

Center reference column

PSALM 132
9 Job 29:14
Is. 61:10
11 Ps. 89:3, 4
11 2 Sam. 7:12
1 Ki. 8:25
11 Heb. *thy belly*
13 Ps. 48:1, 2
14 Ps. 68:16
15 Ps. 147:14
15 Or, *surely*
16 2 Chr. 6:41
16 Hos. 11:12
17 Ezek. 29:21
Luke 1:69
17 1 Ki. 11:36
17 Or, *candle*
18 Ps. 35:26
& 109:29

PSALM 133
1 Gen. 13:8
Heb. 13:1
1 Heb. *even together*
2 Ex. 30:25
3 Deut. 4:48
3 Lev. 25:21
Deut. 28:8
Ps. 42:8

PSALM 134
1 Ps. 135:1, 2
1 1 Chr. 9:33
2 1 Tim. 2:8
2 Or, *in holiness*
3 Ps. 124:8
3 Ps. 128:5
& 135:21

PSALM 135
1 Ps. 113:1 & 134:1
Luke 2:37 — 2
Ps. 116:19 — 2
Ps. 119:68 — 3
Ps. 147:1 — 3
Ex. 19:5 — 4
Deut. 7:6, 7
Ps. 95:3 — 5
& 97:9
Ps. 115:3 — 6
Jer. 10:13 — 7
Job 28:25 — 7
Zech. 10:1
Job 28:22 — 7
Ex. 12:12 — 8
Ps. 78:51
Heb. *from man unto beast* — 8
Ex. 7-10 — 9
Ps. 136:15 — 9
Num. 21:24 — 10
Ps. 136:17
Josh. 12:7 — 11
Ps. 78:55 — 12
& 136:21, 22
Ex. 3:15 — 13
Ps. 102:12
Heb. *to generation and generation* — 13
Deut. 32:36 — 14
Ps. 115:4-8 — 15
Ps. 115:9 — 19
Ps. 134:3 — 21

PSALM 136
Ps. 106:1 — 1
1 Chr. 16:34 — 1
Deut. 10:17 — 2
Ps. 72:18 — 4

5 ᴿTo him that by wisdom made the heavens: for his mercy *endureth* for ever.

6 ᴿTo him that stretched out the earth above the waters: for his mercy *endureth* for ever.

7 ᴿTo him that made great lights: for his mercy *endureth* for ever:

8 ᴿThe sun ᴺto rule by day: for his mercy *endureth* for ever:

9 The moon and stars to rule by night: for his mercy *endureth* for ever.

10 ᴿTo him that smote Egypt in their firstborn: for his mercy *endureth* for ever:

11 ᴿAnd brought out Israel from among them: for his mercy *endureth* for ever:

12 ᴿWith a strong hand, and with a stretched out arm: for his mercy *endureth* for ever.

13 ᴿTo him which divided the Red sea into parts: for his mercy *endureth* for ever:

14 And made Israel to pass through the midst of it: for his mercy *endureth* for ever:

15 ᴿBut ᴺoverthrew Pharaoh and his host in the Red sea: for his mercy *endureth* for ever.

16 ᴿTo him which led his people through the wilderness: for his mercy *endureth* for ever.

17 ᴿTo him which smote great kings: for his mercy *endureth* for ever:

18 ᴿAnd slew famous kings: for his mercy *endureth* for ever:

19 ᴿSī'-hŏn king of the Amorites: for his mercy *endureth* for ever:

20 ᴿAnd Og the king of Bā'-shăn: for his mercy *endureth* for ever:

21 ᴿAnd gave their land for an heritage: for his mercy *endureth* for ever:

22 *Even* an heritage unto Israel his servant: for his mercy *endureth* for ever.

23 Who ᴿremembered us in our low estate: for his mercy *endureth* for ever:

24 And hath redeemed us from our enemies: for his mercy *endureth* for ever.

25 ᴿWho giveth food to all flesh: for his mercy *endureth* for ever.

26 O give thanks unto the God of heaven: for his mercy *endureth* for ever.

PSALM 137

Lament of the exiles in Babylon

BY the rivers of Babylon, there we sat down, yea, we wept, when we remembered Zion.

2 We hanged our harps upon the willows in the midst thereof.

3 For there they that carried us away captive required of us ᴺa song; and they that ᴿwastedᴺ us *required of us* mirth, *saying,* Sing us *one* of the songs of Zion.

4 How shall we sing the LORD's song in a ᴺstrange land?

5 If I forget thee, O Jerusalem, let my right hand forget *her cunning.*

6 If I do not remember thee, let my ᴿtongue cleave to the roof of my mouth; if I prefer not Jerusalem above ᴺmy chief joy.

7 Remember, O LORD, ᴿthe children of Ē'-dom in the day of Jerusalem; who said, ᴺRase *it,* rase *it, even* to the foundation thereof.

8 O daughter of Babylon, ᴿwho art to be ᴺdestroyed; happy *shall he be,* ᴿthatᴺ rewardeth thee as thou hast served us.

9 Happy *shall he be,* that taketh and ᴿdasheth thy little ones against ᴺthe stones.

PSALM 138

God's faithfulness

A Psalm of David.

I WILL praise thee with my whole heart: ᴿbefore the gods will I sing praise unto thee.

2 ᴿI will worship ᴿtoward thy holy temple, and praise thy name for thy lovingkindness and for thy truth: for thou hast ᴿmagnified thy word above all thy name.

3 In the day when I cried thou answeredst me, *and* strengthenedst me *with* strength in my soul.

4 ᴿAll the kings of the earth shall praise thee, O LORD, when they hear the words of thy mouth.

5 Yea, they shall sing in the ways of the LORD: for great *is* the glory of the LORD.

6 ᴿThough the LORD *be* high, yet ᴿhath he respect unto the lowly: but the proud he knoweth afar off.

7 ᴿThough I walk in the midst of trouble, thou wilt revive me: thou shalt stretch forth thine hand against the wrath of mine enemies, and thy right hand shall save me.

8 ᴿThe LORD will perfect *that which* concerneth me: thy mercy, O LORD, *endureth* for ever: ᴿforsake not the works of thine own hands.

PSALM 139

God's perfect knowledge

To the chief Musician, A Psalm of David.

O LORD, ᴿthou hast searched me, and known *me.*

2 ᴿThou knowest my downsitting and mine uprising, thou ᴿunderstandest my thought afar off.

3 ᴿThou ᴺcompassest my path and my lying down, and art acquainted *with* all my ways.

4 For *there is* not a word in my tongue, *but,* lo, O Lᴏʀᴅ, ᴿthou knowest it altogether.

5 Thou hast beset me behind and before, and laid thine hand upon me.

6 ᴿ*Such* knowledge *is* too wonderful for me; it is high, I cannot *attain* unto it.

7 ᴿWhither shall I go from thy spirit? or whither shall I flee from thy presence?

8 ᴿIf I ascend up into heaven, thou *art* there: ᴿif I make my bed in hell, behold, thou *art* there.

9 *If* I take the wings of the morning, *and* dwell in the uttermost parts of the sea;

10 Even there shall thy hand lead me, and thy right hand shall hold me.

11 If I say, Surely the darkness shall cover me; even the night shall be light about me.

12 Yea, ᴿthe darkness ᴺhideth not from thee; but the night shineth as the day: ᴺthe darkness and the light *are* both alike *to thee.*

13 For thou hast possessed my reins: thou hast covered me in my mother's womb.

14 I will praise thee; for I am fearfully *and* wonderfully made: marvellous *are* thy works; and *that* my soul knoweth ᴺright well.

15 ᴿMy ᴺsubstance was not hid from thee, when I was made in secret, *and* curiously wrought in the lowest parts of the earth.

16 Thine eyes did see my substance, yet being unperfect; and in thy book ᴺall *my members* were written, ᴺ*which* in continuance were fashioned, when *as yet there was* none of them.

17 ᴿHow precious also are thy thoughts unto me, O God! how great is the sum of them!

18 *If* I should count them, they are more in number than the sand: when I awake, I am still with thee.

19 Surely thou wilt ᴿslay the wicked, O God: ᴿdepart from me therefore, ye bloody men.

20 For they ᴿspeak against thee wickedly, *and* thine enemies take *thy name* in vain.

21 ᴿDo not I hate them, O Lᴏʀᴅ, that hate thee? and am not I grieved with those that rise up against thee?

22 I hate them with perfect hatred: I count them mine enemies.

23 ᴿSearch me, O God, and know my heart: try me, and know my thoughts:

24 And see if *there be any* ᴺwicked way in me, and ᴿlead me in the way everlasting.

PSALM 139	
2	2 Ki. 19:27
2	Mat. 9:4
	John 2:24
3	Job 31:4
3	Or, *winnowest*
4	Heb. 4:13
6	Job 42:3
	Ps. 40:5
7	Jer. 23:24
	Jonah 1:3
8	Amos 9:2
8	Prov. 15:11
12	Job 34:22
12	Heb. *darkeneth not*
12	Heb. *as is the darkness, so is the light*
14	Heb. *greatly*
15	Job 10:8, 9
15	Or, *strength,* or, *body*
16	Heb. *all of them*
16	Or, what *days they should be fashioned*
17	Ps. 40:5
19	Is. 11:4
19	Ps. 119:115
20	Jude 15
21	2 Chr. 19:2
23	Job 31:6
24	Heb. *way of pain*
24	Ps. 5:8

PSALM 140	
Heb. *man of violences*	1
Ps. 56:6	2
Ps. 58:4	3
Ps. 71:4	4
Jer. 18:22	5
Deut. 32:27	8
Or, *let them not be exalted*	8
Ps. 7:16	9
Ps. 11:6	10
Or, *an evil speaker, a wicked man of violence, be established in the earth: let him be hunted to his overthrow*	11
Ps. 9:4	12

PSALM 141	
Ps. 70:5	1
Rev. 5:8	2
Heb. *directed*	2
Rev. 8:3	2
1 Tim. 2:8	2
Ex. 29:39	2

PSALM 140

Prayer for deliverance

To the chief Musician, A Psalm of David.

DELIVER me, O Lᴏʀᴅ, from the evil man: preserve me from the ᴺviolent man;

2 Which imagine mischiefs in *their* heart; ᴿcontinually are they gathered together *for* war.

3 They have sharpened their tongues like a serpent; ᴿadders' poison *is* under their lips. Sē'-läh.

4 ᴿKeep me, O Lᴏʀᴅ, from the hands of the wicked; preserve me from the violent man; who have purposed to overthrow my goings.

5 ᴿThe proud have hid a snare for me, and cords; they have spread a net by the wayside; they have set gins for me. Sē'-läh.

6 I said unto the Lᴏʀᴅ, Thou *art* my God: hear the voice of my supplications, O Lᴏʀᴅ.

7 O Gᴏᴅ the Lord, the strength of my salvation, thou hast covered my head in the day of battle.

8 Grant not, O Lᴏʀᴅ, the desires of the wicked: further not his wicked device; ᴿ*lest*ᴺ they exalt themselves. Sē'-läh.

9 *As for* the head of those that compass me about, ᴿlet the mischief of their own lips cover them.

10 ᴿLet burning coals fall upon them: let them be cast into the fire; into deep pits, that they rise not up again.

11 Let not ᴺan evil speaker be established in the earth: evil shall hunt the violent man to overthrow *him.*

12 I know that the Lᴏʀᴅ will ᴿmaintain the cause of the afflicted, *and* the right of the poor.

13 Surely the righteous shall give thanks unto thy name: the upright shall dwell in thy presence.

PSALM 141

Prayer for an upright heart

A Psalm of David.

LORD, I cry unto thee: ᴿmake haste unto me; give ear unto my voice, when I cry unto thee.

2 Let ᴿmy prayer be ᴺset forth before thee ᴿ*as* incense; *and* ᴿthe lifting up of my hands *as* ᴿthe evening sacrifice.

3 Set a watch, O Lᴏʀᴅ, before my mouth; keep the door of my lips.

4 Incline not my heart to *any* evil thing, to practise wicked works with men that work

iniquity: [R]and let me not eat of their dainties.
5 [R]Let[N] the righteous smite me; *it shall be* a
kindness: and let him reprove me; *it shall be*
an excellent oil, *which* shall not break my
head: for yet my prayer also *shall be* in their
calamities.
6 When their judges are overthrown in stony
places, they shall hear my words; for they are
sweet.
7 Our bones are scattered at the grave's
mouth, as when one cutteth and cleaveth *wood*
upon the earth.
8 But [R]mine eyes *are* unto thee, O GOD the
Lord: in thee is my trust; [N]leave not my soul
destitute.
9 Keep me from [R]the snares *which* they have
laid for me, and the gins of the workers of
iniquity.
10 [R]Let the wicked fall into their own nets,
whilst that I withal [N]escape.

PSALM 142

Prayer for release from prison

Măs′-chîl of David; A Prayer *when he was in the cave.

I CRIED unto the LORD with my voice; with
my voice unto the LORD did I make my
supplication.
2 [R]I poured out my complaint before him; I
shewed before him my trouble.
3 [R]When my spirit was overwhelmed within
me, then thou knewest my path. [R]In the way
wherein I walked have they privily laid a snare
for me.
4 [R]I[N] looked on *my* right hand, and beheld,
but [R]*there was* no man that would know me:
refuge [N]failed me; no man cared for my soul.
5 I cried unto thee, O LORD: I said, [R]Thou
art my refuge *and* [R]my portion [R]in the land of
the living.
6 Attend unto my cry; for I am [R]brought
very low: deliver me from my persecutors; for
they are stronger than I.
7 Bring my soul out of prison, that I may
praise thy name: [R]the righteous shall compass
me about; [R]for thou shalt deal bountifully with
me.

PSALM 143

Prayer for deliverance from enemies

A Psalm of David.

HEAR my prayer, O LORD, give ear to my
supplications: [R]in thy faithfulness answer me, *and* in thy righteousness.
2 And [R]enter not into judgment with thy
servant: for [R]in thy sight shall no man living
be justified.
3 For the enemy hath persecuted my soul; he
hath smitten my life down to the ground; he
hath made me to dwell in darkness, as those
that have been long dead.
4 [R]Therefore is my spirit overwhelmed
within me; my heart within me is desolate.
5 [R]I remember the days of old; I meditate on
all thy works; I muse on the work of thy
hands.
6 [R]I stretch forth my hands unto thee: [R]my
soul *thirsteth* after thee, as a thirsty land.
Sē′-läh.
7 Hear me speedily, O LORD: my spirit
faileth: hide not thy face from me, [R]lest[N] I be
like unto them that go down into the pit.
8 Cause me to hear thy lovingkindness [R]in
the morning; for in thee do I trust: cause me to
know the way wherein I should walk; for [R]I
lift up my soul unto thee.
9 Deliver me, O LORD, from mine enemies:
I [N]flee unto thee to hide me.
10 [R]Teach me to do thy will; for thou *art* my
God: [R]thy spirit *is* good; lead me into [R]the
land of uprightness.
11 [R]Quicken me, O LORD, for thy name's
sake: for thy righteousness' sake bring my soul
out of trouble.
12 And of thy mercy [R]cut off mine enemies,
and destroy all them that afflict my soul: for I
am thy servant.

PSALM 144

In praise of God's goodness and power

A *Psalm* of David.

BLESSED *be* the LORD [N]my strength,
[R]which teacheth my hands [N]to war, *and*
my fingers to fight:
2 [N]My goodness, and my fortress; my high
tower, and my deliverer; my shield, and *he* in
whom I trust; who subdueth my people under
me.
3 [R]LORD, what *is* man, that thou takest
knowledge of him! *or* the son of man, that
thou makest account of him!
4 [R]Man is like to vanity: [R]his days *are* as a
shadow that passeth away.
5 [R]Bow thy heavens, O LORD, and come
down: [R]touch the mountains, and they shall
smoke.
6 [R]Cast forth lightning, and scatter them:
shoot out thine arrows, and destroy them.
7 Send thine [N]hand from above; rid me, and
deliver me out of great waters, from the hand
of strange children;

PSALM 141
4 Prov. 23:6
5 Prov. 9:8
5 Or, *Let the righteous smite me kindly, and reprove me; let not their precious oil break my head, etc.*
8 Ps. 25:15
8 Heb. *make not my soul bare*
9 Ps. 119:110
10 Ps. 35:8
10 Heb. *pass over*

PSALM 142
* Ps. 57, title
* Or, A Psalm *of David, giving instruction*
* 1 Sam. 22:1
2 Is. 26:16
3 Ps. 143:4
3 Ps. 140:5
4 Ps. 69:20
4 Or, *Look on the right hand, and see*
4 Ps. 31:11
4 Heb. *perished from me*
5 Ps. 46:1
5 Lam. 3:24
5 Ps. 27:13
6 Ps. 116:6
7 Ps. 34:2
7 Ps. 13:6

PSALM 143
1 Ps. 31:1
2 Job 14:3
Ex. 34:7 2
Ps. 77:3 4
Ps. 77:5 5
Ps. 88:9 6
Ps. 63:1 6
Ps. 28:1 7
Or, *for I am become like, etc.* 7
Ps. 46:5 8
Ps. 25:1 8
Heb. *hide me with thee* 9
Ps. 25:4, 5 10
Neh. 9:20 10
Is. 26:10 10
Ps. 119:25 11
Ps. 54:5 12

PSALM 144
Heb. *my rock,* Ps. 18:2, 31 1
2 Sam. 22:35 Ps. 18:34 1
Heb. *to the war, etc.* 1
Or, *My mercy* 2
Job 7:17 Ps. 8:4 Heb. 2:6 3
Job 4:19 4
Ps. 102:11 4
Ps. 18:9 5
Ps. 104:32 5
Ps. 18:13 6
Heb. *hands* 7

8 Whose mouth [R]speaketh vanity, and their right hand *is* a right hand of falsehood.

9 I will [R]sing a new song unto thee, O God: upon a psaltery *and* an instrument of ten strings will I sing praises unto thee.

10 [R]*It is he* that giveth [N]salvation unto kings: who delivereth David his servant from the hurtful sword.

11 Rid me, and deliver me from the hand of strange children, whose mouth speaketh vanity, and their right hand *is* a right hand of falsehood:

12 That our sons *may be* [R]as plants grown up in their youth; *that* our daughters *may be* as corner stones, [N]polished *after* the similitude of a palace:

13 *That* our garners *may be* full, affording [N]all manner of store: *that* our sheep may bring forth thousands and ten thousands in our streets:

14 *That* our oxen *may be* [N]strong to labour; *that there be* no breaking in, nor going out; that *there be* no complaining in our streets.

15 [R]Happy *is that* people, that is in such a case: *yea,* happy *is that* people, whose God *is* the LORD.

PSALM 145

God's greatness and mercy

David's *Psalm of praise.

I WILL extol thee, my God, O king; and I will bless thy name for ever and ever.

2 Every day will I bless thee; and I will praise thy name for ever and ever.

3 [R]Great *is* the LORD, and greatly to be praised; [N]and [R]his greatness *is* unsearchable.

4 [R]One generation shall praise thy works to another, and shall declare thy mighty acts.

5 I will speak of the glorious honour of thy majesty, and of thy wondrous [N]works.

6 And *men* shall speak of the might of thy terrible acts: and I will [N]declare thy greatness.

7 They shall abundantly utter the memory of thy great goodness, and shall sing of thy righteousness.

8 [R]The LORD *is* gracious, and full of compassion; slow to anger, and [N]of great mercy.

9 [R]The LORD *is* good to all: and his tender mercies *are* over all his works.

10 [R]All thy works shall praise thee, O LORD; and thy saints shall bless thee.

11 They shall speak of the glory of thy kingdom, and talk of thy power;

12 To make known to the sons of men his mighty acts, and the glorious majesty of his kingdom.

13 [R]Thy kingdom *is* [N]an everlasting king-

PSALM 144

8	Ps. 12:2
9	Ps. 33:2, 3
10	Ps. 18:50
10	Or, *victory*
12	Ps. 128:3
12	Heb. *cut*
13	Heb. *from kind to kind*
14	Heb. *able to bear burdens,* or, *loaden* with flesh
15	Ps. 33:12

PSALM 145

*	Ps. 100, title
3	Ps. 147:5
3	Heb. *and of his greatness there is no search*
3	Rom. 11:33
4	Is. 38:9
5	Heb. *things,* or, *words*
6	Heb. *declare it*
8	Num. 14:18
8	Heb. *great in mercy*
9	Nah. 1:7
10	Ps. 19:1
13	1 Tim. 1:17
13	Heb. *a kingdom of all ages*

Ps. 146:8	14
Ps. 104:27	15
Or, *look unto thee*	15
Ps. 136:25	15
Ps. 104:21	16
Or, *merciful,* or, *bountiful*	17
Deut. 4:7	18
John 4:24	18
Ps. 31:23	20

PSALM 146

Heb. *Hallelujah*	1
Ps. 103:1	1
Ps. 104:33	2
Is. 2:22	3
Or, *salvation*	3
Eccl. 12:7	4
1 Cor. 2:6	4
Jer. 17:7	5
Rev. 14:7	6
Ps. 103:6	7
Ps. 107:9	7
Ps. 107:10	7
Mat. 9:30	8
Luke 13:13	8
Deut. 10:18	9
Ps. 68:5	
Ps. 147:6	9
Ex. 15:18	10
Ps. 10:10	

PSALM 147

Ps. 92:1	1
Ps. 135:3	1
Ps. 33:1	1

---

dom, and thy dominion *endureth* throughout all generations.

14 The LORD upholdeth all that fall, and [R]raiseth up all *those that be* bowed down.

15 [R]The eyes of all [N]wait upon thee; and [R]thou givest them their meat in due season.

16 Thou openest thine hand, [R]and satisfiest the desire of every living thing.

17 The LORD *is* righteous in all his ways, and [N]holy in all his works.

18 [R]The LORD *is* nigh unto all them that call upon him, to all that call upon him [R]in truth.

19 He will fulfil the desire of them that fear him: he also will hear their cry, and will save them.

20 [R]The LORD preserveth all them that love him: but all the wicked will he destroy.

21 My mouth shall speak the praise of the LORD: and let all flesh bless his holy name for ever and ever.

PSALM 146

Complete trust in God

PRAISE[N] ye the LORD. [R]Praise the LORD, O my soul.

2 [R]While I live will I praise the LORD: I will sing praises unto my God while I have any being.

3 [R]Put not your trust in princes, *nor* in the son of man, in whom *there is* no [N]help.

4 [R]His breath goeth forth, he returneth to his earth; in that very day [R]his thoughts perish.

5 [R]Happy *is* he that *hath* the God of Jacob for his help, whose hope *is* in the LORD his God:

6 [R]Which made heaven, and earth, the sea, and all that therein *is:* which keepeth truth for ever:

7 [R]Which executeth judgment for the oppressed: [R]which giveth food to the hungry. [R]The LORD looseth the prisoners:

8 [R]The LORD openeth *the eyes of* the blind: [R]the LORD raiseth them that are bowed down: the LORD loveth the righteous:

9 [R]The LORD preserveth the strangers; he relieveth the fatherless and widow: [R]but the way of the wicked he turneth upside down.

10 [R]The LORD shall reign for ever, *even* thy God, O Zion, unto all generations. Praise ye the LORD.

PSALM 147

God of power and grace

PRAISE ye the LORD: for [R]*it is* good to sing praises unto our God; [R]for *it is* pleasant; *and* [R]praise is comely.

2 The LORD doth ᴿbuild up Jerusalem: ᴿhe gathereth together the outcasts of Israel.

3 ᴿHe healeth the broken in heart, and bindeth up their ᴺwounds.

4 ᴿHe telleth the number of the stars; he calleth them all by *their* names.

5 ᴿGreat *is* our Lord, and of ᴿgreat power: ᴿhisᴺ understanding *is* infinite.

6 ᴿThe LORD lifteth up the meek: he casteth the wicked down to the ground.

7 Sing unto the LORD with thanksgiving; sing praise upon the harp unto our God:

8 ᴿWho covereth the heaven with clouds, who prepareth rain for the earth, who maketh grass to grow upon the mountains.

9 ᴿHe giveth to the beast his food, *and* ᴿto the young ravens which cry.

10 ᴿHe delighteth not in the strength of the horse: he taketh not pleasure in the legs of a man.

11 The LORD taketh pleasure in them that fear him, in those that hope in his mercy.

12 Praise the LORD, O Jerusalem; praise thy God, O Zion.

13 For he hath strengthened the bars of thy gates; he hath blessed thy children within thee.

14 ᴿHeᴺ maketh peace *in* thy borders, *and* ᴿfilleth thee with the ᴺfinest of the wheat.

15 ᴿHe sendeth forth his commandment *upon* earth: his word runneth very swiftly.

16 ᴿHe giveth snow like wool: he scattereth the hoarfrost like ashes.

17 He casteth forth his ice like morsels: who can stand before his cold?

18 ᴿHe sendeth out his word, and melteth them: he causeth his wind to blow, *and* the waters flow.

19 ᴿHe sheweth ᴺhis word unto Jacob, ᴿhis statutes and his judgments unto Israel.

20 ᴿHe hath not dealt so with any nation: and *as for his* judgments, they have not known them. Praise ye the LORD.

PSALM 148

All creation's praise of God

PRAISEᴺ ye the LORD. Praise ye the LORD from the heavens: praise him in the heights.

2 Praise ye him, all his angels: praise ye him, all his hosts.

3 Praise ye him, sun and moon: praise him, all ye stars of light.

4 Praise him, ᴿye heavens of heavens, and ᴿye waters that *be* above the heavens.

5 Let them praise the name of the LORD: for ᴿhe commanded, and they were created.

6 ᴿHe hath also stablished them for ever and ever: he hath made a decree which shall not pass.

7 Praise the LORD from the earth, ᴿye dragons, and all deeps:

8 Fire, and hail; snow, and vapour; stormy wind ᴿfulfilling his word:

9 ᴿMountains, and all hills; fruitful trees, and all cedars:

10 Beasts, and all cattle; creeping things, and ᴺflying fowl:

11 Kings of the earth, and all people; princes, and all judges of the earth:

12 Both young men, and maidens; old men, and children:

13 Let them praise the name of the LORD: for ᴿhis name alone is ᴺexcellent; ᴿhis glory *is* above the earth and heaven.

14 ᴿHe also exalteth the horn of his people, ᴿthe praise of all his saints; *even* of the children of Israel, ᴿa people near unto him. Praise ye the LORD.

PSALM 149

Praise for God's judgment

PRAISEᴺ ye the LORD. ᴿSing unto the LORD a new song, *and* his praise in the congregation of saints.

2 Let Israel rejoice in ᴿhim that made him: let the children of Zion be joyful in their ᴿKing.

3 ᴿLet them praise his name ᴺin the dance: let them sing praises unto him with the timbrel and harp.

4 For ᴿthe LORD taketh pleasure in his people: ᴿhe will beautify the meek with salvation.

5 Let the saints be joyful in glory: let them ᴿsing aloud upon their beds.

6 *Let* the high *praises* of God *be* ᴺin their mouth, and ᴿa two-edged sword in their hand;

7 To execute vengeance upon the heathen, *and* punishments upon the people;

8 To bind their kings with chains, and their nobles with fetters of iron;

9 ᴿTo execute upon them the judgment written: ᴿthis honour have all his saints. Praise ye the LORD.

PSALM 150

Praise God in his sanctuary

PRAISEᴺ ye the LORD. Praise God in his sanctuary: praise him in the firmament of his power.

2 ᴿPraise him for his mighty acts: praise him according to his excellent ᴿgreatness.

3 Praise him with the sound of the [N]trumpet: praise him with the psaltery and harp.

4 Praise him [R]with the timbrel and dance: praise him with [R]stringed instruments and organs.

PSALM 150
3 Or, *cornet,*
Ps. 98:6
4 Ex. 15:20
4 Ps. 33:2
1 Chr. 15:16   5

5 Praise him upon the loud [R]cymbals: praise him upon the high sounding cymbals.

6 Let every thing that hath breath praise the Lord. Praise ye the Lord.

THE PROVERBS

Much of Proverbs was written by Solomon, but the earliest its present arrangement can be dated is the reign of King Hezekiah, ca. 700 B.C. (cf. 25:1). Although Solomon is credited with 3000 proverbs, only about 900 are preserved in this book. Agur and Lemuel composed those found in the last two chapters.

A proverb, "mashal" in Hebrew, represents common-sense wisdom expressed in a short pithy form. Frequently such self-evident truth was reduced to the verse forms of antithesis or comparison, and in this manner these proverbs became an effective teaching tool covering a diversity of subjects such as chastity, knowledge, morality, friendship, justice, laziness,

and ethical regulations for effective living. Throughout this book there are warnings against sin and the practical admonition that wisdom begins with the fear of God.

The contents of this book are difficult to outline. The following units are apparent in the context:

I. Contrast and comparison of wisdom and folly 1:1 – 9:18
II. Ethical regulations for daily life 10:1 – 22:16
III. The words of the wise 22:17 – 24:34
IV. Sayings of Solomon – a later collection 25:1 – 29:27
V. The words of Agur and Lemuel 30:1 – 31:31

CHAPTER 1

Purpose of the Proverbs

THE [R]proverbs of Solomon the son of David, king of Israel;

2 To know wisdom and instruction; to perceive the words of understanding;

3 To receive the instruction of wisdom, justice, and judgment, and [N]equity;

4 To give subtilty to the simple, to the young man knowledge and [N]discretion.

5 [R]A wise *man* will hear, and will increase learning; and a man of understanding shall attain unto wise counsels:

6 To understand a proverb, and [N]the interpretation; the words of the wise, and their [R]dark sayings.

7 [R]The fear of the Lord *is* [N]the beginning of knowledge: *but* fools despise wisdom and instruction.

Warning against violence

8 [R]My son, hear the instruction of thy father, and forsake not the law of thy mother:

9 For they *shall be* [N]an ornament of grace unto thy head, and chains about thy neck.

10 My son, if sinners entice thee, [R]consent thou not.

11 If they say, Come with us, let us [R]lay wait for blood, let us lurk privily for the innocent without cause:

12 Let us swallow them up alive as the

CHAP. 1
BC 1000
1 1 Ki. 4:32
Eccl. 12:9
3 Heb. *equities*
4 Or, *advisement*
5 ch. 9:9
6 Or, *an eloquent speech*
6 Ps. 78:2
7 Job 28:28
Ps. 111:10
Eccl. 12:13
7 Or, *the principal part*
8 ch. 4:1
9 Heb. *an adding*
10 Gen. 39:7
11 Jer. 5:26

Ps. 28:1   12
Ps. 1:1   15
Ps. 119:101   15
Is. 59:7   16
Heb. *in the eyes*   17
of every thing that
hath a wing
1 Tim. 6:10   19
John 7:37   20
Heb. *Wisdoms,*   20
i.e. *Excellent*
wisdom
Joel 2:28   23
Is. 66:4   24
Jer. 7:13
Zech. 7:11

grave; and whole, [R]as those that go down into the pit:

13 We shall find all precious substance, we shall fill our houses with spoil:

14 Cast in thy lot among us; let us all have one purse:

15 My son, [R]walk not thou in the way with them; [R]refrain thy foot from their path:

16 [R]For their feet run to evil, and make haste to shed blood.

17 Surely in vain the net is spread [N]in the sight of any bird.

18 And they lay wait for their *own* blood; they lurk privily for their *own* lives.

19 [R]So *are* the ways of every one that is greedy of gain; *which* taketh away the life of the owners thereof.

Folly of forsaking wisdom

20 [R]Wisdom[N] crieth without; she uttereth her voice in the streets:

21 She crieth in the chief place of concourse, in the openings of the gates: in the city she uttereth her words, *saying,*

22 How long, ye simple ones, will ye love simplicity? and the scorners delight in their scorning, and fools hate knowledge?

23 Turn you at my reproof: behold, [R]I will pour out my spirit unto you, I will make known my words unto you.

24 [R]Because I have called, and ye refused; I have stretched out my hand, and no man regarded;

25 But ye [R]have set at nought all my counsel, and would none of my reproof:

26 [R]I also will laugh at your calamity; I will mock when your fear cometh;

27 When [R]your fear cometh as desolation, and your destruction cometh as a whirlwind; when distress and anguish cometh upon you.

28 [R]Then shall they call upon me, but I will not answer; they shall seek me early, but they shall not find me:

29 For that they [R]hated knowledge, and did not [R]choose the fear of the LORD:

30 [R]They would none of my counsel: they despised all my reproof.

31 Therefore [R]shall they eat of the fruit of their own way, and be filled with their own devices.

32 For the [N]turning away of the simple shall slay them, and the prosperity of fools shall destroy them.

33 But [R]whoso hearkeneth unto me shall dwell safely, and [R]shall be quiet from fear of evil.

CHAPTER 2

Source and benefits of wisdom

MY son, if thou wilt receive my words, and [R]hide my commandments with thee;

2 So that thou incline thine ear unto wisdom, *and* apply thine heart to understanding;

3 Yea, if thou criest after knowledge, *and* [N]liftest up thy voice for understanding;

4 [R]If thou seekest her as silver, and searchest for her as *for* hid treasures;

5 Then shalt thou understand the fear of the LORD, and find the knowledge of God.

6 [R]For the LORD giveth wisdom: out of his mouth *cometh* knowledge and understanding.

7 He layeth up sound wisdom for the righteous: [R]*he is* a buckler to them that walk uprightly.

8 He keepeth the paths of judgment, and [R]preserveth the way of his saints.

9 Then shalt thou understand righteousness, and judgment, and equity; *yea,* every good path.

10 When wisdom entereth into thine heart, and knowledge is pleasant unto thy soul;

11 Discretion shall preserve thee, [R]understanding shall keep thee:

12 To deliver thee from the way of the evil *man,* from the man that speaketh froward things;

13 Who leave the paths of uprightness, to [R]walk in the ways of darkness;

14 Who [R]rejoice to do evil, *and* [R]delight in the frowardness of the wicked;

15 [R]Whose ways *are* crooked, and *they* froward in their paths:

16 To deliver thee from [R]the strange woman, [R]*even* from the stranger *which* flattereth with her words;

17 [R]Which forsaketh the guide of her youth, and forgetteth the covenant of her God.

18 For [R]her house inclineth unto death, and her paths unto the dead.

19 None that go unto her return again, neither take they hold of the paths of life.

20 That thou mayest walk in the way of good *men,* and keep the paths of the righteous.

21 [R]For the upright shall dwell in the land, and the perfect shall remain in it.

22 [R]But the wicked shall be cut off from the earth, and the transgressors shall be [N]rooted out of it.

CHAPTER 3

Reverence for the LORD

MY son, forget not my law; [R]but let thine heart keep my commandments:

2 For length of days, and [N]long life, and [R]peace, shall they add to thee.

3 Let not mercy and truth forsake thee: [R]bind them about thy neck; [R]write them upon the table of thine heart:

4 [R]So shalt thou find favour and [N]good understanding in the sight of God and man.

5 [R]Trust in the LORD with all thine heart; [R]and lean not unto thine own understanding.

6 [R]In all thy ways acknowledge him, and he shall [R]direct thy paths.

7 [R]Be not wise in thine own eyes: [R]fear the LORD, and depart from evil.

8 It shall be [N]health to thy navel, and [R]marrow[N] to thy bones.

9 [R]Honour the LORD with thy substance, and with the firstfruits of all thine increase:

10 [R]So shall thy barns be filled with plenty, and thy presses shall burst out with new wine.

11 [R]My son, despise not the chastening of the LORD; neither be weary of his correction:

12 For whom the LORD loveth he correcteth; [R]even as a father the son *in whom* he delighteth.

The superior value of wisdom

13 [R]Happy *is* the man *that* findeth wisdom, and [N]the man *that* getteth understanding.

14 [R]For the merchandise of it *is* better than the merchandise of silver, and the gain thereof than fine gold.

CHAP. 1
BC 1000
25 Ps. 107:11
Luke 7:30
26 Ps. 2:4
27 ch. 10:24
28 Job 27:9
Is. 1:15
Jer. 14:12
Ezek. 8:18
Mic. 3:4
Zech. 7:13
Jas. 4:3
29 Job 21:14
29 Ps. 119:173
30 Ps. 81:11
31 Job 4:8
Is. 3:11
Jer. 6:19
32 Or, *ease of the simple*
33 Ps. 25:12
33 Ps. 112:7

CHAP. 2
BC 1000
1 ch. 4:21
3 Heb. *givest thy voice*
4 ch. 3:14
Mat. 13:44
6 1 Ki. 3:9
Jas. 1:5
7 Ps. 84:11
8 1 Sam. 2:9
Ps. 66:9
11 ch. 6:22
13 John 3:19

Jer. 11:15   14
Rom. 1:32   14
Ps. 125:5   15
ch. 5:20   16
ch. 5:3   16
See Mal.   17
2:14, 15
ch. 7:27   18
Ps. 37:29   21
Job 18:17   22
Ps. 37:28
Or, *plucked up* 22

CHAP. 3
BC 1000
Deut. 8:1   1
Heb. *years of life* 2
Ps. 119:165   2
Ex. 13:9   3
Deut. 6:8
2 Cor. 3:3   3
Rom. 14:18   4
Or, *good success* 4
Ps. 37:3, 5   5
Jer. 9:23   5
1 Chr. 28:9   6
Jer. 10:23   6
Rom. 12:16   7
ch. 16:6   7
Heb. *medicine* 8
Job 21:24   8
Heb. *watering, or, moistening* 8
Ex. 22:29   9
Deut. 28:8   10
Job 5:17   11
Ps. 94:12
Deut. 8:5   12
ch. 8:34, 35   13
Heb. *the man that draweth out understanding* 13
Job 28:13   14
Ps. 19:10

15 She *is* more precious than rubies: and ᴿall the things thou canst desire are not to be compared unto her.

16 ᴿLength of days *is* in her right hand; *and* in her left hand riches and honour.

17 ᴿHer ways *are* ways of pleasantness, and all her paths *are* peace.

18 She *is* ᴿa tree of life to them that lay hold upon her: and happy *is every one* that retaineth her.

19 ᴿThe Lᴏʀᴅ by wisdom hath founded the earth; by understanding hath he ᴺestablished the heavens.

20 ᴿBy his knowledge the depths are broken up, and ᴿthe clouds drop down the dew.

Inheritance of honour

21 My son, let not them depart from thine eyes: keep sound wisdom and discretion:

22 So shall they be life unto thy soul, and ᴿgrace to thy neck.

23 ᴿThen shalt thou walk in thy way safely, and thy foot shall not stumble.

24 ᴿWhen thou liest down, thou shalt not be afraid: yea, thou shalt lie down, and thy sleep shall be sweet.

25 ᴿBe not afraid of sudden fear, neither of the desolation of the wicked, when it cometh.

26 For the Lᴏʀᴅ shall be thy confidence, and shall keep thy foot from being taken.

27 ᴿWithhold not good from ᴺthem to whom it is due, when it is in the power of thine hand to do *it.*

28 ᴿSay not unto thy neighbour, Go, and come again, and to morrow I will give; when thou hast it by thee.

29 ᴺDevise not evil against thy neighbour, seeing he dwelleth securely by thee.

30 ᴿStrive not with a man without cause, if he have done thee no harm.

31 ᴿEnvy thou not the oppressor, and choose none of his ways.

32 For the froward *is* abomination to the Lᴏʀᴅ: ᴿbut his secret *is* with the righteous.

33 ᴿThe curse of the Lᴏʀᴅ *is* in the house of the wicked: but ᴿhe blesseth the habitation of the just.

34 ᴿSurely he scorneth the scorners: but he giveth grace unto the lowly.

35 The wise shall inherit glory: but shame ᴺshall be the promotion of fools.

CHAPTER 4

Get wisdom and insight

Hᴇᴀʀ, ᴿye children, the instruction of a father, and attend to know understanding.

CHAP. **3**
BC 1000
15 Mat. 13:44
16 1 Tim. 4:8
17 Mat. 11:29
18 Gen. 2:9
19 Ps. 104:24
19 Or, *prepared*
20 Gen. 1:9
20 Deut. 33:28
Job 36:28
22 ch. 1:9
23 Ps. 37:24
24 Lev. 26:6
Ps. 3:5
25 Ps. 91:5
27 Rom. 13:7
Gal. 6:10
27 Heb. *the owners thereof*
28 Lev. 19:13
29 Or, *Practise no evil*
30 Rom. 12:18
31 Ps. 37:1
32 Ps. 25:14
33 Zech. 5:3
Mal. 2:2
33 Ps. 1:3
34 Jas. 4:6
1 Pet. 5:5
35 Heb. *exalteth the fools*

CHAP. **4**
BC 1000
1 Ps. 34:11

1 Chr. 29:1	3
1 Chr. 28:9	4
Eph. 6:4	
ch. 7:2	4
ch. 2:2, 3	5
2 Thes. 2:10	6
Mat. 13:44	7
Luke 10:42	
1 Sam. 2:30	8
ch. 3:22	9
Or, *she shall compass thee with a crown of glory*	9
ch. 3:2	10
Ps. 18:36	12
Ps. 91:11, 12	12
Ps. 1:1	14
ch. 1:10, 15	
Ps. 36:4	16
Is. 57:20	
Mat. 5:14, 45	18
Phil. 2:15	
2 Sam. 23:4	18
1 Sam. 2:9	19
Is. 59:9, 10	
John 12:35	
ch. 3:3, 21	21
ch. 2:1	21
ch. 3:8 & 12:18	22
Heb. *medicine*	22
Heb. *above all keeping*	23
Heb. *frowardness of mouth, and perverseness of lips*	24

2 For I give you good doctrine, forsake ye not my law.

3 For I was my father's son, ᴿtender and only *beloved* in the sight of my mother.

4 ᴿHe taught me also, and said unto me, Let thine heart retain my words: ᴿkeep my commandments, and live.

5 ᴿGet wisdom, get understanding: forget *it* not; neither decline from the words of my mouth.

6 Forsake her not, and she shall preserve thee: ᴿlove her, and she shall keep thee.

7 ᴿWisdom *is* the principal thing; *therefore* get wisdom: and with all thy getting get understanding.

8 ᴿExalt her, and she shall promote thee: she shall bring thee to honour, when thou dost embrace her.

9 She shall give to thine head ᴿan ornament of grace: ᴺa crown of glory shall she deliver to thee.

Avoid the way of the wicked

10 Hear, O my son, and receive my sayings; ᴿand the years of thy life shall be many.

11 I have taught thee in the way of wisdom; I have led thee in right paths.

12 When thou goest, ᴿthy steps shall not be straitened; ᴿand when thou runnest, thou shalt not stumble.

13 Take fast hold of instruction; let *her* not go: keep her; for she *is* thy life.

14 ᴿEnter not into the path of the wicked, and go not in the way of evil *men.*

15 Avoid it, pass not by it, turn from it, and pass away.

16 ᴿFor they sleep not, except they have done mischief; and their sleep is taken away, unless they cause *some* to fall.

17 For they eat the bread of wickedness, and drink the wine of violence.

18 ᴿBut the path of the just ᴿ*is* as the shining light, that shineth more and more unto the perfect day.

19 ᴿThe way of the wicked *is* as darkness: they know not at what they stumble.

Issues of the heart

20 My son, attend to my words; incline thine ear unto my sayings.

21 ᴿLet them not depart from thine eyes; ᴿkeep them in the midst of thine heart.

22 For they *are* life unto those that find them, and ᴿhealthᴺ to all their flesh.

23 Keep thy heart ᴺwith all diligence; for out of it *are* the issues of life.

24 Put away from thee ᴺa froward mouth, and perverse lips put far from thee.

25 Let thine eyes look right on, and let thine eyelids look straight before thee.

26 Ponder the path of thy feet, and ᴺlet all thy ways be established.

27 ᴿTurn not to the right hand nor to the left: ᴿremove thy foot from evil.

CHAPTER 5

Warning against unchastity

MY son, attend unto my wisdom, *and* bow thine ear to my understanding:

2 That thou mayest regard discretion, and *that* thy lips may ᴿkeep knowledge.

3 ᴿFor the lips of a strange woman drop *as* an honeycomb, and her ᴺmouth *is* ᴿsmoother than oil:

4 But her end is ᴿbitter as wormwood, ᴿsharp as a twoedged sword.

5 ᴿHer feet go down to death; her steps take hold on hell.

6 Lest thou shouldest ponder the path of life, her ways are moveable, *that* thou canst not know *them*.

7 Hear me now therefore, O ye children, and depart not from the words of my mouth.

8 Remove thy way far from her, and come not nigh the door of her house:

9 Lest thou give thine honour unto others, and thy years unto the cruel:

10 Lest strangers be filled with ᴺthy wealth; and thy labours *be* in the house of a stranger;

11 And thou mourn at the last, when thy flesh and thy body are consumed,

12 And say, How have I ᴿhated instruction, and my heart ᴿdespised reproof;

13 And have not obeyed the voice of my teachers, nor inclined mine ear to them that instructed me!

14 I was almost in all evil in the midst of the congregation and assembly.

15 Drink waters out of thine own cistern, and running waters out of thine own well.

16 Let thy fountains be dispersed abroad, *and* rivers of waters in the streets.

17 Let them be only thine own, and not strangers' with thee.

18 Let thy fountain be blessed: and rejoice with ᴿthe wife of thy youth.

19 ᴿ*Let her be as* the loving hind and pleasant roe; let her breasts ᴺsatisfy thee at all times; and ᴺbe thou ravished always with her love.

20 And why wilt thou, my son, be ravished with ᴿa strange woman, and embrace the bosom of a stranger?

21 ᴿFor the ways of man *are* before the eyes of the Lord, and he pondereth all his goings.

22 ᴿHis own iniquities shall take the wicked himself, and he shall be holden with the cords of his ᴺsins.

23 ᴿHe shall die without instruction; and in the greatness of his folly he shall go astray.

CHAPTER 6

Warning against debt

MY son, ᴿif thou be surety for thy friend, *if* thou hast stricken thy hand with a stranger,

2 Thou art snared with the words of thy mouth, thou art taken with the words of thy mouth.

3 Do this now, my son, and deliver thyself, when thou art come into the hand of thy friend; go, humble thyself, ᴺand make sure thy friend.

4 ᴿGive not sleep to thine eyes, nor slumber to thine eyelids.

5 Deliver thyself as a roe from the hand *of the hunter,* and as a bird from the hand of the fowler.

Warning against idleness

6 ᴿGo to the ant, thou sluggard; consider her ways, and be wise:

7 Which having no guide, overseer, or ruler,

8 Provideth her meat in the summer, *and* gathereth her food in the harvest.

9 ᴿHow long wilt thou sleep, O sluggard? when wilt thou arise out of thy sleep?

10 *Yet* a little sleep, a little slumber, a little folding of the hands to sleep:

11 ᴿSo shall thy poverty come as one that travelleth, and thy want as an armed man.

Worthless character traits

12 A naughty person, a wicked man, walketh with a froward mouth.

13 ᴿHe winketh with his eyes, he speaketh with his feet, he teacheth with his fingers;

14 Frowardness *is* in his heart, ᴿhe deviseth mischief continually; ᴿhe ᴺsoweth discord.

15 Therefore shall his calamity come suddenly; suddenly shall he ᴿbe broken ᴿwithout remedy.

16 These six *things* doth the Lord hate: yea, seven *are* an abomination ᴺunto him:

17 ᴿAᴺ proud look, ᴿa lying tongue, and ᴿhands that shed innocent blood,

18 ᴿAn heart that deviseth wicked imaginations, ᴿfeet that be swift in running to mischief,

19 ᴿA false witness *that* speaketh lies, and he ᴿthat soweth discord among brethren.

Foolishness of adultery

20 ᴿMy son, keep thy father's commandment, and forsake not the law of thy mother:

21 ᴿBind them continually upon thine heart, *and* tie them about thy neck.

22 ᴿWhen thou goest, it shall lead thee; when thou sleepest, ᴿit shall keep thee; and *when* thou awakest, it shall talk with thee.

23 ᴿFor the commandment *is* a ᴺlamp; and the law *is* light; and reproofs of instruction *are* the way of life:

24 ᴿTo keep thee from the evil woman, from the flattery ᴺof the tongue of a strange woman.

25 ᴿLust not after her beauty in thine heart; neither let her take thee with her eyelids.

26 For ᴿby means of a whorish woman *a man is brought* to a piece of bread: ᴿand ᴺthe adulteress will ᴿhunt for the precious life.

27 Can a man take fire in his bosom, and his clothes not be burned?

28 Can one go upon hot coals, and his feet not be burned?

29 So he that goeth in to his neighbour's wife; whosoever toucheth her shall not be innocent.

30 *Men* do not despise a thief, if he steal to satisfy his soul when he is hungry;

31 But *if* he be found, ᴿhe shall restore sevenfold; he shall give all the substance of his house.

32 *But* whoso committeth adultery with a woman ᴿlacketh ᴺunderstanding: he *that* doeth it destroyeth his own soul.

33 A wound and dishonour shall he get; and his reproach shall not be wiped away.

34 For jealousy *is* the rage of a man: therefore he will not spare in the day of vengeance.

35 ᴺHe will not regard any ransom; neither will he rest content, though thou givest many gifts.

CHAPTER 7

Wiles of the harlot

MY son, keep my words, and ᴿlay up my commandments with thee.

2 ᴿKeep my commandments, and live; ᴿand my law as the apple of thine eye.

3 ᴿBind them upon thy fingers, write them upon the table of thine heart.

4 Say unto wisdom, Thou *art* my sister; and call understanding *thy* kinswoman:

5 ᴿThat they may keep thee from the strange woman, from the stranger *which* flattereth with her words.

6 For at the window of my house I looked through my casement,

---

CHAP. 6
BC 1000

20 Eph. 6:1
21 ch. 3:3
22 ch. 3:23
22 ch. 2:11
23 Ps. 19:8
23 Or, *candle*
24 ch. 2:16
24 Or, *of the strange tongue*
25 Mat. 5:28
26 ch. 29:3
26 Gen. 39:14
26 Heb. *the woman of a man*, or, *a man's wife*
26 Ezek. 13:18
31 Ex. 22:1
32 ch. 7:7
32 Heb. *heart*
35 Heb. *He will not accept the face of any ransom*

CHAP. 7
BC 1000

1 ch. 2:1
2 Lev. 18:5
ch. 4:4
2 Deut. 32:10
3 Deut. 6:8 & 11:18 & 6:21
5 ch. 2:16 & 5:3

Heb. *the sons*   7
ch. 6:32   7
& 9:4, 16
Job 24:15   9
ch. 9:13   11
1 Tim. 5:13   11
Tit. 2:5
Heb. *she strengthened her face*   13
Heb. *Peace offerings are upon me* 14
Is. 19:9   16
Heb. *in his hand*   20
Or, *the new moon*   20
ch. 5:3   21
Ps. 12:2   21
Heb. *suddenly*   22
Eccl. 9:12   23
Neh. 13:26   26
ch. 2:18 & 5:5   27
& 9:18

CHAP. 8
BC 1000

ch. 1:20 & 9:3   1

---

7 And beheld among the simple ones, I discerned among ᴺthe youths, a young man ᴿvoid of understanding,

8 Passing through the street near her corner; and he went the way to her house,

9 ᴿIn the twilight, in the evening, in the black and dark night:

10 And, behold, there met him a woman *with* the attire of an harlot, and subtil of heart.

11 (ᴿShe *is* loud and stubborn; ᴿher feet abide not in her house:

12 Now *is* she without, now in the streets, and lieth in wait at every corner.)

13 So she caught him, and kissed him, *and* ᴺwith an impudent face said unto him,

14 ᴺ*I have* peace offerings with me; this day have I payed my vows.

15 Therefore came I forth to meet thee, diligently to seek thy face, and I have found thee.

16 I have decked my bed with coverings of tapestry, with carved *works*, with ᴿfine linen of Egypt.

17 I have perfumed my bed with myrrh, aloes, and cinnamon.

18 Come, let us take our fill of love until the morning: let us solace ourselves with loves.

19 For the goodman *is* not at home, he is gone a long journey:

20 He hath taken a bag of money ᴺwith him, *and* will come home at ᴺthe day appointed.

21 With ᴿher much fair speech she caused him to yield, ᴿwith the flattering of her lips she forced him.

22 He goeth after her ᴺstraightway, as an ox goeth to the slaughter, or as a fool to the correction of the stocks;

23 Till a dart strike through his liver; ᴿas a bird hasteth to the snare, and knoweth not that it *is* for his life.

24 Hearken unto me now therefore, O ye children, and attend to the words of my mouth.

25 Let not thine heart decline to her ways, go not astray in her paths.

26 For she hath cast down many wounded: yea, ᴿmany strong *men* have been slain by her.

27 ᴿHer house *is* the way to hell, going down to the chambers of death.

CHAPTER 8

Superior value of wisdom

DOTH not ᴿwisdom cry? and understanding put forth her voice?

2 She standeth in the top of high places, by the way in the places of the paths.

3 She crieth at the gates, at the entry of the city, at the coming in at the doors.

4 Unto you, O men, I call; and my voice *is* to the sons of man.

5 O ye simple, understand wisdom: and, ye fools, be ye of an understanding heart.

6 Hear; for I will speak of ᴿexcellent things; and the opening of my lips *shall be* right things.

7 For my mouth shall speak truth; and wickedness *is* ᴺan abomination to my lips.

8 All the words of my mouth *are* in righteousness; *there is* nothing ᴺfroward or perverse in them.

9 They *are* all plain to him that understandeth, and right to them that find knowledge.

10 Receive my instruction, and not silver; and knowledge rather than choice gold.

11 ᴿFor wisdom *is* better than rubies; and all the things that may be desired are not to be compared to it.

12 I wisdom dwell with ᴺprudence, and find out knowledge of witty inventions.

13 ᴿThe fear of the LORD *is* to hate evil: ᴿpride, and arrogancy, and the evil way, and ᴿthe froward mouth, do I hate.

14 Counsel *is* mine, and sound wisdom: I *am* understanding; ᴿI have strength.

15 ᴿBy me kings reign, and princes decree justice.

16 By me princes rule, and nobles, *even* all the judges of the earth.

17 ᴿI love them that love me; and ᴿthose that seek me early shall find me.

18 ᴿRiches and honour *are* with me; *yea,* durable riches and righteousness.

19 ᴿMy fruit *is* better than gold, yea, than fine gold; and my revenue than choice silver.

20 I ᴺlead in the way of righteousness, in the midst of the paths of judgment:

21 That I may cause those that love me to inherit substance; and I will fill their treasures.

Eternity of wisdom

22 ᴿThe LORD possessed me in the beginning of his way, before his works of old.

23 ᴿI was set up from everlasting, from the beginning, or ever the earth was.

24 When *there were* no depths, I was brought forth; when *there were* no fountains abounding with water.

25 ᴿBefore the mountains were settled, before the hills was I brought forth:

26 While as yet he had not made the earth, nor the ᴺfields, nor ᴺthe highest part of the dust of the world.

27 When he prepared the heavens, I *was* there: when he set ᴺa compass upon the face of the depth:

28 When he established the clouds above: when he strengthened the fountains of the deep:

29 ᴿWhen he gave to the sea his decree, that the waters should not pass his commandment: when ᴿhe appointed the foundations of the earth:

30 ᴿThen I was by him, *as* one brought up *with him:* ᴿand I was daily *his* delight, rejoicing always before him;

31 Rejoicing in the habitable part of his earth; and ᴿmy delights *were* with the sons of men.

Joy of the wise man

32 Now therefore hearken unto me, O ye children: for ᴿblessed *are they that* keep my ways.

33 Hear instruction, and be wise, and refuse it not.

34 ᴿBlessed *is* the man that heareth me, watching daily at my gates, waiting at the posts of my doors.

35 For whoso findeth me findeth life, and shall ᴿobtainᴺ favour of the LORD.

36 But he that sinneth against me ᴿwrongeth his own soul: all they that hate me love death.

CHAPTER 9

Wisdom and folly contrasted

WISDOM hath ᴿbuilded her house, she hath hewn out her seven pillars:

2 ᴿShe hath killed ᴺher beasts; ᴿshe hath mingled her wine; she hath also furnished her table.

3 She hath ᴿsent forth her maidens: ᴿshe crieth ᴿupon the highest places of the city,

4 ᴿWhoso *is* simple, let him turn in hither: *as for* him that wanteth understanding, she saith to him,

5 ᴿCome, eat of my bread, and drink of the wine *which* I have mingled.

6 Forsake the foolish, and live; and go in the way of understanding.

7 He that reproveth a scorner getteth to himself shame: and he that rebuketh a wicked *man* getteth himself a blot.

8 ᴿReprove not a scorner, lest he hate thee: ᴿrebuke a wise man, and he will love thee.

9 Give *instruction* to a wise *man,* and he will be yet wiser: teach a just *man,* ᴿand he will increase in learning.

10 ᴿThe fear of the LORD *is* the beginning of wisdom: and the knowledge of the holy *is* understanding.

11 ᴿFor by me thy days shall be multiplied, and the years of thy life shall be increased.

12 ᴿIf thou be wise, thou shalt be wise for

CHAP. **8**
BC 1000
6 ch. 22:20
7 Heb. *the abomination of my lips*
8 Heb. *wreathed*
11 Job 28:15, etc.
Ps. 19:10 & 119:127
ch. 3:14, 15 & 4:5, 7 & 16:16
12 Or, *subtilty*
13 ch. 16:6
13 ch. 6:17
13 ch. 4:24
14 Eccl. 7:19
15 Dan. 2:21
Rom. 13:1
17 1 Sam. 2:30
Ps. 91:14
John 14:21
17 Jas. 1:5
18 ch. 3:16
Mat. 6:33
19 ver. 10
ch. 3:14
20 Or, *walk*
22 ch. 3:19
23 Ps. 2:6
25 Job 15:7, 8
26 Or, *open places*
26 Or, *the chief part*
27 Or, *a circle*

Gen. 1:9, 10   29
Job 38:10
Jer. 5:22
Job 38:4   29
John 1:1, 2   30
Mat. 3:17   30
Col. 1:13
Ps. 16:3   31
Ps. 119:1, 2   32
Luke 11:28
ch. 3:13, 18   34
ch. 12:2   35
Heb. *bring forth* 35
ch. 20:2   36

CHAP. **9**
BC 1000
Mat. 16:18   1
Eph. 2:20
1 Pet. 2:5
Mat. 22:4   2
Heb. *her killing* 2
ch. 23:30   2
Rom. 10:15   3
ch. 8:1, 2   3
ver. 14   3
Ps. 19:7   4
ch. 6:32
S. of S. 5:1   5
Is. 55:1
John 6:27
Mat. 7:6   8
Ps. 141:5   8
Mat. 13:12   9
Job 28:28   10
ch. 1:7
ch. 3:2, 16   11
Job 35:6, 7   12
ch. 16:26

thyself: but *if* thou scornest, thou alone shalt bear *it*.

13 [R]A foolish woman *is* clamorous: *she is* simple, and knoweth nothing.

14 For she sitteth at the door of her house, on a seat [R]in the high places of the city,

15 To call passengers who go right on their ways:

16 [R]Whoso *is* simple, let him turn in hither: and *as for* him that wanteth understanding, she saith to him,

17 [R]Stolen waters are sweet, and bread [N]*eaten* in secret is pleasant.

18 But he knoweth not that [R]the dead *are* there; *and that* her guests *are* in the depths of hell.

CHAPTER 10

The righteous and the wicked

THE proverbs of Solomon. [R]A wise son maketh a glad father: but a foolish son *is* the heaviness of his mother.

2 [R]Treasures of wickedness profit nothing: [R]but righteousness delivereth from death.

3 [R]The LORD will not suffer the soul of the righteous to famish: but he casteth away [N]the substance of the wicked.

4 [R]He becometh poor that dealeth *with* a slack hand: but [R]the hand of the diligent maketh rich.

5 He that gathereth in summer *is* a wise son: *but* he that sleepeth in harvest *is* [R]a son that causeth shame.

6 Blessings *are* upon the head of the just: but [R]violence covereth the mouth of the wicked.

7 [R]The memory of the just *is* blessed: but the name of the wicked shall rot.

8 The wise in heart will receive commandments: [R]but [N]a prating fool [N]shall fall.

9 [R]He that walketh uprightly walketh surely: but he that perverteth his ways shall be known.

10 [R]He that winketh with the eye causeth sorrow: [R]but a prating fool [N]shall fall.

11 [R]The mouth of a righteous *man is* a well of life: but [R]violence covereth the mouth of the wicked.

12 Hatred stirreth up strifes: but [R]love covereth all sins.

13 In the lips of him that hath understanding wisdom is found: but [R]a rod *is* for the back of him that is void of [N]understanding.

14 Wise *men* lay up knowledge: but [R]the mouth of the foolish *is* near destruction.

15 [R]The rich man's wealth *is* his strong city: the destruction of the poor *is* their poverty.

16 The labour of the righteous *tendeth* to life: the fruit of the wicked to sin.

17 He *is* in the way of life that keepeth instruction: but he that refuseth reproof [N]erreth.

18 He that hideth hatred *with* lying lips, and [R]he that uttereth a slander, *is* a fool.

19 [R]In the multitude of words there wanteth not sin: but [R]he that refraineth his lips *is* wise.

20 The tongue of the just *is as* choice silver: the heart of the wicked *is* little worth.

21 The lips of the righteous feed many: but fools die for want [N]of wisdom.

22 [R]The blessing of the LORD, it maketh rich, and he addeth no sorrow with it.

23 [R]*It is* as sport to a fool to do mischief: but a man of understanding hath wisdom.

24 [R]The fear of the wicked, it shall come upon him: but [R]the desire of the righteous shall be granted.

25 As the whirlwind passeth, [R]so *is* the wicked no *more:* but [R]the righteous *is* an everlasting foundation.

26 As vinegar to the teeth, and as smoke to the eyes, so *is* the sluggard to them that send him.

27 [R]The fear of the LORD [N]prolongeth days: but [R]the years of the wicked shall be shortened.

28 The hope of the righteous *shall be* gladness: but the [R]expectation of the wicked shall perish.

29 The way of the LORD *is* strength to the upright: [R]but destruction *shall be* to the workers of iniquity.

30 [R]The righteous shall never be removed: but the wicked shall not inhabit the earth.

31 [R]The mouth of the just bringeth forth wisdom: but the froward tongue shall be cut out.

32 The lips of the righteous know what is acceptable: but the mouth of the wicked *speaketh* [N]frowardness.

CHAPTER 11

The righteous and the wicked

A[R] FALSE[N] balance *is* abomination to the LORD: but [N]a just weight *is* his delight.

2 [R]*When* pride cometh, then cometh shame: but with the lowly *is* wisdom.

3 [R]The integrity of the upright shall guide them: but the perverseness of transgressors shall destroy them.

4 [R]Riches profit not in the day of wrath: but [R]righteousness delivereth from death.

5 The righteousness of the perfect shall [N]direct his way: but the wicked shall fall by his own wickedness.

6 The righteousness of the upright shall de-

liver them: but ᴿtransgressors shall be taken in *their own* naughtiness.

7 ᴿWhen a wicked man dieth, *his* expectation shall perish: and the hope of unjust *men* perisheth.

8 ᴿThe righteous is delivered out of trouble, and the wicked cometh in his stead.

9 An hypocrite with *his* mouth destroyeth his neighbour: but through knowledge shall the just be delivered.

10 ᴿWhen it goeth well with the righteous, the city rejoiceth: and when the wicked perish, *there is* shouting.

11 ᴿBy the blessing of the upright the city is exalted: but it is overthrown by the mouth of the wicked.

12 He that is ᴺvoid of wisdom despiseth his neighbour: but a man of understanding holdeth his peace.

13 ᴿA ᴺtalebearer revealeth secrets: but he that is of a faithful spirit concealeth the matter.

14 ᴿWhere no counsel *is,* the people fall: but in the multitude of counsellors *there is* safety.

15 ᴿHe that is surety for a stranger ᴺshall smart *for it:* and he that hateth ᴺsuretiship is sure.

16 ᴿA gracious woman retaineth honour: and strong *men* retain riches.

17 ᴿThe merciful man doeth good to his own soul: but *he that is* cruel troubleth his own flesh.

18 The wicked worketh a deceitful work: but ᴿto him that soweth righteousness *shall be* a sure reward.

19 As righteousness *tendeth* to life: so he that pursueth evil *pursueth it* to his own death.

20 They that are of a froward heart *are* abomination to the Lᴏʀᴅ: but *such as are* upright in *their* way *are* his delight.

21 ᴿ*Though* hand *join* in hand, the wicked shall not be unpunished: but ᴿthe seed of the righteous shall be delivered.

22 *As* a jewel of gold in a swine's snout, *so is* a fair woman which ᴺis without discretion.

23 The desire of the righteous *is* only good: *but* the expectation of the wicked ᴿ*is* wrath.

24 There is that ᴿscattereth, and yet increaseth; and *there is* that withholdeth more than is meet, but *it tendeth* to poverty.

25 ᴿTheᴺ liberal soul shall be made fat: ᴿand he that watereth shall be watered also himself.

26 ᴿHe that withholdeth corn, the people shall curse him: but ᴿblessing *shall be* upon the head of him that selleth *it.*

27 He that diligently seeketh good procureth favour: ᴿbut he that seeketh mischief, it shall come unto him.

28 ᴿHe that trusteth in his riches shall fall: but ᴿthe righteous shall flourish as a branch.

29 He that troubleth his own house ᴿshall inherit the wind: and the fool *shall be* servant to the wise of heart.

30 The fruit of the righteous *is* a tree of life; and ᴿhe that ᴺwinneth souls *is* wise.

31 ᴿBehold, the righteous shall be recompensed in the earth: much more the wicked and the sinner.

CHAPTER 12

The righteous and the wicked

WHOSO loveth instruction loveth knowledge: but he that hateth reproof *is* brutish.

2 A good *man* obtaineth favour of the Lᴏʀᴅ: but a man of wicked devices will he condemn.

3 A man shall not be established by wickedness: but the ᴿroot of the righteous shall not be moved.

4 ᴿA virtuous woman *is* a crown to her husband: but she that maketh ashamed *is* ᴿas rottenness in his bones.

5 The thoughts of the righteous *are* right: *but* the counsels of the wicked *are* deceit.

6 ᴿThe words of the wicked *are* to lie in wait for blood: ᴿbut the mouth of the upright shall deliver them.

7 ᴿThe wicked are overthrown, and *are* not: but the house of the righteous shall stand.

8 A man shall be commended according to his wisdom: ᴿbut he that is ᴺof a perverse heart shall be despised.

9 ᴿ*He that is* despised, and hath a servant, *is* better than he that honoureth himself, and lacketh bread.

10 ᴿA righteous *man* regardeth the life of his beast: but the ᴺtender mercies of the wicked *are* cruel.

11 ᴿHe that tilleth his land shall be satisfied with bread: but he that followeth vain *persons* ᴿ*is* void of understanding.

12 The wicked desireth ᴺthe net of evil *men:* but the root of the righteous yieldeth *fruit.*

13 ᴿTheᴺ wicked is snared by the transgression of *his* lips: ᴿbut the just shall come out of trouble.

14 ᴿA man shall be satisfied with good by the fruit of *his* mouth: ᴿand the recompence of a man's hands shall be rendered unto him.

15 ᴿThe way of a fool *is* right in his own eyes: but he that hearkeneth unto counsel *is* wise.

16 ᴿA fool's wrath is ᴺpresently known: but a prudent *man* covereth shame.

17 [R]*He that* speaketh truth sheweth forth righteousness: but a false witness deceit.

18 [R]There is that speaketh like the piercings of a sword: but the tongue of the wise *is* health.

19 The lip of truth shall be established for ever: [R]but a lying tongue *is* but for a moment.

20 Deceit *is* in the heart of them that imagine evil: but to the counsellors of peace *is* joy.

21 There shall no evil happen to the just: but the wicked shall be filled with mischief.

22 [R]Lying lips *are* abomination to the LORD: but they that deal truly *are* his delight.

23 [R]A prudent man concealeth knowledge: but the heart of fools proclaimeth foolishness.

24 [R]The hand of the diligent shall bear rule: but the [N]slothful shall be under tribute.

25 [R]Heaviness in the heart of man maketh it stoop: but [R]a good word maketh it glad.

26 The righteous *is* more [N]excellent than his neighbour: but the way of the wicked seduceth them.

27 The slothful *man* roasteth not that which he took in hunting: but the substance of a diligent man *is* precious.

28 In the way of righteousness *is* life; and *in* the pathway *thereof there is* no death.

CHAPTER 13

The righteous and the wicked

A WISE son *heareth* his father's instruction: [R]but a scorner heareth not rebuke.

2 [R]A man shall eat good by the fruit of *his* mouth: but the soul of the transgressors *shall eat* violence.

3 [R]He that keepeth his mouth keepeth his life: *but* he that openeth wide his lips shall have destruction.

4 [R]The soul of the sluggard desireth, and *hath* nothing: but the soul of the diligent shall be made fat.

5 A righteous *man* hateth lying: but a wicked *man* is loathsome, and cometh to shame.

6 [R]Righteousness keepeth *him that is* upright in the way: but wickedness overthroweth [N]the sinner.

7 [R]There is that maketh himself rich, yet *hath* nothing: *there is* that maketh himself poor, yet *hath* great riches.

8 The ransom of a man's life *are* his riches: but the poor heareth not rebuke.

9 The light of the righteous rejoiceth: [R]but the [N]lamp of the wicked shall be put out.

10 Only by pride cometh contention: but with the well advised *is* wisdom.

11 [R]Wealth *gotten* by vanity shall be dimin-

ished: but he that gathereth [N]by labour shall increase.

12 Hope deferred maketh the heart sick: but [R]*when* the desire cometh, *it is* a tree of life.

13 Whoso [R]despiseth the word shall be destroyed: but he that feareth the commandment [N]shall be rewarded.

14 [R]The law of the wise *is* a fountain of life, to depart from [R]the snares of death.

15 Good understanding giveth favour: but the way of transgressors *is* hard.

16 [R]Every prudent *man* dealeth with knowledge: but a fool [N]layeth open *his* folly.

17 A wicked messenger falleth into mischief: but [R]a[N] faithful ambassador *is* health.

18 Poverty and shame *shall be to* him that refuseth instruction: but [R]he that regardeth reproof shall be honoured.

19 [R]The desire accomplished is sweet to the soul: but *it is* abomination to fools to depart from evil.

20 He that walketh with wise *men* shall be wise: but a companion of fools [N]shall be destroyed.

21 [R]Evil pursueth sinners: but to the righteous good shall be repaid.

22 A good *man* leaveth an inheritance to his children's children: and [R]the wealth of the sinner *is* laid up for the just.

23 [R]Much food *is* in the tillage of the poor: but there is *that is* destroyed for want of judgment.

24 [R]He that spareth his rod hateth his son: but he that loveth him chasteneth him betimes.

25 [R]The righteous eateth to the satisfying of his soul: but the belly of the wicked shall want.

CHAPTER 14

The righteous and the wicked

EVERY wise woman buildeth her house: but the foolish plucketh it down with her hands.

2 He that walketh in his uprightness feareth the LORD: [R]but *he that is* perverse in his ways despiseth him.

3 In the mouth of the foolish *is* a rod of pride: [R]but the lips of the wise shall preserve them.

4 Where no oxen *are,* the crib *is* clean: but much increase *is* by the strength of the ox.

5 [R]A faithful witness will not lie: but a false witness will utter lies.

6 A scorner seeketh wisdom, and *findeth it* not: but [R]knowledge *is* easy unto him that understandeth.

7 Go from the presence of a foolish man,

CHAP. 12	
BC 1000	
17	ch. 14:5
18	Ps. 57:4 & 64:3
19	ch. 19:5, 9
22	Rev. 22:15
23	ch. 13:16
24	ch. 10:4
24	Or, *deceitful*
25	ch. 15:13
25	Is. 50:4
26	Or, *abundant*

CHAP. 13	
BC 1000	
1	Is. 28:15
2	ch. 12:14
3	Ps. 39:1
	ch. 21:23
	Jas. 3:2, etc.
4	ch. 10:4
6	ch. 11:3, 5, 6
6	Heb. *sin*
7	ch. 12:9
9	Job 18:5, 6
	& 21:17
	ch. 24:20
9	Or, *candle*
11	ch. 10:2 & 20:21

Heb. *with the hand*	11
ver. 19	12
2 Chr. 36:16	13
Or, *shall be in peace*	13
ch. 10:11 & 14:27 & 16:22	14
2 Sam. 22:6	14
ch. 12:23 & 15:2	16
Heb. *spreadeth*	16
ch. 25:13	17
Heb. *an ambassador of faithfulness*	17
ch. 15:5, 31	18
ver. 12	19
Heb. *shall be broken*	20
Ps. 32:10	21
Job 27:17	22
ch. 28:8	
Eccl. 2:26	
ch. 12:11	23
ch. 19:18	24
& 22:15	
& 23:13	
& 29:15, 17	
Ps. 34:10	25
& 37:3	

CHAP. 14	
BC 1000	
Rom. 2:4	2
ch. 12:6	3
ver. 25	5
Ex. 20:16 & 23:1	
ch. 6:19 & 12:17	
ch. 8:9 & 17:24	6

when thou perceivest not *in him* the lips of knowledge.

8 The wisdom of the prudent *is* to understand his way: but the folly of fools *is* deceit.

9 [R]Fools make a mock at sin: but among the righteous *there is* favour.

10 The heart knoweth [N]his own bitterness; and a stranger doth not intermeddle with his joy.

11 [R]The house of the wicked shall be overthrown: but the tabernacle of the upright shall flourish.

12 [R]There is a way which seemeth right unto a man, but [R]the end thereof *are* the ways of death.

13 Even in laughter the heart is sorrowful; and [R]the end of that mirth *is* heaviness.

14 The backslider in heart shall be [R]filled with his own ways: and a good man *shall be satisfied* from himself.

15 The simple believeth every word: but the prudent *man* looketh well to his going.

16 [R]A wise *man* feareth, and departeth from evil: but the fool rageth, and is confident.

17 *He that is* soon angry dealeth foolishly: and a man of wicked devices is hated.

18 The simple inherit folly: but the prudent are crowned with knowledge.

19 The evil bow before the good; and the wicked at the gates of the righteous.

20 [R]The poor is hated even of his own neighbour: but [N]the rich *hath* many friends.

21 He that despiseth his neighbour sinneth: [R]but he that hath mercy on the poor, happy *is* he.

22 Do they not err that devise evil? but mercy and truth *shall be* to them that devise good.

23 In all labour there is profit: but the talk of the lips *tendeth* only to penury.

24 The crown of the wise *is* their riches: *but* the foolishness of fools *is* folly.

25 [R]A true witness delivereth souls: but a deceitful *witness* speaketh lies.

26 In the fear of the LORD *is* strong confidence: and his children shall have a place of refuge.

27 [R]The fear of the LORD *is* a fountain of life, to depart from the snares of death.

28 In the multitude of people *is* the king's honour: but in the want of people *is* the destruction of the prince.

29 [R]*He that is* slow to wrath *is* of great understanding: but *he that is* [N]hasty of spirit exalteth folly.

30 A sound heart *is* the life of the flesh: but [R]envy [R]the rottenness of the bones.

31 [R]He that oppresseth the poor reproacheth

[R]his Maker: but he that honoureth him hath mercy on the poor.

32 The wicked is driven away in his wickedness: but [R]the righteous hath hope in his death.

33 Wisdom resteth in the heart of him that hath understanding: but [R]*that which is* in the midst of fools is made known.

34 Righteousness exalteth a nation: but sin *is* a reproach [N]to any people.

35 [R]The king's favour *is* toward a wise servant: but his wrath is *against* him that causeth shame.

CHAPTER 15

The righteous and the wicked

A [R]SOFT answer turneth away wrath: but [R]grievous words stir up anger.

2 The tongue of the wise useth knowledge aright: [R]but the mouth of fools [N]poureth out foolishness.

3 [R]The eyes of the LORD *are* in every place, beholding the evil and the good.

4 [N]A wholesome tongue *is* a tree of life: but perverseness therein *is* a breach in the spirit.

5 [R]A fool despiseth his father's instruction: [R]but he that regardeth reproof is prudent.

6 In the house of the righteous *is* much treasure: but in the revenues of the wicked is trouble.

7 The lips of the wise disperse knowledge: but the heart of the foolish *doeth* not so.

8 [R]The sacrifice of the wicked *is* an abomination to the LORD: but the prayer of the upright *is* his delight.

9 The way of the wicked *is* an abomination unto the LORD: but he loveth him that [R]followeth after righteousness.

10 [N]Correction *is* [R]grievous unto him that forsaketh the way: *and* [R]he that hateth reproof shall die.

11 [R]Hell and destruction *are* before the LORD: how much more then [R]the hearts of the children of men?

12 [R]A scorner loveth not one that reproveth him: neither will he go unto the wise.

13 [R]A merry heart maketh a cheerful countenance: but [R]by sorrow of the heart the spirit is broken.

14 The heart of him that hath understanding seeketh knowledge: but the mouth of fools feedeth on foolishness.

15 All the days of the afflicted *are* evil: [R]but he that is of a merry heart *hath* a continual feast.

16 [R]Better *is* little with the fear of the LORD than great treasure and trouble therewith.

17 ᴿBetter *is* a dinner of herbs where love is, than a stalled ox and hatred therewith.

18 ᴿA wrathful man stirreth up strife: but *he that is* slow to anger appeaseth strife.

19 ᴿThe way of the slothful *man is* as an hedge of thorns: but the way of the righteous ᴺ*is* made plain.

20 ᴿA wise son maketh a glad father: but a foolish man despiseth his mother.

21 ᴿFolly *is* joy to *him that is* ᴺdestitute of wisdom: ᴿbut a man of understanding walketh uprightly.

22 ᴿWithout counsel purposes are disappointed: but in the multitude of counsellors they are established.

23 A man hath joy by the answer of his mouth: and ᴿa word *spoken* ᴺin due season, how good *is it!*

24 ᴿThe way of life *is* above to the wise, that he may depart from hell beneath.

25 ᴿThe Lᴏʀᴅ will destroy the house of the proud: but ᴿhe will establish the border of the widow.

26 ᴿThe thoughts of the wicked *are* an abomination to the Lᴏʀᴅ: ᴿbut *the words* of the pure *are* ᴺpleasant words.

27 ᴿHe that is greedy of gain troubleth his own house; but he that hateth gifts shall live.

28 The heart of the righteous ᴿstudieth to answer: but the mouth of the wicked poureth out evil things.

29 ᴿThe Lᴏʀᴅ *is* far from the wicked: but ᴿhe heareth the prayer of the righteous.

30 The light of the eyes rejoiceth the heart: *and* a good report maketh the bones fat.

31 ᴿThe ear that heareth the reproof of life abideth among the wise.

32 He that refuseth ᴺinstruction despiseth his own soul: but he that ᴺheareth reproof ᴺgetteth understanding.

33 ᴿThe fear of the Lᴏʀᴅ *is* the instruction of wisdom; and ᴿbefore honour *is* humility.

CHAPTER 16

Proverbs concerning conduct

THE ᴿpreparationsᴺ of the heart in man, ᴿand the answer of the tongue, *is* from the Lᴏʀᴅ.

2 ᴿAll the ways of a man *are* clean in his own eyes; but ᴿthe Lᴏʀᴅ weigheth the spirits.

3 ᴿCommitᴺ thy works unto the Lᴏʀᴅ, and thy thoughts shall be established.

4 ᴿThe Lᴏʀᴅ hath made all *things* for himself: ᴿyea, even the wicked for the day of evil.

5 ᴿEvery one *that is* proud in heart *is* an abomination to the Lᴏʀᴅ: ᴿ*though* hand *join* in hand, he shall not be ᴺunpunished.

6 ᴿBy mercy and truth iniquity is purged: and ᴿby the fear of the Lᴏʀᴅ *men* depart from evil.

7 When a man's ways please the Lᴏʀᴅ, he maketh even his enemies to be at peace with him.

8 ᴿBetter *is* a little with righteousness than great revenues without right.

9 ᴿA man's heart deviseth his way: ᴿbut the Lᴏʀᴅ directeth his steps.

10 ᴺA divine sentence *is* in the lips of the king: his mouth transgresseth not in judgment.

11 ᴿA just weight and balance *are* the Lᴏʀᴅ's: ᴺall the weights of the bag *are* his work.

12 *It is* an abomination to kings to commit wickedness: for ᴿthe throne is established by righteousness.

13 ᴿRighteous lips *are* the delight of kings; and they love him that speaketh right.

14 ᴿThe wrath of a king *is as* messengers of death: but a wise man will pacify it.

15 In the light of the king's countenance *is* life; and ᴿhis favour *is* ᴿas a cloud of the latter rain.

16 ᴿHow much better *is it* to get wisdom than gold! and to get understanding rather to be chosen than silver!

17 The highway of the upright *is* to depart from evil: he that keepeth his way preserveth his soul.

18 Pride *goeth* before destruction, and an haughty spirit before a fall.

19 Better *it is to be* of an humble spirit with the lowly, than to divide the spoil with the proud.

20 ᴺHe that handleth a matter wisely shall find good: and whoso ᴿtrusteth in the Lᴏʀᴅ, happy *is* he.

21 The wise in heart shall be called prudent: and the sweetness of the lips increaseth learning.

22 ᴿUnderstanding *is* a wellspring of life unto him that hath it: but the instruction of fools *is* folly.

23 The heart of the wise ᴺteacheth his mouth, and addeth learning to his lips.

24 Pleasant words *are as* an honeycomb, sweet to the soul, and health to the bones.

25 ᴿThere is a way that seemeth right unto a man, but the end thereof *are* the ways of death.

26 ᴿHeᴺ that laboureth laboureth for himself; for his mouth ᴺcraveth it of him.

27 ᴺAn ungodly man diggeth up evil: and in his lips *there is* as a burning fire.

28 ᴿA froward man ᴺsoweth strife: and ᴿa whisperer separateth chief friends.

29 A violent man [R]enticeth his neighbour, and leadeth him into the way *that is* not good.

30 He shutteth his eyes to devise froward things: moving his lips he bringeth evil to pass.

31 [R]The hoary head *is* a crown of glory, *if it* be found in the way of righteousness.

32 [R]*He that is* slow to anger *is* better than the mighty; and he that ruleth his spirit than he that taketh a city.

33 The lot is cast into the lap; but the whole disposing thereof *is* of the LORD.

CHAPTER 17

Proverbs concerning conduct

BETTER *is* [R]a dry morsel, and quietness therewith, than an house full of [N]sacrifices *with* strife.

2 A wise servant shall have rule over [R]a son that causeth shame, and shall have part of the inheritance among the brethren.

3 The fining pot *is* for silver, and the furnace for gold: [R]but the LORD trieth the hearts.

4 A wicked doer giveth heed to false lips; *and* a liar giveth ear to a naughty tongue.

5 [R]Whoso mocketh the poor reproacheth his Maker: *and* he that is glad at calamities shall not be [N]unpunished.

6 Children's children *are* the crown of old men; and the glory of children *are* their fathers.

7 [N]Excellent speech becometh not a fool: much less do [N]lying lips a prince.

8 A gift *is as* [N]a precious stone in the eyes of him that hath it: whithersoever it turneth, it prospereth.

9 [R]He that covereth a transgression [N]seeketh love; but [R]he that repeateth a matter separateth *very* friends.

10 [N]A reproof entereth more into a wise man than an hundred stripes into a fool.

11 An evil *man* seeketh only rebellion: therefore a cruel messenger shall be sent against him.

12 Let [R]a bear robbed of her whelps meet a man, rather than a fool in his folly.

13 Whoso [R]rewardeth evil for good, evil shall not depart from his house.

14 The beginning of strife *is as* when one letteth out water: therefore [R]leave off contention, before it be meddled with.

15 [R]He that justifieth the wicked, and he that condemneth the just, even they both *are* abomination to the LORD.

16 Wherefore *is there* a price in the hand of

a fool to get wisdom, [R]seeing *he hath* no heart *to it*?

17 [R]A friend loveth at all times, and a brother is born for adversity.

18 [R]A man void of [N]understanding striketh hands, *and* becometh surety in the presence of his friend.

19 He loveth transgression that loveth strife: *and* [R]he that exalteth his gate seeketh destruction.

20 [N]He that hath a froward heart findeth no good: and he that hath [R]a perverse tongue falleth into mischief.

21 [R]He that begetteth a fool *doeth it* to his sorrow: and the father of a fool hath no joy.

22 [R]A merry heart doeth good [N]*like* a medicine: [R]but a broken spirit drieth the bones.

23 A wicked *man* taketh a gift out of the bosom [R]to pervert the ways of judgment.

24 [R]Wisdom *is* before him that hath understanding; but the eyes of a fool *are* in the ends of the earth.

25 [R]A foolish son *is* a grief to his father, and bitterness to her that bare him.

26 Also [R]to punish the just *is* not good, *nor* to strike princes for equity.

27 [R]He that hath knowledge spareth his words: *and* a man of understanding is of [N]an excellent spirit.

28 [R]Even a fool, when he holdeth his peace, is counted wise: *and* he that shutteth his lips *is esteemed* a man of understanding.

CHAPTER 18

Proverbs concerning conduct

THROUGH [N]desire a man, having separated himself, seeketh *and* intermeddleth with all wisdom.

2 A fool hath no delight in understanding, but that his heart may discover itself.

3 When the wicked cometh, *then* cometh also contempt, and with ignominy reproach.

4 [R]The words of a man's mouth *are as* deep waters, [R]*and* the wellspring of wisdom *as* a flowing brook.

5 [R]*It is* not good to accept the person of the wicked, to overthrow the righteous in judgment.

6 A fool's lips enter into contention, and his mouth calleth for strokes.

7 [R]A fool's mouth *is* his destruction, and his lips *are* the snare of his soul.

8 [R]The words of a [N]talebearer *are* [N]as wounds, and they go down into the [N]innermost parts of the belly.

9 He also that is slothful in his work is [R]brother to him that is a great waster.

10 ᴿThe name of the Lᴏʀᴅ *is* a strong tower: the righteous runneth into it, and ᴺis safe.

11 ᴿThe rich man's wealth *is* his strong city, and as an high wall in his own conceit.

12 ᴿBefore destruction the heart of man is haughty, and before honour *is* humility.

13 He that ᴺanswereth a matter ᴿbefore he heareth *it,* it *is* folly and shame unto him.

14 The spirit of a man will sustain his infirmity; but a wounded spirit who can bear?

15 The heart of the prudent getteth knowledge; and the ear of the wise seeketh knowledge.

16 ᴿA man's gift maketh room for him, and bringeth him before great men.

17 *He that is* first in his own cause *seemeth* just; but his neighbour cometh and searcheth him.

18 The lot causeth contentions to cease, and parteth between the mighty.

19 A brother offended *is harder to be won* than a strong city: and *their* contentions *are* like the bars of a castle.

20 ᴿA man's belly shall be satisfied with the fruit of his mouth; *and* with the increase of his lips shall he be filled.

21 ᴿDeath and life *are* in the power of the tongue: and they that love it shall eat the fruit thereof.

22 ᴿ*Whoso* findeth a wife findeth a good *thing,* and obtaineth favour of the Lᴏʀᴅ.

23 The poor useth entreaties; but the rich answereth ᴿroughly.

24 A man *that hath* friends must shew himself friendly: ᴿand there is a friend *that* sticketh closer than a brother.

CHAPTER 19

Proverbs concerning conduct

BETTER ᴿ*is* the poor that walketh in his integrity, than *he that is* perverse in his lips, and is a fool.

2 Also, *that* the soul *be* without knowledge, *it is* not good; and he that hasteth with *his* feet sinneth.

3 The foolishness of man perverteth his way: ᴿand his heart fretteth against the Lᴏʀᴅ.

4 ᴿWealth maketh many friends; but the poor is separated from his neighbour.

5 ᴿA false witness shall not be ᴺunpunished, and *he that* speaketh lies shall not escape.

6 ᴿMany will entreat the favour of the prince: and ᴿevery man *is* a friend to ᴺhim that giveth gifts.

7 ᴿAll the brethren of the poor do hate him:

how much more do his friends go ᴿfar from him? he pursueth *them with* words, *yet* they *are* wanting *to him.*

8 He that getteth ᴺwisdom loveth his own soul: he that keepeth understanding ᴿshall find good.

9 ᴿA false witness shall not be unpunished, and *he that* speaketh lies shall perish.

10 Delight is not seemly for a fool; much less ᴿfor a servant to have rule over princes.

11 ᴿThe ᴺdiscretion of a man deferreth his anger; ᴿand *it is* his glory to pass over a transgression.

12 ᴿThe king's wrath *is* as the roaring of a lion; but his favour *is* ᴿas dew upon the grass.

13 ᴿA foolish son *is* the calamity of his father: ᴿand the contentions of a wife *are* a continual dropping.

14 ᴿHouse and riches *are* the inheritance of fathers: and ᴿa prudent wife *is* from the Lᴏʀᴅ.

15 ᴿSlothfulness casteth into a deep sleep; and an idle soul shall ᴿsuffer hunger.

16 ᴿHe that keepeth the commandment keepeth his own soul; *but* he that despiseth his ways shall die.

17 ᴿHe that hath pity upon the poor lendeth unto the Lᴏʀᴅ; and ᴺthat which he hath given will he pay him again.

18 ᴿChasten thy son while there is hope, and let not thy soul spare ᴺfor his crying.

19 A man of great wrath shall suffer punishment: for if thou deliver *him,* yet thou must ᴺdo it again.

20 Hear counsel, and receive instruction, that thou mayest be wise ᴿin thy latter end.

21 *There are* many devices in a man's heart; ᴿnevertheless the counsel of the Lᴏʀᴅ, that shall stand.

22 The desire of a man *is* his kindness: and a poor man *is* better than a liar.

23 ᴿThe fear of the Lᴏʀᴅ *tendeth* to life: and *he that hath it* shall abide satisfied; he shall not be visited with evil.

24 ᴿA slothful *man* hideth his hand in *his* bosom, and will not so much as bring it to his mouth again.

25 Smite a scorner, and the simple ᴿwillᴺ beware: and ᴿreprove one that hath understanding, *and* he will understand knowledge.

26 He that wasteth *his* father, *and* chaseth away *his* mother, is ᴿa son that causeth shame, and bringeth reproach.

27 Cease, my son, to hear the instruction *that causeth* to err from the words of knowledge.

28 ᴺAn ungodly witness scorneth judgment: and ᴿthe mouth of the wicked devoureth iniquity.

29 Judgments are prepared for scorners, ᴿand stripes for the back of fools.

CHAPTER 20

Proverbs concerning conduct

WINE ᴿ*is* a mocker, strong drink *is* raging: and whosoever is deceived thereby is not wise.

2 ᴿThe fear of a king *is* as the roaring of a lion: *whoso* provoketh him to anger ᴿsinneth *against* his own soul.

3 ᴿ*It is* an honour for a man to cease from strife: but every fool will be meddling.

4 ᴿThe sluggard will not plow by reason of the cold; ᴿ*therefore* shall he beg in harvest, and *have* nothing.

5 Counsel in the heart of man *is like* deep water; but a man of understanding will draw it out.

6 ᴿMost men will proclaim every one his own ᴺgoodness: but ᴿa faithful man who can find?

7 ᴿThe just *man* walketh in his integrity: ᴿhis children *are* blessed after him.

8 ᴿA king that sitteth in the throne of judgment scattereth away all evil with his eyes.

9 ᴿWho can say, I have made my heart clean, I am pure from my sin?

10 ᴿDiversᴺ weights, *and* ᴺdivers measures, both of them *are* alike abomination to the LORD.

11 Even a child is ᴿknown by his doings, whether his work *be* pure, and whether *it be* right.

12 ᴿThe hearing ear, and the seeing eye, the LORD hath made even both of them.

13 ᴿLove not sleep, lest thou come to poverty; open thine eyes, *and* thou shalt be satisfied with bread.

14 *It is* naught, *it is* naught, saith the buyer: but when he is gone his way, then he boasteth.

15 There is gold, and a multitude of rubies: but ᴿthe lips of knowledge *are* a precious jewel.

16 ᴿTake his garment that is surety *for* a stranger: and take a pledge of him for a strange woman.

17 ᴿBread of deceit *is* sweet to a man; but afterwards his mouth shall be filled with gravel.

18 ᴿ*Every* purpose is established by counsel: ᴿand with good advice make war.

19 ᴿHe that goeth about *as* a talebearer revealeth secrets: therefore meddle not with him ᴿthat ᴺflattereth with his lips.

20 ᴿWhoso curseth his father or his mother, ᴿhis ᴺlamp shall be put out in obscure darkness.

21 ᴿAn inheritance *may be* gotten hastily at the beginning; ᴿbut the end thereof shall not be blessed.

22 ᴿSay not thou, I will recompense evil; *but* ᴿwait on the LORD, and he shall save thee.

23 ᴿDivers weights *are* an abomination unto the LORD; and ᴺa false balance *is* not good.

24 ᴿMan's goings *are* of the LORD; how can a man then understand his own way?

25 *It is* a snare to the man *who* devoureth *that which is* holy, and ᴿafter vows to make inquiry.

26 ᴿA wise king scattereth the wicked, and bringeth the wheel over them.

27 ᴿThe spirit of man *is* the ᴺcandle of the LORD, searching all the inward parts of the belly.

28 ᴿMercy and truth preserve the king: and his throne is upholden by mercy.

29 The glory of young men *is* their strength: and ᴿthe beauty of old men *is* the gray head.

30 The blueness of a wound ᴺcleanseth away evil: so *do* stripes the inward parts of the belly.

CHAPTER 21

Proverbs concerning conduct

THE king's heart *is* in the hand of the LORD, *as* the rivers of water: he turneth it whithersoever he will.

2 ᴿEvery way of a man *is* right in his own eyes: ᴿbut the LORD pondereth the hearts.

3 ᴿTo do justice and judgment *is* more acceptable to the LORD than sacrifice.

4 ᴿAn high look, and a proud heart, *and* ᴺthe plowing of the wicked, *is* sin.

5 ᴿThe thoughts of the diligent *tend* only to plenteousness; but of every one *that is* hasty only to want.

6 ᴿThe getting of treasures by a lying tongue *is* a vanity tossed to and fro of them that seek death.

7 The robbery of the wicked shall ᴺdestroy them; because they refuse to do judgment.

8 The way of man *is* froward and strange: but *as for* the pure, his work *is* right.

9 *It is* better to dwell in a corner of the housetop, than with ᴺa brawling woman in ᴺa wide house.

10 ᴿThe soul of the wicked desireth evil: his neighbour ᴺfindeth no favour in his eyes.

11 ᴿWhen the scorner is punished, the simple is made wise: and when the wise is instructed, he receiveth knowledge.

12 The righteous *man* wisely considereth the house of the wicked: *but God* overthroweth the wicked for *their* wickedness.

13 ᴿWhoso stoppeth his ears at the cry of the

poor, he also shall cry himself, but shall not be heard.

14 A gift in secret pacifieth anger: and a reward in the bosom strong wrath.

15 *It is* joy to the just to do judgment: but destruction *shall be* to the workers of iniquity.

16 The man that wandereth out of the way of understanding shall remain in the congregation of the dead.

17 He that loveth ᴺpleasure *shall be* a poor man: he that loveth wine and oil shall not be rich.

18 The wicked *shall be* a ransom for the righteous, and the transgressor for the upright.

19 *It is* better to dwell ᴺin the wilderness, than with a contentious and an angry woman.

20 ᴿ*There is* treasure to be desired and oil in the dwelling of the wise; but a foolish man spendeth it up.

21 ᴿHe that followeth after righteousness and mercy findeth life, righteousness, and honour.

22 ᴿA wise *man* scaleth the city of the mighty, and casteth down the strength of the confidence thereof.

23 ᴿWhoso keepeth his mouth and his tongue keepeth his soul from troubles.

24 Proud *and* haughty scorner *is* his name, who dealeth ᴺin proud wrath.

25 The desire of the slothful killeth him; for his hands refuse to labour.

26 He coveteth greedily all the day long: but the righteous giveth and spareth not.

27 ᴿThe sacrifice of the wicked *is* abomination: how much more, *when* he bringeth it ᴺwith a wicked mind?

28 ᴺA false witness shall perish: but the man that heareth speaketh constantly.

29 A wicked man hardeneth his face: but *as for* the upright, he ᴺdirecteth his way.

30 ᴿ*There is* no wisdom nor understanding nor counsel against the LORD.

31 The horse *is* prepared against the day of battle: but ᴿsafetyᴺ *is* of the LORD.

CHAPTER 22

Proverbs concerning conduct

A ᴿGOOD name *is* rather to be chosen than great riches, *and* ᴺloving favour rather than silver and gold.

2 The rich and poor meet together: the LORD *is* the maker of them all.

3 A prudent *man* forseeth the evil, and hideth himself: but the simple pass on, and are punished.

4 ᴺBy humility *and* the fear of the LORD *are* riches, and honour, and life.

5 Thorns *and* snares *are* in the way of the

froward: he that doth keep his soul shall be far from them.

6 ᴿTrainᴺ up a child ᴺin the way he should go: and when he is old, he will not depart from it.

7 The rich ruleth over the poor, and the borrower *is* servant ᴺto the lender.

8 He that soweth iniquity shall reap vanity: ᴺand the rod of his anger shall fail.

9 ᴿHeᴺ that hath a bountiful eye shall be blessed; for he giveth of his bread to the poor.

10 ᴿCast out the scorner, and contention shall go out; yea, strife and reproach shall cease.

11 ᴿHe that loveth pureness of heart, ᴺ*for* the grace of his lips the king *shall be* his friend.

12 The eyes of the LORD preserve knowledge, and he overthroweth ᴺthe words of the transgressor.

13 ᴿThe slothful *man* saith, *There is* a lion without, I shall be slain in the streets.

14 ᴿThe mouth of strange women *is* a deep pit: ᴿhe that is abhorred of the LORD shall fall therein.

15 Foolishness *is* bound in the heart of a child; *but* ᴿthe rod of correction shall drive it far from him.

16 He that oppresseth the poor to increase his *riches, and* he that giveth to the rich, *shall* surely *come* to want.

17 Bow down thine ear, and hear the words of the wise, and apply thine heart unto my knowledge.

18 For *it is* a pleasant thing if thou keep them ᴺwithin thee; they shall withal be fitted in thy lips.

19 That thy trust may be in the LORD, I have made known to thee this day, ᴺeven to thee.

20 Have not I written to thee excellent things in counsels and knowledge,

21 ᴿThat I might make thee know the certainty of the words of truth; ᴿthat thou mightest answer the words of truth ᴺto them that send unto thee?

22 Rob not the poor, because he *is* poor: neither oppress the afflicted in the gate:

23 ᴿFor the LORD will plead their cause, and spoil the soul of those that spoiled them.

24 Make no friendship with an angry man; and with a furious man thou shalt not go:

25 Lest thou learn his ways, and get a snare to thy soul.

26 ᴿBe not thou *one* of them that strike hands, *or* of them that are sureties for debts.

27 If thou hast nothing to pay, why should he take away thy bed from under thee?

28 ᴿRemove not the ancient ᴺlandmark, which thy fathers have set.

29 Seest thou a man diligent in his business? he shall stand before kings; he shall not stand before [N]mean *men*.

CHAPTER 23

Proverbs concerning conduct

WHEN thou sittest to eat with a ruler, consider diligently what *is* before thee:

2 And put a knife to thy throat, if thou *be a* man given to appetite.

3 Be not desirous of his dainties: for they *are* deceitful meat.

4 [R]Labour not to be rich: [R]cease from thine own wisdom.

5 [N]Wilt thou set thine eyes upon that which is not? for *riches* certainly make themselves wings; they fly away as an eagle toward heaven.

6 Eat thou not the bread of *him that hath* [R]an evil eye, neither desire thou his dainty meats:

7 For as he thinketh in his heart, so *is* he: Eat and drink, [R]saith he to thee; but his heart *is* not with thee.

8 The morsel *which* thou hast eaten shalt thou vomit up, and lose thy sweet words.

9 [R]Speak not in the ears of a fool: for he will despise the wisdom of thy words.

10 Remove not the old [N]landmark; and enter not into the fields of the fatherless:

11 [R]For their redeemer *is* mighty; he shall plead their cause with thee.

12 Apply thine heart unto instruction, and thine ears to the words of knowledge.

13 [R]Withhold not correction from the child: for *if* thou beatest him with the rod, he shall not die.

14 Thou shalt beat him with the rod, and shalt deliver his soul from hell.

15 My son, if thine heart be wise, my heart shall rejoice, [N]even mine.

16 Yea, my reins shall rejoice, when thy lips speak right things.

17 [R]Let not thine heart envy sinners: but [R]*be thou* in the fear of the LORD all the day long.

18 [R]For surely there is an [N]end; and thine expectation shall not be cut off.

19 Hear thou, my son, and be wise, and guide thine heart in the way.

20 [R]Be not among winebibbers; among riotous eaters [N]of flesh:

21 For the drunkard and the glutton shall come to poverty: and drowsiness shall clothe *a man* with rags.

22 [R]Hearken unto thy father that begat thee, and despise not thy mother when she is old.

23 [R]Buy the truth, and sell *it* not; *also* wisdom, and instruction, and understanding.

24 [R]The father of the righteous shall greatly rejoice: and he that begetteth a wise *child* shall have joy of him.

25 Thy father and thy mother shall be glad, and she that bare thee shall rejoice.

26 My son, give me thine heart, and let thine eyes observe my ways.

27 [R]For a whore *is* a deep ditch; and a strange woman *is* a narrow pit.

28 [R]She also lieth in wait [N]as *for* a prey, and increaseth the transgressors among men.

29 [R]Who hath woe? who hath sorrow? who hath contentions? who hath babbling? who hath wounds without cause? who [R]hath redness of eyes?

30 [R]They that tarry long at the wine; they that go to seek [R]mixed wine.

31 Look not thou upon the wine when it is red, when it giveth his colour in the cup, *when* it moveth itself aright.

32 At the last it biteth like a serpent, and stingeth like [N]an adder.

33 Thine eyes shall behold strange women, and thine heart shall utter perverse things.

34 Yea, thou shalt be as he that lieth down [N]in the midst of the sea, or as he that lieth upon the top of a mast.

35 [R]They have stricken me, *shalt thou say, and* I was not sick; they have beaten me, *and* [R]I[N] felt *it* not: when shall I awake? I will seek it yet again.

CHAPTER 24

Various warnings and teachings

BE not thou [R]envious against evil men, neither desire to be with them.

2 For their heart studieth destruction, and their lips talk of mischief.

3 Through wisdom is an house builded; and by understanding it is established:

4 And by knowledge shall the chambers be filled with all precious and pleasant riches.

5 [R]A wise man [N]*is* strong; yea, a man of knowledge [N]increaseth strength.

6 [R]For by wise counsel thou shalt make thy war: and in multitude of counsellors *there is* safety.

7 [R]Wisdom *is* too high for a fool: he openeth not his mouth in the gate.

8 He that [R]deviseth to do evil shall be called a mischievous person.

9 The thought of foolishness *is* sin: and the scorner *is* an abomination to men.

10 *If* thou faint in the day of adversity, thy strength *is* [N]small.

Center reference column

CHAP. 22

BC 1000

29 Heb. *obscure men*

CHAP. 23

BC 1000

4 1 Tim. 6:9
4 Rom. 12:16
5 Heb. *Wilt thou cause thine eyes to fly upon*
6 Deut. 15:9
7 Ps. 12:2
9 ch. 9:8
   Mat. 7:6
10 Or, *bound*
11 ch. 22:23
13 ch. 13:24
15 Or, *even I will rejoice*
17 Ps. 37:1
17 ch. 28:14
18 Ps. 37:37
18 Or, *reward*
20 Is. 5:22
20 Heb. *of their flesh*
22 ch. 1:8
   Eph. 6:1, 2

Mat. 13:44 — 23
ch. 10:1 — 24
ch. 22:14 — 27
ch. 7:12 — 28
   Eccl. 7:26
Or, *as a robber* — 28
Is. 5:11, 22 — 29
Gen. 49:12 — 29
Eph. 5:18 — 30
Ps. 75:8 — 30
Or, *a cockatrice* — 32
Heb. *in the heart of the sea* — 34
Jer. 5:3 — 35
Eph. 4:19 — 35
Heb. *I knew it not* — 35

CHAP. 24

BC 1000

Ps. 37:1, etc. & 73:3 — 1
   ch. 3:31
ch. 21:22 — 5
Heb. *is in strength* — 5
Heb. *strengtheneth might* — 5
Luke 14:31 — 6
Ps. 10:5 — 7
Rom. 1:30 — 8
Heb. *narrow* — 10

11 [R]If thou forbear to deliver *them that are* drawn unto death, and *those that are* ready to be slain;

12 If thou sayest, Behold, we knew it not; doth not [R]he that pondereth the heart consider *it?* and he that keepeth thy soul, doth *not* he know *it?* and shall *not* he render to *every* man [R]according to his works?

13 My son, [R]eat thou honey, because *it is* good; and the honeycomb, *which is* sweet [N]to thy taste:

14 [R]So *shall* the knowledge of wisdom *be* unto thy soul: when thou hast found *it,* then there shall be a reward, and thy expectation shall not be cut off.

15 Lay not wait, O wicked *man,* against the dwelling of the righteous; spoil not his resting place:

16 [R]For a just *man* falleth seven times, and riseth up again: [R]but the wicked shall fall into mischief.

17 [R]Rejoice not when thine enemy falleth, and let not thine heart be glad when he stumbleth:

18 Lest the LORD see *it,* and [N]it displease him, and he turn away his wrath from him.

19 [R]Fret[N] not thyself because of evil *men,* neither be thou envious at the wicked;

20 For there shall be no reward to the evil *man;* the [N]candle of the wicked shall be put out.

21 My son, [R]fear thou the LORD and the king: *and* meddle not with [N]them that are given to change:

22 For their calamity shall rise suddenly; and who knoweth the ruin of them both?

23 These *things* also *belong* to the wise. [R]*It is* not good to have respect of persons in judgment.

24 [R]He that saith unto the wicked, Thou *art* righteous; him shall the people curse, nations shall abhor him:

25 But to them that rebuke *him* shall be delight, and [N]a good blessing shall come upon them.

26 *Every man* shall kiss *his* lips [N]that giveth a right answer.

27 [R]Prepare thy work without, and make it fit for thyself in the field; and afterwards build thine house.

28 [R]Be not a witness against thy neighbour without cause; and deceive *not* with thy lips.

29 [R]Say not, I will do so to him as he hath done to me: I will render to the man according to his work.

30 I went by the field of the slothful, and by the vineyard of the man void of understanding;

31 And, lo, [R]it was all grown over with

CHAP. **24**	
BC 1000	
11 Ps. 82:4	
Is. 58:6, 7	
1 John 3:16	
12 ch. 21:2	
12 Ps. 62:12	
13 S. of S. 5:1	
13 Heb. *upon thy palate*	
14 Ps. 19:10	
16 Ps. 34:19	
Mic. 7:8	
16 Esth. 7:10	
Amos 5:2	
17 Job 31:29	
Obad. 12	
18 Heb. *it be evil in his eyes*	
19 Ps. 37:1	
19 Or, *Keep not company with the wicked*	
20 Or, *lamp*	
21 Rom. 13:7	
1 Pet. 2:17	
21 Heb. *changers*	
23 Lev. 19:15	
Deut. 16:19	
24 Is. 5:23	
25 Heb. *a blessing of good*	
26 Heb. *that answereth right words*	
27 1 Ki. 5:17	
28 Eph. 4:25	
29 Mat. 5:39	
31 Gen. 3:18	

Heb. *set my heart*	32
ch. 6:9, etc.	33
Heb. *a man of shield*	34

CHAP. **25**	
BC 700	
1 Ki. 4:32	1
Rom. 11:33	2
Job 29:16	2
Heb. *there is no searching*	3
2 Tim. 2:21	4
ch. 20:8	5
ch. 16:12	5
Heb. *Set not out thy glory*	6
Luke 14:10	7
Mat. 5:25	8
Mat. 5:25	9
Or, *of*	9
ch. 15:23	11
Heb. *spoken upon his wheels*	11
ch. 13:17	13
ch. 20:6	14
Heb. *in a gift of falsehood*	14
Jude 12	14
ch. 15:1	15
ver. 27	16

thorns, *and* nettles had covered the face thereof, and the stone wall thereof was broken down.

32 Then I saw, *and* [N]considered *it* well: I looked upon *it, and* received instruction.

33 [R]*Yet* a little sleep, a little slumber, a little folding of the hands to sleep:

34 So shall thy poverty come *as* one that travelleth; and thy want as [N]an armed man.

CHAPTER 25

About kings

THESE[R] *are* also proverbs of Solomon, which the men of Hĕz-ē-kī′-ăh king of Judah copied out.

2 [R]*It is* the glory of God to conceal a thing: but the honour of kings *is* [R]to search out a matter.

3 The heaven for height, and the earth for depth, and the heart of kings [N]*is* unsearchable.

4 [R]Take away the dross from the silver, and there shall come forth a vessel for the finer.

5 [R]Take away the wicked *from* before the king, and [R]his throne shall be established in righteousness.

6 [N]Put not forth thyself in the presence of the king, and stand not in the place of great *men:*

7 [R]For better *it is* that it be said unto thee, Come up hither; than that thou shouldest be put lower in the presence of the prince whom thine eyes have seen.

On avoiding quarrels

8 [R]Go not forth hastily to strive, lest *thou know not* what to do in the end thereof, when thy neighbour hath put thee to shame.

9 [R]Debate thy cause with thy neighbour *himself;* and discover not a secret [N]to another:

10 Lest he that heareth *it* put thee to shame, and thine infamy turn not away.

11 [R]A word [N]fitly spoken *is like* apples of gold in pictures of silver.

12 *As* an earring of gold, and an ornament of fine gold, *so is* a wise reprover upon an obedient ear.

13 [R]As the cold of snow in the time of harvest, *so is* a faithful messenger to them that send him: for he refresheth the soul of his masters.

14 [R]Whoso boasteth himself [N]of a false gift *is like* [R]clouds and wind without rain.

15 [R]By long forbearing is a prince persuaded, and a soft tongue breaketh the bone.

16 [R]Hast thou found honey? eat so much as is sufficient for thee, lest thou be filled therewith, and vomit it.

17 ᴺWithdraw thy foot from thy neighbour's house; lest he be ᴺweary of thee, and so hate thee.

18 ᴿA man that beareth false witness against his neighbour *is* a maul, and a sword, and a sharp arrow.

19 Confidence in an unfaithful man in time of trouble *is like* a broken tooth, and a foot out of joint.

20 *As* he that taketh away a garment in cold weather, *and as* vinegar upon nitre, so *is* he that ᴿsingeth songs to an heavy heart.

21 ᴿIf thine enemy be hungry, give him bread to eat; and if he be thirsty, give him water to drink:

22 For thou shalt heap coals of fire upon his head, ᴿand the LORD shall reward thee.

23 ᴿTheᴺ north wind driveth away rain: so *doth* an angry countenance ᴿa backbiting tongue.

24 ᴿ*It is* better to dwell in the corner of the housetop, than with a brawling woman and in a wide house.

25 *As* cold waters to a thirsty soul, so *is* good news from a far country.

26 A righteous man falling down before the wicked *is as* a troubled fountain, and a corrupt spring.

27 ᴿ*It is* not good to eat much honey: so *for men* ᴿto search their own glory *is not* glory.

28 ᴿHe that *hath* no rule over his own spirit *is like* a city *that is* broken down, *and* without walls.

CHAPTER 26

Fools, sluggards and talebearers

AS snow in summer, ᴿand as rain in harvest, so honour is not seemly for a fool.

2 As the bird by wandering, as the swallow by flying, so ᴿthe curse causeless shall not come.

3 ᴿA whip for the horse, a bridle for the ass, and a rod for the fool's back.

4 Answer not a fool according to his folly, lest thou also be like unto him.

5 ᴿAnswer a fool according to his folly, lest he be wise in ᴺhis own conceit.

6 He that sendeth a message by the hand of a fool cutteth off the feet, *and* drinketh ᴺdamage.

7 The legs of the lame ᴺare not equal: so *is* a parable in the mouth of fools.

8 ᴺAs he that bindeth a stone in a sling, so *is* he that giveth honour to a fool.

9 *As* a thorn goeth up into the hand of a drunkard, so *is* a parable in the mouth of fools.

CHAP. 25
BC 700
17 Or, *Let thy foot be seldom in thy neighbour's house*
17 Heb. *full of thee*
18 Ps. 57:4
20 Dan. 6:18
21 Mat. 5:44
22 2 Sam. 16:12
23 Job 37:22
23 Or, *The north wind bringeth forth rain: so doth a backbiting tongue an angry countenance*
23 Ps. 101:5
24 ch. 19:13
27 ver. 16
27 ch. 27:2
28 ch. 16:32

CHAP. 26
BC 700
1 1 Sam. 12:17
2 Deut. 23:5
3 Ps. 32:9
5 Mat. 16:1-4
5 Heb. *his own eyes*
6 Or, *violence*
7 Heb. *are lifted up*
8 Or, *As he that putteth a precious stone in an heap of stones*

Or, *A great man grieveth all, and he hireth the fool, he hireth also transgressors*   10
2 Pet. 2:22   11
Ex. 8:15   11
Heb. *iterateth his folly*   11
Rev. 3:17   12
Or, *he is weary*   15
Or, *is enraged*   17
Heb. *flames, or, sparks*   18
Eph. 5:4   19
Heb. *Without wood*   20
Or, *whisperer*   20
Heb. *is silent*   20
ch. 15:18   21
Heb. *chambers*   22
Or, *is known*   24
Ps. 28:3   25
Heb. *maketh his voice gracious*   25
Or, *hatred is covered in secret*   26
Ps. 7:15   27

CHAP. 27
BC 700
Heb. *to morrow day*   1
Heb. *heaviness*   3

10 ᴺThe great *God* that formed all *things* both rewardeth the fool, and rewardeth transgressors.

11 ᴿAs a dog returneth to his vomit, ᴿ*so* a fool ᴺreturneth to his folly.

12 ᴿSeest thou a man wise in his own conceit? *there is* more hope of a fool than of him.

13 The slothful *man* saith, *There is* a lion in the way; a lion *is* in the streets.

14 *As* the door turneth upon his hinges, so *doth* the slothful upon his bed.

15 The slothful hideth his hand in *his* bosom; ᴺit grieveth him to bring it again to his mouth.

16 The sluggard *is* wiser in his own conceit than seven men that can render a reason.

17 He that passeth by, *and* ᴺmeddleth with strife *belonging* not to him, *is like* one that taketh a dog by the ears.

18 As a mad *man* who casteth ᴺfirebrands, arrows, and death,

19 So *is* the man *that* deceiveth his neighbour, and saith, ᴿAm not I in sport?

20 ᴺWhere no wood is, *there* the fire goeth out: so where *there is* no ᴺtalebearer, the strife ᴺceaseth.

21 ᴿAs coals *are* to burning coals, and wood to fire; so *is* a contentious man to kindle strife.

22 The words of a talebearer *are* as wounds, and they go down into the ᴺinnermost parts of the belly.

23 Burning lips and a wicked heart *are like* a potsherd covered with silver dross.

24 He that hateth ᴺdissembleth with his lips, and layeth up deceit within him;

25 ᴿWhen he ᴺspeaketh fair, believe him not: for *there are* seven abominations in his heart.

26 *Whose* ᴺhatred is covered by deceit, his wickedness shall be shewed before the *whole* congregation.

27 ᴿWhoso diggeth a pit shall fall therein: and he that rolleth a stone, it will return upon him.

28 A lying tongue hateth *those that are* afflicted by it; and a flattering mouth worketh ruin.

CHAPTER 27

Self-love and care against offences

BOAST not thyself of ᴺto morrow; for thou knowest not what a day may bring forth.

2 Let another man praise thee, and not thine own mouth; a stranger, and not thine own lips.

3 A stone *is* ᴺheavy, and the sand weighty; but a fool's wrath *is* heavier than them both.

God's People in the Period of the Kings and Prophets

And the king of Israel and Jehoshaphat the king of Judah sat each on his throne, having put on their robes, in a void place in the entrance of the gate of Samaria; and all the prophets prophesied before them."

I KINGS 22:10

The Great King David

AUL'S reign did not please God; so He told Samuel to anoint another man as king over Israel. Samuel went to Bethlehem, to the home of Jesse, in order to examine Jesse's sons. For among these young men he expected to find a suitable person to anoint as the second king of the Jews.

Seven of Jesse's sons passed before Samuel, yet none of them seemed to be the one that God wanted to rule the Jews. Samuel asked Jesse if he had still other sons. Upon learning that the youngest, David, was out in the fields watching the sheep, he had Jesse to send for him. David was ruddy, with beautiful eyes—a very handsome young man. As Samuel gazed at him, the Lord said: "Arise, anoint him: for this is he." So Samuel took the horn of oil and anointed David in the presence of his brothers.

Now, David was not destined to become king of Israel immediately. There were many experiences ahead of him before he would become ruler of his nation. First, he was summoned to the court of King Saul to play the harp. Saul was subject to fits of depression, and music had the power to calm and soothe him. David's harp playing caused Saul to become very fond of him.

During Saul's reign, the Philistines made war on the Israelites. Especially feared by the soldiers of Israel was a Philistine giant named Goliath. One day when Goliath was taunting the Israelites, David begged permission from Saul to go out and fight the giant, even though David was still only a youth. Saul protested; he feared for David's life. But David, remembering experiences that he had survived as a shepherd, said: "The Lord that delivered me out of the paw of the lion, an out of the paw of the bear, he will deliver me out of the hand of this Philistine." Then Saul said: "Go, and the Lord be with thee." Taking a sling and five stones, David went out to meet Goliath; fitting a rock into his sling, he slung it at the giant. The rock struck Goliath in the forehead and killed him.

David became a famous, and very popular, warrior in the army of King Saul. This made Saul angry and jealous of David. In time, David had to flee for his life. Saul and his soldiers tried to capture David, but David always eluded them. During this time, the prophet Samuel died.

War with the Philistines went on and on. Finally, on Mount Gilboa the Philistines overtook Saul and his army and defeated them badly in the year 1004 B.C. Saul's sons, including David's good friend Jonathan, were all killed; and Saul, in despair, killed himself by falling on his sword. When David heard of Saul's death, he was filled with grief.

Then David went to the town of Hebron in Judah; and the men of Judah anointed him as their king. Later, all the tribes of Israel came to David at Hebron and anointed him king of Israel. David was thirty years old when he became king, and he reigned until 965 B.C. During that time, he unified his kingdom and ruled so well that for centuries afterwards the Jews looked back upon his reign as the "golden age" of their nation.

1 Samuel 16:1–1 Kings 2:10.

Tissot

Solomon's Judgment

HEN David was old and death seemed near, he told Zadok the priest and Nathan the prophet to anoint his son Solomon as king of Israel. So a large group of Israelites went to Gihon with Solomon, and there Zadok the priest poured oil from a sacred horn onto Solomon's head, thus anointing him king in the year 965 B.C. This was an exciting moment! Trumpets were blown, and the people shouted: "God save king Solomon!" An atmosphere of great joy prevailed.

Now that his son Solomon was king, David could die with peace of mind. As one last bit of fatherly advice to his son, David said: "I go the way of all the earth: be thou strong therefore, and show thyself a man; and keep the charge of the Lord thy God, to walk in his ways, to keep his statutes, and his commandments, and his judgments, and his testimonies." Then David died and was buried in Bethlehem, which is called "the city of David."

Under Solomon's rule, the kingdom was firmly established. Furthermore, he loved God and worshipped him with many sacrifices. One night, when Solomon had gone to Gibeon to sacrifice, the Lord appeared to him in a dream and said: "Ask what I shall give thee." Solomon replied: "Give thy servant an understanding heart to judge the people, that I may discern between good and bad: for who is able to judge this thy so great a people?" The reply was pleasing to God, and He granted Solomon's wish for a wise and understanding heart.

One day, two women came to Solomon, asking him to resolve a dispute over a child that each claimed as her own. The two women lived in the same house and both gave birth to children during the same week. In the night, however, one of the mothers accidentally smothered her baby by rolling over on it in bed. In desperation she put the dead baby in bed with the other woman while she slept, and took the live baby to be her own. When the other mother awoke the next morning, she was horrified to find that the baby which was lying in bed with her was dead; but upon looking at it more closely, she saw that it was not her child. At that, she and the other woman had a furious argument, with each claiming that the living baby was hers. Finally, they went before King Solomon, asking that he judge between them.

When Solomon had heard what the women had to say, he told one of his court attendants, "Bring me a sword." When the sword had been brought into the king's chamber, he ordered: "Divide the living child in two, and give half to the one, and half to the other." What? Could anyone with human feelings propose such a cruel solution to the problem? The true mother of the child cried out: "O my lord, give her the living child, and in no wise slay it." She would rather have her child alive than dead, even if he would be reared by another woman! But the other woman was spiteful, and totally lacking in love for the child. She said: "Let it be neither mine nor thine, but divide it." Then Solomon ordered that the child be given to the woman who wanted it to be kept alive, for "she is the mother thereof."

As word of Solomon's judgment in this case got around in Israel, the people stood in awe of the king, for they saw that the wisdom of God was truly in him and that he would rule with justice.

1 Kings 1:11–3:28.

Elijah and the Priests of Baal

HEN the famous King Solomon died in 926 B.C., his nation was divided into two parts: the northern kingdom was called Israel, while the southern kingdom took the name of Judah. The separated kingdom was never again reunited.

Some fifty years after Solomon's death, there came to the throne of Israel a man named Ahab. Now Ahab was a rather weak person, married to a dominating woman named Jezebel, daughter of the king of Tyre. Now, the people of Tyre worshipped a nature-god called Baal. Under the influence of his wife Jezebel, King Ahab and the Israelites worshipped Baal, also.

Suddenly, about 860 B.C., a prophet from Tishbe named Elijah rose up in anger against Ahab and Jezebel. He wanted to call the Israelites back to the worship of the one true God. To show Ahab the power of God over nature, and as a punishment for the Israelites' immoral worship of Baal, Elijah promised: "As the Lord God of Israel liveth, before whom I stand, there shall not be dew nor rain these years, but according to my word." Then Elijah had to hide, lest King Ahab kill him, for a great drought settled upon the land.

The Israelites were suffering terribly for lack of water. In the third year of the drought, the Lord told Elijah: "Go, show thyself unto Ahab; and I will send rain upon the earth." So Elijah returned from hiding to seek out King Ahab. When they met, Ahab expressed his anger toward Elijah: "Art thou he that troubleth Israel?" But Elijah told Ahab that it was he who was responsible for Israel's troubles, because he had broken God's commandments and had worshipped Baal. Then Elijah commanded Ahab to have the four hundred and fifty priests of Baal to gather on Mount Carmel.

When the Israelites and the priests of Baal were gathered on the mountain, Elijah spoke out in righteous anger: "How long halt ye between two opinions? if the Lord be God, follow him: but if Baal, then follow him."

Then Elijah proposed a dramatic contest between himself and the priests of Baal. Each would prepare a bull for sacrifice, but not set fire to it. Then they should call upon their respective gods—they upon Baal, he upon God—to consume the sacrifice with fire. All agreed to this test of the power.

First, the priests of Baal cried out to their god, hour after hour, but nothing happened. Then Elijah built an altar to the Lord and put the sacrificial animal on it. He had the people to drench it with water three times; then he prayed for God to consume it with fire, as a proof to the people of his reality and power. "Then the fire of the Lord fell, and consumed the burnt sacrifice." When the Israelites saw what had happened, they fell on their faces and cried out, "The Lord, he is the God; the Lord, he is the God."

Immediately, Elijah ordered the priests of Baal to be seized and killed; and this was done. But when Jezebel heard what Elijah had done, she was furious and vowed to have him killed. So once again Elijah fled for his life. When he was in the desert, hungry and without water, an angel appeared and said: "Arise and eat." And Elijah was strengthened and refreshed by the food and water given him by the angel.

1 Kings 16:29–19:8.

TISSOT

Elisha and the Shunammite Woman

HEN the prophet Elijah was taken from earth, his friend and follower Elisha succeeded him as the greatest of the Hebrew prophets. The sons of the prophets saw in him a spirit akin to that of his master, so they said: "The spirit of Elijah doth rest on Elisha."

One day, Elisha went to the town of Shunem, which was just north of Mount Gilboa in Israel. In this town there lived a wealthy couple who were especially fond of Elisha, and they wanted him to be their guest whenever he was passing through their town. So they built a room in their house for the prophet, furnished with a bed, table, chair, and lamp. On this particular day, Elisha wanted to know what he could do to repay the kindness of the Shunammite woman and her husband. Elisha's servant, Gehazi, told him: "Verily she hath no child, and her husband is old."

Elisha called the woman and told her that, a year later, she would have a son. The woman found it hard to believe that this would happen, but a year later she gave birth to a child, just as Elisha had promised.

When the child had grown to boyhood, he went to the field where his father was reaping grain. Suddenly, he clutched his head in pain and cried out: "My head, my head!" A field hand carried the boy to his mother, who held him on her lap to comfort him; and at noon, the boy died.

The mother's heart must have broken as she gazed at her dead son, but she would not give him up this easily. Rising quickly, she took the child to Elisha's room and laid him on the prophet's bed. Closing the door behind her, she had one of the servants to saddle a donkey and, mounting it, set off in haste to Mount Carmel to see Elisha.

Elisha saw the Shunammite woman before she reached Mount Carmel. The haste with which she was urging the donkey along told him that something was wrong, though he could not guess what it was.

Then the Shunammite woman fell at Elisha's feet and wept in bitter anguish. She sobbed out two painful questions: "Did I desire a son of my lord? Did I not say, do not deceive me?" Guessing what must have happened Elisha sent his servant Gehazi to Shunem, with instructions to lay the prophet's staff upon the face of the child. But this would not satisfy the mother; she refused to leave Elisha. So he returned with her to Shunem.

When Elisha saw the dead child lying on his bed, he closed the door and prayed earnestly to God. Then he lay upon the child, mouth to mouth, eyes to eyes, hands to hands. When he got up, the child sneezed seven times and opened his eyes. Elisha called Gehazi and said: "Call this Shunammite." The servant did as Elisha had commanded him.

Sorrowful but expectant, the Shunammite woman came into the room. Could it really be true? Was her son really alive—breathing—smiling up at her? Elisha spoke gently: "Take up thy son." In gratitude too deep for words, the woman fell at Elisha's feet, bowing to him. Then, her heart full of joy, the woman gathered her son into her arms and went out.

2 Kings 2:1–4:37.

Jonah, the Reluctant Prophet

MONG Israel's enemies, none were hated more bitterly than the Assyrians. For in 721 B.C. they had laid waste the cities of Israel and had taken its people as captives to a foreign land.

How surprised Jonah must have been, then, when he heard God calling him to go to Nineveh, the capital of Assyria, to warn the people of God's anger at their wickedness! Surprise gave way to stubbornness; Jonah did not want to go to Nineveh as God's messenger. So he went to Joppa and boarded a ship for Tarshish—as far away from Nineveh as he could get!

As the ship sailed out onto the sea, however, a great storm came up and it appeared that the ship would sink. The sailors frantically tried to appease the gods that they thought were causing the storm, but with no success. Finally, they decided that Jonah was the cause of the storm. "What shall we do unto thee," they asked him, "that the sea may be calm unto us?" Jonah, unwilling to have all these sailors drown on his account, told them: "Take me up, and cast me forth into the sea; so shall the sea be calm unto you: for I know that for my sake this great tempest is upon you." So they threw Jonah overboard.

Jonah would have drowned in the stormy sea, but "the Lord had prepared a great fish to swallow up Jonah. And Jonah was in the belly of the fish three days and three nights." During that time, Jonah prayed with great earnestness to God; then he was cast upon dry land.

Now Jonah had a second chance to go to Nineveh and prophesy as God had told him to do. Arriving in the city, Jonah began to cry out: "Yet forty days, and Nineveh shall be overthrown!" To Jonah's great surprise, the people of Nineveh—from the king down to the common man—repented of their sins, and fasted as an expression of their sorrow for their wrongdoings. And when God saw this, he decided not to destroy Nineveh.

One would think that Jonah would have been overjoyed at the success of his mission. But the very opposite was true: he was extremely angry. He had prophesied that Nineveh would be destroyed, and he wanted it to be destroyed!

God chided Jonah for his anger, but Jonah continued to be unhappy because Nineveh was not destroyed. So God tried to open Jonah's eyes with an acted-out parable. Jonah was on the outskirts of the city, watching to see what might happen to it. There the sun was bright and hot; so God caused a gourd plant to grow up in one day, the shade of which was a welcome relief for Jonah. The next day, however, worms got onto the gourd plant so that it withered and died. At that, Jonah was beside himself with rage.

Then God said to Jonah: "Thou hast had pity on the gourd, for which thou hast not labored, neither madest it grow; which came up in a night, and perished in a night: and should not I spare Nineveh, that great city, wherein are more than sixscore thousand persons that cannot discern between their right hand and their left hand?"

This story ends with God's question to Jonah. It is a plea for compassion toward one's enemies, and shows that God loves all people.

The Book of Jonah.

Tissot

Jeremiah Foresees Jerusalem's Fall

N the little village of Anathoth, about two miles northeast of Jerusalem, there was born about 625 B.C. a boy named Jeremiah. His father was a priest named Hilkiah. As he grew up, Jeremiah loved the sights and sounds of the countryside; he also became very familiar with the great city of Jerusalem with its beautiful Temple.

When he was in his late teens or early twenties, Jeremiah heard the Lord calling him to be a prophet. The young man felt too young and immature to be a prophet. But God answered him: "Say not, I am a child: for thou shalt go to all that I shall send thee, and whatsoever I command thee thou shalt speak. Be not afraid of their faces: for I am with thee to deliver thee, saith the Lord." With this sense of divine call, Jeremiah undertook his task.

Judah had just crowned a new king, Jehoiakim, in the autumn of 609 B.C., when Jeremiah delivered a startling sermon at the Temple of Solomon in Jerusalem. Speaking for God, he said: "If ye thoroughly amend your ways and your doings; if ye thoroughly execute judgment between a man and his neighbor; if ye oppress not the stranger, the fatherless, and the widow, and shed not innocent blood in this place, neither walk after other gods to your hurt: then will I cause you to dwell in this place, in the land that I gave to your fathers, for ever and ever." But Jeremiah warned that if the people did not repent of their sinful ways, their glorious Temple would be destroyed.

Those who heard Jeremiah were so angry that they wanted to kill him. But he stood his ground with courage, and continued to prophesy. The king of Judah, Jehoiakim, was pompous and proud. Furthermore, he allowed many of the old pagan practices to creep back into the religion of the Jews. Therefore, Jeremiah denounced Jehoiakim severely.

On March 16, 597 B.C., the Babylonians conquered Jerusalem and took the king and many Jews as captives to Babylonia. The Temple was looted of its precious vessels of gold. Then the Babylonian king set Zedekiah on the throne as a puppet ruler. For ten years he was loyal to the Babylonians; but then he began to plot with the Egyptians against Babylonia. Once again the Babylonian armies marched into Judah and beseiged Jerusalem. After a year and a half, in August, 587 B.C., they captured Jerusalem. With terrible vengeance, they burned the Temple and the palace, and broke down the city walls. All the Jews were taken as prisoners to Babylonia.

During Zedekiah's fateful reign, Jeremiah wore a yoke as a symbolic way of saying that it was God's will for Judah to submit to Babylonia's rule, rather than fight against it. "The nations that bring their neck under the yoke of the king of Babylon, and serve him, those will I let remain still in their own land, saith the Lord." This was a most unpopular message; Jeremiah was put in prison for preaching it.

But Jeremiah was not just a prophet of doom. He believed that in the future God would build up the Jewish nation again, if the people would repent and return to God.

The Book of Jeremiah.

REMBRANDT

Esther and Mordecai

IN the days when the Persian Empire extended from India to Ethiopia, there was a great king named Ahasuerus. (This was Hebrew for the name of Xerxes I, who ruled from 485 to 465 B.C.) The king gave a banquet that lasted many days. On the seventh day of of the feast, "when the heart of the king was merry with wine," he commanded that Queen Vashti come in, so that he could show the princes how beautiful she was. But she refused. In anger, the king resolved to get a new queen.

Throughout the kingdom, beautiful young women were sought as possible queens for King Ahasuerus, and were brought to Susa, the capital city of Persia. Now there lived in Susa a Jew named Mordecai, who had been brought as a captive from Judah by the king of Babylonia. Mordecai had adopted as his own daughter a beautiful girl named Esther, whose parents were both dead. When Mordecai heard of the search for a new queen, he took Esther to the palace, as a contestant for the role of queen.

When King Ahasuerus saw Esther, "she obtained grace and favor in his sight more than all the virgins; so that he set the royal crown upon her head, and made her queen instead of Vashti." Even after she was queen, Esther loved and respected her foster-father, Mordecai.

The king's prime minister, whose name was Haman, became very angry with Mordecai because the Jew refused to bow down to him as he passed by. Upon discovering that Mordecai was a Jew, he resolved to destroy all the Jews! He deliberately lied to the king, therefore, and convinced him that the Jews did not keep the laws of the realm and should therefore be destroyed. Letters were sent to all the provinces, setting a date on which the Jews should be massacred.

Mordecai learned of this terrible fate that lay in store for the Jews; he told Esther, and urged her to intercede for her people. At first, Esther was fearful. But Mordecai asked her a thoughtful question: "Who knoweth whether thou art come to the kingdom for such a time as this?" Here was an opportunity to help her people—more than that, a matter of life-or-death! So Esther acted with courage. She promised to plead with the king for the lives of the Jews.

Esther approached the problem in a roundabout manner. First, she prepared an elaborate dinner and invited the king and Haman as the only guests. The king was most pleased, and asked what he might do for her in return. She demurred until after serving the king another fine dinner. Then she told him of Haman's plot to kill the Jews, and revealed that she herself was a Jew. The king was very angry. He had Haman hanged on the very gallows that he had built for Mordecai.

Then Mordecai was made prime minister, second in rank only to the king. He and Esther sent out letters authorizing the Jews to attack the persons who had planned to kill them.

Ever after that time, the Jews have observed two days of feasting, called Purim, as a memorial of the escape of the Jews of Persia from the evil plot of Haman. The ritual of the festival includes the reading of the Book of Esther.

The Book of Esther.

TISSOT

"*And what doth the Lord require of thee, but to do justly, and to love mercy, and to walk humbly with thy God?*"

MICAH 6:8

4 ᴺWrath *is* cruel, and anger *is* outrageous; but who *is* able to stand before ᴺenvy?

5 Open rebuke *is* better than secret love.

6 Faithful *are* the wounds of a friend; but the kisses of an enemy *are* ᴺdeceitful.

7 The full soul ᴺloatheth an honeycomb; but to the hungry soul every bitter thing is sweet.

8 As a bird that wandereth from her nest, so *is* a man that wandereth from his place.

9 Ointment and perfume rejoice the heart: so *doth* the sweetness of a man's friend ᴺby hearty counsel.

10 Thine own friend, and thy father's friend, forsake not; neither go into thy brother's house in the day of thy calamity: *for* ᴿbetter *is* a neighbour *that is* near than a brother far off.

11 My son, be wise, and make my heart glad, ᴿthat I may answer him that reproacheth me.

12 A prudent *man* foreseeth the evil, *and* hideth himself; *but* the simple pass on, *and* are punished.

13 Take his garment that is surety for a stranger, and take a pledge of him for a strange woman.

14 He that blesseth his friend with a loud voice, rising early in the morning, it shall be counted a curse to him.

15 A continual dropping in a very rainy day and a contentious woman are alike.

16 Whosoever hideth her hideth the wind, and the ointment of his right hand, *which* bewrayeth *itself*.

17 Iron sharpeneth iron; so a man sharpeneth the countenance of his friend.

18 ᴿWhoso keepeth the fig tree shall eat the fruit thereof: so he that waiteth on his master shall be honoured.

19 As in water face *answereth* to face, so the heart of man to man.

20 ᴿHell and destruction are ᴺnever full; so ᴿthe eyes of man are never satisfied.

21 ᴿ*As* the fining pot for silver, and the furnace for gold; so *is* a man to his praise.

22 ᴿThough thou shouldest bray a fool in a mortar among wheat with a pestle, *yet* will not his foolishness depart from him.

23 Be thou diligent to know the state of thy flocks, *and* ᴺlook well to thy herds.

24 For ᴺriches *are* not for ever: and doth the crown *endure* ᴺto every generation?

25 ᴿThe hay appeareth, and the tender grass sheweth itself, and herbs of the mountains are gathered.

26 The lambs *are* for thy clothing, and the goats *are* the price of the field.

27 And *thou shalt have* goats' milk enough

for thy food, for the food of thy household, and *for* the ᴺmaintenance for thy maidens.

CHAPTER 28

The wicked versus the righteous

THE ᴿwicked flee when no man pursueth: but the righteous are bold as a lion.

2 For the transgression of a land many *are* the princes thereof: but ᴺby a man of understanding *and* knowledge the state *thereof* shall be prolonged.

3 ᴿA poor man that oppresseth the poor *is* like a sweeping rain ᴺwhich leaveth no food.

4 ᴿThey that forsake the law praise the wicked: ᴿbut such as keep the law contend with them.

5 ᴿEvil men understand not judgment: but ᴿthey that seek the Lord understand all *things*.

6 ᴿBetter *is* the poor that walketh in his uprightness, than *he that is* perverse *in his* ways, though he *be* rich.

7 ᴿWhoso keepeth the law *is* a wise son: but he that ᴺis a companion of riotous *men* shameth his father.

8 ᴿHe that by usury and ᴺunjust gain increaseth his substance, he shall gather it for him that will pity the poor.

9 He that turneth away his ear from hearing the law, ᴿeven his prayer *shall be* abomination.

10 ᴿWhoso causeth the righteous to go astray in an evil way, he shall fall himself into his own pit: ᴿbut the upright shall have good *things* in possession.

11 The rich man *is* wise ᴺin his own conceit; but the poor that hath understanding searcheth him out.

12 ᴿWhen righteous *men* do rejoice, *there is* great glory: but when the wicked rise, a man is ᴺhidden.

13 ᴿHe that covereth his sins shall not prosper: but whoso confesseth and forsaketh *them* shall have mercy.

14 Happy *is* the man ᴿthat feareth alway: ᴿbut he that hardeneth his heart shall fall into mischief.

15 ᴿ*As* a roaring lion, and a ranging bear; ᴿ*so is* a wicked ruler over the poor people.

16 The prince that wanteth understanding *is* also a great oppressor: *but* he that hateth covetousness shall prolong *his* days.

17 ᴿA man that doeth violence to the blood of *any* person shall flee to the pit; let no man stay him.

18 ᴿWhoso walketh uprightly shall be saved:

but ᴿ*he that is* perverse *in his* ways shall fall at once.

19 ᴿHe that tilleth his land shall have plenty of bread: but he that followeth after vain *persons* shall have poverty enough.

20 A faithful man shall abound with blessings: ᴿbut he that maketh haste to be rich shall not be ᴺinnocent.

21 ᴿTo have respect of persons *is* not good: for ᴿfor a piece of bread *that* man will transgress.

22 ᴿHeᴺ that hasteth to be rich *hath* an evil eye, and considereth not that poverty shall come upon him.

23 ᴿHe that rebuketh a man afterwards shall find more favour than he that flattereth with the tongue.

24 Whoso robbeth his father or his mother, and saith, *It is* no transgression; the same ᴿ*is* the companion of ᴺa destroyer.

25 ᴿHe that is of a proud heart stirreth up strife: ᴿbut he that putteth his trust in the LORD shall be made fat.

26 He that trusteth in his own heart is a fool: but whoso walketh wisely, he shall be delivered.

27 ᴿHe that giveth unto the poor shall not lack: but he that hideth his eyes shall have many a curse.

28 ᴿWhen the wicked rise, ᴿmen hide themselves: but when they perish, the righteous increase.

CHAPTER 29

The wicked versus the righteous

ᴿHE,ᴺ that being often reproved hardeneth *his* neck, shall suddenly be destroyed, and that without remedy.

2 ᴿWhen the righteous are ᴺin authority, the people rejoice: but when the wicked beareth rule, ᴿthe people mourn.

3 ᴿWhoso loveth wisdom rejoiceth his father: ᴿbut he that keepeth company with harlots spendeth *his* substance.

4 The king by judgment establisheth the land: but ᴺhe that receiveth gifts overthroweth it.

5 A man that flattereth his neighbour spreadeth a net for his feet.

6 In the transgression of an evil man *there is* a snare: but the righteous doth sing and rejoice.

7 ᴿThe righteous considereth the cause of the poor: *but* the wicked regardeth not to know *it*.

8 ᴿScornful men ᴺbring a city into a snare: but wise *men* ᴿturn away wrath.

9 *If* a wise man contendeth with a foolish man, ᴿwhether he rage or laugh, *there is* no rest.

10 ᴿTheᴺ bloodthirsty hate the upright: but the just seek his soul.

11 A ᴿfool uttereth all his mind: but a wise *man* keepeth it in till afterwards.

12 If a ruler hearken to lies, all his servants *are* wicked.

13 The poor and ᴺthe deceitful man meet together: ᴿthe LORD lighteneth both their eyes.

14 ᴿThe king that faithfully judgeth the poor, his throne shall be established for ever.

15 The rod and reproof give wisdom: but ᴿa child left *to himself* bringeth his mother to shame.

16 When the wicked are multiplied, transgression increaseth: ᴿbut the righteous shall see their fall.

17 ᴿCorrect thy son, and he shall give thee rest; yea, he shall give delight unto thy soul.

18 ᴿWhere *there is* no vision, the people ᴺperish: but ᴿhe that keepeth the law, happy *is* he.

19 A servant will not be corrected by words: for though he understand he will not answer.

20 Seest thou a man *that is* hasty ᴺin his words? ᴿ*there is* more hope of a fool than of him.

21 He that delicately bringeth up his servant from a child shall have him become *his* son at the length.

22 ᴿAn angry man stirreth up strife, and a furious man aboundeth in transgression.

23 ᴿA man's pride shall bring him low: but honour shall uphold the humble in spirit.

24 Whoso is partner with a thief hateth his own soul: ᴿhe heareth cursing, and bewrayeth *it* not.

25 ᴿThe fear of man bringeth a snare: but whoso putteth his trust in the LORD ᴺshall be safe.

26 ᴿMany seek ᴺthe ruler's favour; but *every* man's judgment *cometh* from the LORD.

27 An unjust man *is* an abomination to the just: and *he that is* upright in the way *is* abomination to the wicked.

CHAPTER 30

General observations

THE words of Ā'-gŭr the son of Jā'-kĕh, *even* the prophecy: the man spake unto Ĭ'-thĭ-ĕl, even unto Ĭ'-thĭ-ĕl and Ū'-căl,

2 ᴿSurely I *am* more brutish than *any* man, and have not the understanding of a man.

3 I neither learned wisdom, nor ᴺhave the knowledge of the holy.

4 ᴿWho hath ascended up into heaven, or descended? ᴿwho hath gathered the wind in his fists? who hath bound the waters in a garment? who hath established all the ends of the earth? what is his name, and what is his son's name, if thou canst tell?

5 ᴿEvery word of God is ᴺpure: ᴿhe is a shield unto them that put their trust in him.

6 ᴿAdd thou not unto his words, lest he reprove thee, and thou be found a liar.

7 Two things have I required of thee; ᴺdeny me them not before I die:

8 Remove far from me vanity and lies: give me neither poverty nor riches; ᴿfeed me with food ᴺconvenient for me:

9 ᴿLest I be full, and ᴺdeny thee, and say, Who is the LORD? or lest I be poor, and steal, and take the name of my God in vain.

10 ᴺAccuse not a servant unto his master, lest he curse thee, and thou be found guilty.

11 There is a generation that curseth their father, and doth not bless their mother.

12 There is a generation ᴿthat are pure in their own eyes, and yet is not washed from their filthiness.

13 There is a generation, O how ᴿlofty are their eyes! and their eyelids are lifted up.

14 ᴿThere is a generation, whose teeth are as swords, and their jaw teeth as knives, ᴿto devour the poor from off the earth, and the needy from among men.

15 The horseleach hath two daughters, crying, Give, give. There are three things that are never satisfied, yea, four things say not, ᴺIt is enough:

16 ᴿThe grave; and the barren womb; the earth that is not filled with water; and the fire that saith not, It is enough.

17 ᴿThe eye that mocketh at his father, and despiseth to obey his mother, the ravens of ᴺthe valley shall pick it out, and the young eagles shall eat it.

18 There be three things which are too wonderful for me, yea, four which I know not:

19 The way of an eagle in the air; the way of a serpent upon a rock; the way of a ship in the ᴺmidst of the sea; and the way of a man with a maid.

20 Such is the way of an adulterous woman; she eateth, and wipeth her mouth, and saith, I have done no wickedness.

21 For three things the earth is disquieted, and for four which it cannot bear:

22 ᴿFor a servant when he reigneth; and a fool when he is filled with meat;

23 For an odious woman when she is married; and an handmaid that is heir to her mistress.

24 There be four things which are little upon the earth, but they are ᴺexceeding wise:

25 ᴿThe ants are a people not strong, yet they prepare their meat in the summer;

26 ᴿThe conies are but a feeble folk, yet make they their houses in the rocks;

27 The locusts have no king, yet go they forth all of them ᴺby bands;

28 The spider taketh hold with her hands, and is in kings' palaces.

29 There be three things which go well, yea, four are comely in going:

30 A lion which is strongest among beasts, and turneth not away for any;

31 A ᴺᴺgreyhound; and he goat also; and a king, against whom there is no rising up.

32 If thou hast done foolishly in lifting up thyself, or if thou hast thought evil, ᴿlay thine hand upon thy mouth.

33 Surely the churning of milk bringeth forth butter, and the wringing of the nose bringeth forth blood: so the forcing of wrath bringeth forth strife.

CHAPTER 31

Folly of lust and strong drink

THE words of king Lemuel, the prophecy that his mother taught him.

2 What, my son? and what, ᴿthe son of my womb? and what, the son of my vows?

3 ᴿGive not thy strength unto women, nor thy ways ᴿto that which destroyeth kings.

4 ᴿIt is not for kings, O Lemuel, it is not for kings to drink wine; nor for princes strong drink:

5 ᴿLest they drink, and forget the law, and ᴺpervert the judgment ᴺof any of the afflicted.

6 ᴿGive strong drink unto him that is ready to perish, and wine unto those that be ᴺof heavy hearts.

7 Let him drink, and forget his poverty, and remember his misery no more.

Plea for the righteous

8 ᴿOpen thy mouth for the dumb in the cause of all ᴺsuch as are appointed to destruction.

9 Open thy mouth, ᴿjudge righteously, and ᴿplead the cause of the poor and needy.

The ideal wife and mother

10 ᴿWho can find a virtuous woman? for her price is far above rubies.

11 The heart of her husband doth safely trust in her, so that he shall have no need of spoil.

12 She will do him good and not evil all the days of her life.

CHAP. 30
BC 700
4 John 3:13
4 Job 38:4
Ps. 104:3
Is. 40:12
5 Ps. 12:6
5 Heb. purified
5 Ps. 18:30
6 Deut. 4:2
Rev. 22:18
7 Heb. withhold not from me
8 Mat. 6:11
8 Heb. of my allowance
9 Deut. 8:12
9 Heb. belie thee
10 Heb. Hurt not with thy tongue
12 Luke 18:11
13 Ps. 131:1
ch. 6:17
14 Job 29:17
Ps. 52:2
14 Ps. 14:4
Amos 8:4
15 Heb. Wealth
16 ch. 27:20
Hab. 2:5
17 Gen. 9:22
Lev. 20:9
ch. 20:20
& 23:22
17 Or, the brook
19 Heb. heart
22 ch. 19:10
Eccl. 10:7

Heb. wise, made wise 24
ch. 6:6, etc. 25
Ps. 104:18 26
Heb. gathered together 27
Or, horse 31
Heb. girt in the loins 31
Job 21:5 & 40:4 32
Mic. 7:16

CHAP. 31
BC 1015
Is. 49:15 2
ch. 5:9 3
Deut. 17:17 3
Neh. 13:26
ch. 7:26
Hos. 4:11
Eccl. 10:17 4
Hos. 4:11 5
Heb. alter 5
Heb. of all the sons of affliction 5
Ps. 104:15 6
Heb. bitter of soul, 6
1 Sam. 1:10
See Job 29:15, 16 8
Heb. the sons of destruction 8
Lev. 19:15 9
Deut. 1:16
Job 29:12 9
Is. 1:17
Jer. 22:16
ch. 12:4 & 18:22 & 19:14 10

13 She seeketh wool, and flax, and worketh willingly with her hands.

14 She is like the merchants' ships; she bringeth her food from afar.

15 ᴿShe riseth also while it is yet night, and ᴿgiveth meat to her household, and a portion to her maidens.

16 She considereth a field, and ᴺbuyeth it: with the fruit of her hands she planteth a vineyard.

17 She girdeth her loins with strength, and strengtheneth her arms.

18 ᴺShe perceiveth that her merchandise is good: her candle goeth not out by night.

19 She layeth her hands to the spindle, and her hands hold the distaff.

20 ᴿSheᴺ stretcheth out her hand to the poor; yea, she reacheth forth her hands to the needy.

21 She is not afraid of the snow for her household: for all her household are clothed with ᴺscarlet.

CHAP. **31**
BC 1015
15 Rom. 12:11
15 Luke 12:42
16 Heb. *taketh*
18 Heb. *She tasteth*
20 Eph. 4:28
Heb. 13:16
20 Heb. *She spreadeth*
21 Or, *double garments*

ch. 12:4	**23**
Or, *have gotten riches*	**29**

22 She maketh herself coverings of tapestry; her clothing is silk and purple.

23 ᴿHer husband is known in the gates, when he sitteth among the elders of the land.

24 She maketh fine linen, and selleth it; and delivereth girdles unto the merchant.

25 Strength and honour are her clothing; and she shall rejoice in time to come.

26 She openeth her mouth with wisdom; and in her tongue is the law of kindness.

27 She looketh well to the ways of her household, and eateth not the bread of idleness.

28 Her children arise up, and call her blessed; her husband also, and he praiseth her.

29 Many daughters ᴺhave done virtuously, but thou excellest them all.

30 Favour is deceitful, and beauty is vain: but a woman that feareth the Lᴏʀᴅ, she shall be praised.

31 Give her of the fruit of her hands; and let her own works praise her in the gates.

ECCLESIASTES

OR, THE PREACHER

An extensive investigation of life is the basis for the philosophy expressed in Ecclesiastes. Solomon is associated with this book and may himself have been the author. Some scholars suggest that it was written later by an author who impersonated Solomon. The Jews included Ecclesiastes in the "Megilloth" or books read on feast days. It was publicly read at the Feast of Tabernacles since the author's emphasis on the enjoyment of life made it appropriate reading at this annual season of rejoicing.

The author's investigation of life reflected man's ventures and failures. Although he did not develop a systematic philosophy, he carefully observed life and weighed his experiences from the human "under the sun" perspective. Although everything temporal may be enjoyed to the full, yet they are the mundane and are but for a season.

In his final deliberation the author turns Godward and concludes that all of life should be tempered by the thought of fearing God.

The content lends itself to the following outline:
I. Introduction 1:1–11
II. Temporal things in life examined 1:12–3:22
III. Economic relationship analyzed 4:1–7:29
IV. Man, limited in wisdom, should fear God 8:1–12:14

CHAPTER 1

Theme: vanity of human experience

THE words ᴿof the Preacher, the son of David, king in Jerusalem.

2 ᴿVanity of vanities, saith the Preacher, vanity of vanities; ᴿall is vanity.

3 ᴿWhat profit hath a man of all his labour which he taketh under the sun?

4 *One* generation passeth away, and *another* generation cometh: ᴿbut the earth abideth for ever.

5 ᴿThe sun also ariseth, and the sun goeth down, and ᴺhasteth to his place where he arose.

6 ᴿThe wind goeth toward the south, and turneth about unto the north; it whirleth about

CHAP. **1**
BC 977
1 ver. 12
ch. 7:27
& 12:8-10
2 Ps. 39:5, 6
& 62:9
& 144:4
ch. 12:8
2 Rom. 8:20
3 ch. 2:22
4 Ps. 104:5
& 119:90
5 Ps. 19:4-6
5 Heb. *panteth*
6 John 3:8

Ps. 104:8, 9	**7**
Jer. 5:22	
Heb. *return to go*	**7**
Prov. 27:20	**8**
ch. 3:15	**9**

continually, and the wind returneth again according to his circuits.

7 ᴿAll the rivers run into the sea; yet the sea is not full; unto the place from whence the rivers come, thither they ᴺreturn again.

8 All things are full of labour; man cannot utter it: ᴿthe eye is not satisfied with seeing, nor the ear filled with hearing.

9 ᴿThe thing that hath been, it is that which shall be; and that which is done is that which shall be done: and there is no new thing under the sun.

10 Is there any thing whereof it may be said, See, this is new? it hath been already of old time, which was before us.

11 *There is* no remembrance of former

things; neither shall there be *any* remembrance of *things* that are to come with *those* that shall come after.

Vexation of wisdom

12 [R]I the Preacher was king over Israel in Jerusalem.

13 And I gave my heart to seek and search out by wisdom concerning all *things* that are done under heaven: [R]this sore travail hath God given to the sons of man [N]to be exercised therewith.

14 I have seen all the works that are done under the sun; and, behold, all *is* vanity and vexation of spirit.

15 [R]*That which is* crooked cannot be made straight: and [N]that which is wanting cannot be numbered.

16 I communed with mine own heart, saying, Lo, I am come to great estate, and have gotten [R]more wisdom than all *they* that have been before me in Jerusalem: yea, my heart [N]had great experience of wisdom and knowledge.

17 [R]And I gave my heart to know wisdom, and to know madness and folly: I perceived that this also is vexation of spirit.

18 For [R]in much wisdom *is* much grief: and he that increaseth knowledge increaseth sorrow.

CHAPTER 2

Vanity of pleasure

I[R] SAID in mine heart, Go to now, I will prove thee with mirth, therefore enjoy pleasure: and, behold, [R]this also *is* vanity.

2 I said of laughter, *It is* mad: and of mirth, What doeth it?

3 [R]I sought in mine heart [N]to give myself unto wine, yet acquainting mine heart with wisdom; and to lay hold on folly, till I might see what *was* that good for the sons of men, which they should do under the heaven [N]all the days of their life.

4 I made me great works; I builded me houses; I planted me vineyards:

5 I made me gardens and orchards, and I planted trees in them of all *kind of* fruits:

6 I made me pools of water, to water therewith the wood that bringeth forth trees:

7 I got *me* servants and maidens, and had [N]servants born in my house; also I had great possessions of great and small cattle above all that were in Jerusalem before me:

8 [R]I gathered me also silver and gold, and the peculiar treasure of kings and of the provinces: I gat me men singers and women sing-

ers, and the delights of the sons of men, *as* [N]musical instruments, and that of all sorts.

9 So I was great, and increased more than all that were before me in Jerusalem: also my wisdom remained with me.

10 And whatsoever mine eyes desired I kept not from them, I withheld not my heart from any joy; for my heart rejoiced in all my labour: and [R]this was my portion of all my labour.

11 Then I looked on all the works that my hands had wrought, and on the labour that I had laboured to do: and, behold, all *was* [R]vanity and vexation of spirit, and *there was* no profit under the sun.

Common fate of all

12 And I turned myself to behold wisdom, [R]and madness, and folly: for what *can* the man *do* that cometh after the king? [N]*even* that which hath been already done.

13 Then I saw [N]that wisdom excelleth folly, as far as light excelleth darkness.

14 [R]The wise man's eyes *are* in his head; but the fool walketh in darkness: and I myself perceived also that [R]one event happeneth to them all.

15 Then said I in my heart, As it happeneth to the fool, so it [N]happeneth even to me; and why was I then more wise? Then I said in my heart, that this also *is* vanity.

16 For *there is* no remembrance of the wise more than of the fool for ever; seeing that which now *is* in the days to come shall all be forgotten. And how dieth the wise *man?* as the fool.

17 Therefore I hated life; because the work that is wrought under the sun *is* grievous unto me: for all *is* vanity and vexation of spirit.

Vanity of toil

18 Yea, I hated all my labour which I had [N]taken under the sun: because [R]I should leave it unto the man that shall be after me.

19 And who knoweth whether he shall be a wise *man* or a fool? yet shall he have rule over all my labour wherein I have laboured, and wherein I have shewed myself wise under the sun. This *is* also vanity.

20 Therefore I went about to cause my heart to despair of all the labour which I took under the sun.

21 For there is a man whose labour *is* in wisdom, and in knowledge, and in equity; yet to a man that hath not laboured therein shall he [N]leave it *for* his portion. This also *is* vanity and a great evil.

22 [R]For what hath man of all his labour, and

of the vexation of his heart, wherein he hath laboured under the sun?

23 For all his days *are* ^Rsorrows, and his travail grief; yea, his heart taketh not rest in the night. This is also vanity.

24 ^R*There is* nothing better for a man, *than* that he should eat and drink, and *that* he ^Nshould make his soul enjoy good in his labour. This also I saw, that it *was* from the hand of God.

25 For who can eat, or who else can hasten *hereunto*, more than I?

26 For *God* giveth to a man that *is* good ^Nin his sight wisdom, and knowledge, and joy: but to the sinner he giveth travail, to gather and to heap up, that ^Rhe may give to *him that is* good before God. This also *is* vanity and vexation of spirit.

CHAPTER 3

A season for all things

To every *thing there is* a season, and a ^Rtime to every purpose under the heaven:

2 A time ^Nto be born, and ^Ra time to die; a time to plant, and a time to pluck up *that which is* planted;

3 A time to kill, and a time to heal; a time to break down, and a time to build up;

4 A time to weep, and a time to laugh; a time to mourn, and a time to dance;

5 A time to cast away stones, and a time to gather stones together; a time to embrace, and ^Ra time ^Nto refrain from embracing;

6 A time to ^Nget, and a time to lose; a time to keep, and a time to cast away;

7 A time to rend, and a time to sew; ^Ra time to keep silence, and a time to speak;

8 A time to love, and a time to ^Rhate; a time of war, and a time of peace.

9 ^RWhat profit hath he that worketh in that wherein he laboureth?

God's eternity

10 ^RI have seen the travail, which God hath given to the sons of men to be exercised in it.

11 He hath made every *thing* beautiful in his time: also he hath set the world in their heart, so that ^Rno man can find out the work that God maketh from the beginning to the end.

12 I know that *there is* no good in them, but for *a man* to rejoice, and to do good in his life.

13 And also ^Rthat every man should eat and drink, and enjoy the good of all his labour, it *is* the gift of God.

14 I know that, whatsoever God doeth, it shall be for ever: ^Rnothing can be put to it, nor

---

---

any thing taken from it: and God doeth *it*, that *men* should fear before him.

15 ^RThat which hath been is now; and that which is to be hath already been; and God requireth ^Nthat which is past.

Man's destiny

16 And moreover ^RI saw under the sun the place of judgment, *that* wickedness *was* there; and the place of righteousness, *that* iniquity *was* there.

17 I said in mine heart, ^RGod shall judge the righteous and the wicked: for *there is* ^Ra time there for every purpose and for every work.

18 I said in mine heart concerning the estate of the sons of men, ^Nthat God might manifest them, and that they might see that they themselves are beasts.

19 ^RFor that which befalleth the sons of men befalleth beasts; even one thing befalleth them: as the one dieth, so dieth the other; yea, they have all one breath; so that a man hath no preeminence above a beast: for all *is* vanity.

20 All go unto one place; ^Rall are of the dust, and all turn to dust again.

21 ^RWho knoweth the spirit ^Nof man that ^Ngoeth upward, and the spirit of the beast that goeth downward to the earth?

22 ^RWherefore I perceive that *there is* nothing better, than that a man should rejoice in his own works; for ^Rthat *is* his portion: ^Rfor who shall bring him to see what shall be after him?

CHAPTER 4

Disappointments of life

So I returned, and considered all the ^Roppressions that are done under the sun: and behold the tears of *such as were* oppressed, and they had no comforter; and on the ^Nside of their oppressors *there was* power; but they had no comforter.

2 ^RWherefore I praised the dead which are already dead more than the living which are yet alive.

3 ^RYea, better *is* he than both they, which hath not yet been, who hath not seen the evil work that is done under the sun.

4 Again, I considered all travail, and ^Nevery right work, that ^Nfor this a man is envied of his neighbour. This *is* also vanity and vexation of spirit.

5 ^RThe fool foldeth his hands together, and eateth his own flesh.

6 ^RBetter *is* an handful *with* quietness, than both the hands full *with* travail and vexation of spirit.

7 Then I returned, and I saw vanity under the sun.

8 There is one *alone,* and *there is* not a second; yea, he hath neither child nor brother: yet *is there* no end of all his labour; neither is his ᴿeye satisfied with riches; ᴿneither *saith he,* For whom do I labour, and bereave my soul of good? This *is* also vanity, yea, it *is* a sore travail.

9 Two *are* better than one; because they have a good reward for their labour.

10 For if they fall, the one will lift up his fellow: but woe to him *that is* alone when he falleth; for *he hath* not another to help him up.

11 Again, if two lie together, then they have heat: but how can one be warm *alone?*

12 And if one prevail against him, two shall withstand him; and a threefold cord is not quickly broken.

The wise and the foolish

13 Better *is* a poor and a wise child than an old and foolish king, ᴺwho will no more be admonished.

14 For out of prison he cometh to reign; whereas also *he that is* born in his kingdom becometh poor.

15 I considered all the living which walk under the sun, with the second child that shall stand up in his stead.

16 *There is* no end of all the people, *even* of all that have been before them: they also that come after shall not rejoice in him. Surely this also *is* vanity and vexation of spirit.

CHAPTER 5

KEEP ᴿthy foot when thou goest to the house of God, and be more ready to hear, ᴿthan to give the sacrifice of fools: for they consider not that they do evil.

2 Be not rash with thy mouth, and let not thine heart be hasty to utter *any* ᴺthing before God: for God *is* in heaven, and thou upon earth: therefore let thy words ᴿbe few.

3 For a dream cometh through the multitude of business; and ᴿa fool's voice *is known* by multitude of words.

4 ᴿWhen thou vowest a vow unto God, defer not to pay it; for *he hath* no pleasure in fools: pay that which thou hast vowed.

5 ᴿBetter *is* it that thou shouldest not vow, than that thou shouldest vow and not pay.

6 Suffer not thy mouth to cause thy flesh to sin; ᴿneither say thou before the angel, that it *was* an error: wherefore should God be angry at thy voice, and destroy the work of thine hands?

7 For in the multitude of dreams and many words *there are* also *divers* vanities: but ᴿfear thou God.

Vanity of wealth

8 If thou ᴿseest the oppression of the poor, and violent perverting of judgment and justice in a province, marvel not ᴺat the matter: for ᴿhe that is higher than the highest regardeth; and *there be* higher than they.

9 Moreover the profit of the earth is for all: the king *himself* is served by the field.

10 He that loveth silver shall not be satisfied with silver; nor he that loveth abundance with increase: this *is* also vanity.

11 When goods increase, they are increased that eat them: and what good *is there* to the owners thereof, saving the beholding *of them* with their eyes?

12 The sleep of a labouring man *is* sweet, whether he eat little or much: but the abundance of the rich will not suffer him to sleep.

13 ᴿThere is a sore evil *which* I have seen under the sun, *namely,* riches kept for the owners thereof to their hurt.

14 But those riches perish by evil travail: and he begetteth a son, and *there is* nothing in his hand.

15 ᴿAs he came forth of his mother's womb, naked shall he return to go as he came, and shall take nothing of his labour, which he may carry away in his hand.

16 And this also *is* a sore evil, *that* in all points as he came, so shall he go: and ᴿwhat profit hath he ᴿthat hath laboured for the wind?

17 All his days also ᴿhe eateth in darkness, and *he hath* much sorrow and wrath with his sickness.

Joy of heart

18 Behold *that* which I have seen: ᴿ*it*ᴺ *is* good and comely *for one* to eat and to drink, and to enjoy the good of all his labour that he taketh under the sun ᴺall the days of his life, which God giveth him: ᴿfor it *is* his portion.

19 ᴿEvery man also to whom God hath given riches and wealth, and hath given him power to eat thereof, and to take his portion, and to rejoice in his labour; this *is* the gift of God.

20 ᴺFor he shall not much remember the days of his life; because God answereth *him* in the joy of his heart.

CHAPTER 6

THERE ᴿ is an evil which I have seen under the sun, and it *is* common among men:

2 A man to whom God hath given riches, wealth, and honour, [R]so that he wanteth nothing for his soul of all that he desireth, [R]yet God giveth him not power to eat thereof, but a stranger eateth it: this *is* vanity, and it *is* an evil disease.

3 If a man beget an hundred *children,* and live many years, so that the days of his years be many, and his soul be not filled with good, and [R]also *that* he have no burial; I say, *that* [R]an untimely birth *is* better than he.

4 For he cometh in with vanity, and departeth in darkness, and his name shall be covered with darkness.

5 Moreover he hath not seen the sun, nor known *any thing:* this hath more rest than the other.

6 Yea, though he live a thousand years twice *told,* yet hath he seen no good: do not all go to one place?

7 [R]All the labour of man *is* for his mouth, and yet the [N]appetite is not filled.

8 For what hath the wise more than the fool? what hath the poor, that knoweth to walk before the living?

9 Better *is* the sight of the eyes [N]than the wandering of the desire: this *is* also vanity and vexation of spirit.

10 That which hath been is named already, and it is known that it *is* man: [R]neither may he contend with him that is mightier than he.

11 Seeing there be many things that increase vanity, what *is* man the better?

12 For who knoweth what *is* good for man in *this* life, [N]all the days of his vain life which he spendeth as [R]a shadow? for [R]who can tell a man what shall be after him under the sun?

CHAPTER 7

Wisdom and folly compared

A[R] GOOD name *is* better than precious ointment; and the day of death than the day of one's birth.

2 *It is* better to go to the house of mourning, than to go to the house of feasting: for that *is* the end of all men; and the living will lay *it* to his heart.

3 [N]Sorrow *is* better than laughter: [R]for by the sadness of the countenance the heart is made better.

4 The heart of the wise *is* in the house of mourning; but the heart of fools *is* in the house of mirth.

5 [R]*It is* better to hear the rebuke of the wise, than for a man to hear the song of fools.

6 [R]For as the [N]crackling of thorns under a pot, so *is* the laughter of the fool: this also *is* vanity.

7 Surely oppression maketh a wise man mad; [R]and a gift destroyeth the heart.

8 Better *is* the end of a thing than the beginning thereof: *and* [R]the patient in spirit *is* better than the proud in spirit.

9 [R]Be not hasty in thy spirit to be angry: for anger resteth in the bosom of fools.

10 Say not thou, What is *the cause* that the former days were better than these? for thou dost not inquire [N]wisely concerning this.

11 Wisdom *is* [N]good with an inheritance: and *by it there is* profit [R]to them that see the sun.

12 For wisdom *is* a [N]defence, *and* money *is* a defence: but the excellency of knowledge *is, that* wisdom giveth life to them that have it.

God baffles our wisdom

13 Consider the work of God: for [R]who can make *that* straight, which he hath made crooked?

14 [R]In the day of prosperity be joyful, but in the day of adversity consider: God also hath [N]set the one over against the other, to the end that man should find nothing after him.

15 All *things* have I seen in the days of my vanity: [R]there is a just *man* that perisheth in his righteousness, and there is a wicked *man* that prolongeth *his life* in his wickedness.

16 [R]Be not righteous over much; [R]neither make thyself over wise: why shouldest thou [N]destroy thyself?

17 Be not over much wicked, neither be thou foolish: [R]why shouldest thou die [N]before thy time?

18 *It is* good that thou shoudest take hold of this; yea, also from this withdraw not thine hand: for he that feareth God shall come forth of them all.

19 [R]Wisdom strengtheneth the wise more than ten mighty *men* which are in the city.

20 [R]For *there is* not a just man upon earth, that doeth good, and sinneth not.

21 Also [N]take no heed unto all words that are spoken; lest thou hear thy servant curse thee:

22 For oftentimes also thine own heart knoweth that thou thyself likewise hast cursed others.

23 All this have I proved by wisdom: [R]I said, I will be wise; but it *was* far from me.

24 [R]That which is far off, and [R]exceeding deep, who can find it out?

25 [R]I[N] applied mine heart to know, and to search, and to seek out wisdom, and the reason *of things,* and to know the wickedness of folly, even of foolishness *and* madness:

26 [R]And I find more bitter than death the woman, whose heart *is* snares and nets, *and*

CHAP. **6**
BC 977
2 Job 21:10, etc.
Ps. 17:14 & 73:7
2 Luke 12:20
3 2 Ki. 9:35
Is. 14:19, 20
Jer. 22:19
3 Job 3:16
Ps. 58:8
ch. 4:3
7 Prov. 16:26
7 Heb. *soul*
9 Heb. *than the walking of the soul*
10 Job 9:32
Is. 45:9
Jer. 49:19
12 Heb. *the number of the days of the life of his vanity*
12 Ps. 102:11 & 144:4
Jas. 4:14
12 Ps. 39:6
ch. 8:7

CHAP. **7**
BC 977
1 Prov. 22:1
3 Or, *Anger*
3 2 Cor. 7:10
5 Ps. 141:5
Prov. 15:31
6 ch. 2:2
6 Heb. *sound*

Ex. 23:8   7
Deut. 16:19
Prov. 14:29   8
Prov. 14:17   9
Jas. 1:19
Heb. *out*   10
of wisdom
Or, *as good*   11
as an inheritance,
yea, better too
ch. 11:7   11
Heb. *shadow*   12
Job 12:14   13
ch. 1:15
Deut. 28:47   14
Heb. *made*   14
ch. 8:14   15
Prov. 25:16   16
Rom. 12:3   16
Heb. *be*   16
desolate?
Job 15:32   17
Ps. 55:23
Heb. *not*   17
in thy time?
Prov. 21:22   19
ch. 9:16, 18
1 Ki. 8:46   20
1 John 1:8
Heb. *give not*   21
thine heart
Rom. 1:22   23
Job 28:12   24
1 Tim. 6:16
Rom. 11:33   24
ch. 1:17   25
Heb. *I and*   25
my heart
compassed
Prov. 5:3, 4   26

her hands *as* bands: ᴺwhoso pleaseth God shall escape from her; but the sinner shall be taken by her.

27 Behold, this have I found, saith ᴿthe preacher, ᴺ*counting* one by one, to find out the account:

28 Which yet my soul seeketh, but I find not: ᴿone man among a thousand have I found; but a woman among all those have I not found.

29 Lo, this only have I found, ᴿthat God hath made man upright; but ᴿthey have sought out many inventions.

CHAPTER 8

Obedience to rulers

WHO *is* as the wise *man?* and who knoweth the interpretation of a thing? ᴿa man's wisdom maketh his face to shine, and ᴿtheᴺ boldness of his face shall be changed.

2 I *counsel thee* to keep the king's commandment, ᴿand *that* in regard of the oath of God.

3 ᴿBe not hasty to go out of his sight: stand not in an evil thing; for he doeth whatsoever pleaseth him.

4 Where the word of a king *is, there is* power: and ᴿwho may say unto him, What doest thou?

5 Whoso keepeth the commandment ᴺshall feel no evil thing: and a wise man's heart discerneth both time and judgment.

6 Because ᴿto every purpose there is time and judgment, therefore the misery of man *is* great upon him.

7 ᴿFor he knoweth not that which shall be: for who can tell him ᴺwhen it shall be?

8 ᴿ*There is* no man that hath power over the spirit to retain the spirit; neither *hath he* power in the day of death: and *there is* no ᴺdischarge in *that* war; neither shall wickedness deliver those that are given to it.

9 All this have I seen, and applied my heart unto every work that is done under the sun: *there is* a time wherein one man ruleth over another to his own hurt.

Vanity of wickedness

10 And so I saw the wicked buried, who had come and gone from the place of the holy, and they were forgotten in the city where they had so done: this *is* also vanity.

11 ᴿBecause sentence against an evil work is not executed speedily, therefore the heart of the sons of men is fully set in them to do evil.

12 ᴿThough a sinner do evil an hundred times, and his *days* be prolonged, yet surely I know that ᴿit shall be well with them that fear God, which fear before him:

13 But it shall not be well with the wicked, neither shall he prolong *his* days, *which are* as a shadow; because he feareth not before God.

14 There is a vanity which is done upon the earth; that there be just *men,* unto whom it ᴿhappeneth according to the work of the wicked; again, there be wicked *men,* to whom it happeneth according to the work of the righteous: I said that this also *is* vanity.

15 ᴿThen I commended mirth, because a man hath no better thing under the sun, than to eat, and to drink, and to be merry: for that shall abide with him of his labour the days of his life, which God giveth him under the sun.

Hidden purposes of God

16 When I applied mine heart to know wisdom, and to see the business that is done upon the earth: (for also *there is that* neither day nor night seeth sleep with his eyes:)

17 Then I beheld all the work of God, that ᴿa man cannot find out the work that is done under the sun: because though a man labour to seek *it* out, yet he shall not find *it;* yea further; though a wise *man* think to know *it,* yet shall he not be able to find *it.*

CHAPTER 9

Inequalities of life

FOR all this ᴺI considered in my heart even to declare all this, ᴿthat the righteous, and the wise, and their works, *are* in the hand of God: no man knoweth either love or hatred *by* all *that is* before them.

2 ᴿAll *things come* alike to all: *there is* one event to the righteous, and to the wicked; to the good and to the clean, and to the unclean; to him that sacrificeth, and to him that sacrificeth not: as *is* the good, so *is* the sinner; *and* he that sweareth, as *he* that feareth an oath.

3 This *is* an evil among all *things* that are done under the sun, that *there is* one event unto all: yea, also the heart of the sons of men is full of evil, and madness *is* in their heart while they live, and after that *they go* to the dead.

4 For to him that is joined to all the living there is hope: for a living dog is better than a dead lion.

5 For the living know that they shall die: but ᴿthe dead know not any thing, neither have they any more a reward; for ᴿthe memory of them is forgotten.

6 Also their love, and their hatred, and their envy, is now perished; neither have they any more a portion for ever in any *thing* that is done under the sun.

CHAP. **7**
BC 977
26 Heb. he that is *good before God*
27 ch. 1:1, 2
27 Or, weighing *one thing after another, to find out the reason*
28 Job 33:23
29 Gen. 1:27
29 Gen. 3:6, 7

CHAP. **8**
BC 977
1 Prov. 4:8, 9
Acts 6:15
1 Deut. 28:50
1 Heb. *the strength*
2 1 Chr. 29:24
Ezek. 17:18
3 ch. 10:4
4 Job 34:18
5 Heb. *shall know*
6 ch. 3:1
7 Prov. 24:22
ch. 6:12 & 9:12 & 10:14
7 Or, *how it shall be?*
8 Ps. 49:6, 7
8 Or, *casting off* weapons
11 Ps. 10:6 & 50:21
Is. 26:10
12 Is. 65:20
Rom. 2:5
12 Ps. 37:11, 18, 19
Prov. 1:32, 33
Is. 3:10, 11
Mat. 25:34, 41

Ps. 73:14   14
ch. 2:14 & 7:15 & 9:1-3
ch. 2:24 &   15
3:12, 22 & 5:18 & 9:7
Job 5:9   17
ch. 3:11
Rom. 11:33

CHAP. **9**
BC 977
Heb. *I gave,*   1
or, *set to my heart*
ch. 8:14   1
Job 21:7, etc.   2
Ps. 73:3, 12, 13
Mal. 3:15
Job 14:21   5
Is. 63:16
Job 7:8-10   5
Is. 26:14

7 Go thy way, ^Reat thy bread with joy, and drink thy wine with a merry heart; for God now accepteth thy works.

8 Let thy garments be always white; and let thy head lack no ointment.

9 ^NLive joyfully with the wife whom thou lovest all the days of the life of thy vanity, which he hath given thee under the sun, all the days of thy vanity: ^Rfor that *is* thy portion in *this* life, and in thy labour which thou takest under the sun.

10 Whatsoever thy hand findeth to do, do *it* with thy might; for *there is* no work, nor device, nor knowledge, nor wisdom, in the grave, whither thou goest.

11 I returned, ^Rand saw under the sun, that the race *is* not to the swift, nor the battle to the strong, neither yet bread to the wise, nor yet riches to men of understanding, nor yet favour to men of skill; but time and chance happeneth to them all.

12 For ^Rman also knoweth not his time: as the fishes that are taken in an evil net, and as the birds that are caught in the snare; so *are* the sons of men ^Rsnared in an evil time, when it falleth suddenly upon them.

Excellence of wisdom

13 This wisdom have I seen also under the sun, and it *seemed* great unto me:

14 ^R*There was* a little city, and few men within it; and there came a great king against it, and besieged it, and built great bulwarks against it:

15 Now there was found in it a poor wise man, and he by his wisdom delivered the city; yet no man remembered that same poor man.

16 ^RThen said I, Wisdom *is* better than strength: nevertheless ^Rthe poor man's wisdom *is* despised, and his words are not heard.

17 The words of wise *men are* heard in quiet more than the cry of him that ruleth among fools.

18 ^RWisdom *is* better than weapons of war: but ^Rone sinner destroyeth much good.

CHAPTER 10

Various proverbs

D EAD ^Nflies cause the ointment of the apothecary to send forth a stinking savour: *so doth* a little folly him that is in reputation for wisdom *and* honour.

2 A wise man's heart *is* at his right hand; but a fool's heart at his left.

3 Yea also, when he that is a fool walketh by the way, ^Nhis wisdom faileth *him,* ^Rand he saith to every one *that* he *is* a fool.

4 If the spirit of the ruler rise up against

---

thee, ^Rleave not thy place; for ^Ryielding pacifieth great offences.

5 There is an evil *which* I have seen under the sun, as an error *which* proceedeth ^Nfrom the ruler:

6 ^RFolly is set ^Nin great dignity, and the rich sit in low place.

7 I have seen servants ^Rupon horses, and princes walking as servants upon the earth.

8 ^RHe that diggeth a pit shall fall into it; and whoso breaketh an hedge, a serpent shall bite him.

9 Whoso removeth stones shall be hurt therewith; *and* he that cleaveth wood shall be endangered thereby.

10 If the iron be blunt, and he do not whet the edge, then must he put to more strength: but wisdom *is* profitable to direct.

11 Surely the serpent will bite ^Rwithout enchantment; and ^Na babbler is no better.

12 ^RThe words of a wise man's mouth *are* ^Ngracious; but ^Rthe lips of a fool will swallow up himself.

13 The beginning of the words of his mouth *is* foolishness: and the end of ^Nhis talk *is* mischievous madness.

14 ^RA fool also ^Nis full of words: a man cannot tell what shall be; and ^Rwhat shall be after him, who can tell him?

15 The labour of the foolish wearieth every one of them, because he knoweth not how to go to the city.

16 ^RWoe to thee, O land, when thy king *is* a child, and thy princes eat in the morning!

17 Blessed *art* thou, O land, when thy king *is* the son of nobles, and ^Rthy princes eat in due season, for strength, and not for drunkenness!

18 By much slothfulness the building decayeth; and through idleness of the hands the house droppeth through.

19 A feast is made for laughter, and ^Rwine ^Nmaketh merry: but money answereth all *things*.

20 ^RCurse not the king, no not in thy ^Nthought; and curse not the rich in thy bedchamber: for a bird of the air shall carry the voice, and that which hath wings shall tell the matter.

CHAPTER 11

Stewardship advice

C AST thy bread ^Rupon^N the waters: ^Rfor thou shalt find it after many days.

2 ^RGive a portion ^Rto seven, and also to eight; ^Rfor thou knowest not what evil shall be upon the earth.

3 If the clouds be full of rain, they empty

themselves upon the earth: and if the tree fall toward the south, or toward the north, in the place where the tree falleth, there it shall be.

4 He that observeth the wind shall not sow; and he that regardeth the clouds shall not reap.

5 As ᴿthou knowest not what *is* the way of the spirit, ᴿnor how the bones *do grow* in the womb of her that is with child: even so thou knowest not the works of God who maketh all.

6 In the morning sow thy seed, and in the evening withhold not thine hand: for thou knowest not whether ᴺshall prosper, either this or that, or whether they both *shall be* alike good.

7 Truly the light *is* sweet, and a pleasant *thing it is* for the eyes ᴿto behold the sun:

8 But if a man live many years, *and* rejoice in them all; yet let him remember the days of darkness; for they shall be many. All that cometh *is* vanity.

Advice for youth

9 Rejoice, O young man, in thy youth; and let thy heart cheer thee in the days of thy youth, ᴿand walk in the ways of thine heart, and in the sight of thine eyes: but know thou, that for all these *things* ᴿGod will bring thee into judgment.

10 Therefore remove ᴺsorrow from thy heart, and ᴿput away evil from thy flesh: ᴿfor childhood and youth *are* vanity.

CHAPTER 12

REMEMBER ᴿnow thy Creator in the days of thy youth, while the evil days come not, nor the years draw nigh, ᴿwhen thou shalt say, I have no pleasure in them;

2 While the sun, or the light, or the moon, or the stars, be not darkened, nor the clouds return after the rain:

3 In the day when the keepers of the house shall tremble, and the strong men shall bow

themselves, and ᴺthe grinders cease because they are few, and those that look out of the windows be darkened,

4 And the doors shall be shut in the streets, when the sound of the grinding is low, and he shall rise up at the voice of the bird, and all ᴿthe daughters of musick shall be brought low;

5 Also *when* they shall be afraid of *that which is* high, and fears *shall be* in the way, and the almond tree shall flourish, and the grasshopper shall be a burden, and desire shall fail: because man goeth to ᴿhis long home, and ᴿthe mourners go about the streets:

6 Or ever the silver cord be loosed, or the golden bowl be broken, or the pitcher be broken at the fountain, or the wheel broken at the cistern.

7 ᴿThen shall the dust return to the earth as it was: ᴿand the spirit shall return unto God ᴿwho gave it.

8 ᴿVanity of vanities, saith the preacher; all *is* vanity.

The whole duty of man

9 And moreover, because the preacher was wise, he still taught the people knowledge; yea, he gave good heed, and sought out, *and* ᴿset in order many proverbs.

10 The preacher sought to find out ᴺacceptable words: and *that which was* written *was* upright, *even* words of truth.

11 The words of the wise *are* as goads, and as nails fastened *by* the masters of assemblies, *which* are given from one shepherd.

12 And further, by these, my son, be admonished: of making many books *there is* no end; and ᴿmuch ᴺstudy *is* a weariness of the flesh.

13 ᴺLet us hear the conclusion of the whole matter: ᴿFear God, and keep his commandments: for this *is* the whole *duty* of man.

14 For ᴿGod shall bring every work into judgment, with every secret thing, whether *it be* good, or whether *it be* evil.

THE
SONG OF SOLOMON

The opening statement in the Hebrew text, "the song of songs which is Solomon's" suggests that this may have been the best of the 1005 songs credited to this king of Israel (I Kings 4:32). The name "canticles" is derived from the Latin version.

The love relationship between man and woman is portrayed in this book. The king unsuccessfully woos the Shulamite maiden who yearns for her former lover despite the choral appeals of the court women. Ultimately, she leaves the palace to return to her shepherd lover.

The Israelites read this book annually at the Passover Feast to remind them of God's love for his people. Note the marital love between God and Israel in Is. 50:1; 54:4-5; Jer. 3:1-20; Ezekiel 16 and 23, and Hosea 1-3. This divine-human relation-

ship is emphasized in the New Testament in Mat. 9:15; John 3:29; II Cor. 11:21; Eph. 5:23-32; Rev. 9:7; 21:2, 9; 22:17.

Note the following outline:

CHAPTER 1

THE ᴿsong of songs, which *is* Solomon's.

Longing of the royal bride

2 Let him kiss me with the kisses of his mouth: ᴿfor ᴺthy love *is* better than wine.

3 Because of the savour of thy good ointments thy name *is as* ointment poured forth, therefore do the virgins love thee.

4 ᴿDraw me, ᴿwe will run after thee: the king ᴿhath brought me into his chambers: we will be glad and rejoice in thee, we will remember thy love more than wine: ᴺthe upright love thee.

5 I *am* black, but comely, O ye daughters of Jerusalem, as the tents of Kē'-där, as the curtains of Solomon.

6 Look not upon me, because I *am* black, because the sun hath looked upon me: my mother's children were angry with me; they made me the keeper of the vineyards; *but* mine own vineyard have I not kept.

7 Tell me, O thou whom my soul loveth, where thou feedest, where thou makest *thy flock* to rest at noon: for why should I be ᴺas one that turneth aside by the flocks of thy companions?

8 If thou know not, ᴿO thou fairest among women, go thy way forth by the footsteps of the flock, and feed thy kids beside the shepherds' tents.

The bride and the bridegroom meet

9 I have compared thee, ᴿO my love, ᴿto a company of horses in Pharaoh's chariots.

10 ᴿThy cheeks are comely with rows *of jewels,* thy neck with chains *of gold.*

11 We will make thee borders of gold with studs of silver.

12 While the king *sitteth* at his table, my spikenard sendeth forth the smell thereof.

13 A bundle of myrrh *is* my wellbeloved unto me; he shall lie all night betwixt my breasts.

14 My beloved *is* unto me *as* a cluster of ᴺcamphire in the vineyards of Ĕn-ġē'-dī.

15 ᴿBehold, thou *art* fair, ᴺmy love; behold, thou *art* fair; thou *hast* doves' eyes.

16 Behold, thou *art* fair, my beloved, yea, pleasant: also our bed *is* green.

CHAP. 1
BC 1014

1 1 Ki. 4:32
2 ch. 4:10
2 Heb. *thy loves*
4 Hos. 11:4
John 6:44
& 12:32
4 Phil. 3:12-14
4 Ps. 45:14, 15
John 14:2
Eph. 2:6
4 Or, *they love thee uprightly*
7 Or, *as one that is veiled*
8 ch. 5:9
9 ch. 2:2, 10, 13 & 4:1, 7
John 15:14
9 2 Chr. 1:16
10 Ezek. 16:11
14 Or, *cypress,* ch. 4:13
15 ch. 4:1 & 5:12
15 Or, *my companion*

Or, *galleries*   17

CHAP. 2
BC 1014

Heb. *I delighted and sat down, etc.*   3
Rev. 22:1, 2   3
Heb. *palate*   3
Heb. *house of wine*   4
Heb. *straw me with apples*   5
ch. 8:3   6
ch. 3:5 & 8:4   7
Heb. *I adjure you*   7
ver. 17   9
Heb. *flourishing*   9
ver. 13   10
ver. 10   13
ch. 8:13   14
Ps. 80:13   15
Ezek. 13:4
Luke 13:32

---

17 The beams of our house *are* cedar, *and* our ᴺrafters of fir.

CHAPTER 2

I AM the rose of Shär'-on, *and* the lily of the valleys.

2 As the lily among thorns, so *is* my love among the daughters.

3 As the apple tree among the trees of the wood, so *is* my beloved among the sons. ᴺI sat down under his shadow with great delight, ᴿand his fruit *was* sweet to my ᴺtaste.

4 He brought me to the ᴺbanqueting house, and his banner over me *was* love.

5 Stay me with flagons, ᴺcomfort me with apples: for I *am* sick of love.

6 ᴿHis left hand *is* under my head, and his right hand doth embrace me.

7 ᴿIᴺ charge you, O ye daughters of Jerusalem, by the roes, and by the hinds of the field, that ye stir not up, nor awake *my* love, till he please.

She praises her beloved

8 The voice of my beloved! behold, he cometh leaping upon the mountains, skipping upon the hills.

9 ᴿMy beloved is like a roe or a young hart: behold, he standeth behind our wall, he looketh forth at the windows, ᴺshewing himself through the lattice.

10 My beloved spake, and said unto me, ᴿRise up, my love, my fair one, and come away.

11 For, lo, the winter is past, the rain is over *and* gone;

12 The flowers appear on the earth; the time of the singing *of birds* is come, and the voice of the turtle is heard in our land;

13 The fig tree putteth forth her green figs, and the vines *with* the tender grape give a *good* smell. ᴿArise, my love, my fair one, and come away.

14 O my dove, *that art* in the clefts of the rock, in the secret *places* of the stairs, let me see thy countenance, ᴿlet me hear thy voice; for sweet *is* thy voice, and thy countenance *is* comely.

15 Take us ᴿthe foxes, the little foxes, that spoil the vines: for our vines *have* tender grapes.

16 [R]My beloved *is* mine, and I *am* his: he feedeth among the lilies.

17 [R]Until the day break, and the shadows flee away, turn, my beloved, and be thou [R]like a roe or a young hart upon the mountains [N]of Bether.

CHAPTER 3

Her thoughts in the night

BY [R]night on my bed I sought him whom my soul loveth: I sought him, but I found him not.

2 I will rise now, and go about the city in the streets, and in the broad ways I will seek him whom my soul loveth: I sought him, but I found him not.

3 [R]The watchmen that go about the city found me: *to whom I said,* Saw ye him whom my soul loveth?

4 *It was* but a little that I passed from them, but I found him whom my soul loveth: I held him, and would not let him go, until I had brought him into my mother's house, and into the chamber of her that conceived me.

5 [R]I charge you, O ye daughters of Jerusalem, by the roes, and by the hinds of the field, that ye stir not up, nor awake *my* love, till he please.

Return of the bridegroom

6 [R]Who *is* this that cometh out of the wilderness like pillars of smoke, perfumed with myrrh and frankincense, with all powders of the merchant?

7 Behold his bed, which *is* Solomon's; threescore valiant men *are* about it, of the valiant of Israel.

8 They all hold swords, *being* expert in war: every man *hath* his sword upon his thigh because of fear in the night.

9 King Solomon made himself [N]a chariot of the wood of Lĕb'-ă-nŏn.

10 He made the pillars thereof *of* silver, the bottom thereof *of* gold, the covering of it *of* purple, the midst thereof being paved *with* love, for the daughters of Jerusalem.

11 Go forth, O ye daughters of Zion, and behold king Solomon with the crown wherewith his mother crowned him in the day of his espousals, and in the day of the gladness of his heart.

CHAPTER 4

His praise of the bride

BEHOLD, [R]thou *art* fair, my love; behold, thou *art* fair; thou *hast* doves' eyes

within thy locks: thy hair *is* as a [R]flock of goats, [N]that appear from mount Gilead.

2 [R]Thy teeth *are* like a flock *of sheep that are even* shorn, which came up from the washing; whereof every one bear twins, and none *is* barren among them.

3 Thy lips *are* like a thread of scarlet, and thy speech *is* comely: [R]thy temples *are* like a piece of a pomegranate within thy locks.

4 [R]Thy neck *is* like the tower of David builded [R]for an armoury, whereon there hang a thousand bucklers, all shields of mighty men.

5 [R]Thy two breasts *are* like two young roes that are twins, which feed among the lilies.

6 [R]Until the day [N]break, and the shadows flee away, I will get me to the mountain of myrrh, and to the hill of frankincense.

7 [R]Thou *art* all fair, my love; *there is* no spot in thee.

The true lover's plea

8 Come with me from Lĕb'-ă-nŏn, *my* spouse, with me from Lĕb'-ă-nŏn: look from the top of Ă-ma'-nă, from the top of Shē'-nĭr [R]and Hĕr'-mŏn, from the lions' dens, from the mountains of the leopards.

9 Thou hast [N]ravished my heart, my sister, *my* spouse; thou hast ravished my heart with one of thine eyes, with one chain of thy neck.

10 How fair is thy love, my sister, *my* spouse! [R]how much better is thy love than wine! and the smell of thine ointments than all spices!

11 Thy lips, O *my* spouse, drop *as* the honeycomb: [R]honey and milk *are* under thy tongue; and the smell of thy garments *is* [R]like the smell of Lĕb'-ă-nŏn.

12 A garden [N]inclosed *is* my sister, *my* spouse; a spring shut up, a fountain sealed.

13 Thy plants *are* an orchard of pomegranates, with pleasant fruits; [N]camphire, with spikenard,

14 Spikenard and saffron; calamus and cinnamon, with all trees of frankincense; myrrh and aloes, with all the chief spices:

15 A fountain of gardens, a well of [R]living waters, and streams from Lĕb'-ă-nŏn.

16 Awake, O north wind; and come, thou south; blow upon my garden, *that* the spices thereof may flow out. [R]Let my beloved come into his garden, and eat his pleasant fruits.

CHAPTER 5

I [R]AM come into my garden, my sister, *my* spouse: I have gathered my myrrh with my spice; [R]I have eaten my honeycomb with my honey; I have drunk my wine with my milk:

CHAP. 2
BC 1014
16 ch. 6:3
17 ch. 4:6
17 ver. 9
ch. 8:14
17 Or, *of division*

CHAP. 3
BC 1014
1 Is. 26:9
3 ch. 5:7
5 ch. 2:7
& 8:4
6 ch. 8:5
9 Or, *a bed*

CHAP. 4
BC 1014
1 ch. 1:15
& 5:12

ch. 6:5 | 1
Or, *that eat of, etc.* | 1
ch. 6:6 | 2
ch. 6:7 | 3
ch. 7:4 | 4
Neh. 3:19 | 4
See Prov. 5:19 | 5
ch. 7:3 |
ch. 2:17 | 6
Heb. *breathe* | 6
Eph. 5:27 | 7
Deut. 3:9 | 8
Or, *taken away my heart* | 9
ch. 1:2 | 10
Prov. 24:13, 14 | 11
ch. 5:1 |
Gen. 27:27 | 11
Hos. 14:6, 7 |
Heb. *barred* | 12
Or, *cypress* | 13
John 4:10 | 15
& 7:38 |
ch. 5:1 | 16

CHAP. 5
BC 1014
ch. 4:16 | 1
ch. 4:11 | 1

eat, O ᴿfriends; drink, ᴺyea, drink abundantly, O beloved.

Her troubled dream

2 I sleep, but my heart waketh: *it is* the voice of my beloved ᴿthat knocketh, *saying,* Open to me, my sister, my love, my dove, my undefiled: for my head is filled with dew, *and* my locks with the drops of the night.

3 I have put off my coat; how shall I put it on? I have washed my feet; how shall I defile them?

4 My beloved put in his hand by the hole *of the door,* and my bowels were moved ᴺfor him.

5 I rose up to open to my beloved; and my hands dropped *with* myrrh, and my fingers *with* ᴺsweet smelling myrrh, upon the handles of the lock.

6 I opened to my beloved; but my beloved had withdrawn himself, *and* was gone: my soul failed when he spake: ᴿI sought him, but I could not find him; I called him, but he gave me no answer.

7 ᴿThe watchmen that went about the city found me, they smote me, they wounded me; the keepers of the walls took away my veil from me.

8 I charge you, O daughters of Jerusalem, if ye find my beloved, ᴺthat ye tell him, that I *am* sick of love.

9 What *is* thy beloved more than *another* beloved, ᴿO thou fairest among women? what *is* thy beloved more than *another* beloved, that thou dost so charge us?

10 My beloved *is* white and ruddy, ᴺthe chiefest among ten thousand.

11 His head *is as* the most fine gold, his locks *are* ᴺbushy, *and* black as a raven.

12 ᴿHis eyes *are as the eyes* of doves by the rivers of waters, washed with milk, *and* ᴺfitly set.

13 His cheeks *are as* a bed of spices, *as* ᴺsweet flowers: his lips *like* lilies, dropping sweet smelling myrrh.

14 His hands *are as* gold rings set with the beryl: his belly *is as* bright ivory overlaid *with* sapphires.

15 His legs *are as* pillars of marble, set upon sockets of fine gold: his countenance *is* as Lĕb′-ă-nọn, excellent as the cedars.

16 ᴺHis mouth *is* most sweet: yea, he *is* altogether lovely. This *is* my beloved, and this *is* my friend, O daughters of Jerusalem.

CHAPTER 6

WHITHER is thy beloved gone, ᴿO thou fairest among women? whither is thy

---

---

beloved turned aside? that we may seek him with thee.

2 My beloved is gone down into his garden, to the beds of spices, to feed in the gardens, and to gather lilies.

3 ᴿI *am* my beloved's, and my beloved *is* mine: he feedeth among the lilies.

The bridegroom's fascination

4 Thou *art* beautiful, O my love, as Tĭr′-zăh, comely as Jerusalem, ᴿterrible as *an army* with banners.

5 Turn away thine eyes from me, for ᴺthey have overcome me: thy hair *is* ᴿas a flock of goats that appear from Gilead.

6 ᴿThy teeth *are* as a flock of sheep which go up from the washing, whereof every one beareth twins, and *there is* not one barren among them.

7 ᴿAs a piece of a pomegranate *are* thy temples within thy locks.

8 There are threescore queens, and fourscore concubines, and virgins without number.

9 My dove, my undefiled is *but* one; she *is* the *only* one of her mother, she *is* the choice *one* of her that bare her. The daughters saw her, and blessed her; *yea,* the queens and the concubines, and they praised her.

10 Who *is* she *that* looketh forth as the morning, fair as the moon, clear as the sun, ᴿ*and* terrible as *an army* with banners?

11 I went down into the garden of nuts to see the fruits of the valley, *and* ᴿto see whether the vine flourished, *and* the pomegranates budded.

12 ᴺOr ever I was aware, my soul ᴺmade me *like* the chariots of Ăm-mĭn′-ă-dĭb.

13 Return, return, O Shû′-lă-mīte; return, return, that we may look upon thee. What will ye see in the Shû′-lă-mīte? As it were the company ᴺof two armies.

CHAPTER 7

The bride's dance

HOW beautiful are thy feet with shoes, ᴿO prince's daughter! the joints of thy thighs *are* like jewels, the work of the hands of a cunning workman.

2 Thy navel *is like* a round goblet, *which* wanteth not ᴺliquor: thy belly *is like* an heap of wheat set about with lilies.

3 ᴿThy two breasts *are* like two young roes *that are* twins.

4 ᴿThy neck *is* as a tower of ivory; thine eyes *like* the fishpools in Hĕsh′-bŏn, by the gate of Băth-răb′-bĭm: thy nose *is* as the tower

of Lĕb'-ă-nǫn which looketh toward Damascus.

5 Thine head upon thee *is* like ᴺCarmel, and the hair of thine head like purple; the king *is* ᴺheld in the galleries.

6 How fair and how pleasant art thou, O love, for delights!

7 This thy stature is like to a palm tree, and thy breasts to clusters *of grapes.*

8 I said, I will go up to the palm tree, I will take hold of the boughs thereof: now also thy breasts shall be as clusters of the vine, and the smell of thy nose like apples;

9 And the roof of thy mouth like the best wine for my beloved, that goeth *down* ᴺsweetly, causing the lips ᴺof those that are asleep to speak.

The bride gives her love

10 ᴿI *am* my beloved's, and ᴿhis desire *is* toward me.

11 Come, my beloved, let us go forth into the field; let us lodge in the villages.

12 Let us get up early to the vineyards; let us ᴿsee if the vine flourish, *whether* the tender grape ᴺappear, *and* the pomegranates bud forth: there will I give thee my loves.

13 The ᴿmandrakes give a smell, and at our gates ᴿ*are* all manner of pleasant *fruits,* new and old, *which* I have laid up for thee, O my beloved.

CHAPTER 8

O THAT thou *wert* as my brother, that sucked the breasts of my mother! *when* I should find thee without, I would kiss thee; yea, ᴺI should not be despised.

2 I would lead thee, *and* bring thee into my mother's house, *who* would instruct me: I would cause thee to drink of ᴿspiced wine of the juice of my pomegranate.

3 ᴿHis left hand *should be* under my head, and his right hand should embrace me.

4 ᴿI charge you, O daughters of Jerusalem, ᴺthat ye stir not up, nor awake *my* love, until he please.

Strength of true love

5 ᴿWho *is* this that cometh up from the wilderness, leaning upon her beloved? I raised thee up under the apple tree: there thy mother brought thee forth: there she brought thee forth *that* bare thee.

6 ᴿSet me as a seal upon thine heart, as a seal upon thine arm: for love *is* strong as death; jealousy *is* ᴺcruel as the grave: the coals thereof *are* coals of fire, *which hath* a most vehement flame.

7 Many waters cannot quench love, neither can the floods drown it: ᴿif a man would give all the substance of his house for love, it would utterly be contemned.

8 ᴿWe have a little sister, and she hath no breasts: what shall we do for our sister in the day when she shall be spoken for?

9 If she *be* a wall, we will build upon her a palace of silver: and if she *be* a door, we will inclose her with boards of cedar.

10 I *am* a wall, and my breasts like towers: then was I in his eyes as one that found ᴺfavour.

11 Solomon had a vineyard at Bā'-ăl-hā'-mǒn; ᴿhe let out the vineyard unto keepers; every one for the fruit thereof was to bring a thousand *pieces* of silver.

12 My vineyard, which *is* mine, *is* before me: thou, O Solomon, *must have* a thousand, and those that keep the fruit thereof two hundred.

13 Thou that dwellest in the gardens, the companions hearken to thy voice: ᴿcause me to hear *it.*

14 ᴿMakeᴺ haste, my beloved, and ᴿbe thou like to a roe or to a young hart upon the mountains of spices.

CHAP. 7
BC 1014
5 Or, *crimson*
5 Heb. *bound*
9 Heb. *straightly*
9 Or, *of the ancient*
10 ch. 2:16 & 6:3
10 Ps. 45:11
12 ch. 6:11
12 Heb. *open*
13 Gen. 30:14
13 Mat. 13:52

CHAP. 8
BC 1014
1 Heb. *they should not despise me*
2 Prov. 9:2
3 ch. 2:6

ch. 2:7   4
& 3:5
Heb. *why*   4
should ye stir up, or, *why, etc.*
ch. 3:6   5
Is. 49:16   6
Jer. 22:24
Hag. 2:23
Heb. *hard*   6
Prov. 6:35   7
Ezek. 23:33   8
Heb. *peace*   10
Mat. 21:33   11
ch. 2:14   13
See Rev. 22:17,   14
20
Heb. *Flee away*   14
ch. 2:17   14

THE BOOK OF THE PROPHET

ISAIAH

The book of Isaiah bears the name of the eighth century prophet whose ministry began in 740 B.C. and continued until approximately 685–680. The Dead Sea Scrolls, as well as the New Testament, bear witness to the fact that the entire book was in a single volume as early as the second century B.C.

The message of Isaiah reflects the national and international developments during his ministry. With the Assyrian occupation of Syria in 732 and of the northern Kingdom of Israel (also known as Ephraim) in 722, the pressure extended to the southern Kingdom of Judah. Isaiah predicted God's judgment and the ultimate Babylonian captivity.

Isaiah denounced the sins of his people, warning them of coming judgment, but immediately introduced the prospect of ultimate restoration. He constantly warned the people to trust in God in spite of godless kings who defied the divine anger.

Isaiah assured his peoples success in resisting Assyrian aggression (7–12), but predicted Babylonian captivity (39). Ultimately God's judgment would come upon all nations.

For those who placed their trust in God, Isaiah had a message of assurance and hope. The promise of ultimate restoration would be vested in a mighty ruler (7:14, 9:6–7, 11:1–6) who would establish a wholly righteous kingdom (2:1–5; 11; 35; 60–66). Sin, however, could only be atoned for through the suffering servant (40–53). Isaiah thus assured his people of a three-fold redemption: release from the exile through Cyrus, forgiveness of sin through the suffering servant, and ultimate restoration of the kingdom through the mighty ruler.

Outline of Isaiah:

CHAPTER 1

Israel's sinfulness

THE ᴿvision of Isaiah the son of Amoz, which he saw concerning Judah and Jerusalem in the days of Ŭz-zī′-ăh, Jō′-thăm, Ahaz, *and* Hĕz-ē-kī′-ăh, kings of Judah.

2 ᴿHear, O heavens, and give ear, O earth: for the Lᴏʀᴅ hath spoken, I have nourished and brought up children, and they have rebelled against me.

3 ᴿThe ox knoweth his owner, and the ass his master's crib: *but* Israel ᴿdoth not know, my people doth not consider.

4 Ah sinful nation, a people ᴺladen with iniquity, ᴿa seed of evildoers, children that are corrupters: they have forsaken the Lᴏʀᴅ, they have provoked the Holy One of Israel unto anger, they are ᴺgone away backward.

5 ᴿWhy should ye be stricken any more? ye will ᴺrevolt more and more: the whole head is sick, and the whole heart faint.

6 From the sole of the foot even unto the head *there is* no soundness in it; *but* wounds, and bruises, and putrifying sores: they have not been closed, neither bound up, neither mollified with ᴺointment.

7 ᴿYour country *is* desolate, your cities *are* burned with fire: your land, strangers devour it in your presence, and *it is* desolate, ᴺas overthrown by strangers.

8 And the daughter of Zion is left ᴿas a cottage in a vineyard, as a lodge in a garden of cucumbers, ᴿas a besieged city.

9 ᴿExcept the Lᴏʀᴅ of hosts had left unto us a very small remnant, we should have been as ᴿSodom, *and* we should have been like unto Gō-mŏr′-răh.

True and false worship

10 Hear the word of the Lᴏʀᴅ, ye rulers ᴿof Sodom; give ear unto the law of our God, ye people of Gō-mŏr′-răh.

11 To what purpose *is* the multitude of your ᴿsacrifices unto me? saith the Lᴏʀᴅ: I am full of the burnt offerings of rams, and the fat of fed beasts; and I delight not in the blood of bullocks, or of lambs, or of ᴺhe goats.

12 When ye come ᴿtoᴺ appear before me, who hath required this at your hand, to tread my courts?

13 Bring no more ᴿvain oblations; incense is an abomination unto me; the new moons and sabbaths, ᴿthe calling of assemblies, I cannot away with; *it is* ᴺiniquity, even the solemn meeting.

14 Your ᴿnew moons and your ᴿappointed feasts my soul hateth: they are a trouble unto me; ᴿI am weary to bear *them*.

15 And ᴿwhen ye spread forth your hands, I will hide mine eyes from you: ᴿyea, when ye ᴺmake many prayers, I will not hear: your hands are full of ᴺblood.

16 ᴿWash you, make you clean; put away the evil of your doings from before mine eyes; ᴿcease to do evil;

17 Learn to do well; seek judgment, ᴺrelieve the oppressed, judge the fatherless, plead for the widow.

Obedience or destruction

18 Come now, and ᴿlet us reason together, saith the Lᴏʀᴅ: though your sins be as scarlet, ᴿthey shall be as white as snow; though they be red like crimson, they shall be as wool.

19 If ye be willing and obedient, ye shall eat the good of the land:

20 But if ye refuse and rebel, ye shall be devoured with the sword: ᴿfor the mouth of the Lᴏʀᴅ hath spoken *it*.

The purging and redemption of Zion

21 ᴿHow is the faithful city become an harlot! it was full of judgment; righteousness lodged in it; but now murderers.

22 ᴿThy silver is become dross, thy wine mixed with water:

23 ᴿThy princes *are* rebellious, and ᴿcompanions of thieves: ᴿevery one loveth gifts, and followeth after rewards: they ᴿjudge not the fatherless, neither doth the cause of the widow come unto them.

24 Therefore saith the Lord, the Lᴏʀᴅ of hosts, the mighty One of Israel, Ah, ᴿI will ease me of mine adversaries, and avenge me of mine enemies:

CHAP. 1
BC 760
1 Num. 12:6
2 Jer. 2:12
3 Jer. 8:7
3 Jer. 9:3, 6
4 Heb. of heaviness
4 Mat. 3:7
4 Heb. alienated, or, separated
5 ch. 9:13
5 Heb. increase revolt
6 Or, oil
7 Deut. 28:51
7 Heb. as the overthrow of strangers
8 Job 27:18
8 Jer. 4:17
9 Lam. 3:22
9 Gen. 19:24
10 Deut. 32:32
11 1 Sam. 15:22
11 Heb. great he goats

Ex. 23:17   12
Heb. to be seen   12
Mat. 15:9   13
Joel 1:14   13
Or, grief   13
Num. 28:11   14
Lam. 2:6   14
ch. 43:24   14
Prov. 1:28   15
Mic. 3:4   15
Ps. 66:18   15
Heb. multiply prayer   15
Heb. bloods   15
Jer. 4:14   16
Rom. 12:9   16
Or, righten   17
ch. 43:26   18
Ps. 51:7   18
Rev. 7:14
Tit. 1:2   20
Jer. 2:20   21
Jer. 6:28   22
Hos. 9:15   23
Prov. 29:24   23
Jer. 22:17   23
Ezek. 22:12
Jer. 5:28   23
Zech. 7:10
Deut. 28:63   24

25 And I will turn my hand upon thee, and ᴿpurelyᴺ purge away thy dross, and take away all thy tin:

26 And I will restore thy judges ᴿas at the first, and thy counsellors as at the beginning: afterward ᴿthou shalt be called, The city of righteousness, the faithful city.

27 Zion shall be redeemed with judgment, and ᴺher converts with righteousness.

28 And the ᴿdestructionᴺ of the transgressors and of the sinners *shall be* together, and they that forsake the LORD shall be consumed.

29 For they shall be ashamed of ᴿthe oaks which ye have desired, ᴿand ye shall be confounded for the gardens that ye have chosen.

30 For ye shall be as an oak whose leaf fadeth, and as a garden that hath no water.

31 ᴿAnd the strong shall be ᴿas tow, ᴺand the maker of it as a spark, and they shall both burn together, and none shall quench *them*.

CHAPTER 2

God's reign of peace

THE word that Isaiah the son of Amoz saw concerning Judah and Jerusalem.

2 And ᴿit shall come to pass ᴿin the last days, ᴿ*that* the mountain of the LORD's house shall be ᴺestablished in the top of the mountains, and shall be exalted above the hills; ᴿand all nations shall flow unto it. ★

3 And many people shall go and say, ᴿCome ye, and let us go up to the mountain of the LORD, to the house of the God of Jacob; and he will teach us of his ways, and we will walk in his paths: ᴿfor out of Zion shall go forth the law, and the word of the LORD from Jerusalem. ★

4 And he shall judge among the nations, and shall rebuke many people: and ᴿthey shall beat their swords into plowshares, and their spears into ᴺpruninghooks: nation shall not lift up sword against nation, ᴿneither shall they learn war any more. ★

5 O house of Jacob, come ye, and let us ᴿwalk in the light of the LORD.

Idolatry and pride to be judged

6 Therefore thou hast forsaken thy people the house of Jacob, because they be replenished ᴿfromᴺ the east, and ᴿare soothsayers like the Philistines, ᴿand they ᴺplease themselves in the children of strangers.

7 ᴿTheir land also is full of silver and gold, neither *is there any* end of their treasures; their land is also full of horses, neither *is there any* end of their chariots:

8 ᴿTheir land also is full of idols; they wor-

ship the work of their own hands, that which their own fingers have made:

9 And the mean man boweth down, and the great man humbleth himself: therefore forgive them not.

10 ᴿEnter into the rock, and hide thee in the dust, for fear of the LORD, and for the glory of his majesty.

11 The ᴿlofty looks of man shall be humbled, and the haughtiness of men shall be bowed down, and the LORD alone shall be exalted ᴿin that day.

12 For the day of the LORD of hosts *shall be* upon every *one that is* proud and lofty, and upon every *one that is* lifted up; and he shall be brought low:

13 And upon all ᴿthe cedars of Lĕb´-ă-nŏn, *that are* high and lifted up, and upon all the oaks of Bā´-shăn,

14 And ᴿupon all the high mountains, and upon all the hills *that are* lifted up,

15 And upon every high tower, and upon every fenced wall,

16 ᴿAnd upon all the ships of Tarshish, and upon all ᴺpleasant pictures.

17 ᴿAnd the loftiness of man shall be bowed down, and the haughtiness of men shall be made low: and the LORD alone shall be exalted ᴿin that day.

18 And ᴺthe idols he shall utterly abolish.

19 And they shall go into the ᴿholes of the rocks, and into the caves of ᴺthe earth, ᴿfor fear of the LORD, and for the glory of his majesty, when he ariseth ᴿto shake terribly the earth.

20 In that day a man shall cast ᴺhis idols of silver, and his idols of gold, ᴺwhich they made *each one* for himself to worship, to the moles and to the bats;

21 ᴿTo go into the clefts of the rocks, and into the tops of the ragged rocks, ᴿfor fear of the LORD, and for the glory of his majesty, when he ariseth to shake terribly the earth.

22 ᴿCease ye from man, whose ᴿbreath *is* in his nostrils: for wherein is he to be accounted of?

CHAPTER 3

Judgment of Judah and Jerusalem

FOR, behold, the Lord, the LORD of hosts, ᴿdoth take away from Jerusalem and from Judah ᴿthe stay and the staff, the whole stay of bread, and the whole stay of water,

2 ᴿThe mighty man, and the man of war, the judge, and the prophet, and the prudent, and the ancient,

3 The captain of fifty, and ᴺthe honourable

man, and the counsellor, and the cunning artificer, and the ᴺeloquent orator.

4 And I will give ᴿchildren *to be* their princes, and babes shall rule over them.

5 And the people shall be oppressed, every one by another, and every one by his neighbour: the child shall behave himself proudly against the ancient, and the base against the honourable.

6 When a man shall take hold of his brother of the house of his father, *saying,* Thou hast clothing, be thou our ruler, and *let* this ruin *be* under thy hand:

7 In that day shall he ᴺswear, saying, I will not be an ᴺhealer; for in my house *is* neither bread nor clothing: make me not a ruler of the people.

8 For ᴿJerusalem is ruined, and Judah is fallen: because their tongue and their doings *are* against the Lᴏʀᴅ, to provoke the eyes of his glory.

9 The shew of their countenance doth witness against them; and they declare their sin as ᴿSodom, they hide *it* not. Woe unto their soul! for they have rewarded evil unto themselves.

10 Say ye to the righteous, ᴿthat *it shall be* well *with him:* ᴿfor they shall eat the fruit of their doings.

11 Woe unto the wicked! ᴿ*it shall be* ill *with him:* for the reward of his hands shall be ᴺgiven him.

12 *As for* my people, ᴿchildren *are* their oppressors, and women rule over them. O my people, ᴿtheyᴺ which lead thee cause *thee* to err, and ᴺdestroy the way of thy paths.

Judgment of the elders and princes

13 The Lᴏʀᴅ standeth up ᴿto plead, and standeth to judge the people.

14 The Lᴏʀᴅ will enter into judgment with the ancients of his people, and the princes thereof: for ye have ᴺeaten up ᴿthe vineyard; the spoil of the poor *is* in your houses.

15 What mean ye *that* ye ᴿbeat my people to pieces, and grind the faces of the poor? saith the Lord Gᴏᴅ of hosts.

Judgment of the women

16 Moreover the Lᴏʀᴅ saith, Because the daughters of Zion are haughty, and walk with stretched forth necks and ᴺwanton eyes, walking and ᴺmincing *as* they go, and making a tinkling with their feet:

17 Therefore the Lord will smite with ᴿa scab the crown of the head of the daughters of Zion, and the Lᴏʀᴅ will ᴿdiscoverᴺ their secret parts.

18 In that day the Lord will take away the bravery of *their* tinkling ornaments *about their feet,* and *their* ᴺcauls, and *their* ᴿround tires like the moon,

19 The ᴺchains, and the bracelets, and the ᴺmufflers,

20 The bonnets, and the ornaments of the legs, and the headbands, and the ᴺtablets, and the earrings,

21 The rings, and nose jewels,

22 The changeable suits of apparel, and the mantles, and the wimples, and the crisping pins,

23 The glasses, and the fine linen, and the hoods, and the vails.

24 And it shall come to pass, *that* instead of sweet smell there shall be stink; and instead of a girdle a rent; and instead of well set hair ᴿbaldness; and instead of a stomacher a girding of sackcloth; *and* burning instead of beauty.

25 Thy men shall fall by the sword, and thy ᴺmighty in the war.

26 ᴿAnd her gates shall lament and mourn; and she *being* ᴺᴺdesolate ᴿshall sit upon the ground.

CHAPTER 4

Aɴᴅ ᴿin that day seven women shall take hold of one man, saying, We will ᴿeat our own bread, and wear our own apparel: only ᴺlet us be called by thy name, ᴺto take away ᴿour reproach.

Zion cleansed and glorified

2 In that day shall ᴿthe branch of the Lᴏʀᴅ be ᴺbeautiful and glorious, and the fruit of the earth *shall be* excellent and comely ᴺfor them that are escaped of Israel.

3 And it shall come to pass, *that he that is* left in Zion, and *he that* remaineth in Jerusalem, ᴿshall be called holy, *even* every one that is ᴿwritten ᴺamong the living in Jerusalem:

4 When ᴿthe Lord shall have washed away the filth of the daughters of Zion, and shall have purged the blood of Jerusalem from the midst thereof by the spirit of judgment, and by the spirit of burning.

5 And the Lᴏʀᴅ will create upon every dwelling place of mount Zion, and upon her assemblies, ᴿa cloud and smoke by day, and ᴿthe shining of a flaming fire by night: for ᴺupon all the glory *shall be* ᴺa defence.

6 And there shall be a tabernacle for a shadow in the daytime from the heat, and ᴿfor a place of refuge, and for a covert from storm and from rain.

CHAP. 3
BC 760
3 Or, *skilful of speech*
4 Eccl. 10:16
7 Heb. *lift up the hand,* Gen. 14:22
7 Heb. *binder up*
8 Mic. 3:12
9 Gen. 13:13
10 Eccl. 8:12
10 Ps. 128:2
11 Ps. 11:6
11 Heb. *done to him*
12 ver. 4
12 ch. 9:16
12 Or, *they which call thee blessed*
13 Heb. *swallow up*
13 Mic. 6:2
14 Or, *burnt*
14 Mat. 21:33
15 Mic. 3:2, 3
16 Heb. *deceiving with their eyes*
16 Or, *tripping nicely*
17 Deut. 28:27
17 Jer. 13:22
17 Heb. *make naked*

Or, *networks* 18
Judg. 8:21 18
Or, *sweet balls* 19
Or, *spangled ornaments* 19
Heb. *houses of the soul* 20
ch. 22:12 24
Heb. *might* 25
Jer. 14:2 26
Or, *emptied* 26
Heb. *cleansed* 26
Lam. 2:10 26

CHAP. 4
BC 760
ch. 2:11, 17 1
2 Thes. 3:12 1
Heb. *let thy name be called upon us* 1
Or, *take thou away* 1
Luke 1:25 1
Jer. 23:5 2
Heb. *beauty and glory* 2
Heb. *for the escaping of Israel* 2
ch. 60:21 3
Phil. 4:3 3
Or, *to life* 3
Mal. 3:2, 3 4
Ex. 13:21 5
Zech. 2:5 5
Or, *above* 5
Heb. *a covering* 5
ch. 25:4 6

CHAPTER 5

Parable of the vineyard

NOW will I sing to my wellbeloved a song of my beloved touching ᴿhis vineyard. My wellbeloved hath a vineyard in ᴺa very fruitful hill:

2 And he ᴺfenced it, and gathered out the stones thereof, and planted it with the choicest vine, and built a tower in the midst of it, and also ᴺmade a winepress therein: ᴿand he looked that it should bring forth grapes, and it brought forth wild grapes.

3 And now, O inhabitants of Jerusalem, and men of Judah, ᴿjudge, I pray you, betwixt me and my vineyard.

4 What could have been done more to my vineyard, that I have not done in it? wherefore, when I looked that it should bring forth grapes, brought it forth wild grapes?

5 And now go to; I will tell you what I will do to my vineyard: ᴿI will take away the hedge thereof, and it shall be eaten up; *and* break down the wall thereof, and it shall be trodden down:

6 And I will lay it waste: it shall not be pruned, nor digged; but there shall come up briers and thorns: I will also command the clouds that they rain no rain upon it.

7 For the vineyard of the LORD of hosts *is* the house of Israel, and the men of Judah ᴺhis pleasant plant: and he looked for judgment, but behold ᴺoppression; for righteousness, but behold a cry.

Woes pronounced on seven sins

8 Woe unto them that join ᴿhouse to house, *that* lay field to field, till *there be* no place, that ᴺthey may be placed alone in the midst of the earth!

9 ᴿInᴺ mine ears *said* the LORD of hosts, ᴺOf a truth many houses shall be desolate, *even* great and fair, without inhabitant.

10 Yea, ten acres of vineyard shall yield one ᴿbäth, and the seed of an hō′-mĕr shall yield an ē′-phäh.

11 ᴿWoe unto them that rise up early in the morning, *that* they may follow strong drink; that continue until night, *till* wine ᴺinflame them!

12 And ᴿthe harp, and the viol, the tabret, and pipe, and wine, are in their feasts: but ᴿthey regard not the work of the LORD, neither consider the operation of his hands.

13 ᴿTherefore my people are gone into captivity, because *they have* no knowledge: and ᴺtheir honourable men *are* famished, and their multitude dried up with thirst.

14 Therefore hell hath enlarged herself, and opened her mouth without measure: and their glory, and their multitude, and their pomp, and he that rejoiceth, shall descend into it.

15 And ᴿthe mean man shall be brought down, and the mighty man shall be humbled, and the eyes of the lofty shall be humbled:

16 But the LORD of hosts shall be exalted in judgment, and ᴺᴺGod that is holy shall be sanctified in righteousness.

17 Then shall the lambs feed after their manner, and the waste places of ᴿthe fat ones shall strangers eat.

18 Woe unto them that draw iniquity with cords of vanity, and sin as it were with a cart rope:

19 ᴿThat say, Let him make speed, *and* hasten his work, that we may see *it:* and let the counsel of the Holy One of Israel draw nigh and come, that we may know *it!*

20 Woe unto them that ᴺcall evil good, and good evil; that put darkness for light, and light for darkness; that put bitter for sweet, and sweet for bitter!

21 Woe unto *them that are* ᴿwise in their own eyes, and prudent ᴺin their own sight!

22 Woe unto *them that are* mighty to drink wine, and men of strength to mingle strong drink:

23 Which ᴿjustify the wicked for reward, and take away the righteousness of the righteous from him!

Divine judgment by invasion

24 Therefore ᴿas ᴺthe fire devoureth the stubble, and the flame consumeth the chaff, *so* ᴿtheir root shall be as rottenness, and their blossom shall go up as dust: because they have cast away the law of the LORD of hosts, and despised the word of the Holy One of Israel.

25 ᴿTherefore is the anger of the LORD kindled against his people, and he hath stretched forth his hand against them, and hath smitten them: and ᴿthe hills did tremble, and their carcases *were* ᴺtorn in the midst of the streets. ᴿFor all this his anger is not turned away, but his hand *is* stretched out still.

26 ᴿAnd he will lift up an ensign to the nations from far, and will ᴿhiss unto them from ᴿthe end of the earth: and, behold, ᴿthey shall come with speed swiftly:

27 None shall be weary nor stumble among them; none shall slumber nor sleep; neither ᴿshall the girdle of their loins be loosed, nor the latchet of their shoes be broken:

28 ᴿWhose arrows *are* sharp, and all their

bows bent, their horses' hoofs shall be counted like flint, and their wheels like a whirlwind:

29 Their roaring *shall be* like a lion, they shall roar like young lions: yea, they shall roar, and lay hold of the prey, and shall carry *it* away safe, and none shall deliver *it*.

30 And in that day they shall roar against them like the roaring of the sea: and if *one* ᴿlook unto the land, behold darkness *and* ᴺsorrow, ᴺand the light is darkened in the heavens thereof.

CHAPTER 6

Isaiah's vision and call

IN the year that king ŭz-zī′-ăh died I ᴿsaw also the Lord sitting upon a throne, high and lifted up, and ᴺhis train filled the temple.

2 Above it stood the sĕr′-ă-phĭms: each one had six wings; with twain he covered his face, and ᴿwith twain he covered his feet, and with twain he did fly.

3 And ᴺone cried unto another, and said, ᴿHoly, holy, holy, *is* the Lᴏʀᴅ of hosts: ᴿtheᴺ whole earth *is* full of his glory.

4 And the posts of the ᴺdoor moved at the voice of him that cried, and the house was filled with smoke.

5 Then said I, Woe *is* me! for I am ᴺundone; because I *am* a man of unclean lips, and I dwell in the midst of a people of unclean lips: for mine eyes have seen the King, the Lᴏʀᴅ of hosts.

6 Then flew one of the sĕr′-ă-phĭms unto me, ᴺhaving a live coal in his hand, *which* he had taken with the tongs from off ᴿthe altar:

7 And he ᴿlaidᴺ *it* upon my mouth, and said, Lo, this hath touched thy lips; and thine iniquity is taken away, and thy sin purged.

8 Also I heard the voice of the Lord, saying, Whom shall I send, and who will go for ᴿus? Then said I, ᴺHere *am* I; send me.

9 And he said, Go, and tell this people, Hear ye ᴺᴺindeed, but understand not; and see ye ᴺindeed, but perceive not.

10 Make ᴿthe heart of this people fat, and make their ears heavy, and shut their eyes; ᴿlest they see with their eyes, and hear with their ears, and understand with their heart, and convert, and be healed.

11 Then said I, Lord, how long? And he answered, ᴿUntil the cities be wasted without inhabitant, and the houses without man, and the land be ᴺutterly desolate,

12 ᴿAnd the Lᴏʀᴅ have removed men far away, and *there be* a great forsaking in the midst of the land.

13 But yet in it *shall be* a tenth, ᴺand *it* shall

return, and shall be eaten: as a teil tree, and as an oak, whose ᴺsubstance *is* in them, when they cast *their leaves: so* ᴿthe holy seed *shall be* the substance thereof.

CHAPTER 7

Isaiah's warning to Ahaz

AND it came to pass in the days of Ahaz the son of Jō′-thăm, the son of ŭz-zī′-ăh, king of Judah, *that* Rē′-zĭn the king of Syria, and Pē′-käh the son of Rĕm-ă-lī′-ăh, king of Israel, went up toward Jerusalem to war against it, but could not prevail against it.

2 And it was told the house of David, saying, Syria ᴺis confederate with Ē′-phră-ĭm. And his heart was moved, and the heart of his people, as the trees of the wood are moved with the wind.

3 Then said the Lᴏʀᴅ unto Isaiah, Go forth now to meet Ahaz, thou, and ᴺShē′-ăr-jăsh′-ŭb thy son, at the end of the conduit of the upper pool in the ᴺhighway of the fuller's field;

4 And say unto him, Take heed, and be quiet; fear not, ᴺneither be fainthearted for the two tails of these smoking firebrands, for the fierce anger of Rē′-zĭn with Syria, and of the son of Rĕm-ă-lī′-ăh.

5 Because Syria, Ē′-phră-ĭm, and the son of Rĕm-ă-lī′-ăh, have taken evil counsel against thee, saying,

6 Let us go up against Judah, and ᴺvex it, and let us make a breach therein for us, and set a king in the midst of it, *even* the son of Tā′-bĕ-ăl:

7 Thus saith the Lord Gᴏᴅ, ᴿIt shall not stand, neither shall it come to pass.

8 ᴿFor the head of Syria *is* Damascus, and the head of Damascus *is* Rē′-zĭn; and within threescore and five years shall Ē′-phră-ĭm be broken, ᴺthat it be not a people.

9 And the head of Ē′-phră-ĭm *is* Să-mâr′-ĭ-ă, and the head of Să-mâr′-ĭ-ă *is* Rĕm-ă-lī′-ăh's son. ᴿIfᴺ ye will not believe, surely ye shall not be established.

Sign of Immanuel

10 ᴺMoreover the Lᴏʀᴅ spake again unto Ahaz, saying,

11 ᴿAsk thee a sign of the Lᴏʀᴅ thy God; ᴺask it either in the depth, or in the height above.

12 But Ahaz said, I will not ask, neither will I tempt the Lᴏʀᴅ.

13 And he said, Hear ye now, O house of David; *Is it* a small thing for you to weary men, but will ye weary my God also?

14 Therefore the Lord himself shall give you

CHAP. 5
BC 760
30 ch. 8:22
30 Or, *distress*
30 Or, *when it is light, it shall be dark in the destructions thereof*

CHAP. 6
BC 760
1 John 12:41
1 Or, *the skirts thereof*
2 Ezek. 1:11
3 Heb. *this cried to this*
3 Rev. 4:8
3 Ps. 72:19
3 Heb. *his glory is the fulness of the whole earth*
4 Heb. *thresholds*
5 Heb. *cut off*
6 Heb. *and in his hand a live coal*
6 Rev. 8:3
7 Jer. 1:9
7 Heb. *caused it to touch*
8 Gen. 1:26
8 Heb. *Behold me*
9 Or, *without ceasing, etc.*
9 Heb. *hear ye in hearing, etc.*
9 Heb. *in seeing*
10 Ps. 119:70
10 Jer. 5:21
11 Mic. 3:12
11 Heb. *desolate with desolation*
12 2 Ki. 25:21
13 Or, *when it is returned, and hath been broused*

Or, *stock, or, stem*   13
Ezra 9:2   13

CHAP. 7
BC 742
Heb. *resteth on Ephraim*   2
i.e. *The remnant shall return*   3
Or, *causeway*   3
Heb. *let not thy heart be tender*   4
Or, *waken*   6
ch. 8:10   7
2 Sam. 8:6   8
Heb. *from a people*   8
2 Chr. 20:20   9
Or, *Do ye not believe? it is because ye are not stable*   9
Heb. *And the LORD added to speak*   10
Mat. 12:38   11
Or, *make thy petition deep*   11

a sign; ᴿBehold, a virgin shall conceive, and bear ᴿa son, and ᴺshall call his name ᴿĬm-măn′-ū-ĕl.   ★

15 Butter and honey shall he eat, that he may know to refuse the evil, and choose the good.

16 ᴿFor before the child shall know to refuse the evil, and choose the good, the land that thou abhorrest shall be forsaken of ᴿboth her kings.

17 ᴿThe Lᴏʀᴅ shall bring upon thee, and upon thy people, and upon thy father's house, days that have not come, from the day that ᴿĒ′-phră-ĭm departed from Judah; *even* the king of Assyria.

Devastation of the land foretold

18 And it shall come to pass in that day, *that* the Lᴏʀᴅ ᴿshall hiss for the fly that *is* in the uttermost part of the rivers of Egypt, and for the bee that *is* in the land of Assyria.

19 And they shall come, and shall rest all of them in the desolate valleys, and in ᴿthe holes of the rocks, and upon all thorns, and upon all ᴺbushes.

20 In the same day shall the Lord shave with a ᴿrazor that is hired, *namely,* by them beyond the river, by the king of Assyria, the head, and the hair of the feet: and it shall also consume the beard.

21 And it shall come to pass in that day, *that* a man shall nourish a young cow, and two sheep;

22 And it shall come to pass, for the abundance of milk *that* they shall give he shall eat butter: for butter and honey shall every one eat that is left ᴺin the land.

23 And it shall come to pass in that day, *that* every place shall be, where there were a thousand vines at a thousand silverlings, ᴿit shall *even* be for briers and thorns.

24 With arrows and with bows shall *men* come thither; because all the land shall become briers and thorns.

25 And *on* all hills that shall be digged with the mattock, there shall not come thither the fear of briers and thorns: but it shall be for the sending forth of oxen, and for the treading of lesser cattle.

CHAPTER 8

Defeat of Syria and Israel foretold

MOREOVER the Lᴏʀᴅ said unto me, Take thee a great roll, and ᴿwrite in it with a man's pen concerning ᴺMă′-hĕr-shăl′-ăl-hăsh′-băz.

CHAP. 7
BC 742

14 Mat. 1:23
14 ch. 9:6
14 Or, *thou, O virgin, shalt call:* Gen. 4:1, 25
14 ch. 8:8
16 See ch. 8:4
16 2 Ki. 15:30
17 2 Chr. 28:19
17 1 Ki. 12:16
18 ch. 5:26
19 Jer. 16:16
19 Or, *commendable trees*
20 2 Ki. 16:7
22 Heb. *in the midst of the land*
23 ch. 5:6

CHAP. 8
BC 742

1 Hab. 2:2
1 Heb. *In making speed to the spoil he hasteneth the prey,* or, *Make speed, etc.*

2 Ki. 16:10 — 2
Heb. *approached unto* — 3
ch. 7:16 — 4
2 Ki. 15:29 — 4
Or, *he that is before the king of Assyria shall take away the riches, etc.* — 4
John 9:7 — 6
ch. 7:1, 2 — 6
ch. 30:28 — 8
Heb. *the fulness of the breadth of thy land shall be the stretchings out of his wings* — 8
ch. 7:14 — 8
Joel 3:9 — 9
Or, *yet* — 9
Job 5:12 — 10
ch. 7:7 — 10
ch. 7:14 — 10
Rom. 8:31
Heb. *in strength of hand* — 11
ch. 7:2 — 12
1 Pet. 3:14 — 12
Num. 20:12 — 13
Ps. 76:7 — 13
Luke 12:5
Ezek. 11:16 — 14
Luke 2:34 — 14
Rom. 9:33
1 Pet. 2:8
Mat. 21:44 — 15
Luke 20:18
Rom. 11:25
ch. 54:8 — 17

---

2 And I took unto me faithful witnesses to record, ᴿŪ-rī′-ăh the priest, and Zĕch-ă-rī′-ăh the son of Jĕ-bĕr-ĕ-chī′-ăh.

3 And I ᴺwent unto the prophetess; and she conceived, and bare a son. Then said the Lᴏʀᴅ to me, Call his name Mā′-hĕr-shăl′-ăl-hăsh′-băz.

4 ᴿFor before the child shall have knowledge to cry, My father, and my mother, ᴿtheᴺ riches of Damascus and the spoil of Să-măr′-ĭ-ă shall be taken away before the king of Assyria.

Judah to be spared

5 The Lᴏʀᴅ spake also unto me again, saying,

6 Forasmuch as this people refuseth the waters of ᴿShī-lō′-ăh that go softly, and rejoice ᴿin Rē′-zīn and Rĕm-ă-lī′-ăh's son;

7 Now therefore, behold, the Lord bringeth up upon them the waters of the river, strong and many, *even* the king of Assyria, and all his glory: and he shall come up over all his channels, and go over all his banks:

8 And he shall pass through Judah; he shall overflow and go over, ᴿhe shall reach *even* to the neck; and ᴺthe stretching out of his wings shall fill the breadth of thy land, O ᴿĬm-măn′-ū-ĕl.

Stone of stumbling

9 ᴿAssociate yourselves, O ye people, ᴺand ye shall be broken in pieces; and give ear, all ye of far countries: gird yourselves, and ye shall be broken in pieces; gird yourselves, and ye shall be broken in pieces.

10 ᴿTake counsel together, and it shall come to nought; speak the word, ᴿand it shall not stand: ᴿfor God *is* with us.

11 For the Lᴏʀᴅ spake thus to me ᴺwith a strong hand, and instructed me that I should not walk in the way of this people, saying,

12 Say ye not, A confederacy, to all *them to* whom ᴿthis people shall say, A confederacy; ᴿneither fear ye their fear, nor be afraid.

13 ᴿSanctify the Lᴏʀᴅ of hosts himself; and ᴿlet him *be* your fear, and *let* him *be* your dread.

14 And ᴿhe shall be for a sanctuary; but for ᴿa stone of stumbling and for a rock of offence to both the houses of Israel, for a gin and for a snare to the inhabitants of Jerusalem.   ★

15 And many among them shall ᴿstumble, and fall, and be broken, and be snared, and be taken.

16 Bind up the testimony, seal the law among my disciples.

17 And I will wait upon the Lᴏʀᴅ, that ᴿhid-

eth his face from the house of Jacob, and I ᴿwill look for him.

18 ᴿBehold, I and the children whom the Lᴏʀᴅ hath given me ᴿare for signs and for wonders in Israel from the Lᴏʀᴅ of hosts, which dwelleth in mount Zion.

19 And when they shall say unto you, ᴿSeek unto them that have familiar spirits, and unto wizards ᴿthat peep, and that mutter: should not a people seek unto their God? for the living ᴿto the dead?

20 ᴿTo the law and to the testimony: if they speak not according to this word, *it is* because ᴿ*there is* ᴺno light in them.

21 And they shall pass through it, hardly bestead and hungry: and it shall come to pass, that when they shall be hungry, they shall fret themselves, and ᴿcurse their king and their God, and look upward.

22 And ᴿthey shall look unto the earth; and behold trouble and darkness, ᴿdimness of anguish; and *they shall be* driven to darkness.

CHAPTER 9

Birth of The Prince of Peace

NEVERTHELESS ᴿthe dimness *shall* not *be* such as *was* in her vexation, when at the ᴿfirst he lightly afflicted the land of Zĕ-bū′-lŭn and the land of Năph′-tă-lī, and ᴿafterward did more grievously afflict *her by* the way of the sea, beyond Jordan, in Galilee ᴺof the nations.

2 ᴿThe people that walked in darkness have seen a great light: they that dwell in the land of the shadow of death, upon them hath the light shined.   ★

3 Thou hast multiplied the nation, *and* ᴺnot increased the joy: they joy before thee according to the joy in harvest, *and* as *men* rejoice ᴿwhen they divide the spoil.

4 ᴺFor thou hast broken the yoke of his burden, and ᴿthe staff of his shoulder, the rod of his oppressor, as in the day of ᴿMīd′-ĭ-ăn.

5 ᴺFor every battle of the warrior *is* with confused noise, and garments rolled in blood; ᴿbutᴺ *this* shall be with burning *and* ᴺfuel of fire.

6 ᴿFor unto us a child is born, unto us a ᴿson is given: and ᴿthe government shall be upon his shoulder: and his name shall be called ᴿWonderful, Counsellor, ᴿThe mighty God, The everlasting Father, ᴿThe Prince of Peace.   ★

7 Of the increase of *his* government and

peace ᴿ*there shall be* no end, upon the throne of David, and upon his kingdom, to order it, and to establish it with judgment and with justice from henceforth even for ever. The ᴿzeal of the Lᴏʀᴅ of hosts will perform this. ★

Destruction of arrogant Israel

8 The Lord sent a word into Jacob, and it hath lighted upon Israel.

9 And all the people shall know, *even* Ē′-phră-ĭm and the inhabitant of Să-mâr′-ĭ-ă, that say in the pride and stoutness of heart,

10 The bricks are fallen down, but we will build with hewn stones: the sycomores are cut down, but we will change *them into* cedars.

11 Therefore the Lᴏʀᴅ shall set up the adversaries of Rē′-zīn against him, and ᴺjoin his enemies together;

12 The Syrians before, and the Philistines behind; and they shall devour Israel ᴺwith open mouth. ᴿFor all this his anger is not turned away, but his hand *is* stretched out still.

13 For ᴿthe people turneth not unto him that smiteth them, neither do they seek the Lᴏʀᴅ of hosts.

14 Therefore the Lᴏʀᴅ will cut off from Israel head and tail, branch and rush, ᴿin one day.

15 The ancient and honourable, he *is* the head; and the prophet that teacheth lies, he *is* the tail.

16 For ᴿtheᴺ leaders of this people cause *them* to err; and ᴺ*they that are* led of them *are* ᴺdestroyed.

17 Therefore the Lord ᴿshall have no joy in their young men, neither shall have mercy on their fatherless and widows: for every one *is* an hypocrite and an evildoer, and every mouth speaketh ᴺfolly. ᴿFor all this his anger is not turned away, but his hand *is* stretched out still.

18 For wickedness ᴿburneth as the fire: it shall devour the briers and thorns, and shall kindle in the thickets of the forest, and they shall mount up *like* the lifting up of smoke.

19 Through the wrath of the Lᴏʀᴅ of hosts is ᴿthe land darkened, and the people shall be as the ᴺfuel of the fire: ᴿno man shall spare his brother.

20 And he shall ᴺsnatch on the right hand, and be hungry; and he shall eat on the left hand, ᴿand they shall not be satisfied: ᴿthey shall eat every man the flesh of his own arm:

21 Mă-năs′-sĕh, Ē′-phră-ĭm; and Ē′-phră-ĭm, Mă-năs′-sĕh: *and* they together *shall be* against Judah. ᴿFor all this his anger is not turned away, but his hand *is* stretched out still.

CHAP. 8

BC 742

17 Hab. 2:3
Luke 2:25
18 Heb. 2:13
18 Ps. 71:7
Zech. 3:8
19 1 Sam. 28:8
19 ch. 29:4
19 Ps. 106:28
20 Luke 16:29
20 Mic. 3:6
20 Heb. *no morning*
21 Rev. 16:11
22 ch. 5:30
22 ch. 9:1

CHAP. 9

BC 771

1 ch. 8:22
1 2 Ki. 15:29
2 Chr. 16:4
1 Lev. 26:24
2 Ki. 17:5
1 Chr. 5:26
1 Or, *populous*
2 Mat. 4:16
Eph. 5:8, 14
3 Or, *to him*
3 Judg. 5:30
4 Or, *When thou brakest*
4 ch. 10:5
4 Judg. 7:22
Ps. 83:9
5 Or, *When the whole battle of the warrior was, etc.*
5 ch. 66:15
5 Or, *and it was, etc.*
5 Heb. *meat*
6 ch. 7:14
Luke 2:11
6 John 3:16
6 Mat. 28:18
1 Cor. 15:25
6 Judg. 13:18
6 Tit. 2:13
6 Eph. 2:14

Dan. 2:44   7
Luke 1:32
ch. 37:32   7
Heb. *mingle*   11
Heb. *with whole   12
mouth*
Jer. 4:8   12
Jer. 5:3   13
Rev. 18:8   14
ch. 3:12   16
Or, *they that   16
call them blessed*
Or, *they that   16
are called blessed
of them*
Heb. *swallowed   16
up*
Ps. 147:10   17
Or, *villany*   17
ch. 5:25   17
Mal. 4:1   18
ch. 8:22   19
Heb. *meat*   19
Mic. 7:2, 6   19
Heb. *cut*   20
Lev. 26:26   20
Jer. 19:9   20
ver. 12, 17   21

CHAPTER 10

The fate of oppressors

WOE unto them that ᴿdecree unrighteous decrees, and ᴺthat write grievousness *which* they have prescribed;

2 To turn aside the needy from judgment, and to take away the right from the poor of my people, that widows may be their prey, and *that* they may rob the fatherless!

3 And ᴿwhat will ye do in ᴿthe day of visitation, and in the desolation *which* shall come from far? to whom will ye flee for help? and where will ye leave your glory?

4 Without me they shall bow down under the prisoners, and they shall fall under the slain. ᴿFor all this his anger is not turned away, but his hand *is* stretched out still.

Assyria, instrument of God's judgment

5 ᴺO ᴺAssyrian, ᴿthe rod of mine anger, ᴺand the staff in their hand is mine indignation.

6 I will send him against ᴿan hypocritical nation, and against the people of my wrath will I ᴿgive him a charge, to take the spoil, and to take the prey, and ᴺto tread them down like the mire of the streets.

7 ᴿHowbeit he meaneth not so, neither doth his heart think so; but *it is* in his heart to destroy and cut off nations not a few.

8 ᴿFor he saith, *Are* not my princes altogether kings?

9 *Is* not ᴿCăl'-nō ᴿas Cär-chē'-mĭsh? *is* not Hā'-măth as Arpad? *is* not Să-mâr'-ĭ-ă ᴿas Damascus?

10 As my hand hath found the kingdoms of the idols, and whose graven images did excel them of Jerusalem and of Să-mâr'-ĭ-ă;

11 Shall I not, as I have done unto Să-mâr'-ĭ-ă and her idols, so do to Jerusalem and her idols?

Destruction of Assyria foretold

12 Wherefore it shall come to pass, *that* when the Lord hath performed his whole work ᴿupon mount Zion and on Jerusalem, ᴿI will ᴺpunish the fruit ᴺof the stout heart of the king of Assyria, and the glory of his high looks.

13 ᴿFor he saith, By the strength of my hand I have done *it,* and by my wisdom; for I am prudent: and I have removed the bounds of the people, and have robbed their treasures, and I have put down the inhabitants ᴺlike a valiant *man:*

14 And ᴿmy hand hath found as a nest the

riches of the people: and as one gathereth eggs *that are* left, have I gathered all the earth; and there was none that moved the wing, or opened the mouth, or peeped.

15 Shall ᴿthe axe boast itself against him that heweth therewith? or shall the saw magnify itself against him that shaketh it? ᴺas if the rod should shake *itself* against them that lift it up, *or* as if the staff should lift up ᴺ*itself, as if it were* no wood.

16 Therefore shall the Lord, the Lord of hosts, send among his fat ones leanness; and under his glory he shall kindle a burning like the burning of a fire.

17 And the light of Israel shall be for a fire, and his Holy One for a flame: ᴿand it shall burn and devour his thorns and his briers in one day;

18 And shall consume the glory of his forest, and of ᴿhis fruitful field, ᴺboth soul and body: and they shall be as when a standard-bearer fainteth.

19 And the rest of the trees of his forest shall be ᴺfew, that a child may write them.

Faithful remnant of Jacob

20 And it shall come to pass in that day, *that* the remnant of Israel, and such as are escaped of the house of Jacob, ᴿshall no more again stay upon him that smote them; but shall stay upon the LORD, the Holy One of Israel, in truth.

21 The remnant shall return, *even* the remnant of Jacob, unto the mighty God.

22 ᴿFor though thy people Israel be as the sand of the sea, ᴿyet a remnant ᴺof them shall return: the consumption decreed shall overflow ᴺwith righteousness.

23 ᴿFor the Lord GOD of hosts shall make a consumption, even determined, in the midst of all the land.

24 Therefore thus saith the Lord GOD of hosts, O my people that dwellest in Zion, ᴿbe not afraid of the Assyrian: he shall smite thee with a rod, ᴺand shall lift up his staff against thee, after the manner of ᴿEgypt.

25 For yet a very little while, ᴿand the indignation shall cease, and mine anger in their destruction.

26 And the LORD of hosts shall stir up ᴿa scourge for him according to the slaughter of ᴿMĭd'-ĭ-ăn at the rock of ôr'-ĕb: and ᴿ*as* his rod *was* upon the sea, so shall he lift it up after the manner of Egypt.

27 And it shall come to pass in that day, *that* his burden ᴺshall be taken away from off thy

shoulder, and his yoke from off thy neck, and the yoke shall be destroyed because of ᴿthe anointing.

28 He is come to Aı̄′-ăth, he is passed to Mĭg′-rŏn; at Mĭch′-măsh he hath laid up his carriages:

29 They are gone over ᴿthe passage: they have taken up their lodging at Gē′-bă; Rā′-măh is afraid; ᴿGĭb′-ĕ-ăh of Saul is fled.

30 ᴺLift up thy voice, O daughter ᴿof Găl′-lĭm: cause it to be heard unto ᴿLā′-ı̆sh, O poor Ăn′-ă-thŏth.

31 ᴿMăd-mē′-năh is removed; the inhabitants of Gē′-bĭm gather themselves to flee.

32 As yet shall he remain ᴿat Nob that day: he shall ᴿshake his hand *against* the mount of ᴿthe daughter of Zion, the hill of Jerusalem.

33 Behold, the Lord, the Lᴏʀᴅ of hosts, shall lop the bough with terror: and ᴿthe high ones of stature *shall be* hewn down, and the haughty shall be humbled.

34 And he shall cut down the thickets of the forest with iron, and Lĕb′-ă-nŏn shall fall ᴺby a mighty one.

CHAPTER 11

A Branch out of Jesse's root

AND ᴿthere shall come forth a rod out of the stem of ᴿJesse, and ᴿa Branch shall grow out of his roots: ★

2 ᴿAnd the spirit of the Lᴏʀᴅ shall rest upon him, the spirit of wisdom and understanding, the spirit of counsel and might, the spirit of knowledge and of the fear of the Lᴏʀᴅ;   ★

3 And shall make him of ᴺquick understanding in the fear of the Lᴏʀᴅ: and he shall not judge after the sight of his eyes, neither reprove after the hearing of his ears: ★

4 But ᴿwith righteousness shall he judge the poor, and ᴺreprove with equity for the meek of the earth: and he shall ᴿsmite the earth with the rod of his mouth, and with the breath of his lips shall he slay the wicked.   ★

5 And righteousness shall be the girdle of his loins, and faithfulness the girdle of his reins.   ★

6 ᴿThe wolf also shall dwell with the lamb, and the leopard shall lie down with the kid; and the calf and the young lion and the fatling together; and a little child shall lead them.

7 And the cow and the bear shall feed; their young ones shall lie down together: and the lion shall eat straw like the ox.

8 And the sucking child shall play on the hole of the asp, and the weaned child shall put his hand on the ᴺcockatrice' den.

9 ᴿThey shall not hurt nor destroy in all my

holy mountain: for ᴿthe earth shall be full of the knowledge of the Lᴏʀᴅ, as the waters cover the sea.

Recovery of the remnant

10 ᴿAnd in that day ᴿthere shall be a root of Jesse, which shall stand for an ensign of the people; to it shall the ᴿGentiles seek: and his rest shall be ᴺglorious.   ★

11 And it shall come to pass in that day, *that* the Lord shall set his hand again the second time to recover the remnant of his people, which shall be left, ᴿfrom Assyria, and from Egypt, and from Păth′-rŏs, and from Cŭsh, and from Ē′-lăm, and from Shı̄′-när, and from Hā′-măth, and from the islands of the sea.

12 And he shall set up an ensign for the nations, and shall assemble the outcasts of Israel, and gather together ᴿthe dispersed of Judah from the four ᴺcorners of the earth.

13 ᴿThe envy also of Ē′-phră-ı̆m shall depart, and the adversaries of Judah shall be cut off: Ē′-phră-ı̆m shall not envy Judah, and Judah shall not vex Ē′-phră-ı̆m.

14 But they shall fly upon the shoulders of the Philistines toward the west; they shall spoil ᴺthem of the east together: ᴿtheyᴺ shall lay their hand upon Ē′-dŏm and Moab; ᴺand the children of Ammon shall obey them.

15 And the Lᴏʀᴅ ᴿshall utterly destroy the tongue of the Egyptian sea; and with his mighty wind shall he shake his hand over the river, and shall smite it in the seven streams, ᴿand make *men* go over ᴺdryshod.

16 And ᴿthere shall be an highway for the remnant of his people, which shall be left, from Assyria; ᴿlike as it was to Israel in the day that he came up out of the land of Egypt.

CHAPTER 12

Song of thanksgiving

AND ᴿin that day thou shalt say, O Lᴏʀᴅ, I will praise thee: though thou wast angry with me, thine anger is turned away, and thou comfortedst me.

2 Behold, God *is* my salvation; I will trust, and not be afraid: for the Lᴏʀᴅ ᴿJĕ-Hō′-VăH *is* my ᴿstrength and *my* song; he also is become my salvation.

3 Therefore with joy shall ye draw ᴿwater out of the wells of salvation.

4 And in that day shall ye say, ᴿPraise the Lᴏʀᴅ, ᴺcall upon his name, ᴿdeclare his doings among the people, make mention that his ᴿname is exalted.

5 ᴿSing unto the Lᴏʀᴅ; for he hath done excellent things: this *is* known in all the earth.

6 ᴿCry out and shout, thou ᴺinhabitant of Zion: for great *is* ᴿthe Holy One of Israel in the midst of thee.

CHAPTER 13

Prophecy concerning Babylon

THE ᴿburden of Babylon, which Isaiah the son of Amoz did see.

2 ᴿLift ye up a banner ᴿupon the high mountain, exalt the voice unto them, ᴿshake the hand, that they may go into the gates of the nobles.

3 I have commanded my sanctified ones, I have also called ᴿmy mighty ones for mine anger, *even* them that ᴿrejoice in my highness.

4 The noise of a multitude in the mountains, ᴺlike as of a great people; a tumultuous noise of the kingdoms of nations gathered together: the LORD of hosts mustereth the host of the battle.

5 They come from a far country, from the end of heaven, *even* the LORD, and the weapons of his indignation, to destroy the whole land.

The LORD'S day of judgment

6 Howl ye; ᴿfor the day of the LORD *is* at hand; ᴿit shall come as a destruction from the Almighty.

7 Therefore shall all hands ᴺbe faint, and every man's heart shall melt:

8 And they shall be afraid: ᴿpangs and sorrows shall take hold of them; they shall be in pain as a woman that travaileth: they shall ᴺbe amazed ᴺone at another; their faces *shall be as* ᴺflames.

9 Behold, ᴿthe day of the LORD cometh, cruel both with wrath and fierce anger, to lay the land desolate: and he shall destroy ᴿthe sinners thereof out of it.

10 For the stars of heaven and the constellations thereof shall not give their light: the sun shall be ᴿdarkened in his going forth, and the moon shall not cause her light to shine.

11 And I will punish the world for *their* evil, and the wicked for their iniquity; ᴿand I will cause the arrogancy of the proud to cease, and will lay low the haughtiness of the terrible.

12 I will make a man more precious than fine gold; even a man than the golden wedge of ō'-phĭr.

13 ᴿTherefore I will shake the heavens, and the earth shall remove out of her place, in the wrath of the LORD of hosts, and in ᴿthe day of his fierce anger.

14 And it shall be as the chased roe, and as a sheep that no man taketh up: ᴿthey shall every

man turn to his own people, and flee every one into his own land.

15 Every one that is found shall be thrust through; and every one that is joined *unto them* shall fall by the sword.

16 Their children also shall be ᴿdashed to pieces before their eyes; their houses shall be spoiled, and their wives ravished.

The Medes to destroy Babylon

17 ᴿBehold, I will stir up the Mēdes̀ against them, which shall not regard silver; and *as for* gold, they shall not delight in it.

18 *Their* bows also shall dash the young men to pieces; and they shall have no pity on the fruit of the womb; their eye shall not spare children.

19 ᴿAnd Babylon, the glory of kingdoms, the beauty of the Chăl'-dēēs̀' excellency, shall be ᴺas when God overthrew ᴿSodom and Gō-mŏr'-răh.

20 ᴿIt shall never be inhabited, neither shall it be dwelt in from generation to generation: neither shall the Arabian pitch tent there; neither shall the shepherds make their fold there.

21 ᴿBut ᴺwild beasts of the desert shall lie there; and their houses shall be full of ᴺdoleful creatures; and ᴺᴺowls shall dwell there, and satyrs shall dance there.

22 And ᴺthe wild beasts of the islands shall cry in their ᴺdesolate houses, and dragons in *their* pleasant palaces: ᴿand her time *is* near to come, and her days shall not be prolonged.

CHAPTER 14

Restoration of Israel

FOR the LORD ᴿwill have mercy on Jacob, and ᴿwill yet choose Israel, and set them in their own land: ᴿand the strangers shall be joined with them, and they shall cleave to the house of Jacob.

2 And the people shall take them, ᴿand bring them to their place: and the house of Israel shall possess them in the land of the LORD for servants and handmaids: and they shall take them captives, ᴺwhose captives they were; ᴿand they shall rule over their oppressors.

3 And it shall come to pass in the day that the LORD shall give thee rest from thy sorrow, and from thy fear, and from the hard bondage wherein thou wast made to serve,

Taunt against Babylon's king

4 That thou ᴿshalt take up this ᴺproverb against the king of Babylon, and say, How

hath the oppressor ceased! the ᴿgoldenᴺ city ceased!

5 The Lᴏʀᴅ hath broken ᴿthe staff of the wicked, *and* the sceptre of the rulers.

6 He who smote the people in wrath with ᴺa continual stroke, he that ruled the nations in anger, is persecuted, *and* none hindereth.

7 The whole earth is at rest, *and* is quiet: they break forth into singing.

8 ᴿYea, the fir trees rejoice at thee, *and* the cedars of Lĕb'-ă-nọn, *saying,* Since thou art laid down, no feller is come up against us.

9 ᴿHellᴺ from beneath is moved for thee to meet *thee* at thy coming: it stirreth up the dead for thee, *even* all the ᴺᴺchief ones of the earth; it hath raised up from their thrones all the kings of the nations.

10 All they shall speak and say unto thee, Art thou also become weak as we? art thou become like unto us?

11 Thy pomp is brought down to the grave, *and* the noise of thy viols: the worm is spread under thee, and the worms cover thee.

12 ᴿHow art thou fallen from heaven, ᴺO Lucifer, son of the morning! *how* art thou cut down to the ground, which didst weaken the nations!

13 For thou hast said in thine heart, ᴿI will ascend into heaven, ᴿI will exalt my throne above the stars of God: I will sit also upon the mount of the congregation, ᴿin the sides of the north:

14 I will ascend above the heights of the clouds; ᴿI will be like the most High.

15 Yet thou ᴿshalt be brought down to hell, to the sides of the pit.

16 They that see thee shall narrowly look upon thee, *and* consider thee, *saying, Is* this the man that made the earth to tremble, that did shake kingdoms;

17 *That* made the world as a wilderness, and destroyed the cities thereof; *that* ᴺopened not the house of his prisoners?

18 All the kings of the nations, *even* all of them, lie in glory, every one in his own house.

19 But thou art cast out of thy grave like an abominable branch, *and as* the raiment of those that are slain, thrust through with a sword, that go down to the stones of the pit; as a carcase trodden under feet.

20 Thou shalt not be joined with them in burial, because thou hast destroyed thy land, *and* slain thy people: ᴿthe seed of evildoers shall never be renowned.

21 Prepare slaughter for his children ᴿfor the iniquity of their fathers; that they do not rise, nor possess the land, nor fill the face of the world with cities.

22 For I will rise up against them, saith the Lᴏʀᴅ of hosts, and cut off from Babylon ᴿthe name, and ᴿremnant, ᴿand son, and nephew, saith the Lᴏʀᴅ.

23 ᴿI will also make it a possession for the bittern, and pools of water: and I will sweep it with the besom of destruction, saith the Lᴏʀᴅ of hosts.

The LORD'S purpose to overthrow Assyria

24 The Lᴏʀᴅ of hosts hath sworn, saying, Surely as I have thought, so shall it come to pass; and as I have purposed, *so* shall it stand:

25 That I will break the Assyrian in my land, and upon my mountains tread him under foot: then shall ᴿhis yoke depart from off them, and his burden depart from off their shoulders.

26 This *is* the purpose that is purposed upon the whole earth: and this *is* the hand that is stretched out upon all the nations.

27 For the Lᴏʀᴅ of hosts hath ᴿpurposed, and who shall disannul *it?* and his hand *is* stretched out, and who shall turn it back?

Prophecy concerning Palestina

28 In the year that ᴿking Ahaz died was this burden.

29 Rejoice not thou, whole Palestina, ᴿbecause the rod of him that smote thee is broken: for out of the serpent's root shall come forth a ᴺcockatrice, ᴿand his fruit *shall be* a fiery flying serpent.

30 And the firstborn of the poor shall feed, and the needy shall lie down in safety: and I will kill thy root with famine, and he shall slay thy remnant.

31 Howl, O gate; cry, O city; thou, whole Palestina, *art* dissolved: for there shall come from the north a smoke, and ᴺnone *shall be* alone in his ᴺappointed times.

32 What shall *one* then answer the messengers of the nation? That ᴿthe Lᴏʀᴅ hath founded Zion, and ᴿthe poor of his people shall ᴺtrust in it.

CHAPTER 15

Prophecy concerning Moab

THE ᴿburden of Moab. Because in the night ᴿAr of Moab is laid waste, *and* ᴺbrought to silence; because in the night Kĭr of Moab is laid waste, *and* brought to silence;

2 He is gone up to Bā'-jĭth, and to Dī'-bŏn, the high places, to weep: Moab shall howl over Nē'-bō, and over Mē'-dĕ-bă: ᴿon all their heads *shall be* baldness, *and* every beard cut off.

Center reference column:

CHAP. 14
BC 712
4 Rev. 18:16
4 Or, *exactress of gold*
5 Ps. 125:3
6 Heb. *a stroke without removing*
8 ch. 55:12
  Ezek. 31:16
9 Ezek. 32:21
9 Or, *The grave*
9 Heb. *leaders*
9 Or, *great goats*
12 ch. 34:4
12 Or, *O day star*
13 Mat. 11:23
13 Dan. 8:10
13 Ps. 48:2
14 ch. 47:8
  2 Thes. 2:4
15 Mat. 11:23
17 Or, *did not let his prisoners loose homewards?*
20 Job 18:19
  Ps. 21:10
  & 37:28
  & 109:13
21 Ex. 20:5
  Mat. 23:35

Prov. 10:7   22
Jer. 51:62
1 Ki. 14:10   22
Job 18:19   22
ch. 34:11   23
Zeph. 2:14
ch. 10:27   25
2 Chr. 20:6   27
Job 9:12
& 23:13
Ps. 33:11
Prov. 19:21
& 21:30
ch. 43:13
Dan. 4:31, 35
2 Ki. 16:20   28
2 Chr. 26:6   29
Or, *adder*   29
2 Ki. 18:8   29
Or, *he shall not be alone*   31
Or, *assemblies*   31
Ps. 87:1, 5   32
Zech. 11:11   32
Or, *betake themselves unto it*   32

CHAP. 15
BC 726
Jer. 48:1   1
Num. 21:28   1
Or, *cut off*   1
Lev. 21:5   2

3 In their streets they shall gird themselves with sackcloth: on the tops of their houses, and in their streets, every one shall howl, [N]weeping abundantly.

4 And Hĕsh'-bŏn shall cry, and Ĕl-ĕ-ā'-lēh: their voice shall be heard *even* unto Jā'-hăz: therefore the armed soldiers of Moab shall cry out; his life shall be grievous unto him.

Plight of the fugitives

5 [R]My heart shall cry out for Moab; [N]his fugitives *shall flee* unto Zō'-är, an heifer of three years old: for [R]by the mounting up of Lū'-hĭth with weeping shall they go it up; for in the way of Hŏr-ō-nā'-ĭm they shall raise up a cry of [N]destruction.

6 For the waters [R]of Nimrim shall be [N]desolate: for the hay is withered away, the grass faileth, there is no green thing.

7 Therefore the abundance they have gotten, and that which they have laid up, shall they carry away to the [N]brook of the willows.

8 For the cry is gone round about the borders of Moab; the howling thereof unto ĕg'-lā-ĭm, and the howling thereof unto Bēer-ē'-lĭm.

9 For the waters of Dī'-mŏn shall be full of blood: for I will bring [N]more upon Dī'-mŏn, [R]lions upon him that escapeth of Moab, and upon the remnant of the land.

CHAPTER 16

SEND [R]ye the lamb to the ruler of the land [R]from [N]Sē'-lä to the wilderness, unto the mount of the daughter of Zion.

2 For it shall be, *that,* as a wandering bird [N]cast out of the nest, *so* the daughters of Moab shall be at the fords of [R]Arnon.

3 [N]Take counsel, execute judgment; make thy shadow as the night in the midst of the noonday; hide the outcasts; bewray not him that wandereth.

4 Let mine outcasts dwell with thee, Moab; be thou a covert to them from the face of the spoiler: for the [N]extortioner is at an end, the spoiler ceaseth, [N]the oppressors are consumed out of the land.

5 And in mercy [R]shall the throne be [N]established: and he shall sit upon it in truth in the tabernacle of David, [R]judging, and seeking judgment, and hasting righteousness.

Lament of Moab

6 We have heard of the [R]pride of Moab; *he is* very proud: *even* of his haughtiness, and his pride, and his wrath: [R]*but* his lies *shall* not *be* so.

7 Therefore shall Moab [R]howl for Moab, every one shall howl: for the foundations [R]of

Kĭr-hăr'-ĕ-sĕth shall ye [N]mourn; surely *they are* stricken.

8 For [R]the fields of Hĕsh'-bŏn languish, *and* [R]the vine of Sĭb'-măh: the lords of the heathen have broken down the principal plants thereof, they are come *even* unto Jā'-zĕr, they wandered *through* the wilderness: her branches are [N]stretched out, they are gone over the sea.

9 Therefore I will bewail with the weeping of Jā'-zĕr the vine of Sĭb'-măh: I will water thee with my tears, [R]O Hĕsh'-bŏn, and Ĕl-ĕ-ā'-lēh: for [N]the shouting for thy summer fruits and for thy harvest is fallen.

10 And [R]gladness is taken away, and joy out of the plentiful field; and in the vineyards there shall be no singing, neither shall there be shouting: the treaders shall tread out no wine in *their* presses; I have made *their vintage* shouting to cease.

11 Wherefore [R]my bowels shall sound like an harp for Moab, and mine inward parts for Kĭr-hăr'-ĕsh.

12 And it shall come to pass, when it is seen that Moab is weary on [R]the high place, that he shall come to his sanctuary to pray; but he shall not prevail.

13 This *is* the word that the Lord hath spoken concerning Moab since that time.

14 But now the Lord hath spoken, saying, Within three years, [R]as the years of an hireling, and the glory of Moab shall be contemned, with all that great multitude; and the remnant *shall be* very small *and* [N]feeble

CHAPTER 17

Prophecy concerning Damascus

THE [R]burden of Damascus. Behold, Damascus is taken away from *being* a city, and it shall be a ruinous heap.

2 The cities of Ă-rō'-ĕr *are* forsaken: they shall be for flocks, which shall lie down, and [R]none shall make *them* afraid.

3 [R]The fortress also shall cease from Ē'-phrā-ĭm, and the kingdom from Damascus, and the remnant of Syria: they shall be as the glory of the children of Israel, saith the Lord of hosts.

The humbling of Israel

4 And in that day it shall come to pass, *that* the glory of Jacob shall be made thin, and [R]the fatness of his flesh shall wax lean.

5 [R]And it shall be as when the harvestman gathereth the corn, and reapeth the ears with his arm; and it shall be as he that gathereth ears in the valley of Rĕph'-ā-ĭm.

6 [R]Yet gleaning grapes shall be left in it, as

CHAP. 15
BC 726
3 Heb. *descending into weeping,* or, *coming down with weeping*
5 Jer. 48:31
5 Or, *to the borders thereof, even to Zoar,* as *an heifer*
5 Jer. 48:5
5 Heb. *breaking*
6 Num. 32:36
6 Heb. *desolations*
7 Or, *valley of the Arabians*
9 Heb. *additions*
9 2 Ki. 17:25

CHAP. 16
BC 726
1 2 Ki. 3:4
1 2 Ki. 14:7
1 Or, *Petra:* Heb. *A rock*
2 Or, *a nest forsaken*
2 Num. 21:13
3 Heb. *Bring*
4 Heb. *wringer*
4 Heb. *the treaders down*
5 Luke 1:33
5 Or, *prepared*
5 Ps. 72:2
6 Jer. 48:29
6 ch. 28:15
7 Jer. 48:20
7 2 Ki. 3:25

Or, *mutter*   7
ch. 24:7   8
ver. 9   8
Or, *plucked up*   8
ch. 15:4   9
Or, *the alarm is fallen upon, etc.*   9
ch. 24:8   10
Jer. 48:33
Jer. 48:36   11
ch. 15:2   12
ch. 21:16   14
Or, *not many*   14

CHAP. 17
BC 741
Jer. 49:23   1
Amos 1:3
Zech. 9:1
Jer. 7:33   2
ch. 7:16   3
& 8:4
ch. 10:16   4
Jer. 51:33   5
ch. 24:13   6

the shaking of an olive tree, two *or* three berries in the top of the uppermost bough, four *or* five in the outmost fruitful branches thereof, saith the LORD God of Israel.

7 At that day shall a man [R]look to his Maker, and his eyes shall have respect to the Holy One of Israel.

8 And he shall not look to the altars, the work of his hands, neither shall respect *that* which his fingers have made, either the groves, or the [N]images.

9 In that day shall his strong cities be as a forsaken bough, and an uppermost branch, which they left because of the children of Israel: and there shall be desolation.

10 Because thou hast forgotten [R]the God of thy salvation, and hast not been mindful of the rock of thy strength, therefore shalt thou plant pleasant plants, and shalt set it with strange slips:

11 In the day shalt thou make thy plant to grow, and in the morning shalt thou make thy seed to flourish: *but* the harvest *shall be* [N]a heap in the day of grief and of desperate sorrow.

12 Woe to the [N]multitude of many people, *which* make a noise [R]like the noise of the seas; and to the rushing of nations, *that* make a rushing like the rushing of [N]mighty waters!

13 The nations shall rush like the rushing of many waters: but *God* shall [R]rebuke them, and they shall flee far off, and [R]shall be chased as the chaff of the mountains before the wind, and like [N]a rolling thing before the whirlwind.

14 And behold at eveningtide trouble; *and* before the morning he *is* not. This *is* the portion of them that spoil us, and the lot of them that rob us.

CHAPTER 18

Messengers to Ethiopia

WOE [R]to the land shadowing with wings, which *is* beyond the rivers of Ē-thĭ-ō'-pĭ-ă:

2 That sendeth ambassadors by the sea, even in vessels of bulrushes upon the waters, *saying,* Go, ye swift messengers, to [R]a nation [N]scattered and peeled, to a people terrible from their beginning hitherto; [NN]a nation meted out and trodden down, [N]whose land the rivers have spoiled!

3 All ye inhabitants of the world, and dwellers on the earth, see ye, [R]when he lifteth up an ensign on the mountains; and when he bloweth a trumpet, hear ye.

4 For so the LORD said unto me, I will take my rest, and I will [N]consider in my dwelling

place like a clear heat [N]upon herbs, *and* like a cloud of dew in the heat of harvest.

5 For afore the harvest, when the bud is perfect, and the sour grape is ripening in the flower, he shall both cut off the sprigs with pruning hooks, and take away *and* cut down the branches.

6 They shall be left together unto the fowls of the mountains, and to the beasts of the earth: and the fowls shall summer upon them, and all the beasts of the earth shall winter upon them.

7 In that time [R]shall the present be brought unto the LORD of hosts of a people [N]scattered and peeled, and from a people terrible from their beginning hitherto; a nation meted out and trodden under foot, whose land the rivers have spoiled, to the place of the name of the LORD of hosts, the mount Zion.

CHAPTER 19

Prophecy concerning Egypt

THE [R]burden of Egypt. Behold, the LORD [R]rideth upon a swift cloud, and shall come into Egypt: and [R]the idols of Egypt shall be moved at his presence, and the heart of Egypt shall melt in the midst of it.

2 And I will [R]set[N] the Egyptians against the Egyptians: and they shall fight every one against his brother, and every one against his neighbour; city against city, *and* kingdom against kingdom.

3 And the spirit of Egypt [N]shall fail in the midst thereof; and I will [N]destroy the counsel thereof: and they shall [R]seek to the idols, and to the charmers, and to them that have familiar spirits, and to the wizards.

4 And the Egyptians will I [N]give over [R]into the hand of a cruel lord; and a fierce king shall rule over them, saith the Lord, the LORD of hosts.

5 [R]And the waters shall fail from the sea, and the river shall be wasted and dried up.

6 And they shall turn the rivers far away; *and* the brooks [R]of defence shall be emptied and dried up: the reeds and flags shall wither.

7 The paper reeds by the brooks, by the mouth of the brooks, and every thing sown by the brooks, shall wither, be driven away, [N]and be no *more.*

8 The fishers also shall mourn, and all they that cast angle into the brooks shall lament, and they that spread nets upon the waters shall languish.

9 Moreover they that work in [R]fine flax, and they that weave [N]networks, shall be confounded.

10 And they shall be broken in the ᴺpurposes thereof, all that make sluices *and* ponds ᴺfor fish.

Confusion of the Egyptian princes

11 Surely the princes of ᴿZō'-ăn *are* fools, the counsel of the wise counsellors of Pharaoh is become brutish: how say ye unto Pharaoh, I *am* the son of the wise, the son of ancient kings?

12 ᴿWhere *are* they? where *are* thy wise *men?* and let them tell thee now, and let them know what the Lᴏʀᴅ of hosts hath purposed upon Egypt.

13 The princes of Zō'-ăn are become fools, ᴿthe princes of Nŏph are deceived; they have also seduced Egypt, *even* ᴺᴺ*they that are* the stay of the tribes thereof.

14 The Lᴏʀᴅ hath mingled ᴿa ᴺ perverse spirit in the midst thereof: and they have caused Egypt to err in every work thereof, as a drunken *man* staggereth in his vomit.

15 Neither shall there be *any* work for Egypt, which ᴿthe head or tail, branch or rush, may do.

The LORD'S purpose against Egypt

16 In that day shall Egypt ᴿbe like unto women: and it shall be afraid and fear because of the shaking of the hand of the Lᴏʀᴅ of hosts, ᴿwhich he shaketh over it.

17 And the land of Judah shall be a terror unto Egypt, every one that maketh mention thereof shall be afraid in himself, because of the counsel of the Lᴏʀᴅ of hosts, which he hath determined against it.

18 In that day shall five cities in the land of Egypt ᴿspeak ᴺthe language of Canaan, and swear to the Lᴏʀᴅ of hosts; one shall be called, The city ᴺof destruction.

19 In that day ᴿshall there be an altar to the Lᴏʀᴅ in the midst of the land of Egypt, and a pillar at the border thereof to the Lᴏʀᴅ.

20 And ᴿit shall be for a sign and for a witness unto the Lᴏʀᴅ of hosts in the land of Egypt: for they shall cry unto the Lᴏʀᴅ because of the oppressors, and he shall send them a saviour, and a great one, and he shall deliver them.

21 And the Lᴏʀᴅ shall be known to Egypt, and the Egyptians shall know the Lᴏʀᴅ in that day, and ᴿshall do sacrifice and oblation; yea, they shall vow a vow unto the Lᴏʀᴅ, and perform *it.*

22 And the Lᴏʀᴅ shall smite Egypt: he shall smite and heal *it:* and they shall return *even* to the Lᴏʀᴅ, and he shall be entreated of them, and shall heal them.

23 In that day ᴿshall there be a highway out of Egypt to Assyria, and the Assyrian shall come into Egypt, and the Egyptian into Assyria, and the Egyptians shall serve with the Assyrians.

24 In that day shall Israel be the third with Egypt and with Assyria, *even* a blessing in the midst of the land:

25 Whom the Lᴏʀᴅ of hosts shall bless, saying, Blessed *be* Egypt my people, and Assyria ᴿthe work of my hands, and Israel mine inheritance.

CHAPTER 20

Assyria to conquer Egypt and Ethiopia

IN the year that ᴿTartan came unto Ăsh'-dŏd, (when Sär'-gŏn the king of Assyria sent him,) and fought against Ăsh'-dŏd, and took it;

2 At the same time spake the Lᴏʀᴅ ᴺby Isaiah the son of Amoz, saying, Go and loose ᴿthe sackcloth from off thy loins, and put off thy shoe from thy foot. And he did so, ᴿwalking naked and barefoot.

3 And the Lᴏʀᴅ said, Like as my servant Isaiah hath walked naked and barefoot three years ᴿ*for* a sign and wonder upon Egypt and upon Ē-thĭ-ō'-pĭ-ă;

4 So shall the king of Assyria lead away ᴺthe Egyptians prisoners, and the Ē-thĭ-ō'-pĭ-ăns captives, young and old, naked and barefoot, ᴿeven with *their* buttocks uncovered, to the ᴺshame of Egypt.

5 ᴿAnd they shall be afraid and ashamed of Ē-thĭ-ō'-pĭ-ă their expectation, and of Egypt their glory.

6 And the inhabitant of this ᴺisle shall say in that day, Behold, such *is* our expectation, whither we flee for help to be delivered from the king of Assyria: and how shall we escape?

CHAPTER 21

Defeat of Babylon by Elam and Media

THE burden of the desert of the sea. As ᴿwhirlwinds in the south pass through; *so* it cometh from the desert, from a terrible land.

2 A ᴺgrievous vision is declared unto me; ᴿthe treacherous dealer dealeth treacherously, and the spoiler spoileth. ᴿGo up, O Ē'-lăm: besiege, O Mē'-dĭ-ă; all the sighing thereof have I made to cease.

3 Therefore ᴿare my loins filled with pain: ᴿpangs have taken hold upon me, as the pangs of a woman that travaileth: I was bowed down at the hearing *of it;* I was dismayed at the seeing *of it.*

4 ᴺMy heart panted, fearfulness affrighted

CHAP. 19

BC 714

10 Heb. *foundations*
10 Heb. *of living things*
11 Num. 13:22
12 1 Cor. 1.20
13 Jer. 2:16
13 Or, *governors*
13 Heb. *corners*
14 1 Ki. 22:22
ch. 29:10
14 Heb. *a spirit of perverseness*
15 ch. 9:14
16 Jer. 51:30
Nah. 3:13
16 ch. 11:15
18 Zeph. 3:9
18 Heb. *the lip*
18 Or, *of Heres,* or, *of the sun*
19 Gen. 28:18
Ex. 24:4
Josh. 22:10, 26, 27
20 Josh. 4:20
& 22:27
21 Mal. 1:11

ch. 11:16   23
Ps. 100:3   25
ch. 29:23
Hos. 2:23
Eph. 2:10

CHAP. 20

BC 714

2 Ki. 18:17   1
Heb. *by the hand of Isaiah*   2
Zech. 13:4   2
1 Sam. 19:24   2
Mic. 1:8, 11
ch. 8:18   3
Heb. *the captivity of Egypt*   4
2 Sam. 10:4   4
ch. 3:17
Jer. 13:22
Mic. 1:11
Heb. *nakedness*   4
2 Ki. 18:21   5
Or, *country,*   6
Jer. 47:4

CHAP. 21

BC 714

Zech. 9:14   1
Heb. *hard*   2
ch. 33:1   2
ch. 13:17   2
Jer. 49:34
ch. 15:5   3
& 16:11
ch. 13:8   3
Or, *My mind wandered*   4

me: ^Rthe night of my pleasure hath he ^Nturned into fear unto me.

5 ^RPrepare the table, watch in the watchtower, eat, drink: arise, ye princes, *and* anoint the shield.

6 For thus hath the Lord said unto me, Go, set a watchman, let him declare what he seeth.

7 ^RAnd he saw a chariot *with* a couple of horsemen, a chariot of asses, *and* a chariot of camels; and he hearkened diligently with much heed:

8 And ^Nhe cried, A lion: My lord, I stand continually upon the ^Rwatchtower in the daytime, and I am set in my ward ^Nwhole nights:

9 And, behold, here cometh a chariot of men, *with* a couple of horsemen. And he answered and said, ^RBabylon is fallen, is fallen; and ^Rall the graven images of her gods he hath broken unto the ground.

10 ^RO my threshing, and the ^Ncorn of my floor: that which I have heard of the Lord of hosts, the God of Israel, have I declared unto you.

Prophecy concerning Dumah and Arabia

11 ^RThe burden of Dū′-mäh. He calleth to me out of Sē′-ĭr, Watchman, what of the night? Watchman, what of the night?

12 The watchman said, The morning cometh, and also the night: if ye will inquire, inquire ye: return, come.

13 ^RThe burden upon Arabia. In the forest in Arabia shall ye lodge, O ye travelling companies ^Rof Dē′-dă-nĭm.

14 The inhabitants of the land of Tē′-mă ^Nbrought water to him that was thirsty, they prevented with their bread him that fled.

15 For they fled ^{NN}from the swords, from the drawn sword, and from the bent bow, and from the grievousness of war.

16 For thus hath the Lord said unto me, Within a year, ^Raccording to the years of an hireling, and all the glory of ^RKē′-där shall fail:

17 And the residue of the number of ^Narchers, the mighty men of the children of Kē′-där, shall be diminished: for the Lord God of Israel hath spoken *it*.

CHAPTER 22

The valley of vision

THE burden of the valley of vision. What aileth thee now, that thou art wholly gone up to the housetops?

2 Thou that art full of stirs, a tumultuous city, ^Ra joyous city: thy slain *men are* not slain with the sword, nor dead in battle.

3 All thy rulers are fled together, they are bound ^Nby the archers: all that are found in thee are bound together, *which* have fled from far.

4 Therefore said I, Look away from me; ^RI^N will weep bitterly, labour not to comfort me, because of the spoiling of the daughter of my people.

5 ^RFor *it is* a day of trouble, and of treading down, and of perplexity ^Rby the Lord GOD of hosts in the valley of vision, breaking down the walls, and of crying to the mountains.

6 ^RAnd Ē′-lăm bare the quiver with chariots of men *and* horsemen, and ^RKĭr ^Nuncovered the shield.

7 And it shall come to pass, *that* ^Nthy choicest valleys shall be full of chariots, and the horsemen shall set themselves in array ^Nat the gate.

8 And he discovered the covering of Judah, and thou didst look in that day to the armour ^Rof the house of the forest.

9 ^RYe have seen also the breaches of the city of David, that they are many: and ye gathered together the waters of the lower pool.

10 And ye have numbered the houses of Jerusalem, and the houses have ye broken down to fortify the wall.

11 ^RYe made also a ditch between the two walls for the water of the old pool: but ye have not looked unto the maker thereof, neither had respect unto him that fashioned it long ago.

12 And in that day did the Lord GOD of hosts ^Rcall to weeping, and to mourning, and ^Rto baldness, and to girding with sackcloth:

13 And behold joy and gladness, slaying oxen, and killing sheep, eating flesh, and drinking wine: ^Rlet us eat and drink; for to morrow we shall die.

14 ^RAnd it was revealed in mine ears by the Lord of hosts, Surely this iniquity ^Rshall not be purged from you till ye die, saith the Lord GOD of hosts.

Replacement of Shebna, the steward

15 Thus saith the Lord GOD of hosts, Go, get thee unto this treasurer, *even* unto ^RShĕb′-nă, which *is* over the house, *and say,*

16 What hast thou here? and whom hast thou here, that thou hast hewed thee out a sepulchre here, ^N*as* he ^Rthat heweth him out a sepulchre on high, *and* that graveth an habitation for himself in a rock?

17 Behold, ^Nthe Lord will carry thee away with ^Na mighty captivity, ^Rand will surely cover thee.

18 He will surely violently turn and toss thee *like* a ball into a ^Nlarge country: there shalt

thou dic, and there the chariots of thy glory *shall be* the shame of thy lord's house.

19 And I will drive thee from thy station, and from thy state shall he pull thee down.

20 And it shall come to pass in that day, that I will call my servant ᴿ E-lı'-ă-kım the son of Hıl-kı'-ah:

21 And I will clothe him with thy robe, and strengthen him with thy girdle, and I will commit thy government into his hand: and he shall be a father to the inhabitants of Jerusalem, and to the house of Judah.

22 And the key of the house of David will I lay upon his shoulder; so he shall ᴿ open, and none shall shut; and he shall shut, and none shall open.

23 And I will fasten him *as* ᴿ a nail in a sure place; and he shall be for a glorious throne to his father's house.

24 And they shall hang upon him all the glory of his father's house, the offspring and the issue, all vessels of small quantity, from the vessels of cups, even to all the ᴺ vessels of flagons.

25 In that day, saith the LORD of hosts, shall the nail that is fastened in the sure place be removed, and be cut down, and fall; and the burden that *was* upon it shall be cut off: for the LORD hath spoken *it.*

CHAPTER 23

Prophecy concerning Tyre

THE ᴿ burden of Tyre. Howl, ye ships of Tarshish; for it is laid waste, so that there is no house, no entering in: ᴿ from the land of Chıt'-tım it is revealed to them.

2 Be ᴺ still, ye inhabitants of the isle; thou whom the merchants of Zı'-dŏn, that pass over the sea, have replenished.

3 And by great waters the seed of Sı'-hôr, the harvest of the river, *is* her revenue; and ᴿ she is a mart of nations.

4 Be thou ashamed, O Zı'-dŏn: for the sea hath spoken, *even* the strength of the sea, saying, I travail not, nor bring forth children, neither do I nourish up young men, *nor* bring up virgins.

5 ᴿ As at the report concerning Egypt, *so* shall they be sorely pained at the report of Tyre.

6 Pass ye over to Tarshish; howl, ye inhabitants of the isle.

7 *Is* this your ᴿ joyous *city,* whose antiquity *is* of ancient days? her own feet shall carry her ᴺ afar off to sojourn.

8 Who hath taken this counsel against Tyre, ᴿ the crowning *city,* whose merchants *are*

princes, whose traffickers *are* the honourable of the earth?

9 The LORD of hosts hath purposed it, ᴺ to stain the pride of all glory, *and* to bring into contempt all the honourable of the earth.

10 Pass through thy land as a river, O daughter of Tarshish: *there is* no more ᴺ strength.

11 He stretched out his hand over the sea, he shook the kingdoms: the LORD hath given a commandment ᴺ against ᴺ the merchant *city,* to destroy the ᴺ strong holds thereof.

12 And he said, ᴿ Thou shalt no more rejoice, O thou oppressed virgin, daughter of Zı'-dŏn: arise, ᴿ pass over to Chıt'-tım; there also shalt thou have no rest.

13 Behold the land of the Chăl-dē'-ăns; this people was not, *till* the Assyrian founded it for ᴿ them that dwell in the wilderness: they set up the towers thereof, they raised up the palaces thereof; *and* he brought it to ruin.

14 Howl, ye ships of Tarshish: for your strength is laid waste.

15 And it shall come to pass in that day, that Tyre shall be forgotten seventy years, according to the days of one king: after the end of seventy years ᴺ shall Tyre sing as an harlot.

16 Take an harp, go about the city, thou harlot that hast been forgotten; make sweet melody, sing many songs, that thou mayest be remembered.

17 And it shall come to pass after the end of seventy years, that the LORD will visit Tyre, and she shall turn to her hire, and ᴿ shall commit fornication with all the kingdoms of the world upon the face of the earth.

18 And her merchandise and her hire ᴿ shall be holiness to the LORD: it shall not be treasured nor laid up; for her merchandise shall be for them that dwell before the LORD, to eat sufficiently, and for ᴺ durable clothing.

CHAPTER 24

Desolation of the earth

BEHOLD, the LORD maketh the earth empty, and maketh it waste, and ᴺ turneth it upside down, and scattereth abroad the inhabitants thereof.

2 And it shall be, as with the people, so with the ᴿ priest; ᴺ as with the servant, so with his master; as with the maid, so with her mistress; ᴿ as with the buyer, so with the seller; as with the lender, so with the borrower; as with the taker of usury, so with the giver of usury to him.

3 The land shall be utterly emptied, and ut-

CHAP. 22
BC 712

20	2 Ki. 18:18
22	Job 12:14
23	Ezra 9:8
24	Or, *instruments of viols*

CHAP. 23
BC 715

1	Jer. 25:22 & 47:4 Ezek. 26, & 27, & 28 Amos 1:9 Zech. 9:2, 4
1	ver. 12
2	Heb. *silent*
3	Ezek. 27:3
5	ch. 19:16
7	ch. 22:2
7	Heb. *from afar off*
8	See Ezek. 28:2, 12

★

Heb. *to pollute*	**9**
Heb. *girdle*	**10**
Or, *concerning a merchantman*	**11**
Heb. *Canaan*	**11**
Or, *strengths*	**11**
Rev. 18:22	**12**
ver. 1	**12**
Ps. 72:9	**13**
Heb. *it shall be unto Tyre as the song of an harlot*	**15**
Rev. 17:2	**17**
Zech. 14:20, 21	**18**
Heb. *old*	**18**

CHAP. 24
BC 712

Heb. *perverteth the face thereof*	**1**
Hos. 4:9	**2**
Or, *prince*	**2**
Ezek. 7:12, 13	**2**

terly spoiled: for the LORD hath spoken this word.

4 The earth mourneth *and* fadeth away, the world languisheth *and* fadeth away, ᴺthe haughty people of the earth do languish.

5 ᴿThe earth also is defiled under the inhabitants thereof; because they have transgressed the laws, changed the ordinance, broken the everlasting covenant.

6 Therefore hath ᴿthe curse devoured the earth, and they that dwell therein are desolate: therefore the inhabitants of the earth are burned, and few men left.

7 ᴿThe new wine mourneth, the vine languisheth, all the merryhearted do sigh.

8 The mirth ᴿof tabrets ceaseth, the noise of them that rejoice endeth, the joy of the harp ceaseth.

9 They shall not drink wine with a song; strong drink shall be bitter to them that drink it.

10 The city of confusion is broken down: every house is shut up, that no man may come in.

11 *There is* a crying for wine in the streets; all joy is darkened, the mirth of the land is gone.

12 In the city is left desolation, and the gate is smitten with destruction.

13 When thus it shall be in the midst of the land among the people, ᴿ*there shall be* as the shaking of an olive tree, *and* as the gleaning grapes when the vintage is done.

Premature songs of praise

14 They shall lift up their voice, they shall sing for the majesty of the LORD, they shall cry aloud from the sea.

15 Wherefore glorify ye the LORD in the ᴺfires, *even* ᴿthe name of the LORD God of Israel in the isles of the sea.

16 From the ᴺuttermost part of the earth have we heard songs, *even* glory to the righteous. But I said, ᴺMy leanness, my leanness, woe unto me! ᴿthe treacherous dealers have dealt treacherously; yea, the treacherous dealers have dealt very treacherously.

The earth is utterly broken

17 ᴿFear, and the pit, and the snare, *are* upon thee, O inhabitant of the earth.

18 And it shall come to pass, *that* he who fleeth from the noise of the fear shall fall into the pit; and he that cometh up out of the midst of the pit shall be taken in the snare: for ᴿthe windows from on high are open, and ᴿthe foundations of the earth do shake.

19 ᴿThe earth is utterly broken down, the

earth is clean dissolved, the earth is moved exceedingly.

20 The earth shall ᴿreel to and fro like a drunkard, and shall be removed like a cottage; and the transgression thereof shall be heavy upon it; and it shall fall, and not rise again.

Enthronement of the LORD of hosts

21 And it shall come to pass in that day, *that* the LORD shall ᴺpunish the host of the high ones *that are* on high, ᴿand the kings of the earth upon the earth.

22 And they shall be gathered together, ᴺas prisoners are gathered in the ᴺpit, and shall be shut up in the prison, and after many days shall they be ᴺvisited.

23 Then the ᴿmoon shall be confounded, and the sun ashamed, when the LORD of hosts shall ᴿreign in ᴿmount Zion, and in Jerusalem, and ᴺbefore his ancients gloriously.

CHAPTER 25

Song of praise

O LORD, thou *art* my God; ᴿI will exalt thee, I will praise thy name; ᴿfor thou hast done wonderful *things;* ᴿ*thy* counsels of old *are* faithfulness *and* truth.

2 For thou hast made ᴿof a city an heap; *of* a defenced city a ruin: a palace of strangers to be no city; it shall never be built.

3 Therefore shall the strong people ᴿglorify thee, the city of the terrible nations shall fear thee.

4 For thou hast been a strength to the poor, a strength to the needy in his distress, ᴿa refuge from the storm, a shadow from the heat, when the blast of the terrible ones *is* as a storm *against* the wall.

5 Thou shalt bring down the noise of strangers, as the heat in a dry place; *even* the heat with the shadow of a cloud: the branch of the terrible ones shall be brought low.

Salvation of God's people

6 And in ᴿthis mountain shall ᴿthe LORD of hosts make unto ᴿall people a feast of fat things, a feast of wines on the lees, of fat things full of marrow, of wines on the lees well refined.

7 And he will ᴺdestroy in this mountain the face of the covering ᴺcast over all people, and ᴿthe vail that is spread over all nations.

8 He will ᴿswallow up death in victory; and the Lord GOD will ᴿwipe away tears from off all faces; and the rebuke of his people shall he take away from off all the earth: for the LORD hath spoken *it*.

CHAP. 24
BC 712

4 Heb. *the height of the people*
5 Gen. 3:17
Num. 35:33
6 Mal. 4:6
7 ch. 16:8, 9
Joel 1:10, 12
8 Jer. 7:34
& 16:9
& 25:10
Ezek. 26:13
Hos. 2:11
Rev. 18:22
13 ch. 17:5, 6
15 Or, *valleys*
15 Mal. 1:11
16 Heb. *wing*
16 Heb. *Leanness to me,* or, *My secret to me*
16 Jer. 5:11
17 See Jer. 48:43, 44
18 Gen. 7:11
18 Ps. 18:7
19 Jer. 4:23

ch. 19:14　20
Heb. *visit upon*　21
Ps. 76:12　21
Heb. *with the gathering of prisoners*　22
Or, *dungeon*　22
Or, *found wanting*　22
ch. 13:10　23
& 60:19
Ezek. 32:7
Joel 2:31
& 3:15
Rev. 19:4, 6　23
Heb. 12:22　23
Or, *there shall be glory before his ancients*　23

CHAP. 25
BC 712

Ex. 15:2　1
Ps. 98:1　1
Num. 23:19　1
ch. 21:9　2
& 23:13
Jer. 51:37
Rev. 11:13　3
ch. 4:6　4
ch. 2:2, 3　6
Prov. 9:2　6
Mat. 22:4
Dan. 7:14　6
Mat. 8:11
Heb. *swallow up*　7
Heb. *covered*　7
2 Cor. 3:15　7
Eph. 4:18
Hos. 13:14　8
1 Cor. 15:54　8
Rev. 7:17　8
& 21:4

9 And it shall be said in that day, Lo, this *is* our God; [R]we have waited for him, and he will save us: this *is* the LORD; we have waited for him, [R]we will be glad and rejoice in his salvation.

10 For in this mountain shall the hand of the LORD rest, and Moab shall be [N]trodden down under him, even as straw is [N]trodden down for the dunghill.

11 And he shall spread forth his hands in the midst of them, as he that swimmeth spreadeth forth *his hands* to swim: and he shall bring down their pride together with the spoils of their hands.

12 And the [R]fortress of the high fort of thy walls shall he bring down, lay low, *and* bring to the ground, *even* to the dust.

CHAPTER 26

Song of Judah

IN [R]that day shall this song be sung in the land of Judah; We have a strong city; [R]salvation will *God* appoint *for* walls and bulwarks.

2 [R]Open ye the gates, that the righteous nation which keepeth the [N]truth may enter in.

3 Thou wilt keep *him* in [N]perfect peace, *whose* [N]mind *is* stayed *on thee:* because he trusteth in thee.

4 Trust ye in the LORD for ever: [R]for in the LORD JĔ-HŌ′-VĂH *is* [N]everlasting strength:

5 For he bringeth down them that dwell on high; [R]the lofty city, he layeth it low; he layeth it low, *even* to the ground; he bringeth it *even* to the dust.

6 The foot shall tread it down, *even* the feet of the poor, *and* the steps of the needy.

7 The way of the just *is* uprightness: [R]thou, most upright, dost weigh the path of the just.

8 Yea, [R]in the way of thy judgments, O LORD, have we waited for thee; the desire of *our* soul *is* to thy name, and to the remembrance of thee.

9 [R]With my soul have I desired thee in the night; yea, with my spirit within me will I seek thee early: for when thy judgments *are* in the earth, the inhabitants of the world will learn righteousness.

10 [R]Let favour be shewed to the wicked, *yet* will he not learn righteousness: in [R]the land of uprightness will he deal unjustly, and will not behold the majesty of the LORD.

11 LORD, *when* thy hand is lifted up, [R]they will not see: *but* they shall see, and be ashamed for *their* envy [N]at the people; yea, the fire of thine enemies shall devour them.

12 LORD, thou wilt ordain peace for us: for thou also hast wrought all our works [N]in us.

13 O LORD our God, [R]*other* lords beside thee have had dominion over us: *but* by thee only will we make mention of thy name.

14 *They are* dead, they shall not live; *they are* deceased, they shall not rise: therefore hast thou visited and destroyed them, and made all their memory to perish.

15 Thou hast increased the nation, O LORD, thou hast increased the nation: thou art glorified: thou hadst removed *it* far *unto* all the ends of the earth.

16 LORD, [R]in trouble have they visited thee, they poured out a [N]prayer *when* thy chastening *was* upon them.

17 Like as [R]a woman with child, *that* draweth near the time of her delivery, is in pain, *and* crieth out in her pangs; so have we been in thy sight, O LORD.

18 We have been with child, we have been in pain, we have as it were brought forth wind; we have not wrought any deliverance in the earth; neither have [R]the inhabitants of the world fallen.

19 [R]Thy dead *men* shall live, *together with* my dead body shall they arise. [R]Awake and sing, ye that dwell in dust: for thy dew *is as* the dew of herbs, and the earth shall cast out the dead.

20 Come, my people, [R]enter thou into thy chambers, and shut thy doors about thee: hide thyself as it were [R]for a little moment, until the indignation be overpast.

21 For, behold, the LORD [R]cometh out of his place to punish the inhabitants of the earth for their iniquity: the earth also shall disclose her [N]blood, and shall no more cover her slain.

CHAPTER 27

Punishment of leviathan

IN that day the LORD with his sore and great and strong sword shall punish lē-vī′-ă-thăn the [N]piercing serpent, [R]even lē-vī′-ă-thăn that crooked serpent; and he shall slay [R]the dragon that *is* in the sea.

Prosperity for Israel

2 In that day [R]sing ye unto her, [R]A vineyard of red wine.

3 [R]I the LORD do keep it; I will water it every moment: lest *any* hurt it, I will keep it night and day.

4 Fury *is* not in me: who would set [R]the briers *and* thorns against me in battle? I would [N]go through them, I would burn them together.

CHAP. 25
BC 712
9 Gen. 49:18
Tit. 2:13
9 Ps. 20:5
10 Or, *threshed*
10 Or, *threshed in Madmenah*
12 ch. 26:5

CHAP. 26
BC 712
1 ch. 2:11
1 ch. 60:18
2 Ps. 118:19, 20
2 Heb. *truths*
3 Heb. *peace, peace,* ch. 57:19
3 Or, *thought, or, imagination*
4 ch. 45:17
4 Heb. *the rock of ages,* Deut. 32:4
5 ch. 25:12 & 32:19
7 Ps. 37:23
8 ch. 64:5
9 Ps. 63:6 S. of S. 3:1
10 Eccl. 8:12 Rom. 2:4
10 Ps. 143:10 Ps. 28:5 ch. 5:12
11 Job 34:27
11 Or, *toward thy people*

Or, *for us*   12
2 Chr. 12:8   13
Hos. 5:15   16
Heb. *secret speech*   16
ch. 13:8   17
John 16:21
Ps. 17:14   18
Ezek. 37:1, etc.   19
Dan. 12:2   19
Ex. 12:22, 23   20
Ps. 30:5   20
ch. 54:7, 8
2 Cor. 4:17
Mic. 1:3   21
Jude 14
Heb. *bloods*   21

CHAP. 27
BC 712
Or, *crossing like a bar*   1
Ps. 74:13, 14   1
ch. 51:9   1
Ezek. 29:3 & 32:2
ch. 5:1   2
Ps. 80:8   2
Jer. 2:21
Ps. 121:4, 5   3
2 Sam. 23:6   4
ch. 9:18
Or, *march against*   4

5 Or let him take hold ᴿof my strength, *that* he may ᴿmake peace with me; *and* he shall make peace with me.

6 He shall cause them that come of Jacob ᴿto take root: Israel shall blossom and bud, and fill the face of the world with fruit.

7 Hath he smitten him, ᴺas he smote those that smote him? *or* is he slain according to the slaughter of them that are slain by him?

8 ᴿIn measure, ᴺwhen it shooteth forth, thou wilt debate with it: ᴿheᴺ stayeth his rough wind in the day of the east wind.

9 By this therefore shall the iniquity of Jacob be purged; and this *is* all the fruit to take away his sin; when he maketh all the stones of the altar as chalkstones that are beaten in sunder, the groves and ᴺimages shall not stand up.

10 Yet the defenced city *shall be* desolate, *and* the habitation forsaken, and left like a wilderness: ᴿthere shall the calf feed, and there shall he lie down, and consume the branches thereof.

11 When the boughs thereof are withered, they shall be broken off: the women come, *and* set them on fire: for ᴿit *is* a people of no understanding: therefore he that made them will not have mercy on them, and ᴿhe that formed them will shew them no favour.

12 And it shall come to pass in that day, *that* the LORD shall beat off from the channel of the river unto the stream of Egypt, and ye shall be gathered one by one, O ye children of Israel.

13 ᴿAnd it shall come to pass in that day, ᴿ*that* the great trumpet shall be blown, and they shall come which were ready to perish in the land of Assyria, and the outcasts in the land of Egypt, and shall worship the LORD in the holy mount at Jerusalem.

CHAPTER 28

Woe pronounced on Ephraim

WOE to ᴿthe crown of pride, to the drunkards of Ē'-phră-ĭm, whose ᴿglorious beauty *is* a fading flower, which *are* on the head of the fat valleys of them that are ᴺovercome with wine!

2 Behold, the Lord hath a mighty and strong one, ᴿ*which* as a tempest of hail *and* a destroying storm, as a flood of mighty waters overflowing, shall cast down to the earth with the hand.

3 ᴿThe crown of pride, the drunkards of Ē'-phră-ĭm, shall be trodden ᴺunder feet:

4 And ᴿthe glorious beauty, which *is* on the head of the fat valley, shall be a fading flower, *and* as the hasty fruit before the summer; which *when* he that looketh upon it seeth, while it is yet in his hand he ᴺeateth it up.

CHAP. 27
BC 712
5 ch. 25:4
5 Job 22:21
6 ch. 37:31
Hos. 14:5, 6
7 Heb. *according to the stroke of those*
8 Job 23:6
Ps. 6:1
Jer. 10:24
& 30:11
& 46:28
1 Cor. 10:13
8 Or, *when thou sendest it forth*
8 Ps. 78:38
8 Or, *when he removeth it*
9 Or, *sun images*
10 See ch. 17:2
& 32:14
11 Deut. 32:28
ch. 1:3
Jer. 8:7
11 Deut. 32:18
ch. 43:1, 7
& 44:2, 21, 24
13 ch. 2:11
13 Mat. 24:31
Rev. 11:15

CHAP. 28
BC 725
1 ver. 3
1 ver. 4
1 Heb. *broken*
2 ch. 30:30
Ezek. 13:11
3 ver. 1
3 Heb. *with feet*
4 ver. 1
4 Heb. *swalloweth*

Prov. 20:1	7
Hos. 4:11	
ch. 56:10, 12	7
Jer. 6:10	9
Heb. *the hearing?*	9
Or, *hath been*	10
1 Cor. 14:21	11
Heb. *stammerings of lips*	11
Or, *he hath spoken*	11
Amos 2:4	15
Gen. 49:24	16
Ps. 118:22	
Mat. 21:42	
Acts 4:11	
Rom. 9:33	
& 10:11	
Eph. 2:20	
1 Pet. 2:6-8	
ver. 15	17
Heb. *a treading down to it*	18

Promise of a remnant

5 In that day shall the LORD of hosts be for a crown of glory, and for a diadem of beauty, unto the residue of his people,

6 And for a spirit of judgment to him that sitteth in judgment, and for strength to them that turn the battle to the gate.

Warning to Jerusalem

7 But they also ᴿhave erred through wine, and through strong drink are out of the way; ᴿthe priest and the prophet have erred through strong drink, they are swallowed up of wine, they are out of the way through strong drink; they err in vision, they stumble *in* judgment.

8 For all tables are full of vomit *and* filthiness, *so that there is* no place *clean.*

9 ᴿWhom shall he teach knowledge? and whom shall he make to understand ᴺdoctrine? *them that are* weaned from the milk, *and* drawn from the breasts.

10 For precept ᴺ*must be* upon precept, precept upon precept; line upon line, line upon line; here a little, *and* there a little:

11 For with ᴿstammeringᴺ lips and another tongue ᴺwill he speak to this people.

12 To whom he said, This *is* the rest *wherewith* ye may cause the weary to rest; and this *is* the refreshing: yet they would not hear.

13 But the word of the LORD was unto them precept upon precept, precept upon precept; line upon line, line upon line; here a little, *and* there a little; that they might go, and fall backward, and be broken, and snared, and taken.

14 Wherefore hear the word of the LORD, ye scornful men, that rule this people which *is* in Jerusalem.

15 Because ye have said, We have made a covenant with death, and with hell are we at agreement; when the overflowing scourge shall pass through, it shall not come unto us: ᴿfor we have made lies our refuge, and under falsehood have we hid ourselves:

16 Therefore thus saith the Lord GOD, Behold, I lay in Zion for a foundation ᴿa stone, a tried stone, a precious corner *stone,* a sure foundation: he that believeth shall not make haste. ★

17 Judgment also will I lay to the line, and righteousness to the plummet: and the hail shall sweep away ᴿthe refuge of lies, and the waters shall overflow the hiding place.

18 And your covenant with death shall be disannulled, and your agreement with hell shall not stand; when the overflowing scourge shall pass through, then ye shall be ᴺtrodden down by it.

19 From the time that it goeth forth it shall take you: for morning by morning shall it pass over, by day and by night: and it shall be a vexation only [N]to understand the report.

20 For the bed is shorter than that *a man* can stretch himself *on it:* and the covering narrower than that he can wrap himself *in it.*

21 For the LORD shall rise up as *in* mount [R]Pĕ-rā'-zĭm, he shall be wroth as *in* the valley of [R]Gibeon, that he may do his work, [R]his strange work; and bring to pass his act, his strange act.

22 Now therefore be ye not mockers, lest your bands be made strong: for I have heard from the Lord GOD of hosts [R]a consumption, even determined upon the whole earth.

23 Give ye ear, and hear my voice; hearken, and hear my speech.

24 Doth the plowman plow all day to sow? doth he open and break the clods of his ground?

25 When he hath made plain the face thereof, doth he not cast abroad the fitches, and scatter the cummin, and cast in [N]the principal wheat and the appointed barley and the [N]rie in their [N]place?

26 [N]For his God doth instruct him to discretion, *and* doth teach him.

27 For the fitches are not threshed with a threshing instrument, neither is a cart wheel turned about upon the cummin; but the fitches are beaten out with a staff, and the cummin with a rod.

28 Bread *corn* is bruised; because he will not ever be threshing it, nor break *it with* the wheel of his cart, nor bruise it *with* his horsemen.

29 This also cometh forth from the LORD of hosts, [R]*which* is wonderful in counsel, *and* excellent in working.

CHAPTER 29

Woe pronounced on Jerusalem

WOE [R]to[N] âr'-ĭ-ĕl, to âr'-ĭ-ĕl, [N]the city [R]*where* David dwelt! add ye year to year; let them [N]kill sacrifices.

2 Yet I will distress âr'-ĭ-ĕl, and there shall be heaviness and sorrow: and it shall be unto me as âr'-ĭ-ĕl.

3 And I will camp against thee round about, and will lay siege against thee with a mount, and I will raise forts against thee.

4 And thou shalt be brought down, *and* shalt speak out of the ground, and thy speech shall be low out of the dust, and thy voice shall be, as of one that hath a familiar spirit, [R]out of the ground, and thy speech shall [N]whisper out of the dust.

5 Moreover the multitude of thy [R]strangers shall be like small dust, and the multitude of the terrible ones *shall be* [R]as chaff that passeth away: yea, it shall be [R]at an instant suddenly.

6 [R]Thou shalt be visited of the LORD of hosts with thunder, and with earthquake, and great noise, with storm and tempest, and the flame of devouring fire.

7 [R]And the multitude of all the nations that fight against âr'-ĭ-ĕl, even all that fight against her and her munition, and that distress her, shall be [R]as a dream of a night vision.

8 [R]It shall even be as when an hungry *man* dreameth, and, behold, he eateth; but he awaketh, and his soul is empty: or as when a thirsty man dreameth, and, behold, he drinketh; but he awaketh, and, behold, *he is* faint, and his soul hath appetite: so shall the multitude of all the nations be, that fight against mount Zion.

Spiritual blindness

9 Stay yourselves, and wonder; [N]cry ye out, and cry: [R]they are drunken, [R]but not with wine; they stagger, but not with strong drink.

10 For [R]the LORD hath poured out upon you the spirit of deep sleep, and hath [R]closed your eyes: the prophets and your [N]rulers, [R]the seers hath he covered.

11 And the vision of all is become unto you as the words of a [N]book [R]that is sealed, which *men* deliver to one that is learned, saying, Read this, I pray thee: [R]and he saith, I cannot; for it *is* sealed:

12 And the book is delivered to him that is not learned, saying, Read this, I pray thee: and he saith, I am not learned.

Mere ritualism condemned

13 Wherefore the Lord said, [R]Forasmuch as this people draw near *me* with their mouth, and with their lips do honour me, but have removed their heart far from me, and their fear toward me is taught by [R]the precept of men:

14 [R]Therefore, behold, [N]I will proceed to do a marvellous work among this people, *even* a marvellous work and a wonder: [R]for the wisdom of their wise *men* shall perish, and the understanding of their prudent *men* shall be hid.

Deceit condemned

15 [R]Woe unto them that seek deep to hide their counsel from the LORD, and their works are in the dark, and [R]they say, Who seeth us? and who knoweth us?

16 Surely your turning of things upside down shall be esteemed as the potter's clay: for shall the [R]work say of him that made it,

He made me not? or shall the thing framed say of him that framed it, He had no understanding?

Transformation of Israel

17 *Is* it not yet a very little while, and ^RLĕb′-ă-non shall be turned into a fruitful field, and the fruitful field shall be esteemed as a forest?

18 And ^Rin that day shall the deaf hear the words of the book, and the eyes of the blind shall see out of obscurity, and out of darkness.

19 ^RThe meek also ^Nshall increase *their* joy in the LORD, and ^Rthe poor among men shall rejoice in the Holy One of Israel.

20 For the terrible one is brought to nought, and ^Rthe scorner is consumed, and all that ^Rwatch for iniquity are cut off:

21 That make a man an offender for a word, and ^Rlay a snare for him that reproveth in the gate, and turn aside the just ^Rfor a thing of nought.

22 Therefore thus saith the LORD, ^Rwho redeemed Abraham, concerning the house of Jacob, Jacob shall not now be ashamed, neither shall his face now wax pale.

23 But when he seeth his children, ^Rthe work of mine hands, in the midst of him, they shall sanctify my name, and sanctify the Holy One of Jacob, and shall fear the God of Israel.

24 They also ^Rthat erred in spirit ^Nshall come to understanding, and they that murmured shall learn doctrine.

CHAPTER 30

Vain alliance with Egypt

WOE to the rebellious children, saith the LORD, ^Rthat take counsel, but not of me; and that cover with a covering, but not of my spirit, ^Rthat they may add sin to sin:

2 ^RThat walk to go down into Egypt, and ^Rhave not asked at my mouth; to strengthen themselves in the strength of Pharaoh, and to trust in the shadow of Egypt!

3 ^RTherefore shall the strength of Pharaoh be your shame, and the trust in the shadow of Egypt *your* confusion.

4 For his princes were at ^RZō′-ăn, and his ambassadors came to Hā′-nĕś.

5 ^RThey were all ashamed of a people *that* could not profit them, nor be an help nor profit, but a shame, and also a reproach.

6 ^RThe burden of the beasts of the south: into the land of trouble and anguish, from whence *come* the young and old lion, ^Rthe

viper and fiery flying serpent, they will carry their riches upon the shoulders of young asses, and their treasures upon the bunches of camels, to a people *that* shall not profit *them.*

7 ^RFor the Egyptians shall help in vain, and to no purpose: therefore have I cried ^Nconcerning this, ^RTheir strength *is* to sit still.

Rebellious Israel to be crushed

8 Now go, ^Rwrite it before them in a table, and note it in a book, that it may be for ^Nthe time to come for ever and ever:

9 That ^Rthis *is* a rebellious people, lying children, children *that* will not hear the law of the LORD:

10 ^RWhich say to the seers, See not; and to the prophets, Prophesy not unto us right things, ^Rspeak unto us smooth things, prophesy deceits:

11 Get you out of the way, turn aside out of the path, cause the Holy One of Israel to cease from before us.

12 Wherefore thus saith the Holy One of Israel, Because ye despise this word, and trust in ^Noppression and perverseness, and stay thereon:

13 Therefore this iniquity shall be to you ^Ras a breach ready to fall, swelling out in a high wall, whose breaking ^Rcometh suddenly at an instant.

14 And ^Rhe shall break it as the breaking of ^Nthe potters' vessel that is broken in pieces; he shall not spare: so that there shall not be found in the bursting of it a sherd to take fire from the hearth, or to take water *withal* out of the pit.

15 For thus saith the Lord GOD, the Holy One of Israel; ^RIn returning and rest shall ye be saved; in quietness and in confidence shall be your strength: ^Rand ye would not.

16 But ye said, No; for we will flee upon horses; therefore shall ye flee: and, We will ride upon the swift; therefore shall they that pursue you be swift.

17 ^ROne thousand *shall flee* at the rebuke of one; at the rebuke of five shall ye flee: till ye be left as ^Na beacon upon the top of a mountain, and as an ensign on an hill.

Future restoration of the people

18 And therefore will the LORD wait, that he may be gracious unto you, and therefore will he be exalted, that he may have mercy upon you: for the LORD *is* a God of judgment: ^Rblessed *are* all they that wait for him.

19 For the people ^Rshall dwell in Zion at Jerusalem: thou shalt weep no more: he will

be very gracious unto thee at the voice of thy cry; when he shall hear it, he will answer thee.

20 And *though* the Lord give you ᴿthe bread of adversity, and the water of ᴺaffliction, yet shall not ᴿthy teachers be removed into a corner any more, but thine eyes shall see thy teachers:

21 And thine ears shall hear a word behind thee, saying, This *is* the way, walk ye in it, when ye ᴿturn to the right hand, and when ye turn to the left.

22 ᴿYe shall defile also the covering of ᴺthy graven images of silver, and the ornament of thy molten images of gold: thou shalt ᴺcast them away as a menstruous cloth; ᴿthou shalt say unto it, Get thee hence.

23 ᴿThen shall he give the rain of thy seed, that thou shalt sow the ground withal; and bread of the increase of the earth, and it shall be fat and plenteous: in that day shall thy cattle feed in large pastures.

24 The oxen likewise and the young asses that ear the ground shall eat ᴺᴺclean provender, which hath been winnowed with the shovel and with the fan.

25 And there shall be ᴿupon every high mountain, and upon every ᴺhigh hill, rivers *and* streams of waters in the day of the great slaughter, when the towers fall.

26 Moreover ᴿthe light of the moon shall be as the light of the sun, and the light of the sun shall be sevenfold, as the light of seven days, in the day that the Lᴏʀᴅ bindeth up the breach of his people, and healeth the stroke of their wound.

Punishment of the Assyrians

27 Behold, the name of the Lᴏʀᴅ cometh from far, burning *with* his anger, ᴺand the burden *thereof is* ᴺheavy: his lips are full of indignation, and his tongue as a devouring fire:

28 And ᴿhis breath, as an overflowing stream, ᴿshall reach to the midst of the neck, to sift the nations with the sieve of vanity: and *there shall be* ᴿa bridle in the jaws of the people, causing *them* to err.

29 Ye shall have a song, as in the night *when* a holy solemnity is kept; and gladness of heart, as when one goeth with a pipe to come into ᴿthe mountain of the Lᴏʀᴅ, to the ᴺmighty One of Israel.

30 ᴿAnd the Lᴏʀᴅ shall cause ᴺhis glorious voice to be heard, and shall shew the lighting down of his arm, with the indignation of *his* anger, and *with* the flame of a devouring fire, *with* scattering, and tempest, ᴿand hailstones.

31 For ᴿthrough the voice of the Lᴏʀᴅ shall

the Assyrian be beaten down, ᴿwhich smote with a rod.

32 And ᴺ*in* every place where the grounded staff shall pass, which the Lᴏʀᴅ shall ᴺlay upon him, *it* shall be with tabrets and harps: and in battles of ᴿshaking will he fight ᴺwith it.

33 ᴿFor Tō′-phĕt *is* ordained ᴺof old; yea, for the king it is prepared; he hath made *it* deep *and* large: the pile thereof *is* fire and much wood; the breath of the Lᴏʀᴅ, like a stream of brimstone, doth kindle it.

CHAPTER 31

Folly of reliance on Egypt

WOE to them ᴿthat go down to Egypt for help; and ᴿstay on horses, and trust in chariots, because *they are* many; and in horsemen, because they are very strong; but they look not unto the Holy One of Israel, ᴿneither seek the Lᴏʀᴅ!

2 Yet he also *is* wise, and will bring evil, and ᴿwill not ᴺcall back his words: but will arise against the house of the evildoers, and against the help of them that work iniquity.

3 Now the Egyptians *are* men, and not God; and their horses flesh, and not spirit. When the Lᴏʀᴅ shall stretch out his hand, both he that helpeth shall fall, and he that is holpen shall fall down, and they all shall fail together.

The LORD of hosts to protect Zion

4 For thus hath the Lᴏʀᴅ spoken unto me, ᴿLike as the lion and the young lion roaring on his prey, when a multitude of shepherds is called forth against him, *he* will not be afraid of their voice, nor abase himself for the ᴺnoise of them: so shall the Lᴏʀᴅ of hosts come down to fight for mount Zion, and for the hill thereof.

5 ᴿAs birds flying, so will the Lᴏʀᴅ of hosts defend Jerusalem; defending also he will deliver *it; and* passing over he will preserve *it*.

6 Turn ye unto *him from* whom the children of Israel have deeply revolted.

7 For in that day every man shall ᴿcast away his idols of silver, and ᴺhis idols of gold, which your own hands have made unto you *for* ᴿa sin.

8 Then shall the Assyrian ᴿfall with the sword, not of a mighty man; and the sword, not of a mean man, shall devour him: but he shall flee ᴺfrom the sword, and his young men shall be ᴺᴺdiscomfited.

9 And ᴿheᴺ shall pass over to ᴺhis strong

hold for fear, and his princes shall be afraid of the ensign, saith the LORD, whose fire *is* in Zion, and his furnace in Jerusalem.

CHAPTER 32

Ideal order

BEHOLD, ᴿa king shall reign in righteousness, and princes shall rule in judgment.

2 And a man shall be as an hiding place from the wind, and ᴿa covert from the tempest; as rivers of water in a dry place, as the shadow of a ᴺgreat rock in a weary land.

3 And ᴿthe eyes of them that see shall not be dim, and the ears of them that hear shall hearken.

4 The heart also of the ᴺrash shall understand knowledge, and the tongue of the stammerers shall be ready to speak ᴺplainly.

5 The vile person shall be no more called liberal, nor the churl said *to be* bountiful.

6 For the vile person will speak villany, and his heart will work iniquity, to practise hypocrisy, and to utter error against the LORD, to make empty the soul of the hungry, and he will cause the drink of the thirsty to fail.

7 The instruments also of the churl *are* evil: he deviseth wicked devices to destroy the poor with lying words, even ᴺwhen the needy speaketh right.

8 But the liberal deviseth liberal things; and by liberal things shall he ᴺstand.

Warning to complacent women

9 Rise up, ye women ᴿthat are at ease; hear my voice, ye careless daughters; give ear unto my speech.

10 ᴺMany days and years shall ye be troubled, ye careless women: for the vintage shall fail, the gathering shall not come.

11 Tremble, ye women that are at ease; be troubled, ye careless ones: strip you, and make you bare, and gird *sackcloth* upon *your* loins.

12 They shall lament for the teats, for ᴺthe pleasant fields, for the fruitful vine.

13 ᴿUpon the land of my people shall come up thorns *and* briers; ᴺYea, upon all the houses of joy *in* ᴿthe joyous city:

14 ᴿBecause the palaces shall be forsaken; the multitude of the city shall be left; the ᴺforts and towers shall be for dens for ever, a joy of wild asses, a pasture of flocks;

15 Until ᴿthe spirit be poured upon us from on high, and ᴿthe wilderness be a fruitful field, and the fruitful field be counted for a forest.

16 Then judgment shall dwell in the wilderness, and righteousness remain in the fruitful field.

17 ᴿAnd the work of righteousness shall be peace; and the effect of righteousness quietness and assurance for ever.

18 And my people shall dwell in a peaceable habitation, and in sure dwellings, and in quiet resting places;

19 ᴿWhen it shall hail, coming down ᴿon the forest; ᴺand the city shall be low in a low place.

20 Blessed *are* ye that sow beside all waters, that send forth *thither* the feet of ᴿthe ox and the ass.

CHAPTER 33

The treacherous destroyer

WOE to thee ᴿthat spoilest, and thou *wast* not spoiled; and dealest treacherously, and they dealt not treacherously with thee! ᴿwhen thou shalt cease to spoil, thou shalt be spoiled; *and* when thou shalt make an end to deal treacherously, they shall deal treacherously with thee.

Prayer for salvation

2 O LORD, be gracious unto us; ᴿwe have waited for thee: be thou their arm every morning, our salvation also in the time of trouble.

3 At the noise of the tumult the people fled; at the lifting up of thyself the nations were scattered.

4 And your spoil shall be gathered *like* the gathering of the caterpiller: as the running to and fro of locusts shall he run upon them.

5 ᴿThe LORD is exalted; for he dwelleth on high: he hath filled Zion with judgment and righteousness.

6 And wisdom and knowledge shall be the stability of thy times, *and* strength of ᴺsalvation: the fear of the LORD *is* his treasure.

7 Behold, their ᴺvaliant ones shall cry without: ᴿthe ambassadors of peace shall weep bitterly.

8 ᴿThe highways lie waste, the wayfaring man ceaseth: ᴿhe hath broken the covenant, he hath despised the cities, he regardeth no man.

9 ᴿThe earth mourneth *and* languisheth: Lĕb'-ă-nǫn is ashamed *and* ᴺhewn down: Shâr'-ǫn is like a wilderness; and Bā'-shăn and Carmel shake off *their fruits*.

The LORD brings salvation

10 ᴿNow will I rise, saith the LORD; now will I be exalted; now will I lift up myself.

11 ᴿYe shall conceive chaff, ye shall bring forth stubble: your breath, *as* fire, shall devour you.

12 And the people shall be *as* the burnings

of lime: ᴿ*as* thorns cut up shall they be burned in the fire.

13 Hear, ᴿye *that are* far off, what I have done; and, ye *that are* near, acknowledge my might.

14 The sinners in Zion are afraid; fearfulness hath surprised the hypocrites. Who among us shall dwell with the devouring fire? who among us shall dwell with everlasting burnings?

15 He that ᴿwalketh ᴺrighteously, and speaketh ᴺuprightly; he that despiseth the gain of ᴺoppressions, that shaketh his hands from holding of bribes, that stoppeth his ears from hearing of ᴺblood, and ᴿshutteth his eyes from seeing evil;

16 He shall dwell on ᴺhigh: his place of defence *shall be* the munitions of rocks: bread shall be given him; his waters *shall be* sure.

17 Thine eyes shall see the king in his beauty: they shall behold ᴺthe land that is very far off.

18 Thine heart shall meditate terror. ᴿWhere *is* the scribe? where *is* the ᴺreceiver? where *is* he that counted the towers?

19 ᴿThou shalt not see a fierce people, ᴿa people of a deeper speech than thou canst perceive; of a ᴺstammering tongue, *that thou canst* not understand.

20 ᴿLook upon Zion, the city of our solemnities: thine eyes shall see ᴿJerusalem a quiet habitation, a tabernacle *that* shall not be taken down; ᴿnot one of ᴿthe stakes thereof shall ever be removed, neither shall any of the cords thereof be broken.

21 But there the glorious Lᴏʀᴅ *will be* unto us a place ᴺof broad rivers *and* streams; wherein shall go no galley with oars, neither shall gallant ship pass thereby.

22 For the Lᴏʀᴅ *is* our judge, the Lᴏʀᴅ *is* our ᴿlawgiver,ᴺ ᴿthe Lᴏʀᴅ *is* our king; he will save us.

23 ᴺThy tacklings are loosed; they could not well strengthen their mast, they could not spread the sail: then is the prey of a great spoil divided; the lame take the prey.

24 And the inhabitant shall not say, I am sick: ᴿthe people that dwell therein *shall be* forgiven *their* iniquity.

CHAPTER 34

Judgment of the nations

Cᴏᴍᴇᴿ near, ye nations, to hear; and hearken, ye people: ᴿlet the earth hear, and ᴺall that is therein; the world, and all things that come forth of it.

2 For the indignation of the Lᴏʀᴅ *is* upon all nations, and *his* fury upon all their armies: he

hath utterly destroyed them, he hath delivered them to the slaughter.

3 Their slain also shall be cast out, and ᴿtheir stink shall come up out of their carcases, and the mountains shall be melted with their blood.

4 And ᴿall the host of heaven shall be dissolved, and the heavens shall be rolled together as a scroll: ᴿand all their host shall fall down, as the leaf falleth off from the vine, and as a ᴿfalling *fig* from the fig tree.

Judgment of Idumea

5 For ᴿmy sword shall be bathed in heaven: behold, it ᴿshall come down upon ĭ-dū-mē′-ă, and upon the people of my curse, to judgment.

6 The sword of the Lᴏʀᴅ is filled with blood, it is made fat with fatness, *and* with the blood of lambs and goats, with the fat of the kidneys of rams: for ᴿthe Lᴏʀᴅ hath a sacrifice in Bŏz′-răh, and a great slaughter in the land of ĭ-dū-mē′-ă.

7 And the ᴺunicorns shall come down with them, and the bullocks with the bulls; and their land shall be ᴺsoaked with blood, and their dust made fat with fatness.

8 For *it is* the day of the Lᴏʀᴅ's ᴿvengeance, *and* the year of recompences for the controversy of Zion.

9 ᴿAnd the streams thereof shall be turned into pitch, and the dust thereof into brimstone, and the land thereof shall become burning pitch.

10 It shall not be quenched night nor day; ᴿthe smoke thereof shall go up for ever: ᴿfrom generation to generation it shall lie waste; none shall pass through it for ever and ever.

11 ᴿBut the ᴺcormorant and the bittern shall possess it; the owl also and the raven shall dwell in it: and ᴿhe shall stretch out upon it the line of confusion, and the stones of emptiness.

12 They shall call the nobles thereof to the kingdom, but none *shall be* there, and all her princes shall be nothing.

13 And ᴿthorns shall come up in her palaces, nettles and brambles in the fortresses thereof: and ᴿit shall be an habitation of dragons, *and* a court for ᴺᴺowls.

14 ᴺThe wild beasts of the desert shall also meet with ᴺthe wild beasts of the island, and the satyr shall cry to his fellow; the ᴺscreech owl also shall rest there, and find for herself a place of rest.

15 There shall the great owl make her nest, and lay, and hatch, and gather under her shadow: there shall the vultures also be gathered, every one with her mate.

16 Seek ye out of ᴿthe book of the Lᴏʀᴅ,

and read: no one of these shall fail, none shall want her mate: for my mouth it hath commanded, and his spirit it hath gathered them.

17 And he hath cast the lot for them, and his hand hath divided it unto them by line: they shall possess it for ever, from generation to generation shall they dwell therein.

CHAPTER 35

Joyous restoration of Israel

THE ᴿwilderness and the solitary place shall be glad for them; and the desert shall rejoice, and blossom as the rose.

2 ᴿIt shall blossom abundantly, and rejoice even with joy and singing: the glory of Lĕb'-ă-nọn shall be given unto it, the excellency of Carmel and Shâr'-ọn, they shall see the glory of the LORD, *and* the excellency of our God.

3 ᴿStrengthen ye the weak hands, and confirm the feeble knees.

4 Say to them *that are* of a ᴺfearful heart, Be strong, fear not: behold, your God will come *with* vengeance, *even* God *with* a recompence; he will come and save you. ★

5 Then the ᴿeyes of the blind shall be opened, and ᴿthe ears of the deaf shall be unstopped. ★

6 Then shall the ᴿlame *man* leap as an hart, and the ᴿtongue of the dumb sing: for in the wilderness shall ᴿwaters break out, and streams in the desert. ★

7 And the parched ground shall become a pool, and the thirsty land springs of water: in ᴿthe habitation of dragons, where each lay, *shall be* ᴺgrass with reeds and rushes.

8 And an highway shall be there, and a way, and it shall be called The way of holiness; ᴿthe unclean shall not pass over it; ᴺbut it *shall be* for those: the wayfaring men, though fools, shall not err *therein.*

9 ᴿNo lion shall be there, nor *any* ravenous beast shall go up thereon, it shall not be found there; but the redeemed shall walk *there:*

10 And the ᴿransomed of the LORD shall return, and come to Zion with songs and everlasting joy upon their heads: they shall obtain joy and gladness, and ᴿsorrow and sighing shall flee away.

CHAPTER 36

Sennacherib's demand of surrender

NOW ᴿit came to pass in the fourteenth year of king Hĕz-ē-kī'-ăh, *that* Sĕn-nạch'-ĕr-ĭb king of Assyria came up against all the defenced cities of Judah, and took them.

2 And the king of Assyria sent Răb'-shă-kĕh

CHAP. **35**

BC 713
1 ch. 55:12
2 ch. 32:15
3 Job 4:3, 4
Heb. 12:12
4 Heb. *hasty*
5 ch. 29:18
Mat. 9:27
& 11:5
John 9:6, 7
5 Mat. 11:5
6 Mat. 11:5
& 15:30
John 5:8, 9
Acts 8:7
6 ch. 32:4
Mat. 9:32
& 12:22
6 ch. 41:18
John 7:38
7 ch. 34:13
7 Or, *a court for reeds, etc.*
8 ch. 52:1
Rev. 21:27
8 Or, *for he shall be with them*
9 Lev. 26:6
ch. 11:9
Ezek. 34:25
10 ch. 51:11
10 ch. 25:8
Rev. 7:17
& 21:4

CHAP. **36**

BC 710
1 2 Ki. 18:13, 17
2 Chr. 32:1

Or, *secretary*   3
2 Ki. 18:19, etc.   4
Heb. *a word of lips*   5
Or, *but counsel and strength* are *for the war*   5
Ezek. 29:6, 7   6
Or, *hostages*   8

---

from Lā'-chĭsh to Jerusalem unto king Hĕz-ē-kī'-ăh with a great army. And he stood by the conduit of the upper pool in the highway of the fuller's field.

3 Then came forth unto him Ē-lī'-ă-kĭm, Hĭl-kī'-ăh's son, which was over the house, and Shĕb'-nă the ᴺscribe, and Jō'-ăh, Ā'-săph's son, the recorder.

4 ᴿAnd Răb'-shă-kĕh said unto them, Say ye now to Hĕz-ē-kī'-ăh, Thus saith the great king, the king of Assyria, What confidence *is* this wherein thou trusteth?

5 I say, *sayest thou,* (but *they are but* ᴺvain words) ᴺ*I have* counsel and strength for war: now on whom dost thou trust, that thou rebellest against me?

6 Lo, thou trustest in the ᴿstaff of this broken reed, on Egypt; whereon if a man lean, it will go into his hand, and pierce it: so *is* Pharaoh king of Egypt to all that trust in him.

7 But if thou say to me, We trust in the LORD our God: *is it* not he, whose high places and whose altars Hĕz-ē-kī'-ăh hath taken away, and said to Judah and to Jerusalem, Ye shall worship before this altar?

8 Now therefore give ᴺpledges, I pray thee, to my master the king of Assyria, and I will give thee two thousand horses, if thou be able on thy part to set riders upon them.

9 How then wilt thou turn away the face of one captain of the least of my master's servants, and put thy trust on Egypt for chariots and for horsemen?

10 And am I now come up without the LORD against this land to destroy it? the LORD said unto me, Go up against this land, and destroy it.

11 Then said Ē-lī'-ă-kĭm and Shĕb'-nă and Jō'-ăh unto Răb'-shă-kĕh, Speak, I pray thee, unto thy servants in the Syrian language; for we understand *it:* and speak not to us in the Jews' language, in the ears of the people that *are* on the wall.

12 But Răb'-shă-kĕh said, Hath my master sent me to thy master and to thee to speak these words? *hath he* not *sent me* to the men that sit upon the wall, that they may eat their own dung, and drink their own piss with you?

13 Then Răb'-shă-kĕh stood, and cried with a loud voice in the Jews' language, and said, Hear ye the words of the great king, the king of Assyria.

14 Thus saith the king, Let not Hĕz-ē-kī'-ăh deceive you: for he shall not be able to deliver you.

15 Neither let Hĕz-ē-kī'-ăh make you trust in the LORD, saying, The LORD will surely deliver us: this city shall not be delivered into the hand of the king of Assyria.

16 Hearken not to Hĕz-ē-kī'-ăh: for thus saith the king of Assyria, ᴺᴺMake *an agreement* with me *by* a present, and come out to me: ᴿand eat ye every one of his vine, and every one of his fig tree, and drink ye every one the waters of his own cistern;

17 Until I come and take you away to a land like your own land, a land of corn and wine, a land of bread and vineyards.

18 *Beware* lest Hĕz-ē-kī'-ăh persuade you, saying, The LORD will deliver us. Hath any of the gods of the nations delivered his land out of the hand of the king of Assyria?

19 Where *are* the gods of Hā'-măth and Är'-phăd? where *are* the gods of Sē-phăr-vā'-ĭm? and have they delivered Să-mâr'-ĭ-ă out of my hand?

20 Who *are they* among all the gods of these lands, that have delivered their land out of my hand, that the LORD should deliver Jerusalem out of my hand?

King Hezekiah's reaction

21 But they held their peace, and answered him not a word: for the king's commandment was, saying, Answer him not.

22 Then came Ē-lī'-ă-kĭm, the son of Hĭl-kī'-ăh, that *was* over the household, and Shĕb'-nă the scribe, and Jō'-ăh, the son of Ā'-săph, the recorder, to Hĕz-ē-kī'-ăh with *their* clothes rent, and told him the words of Răb'-shă-kēh.

CHAPTER 37

AND ᴿit came to pass, when king Hĕz-ē-kī'-ăh heard *it,* that he rent his clothes, and covered himself with sackcloth, and went into the house of the LORD.

2 And he sent Ē-lī'-ă-kĭm, who *was* over the household, and Shĕb'-nă the scribe, and the elders of the priests covered with sackcloth, unto Isaiah the prophet the son of Amoz.

3 And they said unto him, Thus saith Hĕz-ē-kī'-ăh, This day *is* a day of trouble, and of rebuke, and of ᴺblasphemy: for the children are come to the birth, and *there is* not strength to bring forth.

4 It may be the LORD thy God will hear the words of Răb'-shă-kēh, whom the king of Assyria his master hath sent to reproach the living God, and will reprove the words which the LORD thy God hath heard: wherefore lift up *thy* prayer for the remnant that is ᴺleft.

Isaiah's advice

5 So the servants of king Hĕz-ē-kī'-ăh came to Isaiah.

6 And Isaiah said unto them, Thus shall ye

CHAP. 36
BC 710
16 Or, *Seek my favour by a present*
16 Heb. *Make with me a blessing*
16 Zech. 3:10

CHAP. 37
BC 710
1 2 Ki. 19:1, etc.
3 Or, *provocation*
4 Heb. *found*

Or, *put a spirit into him* 7
Jer. 49:23 13
Dan. 9:18 17
Heb. *lands* 18
Heb. *given* 19

say unto your master, Thus saith the LORD, Be not afraid of the words that thou hast heard, wherewith the servants of the king of Assyria have blasphemed me.

7 Behold, I will ᴺsend a blast upon him, and he shall hear a rumour, and return to his own land; and I will cause him to fall by the sword in his own land.

Sennacherib's second demand

8 So Răb'-shă-kēh returned, and found the king of Assyria warring against Lĭb'-năh: for he had heard that he was departed from Lā'-chĭsh.

9 And he heard say concerning Tĭr-hā'-kăh king of Ē-thĭ-ō'-pĭ-ă, He is come forth to make war with thee. And when he heard *it,* he sent messengers to Hĕz-ē-kī'-ăh, saying,

10 Thus shall ye speak to Hĕz-ē-kī'-ăh king of Judah, saying, Let not thy God, in whom thou trustest, deceive thee, saying, Jerusalem shall not be given into the hand of the king of Assyria.

11 Behold, thou hast heard what the kings of Assyria have done to all lands by destroying them utterly; and shalt thou be delivered?

12 Have the gods of the nations delivered them which my fathers have destroyed, *as* Gō'-zăn, and Hâr'-ăn, and Rē'-zĕph, and the children of Eden which *were* in Tĕ-lăs'-săr?

13 Where *is* the king of ᴿHā'-măth, and the king of Är'-phăd, and the king of the city of Sē-phăr-vā'-ĭm, Hē'-nă, and Ī'-văh?

Hezekiah's prayer

14 And Hĕz-ē-kī'-ăh received the letter from the hand of the messengers, and read it: and Hĕz-ē-kī'-ăh went up unto the house of the LORD, and spread it before the LORD.

15 And Hĕz-ē-kī'-ăh prayed unto the LORD, saying,

16 O LORD of hosts, God of Israel, that dwellest *between* the chĕr'-ū-bĭms, thou *art* the God, *even* thou alone, of all the kingdoms of the earth: thou hast made heaven and earth.

17 ᴿIncline thine ear, O LORD, and hear; open thine eyes, O LORD, and see: and hear all the words of Sĕn-năch'-ĕr-ĭb, which hath sent to reproach the living God.

18 Of a truth, LORD, the kings of Assyria have laid waste all the ᴺnations, and their countries,

19 And have ᴺcast their gods into the fire: for they *were* no gods, but the work of men's hands, wood and stone: therefore they have destroyed them.

20 Now therefore, O LORD our God, save us from his hand, that all the kingdoms of the

earth may know that thou *art* the Lord, *even* thou only.

Isaiah's message to Hezekiah

21 Then Isaiah the son of Amoz sent unto Hĕz-ē-kī'-ăh, saying, Thus saith the Lord God of Israel, Whereas thou hast prayed to me against Sĕn-nă<u>ch</u>'-ĕr-ĭb king of Assyria:

22 This *is* the word which the Lord hath spoken concerning him; The virgin, the daughter of Zion, hath despised thee, *and* laughed thee to scorn; the daughter of Jerusalem hath shaken her head at thee.

23 Whom hast thou reproached and blasphemed? and against whom hast thou exalted *thy* voice, and lifted up thine eyes on high? *even* against the Holy One of Israel.

24 ᴺBy thy servants hast thou reproached the Lord, and hast said, By the multitude of my chariots am I come up to the height of the mountains, to the sides of Lĕb'-ă-nọn; and I will cut down ᴺthe tall cedars thereof, *and* the choice fir trees thereof: and I will enter into the height of his border, *and* ᴺthe forest of his Carmel.

25 I have digged, and drunk water; and with the sole of my feet have I dried up all the rivers of the ᴺbesieged places.

26 ᴺHast thou not heard long ago, *how* I have done it; *and* of ancient times, that I have formed it? now have I brought it to pass, that thou shouldest be to lay waste defenced cities *into* ruinous heaps.

27 Therefore their inhabitants *were* ᴺof small power, they were dismayed and confounded: they were *as* the grass of the field, and *as* the green herb, *as* the grass on the housetops, and *as corn* blasted before it be grown up.

28 But I know thy ᴺabode, and thy going out, and thy coming in, and thy rage against me.

29 Because thy rage against me, and thy tumult, is come up into mine ears, therefore ᴿwill I put my hook in thy nose, and my bridle in thy lips, and I will turn thee back by the way by which thou camest.

30 And this *shall be* a sign unto thee, Ye shall eat *this* year such as groweth of itself; and the second year that which springeth of the same: and in the third year sow ye, and reap, and plant vineyards, and eat the fruit thereof.

31 And ᴺthe remnant that is escaped of the house of Judah shall again take root downward, and bear fruit upward:

32 For out of Jerusalem shall go forth a remnant, and ᴺthey that escape out of mount Zion: the ᴿzeal of the Lord of hosts shall do this.

Withdrawal and death of Sennacherib

33 Therefore thus saith the Lord concerning the king of Assyria, He shall not come into this city, nor shoot an arrow there, nor come before it with ᴺshields, nor cast a bank against it.

34 By the way that he came, by the same shall he return, and shall not come into this city, saith the Lord.

35 For I will ᴿdefend this city to save it for mine own sake, and for my servant David's sake.

36 Then the ᴿangel of the Lord went forth, and smote in the camp of the Assyrians a hundred and fourscore and five thousand: and when they arose early in the morning, behold, they *were* all dead corpses.

37 So Sĕn-nă<u>ch</u>'-ĕr-ĭb king of Assyria departed, and went and returned, and dwelt at Nĭn'-ĕ-vēh.

38 And it came to pass, as he was worshipping in the house of Nĭs'-rŏ<u>ch</u> his god, that Ă-drăm'-mĕ-lĕ<u>ch</u> and Shă-rē'-zĕr his sons smote him with the sword; and they escaped into the land of ᴺÄr-mē'-nĭ-ă: and Ē'-săr-hăd'-dọn his son reigned in his stead.

CHAPTER 38

Hezekiah's illness

IN ᴿthose days was Hĕz-ē-kī'-ăh sick unto death. And Isaiah the prophet the son of Amoz came unto him, and said unto him, Thus saith the Lord, ᴿSetᴺ thine house in order: for thou shalt die, and not live.

2 Then Hĕz-ē-kī'-ăh turned his face toward the wall, and prayed unto the Lord,

3 And said, ᴿRemember now, O Lord, I beseech thee, how I have walked before thee in truth and with a perfect heart, and have done *that which is* good in thy sight. And Hĕz-ē-kī'-ăh wept ᴺsore.

4 Then came the word of the Lord to Isaiah, saying,

5 Go, and say to Hĕz-ē-kī'-ăh, Thus saith the Lord, the God of David thy father, I have heard thy prayer, I have seen thy tears: behold, I will add unto thy days fifteen years.

6 And I will deliver thee and this city out of the hand of the king of Assyria: and ᴿI will defend this city.

7 And this *shall be* ᴿa sign unto thee from the Lord, that the Lord will do this thing that he hath spoken;

8 Behold, I will bring again the shadow of the degrees, which is gone down in the ᴺsun dial of Ahaz, ten degrees backward. So the

sun returned ten degrees, by which degrees it was gone down.

Psalm of praise after recovery

9 The writing of Hĕz-ē-kī′-ăh king of Judah, when he had been sick, and was recovered of his sickness:

10 I said in the cutting off of my days, I shall go to the gates of the grave: I am deprived of the residue of my years.

11 I said, I shall not see the Lord, *even* the Lord, ᴿin the land of the living: I shall behold man no more with the inhabitants of the world.

12 ᴿMine age is departed, and is removed from me as a shepherd's tent: I have cut off like a weaver my life: he will cut me off ᴺwith pining sickness: from day *even* to night wilt thou make an end of me.

13 I reckoned till morning, *that,* as a lion, so will he break all my bones: from day *even* to night wilt thou make an end of me.

14 Like a crane *or* a swallow, so did I chatter: ᴿI did mourn as a dove: mine eyes fail *with looking* upward: O Lord, I am oppressed; ᴺundertake for me.

15 What shall I say? he hath both spoken unto me, and himself hath done *it:* I shall go softly all my years ᴿin the bitterness of my soul.

16 O Lord, by these *things men* live, and in all these *things is* the life of my spirit: so wilt thou recover me, and make me to live.

17 Behold, ᴺfor peace I had great bitterness: but ᴺthou hast in love to my soul *delivered it* from the pit of corruption: for thou hast cast all my sins behind thy back.

18 For ᴿthe grave cannot praise thee, death can *not* celebrate thee: they that go down into the pit cannot hope for thy truth.

19 The living, the living, he shall praise thee, as I *do* this day: ᴿthe father to the children shall make known thy truth.

20 The Lord *was ready* to save me: therefore we will sing my songs to the stringed instruments all the days of our life in the house of the Lord.

21 For ᴿIsaiah had said, Let them take a lump of figs, and lay *it* for a plaster upon the boil, and he shall recover.

22 ᴿHĕz-ē-kī′-ăh also had said, What *is* the sign that I shall go up to the house of the Lord?

CHAPTER 39

Envoys from Babylon

AT ᴿthat time Mĕr′-ō-dăch-băl′-ă-dăn, the son of Băl′-ă-dăn, king of Babylon, sent

CHAP. **38**
BC 713
11 Ps. 27:13
& 116:9
12 Job 7:6
12 Or, *from the thrum*
14 ch. 59:11
14 Or, *ease me*
15 Job 7:11
17 Or, *on my peace came great bitterness*
17 Heb. *thou hast loved my soul from the pit*
18 Ps. 6:5
& 30:9
& 88:11
& 115:17
Eccl. 9:10
19 Deut. 4:9
& 6:7
Ps. 78:3, 4
21 2 Ki. 20:7
22 2 Ki. 20:8

CHAP. **39**
BC 712
1 2 Ki. 20:12

2 Chr. 32:31	2
Or, *spicery*	2
Or, *jewels*	2
Heb. *vessels, or, instruments*	2
Jer. 20:5	6
Fulfilled, Dan. 1:2, 3	7
1 Sam. 3:18	8

CHAP. **40**
BC 712

Heb. *to the heart*	2
Or, *appointed time*	2
ch. 61:7	2
Mat. 3:3	3
Mal. 3:1	3
Ps. 68:4	3
ch. 45:2	4
Or, *a straight place*	4
Or, *a plain place*	4

letters and a present to Hĕz-ē-kī′-ăh: for he had heard that he had been sick, and was recovered.

2 ᴿAnd Hĕz-ē-kī′-ăh was glad of them, and shewed them the house of his ᴺprecious things, the silver, and the gold, and the spices, and the precious ointment, and all the house of his ᴺᴺarmour, and all that was found in his treasures: there was nothing in his house, nor in all his dominion, that Hĕz-ē-kī′-ăh shewed them not.

3 Then came Isaiah the prophet unto king Hĕz-ē-kī′-ăh, and said unto him, What said these men? and from whence came they unto thee? And Hĕz-ē-kī′-ăh said, They are come from a far country unto me, *even* from Babylon.

4 Then said he, What have they seen in thine house? And Hĕz-ē-kī′-ăh answered, All that *is* in mine house have they seen: there is nothing among my treasures that I have not shewed them.

Isaiah's rebuke

5 Then said Isaiah to Hĕz-ē-kī′-ăh, Hear the word of the Lord of hosts:

6 Behold, the days come, ᴿthat all that *is* in thine house, and *that* which thy fathers have laid up in store until this day, shall be carried to Babylon: nothing shall be left, saith the Lord.

7 And of thy sons that shall issue from thee, which thou shalt beget, shall they take away; and ᴺthey shall be eunuchs in the palace of the king of Babylon.

8 Then said Hĕz-ē-kī′-ăh to Isaiah, ᴿGood *is* the word of the Lord which thou hast spoken. He said moreover, For there shall be peace and truth in my days.

CHAPTER 40

God comforts his people

COMFORT ye, comfort ye my people, saith your God.

2 Speak ye ᴺcomfortably to Jerusalem, and cry unto her, that her ᴺwarfare is accomplished, that her iniquity is pardoned: ᴿfor she hath received of the Lord's hand double for all her sins.

3 ᴿThe voice of him that crieth in the wilderness, ᴿPrepare ye the way of the Lord, ᴿmake straight in the desert a highway for our God. ★

4 Every valley shall be exalted, and every mountain and hill shall be made low: ᴿand the crooked shall be made ᴺstraight, and the rough places ᴺplain:

5 And the glory of the Lord shall be re-

vealed, and all flesh shall see *it* together: for the mouth of the Lord hath spoken *it*.

6 The voice said, Cry. And he said, What shall I cry? [R]All flesh *is* grass, and all the goodliness thereof *is* as the flower of the field:

7 The grass withereth, the flower fadeth: because the spirit of the Lord bloweth upon it: surely the people *is* grass.

8 The grass withereth, the flower fadeth: but [R]the word of our God shall stand for ever.

9 [N]O Zion, that bringest good tidings, get thee up into the high mountain; [N]O Jerusalem, that bringest good tidings, lift up thy voice with strength; lift *it* up, be not afraid; say unto the cities of Judah, Behold your God!

10 Behold, the Lord God will come [N]with strong *hand,* and [R]his arm shall rule for him: behold, [R]his reward *is* with him, and [N]his work before him.　　★

11 He shall [R]feed his flock like a shepherd: he shall gather the lambs with his arm, and carry *them* in his bosom, *and* shall gently lead those [N]that are with young.　　★

God's sovereignty

12 [R]Who hath measured the waters in the hollow of his hand, and meted out heaven with the span, and comprehended the dust of the earth in [N]a measure, and weighed the mountains in scales, and the hills in a balance?

13 [R]Who hath directed the spirit of the Lord, or *being* [N]his counsellor hath taught him?

14 With whom took he counsel, and *who* [N]instructed him, and taught him in the path of judgment, and taught him knowledge, and shewed to him the way of [N]understanding?

15 Behold, the nations *are* as a drop of a bucket, and are counted as the small dust of the balance: behold, he taketh up the isles as a very little thing.

16 And Lĕb'-ă-nọn *is* not sufficient to burn, nor the beasts thereof sufficient for a burnt offering.

17 All nations before him *are* as [R]nothing; and [R]they are counted to him less than nothing, and vanity.

18 To whom then will ye [R]liken God? or what likeness will ye compare unto him?

19 [R]The workman melteth a graven image, and the goldsmith spreadeth it over with gold, and casteth silver chains.

20 He that [N]*is* so impoverished that he hath no oblation chooseth a tree *that* will not rot; he seeketh unto him a cunning workman [R]to prepare a graven image, *that* shall not be moved.

21 [R]Have ye not known? have ye not heard?

hath it not been told you from the beginning? have ye not understood from the foundations of the earth?

22 [N]*It is* he that sitteth upon the circle of the earth, and the inhabitants thereof *are* as grasshoppers; that [R]stretcheth out the heavens as a curtain, and spreadeth them out as a tent to dwell in:

23 That bringeth the [R]princes to nothing; he maketh the judges of the earth as vanity.

24 Yea, they shall not be planted; yea, they shall not be sown: yea, their stock shall not take root in the earth: and he shall also blow upon them, and they shall wither, and the whirlwind shall take them away as stubble.

25 [R]To whom then will ye liken me, or shall I be equal? saith the Holy One.

26 Lift up your eyes on high, and behold who hath created these *things,* that bringeth out their host by number: [R]he calleth them all by names by the greatness of his might, for that *he is* strong in power; not one faileth.

27 Why sayest thou, O Jacob, and speakest, O Israel, My way is hid from the Lord, and my judgment is passed over from my God?

28 Hast thou not known? hast thou not heard, *that* the everlasting God, the Lord, the Creator of the ends of the earth, fainteth not, neither is weary? [R]*there is* no searching of his understanding.

29 He giveth power to the faint; and to *them that have* no might he increaseth strength.

30 Even the youths shall faint and be weary, and the young men shall utterly fall:

31 But they that wait upon the Lord [R]shall [N]renew *their* strength; they shall mount up with wings as eagles; they shall run, and not be weary; *and* they shall walk, and not faint.

CHAPTER 41

God's action among the nations

KEEP[R] silence before me, O islands; and let the people renew *their* strength: let them come near; then let them speak: let us come near together to judgment.

2 Who raised up [N]the righteous *man* [R]from the east, called him to his foot, [R]gave the nations before him, and made *him* rule over kings? he gave *them* as the dust to his sword, *and* as driven stubble to his bow.

3 He pursued them, *and* passed [N]safely; *even* by the way *that* he had not gone with his feet.

4 [R]Who hath wrought and done *it,* calling the generations from the beginning? I the Lord, the [R]first, and with the last; I *am* he.

5 The isles saw *it,* and feared; the ends of the earth were afraid, drew near, and came.

6 ^RThey helped every one his neighbour; and *every one* said to his brother, ^NBe of good courage.

7 ^RSo the carpenter encouraged the ^Ngoldsmith, *and* he that smootheth *with* the hammer ^Nhim that smote the anvil, ^Nsaying, It *is* ready for the sodering: and he fastened it with nails, ^R*that* it should not be moved.

God has chosen Israel

8 But thou, Israel, *art* my servant, Jacob whom I have ^Rchosen, the seed of Abraham my ^Rfriend.

9 *Thou* whom I have taken from the ends of the earth, and called thee from the chief men thereof, and said unto thee, Thou *art* my servant; I have chosen thee, and not cast thee away.

10 ^RFear thou not; ^Rfor I *am* with thee: be not dismayed; for I *am* thy God: I will strengthen thee; yea, I will help thee; yea, I will uphold thee with the right hand of my righteousness.

11 Behold, all they that were incensed against thee shall be ^Rashamed and confounded: they shall be as nothing; and ^Nthey that strive with thee shall perish.

12 Thou shalt seek them, and shalt not find them, *even* ^Nthem that contended with thee: ^Nthey that war against thee shall be as nothing, and as a thing of nought.

13 For I the LORD thy God will hold thy right hand, saying unto thee, Fear not; I will help thee.

14 Fear not, thou worm Jacob, *and* ye ^Nmen of Israel; I will help thee, saith the LORD, and thy redeemer, the Holy One of Israel.

15 Behold, ^RI will make thee a new sharp threshing instrument having ^Nteeth: thou shalt thresh the mountains, and beat *them* small, and shalt make the hills as chaff. ★

16 Thou shalt ^Rfan them, and the wind shall carry them away, and the whirlwind shall scatter them: and thou shalt rejoice in the LORD, *and* ^Rshalt glory in the Holy One of Israel. ★

17 *When* the poor and needy seek water, and *there is* none, *and* their tongue faileth for thirst, I the LORD will hear them, *I* the God of Israel will not forsake them.

18 I will open ^Rrivers in high places, and fountains in the midst of the valleys: I will make the ^Rwilderness a pool of water, and the dry land springs of water.

19 I will plant in the wilderness the cedar,

the shīt'-tăh tree, and the myrtle, and the oil tree; I will set in the desert the fir tree, *and* the pine, and the box tree together:

20 ^RThat they may see, and know, and consider, and understand together, that the hand of the LORD hath done this, and the Holy One of Israel hath created it.

Inadequacy of idolatry

21 ^NProduce your cause, saith the LORD; bring forth your strong *reasons,* saith the King of Jacob.

22 ^RLet them bring *them* forth, and shew us what shall happen: let them shew the former things, what they *be,* that we may ^Nconsider them, and know the latter end of them; or declare us things for to come.

23 ^RShew the things that are to come hereafter, that we may know that ye *are* gods: yea, ^Rdo good, or do evil, that we may be dismayed, and behold *it* together.

24 Behold, ^Rye *are* ^Nof nothing, and your work ^Nof nought: an abomination *is he that* chooseth you.

25 I have raised up *one* from the north, and he shall come: from the rising of the sun ^Rshall he call upon my name: ^Rand he shall come upon princes as *upon* mortar, and as the potter treadeth clay.

26 ^RWho hath declared from the beginning, that we may know? and beforetime, that we may say, *He is* righteous? yea, *there is* none that sheweth, yea, *there is* none that declareth, yea, *there is* none that heareth your words.

27 ^RThe first ^R*shall say* to Zion, Behold, behold them: and I will give to Jerusalem one that bringeth good tidings.

28 ^RFor I beheld, and *there was* no man; even among them, and *there was* no counsellor, that, when I asked of them, could ^Nanswer a word.

29 ^RBehold, they *are* all vanity; their works *are* nothing: their molten images *are* wind and confusion.

CHAPTER 42

Servant of the LORD

BEHOLD ^Rmy servant, whom I uphold; mine elect, *in whom* my soul ^Rdelighteth; ^RI have put my spirit upon him: he shall bring forth judgment to the Gentiles. ★

2 He shall not cry, nor lift up, nor cause his voice to be heard in the street. ★

3 A bruised reed shall he not break, and the ^Nsmoking flax shall he not ^Nquench: he shall bring forth judgment unto truth. ★

CHAP. 41

BC 712

6 ch. 40:19
6 Heb. *Be strong*
7 ch. 40:19
7 Or, *founder*
7 Or, *the smiting*
7 Or, *saying of the soder, It is good*
7 ch. 40:20
8 Deut. 7:6 & 10:15
Ps. 135:4
ch. 43:1
8 2 Chr. 20:7
Jas. 2:23
10 ver. 13, 14
ch. 43:5
10 Deut. 31:6
11 Ex. 23:22
ch. 45:24 & 60:12
Zech. 12:3
11 Heb. *the men of thy strife*
12 Heb. *the men of thy contention*
12 Heb. *the men of thy war*
14 Or, *few men*
15 Mic. 4:13
2 Cor. 10:4
15 Heb. *mouths*
16 Jer. 51:2
16 ch. 45:25
18 ch. 35:6, 7 & 43:19 & 44:3
18 Ps. 107:35

Job 12:9   20
Heb. *Cause to come near*   21
ch. 45:21   22
Heb. *set our heart* upon them   22
ch. 42:9 & 44:7, 8 & 45:3
John 13:19   23
Jer. 10:5   23
Ps. 115:8   24
ch. 44:9
1 Cor. 8:4
Or, *worse than nothing*   24
Or, *worse than of a viper*   24
Ezra 1:2   25
ver. 2   25
ch. 43:9   26
ver. 4   27
ch. 40:9   27
ch. 63:5   28
Heb. *return*   28
ver. 24   29

CHAP. 42

BC 712

ch. 43:10 & 49:3, 6   1
Mat. 12:18
Phil. 2:7
Mat. 3:17 & 17:5   1
Eph. 1:6
ch. 11:2   1
John 3:34
Or, *dimly burning*   3
Heb. *quench it*   3

4 He shall not fail nor be ᴺdiscouraged, till he have set judgment in the earth: ᴿand the isles shall wait for his law.   ★

The mission of the servant

5 Thus saith God the Lᴏʀᴅ, ᴿhe that created the heavens, and stretched them out; he that spread forth the earth, and that which cometh out of it; ᴿhe that giveth breath unto the people upon it, and spirit to them that walk therein:

6 ᴿI the Lᴏʀᴅ have called thee in righteousness, and will hold thine hand, and will keep thee, ᴿand give thee for a covenant of the people, for ᴿa light of the Gentiles;   ★

7 ᴿTo open the blind eyes, to ᴿbring out the prisoners from the prison, *and* them that sit in ᴿdarkness out of the prison house.   ★

8 I *am* the Lᴏʀᴅ: that *is* my name: and my ᴿglory will I not give to another, neither my praise to graven images.

9 Behold, the former things are come to pass, and new things do I declare: before they spring forth I tell you of them.

A new song of praise

10 ᴿSing unto the Lᴏʀᴅ a new song, *and* his praise from the end of the earth, ᴿye that go down to the sea, and ᴺall that is therein; the isles, and the inhabitants thereof.

11 Let the wilderness and the cities thereof lift up *their voice,* the villages *that* Kē'-där doth inhabit: let the inhabitants of the rock sing, let them shout from the top of the mountains.

12 Let them give glory unto the Lᴏʀᴅ, and declare his praise in the islands.

13 The Lᴏʀᴅ shall go forth as a mighty man, he shall stir up jealousy like a man of war: he shall cry, ᴿyea, roar; he shall ᴺprevail against his enemies.

God's impatience with idolaters

14 I have long time holden my peace; I have been still, *and* refrained myself: *now* will I cry like a travailing woman; I will destroy and ᴺdevour at once.

15 I will make waste mountains and hills, and dry up all their herbs; and I will make the rivers islands, and I will dry up the pools.

16 And I will bring the blind by a way *that* they knew not; I will lead them in paths *that* they have not known: I will make darkness light before them, and crooked things ᴺstraight. These things will I do unto them, and not forsake them.

17 They shall be ᴿturned back, they shall be greatly ashamed, that trust in graven images,

---

CHAP. 42
BC 712

4 Heb. *broken*
4 Gen. 49:10
5 ch. 44:24
  Zech. 12:1
5 Acts 17:25
6 ch. 43:1
6 ch. 49:8
6 ch. 49:6
  Luke 2:32
  Acts 13:47
7 ch. 35:5
7 ch. 61:1
  Luke 4:18
  2 Tim. 2:26
  Heb. 2:14
7 ch. 9:2
8 ch. 48:11
10 Ps. 33:3 &
  40:3 & 98:1
10 Ps. 107:23
10 Heb. *the fulness thereof*
13 ch. 31:4
13 Or, *behave himself mightily*
14 Heb. *swallow, or, sup up*
16 Heb. *into straightness*
17 Ps. 97:7
  ch. 1:29
  & 44:11
  & 45:16

ch. 43:8	19
Ezek. 12:2	
See John 9:39, 41	
Rom. 2:21	20
Or, *him*	21
Or, *in snaring all the young men of them*	22
Heb. *a treading*	22
Heb. *for the after time?*	23
2 Ki. 25:9	25
Hos. 7:9	25

CHAP. 43
BC 712

ver. 7	1
ver. 21	1
ch. 44:2, 21	
ch. 44:6	1
ch. 42:6	1
& 45:4	
Ps. 66:12	2
& 91:3, etc.	
Deut. 31:6	2
Dan. 3:25	2
Prov. 11:8	3
& 21:18	
Or, *person*	4
ch. 41:10	5
& 44:2	
Jer. 30:10	
& 46:27, 28	

---

that say to the molten images, Ye *are* our gods.

Spiritual blindness of Israel

18 Hear, ye deaf; and look, ye blind, that ye may see.

19 ᴿWho *is* blind, but my servant? or deaf, as my messenger *that* I sent? who *is* blind as *he that is* perfect, and blind as the Lᴏʀᴅ's servant?

20 Seeing many things, ᴿbut thou observest not; opening the ears, but he heareth not.

21 The Lᴏʀᴅ is well pleased for his righteousness' sake; he will magnify the law, and make ᴺ*it* honourable.

22 But this *is* a people robbed and spoiled; ᴺ*they are* all of them snared in holes, and they are hid in prison houses: they are for a prey, and none delivereth; for ᴺa spoil, and none saith, Restore.

23 Who among you will give ear to this? *who* will hearken and hear ᴺfor the time to come?

24 Who gave Jacob for a spoil, and Israel to the robbers? did not the Lᴏʀᴅ, he against whom we have sinned? for they would not walk in his ways, neither were they obedient unto his law.

25 Therefore he hath poured upon him the fury of his anger, and the strength of battle: ᴿand it hath set him on fire round about, ᴿyet he knew not; and it burned him, yet he laid *it* not to heart.

CHAPTER 43

Redemption of Israel

B UT now thus saith the Lᴏʀᴅ ᴿthat created thee, O Jacob, ᴿand he that formed thee, O Israel, Fear not: ᴿfor I have redeemed thee, ᴿI have called *thee* by thy name; thou *art* mine.

2 ᴿWhen thou passest through the waters, ᴿI *will be* with thee; and through the rivers, they shall not overflow thee: when thou ᴿwalkest through the fire, thou shalt not be burned; neither shall the flame kindle upon thee.

3 For I *am* the Lᴏʀᴅ thy God, the Holy One of Israel, thy Saviour: ᴿI gave Egypt *for* thy ransom, Ē-thǐ-ō'-pǐ-ă and Sē'-bă for thee.

4 Since thou wast precious in my sight, thou hast been honourable, and I have loved thee: therefore will I give men for thee, and people for thy ᴺlife.

5 ᴿFear not: for I *am* with thee: I will bring thy seed from the east, and gather thee from the west;

6 I will say to the north, Give up; and to the south, Keep not back: bring my sons from far, and my daughters from the ends of the earth;

7 *Even* every one that is ᴿcalled by my name: for ᴿI have created him for my glory, ᴿI have formed him; yea, I have made him.

Israel's call to witness

8 ᴿBring forth the blind people that have eyes, and the deaf that have ears.

9 Let all the nations be gathered together, and let the people be assembled: ᴿwho among them can declare this, and shew us former things? let them bring forth their witnesses, that they may be justified: or let them hear, and say, *It is* truth.

10 ᴿYe *are* my witnesses, saith the Lord, ᴿand my servant whom I have chosen: that ye may know and believe me, and understand that I *am* he: ᴿbefore me there was ᴺno God formed, neither shall there be after me.

11 I, *even* I, ᴿ*am* the Lord; and beside me *there is* no saviour.

12 I have declared, and have saved, and I have shewed, when *there was* no ᴿstrange *god* among you: ᴿtherefore ye *are* my witnesses, saith the Lord, that I *am* God.

13 ᴿYea, before the day *was* I *am* he; and *there is* none that can deliver out of my hand: I will work, and who shall ᴿletᴺ it?

Fall of Babylon predicted

14 Thus saith the Lord, your redeemer, the Holy One of Israel; For your sake I have sent to Babylon, and have brought down all their ᴺnobles, and the C̲h̲ăl-dē′-ăns, whose cry *is* in the ships.

15 I *am* the Lord, your Holy One, the creator of Israel, your King.

16 Thus saith the Lord, which ᴿmaketh a way in the sea, and a ᴿpath in the mighty waters;

17 Which ᴿbringeth forth the chariot and horse, the army and the power; they shall lie down together, they shall not rise: they are extinct, they are quenched as tow.

18 ᴿRemember ye not the former things, neither consider the things of old.

19 Behold, I will do a ᴿnew thing; now it shall spring forth; shall ye not know it? ᴿI will even make a way in the wilderness, *and* rivers in the desert.

20 The beast of the field shall honour me, the dragons and the ᴺᴺowls: because ᴿI give waters in the wilderness, *and* rivers in the desert, to give drink to my people, my chosen.

21 ᴿThis people have I formed for myself; they shall shew forth my praise.

Israel's sin of ingratitude

22 But thou hast not called upon me, O Jacob; but thou ᴿhast been weary of me, O Israel.

23 ᴿThou hast not brought me the ᴺsmall cattle of thy burnt offerings; neither hast thou honoured me with thy sacrifices. I have not caused thee to serve with an offering, nor wearied thee with incense.

24 Thou hast bought me no sweet cane with money, neither hast thou ᴺfilled me with the fat of thy sacrifices: but thou hast made me to serve with thy sins, thou hast ᴿwearied me with thine iniquities.

25 I, *even* I, *am* he that ᴿblotteth out thy transgressions ᴿfor mine own sake, ᴿand will not remember thy sins.

26 Put me in remembrance: let us plead together: declare thou, that thou mayest be justified.

27 Thy first father hath sinned, and thy ᴺteachers have transgressed against me.

28 Therefore ᴿI have profaned the ᴺprinces of the sanctuary, ᴿand have given Jacob to the curse, and Israel to reproaches.

CHAPTER 44

One true God

YET now hear, ᴿO Jacob my servant; and Israel, whom I have chosen:

2 Thus saith the Lord that made thee, ᴿand formed thee from the womb, *which* will help thee; Fear not, O Jacob, my servant; and thou, ᴿJĕs-ū′-rŭn, whom I have chosen.

3 For I will ᴿpour water upon him that is thirsty, and floods upon the dry ground: I will pour my spirit upon thy seed, and my blessing upon thine offspring:

4 And they shall spring up *as* among the grass, as willows by the water courses.

5 One shall say, I *am* the Lord's; and another shall call *himself* by the name of Jacob; and another shall subscribe *with* his hand unto the Lord, and surname *himself* by the name of Israel.

6 Thus saith the Lord the King of Israel, and his redeemer the Lord of hosts; ᴿI *am* the first, and I *am* the last; and beside me *there is* no God.

7 And ᴿwho, as I, shall call, and shall declare it, and set it in order for me, since I appointed the ancient people? and the things that are coming, and shall come, let them shew unto them.

8 Fear ye not, neither be afraid: ᴿhave not I told thee from that time, and have declared *it?* ᴿye *are* even my witnesses. Is there a God

beside me? yea, ᴿthere is no ᴺGod; I know not any.

Delusion of men who make gods

9 ᴿThey that make a graven image *are* all of them vanity; and their ᴺdelectable things shall not profit; and they *are* their own witnesses; ᴿthey see not, nor know; that they may be ashamed.

10 Who hath formed a god, or molten a graven image ᴿthat is profitable for nothing?

11 Behold, all his fellows shall be ᴿashamed: and the workmen, they *are* of men: let them all be gathered together, let them stand up; *yet* they shall fear, *and* they shall be ashamed together.

12 ᴿThe smith ᴺwith the tongs both worketh in the coals, and fashioneth it with hammers, and worketh it with the strength of his arms: yea, he is hungry, and his strength faileth: he drinketh no water, and is faint.

13 The carpenter stretcheth out *his* rule; he marketh it out with a line; he fitteth it with planes, and he marketh it out with the compass, and maketh it after the figure of a man, according to the beauty of a man; that it may remain in the house.

14 He heweth him down cedars, and taketh the cypress and the oak, which he ᴺstrengtheneth for himself among the trees of the forest: he planteth an ash, and the rain doth nourish *it*.

15 Then shall it be for a man to burn: for he will take thereof, and warm himself; yea, he kindleth *it*, and baketh bread; yea, he maketh a god, and worshippeth *it;* he maketh it a graven image, and falleth down thereto.

16 He burneth part thereof in the fire; with part thereof he eateth flesh; he roasteth roast, and is satisfied: yea, he warmeth *himself,* and saith, Aha, I am warm, I have seen the fire:

17 And the residue thereof he maketh a god, *even* his graven image: he falleth down unto it, and worshippeth *it,* and prayeth unto it, and saith, Deliver me; for thou *art* my god.

18 ᴿThey have not known nor understood: for ᴿhe hath ᴺshut their eyes, that they cannot see; *and* their hearts, that they cannot understand.

19 And none ᴿconsiderethᴺ in his heart, neither *is there* knowledge nor understanding to say, I have burned part of it in the fire; yea, also I have baked bread upon the coals thereof; I have roasted flesh, and eaten *it:* and shall I make the residue thereof an abomination? shall I fall down to ᴺthe stock of a tree?

20 He feedeth on ashes: ᴿa deceived heart hath turned him aside, that he cannot deliver his soul, nor say, *Is there* not a lie in my right hand?

Glory of God who makes men

21 Remember these, O Jacob and Israel; for ᴿthou *art* my servant: I have formed thee; thou *art* my servant: O Israel, thou shalt not be forgotten of me.

22 ᴿI have blotted out, as a thick cloud, thy transgressions, and, as a cloud, thy sins: return unto me; for ᴿI have redeemed thee.

23 ᴿSing, O ye heavens; for the Lᴏʀᴅ hath done *it:* shout, ye lower parts of the earth: break forth into singing, ye mountains, O forest, and every tree therein: for the Lᴏʀᴅ hath redeemed Jacob, and glorified himself in Israel.

24 Thus saith the Lᴏʀᴅ, ᴿthy redeemer, and ᴿhe that formed thee from the womb, I *am* the Lᴏʀᴅ that maketh all *things;* ᴿthat stretcheth forth the heavens alone; that spreadeth abroad the earth by myself;

25 That ᴿfrustrateth the tokens ᴿof the liars, and maketh diviners mad; that turneth wise *men* backward, ᴿand maketh their knowledge foolish;

26 ᴿThat confirmeth the word of his servant, and performeth the counsel of his messengers; that saith to Jerusalem, Thou shalt be inhabited; and to the cities of Judah, Ye shall be built, and I will raise up the ᴺdecayed places thereof:

27 ᴿThat saith to the deep, Be dry, and I will dry up thy rivers:

28 That saith of Cyrus, *He is* my shepherd, and shall perform all my pleasure: even saying to Jerusalem, ᴿThou shalt be built; and to the temple, Thy foundation shall be laid.

CHAPTER 45

Commission of Cyrus

THUS saith the Lᴏʀᴅ to his anointed, to Cyrus, whose ᴿright hand I ᴺhave holden, ᴿto subdue nations before him; and I will loose the loins of kings, to open before him the two leaved gates; and the gates shall not be shut;

2 I will go before thee, ᴿand make the crooked places straight: ᴿI will break in pieces the gates of brass, and cut in sunder the bars of iron:

3 And I will give thee the treasures of darkness, and hidden riches of secret places, ᴿthat thou mayest know that I, the Lᴏʀᴅ, which ᴿcall *thee* by thy name, *am* the God of Israel.

4 For ᴿJacob my servant's sake, and Israel mine elect, I have even called thee by thy name: I have surnamed thee, though thou hast not known me.

5 I ᴿ*am* the Lᴏʀᴅ, and ᴿ*there is* none else,

there is no God beside me: ^RI girded thee, though thou hast not known me:

6 ^RThat they may know from the rising of the sun, and from the west, that *there is* none beside me. I *am* the LORD, and *there is* none else.

7 I form the light, and create darkness: I make peace, and ^Rcreate evil: I the LORD do all these *things*.

Argument for God's choice

8 ^RDrop down, ye heavens, from above, and let the skies pour down righteousness: let the earth open, and let them bring forth salvation, and let righteousness spring up together; I the LORD have created it.

9 Woe unto him that striveth with ^Rhis Maker! *Let* the potsherd *strive* with the potsherds of the earth. ^RShall the clay say to him that fashioneth it, What makest thou? or thy work, He hath no hands?

10 Woe unto him that saith unto *his* father, What begettest thou? or to the woman, What hast thou brought forth?

11 Thus saith the LORD, the Holy One of Israel, and his Maker, Ask me of things to come concerning ^Rmy sons, and concerning ^Rthe work of my hands command ye me.

12 ^RI have made the earth, and ^Rcreated man upon it: I, *even* my hands, have stretched out the heavens, and ^Rall their host have I commanded.

13 ^RI have raised him up in righteousness, and I will ^Ndirect all his ways: he shall ^Rbuild my city, and he shall let go my captives, ^Rnot for price nor reward, saith the LORD of hosts.

Foreigners' recognition of God

14 Thus saith the LORD, ^RThe labour of Egypt, and merchandise of Ē-thī-ō′-pĭ-ă and of the Să-bē′-ăn̄ṡ, men of stature, shall come over unto thee, and they shall be thine: they shall come after thee; ^Rin chains they shall come over, and they shall fall down unto thee, they shall make supplication unto thee, *saying*, ^RSurely God *is* in thee; and ^Rthere is none else, *there is* no God.

15 Verily thou *art* a God ^Rthat hidest thyself, O God of Israel, the Saviour.

16 They shall be ashamed, and also confounded, all of them: they shall go to confusion together *that are* ^Rmakers of idols.

17 ^RBut Israel shall be saved in the LORD with an everlasting salvation: ye shall not be ashamed nor confounded world without end.

God's design of creation

18 For thus saith the LORD ^Rthat created the heavens; God himself that formed the earth

and made it; he hath established it, he created it not in vain, he formed it to be inhabited: ^RI *am* the LORD; and *there is* none else.

19 I have not spoken in ^Rsecret, in a dark place of the earth: I said not unto the seed of Jacob, Seek ye me in vain: ^RI the LORD speak righteousness, I declare things that are right.

Invitation to the nations

20 Assemble yourselves and come; draw near together, ye *that are* escaped of the nations: ^Rthey have no knowledge that set up the wood of their graven image, and pray unto a god *that* cannot save.

21 Tell ye, and bring *them* near; yea, let them take counsel together: ^Rwho hath declared this from ancient time? *who* hath told it from that time? *have* not I the LORD? ^Rand *there is* no God else beside me; a just God and a Saviour; *there is* none beside me.   ★

22 ^RLook unto me, and be ye saved, all the ends of the earth: for I *am* God, and *there is* none else.

23 ^RI have sworn by myself, the word is gone out of my mouth *in* righteousness, and shall not return, That unto me every ^Rknee shall bow, ^Revery tongue shall swear.

24 ^NSurely, shall *one* say, in the LORD have I ^Rrighteousness^N and strength: *even* to him shall *men* come; and ^Rall that are incensed against him shall be ashamed.

25 ^RIn the LORD shall all the seed of Israel be justified, and ^Rshall glory.

CHAPTER 46

No other like God

BEL ^Rboweth down, Nē′-bō stoopeth, their idols were upon the beasts, and upon the cattle: your carriages *were* heavy loaden; ^Rthey *are* a burden to the weary *beast*.

2 They stoop, they bow down together; they could not deliver the burden, ^Rbut ^Nthemselves are gone into captivity.

3 Hearken unto me, O house of Jacob, and all the remnant of the house of Israel, ^Rwhich are borne *by me* from the belly, which are carried from the womb:

4 And *even* to *your* old age ^RI *am* he; and *even* to hoar hairs ^Rwill I carry *you*: I have made, and I will bear; even I will carry, and will deliver *you*.

5 ^RTo whom will ye liken me, and make *me* equal, and compare me, that we may be like?

6 ^RThey lavish gold out of the bag, and weigh silver in the balance, *and* hire a goldsmith; and he maketh it a god: they fall down, yea, they worship.

7 ^RThey bear him upon the shoulder, they

carry him, and set him in his place, and he standeth; from his place shall he not remove: yea, ᴿone shall cry unto him, yet can he not answer, nor save him out of his trouble.

8 Remember this, and shew yourselves men: ᴿbring *it* again to mind, O ye transgressors.

9 ᴿRemember the former things of old: for I *am* God, and ᴿ*there is* none else; *I am* God, and *there is* none like me,

10 ᴿDeclaring the end from the beginning, and from ancient times *the things* that are not *yet* done, saying, ᴿMy counsel shall stand, and I will do all my pleasure:

11 Calling a ravenous bird ᴿfrom the east, ᴺthe man ᴿthat executeth my counsel from a far country: yea, ᴿI have spoken *it,* I will also bring it to pass; I have purposed *it,* I will also do it.

12 Hearken unto me, ye ᴿstouthearted, ᴿthat *are* far from righteousness:

13 ᴿI bring near my righteousness; it shall not be far off, and my salvation ᴿshall not tarry: and I will place ᴿsalvation in Zion for Israel my glory.

CHAPTER 47

God's judgment of Babylon

COME ᴿdown, and ᴿsit in the dust, O virgin daughter of Babylon, sit on the ground: *there is* no throne, O daughter of the Chăl-dē′-ăns: for thou shalt no more be called tender and delicate.

2 ᴿTake the millstones, and grind meal: uncover thy locks, make bare the leg, uncover the thigh, pass over the rivers.

3 ᴿThy nakedness shall be uncovered, yea, thy shame shall be seen: ᴿI will take vengeance, and I will not meet *thee as* a man.

4 *As for* ᴿour redeemer, the Lᴏʀᴅ of hosts *is* his name, the Holy One of Israel.

5 Sit thou ᴿsilent, and get thee into darkness, O daughter of the Chăl-dē′-ăns: ᴿfor thou shalt no more be called, The lady of kingdoms.

6 ᴿI was wroth with my people, ᴿI have polluted mine inheritance, and given them into thine hand: thou didst shew them no mercy; ᴿupon the ancient hast thou very heavily laid thy yoke.

7 And thou saidst, I shall be ᴿa lady for ever: *so* that thou didst not ᴿlay these *things* to thy heart, ᴿneither didst remember the latter end of it.

8 Therefore hear now this, *thou that art* given to pleasures, that dwellest carelessly, that sayest in thine heart, ᴿI *am,* and none else beside me; ᴿI shall not sit *as* a widow, neither shall I know the loss of children:

9 But ᴿthese two *things* shall come to thee ᴿin a moment in one day, the loss of children, and widowhood: they shall come upon thee in their perfection ᴿfor the multitude of thy sorceries, *and* for the great abundance of thine enchantments.

10 For thou ᴿhast trusted in thy wickedness: ᴿthou hast said, None seeth me. Thy wisdom and thy knowledge, it hath ᴺperverted thee; ᴿand thou hast said in thine heart, I *am,* and none else beside me.

11 Therefore shall evil come upon thee; thou shalt not know ᴺfrom whence it riseth: and mischief shall fall upon thee; thou shalt not be able to ᴺput it off: and ᴿdesolation shall come upon thee suddenly, *which* thou shalt not know.

12 Stand now with thine enchantments, and with the multitude of thy sorceries, wherein thou hast laboured from thy youth; if so be thou shalt be able to profit, if so be thou mayest prevail.

13 ᴿThou art wearied in the multitude of thy counsels. Let now ᴿthe ᴺastrologers, the stargazers, ᴺthe monthly prognosticators, stand up, and save thee from *these things* that shall come upon thee.

14 Behold, they shall be ᴿas stubble; the fire shall burn them; they shall not deliver ᴺthemselves from the power of the flame: *there shall* not *be* a coal to warm at, *nor* fire to sit before it.

15 Thus shall they be unto thee with whom thou hast laboured, *even* ᴿthy merchants, from thy youth: they shall wander every one to his quarter; none shall save thee.

CHAPTER 48

Israel's obstinacy

HEAR ye this, O house of Jacob, which are called by the name of Israel, and ᴿare come forth out of the waters of Judah, ᴿwhich swear by the name of the Lᴏʀᴅ, and make mention of the God of Israel, ᴿ*but* not in truth, nor in righteousness.

2 For they call themselves ᴿof the holy city, and ᴿstay themselves upon the God of Israel; The Lᴏʀᴅ of hosts *is* his name.

3 ᴿI have declared the former things from the beginning; and they went forth out of my mouth, and I shewed them; I did *them* suddenly, ᴿand they came to pass.

4 Because I knew that thou *art* ᴺobstinate, and ᴿthy neck *is* an iron sinew, and thy brow brass;

5 ᴿI have even from the beginning declared *it* to thee; before it came to pass I shewed *it*

Center reference column

CHAP. 46
BC 712

7 ch. 45:20
8 ch. 44:19
9 Deut. 32:7
9 ch. 45:5, 21
10 ch. 45:21
10 Ps. 33:11
Prov. 19:21
Acts 5:39
11 ch. 41:2, 25
11 Heb. *the man of my counsel*
11 ch. 44:28
11 Num. 23:19
12 Ps. 76:5
12 Rom. 10:3
13 Rom. 1:17
13 Hab. 2:3
13 ch. 62:11

CHAP. 47
BC 712

1 Jer. 48:18
1 ch. 3:26
2 Ex. 11:5
Judg. 16:21
Mat. 24:41
3 ch. 3:17 & 20:4
Jer. 13:22
3 Rom. 12:19
4 Jer. 50:34
5 1 Sam. 2:9
5 Dan. 2:37
6 See 2 Sam. 24:14
2 Chr. 28:9
Zech. 1:15
6 ch. 43:28
6 Deut. 28:50
7 Rev. 18:7
7 ch. 46:8
7 Deut. 32:29
8 Zeph. 2:15
8 Rev. 18:7
ch. 51:19   9
1 Thes. 5:3   9
Nah. 3:4   9
Ps. 52:7   10
ch. 29:15   10
Ezek. 8:12
Or, *caused thee*   10
to turn away
ver. 8   10
Heb. *the*   11
morning thereof
Heb. *expiate*   11
1 Thes. 5:3   11
ch. 57:10   13
Dan. 2:2   13
Heb. *viewers of*   13
the heavens
Heb. *that give*   13
knowledge concerning the months
Nah. 1:10   14
Mal. 4:1
Heb. *their souls*   14
Rev. 18:11   15

CHAP. 48
BC 712

Ps. 68:26   1
Deut. 6:13   1
Zeph. 1:5
Jer. 4:2   1
ch. 52:1   2
Mic. 3:11   2
Rom. 2:17
ch. 44:7, 8   3
Josh. 21:45   3
Heb. *hard*   4
Ex. 32:9   4
Deut. 31:27
ver. 3   5

thee: lest thou shouldest say, Mine idol hath done them, and my graven image, and my molten image, hath commanded them.

6 Thou hast heard, see all this; and will not ye declare *it*? I have shewed thee new things from this time, even hidden things, and thou didst not know them.

7 They are created now, and not from the beginning; even before the day when thou heardest them not; lest thou shouldest say, Behold, I knew them.

8 Yea, thou heardest not; yea, thou knewest not; yea, from that time *that* thine ear was not opened: for I knew that thou wouldest deal very treacherously, and wast called ᴿa transgressor from the womb.

9 ᴿFor my name's sake ᴿwill I defer mine anger, and for my praise will I refrain for thee, that I cut thee not off.

10 Behold, ᴿI have refined thee, but not ᴺwith silver; I have chosen thee in the furnace of affliction.

11 ᴿFor mine own sake, *even* for mine own sake, will I do *it*: for ᴿhow should *my name* be polluted? and ᴿI will not give my glory unto another.

Coming doom of Babylon

12 Hearken unto me, O Jacob and Israel, my called; ᴿI *am* he; I *am* the ᴿfirst, I also *am* the last.

13 ᴿMine hand also hath laid the foundation of the earth, and ᴺmy right hand hath spanned the heavens: *when* ᴿI call unto them, they stand up together.

14 All ye, assemble yourselves, and hear; which among them hath declared these *things?* ᴿThe Lᴏʀᴅ hath loved him: ᴿhe will do his pleasure on Babylon, and his arm *shall be on* the Chăl-dē′-ăns.

15 I, *even* I, have spoken; yea, ᴿI have called him: I have brought him, and he shall make his way prosperous.

16 Come ye near unto me, hear ye this; ᴿI have not spoken in secret from the beginning; from the time that it was, there *am* I: and now ᴿthe Lord Gᴏᴅ, and his spirit, hath sent me.

God's plea to Israel

17 Thus saith ᴿthe Lᴏʀᴅ, thy Redeemer, the Holy One of Israel; I *am* the Lᴏʀᴅ thy God which teacheth thee to profit, ᴿwhich leadeth thee by the way *that* thou shouldest go.

18 ᴿO that thou hadst hearkened to my commandments! ᴿthen had thy peace been as a river, and thy righteousness as the waves of the sea:

19 ᴿThy seed also had been as the sand, and

CHAP. 48
BC 712
8 Ps. 58:3
9 Ps. 79:9
& 106:8
Ezek. 20:9
9 Ps. 78:38
10 Ps. 66:10
10 Or, *for silver:*
See Ezek.
22:20-22
11 ver. 9
11 Deut. 32:26
Ezek. 20:9
11 ch. 42:8
12 Deut. 32:39
12 ch. 44:6
Rev. 22:13
13 Ps. 102:25
13 Or, *the palm of my right hand hath spread out*
13 ch. 40:26
14 ch. 45:1
14 ch. 44:28
15 ch. 45:1, 2
16 ch. 45:19
16 Zech. 2:8
17 ch. 43:14
17 Ps. 32:8
18 Deut. 32:20
Ps. 81:13
18 Ps. 119:165
19 Gen. 22:17
Hos. 1:10

Jer. 50:8   20
Ex. 19:4-6   20
ch. 41:17, 18   21
Ex. 17:6   21
Ps. 105:41
ch. 57:21   22

CHAP. 49
BC 712
ch. 41:1   1
Jer. 1:5   1
Mat. 1:20
John 10:36
ch. 11:4   2
Hos. 6:5
Rev. 1:16
ch. 51:16   2
Ps. 45:5   2
ch. 42:1   3
Zech. 3:8
John 15:8   3
Eph. 1:6
Ezek. 3:19   4
Or, *my reward,* 4
ch. 40:10
ver. 1   5
Or, *That Israel may be gathered to him, and I may, etc.*
Mat. 23:37   5
Or, *Art thou lighter than that thou shouldest, etc.* 6
Or, *desolations* 6
Luke 2:32   6
Mat. 26:67   7
Or, *to him that is despised in soul* 7
Ps. 72:10   7
Ps. 69:13   8
2 Cor. 6:2
ch. 42:6   8
Or, *raise up*   8

the offspring of thy bowels like the gravel thereof; his name should not have been cut off nor destroyed from before me.

20 ᴿGo ye forth of Babylon, flee ye from the Chăl-dē′-ăns, with a voice of singing declare ye, tell this, utter it *even* to the end of the earth; say ye, The Lᴏʀᴅ hath ᴿredeemed his servant Jacob.

21 And they ᴿthirsted not *when* he led them through the deserts: he ᴿcaused the waters to flow out of the rock for them: he clave the rock also, and the waters gushed out.

22 ᴿ*There is* no peace, saith the Lᴏʀᴅ, unto the wicked.

CHAPTER 49

The servant's call and commission

LISTEN, ᴿO isles, unto me; and hearken, ye people, from far; ᴿThe Lᴏʀᴅ hath called me from the womb; from the bowels of my mother hath he made mention of my name.

2 And he hath made ᴿmy mouth like a sharp sword; ᴿin the shadow of his hand hath he hid me, and made me ᴿa polished shaft; in his quiver hath he hid me;

3 And said unto me, ᴿThou *art* my servant, O Israel, ᴿin whom I will be glorified.

4 ᴿThen I said, I have laboured in vain, I have spent my strength for nought, and in vain: *yet* surely my judgment *is* with the Lᴏʀᴅ, and ᴺmy work with my God.

5 And now, saith the Lᴏʀᴅ ᴿthat formed me from the womb *to be* his servant, to bring Jacob again to him, ᴺThough Israel ᴿbe not gathered, yet shall I be glorious in the eyes of the Lᴏʀᴅ, and my God shall be my strength.

6 And he said, ᴺIt is a light thing that thou shouldest be my servant to raise up the tribes of Jacob, and to restore the ᴺpreserved of Israel: I will also give thee for a ᴿlight to the Gentiles, that thou mayest be my salvation unto the end of the earth.

7 Thus saith the Lᴏʀᴅ, the Redeemer of Israel, *and* his Holy One, ᴿtoᴺ him whom man despiseth, to him whom the nation abhorreth, to a servant of rulers, ᴿKings shall see and arise, princes also shall worship, because of the Lᴏʀᴅ that is faithful, *and* the Holy One of Israel, and he shall choose thee.   ★

Restoration promised

8 Thus saith the Lᴏʀᴅ, ᴿIn an acceptable time have I heard thee, and in a day of salvation have I helped thee: and I will preserve thee, ᴿand give thee for a covenant of the people, to ᴺestablish the earth, to cause to inherit the desolate heritages;   ★

9 That thou mayest say [R]to the prisoners, Go forth; to them that *are* in darkness, Shew yourselves. They shall feed in the ways, and their pastures *shall be* in all high places.   ★

10 They shall not [R]hunger nor thirst; [R]neither shall the heat nor sun smite them: for he that hath mercy on them [R]shall lead them, even by the springs of water shall he guide them.   ★

11 [R]And I will make all my mountains a way, and my highways shall be exalted.

12 Behold, [R]these shall come from far: and, lo, these from the north and from the west; and these from the land of Sī′-nĭm.

13 [R]Sing, O heavens; and be joyful, O earth; and break forth into singing, O mountains: for the LORD hath comforted his people, and will have mercy upon his afflicted.

Rebuilding of Zion promised

14 [R]But Zion said, The LORD hath forsaken me, and my Lord hath forgotten me.

15 [R]Can a woman forget her sucking child, [N]that she should not have compassion on the son of her womb? yea, they may forget, [R]yet will I not forget thee.

16 Behold, [R]I have graven thee upon the palms of *my* hands; thy walls *are* continually before me.

17 Thy children shall make haste; [R]thy destroyers and they that made thee waste shall go forth of thee.

18 [R]Lift up thine eyes round about, and behold: all these gather themselves together, *and* come to thee. *As* I live, saith the LORD, thou shalt surely clothe thee with them all, [R]as with an ornament, and bind them *on thee*, as a bride *doeth*.

19 For thy waste and thy desolate places, and the land of thy destruction, [R]shall even now be too narrow by reason of the inhabitants, and they that swallowed thee up shall be far away.

20 [R]The children which thou shalt have, [R]after thou hast lost the other, shall say again in thine ears, The place *is* too strait for me: give place to me that I may dwell.

21 Then shalt thou say in thine heart, Who hath begotten me these, seeing I have lost my children, and am desolate, a captive, and removing to and fro? and who hath brought up these? Behold, I was left alone; these, where *had* they *been*?

Israel's honour among the nations

22 [R]Thus saith the Lord GOD, Behold, I will lift up mine hand to the Gentiles, and set up

my standard to the people: and they shall bring thy sons in *their* [N]arms, and thy daughters shall be carried upon *their* shoulders.

23 [R]And kings shall be thy [N]nursing fathers, and their [N]queens thy nursing mothers: they shall bow down to thee with *their* face toward the earth, and [R]lick up the dust of thy feet; and thou shalt know that I *am* the LORD: for [R]they shall not be ashamed that wait for me.

24 [R]Shall the prey be taken from the mighty, or [N]the lawful captive delivered?

25 But thus saith the LORD, Even the [N]captives of the mighty shall be taken away, and the prey of the terrible shall be delivered: for I will contend with him that contendeth with thee, and I will save thy children.

26 And I will [R]feed them that oppress thee with their own flesh; and they shall be drunken with their own [R]blood, as with [N]sweet wine: and all flesh [R]shall know that I the LORD *am* thy Saviour and thy Redeemer, the mighty One of Jacob.

CHAPTER 50

The meaning of God's help

THUS saith the LORD, Where *is* [R]the bill of your mother's divorcement, whom I have put away? or which of my [R]creditors *is it* to whom I have sold you? Behold, for your iniquities [R]have ye sold yourselves, and for your transgressions is your mother put away.

2 Wherefore, when I came, *was there* no man? [R]when I called, *was there* none to answer? [R]Is my hand shortened at all, that it cannot redeem? or have I no power to deliver? behold, [R]at my rebuke I [R]dry up the sea, I make the [R]rivers a wilderness: [R]their fish stinketh, because *there is* no water, and dieth for thirst.

3 [R]I clothe the heavens with blackness, [R]and I make sackcloth their covering.

4 [R]The Lord GOD hath given me the tongue of the learned, that I should know how to speak a word in season to *him that is* [R]weary: he wakeneth morning by morning, he wakeneth mine ear to hear as the learned.

5 The Lord GOD [R]hath opened mine ear, and I was not [R]rebellious, neither turned away back.

6 [R]I gave my back to the smiters, and [R]my cheeks to them that plucked off the hair: I hid not my face from shame and spitting.   ★

7 For the Lord GOD will help me; therefore shall I not be confounded: therefore have [R]I set my face like a flint, and I know that I shall not be ashamed.

CHAP. 49
BC 712
9 Zech. 9:12
10 Rev. 7:16
10 Ps. 121:6
10 Ps. 23:2
11 ch. 40:4
12 ch. 43:5, 6
13 ch. 44:23
14 ch. 40:27
15 Ps. 103:13
Mal. 3:17
Mat. 7:11
15 Heb. *from having compassion*
15 Rom. 11:29
16 Ex. 13:9
S. of S. 8:6
17 ver. 19
18 ch. 60:4
18 Prov. 17:6
19 ch. 54:1, 2
Zech. 10:10
20 ch. 60:4
20 Mat. 3:9
Rom. 11:11
22 ch. 60:4

Heb. *bosom*   22
Ps. 72:11   23
ch. 52:15
& 60:16
Heb. *nourishers*   23
Heb. *princesses*   23
Ps. 72:9   23
Mic. 7:17
Ps. 34:22   23
Rom. 5:5
& 9:33
Mat. 12:29   24
Luke 11:21, 22
Heb. *the   24
captivity of
the just*
Heb. *captivity*   25
ch. 9:20   26
Rev. 14:20   26
& 16:6
Or, *new wine*   26
Ps. 9:16   26
ch. 60:16

CHAP. 50
BC 712
Deut. 24:1   1
Jer. 3:8
Hos. 2:2
2 Ki. 4:1   1
Mat. 18:25
ch. 52:3   1
Prov. 1:24   2
ch. 65:12
Jer. 35:15
Num. 11:23   2
Ps. 106:9   2
Nah. 1:4
Ex. 14:21   2
Josh. 3:16   2
Ex. 7:18   2
Ex. 10:21   3
Rev. 6:12   3
Ex. 4:11   4
Mat. 11:28   4
Ps. 40:6-8   5
Mat. 26:39   5
John 14:31
Heb. 10:5
Mat. 26:67   6
Lam. 3:30   6
Ezek. 3:8, 9   7

8 [R]*He is* near that justifieth me; who will contend with me? let us stand together: who *is* [N]mine adversary? let him come near to me.

9 Behold, the Lord GOD will help me; who *is* he *that* shall condemn me? [R]lo, they all shall wax old as a garment; [R]the moth shall eat them up.

10 Who *is* among you that feareth the LORD, that obeyeth the voice of his servant, that [R]walketh *in* darkness, and hath no light? [R]let him trust in the name of the LORD, and stay upon his God.

11 Behold, all ye that kindle a fire, that compass *yourselves* about with sparks: walk in the light of your fire, and in the sparks *that* ye have kindled. [R]This shall ye have of mine hand; ye shall lie down [R]in sorrow.

CHAPTER 51

God's appeal for Israel's trust

HEARKEN to me, [R]ye that follow after righteousness, ye that seek the LORD: look unto the rock *whence* ye are hewn, and to the hole of the pit *whence* ye are digged.

2 [R]Look unto Abraham your father, and unto Sarah *that* bare you: [R]for I called him alone, and [R]blessed him, and increased him.

3 For the LORD [R]shall comfort Zion: he will comfort all her waste places; and he will make her wilderness like Eden, and her desert [R]like the garden of the LORD; joy and gladness shall be found therein, thanksgiving, and the voice of melody.

4 Hearken unto me, my people; and give ear unto me, O my nation: [R]for a law shall proceed from me, and I will make my judgment to rest [R]for a light of the people.

5 [R]My righteousness *is* near; my salvation is gone forth, [R]and mine arms shall judge the people; [R]the isles shall wait upon me, and [R]on mine arm shall they trust.

6 [R]Lift up your eyes to the heavens, and look upon the earth beneath: for [R]the heavens shall vanish away like smoke, [R]and the earth shall wax old like a garment, and they that dwell therein shall die in like manner: but my salvation shall be for ever, and my righteousness shall not be abolished.

7 [R]Hearken unto me, ye that know righteousness, the people [R]in whose heart *is* my law; [R]fear ye not the reproach of men, neither be ye afraid of their revilings.

8 For [R]the moth shall eat them up like a garment, and the worm shall eat them like wool: but my righteousness shall be for ever,

and my salvation from generation to generation.

Plea for God's continued aid

9 [R]Awake, awake, [R]put on strength, O arm of the LORD; awake, [R]as in the ancient days, in the generations of old. [R]*Art* thou not it that hath cut [R]Rahab, *and* wounded the [R]dragon?

10 *Art* thou not it which hath [R]dried the sea, the waters of the great deep; that hath made the depths of the sea a way for the ransomed to pass over?

11 Therefore [R]the redeemed of the LORD shall return, and come with singing unto Zion; and everlasting joy *shall be* upon their head: they shall obtain gladness and joy; *and* sorrow and mourning shall flee away.

God's comfort to Israel

12 I, *even* I, *am* he [R]that comforteth you: who *art* thou, that thou shouldest be afraid [R]of a man *that* shall die, and of the son of man *which* shall be made [R]as grass;

13 And forgettest the LORD thy maker, [R]that hath stretched forth the heavens, and laid the foundations of the earth; and hast feared continually every day because of the fury of the oppressor, as if he [N]were ready to destroy? [R]and where *is* the fury of the oppressor?

14 The captive exile hasteneth that he may be loosed, [R]and that he should not die in the pit, nor that his bread should fail.

15 But I *am* the LORD thy God, that [R]divided the sea, whose waves roared: The LORD of hosts *is* his name.

16 And [R]I have put my words in thy mouth, and [R]I have covered thee in the shadow of mine hand, [R]that I may plant the heavens, and lay the foundations of the earth, and say unto Zion, Thou *art* my people.

17 [R]Awake, awake, stand up, O Jerusalem, which [R]hast drunk at the hand of the LORD the cup of his fury; [R]thou hast drunken the dregs of the cup of trembling, *and* wrung *them* out.

18 *There is* none to guide her among all the sons *whom* she hath brought forth; neither *is there any* that taketh her by the hand of all the sons *that* she hath brought up.

19 [R]These two *things* [N]are come unto thee; who shall be sorry for thee? desolation, and [N]destruction, and the famine, and the sword: [R]by whom shall I comfort thee?

20 [R]Thy sons have fainted, they lie at the head of all the streets, as a wild bull in a net: they are full of the fury of the LORD, the rebuke of thy God.

CHAP. 50
BC 712
8 Rom. 8:32
8 Heb. *the master of my cause?*
9 Job 13:28
Ps. 102:26
ch. 51:6
9 ch. 51:8
10 Ps. 23:4
10 2 Chr. 20:20
Ps. 20:7
11 John 9:39
11 Ps. 16:4

CHAP. 51
BC 712
1 Rom. 9:30-32
2 Rom. 4:1
Heb. 11:11
2 Gen. 12:1
2 Gen. 24:35
3 ver. 12
ch. 52:9
3 Gen. 13:10
Joel 2:3
4 ch. 2:3
4 ch. 42:6
5 ch. 46:13
Rom. 1:16
5 Ps. 67:4
5 ch. 60:9
5 Rom. 1:16
6 ch. 40:26
6 Ps. 102:26
Mat. 24:35
2 Pet. 3:10
6 ch. 50:9
7 ver. 1
7 Ps. 37:31
7 Mat. 10:28
Acts 5:41
8 ch. 50:9

Ps. 44:23 | 9
Ps. 93:1 | 9
Ps. 44:1 | 9
Job 26:12 | 9
Ps. 87:4 | 9
& 89:10
Ps. 74:13 | 9
Ezek. 29:3
Ex. 14:21 | 10
ch. 43:16
ch. 35:10 | 11
2 Cor. 1:3 | 12
Ps. 118:6 | 12
1 Pet. 1:24 | 12
Ps. 104:2 | 13
Or, *made himself ready* | 13
Job 20:7 | 13
Zech. 9:11 | 14
Job 26:12 | 15
Ps. 74:13
Jer. 31:35
Deut. 18:18 | 16
ch. 59:21
John 3:34
ch. 49:2 | 16
ch. 65:17 | 16
ch. 52:1 | 17
Job 21:20 | 17
Jer. 25:15
See Deut. 28:28, 34 | 17
Ps. 60:3
Ezek. 23:32-34
ch. 47:9 | 19
Heb. *happened* | 19
Heb. *breaking* | 19
Amos 7:2 | 19
Lam. 2:11 | 20

21 Therefore hear now this, thou afflicted, and drunken, ᴿbut not with wine:

22 Thus saith thy Lord the LORD, and thy God ᴿthat pleadeth the cause of his people, Behold, I have taken out of thine hand the cup of trembling, *even* the dregs of the cup of my fury; thou shalt no more drink it again:

23 But ᴿI will put it into the hand of them that afflict thee; ᴿwhich have said to thy soul, Bow down, that we may go over: and thou hast laid thy body as the ground, and as the street, to them that went over.

CHAPTER 52

Call for Zion to awake

AWAKE, ᴿawake; put on thy strength, O Zion; put on thy beautiful garments, O Jerusalem, ᴿthe holy city: for ᴿhenceforth there shall no more come into thee the uncircumcised ᴿand the unclean.

2 ᴿShake thyself from the dust; arise, *and* sit down, O Jerusalem: ᴿloose thyself from the bands of thy neck, O captive daughter of Zion.

3 For thus saith the LORD, ᴿYe have sold yourselves for nought; and ye shall be redeemed without money.

4 For thus saith the Lord GOD, My people went down aforetime into ᴿEgypt to sojourn there; and the Assyrian oppressed them without cause.

5 Now therefore, what have I here, saith the LORD, that my people is taken away for nought? they that rule over them make them to howl, saith the LORD; and my name continually every day *is* ᴿblasphemed.

6 Therefore my people shall know my name: therefore *they shall know* in that day that I *am* he that doth speak: behold, *it is* I.

The servant's good tidings

7 ᴿHow beautiful upon the mountains are the feet of him that bringeth good tidings, that publisheth peace; that bringeth good tidings of good, that publisheth salvation; that saith unto Zion, ᴿThy God reigneth!

8 Thy watchmen shall lift up the voice; with the voice together shall they sing: for they shall see eye to eye, when the LORD shall bring again Zion.

9 Break forth into joy, sing together, ye waste places of Jerusalem: for the LORD hath comforted his people, he hath redeemed Jerusalem.

10 ᴿThe LORD hath made bare his holy arm in the eyes of all the nations; and ᴿall the ends of the earth shall see the salvation of our God.

CHAP. 51	
BC 712	
21	See ver. 17
	Lam. 3:15
22	Jer. 50:34
23	Jer. 25:17
	Zech. 12:2
23	Ps. 66:11

CHAP. 52	
BC 712	
1	ch. 51:9, 17
1	Neh. 11:1
	Mat. 4:5
	Rev. 21:2
1	Nah. 1:15
1	Rev. 21:27
2	ch. 3:26
2	Zech. 2:7
3	Ps. 44:12
4	Gen. 46:6
5	Ezek. 36:20
7	Rom. 10:15
7	Ps. 93:1
10	Ps. 98:2, 3
10	Luke 3:6

ch. 48:20	11
Lev. 22:2	11
Ex. 12:33	12
Mic. 2:13	12
Ex. 14:19	12
Heb. *gather you up*	12
ch. 42:1	13
Or, *prosper,* Jer. 23:5	13
Phil. 2:9	13
Ps. 22:6, 7	14
Ezek. 36:25	15
Eph. 3:5, 9	15

CHAP. 53	
BC 712	
John 12:38	1
Rom. 10:16	
Or, *doctrine?* Heb. *hearing?*	1
Ps. 22:6	3
Heb. 4:15	3
Or, *he hid as it were* his *face from us*	3
Heb. *as an hiding of faces from him,* or, *from us*	3
John 1:10	3
Mat. 8:17	4
Heb. 9:28	
Rom. 4:25	5
Or, *tormented*	5
1 Pet. 2:24	5
Heb. *bruise*	5
Heb. *hath made the iniquity of us all to meet on him*	6
Mat. 26:63	7
Acts 8:32	7
Or, *He was taken away by distress and judgment: but, etc.*	8
Dan. 9:26	8
Heb. was *the stroke upon him*	8
Mat. 27:57	9
Heb. *deaths*	9
1 John 3:5	9

11 ᴿDepart ye, depart ye, go ye out from thence, touch no unclean *thing;* go ye out of the midst of her; ᴿbe ye clean, that bear the vessels of the LORD.

12 For ᴿye shall not go out with haste, nor go by flight: ᴿfor the LORD will go before you; ᴿand the God of Israel *will* ᴺbe your rereward.

13 Behold, ᴿmy servant shall ᴺdeal prudently, ᴿhe shall be exalted and extolled, and be very high.   ★

14 As many were astonied at thee; his ᴿvisage was so marred more than any man, and his form more than the sons of men: ★

15 ᴿSo shall he sprinkle many nations; the kings shall shut their mouths at him: for *that* ᴿwhich had not been told them shall they see; and *that* which they had not heard shall they consider.   ★

CHAPTER 53

The servant's suffering

WHO ᴿhath believed our ᴺᴺreport? and to whom is the arm of the LORD revealed?   ★

2 For he shall grow up before him as a tender plant, and as a root out of a dry ground: he hath no form nor comeliness; and when we shall see him, *there is* no beauty that we should desire him.   ★

3 ᴿHe is despised and rejected of men; a man of sorrows, and ᴿacquainted with grief: and ᴺᴺwe hid as it were *our* faces from him; he was despised, and ᴿwe esteemed him not.★

4 Surely ᴿhe hath borne our griefs, and carried our sorrows: yet we did esteem him stricken, smitten of God, and afflicted.   ★

5 But he *was* ᴿwoundedᴺ for our transgressions, *he was* bruised for our iniquities: the chastisement of our peace *was* upon him; and with his ᴿstripesᴺ we are healed.   ★

6 All we like sheep have gone astray; we have turned every one to his own way; and the LORD ᴺhath laid on him the iniquity of us all. ★

7 He was oppressed, and he was afflicted, yet ᴿhe opened not his mouth: ᴿhe is brought as a lamb to the slaughter, and as a sheep before her shearers is dumb, so he openeth not his mouth.   ★

8 ᴺHe was taken from prison and from judgment: and who shall declare his generation? for ᴿhe was cut off out of the land of the living: for the transgression of my people ᴺwas he stricken.   ★

9 ᴿAnd he made his grave with the wicked, and with the rich in his ᴺdeath; because he had done no violence, neither *was any* ᴿdeceit in his mouth.   ★

10 Yet it pleased the LORD to bruise him; he

hath put *him* to grief: [N]when thou shalt make his soul [R]an offering for sin, he shall see *his* seed, he shall prolong *his* days, and the pleasure of the LORD shall prosper in his hand. ★

11 He shall see of the travail of his soul, *and* shall be satisfied: by his knowledge shall [R]my righteous [R]servant [R]justify many; for he shall bear their iniquities. ★

12 [R]Therefore will I divide him *a portion* with the great, [R]and he shall divide the spoil with the strong; because he hath poured out his soul unto death: and he was [R]numbered with the transgressors; and he bare the sin of many, and [R]made intercession for the transgressors. ★

CHAPTER 54

God's everlasting love

SING,[R] O barren, thou *that* didst not bear; break forth into singing, and cry aloud, thou *that* didst not travail with child: for [R]more *are* the children of the desolate than the children of the married wife, saith the LORD.

2 [R]Enlarge the place of thy tent, and let them stretch forth the curtains of thine habitations: spare not, lengthen thy cords, and strengthen thy stakes;

3 For thou shalt break forth on the right hand and on the left; [R]and thy seed shall inherit the Gentiles, and make the desolate cities to be inhabited.

4 Fear not; for thou shalt not be ashamed: neither be thou confounded; for thou shalt not be put to shame: for thou shalt forget the shame of thy youth, and shalt not remember the reproach of thy widowhood any more.

5 [R]For thy Maker *is* thine husband; the [R]LORD of hosts *is* his name; and thy Redeemer the Holy One of Israel; [R]The God of the whole earth shall he be called.

6 For the LORD [R]hath called thee as a woman forsaken and grieved in spirit, and a wife of youth, when thou wast refused, saith thy God.

7 [R]For a small moment have I forsaken thee; but with great mercies will I gather thee.

8 In a little wrath I hid my face from thee for a moment; [R]but with everlasting kindness will I have mercy on thee, saith the LORD thy Redeemer.

Heritage of the servants of the LORD

9 For this *is as* the waters of [R]Noah unto me: for *as* I have sworn that the waters of Noah should no more go over the earth; so have I sworn that I would not be wroth with thee, nor rebuke thee.

10 For [R]the mountains shall depart, and the

CHAP. **53**
BC 712
10 Or, *when his soul shall make an offering*
10 2 Cor. 5:21
11 1 John 2:1
11 ch. 42:1
11 Rom. 5:18
12 Ps. 2:8
12 Col. 2:15
12 Luke 22:37
12 Luke 23:34

CHAP. **54**
BC 712
1 Gal. 4:27
1 1 Sam. 2:5
2 ch. 49:19, 20
3 ch. 55:5
5 Jer. 3:14
5 Luke 1:32
5 Zech. 14:9
Rom. 3:29
6 ch. 62:4
7 Ps. 30:5
ch. 26:20
& 60:10
2 Cor. 4:17
8 ch. 55:3
Jer. 31:3
9 Gen. 8:21
10 Ps. 46:2
ch. 51:6
Mat. 5:18

Ps. 89:33	10
1 Chr. 29:2	11
Rev. 21:18	
ch. 11:9	13
Jer. 31:34	
John 6:45	
1 Cor. 2:10	
1 Thes. 4:9	
1 John 2:20	
Ps. 119:165	13
ch. 45:24, 25	17

CHAP. **55**
BC 712
John 4:14 ... 1
Mat. 13:44 ... 1
Rev. 3:18
Heb. *weigh* ... 2
Mat. 11:28 ... 3
ch. 54:8 ... 3
& 61:8
Jer. 32:40
2 Sam. 7:8, etc. ... 3
Ps. 89:28
Acts 13:34
John 18:37 ... 4
Rev. 1:5
Jer. 30:9 ... 4
Ezek. 34:23
Dan. 9:25
Hos. 3:5
ch. 52:15 ... 5
Eph. 2:11
ch. 60:5 ... 5
ch. 60:9 ... 5

hills be removed; [R]but my kindness shall not depart from thee, neither shall the covenant of my peace be removed, saith the LORD that hath mercy on thee.

11 O thou afflicted, tossed with tempest, *and* not comforted, behold, I will lay thy stones with [R]fair colours, and lay thy foundations with sapphires.

12 And I will make thy windows of agates, and thy gates of carbuncles, and all thy borders of pleasant stones.

13 And all thy children *shall be* [R]taught of the LORD; and [R]great *shall be* the peace of thy children.

14 In righteousness shalt thou be established: thou shalt be far from oppression; for thou shalt not fear: and from terror; for it shall not come near thee.

15 Behold, they shall surely gather together, *but* not by me: whosoever shall gather together against thee shall fall for thy sake.

16 Behold, I have created the smith that bloweth the coals in the fire, and that bringeth forth an instrument for his work; and I have created the waster to destroy.

17 No weapon that is formed against thee shall prosper; and every tongue *that* shall rise against thee in judgment thou shalt condemn. This *is* the heritage of the servants of the LORD, [R]and their righteousness *is* of me, saith the LORD.

CHAPTER 55

God's call to the unsatisfied

HO, [R]every one that thirsteth, come ye to the waters, and he that hath no money; [R]come ye, buy, and eat; yea, come, buy wine and milk without money and without price.

2 Wherefore do ye [N]spend money for *that which is* not bread? and your labour for *that which* satisfieth not? hearken diligently unto me, and eat ye *that which is* good, and let your soul delight itself in fatness.

3 Incline your ear, and [R]come unto me: hear, and your soul shall live; [R]and I will make an everlasting covenant with you, *even* the [R]sure mercies of David.

4 Behold, I have given him *for* [R]a witness to the people, [R]a leader and commander to the people. ★

5 [R]Behold, thou shalt call a nation *that* thou knowest not, [R]and nations *that* knew not thee shall run unto thee because of the LORD thy God, and for the Holy One of Israel; [R]for he hath glorified thee. ★

God's call to the sinful

6 ^RSeek ye the LORD while he may be found, call ye upon him while he is near:

7 ^RLet the wicked forsake his way, and ^Nthe unrighteous man ^Rhis thoughts: and let him return unto the LORD, ^Rand he will have mercy upon him; and to our God, for ^Nhe will abundantly pardon.

8 ^RFor my thoughts *are* not your thoughts, neither *are* your ways my ways, saith the LORD.

9 ^RFor *as* the heavens are higher than the earth, so are my ways higher than your ways, and my thoughts than your thoughts.

God's everlasting sign

10 For ^Ras the rain cometh down, and the snow from heaven, and returneth not thither, but watereth the earth, and maketh it bring forth and bud, that it may give seed to the sower, and bread to the eater:

11 ^RSo shall my word be that goeth forth out of my mouth: it shall not return unto me void, but it shall accomplish that which I please, and it shall prosper *in the thing* whereto I sent it.

12 ^RFor ye shall go out with joy, and be led forth with peace: the mountains and the hills shall ^Rbreak forth before you into singing, and ^Rall the trees of the field shall clap *their* hands.

13 ^RInstead of ^Rthe thorn shall come up the fir tree, and instead of the brier shall come up the myrtle tree: and it shall be to the LORD ^Rfor a name, for an everlasting sign *that* shall not be cut off.

CHAPTER 56

Admission of proselytes and eunuchs

THUS saith the LORD, Keep ye ^Njudgment, and do justice: ^Rfor my salvation *is* near to come, and my righteousness to be revealed.

2 Blessed *is* the man *that* doeth this, and the son of man *that* layeth hold on it; ^Rthat keepeth the sabbath from polluting it, and keepeth his hand from doing any evil.

3 Neither let ^Rthe son of the stranger, that hath joined himself to the LORD, speak, saying, The LORD hath utterly separated me from his people: neither let the eunuch say, Behold, I *am* a dry tree.

4 For thus saith the LORD unto the eunuchs that keep my sabbaths, and choose *the things* that please me, and take hold of my covenant;

5 Even unto them will I give in ^Rmine house and within my walls a place ^Rand a name bet-

CHAP. **55**
BC 712
6 Ps. 32:6
Mat. 5:25
& 25:11
John 7:34
& 8:21
2 Cor. 6:1
Heb. 3:13
7 ch. 1:16
7 Heb. *the man of iniquity*
7 Zech. 8:17
7 Ps. 130:7
Jer. 3:12
7 Heb. *he will multiply to pardon*
8 2 Sam. 7:19
9 Ps. 103:11
10 Deut. 32:2
11 ch. 54:9
12 ch. 35:10
12 Ps. 98:8
12 1 Chr. 16:33
13 ch. 41:19
13 Mic. 7:4
13 Jer. 13:11

CHAP. **56**	
BC 712	
1 Or, *equity*	
1 Mat. 4:17	
2 ch. 58:13	
3 Acts 8:27	
5 1 Tim. 3:15	
5 1 John 3:1	
ch. 2:2	7
Rom. 12:1	7
Heb. 13:15	
1 Pet. 2:5	
Mat. 21:13	7
Mal. 1:11	7
ch. 11:12	8
John 10:16	8
Heb. *to his gathered*	8
Jer. 12:9	9
Mat. 15:14	10
Phil. 3:2	10
Or, *dreaming, or, talking in their sleep*	10
Mic. 3:11	11
Heb. *strong of appetite*	11
Ezek. 34:2	11
Heb. *know not to be satisfied*	11
Ps. 10:6	12
Prov. 23:35	
Luke 12:19	

CHAP. **57**	
BC 698	
Ps. 12:1	1
Heb. *men of kindness, or, godliness*	1
1 Ki. 14:13	1
Or, *from that which is evil*	1
Or, *go in peace,* Luke 2:29	2
2 Chr. 16:14	2
Or, *before him*	2
Mat. 16:4	3
Or, *among the oaks*	5
2 Ki. 16:4	5
Lev. 18:21	5
2 Ki. 16:3	
Jer. 7:31	
Ezek. 16:20	

ter than of sons and of daughters: I will give them an everlasting name, that shall not be cut off.

6 Also the sons of the stranger, that join themselves to the LORD, to serve him, and to love the name of the LORD, to be his servants, every one that keepeth the sabbath from polluting it, and taketh hold of my covenant;

7 Even them will I ^Rbring to my holy mountain, and make them joyful in my house of prayer: ^Rtheir burnt offerings and their sacrifices *shall be* accepted upon mine altar; for ^Rmine house shall be called an house of prayer ^Rfor all people.

8 The Lord GOD ^Rwhich gathereth the outcasts of Israel saith, ^RYet will I gather *others* to him, ^Nbeside those that are gathered unto him.

Rebuke of faithless leaders

9 ^RAll ye beasts of the field, come to devour, *yea,* all ye beasts in the forest.

10 His watchmen *are* ^Rblind: they are all ignorant, ^Rthey *are* all dumb dogs, they cannot bark; ^Nsleeping, lying down, loving to slumber.

11 Yea, *they are* ^Rgreedy^N dogs *which* ^Rcan^N never have enough, and they *are* shepherds *that* cannot understand: they all look to their own way, every one for his gain, from his quarter.

12 Come ye, *say they,* I will fetch wine, and we will fill ourselves with strong drink; ^Rand to morrow shall be as this day, *and* much more abundant.

CHAPTER 57

THE righteous perisheth, and no man layeth *it* to heart: and ^Rmerciful^N men *are* taken away, ^Rnone considering that the righteous is taken away ^Nfrom the evil *to come.*

2 He shall ^Nenter into peace: they shall rest in ^Rtheir beds, *each one* walking ^N*in* his uprightness.

Idolatry condemned

3 But draw near hither, ^Rye sons of the sorceress, the seed of the adulterer and the whore.

4 Against whom do ye sport yourselves? against whom make ye a wide mouth, *and* draw out the tongue? *are* ye not children of transgression, a seed of falsehood,

5 Enflaming yourselves ^Nwith idols ^Runder every green tree, ^Rslaying the children in the valleys under the clifts of the rocks?

6 Among the smooth *stones* of the stream *is* thy portion; they, they *are* thy lot: even to

them hast thou poured a drink offering, thou hast offered a meat offering. Should I receive comfort in these?

7 [R]Upon a lofty and high mountain hast thou set [R]thy bed: even thither wentest thou up to offer sacrifice.

8 Behind the doors also and the posts hast thou set up thy remembrance: for thou hast discovered *thyself to another* than me, and art gone up; thou hast enlarged thy bed, and [N]made thee *a covenant* with them; [R]thou lovedst their bed [N]where thou sawest *it.*

9 And [R]thou[N] wentest to the king with ointment, and didst increase thy perfumes, and didst send thy messengers far off, and didst debase *thyself even* unto hell.

10 Thou art wearied in the greatness of thy way; [R]*yet* saidst thou not, There is no hope: thou hast found the [N]life of thine hand; therefore thou wast not grieved.

11 And [R]of whom hast thou been afraid or feared, that thou hast lied, and hast not remembered me, nor laid *it* to thy heart? [R]have not I held my peace even of old, and thou fearest me *not?*

12 I will declare thy righteousness, and thy works; for they shall not profit thee.

13 When thou criest, let thy companies deliver thee; but the wind shall carry them all away; vanity shall take *them:* but he that putteth his trust in me shall possess the land, and shall inherit my holy mountain;

No peace for the wicked

14 And shall say, [R]Cast ye up, cast ye up, prepare the way, take up the stumblingblock out of the way of my people.

15 For thus saith the high and lofty One that inhabiteth eternity, [R]whose name *is* Holy; [R]I dwell in the high and holy *place,* [R]with him also *that is* of a contrite and humble spirit, [R]to revive the spirit of the humble, and to revive the heart of the contrite ones.

16 [R]For I will not contend for ever, neither will I be always wroth: for the spirit should fail before me, and the souls [R]*which* I have made.

17 For the iniquity of [R]his covetousness was I wroth, and smote him: [R]I hid me, and was wroth, [R]and he went on [N]frowardly in the way of his heart.

18 I have seen his ways, and [R]will heal him: I will lead him also, and restore comforts unto him and to [R]his mourners.

19 I create [R]the fruit of the lips; Peace, peace [R]to *him that is* far off, and to *him that is* near, saith the LORD; and I will heal him.

20 [R]But the wicked *are* like the troubled sea,

CHAP. 57

BC 698

7 Ezek. 16:16
7 Ezek. 23:41
8 Or, *hewed it for thyself* larger than their's
8 Ezek. 16:26
8 Or, *thou providedst room*
9 Hos. 7:11
9 Or, *thou respectedst the king*
10 Jer. 2:25
10 Or, *living*
11 ch. 51:12
11 Ps. 50:21
14 ch. 40:3
15 Job 6:10
Luke 1:49
15 Zech. 2:13
15 Ps. 34:18 & 51:17
15 Ps. 147:3
16 ch. 61:1
16 Ps. 85:5 & 103:9
Mic. 7:18
16 Num. 16:22
Job 34:14
Heb. 12:9
17 Jer. 6:13
17 ch. 8:17 & 45:15
17 ch. 9:13
17 Heb. *turning away*
18 Jer. 3:22
18 ch. 61:2
19 Heb. 13:15
19 Acts 2:39
Eph. 2:17
20 Job 15:20
Prov. 4:16

ch. 48:22   21

CHAP. 58

BC 698

Heb. *with the throat*   1
Mal. 3:14   3
Lev. 16:29 & 23:27   3
Or, *things wherewith ye grieve others*   3
Heb. *griefs*   3
1 Ki. 21:9   4
Or, *ye fast not as this day*   4
Zech. 7:5   5
Lev. 16:29   5
Or, *to afflict his soul* for *a day?*   5
Esth. 4:3   5
Job 2:8
Dan. 9:3
Neh. 5:10   6
Heb. *the bundles of the yoke*   6
Jer. 34:9   6
Heb. *broken*   6
Ezek. 18:7   7
Mat. 25:35
Or, *afflicted*   7
Job 31:19   7
Gen. 29:14   7
Neh. 5:5
Job 11:17   8
Ex. 14:19   8
ch. 52:12
Heb. *shall gather thee up*   8
Ps. 12:2   9
Heb. *droughts*   11

when it cannot rest, whose waters cast up mire and dirt.

21 [R]*There is* no peace, saith my God, to the wicked.

CHAPTER 58

Wrong way to fast

CRY [N]aloud, spare not, lift up thy voice like a trumpet, and shew my people their transgression, and the house of Jacob their sins.

2 Yet they seek me daily, and delight to know my ways, as a nation that did righteousness, and forsook not the ordinance of their God: they ask of me the ordinances of justice; they take delight in approaching to God.

3 [R]Wherefore have we fasted, *say they,* and thou seest not? *wherefore* have we [R]afflicted our soul, and thou takest no knowledge? Behold, in the day of your fast ye find pleasure, and exact all your [NN]labours.

4 [R]Behold, ye fast for strife and debate, and to smite with the fist of wickedness: [N]ye shall not fast as *ye do this* day, to make your voice to be heard on high.

5 Is it [R]such a fast that I have chosen? [R]a[N] day for a man to afflict his soul? *is it* to bow down his head as a bulrush, and [R]to spread sackcloth and ashes *under him?* wilt thou call this a fast, and an acceptable day to the LORD?

Right way to fast

6 *Is* not this the fast that I have chosen? to loose the bands of wickedness, [R]to undo [N]the heavy burdens, and [R]to let the [N]oppressed go free, and that ye break every yoke?

7 *Is it* not [R]to deal thy bread to the hungry, and that thou bring the poor that are [N]cast out to thy house? [R]when thou seest the naked, that thou cover him; and that thou hide not thyself from [R]thine own flesh?

8 [R]Then shall thy light break forth as the morning, and thine health shall spring forth speedily: and thy righteousness shall go before thee; [R]the glory of the LORD [N]shall be thy rereward.

9 Then shalt thou call, and the LORD shall answer; thou shalt cry, and he shall say, Here I *am.* If thou take away from the midst of thee the yoke, the putting forth of the finger, and [R]speaking vanity;

10 And *if* thou draw out thy soul to the hungry, and satisfy the afflicted soul; then shall thy light rise in obscurity, and thy darkness *be* as the noonday:

11 And the LORD shall guide thee continually, and satisfy thy soul in [N]drought, and

make fat thy bones: and thou shalt be like a watered garden, and like a spring of water, whose waters ᴺfail not.

12 And *they that shall be* of thee ᴿshall build the old waste places: thou shalt raise up the foundations of many generations; and thou shalt be called, The repairer of the breach, The restorer of paths to dwell in.

True observance of the sabbath

13 If ᴿthou turn away thy foot from the sabbath, *from* doing thy pleasure on my holy day; and call the sabbath a delight, the holy of the LORD, honourable; and shalt honour him, not doing thine own ways, nor finding thine own pleasure, nor speaking *thine own* words:

14 ᴿThen shalt thou delight thyself in the LORD; and I will cause thee to ᴿride upon the high places of the earth, and feed thee with the heritage of Jacob thy father: ᴿfor the mouth of the LORD hath spoken *it.*

CHAPTER 59

Sin separates man from God

BEHOLD, the LORD's hand is not ᴿshortened, that it cannot save; neither his ear heavy, that it cannot hear:

2 But your iniquities have separated between you and your God, and your sins ᴺhave hid *his* face from you, that he will not hear.

3 For ᴿyour hands are defiled with blood, and your fingers with iniquity; your lips have spoken lies, your tongue hath muttered perverseness.

4 None calleth for justice, nor *any* pleadeth for truth: they trust in vanity, and speak lies; ᴿthey conceive mischief, and bring forth iniquity.

5 They hatch ᴺcockatrice' eggs, and weave the spider's web: he that eateth of their eggs dieth, and ᴺthat which is crushed breaketh out into a viper.

6 ᴿTheir webs shall not become garments, neither shall they cover themselves with their works: their works *are* works of iniquity, and the act of violence *is* in their hands.

7 ᴿTheir feet run to evil, and they make haste to shed innocent blood: their thoughts *are* thoughts of iniquity; wasting and ᴺdestruction *are* in their paths.

8 The way of peace they know not; and *there is* no ᴺjudgment in their goings: ᴿthey have made them crooked paths: whosoever goeth therein shall not know peace.

9 Therefore is judgment far from us, neither

doth justice overtake us: ᴿwe wait for light, but behold obscurity; for brightness, *but* we walk in darkness.

10 ᴿWe grope for the wall like the blind, and we grope as if *we had* no eyes: we stumble at noonday as in the night; *we are* in desolate places as dead *men.*

11 We roar all like bears, and ᴿmourn sore like doves: we look for judgment, but *there is* none; for salvation, *but* it is far off from us.

12 For our transgressions are multiplied before thee, and our sins testify against us: for our transgressions *are* with us; and *as for* our iniquities, we know them;

13 In transgressing and lying against the LORD, and departing away from our God, speaking oppression and revolt, conceiving and uttering ᴿfrom the heart words of falsehood.

14 And judgment is turned away backward, and justice standeth afar off: for truth is fallen in the street, and equity cannot enter.

15 Yea, truth faileth; and he *that* departeth from evil ᴺmaketh himself a prey: and the LORD saw *it,* and ᴺit displeased him that *there was* no judgment.

God intervenes and redeems

16 ᴿAnd he saw that *there was* no man, and ᴿwondered that *there was* no intercessor: ᴿtherefore his arm brought salvation unto him; and his righteousness, it sustained him.   ★

17 ᴿFor he put on righteousness as a breastplate, and an helmet of salvation upon his head; and he put on the garments of vengeance *for* clothing, and was clad with zeal as a cloak.

18 ᴿAccording to *their* ᴺdeeds, accordingly he will repay, fury to his adversaries, recompence to his enemies; to the islands he will repay recompence.

19 ᴿSo shall they fear the name of the LORD from the west, and his glory from the rising of the sun. When the enemy shall come in ᴿlike a flood, the spirit of the LORD shall ᴺlift up a standard against him.

20 And ᴿthe Redeemer shall come to Zion, and unto them that turn from transgression in Jacob, saith the LORD.   ★

21 ᴿAs for me, this *is* my covenant with them, saith the LORD; My spirit that *is* upon thee, and my words which I have put in thy mouth, shall not depart out of thy mouth, nor out of the mouth of thy seed, nor out of the mouth of thy seed's seed, saith the LORD, from henceforth and for ever.

CHAP. 58
BC 698
11 Heb. *lie,* or, *deceive*
12 ch. 61:4
13 ch. 56:2
14 Job 22:26
14 Deut. 32:13 & 33:29
14 ch. 1:20 & 40:5
Mic. 4:4

CHAP. 59
BC 698
1 Num. 11:23
ch. 50:2
2 Or, *have made him hide*
3 ch. 1:15
4 Job 15:35
Ps. 7:14
5 Or, *adders'*
5 Or, *that which is sprinkled* is as if there brake out a viper
6 Job 8:14
7 Prov. 1:16
Rom. 3:15
7 Heb. *breaking*
8 Or, *right*
8 Ps. 125:5
Prov. 2:15

Jer. 8:15   9
Deut. 28:29   10
Job 5:14
Amos 8:9
ch. 38:14   11
Ezek. 7:16
Mat. 12:34   13
Or, *is accounted mad*   15
Heb. *it was evil in his eyes*   15
Ezek. 22:30   16
Mark 6:6   16
Ps. 98:1   16
ch. 63:5
Eph. 6:14, 17   17
1 Thes. 5:8
ch. 63:6   18
Heb. *recompences*   18
Ps. 113:3   19
Mal. 1:11
Rev. 12:15   19
Or, *put him to flight*   19
Rom. 11:26   20
Heb. 8:10   21
& 10:16

CHAPTER 60

Future glory of Zion

ARISE, ᴿshine;ᴺ for thy light is come, and ᴿthe glory of the LORD is risen upon thee.

2 For, behold, the darkness shall cover the earth, and gross darkness the people: but the LORD shall arise upon thee, and his glory shall be seen upon thee.

3 And the ᴿGentiles shall come to thy light, and kings to the brightness of thy rising. ★

4 ᴿLift up thine eyes round about, and see: all they gather themselves together, ᴿthey come to thee: thy sons shall come from far, and thy daughters shall be nursed at *thy* side.

5 Then thou shalt see, and flow together, and thine heart shall fear, and be enlarged; because ᴿthe ᴺabundance of the sea shall be converted unto thee, the ᴺforces of the Gentiles shall come unto thee.

6 The multitude of camels shall cover thee, the dromedaries of Mĭd′-ĭ-ăn and ᴿĒ′-phäh; all they from ᴿShē′-bă shall come: they shall bring ᴿgold and incense; and they shall shew forth the praises of the LORD.

7 All the flocks of ᴿKē′-där shall be gathered together unto thee, the rams of Nĕ-bāi′-ōth shall minister unto thee: they shall come up with acceptance on mine altar, and ᴿI will glorify the house of my glory.

8 Who *are* these *that* fly as a cloud, and as the doves to their windows?

9 ᴿSurely the isles shall wait for me, and the ships of Tarshish first, ᴿto bring thy sons from far, ᴿtheir silver and their gold with them, ᴿunto the name of the LORD thy God, and to the Holy One of Israel, ᴿbecause he hath glorified thee.

Zion's supremacy among the nations

10 And ᴿthe sons of strangers shall build up thy walls, ᴿand their kings shall minister unto thee: for ᴿin my wrath I smote thee, ᴿbut in my favour have I had mercy on thee.

11 Therefore thy gates ᴿshall be open continually; they shall not be shut day nor night; that *men* may bring unto thee the ᴺforces of the Gentiles, and *that* their kings *may be* brought.

12 ᴿFor the nation and kingdom that will not serve thee shall perish; yea, *those* nations shall be utterly wasted.

13 ᴿThe glory of Lĕb′-ă-nọn shall come unto thee, the fir tree, the pine tree, and the box together, to beautify the place of my sanctu-

ary; and I will make ᴿthe place of my feet glorious.

14 The sons also of them that afflicted thee shall come bending unto thee; and all they that despised thee shall ᴿbow themselves down at the soles of thy feet; and they shall call thee, The city of the LORD, ᴿThe Zion of the Holy One of Israel.

15 Whereas thou hast been forsaken and hated, so that no man went through *thee,* I will make thee an eternal excellency, a joy of many generations.

16 Thou shalt also suck the milk of the Gentiles, ᴿand shalt suck the breast of kings: and thou shalt know that ᴿI the LORD *am* thy Saviour and thy Redeemer, the mighty One of Jacob.

17 For brass I will bring gold, and for iron I will bring silver, and for wood brass, and for stones iron: I will also make thy officers peace, and thine exactors righteousness.

18 Violence shall no more be heard in thy land, wasting nor destruction within thy borders; but thou shalt call ᴿthy walls Salvation, and thy gates Praise.

The LORD, an everlasting light

19 The ᴿsun shall be no more thy light by day; neither for brightness shall the moon give light unto thee: but the LORD shall be unto thee an everlasting light, and ᴿthy God thy glory.

20 ᴿThy sun shall no more go down; neither shall thy moon withdraw itself: for the LORD shall be thine everlasting light, and the days of thy mourning shall be ended.

21 ᴿThy people also *shall be* all righteous: ᴿthey shall inherit the land for ever, ᴿthe branch of my planting, ᴿthe work of my hands, that I may be glorified.

22 ᴿA little one shall become a thousand, and a small one a strong nation: I the LORD will hasten it in his time.

CHAPTER 61

Good tidings to the afflicted

THE ᴿspirit of the Lord GOD *is* upon me; because the LORD ᴿhath anointed me to preach good tidings unto the meek; he hath sent me ᴿto bind up the brokenhearted, to proclaim ᴿliberty to the captives, and the opening of the prison to *them that are* bound; ★

2 ᴿTo proclaim the acceptable year of the LORD, and ᴿthe day of vengeance of our God; ᴿto comfort all that mourn; ★

3 To appoint unto them that mourn in Zion,

Rto give unto them beauty for ashes, the oil of joy for mourning, the garment of praise for the spirit of heaviness; that they might be called trees of righteousness, Rthe planting of the LORD, Rthat he might be glorified.   ★

4 And they shall Rbuild the old wastes, they shall raise up the former desolations, and they shall repair the waste cities, the desolations of many generations.

Israel's double portion

5 And Rstrangers shall stand and feed your flocks, and the sons of the alien *shall be* your plowmen and your vinedressers.

6 RBut ye shall be named the Priests of the LORD: *men* shall call you the Ministers of our God: Rye shall eat the riches of the Gentiles, and in their glory shall ye boast yourselves.

7 RFor your shame *ye shall have* double; and *for* confusion they shall rejoice in their portion: therefore in their land they shall possess the double: everlasting joy shall be unto them.

8 For RI the LORD love judgment, RI hate robbery for burnt offering; and I will direct their work in truth, Rand I will make an everlasting covenant with them.

9 And their seed shall be known among the Gentiles, and their offspring among the people: all that see them shall acknowledge them, Rthat they *are* the seed *which* the LORD hath blessed.

Song of joy

10 RI will greatly rejoice in the LORD, my soul shall be joyful in my God; for Rhe hath clothed me with the garments of salvation, he hath covered me with the robe of righteousness, Ras a bridegroom Ndecketh *himself* with ornaments, and as a bride adorneth *herself* with her jewels.

11 For as the earth bringeth forth her bud, and as the garden causeth the things that are sown in it to spring forth; so the Lord GOD will cause Rrighteousness and Rpraise to spring forth before all the nations.

CHAPTER 62

Restoration of Zion

FOR Zion's sake will I not hold my peace, and for Jerusalem's sake I will not rest, until the righteousness thereof go forth as brightness, and the salvation thereof as a lamp *that* burneth.

2 RAnd the Gentiles shall see thy righteousness, and all kings thy glory: Rand thou shalt

---

CHAP. 61
BC 698
3 Ps. 30:11
3 ch. 60:21
3 John 15:8
4 ch. 49:8
Ezek. 36:33
5 Eph. 2:12
6 Ex. 19:6
ch. 60:17
1 Pet. 2:5
Rev. 1:6
& 5:10
6 ch. 60:5
7 ch. 40:2
Zech. 9:12
8 Ps. 11:7
8 ch. 1:11, 13
8 ch. 55:3
9 ch. 65:23
10 Hab. 3:18
10 Ps. 132:9, 16
10 ch. 49:18
Rev. 21:2
10 Heb. *decketh as a priest*
11 Ps. 72:3 & 85:11
11 ch. 60:18 & 62:7

CHAP. 62
BC 698
2 ch. 60:3
2 See ver. 4, 12

Zech. 9:16   3
Hos. 1:10   4
ch. 49:14   4
& 54:6, 7
ch. 54:1   4
i.e. *My delight is in her*   4
i.e. *Married*   4
Heb. *with the joy of the bridegroom*   5
ch. 65:19   5
Ezek. 3:17   6
Or, *ye that are the LORD'S remembrancers*   6
Heb. *silence*   7
ch. 61:11   7
Zeph. 3:20
Heb. *If I give, etc.*   8
Deut. 28:31   8
Jer. 5:17
See Deut. 12:12   9
& 14:23, 26
& 16:11, 14
ch. 40:3   10
& 57:14
ch. 11:12   10
Zech. 9:9   11
Mat. 21:5
John 12:15
ch. 40:10   11
Rev. 22:12
Or, *recompence*   11
ver. 4   12

CHAP. 63
BC 698
Heb. *decked*   1

---

be called by a new name, which the mouth of the LORD shall name.

3 Thou shalt also be Ra crown of glory in the hand of the LORD, and a royal diadem in the hand of thy God.

4 RThou shalt no more be termed RForsaken; neither shall thy land any more be termed RDesolate: but thou shalt be called NHĕph'-zĭ-bäh, and thy land NBêu'-läh: for the LORD delighteth in thee, and thy land shall be married.

5 For *as* a young man marrieth a virgin, *so* shall thy sons marry thee: and N*as* the bridegroom rejoiceth over the bride, *so* Rshall thy God rejoice over thee.

Zion reassured of God's promises

6 RI have set watchmen upon thy walls, O Jerusalem, *which* shall never hold their peace day nor night: Nye that make mention of the LORD, keep not silence,

7 And give him no Nrest, till he establish, and till he make Jerusalem Ra praise in the earth.

8 The LORD hath sworn by his right hand, and by the arm of his strength, NSurely I will no more Rgive thy corn *to be* meat for thine enemies; and the sons of the stranger shall not drink thy wine, for the which thou hast laboured:

9 But they that have gathered it shall eat it, and praise the LORD; and they that have brought it together shall drink it Rin the courts of my holiness.

Preparation for the return

10 Go through, go through the gates; Rprepare ye the way of the people; cast up, cast up the highway; gather out the stones; Rlift up a standard for the people.

11 Behold, the LORD hath proclaimed unto the end of the world, RSay ye to the daughter of Zion, Behold, thy salvation cometh; behold, his Rreward *is* with him, and his Nwork before him.   ★

12 And they shall call them, The holy people, The redeemed of the LORD: and thou shalt be called, Sought out, A city Rnot forsaken.

CHAPTER 63

Day of vengeance in Edom

WHO *is* this that commeth from Ē'-dom, with dyed garments from Bŏz'-räh? this *that is* Nglorious in his apparel, travelling in the greatness of his strength? I that speak in righteousness, mighty to save.

2 Wherefore ᴿ*art thou* red in thine apparel, and thy garments like him that treadeth in the winefat?

3 I have ᴿtrodden the winepress alone; and of the people *there was* none with me: for I will tread them in mine anger, and trample them in my fury; and their blood shall be sprinkled upon my garments, and I will stain all my raiment.

4 For the ᴿday of vengeance *is* in mine heart, and the year of my redeemed is come.

5 ᴿAnd I looked, and ᴿ*there was* none to help; and I wondered that *there was* none to uphold: therefore mine own ᴿarm brought salvation unto me; and my fury, it upheld me.

6 And I will tread down the people in mine anger, and make them drunk in my fury, and I will bring down their strength to the earth.

God's love recounted

7 I will mention the lovingkindnesses of the LORD, *and* the praises of the LORD, according to all that the LORD hath bestowed on us, and the great goodness toward the house of Israel, which he hath bestowed on them according to his mercies, and according to the multitude of his lovingkindnesses.

8 For he said, Surely they *are* my people, children *that* will not lie: so he was their Saviour.

9 ᴿIn all their affliction he was afflicted, ᴿand the angel of his presence saved them: ᴿin his love and in his pity he redeemed them; and ᴿhe bare them, and carried them all the days of old.

10 But they ᴿrebelled, and ᴿvexed his holy spirit: ᴿtherefore he was turned to be their enemy, *and* he fought against them.

11 Then he remembered the days of old, Moses, *and* his people, *saying,* Where *is* he that ᴿbrought them up out of the sea with the ᴺshepherd of his flock? ᴿwhere *is* he that put his holy spirit within him?

12 That led *them* by the right hand of Moses ᴿwith his glorious arm, ᴿdividing the water before them, to make himself an everlasting name?

13 ᴿThat led them through the deep, as an horse in the wilderness, *that* they should not stumble?

14 As a beast goeth down into the valley, the spirit of the LORD caused him to rest: so didst thou lead thy people, ᴿto make thyself a glorious name.

Prayer for God's return in love

15 ᴿLook down from heaven, and behold ᴿfrom the habitation of thy holiness and of thy glory: where *is* thy zeal and thy strength, ᴺthe sounding ᴿof thy bowels and of thy mercies toward me? are they restrained?

16 ᴿDoubtless thou *art* our father, though Abraham ᴿbe ignorant of us, and Israel acknowledge us not: thou, O LORD, *art* our father, ᴺour redeemer; thy name *is* from everlasting.

17 O LORD, why hast thou ᴿmade us to err from thy ways, *and* ᴿhardened our heart from thy fear? ᴿReturn for thy servants' sake, the tribes of thine inheritance.

18 ᴿThe people of thy holiness have possessed *it* but a little while: ᴿour adversaries have trodden down thy sanctuary.

19 We are *thine:* thou never barest rule over them; ᴺthey were not called by thy name.

CHAPTER 64

OH that thou wouldest ᴿrend the heavens, that thou wouldest come down, that ᴿthe mountains might flow down at thy presence,

2 As *when* ᴺthe melting fire burneth, the fire causeth the waters to boil, to make thy name known to thine adversaries, *that* the nations may tremble at thy presence!

3 When ᴿthou didst terrible things *which* we looked not for, thou camest down, the mountains flowed down at thy presence.

4 For since the beginning of the world ᴿmen have not heard, nor perceived by the ear, neither hath the eye ᴺseen, O God, beside thee, *what* he hath prepared for him that waiteth for him.

5 Thou meetest him that rejoiceth ᴿand worketh righteousness, ᴿ*those that* remember thee in thy ways: behold, thou art wroth; for we have sinned: ᴿin those is continuance, and we shall be saved.

6 But we are all as an unclean *thing,* and all ᴿour righteousnesses *are* as filthy rags; and we all do ᴿfade as a leaf; and our iniquities, like the wind, have taken us away.

7 And *there is* none that calleth upon thy name, that stirreth up himself to take hold of thee: for thou hast hid thy face from us, and hast ᴺconsumed us, ᴺbecause of our iniquities.

8 ᴿBut now, O LORD, thou *art* our father; we *are* the clay, ᴿand thou our potter; and we all *are* ᴿthe work of thy hand.

9 Be not ᴿwroth very sore, O LORD, neither remember iniquity for ever: behold, see, we beseech thee, ᴿwe *are* all thy people.

10 Thy holy cities are a wilderness, Zion is a wilderness, ᴿJerusalem a desolation.

11 ᴿOur holy and our beautiful house, where our fathers praised thee, is burned up with fire: and all ᴿour pleasant things are laid waste.

12 ᴿWilt thou refrain thyself for these *things,* O Lᴏʀᴅ? ᴿwilt thou hold thy peace, and afflict us very sore?

CHAPTER 65

God states his case

I ᴿAM sought of *them that* asked not *for me;* I am found of *them that* sought me not: I said, Behold me, behold me, unto a nation *that* ᴿwas not called by my name.

2 ᴿI have spread out my hands all the day unto a rebellious people, which walketh in a way *that was* not good, after their own thoughts;

3 A people ᴿthat provoketh me to anger continually to my face; ᴿthat sacrificeth in gardens, and burneth incense ᴺupon altars of brick;

4 ᴿWhich remain among the graves, and lodge in the monuments, ᴿwhich eat swine's flesh, and ᴺbroth of abominable *things is in* their vessels;

5 ᴿWhich say, Stand by thyself, come not near to me; for I am holier than thou. These *are* a smoke in my ᴺnose, a fire that burneth all the day.

6 Behold, ᴿ*it is* written before me: ᴿI will not keep silence, ᴿbut will recompense, even recompense into their bosom,

7 Your iniquities, and ᴿthe iniquities of your fathers together, saith the Lᴏʀᴅ, ᴿwhich have burned incense upon the mountains, ᴿand blasphemed me upon the hills: therefore will I measure their former work into their bosom.

The faithful and the idolaters

8 Thus saith the Lᴏʀᴅ, As the new wine is found in the cluster, and *one* saith, Destroy it not; for ᴿa blessing *is* in it: so will I do for my servants' sakes, that I may not destroy them all.

9 And I will bring forth a seed out of Jacob, and out of Judah an inheritor of my mountains: and mine ᴿelect shall inherit it, and my servants shall dwell there.

10 And ᴿShâr'-on shall be a fold of flocks, and ᴿthe valley of Ā'-chôr a place for the herds to lie down in, for my people that have sought me.

11 But ye *are* they that forsake the Lᴏʀᴅ, that forget ᴿmy holy mountain, that prepare ᴿa table for that ᴺtroop, and that furnish the drink offering unto that ᴺnumber.

12 Therefore will I number you to the sword, and ye shall all bow down to the slaughter: ᴿbecause when I called, ye did not

answer; when I spake, ye did not hear; but did evil before mine eyes, and did choose *that* wherein I delighted not.

13 Therefore thus saith the Lord Gᴏᴅ, Behold, my servants shall eat, but ye shall be hungry: behold, my servants shall drink, but ye shall be thirsty: behold, my servants shall rejoice, but ye shall be ashamed:

14 Behold, my servants shall sing for joy of heart, but ye shall cry for sorrow of heart, and ᴿshall howl for ᴺvexation of spirit.

15 And ye shall leave your name ᴿfor a curse unto ᴿmy chosen: for the Lord Gᴏᴅ shall slay thee, and ᴿcall his servants by another name:

16 ᴿThat he who blesseth himself in the earth shall bless himself in the God of truth; and ᴿhe that sweareth in the earth shall swear by the God of truth; because the former troubles are forgotten, and because they are hid from mine eyes.

New heavens and a new earth

17 For, behold, I create ᴿnew heavens and a new earth: and the former shall not be remembered, nor ᴺcome into mind.

18 But be ye glad and rejoice for ever *in that* which I create: for, behold, I create Jerusalem a rejoicing, and her people a joy.

19 And ᴿI will rejoice in Jerusalem, and joy in my people: and the ᴿvoice of weeping shall be no more heard in her, nor the voice of crying.

20 There shall be no more thence an infant of days, nor an old man that hath not filled his days: for the child shall die an hundred years old; ᴿbut the sinner *being* an hundred years old shall be accursed.

21 And they shall build houses, and inhabit *them;* and they shall plant vineyards, and eat the fruit of them.

22 They shall not build, and another inhabit; they shall not plant, and another eat: for ᴿas the days of a tree *are* the days of my people, and ᴿmine elect ᴺshall long enjoy the work of their hands.

23 They shall not labour in vain, ᴿnor bring forth for trouble; for ᴿthey *are* the seed of the blessed of the Lᴏʀᴅ, and their offspring with them.

24 And it shall come to pass, that ᴿbefore they call, I will answer; and while they are yet speaking, I will hear.

25 The ᴿwolf and the lamb shall feed together, and the lion shall eat straw like the bullock: ᴿand dust *shall be* the serpent's meat. They shall not hurt nor destroy in all my holy mountain, saith the Lᴏʀᴅ.

CHAPTER 66

True and false worship

THUS saith the LORD, [R]The heaven *is* my throne, and the earth *is* my footstool: where *is* the house that ye build unto me? and where *is* the place of my rest?

2 For all those *things* hath mine hand made, and all those *things* have been, saith the LORD: [R]but to this *man* will I look, [R]*even* to *him that is* poor and of a contrite spirit, and [R]trembleth at my word.

3 [R]He that killeth an ox *is as if* he slew a man; he that sacrificeth a [N]lamb, *as if* he [R]cut off a dog's neck; he that offereth an oblation, *as if he offered* swine's blood; he that [N]burneth incense, *as if* he blessed an idol. Yea, they have chosen their own ways, and their soul delighteth in their abominations.

4 I also will choose their [N]delusions, and will bring their fears upon them; [R]because when I called, none did answer; when I spake, they did not hear: but they did evil before mine eyes, and chose *that* in which I delighted not.

Birth of a new nation

5 Hear the word of the LORD, [R]ye that tremble at his word; Your brethren that hated you, that cast you out for my name's sake, said, [R]Let the LORD be glorified: but [R]he shall appear to your joy, and they shall be ashamed.

6 A voice of noise from the city, a voice from the temple, a voice of the LORD that rendereth recompence to his enemies.

7 Before she travailed, she brought forth; before her pain came, she was delivered of a man child.

8 Who hath heard such a thing? who hath seen such things? Shall the earth be made to bring forth in one day? *or* shall a nation be born at once? for as soon as Zion travailed, she brought forth her children.

9 Shall I bring to the birth, and not [N]cause to bring forth? saith the LORD: shall I cause to bring forth, and shut *the womb?* saith thy God.

10 Rejoice ye with Jerusalem, and be glad with her, all ye that love her: rejoice for joy with her, all ye that mourn for her:

11 That ye may suck, and be satisfied with the breasts of her consolations; that ye may milk out, and be delighted with the [N]abundance of her glory.

12 For thus saith the LORD, Behold, [R]I will extend peace to her like a river, and the glory of the Gentiles like a flowing stream: then

shall ye [R]suck, ye shall be [R]borne upon *her* sides, and be dandled upon *her* knees.

13 As one whom his mother comforteth, so will I comfort you; and ye shall be comforted in Jerusalem.

14 And when ye see *this,* your heart shall rejoice, and [R]your bones shall flourish like an herb: and the hand of the LORD shall be known toward his servants, and *his* indignation toward his enemies.

Judgment of mankind

15 [R]For, behold, the LORD will come with fire, and with his chariots like a whirlwind, to render his anger with fury, and his rebuke with flames of fire.

16 For by fire and by [R]his sword will the LORD plead with all flesh: and the slain of the LORD shall be many.

17 [R]They that sanctify themselves, and purify themselves in the gardens [N]behind one *tree* in the midst, eating swine's flesh, and the abomination, and the mouse, shall be consumed together, saith the LORD.

18 For I *know* their works and their thoughts: it shall come, that I will gather all nations and tongues; and they shall come, and see my glory.

19 [R]And I will set a sign among them, and I will send those that escape of them unto the nations, *to* Tarshish, Pŭl, and Lud, that draw the bow, *to* Tū'-băl, and Jā'-văn, *to* the isles afar off, that have not heard my fame, neither have seen my glory; [R]and they shall declare my glory among the Gentiles.

20 And they shall bring all your brethren [R]*for* an offering unto the LORD out of all nations upon horses, and in chariots, and in [N]litters, and upon mules, and upon swift beasts, to my holy mountain Jerusalem, saith the LORD, as the children of Israel bring an offering in a clean vessel into the house of the LORD.

21 And I will also take of them for [R]priests *and* for Levites, saith the LORD.

22 For as [R]the new heavens and the new earth, which I will make, shall remain before me, saith the LORD, so shall your seed and your name remain.

23 And [R]it shall come to pass, *that* [N]from one new moon to another, and from one sabbath to another, [R]shall all flesh come to worship before me, saith the LORD.

24 And they shall go forth, and look upon [R]the carcases of the men that have transgressed against me: for their [R]worm shall not die, neither shall their fire be quenched; and they shall be an abhorring unto all flesh.

THE BOOK OF THE PROPHET
JEREMIAH

The book of Jeremiah has preserved the messages and writings of the prophet who served as God's messenger throughout the last four decades of the kingdom of Judah, 627–586 B.C. With the decline of Assyrian power after 650 B.C., Josiah had the opportunity to assert himself politically and religiously. By 605 B.C., the Babylonians advanced to Palestine and ultimately the city with its temple was destroyed.

Jeremiah's warning that judgment was coming was favorably received until 609 B.C., the date when Josiah was killed in battle at Megiddo. After that many of the civil and religious leaders openly opposed Jeremiah. As a messenger of God faithfully warning his people, he was subjected to much suffering and narrowly escaped death as the pressures mounted. His message was primarily concerned with the national and international involvements facing his people at that time. He assures them, however, that they would be restored after 70 years of Babylonian captivity. Likewise, he predicts the ultimate restoration of Israel (ch. 31).

Since this book is not arranged in chronological order it is difficult to outline. It may be divided as follows:

CHAPTER 1

Call of Jeremiah

THE words of Jeremiah the son of Hĭl-kī'-ăh, of the priests that were ᴿin Ăn'-ă-thŏth in the land of Benjamin:

2 To whom the word of the LORD came in the days of Jō-sī'-ăh the son of Amon king of Judah, ᴿin the thirteenth year of his reign.

3 It came also in the days of Jĕ-hoi'-ă-kĭm the son of Jō-sī'-ăh king of Judah, ᴿunto the end of the eleventh year of Zĕd-ē-kī'-ăh the son of Jō-sī'-ăh king of Judah, ᴿunto the carrying away of Jerusalem captive ᴿin the fifth month.

4 Then the word of the LORD came unto me, saying,

5 Before I ᴿformed thee in the belly ᴿI knew thee; and before thou camest forth out of the womb I ᴿsanctified thee, and I ᴺordained thee a prophet unto the nations.

6 Then said I, ᴿAh, Lord GOD! behold, I cannot speak: for I am a child.

7 But the LORD said unto me, Say not, I am a child: for thou shalt go to all that I shall send thee, and ᴿwhatsoever I command thee thou shalt speak.

8 ᴿBe not afraid of their faces: for ᴿI am with thee to deliver thee, saith the LORD.

9 Then the LORD put forth his hand, and ᴿtouched my mouth. And the LORD said unto me, Behold, I have ᴿput my words in thy mouth.

10 ᴿSee, I have this day set thee over the nations and over the kingdoms, to ᴿroot out, and to pull down, and to destroy, and to throw down, to build, and to plant.

Vision of the almond rod

11 Moreover the word of the LORD came unto me, saying, Jeremiah, what seest thou? And I said, I see a rod of an almond tree.

12 Then said the LORD unto me, Thou hast well seen: for I will hasten my word to perform it.

Vision of the boiling pot

13 And the word of the LORD came unto me the second time, saying, What seest thou? And I said, I see ᴿa seething pot; and the face thereof is ᴺtoward the north.

14 Then the LORD said unto me, Out of the ᴿnorth an evil ᴺshall break forth upon all the inhabitants of the land.

15 For, lo, I will ᴿcall all the families of the kingdoms of the north, saith the LORD; and they shall come, and they shall ᴿset every one his throne at the entering of the gates of Jerusalem, and against all the walls thereof round about, and against all the cities of Judah.

16 And I will utter my judgments against them touching all their wickedness, ᴿwho have forsaken me, and have burned incense unto other gods, and worshipped the works of their own hands.

17 Thou therefore ᴿgird up thy loins, and arise, and speak unto them all that I command thee: ᴿbe not dismayed at their faces, lest I ᴺconfound thee before them.

18 For, behold, I have made thee this day ᴿa defenced city, and an iron pillar, and brasen walls against the whole land, against the kings of Judah, against the princes thereof, against the priests thereof, and against the people of the land.

CHAP. 1
BC 629
1 Josh. 21:18
1 Chr. 6:60
ch. 32:7, 8
2 ch. 25:3
3 ch. 39:2
3 ch. 52:12
3 2 Ki. 25:8
5 Is. 49:1, 5
5 Ex. 33:12
5 Luke 1:15
Gal. 1:15
5 Heb. *gave*
6 Ex. 4:10
& 6:12, 30
7 Num. 22:20, 38
Mat. 28:20
8 Ezek. 2:6
& 3:9
8 Ex. 3:12
Deut. 31:6
Josh. 1:5
Heb. 13:6
9 Is. 6:7
9 Is. 51:16
ch. 5:14
10 1 Ki. 19:17
10 ch. 18:7
2 Cor. 10:4
Ezek. 11:3 — 13
& 24:3
Heb. *from the face of the north* — 13
ch. 6:1 — 14
Heb. *shall be opened* — 14
ch. 6:22 — 15
ch. 39:3 — 15
Deut. 28:20 — 16
ch. 17:13
2 Ki. 4:29 — 17
Job 38:3
Luke 12:35
1 Pet. 1:13
Ex. 3:12 — 17
Ezek. 2:6
Or, *break to pieces* — 17
Is. 50:7 — 18
ch. 6:27
& 15:20

19 And they shall fight against thee; but they shall not prevail against thee; ^Rfor I *am* with thee, saith the LORD, to deliver thee.

CHAPTER 2

Israel's early devotion

MOREOVER the word of the LORD came to me, saying,

2 Go and cry in the ears of Jerusalem, saying, Thus saith the LORD; I remember ^Nthee, the kindness of thy ^Ryouth, the love of thine espousals, ^Rwhen thou wentest after me in the wilderness, in a land *that was* not sown.

3 ^RIsrael *was* holiness unto the LORD, *and* ^Rthe firstfruits of his increase: ^Rall that devour him shall offend; evil shall come upon them, saith the LORD.

Israel's apostasy

4 Hear ye the word of the LORD, O house of Jacob, and all the families of the house of Israel:

5 Thus saith the LORD, ^RWhat iniquity have your fathers found in me, that they are gone far from me, ^Rand have walked after vanity, and are become vain?

6 Neither said they, Where *is* the LORD that ^Rbrought us up out of the land of Egypt, that led us through ^Rthe wilderness, through a land of deserts and of pits, through a land of drought, and of the shadow of death, through a land that no man passed through, and where no man dwelt?

7 And I brought you into ^Ra^N plentiful country, to eat the fruit thereof and the goodness thereof; but when ye entered, ye ^Rdefiled my land, and made mine heritage an abomination.

8 The priests said not, Where *is* the LORD? and they that handle the ^Rlaw knew me not: the pastors also transgressed against me, ^Rand the prophets prophesied by Bā'-ăl, and walked after *things that* do not profit.

9 Wherefore ^RI will yet plead with you, saith the LORD, and with your children's children will I plead.

10 For pass ^Nover the isles of Chĭt'-tĭm, and see; and send unto Kē'-där, and consider diligently, and see if there be such a thing.

11 ^RHath a nation changed *their* gods, which *are* ^Ryet no gods? ^Rbut my people have changed their glory for *that which* doth not profit.

12 Be astonished, O ye heavens, at this, and be horribly afraid, be ye very desolate, saith the LORD.

13 For my people have committed two evils; they have forsaken me the ^Rfountain of living waters, *and* hewed them out cisterns, broken cisterns, that can hold no water.

Results of apostasy

14 *Is* Israel ^Ra servant? *is* he a homeborn *slave?* why is he ^Nspoiled?

15 ^RThe young lions roared upon him, *and* ^Nyelled, and they made his land waste: his cities are burned without inhabitant.

16 Also the children of Nŏph and ^RTă-hăp'-ă-nēś ^Nhave broken the crown of thy head.

17 ^RHast thou not procured this unto thyself, in that thou hast forsaken the LORD thy God, when ^Rhe led thee by the way?

18 And now what hast thou to do ^Rin the way of Egypt, to drink the waters of ^RSĭ'-hôr? or what hast thou to do in the way of Assyria, to drink the waters of the river?

19 Thine own wickedness shall correct thee, and thy backslidings shall reprove thee: know therefore and see that *it is* an evil *thing* and bitter, that thou hast forsaken the LORD thy God, and that my fear *is* not in thee, saith the Lord GOD of hosts.

Israel's idolatry

20 For of old time I have broken thy yoke, *and* burst thy bands; and ^Rthou saidst, I will not ^Ntransgress; when ^Rupon every high hill and under every green tree thou wanderest, ^Rplaying the harlot.

21 Yet I had ^Rplanted thee a noble vine, wholly a right seed: how then art thou turned into ^Rthe degenerate plant of a strange vine unto me?

22 For though thou wash thee with nitre, and take thee much soap, *yet* thine iniquity is marked before me, saith the Lord GOD.

23 ^RHow canst thou say, I am not polluted, I have not gone after Bā'-ă-lĭm? see thy way in the valley, know what thou hast done: ^N*thou art* a swift dromedary traversing her ways;

24 ^NA wild ass ^Nused to the wilderness, *that* snuffeth up the wind at ^Nher pleasure; in her occasion who can ^Nturn her away? all they that seek her will not weary themselves; in her month they shall find her.

25 Withhold thy foot from being unshod, and thy throat from thirst: but thou saidst, ^NThere is no hope: no; for I have loved ^Rstrangers, and after them will I go.

26 As the thief is ashamed when he is found, so is the house of Israel ashamed; they, their

kings, their princes, and their priests, and their prophets,

27 Saying to a stock, Thou *art* my father; and to a stone, Thou hast ᴺbrought me forth: for they have turned ᴺ*their* back unto me, and not *their* face: but in the time of their ᴿtrouble they will say, Arise, and save us.

28 But ᴿwhere *are* thy gods that thou hast made thee? let them arise, if they ᴿcan save thee in the time of thy ᴺtrouble: for ᴿ*according to* the number of thy cities are thy gods, O Judah.

Israel's incorrigibility

29 Wherefore will ye plead with me? ye all have transgressed against me, saith the LORD.

30 In vain have I ᴿsmitten your children; they received no correction: your own sword hath ᴿdevoured your prophets, like a destroying lion.

31 O generation, see ye the word of the LORD. Have I been a wilderness unto Israel? a land of darkness? wherefore say my people, ᴺWe are lords; ᴿwe will come no more unto thee?

32 Can a maid forget her ornaments, *or* a bride her attire? yet my people ᴿhave forgotten me days without number.

Israel's harlotry

33 Why trimmest thou thy way to seek love? therefore hast thou also taught the wicked ones thy ways.

34 Also in thy skirts is found ᴿthe blood of the souls of the poor innocents: I have not found it by ᴺsecret search, but upon all these.

35 ᴿYet thou sayest, Because I am innocent, surely his anger shall turn from me. Behold, ᴿI will plead with thee, ᴿbecause thou sayest, I have not sinned.

36 ᴿWhy gaddest thou about so much to change thy way? ᴿthou also shalt be ashamed of Egypt, ᴿas thou wast ashamed of Assyria.

37 Yea, thou shalt go forth from him, and ᴿthine hands upon thine head: for the LORD hath rejected thy confidences, and thou shalt not prosper in them.

CHAPTER 3

THEY ᴺsay, If a man put away his wife, and she go from him, and become another man's, ᴿshall he return unto her again? shall not that ᴿland be greatly polluted? but thou hast ᴿplayed the harlot with many lovers; ᴿyet return again to me, saith the LORD.

2 Lift up thine eyes unto ᴿthe high places, and see where thou hast not been lien with. ᴿIn the ways hast thou sat for them, as the

---

CHAP. 2
BC 629
27 Or, *begotten me*
27 Heb. *the hinder part of the neck*
27 Is. 26:16
28 Judg. 10:14
28 Heb. *evil*
28 ch. 11:13
30 Is. 9:13
30 Acts 7:52
31 Heb. *We have dominion*
31 Deut. 32:15
32 Ps. 106:21
34 Ps. 106:38
34 Heb. *digging*
35 ver. 23, 29
35 ver. 9
35 Prov. 28:13
36 Hos. 12:1
36 Is. 30:3
36 2 Chr. 28:16
37 2 Sam. 13:19

CHAP. 3
BC 629
1 Heb. *Saying*
1 Deut. 24:4
1 ch. 2:7
1 ch. 2:20
Ezek. 16:26
1 Zech. 1:3
2 Deut. 12:2
2 Prov. 23:28

ch. 2:7	2
Lev. 26:19	3
Zeph. 3:5	3
Prov. 2:17	4
Hos. 2:15	4
Ps. 103:9	5
Is. 57:16	
ch. 7:24	6
ch. 2:20	6
2 Ki. 17:13	7
Ezek. 16:46	7
Ezek. 23:9	8
2 Ki. 17:6	8
Ezek. 23:11	8
Or, *fame*	9
ch. 2:7	9
ch. 2:27	9
Hos. 7:14	10
Heb. *in falsehood*	10
Ezek. 16:51	11
2 Ki. 17:6	12
Ps. 86:15	12
Deut. 30:1	13
Ezek. 16:15	13
ch. 2:25	13
Deut. 12:2	13
Hos. 2:19	14
Rom. 11:5	14
Ezek. 34:23	15
Eph. 4:11	
Acts 20:28	15

Arabian in the wilderness; ᴿand thou hast polluted the land with thy whoredoms and with thy wickedness.

3 Therefore the ᴿshowers have been withholden, and there hath been no latter rain; and thou hadst a ᴿwhore's forehead, thou refusedst to be ashamed.

4 Wilt thou not from this time cry unto me, My father, thou *art* ᴿthe guide of ᴿmy youth?

5 ᴿWill he reserve *his* anger for ever? will he keep *it* to the end? Behold, thou hast spoken and done evil things as thou couldest.

Both Judah and Israel alike

6 The LORD said also unto me in the days of Jō-sī'-ăh the king, Hast thou seen *that* which ᴿbacksliding Israel hath done? she is ᴿgone up upon every high mountain and under every green tree, and there hath played the harlot.

7 ᴿAnd I said after she had done all these *things*, Turn thou unto me. But she returned not. And her treacherous ᴿsister Judah saw *it*.

8 And I saw, when ᴿfor all the causes whereby backsliding Israel committed adultery I had ᴿput her away, and given her a bill of divorce; ᴿyet her treacherous sister Judah feared not, but went and played the harlot also.

9 And it came to pass through the ᴺlightness of her whoredom, that she ᴿdefiled the land, and committed adultery with ᴿstones and with stocks.

10 And yet for all this her treacherous sister Judah hath not turned unto me ᴿwith her whole heart, but ᴺfeignedly, saith the LORD.

11 And the LORD said unto me, ᴿThe backsliding Israel hath justified herself more than treacherous Judah.

Call for Israel's repentance

12 Go and proclaim these words toward ᴿthe north, and say, Return, thou backsliding Israel, saith the LORD; *and* I will not cause mine anger to fall upon you: for I *am* ᴿmerciful, saith the LORD, *and* I will not keep *anger* for ever.

13 ᴿOnly acknowledge thine iniquity, that thou hast transgressed against the LORD thy God, and hast ᴿscattered thy ways to the ᴿstrangers ᴿunder every green tree, and ye have not obeyed my voice, saith the LORD.

14 Turn, O backsliding children, saith the LORD; ᴿfor I am married unto you: and I will take you ᴿone of a city, and two of a family, and I will bring you to Zion:

15 And I will give you ᴿpastors according to mine heart, which shall ᴿfeed you with knowledge and understanding.

16 And it shall come to pass, when ye be multiplied and increased in the land, in those days, saith the LORD, they shall say no more, The ark of the covenant of the LORD: ᴿneither shall it ᴺcome to mind: neither shall they remember it; neither shall they visit *it; neither* shall ᴺ*that* be done any more.

17 At that time they shall call Jerusalem the throne of the LORD; and all the nations shall be gathered unto it, ᴿto the name of the LORD, to Jerusalem: neither shall they ᴿwalk any more after the ᴺimagination of their evil heart.

18 In those days ᴿthe house of Judah shall walk ᴺwith the house of Israel, and they shall come together out of the land of ᴿthe north to ᴿthe land that I have ᴺgiven for an inheritance unto your fathers.

19 But I said, How shall I put thee among the children, and give thee ᴿa ᴺpleasant land, ᴺa goodly heritage of the hosts of nations? and I said, Thou shalt call me, ᴿMy father; and shalt not turn away ᴺfrom me.

20 Surely *as* a wife treacherously departeth from her ᴺhusband, so ᴿhave ye dealt treacherously with me, O house of Israel, saith the LORD.

Israel's lament

21 A voice was heard upon ᴿthe high places, weeping *and* supplications of the children of Israel: for they have perverted their way, *and* they have forgotten the LORD their God.

22 ᴿReturn, ye backsliding children, *and* ᴿI will heal your backslidings. Behold, we come unto thee; for thou *art* the LORD our God.

23 ᴿTruly in vain *is salvation hoped for* from the hills, *and from* the multitude of mountains: ᴿtruly in the LORD our God *is* the salvation of Israel.

24 ᴿFor shame hath devoured the labour of our fathers from our youth; their flocks and their herds, their sons and their daughters.

25 We lie down in our shame, and our confusion covereth us: ᴿfor we have sinned against the LORD our God, we and our fathers, from our youth even unto this day, and ᴿhave not obeyed the voice of the LORD our God.

CHAPTER 4

Conditions of restoration

IF thou wilt return, O Israel, saith the LORD, ᴿreturn unto me: and if thou wilt put away thine abominations out of my sight, then shalt thou not remove.

2 ᴿAnd thou shalt swear, The LORD liveth, ᴿin truth, in judgment, and in righteousness;

CHAP. 3
BC 629
16 Is. 65:17
16 Heb. *come upon the heart*
16 Or, *it be magnified*
17 Is. 60:9
17 ch. 11:8
17 Or, *stubbornness*
18 Is. 11:13
Hos. 1:11
18 Or, *to*
18 ch. 31:8
18 Amos 9:15
18 Or, *caused your fathers to possess*
19 Ps. 106:24
19 Heb. *land of desire*
19 Heb. *an heritage of glory, or, beauty*
19 Is. 63:16
19 Heb. *from after me*
20 Heb. *friend*
20 Is. 48:8
21 Is. 15:2
22 ver. 14
Hos. 14:1
22 Hos. 6:1 & 14:4
23 Ps. 121:1, 2
23 Ps. 3:8
24 ch. 11:13
Hos. 9:10
25 Ezra 9:7
25 ch. 22:21

CHAP. 4
BC 612
1 ch. 3:1, 22
Joel 2:12
2 Deut. 10:20
Is. 45:23 & 65:16
See ch. 5:2
2 Is. 48:1
Zech. 8:8

Gen. 22:18   2
Ps. 72:17
1 Cor. 1:31   2
Hos. 10:12   3
Mat. 13:7   3
Deut. 10:16   4
ch. 9:26
Rom. 2:28
ch. 8:14   5
Or, *strengthen* 6
ch. 1:13-15   6
& 6:1, 22
Heb. *breaking*   6
2 Ki. 24:1   7
ch. 5:6
Dan. 7:4
ch. 25:9   7
Is. 1:7   7
Is. 22:12   8
Ezek. 14:9   10
2 Thes. 2:11
ch. 14:13   10
ch. 51:1   11
Ezek. 17:10
Or, *a fuller wind than those* 12
ch. 1:16   12
Heb. *utter judgments* 12
Is. 5:28   13
Deut. 28:49   13
Hos. 8:1
Hab. 1:8
Is. 1:16   14
Jas. 4:8
ch. 8:16   15

ᴿand the nations shall bless themselves in him, and in him shall they ᴿglory.

3 For thus saith the LORD to the men of Judah and Jerusalem, ᴿBreak up your fallow ground, and ᴿsow not among thorns.

4 ᴿCircumcise yourselves to the LORD, and take away the foreskins of your heart, ye men of Judah and inhabitants of Jerusalem: lest my fury come forth like fire, and burn that none can quench *it,* because of the evil of your doings.

Destruction from the north

5 Declare ye in Judah, and publish in Jerusalem; and say, Blow ye the trumpet in the land: cry, gather together, and say, ᴿAssemble yourselves, and let us go into the defenced cities.

6 Set up the standard toward Zion: ᴺretire, stay not: for I will bring evil from the ᴿnorth, and a great ᴺdestruction.

7 ᴿThe lion is come up from his thicket, and ᴿthe destroyer of the Gentiles is on his way; he is gone forth from his place ᴿto make thy land desolate; *and* thy cities shall be laid waste, without an inhabitant.

8 For this ᴿgird you with sackcloth, lament and howl: for the fierce anger of the LORD is not turned back from us.

9 And it shall come to pass at that day, saith the LORD, *that* the heart of the king shall perish, and the heart of the princes; and the priests shall be astonished, and the prophets shall wonder.

10 Then said I, Ah, Lord GOD! ᴿsurely thou hast greatly deceived this people and Jerusalem, ᴿsaying, Ye shall have peace; whereas the sword reacheth unto the soul.

11 At that time shall it be said to this people and to Jerusalem, ᴿA dry wind of the high places in the wilderness toward the daughter of my people, not to fan, nor to cleanse,

12 *Even* ᴺa full wind from those *places* shall come unto me: now also ᴿwill I ᴺgive sentence against them.

13 Behold, he shall come up as clouds, and ᴿhis chariots *shall be* as a whirlwind: ᴿhis horses are swifter than eagles. Woe unto us! for we are spoiled.

14 O Jerusalem, ᴿwash thine heart from wickedness, that thou mayest be saved. How long shall thy vain thoughts lodge within thee?

15 For a voice declareth ᴿfrom Dan, and publisheth affliction from mount Ē'-phră-ĭm.

16 Make ye mention to the nations; behold, publish against Jerusalem, *that* watchers come from a far country, and give out their voice against the cities of Judah.

17 ᴿAs keepers of a field, are they against her round about; because she hath been rebellious against me, saith the LORD.

18 ᴿThy way and thy doings have procured these *things* unto thee; this *is* thy wickedness, because it is bitter, because it reacheth unto thine heart.

19 My ᴿbowels, my bowels! I am pained at ᴺmy very heart; my heart maketh a noise in me; I cannot hold my peace, because thou hast heard, O my soul, the sound of the trumpet, the alarm of war.

20 ᴿDestruction upon destruction is cried; for the whole land is spoiled: suddenly are ᴿmy tents spoiled, *and* my curtains in a moment.

21 How long shall I see the standard, *and* hear the sound of the trumpet?

22 For my people *is* foolish, they have not known me; they *are* sottish children, and they have none understanding: ᴿthey *are* wise to do evil, but to do good they have no knowledge.

Desolation of the land

23 ᴿI beheld the earth, and, lo, *it was* ᴿwithout form, and void; and the heavens, and they *had* no light.

24 ᴿI beheld the mountains, and, lo, they trembled, and all the hills moved lightly.

25 I beheld, and, lo, *there was* no man, and ᴿall the birds of the heavens were fled.

26 I beheld, and, lo, the fruitful place *was* a wilderness, and all the cities thereof were broken down at the presence of the LORD, *and* by his fierce anger.

27 For thus hath the LORD said, The whole land shall be desolate; ᴿyet will I not make a full end.

28 For this ᴿshall the earth mourn, and ᴿthe heavens above be black: because I have spoken *it,* I have purposed *it,* and ᴿwill not repent, neither will I turn back from it.

29 The whole city shall flee for the noise of the horsemen and bowmen; they shall go into thickets, and climb up upon the rocks: every city *shall be* forsaken, and not a man dwell therein.

30 And *when* thou *art* spoiled, what wilt thou do? Though thou clothest thyself with crimson, though thou deckest thee with ornaments of gold, ᴿthough thou rentest thy ᴺface with painting, in vain shalt thou make thyself fair; ᴿthy lovers will despise thee, they will seek thy life.

31 For I have heard a voice as of a woman in travail, *and* the anguish as of her that bringeth forth her first child, the voice of the

daughter of Zion, *that* bewaileth herself, *that* ᴿspreadeth her hands, *saying,* Woe *is* me now! for my soul is wearied because of murderers.

CHAPTER 5

Perversion of justice in Jerusalem

RUN ye to and fro through the streets of Jerusalem, and see now, and know, and seek in the broad places thereof, ᴿif ye can find a man, ᴿif there be *any* that executeth judgment, that seeketh the truth; ᴿand I will pardon it.

2 And ᴿthough they say, ᴿThe LORD liveth; surely they ᴿswear falsely.

3 O LORD, *are* not ᴿthine eyes upon the truth? thou hast ᴿstricken them, but they have not grieved; thou hast consumed them, *but* ᴿthey have refused to receive correction: they have made their faces harder than a rock; they have refused to return.

4 Therefore I said, Surely these *are* poor; they are foolish: for ᴿthey know not the way of the LORD, *nor* the judgment of their God.

5 I will get me unto the great men, and will speak unto them; for ᴿthey have known the way of the LORD, *and* the judgment of their God: but these have altogether ᴿbroken the yoke, *and* burst the bonds.

6 Wherefore ᴿa lion out of the forest shall slay them, ᴿ*and* a wolf of the ᴺevenings shall spoil them, ᴿa leopard shall watch over their cities: every one that goeth out thence shall be torn in pieces: because their transgressions are many, *and* their backslidings ᴺare increased.

Total corruption in Judah

7 How shall I pardon thee for this? thy children have forsaken me, and ᴿsworn by *them* ᴿ*that are* no gods: ᴿwhen I had fed them to the full, they then committed adultery, and assembled themselves by troops in the harlots' houses.

8 ᴿThey were *as* fed horses in the morning: every one neighed after his neighbour's wife.

9 ᴿShall I not visit for these *things?* saith the LORD: ᴿand shall not my soul be avenged on such a nation as this?

10 ᴿGo ye up upon her walls, and destroy; ᴿbut make not a full end: take away her batlements; for they *are* not the LORD's.

11 For ᴿthe house of Israel and the house of Judah have dealt very treacherously against me, saith the LORD.

12 ᴿThey have belied the LORD, and said, ᴿ*It is* not he; neither shall evil come upon us; ᴿneither shall we see sword nor famine:

13 And the prophets shall become wind, and the word *is* not in them: thus shall it be done unto them.

God's judgment

14 Wherefore thus saith the LORD God of hosts, Because ye speak this word, ᴿbehold, I will make my words in thy mouth fire, and this people wood, and it shall devour them.

15 Lo, I will bring a ᴿnation upon you ᴿfrom far, O house of Israel, saith the LORD: it *is* a mighty nation, it *is* an ancient nation, a nation whose language thou knowest not, neither understandest what they say.

16 Their quiver *is* as an open sepulchre, they *are* all mighty men.

17 And they shall eat up thine ᴿharvest, and thy bread, *which* thy sons and thy daughters should eat: they shall eat up thy flocks and thine herds: they shall eat up thy vines and thy fig trees: they shall impoverish thy fenced cities, wherein thou trustedst, with the sword.

A remnant for remembrance

18 Nevertheless in those days, saith the LORD, I ᴿwill not make a full end with you.

19 And it shall come to pass, when ye shall say, ᴿWherefore doeth the LORD our God all these *things* unto us? then shalt thou answer them, Like as ye have ᴿforsaken me, and served strange gods in your land, so ᴿshall ye serve strangers in a land *that is* not yours.

20 Declare this in the house of Jacob, and publish it in Judah, saying,

21 Hear now this, O ᴿfoolish people, and without ᴺunderstanding; which have eyes, and see not; which have ears, and hear not:

22 ᴿFear ye not me? saith the LORD: will ye not tremble at my presence, which have placed the sand *for* the ᴿbound of the sea by a perpetual decree, that it cannot pass it: and though the waves thereof toss themselves, yet can they not prevail; though they roar, yet can they not pass over it?

23 But this people hath a revolting and a rebellious heart; they are revolted and gone.

24 Neither say they in their heart, Let us now fear the LORD our God, ᴿthat giveth rain, both the ᴿformer and the latter, in his season: ᴿhe reserveth unto us the appointed weeks of the harvest.

25 ᴿYour iniquities have turned away these *things,* and your sins have withholden good *things* from you.

26 For among my people are found wicked *men:* ᴺthey ᴿlay wait, as he that setteth snares; they set a trap, they catch men.

CHAP. 5
BC 612

14 ch. 1:9
15 Deut. 28:49
Is. 5:26
ch. 1:15 & 6:22
15 Is. 39:3
ch. 4:16
17 Lev. 26:16
Deut. 28:31, 33
18 ch. 4:27
19 Deut. 29:24, etc.
1 Ki. 9:8, 9
ch. 13:22 & 16:10
19 ch. 2:13
19 Deut. 28:48
21 Is. 6:9
Ezek. 12:2
Mat. 13:14
John 12:40
Acts 28:26
Rom. 11:8
21 Heb. *heart*
22 Rev. 15:4
22 Job 26:10
Prov. 8:29
24 Ps. 147:8
Acts 14:17
24 Joel 2:23
24 Gen. 8:22
25 ch. 3:3
26 Or, *they pry as fowlers lie in wait*
26 Prov. 1:11
Hab. 1:15

Or, *coop*   27
Deut. 32:15   28
Is. 1:23   28
Zech. 7:10
Job 12:6   28
Ps. 73:12
Mal. 3:5   29
Or, *Astonishment and filthiness*   30
Hos. 6:10   30
ch. 14:14   31
& 23:25, 26
Ezek. 13:6
Or, *take into their hands*   31
Mic. 2:11   31

CHAP. 6
BC 612

Neh. 3:14   1
ch. 4:6   1
Or, *dwelling at home*   2
2 Ki. 25:1   3
Joel 3:9   4
ch. 15:8   4
Or, *pour out the engine of shot*   5
Is. 57:20   7
Ps. 55:9   7
ch. 20:8
Ezek. 7:11
Hos. 9:12   8
Heb. *be loosed,* 8
or, *disjointed*
Acts 7:51   10
See Ex. 6:12

---

27 As a ᴺcage is full of birds, so *are* their houses full of deceit: therefore they are become great, and waxen rich.

28 They are waxen ᴿfat, they shine: yea, they overpass the deeds of the wicked: they judge not ᴿthe cause, the cause of the fatherless, ᴿyet they prosper; and the right of the needy do they not judge.

29 ᴿShall I not visit for these *things?* saith the LORD: shall not my soul be avenged on such a nation as this?

30 ᴺA wonderful and ᴿhorrible thing is committed in the land;

31 The prophets prophesy ᴿfalsely, and the priests ᴺbear rule by their means; and my people ᴿlove *to have it* so: and what will ye do in the end thereof?

CHAPTER 6

Threatened siege of Jerusalem

O YE children of Benjamin, gather yourselves to flee out of the midst of Jerusalem, and blow the trumpet in Tĕ-kō′-ă, and set up a sign of fire in ᴿBĕth-hăc′-cĕr-ĕm: ᴿfor evil appeareth out of the north, and great destruction.

2 I have likened the daughter of Zion to a ᴺcomely and delicate *woman.*

3 The shepherds with their flocks shall come unto her; ᴿthey shall pitch *their* tents against her round about; they shall feed every one in his place.

4 ᴿPrepare ye war against her; arise, and let us go up ᴿat noon. Woe unto us! for the day goeth away, for the shadows of the evening are stretched out.

5 Arise, and let us go by night, and let us destroy her palaces.

6 For thus hath the LORD of hosts said, Hew ye down trees, and ᴺcast a mount against Jerusalem: this *is* the city to be visited; she *is* wholly oppression in the midst of her.

7 ᴿAs a fountain casteth out her waters, so she casteth out her wickedness: ᴿviolence and spoil is heard in her; before me continually *is* grief and wounds.

8 Be thou instructed, O Jerusalem, lest ᴿmy soul ᴺdepart from thee; lest I make thee desolate, a land not inhabited.

9 Thus saith the LORD of hosts, They shall throughly glean the remnant of Israel as a vine: turn back thine hand as a grapegatherer into the baskets.

10 To whom shall I speak, and give warning, that they may hear? behold, their ᴿear *is* uncircumcised, and they cannot hearken: be-

hold, ᴿthe word of the LORD is unto them a reproach; they have no delight in it.

11 Therefore I am full of the fury of the LORD; ᴿI am weary with holding in: I will pour it out ᴿupon the children abroad, and upon the assembly of young men together: for even the husband with the wife shall be taken, the aged with *him that is* full of days.

12 And ᴿtheir houses shall be turned unto others, *with their* fields and wives together: for I will stretch out my hand upon the inhabitants of the land, saith the LORD.

13 For from the least of them even unto the greatest of them every one *is* given to ᴿcovetousness; and from the prophet even unto the priest every one dealeth falsely.

14 They have ᴿhealed also the ᴺhurt *of the daughter* of my people slightly, ᴿsaying, Peace, peace; when *there is* no peace.

15 Were they ᴿashamed when they had committed abomination? nay, they were not at all ashamed, neither could they blush: therefore they shall fall among them that fall: at the time *that* I visit them they shall be cast down, saith the LORD.

Warnings not heeded

16 Thus saith the LORD, Stand ye in the ways, and see, and ask for the ᴿold paths, where *is* the good way, and walk therein, and ye shall find ᴿrest for your souls. But they said, We will not walk *therein.*

17 Also I set ᴿwatchmen over you, *saying,* Hearken to the sound of the trumpet. But they said, We will not hearken.

18 Therefore hear, ye nations, and know, O congregation, what *is* among them.

19 ᴿHear, O earth: behold, I will bring evil upon this people, *even* ᴿthe fruit of their thoughts, because they have not hearkened unto my words, nor to my law, but rejected it.

20 ᴿTo what purpose cometh there to me incense ᴿfrom Shē′-bă, and the sweet cane from a far country? ᴿyour burnt offerings *are* not acceptable, nor your sacrifices sweet unto me.

21 Therefore thus saith the LORD, Behold, I will lay stumblingblocks before this people, and the fathers and the sons together shall fall upon them; the neighbour and his friend shall perish.

Destruction from the north

22 Thus saith the LORD, Behold, a people cometh from the ᴿnorth country, and a great nation shall be raised from the sides of the earth.

23 They shall lay hold on bow and spear;

they *are* cruel, and have no mercy; their voice ᴿroareth like the sea; and they ride upon horses, set in array as men for war against thee, O daughter of Zion.

24 We have heard the fame thereof: our hands wax feeble: ᴿanguish hath taken hold of us, *and* pain, as of a woman in travail.

25 Go not forth into the field, nor walk by the way; for the sword of the enemy *and* fear *is* on every side.

26 O daughter of my people, ᴿgird *thee* with sackcloth, ᴿand wallow thyself in ashes: ᴿmake thee mourning, *as for* an only son, most bitter lamentation: for the spoiler shall suddenly come upon us.

27 I have set thee *for* a tower *and* ᴿa fortress among my people, that thou mayest know and try their way.

28 ᴿThey *are* all grievous revolters, ᴿwalking with slanders: *they are* ᴿbrass and iron; they *are* all corrupters.

29 The bellows are burned, the lead is consumed of the fire; the founder melteth in vain: for the wicked are not plucked away.

30 ᴿReprobateᴺ silver shall *men* call them, because the LORD hath rejected them.

CHAPTER 7

Jeremiah's sermon at the temple

THE word that came to Jeremiah from the LORD, saying,

2 ᴿStand in the gate of the LORD's house, and proclaim there this word, and say, Hear the word of the LORD, all *ye of* Judah, that enter in at these gates to worship the LORD.

3 Thus saith the LORD of hosts, the God of Israel, ᴿAmend your ways and your doings, and I will cause you to dwell in this place.

4 ᴿTrust ye not in lying words, saying, The temple of the LORD, The temple of the LORD, The temple of the LORD, *are* these.

5 For if ye throughly amend your ways and your doings; if ye throughly ᴿexecute judgment between a man and his neighbour;

6 *If* ye oppress not the stranger, the fatherless, and the widow, and shed not innocent blood in this place, ᴿneither walk after other gods to your hurt:

7 ᴿThen will I cause you to dwell in this place, in ᴿthe land that I gave to your fathers, for ever and ever.

8 Behold, ᴿye trust in ᴿlying words, that cannot profit.

9 ᴿWill ye steal, murder, and commit adultery, and swear falsely, and burn incense unto Bā′-ăl, and ᴿwalk after other gods whom ye know not;

10 ^RAnd come and stand before me in this house, ^Rwhich^N is called by my name, and say, We are delivered to do all these abominations?

11 Is ^Rthis house, which is called by my name, become a ^Rden of robbers in your eyes? Behold, even I have seen *it,* saith the LORD.

12 But go ye now unto ^Rmy place which *was* in Shi'-lōh, ^Rwhere I set my name at the first, and see ^Rwhat I did to it for the wickedness of my people Israel.

13 And now, because ye have done all these works, saith the LORD, and I spake unto you, ^Rrising up early and speaking, but ye heard not; and I ^Rcalled you, but ye answered not;

14 Therefore will I do unto *this* house, which is called by my name, wherein ye trust, and unto the place which I gave to you and to your fathers, as I have done to ^RShi'-lōh.

15 And I will cast you out of my sight, ^Ras I have cast out all your brethren, ^Reven the whole seed of Ē'-phră-ĭm.

Judah's false worship

16 Therefore ^Rpray not thou for this people, neither lift up cry nor prayer for them, neither make intercession to me: ^Rfor I will not hear thee.

17 Seest thou not what they do in the cities of Judah and in the streets of Jerusalem?

18 ^RThe children gather wood, and the fathers kindle the fire, and the women knead *their* dough, to make cakes to the ^Nqueen of heaven, and to ^Rpour out drink offerings unto other gods, that they may provoke me to anger.

19 ^RDo they provoke me to anger? saith the LORD: *do they* not *provoke* themselves to the confusion of their own faces?

20 Therefore thus saith the Lord GOD; Behold, mine anger and my fury shall be poured out upon this place, upon man, and upon beast, and upon the trees of the field, and upon the fruit of the ground; and it shall burn, and shall not be quenched.

Judah ignores the prophets

21 Thus saith the LORD of hosts, the God of Israel; ^RPut your burnt offerings unto your sacrifices, and eat flesh.

22 ^RFor I spake not unto your fathers, nor commanded them in the day that I brought them out of the land of Egypt, ^Nconcerning burnt offerings or sacrifices:

23 But this thing commanded I them, saying, ^RObey my voice, and ^RI will be your God, and ye shall be my people: and walk ye in all the ways that I have commanded you, that it may be well unto you.

24 ^RBut they hearkened not, nor inclined their ear, but ^Rwalked in the counsels *and* in the ^Nimagination of their evil heart, and ^Rwent^N backward, and not forward.

25 Since the day that your fathers came forth out of the land of Egypt unto this day I have even ^Rsent unto you all my servants the prophets, ^Rdaily rising up early and sending *them:*

26 ^RYet they hearkened not unto me, nor inclined their ear, but ^Rhardened their neck: ^Rthey did worse than their fathers.

27 Therefore ^Rthou shalt speak all these words unto them; but they will not hearken to thee: thou shalt also call unto them; but they will not answer thee.

28 But thou shalt say unto them, This *is* a nation that obeyeth not the voice of the LORD their God, ^Rnor receiveth ^Ncorrection: ^Rtruth is perished, and is cut off from their mouth.

29 ^RCut off thine hair, *O Jerusalem,* and cast *it* away, and take up a lamentation on high places; for the LORD hath rejected and forsaken the generation of his wrath.

Impending destruction of Judah

30 For the children of Judah have done evil in my sight, saith the LORD: ^Rthey have set their abominations in the house which is called by my name, to pollute it.

31 And they have built the ^Rhigh places of Tō'-phĕt, which *is* in the valley of the son of Hĭn'-nŏm, to ^Rburn their sons and their daughters in the fire; ^Rwhich I commanded *them* not, neither ^Ncame it into my heart.

32 Therefore, behold, ^Rthe days come, saith the LORD, that it shall no more be called Tō'-phĕt, nor the valley of the son of Hĭn'-nŏm, but the valley of slaughter: ^Rfor they shall bury in Tō'-phĕt, till there be no place.

33 And the ^Rcarcases of this people shall be meat for the fowls of the heaven, and for the beasts of the earth; and none shall fray *them* away.

34 Then will I cause to ^Rcease from the cities of Judah, and from the streets of Jerusalem, the voice of mirth, and the voice of gladness, the voice of the bridegroom, and the voice of the bride: for ^Rthe land shall be desolate.

CHAPTER 8

AT that time, saith the LORD, they shall bring out the bones of the kings of Judah, and the bones of his princes, and the bones of the priests, and the bones of the prophets, and the bones of the inhabitants of Jerusalem, out of their graves:

CHAP. **7**
BC 600
10 Ezek. 23:39
10 ver. 11, 14
ch. 32:34 & 34:15
10 Heb. *whereupon my name is called*
11 Is 56:7
11 Mat. 21:13
Mark 11:17
Luke 19:46
12 Josh. 18:1
Judg. 18·31
12 Deut. 12:11
12 1 Sam. 4:10
Ps. 78:60
ch. 26:6
13 2 Chr. 36:15
ch. 11:7
13 Prov. 1:24
Is. 65:12 & 66:4
14 1 Sam. 4:10
Ps. 78:60
15 2 Ki. 17:23
15 Ps. 78:67
16 Ex. 32:10
16 ch. 15:1
18 ch. 44:17
18 Or, *frame,* or, *workmanship of heaven*
18 ch. 19:13
19 Deut. 32:16, 21
21 Is. 1:11
Amos 5:21
Hos. 8:13
22 1 Sam. 15:22
Ps. 51:16
Hos. 6:6
22 Heb. *concerning the matter of*
23 Ex. 15:26
Deut. 6:3
23 Ex. 19:5
Lev. 26:12

Ps. 81:11   24
Ps. 81:12   24
Or, *stubbornness* 24
ch. 32:33   24
Heb. *were*   24
2 Chr. 36:15   25
ver. 13   25
ch. 11:8   26
Neh. 9:17   26
ch. 16:12   26
Ezek. 2:7   27
ch. 5:3   28
Or, *instruction* 28
ch. 9:3   28
Job 1:20   29
Is. 15:2
Mic. 1:16
2 Ki. 21:4   30
2 Chr. 33:4
Ezek. 7:20
Dan. 9:27
2 Ki. 23:10   31
Ps. 106:38   31
Deut. 17:3   31
Heb. *came it upon my heart*   31
ch. 19:6   32
2 Ki. 23:10   32
ch. 19:11
Deut. 28:26   33
Is. 24:7, 8   34
Ezek. 26:13
Hos. 2:11
Rev. 18:23
Lev. 26:33   34

2 And they shall spread them before the sun, and the moon, and all the host of heaven, whom they have loved, and whom they have served, and after whom they have walked, and whom they have sought, and [R]whom they have worshipped: they shall not be gathered, [R]nor be buried; they shall be for dung upon the face of the earth.

3 And [R]death shall be chosen rather than life by all the residue of them that remain of this evil family, which remain in all the places whither I have driven them, saith the LORD of hosts.

Judah's perpetual backsliding

4 Moreover thou shalt say unto them, Thus saith the LORD; Shall they fall, and not arise? shall he turn away, and not return?

5 Why *then* is this people of Jerusalem [R]slidden back by a perpetual backsliding? [R]they hold fast deceit, [R]they refuse to return.

6 [R]I hearkened and heard, *but* they spake not aright: no man repented him of his wickedness, saying, What have I done? every one turned to his course, as the horse rusheth into the battle.

7 Yea, [R]the stork in the heaven knoweth her appointed times; and [R]the turtle and the crane and the swallow observe the time of their coming; but [R]my people know not the judgment of the LORD.

8 How do ye say, We *are* wise, [R]and the law of the LORD *is* with us? Lo, certainly [N]in vain made he *it;* the pen of the scribes *is* in vain.

9 [R]The[N] wise *men* are ashamed, they are dismayed and taken: lo, they have rejected the word of the LORD; and [N]what wisdom *is* in them?

10 Therefore [R]will I give their wives unto others, *and* their fields to them that shall inherit *them:* for every one from the least even unto the greatest is given to [R]covetousness, from the prophet even unto the priest every one dealeth falsely.

11 For they have [R]healed the hurt of the daughter of my people slightly, saying, [R]Peace, peace; when *there is* no peace.

12 Were they [R]ashamed when they had committed abomination? nay, they were not at all ashamed, neither could they blush: therefore shall they fall among them that fall: in the time of their visitation they shall be cast down, saith the LORD.

13 [N]I will surely consume them, saith the LORD: *there shall be* no grapes [R]on the vine, nor figs on the [R]fig tree, and the leaf shall fade; and *the things that* I have given them shall pass away from them.

14 Why do we sit still? [R]assemble yourselves, and let us enter into the defenced cities, and let us be silent there: for the LORD our God hath put us to silence, and given us [R]water of [N]gall to drink, because we have sinned against the LORD.

15 We [R]looked for peace, but no good *came; and* for a time of health, and behold trouble!

16 The snorting of his horses was heard from [R]Dan: the whole land trembled at the sound of the neighing of his [R]strong ones; for they are come, and have devoured the land, and [N]all that is in it; the city, and those that dwell therein.

17 For, behold, I will send serpents, cockatrices, among you, which *will* not *be* [R]charmed, and they shall bite you, saith the LORD.

Jeremiah's lament for Jerusalem

18 *When* I would comfort myself against sorrow, my heart *is* faint [N]in me.

19 Behold the voice of the cry of the daughter of my people [N]because of them that dwell in [R]a far country: *Is* not the LORD in Zion? *is* not her king in her? Why have they provoked me to anger with their graven images, *and* with strange vanities?

20 The harvest is past, the summer is ended, and we are not saved.

21 [R]For the hurt of the daughter of my people am I hurt; I am [R]black; astonishment hath taken hold on me.

22 *Is there* no [R]balm in Gilead; *is there* no physician there? why then is not the health of the daughter of my people [N]recovered?

CHAPTER 9

O H [R]that[N] my head were waters, and mine eyes a fountain of tears, that I might weep day and night for the slain of the daughter of my people!

2 Oh that I had in the wilderness a lodging place of wayfaring men; that I might leave my people, and go from them! for [R]they *be* all adulterers, an assembly of treacherous men.

3 And [R]they bend their tongues *like* their bow *for* lies: but they are not valiant for the truth upon the earth; for they proceed from evil to evil, and they [R]know not me, saith the LORD.

4 [R]Take ye heed every one of his [N]neighbour, and trust ye not in any brother: for every brother will utterly supplant, and every neighbour will [R]walk with slanders.

5 And they will [N]deceive every one his neighbour, and will not speak the truth: they

have taught their tongue to speak lies, *and* weary themselves to commit iniquity.

6 Thine habitation *is* in the midst of deceit; through deceit they refuse to know me, saith the LORD.

7 Therefore thus saith the LORD of hosts, Behold, ᴿI will melt them, and try them; ᴿfor how shall I do for the daughter of my people?

8 Their tongue *is as* an arrow shot out; it speaketh ᴿdeceit: *one* speaketh ᴿpeaceably to his neighbour with his mouth, but ᴺin heart he layeth ᴺhis wait.

9 ᴿShall I not visit them for these *things?* saith the LORD: shall not my soul be avenged on such a nation as this?

10 For the mountains will I take up a weeping and wailing, and ᴿfor the ᴺhabitations of the wilderness a lamentation, because they are ᴺburned up, so that none can pass through *them;* neither can *men* hear the voice of the cattle; ᴿbothᴺ the fowl of the heavens and the beast are fled; they are gone.

11 And I will make Jerusalem ᴿheaps, *and* ᴿa den of dragons; and I will make the cities of Judah ᴺdesolate, without an inhabitant.

God's justice explained

12 ᴿWho *is* the wise man, that may understand this? and *who is he* to whom the mouth of the LORD hath spoken, that he may declare it, for what the land perisheth *and* is burned up like a wilderness, that none passeth through?

13 And the LORD saith, Because they have forsaken my law which I set before them, and have not obeyed my voice, neither walked therein;

14 But have ᴿwalked after the ᴺimagination of their own heart, and after Bā'-ă-lĭm, ᴿwhich their fathers taught them:

15 Therefore thus saith the LORD of hosts, the God of Israel; Behold, I will ᴿfeed them, *even* this people, ᴿwith wormwood, and give them water of gall to drink.

16 I will ᴿscatter them also among the heathen, whom neither they nor their fathers have known: ᴿand I will send a sword after them, till I have consumed them.

Professional mourners called

17 Thus saith the LORD of hosts, Consider ye, and call for ᴿthe mourning women, that they may come; and send for cunning *women,* that they may come:

18 And let them make haste, and take up a wailing for us, that ᴿour eyes may run down with tears, and our eyelids gush out with waters.

19 For a voice of wailing is heard out of

CHAP. **9**
BC 600
7 Is. 1:25
7 Hos. 11:8
8 Ps. 12:2
8 Ps. 55:21
8 Heb. *in the midst of him*
8 Or, *wait for him*
9 ch. 5:9, 29
10 Hos. 4:3
10 Or, *pastures*
10 Or, *desolate*
10 ch. 4:25
10 Heb. *from the fowl even to, etc.*
11 Is. 25:2
11 Is. 13:22 & 34:13
11 Heb. *desolation*
12 Hos. 14:9
14 ch. 7:24
14 Or, *stubbornness*
14 Gal. 1:14
15 Ps. 80:5
15 ch. 8:14
Lam. 3:19
16 Lev. 26:33
Deut. 28:64
16 Lev. 26:33
ch. 44:27
Ezek. 5:2
17 2 Chr. 35:25
Job 3:8
Eccl. 12:5
Amos 5:16
Mat. 9:23
18 ch. 14:17

Lev. 18:28	**19**
ch. 6:11	**21**
ch. 8:2	**22**
Eccl. 9:11	**23**
1 Cor. 1:31	**24**
2 Cor. 10:17	
Mic. 7:18	**24**
Rom. 2:8, 9	**25**
Heb. *visit upon*	**25**
Heb. *cut off into*	**26**
corners, or, *having the corners of their hair polled*	
ch. 25:23	**26**
Lev. 26:41	**26**
Rom. 2:28	

CHAP. **10**
BC 600
Lev. 18:3 ... **2**
Heb. *statutes,* or, **3** *ordinances are vanity*
Is. 40:19 **3** & 45:20
Is. 41:7 **4**
Ps. 115:5 **5**
Ps. 115:7 **5**
Is. 46:1, 7
Is. 41:23 **5**
Ex. 15:11 **6**
Ps. 86:8, 10

Zion, How are we spoiled! we are greatly confounded, because we have forsaken the land, because ᴿour dwellings have cast *us* out.

20 Yet hear the word of the LORD, O ye women, and let your ear receive the word of his mouth, and teach your daughters wailing, and every one her neighbour lamentation.

21 For death is come up into our windows, *and* is entered into our palaces, to cut off ᴿthe children from without, *and* the young men from the streets.

22 Speak, Thus saith the LORD, Even the carcases of men shall fall ᴿas dung upon the open field, and as the handful after the harvestman, and none shall gather *them.*

Man's true glory

23 Thus saith the LORD, ᴿLet not the wise *man* glory in his wisdom, neither let the mighty *man* glory in his might, let not the rich *man* glory in his riches:

24 But ᴿlet him that glorieth glory in this, that he understandeth and knoweth me, that I *am* the LORD which exercise lovingkindness, judgment, and righteousness, in the earth: ᴿfor in these *things* I delight, saith the LORD.

25 Behold, the days come, saith the LORD, that ᴿI will ᴺpunish all *them which are* circumcised with the uncircumcised;

26 Egypt, and Judah, and Ē'-dǫm, and the children of Ammon, and Moab, and all *that are* ᴺin the ᴿutmost corners, that dwell in the wilderness: for all *these* nations *are* uncircumcised, and all the house of Israel *are* ᴿuncircumcised in the heart.

CHAPTER 10
Folly of idolatry

HEAR ye the word which the LORD speaketh unto you, O house of Israel:

2 Thus saith the LORD, ᴿLearn not the way of the heathen, and be not dismayed at the signs of heaven; for the heathen are dismayed at them.

3 For the ᴺcustoms of the people *are* vain: for ᴿone cutteth a tree out of the forest, the work of the hands of the workman, with the axe.

4 They deck it with silver and with gold; they ᴿfasten it with nails and with hammers, that it move not.

5 They *are* upright as the palm tree, ᴿbut speak not: they must needs be ᴿborne, because they cannot go. Be not afraid of them; for ᴿthey cannot do evil, neither also *is it* in them to do good.

6 Forasmuch as *there is* none ᴿlike unto

thee, O Lord; thou *art* great, and thy name *is* great in might.

7 ᴿWho would not fear thee, O King of nations? for to thee doth it appertain: forasmuch as ᴿamong all the wise *men* of the nations, and in all their kingdoms, *there is* none like unto thee.

8 But they are ᴺaltogether ᴿbrutish and foolish: the stock *is* a doctrine of vanities.

9 Silver spread into plates is brought from Tarshish, and ᴿgold from Ū'-phăz, the work of the workman, and of the hands of the founder: blue and purple *is* their clothing: they *are* all ᴿthe work of cunning *men.*

10 But the Lord *is* the ᴺtrue God, he *is* ᴿthe living God, and an ᴿeverlastingᴺ king: at his wrath the earth shall tremble, and the nations shall not be able to abide his indignation.

11 Thus shall ye say unto them, ᴿThe gods that have not made the heavens and the earth, *even* ᴿthey shall perish from the earth, and from under these heavens.

12 He ᴿhath made the earth by his power, he hath ᴿestablished the world by his wisdom, and ᴿhath stretched out the heavens by his discretion.

13 ᴿWhen he uttereth his voice, *there is* a ᴺmultitude of waters in the heavens, and ᴿhe causeth the vapours to ascend from the ends of the earth; he maketh lightnings ᴺwith rain, and bringeth forth the wind out of his treasures.

14 ᴿEvery man ᴺis ᴿbrutish in *his* knowledge: ᴿevery founder is confounded by the graven image: ᴿfor his molten image *is* falsehood, and *there is* no breath in them.

15 They *are* vanity, *and* the work of errors: in the time of their visitation they shall perish.

16 ᴿThe portion of Jacob *is* not like them: for he *is* the former of all *things;* and ᴿIsrael *is* the rod of his inheritance: ᴿThe Lord of hosts *is* his name.

Exile predicted

17 ᴿGather up thy wares out of the land, O ᴺinhabitant of the fortress.

18 For thus saith the Lord, Behold, I will ᴿsling out the inhabitants of the land at this once, and will distress them, ᴿthat they may find *it so.*

19 ᴿWoe is me for my hurt! my wound is grievous: but I said, ᴿTruly this *is* a grief, and ᴿI must bear it.

20 ᴿMy tabernacle is spoiled, and all my cords are broken: my children are gone forth of me, and they *are* not: *there is* none to stretch forth my tent any more, and to set up my curtains.

21 For the pastors are become brutish, and have not sought the Lord: therefore they shall

not prosper, and all their flocks shall be scattered.

22 Behold, the noise of the bruit is come, and a great commotion out of the ᴿnorth country, to make the cities of Judah desolate, *and* a ᴿden of dragons.

23 O Lord, I know that the ᴿway of man *is* not in himself: *it is* not in man that walketh to direct his steps.

24 O Lord, ᴿcorrect me, but with judgment; not in thine anger, lest thou ᴺbring me to nothing.

25 ᴿPour out thy fury upon the heathen ᴿthat know thee not, and upon the families that call not on thy name: for they have eaten up Jacob, and ᴿdevoured him, and consumed him, and have made his habitation desolate.

CHAPTER 11

The covenant broken

THE word that came to Jeremiah from the Lord, saying,

2 Hear ye the words of this covenant, and speak unto the men of Judah, and to the inhabitants of Jerusalem;

3 And say thou unto them, Thus saith the Lord God of Israel; ᴿCursed *be* the man that obeyeth not the words of this covenant,

4 Which I commanded your fathers in the day *that* I brought them forth out of the land of Egypt, ᴿfrom the iron furnace, saying, ᴿObey my voice, and do them, according to all which I command you: so shall ye be my people, and I will be your God:

5 That I may perform the ᴿoath which I have sworn unto your fathers, to give them a land flowing with milk and honey, as *it is* this day. Then answered I, and said, ᴺSo be it, O Lord.

6 Then the Lord said unto me, Proclaim all these words in the cities of Judah, and in the streets of Jerusalem, saying, Hear ye the words of this covenant, ᴿand do them.

7 For I earnestly protested unto your fathers in the day *that* I brought them up out of the land of Egypt, *even* unto this day, ᴿrising early and protesting, saying, Obey my voice.

8 ᴿYet they obeyed not, nor inclined their ear, but ᴿwalked every one in the ᴺimagination of their evil heart: therefore I will bring upon them all the words of this covenant, which I commanded *them* to do; but they did *them* not.

9 And the Lord said unto me, ᴿA conspiracy is found among the men of Judah, and among the inhabitants of Jerusalem.

10 They are turned back to ᴿthe iniquities of their forefathers, which refused to hear my

words; and they went after other gods to serve them: the house of Israel and the house of Judah have broken my covenant which I made with their fathers.

11 Therefore thus saith the LORD, Behold, I will bring evil upon them, which they shall not be able [N]to escape; and [R]though they shall cry unto me, I will not hearken unto them.

12 Then shall the cities of Judah and inhabitants of Jerusalem go, and [R]cry unto the gods unto whom they offer incense: but they shall not save them at all in the time of their [N]trouble.

13 For *according to* the number of thy [R]cities were thy gods, O Judah; and *according to* the number of the streets of Jerusalem have ye set up altars to *that* [N]shameful thing, *even* altars to burn incense unto Bā'-ǎl.

14 Therefore [R]pray not thou for this people, neither lift up a cry or prayer for them: for I will not hear *them* in the time that they cry unto me for their [N]trouble.

15 [R]What[N] hath my beloved to do in mine house, *seeing* she hath [R]wrought lewdness with many, and [R]the holy flesh is passed from thee? [N]when thou doest evil, then thou [R]rejoicest.

16 The LORD called thy name, [R]A green olive tree, fair, *and* of goodly fruit: with the noise of a great tumult he hath kindled fire upon it, and the branches of it are broken.

17 For the LORD of hosts, [R]that planted thee, hath pronounced evil against thee, for the evil of the house of Israel and of the house of Judah, which they have done against themselves to provoke me to anger in offering incense unto Bā'-ǎl.

Scheme against Jeremiah

18 And the LORD hath given me knowledge *of it,* and I know *it:* then thou shewedst me their doings.

19 But I *was* like a lamb *or* an ox *that* is brought to the slaughter; and I knew not that they had devised devices against me, *saying,* Let us destroy [N]the tree with the fruit thereof, [R]and let us cut him off from [R]the land of the living, that his name may be no more remembered.

20 But, O LORD of hosts, that judgest righteously, that [R]triest the reins and the heart, let me see thy vengeance on them: for unto thee have I revealed my cause.

21 Therefore thus saith the LORD of the men of Ăn'-ǎ-thŏth, [R]that seek thy life, saying, [R]Prophesy not in the name of the LORD, that thou die not by our hand:

22 Therefore thus saith the LORD of hosts, Behold, I will [N]punish them: the young men

shall die by the sword; their sons and their daughters shall die by famine:

23 And there shall be no remnant of them: for I will bring evil upon the men of Ăn'-ǎ-thŏth, *even* [R]the year of their visitation.

CHAPTER 12

Jeremiah's complaint

RIGHTEOUS [R]*art* thou, O LORD, when I plead with thee: yet [N]let me talk with thee of *thy* judgments: [R]Wherefore doth the way of the wicked prosper? *wherefore* are all they happy that deal very treacherously?

2 Thou hast planted them, yea, they have taken root: [N]they grow, yea, they bring forth fruit: [R]thou *art* near in their mouth, and far from their reins.

3 But thou, O LORD, [R]knowest me: thou hast seen me, and [R]tried mine heart [N]toward thee: pull them out like sheep for the slaughter, and prepare them for [R]the day of slaughter.

4 How long shall [R]the land mourn, and the herbs of every field wither, [R]for the wickedness of them that dwell therein? [R]the beasts are consumed, and the birds; because they said, He shall not see our last end.

God's reply

5 If thou hast run with the footmen, and they have wearied thee, then how canst thou contend with horses? and *if* in the land of peace, *wherein* thou trustedst, *they wearied thee,* then how wilt thou do in [R]the swelling of Jordan?

6 For even [R]thy brethren, and the house of thy father, even they have dealt treacherously with thee; yea, [N]they have called a multitude after thee: [R]believe them not, though they speak [N]fair words unto thee.

7 I have forsaken mine house, I have left mine heritage; I have given [N]the dearly beloved of my soul into the hand of her enemies.

8 Mine heritage is unto me as a lion in the forest; it [NN]crieth out against me: therefore have I hated it.

9 Mine heritage *is* unto me *as* a [N]speckled bird, the birds round about *are* against her; come ye, assemble all the beasts of the field, [R]come[N] to devour.

10 Many [R]pastors have destroyed [R]my vineyard, they have [R]trodden my portion under foot, they have made my [N]pleasant portion a desolate wilderness.

11 They have made it desolate, *and being* desolate [R]it mourneth unto me; the whole land is made desolate, because [R]no man layeth *it* to heart.

12 The spoilers are come upon all high places through the wilderness: for the sword of

the LORD shall devour from the *one* end of the land even to the *other* end of the land: no flesh shall have peace.

13 ᴿThey have sown wheat, but shall reap thorns: they have put themselves to pain, *but* shall not profit: and ᴺthey shall be ashamed of your revenues because of the fierce anger of the LORD.

Conditional restoration

14 Thus saith the LORD against all mine evil neighbours, that ᴿtouch the inheritance which I have caused my people Israel to inherit; Behold, I will ᴿpluck them out of their land, and pluck out the house of Judah from among them.

15 ᴿAnd it shall come to pass, after that I have plucked them out I will return, and have compassion on them, ᴿand will bring them again, every man to his heritage, and every man to his land.

16 And it shall come to pass, if they will diligently learn the ways of my people, ᴿto swear by my name, The LORD liveth; as they taught my people to swear by Bā'-ăl; then shall they be ᴿbuilt in the midst of my people.

17 But if they will not ᴿobey, I will utterly pluck up and destroy that nation, saith the LORD.

CHAPTER 13

Sign of the linen waist girdle

THUS saith the LORD unto me, Go and get thee a linen girdle, and put it upon thy loins, and put it not in water.

2 So I got a girdle according to the word of the LORD, and put *it* on my loins.

3 And the word of the LORD came unto me the second time, saying,

4 Take the girdle that thou hast got, which *is* upon thy loins, and arise, go to Ēu-phrā'-tēś, and hide it there in a hole of the rock.

5 So I went, and hid it by Ēu-phrā'-tēś, as the LORD commanded me.

6 And it came to pass after many days, that the LORD said unto me, Arise, go to Ēu-phrā'-tēś, and take the girdle from thence, which I commanded thee to hide there.

7 Then I went to Ēu-phrā'-tēś, and digged, and took the girdle from the place where I had hid it: and, behold, the girdle was marred, it was profitable for nothing.

8 Then the word of the LORD came unto me, saying,

9 Thus saith the LORD, After this manner ᴿwill I mar the pride of Judah, and the great pride of Jerusalem.

CHAP. 12
BC 608
13 Lev. 26:16
Deut. 28:38
Mic. 6:15
Hag. 1:6
13 Or, *ye*
14 Zech. 2:8
14 Deut. 30:3
ch. 32:37
15 Ezek. 28:25
15 Amos 9:14
16 ch. 4:2
16 Eph. 2:20, 21
1 Pet. 2:5
17 Is. 60:12

CHAP. 13
BC 602
9 Lev. 26:19

ch. 9:14 & 11:8	10
& 16:12	
Or, *stubbornness*	10
Ex. 19:5	11
ch. 33:9	11
Is. 51:17, 21	13
& 63:6	
ch. 25:27 & 51:7	
Ps. 2:9	14
Heb. *a man*	14
against his brother	
Heb. *from*	14
destroying them	
Is. 5:30 & 8:22	16
Amos 8:9	
Is. 59:9	16
Ps. 44:19	16
ch. 9:1 & 14:17	17
Lam. 1:2, 16	
& 2:18	
2 Ki. 24:12	18
ch. 22:26	
Or, *head tires*	18
ch. 6:22	20
Heb. *visit upon*	21
ch. 6:24	21

10 This evil people, which refuse to hear my words, which ᴿwalk in the ᴺimagination of their heart, and walk after other gods, to serve them, and to worship them, shall even be as this girdle, which is good for nothing.

11 For as the girdle cleaveth to the loins of a man, so have I caused to cleave unto me the whole house of Israel and the whole house of Judah, saith the LORD; that ᴿthey might be unto me for a people, and ᴿfor a name, and for a praise, and for a glory: but they would not hear.

Sign of the wine jars

12 Therefore thou shalt speak unto them this word; Thus saith the LORD God of Israel, Every bottle shall be filled with wine: and they shall say unto thee, Do we not certainly know that every bottle shall be filled with wine?

13 Then shalt thou say unto them, Thus saith the LORD, Behold, I will fill all the inhabitants of this land, even the kings that sit upon David's throne, and the priests, and the prophets, and all the inhabitants of Jerusalem, ᴿwith drunkenness.

14 And ᴿI will dash them ᴺone against another, even the fathers and the sons together, saith the LORD: I will not pity, nor spare, nor have mercy, ᴺbut destroy them.

Judah's pride and shame

15 Hear ye, and give ear; be not proud: for the LORD hath spoken.

16 Give glory to the LORD your God, before he cause ᴿdarkness, and before your feet stumble upon the dark mountains, and, while ye ᴿlook for light, he turn it into ᴿthe shadow of death, *and* make *it* gross darkness.

17 But if ye will not hear it, my soul shall weep in secret places for *your* pride; and ᴿmine eye shall weep sore, and run down with tears, because the LORD's flock is carried away captive.

18 Say unto ᴿthe king and to the queen, Humble yourselves, sit down: for your ᴺprincipalities shall come down, *even* the crown of your glory.

19 The cities of the south shall be shut up, and none shall open *them:* Judah shall be carried away captive all of it, it shall be wholly carried away captive.

20 Lift up your eyes, and behold them ᴿthat come from the north: where *is* the flock *that* was given thee, thy beautiful flock?

21 What wilt thou say when he shall ᴺpunish thee? for thou hast taught them *to be* captains, *and* as chief over thee: shall not ᴿsorrows take thee, as a woman in travail?

22 And if thou say in thine heart, ᴿWherefore come these things upon me? For the greatness of thine iniquity are ᴿthy skirts discovered, *and* thy heels ᴺmade bare.

23 Can the Ē-thĭ-ō′-pĭ-ăn change his skin, or the leopard his spots? *then* may ye also do good, that are ᴺaccustomed to do evil.

24 Therefore will I scatter them ᴿas the stubble that passeth away by the wind of the wilderness.

25 ᴿThis *is* thy lot, the portion of thy measures from me, saith the Lᴏʀᴅ; because thou hast forgotten me, and trusted in ᴿfalsehood.

26 Therefore ᴿwill I discover thy skirts upon thy face, that thy shame may appear.

27 I have seen thine adulteries, and thy ᴿneighings, the lewdness of thy whoredom, *and* thine abominations ᴿon the hills in the fields. Woe unto thee, O Jerusalem! wilt thou not be made clean? ᴺwhen *shall it* once *be?*

CHAPTER 14

Judah beyond deliverance

THE word of the Lᴏʀᴅ that came to Jeremiah concerning ᴺthe dearth.

2 Judah mourneth, and ᴿthe gates thereof languish; they are ᴿblack unto the ground; and ᴿthe cry of Jerusalem is gone up.

3 And their nobles have sent their little ones to the waters: they came to the pits, *and* found no water; they returned with their vessels empty; they were ᴿashamed and confounded, ᴿand covered their heads.

4 Because the ground is chapt, for there was no rain in the earth, the plowmen were ashamed, they covered their heads.

5 Yea, the hind also calved in the field, and forsook *it,* because there was no grass.

6 And ᴿthe wild asses did stand in the high places, they snuffed up the wind like dragons; their eyes did fail, because *there was* no grass.

7 O Lᴏʀᴅ, though our iniquities testify against us, do thou *it* ᴿfor thy name's sake: for our backslidings are many; we have sinned against thee.

8 ᴿO the hope of Israel, the saviour thereof in time of trouble, why shouldest thou be as a stranger in the land, and as a wayfaring man *that* turneth aside to tarry for a night?

9 Why shouldest thou be as a man astonied, as a mighty man ᴿ*that* cannot save? yet thou, O Lᴏʀᴅ, ᴿ*art* in the midst of us, and ᴺwe are called by thy name; leave us not.

10 Thus saith the Lᴏʀᴅ unto this people, ᴿThus have they loved to wander, they have not refrained their feet, therefore the Lᴏʀᴅ

doth not accept them; ᴿhe will now remember their iniquity, and visit their sins.

11 Then said the Lᴏʀᴅ unto me, ᴿPray not for this people for *their* good.

12 ᴿWhen they fast, I will not hear their cry; and ᴿwhen they offer burnt offering and an oblation, I will not accept them: but ᴿI will consume them by the sword, and by the famine, and by the pestilence.

13 ᴿThen said I, Ah, Lord Gᴏᴅ! behold, the prophets say unto them, Ye shall not see the sword, neither shall ye have famine; but I will give you ᴺassured peace in this place.

14 Then the Lᴏʀᴅ said unto me, ᴿThe prophets prophesy lies in my name: ᴿI sent them not, neither have I commanded them, neither spake unto them: they prophesy unto you a false vision and divination, and a thing of nought, and the deceit of their heart.

15 Therefore thus saith the Lᴏʀᴅ concerning the prophets that prophesy in my name, and I sent them not, ᴿyet they say, Sword and famine shall not be in this land; By sword and famine shall those prophets be consumed.

16 And the people to whom they prophesy shall be cast out in the streets of Jerusalem because of the famine and the sword; ᴿand they shall have none to bury them, them, their wives, nor their sons, nor their daughters: for I will pour their wickedness upon them.

17 Therefore thou shalt say this word unto them; ᴿLet mine eyes run down with tears night and day, and let them not cease: ᴿfor the virgin daughter of my people is broken with a great breach, with a very grievous blow.

18 If I go forth into ᴿthe field, then behold the slain with the sword! and if I enter into the city, then behold them that are sick with famine! yea, both the prophet and the priest ᴺgo about into a land that they know not.

Confession of Judah's sin

19 ᴿHast thou utterly rejected Judah? hath thy soul lothed Zion? why hast thou smitten us, and ᴿ*there is* no healing for us? ᴿwe looked for peace, and *there is* no good; and for the time of healing, and behold trouble!

20 We acknowledge, O Lᴏʀᴅ, our wickedness, *and* the iniquity of our fathers: for ᴿwe have sinned against thee.

21 Do not abhor *us,* for thy name's sake, do not disgrace the throne of thy glory: ᴿremember, break not thy covenant with us.

22 ᴿAre there *any* among ᴿthe vanities of the Gentiles that can cause rain? or can the heavens give showers? ᴿ*art* not thou he, O Lᴏʀᴅ our God? therefore we will wait upon thee: for thou hast made all these *things.*

CHAPTER 15

God's final rejection

THEN said the LORD unto me, [R]Though [R]Moses and [R]Samuel stood before me, *yet* my mind *could* not *be* toward this people: cast *them* out of my sight, and let them go forth.

2 And it shall come to pass, if they say unto thee, Whither shall we go forth? then thou shalt tell them, Thus saith the LORD; [R]Such as *are* for death, to death; and such as *are* for the sword, to the sword; and such as *are* for the famine, to the famine; and such as *are* for the captivity, to the captivity.

3 And I will [R]appoint over them four [N]kinds, saith the LORD: the sword to slay, and the dogs to tear, and [R]the fowls of the heaven, and the beasts of the earth, to devour and destroy.

4 And [N]I will cause them to be [R]removed into all kingdoms of the earth, because of [R]Mă-năs′-sēh the son of Hĕz-ē-kī′-ăh king of Judah, for *that* which he did in Jerusalem.

5 For who shall have pity upon thee, O Jerusalem? or who shall bemoan thee? or who shall go aside [N]to ask how thou doest?

6 [R]Thou hast forsaken me, saith the LORD, thou art [R]gone backward: therefore will I stretch out my hand against thee, and destroy thee; [R]I am weary with repenting.

7 And I will fan them with a fan in the gates of the land; I will bereave *them* of [N]children, I will destroy my people, *since* they return not from their ways.

8 Their widows are increased to me above the sand of the seas: I have brought upon them [N]against the mother of the young men a spoiler at noonday: I have caused *him* to fall upon it suddenly, and terrors upon the city.

9 [R]She that hath borne seven languisheth: she hath given up the ghost; [R]her sun is gone down while *it was* yet day: she hath been ashamed and confounded: and the residue of them will I deliver to the sword before their enemies, saith the LORD.

Jeremiah's self-pity

10 [R]Woe is me, my mother, that thou hast borne me a man of strife and a man of contention to the whole earth! I have neither lent on usury, nor men have lent to me on usury; *yet* every one of them doth curse me.

11 The LORD said, Verily it shall be well with thy remnant; verily [N]I will cause [R]the enemy to entreat thee *well* in the time of evil and in the time of affliction.

12 Shall iron break the northern iron and the steel?

13 Thy substance and thy treasures will I give to the [R]spoil without price, and *that* for all thy sins, even in all thy borders.

14 And I will make *thee* to pass with thine enemies [R]into a land *which* thou knowest not: for a [R]fire is kindled in mine anger, *which* shall burn upon you.

15 O LORD, [R]thou knowest: remember me, and visit me, and [R]revenge me of my persecutors; take me not away in thy longsuffering: know that [R]for thy sake I have suffered rebuke.

16 Thy words were found, and I did [R]eat them; and [R]thy word was unto me the joy and rejoicing of mine heart: for [N]I am called by thy name, O LORD God of hosts.

17 [R]I sat not in the assembly of the mockers, nor rejoiced; I sat alone because of thy hand: for thou hast filled me with indignation.

18 Why is my [R]pain perpetual, and my wound incurable, *which* refuseth to be healed? wilt thou be altogether unto me [R]as a liar, *and as* waters *that* [N]fail?

God's promise to Jeremiah

19 Therefore thus saith the LORD, [R]If thou return, then will I bring thee again, *and* thou shalt [R]stand before me: and if thou [R]take forth the precious from the vile, thou shalt be as my mouth: let them return unto thee; but return not thou unto them.

20 And I will make thee unto this people a fenced brasen wall: and they shall fight against thee, but [R]they shall not prevail against thee: for *I am* with thee to save thee and to deliver thee, saith the LORD.

21 And I will deliver thee out of the hand of the wicked, and I will redeem thee out of the hand of the terrible.

CHAPTER 16

Threat of exile

THE word of the LORD came also unto me, saying,

2 Thou shalt not take thee a wife, neither shalt thou have sons or daughters in this place.

3 For thus saith the LORD concerning the sons and concerning the daughters that are born in this place, and concerning their mothers that bare them, and concerning their fathers that begat them in this land;

4 They shall die of [R]grievous deaths; they shall not be [R]lamented; neither shall they be buried; *but* they shall be [R]as dung upon the face of the earth: and they shall be consumed by the sword, and by famine; and their [R]car-

cases shall be meat for the fowls of heaven, and for the beasts of the earth.

5 For thus saith the LORD, ^REnter not into the house of ^Nmourning, neither go to lament nor bemoan them: for I have taken away my peace from this people, saith the LORD, *even* lovingkindness and mercies.

6 Both the great and the small shall die in this land: they shall not be buried, ^Rneither shall *men* lament for them, nor ^Rcut themselves, nor ^Rmake themselves bald for them:

7 Neither shall *men* ^Ntear *themselves* for them in mourning, to comfort them for the dead; neither shall *men* give them the cup of consolation to ^Rdrink for their father or for their mother.

8 Thou shalt not also go into the house of feasting, to sit with them to eat and to drink.

9 For thus saith the LORD of hosts, the God of Israel; Behold, ^RI will cause to cease out of this place in your eyes, and in your days, the voice of mirth, and the voice of gladness, the voice of the bridegroom, and the voice of the bride.

10 And it shall come to pass, when thou shalt shew this people all these words, and they shall say unto thee, ^RWherefore hath the LORD pronounced all this great evil against us? or what *is* our iniquity? or what *is* our sin that we have committed against the LORD our God?

11 Then shalt thou say unto them, ^RBecause your fathers have forsaken me, saith the LORD, and have walked after other gods, and have served them, and have worshipped them, and have forsaken me, and have not kept my law;

12 And ye have done ^Rworse than your fathers; for, behold, ^Rye walk every one after the ^Nimagination of his evil heart, that they may not hearken unto me:

13 ^RTherefore will I cast you out of this land ^Rinto a land that ye know not, *neither* ye nor your fathers; and there shall ye serve other gods day and night; where I will not shew you favour.

Promise of return

14 Therefore, behold, the ^Rdays come, saith the LORD, that it shall no more be said, The LORD liveth, that brought up the children of Israel out of the land of Egypt;

15 But, The LORD liveth, that brought up the children of Israel from the land of the north, and from all the lands whither he had driven them: and ^RI will bring them again into their land that I gave unto their fathers.

16 Behold, I will send for many ^Rfishers, saith the LORD, and they shall fish them; and

after will I send for many hunters, and they shall hunt them from every mountain, and from every hill, and out of the holes of the rocks.

17 For mine ^Reyes *are* upon all their ways: they are not hid from my face, neither is their iniquity hid from mine eyes.

18 And first I will recompense their iniquity and their sin ^Rdouble; because ^Rthey have defiled my land, they have filled mine inheritance with the carcases of their detestable and abominable things.

19 O LORD, ^Rmy strength, and my fortress, and ^Rmy refuge in the day of affliction, the Gentiles shall come unto thee from the ends of the earth, and shall say, Surely our fathers have inherited lies, vanity, and *things* ^Rwherein *there is* no profit.

20 Shall a man make gods unto himself, and ^Rthey *are* no gods?

21 Therefore, behold, I will this once cause them to know, I will cause them to know mine hand and my might; and they shall know that ^Rmy name *is* ^NThe LORD.

CHAPTER 17

The sin of Judah punished

THE sin of Judah *is* written with a ^Rpen of iron, *and* with the ^Npoint of a diamond: *it is* ^Rgraven upon the table of their heart, and upon the horns of your altars;

2 Whilst their children remember their altars and their ^Rgroves by the green trees upon the high hills.

3 O my mountain in the field, I will give thy substance *and* all thy treasures to the spoil, *and* thy high places for sin, throughout all thy borders.

4 And thou, even ^Nthyself, shalt discontinue from thine heritage that I gave thee; and I will cause thee to serve thine enemies in ^Rthe land which thou knowest not: for ^Rye have kindled a fire in mine anger, *which* shall burn for ever.

Trust in God

5 Thus saith the LORD; ^RCursed *be* the man that trusteth in man, and maketh ^Rflesh his arm, and whose heart departeth from the LORD.

6 For he shall be ^Rlike the heath in the desert, and ^Rshall not see when good cometh; but shall inhabit the parched places in the wilderness, ^Rin a salt land and not inhabited.

7 ^RBlessed *is* the man that trusteth in the LORD, and whose hope the LORD is.

8 For he shall be ^Ras a tree planted by the waters, and *that* spreadeth out her roots by the

Center reference column

CHAP. 16
BC 601

5 Ezek. 24:17, 22, 23
5 Or, *mourning feast*
6 ch. 22:18
6 Lev. 19:28 Deut. 14:1 ch. 41:5 & 47:5
6 Is. 22:12 ch. 7:29
7 Or, *break bread for them,* as Ezek. 24:17 Hos. 9:4 See Deut. 26:14 Job 42:11
7 Prov. 31:6
9 Is. 24:7, 8 Ezek. 26:13 Hos. 2:11 Rev. 18:23
10 Deut. 29:24 ch. 5:19
11 Deut. 29:25 ch. 22:9
12 ch. 7:26
12 ch. 13:10
12 Or, *stubbornness*
13 Deut. 4:26 & 28:36, 63
13 ch. 15:14
14 Is. 43:18 ch. 23:7, 8
15 ch. 24:6 & 30:3 & 32:37
16 Amos 4:2 Hab. 1:15

Job 34:21   17
Prov. 5:21 & 15:3 ch. 32:19
Is. 40:2   18
ch. 17:18
Ezek. 43:7   18
Ps. 18:2   19
ch. 17:17   19
Is. 44:10   19
ch. 10:5
Is. 37:19   20
ch. 2:11
Gal. 4:8
Ex. 15:3   21
ch. 33:2
Amos 5:8
Or, *JEHOVAH,*   21
Ps. 83:18

CHAP. 17
BC 601

Job 19:24   1
Heb. *nail*   1
Prov. 3:3   1
2 Cor. 3:3
Judg. 3:7   2
2 Chr. 24:18
Heb. *in thyself*   4
ch. 16:13   4
ch. 15:14   4
Is. 30:1, 2   5 & 31:1
See Is. 31:3   5
ch. 48:6   6
Job 20:17   6
Deut. 29:23   6
Ps. 2:12   7 & 34:8
Is. 30:18
Job 8:16   8
Ps. 1:3

river, and shall not see when heat cometh, but her leaf shall be green; and shall not be careful in the year of ᴺdrought, neither shall cease from yielding fruit.

9 The heart *is* deceitful above all *things,* and desperately wicked: who can know it?

10 I the LORD ᴿsearch the heart, *I* try the reins, ᴿeven to give every man according to his ways, *and* according to the fruit of his doings.

11 *As* the partridge ᴺsitteth *on eggs,* and hatcheth *them* not; *so* he that getteth riches, and not by right, ᴿshall leave them in the midst of his days, and at his end shall be ᴿa fool.

12 A glorious high throne from the beginning *is* the place of our sanctuary.

13 O LORD, ᴿthe hope of Israel, ᴿall that forsake thee shall be ashamed, *and* they that depart from me shall be ᴿwritten in the earth, because they have forsaken the LORD, the ᴿfountain of living waters.

Jeremiah pleads for God's help

14 Heal me, O LORD, and I shall be healed; save me, and I shall be saved: for ᴿthou *art* my praise.

15 Behold, they say unto me, ᴿWhere *is* the word of the LORD? let it come now.

16 As for me, ᴿI have not hastened from *being* a pastor ᴺto follow thee: neither have I desired the woeful day; thou knowest: that which came out of my lips was *right* before thee.

17 Be not a terror unto me: ᴿthou *art* my hope in the day of evil.

18 ᴿLet them be confounded that persecute me, but ᴿlet not me be confounded: let them be dismayed, but let not me be dismayed: bring upon them the day of evil, and ᴿdestroyᴺ them with double destruction.

Prophecy concerning the sabbath

19 Thus said the LORD unto me; Go and stand in the gate of the children of the people, whereby the kings of Judah come in, and by the which they go out, and in all the gates of Jerusalem;

20 And say unto them, ᴿHear ye the word of the LORD, ye kings of Judah, and all Judah, and all the inhabitants of Jerusalem, that enter in by these gates:

21 Thus saith the LORD; ᴿTake heed to yourselves, and bear no burden on the sabbath day, nor bring *it* in by the gates of Jerusalem;

22 Neither carry forth a burden out of your houses on the sabbath day, neither do ye any work, but hallow ye the sabbath day, as I ᴿcommanded your fathers.

23 ᴿBut they obeyed not, neither inclined their ear, but made their neck stiff, that they might not hear, nor receive instruction.

24 And it shall come to pass, if ye diligently hearken unto me, saith the LORD, to bring in no burden through the gates of this city on the sabbath day, but hallow the sabbath day, to do no work therein;

25 ᴿThen shall there enter into the gates of this city kings and princes sitting upon the throne of David, riding in chariots and on horses, they, and their princes, the men of Judah, and the inhabitants of Jerusalem: and this city shall remain for ever.

26 And they shall come from the cities of Judah, and from ᴿthe places about Jerusalem, and from the land of Benjamin, and from ᴿthe plain, and from the mountains, and from ᴿthe south, bringing burnt offerings, and sacrifices, and meat offerings, and incense, and bringing ᴿsacrifices of praise, unto the house of the LORD.

27 But if ye will not hearken unto me to hallow the sabbath day, and not to bear a burden, even entering in at the gates of Jerusalem on the sabbath day; then ᴿwill I kindle a fire in the gates thereof, ᴿand it shall devour the palaces of Jerusalem, and it shall not be quenched.

CHAPTER 18

Sign of the potter and the clay

THE word which came to Jeremiah from the LORD, saying,

2 Arise, and go down to the potter's house, and there I will cause thee to hear my words.

3 Then I went down to the potter's house, and, behold, he wrought a work on the ᴺwheels.

4 And the vessel ᴺthat he made of clay was marred in the hand of the potter: so he ᴺmade it again another vessel, as seemed good to the potter to make *it.*

5 Then the word of the LORD came to me, saying,

6 O house of Israel, ᴿcannot I do with you as this potter? saith the LORD. Behold, ᴿas the clay *is* in the potter's hand, so *are* ye in mine hand, O house of Israel.

7 *At what* instant I shall speak concerning a nation, and concerning a kingdom, to ᴿpluck up, and to pull down, and to destroy *it;*

8 ᴿIf that nation, against whom I have pronounced, turn from their evil, ᴿI will repent of the evil that I thought to do unto them.

9 And *at what* instant I shall speak concern-

ing a nation, and concerning a kingdom, to build and to plant *it;*

10 If it do evil in my sight, that it obey not my voice, then I will repent of the good, wherewith I said I would benefit them.

11 Now therefore go to, speak to the men of Judah, and to the inhabitants of Jerusalem, saying, Thus saith the LORD; Behold, I frame evil against you, and devise a device against you: ᴿreturn ye now every one from his evil way, and make your ways and your doings good.

Stubborn rebellion

12 And they said, ᴿThere is no hope: but we will walk after our own devices, and we will every one do the imagination of his evil heart.

13 Therefore thus saith the LORD; ᴿAsk ye now among the heathen, who hath heard such things: the virgin of Israel hath done ᴿa very horrible thing.

14 Will *a man* leave ᴺthe snow of Lĕb'-ă-non *which cometh* from the rock of the field? *or* shall the cold flowing waters that come from another place be forsaken?

15 Because my people hath forgotten ᴿme, they have burned incense to vanity, and they have caused them to stumble in their ways *from* the ᴿancient paths, to walk in paths, *in* a way not cast up;

16 To make their land ᴿdesolate, *and* a perpetual ᴿhissing; every one that passeth thereby shall be astonished, and wag his head.

17 ᴿI will scatter them ᴿas with an east wind before the enemy; ᴿI will shew them the back, and not the face, in the day of their calamity.

Plot against Jeremiah and his plea

18 Then said they, ᴿCome, and let us devise devices against Jeremiah; ᴿfor the law shall not perish from the priest, nor counsel from the wise, nor the word from the prophet. Come, and let us smite him ᴺwith the tongue, and let us not give heed to any of his words.

19 Give heed to me, O LORD, and hearken to the voice of them that contend with me.

20 ᴿShall evil be recompensed for good? for ᴿthey have digged a pit for my soul. Remember that I stood before thee to speak good for them, *and* to turn away thy wrath from them.

21 Therefore ᴿdeliver up their children to the famine, and ᴺpour out their *blood* by the force of the sword; and let their wives be bereaved of their children, and *be* widows; and let their men be put to death; *let* their young men *be* slain by the sword in battle.

22 Let a cry be heard from their houses, when thou shalt bring a troop suddenly upon

them: for ᴿthey have digged a pit to take me, and hid snares for my feet.

23 Yet, LORD, thou knowest all their counsel against me ᴺto slay *me:* ᴿforgive not their iniquity, neither blot out their sin from thy sight, but let them be overthrown before thee; deal *thus* with them in the time of thine anger.

CHAPTER 19

Sign of the broken bottle

THUS saith the LORD, Go and get a potter's earthen bottle, and *take* of the ancients of the people, and of the ancients of the priests;

2 And go forth unto ᴿthe valley of the son of Hĭn'-nom, which *is* by the entry of ᴺthe east gate, and proclaim there the words that I shall tell thee,

3 ᴿAnd say, Hear ye the word of the LORD, O kings of Judah, and inhabitants of Jerusalem; Thus saith the LORD of hosts, the God of Israel; Behold, I will bring evil upon this place, the which whosoever heareth, his ears shall ᴿtingle.

4 Because they ᴿhave forsaken me, and have estranged this place, and have burned incense in it unto other gods, whom neither they nor their fathers have known, nor the kings of Judah, and have filled this place with ᴿthe blood of innocents;

5 ᴿThey have built also the high places of Bā'-ăl, to burn their sons with fire *for* burnt offerings unto Bā'-ăl, ᴿwhich I commanded not, nor spake *it,* neither came *it* into my mind:

6 Therefore, behold, the days come, saith the LORD, that this place shall no more be called Tō'-phĕt, nor ᴿThe valley of the son of Hĭn'-nom, but The valley of slaughter.

7 And I will make void the counsel of Judah and Jerusalem in this place; ᴿand I will cause them to fall by the sword before their enemies, and by the hands of them that seek their lives: and their ᴿcarcases will I give to be meat for the fowls of the heaven, and for the beasts of the earth.

8 And I will make this city ᴿdesolate, and an hissing; every one that passeth thereby shall be astonished and hiss because of all the plagues thereof.

9 And I will cause them to eat the ᴿflesh of their sons and the flesh of their daughters, and they shall eat every one the flesh of his friend in the siege and straitness, wherewith their enemies, and they that seek their lives, shall straiten them.

CHAP. 18

BC 605

11 2 Ki. 17:13
ch. 7:3
12 ch. 2:25
13 ch. 2:10
1 Cor. 5:1
13 ch. 5:30
14 Or, *my fields for a rock,* or for *the snow of Lebanon? shall the running waters be forsaken for the strange cold waters?*
15 ch. 2:13, 32
15 ch. 6:16
16 ch. 19:8
16 1 Ki. 9:8
Lam. 2:15
Mic. 6:16
17 ch. 13:24
17 Ps. 48:7
17 See ch. 2:27
18 ch. 11:19
18 Lev. 10:11
Mal. 2:7
John 7:48
18 Or, *for the tongue*
20 Ps. 109:4
20 ver. 22
Ps. 35:7
21 Ps. 109:9
21 Heb. *pour them out*

ver. 20   22
Heb. *for death* 23
Ps. 35:4   23
& 109:14
ch. 11:20

CHAP. 19

BC 605

Josh. 15:8   2
2 Ki. 23:10
Heb. *the sun gate* 2
ch. 17:20   3
1 Sam. 3:11   3
2 Ki. 21:12
Deut. 28:20   4
Is. 65:11
2 Ki. 21:16   4
ch. 2:34
ch. 7:31   5
& 32:35
Lev. 18:21   5
Josh. 15:8   6
Lev. 26:17   7
Deut. 28:25
Ps. 79:2   7
ch. 7:33
& 16:4
& 34:20
ch. 18:16   8
& 49:13
& 50:13
Lev. 26:29   9
Deut. 28:53
Is. 9:20
Lam. 4:10

10 ᴿThen shalt thou break the bottle in the sight of the men that go with thee,

11 And shalt say unto them, Thus saith the LORD of hosts; ᴿEven so will I break this people and this city, as *one* breaketh a potter's vessel, that cannot ᴺbe made whole again: and they shall ᴿbury *them* in Tō'-phĕt, till *there be* no place to bury.

12 Thus will I do unto this place, saith the LORD, and to the inhabitants thereof, and *even* make this city as Tō'-phĕt:

13 And the houses of Jerusalem, and the houses of the kings of Judah, shall be defiled ᴿas the place of Tō'-phĕt, because of all the houses upon whose ᴿroofs they have burned incense unto all the host of heaven, and ᴿhave poured out drink offerings unto other gods.

14 Then came Jeremiah from Tō'-phĕt, whither the LORD had sent him to prophesy; and he stood in ᴿthe court of the LORD's house; and said to all the people,

15 Thus saith the LORD of hosts, the God of Israel; Behold, I will bring upon this city and upon all her towns all the evil that I have pronounced against it, because ᴿthey have hardened their necks, that they might not hear my words.

CHAPTER 20

Jeremiah's beating and prophecy

N OW Păsh'-ùr the son of ᴿĭm'-mer the priest, who *was* also chief governor in the house of the LORD, heard that Jeremiah prophesied these things.

2 Then Păsh'-ùr smote Jeremiah the prophet, and put him in the stocks that *were* in the high gate of Benjamin, which *was* by the house of the LORD.

3 And it came to pass on the morrow, that Păsh'-ùr brought forth Jeremiah out of the stocks. Then said Jeremiah unto him, The LORD hath not called thy name Păsh'-ùr, but ᴺMā'-gôr-mĭs-sā'-bĭb.

4 For thus saith the LORD, Behold, I will make thee a terror to thyself, and to all thy friends: and they shall fall by the sword of their enemies, and thine eyes shall behold *it*: and I will give all Judah into the hand of the king of Babylon, and he shall carry them captive into Babylon, and shall slay them with the sword.

5 Moreover I ᴿwill deliver all the strength of this city, and all the labours thereof, and all the precious things thereof, and all the treasures of the kings of Judah will I give into the

hand of their enemies, which shall spoil them, and take them, and carry them to Babylon.

6 And thou, Păsh'-ùr, and all that dwell in thine house shall go into captivity: and thou shalt come to Babylon, and there thou shalt die, and shalt be buried there, thou, and all thy friends, to whom thou hast ᴿprophesied lies.

Jeremiah bewails his lot

7 O LORD, thou hast deceived me, and I was ᴺdeceived: ᴿthou art stronger than I, and hast prevailed: ᴿI am in derision daily, every one mocketh me.

8 For since I spake, I cried out, ᴿI cried violence and spoil; because the word of the LORD was made a reproach unto me, and a derision, daily.

9 Then I said, I will not make mention of him, nor speak any more in his name. But *his word* was in mine heart as a ᴿburning fire shut up in my bones, and I was weary with forbearing, and ᴿI could not *stay*.

10 ᴿFor I heard the defaming of many, fear on every side. Report, *say they,* and we will report it. ᴿAllᴺ my familiars watched for my halting, *saying,* Peradventure he will be enticed, and we shall prevail against him, and we shall take our revenge on him.

11 But the LORD *is* with me as a mighty terrible one: therefore my persecutors shall stumble, and they shall not ᴿprevail: they shall be greatly ashamed; for they shall not prosper: *their* ᴿeverlasting confusion shall never be forgotten.

12 But, O LORD of hosts, that ᴿtriest the righteous, *and* seest the reins and the heart, ᴿlet me see thy vengeance on them: for unto thee have I opened my cause.

13 Sing unto the LORD, praise ye the LORD: for ᴿhe hath delivered the soul of the poor from the hand of evildoers.

14 ᴿCursed *be* the day wherein I was born: let not the day wherein my mother bare me be blessed.

15 Cursed *be* the man who brought tidings to my father, saying, A man child is born unto thee; making him very glad.

16 And let that man be as the cities which the LORD ᴿoverthrew, and repented not: and let him ᴿhear the cry in the morning, and the shouting at noontide;

17 ᴿBecause he slew me not from the womb; or that my mother might have been my grave, and her womb *to be* always great *with me*.

18 ᴿWherefore came I forth out of the womb to ᴿsee labour and sorrow, that my days should be consumed with shame?

CHAPTER 21

Prophecy against king Zedekiah

THE word which came unto Jeremiah from the LORD, when king Zĕd-e-kī′-ăh sent unto him ᴿPăsh′-ùr the son of Mĕl-chī′-ăh, and ᴿZĕph-ă-nī′-ăh the son of Mā-ă-sēi′-ăh the priest, saying,

2 ᴿInquire, I pray thee, of the LORD for us; for Nĕb-ū-chăd-rĕz′-zär king of Babylon maketh war against us; if so be that the LORD will deal with us according to all his wondrous works, that he may go up from us.

3 Then said Jeremiah unto them, Thus shall ye say to Zĕd-e-kī′-ăh:

4 Thus saith the LORD God of Israel; Behold, I will turn back the weapons of war that *are* in your hands, wherewith ye fight against the king of Babylon, and *against* the Chăl-dē′-ăns, which besiege you without the walls, and ᴿI will assemble them into the midst of this city.

5 And I myself will fight against you with an ᴿoutstretched hand and with a strong arm, even in anger, and in fury, and in great wrath.

6 And I will smite the inhabitants of this city, both man and beast: they shall die of a great pestilence.

7 And afterward, saith the LORD, ᴿI will deliver Zĕd-e-kī′-ăh king of Judah, and his servants, and the people, and such as are left in this city from the pestilence, from the sword, and from the famine, into the hand of Nĕb-ū-chăd-rĕz′-zär king of Babylon, and into the hand of their enemies, and into the hand of those that seek their life: and he shall smite them with the edge of the sword; ᴿhe shall not spare them, neither have pity, nor have mercy.

8 And unto this people thou shalt say, Thus saith the LORD; Behold, ᴿI set before you the way of life, and the way of death.

9 He that ᴿabideth in this city shall die by the sword, and by the famine, and by the pestilence: but he that goeth out, and falleth to the Chăl-dē′-ăns that besiege you, he shall live, and ᴿhis life shall be unto him for a prey.

10 For I have ᴿset my face against this city for evil, and not for good, saith the LORD: ᴿit shall be given into the hand of the king of Babylon, and he shall ᴿburn it with fire.

11 And touching the house of the king of Judah, *say,* Hear ye the word of the LORD;

12 O house of David, thus saith the LORD; ᴿExecuteᴺ judgment ᴿin the morning, and deliver *him that is* spoiled out of the hand of the oppressor, lest my fury go out like fire, and

burn that none can quench *it,* because of the evil of your doings.

13 Behold, ᴿI *am* against thee, O ᴺinhabitant of the valley, *and* rock of the plain, saith the LORD; which say, ᴿWho shall come down against us? or who shall enter into our habitations?

14 But I will ᴺpunish you according to the ᴿfruit of your doings, saith the LORD: and I will kindle a fire in the forest thereof, and ᴿit shall devour all things round about it.

CHAPTER 22

Warning against injustice and violence

THUS saith the LORD; Go down to the house of the king of Judah, and speak there this word,

2 And say, ᴿHear the word of the LORD, O king of Judah, that sittest upon the throne of David, thou, and thy servants, and thy people that enter in by these gates:

3 Thus saith the LORD; ᴿExecute ye judgment and righteousness, and deliver the spoiled out of the hand of the oppressor: and do no wrong, do no violence to the stranger, the fatherless, nor the widow, neither shed innocent blood in this place.

4 For if ye do this thing indeed, ᴿthen shall there enter in by the gates of this house kings sitting ᴺupon the throne of David, riding in chariots and on horses, he, and his servants, and his people.

5 But if ye will not hear these words, ᴿI swear by myself, saith the LORD, that this house shall become a desolation.

6 For thus saith the LORD unto the king's house of Judah; Thou *art* Gilead unto me, *and* the head of Lĕb′-ă-non: *yet* surely I will make thee a wilderness, *and* cities *which* are not inhabited.

7 And I will prepare destroyers against thee, every one with his weapons: and they shall cut down ᴿthy choice cedars, ᴿand cast *them* into the fire.

8 And many nations shall pass by this city, and they shall say every man to his neighbour, ᴿWherefore hath the LORD done thus unto this great city?

9 Then they shall answer, ᴿBecause they have forsaken the covenant of the LORD their God, and worshipped other gods, and served them.

10 Weep ye not for ᴿthe dead, neither bemoan him: *but* weep sore for him ᴿthat goeth away: for he shall return no more, nor see his native country.

Prophecy against Shallum

11 For thus saith the LORD touching ᴿShăl′-lŭm the son of Jō-sī′-ăh king of Judah, which reigned instead of Jō-sī′-ăh his father, ᴿwhich went forth out of this place; He shall not return thither any more:

12 But he shall die in the place whither they have led him captive, and shall see this land no more.

13 ᴿWoe unto him that buildeth his house by unrighteousness, and his chambers by wrong; ᴿ*that* useth his neighbour's service without wages, and giveth him not for his work;

14 That saith, I will build me a wide house and ᴺlarge chambers, and cutteth him out ᴺwindows; and *it is* ceiled with cedar, and painted with vermilion.

15 Shalt thou reign, because thou closest *thyself* in cedar? did not thy father eat and drink, and do judgment and justice, *and then* ᴿ*it was* well with him?

16 He judged the cause of the poor and needy; then *it was* well *with him: was* not this to know me? saith the LORD.

17 ᴿBut thine eyes and thine heart *are* not but for thy covetousness, and for to shed innocent blood, and for oppression, and for ᴺviolence, to do *it*.

Prophecy against Jehoiakim

18 Therefore thus saith the LORD concerning Jĕ-hoĭ′-ă-kĭm the son of Jō-sī′-ăh king of Judah; ᴿThey shall not lament for him, *saying,* ᴿAh my brother! or, Ah sister! they shall not lament for him, *saying,* Ah lord! or, Ah his glory!

19 ᴿHe shall be buried with the burial of an ass, drawn and cast forth beyond the gates of Jerusalem.

20 Go up to Lĕb′-ă-nọn, and cry; and lift up thy voice in Bā′-shăn, and cry from the passages: for all thy lovers are destroyed.

21 I spake unto thee in thy ᴺprosperity; *but* thou saidst, I will not hear. ᴿThis *hath been* thy manner from thy youth, that thou obeyedst not my voice.

22 The wind shall eat up all ᴿthy pastors, and thy lovers shall go into captivity: surely then shalt thou be ashamed and confounded for all thy wickedness.

23 O ᴺinhabitant of Lĕb′-ă-nọn, that makest thy nest in the cedars, how gracious shalt thou be when pangs come upon thee, ᴿthe pain as of a woman in travail!

24 *As* I live, saith the LORD, ᴿthough Cō-nī′-ăh the son of Jĕ-hoĭ′-ă-kĭm king of Judah ᴿwere the signet upon my right hand, yet would I pluck thee thence;

CHAP. 22
BC 609
11 See 1 Chr. 3:15, with
2 Ki. 23:30
11 2 Ki. 23:34
13 ver. 18
2 Ki. 23:35
13 Lev. 19:13
Deut. 24:14, 15
Mic. 3:10
Hab. 2:9
Jas. 5:4
14 Heb. *through-aired*
14 Or, *my windows*
15 Ps. 128:2
Is. 3:10
17 Ezek. 19:6
17 Or, *incursion*
18 ch. 16:4, 6
18 See 1 Ki. 13:30, Fulfilled
19 2 Chr. 36:6
ch. 36:30
21 Heb. *prosperities*
21 ch. 3:25
& 7:23, etc.
22 ch. 23:1
23 Heb. *inhabitress*
23 ch. 6:24
24 See 2 Ki. 24:6, 8
1 Chr. 3:16
ch. 37:1
24 S. of S. 8:6
Hag. 2:23

ch. 34:20   25
2 Ki. 24:15   26
2 Chr. 36:10
Heb. *lift*   27
up their mind
Ps. 31:12   28
ch. 48:38
Hos. 8:8
Deut. 32:1   29
Is. 1:2
& 34:1
Mic. 1:2
See 1 Chr. 3:16, 30
17
Mat. 1:12
ch. 36:30   30

CHAP. 23
BC 599
ch. 10:21   1
& 22:22
Ezek. 34:2
Ex. 32:34   2
ch. 32:37   3
Ezek. 34:13
ch. 3:15   4
Ezek. 34:23
Is. 4:2   5
& 11:1
& 40:10, 11
ch. 33:14
Dan. 9:24
Zech. 6:12
John 1:45
Ps. 72:2   5
Is. 9:7
& 32:1, 18
Deut. 33:28   6
Zech. 14:11
ch. 32:37   6
ch. 33:16   6
1 Cor. 1:30
Heb. *Jehovah-tsidkenu*
ch. 16:14   7

---

25 ᴿAnd I will give thee into the hand of them that seek thy life, and into the hand *of them* whose face thou fearest, even into the hand of Nĕb-ū-chăd-rĕz′-zär king of Babylon, and into the hand of the Chăl-dē′-ăns.

26 ᴿAnd I will cast thee out, and thy mother that bare thee, into another country, where ye were not born; and there shall ye die.

27 But to the land whereunto they ᴺdesire to return, thither shall they not return.

28 *Is* this man Cō-nī′-ăh a despised broken idol? *is he* ᴿa vessel wherein *is* no pleasure? wherefore are they cast out, he and his seed, and are cast into a land which they know not?

29 ᴿO earth, earth, earth, hear the word of the LORD.

30 Thus saith the LORD, Write ye this man ᴿchildless, a man *that* shall not prosper in his days: for no man of his seed shall prosper, ᴿsitting upon the throne of David, and ruling any more in Judah.

CHAPTER 23

Righteous king for the remnant

WOE ᴿbe unto the pastors that destroy and scatter the sheep of my pasture! saith the LORD.

2 Therefore thus saith the LORD God of Israel against the pastors that feed my people; Ye have scattered my flock, and driven them away, and have not visited them: ᴿbehold, I will visit upon you the evil of your doings, saith the LORD.

3 And ᴿI will gather the remnant of my flock out of all countries whither I have driven them, and will bring them again to their folds; and they shall be fruitful and increase.

4 And I will set up ᴿshepherds over them which shall feed them: and they shall fear no more, nor be dismayed, neither shall they be lacking, saith the LORD.

5 Behold, ᴿthe days come, saith the LORD, that I will raise unto David a righteous Branch, and a King shall reign and prosper, ᴿand shall execute judgment and justice in the earth.   ★

6 ᴿIn his days Judah shall be saved, and Israel ᴿshall dwell safely: and ᴿthis *is* his name whereby he shall be called, ᴺTHE LORD OUR RIGHTEOUSNESS.   ★

7 Therefore, behold, ᴿthe days come, saith the LORD, that they shall no more say, The LORD liveth, which brought up the children of Israel out of the land of Egypt;

8 But, The LORD liveth, which brought up and which led the seed of the house of Israel

out of the north country, ᴿand from all countries whither I had driven them; and they shall dwell in their own land.

Ungodly prophets and priests

9 Mine heart within me is broken because of the prophets; ᴿall my bones shake; I am like a drunken man, and like a man whom wine hath overcome, because of the LORD, and because of the words of his holiness.

10 For ᴿthe land is full of adulterers; for ᴿbecause of ᴺswearing the land mourneth; ᴿthe pleasant places of the wilderness are dried up, and their ᴺcourse is evil, and their force *is* not right.

11 For ᴿboth prophet and priest are profane; yea, ᴿin my house have I found their wickedness, saith the LORD.

12 ᴿWherefore their way shall be unto them as slippery *ways* in the darkness: they shall be driven on, and fall therein: for I ᴿwill bring evil upon them, *even* the year of their visitation, saith the LORD.

13 And I have seen ᴺᴺfolly in the prophets of Să-mâr'-ĭ-ă; ᴿthey prophesied in Bā'-ăl, and ᴿcaused my people Israel to err.

14 I have seen also in the prophets of Jerusalem ᴺan horrible thing: ᴿthey commit adultery, and ᴿwalk in lies: they ᴿstrengthen also the hands of evildoers, that none doth return from his wickedness: they are all of them unto me as ᴿSodom, and the inhabitants thereof as Gŏ-mŏr'-răh.

15 Therefore thus saith the LORD of hosts concerning the prophets; Behold, I will feed them with ᴿwormwood, and make them drink the water of gall: for from the prophets of Jerusalem is ᴺprofaneness gone forth into all the land.

16 Thus saith the LORD of hosts, Hearken not unto the words of the prophets that prophesy unto you: they make you vain: ᴿthey speak a vision of their own heart, *and* not out of the mouth of the LORD.

17 They say still unto them that despise me, The LORD hath said, ᴿYe shall have peace; and they say unto every one that walketh after the ᴺimagination of his own heart, ᴿNo evil shall come upon you.

18 For ᴿwho hath stood in the ᴺcounsel of the LORD, and hath perceived and heard his word? who hath marked his word, and heard *it?*

19 Behold, a ᴿwhirlwind of the LORD is gone forth in fury, even a grievous whirlwind: it shall fall grievously upon the head of the wicked.

20 The ᴿanger of the LORD shall not return, until he have executed, and till he have per-

CHAP. 23
BC 599

8 Is. 43:5, 6
9 See Hab. 3:16
10 ch. 9:2
10 Hos. 4:2, 3
10 Or, *cursing*
10 ch. 9:10
10 Or, *violence*
11 Zeph. 3:4
11 ch. 7:30
Ezek. 8:11
& 23:39
12 Ps. 35:6
Prov. 4:19
ch. 13:16
12 ch. 11:23
13 Or, *an absurd thing*
13 Heb. *unsavoury*
13 ch. 2:8
13 Is. 9:16
14 Or, *filthiness*
14 ch. 29:23
14 ver. 26
14 Ezek. 13:22
14 Is. 1:9, 10
15 ch. 9:15
15 Or, *hypocrisy*
16 ch. 14:14
17 ch. 8:11
Ezek. 13:10
Zech. 10:2
17 Or, *stubbornness*
17 Mic. 3:11
18 Job 15:8
1 Cor. 2:16
18 Or, *secret*
19 ch. 25:32
& 30:23
20 ch. 30:24

Gen. 49:1   20
ch. 14:14   21
ver. 18   22
ch. 25:5   22
Ps. 139:7   24
Amos 9:2, 3
1 Ki. 8:27   24
Ps. 139:7
Judg. 3:7   27
Heb. *with*   28
whom is
Deut. 18:20   30
ch. 14:14, 15
Or, *that*   31
smooth their
tongues
Zeph. 3:4   32
Mal. 1:1   33
ver. 39   33
Heb. *visit upon* 34

formed the thoughts of his heart: ᴿin the latter days ye shall consider it perfectly.

21 ᴿI have not sent these prophets, yet they ran: I have not spoken to them, yet they prophesied.

22 But if they had ᴿstood in my counsel, and had caused my people to hear my words, then they should have ᴿturned them from their evil way, and from the evil of their doings.

Self-appointed prophets

23 *Am* I a God at hand, saith the LORD, and not a God afar off?

24 Can any ᴿhide himself in secret places that I shall not see him? saith the LORD. ᴿDo not I fill heaven and earth? saith the LORD.

25 I have heard what the prophets said, that prophesy lies in my name, saying, I have dreamed, I have dreamed.

26 How long shall *this* be in the heart of the prophets that prophesy lies? yea, *they are* prophets of the deceit of their own heart;

27 Which think to cause my people to forget my name by their dreams which they tell every man to his neighbour, ᴿas their fathers have forgotten my name for Bā'-ăl.

28 The prophet ᴺthat hath a dream, let him tell a dream; and he that hath my word, let him speak my word faithfully. What *is* the chaff to the wheat? saith the LORD.

29 *Is* not my word like as a fire? saith the LORD; and like a hammer *that* breaketh the rock in pieces?

30 Therefore, behold, ᴿI *am* against the prophets, saith the LORD, that steal my words every one from his neighbour.

31 Behold, I *am* against the prophets, saith the LORD, ᴺthat use their tongues, and say, He saith.

32 Behold, I *am* against them that prophesy false dreams, saith the LORD, and do tell them, and cause my people to err by their lies, and by ᴿtheir lightness; yet I sent them not, nor commanded them: therefore they shall not profit this people at all, saith the LORD.

33 And when this people, or the prophet, or a priest, shall ask thee, saying, What *is* ᴿthe burden of the LORD? thou shalt then say unto them, What burden? ᴿI will even forsake you, saith the LORD.

34 And *as for* the prophet, and the priest, and the people, that shall say, The burden of the LORD, I will even ᴺpunish that man and his house.

35 Thus shall ye say every one to his neighbour, and every one to his brother, What hath the LORD answered? and, What hath the LORD spoken?

36 And the burden of the LORD shall ye

mention no more: for every man's word shall be his burden; for ye have perverted the words of the living God, of the LORD of hosts our God.

37 Thus shalt thou say to the prophet, What hath the LORD answered thee? and, What hath the LORD spoken?

38 But since ye say, The burden of the LORD; therefore thus saith the LORD; Because ye say this word, The burden of the LORD, and I have sent unto you, saying, Ye shall not say, The burden of the LORD;

39 Therefore, behold, I, even I, R will utterly forget you, and R I will forsake you, and the city that I gave you and your fathers, *and cast you* out of my presence:

40 And I will bring R an everlasting reproach upon you, and a perpetual shame, which shall not be forgotten.

CHAPTER 24

Vision of two baskets of figs

THE R LORD shewed me, and, behold, two baskets of figs *were* set before the temple of the LORD, after that Nĕb-ū-chăd-rĕz'-zär R king of Babylon had carried away captive R Jĕc-ō-nī'-ăh the son of Jĕ-hoī'-ă-kĭm king of Judah, and the princes of Judah, with the carpenters and smiths, from Jerusalem, and had brought them to Babylon.

2 One basket *had* very good figs, *even* like the figs *that are* first ripe: and the other basket *had* very naughty figs, which could not be eaten, N they were so bad.

3 Then said the LORD unto me, What seest thou, Jeremiah? And I said, Figs; the good figs, very good; and the evil, very evil, that cannot be eaten, they are so evil.

4 Again the word of the LORD came unto me, saying,

5 Thus saith the LORD, the God of Israel; Like these good figs, so will I acknowledge N them that are carried away captive of Judah, whom I have sent out of this place into the land of the Chăl-dē'-ăns for *their* good.

6 For I will set mine eyes upon them for good, and R I will bring them again to this land: and R I will build them, and not pull *them* down; and I will plant them, and not pluck *them* up.

7 And I will give them R an heart to know me, that I *am* the LORD: and they shall be R my people, and I will be their God: for they shall return unto me R with their whole heart.

8 And as the evil R figs, which cannot be eaten, they are so evil; surely thus saith the LORD, So will I give Zĕd-ē-kī'-ăh the king of

Judah, and his princes, and the residue of Jerusalem, that remain in this land, and R them that dwell in the land of Egypt:

9 And I will deliver them N to R be removed into all the kingdoms of the earth for *their* hurt, R *to be* a reproach and a proverb, a taunt and a curse, in all places whither I shall drive them.

10 And I will send the sword, the famine, and the pestilence, among them, till they be consumed from off the land that I gave unto them and to their fathers.

CHAPTER 25

Seventy years in Babylon

THE word that came to Jeremiah concerning all the people of Judah R in the fourth year of Jĕ-hoī'-ă-kĭm the son of Jō-sī'-ăh king of Judah, that *was* the first year of Nĕb-ū-chăd-rĕz'-zär king of Babylon;

2 The which Jeremiah the prophet spake unto all the people of Judah, and to all the inhabitants of Jerusalem, saying,

3 R From the thirteenth year of Jō-sī'-ăh the son of Amon king of Judah, even unto this day, that *is* the three and twentieth year, the word of the LORD hath come unto me, and I have spoken unto you, rising early and speaking; R but ye have not hearkened.

4 And the LORD hath sent unto you all his servants the prophets, R rising early and sending *them;* but ye have not hearkened, nor inclined your ear to hear.

5 They said, R Turn ye again now every one from his evil way, and from the evil of your doings, and dwell in the land that the LORD hath given unto you and to your fathers for ever and ever:

6 And go not after other gods to serve them, and to worship them, and provoke me not to anger with the works of your hands; and I will do you no hurt.

7 Yet ye have not hearkened unto me, saith the LORD; that ye might R provoke me to anger with the works of your hands to your own hurt.

8 Therefore thus saith the LORD of hosts; Because ye have not heard my words,

9 Behold, I will send and take R all the families of the north, saith the LORD, and Nĕb-ū-chăd-rĕz'-zär the king of Babylon, R my servant, and will bring them against this land, and against the inhabitants thereof, and against all these nations round about, and will utterly destroy them, and R make them an astonishment, and an hissing, and perpetual desolations.

CHAP. **23**
BC 599
39 Hos. 4:6
39 ver. 33
40 ch. 20:11

CHAP. **24**
BC 598
1 Amos 7:1, 4 & 8:1
1 2 Ki. 24:12, etc. 2 Chr. 36:10
1 See ch. 22:24, etc. & 29:2
2 Heb. *for badness*
5 Heb. *the captivity*
6 ch. 12:15 & 29:10
6 ch. 32:41 & 33:7 & 42:10
7 Deut. 30:6 ch. 32:39 Ezek. 11:19 & 36:26, 27
7 ch. 30:22 & 31:33 & 32:38
7 ch. 29:13
8 ch. 29:17

See ch. 43, & 44	**8**
Heb. *for removing,* or, *vexation*	**9**
Deut. 28:25, 37 1 Ki. 9:7 2 Chr. 7:20 ch. 15:4 & 29:18 & 34:17 Ps. 44:13, 14	**9**

CHAP. **25**
BC 606
ch. 36:1 ... **1**
ch. 1:2 ... **3**
ch. 7:13 & 11:7, 8, 10 ... **3**
ch. 7:13, 25 ... **4**
ch. 18:11 ... **5**
Jonah 3:8 Deut. 32:21 ... **7**
ch. 1:15 ... **9**
ch. 27:6 ... **9**
Is. 45:1 ch. 18:16 ... **9**

10 Moreover [N]I will take from them the [R]voice of mirth, and the voice of gladness, the voice of the bridegroom, and the voice of the bride, [R]the sound of the millstones, and the light of the candle.

11 And this whole land shall be a desolation, *and* an astonishment; and these nations shall serve the king of Babylon seventy years.

12 And it shall come to pass, [R]when [R]seventy years are accomplished, *that* I will [N]punish the king of Babylon, and that nation, saith the Lord, for their iniquity, and the land of the Chăl-dē′-ăns, [R]and will make it perpetual desolations.

13 And I will bring upon that land all my words which I have pronounced against it, *even* all that is written in this book, which Jeremiah hath prophesied against all the nations.

14 [R]For many nations [R]and great kings shall [R]serve themselves of them also: [R]and I will recompense them according to their deeds, and according to the works of their own hands.

Wine of wrath

15 For thus saith the Lord God of Israel unto me; Take the [R]wine cup of this fury at my hand, and cause all the nations, to whom I send thee, to drink it.

16 And [R]they shall drink, and be moved, and be mad, because of the sword that I will send among them.

17 Then took I the cup at the Lord's hand, and made all the nations to drink, unto whom the Lord had sent me:

18 *To wit,* Jerusalem, and the cities of Judah, and the kings thereof, and the princes thereof, to make them [R]a desolation, an astonishment, an hissing, and [R]a curse; as *it is* this day;

19 Pharaoh king of Egypt, and his servants, and his princes, and all his people;

20 And all the mingled people, and all the kings of [R]the land of Uz, and all the kings of the land of the Philistines, and Ăsh′-kĕ-lŏn, and Azzah, and ĕk′-rŏn, and [R]the remnant of Ăsh′-dŏd,

21 [R]Ē′-dǫm, and Moab, and the children of Ammon,

22 And all the kings of [R]Tȳ′-rŭs, and all the kings of Zī′-dŏn, and the kings of the [N]isles which *are* beyond the [R]sea,

23 [R]Dē′-dăn, and Tē′-mă, and Buz, and all [N]*that are* in the utmost corners,

24 And all the kings of Arabia, and all the kings of the [R]mingled people that dwell in the desert,

25 And all the kings of Zimri, and all the

kings of Ē′-lăm, and all the kings of the Mēdeś,

26 [R]And all the kings of the north, far and near, one with another, and all the kingdoms of the world, which *are* upon the face of the earth: and the king of Shē′-shăch shall drink after them.

27 Therefore thou shalt say unto them, Thus saith the Lord of hosts, the God of Israel; [R]Drink ye, and [R]be drunken, and spue, and fall, and rise no more, because of the sword which I will send among you.

28 And it shall be, if they refuse to take the cup at thine hand to drink, then shalt thou say unto them, Thus saith the Lord of hosts; Ye shall certainly drink.

29 For, lo, [R]I begin to bring evil on the city [R]which[N] is called by my name, and should ye be utterly unpunished? Ye shall not be unpunished: for [R]I will call for a sword upon all the inhabitants of the earth, saith the Lord of hosts.

Judgment of all flesh

30 Therefore prophesy thou against them all these words, and say unto them, The Lord shall [R]roar from on high, and utter his voice from [R]his holy habitation; he shall mightily roar upon [R]his habitation; he shall give [R]a shout, as they that tread *the grapes,* against all the inhabitants of the earth.

31 A noise shall come *even* to the ends of the earth; for the Lord hath [R]a controversy with the nations, [R]he will plead with all flesh; he will give them *that are* wicked to the sword, saith the Lord.

32 Thus saith the Lord of hosts, Behold, evil shall go forth from nation to nation, and [R]a great whirlwind shall be raised up from the coasts of the earth.

33 [R]And the slain of the Lord shall be at that day from *one* end of the earth even unto the *other* end of the earth: they shall not be [R]lamented, [R]neither gathered, nor buried; they shall be dung upon the ground.

34 [R]Howl, ye shepherds, and cry; and wallow yourselves *in the ashes,* ye principal of the flock: for [N]the days of your slaughter and of your dispersions are accomplished; and ye shall fall like [N]a pleasant vessel.

35 And [N]the shepherds shall have no way to flee, nor the principal of the flock to escape.

36 A voice of the cry of the shepherds, and an howling of the principal of the flock, *shall be heard:* for the Lord hath spoiled their pasture.

37 And the peaceable habitations are cut down because of the fierce anger of the Lord.

38 He hath forsaken his covert, as the lion: for their land is ^Ndesolate because of the fierceness of the oppressor, and because of his fierce anger.

CHAPTER 26

Jeremiah's prophecy and trial

IN the beginning of the reign of Jĕ-hoi′-ă-kīm the son of Jō-si′-ăh king of Judah came this word from the LORD, saying,

2 Thus saith the LORD; Stand in ^Rthe court of the LORD's house, and speak unto all the cities of Judah, which come to worship in the LORD's house, ^Rall the words that I command thee to speak unto them; ^Rdiminish not a word:

3 ^RIf so be they will hearken, and turn every man from his evil way, that I may ^Rrepent me of the evil, which I purpose to do unto them because of the evil of their doings.

4 And thou shalt say unto them, Thus saith the LORD; ^RIf ye will not hearken to me, to walk in my law, which I have set before you,

5 To hearken to the words of my servants the prophets, ^Rwhom I sent unto you, both rising up early, and sending *them,* but ye have not hearkened;

6 Then will I make this house like ^RShi′-lōh, and will make this city ^Ra curse to all the nations of the earth.

7 So the priests and the prophets and all the people heard Jeremiah speaking these words in the house of the LORD.

8 Now it came to pass, when Jeremiah had made an end of speaking all that the LORD had commanded *him* to speak unto all the people, that the priests and the prophets and all the people took him, saying, Thou shalt surely die.

9 Why hast thou prophesied in the name of the LORD, saying, This house shall be like Shi′-lōh, and this city shall be desolate without an inhabitant? And all the people were gathered against Jeremiah in the house of the LORD.

10 When the princes of Judah heard these things, then they came up from the king's house unto the house of the LORD, and sat down ^Nin the entry of the new gate of the LORD's *house.*

11 Then spake the priests and the prophets unto the princes and to all the people, saying, ^NThis man *is* worthy to die; ^Rfor he hath prophesied against this city, as ye have heard with your ears.

12 Then spake Jeremiah unto all the princes

and to all the people, saying, The LORD sent me to prophesy against this house and against this city all the words that ye have heard.

13 Therefore now ^Ramend your ways and your doings, and obey the voice of the LORD your God; and the LORD will ^Rrepent him of the evil that he hath pronounced against you.

14 As for me, behold, ^RI *am* in your hand: do with me ^Nas seemeth good and meet unto you.

15 But know ye for certain, that if ye put me to death, ye shall surely bring innocent blood upon yourselves, and upon this city, and upon the inhabitants thereof: for of a truth the LORD hath sent me unto you to speak all these words in your ears.

16 Then said the princes and all the people unto the priests and to the prophets; This man *is* not worthy to die: for he hath spoken to us in the name of the LORD our God.

17 ^RThen rose up certain of the elders of the land, and spake to all the assembly of the people, saying,

18 ^RMī′-căh the Mō-răs′-thīte prophesied in the days of Hĕz-ē-kī′-ăh king of Judah, and spake to all the people of Judah, saying, Thus saith the LORD of hosts; ^RZion shall be plowed *like* a field, and Jerusalem shall become heaps, and the mountain of the house as the high places of a forest.

19 Did Hĕz-ē-kī′-ăh king of Judah and all Judah put him at all to death? ^Rdid he not fear the LORD, and besought ^Nthe LORD, and the LORD ^Rrepented him of the evil which he had pronounced against them? ^RThus might we procure great evil against our souls.

Death to Urijah

20 And there was also a man that prophesied in the name of the LORD, Ū-rī′-jăh the son of Shĕm-ai′-ăh of Kīr′-jăth-jē′-ă-rĭm, who prophesied against this city and against this land according to all the words of Jeremiah:

21 And when Jĕ-hoi′-ă-kīm the king, with all his mighty men, and all the princes, heard his words, the king sought to put him to death: but when Ū-rī′-jăh heard it, he was afraid, and fled, and went into Egypt;

22 And Jĕ-hoi′-ă-kīm the king sent men into Egypt, *namely,* ĕl-nā′-thăn the son of Ăch′-bôr, and *certain* men with him into Egypt.

23 And they fetched forth Ū-rī′-jăh out of Egypt, and brought him unto Jĕ-hoi′-ă-kīm the king; who slew him with the sword, and cast his dead body into the graves of the ^Ncommon people.

24 Nevertheless ^Rthe hand of Ă-hī′-kăm the son of Shā′-phăn was with Jeremiah, that they

CHAP. **25**
BC 606
38 Heb. *a desolation*

CHAP. **26**
BC 609
2 ch. 19:14
2 Ezek. 3:10
Mat. 28:20
2 Acts 20:27
3 ch. 36:3
3 ch. 18:8
Jonah 3:8, 9
4 Lev. 26:14, etc.
Deut. 28:15
5 ch. 7:13, 25
& 11:7
& 25:3, 4
6 1 Sam. 4:10, 11
Ps. 78:60
ch. 7:12, 14
6 Is. 65:15
ch. 24:9
10 Or, *at the door*
11 Heb. *The judgment of death* is *for this man*
11 ch. 38:4

ch. 7:3   13
ver. 3, 19   13
ch. 38:5   14
Heb. *as it is good and right in your eyes*   14
See Acts 5:34, etc.   17
Mic. 1:1   18
Mic. 3:12   18
2 Chr. 32:26   19
Heb. *the face of the LORD*   19
Ex. 32:14   19
2 Sam. 24:16
Acts 5:39   19
Heb. *sons of the people*   23
2 Ki. 22:12, 14   24
ch. 39:14

should not give him into the hand of the people to put him to death.

CHAPTER 27

Submission to Babylon urged

IN the beginning of the reign of Jĕ-hŏi'-ă-kĭm the son of Jō-sī'-ăh Rking of Judah came this word unto Jeremiah from the LORD, saying,

2 Thus Nsaith the LORD to me; Make thee bonds and yokes, Rand put them upon thy neck,

3 And send them to the king of Ē'-dŏm, and to the king of Moab, and to the king of the Ammonites, and to the king of Tȳ'-rŭs, and to the king of Zĭ'-dŏn, by the hand of the messengers which come to Jerusalem unto Zĕd-ē-kī'-ăh king of Judah;

4 And command them Nto say unto their masters, Thus saith the LORD of hosts, the God of Israel; Thus shall ye say unto your masters;

5 RI have made the earth, the man and the beast that *are* upon the ground, by my great power and by my outstretched arm, and Rhave given it unto whom it seemed meet unto me.

6 RAnd now have I given all these lands into the hand of Nĕb-ū-chăd-nĕz'-zär the king of Babylon, Rmy servant; and Rthe beasts of the field have I given him also to serve him.

7 RAnd all nations shall serve him, and his son, and his son's son, Runtil the very time of his land come: Rand then many nations and great kings shall serve themselves of him.

8 And it shall come to pass, *that* the nation and kingdom which will not serve the same Nĕb-ū-chăd-nĕz'-zär the king of Babylon, and that will not put their neck under the yoke of the king of Babylon, that nation will I punish, saith the LORD, with the sword, and with the famine, and with the pestilence, until I have consumed them by his hand.

9 Therefore hearken not ye to your prophets, nor to your diviners, nor to your Ndreamers, nor to your enchanters, nor to your sorcerers, which speak unto you, saying, Ye shall not serve the king of Babylon:

10 RFor they prophesy a lie unto you, to remove you far from your land; and that I should drive you out, and ye should perish.

11 But the nations that bring their neck under the yoke of the king of Babylon, and serve him, those will I let remain still in their own land, saith the LORD; and they shall till it, and dwell therein.

12 I spake also to RZĕd-ē-kī'-ăh king of Judah according to all these words, saying,

Bring your necks under the yoke of the king of Babylon, and serve him and his people, and live.

13 RWhy will ye die, thou and thy people, by the sword, by the famine, and by the pestilence, as the LORD hath spoken against the nation that will not serve the king of Babylon?

14 Therefore hearken not unto the words of the prophets that speak unto you, saying, Ye shall not serve the king of Babylon: for they prophesy Ra lie unto you.

15 For I have not sent them, saith the LORD, yet they prophesy Na lie in my name; that I might drive you out, and that ye might perish, ye, and the prophets that prophesy unto you.

16 Also I spake to the priests and to all this people, saying, Thus saith the LORD; Hearken not to the words of your prophets that prophesy unto you saying, Behold, Rthe vessels of the LORD's house shall now shortly be brought again from Babylon: for they prophesy a lie unto you.

17 Hearken not unto them; serve the king of Babylon, and live: wherefore should this city be laid waste?

18 But if they *be* prophets, and if the word of the LORD be with them, let them now make intercession to the LORD of hosts, that the vessels which are left in the house of the LORD, and *in* the house of the king of Judah, and at Jerusalem, go not to Babylon.

19 For thus saith the LORD of hosts Rconcerning the pillars, and concerning the sea, and concerning the bases, and concerning the residue of the vessels that remain in this city,

20 Which Nĕb-ū-chăd-nĕz'-zär king of Babylon took not, when he carried away Rcaptive Jĕc-ō-nī'-ăh the son of Jĕ-hŏi'-ă-kĭm king of Judah from Jerusalem to Babylon, and all the nobles of Judah and Jerusalem;

21 Yea, thus saith the LORD of hosts, the God of Israel, concerning the vessels that remain *in* the house of the LORD, and *in* the house of the king of Judah and of Jerusalem;

22 They shall be Rcarried to Babylon, and there shall they be until the day that I Rvisit them, saith the LORD; then Rwill I bring them up, and restore them to this place.

CHAPTER 28

Hananiah's false prophecy and death

AND Rit came to pass the same year, in the beginning of the reign of Zĕd-ē-kī'-ăh king of Judah, in the fourth year, *and* in the fifth month, *that* Hăn-ă-nī'-ăh the son of Ā'-zŭr the prophet, which *was* of Gibeon, spake unto

me in the house of the LORD, in the presence of the priests and of all the people, saying,

2 Thus speaketh the LORD of hosts, the God of Israel, saying, I have broken [R]the yoke of the king of Babylon.

3 [R]Within [N]two full years will I bring again into this place all the vessels of the LORD's house, that Něb-ū-chăd-něz'-zär king of Babylon took away from this place, and carried them to Babylon:

4 And I will bring again to this place Jĕc-ō-nī'-ăh the son of Jĕ-hoī'-ă-kĭm king of Judah, with all the [N]captives of Judah, that went into Babylon, saith the LORD: for I will break the yoke of the king of Babylon.

5 Then the prophet Jeremiah said unto the prophet Hăn-ă-nī'-ăh in the presence of the priests, and in the presence of all the people that stood in the house of the LORD,

6 Even the prophet Jeremiah said, [R]Ä'-měn: the LORD do so: the LORD perform thy words which thou hast prophesied, to bring again the vessels of the LORD's house, and all that is carried away captive, from Babylon into this place.

7 Nevertheless hear thou now this word that I speak in thine ears, and in the ears of all the people;

8 The prophets that have been before me and before thee of old prophesied both against many countries, and against great kingdoms, of war, and of evil, and of pestilence.

9 [R]The prophet which prophesieth of peace, when the word of the prophet shall come to pass, then shall the prophet be known, that the LORD hath truly sent him.

10 Then Hăn-ă-nī'-ăh the prophet took the [R]yoke from off the prophet Jeremiah's neck, and brake it.

11 And Hăn-ă-nī'-ăh spake in the presence of all the people, saying, Thus saith the LORD; Even so will I break the yoke of Něb-ū-chăd-něz'-zär king of Babylon [R]from the neck of all nations within the space of two full years. And the prophet Jeremiah went his way.

12 Then the word of the LORD came unto Jeremiah the prophet, after that Hăn-ă-nī'-ăh the prophet had broken the yoke from off the neck of the prophet Jeremiah, saying,

13 Go and tell Hăn-ă-nī'-ăh, saying, Thus saith the LORD; Thou hast broken the yokes of wood; but thou shalt make for them yokes of iron.

14 For thus saith the LORD of hosts, the God of Israel; [R]I have put a yoke of iron upon the neck of all these nations, that they may serve Něb-ū-chăd-něz'-zär king of Babylon; and they

CHAP. 28
BC 596
2 ch. 27:12
3 ch. 27:16
3 Heb. two years of days
4 Heb. captivity
6 1 Ki. 1:36
9 Deut. 18:22
10 ch. 27:2
11 ch. 27:7
14 Deut. 28:48
   ch. 27:7

ch. 27:6   14
ch. 29:31   15
Ezek. 13:22
Deut. 13:5   16
ch. 29:32
Heb. revolt   16

CHAP. 29
BC 599
2 Ki. 24:12, etc.   2
ch. 22:26 & 28:4
Or, chamberlains   2
ver. 28   5
Ezra 6:10   7
1 Tim. 2:2
ch. 14:14 & 23:21   8
& 27:14, 15
Eph. 5:6
ver. 31   9
Heb. in a lie   9
2 Chr. 36:21, 22   10
Ezra 1:1
ch. 25:12 & 27:22
Dan. 9:2

shall serve him: and [R]I have given him the beasts of the field also.

15 Then said the prophet Jeremiah unto Hăn-ă-nī'-ăh the prophet, Hear now, Hăn-ă-nī'-ăh; The LORD hath not sent thee; but [R]thou makest this people to trust in a lie.

16 Therefore thus saith the LORD; Behold, I will cast thee from off the face of the earth: this year thou shalt die, because thou hast taught [R]rebellion[N] against the LORD.

17 So Hăn-ă-nī'-ăh the prophet died the same year in the seventh month.

CHAPTER 29

Letter to the exiles

NOW these are the words of the letter that Jeremiah the prophet sent from Jerusalem unto the residue of the elders which were carried away captives, and to the priests, and to the prophets, and to all the people whom Něb-ū-chăd-něz'-zär had carried away captive from Jerusalem to Babylon;

2 (After that [R]Jĕc-ō-nī'-ăh the king, and the queen, and the [N]eunuchs, the princes of Judah and Jerusalem, and the carpenters, and the smiths, were departed from Jerusalem;)

3 By the hand of ĕl-ā'-săh the son of Shā'-phăn, and Gĕm-ă-rī'-ăh the son of Hĭl-kī'-ăh, (whom Zĕd-ē-kī'-ăh king of Judah sent unto Babylon to Něb-ū-chăd-něz'-zär king of Babylon) saying,

4 Thus saith the LORD of hosts, the God of Israel, unto all that are carried away captives, whom I have caused to be carried away from Jerusalem unto Babylon;

5 [R]Build ye houses, and dwell in them; and plant gardens, and eat the fruit of them;

6 Take ye wives, and beget sons and daughters; and take wives for your sons, and give your daughters to husbands, that they may bear sons and daughters; that ye may be increased there, and not diminished.

7 And seek the peace of the city whither I have caused you to be carried away captives, [R]and pray unto the LORD for it: for in the peace thereof shall ye have peace.

8 For thus saith the LORD of hosts, the God of Israel; Let not your prophets and your diviners, that be in the midst of you, [R]deceive you, neither hearken to your dreams which ye cause to be dreamed.

9 [R]For they prophesy [N]falsely unto you in my name: I have not sent them, saith the LORD.

10 For thus saith the LORD, That after [R]seventy years be accomplished at Babylon I will

visit you, and perform my good word toward you, in causing you to return to this place.

11 For I know the thoughts that I think toward you, saith the LORD, thoughts of peace, and not of evil, to give you an ᴺexpected end.

12 Then shall ye ᴿcall upon me, and ye shall go and pray unto me, and I will hearken unto you.

13 And ᴿye shall seek me, and find *me,* when ye shall search for me ᴿwith all your heart.

14 And ᴿI will be found of you, saith the LORD: and I will turn away your captivity, and ᴿI will gather you from all the nations, and from all the places whither I have driven you, saith the LORD; and I will bring you again into the place whence I caused you to be carried away captive.

15 Because ye have said, The LORD hath raised us up prophets in Babylon;

16 *Know* that thus saith the LORD of the king that sitteth upon the throne of David, and of all the people that dwelleth in this city, *and* of your brethren that are not gone forth with you into captivity;

17 Thus saith the LORD of hosts; Behold, I will send upon them the sword, the famine, and the pestilence, and will make them like ᴿvile figs, that cannot be eaten, they are so evil.

18 And I will persecute them with the sword, with the famine, and with the pestilence, and ᴿwill deliver them to be removed to all the kingdoms of the earth, ᴺto be ᴿa curse, and an astonishment, and an hissing, and a reproach, among all the nations whither I have driven them:

19 Because they have not hearkened to my words, saith the LORD, which ᴿI sent unto them by my servants the prophets, rising up early and sending *them;* but ye would not hear, saith the LORD.

20 Hear ye therefore the word of the LORD, all ye of the captivity, whom I have sent from Jerusalem to Babylon:

21 Thus saith the LORD of hosts, the God of Israel, of Ahab the son of Kō-lāi'-ăh, and of Zĕd-e-kī'-ăh the son of Mā-a-sēi'-ăh, which prophesy a lie unto you in my name; Behold, I will deliver them into the hand of Nĕb-ū-chăd-rĕz'-zär king of Babylon; and he shall slay them before your eyes;

22 ᴿAnd of them shall be taken up a curse by all the captivity of Judah which *are* in Babylon, saying, The LORD make thee like Zĕd-e-kī'-ăh and like Ahab, ᴿwhom the king of Babylon roasted in the fire;

23 Because ᴿthey have committed villany in

CHAP. 29
BC 599
11 Heb. *end and*
expectation
12 Dan. 9:3, etc.
13 Lev. 26:39,
40, etc.
Deut. 30:1, etc.
13 ch. 24:7
14 Deut. 4:7
Ps. 32:6 & 46:1
Is. 55:6
14 ch. 23:3, 8
& 30:3 & 32:37
17 ch. 24:8
18 Deut. 28:25
2 Chr. 29:8
ch. 15:4 & 24:9
& 34:17
18 Heb. *for a curse*
18 ch. 26:6 & 42:18
19 ch. 25:4 & 32:33
22 See Gen. 48:20
Is. 65:15
22 Dan. 3:6
23 ch. 23:14

Or, *dreamer*	24
2 Ki. 25:18	25
ch. 21:1	
ch. 20:1	26
2 Ki. 9:11	26
Acts 26:24	
ch. 20:2	26
ver. 5	28
ch. 28:15	31
ch. 28:16	32
Heb. *revolt*	32

CHAP. 30
BC 606
ver. 18 3
ch. 32:44
Ezek. 39:25
Amos 9:14, 15
ch. 16:15 3

Israel, and have committed adultery with their neighbours' wives, and have spoken lying words in my name, which I have not commanded them; even I know, and *am* a witness, saith the LORD.

24 *Thus* shalt thou also speak to Shĕm-āī'-ăh the ᴺNĕ-hĕl'-ă-mīte, saying,

25 Thus speaketh the LORD of hosts, the God of Israel, saying, Because thou hast sent letters in thy name unto all the people that *are* at Jerusalem, ᴿand to Zĕph-ă-nī'-ăh the son of Mā-ă-sēi'-ăh the priest, and to all the priests, saying,

26 The LORD hath made thee priest in the stead of Jĕ-hoi'-ă-dä the priest, that ye should be ᴿofficers in the house of the LORD, for every man *that is* ᴿmad, and maketh himself a prophet, that thou shouldest ᴿput him in prison, and in the stocks.

27 Now therefore why hast thou not reproved Jeremiah of Ăn'-ă-thŏth, which maketh himself a prophet to you?

28 For therefore he sent unto us *in* Babylon, saying, This *captivity is* long: ᴿbuild ye houses, and dwell *in them;* and plant gardens, and eat the fruit of them.

29 And Zĕph-ă-nī'-ăh the priest read this letter in the ears of Jeremiah the prophet.

30 Then came the word of the LORD unto Jeremiah, saying,

31 Send to all them of the captivity, saying, Thus saith the LORD concerning Shĕm-āī'-ăh the Nĕ-hĕl'-ă-mīte; Because that Shĕm-āī'-ăh hath prophesied unto you, ᴿand I sent him not, and he caused you to trust in a lie:

32 Therefore thus saith the LORD; Behold, I will punish Shĕm-āī'-ăh the Nĕ-hĕl'-ă-mīte, and his seed: he shall not have a man to dwell among this people; neither shall he behold the good that I will do for my people, saith the LORD; ᴿbecause he hath taught ᴺrebellion against the LORD.

CHAPTER 30

Restoration promised

THE word that came to Jeremiah from the LORD, saying,

2 Thus speaketh the LORD God of Israel, saying, Write thee all the words that I have spoken unto thee in a book.

3 For, lo, the days come, saith the LORD, that ᴿI will bring again the captivity of my people Israel and Judah, saith the LORD: ᴿand I will cause them to return to the land that I gave to their fathers, and they shall possess it.

4 And these *are* the words that the LORD spake concerning Israel and concerning Judah.

5 For thus saith the Lord; We have heard a voice of trembling, ᴺof fear, and not of peace.

6 Ask ye now, and see whether ᴺa man doth travail with child? wherefore do I see every man with his hands on his loins, ᴿas a woman in travail, and all faces are turned into paleness?

7 ᴿAlas! for that day *is* great, ᴿso that none *is* like it: it *is* even the time of Jacob's trouble; but he shall be saved out of it.

8 For it shall come to pass in that day, saith the Lord of hosts, *that* I will break his yoke from off thy neck, and will burst thy bonds, and strangers shall no more serve themselves of him:

9 But they shall serve the Lord their God, and ᴿDavid their king, whom I will ᴿraise up unto them.   ★

Israel's chastening

10 Therefore ᴿfear thou not, O my servant Jacob, saith the Lord; neither be dismayed, O Israel: for, lo, I will save thee from afar, and thy seed ᴿfrom the land of their captivity; and Jacob shall return, and shall be in rest, and be quiet, and none shall make *him* afraid.

11 For I *am* with thee, saith the Lord, to save thee: ᴿthough I make a full end of all nations whither I have scattered thee, ᴿyet will I not make a full end of thee: but I will correct thee ᴿin measure, and will not leave thee altogether unpunished.

12 For thus saith the Lord, ᴿThy bruise *is* incurable, *and* thy wound *is* grievous.

13 *There is* none to plead thy cause, ᴺthat thou mayest be bound up: ᴿthou hast no healing medicines.

14 ᴿAll thy lovers have forgotten thee; they seek thee not; for I have wounded thee with the wound ᴿof an enemy, with the chastisement ᴿof a cruel one, for the multitude of thine iniquity; ᴿ*because* thy sins were increased.

15 Why ᴿcriest thou for thine affliction? thy sorrow *is* incurable for the multitude of thine iniquity: *because* thy sins were increased, I have done these things unto thee.

16 Therefore all they that devour thee ᴿshall be devoured; and all thine adversaries, every one of them, shall go into captivity; and they that spoil thee shall be a spoil, and all that prey upon thee will I give for a prey.

17 ᴿFor I will restore health unto thee, and I will heal thee of thy wounds, saith the Lord; because they called thee an Outcast, *saying,* This *is* Zion, whom no man seeketh after.

CHAP. 30

BC 606

5 Or, there is *fear, and not peace*
6 Heb. *a male*
6 ch. 4:31 & 6:24
7 Joel 2:11, 31
Amos 5:18
Zeph. 1:14, etc.
7 Dan. 12:1
9 Is. 55:3, 4
Ezek. 34:23
& 37:24
Hos. 3:5
9 Luke 1:69
Acts 2:30 & 13:23
10 Is. 41:13
& 43:5 & 44:2
ch. 46:27, 28
10 ch. 3:18
11 Amos 9:8
11 ch. 4:27
11 Ps. 6:1
Is. 27:8
ch. 10:24 & 46:28
12 2 Chr. 36:16
ch. 15:18
13 Heb. *for binding up,* or, *pressing*
13 ch. 8:22
14 Lam. 1:2
14 Job 13:24
& 16:9 & 19:11
14 Job 30:21
14 ch. 5:6
15 ch. 15:18
16 Ex. 23:22
Is. 33:1 & 41:11
ch. 10:25
17 ch. 33:6

ver. 3   **18**
ch. 33:7, 11
Ps. 102:13   **18**
Or, *little hill*   **18**
Is. 51:11   **19**
Zech. 10:8   **19**
Is. 1:26   **20**
Gen. 49:10   **21**
Num. 16:5   **21**
ch. 31:1, 33   **22**
ch. 23:19   **23**
& 25:32
Heb. *cutting*   **23**
Or, *remain*   **23**
Gen. 49:1   **24**

CHAP. 31

BC 606

ch. 30:24   **1**
ch. 30:22   **1**
Num. 10:33   **2**
Deut. 1:33
Ps. 95:11
Is. 63:14
Heb. *from afar*   **3**
Mal. 1:2   **3**
Rom. 11:28   **3**
Or, *have I extended lovingkindness unto thee*
Hos. 11:4   **3**
ch. 33:7   **4**
Ex. 15:20   **4**
Judg. 11:34
Ps. 149:3
Or, *timbrels*   **4**
Is. 65:21   **5**
Amos 9:14
Heb. *profane them,*   **5**
Deut. 20:6

"Ye shall be my people"

18 Thus saith the Lord; Behold, ᴿI will bring again the captivity of Jacob's tents, and ᴿhave mercy on his dwelling places; and the city shall be builded upon her own ᴺheap, and the palace shall remain after the manner thereof.

19 And ᴿout of them shall proceed thanksgiving and the voice of them that make merry: ᴿand I will multiply them, and they shall not be few; I will also glorify them, and they shall not be small.

20 Their children also shall be ᴿas aforetime, and their congregation shall be established before me, and I will punish all that oppress them.

21 And their nobles shall be of themselves, ᴿand their governor shall proceed from the midst of them; and I will ᴿcause him to draw near, and he shall approach unto me: for who *is* this that engaged his heart to approach unto me? saith the Lord.

22 And ye shall be ᴿmy people, and I will be your God.

Restoration of Israel promised

23 Behold, the ᴿwhirlwind of the Lord goeth forth with fury, a ᴺcontinuing whirlwind: it shall ᴺfall with pain upon the head of the wicked.

24 The fierce anger of the Lord shall not return, until he have done *it,* and until he have performed the intents of his heart: ᴿin the latter days ye shall consider it.

CHAPTER 31

AT ᴿthe same time, saith the Lord, ᴿwill I be the God of all the families of Israel, and they shall be my people.

2 Thus saith the Lord, The people *which were* left of the sword found grace in the wilderness; *even* Israel, when ᴿI went to cause him to rest.

3 The Lord hath appeared ᴺof old unto me, *saying,* Yea, ᴿI have loved thee with ᴿan everlasting love: therefore ᴺwith lovingkindness have I ᴿdrawn thee.

4 Again ᴿI will build thee, and thou shalt be built, O virgin of Israel: thou shalt again be adorned with thy ᴿtabrets,ᴺ and shalt go forth in the dances of them that make merry.

5 ᴿThou shalt yet plant vines upon the mountains of Să-mâr′-ĭ-ă: the planters shall plant, and shall ᴺeat *them* as common things.

6 For there shall be a day, *that* the watchmen upon the mount Ē′-phră-ĭm shall cry,

R Arise ye, and let us go up to Zion unto the LORD our God.

7 For thus saith the LORD; R Sing with gladness for Jacob, and shout among the chief of the nations: publish ye, praise ye, and say, O LORD, save thy people, the remnant of Israel.

8 Behold, I will bring them R from the north country, and R gather them from the coasts of the earth, *and* with them the blind and the lame, the woman with child and her that travaileth with child together: a great company shall return thither.

9 R They shall come with weeping, and with N supplications will I lead them: I will cause them to walk R by the rivers of waters in a straight way, wherein they shall not stumble: for I am a father to Israel, and Ē'-phră-ĭm *is* my R firstborn.

10 Hear the word of the LORD, O ye nations, and declare *it* in the isles afar off, and say, He that scattered Israel R will gather him, and keep him, as a shepherd *doth* his flock.

11 For R the LORD hath redeemed Jacob, and ransomed him R from the hand of *him that was* stronger than he.

12 Therefore they shall come and sing in R the height of Zion, and shall flow together to R the goodness of the LORD, for wheat, and for wine, and for oil, and for the young of the flock and of the herd: and their soul shall be as a R watered garden; R and they shall not sorrow any more at all.

13 Then shall the virgin rejoice in the dance, both young men and old together: for I will turn their mourning into joy, and will comfort them, and make them rejoice from their sorrow.

14 And I will satiate the soul of the priests with fatness, and my people shall be satisfied with my goodness, saith the LORD.

God remembers Ephraim

15 Thus saith the LORD; R A voice was heard in R Rā'-mǎh, lamentation, *and* bitter weeping; Rahel weeping for her children refused to be comforted for her children, because R they *were* not.   ★

16 Thus saith the LORD; Refrain thy voice from weeping, and thine eyes from tears: for thy work shall be rewarded, saith the LORD; and R they shall come again from the land of the enemy.

17 And there is hope in thine end, saith the LORD, that thy children shall come again to their own border.

18 I have surely heard Ē'-phră-ĭm bemoaning himself *thus;* Thou hast chastised me, and I

CHAP. **31**
BC 606

6 Is. 2:3
Mic. 4:2
7 Is. 12:5, 6
8 ch. 3:12, 18
& 23:8
8 Ezek. 20:34, 41
& 34:13
9 ch. 50:4
9 Or, *favours,*
Zech. 12:10
9 Is. 35:8 & 43:19
& 49:10, 11
9 Ex. 4:22
10 Is. 40:11
Ezek. 34:12-14
11 Is. 44:23
& 48:20
11 Is. 49:24
12 Ezek. 17:23
12 Hos. 3:5
12 Is. 58:11
12 Is. 35:10
& 65:19
Rev. 21:4
15 Mat. 2:17, 18
15 Josh. 18:25
15 Gen. 42:13
16 ver. 4, 5
Ezra 1:5
Hos. 1:11

Lam. 5:21   18
Deut. 30:2   19
Deut. 32:36   20
Is. 63:15
Hos. 11:8
Heb. *sound*   20
Is. 57:18   20
Hos. 14:4
ch. 50:5   21
ch. 2:18, 23, 36   22
ch. 3:6, 8,   22
  11, 12, 14, 22
Ps. 122:5-8   23
Is. 1:26
Zech. 8:3   23
ch. 33:12   24
Ezek. 36:9-11   27
ch. 44:27   28
ch. 1:10 & 18:7   28
ch. 24:6   28
Ezek. 18:2, 3   29
Gal. 6:5, 7   30
ch. 32:40   31
& 33:14
Ezek. 37:26
Heb. 8:8-12
& 10:16, 17

was chastised, as a bullock unaccustomed *to the yoke:* R turn thou me, and I shall be turned; for thou *art* the LORD my God.

19 Surely R after that I was turned, I repented; and after that I was instructed, I smote upon *my* thigh: I was ashamed, yea, even confounded, because I did bear the reproach of my youth.

20 *Is* Ē'-phră-ĭm my dear son? *is he* a pleasant child? for since I spake against him, I do earnestly remember him still: R therefore my bowels N are troubled for him; R I will surely have mercy upon him, saith the LORD.

21 Set thee up waymarks, make thee high heaps: R set thine heart toward the highway, *even* the way *which* thou wentest: turn again, O virgin of Israel, turn again to these thy cities.

22 How long wilt thou R go about, O thou R backsliding daughter? for the LORD hath created a new thing in the earth, A woman shall compass a man.

Judah's praise

23 Thus saith the LORD of hosts, the God of Israel; As yet they shall use this speech in the land of Judah and in the cities thereof, when I shall bring again their captivity; R The LORD bless thee, O habitation of justice, *and* R mountain of holiness.

24 And there shall dwell in Judah itself, and R in all the cities thereof together, husbandmen, and they *that* go forth with flocks.

25 For I have satiated the weary soul, and I have replenished every sorrowful soul.

26 Upon this I awaked, and beheld; and my sleep was sweet unto me.

The new covenant for Israel and Judah

27 Behold, the days come, saith the LORD, that R I will sow the house of Israel and the house of Judah with the seed of man, and with the seed of beast.

28 And it shall come to pass, *that* like as I have R watched over them, R to pluck up, and to break down, and to throw down, and to destroy, and to afflict; so will I watch over them, R to build, and to plant, saith the LORD.

29 R In those days they shall say no more, The fathers have eaten a sour grape, and the children's teeth are set on edge.

30 R But every one shall die for his own iniquity: every man that eateth the sour grape, his teeth shall be set on edge.

31 Behold, the R days come, saith the LORD, that I will make a new covenant with the house of Israel, and with the house of Judah:

32 Not according to the covenant that I made with their fathers in the day *that* [R]I took them by the hand to bring them out of the land of Egypt; which my covenant they brake, [N]although I was an husband unto them, saith the LORD:

33 [R]But this *shall be* the covenant that I will make with the house of Israel; After those days, saith the LORD, [R]I will put my law in their inward parts, and write it in their hearts; [R]and will be their God, and they shall be my people.

34 And they shall teach no more every man his neighbour, and every man his brother, saying, Know the LORD: for [R]they shall all know me, from the least of them unto the greatest of them, saith the LORD: for [R]I will forgive their iniquity, and I will remember their sin no more.

35 Thus saith the LORD, [R]which giveth the sun for a light by day, *and* the ordinances of the moon and of the stars for a light by night, which divideth [R]the sea when the waves thereof roar; [R]The LORD of hosts *is* his name:

36 [R]If those ordinances depart from before me, saith the LORD, *then* the seed of Israel also shall cease from being a nation before me for ever.

37 Thus saith the LORD; [R]If heaven above can be measured, and the foundations of the earth searched out beneath, I will also cast off all the seed of Israel for all that they have done, saith the LORD.

Rebuilding of Jerusalem promised

38 Behold, the days come, saith the LORD, that the city shall be built to the LORD [R]from the tower of Hăn'-ă-nĕel unto the gate of the corner.

39 And [R]the measuring line shall yet go forth over against it upon the hill Gâr'-ĕb, and shall compass about to Gō'-ăth.

40 And the whole valley of the dead bodies, and of the ashes, and all the fields unto the brook of Kī'-drŏn, [R]unto the corner of the horse gate toward the east, [R]*shall be* holy unto the LORD; it shall not be plucked up, nor thrown down any more for ever.

CHAPTER 32

Jeremiah buys a field

THE word that came to Jeremiah from the LORD [R]in the tenth year of Zĕd-ē-kī'-ăh king of Judah, which *was* the eighteenth year of Nĕb-ū-chăd-rĕz'-zăr.

2 For then the king of Babylon's army be-

CHAP. 31

BC 606

32 Deut. 1:31
32 Or, *should I have continued an husband unto them?*
33 ch. 32:40
33 Ps. 40:8
Ezek. 11:19
& 36:26, 27
33 ch. 24:7
& 30:22 & 32:38
34 Is. 54:13
John 6:45
1 Cor. 2:10
1 John 2:20
34 ch. 33:8 & 50:20
Mic. 7:18
Acts 10:43
& 13:39
Rom. 11:27
35 Gen. 1:16
Ps. 72:5, 17
& 89:2, 36
& 119:91
35 Is. 51:15
35 ch. 10:16
36 Ps. 148:6
Is. 54:9, 10
ch. 33:20
37 ch. 33:22
38 Neh. 3:1
Zech. 14:10
39 Ezek. 40:8
Zech. 2:1
40 2 Chr. 23:15
Neh. 3:28
40 Joel 3:17

CHAP. 32

BC 590

1 2 Ki. 25:1
ch. 39:1

Neh. 3:25　　2
ch. 33:1
& 37:21 & 39:14
ch. 34:2　　3
ch. 34:3　　4
& 38:18, 23
& 39:5 & 52:9
ch. 27:22　　5
ch. 21:4 & 33:5　5
Lev. 25:24, 25, 32　7
Ruth 4:4
Gen. 23:16　　9
Zech. 11:12
Or, *seven shekels*　9
and ten pieces
of silver
Heb. *wrote*　　10
in the book
ch. 36:4　　12
See Is. 8:2　　12

---

sieged Jerusalem: and Jeremiah the prophet was shut up [R]in the court of the prison, which *was* in the king of Judah's house.

3 For Zĕd-ē-kī'-ăh king of Judah had shut him up, saying, Wherefore dost thou prophesy, and say, Thus saith the LORD, [R]Behold, I will give this city into the hand of the king of Babylon, and he shall take it;

4 And Zĕd-ē-kī'-ăh king of Judah [R]shall not escape out of the hand of the Chăl-dē'-ăns, but shall surely be delivered into the hand of the king of Babylon, and shall speak with him mouth to mouth, and his eyes shall behold his eyes;

5 And he shall lead Zĕd-ē-kī'-ăh to Babylon, and there shall he be [R]until I visit him, saith the LORD: [R]though ye fight with the Chăl-dē'-ăns, ye shall not prosper.

6 And Jeremiah said, The word of the LORD came unto me, saying,

7 Behold, Hăn'-ă-mĕel the son of Shăl'-lŭm thine uncle shall come unto thee, saying, Buy thee my field that *is* in Ăn'-ă-thōth: for the [R]right of redemption *is* thine to buy *it*.

8 So Hăn'-ă-mĕel mine uncle's son came to me in the court of the prison according to the word of the LORD, and said unto me, Buy my field, I pray thee, that *is* in Ăn'-ă-thōth, which *is* in the country of Benjamin: for the right of inheritance *is* thine, and the redemption *is* thine; buy *it* for thyself. Then I knew that this *was* the word of the LORD.

9 And I bought the field of Hăn'-ă-mĕel my uncle's son, that *was* in Ăn'-ă-thōth, and [R]weighed him the money, *even* [N]seventeen shē'-kĕls of silver.

10 And I [N]subscribed the evidence, and sealed *it,* and took witnesses, and weighed *him* the money in the balances.

11 So I took the evidence of the purchase, *both* that which was sealed *according* to the law and custom, and that which was open:

12 And I gave the evidence of the purchase unto [R]Bâr'-ŭch the son of Nē-rī'-ăh, the son of Mā-ă-sĕi'-ăh, in the sight of Hăn'-ă-mĕel mine uncle's *son,* and in the presence of the [R]witnesses that subscribed the book of the purchase, before all the Jews that sat in the court of the prison.

13 And I charged Bâr'-ŭch before them, saying,

14 Thus saith the LORD of hosts, the God of Israel; Take these evidences, this evidence of the purchase, both which is sealed, and this evidence which is open; and put them in an earthen vessel, that they may continue many days.

15 For thus saith the LORD of hosts, the God

of Israel; Houses and fields and vineyards R shall be possessed again in this land.

Jeremiah's prayer

16 Now when I had delivered the evidence of the purchase unto Bâr'-ŭch the son of Nē-rī'-ăh, I prayed unto the LORD, saying,

17 Ah Lord GOD! behold, R thou hast made the heaven and the earth by thy great power and stretched out arm, *and* R there is nothing N too hard for thee:

18 Thou shewest R lovingkindness unto thousands, and recompensest the iniquity of the fathers into the bosom of their children after them: the Great, R the Mighty God, R the LORD of hosts, *is* his name,

19 R Great in counsel, and mighty in N work: for thine R eyes *are* open upon all the ways of the sons of men: R to give every one according to his ways, and according to the fruit of his doings:

20 Which hast set signs and wonders in the land of Egypt, *even* unto this day, and in Israel, and among *other* men; and hast made thee R a name, as at this day;

21 And R hast brought forth thy people Israel out of the land of Egypt with signs, and with wonders, and with a strong hand, and with a stretched out arm, and with great terror;

22 And hast given them this land, which thou didst swear to their fathers to give them, R a land flowing with milk and honey;

23 And they came in, and possessed it; but R they obeyed not thy voice, neither walked in thy law; they have done nothing of all that thou commandedst them to do: therefore thou hast caused all this evil to come upon them:

24 Behold the N mounts, they are come unto the city to take it; and the city R is given into the hand of the Chăl-dē'-ăns, that fight against it, because of R the sword, and of the famine, and of the pestilence: and what thou hast spoken is come to pass; and, behold, thou seest *it*.

25 And thou hast said unto me, O Lord GOD, Buy thee the field for money, and take witnesses; N for R the city is given into the hand of the Chăl-dē'-ăns.

God's answer

26 Then came the word of the LORD unto Jeremiah, saying,

27 Behold, I *am* the LORD, the R God of all flesh: R is there any thing too hard for me?

28 Therefore thus saith the LORD; Behold, R I will give this city into the hand of the Chăl-dē'-ăns, and into the hand of Nĕb-ū-chăd-rĕz'-zär king of Babylon, and he shall take it:

CHAP. **32**	
BC 590	
15 ver. 37, 43	
17 2 Ki. 19:15	
17 ver. 27	
Gen. 18:14	
Luke 1:37	
17 Or, *hid*	
from thee	
18 Ex. 20:6 & 34:7	
Deut. 5:9, 10	
18 Is. 9:6	
18 ch. 10:16	
19 Is. 28:29	
19 Heb. *doing*	
19 Job 34:21	
Ps. 33:13	
Prov. 5:21	
19 ch. 17:10	
20 Ex. 9:16	
1 Chr. 17:21	
Is. 63:12	
Dan. 9:15	
21 Ex. 6:6	
2 Sam. 7:23	
1 Chr. 17:21	
Ps. 136:11, 12	
22 Ex. 3:8, 17	
ch. 11:5	
23 Neh. 9:26	
ch. 11:8	
Dan. 9:10-14	
24 Or, *engines of*	
shot, ch. 33:4	
24 ver. 25, 36	
24 ch. 14:12	
25 Or, *though*	
25 ver. 24	
27 Num. 16:22	
27 ver. 17	
28 ver. 3	
ch. 21:10	29
& 37:8, 10	
ch. 19:13	29
ch. 2:7 & 3:25	30
& 7:22-26	
Ezek. 20:28	
Heb. *for*	31
my anger	
2 Ki. 24:3	31
Is. 1:4, 6	32
Dan. 9:8	
ch. 2:27 & 7:24	33
Heb. *neck*	33
ch. 7:13	33
ch. 23:11	34
Ezek. 8:5, 6	
ch. 7:31 & 19:5	35
Lev. 18:21	35
1 Ki. 11:33	
ch. 7:31	35
ver. 24	36
Deut. 30:3	37
ch. 23:3 & 29:14	
Ezek. 37:21	
ch. 33:16	37
ch. 24:7	38
& 30:22	
& 31:33	
ch. 24:7	39
Ezek. 11:19	
Heb. *all days*	39
Is. 55:3	40
ch. 31:31	
Heb. *from*	40
after them	
ch. 31:33	40
Deut. 30:9	41
Zeph. 3:17	
ch. 24:6 & 31:28	41
Amos 9:15	
Heb. *in truth,*	41
or, stability	

29 And the Chăl-dē'-ăns, that fight against this city, shall come and R set fire on this city, and burn it with the houses, R upon whose roofs they have offered incense unto Bā'-ăl, and poured out drink offerings unto other gods, to provoke me to anger.

30 For the children of Israel and the children of Judah R have only done evil before me from their youth: for the children of Israel have only provoked me to anger with the work of their hands, saith the LORD.

31 For this city hath been to me *as* N a provocation of mine anger and of my fury from the day that they built it even unto this day; R that I should remove it from before my face,

32 Because of all the evil of the children of Israel and of the children of Judah, which they have done to provoke me to anger, R they, their kings, their princes, their priests, and their prophets, and the men of Judah, and the inhabitants of Jerusalem.

33 And they have turned unto me the R back, N and not the face: though I taught them, R rising up early and teaching *them*, yet they have not hearkened to receive instruction.

34 But they R set their abominations in the house, which is called by my name, to defile it.

35 And they built the high places of Bā'-ăl, which *are* in the valley of the son of Hĭn'-nŏm, to R cause their sons and their daughters to pass through *the fire* unto R Molech; R which I commanded them not, neither came it into my mind, that they should do this abomination, to cause Judah to sin.

36 And now therefore thus saith the LORD, the God of Israel, concerning this city, whereof ye say, R It shall be delivered into the hand of the king of Babylon by the sword, and by the famine, and by the pestilence;

37 Behold, I will R gather them out of all countries, whither I have driven them in mine anger, and in my fury, and in great wrath; and I will bring them again unto this place, and I will cause them R to dwell safely:

38 And they shall be R my people, and I will be their God:

39 And I will R give them one heart, and one way, that they may fear me N for ever, for the good of them, and of their children after them:

40 And R I will make an everlasting covenant with them, that I will not turn away N from them, to do them good; but R I will put my fear in their hearts, that they shall not depart from me.

41 Yea, R I will rejoice over them to do them good, and R I will plant them in this land N assuredly with my whole heart and with my whole soul.

42 For thus saith the LORD; [R]Like as I have brought all this great evil upon this people, so will I bring upon them all the good that I have promised them.

43 And [R]fields shall be bought in this land, [R]whereof ye say, *It is* desolate without man or beast; it is given into the hand of the Chăl-dē'-ăns.

44 Men shall buy fields for money, and subscribe evidences, and seal *them,* and take witnesses in [R]the land of Benjamin, and in the places about Jerusalem, and in the cities of Judah, and in the cities of the mountains, and in the cities of the valley, and in the cities of the south: for [R]I will cause their captivity to return, saith the LORD.

CHAPTER 33

Restoration of Judah foretold

MOREOVER the word of the LORD came unto Jeremiah the second time, while he was yet [R]shut up in the court of the prison, saying,

2 Thus saith the LORD the [R]maker thereof, the LORD that formed it, to establish it; [R]the[N] LORD *is* his name;

3 [R]Call unto me, and I will answer thee, and shew thee great and [N]mighty things, which thou knowest not.

4 For thus saith the LORD, the God of Israel, concerning the houses of this city, and concerning the houses of the kings of Judah, which are thrown down by [R]the mounts, and by the sword;

5 [R]They come to fight with the Chăl-dē'-ăns, but *it is* to fill them with the dead bodies of men, whom I have slain in mine anger and in my fury, and for all whose wickedness I have hid my face from this city.

6 Behold, [R]I will bring it health and cure, and I will cure them, and will reveal unto them the abundance of peace and truth.

7 And [R]I will cause the captivity of Judah and the captivity of Israel to return, and will build them, [R]as at the first.

8 And I will [R]cleanse them from all their iniquity, whereby they have sinned against me; and I will [R]pardon all their iniquities, whereby they have sinned, and whereby they have transgressed against me.

9 [R]And it shall be to me a name of joy, a praise and an honour before all the nations of the earth, which shall hear all the good that I do unto them: and they shall [R]fear and tremble for all the goodness and for all the prosperity that I procure unto it.

CHAP. **32**
BC 590
42 ch. 31:28
43 ver. 15
43 ch. 33:10
44 ch. 17:26
44 ch. 33:7, 11

CHAP. **33**
BC 590
1 ch. 32:2, 3
2 Is. 37:26
2 Ex. 15:3
Amos 5:8 & 9:6
2 Or, *JEHOVAH*
3 Ps. 91:15
ch. 29:12
3 Or, *hidden,*
Is. 48:6
4 ch. 32:24
5 ch. 32:5
6 ch. 30:17
7 ch. 30:3 & 32:44
7 Is. 1:26
ch. 24:6 & 30:20
& 31:4, 28 & 42:10
8 Ezek. 36:25
Zech. 13:1
Heb. 9:13, 14
8 ch. 31:34
Mic. 7:18
9 Is. 62:7
ch. 13:11
9 Is. 60:5

ch. 32:43	10
ch. 7:34 & 16:9	11
& 25:10	
Rev. 18:23	
1 Chr. 16:8	11
2 Chr. 5:13	
Ezra 3:11	
Ps. 136:1	
Is. 12:4	
Lev. 7:12	11
Ps. 107:22	
& 116:17	
ver. 7	11
Is. 65:10	12
ch. 31:24 & 50:19	
ch. 17:26	13
& 32:44	
Lev. 27:32	13
ch. 23:5	14
& 31:27, 31	
ch. 29:10	14
Is. 4:2 & 11:1	15
ch. 23:5	
Heb. *Jehovah-*	16
tsidkenu	
Heb. *There shall*	17
not be cut	
off from David	
2 Sam. 7:16	17
1 Ki. 2:4	
Ps. 89:29	
Luke 1:32	
Rom. 12:1	18
& 15:16	
1 Pet. 2:5, 9	
Rev. 1:6	
ver. 25	20
Ps. 89:37	
Is. 54:9	
ch. 31:36	
Ps. 89:34	21
Gen. 15:5	22

10 Thus saith the LORD; Again there shall be heard in this place, [R]which ye say *shall be* desolate without man and without beast, *even* in the cities of Judah, and in the streets of Jerusalem, that are desolate, without man, and without inhabitant, and without beast,

11 The [R]voice of joy, and the voice of gladness, the voice of the bridegroom, and the voice of the bride, the voice of them that shall say, [R]Praise the LORD of hosts: for the LORD *is* good; for his mercy *endureth* for ever: *and* of them that shall bring [R]the sacrifice of praise into the house of the LORD. For [R]I will cause to return the captivity of the land, as at the first, saith the LORD.

12 Thus saith the LORD of hosts; [R]Again in this place, which is desolate without man and without beast, and in all the cities thereof, shall be an habitation of shepherds causing *their* flocks to lie down.

13 [R]In the cities of the mountains, in the cities of the vale, and in the cities of the south, and in the land of Benjamin, and in the places about Jerusalem, and in the cities of Judah, shall the flocks [R]pass again under the hands of him that telleth *them,* saith the LORD.

Promises to David to be honoured

14 [R]Behold, the days come, saith the LORD, that [R]I will perform that good thing which I have promised unto the house of Israel and to the house of Judah.

15 In those days, and at that time, will I cause the [R]Branch of righteousness to grow up unto David; and he shall execute judgment and righteousness in the land.   ★

16 In those days shall Judah be saved, and Jerusalem shall dwell safely: and this *is the name* wherewith she shall be called, [N]The LORD our righteousness.   ★

17 For thus saith the LORD; [N]David shall never [R]want a man to sit upon the throne of the house of Israel;

18 Neither shall the priests the Levites want a man before me to [R]offer burnt offerings, and to kindle meat offerings, and to do sacrifice continually.

19 And the word of the LORD came unto Jeremiah, saying,

20 Thus saith the LORD; [R]If ye can break my covenant of the day, and my covenant of the night, and that there should not be day and night in their season;

21 *Then* may also [R]my covenant be broken with David my servant, that he should not have a son to reign upon his throne; and with the Levites the priests, my ministers.

22 As [R]the host of heaven cannot be num-

bered, neither the sand of the sea measured: so will I multiply the seed of David my servant, and the Levites that minister unto me.

23 Moreover the word of the LORD came to Jeremiah, saying,

24 Considerest thou not what this people have spoken, saying, ^RThe two families which the LORD hath chosen, he hath even cast them off? thus they have despised my people, that they should be no more a nation before them.

25 Thus saith the LORD; If ^Rmy covenant *be* not with day and night, *and if* I have not ^Rappointed the ordinances of heaven and earth;

26 ^RThen will I cast away the seed of Jacob, and David my servant, *so* that I will not take *any* of his seed *to be* rulers over the seed of Abraham, Isaac, and Jacob: for ^RI will cause their captivity to return, and have mercy on them.

CHAPTER 34

Jeremiah warns Zedekiah

THE word which came unto Jeremiah from the LORD, ^Rwhen Nĕb-ū-chăd-nĕz′-zär king of Babylon, and all his army, and ^Rall the kingdoms of the earth ^Nof his dominion, and all the people, fought against Jerusalem, and against all the cities thereof, saying,

2 Thus saith the LORD, the God of Israel; Go and speak to Zĕd-ē-kī′-ăh king of Judah, and tell him, Thus saith the LORD; Behold, ^RI will give this city into the hand of the king of Babylon, and ^Rhe shall burn it with fire:

3 And ^Rthou shalt not escape out of his hand, but shalt surely be taken, and delivered into his hand; and thine eyes shall behold the eyes of the king of Babylon, and ^Nhe shall speak with thee mouth to mouth, and thou shalt go to Babylon.

4 Yet hear the word of the LORD, O Zĕd-ē-kī′-ăh king of Judah; Thus saith the LORD of thee, Thou shalt not die by the sword:

5 *But* thou shalt die in peace: and with ^Rthe burnings of thy fathers, the former kings which were before thee, ^Rso shall they burn *odours* for thee; and ^Rthey will lament thee, *saying,* Ah lord! for I have pronounced the word, saith the LORD.

6 Then Jeremiah the prophet spake all these words unto Zĕd-ē-kī′-ăh king of Judah in Jerusalem,

7 When the king of Babylon's army fought against Jerusalem, and against all the cities of Judah that were left, against Lā′-chĭsh, and against Ă-zē′-kăh: for ^Rthese defenced cities remained of the cities of Judah.

CHAP. **33**
BC 590
23 ver. 21, 22
25 ver. 20
Gen. 8:22
25 Ps. 74:16
& 104:19
ch. 31:35, 36
26 ch. 31:37
26 ver. 7, 11
Ezra 2:1

CHAP. **34**
BC 591
1 2 Ki. 25:1
ch. 39:1 & 52:4
1 ch. 1:15
1 Heb. *the dominion of his hand*
2 ch. 21:10
& 32:3, 28
2 ver. 22
ch. 32:29
3 ch. 32:4
3 Heb. *his mouth shall speak to thy mouth*
5 2 Chr. 16:14
& 21:19
5 Dan. 2:46
5 See ch. 22:18
7 2 Ki. 18:13
& 19:8
2 Chr. 11:5, 9

ver. 14	8
Ex. 21:2	
Lev. 25:10	
Neh. 5:11	9
Lev. 25:39-46	9
See ver. 21	11
ch. 37:5	
Ex. 21:2 & 23:10	14
Deut. 15:12	
Or, *hath sold himself*	14
Heb. *to day*	15
2 Ki. 23:3	15
Neh. 10:29	
ch. 7:10	15
Heb. *whereupon my name is called*	15
Ex. 20:7	16
Lev. 19:12	
Mat. 7:2	17
Gal. 6:7	
Jas. 2:13	
ch. 32:24, 36	17
Heb. *for a removing*	17
Deut. 28:25, 64	17
ch. 29:18	
See Gen. 15:10, 17	18

Proclamation of liberty broken

8 *This is* the word that came unto Jeremiah from the LORD, after that the king Zĕd-ē-kī′-ăh had made a covenant with all the people which *were* at Jerusalem, to proclaim ^Rliberty unto them;

9 ^RThat every man should let his manservant, and every man his maidservant, *being* an Hebrew or an Hebrewess, go free; ^Rthat none should serve himself of them, *to wit,* of a Jew his brother.

10 Now when all the princes, and all the people, which had entered into the covenant, heard that every one should let his manservant, and every one his maidservant, go free, that none should serve themselves of them any more, then they obeyed, and let *them* go.

11 But ^Rafterward they turned, and caused the servants and the handmaids, whom they had let go free, to return, and brought them into subjection for servants and for handmaids.

12 Therefore the word of the LORD came to Jeremiah from the LORD, saying,

13 Thus saith the LORD, the God of Israel; I made a covenant with your fathers in the day that I brought them forth out of the land of Egypt, out of the house of bondmen, saying,

14 At the end of ^Rseven years let ye go every man his brother an Hebrew, which ^Nhath been sold unto thee; and when he hath served thee six years, thou shalt let him go free from thee: but your fathers hearkened not unto me, neither inclined their ear.

15 And ye were ^Nnow turned, and had done right in my sight, in proclaiming liberty every man to his neighbour; and ye had ^Rmade a covenant before me ^Rin the house ^Nwhich is called by my name:

16 But ye turned and ^Rpolluted my name, and caused every man his servant, and every man his handmaid, whom ye had set at liberty at their pleasure, to return, and brought them into subjection, to be unto you for servants and for handmaids.

17 Therefore thus saith the LORD; Ye have not hearkened unto me, in proclaiming liberty, every one to his brother, and every man to his neighbour: ^Rbehold, I proclaim a liberty for you, saith the LORD, ^Rto the sword, to the pestilence, and to the famine; and I will make you ^Nto be ^Rremoved into all the kingdoms of the earth.

18 And I will give the men that have transgressed my covenant, which have not performed the words of the covenant which they had made before me, when ^Rthey cut the calf in twain, and passed between the parts thereof,

19 The princes of Judah, and the princes of Jerusalem, the eunuchs, and the priests, and all the people of the land, which passed between the parts of the calf;

20 I will even give them into the hand of their enemies, and into the hand of them that seek their life: and their ᴿdead bodies shall be for meat unto the fowls of the heaven, and to the beasts of the earth.

21 And Zĕd-ē-kī′-ăh king of Judah and his princes will I give into the hand of their enemies, and into the hand of them that seek their life, and into the hand of the king of Babylon's army, ᴿwhich are gone up from you.

22 ᴿBehold, I will command, saith the LORD, and cause them to return to this city; and they shall fight against it, ᴿand take it, and burn it with fire: and ᴿI will make the cities of Judah a desolation without an inhabitant.

CHAPTER 35

The faithful Rechabites

THE word which came unto Jeremiah from the LORD in the days of Jĕ-hoî′-ă-kĭm the son of Jō-sī′-ăh king of Judah, saying,

2 Go unto the house of the ᴿRē′-chăb-ītes, and speak unto them, and bring them into the house of the LORD, into one of ᴿthe chambers, and give them wine to drink.

3 Then I took Jā-ăz-ă-nī′-ăh the son of Jeremiah, the son of Hă-băz-ĭ-nī′-ăh, and his brethren, and all his sons, and the whole house of the Rē′-chăb-ītes;

4 And I brought them into the house of the LORD, into the chamber of the sons of Hā′-năn, the son of Ĭg-dă-lī′-ăh, a man of God, which was by the chamber of the princes, which was above the chamber of Mā-ă-sē̂i′-ăh the son of Shăl′-lŭm, ᴿthe keeper of the ᴺdoor:

5 And I set before the sons of the house of the Rē′-chăb-ītes pots full of wine, and cups, and I said unto them, Drink ye wine.

6 But they said, We will drink no wine: for ᴿJŏn′-ă-dăb the son of Rē′-chăb our father commanded us, saying, Ye shall drink no wine, neither ye, nor your sons for ever:

7 Neither shall ye build house, nor sow seed, nor plant vineyard, nor have any: but all your days ye shall dwell in tents; ᴿthat ye may live many days in the land where ye be strangers.

8 Thus have we obeyed the voice of Jŏn′-ă-dăb the son of Rē′-chăb our father in all that he hath charged us, to drink no wine all our days, we, our wives, our sons, nor our daughters;

9 Nor to build houses for us to dwell in: neither have we vineyard, nor field, nor seed:

10 But we have dwelt in tents, and have

obeyed, and done according to all that Jŏn′-ă-dăb our father commanded us.

11 But it came to pass, when Nĕb-ū-chăd-rĕz′-zär king of Babylon came up into the land, that we said, Come, and let us go to Jerusalem for fear of the army of the Chăl-dē′-ăns, and for fear of the army of the Syrians: so we dwell at Jerusalem.

Unfaithful Judah

12 Then came the word of the LORD unto Jeremiah, saying,

13 Thus saith the LORD of hosts, the God of Israel; Go and tell the men of Judah and the inhabitants of Jerusalem, Will ye not ᴿreceive instruction to hearken to my words? saith the LORD.

14 The words of Jŏn′-ă-dăb the son of Rē′-chăb, that he commanded his sons not to drink wine, are performed; for unto this day they drink none, but obey their father's commandment: ᴿnotwithstanding I have spoken unto you, ᴿrising early and speaking; but ye hearkened not unto me.

15 I have sent also unto you all my servants the prophets, rising up early and sending them, saying, ᴿReturn ye now every man from his evil way, and amend your doings, and go not after other gods to serve them, and ye shall dwell in the land which I have given to you and to your fathers: but ye have not inclined your ear, nor hearkened unto me.

16 Because the sons of Jŏn′-ă-dăb the son of Rē′-chăb have performed the commandment of their father, which he commanded them; but this people hath not hearkened unto me:

17 Therefore thus saith the LORD God of hosts, the God of Israel; Behold, I will bring upon Judah and upon all the inhabitants of Jerusalem all the evil that I have pronounced against them: ᴿbecause I have spoken unto them, but they have not heard; and I have called unto them, but they have not answered.

18 And Jeremiah said unto the house of the Rē′-chăb-ītes, Thus saith the LORD of hosts, the God of Israel; Because ye have obeyed the commandment of Jŏn′-ă-dăb your father, and kept all his precepts, and done according unto all that he hath commanded you:

19 Therefore thus saith the LORD of hosts, the God of Israel; ᴺJŏn′-ă-dăb the son of Rē′-chăb shall not want a man to ᴿstand before me for ever.

CHAPTER 36

Baruch transcribes Jeremiah's prophecy

AND it came to pass in the fourth year of Jĕ-hoî′-ă-kĭm the son of Jō-sī′-ăh king of

Judah, *that* this word came unto Jeremiah from the Lord, saying,

2 Take thee a ^Rroll of a book, and ^Rwrite therein all the words that I have spoken unto thee against Israel, and against Judah, and against ^Rall the nations, from the day I spake unto thee, from the days of ^RJō-sī′-ăh, even unto this day.

3 ^RIt may be that the house of Judah will hear all the evil which I purpose to do unto them; that they may ^Rreturn every man from his evil way; that I may forgive their iniquity and their sin.

4 Then Jeremiah ^Rcalled Bâr′-ŭch the son of Nē-rī′-ăh: and ^RBâr′-ŭch wrote from the mouth of Jeremiah all the words of the Lord, which he had spoken unto him, upon a roll of a book.

5 And Jeremiah commanded Bâr′-ŭch, saying, I *am* shut up; I cannot go into the house of the Lord:

6 Therefore go thou, and read in the roll, which thou hast written from my mouth, the words of the Lord in the ears of the people in the Lord's house upon ^Rthe fasting day: and also thou shalt read them in the ears of all Judah that come out of their cities.

7 ^RIt may be ^Nthey will present their supplication before the Lord, and will return every one from his evil way: for great *is* the anger and the fury that the Lord hath pronounced against this people.

8 And Bâr′-ŭch the son of Nē-rī′-ăh did according to all that Jeremiah the prophet commanded him, reading in the book the words of the Lord in the Lord's house.

Baruch reads the roll

9 And it came to pass in the fifth year of Jĕ-hoi′-ă-kĭm the son of Jō-sī′-ăh king of Judah, in the ninth month, *that* they proclaimed a fast before the Lord to all the people in Jerusalem, and to all the people that came from the cities of Judah unto Jerusalem.

10 Then read Bâr′-ŭch in the book the words of Jeremiah in the house of the Lord, in the chamber of Gĕm-ă-rī′-ăh the son of Shā′-phăn the scribe, in the higher court, at the ^Rentry^N of the new gate of the Lord's house, in the ears of all the people.

11 When Mī-chāi′-ăh the son of Gĕm-ă-rī′-ăh, the son of Shā′-phăn, had heard out of the book all the words of the Lord,

12 Then he went down into the king's house, into the scribe's chamber: and, lo, all the princes sat there, *even* Ē-lī′-shă-mă the scribe, and Dĕl-āi′-ăh the son of Shĕm-āi′-ăh, and ĕl-nā′-thăn the son of Ăch′-bôr, and Gĕm-ă-rī′-ăh the son of Shā′-phăn, and Zĕd-

CHAP. 36
BC 607
2 Is. 8:1
Ezek. 2:9
Zech. 5:1
2 ch. 30:2
2 ch. 25:15, etc.
2 ch. 25:3
3 ver. 7
ch. 26:3
3 ch. 18:8
Jonah 3:8
4 ch. 32:12
4 See ch. 45:1
6 Lev. 16:29
& 23:27-32
Acts 27:9
7 ver. 3
7 Heb. *their supplications shall fall*
10 ch. 26:10
10 Or, *door*

ē-kī′-ăh the son of Hăn-ă-nī′-ăh, and all the princes.

13 Then Mī-chāi′-ăh declared unto them all the words that he had heard, when Bâr′-ŭch read the book in the ears of the people.

14 Therefore all the princes sent Jĕ-hū′-dī the son of Nĕth-ă-nī′-ăh, the son of Shĕl-ē-mī′-ăh, the son of Cū′-shī, unto Bâr′-ŭch, saying, Take in thine hand the roll wherein thou hast read in the ears of the people, and come. So Bâr′-ŭch the son of Nē-rī′-ăh took the roll in his hand, and came unto them.

15 And they said unto him, Sit down now, and read it in our ears. So Bâr′-ŭch read *it* in their ears.

16 Now it came to pass, when they had heard all the words, they were afraid both one and other, and said unto Bâr′-ŭch, We will surely tell the king of all these words.

17 And they asked Bâr′-ŭch, saying, Tell us now, How didst thou write all these words at his mouth?

18 Then Bâr′-ŭch answered them, He pronounced all these words unto me with his mouth, and I wrote *them* with ink in the book.

19 Then said the princes unto Bâr′-ŭch, Go, hide thee, thou and Jeremiah; and let no man know where ye be.

The king burns the roll

20 And they went in to the king into the court, but they laid up the roll in the chamber of Ē-lī′-shă-mă the scribe, and told all the words in the ears of the king.

21 So the king sent Jĕ-hū′-dī to fetch the roll: and he took it out of Ē-lī′-shă-mă the scribe's chamber. And Jĕ-hū′-dī read it in the ears of the king, and in the ears of all the princes which stood beside the king.

22 Now the king sat in ^Rthe winterhouse in the ninth month: and *there was a fire* on the hearth burning before him.

23 And it came to pass, *that* when Jĕ-hū′-dī had read three or four leaves, he cut it with the penknife, and cast *it* into the fire that *was* on the hearth, until all the roll was consumed in the fire that *was* on the hearth.

24 Yet they were not afraid, nor ^Rrent their garments, *neither* the king, nor any of his servants that heard all these words.

25 Nevertheless ĕl-nā′-thăn and Dĕl-āi′-ăh and Gĕm-ă-rī′-ăh had made intercession to the king that he would not burn the roll: but he would not hear them.

26 But the king commanded Jĕ-răh′-mēĕl the son ^Nof Hăm′-mĕ-lĕch, and Sĕ-rāi′-ăh the son of Ăz′-rī-ĕl, and Shĕl-ē-mī′-ăh the son of Ăb′-dēĕl, to take Bâr′-ŭch the scribe and

See Amos 3:15 22
2 Ki. 22:11 24
Is. 36:22
& 37:1
Or, *of the king* 26

Jeremiah the prophet: but the LORD hid them.

27 Then the word of the LORD came to Jeremiah, after that the king had burned the roll, and the words which Bâr'-ŭch wrote at the mouth of Jeremiah, saying,

28 Take thee again another roll, and write in it all the former words that were in the first roll, which Jĕ-hoi'-ă-kĭm the king of Judah hath burned.

29 And thou shalt say to Jĕ-hoi'-ă-kĭm king of Judah, Thus saith the LORD; Thou hast burned this roll, saying, Why hast thou written therein, saying, The king of Babylon shall certainly come and destroy this land, and shall cause to cease from thence man and beast?

30 Therefore thus saith the LORD of Jĕ-hoi'-ă-kĭm king of Judah; ᴿHe shall have none to sit upon the throne of David: and his dead body shall be ᴿcast out in the day to the heat, and in the night to the frost.

31 And I will ᴺpunish him and his seed and his servants for their iniquity; and I will bring upon them, and upon the inhabitants of Jerusalem, and upon the men of Judah, all the evil that I have pronounced against them; but they hearkened not.

The second roll prepared

32 Then took Jeremiah another roll, and gave it to Bâr'-ŭch the scribe, the son of Nē-rī'-ăh; who wrote therein from the mouth of Jeremiah all the words of the book which Jĕ-hoi'-ă-kĭm king of Judah had burned in the fire: and there were added besides unto them many ᴺlike words.

CHAPTER 37

Retreat of the Chaldeans

AND king ᴿZĕd-ē-kī'-ăh the son of Jō-sī'-ăh reigned instead of Cō-nī'-ăh the son of Jĕ-hoi'-ă-kĭm, whom Nĕb-ū-chăd-rĕz'-zär king of Babylon made king in the land of Judah.

2 ᴿBut neither he, nor his servants, nor the people of the land, did hearken unto the words of the LORD, which he spake ᴺby the prophet Jeremiah.

3 And Zĕd-ē-kī'-ăh the king sent Jĕ-hū'-căl the son of Shĕl-ē-mī'-ăh and ᴿZĕph-ă-nī'-ăh the son of Mā-ă-sêī'-ăh the priest to the prophet Jeremiah, saying, Pray now unto the LORD our God for us.

4 Now Jeremiah came in and went out among the people: for they had not put him into prison.

5 Then ᴿPharaoh's army was come forth out of Egypt: ᴿand when the Chăl-dē'-ăns that besieged Jerusalem heard tidings of them, they departed from Jerusalem.

CHAP. 36
BC 607
30 ch. 22:30
30 ch. 22:19
31 Heb. visit upon, ch. 23:34
32 Heb. as they

CHAP. 37
BC 590
1 2 Ki. 24:17
2 Chr. 36:10
ch. 22:24
2 2 Chr. 36:12, 14
2 Heb. by the hand of the prophet
3 ch. 21:1, 2 & 29:25 & 52:24
5 See 2 Ki. 24:7
Ezek. 17:15
5 ver. 11
ch. 34:21

ch. 21:2   7
ch. 34:22   8
Heb. souls   9
ch. 21:4, 5   10
Heb. thrust through   10
ver. 5   11
Heb. made to ascend   11
Or, to slip away from thence in the midst of the people   12
Heb. falsehood, or, a lie   14
ch. 38:26   15
ch. 38:6   16
Or, cells   16
Heb. let my supplication fall   20

6 Then came the word of the LORD unto the prophet Jeremiah, saying,

7 Thus saith the LORD, the God of Israel; Thus shall ye say to the king of Judah, ᴿthat sent you unto me to inquire of me; Behold, Pharaoh's army, which is come forth to help you, shall return to Egypt into their own land.

8 ᴿAnd the Chăl-dē'-ăns shall come again, and fight against this city, and take it, and burn it with fire.

9 Thus saith the LORD; Deceive not ᴺyourselves, saying, The Chăl-dē'-ăns shall surely depart from us: for they shall not depart.

10 ᴿFor though ye had smitten the whole army of the Chăl-dē'-ăns that fight against you, and there remained but ᴺwounded men among them, yet should they rise up every man in his tent, and burn this city with fire.

Jeremiah imprisoned

11 ᴿAnd it came to pass, that when the army of the Chăl-dē'-ăns was ᴺbroken up from Jerusalem for fear of Pharaoh's army,

12 Then Jeremiah went forth out of Jerusalem to go into the land of Benjamin, ᴺto separate himself thence in the midst of the people.

13 And when he was in the gate of Benjamin, a captain of the ward was there, whose name was ī-rī'-jăh, the son of Shĕl-ē-mī'-ăh, the son of Hăn-ă-nī'-ăh; and he took Jeremiah the prophet, saying, Thou fallest away to the Chăl-dē'-ăns.

14 Then said Jeremiah, It is ᴺfalse; I fall not away to the Chăl-dē'-ăns. But he hearkened not to him: so ī-rī'-jăh took Jeremiah, and brought him to the princes.

15 Wherefore the princes were wroth with Jeremiah, and smote him, ᴿand put him in prison in the house of Jonathan the scribe: for they had made that the prison.

16 When Jeremiah was entered into ᴿthe dungeon, and into the ᴺcabins, and Jeremiah had remained there many days;

17 Then Zĕd-ē-kī'-ăh the king sent, and took him out: and the king asked him secretly in his house, and said, Is there any word from the LORD? And Jeremiah said, There is: for, said he, thou shalt be delivered into the hand of the king of Babylon.

18 Moreover Jeremiah said unto king Zĕd-ē-kī'-ăh, What have I offended against thee, or against thy servants, or against this people, that ye have put me in prison?

19 Where are now your prophets which prophesied unto you, saying, The king of Babylon shall not come against you, nor against this land?

20 Therefore hear now, I pray thee, O my lord the king: ᴺlet my supplication, I pray

thee, be accepted before thee; that thou cause me not to return to the house of Jonathan the scribe, lest I die there.

21 Then Zĕd-e-kī'-ăh the king commanded that they should commit Jeremiah ᴿinto the court of the prison, and that they should give him daily a piece of bread out of the bakers' street, ᴿuntil all the bread in the city were spent. Thus Jeremiah remained in the court of the prison.

CHAPTER 38

Jeremiah rescued from starvation

THEN Shĕph-ă-tī'-ăh the son of Măt'-tăn, and Gĕd-ă-lī'-ăh the son of Păsh'-ŭr, and ᴿJû'-căl the son of Shĕl-e-mī'-ăh, and ᴿPăsh'-ŭr the son of Măl-chī'-ăh, ᴿheard the words that Jeremiah had spoken unto all the people, saying,

2 Thus saith the LORD, ᴿHe that remaineth in this city shall die by the sword, by the famine, and by the pestilence: but he that goeth forth to the Chăl-dē'-ăns shall live; for he shall have his life for a prey, and shall live.

3 Thus saith the LORD, ᴿThis city shall surely be given into the hand of the king of Babylon's army, which shall take it.

4 Therefore the princes said unto the king, We beseech thee, ᴿlet this man be put to death: for thus he weakeneth the hands of the men of war that remain in this city, and the hands of all the people, in speaking such words unto them: for this man seeketh not the ᴺwelfare of this people, but the hurt.

5 Then Zĕd-e-kī'-ăh the king said, Behold, he *is* in your hand: for the king *is* not *he that* can do *any* thing against you..

6 ᴿThen took they Jeremiah, and cast him into the dungeon of Măl-chī'-ăh the son ᴺof Hăm'-mĕ-lĕch, that *was* in the court of the prison: and they let down Jeremiah with cords. And in the dungeon *there was* no water, but mire: so Jeremiah sunk in the mire.

7 ᴿNow when E'-bĕd-mĕl'-ĕch the E-thi-ō'-pī-ăn, one of the eunuchs which was in the king's house, heard that they had put Jeremiah in the dungeon; the king then sitting in the gate of Benjamin;

8 E'-bĕd-mĕl'-ĕch went forth out of the king's house, and spake to the king, saying,

9 My lord the king, these men have done evil in all that they have done to Jeremiah the prophet, whom they have cast into the dungeon; and ᴺhe is like to die for hunger in the place where he is: for *there is* no more bread in the city.

10 Then the king commanded E'-bĕd-mĕl'-

ĕch the E-thi-ō'-pī-ăn, saying, Take from hence thirty men ᴺwith thee, and take up Jeremiah the prophet out of the dungeon, before he die.

11 So E'-bĕd-mĕl'-ĕch took the men with him, and went into the house of the king under the treasury, and took thence old cast clouts and old rotten rags, and let them down by cords into the dungeon to Jeremiah.

12 And E'-bĕd-mĕl'-ĕch the E-thi-ō'-pī-ăn said unto Jeremiah, Put now *these* old cast clouts and rotten rags under thine armholes under the cords. And Jeremiah did so.

13 ᴿSo they drew up Jeremiah with cords, and took him up out of the dungeon: and Jeremiah remained ᴿin the court of the prison.

The king's audience with Jeremiah

14 Then Zĕd-e-kī'-ăh the king sent, and took Jeremiah the prophet unto him into the ᴺthird entry that *is* in the house of the LORD: and the king said unto Jeremiah, I will ask thee a thing; hide nothing from me.

15 Then Jeremiah said unto Zĕd-e-kī'-ăh, If I declare *it* unto thee, wilt thou not surely put me to death? and if I give thee counsel, wilt thou not hearken unto me?

16 So Zĕd-e-kī'-ăh the king sware secretly unto Jeremiah, saying, *As* the LORD liveth, ᴿthat made us this soul, I will not put thee to death, neither will I give thee into the hand of these men that seek thy life.

17 Then said Jeremiah unto Zĕd-e-kī'-ăh, Thus saith the LORD, the God of hosts, the God of Israel; If thou wilt assuredly ᴿgo forth ᴿunto the king of Babylon's princes, then thy soul shall live, and this city shall not be burned with fire; and thou shalt live, and thine house:

18 But if thou wilt not go forth to the king of Babylon's princes, then shall this city be given into the hand of the Chăl-dē'-ăns, and they shall burn it with fire, and ᴿthou shalt not escape out of their hand.

19 And Zĕd-e-kī'-ăh the king said unto Jeremiah, I am afraid of the Jews that are fallen to the Chăl-dē'-ăns, lest they deliver me into their hand, and they ᴿmock me.

20 But Jeremiah said, They shall not deliver *thee.* Obey, I beseech thee, the voice of the LORD, which I speak unto thee: so it shall be well unto thee, and thy soul shall live.

21 But if thou refuse to go forth, this *is* the word that the LORD hath shewed me:

22 And, behold, all the women that are left in the king of Judah's house *shall be* brought forth to the king of Babylon's princes, and those *women* shall say, ᴺThy friends have set thee on, and have prevailed against thee: thy

feet are sunk in the mire, *and* they are turned away back.

23 So they shall bring out all thy wives and ᴿthy children to the Chăl-dē'-ăns: and thou shalt not escape out of their hand, but shalt be taken by the hand of the king of Babylon: and ᴺthou shalt cause this city to be burned with fire.

24 Then said Zĕd-ē-kī'-ăh unto Jeremiah, Let no man know of these words, and thou shalt not die.

25 But if the princes hear that I have talked with thee, and they come unto thee, and say unto thee, Declare unto us now what thou hast said unto the king, hide it not from us, and we will not put thee to death; also what the king said unto thee:

26 Then thou shalt say unto them, ᴿI presented my supplication before the king, that he would not cause me to return ᴿto Jonathan's house, to die there.

27 Then came all the princes unto Jeremiah, and asked him: and he told them according to all these words that the king had commanded. So ᴺthey left off speaking with him; for the matter was not perceived.

28 So ᴿJeremiah abode in the court of the prison until the day that Jerusalem was taken: and he was *there* when Jerusalem was taken.

CHAPTER 39

Jerusalem's fall and Zedekiah's fate

IN the ᴿninth year of Zĕd-ē-kī'-ăh king of Judah, in the tenth month, came Nĕb-ū-chăd-rĕz'-zär king of Babylon and all his army against Jerusalem, and they besieged it.

2 *And* in the eleventh year of Zĕd-ē-kī'-ăh, in the fourth month, the ninth *day* of the month, the city was broken up.

3 ᴿAnd all the princes of the king of Babylon came in, and sat in the middle gate, *even* Nĕr'-găl-shă-rē'-zĕr, Săm'-gär-nē'-bō, Sär'-sĕ-chīm, Răb'-să-rīs, Nĕr'-găl-shă-rē'-zĕr, Rabmag, with all the residue of the princes of the king of Babylon.

4 ᴿAnd it came to pass, *that* when Zĕd-ē-kī'-ăh the king of Judah saw them, and all the men of war, then they fled, and went forth out of the city by night, by the way of the king's garden, by the gate betwixt the two walls: and he went out the way of the plain.

5 But the Chăl-dē'-ăns' army pursued after them, and ᴿovertook Zĕd-ē-kī'-ăh in the plains of Jericho: and when they had taken him, they brought him up to Nĕb-ū-chăd-nĕz'-zär king of Babylon to ᴿRĭb'-läh in the land of Hā'-măth, where he ᴺgave judgment upon him.

6 Then the king of Babylon slew the sons of

Zĕd-ē-kī'-ăh in Rĭb'-läh before his eyes: also the king of Babylon slew all the nobles of Judah.

7 Moreover ᴿhe put out Zĕd-ē-kī'-ăh's eyes, and bound him ᴺwith chains, to carry him to Babylon.

8 ᴿAnd the Chăl-dē'-ăns burned the king's house, and the houses of the people, with fire, and brake down the walls of Jerusalem.

9 ᴿThen Nĕb-ū'-zär-ăd'-ăn the ᴺᴺcaptain of the guard carried away captive into Babylon the remnant of the people that remained in the city, and those that fell away, that fell to him, with the rest of the people that remained.

10 But Nĕb-ū'-zär-ăd'-ăn the captain of the guard left of the poor of the people, which had nothing, in the land of Judah, and gave them vineyards and fields ᴺat the same time.

Nebuchadrezzar's treatment of Jeremiah

11 Now Nĕb-ū-chăd-rĕz'-zär king of Babylon gave charge concerning Jeremiah ᴺto Nĕb-ū'-zär-ăd'-ăn the captain of the guard, saying,

12 Take him, and ᴺlook well to him, and do him no harm; but do unto him even as he shall say unto thee.

13 So Nĕb-ū'-zär-ăd'-ăn the captain of the guard sent, and Nĕb-ū-shăs'-băn, Răb'-să-rīs, and Nĕr'-găl-shă-rē'-zĕr, Rabmag, and all the king of Babylon's princes;

14 Even they sent, ᴿand took Jeremiah out of the court of the prison, and committed him ᴿunto Gĕd-ă-lī'-ăh the son of ᴿĂ-hī'-kăm the son of Shā'-phăn, that he should carry him home: so he dwelt among the people.

15 Now the word of the LORD came unto Jeremiah, while he was shut up in the court of the prison, saying,

16 Go and speak to ᴿĒ'-bĕd-mĕl'-ĕch the Ē-thī-ō'-pī-ăn, saying, Thus saith the LORD of hosts, the God of Israel; Behold, ᴿI will bring my words upon this city for evil, and not for good; and they shall be *accomplished* in that day before thee.

17 But I will deliver thee in that day, saith the LORD: and thou shalt not be given into the hand of the men of whom thou *art* afraid.

18 For I will surely deliver thee, and thou shalt not fall by the sword, but ᴿthy life shall be for a prey unto thee: ᴿbecause thou hast put thy trust in me, saith the LORD.

CHAPTER 40

Jeremiah stays in Judah

THE word that came to Jeremiah from the LORD, ᴿafter that Nĕb-ū'-zär-ăd'-ăn the captain of the guard had let him go from Rā'-

măh, when he had taken him being bound in ᴺchains among all that were carried away captive of Jerusalem and Judah, which were carried away captive unto Babylon.

2 And the captain of the guard took Jeremiah, and ᴿsaid unto him, The Lᴏʀᴅ thy God hath pronounced this evil upon this place.

3 Now the Lᴏʀᴅ hath brought *it,* and done according as he hath said: ᴿbecause ye have sinned against the Lᴏʀᴅ, and have not obeyed his voice, therefore this thing is come upon you.

4 And now, behold, I loose thee this day from the chains which ᴺ*were* upon thine hand. ᴿIf it seem good unto thee to come with me into Babylon, come; and ᴺI will look well unto thee: but if it seem ill unto thee to come with me into Babylon, forbear: behold, ᴿall the land *is* before thee: whither it seemeth good and convenient for thee to go, thither go.

5 Now while he was not yet gone back, *he said,* Go back also to Gĕd-å-lī′-åh the son of Å-hī′-kăm the son of Shā′-phăn, ᴿwhom the king of Babylon hath made governor over the cities of Judah, and dwell with him among the people: or go wheresoever it seemeth convenient unto thee to go. So the captain of the guard gave him victuals and a reward, and let him go.

6 ᴿThen went Jeremiah unto Gĕd-å-lī′-åh the son of Å-hī′-kăm to ᴿMizpah; and dwelt with him among the people that were left in the land.

Gedaliah made governor

7 ᴿNow when all the captains of the forces which *were* in the fields, *even* they and their men, heard that the king of Babylon had made Gĕd-å-lī′-åh the son of Å-hī′-kăm governor in the land, and had committed unto him men, and women, and children, and of ᴿthe poor of the land, of them that were not carried away captive to Babylon;

8 Then they came to Gĕd-å-lī′-åh to Mizpah, ᴿeven ĭsh′-mā-ĕl the son of Nĕth-å-nī′-åh, and Jō-hā′-năn and Jonathan the sons of Kā-rē′-åh, and Sĕ-rāī′-åh the son of Tăn-hū′-mĕth, and the sons of Ē′-phāī the Nĕ-tŏph′-å-thīte, and Jĕz-å-nī′-åh the son of a Mā-ă<u>ch</u>′-å-thīte, they and their men.

9 And Gĕd-å-lī′-åh the son of Å-hī′-kăm the son of Shā′-phăn sware unto them and to their men, saying, Fear not ᴺto serve the <u>Ch</u>ăl-dē′-ăns: dwell in the land, and serve the king of Babylon, and it shall be well with you.

10 As for me, behold, I will dwell at Mizpah to serve the <u>Ch</u>ăl-dē′-ăns, which will come unto us: but ye, gather ye wine, and summer fruits, and oil, and put *them* in your vessels,

CHAP. **40**

BC 588

1 Or, *manicles*
2 ch. 50:7
3 Deut. 29:24, 25
Dan. 9:11
4 Or, *are upon thine hand*
4 ch. 39:12
4 Heb. *I will set mine eye upon thee*
4 Gen. 20:15
5 See ch. 41:10
6 ch. 39:14
6 Judg. 20:1
7 2 Ki. 25:23, etc.
7 ch. 39:10
8 ch. 41:1
9 Heb. *to stand before:* and ver. 10
Deut. 1:38

See ch. 41:10   **14**
Heb. *to strike thee in soul?*   **14**

CHAP. **41**

BC 588

2 Ki. 25:25   **1**
ch. 40:6, 8
2 Ki. 25:25   **2**

and dwell in your cities that ye have taken.

11 Likewise when all the Jews that *were* in Moab, and among the Ammonites, and in Ē′-dŏm, and that *were* in all the countries, heard that the king of Babylon had left a remnant of Judah, and that he had set over them Gĕd-å-lī′-åh the son of Å-hī′-kăm the son of Shā′-phăn;

12 Even all the Jews returned out of all places whither they were driven, and came to the land of Judah, to Gĕd-å-lī′-åh, unto Mizpah, and gathered wine and summer fruits very much.

Plot against Gedaliah's life

13 Moreover Jō-hā′-năn the son of Kā-rē′-åh, and all the captains of the forces that *were* in the fields, came to Gĕd-å-lī′-åh to Mizpah,

14 And said unto him, Dost thou certainly know that ᴿBā′-å-lĭs the king of the Ammonites hath sent ĭsh′-mā-ĕl the son of Nĕth-å-nī′-åh ᴺto slay thee? But Gĕd-å-lī′-åh the son of Å-hī′-kăm believed them not.

15 Then Jō-hā′-năn the son of Kā-rē′-åh spake to Gĕd-å-lī′-åh in Mizpah secretly, saying, Let me go, I pray thee, and I will slay ĭsh′-mā-ĕl the son of Nĕth-å-nī′-åh, and no man shall know *it:* wherefore should he slay thee, that all the Jews which are gathered unto thee should be scattered, and the remnant in Judah perish?

16 But Gĕd-å-lī′-åh the son of Å-hī′-kăm said unto Jō-hā′-năn the son of Kā-rē′-åh, Thou shalt not do this thing: for thou speakest falsely of ĭsh′-mā-ĕl.

CHAPTER 41

NOW it came to pass in the seventh month, ᴿ*that* ĭsh′-mā-ĕl the son of Nĕth-å-nī′-åh the son of Ē-lī′-shå-mă, of the seed royal, and the princes of the king, even ten men with him, came unto Gĕd-å-lī′-åh the son of Å-hī′-kăm to Mizpah; and there they did eat bread together in Mizpah.

2 Then arose ĭsh′-mā-ĕl the son of Nĕth-å-nī′-åh, and the ten men that were with him, and ᴿsmote Gĕd-å-lī′-åh the son of Å-hī′-kăm the son of Shā′-phăn with the sword, and slew him, whom the king of Babylon had made governor over the land.

3 ĭsh′-mā-ĕl also slew all the Jews that were with him, *even* with Gĕd-å-lī′-åh, at Mizpah, and the <u>Ch</u>ăl-dē′-ăns that were found there, *and* the men of war.

Johanan rescues the people of Mizpah

4 And it came to pass the second day after he had slain Gĕd-å-lī′-åh, and no man knew *it,*

5 That there came certain from Shē'-chĕm, from Shī'-lōh, and from Să-mâr'-ĭ-ă, *even* fourscore men, ᴿhaving their beards shaven, and their clothes rent, and having cut themselves, with offerings and incense in their hand, to bring *them* to ᴿthe house of the LORD.

6 And ĭsh'-mā-ĕl the son of Nĕth-ă-nī'-ăh went forth from Mizpah to meet them, ᴺweeping all along as he went: and it came to pass, as he met them, he said unto them, Come to Gĕd-ă-lī'-ăh the son of Ă-hī'-kăm.

7 And it was *so,* when they came into the midst of the city, that ĭsh'-mā-ĕl the son of Nĕth-ă-nī'-ăh slew them, *and cast them* into the midst of the pit, he, and the men that *were* with him.

8 But ten men were found among them that said unto ĭsh'-mā-ĕl, Slay us not: for we have treasures in the field, of wheat, and of barley, and of oil, and of honey. So he forbare, and slew them not among their brethren.

9 Now the pit wherein ĭsh'-mā-ĕl had cast all the dead bodies of the men, whom he had slain ᴺᴺbecause of Gĕd-ă-lī'-ăh, *was it* ᴿwhich Ā'-să the king had made for fear of Bā-ash'-ă king of Israel: *and* ĭsh'-mā-ĕl the son of Nĕth-ă-nī'-ăh filled it with *them that were* slain.

10 Then ĭsh'-mā-ĕl carried away captive all the residue of the people that *were* in Mizpah, ᴿ*even* the king's daughters, and all the people that remained in Mizpah, ᴿwhom Nĕb-ū'-zär-ăd'-ăn the captain of the guard had committed to Gĕd-ă-lī'-ăh the son of Ă-hī'-kăm: and ĭsh'-mā-ĕl the son of Nĕth-ă-nī'-ăh carried them away captive, and departed to go over to ᴿthe Ammonites.

11 But when Jō-hā'-năn the son of Kă-rē'-ăh, and all ᴿthe captains of the forces that *were* with him, heard of all the evil that ĭsh'-mā-ĕl the son of Nĕth-ă-nī'-ăh had done,

12 Then they took all the men, and went to fight with ĭsh'-mā-ĕl the son of Nĕth-ă-nī'-ăh, and found him by ᴿthe great waters that *are* in Gibeon.

13 Now it came to pass, *that* when all the people which *were* with ĭsh'-mā-ĕl saw Jō-hā'-năn the son of Kă-rē'-ăh, and all the captains of the forces that *were* with him, then they were glad.

14 So all the people that ĭsh'-mā-ĕl had carried away captive from Mizpah cast about and returned, and went unto Jō-hā'-năn the son of Kă-rē'-ăh.

15 But ĭsh'-mā-ĕl the son of Nĕth-ă-nī'-ăh escaped from Jō-hā'-năn with eight men, and went to the Ammonites.

16 Then took Jō-hā'-năn the son of Kă-rē'-ăh, and all the captains of the forces

that *were* with him, all the remnant of the people whom he had recovered from ĭsh'-mā-ĕl the son of Nĕth-ă-nī'-ăh, from Mizpah, after *that* he had slain Gĕd-ă-lī'-ăh the son of Ă-hī'-kăm, *even* mighty men of war, and the women, and the children, and the eunuchs, whom he had brought again from Gibeon:

17 And they departed, and dwelt in the habitation of ᴿChĭm'-hăm, which is by Beth-le-hem, to go to enter into Egypt,

18 Because of the Chăl-dē'-ăns: for they were afraid of them, because ĭsh'-mā-ĕl the son of Nĕth-ă-nī'-ăh had slain Gĕd-ă-lī'-ăh the son of Ă-hī'-kăm, ᴿwhom the king of Babylon made governor in the land.

CHAPTER 42

Jeremiah counsels against flight

THEN all the captains of the forces, ᴿand Jō-hā'-năn the son of Kă-rē'-ăh, and Jĕz-ă-nī'-ăh the son of Hō-shāi'-ăh, and all the people from the least even unto the greatest, came near,

2 And said unto Jeremiah the prophet, ᴺLet, we beseech thee, our supplication be accepted before thee, and ᴿpray for us unto the LORD thy God, *even* for all this remnant; (for we are left *but* ᴿa few of many, as thine eyes do behold us:)

3 That the LORD thy God may shew us ᴿthe way wherein we may walk, and the thing that we may do.

4 Then Jeremiah the prophet said unto them, I have heard *you;* behold, I will pray unto the LORD your God according to your words; and it shall come to pass, *that* ᴿwhatsoever thing the LORD shall answer you, I will declare *it* unto you; I will ᴿkeep nothing back from you.

5 Then they said to Jeremiah, ᴿThe LORD be a true and faithful witness between us, if we do not even according to all things for the which the LORD thy God shall send thee to us.

6 Whether *it be* good, or whether *it be* evil, we will obey the voice of the LORD our God, to whom we send thee; ᴿthat it may be well with us, when we obey the voice of the LORD our God.

7 And it came to pass after ten days, that the word of the LORD came unto Jeremiah.

8 Then called he Jō-hā'-năn the son of Kă-rē'-ăh, and all the captains of the forces which *were* with him, and all the people from the least even to the greatest,

9 And said unto them, Thus saith the LORD, the God of Israel, unto whom ye sent me to present your supplication before him;

CHAP. 41
BC 588
5 Lev. 19:27, 28
Deut. 14:1
Is. 15:2
5 See 1 Sam. 1:7
2 Ki. 25:9
6 Heb. *in going and weeping*
9 Or, *near Gedaliah*
9 Heb. *by the hand, or, by the side of Gedaliah*
9 1 Ki. 15:22
2 Chr. 16:6
10 ch. 43:6
10 ch. 40:7
10 ch. 40:14
11 ch. 40:7, 8, 13
12 2 Sam. 2:13

2 Sam. 19:37, 38 17
ch. 40:5   18

CHAP. 42
BC 588
ch. 40:8, 13
& 41:11   1
Or, *Let our supplication fall before thee* 2
1 Sam. 7:8
& 12:19   2
Is. 37:4
Jas. 5:16
Lev. 26:22   2
Ezra 8:21   3
1 Ki. 22:14   4
1 Sam. 3:18   4
Acts 20:20
Gen. 31:50   5
Deut. 6:3   6
ch. 7:23

10 If ye will still abide in this land, then ᴿwill I build you, and not pull *you* down, and I will plant you, and not pluck *you* up: for I ᴿrepent me of the evil that I have done unto you.

11 Be not afraid of the king of Babylon, of whom ye are afraid; be not afraid of him, saith the Lᴏʀᴅ: ᴿfor I *am* with you to save you, and to deliver you from his hand.

12 And ᴿI will shew mercies unto you, that he may have mercy upon you, and cause you to return to your own land.

13 But if ᴿye say, We will not dwell in this land, neither obey the voice of the Lᴏʀᴅ your God,

14 Saying, No; but we will go into the land of Egypt, where we shall see no war, nor hear the sound of the trumpet, nor have hunger of bread; and there will we dwell:

15 And now therefore hear the word of the Lᴏʀᴅ, ye remnant of Judah; Thus saith the Lᴏʀᴅ of hosts, the God of Israel; If ye ᴿwholly set ᴿyour faces to enter into Egypt, and go to sojourn there;

16 Then it shall come to pass, *that* the sword, which ye feared, shall overtake you there in the land of Egypt, and the famine, whereof ye were afraid, ᴺshall follow close after you there in Egypt; and there ye shall die.

17 ᴺSo shall it be with all the men that set their faces to go into Egypt to sojourn there; they shall die ᴿby the sword, by the famine, and by the pestilence: and ᴿnone of them shall remain or escape from the evil that I will bring upon them.

18 For thus saith the Lᴏʀᴅ of hosts, the God of Israel; As mine anger and my fury hath been ᴿpoured forth upon the inhabitants of Jerusalem; so shall my fury be poured forth upon you, when ye shall enter into Egypt: and ᴿye shall be an execration, and an astonishment, and a curse, and a reproach; and ye shall see this place no more.

19 The Lᴏʀᴅ hath said concerning you, O ye remnant of Judah; ᴿGo ye not into Egypt: know certainly that I have ᴺadmonished you this day.

20 For ᴺye dissembled in your hearts, when ye sent me unto the Lᴏʀᴅ your God, saying, Pray for us unto the Lᴏʀᴅ our God; and according unto all that the Lᴏʀᴅ our God shall say, so declare unto us, and we will do *it*.

21 And *now* I have this day declared *it* to you; but ye have not obeyed the voice of the Lᴏʀᴅ your God, nor any *thing* for the which he hath sent me unto you.

22 Now therefore know certainly that ᴿye shall die by the sword, by the famine, and by

the pestilence, in the place whither ye desire ᴺto go *and* to sojourn.

CHAPTER 43

The remnant flees to Egypt

AND it came to pass, *that* when Jeremiah had made an end of speaking unto all the people all the words of the Lᴏʀᴅ their God, for which the Lᴏʀᴅ their God had sent him to them, *even* all these words,

2 ᴿThen spake ăz-ă-rī´-ăh the son of Hō-shăī´-ăh, and Jō-hā´-năn the son of Kă-rē´-ăh, and all the proud men, saying unto Jeremiah, Thou speakest falsely: the Lᴏʀᴅ our God hath not sent thee to say, Go not into Egypt to sojourn there:

3 But Băr´-ŭch the son of Nē-rī´-ăh setteth thee on against us, for to deliver us into the hand of the Chăl-dē´-ăns, that they might put us to death, and carry us away captives into Babylon.

4 So Jō-hā´-năn the son of Kă-rē´-ăh, and all the captains of the forces, and all the people, obeyed not the voice of the Lᴏʀᴅ, to dwell in the land of Judah.

5 But Jō-hā´-năn the son of Kă-rē´-ăh, and all the captains of the forces, took ᴿall the remnant of Judah, that were returned from all nations, whither they had been driven, to dwell in the land of Judah;

6 *Even* men, and women, and children, ᴿand the king's daughters, ᴿand every person that Nĕb-ū´-zăr-ăd´-ăn the captain of the guard had left with Gĕd-ă-lī´-ăh the son of Ă-hī´-kăm the son of Shā´-phăn, and Jeremiah the prophet, and Băr´-ŭch the son of Nē-rī´-ăh.

7 So they came into the land of Egypt: for they obeyed not the voice of the Lᴏʀᴅ: thus came they *even* to ᴿTăh´-păn-hĕs̀.

8 Then came the word of the Lᴏʀᴅ unto Jeremiah in Tăh´-păn-hĕs̀, saying,

9 Take great stones in thine hand, and hide them in the clay in the brickkiln, which *is* at the entry of Pharaoh's house in Tăh´-păn-hĕs̀, in the sight of the men of Judah;

10 And say unto them, Thus saith the Lᴏʀᴅ of hosts, the God of Israel; Behold, I will send and take Nĕb-ū-chăd-rĕz´-zăr the king of Babylon, ᴿmy servant, and will set his throne upon these stones that I have hid; and he shall spread his royal pavilion over them.

11 ᴿAnd when he cometh, he shall smite the land of Egypt, *and deliver* ᴿsuch *as are* for death to death; and such *as are* for captivity to captivity; and such *as are* for the sword to the sword.

12 And I will kindle a fire in the houses of

Rthe gods of Egypt; and he shall burn them, and carry them away captives: and he shall array himself with the land of Egypt, as a shepherd putteth on his garment; and he shall go forth from thence in peace.

13 He shall break also the Nimages of NBĕth-shē′-mĕsh, that *is* in the land of Egypt; and the houses of the gods of the Egyptians shall he burn with fire.

CHAPTER 44

The remnant rebuked by Jeremiah

THE word that came to Jeremiah concerning all the Jews which dwell in the land of Egypt, which dwell at RMĭg′-dŏl, and at RTäh′-păn-hēs, and at RNŏph, and in the country of Păth′-rŏs, saying,

2 Thus saith the LORD of hosts, the God of Israel; Ye have seen all the evil that I have brought upon Jerusalem, and upon all the cities of Judah; and, behold, this day they *are* Ra desolation, and no man dwelleth therein,

3 Because of their wickedness which they have committed to provoke me to anger, in that they went Rto burn incense, *and* to Rserve other gods, whom they knew not, *neither* they, ye, nor your fathers.

4 Howbeit RI sent unto you all my servants the prophets, rising early and sending *them,* saying, Oh, do not this abominable thing that I hate.

5 But they hearkened not, nor inclined their ear to turn from their wickedness, to burn no incense unto other gods.

6 Wherefore my fury and mine anger was poured forth, and was kindled in the cities of Judah and in the streets of Jerusalem; and they are wasted *and* desolate, as at this day.

7 Therefore now thus saith the LORD, the God of hosts, the God of Israel; Wherefore commit ye *this* great evil Ragainst your souls, to cut off from you man and woman, child and suckling, Nout of Judah, to leave you none to remain;

8 In that ye Rprovoke me unto wrath with the works of your hands, burning incense unto other gods in the land of Egypt, whither ye be gone to dwell, that ye might cut yourselves off, and that ye might be Ra curse and a reproach among all the nations of the earth?

9 Have ye forgotten the Nwickedness of your fathers, and the wickedness of the kings of Judah, and the wickedness of their wives, and your own wickedness, and the wickedness of your wives, which they have committed in the

land of Judah, and in the streets of Jerusalem?

10 They are not Nhumbled *even* unto this day, neither have they Rfeared, nor walked in my law, nor in my statutes, that I set before you and before your fathers.

11 Therefore thus saith the LORD of hosts, the God of Israel; Behold, RI will set my face against you for evil, and to cut off all Judah.

12 And I will take the remnant of Judah, that have set their faces to go into the land of Egypt to sojourn there, and Rthey shall all be consumed, *and* fall in the land of Egypt; they shall *even* be consumed by the sword *and* by the famine: they shall die, from the least even unto the greatest, by the sword and by the famine: and Rthey shall be an execration, *and* an astonishment, and a curse, and a reproach.

13 RFor I will punish them that dwell in the land of Egypt, as I have punished Jerusalem, by the sword, by the famine, and by the pestilence:

14 So that none of the remnant of Judah, which are gone into the land of Egypt to sojourn there, shall escape or remain, that they should return into the land of Judah, to the which they Nhave a desire to return to dwell there: for Rnone shall return but such as shall escape.

Defiance of the people

15 Then all the men which knew that their wives had burned incense unto other gods, and all the women that stood by, a great multitude, even all the people that dwelt in the land of Egypt, in Păth′-rŏs, answered Jeremiah, saying,

16 *As for* the word that thou hast spoken unto us in the name of the LORD, Rwe will not hearken unto thee.

17 But we will certainly do Rwhatsoever thing goeth forth out of our own mouth, to burn incense unto the Rqueen N of heaven, and to pour out drink offerings unto her, as we have done, we, and our fathers, our kings, and our princes, in the cities of Judah, and in the streets of Jerusalem: for *then* had we plenty of Nvictuals, and were well, and saw no evil.

18 But since we left off to burn incense to the queen of heaven, and to pour out drink offerings unto her, we have wanted all *things,* and have been consumed by the sword and by the famine.

19 RAnd when we burned incense to the queen of heaven, and poured out drink offerings unto her, did we make her cakes to worship her, and pour out drink offerings unto her, without our Nmen?

CHAP. 43
BC 588
12 ch. 46:25
13 Heb. *statues,* or, *standing images*
13 Or, *The house of the sun*

CHAP. 44
BC 587
1 Ex. 14:2
ch. 46:14
1 ch. 43:7
1 Is. 19:13
2 ch. 9:11 & 34:22
3 ch. 19:4
3 Deut. 13:6 & 32:17
4 2 Chr. 36:15
ch. 7:25 & 25:4 & 26:5 & 29:19
7 Num. 16:38
ch. 7:19
7 Heb. *out of the midst of Judah*
8 ch. 25:6, 7
8 ver. 12
ch. 42:18
9 Heb. *wickednesses,* or, *punishments, etc.*

Heb. *contrite,* Ps. 51:17	10
Prov. 28:14	10
Lev. 17:10 & 20:5, 6	11
ch. 21:10	
Amos 9:4	
ch. 42:15-17, 22	12
ch. 42:18	12
ch. 43:11	13
Heb. *lift up their soul*	14
ver. 28	14
ch. 6:16	16
See ver. 25	17
Num. 30:12	
Deut. 23:23	
Judg. 11:36	
ch. 7:18	17
Or, *frame of heaven*	17
Heb. *bread*	17
ch. 7:18	19
Or, *husbands?*	19

Jeremiah prophesies punishment

20 Then Jeremiah said unto all the people, to the men, and to the women, and to all the people which had given him *that* answer, saying,

21 The incense that ye burned in the cities of Judah, and in the streets of Jerusalem, ye, and your fathers, your kings, and your princes, and the people of the land, did not the LORD remember them, and came it *not* into his mind?

22 So that the LORD could no longer bear, because of the evil of your doings, *and* because of the abominations which ye have committed; therefore is your land ᴿa desolation, and an astonishment, and a curse, without an inhabitant, ᴿas at this day.

23 Because ye have burned incense, and because ye have sinned against the LORD, and have not obeyed the voice of the LORD, nor walked in his law, nor in his statutes, nor in his testimonies; ᴿtherefore this evil is happened unto you, as at this day.

24 Moreover Jeremiah said unto all the people, and to all the women, Hear the word of the LORD, all Judah ᴿthat *are* in the land of Egypt:

25 Thus saith the LORD of hosts, the God of Israel, saying; ᴿYe and your wives have both spoken with your mouths, and fulfilled with your hand, saying, We will surely perform our vows that we have vowed, to burn incense to the queen of heaven, and to pour out drink offerings unto her: ye will surely accomplish your vows, and surely perform your vows.

26 Therefore hear ye the word of the LORD, all Judah that dwell in the land of Egypt; Behold, ᴿI have sworn by my great name, saith the LORD, that ᴿmy name shall no more be named in the mouth of any man of Judah in all the land of Egypt, saying, The Lord GOD liveth.

27 ᴿBehold, I will watch over them for evil, and not for good: and all the men of Judah that *are* in the land of Egypt ᴿshall be consumed by the sword and by the famine, until there be an end of them.

28 Yet ᴿa small number that escape the sword shall return out of the land of Egypt into the land of Judah, and all the remnant of Judah, that are gone into the land of Egypt to sojourn there, shall know whose ᴿwords shall stand, ᴺmine, or theirs.

29 And this *shall be* a sign unto you, saith the LORD, that I will punish you in this place, that ye may know that my words shall surely stand against you for evil:

30 Thus saith the LORD; Behold, ᴿI will give Phâr'-āōh-hŏph'-rǎ king of Egypt into the hand of his enemies, and into the hand of them that seek his life; as I gave ᴿZĕd-ē-kī'-ăh king of Judah into the hand of Nĕb-ū-chăd-rĕz'-zăr king of Babylon, his enemy, and that sought his life.

CHAPTER 45

Consolation for Baruch

THE ᴿword that Jeremiah the prophet spake unto Bâr'-ŭch the son of Nē-rī'-ăh, when he had written these words in a book at the mouth of Jeremiah, in the fourth year of Jĕhoî'-ă-kĭm the son of Jō-sī'-ăh king of Judah, saying,

2 Thus saith the LORD, the God of Israel, unto thee, O Bâr'-ŭch;

3 Thou didst say, Woe is me now! for the LORD hath added grief to my sorrow; I fainted in my sighing, and I find no rest.

4 Thus shalt thou say unto him, The LORD saith thus; Behold, ᴿ*that* which I have built will I break down, and that which I have planted I will pluck up, even this whole land.

5 And seekest thou great things for thyself? seek *them* not: for, behold, ᴿI will bring evil upon all flesh, saith the LORD: but thy life will I give unto thee ᴿfor a prey in all places whither thou goest.

CHAPTER 46

Prophecy concerning Egypt

THE word of the LORD which came to Jeremiah the prophet against ᴿthe Gentiles;

2 Against Egypt, ᴿagainst the army of Phâr'-āōh-nē'-chō king of Egypt, which was by the river ᴱu-phrā'-tēs in Cär-chē'-mĭsh, which Nĕb-ū-chăd-rĕz'-zăr king of Babylon smote in the fourth year of Jĕ-hoî'-ă-kĭm the son of Jō-sī'-ăh king of Judah.

3 ᴿOrder ye the buckler and shield, and draw near to battle.

4 Harness the horses; and get up, ye horsemen, and stand forth with *your* helmets; furbish the spears, *and* put on the brigandines.

5 Wherefore have I seen them dismayed *and* turned away back? and their mighty ones are ᴺbeaten down, and are ᴺfled apace, and look not back: *for* ᴿfear *was* round about, saith the LORD.

6 Let not the swift flee away, nor the mighty man escape; they shall ᴿstumble, and fall toward the north by the river ᴱu-phrā'-tēs.

7 Who *is* this *that* cometh up ᴿas a flood, whose waters are moved as the rivers?

8 Egypt riseth up like a flood, and *his* waters are moved like the rivers; and he saith, I will go up, *and* will cover the earth; I will destroy the city and the inhabitants thereof.

9 Come up, ye horses; and rage, ye chariots; and let the mighty men come forth; ᴺthe Ē-thĭ-ō'-pĭ-ăns and ᴺthe Lĭb'-y̆-ăns, that handle the shield; and the Ly̆d'-ĭ-ăns, ᴿthat handle *and* bend the bow.

10 For this *is* ᴿthe day of the Lord Gᴏᴅ of hosts, a day of vengeance, that he may avenge him of his adversaries: and ᴿthe sword shall devour, and it shall be satiate and made drunk with their blood: for the Lord Gᴏᴅ of hosts ᴿhath a sacrifice in the north country by the river Ēu-phrā'-tēś.

11 ᴿGo up into Gilead, and take balm, ᴿO virgin, the daughter of Egypt: in vain shalt thou use many medicines; *for* ᴿthouᴺ shalt not be cured.

12 The nations have heard of thy shame, and thy cry hath filled the land: for the mighty man hath stumbled against the mighty, *and* they are fallen both together.

13 The word that the Lᴏʀᴅ spake to Jeremiah the prophet, how Nĕb-ū-chăd-rĕz'-zär king of Babylon should come *and* ᴿsmite the land of Egypt.

14 Declare ye in Egypt, and publish in Mĭg'-dŏl, and publish in Nŏph and in Täh'-păn-hēś: say ye, ᴿStand fast, and prepare thee; for ᴿthe sword shall devour round about thee.

15 Why are thy valiant *men* swept away? they stood not, because the Lᴏʀᴅ did drive them.

16 He ᴺmade many to fall, yea, ᴿone fell upon another: and they said, Arise, and let us go again to our own people, and to the land of our nativity, from the oppressing sword.

17 They did cry there, Pharaoh king of Egypt *is but* a noise; he hath passed the time appointed.

18 *As* I live, saith the King, ᴿwhose name *is* the Lᴏʀᴅ of hosts, Surely as Tā'-bôr *is* among the mountains, and as Carmel by the sea, *so* shall he come.

19 O ᴿthou daughter dwelling in Egypt, ᴺfurnish thyself ᴿto go into captivity: for Nŏph shall be waste and desolate without an inhabitant.

20 Egypt *is like* a very fair ᴿheifer, *but* destruction cometh; it cometh ᴿout of the north.

21 Also her hired men *are* in the midst of her like ᴺfatted bullocks; for they also are turned back, *and* are fled away together: they

did not stand, because ᴿthe day of their calamity was come upon them, *and* the time of their visitation.

22 ᴿThe voice thereof shall go like a serpent; for they shall march with an army, and come against her with axes, as hewers of wood.

23 They shall ᴿcut down her forest, saith the Lᴏʀᴅ, though it cannot be searched; because they are more than ᴿthe grasshoppers, and *are* innumerable.

24 The daughter of Egypt shall be confounded; she shall be delivered into the hand of ᴿthe people of the north.

25 The Lᴏʀᴅ of hosts, the God of Israel, saith; Behold, I will punish the ᴺᴺmultitude of ᴿNo, and Pharaoh, and Egypt, ᴿwith their gods, and their kings; even Pharaoh, and *all* them that trust in him:

26 ᴿAnd I will deliver them into the hand of those that seek their lives, and into the hand of Nĕb-ū-chăd-rĕz'-zär king of Babylon, and into the hand of his servants: and ᴿafterward it shall be inhabited, as in the days of old, saith the Lᴏʀᴅ.

27 ᴿBut fear not thou, O my servant Jacob, and be not dismayed, O Israel: for, behold, I will save thee from afar off, and thy seed from the land of their captivity; and Jacob shall return, and be in rest and at ease, and none shall make *him* afraid.

28 Fear thou not, O Jacob my servant, saith the Lᴏʀᴅ: for I *am* with thee; for I will make a full end of all the nations whither I have driven thee: but I will not make ᴿa full end of thee, but correct thee in measure; yet will I ᴺnot leave thee wholly unpunished.

CHAPTER 47

Prophecy concerning Philistia

THE word of the Lᴏʀᴅ that came to Jeremiah the prophet ᴿagainst the Philistines, ᴿbefore that Pharaoh smote ᴺGā'-ză.

2 Thus saith the Lᴏʀᴅ; Behold, ᴿwaters rise up ᴿout of the north, and shall be an overflowing flood, and shall overflow the land, and ᴺall that is therein; the city, and them that dwell therein: then the men shall cry, and all the inhabitants of the land shall howl.

3 At the ᴿnoise of the stamping of the hoofs of his strong *horses,* at the rushing of his chariots, *and at* the rumbling of his wheels, the fathers shall not look back to *their* children for feebleness of hands;

4 Because of the day that cometh to spoil all the Philistines, *and* to cut off from ᴿTy̆'-rŭs and Zī'-dŏn every helper that remaineth: for

the LORD will spoil the Philistines, ^Rthe remnant of ^Nthe country of ^RCăph′-tôr.

5 ^RBaldness is come upon Gā′-ză; ^RĂsh′-kĕ-lon is cut off *with* the remnant of their valley: how long wilt thou cut thyself?

6 O thou ^Rsword of the LORD, how long *will it be* ere thou be quiet? ^Nput up thyself into thy scabbard, rest, and be still.

7 ^NHow can it be quiet, seeing the LORD hath ^Rgiven it a charge against Ăsh′-kĕ-lon, and against the sea shore? there hath he ^Rappointed it.

CHAPTER 48

Prophecy concerning Moab

AGAINST ^RMoab thus saith the LORD of hosts, the God of Israel; Woe unto ^RNē′-bō! for it is spoiled: ^RKĭr-ĭ-ă-thā′-ĭm is confounded *and* taken: ^NMĭs′-găb is confounded and dismayed.

2 ^R*There shall be* no more praise of Moab: in ^RHĕsh′-bŏn they have devised evil against it; come, and let us cut it off from *being* a nation. Also thou shalt ^Nbe cut down, O Măd′-mĕn; the sword shall ^Npursue thee.

3 A voice of crying *shall be* from Hŏr-ō-nā′-ĭm, spoiling and great destruction.

4 Moab is destroyed; her little ones have caused a cry to be heard.

5 ^RFor in the going up of Lū′-hĭth ^Ncontinual weeping shall go up; for in the going down of Hŏr-ō-nā′-ĭm the enemies have heard a cry of destruction.

6 Flee, save your lives, and be like ^Nthe ^Rheath in the wilderness.

7 For because thou hast trusted in thy works and in thy treasures, thou shalt also be taken: and ^RChē′-mŏsh shall go forth into captivity *with* his ^Rpriests and his princes together.

8 And ^Rthe spoiler shall come upon every city, and no city shall escape: the valley also shall perish, and the plain shall be destroyed, as the LORD hath spoken.

9 ^RGive wings unto Moab, that it may flee and get away: for the cities thereof shall be desolate, without any to dwell therein.

10 ^RCursed *be* he that doeth the work of the LORD ^Ndeceitfully, and cursed *be* he that keepeth back his sword from blood.

11 Moab hath been at ease from his youth, and he ^Rhath settled on his lees, and hath not been emptied from vessel to vessel, neither hath he gone into captivity: therefore his taste ^Nremained in him, and his scent is not changed.

12 Therefore, behold, the days come, saith

	CHAP. 47	
	BC 600	
4	Ezek. 25:16	
4	Heb. *the isle*	
4	Gen. 10:14	
5	Mic. 1:16	
5	ch. 25:20	
6	Ezek. 21:3	
6	Heb. *gather thyself*	
7	Heb. *How canst thou*	
7	Ezek. 14:17	
7	Mic. 6:9	

	CHAP. 48	
	BC 600	
1	Is. 15, & 16	
1	Is. 15:2	
1	Num. 32:37	
1	Or, *The high place*	
2	Is. 16:14	
2	Is. 15:4	
2	Or, *be brought to silence*, Is. 15:1	
2	Heb. *go after thee*	
5	Is. 15:5	
5	Heb. *weeping with weeping*	
6	Or, *a naked tree*	
6	ch. 17:6	
7	Num. 21:29 Judg. 11:24 Is. 46:1, 2	
7	ch. 49:3	
8	ch. 6:26	
9	Ps. 55:6	
10	Judg. 5:23 1 Sam. 15:3 1 Ki. 20:42	
10	Or, *negligently*	
11	Zeph. 1:12	
11	Heb. *stood*	

1 Ki. 11:7		13
Hos. 10:6		13
1 Ki. 12:29		13
Is. 16:6		14
ver. 8, 9, 18		15
Heb. *the choice of*		15
ch. 50:27		15
ch. 46:18		15
Is. 9:4 & 14:4, 5		17
Is. 47:1		18
Num. 21:30		18
Is. 15:2		
ver. 8		18
Heb. *inhabitress*		19
Deut. 2:36		19
1 Sam. 4:13		19
Is. 16:7		20
Num. 21:13		20
ver. 8		21
Amos 2:2		24
Ps. 75:10		25
Ezek. 30:21		25
ch. 25:15		26
Zeph. 2:8		27
ch. 2:26		27
Or, *movedst thyself*		27
Ps. 55:6, 7		28
S. of S. 2:14		28
Is. 16:6, etc.		29
Is. 16:6		30
ch. 50:36		30
Or, *those on whom he stayeth* (Heb. *his bars*) *do not right*		30
Is. 15:5		31

the LORD, that I will send unto him wanderers, that shall cause him to wander, and shall empty his vessels, and break their bottles.

13 And Moab shall be ashamed of ^RChē′-mŏsh, as the house of Israel ^Rwas ashamed of ^RBeth-el their confidence.

14 How say ye, ^RWe *are* mighty and strong men for the war?

15 ^RMoab is spoiled, and gone up *out of* her cities, and ^Nhis chosen young men are ^Rgone down to the slaughter, saith ^Rthe King, whose name *is* the LORD of hosts.

16 The calamity of Moab *is* near to come, and his affliction hasteth fast.

17 All ye that are about him, bemoan him; and all ye that know his name, say, ^RHow is the strong staff broken, *and* the beautiful rod!

18 ^RThou daughter that dost inhabit ^RDī′-bŏn, come down from *thy* glory, and sit in thirst; for ^Rthe spoiler of Moab shall come upon thee, *and* he shall destroy thy strong holds.

19 O ^Ninhabitant of ^RĂ-rō′-ĕr, ^Rstand by the way, and espy; ask him that fleeth, and her that escapeth, *and* say, What is done?

20 Moab is confounded; for it is broken down: ^Rhowl and cry; tell ye it in ^RArnon, that Moab is spoiled,

21 And judgment is come upon ^Rthe plain country; upon Hō′-lŏn, and upon Jā-hā′-zăh, and upon Mĕph′-ā-ăth,

22 And upon Dī′-bŏn, and upon Nē′-bō, and upon Bĕth-dĭb-lă-thā′-ĭm,

23 And upon Kĭr-ĭ-ă-thā′-ĭm, and upon Bĕth-găm′-ŭl, and upon Bĕth-mē′-ŏn,

24 And upon ^RKĕr′-ĭ-ōth, and upon Bŏz′-răh, and upon all the cities of the land of Moab, far or near.

25 ^RThe horn of Moab is cut off, and his ^Rarm is broken, saith the LORD.

26 ^RMake ye him drunken: for he magnified *himself* against the LORD: Moab also shall wallow in his vomit, and he also shall be in derision.

27 For ^Rwas not Israel a derision unto thee? ^Rwas he found among thieves? for since thou spakest of him, thou ^Nskippedst for joy.

28 O ye that dwell in Moab, leave the cities, and ^Rdwell in the rock, and be like ^Rthe dove *that* maketh her nest in the sides of the hole's mouth.

29 We have heard the ^Rpride of Moab, (he is exceeding proud) his loftiness, and his arrogancy, and his pride, and the haughtiness of his heart.

30 I know his wrath, saith the LORD; but *it* shall not *be* so; ^Rhis^N lies shall not so effect *it*.

31 Therefore ^Rwill I howl for Moab, and I

will cry out for all Moab; *mine heart* shall mourn for the men of Kĭr-hē'-rĕś.

32 ᴿO vine of Sĭb'-mäh, I will weep for thee with the weeping of Jā'-zĕr: thy plants are gone over the sea, they reach *even* to the sea of Jā'-zĕr: the spoiler is fallen upon thy summer fruits and upon thy vintage.

33 And ᴿjoy and gladness is taken from the plentiful field, and from the land of Moab; and I have caused wine to fail from the winepresses: none shall tread with shouting; *their* shouting *shall be* no shouting.

34 ᴿFrom the cry of Hĕsh'-bŏn *even* unto Ĕl-ĕ-ā'-lĕh, *and even* unto Jā'-hăz, have they uttered their voice, ᴿfrom Zō'-är *even* unto Hŏr-ō-nā'-ĭm, *as* an heifer of three years old: for the waters also of Nimrim shall be ᴺdesolate.

35 Moreover I will cause to cease in Moab, saith the Lᴏʀᴅ, ᴿhim that offereth in the high places, and him that burneth incense to his gods.

36 Therefore ᴿmine heart shall sound for Moab like pipes, and mine heart shall sound like pipes for the men of Kĭr-hē'-rĕś: because ᴿthe riches *that* he hath gotten are perished.

37 For ᴿevery head *shall be* bald, and every beard ᴺclipped: upon all the hands *shall be* cuttings, and ᴿupon the loins sackcloth.

38 *There shall be* lamentation generally upon all the housetops of Moab, and in the streets thereof: for I have broken Moab like ᴿa vessel wherein *is* no pleasure, saith the Lᴏʀᴅ.

39 They shall howl, *saying,* How is it broken down! how hath Moab turned the ᴺback with shame! so shall Moab be a derision and a dismaying to all them about him.

40 For thus saith the Lᴏʀᴅ; Behold, ᴿhe shall fly as an eagle, and shall ᴿspread his wings over Moab.

41 ᴿKĕr'-ĭ-ŏthᴺ is taken, and the strong holds are surprised, and ᴿthe mighty men's hearts in Moab at that day shall be as the heart of a woman in her pangs.

42 And Moab shall be destroyed ᴿfrom *being* a people, because he hath magnified *himself* against the Lᴏʀᴅ.

43 ᴿFear, and the pit, and the snare, *shall be* upon thee, O inhabitant of Moab, saith the Lᴏʀᴅ.

44 He that fleeth from the fear shall fall into the pit; and he that getteth up out of the pit shall be taken in the snare: for ᴿI will bring upon it, *even* upon Moab, the year of their visitation, saith the Lᴏʀᴅ.

45 They that fled stood under the shadow of Hĕsh'-bŏn because of the force: but ᴿa fire shall come forth out of Hĕsh'-bŏn, and a flame

from the midst of Sī'-hŏn, and ᴿshall devour the corner of Moab, and the crown of the head of the ᴺtumultuous ones.

46 ᴿWoe be unto thee, O Moab! the people of Chē'-mŏsh perisheth: for thy sons are taken ᴺcaptives, and thy daughters captives.

47 Yet will I bring again the captivity of Moab ᴿin the latter days, saith the Lᴏʀᴅ. Thus far *is* the judgment of Moab.

CHAPTER 49

Prophecy concerning Ammon

CONCERNINGᴺ ᴿthe Ammonites, thus saith the Lᴏʀᴅ; Hath Israel no sons? hath he no heir? why *then* doth ᴺtheir king inherit ᴿGad, and his people dwell in his cities?

2 Therefore, behold, the days come, saith the Lᴏʀᴅ, that I will cause an alarm of war to be heard in ᴿRăb'-băh of the Ammonites; and it shall be a desolate heap, and her daughters shall be burned with fire: then shall Israel be heir unto them that were his heirs, saith the Lᴏʀᴅ.

3 Howl, O Hĕsh'-bŏn, for Ā'-ī is spoiled: cry, ye daughters of Răb'-băh, ᴿgird you with sackcloth; lament, and run to and fro by the hedges; for ᴺtheir king shall go into captivity, *and* his ᴿpriests and his princes together.

4 Wherefore gloriest thou in the valleys, ᴺthy flowing valley, O ᴿbacksliding daughter? that trusted in her treasures, ᴿ*saying,* Who shall come unto me?

5 Behold, I will bring a fear upon thee, saith the Lord Gᴏᴅ of hosts, from all those that be about thee; and ye shall be driven out every man right forth; and none shall gather up him that wandereth.

6 And ᴿafterward I will bring again the captivity of the children of Ammon, saith the Lᴏʀᴅ.

Prophecy concerning Edom

7 ᴿConcerning Ē'-dŏm, thus saith the Lᴏʀᴅ of hosts; ᴿ*Is* wisdom no more in Tē'-măn? ᴿis counsel perished from the prudent? is their wisdom vanished?

8 ᴿFlee ye, ᴺturn back, dwell deep, O inhabitants of ᴿDē'-dăn; for I will bring the calamity of Esau upon him, the time *that* I will visit him.

9 If ᴿgrapegatherers come to thee, would they not leave *some* gleaning grapes? if thieves by night, they will destroy ᴺtill they have enough.

10 ᴿBut I have made Esau bare, I have un-

covered his secret places, and he shall not be able to hide himself: his seed is spoiled, and his brethren, and his neighbours, and ᴿhe *is* not.

11 Leave thy fatherless children, I will preserve *them* alive; and let thy widows trust in me.

12 For thus saith the LORD; Behold, ᴿthey whose judgment *was* not to drink of the cup have assuredly drunken; and *art* thou he *that* shall altogether go unpunished? thou shalt not go unpunished, but thou shalt surely drink *of it*.

13 For ᴿI have sworn by myself, saith the LORD, that ᴿBŏz′-răh shall become a desolation, a reproach, a waste, and a curse; and all the cities thereof shall be perpetual wastes.

14 I have heard a ᴿrumour from the LORD, and an ambassador is sent unto the heathen, *saying,* Gather ye together, and come against her, and rise up to the battle.

15 For, lo, I will make thee small among the heathen, *and* despised among men.

16 Thy terribleness hath deceived thee, *and* the pride of thine heart, O thou that dwellest in the clefts of the rock, that holdest the height of the hill: ᴿthough thou shouldest make thy ᴿnest as high as the eagle, ᴿI will bring thee down from thence, saith the LORD.

17 Also Ē′-dǫm shall be a desolation: ᴿevery one that goeth by it shall be astonished, and shall hiss at all the plagues thereof.

18 ᴿAs in the overthrow of Sodom and Gō-mŏr′-răh and the neighbour *cities* thereof, saith the LORD, no man shall abide there, neither shall a son of man dwell in it.

19 ᴿBehold, he shall come up like a lion from ᴿthe swelling of Jordan against the habitation of the strong: but I will suddenly make him run away from her: and who *is* a chosen *man, that* I may appoint over her? for ᴿwho *is* like me? and who will ᴺappoint me the time? and ᴿwho *is* that shepherd that will stand before me?

20 ᴿTherefore hear the counsel of the LORD, that he hath taken against Ē′-dǫm; and his purposes, that he hath purposed against the inhabitants of Tē′-măn: Surely the least of the flock shall draw them out: surely he shall make their habitations desolate with them.

21 ᴿThe earth is moved at the noise of their fall, at the cry the noise thereof was heard in the ᴺRed sea.

22 Behold, ᴿhe shall come up and fly as the eagle, and spread his wings over Bŏz′-răh: and at that day shall the heart of the mighty men of Ē′-dǫm be as the heart of a woman in her pangs.

Prophecy concerning Damascus

23 ᴿConcerning Damascus. Hā′-măth is confounded, and Arpad: for they have heard evil tidings: they are ᴺfainthearted; ᴿ*there is* sorrow ᴺon the sea; it cannot be quiet.

24 Damascus is waxed feeble, *and* turneth herself to flee, and fear hath seized on *her:* ᴿanguish and sorrows have taken her, as a woman in travail.

25 How is ᴿthe city of praise not left, the city of my joy!

26 ᴿTherefore her young men shall fall in her streets, and all the men of war shall be cut off in that day, saith the LORD of hosts.

27 And I will kindle a ᴿfire in the wall of Damascus, and it shall consume the palaces of Bĕn-hā′-dăd.

Prophecies concerning Kedar and Hazor

28 ᴿConcerning Kē′-där, and concerning the kingdoms of Hā′-zôr, which Nĕb-ū-chăd-rĕz′-zär king of Babylon shall smite, thus saith the LORD; Arise ye, go up to Kē′-där, and spoil ᴿthe men of the east.

29 Their ᴿtents and their flocks shall they take away: they shall take to themselves their curtains, and all their vessels, and their camels; and they shall cry unto them, ᴿFear *is* on every side.

30 ᴿFlee, ᴺget you far off, dwell deep, O ye inhabitants of Hā′-zôr, saith the LORD; for Nĕb-ū-chăd-rĕz′-zär king of Babylon hath taken counsel against you, and hath conceived a purpose against you.

31 Arise, get you up unto ᴿthe ᴺwealthy nation, that dwelleth without care, saith the LORD, which have neither gates nor bars, *which* ᴿdwell alone.

32 And their camels shall be a booty, and the multitude of their cattle a spoil: and I will scatter into all winds them *that are* ᴺin the utmost corners; and I will bring their calamity from all sides thereof, saith the LORD.

33 And Hā′-zôr ᴿshall be a dwelling for dragons, *and* a desolation for ever: ᴿthere shall no man abide there, nor *any* son of man dwell in it.

Prophecy concerning Elam

34 The word of the LORD that came to Jeremiah the prophet against ᴿĒ′-lăm in the beginning of the reign of Zĕd-ē-kī′-ăh king of Judah, saying,

35 Thus saith the LORD of hosts; Behold, I will break ᴿthe bow of Ē′-lăm, the chief of their might.

36 And upon Ē'-lăm will I bring the four winds from the four quarters of heaven, and ᴿwill scatter them toward all those winds; and there shall be no nation whither the outcasts of Ē'-lăm shall not come.

37 For I will cause Ē'-lăm to be dismayed before their enemies, and before them that seek their life: and I will bring evil upon them, *even* my fierce anger, saith the LORD; ᴿand I will send the sword after them, till I have consumed them:

38 And I will ᴿset my throne in Ē'-lăm, and will destroy from thence the king and the princes, saith the LORD.

39 But it shall come to pass ᴿin the latter days, *that* I will bring again the captivity of Ē'-lăm, saith the LORD.

CHAPTER 50

Prophecy concerning Babylon

THE word that the LORD spake ᴿagainst Babylon *and* against the land of the Chăl-dē'-ăns ᴺby Jeremiah the prophet.

2 Declare ye among the nations, and publish, and ᴺset up a standard; publish, *and* conceal not: say, Babylon is taken, ᴿBel is confounded, Mĕr'-ō-dăch is broken in pieces; ᴿher idols are confounded, her images are broken in pieces.

3 ᴿFor out of the north there cometh up ᴿa nation against her, which shall make her land desolate, and none shall dwell therein: they shall remove, they shall depart, both man and beast.

Penitent Israel to seek God

4 In those days, and in that time, saith the LORD, the children of Israel shall come, ᴿthey and the children of Judah together, ᴿgoing and weeping: they shall go, ᴿand seek the LORD their God.

5 They shall ask the way to Zion with their faces thitherward, *saying,* Come, and let us join ourselves to the LORD in ᴿa perpetual covenant *that* shall not be forgotten.

6 My people hath been ᴿlost sheep: their shepherds have caused them to go astray, they have turned them away *on* ᴿthe mountains: they have gone from mountain to hill, they have forgotten their ᴺrestingplace.

7 All that found them have ᴿdevoured them: and ᴿtheir adversaries said, ᴿWe offend not, because they have sinned against the LORD, ᴿthe habitation of justice, even the LORD, ᴿthe hope of their fathers.

The coming plunder of Babylon

8 ᴿRemove out of the midst of Babylon, and go forth out of the land of the Chăl-dē'-ăns, and be as the he goats before the flocks.

9 ᴿFor, lo, I will raise and cause to come up against Babylon an assembly of great nations from the north country: and they shall set themselves in array against her; from thence she shall be taken: their arrows *shall be* as of a mighty ᴺexpert man; ᴿnone shall return in vain.

10 And Chăl-dē'-ă shall be a spoil: ᴿall that spoil her shall be satisfied, saith the LORD.

11 ᴿBecause ye were glad, because ye rejoiced, O ye destroyers of mine heritage, because ye are grown ᴺfat ᴿas the heifer at grass, and ᴺbellow as bulls;

12 Your mother shall be sore confounded; she that bare you shall be ashamed: behold, the hindermost of the nations *shall be* a wilderness, a dry land, and a desert.

13 Because of the wrath of the LORD it shall not be inhabited, ᴿbut it shall be wholly desolate: ᴿevery one that goeth by Babylon shall be astonished, and hiss at all her plagues.

14 ᴿPut yourselves in array against Babylon round about: all ye ᴿthat bend the bow, shoot at her, spare no arrows: for she hath sinned against the LORD.

15 Shout against her round about: she hath ᴿgiven her hand: her foundations are fallen, ᴿher walls are thrown down: for ᴿit *is* the vengeance of the LORD: take vengeance upon her; as she hath done, do unto her.

16 Cut off the sower from Babylon, and him that handleth the ᴺsickle in the time of harvest: for fear of the oppressing sword ᴿthey shall turn every one to his people, and they shall flee every one to his own land.

Restoration and pardon of Israel

17 Israel *is* ᴿa scattered sheep; ᴿthe lions have driven *him* away: first ᴿthe king of Assyria hath devoured him; and last this ᴿNĕb-ū-chăd-rĕz'-zär king of Babylon hath broken his bones.

18 Therefore thus saith the LORD of hosts, the God of Israel; Behold, I will punish the king of Babylon and his land, as I have punished the king of Assyria.

19 ᴿAnd I will bring Israel again to his habitation, and he shall feed on Carmel and Bā'-shăn, and his soul shall be satisfied upon mount Ē'-phră-ĭm and Gilead.

20 In those days, and in that time, saith the LORD, ᴿthe iniquity of Israel shall be sought

for, and *there shall be* none; and the sins of Judah, and they shall not be found: for I will pardon them [R]whom I reserve.

The coming slaughter of Babylon

21 Go up against the land [N]of Mĕr-ă-thā′-ĭm, *even* against it, and against the inhabitants of [R]Pē′-kŏd:[N] waste and utterly destroy after them, saith the LORD, and do [R]according to all that I have commanded thee.

22 [R]A sound of battle *is* in the land, and of great destruction.

23 How is [R]the hammer of the whole earth cut asunder and broken! how is Babylon become a desolation among the nations!

24 I have laid a snare for thee, and thou art also taken, O Babylon, [R]and thou wast not aware: thou art found, and also caught, because thou hast striven against the LORD.

25 The LORD hath opened his armoury, and hath brought forth [R]the weapons of his indignation: for this *is* the work of the Lord GOD of hosts in the land of the Chăl-dē′-ăns.

26 Come against her [N]from the utmost border, open her storehouses: [N]cast her up as heaps, and destroy her utterly: let nothing of her be left.

27 Slay all her [R]bullocks; let them go down to the slaughter: woe unto them! for their day is come, the time of [R]their visitation.

28 The voice of them that flee and escape out of the land of Babylon, [R]to declare in Zion the vengeance of the LORD our God, the vengeance of his temple.

29 Call together the archers against Babylon: [R]all ye that bend the bow, camp against it round about; let none thereof escape: [R]recompense her according to her work; according to all that she hath done, do unto her: [R]for she hath been proud against the LORD, against the Holy One of Israel.

30 [R]Therefore shall her young men fall in the streets, and all her men of war shall be cut off in that day, saith the LORD.

31 Behold, I *am* against thee, O thou [N]most proud, saith the Lord GOD of hosts: for [R]thy day is come, the time *that* I will visit thee.

32 And [N]the most proud shall stumble and fall, and none shall raise him up: and [R]I will kindle a fire in his cities, and it shall devour all round about him.

Israel's Redeemer is strong

33 Thus saith the LORD of hosts; The children of Israel and the children of Judah *were* oppressed together: and all that took them

captives held them fast; they refused to let them go.

34 [R]Their Redeemer *is* strong; [R]the LORD of hosts *is* his name: he shall throughly plead their cause, that he may give rest to the land, and disquiet the inhabitants of Babylon.

War and the desolation of Babylon

35 A sword *is* upon the Chăl-dē′-ăns, saith the LORD, and upon the inhabitants of Babylon, and [R]upon her princes, and upon [R]her wise *men*.

36 A sword *is* [R]upon the [NN]liars; and they shall dote: a sword *is* upon her mighty men; and they shall be dismayed.

37 A sword *is* upon their horses, and upon their chariots, and upon all [R]the mingled people that *are* in the midst of her; and [R]they shall become as women: a sword *is* upon her treasures; and they shall be robbed.

38 [R]A drought *is* upon her waters; and they shall be dried up: for it *is* the land of [R]graven images, and they are mad upon *their* idols.

39 [R]Therefore the wild beasts of the desert with the wild beasts of the islands shall dwell *there,* and the owls shall dwell therein: [R]and it shall be no more inhabited for ever; neither shall it be dwelt in from generation to generation.

40 [R]As God overthrew Sodom and Gō-mŏr′-răh and the neighbour *cities* thereof, saith the LORD; *so* shall no man abide there, neither shall any son of man dwell therein.

41 [R]Behold, a people shall come from the north, and a great nation, and many kings shall be raised up from the coasts of the earth.

42 [R]They shall hold the bow and the lance: [R]they *are* cruel, and will not shew mercy: [R]their voice shall roar like the sea, and they shall ride upon horses, *every one* put in array, like a man to the battle, against thee, O daughter of Babylon.

43 The king of Babylon hath heard the report of them, and his hands waxed feeble: anguish took hold of him, *and* pangs as of a woman in travail.

44 [R]Behold, he shall come up like a lion from the swelling of Jordan unto the habitation of the strong: but I will make them suddenly run away from her: and who *is* a chosen *man, that* I may appoint over her? for who *is* like me? and who will [N]appoint me the time? and [R]who *is* that shepherd that will stand before me?

45 Therefore hear ye [R]the counsel of the LORD, that he hath taken against Babylon; and his purposes, that he hath purposed against the

CHAP. **50**
BC 595

20	Is. 1:9
21	Or, *of the rebels*
21	Ezek. 23:23
21	Or, *Visitation*
21	See 2 Sam. 16:11
	2 Ki. 18:25
	2 Chr. 36:23
	Is. 10:6 & 44:28
	& 48:14
22	ch. 51:54
23	Is. 14:6
	ch. 51:20
24	ch. 51:8, 31
	Dan. 5:30
25	Is. 13:5
26	Heb. *from the end*
26	Or, *tread her*
27	Ps. 22:12
	Is. 34:7
	ch. 46:21
27	ch. 48:44
28	ch. 51:10
29	ver. 14
29	ver. 15
	ch. 51:56
	Rev. 18:6
29	Is. 47:10
30	ch. 49:26 & 51:4
31	Heb. *pride*
31	ver. 27
32	Heb. *pride*
32	ch. 21:14

Rev. 18:8	34
Is. 47:4	34
Dan. 5:30	35
Is. 47:13	35
Is. 44:25	36
ch. 48:30	
Or, *chief stays*	36
Heb. *bars*	36
ch. 25:20	37
Ezek. 30:5	
ch. 51:30	37
Nah. 3:13	
Is. 44:27	38
ch. 51:36	
Rev. 16:12	
ver. 2	38
Is. 13:21, 22	39
& 34:14	
ch. 51:37	
Rev. 18:2	
Is. 13:20	39
ch. 25:12	
Gen. 19:25	40
Is. 13:19	
ch. 51:26	
ver. 9	41
ch. 6:22 & 25:14	
& 51:27	
Rev. 17:16	
ch. 6:23	42
Is. 13:18	42
Is. 5:30	42
ch. 49:19	44
Or, *convent me to plead?*	44
Job 41:10	44
ch. 49:19	
Is. 14:24	45
ch. 51:11	

land of the Chăl-dē'-ăns: Surely the least of the flock shall draw them out: surely he shall make *their* habitation desolate with them.

46 ^RAt the noise of the taking of Babylon the earth is moved, and the cry is heard among the nations.

CHAPTER 51

Judgment of guilty Babylon

THUS saith the LORD; Behold, I will raise up against Babylon, and against them that dwell in the ^Nmidst of them that rise up against me, ^Ra destroying wind;

2 And will send unto Babylon ^Rfanners, that shall fan her, and shall empty her land: ^Rfor in the day of trouble they shall be against her round about.

3 Against *him that* bendeth ^Rlet the archer bend his bow, and against *him that* lifteth himself up in his brigandine: and spare ye not her young men; ^Rdestroy ye utterly all her host.

4 Thus the slain shall fall in the land of the Chăl-dē'-ăns, ^Rand *they that are* thrust through in her streets.

5 For Israel *hath* not *been* forsaken, nor Judah of his God, of the LORD of hosts; though their land was filled with sin against the Holy One of Israel.

6 ^RFlee out of the midst of Babylon, and deliver every man his soul: be not cut off in her iniquity; for ^Rthis *is* the time of the LORD's vengeance; ^Rhe will render unto her a recompence.

7 ^RBabylon *hath been* a golden cup in the LORD's hand, that made all the earth drunken: ^Rthe nations have drunken of her wine; therefore the nations ^Rare mad.

8 Babylon is suddenly ^Rfallen and destroyed: ^Rhowl for her; ^Rtake balm for her pain, if so be she may be healed.

9 We would have healed Babylon, but she is not healed: forsake her, and ^Rlet us go every one into his own country: ^Rfor her judgment reacheth unto heaven, and is lifted up *even* to the skies.

10 The LORD hath ^Rbrought forth our righteousness: come, and let us ^Rdeclare in Zion the work of the LORD our God.

The Medes to execute judgment

11 ^RMake ^Nbright the arrows; gather the shields: ^Rthe LORD hath raised up the spirit of the kings of the Mēdes: ^Rfor his device *is* against Babylon, to destroy it; because it *is* ^Rthe vengeance of the LORD, the vengeance of his temple.

	CHAP. **50**
	BC 595
46	Rev. 18:9

	CHAP. **51**
	BC 595
1	Heb. *heart*
1	2 Ki. 19:7
	ch. 4:11
2	ch. 15:7
2	ch. 50:14
3	ch. 50:14
3	ch. 50:21
4	ch. 49:26
	& 50:30, 37
6	ch. 50:8
	Rev. 18:4
6	ch. 50:15
6	ch. 25:14
7	Rev. 17:4
7	Rev. 14:8
7	ch. 25:16
8	Is. 21:9
	Rev. 14:8 & 18:2
8	ch. 48:20
	Rev. 18:9, 11, 19
8	ch. 46:11
9	Is. 13:14
	ch. 50:16
9	Rev. 18:5
10	Ps. 37:6
10	ch. 50:28
11	ch. 46:4
11	Heb. *pure*
11	ver. 28
	Is. 13:17
11	ch. 50:45
11	ch. 50:28

Nah. 2:1 & 3:14	12
Heb. *liers in wait*	12
Rev. 17:1, 15	13
ch. 49:13	14
Amos 6:8	
Heb. *by his soul*	14
Nah. 3:15	14
Heb. *utter*	14
ch. 50:15	14
Gen. 1:1, 6	15
ch. 10:12, etc.	
Job 9:8	15
Ps. 104:2	
Is. 40:22	
Or, *noise*	16
Ps. 135:7	16
ch. 10:14	17
Or, *is more brutish than to know*	17
ch. 50:2	17
ch. 10:15	18
ch. 10:16	19
Is. 10:5, 15	20
ch. 50:23	
Or, *in thee*, or, *by thee*	20
2 Chr. 36:17	22
ch. 50:15	24
Is. 13:2	25
Zech. 4:7	
Rev. 8:8	25
ch. 50:40	26

12 ^RSet up the standard upon the walls of Babylon, make the watch strong, set up the watchmen, prepare the ^Nambushes: for the LORD hath both devised and done that which he spake against the inhabitants of Babylon.

13 ^RO thou that dwellest upon many waters, abundant in treasures, thine end is come, *and* the measure of thy covetousness.

14 ^RThe LORD of hosts hath sworn ^Nby himself, *saying,* Surely I will fill thee with men, ^Ras with caterpillers; and they shall ^Nlift ^Rup a shout against thee.

15 ^RHe hath made the earth by his power, he hath established the world by his wisdom, and ^Rhath stretched out the heaven by his understanding.

16 When he uttereth *his* voice, *there is* a ^Nmultitude of waters in the heavens; and ^Rhe causeth the vapours to ascend from the ends of the earth: he maketh lightnings with rain, and bringeth forth the wind out of his treasures.

17 ^REvery man ^Nis brutish by *his* knowledge; every founder is confounded by the graven image: ^Rfor his molten image *is* falsehood, and *there is* no breath in them.

18 ^RThey *are* vanity, the work of errors: in the time of their visitation they shall perish.

19 ^RThe portion of Jacob *is* not like them; for he *is* the former of all things: and *Israel is* the rod of his inheritance: the LORD of hosts *is* his name.

20 ^RThou *art* my battle axe *and* weapons of war: for ^Nwith thee will I break in pieces the nations, and with thee will I destroy kingdoms;

21 And with thee will I break in pieces the horse and his rider; and with thee will I break in pieces the chariot and his rider;

22 With thee also will I break in pieces man and woman; and with thee will I break in pieces ^Rold and young; and with thee will I break in pieces the young man and the maid;

23 I will also break in pieces with thee the shepherd and his flock; and with thee will I break in pieces the husbandman and his yoke of oxen; and with thee will I break in pieces captains and rulers.

24 ^RAnd I will render unto Babylon and to all the inhabitants of Chăl-dē'-ă all their evil that they have done in Zion in your sight, saith the LORD.

25 Behold, I *am* against thee, ^RO destroying mountain, saith the LORD, which destroyest all the earth: and I will stretch out mine hand upon thee, and roll thee down from the rocks, ^Rand will make thee a burnt mountain.

26 And they shall not take of thee a stone for a corner, nor a stone for foundations; ^Rbut

thou shalt be ᴺdesolate for ever, saith the LORD.

27 ᴿSet ye up a standard in the land, blow the trumpet among the nations, ᴿprepare the nations against her, call together against her ᴿthe kingdoms of Ăr'-ă-răt, Mĭn'-nĭ, and Ăsh-chē'-năz; appoint a captain against her; cause the horses to come up as the rough caterpillers.

28 Prepare against her the nations with ᴿthe kings of the Mēdeś, the captains thereof, and all the rulers thereof, and all the land of his dominion.

29 And the land shall tremble and sorrow: for every purpose of the LORD shall be performed against Babylon, ᴿto make the land of Babylon a desolation without an inhabitant.

30 The mighty men of Babylon have forborne to fight, they have remained in *their* holds: their might hath failed; ᴿthey became as women: they have burned her dwelling places; ᴿher bars are broken.

31 ᴿOne post shall run to meet another, and one messenger to meet another, to shew the king of Babylon that his city is taken at *one* end,

32 And that ᴿthe passages are stopped, and the reeds they have burned with fire, and the men of war are affrighted.

33 For thus saith the LORD of hosts, the God of Israel; The daughter of Babylon *is* ᴿlike a threshingfloor, ᴿ*it*ᴺ *is* time to thresh her: yet a little while, ᴿand the time of her harvest shall come.

The LORD avenges Jerusalem

34 Nĕb-ū-chăd-rĕz'-zär the king of Babylon hath ᴿdevoured me, he hath crushed me, he hath made me an empty vessel, he hath swallowed me up like a dragon, he hath filled his belly with my delicates, he hath cast me out.

35 ᴺThe violence done to me and to my ᴺflesh *be* upon Babylon, shall the ᴺinhabitant of Zion say; and my blood upon the inhabitants of Chăl-dē'-ă, shall Jerusalem say.

36 Therefore thus saith the LORD; Behold, ᴿI will plead thy cause, and take vengeance for thee; ᴿand I will dry up her sea, and make her springs dry.

37 ᴿAnd Babylon shall become heaps, a dwelling place for dragons, ᴿan astonishment, and an hissing, without an inhabitant.

38 They shall roar together like lions: they shall ᴺyell as lions' whelps.

39 In their heat I will make their feasts, and ᴿI will make them drunken, that they may rejoice, and sleep a perpetual sleep, and not wake, saith the LORD.

40 I will bring them down like lambs to the slaughter, like rams with he goats.

41 How is ᴿShē'-shăch taken! and how is ᴿthe praise of the whole earth surprised! how is Babylon become an astonishment among the nations!

42 ᴿThe sea is come up upon Babylon: she is covered with the multitude of the waves thereof.

43 ᴿHer cities are a desolation, a dry land, and a wilderness, a land wherein no man dwelleth, neither doth *any* son of man pass thereby.

44 ᴿAnd I will punish Bel in Babylon, and I will bring forth out of his mouth that which he hath swallowed up: and the nations shall not flow together any more unto him: yea, ᴿthe wall of Babylon shall fall.

45 ᴿMy people, go ye out of the midst of her, and deliver ye every man his soul from the fierce anger of the LORD.

46 And ᴺlest your heart faint, and ye fear ᴿfor the rumour that shall be heard in the land; a rumour shall both come *one* year, and after that in *another* year *shall come* a rumour, and violence in the land, ruler against ruler.

47 Therefore, behold, the days come, that ᴿI will ᴺdo judgment upon the graven images of Babylon: and her whole land shall be confounded, and all her slain shall fall in the midst of her.

48 Then ᴿthe heaven and the earth, and all that *is* therein, shall sing for Babylon: ᴿfor the spoilers shall come unto her from the north, saith the LORD.

49 ᴺAs Babylon *hath caused* the slain of Israel to fall, so at Babylon shall fall the slain of all ᴺthe earth.

50 ᴿYe that have escaped the sword, go away, stand not still: remember the LORD afar off, and let Jerusalem come into your mind.

51 ᴿWe are confounded, because we have heard reproach: shame hath covered our faces: for strangers are come into the sanctuaries of the LORD's house.

52 Wherefore, behold, the days come, saith the LORD, ᴿthat I will do judgment upon her graven images: and through all her land the wounded shall groan.

53 ᴿThough Babylon should mount up to heaven, and though she should fortify the height of her strength, *yet* from me shall spoilers come unto her, saith the LORD.

The noise of destruction

54 ᴿA sound of a cry *cometh* from Babylon, and great destruction from the land of the Chăl-dē'-ăns:

55 Because the LORD hath spoiled Babylon, and destroyed out of her the great voice; when her waves do roar like great waters, a noise of their voice is uttered:

56 Because the spoiler is come upon her, *even* upon Babylon, and her mighty men are taken, every one of their bows is broken: [R]for the LORD God of recompences shall surely requite.

57 [R]And I will make drunk her princes, and her wise *men,* her captains, and her rulers, and her mighty men: and they shall sleep a perpetual sleep, and not wake, saith [R]the King, whose name *is* the LORD of hosts.

58 Thus saith the LORD of hosts; [R]The[N] broad walls of Babylon shall be utterly [N]broken, and her high gates shall be burned with fire; and [R]the people shall labour in vain, and the folk in the fire, and they shall be weary.

Instructions to the Babylonian exiles

59 The word which Jeremiah the prophet commanded Sĕ-raī'-ăh the son of Nē-rī'-ăh, the son of Mā-ă-seī'-ăh, when he went [N]with Zĕd-ē-kī'-ăh the king of Judah into Babylon in the fourth year of his reign. And *this* Sĕ-raī'-ăh *was* a [N]quiet prince.

60 So Jeremiah wrote in a book all the evil that should come upon Babylon, *even* all these words that are written against Babylon.

61 And Jeremiah said to Sĕ-raī'-ăh, When thou comest to Babylon, and shalt see, and shalt read all these words;

62 Then shalt thou say, O LORD, thou hast spoken against this place, to cut it off, that [R]none shall remain in it, neither man nor beast, but that it shall be [N]desolate for ever.

63 And it shall be, when thou hast made an end of reading this book, [R]*that* thou shalt bind a stone to it, and cast it into the midst of Eū-phrā'-tĕś:

64 And thou shalt say, Thus shall Babylon sink, and shall not rise from the evil that I will bring upon her: [R]and they shall be weary. Thus far *are* the words of Jeremiah.

CHAPTER 52

Capture of Jerusalem

ZĕD-Ē-KĪ'-ĂH *was* [R]one and twenty years old when he [N]began to reign, and he reigned eleven years in Jerusalem. And his mother's name *was* Hă-mū'-tăl the daughter of Jeremiah of Lĭb'-năh.

2 And he did *that which was* evil in the eyes of the LORD, according to all that Jĕ-hoī'-ă-kĭm had done.

3 For through the anger of the LORD it came to pass in Jerusalem and Judah, till he had cast

them out from his presence, that Zĕd-ē-kī'-ăh rebelled against the king of Babylon.

4 And it came to pass in the [R]ninth year of his reign, in the tenth month, in the tenth *day* of the month, *that* Nĕb-ū-chăd-rĕz'-zär king of Babylon came, he and all his army, against Jerusalem, and pitched against it, and built forts against it round about.

5 So the city was besieged unto the eleventh year of king Zĕd-ē-kī'-ăh.

6 And in the fourth month, in the ninth *day* of the month, the famine was sore in the city, so that there was no bread for the people of the land.

7 Then the city was broken up, and all the men of war fled, and went forth out of the city by night by the way of the gate between the two walls, which *was* by the king's garden; (now the Chăl-dē'-ăns *were* by the city round about:) and they went by the way of the plain.

8 But the army of the Chăl-dē'-ăns pursued after the king, and overtook Zĕd-ē-kī'-ăh in the plains of Jericho; and all his army was scattered from him.

9 [R]Then they took the king, and carried him up unto the king of Babylon to Rĭb'-läh in the land of Hā'-măth; where he gave judgment upon him.

10 [R]And the king of Babylon slew the sons of Zĕd-ē-kī'-ăh before his eyes: he slew also all the princes of Judah in Rĭb'-läh.

11 Then he [N]put out the eyes of Zĕd-ē-kī'-ăh; and the king of Babylon bound him in [N]chains, and carried him to Babylon, and put him in [N]prison till the day of his death.

Jerusalem destroyed

12 [R]Now in the fifth month, in the tenth *day* of the month, [R]which *was* the nineteenth year of Nĕb-ū-chăd-rĕz'-zär king of Babylon, [R]came Nĕb-ū'-zär-ăd'-ăn, [NN]captain of the guard, *which* [N]served the king of Babylon, into Jerusalem,

13 And burned the house of the LORD, and the king's house; and all the houses of Jerusalem, and all the houses of the great *men,* burned he with fire:

14 And all the army of the Chăl-dē'-ăns, that *were* with the captain of the guard, brake down all the walls of Jerusalem round about.

15 [R]Then Nĕb-ū'-zär-ăd'-ăn the captain of the guard carried away captive *certain* of the poor of the people, and the residue of the people that remained in the city, and those that fell away, that fell to the king of Babylon, and the rest of the multitude.

16 But Nĕb-ū'-zär-ăd'-ăn the captain of the guard left *certain* of the poor of the land for vinedressers and for husbandmen.

17 ᴿAlso the ᴿpillars of brass that *were* in the house of the Lᴏʀᴅ, and the bases, and the brasen sea that *was* in the house of the Lᴏʀᴅ, the Chăl-dē′-ăns brake, and carried all the brass of them to Babylon.

18 ᴿThe caldrons also, and the ᴺshovels, and the snuffers, and the ᴺbowls, and the spoons, and all the vessels of brass wherewith they ministered, took they away.

19 And the basins, and the ᴺfirepans, and the bowls, and the caldrons, and the candlesticks, and the spoons, and the cups; *that* which *was* of gold *in* gold, and *that* which *was* of silver *in* silver, took the captain of the guard away.

20 The two pillars, one sea, and twelve brasen bulls that *were* under the bases, which king Solomon had made in the house of the Lᴏʀᴅ: ᴿthe ᴺ brass of all these vessels was without weight.

21 And *concerning* the ᴿpillars, the height of one pillar *was* eighteen cubits; and a ᴺfillet of twelve cubits did compass it; and the thickness thereof *was* four fingers: *it was* hollow.

22 And a chapiter of brass *was* upon it; and the height of one chapiter *was* five cubits, with network and pomegranates upon the chapiters round about, all *of* brass. The second pillar also and the pomegranates *were* like unto these.

23 And there were ninety and six pomegranates on a side; *and* ᴿall the pomegranates upon the network *were* an hundred round about.

24 And ᴿthe captain of the guard took Sĕ-rai′-ăh the chief priest, ᴿand Zĕph-ă-nī′-ăh the second priest, and the three keepers of the ᴺdoor:

25 He took also out of the city an eunuch, which had the charge of the men of war; and seven men of them that ᴺwere near the king's person, which were found in the city; and the ᴺprincipal scribe of the host, who mustered the people of the land; and threescore

CHAP. 52	
BC 588	
17 ch. 27:19	
17 See 1 Ki.	
7:15, 23, 27, 50	
18 Ex. 27:3	
2 Ki. 25:14-16	
18 Or, *instruments*	
to remove	
the ashes	
18 Or, *basins*	
19 Or, *censers*	
20 1 Ki. 7:47	
20 Heb. *their brass*	
21 1 Ki. 7:15	
2 Ki. 25:17	
2 Chr. 3:15	
21 Heb. *thread*	
23 See 1 Ki. 7:20	
24 2 Ki. 25:18	
24 ch. 21:1 & 29:5	
24 Heb. *threshold*	
25 Heb. *saw*	
the face of the king	
25 Or, *scribe of the*	
captain of the host	

2 Ki. 24:2	**28**
See 2 Ki. 24:12	**28**
See 2 Ki. 24:14	**28**
See ver. 12	**29**
ch. 39:9	
Heb. *souls*	**29**
2 Ki. 25:27-30	**31**
Gen. 40:13, 20	**31**
Heb. *good things*	**32**
with him	
2 Sam. 9:13	**33**
Heb. *the matter*	**34**
of the day	
in his day	

men of the people of the land, that were found in the midst of the city.

26 So Nĕb-ū′-zăr-ăd′-ăn the captain of the guard took them, and brought them to the king of Babylon to Rĭb′-lăh.

27 And the king of Babylon smote them, and put them to death in Rĭb′-lăh in the land of Hā′-măth. Thus Judah was carried away captive out of his own land.

28 ᴿThis *is* the people whom Nĕb-ū-chăd-rĕz′-zăr carried away captive: in the ᴿseventh year ᴿthree thousand Jews and three and twenty:

29 ᴿIn the eighteenth year of Nĕb-ū-chăd-rĕz′-zăr he carried away captive from Jerusalem eight hundred thirty and two ᴺpersons:

30 In the three and twentieth year of Nĕb-ū-chăd-rĕz′-zăr Nĕb-ū′-zăr-ăd′-ăn the captain of the guard carried away captive of the Jews seven hundred forty and five persons: all the persons *were* four thousand and six hundred.

Pardon of Jehoiachin

31 ᴿAnd it came to pass in the seven and thirtieth year of the captivity of Jĕ-hoi′-ă-chĭn king of Judah, in the twelfth month, in the five and twentieth *day* of the month, *that* Ē′-vĭl-mĕr′-ō-dăch king of Babylon in the *first* year of his reign ᴿlifted up the head of Jĕ-hoi′-ă-chĭn king of Judah, and brought him forth out of prison,

32 And spake ᴺkindly unto him, and set his throne above the throne of the kings that *were* with him in Babylon,

33 And changed his prison garments: ᴿand he did continually eat bread before him all the days of his life.

34 And *for* his diet, there was a continual diet given him of the king of Babylon, ᴺevery day a portion until the day of his death, all the days of his life.

THE LAMENTATIONS

OF JEREMIAH

Lamentations reflects the sorrows and grief of an author who lamented the fall of Jerusalem. Scholarship generally assigns this book to the time of Jerusalem's destruction in 586 B.C. The Talmud, Septuagint, the church fathers considered Jeremiah to be the author.

The capitulation of the kingdom of Judah to the Babylonians, who reduced Jerusalem with its temple to ruins, represents the epitome of divine judgment on God's chosen people. The author of Lamentations reflects on God's providence with His people, acknowledges God's righteousness, and finds hope in confessing the sins of his people.

CHAPTER 1

Loneliness of desolate Zion

HOW doth the city sit solitary, *that was* full of people! [R]*how* is she become as a widow! she *that was* great among the nations, *and* princess among the provinces, *how* is she become tributary!

2 She [R]weepeth sore in the [R]night, and her tears *are* on her cheeks: among all her lovers she hath none to comfort *her:* all her friends have dealt treacherously with her, they are become her enemies.

3 Judah is gone into captivity because of affliction, and [N]because of great servitude: [R]she dwelleth among the heathen, she findeth no rest: all her persecutors overtook her between the straits.

4 The ways of Zion do mourn, because none come to the solemn feasts: all her gates are desolate: her priests sigh, her virgins are afflicted, and she *is* in bitterness.

5 Her adversaries [R]are the chief, her enemies prosper; for the LORD hath afflicted her [R]for the multitude of her transgressions: her [R]children are gone into captivity before the enemy.

6 And from the daughter of Zion all her beauty is departed: her princes are become like harts *that* find no pasture, and they are gone without strength before the pursuer.

7 Jerusalem remembered in the days of her affliction and of her miseries all her [N]pleasant things that she had in the days of old, when her people fell into the hand of the enemy, and none did help her: the adversaries saw her, *and* did mock at her sabbaths.

Desolation due to sin

8 [R]Jerusalem hath grievously sinned; therefore she [N]is removed: all that honoured her despise her, because [R]they have seen her nakedness: yea, she sigheth, and turneth backward.

9 Her filthiness *is* in her skirts; she [R]remembereth not her last end; therefore she came down wonderfully: [R]she had no comforter. O LORD, behold my affliction: for the enemy hath magnified *himself.*

10 The adversary hath spread out his hand upon [R]all her [N]pleasant things: for she hath seen *that* [R]the heathen entered into her sanctuary, whom thou didst command *that* [R]they should not enter into thy congregation.

11 All her people sigh, [R]they seek bread; they have given their pleasant things for meat [N]to relieve the soul: see, O LORD, and consider; for I am become vile.

12 [N]*Is* it nothing to you, all ye that [N]pass by? behold, and see [R]if there be any sorrow

like unto my sorrow, which is done unto me, wherewith the LORD hath afflicted *me* in the day of his fierce anger.

13 From above hath he sent fire into my bones, and it prevaileth against them: he hath [R]spread a net for my feet, he hath turned me back: he hath made me desolate *and* faint all the day.

14 [R]The yoke of my transgressions is bound by his hand: they are wreathed, *and* come up upon my neck: he hath made my strength to fall, the Lord hath delivered me into *their* hands, *from whom* I am not able to rise up.

15 The Lord hath trodden under foot all my mighty *men* in the midst of me: he hath called an assembly against me to crush my young men: [R]the Lord hath trodden [N]the virgin, the daughter of Judah, *as* in a winepress.

16 For these *things* I weep; [R]mine eye, mine eye runneth down with water, because [R]the comforter that should [N]relieve my soul is far from me: my children are desolate, because the enemy prevailed.

17 [R]Zion spreadeth forth her hands, *and* [R]*there is* none to comfort her: the LORD hath commanded concerning Jacob, *that* his adversaries *should be* round about him: Jerusalem is as a menstruous woman among them.

The LORD'S judgment is just

18 The LORD is [R]righteous; for I have [R]rebelled against his [N]commandment: hear, I pray you, all people, and behold my sorrow: my virgins and my young men are gone into captivity.

19 I called for my lovers, *but* [R]they deceived me: my priests and mine elders gave up the ghost in the city, [R]while they sought their meat to relieve their souls.

20 Behold, O LORD; for I *am* in distress: my [R]bowels are troubled; mine heart is turned within me; for I have grievously rebelled: [R]abroad the sword bereaveth, at home *there is* as death.

21 They have heard that I sigh: [R]*there is* none to comfort me: all mine enemies have heard of my trouble; they are glad that thou hast done *it:* thou wilt bring [R]the day *that* thou hast [N]called, and they shall be like unto me.

22 [R]Let all their wickedness come before thee; and do unto them, as thou hast done unto me for all my transgressions: for my sighs *are* many, and [R]my heart *is* faint.

CHAPTER 2

The LORD'S anger against Zion

HOW hath the Lord covered the daughter of Zion with a cloud in his anger, [R]*and*

CHAP. 1
BC 588
1 Is. 47:7, 8
2 Jer. 13:17
2 Job 7:3
3 Heb. *for the greatness of servitude*
3 ch. 2:9
5 Deut. 28:43
5 Jer. 30:14
Dan. 9:7
5 Jer. 52:28
7 Or, *desirable*
8 1 Ki. 8:46
8 Heb. *is become a removing,* or, *wandering*
8 Jer. 13:22
Ezek. 16:37
Hos. 2:10
9 Deut. 32:29
Is. 47:7
9 ver. 2, 17, 21
10 ver. 7
10 Or, *desirable*
10 Jer. 51:51
10 Deut. 23:3
Neh. 13:1
11 Jer. 38:9 & 52:6
11 Or, *to make the soul to come again*
12 Or, *It is nothing*
12 Heb. *pass by the way?*
12 Dan. 9:12

Ezek. 12:13   13
Deut. 28:48   14
Is. 63:3   15
Rev. 14:19
Or, *the winepress* 15 *of the virgin, etc.*
Jer. 13:17   16
ch. 2:18
ver. 2, 9   16
Heb. *bring back* 16
Jer. 4:31   17
ver. 2, 9   17
Neh. 9:33   18
Dan. 9:7, 14
1 Sam. 12:14   18
Heb. *mouth*   18
ver. 2   19
Jer. 30:14
ver. 11   19
Job 30:27   20
Is. 16:11
Jer. 4:19
Hos. 11:8
Deut. 32:25   20
Ezek. 7:15
ver. 2   21
Is. 13, etc.   21
Jer. 46, etc.
Or, *proclaimed* 21
Ps. 109:15   22
ch. 5:17   22

CHAP. 2
BC 588
Mat. 11:23   1

cast down from heaven unto the earth ᴿthe beauty of Israel, and remembered not ᴿhis footstool in the day of his anger!

2 The Lord hath swallowed up all the habitations of Jacob, and hath not pitied: he hath thrown down in his wrath the strong holds of the daughter of Judah; he hath ᴺbrought *them* down to the ground: ᴿhe hath polluted the kingdom and the princes thereof.

3 He hath cut off in *his* fierce anger all the horn of Israel: ᴿhe hath drawn back his right hand from before the enemy, ᴿand he burned against Jacob like a flaming fire, *which* devoureth round about.

4 ᴿHe hath bent his bow like an enemy: he stood with his right hand as an adversary, and slew ᴿall ᴺ *that were* pleasant to the eye in the tabernacle of the daughter of Zion: he poured out his fury like fire.

5 ᴿThe Lord was as an enemy: he hath swallowed up Israel, ᴿhe hath swallowed up all her palaces: he hath destroyed his strong holds, and hath increased in the daughter of Judah mourning and lamentation.

6 And he hath violently ᴿtaken away his ᴺtabernacle, ᴿas *if it were of* a garden: he hath destroyed his places of the assembly: ᴿthe LORD hath caused the solemn feasts and sabbaths to be forgotten in Zion, and hath despised in the indignation of his anger the king and the priests.

7 The Lord hath cast off his altar, he hath abhorred his sanctuary, he hath ᴺgiven up into the hand of the enemy the walls of her palaces; ᴿthey have made a noise in the house of the LORD, as in the day of a solemn feast.

8 The LORD hath purposed to destroy the wall of the daughter of Zion: ᴿhe hath stretched out a line, he hath not withdrawn his hand from ᴺdestroying: therefore he made the rampart and the wall to lament; they languished together.

9 Her gates are sunk into the ground; he hath destroyed and ᴿbroken her bars: ᴿher king and her princes *are* among the Gentiles: ᴿthe law *is* no *more;* her ᴿprophets also find no vision from the LORD.

10 The elders of the daughter of Zion ᴿsit upon the ground, *and* keep silence: they have ᴿcast up dust upon their heads; they have ᴿgirded themselves with sackcloth: the virgins of Jerusalem hang down their heads to the ground.

11 ᴿMine eyes do fail with tears, ᴿmy bowels are troubled, ᴿmy liver is poured upon the earth, for the destruction of the daughter of my people; because ᴿthe children and the sucklings ᴺswoon in the streets of the city.

12 They say to their mothers, Where *is* corn

and wine? when they swooned as the wounded in the streets of the city, when their soul was poured out into their mothers' bosom.

13 What thing shall I take to witness for thee? ᴿwhat thing shall I liken to thee, O daughter of Jerusalem? what shall I equal to thee, that I may comfort thee, O virgin daughter of Zion? for thy breach *is* great like the sea: who can heal thee?

14 Thy ᴿprophets have seen vain and foolish things for thee: and they have not ᴿdiscovered thine iniquity, to turn away thy captivity; but have seen for thee false burdens and causes of banishment.

The enemy rejoices

15 All that pass ᴺby ᴿclap *their* hands at thee; they hiss ᴿand wag their head at the daughter of Jerusalem, *saying, Is* this the city that *men* call ᴿThe perfection of beauty, The joy of the whole earth?

16 ᴿAll thine enemies have opened their mouth against thee: they hiss and gnash the teeth: they say, ᴿWe have swallowed *her* up: certainly this *is* the day that we looked for; we have found, ᴿwe have seen *it.*

17 The LORD hath done *that* which he had ᴿdevised; he hath fulfilled his word that he had commanded in the days of old: he hath thrown down, and hath not pitied: and he hath caused *thine* enemy to ᴿrejoice over thee, he hath set up the horn of thine adversaries.

Misery of the vanquished people

18 Their heart cried unto the Lord, O wall of the daughter of Zion, ᴿlet tears run down like a river day and night: give thyself no rest; let not the apple of thine eye cease.

19 Arise, ᴿcry out in the night: in the beginning of the watches ᴿpour out thine heart like water before the face of the Lord: lift up thy hands toward him for the life of thy young children, that faint for hunger ᴿin the top of every street.

20 Behold, O LORD, and consider to whom thou hast done this. ᴿShall the women eat their fruit, *and* children ᴺof a span long? ᴿshall the priest and the prophet be slain in the sanctuary of the Lord?

21 ᴿThe young and the old lie on the ground in the streets: my virgins and my young men are fallen by the sword; thou hast slain *them* in the day of thine anger; ᴿthou hast killed, *and* not pitied.

22 Thou hast called as in a solemn day ᴿmy terrors round about, so that in the day of the LORD's anger none escaped nor remained: ᴿthose that I have swaddled and brought up hath mine enemy consumed.

CHAPTER 3

Jeremiah's personal affliction

I AM the man *that* hath seen affliction by the rod of his wrath.

2 He hath led me, and brought *me into* darkness, but not *into* light.

3 Surely against me is he turned; he turneth his hand *against me* all the day.

4 [R]My flesh and my skin hath he made old; he hath [R]broken my bones.

5 He hath builded against me, and compassed *me* with gall and travail.

6 [R]He hath set me in dark places, as *they that be* dead of old.

7 [R]He hath hedged me about, that I cannot get out: he hath made my chain heavy.

8 Also [R]when I cry and shout, he shutteth out my prayer.

9 He hath inclosed my ways with hewn stone, he hath made my paths crooked.

10 [R]He *was* unto me *as* a bear lying in wait, *and as* a lion in secret places.

11 He hath turned aside my ways, and [R]pulled me in pieces: he hath made me desolate.

12 He hath bent his bow, and [R]set me as a mark for the arrow.

13 He hath caused [R]the [N]arrows of his quiver to enter into my reins.

14 I was a [R]derision to all my people; *and* [R]their song all the day.

15 [R]He hath filled me with [N]bitterness, he hath made me drunken with wormwood.

16 He hath also broken my teeth [R]with gravel stones, he hath [N]covered me with ashes.

17 And thou hast removed my soul far off from peace: I forgat [N]prosperity.

18 [R]And I said, My strength and my hope is perished from the LORD:

19 [N]Remembering mine affliction and my misery, [R]the wormwood and the gall.

20 My soul hath *them* still in remembrance, and is [N]humbled in me.

21 This I [N]recall to my mind, therefore have I hope.

22 [R]*It is of* the LORD's mercies that we are not consumed, because his compassions fail not.

23 *They are* new [R]every morning: great *is* thy faithfulness.

24 The LORD *is* my [R]portion, saith my soul; therefore will I hope in him.

25 The LORD *is* good unto them that [R]wait for him, to the soul *that* seeketh him.

26 *It is* good that *a man* should both hope [R]and quietly wait for the salvation of the LORD.

27 [R]*It is* good for a man that he bear the yoke in his youth.

28 [R]He sitteth alone and keepeth silence, because he hath borne *it* upon him.

29 [R]He putteth his mouth in the dust; if so be there may be hope.

30 [R]He giveth *his* cheek to him that smiteth him: he is filled full with reproach.

31 [R]For the Lord will not cast off for ever:

32 But though he cause grief, yet will he have compassion according to the multitude of his mercies.

33 For [R]he doth not afflict [N]willingly nor grieve the children of men.

34 To crush under his feet all the prisoners of the earth,

35 To turn aside the right of a man before the face of [N]the most High,

36 To subvert a man in his cause, [R]the Lord [N]approveth not.

37 Who *is* he [R]that saith, and it cometh to pass, *when* the Lord commandeth *it* not?

38 Out of the mouth of the most High proceedeth not [R]evil and good?

39 [R]Wherefore doth a living man [N]complain, [R]a man for the punishment of his sins?

Exhortation to return to the LORD

40 Let us search and try our ways, and turn again to the LORD.

41 [R]Let us lift up our heart with *our* hands unto God in the heavens.

42 [R]We have transgressed and have rebelled: thou hast not pardoned.

43 Thou hast covered with anger, and persecuted us: thou hast slain, thou hast not pitied.

44 Thou hast covered thyself with a cloud, [R]that *our* prayer should not pass through.

45 Thou hast made us *as* the [R]offscouring and refuse in the midst of the people.

46 [R]All our enemies have opened their mouths against us.

47 [R]Fear and a snare is come upon us, [R]desolation and destruction.

48 [R]Mine eye runneth down with rivers of water for the destruction of the daughter of my people.

49 [R]Mine eye trickleth down, and ceaseth not, without any intermission,

50 Till the LORD [R]look down, and behold from heaven.

51 Mine eye affecteth [N]mine heart [N]because of all the daughters of my city.

Jeremiah's misfortunes

52 Mine enemies chased me sore, like a bird, [R]without cause.

CHAP. 3

BC 588

4	Job 16:8
5	Ps. 51:8
	Is. 38:13
6	Ps. 88:5, 6
7	Hos. 2:6
8	Job 30:20
10	Is. 38:13
	Hos. 5:14
11	Hos. 6:1
12	Job 7:20
	Ps. 38:2
13	Job 6:4
13	Heb. *sons*
14	Jer. 20:7
14	Job 30:9
	Ps. 69:12
15	Jer. 9:15
15	Heb. *bitternesses*
16	Prov. 20:17
16	Or, *rolled me in the ashes*
17	Heb. *good*
18	Ps. 31:22
19	Or, *Remember*
19	Jer. 9:15
20	Heb. *bowed*
21	Heb. *make to return to my heart*
22	Mal. 3:6
23	Is. 33:2
24	Ps. 16:5
25	Is. 30:18
	Mic. 7:7
26	Ps. 37:7

Ps. 94:12	27
Jer. 15:17	28
Job 42:6	29
Is. 50:6	30
Mat. 5:39	
Ps. 94:14	31
Ezek. 33:11	33
Heb. *from his heart*	33
Or, *a superior*	35
Hab. 1:13	36
Or, *seeth not*	36
Ps. 33:9	37
Job 2:10	38
Amos 3:6	
Prov. 19:3	39
Or, *murmur*	39
Mic. 7:9	39
Ps. 86:4	41
Dan. 9:5	42
ver. 8	44
1 Cor. 4:13	45
ch. 2:16	46
Is. 24:17	47
Is. 51:19	47
Jer. 4:19	48
Ps. 77:2	49
Is. 63:15	50
Heb. *my soul*	51
Or, *more than all*	51
Ps. 35:7	52

53 They have cut off my life ᴿin the dungeon, and ᴿcast a stone upon me.

54 ᴿWaters flowed over mine head; *then* ᴿI said, I am cut off.

55 ᴿI called upon thy name, O Lᴏʀᴅ, out of the low dungeon.

56 ᴿThou hast heard my voice: hide not thine ear at my breathing, at my cry.

57 Thou ᴿdrewest near in the day *that* I called upon thee: thou saidst, Fear not.

58 O Lord, thou hast ᴿpleaded the causes of my soul; ᴿthou hast redeemed my life.

59 O Lᴏʀᴅ, thou hast seen my wrong: ᴿjudge thou my cause.

60 Thou hast seen all their vengeance *and* all their ᴿimaginations against me.

61 Thou hast heard their reproach, O Lᴏʀᴅ, *and* all their imaginations against me;

62 The lips of those that rose up against me, and their device against me all the day.

63 Behold their ᴿsitting down, and their rising up; I *am* their musick.

64 ᴿRender unto them a recompence, O Lᴏʀᴅ, according to the work of their hands.

65 Give them ᴺsorrow of heart, thy curse unto them.

66 Persecute and destroy them in anger ᴿfrom under the ᴿheavens of the Lᴏʀᴅ.

CHAPTER 4

Distress of the siege

Hᴏᴡ is the gold become dim! *how* is the most fine gold changed! the stones of the sanctuary are poured out ᴿin the top of every street.

2 The precious sons of Zion, comparable to fine gold, how are they esteemed ᴿas earthen pitchers, the work of the hands of the potter!

3 Even the ᴺsea monsters draw out the breast, they give suck to their young ones: the daughter of my people *is become* cruel, ᴿlike the ostriches in the wilderness.

4 ᴿThe tongue of the sucking child cleaveth to the roof of his mouth for thirst: ᴿthe young children ask bread, *and* no man breaketh *it* unto them.

5 They that did feed delicately are desolate in the streets: they that were brought up in scarlet ᴿembrace dunghills.

6 For the ᴺpunishment of the iniquity of the daughter of my people is greater than the punishment of the sin of Sodom, that was ᴿoverthrown as in a moment, and no hands stayed on her.

7 Her Nazarites were purer than snow, they were whiter than milk, they were more ruddy

CHAP. 3
BC 588
53 Jer. 37:16
53 Dan. 6:17
54 Ps. 69:2
54 Is. 38:10
55 Ps. 130:1
56 Ps. 3:4
57 Jas. 4:8
58 Ps. 35:1
Jer. 51:36
58 Ps. 71:23
59 Ps. 9:4
60 Jer. 11:19
63 Ps. 139:2
64 Ps. 28:4
Jer. 11:20
65 Or, *obstinacy of heart*
66 Deut. 25:19
Jer. 10:11
66 Ps. 8:3

CHAP. 4
BC 588
1 ch. 2:19
2 Is. 30:14
Jer. 19:11
3 Or, *sea calves*
3 Job 39:14
4 Ps. 22:15
4 See ch. 2:11, 12
5 Job 24:8
6 Or, *iniquity*
6 Gen. 19:25

ch. 5:10	8
Joel 2:6	
Nah. 2:10	
Heb. *darker than blackness*	8
Ps. 102:5	8
Heb. *flow out*	9
ch. 2:20	10
Is. 49:15	10
Deut. 28:57	10
Jer. 7:20	11
Deut. 32:22	11
Jer. 6:13	13
Ezek. 22:26	
Mat. 23:31	13
Jer. 2:34	14
Num. 19:16	14
Or, *in that they could not but touch*	14
Or, *ye polluted*	15
Lev. 13:45	15
Or, *face*	16
ch. 5:12	16
2 Ki. 24:7	17
Is. 20:5	
Jer. 37:7	
2 Ki. 25:4	18
Ezek. 7:2, 3	18
Deut. 28:49	19
Gen. 2:7	20
Jer. 52:9	20
Ezek. 12:13	
Jer. 25:15	21
Obad. 10	

in body than rubies, their polishing *was* of sapphire:

8 Their visage is ᴿblackerᴺ than a coal; they are not known in the streets: ᴿtheir skin cleaveth to their bones; it is withered, it is become like a stick.

9 *They that be* slain with the sword are better than *they that be* slain with hunger: for these ᴺpine away, stricken through for *want of* the fruits of the field.

10 ᴿThe hands of the ᴿpitiful women have sodden their own children: they were their ᴿmeat in the destruction of the daughter of my people.

11 The Lᴏʀᴅ hath accomplished his fury; ᴿhe hath poured out his fierce anger, and ᴿhath kindled a fire in Zion, and it hath devoured the foundations thereof.

Incredibility of Jerusalem's fall

12 The kings of the earth, and all the inhabitants of the world, would not have believed that the adversary and the enemy should have entered into the gates of Jerusalem.

13 ᴿFor the sins of her prophets, *and* the iniquities of her priests, ᴿthat have shed the blood of the just in the midst of her,

14 They have wandered *as* blind *men* in the streets, ᴿthey have polluted themselves with blood, ᴿsoᴺ that men could not touch their garments.

15 They cried unto them, Depart ye; ᴺ*It is* ᴿunclean; depart, depart, touch not: when they fled away and wandered, they said among the heathen, They shall no more sojourn *there*.

16 The ᴺanger of the Lᴏʀᴅ hath divided them; he will no more regard them: ᴿthey respected not the persons of the priests, they favoured not the elders.

17 As for us, ᴿour eyes as yet failed for our vain help: in our watching we have watched for a nation *that* could not save *us*.

18 ᴿThey hunt our steps, that we cannot go in our streets: our end is near, our days are fulfilled; for ᴿour end is come.

19 Our persecutors are ᴿswifter than the eagles of the heaven: they pursued us upon the mountains, they laid wait for us in the wilderness.

20 The ᴿbreath of our nostrils, the anointed of the Lᴏʀᴅ, ᴿwas taken in their pits, of whom we said, Under his shadow we shall live among the heathen.

21 Rejoice and be glad, O daughter of E̅'-dᴏm, that dwellest in the land of Uz; ᴿthe cup also shall pass through unto thee: thou shalt be drunken, and shalt make thyself naked.

22 ᴿTheᴺ punishment of thine iniquity is accomplished, O daughter of Zion; he will no more carry thee away into captivity: ᴿhe will visit thine iniquity, O daughter of Ē'-dom; he will ᴺdiscover thy sins.

CHAPTER 5

Prayer for restoration

REMEMBER,ᴿ O Lord, what is come upon us: consider, and behold ᴿour reproach.

2 ᴿOur inheritance is turned to strangers, our houses to aliens.

3 We are orphans and fatherless, our mothers *are* as widows.

4 We have drunken our water for money; our wood ᴺis sold unto us.

5 ᴿOurᴺ necks *are* under persecution: we labour, *and* have no rest.

6 ᴿWe have given the hand ᴿto the Egyptians, *and to* the Assyrians, to be satisfied with bread.

7 ᴿOur fathers have sinned, *and are* not; and we have borne their iniquities.

8 Servants have ruled over us: *there is* none that doth deliver *us* out of their hand.

CHAP. 4
BC 588
22 Is. 40:2
22 Or, *Thine iniquity*
22 Ps. 137:7
22 Or, *carry* thee *captive for thy sins*

CHAP. 5
BC 588
1 Ps. 89:50
1 Ps. 79:4
ch. 2:15
2 Ps. 79:1
4 Heb. *cometh for price*
5 Jer. 28:14
5 Heb. *on our necks are we persecuted*
6 Gen. 24:2
6 Hos. 12:1
7 Jer. 31:29

Or, *terrors,* or, *storms*	10
Ps. 89:39	16
Heb. *The crown of our head is fallen*	16
Ps. 6:7	17
Ps. 9:7	19
Ps. 45:6	19
Ps. 13:1	20
Heb. *for length of days?*	20
Or, *For wilt thou utterly reject us?*	22

9 We gat our bread with *the peril of* our lives because of the sword of the wilderness.

10 Our skin was black like an oven because of the ᴺterrible famine.

11 They ravished the women in Zion, *and* the maids in the cities of Judah.

12 Princes are hanged up by their hand: the faces of elders were not honoured.

13 They took the young men to grind, and the children fell under the wood.

14 The elders have ceased from the gate, the young men from their musick.

15 The joy of our heart is ceased; our dance is turned into mourning.

16 ᴿTheᴺ crown is fallen *from* our head: woe unto us, that we have sinned!

17 For this our heart is faint; ᴿfor these *things* our eyes are dim.

18 Because of the mountain of Zion, which is desolate, the foxes walk upon it.

19 Thou, O Lord, ᴿremainest for ever; ᴿthy throne from generation to generation.

20 ᴿWherefore dost thou forget us for ever, *and* forsake us ᴺso long time?

21 Turn thou us unto thee, O Lord, and we shall be turned; renew our days as of old.

22 ᴺBut thou hast utterly rejected us; thou art very wroth against us.

THE BOOK OF THE PROPHET

EZEKIEL

The prophet Ezekiel has been traditionally credited with writing the book that bears his name. Born in Jerusalem into a priestly family, Ezekiel was taken captive at the age of 25 in 597 B.C. In the environs of Babylon he was called to be a prophet. His last message is dated in 571 B.C.

Living in exile, Ezekiel was commissioned to be a watchman to his people. From 593 B.C. until Jerusalem fell in 586 B.C. he warned his fellow exiles about the doom of their native city. He graphically portrayed the sin and guilt of his people and the impending judgment awaiting the false prophets. After Jerusalem fell, his whole message was one of encouragement and hope. God, who had sent judgment, was also the shepherd of Israel who would ultimately restore His chosen people to their own land, supreme over all nations. The glory of God, which abandoned Jerusalem, would return to the restored temple.

Outline:

I. Ezekiel's commission as a prophet   1:1–3:21
II. Jerusalem doomed and abandoned   3:22–11:25
III. Leaders and people condemned   12:1–19:14
IV. The reason for condemnation   20:1–24:27
V. Foreign nations in prophecy   25:1–32:32
VI. God's promises to Israel   33:1–39:29
VII. The restored state of Israel   40:1–48:35

CHAPTER 1

In Babylon with the exiles

NOW it came to pass in the thirtieth year, in the fourth *month,* in the fifth *day* of the month, as I *was* among the ᴺcaptives ᴿby the river of Chē'-bär, *that* ᴿthe heavens were opened, and I saw ᴿvisions of God.

2 In the fifth *day* of the month, which *was* the fifth year of ᴿking Jĕ-hoi'-ă-chin's captivity,

CHAP. 1
BC 595
1 Heb. *captivity*
1 ch. 3:15, 23
1 Mat. 3:16
1 ch. 8:3
2 2 Ki. 24:12

Heb. *Jehezkel*	3
1 Ki. 18:46	3
Jer. 23:19	4
Jer. 1:14	4
Heb. *catching itself*	4

3 The word of the Lord came expressly unto ᴺĒ-zĕk'-ĭĕl the priest, the son of Bū'-zī, in the land of the Chăl-dē'-ăns by the river Chē'-bär; and ᴿthe hand of the Lord was there upon him.

Vision of four living creatures

4 And I looked, and, behold, ᴿa whirlwind came ᴿout of the north, a great cloud, and a fire ᴺinfolding itself, and a brightness *was*

about it, and out of the midst thereof as the colour of amber, out of the midst of the fire.

5 [R]Also out of the midst thereof *came* the likeness of four living creatures. And [R]this *was* their appearance; they had [R]the likeness of a man.

6 And every one had four faces, and every one had four wings.

7 And their feet *were* [N]straight feet; and the sole of their feet *was* like the sole of a calf's foot: and they sparkled [R]like the colour of burnished brass.

8 [R]And *they had* the hands of a man under their wings on their four sides; and they four had their faces and their wings.

9 [R]Their wings *were* joined one to another; [R]they turned not when they went; they went every one straight forward.

10 As for [R]the likeness of their faces, they four [R]had the face of a man, [R]and the face of a lion, on the right side: [R]and they four had the face of an ox on the left side; [R]they four also had the face of an eagle.

11 Thus *were* their faces: and their wings *were* [N]stretched upward; two *wings* of every one *were* joined one to another, and [R]two covered their bodies.

12 And [R]they went every one straight forward: [R]whither the spirit was to go, they went; *and* they turned not when they went.

13 As for the likeness of the living creatures, their appearance *was* like burning coals of fire, [R]*and* like the appearance of lamps: it went up and down among the living creatures; and the fire was bright, and out of the fire went forth lightning.

14 And the living creatures ran and returned [R]as the appearance of a flash of lightning.

Vision of the four wheels

15 Now as I beheld the living creatures, behold [R]one wheel upon the earth by the living creatures, with his four faces.

16 [R]The appearance of the wheels and their work *was* [R]like unto the colour of a beryl: and they four had one likeness: and their appearance and their work *was* as it were a wheel in the middle of a wheel.

17 When they went, they went upon their four sides: [R]*and* they turned not when they went.

18 As for their rings, they were so high that they were dreadful; and their [N]rings *were* [R]full of eyes round about them four.

19 And [R]when the living creatures went, the wheels went by them: and when the living creatures were lifted up from the earth, the wheels were lifted up.

20 [R]Whithersoever the spirit was to go, they went, thither *was their* spirit to go; and the wheels were lifted up over against them: [R]for the spirit [N]of the living creature *was* in the wheels.

21 [R]When those went, *these* went; and when those stood, *these* stood; and when those were lifted up from the earth, the wheels were lifted up over against them: for the spirit [N]of the living creature *was* in the wheels.

Vision of the glory of the LORD

22 [R]And the likeness of the firmament upon the heads of the living creature *was* as the colour of the terrible crystal, stretched forth over their heads above.

23 And under the firmament *were* their wings straight, the one toward the other: every one had two, which covered on this side, and every one had two, which covered on that side, their bodies.

24 [R]And when they went, I heard the noise of their wings, [R]like the noise of great waters, as [R]the voice of the Almighty, the voice of speech, as the noise of an host: when they stood, they let down their wings.

25 And there was a voice from the firmament that *was* over their heads, when they stood, *and* had let down their wings.

26 [R]And above the firmament that *was* over their heads *was* the likeness of a throne, [R]as the appearance of a sapphire stone: and upon the likeness of the throne *was* the likeness as the appearance of a man above upon it.

27 [R]And I saw as the colour of amber, as the appearance of fire round about within it, from the appearance of his loins even upward, and from the appearance of his loins even downward, I saw as it were the appearance of fire, and it had brightness round about.

28 [R]As the appearance of the bow that is in the cloud in the day of rain, so *was* the appearance of the brightness round about. [R]This *was* the appearance of the likeness of the glory of the LORD. And when I saw *it,* [R]I fell upon my face, and I heard a voice of one that spake.

CHAPTER 2

Ezekiel's call

AND he said unto me, Son of man, [R]stand upon thy feet, and I will speak unto thee.

2 And [R]the spirit entered into me when he spake unto me, and set me upon my feet, that I heard him that spake unto me.

3 And he said unto me, Son of man, I send thee to the children of Israel, to a rebellious

ᴺnation that hath rebelled against me: ᴿthey and their fathers have transgressed against me, *even* unto this very day.

4 ᴿFor *they are* ᴺimpudent children and stiffhearted. I do send thee unto them; and thou shalt say unto them, Thus saith the Lord GOD.

5 ᴿAnd they, whether they will hear, or whether they will forbear, (for they *are* a rebellious house,) yet ᴿshall know that there hath been a prophet among them.

6 And thou, son of man, ᴿbe not afraid of them, neither be afraid of their words, though ᴿbriersᴺ and thorns *be* with thee, and thou dost dwell among scorpions: ᴿbe not afraid of their words, nor be dismayed at their looks, ᴿthough they *be* a rebellious house.

7 ᴿAnd thou shalt speak my words unto them, ᴿwhether they will hear, or whether they will forbear: for they *are* ᴺmost rebellious.

Ezekiel eats the roll

8 But thou, son of man, hear what I say unto thee; Be not thou rebellious like that rebellious house: open thy mouth, and ᴿeat that I give thee.

9 And when I looked, behold, ᴿan hand *was* sent unto me; and, lo, ᴿa roll of a book *was* therein;

10 And he spread it before me; and it *was* written within and without: and *there was* written therein lamentations, and mourning, and woe.

CHAPTER 3

MOREOVER he said unto me, Son of man, eat that thou findest; ᴿeat this roll, and go speak unto the house of Israel.

2 So I opened my mouth, and he caused me to eat that roll.

3 And he said unto me, Son of man, cause thy belly to eat, and fill thy bowels with this roll that I give thee. Then did I ᴿeat *it;* and it was in my mouth ᴿas honey for sweetness.

Mission to the exiles at Telabib

4 And he said unto me, Son of man, go, get thee unto the house of Israel, and speak with my words unto them.

5 For thou *art* not sent to a people ᴺof a strange speech and of an hard language, *but* to the house of Israel;

6 Not to many people ᴺof a strange speech and of an hard language, whose words thou canst not understand. ᴺSurely, ᴿhad I sent thee to them, they would have hearkened unto thee.

7 But the house of Israel will not hearken unto thee; ᴿfor they will not hearken unto me:

CHAP. **2**
BC 595
3 Heb. *nations*
3 Jer. 3:25
ch. 20:18, 21, 30
4 ch. 3:7
4 Heb. *hard of face*
5 ch. 3:11, 26, 27
5 ch. 33:33
6 Jer. 1:8, 17
Luke 12:4
6 Is. 9:18
Jer. 6:28
Mic. 7:4
6 Or, *rebels*
6 ch. 3:9
1 Pet. 3:14
6 ch. 3:9, 26, 27
7 Jer. 1:7, 17
7 ver. 5
7 Heb. *rebellion*
8 Rev. 10:9
9 Jer. 1:9
ch. 8:3
9 ch. 3:1

CHAP. **3**
BC 595
1 ch. 2:8, 9
3 Rev. 10:9
See Jer. 15:16
3 Ps. 19:10
& 119:103
5 Heb. *deep of lip, and heavy of tongue,* ver. 6
6 Heb. *deep of lip, and heavy of language*
6 Or, *If I had sent thee, etc., would they not have hearkened unto thee?*
6 Mat. 11:21
7 John 15:20

ch. 2:4   7
Heb. *stiff*   7
of forehead and hard of heart
Is. 50:7   9
Jer. 1:18
Mic. 3:8
Jer. 1:8, 17   9
ch. 2:6
ch. 2:5, 7   11
ch. 8:3   12
1 Ki. 18:12
Acts 8:39
Heb. *kissed*   13
ver. 12   14
ch. 8:3
Heb. *bitter*   14
Heb. *hot anger*   14
2 Ki. 3:15   14
ch. 1:3 & 8:1
Job 2:13   15
Ps. 137:1
ch. 33:7-9   17
Is. 52:8 & 56:10   17
Jer. 6:17
ch. 33:6   18
John 8:21
Is. 49:4, 5   19
Acts 20:26
ch. 18:24   20
& 33:12, 13
Heb. *right-*   20
eousnesses

ᴿfor all the house of Israel *are* ᴺimpudent and hardhearted.

8 Behold, I have made thy face strong against their faces, and thy forehead strong against their foreheads.

9 ᴿAs an adamant harder than flint have I made thy forehead: ᴿfear them not, neither be dismayed at their looks, though they *be* a rebellious house.

10 Moreover he said unto me, Son of man, all my words that I shall speak unto thee receive in thine heart, and hear with thine ears.

11 And go, get thee to them of the captivity, unto the children of thy people, and speak unto them, and tell them, ᴿThus saith the Lord GOD; whether they will hear, or whether they will forbear.

12 Then ᴿthe spirit took me up, and I heard behind me a voice of a great rushing, *saying,* Blessed *be* the glory of the LORD from his place.

13 *I heard* also the noise of the wings of the living creatures that ᴺtouched one another, and the noise of the wheels over against them, and a noise of a great rushing.

14 So ᴿthe spirit lifted me up, and took me away, and I went ᴺin bitterness, in the ᴺheat of my spirit; but ᴿthe hand of the LORD was strong upon me.

15 Then I came to them of the captivity at Tĕl-ā′-bĭb, that dwelt by the river of Chē′-bär, and ᴿI sat where they sat, and remained there astonished among them seven days.

Prophet as watchman

16 And it came to pass at the end of seven days, that the word of the LORD came unto me, saying,

17 ᴿSon of man, I have made thee ᴿa watchman unto the house of Israel: therefore hear the word at my mouth, and give them warning from me.

18 When I say unto the wicked, Thou shalt surely die; and thou givest him not warning, nor speakest to warn the wicked from his wicked way, to save his life; the same wicked *man* ᴿshall die in his iniquity; but his blood will I require at thine hand.

19 Yet if thou warn the wicked, and he turn not from his wickedness, nor from his wicked way, he shall die in his iniquity; ᴿbut thou hast delivered thy soul.

20 Again, When a ᴿrighteous *man* doth turn from his ᴺrighteousness, and commit iniquity, and I lay a stumblingblock before him, he shall die: because thou hast not given him warning, he shall die in his sin, and his righteousness which he hath done shall not be re-

membered; but his blood will I require at thine hand.

21 Nevertheless if thou warn the righteous *man,* that the righteous sin not, and he doth not sin, he shall surely live, because he is warned; also thou hast delivered thy soul.

Prophet to be bound and stricken dumb

22 ᴿAnd the hand of the LORD was there upon me; and he said unto me, Arise, go forth ᴿinto the plain, and I will there talk with thee.

23 Then I arose, and went forth into the plain: and, behold, ᴿthe glory of the LORD stood there, as the glory which I ᴿsaw by the river of Chē′-bär: ᴿand I fell on my face.

24 Then ᴿthe spirit entered into me, and set me upon my feet, and spake with me, and said unto me, Go, shut thyself within thine house.

25 But thou, O son of man, behold, ᴿthey shall put bands upon thee, and shall bind thee with them, and thou shalt not go out among them:

26 And ᴿI will make thy tongue cleave to the roof of thy mouth, that thou shalt be dumb, and shalt not be to them ᴺa reprover: ᴿfor they *are* a rebellious house.

27 ᴿBut when I speak with thee, I will open thy mouth, and thou shalt say unto them, ᴿThus saith the Lord GOD; He that heareth, let him hear; and he that forbeareth, let him forbear: for they *are* a rebellious house.

CHAPTER 4

Signs of the siege and exile

THOU also, son of man, take thee a tile, and lay it before thee, and portray upon it the city, *even* Jerusalem:

2 And lay siege against it, and build a fort against it, and cast a mount against it; set the camp also against it, and set ᴺbattering rams against it round about.

3 Moreover take thou unto thee ᴺan iron pan, and set it *for* a wall of iron between thee and the city: and set thy face against it, and it shall be besieged, and thou shalt lay siege against it. ᴿThis *shall be* a sign to the house of Israel.

4 Lie thou also upon thy left side, and lay the iniquity of the house of Israel upon it: *according* to the number of the days that thou shalt lie upon it thou shalt bear their iniquity.

5 For I have laid upon thee the years of their iniquity, according to the number of the days, three hundred and ninety days: ᴿso shalt thou bear the iniquity of the house of Israel.

6 And when thou hast accomplished them, lie again on thy right side, and thou shalt bear

the iniquity of the house of Judah forty days: I have appointed thee ᴺeach day for a year.

7 Therefore thou shalt set thy face toward the siege of Jerusalem, and thine arm *shall be* uncovered, and thou shalt prophesy against it.

8 ᴿAnd, behold, I will lay bands upon thee, and thou shalt not turn thee ᴺfrom one side to another, till thou hast ended the days of thy siege.

9 Take thou also unto thee wheat, and barley, and beans, and lentiles, and millet, and ᴺfitches, and put them in one vessel, and make thee bread thereof, *according* to the number of the days that thou shalt lie upon thy side, three hundred and ninety days shalt thou eat thereof.

10 And thy meat which thou shalt eat *shall be* by weight, twenty shē′-kĕls a day: from time to time shalt thou eat it.

11 Thou shalt drink also water by measure, the sixth part of an hīn: from time to time shalt thou drink.

12 And thou shalt eat it *as* barley cakes, and thou shalt bake it with dung that cometh out of man, in their sight.

13 And the LORD said, Even thus ᴿshall the children of Israel eat their defiled bread among the Gentiles, whither I will drive them.

14 Then said I, ᴿAh Lord GOD! behold, my soul hath not been polluted: for from my youth up even till now have I not eaten of ᴿthat which dieth of itself, or is torn in pieces; neither came there ᴿabominable flesh into my mouth.

15 Then he said unto me, Lo, I have given thee cow's dung for man's dung, and thou shalt prepare thy bread therewith.

16 Moreover he said unto me, Son of man, behold, I will break the ᴿstaff of bread in Jerusalem: and they shall ᴿeat bread by weight, and with care; and they shall ᴿdrink water by measure, and with astonishment:

17 That they may want bread and water, and be astonied one with another, and ᴿconsume away for their iniquity.

CHAPTER 5

Sign of Jerusalem's fall

AND thou, son of man, take thee a sharp knife, take thee a barber's razor, ᴿand cause *it* to pass upon thine head and upon thy beard: then take thee balances to weigh, and divide the *hair.*

2 ᴿThou shalt burn with fire a third part in the midst of ᴿthe city, when ᴿthe days of the siege are fulfilled: and thou shalt take a third part, *and* smite about it with a knife: and a

third part thou shalt scatter in the wind; and I will draw out a sword after them.

3 ᴿThou shalt also take thereof a few in number, and bind them in thy ᴺskirts.

4 Then take of them again, and ᴿcast them into the midst of the fire, and burn them in the fire; *for* thereof shall a fire come forth into all the house of Israel.

5 Thus saith the Lord Goᴅ; This *is* Jerusalem: I have set it in the midst of the nations and countries *that are* round about her.

6 And she hath changed my judgments into wickedness more than the nations, and my statutes more than the countries that *are* round about her: for they have refused my judgments and my statutes, they have not walked in them.

7 Therefore thus saith the Lord Goᴅ; Because ye multiplied more than the nations that *are* round about you, *and* have not walked in my statutes, neither have kept my judgments, ᴿneither have done according to the judgments of the nations that *are* round about you;

8 Therefore thus saith the Lord Goᴅ; Behold, I, even I, *am* against thee, and will execute judgments in the midst of thee in the sight of the nations.

9 ᴿAnd I will do in thee that which I have not done, and whereunto I will not do any more the like, because of all thine abominations.

10 Therefore the fathers ᴿshall eat the sons in the midst of thee, and the sons shall eat their fathers; and I will execute judgments in thee, and the whole remnant of thee will I ᴿscatter into all the winds.

11 Wherefore, *as* I live, saith the Lord Goᴅ; Surely, because thou hast ᴿdefiled my sanctuary with all thy ᴿdetestable things, and with all thine abominations, therefore will I also diminish *thee;* ᴿneither shall mine eye spare, neither will I have any pity.

12 ᴿA third part of thee shall die with the pestilence, and with famine shall they be consumed in the midst of thee: and a third part shall fall by the sword round about thee; and ᴿI will scatter a third part into all the winds, and ᴿI will draw out a sword after them.

13 Thus shall mine anger ᴿbe accomplished, and I will ᴿcause my fury to rest upon them, ᴿand I will be comforted: ᴿand they shall know that I the Loʀᴅ have spoken *it* in my zeal, when I have accomplished my fury in them.

14 Moreover ᴿI will make thee waste, and a reproach among the nations that *are* round about thee, in the sight of all that pass by.

15 So it shall be a ᴿreproach and a taunt, an

instruction and an astonishment unto the nations that *are* round about thee, when I shall execute judgments in thee in anger and in fury and in ᴿfurious rebukes. I the Loʀᴅ have spoken *it.*

16 When I shall ᴿsend upon them the evil arrows of famine, which shall be for *their* destruction, *and* which I will send to destroy you: and I will increase the famine upon you, and will break your ᴿstaff of bread:

17 So will I send upon you famine and ᴿevil beasts, and they shall bereave thee; and ᴿpestilence and blood shall pass through thee; and I will bring the sword upon thee. I the Loʀᴅ have spoken *it.*

CHAPTER 6

Doom of pagan altars

AND the word of the Loʀᴅ came unto me, saying,

2 Son of man, ᴿset thy face toward the ᴿmountains of Israel, and prophesy against them,

3 And say, Ye mountains of Israel, hear the word of the Lord Goᴅ; Thus saith the Lord Goᴅ to the mountains, and to the hills, to the rivers, and to the valleys; Behold, I, *even* I, will bring a sword upon you, and ᴿI will destroy your high places.

4 And your altars shall be desolate, and your ᴺimages shall be broken: and ᴿI will cast down your slain *men* before your idols.

5 And I will ᴺlay the dead carcases of the children of Israel before their idols; and I will scatter your bones round about your altars.

6 In all your dwelling places the cities shall be laid waste, and the high places shall be desolate; that your altars may be laid waste and made desolate, and your idols may be broken and cease, and your images may be cut down, and your works may be abolished.

7 And the slain shall fall in the midst of you, and ᴿye shall know that I *am* the Loʀᴅ.

Remnant for remembrance

8 ᴿYet will I leave a remnant, that ye may have *some* that shall escape the sword among the nations, when ye shall be scattered through the countries.

9 And they that escape of you shall remember me among the nations whither they shall be carried captives, because ᴿI am broken with their whorish heart, which hath departed from me, and ᴿwith their eyes, which go a whoring after their idols: and ᴿthey shall lothe themselves for the evils which they have committed in all their abominations.

10 And they shall know that I *am* the LORD, *and that* I have not said in vain that I would do this evil unto them.

Desolation of the land

11 Thus saith the Lord GOD; Smite [R]with thine hand, and stamp with thy foot, and say, Alas for all the evil abominations of the house of Israel! [R]for they shall fall by the sword, by the famine, and by the pestilence.

12 He that is far off shall die of the pestilence; and he that is near shall fall by the sword; and he that remaineth and is besieged shall die by the famine: [R]thus will I accomplish my fury upon them.

13 Then [R]shall ye know that I *am* the LORD, when their slain *men* shall be among their idols round about their altars, [R]upon every high hill, [R]in all the tops of the mountains, and [R]under every green tree, and under every thick oak, the place where they did offer sweet savour to all their idols.

14 So will I [R]stretch out my hand upon them, and make the land desolate, yea, [N]more desolate than the wilderness toward [R]Dĭb'-lăth, in all their habitations: and they shall know that I *am* the LORD.

CHAPTER 7

Disaster at the end

MOREOVER the word of the LORD came unto me, saying,

2 Also, thou son of man, thus saith the Lord GOD unto the land of Israel; [R]An end, the end is come upon the four corners of the land.

3 Now *is* the end *come* upon thee, and I will send mine anger upon thee, and will judge thee according to thy ways, and will [N]recompense upon thee all thine abominations.

4 And [R]mine eye shall not spare thee, neither will I have pity: but I will recompense thy ways upon thee, and thine abominations shall be in the midst of thee: [R]and ye shall know that I *am* the LORD.

5 Thus saith the Lord GOD; An evil, an only evil, behold, is come.

6 An end is come, the end is come: it [N]watcheth for thee; behold, it is come.

7 [R]The morning is come unto thee, O thou that dwellest in the land: [R]the time is come, the day of trouble *is* near, and not the [N]sounding again of the mountains.

8 Now will I shortly [R]pour out my fury upon thee, and accomplish mine anger upon thee: and I will judge thee according to thy ways, and will recompense thee for all thine abominations.

9 And mine eye shall not spare, neither will I have pity: I will recompense [N]thee according to thy ways and thine abominations *that* are in the midst of thee; and ye shall know that I *am* the LORD that smiteth.

10 Behold the day, behold, it is come: [R]the morning is gone forth; the rod hath blossomed, pride hath budded.

11 [R]Violence is risen up into a rod of wickedness: none of them *shall remain,* nor of their [N]multitude, nor of any of [N]theirs: [R]neither *shall there be* wailing for them.

12 The time is come, the day draweth near: let not the buyer rejoice, nor the seller mourn: for wrath *is* upon all the multitude thereof.

13 For the seller shall not return to that which is sold, [N]although they were yet alive: for the vision *is* touching the whole multitude thereof, *which* shall not return; neither shall any strengthen himself [N]in [N]the iniquity of his life.

The sword without and famine within

14 They have blown the trumpet, even to make all ready; but none goeth to the battle: for my wrath *is* upon all the multitude thereof.

15 [R]The sword *is* without, and the pestilence and the famine within: he that *is* in the field shall die with the sword; and he that *is* in the city, famine and pestilence shall devour him.

16 But they that escape of them shall escape, and shall be on the mountains like doves of the valleys, all of them mourning, every one for his iniquity.

17 All [R]hands shall be feeble, and all knees shall [N]be weak *as* water.

18 They shall also [R]gird *themselves* with sackcloth, and horror shall cover them; and shame *shall be* upon all faces, and baldness upon all their heads.

19 They shall cast their silver in the streets, and their gold shall be [N]removed: their [R]silver and their gold shall not be able to deliver them in the day of the wrath of the LORD: they shall not satisfy their souls, neither fill their bowels: [N]because it is the stumblingblock of their iniquity.

20 As for the beauty of his ornament, he set it in majesty: [R]but they made the images of their abominations *and* of their detestable things therein: therefore have I [N]set it far from them.

21 And I will give it into the hands of the strangers for a prey, and to the wicked of the earth for a spoil; and they shall pollute it.

22 My face will I turn also from them, and they shall pollute my secret *place:* for the [N]robbers shall enter into it, and defile it.

23 Make a chain: for [R]the land is full of bloody crimes, and the city is full of violence.

24 Wherefore I will bring the worst of the heathen, and they shall possess their houses: I will also make the pomp of the strong to cease; and [N]their holy places shall be defiled.

25 [N]Destruction cometh; and they shall seek peace, and *there shall be* none.

26 [R]Mischief shall come upon mischief, and rumour shall be upon rumour; [R]then shall they seek a vision of the prophet; but the law shall perish from the priest, and counsel from the ancients.

27 The king shall mourn, and the prince shall be clothed with desolation, and the hands of the people of the land shall be troubled: I will do unto them after their way, and [N]according to their deserts will I judge them; and they shall know that I *am* the LORD.

CHAPTER 8

Visions of abominations in the temple

AND it came to pass in the sixth year, in the sixth *month,* in the fifth *day* of the month, *as* I sat in mine house, and [R]the elders of Judah sat before me, that [R]the hand of the Lord GOD fell there upon me.

2 [R]Then I beheld, and lo a likeness as the appearance of fire: from the appearance of his loins even downward, fire; and from his loins even upward, as the appearance of brightness, [R]as the colour of amber.

3 And he [R]put forth the form of an hand, and took me by a lock of mine head; and [R]the spirit lifted me up between the earth and the heaven, and [R]brought me in the visions of God to Jerusalem, to the door of the inner gate that looketh toward the north; [R]where *was* the seat of the image of jealousy, which [R]provoketh to jealousy.

4 And, behold, the glory of the God of Israel *was* there, according to the vision that I [R]saw in the plain.

5 Then said he unto me, Son of man, lift up thine eyes now the way toward the north. So I lifted up mine eyes the way toward the north, and behold northward at the gate of the altar this image of jealousy in the entry.

6 He said furthermore unto me, Son of man, seest thou what they do? *even* the great abominations that the house of Israel committeth here, that I should go far off from my sanctuary? but turn thee yet again, *and* thou shalt see greater abominations.

7 And he brought me to the door of the court; and when I looked, behold a hole in the wall.

8 Then said he unto me, Son of man, dig now in the wall: and when I had digged in the wall, behold a door.

9 And he said unto me, Go in, and behold the wicked abominations that they do here.

10 So I went in and saw; and behold every form of creeping things, and abominable beasts, and all the idols of the house of Israel, portrayed upon the wall round about.

11 And there stood before them seventy men of the ancients of the house of Israel, and in the midst of them stood Jā-ăz-ă-nī′-ăh the son of Shā′-phăn, with every man his censer in his hand; and a thick cloud of incense went up.

12 Then said he unto me, Son of man, hast thou seen what the ancients of the house of Israel do in the dark, every man in the chambers of his imagery? for they say, [R]The LORD seeth us not; the LORD hath forsaken the earth.

13 He said also unto me, Turn thee yet again, *and* thou shalt see greater abominations that they do.

14 Then he brought me to the door of the gate of the LORD's house which *was* toward the north; and, behold, there sat women weeping for Tăm′-mŭz.

15 Then said he unto me, Hast thou seen *this,* O son of man? turn thee yet again, *and* thou shalt see greater abominations than these.

16 And he brought me into the inner court of the LORD's house, and, behold, at the door of the temple of the LORD, [R]between the porch and the altar, [R]*were* about five and twenty men, [R]with their backs toward the temple of the LORD, and their faces toward the east; and they worshipped [R]the sun toward the east.

17 Then he said unto me, Hast thou seen *this,* O son of man? [N]Is it a light thing to the house of Judah that they commit the abominations which they commit here? for they have [R]filled the land with violence, and have returned to provoke me to anger: and, lo, they put the branch to their nose.

18 [R]Therefore will I also deal in fury: mine [R]eye shall not spare, neither will I have pity: and though they [R]cry in mine ears with a loud voice, *yet* will I not hear them.

CHAPTER 9

Executioners of the city

HE cried also in mine ears with a loud voice, saying, Cause them that have charge over the city to draw near, even every man *with* his destroying weapon in his hand.

2 And, behold, six men came from the way of the higher gate, [N]which lieth toward the north, and every man [N]a slaughter weapon in

---

CHAP. 7
BC 594

23 2 Ki. 21:16
24 Or, *they shall inherit their holy places*
25 Heb. *Cutting off*
26 Deut. 32:23
    Jer. 4:20
26 Ps. 74:9
    ch. 20:1, 3
27 Heb. *with their judgments*

CHAP. 8
BC 594

1 ch. 14:1 & 20:1 & 33:31
1 ch. 1:3 & 3:22
2 ch. 1:26, 27
2 ch. 1:4
3 Dan. 5:5
3 ch. 3:14
3 ch. 11:1, 24 & 40:2
3 Jer. 7:30 & 32:34 ch. 5:11
3 Deut. 32:16, 21
4 ch. 1:28 & 3:22, 23

ch. 9:9   12
Joel 2:17   16
ch. 11:1   16
Jer. 2:27   16
  & 32:33
Deut. 4:19   16
2 Ki. 23:5, 11   16
Job 31:26
Jer. 44:17
Or, *Is there any thing lighter than to commit*   17
ch. 9:9   17
ch. 5:13   18
  & 16:42 & 24:13
ch. 5:11 & 7:4, 9   18
  & 9:5, 10
Prov. 1:28   18
Is. 1:15
Jer. 11:11 & 14:12
Mic. 3:4
Zech. 7:13

CHAP. 9
BC 594

Heb. *which is turned*   2
Heb. *a weapon of his breaking in pieces*   2

his hand; [R]and one man among them *was* clothed with linen, with a writer's inkhorn [N]by his side: and they went in, and stood beside the brasen altar.

Marking those to be spared

3 And [R]the glory of the God of Israel was gone up from the cherub, whereupon he was, to the threshold of the house. And he called to the man clothed with linen, which *had* the writer's inkhorn by his side;

4 And the LORD said unto him, Go through the midst of the city, through the midst of Jerusalem, and [N]set [R]a mark upon the foreheads of the men [R]that sigh and that cry for all the abominations that be done in the midst thereof.

5 And to the others he said in [N]mine hearing, Go ye after him through the city, and smite: [R]let not your eye spare, neither have ye pity:

6 [R]Slay [N]utterly old *and* young, both maids, and little children, and women: but [R]come not near any man upon whom *is* the mark; and [R]begin at my sanctuary. [R]Then they began at the ancient men which *were* before the house.

7 And he said unto them, Defile the house, and fill the courts with the slain: go ye forth. And they went forth, and slew in the city.

Intercession of the prophet

8 And it came to pass, while they were slaying them, and I was left, that I [R]fell upon my face, and cried, and said, [R]Ah Lord GOD! wilt thou destroy all the residue of Israel in thy pouring out of thy fury upon Jerusalem?

9 Then said he unto me, The iniquity of the house of Israel and Judah *is* exceeding great, and [R]the land is [N]full of blood, and the city full of [N]perverseness: for they say, [R]The LORD hath forsaken the earth, and [R]the LORD seeth not.

10 And as for me also, mine [R]eye shall not spare, neither will I have pity, *but* [R]I will recompense their way upon their head.

11 And, behold, the man clothed with linen, which *had* the inkhorn by his side, [N]reported the matter, saying, I have done as thou hast commanded me.

CHAPTER 10

Fire scattered over the city

THEN I looked, and, behold, in the [R]firmament that was above the head of the chĕr′-ū-bĭms there appeared over them as it were a sapphire stone, as the appearance of the likeness of a throne.

2 [R]And he spake unto the man clothed with linen, and said, Go in between the wheels, *even* under the cherub, and fill [N]thine hand with [R]coals of fire from between the chĕr′-ū-bĭms, and [R]scatter *them* over the city. And he went in in my sight.

3 Now the chĕr′-ū-bĭms stood on the right side of the house, when the man went in; and the cloud filled the inner court.

4 [R]Then the glory of the LORD [N]went up from the cherub, *and stood* over the threshold of the house; and [R]the house was filled with the cloud, and the court was full of the brightness of the LORD's glory.

5 And the [R]sound of the chĕr′-ū-bĭms' wings was heard *even* to the outer court, as [R]the voice of the Almighty God when he speaketh.

6 And it came to pass, *that* when he had commanded the man clothed with linen, saying, Take fire from between the wheels, from between the chĕr′-ū-bĭms; then he went in, and stood beside the wheels.

7 And *one* cherub [N]stretched forth his hand from between the chĕr′-ū-bĭms unto the fire that *was* between the chĕr′-ū-bĭms, and took *thereof,* and put *it* into the hands of *him that was* clothed with linen: who took *it,* and went out.

8 [R]And there appeared in the chĕr′-ū-bĭms the form of a man's hand under their wings.

9 [R]And when I looked, behold the four wheels by the chĕr′-ū-bĭms, one wheel by one cherub, and another wheel by another cherub: and the appearance of the wheels *was* as the colour of a [R]beryl stone.

10 And *as for* their appearances, they four had one likeness, as if a wheel had been in the midst of a wheel.

11 [R]When they went, they went upon their four sides; they turned not as they went, but to the place whither the head looked they followed it; they turned not as they went.

12 And their whole [N]body, and their backs, and their hands, and their wings, and the wheels, *were* full of eyes round about, *even* the wheels that they four had.

13 As for the wheels, [N]it was cried unto them in my hearing, O wheel.

14 [R]And every one had four faces: the first face *was* the face of a cherub, and the second face *was* the face of a man, and the third the face of a lion, and the fourth the face of an eagle.

15 And the chĕr′-ū-bĭms were lifted up. This *is* [R]the living creature that I saw by the river of Chē′-bär.

16 [R]And when the chĕr′-ū-bĭms went, the wheels went by them: and when the chĕr′-

ū-bĭms lifted up their wings to mount up from the earth, the same wheels also turned not from beside them.

17 ᴿWhen they stood, *these* stood; and when they were lifted up, *these* lifted up themselves *also:* for the spirit ᴺof the living creature *was* in them.

Glory of the LORD departs

18 Then ᴿthe glory of the LORD ᴿdeparted from off the threshold of the house, and stood over the chĕr′-ū-bĭms.

19 And ᴿthe chĕr′-ū-bĭms lifted up their wings, and mounted up from the earth in my sight: when they went out, the wheels also *were* beside them, and *every one* stood at the door of the east gate of the LORD's house; and the glory of the God of Israel *was* over them above.

20 ᴿThis *is* the living creature that I saw under the God of Israel ᴿby the river of Chē′-bär; and I knew that they *were* the chĕr′-ū-bĭms.

21 ᴿEvery one had four faces apiece, and every one four wings; and the likeness of the hands of a man *was* under their wings.

22 And ᴿthe likeness of their faces *was* the same faces which I saw by the river of Chē′-bär, their appearances and themselves: ᴿthey went every one straight forward.

CHAPTER 11

Judgment of the wicked princes

MOREOVER ᴿthe spirit lifted me up, and brought me unto ᴿthe east gate of the LORD's house, which looketh eastward: and behold ᴿat the door of the gate five and twenty men; among whom I saw Jā-ăz-ă-nī′-ăh the son of Ā′-zùr, and Pĕl-ă-tī′-ăh the son of Bĕ-nāi′-ăh, princes of the people.

2 Then said he unto me, Son of man, these *are* the men that devise mischief, and give wicked counsel in this city:

3 Which say, ᴺ*It is* not ᴿnear; let us build houses: ᴿthis *city is* the caldron, and we *be* the flesh.

4 Therefore prophesy against them, prophesy, O son of man.

5 And ᴿthe spirit of the LORD fell upon me, and said unto me, Speak; Thus saith the LORD; Thus have ye said, O house of Israel: for I know the things that come into your mind, *every one of* them.

6 ᴿYe have multiplied your slain in this city, and ye have filled the streets thereof with the slain.

7 Therefore thus saith the Lord GOD; ᴿYour

slain whom ye have laid in the midst of it, they *are* the flesh, and this *city is* the caldron: ᴿbut I will bring you forth out of the midst of it.

8 Ye have feared the sword; and I will bring a sword upon you, saith the Lord GOD.

9 And I will bring you out of the midst thereof, and deliver you into the hands of strangers, and ᴿwill execute judgments among you.

10 ᴿYe shall fall by the sword; I will judge you in ᴿthe border of Israel; ᴿand ye shall know that I *am* the LORD.

11 ᴿThis *city* shall not be your caldron, neither shall ye be the flesh in the midst thereof; *but* I will judge you in the border of Israel:

12 And ᴿye shall know that I *am* the LORD: ᴺfor ye have not walked in my statutes, neither executed my judgments, but ᴿhave done after the manners of the heathen that *are* round about you.

13 And it came to pass, when I prophesied, that ᴿPĕl-ă-tī′-ăh the son of Bĕ-nāi′-ăh died. Then ᴿfell I down upon my face, and cried with a loud voice, and said, Ah Lord GOD! wilt thou make a full end of the remnant of Israel?

Restoration of the exiles

14 Again the word of the LORD came unto me, saying,

15 Son of man, thy brethren, *even* thy brethren, the men of thy kindred, and all the house of Israel wholly, *are* they unto whom the inhabitants of Jerusalem have said, Get you far from the LORD: unto us is this land given in possession.

16 Therefore say, Thus saith the Lord GOD; Although I have cast them far off among the heathen, and although I have scattered them among the countries, ᴿyet will I be to them as a little sanctuary in the countries where they shall come.

17 Therefore say, Thus saith the Lord GOD; ᴿI will even gather you from the people, and assemble you out of the countries where ye have been scattered, and I will give you the land of Israel.

18 And they shall come thither, and ᴿthey shall take away all the detestable things thereof and all the abominations thereof from thence.

19 And ᴿI will give them one heart, and I will put ᴿa new spirit within you; and I will take ᴿthe stony heart out of their flesh, and will give them an heart of flesh:

20 ᴿThat they may walk in my statutes, and keep mine ordinances, and do them: ᴿand they

shall be my people, and I will be their God.

21 But *as for them* whose heart walketh after the heart of their detestable things and their abominations, ᴿI will recompense their way upon their own heads, saith the Lord GOD.

Glory of the LORD leaves the city

22 Then did the chĕr′-ū-bĭms ᴿlift up their wings, and the wheels beside them; and the glory of the God of Israel *was* over them above.

23 And ᴿthe glory of the LORD went up from the midst of the city, and stood ᴿupon the mountain ᴿwhich *is* on the east side of the city.

24 Afterwards ᴿthe spirit took me up, and brought me in a vision by the spirit of God into Chăl-dē′-ă, to them of the captivity. So the vision that I had seen went up from me.

25 Then I spake unto them of the captivity all the things that the LORD had shewed me.

CHAPTER 12

Oracle of the prince and people

THE word of the LORD also came unto me, saying,

2 Son of man, thou dwellest in the midst of ᴿa rebellious house, which ᴿhave eyes to see, and see not; they have ears to hear, and hear not: ᴿfor they *are* a rebellious house.

3 Therefore, thou son of man, prepare thee ᴺstuff for removing, and remove by day in their sight; and thou shalt remove from thy place to another place in their sight: it may be they will consider, though they *be* a rebellious house.

4 Then shalt thou bring forth thy stuff by day in their sight, as stuff for removing: and thou shalt go forth at even in their sight, ᴺas they that go forth into captivity.

5 ᴺDig thou through the wall in their sight, and carry out thereby.

6 In their sight shalt thou bear *it* upon *thy* shoulders, *and* carry *it* forth in the twilight: thou shalt cover thy face, that thou see not the ground: ᴿfor I have set thee *for* a sign unto the house of Israel.

7 And I did so as I was commanded: I brought forth my stuff by day, as stuff for captivity, and in the even I ᴺdigged through the wall with mine hand; I brought *it* forth in the twilight, *and* I bare *it* upon *my* shoulder in their sight.

8 And in the morning came the word of the LORD unto me, saying,

9 Son of man, hath not the house of Israel,

CHAP. 11

BC 594

21 ch. 9:10 & 22:31
22 ch. 1:19 & 10:19
23 ch. 8:4 & 9:3
& 10:4, 18 & 43:4
23 See Zech. 14:4
23 ch. 43:2
24 ch. 8:3

CHAP. 12

BC 594

2 ch. 2:3, 6-8
& 3:26, 27
2 Is. 6:9 & 42:20
Jer. 5:21
Mat. 13:13, 14
2 ch. 2:5
3 Or, *instruments*
4 Heb. *as the goings forth of captivity*
5 Heb. *Dig for thee*
6 ver. 11
Is. 8:18
ch. 4:3 & 24:24
7 Heb. *digged for me*

ch. 2:5   **9**
ch. 17:12 & 24:19   **9**
Mal. 1:1   **10**
ver. 6   **11**
2 Ki. 25:4, 5, 7   **11**
Heb. *by removing go into captivity*
Jer. 39:4   **12**
Job 19:6   **13**
Jer. 52:9
Lam. 1:13
ch. 17:20
2 Ki. 25:7   **13**
Jer. 52:11
ch. 17:16
2 Ki. 25:4   **14**
ch. 5:10
ch. 5:2, 12   **14**
ver. 16, 20   **15**
Ps. 9:16
ch. 6:7, 14
& 11:10
ch. 6:8-10   **16**
Heb. *men of number*   **16**
ch. 4:16   **18**
Zech. 7:14   **19**
Heb. *the fulness thereof*   **19**
Ps. 107:34   **19**
ver. 27   **22**
ch. 11:3
Amos 6:3
2 Pet. 3:4
Joel 2:1   **23**
Zeph. 1:14

ᴿthe rebellious house, said unto thee, ᴿWhat doest thou?

10 Say thou unto them, Thus saith the Lord GOD; This ᴿburden *concerneth* the prince in Jerusalem, and all the house of Israel that *are* among them.

11 Say, ᴿI *am* your sign: like as I have done, so shall it be done unto them: ᴿtheyᴺ shall remove *and* go into captivity.

12 And ᴿthe prince that *is* among them shall bear upon *his* shoulder in the twilight, and shall go forth: they shall dig through the wall to carry out thereby: he shall cover his face, that he see not the ground with *his* eyes.

13 My ᴿnet also will I spread upon him, and he shall be taken in my snare: and ᴿI will bring him to Babylon *to* the land of the Chăl-dē′-ăns; yet shall he not see it, though he shall die there.

14 And ᴿI will scatter toward every wind all that *are* about him to help him, and all his bands; and ᴿI will draw out the sword after them.

15 ᴿAnd they shall know that I *am* the LORD, when I shall scatter them among the nations, and disperse them in the countries.

16 ᴿBut I will leave ᴺa few men of them from the sword, from the famine, and from the pestilence; that they may declare all their abominations among the heathen whither they come; and they shall know that I *am* the LORD.

17 Moreover the word of the LORD came to me, saying,

18 Son of man, ᴿeat thy bread with quaking, and drink thy water with trembling and with carefulness;

19 And say unto the people of the land, Thus saith the Lord GOD of the inhabitants of Jerusalem, *and* of the land of Israel; They shall eat their bread with carefulness, and drink their water with astonishment, that her land may ᴿbe desolate from ᴺall that is therein, ᴿbecause of the violence of all them that dwell therein.

20 And the cities that are inhabited shall be laid waste, and the land shall be desolate; and ye shall know that I *am* the LORD.

21 And the word of the LORD came unto me, saying,

22 Son of man, what *is* that proverb *that* ye have in the land of Israel, saying, ᴿThe days are prolonged, and every vision faileth?

23 Tell them therefore, Thus saith the Lord GOD; I will make this proverb to cease, and they shall no more use it as a proverb in Israel; but say unto them, ᴿThe days are at hand, and the effect of every vision.

24 For ᴿthere shall be no more any ᴿvain vision nor flattering divination within the house of Israel.

25 For I *am* the LORD: I will speak, and ᴿthe word that I shall speak shall come to pass; it shall be no more prolonged: for in your days, O rebellious house, will I say the word, and will perform it, saith the Lord GOD.

26 Again the word of the LORD came to me, saying,

27 ᴿSon of man, behold, *they of* the house of Israel say, The vision that he seeth *is* for many days *to come,* and he prophesieth of the times *that are* far off.

28 ᴿTherefore say unto them, Thus saith the Lord GOD; There shall none of my words be prolonged any more, but the word which I have spoken shall be done, saith the Lord GOD.

CHAPTER 13

False prophets condemned

AND the word of the LORD came unto me, saying,

2 Son of man, prophesy against the prophets of Israel that prophesy, and say thou unto ᴿthemᴺ that prophesy out of their own ᴿhearts, Hear ye the word of the LORD;

3 Thus saith the Lord GOD; Woe unto the foolish prophets, that ᴺfollow their own spirit, ᴺand have seen nothing!

4 O Israel, thy prophets are ᴿlike the foxes in the deserts.

5 Ye ᴿhave not gone up into the ᴺgaps, neither ᴺmade up the hedge for the house of Israel to stand in the battle in the day of the LORD.

6 ᴿThey have seen vanity and lying divination, saying, The LORD saith: and the LORD hath not sent them: and they have made *others* to hope that they would confirm the word.

7 Have ye not seen a vain vision, and have ye not spoken a lying divination, whereas ye say, The LORD saith *it;* albeit I have not spoken?

8 Therefore thus saith the Lord GOD; Because ye have spoken vanity, and seen lies, therefore, behold, I *am* against you, saith the Lord GOD.

9 And mine hand shall be upon the prophets that see vanity, and that divine lies: they shall not be in the ᴺassembly of my people, ᴿneither shall they be written in the writing of the house of Israel, ᴿneither shall they enter into the land of Israel; ᴿand ye shall know that I *am* the Lord GOD.

10 Because, even because they have seduced my people, saying, ᴿPeace; and *there was* no peace; and one built up ᴺa wall, and, lo, others ᴿdaubed it with untempered *mortar:*

11 Say unto them which daub *it* with untempered *mortar,* that it shall fall: ᴿthere shall be an overflowing shower; and ye, O great hailstones, shall fall; and a stormy wind shall rend *it.*

12 Lo, when the wall is fallen, shall it not be said unto you, Where *is* the daubing wherewith ye have daubed *it?*

13 Therefore thus saith the Lord GOD; I will even rend *it* with a stormy wind in my fury; and there shall be an overflowing shower in mine anger, and great hailstones in *my* fury to consume *it.*

14 So will I break down the wall that ye have daubed with untempered *mortar,* and bring it down to the ground, so that the foundation thereof shall be discovered, and it shall fall, and ye shall be consumed in the midst thereof: ᴿand ye shall know that I *am* the LORD.

15 Thus will I accomplish my wrath upon the wall, and upon them that have daubed it with untempered *mortar,* and will say unto you, The wall *is* no *more,* neither they that daubed it;

16 *To wit,* the prophets of Israel which prophesy concerning Jerusalem, and which ᴿsee visions of peace for her, and *there is* no peace, saith the Lord GOD.

Prophetesses denounced

17 Likewise, thou son of man, ᴿset thy face against the daughters of thy people, ᴿwhich prophesy out of their own heart; and prophesy thou against them,

18 And say, Thus saith the Lord GOD; Woe to the *women* that sew pillows to all ᴺarmholes, and make kerchiefs upon the head of every stature to hunt souls! Will ye ᴿhunt the souls of my people, and will ye save the souls alive *that come* unto you?

19 And will ye pollute me among my people ᴿfor handfuls of barley and for pieces of bread, to slay the souls that should not die, and to save the souls alive that should not live, by your lying to my people that hear *your* lies?

20 Wherefore thus saith the Lord GOD; Behold, I *am* against your pillows, wherewith ye there hunt the souls ᴺto make *them* fly, and I will tear them from your arms, and will let the souls go, *even* the souls that ye hunt to make *them* fly.

21 Your kerchiefs also will I tear, and deliver my people out of your hand, and they

shall be no more in your hand to be hunted; [R]and ye shall know that I *am* the LORD.

22 Because with lies ye have made the heart of the righteous sad, whom I have not made sad; and [R]strengthened the hands of the wicked, that he should not return from his wicked way, [NN]by promising him life:

23 Therefore [R]ye shall see no more vanity, nor divine divinations: for I will deliver my people out of your hand: and ye shall know that I *am* the LORD.

CHAPTER 14

Answer to the inquiring idolaters

THEN [R]came certain of the elders of Israel unto me, and sat before me.

2 And the word of the LORD came unto me, saying,

3 Son of man, these men have set up their idols in their heart, and put [R]the stumblingblock of their iniquity before their face: [R]should I be inquired of at all by them?

4 Therefore speak unto them, and say unto them, Thus saith the Lord GOD; Every man of the house of Israel that setteth up his idols in his heart, and putteth the stumblingblock of his iniquity before his face, and cometh to the prophet; I the LORD will answer him that cometh according to the multitude of his idols;

5 That I may take the house of Israel in their own heart, because they are all estranged from me through their idols.

6 Therefore say unto the house of Israel, Thus saith the Lord GOD; Repent, and turn [N]*yourselves* from your idols; and turn away your faces from all your abominations.

7 For every one of the house of Israel, or of the stranger that sojourneth in Israel, which separateth himself from me, and setteth up his idols in his heart, and putteth the stumblingblock of his iniquity before his face, and cometh to a prophet to inquire of him concerning me; I the LORD will answer him by myself:

8 And [R]I will set my face against that man, and will make him a [R]sign and a proverb, and I will cut him off from the midst of my people; [R]and ye shall know that I *am* the LORD.

9 And if the prophet be deceived when he hath spoken a thing, I the LORD [R]have deceived that prophet, and I will stretch out my hand upon him, and will destroy him from the midst of my people Israel.

10 And they shall bear the punishment of their iniquity: the punishment of the prophet shall be even as the punishment of him that seeketh *unto him;*

11 That the house of Israel may [R]go no more astray from me, neither be polluted any more with all their transgressions; [R]but that they may be my people, and I may be their God, saith the Lord GOD.

Only the righteous escape judgment

12 The word of the LORD came again to me, saying,

13 Son of man, when the land sinneth against me by trespassing grievously, then will I stretch out mine hand upon it, and will break the [R]staff of the bread thereof, and will send famine upon it, and will cut off man and beast from it:

14 [R]Though these three men, Noah, Daniel, and Job, were in it, they should deliver *but* their own souls [R]by their righteousness, saith the Lord GOD.

15 If I cause [R]noisome beasts to pass through the land, and they [N]spoil it, so that it be desolate, that no man may pass through because of the beasts:

16 [R]*Though* these three men *were* [N]in it, *as* I live, saith the Lord GOD, they shall deliver neither sons nor daughters; they only shall be delivered, but the land shall be desolate.

17 Or *if* [R]I bring a sword upon that land, and say, Sword, go through the land; so that I [R]cut off man and beast from it:

18 [R]Though these three men *were* in it, *as* I live, saith the Lord GOD, they shall deliver neither sons nor daughters, but they only shall be delivered themselves.

19 Or *if* I send [R]a pestilence into that land, and [R]pour out my fury upon it in blood, to cut off from it man and beast:

20 [R]Though Noah, Daniel, and Job, *were* in it, *as* I live, saith the Lord GOD, they shall deliver neither son nor daughter; they shall *but* deliver their own souls by their righteousness.

21 For thus saith the Lord GOD; [N]How much more when [R]I send my four sore judgments upon Jerusalem, the sword, and the famine, and the noisome beast, and the pestilence, to cut off from it man and beast?

22 [R]Yet, behold, therein shall be left a remnant that shall be brought forth, *both* sons and daughters: behold, they shall come forth unto you, and [R]ye shall see their way and their doings: and ye shall be comforted concerning the evil that I have brought upon Jerusalem, *even* concerning all that I have brought upon it.

23 And they shall comfort you, when ye see their ways and their doings: and ye shall know that I have not done [R]without cause all that I have done in it, saith the Lord GOD.

CHAPTER 15

Parable of the vine

AND the word of the LORD came unto me,
saying,
2 Son of man, What is the vine tree more
than any tree, *or than* a branch which is
among the trees of the forest?
3 Shall wood be taken thereof to do any
work? or will *men* take a pin of it to hang any
vessel thereon?
4 Behold, [R]it is cast into the fire for fuel; the
fire devoureth both the ends of it, and the
midst of it is burned. [N]Is it meet for *any* work?
5 Behold, when it was whole, it was [N]meet
for no work: how much less shall it be meet
yet for *any* work, when the fire hath devoured
it, and it is burned?
6 Therefore thus saith the Lord GOD; As the
vine tree among the trees of the forest, which I
have given to the fire for fuel, so will I give
the inhabitants of Jerusalem.
7 And [R]I will set my face against them;
[R]they shall go out from *one* fire, and *another*
fire shall devour them; [R]and ye shall know that
I *am* the LORD, when I set my face against
them.
8 And I will make the land desolate, because
they have [N]committed a trespass, saith the
Lord GOD.

CHAPTER 16

Adoption of the infant Israel

AGAIN the word of the LORD came unto
me, saying,
2 Son of man, [R]cause Jerusalem to know her
abominations,
3 And say, Thus saith the Lord GOD unto
Jerusalem; Thy [N]birth [R]and thy nativity *is* of
the land of Canaan; [R]thy father *was* an
Amorite, and thy mother an Hittite.
4 And *as for* thy nativity, [R]in the day thou
wast born thy navel was not cut, neither wast
thou washed in water [N]to supple *thee;* thou
wast not salted at all, nor swaddled at all.
5 None eye pitied thee, to do any of these
unto thee, to have compassion upon thee; but
thou wast cast out in the open field, to the loth-
ing of thy person, in the day that thou wast
born.
6 And when I passed by thee, and saw thee
[N]polluted in thine own blood, I said unto thee
when thou wast in thy blood, Live; yea, I said
unto thee *when thou wast* in thy blood, Live.
7 [R]I have [N]caused thee to multiply as the
bud of the field, and thou hast increased and
waxen great, and thou art come to [N]excellent
ornaments: *thy* breasts are fashioned, and thine
hair is grown, whereas thou *wast* naked and
bare.

Marriage of the maiden Israel

8 Now when I passed by thee, and looked
upon thee, behold, thy time *was* the time of
love; [R]and I spread my skirt over thee, and
covered thy nakedness: yea, I sware unto thee,
and entered into a covenant with thee, saith
the Lord GOD, and [R]thou becamest mine.
9 Then washed I thee with water; yea, I
throughly washed away thy [N]blood from thee,
and I anointed thee with oil.
10 I clothed thee also with broidered work,
and shod thee with badgers' skin, and I girded
thee about with fine linen, and I covered thee
with silk.
11 I decked thee also with ornaments, and I
[R]put bracelets upon thy hands, [R]and a chain on
thy neck.
12 And I put a jewel on thy [N]forehead, and
earrings in thine ears, and a beautiful crown
upon thine head.
13 Thus wast thou decked with gold and
silver; and thy raiment *was of* fine linen, and
silk, and broidered work; [R]thou didst eat fine
flour, and honey, and oil: and thou wast exceeding [R]beautiful, and thou didst prosper into
a kingdom.
14 And [R]thy renown went forth among the
heathen for thy beauty: for it *was* perfect
through my comeliness, which I had put upon
thee, saith the Lord GOD.

Infidelity of the wife Israel

15 [R]But thou didst trust in thine own beauty,
[R]and playedst the harlot because of thy renown, and pouredst out thy fornications on
every one that passed by; his it was.
16 [R]And of thy garments thou didst take,
and deckedst thy high places with divers colours, and playedst the harlot thereupon: *the
like things* shall not come, neither shall it be
so.
17 Thou hast also taken thy fair jewels of
my gold and of my silver, which I had given
thee, and madest to thyself images [N]of men,
and didst commit whoredom with them,
18 And tookest thy broidered garments, and
coveredst them: and thou hast set mine oil and
mine incense before them.
19 [R]My meat also which I gave thee, fine
flour, and oil, and honey, *wherewith* I fed thee,
thou hast even set it before them for [N]a sweet
savour: and *thus* it was, saith the Lord GOD.
20 [R]Moreover thou hast taken thy sons and
thy daughters, whom thou hast borne unto me,

CHAP. 15
BC 594
4 John 15:6
4 Heb. *Will it prosper?*
5 Heb. *made* fit
7 Lev. 17:10 ch. 14:8
7 Is. 24:18
7 ch. 7:4
8 Heb. *trespassed a trespass*

CHAP. 16
BC 594
2 ch. 20:4 & 22:2
3 Heb. *cutting out,* or, *habitation*
3 ch. 21:30
3 ver. 45
4 Hos. 2:3
4 Or, *when I looked* upon thee
6 Or, *trodden under foot*
7 Ex. 1:7
7 Heb. *made thee a million*
7 Heb. *ornament of ornaments*

Ruth 3:9 8
Ex. 19:5 Jer. 2:2 8
Heb. *bloods* 9
Gen. 24:22 11
Prov. 1:9 11
Heb. *nose:* See Is. 3:21 12
Deut. 32:13, 14 13
Ps. 48:2 13
Lam. 2:15 14
Deut. 32:15 Jer. 7:4 Mic. 3:11 15
Is. 1:21 & 57:8 Jer. 2:20 & 3:2, 6, 20 ch. 23:3, 8 15
2 Ki. 23:7 ch. 7:20 Hos. 2:8 16
Heb. *of a male* 17
Hos. 2:8 19
Heb. *a savour of rest* 19
2 Ki. 16:3 Ps. 106:37 Is. 57:5 Jer. 7:31 ch. 20:26 20

and these hast thou sacrificed unto them ᴺto be devoured. *Is this* of thy whoredoms a small matter,

21 That thou hast slain my children, and delivered them to cause them to pass through *the fire* for them?

22 And in all thine abominations and thy whoredoms thou hast not remembered the days of thy ᴿyouth, ᴿwhen thou wast naked and bare, *and* wast polluted in thy blood.

23 And it came to pass after all thy wickedness, (woe, woe unto thee! saith the Lord GOD;)

24 *That* ᴿthou hast also built unto thee an ᴺeminent place, and ᴿhast made thee an high place in every street.

25 Thou hast built thy high place ᴿat every head of the way, and hast made thy beauty to be abhorred, and hast opened thy feet to every one that passed by, and multiplied thy whoredoms.

26 Thou hast also committed fornication with ᴿthe Egyptians thy neighbours, great of flesh; and hast increased thy whoredoms, to provoke me to anger.

27 Behold, therefore I have stretched out my hand over thee, and have diminished thine ordinary *food*, and delivered thee unto the will of them that hate thee, ᴿthe ᴺdaughters of the Philistines, which are ashamed of thy lewd way.

28 Thou hast played the whore also with the Assyrians, because thou wast unsatiable; yea, thou hast played the harlot with them, and yet couldest not be satisfied.

29 Thou hast moreover multiplied thy fornication in the land of Canaan ᴿunto Chăl-dē′-ă; and yet thou wast not satisfied herewith.

30 How weak is thine heart, saith the Lord GOD, seeing thou doest all these *things*, the work of an imperious whorish woman;

31 ᴺIn that ᴿthou buildest thine eminent place in the head of every way, and makest thine high place in every street; and hast not been as an harlot, in that thou scornest hire;

32 *But as* a wife that committeth adultery, *which* taketh strangers instead of her husband!

33 They give gifts to all whores: but ᴿthou givest thy gifts to all thy lovers, and ᴺhirest them, that they may come unto thee on every side for thy whoredom.

34 And the contrary is in thee from *other* women in thy whoredoms, whereas none followeth thee to commit whoredoms: and in that thou givest a reward, and no reward is given unto thee, therefore thou art contrary.

CHAP. 16
BC 594
20 Heb. *to devour*
22 ver. 43, 60
Jer. 2:2
Hos. 11:1
22 ver. 4, 5, 6
24 ver. 31
24 Or,
brothel house
24 Is. 57:5, 7
Jer. 2:20 & 3:2
25 Prov. 9:14
26 ch. 8:10, 14
27 ver. 57
2 Chr. 28:18
27 Or, *cities*
29 ch. 23:14
31 Or, *In thy daughters is thine, etc.*
31 ver. 24, 39
33 Is. 30:6
Hos. 8:9
33 Heb. *bribest*

ver. 20   36
Jer. 2:34
Jer. 13:22, 26   37
Lam. 1:8
ch. 23:9, 10, 22, 29
Hos. 2:10 & 8:10
Nah. 3:5
Heb. *with judgments of*   38
Lev. 20:10   38
Deut. 22:22
ch. 23:45
See ver. 20, 36 38
Gen. 9:6
Ex. 21:12
ver. 24, 31   39
ch. 23:26   39
Hos. 2:3
Heb. *instruments of thine ornament*   39
ch. 23:46   40
John 8:5, 7   40
Deut. 13:16   41
2 Ki. 25:9
Jer. 39:8 & 52:13
ch. 5:8   41
& 23:10, 48
ch. 23:27   41
ch. 5:13   42
ver. 22   43
Ps. 78:42
ch. 9:10 & 11:21 43
& 22:31
ver. 3   45
Deut. 32:32   46
Is. 1:10
Heb. *lesser than thou*   46
Or, *that was lothed as a small thing*   47

35 Wherefore, O harlot, hear the word of the LORD:

36 Thus saith the Lord GOD; Because thy filthiness was poured out, and thy nakedness discovered through thy whoredoms with thy lovers, and with all the idols of thy abominations, and by ᴿthe blood of thy children, which thou didst give unto them;

37 Behold, therefore ᴿI will gather all thy lovers, with whom thou hast taken pleasure, and all *them* that thou hast loved, with all *them* that thou hast hated; I will even gather them round about against thee, and will discover thy nakedness unto them, that they may see all thy nakedness.

38 And I will judge thee, ᴺas ᴿwomen that break wedlock and ᴿshed blood are judged; and I will give thee blood in fury and jealousy.

39 And I will also give thee into their hand, and they shall throw down ᴿthine eminent place, and shall break down thy high places: ᴿthey shall strip thee also of thy clothes, and shall take ᴺthy fair jewels, and leave thee naked and bare.

40 ᴿThey shall also bring up a company against thee, ᴿand they shall stone thee with stones, and thrust thee through with their swords.

41 And they shall ᴿburn thine houses with fire, and ᴿexecute judgments upon thee in the sight of many women: and I will cause thee to ᴿcease from playing the harlot, and thou also shalt give no hire any more.

42 So ᴿwill I make my fury toward thee to rest, and my jealousy shall depart from thee, and I will be quiet, and will be no more angry.

43 Because ᴿthou hast not remembered the days of thy youth, but hast fretted me in all these *things;* behold, therefore ᴿI also will recompense thy way upon *thine* head, saith the Lord GOD: and thou shalt not commit this lewdness above all thine abominations.

44 Behold, every one that useth proverbs shall use *this* proverb against thee, saying, As *is* the mother, *so is* her daughter.

45 Thou *art* thy mother's daughter, that loatheth her husband and her children; and thou *art* the sister of thy sisters, which lothed their husbands and their children: ᴿyour mother *was* an Hittite, and your father an Amorite.

46 And thine elder sister *is* Să-mâr′-ĭ-ă, she and her daughters that dwell at thy left hand: and ᴿthyᴺ younger sister, that dwelleth at thy right hand, *is* Sodom and her daughters.

47 Yet hast thou not walked after their ways, nor done after their abominations: but, ᴺas *if*

that were a very little *thing,* ᴿthou wast corrupted more than they in all thy ways.

48 *As* I live, saith the Lord GOD, ᴿSodom thy sister hath not done, she nor her daughters, as thou hast done, thou and thy daughters.

49 Behold, this was the iniquity of thy sister Sodom, pride, ᴿfulness of bread, and abundance of idleness was in her and in her daughters, neither did she strengthen the hand of the poor and needy.

50 And they were haughty, and ᴿcommitted abomination before me: therefore ᴿI took them away as I saw *good.*

51 Neither hath Să-mâr'-ĭ-ă committed half of thy sins; but thou hast multiplied thine abominations more than they, and ᴿhast justified thy sisters in all thine abominations which thou hast done.

52 Thou also, which hast judged thy sisters, bear thine own shame for thy sins that thou hast committed more abominable than they: they are more righteous than thou: yea, be thou confounded also, and bear thy shame, in that thou hast justified thy sisters.

Promise of restoration

53 ᴿWhen I shall bring again their captivity, ᴿthe captivity of Sodom and her daughters, and the captivity of Să-mâr'-ĭ-ă and her daughters, then *will I bring again* the captivity of thy captives in the midst of them:

54 That thou mayest bear thine own shame, and mayest be confounded in all that thou hast done, in that thou art ᴿa comfort unto them.

55 When thy sisters, Sodom and her daughters, shall return to their former estate, and Să-mâr'-ĭ-ă and her daughters shall return to their former estate, then thou and thy daughters shall return to your former estate.

56 For thy sister Sodom was not ᴺmentioned by thy mouth in the day of thy ᴺpride,

57 Before thy wickedness was discovered, as at the time of *thy* ᴿreproach of the daughters of ᴺSyria, and all *that are* round about her, ᴿthe daughters of the Philistines, which ᴺdespise thee round about.

58 ᴿThou hast ᴺborne thy lewdness and thine abominations, saith the LORD.

59 For thus saith the Lord GOD; I will even deal with thee as thou hast done, which hast ᴿdespised ᴿthe oath in breaking the covenant.

60 Nevertheless I will ᴿremember my covenant with thee in the days of thy youth, and I will establish unto thee ᴿan everlasting covenant.

61 Then ᴿthou shalt remember thy ways, and be ashamed, when thou shalt receive thy sisters, thine elder and thy younger: and I will

give them unto thee for ᴿdaughters, ᴿbut not by thy covenant.

62 ᴿAnd I will establish my covenant with thee; and thou shalt know that I *am* the LORD:

63 That thou mayest remember, and be confounded, ᴿand never open thy mouth any more because of thy shame, when I am pacified toward thee for all that thou hast done, saith the Lord GOD.

CHAPTER 17

Riddle of the great eagle

AND the word of the LORD came unto me, saying,

2 Son of man, put forth a riddle, and speak a parable unto the house of Israel;

3 And say, Thus saith the Lord GOD; ᴿA great eagle with great wings, longwinged, full of feathers, which had ᴺdivers colours, came unto Lĕb'-ă-nọn, and ᴿtook the highest branch of the cedar:

4 He cropped off the top of his young twigs, and carried it into a land of traffick; he set it in a city of merchants.

5 He took also of the seed of the land, and ᴺplanted it in ᴿa fruitful field; he placed *it* by great waters, *and* set it ᴿas a willow tree.

6 And it grew, and became a spreading vine ᴿof low stature, whose branches turned toward him, and the roots thereof were under him: so it became a vine, and brought forth branches, and shot forth sprigs.

7 There was also another great eagle with great wings and many feathers: and, behold, ᴿthis vine did bend her roots toward him, and shot forth her branches toward him, that he might water it by the furrows of her plantation.

8 It was planted in a good ᴺsoil by great waters, that it might bring forth branches, and that it might bear fruit, that it might be a goodly vine.

9 Say thou, Thus saith the Lord GOD; Shall it prosper? ᴿshall he not pull up the roots thereof, and cut off the fruit thereof, that it wither? it shall wither in all the leaves of her spring, even without great power or many people to pluck it up by the roots thereof.

10 Yea, behold, *being* planted, shall it prosper? ᴿshall it not utterly wither, when the east wind toucheth it? it shall wither in the furrows where it grew.

Explanation of the riddle

11 Moreover the word of the LORD came unto me, saying,

12 Say now to ᴿthe rebellious house, Know

ye not what these *things mean?* tell *them,* Behold, [R]the king of Babylon is come to Jerusalem, and hath taken the king thereof, and the princes thereof, and led them with him to Babylon;

13 [R]And hath taken of the king's seed, and made a covenant with him, [R]and hath [N]taken an oath of him: he hath also taken the mighty of the land:

14 That the kingdom might be [R]base, that it might not lift itself up, [N]*but* that by keeping of his covenant it might stand.

15 But [R]he rebelled against him in sending his ambassadors into Egypt, [R]that they might give him horses and much people. [R]Shall he prosper? shall he escape that doeth such *things?* or shall he break the covenant, and be delivered?

16 *As* I live, saith the Lord GOD, surely [R]in the place *where* the king *dwelleth* that made him king, whose oath he despised, and whose covenant he brake, *even* with him in the midst of Babylon he shall die.

17 [R]Neither shall Pharaoh with *his* mighty army and great company make for him in the war, [R]by casting up mounts, and building forts, to cut off many persons:

18 Seeing he despised the oath by breaking the covenant, when, lo, he had [R]given his hand, and hath done all these *things,* he shall not escape.

19 Therefore thus saith the Lord GOD; *As* I live, surely mine oath that he hath despised, and my covenant that he hath broken, even it will I recompense upon his own head.

20 And I will [R]spread my net upon him, and he shall be taken in my snare, and I will bring him to Babylon, and [R]will plead with him there for his trespass that he hath trespassed against me.

21 And [R]all his fugitives with all his bands shall fall by the sword, and they that remain shall be scattered toward all winds: and ye shall know that I the LORD have spoken *it.*

22 Thus saith the Lord GOD; I will also take of the highest [R]branch of the high cedar, and will set *it;* I will crop off from the top of his young twigs [R]a tender one, and will [R]plant *it* upon an high mountain and eminent:

23 [R]In the mountain of the height of Israel will I plant it: and it shall bring forth boughs, and bear fruit, and be a goodly cedar: and [R]under it shall dwell all fowl of every wing; in the shadow of the branches thereof shall they dwell.

24 And all the trees of the field shall know that I the LORD [R]have brought down the high tree, have exalted the low tree, have dried up

the green tree, and have made the dry tree to flourish: [R]I the LORD have spoken and have done *it.*

CHAPTER 18

Moral responsibility

THE word of the LORD came unto me again, saying,

2 What mean ye, that ye use this proverb concerning the land of Israel, saying, The [R]fathers have eaten sour grapes, and the children's teeth are set on edge?

3 *As* I live, saith the Lord GOD, ye shall not have *occasion* any more to use this proverb in Israel.

4 Behold, all souls are mine; as the soul of the father, so also the soul of the son is mine: [R]the soul that sinneth, it shall die.

5 But if a man be just, and do [N]that which is lawful and right,

6 [R]*And* hath not eaten upon the mountains, neither hath lifted up his eyes to the idols of the house of Israel, neither hath [R]defiled his neighbour's wife, neither hath come near to [R]a menstruous woman,

7 And hath not [R]oppressed any, *but* hath restored to the debtor his [R]pledge, hath spoiled none by violence, hath [R]given his bread to the hungry, and hath covered the naked with a garment;

8 He *that* hath not given forth upon [R]usury, neither hath taken any increase, *that* hath withdrawn his hand from iniquity, [R]hath executed true judgment between man and man,

9 Hath walked in my statutes, and hath kept my judgments, to deal truly; he *is* just, he shall surely [R]live, saith the Lord GOD.

10 If he beget a son *that is* a [N]robber, [R]a shedder of blood, and [N]*that* doeth the like to *any* one of these *things,*

11 And that doeth not any of those *duties,* but even hath eaten upon the mountains, and defiled his neighbour's wife,

12 Hath oppressed the poor and needy, hath spoiled by violence, hath not restored the pledge, and hath lifted up his eyes to the idols, hath [R]committed abomination,

13 Hath given forth upon usury, and hath taken increase: shall he then live? he shall not live: he hath done all these abominations; he shall surely die; [R]his [N]blood shall be upon him.

14 Now, lo, *if* he beget a son, that seeth all his father's sins which he hath done, and considereth, and doeth not such like,

15 [R]*That* hath not eaten upon the mountains, neither hath lifted up his eyes to the idols of

---

Center reference column:

CHAP. 17	
BC 594	
12	ver. 3
12	2 Ki. 24:11-16
13	2 Ki. 24:17
13	2 Chr. 36:13
13	Heb. *brought him to an oath*
14	ver. 6
	ch. 29:14
14	Heb. *to keep his covenant, to stand to it*
15	2 Ki. 24:20
	2 Chr. 36:13
15	Deut. 17:16
	Is. 31:1, 3
	& 36:6, 9
15	ver. 9
16	Jer. 32:5 & 34:3
	ch. 12:13
17	Jer. 37:7
17	Jer. 52:4
18	1 Chr. 29:24
	Lam. 5:6
20	ch. 12:13
20	ch. 20:36
21	ch. 12:14
22	Is. 11:1
	Jer. 23:5
	Zech. 3:8
22	Is. 53:2
22	Ps. 2:6
23	Is. 2:2, 3
23	See ch. 31:6
	Dan. 4:12
24	Luke 1:52
ch. 22:14	24

CHAP. 18	
BC 594	
Jer. 31:29	2
Lam. 5:7	
Rom. 6:23	4
Heb. *judgment and justice*	5
ch. 22:9	6
Lev. 18:20	6
& 20:10	
Lev. 18:19	6
& 20:18	
Ex. 22:21	7
Lev. 19:15 & 25:14	
Ex. 22:26	7
Deut. 24:12	
Deut. 15:7	7
Is. 58:7	
Mat. 25:35	
Ex. 22:25	8
Lev. 25:36	
Deut. 23:19	
Neh. 5:7	
Ps. 15:5	
Deut. 1:16	8
Zech. 8:16	
ch. 20:11	9
Amos 5:4	
Or, *breaker up of an house*	10
Gen. 9:6	10
Ex. 21:12	
Num. 35:31	
Or, *that doeth to his brother besides any of these*	10
ch. 8:6, 17	12
Lev. 20:9, 11-13, 16, 27	13
ch. 3:18	
Acts 18:6	
Heb. *bloods*	13
ver. 6, etc.	15

the house of Israel, hath not defiled his neighbour's wife,

16 Neither hath oppressed any, ᴺhath not withholden the pledge, neither hath spoiled by violence, *but* hath given his bread to the hungry, and hath covered the naked with a garment,

17 *That* hath taken off his hand from the poor, *that* hath not received usury nor increase, hath executed my judgments, hath walked in my statutes; he shall not die for the iniquity of his father, he shall surely live.

18 *As for* his father, because he cruelly oppressed, spoiled his brother by violence, and did *that* which *is* not good among his people, lo, even ᴿhe shall die in his iniquity.

19 Yet say ye, Why? ᴿdoth not the son bear the iniquity of the father? When the son hath done that which is lawful and right, *and* hath kept all my statutes, and hath done them, he shall surely live.

20 ᴿThe soul that sinneth, it shall die. ᴿThe son shall not bear the iniquity of the father, neither shall the father bear the iniquity of the son: ᴿthe righteousness of the righteous shall be upon him, ᴿand the wickedness of the wicked shall be upon him.

Forgiveness for the repentant

21 But ᴿif the wicked will turn from all his sins that he hath committed, and keep all my statutes, and do that which is lawful and right, he shall surely live, he shall not die.

22 ᴿAll his transgressions that he hath committed, they shall not be mentioned unto him: in his righteousness that he hath done he shall live.

23 ᴿHave I any pleasure at all that the wicked should die? saith the Lord Goᴅ: *and* not that he should return from his ways, and live?

24 But ᴿwhen the righteous turneth away from his righteousness, and committeth iniquity, *and* doeth according to all the abominations that the wicked *man* doeth, shall he live? ᴿAll his righteousness that he hath done shall not be mentioned: in his trespass that he hath trespassed, and in his sin that he hath sinned, in them shall he die.

25 Yet ye say, ᴿThe way of the Lord is not equal. Hear now, O house of Israel; Is not my way equal? are not your ways unequal?

26 ᴿWhen a righteous *man* turneth away from his righteousness, and committeth iniquity, and dieth in them; for his iniquity that he hath done shall he die.

27 Again, ᴿwhen the wicked *man* turneth away from his wickedness that he hath committed, and doeth that which is lawful and right, he shall save his soul alive.

28 Because he ᴿconsidereth, and turneth away from all his transgressions that he hath committed, he shall surely live, he shall not die.

29 ᴿYet saith the house of Israel, The way of the Lord is not equal. O house of Israel, are not my ways equal? are not your ways unequal?

Appeal for Israel to repent

30 ᴿTherefore I will judge you, O house of Israel, every one according to his ways, saith the Lord Goᴅ. ᴿRepent, and turn ᴺ*yourselves* from all your transgressions; so iniquity shall not be your ruin.

31 ᴿCast away from you all your transgressions, whereby ye have transgressed; and make you a ᴿnew heart and a new spirit: for why will ye die, O house of Israel?

32 For ᴿI have no pleasure in the death of him that dieth, saith the Lord Goᴅ: wherefore turn ᴺ*yourselves,* and live ye.

CHAPTER 19

Lamentation for Israel's princes

MOREOVER ᴿtake thou up a lamentation for the princes of Israel,

2 And say, What *is* thy mother? A lioness: she lay down among lions, she nourished her whelps among young lions.

3 And she brought up one of her whelps: ᴿit became a young lion, and it learned to catch the prey; it devoured men.

4 The nations also heard of him; he was taken in their pit, and they brought him with chains unto the land of ᴿEgypt.

5 Now when she saw that she had waited, *and* her hope was lost, then she took ᴿanother of her whelps, *and* made him a young lion.

6 ᴿAnd he went up and down among the lions, ᴿhe became a young lion, and learned to catch the prey, *and* devoured men.

7 And he knew ᴺtheir desolate palaces, and he laid waste their cities; and the land was desolate, and the fulness thereof, by the noise of his roaring.

8 ᴿThen the nations set against him on every side from the provinces, and spread their net over him: ᴿhe was taken in their pit.

9 ᴿAnd they put him in ward ᴺin chains, and brought him to the king of Babylon: they brought him into holds, that his voice should no more be heard upon ᴿthe mountains of Israel.

10 Thy mother *is* ᴿlike a vine ᴺin thy blood,

planted by the waters: she was ᴿfruitful and full of branches by reason of many waters.

11 And she had strong rods for the sceptres of them that bare rule, and her ᴿstature was exalted among the thick branches, and she appeared in her height with the multitude of her branches.

12 But she was plucked up in fury, she was cast down to the ground, and the ᴿeast wind dried up her fruit: her strong rods were broken and withered; the fire consumed them.

13 And now she *is* planted in the wilderness, in a dry and thirsty ground.

14 ᴿAnd fire is gone out of a rod of her branches, *which* hath devoured her fruit, so that she hath no strong rod *to be* a sceptre to rule. ᴿThis *is* a lamentation, and shall be for a lamentation.

CHAPTER 20

Israel's rebellion in Egypt

AND it came to pass in the seventh year, in the fifth *month,* the tenth *day* of the month, *that* ᴿcertain of the elders of Israel came to inquire of the LORD, and sat before me.

2 Then came the word of the LORD unto me, saying,

3 Son of man, speak unto the elders of Israel, and say unto them, Thus saith the Lord GOD; Are ye come to inquire of me? *As* I live, saith the Lord GOD, ᴿI will not be inquired of by you.

4 Wilt thou ᴿjudgeᴺ them, son of man, wilt thou judge *them?* ᴿcause them to know the abominations of their fathers:

5 And say unto them, Thus saith the Lord GOD; In the day when ᴿI chose Israel, and ᴺlifted up mine hand unto the seed of the house of Jacob, and made myself ᴿknown unto them in the land of Egypt, when I lifted up mine hand unto them, saying, ᴿI *am* the LORD your God;

6 In the day *that* I lifted up mine hand unto them, ᴿto bring them forth of the land of Egypt into a land that I had espied for them, flowing with milk and honey, ᴿwhich *is* the glory of all lands:

7 Then said I unto them, ᴿCast ye away every man ᴿthe abominations of his eyes, and defile not yourselves with ᴿthe idols of Egypt: I *am* the LORD your God.

8 But they rebelled against me, and would not hearken unto me: they did not every man cast away the abominations of their eyes, neither did they forsake the idols of Egypt: then I

said, I will ᴿpour out my fury upon them, to accomplish my anger against them in the midst of the land of Egypt.

Israel's rebellion in the wilderness

9 ᴿBut I wrought for my name's sake, that it should not be polluted before the heathen, among whom they *were,* in whose sight I made myself known unto them, in bringing them forth out of the land of Egypt.

10 Wherefore I ᴿcaused them to go forth out of the land of Egypt, and brought them into the wilderness.

11 ᴿAnd I gave them my statutes, and ᴺshewed them my judgments, ᴿwhich *if* a man do, he shall even live in them.

12 Moreover also I gave them my ᴿsabbaths, to be a sign between me and them, that they might know that I *am* the LORD that sanctify them.

13 But the house of Israel ᴿrebelled against me in the wilderness: they walked not in my statutes, and they ᴿdespised my judgments, which *if* a man do, he shall even live in them; and my sabbaths they greatly ᴿpolluted: then I said, I would pour out my fury upon them in the ᴿwilderness, to consume them.

14 ᴿBut I wrought for my name's sake, that it should not be polluted before the heathen, in whose sight I brought them out.

15 Yet also ᴿI lifted up my hand unto them in the wilderness, that I would not bring them into the land which I had given *them,* flowing with milk and honey, ᴿwhich *is* the glory of all lands;

16 ᴿBecause they despised my judgments, and walked not in my statutes, but polluted my sabbaths: for ᴿtheir heart went after their idols.

17 ᴿNevertheless mine eye spared them from destroying them, neither did I make an end of them in the wilderness.

18 But I said unto their children in the wilderness, Walk ye not in the statutes of your fathers, neither observe their judgments, nor defile yourselves with their idols:

19 I *am* the LORD your God; ᴿwalk in my statutes, and keep my judgments, and do them;

20 ᴿAnd hallow my sabbaths; and they shall be a sign between me and you, that ye may know that I *am* the LORD your God.

21 Notwithstanding ᴿthe children rebelled against me: they walked not in my statutes, neither kept my judgments to do them, ᴿwhich *if* a man do, he shall even live in them; they polluted my sabbaths: then I said, ᴿI would pour out my fury upon them, to accomplish my anger against them in the wilderness.

22 ᴿNevertheless I withdrew mine hand, and

CHAP. **19**

BC 594

10 Deut. 8:7-9
11 ch. 31:3
Dan. 4:11
12 ch. 17:10
Hos. 13:15
14 Judg. 9:15
2 Ki. 24.20
ch. 17:18
14 Lam. 4:20

CHAP. **20**

BC 593

1 ch. 8:1
3 ch. 14:3
4 ch. 22:2
4 Or, *plead for them*
4 ch. 16:2
5 Ex. 6:7
Deut. 7:6
5 Or, *sware,* ver. 6, etc.
Ex. 6:8
5 Ex. 3:8 & 4:31
Deut. 4:34
5 Ex. 20:2
6 Ex. 3:8, 17
Deut. 8:7-9
Jer. 32:22
6 ver. 15
Ps. 48:2
Dan. 8:9
Zech. 7:14
7 ch. 18:31
7 2 Chr. 15:8
7 Lev. 18:3
Deut. 29:16
Josh. 24:14

ch. 7:8   **8**
Num. 14:13, etc. **9**
ch. 36:21, 22
Ex. 13:18   **10**
Deut. 4:8   **11**
Neh. 9:13
Ps. 147:19
Heb. *made them* **11**
to know
Lev. 18:5   **11**
Rom. 10:5
Gal. 3:12
Ex. 20:8   **12**
Deut. 5:12
Neh. 9:14
Num. 14:22 **13**
Ps. 78:40
& 95:8-10
Prov. 1:25 **13**
Ex. 16:27 **13**
Num. 14:29 **13**
Ps. 106:23
ver. 9, 22 **14**
Num. 14:28 **15**
Ps. 95:11
& 106:26
ver. 6 **15**
ver. 13, 24 **16**
Num. 15:39 **16**
Ps. 78:37
Amos 5:25
Acts 7:42
Ps. 78:38 **17**
Deut. 5:32 **19**
& 6, & 7, & 8,
& 10, & 11, & 12
Jer. 17:22 **20**
Num. 25:1 **21**
Deut. 9:23
ver. 11, 13 **21**
ver. 8, 13 **21**
ver. 17 **22**

ᴿwrought for my name's sake, that it should not be polluted in the sight of the heathen, in whose sight I brought them forth.

23 I lifted up mine hand unto them also in the wilderness, that ᴿI would scatter them among the heathen, and disperse them through the countries;

24 ᴿBecause they had not executed my judgments, but had despised my statutes, and had polluted my sabbaths, and ᴿtheir eyes were after their fathers' idols.

25 Wherefore ᴿI gave them also statutes *that were* not good, and judgments whereby they should not live;

26 And I polluted them in their own gifts, in that they caused to pass ᴿthrough *the fire* all that openeth the womb, that I might make them desolate, to the end that they ᴿmight know that I *am* the LORD.

Israel's continuing idolatry

27 Therefore, son of man, speak unto the house of Israel, and say unto them, Thus saith the Lord GOD; Yet in this your fathers have ᴿblasphemed me, in that they have ᴺcommitted a trespass against me.

28 *For* when I had brought them into the land, *for* the which I lifted up mine hand to give it to them, then ᴿthey saw every high hill, and all the thick trees, and they offered there their sacrifices, and there they presented the provocation of their offering: there also they made their ᴿsweet savour, and poured out there their drink offerings.

29 Then ᴺI said unto them, What *is* the high place whereunto ye go? And the name thereof is called Bāʹ-măh unto this day.

30 Wherefore say unto the house of Israel, Thus saith the Lord GOD; Are ye polluted after the manner of your fathers? and commit ye whoredom after their abominations?

31 For when ye offer ᴿyour gifts, when ye make your sons to pass through the fire, ye pollute yourselves with all your idols, even unto this day: and shall I be inquired of by you, O house of Israel? *As* I live, saith the Lord GOD, I will not be inquired of by you.

32 And that ᴿwhich cometh into your mind shall not be at all, that ye say, We will be as the heathen, as the families of the countries, to serve wood and stone.

Purge of the rebels

33 *As* I live, saith the Lord GOD, surely with a mighty hand, and ᴿwith a stretched out arm, and with fury poured out, will I rule over you:

34 And I will bring you out from the people, and will gather you out of the countries

wherein ye are scattered, with a mighty hand, and with a stretched out arm, and with fury poured out.

35 And I will bring you into the wilderness of the people, and there ᴿwill I plead with you face to face.

36 ᴿLike as I pleaded with your fathers in the wilderness of the land of Egypt, so will I plead with you, saith the Lord GOD.

37 And I will cause you to ᴿpass under the rod, and I will bring you into ᴺthe bond of the covenant:

38 And ᴿI will purge out from among you the rebels, and them that transgress against me: I will bring them forth out of the country where they sojourn, and ᴿthey shall not enter into the land of Israel: and ye shall know that I *am* the LORD.

39 As for you, O house of Israel, thus saith the Lord GOD; ᴿGo ye, serve ye every one his idols, and hereafter *also,* if ye will not hearken unto me: ᴿbut pollute ye my holy name no more with your gifts, and with your idols.

40 For ᴿin mine holy mountain, in the mountain of the height of Israel, saith the Lord GOD, there shall all the house of Israel, all of them in the land, serve me: there ᴿwill I accept them, and there will I require your offerings, and the ᴺfirstfruits of your oblations, with all your holy things.

41 I will accept you with your ᴿsweetᴺ savour, when I bring you out from the people, and gather you out of the countries wherein ye have been scattered; and I will be sanctified in you before the heathen.

42 ᴿAnd ye shall know that I *am* the LORD, ᴿwhen I shall bring you into the land of Israel, into the country *for* the which I lifted up mine hand to give it to your fathers.

43 And ᴿthere shall ye remember your ways, and all your doings, wherein ye have been defiled; and ᴿye shall lothe yourselves in your own sight for all your evils that ye have committed.

44 ᴿAnd ye shall know that I *am* the LORD, when I have wrought with you ᴿfor my name's sake, not according to your wicked ways, nor according to your corrupt doings, O ye house of Israel, saith the Lord GOD.

Prophecy against the south

45 Moreover the word of the LORD came unto me, saying,

46 ᴿSon of man, set thy face toward the south, and drop *thy word* toward the south, and prophesy against the forest of the south field;

47 And say to the forest of the south, Hear

the word of the LORD; Thus saith the Lord GOD; Behold, ᴿI will kindle a fire in thee, and it shall devour ᴿevery green tree in thee, and every dry tree: the flaming flame shall not be quenched, and all faces ᴿfrom the south to the north shall be burned therein.

48 And all flesh shall see that I the LORD have kindled it: it shall not be quenched.

49 Then said I, Ah Lord GOD! they say of me, Doth he not speak parables?

CHAPTER 21

Prophecy against Jerusalem

AND the word of the LORD came unto me, saying,

2 ᴿSon of man, set thy face toward Jerusalem, and ᴿdrop *thy word* toward the holy places, and prophesy against the land of Israel,

3 And say to the land of Israel, Thus saith the LORD; Behold, I *am* against thee, and will draw forth my sword out of his sheath, and will cut off from thee ᴿthe righteous and the wicked.

4 Seeing then that I will cut off from thee the righteous and the wicked, therefore shall my sword go forth out of his sheath against all flesh ᴿfrom the south to the north:

5 That all flesh may know that I the LORD have drawn forth my sword out of his sheath: it ᴿshall not return any more.

6 ᴿSigh therefore, thou son of man, with the breaking of *thy* loins; and with bitterness sigh before their eyes.

7 And it shall be, when they say unto thee, Wherefore sighest thou? that thou shalt answer, For the tidings; because it cometh: and every heart shall melt, and ᴿall hands shall be feeble, and every spirit shall faint, and all knees ᴺshall be weak *as* water: behold, it cometh, and shall be brought to pass, saith the Lord GOD.

The sharpened sword

8 Again the word of the LORD came unto me, saying,

9 Son of man, prophesy, and say, Thus saith the LORD; Say, ᴿA sword, a sword is sharpened, and also furbished:

10 It is sharpened to make a sore slaughter; it is furbished that it may glitter: should we then make mirth? ᴺit contemneth the rod of my son, *as* every tree.

11 And he hath given it to be furbished, that it may be handled: this sword is sharpened, and it is furbished, to give it into the hand of ᴿthe slayer.

12 Cry and howl, son of man: for it shall be upon my people, it *shall be* upon all the princes of Israel: ᴺterrors by reason of the sword shall be upon my people: ᴿsmite therefore upon *thy* thigh.

13 ᴺBecause *it is* ᴿa trial, and what if *the sword* contemn even the rod? ᴿit shall be no *more,* saith the Lord GOD.

14 Thou therefore, son of man, prophesy, and ᴿsmite *thine* ᴺhands together, and let the sword be doubled the third time, the sword of the slain: it *is* the sword of the great *men that are* slain, which entereth into their ᴿprivy chambers.

15 I have set the ᴺpoint of the sword against all their gates, that *their* heart may faint, and *their* ruins be multiplied: ah! ᴿ*it is* made bright, *it is* ᴺwrapped up for the slaughter.

16 ᴿGo thee one way or other, *either* on the right hand, ᴺor on the left, whithersoever thy face *is* set.

17 I will also ᴿsmite mine hands together, and ᴿI will cause my fury to rest: I the LORD have said *it.*

The sword of Babylon against Jerusalem

18 The word of the LORD came unto me again, saying,

19 Also, thou son of man, appoint thee two ways, that the sword of the king of Babylon may come: both twain shall come forth out of one land: and choose thou a place, choose *it* at the head of the way to the city.

20 Appoint a way, that the sword may come to ᴿRăb'-băth of the Ammonites, and to Judah in Jerusalem the defenced.

21 For the king of Babylon stood at the ᴺparting of the way, at the head of the two ways, to use divination: he made *his* ᴺarrows bright, he consulted with ᴺimages, he looked in the liver.

22 At his right hand was the divination for Jerusalem, to appoint ᴺᴺcaptains, to open the mouth in the slaughter, to ᴿlift up the voice with shouting, ᴿto appoint *battering* rams against the gates, to cast a mount, *and* to build a fort.

23 And it shall be unto them as a false divination in their sight, ᴺto them that ᴿhave sworn oaths: but he will call to remembrance the iniquity, that they may be taken.

24 Therefore thus saith the Lord GOD; Because ye have made your iniquity to be remembered, in that your transgressions are discovered, so that in all your doings your sins do appear; because, *I say,* that ye are come to remembrance, ye shall be taken with the hand.

25 And thou, ᴿprofane wicked prince of Is-

rael, ^Rwhose day is come, when iniquity *shall have* an end,

26 Thus saith the Lord GOD; Remove the diadem, and take off the crown: this *shall* not *be* the same: ^Rexalt *him that is* low, and abase *him that is* high.

27 ^NI will overturn, overturn, overturn, it: ^Rand it shall be no *more,* until he come whose right it is; and I will give it *him.*

The sword of Babylon against Ammon

28 And thou, son of man, prophesy and say, Thus saith the Lord GOD ^Rconcerning the Ammonites, and concerning their reproach; even say thou, The sword, the sword *is* drawn: for the slaughter *it is* furbished, to consume because of the glittering:

29 Whiles they ^Rsee vanity unto thee, whiles they divine a lie unto thee, to bring thee upon the necks of *them that are* slain, of the wicked, ^Rwhose day is come, when their iniquity *shall have* an end.

30 ^RShall^N I cause *it* to return into his sheath? ^RI will judge thee in the place where thou wast created, ^Rin the land of thy nativity.

31 And I will ^Rpour out mine indignation upon thee, I will ^Rblow against thee in the fire of my wrath, and deliver thee into the hand of ^Nbrutish men, *and* skilful to destroy.

32 Thou shalt be for fuel to the fire; thy blood shall be in the midst of the land; ^Rthou shalt be no *more* remembered: for I the LORD have spoken *it.*

CHAPTER 22

Abominable deeds of Jerusalem

MOREOVER the word of the LORD came unto me, saying,

2 Now, thou son of man, ^Rwilt thou ^Njudge, wilt thou judge ^Rthe ^Nbloody city? yea, thou shalt ^Nshew her all her abominations.

3 Then say thou, Thus saith the Lord GOD, The city sheddeth blood in the midst of it, that her time may come, and maketh idols against herself to defile herself.

4 Thou art become guilty in thy blood that thou hast ^Rshed; and hast defiled thyself in thine idols which thou hast made; and thou hast caused thy days to draw near, and art come *even* unto thy years: ^Rtherefore have I made thee a reproach unto the heathen, and a mocking to all countries.

5 *Those that be* near, and *those that be* far from thee, shall mock thee, *which art* ^Ninfamous *and* much vexed.

6 Behold, ^Rthe princes of Israel, every one were in thee to their ^Npower to shed blood.

7 In thee have they ^Rset light by father and mother: in the midst of thee have they ^Rdealt by ^Noppression with the stranger: in thee have they vexed the fatherless and the widow.

8 Thou hast despised mine holy things, and hast ^Rprofaned my sabbaths.

9 In thee are ^Rmen^N that carry tales to shed blood: ^Rand in thee they eat upon the mountains: in the midst of thee they commit lewdness.

10 In thee have they ^Rdiscovered their fathers' nakedness: in thee have they humbled her that was ^Rset apart for pollution.

11 And ^None hath committed abomination ^Rwith his neighbour's wife; and ^Nanother ^Rhath ^Nlewdly defiled his daughter in law; and another in thee hath humbled his ^Rsister, his father's daughter.

12 In thee ^Rhave they taken gifts to shed blood; ^Rthou hast taken usury and increase, and thou hast greedily gained of thy neighbours by extortion, and ^Rhast forgotten me, saith the Lord GOD.

Judgment of the LORD

13 Behold, therefore I have ^Rsmitten mine hand at thy dishonest gain which thou hast made, and at thy blood which hath been in the midst of thee.

14 ^RCan thine heart endure, or can thine hands be strong, in the days that I shall deal with thee? ^RI the LORD have spoken *it,* and will do *it.*

15 And ^RI will scatter thee among the heathen, and disperse thee in the countries, and ^Rwill consume thy filthiness out of thee.

16 And thou ^Nshalt take thine inheritance in thyself in the sight of the heathen, and ^Rthou shalt know that I *am* the LORD.

Israel's dross to be refined

17 And the word of the LORD came unto me, saying,

18 Son of man, ^Rthe house of Israel is to me become dross: all they *are* brass, and tin, and iron, and lead, in the midst of the furnace; they are *even* the ^Ndross of silver.

19 Therefore thus saith the Lord GOD; Because ye are all become dross, behold, therefore I will gather you into the midst of Jerusalem.

20 ^N*As* they gather silver, and brass, and iron, and lead, and tin, into the midst of the furnace, to blow the fire upon it, to melt *it;* so will I gather *you* in mine anger and in my fury, and I will leave *you there,* and melt you.

21 Yea, I will gather you, and blow upon you in the fire of my wrath, and ye shall be melted in the midst thereof.

22 As silver is melted in the midst of the furnace, so shall ye be melted in the midst thereof; and ye shall know that I the LORD have [R]poured out my fury upon you.

23 And the word of the LORD came unto me, saying,

24 Son of man, say unto her, Thou *art* the land that is not cleansed, nor rained upon in the day of indignation.

25 [R]*There is* a conspiracy of her prophets in the midst thereof, like a roaring lion ravening the prey; they [R]have devoured souls; [R]they have taken the treasure and precious things; they have made her many widows in the midst thereof.

26 [R]Her priests have [N]violated my law, and have [R]profaned mine holy things: they have put no [R]difference between the holy and profane, neither have they shewed *difference* between the unclean and the clean, and have hid their eyes from my sabbaths, and I am profaned among them.

27 Her [R]princes in the midst thereof *are* like wolves ravening the prey, to shed blood, *and* to destroy souls, to get dishonest gain.

28 And [R]her prophets have daubed them with untempered *mortar,* [R]seeing vanity, and divining lies unto them, saying, Thus saith the Lord GOD, when the LORD hath not spoken.

29 The people of the land have used [N]oppression, and exercised robbery, and have vexed the poor and needy: yea, they have [R]oppressed the stranger [N]wrongfully.

30 [R]And I sought for a man among them, that should [R]make up the hedge, and [R]stand·in the gap before me for the land, that I should not destroy it: but I found none.

31 Therefore have I [R]poured out mine indignation upon them; I have consumed them with the fire of my wrath: [R]their own way have I recompensed upon their heads, saith the Lord GOD.

CHAPTER 23

Parable of the two sisters

THE word of the LORD came again unto me, saying,

2 Son of man, there were [R]two women, the daughters of one mother:

3 And [R]they committed whoredoms in Egypt; they committed whoredoms in [R]their youth: there were their breasts pressed, and there they bruised the teats of their virginity.

4 And the names of them *were* Ă-hō'-lăh the elder, and Ă-hŏl'-ĭ-băh her sister: and [R]they were mine, and they bare sons and daughters. Thus *were* their names; Să-mâr'-ĭ-ă *is* [N]Ă-hō'-lăh, and Jerusalem [N]Ă-hŏl'-ĭ-băh.

Infidelity of Samaria

5 And Ă-hō'-lăh played the harlot when she was mine; and she doted on her lovers, on [R]the Assyrians *her* neighbours,

6 *Which were* clothed with blue, captains and rulers, all of them desirable young men, horsemen riding upon horses.

7 Thus she [N]committed her whoredoms with them, with all them *that were* [N]the chosen men of Assyria, and with all on whom she doted: with all their idols she defiled herself.

8 Neither left she her whoredoms *brought* [R]from Egypt: for in her youth they lay with her, and they bruised the breasts of her virginity, and poured their whoredom upon her.

9 Wherefore I have delivered her into the hand of her lovers, into the hand of the [R]Assyrians, upon whom she doted.

10 These discovered her nakedness: they took her sons and her daughters, and slew her with the sword: and she became [N]famous among women; for they had executed judgment upon her.

Infidelity of Jerusalem

11 And [R]when her sister Ă-hŏl'-ĭ-băh saw *this,* [R]she [N] was more corrupt in her inordinate love than she, and in her whoredoms [N]more than her sister in *her* whoredoms.

12 She doted upon the [R]Assyrians *her* neighbours, [R]captains and rulers clothed most gorgeously, horsemen riding upon horses, all of them desirable young men.

13 Then I saw that she was defiled, *that* they *took* both one way,

14 And *that* she increased her whoredoms: for when she saw men portrayed upon the wall, the images of the Chăl-dē'-ăns portrayed with vermilion,

15 Girded with girdles upon their loins, exceeding in dyed attire upon their heads, all of them princes to look to, after the manner of the Babylonians of Chăl-dē'-ă, the land of their nativity:

16 [R]And [N]as soon as she saw them with her eyes, she doted upon them, and sent messengers unto them into Chăl-dē'-ă.

17 And the [N]Babylonians came to her into the bed of love, and they defiled her with their whoredom, and she was polluted with them, and [R]her mind was [N]alienated from them.

18 So she discovered her whoredoms, and discovered her nakedness: then [R]my mind was alienated from her, like as my mind was alienated from her sister.

19 Yet she multiplied her whoredoms, in calling to remembrance the days of her youth,

^Rwherein she had played the harlot in the land of Egypt.

20 For she doted upon their paramours, whose flesh *is as* the flesh of asses, and whose issue *is like* the issue of horses.

21 Thus thou calledst to remembrance the lewdness of thy youth, in bruising thy teats by the Egyptians for the paps of thy youth.

Punishment of Jerusalem

22 Therefore, O Ă-hŏl′-ĭ-băh, thus saith the Lord GOD; ^RBehold, I will raise up thy lovers against thee, from whom thy mind is alienated, and I will bring them against thee on every side;

23 The Babylonians, and all the Chăl-dē′-ăns, ^RPē′-kŏd, and Shō′-ă, and Kō′-ă, *and* all the Assyrians with them: ^Rall of them desirable young men, captains and rulers, great lords and renowned, all of them riding upon horses.

24 And they shall come against thee with chariots, wagons, and wheels, and with an assembly of people, *which* shall set against thee buckler and shield and helmet round about: and I will set judgment before them, and they shall judge thee according to their judgments.

25 And I will set my jealousy against thee, and they shall deal furiously with thee: they shall take away thy nose and thine ears; and thy remnant shall fall by the sword: they shall take thy sons and thy daughters; and thy residue shall be devoured by the fire.

26 ^RThey shall also strip thee out of thy clothes, and take away thy ^Nfair jewels.

27 Thus ^Rwill I make thy lewdness to cease from thee, and thy ^Rwhoredom *brought* from the land of Egypt: so that thou shalt not lift up thine eyes unto them, nor remember Egypt any more.

28 For thus saith the Lord GOD; Behold, I will deliver thee into the hand *of them* ^Rwhom thou hatest, into the hand *of them* ^Rfrom whom thy mind is alienated:

29 And they shall deal with thee hatefully, and shall take away all thy labour, and ^Rshall leave thee naked and bare: and the nakedness of thy whoredoms shall be discovered, both thy lewdness and thy whoredoms.

30 I will do these *things* unto thee, because thou hast ^Rgone a whoring after the heathen, *and* because thou art polluted with their idols.

31 Thou hast walked in the way of thy sister; therefore will I give her ^Rcup into thine hand.

32 Thus saith the Lord GOD; Thou shalt

drink of thy sister's cup deep and large: ^Rthou shalt be laughed to scorn and had in derision; it containeth much.

33 Thou shalt be filled with drunkenness and sorrow, with the cup of astonishment and desolation, with the cup of thy sister Să-mâr′-ĭ-ă.

34 Thou shalt ^Reven drink it and suck *it* out, and thou shalt break the sherds thereof, and pluck off thine own breasts: for I have spoken *it*, saith the Lord GOD.

35 Therefore thus saith the Lord GOD; Because thou ^Rhast forgotten me, and ^Rcast me behind thy back, therefore bear thou also thy lewdness and thy whoredoms.

Judgment upon Samaria and Jerusalem

36 The LORD said moreover unto me; Son of man, wilt thou ^Rjudge^N Ă-hō′-lăh and Ă-hŏl′-ĭ-băh? yea, ^Rdeclare unto them their abominations;

37 That they have committed adultery, and ^Rblood *is* in their hands, and with their idols have they committed adultery, and have also caused their sons, ^Rwhom they bare unto me, to pass for them through *the fire,* to devour *them.*

38 Moreover this they have done unto me: they have defiled my sanctuary in the same day, and ^Rhave profaned my sabbaths.

39 For when they had slain their children to their idols, then they came the same day into my sanctuary to profane it; and, lo, ^Rthus have they done in the midst of mine house.

40 And furthermore, that ye have sent for men ^Nto come from far, ^Runto whom a messenger *was* sent; and, lo, they came: for whom thou didst ^Rwash thyself, ^Rpaintedst thy eyes, and deckedst thyself with ornaments,

41 And satest upon a ^Nstately ^Rbed, and a table prepared before it, ^Rwhereupon thou hast set mine incense and mine oil.

42 And a voice of a multitude being at ease *was* with her: and with the men ^Nof the common sort *were* brought ^NSă-bē′-ăns from the wilderness, which put bracelets upon their hands, and beautiful crowns upon their heads.

43 Then said I unto *her that was* old in adulteries, Will they now commit ^Nwhoredoms with her, and she *with them?*

44 Yet they went in unto her, as they go in unto a woman that playeth the harlot: so went they in unto Ă-hō′-lăh and unto Ă-hŏl′-ĭ-băh, the lewd women.

45 And the righteous men, they shall ^Rjudge them after the manner of adulteresses, and after the manner of women that shed blood; because they *are* adulteresses, and ^Rblood *is* in their hands.

46 For thus saith the Lord GOD; R I will bring up a company upon them, and will give them N to be removed and spoiled.

47 R And the company shall stone them with stones, and N dispatch them with their swords; R they shall slay their sons and their daughters, and burn up their houses with fire.

48 Thus R will I cause lewdness to cease out of the land, R that all women may be taught not to do after your lewdness.

49 And they shall recompense your lewdness upon you, and ye shall R bear the sins of your idols: R and ye shall know that I *am* the Lord GOD.

CHAPTER 24

Parable of the boiling pot

AGAIN in the ninth year, in the tenth month, in the tenth *day* of the month, the word of the LORD came unto me, saying,

2 Son of man, write thee the name of the day, *even* of this same day: the king of Babylon set himself against Jerusalem R this same day.

3 R And utter a parable unto the rebellious house, and say unto them, Thus saith the Lord GOD; R Set on a pot, set *it* on, and also pour water into it:

4 Gather the pieces thereof into it, *even* every good piece, the thigh, and the shoulder; fill *it* with the choice bones.

5 Take the choice of the flock, and N burn also the bones under it, *and* make it boil well, and let them seethe the bones of it therein.

Parable of the rusted pot

6 Wherefore thus saith the Lord GOD; Woe to R the bloody city, to the pot whose scum *is* therein, and whose scum is not gone out of it! bring it out piece by piece; let no R lot fall upon it.

7 For her blood is in the midst of her; she set it upon the top of a rock; R she poured it not upon the ground, to cover it with dust;

8 That it might cause fury to come up to take vengeance; R I have set her blood upon the top of a rock, that it should not be covered.

9 Therefore thus saith the Lord GOD; R Woe to the bloody city! I will even make the pile for fire great.

10 Heap on wood, kindle the fire, consume the flesh, and spice it well, and let the bones be burned.

11 Then set it empty upon the coals thereof, that the brass of it may be hot, and may burn, and *that* R the filthiness of it may be molten in it, *that* the scum of it may be consumed.

CHAP. 23
BC 593

46 ch. 16:40
46 Heb. *for a removing and spoil*
47 ch. 16:40
47 Or, *single them out*
47 2 Chr. 36:17, 19 ch. 24:21
48 ch. 22:15
48 Deut. 13:11 2 Pet. 2:6
49 ver. 35
49 ch. 20:38, 42, 44 & 25:5

CHAP. 24
BC 590

2 2 Ki. 25:1 Jer. 39:1 & 52:4
3 ch. 17:12
3 See Jer. 1:13 ch. 11:3
5 Or, *heap*
6 ch. 22:3
6 See 2 Sam. 8:2 Joel 3:3 Obad. 11 Nah. 3:10
7 Lev. 17:13 Deut. 12:16
8 Mat. 7:2
9 ver. 6 Hab. 2:12
11 ch. 22:15

ch. 8:18   **13**
1 Sam. 15:29   **14**
ch. 5:11   **14**
Heb. *go*   **16**
Heb. *Be silent*   **17**
Jer. 16:5   **17**
See Lev. 10:6 & 21:10 **17**
2 Sam. 15:30   **17**
Mic. 3:7   **17**
Heb. *upper lip*, ver. 22 **17**
Lev. 13:45
ch. 12:9 & 37:18   **19**
Jer. 7:14   **21**
ch. 7:20
Heb. *the pity of your soul* **21**
ch. 23:47   **21**
ver. 17   **22**
Jer. 16:6, 7
Job 27:15   **23**
Ps. 78:64
Lev. 26:39   **23**
Is. 20:3   **24**
ch. 4:3 & 12:6, 11   **24**
Jer. 17:15
John 13:19 & 14:29
ch. 6:7 & 25:5   **24**
ver. 21   **25**
Heb. *the lifting up of their soul* **25**
ch. 33:21   **26**

12 She hath wearied *herself* with lies, and her great scum went not forth out of her: her scum *shall be* in the fire.

13 In thy filthiness *is* lewdness: because I have purged thee, and thou wast not purged, thou shalt not be purged from thy filthiness any more, R till I have caused my fury to rest upon thee.

14 R I the LORD have spoken *it:* it shall come to pass, and I will do *it;* I will not go back, R neither will I spare, neither will I repent; according to thy ways, and according to thy doings, shall they judge thee, saith the Lord GOD.

Death of Ezekiel's wife

15 Also the word of the LORD came unto me, saying,

16 Son of man, behold, I take away from thee the desire of thine eyes with a stroke: yet neither shalt thou mourn nor weep, neither shall thy tears N run down.

17 N Forbear to cry, R make no mourning for the dead, R bind the tire of thine head upon thee, and R put on thy shoes upon thy feet, and R cover not *thy* N lips, and eat not the bread of men.

18 So I spake unto the people in the morning: and at even my wife died; and I did in the morning as I was commanded.

19 And the people said unto me, R Wilt thou not tell us what these *things are* to us, that thou doest *so?*

20 Then I answered them, The word of the LORD came unto me, saying,

21 Speak unto the house of Israel, Thus saith the Lord GOD; Behold, R I will profane my sanctuary, the excellency of your strength, the desire of your eyes, and N that which your soul pitieth; R and your sons and your daughters whom ye have left shall fall by the sword.

22 And ye shall do as I have done: R ye shall not cover *your* lips, nor eat the bread of men.

23 And your tires *shall be* upon your heads, and your shoes upon your feet: R ye shall not mourn nor weep; but R ye shall pine away for your iniquities, and mourn one toward another.

24 Thus R E-zek'-i̯el is unto you a sign: according to all that he hath done shall ye do: R and when this cometh, R ye shall know that I *am* the Lord GOD.

25 Also, thou son of man, *shall it* not *be* in the day when I take from them R their strength, the joy of their glory, the desire of their eyes, and N that whereupon they set their minds, their sons and their daughters,

26 *That* R he that escapeth in that day shall

come unto thee, to cause *thee* to hear *it* with *thine* ears?

27 ᴿIn that day shall thy mouth be opened to him which is escaped, and thou shalt speak, and be no more dumb: and thou shalt be a sign unto them; and they shall know that I *am* the Lᴏʀᴅ.

CHAPTER 25

Prophecy against Ammon

THE word of the Lᴏʀᴅ came again unto me, saying,

2 Son of man, ᴿset thy face ᴿagainst the Ammonites, and prophesy against them;

3 And say unto the Ammonites, Hear the word of the Lord Gᴏᴅ; Thus saith the Lord Gᴏᴅ; ᴿBecause thou saidst, Aha, against my sanctuary, when it was profaned; and against the land of Israel, when it was desolate; and against the house of Judah, when they went into captivity;

4 Behold, therefore I will deliver thee to the ᴺmen of the east for a possession, and they shall set their palaces in thee, and make their dwellings in thee: they shall eat thy fruit, and they shall drink thy milk.

5 And I will make ᴿRăb'-băh ᴿa stable for camels, and the Ammonites a couching place for flocks: ᴿand ye shall know that I *am* the Lᴏʀᴅ.

6 For thus saith the Lord Gᴏᴅ; Because thou ᴿhast clapped *thine* ᴺhands, and stamped with the ᴺfeet, and ᴿrejoiced in ᴺheart with all thy despite against the land of Israel;

7 Behold, therefore I will ᴿstretch out mine hand upon thee, and will deliver thee for ᴺa spoil to the heathen; and I will cut thee off from the people, and I will cause thee to perish out of the countries: I will destroy thee; and thou shalt know that I *am* the Lᴏʀᴅ.

Prophecy against Moab

8 Thus saith the Lord Gᴏᴅ; Because that ᴿMoab and ᴿSē'-ĭr do say, Behold, the house of Judah *is* like unto all the heathen;

9 Therefore, behold, I will open the ᴺside of Moab from the cities, from his cities *which are* on his frontiers, the glory of the country, Běth-jěsh'-ĭ-mōth, Bā'-ăl-mē'-ọn, and Kĭr-ĭ-ă-thā'-ĭm,

10 ᴿUnto the men of the east ᴺwith the Ammonites, and will give them in possession, that the Ammonites ᴿmay not be remembered among the nations.

11 And I will execute judgments upon Moab; and they shall know that I *am* the Lᴏʀᴅ.

Prophecy against Edom

12 Thus saith the Lord Gᴏᴅ; ᴿBecause that Ē'-dọm hath dealt against the house of Judah ᴺby taking vengeance, and hath greatly offended, and revenged himself upon them;

13 Therefore thus saith the Lord Gᴏᴅ; I will also stretch out mine hand upon Ē'-dọm, and will cut off man and beast from it; and I will make it desolate from Tē'-măn; and ᴺthey of Dē'-dăn shall fall by the sword.

14 And ᴿI will lay my vengeance upon Ē'-dọm by the hand of my people Israel: and they shall do in Ē'-dọm according to mine anger and according to my fury; and they shall know my vengeance, saith the Lord Gᴏᴅ.

Prophecy against Philistia

15 Thus saith the Lord Gᴏᴅ; ᴿBecause ᴿthe Philistines have dealt by revenge, and have taken vengeance with a despiteful heart, to destroy *it* ᴺfor the old hatred;

16 Therefore thus saith the Lord Gᴏᴅ; Behold, ᴿI will stretch out mine hand upon the Philistines, and I will cut off the ᴿChĕr'-ĕ-thĭms, ᴿand destroy the remnant of the ᴺsea coast.

17 And I will ᴿexecute great ᴺvengeance upon them with furious rebukes; ᴿand they shall know that I *am* the Lᴏʀᴅ, when I shall lay my vengeance upon them.

CHAPTER 26

Prophecy against Tyrus

AND it came to pass in the eleventh year, in the first *day* of the month, *that* the word of the Lᴏʀᴅ came unto me, saying,

2 Son of man, ᴿbecause that Tȳ'-rŭs hath said against Jerusalem, ᴿAha, she is broken *that was* the gates of the people: she is turned unto me: I shall be replenished, *now* she is laid waste:

3 Therefore thus saith the Lord Gᴏᴅ; Behold, I *am* against thee, O Tȳ'-rŭs, and will cause many nations to come up against thee, as the sea causeth his waves to come up.

4 And they shall destroy the walls of Tȳ'-rŭs, and break down her towers: I will also scrape her dust from her, and ᴿmake her like the top of a rock.

5 It shall be *a place for* the spreading of nets ᴿin the midst of the sea: for I have spoken *it,* saith the Lord Gᴏᴅ: and it shall become a spoil to the nations.

6 And her daughters which *are* in the field shall be slain by the sword; ᴿand they shall know that I *am* the Lᴏʀᴅ.

7 For thus saith the Lord Gᴏᴅ; Behold, I will bring upon Tȳ'-rŭs Nĕb-ū-chăd-rĕz'-zär

king of Babylon, ᴿa king of kings, from the north, with horses, and with chariots, and with horsemen, and companies, and much people.

8 He shall slay with the sword thy daughters in the field: and he shall ᴿmake a fort against thee, and ᴺcast a mount against thee, and lift up the buckler against thee.

9 And he shall set engines of war against thy walls, and with his axes he shall break down thy towers.

10 By reason of the abundance of his horses their dust shall cover thee: thy walls shall shake at the noise of the horsemen, and of the wheels, and of the chariots, when he shall enter into thy gates, ᴺas men enter into a city wherein is made a breach.

11 With the hoofs of his horses shall he tread down all thy streets: he shall slay thy people by the sword, and thy strong garrisons shall go down to the ground.

12 And they shall make a spoil of thy riches, and make a prey of thy merchandise: and they shall break down thy walls, and destroy ᴺthy pleasant houses: and they shall lay thy stones and thy timber and thy dust in the midst of the water.

13 ᴿAnd I will cause the noise of ᴿthy songs to cease; and the sound of thy harps shall be no more heard.

14 And ᴿI will make thee like the top of a rock: thou shalt be *a place* to spread nets upon; thou shalt be built no more: for I the Lᴏʀᴅ have spoken *it,* saith the Lord Gᴏᴅ.

15 Thus saith the Lord Gᴏᴅ to Tў′-rŭs; Shall not the isles ᴿshake at the sound of thy fall, when the wounded cry, when the slaughter is made in the midst of thee?

16 Then all the ᴿprinces of the sea shall ᴿcome down from their thrones, and lay away their robes, and put off their broidered garments: they shall clothe themselves with ᴺtrembling; ᴿthey shall sit upon the ground, and ᴿshall tremble at *every* moment, and ᴿbe astonished at thee.

17 And they shall take up a ᴿlamentation for thee, and say to thee, How art thou destroyed, *that wast* inhabited ᴺof seafaring men, the renowned city, which wast ᴿstrong in the sea, she and her inhabitants, which cause their terror *to be* on all that haunt it!

18 Now shall ᴿthe isles tremble in the day of thy fall; yea, the isles that *are* in the sea shall be troubled at thy departure.

19 For thus saith the Lord Gᴏᴅ; When I shall make thee a desolate city, like the cities that are not inhabited; when I shall bring up the deep upon thee, and great waters shall cover thee;

20 When I shall bring thee down ᴿwith them

that descend into the pit, with the people of old time, and shall set thee in the low parts of the earth, in places desolate of old, with them that go down to the pit, that thou be not inhabited; and I shall set glory ᴿin the land of the living;

21 ᴿI will make thee ᴺa terror, and thou *shalt be* no *more:* ᴿthough thou be sought for, yet shalt thou never be found again, saith the Lord Gᴏᴅ.

CHAPTER 27

Lament over Tyrus

THE word of the Lᴏʀᴅ came again unto me, saying,

2 Now, thou son of man, ᴿtake up a lamentation for Tў′-rŭs;

3 And say unto Tў′-rŭs, ᴿO thou that art situate at the entry of the sea, *which art* ᴿa merchant of the people for many isles, Thus saith the Lord Gᴏᴅ; O Tў′-rŭs, thou hast said, ᴿI *am* ᴺof perfect beauty.

4 Thy borders *are* in the ᴺmidst of the seas, thy builders have perfected thy beauty.

5 They have ᴺmade all thy *ship* boards of fir trees of ᴿSē′-nīr: they have taken cedars from Lĕb′-ă-nọn to make masts for thee.

6 *Of* the oaks of Bā′-shăn have they made thine oars; ᴺᴺthe company of the Ashurites have made thy benches *of* ivory, *brought* out of ᴿthe isles of C̲h̲ĭt′-tĭm.

7 Fine linen with broidered work from Egypt was that which thou spreadest forth to be thy sail; ᴺblue and purple from the isles of Ē-lī′-shăh was that which covered thee.

8 The inhabitants of Zī′-dŏn and Arvad were thy mariners: thy wise *men,* O Tў′-rŭs, *that* were in thee, were thy pilots.

9 The ancients of ᴿGē′-băl and the wise *men* thereof were in thee thy ᴺᴺcalkers: all the ships of the sea with their mariners were in thee to occupy thy merchandise.

10 They of Persia and of Lud and of Phŭt were in thine army, thy men of war: they hanged the shield and helmet in thee; they set forth thy comeliness.

11 The men of Arvad with thine army *were* upon thy walls round about, and the Găm′-mă-dĭms were in thy towers: they hanged their shields upon thy walls round about; they have made ᴿthy beauty perfect.

12 ᴿTarshish *was* thy merchant by reason of the multitude of all *kind of* riches; with silver, iron, tin, and lead, they traded in thy fairs.

13 ᴿJā′-văn, Tū′-băl, and Mē′-she̲c̲h̲, they *were* thy merchants: they traded ᴿthe persons of men and vessels of brass in thy ᴺmarket.

14 They of the house of ᴿTō-gär′-măh traded

in thy fairs with horses and horsemen and mules.

15 The men of ᴿDē'-dăn *were* thy merchants; many isles *were* the merchandise of thine hand: they brought thee *for* a present horns of ivory and ebony.

16 Syria *was* thy merchant by reason of the multitude of ᴺthe wares of thy making: they occupied in thy fairs with emeralds, purple, and broidered work, and fine linen, and coral, and ᴺagate.

17 Judah, and the land of Israel, they *were* thy merchants: they traded in thy market wheat of ᴿMĭn'-nĭth, and Păn'-năg, and honey, and oil, and ᴿbalm.ᴺ

18 Damascus *was* thy merchant in the multitude of the wares of thy making, for the multitude of all riches; in the wine of Hĕl'-bŏn, and white wool.

19 Dan also and Jā'-văn ᴺgoing to and fro occupied in thy fairs: bright iron, cassia, and calamus, were in thy market.

20 ᴿDē'-dăn *was* thy merchant in ᴺprecious clothes for chariots.

21 Arabia, and all the princes of ᴿKē'-där, ᴺthey occupied with thee in lambs, and rams, and goats: in these *were they* thy merchants.

22 The merchants of ᴿShē'-bă and Rā'-ă-mäh, they *were* thy merchants: they occupied in thy fairs with chief of all spices, and with all precious stones, and gold.

23 ᴿHâr'-ăn, and Căn'-nēh, and Eden, the merchants of ᴿShē'-bă, Ăssh'-ŭr, *and* Chīl'-măd, *were* thy merchants.

24 These *were* thy merchants in ᴺall sorts *of things,* in blue ᴺclothes, and broidered work, and in chests of rich apparel, bound with cords, and made of cedar, among thy merchandise.

25 ᴿThe ships of Tarshish did sing of thee in thy market: and thou wast replenished, and made very glorious ᴿin the midst of the seas.

26 Thy rowers have brought thee into great waters: ᴿthe east wind hath broken thee in the ᴺmidst of the seas.

27 Thy ᴿriches, and thy fairs, thy merchandise, thy mariners, and thy pilots, thy calkers, and the occupiers of thy merchandise, and all thy men of war, that *are* in thee, ᴺand in all thy company which *is* in the midst of thee, shall fall into the ᴺmidst of the seas in the day of thy ruin.

28 The ᴺsuburbsᴿ shall shake at the sound of the cry of thy pilots.

29 And ᴿall that handle the oar, the mariners, *and* all the pilots of the sea, shall come down from their ships, they shall stand upon the land;

30 And shall cause their voice to be heard against thee, and shall cry bitterly, and shall ᴿcast up dust upon their heads, they ᴿshall wallow themselves in the ashes:

31 And they shall ᴿmake themselves utterly bald for thee, and gird them with sackcloth, and they shall weep for thee with bitterness of heart *and* bitter wailing.

32 And in their wailing they shall ᴿtake up a lamentation for thee, and lament over thee, *saying,* ᴿWhat *city is* like Tȳ'-rŭs, like the destroyed in the midst of the sea?

33 ᴿWhen thy wares went forth out of the seas, thou filledst many people; thou didst enrich the kings of the earth with the multitude of thy riches and of thy merchandise.

34 In the time *when* ᴿthou shalt be broken by the seas in the depths of the waters ᴿthy merchandise and all thy company in the midst of thee shall fall.

35 ᴿAll the inhabitants of the isles shall be astonished at thee, and their kings shall be sore afraid, they shall be troubled in *their* countenance.

36 The merchants among the people ᴿshall hiss at thee; ᴿthou shalt be ᴺa terror, and ᴺnever *shalt be* any more.

CHAPTER 28

Fall of the prince of Tyrus

THE word of the Lᴏʀᴅ came again unto me, saying,

2 Son of man, say unto the prince of Tȳ'-rŭs, Thus saith the Lord Gᴏᴅ; Because thine heart *is* lifted up, and ᴿthou hast said, I *am* a God, I sit *in* the seat of God, ᴿin the ᴺmidst of the seas; ᴿyet thou *art* a man, and not God, though thou set thine heart as the heart of God:

3 Behold, ᴿthou *art* wiser than Daniel; there is no secret that they can hide from thee:

4 With thy wisdom and with thine understanding thou hast gotten thee riches, and hast gotten gold and silver into thy treasures:

5 ᴿByᴺ thy great wisdom *and* by thy traffick hast thou increased thy riches, and thine heart is lifted up because of thy riches:

6 Therefore thus saith the Lord Gᴏᴅ; Because thou hast set thine heart as the heart of God;

7 Behold, therefore I will bring strangers upon thee, ᴿthe terrible of the nations: and they shall draw their swords against the beauty of thy wisdom, and they shall defile thy brightness.

8 They shall bring thee down to the pit, and

thou shalt die the deaths of *them that are* slain in the midst of the seas.

9 Wilt thou yet ᴿsay before him that slayeth thee, I *am* God? but thou *shalt be* a man, and no God, in the hand of him that ᴺslayeth thee.

10 Thou shalt die the deaths of ᴿthe uncircumcised by the hand of strangers: for I have spoken *it,* saith the Lord God.

Lament over his fall

11 Moreover the word of the Lord came unto me, saying,

12 Son of man, ᴿtake up a lamentation upon the king of Tȳ'-rŭs, and say unto him, Thus saith the Lord God; ᴿThou sealest up the sum, full of wisdom, and perfect in beauty.

13 Thou hast been in ᴿEden the garden of God; every precious stone *was* thy covering, the ᴺsardius, topaz, and the diamond, the ᴺberyl, the onyx, and the jasper, the sapphire, the ᴺemerald, and the carbuncle, and gold: the workmanship of ᴿthy tabrets and of thy pipes was prepared in thee in the day that thou wast created.

14 Thou *art* the anointed ᴿcherub that covereth; and I have set thee *so:* thou wast upon ᴿthe holy mountain of God; thou hast walked up and down in the midst of the stones of fire.

15 Thou *wast* perfect in thy ways from the day that thou wast created, till iniquity was found in thee.

16 By the multitude of thy merchandise they have filled the midst of thee with violence, and thou hast sinned: therefore I will cast thee as profane out of the mountain of God: and I will destroy thee, ᴿO covering cherub, from the midst of the stones of fire.

17 ᴿThine heart was lifted up because of thy beauty, thou hast corrupted thy wisdom by reason of thy brightness: I will cast thee to the ground, I will lay thee before kings, that they may behold thee.

18 Thou hast defiled thy sanctuaries by the multitude of thine iniquities, by the iniquity of thy traffick; therefore will I bring forth a fire from the midst of thee, it shall devour thee, and I will bring thee to ashes upon the earth in the sight of all them that behold thee.

19 All they that know thee among the people shall be astonished at thee: ᴿthou shalt be ᴺa terror, and never *shalt* thou *be* any more.

Prophecy against Zidon

20 Again the word of the Lord came unto me, saying,

21 Son of man, ᴿset thy face ᴿagainst Zī'-dŏn, and prophesy against it,

22 And say, Thus saith the Lord God; ᴿBe-

hold, I *am* against thee, O Zī'-dŏn; and I will be glorified in the midst of thee: and ᴿthey shall know that I *am* the Lord, when I shall have executed judgments in her, and shall be ᴿsanctified in her.

23 ᴿFor I will send into her pestilence, and blood into her street; and the wounded shall be judged in the midst of her by the sword upon her on every side; and they shall know that I *am* the Lord.

24 And there shall be no more ᴿa pricking brier unto the house of Israel, nor *any* grieving thorn of all *that are* round about them, that despised them; and they shall know that I *am* the Lord God.

Restoration of Israel foretold

25 Thus saith the Lord God; When I shall have ᴿgathered the house of Israel from the people among whom they are scattered, and shall be ᴿsanctified in them in the sight of the heathen, then shall they dwell in their land that I have given to my servant Jacob.

26 And they shall ᴿdwell ᴺsafely therein, and shall ᴿbuild houses, and ᴿplant vineyards; yea, they shall dwell with confidence, when I have executed judgments upon all those that ᴺdespise them round about them; and they shall know that I *am* the Lord their God.

CHAPTER 29

Prophecy against Egypt

IN the tenth year, in the tenth *month,* in the twelfth *day* of the month, the word of the Lord came unto me, saying,

2 Son of man, ᴿset thy face against Pharaoh king of Egypt, and prophesy against him, and ᴿagainst all Egypt:

3 Speak, and say, Thus saith the Lord God; ᴿBehold, I *am* against thee, Pharaoh king of Egypt, the great ᴿdragon that lieth in the midst of his rivers, ᴿwhich hath said, My river *is* mine own, and I have made *it* for myself.

4 But ᴿI will put hooks in thy jaws, and I will cause the fish of thy rivers to stick unto thy scales, and I will bring thee up out of the midst of thy rivers, and all the fish of thy rivers shall stick unto thy scales.

5 And I will leave thee *thrown* into the wilderness, thee and all the fish of thy rivers: thou shalt fall upon the ᴺopen fields; ᴿthou shalt not be brought together, nor gathered: ᴿI have given thee for meat to the beasts of the field and to the fowls of the heaven.

6 And all the inhabitants of Egypt shall know that I *am* the Lord, because they have been a ᴿstaff of reed to the house of Israel.

7 ᴿWhen they took hold of thee by thy hand, thou didst break, and rend all their shoulder: and when they leaned upon thee, thou brakest, and madest all their loins to be at a stand.

8 Therefore thus saith the Lord GOD; Behold, I will bring ᴿa sword upon thee, and cut off man and beast out of thee.

9 And the land of Egypt shall be desolate and waste; and they shall know that I *am* the LORD: because he hath said, The river *is* mine, and I have made *it*.

10 Behold, therefore I *am* against thee, and against thy rivers, ᴿand I will make the land of Egypt ᴺutterly waste *and* desolate, ᴿfromᴺ the tower of ᴺSȳ-ē′-nē even unto the border of Ē-thĭ-ō′-pĭ-ă.

11 ᴿNo foot of man shall pass through it, nor foot of beast shall pass through it, neither shall it be inhabited forty years.

12 ᴿAnd I will make the land of Egypt desolate in the midst of the countries *that are* desolate, and her cities among the cities *that are* laid waste shall be desolate forty years: and I will scatter the Egyptians among the nations, and will disperse them through the countries.

13 Yet thus saith the Lord GOD; At the ᴿend of forty years will I gather the Egyptians from the people whither they were scattered:

14 And I will bring again the captivity of Egypt, and will cause them to return *into* the land of Păth′-rŏs, into the land of their ᴺhabitation; and they shall be there a ᴿbaseᴺ kingdom.

15 It shall be the basest of the kingdoms; neither shall it exalt itself any more above the nations: for I will diminish them, that they shall no more rule over the nations.

16 And it shall be no more ᴿthe confidence of the house of Israel, which bringeth *their* iniquity to remembrance, when they shall look after them: but they shall know that I *am* the Lord GOD.

Babylon to be recompensed

17 And it came to pass in the seven and twentieth year, in the first *month*, in the first *day* of the month, the word of the LORD came unto me, saying,

18 Son of man, ᴿNĕb-ū-chăd-rĕz′-zär king of Babylon caused his army to serve a great service against Tȳ′-rŭs: every head *was* made bald, and every shoulder *was* peeled: yet had he no wages, nor his army, for Tȳ′-rŭs, for the service that he had served against it:

19 Therefore thus saith the Lord GOD; Behold, I will give the land of Egypt unto

Nĕb-ū-chăd-rĕz′-zär king of Babylon; and he shall take her multitude, and ᴺtake her spoil, and take her prey; and it shall be the wages for his army.

20 I have given him the land of Egypt ᴺ*for* his labour wherewith he ᴿserved against it, because they wrought for me, saith the Lord GOD.

21 In that day ᴿwill I cause the horn of the house of Israel to bud forth, and I will give thee ᴿthe opening of the mouth in the midst of them; and they shall know that I *am* the LORD.

CHAPTER 30

Egypt and her allies doomed

THE word of the LORD came again unto me, saying,

2 Son of man, prophesy and say, Thus saith the Lord GOD; ᴿHowl ye, Woe worth the day!

3 For ᴿthe day *is* near, even the day of the LORD *is* near, a cloudy day; it shall be the time of the heathen.

4 And the sword shall come upon Egypt, and great ᴺpain shall be in Ē-thĭ-ō′-pĭ-ă, when the slain shall fall in Egypt, and they ᴿshall take away her multitude, and ᴿher foundations shall be broken down.

5 Ē-thĭ-ō′-pĭ-ă, and ᴺLĭb′-ў-ă, and Lydia, and ᴿall the mingled people, and Chŭb, and the ᴺmen of the land that is in league, shall fall with them by the sword.

6 Thus saith the LORD; They also that uphold Egypt shall fall; and the pride of her power shall come down: ᴿfromᴺ the tower of Sȳ-ē′-nē shall they fall in it by the sword, saith the Lord GOD.

7 ᴿAnd they shall be desolate in the midst of the countries *that are* desolate, and her cities shall be in the midst of the cities *that are* wasted.

8 And they shall know that I *am* the LORD, when I have set a fire in Egypt, and *when* all her helpers shall be ᴺdestroyed.

9 In that day ᴿshall messengers go forth from me in ships to make the careless Ē-thĭ-ō′-pĭ-ăns afraid, and great pain shall come upon them, as in the day of Egypt: for, lo, it cometh.

10 Thus saith the Lord GOD; ᴿI will also make the multitude of Egypt to cease by the hand of Nĕb-ū-chăd-rĕz′-zär king of Babylon.

11 He and his people with him, ᴿthe terrible of the nations, shall be brought to destroy the land: and they shall draw their swords against Egypt, and fill the land with the slain.

12 And ᴿI will make the rivers ᴺdry, and

CHAP. 29
BC 589

7 Jer. 37:5, 7, 11
  ch. 17:17
8 ch. 14:17
  & 32:11-13
10 ch. 30:12
10 Heb. *wastes of waste*
10 ch. 30:6
10 Or, *from Migdol to Syene*, Ex. 14:2
  Jer. 44:1
10 Heb. *Seveneh*
11 ch. 32:13
12 ch. 30:7, 26
13 Is. 19:23
  Jer. 46:26
14 Or, *birth*
14 ch. 17:6, 14
14 Heb. *low*
16 Is. 30:2, 3 & 36:4, 6
18 Jer. 27:6
  ch. 26:7, 8

Heb. *spoil her spoil, and prey her prey* 19
Or, *for his hire* 20
Jer. 25:9 20
Ps. 132:17 21
ch. 24:27 21

CHAP. 30
BC 572

Is. 13:6 2
ch. 7:7, 12 3
Joel 2:1
Zeph. 1:7
Or, *fear* 4
ch. 29:19 4
Jer. 50:15 4
Heb. *Phut*, ch. 27:10 5
Jer. 25:20, 24 5
Heb. *children* 5
ch. 29:10 6
Or, *from Migdol to Syene* 6
ch. 29:12 7
Heb. *broken* 8
Is. 18:1, 2 9
ch. 29:19 10
ch. 28:7 11
Is. 19:5, 6 12
Heb. *drought* 12

Rsell the land into the hand of the wicked: and I will make the land waste, and Nall that is therein, by the hand of strangers: I the LORD have spoken it.

13 Thus saith the Lord GOD; I will also Rdestroy the idols, and I will cause their images to cease out of Nŏph; Rand there shall be no more a prince of the land of Egypt: Rand I will put a fear in the land of Egypt.

14 And I will make RPăth'-rŏs desolate, and will set fire in RZō'-ăn,N Rand will execute jŭdgments in No.

15 And I will pour my fury upon NSin, the strength of Egypt; and RI will cut off the multitude of No.

16 And I will Rset fire in Egypt: Sin shall have great pain, and No shall be rent asunder, and Nŏph shall have distresses daily.

17 The young men of NĀ'-vĕn and of NPī-bē'-sĕth shall fall by the sword: and these cities shall go into captivity.

18 RAt Tĕ-hăph'-nĕ-hēś also the day shall be Ndarkened, when I shall break there the yokes of Egypt: and the pomp of her strength shall cease in her: as for her, a cloud shall cover her, and her daughters shall go into captivity.

19 Thus will I execute judgments in Egypt: and they shall know that I am the LORD.

Pharaoh's arm broken

20 And it came to pass in the eleventh year, in the first month, in the seventh day of the month, that the word of the LORD came unto me, saying,

21 Son of man, I have Rbroken the arm of Pharaoh king of Egypt; and, lo, Rit shall not be bound up to be healed, to put a roller to bind it, to make it strong to hold the sword.

22 Therefore thus saith the Lord GOD; Behold, I am against Pharaoh king of Egypt, and will Rbreak his arms, the strong, and that which was broken; and I will cause the sword to fall out of his hand.

23 RAnd I will scatter the Egyptians among the nations, and will disperse them through the countries.

24 And I will strengthen the arms of the king of Babylon, and put my sword in his hand: but I will break Pharaoh's arms, and he shall groan before him with the groanings of a deadly wounded man.

25 But I will strengthen the arms of the king of Babylon, and the arms of Pharaoh shall fall down; and Rthey shall know that I am the LORD, when I shall put my sword into the hand of the king of Babylon, and he shall stretch it out upon the land of Egypt.

26 RAnd I will scatter the Egyptians among the nations, and disperse them among the countries; and they shall know that I am the LORD.

CHAPTER 31

Allegory of Pharaoh's fall

AND it came to pass in the eleventh year, in the third month, in the first day of the month, that the word of the LORD came unto me, saying,

2 Son of man, speak unto Pharaoh king of Egypt, and to his multitude; RWhom art thou like in thy greatness?

3 RBehold, the Assyrian was a cedar in Lĕb'-ă-nŏn Nwith fair branches, and with a shadowing shroud, and of an high stature; and his top was among the thick boughs.

4 RThe waters Nmade him great, the deep Nset him up on high with her rivers running round about his plants, and sent out her Nlittle rivers unto all the trees of the field.

5 Therefore Rhis height was exalted above all the trees of the field, and his boughs were multiplied, and his branches became long because of the multitude of waters, Nwhen he shot forth.

6 All the Rfowls of heaven made their nests in his boughs, and under his branches did all the beasts of the field bring forth their young, and under his shadow dwelt all great nations.

7 Thus was he fair in his greatness, in the length of his branches: for his root was by great waters.

8 The cedars in the Rgarden of God could not hide him: the fir trees were not like his boughs, and the chesnut trees were not like his branches; nor any tree in the garden of God was like unto him in his beauty.

9 I have made him fair by the multitude of his branches: so that all the trees of Eden, that were in the garden of God, envied him.

10 Therefore thus saith the Lord GOD; Because thou hast lifted up thyself in height, and he hath shot up his top among the thick boughs, and Rhis heart is lifted up in his height;

11 I have therefore delivered him into the hand of the mighty one of the heathen; Nhe shall surely deal with him: I have driven him out for his wickedness.

12 And strangers, Rthe terrible of the nations, have cut him off, and have left him: Rupon the mountains and in all the valleys his branches are fallen, and his boughs are broken by all the rivers of the land; and all the people

of the earth are gone down from his shadow, and have left him.

13 ᴿUpon his ruin shall all the fowls of the heaven remain, and all the beasts of the field shall be upon his branches:

14 To the end that none of all the trees by the waters exalt themselves for their height, neither shoot up their top among the thick boughs, neither their trees ᴺstand up in their height, all that drink water: for ᴿthey are all delivered unto death, ᴿto the nether parts of the earth, in the midst of the children of men, with them that go down to the pit.

15 Thus saith the Lord GOD; In the day when he went down to the grave I caused a mourning: I covered the deep for him, and I restrained the floods thereof, and the great waters were stayed: and I caused Lĕb′-ă-nǫn ᴺto mourn for him, and all the trees of the field fainted for him.

16 I made the nations to ᴿshake at the sound of his fall, when I ᴿcast him down to hell with them that descend into the pit: and ᴿall the trees of Eden, the choice and best of Lĕb′-ă-nǫn, all that drink water, ᴿshall be comforted in the nether parts of the earth.

17 They also went down into hell with him unto *them that be* slain with the sword; and *they that were* his arm, *that* ᴿdwelt under his shadow in the midst of the heathen.

18 ᴿTo whom art thou thus like in glory and in greatness among the trees of Eden? yet shalt thou be brought down with the trees of Eden unto the nether parts of the earth: ᴿthou shalt lie in the midst of the uncircumcised with *them that be* slain by the sword. This *is* Pharaoh and all his multitude, saith the Lord GOD.

CHAPTER 32

Lamentation over Pharaoh's fall

AND it came to pass in the twelfth year, in the twelfth month, in the first *day* of the month, *that* the word of the LORD came unto me, saying,

2 Son of man, ᴿtake up a lamentation for Pharaoh king of Egypt, and say unto him, ᴿThou art like a young lion of the nations, ᴿand thou *art* as a ᴺwhale in the seas: and thou camest forth with thy rivers, and troubledst the waters with thy feet, and ᴿfouledst their rivers.

3 Thus saith the Lord GOD; I will therefore ᴿspread out my net over thee with a company of many people; and they shall bring thee up in my net.

4 Then ᴿwill I leave thee upon the land, I will cast thee forth upon the open field, and ᴿwill cause all the fowls of the heaven to re-

main upon thee, and I will fill the beasts of the whole earth with thee.

5 And I will lay thy flesh ᴿupon the mountains, and fill the valleys with thy height.

6 I will also water with thy blood ᴺthe land wherein thou swimmest, *even* to the mountains; and the rivers shall be full of thee.

7 And when I shall ᴺput thee out, ᴿI will cover the heaven, and make the stars thereof dark; I will cover the sun with a cloud, and the moon shall not give her light.

8 All the ᴺbright lights of heaven will I make ᴺdark over thee, and set darkness upon thy land, saith the Lord GOD.

9 I will also ᴺvex the hearts of many people, when I shall bring thy destruction among the nations, into the countries which thou hast not known.

10 Yea, I will make many people amazed at thee, and their kings shall be horribly afraid for thee, when I shall brandish my sword before them; and ᴿthey shall tremble at *every* moment, every man for his own life, in the day of thy fall.

11 ᴿFor thus saith the Lord GOD; The sword of the king of Babylon shall come upon thee.

12 By the swords of the mighty will I cause thy multitude to fall, ᴿthe terrible of the nations, all of them: and ᴿthey shall spoil the pomp of Egypt, and all the multitude thereof shall be destroyed.

13 I will destroy also all the beasts thereof from beside the great waters; ᴿneither shall the foot of man trouble them any more, nor the hoofs of beasts trouble them.

14 Then will I make their waters deep, and cause their rivers to run like oil, saith the Lord GOD.

15 When I shall make the land of Egypt desolate, and the country shall be ᴺdestitute of that whereof it was full, when I shall smite all them that dwell therein, ᴿthen shall they know that I *am* the LORD.

16 This *is* the ᴿlamentation wherewith they shall lament her: the daughters of the nations shall lament her: they shall lament for her, *even* for Egypt, and for all her multitude, saith the Lord GOD.

Lamentation over Egypt

17 It came to pass also in the twelfth year, in the fifteenth *day* of the month, *that* the word of the LORD came unto me, saying,

18 Son of man, wail for the multitude of Egypt, and ᴿcast them down, *even* her, and the daughters of the famous nations, unto the nether parts of the earth, with them that go down into the pit.

19 ᴿWhom dost thou pass in beauty? ᴿgo

down, and be thou laid with the uncircumcised.

20 They shall fall in the midst of *them that are* slain by the sword: ᴺshe is delivered to the sword: draw her and all her multitudes.

21 ᴿThe strong among the mighty shall speak to him out of the midst of hell with them that help him: they are ᴿgone down, they lie uncircumcised, slain by the sword.

22 Ăssh′-ùr *is* there and all her company: his graves *are* about him: all of them slain, fallen by the sword:

23 ᴿWhose graves are set in the sides of the pit, and her company is round about her grave: all of them slain, fallen by the sword, which ᴿcaused ᴺterror in the land of the living.

24 There *is* ᴿĒ′-lăm and all her multitude round about her grave, all of them slain, fallen by the sword, which are ᴿgone down uncircumcised into the nether parts of the earth, ᴿwhich caused their terror in the land of the living; yet have they borne their shame with them that go down to the pit.

25 They have set her a bed in the midst of the slain with all her multitude: her graves *are* round about him: all of them uncircumcised, slain by the sword: though their terror was caused in the land of the living, yet have they borne their shame with them that go down to the pit: he is put in the midst of *them that be* slain.

26 There *is* ᴿMē′-shĕ<u>ch</u>, Tū′-băl, and all her multitude: her graves *are* round about him: all of them ᴿuncircumcised, slain by the sword, though they caused their terror in the land of the living.

27 ᴿAnd they shall not lie with the mighty *that are* fallen of the uncircumcised, which are gone down to hell ᴺwith their weapons of war: and they have laid their swords under their heads, but their iniquities shall be upon their bones, though *they were* the terror of the mighty in the land of the living.

28 Yea, thou shalt be broken in the midst of the uncircumcised, and shalt lie with *them that are* slain with the sword.

29 There *is* ᴿĒ′-d<u>o</u>m, her kings, and all her princes, which with their might are ᴺlaid by *them that were* slain by the sword: they shall lie with the uncircumcised, and with them that go down to the pit.

30 ᴿThere *be* the princes of the north, all of them, and all the ᴿZĭ-dō′-nĭ-ăns, which are gone down with the slain; with their terror they are ashamed of their might; and they lie uncircumcised with *them that be* slain by the sword, and bear their shame with them that go down to the pit.

31 Pharaoh shall see them, and shall be

ᴿcomforted over all his multitude, *even* Pharaoh and all his army slain by the sword, saith the Lord Gᴏᴅ.

32 For I have caused my terror in the land of the living: and he shall be laid in the midst of the uncircumcised with *them that are* slain with the sword, *even* Pharaoh and all his multitude, saith the Lord Gᴏᴅ.

CHAPTER 33

The prophet as watchman

AGAIN the word of the Lᴏʀᴅ came unto me, saying,

2 Son of man, speak to ᴿthe children of thy people, and say unto them, ᴿWhenᴺ I bring the sword upon a land, if the people of the land take a man of their coasts, and set him for their ᴿwatchman:

3 If when he seeth the sword come upon the land, he blow the trumpet, and warn the people;

4 Then ᴺwhosoever heareth the sound of the trumpet, and taketh not warning; if the sword come, and take him away, ᴿhis blood shall be upon his own head.

5 He heard the sound of the trumpet, and took not warning; his blood shall be upon him. But he that taketh warning shall deliver his soul.

6 But if the watchman see the sword come, and blow not the trumpet, and the people be not warned; if the sword come, and take *any* person from among them, ᴿhe is taken away in his iniquity; but his blood will I require at the watchman's hand.

7 ᴿSo thou, O son of man, I have set thee a watchman unto the house of Israel; therefore thou shalt hear the word at my mouth, and warn them from me.

8 When I say unto the wicked, O wicked *man,* thou shalt surely die; if thou dost not speak to warn the wicked from his way, that wicked *man* shall die in his iniquity; but his blood will I require at thine hand.

9 Nevertheless, if thou warn the wicked of his way to turn from it; if he do not turn from his way, he shall die in his iniquity; but thou hast delivered thy soul.

God's righteous judgment

10 Therefore, O thou son of man, speak unto the house of Israel; Thus ye speak, saying, If our transgressions and our sins *be* upon us, and we ᴿpine away in them, ᴿhow should we then live?

11 Say unto them, *As* I live, saith the Lord Gᴏᴅ, ᴿI have no pleasure in the death of the wicked; but that the wicked turn from his way

and live: turn ye, turn ye from your evil ways; for ᴿwhy will ye die, O house of Israel?

12 Therefore, thou son of man, say unto the children of thy people, The ᴿrighteousness of the righteous shall not deliver him in the day of his transgression: as for the wickedness of the wicked, ᴿhe shall not fall thereby in the day that he turneth from his wickedness: neither shall the righteous be able to live for his *righteousness* in the day that he sinneth.

13 When I shall say to the righteous, *that* he shall surely live; ᴿif he trust to his own righteousness, and commit iniquity, all his righteousnesses shall not be remembered, but for his iniquity that he hath committed, he shall die for it.

14 Again, ᴿwhen I say unto the wicked, Thou shalt surely die; if he turn from his sin, and do ᴺthat which is lawful and right;

15 *If* the wicked ᴿrestore the pledge, ᴿgive again that he had robbed, walk in ᴿthe statutes of life, without committing iniquity; he shall surely live, he shall not die.

16 ᴿNone of his sins that he hath committed shall be mentioned unto him: he hath done that which is lawful and right: he shall surely live.

17 ᴿYet the children of thy people say, The way of the Lord is not equal: but as for them, their way is not equal.

18 ᴿWhen the righteous turneth from his righteousness, and committeth iniquity, he shall even die thereby.

19 But if the wicked turn from his wickedness, and do that which is lawful and right, he shall live thereby.

20 Yet ye say, ᴿThe way of the Lord is not equal. O ye house of Israel, I will judge you every one after his ways.

Report of Jerusalem's fall

21 And it came to pass in the twelfth year ᴿof our captivity, in the tenth *month,* in the fifth *day* of the month, ᴿ*that* one that had escaped out of Jerusalem came unto me, saying, ᴿThe city is smitten.

22 Now ᴿthe hand of the LORD was upon me in the evening, afore he that was escaped came; and had opened my mouth, until he came to me in the morning; ᴿand my mouth was opened, and I was no more dumb.

Desolation of the land predicted

23 Then the word of the LORD came unto me, saying,

24 Son of man, ᴿthey that inhabit those ᴿwastes of the land of Israel speak, saying, ᴿAbraham was one, and he inherited the land:

ᴿbut we *are* many; the land is given us for inheritance.

25 Wherefore say unto them, Thus saith the Lord GOD; ᴿYe eat with the blood, and ᴿlift up your eyes toward your idols, and ᴿshed blood: and shall ye possess the land?

26 Ye stand upon your sword, ye work abomination, and ye ᴿdefile every one his neighbour's wife: and shall ye possess the land?

27 Say thou thus unto them, Thus saith the Lord GOD; *As* I live, surely ᴿthey that *are* in the wastes shall fall by the sword, and him that *is* in the open field ᴿwill I give to the beasts ᴺto be devoured, and they that *be* in the forts and ᴿin the caves shall die of the pestilence.

28 ᴿFor I will lay the land ᴺmost desolate, and the ᴿpomp of her strength shall cease; and ᴿthe mountains of Israel shall be desolate, that none shall pass through.

29 Then shall they know that I *am* the LORD, when I have laid the land most desolate because of all their abominations which they have committed.

Ezekiel's false popularity

30 Also, thou son of man, the children of thy people still are talking ᴺagainst thee by the walls and in the doors of the houses, and ᴿspeak one to another, every one to his brother, saying, Come, I pray you, and hear what is the word that cometh forth from the LORD.

31 And ᴿthey come unto thee ᴺas the people cometh, and ᴺthey ᴿsit before thee *as* my people, and they hear thy words, but they will not do them: ᴿfor with their mouth ᴺthey shew much love, *but* ᴿtheir heart goeth after their covetousness.

32 And, lo, thou *art* unto them as ᴺa very lovely song of one that hath a pleasant voice, and can play well on an instrument: for they hear thy words, but they do them not.

33 ᴿAnd when this cometh to pass, (lo, it will come,) then ᴿshall they know that a prophet hath been among them.

CHAPTER 34

God's concern for His flock

AND the word of the LORD came unto me, saying,

2 Son of man, prophesy against the shepherds of Israel, prophesy, and say unto them, Thus saith the Lord GOD unto the shepherds; ᴿWoe *be* to the shepherds of Israel that do

feed themselves! should not the shepherds feed the flocks?

3 ᴿYe eat the fat, and ye clothe you with the wool, ye kill them that are fed: *but* ye feed not the flock.

4 ᴿThe diseased have ye not strengthened, neither have ye healed that which was sick, neither have ye bound up *that which was* broken, neither have ye brought again that which was driven away, neither have ye ᴿsought that which was lost; but with ᴿforce and with cruelty have ye ruled them.

5 ᴿAnd they were ᴿscattered, ᴺbecause *there is* no shepherd: ᴿand they became meat to all the beasts of the field, when they were scattered.

6 My sheep wandered through all the mountains, and upon every high hill: yea, my flock was scattered upon all the face of the earth, and none did search or seek *after them.*

7 Therefore, ye shepherds, hear the word of the Lᴏʀᴅ;

8 *As* I live, saith the Lord Gᴏᴅ, surely because my flock became a prey, and my flock ᴿbecame meat to every beast of the field, because *there was* no shepherd, neither did my shepherds search for my flock, ᴿbut the shepherds fed themselves, and fed not my flock;

9 Therefore, O ye shepherds, hear the word of the Lᴏʀᴅ;

10 Thus saith the Lord Gᴏᴅ; Behold, I *am* against the shepherds; and ᴿI will require my flock at their hand, and cause them to cease from feeding the flock; neither shall the shepherds ᴿfeed themselves any more; for I will deliver my flock from their mouth, that they may not be meat for them.

11 For thus saith the Lord Gᴏᴅ; Behold, I, *even* I, will both search my sheep, and seek them out.

12 ᴺAs a shepherd seeketh out his flock in the day that he is among his sheep *that are* scattered; so will I seek out my sheep, and will deliver them out of all places where they have been scattered in ᴿthe cloudy and dark day.

13 And ᴿI will bring them out from the people, and gather them from the countries, and will bring them to their own land, and feed them upon the mountains of Israel by the rivers, and in all the inhabited places of the country.

14 ᴿI will feed them in a good pasture, and upon the high mountains of Israel shall their fold be: ᴿthere shall they lie in a good fold, and *in* a fat pasture shall they feed upon the mountains of Israel.

15 I will feed my flock, and I will cause them to lie down, saith the Lord Gᴏᴅ.

16 ᴿI will seek that which was lost, and bring again that which was driven away, and will bind up *that which was* broken, and will strengthen that which was sick: but I will destroy ᴿthe fat and the strong; I will feed them ᴿwith judgment.

17 And *as for* you, O my flock, thus saith the Lord Gᴏᴅ; ᴿBehold, I judge between ᴺcattle and cattle, between the rams and the ᴺhe goats.

18 *Seemeth it* a small thing unto you to have eaten up the good pasture, but ye must tread down with your feet the residue of your pastures? and to have drunk of the deep waters, but ye must foul the residue with your feet?

19 And *as for* my flock, they eat that which ye have trodden with your feet; and they drink that which ye have fouled with your feet.

20 Therefore thus saith the Lord Gᴏᴅ unto them; ᴿBehold, I, *even* I, will judge between the fat cattle and between the lean cattle.

21 Because ye have thrust with side and with shoulder, and pushed all the diseased with your horns, till ye have scattered them abroad;

22 Therefore will I save my flock, and they shall no more be a prey; and I will judge between cattle and cattle.

23 And I will set up one ᴿshepherd over them, and he shall feed them, ᴿ*even* my servant David; he shall feed them, and he shall be their shepherd.   ★

24 And ᴿI the Lᴏʀᴅ will be their God, and my servant David ᴿa prince among them; I the Lᴏʀᴅ have spoken *it*.   ★

Covenant of peace

25 And ᴿI will make with them a covenant of peace, and ᴿwill cause the evil beasts to cease out of the land: and they ᴿshall dwell safely in the wilderness, and sleep in the woods.

26 And I will make them and the places round about ᴿmy hill ᴿa blessing; and I will ᴿcause the shower to come down in his season; there shall be ᴿshowers of blessing.

27 And ᴿthe tree of the field shall yield her fruit, and the earth shall yield her increase, and they shall be safe in their land, and shall know that I *am* the Lᴏʀᴅ, when I have ᴿbroken the bands of their yoke, and delivered them out of the hand of those that ᴿserved themselves of them.

28 And they shall no more be a prey to the heathen, neither shall the beast of the land devour them; but ᴿthey shall dwell safely, and none shall make *them* afraid.

29 And I will raise up for them a ᴿplant ᴺof renown, and they shall be no more ᴺconsumed

CHAP. **34**
BC 587
3 Is. 56:11
  Zech. 11:16
4 Zech. 11:16
4 Luke 15:4
4 1 Pet. 5:3
5 ch. 33:21
5 1 Ki. 22:17
  Mat. 9:36
5 Or, *without a shepherd,*
5 Is. 56:9
8 ver. 5, 6
8 ver. 2, 10
10 ch. 3:18
  Heb. 13:17
10 ver. 2, 8
12 Heb. *According to the seeking*
12 ch. 30:3
13 Is. 65:9, 10
  Jer. 23:3
14 Ps. 23:2
14 Jer. 33:12

Is. 40:11   16
Mic. 4:6
Mat. 18:11
Luke 5:32
Is. 10:16   16
Amos 4:1
Jer. 10:24   16
ch. 20:37   17
Mat. 25:32
Heb. *small cattle* 17
of lambs and kids
Heb. *great*   17
he goats
ver. 17   20
Is. 40:11   23
John 10:11
Heb. 13:20
1 Pet. 2:25
Jer. 30:9   23
Hos. 3:5
Ex. 29:45   24
ch. 37:22   24
ch. 37:26   25
Lev. 26:6   25
Is. 11:6-9
Hos. 2:18
Jer. 23:6   25
Is. 56:7   26
Gen. 12:2   26
Is. 19:24
Zech. 8:13
Lev. 26:4   26
Ps. 68:9   26
Lev. 26:4   27
Ps. 85:12
Is. 4:2
Jer. 2:20   27
Jer. 25:14   27
Jer. 30:10   28
Is. 11:1   29
Or, *for renown*   29
Heb. *taken away* 29

with hunger in the land, ᴿneither bear the shame of the heathen any more.

30 Thus shall they know that ᴿI the LORD their God *am* with them, and *that* they, *even* the house of Israel, *are* my people, saith the Lord GOD.

31 And ye my ᴿflock, the flock of my pasture, *are* men, *and* I *am* your God, saith the Lord GOD.

CHAPTER 35

Prophecy against mount Seir

MOREOVER the word of the LORD came unto me, saying,

2 Son of man, set thy face against ᴿmount Sē′-ĭr, and ᴿprophesy against it,

3 And say unto it, Thus saith the Lord GOD; Behold, O mount Sē′-ĭr, I *am* against thee, and ᴿI will stretch out mine hand against thee, and I will make thee ᴺmost desolate.

4 I will lay thy cities waste, and thou shalt be desolate, and thou shalt know that I *am* the LORD.

5 ᴿBecause thou hast had a ᴺperpetual hatred, and hast ᴺshed *the blood of* the children of Israel by the ᴺforce of the sword in the time of their calamity, ᴿin the time *that their* iniquity *had* an end:

6 Therefore, *as* I live, saith the Lord GOD, I will prepare thee unto blood, and blood shall pursue thee: ᴿsith thou hast not hated blood, even blood shall pursue thee.

7 Thus will I make mount Sē′-ĭr ᴺmost desolate, and cut off from it ᴿhim that passeth out and him that returneth.

8 And I will fill his mountains with his slain *men:* in thy hills, and in thy valleys, and in all thy rivers, shall they fall that are slain with the sword.

9 ᴿI will make thee perpetual desolations, and thy cities shall not return: ᴿand ye shall know that I *am* the LORD.

10 Because thou hast said, These two nations and these two countries shall be mine, and we will ᴿpossess it; ᴺwhereas ᴿthe LORD was there:

11 Therefore, *as* I live, saith the Lord GOD, I will even do ᴿaccording to thine anger, and according to thine envy which thou hast used out of thy hatred against them; and I will make myself known among them, when I have judged thee.

12 ᴿAnd thou shalt know that I *am* the LORD, *and that* I have heard all thy blasphemies which thou hast spoken against the mountains of Israel, saying, They are laid desolate, they are given us ᴺto consume.

13 Thus ᴿwith your mouth ye have ᴺboasted against me, and have multiplied your words against me: I have heard *them.*

14 Thus saith the Lord GOD; ᴿWhen the whole earth rejoiceth, I will make thee desolate.

15 ᴿAs thou didst rejoice at the inheritance of the house of Israel, because it was desolate, so will I do unto thee: thou shalt be desolate, O mount Sē′-ĭr, and all ĭ-dū-mē′-ă, *even* all of it: and they shall know that I *am* the LORD.

CHAPTER 36

Judgment on Israel's enemies

ALSO, thou son of man, prophesy unto the ᴿmountains of Israel, and say, Ye mountains of Israel, hear the word of the LORD:

2 Thus saith the Lord GOD; Because ᴿthe enemy hath said against you, Aha, ᴿeven the ancient high places ᴿare ours in possession:

3 Therefore prophesy and say, Thus saith the Lord GOD; ᴺBecause they have made *you* desolate, and swallowed you up on every side, that ye might be a possession unto the residue of the heathen, ᴿand ᴺye are taken up in the lips of talkers, and *are* an infamy of the people:

4 Therefore, ye mountains of Israel, hear the word of the Lord GOD; Thus saith the Lord GOD to the mountains, and to the hills, to the ᴺrivers, and to the valleys, to the desolate wastes, and to the cities that are forsaken, which ᴿbecame a prey and ᴿderision to the residue of the heathen that *are* round about;

5 Therefore thus saith the Lord GOD; ᴿSurely in the fire of my jealousy have I spoken against the residue of the heathen, and against all ĭ-dū-mē′-ă, ᴿwhich have appointed my land into their possession with the joy of all *their* heart, with despiteful minds, to cast it out for a prey.

6 Prophesy therefore concerning the land of Israel, and say unto the mountains, and to the hills, to the rivers, and to the valleys, Thus saith the Lord GOD; Behold, I have spoken in my jealousy and in my fury, because ye have ᴿborne the shame of the heathen:

7 Therefore thus saith the Lord GOD; I have ᴿlifted up mine hand, Surely the heathen that *are* about you, they shall bear their shame.

8 But ye, O mountains of Israel, ye shall shoot forth your branches, and yield your fruit to my people of Israel; for they are at hand to come.

9 For, behold, I *am* for you, and I will turn unto you, and ye shall be tilled and sown:

CHAP. 34
BC 587
29 ch. 36:3, 6
30 ver. 24
31 Ps. 100:3
John 10:11

CHAP. 35
BC 587
2 Deut. 2:5
2 Amos 1:11
3 ch. 6:14
3 Heb. *desolation and desolation*
5 ch. 25:12
5 Or, *hatred of old*
5 Heb. *poured out the children*
5 Heb. *hands*
5 Ps. 137:7
Dan. 9:24
6 Ps. 109:17
7 Heb. *desolation and desolation*
7 Judg. 5:6
9 Jer. 49:17
9 ch. 36:11
10 Ps. 83:4, 12
10 Or, *though the LORD was there*
10 Ps. 48:1, 3
ch. 48:35
11 Mat. 7:2
Jas. 2:13
12 Ps. 9:16
12 Heb. *to devour*

1 Sam. 2:3   **13**
Heb. *magnified* **13**
Is. 65:13   **14**
Obad. 12, 15   **15**

CHAP. 36
BC 587
ch. 6:2, 3   **1**
ch. 25:3   **2**
Deut. 32:13   **2**
ch. 35:10   **2**
Heb. *Because for because* **3**
Deut. 28:37   **3**
Or, *ye are made to come upon the lip of the tongue*   **3**
Or, *bottoms, or, dales*   **4**
ch. 34:28   **4**
Ps. 79:4   **4**
Deut. 4:24   **5**
ch. 38:19
ch. 35:10, 12   **5**
ver. 15   **6**
Ps. 123:3, 4
ch. 34:29
ch. 20:5   **7**

10 And I will multiply men upon you, all the house of Israel, *even* all of it: and the cities shall be inhabited, and ᴿthe wastes shall be builded:

11 And ᴿI will multiply upon you man and beast; and they shall increase and bring fruit: and I will settle you after your old estates, and will do better *unto you* than at your beginnings: ᴿand ye shall know that I *am* the Lᴏʀᴅ.

12 Yea, I will cause men to walk upon you, *even* my people Israel; ᴿand they shall possess thee, and thou shalt be their inheritance, and thou shalt no more henceforth ᴿbereave them *of men*.

13 Thus saith the Lord Gᴏᴅ; Because they say unto you, ᴿThou *land* devourest up men, and hast bereaved thy nations;

14 Therefore thou shalt devour men no more, neither ᴺbereave thy nations any more, saith the Lord Gᴏᴅ.

15 ᴿNeither will I cause *men* to hear in thee the shame of the heathen any more, neither shalt thou bear the reproach of the people any more, neither shalt thou cause thy nations to fall any more, saith the Lord Gᴏᴅ.

16 Moreover the word of the Lᴏʀᴅ came unto me, saying,

17 Son of man, when the house of Israel dwelt in their own land, ᴿthey defiled it by their own way and by their doings: their way was before me as ᴿthe uncleanness of a removed woman.

18 Wherefore I poured my fury upon them ᴿfor the blood that they had shed upon the land, and for their idols *wherewith* they had polluted it:

19 And I scattered them among the heathen, and they were dispersed through the countries: ᴿaccording to their way and according to their doings I judged them.

20 And when they entered unto the heathen, whither they went, they ᴿprofaned my holy name, when they said to them, These *are* the people of the Lᴏʀᴅ, and are gone forth out of his land.

21 But I had pity ᴿfor mine holy name, which the house of Israel had profaned among the heathen, whither they went.

A new heart and a new spirit

22 Therefore say unto the house of Israel, Thus saith the Lord Gᴏᴅ; I do not *this* for your sakes, O house of Israel, ᴿbut for mine holy name's sake, which ye have profaned among the heathen, whither ye went.

23 And I will sanctify my great name, which was profaned among the heathen, which ye have profaned in the midst of them; and the

heathen shall know that I *am* the Lᴏʀᴅ, saith the Lord Gᴏᴅ, when I shall be ᴿsanctified in you before ᴺtheir eyes.

24 For ᴿI will take you from among the heathen, and gather you out of all countries, and will bring you into your own land.

25 ᴿThen will I sprinkle clean water upon you, and ye shall be clean: ᴿfrom all your filthiness, and from all your idols, will I cleanse you.

26 A ᴿnew heart also will I give you, and a new spirit will I put within you: and I will take away the stony heart out of your flesh, and I will give you an heart of flesh.

27 And I will put my ᴿspirit within you, and cause you to walk in my statutes, and ye shall keep my judgments, and do *them*.

28 ᴿAnd ye shall dwell in the land that I gave to your fathers; ᴿand ye shall be my people, and I will be your God.

29 I will also ᴿsave you from all your uncleannesses: and ᴿI will call for the corn, and will increase it, and ᴿlay no famine upon you.

30 ᴿAnd I will multiply the fruit of the tree, and the increase of the field, that ye shall receive no more reproach of famine among the heathen.

31 Then ᴿshall ye remember your own evil ways, and your doings that *were* not good, and ᴿshall lothe yourselves in your own sight for your iniquities and for your abominations.

32 ᴿNot for your sakes do I *this,* saith the Lord Gᴏᴅ, be it known unto you: be ashamed and confounded for your own ways, O house of Israel.

Restoration of Israel promised

33 Thus saith the Lord Gᴏᴅ; In the day that I shall have cleansed you from all your iniquities I will also cause *you* to dwell in the cities, ᴿand the wastes shall be builded.

34 And the desolate land shall be tilled, whereas it lay desolate in the sight of all that passed by.

35 And they shall say, This land that was desolate is become like the garden of ᴿEden; and the waste and desolate and ruined cities *are become* fenced, *and* are inhabited.

36 Then the heathen that are left round about you shall know that I the Lᴏʀᴅ build the ruined *places, and* plant that that was desolate: ᴿI the Lᴏʀᴅ have spoken *it,* and I will do *it*.

37 Thus saith the Lord Gᴏᴅ; ᴿI will yet *for* this be inquired of by the house of Israel, to do *it* for them; I will ᴿincrease them with men like a flock.

38 As the ᴺholy flock, as the flock of Jerusalem in her solemn feasts; so shall the waste

CHAP. **36**

BC 587

10 ver. 33
Is. 58:12 & 61:4
Amos 9:14
11 Jer. 31:27
& 33:12
11 ch. 35:9
& 37:6, 13
12 Obad. 17, etc.
12 See Jer. 15:7
13 Num. 13:32
14 Or, *cause to fall*
15 ch. 34:29
17 Lev. 18:25, 27, 28
Jer. 2:7
17 Lev. 15:19, etc.
18 ch. 16:36, 38
& 23:37
19 ch. 7:3 & 18:30
& 39:24
20 Is. 52:5
Rom. 2:24
21 ch. 20:9, 14
22 Ps. 106:8

ch. 20:41 & 28:22	23
Or, *your*	23
ch. 34:13 & 37:21	24
Is. 52:15 Heb. 10:22	25
Jer. 33:8	25
Jer. 32:39 ch. 11:19	26
ch. 11:19 & 37:14	27
ch. 28:25 & 37:25	28
Jer. 30:22 ch. 11:20 & 37:27	28
Mat. 1:21 Rom. 11:26	29
See Ps. 105:16	29
ch. 34:29	29
ch. 34:27	30
ch. 16:61, 63	31
Lev. 26:39 ch. 6:9 & 20:43	31
ver. 22 Deut. 9:5	32
ver. 10	33
Is. 51:3 ch. 28:13 Joel 2:3	35
ch. 17:24 & 22:14 & 37:14	36
See ch. 14:3 & 20:3, 31	37
ver. 10	37
Heb. *flock of holy things*	38

cities be filled with flocks of men: and they shall know that I *am* the LORD.

CHAPTER 37

The valley of dry bones

THE ᴿhand of the LORD was upon me, and carried me out ᴿin the spirit of the LORD, and set me down in the midst of the valley which *was* full of bones,

2 And caused me to pass by them round about: and, behold, *there were* very many in the open ᴺvalley; and, lo, *they were* very dry.

3 And he said unto me, Son of man, can these bones live? And I answered, O Lord GOD, ᴿthou knowest.

4 Again he said unto me, Prophesy upon these bones, and say unto them, O ye dry bones, hear the word of the LORD.

5 Thus saith the Lord GOD unto these bones; Behold, I will ᴿcause breath to enter into you, and ye shall live:

6 And I will lay sinews upon you, and will bring up flesh upon you, and cover you with skin, and put breath in you, and ye shall live; ᴿand ye shall know that I *am* the LORD.

7 So I prophesied as I was commanded: and as I prophesied, there was a noise, and behold a shaking, and the bones came together, bone to his bone.

8 And when I beheld, lo, the sinews and the flesh came up upon them, and the skin covered them above: but *there was* no breath in them.

9 Then said he unto me, Prophesy unto the ᴺwind, prophesy, son of man, and say to the wind, Thus saith the Lord GOD; ᴿCome from the four winds, O breath, and breathe upon these slain, that they may live.

10 So I prophesied as he commanded me, ᴿand the breath came into them, and they lived, and stood up upon their feet, an exceeding great army.

11 Then he said unto me, Son of man, these bones are the whole house of Israel: behold, they say, ᴿOur bones are dried, and our hope is lost: we are cut off for our parts.

12 Therefore prophesy and say unto them, Thus saith the Lord GOD; Behold, ᴿO my people, I will open your graves, and cause you to come up out of your graves, and ᴿbring you into the land of Israel.

13 And ye shall know that I *am* the LORD, when I have opened your graves, O my people, and brought you up out of your graves,

14 And ᴿshall put my spirit in you, and ye shall live, and I shall place you in your own land: then shall ye know that I the LORD have spoken *it*, and performed *it*, saith the LORD.

CHAP. **37**

BC 587

1 ch. 1:3
1 ch. 3:14 & 8:3
& 11:24
Luke 4:1
2 Or, *champaign*
3 Deut. 32:39
1 Sam. 2:6
John 5:21
Rom. 4:17
2 Cor. 1:9
5 ver. 9
Ps. 104:30
6 ch. 6:7 & 35:12
Joel 2:27 & 3:17
9 Or, *breath*
9 ver. 5
Ps. 104:30
10 Rev. 11:11
11 Ps. 141:7
Is. 49:14
12 Is. 26:19
Hos. 13:14
12 ver. 25
ch. 36:24
14 ch. 36:27

See   16
Num. 17:2
2 Chr. 11:12, 13, 16
16 & 15:9
& 30:11, 18
See   17
ver. 22, 24
ch. 12:9 & 24:19 18
Zech. 10:6   19
ver. 16, 17   19
ch. 12:3   20
ch. 36:24   21
Is. 11:13   22
Jer. 3:18
Hos. 1:11
ch. 34:23   22
John 10:16
ch. 36:25   23
ch. 36:28   23
Is. 40:11   24
Jer. 23:5
Luke 1:32
John 10:16   24
ch. 36:27   24
ch. 36:28   25
Is. 60:21   25
Joel 3:20
Amos 9:15
John 12:34   25
Ps. 89:3   26
Is. 55:3
Jer. 32:40
ch. 36:10   26
2 Cor. 6:16   26

Reunion of Judah and Israel

15 The word of the LORD came again unto me, saying,

16 Moreover, thou son of man, ᴿtake thee one stick, and write upon it, For Judah, and for ᴿthe children of Israel his companions: then take another stick, and write upon it, For Joseph, the stick of Ē'-phră-ĭm, and *for* all the house of Israel his companions:

17 And ᴿjoin them one to another into one stick; and they shall become one in thine hand.

18 And when the children of thy people shall speak unto thee, saying, ᴿWilt thou not shew us what thou *meanest* by these?

19 ᴿSay unto them, Thus saith the Lord GOD; Behold, I will take ᴿthe stick of Joseph, which *is* in the hand of Ē'-phră-ĭm, and the tribes of Israel his fellows, and will put them with him, *even* with the stick of Judah, and make them one stick, and they shall be one in mine hand.

20 And the sticks whereon thou writest shall be in thine hand ᴿbefore their eyes.

21 And say unto them, Thus saith the Lord GOD; Behold, ᴿI will take the children of Israel from among the heathen, whither they be gone, and will gather them on every side, and bring them into their own land:

22 And ᴿI will make them one nation in the land upon the mountains of Israel; and ᴿone king shall be king to them all: and they shall be no more two nations, neither shall they be divided into two kingdoms any more at all:

23 ᴿNeither shall they defile themselves any more with their idols, nor with their detestable things, nor with any of their transgressions: but ᴿI will save them out of all their dwelling places, wherein they have sinned, and will cleanse them: so shall they be my people, and I will be their God.

The Davidic line to continue

24 And ᴿDavid my servant *shall be* king over them; and ᴿthey all shall have one shepherd: ᴿthey shall also walk in my judgments, and observe my statutes, and do them.   ★

25 ᴿAnd they shall dwell in the land that I have given unto Jacob my servant, wherein your fathers have dwelt; and they shall dwell therein, *even* they, and their children, and their children's children ᴿfor ever: and ᴿmy servant David *shall be* their prince for ever.   ★

26 Moreover I will make a ᴿcovenant of peace with them; it shall be an everlasting covenant with them: and I will place them, and ᴿmultiply them, and will set my ᴿsanctuary in the midst of them for evermore.

27 ᴿMy tabernacle also shall be with them: yea, I will be ᴿtheir God, and they shall be my people.

28 ᴿAnd the heathen shall know that I the LORD do ᴿsanctify Israel, when my sanctuary shall be in the midst of them for evermore.

CHAPTER 38

Prophecy against Gog

AND the word of the LORD came unto me, saying,

2 ᴿSon of man, ᴿset thy face against ᴿGog, the land of Mā′-gŏg, ᴺthe chief prince of ᴿMē′-shĕch and Tū′-băl, and prophesy against him,

3 And say, Thus saith the Lord GOD; Behold, I *am* against thee, O Gog, the chief prince of Mē′-shĕch and Tū′-băl:

4 And ᴿI will turn thee back, and put hooks into thy jaws, and I will bring thee forth, and all thine army, horses and horsemen, ᴿall of them clothed with all sorts *of armour, even* a great company *with* bucklers and shields, all of them handling swords:

5 Persia, Ē-thi-ō′-pī-ȧ, and ᴺLĭb′-ў-ȧ with them; all of them with shield and helmet:

6 ᴿGō′-mĕr, and all his bands; the house of ᴿTō-gär′-măh of the north quarters, and all his bands: *and* many people with thee.

7 ᴿBe thou prepared, and prepare for thyself, thou, and all thy company that are assembled unto thee, and be thou a guard unto them.

8 ᴿAfter many days ᴿthou shalt be visited: in the latter years thou shalt come into the land *that is* brought back from the sword, ᴿ*and is* gathered out of many people, against ᴿthe mountains of Israel, which have been always waste: but it is brought forth out of the nations, and they shall ᴿdwell safely all of them.

9 Thou shalt ascend and come ᴿlike a storm, thou shalt be ᴿlike a cloud to cover the land, thou, and all thy bands, and many people with thee.

10 Thus saith the Lord GOD; It shall also come to pass, *that* at the same time shall things come into thy mind, and thou shalt ᴺthink an evil thought:

11 And thou shalt say, I will go up to the land of unwalled villages; I will ᴿgo to them that are at rest, ᴿthat dwell ᴺsafely, all of them dwelling without walls, and having neither bars nor gates,

12 ᴺTo take a spoil, and to take a prey; to turn thine hand upon the desolate places *that are now* inhabited, ᴿand upon the people *that are* gathered out of the nations, which have

gotten cattle and goods, that dwell in the ᴺmidst of the land.

13 ᴿShē′-bȧ, and ᴿDē′-dăn, and the merchants ᴿof Tarshish, with all ᴿthe young lions thereof, shall say unto thee, Art thou come to take a spoil? hast thou gathered thy company to take a prey? to carry away silver and gold, to take away cattle and goods, to take a great spoil?

14 Therefore, son of man, prophesy and say unto Gog, Thus saith the Lord GOD; ᴿIn that day when my people of Israel ᴿdwelleth safely, shalt thou not know *it*?

15 ᴿAnd thou shalt come from thy place out of the north parts, thou, ᴿand many people with thee, all of them riding upon horses, a great company, and a mighty army:

16 ᴿAnd thou shalt come up against my people of Israel, as a cloud to cover the land; ᴿit shall be in the latter days, and I will bring thee against my land, that the heathen may know me, when I shall be sanctified in thee, O Gog, before their eyes.

Defeat of Gog foretold

17 Thus saith the Lord GOD; *Art* thou he of whom I have spoken in old time ᴺby my servants the prophets of Israel, which prophesied in those days *many* years that I would bring thee against them?

18 And it shall come to pass at the same time when Gog shall come against the land of Israel, saith the Lord GOD, *that* my fury shall come up in my face.

19 For ᴿin my jealousy ᴿ*and* in the fire of my wrath have I spoken, ᴿSurely in that day there shall be a great shaking in the land of Israel;

20 So that ᴿthe fishes of the sea, and the fowls of the heaven, and the beasts of the field, and all creeping things that creep upon the earth, and all the men that *are* upon the face of the earth, shall shake at my presence, ᴿand the mountains shall be thrown down, and the ᴺsteep places shall fall, and every wall shall fall to the ground.

21 And I will ᴿcall for ᴿa sword against him throughout all my mountains, saith the Lord GOD: ᴿevery man's sword shall be against his brother.

22 And I will ᴿplead against him with ᴿpestilence and with blood; and ᴿI will rain upon him, and upon his bands, and upon the many people that *are* with him, an overflowing rain, and ᴿgreat hailstones, fire, and brimstone.

23 Thus will I magnify myself, and ᴿsanctify myself; ᴿand I will be known in the eyes

of many nations, and they shall know that I *am* the LORD.

CHAPTER 39

Second prophecy against Gog

THEREFORE, ᴿthou son of man, prophesy against Gog, and say, Thus saith the Lord GOD; Behold, I *am* against thee, O Gog, the chief prince of Mē′-shĕch and Tū′-bǎl:

2 And I will turn thee back, and ᴺleave but the sixth part of thee, ᴿand will cause thee to come up from ᴺthe north parts, and will bring thee upon the mountains of Israel:

3 And I will smite thy bow out of thy left hand, and will cause thine arrows to fall out of thy right hand.

4 ᴿThou shalt fall upon the mountains of Israel, thou, and all thy bands, and the people that *is* with thee: ᴿI will give thee unto the ravenous birds of every ᴺsort, and *to* the beasts of the field ᴺto be devoured.

5 Thou shalt fall upon ᴺthe open field: for I have spoken *it,* saith the Lord GOD.

6 ᴿAnd I will send a fire on Mā′-gŏg, and among them that dwell ᴺcarelessly in ᴿthe isles: and they shall know that I *am* the LORD.

7 ᴿSo will I make my holy name known in the midst of my people Israel; and I will not *let them* ᴿpollute my holy name any more: ᴿand the heathen shall know that I *am* the LORD, the Holy One in Israel.

8 ᴿBehold, it is come, and it is done, saith the Lord GOD; this *is* the day ᴿwhereof I have spoken.

9 And they that dwell in the cities of Israel shall go forth, and shall set on fire and burn the weapons, both the shields and the bucklers, the bows and the arrows, and the ᴺhandstaves, and the spears, and they shall ᴺburn them with fire seven years:

10 So that they shall take no wood out of the field, neither cut down *any* out of the forests; for they shall burn the weapons with fire: ᴿand they shall spoil those that spoiled them, and rob those that robbed them, saith the Lord GOD.

11 And it shall come to pass in that day, *that* I will give unto Gog a place there of graves in Israel, the valley of the passengers on the east of the sea: and it shall stop the ᴺnoses of the passengers: and there shall they bury Gog and all his multitude: and they shall call *it* The valley of ᴺHā′-mŏn-gŏg.

12 And seven months shall the house of Israel be burying of them, ᴿthat they may cleanse the land.

13 Yea, all the people of the land shall bury *them;* and it shall be to them a renown the day

that ᴿI shall be glorified, saith the Lord GOD.

14 And they shall sever out ᴺmen of continual employment, passing through the land to bury with the passengers those that remain upon the face of the earth, ᴿto cleanse it: after the end of seven months shall they search.

15 And the passengers *that* pass through the land, when *any* seeth a man's bone, then shall he ᴺset up a sign by it, till the buriers have buried it in the valley of Hā′-mŏn-gŏg.

16 And also the name of the city *shall be* ᴺHă-mō′-näh. Thus shall they ᴿcleanse the land.

Summons to the sacrificial feast

17 And, thou son of man, thus saith the Lord GOD; ᴿSpeak ᴺunto every feathered fowl, and to every beast of the field, ᴿAssemble yourselves, and come; gather yourselves on every side to my ᴺsacrifice that I do sacrifice for you, *even* a great sacrifice ᴿupon the mountains of Israel, that ye may eat flesh, and drink blood.

18 ᴿYe shall eat the flesh of the mighty, and drink the blood of the princes of the earth, of rams, of lambs, and of ᴺgoats, of bullocks, all of them ᴿfatlings of Bā′-shăn.

19 And ye shall eat fat till ye be full, and drink blood till ye be drunken, of my sacrifice which I have sacrificed for you.

20 ᴿThus ye shall be filled at my table with horses and chariots, ᴿwith mighty men, and with all men of war, saith the Lord GOD.

21 ᴿAnd I will set my glory among the heathen, and all the heathen shall see my judgment that I have executed, and ᴿmy hand that I have laid upon them.

22 ᴿSo the house of Israel shall know that I *am* the LORD their God from that day and forward.

23 ᴿAnd the heathen shall know that the house of Israel went into captivity for their iniquity: because they trespassed against me, therefore ᴿhid I my face from them, and ᴿgave them into the hand of their enemies: so fell they all by the sword.

24 ᴿAccording to their uncleanness and according to their transgressions have I done unto them, and hid my face from them.

Return of the exiles

25 Therefore thus saith the Lord GOD; ᴿNow will I bring again the captivity of Jacob, and have mercy upon the ᴿwhole house of Israel, and will be jealous for my holy name;

26 ᴿAfter that they have borne their shame, and all their trespasses whereby they have trespassed against me, when they ᴿdwelt safely in their land, and none made *them* afraid.

27 ᴿWhen I have brought them again from the people, and gathered them out of their enemies' lands, and ᴿam sanctified in them in the sight of many nations;

28 ᴿThen shall they know that I *am* the Lᴏʀᴅ their God, ᴺwhich caused them to be led into captivity among the heathen: but I have gathered them unto their own land, and have left none of them any more there.

29 ᴿNeither will I hide my face any more from them: for I have ᴿpoured out my spirit upon the house of Israel, saith the Lord Gᴏᴅ.

CHAPTER 40

Vision of the new Israel

IN the five and twentieth year of our captivity, in the beginning of the year, in the tenth *day* of the month, in the fourteenth year after that ᴿthe city was smitten, in the selfsame day ᴿthe hand of the Lᴏʀᴅ was upon me, and brought me thither.

2 ᴿIn the visions of God brought he me into the land of Israel, and ᴿset me upon a very high mountain, ᴺby which *was* as the frame of a city on the south.

3 And he brought me thither, and, behold, *there was* a man, whose appearance *was* ᴿlike the appearance of brass, ᴿwith a line of flax in his hand, ᴿand a measuring reed; and he stood in the gate.

4 And the man said unto me, ᴿSon of man, behold with thine eyes, and hear with thine ears, and set thine heart upon all that I shall shew thee; for to the intent that I might shew *them* unto thee *art* thou brought hither: ᴿdeclare all that thou seest to the house of Israel.

Measurements of the temple

5 And behold ᴿa wall on the outside of the house round about, and in the man's hand a measuring reed of six cubits *long* by the cubit and an hand breadth: so he measured the breadth of the building, one reed; and the height, one reed.

6 Then came he unto the gate ᴺwhich looketh toward the east, and went up the stairs thereof, and measured the threshold of the gate, *which was* one reed broad; and the other threshold *of the gate, which was* one reed broad.

7 And *every* little chamber *was* one reed long, and one reed broad; and between the little chambers *were* five cubits; and the threshold of the gate by the porch of the gate within *was* one reed.

8 He measured also the porch of the gate within, one reed.

9 Then measured he the porch of the gate, eight cubits; and the posts thereof, two cubits; and the porch of the gate *was* inward.

10 And the little chambers of the gate eastward *were* three on this side, and three on that side; they three *were* of one measure: and the posts had one measure on this side and on that side.

11 And he measured the breadth of the entry of the gate, ten cubits; *and* the length of the gate, thirteen cubits.

12 The ᴺspace also before the little chambers *was* one cubit *on this side,* and the space *was* one cubit on that side: and the little chambers *were* six cubits on this side, and six cubits on that side.

13 He measured then the gate from the roof of *one* little chamber to the roof of another: the breadth *was* five and twenty cubits, door against door.

14 He made also posts of threescore cubits, even unto the post of the court round about the gate.

15 And from the face of the gate of the entrance unto the face of the porch of the inner gate *were* fifty cubits.

16 And *there were* ᴿnarrowᴺ windows to the little chambers, and to their posts within the gate round about, and likewise to the ᴺarches: and windows *were* round about ᴺinward: and upon *each* post *were* palm trees.

The outward courts and the gates

17 Then brought he me into ᴿthe outward court, and, lo, *there were* ᴿchambers, and a pavement made for the court round about: ᴿthirty chambers *were* upon the pavement.

18 And the pavement by the side of the gates over against the length of the gates *was* the lower pavement.

19 Then he measured the breadth from the forefront of the lower gate unto the forefront of the inner court ᴺwithout, an hundred cubits eastward and northward.

20 And the gate of the outward court ᴺthat looked toward the north, he measured the length thereof, and the breadth thereof.

21 And the little chambers thereof *were* three on this side and three on that side; and the posts thereof and the ᴺarches thereof were after the measure of the first gate: the length thereof *was* fifty cubits, and the breadth five and twenty cubits.

22 And their windows, and their arches, and their palm trees, *were* after the measure of the gate that looketh toward the east; and they went up unto it by seven steps; and the arches thereof *were* before them.

23 And the gate of the inner court *was* over

against the gate toward the north, and toward the east; and he measured from gate to gate an hundred cubits.

24 After that he brought me toward the south, and behold a gate toward the south: and he measured the posts thereof and the arches thereof according to these measures.

25 And *there were* windows in it and in the arches thereof round about, like those windows: the length *was* fifty cubits, and the breadth five and twenty cubits.

26 And *there were* seven steps to go up to it, and the arches thereof *were* before them: and it had palm trees, one on this side, and another on that side, upon the posts thereof.

27 And *there was* a gate in the inner court toward the south: and he measured from gate to gate toward the south an hundred cubits.

The inner court

28 And he brought me to the inner court by the south gate: and he measured the south gate according to these measures;

29 And the little chambers thereof, and the posts thereof, and the arches thereof, according to these measures: and *there were* windows in it and in the arches thereof round about: *it was* fifty cubits long, and five and twenty cubits broad.

30 And the arches round about *were* ᴿfive and twenty cubits long, and five cubits ᴺbroad.

31 And the arches thereof *were* toward the utter court; and palm trees *were* upon the posts thereof: and the going up to it *had* eight steps.

32 And he brought me into the inner court toward the east: and he measured the gate according to these measures.

33 And the little chambers thereof, and the posts thereof, and the arches thereof, *were* according to these measures: and *there were* windows therein and in the arches thereof round about: *it was* fifty cubits long, and five and twenty cubits broad.

34 And the arches thereof *were* toward the outward court; and palm trees *were* upon the posts thereof, on this side, and on that side: and the going up to it *had* eight steps.

35 And he brought me to the north gate, and measured *it* according to these measures;

36 The little chambers thereof, the posts thereof, and the arches thereof, and the windows to it round about: the length *was* fifty cubits, and the breadth five and twenty cubits.

37 And the posts thereof *were* toward the utter court; and palm trees *were* upon the posts thereof, on this side, and on that side: and the going up to it *had* eight steps.

CHAP. **40**
BC 574
30 See ver. 21, 25, 33, 36
30 Heb. *breadth*

Lev. 4:2, 3   **39**
Lev. 5:6   **39**
& 6:6 & 7:1
Or, *at the step*   **40**
Or, *endirons,* or,   **43**
  the two hearth-stones
1 Chr. 6:31   **44**
Lev. 8:35   **45**
Num. 3:27, 28, 32, 38 & 18:5
1 Chr. 9:23
2 Chr. 13:11
Ps. 134:1
Or, *ward,*   **45**
  or, *ordinance,* ver. 46
Num. 18:5   **46**
  ch. 44:15
1 Ki. 2:35   **46**
  ch. 43:19
  & 44:15, 16
1 Ki. 6:3   **49**
1 Ki. 7:21   **49**

The vestibule

38 And the chambers and the entries thereof *were* by the posts of the gates, where they washed the burnt offering.

39 And in the porch of the gate *were* two tables on this side, and two tables on that side, to slay thereon the burnt offering and ᴿthe sin offering and ᴿthe trespass offering.

40 And at the side without, ᴺas one goeth up to the entry of the north gate, *were* two tables; and on the other side, which *was* at the porch of the gate, *were* two tables.

41 Four tables *were* on this side, and four tables on that side, by the side of the gate; eight tables, whereupon they slew *their sacrifices.*

42 And the four tables *were* of hewn stone for the burnt offering, of a cubit and an half long, and a cubit and an half broad, and one cubit high: whereupon also they laid the instruments wherewith they slew the burnt offering and the sacrifice.

43 And within *were* ᴺhooks, an hand broad, fastened round about: and upon the tables *was* the flesh of the offering.

44 And without the inner gate *were* the chambers of ᴿthe singers in the inner court, which *was* at the side of the north gate; and their prospect *was* toward the south: one at the side of the east gate *having* the prospect toward the north.

45 And he said unto me, This chamber, whose prospect *is* toward the south, *is* for the priests, ᴿthe keepers of the ᴺcharge of the house.

46 And the chamber whose prospect *is* toward the north *is* for the priests, ᴿthe keepers of the charge of the altar: these *are* the sons of ᴿZā′-dŏk among the sons of Levi, which come near to the LORD to minister unto him.

47 So he measured the court, an hundred cubits long, and an hundred cubits broad, foursquare; and the altar *that was* before the house.

48 And he brought me to the porch of the house, and measured *each* post of the porch, five cubits on this side, and five cubits on that side: and the breadth of the gate *was* three cubits on this side, and three cubits on that side.

49 ᴿThe length of the porch *was* twenty cubits, and the breadth eleven cubits; and *he brought me* by the steps whereby they went up to it: and *there were* ᴿpillars by the posts, one on this side, and another on that side.

CHAPTER 41

The nave and the most holy place

AFTERWARD he brought me to the temple, and measured the posts, six cubits broad on the one side, and six cubits broad on the other side, *which was* the breadth of the tabernacle.

2 And the breadth of the ᴺdoor *was* ten cubits; and the sides of the door *were* five cubits on the one side, and five cubits on the other side: and he measured the length thereof, forty cubits: and the breadth, twenty cubits.

3 Then went he inward, and measured the post of the door, two cubits; and the door, six cubits; and the breadth of the door, seven cubits.

4 So ᴿhe measured the length thereof, twenty cubits; and the breadth, twenty cubits, before the temple: and he said unto me, This *is* the most holy *place.*

The temple walls

5 After he measured the wall of the house, six cubits; and the breadth of *every* side chamber, four cubits, round about the house on every side.

6 ᴿAnd the side chambers *were* three, ᴺone over another, and ᴺthirty in order; and they entered into the wall which *was* of the house for the side chambers round about, that they might ᴺhave hold, but they had not hold in the wall of the house.

7 And ᴿ*there*ᴺ *was* an enlarging, and a winding about still upward to the side chambers: for the winding about of the house went still upward round about the house: therefore the breadth of the house *was still* upward, and so increased *from* the lowest *chamber* to the highest by the midst.

8 I saw also the height of the house round about: the foundations of the side chambers *were* ᴿa full reed of six great cubits.

9 The thickness of the wall, which *was* for the side chamber without, *was* five cubits: and *that* which *was* left *was* the place of the side chambers that *were* within.

10 And between the chambers *was* the wideness of twenty cubits round about the house on every side.

11 And the doors of the side chambers *were* toward *the place that was* left, one door toward the north, and another door toward the south: and the breadth of the place that was left *was* five cubits round about.

12 Now the building that *was* before the separate place at the end toward the west *was*

seventy cubits broad; and the wall of the building *was* five cubits thick round about, and the length thereof ninety cubits.

13 So he measured the house, an hundred cubits long; and the separate place, and the building, with the walls thereof, an hundred cubits long;

14 Also the breadth of the face of the house, and of the separate place toward the east, an hundred cubits.

The furnishings

15 And he measured the length of the building over against the separate place which *was* behind it, and the ᴺgalleries thereof on the one side and on the other side, an hundred cubits, with the inner temple, and the porches of the court;

16 The door posts, and ᴿthe narrow windows, and the galleries round about on their three stories, over against the door, ᴺceiled with wood round about, ᴺand from the ground up to the windows, and the windows *were* covered;

17 To that above the door, even unto the inner house, and without, and by all the wall round about within and without, by ᴺmeasure.

18 And *it was* made ᴿwith chĕr'-ū-bĭms and palm trees, so that a palm tree *was* between a cherub and a cherub; and *every* cherub had two faces;

19 ᴿSo that the face of a man *was* toward the palm tree on the one side, and the face of a young lion toward the palm tree on the other side: *it was* made through all the house round about.

20 From the ground unto above the door *were* chĕr'-ū-bĭms and palm trees made, and *on* the wall of the temple.

21 The ᴺposts of the temple *were* squared, *and* the face of the sanctuary; the appearance *of the one* as the appearance *of the other.*

22 ᴿThe altar of wood *was* three cubits high, and the length thereof two cubits; and the corners thereof, and the length thereof, and the walls thereof, *were* of wood: and he said unto me, This *is* ᴿthe table that *is* ᴿbefore the LORD.

23 ᴿAnd the temple and the sanctuary had two doors.

24 And the doors had two leaves *apiece,* two turning leaves; two *leaves* for the one door, and two leaves for the other *door.*

25 And *there were* made on them, on the doors of the temple, chĕr'-ū-bĭms and palm trees, like as *were* made upon the walls; and

CHAP. 41
BC 574

2 Or, *entrance*
4 1 Ki. 6:20
2 Chr. 3:8
6 1 Ki. 6:5, 6
6 Heb. *side chamber over side chamber*
6 Or, *three and thirty times, or, foot*
6 Heb. *be holden*
7 1 Ki. 6:8
7 Heb. *it was made broader, and went round*
8 ch. 40:5

Or, *several walks,* or, *walks with pillars* 15
ver. 26
ch. 40:16 16
Heb. *ceiling of wood* 16
Or, *and the ground unto the windows* 16
Heb. *measures* 17
1 Ki. 6:29 18
See ch. 1:10 19
Heb. *post* 21
Ex. 30:1 22
ch. 44:16 22
Mal. 1:7, 12
Ex. 30:8 22
1 Ki. 6:31-35 23

there were thick planks upon the face of the porch without.

26 And *there were* ᴿnarrow windows and palm trees on the one side and on the other side, on the sides of the porch, and *upon* the side chambers of the house, and thick planks.

CHAPTER 42

The priests' chambers

THEN he brought me forth into the utter court, the way toward the north: and he brought me into ᴿthe chamber that *was* over against the separate place, and which *was* before the building toward the north.

2 Before the length of an hundred cubits *was* the north door, and the breadth *was* fifty cubits.

3 Over against the twenty *cubits* which *were* for the inner court, and over against the pavement which *was* for the utter court, *was* ᴿgallery against gallery in three *stories.*

4 And before the chambers *was* a walk of ten cubits breadth inward, a way of one cubit; and their doors toward the north.

5 Now the upper chambers *were* shorter: for the galleries ᴺwere higher than these, ᴺthan the lower, and than the middlemost of the building.

6 For they *were* in three *stories,* but had not pillars as the pillars of the courts: therefore *the building* was straitened more than the lowest and the middlemost from the ground.

7 And the wall that *was* without over against the chambers, toward the utter court on the forepart of the chambers, the length thereof *was* fifty cubits.

8 For the length of the chambers that *were* in the utter court *was* fifty cubits: and, lo, before the temple *were* an hundred cubits.

9 And ᴺfrom under these chambers *was* ᴺthe entry on the east side, ᴺas one goeth into them from the utter court.

10 The chambers *were* in the thickness of the wall of the court toward the east, over against the separate place, and over against the building.

11 And ᴿthe way before them *was* like the appearance of the chambers which *were* toward the north, as long as they, *and* as broad as they: and all their goings out *were* both according to their fashions, and according to their doors.

12 And according to the doors of the chambers that *were* toward the south *was* a door in the head of the way, *even* the way directly before the wall toward the east, as one entereth into them.

13 Then said he unto me, The north chambers *and* the south chambers, which *are* before the separate place, they *be* holy chambers, where the priests that approach unto the Lᴏʀᴅ ᴿshall eat the most holy things: there shall they lay the most holy things, and ᴿthe meat offering, and the sin offering, and the trespass offering; for the place *is* holy.

14 ᴿWhen the priests enter therein, then shall they not go out of the holy *place* into the utter court, but there they shall lay their garments wherein they minister; for they *are* holy; and shall put on other garments, and shall approach to *those things* which *are* for the people.

Over-all measurements

15 Now when he had made an end of measuring the inner house, he brought me forth toward the gate whose prospect *is* toward the east, and measured it round about.

16 He measured the east ᴺside with the measuring reed, five hundred reeds, with the measuring reed round about.

17 He measured the north side, five hundred reeds, with the measuring reed round about.

18 He measured the south side, five hundred reeds, with the measuring reed.

19 He turned about to the west side, *and* measured five hundred reeds with the measuring reed.

20 He measured it by the four sides: ᴿit had a wall round about, ᴿfive hundred *reeds* long, and five hundred broad, to make a separation between the sanctuary and the profane place.

CHAPTER 43

The glory of the LORD fills the temple

AFTERWARD he brought me to the gate, *even* the gate ᴿthat looketh toward the east:

2 ᴿAnd, behold, the glory of the God of Israel came from the way of the east: and ᴿhis voice *was* like a noise of many waters: ᴿand the earth shined with his glory.

3 And *it was* ᴿaccording to the appearance of the vision which I saw, *even* according to the vision that I saw ᴺwhen I came ᴿto destroy the city: and the visions *were* like the vision that I saw ᴿby the river Chē'-bär; and I fell upon my face.

4 ᴿAnd the glory of the Lᴏʀᴅ came into the house by the way of the gate whose prospect *is* toward the east.

5 ᴿSo the spirit took me up, and brought me into the inner court; and, behold, ᴿthe glory of the Lᴏʀᴅ filled the house.

6 And I heard *him* speaking unto me out of the house; and ᴿthe man stood by me.

7 And he said unto me, Son of man, ᴿthe place of my throne, and ᴿthe place of the soles of my feet, ᴿwhere I will dwell in the midst of the children of Israel for ever, and my holy name, shall the house of Israel ᴿno more defile, *neither* they, nor their kings, by their whoredom, nor by ᴿthe carcases of their kings in their high places.

8 ᴿIn their setting of their threshold by my thresholds, and their post by my posts, ᴺand the wall between me and them, they have even defiled my holy name by their abominations that they have committed: wherefore I have consumed them in mine anger.

9 Now let them put away their whoredom, and ᴿthe carcases of their kings, far from me, ᴿand I will dwell in the midst of them for ever.

The law of the temple

10 Thou son of man, ᴿshew the house to the house of Israel, that they may be ashamed of their iniquities: and let them measure the ᴺpattern.

11 And if they be ashamed of all that they have done, shew them the form of the house, and the fashion thereof, and the goings out thereof, and the comings in thereof, and all the forms thereof, and all the ordinances thereof, and all the forms thereof, and all the laws thereof: and write *it* in their sight, that they may keep the whole form thereof, and all the ordinances thereof, and do them.

12 This *is* the law of the house; Upon ᴿthe top of the mountain the whole limit thereof round about *shall be* most holy. Behold, this *is* the law of the house.

Size and ordinances of the altar

13 And these *are* the measures of the altar after the cubits: ᴿThe cubit *is* a cubit and an hand breadth; even the ᴺbottom *shall be* a cubit, and the breadth a cubit, and the border thereof by the ᴺedge thereof round about *shall be* a span: and this *shall be* the higher place of the altar.

14 And from the bottom *upon* the ground *even* to the lower settle *shall be* two cubits, and the breadth one cubit; and from the lesser settle *even* to the greater settle *shall be* four cubits, and the breadth *one* cubit.

15 So ᴺthe altar *shall be* four cubits; and from ᴺthe altar and upward *shall be* four horns.

16 And the altar *shall be* twelve *cubits* long,

twelve broad, square in the four squares thereof.

17 And the settle *shall be* fourteen *cubits* long and fourteen broad in the four squares thereof; and the border about it *shall be* half a cubit; and the bottom thereof *shall be* a cubit about; and ᴿhis stairs shall look toward the east.

18 And he said unto me, Son of man, thus saith the Lord GOD; These *are* the ordinances of the altar in the day when they shall make it, to offer burnt offerings thereon, and to ᴿsprinkle blood thereon.

19 And thou shalt give to ᴿthe priests the Levites that be of the seed of Zā′-dŏk, which approach unto me, to minister unto me, saith the Lord GOD, ᴿa young bullock for a sin offering.

20 And thou shalt take of the blood thereof, and put *it* on the four horns of it, and on the four corners of the settle, and upon the border round about: thus shalt thou cleanse and purge it.

21 Thou shalt take the bullock also of the sin offering, and he ᴿshall burn it in the appointed place of the house, ᴿwithout the sanctuary.

22 And on the second day thou shalt offer a kid of the goats without blemish for a sin offering; and they shall cleanse the altar, as they did cleanse *it* with the bullock.

23 When thou hast made an end of cleansing *it,* thou shalt offer a young bullock without blemish, and a ram out of the flock without blemish.

24 And thou shalt offer them before the LORD, ᴿand the priests shall cast salt upon them, and they shall offer them up *for* a burnt offering unto the LORD.

25 ᴿSeven days shalt thou prepare every day a goat *for* a sin offering: they shall also prepare a young bullock, and a ram out of the flock, without blemish.

26 Seven days shall they purge the altar and purify it; and they shall ᴺconsecrate themselves.

27 ᴿAnd when these days are expired, it shall be, *that* upon the eighth day, and *so* forward, the priests shall make your burnt offerings upon the altar, and your ᴺpeace offerings; and I will ᴿaccept you, saith the Lord GOD.

CHAPTER 44

Ordinance about entrance to the temple

THEN he brought me back the way of the gate of the outward sanctuary ᴿwhich looketh toward the east; and it *was* shut.

CHAP. 43
BC 574
6 ch. 40:3
7 Ps. 99:1
7 1 Chr. 28:2
Ps. 99:5
7 Ex. 29:45
Ps. 68:16
& 132:14
Joel 3:17
John 1:14
2 Cor. 6:16
7 ch. 39:7
7 Lev. 26:30
Jer. 16:18
8 See 2 Ki. 16:14
& 21:4, 5, 7
ch. 8:3 & 23:39
& 44:7
8 Or, *for there was but a wall between me and them*
9 ver. 7
9 ver. 7
10 ch. 40:4
10 Or, *sum, or, number*
12 ch. 40:2
13 ch. 41:8
13 Heb. *bosom*
13 Heb. *lip*
15 Heb. *Harel, i.e. the mountain of God*
15 Heb. *Ariel, i.e. the lion of God*

See Ex. 20:26   17
Lev. 1:5   18
ch. 44:16   19
Ex. 29:10   19
Lev. 8:14
ch. 45:18
Ex. 29:14   21
Heb. 13:11   21
Lev. 2:13   24
Ex. 29:35   25
Lev. 8:33
Heb. *fill their hands,*   26
Ex. 29:24
Lev. 9:1   27
Or, *thank offerings*
ch. 20:40, 41   27
Rom. 12:1
1 Pet. 2:5

CHAP. 44
BC 574
ch. 43:1   1

2 Then said the LORD unto me; This gate shall be shut, it shall not be opened, and no man shall enter in by it; [R]because the LORD, the God of Israel, hath entered in by it, therefore it shall be shut.

3 *It is* for the prince; the prince, he shall sit in it to [R]eat bread before the LORD; [R]he shall enter by the way of the porch of *that* gate, and shall go out by the way of the same.

4 Then brought he me the way of the north gate before the house: and I looked, and, [R]behold, the glory of the LORD filled the house of the LORD: [R]and I fell upon my face.

5 And the LORD said unto me, [R]Son of man, [N]mark well, and behold with thine eyes, and hear with thine ears all that I say unto thee concerning all the ordinances of the house of the LORD, and all the laws thereof; and mark well the entering in of the house, with every going forth of the sanctuary.

6 And thou shalt say to the [R]rebellious, *even* to the house of Israel, Thus saith the Lord GOD; O ye house of Israel, [R]let it suffice you of all your abominations,

7 [R]In that ye have brought *into my sanctuary* [R]strangers,[N] [R]uncircumcised in heart, and uncircumcised in flesh, to be in my sanctuary, to pollute it, *even* my house, when ye offer [R]my bread, [R]the fat and the blood, and they have broken my covenant because of all your abominations.

8 And ye have not [R]kept the charge of mine holy things: but ye have set keepers of my [N]charge in my sanctuary for yourselves.

Idolatrous Levites

9 Thus saith the Lord GOD; [R]No stranger, uncircumcised in heart, nor uncircumcised in flesh, shall enter into my sanctuary, of any stranger that *is* among the childen of Israel.

10 [R]And the Levites that are gone away far from me, when Israel went astray, which went astray away from me after their idols; they shall even bear their iniquity.

11 Yet they shall be ministers in my sanctuary, [R]*having* charge at the gates of the house, and ministering to the house: [R]they shall slay the burnt offering and the sacrifice for the people, and [R]they shall stand before them to minister unto them.

12 Because they ministered unto them before their idols, and [R]caused[N] the house of Israel to fall into iniquity; therefore have I [R]lifted up mine hand against them, saith the Lord GOD, and they shall bear their iniquity.

13 [R]And they shall not come near unto me, to do the office of a priest unto me, nor to come near to any of my holy things, in the most holy *place*: but they shall [R]bear their

shame, and their abominations which they have committed.

14 But I will make them [R]keepers of the charge of the house, for all the service thereof, and for all that shall be done therein.

Ministers of the sanctuary

15 [R]But the priests the Levites, [R]the sons of Zā'-dŏk, that kept the charge of my sanctuary [R]when the children of Israel went astray from me, they shall come near to me to minister unto me, and they [R]shall stand before me to offer unto me [R]the fat and the blood, saith the Lord GOD:

16 They shall enter into my sanctuary, and they shall come near to [R]my table, to minister unto me, and they shall keep my charge.

17 And it shall come to pass, *that* when they enter in at the gates of the inner court, [R]they shall be clothed with linen garments; and no wool shall come upon them, whiles they minister in the gates of the inner court, and within.

18 [R]They shall have linen bonnets upon their heads, and shall have linen breeches upon their loins; they shall not gird *themselves* [NN]with any thing that causeth sweat.

19 And when they go forth into the utter court, *even* into the utter court to the people, [R]they shall put off their garments wherein they ministered, and lay them in the holy chambers, and they shall put on other garments; and they shall [R]not sanctify the people with their garments.

20 [R]Neither shall they shave their heads, nor suffer their locks to grow long; they shall only poll their heads.

21 [R]Neither shall any priest drink wine, when they enter into the inner court.

22 Neither shall they take for their wives a [R]widow, nor her that is [N]put away: but they shall take maidens of the seed of the house of Israel, or a widow [N]that had a priest before.

23 And [R]they shall teach my people *the difference* between the holy and profane, and cause them to discern between the unclean and the clean.

24 And [R]in controversy they shall stand in judgment; *and* they shall judge it according to my judgments: and they shall keep my laws and my statutes in all mine assemblies; [R]and they shall hallow my sabbaths.

25 And they shall come at no dead person to defile themselves: but for father, or for mother, or for son, or for daughter, for brother, or for sister that hath had no husband, they may defile themselves.

26 And [R]after he is cleansed, they shall reckon unto him seven days.

27 And in the day that he goeth into the

sanctuary, Runto the inner court, to minister in the sanctuary, Rhe shall offer his sin offering, saith the Lord GOD.

28 And it shall be unto them for an inheritance: I Ram their inheritance: and ye shall give them no possession in Israel: I am their possession.

29 RThey shall eat the meat offering, and the sin offering, and the trespass offering; and Revery Ndedicated thing in Israel shall be theirs.

30 And the Rfirst N of all the firstfruits of all things, and every oblation of all, of every sort of your oblations, shall be the priest's: ye Rshall also give unto the priest the first of your dough, Rthat he may cause the blessing to rest in thine house.

31 The priests shall not eat of any thing that is Rdead of itself, or torn, whether it be fowl or beast.

CHAPTER 45

Apportionment of the LORD'S land

MOREOVER, Nwhen ye shall Rdivide by lot the land for inheritance, ye shall Roffer an oblation unto the LORD, Nan holy portion of the land: the length shall be the length of five and twenty thousand reeds, and the breadth shall be ten thousand. This shall be holy in all the borders thereof round about.

2 Of this there shall be for the sanctuary five hundred in length, with five hundred in breadth, square round about; and fifty cubits round about for the Nsuburbs thereof.

3 And of this measure shalt thou measure the length of five and twenty thousand, and the breadth of ten thousand: Rand in it shall be the sanctuary and the most holy place.

4 RThe holy portion of the land shall be for the priests the ministers of the sanctuary, which shall come near to minister unto the LORD: and it shall be a place for their houses, and an holy place for the sanctuary.

5 RAnd the five and twenty thousand of length, and the ten thousand of breadth, shall also the Levites, the ministers of the house, have for themselves, for a possession for Rtwenty chambers.

6 RAnd ye shall appoint the possession of the city five thousand broad, and five and twenty thousand long, over against the oblation of the holy portion: it shall be for the whole house of Israel.

7 RAnd a portion shall be for the prince on the one side and on the other side of the oblation of the holy portion, and of the possession of the city, before the oblation of the holy portion, and before the possession of the city,

from the west side westward, and from the east side eastward: and the length shall be over against one of the portions, from the west border unto the east border.

8 In the land shall be his possession in Israel: and Rmy princes shall no more oppress my people; and the rest of the land shall they give to the house of Israel according to their tribes.

Duties of the princes

9 Thus saith the Lord GOD; RLet it suffice you, O princes of Israel: Rremove violence and spoil, and execute judgment and justice, take away your Nexactions from my people, saith the Lord GOD.

10 Ye shall have just Rbalances, and a just ē'-phäh, and a just bäth.

11 The ē'-phäh and the bäth shall be of one measure, that the bäth may contain the tenth part of an hō'-mer, and the ē'-phäh the tenth part of an hō'-mer: the measure thereof shall be after the hō'-mer.

12 And the Rshē'-kel shall be twenty gē'-rähs: twenty shē'-kels, five and twenty shē'-kels, fifteen shē'-kels, shall be your mā'-neh.

Required offerings

13 This is the oblation that ye shall offer; the sixth part of an ē'-phäh of an hō'-mer of wheat, and ye shall give the sixth part of an ē'-phäh of an hō'-mer of barley:

14 Concerning the ordinance of oil, the bäth of oil, ye shall offer the tenth part of a bäth out of the côr, which is an hō'-mer of ten bäths; for ten bäths are an hō'-mer:

15 And one Nlamb out of the flock, out of two hundred, out of the fat pastures of Israel; for a meat offering, and for a burnt offering, and for Npeace offerings, Rto make reconciliation for them, saith the Lord GOD.

16 All the people of the land Nshall give this oblation Nfor the prince in Israel.

17 And it shall be the prince's part to give burnt offerings, and meat offerings, and drink offerings, in the feasts, and in the new moons, and in the sabbaths, in all solemnities of the house of Israel: he shall prepare the sin offering, and the meat offering, and the burnt offering, and the Npeace offerings, to make reconciliation for the house of Israel.

18 Thus saith the Lord GOD; In the first month, in the first day of the month, thou shalt take a young bullock without blemish, and Rcleanse the sanctuary:

19 RAnd the priest shall take of the blood of the sin offering, and put it upon the posts of the house, and upon the four corners of the

Center reference column

CHAP. 44
BC 574

27	ver. 17
27	Lev. 4:3
28	Num. 18:20
	Deut. 10:9
	& 18:1, 2
	Josh. 13:14
29	Lev. 7:6
29	Lev. 27:21, 28,
	compared with
	Num. 18:14
29	Or, devoted
30	Ex. 13:2
	& 22:29 & 23:19
	Num. 3:13 & 18:12
30	Or, chief
30	Num. 15:20
	Neh. 10:37
30	Prov. 3:9
	Mal. 3:10
31	Ex. 22:31
	Lev. 22:8

CHAP. 45
BC 574

1	Heb. when ye cause the land to fall
1	ch. 47:22
1	ch. 48:8
1	Heb. holiness
2	Or, void places
3	ch. 48:10
4	ver. 1
5	ch. 48:13
5	See ch. 40:17
6	ch. 48:15
7	ch. 48:21

See Jer. 22:17	8
ch. 22:27 & 46:18	
ch. 44:6	9
Jer. 22:3	9
Heb. expulsions	9
Lev. 19:35, 36	10
Prov. 11:1	
Ex. 30:13	12
Lev. 27:25	
Num. 3:47	
Or, kid	15
Or, thank offerings	15
Lev. 1:4	15
Heb. shall be for	16
Or, with	16
Or, thank offerings	17
Lev. 16:16	18
ch. 43:20	19

settle of the altar, and upon the posts of the gate of the inner court.

20 And so thou shalt do the seventh *day* of the month ᴿfor every one that erreth, and for *him that is* simple: so shall ye reconcile the house.

21 ᴿIn the first *month,* in the fourteenth day of the month, ye shall have the passover, a feast of seven days; unleavened bread shall be eaten.

22 And upon that day shall the prince prepare for himself and for all the people of the land ᴿa bullock *for* a sin offering.

23 And ᴿseven days of the feast he shall prepare a burnt offering to the LORD, seven bullocks and seven rams without blemish daily the seven days; ᴿand a kid of the goats daily *for* a sin offering.

24 ᴿAnd he shall prepare a meat offering of an ē'-phäh for a bullock, and an ē'-phäh for a ram, and an hĭn of oil for an ē'-phäh.

25 In the seventh *month,* in the fifteenth day of the month, shall he do the like in the ᴿfeast of the seven days, according to the sin offering, according to the burnt offering, and according to the meat offering, and according to the oil.

CHAPTER 46

Sabbaths and new moons

THUS saith the Lord GOD; The gate of the inner court that looketh toward the east shall be shut the six working days; but on the sabbath it shall be opened, and in the day of the new moon it shall be opened.

2 ᴿAnd the prince shall enter by the way of the porch of *that* gate without, and shall stand by the post of the gate, and the priests shall prepare his burnt offering and his peace offerings, and he shall worship at the threshold of the gate: then he shall go forth; but the gate shall not be shut until the evening.

3 Likewise the people of the land shall worship at the door of this gate before the LORD in the sabbaths and in the new moons.

4 And the burnt offering that ᴿthe prince shall offer unto the LORD in the sabbath day *shall be* six lambs without blemish, and a ram without blemish.

5 ᴿAnd the meat offering *shall be* an ē'-phäh for a ram, and the meat offering for the lambs ᴺas he shall be able to give, and an hĭn of oil to an ē'-phäh.

6 And in the day of the new moon *it shall be* a young bullock without blemish, and six lambs, and a ram: they shall be without blemish.

CHAP. **45**
BC 574
20 Lev. 4:27
21 Ex. 12:18
Lev. 23:5, 6
Num. 9:2, 3
& 28:16, 17
Deut. 16:1, etc.
22 Lev. 4:14
23 Lev. 23:8
23 See Num.
28:15, 22, 30
& 29:5, 11,
16, 19, etc.
24 ch. 46:5, 7
25 Lev. 23:34
Num. 29:12
Deut. 16:13

CHAP. **46**
BC 574
2 ver. 8
ch. 44:3
4 ch. 45:17
5 ver. 7, 11
ch. 45:24
5 Heb. *the gift of his hand,* Deut. 16:17

ver. 2	8
Ex. 23:14-17	9
Deut. 16:16	
ver. 5	11
ver. 2	12
ch. 44:3	
Ex. 29:38	13
Num. 28:3	
Heb. *a son of his year*	13
Heb. *morning by morning*	13
Lev. 25:10	17

7 And he shall prepare a meat offering, an ē'-phäh for a bullock, and an ē'-phäh for a ram, and for the lambs according as his hand shall attain unto, and an hĭn of oil to an ē'-phäh.

Ritual laws

8 ᴿAnd when the prince shall enter, he shall go in by the way of the porch of *that* gate, and he shall go forth by the way thereof.

9 But when the people of the land ᴿshall come before the LORD in the solemn feasts, he that entereth in by the way of the north gate to worship shall go out by the way of the south gate; and he that entereth by the way of the south gate shall go forth by the way of the north gate: he shall not return by the way of the gate whereby he came in, but shall go forth over against it.

10 And the prince in the midst of them, when they go in, shall go in; and when they go forth, shall go forth.

11 And in the feasts and in the solemnities ᴿthe meat offering shall be an ē'-phäh to a bullock, and an ē'-phäh to a ram, and to the lambs as he is able to give, and an hĭn of oil to an ē'-phäh.

12 Now when the prince shall prepare a voluntary burnt offering or peace offerings voluntarily unto the LORD, ᴿ*one* shall then open him the gate that looketh toward the east, and he shall prepare his burnt offering and his peace offerings, as he did on the sabbath day: then he shall go forth; and after his going forth *one* shall shut the gate.

13 ᴿThou shalt daily prepare a burnt offering unto the LORD *of* a lamb ᴺof the first year without blemish: thou shalt prepare it ᴺevery morning.

14 And thou shalt prepare a meat offering for it every morning, the sixth part of an ē'-phäh, and the third part of an hĭn of oil, to temper with the fine flour; a meat offering continually by a perpetual ordinance unto the LORD.

15 Thus shall they prepare the lamb, and the meat offering, and the oil, every morning *for* a continual burnt offering.

Inheritance laws

16 Thus saith the Lord GOD; If the prince give a gift unto any of his sons, the inheritance thereof shall be his sons'; it *shall be* their possession by inheritance.

17 But if he give a gift of his inheritance to one of his servants, then it shall be his to ᴿthe year of liberty; after it shall return to the prince: but his inheritance shall be his sons' for them.

18 Moreover ᴿthe prince shall not take of the people's inheritance by oppression, to thrust them out of their possession; *but* he shall give his sons inheritance out of his own possession: that my people be not scattered every man from his possession.

Rooms for preparation of offerings

19 After he brought me through the entry, which *was* at the side of the gate, into the holy chambers of the priests, which looked toward the north: and, behold, there *was* a place on the two sides westward.

20 Then said he unto me, This *is* the place where the priests shall ᴿboil the trespass offering and the sin offering, where they shall ᴿbake the meat offering; that they bear *them* not out into the utter court, ᴿto sanctify the people.

21 Then he brought me forth into the utter court, and caused me to pass by the four corners of the court; and, behold, ᴺin every corner of the court *there was* a court.

22 In the four corners of the court *there were* courts ᴺjoined of forty *cubits* long and thirty broad: these four ᴺcorners *were* of one measure.

23 And *there was* a row *of building* round about in them, round about them four, and *it was* made with boiling places under the rows round about.

24 Then said he unto me, These *are* the places of them that boil, where the ministers of the house shall ᴿboil the sacrifice of the people.

CHAPTER 47

The river flowing from the temple

AFTERWARD he brought me again unto the door of the house; and, behold, ᴿwaters issued out from under the threshold of the house eastward: for the forefront of the house *stood toward* the east, and the waters came down from under from the right side of the house, at the south *side* of the altar.

2 Then brought he me out of the way of the gate northward, and led me about the way without unto the utter gate by the way that looketh eastward; and, behold, there ran out waters on the right side.

3 And when ᴿthe man that had the line in his hand went forth eastward, he measured a thousand cubits, and he brought me through the waters; the ᴺwaters *were* to the ancles.

4 Again he measured a thousand, and brought me through the waters; the waters *were* to the knees. Again he measured a thou-

sand, and brought me through; the waters *were* to the loins.

5 Afterward he measured a thousand; *and it was* a river that I could not pass over: for the waters were risen, ᴺwaters to swim in, a river that could not be passed over.

6 And he said unto me, Son of man, hast thou seen *this?* Then he brought me, and caused me to return to the brink of the river.

7 Now when I had returned, behold, at the ᴺbank of the river *were* very many ᴿtrees on the one side and on the other.

8 Then said he unto me, These waters issue out toward the east country, and go down into the ᴺdesert, and go into the sea: *which being* brought forth into the sea, the waters shall be healed.

9 And it shall come to pass, *that* every thing that liveth, which moveth, whithersoever the ᴺrivers shall come, shall live: and there shall be a very great multitude of fish, because these waters shall come thither: for they shall be healed; and every thing shall live whither the river cometh.

10 And it shall come to pass, *that* the fishers shall stand upon it from Ĕn-gĕ̄'-dī even unto Ĕn-ĕg'-lā-ĭm; they shall be a *place* to spread forth nets; their fish shall be according to their kinds, as the fish ᴿof the great sea, exceeding many.

11 But the miry places thereof and the marishes thereof ᴺshall not be healed; they shall be given to salt.

12 And ᴿby the river upon the bank thereof, on this side and on that side, ᴺshall grow all trees for meat, ᴿwhose leaf shall not fade, neither shall the fruit thereof be consumed: it shall bring forth ᴺnew fruit according to his months, because their waters they issued out of the sanctuary: and the fruit thereof shall be for meat, and the leaf thereof ᴺfor ᴿmedicine.

Boundaries of the land

13 Thus saith the Lord GOD; This *shall be* the border, whereby ye shall inherit the land according to the twelve tribes of Israel: ᴿJoseph *shall have two* portions.

14 And ye shall inherit it, one as well as another: *concerning* the which I ᴿliftedᴺ up mine hand to give it unto your fathers: and this land shall ᴿfall unto you for inheritance.

15 And this *shall be* the border of the land toward the north side, from the great sea, ᴿthe way of Hĕth'-lŏn, as men go to ᴿZē'-dăd;

16 ᴿHā'-măth, ᴿBĕ-rō'-thăh, Sĭb'-ră-ĭm, which *is* between the border of Damascus and the border of Hā'-măth; ᴺHā'-zär-hăt'-tī-cŏn, which *is* by the coast of Hau'-răn.

17 And the border from the sea shall be [R]Hā'-zär-ē'-năn, the border of Damascus, and the north northward, and the border of Hā'-măth. And *this is* the north side.

18 And the east side ye shall measure [N]from Haū'-răn, and from Damascus, and from Gilead, and from the land of Israel *by* Jordan, from the border unto the east sea. And *this is* the east side.

19 And the south side southward, from Tā'-mär *even* to [R]the waters of [N]strife *in* Kā'-dĕsh, the [N]river to the great sea. And *this is* [N]the south side southward.

20 The west side also *shall be* the great sea from the border, till a man come over against Hā'-măth. This *is* the west side.

Allotment for aliens

21 So shall ye divide this land unto you according to the tribes of Israel.

22 And it shall come to pass, *that* ye shall divide it by lot for an inheritance unto you, [R]and to the strangers that sojourn among you, which shall beget children among you: [R]and they shall be unto you as born in the country among the children of Israel; they shall have inheritance with you among the tribes of Israel.

23 And it shall come to pass, *that* in what tribe the stranger sojourneth, there shall ye give *him* his inheritance, saith the Lord GOD.

CHAPTER 48

Division of the northern portion

NOW these *are* the names of the tribes. [R]From the north end to the coast of the way of Hĕth'-lŏn, as one goeth to Hā'-măth, Hā'-zär-ē'-năn, the border of Damascus northward, to the coast of Hā'-măth; for these are his sides east *and* west; [N]a *portion for* Dan.

2 And by the border of Dan, from the east side unto the west side, a *portion for* Asher.

3 And by the border of Asher, from the east side even unto the west side, a *portion for* Năph'-tă-lī.

4 And by the border of Năph'-tă-lī, from the east side unto the west side, a *portion for* Mă-năs'-sēh.

5 And by the border of Mă-năs'-sēh, from the east side unto the west side, a *portion for* Ē'-phră-ĭm.

6 And by the border of Ē'-phră-ĭm, from the east side even unto the west side, a *portion for* Reuben.

7 And by the border of Reuben, from the

east side unto the west side, a *portion for* Judah.

The LORD'S portion

8 And by the border of Judah, from the east side unto the west side, shall be [R]the offering which ye shall offer of five and twenty thousand *reeds in* breadth, and *in* length as one of the *other* parts, from the east side unto the west side: and the sanctuary shall be in the midst of it.

9 The oblation that ye shall offer unto the LORD *shall be* of five and twenty thousand in length, and of ten thousand in breadth.

10 And for them, *even* for the priests, shall be *this* holy oblation; toward the north five and twenty thousand *in length,* and toward the west ten thousand in breadth, and toward the east ten thousand in breadth, and toward the south five and twenty thousand in length: and the sanctuary of the LORD shall be in the midst thereof.

11 [R]*It*[N] *shall be* for the priests that are sanctified of the sons of Zā'-dŏk; which have kept my [N]charge, which went not astray when the children of Israel went astray, [R]as the Levites went astray.

12 And *this* oblation of the land that is offered shall be unto them a thing most holy by the border of the Levites.

13 And over against the border of the priests the Levites *shall have* five and twenty thousand in length, and ten thousand in breadth: all the length *shall be* five and twenty thousand, and the breadth ten thousand.

14 [R]And they shall not sell of it, neither exchange, nor alienate the firstfruits of the land: for *it is* holy unto the LORD.

15 [R]And the five thousand, that are left in the breadth over against the five and twenty thousand, shall be [R]a profane *place* for the city, for dwelling, and for suburbs: and the city shall be in the midst thereof.

16 And these *shall be* the measures thereof; the north side four thousand and five hundred, and the south side four thousand and five hundred, and on the east side four thousand and five hundred, and the west side four thousand and five hundred.

17 And the suburbs of the city shall be toward the north two hundred and fifty, and toward the south two hundred and fifty, and toward the east two hundred and fifty, and toward the west two hundred and fifty.

18 And the residue in length over against the oblation of the holy *portion shall be* ten thou-

sand eastward, and ten thousand westward: and it shall be over against the oblation of the holy *portion;* and the increase thereof shall be for food unto them that serve the city.

19 [R]And they that serve the city shall serve it out of all the tribes of Israel.

20 All the oblation *shall be* five and twenty thousand by five and twenty thousand: ye shall offer the holy oblation foursquare, with the possession of the city.

21 [R]And the residue *shall be* for the prince, on the one side and on the other of the holy oblation, and of the possession of the city, over against the five and twenty thousand of the oblation toward the east border, and westward over against the five and twenty thousand toward the west border, over against the portions for the prince: and it shall be the holy oblation; [R]and the sanctuary of the house *shall be* in the midst thereof.

22 Moreover from the possession of the Levites, and from the possession of the city, *being* in the midst *of that* which is the prince's, between the border of Judah and the border of Benjamin, shall be for the prince.

Division of the southern portion

23 As for the rest of the tribes, from the east side unto the west side, Benjamin *shall have* [N]a *portion.*

24 And by the border of Benjamin, from the east side unto the west side, Simeon *shall have* a *portion.*

25 And by the border of Simeon, from the east side unto the west side, ĭs'-să-chär a *portion.*

26 And by the border of Ĭs'-să-chär, from the east side unto the west side, Zĕ-bū'-lŭn a *portion.*

27 And by the border of Zĕ-bū'-lŭn, from the east side unto the west side, Gad a *portion.*

28 And by the border of Gad, at the south side southward, thc border shall be even from Tā'-mär *unto* [R]the waters of [N]strife *in* Kā'-dĕsh, *and* to the river toward the great sea.

29 [R]This *is* the land which ye shall divide by lot unto the tribes of Israel for inheritance, and these *are* their portions, saith the Lord GOD.

Name of the city and its gates

30 And these *are* the goings out of the city on the north side, four thousand and five hundred measures.

31 [R]And the gates of the city *shall be* after the names of the tribes of Israel: three gates northward; one gate of Reuben, one gate of Judah, one gate of Levi.

32 And at the east side four thousand and five hundred: and three gates; and one gate of Joseph, one gate of Benjamin, one gate of Dan.

33 And at the south side four thousand and five hundred measures: and three gates; one gate of Simeon, one gate of ĭs'-să-chär, one gate of Zĕ-bū'-lŭn.

34 At the west side four thousand and five hundred, *with* their three gates; one gate of Gad, one gate of Asher, one gate of Năph'-tă-lī.

35 *It was* round about eighteen thousand *measures:* [R]and the name of the city from *that* day *shall be,* [R]The[N] LORD *is* there.

CHAP. 48
BC 574
19 ch. 45:6
21 ch. 45:7
21 ver. 8, 10
23 Heb. *one portion*

ch. 47:19 **28**
Heb. *Meribah-kadesh* **28**
ch. 47:14, 21, 22 **29**
Rev. 21:12, etc. **31**
Jer. 33:16 **35**
Jer. 3:17 **35**
Joel 3:21
Zech. 2:10
Rcv. 21:3 & 22:3
Heb. *Jehovah-shammah:* **35**
See Ex. 17:15
Judg. 6:24

THE BOOK OF DANIEL

The authorship of Daniel has been traditionally assigned to Daniel himself who lived in the sixth century B.C. Jesus attributed it to Daniel the prophet. Scholars who credit this book to a second century author deny its prophetic nature and reassign its historical setting.

Daniel rose to a high position of responsibility in 604 B.C., the second year of his captivity. He served under Nebuchadnezzar and continued into the reign of Cyrus, King of Persia, who conquered Babylon in 539 B.C. Whereas the first six chapters, written in third person, tell of the personal experiences of Daniel and his three friends, the last six chapters are written in the first person with Daniel himself being the channel of revelation. Linguistically the book is divided as follows: Hebrew: 1:1–2:4a; 8:1–12:13, and Aramaic: 2:4b–7:28. Daniel was equally familiar with both languages.

Even though Daniel was vitally involved in international

affairs, he had a genuine concern for the future prospects of his nation Israel. For a better understanding of the book of Daniel a chronological analysis is most significant:

I. Experiences during Nebuchadnezzar's reign
605–561 B.C.
From captivity to rulership 1:1–2:49
Religious test of Daniel's three friends 3:1–30
The king's humiliation 4:1–37
II. The Nabonidus-Belshazzar period 556–539 B.C.
Succession of kingdoms 7:1–28
Identification of kingdoms 8:1–27
The fall of Babylon 5:1–30
III. In the days of Cyrus 539–536 B.C.
Prayer and revelation 9:1–27
Daniel's religion tested 5:31–6:28
The final revelation and message 10:1–12:13

CHAPTER 1

Daniel in the king's court

IN the third year of the reign of Jĕ-hoĭ'-ă-kĭm king of Judah ᴿcame Nĕb-ū-chăd-nĕz'-zär king of Babylon unto Jerusalem, and besieged it.

2 And the Lord gave Jĕ-hoĭ'-ă-kĭm king of Judah into his hand, with ᴿpart of the vessels of the house of God: which he carried ᴿinto the land of Shī'-när to the house of his god; ᴿand he brought the vessels into the treasure house of his god.

3 And the king spake unto Ăsh'-pē-năz the master of his eunuchs, that he should bring ᴿcertain of the children of Israel, and of the king's seed, and of the princes;

4 Children ᴿin whom *was* no blemish, but well favoured, and skilful in all wisdom, and cunning in knowledge, and understanding science, and such as *had* ability in them to stand in the king's palace, and ᴿwhom they might teach the learning and the tongue of the Chăl-dē'-ăns.

5 And the king appointed them a daily provision of the king's meat, and of ᴺthe wine which he drank: so nourishing them three years, that at the end thereof they might ᴿstand before the king.

6 Now among these were of the children of Judah, Daniel, Hăn-ă-nī'-ăh, Mī'-shā-ĕl, and Ăz-ă-rī'-ăh:

7 ᴿUnto whom the prince of the eunuchs gave names: ᴿfor he gave unto Daniel *the name* of Bĕl-tē-shăz'-zär; and to Hăn-ă-nī'-ăh, of Shā'-drăch; and to Mī'-shā-ĕl, of Mē'-shăch; and to Ăz-ă-rī'-ăh, of Ă-bĕd'-nĕ-gō.

Refusal to eat the king's food

8 But Daniel purposed in his heart that he would not defile himself ᴿwith the portion of the king's meat, nor with the wine which he drank: therefore he requested of the prince of the eunuchs that he might not defile himself.

9 Now ᴿGod had brought Daniel into favour and tender love with the prince of the eunuchs.

10 And the prince of the eunuchs said unto Daniel, I fear my lord the king, who hath appointed your meat and your drink: for why should he see your faces ᴺworse liking than the children which *are* of your ᴺsort? then shall ye make *me* endanger my head to the king.

11 Then said Daniel to ᴺMĕl'-zär, whom the prince of the eunuchs had set over Daniel, Hăn-ă-nī'-ăh, Mī'-shā-ĕl, and Ăz-ă-rī'-ăh,

12 Prove thy servants, I beseech thee, ten

days; and let them give us ᴺpulse ᴺto eat, and water to drink.

13 Then let our countenances be looked upon before thee, and the countenance of the children that eat of the portion of the king's meat: and as thou seest, deal with thy servants.

14 So he consented to them in this matter, and proved them ten days.

15 And at the end of ten days their countenances appeared fairer and fatter in flesh than all the children which did eat the portion of the king's meat.

16 Thus Mĕl'-zär took away the portion of their meat, and the wine that they should drink; and gave them pulse.

Daniel's superiority

17 As for these four children, ᴿGod gave them ᴿknowledge and skill in all learning and wisdom: and ᴺDaniel had ᴿunderstanding in all visions and dreams.

18 Now at the end of the days that the king had said he should bring them in, then the prince of the eunuchs brought them in before Nĕb-ū-chăd-nĕz'-zär.

19 And the king communed with them; and among them all was found none like Daniel, Hăn-ă-nī'-ăh, Mī'-shā-ĕl, and Ăz-ă-rī'-ăh: therefore ᴿstood they before the king.

20 ᴿAnd in all matters of ᴺwisdom *and* understanding, that the king inquired of them, he found them ten times better than all the magicians *and* astrologers that *were* in all his realm.

21 ᴿAnd Daniel continued *even* unto the first year of king Cyrus.

CHAPTER 2

Nebuchadnezzar forgets his dream

AND in the second year of the reign of Nĕb-ū-chăd-nĕz'-zär Nĕb-ū-chăd-nĕz'-zär dreamed dreams, ᴿwherewith his spirit was troubled, and ᴿhis sleep brake from him.

2 ᴿThen the king commanded to call the magicians, and the astrologers, and the sorcerers, and the Chăl-dē'-ăns, for to shew the king his dreams. So they came and stood before the king.

3 And the king said unto them, I have dreamed a dream, and my spirit was troubled to know the dream.

4 Then spake the Chăl-dē'-ăns to the king in Sўr'-ĭ-ăck, ᴿO king, live for ever: tell thy servants the dream, and we will shew the interpretation.

5 The king answered and said to the Chăl-dē'-ăns, The thing is gone from me: if ye will not make known unto me the dream, with the

interpretation thereof, ye shall be ᴿcutᴺ in pieces, and your houses shall be made a dunghill.

6 ᴿBut if ye shew the dream, and the interpretation thereof, ye shall receive of me gifts and ᴺrewards and great honour: therefore shew me the dream, and the interpretation thereof.

7 They answered again and said, Let the king tell his servants the dream, and we will shew the interpretation of it.

8 The king answered and said, I know of certainty that ye would ᴺgain the time, because ye see the thing is gone from me.

9 But if ye will not make known unto me the dream, *there is but* one decree for you: for ye have prepared lying and corrupt words to speak before me, till the time be changed: therefore tell me the dream, and I shall know that ye can shew me the interpretation thereof.

10 The Chăl-dē'-ăns answered before the king, and said, There is not a man upon the earth that can shew the king's matter: therefore *there is* no king, lord, nor ruler, *that* asked such things at any magician, or astrologer, or Chăl-dē'-ăn.

11 And *it is* a rare thing that the king requireth, and there is none other that can shew it before the king, ᴿexcept the gods, whose dwelling is not with flesh.

12 For this cause the king was angry and very furious, and commanded to destroy all the wise *men* of Babylon.

13 And the decree went forth that the wise *men* should be slain; and they sought Daniel and his fellows to be slain.

14 Then Daniel ᴺanswered with counsel and wisdom to Ăr'-ĭ-ŏch the ᴺᴺcaptain of the king's guard, which was gone forth to slay the wise *men* of Babylon:

15 He answered and said to Ăr'-ĭ-ŏch the king's captain, Why *is* the decree *so* hasty from the king? Then Ăr'-ĭ-ŏch made the thing known to Daniel.

16 Then Daniel went in, and desired of the king that he would give him time, and that he would shew the king the interpretation.

17 Then Daniel went to his house, and made the thing known to Hăn-ă-nī'-ăh, Mī'-shā-ĕl, and Ăz-ă-rī'-ăh, his companions:

18 ᴿThat they would desire mercies ᴺof the God of heaven concerning this secret; ᴺthat Daniel and his fellows should not perish with the rest of the wise *men* of Babylon.

It is revealed to Daniel

19 Then was the secret revealed unto Daniel ᴿin a night vision. Then Daniel blessed the God of heaven.

CHAP. 2
BC 603
5 2 Ki. 10:27
Ezra 6:11
ch. 3:29
5 Chald. *made pieces*
6 ch. 5:16
6 Or, *fee*, ver. 48
ch. 5:17
8 Chald. *buy*, Eph. 5:16
11 ch. 5:11
14 Chald. *returned*
14 Or, *chief marshal*
14 Chald. *chief of the executioners, or, slaughtermen*
18 Mat. 18:19
18 Chald. *from before God*
18 Or, *that they should not destroy Daniel, etc.*
19 Num. 12:6
Job 33:15

Ps. 113:2   20
Jer. 32:19   20
Esth. 1:13   21
Job 12:18   21
Ps. 75:6, 7
Jer. 27:5
Jas. 1:5   21
Job 12:22   22
Ps. 25:14
Ps. 139:11   22
Heb. 4:13
ch. 5:11, 14   22
ver. 18   23
Chald. *That I have found*   25
Chald. *children of the captivity of Judah*   25
Gen. 40:8   28
Amos 4:13
Chald. *hath made known*   28
Gen. 49:1   28
Chald. *came up*   29
ver. 22, 28   29
Acts 3:12   30
Or, *but for the intent that the interpretation may be made known to the king*   30
ver. 47   30
Chald. *wast seeing*   31
See ver. 38, etc.   32
Or, *sides*   32

20 Daniel answered and said, ᴿBlessed be the name of God for ever and ever: ᴿfor wisdom and might are his:

21 And he changeth ᴿthe times and the seasons: ᴿhe removeth kings, and setteth up kings: ᴿhe giveth wisdom unto the wise, and knowledge to them that know understanding:

22 ᴿHe revealeth the deep and secret things: ᴿhe knoweth what *is* in the darkness, and ᴿthe light dwelleth with him.

23 I thank thee, and praise thee, O thou God of my fathers, who hast given me wisdom and might, and hast made known unto me now what we ᴿdesired of thee: for thou hast *now* made known unto us the king's matter.

24 Therefore Daniel went in unto Ăr'-ĭ-ŏch, whom the king had ordained to destroy the wise *men* of Babylon: he went and said thus unto him; Destroy not the wise *men* of Babylon: bring me in before the king, and I will shew unto the king the interpretation.

25 Then Ăr'-ĭ-ŏch brought in Daniel before the king in haste, and said thus unto him, ᴺI have found a man of the ᴺcaptives of Judah, that will make known unto the king the interpretation.

26 The king answered and said to Daniel, whose name *was* Bĕl-tē-shăz'-zär, Art thou able to make known unto me the dream which I have seen, and the interpretation thereof?

27 Daniel answered in the presence of the king, and said, The secret which the king hath demanded cannot the wise *men*, the astrologers, the magicians, the soothsayers, shew unto the king;

28 ᴿBut there is a God in heaven that revealeth secrets, and ᴺmaketh known to the king Nĕb-ū-chăd-nĕz'-zär ᴿwhat shall be in the latter days. Thy dream, and the visions of thy head upon thy bed, are these;

29 As for thee, O king, thy thoughts ᴺcame *into thy mind* upon thy bed, what should come to pass hereafter: ᴿand he that revealeth secrets maketh known to thee what shall come to pass.

30 ᴿBut as for me, this secret is not revealed to me for *any* wisdom that I have more than any living, ᴺbut for *their* sakes that shall make known the interpretation to the king, ᴿand that thou mightest know the thoughts of thy heart.

31 Thou, O king, ᴺsawest, and behold a great image. This great image, whose brightness *was* excellent, stood before thee; and the form thereof *was* terrible.

32 ᴿThis image's head *was* of fine gold, his breast and his arms of silver, his belly and his ᴺthighs of brass,

33 His legs of iron, his feet part of iron and part of clay.

34 Thou sawest till that a stone was cut out ᴿwithoutᴺ hands, which smote the image upon his feet *that were* of iron and clay, and brake them to pieces.

35 Then was the iron, the clay, the brass, the silver, and the gold, broken to pieces together, and became ᴿlike the chaff of the summer threshingfloors; and the wind carried them away, that ᴿno place was found for them: and the stone that smote the image ᴿbecame a great mountain, ᴿand filled the whole earth.

Daniel interprets the dream

36 This *is* the dream; and we will tell the interpretation thereof before the king.

37 ᴿThou, O king, *art* a king of kings: ᴿfor the God of heaven hath given thee a kingdom, power, and strength, and glory.

38 ᴿAnd wheresoever the children of men dwell, the beasts of the field and the fowls of the heaven hath he given into thine hand, and hath made thee ruler over them all. ᴿThou *art* this head of gold.

39 And after thee shall arise ᴿanother kingdom ᴿinferior to thee, and another third kingdom of brass, which shall bear rule over all the earth.

40 And ᴿthe fourth kingdom shall be strong as iron: forasmuch as iron breaketh in pieces and subdueth all *things:* and as iron that breaketh all these, shall it break in pieces and bruise.

41 And whereas thou sawest the feet and toes, part of potters' clay, and part of iron, the kingdom shall be divided; but there shall be in it of the strength of the iron, forasmuch as thou sawest the iron mixed with miry clay.

42 And *as* the toes of the feet *were* part of iron, and part of clay, *so* the kingdom shall be partly strong, and partly ᴺbroken.

43 And whereas thou sawest iron mixed with miry clay, they shall mingle themselves with the seed of men: but they shall not cleave ᴺone to another, even as iron is not mixed with clay.

44 And in ᴺthe days of these kings ᴿshall the God of heaven set up a kingdom, ᴿwhich shall never be destroyed: and the ᴺkingdom shall not be left to other people, ᴿbut it shall break in pieces and consume all these kingdoms, and it shall stand for ever. ★

45 ᴿForasmuch as thou sawest that the stone was cut out of the mountain ᴺwithout hands, and that it brake in pieces the iron, the brass, the clay, the silver, and the gold; the great God hath made known to the king what shall

come to pass ᴺhereafter: and the dream *is* certain, and the interpretation thereof sure. ★

Daniel honoured

46 ᴿThen the king Nĕb-ū-chăd-nĕz'-zär fell upon his face, and worshipped Daniel, and commanded that they should offer an oblation ᴿand sweet odours unto him.

47 The king answered unto Daniel, and said, Of a truth *it is,* that your God *is* a God of gods, and a Lord of kings, and a revealer of secrets, seeing thou couldest reveal this secret.

48 Then the king made Daniel a great man, ᴿand gave him many great gifts, and made him ruler over the whole province of Babylon, and ᴿchief of the governors over all the wise *men* of Babylon.

49 Then Daniel requested of the king, ᴿand he set Shā'-drăch, Mē'-shăch, and Ă-bĕd'-nĕ-gō, over the affairs of the province of Babylon: but Daniel ᴿsat in the gate of the king.

CHAPTER 3

Nebuchadnezzar's image of gold

NĕB-Ū-cHăD-NĕZ'-ZäR the king made an image of gold, whose height *was* threescore cubits, *and* the breadth thereof six cubits: he set it up in the plain of Dū'-rä, in the province of Babylon.

2 Then Nĕb-ū-chăd-nĕz'-zär the king sent to gather together the princes, the governors, and the captains, the judges, the treasurers, the counsellors, the sheriffs, and all the rulers of the provinces, to come to the dedication of the image which Nĕb-ū-chăd-nĕz'-zär the king had set up.

3 Then the princes, the governors, and captains, the judges, the treasurers, the counsellors, the sheriffs, and all the rulers of the provinces, were gathered together unto the dedication of the image that Nĕb-ū-chăd-nĕz'-zär the king had set up; and they stood before the image that Nĕb-ū-chăd-nĕz'-zär had set up.

4 Then an herald cried ᴺaloud, To you ᴺit is commanded, ᴿO people, nations, and languages,

5 *That* at what time ye hear the sound of the cornet, flute, harp, sackbut, psaltery, ᴺ ᴺdulcimer, and all kinds of musick, ye fall down and worship the golden image that Nĕb-ū-chăd-nĕz'-zär the king hath set up:

6 And whoso falleth not down and worshippeth shall the same hour ᴿbe cast into the midst of a burning fiery furnace.

7 Therefore at that time, when all the people heard the sound of the cornet, flute, harp,

CHAP. 2
BC 603
34 Zech. 4:6
2 Cor. 5:1
Heb. 9:24
34 Or, *which was not in hands:* as ver. 45
35 Hos. 13:3
35 Ps. 37:10, 36
35 Is. 2:2, 3
35 Ps. 80:9
37 Ezra 7:12
Is. 47:5
Jer. 27:6, 7
Ezek. 26:7
Hos. 8:10
37 Ezra 1:2
38 ch. 4:21, 22
Jer. 27:6
38 ver. 32
39 ch. 5:28, 31
39 ver. 32
40 ch. 7:7, 23
42 Or, *brittle*
43 Chald. *this with this*
44 Chald. *their days*
44 ver. 28
44 ch. 4:3, 34 & 6:26 & 7:14, 27
Mic. 4:7
Luke 1:32, 33
44 Chald. *kingdom thereof*
44 Ps. 2:9
Is. 60:12
1 Cor. 15:24
45 ver. 35
Is. 28:16
45 Or, *which was not in hand*

Chald. *after this* 45
See Acts 10:25 46
& 14:13 & 28:6
Ezra 6:10 46
ver. 6 48
ch. 4:9 & 5:11 48
ch. 3:12 49
Esth. 2:19, 21 49
& 3:2

CHAP. 3
BC 580
Chald. *with might* 4
Chald. *they command* 4
ch. 4:1 & 6:25 4
Or, *singing* 5
Chald. *symphony* 5
Jer. 29:22 6
Rev. 13:15

sackbut, psaltery, and all kinds of musick, all the people, the nations, and the languages, fell down *and* worshipped the golden image that Nĕb-ū-chăd-nĕz'-zär the king had set up.

Malicious accusation

8 Wherefore at that time certain Chăl-dē'-ăns ᴿcame near, and accused the Jews.

9 They spake and said to the king Nĕb-ū-chăd-nĕz'-zär, ᴿO king, live for ever.

10 Thou, O king, hast made a decree, that every man that shall hear the sound of the cornet, flute, harp, sackbut, psaltery, and dulcimer, and all kinds of musick, shall fall down and worship the golden image:

11 And whoso falleth not down and worshippeth, *that* he should be cast into the midst of a burning fiery furnace.

12 ᴿThere are certain Jews whom thou hast set over the affairs of the province of Babylon, Shā'-drăch, Mē'-shăch, and Ă-bĕd'-nĕ-gō; these men, O king, ᴺhave not regarded thee: they serve not thy gods, nor worship the golden image which thou hast set up.

13 Then Nĕb-ū-chăd-nĕz'-zär in *his* rage and fury commanded to bring Shā'-drăch, Mē'-shăch, and Ă-bĕd'-nĕ-gō. Then they brought these men before the king.

14 Nĕb-ū-chăd-nĕz'-zär spake and said unto them, *Is it* ᴺtrue, O Shā'-drăch, Mē'-shăch, and Ă-bĕd'-nĕ-gō, do not ye serve my gods, nor worship the golden image which I have set up?

15 Now if ye be ready that at what time ye hear the sound of the cornet, flute, harp, sackbut, psaltery, and dulcimer, and all kinds of musick, ye fall down and worship the image which I have made; ᴿ*well:* but if ye worship not, ye shall be cast the same hour into the midst of a burning fiery furnace; ᴿand who *is* that God that shall deliver you out of my hands?

The fiery furnace

16 Shā'-drăch, Mē'-shăch, and Ă-bĕd'-nĕ-gō, answered and said to the king, O Nĕb-ū-chăd-nĕz'-zär, ᴿwe *are* not careful to answer thee in this matter.

17 If it be *so,* our God whom we serve is able to deliver us from the burning fiery furnace, and he will deliver *us* out of thine hand, O king.

18 But if not, be it known unto thee, O king, that we will not serve thy gods, nor worship the golden image which thou hast set up.

19 Then was Nĕb-ū-chăd-nĕz'-zär ᴺfull of fury, and the form of his visage was changed against Shā'-drăch, Mē'-shăch, and Ă-bĕd'-

CHAP. **3**
BC 580
8 ch. 6:12
9 ch. 2:4 & 5:10
& 6:6, 21
12 ch. 2:49
12 Chald. *have set no regard upon thee*
14 Or, *of purpose,* as Ex. 21:13
15 As Ex. 32:32
Luke 13:9
15 Ex. 5:2
2 Ki. 18:35
16 Mat. 10:19
19 Chald. *filled*

Chald. *mighty of strength* 20
Or, *mantles* 21
Or, *turbans* 21
Chald. *word* 22
Or, *spark* 22
Or, *governors* 24
Is. 43:2 25
Chald. *there is no hurt in them* 25
ver. 28 25
Job 1:6 & 38:7
Ps. 34:7
Chald. *door* 26
Heb. 11:34 27
Ps. 34:7, 8 28
Jer. 17:7
ch. 6:22, 23
ch. 6:26
Chald. *a decree is made by me* 29
Chald. *error* 29
ch. 2:5 29
Chald. *made pieces* 29
ch. 6:27 29

nĕ-gō: *therefore* he spake, and commanded that they should heat the furnace one seven times more than it was wont to be heated.

20 And he commanded the ᴺmost mighty men that *were* in his army to bind Shā'-drăch, Mē'-shăch, and Ă-bĕd'-nĕ-gō, *and* to cast *them* into the burning fiery furnace.

21 Then these men were bound in their ᴺcoats, their hosen, and their ᴺhats, and their *other* garments, and were cast into the midst of the burning fiery furnace.

22 Therefore because the king's ᴺcommandment was urgent, and the furnace exceeding hot, the ᴺflame of the fire slew those men that took up Shā'-drăch, Mē'-shăch, and Ă-bĕd'-nĕ-gō.

23 And these three men, Shā'-drăch, Mē'-shăch, and Ă-bĕd'-nĕ-gō, fell down bound into the midst of the burning fiery furnace.

24 Then Nĕb-ū-chăd-nĕz'-zär the king was astonied, and rose up in haste, *and* spake, and said unto his ᴺcounsellors, Did not we cast three men bound into the midst of the fire? They answered and said unto the king, True, O king.

25 He answered and said, Lo, I see four men loose, ᴿwalking in the midst of the fire, and ᴺthey have no hurt; and the form of the fourth is like ᴿthe Son of God.

26 Then Nĕb-ū-chăd-nĕz'-zär came near to the ᴺmouth of the burning fiery furnace, *and* spake, and said, Shā'-drăch, Mē'-shăch, and Ă-bĕd'-nĕ-gō, ye servants of the most high God, come forth, and come *hither.* Then Shā'-drăch, Mē'-shăch, and Ă-bĕd'-nĕ-gō, came forth of the midst of the fire.

27 And the princes, governors, and captains, and the king's counsellors, being gathered together, saw these men, ᴿupon whose bodies the fire had no power, nor was an hair of their head singed, neither were their coats changed, nor the smell of fire had passed on them.

28 *Then* Nĕb-ū-chăd-nĕz'-zär spake, and said, Blessed *be* the God of Shā'-drăch, Mē'-shăch, and Ă-bĕd'-nĕ-gō, who hath sent his angel, and delivered his servants that ᴿtrusted in him, and have changed the king's word, and yielded their bodies, that they might not serve nor worship any god, except their own God.

29 ᴿTherefore ᴺI make a decree, That every people, nation, and language, which speak ᴺany thing amiss against the God of Shā'-drăch, Mē'-shăch, and Ă-bĕd'-nĕ-gō, shall be ᴿcutᴺ in pieces, and their houses shall be made a dunghill: ᴿbecause there is no other God that can deliver after this sort.

30 Then the king ^Npromoted Shā'-drăch, Mē'-shăch, and Ă-bĕd'-nĕ-gō, in the province of Babylon.

CHAPTER 4

Nebuchadnezzar's dream of a tree

NĔB-Ū-CHĂD-NĔZ'-ZäR the king, ^Runto all people, nations, and languages, that dwell in all the earth; Peace be multiplied unto you.

2 ^NI thought it good to shew the signs and wonders ^Rthat the high God hath wrought toward me.

3 ^RHow great *are* his signs! and how mighty *are* his wonders! his kingdom *is* ^Ran everlasting kingdom, and his dominion *is* from generation to generation.

4 I Nĕb-ū-chăd-nĕz'-zär was at rest in mine house, and flourishing in my palace:

5 I saw a dream which made me afraid, ^Rand the thoughts upon my bed and the visions of my head ^Rtroubled me.

6 Therefore made I a decree to bring in all the wise *men* of Babylon before me, that they might make known unto me the interpretation of the dream.

7 ^RThen came in the magicians, the astrologers, the Chăl-dē'-ăns, and the soothsayers: and I told the dream before them; but they did not make known unto me the interpretation thereof.

8 But at the last Daniel came in before me, ^Rwhose name *was* Bĕl-tē-shăz'-zär, according to the name of my god, ^Rand in whom *is* the spirit of the holy gods: and before him I told the dream, *saying,*

9 O Bĕl-tē-shăz'-zär, ^Rmaster of the magicians, because I know that the spirit of the holy gods *is* in thee, and no secret troubleth thee, tell me the visions of my dream that I have seen, and the interpretation thereof.

10 Thus *were* the visions of mine head in my bed; ^NI saw, and behold ^Ra tree in the midst of the earth, and the height thereof *was* great.

11 The tree grew, and was strong, and the height thereof reached unto heaven, and the sight thereof to the end of all the earth:

12 The leaves thereof *were* fair, and the fruit thereof much, and in it *was* meat for all: ^Rthe beasts of the field had shadow under it, and the fowls of the heaven dwelt in the boughs thereof, and all flesh was fed of it.

13 I saw in the visions of my head upon my bed, and, behold, ^Ra watcher and ^Ran holy one came down from heaven;

14 He cried ^Naloud, and said thus, ^RHew

CHAP. 3

BC 580

30 Chald. *made to prosper*

CHAP. 4

BC 570

1 ch. 3:4 & 6:25
2 Chald. *It was seemly before me*
2 ch. 3:26
3 ch. 6:27
3 ver. 34
ch. 2:44 & 6:26
5 ch. 2:28, 29
5 ch. 2:1
7 ch. 2:2
8 ch. 1:7
8 ver. 18
Is. 63:11
ch. 2:11 & 5:11, 14
9 ch. 2:48 & 5:11
10 Chald. *I was seeing*
10 ver. 20
Ezek. 31:3, etc.
12 Ezek. 17:23 & 31:6
See Lam. 4:20
13 ver. 17, 23
13 Deut. 33:2
ch. 8:13
Zech. 14:5
Jude 14
14 Chald. *with might*
14 Mat. 3:10

Ezek. 31:12   **14**
ch. 11:13 & 12:7 **16**
Ps. 9:16   **17**
ver. 25, 32   **17**
ch. 2:21 & 5:21
Gen. 41:8, 15   **18**
ch. 5:8, 15
ver. 8   **18**
ver. 8   **19**
See 2 Sam. 18:32 **19**
Jer. 29:7
ver. 10, 11, 12 **20**
ch. 2:38   **22**
Jer. 27:6-8   **22**
ver. 13   **23**
ch. 5:21   **23**

---

down the tree, and cut off his branches, shake off his leaves, and scatter his fruit: ^Rlet the beasts get away from under it, and the fowls from his branches:

15 Nevertheless leave the stump of his roots in the earth, even with a band of iron and brass, in the tender grass of the field; and let it be wet with the dew of heaven, and *let* his portion *be* with the beasts in the grass of the earth:

16 Let his heart be changed from man's, and let a beast's heart be given unto him; and let seven ^Rtimes pass over him.

17 This matter *is* by the decree of the watchers, and the demand by the word of the holy ones: to the intent ^Rthat the living may know ^Rthat the most High ruleth in the kingdom of men, and giveth it to whomsoever he will, and setteth up over it the basest of men.

18 This dream I king Nĕb-ū-chăd-nĕz'-zär have seen. Now thou, O Bĕl-tē-shăz'-zär, declare the interpretation thereof, ^Rforasmuch as all the wise *men* of my kingdom are not able to make known unto me the interpretation: but thou *art* able; ^Rfor the spirit of the holy gods *is* in thee.

Daniel's interpretation

19 Then Daniel, ^Rwhose name *was* Bĕl-tē-shăz'-zär, was astonied for one hour, and his thoughts troubled him. The king spake, and said, Bĕl-tē-shăz'-zär, let not the dream, or the interpretation thereof, trouble thee. Bĕl-tē-shăz'-zär answered and said, My lord, ^Rthe dream *be* to them that hate thee, and the interpretation thereof to thine enemies.

20 ^RThe tree that thou sawest, which grew, and was strong, whose height reached unto the heaven, and the sight thereof to all the earth;

21 Whose leaves *were* fair, and the fruit thereof much, and in it *was* meat for all; under which the beasts of the field dwelt, and upon whose branches the fowls of the heaven had their habitation:

22 ^RIt *is* thou, O king, that art grown and become strong: for thy greatness is grown, and reacheth unto heaven, ^Rand thy dominion to the end of the earth.

23 ^RAnd whereas the king saw a watcher and an holy one coming down from heaven, and saying, Hew the tree down, and destroy it; yet leave the stump of the roots thereof in the earth, even with a band of iron and brass, in the tender grass of the field; and let it be wet with the dew of heaven, ^Rand *let* his portion *be* with the beasts of the field, till seven times pass over him;

24 This *is* the interpretation, O king, and

this *is* the decree of the most High, which is come upon my lord the king:

25 That they shall ᴿdrive thee from men, and thy dwelling shall be with the beasts of the field, and they shall make thee ᴿto eat grass as oxen, and they shall wet thee with the dew of heaven, and seven times shall pass over thee, ᴿtill thou know that the most High ruleth in the kingdom of men, and ᴿgiveth it to whomsoever he will.

26 And whereas they commanded to leave the stump of the tree roots; thy kingdom shall be sure unto thee, after that thou shalt have known that the ᴿheavens do rule.

27 Wherefore, O king, let my counsel be acceptable unto thee, and ᴿbreak off thy sins by righteousness, and thine iniquities by shewing mercy to the poor; ᴿif it may be ᴿaᴺ lengthening of thy tranquillity.

The dream fulfilled

28 All this came upon the king Nĕb-ū- chăd-nĕz′-zär.

29 At the end of twelve months he walked ᴺin the palace of the kingdom of Babylon.

30 The king ᴿspake, and said, Is not this great Babylon, that I have built for the house of the kingdom by the might of my power, and for the honour of my majesty?

31 ᴿWhile the word *was* in the king's mouth, there fell ᴿa voice from heaven, *saying,* O king Nĕb-ū-chăd-nĕz′-zär, to thee it is spoken; The kingdom is departed from thee.

32 And ᴿthey shall drive thee from men, and thy dwelling *shall be* with the beasts of the field: they shall make thee to eat grass as oxen, and seven times shall pass over thee, until thou know that the most High ruleth in the kingdom of men, and giveth it to whomsoever he will.

33 The same hour was the thing fulfilled upon Nĕb-ū-chăd-nĕz′-zär: and he was driven from men, and did eat grass as oxen, and his body was wet with the dew of heaven, till his hairs were grown like eagles' *feathers,* and his nails like birds' *claws.*

34 And ᴿat the end of the days I Nĕb-ū- chăd-nĕz′-zär lifted up mine eyes unto heaven, and mine understanding returned unto me, and I blessed the most High, and I praised and honoured him ᴿthat liveth for ever, whose dominion *is* ᴿan everlasting dominion, and his kingdom *is* from generation to generation:

35 And ᴿall the inhabitants of the earth *are* reputed as nothing: and ᴿhe doeth according to his will in the army of heaven, and *among* the inhabitants of the earth: and ᴿnone can stay his hand, or say unto him, ᴿWhat doest thou?

CHAP. 4	
BC 570	
25 ver. 32	
ch. 5:21, etc.	
25 Ps. 106:20	
25 ver. 17, 32	
Ps. 83:18	
25 Jer. 27:5	
26 Mat. 21:25	
Luke 15:18	
27 1 Pet. 4:8	
27 Ps. 41:1	
27 1 Ki. 21:29	
27 Or, *an healing of thine error*	
29 Or, *upon*	
30 Prov. 16:18	
ch. 5:20	
31 ch. 5:5	
Luke 12:20	
31 ver. 24	
32 ver. 25	
34 ver. 26	
34 ch. 12:7	
Rev. 4:10	
34 Ps. 10:16	
ch. 2:44	
Mic. 4:7	
Luke 1:33	
35 Is. 40:15	
35 Ps. 115:3 & 135:6	
35 Job 34:29	
35 Job 9:12	
Rom. 9:20	
Is. 45:9	
ver. 26	**36**
Job 42:12	**36**
Prov. 22:4	
Mat. 6:33	
Ps. 33:4	**37**
Rev. 15:3	
Ex. 18:11	**37**
ch. 5:20	

CHAP. 5	
BC 538	
Esth. 1:3	**1**
ch. 1:2	**2**
Jer. 52:19	
Or, *grandfather:* as ver. 11, 13	**2**
2 Sam. 9:7	
Jer. 27:7	
Chald. *brought forth*	**2**
Rev. 9:20	**4**
ch. 4:31	**5**
Chald. *brightnesses,* ver. 9	**6**
Chald. *changed it*	**6**
Or, *girdles,* Is. 5:27	**6**
Chald. *bindings, or, knots* Nah. 2:10	**6**
ch. 4:6	**7**
Chald. *with might* Is. 47:13	**7**
Or, *purple*	**7**
ch. 6:2	**7**
ch. 2:27	**8**
ch. 2:1	**9**
Chald. *brightnesses*	**9**

36 At the same time my reason returned unto me; ᴿand for the glory of my kingdom, mine honour and brightness returned unto me; and my counsellors and my lords sought unto me; and I was established in my kingdom, and excellent majesty was ᴿadded unto me.

37 Now I Nĕb-ū-chăd-nĕz′-zär praise and extol and honour the King of heaven, ᴿall whose works *are* truth, and his ways judgment: ᴿand those that walk in pride he is able to abase.

CHAPTER 5

The great banquet

Bĕl-SHăZ′-ZäR the king made a great feast to a thousand of his lords, and drank wine before the thousand.

2 Bĕl-shăz′-zär, whiles he tasted the wine, commanded to bring the golden and silver vessels ᴿwhich his ᴺfather Nĕb-ū-chăd-nĕz′-zär had ᴺtaken out of the temple which *was* in Jerusalem; that the king, and his princes, his wives, and his concubines, might drink therein.

3 Then they brought the golden vessels that were taken out of the temple of the house of God which *was* at Jerusalem; and the king, and his princes, his wives, and his concubines, drank in them.

4 They drank wine, ᴿand praised the gods of gold, and of silver, of brass, of iron, of wood, and of stone.

Handwriting on the wall

5 ᴿIn the same hour came forth fingers of a man's hand, and wrote over against the candlestick upon the plaster of the wall of the king's palace: and the king saw the part of the hand that wrote.

6 Then the king's ᴺcountenance ᴺwas changed, and his thoughts troubled him, so that the ᴺᴺjoints of his loins were loosed, and his ᴿknees smote one against another.

7 ᴿThe king cried ᴺaloud to bring in ᴿthe astrologers, the Chăl-dē′-ăns, and the soothsayers. *And* the king spake, and said to the wise *men* of Babylon, Whosoever shall read this writing, and shew me the interpretation thereof, shall be clothed with ᴺscarlet, and *have* a chain of gold about his neck, ᴿand shall be the third ruler in the kingdom.

8 Then came in all the king's wise *men:* ᴿbut they could not read the writing, nor make known to the king the interpretation thereof.

9 Then was king Bĕl-shăz′-zär greatly ᴿtroubled, and his ᴺcountenance was changed in him, and his lords were astonied.

Daniel offered gifts

10 *Now* the queen, by reason of the words of the king and his lords, came into the banquet house: *and* the queen spake and said, O King, live for ever: let not thy thoughts trouble thee, nor let thy countenance be changed:

11 ᴿThere is a man in thy kingdom, in whom *is* the spirit of the holy gods; and in the days of thy ᴺfather light and understanding and wisdom, like the wisdom of the gods, was found in him; whom the king Nĕb-ū-chăd-nĕz′-zär·thy ᴺfather, the king, *I say,* thy father, made ᴿmaster of the magicians, astrologers, Chăl-dē′-ăns, *and* soothsayers;

12 ᴿForasmuch as an excellent spirit, and knowledge, and understanding, ᴺinterpreting of dreams, and shewing of hard sentences, and ᴺdissolving of ᴺdoubts, were found in the same Daniel, ᴿwhom the king named Bĕl-tē-shăz′-zär: now let Daniel be called, and he will shew the interpretation.

13 Then was Daniel brought in before the king. *And* the king spake and said unto Daniel, *Art* thou that Daniel, which *art* of the children of the captivity of Judah, whom the king my ᴺfather brought out of Jewry?

14 I have even heard of thee, that ᴿthe spirit of the gods *is* in thee, and *that* light and understanding and excellent wisdom is found in thee.

15 And now ᴿthe wise *men,* the astrologers, have been brought in before me, that they should read this writing, and make known unto me the interpretation thereof: but they could not shew the interpretation of the thing:

16 And I have heard of thee, that thou canst ᴺmake interpretations, and dissolve doubts: ᴿnow if thou canst read the writing, and make known to me the interpretation thereof, thou shalt be clothed with scarlet, and *have* a chain of gold about thy neck, and shalt be the third ruler in the kingdom.

Daniel refuses the gifts

17 Then Daniel answered and said before the king, Let thy gifts be to thyself, and give thy ᴺrewards to another; yet I will read the writing unto the king, and make known to him the interpretation.

18 O thou king, ᴿthe most high God gave Nĕb-ū-chăd-nĕz′-zär thy father a kingdom and majesty, and glory, and honour:

19 And for the majesty that he gave him, ᴿall people, nations, and languages, trembled and feared before him: whom he would he slew; and whom he would he kept alive; and whom he would he set up; and whom he would he put down.

20 ᴿBut when his heart was lifted up, and his mind hardened ᴺin pride, he was ᴺdeposed from his kingly throne, and they took his glory from him:

21 And he was ᴿdriven from the sons of men; and ᴺhis heart was made like the beasts, and his dwelling *was* with the wild asses: they fed him with grass like oxen, and his body was wet with the dew of heaven; ᴿtill he knew that the most high God ruled in the kingdom of men, and *that* he appointeth over it whomsoever he will.

22 And thou his son, O Bĕl-shăz′-zär, ᴿhast not humbled thine heart, though thou knewest all this;

23 ᴿBut hast lifted up thyself against the Lord of heaven; and they have brought the vessels of his house before thee, and thou, and thy lords, thy wives, and thy concubines, have drunk wine in them; and thou hast praised the gods of silver, and gold, of brass, iron, wood, and stone, ᴿwhich see not, nor hear, nor know: and the God in whose hand thy breath *is,* ᴿand whose *are* all thy ways, hast thou not glorified:

Interpretation of the writing

24 Then was the part of the hand sent from him; and this writing was written.

25 And this *is* the writing that was written, MĒ′-NĒ, MĒ′-NĒ, TĒ′-KĔl, Ū-PHÄR′-SĬN.

26 This *is* the interpretation of the thing: MĒ′-NĒ; God hath numbered thy kingdom, and finished it.

27 TĒ′-KĔl; ᴿThou art weighed in the balances, and art found wanting.

28 PĒ′-RĔś; Thy kingdom is divided, and given to the ᴿMēdeś and ᴿPersians.

29 Then commanded Bĕl-shăz′-zär, and they clothed Daniel with scarlet, and *put* a chain of gold about his neck, and made a proclamation concerning him, ᴿthat he should be the third ruler in the kingdom.

30 ᴿIn that night was Bĕl-shăz′-zär the king of the Chăl-dē′-ăns slain.

31 ᴿAnd Dă-rī′-ŭs the Mē′-dĭ-ăn took the kingdom, ᴺ*being* ᴺabout threescore and two years old.

CHAPTER 6

Plot to ensnare Daniel

IT pleased Dă-rī′-ŭs to set over the kingdom an hundred and twenty princes, which should be over the whole kingdom;

2 And over these three presidents; of whom Daniel *was* first: that the princes might give accounts unto them, and the king should have no damage.

3 Then this Daniel was preferred above the presidents and princes, [R]because an excellent spirit *was* in him; and the king thought to set him over the whole realm.

4 [R]Then the presidents and princes sought to find occasion against Daniel concerning the kingdom; but they could find none occasion nor fault; forasmuch as he *was* faithful, neither was there any error or fault found in him.

5 Then said these men, We shall not find any occasion against this Daniel, except we find *it* against him concerning the law of his God.

6 Then these presidents and princes [N]assembled together to the king, and said thus unto him, [R]King Dă-rī'-ŭs, live for ever.

7 All the presidents of the kingdom, the governors, and the princes, the counsellors, and the captains, have consulted together to establish a royal statute, and to make a firm [N]decree, that whosoever shall ask a petition of any God or man for thirty days, save of thee, O king, he shall be cast into the den of lions.

8 Now, O king, establish the decree, and sign the writing, that it be not changed, according to the [R]law of the Mēdeṡ and Persians, which [N]altereth not.

9 Wherefore king Dă-rī'-ŭs signed the writing and the decree.

10 Now when Daniel knew that the writing was signed, he went into his house; and his windows being open in his chamber [R]toward Jerusalem, he kneeled upon his knees [R]three times a day, and prayed, and gave thanks before his God, as he did aforetime.

11 Then these men assembled, and found Daniel praying and making supplication before his God.

12 [R]Then they came near, and spake before the king concerning the king's decree; Hast thou not signed a decree, that every man that shall ask *a petition* of any God or man within thirty days, save of thee, O king, shall be cast into the den of lions? The king answered and said, The thing *is* true, [R]according to the law of the Mēdeṡ and Persians, which altereth not.

13 Then answered they and said before the king, That Daniel, [R]which *is* of the children of the captivity of Judah, [R]regardeth not thee, O king, nor the decree that thou hast signed, but maketh his petition three times a day.

14 Then the king, when he heard *these* words, [R]was sore displeased with himself, and set *his* heart on Daniel to deliver him: and he laboured till the going down of the sun to deliver him.

15 Then these men assembled unto the king, and said unto the king, Know, O king, that [R]the law of the Mēdeṡ and Persians *is*, That

no decree nor statute which the king establisheth may be changed.

Daniel in the lions' den

16 Then the king commanded, and they brought Daniel, and cast *him* into the den of lions. *Now* the king spake and said unto Daniel, Thy God whom thou servest continually, he will deliver thee.

17 [R]And a stone was brought, and laid upon the mouth of the den; [R]and the king sealed it with his own signet, and with the signet of his lords; that the purpose might not be changed concerning Daniel.

18 Then the king went to his palace, and passed the night fasting: neither were [N]instruments of musick brought before him: [R]and his sleep went from him.

19 Then the king arose very early in the morning, and went in haste unto the den of lions.

20 And when he came to the den, he cried with a lamentable voice unto Daniel: *and* the king spake and said to Daniel, O Daniel, servant of the living God, [R]is thy God, whom thou servest continually, able to deliver thee from the lions?

21 Then said Daniel unto the king, [R]O king, live for ever.

22 [R]My God hath sent his angel, and hath [R]shut the lions' mouths, that they have not hurt me: forasmuch as before him innocency was found in me; and also before thee, O king, have I done no hurt.

23 Then was the king exceeding glad for him, and commanded that they should take Daniel up out of the den. So Daniel was taken up out of the den, and no manner of hurt was found upon him, [R]because he believed in his God.

24 And the king commanded, [R]and they brought those men which had accused Daniel, and they cast *them* into the den of lions, them, [R]their children, and their wives; and the lions had the mastery of them, and brake all their bones in pieces or ever they came at the bottom of the den.

Darius issues new decree

25 [R]Then king Dă-rī'-ŭs wrote unto all people, nations, and languages, that dwell in all the earth; Peace be multiplied unto you.

26 [R]I make a decree, That in every dominion of my kingdom men [R]tremble and fear before the God of Daniel: [R]for he *is* the living God, and stedfast for ever, and his kingdom *that* which shall not be [R]destroyed, and his dominion *shall be even* unto the end.

27 He delivereth and rescueth, ᴿand he worketh signs and wonders in heaven and in earth, who hath delivered Daniel from the ᴺpower of the lions.

28 So this Daniel prospered in the reign of Dă-rī′-ŭs, ᴿand in the reign of ᴿCyrus the Persian.

CHAPTER 7

Daniel's dream of four beasts

IN the first year of Bĕl-shăz′-zär king of Babylon ᴿDaniel ᴺhad a dream and ᴿvisions of his head upon his bed: then he wrote the dream, and told the sum of the ᴺmatters.

2 Daniel spake and said, I saw in my vision by night, and, behold, the four winds of the heaven strove upon the great sea

3 And four great beasts ᴿcame up from the sea, diverse one from another.

4 The first was ᴿlike a lion, and had eagle's wings: I beheld till the wings thereof were plucked, ᴺand it was lifted up from the earth, and made stand upon the feet as a man, and a man's heart was given to it.

5 ᴿAnd behold another beast, a second, like to a bear, and ᴺit raised up itself on one side, and it had three ribs in the mouth of it between the teeth of it: and they said thus unto it, Arise, devour much flesh.

6 After this I beheld, and lo another, like a leopard, which had upon the back of it four wings of a fowl; the beast had also ᴿfour heads; and dominion was given to it.

7 After this I saw in the night visions, and behold ᴿa fourth beast, dreadful and terrible, and strong exceedingly; and it had great iron teeth: it devoured and brake in pieces, and stamped the residue with the feet of it: and it was diverse from all the beasts that were before it; ᴿand it had ten horns.

8 I considered the horns, and, behold, ᴿthere came up among them another little horn, before whom there were three of the first horns plucked up by the roots: and, behold, in this horn were eyes like the eyes ᴿof man, ᴿand a mouth speaking great things.

9 ᴿI beheld till the thrones were cast down, and ᴿthe Ancient of days did sit, ᴿwhose garment was white as snow, and the hair of his head like the pure wool: his throne was like the fiery flame, ᴿand his wheels as burning fire.

10 ᴿA fiery stream issued and came forth from before him: ᴿthousand thousands ministered unto him, and ten thousand times ten thousand stood before him: ᴿthe judgment was set, and the books were opened.

11 I beheld then because of the voice of the great words which the horn spake: ᴿI beheld even till the beast was slain, and his body destroyed, and given to the burning flame.

12 As concerning the rest of the beasts, they had their dominion taken away: yet ᴺtheir lives were prolonged for a season and time.

13 I saw in the night visions, and, behold, ᴿone like the Son of man came with the clouds of heaven, and came to the Ancient of days, and they brought him near before him.

14 ᴿAnd there was given him dominion, and glory, and a kingdom, that all ᴿpeople, nations, and languages, should serve him: his dominion is ᴿan everlasting dominion, which shall not pass away, and his kingdom that which shall not be destroyed.   ★

Meaning of the dream

15 I Daniel was grieved in my spirit in the midst of my ᴺbody, and the visions of my head troubled me.

16 I came near unto one of them that stood by, and asked him the truth of all this. So he told me, and made me know the interpretation of the things.

17 These great beasts, which are four, are four kings, which shall arise out of the earth.

18 But ᴿthe saints of the ᴺmost High shall take the kingdom, and possess the kingdom for ever, even for ever and ever.

19 Then I would know the truth of the fourth beast, which was diverse ᴺfrom all the others, exceeding dreadful, whose teeth were of iron, and his nails of brass; which devoured, brake in pieces, and stamped the residue with his feet;

20 And of the ten horns that were in his head, and of the other which came up, and before whom three fell; even of that horn that had eyes, and a mouth that spake very great things, whose look was more stout than his fellows.

21 I beheld, ᴿand the same horn made war with the saints, and prevailed against them;

22 Until the Ancient of days came, ᴿand judgment was given to the saints of the most High; and the time came that the saints possessed the kingdom.

23 Thus he said, The fourth beast shall be ᴿthe fourth kingdom upon earth, which shall be diverse from all kingdoms, and shall devour the whole earth, and shall tread it down, and break it in pieces.

24 ᴿAnd the ten horns out of this kingdom are ten kings that shall arise: and another shall rise after them; and he shall be diverse from the first, and he shall subdue three kings.

25 ᴿAnd he shall speak great words against

Center reference column

CHAP. 6
BC 538
27 ch. 4:3
27 Heb. hand
28 ch. 1:21
28 Ezra 1:1, 2

CHAP. 7
BC 555
1 Num. 12:6
Amos 3:7
1 Chald. saw
1 ch. 2:28
1 Or, words
3 Rev. 13:1
4 Deut. 28:49
2 Sam. 1:23
Jer. 48:40
Ezek. 17:3
Hab. 1:8
4 Or, wherewith
5 ch. 2:39
5 Or, it raised up one dominion
6 ch. 8:8, 22
7 ch. 2:40
7 ch. 2:41
Rev. 13:1
8 ch. 8:9
8 Rev. 9:7
8 Ps. 12:3
Rev. 13:5
9 Rev. 20:4
9 Ps. 90:2
9 Ps. 104:2
Rev. 1:14
9 Ezek. 1:15
10 Ps. 50:3
Is. 30:33 & 66:15
10 1 Ki. 22:19
Ps. 68:17
Rev. 5:11
10 Rev. 20:4

Rev. 19:20   11
Chald. a   12
prolonging in
life was given them
Ezek. 1:26   13
Mat. 24:30
Rev. 1:7
Ps. 2:6-8   14
Mat. 28:18
John 3:35
1 Cor. 15:27
Eph. 1:22
ch. 3:4   14
Ps. 145:13   14
Mic. 4:7
Luke 1:33
John 12:34
Heb. 12:28
Chald. sheath   15
Is. 60:12   18
2 Tim. 2:11
Rev. 2:26
Chald. high ones,   18
i.e. things,
or, places
Chald. from   19
all those
Rev. 17:14   21
Rev. 1:6   22
ch. 2:40   23
Rev. 17:12   24
Is. 37:23   25

the most High, and shall ᴿwear out the saints of the most High, and ᴿthink to change times and laws: and ᴿthey shall be given into his hand ᴿuntil a time and times and the dividing of time.

26 ᴿBut the judgment shall sit, and they shall take away his dominion, to consume and to destroy *it* unto the end.

27 And the ᴿkingdom and dominion, and the greatness of the kingdom under the whole heaven, shall be given to the people of the saints of the most High, ᴿwhose kingdom *is* an everlasting kingdom, ᴿand all ᴺdominions shall serve and obey him.

28 Hitherto *is* the end of the matter. As for me Daniel, ᴿmy cogitations much troubled me, and my countenance changed in me: but I ᴿkept the matter in my heart.

CHAPTER 8

Vision of the ram, he goat, and horn

IN the third year of the reign of king Bĕl-shăz'-zär a vison appeared unto me, *even unto* me Daniel, after that which appeared unto me ᴿat the first.

2 And I saw in a vision; and it came to pass, when I saw, that I *was* at ᴿShû'-shăn *in* the palace, which *is* in the province of Ē'-lăm; and I saw in a vision, and I was by the river of ū'-lăi.

3 Then I lifted up mine eyes, and saw, and, behold, there stood before the river a ram which had *two* horns: and the *two* horns *were* high; but one *was* higher than ᴺthe other, and the higher came up last.

4 I saw the ram pushing westward, and northward, and southward; so that no beasts might stand before him, neither *was there any* that could deliver out of his hand; ᴿbut he did according to his will, and became great.

5 And as I was considering, behold, an he goat came from the west on the face of the whole earth, and ᴺtouched not the ground: and the goat *had* ᴺa notable horn between his eyes.

6 And he came to the ram that had *two* horns, which I had seen standing before the river, and ran unto him in the fury of his power.

7 And I saw him come close unto the ram, and he was moved with choler against him, and smote the ram, and brake his two horns: and there was no power in the ram to stand before him, but he cast him down to the ground, and stamped upon him: and there was none that could deliver the ram out of his hand.

8 Therefore the he goat waxed very great: and when he was strong, the great horn was

broken; and for it came up ᴿfour notable ones toward the four winds of heaven.

9 ᴿAnd out of one of them came forth a little horn, which waxed exceeding great, ᴿtoward the south, and toward the east, and toward the ᴿpleasant *land*.

10 ᴿAnd it waxed great, *even* ᴺto ᴿthe host of heaven; and ᴿit cast down *some* of the host and of the stars to the ground, and stamped upon them.

11 Yea, ᴿhe magnified *himself* even ᴺto ᴿthe prince of the host, ᴿand ᴺby him ᴿthe daily *sacrifice* was taken away, and the place of his sanctuary was cast down.

12 And ᴿan ᴺ host was given *him* against the daily *sacrifice* by reason of transgression, and it cast down ᴿthe truth to the ground; and it ᴿpractised, and prospered.

13 Then I heard ᴿone saint speaking, and another saint said unto ᴺᴺthat certain *saint* which spake, How long *shall be* the vision *concerning* the daily *sacrifice,* and the transgression ᴺof desolation, to give both the sanctuary and the host to be trodden under foot?

14 And he said unto me, Unto two thousand and three hundred ᴺdays; then shall the sanctuary be ᴺcleansed.

Meaning of the vision

15 And it came to pass, when I, *even* I Daniel, had seen the vision, and ᴿsought for the meaning, then, behold, there stood before me ᴿas the appearance of a man.

16 And I heard a man's voice ᴿbetween *the banks of* ū'-lăi, which called, and said, ᴿGabriel, make this *man* to understand the vision.

17 So he came near where I stood: and when he came, I was afraid, and ᴿfell upon my face: but he said unto me, Understand, O son of man: for at the time of the end *shall be* the vision.

18 ᴿNow as he was speaking with me, I was in a deep sleep on my face toward the ground: ᴿbut he touched me, and ᴺset me upright.

19 And he said, Behold, I will make thee know what shall be in the last end of the indignation: ᴿfor at the time appointed the end *shall be.*

20 The ram which thou sawest having *two* horns *are* the kings of Mē'-dĭ-ă and Persia.

21 And the rough goat *is* the king of Grecia: and the great horn that *is* between his eyes ᴿ*is* the first king.

22 ᴿNow that being broken, whereas four stood up for it, four kingdoms shall stand up out of the nation, but not in his power.

23 And in the latter time of their kingdom, when the transgressors ᴺare come to the full, a

king ᴿof fierce countenance, and understanding dark sentences, shall stand up.

24 And his power shall be mighty, ᴿbut not by his own power: and he shall destroy wonderfully, ᴿand shall prosper, and practise, ᴿand shall destroy the mighty and the ᴺholy people.

25 And ᴿthrough his policy also he shall cause craft to prosper in his hand; ᴿand he shall magnify *himself* in his heart, and by ᴺpeace shall destroy many: ᴿhe shall also stand up against the Prince of princes; but he shall be ᴿbroken without hand.

26 And the vision of the evening and the morning which was told *is* true: ᴿwherefore shut thou up the vision; for it *shall be* for many days.

27 ᴿAnd I Daniel fainted, and was sick *certain* days; afterward I rose up, and did the king's business; and I was astonished at the vision, but none understood *it*.

CHAPTER 9

Seventy years of exile

IN the first year ᴿof Dă-rī′-ŭs the son of Ă-hăs̀-ū-ē′-rŭs, of the seed of the Mēdes̀, which was made king over the realm of the Chăl-dē′-ăns;

2 In the first year of his reign I Daniel understood by books the number of the years, whereof the word of the LORD came to ᴿJeremiah the prophet, that he would accomplish seventy years in the desolations of Jerusalem.

Daniel's prayer

3 ᴿAnd I set my face unto the Lord God, to seek by prayer and supplications, with fasting, and sackcloth, and ashes:

4 And I prayed unto the LORD my God, and made my confession, and said, O ᴿLord, the great and dreadful God, keeping the covenant and mercy to them that love him, and to them that keep his commandments;

5 ᴿWe have sinned, and have committed iniquity, and have done wickedly, and have rebelled, even by departing from thy precepts and from thy judgments:

6 ᴿNeither have we hearkened unto thy servants the prophets, which spake in thy name to our kings, our princes, and our fathers, and to all the people of the land.

7 O Lord, ᴿrighteousness ᴺ*belongeth* unto thee, but unto us confusion of faces, as at this day; to the men of Judah, and to the inhabitants of Jerusalem, and unto all Israel, *that are* near, and *that are* far off, through all the

countries whither thou hast driven them, because of their trespass that they have trespassed against thee.

8 O Lord, to us *belongeth* confusion of face, to our kings, to our princes, and to our fathers, because we have sinned against thee.

9 ᴿTo the Lord our God *belong* mercies and forgivenesses, though we have rebelled against him;

10 Neither have we obeyed the voice of the LORD our God, to walk in his laws, which he set before us by his servants the prophets.

11 Yea, ᴿall Israel have transgressed thy law, even by departing, that they might not obey thy voice; therefore the curse is poured upon us, and the oath that *is* written in the ᴿlaw of Moses the servant of God, because we have sinned against him.

12 And he hath ᴿconfirmed his words, which he spake against us, and against our judges that judged us, by bringing upon us a great evil: ᴿfor under the whole heaven hath not been done as hath been done upon Jerusalem.

13 ᴿAs *it is* written in the law of Moses, all this evil is come upon us: ᴿyet ᴺmade we not our prayer before the LORD our God, that we might turn from our iniquities, and understand thy truth.

14 Therefore hath the LORD ᴿwatched upon the evil, and brought it upon us: for ᴿthe LORD our God *is* righteous in all his works which he doeth: for we obeyed not his voice.

15 And now, O Lord our God, ᴿthat hast brought thy people forth out of the land of Egypt with a mighty hand, and hast ᴺgotten thee ᴿrenown, as at this day; we have sinned, we have done wickedly.

16 O Lord, ᴿaccording to all thy righteousness, I beseech thee, let thine anger and thy fury be turned away from thy city Jerusalem, ᴿthy holy mountain: because for our sins, ᴿand for the iniquities of our fathers, ᴿJerusalem and thy people ᴿ*are become* a reproach to all *that are* about us.

17 Now therefore, O our God, hear the prayer of thy servant, and his supplications, ᴿand cause thy face to shine upon thy sanctuary ᴿthat is desolate, ᴿfor the Lord's sake.

18 ᴿO my God, incline thine ear, and hear; open thine eyes, ᴿand behold our desolations, and the city ᴿwhichᴺ is called by thy name: for we do not ᴺpresent our supplications before thee for our righteousnesses, but for thy great mercies.

19 O Lord, hear; O Lord, forgive; O Lord, hearken and do; defer not, for thine own sake, O my God: for thy city and thy people are called by thy name.

Answer to the prayer

20 And whiles I *was* speaking, and praying, and confessing my sin and the sin of my people Israel, and presenting my supplication before the LORD my God for the holy mountain of my God;

21 Yea, whiles I *was* speaking in prayer, even the man [R]Gabriel, whom I had seen in the vision at the beginning, being caused to fly [N]swiftly, touched me about the time of the evening oblation.

22 And he informed *me,* and talked with me, and said, O Daniel, I am now come forth [N]to give thee skill and understanding.

23 At the beginning of thy supplications the [N]commandment came forth, and I am come to shew *thee;* for thou *art* [N]greatly beloved: therefore [R]understand the matter, and consider the vision.

24 Seventy weeks are determined upon thy people and upon thy holy city, [N]to finish the transgression, and [N]to make an end of sins, [R]and to make reconciliation for iniquity, [R]and to bring in everlasting righteousness, and to seal up the vision and [N]prophecy, [R]and to anoint the most Holy. ★

25 Know therefore and understand, *that* from the going forth of the commandment to restore and to build Jerusalem unto [R]the Messiah [R]the Prince *shall be* seven weeks, and threescore and two weeks: the street shall be built again, and the wall, even in troublous times. ★

26 And after threescore and two weeks [R]shall Messiah be cut off, [R]but[N] not for himself: [N]and [R]the people of the prince that shall come [R]shall destroy the city and the sanctuary; and the end thereof *shall be* with a flood, and unto the end of the war desolations are determined. ★

27 And he shall confirm [R]the[N] covenant with [R]many for one week: and in the midst of the week he shall cause the sacrifice and the oblation to cease, and for the overspreading of abominations he shall make *it* desolate, [R]even until the consummation, and that determined shall be poured upon the desolate.

CHAPTER 10

Daniel's vision by the river

IN the third year of Cyrus king of Persia a thing was revealed unto Daniel, whose name was called Bĕl-tē-shăz′-zăr; and the thing *was* true, but the time appointed *was* [N]long: and he understood the thing, and had understanding of the vision.

CHAP. 9

BC 538

21 ch. 8:16
21 Heb. *with weariness,* or, *flight*
22 Heb. *to make thee skilful of understanding*
23 Heb. *word*
23 Heb. a man *of desires*
23 Mat. 24:15
24 Or, *to restrain*
24 Or, *to seal up*
24 Is. 53:10
24 Rev. 14:6
24 Heb. *prophet*
24 Ps. 45:7
25 John 1:41
25 Is. 55:4
26 Is. 53:8
26 1 Pet. 2:21
26 Or, *and shall have nothing*
26 Or, *and [the Jews] they shall be no more his people,* ch. 11:17, or, *and the prince's [Messiah's,* ver. 25] *future people*
26 Mat. 22:7
26 Luke 19:44
27 Is. 42:6
27 Or, *a*
27 Mat. 26:28
27 ch. 11:36

CHAP. 10

BC 534

1 Heb. *great*

Heb. *weeks of days* **2**
Heb. *bread of desires* **3**
Heb. *one man* **5**
Rev. 1:13 **5**
Rev. 1:15 **6**
Or, *vigour* **8**
ch. 9:21 **10**
Heb. *moved* **10**
ch. 9:23 **11**
Heb. *a man of desires* **11**
Heb. *stand upon thy standing* **11**
Rev. 1:17 **12**
ch. 9:3, 4, 22, 23 Acts 10:4 **12**
ver. 20 **13**
ver. 21 ch. 12:1 Jude 9 Rev. 12:7 **13**
Or, *the first* **13**
Gen. 49:1 ch. 2:28 **14**
ver. 1 ch. 8:26 Hab. 2:3 **14**
ver. 9 ch. 8:18 **15**
ch. 8:15 **16**
ver. 10 Jer. 1:9 **16**

2 In those days I Daniel was mourning three [N]full weeks.

3 I ate no [N]pleasant bread, neither came flesh nor wine in my mouth, neither did I anoint myself at all, till three whole weeks were fulfilled.

4 And in the four and twentieth day of the first month, as I was by the side of the great river, which *is* Hĭd′-dĕ-kĕl;

5 Then I lifted up mine eyes, and looked, and behold [N]a certain man clothed in linen, whose loins *were* [R]girded with fine gold of Ū′-phăz:

6 His body also *was* like the beryl, and his face as the appearance of lightning, and his eyes as lamps of fire, and his arms and his feet like in colour to polished brass, [R]and the voice of his words like the voice of a multitude.

7 And I Daniel alone saw the vision: for the men that were with me saw not the vision; but a great quaking fell upon them, so that they fled to hide themselves.

8 Therefore I was left alone, and saw this great vision, and there remained no strength in me: for my [N]comeliness was turned in me into corruption, and I retained no strength.

9 Yet heard I the voice of his words: and when I heard the voice of his words, then was I in a deep sleep on my face, and my face toward the ground.

10 [R]And, behold, an hand touched me, which [N]set me upon my knees and *upon* the palms of my hands.

11 And he said unto me, O Daniel, [R]a[N] man greatly beloved, understand the words that I speak unto thee, and [N]stand upright: for unto thee am I now sent. And when he had spoken this word unto me, I stood trembling.

12 Then said he unto me, [R]Fear not, Daniel: for from the first day that thou didst set thine heart to understand, and to chasten thyself before thy God, [R]thy words were heard, and I am come for thy words.

13 [R]But the prince of the kingdom of Persia withstood me one and twenty days: but, lo, [R]Michael, [N]one of the chief princes, came to help me; and I remained there with the kings of Persia.

14 Now I am come to make thee understand what shall befall thy people [R]in the latter days: [R]for yet the vision *is* for *many* days.

15 And when he had spoken such words unto me, [R]I set my face toward the ground, and I became dumb.

16 And, behold, [R]*one* like the similitude of the sons of men [R]touched my lips: then I opened my mouth, and spake, and said unto him that stood before me, O my lord, by the

vision ᴿmy sorrows are turned upon me, and I have retained no strength.

17 For how can ᴺthe servant of this my lord talk with this my lord? for as for me, straightway there remained no strength in me, neither is there breath left in me.

18 Then there came again and touched me *one* like the appearance of a man, and he strengthened me,

19 ᴿAnd said, O man greatly beloved, ᴿfear not: peace *be* unto thee, be strong, yea, be strong. And when he had spoken unto me, I was strengthened, and said, Let my lord speak; for thou hast strengthened me.

20 Then said he, Knowest thou wherefore I come unto thee? and now will I return to fight ᴿwith the prince of Persia: and when I am gone forth, lo, the prince of Grecia shall come.

21 But I will shew thee that which is noted in the scripture of truth: and *there is* none that ᴺholdeth with me in these things, ᴿbut Michael your prince.

CHAPTER 11

ALSO I ᴿin the first year of ᴿDă-rī'-ŭs the Mēde, *even* I, stood to confirm and to strengthen him.

Kingdoms of Persia and Grecia

2 And now will I shew thee the truth. Behold, there shall stand up yet three kings in Persia; and the fourth shall be far richer than *they* all: and by his strength through his riches he shall stir up all against the realm of Grecia.

3 And ᴿa mighty king shall stand up, that shall rule with great dominion, and ᴿdo according to his will.

4 And when he shall stand up, ᴿhis kingdom shall be broken, and shall be divided toward the four winds of heaven; and not to his posterity, ᴿnor according to his dominion which he ruled: for his kingdom shall be plucked up, even for others beside those.

5 And the king of the south shall be strong, and *one* of his princes; and he shall be strong above him, and have dominion; his dominion *shall be* a great dominion.

6 And in the end of years they ᴺshall join themselves together; for the king's daughter of the south shall come to the king of the north to make ᴺan agreement: but she shall not retain the power of the arm; neither shall he stand, nor his arm: but she shall be given up, and they that brought her, and ᴺhe that begat her, and he that strengthened her in *these* times.

7 But out of a branch of her roots shall *one* stand up ᴺin his estate, which shall come with

CHAP. 10
BC 534

16 ver. 8
17 Or, *this servant of my lord*
19 ver. 11
19 Judg. 6:23
20 ver. 13
21 Heb. *strengtheneth himself*
21 ver. 13
Jude 9
Rev. 12:7

CHAP. 11
BC 534

1 ch. 9:1
1 ch. 5:31
3 ch. 7:6 & 8:5
3 ver. 16, 36
ch. 8:4
4 ch. 8:8
4 ch. 8:22
6 Heb. *shall associate themselves*
6 Heb. *rights*
6 Or, *whom she brought forth*
7 Or, *in his place,* or, *office,* ver. 20

Heb. *vessels of their desire*	8
Or, *shall war*	10
Is. 8:8	10
ch. 9:26	10
Or, *then shall he be stirred up again* ver. 7	10
Heb. *at the end of times, even years,* ch. 4:16 & 12:7	13
Heb. *the children of robbers*	14
Heb. *the city of munitions*	15
Heb. *the people of his choices*	15
ch. 8:4, 7	16
Josh. 1:5	16
Heb. *the land of ornament*	16
Or, *goodly*	16
2 Chr. 20:3	17
Or, *much uprightness:* or, *equal conditions*	17
Heb. *to corrupt*	17
ch. 9:26	17
Heb. *for him*	18
Heb. *his*	18
Ps. 37:36	19

an army, and shall enter into the fortress of the king of the north, and shall deal against them, and shall prevail:

8 And shall also carry captives into Egypt their gods, with their princes, *and* with ᴺtheir precious vessels of silver and of gold; and he shall continue *more* years than the king of the north.

9 So the king of the south shall come into *his* kingdom, and shall return into his own land.

10 But his sons ᴺshall be stirred up, and shall assemble a multitude of great forces: and *one* shall certainly come, ᴿand overflow, and pass through: ᴺthen shall he return, and be stirred up, ᴿ*even* to his fortress.

11 And the king of the south shall be moved with choler, and shall come forth and fight with him, *even* with the king of the north: and he shall set forth a great multitude; but the multitude shall be given into his hand.

12 *And* when he hath taken away the multitude, his heart shall be lifted up; and he shall cast down *many* ten thousands: but he shall not be strengthened *by it.*

13 For the king of the north shall return, and shall set forth a multitude greater than the former, and shall certainly come ᴺafter certain years with a great army and with much riches.

14 And in those times there shall many stand up against the king of the south: also ᴺthe robbers of thy people shall exalt themselves to establish the vision; but they shall fall.

15 So the king of the north shall come, and cast up a mount, and take ᴺthe most fenced cities: and the arms of the south shall not withstand, neither ᴺhis chosen people, neither *shall there be any* strength to withstand.

16 But he that cometh against him ᴿshall do according to his own will, and ᴿnone shall stand before him: and he shall stand in ᴺthe ᴺglorious land, which by his hand shall be consumed.

17 He shall also ᴿset his face to enter with the strength of his whole kingdom, and ᴺupright ones with him; thus shall he do: and he shall give him the daughter of women, ᴺcorrupting her: but she shall not stand *on his side,* ᴿneither be for him.

18 After this shall he turn his face unto the isles, and shall take many: but a prince ᴺfor his own behalf shall cause ᴺthe reproach offered by him to cease; without his own reproach he shall cause *it* to turn upon him.

19 Then he shall turn his face toward the fort of his own land: but he shall stumble and fall, ᴿand not be found.

A contemptible plunderer

20 Then shall stand up ᴺin his estate ᴺa raiser of taxes *in* the glory of the kingdom: but within few days he shall be destroyed, neither in ᴺanger, nor in battle.

21 And ᴺin his estate ᴿshall stand up a vile person, to whom they shall not give the honour of the kingdom: but he shall come in peaceably, and obtain the kingdom by flatteries.

22 And with the arms of a flood shall they be overflown from before him, and shall be broken; ᴿyea, also the prince of the covenant.

23 And after the league *made* with him ᴿhe shall work deceitfully: for he shall come up, and shall become strong with a small people.

24 He shall enter ᴺpeaceably even upon the fattest places of the province; and he shall do *that* which his fathers have not done, nor his fathers' fathers; he shall scatter among them the prey, and spoil, and riches: *yea,* and he shall ᴺforecast his devices against the strong holds, even for a time.

25 And he shall stir up his power and his courage against the king of the south with a great army; and the king of the south shall be stirred up to battle with a very great and mighty army; but he shall not stand: for they shall forecast devices against him.

26 Yea, they that feed of the portion of his meat shall destroy him, and his army shall overflow: and many shall fall down slain.

27 And both these kings' ᴺhearts *shall be* to do mischief, and they shall speak lies at one table; but it shall not prosper: for yet the end *shall be* at the time appointed.

28 Then shall he return into his land with great riches; and his heart *shall be* against the holy covenant; and he shall do *exploits,* and return to his own land.

29 At the time appointed he shall return, and come toward the south; but it shall not be as the former, or as the latter.

30 ᴿFor the ships of Chĭt'-tĭm shall come against him: therefore he shall be grieved, and return, and have indignation against the holy covenant: so shall he do; he shall even return, and have intelligence with them that forsake the holy covenant.

31 And arms shall stand on his part, ᴿand they shall pollute the sanctuary of strength, and shall take away the daily *sacrifice,* and they shall place the abomination that ᴺmaketh desolate.

32 And such as do wickedly against the covenant shall he ᴺcorrupt by flatteries: but the people that do know their God shall be strong, and do *exploits.*

33 And they that understand among the people shall instruct many: yet they shall fall by the sword, and by flame, by captivity, and by spoil, *many* days.

34 Now when they shall fall, they shall be holpen with a little help: but many shall cleave to them with flatteries.

35 And *some* of them of understanding shall fall, ᴿto try ᴺthem, and to purge, and to make *them* white, *even* to the time of the end: because *it is* yet for a time appointed.

36 And the king shall do according to his will; and he shall ᴿexalt himself, and magnify himself above every god, and shall speak marvellous things against the God of gods, and shall prosper till the indignation be accomplished: for that that is determined shall be done.

37 Neither shall he regard the God of his fathers, nor the desire of women, ᴿnor regard any god: for he shall magnify himself above all.

38 But ᴺin his ᴺestate shall he honour the God of ᴺᴺforces: and a god whom his fathers knew not shall be honour with gold, and silver, and with precious stones, and ᴺpleasant things.

39 Thus shall he do in the ᴺmost strong holds with a strange god, whom he shall acknowledge *and* increase with glory: and he shall cause them to rule over many, and shall divide the land for ᴺgain.

The time of the end

40 And at the time of the end shall the king of the south push at him: and the king of the north shall come against him ᴿlike a whirlwind, with chariots, ᴿand with horsemen, and with many ships; and he shall enter into the countries, and shall overflow and pass over.

41 He shall enter also into the ᴺᴺglorious land, and many *countries* shall be overthrown: but these shall escape out of his hand, ᴿ*even* Ē'-dọm, and Moab, and the chief of the children of Ammon.

42 He shall ᴺstretch forth his hand also upon the countries: and the land of Egypt shall not escape.

43 But he shall have power over the treasures of gold and of silver, and over all the precious things of Egypt: and the Lĭb'-ў-ăns and the Ē-thĭ-ō'-pĭ-ăns *shall be* ᴿat his steps.

44 But tidings out of the east and out of the north shall trouble him: therefore he shall go forth with great fury to destroy, and utterly to make away many.

45 And he shall plant the tabernacles of his palace between the seas in ᴿthe ᴺᴺglorious

holy mountain; ^Ryet he shall come to his end, and none shall help him.

CHAPTER 12

Time of trouble for the Jews

AND at that time shall Michael stand up, the great prince which standeth for the children of thy people: ^Rand there shall be a time of trouble, such as never was since there was a nation *even* to that same time: and at that time thy people ^Rshall be delivered, every one that shall be found ^Rwritten in the book.

2 And many of them that sleep in the dust of the earth shall awake, ^Rsome to everlasting life, and some to shame ^R*and* everlasting contempt.

3 And they that be ^Nwise shall ^Rshine as the brightness of the firmament; ^Rand they that turn many to righteousness ^Ras the stars for ever and ever.

4 But thou, O Daniel, ^Rshut up the words, and seal the book, *even* to the time of the end: many shall run to and fro, and knowledge shall be increased.

Prophecy sealed until the end

5 Then I Daniel looked, and, behold, there stood other two, the one on this side of the ^Nbank of the river, and the other on that side of the bank ^Rof the river.

6 And *one* said to the man clothed in linen, which *was* ^Nupon the waters of the river, ^RHow long *shall it be to* the end of these wonders?

7 And I heard the man clothed in linen, which *was* upon the waters of the river, when he ^Rheld up his right hand and his left hand unto heaven, and sware by him ^Rthat liveth for ever ^Rthat *it shall be* for a time, times, and ^Nan half; ^Rand when he shall have accomplished to scatter the power of ^Rthe holy people, all these *things* shall be finished.

8 And I heard, but I understood not: then said I, O my Lord, what *shall be* the end of these *things?*

9 And he said, Go thy way, Daniel: for the words *are* closed up and sealed till the time of the end.

10 ^RMany shall be purified, and made white, and tried; ^Rbut the wicked shall do wickedly: and none of the wicked shall understand; but ^Rthe wise shall understand.

11 And from the time *that* the daily *sacrifice* shall be taken away, and ^Nthe abomination that ^Nmaketh desolate set up, *there shall be* a thousand two hundred and ninety days.

12 Blessed *is* he that waiteth, and cometh to the thousand three hundred and five and thirty days.

13 But go thou thy way till the end *be:* ^Rfor ^Nthou shalt rest, ^Rand stand in thy lot at the end of the days.

CHAP. 11
BC 534
45 Rev. 19:20

CHAP. 12
BC 534

1	Is. 26:20
	Jer. 30:7
	Rev. 16:18
1	Rom. 11:26
1	Ex. 32:32
	Ps. 56:8
2	Mat. 25:46
	John 5:28
	Acts 24:15
2	Is. 66:24
	Rom. 9:21
3	Or, *teachers*
3	Mat. 13:43
3	Jas. 5:20
3	1 Cor. 15:41
4	Rev. 22:10
5	Heb. *lip*
5	ch. 10:4

Or, *from above*	6
ch. 8:13	6
Deut. 32:40	7
ch. 4:34	7
ch. 7:25	7
Or, *part*	7
Luke 21:24	7
ch. 8:24	7
Zech. 13:9	10
Hos. 14:9	10
John 8:47	10
Heb. *to set up the abomination, etc.*	11
Or, *astonisheth*	11
Rev. 14:13	13
Or, *and thou, etc.*	13
Ps. 1:5	13

HOSEA

Hosea is considered to be the author of the book bearing his name. He began his ministry about 760 B.C. and continued toward the end of the eighth century. His marital experience provided the basis for his message in which he warned the Israelites of their unfaithfulness. Vividly, he portrayed God's love for backsliding Israel.

Outline for further study:

  I. Hosea's experience and message   1:1 – 3:5
 II. Israel's sins and impending judgment   4:1 – 10:15
III. God's love, judgment and mercy   11:1 – 14:9

CHAPTER 1

Hosea's marriage and children

THE word of the LORD that came unto Hō-sē′-ă, the son of Bēēr′-ī, in the days of ŭz-zī′-ăh, Jō′-thăm, Ahaz, *and* Hĕz-ē-kī′-ăh, kings of Judah, and in the days of Jĕr-ŏ-bō′-ăm the son of Jō′-ăsh, king of Israel.

2 The beginning of the word of the LORD by Hō-sē′-ă. And the LORD said to Hō-sē′-ă, ^RGo, take unto thee a wife of whoredoms and children of whoredoms: for ^Rthe land hath committed great whoredom, *departing* from the LORD.

3 So he went and took Gō′-mĕr the daughter of Dĭb-lā′-ĭm; which conceived, and bare him a son.

4 And the LORD said unto him, Call his name Jĕz′-rēēl; for yet a little *while,* ^Rand I will ^Navenge the blood of Jĕz′-rēēl upon the house of Jehu, ^Rand will cause to cease the kingdom of the house of Israel.

5 ^RAnd it shall come to pass at that day, that I will break the bow of Israel in the valley of Jĕz′-rēēl.

6 And she conceived again, and bare a daughter. And *God* said unto him, Call her name ^NLō-rŭ-hä′-măh: ^Rfor ^NI will no more

CHAP. 1
BC 785

2	ch. 3:1
2	Deut. 31:16
	Ps. 73:27
	Jer. 2:13
	Ezek. 23:3, etc.

2 Ki. 10:11	4
Heb. *visit*	4
2 Ki. 15:10	4
2 Ki. 15:29	5
i.e. *Not having obtained mercy*	6
2 Ki. 17:6	6
Heb. *I will not add any more to*	6

have mercy upon the house of Israel; ^Nbut I will utterly take them away.

7 ^RBut I will have mercy upon the house of Judah, and will save them by the LORD their God, and ^Rwill not save them by bow, nor by sword, nor by battle, by horses, nor by horsemen.

8 Now when she had weaned Lō-rû-hä′-mäh, she conceived, and bare a son.

9 Then said *God,* Call his name ^NLō-ăm′-mĭ: for ye *are* not my people, and I will not be your *God.*

10 Yet ^Rthe number of the children of Israel shall be as the sand of the sea, which cannot be measured nor numbered; ^Rand it shall come to pass, *that* ^Nin the place where it was said unto them, Ye *are* not my people, *there* it shall be said unto them, *Ye are* ^Rthe sons of the living God.

11 ^RThen shall the children of Judah and the children of Israel be gathered together, and appoint themselves one head, and they shall come up out of the land: for great *shall be* the day of Jĕz′-rĕel.

CHAPTER 2

Adultery and judgment

SAY ye unto your brethren, ^NĂm′-mĭ; and to your sisters, ^NRû-hä′-mäh.

2 Plead with your mother, plead: for ^Rshe *is* not my wife, neither *am* I her husband: let her therefore put away her ^Rwhoredoms out of her sight, and her adulteries from between her breasts;

3 Lest ^RI strip her naked, and set her as in the day that she was ^Rborn, and make her as a wilderness, and set her like a dry land, and slay her with ^Rthirst.

4 And I will not have mercy upon her children; for they *be* the ^Rchildren of whoredoms.

5 For their mother hath played the harlot: she that conceived them hath done shamefully: for she said, I will go after my lovers, ^Rthat give *me* my bread and my water, my wool and my flax, mine oil and my ^Ndrink.

6 Therefore, behold, ^RI will hedge up thy way with thorns, and ^Nmake a wall, that she shall not find her paths.

7 And she shall follow after her lovers, but she shall not overtake them; and she shall seek them, but shall not find *them:* then shall she say, ^RI will go and return to my ^Rfirst husband; for then *was it* better with me than now.

8 For she did not ^Rknow that I gave her corn, and ^Nwine, and oil, and multiplied her silver and gold, ^N*which* they prepared for Bā′-ăl.

CHAP. 1
BC 785
6 Or, *that I should altogether pardon them*
7 2 Ki. 19:35
7 Zech. 4:6
9 i.e. *Not my people*
10 Gen. 32:12
10 1 Pet. 2:10
10 Or, *instead of that*
10 John 1:12
11 Is. 11:12

CHAP. 2
BC 785
1 i.e. *My people*
1 i.e. *Having obtained mercy*
2 Is. 50:1
2 Ezek. 16:25
3 Jer. 13:22
3 Ezek. 16:4
3 Amos 8:11
4 John 8:41
5 ver. 8, 12
5 Heb. *drinks*
6 Lam. 3:7, 9
6 Heb. *wall a wall*
7 Luke 15:18
7 Ezek. 16:8
8 Is. 1:3
8 Heb. *new wine*
8 Or, *wherewith they made Baal*

Or, *take away*	9
Ezek. 16:37	10
Heb. *folly,* or, *villany*	10
Amos 8:10	11
Heb. *make desolate*	12
Or, *friendly*	14
Heb. *to her heart*	14
Josh. 7:26	15
Jer. 2:2	15
Ezek. 16:8	
Ex. 15:1	15
i.e. *My husband*	16
i.e. *My lord*	16
Ex. 23:13	17
Ps. 16:4	
Job 5:23	18
Is. 2:4	18
Lev. 26:5	18
Jer. 23:6	
Jer. 31:33	20
John 17:3	
Zech. 8:12	21
Jer. 31:27	23
ch. 1:6	23
ch. 1:10	23

9 Therefore will I return, and take away my corn in the time thereof, and my wine in the season thereof, and will ^Nrecover my wool and my flax *given* to cover her nakedness.

10 And now ^Rwill I discover her ^Nlewdness in the sight of her lovers, and none shall deliver her out of mine hand.

11 ^RI will also cause all her mirth to cease, her feast days, her new moons, and her sabbaths, and all her solemn feasts.

12 And I will ^Ndestroy her vines and her fig trees, whereof she hath said, These *are* my rewards that my lovers have given me: and I will make them a forest, and the beasts of the field shall eat them.

13 And I will visit upon her the days of Bā′-ă-lĭm, wherein she burned incense to them, and she decked herself with her earrings and her jewels, and she went after her lovers, and forgat me, saith the LORD.

Restoration and renewal promised

14 Therefore, behold, I will allure her, and bring her into the wilderness, and speak ^{NN}comfortably unto her.

15 And I will give her her vineyards from thence, and ^Rthe valley of Ā′-chôr for a door of hope: and she shall sing there, as in ^Rthe days of her youth, and ^Ras in the day when she came up out of the land of Egypt.

16 And it shall be at that day, saith the LORD, *that* thou shalt call me ^NĬsh′-ĭ; and shalt call me no more ^NBā′-ă-lĭ.

17 For ^RI will take away the names of Bā′-ă-lĭm out of her mouth, and they shall no more be remembered by their name.

18 And in that day will I make a ^Rcovenant for them with the beasts of the field, and with the fowls of heaven, and *with* the creeping things of the ground: and ^RI will break the bow and the sword and the battle out of the earth, and will make them to ^Rlie down safely.

19 And I will betroth thee unto me for ever; yea, I will betroth thee unto me in righteousness, and in judgment, and in lovingkindness, and in mercies.

20 I will even betroth thee unto me in faithfulness: and ^Rthou shalt know the LORD.

21 And it shall come to pass in that day, ^RI will hear, saith the LORD, I will hear the heavens, and they shall hear the earth;

22 And the earth shall hear the corn, and the wine, and the oil; and they shall hear Jĕz′-rĕel.

23 And ^RI will sow her unto me in the earth; ^Rand I will have mercy upon her that had not obtained mercy; and I ^Rwill say to *them which were* not my people, Thou *art* my people; and they shall say, *Thou art* my God.

CHAPTER 3

Redemption and restoration

THEN said the LORD unto me, ^RGo yet, love a woman beloved of *her* ^Rfriend, yet an adulteress, according to the love of the LORD toward the children of Israel, who look to other gods, and love flagons ^Nof wine.

2 So I bought her to me for fifteen *pieces* of silver, and *for* an hō'-mĕr of barley, and an ^Nhalf hō'-mĕr of barley:

3 And I said unto her, Thou shalt ^Rabide for me many days; thou shalt not play the harlot, and thou shalt not be for *another* man: so *will* I also *be* for thee.

4 For the children of Israel shall abide many days ^Rwithout a king, and without a prince, and without a sacrifice, and without ^Nan image, and without an ^Rē'-phŏd, and *without* ^Rtĕr'-ă-phīm:

5 Afterward shall the children of Israel return, and ^Rseek the LORD their God, and ^RDavid their king; and shall fear the LORD and his goodness in the ^Rlatter days.   ★

CHAPTER 4

Moral decay of the people and priests

HEAR the word of the LORD, ye children of Israel: for the LORD hath a ^Rcontroversy with the inhabitants of the land, because *there is* no truth, nor mercy, nor ^Rknowledge of God in the land.

2 By swearing, and lying, and killing, and stealing, and committing adultery, they break out, and ^Nblood toucheth blood.

3 Therefore ^Rshall the land mourn, and ^Revery one that dwelleth therein shall languish, with the beasts of the field, and with the fowls of heaven; yea, the fishes of the sea also shall be taken away.

4 Yet let no man strive, nor reprove another: for thy people *are* as they ^Rthat strive with the priest.

5 Therefore shalt thou fall ^Rin the day, and the prophet also shall fall with thee in the night, and I will ^Ndestroy thy mother.

6 ^RMy people are ^Ndestroyed for lack of knowledge: because thou hast rejected knowledge, I will also reject thee, that thou shalt be no priest to me: seeing thou hast forgotten the law of thy God, I will also forget thy children.

7 As they were increased, so they sinned against me: ^R*therefore* will I change their glory into shame.

8 They eat up the sin of my people, and they ^Nset their heart on their iniquity.

9 And there shall be, ^Rlike people, like priest: and I will ^Npunish them for their ways, and ^Nreward them their doings.

10 For ^Rthey shall eat, and not have enough: they shall commit whoredom, and shall not increase: because they have left off to take heed to the LORD.

Israel's idolatry

11 Whoredom and wine and new wine ^Rtake away the heart.

12 My people ask counsel at their ^Rstocks, and their staff declareth unto them: for ^Rthe spirit of whoredoms hath caused *them* to err, and they have gone a whoring from under their God.

13 ^RThey sacrifice upon the tops of the mountains, and burn incense upon the hills, under oaks and poplars and elms, because the shadow thereof *is* good: ^Rtherefore your daughters shall commit whoredom, and your spouses shall commit adultery.

14 ^NI will not punish your daughters when they commit whoredom, nor your spouses when they commit adultery: for themselves are separated with whores, and they sacrifice with harlots: therefore the people *that* doth not understand shall ^Nfall.

15 Though thou, Israel, play the harlot, *yet* let not Judah offend; ^Rand come not ye unto Gĭl'-găl, neither go ye up to ^RBĕth-ā'-vĕn, ^Rnor swear, The LORD liveth.

16 For Israel ^Rslideth back as a backsliding heifer: now the LORD will feed them as a lamb in a large place.

17 Ē'-phră-ĭm *is* joined to idols: ^Rlet him alone.

18 Their drink ^Nis sour: they have committed whoredom continually: ^Rher ^Nrulers *with* shame do love, Give ye.

19 ^RThe wind hath bound her up in her wings, and ^Rthey shall be ashamed because of their sacrifices.

CHAPTER 5

Judgment against the priests and king

HEAR ye this, O priests; and hearken, ye house of Israel; and give ye ear, O house of the king; for judgment *is* toward you, because ^Rye have been a snare on Mizpah, and a net spread upon Tā'-bôr.

2 And the revolters are ^Rprofound to make slaughter, ^Nthough I *have been* ^Na rebuker of them all.

3 ^RI know Ē'-phră-ĭm, and Israel is not hid from me: for now, O Ē'-phră-ĭm, ^Rthou committest whoredom, *and* Israel is defiled.

4 ᴺᴺThey will not frame their doings to turn unto their God: for ᴿthe spirit of whoredoms *is* in the midst of them, and they have not known the Lᴏʀᴅ.

5 And the pride of Israel doth testify to his face: therefore shall Israel and Ē'-phră-ĭm fall in their iniquity; Judah also shall fall with them.

6 ᴿThey shall go with their flocks and with their herds to seek the Lᴏʀᴅ; but they shall not find *him;* he hath withdrawn himself from them.

7 They have ᴿdealt treacherously against the Lᴏʀᴅ: for they have begotten strange children: now shall a month devour them with their portions.

Punishment of Ephraim and Judah

8 ᴿBlow ye the cornet in Gĭb'-ĕ-ăh, *and* the trumpet in Rā'-măh: ᴿcry aloud *at* ᴿBĕth-ā'-vĕn, after thee, O Benjamin.

9 Ē'-phră-ĭm shall be desolate in the day of rebuke: among the tribes of Israel have I made known that which shall surely be.

10 The princes of Judah were like them that ᴿremove the bound: *therefore* I will pour out my wrath upon them like water.

11 Ē'-phră-ĭm *is* ᴿoppressed *and* broken in judgment, because he willingly walked after ᴿthe commandment.

12 Therefore *will* I *be* unto Ē'-phră-ĭm as a moth, and to the house of Judah ᴿas ᴺrottenness.

13 When Ē'-phră-ĭm saw his sickness, and Judah *saw* his ᴿwound, then went Ē'-phră-ĭm ᴿto the Assyrian, and sent ᴺto king Jâr'-ĕb: yet could he not heal you, nor cure you of your wound.

14 For ᴿI *will be* unto Ē'-phră-ĭm as a lion, and as a young lion to the house of Judah: ᴿI, *even* I, will tear and go away; I will take away, and none shall rescue *him.*

God will await Israel's repentance

15 I will go *and* return to my place, ᴺtill they acknowledge their offence, and seek my face: in their affliction they will seek me early.

CHAPTER 6

COME, and let us return unto the Lᴏʀᴅ: for ᴿhe hath torn, and ᴿhe will heal us; he hath smitten, and he will bind us up.

2 ᴿAfter two days will he revive us: in the third day he will raise us up, and we shall live in his sight.

3 ᴿThen shall we know, *if* we follow on to know the Lᴏʀᴅ: his going forth is prepared ᴿas the morning; and ᴿhe shall come unto us

ᴿas the rain, as the latter *and* former rain unto the earth.

4 O Ē'-phră-ĭm, what shall I do unto thee? O Judah, what shall I do unto thee? for your ᴺgoodness *is* as a morning cloud, and as the early dew it goeth away.

5 Therefore have I hewed *them* by the prophets; I have slain them by ᴿthe words of my mouth: ᴺand thy judgments *are as* the light *that* goeth forth.

6 For I desired ᴿmercy, and ᴿnot sacrifice; and the ᴿknowledge of God more than burnt offerings.

7 But they ᴺlike men have transgressed the covenant: there have they dealt treacherously against me.

8 Gilead *is* a city of them that work iniquity, *and is* ᴺpolluted with blood.

9 And as troops of robbers wait for a man, *so* the company of priests murder in the way ᴺby consent: for they commit ᴺlewdness.

10 I have seen an horrible thing in the house of Israel: there *is* the whoredom of Ē'-phră-ĭm, Israel is defiled.

11 Also, O Judah, he hath set an harvest for thee, when I returned the captivity of my people.

CHAPTER 7

Corruption and wickedness of Israel

WHEN I would have healed Israel, then the iniquity of Ē'-phră-ĭm was discovered, and the ᴺwickedness of Să-mâr'-ĭ-ă: for ᴿthey commit falsehood; and the thief cometh in, *and* the troop of robbers ᴺspoileth without.

2 And they ᴺconsider not in their hearts *that* I ᴿremember all their wickedness: now their own doings have beset them about; they are before my face.

3 They make the king glad with their wickedness, and the princes ᴿwith their lies.

4 ᴿThey *are* all adulterers, as an oven heated by the baker, ᴺwho ceaseth ᴺfrom raising after he hath kneaded the dough, until it be leavened.

5 In the day of our king the princes have made *him* sick ᴺwith bottles of wine; he stretched out his hand with scorners.

6 For they have ᴺmade ready their heart like an oven, whiles they lie in wait: their baker sleepeth all the night; in the morning it burneth as a flaming fire.

7 They are all hot as an oven, and have devoured their judges; all their kings are fallen: ᴿ*there is* none among them that calleth unto me.

8 Ē'-phră-ĭm, he ᴿhath mixed himself among the people; Ē'-phră-ĭm is a cake not turned.

CHAP. 5
BC 780
4 Heb. *They will not give*
4 Or, *Their doings will not suffer them*
4 ch. 4:12
6 Prov. 1:28
7 Jer. 3:20
8 Joel 2:1
8 Is. 10:30
8 Josh. 7:2
10 Deut. 19:14
11 Deut. 28:33
11 Mic. 6:16
12 Prov. 12:4
12 Or, *a worm*
13 Jer. 30:12
13 2 Ki. 15:19
13 Or, *to the king of Jareb:* or, *to the king* that *should plead*
14 Lam. 3:10
14 Ps. 50:22
15 Heb. *till they be guilty*

CHAP. 6
BC 780
1 Deut. 32:39
1 Jer. 30:17
2 1 Cor. 15:4
3 Is. 54:13
3 2 Sam. 23:4
3 Ps. 72:6

Job 29:23   3
Or, *mercy,* or, *kindness*   4
Jer. 23:29   5
Or, *that thy judgments might be, etc.*   5
Mat. 9:13   6
Is. 1:11   6
John 17:3   6
Or, *like Adam,* Job 31:33   7
Or, *cunning for blood*   8
Heb. *with one shoulder,* or, *to Shechem*   9
Or, *enormity*   9

CHAP. 7
BC 780
Heb. *evils*   1
ch. 5:1   1
Heb. *strippeth*   1
Heb. *say not to*   2
Jer. 17:1   2
Rom. 1:32   3
Jer. 9:2   4
Or, *the raiser will cease*   4
Or, *from waking*   4
Or, *with heat through wine*   5
Or, *applied*   6
Is. 64:7   7
Ps. 106:35   8

9 [R]Strangers have devoured his strength, and he knoweth *it* not: yea, gray hairs are [N]here and there upon him, yet he knoweth not.

10 And the [R]pride of Israel testifieth to his face: and [R]they do not return to the LORD their God, nor seek him for all this.

Ephraim's misplaced trust

11 [R]E'-phră-ĭm also is like a silly dove without heart: [R]they call to Egypt, they go to Assyria.

12 When they shall go, I will spread my net upon them; I will bring them down as the fowls of the heaven; I will chastise them, [R]as their congregation hath heard.

13 Woe unto them! for they have fled from me: [N]destruction unto them! because they have transgressed against me: though [R]I have redeemed them, yet they have spoken lies against me.

14 [R]And they have not cried unto me with their heart, when they howled upon their beds: they assemble themselves for corn and wine, *and* they rebel against me.

15 Though I [N]have bound *and* strengthened their arms, yet do they imagine mischief against me.

16 They return, *but* not to the most High: [R]they are like a deceitful bow: their princes shall fall by the sword for the [R]rage of their tongue: this *shall be* their derision [R]in the land of Egypt.

CHAPTER 8

SET the trumpet to [N]thy mouth. *He shall come* [R]as an eagle against the house of the LORD, because they have transgressed my covenant, and trespassed against my law.

2 [R]Israel shall cry unto me, My God, [R]we know thee.

3 Israel hath cast off *the thing that is* good: the enemy shall pursue him.

Unauthorized kings

4 [R]They have set up kings, but not by me: they have made princes, and I knew *it* not: of their silver and their gold have they made them idols, that they may be cut off.

5 Thy calf, O Să-mâr'-ĭ-ă, hath cast *thee* off; mine anger is kindled against them: [R]how long *will it be* ere they attain to innocency?

6 For from Israel *was* it also: the workman made it; therefore it *is* not God: but the calf of Să-mâr'-ĭ-ă shall be broken in pieces.

Useless foreign alliances

7 For [R]they have sown the wind, and they shall reap the whirlwind: it hath no [N]stalk: the

bud shall yield no meal: if so be it yield, the strangers shall swallow it up.

8 [R]Israel is swallowed up: now shall they be among the Gentiles [R]as a vessel wherein *is* no pleasure.

9 For they are gone up to Assyria, [R]a wild ass alone by himself: E'-phră-ĭm [R]hath hired [N]lovers.

10 Yea, though they have hired among the nations, now [R]will I gather them, and they shall [N]sorrow [N]a little for the burden of [R]the king of princes.

Altars for sinning

11 Because E'-phră-ĭm hath made many altars to sin, altars shall be unto him to sin.

12 I have written to him [R]the great things of my law, *but* they were counted as a strange thing.

13 [R]They[N] sacrifice flesh *for* the sacrifices of mine offerings, and eat *it;* [R]but the LORD accepteth them not; now will he remember their iniquity, and visit their sins: they shall return to Egypt.

14 [R]For Israel hath forgotten [R]his Maker, and buildeth temples; and Judah hath multiplied fenced cities: but [R]I will send a fire upon his cities, and it shall devour the palaces thereof.

CHAPTER 9

Exile predicted

REJOICE not, O Israel, for joy, as *other* people: for thou hast gone a whoring from thy God, thou hast loved a [R]reward [N]upon every cornfloor.

2 The floor and the [N]winepress shall not feed them, and the new wine shall fail in her.

3 They shall not dwell in [R]the LORD's land; [R]but E'-phră-ĭm shall return to Egypt, and [R]they shall eat unclean *things* in Assyria.

4 They shall not offer wine *offerings* to the LORD, [R]neither shall they be pleasing unto him: their sacrifices *shall be* unto them as the bread of mourners; all that eat thereof shall be polluted: for their bread for their soul shall not come into the house of the LORD.

5 What will ye do in the solemn day, and in the day of the feast of the LORD?

6 For, lo, they are gone because of [N]destruction: Egypt shall gather them up, Mĕm'-phĭs shall bury them: [N][N]the pleasant *places* for their silver, nettles shall possess them: thorns *shall be* in their tabernacles.

Ridicule of the prophet

7 The days of visitation are come, the days of recompence are come; Israel shall know *it:*

the prophet *is* a fool, ᴿthe ᴺspiritual man *is* mad, for the multitude of thine iniquity, and the great hatred.

8 The watchman of Ē'-phrā-ĭm *was* with my God: *but* the prophet *is* a snare of a fowler in all his ways, *and* hatred ᴺin the house of his God.

9 ᴿThey have deeply corrupted *themselves*, as in the days of ᴿGĭb'-ĕ-ăh: *therefore* he will remember their iniquity, he will visit their sins.

Punishment for Israel's infidelity

10 I found Israel like grapes in the wilderness; I saw your fathers as the firstripe in the fig tree at her first time: *but* they went to ᴿBā'-ăl-pē'-ôr, and separated themselves unto *that* shame; ᴿand *their* abominations were according as they loved.

11 *As for* Ē'-phrā-ĭm, thcir glory shall fly away like a bird, from the birth, and from the womb, and from the conception.

12 Though they bring up their children, yet will I bereave them, *that there shall* not *be* a man *left:* yea, ᴿwoe also to them when I depart from them!

13 Ē'-phrā-ĭm, ᴿas I saw Tȳ'-rŭs, *is* planted in a pleasant place: but Ē'-phrā-ĭm shall bring forth his children to the murderer.

14 Give them, O Lᴏʀᴅ: what wilt thou give? give them ᴿa ᴺmiscarrying womb and dry breasts.

15 All their wickedness *is* in Gĭl'-găl: for there I hated them: for the wickedness of their doings I will drive them out of mine house, I will love thcm no more: ᴿall their princes *are* revolters.

16 Ē'-phrā-ĭm is smitten, their root is dried up, they shall bear no fruit: yea, though they bring forth, yet will I slay *even* ᴺthe beloved *fruit* of their womb.

17 My God will cast them away, because they did not hearken unto him: and they shall be wanderers among the nations.

CHAPTER 10

Destruction of idols and altars

ISRAEL *is* ᴿanᴺ empty vine, he bringeth forth fruit unto himself: according to the multitude of his fruit ᴿhe hath increased the altars; according to the goodness of his land they have made goodly ᴺimages.

2 ᴺTheir heart is ᴿdivided; now shall they be found faulty: he shall ᴺbreak down their altars, he shall spoil their images.

3 For now they shall say, We have no king, because we feared not the Lᴏʀᴅ; what then should a king do to us?

4 They have spoken words, swearing falsely in making a covenant: thùs judgment springeth up ᴿas hemlock in the furrows of the field.

5 The inhabitants of Să-mâr'-ĭ-ă shall fear because of the calves of Bĕth-ā'-vĕn: for the people thereof shall mourn over it, and ᴺthe priests thereof *that* rejoiced on it, for the glory thereof, because it is departed from it.

6 It shall be also carried unto Assyria *for* a present to king Jâr'-ĕb: Ē'-phrā-ĭm shall receive shame, and Israel shall be ashamed of his own counsel.

7 *As for* Să-mâr'-ĭ-ă, her king is cut off as the foam upon ᴺthe water.

8 The high places also of Ā'-vĕn, ᴿthe sin of Israel, shall be destroyed: the thorn and the thistle shall come up on their altars; ᴿand they shall say to the mountains, Cover us; and to the hills, Fall on us.

Destruction by war

9 O Israel, thou hast sinned from the days of Gĭb'-ĕ-ăh: there they stood: the battle in Gĭb'-ĕ-ăh against the children of iniquity did not overtake them.

10 *It is* in my desire that I should chastise them; and ᴿthe people shall be gathered against them, ᴺwhen they shall bind themselves in their two furrows.

11 And Ē'-phrā-ĭm *is* as ᴿan heifer *that is* taught, *and* loveth to tread out *the corn;* but I passed over upon ᴺher fair neck: I will make Ē'-phrā-ĭm to ride; Judah shall plow, *and* Jacob shall break his clods.

12 Sow to yourselves in righteousness, reap in mercy; ᴿbreak up your fallow ground: for *it is* time to seek the Lᴏʀᴅ, till he come and rain righteousness upon you.

13 ᴿYe have plowed wickedness, ye have reaped iniquity; ye have eaten the fruit of lies: because thou didst trust in thy way, in the multitude of thy mighty men.

14 Therefore shall a tumult arise among thy people, and all thy fortresses shall be spoiled, as Shăl'-măn spoiled Bĕth-är'-bĕl in the day of battle: the mother was dashed in pieces upon *her* children.

15 So shall Beth-el do unto you because of ᴺyour great wickedness: in a morning shall the king of Israel utterly be cut off.

CHAPTER 11

God's love for Israel

WHEN Israel *was* a child, then I loved him, and ᴿcalled my ᴿson out of Egypt.   ★

2 *As* they called them, so they went from

them: they sacrificed unto Bā́-ă-lĭm, and burned incense to graven images.

3 ᴿI taught Ḗ-phră-ĭm also to go, taking them by their arms; but they knew not that ᴿI healed them.

4 I drew them with cords of a man, with bands of love: and ᴿI was to them as they that ᴺtake off the yoke on their jaws, and ᴿI laid meat unto them.

5 He shall not return into the land of Egypt, but the Assyrian shall be his king, because they refused to return.

6 And the sword shall abide on his cities, and shall consume his branches, and devour *them,* because of their own counsels.

7 And my people are bent to ᴿbacksliding from me: though they called them to the most High, ᴺnone at all would exalt *him.*

God's promise of forgiveness

8 ᴿHow shall I give thee up, Ḗ-phră-ĭm? *how* shall I deliver thee, Israel? how shall I make thee as ᴿĂd́-măh? *how* shall I set thee as Zĕ-bṓ-ĭm? mine heart is turned within me, my repentings are kindled together.

9 I will not execute the fierceness of mine anger, I will not return to destroy Ḗ-phră-ĭm: ᴿfor I *am* God, and not man; the Holy One in the midst of thee: and I will not enter into the city.

10 They shall walk after the LORD: ᴿhe shall roar like a lion: when he shall roar, then the children shall tremble from the west.

11 They shall tremble as a bird out of Egypt, ᴿand as a dove out of the land of Assyria: ᴿand I will place them in their houses, saith the LORD.

Israel's history of sin

12 Ḗ-phră-ĭm compasseth me about with lies, and the house of Israel with deceit: but Judah yet ruleth with God, and is faithful ᴺwith the saints.

CHAPTER 12

Ḗ-PHRĂ-ĬM feedeth on wind, and followeth after the east wind: he daily increaseth lies and desolation; ᴿand they do make a covenant with the Assyrians, and ᴿoil is carried into Egypt.

2 ᴿThe LORD hath also a controversy with Judah, and will ᴺpunish Jacob according to his ways; according to his doings will he recompense him.

3 He took his brother ᴿby the heel in the womb, and by his strength he ᴿhadᴺ power with God:

4 Yea, he had power over the angel, and

prevailed: he wept, and made supplication unto him: he found him *in* ᴿBeth-el, and there he spake with us;

5 Even the LORD God of hosts; the LORD *is* his ᴿmemorial.

6 ᴿTherefore turn thou to thy God: keep mercy and judgment, and wait on thy God continually.

7 *He is* ᴺa merchant, ᴿthe balances of deceit *are* in his hand: he loveth to ᴺoppress.

8 And Ḗ-phră-ĭm said, ᴿYet I am become rich, I have found me out substance: ᴺ*in* all my labours they shall find none iniquity in me ᴺthat *were* sin.

9 And I *that am* the LORD thy God from the land of Egypt ᴿwill yet make thee to dwell in tabernacles, as in the days of the solemn feast.

10 ᴿI have also spoken by the prophets, and I have multiplied visions, and used similitudes, ᴺby the ministry of the prophets.

11 *Is there* iniquity *in* Gilead? surely they are vanity: they sacrifice bullocks in Gĭĺ-găl; yea, their altars *are* as heaps in the furrows of the fields.

12 And Jacob ᴿfled into the country of Syria, and Israel served for a wife, and for a wife he kept *sheep.*

13 ᴿAnd by a prophet the LORD brought Israel out of Egypt, and by a prophet was he preserved.

14 Ḗ-phră-ĭm provoked *him* to anger ᴺmost bitterly: therefore shall he leave his ᴺblood upon him, ᴿand his reproach shall his Lord return unto him.

CHAPTER 13

God's glory departs

WHEN Ḗ-phră-ĭm spake trembling, he exalted himself in Israel; but when he offended in Bā́-ăl, he died.

2 And now ᴺthey sin more and more, and have made them molten images of their silver, *and* idols according to their own understanding, all of it the work of the craftsmen: they say of them, Let ᴺthe men that sacrifice kiss the calves.

3 Therefore they shall be as the morning cloud, and as the early dew that passeth away, ᴿas the chaff *that* is driven with the whirlwind out of the floor, and as the smoke out of the chimney.

4 Yet ᴿI *am* the LORD thy God from the land of Egypt, and thou shalt know no god but me: for ᴿ*there is* no saviour beside me.

5 ᴿI did know thee in the wilderness, ᴿin the land of ᴺgreat drought.

6 ᴿAccording to their pasture, so were they

filled; they were filled, and their heart was exalted; therefore have they forgotten me.

7 Therefore [R]I will be unto them as a lion: as [R]a leopard by the way will I observe *them:*

8 I will meet them [R]as a bear *that is* bereaved *of her whelps,* and will rend the caul of their heart, and there will I devour them like a lion: [N]the wild beast shall tear them.

9 O Israel, thou hast destroyed thyself; but in me [N]*is* thine help.

10 [N]I will be thy king: [R]where *is any other* that may save thee in all thy cities? and thy judges of whom [R]thou saidst, Give me a king and princes?

11 [R]I gave thee a king in mine anger, and took *him* away in my wrath.

12 [R]The iniquity of Ē'-phră-ĭm *is* bound up; his sin *is* hid.

13 [R]The sorrows of a travailing woman shall come upon him: he *is* an unwise son; for he should not stay [N]long in *the place of* the breaking forth of children.

14 I will ransom them from [N]the power of the grave; I will redeem them from death: [R]O death, I will be thy plagues; O grave, I will be thy destruction: [R]repentance shall be hid from mine eyes.

15 Though he be fruitful among *his* brethren, [R]an east wind shall come, the wind of the LORD shall come up from the wilderness, and his spring shall become dry, and his fountain shall be dried up: he shall spoil the treasure of all [N]pleasant vessels.

16 Să-mâr'-ĭ-ă shall become desolate; for she hath rebelled against her God: [R]they shall fall by the sword: their infants shall be dashed in pieces, and their women with child shall be ripped up.

CHAP. **13**	
BC 725	
7 Lam. 3:10	
7 Jer. 5:6	
8 2 Sam. 17:8	
8 Heb. *the beast of the field*	
9 Heb. *in thy help*	
10 Rather, *Where is thy king?* King Hoshea being then in prison, 2 Ki. 17:4	
10 Deut. 32:38	
10 1 Sam. 8:5	
11 1 Sam. 8:7	
12 Deut. 32:34	
13 Is. 13:8	
13 Heb. *a time*	
14 Heb. *the hand*	
14 1 Cor. 15:54	
14 Jer. 15:6	
15 Jer. 4:11	
15 Heb. *vessels of desire*	
16 2 Ki. 8:12	

CHAP. **14**	
BC 725	
Joel 2:13	1
Or, *give good*	2
Heb. 13:15	2
Ps. 33:17	3
Ps. 10:14	3
Prov. 19:12	5
Or, *blossom*	5
Heb. *strike*	5
Heb. *shall go*	6
Ps. 52:8	6
Gen. 27:27	6
Jer. 15:6	7
Or, *blossom*	7
Or, *memorial*	7
Prov. 10:29	9

CHAPTER 14

Call for Israel to repent

O ISRAEL, [R]return unto the LORD thy God; for thou hast fallen by thine iniquity.

2 Take with you words, and turn to the LORD: say unto him, Take away all iniquity, and [N]receive *us* graciously: so will we render the [R]calves of our lips.

3 Ăssh'-ŭr shall not save us; [R]we will not ride upon horses: neither will we say any more to the work of our hands, *Ye are* our gods: [R]for in thee the fatherless findeth mercy.

God's promise of restoration

4 I will heal their backsliding, I will love them freely: for mine anger is turned away from him.

5 I will be as [R]the dew unto Israel: he shall [N]grow as the lily, and [N]cast forth his roots as Lĕb'-ă-nọn.

6 His branches [N]shall spread, and [R]his beauty shall be as the olive tree, and [R]his smell as Lĕb'-ă-nọn.

7 [R]They that dwell under his shadow shall return; they shall revive *as* the corn, and [N]grow as the vine: the [N]scent thereof *shall be* as the wine of Lĕb'-ă-nọn.

8 Ē'-phră-ĭm *shall say,* What have I to do any more with idols? I have heard *him,* and observed him: I *am* like a green fir tree. From me is thy fruit found.

A word to the wise

9 Who *is* wise, and he shall understand these *things?* prudent, and he shall know them? for [R]the ways of the LORD *are* right, and the just shall walk in them: but the transgressors shall fall therein.

JOEL

Little is known about Joel. A probable date for his ministry is during the reign of Joash, king of Judah, 835–796 B.C. After a locust plague Joel warned his people of a greater devastation in the crucial day of the Lord which would bring world wide judgment. Cf. 2:28 ff. with Acts 2:16ff. Ultimately Israel would triumph over heathen nations.

I. The devastation by locusts   1:1–12
II. The prophet's concern for his people   1:13–2:17
III. God's promise of restoration   2:18–3:21

CHAPTER 1

The plague of locusts

T HE word of the LORD that came to Jō'-ĕl the son of Pĕ-thū'-ĕl.

2 Hear this, ye old men, and give ear, all ye

CHAP. **1**	
BC 800	
ch. 2:2	2
Ps. 78:4	3
Deut. 28:38	4
Heb. *The residue of the palmerworm*	4

inhabitants of the land. [R]Hath this been in your days, or even in the days of your fathers?

3 [R]Tell ye your children of it, and *let* your children *tell* their children, and their children another generation.

4 [R]That[N] which the palmerworm hath left

hath the locust eaten; and that which the locust hath left hath the cankerworm eaten; and that which the cankerworm hath left hath the caterpiller eaten.

5 Awake, ye drunkards, and weep; and howl, all ye drinkers of wine, because of the new wine; ʀfor it is cut off from your mouth.

6 For ʀa nation is come up upon my land, strong, and without number, ʀwhose teeth *are* the teeth of a lion, and he hath the cheek teeth of a great lion.

7 He hath ʀlaid my vine waste, and ᴺbarked my fig tree: he hath made it clean bare, and cast *it* away; the branches thereof are made white.

8 ʀLament like a virgin girded with sackcloth for ʀthe husband of her youth.

9 ʀThe meat offering and the drink offering is cut off from the house of the Lord; the priests, the Lord's ministers, mourn.

10 The field is wasted, ʀthe land mourneth; for the corn is wasted: ʀthe new wine is ᴺdried up, the oil languisheth.

The drought

11 ʀBe ye ashamed, O ye husbandmen; howl, O ye vinedressers, for the wheat and for the barley; because the harvest of the field is perished.

12 ʀThe vine is dried up, and the fig tree languisheth; the pomegranate tree, the palm tree also, and the apple tree, *even* all the trees of the field, are withered: because ʀjoy is withered away from the sons of men.

13 ʀGird yourselves, and lament, ye priests: howl, ye ministers of the altar: come, lie all night in sackcloth, ye ministers of my God: for the meat offering and the drink offering is withholden from the house of your God.

14 ʀSanctify ye a fast, call ʀa ᴺsolemn assembly, gather the elders *and* ʀall the inhabitants of the land *into* the house of the Lord your God, and cry unto the Lord,

15 ʀAlas for the day! for ʀthe day of the Lord *is* at hand, and as a destruction from the Almighty shall it come.

16 Is not the meat cut off before our eyes, *yea,* ʀjoy and gladness from the house of our God?

17 The ᴺseed is rotten under their clods, the garners are laid desolate, the barns are broken down; for the corn is withered.

18 How do ʀthe beasts groan! the herds of cattle are perplexed, because they have no pasture; yea, the flocks of sheep are made desolate.

19 O Lord, ʀto thee will I cry: for ʀthe fire

CHAP. 1
BC 800
5 Is. 32:10
6 Prov. 30:25
6 Rev. 9:8
7 Is. 5:6
7 Heb. laid *my fig tree for a barking*
8 Is. 22:12
8 Prov. 2:17
Jer. 3:4
9 ch. 2:14
10 Jer. 12:11
10 Is. 24:7
10 Or, *ashamed*
11 Jer. 14:3, 4
12 ver. 10
12 Is. 24:11
Jer. 48:33
13 Jer. 4:8
14 2 Chr. 20:3
14 Lev. 23:36
14 Or, *day of restraint*
14 2 Chr. 20:13
15 Jer. 30:7
15 Is. 13:6, 9
16 See Deut. 12:6, 7
17 Heb. *grains*
18 Hos. 4:3
19 Ps. 50:15
19 Jer. 9:10

Or, *habitations*   19
Job 38:41   20
Ps. 104:21
1 Ki. 17:7   20

CHAP. 2
BC 800
Jer. 4:5   1
Or, *cornet*   1
Num. 10:5   1
Obad. 15   1
Zeph. 1:14
Amos 5:18   2
ch. 1:6   2
Ex. 10:14   2
Heb. *of generation and generation*   2
Gen. 2:8   3
Is. 51:3
Zech. 7:14   3
Rev. 9:7   4
Rev. 9:9   5
Jer. 8:21   6
Lam. 4:8
Nah. 2:10
Heb. *pot*   6
Or, *dart*   8
Jer. 9:21   9
John 10:1   9
Ps. 18:7   10
Is. 13:10   10
Mat. 24:29
Jer. 25:30   11
Jer. 50:34   11
Rev. 18:8
Jer. 30:7   11
Amos 5:18
Zeph. 1:15
Mal. 3:2   11

hath devoured the ᴺpastures of the wilderness, and the flame hath burned all the trees of the field.

20 The beasts of the field ʀcry also unto thee: for ʀthe rivers of waters are dried up, and the fire hath devoured the pastures of the wilderness.

CHAPTER 2

The day of the LORD

ʙLOWʀ ye the ᴺtrumpet in Zion, and ʀsound an alarm in my holy mountain: let all the inhabitants of the land tremble: for ʀthe day of the Lord cometh, for *it is* nigh at hand;

2 ʀA day of darkness and of gloominess, a day of clouds and of thick darkness, as the morning spread upon the mountains: ʀa great people and a strong; ʀthere hath not been ever the like, neither shall be any more after it, *even* to the years ᴺof many generations.

3 A fire devoureth before them; and behind them a flame burneth: the land *is* as ʀthe garden of Eden before them, ʀand behind them a desolate wilderness; yea, and nothing shall escape them.

4 ʀThe appearance of them *is* as the appearance of horses; and as horsemen, so shall they run.

5 ʀLike the noise of chariots on the tops of mountains shall they leap, like the noise of a flame of fire that devoureth the stubble, as a strong people set in battle array.

6 Before their face the people shall be much pained: ʀall faces shall gather ᴺblackness.

7 They shall run like mighty men; they shall climb the wall like men of war; and they shall march every one on his ways, and they shall not break their ranks:

8 Neither shall one thrust another; they shall walk every one in his path: and *when* they fall upon the ᴺsword, they shall not be wounded.

9 They shall run to and fro in the city; they shall run upon the wall, they shall climb up upon the houses; they shall ʀenter in at the windows ʀlike a thief.

10 ʀThe earth shall quake before them; the heavens shall tremble: ʀthe sun and the moon shall be dark, and the stars shall withdraw their shining:

11 ʀAnd the Lord shall utter his voice before his army: for his camp *is* very great: ʀfor *he is* strong that executeth his word: for the ʀday of the Lord *is* great and very terrible; and ʀwho can abide it?

Call to repentance

12 Therefore also now, saith the LORD, ᴿturn ye *even* to me with all your heart, and with fasting, and with weeping, and with mourning:

13 And ᴿrend your heart, and not ᴿyour garments, and turn unto the LORD your God: for he *is* ᴿgracious and merciful, slow to anger, and of great kindness, and repenteth him of the evil.

14 ᴿWho knoweth *if* he will return and repent, and leave ᴿa blessing behind him; *even* ᴿa meat offering and a drink offering unto the LORD your God?

15 ᴿBlow the trumpet in Zion, ᴿsanctify a fast, call a solemn assembly:

16 Gather the people, ᴿsanctify the congregation, assemble the elders, gather the children, and those that suck the breasts: ᴿlet the bridegroom go forth of his chamber, and the bride out of her closet.

17 Let the priests, the ministers of the LORD, weep ᴿbetween the porch and the altar, and let them say, ᴿSpare thy people, O LORD, and give not thine heritage to reproach, that the heathen should ᴺrule over them: ᴿwherefore should they say among the people, Where *is* their God?

God's promise of deliverance

18 Then will the LORD ᴿbe jealous for his land, ᴿand pity his people.

19 Yea, the LORD will answer and say unto his people, Behold, I will send you ᴿcorn, and wine, and oil, and ye shall be satisfied therewith: and I will no more make you a reproach among the heathen:

20 But ᴿI will remove far off from you ᴿthe northern *army,* and will drive him into a land barren and desolate, with his face toward the east sea, and his hinder part ᴿtoward the utmost sea, and his stink shall come up, and his ill savour shall come up, because ᴺhe hath done great things.

21 Fear not, O land; be glad and rejoice: for the LORD will do great things.

22 Be not afraid, ye beasts of the field: for ᴿthe pastures of the wilderness do spring, for the tree beareth her fruit, the fig tree and the vine do yield their strength.

23 Be glad then, ye children of Zion, and ᴿrejoice in the LORD your God: for he hath given you ᴺthe former rain ᴺmoderately, and he ᴿwill cause to come down for you the rain, the former rain, and the latter rain in the first *month.*

24 And the floors shall be full of wheat, and

the vats shall overflow with wine and oil.

25 And I will restore to you the years ᴿthat the locust hath eaten, the cankerworm, and the caterpiller, and the palmerworm, my great army which I sent among you.

26 And ye shall ᴿeat in plenty, and be satisfied, and praise the name of the LORD your God, that hath dealt wondrously with you: and my people shall never be ashamed.

27 And ye shall know that I *am* ᴿin the midst of Israel, and *that* ᴿI *am* the LORD your God, and none else: and my people shall never be ashamed.

The outpouring of God's spirit

28 ᴿAnd it shall come to pass afterward, *that* I ᴿwill pour out my spirit upon all flesh; ᴿand your sons and ᴿyour daughters shall prophesy, your old men shall dream dreams, your young men shall see visions:

29 And also upon ᴿthe servants and upon the handmaids in those days will I pour out my spirit.

30 And ᴿI will shew wonders in the heavens and in the earth, blood, and fire, and pillars of smoke.

31 ᴿThe sun shall be turned into darkness, and the moon into blood, ᴿbefore the great and the terrible day of the LORD come.

32 And it shall come to pass, *that* ᴿwhosoever shall call on the name of the LORD shall be delivered: for ᴿin mount Zion and in Jerusalem shall be deliverance, as the LORD hath said, and in ᴿthe remnant whom the LORD shall call.

CHAPTER 3

Judgment on the nations

FOR, behold, ᴿin those days, and in that time, when I shall bring again the captivity of Judah and Jerusalem,

2 ᴿI will also gather all nations, and will bring them down into the valley of Jĕ-hŏsh′-ă-phăt, and ᴿwill plead with them there for my people and *for* my heritage Israel, whom they have scattered among the nations, and parted my land.

3 And they have ᴿcast lots for my people; and have given a boy for an harlot, and sold a girl for wine, that they might drink.

4 Yea, and what have ye to do with me, ᴿO Tyre, and Zī′-dŏn, and all the coasts of Palestine? will ye render me a recompence? and if ye recompense me, swiftly *and* speedily will I return your recompence upon your own head;

5 Because ye have taken my silver and my

gold, and have carried into your temples my goodly ᴺpleasant things:

6 The children also of Judah and the children of Jerusalem have ye sold unto ᴺthe Grecians, that ye might remove them far from their border.

7 Behold, ᴿI will raise them out of the place whither ye have sold them, and will return your recompence upon your own head:

8 And I will sell your sons and your daughters into the hand of the children of Judah, and they shall sell them to the ᴿSă-bē'-ănś, to a people ᴿfar off: for the LORD hath spoken *it*.

The valley of decision

9 ᴿProclaim ye this among the Gentiles; ᴺPrepare war, wake up the mighty men, let all the men of war draw near; let them come up:

10 ᴿBeat your plowshares into swords, and your ᴺpruninghooks into spears: ᴿlet the weak say, I *am* strong.

11 Assemble yourselves, and come, all ye heathen, and gather yourselves together round about: thither ᴺcause ᴿthy mighty ones to come down, O LORD.

12 Let the heathen be wakened, and come up to the valley of Jĕ-hŏsh'-ă-phăt: for there will I sit to ᴿjudge all the heathen round about.

13 ᴿPut ye in the sickle, for ᴿthe harvest is ripe: come, get you down: for the ᴿpress is full, the vats overflow; for their wickedness *is* great.

14 Multitudes, multitudes in the valley of ᴺdecision: for ᴿthe day of the LORD *is* near in the valley of decision.

15 The sun and the moon shall be darkened, and the stars shall withdraw their shining.

16 The LORD also shall roar out of Zion, and utter his voice from Jerusalem; and the heavens and the earth shall shake: ᴿbut the LORD *will be* the ᴺhope of his people, and the strength of the children of Israel.

Future of Judah

17 So shall ye know that I *am* the LORD your God dwelling in Zion, my holy mountain: then shall Jerusalem be ᴺholy, and there shall no strangers pass through her any more.

18 And it shall come to pass in that day, *that* the mountains shall drop down new wine, and the hills shall flow with milk, and all the rivers of Judah shall ᴺflow with waters, and a fountain shall come forth of the house of the LORD, and shall water the valley of Shĭt'-tĭm.

19 Egypt shall be a desolation, and Ē'-dŏm shall be a desolate wilderness, for the violence *against* the children of Judah, because they have shed innocent blood in their land.

20 But Judah shall ᴺdwell for ever, and Jerusalem from generation to generation.

21 For I will ᴿcleanse their blood *that* I have not cleansed: ᴺfor the LORD dwelleth in Zion.

CHAP. 3
BC 800
5 Heb. *desirable:*
Dan. 11:38
6 Heb. *the sons of the Grecians*
7 Is. 43:5, 6
Jer. 23:8
8 Ezek. 23:42
8 Jer. 6:20
9 Ezek. 38:7
9 Heb. *Sanctify*
10 Is. 2:4
Mic. 4:3
10 Or, *scythes*
10 Zech. 12:8
11 Or, *the LORD shall bring down*
11 Ps. 103:20
Is. 13:3
12 Ps. 96:13
Is. 2:4
13 Mat. 13:39
Rev. 14:15
13 Jer. 51:33
13 Is. 63:3
Rev. 14:19

Or, *concision*, or, 14
threshing
ch. 2:1   14
Is. 51:5, 6   16
Heb. *place of*   16
repair, or,
harbour
Heb. *holiness*   17
Heb. *go*   18
Or, *abide*   20
Is. 4:4   21
Or, *even I the*   21
LORD that dwelleth in Zion

AMOS

The author of the book of Amos came from Tekoa to deliver God's message in the northern kingdom of Israel. His ministry began about 760 B.C. and may have lasted less than a decade. Amos boldly denounced the social evils prevailing in apostate, self-complacent, prosperous Israel. He warns of judgment to come.

   I. God's judgment on nations   1:1 – 2:16
  II. Israel's condemnation – five visions   3:1 – 9:10
 III. Restoration promised   9:11 – 15

CHAPTER 1

Amos's time and background

THE words of Amos, who was among the herdmen of ᴿTĕ-kō'-ă, which he saw concerning Israel in the days of ŭz-zī'-ăh king of Judah, and in the days of ᴿJĕr-ŏ-bō'-ăm the son of Jō'-ăsh king of Israel, two years before the ᴿearthquake.

2 And he said, The LORD will ᴿroar from Zion, and utter his voice from Jerusalem; and the habitations of the shepherds shall mourn, and the top of ᴿCarmel shall wither.

Prophecy against Damascus

3 Thus saith the LORD; For three transgressions of ᴿDamascus, ᴺand for four, I will not ᴺturn away *the punishment* thereof; because they have threshed Gilead with threshing instruments of iron:

4 ᴿBut I will send a fire into the house of Hă-zā'-ĕl, which shall devour the palaces of Bĕn-hā'-dăd.

5 I will break also the ᴿbar of Damascus, and cut off the inhabitant from ᴺthe plain of Ā'-vĕn, and him that holdeth the sceptre from

---

CHAP. 1
BC 787
1 2 Sam. 14:2
1 ch. 7:10
1 Zech. 14:5
2 Joel 3:16
2 1 Sam. 25:2
Is. 33:9

Is. 8:4   3
Or, *yea, for four*   3
Or, *convert it*, or,   3
let it be quiet
Jer. 17:27   4
Jer. 51:30   5
Or, *Bikathaven*   5

Nthe house of Eden: and the people of Syria shall go into captivity unto Kĭr, saith the LORD.

Prophecy against Gaza and Tyrus

6 Thus saith the LORD; For three transgressions of RGā'-ză, and for four, I will not turn away *the punishment* thereof; because they Ncarried away captive the whole captivity, to deliver *them* up to Ē'-dom:

7 RBut I will send a fire on the wall of Gā'-ză, which shall devour the palaces thereof:

8 And I will cut off the inhabitant Rfrom Ăsh'-dŏd, and him that holdeth the sceptre from ăsh'-kĕ-lon, and I will Rturn mine hand against ĕk'-rŏn: and Rthe remnant of the Philistines shall perish, saith the Lord GOD.

9 Thus saith the LORD; For three transgressions of RTȳ'-rŭs, and for four, I will not turn away *the punishment* thereof; because they delivered up the whole captivity to Ē'-dom, and remembered not Nthe brotherly covenant:

10 But I will send a fire on the wall of Tȳ'-rŭs, which shall devour the palaces thereof.

Prophecy against Edom and Ammon

11 Thus saith the LORD; For three transgressions of RĒ'-dom, and for four, I will not turn away *the punishment* thereof; because he did pursue his brother with the sword, and Ndid cast off all pity, and his anger did tear perpetually, and he kept his wrath for ever:

12 But RI will send a fire upon Tē'-măn, which shall devour the palaces of Bŏz'-răh.

13 Thus saith the LORD; For three transgressions of Rthe children of Ammon, and for four, I will not turn away *the punishment* thereof; because they have Nripped up the women with child of Gilead, that they might enlarge their border:

14 But I will kindle a fire in the wall of RRăb'-băh, and it shall devour the palaces thereof, Rwith shouting in the day of battle, with a tempest in the day of the whirlwind:

15 And Rtheir king shall go into captivity, he and his princes together, saith the LORD.

CHAPTER 2

Prophecy against Moab

THUS saith the LORD; For three transgressions of Moab, and for four, I will not turn away *the punishment* thereof; because he Rburned the bones of the king of Ē'-dom into lime:

2 But I will send a fire upon Moab, and it

CHAP. 1
BC 787
5 Or, *Betheden*
6 Jer. 47:4, 5
6 Or, *carried them away with an entire captivity*
7 Jer. 47:1
8 Zeph. 2:4
8 Ps. 81:14
8 Ezek. 25:16
9 Is. 23:1
9 Heb. *the covenant of brethren,* 1 Ki. 5:1
11 Is. 21:11 Jer. 49:8
11 Heb. *corrupted his compassions*
12 Obad. 9, 10
13 Jer. 49:1 Ezek. 25:2
13 Or, *divided the mountains*
14 Deut. 3:11
14 ch. 2:2
15 Jer. 49:3

CHAP. 2
BC 787
1 2 Ki. 3:27

Jer. 48:41   2
Num. 24:17   3
Jer. 48:7
Lev. 26:14   4
Is. 28:15   4
Jer. 16:19
Ezek. 20:13, 16, 18   4
Jer. 17:27   5
Hos. 8:14
Is. 29:21   6
ch. 5:12   7
Ezek. 22:11   7
Or, *young woman*   7
Lev. 20:3   7
Ex. 22:26   8
1 Cor. 8:10   8
Or, *such as have fined,* or, *mulcted*   8
Num. 21:24   9
Deut. 2:31
Is. 5:24   9
Mal. 4:1
Ex. 12:51   10
Deut. 2:7   10
Num. 6:2   11
Judg. 13:5
Is. 30:10   12
Jer. 11:21
Mic. 2:6
Is. 1:14   13
Or, *I will press your place, as a cart full of sheaves presseth*   13
Jer. 9:23   14
Ps. 33:16   14
Heb. *his soul,* or, *life*   14

---

shall devour the palaces of RKer'-ĭ-ōth: and Moab shall die with tumult, with shouting, *and* with the sound of the trumpet:

3 And I will cut off Rthe judge from the midst thereof, and will slay all the princes thereof with him, saith the LORD.

Prophecy against Judah

4 Thus saith the LORD; For three transgressions of Judah, and for four, I will not turn away *the punishment* thereof; Rbecause they have despised the law of the LORD, and have not kept his commandments, and Rtheir lies caused them to err, Rafter the which their fathers have walked:

5 RBut I will send a fire upon Judah, and it shall devour the palaces of Jerusalem.

Prophecy against Israel

6 Thus saith the LORD; For three transgressions of Israel, and for four, I will not turn away *the punishment* thereof; because Rthey sold the righteous for silver, and the poor for a pair of shoes;

7 That pant after the dust of the earth on the head of the poor, and Rturn aside the way of the meek: Rand a man and his father will go in unto the *same* Nmaid, Rto profane my holy name:

8 And they lay *themselves* down upon clothes Rlaid to pledge Rby every altar, and they drink the wine of Nthe condemned *in* the house of their god.

9 Yet destroyed I the RAmorite before them, whose height *was* like the height of the cedars, and he *was* strong as the oaks; yet I Rdestroyed his fruit from above, and his roots from beneath.

10 Also RI brought you up from the land of Egypt, and Rled you forty years through the wilderness, to possess the land of the Amorite.

11 And I raised up of your sons for prophets, and of your young men for RNazarites. *Is it* not even thus, O ye children of Israel? saith the LORD.

12 But ye gave the Nazarites wine to drink; and commanded the prophets, Rsaying, Prophesy not.

13 RBehold, NI am pressed under you, as a cart is pressed *that is* full of sheaves.

14 RTherefore the flight shall perish from the swift, and the strong shall not strengthen his force, Rneither shall the mighty deliver Nhimself:

15 Neither shall he stand that handleth the bow; and *he that is* swift of foot shall not deliver *himself:* neither shall he that rideth the horse deliver himself.

16 *And he that is* ^Ncourageous among the mighty shall flee away naked in that day, saith the Lord.

CHAPTER 3

God has spoken to the prophets

HEAR this word that the Lord hath spoken against you, O children of Israel, against the whole family which I brought up from the land of Egypt, saying,

2 ^RYou only have I known of all the families of the earth: ^Rtherefore I will ^Npunish you for all your iniquities.

3 Can two walk together, except they be agreed?

4 Will a lion roar in the forest, when he hath no prey? will a young lion ^Ncry out of his den, if he have taken nothing?

5 Can a bird fall in a snare upon the earth, where no gin *is* for him? shall *one* take up a snare from the earth, and have taken nothing at all?

6 Shall a trumpet be blown in the city, and the people ^Nnot be afraid? ^Rshall there be evil in a city, ^Nand the Lord hath not done *it?*

7 Surely the Lord God will do nothing, but ^Rhe revealeth his secret unto his servants the prophets.

8 The lion hath roared, who will not fear? the Lord God hath spoken, ^Rwho can but prophesy?

Punishment of Israel

9 Publish in the palaces at Ăsh'-dŏd, and in the palaces in the land of Egypt, and say, Assemble yourselves upon the mountains of Să-mâr'-ĭ-ă, and behold the great tumults in the midst thereof, and the ^Noppressed in the midst thereof.

10 For they ^Rknow not to do right, saith the Lord, who store up violence and ^Nrobbery in their palaces.

11 Therefore thus saith the Lord God; An adversary *there shall be* even round about the land; and he shall bring down thy strength from thee, and thy palaces shall be spoiled.

12 Thus saith the Lord; As the shepherd ^Ntaketh out of the mouth of the lion two legs, or a piece of an ear; so shall the children of Israel be taken out that dwell in Să-mâr'-ĭ-ă in the corner of a bed, and ^Nin Damascus *in a* couch.

13 Hear ye, and testify in the house of Jacob, saith the Lord God, the God of hosts,

14 That in the day that I shall ^Nvisit the transgressions of Israel upon him I will also

visit the altars of Beth-el: and the horns of the altar shall be cut off, and fall to the ground.

15 And I will smite ^Rthe winter house with ^Rthe summer house; and ^Rthe houses of ivory shall perish, and the great houses shall have an end, saith the Lord.

CHAPTER 4

Greed of the women

HEAR this word, ye ^Rkine of Bā'-shăn, that *are* in the mountain of Să-mâr'-ĭ-ă, which oppress the poor, which crush the needy, which say to their masters, Bring, and let us drink.

2 ^RThe Lord God hath sworn by his holiness, that, lo, the days shall come upon you, that he will take you away ^Rwith hooks, and your posterity with fishhooks.

3 And ^Rye shall go out at the breaches, every *cow at that which is* before her; and ^Nye shall cast *them* into the palace, saith the Lord.

Hypocritical worship

4 ^RCome to Beth-el, and transgress; at ^RGĭl'-găl multiply transgression; and ^Rbring your sacrifices every morning, ^R*and* your tithes after ^Nthree years:

5 ^RAnd ^Noffer a sacrifice of thanksgiving with leaven, and proclaim *and* publish ^Rthe free offerings: for ^Nthis liketh you, O ye children of Israel, saith the Lord God.

God's chastening rejected

6 And I also have given you cleanness of teeth in all your cities, and want of bread in all your places: ^Ryet have ye not returned unto me, saith the Lord.

7 And also I have withholden the rain from you, when *there were* yet three months to the harvest: and I caused it to rain upon one city, and caused it not to rain upon another city: one piece was rained upon, and the piece whereupon it rained not withered.

8 So two *or* three cities wandered unto one city, to drink water; but they were not satisfied: yet have ye not returned unto me, saith the Lord.

9 ^RI have smitten you with blasting and mildew: ^Nwhen your gardens and your vineyards and your fig trees and your olive trees increased, ^Rthe palmerworm devoured *them:* yet have ye not returned unto me, saith the Lord.

10 I have sent among you the pestilence ^Rafter^N the manner of Egypt: your young men have I slain with the sword, ^Nand have taken away your horses; and I have made the stink

of your camps to come up unto your nostrils: yet have ye not returned unto me, saith the LORD.

11 I have overthrown *some* of you, as God overthrew ᴿSodom and Gō-mŏr'-răh, and ye were as a firebrand plucked out of the burning: yet have ye not returned unto me, saith the LORD.

12 Therefore thus will I do unto thee, O Israel: *and* because I will do this unto thee, ᴿprepare to meet thy God, O Israel.

13 For, lo, he that formeth the mountains, and createth the ᴺwind, ᴿand declareth unto man what *is* his thought, that maketh the morning darkness, ᴿand treadeth upon the high places of the earth, ᴿThe LORD, The God of hosts, *is* his name.

CHAPTER 5

Lamentation for Israel

HEAR ye this word which I ᴿtake up against you, *even* a lamentation, O house of Israel.

2 The virgin of Israel is fallen; she shall no more rise: she is forsaken upon her land; *there is* none to raise her up.

3 For thus saith the Lord GOD; The city that went out *by* a thousand shall leave an hundred, and that which went forth *by* an hundred shall leave ten, to the house of Israel.

Call to repentance

4 For thus saith the LORD unto the house of Israel, ᴿSeek ye me, ᴿand ye shall live:

5 But seek not ᴿBeth-el, nor enter into Gĭl'-găl, and pass not to ᴿBē̆er-shē'-bă: for Gĭl'-găl shall surely go into captivity, and ᴿBeth-el shall come to nought.

6 Seek the LORD, and ye shall live; lest he break out like fire in the house of Joseph, and devour *it,* and *there be* none to quench *it* in Beth-el.

7 Ye who ᴿturn judgment to wormwood, and leave off righteousness in the earth,

8 *Seek him* that maketh the ᴿseven stars and ō-rī'-ǫn, and turneth the shadow of death into the morning, ᴿand maketh the day dark with night: that ᴿcalleth for the waters of the sea, and poureth them out upon the face of the earth: ᴿThe LORD *is* his name:

9 That strengtheneth the ᴺspoiled against the strong, so that the spoiled shall come against the fortress.

Perversion of truth and justice

10 ᴿThey hate him that rebuketh in the gate, and they ᴿabhor him that speaketh uprightly.

11 Forasmuch therefore as your treading *is* upon the poor, and ye take from him burdens of wheat: ᴿye have built houses of hewn stone, but ye shall not dwell in them; ye have planted ᴺpleasant vineyards, but ye shall not drink wine of them.

12 For I know your manifold transgressions and your mighty sins: ᴿthey afflict the just, they take ᴺa bribe, and they ᴿturn aside the poor in the gate *from their right.*

13 Therefore ᴿthe prudent shall keep silence in that time; for it *is* an evil time.

Call to establish justice

14 Seek good, and not evil, that ye may live: and so the LORD, the God of hosts, shall be with you, ᴿas ye have spoken.

15 ᴿHate the evil, and love the good, and establish judgment in the gate: ᴿit may be that the LORD God of hosts will be gracious unto the remnant of Joseph.

16 Therefore the LORD, the God of hosts, the Lord, saith thus; Wailing *shall be* in all streets; and they shall say in all the highways, Alas! alas! and they shall call the husbandman to mourning, and ᴿsuch as are skilful of lamentation to wailing.

17 And in all vineyards *shall be* wailing: for ᴿI will pass through thee, saith the LORD.

18 ᴿWoe unto you that desire the day of the LORD! to what end *is* it for you? ᴿthe day of the LORD *is* darkness, and not light.

19 ᴿAs if a man did flee from a lion, and a bear met him; or went into the house, and leaned his hand on the wall, and a serpent bit him.

20 *Shall* not the day of the LORD *be* darkness, and not light? even very dark, and no brightness in it?

21 ᴿI hate, I despise your feast days, and ᴿI will not ᴺsmell in your solemn assemblies.

22 ᴿThough ye offer me burnt offerings and your meat offerings, I will not accept *them:* neither will I regard the ᴺpeace offerings of your fat beasts.

23 Take thou away from me the noise of thy songs; for I will not hear the melody of thy viols.

24 ᴿBut let judgment ᴺrun down as waters, and righteousness as a mighty stream.

The coming oppression and exile

25 ᴿHave ye offered unto me sacrifices and offerings in the wilderness forty years, O house of Israel?

26 But ye have borne ᴺthe tabernacle ᴿof your Moloch and Chī'-ŭn your images, the star of your god, which ye made to yourselves.

27 Therefore will I cause you to go into captivity Rbeyond Damascus, saith the LORD, Rwhose name *is* The God of hosts.

CHAPTER 6

WOE Rto them *that* Nare at ease in Zion, and trust in the mountain of Să-mâr′-ĭ-ă, *which are* named Rchief N of the nations, to whom the house of Israel came!

2 RPass ye unto RCăl′-nēh, and see; and from thence go ye to RHā′-măth the great: then go down to Gath of the Philstines: R*be they* better than these kingdoms? or their border greater than your border?

3 Ye that Rput far away the Revil day, Rand cause Rthe Nseat of violence to come near;

4 That lie upon beds of ivory, and Nstretch themselves upon their couches, and eat the lambs out of the flock, and the calves out of the midst of the stall;

5 RThat Nchant to the sound of the viol, *and* invent to themselves instruments of musick, Rlike David;

6 That drink Nwine in bowls, and anoint themselves with the chief ointments: Rbut they are not grieved for the Naffliction of Joseph.

7 Therefore now shall they go captive with the first that go captive, and the banquet of them that stretched themselves shall be removed.

8 RThe Lord GOD hath sworn by himself, saith the LORD the God of hosts, I abhor Rthe excellency of Jacob, and hate his palaces: therefore will I deliver up the city with all Nthat is therein.

9 And it shall come to pass, if there remain ten men in one house, that they shall die.

10 And a man's uncle shall take him up, and he that burneth him, to bring out the bones out of the house, and shall say unto him that *is* by the sides of the house, *Is there* yet *any* with thee? and he shall say, No. Then shall he say, RHold thy tongue: Rfor Nwe may not make mention of the name of the LORD.

11 For, behold, Rthe Lord commandeth, Rand he will smite the great house with Nbreaches, and the little house with clefts.

12 Shall horses run upon the rock? will *one* plow *there* with oxen? for Rye have turned judgment into gall, and the fruit of righteousness into hemlock:

13 Ye which rejoice in a thing of nought, which say, Have we not taken to us horns by our own strength?

14 But, behold, RI will raise up against you a nation, O house of Israel, saith the LORD the God of hosts; and they shall afflict you from the Rentering in of Hē′-măth unto the Nriver of the wilderness.

CHAPTER 7

Grasshoppers, fire, and plumbline

THUS hath the Lord GOD shewed unto me; and, behold, he formed Ngrasshoppers in the beginning of the shooting up of the latter growth; and, lo, *it was* the latter growth after the king's mowings.

2 And it came to pass, *that* when they had made an end of eating the grass of the land, then I said, O Lord GOD, forgive, I beseech thee: Rby N whom shall Jacob arise? for he *is* small.

3 RThe LORD repented for this: It shall not be, saith the LORD.

4 Thus hath the Lord GOD shewed unto me: and, behold, the Lord GOD called to contend by fire, and it devoured the great deep, and did eat up a part.

5 Then said I, O Lord GOD, cease, I beseech thee: Rby whom shall Jacob arise? for he *is* small.

6 The LORD repented for this: This also shall not be, saith the Lord GOD.

7 Thus he shewed me: and, behold, the Lord stood upon a wall *made* by a plumbline, with a plumbline in his hand.

8 And the LORD said unto me, Amos, what seest thou? And I said, A plumbline. Then said the Lord, Behold, RI will set a plumbline in the midst of my people Israel: RI will not again pass by them any more:

9 RAnd the high places of Isaac shall be desolate, and the sanctuaries of Israel shall be laid waste; and RI will rise against the house of Jĕr-ŏ-bō′-ăm with the sword.

Amos commanded to leave Bethel

10 Then Ăm-ă-zī′-ăh Rthe priest of Beth-el sent to RJĕr-ŏ-bō′-ăm king of Israel, saying, Amos hath conspired against thee in the midst of the house of Israel: the land is not able to bear all his words.

11 For thus Amos saith, Jĕr-ŏ-bō′-ăm shall die by the sword, and Israel shall surely be led away captive out of their own land.

12 Also Ăm-ă-zī′-ăh said unto Amos, O thou seer, go, flee thee away into the land of Judah, and there eat bread, and prophesy there:

13 But Rprophesy not again any more at Beth-el: Rfor it *is* the king's Nchapel, and it *is* the Nking's court.

Amos replies

14 Then answered Amos, and said to Ăm-ă-zī′-ăh, I *was* no prophet, neither *was* I Ra prophet's son; Rbut I *was* an herdman, and a gatherer of Nsycomore fruit:

15 And the LORD took me Nas I followed the

flock, and the LORD said unto me, Go, prophesy unto my people Israel.

16 Now therefore hear thou the word of the LORD: Thou sayest, Prophesy not against Israel, and ᴿdrop not *thy word* against the house of Isaac.

17 ᴿTherefore thus saith the LORD; ᴿThy wife shall be an harlot in the city, and thy sons and thy daughters shall fall by the sword, and thy land shall be divided by line; and thou shalt die in a polluted land: and Israel shall surely go into captivity forth of his land.

CHAPTER 8

Vison of a basket of summer fruit

THUS hath the Lord GOD shewed unto me: and behold a basket of summer fruit.

2 And he said, Amos, what seest thou? And I said, A basket of summer fruit. Then said the LORD unto me, ᴿThe end is come upon my people of Israel; ᴿI will not again pass by them any more.

3 And ᴿthe songs of the temple ᴺshall be howlings in that day, saith the Lord GOD: *there shall be* many dead bodies in every place; ᴿthey shall cast *them* forth ᴺwith silence.

Judgment against deceitful merchants

4 Hear this, O ye that ᴿswallow up the needy, even to make the poor of the land to fail,

5 Saying, When will the ᴺnew moon be gone, that we may sell corn? and ᴿthe sabbath, that we may ᴺset forth wheat, ᴿmaking the ē'-phäh small, and the shē'-kĕl great, and ᴺfalsifying the balances by deceit?

6 That we may buy the poor for ᴿsilver, and the needy for a pair of shoes; *yea,* and sell the refuse of the wheat?

7 The LORD hath sworn by ᴿthe excellency of Jacob, Surely ᴿI will never forget any of their works.

8 ᴿShall not the land tremble for this, and every one mourn that dwelleth therein? and it shall rise up wholly as a flood; and it shall be cast out and drowned, ᴿas *by* the flood of Egypt.

Day of mourning for spiritual famine

9 And it shall come to pass in that day, saith the Lord GOD, ᴿthat I will cause the sun to go down at noon, and I will darken the earth in the clear day:

10 And I will turn your feasts into mourning, and all your songs into lamentation; ᴿand I will bring up sackcloth upon all loins, and baldness upon every head; ᴿand I will make it

---

CHAP. **7**
BC 787
16 Ezek. 21:2
Mic. 2:6
17 Jer. 28:12
& 29:21, 32
17 Is. 13:16
Lam. 5:11
Hos. 4:13
Zech. 14:2

CHAP. **8**
BC 787
2 Ezek. 7:2
2 ch. 7:8
3 ch. 5:23
3 Heb. *shall howl*
3 ch. 6:9, 10
3 Heb. *be silent*
4 Ps. 14:4
Prov. 30:14
5 Or, *month*
5 Neh. 13:15
5 Heb. *open*
5 Mic. 6:10
5 Heb. *perverting the balances of deceit*
6 ch. 2:6
7 ch. 6:8
7 Hos. 8:13
8 Hos. 4:3
8 ch. 9:5
9 Job 5:14
Is. 13:10
& 59:9, 10
Jer. 15:9
Mic. 3:6
10 Is. 15:2, 3
Jer. 48:37
Ezek. 27:31
10 Jer. 6:26
Zech. 12:10

1 Sam. 3:1 **11**
Ps. 74:9
Ezek. 7:26
Hos. 4:15 **14**
Deut. 34:3 **14**
Heb. *way:* **14**
Acts 9:2 &
19:9, 23 &
24:14
ch. 5:5 **14**

CHAP. **9**
BC 787
Or, *chapter, or,* **1**
knop
Ps. 68:21 **1**
Hab. 3:13
Or, *wound them* **1**
ch. 2:14 **1**
Ps. 139:8 **2**
Jer. 51:53 **2**
Lev. 26:33 **4**
Lev. 17:10 **4**
Mic. 1:4 **5**
ch. 8:8 **5**
Ps. 104:3 **6**
Or, *spheres* **6**
Heb. *ascensions* **6**
Or, *bundle* **6**
ch. 5:8 **6**
ch. 4:13 **6**
Jer. 47:4 **7**
Deut. 2:23 **7**
Jer. 47:4
ch. 1:5 **7**
ver. 4 **8**
Jer. 30:11
Obad. 16, 17 **8**

---

as the mourning of an only *son,* and the end thereof as a bitter day.

11 Behold, the days come, saith the Lord GOD, that I will send a famine in the land, not a famine of bread, nor a thirst for water, but ᴿof hearing the words of the LORD:

12 And they shall wander from sea to sea, and from the north even to the east, they shall run to and fro to seek the word of the LORD, and shall not find *it.*

13 In that day shall the fair virgins and young men faint for thirst.

14 They that ᴿswear by ᴿthe sin of Să-mär'-ĭ-ă, and say, Thy god, O Dan, liveth; and, The ᴺmanner of ᴿBēĕr-shē'-bă liveth; even they shall fall, and never rise up again.

CHAPTER 9

Vision of God destroying the idolaters

I SAW the Lord standing upon the altar: and he said, Smite the ᴺlintel of the door, that the posts may shake: and ᴿcutᴺ them in the head, all of them; and I will slay the last of them with the sword: ᴿhe that fleeth of them shall not flee away, and he that escapeth of them shall not be delivered.

2 ᴿThough they dig into hell, thence shall mine hand take them; ᴿthough they climb up to heaven, thence will I bring them down:

3 And though they hide themselves in the top of Carmel, I will search and take them out thence; and though they be hid from my sight in the bottom of the sea, thence will I command the serpent, and he shall bite them:

4 And though they go into captivity before their enemies, ᴿthence will I command the sword, and it shall slay them: and ᴿI will set mine eyes upon them for evil, and not for good.

The LORD will save a remnant

5 And the Lord GOD of hosts *is* he that toucheth the land, and it shall ᴿmelt, ᴿand all that dwell therein shall mourn: and it shall rise up wholly like a flood; and shall be drowned, as *by* the flood of Egypt.

6 *It is* he that buildeth his ᴿstoriesᴺᴺ in the heaven, and hath founded his ᴺtroop in the earth; he that ᴿcalleth for the waters of the sea, and poureth them out upon the face of the earth: ᴿThe LORD *is* his name.

7 *Are* ye not as children of the Ē-thĭ-ō'-pĭ-ăns unto me, O children of Israel? saith the LORD. Have not I brought up Israel out of the land of Egypt? and the ᴿPhilistines from ᴿCăph'-tôr, and the Syrians from ᴿKĭr?

8 Behold, ᴿthe eyes of the Lord GOD *are* upon the sinful kingdom, and I ᴿwill destroy it

from off the face of the earth; saving that I will not utterly destroy the house of Jacob, saith the LORD.

9 For, lo, I will command, and I will ᴺsift the house of Israel among all nations, like as *corn* is sifted in a sieve, yet shall not the least ᴺgrain fall upon the earth.

10 All the sinners of my people shall die by the sword, ᴿwhich say, The evil shall not overtake nor prevent us.

Restoration promised

11 ᴿIn that day will I raise up the tabernacle of David that is fallen, and ᴺclose up the breaches thereof; and I will raise up his ruins, and I will build it as in the days of old:

12 ᴿThat they may possess the remnant of

CHAP. **9**	
BC 787	
9 Heb. *cause to move*	
9 Heb. *stone*	
10 ch. 6:3	
11 Acts 15:16	
11 Heb. *hedge, or, wall*	
12 Obad. 19	
12 Num. 24:18	
12 Heb. *upon whom my name is called*	
Lev. 26:5	13
Heb. *draweth forth*	13
Joel 3:18	13
Or, *new wine*	13
Jer. 30:3	14
Is. 61:4	14
Ezek. 34:28	15

ᴿE′-dom, and of all the heathen, ᴺwhich are called by my name, saith the LORD that doeth this.

13 Behold, ᴿthe days come, saith the LORD, that the plowman shall overtake the reaper, and the treader of grapes him that ᴺsoweth seed; ᴿand the mountains shall drop ᴺsweet wine, and all the hills shall melt.

14 ᴿAnd I will bring again the captivity of my people of Israel, and ᴿthey shall build the waste cities, and inhabit *them;* and they shall plant vineyards, and drink the wine thereof; they shall also make gardens, and eat the fruit of them.

15 And I will plant them upon their land, and ᴿthey shall no more be pulled up out of their land which I have given them, saith the LORD thy God.

OBADIAH

The prophet Obadiah, about whom nothing is known, in all likelihood was the author of the fourth book of the minor prophets. The message primarily is a rebuke for Edom, which apparently prided itself in being more fortunate than Judah. This may be in response to an Edomite attack on Jehoram, II Chron. 21:16, 17 or on Ahaz, II Chron. 28:17.

OUTLINE:
   I. Edom's security—Judah's calamity   vss. 1–14
  II. Edom's fate—Judah's triumph   vss. 15–21

The destruction of Edom

THE vision of ō-bă-dī′-ăh. Thus saith the Lord GOD ᴿconcerning E′-dom; ᴿWe have heard a rumour from the LORD, and an ambassador is sent among the heathen, Arise ye, and let us rise up against her in battle.

2 Behold, I have made thee small among the heathen: thou art greatly despised.

3 The pride of thine heart hath deceived thee, thou that dwellest in the clefts of the rock, whose habitation *is* high; ᴿthat saith in his heart, Who shall bring me down to the ground?

4 ᴿThough thou exalt *thyself* as the eagle, and though thou ᴿset thy nest among the stars, thence will I bring thee down, saith the LORD.

5 If ᴿthieves came to thee, if robbers by night, (how art thou cut off!) would they not have stolen till they had enough? if the grape-gatherers came to thee, ᴿwould they not leave ᴺ*some* grapes?

6 How are *the things* of Esau searched out! *how* are his hidden things sought up!

7 All the men of thy confederacy have

BC 587	
1 Is. 21:11	
Ezek. 25:12	
Joel 3:19	
Mal. 1:3	
1 Jer. 49:14	
3 Is. 14:13-15	
Rev. 18:7	
4 Job 20:6	
4 Hab. 2:9	
5 Jer. 49:9	
5 Deut. 24:21	
5 Or, *gleanings?*	
Jer. 38:22	7
Heb. *the men of thy peace*	7
Heb. *the men of thy bread*	7
Is. 19:11	7
Or, *of it*	7
Job 5:12	8
Is. 29:14	
Ps. 76:5	9
Jer. 49:7	9
Gen. 27:41	10
Ezek. 35:9	10
Or, *carried away his substance*	11
Nah. 3:10	11
Or, *do not behold, etc.*	12
Mic. 4:11	12
Prov. 17:5	12

brought thee *even* to the border: ᴿtheᴺ men that were at peace with thee have deceived thee, *and* prevailed against thee; ᴺ*they that eat thy bread have laid a wound under thee:* ᴿ*there is* none understanding ᴺin him.

8 ᴿShall I not in that day, saith the LORD, even destroy the wise *men* out of E′-dom, and understanding out of the mount of Esau?

9 And thy ᴿmighty *men,* O ᴿTē′-măn, shall be dismayed, to the end that every one of the mount of Esau may be cut off by slaughter.

Cause of the judgment

10 For *thy* ᴿviolence against thy brother Jacob shame shall cover thee, and ᴿthou shalt be cut off for ever.

11 In the day that thou stoodest on the other side, in the day that the strangers ᴺcarried away captive his forces, and foreigners entered into his gates, and ᴿcast lots upon Jerusalem, even thou *wast* as one of them.

12 But ᴺthou shouldest not have ᴿlooked on the day of thy brother in the day that he became a stranger; neither shouldest thou have ᴿrejoiced over the children of Judah in the day of their destruction; neither shouldest

thou have ᴺspoken proudly in the day of distress.

13 Thou shouldest not have entered into the gate of my people in the day of their calamity; yea, thou shouldest not have looked on their affliction in the day of their calamity, nor have laid *hands* on their ᴺsubstance in the day of their calamity;

14 Neither shouldest thou have stood in the crossway, to cut off those of his that did escape; neither shouldest thou have ᴺdelivered up those of his that did remain in the day of distress.

Judgment upon all nations

15 ᴿFor the day of the Lᴏʀᴅ *is* near upon all the heathen: ᴿas thou hast done, it shall be done unto thee: thy reward shall return upon thine own head.

16 ᴿFor as ye have drunk upon my holy mountain, *so* shall all the heathen drink continually, yea, they shall drink, and they shall ᴺswallow down, and they shall be as though they had not been.

Restoration of all Israel

17 But upon mount Zion ᴿshall be ᴺdeliverance, and ᴺthere shall be holiness; and the house of Jacob shall possess their possessions.

18 And the house of Jacob ᴿshall be a fire, and the house of Joseph a flame, and the house of Esau for stubble, and they shall kindle in them, and devour them; and there shall not be *any* remaining of the house of Esau; for the Lᴏʀᴅ hath spoken *it*.

19 And *they of* the south shall possess the mount of Esau; ᴿand *they of* the plain the Philistines: and they shall possess the fields of Ē′-phră-ĭm, and the fields of Să-mâr′-ĭ-ă: and Benjamin *shall possess* Gilead.

20 And the captivity of this host of the children of Israel *shall possess* that of the Canaanites, *even* ᴿunto Zăr′-ĕ-phăth; and the captivity of Jerusalem, ᴺwhich *is* in Sĕ-phâr′-ăd, ᴿshall possess the cities of the south.

21 And ᴿsaviours shall come up on mount Zion to judge the mount of Esau; and the ᴿkingdom shall be the Lᴏʀᴅ's.

BC 587	
12 Heb. *magnified thy mouth*	
13 Or, *forces*	
14 Or, *shut up,* Ps. 31:8	
15 Ezek. 30:3	
15 Hab. 2:8	
16 Joel 3:17	
16 Or, *sup up*	
Amos 9:8	17
Or, *they that escape*	17
Or, *it shall be holy*	17
Zech. 12:6	18
Zeph. 2:7	19
1 Ki. 17:9	20
Or, *shall possess that which is in Sepharad*	20
Jer. 32:44	20
Jas. 5:20	21
Rev. 11:15	21

JONAH

Nowhere is the author of the book of Jonah clearly identified. It may have been written by Jonah the son of Amittai who is the central character. Among the minor prophets, this book is distinctive as a narrative telling of Jonah's personal experience. If Jonah is identified with the prophet bearing the same name in II Kings 14:25, then he can be dated approximately from 800–750 B.C. Note the references by Jesus to Jonah: Matt. 12:39–41 and Luke 11:29–30.

OUTLINE:
    I. Jonah's disobedience and return   1:1–2:10
    II. The Ninevites heed Jonah's warning   3:1–10
    III. Jonah's anger—God's mercy   4:1–11

CHAPTER 1

Jonah's disobedience

Nᴏᴡ the word of the Lᴏʀᴅ came unto ᴺJonah the son of Ă-mĭt′-tāĭ, saying,

2 Arise, go to Nĭn′-ē-vēh, that ᴿgreat city, and cry against it; for ᴿtheir wickedness is come up before me.

3 But Jonah rose up to flee unto Tarshish from the presence of the Lᴏʀᴅ, and went down to ᴿJoppa; and he found a ship going to Tarshish: so he paid the fare thereof, and went down into it, to go with them unto Tarshish ᴿfrom the presence of the Lᴏʀᴅ.

4 But ᴿthe Lᴏʀᴅ ᴺsent out a great wind into the sea, and there was a mighty tempest in the sea, so that the ship was ᴺlike to be broken.

5 Then the mariners were afraid, and cried every man unto his god, and cast forth the wares that *were* in the ship into the sea, to lighten *it* of them. But Jonah was gone down ᴿinto the sides of the ship; and he lay, and was fast asleep.

6 So the shipmaster came to him, and said unto him, What meanest thou, O sleeper? arise, ᴿcall upon thy God, ᴿif so be that God will think upon us, that we perish not.

Jonah thrown into the sea

7 And they said every one to his fellow, Come, and let us ᴿcast lots, that we may know for whose cause this evil *is* upon us. So they cast lots, and the lot fell upon Jonah.

8 Then said they unto him, ᴿTell us, we pray thee, for whose cause this evil *is* upon us; What *is* thine occupation? and whence comest thou? what *is* thy country? and of what people *art* thou?

CHAP. 1	
BC 862	
1 Called, Mat. 12:39, *Jonas*	
2 Gen. 10:11	
2 Gen. 18:20	
3 Josh. 19:46	
3 Gen. 4:16	
4 Ps. 107:25	
4 Heb. *cast forth*	
4 Heb. *thought to be broken*	
1 Sam. 24:3	5
Ps. 107:28	6
Joel 2:14	6
Josh. 7:14 1 Sam. 14:41	7
Josh. 7:19	8

9 And he said unto them, I *am* an Hebrew; and I fear [N]the LORD, the God of heaven, [R]which hath made the sea and the dry *land*.

10 Then were the men [N]exceedingly afraid, and said unto him, Why hast thou done this? For the men knew that he fled from the presence of the LORD, because he had told them.

11 Then said they unto him, What shall we do unto thee, that the sea [N]may be calm unto us? for the sea [NN]wrought, and was tempestuous.

12 And he said unto them, [R]Take me up, and cast me forth into the sea; so shall the sea be calm unto you: for I know that for my sake this great tempest *is* upon you.

13 Nevertheless the men [N]rowed hard to bring *it* to the land; [R]but they could not: for the sea wrought, and was tempestuous against them.

14 Wherefore they cried unto the LORD, and said, We beseech thee, O LORD, we beseech thee, let us not perish for this man's life, and [R]lay not upon us innocent blood: for thou, O LORD, [R]hast done as it pleased thee.

15 So they took up Jonah, and cast him forth into the sea: [R]and the sea [N]ceased from her raging.

16 Then the men [R]feared the LORD exceedingly, and [N]offered a sacrifice unto the LORD, and made vows.

Jonah's ordeal and prayer

17 Now the LORD had prepared a great fish to swallow up Jonah. And [R]Jonah was in the [N]belly of the fish three days and three nights.

CHAPTER 2

THEN Jonah prayed unto the LORD his God out of the fish's belly,

2 And said, I [R]cried [N]by reason of mine affliction unto the LORD, [R]and he heard me; out of the belly of [N]hell cried I, *and* thou heardest my voice.

3 [R]For thou hadst cast me into the deep, in the [N]midst of the seas; and the floods compassed me about: [R]all thy billows and thy waves passed over me.

4 [R]Then I said, I am cast out of thy sight; yet I will look again [R]toward thy holy temple.

5 The [R]waters compassed me about, *even* to the soul: the depth closed me round about, the weeds were wrapped about my head.

6 I went down to the [N]bottoms of the mountains; the earth with her bars *was* about me for ever: yet hast thou brought up my life [R]from [N]corruption, O LORD my God.

7 When my soul fainted within me I remembered the LORD: [R]and my prayer came in unto thee, into thine holy temple.

CHAP. 1
BC 862
9 Or, *JEHOVAH*
9 Ps. 146:6
Acts 17:24
10 Heb. *with great fear*
11 Heb. *may be silent from us*
11 Or, *grew more and more tempestuous*
11 Heb. *went*
12 John 11:50
13 Heb. *digged*
13 Prov. 21:30
14 Deut. 21:8
14 Ps. 115:3
15 Ps. 89:9
Luke 8:24
15 Heb. *stood*
16 Mark 4:41
Acts 5:11
16 Heb. *sacrificed a sacrifice unto the LORD, and vowed vows*
17 Mat. 12:40
Luke 11:30
17 Heb. *bowels*

CHAP. 2
BC 862
2 Ps. 120:1
Lam. 3:55
2 Or, *out of mine affliction*
2 Ps. 65:2
2 Or, *the grave*, Is. 14:9
3 Ps. 88:6
3 Heb. *heart*
3 Ps. 42:7
4 Ps. 31:22
4 1 Ki. 8:38
5 Ps. 69:1
Lam. 3:54
6 Heb. *cuttings off*
6 Ps. 16:10
6 Or, *the pit*
7 Ps. 18:6

2 Ki. 17:15   8
Jer. 10:8
Ps. 50:14   9
Hos. 14:2
Ps. 3:8   9

CHAP. 3
BC 862
Heb. *of*   3
God: Gen. 30:8
Ps. 36:6
Deut. 18:22   4
Mat. 12:41   5
Luke 11:32
Job 2:8   6
2 Chr. 20:3   7
Joel 2:15
Heb. *said*   7
Heb. *great men*   7
Is. 58:6   8
Is. 59:6   8
2 Sam. 12:22   9
Joel 2:14
Jer. 18:8   10
Amos 7:3, 6

CHAP. 4
BC 862
ch. 1:3   2

8 They that observe [R]lying vanities forsake their own mercy.

9 But I will [R]sacrifice unto thee with the voice of thanksgiving; I will pay *that* that I have vowed. [R]Salvation *is* of the LORD.

10 And the LORD spake unto the fish, and it vomited out Jonah upon the dry *land*.

CHAPTER 3

Jonah's obedience and the result

AND the word of the LORD came unto Jonah the second time, saying,

2 Arise, go unto Nĭn'-ĕ-vēh, that great city, and preach unto it the preaching that I bid thee.

3 So Jonah arose, and went unto Nĭn'-ĕ-vēh, according to the word of the LORD. Now Nĭn'-ĕ-vēh was an [N]exceeding great city of three days' journey.

4 And Jonah began to enter into the city a day's journey, and [R]he cried, and said, Yet forty days, and Nĭn'-ĕ-vēh shall be overthrown.

5 So the people of Nĭn'-ĕ-vēh [R]believed God, and proclaimed a fast, and put on sackcloth, from the greatest of them even to the least of them.

6 For word came unto the king of Nĭn'-ĕ-vēh, and he arose from his throne, and he laid his robe from him, and covered *him* with sackcloth, [R]and sat in ashes.

7 [R]And he caused *it* to be proclaimed and [N]published through Nĭn'-ĕ-vēh by the decree of the king and his [N]nobles, saying, Let neither man nor beast, herd nor flock, taste any thing: let them not feed, nor drink water:

8 But let man and beast be covered with sackcloth, and cry mightily unto God: yea, [R]let them turn every one from his evil way, and from [R]the violence that *is* in their hands.

9 [R]Who can tell *if* God will turn and repent, and turn away from his fierce anger, that we perish not?

10 [R]And God saw their works, that they turned from their evil way; and God repented of the evil, that he had said that he would do unto them; and he did *it* not.

CHAPTER 4

Jonah's anger

BUT it displeased Jonah exceedingly, and he was very angry.

2 And he prayed unto the LORD, and said, I pray thee, O LORD, *was* not this my saying, when I was yet in my country? Therefore I [R]fled before unto Tarshish: for I knew that

thou *art* a ᴿgracious God, and merciful, slow to anger, and of great kindness, and repentest thee of the evil.

3 ᴿTherefore now, O Lᴏʀᴅ, take, I beseech thee, my life from me; for ᴿ*it is* better for me to die than to live.

4 Then said the Lᴏʀᴅ, ᴺDoest thou well to be angry?

5 So Jonah went out of the city, and sat on the east side of the city, and there made him a booth, and sat under it in the shadow, till he might see what would become of the city.

God's reproof

6 And the Lᴏʀᴅ God prepared a ᴺᴺgourd, and made *it* to come up over Jonah, that it might be a shadow over his head, to deliver him from his grief. So Jonah ᴺwas exceeding glad of the gourd.

7 But God prepared a worm when the morn-

ing rose the next day, and it smote the gourd that it withered.

8 And it came to pass, when the sun did arise, that God prepared a ᴺvehement east wind; and the sun beat upon the head of Jonah, that he fainted, and wished in himself to die, and said, ᴿ*It is* better for me to die than to live.

9 And God said to Jonah, ᴺDoest thou well to be angry for the gourd? And he said, ᴺI do well to be angry, *even* unto death.

10 Then said the Lᴏʀᴅ, Thou hast ᴺhad pity on the gourd, for the which thou hast not laboured, neither madest it grow; which ᴺcame up in a night, and perished in a night:

11 And should not I spare Nĭn'-ĕ-vēh, ᴿthat great city, wherein are more than sixscore thousand persons ᴿthat cannot discern between their right hand and their left hand; and *also* much ᴿcattle?

CHAP. 4
BC 862
2 Ex. 34:6
Ps. 86:5
Joel 2:13
3 1 Ki. 19:4
3 ver. 8
4 Or, *Art thou greatly angry?*
6 Or, *palmcrist*
6 Heb. *Kikajon*
6 Heb. *rejoiced with great joy*
Or, *silent* 8
ver. 3 8
Or, *Art thou greatly angry?* 9
Or, *I am greatly angry* 9
Or, *spared* 10
Heb. *was the son of the night* 10
ch. 1:2 & 3:2, 3 11
Deut. 1:39 11
Ps. 36:6 11
& 145:9

MICAH

Micah, who lived in Moresheth-gath, located some thirty miles from Jerusalem, had a message for both Judah and Israel. Being contemporary with Isaiah and Hosea, Micah lived in the last half of the eighth century. Boldly this prophet pronounced judgment on the capital cities, the leaders, and the people. In contrast to the message of doom, he offered one of hope of restoration vested in a mighty leader whose birthplace is Bethlehem.

OUTLINE:

CHAPTER 1

Judgment on Israel and Judah

Tᴴᴇ word of the Lᴏʀᴅ that came to ᴿMī'-căh the Mō-răs'-thīte in the days of Jō'-thăm, Ahaz, *and* Hĕz-ē-kī'-ăh, kings of Judah, which he saw concerning Să-mâr'-ĭ-ă and Jerusalem.

2 ᴺHear, all ye people; hearken, O earth, and all that therein is: and let the Lord Gᴏᴅ be witness against you, the Lord from ᴿhis holy temple.

3 For, behold, the Lᴏʀᴅ cometh forth out of his place, and will come down, and tread upon the high places of the earth.

4 And ᴿthe mountains shall be molten under him, and the valleys shall be cleft, as wax before the fire, *and* as the waters *that are* poured down ᴺa steep place.

5 For the transgression of Jacob *is* all this, and for the sins of the house of Israel. What *is* the transgression of Jacob? *is it* not Să-mâr'-ĭ-ă? and what *are* the high places of Judah? *are they* not Jerusalem?

CHAP. 1
BC 750
1 Jer. 26:18
2 Heb. *Hear, ye people, all of them*
2 Ps. 11:4
4 Amos 9:5
4 Heb. *a descent*
2 Ki. 19:25 6
Ezek. 13:14 6
Hos. 2:5 7
Ps. 102:6 8
Heb. *daughters of the owl* 8
Or, *she is grievously sick of her wounds* 9
2 Ki. 18:13 9
2 Sam. 1:20 10
i.e. *Dust* 10
Or, *thou that dwellest fairly* 11
Heb. *inhabitress* 11

6 Therefore I will make Să-mâr'-ĭ-ă ᴿas an heap of the field, *and* as plantings of a vineyard: and I will pour down the stones thereof into the valley, and I will ᴿdiscover the foundations thereof.

7 And all the graven images thereof shall be beaten to pieces, and all the ᴿhires thereof shall be burned with the fire, and all the idols thereof will I lay desolate: for she gathered *it* of the hire of an harlot, and they shall return to the hire of an harlot.

Micah's lament

8 Therefore I will wail and howl, I will go stripped and naked: ᴿI will make a wailing like the dragons, and mourning as the ᴺowls.

9 For ᴺher wound *is* incurable; for ᴿit is come unto Judah; he is come unto the gate of my people, *even* to Jerusalem.

10 ᴿDeclare ye *it* not at Gath, weep ye not at all: in the house of ᴺĂph'-răh roll thyself in the dust.

11 Pass ye away, ᴺthou ᴺinhabitant of

Sā'-phĭr, having thy shame naked: the inhabitant of ^NZā'-ă-năn came not forth in the mourning of ^NBĕth-ē'-zĕl; he shall receive of you his standing.

12 For the inhabitant of Mâr'-ōth ^Nwaited carefully for good: but ^Revil came down from the LORD unto the gate of Jerusalem.

13 O thou inhabitant of ^RLā'-chĭsh, bind the chariot to the swift beast: she *is* the beginning of the sin to the daughter of Zion: for the transgressions of Israel were found in thee.

14 Therefore shalt thou ^Rgive presents ^Nto Mō'-rĕsh-ĕth-găth: the houses of ^RĂch'-zĭb^N *shall be* a lie to the kings of Israel.

15 Yet will I bring an heir unto thee, O inhabitant of ^RMă-rē'-shäh: ^Nhe shall come unto ^RAdullam the glory of Israel.

16 Make thee ^Rbald, and poll thee for thy ^Rdelicate children; enlarge thy baldness as the eagle; for they are gone into captivity from thee.

CHAPTER 2

Oppression of the people and prophets

WOE to them that devise iniquity, and work evil upon their beds! when the morning is light, they practise it, because it is in the power of their hand.

2 And they covet fields, and take *them* by violence; and houses, and take *them* away: so they ^Noppress a man and his house, even a man and his heritage.

3 Therefore thus saith the LORD; Behold, against this family do I devise an evil, from which ye shall not remove your necks; neither shall ye go haughtily: for this time *is* evil.

4 In that day shall *one* take up a parable against you, and ^Rlament^N with a doleful lamentation, *and* say, We be utterly spoiled: he hath changed the portion of my people: how hath he removed *it* from me! ^Nturning away he hath divided our fields.

5 Therefore thou shalt have none that shall cast a cord by lot in the congregation of the LORD.

6 ^{NN}Prophesy ye not, *say they to them that* prophesy: they shall not prophesy to them, *that* they shall not take shame.

7 O *thou that art* named the house of Jacob, is the spirit of the LORD ^Nstraitened? *are* these his doings? do not my words do good to him that walketh ^Nuprightly?

8 Even ^Nof late my people is risen up as an enemy: ye pull off the robe ^Nwith the garment from them that pass by securely as men averse from war.

9 The ^Nwomen of my people have ye cast out from their pleasant houses; from their

children have ye taken away my glory for ever.

10 Arise ye, and depart; for this *is* not *your* ^Rrest: because it is ^Rpolluted, it shall destroy *you*, even with a sore destruction.

11 If a man ^Nwalking in the spirit and falsehood do lie, *saying,* I will prophesy unto thee of wine and of strong drink; he shall even be the prophet of this people.

Promise of a remnant

12 ^RI will surely assemble, O Jacob, all of thee; I will surely gather the remnant of Israel; I will put them together ^Ras the sheep of Bŏz'-räh, as the flock in the midst of their fold: ^Rthey shall make great noise by reason of *the multitude of* men.

13 The breaker is come up before them: they have broken up, and have passed through the gate, and are gone out by it: and ^Rtheir king shall pass before them, ^Rand the LORD on the head of them.

CHAPTER 3

Denunciation of the prophets

AND I said, Hear, I pray you, O heads of Jacob, and ye princes of the house of Israel; ^R*Is it* not for you to know judgment?

2 Who hate the good, and love the evil; who pluck off their skin from off them, and their flesh from off their bones;

3 Who also ^Reat the flesh of my people, and flay their skin from off them; and they break their bones, and chop them in pieces, as for the pot, and ^Ras flesh within the caldron.

4 Then ^Rshall they cry unto the LORD, but he will not hear them: he will even hide his face from them at that time, as they have behaved themselves ill in their doings.

5 Thus saith the LORD ^Rconcerning the prophets that make my people err, that ^Rbite with their teeth, and cry, Peace; and ^Rhe that putteth not into their mouths, they even prepare war against him.

6 ^RTherefore night *shall be* unto you, ^Nthat ye shall not have a vision; and it shall be dark unto you, ^Nthat ye shall not divine; ^Rand the sun shall go down over the prophets, and the day shall be dark over them.

7 Then shall the seers be ashamed, and the diviners confounded: yea, they shall all cover their ^Nlips; ^Rfor *there is* no answer of God.

8 But truly I am full of power by the spirit of the LORD, and of judgment, and of might, ^Rto declare unto Jacob his transgression, and to Israel his sin.

9 Hear this, I pray you, ye heads of the house of Jacob, and princes of the house of

Center reference column

CHAP. 1
BC 750

11 Or, *the country of flocks*
12 Or, *was grieved*
12 Amos 3:6
13 2 Ki. 18:14
14 2 Sam. 8:2
2 Ki. 18:14
14 Or, *for*
14 Josh. 15:44
14 i.e. *a lie*
15 Josh. 15:44
15 Or, *the glory of Israel shall come, etc.*
15 2 Chr. 11:7
16 Job 1:20
Is. 15:2
Jer. 7:29
16 Lam. 4:5

CHAP. 2
BC 730

2 Or, *defraud*
4 2 Sam. 1:17
4 Heb. *with a lamentation of lamentations*
4 Or, *instead of restoring*
6 Or, *Prophesy not as they prophesy*
6 Heb. *Drop, etc.,* Ezek. 21:2
7 Or, *shortened?*
7 Heb. *upright?*
8 Heb. *yesterday*
8 Heb. *over against a garment*
9 Or, *wives*

Deut. 12:9　　10
Lev. 18:25　　10
Jer. 3:2
Or, *walk with the wind, and lie falsely*　　11
ch. 4:6, 7　　12
Jer. 31:10　　12
Ezek. 36:37　　12
Hos. 3:5　　13
Is. 52:12　　13

CHAP. 3
BC 710

Jer. 5:4, 5　　1
Ps. 14:4　　3
Ezek. 11:3　　3
Ps. 18:41　　4
Prov. 1:28
Is. 1:15
Is. 56:10, 11　　5
Ezek. 13:10
Mat. 7:15　　5
Ezek. 13:18　　5
Is..8:20　　6
Ezek. 13:23
Heb. *from a vision*　　6
Heb. *from divining*　　6
Heb. *upper lip*　　7
Amos 8:11　　7
Is. 58:1　　8

Israel, that abhor judgment, and pervert all equity.

10 [R]They build up Zion with [R]blood,[N] and Jerusalem with iniquity.

11 [R]The heads thereof judge for reward, and [R]the priests thereof teach for hire, and the prophets thereof divine for money: [R]yet will they lean upon the LORD, [N]and say, *Is* not the LORD among us? none evil can come upon us.

12 Therefore shall Zion for your sake be [R]plowed *as* a field, [R]and Jerusalem shall become heaps, and [R]the mountain of the house as the high places of the forest.

CHAPTER 4

Promise of a reign of peace

BUT [R]in the last days it shall come to pass, *that* the mountain of the house of the LORD shall be established in the top of the mountains, and it shall be exalted above the hills; and people shall flow unto it.

2 And many nations shall come, and say, Come, and let us go up to the mountain of the LORD, and to the house of the God of Jacob; and he will teach us of his ways, and we will walk in his paths: for the law shall go forth of Zion, and the word of the LORD from Jerusalem.

3 And he shall judge among many people, and rebuke strong nations afar off; and they shall beat their swords into [R]plowshares, and their spears into [N]pruninghooks: nation shall not lift up a sword against nation, [R]neither shall they learn war any more.

4 [R]But they shall sit every man under his vine and under his fig tree; and none shall make *them* afraid: for the mouth of the LORD of hosts hath spoken *it*.

5 For all people will walk every one in the name of his god, and [R]we will walk in the name of the LORD our God for ever and ever.

Rescue and restoration of Zion

6 In that day, saith the LORD, [R]will I assemble her that halteth, [R]and I will gather her that is driven out, and her that I have afflicted;

7 And I will make her that halted [R]a remnant, and her that was cast far off a strong nation: and the LORD [R]shall reign over them in mount Zion from henceforth, even for ever.

8 And thou, O tower of [N]the flock, the strong hold of the daughter of Zion, unto thee shall it come, even the first dominion; the kingdom shall come to the daughter of Jerusalem.

9 Now why dost thou cry out aloud? *is there* no king in thee? is thy counsellor per-

ished? for [R]pangs have taken thee as a woman in travail.

10 Be in pain, and labour to bring forth, O daughter of Zion, like a woman in travail: for now shalt thou go forth out of the city, and thou shalt dwell in the field, and thou shalt go *even* to Babylon; there shalt thou be delivered; there the LORD shall redeem thee from the hand of thine enemies.

11 [R]Now also many nations are gathered against thee, that say, Let her be defiled, and let our eye [R]look upon Zion.

12 But they know not [R]the thoughts of the LORD, neither understand they his counsel: for he shall gather them [R]as the sheaves into the floor.

13 [R]Arise and thresh, O daughter of Zion: for I will make thine horn iron, and I will make thy hoofs brass: and thou shalt [R]beat in pieces many people: [R]and I will consecrate their gain unto the LORD, and their substance unto [R]the Lord of the whole earth.

CHAPTER 5

Promise of a ruler from Bethlehem

NOW gather thyself in troops, O daughter of troops: he hath laid siege against us: they shall [R]smite the judge of Israel with a rod upon the cheek.

2 But thou, [R]Beth-lehem ĕph'-ră-tăh, *though* thou be little [R]among the [R]thousands of Judah, *yet* out of thee shall he come forth unto me *that is* to be [R]ruler in Israel; [R]whose goings forth *have been* from of old, from [N]everlasting. ★

3 Therefore will he give them up, until the time *that* [R]she which travaileth hath brought forth: then [R]the remnant of his brethren shall return unto the children of Israel.

4 And he shall stand and [R]feed[N] in the strength of the LORD, in the majesty of the name of the LORD his God; and they shall abide: for now [R]shall he be great unto the ends of the earth.

Deliverance from Assyria

5 And this *man* [R]shall be the peace, when the Assyrian shall come into our land: and when he shall tread in our palaces, then shall we raise against him seven shepherds, and eight [N]principal men.

6 And they shall [N]waste the land of Assyria with the sword, and the land of [R]Nimrod [N]in the entrances thereof: thus shall he [R]deliver *us* from the Assyrian, when he cometh into our land, and when he treadeth within our borders.

7 And [R]the remnant of Jacob shall be in the midst of many people [R]as a dew from the

Center reference column

CHAP. 3
BC 710
10 Jer. 22:13
10 Ezek. 22:27
Zeph. 3:3
10 Heb. *bloods*
11 Is. 1:23
Ezek. 22:12
11 Jer. 6:13
11 Is. 48:2
Jer. 7:4
11 Heb. *saying*
12 Jer. 26:18
12 Ps. 79:1
12 ch. 4:2

CHAP. 4
BC 710
1 Ezek. 17:22
3 Is. 2:4
Joel 3:10
3 Or, *scythes*
3 Ps. 72:7
4 1 Ki. 4:26
Zech. 3:10
5 Zech. 10:12
6 Ezek. 34:16
6 Ps. 147:2
Ezek. 34:13
7 ch. 2:12
7 Is. 9:6
Dan. 7:14
Luke 1:33
Rev. 11:15
8 Or, *Edar:*
Gen. 35:21
9 Jer. 8:19

Is. 13:8   9
Jer. 30:6
Lam. 2:16   11
Obad. 12   11
Is. 55:8   12
Is. 21:10   12
Jer. 51:33   13
Dan. 2:44   13
Is. 18:7   13
Zech. 4:14   13

CHAP. 5
BC 710
Lam. 3:30   1
Mat. 2:6   2
John 7:42
1 Sam. 23:23   2
Ex. 18:25   2
Gen. 49:10   2
Is. 9:6   2
Ps. 90:2   2
John 1:1   2
Heb. *the days of eternity*   2
ch. 4:10   3
ch. 4:7   3
Is. 40:11   4
Ezek. 34:23
Or, *rule*   4
Ps. 72:8   4
Is. 52:13
Zech. 9:10
Ps. 72:7   5
Is. 9:6
Heb. *princes of men*   5
Heb. *eat up*   6
Gen. 10:8   6
Or, *with her own naked swords*   6
Luke 1:71   6
ver. 3   7
Deut. 32:2   7
Ps. 72:6

LORD, as the showers upon the grass, that tarrieth not for man, nor waiteth for the sons of men.

8 And the remnant of Jacob shall be among the Gentiles in the midst of many people as a lion among the beasts of the forest, as a young lion among the flocks of ᴺsheep: who, if he go through, both treadeth down, and teareth in pieces, and none can deliver.

9 Thine hand shall be lifted up upon thine adversaries, and all thine enemies shall be cut off.

Removal of fortresses, and idols

10 ᴿAnd it shall come to pass in that day, saith the LORD, that I will cut off thy horses out of the midst of thee, and I will destroy thy chariots:

11 And I will cut off the cities of thy land, and throw down all thy strong holds:

12 And I will cut off witchcrafts out of thine hand; and thou shalt have no *more* ᴿsoothsayers:

13 ᴿThy graven images also will I cut off, and thy ᴺstanding images out of the midst of thee; and thou shalt ᴿno more worship the work of thine hands.

14 And I will pluck up thy groves out of the midst of thee: so will I destroy thy ᴺcities.

15 And I will ᴿexecute vengeance in anger and fury upon the heathen, such as they have not heard.

CHAPTER 6

The LORD'S requirements

HEAR ye now what the LORD saith; Arise, contend thou ᴺbefore the mountains, and let the hills hear thy voice.

2 ᴿHear ye, O mountains, ᴿthe LORD's controversy, and ye strong foundations of the earth: for ᴿthe LORD hath a controversy with his people, and he will plead with Israel.

3 O my people, ᴿwhat have I done unto thee? and wherein have I wearied thee? testify against me.

4 ᴿFor I brought thee up out of the land of Egypt, and redeemed thee out of the house of servants; and I sent before thee Moses, Aaron, and Miriam.

5 O my people, remember now what ᴿBalak king of Moab consulted, and what Bā'-lăãm the son of Bē'-ôr answered him from ᴿShĭt'-tĭm unto Gĭl'-găl; that ye may know ᴿthe righteousness of the LORD.

6 Wherewith shall I come before the LORD, *and* bow myself before the high God? shall I come before him with burnt offerings, with calves ᴺof a year old?

CHAP. 5
BC 710
8 Or, *goats*
10 Zech. 9:10
12 Is. 2:6
13 Zech. 13:2
13 Or, *statues*
13 Is. 2:8
14 Or, *enemies*
15 2 Thes. 1:8

CHAP. 6
BC 710
1 Or, *with*
2 Ps. 50:1, 4
2 Hos. 12:2
2 Is. 1:18
3 Jer. 2:5, 31
4 Deut. 4:20
5 Num. 22:5
Josh. 24:9
5 Num. 25:1
5 Judg. 5:11
6 Heb. *sons of a year?*

Ps. 50:9   7
Is. 1:11
Job 29:6   7
2 Ki. 16:3   7
Ezek. 23:37
Heb. *belly*   7
Deut. 10:12   8
1 Sam. 15:22
Gen. 18:19   8
Is. 1:17
Heb. *humble*   8
thyself *to walk*
Or, *thy name*   9
shall see that which is
Or, Is there *yet*   10
unto every man an house of the wicked, etc.
Heb. *measure*   10
of leanness,
Amos 8:5
Or, *Shall I be*   11
pure with, etc.
Hos. 12:7   11
Jer. 9:3, 5   12
Lev. 26:16   13
Ps. 107:17
Lev. 26:26   14
Amos 5:11   15
Or, *he doth much* 16
keep the, etc.
1 Ki. 16:25   16
Hos. 5:11   16
Or, *astonishment* 16
Is. 25:8   16

CHAP. 7
BC 710
Heb. *the*   1
gatherings of summer
Is. 17:6   1
Is. 28:4   1
Ps. 12:1   2
Is. 57:1
Or, *godly, or,*   2
merciful
Hab. 1:15   2

7 ᴿWill the LORD be pleased with thousands of rams, *or* with ten thousands of ᴿrivers of oil? ᴿshall I give my firstborn *for* my transgression, the fruit of my ᴺbody *for* the sin of my soul?

8 He hath ᴿshewed thee, O man, what *is* good; and what doth the LORD require of thee, but ᴿto do justly, and to love mercy, and to ᴺwalk humbly with thy God?

Corruption of Israel

9 The LORD's voice crieth unto the city, and ᴺ*the man of* wisdom shall see thy name: hear ye the rod, and who hath appointed it.

10 ᴺAre there yet the treasures of wickedness in the house of the wicked, and the ᴺscant measure *that is* abominable?

11 ᴺShall I count *them* pure with ᴿthe wicked balances, and with the bag of deceitful weights?

12 For the rich men thereof are full of violence, and the inhabitants thereof have spoken lies, and ᴿtheir tongue *is* deceitful in their mouth.

13 Therefore also will I ᴿmake *thee* sick in smiting thee, in making *thee* desolate because of thy sins.

14 ᴿThou shalt eat, but not be satisfied; and thy casting down *shall be* in the midst of thee; and thou shalt take hold, but shalt not deliver; and *that* which thou deliverest will I give up to the sword.

15 Thou shalt ᴿsow, but thou shalt not reap; thou shalt tread the olives, but thou shalt not anoint thee with oil; and sweet wine, but shalt not drink wine.

16 For ᴺthe statutes of ᴿOmri are ᴿkept, and all the works of the house of Ahab, and ye walk in their counsels; that I should make thee a ᴺdesolation, and the inhabitants thereof an hissing: therefore ye shall bear the ᴿreproach of my people.

CHAPTER 7

Lament of Israel's moral depravity

WOE is me! for I am as ᴺwhen they have gathered the summer fruits, as ᴿthe grapegleanings of the vintage: *there is* no cluster to eat: ᴿmy soul desired the firstripe fruit.

2 The ᴿgoodᴺ *man* is perished out of the earth: and *there is* none upright among men: they all lie in wait for blood; ᴿthey hunt every man his brother with a net.

3 That they may do evil with both hands earnestly, the prince asketh, and the judge *asketh* for a reward; and the great *man,* he ut-

tereth ᴺhis mischievous desire: so they wrap it up.

4 The best of them ᴿ*is* as a brier: the most upright *is sharper* than a thorn hedge: the day of thy watchmen *and* thy visitation cometh; now shall be their perplexity.

5 Trust ye not in a friend, put ye not confidence in a guide: keep the doors of thy mouth from her that lieth in thy bosom.

6 For ᴿthe son dishonoureth the father, the daughter riseth up against her mother, the daughter in law against her mother in law; a man's enemies *are* the men of his own house.

Salvation from God

7 Therefore I will look unto the LORD; I will wait for the God of my salvation: my God will hear me.

8 ᴿRejoice not against me, O mine enemy: ᴿwhen I fall, I shall arise; when I sit in darkness, the LORD *shall be* a light unto me.

9 ᴿI will bear the indignation of the LORD, because I have sinned against him, until he plead my cause, and execute judgment for me: he will bring me forth to the light, *and* I shall behold his righteousness.

10 ᴺThen *she that is* mine enemy shall see *it,* and ᴿshame shall cover her which said unto me, ᴿWhere is the LORD thy God? mine eyes shall behold her: now ᴺshall she be trodden down as the mire of the streets.

Restoration of a pardoned Israel

11 *In* the day that thy walls are to be built, *in* that day shall the decree be far removed.

CHAP. 7

BC 710

3 Heb. *the mischief of his soul*
4 Ezek. 2:6
Is. 55:13
6 Mat. 10:21
8 Prov. 24:17
8 Ps. 37:24
Prov. 24:16
9 Lam. 3:39
10 Or, *And thou wilt see her that is mine enemy, and cover her with shame*
10 Ps. 35:26
10 Ps. 42:3
10 Heb. *she shall be for a treading down*

Is. 11:16   12
Or, *even to*   12
Or, *After that it hath been*   13
Jer. 21:14   13
Or, *Rule,*   14
Ps. 28:9
Is. 37:24   14
Ps. 68:22   15
Is. 26:11   16
Job 21:5   16
Ps. 72:9   17
Is. 49:23
Ps. 18:45   17
Or, *creeping things*   17
Ex. 15:11   18
Ex. 34:6   18
Jer. 50:20
ch. 4:7   18
Ps. 103:9   18
Is. 57:16
Luke 1:72   20
Ps. 105:9   20

---

12 *In* that day *also* ᴿhe shall come even to thee from Assyria, ᴺand *from* the fortified cities, and from the fortress even to the river, and from sea to sea, and *from* mountain to mountain.

13 ᴺNotwithstanding the land shall be desolate because of them that dwell therein, ᴿfor the fruit of their doings.

14 ᴺFeed thy people with thy rod, the flock of thine heritage, which dwell solitarily *in* ᴿthe wood, in the midst of Carmel: let them feed *in* Bā′-shăn and Gilead, as in the days of old.

15 ᴿAccording to the days of thy coming out of the land of Egypt will I shew unto him marvellous *things.*

16 The nations ᴿshall see and be confounded at all their might: ᴿthey shall lay *their* hand upon *their* mouth, their ears shall be deaf.

17 They shall lick the ᴿdust like a serpent, ᴿthey shall move out of their holes like ᴺworms of the earth: they shall be afraid of the LORD our God, and shall fear because of thee.

18 ᴿWho *is* a God like unto thee, that ᴿpardoneth iniquity, and passeth by the transgression of ᴿthe remnant of his heritage? ᴿhe retaineth not his anger for ever, because he delighteth *in* mercy.

19 He will turn again, he will have compassion upon us; he will subdue our iniquities; and thou wilt cast all their sins into the depths of the sea.

20 ᴿThou wilt perform the truth to Jacob, *and* the mercy to Abraham, ᴿwhich thou hast sworn unto our fathers from the days of old.

NAHUM

Nahum, a native of Elkosh, prophesied after the sack of No (i.e., No-amon or Thebes, 3:8) by the Assyrians and before the fall of Nineveh in 612 B.C. to the Medo-Babylonian armies. A century and a half later than Jonah's warning, the prophet Nahum portrayed the terrible judgment about to fall on the Assyrian capital.

OUTLINE:

   I. God's majesty in judgment and mercy   1:1 – 14
  II. Siege and destruction of Nineveh   1:15 – 2:13
 III. The sins of Nineveh   3:1 – 19

CHAPTER 1

God's vengeance on his adversaries

THE burden ᴿof Nĭn′-ĕ-vĕh. The book of the vision of Nahum the ĕl′-kō-shīte.

2 ᴺGod *is* ᴿjealous, and the LORD revengeth; the LORD revengeth, and *is* furious; the LORD will take vengeance on his adversaries, and he reserveth *wrath* for his enemies.

CHAP. 1

BC 713

1 Zeph. 2:13
2 Or, *The LORD is a jealous God, and a revenger*
2 Ex. 20:5

Ex. 34:6, 7   3
Job 9:4   3
Ps. 18:7   3
Mat. 8:26   4
Is. 33:9   4

---

3 The LORD *is* ᴿslow to anger, and ᴿgreat in power, and will not at all acquit *the wicked:* ᴿthe LORD *hath* his way in the whirlwind and in the storm, and the clouds *are* the dust of his feet.

4 ᴿHe rebuketh the sea, and maketh it dry, and drieth up all the rivers: ᴿBā′-shăn languisheth, and Carmel, and the flower of Lĕb′-ă-non languisheth.

5 The mountains quake at him, and the hills melt, and the earth is burned at his presence, yea, the world, and all that dwell therein.

6 Who can stand before his indignation? and ᴿwho can ᴺabide in the fierceness of his anger? his fury is poured out like fire, and the rocks are thrown down by him.

7 ᴿThe Lᴏʀᴅ is good, a ᴺstrong hold in the day of trouble; and he knoweth them that trust in him.

8 But with an overrunning flood he will make an utter end of the place thereof, and darkness shall pursue his enemies.

9 ᴿWhat do ye imagine against the Lᴏʀᴅ? ᴿhe will make an utter end: affliction shall not rise up the second time.

10 For while they be folden together ᴿas thorns, ᴿand while they are drunken as drunkards, ᴿthey shall be devoured as stubble fully dry.

11 There is one come out of thee, that imagineth evil against the Lᴏʀᴅ, ᴺa wicked counsellor.

God's good tidings

12 Thus saith the Lᴏʀᴅ; ᴺThough they be quiet, and likewise many, yet thus shall they be ᴺcut down, when he shall pass through. Though I have afflicted thee, I will afflict thee no more.

13 For now will I break his yoke from off thee, and will burst thy bonds in sunder.

14 And the Lᴏʀᴅ hath given a commandment concerning thee, that no more of thy name be sown: out of the house of thy gods will I cut off the graven image and the molten image: I will make thy grave; for thou art vile.

15 Behold upon the mountains the feet of him that bringeth good tidings, that publisheth peace! O Judah, ᴺkeep thy solemn feasts, perform thy vows: for ᴺthe wicked shall no more pass through thee; he is utterly cut off.

CHAPTER 2

The fall of Nineveh

HE ᴺthat dasheth in pieces is come up before thy face: keep the munition, watch the way, make thy loins strong, fortify thy power mightily.

2 For the Lᴏʀᴅ hath turned away ᴺthe excellency of Jacob, as the excellency of Israel: for the emptiers have emptied them out, and marred their vine branches.

3 The shield of his mighty men is made red, the valiant men are ᴺin scarlet: the chariots shall be with ᴺflaming torches in the day of his preparation, and the fir trees shall be terribly shaken.

CHAP. 1

BC 713

6 Mal. 3:2
6 Heb. stand up
7 Jer. 33:11
7 Or, strength
9 Ps. 2:1
9 1 Sam. 3:12
10 2 Sam. 23:6
10 ch. 3:11
10 Mal. 4:1
11 Heb. a counsellor of Belial
12 Or, If they would have been at peace, so should they have been many, and so should they have been shorn, and he should have passed away
12 Heb. shorn
15 Heb. feast
15 Heb. Belial

CHAP. 2

BC 713

1 Or, The disperser, or, hammer
2 Or, the pride of Jacob as the pride of Israel
3 Or, dyed
3 Or, fiery

Heb. their show   4
Or, gallants   5
Heb. covering, or,   5
  coverer
Or, molten   6
Or, that which   7
  was established,
  or, there was a
  stand made
Or, discovered   7
Or, from the   8
  days that she
  hath been
Or, cause them   8
  to turn
Or, and their   9
  infinite store
Heb. vessels of   9
  desire

CHAP. 3

BC 713

Heb. city of   1
  bloods
Heb. the flame   3
  of the sword,
  and the lightning
  of the spear
Is. 47:9, 12   4

---

4 The chariots shall rage in the streets, they shall justle one against another in the broad ways: ᴺthey shall seem like torches, they shall run like the lightnings.

5 He shall recount his ᴺworthies: they shall stumble in their walk; they shall make haste to the wall thereof, and the ᴺdefence shall be prepared.

6 The gates of the rivers shall be opened, and the palace shall be ᴺdissolved.

7 And ᴺHŭz'-zăb shall be ᴺled away captive, she shall be brought up, and her maids shall lead her as with the voice of doves, tabering upon their breasts.

8 But Nĭn'-ĕ-vēh is ᴺof old like a pool of water: yet they shall flee away. Stand, stand, shall they cry; but none shall ᴺlook back.

9 Take ye the spoil of silver, take the spoil of gold: ᴺfor there is none end of the store and glory out of all the ᴺpleasant furniture.

10 She is empty, and void, and waste: and the heart melteth, and the knees smite together, and much pain is in all loins, and the faces of them all gather blackness.

11 Where is the dwelling of the lions, and the feedingplace of the young lions, where the lion, even the old lion, walked, and the lion's whelp, and none made them afraid?

12 The lion did tear in pieces enough for his whelps, and strangled for his lionesses, and filled his holes with prey, and his dens with ravin.

The LORD is against Nineveh

13 Behold, I am against thee, saith the Lᴏʀᴅ of hosts, and I will burn her chariots in the smoke, and the sword shall devour thy young lions: and I will cut off thy prey from the earth, and the voice of thy messengers shall no more be heard.

CHAPTER 3

WOE to the ᴺbloody city! it is all full of lies and robbery; the prey departeth not;

2 The noise of a whip, and the noise of the rattling of the wheels, and of the pransing horses, and of the jumping chariots.

3 The horseman lifteth up both ᴺthe bright sword and the glittering spear: and there is a multitude of slain, and a great number of carcases; and there is none end of their corpses; they stumble upon their corpses:

4 Because of the multitude of the whoredoms of the wellfavoured harlot, ᴿthe mistress of witchcrafts, that selleth nations through her whoredoms, and families through her witchcrafts.

5 ᴿBehold, I *am* against thee, saith the LORD of hosts; and ᴿI will discover thy skirts upon thy face, and I will shew the nations thy nakedness, and the kingdoms thy shame.

6 And I will cast abominable filth upon thee, and make thee vile, and will set thee as ᴿa gazingstock.

7 And it shall come to pass, *that* all they that look upon thee ᴿshall flee from thee, and say, Nĭn'-ĕ-vēh is laid waste: ᴿwho will bemoan her? whence shall I seek comforters for thee?

Nineveh taunted

8 ᴿArt thou better than ᴺᴺpopulous ᴿNo, that was situate among the rivers, *that had* the waters round about it, whose rampart *was* the sea, *and* her wall *was* from the sea?

9 Ē-thĭ-ō'-pĭ-ă and Egypt *were* her strength, and *it was* infinite; Pŭt and Lū'-bĭm were ᴺthy helpers.

10 Yet *was* she carried away, she went into captivity: ᴿher young children also were dashed in pieces ᴿat the top of all the streets: and they ᴿcast lots for her honourable men, and all her great men were bound in chains.

11 Thou also shalt be ᴿdrunken: thou shalt be hid, thou also shalt seek strength because of the enemy.

12 All thy strong holds *shall be like* ᴿfig trees with the firstripe figs: if they be shaken,

CHAP. 3
BC 713
5 ch. 2:13
5 Is. 47:2, 3
6 Heb. 10:33
7 Rev. 18:10
7 Jer. 15:5
8 Amos 6:2
8 Or, *nourishing*
8 Heb. *No Amon*
8 Jer. 46:25
9 Heb. *in thy help*
10 Ps. 137:9
Is. 13:16
Hos. 13:16
10 Lam. 2:19
10 Joel 3:3
Obad. 11
11 Jer. 25:17
ch. 1:10
12 Rev. 6:13

Jer. 50:37	13
Ps. 147:13	13
Jer. 51:30	
ch. 2:1	14
Joel 1:4	15
Or, *spreadeth himself*	16
Rev. 9:7	17
Ex. 15:16	18
Ps. 76:6	
Jer. 50:18	18
Ezek. 31:3	
Or, *valiant ones*	18
1 Ki. 22:17	18
Heb. *wrinkling*	19
Mic. 1:9	19
Lam. 2:15	19
Zeph. 2:15	

they shall even fall into the mouth of the eater.

13 Behold, ᴿthy people in the midst of thee *are* women: the gates of thy land shall be set wide open unto thine enemies: the fire shall devour thy ᴿbars.

14 Draw thee waters for the siege, ᴿfortify thy strong holds: go into clay, and tread the mortar, make strong the brickkiln.

15 There shall the fire devour thee; the sword shall cut thee off, it shall eat thee up like ᴿthe cankerworm: make thyself many as the cankerworm, make thyself many as the locusts.

16 Thou hast multiplied thy merchants above the stars of heaven: the cankerworm ᴺspoileth, and flieth away.

17 ᴿThy crowned *are* as the locusts, and thy captains as the great grasshoppers, which camp in the hedges in the cold day, *but* when the sun ariseth they flee away, and their place is not known where they *are*.

18 ᴿThy shepherds slumber, O ᴿking of Assyria: thy ᴺnobles shall dwell *in the dust*: thy people is ᴿscattered upon the mountains, and no man gathereth *them*.

19 *There is* no ᴺhealing of thy bruise; ᴿthy wound is grievous: ᴿall that hear the bruit of thee shall clap the hands over thee: for upon whom hath not thy wickedness passed continually?

HABAKKUK

Toward the end of the seventh century Habakkuk was active in Judah. His book is unique as a dialogue between the prophet and God. Habakkuk observes the injustice prevailing in Judah and wonders how a just God could tolerate such evil. When told that the godless Chaldeans will invade Judah, the prophet is again perplexed. This heathen nation will ultimately be destroyed and God's people will prosper. Habakkuk concludes with a prayer of praise.

OUTLINE:

CHAPTER 1

Habakkuk's plaintive question

THE burden which Hă-băk'-kŭk the prophet did see.

2 O LORD, how long shall I cry, ᴿand thou wilt not hear! *even* cry out unto thee *of* violence, and thou wilt not save!

3 Why dost thou shew me iniquity, and cause *me* to behold grievance? for spoiling and violence *are* before me: and there are *that* raise up strife and contention.

CHAP. 1
BC 626
2 Lam. 3:8

Jer. 12:1	4
Or, *wrested*	4
Is. 29:14	5
Fulfilled,	6
2 Chr. 36:6	

4 Therefore the law is slacked, and judgment doth never go forth: for the ᴿwicked doth compass about the righteous; therefore ᴺwrong judgment proceedeth.

God's answer

5 ᴿBehold ye among the heathen, and regard, and wonder marvellously: for *I* will work a work in your days, *which* ye will not believe, though it be told *you*.

6 For, lo, ᴺI raise up the Chăl-dē'-ăns, *that* bitter and hasty nation, which shall march

through the ᴺbreadth of the land, to possess the dwelling places *that are* not theirs.

7 They *are* terrible and dreadful: ᴺtheir judgment and their dignity shall proceed of themselves.

8 Their horses also are swifter than the leopards, and are more ᴺfierce than the evening wolves: and their horsemen shall spread themselves, and their horsemen shall come from far; they shall fly as the eagle *that* hasteth to eat.

9 They shall come all for violence: ᴺᴺtheir faces shall sup up *as* the east wind, and they shall gather the captivity as the sand.

10 And they shall scoff at the kings, and the princes shall be a scorn unto them: they shall deride every strong hold; for they shall heap dust, and take it.

11 Then shall *his* mind change, and he shall pass over, and offend, ᴿimputing this his power unto his god.

Habakkuk's continued complaint

12 *Art* thou not from everlasting, O LORD my God, mine Holy One? we shall not die. O LORD, ᴿthou hast ordained them for judgment; and, O ᴺmighty God, thou hast ᴺestablished them for correction.

13 *Thou art* of purer eyes than to behold evil, and canst not look on ᴺiniquity: wherefore lookest thou upon them that deal treacherously, *and* holdest thy tongue when the wicked devoureth *the man that is* more righteous than he?

14 And makest men as the fishes of the sea, as the ᴺcreeping things, *that have* no ruler over them?

15 They take up all of them with the angle, they catch them in their net, and gather them in their ᴺdrag: therefore they rejoice and are glad.

16 Therefore ᴿthey sacrifice unto their net, and burn incense unto their drag; because by them their portion *is* fat, and their meat ᴺᴺplenteous.

17 Shall they therefore empty their net, and not spare continually to slay the nations?

CHAPTER 2

I WILL ᴿstand upon my watch, and set me upon the ᴺtower, and will watch to see what he will say ᴺunto me, and what I shall answer ᴺᴺwhen I am reproved.

God's assurance for the upright

2 And the LORD answered me, and said, ᴿWrite the vision, and make *it* plain upon tables, that he may run that readeth it.

3 For ᴿthe vision *is* yet for an appointed time, but at the end it shall speak, and not lie: though it tarry, wait for it; because it will ᴿsurely come, it will not tarry.

4 Behold, his soul *which* is lifted up is not upright in him: but the ᴿjust shall live by his faith.

5 ᴺYea also, because he transgresseth by wine, *he is* a proud man, neither keepeth at home, who enlargeth his desire as hell, and *is* as death, and cannot be satisfied, but gathereth unto him all nations, and heapeth unto him all people:

Woes upon the tyrant

6 Shall not all these take up a parable against him, and a taunting proverb against him, and say, ᴺWoe to him that increaseth *that which is* not his! how long? and to him that ladeth himself with thick clay!

7 Shall they not rise up suddenly that shall bite thee, and awake that shall vex thee, and thou shalt be for booties unto them?

8 ᴿBecause thou hast spoiled many nations, all the remnant of the people shall spoil thee; because of men's ᴺblood, and *for* the violence of the land, of the city, and of all that dwell therein.

9 Woe to him that ᴺcoveteth an evil covetousness to his house, that he may ᴿset his nest on high, that he may be delivered from the ᴺpower of evil!

10 Thou hast consulted shame to thy house by cutting off many people, and hast sinned *against* thy soul.

11 For the stone shall cry out of the wall, and the ᴺbeam out of the timber shall ᴺanswer it.

12 Woe to him that buildeth a town with ᴺblood, and stablisheth a city by iniquity!

13 Behold, *is it* not of the LORD of hosts that the people shall labour in the very fire, and the people shall weary themselves ᴺfor very vanity?

14 For the earth shall be filled ᴺwith the knowledge of the glory of the LORD, as the waters cover the sea.

15 Woe unto him that giveth his neighbour drink, that puttest thy ᴿbottle to *him,* and makest *him* drunken also, that thou mayest look on their nakedness!

16 Thou art filled ᴺwith shame for glory: drink thou also, and let thy foreskin be uncovered: the cup of the LORD's right hand shall be turned unto thee, and shameful spewing *shall be* on thy glory.

17 For the violence of Lĕb'-ă-nọn shall cover thee, and the spoil of beasts, *which*

made them afraid, because of men's blood, and for the violence of the land, of the city, and of all that dwell therein.

Idols unprofitable

18 What profiteth the graven image that the maker thereof hath graven it; the molten image, and a teacher of lies, that ᴺthe maker of his work trusteth therein, to make dumb idols?

19 Woe unto him that saith to the wood, Awake; to the dumb stone, Arise, it shall teach! Behold, it *is* laid over with gold and silver, and *there is* no breath at all in the midst of it.

20 But the LORD *is* in his holy temple: ᴺlet all the earth keep silence before him.

CHAPTER 3

Song of God's glory and might

A PRAYER of Hă-băk′-kŭk the prophet ᴺupon Shĭg-ĭ-ō′-nŏth.

2 O LORD, I have heard ᴺthy speech, *and* was afraid: O LORD, ᴺrevive thy work in the midst of the years, in the midst of the years make known; in wrath remember mercy.

3 God came from ᴺTē′-măn, and the Holy One from mount Pâr′-ăn. Sē′-läh. His glory covered the heavens, and the earth was full of his praise.

4 And *his* brightness was as the light; he had ᴺhorns *coming* out of his hand: and there *was* the hiding of his power.

5 Before him went the pestilence, and ᴺburning coals went forth at his feet.

6 He stood, and measured the earth: he beheld, and drove asunder the nations; ᴿand the everlasting mountains were scattered, the perpetual hills did bow: his ways *are* everlasting.

7 I saw the tents of ᴺCū′-shăn ᴺin affliction: *and* the curtains of the land of Mĭd′-ĭ-ăn did tremble.

8 Was the LORD displeased against the rivers? *was* thine anger against the rivers? *was* thy wrath against the sea, that thou didst ride

---

CHAP. **2**
BC 626

18 Heb. *the fashioner of his fashion*
20 Heb. *be silent all the earth before him*

CHAP. **3**
BC 626

1 Or, *according to variable songs, or, tunes, called in Hebrew, Shigionoth*
2 Heb. *thy report, or, thy hearing*
2 Or, *preserve alive*
3 Or, *the south*
4 Or, *bright beams out of his side*
5 Or, *burning diseases*
6 Nah. 1:5
7 Or, *Ethiopia*
7 Or, *under affliction, or, vanity*

Or, *thy chariots were salvation?* 8
Or, *Thou didst cleave the rivers of the earth* 9
Ex. 14:22 10
Or, *thine arrows walked in the light, etc.* 11
Heb. *making naked* 13
Heb. *were tempestuous* 14
Ps. 77:19 15
Or, *mud* 15
Ps. 119:120 16
Or, *cut them in pieces* 16
Heb. *lie* 17
2 Sam. 22:34 19
Deut. 32:13 19
Heb. *Neginoth, Ps. 4, title* 19

---

upon thine horses *and* ᴺthy chariots of salvation?

9 Thy bow was made quite naked, *according* to the oaths of the tribes, *even thy* word. Sē′-läh. ᴺThou didst cleave the earth with rivers.

10 The mountains saw thee, *and* they trembled: the overflowing of the water passed by: the deep uttered his voice, *and* ᴿlifted up his hands on high.

11 The sun *and* moon stood still in their habitation: ᴺat the light of thine arrows they went, *and* at the shining of thy glittering spear.

12 Thou didst march through the land in indignation, thou didst thresh the heathen in anger.

13 Thou wentest forth for the salvation of thy people, *even* for salvation with thine anointed; thou woundedst the head out of the house of the wicked, ᴺby discovering the foundation unto the neck. Sē′-läh.

14 Thou didst strike through with his staves the head of his villages: they ᴺcame out as a whirlwind to scatter me: their rejoicing *was* as to devour the poor secretly.

15 ᴿThou didst walk through the sea with thine horses, *through* the ᴺheap of great waters.

Song of faith

16 When I heard, ᴿmy belly trembled; my lips quivered at the voice: rottenness entered into my bones, and I trembled in myself, that I might rest in the day of trouble: when he cometh up unto the people, he will ᴺinvade them with his troops.

17 Although the fig tree shall not blossom, neither *shall* fruit *be* in the vines; the labour of the olive shall ᴺfail, and the fields shall yield no meat; the flock shall be cut off from the fold, and *there shall be* no herd in the stalls:

18 Yet I will rejoice in the LORD, I will joy in the God of my salvation.

19 The LORD God *is* my strength, and he will make my feet like ᴿhinds' *feet,* and he will make me to ᴿwalk upon mine high places. To the chief singer on my ᴺstringed instruments.

ZEPHANIAH

Zephaniah was active during the reign of Josiah. He may have been contemporary with Nahum, Habakkuk, and Jeremiah. If Hizkiah, noted in 1:1, is King Hezekiah, then Zephaniah is of royal blood. By warning his people that the day of the LORD is near, Zephaniah may have stimulated the great reformation during Josiah's reign.

OUTLINE:

I. God's judgment on Jerusalem   1:1 – 2:3
II. Surrounding cities and nations judged   2:4 – 15
III. Jerusalem judged and restored   3:1 – 20

CHAPTER 1

Zephaniah's ancestry

THE word of the LORD which came unto Zĕph-ȧ-nī′-ăh the son of Cū′-shī, the son of Gĕd-ȧ-lī′-ăh, the son of Ăm-ȧ-rī′-ăh, the son of Hīz-kī′-ăh, in the days of Jō-sī′-ăh the son of Amon, king of Judah.

Universal judgment

2 ᴺI will utterly consume all *things* from off ᴺthe land, saith the LORD.

3 ᴿI will consume man and beast; I will consume the fowls of the heaven, and the fishes of the sea, and the ᴺstumblingblocks with the wicked; and I will cut off man from off the land, saith the LORD.

Judgment of Judah

4 I will also stretch out mine hand upon Judah, and upon all the inhabitants of Jerusalem; and I will cut off the remnant of Bā′-ăl from this place, *and* the name of ᴿthe Chĕm′-ȧ-rīms with the priests;

5 And them ᴿthat worship the host of heaven upon the housetops; and them that worship *and* that swear ᴺby the LORD, and that swear ᴿby Măl′-chăm;

6 And ᴿthem that are turned back from the LORD; and *those* that ᴿhave not sought the LORD, nor inquired for him.

The day of the LORD'S judgment

7 ᴿHold thy peace at the presence of the Lord GOD: ᴿfor the day of the LORD *is* at hand: for ᴿthe LORD hath prepared a sacrifice, he hath ᴺbid his guests.

8 And it shall come to pass in the day of the LORD's sacrifice, that I will ᴺpunish ᴿthe princes, and the king's children, and all such as are clothed with strange apparel.

9 In the same day also will I punish all those that leap on the threshold, which fill their masters' houses with violence and deceit.

10 And it shall come to pass in that day, saith the LORD, *that there shall be* the noise of a cry from ᴿthe fish gate, and an howling from the second, and a great crashing from the hills.

11 ᴿHowl, ye inhabitants of Măk′-tĕsh, for all the merchant people are cut down; all they that bear silver are cut off.

12 And it shall come to pass at that time, *that* I will search Jerusalem with candles, and punish the men that are ᴿsettledᴺ on their lees: ᴿthat say in their heart, The LORD will not do good, neither will he do evil.

13 Therefore their goods shall become a

booty, and their houses a desolation: they shall also build houses, but ᴿnot inhabit *them;* and they shall plant vineyards, but ᴿnot drink the wine thereof.

14 ᴿThe great day of the LORD *is* near, *it is* near, and hasteth greatly, *even* the voice of the day of the LORD: the mighty man shall cry there bitterly.

15 ᴿThat day *is* a day of wrath, a day of trouble and distress, a day of wasteness and desolation, a day of darkness and gloominess, a day of clouds and thick darkness,

16 A day of ᴿthe trumpet and alarm against the fenced cities, and against the high towers.

17 And I will bring distress upon men, that they shall ᴿwalk like blind men, because they have sinned against the LORD: and ᴿtheir blood shall be poured out as dust, and their flesh ᴿas the dung.

18 ᴿNeither their silver nor their gold shall be able to deliver them in the day of the LORD's wrath; but the whole land shall be ᴿdevoured by the fire of his jealousy: for ᴿhe shall make even a speedy riddance of all them that dwell in the land.

CHAPTER 2

Final warning

GATHERᴿ yourselves together, yea, gather together, O nation ᴺnot desired;

2 Before the decree bring forth, *before* the day pass ᴿas the chaff, before ᴿthe fierce anger of the LORD come upon you, before the day of the LORD's anger come upon you.

3 ᴿSeek ye the LORD, ᴿall ye meek of the earth, which have wrought his judgment; seek righteousness, seek meekness: ᴿit may be ye shall be hid in the day of the LORD's anger.

Judgment of Philistia

4 For ᴿGā′-ză shall be forsaken, and Ăsh′-kĕ-lon a desolation: they shall drive out Ăsh′-dŏd ᴿat the noon day, and ĕk′-rŏn shall be rooted up.

5 Woe unto the inhabitants of ᴿthe sea coast, the nation of the Chĕr′-ĕ-thītes! the word of the LORD *is* against you; O ᴿCanaan, the land of the Philistines, I will even destroy thee, that there shall be no inhabitant.

6 And the sea coast shall be dwellings *and* cottages for shepherds, ᴿand folds for flocks.

7 And the coast shall be for ᴿthe remnant of the house of Judah; they shall feed thereupon: in the houses of Ăsh′-kĕ-lon shall they lie down in the evening: ᴺfor the LORD their God shall ᴿvisit them, and ᴿturn away their captivity.

CHAP. 1
BC 630

2 Heb. *By taking away I will make an end*
2 Heb. *the face of the land*
3 Hos. 4:3
3 Or, *idols*
4 Hos. 10:5
5 2 Ki. 23:12
5 Or, *to the LORD*
5 Josh. 23:7
6 Is. 1:4
  Jer. 2:13
6 Hos. 7:7
7 Hab. 2:20
  Zech. 2:13
7 Is. 13:6
7 Is. 34:6
  Jer. 46:10
7 Heb. *sanctified, or, prepared*
8 Heb. *visit upon*
8 Jer. 39:6
10 2 Chr. 33:14
11 Jas. 5:1
12 Jer. 48:11
12 Heb. *curded, or, thickened*
12 Ps. 94:7

Amos 5:11   13
Mic. 6:15   13
Joel 2:1, 11   14
Is. 22:5   15
  Jer. 30:7
Jer. 4:19   16
Deut. 28:29   17
Ps. 79:3   17
Jer. 9:22   17
Ezek. 7:19   18
  ch. 3:8   18
  ver. 2, 3   18

CHAP. 2
BC 630

Joel 2:16   1
Or, *not desirous* 1
Job 21:18   2
  Is. 17:13
2 Ki. 23:26   2
Amos 5:6   3
Ps. 76:9   3
Amos 5:15   3
Zech. 9:5, 6   4
Jer. 6:4   4
Ezek. 25:16   5
Josh. 13:3   5
Is. 17:2   6
Mic. 5:7, 8   7
Or, *when, etc.*   7
Luke 1:68   7
Jer. 29:14   7

Judgment of Moab and Ethiopia

8 ᴿI have heard the reproach of Moab, and ᴿthe revilings of the children of Ammon, whereby they have reproached my people, and ᴿmagnified *themselves* against their border.

9 Therefore *as* I live, saith the Lᴏʀᴅ of hosts, the God of Israel, Surely ᴿMoab shall be as Sodom, and ᴿthe children of Ammon as Gō-mŏr'-răh, ᴿ*even* the breeding of nettles, and saltpits, and a perpetual desolation: ᴿthe residue of my people shall spoil them, and the remnant of my people shall possess them.

10 This shall they have ᴿfor their pride, because they have reproached and magnified *themselves* against the people of the Lᴏʀᴅ of hosts.

11 The Lᴏʀᴅ *will be* terrible unto them: for he will ᴺfamish all the gods of the earth; ᴿand *men* shall worship him, every one from his place, *even* all ᴿthe isles of the heathen.

12 ᴿYe Ē-thĭ-ō'-pĭ-ăns also, ye *shall be* slain by ᴿmy sword.

Judgment of Assyria

13 And he will stretch out his hand against the north, and ᴿdestroy Assyria; and will make Nĭn'-ĕ-vēh a desolation, *and* dry like a wilderness.

14 And ᴿflocks shall lie down in the midst of her, all ᴿthe beasts of the nations: both the ᴿcormorantᴺ and the bittern shall lodge in the ᴺupper lintels of it; *their* voice shall sing in the windows; desolation *shall be* in the thresholds: ᴺfor he shall uncover the ᴿcedar work.

15 This *is* the rejoicing city ᴿthat dwelt carelessly, ᴿthat said in her heart, I *am,* and *there is* none beside me: how is she become a desolation, a place for beasts to lie down in! every one that passeth by her ᴿshall hiss, *and* ᴿwag his hand.

CHAPTER 3

Jerusalem reproved for sin

Wᴏᴇ to ᴺᴺher that is filthy and polluted, to the oppressing city!

2 She ᴿobeyed not the voice; she ᴿreceived not ᴺcorrection; she trusted not in the Lᴏʀᴅ; she drew not near to her God.

3 ᴿHer princes within her *are* roaring lions; her judges *are* ᴿevening wolves; they gnaw not the bones till the morrow.

4 Her ᴿprophets *are* light *and* treacherous persons: her priests have polluted the sanctuary, they have done ᴿviolence to the law.

5 ᴿThe just Lᴏʀᴅ ᴿ*is* in the midst thereof;

he will not do iniquity: ᴺevery morning doth he bring his judgment to light, he faileth not; but ᴿthe unjust knoweth no shame.

6 I have cut off the nations: their ᴺtowers are desolate; I made their streets waste, that none passeth by: their cities are destroyed, so that there is no man, that there is none inhabitant.

7 ᴿI said, Surely thou wilt fear me, thou wilt receive instruction; so their dwelling should not be cut off, howsoever I punished them: but they rose early, *and* ᴿcorrupted all their doings.

Purging of the nations

8 Therefore ᴿwait ye upon me, saith the Lᴏʀᴅ, until the day that I rise up to the prey: for my determination *is* to ᴿgather the nations, that I may assemble the kingdoms, to pour upon them mine indignation, *even* all my fierce anger: for all the earth ᴿshall be devoured with the fire of my jealousy.

9 For then will I turn to the people ᴿa pure ᴺlanguage, that they may all call upon the name of the Lᴏʀᴅ, to serve him with one ᴺconsent.

10 ᴿFrom beyond the rivers of Ē-thĭ-ō'-pĭ-ă my suppliants, *even* the daughter of my dispersed, shall bring mine offering.

Purging of Judah

11 In that day shalt thou not be ashamed for all thy doings, wherein thou hast transgressed against me: for then I will take away out of the midst of thee them that ᴿrejoice in thy pride, and thou shalt no more be haughty ᴺbecause of my holy mountain.

12 I will also leave in the midst of thee ᴿan afflicted and poor people, and they shall trust in the name of the Lᴏʀᴅ.

13 ᴿThe remnant of Israel ᴿshall not do iniquity, ᴿnor speak lies; neither shall a deceitful tongue be found in their mouth: for ᴿthey shall feed and lie down, and none shall make *them* afraid.

Exultation of Jerusalem

14 ᴿSing, O daughter of Zion; shout, O Israel; be glad and rejoice with all the heart, O daughter of Jerusalem.

15 The Lᴏʀᴅ hath taken away thy judgments, he hath cast out thine enemy: ᴿthe king of Israel, *even* the Lᴏʀᴅ, ᴿ*is* in the midst of thee: thou shalt not see evil any more.

16 In that day ᴿit shall be said to Jerusalem, Fear thou not: *and* to Zion, ᴿLet not thine hands be ᴺslack.

17 The Lᴏʀᴅ thy God ᴿin the midst of thee *is* mighty; he will save, ᴿhe will rejoice over

thee with joy; [N]he will rest in his love, he will joy over thee with singing.

18 I will gather *them that* [R]*are* sorrowful for the solemn assembly, *who* are of thee, *to whom* [N]the reproach of it *was* a burden.

19 Behold, at that time I will undo all that afflict thee: and I will save her that halteth, and gather her that was driven out; and [N]I will

get them praise and fame in every land where they have been put to shame.

20 At that time [R]will I bring you *again,* even in the time that I gather you: for I will make you a name and a praise among all people of the earth, when I turn back your captivity before your eyes, saith the LORD.

HAGGAI

Haggai's messages were delivered to the Jews in Jerusalem during the last half of the year 520 B.C. The rebuilding of the temple had been delayed for eighteen years when Haggai aroused his people to renewed activity. In four brief messages Haggai encourages the builders, who completed the temple by 515 B.C.

OUTLINE:
I. People stirred to action　1:1 – 15
II. The greater glory of the new temple　2:1 – 9
III. Blessings assured　2:10 – 19
IV. Zerubbabel, God's servant　2:20 – 23

CHAPTER 1

Reproach for indifference

IN [R]the second year of Dă-rī′-ŭs the king, in the sixth month, in the first day of the month, came the word of the LORD [N]by Hăg′-gāi the prophet unto [R]Zĕ-rŭb′-bă-bĕl the son of Shē-ăl′-tī-ĕl, [N]governor of Judah, and to [R]Joshua the son of [R]Jŏs′-ĕ-dĕch, the high priest, saying,

2 Thus speaketh the LORD of hosts, saying, This people say, The time is not come, the time that the LORD's house should be built.

3 Then came the word of the LORD [R]by Hăg′-gāi the prophet, saying,

4 [R]*Is it* time for you, O ye, to dwell in your ceiled houses, and this house *lie* waste?

5 Now therefore thus saith the LORD of hosts; [R]Consider[N] your ways.

6 Ye have [R]sown much, and bring in little; ye eat, but ye have not enough; ye drink, but ye are not filled with drink; ye clothe you, but there is none warm; and [R]he that earneth wages earneth wages *to put it* into a bag [N]with holes.

7 Thus saith the LORD of hosts; Consider your ways.

8 Go up to the mountain, and bring wood, and build the house; and I will take pleasure in it, and I will be glorified, saith the LORD.

9 [R]Ye looked for much, and, lo, *it came* to little; and when ye brought *it* home, [R]I did [N]blow upon it. Why? saith the LORD of hosts. Because of mine house that *is* waste, and ye run every man unto his own house.

10 Therefore [R]the heaven over you is stayed from dew, and the earth is stayed *from* her fruit.

11 And I [R]called for a drought upon the land, and upon the mountains, and upon the corn, and upon the new wine, and upon the oil, and upon *that* which the ground bringeth forth, and upon men, and upon cattle, and [R]upon all the labour of the hands.

Temple rebuilding begun

12 [R]Then Zĕ-rŭb′-bă-bĕl the son of Shē-ăl′-tī-ĕl, and Joshua the son of Jŏs′-ĕ-dĕch, the high priest, with all the remnant of the people, obeyed the voice of the LORD their God, and the words of Hăg′-gāi the prophet, as the LORD their God had sent him, and the people did fear before the LORD.

13 Then spake Hăg′-gāi the LORD's messenger in the LORD's message unto the people, saying, [R]I *am* with you, saith the LORD.

14 And [R]the LORD stirred up the spirit of Zĕ-rŭb′-bă-bĕl the son of Shē-ăl′-tī-ĕl, [R]governor of Judah, and the spirit of Joshua the son of Jŏs′-ĕ-dĕch, the high priest, and the spirit of all the remnant of the people; [R]and they came and did work in the house of the LORD of hosts, their God,

15 In the four and twentieth day of the sixth month, in the second year of Dă-rī′-ŭs the king.

CHAPTER 2

Encouragement to the builders

IN the seventh *month,* in the one and twentieth *day* of the month, came the word of the LORD [N]by the prophet Hăg′-gāi, saying,

2 Speak now to Zĕ-rŭb′-bă-bĕl the son of Shē-ăl′-tī-ĕl, governor of Judah, and to Joshua the son of Jŏs′-ĕ-dĕch, the high priest, and to

the residue of the people, saying,

3 ᴿWho *is* left among you that saw this house in her first glory? and how do ye see it now? ᴿ*is it* not in your eyes in comparison of it as nothing?

4 Yet now ᴿbe strong, O Zĕ-rŭb′-bă-bĕl, saith the LORD; and be strong, O Joshua, son of Jŏs′-ĕ-dĕch, the high priest; and be strong, all ye people of the land, saith the LORD, and work: for I *am* with you, saith the LORD of hosts:

5 ᴿ*According to* the word that I covenanted with you when ye came out of Egypt, so ᴿmy spirit remaineth among you: fear ye not.

6 For thus saith the LORD of hosts; ᴿYet once, it *is* a little while, and ᴿI will shake the heavens, and the earth, and the sea, and the dry *land;*

7 And I will shake all nations, ᴿand the desire of all nations shall come: and I will fill this house with glory, saith the LORD of hosts. ★

8 The silver *is* mine, and the gold *is* mine, saith the LORD of hosts.

9 ᴿThe glory of this latter house shall be greater than of the former, saith the LORD of hosts: and in this place will I give ᴿpeace, saith the LORD of hosts.

Uncleanness and chastening

10 In the four and twentieth *day* of the ninth *month,* in the second year of Dă-rī′-ŭs, came the word of the LORD by Hăg′-gâi the prophet, saying,

11 Thus saith the LORD of hosts; ᴿAsk now the priests *concerning* the law, saying,

12 If one bear holy flesh in the skirt of his garment, and with his skirt do touch bread, or pottage, or wine, or oil, or any meat, shall it be holy? And the priests answered and said, No.

13 Then said Hăg′-gâi, If *one that is* ᴿunclean by a dead body touch any of these, shall it be unclean? And the priests answered and said, It shall be unclean.

CHAP. 2
BC 520
3 Ezra 3:12
3 Zech. 4:10
4 Zech. 8:9
5 Ex. 29:45, 46
5 Neh. 9:20
Is. 63:11
6 ver. 21
Heb. 12:26
6 Joel 3:16
7 Gen. 49:10
Mal. 3:1
9 John 1:14
9 Ps. 85:8, 9
Luke 2:14
Eph. 2:14
11 Lev. 10:10, 11
Deut. 33:10
Mal. 2:7
13 Num. 19:11

Tit. 1:15	14
ch. 1:5	15
ch. 1:6, 9	16
Zech. 8:10	
Deut. 28:22	17
1 Ki. 8:37	
Amos 4:9	
ch. 1:9	
ch. 1:11	17
Jer. 5:3	17
Amos 4:6, 8-11	
Zech. 8:9	18
Zech. 8:12	19
ch. 1:14	21
ver. 6, 7	21
Dan. 2:44	22
Mic. 5:10	22
Zech. 9:10	
S. of S. 8:6	23
Jer. 22:24	
Is. 42:1	23
& 43:10	

14 Then answered Hăg′-gâi, and said, ᴿSo *is* this people, and so *is* this nation before me, saith the LORD; and so *is* every work of their hands; and that which they offer there *is* unclean.

15 And now, I pray you, ᴿconsider from this day and upward, from before a stone was laid upon a stone in the temple of the LORD:

16 Since those *days* were, ᴿwhen *one* came to an heap of twenty *measures,* there were *but* ten: when *one* came to the pressfat for to draw out fifty *vessels* out of the press, there were *but* twenty.

17 ᴿI smote you with blasting and with mildew and with hail ᴿin all the labours of your hands; ᴿyet ye *turned* not to me, saith the LORD.

18 Consider now from this day and upward, from the four and twentieth day of the ninth *month, even* from ᴿthe day that the foundation of the LORD's temple was laid, consider *it.*

19 ᴿIs the seed yet in the barn? yea, as yet the vine, and the fig tree, and the pomegranate, and the olive tree, hath not brought forth: from this day will I bless *you.*

Messianic kingship

20 And again the word of the LORD came unto Hăg′-gâi in the four and twentieth *day* of the month, saying,

21 Speak to Zĕ-rŭb′-bă-bĕl, ᴿgovernor of Judah, saying, ᴿI will shake the heavens and the earth;

22 And ᴿI will overthrow the throne of kingdoms, and I will destroy the strength of the kingdoms of the heathen; and ᴿI will overthrow the chariots, and those that ride in them; and the horses and their riders shall come down, every one by the sword of his brother.

23 In that day, saith the LORD of hosts, will I take thee, O Zĕ-rŭb′-bă-bĕl, my servant, the son of Shē-ăl′-tĭ-ĕl, saith the LORD, ᴿand will make thee as a signet: for ᴿI have chosen thee, saith the LORD of hosts.

ZECHARIAH

The prophet Zechariah began his ministry two months later than his contemporary Haggai. The series of visions in chapters 1–8 were the basis for encouraging the Jews in rebuilding the temple. God has a long range plan for His people. In chapters 9–14 the coming of the Messiah and the establishment of the ultimate kingdom are vividly projected.

OUTLINE:

I. The series of visions   1:1–6:15
II. Should the people fast?   7:1–8:23
III. The Messiah and his kingdom   9:1–14:21

CHAPTER 1

Call for repentance

IN the eighth month, ᴿin the second year of Dă-rī'-ŭs, came the word of the LORD ᴿunto Zĕch-ȧ-rī'-ăh, the son of Bĕr-ē-chī'-ăh, the son of Ĭd'-dō the prophet, saying,

2 The LORD hath been ᴺsore displeased with your fathers.

3 Therefore say thou unto them, Thus saith the LORD of hosts; Turn ᴿye unto me, saith the LORD of hosts, and I will turn unto you, saith the LORD of hosts.

4 Be ye not as your fathers, ᴿunto whom the former prophets have cried, saying, Thus saith the LORD of hosts; ᴿTurn ye now from your evil ways, and *from* your evil doings: but they did not hear, nor hearken unto me, saith the LORD.

5 Your fathers, where *are* they? and the prophets, do they live for ever?

6 But ᴿmy words and my statutes, which I commanded my servants the prophets, did they not ᴺtake hold of your fathers? and they returned and said, ᴿLike as the LORD of hosts thought to do unto us, according to our ways, and according to our doings, so hath he dealt with us.

Vision of the horses

7 Upon the four and twentieth day of the eleventh month, which *is* the month Sē'-băt, in the second year of Dă-rī'-ŭs, came the word of the LORD unto Zĕch-ȧ-rī'-ăh, the son of Bĕr-ē-chī'-ăh, the son of Ĭd'-dō the prophet, saying,

8 I saw by night, and behold ᴿa man riding upon a red horse, and he stood among the myrtle trees that *were* in the bottom; and behind him *were there* ᴿred horses, ᴺspeckled, and white.

9 Then said I, O my lord, what *are* these? And the angel that talked with me said unto me, I will shew thee what these *be*.

10 And the man that stood among the myrtle trees answered and said, ᴿThese *are they* whom the LORD hath sent to walk to and fro through the earth.

11 ᴿAnd they answered the angel of the LORD that stood among the myrtle trees, and said, We have walked to and fro through the earth, and, behold, all the earth sitteth still, and is at rest.

12 Then the angel of the LORD answered and said, O LORD of hosts, how long wilt thou not have mercy on Jerusalem and on the cities of Judah, against which thou hast had indignation ᴿthese threescore and ten years?

13 And the LORD answered the angel that talked with me *with* ᴿgood words *and* comfortable words.

14 So the angel that communed with me said unto me, Cry thou, saying, Thus saith the LORD of hosts; I am ᴿjealous for Jerusalem and for Zion with a great jealousy.

15 And I am very sore displeased with the heathen *that are* at ease: for ᴿI was but a little displeased, and they helped forward the affliction.

16 Therefore thus saith the LORD; ᴿI am returned to Jerusalem with mercies: my house shall be built in it, saith the LORD of hosts, and ᴿa line shall be stretched forth upon Jerusalem.

17 Cry yet, saying, Thus saith the LORD of hosts; My cities through ᴺprosperity shall yet be spread abroad; ᴿand the LORD shall yet comfort Zion, and ᴿshall yet choose Jerusalem.

Four horns and four carpenters

18 Then lifted I up mine eyes, and saw, and behold four horns.

19 And I said unto the angel that talked with me, What *be* these? And he answered me, ᴿThese *are* the horns which have scattered Judah, Israel, and Jerusalem.

20 And the LORD shewed me four carpenters.

21 Then said I, What come these to do? And he spake, saying, These *are* the horns which have scattered Judah, so that no man did lift up his head: but these are come to fray them, to cast out the horns of the Gentiles, which ᴿlifted up *their* horn over the land of Judah to scatter it.

CHAPTER 2

The measuring line

I LIFTED up mine eyes again, and looked, and behold ᴿa man with a measuring line in his hand.

2 Then said I, Whither goest thou? And he said unto me, ᴿTo measure Jerusalem, to see what *is* the breadth thereof, and what *is* the length thereof.

3 And, behold, the angel that talked with me went forth, and another angel went out to meet him,

4 And said unto him, Run, speak to this young man, saying, ᴿJerusalem shall be inhabited *as* towns without walls for the multitude of men and cattle therein:

5 For I, saith the LORD, will be unto her ᴿa wall of fire round about, ᴿand will be the glory in the midst of her.

6 Ho, ho, *come forth*, and flee ᴿfrom the

land of the north, saith the LORD: for I have [R]spread you abroad as the four winds of the heaven, saith the LORD.

7 [R]Deliver thyself, O Zion, that dwellest *with* the daughter of Babylon.

8 For thus saith the LORD of hosts; After the glory hath he sent me unto the nations which spoiled you: for he that [R]toucheth you toucheth the apple of his eye.

9 For, behold, I will [R]shake mine hand upon them, and they shall be a spoil to their servants: and [R]ye shall know that the LORD of hosts hath sent me.

10 [R]Sing and rejoice, O daughter of Zion: for, lo, I come, and I [R]will dwell in the midst of thee, saith the LORD.

11 [R]And many nations shall be joined to the LORD [R]in that day, and shall be [R]my people: and I will dwell in the midst of thee, and [R]thou shalt know that the LORD of hosts hath sent me unto thee.

12 And the LORD shall [R]inherit Judah his portion in the holy land, and [R]shall choose Jerusalem again.

13 [R]Be silent, O all flesh, before the LORD: for he is raised up [R]out of [N]his holy habitation.

CHAPTER 3

The high priest Joshua

AND he shewed me [R]Joshua the high priest standing before the angel of the LORD, and [R]Satan[N] standing at his right hand [N]to resist him.

2 And the LORD said unto Satan, [R]The LORD rebuke thee, O Satan; even the LORD that [R]hath chosen Jerusalem rebuke thee: [R]*is* not this a brand plucked out of the fire?

3 Now Joshua was clothed with [R]filthy garments, and stood before the angel.

4 And he answered and spake unto those that stood before him, saying, Take away the filthy garments from him. And unto him he said, Behold, I have caused thine iniquity to pass from thee, [R]and I will clothe thee with change of raiment.

5 And I said, Let them set a fair [R]mitre upon his head. So they set a fair mitre upon his head, and clothed him with garments. And the angel of the LORD stood by.

6 And the angel of the LORD protested unto Joshua, saying,

7 Thus saith the LORD of hosts; If thou wilt walk in my ways, and if thou wilt [R]keep my [N]charge, then thou shalt also [R]judge my house, and shalt also keep my courts, and I will give thee [N]places to walk among these that [R]stand by.

8 Hear now, O Joshua the high priest, thou,

and thy fellows that sit before thee: for they *are* [R]men[N] wondered at: for, behold, I will bring forth [R]my servant the [R]BRANCH.   ★

9 For behold the stone that I have laid before Joshua; [R]upon one stone *shall be* [R]seven eyes: behold, I will engrave the graving thereof, saith the LORD of hosts, and [R]I will remove the iniquity of that land in one day.

10 [R]In that day, saith the LORD of hosts, shall ye call every man his neighbour [R]under the vine and under the fig tree.

CHAPTER 4

The golden candlestick

AND [R]the angel that talked with me came again, and waked me, [R]as a man that is wakened out of his sleep,

2 And said unto me, What seest thou? And I said, I have looked, and behold [R]a candlestick all *of* gold, [N]with a bowl upon the top of it, [R]and his seven lamps thereon, and [N]seven pipes to the seven lamps, which *are* upon the top thereof:

3 [R]And two olive trees by it, one upon the right *side* of the bowl, and the other upon the left *side* thereof.

4 So I answered and spake to the angel that talked with me, saying, What *are* these, my lord?

5 Then the angel that talked with me answered and said unto me, Knowest thou not what these be? And I said, No, my lord.

6 Then he answered and spake unto me, saying, This *is* the word of the LORD unto Zĕ-rŭb′-bă-bĕl, saying, [R]Not by [N]might, nor by power, but by my spirit, saith the LORD of hosts.

7 Who *art* thou, [R]O great mountain? before Zĕ-rŭb′-bă-bĕl *thou shalt become* a plain: and he shall bring forth [R]the headstone *thereof* [R]*with* shoutings, *crying,* Grace, grace unto it.

8 Moreover the word of the LORD came unto me, saying,

9 The hands of Zĕ-rŭb′-bă-bĕl [R]have laid the foundation of this house; his hands [R]shall also finish it; and [R]thou shalt know that the [R]LORD of hosts hath sent me unto you.

10 For who hath despised the day of [R]small things? [N]for they shall rejoice, and shall see the [N]plummet in the hand of Zĕ-rŭb′-bă-bĕl *with* those seven; [R]they *are* the eyes of the LORD, which run to and fro through the whole earth.

11 Then answered I, and said unto him, What *are* these [R]two olive trees upon the right *side* of the candlestick and upon the left *side* thereof?

12 And I answered again, and said unto him,

What *be these* two olive branches which
^Nthrough the two golden pipes ^Nempty ^Nthe
golden *oil* out of themselves?

13 And he answered me and said, Knowest
thou not what these *be?* And I said, No, my
lord.

14 Then said he, ^RThese *are* the two
^Nanointed ones, ^Rthat stand by ^Rthe Lord of
the whole earth.

CHAPTER 5

A flying roll

THEN I turned, and lifted up mine eyes,
and looked, and behold a flying ^Rroll.

2 And he said unto me, What seest thou?
And I answered, I see a flying roll; the length
thereof *is* twenty cubits, and the breadth
thereof ten cubits.

3 Then said he unto me, This *is* the ^Rcurse
that goeth forth over the face of the whole
earth: for ^Nevery one that stealeth shall be cut
off *as* on this side according to it; and every
one that sweareth shall be cut off *as* on that
side according to it.

4 I will bring it forth, saith the LORD of
hosts, and it shall enter into the house of the
thief, and into the house of ^Rhim that sweareth
falsely by my name: and it shall remain in the
midst of his house, and ^Rshall consume it with
the timber thereof and the stones thereof.

The woman in the ephah

5 Then the angel that talked with me went
forth, and said unto me, Lift up now thine
eyes, and see what *is* this that goeth forth.

6 And I said, What *is* it? And he said, This
is an ē'-phäh that goeth forth. He said moreover, This *is* their resemblance through all the
earth.

7 And, behold, there was lifted up a ^Ntalent
of lead: and this *is* a woman that sitteth in the
midst of the ē'-phäh.

8 And he said, This *is* wickedness. And he
cast it into the midst of the ē'-phäh; and he
cast the weight of lead upon the mouth
thereof.

9 Then lifted I up mine eyes, and looked,
and, behold, there came out two women, and
the wind *was* in their wings; for they had
wings like the wings of a stork: and they lifted
up the ē'-phäh between the earth and the
heaven.

10 Then said I to the angel that talked with
me, Whither do these bear the ē'-phäh?

11 And he said unto me, To ^Rbuild it an
house in ^Rthe land of Shī'-när: and it shall be
established, and set there upon her own base.

CHAP. **4**
BC 519

12 Heb. *by the hand*
12 Or, *empty out of themselves* oil into *the gold*
12 Heb. *the gold*
14 Rev. 11:4
14 Heb. *sons of oil*
14 ch. 3:7
14 See Josh. 3:11, 13 ch. 6:5

CHAP. **5**
BC 519

1 Ezek. 2:9
3 Mal. 4:6
3 Or, *every one of this people that stealeth holdeth* himself *guiltless as it* doth
4 Lev. 19:12 ch. 8:17 Mal. 3:5
4 See Lev. 14:45
7 Or, *weighty piece*
11 Jer. 29:5, 28
11 Gen. 10:10

CHAP. **6**
BC 519

ch. 1:8	2
Rev. 6:5	2
Or, *strong*	3
ch. 5:10	4
Ps. 104:4	5
Heb. 1:7, 14	
Or, *winds*	5
1 Ki. 22:19	5
Dan. 7:10	
ch. 4:14	
Luke 1:19	
Jer. 1:14	6
Gen. 13:17	7
ch. 1:10	
Eccl. 10:4	8
Ex. 29:6	11
Luke 1:78	12
John 1:45	12
ch. 3:8	12
Or, *branch up from under him*	12
Mat. 16:18	12
Eph. 2:20	
Heb. 3:3	
Is. 22:24	13
Ps. 110:4	13
Heb. 3:1	
Ex. 12:14	14
Mark 14:9	
Is. 57:19	15
Eph. 2:13	

CHAPTER 6

Four chariots

AND I turned, and lifted up mine eyes, and
looked, and, behold, there came four
chariots out from between two mountains; and
the mountains *were* mountains of brass.

2 In the first chariot *were* ^Rred horses; and in
the second chariot ^Rblack horses;

3 And in the third chariot white horses; and
in the fourth chariot grisled and ^Nbay horses.

4 Then I answered ^Rand said unto the angel
that talked with me, What *are* these, my lord?

5 And the angel answered and said unto me,
^RThese *are* the four ^Nspirits of the heavens,
which go forth from ^Rstanding before the Lord
of all the earth.

6 The black horses which *are* therein go
forth into ^Rthe north country; and the white go
forth after them; and the grisled go forth toward the south country.

7 And the bay went forth, and sought to go
that they might ^Rwalk to and fro through the
earth: and he said, Get you hence, walk to and
fro through the earth. So they walked to and
fro through the earth.

8 Then cried he upon me, and spake unto
me, saying, Behold, these that go toward the
north country have quieted my ^Rspirit in the
north country.

Coronation of Joshua

9 And the word of the LORD came unto me,
saying,

10 Take of *them of* the captivity, *even* of
Hĕl'-dâi, of Tō-bī'-jäh, and of Jĕ-dâi'-ăh,
which are come from Babylon, and come thou
the same day, and go into the house of Jō-sī'-
ăh the son of Zĕph-ă-nī'-ăh;

11 Then take silver and gold, and make
^Rcrowns, and set *them* upon the head of
Joshua the son of Jŏs'-ĕ-dĕch, the high priest;

12 And speak unto him, saying, Thus
speaketh the LORD of hosts, saying, Behold
^Rthe man whose name *is* The ^RBRANCH;
and he shall ^Ngrow up out of his place, ^Rand
he shall build the temple of the LORD: ★

13 Even he shall build the temple of the
LORD; and he ^Rshall bear the glory, and shall
sit and rule upon his throne; and ^Rhe shall be a
priest upon his throne: and the counsel of
peace shall be between them both.   ★

14 And the crowns shall be to Hē'-lĕm, and
to Tō-bī'-jäh, and to Jĕ-dâi'-ăh, and to Hen the
son of Zĕph-ă-nī'-ăh, ^Rfor a memorial in the
temple of the LORD.

15 And ^Rthey *that are* far off shall come and
build in the temple of the LORD, and ye shall

know that the LORD of hosts hath sent me unto you. And *this* shall come to pass, if ye will diligently obey the voice of the LORD your God.

CHAPTER 7

Question about the fasts

AND it came to pass in the fourth year of king Dă-rī′-ŭs, *that* the word of the LORD came unto Zĕch-ă-rī′-ăh in the fourth *day* of the ninth month, *even* in Chĭś′-lĕû;

2 When they had sent unto the house of God Shĕr-ē′-zĕr and Rē′-gĕm-mĕl′-ĕch, and their men, ᴺto pray before the LORD,

3 *And* to ᴿspeak unto the priests which *were* in the house of the LORD of hosts, and to the prophets, saying, Should I weep in ᴿthe fifth month, separating myself, as I have done these so many years?

4 Then came the word of the LORD of hosts unto me, saying,

5 Speak unto all the people of the land, and to the priests, saying, When ye ᴿfasted and mourned in the fifth ᴿand seventh *month*, ᴿeven those seventy years, did ye at all fast ᴿunto me, *even* to me?

6 And when ye did eat, and when ye did drink, ᴺdid not ye eat *for yourselves,* and drink *for yourselves?*

7 ᴺ*Should* ye not *hear* the words which the LORD hath cried ᴺby the former prophets, when Jerusalem was inhabited and in prosperity, and the cities thereof round about her, when *men* inhabited ᴿthe south and the plain?

Causes of the exile

8 And the word of the LORD came unto Zĕch-ă-rī′-ăh, saying,

9 Thus speaketh the LORD of hosts, saying, ᴿExecuteᴺ true judgment, and shew mercy and compassions every man to his brother:

10 And ᴿoppress not the widow, nor the fatherless, the stranger, nor the poor; ᴿand let none of you imagine evil against his brother in your heart.

11 But they refused to hearken, and ᴿpulledᴺ away the shoulder, and ᴿstoppedᴺ their ears, that they should not hear.

12 Yea, they made their ᴿhearts *as* an adamant stone, ᴿlest they should hear the law, and the words which the LORD of hosts hath sent in his spirit ᴺby the former prophets: ᴿtherefore came a great wrath from the LORD of hosts.

13 Therefore it is come to pass, *that* as he cried, and they would not hear; so ᴿthey cried, and I would not hear, saith the LORD of hosts:

14 But ᴿI scattered them with a whirlwind among all the nations whom they knew not. Thus the land was desolate after them, that no man passed through nor returned: for they laid the ᴺpleasant land desolate.

CHAPTER 8

Promises concerning restoration

AGAIN the word of the LORD of hosts came *to me,* saying,

2 Thus saith the LORD of hosts; ᴿI was jealous for Zion with great jealousy, and I was jealous for her with great fury.

3 Thus saith the LORD; I am returned unto Zion, and will dwell in the midst of Jerusalem: and Jerusalem ᴿshall be called a city of truth; and ᴿthe mountain of the LORD of hosts ᴿthe holy mountain.

4 Thus saith the LORD of hosts; ᴿThere shall yet old men and old women dwell in the streets of Jerusalem, and every man with his staff in his hand ᴺfor very age.

5 And the streets of the city shall be full of boys and girls playing in the streets thereof.

6 Thus saith the LORD of hosts; If it be ᴺmarvellous in the eyes of the remnant of this people in these days, ᴿshould it also be marvellous in mine eyes? saith the LORD of hosts.

7 Thus saith the LORD of hosts; Behold, ᴿI will save my people from the east country, and from ᴺthe west country;

8 And I will bring them, and they shall dwell in the midst of Jerusalem: ᴿand they shall be my people, and I will be their God, ᴿin truth and in righteousness.

9 Thus saith the LORD of hosts; ᴿLet your hands be strong, ye that hear in these days these words by the mouth of ᴿthe prophets, which *were* in ᴿthe day *that* the foundation of the house of the LORD of hosts was laid, that the temple might be built.

10 For before these days ᴺthere was no ᴿhire for man, nor any hire for beast; neither *was there any* peace to him that went out or came in because of the affliction: for I set all men every one against his neighbour.

11 But now I *will* not *be* unto the residue of this people as in the former days, saith the LORD of hosts.

12 ᴿFor the seed *shall be* ᴺprosperous; the vine shall give her fruit, and ᴿthe ground shall give her increase, and ᴿthe heavens shall give their dew; and I will cause the remnant of this people to possess all these *things.*

13 And it shall come to pass, *that* as ye were ᴿa curse among the heathen, O house of Judah, and house of Israel; so will I save you,

and ᴿye shall be a blessing: fear not, *but* let your hands be strong.

14 For thus saith the LORD of hosts; ᴿAs I thought to punish you, when your fathers provoked me to wrath, saith the LORD of hosts, ᴿand I repented not:

15 So again have I thought in these days to do well unto Jerusalem and to the house of Judah: fear ye not.

Conditions of the restoration

16 These *are* the things that ye shall do; ᴿSpeak ye every man the truth to his neighbour; ᴺexecute the judgment of truth and peace in your gates:

17 ᴿAnd let none of you imagine evil in your hearts against his neighbour; and love no false oath: for all these *are things* that I hate, saith the LORD.

Answer to the question about fasts

18 And the word of the LORD of hosts came unto me, saying,

19 Thus saith the LORD of hosts; ᴿThe fast of the fourth *month,* ᴿand the fast of the fifth, ᴿand the fast of the seventh, ᴿand the fast of the tenth, shall be to the house of Judah ᴿjoy and gladness, and cheerful ᴺfeasts; ᴿtherefore love the truth and peace.

Nations to seek God

20 Thus saith the LORD of hosts; *It shall* yet *come to pass,* that there shall come people, and the inhabitants of many cities:

21 And the inhabitants of one *city* shall go to another, saying, ᴿLet us go ᴺᴺspeedily ᴺto pray before the LORD, and to seek the LORD of hosts: I will go also.

22 Yea, ᴿmany people and strong nations shall come to seek the LORD of hosts in Jerusalem, and to pray before the LORD.

23 Thus saith the LORD of hosts; In those days *it shall come to pass,* that ten men shall ᴿtake hold out of all languages of the nations, even shall take hold of the skirt of him that is a Jew, saying, We will go with you: for we have heard ᴿthat God *is* with you.

CHAPTER 9

Judgment on surrounding nations

THE ᴿburden of the word of the LORD in the land of Hā′-dra<u>ch</u>, and ᴿDamascus *shall be* the rest thereof: when ᴿthe eyes of man, as of all the tribes of Israel, *shall be* toward the LORD.

2 And ᴿHā′-măth also shall border thereby; ᴿTȳ′-rŭs, and ᴿZĭ′-dŏn, though it be very ᴿwise.

CHAP. **8**
BC 518
13 Gen. 12:2
14 Ruth 4:11
14 Jer. 31:28
14 2 Chr. 36:16
16 Eph. 4:25
16 Heb. *judge truth, and the judgment of peace*
17 Prov. 3:29
19 Jer. 52:6
19 Jer. 52:12
19 2 Ki. 25:25
Jer. 41:1, 2
19 Jer. 52:4
19 Esth. 8:17
19 Or, *solemn, or, set times*
19 ver. 16
21 Is. 2:3
Mic. 4:1, 2
21 Or, *continually*
21 Heb. *going*
21 Heb. *to entreat the face of the LORD*
22 Is. 60:3, etc.
23 Is. 3:6
23 1 Cor. 14:25

CHAP. **9**
BC 487
1 Jer. 23:33
1 Amos 1:3
1 2 Chr. 20:12
Ps. 145:15
2 Jer. 49:23
2 Is. 23
Ezek. 26
2 1 Ki. 17:9
2 Ezek. 28:3

Is. 23:1   4
Ezek. 26:17   4
Amos 1:8   6
Heb. *bloods*   7
Ps. 34:7   8
ch. 2:10   9
Jer. 23:5   9
  Luke 19:38
Or, *saving himself*   9
Hos. 1:7   10
  Mic. 5:10
Or, *whose covenant is by blood,*   11
  Ex. 24:8
Is. 42:7   11
Is. 49:9   12
Ps. 18:14   14
Is. 21:1   14
Or, *subdue the stones of the sling*   15
Or, *shall fill both the bowls, etc.*
Is. 62:3   16
Mal. 3:17
Is. 11:12   16

3 And Tȳ′-rŭs did build herself a strong hold, and heaped up silver as the dust, and fine gold as the mire of the streets.

4 Behold, ᴿthe Lord will cast her out, and he will smite ᴿher power in the sea; and she shall be devoured with fire.

5 Ăsh′-kĕ-lon shall see *it,* and fear; Gā′-ză also *shall see it,* and be very sorrowful, and ĕk′-rŏn; for her expectation shall be ashamed; and the king shall perish from Gā′-ză, and Ăsh′-kĕ-lon shall not be inhabited.

6 And a bastard shall dwell ᴿin Ăsh′-dŏd, and I will cut off the pride of the Philistines.

7 And I will take away his ᴺblood out of his mouth, and his abominations from between his teeth: but he that remaineth, even he, *shall be* for our God, and he shall be as a governor in Judah, and ĕk′-rŏn as a Jĕb′-ū-sĭte.

8 And ᴿI will encamp about mine house because of the army, because of him that passeth by, and because of him that returneth: and no oppressor shall pass through them any more: for now have I seen with mine eyes.

Restoration under the humble King

9 ᴿRejoice greatly, O daughter of Zion; shout, O daughter of Jerusalem: behold, ᴿthy King cometh unto thee: he *is* just, and ᴺhaving salvation; lowly, and riding upon an ass, and upon a colt the foal of an ass.   ★

10 And I ᴿwill cut off the chariot from Ē′-phră-ĭm, and the horse from Jerusalem, and the battle bow shall be cut off: and he shall speak peace unto the heathen: and his dominion *shall be* from sea *even* to sea, and from the river *even* to the ends of the earth.   ★

11 As for thee also, ᴺby the blood of thy covenant I have sent forth thy ᴿprisoners out of the pit wherein *is* no water.

12 Turn you to the strong hold, ᴿye prisoners of hope: even to day do I declare *that* I will render double unto thee;

13 When I have bent Judah for me, filled the bow with Ē′-phră-ĭm, and raised up thy sons, O Zion, against thy sons, O Greece, and made thee as the sword of a mighty man.

14 And the LORD shall be seen over them, and ᴿhis arrow shall go forth as the lightning: and the Lord GOD shall blow the trumpet and shall go ᴿwith whirlwinds of the south.

15 The LORD of hosts shall defend them; and they shall devour, and ᴺsubdue with sling stones; and they shall drink, *and* make a noise as through wine; and they ᴺshall be filled like bowls, *and* as the corners of the altar.

16 And the LORD their God shall save them in that day as the flock of his people: for ᴿthey *shall be as* the stones of a crown, ᴿlifted up as an ensign upon his land.

17 For ᴿhow great *is* his goodness, and how great *is* his beauty! ᴿcorn shall make the young men ᴺcheerful, and new wine the maids.

CHAPTER 10

Redemption of God's people

ASK ye ᴿof the Lᴏʀᴅ ᴿrain ᴿin the time of the latter rain; *so* the Lᴏʀᴅ shall make ᴺbright clouds, and give them showers of rain, to every one grass in the field.

2 For the ᴿidolsᴺ have spoken vanity, and the diviners have seen a lie, and have told false dreams; they ᴿcomfort in vain: therefore they went their way as a flock, they ᴺwere troubled, ᴿbecause *there was* no shepherd.

3 Mine anger was kindled against the shepherds, ᴿand I ᴺpunished the goats: for the Lᴏʀᴅ of hosts ᴿhath visited his flock the house of Judah, and ᴿhath made them as his goodly horse in the battle.

4 Out of him came forth ᴿthe corner, out of him ᴿthe nail, out of him the battle bow, out of him every oppressor together.

5 And they shall be as mighty *men,* which ᴿtread down *their enemies* in the mire of the streets in the battle: and they shall fight, because the Lᴏʀᴅ *is* with them, and ᴺthe riders on horses shall be confounded.

6 And I will strengthen the house of Judah, and I will save the house of Joseph, and ᴿI will bring them again to place them; for I ᴿhave mercy upon them: and they shall be as though I had not cast them off: for I *am* the Lᴏʀᴅ their God, and ᴿwill hear them.

7 And *they of* E̅'-phră-ĭm shall be like a mighty *man,* and their ᴿheart shall rejoice as through wine: yea, their children shall see *it,* and be glad; their heart shall rejoice in the Lᴏʀᴅ.

8 I will ᴿhiss for them, and gather them; for I have redeemed them: ᴿand they shall increase as they have increased.

9 And ᴿI will sow them among the people: and they shall ᴿremember me in far countries; and they shall live with their children, and turn again.

10 ᴿI will bring them again also out of the land of Egypt, and gather them out of Assyria; and I will bring them into the land of Gilead and Lĕb'-ă-nọn; and ᴿ*place* shall not be found for them.

11 ᴿAnd he shall pass through the sea with affliction, and shall smite the waves in the sea, and all the deeps of the river shall dry up: and ᴿthe pride of Assyria shall be brought down, and ᴿthe sceptre of Egypt shall depart away.

12 And I will strengthen them in the Lᴏʀᴅ;

and ᴿthey shall walk up and down in his name, saith the Lᴏʀᴅ.

CHAPTER 11

A day of visitation

OPEN ᴿthy doors, O Lĕb'-ă-nọn, that the fire may devour thy cedars.

2 Howl, fir tree; for the cedar is fallen; because the ᴺmighty are spoiled: howl, O ye oaks of Bā'-shăn; ᴿfor ᴺthe forest of the vintage is come down.

3 *There is* a voice of the howling of the shepherds; for their glory is spoiled: a voice of the roaring of young lions; for the pride of Jordan is spoiled.

Allegory of the shepherds

4 Thus saith the Lᴏʀᴅ my God; Feed the flock of the slaughter;

5 Whose possessors slay them, and ᴿhold themselves not guilty: and they that sell them ᴿsay, Blessed *be* the Lᴏʀᴅ; for I am rich: and their own shepherds pity them not.

6 For I will no more pity the inhabitants of the land, saith the Lᴏʀᴅ: but, lo, I will ᴺdeliver the men every one into his neighbour's hand, and into the hand of his king: and they shall smite the land, and out of their hand I will not deliver *them.*

7 And I will feed the flock of slaughter, ᴺ*even* you, ᴿO poor of the flock. And I took unto me two staves; the one I called Beauty, and the other I called ᴺBands; and I fed the flock.

8 Three shepherds also I cut off ᴿin one month; and my soul ᴺloathed them, and their soul also abhorred me.

9 Then said I, I will not feed you: ᴿthat that dieth, let it die; and that that is to be cut off, let it be cut off; and let the rest eat every one the flesh ᴺof another.

10 And I took my staff, *even* Beauty, and cut it asunder, that I might break my covenant which I had made with all the people.

11 And it was broken in that day: and ᴺso ᴿthe poor of the flock that waited upon me knew that it *was* the word of the Lᴏʀᴅ.

12 And I said unto them, ᴺIf ye think good, give *me* my price; and if not, forbear. So they ᴿweighed for my price thirty *pieces* of silver. ★

13 And the Lᴏʀᴅ said unto me, Cast it unto the ᴿpotter: a goodly price that I was prised at of them. And I took the thirty *pieces* of silver, and cast them to the potter in the house of the Lᴏʀᴅ.   ★

14 Then I cut asunder mine other staff, *even* ᴺBands, that I might break the brotherhood between Judah and Israel.

15 And the LORD said unto me, RTake unto thee yet the instruments of a foolish shepherd.

16 For, lo, I will raise up a shepherd in the land, *which* shall not visit those that be Ncut off, neither shall seek the young one, nor heal that that is broken, nor Nfeed that that standeth still: but he shall eat the flesh of the fat, and tear their claws in pieces.

17 RWoe to the idol shepherd that leaveth the flock! the sword *shall be* upon his arm, and upon his right eye: his arm shall be clean dried up, and his right eye shall be utterly darkened.

CHAPTER 12

Siege of Jerusalem

THE burden of the word of the LORD for Israel, saith the LORD, Rwhich stretcheth forth the heavens, and layeth the foundation of the earth, and Rformeth the spirit of man within him.

2 Behold, I will make Jerusalem Ra cup of Ntrembling unto all the people round about, Nwhen they shall be in the siege both against Judah *and* against Jerusalem.

3 RAnd in that day will I make Jerusalem Ra burdensome stone for all people: all that burden themselves with it shall be cut in pieces, though all the people of the earth be gathered together against it.

4 In that day, saith the LORD, RI will smite every horse with astonishment, and his rider with madness: and I will open mine eyes upon the house of Judah, and will smite every horse of the people with blindness.

5 And the governors of Judah shall say in their heart, NThe inhabitants of Jerusalem *shall be* my strength in the LORD of hosts their God.

Restoration of Judah

6 In that day will I make the governors of Judah Rlike an hearth of fire among the wood, and like a torch of fire in a sheaf; and they shall devour all the people round about, on the right hand and on the left: and Jerusalem shall be inhabited again in her own place, *even* in Jerusalem.

7 The LORD also shall save the tents of Judah first, that the glory of the house of David and the glory of the inhabitants of Jerusalem do not magnify *themselves* against Judah.

8 In that day shall the LORD defend the inhabitants of Jerusalem; and he that is NNfeeble among them at that day shall be as David; and the house of David *shall be* as God, as the angel of the LORD before them.

9 And it shall come to pass in that day, *that*

I will seek to Rdestroy all the nations that come against Jerusalem.

10 RAnd I will pour upon the house of David, and upon the inhabitants of Jerusalem, the spirit of grace and of supplications: and they shall Rlook upon me whom they have pierced, and they shall mourn for him, Ras one mourneth for *his* only *son,* and shall be in bitterness for him, as one that is in bitterness for *his* firstborn.　　★

11 In that day shall there be a great Rmourning in Jerusalem, Ras the mourning of Hā-dăd-rĭm′-mon in the valley of Mĕ-gĭd′-don.

12 RAnd the land shall mourn, Nevery family apart; the family of the house of David apart, and their wives apart; the family of the house of RNathan apart, and their wives apart;

13 The family of the house of Levi apart, and their wives apart; the family Nof Shĭm′-ĕ-i apart, and their wives apart;

14 All the families that remain, every family apart, and their wives apart.

CHAPTER 13

Fountain of purification

IN that day there shall be Ra fountain opened to the house of David and to the inhabitants of Jerusalem for sin and for Nuncleanness.　　★

2 And it shall come to pass in that day, saith the LORD of hosts, *that* I will Rcut off the names of the idols out of the land, and they shall no more be remembered: and also I will cause Rthe prophets and the unclean spirit to pass out of the land.

3 And it shall come to pass, *that* when any shall yet prophesy, then his father and his mother that begat him shall say unto him, Thou shalt not live; for thou speakest lies in the name of the LORD: and his father and his mother that begat him Rshall thrust him through when he prophesieth.

4 And it shall come to pass in that day, *that* Rthe prophets shall be ashamed every one of his vision, when he hath prophesied; neither shall they wear RaN rough garment Nto deceive:

5 RBut he shall say, I *am* no prophet, I *am* an husbandman; for man taught me to keep cattle from my youth.

6 And *one* shall say unto him, What *are* these wounds in thine hands? Then he shall answer, *Those* with which I was wounded *in* the house of my friends.　　★

Sword against the shepherd

7 Awake, O sword, against Rmy shepherd, and against the man Rthat is my fellow, saith the LORD of hosts: Rsmite the shepherd, and

the sheep shall be scattered: and I will turn mine hand upon ᴿthe little ones.   ★

8 And it shall come to pass, *that* in all the land, saith the LORD, two parts therein shall be cut off *and* die; ᴿbut the third shall be left therein.

9 And I will bring the third part ᴿthrough the fire, and will ᴿrefine them as silver is refined, and will try them as gold is tried: ᴿthey shall call on my name, and I will hear them: ᴿI will say, It *is* my people: and they shall say, The LORD *is* my God.

CHAPTER 14

The day of the LORD

BEHOLD, ᴿthe day of the LORD cometh, and thy spoil shall be divided in the midst of thee.

2 For ᴿI will gather all nations against Jerusalem to battle; and the city shall be taken, and the houses rifled, and the women ravished; and half of the city shall go forth into captivity, and the residue of the people shall not be cut off from the city.

3 Then shall the LORD go forth, and fight against those nations, as when he fought in the day of battle.

4 And his feet shall stand in that day ᴿupon the mount of Olives, which *is* before Jerusalem on the east, and the mount of Olives shall cleave in the midst thereof toward the east and toward the west, ᴿ*and there shall be* a very great valley; and half of the mountain shall remove toward the north, and half of it toward the south.   ★

5 And ye shall flee *to* the valley of ᴺthe mountains; ᴺfor the valley of the mountains shall reach unto Ā′-zăl: yea, ye shall flee, like as ye fled from before the ᴿearthquake in the days of ŭz′-zī′-ăh king of Judah: ᴿand the LORD my God shall come, *and* ᴿall the saints with thee.

6 And it shall come to pass in that day, ᴺ*that* the light shall not be ᴺclear, *nor* ᴺdark:

7 But ᴺit shall be one day ᴿwhich shall be known to the LORD, not day, nor night: but it shall come to pass, *that* at ᴿevening time it shall be light.

8 And it shall be in that day, *that* living ᴿwaters shall go out from Jerusalem; half of them toward the ᴺformer sea, and half of them toward the hinder sea: in summer and in winter shall it be.

Universal reign of the LORD

9 And the LORD shall be ᴿking over all the earth: in that day shall there be ᴿone LORD, and his name one.

CHAP.	13
BC 487	
7	Luke 12:32
8	Rom. 11:5
8	Is. 48:10
9	1 Pet. 1:6
9	Ps. 50:15
9	Jer. 30:22

CHAP.	14
BC 487	
1	Is. 13:9
2	Joel 3:2
4	Ezek. 11:23
4	Joel 3:12
5	Or, *my mountains*
5	Or, *when he shall touch the valley of the mountains to the place he separated*
5	Amos 1:1
5	Mat. 24:30
5	Joel 3:11
6	i.e. it shall not be clear in some places of the world
6	Heb. *precious*
6	Heb. *thickness*
7	Or, *the day shall be one*
7	Mat. 24:36
7	Is. 30:26
8	Ezek. 47:1
8	Or, *eastern*, Joel 2:20
9	Rev. 11:15
9	Eph. 4:5, 6

Or, *compassed*	10
ch. 12:6	10
Or, *shall abide*	10
Neh. 3:1	10
Jer. 31:40	11
Jer. 23:6	11
Or, *shall abide*	11
1 Sam. 14:15, 20	13
Judg. 7:22	13
2 Chr. 20:23	
Ezek. 38:21	
Or, *thou also, O Judah, shalt*	14
Or, *against*	14
Ezek. 39:10, 17, etc.	14
ver. 12	15
Is. 60:6 & 66:23	16
Lev. 23:34	16
Neh. 8:14	
Hos. 12:9	
John 7:2	
Is. 60:12	17
Deut. 11:10	18
Heb. *upon whom there is not*	18
Or, *sin*	19
Or, *bridles*	20
Is. 23:18	20
Is. 35:8	21
Joel 3:17	
Rev. 21:27 & 22:15	
Eph. 2:19-22	21

10 All the land shall be ᴺturned as a plain from Gē′-bă to Rĭm′-mon south of Jerusalem: and it shall be lifted up, and ᴿinhabitedᴺ in her place, from Benjamin's gate unto the place of the first gate, unto the corner gate, ᴿand *from* the tower of Hăn′-ă-nēĕl unto the king's winepresses.

11 And *men* shall dwell in it, and there shall be ᴿno more utter destruction; ᴿbut Jerusalem ᴺshall be safely inhabited.

12 And this shall be the plague wherewith the LORD will smite all the people that have fought against Jerusalem; Their flesh shall consume away while they stand upon their feet, and their eyes shall consume away in their holes, and their tongue shall consume away in their mouth.

13 And it shall come to pass in that day, *that* ᴿa great tumult from the LORD shall be among them; and they shall lay hold every one on the hand of his neighbour, and ᴿhis hand shall rise up against the hand of his neighbour.

14 And ᴺJudah also shall fight ᴺat Jerusalem; ᴿand the wealth of all the heathen round about shall be gathered together, gold, and silver, and apparel, in great abundance.

15 And ᴿso shall be the plague of the horse, of the mule, of the camel, and of the ass, and of all the beasts that shall be in these tents, as this plague.

16 And it shall come to pass, *that* every one that is left of all the nations which came against Jerusalem shall even ᴿgo up from year to year to worship the King, the LORD of hosts, and to keep ᴿthe feast of tabernacles.

17 ᴿAnd it shall be, *that* whoso will not come up of *all* the families of the earth unto Jerusalem to worship the King, the LORD of hosts, even upon them shall be no rain.

18 And if the family of Egypt go not up, and come not, ᴿthatᴺ *have* no *rain;* there shall be the plague, wherewith the LORD will smite the heathen that come not up to keep the feast of tabernacles.

19 This shall be the ᴺpunishment of Egypt, and the punishment of all nations that come not up to keep the feast of tabernacles.

20 In that day shall there be upon the ᴺbells of the horses, ᴿHOLINESS UNTO THE LORD; and the pots in the LORD'S house shall be like the bowls before the altar.

21 Yea, every pot in Jerusalem and in Judah shall be holiness unto the LORD of hosts: and all they that sacrifice shall come and take of them, and seethe therein: and in that day there shall be no more the ᴿCanaanite in ᴿthe house of the LORD of hosts.

MALACHI

The prophet Malachi traditionally is considered the last of God's prophetic messengers. He was active during the last half of the fifth century B.C. As a contemporary of Nehemiah, Malachi voiced his opposition to the abuses prevalent in Judah. He was concerned about their apostasy and indifference. He warned them of judgment to come.

OUTLINE:

I. Israel indifferent to God's favour 1:1–14
II. Unfaithfulness rebuked 2:1–16
III. Accountability to God 2:17–4:6

CHAPTER 1

God's love

THE burden of the word of the LORD to Israel ᴺby Măl'-ă-chī.

2 ᴿI have loved you, saith the LORD. Yet ye say, Wherein hast thou loved us? *Was* not Esau Jacob's brother? saith the LORD: yet ᴿI loved Jacob,

3 And I hated Esau, and ᴿlaid his mountains and his heritage waste for the dragons of the wilderness.

4 Whereas Ē'-dom saith, We are impoverished, but we will return and build the desolate places; thus saith the LORD of hosts, They shall build, but I will throw down; and they shall call them, The border of wickedness, and, The people against whom the LORD hath indignation for ever.

5 And your eyes shall see, and ye shall say, ᴿThe LORD will be magnified ᴺᴺfrom the border of Israel.

Judah's dishonour

6 A son ᴿhonoureth *his* father, and a servant his master: ᴿif then I *be* a father, where *is* mine honour? and if I *be* a master, where *is* my fear? saith the LORD of hosts unto you, O priests, that despise my name. ᴿAnd ye say, Wherein have we despised thy name?

Polluted offerings

.7 ᴺYe offer ᴿpolluted bread upon mine altar; and ye say, Wherein have we polluted thee? In that ye say, ᴿThe table of the LORD *is* contemptible.

8 And ᴿif ye offer the blind ᴺfor sacrifice, *is it* not evil? and if ye offer the lame and sick, *is it* not evil? offer it now unto thy governor; will he be pleased with thee, or ᴿaccept thy person? saith the LORD of hosts.

9 And now, I pray you, beseech ᴺGod that he will be gracious unto us: ᴿthis hath been ᴺby your means: will he regard your persons? saith the LORD of hosts.

10 Who *is there* even among you that would

shut the doors *for nought?* ᴿneither do ye kindle *fire* on mine altar for nought. I have no pleasure in you, saith the LORD of hosts, ᴿneither will I accept an offering at your hand.

11 For ᴿfrom the rising of the sun even unto the going down of the same my name *shall be* great ᴿamong the Gentiles; ᴿand in every place ᴿincense *shall be* offered unto my name, and a pure offering: ᴿfor my name *shall be* great among the heathen, saith the LORD of hosts.

12 But ye have profaned it, in that ye say, ᴿThe table of the LORD *is* polluted; and the fruit thereof, *even* his meat, *is* contemptible.

13 Ye said also, Behold, what a weariness *is it!* ᴺand ye have snuffed at it, saith the LORD of hosts; and ye brought *that which was* torn, and the lame, and the sick; thus ye brought an offering: ᴿshould I accept this of your hand? saith the LORD.

14 But cursed *be* ᴿthe deceiver, ᴺwhich hath in his flock a male, and voweth, and sacrificeth unto the Lord a corrupt thing: for ᴿI *am* a great King, saith the LORD of hosts, and my name *is* dreadful among the heathen.

CHAPTER 2

AND now, O ye priests, this commandment *is* for you.

2 ᴿIf ye will not hear, and if ye will not lay *it* to heart, to give glory unto my name, saith the LORD of hosts, I will even send a curse upon you, and I will curse your blessings: yea, I have cursed them already, because ye do not lay *it* to heart.

3 Behold, I will ᴺcorrupt your seed, and ᴺspread dung upon your faces, *even* the dung of your solemn feasts; and ᴺone shall ᴿtake you away with it.

The covenant profaned

4 And ye shall know that I have sent this commandment unto you, that my covenant might be with Levi, saith the LORD of hosts.

5 ᴿMy covenant was with him of life and peace; and I gave them to him ᴿfor the fear

CHAP. 1
BC 397
1 Heb. *by the hand of Malachi*
2 Deut. 7:8 & 10:15
2 Rom. 9:13
3 Jer. 49:18 Ezek. 35:3 Obad. 10
5 Ps. 35:27
5 Or, *upon*
5 Heb. *from upon*
6 Ex. 20:12
6 Luke 6:46
6 ch. 2:14
7 Or, *Bring unto, etc.*
7 Deut. 15:21
7 Ezek. 41:22
8 Lev. 22:22
8 Heb. *to sacrifice*
8 Job 42:8
9 Heb. *the face of God*
9 Hos. 13:9
9 Heb. *from your hand*

1 Cor. 9:13   10
Is. 1:11   10
Is. 59:19   11
Is. 60:3, 5   11
1 Tim. 2:8   11
Rev. 8:3   11
Is. 66:19   11
ver. 7   12
Or, *whereas ye might have blown it away*   13
Lev. 22:20   13
ver. 8   14
Or, *in whose flock is*   14
Ps. 47:2   14
1 Tim. 6:15

CHAP. 2
BC 397
Deut. 28:15   2
Or, *reprove*   3
Heb. *scatter*   3
Or, *it shall take you away to it*   3
1 Ki. 14:10   3
Num. 25:12   5
Ezek. 34:25
Deut. 33:9   5

wherewith he feared me, and was afraid before my name.

6 ᴿThe law of truth was in his mouth, and iniquity was not found in his lips: he walked with me in peace and equity, and did ᴿturn many away from iniquity.

7 ᴿFor the priest's lips should keep knowledge, and they should seek the law at his mouth: ᴿfor he *is* the messenger of the LORD of hosts.

8 But ye are departed out of the way; ye ᴿhave caused many to ᴺstumble at the law; ᴿye have corrupted the covenant of Levi, saith the LORD of hosts.

9 Therefore ᴿhave I also made you contemptible and base before all the people, according as ye have not kept my ways, but ᴺᴺhave been partial in the law.

10 ᴿHave we not all one father? ᴿhath not one God created us? why do we deal treacherously every man against his brother, by profaning the covenant of our fathers?

11 Judah hath dealt treacherously, and an abomination is committed in Israel and in Jerusalem; for Judah hath profaned the holiness of the LORD which he ᴺloved, ᴿand hath married the daughter of a strange god.

12 The LORD will cut off the man that doeth this, ᴺthe master and the scholar, out of the tabernacles of Jacob, ᴿand him that offereth an offering unto the LORD of hosts.

13 And this have ye done again, covering the altar of the LORD with tears, with weeping, and with crying out, insomuch that he regardeth not the offering any more, or receiveth *it* with good will at your hand.

14 Yet ye say, Wherefore? Because the LORD hath been witness between thee and ᴿthe wife of thy youth, against whom thou hast dealt treacherously: ᴿyet *is* she thy companion, and the wife of thy covenant.

15 And ᴿdid not he make one? Yet had he the ᴺresidue of the spirit. And wherefore one? That he might seek ᴿaᴺ godly seed. Therefore take heed to your spirit, and let none deal ᴺtreacherously against the wife of his youth.

16 For ᴿthe LORD, the God of Israel, saith ᴺthat he hateth ᴺputting away: for *one* covereth violence with his garment, saith the LORD of hosts: therefore take heed to your spirit, that ye deal not treacherously.

Justice forsaken

17 ᴿYe have wearied the LORD with your words. Yet ye say, Wherein have we wearied *him?* When ye say, Every one that doeth evil

---

CHAP. 2

BC 397

6 Deut. 33:10
6 Jer. 23:22
Jas. 5:20
7 Deut. 17:9
7 Gal. 4:14
8 Jer. 18:15
8 Or, *fall in the law*
8 Neh. 13:29
9 1 Sam. 2:30
9 Or, *lifted up the face against*
9 Heb. *accepted faces*
10 1 Cor. 8:6
10 Job 31:15
11 Or, *ought to love*
11 Ezra 9:1
Neh. 13:23
12 Or, *him that waketh, and him that answereth*
12 Neh. 13:29
14 Prov. 5:18
14 Prov. 2:17
15 Mat. 19:4
15 Or, *excellency*
15 Ezra 9:2
1 Cor. 7:14
15 Heb. *a seed of God*
15 Or, *unfaithfully*
16 Deut. 24:1
Mat. 5:32
16 Or, *if he hate her, put her away*
16 Heb. *to put away*
17 Is. 43:24

CHAP. 3

BC 397

Mat. 11:10	1
Luke 1:76	
Is. 40:3	1
Is. 63:9	1
Hag. 2:7	1
ch. 4:1	2
Rev. 6:17	2
Is. 4:4	2
Mat. 3:10	
Is. 1:25	3
1 Pet. 2:5	3
ch. 1:11	4
Or, *ancient*	4
Zech. 5:4	5
Jas. 5:4	
Or, *defraud*	5
Num. 23:19	6
Rom. 11:29	
Jas. 1:17	
Lam. 3:22	6
Acts 7:51	7
Zech. 1:3	7
ch. 1:6	7
Neh. 13:10	8
Prov. 3:9	10
1 Chr. 26:20	10
2 Chr. 31:11	
Neh. 10:38	
Gen. 7:11	10
2 Ki. 7:2	
2 Chr. 31:10	10
Heb. *empty out*	10
Amos 4:9	11
Heb. *corrupt*	11

---

is good in the sight of the LORD, and he delighteth in them; or Where *is* the God of judgment?

CHAPTER 3

BEHOLD, ᴿI will send my messenger, and he shall ᴿprepare the way before me: and the Lord, whom ye seek, shall suddenly come to his temple, ᴿeven the messenger of the covenant, whom ye delight in: behold, ᴿhe shall come, saith the LORD of hosts.   ★

2 But who may abide ᴿthe day of his coming? and ᴿwho shall stand when he appeareth? for ᴿhe *is* like a refiner's fire, and like fullers' soap:

3 And ᴿhe shall sit *as* a refiner and purifier of silver: and he shall purify the sons of Levi, and purge them as gold and silver, that they may ᴿoffer unto the LORD an offering in righteousness.

4 Then ᴿshall the offering of Judah and Jerusalem be pleasant unto the LORD, as in the days of old, and as in ᴺformer years.

5 And I will come near to you to judgment; and I will be a swift witness against the sorcerers, and against the adulterers, ᴿand against false swearers, and against those that ᴺoppress the hireling in *his* wages, the widow, and the fatherless, and that turn aside the stranger *from his right,* and fear not me, saith the LORD of hosts.

Tithing neglected

6 For I *am* the LORD, ᴿI change not; ᴿtherefore ye sons of Jacob are not consumed.

7 Even from the days of ᴿyour fathers ye are gone away from mine ordinances, and have not kept *them.* ᴿReturn unto me, and I will return unto you, saith the LORD of hosts. ᴿBut ye said, Wherein shall we return?

8 Will a man rob God? Yet ye have robbed me. But ye say, Wherein have we robbed thee? ᴿIn tithes and offerings.

9 Ye *are* cursed with a curse: for ye have robbed me, *even* this whole nation.

10 ᴿBring ye all the tithes into ᴿthe storehouse, that there may be meat in mine house, and prove me now herewith, saith the LORD of hosts, if I will not open you the ᴿwindows of heaven, and ᴿpourᴺ you out a blessing, that *there shall* not *be room* enough *to receive it.*

11 And I will rebuke ᴿthe devourer for your sakes, and he shall not ᴺdestroy the fruits of your ground; neither shall your vine cast her fruit before the time in the field, saith the LORD of hosts.

12 And all nations shall call you blessed: for

ye shall be ᴿa delightsome land, saith the LORD of hosts.

The righteous and the wicked

13 ᴿYour words have been stout against me, saith the LORD. Yet ye say, What have we spoken *so much* against thee?

14 ᴿYe have said, It *is* vain to serve God: and what profit *is it* that we have kept ᴺhis ordinance, and that we have walked ᴺmournfully before the LORD of hosts?

15 And now ᴿwe call the proud happy; yea, they that work wickedness ᴺare set up; yea, *they that* ᴿtempt God are even delivered.

16 Then they ᴿthat feared the LORD ᴿspake often one to another: and the LORD hearkened, and heard *it,* and ᴿa book of remembrance was written before him for them that feared the LORD, and that thought upon his name.

17 And ᴿthey shall be mine, saith the LORD of hosts, in that day when I make up my ᴿjewels;ᴺ and ᴿI will spare them, as a man spareth his own son that serveth him.

18 ᴿThen shall ye return, and discern between the righteous and the wicked, between him that serveth God and him that serveth him not.

CHAP. **3**	
BC 397	
12	Dan. 8:9
13	ch. 2:17
14	Job 21:14
14	Heb. *his observation*
14	Heb. *in black*
15	Ps. 73:12
15	Heb. *are built*
15	Ps. 95:9
16	Ps. 66:16
16	Heb. 3:13
16	Ps. 56:8
17	Ex. 19:5
17	Is. 62:3
17	Or, *special treasure*
17	Ps. 103:13
18	Ps. 58:11

CHAP. **4**		
BC 397		
Joel 2:31		1
ch. 3:18		1
Obad. 18		1
Amos 2:9		1
ch. 3:16		2
Luke 1:78		2
Mic. 7:10		3
Ex. 20:3		4
Deut. 4:10		4
Ps. 147:19		4
Mat. 11:14		5
Joel 2:31		5
Zech. 14:12		6
Zech. 5:3		6

CHAPTER 4

FOR, behold, ᴿthe day cometh, that shall burn as an oven; and all ᴿthe proud, yea, and all that do wickedly, shall be ᴿstubble: and the day that cometh shall burn them up, saith the LORD of hosts, that it shall ᴿleave them neither root nor branch.

2 But unto you that ᴿfear my name shall the ᴿSun of righteousness arise with healing in his wings; and ye shall go forth, and grow up as calves of the stall.

3 ᴿAnd ye shall tread down the wicked; for they shall be ashes under the soles of your feet in the day that I shall do *this,* saith the LORD of hosts.

Command to obey

4 Remember ye the ᴿlaw of Moses my servant, which I commanded unto him ᴿin Hôr′-ĕb for all Israel, *with* ᴿthe statutes and judgments.

5 Behold, I will send you ᴿĒ-lī′-jăh the prophet ᴿbefore the coming of the great and dreadful day of the LORD:

6 And he shall turn the heart of the fathers to the children, and the heart of the children to their fathers, lest I come and ᴿsmite the earth with ᴿa curse.

THE END OF THE PROPHETS

History of the Hebrew People

400 B.C. to 9 A.D.

including the development of the Jewish Religion

THE INTERTESTAMENTAL HISTORY OF THE JEWISH RELIGION

Introduction

The Bible is silent concerning the events of the four hundred years between the prophecies of Malachi, which were pronounced to the Jews just returned from exile, and the incarnation of the Messiah. Yet we know from secular history, from the apocryphal books, and even from the New Testament that during this period dynamic and far-reaching changes occurred in both the political and religious spheres of Israel—changes that prepared the way for the coming of Jesus Christ "in the fullness of time."

During these intervening centuries, political control of Palestine and of most of the Mediterranean world had passed from Persia to Rome, from East to West. At the time of Malachi, Palestine was thinly populated by a straggly group of newly returned exiles. Most of them were poor, and both city and countryside bore the marks of long desolation. By New Testament times, Palestine was a populous, heavily cultivated, prosperous country. Greek had replaced Hebrew as the language of literature, and Aramaic was commonly spoken throughout the Middle East.

In the New Testament we meet many aspects of Jewish religion that arose during this intertestamental period—the synagogue, scribes, Pharisees and Sadducees, the Sanhedrin, well-defined belief in immortality and the resurrection, and a concentration on separation, legalism, and nationalism.

Political History

To understand how and why these political and religious changes came about, it is important to be familiar with the political history of the intertestamental period—to understand the changes that were imposed on Israel by outside forces and how the Jewish people reacted.

The following chronological chart should prove helpful in sorting out the details of this period:

587 B.C.	Jerusalem destroyed and the people carried to Babylon
538 B.C.	Return of exiles under Zerubbabel
457 B.C.	Second return of exiles (under Ezra)
444 B.C.	Nehemiah's return
400 B.C.?	Malachi's prophecies
332 B.C.	Jerusalem captured by Alexander the Great
168 B.C.	Temple polluted by Antiochus IV (Epiphanes)
165 B.C.	Purification of the temple by Judas Maccabeus
142 B.C.	Independence granted by Syrians
135-106 B.C.	John Hyrcanus rules—Samaritans and Idumeans conquered
63 B.C.	First capture of Jerusalem by Romans
37 B.C.	Second capture of Jerusalem by Romans
6 B.C.	Birth of Jesus
4 B.C.	Death of Herod
A.D. 70	Jerusalem destroyed by Titus

Babylonian Exile

The Old Testament history of the people of Israel is a continuous cycle of rebellion and idolatry, punishment at the hands of a Canaanite nation, repentance, and a relapse into sin. This cycle reached its climax when the kingdom of Judah was conquered by Nebuchadnezzar and the people were carried off into captivity. The despair of the Jews in exile is beautifully expressed in Psalm 137: "By the rivers of Babylon, there we sat down, yea, we wept, when we remembered Zion. . . . If I forget thee, O Jerusalem, let my right hand forget her cunning. If I do not remember thee, let my tongue cleave to the roof of my mouth."

Many of these exiled Jews sought to maintain their national unity by forming a separate religious community, marked by faithfulness to God's law, prayer, Sabbath observance, and a determination to guard their place as God's special people. These emphases formed the historical beginnings of New Testament and post-biblical Judaism.

Persian Period

In 539 B.C. the Persian Cyrus conquered Babylon. He reversed the practice of assimilating and homogenizing captive peoples by extending toleration to all religious groups and encouraging captives to return to their homeland. In 538 B.C. he issued an edict allowing the Jews to return to Palestine. According to Ezra 2:2-67 more than 50,000 took advantage of this opportunity, returning in three groups: one led by Zerubbabel in 538 B.C., the second led by Ezra in 457 B.C., and the third led by Nehemiah in 444 B.C.

After the return of these exiles, two distinct changes can be seen in Israelite history. They came back with a new name—Jews (from Judeans), which before had applied only to the tribe of Judah. Also, because of the experience of captivity and exile, combined with the new emphasis on separation and national identity, from this point on, there was never again any danger of a relapse into idol-worship.

The returning Jews faced an extremely difficult task. The area around Jerusalem had lain waste for fifty years; the city was totally destroyed; and they were surrounded by people who opposed their rebuilding efforts. The hostility of these people had been aroused by the determination of the Jews to keep themselves pure and separate.

Soon after the return, public worship was restored and an altar was erected. But the opposition of the Samaritans halted all work on rebuilding the temple. The strong leadership of Zerubbabel, Joshua the high priest, and the prophet Haggai finally got the project underway again in 520 B.C. and the temple was finished and dedicated in 516 B.C. It provided a center for the religious fervor of the Jews and a tangible symbol of their nationalistic hope.

Ezra and Nehemiah

In 457 B.C. Ezra, a scribe of the law, asked permission from Artaxerxes to lead a group of Jews to Palestine. On reaching Jerusalem he was appalled to find that many of the residents had defiled themeslves by marrying unbelievers. After prayer and confession, Ezra was able to persuade the priests to put away their foreign wives. Other religious reforms, however, were not instituted until the arrival of Nehemiah.

Nehemiah, a cupbearer to Artaxerxes, was shocked to hear a report from Jerusalem that, even though the temple had been rebuilt, the law was not being kept, sacrifices were not made, and the walls of Jerusalem were still in ruin. He sought and received a leave of absence from the king to go to Jerusalem and supervise the rebuilding of the walls.

Nehemiah provided the necessary leadership and impetus to inspire the people to repair the wall in spite of opposition from surrounding enemies. Breaches in the wall were repaired in fifty-two days and final completion of the walls was accomplished in two years.

As resident governor Nehemiah did much to improve the religious and social conditions of the people. Ezra was appointed to institute religious reforms. The reading of the law, as recorded in Nehemiah 8, was received with repentance and promises to keep God's covenant and maintain separation from non-Jews.

Although the devotion of the Jews to God's law was necessary and admirable, in time religious truth became dogmatized and was reduced to rules and doctrine. The spirit was missing and legalism stepped in to become the standard of faithfulness to God.

The prophecies of Malachi in about 400 B.C. mark the end of the Old Testament period. From this time to the coming of Alexander the Great, the Jews lived in peace under Persian rule.

Greek Period

Alexander ascended the Macedonian throne at his father's death in 336 B.C., at the age of twenty. As a youth Alexander had been tutored by the Greek philosopher Aristotle. From him Alexander came to know and love Greek culture and civilization. As ruler and conqueror, one of his purposes was to spread this culture throughout the world.

In 335 Alexander conquered Greece and in 334 he moved east into Asia to conquer the Persian Empire. Going through Asia Minor in about a year and a half, he met a large Persian army under Darius. In spite of being several times larger than Alexander's army, the Persians were put to flight.

Alexander then moved down the eastern coast of the Mediterranean, taking Jerusalem in 332. That same year he entered Egypt where he was welcomed as a liberator. From Egypt he moved east again, completing his conquest of the Persian Empire by 331. From 330 to 325 he continued east, conquering his way to India and into China. He then returned to Babylon, reaching it in 323. He contracted malaria there and died at the age of 33, having conquered and ruled over a larger territory than any man before him.

Under Greek rule, the Jews in Palestine were allowed to keep the religious and cultural freedom they had had under the Persians. Jews in other areas, notably Egypt, also thrived and gained importance, existing as separate communities under their own laws.

Along with his military conquests, Alexander the Great spread Greek civilization and language, attempting to unite East and West as partners in a common culture. This was very important in future Jewish history, as two parties grew out of the conflict between Greek and Jewish culture. The "Hellenists" accepted and accommodated themselves to the Greek way of life while the "Hasidim" (the name means "pious ones") sought to maintain the separateness of the Jews and faithfulness to God's law.

The Ptolemys

Alexander's death was followed by the power struggle among his family and generals. The empire was finally divided in four parts, each one ruled by one of four generals, thus fulfilling the prophecy of Daniel 11:4: "And when he shall stand up, his kingdom shall be broken, and shall be divided toward the four winds of heaven."

Ptolemy took over Egypt with Seleucus as his subordinate. In 312 Seleucus broke away and established the Seleucid dynasty in the Syro-Mestopotamian area. Palestine subsequently was involved in a tug-of-war between the two powers. The Ptolemies held Palestine for more than a century, but when Antiochus III came to power in the Seleucid dynasty, a twenty-year struggle began with Antiochus III finally defeating the young Ptolemy V in 198 B.C.

During Ptolemaic rule the Jews fared well under a benevolent policy of toleration. In Alexandria, a group of Jewish scholars translated the Pentateuch into Greek, probably around the time of Ptolemy II. Translation of the remaining Jewish Scriptures followed, with the work being finished about 150 B.C. This translation, commonly known as the Septuagint, served as a bond to unite the Jews of the Dispersion and helped spread Judaism throughout the Greek-speaking world. It was also during this time that the synagogue became a center of worship in many towns and villages, both throughout the Dispersion and in Palestine itself.

The Seleucids

Antiochus III generally followed a benevolent policy toward Palestine. His successor was Seleucus III, who was succeeded in turn by Antiochus IV. Antiochus intended to fully Hellenize the Jews—by force if necessary. He alienated many of his subjects early in his reign by taking on the title "Epiphanes," meaning "the manifest god." (He was eventually nicknamed "Epimanes" meaning "madman.")

At the time Antiochus took the throne, Onias III held the office of high priest. He was supplanted by his younger brother, Joshua (better known by his Greek name Jason), who had offered Antiochus a bribe for the position—as well as a pledge to pursue Antiochus's efforts at Hellenization. Later Jason was himself deposed and replaced by Menelaus, who also had Onias, the legitimate high priest, murdered. Faithful Jews were appalled by this profaning of the high priestly office.

While Antiochus was campaigning in Egypt, Jason took advantage of this chance to reestablish himself. Antiochus returned and reinstated Menelaus. However, at this point the Jews rebelled and refused to accept Menelaus. Rioting broke out and was put down with bloody reprisals. Thousands of Jews were killed or sold into slavery and the temple was ransacked.

In 168 B.C. Antiochus issued a decree forbidding all expressions of Jewish worship—circumcision, sacrifices, Sabbath observance, possession of copies of the law. The

temple was rededicated to Zeus and profaned by the sacrifice of pigs on the altar. Horrible persecutions faced Jews who broke Antiochus's law.

Maccabean Revolt

Antiochus also ordered that a pig be sacrificed in every town and village in Palestine with a Jewish volunteer actually slaying the animal. Jewish resistance came to a head in the village of Modein when Mattathias, the local priest, refused to participate in the sacrifice. Filled with rage, he killed both the Jew who had volunteered to make the sacrifice and the Syrian official in charge. With this act, the period known as the Maccabean revolt began. A complete history of this period can be found in the apocryphal books of 1 and 2 Maccabees.

With his five sons Mattathias fled to the hills of the Judean wilderness, calling on the faithful to join him in guerilla warfare against the Syrians. Though at first the group was small, it kept growing with the addition of many of the "Hasidim."

Judas Maccabeus

Mattathias died in 166 B.C. and leadership of the rebels was taken over by his son Judas, who was nicknamed "Maccabeus," or "the Hammerer." At first these Jews confined their revolt to surprise attacks on small towns, instituting instant religious reform by destroying pagan altars, circumcising Hellenistic Jews, and reestablishing synagogues. Under Judas the revolt soon spread to all-out warfare against Lysias, Antiochus's representative.

After several decisive victories, Lysias and Judas negotiated peace and the Jews were granted the right to reoccupy Jerusalem, except for the fortified height of Akra, and to reinstitute temple worship. Judas cleansed the temple of its pollution and erected a new altar; in 165 B.C. the temple was rededicated. This event is celebrated annually by the Jews in the Feast of Dedication, or "Hanukkah."

With Jerusalem secured, Judas extended his authority over the surrounding area, winning campaigns in Galilee and to the east and south of Jerusalem against Gentile nations—Idumeans, Edomites, Ammonites. During this time Antiochus IV died and was succeeded by his seven-year-old son, Antiochus V, with his general Philip appointed as regent and guardian.

This gave Judas an opportunity to attack Akra, the Syrian fortress overlooking the temple. He laid siege to it and again he and Lysias faced each other in battle. During this battle, Eleazar, one of Judas's brothers, was crushed to death when an elephant he killed fell on him.

Lysias defeated Judas overwhelmingly, forcing him and his followers to retreat to Jerusalem and take refuge in the temple fortress. Lysias, however, was unable to follow up his victory because he received word that Philip was on his way to take over the government. Lysias was forced to make a quick peace with Judas, offering a general amnesty and guaranteeing the Jews freedom of religion. He deposed the high priest, Menelaus, had him put to death, and installed in his place Alcimus, who was of the high-priestly line, though he was also a Hellenist.

At this time Judas was defeated by the Hasidim, who formed a major part of his army. They were interested only in religious freedom, and once that had been gained they refused to continue to fight for Judas's political aspirations.

Judas had opposed the appointment of Alcimus to the high-priestly office and apparently drove him out of Jerusalem. Alcimus turned for help to Syria. Demetrius I, a nephew of Antiochus IV, was now the king, having murdered both Lysias and Antiochus V. Demetrius sent a strong military escort to Jerusalem under his general Bacchides, and Judas was forced to flee the city. The Hasidim accepted and trusted Alcimus, but he treacherously massacred sixty of them. So they turned against him and returned to Judas. Alcimus again appealed for protection to Demetrius, who sent an army under his general Nicanor. When Judas and Nicanor met in battle near the village of Adasa, Nicanor was killed and his army soundly defeated.

At this stage Judas, seeking to strengthen his position, sent two ambassadors, Eupolemos and Jason, to Rome to establish a treaty of mutual support. The treaty was concluded, but before the Syrians received Rome's warning not to interfere with Judas, Demetrius had sent out Bacchides with a large army to avenge Nicanor's defeat. Many of Judas's followers fled when they saw the size and might of the Syrian forces. In the ensuing battle at Elasa, Judas was slain and what was left of his army fled to the wilderness of Judea.

Jonathan

Another of Judas's brothers was killed at this time, leaving two—Simon and Jonathan. Jonathan became the leader of the rebels, and for a time they confined themselves to guerrilla raids again, slowly retaking most of Judea from the Syrians, except for Jerusalem.

With the death of Judas and the weakening of Maccabean power, the Hellenists regained control of Jewish affairs. Alcimus, the high priest, renewed the Hellenization of the Jewish religion, going so far as to tear down the partition of the temple separating the court of the Jews from the court of the Gentiles. He died a short time later, and this was considered a punishment from God by the Hasidim. For the next seven years the office of high priest was vacant.

After the death of Alcimus, Bacchides withdrew to Antioch. Two years later he returned to Jerusalem at the request of the Hellenists. His army was defeated in the wilderness of Judea by the Maccabees. Angry at the Hellenists for bringing him into such a position, Bacchides turned against them and made peace with Jonathan.

Jonathan established his headquarters just north of Jerusalem and proceeded to punish the Hellenists and increase his own power and influence. His chance to regain Jerusalem and become even more powerful came in 153 B.C., when Alexander Balas, claiming to be a son of Antiochus Epiphanes, challenged Demetrius I's right to the throne of Syria. Playing off one claimant against the other for his military support, Jonathan first accepted Demetrius's concessions and was able to take over all of Jerusalem except the Akra. Then he switched his support to Balas, who offered him the dual power of high priest and ruler of the Jews.

Balas finally won the throne, defeating and killing Demetrius. But he didn't remain king for long—he was challenged by Demetrius's son, Demetrius II, and was defeated and killed in 145 B.C. While this struggle for the Syrian throne was going on, Judas strengthened his own position by extending his territory to the south and to the west.

From a righteous crusade against religious oppression and persecution, the war of the Maccabees had changed to a struggle for personal ambition. Jonathan gained far more with his political intrigue than his brother Judas had ever won in war.

Jonathan became more and more deeply involved in the dynastic struggles of the Seleucids, dangerously playing off one pretender against another. In 143 B.C. he was tricked by Tryphon, a Syrian general supporting Antiochus VI, into meeting with him at the town of Ptolemais. Tryphon treacherously captured Jonathan and killed the men accompanying him. Tryphon then bargained with Jonathan's brother Simon for his release, but Tryphon broke his promise to release Jonathan in exchange for two hostages and 100 talents of silver. Instead he murdered Jonathan. Simon, the last remaining son of Mattathias, became the leader of the Maccabees.

Political Independence

When Simon took over as high priest and ruler of the Jews, Syria was divided between the supporters of Antiochus VI and the supporters of Demetrius II. Both were eager for Jewish military support and recognition, and Simon was able to conclude a peace treaty with Demetrius, guaranteeing full Jewish independence and immunity from taxation. So in 142 B.C. the long struggle of the Maccabees was finally won.

Simon's rule was fairly peaceful. One of his greatest accomplishments was to unify the various parties of the Jewish people. He was confirmed by the Jewish council of state (the forerunner of the Sanhedrin) in his offices of high priest and ruler, with hereditary rights going to his descendants. The weakness of Syria enabled Simon to take the last remaining Syrian strongholds in Judea—Joppa, Gazara, Bethsura, and finally the Akra. He also negotiated a treaty with Rome, guaranteeing complete freedom of worship for the Jews.

In 135 B.C. Simon and two of his sons, Mattathias and Judas, were murdered by his son-in-law, Ptolemy (no relation to the Egyptian Ptolemys). A third son, John Hyrcanus, escaped and assumed his father's offices. His rule was the beginning of the Hasmonean dynasty, named for an ancestor of the Maccabees, Asmoneus.

Hasmoneans

In the very first year of Hyrcanus's rule, the Syrians attacked Jerusalem and placed it under siege. The Jews were forced to accept their terms—surrendering their arms, making heavy indemnity payments, and handing over hostages. However, further power struggles for the Syrian throne enabled Hyrcanus to regain independence. He extended his territory so that it was almost as large as Solomon's kingdom. His main military campaigns were against the Samaritans and Idumeans. The Samaritan temple on Mount Gerizim was destroyed, and the Idumeans were forced to accept the Jewish religion and to be circumcised.

Hyrcanus was the first Jewish ruler to mint coins bearing his own name. This and other expressions of his authority alienated some of the Jewish people, especially the Hasidim. It was evident that Hyrcanus was becoming more and more Hellenistic, increasing the worldliness of the high priestly office and assuming more power and authority for himself. He departed drastically from the ideals of the early Maccabees.

The existence of several of the Jewish sects can be dated to this period of Jewish history. The Pharisees and Essenes both came out of the Hasidim and the Sadducees were an outgrowth of the Hellenists. Hyrcanus supported the Pharisees at first but gradually moved toward the more political and aristocratic Sadducees.

Before John Hyrcanus died in 106 B.C., he declared that his wife should succeed him as ruler and that their oldest son Aristobulus should serve as high priest. Aristobulus, seeking civil as well as religious power, imprisoned three of his brothers and his mother and let all of them starve to death, except for the youngest brother. Another brother, Antigonus, was spared for a while, but finally Aristobulus had him murdered too. It was said that his remorse caused his own death within a year.

After the death of Aristobulus, his widow, Alexandra, freed his youngest brother, Alexander Jannaeus, from prison and married him. Jannaeus succeeded his brother as high priest and ruler and was the first of the Hasmoneans to take on himself the title of king. He was a cruel ruler, ruthlessly murdering those who opposed him. During his reign the antagonism between the Pharisees and the Hasmoneans reached its climax.

The trouble broke out into open rebellion during the Feast of Tabernacles at which Jannaeus was officiating as high priest, when he contemptuously poured out a libation of wine at his own feet instead of on the altar. The enraged worshipers pelted him with the citrons they were carrying in honor of the feast. Jannaeus set loose his soldiers on the people and some six thousand of them were massacred.

Six years of civil war followed. The Pharisees asked for help from the Syrian king, Demetrius III. Here the descendants of the Hasidim and the descendant of Antiochus Epiphanes joined together to fight the descendant of the Maccabees! Jannaeus was defeated and forced to flee to the Judean hills. However at this point six thousand Jews, fearing Syrian control even more, turned from them to help Jannaeus. Demetrius then withdrew his Syrian forces and Jannaeus reestablished his authority. He hunted down and captured the leaders of the rebellion and crucified eight hundred of them at a banquet celebrating his victory.

Alexander Jannaeus died in 76 B.C. at the age of forty-nine and left his widow, Alexandra, to rule in his place. Her brother, Simon ben Shetech, had been one of the leaders of Pharisaic opposition to Jannaeus. Tradition has it that Jannaeus repented on his deathbed and advised his wife to support the Pharisees and follow their advice in her rule.

By favoring the Pharisees and gaining their support, Alexandra restored peace and prosperity to the Jewish nation. One of the most important reforms instituted during her rule was compulsory education for all boys, consisting chiefly of the study of biblical law but providing also general elementary training.

When Alexandra died, Hyrcanus, her older son who was already serving as high priest, succeeded her to the throne. His brother, Aristobulus II, challenged his authority, defeated him in battle, and forced him to abdicate both his high priestly and ruling offices.

Weak and cowardly, Hyrcanus easily yielded to his brother. But Antipater, the governor of Idumea, was afraid that Aristobulus would deprive him of his position, and so he persuaded Hyrcanus to attempt to regain the throne. Aretas, the Nabatean king, joined them in attacking Aristobulus. Aristobulus was defeated and fled to Jerusalem, where he was besieged in the temple area.

Civil war ensued from 65-63 B.C., when both brothers appealed to Rome, giving Pompey the opportunity he had been looking for to interfere in the affairs of Palestine.

After various negotiations and struggles, Pompey attacked Jerusalem. Hyrcanus's followers surrendered and opened the city gates to him, but Aristobulus's supporters fled to the temple and withstood a siege of three months.

When the temple area finally was taken, twelve thousand Jews were massacred, and Pompey himself desecrated the temple by marching into the Holy of Holies.

Hyrcanus was named high priest and "ethnarch" (ruler), but he served under Rome. In spite of further attempts to regain Jewish independence, Hasmonean rule had come to an end. The nation was greatly reduced in size and the high priest served as the dependent of a foreign power.

Roman Rule

Under the Romans, the Jews were generally treated fairly, though they were always kept in submission. They were granted freedom of religion and were required to pay only a small tribute; the Sanhedrin was granted the power to rule on minor civil and religious cases as a judicial body. It also had some legislative powers.

Palestine was divided up into districts—Galilee, Judea, Samaria, Idumea, and Perea. Antipater, who had been governor of Idumea, won the favor of Caesar by supporting him against Pompey and was made procurator of Judea. He also gained positions for his two sons, making Phasael the military governor of Judea and Herod the tetrarch of Galilee.

In the next twenty years power struggles in Rome were reflected in Palestine as Antipater and his sons fought for power with the remaining Hasmoneans—Aristobulus II and his sons, Antigonus and Aristobulus III.

Antipater himself was murdered in 43 B.C. and his son Phasael was captured and committed suicide.

Herod the Great

In 40 B.C. the kingship of Judea was conferred on Herod (known through history as "the Great"); in 31 B.C. Caesar Augustus extended his realm to include practically all of Palestine. His administration of the Jews was strong and efficient. Many new buildings were constructed; the best known, of course, is Herod's temple, begun in 20 B.C. and actually finished only six years before the Romans destroyed Jerusalem in A.D. 70. All evidence is that this was a truly magnificent structure. It was constructed of white marble and its eastern front was covered with gold plates to reflect the rays of the rising sun.

Most of Herod's rule was marked by peace, yet he was a cruel and ruthless man who did not hesitate to murder anyone who presented a threat to his power. During his reign he exterminated the remaining Hasmoneans—Hyrcanus, Antigonus, and the young Aristobulus—most of the Sanhedrin, his favorite wife, Mariamne, three of his sons and three hundred of their supporters, two of his brothers-in-law and many others. It was this Herod who murdered the innocent children of Bethlehem.

Herod died in 4 B.C., and his kingdom was divided among three of his sons. Archelaus ruled Judea, Samaria, and Idumea from A.D. 6-9; at his death Judea passed into the hands of Roman procurators, one of whom was Pontius Pilate. Herod Antipas ruled Galilee and Perea. It was he who murdered John the Baptist and before whom Jesus appeared on Good Friday morning (Luke 23:7-12). The third son, Philip, ruled the area to the east and northeast of Galilee.

The death of Herod the Great, which occurred shortly after the birth of Jesus Christ, marks the end of the intertestamental period. Many of the features of this time in history prepared the way for the coming of Jesus. The Jews had returned to faithfulness to God's covenant and many of them were looking for the long-promised Messiah.

The influence of the Greeks had resulted in a language understood and spoken by most of the Mediterranean world. And the rule of the Romans brought peace to this troubled area, which enabled the disciples to travel widely, spreading the good news of the gospel.

Features of Judaism

The term "Judaism" is generally used to refer to the Jewish religion from the New Testament period on, to distinguish it from the religion of the Old Testament.

Probably the most important influence on the Jews during the intertestamental period was their exposure to other cultures. New ideas and customs brought change on the one hand and a determination to hold to their faith and keep themselves separate on the other. This led to such developments as synagogues, scribes, and religious sects, which will be discussed individually.

Synagogues

The survival of the Jewish religion after the destruction of the temple in A.D. 70 is due in large part to the institution of synagogues. The synagogue began during the Babylonian Exile. As was pointed out before, many of the Jews in Babylon gathered together as a community to maintain their separateness as God's chosen people and faithfulness to the law.

The new devotion of Jews to obedience to God led to a need for studying His law. Although at first, of course, there was no formally organized synagogue it came out of this need. Its actual development is hard to trace. Gatherings at the time of Ezra were an early beginning and by the third century B.C. there were definitely synagogues in existence.

Further development of the synagogue came with the Dispersion. During the Greek period of intertestamental history there were strong, independent communities of Jews in many foreign cities, especially in Egypt, Asia Minor, and Greece. Deprived of temple worship, these Jews needed a religious center to serve as a place of both worship and instruction. In Palestine itself the synagogue became common during the Maccabean period as a center for preserving faith and tradition.

By the time of Christ, synagogues had a fixed place in every Jewish community. In the New Testament we frequently read of Jesus attending the synagogue on the Sabbath "as his custom was" (Luke 4:16). When Paul made his missionary journeys, he always started by preaching to the Jews in the local synagogue.

There was no conflict between the synagogues and the temple. The synagogues were local and were more directed to teaching than to worship. But the temple was the national center—it represented the Jewish religion. It was at the temple that sacrifices were made and the priests fulfilled their various functions. All faithful Jews tried to go to Jerusalem at least once a year to worship at the temple during one of the great feasts. It was for this reason that so many Jews and proselytes from different countries were in Jerusalem at Pentecost.

There were three key elements in synagogue worship: prayer, reading of the law and the prophets, and a homily (what we would call a sermon). The service uusally opened with the Shema: "Hear, O Israel: The Lord our God is one Lord: and thou shalt love the Lord thy God with all thine heart, and with all thy soul, and with all thy might" (Deuteronomy 6:4,5). This was followed by other prayers of blessing and thanksgiving.

Then the leader of the synagogue—a layman—would

call on a member of the congregation to read. At some point a fixed system of law reading was established so the entire law would be covered in three years. A reading from the prophets usually followed the law. These readings were often accompanied by a translation into the vernacular—either Aramaic or Greek.

The sermon was delivered by members of the congregation who either had special training or were known for their knowledge and piety. It was commonly based on the reading from the prophets. There was no appointed preacher, and a visiting priest, scribe, or teacher would often be invited to participate, as Paul did in the synagogues of the Dispersion.

Another function of the synagogue was as a teaching organization. Since the primary responsibility of adults in the synagogue was to read the Torah (the law), during the week the synagogue was used as a school where boys of the community were taught to read Hebrew.

The synagogue had an important place in Jewish life (and still does). It promoted piety and faithfulness to God, offered a place for exchanging ideas, and preserved Jewish faith and traditions. It also served as the model for Christian churches and worship services.

Scribes

The emphasis on the law led to another development—that of men who studied the law and skilled in its interpretation. These men, called scribes, were the natural successors to Ezra, who is described in Ezra 7:6 as "a ready scribe in the law of Moses." His function was to instruct the Jews returned from Exile in God's law: "For Ezra had prepared his heart to seek the law of the Lord, and to do it, and to teach in Israel statutes and judgments" (Ezra 7:10).

The scribes of intertestamental and New Testament times devoted themselves to studying and interpreting the law and teaching. The influence of Hellenism during this period brought new customs and ideas that caused questions about the meaning of the law. So the scribes actually functioned as jurists, answering legal questions about how the law should be related to everyday life. The teachings and interpretations of the scribes gradually developed into an oral tradition of law that was accepted as being as authoritative as the Torah itself. Meanwhile the scribes themselves gained more and more authority until they were second only to the priests.

There seems to have been a close relationship between the scribes and the priests. Originally the study and interpretation of the law had been left to the priests, but gradually a cleavage developed between the temple and the law. It was not that the priests were no longer interested in the law, but generally they directed their attention more to political questions, leaving study of the law to the scribes.

The scribes did not form a separate party in Palestine but were members of both major sects—Pharisees and Sadducees. In the Book of Acts there is a reference to "the scribes that were of the Pharisees' part" (23:9). Probably the majority of them were Pharisees, since in the New Testament they usually appear in close association.

Sanhedrin

The Sanhedrin was the ruling body of the Jews, having its origin in the traditional council of elders. It was made up of seventy-two men, with the high priest serving as its head. It is not known how the members were selected, but they were drawn from the priests, the scribes, and the elders. Both Pharisees and Sadducees were represented.

During the Roman period the Sanhedrin controlled most of the internal affairs of Palestine. Apparently its authority was recognized even by Jews of the Dispersion. It served as both a judicial and a legislative body, administering all affairs for which authority had been granted by the Roman procurator.

The Sanhedrin was the highest court in the land and served as the final court of appeal for both civil and criminal cases. It maintained its own officers who could carry out arrests. It could pass a sentence of death but could not carry out the execution without the confirmation of the Roman procurator. The stoning of Stephen which was carried out by the Sanhedrin was therefore illegal. The Sanhedrin passed out of existence with the destruction of Jerusalem in A.D. 70.

Temple Worship

The temple in Jerusalem was always the center of the Jewish religion. In the intertestamental period the new emphasis on faithfulness to the law gave even more prominence to the temple rituals.

After the return from Exile and the new functions of the scribes, the priests were no longer considered the guardians of the law. Their authority became limited to the proper execution of temple rituals and sacrifices. They were headed by the high priest, who exercised both political and religious authority in his dual role as head of the Sanhedrin and of temple worship.

The Levites who at one time formed the priestly body, were responsible for various tasks associated with the temple ritual. They were the singers and doorkeepers and carried out other more menial work.

The priests and Levites were divided into twenty-four "courses." Each course was on duty for a week at a time and conducted the daily rituals during its week of responsibility. Daily worship consisted of two services—one in the morning and one in the evening. Worship began by killing the lamb for the offering of burnt sacrifice. Then the officiating priest went into the court where the worshipers were assembled and the Shema and the ten commandments were recited.

This was followed by the incense offering and the blessing: "The Lord bless thee and keep thee: the Lord make his face shine upon thee and be gracious unto thee: the Lord lift up his countenance upon thee, and give thee peace" (Numbers 6:24-26). The sacrificial lamb was then burned and the meat offering and drink offering were made. The service was concluded by the singing of the Psalm for the day by the Levites. Each Psalm was divided into three sections; at the end of each section trumpets were sounded, and the people prostrated themselves in worship. Sabbath services were essentially the same, but there were more offerings and readings from Scripture.

The religious festivals celebrated during intertestamental and New Testament times were the same as in the Old Testament: the Passover, Pentecost, Feast of Tabernacles, Day of Atonement, etc. Also two others had been added: the Feast of Purim, which commemorated the deliverance of the Jews by Esther from Haman's plot (Esther 9:1-10) and the Feast of Dedication, which celebrated the cleansing of the temple by Judas Maccabeus.

Jewish Sects

During the Greek and Maccabean periods two opposing parties arose within Palestine: the Hasidim and the Hellenists—those who strove to remain faithful to the Jewish

faith and traditions and those who wanted to accept and accommodate themselves to Greek customs.

Gradually, however, especially in the Hasmonean period, this distinction became less clear and other sects arose. The Hasidim were satisfied when they achieved religious freedom, and they were not concerned at all with political matters.

Pharisees

By far the largest and most important sect was the Pharisees. They had their roots in the Hasidim and their name means "separated." Like the Hasidim they emphasized faithfulness to the law and separation from non-Jews, but they were more willing to adjust to changing situations.

The exact history of the Pharisees is difficult to trace but the name first occurred during the reign of John Hyrcanus (about 135 B.C.). As was noted in the history of the Hasmoneans, he originally supported the Pharisees but turned against them because they were more interested in the law than in Jewish nationalism. During the reign of Alexander Jannaeus, the Pharisees revolted against him and he was temporarily exiled. When he put down the revolt he killed six thousand of the Pharisees. On another occasion he crucified some eight hundred of them.

When Jannaeus died, tradition has it, he advised his queen to side with the Pharisees. She did so, and during her reign the Pharisees became increasingly powerful. They were very influential and popular with the common people because of their piety. The Sanhedrin, the ruling body of the Jews, included many Pharisees. Even though they did not constitute a majority, their influence with the masses gave them a great deal of power and increased their authority.

The basis of Pharisaism lies in the post-exilic tendencies of legalism and nationalism. The study and interpretation of the law and the need for the Jews to maintain their identity over against the influence of pagan customs and ideas evolved into the ideals held by the Pharisees. They believed that perfect obedience to the law would bring the coming of the Messiah. Yet, sadly, their very legalism blinded them to the truth that Jesus was the Messiah.

The Pharisees were distinctive in both life style and dress. Jesus said of them, "All their works they do for to be seen of men: they make broad their phylacteries, and enlarge the borders of the garments" (Matthew 23:5). The phylacteries were leather boxes, containing part of the law, which were wrapped around the forehead and arms. "The borders of their garments" apparently refers to the fringes of their robes, which they wore very long to indicate their piety.

The Pharisees lived in a world separated from other people by their strict adherence to the law, performing all its requirements exactly and even going beyond what was required so as to avoid accidentally violating the law. They paid tithes exactly, even on such minor things as spices; they avoided any contact with death so they would not defile themselves; they kept the Sabbath strictly, developing exact rules on what constituted work; they practiced ceremonial washings; they refused to associate with Gentiles or with any Jews whom they considered "sinners."

In view of their separatism, a surprising feature of the Pharisees was their missionary zeal. They were well known for their proselytizing efforts and are generally credited with having proselytized the Idumeans.

The Pharisees had a great deal of influence on the development of the Jewish religion. They introduced new ideas by interpreting the Old Testament and developing such doctrines as the resurrection of the dead and punishment for the wicked. It was the Pharisees who upheld oral tradition and expanded the law to include their own interpretations of it. Their motives were certainly honorable—by studying and intrepreting the law they sought God's will in answer to the problem of their day. Yet their rigidity placed a large burden on the common people.

Jesus obviously respected the teachings of the Pharisees but criticized them for not following them themselves. He advised the Jew: "All therefore whatsoever they bid you observe, that observe and do; but do not ye after their works: for they say and do not" (Matthew 23:3). By New Testament times the Pharisees had lost the spirit of the law and the covenant and held only to its form. For them religion had become external rather than a matter of the heart.

Sadducees

The second most important party among the Jews was that of the Sadducees. Although they were fewer in number than the Pharisees and less popular with the people, nevertheless they exerted a great deal of power and authority because of the makeup of their group. Most of the members were wealthy aristocrats—men of the upper classes who controlled the religious, economic, and governmental aspects of Jewish life. Because the high priest and other high-ranking priestly officials were usually Sadducees, the Sadducees also controlled the Sanhedrin.

Like the Pharisees, the Sadducees originated during the time of the Maccabees. They started out as primarily a religious group. However because of the intermingling of politics and religion in Jewish national affairs, this distinction became impossible to maintain; so the Sadducees gradually assumed a religious character that put them in opposition to the Pharisees. Their main emphasis was on the function of the temple—especially the sacrifices.

The Sadducees are generally known as defenders of the status quo. They supported the Hasmoneans and were in a favorable position during most of the Hasmonean rule. In a way the Sadducees can be said to have come out of the Hellenistic movement, since they tended to accommodate themselves to situations as they were, rather than putting themselves in opposition to them. Yet sympathy for the Hellenistic culture was not one of their distinguishing marks.

The Sadducees rejected the teaching of the Pharisees that oral tradition was equal in authority to the law. As a result they held that their obligations were only to the written word and they did not follow the laws of the Pharisees. They also denied doctrines that had been developed by interpreting the law—for example, resurrection from the dead and the existence of angels and demons. Over against the Pharisees' emphasis on providence, they maintained that man was free to choose as he pleased.

The origin of the name Sadducees is uncertain. There are many theories. The most commonly held one is that the name is derived from Zadok, who originated the high priestly line which held the office up to the Babylonian captivity. According to this theory, the Sadducees took this name because they claimed to belong to the true priestly line.

Essenes

The Essenes are another group whose roots lie in the Hasidim of the Maccabean period. In fact the name Es-

sene is probably a Greek form of Hasidim. The Essenes were devoted to study of the Scriptures and separation from the world. Some of them lived in Jerusalem or in small villages of Judea; but basically they were an ascetic group, and most of them withdrew from society and formed monastic communities in the Dead Sea desert. They were marked by love and faithfulness to their fellow members.

The Essenes were very much concerned with ritual contamination—not only by uncleanness as defined in the law, or by contact with Gentiles, but also by contact with non-Essene Jews. To avoid contamination by going to the temple in person, they usually sent their gifts. And if they did go there, apparently there was a special gate for their exclusive use.

The law was interpreted strictly. For example, on the Sabbath work of any kind was absolutely prohibiting—including going to the temple. There were also special rules of the community, and disobedience resulted in being banished.

Apparently celibacy was the rule in Essene communities, but the members adopted children, bringing them up in the way of the Essenes. However at least one group allowed three-year trial marriages, which would be finalized if a child was conceived during the trial period.

One of the distinctive features of the communities were the ritual washings. Each day, before their communal meal, all the members would bathe together in a special pool constructed for this purpose. The rule was that they had to be totally immersed. This bath took on a special meaning on the day of Pentecost, which was their holiest day. On this day the members of the sect repeated their vows and renewed their covenant. The bath served as a seal of their vows.

The communal meal served several functions. It was presided over by a priest, who blessed and distributed the food. This meal was an expression of unity and interdependence, but more importantly, it anticipated the feast they would partake in at the coming of the Messiah.

It was not easy to enter an Essene community. The novitiate had to pass through three stages that tested his faithfulness before he could become a full member. The first stage consisted of a year of probation, during which the newcomer remained outside the sect. He could not wear their special clothing or participate in the ritual baths and communal meals. At the end of this year, after repenting of his sins, he took a ritual bath and became a provisional member. He could then participate in the daily sacred bath.

After two more years of study and testing, the new member had to pass examinations and submit to a vote of the community. If he passed, he had to take a vow to be faithful to the community and not to divulge its doctrines to anyone. He then became a full member and was allowed to participate in the daily sacred meal. This was followed by one more year of probation.

Many scholars believe that the Qumran community of the Dead Sea Scrolls was actually an Essene community. Those scrolls tell us quite a bit about the daily life of the Essenes. Their daily activities were scheduled according to the rising and setting of the sun. They got up at dawn and offered prayer, facing the rising sun. The rest of the morning they worked at their assigned tasks. At noon they gathered together for the ritual bath, followed by the sacred communal meal. Afternoon again was given to their work and in the evening the members devoted themselves to the study of Scripture.

The Essene communities were based in large part on their eschatological hopes. They thought they were living in the last times and that the coming of the Messiah with His kingdom of light was imminent. They believed their withdrawal into the desert would help prepare a way for the Messiah. Their purity of life was designed to fulfill Isaiah's command, "Prepare ye the way of the Lord, make straight in the desert a highway for our God" (Isaiah 40:3).

Zealots

The fourth party of intertestamental times was the Zealots, who trace their beginnings to Roman rule over Palestine. They followed the Maccabean spirit of revolt against pagan rule over their country. They expressed their zeal for God's law by resistance to the Romans, often resorting to violence and assassination. One of the twelve disciples, Simon the Zealot, was a member of this party.

The Zealots led several unsuccessful revolts against Roman rule, but their movement was crushed when the Romans destroyed Jerusalem in A.D. 70 and took the last stronghold of the Zealots at Masada. This event also marked the scattering of the Jews and the end of temple worship.

Doctrines

Most of what we know about the distinctive doctrines of this period comes from the books of the Apocrypha, which will be discussed later. These doctrines developed from the new emphasis on faithfulness to God's covenant and from the interpretation of Old Testament Scriptures by the scribes and Pharisees.

Theology

The Babylonian captivity taught the Jews that their God was powerful and transcendent. He did not control just their nation but was the God in control of all nations. It was He who governed the entire world. He was not only the God of Israel but also the God of Babylon, Persia, Greece, and Rome. He was the God of the created world and of the stars of the heavens. Everything that happened was in His hands.

This understanding of God's power and authority led to a new reverence. The Jews of the intertestamental and New Testament periods were very hesitant to use God's name directly. Instead they used such terms as "heaven," "the Holy One," and "the Name."

Angels and Demons

Another development was the emphasis on angels as the intermediaries between God and man, since it was believed that God was too high to be directly involved with man.

In the Old Testament God is often referred to as helping Israel in its battles. However, apocryphal literature usually places angels in this position of fighting for the children of Israel. A number of angels are given proper names—Phanuel, Uriel, Raphael, Raguel, Michael, Saraquael, Gabriel, and Remiel. Other terms used for angels were "sons of God," "holy ones," and "watchers."

The function of the angels as described in the Apocrypha is twofold: to praise God and to carry messages between God and man. Angels served as guardians for particular nations and individuals. Thus Michael was the guardian angel for Israel. The angels were also divided into a hierarchy with archangels, cherubim, seraphim, etc.

Demons, or evil spirits, also have a prominent place in

apocryphal literature. They were thought to be the offspring of fallen angels and the "daughters of men." The evil spirits were responsible for evil in the world and for leading men astray. Their ruler is alternately known as Beliar or Belial, Asmodeus, Azazel, and Mastemus.

Some of what the Apocrypha teaches about angels and demons reflects the truths of the Old Testament. But it goes beyond that, because out of these beliefs came a doctrine that was close to dualism. Good was under the control of God and the angels, and evil was in the power of Satan and his demons. Evil and good were in constant conflict in this life until a final battle when God would be victorious and establish the kingdom of light.

The Kingdom of God

Influenced by Isaiah's passages about the messianic kingdom (Isaiah 11 and 65), the Jews expected a kingdom established by God in which evil would be banished and the nation of Israel would be vindicated. This kingdom would be established by the coming Messiah, God's anointed one.

The Jewish beliefs of the kingdom of God and the coming of the Messiah contained elements of both truth and error. Yet taken generally they should be recognized as forerunners of Christian truths.

At first the writings about the kingdom seemed to be an expectation of nothing more than Israel's victory over its enemies, the foreign powers that ruled over and oppressed the nation. This kingdom was earthly and political—Israel would be reestablished as a world power and restored to its rightful place.

Gradually, however, this belief developed into an everlasting kingdom where evil was completely overcome and forever banished. The enemy was no longer a specific worldly power but the demonic forces of evil, which would be overcome by God and His angels. He would deliver not just Israel but the entire universe from the power of Satan. Creation would be restored to the age of Paradise. All the righteous would be resurrected to new life in the kingdom, which would be a kingdom of happiness and peace.

Resurrection From the Dead

The Apocrypha generally reflects a belief in Sheol, an intermediate stage of waiting for the spirits of all the dead. This belief was also prominent in the Old Testament: "The dead know not any thing, neither have they any more a reward; for the memory of them is forgotten. . . . for there is no work, nor device, nor knowledge, nor wisdom, in the grave [Sheol], whither thou goest" (Ecclesiastes 9:5,10). The Old Testament reflects some hope in immortality, for example by David and Job. It is also clearly taught in at least two passages. "Thy dead men shall live, together with my dead body shall they arise. Awake and sing, ye that dwell in dust: for thy dew is as the dew of herbs, and the earth shall cast out the dead" (Isaiah 26:19). "And many of them sleep in the dust of the earth shall awake, some to everlasting life, and some to share and everlasting contempt" (Daniel 12:2).

But during the intertestamental period the belief in the resurrection of the body became more pronounced. All those who died would rise again to be judged by God. The righteous would be rewarded with a place in the kingdom and the wicked would be punished with eternal torment in the fires of Gehenna.

The apocryphal books also show a change in Sheol. Once thought of as a shadowy place of waiting without distinction between the righteous and the wicked, it eventually became a place of reward and punishment in anticipation of future judgment.

The Messiah

The Messiah who would come to establish the kingdom of God was a prominent feature of intertestamental doctrine. At first he was thought of as an earthly king, a man who would lead the forces of Israel to triumph and rule over the nation. In later writings, however, he is described as a transcendent being—not really God Himself but somehow exalted above men. He would have both kingly and priestly functions in the new kingdom.

This image is an imperfect picture of the true Messiah. The doctrine of the kingdom had elements of truth, yet it, too, was incomplete. Still, these beliefs helped prepare the way for the coming of Christ, whose kingdom rules now in the hearts of believers and who will reign forever in His perfect kingdom.

Torah

The basis of Judaism lies in the devotion of the people to the Torah, or the law. Actually Torah means more than just the law of Moses; it includes the oral traditions of the scribes as well. The scrolls of the Torah became the actual physical symbol of the Jewish faith. Although in New Testament times legalism and outward observance were frequently criticized by Jesus, the intertestamental literature lays great stress on piety, devotion to God, and a love for the law.

In the intertestamental period the stress was on strict obedience to the requirements of the law as the only way to obtain life in the new kingdom. Instead of being an act of thanksgiving to a gracious God, obedience became the means for pleasing God and obtaining His divine favor.

The importance of obedience to the law created a need for interpretation so that it would be clear exactly what was required. This led to the functions of the scribes and the development of oral tradition. It was also necessary to have an intimate knowledge of the law. The synagogues developed out of this need.

Sources

Much of our information about this period in Jewish history comes from the books of the Apocrypha. They will be discussed in detail. There are several other important sources as well. One of these is Josephus, a Jewish historian who lived during the time of the apostles. His two books are *The Jewish War* and *Jewish Antiquities*. They cannot be relied on completely because he was not always accurate, yet these books give the most history we have of the history and religion of the intertestamental period.

Another source of information is Philo, a Jewish philosopher who represented the Hellenistic viewpoint. He also was a contemporary of Jesus and the apostles. His books are mostly philosophical and they help us ascertain the character of Judaism in the Dispersion.

The Apocrypha

The Apocrypha is the term commonly used to identify a group of fifteen books written during the period between 200 B.C. and A.D. 100. Currently this group of books is published in one volume with the Old and New Testaments. The books in the Apocrypha are as follows:
1. I Esdras
2. II Esdras
3. Tobit
4. Judith

5. The Additions to the Book of Esther
6. The Wisdom of Solomon
7. Ecclesiasticus, or The Wisdom of Jesus the Son of Sirach
8. Baruch
9. The Letter of Jeremiah
10. The Prayer of Azariah and the Song of the Three Young Men
11. Susanna
12. Bel and the Dragon
13. The Prayer of Manasseh
14. I Maccabees
15. II Maccabees

The Jews never recognized any of these books as part of the Old Testament canon. They regarded the Old Testament as canonical or authoritative because it had come to them through the prophets who had been divinely called to communicate God's message. This succession of prophets had been broken about 400 B.C., according to Josephus, with Malachi as the last prophet. Any literature produced after that time was not recognized by the Jews as canonical since the authors were not acknowledged as prophets. The distinctive phrase "Thus saith the Lord" was missing and consequently the writings lacked the stamp of authority.

The absence of the gift of prophecy in this post-Malachi era, often known as the four hundred silent years, is reflected in I Maccabees 4:46; 9:27; and 14:41. Josephus asserted rather forcefully that the Jews regarded twenty-two books (thirty-nine in English) as inspired and God-given and that the Jews would be willing to die if need be for this canon of prophetic literature.

The New Testament reflects agreement with the Jews that only these twenty-two books composed the Jewish canon. Although there are occasional allusions to the apocryphal literature, no direct quotations are found in the New Testament. Hundreds of quotations, however, occur throughout the New Testament making use of most of the twenty-two or thirty-nine books known as the Old Testament.

Jesus in His teaching concurred with the prevailing idea that only the Old Testament books and not the apocryphal literature provided the basic authority on which matters of eternal import should be decided. Jesus came to fulfill the "law and the prophets"—a term commonly used in the New Testament to identify the Old Testament collection of canonical scrolls—and repeatedly appealed to them in His dialogue with the religious leaders of His day. There is no evidence to suggest that there was any difference of opinion between Jesus and the religious teachers regarding the limits of the literature which the Jews considered as part of the canon and of prophetic origin.

Trained under Gamaliel in the foremost center of Jewish learning in Jerusalem, Paul in his writings likewise reflected the viewpoint that only the Old Testament was the canon of the Jews. This was evident when he was on trial for his life before Felix, the Roman governor in Caesarea. In the presence of his accusers Paul asserted that he was in full agreement with them in all that was "written in the law and in the prophets" (Acts 24:14). Nowhere in his writing did Paul accord the authority to any of the apocryphal books that he repeatedly gave to the Old Testament canon of the Jews.

It is significant that Paul recognized that the Jews were the recipients of this divine revelation known as the Old Testament; he wrote that to the Jews were "committed the oracles of God" (Romans 3:2). The church was not the authority in this matter. It was a fact of history that this revelation or communication of God, now in written form, had in the providence of God been entrusted to the Jews. When Paul wrote this letter to the Romans, the Jewish Old Testament canon also had the stamp of approval of Christ and the apostles. Since that time no additional literature has ever been recognized by the Jews as having the authority accorded the Old Testament. It is the Jewish canon—and this canon alone as far as the Old Testament is concerned—that has been regarded as canonical by the entire church throughout the centuries since that time.

That more literature would be recognized as canonical with the coming of Jesus Christ seemed to be a normal development. Since Jesus came as a prophet, breaking the four hundred years of silence, it was recognized that Jesus represented the continuation of divine revelation that had been initiated through the prophets. Jesus came to fulfill the "law and the prophets." This was recognized by the author of Hebrews in his opening words when he said, "God who . . . spake in time past unto the fathers by the prophets, hath in these last days spoken unto us by his Son . . ." (1:1,2). Since Jesus represented the complement and the climax of God's revelation to man, it follows that the literature that pertained directly to the life and teachings of Jesus Christ should gain recognition on the same level of authority as the canon of the Jews, which was regarded as of divine origin. Since the Jews in the course of time did not recognize Jesus as divine and the Christian church did, the literature concerning Jesus did not gain canonical recognition by the Jews.

The cleavage between the Jews and the Christian church developed in the early centuries of the Christian era. Paul in his missionary activities entered synagogue after synagogue reasoning out of the Scriptures that Jesus was the Christ (Acts 17:1-4). Very likely Paul often used the Greek version of the Old Testament, commonly known as the Septuagint or LXX. The Jews apparently reacted to this missionizing approach by the Christian church, which became predominantly Gentile, by reverting primarily to the Hebrew canon which they carefully transmitted on scrolls in the Hebrew language (especially after the destruction of Jerusalem in A.D. 70). The Christian church continued to use the Septuagint together with the New Testament literature which was also in the Greek language.

How did the Apocrypha gain acceptance by a segment of the Christian church? This development in church history is rather significant, since the Roman Catholic Church in the twentieth century accepts as fully canonical the group of books listed above (except the Prayer of Manasseh and I and II Esdras), commonly called the Apocrypha. Modern Roman Catholic scholars prefer to use the distinction made by Sixtus of Sienna in A.D. 1566 in identifying these additional books as canonical or "Deuterocanonical," meaning that they were added to the canon at a later time. The Old Testament, which is held to be canonical by the Jews and by the entire church, they identify as "protocanonical." The Prayer of Manasseh and I and II Esdras, as well as other literature which was written from about 200 B.C. to A.D. 200, the Roman Catholics identify as "apocryphal." (Protestants identify this literature as pseudopigraphical.)

The Greek versions of the Old Testament—the earliest manuscripts available are from the fourth and fifth centuries A.D.—contain the Apocrypha with the exception of

II Esdras. How these came to be bound in the Old Testament volume is not definitely known. In the second century of the Christian era the codex, or book form, seems to have replaced scrolls for the circulation of the Gospels. Probably in the course of time the Old Testament was transferred from scrolls to books, whereas the Jews definitely continued to use scrolls for the transmission of the Hebrew text throughout the first millennium A.D. Since the apocryphal books were quoted by the church fathers and probably read publicly in the churches, it may well be that for practical reasons they were included in the bound volumes of the Greek versions of the Old Testament in the fourth and fifth centuries. The fact that they were included does not warrant the conclusion that they were considered to be canonical, just as their inclusion in modern times does not mean that these books are canonical.

Generally speaking, church leaders and Christian scholars have clearly recognized that the Apocrypha was not part of the canonical Old Testament. Melito, Bishop of Sardis near the end of the second century A.D., definitely asserted that the Old Testament canon was composed of twenty-two books. Origen, one of the most learned Greek fathers in the third century, likewise recognized a canon of twenty-two books as held by the Jews. Tertullian, the Latin father of this early period, speaks of twenty-four books (listing Ruth and Lamentations as separate books). Jerome, who was asked by Pope Damasus to translate the Old Testament into Latin, recognized only these twenty-two or twenty-four. It was not his intention to translate the books in the Apocrypha but he did so because of pressure, and he indicated in his prefaces that these books were in a separate category. In his writings he repeatedly distinguished between the books that are canonical and those that are not.

Augustine was present at the councils of Hippo in A.D. 393 and Carthage in A.D. 397. It is reasonable to consider that the lists of books approved at these councils were composed of literature that was of a theistic nature and recommended for reading. On this basis the Apocrypha could be included, but this does not necessarily give them canonical recognition unless there is supporting evidence.

Augustine made it clear in his writings that the books of the Maccabees, Judith, and others were not considered as authoritative or included in the canon of the Jews received by the church.

In the course of centuries, however, the Latin Bible copyists were careless in transmitting the prefaces to the apocryphal books made by Jerome in which he pointed out that these books were not canonical. With these prefaces omitted, the church began to regard these apocryphal books as part of the Scriptures. Among those who expressed concern on this matter was Cardinal Cajetan, an eminent theologian at Rome in the early seventeenth century. In the preface to his commentary on Hebrews, he asserted that Jerome made a clear distinction between the canonical and noncanonical books. In the *Complutensian Polyglott,* which was published before the Council of Trent convened in 1546, and dedicated to Pope Leo X, Cardinal Ximenes, the Archbishop of Toledo in Spain, made some significant observations in the preface. In regard to the apocryphal books, which were printed only in Greek and not in Hebrew in this Polyglott, he stated that these books were received by the church for edification rather than for confirming the authority of ecclesiastical doctrines.

In A.D. 1546 the Council of Trent decreed that the list of books commonly known today as the Apocrypha (excluding the Prayer of Manasseh and I and II Esdras) were part of the canon of Holy Scripture. The decision seemed to be based on popular usage—these books with some exceptions were included in the early versions, they were read in public services, and were quoted by the church fathers. Had the members of the Council of Trent given careful consideration to the facts of history, especially the well-recognized fact that neither the Jews nor Jesus and the apostles included the Apocrypha in the canon, they might have come to a different conclusion.

Beyond the historical evidence concerning the acceptance of the Apocrypha is the question of authority. Is the church vested with authority to decide what the content of the canon should be? Or should the church, in regard to the Old Testament literature, recognize what Jesus and the apostles and the Jews, to whom the Old Testament revelation was given, considered canonical?

The Seleucid Kings

(with the years they ruled)

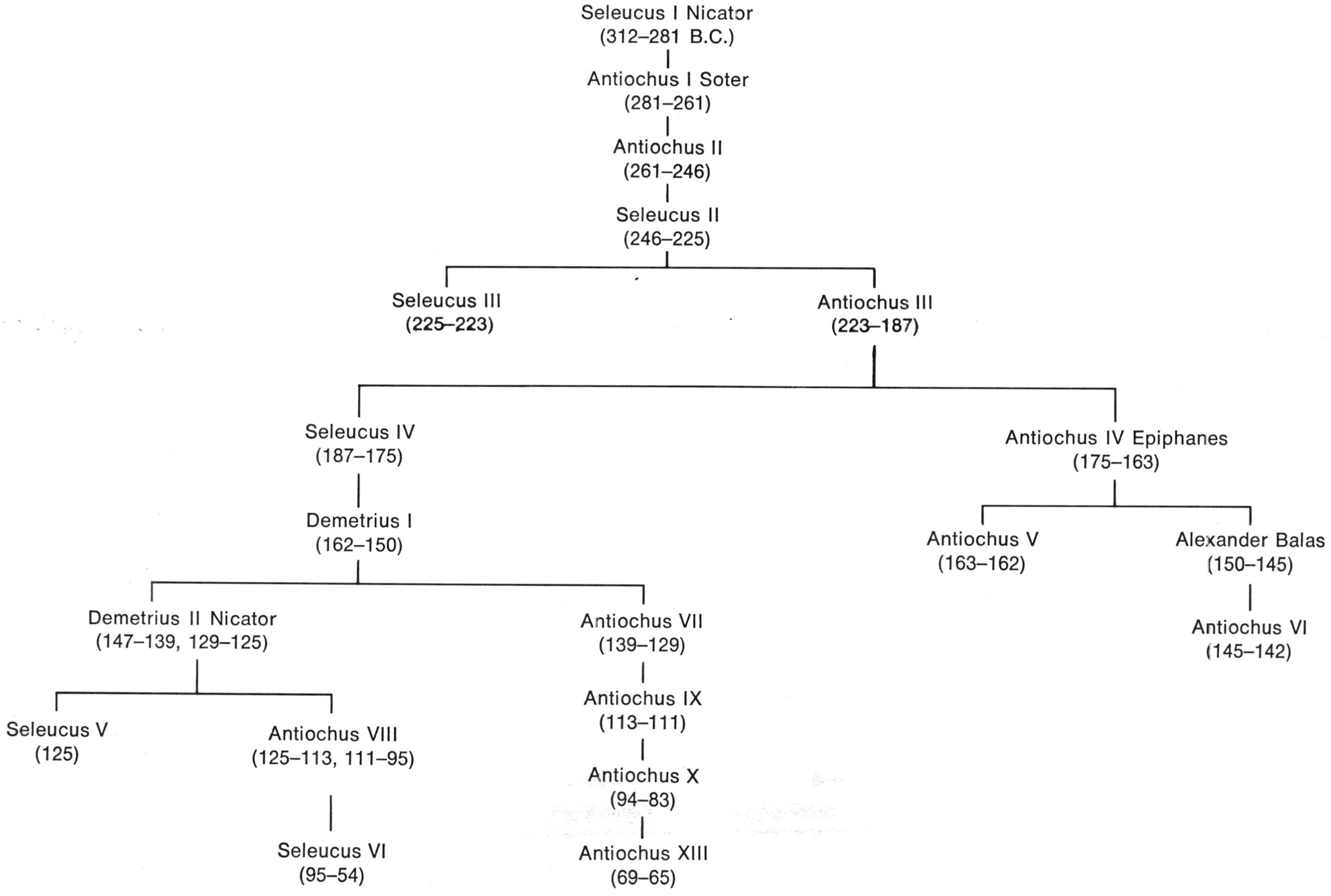

Seleucus I Nicator
(312–281 B.C.)

Antiochus I Soter
(281–261)

Antiochus II
(261–246)

Seleucus II
(246–225)

Seleucus III
(225–223)

Antiochus III
(223–187)

Seleucus IV
(187–175)

Demetrius I
(162–150)

Antiochus IV Epiphanes
(175–163)

Antiochus V
(163–162)

Alexander Balas
(150–145)

Antiochus VI
(145–142)

Antiochus VII
(139–129)

Antiochus IX
(113–111)

Antiochus X
(94–83)

Antiochus XIII
(69–65)

Demetrius II Nicator
(147–139, 129–125)

Antiochus VIII
(125–113, 111–95)

Seleucus VI
(95–54)

Seleucus V
(125)

The Maccabees and Hasmoneans

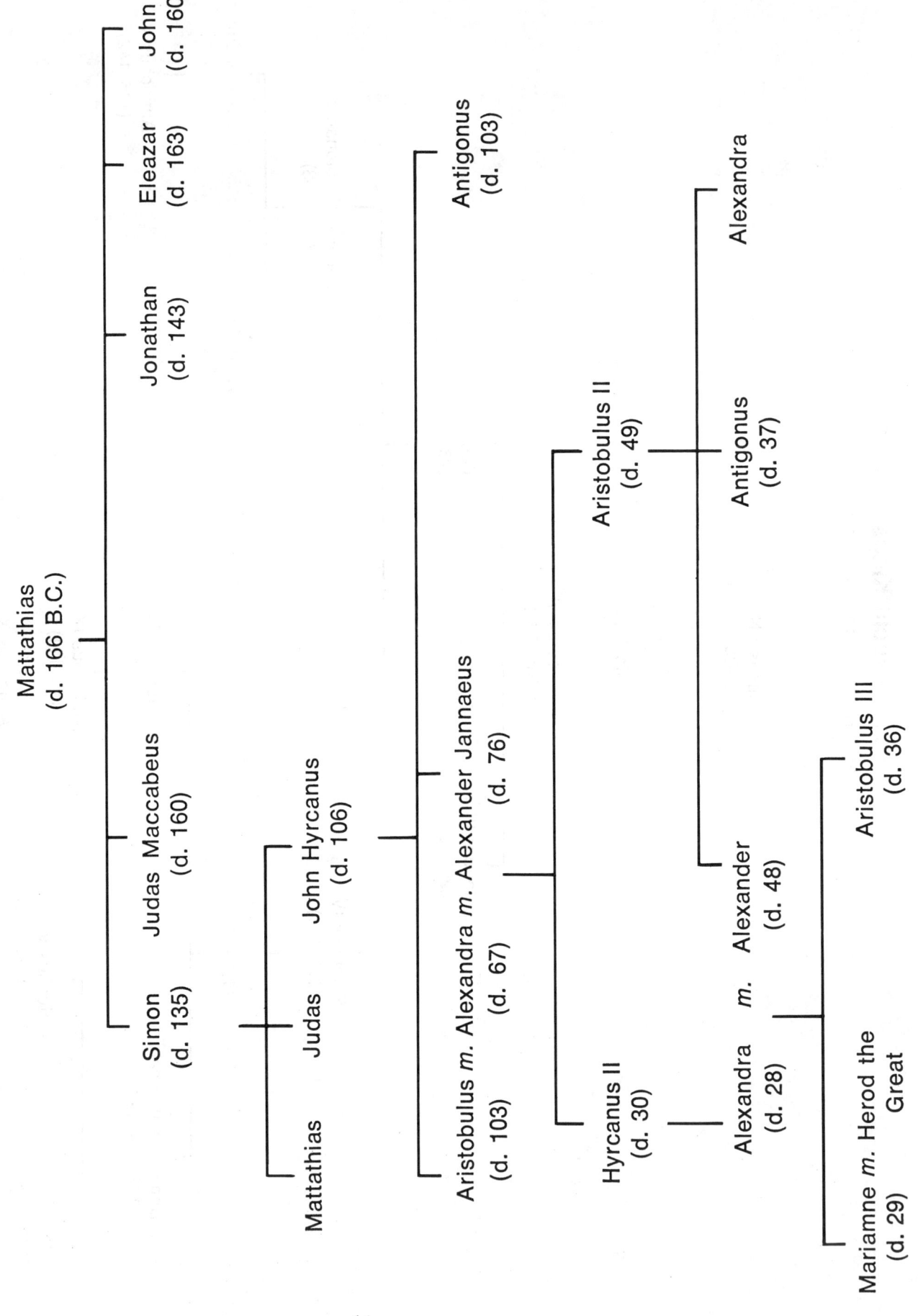

The Herodian Family

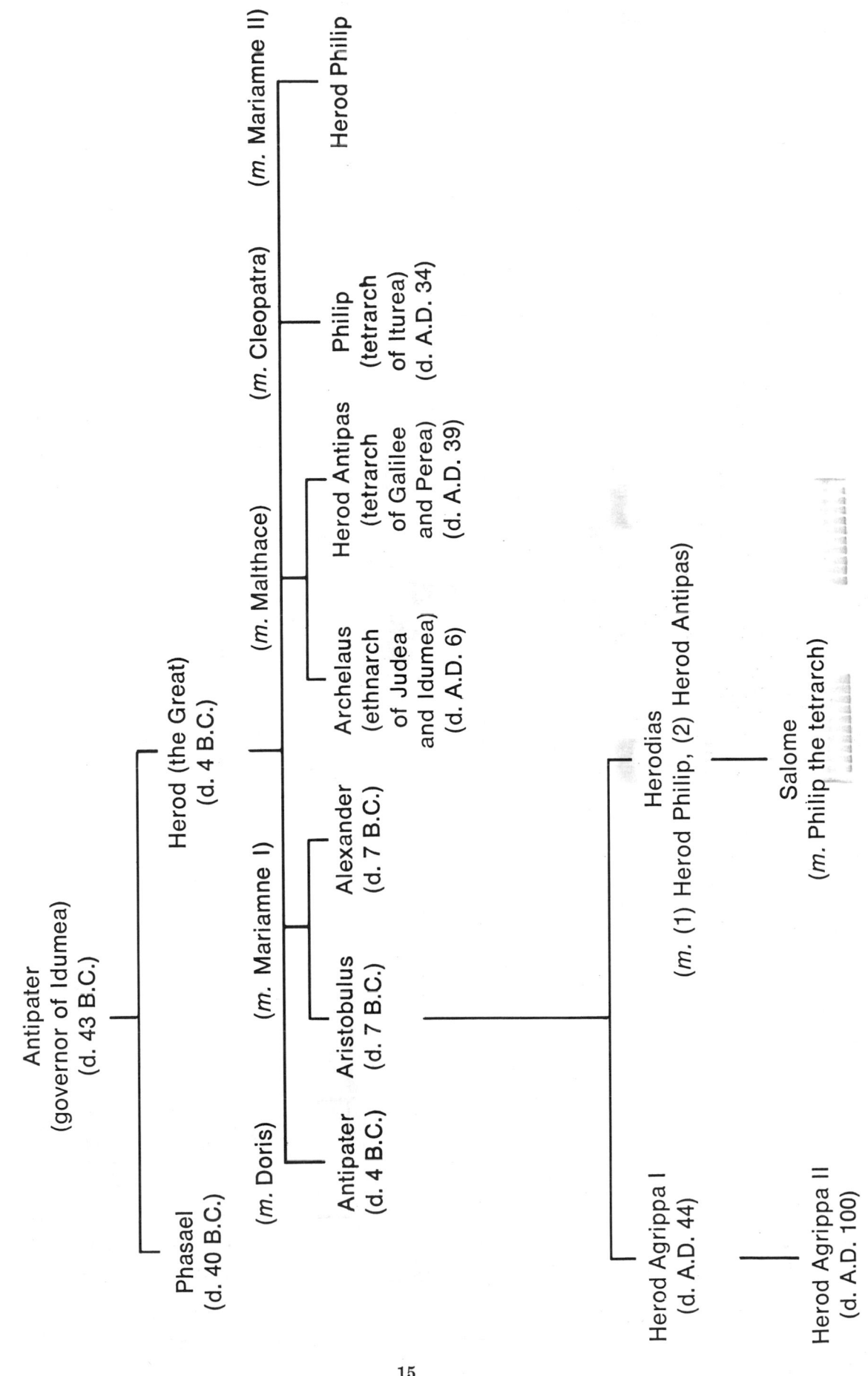

Antipater
(governor of Idumea)
(d. 43 B.C.)

Phasael
(d. 40 B.C.)

Herod (the Great)
(d. 4 B.C.)

(m. Doris)

(m. Mariamne I)

(m. Malthace)

(m. Cleopatra)

(m. Mariamne II)

Antipater
(d. 4 B.C.)

Aristobulus
(d. 7 B.C.)

Alexander
(d. 7 B.C.)

Archelaus
(ethnarch
of Judea
and Idumea)
(d. A.D. 6)

Herod Antipas
(tetrarch
of Galilee
and Perea)
(d. A.D. 39)

Philip
(tetrarch
of Iturea)
(d. A.D. 34)

Herod Philip

Herodias
(m. (1) Herod Philip, (2) Herod Antipas)

Salome
(m. Philip the tetrarch)

Herod Agrippa I
(d. A.D. 44)

Herod Agrippa II
(d. A.D. 100)

Herod's Temple

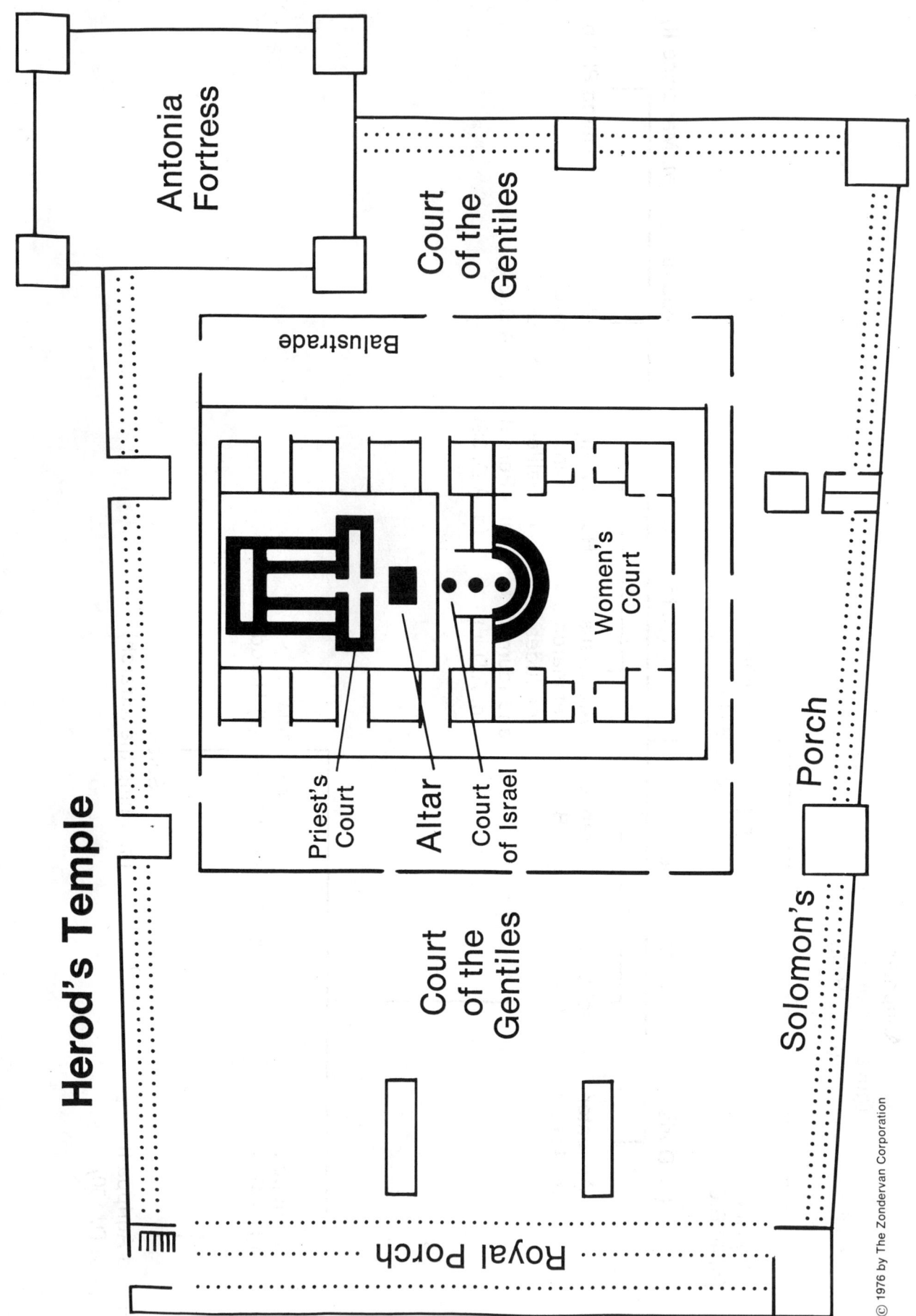

Antonia Fortress

Court of the Gentiles

Balustrade

Priest's Court

Altar

Court of Israel

Women's Court

Court of the Gentiles

Solomon's Porch

Royal Porch

16

The Family Record of

Husband _____

Wife _____

Who were united in Holy Matrimony

At _____
(church or place)

On _____
(date)

By _____

Witnessed by _____

_____

_____

_____

_____

Husband's Genealogy

FATHER
_____
_____
_____
_____
_____

FATHER
_____
_____
_____
_____
_____

MOTHER
_____
_____
_____
_____
_____

NAME
_____
DATE BIRTH
_____
PLACE
_____
BROTHERS, SISTERS
_____
_____
_____
_____
_____

FATHER
_____
_____
_____
_____
_____

MOTHER
_____
_____
_____
_____
_____

MOTHER
_____
_____
_____
_____
_____

FATHER

MOTHER

FATHER

MOTHER

FATHER

MOTHER

FATHER

MOTHER

FATHER

MOTHER

FATHER

MOTHER

FATHER

MOTHER

FATHER

MOTHER

FATHER

MOTHER

FATHER

MOTHER

FATHER

MOTHER

FATHER

MOTHER

FATHER

MOTHER

FATHER

MOTHER

FATHER

MOTHER

FATHER

MOTHER

FATHER

MOTHER

FATHER

MOTHER

FATHER

MOTHER

FATHER

MOTHER

FATHER

MOTHER

FATHER

MOTHER

FATHER

MOTHER

FATHER

MOTHER

FATHER

MOTHER

FATHER

MOTHER

FATHER

MOTHER

FATHER

MOTHER

FATHER

MOTHER

Wife's Genealogy

FATHER
_____
_____
_____
_____
_____
_____
_____

FATHER
_____
_____
_____
_____
_____
_____

MOTHER
_____
_____
_____
_____
_____
_____
_____
_____

NAME
_____
DATE BIRTH
_____
PLACE
_____
BROTHERS, SISTERS
_____
_____
_____
_____
_____
_____

FATHER
_____
_____
_____
_____
_____
_____
_____

MOTHER
_____
_____
_____
_____
_____
_____
_____

MOTHER
_____
_____
_____
_____
_____
_____
_____
_____

FATHER

MOTHER

FATHER

MOTHER

FATHER

MOTHER

FATHER

MOTHER

FATHER

MOTHER

FATHER

MOTHER

FATHER

MOTHER

FATHER

MOTHER

FATHER

MOTHER

FATHER

MOTHER

FATHER

MOTHER

FATHER

MOTHER

FATHER

MOTHER

FATHER

MOTHER

FATHER

MOTHER

FATHER

MOTHER

FATHER

MOTHER

FATHER

MOTHER

FATHER

MOTHER

FATHER

MOTHER

FATHER

MOTHER

FATHER

MOTHER

FATHER

MOTHER

FATHER

MOTHER

FATHER

MOTHER

FATHER

MOTHER

FATHER

MOTHER

FATHER

MOTHER

FATHER

MOTHER

Children

_____

_____

_____

_____

_____

_____

_____

_____

_____

_____

_____

_____

Marriages

_____

_____

_____

_____

_____

_____

_____

_____

_____

_____

_____

Military Records

Deaths

_____

_____

_____

_____

_____

_____

_____

_____

_____

_____

_____

_____

Family Records

_____

_____

_____

_____

_____

_____

_____

_____

_____

_____

_____

Family Records

_____

_____

_____

_____

_____

_____

_____

_____

_____

_____

_____

_____

Family Records

_____

_____

_____

_____

_____

_____

_____

_____

_____

_____

_____

_____

_____

Family Records

_____

_____

_____

_____

_____

_____

_____

_____

_____

_____

_____

_____

Family Records

_____

_____

_____

_____

_____

_____

_____

_____

_____

_____

_____

_____

Family Records

_____

_____

_____

_____

_____

_____

_____

_____

_____

_____

_____

_____

Family Records

_____

_____

_____

_____

_____

_____

_____

_____

_____

_____

_____

_____

The
New Testament

of Our Lord and Saviour

Jesus Christ

TRANSLATED OUT OF
THE ORIGINAL GREEK AND WITH THE FORMER
TRANSLATIONS DILIGENTLY COMPARED
AND REVISED

With all the words recorded therein
as having been spoken by Our Lord
printed in red

THE GOSPEL ACCORDING TO
ST. MATTHEW

From at least the second century A.D., the first Gospel has been ascribed to Matthew, the publican, tax-collector and disciple. Its position as the opening book of the New Testament is appropriate, for it breathes the atmosphere of the Old Testament and thus provides a transition from Old Covenant to New. A number of the Old Testament themes are reinterpreted and interwoven in Matthew's presentation of Jesus as the Messiah: (1) the fulfillment theme, emphasizing Old Testament prophecies of Christ and the close bond between the faith of Israel and Christianity; (2) the corporate personality theme, portraying the career of Jesus as a recapitulation of the experiences of ancient Israel; (3) the new exodus theme, presenting Christian redemption within the framework of the old exodus; (4) the new Israel theme, showing the continuity between God's past and present activity. Although Matthew is certainly Jewish in interest and emphasis, the Gospel carries a note of universalism (e.g., 28:19–20) and seeks to present Christianity as much more comprehensive than Judaism. The author gives a carefully structured portrayal of the life, character, and work of Jesus. The most obvious feature of this structure is the alternation of five blocks of narrative with four groupings of discourse, followed by accounts of the Passion and Resurrection. The gospel almost certainly originated in Palestine, probably being finally composed in Jerusalem or Antioch. Some scholars, noting the high development of doctrine, have dated the work as late as the period A.D. 80–100; others believe it could have been written as early as A.D. 60–70.

OUTLINE OF THE BOOK:

I. Birth and Infancy of Jesus 1:1–2:23
II. Prelude to the Ministry of Jesus 3:1–4:11
III. The Ministry of Jesus 4:12–25:46
IV. Passion and Resurrection Accounts 26:1–28:15
V. Jesus in Galilee: the Great Commission 28:16–20

CHAPTER 1

The genealogy of Jesus Christ

THE book of the ᴿgeneration of Jesus Christ, ᴿthe son of David, ᴿthe son of Abraham.

2 ᴿAbraham begat Isaac; and ᴿIsaac begat Jacob; and ᴿJacob begat Judas and his brethren;

3 And ᴿJudas begat Phâr′-ĕś and Zâr′-ă of Thā′-mär; and ᴿPhâr′-ĕś begat Ĕś′-rŏm; and Ĕś′-rŏm begat âr′-ăm;

4 And âr′-ăm begat Ă-mĭn′-ă-dăb; and Ă-mĭn′-ă-dăb begat Nā-ăs′-sŏn; and Nā-ăs′-sŏn begat Săl′-mŏn;

5 And Săl′-mŏn begat Bō′-ŏz of Rā′-chăb; and Bō′-ŏz begat ō′-bĕd of Ruth; and ō′-bĕd begat Jesse;

6 And ᴿJesse begat David the king; and ᴿDavid the king begat Solomon of her *that had been the wife* of Ū-rī′-ăs;

7 And ᴿSolomon begat Rō-bō′-ăm; and Rō-bō′-ăm begat Ă-bī′-ă; and Ă-bī′-ă begat Ā′-să;

8 And Ā′-să begat Jŏs′-ă-phăt; and Jŏs′-ă-phăt begat Joram; and Joram begat ō-zī′-ăs;

9 And ō-zī′-ăs begat Jō′-ă-thăm; and Jō′-ă-thăm begat Ā′-chăz; and Ā′-chăz begat ĕz-ē-kī′-ăs;

10 And ᴿĔz-ē-kī′-ăs begat Mă-năs′-sĕś; and Mă-năs′-sĕś begat Amon; and Amon begat Jō-sī′-ăs;

11 And ᴿJō-sī′-ăsᴺ begat Jĕch-ō-nī′-ăs and his brethren, about the time they were ᴿcarried away to Babylon:

12 And after they were brought to Babylon, ᴿJĕch-ō-nī′-ăs begat Să-lā′-thĭ-ĕl; and Să-lā′-thĭ-ĕl begat ᴿZŏ-rŏb′-ă-bĕl;

13 And Zŏ-rŏb′-ă-bĕl begat Ă-bī′-ŭd; and Ă-bī′-ŭd begat Ē-lī′-ă-kĭm; and Ē-lī′-ă-kĭm begat Ā′-zôr;

14 And Ā′-zôr begat Sā′-dŏc; and Sā′-dŏc begat Ā′-chĭm; and Ā′-chĭm begat Ē-lī′-ŭd;

15 And Ē-lī′-ŭd begat Ĕl-ē-ā′-zär; and Ĕl-ē-ā′-zär begat Măt′-thăn; and Măt′-thăn begat Jacob;

16 And Jacob begat Joseph the husband of Mary, of whom was born Jesus, who is called Christ.

17 So all the generations from Abraham to David *are* fourteen generations; and from David until the carrying away into Babylon *are* fourteen generations; and from the carrying away into Babylon unto Christ *are* fourteen generations.

The annunciation to Joseph

18 Now the ᴿbirth of Jesus Christ was on this wise: When as his mother Mary was espoused to Joseph, before they came together, she was found with child ᴿof the Holy Ghost.

19 Then Joseph her husband, being a just *man,* and not willing ᴿto make her a publick example, was minded to put her away privily.

20 But while he thought on these things, behold, the angel of the Lord appeared unto him in a dream, saying, Joseph, thou son of David, fear not to take unto thee Mary thy wife: ᴿfor that which is ᴺconceived in her is of the Holy Ghost.

Cross-reference column:

CHAP. 1

1 Luke 3:23
1 Ps. 132:11
Is. 11:1
Jer. 23:5
ch. 22:42
John 7:42
Acts 2:30
Rom. 1:3
1 Gen. 12:3
2 Gen. 21:2
2 Gen. 25:26
3 Gen. 38:27
3 Ruth 4:18
1 Chr. 2:5
6 1 Sam. 16:1
  & 17:12
6 2 Sam. 12:24
7 1 Chr. 3:10
10 2 Ki. 20:21
1 Chr. 3:13
11 See 1 Chr. 3:15, 16
11 Some read *Josias begat Jakim, and Jakim begat Jechonias*
11 2 Ki. 24:14-16 & 25:11
2 Chr. 36:10
Jer. 27:20
& 52:11, 15
Dan. 1:2

1 Chr. 3:17 12
Ezra 3:2 12
Neh. 12:1
Hag. 1:1
Luke 1:27 18
Luke 1:35 18
Deut. 24:1 19
Luke 1:35 20
Gr. *begotten* 20

21 ᴿAnd she shall bring forth a son, and thou shalt call his name ᴺJESUS: for ᴿhe shall save his people from their sins.

22 Now all this was done, that it might be fulfilled which was spoken of the Lord by the prophet, saying,

23 ᴿBehold, a virgin shall be with child, and shall bring forth a son, and ᴺthey shall call his name ĕm-măn′-ū-ĕl, which being interpreted is, God with us.

24 Then Joseph being raised from sleep did as the angel of the Lord had bidden him, and took unto him his wife:

25 And knew her not till she had brought forth ᴿher firstborn son: and he called his name JESUS.

CHAPTER 2

Visit of the wise men

NOW when ᴿJesus was born in Bethlehem of Judæa in the days of Herod the king, behold, there came wise men ᴿfrom the east to Jerusalem,

2 Saying, ᴿWhere is he that is born King of the Jews? for we have seen ᴿhis star in the east, and are come to worship him.

3 When Herod the king had heard *these things,* he was troubled, and all Jerusalem with him.

4 And when he had gathered all ᴿthe chief priests and ᴿscribes of the people together, ᴿhe demanded of them where Christ should be born.

5 And they said unto him, In Bethlehem of Judæa: for thus it is written by the prophet,

6 ᴿAnd thou Bethlehem, *in* the land of Judah, art not the least among the princes of Judah: for out of thee shall come a Governor, ᴿthat shall ᴺrule my people Israel.

7 Then Herod, when he had privily called the wise men, inquired of them diligently what time the star appeared.

8 And he sent them to Bethlehem, and said, Go and search diligently for the young child; and when ye have found *him,* bring me word again, that I may come and worship him also.

9 When they had heard the king, they departed; and, lo, the star, which they saw in the east, went before them, till it came and stood over where the young child was.

10 When they saw the star, they rejoiced with exceeding great joy.

11 And when they were come into the house, they saw the young child with Mary his mother, and fell down, and worshipped him:

and when they had opened their treasures, ᴿthey ᴺpresented unto him gifts; gold, and frankincense, and myrrh.

12 And being warned of God ᴿin a dream that they should not return to Herod, they departed into their own country another way.

Flight into Egypt

13 And when they were departed, behold, the angel of the Lord appeareth to Joseph in a dream, saying, Arise, and take the young child and his mother, and flee into Egypt, and be thou there until I bring thee word: for Herod will seek the young child to destroy him.

14 When he arose, he took the young child and his mother by night, and departed into Egypt:

15 And was there until the death of Herod: that it might be fulfilled which was spoken of the Lord by the prophet, saying, ᴿOut of Egypt have I called my son.

Slaughter of Bethlehem's babies

16 Then Herod, when he saw that he was mocked of the wise men, was exceeding wroth, and sent forth, and slew all the children that were in Bethlehem, and in all the coasts thereof, from two years old and under, according to the time which he had diligently inquired of the wise men.

17 Then was fulfilled that which was spoken by ᴿJeremy the prophet, saying,

18 In Rā′-mă was there a voice heard, lamentation, and weeping, and great mourning, Rachel weeping *for* her children, and would not be comforted, because they are not.

Return from Egypt

19 But when Herod was dead, behold, an angel of the Lord appeareth in a dream to Joseph in Egypt,

20 Saying, Arise, and take the young child and his mother, and go into the land of Israel: for they are dead which sought the young child's life.

21 And he arose, and took the young child and his mother, and came into the land of Israel.

22 But when he heard that Ăr-chĕ-lā′-ŭs did reign in Judæa in the room of his father Herod, he was afraid to go thither: notwithstanding, being warned of God in a dream, he turned aside ᴿinto the parts of Galilee:

23 And he came and dwelt in a city called ᴿNazareth: that it might be fulfilled ᴿwhich was spoken by the prophets, He shall be called a Nazarene.

CHAP. 1

21 Luke 1:31
21 i.e. *Saviour*
21 Acts 4:12
  & 5:31
  & 13:23, 38
23 Is. 7:14
23 Or, *his name shall be called*
25 Ex. 13:2
  Luke 2:7, 21

CHAP. 2

The Fourth Year before the Common Account called Anno Domini
1 Luke 2:4, 6
1 Gen. 25:6
1 Ki. 4:30
2 Luke 2:11
2 Num. 24:17
  Is. 60:3
4 2 Chr. 36:14
4 2 Chr. 34:13
4 Mal. 2:7
6 John 7:42
6 Rev. 2:27
6 Or, *feed*

Ps. 72:10   11
Is. 60:6
Or, *offered*   11
ch. 1:20   12
Hos. 11:1   15
Jer. 31:15   17
ch. 3:13   22
  Luke 2:39
John 1:45   23
Judg. 13:5   23

CHAPTER 3

The ministry of John the Baptist

IN those days came ᴿJohn the Baptist, preaching ᴿin the wilderness of Judæa,

2 And saying, Repent ye: for ᴿthe kingdom of heaven is at hand.

3 For this is he that was spoken of by the prophet Ē-śāi′-ăs, saying, ᴿThe voice of one crying in the wilderness, ᴿPrepare ye the way of the Lord, make his paths straight.

4 And ᴿthe same John had his raiment of camel's hair, and a leathern girdle about his loins; and his meat was ᴿlocusts and ᴿwild honey.

5 ᴿThen went out to him Jerusalem, and all Judæa, and all the region round about Jordan,

6 ᴿAnd were baptized of him in Jordan, confessing their sins.

7 But when he saw many of the Pharisees and Săd′-dū-çēeś come to his baptism, he said unto them, ᴿO generation of vipers, who hath warned you to flee from ᴿthe wrath to come?

8 Bring forth therefore fruits meet for repentance:

9 And think not to say within yourselves, ᴿWe have Abraham to *our* father: for I say unto you, that God is able of these stones to raise up children unto Abraham.

10 And now also the axe is laid unto the root of the trees: ᴿtherefore every tree which bringeth not forth good fruit is hewn down, and cast into the fire.

11 ᴿI indeed baptize you with water unto repentance: but he that cometh after me is mightier than I, whose shoes I am not worthy to bear: ᴿhe shall baptize you with the Holy Ghost, and *with* fire:

12 ᴿWhose fan *is* in his hand, and he will throughly purge his floor, and gather his wheat into the garner; but he will ᴿburn up the chaff with unquenchable fire.

The baptism of Jesus

13 ᴿThen cometh Jesus ᴿfrom Galilee to Jordan unto John, to be baptized of him.

14 But John forbad him, saying, I have need to be baptized of thee, and comest thou to me?

15 And Jesus answering said unto him, Suffer *it to be so* now: for thus it becometh us to fulfill all righteousness. Then he suffered him.

16 ᴿAnd Jesus, when he was baptized, went up straightway out of the water: and, lo, the heavens were opened unto him, and he saw ᴿthe Spirit of God descending like a dove, and lighting upon him:

17 ᴿAnd lo a voice from heaven, saying,

ᴿThis is my beloved Son, in whom I am well pleased.

CHAPTER 4

The temptation of Jesus

THEN was ᴿJesus led up of ᴿthe Spirit into the wilderness to be tempted of the devil.

2 And when he had fasted forty days and forty nights, he was afterward an hungred.

3 And when the tempter came to him, he said, If thou be the Son of God, command that these stones be made bread.

4 But he answered and said, It is written, ᴿMan shall not live by bread alone, but by every word that proceedeth out of the mouth of God.

5 Then the devil taketh him up ᴿinto the holy city, and setteth him on a pinnacle of the temple,

6 And saith unto him, If thou be the Son of God, cast thyself down: for it is written, ᴿHe shall give his angels charge concerning thee: and in *their* hands they shall bear thee up, lest at any time thou dash thy foot against a stone.

7 Jesus said unto him, It is written again, ᴿThou shalt not tempt the Lord thy God.

8 Again, the devil taketh him up into an exceeding high mountain, and sheweth him all the kingdoms of the world, and the glory of them;

9 And saith unto him, All these things will I give thee, if thou wilt fall down and worship me.

10 Then saith Jesus unto him, Get thee hence, Satan: for it is written, ᴿThou shalt worship the Lord thy God, and him only shalt thou serve.

11 Then the devil leaveth him, and, behold, ᴿangels came and ministered unto him.

Beginning of Jesus' preaching

12 ᴿNow when Jesus had heard that John was ᴺcast into prison, he departed into Galilee;

13 And leaving Nazareth, he came and dwelt in Că-pĕr′-nă-ŭm, which is upon the sea coast, in the borders of Ză-bū′-lon and Nĕph′-thă-līm:

14 That it might be fulfilled which was spoken by Ē-śāi′-ăs the prophet, saying,

15 ᴿThe land of Ză-bū′-lon, and the land of Nĕph′-thă-līm, *by* the way of the sea, beyond Jordan, Galilee of the Gentiles;

16 ᴿThe people which sat in darkness saw great light; and to them which sat in the region and shadow of death light is sprung up.

CHAP. **3**

AD 26

1 Mark 1:4
Luke 3:2, 3
1 Josh. 14:10
2 Dan. 2:44
ch. 4:17
3 Is. 40:3
Luke 3:4
John 1:23
3 Luke 1:76
4 Mark 1:6
2 Ki. 1:8
4 Lev. 11:22
4 1 Sam. 14:25, 26
5 Mark 1:5
Luke 3:7
6 Acts 19:4, 18
7 ch. 12:34
Luke 3:7-9
7 Rom. 5:9
1 Thes. 1:10
9 John 8:33
Acts 13:26
Rom. 4:1, 11, 16
10 ch. 7:19
Luke 13:7, 9
John 15:6
11 Mark 1:8
Luke 3:16
Acts 1:5
11 Is. 4:4
Acts 2:3, 4
1 Cor. 12:13
12 Mal. 3:3
12 Mal. 4:1
ch. 13:30
13 Mark 1:9
Luke 3:21
13 ch. 2:22
16 Mark 1:10
16 Is. 11:2
Luke 3:22
John 1:32
17 John 12:28

Ps. 2:7   17
Mark 1:11
Luke 9:35
Col. 1:13

CHAP. **4**

AD 26

Mark 1:12   1
Luke 4:1
Ezek. 3:14   1
Acts 8:39
Deut. 8:3   4
Neh. 11:1   5
ch. 27:53
Ps. 91:11   6
Deut. 6:16   7
Deut. 6:13   10
& 10:20
Josh. 24:14
1 Sam. 7:3
Heb. 1:14   11
Mark 1:14   12
Luke 3:20
& 4:14, 31
John 4:43
Or, *delivered up*   12
Is. 9:1, 2   15
Is. 42:7   16
Luke 2:32

17 ᴿFrom that time Jesus began to preach, and to say, ᴿRepent: for the kingdom of heaven is at hand.

Call of the first disciples

18 ᴿAnd Jesus, walking by the sea of Galilee, saw two brethren, Simon ᴿcalled Peter, and Andrew his brother, casting a net into the sea: for they were fishers.

19 And he saith unto them, Follow me, and ᴿI will make you fishers of men.

20 ᴿAnd they straightway left *their* nets, and followed him.

21 ᴿAnd going on from thence, he saw other two brethren, James *the son* of Zĕb′-ĕ-dēē, and John his brother, in a ship with Zĕb′-ĕ-dēē their father, mending their nets; and he called them.

22 And they immediately left the ship and their father, and followed him.

Ministry in Galilee

23 And Jesus went about all Galilee, ᴿteaching in their synagogues, and preaching ᴿthe gospel of the kingdom, ᴿand healing all manner of sickness and all manner of disease among the people.

24 And his fame went throughout all Syria: and they brought unto him all sick people that were taken with divers diseases and torments, and those which were possessed with devils, and those which were lunatic, and those that had the palsy; and he healed them.

25 ᴿAnd there followed him great multitudes of people from Galilee, and *from* Dĕ-căp′-ŏ-lĭs, and *from* Jerusalem, and *from* Judæa, and *from* beyond Jordan.

CHAPTER 5

The sermon on the mount

AND seeing the multitudes, ᴿhe went up into a mountain: and when he was set, his disciples came unto him:

2 And he opened his mouth, and taught them, saying,

The beatitudes

3 ᴿBlessed *are* the poor in spirit: for theirs is the kingdom of heaven.

4 ᴿBlessed *are* they that mourn: for they shall be comforted.

5 ᴿBlessed *are* the meek: for ᴿthey shall inherit the earth.

6 Blessed *are* they which do hunger and thirst after righteousness: ᴿfor they shall be filled.

CHAP. **4**	
AD 26	
17	Mark 1:14
17	ch. 3:2
	& 10:7
18	Mark 1:16-18
	Luke 5:2
18	John 1:42
19	Luke 5:10
20	Mark 10:28
	Luke 18:28
21	Mark 1:19
	Luke 5:10
23	ch. 9:35
	Mark 1:21, 39
	Luke 1:44
23	ch. 24:14
	Mark 1:14
23	Mark 1:34
25	Mark 3:7

CHAP. **5**	
AD 31	
1	Mark 3:13
3	Luke 6:20
	See Ps. 51:17
	Prov. 16:19
	& 29:23
	Is. 57:15
	& 66:2
4	Is. 61:2, 3
	Luke 6:21
	John 16:20
	2 Cor. 1:7
	Rev. 21:4
5	Ps. 37:11
5	Rom. 4:13
6	Is. 55:1
	& 65:13

Ps. 41:1	7
Mark 11:25	
Ps. 15:2	8
Heb. 12:14	
1 Cor. 13:12	8
2 Cor. 4:17	10
1 Pet. 3:14	
Luke 6:22	11
1 Pet. 4:14	11
Gr. *lying*	11
Luke 6:23	12
Acts 5:41	
1 Pet. 4:13	
Neh. 9:26	12
Acts 7:52	
Mark 9:50	13
Luke 14:34	
Prov. 4:18	14
Phil. 2:15	
Mark 4:21	15
Luke 8:16	
The word in the	15
original signifieth	
a measure	
containing about	
a pint less than a	
peck	
1 Pet. 2:12	16
John 15:8	16
1 Cor. 14:25	
Rom. 10:4	17
Luke 16:17	18
Jas. 2:10	19
Rom. 10:3	20
Or, *to them*	21
Ex. 20:13	21
1 John 3:15	22

7 Blessed *are* the merciful: ᴿfor they shall obtain mercy.

8 ᴿBlessed *are* the pure in heart: for ᴿthey shall see God.

9 Blessed *are* the peacemakers: for they shall be called the children of God.

10 ᴿBlessed *are* they which are persecuted for righteousness' sake: for theirs is the kingdom of heaven.

11 ᴿBlessed are ye, when *men* shall revile you, and persecute *you,* and shall say all manner of ᴿevil against you ᴺfalsely, for my sake.

12 ᴿRejoice, and be exceeding glad: for great *is* your reward in heaven: for ᴿso persecuted they the prophets which were before you.

Believers as salt and light

13 Ye are the salt of the earth: ᴿbut if the salt have lost his savour, wherewith shall it be salted? it is thenceforth good for nothing, but to be cast out, and to be trodden under foot of men.

14 Ye are the light of the world. A city that is set on an hill cannot be hid.

15 Neither do men ᴿlight a candle, and put it under ᴺa bushel, but on a candlestick; and it giveth light unto all that are in the house.

16 Let your light so shine before men, ᴿthat they may see your good works, and ᴿglorify your Father which is in heaven.

The law and the prophets fulfilled

17 ᴿThink not that I am come to destroy the law, or the prophets: I am not come to destroy, but to fulfill.

18 For verily I say unto you, ᴿTill heaven and earth pass, one jot or one tittle shall in no wise pass from the law, till all be fulfilled.

19 ᴿWhosoever therefore shall break one of these least commandments, and shall teach men so, he shall be called the least in the kingdom of heaven: but whosoever shall do and teach *them,* the same shall be called great in the kingdom of heaven.

20 For I say unto you, That except your righteousness shall exceed ᴿ*the righteousness* of the scribes and Pharisees, ye shall in no case enter into the kingdom of heaven.

Anger and reconciliation

21 Ye have heard that it was said ᴺby them of old time, ᴿThou shalt not kill; and whosoever shall kill shall be in danger of the judgment:

22 But I say unto you, That ᴿwhosoever is angry with his brother without a cause shall be in danger of the judgment: and whosoever

shall say to his brother, ^RRā′-că, ^Nshall be in danger of the council: but whosoever shall say, Thou fool, shall be in danger of hell fire.

23 Therefore ^Rif thou bring thy gift to the altar, and there rememberest that thy brother hath aught against thee;

24 ^RLeave there thy gift before the altar, and go thy way; first be reconciled to thy brother, and then come and offer thy gift.

25 ^RAgree with thine adversary quickly, ^Rwhiles thou art in the way with him; lest at any time the adversary deliver thee to the judge, and the judge deliver thee to the officer, and thou be cast into prison.

26 Verily I say unto thee, Thou shalt by no means come out thence, till thou hast paid the uttermost farthing.

Adultery and divorce

27 Ye have heard that it was said by them of old time, ^RThou shalt not commit adultery:

28 But I say unto you, That whosoever ^Rlooketh on a woman to lust after her hath committed adultery with her already in his heart.

29 ^RAnd if thy right eye ^Noffend thee, ^Rpluck it out, and cast *it* from thee: for it is profitable for thee that one of thy members should perish, and not *that* thy whole body should be cast into hell.

30 And if thy right hand offend thee, cut it off, and cast *it* from thee: for it is profitable for thee that one of thy members should perish, and not *that* thy whole body should be cast into hell.

31 It hath been said, ^RWhosoever shall put away his wife, let him give her a writing of divorcement:

32 But I say unto you, That ^Rwhosoever shall put away his wife, saving for the cause of fornication, causeth her to commit adultery: and whosoever shall marry her that is divorced committeth adultery.

The law of oaths

33 Again, ye have heard that ^Rit hath been said by them of old time, ^RThou shalt not forswear thyself, but ^Rshalt perform unto the Lord thine oaths:

34 But I say unto you, ^RSwear not at all; neither by heaven; for it is ^RGod's throne:

35 Nor by the earth; for it is his footstool: neither by Jerusalem; for it is ^Rthe city of the great King.

36 Neither shalt thou swear by thy head, because thou canst not make one hair white or black.

37 ^RBut let your communication be, Yea,

yea; Nay, nay: for whatsoever is more than these cometh of evil.

Return good for evil

38 Ye have heard that it hath been said, ^RAn eye for an eye, and a tooth for a tooth:

39 But I say unto you, ^RThat ye resist not evil: ^Rbut whosoever shall smite thee on thy right cheek, turn to him the other also.

40 And if any man will sue thee at the law, and take away thy coat, let him have *thy* cloak also.

41 And whosoever ^Rshall compel thee to go a mile, go with him twain.

42 Give to him that asketh thee, and ^Rfrom him that would borrow of thee turn not thou away.

The law of love

43 Ye have heard that it hath been said, ^RThou shalt love thy neighbour, ^Rand hate thine enemy.

44 But I say unto you, ^RLove your enemies, bless them that curse you, do good to them that hate you, and pray ^Rfor them which despitefully use you, and persecute you;

45 That ye may be the children of your Father which is in heaven: for ^Rhe maketh his sun to rise on the evil and on the good, and sendeth rain on the just and on the unjust.

46 ^RFor if ye love them which love you, what reward have ye? do not even the publicans the same?

47 And if ye salute your brethren only, what do ye more *than others?* do not even the publicans so?

48 ^RBe ye therefore perfect, even ^Ras your Father which is in heaven is perfect.

CHAPTER 6

True piety

TAKE heed that ye do not your ^Nalms before men, to be seen of them: otherwise ye have no reward ^Nof your Father which is in heaven.

2 Therefore ^Rwhen thou doest *thine* alms, ^Ndo not sound a trumpet before thee, as the hypocrites do in the synagogues and in the streets, that they may have glory of men. Verily I say unto you, They have their reward.

3 But when thou doest alms, let not thy left hand know what thy right hand doeth:

4 That thine alms may be in secret: and thy Father which seeth in secret himself ^Rshall reward thee openly.

5 And when thou prayest, thou shalt not be as the hypocrites *are:* for they love to pray

---

standing in the synagogues and in the corners of the streets, that they may be seen of men. Verily I say unto you, They have their reward.

6 But thou, when thou prayest, ᴿenter into thy closet, and when thou hast shut thy door, pray to thy Father which is in secret; and thy Father which seeth in secret shall reward thee openly.

7 But when ye pray, ᴿuse not vain repetitions, as the heathen *do:* ᴿfor they think that they shall be heard for their much speaking.

8 Be not ye therefore like unto them: for your Father knoweth what things ye have need of, before ye ask him.

The Lord's prayer

9 After this manner therefore pray ye: ᴿOur Father which art in heaven, Hallowed be thy name.

10 Thy kingdom come. ᴿThy will be done in earth, ᴿas *it is* in heaven.

11 Give us this day our ᴿdaily bread.

12 And ᴿforgive us our debts, as we forgive our debtors.

13 ᴿAnd lead us not into temptation, but ᴿdeliver us from evil: ᴿFor thine is the kingdom, and the power, and the glory, for ever. Ä'-měn.

14 ᴿFor if ye forgive men their trespasses, your heavenly Father will also forgive you:

15 But ᴿif ye forgive not men their trespasses, neither will your Father forgive your trespasses.

Fasting

16 Moreover ᴿwhen ye fast, be not, as the hypocrites, of a sad countenance: for they disfigure their faces, that they may appear unto men to fast. Verily I say unto you, They have their reward.

17 But thou, when thou fastest, ᴿanoint thine head, and wash thy face;

18 That thou appear not unto men to fast, but unto thy Father which is in secret: and thy Father, which seeth in secret, shall reward thee openly.

Loyalties and integrity

19 ᴿLay not up for yourselves treasures upon earth, where moth and rust doth corrupt, and where thieves break through and steal:

20 ᴿBut lay up for yourselves treasures in heaven, where neither moth nor rust doth corrupt, and where thieves do not break through nor steal:

21 For where your treasure is, there will your heart be also.

22 ᴿThe light of the body is the eye: if

therefore thine eye be single, thy whole body shall be full of light.

23 But if thine eye be evil, thy whole body shall be full of darkness. If therefore the light that is in thee be darkness, how great *is* that darkness!

24 ᴿNo man can serve two masters: for either he will hate the one, and love the other; or else he will hold to the one, and despise the other. ᴿYe cannot serve God and mammon.

Trust is better than anxiety

25 Therefore I say unto you, ᴿTake no thought for your life, what ye shall eat, or what ye shall drink; nor yet for your body, what ye shall put on. Is not the life more than meat, and the body than raiment?

26 ᴿBehold the fowls of the air: for they sow not, neither do they reap, nor gather into barns; yet your heavenly Father feedeth them. Are ye not much better than they?

27 Which of you by taking thought can add one cubit unto his stature?

28 And why take ye thought for raiment? Consider the lilies of the field, how they grow; they toil not, neither do they spin:

29 And yet I say unto you, That even Solomon in all his glory was not arrayed like one of these.

30 Wherefore, if God so clothe the grass of the field, which to day is, and to morrow is cast into the oven, *shall he* not much more *clothe* you, O ye of little faith?

31 Therefore take no thought, saying, What shall we eat? or, What shall we drink? or, Wherewithal shall we be clothed?

32 (For after all these things do the Gentiles seek:) for your heavenly Father knoweth that ye have need of all these things.

33 But ᴿseek ye first the kingdom of God, and his righteousness; and all these things shall be added unto you.

34 Take therefore no thought for the morrow: for the morrow shall take thought for the things of itself. Sufficent unto the day *is* the evil thereof.

CHAPTER 7

Judgment and hypocrisy

JUDGEᴿ not, that ye be not judged.

2 For with what judgment ye judge, ye shall be judged: ᴿand with what measure ye mete, it shall be measured to you again.

3 ᴿAnd why beholdest thou the mote that is in thy brother's eye, but considerest not the beam that is in thine own eye?

CHAP. **6**
AD 31
6 2 Ki. 4:33
7 Eccl. 5:2
7 1 Ki. 18:26
9 Luke 11:2
10 ch. 26:39
Acts 21:14
10 Ps. 103:20
11 See Job 23:12
Prov. 30:8
12 ch. 18:21
13 ch. 26:41
1 Cor. 10:13
2 Pet. 2:9
Rev. 3:10
13 John 17:15
14 Matt 11:25
Eph. 4:32
Col. 3:13
15 ch. 18:35
Jas. 2:13
16 Is. 58:5
17 Ruth 3:3
Dan. 10:3
19 Prov. 23:4
1 Tim. 6:17
Heb. 13:5
Jas. 5:1
20 ch. 19:21
Luke 12:33
& 18:22
1 Tim. 6:19
1 Pet. 1:4
22 Luke 11:34

Luke 16:13   24
Gal. 1:10   24
1 Tim. 6:17
Jas. 4:4
1 John 2:15
Ps. 55:22   25
Luke 12:22
Phil. 4:6
1 Pet. 5:7
Job 38:41   26
Ps. 147:9
Luke 12:24
See 1 Ki. 3:13   33
Ps. 37:25
Mark 10:30
Luke 12:31
1 Tim. 4:8

CHAP. **7**
AD 31
Luke 6:37   1
Rom. 14:3
1 Cor. 4:3
Jas. 4:11
Mark 4:24   2
Luke 6:38
Luke 6:41   3

4 Or how wilt thou say to thy brother, Let me pull out the mote out of thine eye; and, behold, a beam *is* in thine own eye?

5 Thou hyprocrite, first cast out the beam out of thine own eye; and then shalt thou see clearly to cast out the mote out of thy brother's eye.

6 ᴿGive not that which is holy unto the dogs, neither cast ye your pearls before swine, lest they trample them under their feet, and turn again and rend you.

Prayer and the golden rule

7 ᴿAsk, and it shall be given you; seek, and ye shall find; knock, and it shall be opened unto you:

8 For ᴿevery one that asketh receiveth; and he that seeketh findeth; and to him that knock-eth it shall be opened.

9 ᴿOr what man is there of you, whom if his son ask bread, will he give him a stone?

10 Or if he ask a fish, will he give him a serpent?

11 If ye then, ᴿbeing evil, know how to give good gifts unto your children, how much more shall your Father which is in heaven give good things to them that ask him?

12 Therefore all things ᴿwhatsoever ye would that men should do to you, do ye even so to them: for ᴿthis is the law and the prophets.

The narrow and wide gates

13 ᴿEnter ye in at the strait gate: for wide *is* the gate, and broad *is* the way, that leadeth to destruction, and many there be which go in thereat:

14 ᴺBecause strait *is* the gate, and narrow *is* the way, which leadeth unto life, and few there be that find it.

False prophets

15 ᴿBeware of false prophets, ᴿwhich come to you in sheep's clothing, but inwardly they are ᴿravening wolves.

16 ᴿYe shall know them by their fruits. ᴿDo men gather grapes of thorns, or figs of thistles?

17 Even so ᴿevery good tree bringeth forth good fruit; but a corrupt tree bringeth forth evil fruit.

18 A good tree cannot bring forth evil fruit, neither *can* a corrupt tree bring forth good fruit.

19 ᴿEvery tree that bringeth not forth good fruit is hewn down, and cast into the fire.

20 Wherefore by their fruits ye shall know them.

CHAP. 7
AD 31
6 Prov. 9:7, 8
& 23:9
Acts 13:45
7 ch. 21:22
Mark 11:24
Luke 11:9
& 18:1
John 14:13
& 15:7 &
16:23, 24
Jas. 1:5, 6
1 John 3:22
& 5:14, 15
8 Prov. 8:17
Jer. 29:12
9 Luke 11:11
11 Gen. 6:5
& 8:21
12 Luke 6:31
12 Lev. 19:18
ch. 22:40
Rom. 13:8
Gal. 5:14
1 Tim. 1:5
13 Luke 13:24
14 Or, *How*
15 Deut. 13:3
Jer. 23:16
ch. 24:4, 5
Mark 13:22
Rom. 16:17
Eph. 5:6
Col. 2:8
2 Pet. 2:1
1 John 4:1
15 Mic. 3:5
2 Tim. 3:5
15 Acts 20:29
16 ver. 20
16 Luke 6:43
17 Jer. 11:19
ch. 12:33
19 ch. 3:10
Luke 3:9
John 15:2

Hos. 8:2   **21**
ch. 25:11
Luke 6:46
& 13:25
Acts 19:13
Rom. 2:13
Jas. 1:22
Num. 24:4   **22**
John 11:51
1 Cor. 13:2
ch. 25:12   **23**
Luke 13:25
2 Tim. 2:19
Ps. 5:5 & 6:8   **23**
ch. 25:41
Luke 6:47, etc.   **24**
ch. 13:54   **28**
Mark 1:22 & 6:2
Luke 4:32
John 7:46   **29**

CHAP. 8
AD 31
Mark 1:40, etc.   **2**
Luke 5:12, etc.
ch. 9:30   **4**
Mark 5:43
Lev. 14:3, 4, 10   **4**
Luke 5:14
Luke 7:1, etc.   **5**

Doers of the word

21 Not every one that saith unto me, ᴿLord, Lord, shall enter into the kingdom of heaven; but he that doeth the will of my Father which is in heaven.

22 Many will say to me in that day, Lord, Lord, have we ᴿnot prophesied in thy name? and in thy name have cast out devils? and in thy name done many wonderful works?

23 And ᴿthen will I profess unto them, I never knew you: ᴿdepart from me, ye that work iniquity.

24 Therefore ᴿwhosoever heareth these sayings of mine, and doeth them, I will liken him unto a wise man, which built his house upon a rock:

25 And the rain descended, and the floods came, and the winds blew, and beat upon that house; and it fell not: for it was founded upon a rock.

26 And every one that heareth these sayings of mine, and doeth them not, shall be likened unto a foolish man, which built his house upon the sand:

27 And the rain descended, and the floods came, and the winds blew, and beat upon that house; and it fell: and great was the fall of it.

28 And it came to pass, when Jesus had ended these sayings, ᴿthe people were astonished at his doctrine:

29 ᴿFor he taught them as *one* having authority, and not as the scribes.

CHAPTER 8

Cleansing the leper

Wʜᴇɴ he was come down from the mountain, great multitudes followed him.

2 ᴿAnd, behold, there came a leper and worshipped him, saying, Lord, if thou wilt, thou canst make me clean.

3 And Jesus put forth *his* hand, and touched him, saying, I will; be thou clean. And immediately his leprosy was cleansed.

4 And Jesus saith unto him, ᴿSee thou tell no man; but go thy way, shew thyself to the priest, and offer the gift that ᴿMoses commanded, for a testimony unto them.

Healing the centurion's servant

5 ᴿAnd when Jesus was entered into Că-pĕr'-nă-ŭm, there came unto him a centurion, beseeching him,

6 And saying, Lord, my servant lieth at home sick of the palsy, grievously tormented.

7 And Jesus saith unto him, I will come and heal him.

8 The centurion answered and said, Lord, ᴿI am not worthy that thou shouldest come under my roof: but ᴿspeak the word only, and my servant shall be healed.

9 For I am a man under authority, having soldiers under me: and I say to this *man,* Go, and he goeth; and to another, Come, and he cometh; and to my servant, Do this, and he doeth *it.*

10 When Jesus heard *it,* he marvelled, and said to them that followed, Verily I say unto you, I have not found so great faith, no, not in Israel.

11 And I say unto you, That ᴿmany shall come from the east and west, and shall sit down with Abraham, and Isaac, and Jacob, in the kingdom of heaven.

12 But ᴿthe children of the kingdom ᴿshall be cast out into outer darkness: there shall be weeping and gnashing of teeth.

13 And Jesus said unto the centurion, Go thy way; and as thou hast believed, *so* be it done unto thee. And his servant was healed in the selfsame hour.

14 ᴿAnd when Jesus was come into Peter's house, he saw ᴿhis wife's mother laid, and sick of a fever.

Healing Peter's mother in law

15 And he touched her hand, and the fever left her: and she arose, and ministered unto them.

16 ᴿWhen the even was come, they brought unto him many that were possessed with devils: and he cast out the spirits with *his* word, and healed all that were sick:

17 That it might be fulfilled which was spoken by Ē-śaī'-ăs the prophet, saying, ᴿHimself took our infirmities, and bare *our* sicknesses.

Conditions of discipleship

18 Now when Jesus saw great multitudes about him, he gave commandment to depart unto the other side.

19 ᴿAnd a certain scribe came, and said unto him, Master, I will follow thee whithersoever thou goest.

20 And Jesus saith unto him, The foxes have holes, and the birds of the air *have* nests; but the Son of man hath not where to lay *his* head.

21 ᴿAnd another of his disciples said unto him, Lord, ᴿsuffer me first to go and bury my father.

22 But Jesus said unto him, Follow me; and let the dead bury their dead.

CHAP. 8

AD 31

8 Luke 15:19, 21
8 Ps. 107:20
11 Gen. 12:3
Is. 2:2, 3 & 11:10
Mal. 1:11
Luke 13:29
Acts 10:45
& 11:18
& 14:27
Rom. 15:9, etc.
Eph. 3:6
12 ch. 21:43
12 ch. 13:42, 50
& 22:13 & 24:51
& 25:30
Luke 13:28
2 Pet. 2:17
Jude 13
14 Mark 1:29-31
Luke 4:38, 39
14 1 Cor. 9:5
16 Mark 1:32, etc.
Luke 4:40, 41
17 Is. 53:4
1 Pet. 2:24
19 Luke 9:57, 58
21 Luke 9:59, 60
21 See 1 Ki. 19:20

Mark 4:37, etc.   24
Luke 8:23, etc.
Ps. 65:7   26
& 89:9
& 107:29
Mark 5:1, etc.   28
Luke 8:26, etc.
See Deut. 5:25   34
1 Ki. 17:18
Luke 5:8
Acts 16:39

CHAP. 9

AD 31

ch. 4:13   1
Mark 2:3   2
Luke 5:18
ch. 8:10   2

Jesus stills the storm

23 And when he was entered into a ship, his disciples followed him.

24 ᴿAnd, behold, there arose a great tempest in the sea, insomuch that the ship was covered with the waves: but he was asleep.

25 And his disciples came to *him,* and awoke him, saying, Lord, save us: we perish.

26 And he saith unto them, Why are ye fearful, O ye of little faith? Then ᴿhe arose, and rebuked the winds and the sea; and there was a great calm.

27 But the men marvelled, saying, What manner of man is this, that even the winds and the sea obey him!

Casting out demons

28 ᴿAnd when he was come to the other side into the country of the Gĕr'-gĕ-sēneś, there met him two possessed with devils, coming out of the tombs, exceeding fierce, so that no man might pass by that way.

29 And, behold, they cried out, saying, What have we to do with thee, Jesus, thou Son of God? art thou come hither to torment us before the time?

30 And there was a good way off from them an herd of many swine feeding.

31 So the devils besought him, saying, If thou cast us out, suffer us to go away into the herd of swine.

32 And he said unto them, Go. And when they were come out, they went into the herd of swine: and, behold, the whole herd of swine ran violently down a steep place into the sea, and perished in the waters.

33 And they that kept them fled, and went their ways into the city, and told every thing, and what was befallen to the possessed of the devils.

34 And, behold, the whole city came out to meet Jesus: and when they saw him, ᴿthey besought *him* that he would depart out of their coasts.

CHAPTER 9

Curing the paralytic

AND he entered into a ship, and passed over, ᴿand came into his own city.

2 ᴿAnd, behold, they brought to him a man sick of the palsy, lying on a bed: ᴿand Jesus seeing their faith said unto the sick of the palsy; Son, be of good cheer; thy sins be forgiven thee.

3 And, behold, certain of the scribes said within themselves, This *man* blasphemeth.

4 And Jesus ᴿknowing their thoughts said, Wherefore think ye evil in your hearts?

5 For whether is easier, to say, *Thy* sins be forgiven thee; or to say, Arise, and walk?

6 But that ye may know that the Son of man hath power on earth to forgive sins, (then saith he to the sick of the palsy,) Arise, take up thy bed, and go unto thine house.

7 And he arose, and departed to his house.

8 But when the multitudes saw *it,* they marvelled, and glorified God, which had given such power unto men.

The call of Matthew

9 ᴿAnd as Jesus passed forth from thence, he saw a man, named Matthew, sitting at the receipt of custom: and he saith unto him, Follow me. And he arose, and followed him.

10 ᴿAnd it came to pass, as Jesus sat at meat in the house, behold, many publicans and sinners came and sat down with him and his disciples.

11 And when the Pharisees saw *it,* they said unto his disciples, Why eateth your Master with ᴿpublicans and ᴿsinners?

12 But when Jesus heard *that,* he said unto them, They that be whole need not a physician, but they that are sick.

13 But go ye and learn what *that* meaneth, ᴿI will have mercy, and not sacrifice: for I am not come to call the righteous, ᴿbut sinners to repentance.

Question about fasting

14 Then came to him the disciples of John, saying, ᴿWhy do we and the Pharisees fast oft, but thy disciples fast not?

15 And Jesus said unto them, Can ᴿthe children of the bridechamber mourn, as long as the bridegroom is with them? but the days will come, when the bridegroom shall be taken from them, and ᴿthen shall they fast.

16 No man putteth a piece of ᴺnew cloth unto an old garment, for that which is put in to fill it up taketh from the garment, and the rent is made worse.

17 Neither do men put new wine into old bottles: else the bottles break, and the wine runneth out, and the bottles perish: but they put new wine into new bottles, and both are preserved.

Raising of the ruler's daughter

18 ᴿWhile he spake these things unto them, behold, there came a certain ruler, and wor-

---

CHAP. **9**

AD 31

4 Ps. 139:2
ch. 12:25
Mark 12:15
Luke 5:22
& 6:8
& 9:47
& 11:17
9 Mark 2:14
Luke 5:27
10 Mark 2:15, etc.
Luke 5:29, etc.
11 ch. 11:19
Luke 5:30
& 15:2
11 Gal. 2:15
13 Hos. 6:6
Mic. 6:6-8
ch. 12:7
13 1 Tim. 1:15
14 Mark 2:18, etc.
Luke 5:33, etc.
& 18:12
15 John 3:29
15 Acts 13:2, 3
& 14:23
1 Cor. 7:5
16 Or, *raw,* or, *unwrought cloth*
18 Mark 5:22, etc.
Luke 8:41, etc.

Mark 5:25   **20**
Luke 8:43
Luke 7:50   **22**
& 8:48
& 17:19
& 18:42
Mark 5:38   **23**
Luke 8:51
See 2 Chr. 35:25 **23**
Acts 20:10   **24**
Or, *this fame*   **26**
ch. 15:22   **27**
Mark 10:47
Luke 18:38
ch. 8:4   **30**
Luke 5:14
Mark 7:36   **31**
ch. 12:22   **32**
Luke 11:14
ch. 12:24   **34**
Luke 11:15
ch. 4:23   **35**
Mark 6:35   **36**

---

shipped him, saying, My daughter is even now dead: but come and lay thy hand upon her, and she shall live.

19 And Jesus arose, and followed him, and *so did* his disciples.

20 ᴿAnd, behold, a woman, which was diseased with an issue of blood twelve years, came behind *him,* and touched the hem of his garment:

21 For she said within herself, If I may but touch his garment, I shall be whole.

22 But Jesus turned him about, and when he saw her, he said, Daughter, be of good comfort; ᴿthy faith hath made thee whole. And the woman was made whole from that hour.

23 ᴿAnd when Jesus came into the ruler's house, and saw ᴿthe minstrels and the people making a noise,

24 He said unto them, ᴿGive place: for the maid is not dead, but sleepeth. And they laughed him to scorn.

25 But when the people were put forth, he went in, and took her by the hand, and the maid arose.

26 And ᴺthe fame hereof went abroad into all that land.

Healing the blind and the dumb

27 And when Jesus departed thence, two blind men followed him, crying, and saying, ᴿ*Thou* son of David, have mercy on us.

28 And when he was come into the house, the blind men came to him: and Jesus saith unto them, Believe ye that I am able to do this? They said unto him, Yea, Lord.

29 Then touched he their eyes, saying, According to your faith be it unto you.

30 And their eyes were opened; and Jesus straitly charged them, saying, ᴿSee *that* no man know *it.*

31 ᴿBut they, when they were departed, spread abroad his fame in all that country.

32 ᴿAs they went out, behold, they brought to him a dumb man possessed with a devil.

33 And when the devil was cast out, the dumb spake: and the multitudes marvelled, saying, It was never so seen in Israel.

34 But the Pharisees said, ᴿHe casteth out devils through the prince of the devils.

The need for workers

35 And Jesus went about all the cities and villages, ᴿteaching in their synagogues, and preaching the gospel of the kingdom, and healing every sickness and every disease among the people.

36 ᴿBut when he saw the multitudes, he was

moved with compassion on them, because they ᴺfainted, and were scattered abroad, ᴿas sheep having no shepherd.

37 Then saith he unto his disciples, ᴿThe harvest truly *is* plenteous, but the labourers *are* few;

38 ᴿPray ye therefore the Lord of the harvest, that he will send forth labourers into his harvest.

CHAPTER 10

Disciples named and commissioned

AND ᴿwhen he had called unto *him* his twelve disciples, he gave them power ᴺagainst unclean spirits, to cast them out, and to heal all manner of sickness and all manner of disease.

2 Now the names of the twelve apostles are these; The first, Simon, ᴿwho is called Peter, and Andrew his brother; James *the son* of Zĕb'-ĕ-dĕē, and John his brother;

3 Philip, and Bartholomew; Thomas, and Matthew the publican; James *the son* of Ăl-phæ'-ŭs, and Lĕb-bæ'-ŭs, whose surname was Thăd-dæ'-ŭs;

4 ᴿSimon the Canaanite, and Judas ᴿIscariot, who also betrayed him.

5 These twelve Jesus sent forth, and commanded them, saying, ᴿGo not into the way of the Gentiles, and into *any* city of ᴿthe Să-măr'-ĭ-tăns enter ye not:

6 ᴿBut go rather to the ᴿlost sheep of the house of Israel.

7 ᴿAnd as ye go, preach, saying, ᴿThe kingdom of heaven is at hand.

8 Heal the sick, cleanse the lepers, raise the dead, cast out devils: ᴿfreely ye have received, freely give.

9 ᴿProvideᴺ neither gold, nor silver, nor ᴿbrass in your purses,

10 Nor scrip for *your* journey, neither two coats, neither shoes, nor yet ᴺstaves: ᴿfor the workman is worthy of his meat.

11 ᴿAnd into whatsoever city or town ye shall enter, inquire who in it is worthy; and there abide till ye go thence.

12 And when ye come into an house, salute it.

13 ᴿAnd if the house be worthy, let your peace come upon it: ᴿbut if it be not worthy, let your peace return to you.

14 ᴿAnd whosoever shall not receive you, nor hear your words, when ye depart out of that house or city, ᴿshake off the dust of your feet.

15 Verily I say unto you, ᴿIt shall be more tolerable for the land of Sodom and Gō-mŏr'-

rhă in the day of judgment, than for that city.

Persecution expected

16 ᴿBehold, I send you forth as sheep in the midst of wolves: ᴿbe ye therefore wise as serpents, and ᴿharmlessᴺ as doves.

17 But beware of men: for ᴿthey will deliver you up to the councils, and ᴿthey will scourge you in their synagogues;

18 And ᴿye shall be brought before governors and kings for my sake, for a testimony against them and the Gentiles.

19 ᴿBut when they deliver you up, take no thought how or what ye shall speak: for ᴿit shall be given you in that same hour what ye shall speak.

20 ᴿFor it is not ye that speak, but the Spirit of your Father which speaketh in you.

21 ᴿAnd the brother shall deliver up the brother to death, and the father the child: and the children shall rise up against *their* parents, and cause them to be put to death.

22 And ᴿye shall be hated of all *men* for my name's sake: ᴿbut he that endureth to the end shall be saved.

23 But ᴿwhen they persecute you in this city, flee ye into another: for verily I say unto you, Ye shall not ᴺhave gone over the cities of Israel, ᴿtill the Son of man be come.

Encouraging the twelve

24 ᴿThe disciple is not above *his* master, nor the servant above his lord.

25 It is enough for the disciple that he be as his master, and the servant as his lord. If ᴿthey have called the master of the house ᴺBē-ĕl'-zĕ-bŭb, how much more *shall they call* them of his household?

26 Fear them not therefore: ᴿfor there is nothing covered, that shall not be revealed; and hid, that shall not be known.

27 What I tell you in darkness, *that* speak ye in light: and what ye hear in the ear, *that* preach ye upon the housetops.

28 ᴿAnd fear not them which kill the body, but are not able to kill the soul: but rather fear him which is able to destroy both soul and body in hell.

29 Are not two sparrows sold for a ᴺfarthing? and one of them shall not fall on the ground without your Father.

30 ᴿBut the very hairs of your head are all numbered.

31 Fear ye not therefore, ye are of more value than many sparrows.

32 ᴿWhosoever therefore shall confess me before men, ᴿhim will I confess also before my Father which is in heaven.

CHAP. 9 — AD 31
36 Or, *were tired and lay down*
36 Num. 27:17
1 Ki. 22:17
37 Luke 10:2
John 4:35
38 2 Thes. 3:1

CHAP. 10 — AD 31
1 Mark 3:13; Luke 6:13
1 Or, *over*
2 John 1:42
4 Luke 6:15; Acts 1:13; John 13:26
5 ch. 4:15
5 John 4:9
6 ch. 15:24; Acts 13:46
6 Is. 53:6; Jer. 50:6
7 Luke 9:2
7 ch. 3:2; Luke 10:9
8 Acts 8:18
9 1 Sam. 9:7; Mark 6:8
9 Or, *Get*
9 Mark 6:8
10 Gr. *a staff*
10 Luke 10:7; 1 Tim. 5:18
11 Luke 10:8
13 Luke 10:5
13 Ps. 35:13
14 Mark 6:11; Luke 9:5
14 Neh. 5:13; Acts 13:51
15 ch. 11:22
16 Luke 10:3; Eph. 5:15; Phil. 2:15; Or, *simple*
17 Mark 13:9; Luke 12:11
17 Acts 5:40
18 Acts 12:1; 2 Tim. 4:16
19 Luke 21:14; Ex. 4:12; Jer. 1:7
20 2 Sam. 23:2
21 Mic. 7:6; Luke 21:16
22 Luke 21:17
22 Dan. 12:12; Mark 13:13
23 ch. 2:13; Acts 8:1
23 Or, *end*
23 ch. 16:28
24 Luke 6:40; John 15:20
25 Mark 3:22; John 8:48
25 Gr. *Beelzebul*
26 Mark 4:22; Luke 8:17
28 Luke 12:4; 1 Pet. 3:14
29 *It is in value halfpenny farthing in the original, as being the tenth part of the Roman penny*
30 1 Sam. 14:45; Luke 21:18
32 Luke 12:8; Rom. 10:9
32 Rev. 3:5

33 ᴿBut whosoever shall deny me before men, him will I also deny before my Father which is in heaven.

34 ᴿThink not that I am come to send peace on earth: I came not to send peace, but a sword.

35 For I am come to set a man at variance ᴿagainst his father, and the daughter against her mother, and the daughter in law against her mother in law.

36 And ᴿa man's foes *shall be* they of his own household.

37 ᴿHe that loveth father or mother more than me is not worthy of me: and he that loveth son or daughter more than me is not worthy of me.

38 ᴿAnd he that taketh not his cross, and followeth after me, is not worthy of me.

39 ᴿHe that findeth his life shall lose it: and he that loseth his life for my sake shall find it.

40 ᴿHe that receiveth you receiveth me, and he that receiveth me receiveth him that sent me.

41 ᴿHe that receiveth a prophet in the name of a prophet shall receive a prophet's reward; and he that receiveth a righteous man in the name of a righteous man shall receive a righteous man's reward.

42 ᴿAnd whosoever shall give to drink unto one of these little ones a cup of cold *water* only in the name of a disciple, verily I say unto you, he shall in no wise lose his reward.

CHAPTER 11

AND it came to pass, when Jesus had made an end of commanding his twelve disciples, he departed thence to teach and to preach in their cities.

Jesus and John the Baptist

2 ᴿNow when John had heard ᴿin the prison the works of Christ, he sent two of his disciples,

3 And said unto him, Art thou ᴿhe that should come, or do we look for another?

4 Jesus answered and said unto them, Go and shew John again those things which ye do hear and see:

5 ᴿThe blind receive their sight, and the lame walk, the lepers are cleansed, and the deaf hear, the dead are raised up, and ᴿthe poor have the gospel preached to them.

6 And blessed is *he,* whosoever shall not ᴿbe offended in me.

7 ᴿAnd as they departed, Jesus began to say unto the multitudes concerning John, What went ye out into the wilderness to see? ᴿA reed shaken with the wind?

8 But what went ye out for to see? A man

clothed in soft raiment? behold, they that wear soft *clothing* are in kings' houses.

9 But what went ye out for to see? A prophet? yea, I say unto you, ᴿand more than a prophet.

10 For this is *he,* of whom it is written, ᴿBehold, I send my messenger before thy face, which shall prepare thy way before thee.

11 Verily I say unto you, Among them that are born of women there hath not risen a greater than John the Baptist: notwithstanding he that is least in the kingdom of heaven is greater than he.

12 ᴿAnd from the days of John the Baptist until now the kingdom of heaven ᴺsuffereth violence, and the violent take it by force.

13 ᴿFor all the prophets and the law prophesied until John.

14 And if ye will receive *it,* this is ᴿE-lī′-ăs, which was for to come.

15 ᴿHe that hath ears to hear, let him hear.

16 ᴿBut whereunto shall I liken this generation? It is like unto children sitting in the markets, and calling unto their fellows,

17 And saying, We have piped unto you, and ye have not danced; we have mourned unto you, and ye have not lamented.

18 For John came neither eating nor drinking, and they say, He hath a devil.

19 The Son of man came eating and drinking, and they say, Behold a man gluttonous, and a winebibber, ᴿa friend of publicans and sinners. ᴿBut wisdom is justified of her children.

Judgment of the impenitent

20 ᴿThen began he to upbraid the cities wherein most of his mighty works were done, because they repented not:

21 Woe unto thee, Chō-rā′-zĭn! woe unto thee, Běth-sā′-ĭ-dă! for if the mighty works, which were done in you, had been done in Tyre and Sī′-dŏn, they would have repented long ago ᴿin sackcloth and ashes.

22 But I say unto you, ᴿIt shall be more tolerable for Tyre and Sī′-dŏn at the day of judgment, than for you.

23 And thou, Că-pĕr′-nă-ŭm, ᴿwhich art exalted unto heaven, shalt be brought down to hell: for if the mighty works, which have been done in thee, had been done in Sodom, it would have remained until this day.

24 But I say unto you, ᴿThat it shall be more tolerable for the land of Sodom in the day of judgment, than for thee.

Revealer of the Father

25 ᴿAt that time Jesus answered and said, I thank thee, O Father, Lord of heaven and

---

CHAP. 10

AD 31

33 Luke 9:26
2 Tim. 2:12
34 Luke 12:49
35 Mic. 7:6
36 Ps. 41:9
 & 55:13
 John 13:18
37 Luke 14:26
38 Mark 8:34
39 Luke 17:33
 John 12:25
40 Luke 9:48
 John 12:44
 Gal. 4:14
41 1 Ki. 17:10
 2 Ki. 4:8
42 ch. 25:40
 Mark 9:41
 Heb. 6:10

CHAP. 11

AD 31

2 Luke 7:18
2 ch. 14:3
3 Gen. 49:10
 Num. 24:17
 Dan. 9:24
 John 6:14
5 Is. 29:18
 & 35:4-6
 John 2:23
5 Ps. 22:26
 Is. 61:1
 Luke 4:18
 Jas. 2:5
6 Is. 8:14, 15
 Rom. 9:32
 1 Pet. 2:8
7 Luke 7:24
7 Eph. 4:14

Luke 1:76   9
Mal. 3:1   10
 Mark 1:2
 Luke 1:76
Luke 16:16   12
Or, *is gotten*   12
 by force, and they
 that thrust men
Mal. 4:6   13
Mal. 4:5   14
 Luke 1:17
ch. 13:9   15
 Luke 8:8
 Rev. 2:7, 11, 17,
 29 & 3:6, 13
Luke 7:31   16
ch. 9:10   19
Luke 7:35   19
Luke 10:18   20
Jonah 3:7   21
ver. 24   22
 ch. 10:15
See Is. 14:13   23
 Lam. 2:1
ch. 10:15   24
Luke 10:21   25

earth, because ᴿthou hast hid these things from the wise and prudent, ᴿand hast revealed them unto babes.

26 Even so, Father: for so it seemed good in thy sight.

27 ᴿAll things are delivered unto me of my Father: and no man knoweth the Son, but the Father; ᴿneither knoweth any man the Father, save the Son, and *he* to whomsoever the Son will reveal *him*.

28 Come unto me, all *ye* that labour and are heavy laden, and I will give you rest.

29 Take my yoke upon you, ᴿand learn of me; for I am meek and ᴿlowly in heart: ᴿand ye shall find rest unto your souls.

30 ᴿFor my yoke *is* easy, and my burden is light.

CHAPTER 12

Lord of the sabbath

AT that time ᴿJesus went on the sabbath day through the corn; and his disciples were an hungred, and began to pluck the ears of corn, and to eat.

2 But when the Pharisees saw *it,* they said unto him, Behold, thy disciples do that which is not lawful to do upon the sabbath day.

3 But he said unto them, Have ye not read ᴿwhat David did, when he was an hungred, and they that were with him;

4 How he entered into the house of God, and did eat ᴿthe shewbread, which was not lawful for him to eat, neither for them which were with him, ᴿbut only for the priests?

5 Or have ye not read in the ᴿlaw, how that on the sabbath days the priests in the temple profane the sabbath, and are blameless?

6 But I say unto you, That in this place is ᴿ*one* greater than the temple.

7 But if ye had known what *this* meaneth, ᴿI will have mercy, and not sacrifice, ye would not have condemned the guiltless.

8 For the Son of man is Lord even of the sabbath day.

9 ᴿAnd when he was departed thence, he went into their synagogue:

10 And, behold, there was a man which had *his* hand withered. And they asked him, saying, ᴿIs it lawful to heal on the sabbath days? that they might accuse him.

11 And he said unto them, What man shall there be among you, that shall have one sheep, and ᴿif it fall into a pit on the sabbath day, will he not lay hold on it, and lift *it* out?

12 How much then is a man better than a sheep? Wherefore it is lawful to do well on the sabbath days.

13 Then saith he to the man, Stretch forth thine hand. And he stretched *it* forth; and it was restored whole, like as the other.

14 Then ᴿthe Pharisees went out, and ᴺheld a council against him, how they might destroy him.

His healing fulfills the prophecy

15 But when Jesus knew *it,* ᴿhe withdrew himself from thence: ᴿand great multitudes followed him, and he healed them all;

16 And ᴿcharged them that they should not make him known:

17 That it might be fulfilled which was spoken by Ē-śaī'-ăs the prophet, saying,

18 ᴿBehold my servant, whom I have chosen; my beloved, ᴿin whom my soul is well pleased: I will put my spirit upon him, and he shall shew judgment to the Gentiles.

19 He shall not strive, nor cry; neither shall any man hear his voice in the streets.

20 A bruised reed shall he not break, and smoking flax shall he not quench, till he send forth judgment unto victory.

21 And in his name shall the Gentiles trust.

Jesus rebukes the Pharisees

22 ᴿThen was brought unto him one possessed with a devil, blind, and dumb: and he healed him, insomuch that the blind and dumb both spake and saw.

23 And all the people were amazed, and said, Is not this the son of David?

24 ᴿBut when the Pharisees heard *it,* they said, This *fellow* doth not cast out devils, but by ᴺBē-ĕl'-zĕ-bŭb the prince of the devils.

25 And Jesus ᴿknew their thoughts, and said unto them, Every kingdom divided against itself is brought to desolation; and every city or house divided against itself shall not stand:

26 And if Satan cast out Satan, he is divided against himself; how shall then his kingdom stand?

27 And if I by Bē-ĕl'-zĕ-bŭb cast out devils, by whom do your children cast *them* out? therefore they shall be your judges.

28 But if I cast out devils by the Spirit of God, then ᴿthe kingdom of God is come unto you.

29 ᴿOr else how can one enter into a strong man's house, and spoil his goods, except he first bind the strong man? and then he will spoil his house.

30 He that is not with me is against me; and he that gathereth not with me scattereth abroad.

31 Wherefore I say unto you, ᴿAll manner of sin and blasphemy shall be forgiven

CHAP. 11
AD 31

25 Ps. 8:2
1 Cor. 1:19
& 2:8
2 Cor. 3:14
25 ch. 16:17
27 ch. 28:18
Luke 10:22
John 3:35 & 13:3
& 17:2
1 Cor. 15:27
27 John 1:18
& 6:46 & 10:15
29 John 13:15
Phil. 2:5
1 Pet. 2:21
1 John 2:6
29 Zech. 9:9
Phil. 2:7, 8
29·Jer. 6:16
30 1 John 5:3

CHAP. 12
AD 31

1 Deut. 23:25
Mark 2:23
Luke 6:1
3 1 Sam. 21:6
4 Ex. 25:30
Lev. 24:5
4 Ex. 29:32
Lev. 8:31 & 24:9
5 Num. 28:9
John 7:22
6 2 Chr. 6:18
Mal. 3:1
7 Hos. 6:6
Mic. 6:6-8
ch. 9:13
9 Mark 3:1
Luke 6:6
10 Luke 13:14
& 14:3
John 9:16
11 Deut. 22:4

ch. 27:1   14
Mark 3:6
Luke 6:11
John 5:18
& 10:39 & 11:53
Or, *took
counsel*   14
See ch. 10:23   15
Mark 3:7
ch. 19:2   15
ch. 9:30   16
Is. 42:1   18
ch. 3:17   18
& 17:5
See ch. 9:32   22
Mark 3:11
Luke 11:14
ch. 9:34   24
Mark 3:22
Luke 11:15
Gr. *Beelzebul,*   24
ver. 27
ch. 9:4   25
John 2:25
Rev. 2:23
Dan. 2:44   28
& 7:14
Luke 1:33
& 11:20
& 17:20, 21
Is. 49:24   29
Luke 11:21-23
Mark 3:28   31
Luke 12:10
Heb. 6:4
& 10:26, 29
1 John 5:16

men: ᴿbut the blasphemy *against* the *Holy Ghost* shall not be forgiven unto men.

32 And whosoever ᴿspeaketh a word against the Son of man, ᴿit shall be forgiven him: but whosoever speaketh against the Holy Ghost, it shall not be forgiven him, neither in this world, neither in the *world* to come.

33 Either make the tree good, and ᴿhis fruit good; or else make the tree corrupt, and his fruit corrupt: for the tree is known by *his* fruit.

34 O ᴿgeneration of vipers, how can ye, being evil, speak good things? ᴿfor out of the abundance of the heart the mouth speaketh.

35 A good man out of the good treasure of the heart bringeth forth good things: and an evil man out of the evil treasure bringeth forth evil things.

36 But I say unto you, That every idle word that men shall speak, they shall give account thereof in the day of judgment.

37 For by thy words thou shalt be justified, and by thy words thou shalt be condemned.

The sign of Jonas

38 ᴿThen certain of the scribes and of the Pharisees answered, saying, Master, we would see a sign from thee.

39 But he answered and said unto them, An evil and ᴿadulterous generation seeketh after a sign; and there shall no sign be given to it, but the sign of the prophet Jonas:

40 ᴿFor as Jonas was three days and three nights in the whale's belly; so shall the Son of man be three days and three nights in the heart of the earth.

41 ᴿThe men of Nĭn′-ĕ-vēh shall rise in judgment with this generation, and ᴿshall condemn it: ᴿbecause they repented at the preaching of Jonas; and, behold, a greater than Jonas *is* here.

42 ᴿThe queen of the south shall rise up in the judgment with this generation, and shall condemn it: for she came from the uttermost parts of the earth to hear the wisdom of Solomon; and, behold, a greater than Solomon *is* here.

This wicked generation

43 ᴿWhen the unclean spirit is gone out of a man, ᴿhe walketh through dry places, seeking rest, and findeth none.

44 Then he saith, I will return into my house from whence I came out; and when he is come, he findeth *it* empty, swept, and garnished.

45 Then goeth he, and taketh with himself seven other spirits more wicked than himself, and they enter in and dwell there: ᴿand the last

state of that man is worse than the first. Even so shall it be also unto this wicked generation.

Jesus' true kindred

46 While he yet talked to the people, ᴿbehold, *his* mother and ᴿhis brethren stood without, desiring to speak with him.

47 Then one said unto him, Behold, thy mother and thy brethren stand without, desiring to speak with thee.

48 But he answered and said unto him that told him, Who is my mother? and who are my brethren?

49 And he stretched forth his hand toward his disciples, and said, Behold my mother and my brethren!

50 For ᴿwhosoever shall do the will of my Father which is in heaven, the same is my brother, and sister, and mother.

CHAPTER 13

Parable of the sower

THE same day went Jesus out of the house, ᴿand sat by the sea side.

2 ᴿAnd great multitudes were gathered together unto him, so that ᴿhe went into a ship, and sat; and the whole multitude stood on the shore.

3 And he spake many things unto them in parables, saying, ᴿBehold, a sower went forth to sow;

4 And when he sowed, some *seeds* fell by the way side, and the fowls came and devoured them up:

5 Some fell upon stony places, where they had not much earth: and forthwith they sprung up, because they had no deepness of earth:

6 And when the sun was up, they were scorched; and because they had no root, they withered away.

7 And some fell among thorns; and the thorns sprung up, and choked them:

8 But other fell into good ground, and brought forth fruit, some ᴿan hundredfold, some sixtyfold, some thirtyfold.

9 ᴿWho hath ears to hear, let him hear.

The reason for parables

10 And the disciples came, and said unto him, Why speakest thou unto them in parables?

11 He answered and said unto them, Because ᴿit is given unto you to know the mysteries of the kingdom of heaven, but to them it is not given.

12 ᴿFor whosoever hath, to him shall be given, and he shall have more abundance: but

CHAP. 12
AD 31
31 Acts 7:51
32 ch. 11:19
& 13:55
John 7:12, 52
32 1 Tim. 1:13
33 ch. 7:17
Luke 6:43
34 ch. 3:7
& 23:33
34 Luke 6:45
38 ch. 16:1
Mark 8:11
Luke 11:16
John 2:18
1 Cor. 1:22
39 Is. 57:3
ch. 16:4
Mark 8:38
John 4:48
40 Jonah 1:17
41 Luke 11:32
41 See Jer. 3:11
Ezek. 16:51
Rom. 2:27
41 Jonah 3:5
42 1 Ki. 10:1
2 Chr. 9:1
Luke 11:31
43 Luke 11:24
43 Job 1:7
1 Pet. 5:8
45 Heb. 6:4
& 10:26
2 Pet. 2:20-22

Mark 3:31   46
Luke 8:19-21
ch. 13:55   46
Mark 6:3
John 2:12
& 7:3, 5
Acts 1:14
1 Cor. 9:5
Gal. 1:19
See John 15:14   50
Gal. 5:6
& 6:15
Col. 3:11
Heb. 2:11

CHAP. 13
AD 31
Mark 4:1   1
Luke 8:4   2
Luke 5:3   2
Luke 8:5   3
Gen. 26:12   8
ch. 11:15   9
Mark 4:9
ch. 11:25   11
& 16:17
Mark 4:11
1 Cor. 2:10
1 John 2:27
ch. 25:29   12
Mark 4:25
Luke 8:18
& 19:26

whosoever hath not, from him shall be taken away even that he hath.

13 Therefore speak I to them in parables: because they seeing see not; and hearing they hear not, neither do they understand.

14 And in them is fulfilled the prophecy of Ē-śāi′-ǎs, which saith, ᴿBy hearing ye shall hear, and shall not understand; and seeing ye shall see, and shall not perceive:

15 For this people's heart is waxed gross, and *their* ears ᴿare dull of hearing, and their eyes they have closed; lest at any time they should see with *their* eyes, and hear with *their* ears, and should understand with *their* heart, and should be converted, and I should heal them.

16 But ᴿblessed *are* your eyes, for they see: and your ears, for they hear.

17 For verily I say unto you, ᴿThat many prophets and righteous *men* have desired to see *those things* which ye see, and have not seen *them;* and to hear *those things* which ye hear, and have not heard *them.*

Parable of the sower explained

18 ᴿHear ye therefore the parable of the sower.

19 When any one heareth the word ᴿof the kingdom, and understandeth *it* not, then cometh the wicked *one,* and catcheth away that which was sown in his heart. This is he which received seed by the way side.

20 But he that received the seed into stony places, the same is he that heareth the word, and anon ᴿwith joy receiveth it;

21 Yet hath he not root in himself, but dureth for a while: for when tribulation or persecution ariseth because of the word, by and by ᴿhe is offended.

22 ᴿHe also that received seed ᴿamong the thorns is he that heareth the word; and the care of this world, and the deceitfulness of riches, choke the word, and he becometh unfruitful.

23 But he that received seed into the good ground is he that heareth the word, and understandeth *it;* which also beareth fruit, and bringeth forth, some an hundredfold, some sixty, some thirty.

Tares, mustard seed, and leaven

24 Another parable put he forth unto them, saying, The kingdom of heaven is likened unto a man which sowed good seed in his field:

25 But while men slept, his enemy came and sowed tares among the wheat, and went his way.

26 But when the blade was sprung up, and

CHAP. **13**
AD 31
14 Is. 6:9
Ezek. 12:2
Mark 4:12
Luke 8:10
John 12:40
Acts 28:26, 27
Rom. 11:8
2 Cor. 3:14, 15
15 Heb. 5:11
16 ch. 16:17
Luke 10:23, 24
John 20:29
17 Heb. 11:13
1 Pet. 1:10, 11
18 Mark 4:14
Luke 8:11
19 ch. 4:23
20 Is. 58:2
Ezek. 33:31, 32
John 5:35
21 ch. 11:6
2 Tim. 1:15
22 ch. 19:23
Mark 10:23
Luke 18:24
1 Tim. 6:9
2 Tim. 4:10
22 Jer. 4:3

ch. 3:12   30
Is. 2:2, 3   31
Mic. 4:1
Mark 4:30
Luke 13:18
Luke 13:20, etc.   33
The word in the   33
Greek is *a measure containing about a peck and a half, wanting a little more than a pint*
Mark 4:33   34
Ps. 78:2   35
Rom. 16:25, 26   35
1 Cor. 2:7
Eph. 3:9
Col. 1:26
ch. 24:14   38
& 28:19
Mark 16:15
Luke 24:47
Rom. 10:18
Col. 1:6
Gen. 3:15   38
John 8:44
Acts 13:10
1 John 3:8
Joel 3:13   39
Rev. 14:15
ch. 18:7   41
2 Pet. 2:1, 2
Or, *scandals*   41
ch. 3:12   42
Rev. 19:20
& 20:10
ver. 50   42
ch. 8:12

brought forth fruit, then appeared the tares also.

27 So the servants of the householder came and said unto him, Sir, didst not thou sow good seed in thy field? from whence then hath it tares?

28 He said unto them, An enemy hath done this. The servants said unto him, Wilt thou then that we go and gather them up?

29 But he said, Nay; lest while ye gather up the tares, ye root up also the wheat with them.

30 Let both grow together until the harvest: and in the time of harvest I will say to the reapers, Gather ye together first the tares, and bind them in bundles to burn them: but ᴿgather the wheat into my barn.

31 Another parable put he forth unto them, saying, ᴿThe kingdom of heaven is like to a grain of mustard seed, which a man took, and sowed in his field:

32 Which indeed is the least of all seeds: but when it is grown, it is the greatest among herbs, and becometh a tree, so that the birds of the air come and lodge in the branches thereof.

33 ᴿAnother parable spake he unto them; The kingdom of heaven is like unto leaven, which a woman took, and hid in three ᴺmeasures of meal, till the whole was leavened.

34 ᴿAll these things spake Jesus unto the multitude in parables; and without a parable spake he not unto them:

35 That it might be fulfilled which was spoken by the prophet, saying, ᴿI will open my mouth in parables; ᴿI will utter things which have been kept secret from the foundation of the world.

36 Then Jesus sent the multitude away, and went into the house: and his disciples came unto him, saying, Declare unto us the parable of the tares of the field.

37 He answered and said unto them, He that soweth the good seed is the Son of man;

38 ᴿThe field is the world; the good seed are the children of the kingdom; but the tares are ᴿthe children of the wicked *one;*

39 The enemy that sowed them is the devil; ᴿthe harvest is the end of the world; and the reapers are the angels.

40 As therefore the tares are gathered and burned in the fire; so shall it be in the end of this world.

41 The Son of man shall send forth his angels, ᴿand they shall gather out of his kingdom all ᴺthings that offend, and them which do iniquity;

42 ᴿAnd shall cast them into a furnace of fire: ᴿthere shall be wailing and gnashing of teeth.

43 ᴿThen shall the righteous shine forth as the sun in the kingdom of their Father. ᴿWho hath ears to hear, let him hear.

Hidden treasure, pearl, and net

44 Again, the kingdom of heaven is like unto treasure hid in a field; the which when a man hath found, he hideth, and for joy thereof goeth and ᴿselleth all that he hath, and ᴿbuyeth that field.

45 Again, the kingdom of heaven is like unto a merchant man, seeking goodly pearls:

46 Who, when he had found ᴿone pearl of great price, went and sold all that he had, and bought it.

47 Again, the kingdom of heaven is like unto a net, that was cast into the sea, and ᴿgathered of every kind:

48 Which, when it was full, they drew to shore, and sat down, and gathered the good into vessels, but cast the bad away.

49 So shall it be at the end of the world: the angels shall come forth, and ᴿsever the wicked from among the just,

50 And shall cast them into the furnace of fire: there shall be wailing and gnashing of teeth.

Responsibility of discipleship

51 Jesus saith unto them, Have ye understood all these things? They say unto him, Yea, Lord.

52 Then said he unto them, Therefore every scribe *which is* instructed unto the kingdom of heaven is like unto a man *that is* an householder, which bringeth forth out of his treasure ᴿ*things* new and old.

Rejection of Jesus at Nazareth

53 And it came to pass, *that* when Jesus had finished these parables, he departed thence.

54 ᴿAnd when he was come into his own country, he taught them in their synagogue, insomuch that they were astonished, and said, Whence hath this *man* this wisdom, and *these* mighty works?

55 ᴿIs not this the carpenter's son? is not his mother called Mary? and ᴿhis brethren, ᴿJames, and Jō'-sĕŝ, and Simon, and Judas?

56 And his sisters, are they not all with us? Whence then hath this *man* all these things?

57 And they ᴿwere offended in him. But Jesus said unto them, ᴿA prophet is not without honour, save in his own country, and in his own house.

58 And ᴿhe did not many mighty works there because of their unbelief.

CHAP. 13
AD 31
43 Dan. 12:3
1 Cor. 15:42, 43, 58
43 ver. 9
44 Phil. 3:7, 8
44 Is. 55:1
Rev. 3:18
46 Prov. 2:4
& 3:14, 15
& 8:10, 19
47 ch. 22:10
49 ch. 25:32
52 S. of S. 7:13
54 ch. 2:23
Mark 6:1
Luke 4:16
55 Is. 49:7
Mark 6:3
Luke 3:23
John 6:42
55 ch. 12:46
55 Mark 15:40
57 ch. 11:6
Mark 6:3, 4
57 Luke 4:24
John 4:44
58 Mark 6:5, 6

CHAP. 14
AD 32
Mark 6:14 — 1
Luke 9:7
Or, *are* — 2
wrought by him
Mark 6:17 — 3
Luke 3:19, 20
Lev. 18:16 — 4
& 20:21
ch. 21:26 — 5
Luke 20:6
Gr. *in the midst* — 6
ch. 10:23 — 13
& 12:15
Mark 6:32
Luke 9:10
John 6:1, 2
ch. 9:36 — 14
Mark 6:34
Mark 6:35 — 15
Luke 9:12
John 6:5
ch. 15:36 — 19

CHAPTER 14

John the Baptist beheaded

AT that time ᴿHerod the tē′-trärch heard of the fame of Jesus,

2 And said unto his servants, This is John the Baptist; he is risen from the dead; and therefore mighty works ᴺdo shew forth themselves in him.

3 ᴿFor Herod had laid hold on John, and bound him, and put *him* in prison for Hĕ-rō′-dĭ-ăs′ sake, his brother Philip's wife.

4 For John said unto him, ᴿIt is not lawful for thee to have her.

5 And when he would have put him to death, he feared the multitude, ᴿbecause they counted him as a prophet.

6 But when Herod's birthday was kept, the daughter of Hĕ-rō′-dĭ-ăs danced ᴺbefore them, and pleased Herod.

7 Whereupon he promised with an oath to give her whatsoever she would ask.

8 And she, being before instructed of her mother, said, Give me here John Baptist's head in a charger.

9 And the king was sorry: nevertheless for the oath's sake, and them which sat with him at meat, he commanded *it* to be given *her*.

10 And he sent, and beheaded John in the prison.

11 And his head was brought in a charger, and given to the damsel: and she brought *it* to her mother.

12 And his disciples came, and took up the body, and buried it, and went and told Jesus.

Feeding the five thousand

13 ᴿWhen Jesus heard *of it,* he departed thence by ship into a desert place apart: and when the people had heard *thereof,* they followed him on foot out of the cities.

14 And Jesus went forth, and saw a great multitude, and ᴿwas moved with compassion toward them, and he healed their sick.

15 ᴿAnd when it was evening, his disciples came to him, saying, This is a desert place, and the time is now past; send the multitude away, that they may go into the villages, and buy themselves victuals.

16 But Jesus said unto them, They need not depart; give ye them to eat.

17 And they say unto him, We have here but five loaves, and two fishes.

18 He said, Bring them hither to me.

19 And he commanded the multitude to sit down on the grass, and took the five loaves, and the two fishes, and looking up to heaven, ᴿhe blessed, and brake, and gave the loaves to

his disciples, and the disciples to the multitude.

20 And they did all eat, and were filled: and they took up of the fragments that remained twelve baskets full.

21 And they that had eaten were about five thousand men, beside women and children.

Jesus walks on the water

22 And straightway Jesus constrained his disciples to get into a ship, and to go before him unto the other side, while he sent the multitudes away.

23 ᴿAnd when he had sent the multitudes away, he went up into a mountain apart to pray: ᴿand when the evening was come, he was there alone.

24 But the ship was now in the midst of the sea, tossed with waves: for the wind was contrary.

25 And in the fourth watch of the night Jesus went unto them, walking on the sea.

26 And when the disciples saw him ᴿwalking on the sea, they were troubled, saying, It is a spirit; and they cried out for fear.

27 But straightway Jesus spake unto them, saying,Be of good cheer; it is I; be not afraid.

28 And Peter answered him and said, Lord, if it be thou, bid me come unto thee on the water.

29 And he said,Come. And when Peter was come down out of the ship, he walked on the water, to go to Jesus.

30 But when he saw the wind ᴺboisterous, he was afraid; and beginning to sink, he cried, saying, Lord, save me.

31 And immediately Jesus stretched forth *his* hand, and caught him, and said unto him, O thou of little faith, wherefore didst thou doubt?

32 And when they were come into the ship, the wind ceased.

33 Then they that were in the ship came and worshipped him, saying, Of a truth ᴿthou art the Son of God.

34 ᴿAnd when they were gone over, they came into the land of Gĕn-nĕś'-ă-rĕt.

35 And when the men of that place had knowledge of him, they sent out into all that country round about, and brought unto him all that were diseased;

36 And besought him that they might only touch the hem of his garment: and ᴿas many as touched were made perfectly whole.

CHAPTER 15

Ceremonial and real defilement

THEN ᴿcame to Jesus scribes and Pharisees, which were of Jerusalem, saying,

---

CHAP. 14
AD 32
23 Mark 6:46
23 John 6:16
26 Job 9:8
30 Or, *strong*
33 Ps. 2:7
ch. 16:16
& 26:63
Mark 1:1
Luke 4:41
John 1:49
& 6:69
& 11:27
Acts 8:37
Rom. 1:4
34 Mark 6:53
36 ch. 9:20
Mark 3:10
Luke 6:19
Acts 19:12

CHAP. 15
AD 32
1 Mark 7:1

Mark 7:5	2
Ex. 20:12	4
Lev. 19:3	
Deut. 5:16	
Prov. 23:22	
Eph. 6:2	
Ex. 21:17	4
Lev. 20:9	
Deut. 27:16	
Prov. 20:20	
& 30:17	
Mark 7:11, 12	5
Mark 7:6	7
Is. 29:13	8
Ezek. 33:31	
Is. 29:13	9
Col. 2:18-22	
Tit. 1:14	
Mark 7:14	10
Acts 10:15	11
Rom. 14:14, 17, 20	
1 Tim. 4:4	
Tit. 1:15	
John 15:2	13
1 Cor. 3:12, etc.	
Is. 9:16	14
Mal. 2:8	
ch. 23:16	
Luke 6:39	
Mark 7:17	15
ch. 16:9	16
Mark 7:18	
1 Cor. 6:13	17
Jas. 3:6	18
Gen. 6:5 & 8:21	19
Prov. 6:14	
Jer. 17:9	
Mark 7:21	
Mark 7:24	21

---

2 ᴿWhy do thy disciples transgress the tradition of the elders? for they wash not their hands when they eat bread.

3 But he answered and said unto them,Why do ye also transgress the commandment of God by your tradition?

4 For God commanded, saying, ᴿHonour thy father and mother: and, ᴿHe that curseth father or mother, let him die the death.

5 But ye say, Whosoever shall say to *his* father or *his* mother, ᴿ*It is* a gift, by whatsoever thou mightest be profited by me;

6 And honour not his father or his mother, *he shall be free.* Thus have ye made the commandment of God of none effect by your tradition.

7 *Ye* ᴿhypocrites, well did Ē-śâi'-ăs prophesy of you, saying,

8 ᴿThis people draweth nigh unto me with their mouth, and honoureth me with *their* lips; but their heart is far from me.

9 But in vain they do worship me, ᴿteaching *for* doctrines the commandments of men.

10 ᴿAnd he called the multitude, and said unto them,Hear, and understand:

11 ᴿNot that which goeth into the mouth defileth a man; but that which cometh out of the mouth, this defileth a man.

12 Then came his disciples, and said unto him, Knowest thou that the Pharisees were offended, after they heard this saying?

13 But he answered and said, ᴿEvery plant, which my heavenly Father hath not planted, shall be rooted up.

14 Let them alone: ᴿthey be blind leaders of the blind. And if the blind lead the blind, both shall fall into the ditch.

15 ᴿThen answered Peter and said unto him, Declare unto us this parable.

16 And Jesus said, ᴿAre ye also yet without understanding?

17 Do not ye yet understand, that ᴿwhatsoever entereth in at the mouth goeth into the belly, and is cast out into the draught?

18 But ᴿthose things which proceed out of the mouth come forth from the heart; and they defile the man.

19 ᴿFor out of the heart proceed evil thoughts, murders, adulteries, fornications, thefts, false witness, blasphemies:

20 These are *the things* which defile a man: but to eat with unwashen hands defileth not a man.

Faith of the Canaanite woman

21 ᴿThen Jesus went thence, and departed into the coasts of Tyre and śī'-dŏn.

22 And, behold, a woman of Canaan came out of the same coasts, and cried unto him,

saying, Have mercy on me, O Lord, *thou* son of David; my daughter is grievously vexed with a devil.

23 But he answered her not a word. And his disciples came and besought him, saying, Send her away; for she crieth after us.

24 But he answered and said, [R]I am not sent but unto the lost sheep of the house of Israel.

25 Then came she and worshipped him, saying, Lord, help me.

26 But he answered and said, It is not meet to take the children's bread, and to cast *it* to [R]dogs.

27 And she said, Truth, Lord: yet the dogs eat of the crumbs which fall from their masters' table.

28 Then Jesus answered and said unto her, O woman, great *is* thy faith: be it unto thee even as thou wilt. And her daughter was made whole from that very hour.

Healing of many

29 [R]And Jesus departed from thence, and came nigh [R]unto the sea of Galilee; and went up into a mountain, and sat down there.

30 [R]And great multitudes came unto him, having with them *those that were* lame, blind, dumb, maimed, and many others, and cast them down at Jesus' feet; and he healed them:

31 Insomuch that the multitude wondered, when they saw the dumb to speak, the maimed to be whole, the lame to walk, and the blind to see: and they glorified the God of Israel.

Feeding the four thousand

32 [R]Then Jesus called his disciples *unto him,* and said, I have compassion on the multitude, because they continue with me now three days, and have nothing to eat: and I will not send them away fasting, lest they faint in the way.

33 [R]And his disciples say unto him, Whence should we have so much bread in the wilderness, as to fill so great a multitude?

34 And Jesus saith unto them, How many loaves have ye? And they said, Seven, and a few little fishes.

35 And he commanded the multitude to sit down on the ground.

36 And [R]he took the seven loaves and the fishes, and [R]gave thanks, and brake *them,* and gave to his disciples, and the disciples to the multitude.

37 And they did all eat, and were filled: and they took up of the broken *meat* that was left seven baskets full.

38 And they that did eat were four thousand men, beside women and children.

39 [R]And he sent away the multitude, and took ship, and came into the coasts of Măg'-dă-lă.

CHAPTER 16

Leaven of the Pharisees and Sadducees

THE [R]Pharisees also with the Săd'-dū-çēēś came, and tempting desired him that he would shew them a sign from heaven.

2 He answered and said unto them, When it is evening, ye say, *It will be* fair weather: for the sky is red.

3 And in the morning, *It will be* foul weather to day: for the sky is red and lowring. O *ye* hypocrites, ye can discern the face of the sky; but can ye not *discern* the signs of the times?

4 [R]A wicked and adulterous generation seeketh after a sign; and there shall no sign be given unto it, but the sign of the prophet Jonas. And he left them, and departed.

5 And [R]when his disciples were come to the other side, they had forgotten to take bread.

6 Then Jesus said unto them, [R]Take heed and beware of the leaven of the Pharisees and of the Săd'-dū-çēēś.

7 And they reasoned among themselves, saying, *It is* because we have taken no bread.

8 *Which* when Jesus perceived, he said unto them, O ye of little faith, why reason ye among yourselves, because ye have brought no bread?

9 [R]Do ye not yet understand, neither remember the five loaves of the five thousand, and how many baskets ye took up?

10 [R]Neither the seven loaves of the four thousand, and how many baskets ye took up?

11 How is it that ye do not understand that I spake *it* not to you concerning bread, that ye should beware of the leaven of the Pharisees and of the Săd'-dū-çēēś?

12 Then understood they how that he bade *them* not beware of the leaven of bread, but of the doctrine of the Pharisees and of the Săd'-dū-çēēś.

Peter's confession

13 When Jesus came into the coasts of Cæ-să-rē'-ă Philippi, he asked his disciples, saying, [R]Whom do men say that I the Son of man am?

14 And they said, [R]Some *say that thou art* John the Baptist: some, Ē-lī'-ăs; and others, Jeremias, or one of the prophets.

15 He saith unto them, But whom say ye that I am?

16 And Simon Peter answered and said,

ᴿThou art the Christ, the Son of the living God.

17 And Jesus answered and said unto him, Blessed art thou, Simon Bär-jō'-nă: ᴿfor flesh and blood hath not revealed *it* unto thee, but ᴿmy Father which is in heaven.

18 And I say also unto thee, That ᴿthou art Peter, and ᴿupon this rock I will build my church; and ᴿthe gates of hell shall not prevail against it.

19 ᴿAnd I will give unto thee the keys of the kingdom of heaven: and whatsoever thou shalt bind on earth shall be bound in heaven: and whatsoever thou shalt loose on earth shall be loosed in heaven.

20 ᴿThen charged he his disciples that they should tell no man that he was Jesus the Christ.

The way of the cross

21 From that time forth began Jesus ᴿto shew unto his disciples, how that he must go unto Jerusalem, and suffer many things of the elders and chief priests and scribes, and be killed, and be raised again the third day.

22 Then Peter took him, and began to rebuke him, saying, ᴺBe it far from thee, Lord: this shall not be unto thee.

23 But he turned, and said unto Peter, Get thee behind me, ᴿSatan: ᴿthou art an offence unto me: for thou savourest not the things that be of God, but those that be of men.

24 ᴿThen said Jesus unto his disciples, If any *man* will come after me, let him deny himself, and take up his cross, and follow me.

25 For ᴿwhosoever will save his life shall lose it: and whosoever will lose his life for my sake shall find it.

26 For what is a man profited, if he shall gain the whole world, and lose his own soul? or ᴿwhat shall a man give in exchange for his soul?

27 For ᴿthe Son of man shall come in the glory of his Father ᴿwith his angels; ᴿand then he shall reward every man according to his works.

28 Verily I say unto you, ᴿThere be some standing here, which shall not taste of death, till they see the Son of man coming in his kingdom.

CHAPTER 17

The transfiguration

AND ᴿafter six days Jesus taketh Peter, James, and John his brother, and bringeth them up into an high mountain apart,

2 And was transfigured before them: and his

CHAP. 16

AD 32

16 ch. 14:33
Mark 8:29
Luke 9:20
John 6:69
Acts 8:37
1 John 4:15
17 Eph. 2:8
17 1 Cor. 2:10
18 John 1:42
18 Eph. 2:20
Rev. 21:14
18 Job 33:17
Ps. 9:13
Is. 38:10
19 ch. 18:18
John 20:23
20 ch. 17:9
Luke 9:21
21 ch. 20:17
Mark 8:31
Luke 9:22 & 18:31
22 Gr. *Pity thyself*
23 See 2 Sam. 10:22
23 Rom. 8:7
24 Mark 8:34
Luke 9:23
Acts 14:22
2 Tim. 3:12
25 Luke 17:33
John 12:25
26 Ps. 49:7, 8
27 ch. 26:64
Mark 8:38
Luke 9:26
27 Dan. 7:10
Zech. 14:5
Jude 14
27 Job 34:11
Ps. 62:12
Prov. 24:12
Rom. 2:6
1 Pet. 1:17
28 Mark 9:1
Luke 9:27

CHAP. 17

AD 32

1 Mark 9:2
Luke 9:28

2 Pet. 1:17   5
ch. 3:17   5
Mark 1:11
Luke 3:22
Is. 42:1   5
Deut. 18:15, 19   5
Acts 3:22, 23
2 Pet. 1:18   6
Dan. 8:18   7
& 9:21 & 10:10, 18
ch. 16:20   9
Mark 8:30
Mal. 4:5   10
ch. 11:14
Mark 9:11
Mal. 4:6   11
Luke 1:16, 17
Acts 3:21
ch. 11:14   12
Mark 9:12, 13
ch. 14:3, 10   12
ch. 16:21   12
ch. 11:14   13
Mark 9:14   14
Luke 9:37
ch. 21:21   20
Mark 11:23
Luke 17:6

---

face did shine as the sun, and his raiment was white as the light.

3 And, behold, there appeared unto them Moses and Ē-lĭ'-ăs talking with him.

4 Then answered Peter, and said unto Jesus, Lord, it is good for us to be here: if thou wilt, let us make here three tabernacles; one for thee, and one for Moses, and one for Ē-lĭ'-ăs.

5 ᴿWhile he yet spake, behold, a bright cloud overshadowed them: and behold a voice out of the cloud, which said, ᴿThis is my beloved Son, ᴿin whom I am well pleased; ᴿhear ye him.

6 ᴿAnd when the disciples heard *it*, they fell on their face, and were sore afraid.

7 And Jesus came and ᴿtouched them, and said, Arise, and be not afraid.

8 And when they had lifted up their eyes, they saw no man, save Jesus only.

John the Baptist likened to Elias

9 And as they came down from the mountain, ᴿJesus charged them, saying, Tell the vision to no man, until the Son of man be risen again from the dead.

10 And his disciples asked him, saying, ᴿWhy then say the scribes that Ē-lĭ'-ăs must first come?

11 And Jesus answered and said unto them, Ē-lĭ'-ăs truly shall first come, and ᴿrestore all things.

12 ᴿBut I say unto you, That Ē-lĭ'-ăs is come already, and they knew him not, but ᴿhave done unto him whatsoever they listed. Likewise ᴿshall also the Son of man suffer of them.

13 ᴿThen the disciples understood that he spake unto them of John the Baptist.

Disciples' inability to cure

14 ᴿAnd when they were come to the multitude, there came to him a *certain* man, kneeling down to him, and saying,

15 Lord, have mercy on my son: for he is lunatic, and sore vexed: for ofttimes he falleth into the fire, and oft into the water.

16 And I brought him to thy disciples, and they could not cure him.

17 Then Jesus answered and said, O faithless and perverse generation, how long shall I be with you? how long shall I suffer you? bring him hither to me.

18 And Jesus rebuked the devil; and he departed out of him: and the child was cured from that very hour.

19 Then came the disciples to Jesus apart, and said, Why could not we cast him out?

20 And Jesus said unto them, Because of your unbelief: for verily I say unto you, ᴿIf ye

have faith as a grain of mustard seed, ye shall say unto this mountain, Remove hence to yonder place; and it shall remove; and nothing shall be impossible unto you.

21 Howbeit this kind goeth not out but by prayer and fasting.

His death and resurrection foretold

22 ^RAnd while they abode in Galilee, Jesus said unto them, The Son of man shall be betrayed into the hands of men:

23 And they shall kill him, and the third day he shall be raised again. And they were exceeding sorry.

Miracle of the tribute money

24 And ^Rwhen they were come to Că-pĕr′-nă-ŭm, they that received ^Ntribute *money* came to Peter, and said, Doth not your master pay tribute?

25 He saith, Yes. And when he was come into the house, Jesus prevented him, saying, What thinkest thou, Simon? of whom do the kings of the earth take custom or tribute? of their own children, or of strangers?

26 Peter saith unto him, Of strangers. Jesus saith unto him, Then are the children free.

27 Notwithstanding, lest we should offend them, go thou to the sea, and cast an hook, and take up the fish that first cometh up; and when thou hast opened his mouth, thou shalt find ^Na piece of money: that take, and give unto them for me and thee.

CHAPTER 18

Greatest in the kingdom

AT ^Rthe same time came the disciples unto Jesus, saying, Who is the greatest in the kingdom of heaven?

2 And Jesus called a little child unto him, and set him in the midst of them,

3 And said, Verily I say unto you, ^RExcept ye be converted, and become as little children, ye shall not enter into the kingdom of heaven.

4 ^RWhosoever therefore shall humble himself as this little child, the same is greatest in the kingdom of heaven.

5 And ^Rwhoso shall receive one such little child in my name receiveth me.

6 ^RBut whoso shall offend one of these little ones which believe in me, it were better for him that a millstone were hanged about his neck, and *that* he were drowned in the depth of the sea.

7 Woe unto the world because of offences! for ^Rit must needs be that offences come; but

^Rwoe to that man by whom the offence cometh!

8 ^RWherefore if thy hand or thy foot offend thee, cut them off, and cast *them* from thee: it is better for thee to enter into life halt or maimed, rather than having two hands or two feet to be cast into everlasting fire.

9 And if thine eye offend thee, pluck it out, and cast *it* from thee: it is better for thee to enter into life with one eye, rather than having two eyes to be cast into hell fire.

Parable of the lost sheep

10 Take heed that ye despise not one of these little ones; for I say unto you, That in heaven ^Rtheir angels do always ^Rbehold the face of my Father which is in heaven.

11 ^RFor the Son of man is come to save that which was lost.

12 ^RHow think ye? if a man have an hundred sheep, and one of them be gone astray, doth he not leave the ninety and nine, and goeth into the mountains, and seeketh that which is gone astray?

13 And if so be that he find it, verily I say unto you, he rejoiceth more of that *sheep,* than of the ninety and nine which went not astray.

14 Even so it is not the will of your Father which is in heaven, that one of these little ones should perish.

Treatment of offenders

15 Moreover ^Rif thy brother shall trespass against thee, go and tell him his fault between thee and him alone: if he shall hear thee, ^Rthou hast gained thy brother.

16 But if he will not hear *thee, then* take with thee one or two more, that in ^Rthe mouth of two or three witnesses every word may be established.

17 And if he shall neglect to hear them, tell *it* unto the church: but if he neglect to hear the church, let him be unto thee as an ^Rheathen man and a publican.

18 Verily I say unto you, ^RWhatsoever ye shall bind on earth shall be bound in heaven: and whatsoever ye shall loose on earth shall be loosed in heaven.

19 ^RAgain I say unto you, That if two of you shall agree on earth as touching any thing that they shall ask, ^Rit shall be done for them of my Father which is in heaven.

20 For where two or three are gathered together in my name, there am I in the midst of them.

21 Then came Peter to him, and said, Lord, how oft shall my brother sin against me, and I forgive him? ^Rtill seven times?

CHAP. 17
AD 32
22 ch. 16:21
& 20:17
Mark 8:31
& 9:30, 31
& 10:33
Luke 9:22, 44
& 18:31 & 24:6, 7
24 Mark 9:33
24 Called in the original, *didrachma,* being in value fifteen pence: See Ex. 30:13 & 33:26
27 Or, *a stater:* It is half an ounce of silver, in value, *2s. 6d.* after *5s.* the ounce

CHAP. 18
AD 32
1 Mark 9:33
Luke 9:46
& 22:24
3 Ps. 131:2
ch. 19:14
Mark 10:14
Luke 18:16
1 Cor. 14:20
1 Pet. 2:2
4 ch. 20:27
& 23:11
5 ch. 10:42
Luke 9:48
6 Mark 9:42
Luke 17:1, 2
7 Luke 17:1
1 Cor. 11:19

ch. 26:24 — 7
ch. 5:29, 30 — 8
Mark 9:43, 45
Ps. 34:7 — 10
Zech. 13:7
Heb. 1:14
Esth. 1:14 — 10
Luke 1:19
Luke 9:56 — 11
& 19:10
John 3:17
& 12:47
Luke 15:4 — 12
Lev. 19:17 — 15
Luke 17:3
Jas. 5:20 — 15
1 Pet. 3:1
Deut. 17:6 — 16
& 19:15
John 8:17
2 Cor. 13:1
Heb. 10:28
Rom. 16:17 — 17
1 Cor. 5:9
2 Thes. 3:6, 14
2 John 10
ch. 16:19 — 18
John 20:23
1 Cor. 5:4
ch. 5:24 — 19
1 John 3:22 — 19
& 5:14
Luke 17:4 — 21

22 Jesus saith unto him, I say not unto thee, Until seven times: [R]but, Until seventy times seven.

Parable of the unforgiving servant

23 Therefore is the kingdom of heaven likened unto a certain king, which would take account of his servants.

24 And when he had begun to reckon, one was brought unto him, which owed him ten thousand [N]talents.

25 But forasmuch as he had not to pay, his lord commanded him [R]to be sold, and his wife, and children, and all that he had, and payment to be made.

26 The servant therefore fell down, and [N]worshipped him, saying, Lord, have patience with me, and I will pay thee all.

27 Then the lord of that servant was moved with compassion, and loosed him, and forgave him the debt.

28 But the same servant went out, and found one of his fellowservants, which owed him an hundred [N]pence: and he laid hands on him, and took *him* by the throat, saying, Pay me that thou owest.

29 And his fellowservant fell down at his feet, and besought him, saying, Have patience with me, and I will pay thee all.

30 And he would not: but went and cast him into prison, till he should pay the debt.

31 So when his fellowservants saw what was done, they were very sorry, and came and told unto their lord all that was done.

32 Then his lord, after that he had called him, said unto him, O thou wicked servant, I forgave thee all that debt, because thou desiredst me:

33 Shouldest not thou also have had compassion on thy fellowservant, even as I had pity on thee?

34 And his lord was wroth, and delivered him to the tormentors, till he should pay all that was due unto him.

35 [R]So likewise shall my heavenly Father do also unto you, if ye from your hearts forgive not every one his brother their trespasses.

CHAPTER 19

Jesus goes to Judæa

AND it came to pass, [R]*that* when Jesus had finished these sayings, he departed from Galilee, and came into the coasts of Judæa beyond Jordan;

2 [R]And great multitudes followed him; and he healed them there.

CHAP. **18**

AD 32

22 ch. 6:14
Mark 11:25
Col. 3:13
24 *A talent is 750 ounces of silver, which after five shillings the ounce is 187l. 10s.*
25 2 Ki. 4:1
Neh. 5:8
26 Or, *besought him*
28 *The Roman penny is the eighth part of an ounce, which after five shillings the ounce is seven pence halfpenny,* ch. 20:2
35 Prov. 21:13
ch. 6:12
Mark 11:26
Jas. 2:13

CHAP. **19**

AD 33

1 Mark 10:1
John 10:40
2 ch. 12:15

Gen. 1:27   4
& 5:2
Mal. 2:15
Gen. 2:24   5
Mark 10:5-9
Eph. 5:31
1 Cor. 6:16   5
& 7:2
Deut. 24:1   7
ch. 5:31
ch. 5:32   9
Mark 10:11
Luke 16:18
1 Cor. 7:10
Prov. 21:19   10
1 Cor. 7:2, 7, 9, 17   11
1 Cor. 7:32   12
& 9:5, 15
Mark 10:13   13
Luke 18:15
ch. 18:3   14
Mark 10:17   16
Luke 18:18
Luke 10:25   16

Teaching on marriage

3 The Pharisees also came unto him, tempting him, and saying unto him, Is it lawful for a man to put away his wife for every cause?

4 And he answered and said unto them, Have ye not read, [R]that he which made *them* at the beginning made them male and female,

5 And said, [R]For this cause shall a man leave father and mother, and shall cleave to his wife: and [R]they twain shall be one flesh?

6 Wherefore they are no more twain, but one flesh. What therefore God hath joined together, let not man put asunder.

7 They say unto him, [R]Why did Moses then command to give a writing of divorcement, and to put her away?

8 He saith unto them, Moses because of the hardness of your hearts suffered you to put away your wives: but from the beginning it was not so.

9 [R]And I say unto you, Whosoever shall put away his wife, except *it be* for fornication, and shall marry another, committeth adultery: and whoso marrieth her which is put away doth commit adultery.

10 His disciples say unto him, [R]If the case of the man be so with *his* wife, it is not good to marry.

11 But he said unto them, [R]All *men* cannot receive this saying, save *they* to whom it is given.

12 For there are some eunuchs, which were so born from *their* mother's womb: and there are some eunuchs, which were made eunuchs of men: and [R]there be eunuchs, which have made themselves eunuchs for the kingdom of heaven's sake. He that is able to receive *it*, let him receive *it*.

Jesus blesses the children

13 [R]Then were there brought unto him little children, that he should put *his* hands on them, and pray: and the disciples rebuked them.

14 But Jesus said, Suffer little children, and forbid them not, to come unto me: for [R]of such is the kingdom of heaven.

15 And he laid *his* hands on them, and departed thence.

The rich young ruler

16 [R]And, behold, one came and said unto him, [R]Good Master, what good thing shall I do, that I may have eternal life?

17 And he said unto him, Why callest thou me good? *there is* none good but one, *that is,* God: but if thou wilt enter into life, keep the commandments.

18 He saith unto him, Which? Jesus said, [R]Thou shalt do no murder, Thou shalt not commit adultery, Thou shalt not steal, Thou shalt not bear false witness,

19 [R]Honour thy father and *thy* mother: and, [R]Thou shalt love thy neighbour as thyself.

20 The young man saith unto him, All these things have I kept from my youth up: what lack I yet?

21 Jesus said unto him, If thou wilt be perfect, [R]go *and* sell that thou hast, and give to the poor, and thou shalt have treasure in heaven: and come *and* follow me.

22 But when the young man heard that saying, he went away sorrowful: for he had great possessions.

Rewards of discipleship

23 Then said Jesus unto his disciples, Verily I say unto you, That [R]a rich man shall hardly enter into the kingdom of heaven.

24 And again I say unto you, It is easier for a camel to go through the eye of a needle, than for a rich man to enter into the kingdom of God.

25 When his disciples heard *it,* they were exceedingly amazed, saying, Who then can be saved?

26 But Jesus beheld *them,* and said unto them, With men this is impossible; but [R]with God all things are possible.

27 Then answered Peter and said unto him, Behold, [R]we have forsaken all, and followed thee; what shall we have therefore?

28 And Jesus said unto them, Verily I say unto you, That ye which have followed me, in the regeneration when the Son of man shall sit in the throne of his glory, [R]ye also shall sit upon twelve thrones, judging the twelve tribes of Israel.

29 [R]And every one that hath forsaken houses, or brethren, or sisters, or father, or mother, or wife, or children, or lands, for my name's sake, shall receive an hundredfold, and shall inherit everlasting life.

30 [R]But many *that are* first shall be last; and the last *shall be* first.

CHAPTER 20

The labourers in the vineyard

FOR the kingdom of heaven is like unto a man *that is* an householder, which went out early in the morning to hire labourers into his vineyard.

2 And when he had agreed with the labourers for a [N]penny a day, he sent them into his vineyard.

CHAP. 19

AD 33

18 Ex. 20:13
Deut. 5:17
19 ch. 15:4
19 Lev. 19:18
ch. 22:39
Rom. 13:9
Gal. 5:14
Jas. 2:8
21 ch. 6:20
Luke 12:33
& 16:9
Acts 2:45
& 4:34, 35
1 Tim. 6:18, 19
23 ch. 13:22
Mark 10:24
1 Cor. 1:26
1 Tim. 6:9
26 Gen. 18:14
Job 42:2
Jer. 32:17
Zech. 8:6
Luke 1:37
& 18:27
27 Deut. 33:9
ch. 4:20
Luke 5:11
28 ch. 20:21
Luke 22:28-30
1 Cor. 6:2
Rev. 2:26
29 Mark 10:29, 30
Luke 18:29, 30
30 ch. 20:16
& 21:31, 32
Mark 10:31
Luke 13:30

CHAP. 20

AD 33

2 *The Roman penny is the eighth part of an ounce, which after five shillings the ounce is seven pence halfpenny,* ch. 18:28

Or, *have* 12
continued
one hour
only
Rom. 9:21 15
Deut. 15:9 15
Prov. 23:6
ch. 6:23
ch. 19:30 16
ch. 22:14 16
Mark 10:32 17
Luke 18:31
John 12:12
ch. 16:21 18
ch. 27:2 19
Mark 15:1, 16, etc.
Luke 23:1
John 18:28, etc.
Acts 3:13
Mark 10:35 20
ch. 4:21 20

3 And he went out about the third hour, and saw others standing idle in the marketplace,

4 And said unto them; Go ye also into the vineyard, and whatsoever is right I will give you. And they went their way.

5 Again he went out about the sixth and ninth hour, and did likewise.

6 And about the eleventh hour he went out, and found others standing idle, and saith unto them, Why stand ye here all the day idle?

7 They say unto him, Because no man hath hired us. He saith unto them, Go ye also into the vineyard; and whatsoever is right, *that* shall ye receive.

8 So when even was come, the lord of the vineyard saith unto his steward, Call the labourers, and give them *their* hire, beginning from the last unto the first.

9 And when they came that *were hired* about the eleventh hour, they received every man a penny.

10 But when the first came, they supposed that they should have received more; and they likewise received every man a penny.

11 And when they had received *it,* they murmured against the goodman of the house,

12 Saying, These last [N]have wrought *but* one hour, and thou hast made them equal unto us, which have borne the burden and heat of the day.

13 But he answered one of them, and said, Friend, I do thee no wrong: didst not thou agree with me for a penny?

14 Take *that* thine *is,* and go thy way: I will give unto this last, even as unto thee.

15 [R]Is it not lawful for me to do what I will with mine own? [R]Is thine eye evil, because I am good?

16 [R]So the last shall be first, and the first last: [R]for many be called, but few chosen.

His passion foretold

17 [R]And Jesus going up to Jerusalem took the twelve disciples apart in the way, and said unto them,

18 [R]Behold, we go up to Jerusalem; and the Son of man shall be betrayed unto the chief priests and unto the scribes, and they shall condemn him to death,

19 [R]And shall deliver him to the Gentiles to mock, and to scourge, and to crucify *him:* and the third day he shall rise again.

True greatness

20 [R]Then came to him the mother of [R]Zĕb'-ĕ-dĕe's children with her sons, worshipping *him,* and desiring a certain thing of him.

21 And he said unto her, What wilt thou?

She saith unto him, Grant that these my two sons [R]may sit, the one on thy right hand, and the other on the left, in thy kingdom.

22 But Jesus answered and said, Ye know not what ye ask. Are ye able to drink of [R]the cup that I shall drink of, and to be baptized with [R]the baptism that I am baptized with? They say unto him, We are able.

23 And he saith unto them, [R]Ye shall drink indeed of my cup, and be baptized with the baptism that I am baptized with: but to sit on my right hand, and on my left, is not mine to [R]give, but *it shall be given to them* for whom it is prepared of my Father.

24 [R]And when the ten heard *it,* they were moved with indignation against the two brethren.

25 But Jesus called them *unto him,* and said, Ye know that the princes of the Gentiles exercise dominion over them, and they that are great exercise authority upon them.

26 But [R]it shall not be so among you: but [R]whosoever will be great among you, let him be your minister;

27 [R]And whosoever will be chief among you, let him be your servant:

28 [R]Even as the [R]Son of man came not to be ministered unto, [R]but to minister, and [R]to give his life a ransom [R]for many.

Two blind men healed

29 [R]And as they departed from Jericho, a great multitude followed him.

30 And, behold, [R]two blind men sitting by the way side, when they heard that Jesus passed by, cried out, saying, Have mercy on us, O Lord, *thou* son of David.

31 And the multitude rebuked them, because they should hold their peace: but they cried the more, saying, Have mercy on us, O Lord, *thou* son of David.

32 And Jesus stood still, and called them, and said, What will ye that I shall do unto you?

33 They say unto him, Lord, that our eyes may be opened.

34 So Jesus had compassion *on them,* and touched their eyes: and immediately their eyes received sight, and they followed him.

CHAPTER 21

Triumphal entry into Jerusalem

AND [R]when they drew nigh unto Jerusalem, and were come to Bĕth'-phă-ġē, unto [R]the mount of Olives, then sent Jesus two disciples,

2 Saying unto them, Go into the village over

CHAP. 20
AD 33
21 ch. 19:28
22 ch. 26:39, 42
Mark 14:36
Luke 22:42
John 18:11
22 Luke 12:50
23 Acts 12:2
Rom. 8:17
2 Cor. 1:7
Rev. 1:9
23 ch. 24:34
24 Mark 10:41
Luke 22:24, 25
26 1 Pet. 5:3
26 ch. 23:11
Mark 9:35
& 10:43
27 ch. 18:4
28 John 13:4
28 Phil. 2:7
28 Luke 22:27
John 13:14
28 Is. 53:10, 11
Dan. 9:24, 26
John 11:51, 52
1 Tim. 2:6
Tit. 2:14
1 Pet. 1:19
28 ch. 26:28
Rom. 5:15, 19
Heb. 9:28
29 Mark 10:46
Luke 18:35
30 ch. 9:27

CHAP. 21
AD 33
1 Mark 11:1
Luke 19:29
1 Zech. 14:4

Is. 62:11   **5**
Zech. 9:9
John 12:15
Mark 11:4   **6**
2 Ki. 9:13   **7**
See Lev. 23:40   **8**
John 12:13
Ps. 118:25   **9**
Ps. 118:26   **9**
ch. 23:39
Mark 11:15   **10**
Luke 19:45
John 2:13, 15
ch. 2:23   **11**
Luke 7:16
John 6:14
& 7:40 & 9:17
Mark 11:11   **12**
Luke 19:45
John 2:15
Deut. 14:25   **12**
Is. 56:7   **13**
Jer. 7:11   **13**
Mark 11:17
Luke 19:46
Ps. 8:2   **16**
Mark 11:11   **17**
John 11:18
Mark 11:12   **18**

---

against you, and straightway ye shall find an ass tied, and a colt with her: loose *them,* and bring *them* unto me.

3 And if any *man* say aught unto you, ye shall say, The Lord hath need of them; and straightway he will send them.

4 All this was done, that it might be fulfilled which was spoken by the prophet, saying,

5 [R]Tell ye the daughter of Sī'-ọn, Behold, thy King cometh unto thee, meek, and sitting upon an ass, and a colt the foal of an ass.

6 [R]And the disciples went, and did as Jesus commanded them,

7 And brought the ass, and the colt, and [R]put on them their clothes, and they set *him* thereon.

8 And a very great multitude spread their garments in the way; [R]others cut down branches from the trees, and strawed *them* in the way.

9 And the multitudes that went before, and that followed, cried, saying, [R]Hō-săn'-nă to the son of David: [R]Blessed *is* he that cometh in the name of the Lord; Hō-săn'-nă in the highest.

10 [R]And when he was come into Jerusalem, all the city was moved, saying, Who is this?

11 And the multitude said, This is Jesus [R]the prophet of Nazareth of Galilee.

Cleansing the temple

12 [R]And Jesus went into the temple of God, and cast out all them that sold and bought in the temple, and overthrew the tables of the [R]moneychangers, and the seats of them that sold doves,

13 And said unto them, It is written, [R]My house shall be called the house of prayer; [R]but ye have made it a den of thieves.

14 And the blind and the lame came to him in the temple; and he healed them.

15 And when the chief priests and scribes saw the wonderful things that he did, and the children crying in the temple, and saying, Hō-săn'-nă to the son of David; they were sore displeased,

16 And said unto him, Hearest thou what these say? And Jesus saith unto them, Yea; have ye never read, [R]Out of the mouth of babes and sucklings thou hast perfected praise?

17 And he left them, and went out of the city into [R]Bethany; and he lodged there.

The fruitless fig tree

18 [R]Now in the morning as he returned into the city, he hungered.

19 ᴿAnd when he saw ᴺa fig tree in the way, he came to it, and found nothing thereon, but leaves only, and said unto it, Let no fruit grow on thee henceforward for ever. And presently the fig tree withered away.

20 ᴿAnd when the disciples saw *it*, they marvelled, saying, How soon is the fig tree withered away!

21 Jesus answered and said unto them, Verily I say unto you, ᴿIf ye have faith, and ᴿdoubt not, ye shall not only do this *which is done* to the fig tree, ᴿbut also if ye shall say unto this mountain, Be thou removed, and be thou cast into the sea; it shall be done.

22 And ᴿall things, whatsoever ye shall ask in prayer, believing, ye shall receive.

The question about authority

23 ᴿAnd when he was come into the temple, the chief priests and the elders of the people came unto him as he was teaching, and ᴿsaid, By what authority doest thou these things? and who gave thee this authority?

24 And Jesus answered and said unto them, I also will ask you one thing, which if ye tell me, I in like wise will tell you by what authority I do these things.

25 The baptism of John, whence was it? from heaven, or of men? And they reasoned with themselves, saying, If we shall say, From heaven; he will say unto us, Why did ye not then believe him?

26 But if we shall say, Of men; we fear the people; ᴿfor all hold John as a prophet.

27 And they answered Jesus, and said, We cannot tell. And he said unto them, Neither tell I you by what authority I do these things.

Parable of the two sons

28 But what think ye? A *certain* man had two sons; and he came to the first, and said, Son, go work to day in my vineyard.

29 He answered and said, I will not: but afterward he repented, and went.

30 And he came to the second, and said likewise. And he answered and said, I *go*, sir: and went not.

31 Whether of them twain did the will of *his* father? They say unto him, The first. Jesus saith unto them, ᴿVerily I say unto you, That the publicans and the harlots go into the kingdom of God before you.

32 For ᴿJohn came unto you in the way of righteousness, and ye believed him not: ᴿbut the publicans and the harlots believed him: and ye, when ye had seen *it*, repented not afterward, that ye might believe him.

Parable of the wicked husbandmen

33 Hear another parable: There was a certain householder, ᴿwhich planted a vineyard, and hedged it round about, and digged a winepress in it, and built a tower, and let it out to husbandmen, and ᴿwent into a far country:

34 And when the time of the fruit drew near, he sent his servants to the husbandmen, ᴿthat they might receive the fruits of it.

35 ᴿAnd the husbandmen took his servants, and beat one, and killed another, and stoned another.

36 Again, he sent other servants more than the first: and they did unto them likewise.

37 But last of all he sent unto them his son, saying, They will reverence my son.

38 But when the husbandmen saw the son, they said among themselves, ᴿThis is the heir; ᴿcome, let us kill him, and let us seize on his inheritance.

39 ᴿAnd they caught him, and cast *him* out of the vineyard, and slew *him*.

40 When the lord therefore of the vineyard cometh, what will he do unto those husbandmen?

41 ᴿThey say unto him, ᴿHe will miserably destroy those wicked men, ᴿand will let out *his* vineyard unto other husbandmen, which shall render him the fruits in their seasons.

42 Jesus saith unto them, ᴿDid ye never read in the scriptures, The stone which the builders rejected, the same is become the head of the corner: this is the Lord's doing, and it is marvellous in our eyes?

43 Therefore say I unto you, ᴿThe kingdom of God shall be taken from you, and given to a nation bringing forth the fruits thereof.

44 And whosoever ᴿshall fall on this stone shall be broken: but on whomsoever it shall fall, ᴿit will grind him to powder.

45 And when the chief priests and Pharisees had heard his parables, they perceived that he spake of them.

46 But when they sought to lay hands on him, they feared the multitude, because ᴿthey took him for a prophet.

CHAPTER 22

Parable of the marriage feast

AND Jesus answered ᴿand spake unto them again by parables, and said,

2 The kingdom of heaven is like unto a certain king, which made a marriage for his son,

3 And sent forth his servants to call them that were bidden to the wedding: and they would not come.

4 Again, he sent forth other servants, saying,

Tell them which are bidden, Behold, I have prepared my dinner: ᴿmy oxen and *my* fatlings *are* killed, and all things *are* ready: come unto the marriage.

5 But they made light of *it,* and went their ways, one to his farm, another to his merchandise:

6 And the remnant took his servants, and entreated *them* spitefully, and slew *them.*

7 But when the king heard *thereof,* he was wroth: and he sent forth ᴿhis armies, and destroyed those murderers, and burned up their city.

8 Then saith he to his servants, The wedding is ready, but they which were bidden were not ᴿworthy.

9 Go ye therefore into the highways, and as many as ye shall find, bid to the marriage.

10 So those servants went out into the highways, and ᴿgathered together all as many as they found, both bad and good: and the wedding was furnished with guests.

11 And when the king came in to see the guests, he saw there a man ᴿwhich had not on a wedding garment:

12 And he saith unto him, Friend, how camest thou in hither not having a wedding garment? And he was speechless.

13 Then said the king to the servants, Bind him hand and foot, and take him away, and cast *him* ᴿinto outer darkness; there shall be weeping and gnashing of teeth.

14 ᴿFor many are called, but few *are* chosen.

The tribute money

15 ᴿThen went the Pharisees, and took counsel how they might entangle him in *his* talk.

16 And they sent out unto him their disciples with the Hĕ-rō′-dĭ-ăns, saying, Master, we know that thou art true, and teachest the way of God in truth, neither carest thou for any *man:* for thou regardest not the person of men.

17 Tell us therefore, What thinkest thou? Is it lawful to give tribute unto Cæsar, or not?

18 But Jesus perceived their wickedness, and said, Why tempt ye me, *ye* hypocrites?

19 Shew me the tribute money. And they brought unto him a ᴺpenny.

20 And he saith unto them, Whose *is* this image and ᴺsuperscription?

21 They say unto him, Cæsar's. Then saith he unto them, ᴿRender therefore unto Cæsar the things which are Cæsar's; and unto God the things that are God's.

22 When they had heard *these words,* they marvelled, and left him, and went their way.

Question about the resurrection

23 ᴿThe same day came to him the Săd′-dū-çėėś, ᴿwhich say that there is no resurrection, and asked him,

24 Saying, Master, ᴿMoses said, If a man die, having no children, his brother shall marry his wife, and raise up seed unto his brother.

25 Now there were with us seven brethren: and the first, when he had married a wife, deceased, and, having no issue, left his wife unto his brother:

26 Likewise the second also, and the third, unto the ᴺseventh.

27 And last of all the woman died also.

28 Therefore in the resurrection whose wife shall she be of the seven? for they all had her.

29 Jesus answered and said unto them, Ye do err, ᴿnot knowing the scriptures, nor the power of God.

30 For in the resurrection they neither marry, nor are given in marriage, but ᴿare as the angels of God in heaven.

31 But as touching the resurrection of the dead, have ye not read that which was spoken unto you by God, saying,

32 ᴿI am the God of Abraham, and the God of Isaac, and the God of Jacob? God is not the God of the dead, but of the living.

33 And when the multitude heard *this,* ᴿthey were astonished at his doctrine.

Question about the great commandment

34 ᴿBut when the Pharisees had heard that he had put the Săd′-dū-çėėś to silence, they were gathered together.

35 Then one of them, *which was* ᴿa lawyer, asked *him a question,* tempting him, and saying,

36 Master, which *is* the great commandment in the law?

37 Jesus said unto him, ᴿThou shalt love the Lord thy God with all thy heart, and with all thy soul, and with all thy mind.

38 This is the first and great commandment.

39 And the second *is* like unto it, ᴿThou shalt love thy neighbour as thyself.

40 ᴿOn these two commandments hang all the law and the prophets.

Christ's unanswerable question

41 ᴿWhile the Pharisees were gathered together, Jesus asked them,

42 Saying, What think ye of Christ? whose son is he? They say unto him, *The son* of David.

43 He saith unto them, How then doth David in spirit call him Lord, saying,

44 ᴿThe Lᴏʀᴅ said unto my Lord, Sit thou on my right hand, till I make thine enemies thy footstool?

45 If David then call him Lord, how is he his son?

46 ᴿAnd no man was able to answer him a word, ᴿneither durst any *man* from that day forth ask him any more *questions.*

CHAPTER 23

Warning against the Pharisees

THEN spake Jesus to the multitude, and to his disciples,

2 Saying, ᴿThe scribes and the Pharisees sit in Moses' seat:

3 All therefore whatsoever they bid you observe, *that* observe and do; but do not ye after their works: for ᴿthey say, and do not.

4 ᴿFor they bind heavy burdens and grievous to be borne, and lay *them* on men's shoulders; but they *themselves* will not move them with one of their fingers.

5 But ᴿall their works they do for to be seen of men: ᴿthey make broad their phylacteries, and enlarge the borders of their garments,

6 ᴿAnd love the uppermost rooms at feasts, and the chief seats in the synagogues,

7 And greetings in the markets, and to be called of men, Rabbi, Rabbi.

8 ᴿBut be not ye called Rabbi: for one is your Master, *even* Christ; and all ye are brethren.

9 And call no *man* your father upon the earth: ᴿfor one is your Father, which is in heaven.

10 Neither be ye called masters: for one is your Master, *even* Christ.

11 But ᴿhe that is greatest among you shall be your servant.

12 ᴿAnd whosoever shall exalt himself shall be abased; and he that shall humble himself shall be exalted.

Woes pronounced on the Pharisees

13 But ᴿwoe unto you, scribes and Pharisees, hypocrites! for ye shut up the kingdom of heaven against men: for ye neither go in *yourselves,* neither suffer ye them that are entering to go in.

14 Woe unto you, scribes and Pharisees, hypocrites! ᴿfor ye devour widows' houses, and for a pretence make long prayer: therefore ye shall receive the greater damnation.

15 Woe unto you, scribes and Pharisees, hypocrites! for ye compass sea and land to make one proselyte, and when he is made, ye make him twofold more the child of hell than yourselves.

16 Woe unto you, ᴿye blind guides, which say, ᴿWhosoever shall swear by the temple, it is nothing; but whosoever shall swear by the gold of the temple, he is a debtor!

17 *Ye* fools and blind: for whether is greater, the gold, ᴿor the temple that sanctifieth the gold?

18 And, Whosoever shall swear by the altar, it is nothing; but whosoever sweareth by the gift that is upon it, he is ᴺguilty.

19 *Ye* fools and blind: for whether *is* greater, the gift, or ᴿthe altar that sanctifieth the gift?

20 Whoso therefore shall swear by the altar, sweareth by it, and by all things thereon.

21 And whoso shall swear by the temple, sweareth by it, and by ᴿhim that dwelleth therein.

22 And he that shall swear by heaven, sweareth by ᴿthe throne of God, and by him that sitteth thereon.

23 Woe unto you, scribes and Pharisees, hypocrites! ᴿfor ye pay tithe of mint and ᴺanise and cummin, and ᴿhave omitted the weightier *matters* of the law, judgment, mercy, and faith: these ought ye to have done, and not to leave the other undone.

24 *Ye* blind guides, which strain at a gnat, and swallow a camel.

25 Woe unto you, scribes and Pharisees, hypocrites! ᴿfor ye make clean the outside of the cup and of the platter, but within they are full of extortion and excess.

26 *Thou* blind Pharisee, cleanse first that *which is* within the cup and platter, that the outside of them may be clean also.

27 Woe unto you, scribes and Pharisees, hypocrites! ᴿfor ye are like unto whited sepulchres, which indeed appear beautiful outward, but are within full of dead *men's* bones, and of all uncleanness.

28 Even so ye also outwardly appear righteous unto men, but within ye are full of hypocrisy and iniquity.

29 ᴿWoe unto you, scribes and Pharisees, hypocrites! because ye build the tombs of the prophets, and garnish the sepulchres of the righteous,

30 And say, If we had been in the days of our fathers, we would not have been partakers with them in the blood of the prophets.

31 Wherefore ye be witnesses unto yourselves, that ᴿye are the children of them which killed the prophets.

32 ᴿFill ye up then the measure of your fathers.

33 *Ye* serpents, *ye* ᴿgeneration of vipers, how can ye escape the damnation of hell?

34 ᴿWherefore, behold, I send unto you prophets, and wise men, and scribes: and

ᴿ*some* of them ye shall kill and crucify; and ᴿ*some* of them shall ye scourge in your synagogues, and persecute *them* from city to city:

35 ᴿThat upon you may come all the righteous blood shed upon the earth, ᴿfrom the blood of righteous Abel unto ᴿthe blood of Zăch-ă-rī′-ăs son of Băr-ă-chī′-ăs, whom ye slew between the temple and the altar.

36 Verily I say unto you, All these things shall come upon this generation.

Lament over Jerusalem

37 ᴿO Jerusalem, Jerusalem, *thou* that killest the prophets, ᴿand stonest them which are sent unto thee, how often would ᴿI have gathered thy children together, even as a hen gathereth her chickens ᴿunder *her* wings, and ye would not!

38 Behold, your house is left unto you desolate.

39 For I say unto you, Ye shall not see me henceforth, till ye shall say, ᴿBlessed *is* he that cometh in the name of the Lord.

CHAPTER 24

Sufferings before the end

AND ᴿJesus went out, and departed from the temple: and his disciples came to *him* for to shew him the buildings of the temple.

2 And Jesus said unto them, See ye not all these things? verily I say unto you, ᴿThere shall not be left here one stone upon another, that shall not be thrown down.

3 And as he sat upon the mount of Olives, ᴿthe disciples came unto him privately, saying, ᴿTell us, when shall these things be? and what *shall be* the sign of thy coming, and of the end of the world?

4 And Jesus answered and said unto them, ᴿTake heed that no man deceive you.

5 For ᴿmany shall come in my name, saying, I am Christ; ᴿand shall deceive many.

6 And ye shall hear of wars and rumours of wars: see that ye be not troubled: for all *these things* must come to pass, but the end is not yet.

7 For ᴿnation shall rise against nation, and kingdom against kingdom: and there shall be famines, and pestilences, and earthquakes, in divers places.

8 All these *are* the beginning of sorrows.

9 ᴿThen shall they deliver you up to be afflicted, and shall kill you: and ye shall be hated of all nations for my name's sake.

10 And then shall many ᴿbe offended, and shall betray one another, and shall hate one another.

11 And ᴿmany false prophets shall rise, and ᴿshall deceive many.

12 And because iniquity shall abound, the love of many shall wax cold.

13 ᴿBut he that shall endure unto the end, the same shall be saved.

14 And this ᴿgospel of the kingdom ᴿshall be preached in all the world for a witness unto all nations; and then shall the end come.

Tribulation at the end

15 ᴿWhen ye therefore shall see the abomination of desolation, spoken of by ᴿDaniel the prophet, stand in the holy place, (ᴿwhoso readeth, let him understand:)

16 Then let them which be in Judæa flee into the mountains:

17 Let him which is on the housetop not come down to take any thing out of his house:

18 Neither let him which is in the field return back to take his clothes.

19 And ᴿwoe unto them that are with child, and to them that give suck in those days!

20 But pray ye that your flight be not in the winter, neither on the sabbath day:

21 For ᴿthen shall be great tribulation, such as was not since the beginning of the world to this time, no, nor ever shall be.

22 And except those days should be shortened, there should no flesh be saved: ᴿbut for the elect's sake those days shall be shortened.

23 ᴿThen if any man shall say unto you, Lo, here *is* Christ, or there; believe *it* not.

24 For ᴿthere shall arise false Christs, and false prophets, and shall shew great signs and wonders; insomuch that, ᴿif *it were* possible, they shall deceive the very elect.

25 Behold, I have told you before.

26 Wherefore if they shall say unto you, Behold, he is in the desert; go not forth: behold, *he is* in the secret chambers; believe *it* not.

27 ᴿFor as the lightning cometh out of the east, and shineth even unto the west; so shall also the coming of the Son of man be.

28 ᴿFor wheresoever the carcase is, there will the eagles be gathered together.

Coming of the Son of man

29 ᴿImmediately after the tribulation of those days ᴿshall the sun be darkened, and the moon shall not give her light, and the stars shall fall from heaven, and the powers of the heavens shall be shaken:

30 ᴿAnd then shall appear the sign of the Son of man in heaven: ᴿand then shall all the tribes of the earth mourn, ᴿand they shall see the Son of man coming in the clouds of heaven with power and great glory.

31 ᴿAnd he shall send his angels ᴺwith a great sound of a trumpet, and they shall gather together his elect from the four winds, from one end of heaven to the other.

Exhortation to readiness

32 Now learn ᴿa parable of the fig tree; When his branch is yet tender, and putteth forth leaves, ye know that summer is nigh:

33 So likewise ye, when ye shall see all these things, know ᴿthat ᴺit is near, even at the doors.

34 Verily I say unto you, ᴿThis generation shall not pass, till all these things be fulfilled.

35 ᴿHeaven and earth shall pass away, but my words shall not pass away.

36 ᴿBut of that day and hour knoweth no man, no, not the angels of heaven, ᴿbut my Father only.

37 But as the days of Nō'-ē were, so shall also the coming of the Son of man be.

38 ᴿFor as in the days that were before the flood they were eating and drinking, marrying and giving in marriage, until the day that Nō'-ē entered into the ark,

39 And knew not until the flood came, and took them all away; so shall also the coming of the Son of man be.

40 ᴿThen shall two be in the field; the one shall be taken, and the other left.

41 Two women shall be grinding at the mill; the one shall be taken, and the other left.

42 ᴿWatch therefore: for ye know not what hour your Lord doth come.

43 ᴿBut know this, that if the goodman of the house had known in what watch the thief would come, he would have watched, and would not have suffered his house to be broken up.

44 ᴿTherefore be ye also ready: for in such an hour as ye think not the Son of man cometh.

45 ᴿWho then is a faithful and wise servant, whom his lord hath made ruler over his household, to give them meat in due season?

46 ᴿBlessed is that servant, whom his lord when he cometh shall find so doing.

47 Verily I say unto you, That ᴿhe shall make him ruler over all his goods.

48 But and if that evil servant shall say in his heart, My lord delayeth his coming;

49 And shall begin to smite his fellowservants, and to eat and drink with the drunken;

50 The lord of that servant shall come in a day when he looketh not for him, and in an hour that he is not aware of,

51 And shall ᴺcut him asunder, and appoint him his portion with the hypocrites: ᴿthere shall be weeping and gnashing of teeth.

CHAPTER 25

The wise and foolish virgins

THEN shall the kingdom of heaven be likened unto ten virgins, which took their lamps, and went forth to meet ᴿthe bridegroom.

2 ᴿAnd five of them were wise, and five were foolish.

3 They that were foolish took their lamps, and took no oil with them:

4 But the wise took oil in their vessels with their lamps.

5 While the bridegroom tarried, ᴿthey all slumbered and slept.

6 And at midnight ᴿthere was a cry made, Behold, the bridegroom cometh; go ye out to meet him.

7 Then all those virgins arose, and ᴿtrimmed their lamps.

8 And the foolish said unto the wise, Give us of your oil; for our lamps are ᴺgone out.

9 But the wise answered, saying, Not so; lest there be not enough for us and you: but go ye rather to them that sell, and buy for yourselves.

10 And while they went to buy, the bridegroom came; and they that were ready went in with him to the marriage: and ᴿthe door was shut.

11 Afterward came also the other virgins, saying, ᴿLord, Lord, open to us.

12 But he answered and said, Verily I say unto you, ᴿI know you not.

13 ᴿWatch therefore, for ye know neither the day nor the hour wherein the Son of man cometh.

Parable of the talents

14 ᴿFor the kingdom of heaven is ᴿas a man travelling into a far country, who called his own servants, and delivered unto them his goods.

15 And unto one he gave five ᴺtalents, to another two, and to another one; ᴿto every man according to his several ability; and straightway took his journey.

16 Then he that had received the five talents went and traded with the same, and made them other five talents.

17 And likewise he that had received two, he also gained other two.

18 But he that had received one went and digged in the earth, and hid his lord's money.

19 After a long time the lord of those servants cometh, and reckoneth with them.

20 And so he that had received five talents came and brought other five talents, saying, Lord, thou deliveredst unto me five talents:

behold, I have gained beside them five talents more.

21 His lord said unto him, Well done, *thou* good and faithful servant: thou hast been faithful over a few things, ᴿI will make thee ruler over many things: enter thou into ᴿthe joy of thy lord.

22 He also that had received two talents came and said, Lord, thou deliveredst unto me two talents: behold, I have gained two other talents beside them.

23 His lord said unto him, ᴿWell done, good and faithful servant; thou hast been faithful over a few things, I will make thee ruler over many things: enter thou into the joy of thy lord.

24 Then he which had received the one talent came and said, Lord, I knew thee that thou art an hard man, reaping where thou hast not sown, and gathering where thou hast not strawed:

25 And I was afraid, and went and hid thy talent in the earth: lo, *there* thou hast *that is* thine.

26 His lord answered and said unto him, *Thou* wicked and slothful servant, thou knewest that I reap where I sowed not, and gather where I have not strawed:

27 Thou oughtest therefore to have put my money to the exchangers, and *then* at my coming I should have received mine own with usury.

28 Take therefore the talent from him, and give *it* unto him which hath ten talents.

29 ᴿFor unto every one that hath shall be given, and he shall have abundance: but from him that hath not shall be taken away even that which he hath.

30 And cast ye the unprofitable servant ᴿinto outer darkness: there shall be weeping and gnashing of teeth.

Parable of the last judgment

31 ᴿWhen the Son of man shall come in his glory, and all the holy angels with him, then shall he sit upon the throne of his glory:

32 And ᴿbefore him shall be gathered all nations: and ᴿhe shall separate them one from another, as a shepherd divideth *his* sheep from the goats:

33 And he shall set the sheep on his right hand, but the goats on the left.

34 Then shall the King say unto them on his right hand, Come, ye blessed of my Father, ᴿinherit the kingdom ᴿprepared for you from the foundation of the world:

35 ᴿFor I was an hungred, and ye gave me meat: I was thirsty, and ye gave me drink: ᴿI was a stranger, and ye took me in:

36 ᴿNaked, and ye clothed me: I was sick, and ye visited me: ᴿI was in prison, and ye came unto me.

37 Then shall the righteous answer him, saying, Lord, when saw we thee an hungred, and fed *thee?* or thirsty, and gave *thee* drink?

38 When saw we thee a stranger, and took *thee* in? or naked, and clothed *thee?*

39 Or when saw we thee sick, or in prison, and came unto thee?

40 And the King shall answer and say unto them, Verily I say unto you, ᴿInasmuch as ye have done *it* unto one of the least of these my brethren, ye have done *it* unto me.

41 Then shall he say also unto them on the left hand, ᴿDepart from me, ye cursed, ᴿinto everlasting fire, prepared for ᴿthe devil and his angels:

42 For I was an hungred, and ye gave me no meat: I was thirsty, and ye gave me no drink:

43 I was a stranger, and ye took me not in: naked, and ye clothed me not: sick, and in prison, and ye visited me not.

44 Then shall they also answer him, saying, Lord, when saw we thee an hungred, or athirst, or a stranger, or naked, or sick, or in prison, and did not minister unto thee?

45 Then shall he answer them, saying, Verily I say unto you, ᴿInasmuch as ye did *it* not to one of the least of these, ye did *it* not to me.

46 And ᴿthese shall go away into everlasting punishment: but the righteous into life eternal.

CHAPTER 26

Plot to kill Jesus

AND it came to pass, when Jesus had finished all these sayings, he said unto his disciples,

2 ᴿYe know that after two days is *the feast of* the passover, and the Son of man is betrayed to be crucified.

3 ᴿThen assembled together the chief priests, and the scribes, and the elders of the people, unto the palace of the high priest, who was called Cāi'-ȧ-phȧs,

4 And consulted that they might take Jesus by subtilty, and kill *him*.

5 But they said, Not on the feast *day*, lest there be an uproar among the people.

The anointing at Bethany

6 ᴿNow when Jesus was in ᴿBethany, in the house of Simon the leper,

7 There came unto him a woman having an alabaster box of very precious ointment, and poured it on his head, as he sat *at meat*.

8 ᴿBut when his disciples saw *it*, they had

CHAP. 25

AD 33

21 ver. 34, 46
ch. 24:47
Luke 12:44
& 22:29, 30
21 2 Tim. 2:12
Heb. 12:2
1 Pet. 1:8
23 ver. 21
29 ch. 13:12
Mark 4:25
Luke 8:18
& 10:26
John 15:2
30 ch. 8:12
& 24:51
31 Zech. 14:5
ch. 16:27
& 19:28
Mark 8:38
Acts 1:11
1 Thes. 4:16
2 Thes. 1:7
Jude 14
Rev. 1:7
32 Rom. 14:10
2 Cor. 5:10
Rev. 20:12
32 Ezek. 20:38
34 Rom. 8:17
1 Pet. 1:4, 9
& 3:9
Rev. 21:7
34 ch. 20:23
Mark 10:40
1 Cor. 2:9
Heb. 11:16
35 Is. 58:7
Ezek. 18:7
Jas. 1:27
35 Heb. 13:2
3 John 5

Jas. 2:15, 16   **36**
2 Tim. 1:16   **36**
Prov. 14:31   **40**
& 19:17
ch. 10:42
Mark 9:41
Heb. 6:10
Ps. 6:8   **41**
ch. 7:23
Luke 13:27
ch. 13:40, 42   **41**
2 Pet. 2:4   **41**
Jude 6
Prov. 14:31   **45**
& 17:5
Zech. 2:8
Acts 9:5
Dan. 12:2   **46**
John 5:29
Rom. 2:7, etc.

CHAP. 26

AD 33

Mark 14:1   **2**
Luke 22:1
John 13:1
Ps. 2:2   **3**
John 11:47
Acts 4:25, etc.
Mark 14:3   **6**
John 11:1, 2
& 12:3
ch. 21:17
John 12:4   **8**

indignation, saying, To what purpose *is* this waste?

9 For this ointment might have been sold for much, and given to the poor.

10 When Jesus understood *it,* he said unto them, Why trouble ye the woman? for she hath wrought a good work upon me.

11 [R]For ye have the poor always with you; but [R]me ye have not always.

12 For in that she hath poured this ointment on my body, she did *it* for my burial.

13 Verily I say unto you, Wheresoever this gospel shall be preached in the whole world, *there* shall also this, that this woman hath done, be told for a memorial of her.

The treachery of Judas

14 [R]Then one of the twelve, called [R]Judas Iscariot, went unto the chief priests,

15 And said *unto them,* [R]What will ye give me, and I will deliver him unto you? And they covenanted with him for thirty pieces of silver.

16 And from that time he sought opportunity to betray him.

The last supper

17 [R]Now the first *day* of the *feast of* unleavened bread the disciples came to Jesus, saying unto him, Where wilt thou that we prepare for thee to eat the passover?

18 And he said, Go into the city to such a man, and say unto him, The Master saith, My time is at hand; I will keep the passover at thy house with my disciples.

19 And the disciples did as Jesus had appointed them; and they made ready the passover.

20 [R]Now when the even was come, he sat down with the twelve.

21 And as they did eat, he said, Verily I say unto you, that one of you shall betray me.

22 And they were exceeding sorrowful, and began every one of them to say unto him, Lord, is it I?

23 And he answered and said, [R]He that dippeth *his* hand with me in the dish, the same shall betray me.

24 The Son of man goeth [R]as it is written of him: but [R]woe unto that man by whom the Son of man is betrayed! it had been good for that man if he had not been born.

25 Then Judas, which betrayed him, answered and said, Master, is it I? He said unto him, Thou hast said.

26 [R]And as they were eating, [R]Jesus took bread, and [N]blessed *it,* and brake *it,* and gave *it* to the disciples, and said, Take, eat; [R]this is my body.

27 And he took the cup, and gave thanks,

and gave *it* to them, saying, [R]Drink ye all of it;

28 For [R]this is my blood [R]of the new testament, which is shed [R]for many for the remission of sins.

29 But [R]I say unto you, I will not drink henceforth of this fruit of the vine, [R]until that day when I drink it new with you in my Father's kingdom.

Peter's denial foretold

30 [R]And when they had sung an [N]hymn, they went out into the mount of Olives.

31 Then saith Jesus unto them, [R]All ye shall [R]be offended because of me this night: for it is written, [R]I will smite the shepherd, and the sheep of the flock shall be scattered abroad.

32 But after I am risen again, [R]I will go before you into Galilee.

33 Peter answered and said unto him, Though all *men* shall be offended because of thee, *yet* will I never be offended.

34 Jesus said unto him, [R]Verily I say unto thee, That this night, before the cock crow, thou shalt deny me thrice.

35 Peter said unto him, Though I should die with thee, yet will I not deny thee. Likewise also said all the disciples.

Jesus in Gethsemane

36 [R]Then cometh Jesus with them unto a place called Găth-sĕm′-ă-nē, and saith unto the disciples, Sit ye here, while I go and pray yonder.

37 And he took with him Peter and [R]the two sons of Zĕb′-ĕ-dĕe, and began to be sorrowful and very heavy.

38 Then saith he unto them, [R]My soul is exceeding sorrowful, even unto death: tarry ye here, and watch with me.

39 And he went a little farther, and fell on his face, and [R]prayed, saying, [R]O my Father, if it be possible, [R]let this cup pass from me: nevertheless [R]not as I will, but as thou *wilt.*

40 And he cometh unto the disciples, and findeth them asleep, and saith unto Peter, What, could ye not watch with me one hour?

41 [R]Watch and pray, that ye enter not into temptation: the spirit indeed *is* willing, but the flesh *is* weak.

42 He went away again the second time, and prayed, saying, O my Father, if this cup may not pass away from me, except I drink it, thy will be done.

43 And he came and found them asleep again: for their eyes were heavy.

44 And he left them, and went away again, and prayed the third time, saying the same words.

CHAP. **26**
AD 33
11 Deut. 15:11
John 12:8
11 See ch. 18:20
& 28:20
John 13:33
& 14:19
& 16:5, 28
& 17:11
14 Mark 14:10
Luke 22:3
John 13:2, 30
14 ch. 10:4
15 Zech. 11:12
ch. 27:3
17 Ex. 12:6, 18
Mark 14:12
Luke 22:7
20 Mark 14:17-21
Luke 22:14
John 13:21
23 Ps. 41:9
Luke 22:21
John 13:18
24 Ps. 22
Dan. 9:26
Mark 9:12
Luke 24:25, 26, 46
Acts 17:2, 3
& 26:22, 23
1 Cor. 15:3
24 John 17:12
26 Mark 14:22
Luke 22:19
26 1 Cor. 11:23
26 Many Greek copies have, *gave thanks:* See Mark 6:41
26 1 Cor. 10:16

Mark 14:23   27
See Ex. 24:8   28
Lev. 17:11
Jer. 31:31   28
ch. 20:28   28
Rom. 5:15
Heb. 9:22
Mark 14:26   29
Luke 22:18
Acts 10:41   29
Mark 14:26   30
Or, *psalm*   30
Mark 14:27   31
John 16:32
ch. 11:6   31
Zech. 13:7   31
ch. 28:7, 10   32
Mark 14:28
& 16:7
Mark 14:30   34
Luke 22:34
John 13:38
Mark 14:32-35   36
Luke 22:39
John 18:1
ch. 4:21   37
John 12:27   38
Mark 14:36   39
Luke 22:42
Heb. 5:7
John 12:27   39
ch. 20:22   39
John 5:30   39
& 6:38
Phil. 2:8
Mark 14:33   41
& 14:38
Luke 22:40, 46
Eph. 6:18

45 Then cometh he to his disciples, and saith unto them, Sleep on now, and take *your* rest: behold, the hour is at hand, and the Son of man is betrayed into the hands of sinners.

46 Rise, let us be going: behold, he is at hand that doth betray me.

Jesus betrayed and arrested

47 And ᴿwhile he yet spake, lo, Judas, one of the twelve, came, and with him a great multitude with swords and staves, from the chief priests and elders of the people.

48 Now he that betrayed him gave them a sign, saying, Whomsoever I shall kiss, that same is he: hold him fast.

49 And forthwith he came to Jesus, and said, Hail, master; ᴿand kissed him.

50 And Jesus said unto him, ᴿFriend, wherefore art thou come? Then came they, and laid hands on Jesus, and took him.

51 And, behold, ᴿone of them which were with Jesus stretched out *his* hand, and drew his sword, and struck a servant of the high priest's, and smote off his ear.

52 Then said Jesus unto him, Put up again thy sword into his place: ᴿfor all they that take the sword shall perish with the sword.

53 Thinkest thou that I cannot now pray to my Father, and he shall presently give me ᴿmore that twelve legions of angels?

54 But how then shall the scriptures be fulfilled, ᴿthat thus it must be?

55 In that same hour said Jesus to the multitudes, Are ye come out as against a thief with swords and staves for to take me? I sat daily with you teaching in the temple, and ye laid no hold on me.

56 But all this was done, that the ᴿscriptures of the prophets might be fulfilled. Then ᴿall the disciples forsook him, and fled.

Jesus before Caiaphas

57 ᴿAnd they that had laid hold on Jesus led *him* away to Cāi'-ă-phăs the high priest, where the scribes and the elders were assembled.

58 But Peter followed him afar off unto the high priest's palace, and went in, and sat with the servants, to see the end.

59 Now the chief priests, and elders, and all the council, sought false witness against Jesus, to put him to death;

60 But found none: yea, though ᴿmany false witnesses came, *yet* found they none. At the last came ᴿtwo false witnesses,

61 And said, This *fellow* said, ᴿI am able to destroy the temple of God, and to build it in three days.

62 ᴿAnd the high priest arose, and said unto him, Answerest thou nothing? what

is it which these witness against thee?

63 But ᴿJesus held his peace. And the high priest answered and said unto him, ᴿI adjure thee by the living God, that thou tell us whether thou be the Christ, the Son of God.

64 Jesus saith unto him, Thou hast said: nevertheless I say unto you, ᴿHereafter shall ye see the Son of man ᴿsitting on the right hand of power, and coming in the clouds of heaven.

65 ᴿThen the high priest rent his clothes, saying, He hath spoken blasphemy; what further need have we of witnesses? behold, now ye have heard his blasphemy.

66 What think ye? They answered and said, ᴿHe is guilty of death.

67 ᴿThen did they spit in his face, and buffeted him; and ᴿothers smote *him* with ᴺthe palms of their hands,

68 Saying, ᴿProphesy unto us, thou Christ, Who is he that smote thee?

Peter's denial of Jesus

69 ᴿNow Peter sat without in the palace: and a damsel came unto him, saying, Thou also wast with Jesus of Galilee.

70 But he denied before *them* all, saying, I know not what thou sayest.

71 And when he was gone out into the porch, another *maid* saw him, and said unto them that were there, This *fellow* was also with Jesus of Nazareth.

72 And again he denied with an oath, I do not know the man.

73 And after a while came unto *him* they that stood by, and said to Peter, Surely thou also art *one* of them; for thy ᴿspeech bewrayeth thee.

74 Then ᴿbegan he to curse and to swear, *saying,* I know not the man. And immediately the cock crew.

75 And Peter remembered the word of Jesus, which said unto him, ᴿBefore the cock crow, thou shalt deny me thrice. And he went out, and wept bitterly.

CHAPTER 27

Jesus delivered to Pilate

WHEN the morning was come, ᴿall the chief priests and elders of the people took counsel against Jesus to put him to death:

2 And when they had bound him, they led *him* away, and ᴿdelivered him to Pontius Pilate the governor.

The death of Judas

3 ᴿThen Judas, which had betrayed him, when he saw that he was condemned, repented

CHAP. 26	
AD 33	
47 Mark 14:43	
Luke 22:47	
John 18:3	
Acts 1:16	
49 2 Sam. 20:9	
50 Ps. 41:9	
& 55:13	
51 John 18:10	
52 Gen. 9:6	
Rev. 13:10	
53 2 Ki. 6:17	
Dan. 7:10	
54 ver. 24	
Is. 53:7, etc.	
Luke 24:25, 44, 46	
56 Lam. 4:20	
56 See John 18:15	
57 Mark 14:53	
Luke 22:54	
John 18:12, 13, 24	
60 Ps. 27:12	
& 35:11	
Mark 14:55	
Acts 6:13	
60 Deut. 19:15	
61 ch. 27:40	
John 2:19	
62 Mark 14:60	

Is. 53:7	63
ch. 27:12	63
Lev. 5:1	63
1 Sam. 14:24, 26	
Dan. 7:13	64
ch. 16:27	
& 24:30	
& 25:31	
Luke 21:27	
John 1:51	
Rom. 14:10	
1 Thes. 4:16	
Rev. 1:7	
Ps. 110:1	64
Acts 7:55	
2 Ki. 18:37	65
Lev. 24:16	66
John 19:7	
Is. 50:6	67
& 53:3	
ch. 27:30	
Luke 22:63	67
Or, *rods*	67
Mark 14:65	68
Luke 22:64	
Mark 14:66	69
Luke 22:55	
John 18:16, 17, 25	
Luke 22:59	73
Mark 14:71	74
ver. 34	75
Luke 22:61	
John 13:38	

CHAP. 27	
AD 33	
Ps. 2:2	1
Mark 15:1	
Luke 22:66	
& 23:1	
John 18:28	
ch. 20:19	2
Acts 3:13	
ch. 26:14	3

himself, and brought again the thirty pieces of silver to the chief priests and elders,

4 Saying, I have sinned in that I have betrayed the innocent blood. And they said, What *is that* to us? see thou *to that.*

5 And he cast down the pieces of silver in the temple, ᴿand departed, and went and hanged himself.

6 And the chief priests took the silver pieces, and said, It is not lawful for to put them into the treasury, because it is the price of blood.

7 And they took counsel, and bought with them the potter's field, to bury strangers in.

8 Wherefore that field was called, ᴿThe field of blood, unto this day.

9 Then was fulfilled that which was spoken by Jeremy the prophet, saying, ᴿAnd they took the thirty pieces of silver, the price of him that was valued, ᴺwhom they of the children of Israel did value;

10 And gave them for the potter's field, as the Lord appointed me.

Jesus before Pilate

11 And Jesus stood before the governor: ᴿand the governor asked him, saying, Art thou the King of the Jews? And Jesus said unto him, ᴿThou sayest.

12 And when he was accused of the chief priests and elders, ᴿhe answered nothing.

13 Then said Pilate unto him, ᴿHearest thou not how many things they witness against thee?

14 And he answered him to never a word; insomuch that the governor marvelled greatly.

15 ᴿNow at *that* feast the governor was wont to release unto the people a prisoner, whom they would.

16 And they had then a notable prisoner, called Bär-ăb′-băs.

17 Therefore when they were gathered together, Pilate said unto them, Whom will ye that I release unto you? Bär-ăb′-băs, or Jesus which is called Christ?

18 For he knew that for envy they had delivered him.

19 When he was set down on the judgment seat, his wife sent unto him, saying, Have thou nothing to do with that just man: for I have suffered many things this day in a dream because of him.

20 ᴿBut the chief priests and elders persuaded the multitude that they should ask Bär-ăb′-băs, and destroy Jesus.

21 The governor answered and said unto them, Whether of the twain will ye that I release unto you? They said, Bär-ăb′-băs.

22 Pilate saith unto them, What shall I do then with Jesus which is called Christ? *They* all say unto him, Let him be crucified.

23 And the governor said, Why, what evil hath he done? But they cried out the more, saying, Let him be crucified.

24 When Pilate saw that he could prevail nothing, but *that* rather a tumult was made, he ᴿtook water, and washed *his* hands before the multitude, saying, I am innocent of the blood of this just person: see ye *to it.*

25 Then answered all the people, and said, ᴿHis blood *be* on us, and on our children.

26 Then released he Bär-ăb′-băs unto them: and when ᴿhe had scourged Jesus, he delivered *him* to be crucified.

Jesus mocked by the soldiers

27 ᴿThen the soldiers of the governor took Jesus into the ᴺcommon hall, and gathered unto him the whole band *of soldiers.*

28 And they stripped him, and ᴿput on him a scarlet robe.

29 ᴿAnd when they had plaited a crown of thorns, they put *it* upon his head, and a reed in his right hand: and they bowed the knee before him, and mocked him, saying, Hail, King of the Jews!

30 And ᴿthey spit upon him, and took the reed, and smote him on the head.

31 And after that they had mocked him, they took the robe off from him, and put his own raiment on him, ᴿand led him away to crucify *him.*

The crucifixion

32 ᴿAnd as they came out, ᴿthey found a man of Çȳ-rē′-nē, Simon by name: him they compelled to bear his cross.

33 ᴿAnd when they were come unto a place called Gŏl′-gŏ-thă, that is to say, a place of a skull,

34 ᴿThey gave him vinegar to drink mingled with gall: and when he had tasted *thereof,* he would not drink.

35 ᴿAnd they crucified him, and parted his garments, casting lots: that it might be fulfilled which was spoken by the prophet, ᴿThey parted my garments among them, and upon my vesture did they cast lots.

36 ᴿAnd sitting down they watched him there;

37 And ᴿset up over his head his accusation written, THIS IS JESUS THE KING OF THE JEWS.

38 ᴿThen were there two thieves crucified with him, one on the right hand, and another on the left.

39 And ᴿthey that passed by reviled him, wagging their heads,

CHAP. 27
AD 33
5 2 Sam. 17:23
Acts 1:18
8 Acts 1:19
9 Zech. 11:12
9 Or, *whom they bought of the children of Israel*
11 Mark 15:2
Luke 23:3
John 18:33
11 John 18:37
1 Tim. 6:13
12 ch. 26:63
John 19:9
13 ch. 26:62
John 19:10
15 Mark 15:6
Luke 23:17
John 18:39
20 Mark 15:11
Luke 23:18
John 18:40
Acts 3:14

Deut. 21:6   24
Deut. 19:10   25
Josh. 2:19
2 Sam. 1:16
1 Ki. 2:32
Acts 5:28
Is. 53:5   26
Mark 15:15
Luke 23:16, 24, 25
John 19:1, 16
Mark 15:16   27
John 19:2
Or, *governor's house*   27
Luke 23:11   28
Ps. 69:19   29
Is. 53:3
Is. 50:6   30
ch. 26:67
Is. 53:7   31
Num. 15:35   32
1 Ki. 21:13
Acts 7:58
Heb. 13:12
Mark 15:21   32
Luke 23:26
Mark 15:22   33
Luke 23:33
John 19:17
See ver. 48   34
Ps. 69:21
Mark 15:24   35
Luke 23:34
John 19:24
Ps. 22:18   35
ver. 54   36
Mark 15:26   37
Luke 23:38
John 19:19
Is. 53:12   38
Mark 15:27
Luke 23:32, 33
John 19:18
Ps. 22:7   39
& 109:25
Mark 15:29
Luke 23:35

40 And saying, ᴿThou that destroyest the temple, and buildest *it* in three days, save thyself. ᴿIf thou be the Son of God, come down from the cross.

41 Likewise also the chief priests mocking *him,* with the scribes and elders, said,

42 He saved others; himself he cannot save. If he be the King of Israel, let him now come down from the cross, and we will believe him.

43 ᴿHe trusted in God; let him deliver him now, if he will have him: for he said, I am the Son of God.

44 ᴿThe thieves also, which were crucified with him, cast the same in his teeth.

The death of Jesus

45 ᴿNow from the sixth hour there was darkness over all the land unto the ninth hour.

46 And about the ninth hour ᴿJesus cried with a loud voice, saying, Ē'-lī, Ē'-lī, lä'-mä sȧ-bǎch'-thȧ-nī? that is to say, ᴿMy God, my God, why hast thou forsaken me?

47 Some of them that stood there, when they heard *that,* said, This *man* calleth for Ē-lī'-ȧs.

48 And straightway one of them ran, and took a sponge, ᴿand filled *it* with vinegar, and put *it* on a reed, and gave him to drink.

49 The rest said, Let be, let us see whether Ē-lī'-ȧs will come to save him.

50 ᴿJesus, when he had cried again with a loud voice, yielded up the ghost.

The centurion's confession

51 And, behold, ᴿthe veil of the temple was rent in twain from the top to the bottom; and the earth did quake, and the rocks rent;

52 And the graves were opened; and many bodies of the saints which slept arose,

53 And came out of the graves after his resurrection, and went into the holy city, and appeared unto many.

54 ᴿNow when the centurion, and they that were with him, watching Jesus, saw the earthquake, and those things that were done, they feared greatly, saying, Truly this was the Son of God.

The burial in Joseph's tomb

55 And many women were there beholding afar off, ᴿwhich followed Jesus from Galilee, ministering unto him:

56 ᴿAmong which was Mary Mǎg'-dȧ-lēne, and Mary the mother of James and Jō'-sės, and the mother of Zěb'-ě-dēe's children.

57 ᴿWhen the even was come, there came a rich man of Ǎr-ĭm-ȧ-thæ'-ȧ, named Joseph, who also himself was Jesus' disciple:

58 He went to Pilate, and begged the body

CHAP. 27	
AD 33	
40 ch. 26:61	
John 2:19	
40 ch. 26:63	
43 Ps. 22:8	
44 Mark 15:32	
Luke 23:39	
45 Amos 8:9	
Mark 15:33	
Luke 23:44	
46 Heb. 5:7	
46 Ps. 22:1	
48 Ps. 69:21	
Mark 15:36	
Luke 23:36	
John 19:29	
50 Mark 15:37	
Luke 23:46	
51 Ex. 26:31	
2 Chr. 3:14	
Mark 15:38	
Luke 23:45	
54 ver. 36	
Mark 15:39	
Luke 23:47	
55 Luke 8:2, 3	
56 Mark 15:40	
57 Mark 15:42	
Luke 23:50	
John 19:38	

Is. 53:9	60
ch. 16:21	63
& 17:23	
& 20:19	
& 26:61	
Mark 8:31	
& 10:34	
Luke 9:22	
& 13:33	
& 24:6, 7	
John 2:19	
Dan. 6:17	66

CHAP. 28	
AD 33	
Mark 16:1	1
Luke 24:1	
John 20:1	
ch. 27:56	1
Or, *had been*	2
See Mark 16:5	2
Luke 24:4	
John 20:12	
Dan. 10:6	3
ch. 12:40	6
& 16:21	
& 17:23	
& 20:19	
ch. 26:32	7
Mark 16:7	
See Mark 16:9	9
John 20:14	

of Jesus. Then Pilate commanded the body to be delivered.

59 And when Joseph had taken the body, he wrapped it in a clean linen cloth,

60 And ᴿlaid it in his own new tomb, which he had hewn out in the rock: and he rolled a great stone to the door of the sepulchre, and departed.

61 And there was Mary Mǎg'-dȧ-lēne, and the other Mary, sitting over against the sepulchre.

The tomb sealed and guarded

62 Now the next day, that followed the day of the preparation, the chief priests and Pharisees came together unto Pilate,

63 Saying, Sir, we remember that that deceiver said, while he was yet alive, ᴿAfter three days I will rise again.

64 Command therefore that the sepulchre be made sure until the third day, lest his disciples come by night, and steal him away, and say unto the people, He is risen from the dead: so the last error shall be worse than the first.

65 Pilate said unto them, Ye have a watch: go your way, make *it* as sure as ye can.

66 So they went, and made the sepulchre sure, ᴿsealing the stone, and setting a watch.

CHAPTER 28

The resurrection of Christ

IN the ᴿend of the sabbath, as it began to dawn toward the first *day* of the week, came Mary Mǎg'-dȧ-lēne ᴿand the other Mary to see the sepulchre.

2 And, behold, ᴺwas a great earthquake: for ᴿthe angel of the Lord descended from heaven, and came and rolled back the stone from the door, and sat upon it.

3 ᴿHis countenance was like lightning, and his raiment white as snow:

4 And for fear of him the keepers did shake, and became as dead *men.*

5 And the angel answered and said unto the women, Fear not ye: for I know that ye seek Jesus, which was crucified.

6 He is not here: for he is risen, ᴿas he said. Come, see the place where the Lord lay.

7 And go quickly, and tell his disciples that he is risen from the dead; and, behold, ᴿhe goeth before you into Galilee; there shall ye see him: lo, I have told you.

8 And they departed quickly from the sepulchre with fear and great joy; and did run to bring his disciples word.

9 And as they went to tell his disciples, behold, ᴿJesus met them, saying, All hail. And

they came and held him by the feet, and worshipped him.

10 Then said Jesus unto them, Be not afraid: go tell ^Rmy brethren that they go into Galilee, and there shall they see me.

The Pharisees bribe the soldiers

11 Now when they were going, behold, some of the watch came into the city, and shewed unto the chief priests all the things that were done.

12 And when they were assembled with the elders, and had taken counsel, they gave large money unto the soldiers,

13 Saying, Say ye, His disciples came by night, and stole him *away* while we slept.

14 And if this come to the governor's ears, we will persuade him, and secure you.

15 So they took the money, and did as they

CHAP. 28
AD 33
10 See John 20:17
Rom. 8:29
Heb. 2:11
ver. 7   **16**
ch. 26:32
Dan. 7:13, 14   **18**
ch. 11:27
Luke 1:32
John 3:35
Acts 2:36
Rom. 14:9
1 Cor. 15:27
Eph. 1:10, 21
Mark 16:15   **19**
Is. 52:10   **19**
Luke 24:47
Acts 2:38, 39
Rom. 10:18
Or, *make*   **19**
disciples, or,
Christians of
all nations
Acts 2:42   **20**

were taught: and this saying is commonly reported among the Jews until this day.

The great commission

16 Then the eleven disciples went away into Galilee, into a mountain ^Rwhere Jesus had appointed them.

17 And when they saw him, they worshipped him: but some doubted.

18 And Jesus came and spake unto them, saying, ^RAll power is given unto me in heaven and in earth.

19 ^RGo ye therefore, and ^Rteach^N all nations, baptizing them in the name of the Father, and of the Son, and of the Holy Ghost:

20 ^RTeaching them to observe all things whatsoever I have commanded you: and, lo, I am with you alway, *even* unto the end of the world. Ä'-mĕn.

THE GOSPEL ACCORDING TO
ST. MARK

There is abundant early Christian testimony that the second Gospel was written by Mark, based on the preaching of Peter, and originated in Rome. Although "Marcus" was a common name, the comments of the early Church Fathers indicate that the author was to be identified with "John Mark," the nephew of Barnabas and associate of Peter. That the figure of Peter stands behind the Gospel suggests why it was accepted as canonical; Mark was considered a channel for the apostolic proclamation. That it was written in Rome, and further, that it was directed to Gentile Christians, is substantiated by its Latin forms of expression, its infrequent use of the Old Testament, and its repeated explanations of Jewish customs and expressions. Mark's Gospel is a gospel of action. A general air of breathlessness and a crudity of style dominate. It presents Jesus in dramatic episodes climaxing in the cross, with the teachings of the Lord occupying a minor role. It is a gospel, a proclamation of the good news of divine redemption; not

strictly a biography and not primarily concerned with chronology. Yet the fact that both Matthew and Luke probably used it as a framework for their own presentations speaks strongly for its historical authenticity, its basic chronological reliability, and its apostolic authority. Since its eschatology (Mark 13) is considered general and its doctrinal content elemental, most scholars date the Gospel about A.D. 65–60. Others, arguing for a pre-A.D. 70 date for Luke–Acts and accepting the priority of Mark among the Synoptic Gospels, date it in the 50's or early 60's.

OUTLINE OF THE BOOK:
  I. The Period of Preparation   1:1–13
 II. The Galilean Ministry   1:14–9:50
III. The Perean Ministry   10:1–52
IV. Passion Week   11:1–15:47
 V. The Resurrection   16:1–20

CHAPTER 1

The preaching of John the Baptist

THE beginning of the gospel of Jesus Christ, ^Rthe Son of God;

2 As it is written in the prophets, ^RBehold, I send my messenger before thy face, which shall prepare thy way before thee.

3 ^RThe voice of one crying in the wilderness, Prepare ye the way of the Lord, make his paths straight.

4 ^RJohn did baptize in the wilderness, and preach the baptism of repentance ^Nfor the remission of sins.

5 ^RAnd there went out unto him all the land of Judæa, and they of Jerusalem, and were all

CHAP. 1
AD 26
1 Mat. 14:33
Luke 1:35
2 Mal. 3:1
Mat. 11:10
Luke 7:27
3 Is. 40:3
Mat. 3:3
Luke 3:4
4 Mat. 3:1
Luke 3:3
4 Or, *unto*
5 Mat. 3:5
Mat. 3:4   **6**
Mat. 3:11   **7**
Acts 13:25
Acts 1:5 &   **8**
11:16 & 19:4
Is. 44:3   **8**
Acts 2:4 & 10:45
Mat. 3:13   **9**

baptized of him in the river of Jordan, confessing their sins.

6 And John was ^Rclothed with camel's hair, and with a girdle of a skin about his loins; and he did eat locusts and wild honey;

7 And preached, saying, ^RThere cometh one mightier than I after me, the latchet of whose shoes I am not worthy to stoop down and unloose.

8 ^RI indeed have baptized you with water: but he shall baptize you ^Rwith the Holy Ghost.

The baptism of Jesus

9 ^RAnd it came to pass in those days, that Jesus came from Nazareth of Galilee, and was baptized of John in Jordan.

10 [R]And straightway coming up out of the water, he saw the heavens [N]opened, and the Spirit like a dove descending upon him:

11 And there came a voice from heaven, *saying,* [R]Thou art my beloved Son, in whom I am well pleased.

The temptation of Jesus

12 [R]And immediately the Spirit driveth him into the wilderness.

13 And he was there in the wilderness forty days, tempted of Satan; and was with the wild beasts; [R]and the angels ministered unto him.

Jesus begins His ministry

14 [R]Now after that John was put in prison, Jesus came into Galilee, [R]preaching the gospel of the kingdom of God,

15 And saying, [R]The time is fulfilled, and [R]the kingdom of God is at hand: repent ye, and believe the gospel.

Call of the first disciples

16 [R]Now as he walked by the sea of Galilee, he saw Simon and Andrew his brother casting a net into the sea: for they were fishers.

17 And Jesus said unto them, Come ye after me, and I will make you to become fishers of men.

18 And straightway [R]they forsook their nets, and followed him.

19 [R]And when he had gone a little farther thence, he saw James the *son* of Zĕb'-ĕ-dĕe, and John his brother, who also were in the ship mending their nets.

20 And straightway he called them: and they left their father Zĕb'-ĕ-dĕe in the ship with the hired servants, and went after him.

The unclean spirit cast out

21 [R]And they went into Că-pĕr'-nă-ŭm; and straightway on the sabbath day he entered into the synagogue, and taught.

22 [R]And they were astonished at his doctrine: for he taught them as one that had authority, and not as the scribes.

23 And there was in their synagogue a man with an unclean spirit; and he cried out,

24 Saying, Let *us* alone; [R]what have we to do with thee, thou Jesus of Nazareth? art thou come to destroy us? I know thee who thou art, the Holy One of God.

25 And Jesus [R]rebuked him, saying, Hold thy peace, and come out of him.

26 And when the unclean spirit [R]had torn him, and cried with a loud voice, he came out of him.

CHAP. 1
AD 26
10 Mat. 3:16
John 1:32
10 Or, *cloven,*
or, *rent*
11 Ps. 2:7
Mat. 3:17
ch. 9:7
12 Mat. 4:1
13 Mat. 4:11
14 Mat. 4:12
14 Mat. 4:23
15 Dan. 9:25
Gal. 4:4
Eph. 1:10
15 Mat. 3:2
& 4:17
16 Mat. 4:18
Luke 5:4
18 Mat. 19:27
Luke 4:40
21 Mat. 4:13
Luke 4:31
22 Mat. 7:28
24 Mat. 8:29
25 ver. 34
26 ch. 9:20

Mat. 8:14   **29**
Luke 4:38
Mat. 8:16   **32**
Luke 4:40
ch. 3:12   **34**
Luke 4:41
See Acts 16:17, **18**
Or, *to say that* **34**
they knew him
Luke 4:42   **35**
Luke 4:43   **38**
Is. 61:1   **38**
John 16:28
& 17:4
Mat. 4:23   **39**
Luke 4:44
Mat. 8:2   **40**
Luke 5:12

27 And they were all amazed, insomuch that they questioned among themselves, saying, What thing is this? what new doctrine *is* this? for with authority commandeth he even the unclean spirits, and they do obey him.

28 And immediately his fame spread abroad throughout all the region round about Galilee.

Healing Peter's mother in law

29 [R]And forthwith, when they were come out of the synagogue, they entered into the house of Simon and Andrew, with James and John.

30 But Simon's wife's mother lay sick of a fever, and anon they tell him of her.

31 And he came and took her by the hand, and lifted her up; and immediately the fever left her, and she ministered unto them.

Healings at sunset

32 [R]And at even, when the sun did set, they brought unto him all that were diseased, and them that were possessed with devils.

33 And all the city was gathered together at the door.

34 And he healed many that were sick of divers diseases, and cast out many devils; and [R]suffered not the devils [N]to speak, because they knew him.

Jesus prays and preaches

35 And [R]in the morning, rising up a great while before day, he went out, and departed into a solitary place, and there prayed.

36 And Simon and they that were with him followed after him.

37 And when they had found him, they said unto him, All *men* seek for thee.

38 And he said unto them, [R]Let us go into the next towns, that I may preach there also: for [R]therefore came I forth.

39 [R]And he preached in their synagogues throughout all Galilee and cast out devils.

Cleansing the leper

40 [R]And there came a leper to him, beseeching him, and kneeling down to him, and saying unto him, If thou wilt, thou canst make me clean.

41 And Jesus, moved with compassion, put forth *his* hand, and touched him, and saith unto him, I will; be thou clean.

42 And as soon as he had spoken, immediately the leprosy departed from him, and he was cleansed.

43 And he straitly charged him, and forthwith sent him away;

44 And saith unto him, See thou say nothing to any man: but go thy way, shew thyself to the priest, and offer for thy cleansing those things ᴿwhich Moses commanded, for a testimony unto them.

45 ᴿBut he went out, and began to publish *it* much, and to blaze abroad the matter, insomuch that Jesus could no more openly enter into the city, but was without in desert places: ᴿand they came to him from every quarter.

CHAPTER 2

The paralytic forgiven and healed

AND again ᴿhe entered into Că-pĕr'-nă-ŭm after *some* days; and it was noised that he was in the house.

2 And straightway many were gathered together, insomuch that there was no room to receive *them,* no, not so much as about the door: and he preached the word unto them.

3 And they come unto him, bringing one sick of the palsy, which was borne of four.

4 And when they could not come nigh unto him for the press, they uncovered the roof where he was: and when they had broken *it* up, they let down the bed wherein the sick of the palsy lay.

5 When Jesus saw their faith, he said unto the sick of the palsy, Son, thy sins be forgiven thee.

6 But there were certain of the scribes sitting there, and reasoning in their hearts,

7 Why doth this *man* thus speak blasphemies? ᴿwho can forgive sins but God only?

8 And immediately when Jesus perceived in his spirit that they so reasoned within themselves, he said unto them, Why reason ye these things in your hearts?

9 ᴿWhether is it easier to say to the sick of the palsy, *Thy* sins be forgiven thee; or to say, Arise, and take up thy bed, and walk?

10 But that ye may know that the Son of man hath power on earth to forgive sins, (he saith to the sick of the palsy,)

11 I say unto thee, Arise, and take up thy bed, and go thy way into thine house.

12 And immediately he arose, took up the bed, and went forth before them all; insomuch that they were all amazed, and glorified God, saying, We never saw it on this fashion.

Call of Levi, and Levi's banquet

13 ᴿAnd he went forth again by the sea side; and all the multitude resorted unto him, and he taught them.

14 ᴿAnd as he passed by, he saw Levi the *son* of Ăl-phæ'-ŭs sitting ᴺat the receipt of custom, and said unto him, Follow me. And he arose and followed him.

15 ᴿAnd it came to pass, that, as Jesus sat at meat in his house, many publicans and sinners sat also together with Jesus and his disciples: for there were many, and they followed him.

16 And when the scribes and Pharisees saw him eat with publicans and sinners, they said unto his disciples, How is it that he eateth and drinketh with publicans and sinners?

17 When Jesus heard *it,* he saith unto them, ᴿThey that are whole have no need of the physician, but they that are sick: I came not to call the righteous, but sinners to repentance.

Question about fasting

18 ᴿAnd the disciples of John and of the Pharisees used to fast: and they come and say unto him, Why do the disciples of John and of the Pharisees fast, but thy disciples fast not?

19 And Jesus said unto them, Can the children of the bridechamber fast, while the bridegroom is with them? as long as they have the bridegroom with them, they cannot fast.

20 But the days will come, when the bridegroom shall be taken away from them, and then shall they fast in those days.

21 No man also seweth a piece of ᴺnew cloth on an old garment: else the new piece that filled it up taketh away from the old, and the rent is made worse.

22 And no man putteth new wine into old bottles: else the new wine doth burst the bottles, and the wine is spilled, and the bottles will be marred: but new wine must be put into new bottles.

Lord of the sabbath

23 ᴿAnd it came to pass, that he went through the corn fields on the sabbath day; and his disciples began, as they went, ᴿto pluck the ears of corn.

24 And the Pharisees said unto him, Behold, why do they on the sabbath day that which is not lawful?

25 And he said unto them, Have ye never read ᴿwhat David did, when he had need, and was an hungred, he, and they that were with him?

26 How he went into the house of God in the days of Ă-bī'-ă-thär the high priest, and did eat the shewbread, ᴿwhich is not lawful to eat but for the priests, and gave also to them which were with him?

27 And he said unto them, The sabbath was made for man, and not man for the sabbath:

28 Therefore ᴿthe Son of man is Lord also of the sabbath.

CHAP. 1
AD 26
44 Lev. 14:3, 4, 10
45 Luke 5:15
45 ch. 2:13

CHAP. 2
AD 31
1 Mat. 9:1
7 Job 14:4
  Is. 43:25
9 Mat. 9:5
13 Mat. 9:9
14 Mat. 9:9
  Luke 5:27
14 Or, *at the place where the custom was received*

Mat. 9:10   15
Mat. 9:12, 13   17
& 18:11
Luke 5:31, 32
& 19:10
1 Tim. 1:15
Mat. 9:14   18
Luke 5:33
Or, *raw, or, unwrought*   21
Mat. 12:1   23
Luke 6:1
Deut. 23:25   23
1 Sam. 21:6   25
Ex. 29:32, 33   26
Lev. 24:9
Mat. 12:8   28

CHAPTER 3

AND ᴿhe entered again into the synagogue; and there was a man there which had a withered hand.

2 And they watched him, whether he would heal him on the sabbath day; that they might accuse him.

3 And he saith unto the man which had the withered hand, ᴺStand forth.

4 And he saith unto them, Is it lawful to do good on the sabbath days, or to do evil? to save life, or to kill? But they held their peace.

5 And when he had looked round about on them with anger, being grieved for the ᴺhardness of their hearts, he saith unto the man, Stretch forth thine hand. And he stretched *it* out: and his hand was restored whole as the other.

6 ᴿAnd the Pharisees went forth, and straightway took counsel with ᴿthe Hĕ-rō′-dĭ-ăns against him, how they might destroy him.

Ministry by the sea

7 But Jesus withdrew himself with his disciples to the sea: and a great multitude from Galilee followed him, ᴿand from Judæa,

8 And from Jerusalem, and from ĭ-dū-mæ′-ă, and *from* beyond Jordan; and they about Tyre and Sĭ′-dŏn, a great multitude, when they had heard what great things he did, came unto him.

9 And he spake to his disciples, that a small ship should wait on him because of the multitude, lest they should throng him.

10 For he had healed many; insomuch that they ᴺpressed upon him for to touch him, as many as had plagues.

11 ᴿAnd unclean spirits, when they saw him, fell down before him, and cried, saying, ᴿThou art the Son of God.

12 And ᴿhe straitly charged them that they should not make him known.

Ordaining of the twelve disciples

13 ᴿAnd he goeth up into a mountain, and calleth *unto him* whom he would: and they came unto him.

14 And he ordained twelve, that they should be with him, and that he might send them forth to preach,

15 And to have power to heal sicknesses, and to cast out devils:

16 And Simon ᴿhe surnamed Peter;

17 And James the *son* of Zĕb′-ĕ-dĕe, and John the brother of James; and he surnamed them Bō-ăn-ĕr′-ġĕs, which is, The sons of thunder:

18 And Andrew, and Philip, and Bartholo-

mew, and Matthew, and Thomas, and James the *son* of Ăl-phæ′-ŭs, and Thăd-dæ′-ŭs, and Simon the Canaanite,

19 And Judas Iscariot, which also betrayed him: and they went ᴺinto an house.

20 And the multitude cometh together again, ᴿso that they could not so much as eat bread.

21 And when his ᴺfriends hear *of it,* they went out to lay hold on him: ᴿfor they said, He is beside himself.

22 And the scribes which came down from Jerusalem said, ᴿHe hath Bē-ĕl′-zĕ-bŭb, and by the prince of the devils casteth he out devils.

23 ᴿAnd he called them *unto him,* and said unto them in parables, How can Satan cast out Satan?

24 And if a kingdom be divided against itself, that kingdom cannot stand.

25 And if a house be divided against itself, that house cannot stand.

26 And if Satan rise up against himself, and be divided, he cannot stand, but hath an end.

27 ᴿNo man can enter into a strong man's house, and spoil his goods, except he will first bind the strong man; and then he will spoil his house.

The unforgivable sin

28 ᴿVerily I say unto you, All sins shall be forgiven unto the sons of men, and blasphemies wherewith soever they shall blaspheme:

29 But he that shall blaspheme against the Holy Ghost hath never forgiveness, but is in danger of eternal damnation:

30 Because they said, He hath an unclean spirit.

Jesus' true kindred

31 ᴿThere came then his brethren and his mother, and, standing without, sent unto him, calling him.

32 And the multitude sat about him, and they said unto him, Behold, thy mother and thy brethren without seek for thee.

33 And he answered them, saying, Who is my mother, or my brethren?

34 And he looked round about on them which sat about him, and said, Behold my mother and my brethren!

35 For whosoever shall do the will of God, the same is my brother, and my sister, and mother.

CHAPTER 4

Parable of the sower

AND ᴿhe began again to teach by the sea side: and there was gathered unto him a

CHAP. 3
AD 31
1 Mat. 12:9
  Luke 6:6
3 Gr. *Arise, stand forth in the midst*
5 Or, *blindness*
6 Mat. 12:14
6 Mat. 22:16
7 Luke 6:17
10 Or, *rushed*
11 ch. 1:23, 24
  Luke 4:41
11 Mat. 14:33
  ch. 1:1
12 Mat. 12:16
  ch. 1:25, 34
13 Mat. 10:1
  Luke 6:12
  & 9:1
16 John 1:42

Or, *home*   19
ch. 6:31   20
Or, *kinsmen*   21
John 7:5   21
 & 10:20
Mat. 9:34   22
 & 10:25
Luke 11:15
John 7:20
 & 8:48, 52
 & 10:20
Mat. 12:25   23
Is. 49:24   27
Mat. 12:29
Mat. 12:31   28
Luke 12:10
1 John 5:16
Mat. 12:46   31
Luke 8:19

CHAP. 4
AD 31
Mat. 13:1   1
Luke 8:4

great multitude, so that he entered into a ship, and sat in the sea; and the whole multitude was by the sea on the land.

2 And he taught them many things by parables, ᴿand said unto them in his doctrine,

3 Hearken; Behold, there went out a sower to sow:

4 And it came to pass, as he sowed, some fell by the way side, and the fowls of the air came and devoured it up.

5 And some fell on stony ground, where it had not much earth; and immediately it sprang up, because it had no depth of earth:

6 But when the sun was up, it was scorched; and because it had no root, it withered away.

7 And some fell among thorns, and the thorns grew up, and choked it, and it yielded no fruit.

8 And other fell on good ground, ᴿand did yield fruit that sprang up and increased; and brought forth, some thirty, and some sixty, and some an hundred.

9 And he said unto them, He that hath ears to hear, let him hear.

10 ᴿAnd when he was alone, they that were about him with the twelve asked of him the parable.

11 And he said unto them, Unto you it is given to know the mystery of the kingdom of God: but unto ᴿthem that are without, all *these* things are done in parables:

12 ᴿThat seeing they may see, and not perceive; and hearing they may hear, and not understand; lest at any time they should be converted, and *their* sins should be forgiven them.

13 And he said unto them, Know ye not this parable? and how then will ye know all parables?

Parable explained

14 ᴿThe sower soweth the word.

15 And these are they by the way side, where the word is sown; but when they have heard, Satan cometh immediately, and taketh away the word that was sown in their hearts.

16 And these are they likewise which are sown on stony ground; who, when they have heard the word, immediately receive it with gladness;

17 And have no root in themselves, and so endure but for a time: afterward, when affliction or persecution ariseth for the word's sake, immediately they are offended.

18 And these are they which are sown among thorns; such as hear the word,

19 And the cares of this world, ᴿand the deceitfulness of riches, and the lusts of other

CHAP. **4**
AD 31
2 ch. 12:38
8 John 15:5
Col. 1:6
10 Mat. 13:10
Luke 8:9, etc.
11 1 Cor. 5:12
Col. 4:5
1 Thes. 4:12
1 Tim. 3:7
12 Is. 6:9
Mat. 13:14
Luke 8:10
John 12:40
Acts 28:26
Rom. 11:8
14 Mat. 13:19
19 1 Tim. 6:9, 17

Mat. 5:15   21
Luke 8:16
& 11:33
The word in   21
the original
signifieth a less
measure, as
Mat. 5:15
Mat. 10:26   22
ver. 9   23
Mat. 11:15
Mat. 7:2   24
Luke 6:38
Mat. 13:12   25
& 25:29
Luke 8:18
& 19:26
Mat. 13:24   26
Or, *ripe*   29
Rev. 14:15   29
Mat. 13:31   30
Luke 13:18
Acts 2:41
& 4:4 & 5:14
& 19:20
Mat. 13:34   33
John 16:12
Mat. 8:18, 23   35
Luke 8:22

things entering in, choke the word, and it becometh unfruitful.

20 And these are they which are sown on good ground; such as hear the word, and receive *it,* and bring forth fruit, some thirtyfold, some sixty, and some an hundred.

21 ᴿAnd he said unto them, Is a candle brought to be put under a ᴺbushel, or under a bed? and not to be set on a candlestick?

22 ᴿFor there is nothing hid, which shall not be manifested; neither was any thing kept secret, but that it should come abroad.

23 ᴿIf any man have ears to hear, let him hear.

24 And he said unto them, Take heed what ye hear: ᴿwith what measure ye mete, it shall be measured to you: and unto you that hear shall more be given.

25 ᴿFor he that hath, to him shall be given: and he that hath not, from him shall be taken even that which he hath.

26 And he said, ᴿSo is the kingdom of God, as if a man should cast seed into the ground;

27 And should sleep, and rise night and day, and the seed should spring and grow up, he knoweth not how.

28 For the earth bringeth forth fruit of herself; first the blade, then the ear, after that the full corn in the ear.

29 But when the fruit is ᴺbrought forth, immediately ᴿhe putteth in the sickle, because the harvest is come.

The parable of the mustard seed

30 And he said, ᴿWhereunto shall we liken the kingdom of God? or with what comparison shall we compare it?

31 *It is* like a grain of mustard seed, which, when it is sown in the earth, is less than all the seeds that be in the earth:

32 But when it is sown, it groweth up, and becometh greater than all herbs, and shooteth out great branches; so that the fowls of the air may lodge under the shadow of it.

33 ᴿAnd with many such parables spake he the word unto them, as they were able to hear *it.*

34 But without a parable spake he not unto them: and when they were alone, he expounded all things to his disciples.

Jesus stills the storm

35 ᴿAnd the same day, when the even was come, he saith unto them, Let us pass over unto the other side.

36 And when they had sent away the multitude, they took him even as he was in the ship. And there were also with him other little ships.

37 And there arose a great storm of wind, and the waves beat into the ship, so that it was now full.

38 And he was in the hinder part of the ship, asleep on a pillow: and they awake him, and say unto him, Master, carest thou not that we perish?

39 And he arose, and rebuked the wind, and said unto the sea, Peace, be still. And the wind ceased, and there was a great calm.

40 And he said unto them, Why are ye so fearful? how is it that ye have no faith?

41 And they feared exceedingly, and said one to another, What manner of man is this, that even the wind and the sea obey him?

CHAPTER 5

The demoniac healed

AND ᴿthey came over unto the other side of the sea, into the country of the Găd′-ă-rēnes.

2 And when he was come out of the ship, immediately there met him out of the tombs a man with an unclean spirit,

3 Who had *his* dwelling among the tombs; and no man could bind him, no, not with chains:

4 Because that he had been often bound with fetters and chains, and the chains had been plucked asunder by him, and the fetters broken in pieces: neither could any *man* tame him.

5 And always, night and day, he was in the mountains, and in the tombs, crying, and cutting himself with stones.

6 But when he saw Jesus afar off, he ran and worshipped him,

7 And cried with a loud voice, and said, What have I to do with thee, Jesus, *thou* Son of the most high God? I adjure thee by God, that thou torment me not.

8 For he said unto him, Come out of the man, *thou* unclean spirit.

9 And he asked him, What *is* thy name? And he answered, saying, My name *is* Legion: for we are many.

10 And he besought him much that he would not send them away out of the country.

11 Now there was there nigh unto the mountains a great herd of swine feeding.

12 And all the devils besought him, saying, Send us into the swine, that we may enter into them.

13 And forthwith Jesus gave them leave. And the unclean spirits went out, and entered into the swine: and the herd ran violently down a steep place into the sea, (they were about two thousand;) and were choked in the sea.

CHAP. **5**
AD 31
1 Mat. 8:28
Luke 8:26

Mat. 8:34   **17**
Acts 16:39
Luke 8:38   **18**
Mat. 9:1   **21**
 Luke 8:40
Mat. 9:18   **22**
 Luke 8:41
Lev. 15:25   **25**
Mat. 9:20
Luke 6:19   **30**
 & 8:46

14 And they that fed the swine fled, and told *it* in the city, and in the country. And they went out to see what it was that was done.

15 And they come to Jesus, and see him that was possessed with the devil, and had the legion, sitting, and clothed, and in his right mind: and they were afraid.

16 And they that saw *it* told them how it befell to him that was possessed with the devil, and *also* concerning the swine.

17 And ᴿthey began to pray him to depart out of their coasts.

18 And when he was come into the ship, ᴿhe that had been possessed with the devil prayed him that he might be with him.

19 Howbeit Jesus suffered him not, but saith unto him, Go home to thy friends, and tell them how great things the Lord hath done for thee, and hath had compassion on thee.

20 And he departed, and began to publish in Dĕ-căp′-ŏ-lĭs how great things Jesus had done for him: and all *men* did marvel.

The woman who touched His garment

21 ᴿAnd when Jesus was passed over again by ship unto the other side, much people gathered unto him: and he was nigh unto the sea.

22 ᴿAnd, behold, there cometh one of the rulers of the synagogue, Jā-ī′-rŭs by name; and when he saw him, he fell at his feet,

23 And besought him greatly, saying, My little daughter lieth at the point of death: *I pray thee,* come and lay thy hands on her, that she may be healed; and she shall live.

24 And *Jesus* went with him; and much people followed him, and thronged him.

25 And a certain woman, ᴿwhich had an issue of blood twelve years,

26 And had suffered many things of many physicians, and had spent all that she had, and was nothing bettered, but rather grew worse,

27 When she had heard of Jesus, came in the press behind, and touched his garment.

28 For she said, If I may touch but his clothes, I shall be whole.

29 And straightway the fountain of her blood was dried up; and she felt in *her* body that she was healed of that plague.

30 And Jesus, immediately knowing in himself that ᴿvirtue had gone out of him, turned him about in the press, and said, Who touched my clothes?

31 And his disciples said unto him, Thou seest the multitude thronging thee, and sayest thou, Who touched me?

32 And he looked round about to see her that had done this thing.

33 But the woman fearing and trembling,

knowing what was done in her, came and fell down before him, and told him all the truth.

34 And he said unto her, Daughter, ^Rthy faith hath made thee whole; go in peace, and be whole of thy plague.

Raising of the ruler's daughter

35 ^RWhile he yet spake, there came from the ruler of the synagogue's *house certain* which said, Thy daughter is dead: why troublest thou the Master any further?

36 As soon as Jesus heard the word that was spoken, he saith unto the ruler of the synagogue, Be not afraid, only believe.

37 And he suffered no man to follow him, save Peter, and James, and John the brother of James.

38 And he cometh to the house of the ruler of the synagogue, and seeth the tumult, and them that wept and wailed greatly.

39 And when he was come in, he saith unto them, Why make ye this ado, and weep? the damsel is not dead, but ^Rsleepeth.

40 And they laughed him to scorn. ^RBut when he had put them all out, he taketh the father and the mother of the damsel, and them that were with him, and entereth in where the damsel was lying.

41 And he took the damsel by the hand, and said unto her, Tăl'-ĭ-thă cū'-mī; which is, being interpreted, Damsel, I say unto thee, arise.

42 And straightway the damsel arose, and walked; for she was *of the age* of twelve years. And they were astonished with a great astonishment.

43 And ^Rhe charged them straitly that no man should know it; and commanded that something should be given her to eat.

CHAPTER 6

Jesus' rejection at Nazareth

AND ^Rhe went out from thence, and came into his own country; and his disciples follow him.

2 And when the sabbath day was come, he began to teach in the synagogue: and many hearing *him* were astonished, saying, ^RFrom whence hath this *man* these things? and what wisdom *is* this which is given unto him, that even such mighty works are wrought by his hands?

3 Is not this the carpenter, the son of Mary, ^Rthe brother of James, and Jō'-sĕś, and of Judah, and Simon? and are not his sisters here with us? And they ^Rwere offended at him.

4 But Jesus said unto them, ^RA prophet is

not without honour, but in his own country, and among his own kin, and in his own house.

5 ^RAnd he could there do no mighty work, save that he laid his hands upon a few sick folk, and healed *them*.

6 And ^Rhe marvelled because of their unbelief. ^RAnd he went round about the villages, teaching.

The mission of the twelve

7 ^RAnd he called *unto him* the twelve, and began to send them forth by two and two; and gave them power over unclean spirits;

8 And commanded them that they should take nothing for *their* journey, save a staff only; no scrip, no bread, no ^Nmoney in *their* purse:

9 But ^Rbe shod with sandals; and not put on two coats.

10 ^RAnd he said unto them, In what place soever ye enter into an house, there abide till ye depart from that place.

11 ^RAnd whosoever shall not receive you, nor hear you, when ye depart thence, ^Rshake off the dust under your feet for a testimony against them. Verily I say unto you, It shall be more tolerable for Sodom ^Nand Gō-mŏr'-rhă in the day of judgment, than for that city.

12 And they went out, and preached that men should repent.

13 And they cast out many devils, ^Rand anointed with oil many that were sick, and healed *them*.

John the Baptist beheaded

14 ^RAnd king Herod heard *of him;* (for his name was spread abroad:) and he said, That John the Baptist was risen from the dead, and therefore mighty works do shew forth themselves in him.

15 ^ROthers said, That it is Ē-lī'-ăs. And others said, That it is a prophet, or as one of the prophets.

16 ^RBut when Herod heard *thereof,* he said, It is John, whom I beheaded: he is risen from the dead.

17 For Herod himself had sent forth and laid hold upon John, and bound him in prison for Hĕ-rō'-dĭ-ăs' sake, his brother Philip's wife: for he had married her.

18 For John had said unto Herod, ^RIt is not lawful for thee to have thy brother's wife.

19 Therefore Hĕ-rō'-dĭ-ăs had ^Na quarrel against him, and would have killed him; but she could not:

20 For Herod ^Rfeared John, knowing that he was a just man and an holy, and ^Nobserved him; and when he heard him, he did many things, and heard him gladly.

CHAP. **5**

AD 31
34 Mat. 9:22
ch. 10:52
Acts 14:9
35 Luke 8:49
39 John 11:11
40 Acts 9:40
43 Mat. 8:4
& 9:30 & 12:16
& 17:9
ch. 3:12
Luke 5:14

CHAP. **6**

AD 31
1 Mat. 13:54
Luke 4:16
2 John 6:42
3 See Mat. 12:46
Gal. 1:19
3 Mat. 11:6
4 Mat. 13:57
John 4:44

See Gen. 19:22 **5**
& 32:25
Mat. 13:58
ch. 9:23
Is. 59:16 **6**
Mat. 9:35 **6**
Luke 13:22
Mat. 10:1 **7**
ch. 3:13, 14
Luke 9:1
The word **8**
signifieth
*a piece of brass
money, in value
somewhat less
than a farthing,*
Mat. 10:9: but
here it is taken
in general for
money,
Luke 9:3
Gen. 40:20 **9**
Mat. 10:11 **10**
Luke 9:4
& 10:7, 8
Mat. 10:14 **11**
Luke 10:10
Acts 13:51 **11**
& 18:6
Gr. *or* **11**
Jas. 5:14 **13**
Mat. 14:1 **14**
Luke 9:7
Mat. 16:14 **15**
ch. 8:28
Mat. 14:2 **16**
Luke 3:19
Lev. 18:16 **18**
& 20:21
Or, *an inward* **19**
grudge
Mat. 14:5 **20**
& 21:26
Or, *kept* **20**
him, or,
saved him

21 R And when a convenient day was come, that Herod R on his birthday made a supper to his lords, high captains, and chief *estates* of Galilee;

22 And when the daughter of the said Hĕ-rō′-dĭ-ăs came in, and danced, and pleased Herod and them that sat with him, the king said unto the damsel, Ask of me whatsoever thou wilt, and I will give *it* thee.

23 And he sware unto her, R Whatsoever thou shalt ask of me, I will give *it* thee, unto the half of my kingdom.

24 And she went forth, and said unto her mother, What shall I ask? And she said, The head of John the Baptist.

25 And she came in straightway with haste unto the king, and asked, saying, I will that thou give me by and by in a charger the head of John the Baptist.

26 R And the king was exceeding sorry; *yet* for his oath's sake, and for their sakes which sat with him, he would not reject her.

27 And immediately the king sent N an executioner, and commanded his head to be brought: and he went and beheaded him in the prison,

28 And brought his head in a charger, and gave it to the damsel: and the damsel gave it to her mother.

29 And when his disciples heard *of it,* they came and took up his corpse, and laid it in a tomb.

Feeding the five thousand

30 R And the apostles gathered themselves together unto Jesus, and told him all things, both what they had done, and what they had taught.

31 R And he said unto them, Come ye yourselves apart into a desert place, and rest a while: for R there were many coming and going, and they had no leisure so much as to eat.

32 R And they departed into a desert place by ship privately.

33 And the people saw them departing, and many knew him, and ran afoot thither out of all cities, and outwent them, and came together unto him.

34 R And Jesus, when he came out, saw much people, and was moved with compassion toward them, because they were as sheep not having a shepherd: and R he began to teach them many things.

35 R And when the day was now far spent, his disciples came unto him, and said, This is a desert place, and now the time *is* far passed:

36 Send them away, that they may go into the country round about, and into the villages,

CHAP. 6
AD 31
21 Mat. 14:6
21 Gen. 40:20
23 Esth. 5:3, 6
& 7:2
26 Mat. 14:9
27 Or, *one of his guard*
30 Luke 9:10
31 Mat. 14:13
31 ch. 3:20
32 Mat. 14:13
34 Mat. 9:36
& 14:14
34 Luke 9:11
35 Mat. 14:15
Luke 9:12

Num. 11:13, 22   37
2 Ki. 4:43
The Roman   37
penny is seven-
pence halfpenny:
as Mat. 18:28
Mat. 14:17   38
Luke 9:13
John 6:9
See Mat. 15:34
ch. 8:5
1 Sam. 9:13   41
Mat. 26:26
Mat. 14:22   45
John 6:17
Or, *over against*   45
Bethsaida
See Luke 24:28   48
ch. 8:17, 18   52
ch. 3:5   52
& 16:14
Mat. 14:34   53

and buy themselves bread: for they have nothing to eat.

37 He answered and said unto them, Give ye them to eat. And they say unto him, R Shall we go and buy two hundred N pennyworth of bread, and give them to eat?

38 He saith unto them, How many loaves have ye? go and see. And when they knew, they say, R Five, and two fishes.

39 And he commanded them to make all sit down by companies upon the green grass.

40 And they sat down in ranks, by hundreds, and by fifties.

41 And when he had taken the five loaves and the two fishes, he looked up to heaven, R and blessed, and brake the loaves, and gave *them* to his disciples to set before them; and the two fishes divided he among them all.

42 And they did all eat, and were filled.

43 And they took up twelve baskets full of the fragments, and of the fishes.

44 And they that did eat of the loaves were about five thousand men.

Jesus walks on the water

45 R And straightway he constrained his disciples to get into the ship, and to go to the other side before N unto Bĕth-sā′-ĭ-dă, while he sent away the people.

46 And when he had sent them away, he departed into a mountain to pray.

47 R And when even was come, the ship was in the midst of the sea, and he alone on the land.

48 And he saw them toiling in rowing; for the wind was contrary unto them: and about the fourth watch of the night he cometh unto them, walking upon the sea, and R would have passed by them.

49 But when they saw him walking upon the sea, they supposed it had been a spirit, and cried out:

50 For they all saw him, and were troubled. And immediately he talked with them, and saith unto them, Be of good cheer: it is I; be not afraid.

51 And he went up unto them into the ship; and the wind ceased: and they were sore amazed in themselves beyond measure, and wondered.

52 For R they considered not *the miracle* of the loaves: for their R heart was hardened.

Jesus' ministry at Gennesaret

53 R And when they had passed over, they came into the land of Gĕn-nĕs′-ă-rĕt, and drew to the shore.

54 And when they were come out of the ship, straightway they knew him,

55 And ran through that whole region round about, and began to carry about in beds those that were sick, where they heard he was.

56 And whithersoever he entered, into villages, or cities, or country, they laid the sick in the streets, and besought him that [R]they might touch if it were but the border of his garment: and as many as touched [N]him were made whole.

CHAPTER 7

Ceremonial and real defilement

THEN [R]came together unto him the Pharisees, and certain of the scribes, which came from Jerusalem.

2 And when they saw some of his disciples eat bread with [N]defiled, that is to say, with unwashen, hands, they found fault.

3 For the Pharisees, and all the Jews, except they wash *their* hands [N]oft, eat not, holding the tradition of the elders.

4 And *when they come* from the market, except they wash, they eat not. And many other things there be, which they have received to hold, *as* the washing of cups, and [N]pots, brasen vessels, and of [N]tables.

5 [R]Then the Pharisees and scribes asked him, Why walk not thy disciples according to the tradition of the elders, but eat bread with unwashen hands?

6 He answered and said unto them, Well hath Ē-śái′-ăs prophesied of you hypocrites, as it is written, [R]This people honoureth me with *their* lips, but their heart is far from me.

7 Howbeit in vain do they worship me, teaching *for* doctrines the commandments of men.

8 For laying aside the commandment of God, ye hold the tradition of men, *as* the washing of pots and cups: and many other such like things ye do.

9 And he said unto them, Full well ye [N]reject the commandment of God, that ye may keep your own tradition.

10 For Moses said, [R]Honour thy father and thy mother; and, [R]Whoso curseth father or mother, let him die the death:

11 But ye say, If a man shall say to his father or mother, *It is* [R]Côr′-băn, that is to say, a gift, by whatsoever thou mightest be profited by me; *he shall be free.*

12 And ye suffer him no more to do aught for his father or his mother;

13 Making the word of God of none effect through your tradition, which he have delivered: and many such like things do ye.

14 [R]And when he had called all the people *unto him,* he said unto them, Hearken unto me every one *of you,* and understand:

15 There is nothing from without a man, that entering into him can defile him: but the things which come out of him, those are they that defile the man.

16 [R]If any man have ears to hear, let him hear.

17 [R]And when he was entered into the house from the people, his disciples asked him concerning the parable.

18 And he saith unto them, Are ye so without understanding also? Do ye not perceive, that whatsoever thing from without entereth into the man, *it* cannot defile him;

19 Because it entereth not into his heart, but into the belly, and goeth out into the draught, purging all meats?

20 And he said, That which cometh out of the man, that defileth the man.

21 [R]For from within, out of the heart of men, proceed evil thoughts, adulteries, fornications, murders,

22 Thefts, [N]covetousness, wickedness, deceit, lasciviousness, an evil eye, blasphemy, pride, foolishness:

23 All these evil things come from within, and defile the man.

Faith of the Syrophenician woman

24 [R]And from thence he arose, and went into the borders of Tyre and Śī′-dŏn, and entered into an house, and would have no man know *it:* but he could not be hid.

25 For a *certain* woman, whose young daughter had an unclean spirit, heard of him, and came and fell at his feet:

26 The woman was a [N]Greek, a Sȳ-rō-phē-nĭç′-ĭ-ăn by nation; and she besought him that he would cast forth the devil out of her daughter.

27 But Jesus said unto her, Let the children first be filled: for it is not meet to take the children's bread, and to cast *it* unto the dogs.

28 And she answered and said unto him, Yes, Lord: yet the dogs under the table eat of the children's crumbs.

29 And he said unto her, For this saying go thy way; the devil is gone out of thy daughter.

30 And when she was come to her house, she found the devil gone out, and her daughter laid upon the bed.

Healing of the deaf-mute

31 [R]And again, departing from the coasts of Tyre and Śī′-dŏn, he came unto the sea of Galilee, through the midst of the coasts of Dĕ-căp′-ŏ-lĭs.

32 And [R]they bring unto him one that was deaf, and had an impediment in his speech; and they beseech him to put his hand upon him.

CHAP. 6
AD 31
56 Mat. 9:20
ch. 5:27, 28
Acts 19:12
56 Or, *it*

CHAP. 7
AD 32
1 Mat. 15:1
2 Or, *common*
3 Or, *diligently:* in the original, *with the fist* Theophylact, *up to the elbow*
4 Sextarius is about a pint and a half
4 Or, *beds*
5 Mat. 15:2
6 Is. 29:13
9 Or, *frustrate*
10 Ex. 20:12
Deut. 5:16
Mat. 15:4
10 Ex. 21:17
Lev. 20:9
Prov. 20:20
11 Mat. 15:5 & 23:18
14 Mat. 15:10

Mat. 11:16   16
Mat. 15:15   17
Gen. 6:5   21
& 8:21
Mat. 15:19
Gr. *covetousnesses, wickednesses*   22
Mat. 15:21   24
Or, *Gentile* 26
Mat. 15:29   31
Mat. 9:32   32
Luke 11:14

33 And he took him aside from the multitude, and put his fingers into his ears, and ^Rhe spit, and touched his tongue;

34 And ^Rlooking up to heaven, ^Rhe sighed, and saith unto him, Ĕph′-phă-thă, that is, Be opened.

35 ^RAnd straightway his ears were opened, and the string of his tongue was loosed, and he spake plain.

36 And ^Rhe charged them that they should tell no man: but the more he charged them, so much the more a great deal they published *it;*

37 And were beyond measure astonished, saying, He hath done all things well: he maketh both the deaf to hear, and the dumb to speak.

CHAPTER 8

Feeding the four thousand

IN those days ^Rthe multitude being very great, and having nothing to eat, Jesus called his disciples *unto him,* and saith unto them,

2 I have compassion on the multitude, because they have now been with me three days, and have nothing to eat:

3 And if I send them away fasting to their own houses, they will faint by the way: for divers of them came from far.

4 And his disciples answered him, From whence can a man satisfy these *men* with bread here in the wilderness?

5 ^RAnd he asked them, How many loaves have ye? And they said, Seven.

6 And he commanded the people to sit down on the ground: and he took the seven loaves, and gave thanks, and brake, and gave to his disciples to set before *them;* and they did set *them* before the people.

7 And they had a few small fishes: and ^Rhe blessed, and commanded to set them also before *them.*

8 So they did eat, and were filled: and they took up of the broken *meat* that was left seven baskets.

9 And they that had eaten were about four thousand: and he sent them away.

10 And ^Rstraightway he entered into a ship with his disciples, and came into the parts of Dăl-mă-nū′-thă.

The leaven of the Pharisees

11 ^RAnd the Pharisees came forth, and began to question with him, seeking of him a sign from heaven, tempting him.

12 And he sighed deeply in his spirit, and

saith, Why doth this generation seek after a sign? verily I say unto you, There shall no sign be given unto this generation.

13 And he left them, and entering into the ship again departed to the other side.

14 ^RNow *the disciples* had forgotten to take bread, neither had they in the ship with them more than one loaf.

15 ^RAnd he charged them, saying, Take heed, beware of the leaven of the Pharisees, and *of* the leaven of Herod.

16 And they reasoned among themselves, saying, *It is* because we have no bread.

17 And when Jesus knew *it,* he saith unto them, Why reason ye, because ye have no bread? ^Rperceive ye not yet, neither understand? have ye your heart yet hardened?

18 Having eyes, see ye not? and having ears, hear ye not? and do ye not remember?

19 ^RWhen I brake the five loaves among five thousand, how many baskets full of fragments took ye up? They say unto him, Twelve.

20 And ^Rwhen the seven among four thousand, how many baskets full of fragments took ye up? And they said, Seven.

21 And he said unto them, How is it that ^Rye do not understand?

Healing the blind man at Bethsaida

22 And he cometh to Bĕth-sā′-ĭ-dă; and they bring a blind man unto him, and besought him to touch him.

23 And he took the blind man by the hand, and led him out of the town; and when ^Rhe had spit on his eyes, and put his hands upon him, he asked him if he saw aught.

24 And he looked up, and said, I see men as trees, walking.

25 After that he put *his* hands again upon his eyes, and made him look up: and he was restored, and saw every man clearly.

26 And he sent him away to his house, saying, Neither go into the town, ^Rnor tell *it* to any in the town.

Peter's confession

27 ^RAnd Jesus went out, and his disciples, into the towns of Çæ-să-rē′-ă Philippi: and by the way he asked his disciples, saying unto them, Whom do men say that I am?

28 And they answered, ^RJohn the Baptist: but some *say,* Ē-lī′-ăs; and others, One of the prophets.

29 And he saith unto them, But whom say ye that I am? And Peter answereth and saith unto him, ^RThou art the Christ.

30 ^RAnd he charged them that they should tell no man of him.

Center reference column:

CHAP. 7
AD 32
33 ch. 8:23
   John 9:6
34 ch. 6:41
   John 11:41
   & 17:1
34 John 11:33, 38
35 Is. 35:5, 6
36 ch. 5:43

CHAP. 8
AD 32
1 Mat. 15:32
5 Mat. 15:34
See ch. 6:38
7 Mat. 14:19
   ch. 6:41
10 Mat. 15:39
11 Mat. 12:38
   & 16:1
   John 6:30

Mat. 15:5	14
Mat. 16:6	15
Luke 12:1	
ch. 6:52	17
Mat. 14:20	19
ch. 6:43	
Luke 9:17	
John 6:13	
ver. 8	20
Mat. 15:37	
ver. 17	21
ch. 6:52	
ch. 7:33	23
Mat. 8:4	26
ch. 5:43	
Mat. 16:13	27
Luke 9:18	
Mat. 14:2	28
Mat. 16:16	29
John 6:69	
& 11:27	
Mat. 16:20	30

The way of the cross

31 And ᴿhe began to teach them, that the Son of man must suffer many things, and be rejected of the elders, and *of* the chief priests, and scribes, and be killed, and after three days rise again.

32 And he spake that saying openly. And Peter took him, and began to rebuke him.

33 But when he had turned about and looked on his disciples, he rebuked Peter, saying, Get thee behind me, Satan: for thou savourest not the things that be of God, but the things that be of men.

34 And when he had called the people *unto him* with his disciples also, he said unto them, ᴿWhosoever will come after me, let him deny himself, and take up his cross, and follow me.

35 For ᴿwhosoever will save his life shall lose it; but whosoever shall lose his life for my sake and the gospel's, the same shall save it.

36 For what shall it profit a man, if he shall gain the whole world, and lose his own soul?

37 Or what shall a man give in exchange for his soul?

38 ᴿWhosoever therefore ᴿshall be ashamed of me and of my words in this adulterous and sinful generation; of him also shall the Son of man be ashamed, when he cometh in the glory of his Father with the holy angels.

CHAPTER 9

AND he said unto them, ᴿVerily I say unto you, That there be some of them that stand here, which shall not taste of death, till they have seen ᴿthe kingdom of God come with power.

The transfiguration

2 ᴿAnd after six days Jesus taketh *with him* Peter, and James, and John, and leadeth them up into an high mountain apart by themselves: and he was transfigured before them.

3 And his raiment became shining, exceeding ᴿwhite as snow; so as no fuller on earth can white them.

4 And there appeared unto them Ē-lī′-ăs with Moses: and they were talking with Jesus.

5 And Peter answered and said to Jesus, Master, it is good for us to be here: and let us make three tabernacles; one for thee, and one for Moses, and one for Ē-lī′-ăs.

6 For he wist not what to say; for they were sore afraid.

7 And there was a cloud that overshadowed them: and a voice came out of the cloud, saying, This is my beloved Son: hear him.

8 And suddenly, when they had looked

CHAP. **8**

AD 32
31 Mat. 16:21
& 17:22
Luke 9:22
34 Mat. 10:38
& 16:24
Luke 9:23
& 14:27
35 John 12:25
38 Mat. 10:33
Luke 9:26
& 12:9
38 See Rom. 1:16
2 Tim. 1:8 & 2:12

CHAP. **9**

AD 32
1 Mat. 16:28
Luke 9:27
1 Mat. 24:30
2 Mat. 17:1
Luke 9:28
3 Dan. 7:9

Mat. 17:9   **9**
Mal. 4:5   **11**
Mat. 17:10
Ps. 22:6   **12**
Is. 53:2, etc.
Dan. 9:26
Luke 23:11   **12**
Phil. 2:7
Mat. 11:14   **13**
& 17:12
Luke 1:17
Mat. 17:14   **14**
Luke 9:37
Or, *among*   **16**
yourselves?
Mat. 17:14   **17**
Luke 9:38
Or, *dasheth him* **18**
ch. 1:26   **20**
Luke 9:42
Mat. 17:20   **23**
ch. 11:23
Luke 17:6
John 11:40

round about, they saw no man any more, save Jesus only with themselves.

9 ᴿAnd as they came down from the mountain, he charged them that they should tell no man what things they had seen, till the Son of man were risen from the dead.

10 And they kept that saying with themselves, questioning one with another what the rising from the dead should mean.

11 And they asked him, saying, Why say the scribes ᴿthat Ē-lī′-ăs must first come?

12 And he answered and told them, Ē-lī′-ăs verily cometh first, and restoreth all things; and ᴿhow it is written of the Son of man, that he must suffer many things, and ᴿbe set at nought.

13 But I say unto you, That ᴿĒ-lī′-ăs is indeed come, and they have done unto him whatsoever they listed, as it is written of him.

Impotence of the disciples

14 ᴿAnd when he came to *his* disciples, he saw a great multitude about them, and the scribes questioning with them.

15 And straightway all the people, when they beheld him, were greatly amazed, and running to *him* saluted him.

16 And he asked the scribes, What question ye ᴺwith them?

17 And ᴿone of the multitude answered and said, Master, I have brought unto thee my son, which hath a dumb spirit;

18 And wheresoever he taketh him, he ᴺteareth him: and he foameth, and gnasheth with his teeth, and pineth away: and I spake to thy disciples that they should cast him out; and they could not.

19 He answereth him, and saith, O faithless generation, how long shall I be with you? how long shall I suffer you? bring him unto me.

20 And they brought him unto him: and ᴿwhen he saw him, straightway the spirit tare him; and he fell on the ground, and wallowed foaming.

21 And he asked his father, How long is it ago since this came unto him? And he said, Of a child.

22 And ofttimes it hath cast him into the fire, and into the waters, to destroy him: but if thou canst do any thing, have compassion on us, and help us.

23 Jesus said unto him, ᴿIf thou canst believe, all things *are* possible to him that believeth.

24 And straightway the father of the child cried out, and said with tears, Lord, I believe; help thou mine unbelief.

25 When Jesus saw that the people came

running together, he rebuked the foul spirit, saying unto him,*Thou* dumb and deaf spirit, I charge thee, come out of him, and enter no more into him.

26 And *the spirit* cried, and rent him sore, and came out of him: and he was as one dead; insomuch that many said, He is dead.

27 But Jesus took him by the hand, and lifted him up; and he arose.

28 ᴿAnd when he was come into the house, his disciples asked him privately, Why could not we cast him out?

29 And he said unto them, This kind can come forth by nothing, but by prayer and fasting.

Jesus speaks of His death

30 And they departed thence, and passed through Galilee; and he would not that any man should know *it*.

31 ᴿFor he taught his disciples, and said unto them, The Son of man is delivered into the hands of men, and they shall kill him; and after that he is killed, he shall rise the third day.

32 But they understood not that saying, and were afraid to ask him.

Who is the greatest?

33 ᴿAnd he came to Că-pĕr′-nă-ŭm: and being in the house he asked them, What was it that ye disputed among yourselves by the way?

34 But they held their peace: for by the way they had disputed among themselves, who *should be* the greatest.

35 And he sat down, and called the twelve, and saith unto them, ᴿIf any man desire to be first, *the same* shall be last of all, and servant of all.

36 And ᴿhe took a child, and set him in the midst of them: and when he had taken him in his arms, he said unto them,

37 Whosoever shall receive one of such children in my name, receiveth me: and ᴿwhosoever shall receive me, receiveth not me, but him that sent me.

38 ᴿAnd John answered him, saying, Master, we saw one casting out devils in thy name, and he followeth not us: and we forbad him, because he followeth not us.

39 But Jesus said, Forbid him not: ᴿfor there is no man which shall do a miracle in my name, that can lightly speak evil of me.

40 For ᴿhe that is not against us is on our part.

41 ᴿFor whosoever shall give you a cup of

water to drink in my name, because ye belong to Christ, verily I say unto you, he shall not lose his reward.

42 ᴿAnd whosoever shall offend one of *these* little ones that believe in me, it is better for him that a millstone were hanged about his neck, and he were cast into the sea.

43 ᴿAnd if thy hand ᴺoffend thee, cut it off: it is better for thee to enter into life maimed, than having two hands to go into hell, into the fire that never shall be quenched:

44 ᴿWhere their worm dieth not, and the fire is not quenched.

45 And if thy foot offend thee, cut it off: it is better for thee to enter halt into life, than having two feet to be cast into hell, into the fire that never shall be quenched:

46 Where their worm dieth not, and the fire is not quenched.

47 And if thine eye ᴺoffend thee, pluck it out: it is better for thee to enter into the kingdom of God with one eye, than having two eyes to be cast into hell fire:

48 Where their worm dieth not, and the fire is not quenched.

49 For every one shall be salted with fire, ᴿand every sacrifice shall be salted with salt.

50 ᴿSalt *is* good: but if the salt have lost his saltness, wherewith will ye season it? ᴿHave salt in yourselves, and ᴿhave peace one with another.

CHAPTER 10

Teaching about marriage

AND ᴿhe arose from thence, and cometh into the coasts of Judæa by the farther side of Jordan: and the people resort unto him again; and, as he was wont, he taught them again.

2 ᴿAnd the Pharisees came to him, and asked him, Is it lawful for a man to put away *his* wife? tempting him.

3 And he answered and said unto them, What did Moses command you?

4 And they said, ᴿMoses suffered to write a bill of divorcement, and to put *her* away.

5 And Jesus answered and said unto them, For the hardness of your heart he wrote you this precept.

6 But from the beginning of the creation ᴿGod made them male and female.

7 ᴿFor this cause shall a man leave his father and mother, and cleave to his wife;

8 And they twain shall be one flesh: so then they are no more twain, but one flesh.

CHAP. 9	
AD 32	
28	Mat. 17:19
31	Mat. 17:22
	Luke 9:44
33	Mat. 18:1
	Luke 9:46
	& 22:24
35	Mat. 20:26, 27
	ch. 10:43
36	Mat. 18:2
	ch. 10:16
37	Mat. 10:40
	Luke 9:48
38	Num. 11:28
	Luke 9:49
39	1 Cor. 12:3
40	See Mat. 12:30
41	Mat. 10:42

Mat. 18:6	42
Luke 17:1	
Deut. 13:6	43
Mat. 5:29	
& 18:8	
Or, *cause thee*	43
to offend,	
ver. 45, 47	
Is. 66:24	44
Or, *cause thee*	47
to offend	
Lev. 2:13	49
Ezek. 43:24	
Mat. 5:13	50
Luke 14:34	
Eph. 4:29	50
Col. 4:6	
Rom. 12:18	50
& 14:19	
2 Cor. 13:11	
Heb. 12:14	

CHAP. 10	
AD 33	
Mat. 19:1	1
John 10:40	
& 11:7	
Mat. 19:3	2
Deut. 24:1	4
Mat. 5:31	
& 19:7	
Gen. 1:27	6
& 5:2	
Gen. 2:24	7
1 Cor. 6:16	
Eph. 5:31	

9 What therefore God hath joined together, let not man put asunder.

10 And in the house his disciples asked him again of the same *matter*.

11 And he saith unto them, [R]Whosoever shall put away his wife, and marry another, committeth adultery against her.

12 And if a woman shall put away her husband, and be married to another, she committeth adultery.

Jesus blesses the children

13 [R]And they brought young children to him, that he should touch them: and *his* disciples rebuked those that brought *them*.

14 But when Jesus saw *it,* he was much displeased, and said unto them, Suffer the little children to come unto me, and forbid them not: for [R]of such is the kingdom of God.

15 Verily I say unto you, [R]Whosoever shall not receive the kingdom of God as a little child, he shall not enter therein.

16 And he took them up in his arms, put *his* hands upon them, and blessed them.

The rich young man

17 [R]And when he was gone forth into the way, there came one running, and kneeled to him, and asked him, Good Master, what shall I do that I may inherit eternal life?

18 And Jesus said unto him, Why callest thou me good? *there is* none good but one, *that is,* God.

19 Thou knowest the commandments, [R]Do not commit adultery, Do not kill, Do not steal, Do not bear false witness, Defraud not, Honour thy father and mother.

20 And he answered and said unto him, Master, all these have I observed from my youth.

21 Then Jesus beholding him loved him, and said unto him, One thing thou lackest: go thy way, sell whatsoever thou hast, and give to the poor, and thou shalt have [R]treasure in heaven: and come, take up the cross, and follow me.

22 And he was sad at that saying, and went away grieved: for he had great possessions.

The perils of riches

23 [R]And Jesus looked round about, and saith unto his disciples, How hardly shall they that have riches enter into the kingdom of God!

24 And the disciples were astonished at his words. But Jesus answereth again, and saith unto them, Children, how hard is it for them [R]that trust in riches to enter into the kingdom of God!

25 It is easier for a camel to go through the eye of a needle, than for a rich man to enter into the kingdom of God.

26 And they were astonished out of measure, saying among themselves, Who then can be saved?

27 And Jesus looking upon them saith, With men *it is* impossible, but not with God: for [R]with God all things are possible.

Rewards of discipleship

28 [R]Then Peter began to say unto him, Lo, we have left all, and have followed thee.

29 And Jesus answered and said, Verily I say unto you, There is no man that hath left house, or brethren, or sisters, or father, or mother, or wife, or children, or lands, for my sake, and the gospel's,

30 [R]But he shall receive an hundredfold now in this time, houses, and brethren, and sisters, and mothers, and children, and lands, with persecutions; and in the world to come eternal life.

31 [R]But many *that are* first shall be last; and the last first.

His death and resurrection foretold

32 [R]And they were in the way going up to Jerusalem; and Jesus went before them: and they were amazed; and as they followed, they were afraid. [R]And he took again the twelve, and began to tell them what things should happen unto him,

33 *Saying,* Behold, we go up to Jerusalem; and the Son of man shall be delivered unto the chief priests, and unto the scribes; and they shall condemn him to death, and shall deliver him to the Gentiles:

34 And they shall mock him, and shall scourge him, and shall spit upon him, and shall kill him: and the third day he shall rise again.

Request of James and John

35 [R]And James and John, the sons of Zĕb'-ĕ-dēē, come unto him, saying, Master, we would that thou shouldest do for us whatsoever we shall desire.

36 And he said unto them, What would ye that I should do for you?

37 They said unto him, Grant unto us that we may sit, one on thy right hand, and the other on thy left hand, in thy glory.

38 But Jesus said unto them, Ye know not what ye ask: can ye drink of the cup that I drink of? and be baptized with the baptism that I am baptized with?

Center reference column:

CHAP. **10**
AD 33
11 Mat. 5:32
& 19:9
Luke 16:18
Rom. 7:3
1 Cor. 7:10, 11
13 Mat. 19:13
Luke 18:15
14 1 Cor. 14:20
1 Pet. 2:2
15 Mat. 18:3
17 Mat. 19:16
Luke 18:18
19 Ex. 20
Rom. 13:9
21 Mat. 6:19, 20
& 19:21
Luke 12:33
& 16:9
23 Mat. 19:23
Luke 18:24
24 Job 31:24
Ps. 52:7
& 62:10
1 Tim. 6:17

Jer. 32:17   **27**
Mat. 19:26
Luke 1:37
Mat. 19:27   **28**
Luke 18:28
2 Chr. 25:9   **30**
Luke 18:30
Mat. 19:30   **31**
& 20:16
Luke 13:30
Mat. 20:17   **32**
Luke 18:31
ch. 8:31   **32**
& 9:31
Luke 9:22
& 18:31
Mat. 20:20   **35**

39 And they said unto him, We can. And Jesus said unto them, Ye shall indeed drink of the cup that I drink of; and with the baptism that I am baptized withal shall ye be baptized:

40 But to sit on my right hand and on my left hand is not mine to give; but *it shall be given to them* for whom it is prepared.

41 ᴿAnd when the ten heard *it*, they began to be much displeased with James and John.

42 But Jesus called them *to him*, and saith unto them, ᴿYe know that they which ᴺare accounted to rule over the Gentiles exercise lordship over them; and their great ones exercise authority upon them.

43 ᴿBut so shall it not be among you: but whosoever will be great among you, shall be your minister:

44 And whosoever of you will be the chiefest, shall be servant of all.

45 For even ᴿthe Son of man came not to be ministered unto, but to minister, and ᴿto give his life a ransom for many.

Healing of blind Bartimæus

46 ᴿAnd they came to Jericho: and as he went out of Jericho with his disciples and a great number of people, blind Bär-tĭ-mæ'-ŭs, the son of Tĭ-mæ'-ŭs, sat by the highway side begging.

47 And when he heard that it was Jesus of Nazareth, he began to cry out, and say, Jesus, *thou* son of David, have mercy on me.

48 And many charged him that he should hold his peace: but he cried the more a great deal, *Thou* son of David, have mercy on me.

49 And Jesus stood still, and commanded him to be called. And they call the blind man, saying unto him, Be of good comfort, rise; he calleth thee.

50 And he, casting away his garment, rose, and came to Jesus.

51 And Jesus answered and said unto him, What wilt thou that I should do unto thee? The blind man said unto him, Lord, that I might receive my sight.

52 And Jesus said unto him, Go thy way; ᴿthy faith hath ᴺmade thee whole. And immediately he received his sight, and followed Jesus in the way.

CHAPTER 11

The triumphal entry

AND ᴿwhen they came nigh to Jerusalem, unto Bĕth'-phă-ġē and Bethany, at the

CHAP. **10**
AD 33
41 Mat. 20:24
42 Luke 22:25
42 Or, *think good*
43 Mat. 20:26, 28
ch. 9:35
Luke 9:48
45 John 13:14
Phil. 2:7
45 Mat. 20:28
1 Tim. 2:6
Tit. 2:14
46 Mat. 20:29
Luke 18:35
52 Mat. 9:22
ch. 5:34
52 Or, *saved thee*

CHAP. **11**
AD 33
1 Mat. 21:1
Luke 19:45
John 2:14

Mat. 21:8　　**8**
Ps. 118:26　**9**
Ps. 148:1　　**10**
Mat. 21:12　**11**
Mat. 21:18　**12**
Mat. 21:10　**13**
Mat. 21:12　**15**
Luke 19:45
John 2:14
Is. 56:7　　　**17**
Or, *an house of prayer for all nations?*　**17**

mount of Olives, he sendeth forth two of his disciples,

2 And saith unto them, Go your way into the village over against you: and as soon as ye be entered into it, ye shall find a colt tied, whereon never man sat; loose him, and bring *him*.

3 And if any man say unto you, Why do ye this? say ye that the Lord hath need of him; and straightway he will send him hither.

4 And they went their way, and found the colt tied by the door without in a place where two ways met; and they loose him.

5 And certain of them that stood there said unto them, What do ye, loosing the colt?

6 And they said unto them even as Jesus had commanded: and they let them go.

7 And they brought the colt to Jesus, and cast their garments on him; and he sat upon him.

8 ᴿAnd many spread their garments in the way: and others cut down branches off the trees, and strawed *them* in the way.

9 And they that went before, and they that followed, cried, saying, ᴿHō-săn'-nă; Blessed *is* he that cometh in the name of the Lord:

10 Blessed *be* the kingdom of our father David, that cometh in the name of the Lord: ᴿHō-săn'-nă in the highest.

11 ᴿAnd Jesus entered into Jerusalem, and into the temple: and when he had looked round about upon all things, and now the eventide was come, he went out unto Bethany with the twelve.

The fruitless fig tree

12 ᴿAnd on the morrow, when they were come from Bethany, he was hungry:

13 ᴿAnd seeing a fig tree afar off having leaves, he came, if haply he might find any thing thereon: and when he came to it, he found nothing but leaves; for the time of figs was not *yet*.

14 And Jesus answered and said unto it, No man eat fruit of thee hereafter for ever. And his disciples heard *it*.

Cleansing the temple

15 ᴿAnd they come to Jerusalem: and Jesus went into the temple, and began to cast out them that sold and bought in the temple, and overthrew the tables of the moneychangers, and the seats of them that sold doves;

16 And would not suffer that any man should carry *any* vessel through the temple.

17 And he taught, saying unto them, Is it not written, ᴿMy house shall be called ᴺof all na-

tions the house of prayer? but ᴿye have made it a den of thieves.

18 And ᴿthe scribes and chief priests heard *it,* and sought how they might destroy him: for they feared him, because ᴿall the people was astonished at his doctrine.

19 And when even was come, he went out of the city.

The power of faith

20 ᴿAnd in the morning, as they passed by, they saw the fig tree dried up from the roots.

21 And Peter calling to remembrance saith unto him, Master, behold, the fig tree which thou cursedst is withered away.

22 And Jesus answering saith unto them, ᴺHave faith in God.

23 For ᴿverily I say unto you, That whosoever shall say unto this mountain, Be thou removed, and be thou cast into the sea; and shall not doubt in his heart, but shall believe that those things which he saith shall come to pass; he shall have whatsoever he saith.

24 Therefore I say unto you, ᴿWhat things soever ye desire, when ye pray, believe that ye receive *them,* and ye shall have *them.*

25 And when ye stand praying, ᴿforgive, if ye have aught against any: that your Father also which is in heaven may forgive you your trespasses.

26 But ᴿif ye do not forgive, neither will your Father which is in heaven forgive your trespasses.

The question about authority

27 And they come again to Jerusalem: ᴿand as he was walking in the temple, there come to him the chief priests, and the scribes, and the elders,

28 And say unto him, By what authority doest thou these things? and who gave thee this authority to do these things?

29 And Jesus answered and said unto them, I will also ask of you one ᴺquestion, and answer me, and I will tell you by what authority I do these things.

30 The baptism of John, was *it* from heaven, or of men? answer me.

31 And they reasoned with themselves, saying, If we shall say, From heaven; he will say, Why then did ye not believe him?

32 But if we shall say, Of men; they feared the people: for ᴿall *men* counted John, that he was a prophet indeed.

33 And they answered and said unto Jesus, We cannot tell. And Jesus answering saith

---

CHAP. 11

AD 33

17 Jer. 7:11
18 Mat. 21:45, 46
Luke 19:47
18 Mat. 7:28
ch. 1:22
Luke 4:32
20 Mat. 21:19
22 Or, *Have the faith of God*
23 Mat. 17:20
& 21:21
Luke 17:6
24 Mat. 7:7
Luke 11:9
John 14:13
& 15:7
& 16:24
Jas. 1:5, 6
25 Mat. 6:14
Col. 3:13
26 Mat. 18:35
27 Mat. 21:23
Luke 20:1
29 Or, *thing*
32 Mat. 3:5
& 14:5
ch. 6:20

CHAP. 12

AD 33

Mat. 21:33   **1**
Luke 20:9
Ps. 118:22   **10**
Mat. 21:45, 46   **12**
ch. 11:18
John 7:25, 30, 44
Mat. 22:15   **13**
Luke 20:20

---

unto them, Neither do I tell you by what authority I do these things.

CHAPTER 12

Parable of the wicked husbandmen

AND ᴿhe began to speak unto them by parables. A *certain* man planted a vineyard, and set an hedge about *it,* and digged *a place for* the winefat, and built a tower, and let it out to husbandmen, and went into a far country.

2 And at the season he sent to the husbandmen a servant, that he might receive from the husbandmen of the fruit of the vineyard.

3 And they caught *him,* and beat him, and sent *him* away empty.

4 And again he sent unto them another servant; and at him they cast stones, and wounded *him* in the head, and sent *him* away shamefully handled.

5 And again he sent another; and him they killed, and many others; beating some, and killing some.

6 Having yet therefore one son, his wellbeloved, he sent him also last unto them, saying, They will reverence my son.

7 But those husbandmen said among themselves, This is the heir; come, let us kill him, and the inheritance shall be ours.

8 And they took him, and killed *him,* and cast *him* out of the vineyard.

9 What shall therefore the lord of the vineyard do? he will come and destroy the husbandmen, and will give the vineyard unto others.

10 And have ye not read this scripture; ᴿThe stone which the builders rejected is become the head of the corner:

11 This was the Lord's doing, and it is marvellous in our eyes?

12 ᴿAnd they sought to lay hold on him, but feared the people: for they knew that he had spoken the parable against them: and they left him, and went their way.

The tribute money

13 ᴿAnd they send unto him certain of the Pharisees and of the Hĕ-rō′-dĭ-ăns, to catch him in *his* words.

14 And when they were come, they say unto him, Master, we know that thou art true, and carest for no man: for thou regardest not the person of men, but teachest the way of God in truth: Is it lawful to give tribute to Cæsar, or not?

15 Shall we give, or shall we not give? But he, knowing their hypocrisy, said unto them,

Why tempt ye me? bring me a ᴺpenny, that I may see *it.*

16 And they brought *it.* And he saith unto them, Whose *is* this image and superscription? And they said unto him, Cæsar's.

17 And Jesus answering said unto them, Render to Cæsar the things that are Cæsar's, and to God the things that are God's. And they marvelled at him.

Question about resurrection

18 ᴿThen come unto him the Săd'-dŭ-çêês, ᴿwhich say there is no resurrection; and they asked him, saying,

19 Master, ᴿMoses wrote unto us, If a man's brother die, and leave *his* wife *behind him,* and leave no children, that his brother should take his wife, and raise up seed unto his brother.

20 Now there were seven brethren: and the first took a wife, and dying left no seed.

21 And the second took her, and died, neither left he any seed: and the third likewise.

22 And the seven had her, and left no seed: last of all the woman died also.

23 In the resurrection therefore, when they shall rise, whose wife shall she be of them? for the seven had her to wife.

24 And Jesus answering said unto them, Do ye not therefore err, because ye know not the scriptures, neither the power of God?

25 For when they shall rise from the dead, they neither marry, nor are given in marriage; but ᴿare as the angels which are in heaven.

26 And as touching the dead, that they rise: have ye not read in the book of Moses, how in the bush God spake unto him, saying, ᴿI *am* the God of Abraham, and the God of Isaac, and the God of Jacob?

27 He is not the God of the dead, but the God of the living: ye therefore do greatly err.

First of all commandments

28 ᴿAnd one of the scribes came, and having heard them reasoning together, and perceiving that he had answered them well, asked him, Which is the first commandment of all?

29 And Jesus answered him, The first of all the commandments *is,* ᴿHear, O Israel; The Lord our God is one Lord:

30 And thou shalt love the Lord thy God with all thy heart, and with all thy soul, and with all thy mind, and with all thy strength: this *is* the first commandment.

31 And the second *is* like, *namely* this, ᴿThou shalt love thy neighbour as thyself. There is none other commandment greater than these.

32 And the scribe said unto him, Well,

Master, thou hast said the truth: for there is one God; ᴿand there is none other but he:

33 And to love him with all the heart, and with all the understanding, and with all the soul, and with all the strength, and to love *his* neighbour as himself, ᴿis more than all whole burnt offerings and sacrifices.

34 And when Jesus saw that he answered discreetly, he said unto him, Thou art not far from the kingdom of God. ᴿAnd no man after that durst ask him *any question.*

35 ᴿAnd Jesus answered and said, while he taught in the temple, How say the scribes that Christ is the son of David?

36 For David himself said ᴿby the Holy Ghost, ᴿThe Lᴏʀᴅ said to my Lord, Sit thou on my right hand, till I make thine enemies thy footstool.

37 David therefore himself calleth him Lord; and whence is he *then* his son? And the common people heard him gladly.

38 And ᴿhe said unto them in his doctrine, ᴿBeware of the scribes, which love to go in long clothing, and ᴿ*love* salutations in the marketplaces,

39 And the chief seats in the synagogues, and the uppermost rooms at feasts:

40 ᴿWhich devour widows' houses, and for a pretence make long prayers: these shall receive greater damnation.

The widow's mites

41 ᴿAnd Jesus sat over against the treasury, and beheld how the people cast ᴺmoney ᴿinto the treasury: and many that were rich cast in much.

42 And there came a certain poor widow, and she threw in two ᴺmites, which make a farthing.

43 And he called *unto him* his disciples, and saith unto them, Verily I say unto you, That ᴿthis poor widow hath cast more in, than all they which have cast into the treasury:

44 For all *they* did cast in of their abundance; but she of her want did cast in all that she had, ᴿ*even* all her living.

CHAPTER 13

Signs before the end

AND ᴿas he went out of the temple, one of his disciples saith unto him, Master, see what manner of stones and what buildings *are here!*

2 And Jesus answering said unto him, Seest thou these great buildings? ᴿthere shall not be left one stone upon another, that shall not be thrown down.

Center reference column

CHAP. 12

AD 33

15 Valuing of our money seven pence halfpenny, as
Mat. 18:28
18 Mat. 22:23
Luke 20:27
18 Acts 23:8
19 Deut. 25:5
25 1 Cor. 15:42, 49, 52
26 Ex. 3:6
28 Mat. 22:35
29 Deut. 6:4
Luke 10:27
31 Lev. 19:18
Mat. 22:39
Rom. 13:9
Gal. 5:14
Jas. 2:8

Deut. 4:39	32
Is. 45:6, 14 & 46:9	
1 Sam. 15:22	33
Hos. 6:6	
Mic. 6:6-8	
Mat. 22:46	34
Mat. 22:41	35
Luke 20:41	
2 Sam. 23:2	36
Ps. 110:1	36
ch. 4:2	38
Mat. 23:1, etc.	38
Luke 20:46	
Luke 11:43	38
Mat. 23:14	40
Luke 21:1	41
A piece of brass money: See Mat. 10:9	41
2 Ki. 12:9	41
It is the seventh part of one piece of that brass money	42
2 Cor. 8:12	43
Deut. 24:6	44
1 John 3:17	

CHAP. 13

AD 33

Mat. 24:1	1
Luke 21:5	
Luke 19:44	2

3 And as he sat upon the mount of Olives over against the temple, Peter and James and John and Andrew asked him privately,

4 ᴿTell us, when shall these things be? and what *shall be* the sign when all these things shall be fulfilled?

5 And Jesus answering them began to say, ᴿTake heed lest any *man* deceive you:

6 For many shall come in my name, saying, I am *Christ;* and shall deceive many.

7 And when ye shall hear of wars and rumours of wars, be ye not troubled: for *such things* must needs be; but the end *shall* not *be* yet.

8 For nation shall rise against nation, and kingdom against kingdom: and there shall be earthquakes in divers places, and there shall be famines and troubles: ᴿthese *are* the beginnings of ᴺsorrows.

Sufferings before the end

9 But ᴿtake heed to yourselves: for they shall deliver you up to councils; and in the synagogues ye shall be beaten: and ye shall be brought before rulers and kings for my sake, for a testimony against them.

10 And ᴿthe gospel must first be published among all nations.

11 ᴿBut when they shall lead *you,* and deliver you up, take no thought beforehand what ye shall speak, neither do ye premeditate: but whatsoever shall be given you in that hour, that speak ye: for it is not ye that speak, ᴿbut the Holy Ghost.

12 Now ᴿthe brother shall betray the brother to death, and the father the son; and children shall rise up against *their* parents, and shall cause them to be put to death.

13 ᴿAnd ye shall be hated of all *men* for my name's sake: but ᴿhe that shall endure unto the end, the same shall be saved.

Tribulation at the end

14 ᴿBut when ye shall see the abomination of desolation, ᴿspoken of by Daniel the prophet, standing where it ought not, (let him that readeth understand,) then ᴿlet them that be in Judæa flee to the mountains:

15 And let him that is on the housetop not go down into the house, neither enter *therein,* to take any thing out of his house:

16 And let him that is in the field not turn back again for to take up his garment.

17 ᴿBut woe to them that are with child, and to them that give suck in those days!

18 And pray ye that your flight be not in the winter.

19 ᴿFor *in* those days shall be affliction,

such as was not from the beginning of the creation which God created unto this time, neither shall be.

20 And except that the Lord had shortened those days, no flesh should be saved: but for the elect's sake, whom he hath chosen, he hath shortened the days.

21 ᴿAnd then if any man shall say to you, Lo, here *is* Christ; or, lo, *he is* there; believe *him* not:

22 For false Christs and false prophets shall rise, and shall shew signs and wonders, to seduce, if *it were* possible, even the elect.

23 But ᴿtake ye heed: behold, I have foretold you all things.

Coming of the Son of man

24 ᴿBut in those days, after that tribulation, the sun shall be darkened, and the moon shall not give her light,

25 And the stars of heaven shall fall, and the powers that are in heaven shall be shaken.

26 ᴿAnd then shall they see the Son of man coming in the clouds with great power and glory.

27 And then shall he send his angels, and shall gather together his elect from the four winds, from the uttermost part of the earth to the uttermost part of heaven.

28 ᴿNow learn a parable of the fig tree; When her branch is yet tender, and putteth forth leaves, ye know that summer is near:

29 So ye in like manner, when ye shall see these things come to pass, know that it is nigh, *even* at the doors.

30 Verily I say unto you, that this generation shall not pass, till all these things be done.

31 Heaven and earth shall pass away: but ᴿmy words shall not pass away.

Exhortation to watchfulness

32 But of that day and *that* hour knoweth no man, no, not the angels which are in heaven, neither the Son, but the Father.

33 ᴿTake ye heed, watch and pray: for ye know not when the time is.

34 ᴿ*For the Son of man is* as a man taking a far journey, who left his house, and gave authority to his servants, and to every man his work, and commanded the porter to watch.

35 ᴿWatch ye therefore: for ye know not when the master of the house cometh, at even, or at midnight, or at the cockcrowing, or in the morning:

36 Lest coming suddenly he find you sleeping.

37 And what I say unto you I say unto all, Watch.

CHAPTER 14

Plot to kill Jesus

AFTER [R]two days was *the feast of* the
passover, and of unleavened bread: and
the chief priests and the scribes sought how
they might take him by craft, and put *him* to
death.

2 But they said, Not on the feast *day,* lest
there be an uproar of the people.

The anointing at Bethany

3 [R]And being in Bethany in the house of
Simon the leper, as he sat at meat, there came
a woman having an alabaster box of ointment
of [N]spikenard very precious; and she brake the
box, and poured *it* on his head.

4 And there were some that had indignation
within themselves, and said, Why was this
waste of the ointment made?

5 For it might have been sold for more than
three hundred [R]pence, and have been given to
the poor. And they murmured against her.

6 And Jesus said, Let her alone; why trouble
ye her? she hath wrought a good work on me.

7 For ye have the poor with you always, and
whensoever ye will ye may do them good: but
me ye have not always.

8 She hath done what she could: she is come
aforehand to anoint my body to the burying.

9 Verily I say unto you, Wheresoever this
gospel shall be preached throughout the whole
world, *this* also that she hath done shall be
spoken of for a memorial of her.

Judas' treachery

10 [R]And Judas Iscariot, one of the twelve,
went unto the chief priests, to betray him unto
them.

11 And when they heard *it,* they were glad,
and promised to give him money. And he
sought how he might conveniently betray him.

The last supper

12 [R]And the first day of unleavened bread,
when they [N]killed the passover, his disciples
said unto him, Where wilt thou that we go and
prepare that thou mayest eat the passover?

13 And he sendeth forth two of his disciples,
and saith unto them, Go ye into the city, and
there shall meet you a man bearing a pitcher
of water: follow him.

14 And wheresoever he shall go in, say ye to
the goodman of the house, The Master saith,
Where is the guestchamber, where I shall eat
the passover with my disciples?

15 And he will shew you a large upper room
furnished *and* prepared: there make ready for
us.

16 And his disciples went forth, and came
into the city, and found as he had said unto
them: and they made ready the passover.

17 [R]And in the evening he cometh with the
twelve.

18 And as they sat and did eat, Jesus said,
Verily I say unto you, One of you which eateth with me shall betray me.

19 And they began to be sorrowful, and to
say unto him one by one, *Is* it I? and another
said, Is it I?

20 And he answered and said unto them, *It
is* one of the twelve, that dippeth with me in
the dish.

21 [R]The Son of man indeed goeth, as it is
written of him: but woe to that man by whom
the Son of man is betrayed! good were it for
that man if he had never been born.

22 [R]And as they did eat, Jesus took bread,
and blessed, and brake *it,* and gave to them,
and said, Take, eat: this is my body.

23 And he took the cup, and when he had
given thanks, he gave *it* to them: and they all
drank of it.

24 And he said unto them, This is my blood
of the new testament, which is shed for many.

25 Verily I say unto you, I will drink no
more of the fruit of the vine, until that day that
I drink it new in the kingdom of God.

Peter's denial foretold

26 [R]And when they had sung an [N]hymn,
they went out into the mount of Olives.

27 [R]And Jesus saith unto them, All ye shall
be offended because of me this night: for it is
written, [R]I will smite the shepherd, and the
sheep shall be scattered.

28 But [R]after that I am risen, I will go before
you into Galilee.

29 [R]But Peter said unto him, Although all
shall be offended, yet *will* not I.

30 And Jesus saith unto him, Verily I say
unto thee, That this day, *even* in this night,
before the cock crow twice, thou shalt deny
me thrice.

31 But he spake the more vehemently, If I
should die with thee, I will not deny thee in
any wise. Likewise also said they all.

Jesus prays in Gethsemane

32 [R]And they came to a place which was
named Gĕth-sĕm´-ă-nē: and he saith to his
disciples, Sit ye here, while I shall pray.

33 And he taketh with him Peter and James
and John, and began to be sore amazed, and to
be very heavy;

34 And saith unto them, [R]My soul is exceeding sorrowful unto death: tarry ye here,
and watch.

35 And he went forward a little, and fell on the ground, and prayed that, if it were possible, the hour might pass from him.

36 And he said, [R]Abba, Father, [R]all things *are* possible unto thee; take away this cup from me: [R]nevertheless not what I will, but what thou wilt.

37 And he cometh, and findeth them sleeping, and saith unto Peter, Simon, sleepest thou? couldest not thou watch one hour?

38 Watch ye and pray, lest ye enter into temptation. [R]The spirit truly *is* ready, but the flesh *is* weak.

39 And again he went away, and prayed, and spake the same words.

40 And when he returned, he found them asleep again, (for their eyes were heavy,) neither wist they what to answer him.

41 And he cometh the third time, and saith unto them, Sleep on now, and take *your* rest: it is enough, [R]the hour is come; behold, the Son of man is betrayed into the hands of sinners.

42 [R]Rise up, let us go; lo, he that betrayeth me is at hand.

Jesus betrayed and arrested

43 [R]And immediately, while he yet spake, cometh Judas, one of the twelve, and with him a great multitude with swords and staves, from the chief priests and the scribes and the elders.

44 And he that betrayed him had given them a token, saying, Whomsoever I shall kiss, that same is he; take him, and lead *him* away safely.

45 And as soon as he was come, he goeth straightway to him, and saith, Master, master; and kissed him.

46 And they laid their hands on him, and took him.

47 And one of them that stood by drew a sword, and smote a servant of the high priest, and cut off his ear.

48 [R]And Jesus answered and said unto them, Are ye come out, as against a thief, with swords and *with* staves to take me?

49 I was daily with you in the temple teaching, and ye took me not: but [R]the scriptures must be fulfilled.

50 [R]And they all forsook him, and fled.

51 And there followed him a certain young man, having a linen cloth cast about *his* naked *body;* and the young men laid hold on him:

52 And he left the linen cloth, and fled from them naked.

Jesus before the high priest

53 [R]And they led Jesus away to the high priest: and with him were assembled all the chief priests and the elders and the scribes.

54 And Peter followed him afar off, even into the palace of the high priest: and he sat with the servants, and warmed himself at the fire.

55 [R]And the chief priests and all the council sought for witness against Jesus to put him to death; and found none.

56 For many bare false witness against him, but their witness agreed not together.

57 And there arose certain, and bare false witness against him, saying,

58 We heard him say, [R]I will destroy this temple that is made with hands, and within three days I will build another made without hands.

59 But neither so did their witness agree together.

60 [R]And the high priest stood up in the midst, and asked Jesus, saying, Answerest thou nothing? what *is it which* these witness against thee?

61 But [R]he held his peace, and answered nothing. [R]Again the high priest asked him, and said unto him, Art thou the Christ, the Son of the Blessed?

62 And Jesus said, I am: [R]and ye shall see the Son of man sitting on the right hand of power, and coming in the clouds of heaven.

63 Then the high priest rent his clothes, and saith, What need we any further witnesses?

64 Ye have heard the blasphemy: what think ye? And they all condemned him to be guilty of death.

65 And some began to spit on him, and to cover his face, and to buffet him, and to say unto him, Prophesy: and the servants did strike him with the palms of their hands.

Peter's denial of Jesus

66 [R]And as Peter was beneath in the palace, there cometh one of the maids of the high priest:

67 And when she saw Peter warming himself, she looked upon him, and said, And thou also wast with Jesus of Nazareth.

68 But he denied, saying, I know not, neither understand I what thou sayest. And he went out into the porch; and the cock crew.

69 [R]And a maid saw him again, and began to say to them that stood by, This is *one* of them.

70 And he denied it again. [R]And a little after, they that stood by said again to Peter, Surely thou art *one* of them: [R]for thou art a Galilæan, and thy speech agreeth *thereto*.

71 But he began to curse and to swear, *saying,* I know not this man of whom ye speak.

72 [R]And the second time the cock crew. And Peter called to mind the word that Jesus

CHAP. 14
AD 33
36 Rom. 8:15
Gal. 4:6
36 Heb. 5:7
36 John 5:30
& 6:38
38 Rom. 7:23
Gal. 5:17
41 John 13:1
42 Mat. 26:46
John 18:1, 2
43 Mat. 26:47
Luke 22:47
John 18:3
48 Mat. 26:55
Luke 22:52
49 Ps. 22:6
Is. 53:7, etc.
Luke 22:37
& 24:44
50 ver. 27
Ps. 88:8
53 Mat. 26:57
Luke 22:54
John 18:13

Mat. 26:59   55
ch. 15:29   58
John 2:19
Mat. 26:62   60
Is. 53:7   61
Mat. 26:63   61
Mat. 24:30   62
& 26:64
Luke 22:69
Mat. 26:58, 69 66
Luke 22:55
John 18:16
Mat. 26:71   69
Luke 22:58
John 18:25
Mat. 26:73   70
Luke 22:59
John 18:26
Acts 2:7   70
Mat. 26:75   72

said unto him, Before the cock crow twice, thou shalt deny me thrice. And ᴺwhen he thought thereon, he wept.

CHAPTER 15

Jesus before Pilate

AND ᴿstraightway in the morning the chief priests held a consultation with the elders and scribes and the whole council, and bound Jesus, and carried *him* away, and delivered *him* to Pilate.

2 ᴿAnd Pilate asked him, Art thou the King of the Jews? And he answering said unto him, Thou sayest *it*.

3 And the chief priests accused him of many things: but he answered nothing.

4 ᴿAnd Pilate asked him again, saying, Answerest thou nothing? behold how many things they witness against thee.

5 ᴿBut Jesus yet answered nothing; so that Pilate marvelled.

6 Now ᴿat *that* feast he released unto them one prisoner, whomsoever they desired.

7 And there was *one* named Bär-ăb'-băs, *which lay* bound with them that had made insurrection with him, who had committed murder in the insurrection.

8 And the multitude crying aloud began to desire *him to do* as he had ever done unto them.

9 But Pilate answered them, saying, Will ye that I release unto you the King of the Jews?

10 For he knew that the chief priests had delivered him for envy.

11 But ᴿthe chief priests moved the people, that he should rather release Bär-ăb'-băs unto them.

12 And Pilate answered and said again unto them, What will ye then that I shall do *unto him* whom ye call the King of the Jews?

13 And they cried out again, Crucify him.

14 Then Pilate said unto them, Why, what evil hath he done? And they cried out the more exceedingly, Crucify him.

15 ᴿAnd *so* Pilate, willing to content the people, released Bär-ăb'-băs unto them, and delivered Jesus, when he had scourged *him,* to be crucified.

The soldiers mock Jesus

16 ᴿAnd the soldiers led him away into the hall, called Prae-tôr'-ĭ-ŭm; and they call together the whole band.

17 And they clothed him with purple, and plaited a crown of thorns, and put it about his *head,*

18 And began to salute him, Hail, King of the Jews!

19 And they smote him on the head with a reed, and did spit upon him, and bowing *their* knees worshipped him.

20 And when they had mocked him, they took off the purple from him, and put his own clothes on him, and led him out to crucify him.

The crucifixion

21 ᴿAnd they compel one Simon a Çy-rē'-nĭ-ăn, who passed by, coming out of the country, the father of Alexander and Rufus, to bear his cross.

22 ᴿAnd they bring him unto the place Gŏl'-gŏ-thä, which is, being interpreted, The place of a skull.

23 ᴿAnd they gave him to drink wine mingled with myrrh: but he received *it* not.

24 And when they had crucified him, ᴿthey parted his garments, casting lots upon them, what every man should take.

25 And ᴿit was the third hour, and they crucified him.

26 And ᴿthe superscription of his accusation was written over, THE KING OF THE JEWS.

27 And ᴿwith him they crucify two thieves; the one on his right hand, and the other on his left.

28 And the scripture was fulfilled, which saith, ᴿAnd he was numbered with the transgressors.

29 And ᴿthey that passed by railed on him, wagging their heads, and saying, Ah, ᴿthou that destroyest the temple, and buildest *it* in three days,

30 Save thyself, and come down from the cross.

31 Likewise also the chief priests mocking said among themselves with the scribes, He saved others; himself he cannot save.

32 Let Christ the King of Israel descend now from the cross, that we may see and believe. And ᴿthey that were crucified with him reviled him.

The death of Jesus

33 And ᴿwhen the sixth hour was come, there was darkness over the whole land until the ninth hour.

34 And at the ninth hour Jesus cried with a loud voice, saying, ᴿĒ-lō-ī, Ē-lō-ī, lä'-mä să-băch'-thă-nī? which is, being interpreted, My God, my God, why hast thou forsaken me?

35 And some of them that stood by, when

CHAP. 14	
AD 33	
72 Or, *he wept abundantly,* or, *he began to weep*	
CHAP. 15	
AD 33	
1 Ps. 2:2	
Mat. 27:1	
Luke 22:66 & 23:1	
John 18:28	
Acts 3:13 & 4:26	
2 Mat. 27:11	
4 Mat. 27:13	
5 Is. 53:7	
John 19:9	
6 Mat. 27:15	
Luke 23:17	
John 18:39	
11 Mat. 27:20	
Acts 3:14	
15 Mat. 27:26	
John 19:1, 16	
16 Mat. 27:27	
Mat. 27:32	21
Luke 23:26	
Mat. 27:33	22
Luke 23:33	
John 19:17	
Mat. 27:34	23
Ps. 22:18	24
Luke 23:34	
John 19:23	
See Mat. 27:45	25
Luke 23:44	
John 19:14	
Mat. 27:37	26
John 19:19	
Mat. 27:38	27
Is. 53:12	28
Luke 22:37	
Ps. 22:7	29
ch. 14:58	29
John 2:19	
Mat. 27:44	32
Luke 23:39	
Mat. 27:45	33
Luke 23:44	
Ps. 22:1	34
Mat. 27:46	

they heard *it,* said, Behold, he calleth Ē-lī'-ăs.

36 And ᴿone ran and filled a sponge full of vinegar, and put *it* on a reed, and ᴿgave him to drink, saying, Let alone; let us see whether Ē-lī'-ăs will come to take him down.

37 ᴿAnd Jesus cried with a loud voice, and gave up the ghost.

38 And ᴿthe veil of the temple was rent in twain from the top to the bottom.

39 And ᴿwhen the centurion, which stood over against him, saw that he so cried out, and gave up the ghost, he said, Truly this man was the Son of God.

40 ᴿThere were also women looking on ᴿafar off: among whom was Mary Măg'-dă-lēne, and Mary the mother of James the less and of Jō'-sĕś, and Să-lō'-mē;

41 (Who also, when he was in Galilee, ᴿfollowed him, and ministered unto him;) and many other women which came up with him unto Jerusalem.

The burial in Joseph's tomb

42 ᴿAnd now when the even was come, because it was the preparation, that is, the day before the sabbath,

43 Joseph of Ăr-ĭm-ă-thæ'-ă, an honourable counsellor, which also ᴿwaited for the kingdom of God, came, and went in boldly unto Pilate, and craved the body of Jesus.

44 And Pilate marvelled if he were already dead: and calling *unto him* the centurion, he asked him whether he had been any while dead.

45 And when he knew *it* of the centurion, he gave the body to Joseph.

46 ᴿAnd he bought fine linen, and took him down, and wrapped him in the linen, and laid him in a sepulchre which was hewn out of a rock, and rolled a stone unto the door of the sepulchre.

47 And Mary Măg'-dă-lēne and Mary *the mother* of Jō'-sĕś beheld where he was laid.

CHAPTER 16

The resurrection of Christ

AND ᴿwhen the sabbath was past, Mary Măg'-dă-lēne, and Mary the *mother* of James, and Să-lō'-mē, ᴿhad bought sweet spices, that they might come and anoint him.

2 ᴿAnd very early in the morning the first *day* of the week, they came unto the sepulchre at the rising of the sun.

3 And they said among themselves, Who shall roll us away the stone from the door of the sepulchre?

CHAP. 15
AD 33
36 Mat. 27:48
John 19:29
36 Ps. 69:21
37 Mat. 27:50
Luke 23:46
John 19:30
38 Mat. 27:51
Luke 23:45
39 Mat. 27:54
Luke 23:47
40 Mat. 27:55
Luke 23:49
40 Ps. 38:11
41 Luke 8:2, 3
42 Mat. 27:57
Luke 23:50
John 19:38
43 Luke 2:25, 38
46 Mat. 27:59, 60
Luke 23:53
John 19:40

CHAP. 16
AD 33
1 Mat. 28:1
Luke 24:1
John 20:1
1 Luke 23:56
2 Luke 24:1
John 20:1

Luke 24:3	5
John 20:11	
Mat. 28:5	6
Mat. 26:32	7
ch. 14:28	
Mat. 28:8	8
Luke 24:9	
Luke 8:2	9
Luke 24:10	10
John 20:18	
Luke 24:11	11
Luke 24:13	12
Luke 24:36	14
John 20:19	
1 Cor. 15:5	
Or, *together*	14
Mat. 28:19	15
John 15:16	
Col. 1:23	15
John 3:18	16
Acts 2:38	
& 16:30-32	
Rom. 10:9	
1 Pet. 3:21	
John 12:48	16
Luke 10:17	17
Acts 5:16	
Acts 2:4	17
1 Cor. 12:10	
Luke 10:19	18
Acts 28:5	
Acts 5:15	18
Jas. 5:14	
Acts 1:2, 3	19
Luke 24:51	19
Ps. 110:1	19
Acts 7:55	
Acts 5:12	20
1 Cor. 2:4, 5	
Heb. 2:4	

4 And when they looked, they saw that the stone was rolled away: for it was very great.

5 ᴿAnd entering into the sepulchre, they saw a young man sitting on the right side, clothed in a long white garment; and they were affrighted.

6 ᴿAnd he saith unto them, Be not affrighted: Ye seek Jesus of Nazareth, which was crucified: he is risen; he is not here: behold the place where they laid him.

7 But go your way, tell his disciples and Peter that he goeth before you into Galilee: there shall ye see him, ᴿas he said unto you.

8 And they went out quickly, and fled from the sepulchre; for they trembled and were amazed: ᴿneither said they any thing to any *man;* for they were afraid.

9 Now when *Jesus* was risen early the first *day* of the week, he appeared first to Mary Măg'-dă-lēne, ᴿout of whom he had cast seven devils.

10 ᴿAnd she went and told them that had been with him, as they mourned and wept.

11 ᴿAnd they, when they had heard that he was alive, and had been seen of her, believed not.

12 After that he appeared in another form ᴿunto two of them, as they walked, and went into the country.

13 And they went and told *it* unto the residue: neither believed they them.

The great commission

14 ᴿAfterward he appeared unto the eleven as they sat ᴺat meat, and upbraided them with their unbelief and hardness of heart, because they believed not them which had seen him after he was risen.

15 ᴿAnd he said unto them, Go ye into all the world, ᴿand preach the gospel to every creature.

16 ᴿHe that believeth and is baptized shall be saved; ᴿbut he that believeth not shall be damned.

17 And these signs shall follow them that believe; ᴿIn my name shall they cast out devils; ᴿthey shall speak with new tongues;

18 ᴿThey shall take up serpents; and if they drink any deadly thing, it shall not hurt them; ᴿthey shall lay hands on the sick, and they shall recover.

19 So then ᴿafter the Lord had spoken unto them, he was ᴿreceived up into heaven, and ᴿsat on the right hand of God.

20 And they went forth, and preached every where, the Lord working with *them,* ᴿand confirming the word with signs following. Ä'-měn.

THE GOSPEL ACCORDING TO
ST. LUKE

The third Gospel opens with a preface (1:1–4), the only example of its kind in the New Testament. From the preface we can deduce that the author was not an eyewitness of the events described, but nonetheless considers his account reliable since he based it upon information received from eyewitnesses. He acknowledges that others have written accounts of the character and life of Jesus, implies that he had access to these earlier narratives, and suggests that for some reason they were unsatisfactory for his purpose. He identifies his addressee by name, Theophilus, and by the added designation, "most excellent," probably meant to signify a Roman of some status. He states his purpose to be the orderly presentation of the origins of Christianity. The classical style throughout suggests that this work was intended for a public with some literary taste. In his emphasis on historical order, the author has been aptly called the "first Christian historian." Although theological concerns control his purpose and the selection of data, he seeks to be comprehensive in his treatment and to tie the events of redemptive history to secular history. Notices of time and place are frequent, and biographical interest is pronounced. Early Christian tradition unanimously ascribes the third Gospel to Luke, Paul's "beloved physician" (Col. 4:14), and considers the work apostolic because of Luke's association with Paul. Many date the Gospel between A.D. 75 and 85; others place it in the early 60's. Probably it was composed in Caesarea during Paul's two year imprisonment there, and finally issued in Rome.

OUTLINE OF THE BOOK:
  I. Preface 1:1–4
  II. Infancy and Preparation 1:5–4:13
  III. The Galilean Ministry 4:14–9:50
  IV. The Perean and Judean Ministry 9:51–19:27
  V. The Last Days in Jerusalem 19:28–21:38
  VI. The Passion Narrative 22:1–23:56
  VII. The Resurrection Account 24:1–53

CHAPTER 1

Preface

FORASMUCH as many have taken in hand to set forth in order a declaration of those things which are most surely believed among us,

2 ᴿEven as they delivered them unto us, which ᴿfrom the beginning were eyewitnesses, and ministers of the word;

3 ᴿIt seemed good to me also, having had perfect understanding of all things from the very first, to write unto thee ᴿin order, ᴿmost excellent Thē-ŏph'-ĭ-lŭs,

4 ᴿThat thou mightest know the certainty of those things, wherein thou hast been instructed.

The birth of John foretold

5 THERE was ᴿin the days of Herod, the king of Judæa, a certain priest named Zăch-ă-rī'-ăs, ᴿof the course of Ă-bī'-ă: and his wife was of the daughters of Aaron, and her name was Elisabeth.

6 And they were both ᴿrighteous before God, walking in all the commandments and ordinances of the Lord blameless.

7 And they had no child, because that Elisabeth was barren, and they both were now well stricken in years.

8 And it came to pass, that while he executed the priest's office before God ᴿin the order of his course,

9 According to the custom of the priest's office, his lot was ᴿto burn incense when he went into the temple of the Lord.

10 ᴿAnd the whole multitude of the people were praying without at the time of incense.

11 And there appeared unto him an angel of the Lord standing on the right side of ᴿthe altar of incense.

12 And when Zăch-ă-rī'-ăs saw him, ᴿhe was troubled, and fear fell upon him.

13 But the angel said unto him, Fear not, Zăch-ă-rī'-ăs: for thy prayer is heard; and thy wife Elisabeth shall bear thee a son, and ᴿthou shalt call his name John.

14 And thou shalt have joy and gladness; and ᴿmany shall rejoice at his birth.

15 For he shall be great in the sight of the Lord, and ᴿshall drink neither wine nor strong drink; and he shall be filled with the Holy Ghost, ᴿeven from his mother's womb.

16 ᴿAnd many of the children of Israel shall he turn to the Lord their God.

17 ᴿAnd he shall go before him in the spirit and power of Ē-lī'-ăs, to turn the hearts of the fathers to the children, and the disobedient ᴺto the wisdom of the just; to make ready a people prepared for the Lord.

18 And Zăch-ă-rī'-ăs said unto the angel, ᴿWhereby shall I know this? for I am an old man, and my wife well stricken in years.

19 And the angel answering said unto him, I am ᴿGabriel, that stand in the presence of God; and am sent to speak unto thee, and to shew thee these glad tidings.

20 And, behold, ᴿthou shalt be dumb, and not able to speak, until the day that these things shall be performed, because thou be-

CHAP. 1
Before the Common Account called Anno Domini the sixth Year

2 Heb. 2:3
1 Pet. 5:1
2 Mark 1:1
John 15:27
3 Acts 15:19
1 Cor. 7:40
3 Acts 11:4
3 Acts 1:1
4 John 20:31
5 Mat. 2:1
5 1 Chr. 24:10
Neh. 12:5
6 Gen. 7:1
1 Ki. 9:4
2 Ki. 20:3
8 1 Chr. 24:19
2 Chr. 8:14
9 Ex. 30:7, 8
1 Chr. 23:13

Lev. 16:17   10
Ex. 30:1   11
Judg. 6:22   12
& 13:22
Dan. 10:8
ch. 2:9
ver. 60, 63   13
ver. 58   14
Num. 6:3   15
Judg. 13:4
ch. 7:33
Jer. 1:5   15
Gal. 1:15
Mal. 4:5, 6   16
Mal. 4:5   17
Mat. 11:14
Mark 9:12
Or, by   17
Gen. 17:17   18
Dan. 8:16   19
& 9:21-23
Mat. 18:10
Ezek. 3:26   20
& 24:27

lievest not my words, which shall be fulfilled in their season.

21 And the people waited for Zăch-ă-rī'-ăs, and marvelled that he tarried so long in the temple.

22 And when he came out, he could not speak unto them: and they perceived that he had seen a vision in the temple: for he beckoned unto them, and remained speechless.

23 And it came to pass, that, as soon as ᴿthe days of his ministration were accomplished, he departed to his own house.

24 And after those days his wife Elisabeth conceived, and hid herself five months, saying,

25 Thus hath the Lord dealt with me in the days wherein he looked on *me,* to ᴿtake away my reproach among men.

The annunciation to Mary

26 And in the sixth month the angel Gabriel was sent from God unto a city of Galilee, named Nazareth,

27 To a virgin ᴿespoused to a man whose name was Joseph, of the house of David; and the virgin's name *was* Mary.

28 And the angel came in unto her, and said, ᴿHail, *thou that art* ᴺhighly favoured, ᴿthe Lord *is* with thee: blessed *art* thou among women.

29 And when she saw *him,* ᴿshe was troubled at his saying, and cast in her mind what manner of salutation this should be.

30 And the angel said unto her, Fear not, Mary: for thou hast found favour with God.

31 ᴿAnd, behold, thou shalt conceive in thy womb, and bring forth a son, and ᴿshalt call his name JESUS.

32 He shall be great, ᴿand shall be called the Son of the Highest: and ᴿthe Lord God shall give unto him the throne of his father David:

33 ᴿAnd he shall reign over the house of Jacob for ever; and of his kingdom there shall be no end.

34 Then said Mary unto the angel, How shall this be, seeing I know not a man?

35 And the angel answered and said unto her, ᴿThe Holy Ghost shall come upon thee, and the power of the Highest shall overshadow thee: therefore also that holy thing which shall be born of thee shall be called ᴿthe Son of God.

36 And, behold, thy cousin Elisabeth, she hath also conceived a son in her old age: and this is the sixth month with her, who was called barren.

37 For ᴿwith God nothing shall be impossible.

38 And Mary said, Behold the handmaid of

the Lord; be it unto me according to thy word. And the angel departed from her.

Mary visits Elisabeth

39 And Mary arose in those days, and went into the hill country with haste, ᴿinto a city of Judah;

40 And entered into the house of Zăch-ă-rī'-ăs, and saluted Elisabeth.

41 And it came to pass, that, when Elisabeth heard the salutation of Mary, the babe leaped in her womb; and Elisabeth was filled with the Holy Ghost:

42 And she spake out with a loud voice, and said, ᴿBlessed *art* thou among women, and blessed *is* the fruit of thy womb.

43 And whence *is* this to me, that the mother of my Lord should come to me?

44 For, lo, as soon as the voice of thy salutation sounded in mine ears, the babe leaped in my womb for joy.

45 And blessed *is* she ᴺthat believed: for there shall be a performance of those things which were told her from the Lord.

46 And Mary said,

Mary magnifies the Lord

ᴿMy soul doth magnify the Lord,

47 And my spirit hath rejoiced in God my Saviour.

48 For ᴿhe hath regarded the low estate of his handmaiden: for, behold, from henceforth ᴿall generations shall call me blessed.

49 For he that is mighty ᴿhath done to me great things; and ᴿholy *is* his name.

50 And ᴿhis mercy *is* on them that fear him from generation to generation.

51 ᴿHe hath shewed strength with his arm; ᴿhe hath scattered the proud in the imagination of their hearts.

52 ᴿHe hath put down the mighty from *their* seats, and exalted them of low degree.

53 ᴿHe hath filled the hungry with good things; and the rich he hath sent empty away.

54 He hath holpen his servant Israel, ᴿin remembrance of *his* mercy;

55 ᴿAs he spake to our fathers, to Abraham, and to his seed for ever.

56 And Mary abode with her about three months, and returned to her own house.

The birth of John the Baptist

57 Now Elisabeth's full time came that she should be delivered; and she brought forth a son.

58 And her neighbours and her cousins heard how the Lord had shewed great mercy upon her; and they rejoiced with her.

CHAP. 1

Before the Common Account called Anno Domini the sixth Year

23 2 Ki. 11:5
1 Chr. 9:25
25 Gen. 30:23
Is. 4:1 & 54:1, 4
27 Mat. 1:18
ch. 2:4, 5
28 Dan. 9:23
& 10:19
28 Or, *graciously accepted,* or, *much graced:* See ver. 30
28 Judg. 6:12
29 ver. 12
31 Is. 7:14
Mat. 1:21
31 ch. 2:21
32 Mark 5:7
32 2 Sam. 7:11
Ps. 132:11
Is. 9:6, 7 & 16:5
Jer. 23:5
33 Dan. 2:44
Obad. 21
Mic. 4:7
John 12:34
Heb. 1:8
35 Mat. 1:20
35 Mat. 14:33
Mark 1:1
John 1:34
& 20:31
Acts 8:37
Rom. 1:4
37 Gen. 18:14
Jer. 32:17
Mat. 19:26
Mark 10:27
ch. 18:27
Rom. 4:21

Josh. 21:9   **39**
Judg. 5:24   **43**
Or, *which*   **45**
believed that there
1 Sam. 2:1   **46**
Ps. 34:2, 3
Hab. 3:18
1 Sam. 1:11   **48**
Ps. 138:6
ch. 11:27   **48**
Ps. 71:19   **49**
& 126:2, 3
Ps. 111:9   **49**
Gen. 17:7   **50**
Ex. 20:6
Ps. 103:17
Ps. 98:1   **51**
& 118:15
Is. 40:10
Ps. 33:10   **51**
1 Pet. 5:5
1 Sam. 2:6   **52**
Job 5:11
Ps. 113:6
1 Sam. 2:5   **53**
Ps. 34:10
Ps. 98:3   **54**
Jer. 31:3
Gen. 17:19   **55**
Ps. 132:11
Gal. 3:16

59 And it came to pass, that ᴿon the eighth day they came to circumcise the child; and they called him Zăch-ă-rī′-ăs, after the name of his father.

60 And his mother answered and said, ᴿNot *so;* but he shall be called John.

61 And they said unto her, There is none of thy kindred that is called by this name.

62 And they made signs to his father, how he would have him called.

63 And he asked for a writing table, and wrote, saying, His name is John. And they marvelled all.

64 And his mouth was opened immediately, and his tongue *loosed,* and he spake, and praised God.

65 And fear came on all that dwelt round about them: and all these ᴺsayings were noised abroad throughout all the hill country of Judæa.

66 And all they that heard *them* ᴿlaid *them* up in their hearts, saying, What manner of child shall this be! And ᴿthe hand of the Lord was with him.

Zacharias' prophecy

67 And his father Zăch-ă-rī′-ăs ᴿwas filled with the Holy Ghost, and prophesied, saying,

68 ᴿBlessed *be* the Lord God of Israel; for ᴿhe hath visited and redeemed his people,

69 ᴿAnd hath raised up an horn of salvation for us in the house of his servant David;

70 ᴿAs he spake by the mouth of his holy prophets, which have been since the world began:

71 That we should be saved from our enemies, and from the hand of all that hate us;

72 ᴿTo perform the mercy *promised* to our fathers, and to remember his holy covenant;

73 ᴿThe oath which he sware to our father Abraham,

74 That he would grant unto us, that we being delivered out of the hand of our enemies might ᴿserve him without fear,

75 ᴿIn holiness and righteousness before him, all the days of our life.

76 And thou, child, shalt be called the prophet of the Highest: for ᴿthou shalt go before the face of the Lord to prepare his ways;

77 To give knowledge of salvation unto his people ᴿbyᴺ the remission of their sins,

78 Through the ᴺtender mercy of our God; whereby the ᴺdayspring from on high hath visited us,

79 ᴿTo give light to them that sit in darkness and *in* the shadow of death, to guide our feet into the way of peace.

CHAP. 1
Before the Common Account called Anno Domini the sixth Year
59 Gen. 17:12
Lev. 12:3
60 ver. 13
65 Or, *things*
66 ch. 2:19
66 Gen. 39:2
Ps. 80:17
67 Joel 2:28
68 1 Ki. 1:48
Ps. 41:13
68 Ex. 3:16
Ps. 111:9
69 Ps. 132:17
70 Jer. 23:5
Dan. 9:24
72 Lev. 26:42
Ezek. 16:60
73 Gen. 12:3
Heb. 6:13
74 Rom. 6:18
Heb. 9:14
75 Jer. 32:39
Eph. 4:24
76 Is. 40:3
Mat. 11:10
77 Mark 1:4
77 Or, *for*
78 Or, *bowels of the mercy*
78 Or, *sunrising,* or, *branch,* Num. 24:17
79 Is. 9:2
Mat. 4:16

ch. 2:40	80
Mat. 3:1	80

CHAP. 2	
Before the Common Account called Anno Domini the fifth Year	
Or, *inrolled*	1
Acts 5:37	2
1 Sam. 16:1	4
John 7:42	
Mat. 1:16	4
Mat. 1:18	5
Mat. 1:25	7
Or, *the night watches*	8
ch. 1:12	9
Gen. 12:3	10
Mat. 28:19	
Mark 1:15	
Is. 9:6	11
Mat. 1:21	11
Mat. 1:16	11
Acts 2:36	
Gen. 28:12	13
Dan. 7:10	
Rev. 5:11	
ch. 19:38	14
Eph. 1:6	
Is. 57:19	14
Rom. 5:1	
Col. 1:20	
John 3:16	14
Eph. 2:4, 7	
2 Thes. 2:16	
1 John 4:9	
Gr. *the men the shepherds*	15

80 And ᴿthe child grew, and waxed strong in spirit, and ᴿwas in the deserts till the day of his shewing unto Israel.

CHAPTER 2

The birth of Jesus

AND it came to pass in those days, that there went out a decree from Cæsar Augustus, that all the world should be ᴺtaxed.

2 (ᴿ*And* this taxing was first made when Çy̆-rē′-nĭ-ŭs was governor of Syria.)

3 And all went to be taxed, every one into his own city.

4 And Joseph also went up from Galilee, out of the city of Nazareth, into Judæa, unto ᴿthe city of David, which is called Bethlehem; (ᴿbecause he was of the house and lineage of David:)

5 To be taxed with Mary ᴿhis espoused wife, being great with child.

6 And so it was, that, while they were there, the days were accomplished that she should be delivered.

7 And ᴿshe brought forth her firstborn son, and wrapped him in swaddling clothes, and laid him in a manger; because there was no room for them in the inn.

The shepherds and the angels

8 And there were in the same country shepherds abiding in the field, keeping ᴺwatch over their flock by night.

9 And, lo, the angel of the Lord came upon them, and the glory of the Lord shone round about them: ᴿand they were sore afraid.

10 And the angel said unto them, Fear not: for, behold, I bring you good tidings of great joy, ᴿwhich shall be to all people.

11 ᴿFor unto you is born this day in the city of David ᴿa Saviour, ᴿwhich is Christ the Lord.

12 And this *shall be* a sign unto you; Ye shall find the babe wrapped in swaddling clothes, lying in a manger.

13 ᴿAnd suddenly there was with the angel a multitude of the heavenly host praising God, and saying,

14 ᴿGlory to God in the highest, and on earth ᴿpeace, ᴿgood will toward men.

15 And it came to pass, as the angels were gone away from them into heaven, ᴺthe shepherds said one to another, Let us now go even unto Bethlehem, and see this thing which is come to pass, which the Lord hath made known unto us.

16 And they came with haste, and found

Mary, and Joseph, and the babe lying in a manger.

17 And when they had seen *it,* they made known abroad the saying which was told them concerning this child.

18 And all they that heard *it* wondered at those things which were told them by the shepherds.

19 [R]But Mary kept all these things, and pondered *them* in her heart.

20 And the shepherds returned, glorifying and praising God for all the things that they had heard and seen, as it was told unto them.

21 [R]And when eight days were accomplished for the circumcising of the child, his name was called [R]JESUS, which was so named of the angel before he was conceived in the womb.

Presentation in the temple

22 And when [R]the days of her purification according to the law of Moses were accomplished, they brought him to Jerusalem, to present *him* to the Lord;

23 (As it is written in the law of the Lord, [R]Every male that openeth the womb shall be called holy to the Lord;)

24 And to offer a sacrifice according to [R]that which is said in the law of the Lord, A pair of turtledoves, or two young pigeons.

25 And, behold, there was a man in Jerusalem, whose name *was* Simeon; and the same man *was* just and devout, [R]waiting for the consolation of Israel: and the Holy Ghost was upon him.

26 And it was revealed unto him by the Holy Ghost, that he should not [R]see death, before he had seen the Lord's Christ.

27 And he came [R]by the Spirit into the temple: and when the parents brought in the child Jesus, to do for him after the custom of the law,

28 Then took he him up in his arms, and blessed God, and said,

Simeon and Anna give thanks

29 Lord, [R]now lettest thou thy servant depart in peace, according to thy word:

30 For mine eyes [R]have seen thy salvation,

31 Which thou hast prepared before the face of all people;

32 [R]A light to lighten the Gentiles, and the glory of thy people Israel.

33 And Joseph and his mother marvelled at those things which were spoken of him.

34 And Simeon blessed them, and said unto Mary his mother, Behold, this *child* is set for

the [R]fall and rising again of many in Israel; and for [R]a sign which shall be spoken against;

35 (Yea, [R]a sword shall pierce through thy own soul also,) that the thoughts of many hearts may be revealed.

36 And there was one Anna, a prophetess, the daughter of Phă-nū′-ĕl, of the tribe of Ā′-sĕr: she was of a great age, and had lived with an husband seven years from her virginity;

37 And she *was* a widow of about fourscore and four years, which departed not from the temple, but served *God* with fastings and prayers [R]night and day.

38 And she coming in that instant gave thanks likewise unto the Lord, and spake of him to all them that [R]looked for redemption in [N]Jerusalem.

39 And when they had performed all things according to the law of the Lord, they returned into Galilee, to their own city Nazareth.

40 [R]And the child grew, and waxed strong in spirit, filled with wisdom: and the grace of God was upon him.

The boy Jesus in the temple

41 Now his parents went to Jerusalem [R]every year at the feast of the passover.

42 And when he was twelve years old, they went up to Jerusalem after the custom of the feast.

43 And when they had fulfilled the days, as they returned, the child Jesus tarried behind in Jerusalem; and Joseph and his mother knew not *of it.*

44 But they, supposing him to have been in the company, went a day's journey; and they sought him among *their* kinsfolk and acquaintance.

45 And when they found him not, they turned back again to Jerusalem, seeking him.

46 And it came to pass, that after three days they found him in the temple, sitting in the midst of the doctors, both hearing them, and asking them questions.

47 And [R]all that heard him were astonished at his understanding and answers.

48 And when they saw him, they were amazed: and his mother said unto him, Son, why hast thou thus dealt with us? behold, thy father and I have sought thee sorrowing.

49 And he said unto them, How is it that ye sought me? wist ye not that I must be about [R]my Father's business?

50 And [R]they understood not the saying which he spake unto them.

51 And he went down with them, and came to Nazareth, and was subject unto them: but

CHAP. 2

Before the Common Account called Anno Domini the fifth Year

19 Gen. 37:11
ch. 1:66
21 Gen. 17:12
Lev. 12:3
ch. 1:59
21 Mat. 1:21, 25
ch. 1:31
22 Lev. 12:2
23 Ex. 13:2
& 22:29
Num. 3:13
24 Lev. 12:2
25 ver. 38
Is. 40:1
Mark 15:43
26 Ps. 89:48
Heb. 11:5
27 Mat. 4:1
29 Gen. 46:30
Phil. 1:23
30 Is. 52:10
32 Is. 9:2 & 42:6
& 49:6 & 60:1-3
Mat. 4:16
Acts 13:47
& 28:28

Is. 8:14   **34**
Hos. 14:9
Mat. 21:44
Rom. 9:32
1 Cor. 1:23
2 Cor. 2:16
1 Pet. 2:7, 8
Acts 28:22   **34**
Ps. 42:10   **35**
Acts 26:7   **37**
1 Tim. 5:5
ver. 25   **38**
Mark 15:43
ch. 24:21
Or, *Israel*   **38**
ver. 52   **40**
ch. 1:80
Ex. 23:15, 17   **41**
& 34:23
Deut. 16:1, 16
Mat. 7:28   **47**
Mark 1:22
ch. 4:22, 32
John 7:15, 46
John 2:16   **49**
ch. 9:45 & 18:34   **50**

his mother ᴿkept all these sayings in her heart.

52 And Jesus ᴿincreased in wisdom and ᴺstature, and in favour with God and man.

CHAPTER 3

The preaching of John the Baptist

NOW in the fifteenth year of the reign of Tī-bē′-rĭ-ŭs Cæsar, Pontius Pilate being governor of Judæa, and Herod being tē′-trärch of Galilee, and his brother Philip tē′-trärch of ī-tū-ræ′-ă and of the region of Trăch-ō-nī′-tĭs, and Lȳ-sā′-nĭ-ăs the tē′-trärch of Ăb-ĭ-lē′-nē,

2 ᴿĂn′-năs and Cāi′-ă-phăs being the high priests, the word of God came unto John the son of Zăch-ă-rī′-ăs in the wilderness.

3 ᴿAnd he came into all the country about Jordan, preaching the baptism of repentance ᴿfor the remission of sins;

4 As it is written in the book of the words of Ē-śāi′-ăs the prophet, saying, ᴿThe voice of one crying in the wilderness, Prepare ye the way of the Lord, make his paths straight.

5 Every valley shall be filled, and every mountain and hill shall be brought low; and the crooked shall be made straight, and the rough ways *shall be* made smooth;

6 And ᴿall flesh shall see the salvation of God.

7 Then said he to the multitude that came forth to be baptized of him, ᴿO generation of vipers, who hath warned you to flee from the wrath to come?

8 Bring forth therefore fruits ᴺworthy of repentance, and begin not to say within yourselves, We have Abraham to *our* father: for I say unto you, That God is able of these stones to raise up children unto Abraham.

9 And now also the axe is laid unto the root of the trees: ᴿevery tree therefore which bringeth not forth good fruit is hewn down, and cast into the fire.

10 And the people asked him, saying, ᴿWhat shall we do then?

11 He answereth and saith unto them, ᴿHe that hath two coats, let him impart to him that hath none; and he that hath meat, let him do likewise.

12 Then ᴿcame also publicans to be baptized, and said unto him, Master, what shall we do?

13 And he said unto them, ᴿExact no more than that which is appointed you.

14 And the soldiers likewise demanded of him, saying, And what shall we do? And he said unto them, ᴺDo violence to no man, ᴿneither accuse *any* falsely; and be content with your ᴺwages.

15 And as the people were ᴺin expectation,

and all men ᴺmused in their hearts of John, whether he were the Christ, or not;

16 John answered, saying unto *them* all, ᴿI indeed baptize you with water; but one mightier than I cometh, the latchet of whose shoes I am not worthy to unloose: he shall baptize you with the Holy Ghost and with fire:

17 Whose fan *is* in his hand, and he will throughly purge his floor, and ᴿwill gather the wheat into his garner; but the chaff he will burn with fire unquenchable.

18 And many other things in his exhortation preached he unto the people.

19 ᴿBut Herod the tē′-trärch, being reproved by him for Hē-rō′-dĭ-ăs his brother Philip's wife, and for all the evils which Herod had done,

20 Added yet this above all, that he shut up John in prison.

John baptizes Jesus

21 Now when all the people were baptized, ᴿit came to pass, that Jesus also being baptized, and praying, the heaven was opened,

22 And the Holy Ghost descended in a bodily shape like a dove upon him, and a voice came from heaven, which said, Thou art my beloved Son; in thee I am well pleased.

The genealogy of Jesus

23 And Jesus himself began to be ᴿabout thirty years of age, being (as was supposed) ᴿthe son of Joseph, which was *the son* of Hē′-lī,

24 Which was *the son* of Măt′-thăt, which was *the son* of Levi, which was *the son* of Mĕl′-chī, which was *the son* of Jăn′-nă, which was *the son* of Joseph,

25 Which was *the son* of Măt-tă-thī′-ăs, which was *the son* of Amos, which was *the son* of Nā′-ŭm, which was *the son* of Ĕś′-lī, which was *the son* of Năg′-gē,

26 Which was *the son* of Mā′-ăth, which was *the son* of Măt-tă-thī′-ăs, which was *the son* of Sĕm′-ĕ-ī, which was *the son* of Joseph, which was *the son* of Judah,

27 Which was *the son* of Jō-ăn′-nă, which was *the son* of Rhē′-să, which was *the son* of Zō-rŏb′-ă-bĕl, which was *the son* of Să-lā-thĭ-ĕl, which was *the son* of Nē′-rī,

28 Which was *the son* of Mĕl′-chī, which was *the son* of Ăd′-dī, which was *the son* of Cō′-săm, which was *the son* of ĕl-mō′-dăm, which was *the son* of Er,

29 Which was *the son* of Jō′-sē, which was *the son* of Ĕl-ĭ-ē′-zĕr, which was *the son* of Jō′-rĭm, which was *the son* of Măt′-thăt, which was *the son* of Levi,

30 Which was *the son* of Simeon, which was

CHAP. 2

Before the Common Account called Anno Domini the fifth Year

51 ver. 19
Dan. 7:28
52 ver. 40
1 Sam. 2:26
52 Or, *age*

CHAP. 3

AD 26
2 John 11:49, 51
& 18:13
Acts 4:6
3 Mat. 3:1
Mark 1:4
3 ch. 1:77
4 Is. 40:3
Mat. 3:3
Mark 1:3
John 1:23
6 Ps. 98:2
Is. 52:10
ch. 2:10
7 Mat. 3:7
8 Or, *meet for*
9 Mat. 7:19
10 Acts 2:37
11 ch. 11:41
2 Cor. 8:14
Jas. 2:15, 16
1 John 3:17
& 4:20
12 Mat. 21:32
ch. 7:29
13 ch. 19:8
14 Or, *Put no man in fear*
14 Ex. 23:1
Lev. 19:11
14 Or, *allowance*

Or, *in suspense* 15
Or, *reasoned,* 15
or, *debated*
Mat. 3:11 16
Mic. 4:12 17
Mat. 13:30
Mat. 14:3 19
Mark 6:17
Mat. 3:13 21
John 1:32
See Num. 4:3, 23
35, 39, 43, 47
Mat. 13:55 23
John 6:42

The Early Life of Jesus

"*And the child grew, and waxed strong in spirit, filled with wisdom; and the grace of God was upon him.*"

LUKE 2:40

ANY great events have their beginning quietly, privately, almost completely unnoticed by the world. So it was with the birth of Jesus. The remarkable good news that God would make his dwelling with men and walk among them in human flesh for their salvation was announced first to a young woman named Mary, in the little town of Nazareth in Galilee.

Mary was a young unmarried woman, a virgin, engaged to a carpenter named Joseph. One can understand why she would be startled, therefore, when the angel Gabriel suddenly appeared to her and spoke to her: "Hail, thou that art highly favored, the Lord is with thee: blessed art thou among women." What could this possibly mean? Mary asked herself.

The angel, seeing Mary's troubled expression, spoke reassuringly: "Fear not, Mary: for thou hast found favor with God. And behold, thou shalt conceive in thy womb, and bring forth a son, and shalt call his name Jesus." The very name of her child pointed to his great mission in life, for "Jesus" is the Greek rendering of the Jewish name "Joshua," which means "The Lord is salvation."

Then the angel spoke even more exciting words, a promise that Mary's son would be the Messiah for whom the Jews had waited in hope:

"He shall be great, and shall be called the Son of the Highest;
And the Lord God shall give unto him the throne of his father David:
And he shall reign over the house of Jacob for ever;
And of his kingdom there shall be no end."

Mary found it hard to understand how all this could be happening to her. Why, she was not even married! So she asked the angel: "How shall this be, seeing I know not a man?"

Gabriel's answer to her question was breath-taking: The Spirit of God, the Holy Ghost, would be the father of her child. Mary must have been overcome with awe as she heard the angel's explanation: "The Holy Ghost shall come upon thee, and the power of the Highest shall overshadow thee: therefore also that holy thing which shall be born of thee shall be called the Son of God."

The Son of God! Now Mary could understand why the angel had called her "highly favored" and "blessed among women." She could never have imagined that life held in store for her such a high and holy mission as to be the mother of Jesus, the Son of God.

Mary could not know immediately all that it would mean to be the mother of Jesus, but one thing she did know: She was committed to living by the will of God. So her reply was one of obedience to the divine plan: "Behold the handmaid of the Lord; be it unto me according to thy word." And with that, "the angel departed from her."

Luke 1:26–38.

BLOCH

The Visit to Elizabeth

OOD news must be shared. The news which Mary had to tell was so personal and so wonderful that it could be shared only with someone very close and dear to her. Mary remembered what the angel had told her: Her cousin Elizabeth was expecting a baby also. So Mary left promptly for the home of Zechariah and Elizabeth, which was located in the hill country of Judah.

When Mary arrived at the home and greeted her cousin, Elizabeth was deeply moved. She felt inspired by God to speak to Mary in exultation: "Blessed art thou among women, and blessed is the fruit of thy womb." Then, leaping in imagination to the day when Mary's child, the Messiah, would be born, Elizabeth asked: "Whence is this to me, that the mother of my Lord should come to me?" Because of her religious sensitivity, Elizabeth realized what wonderful events were taking place, and in true humility felt her human unworthiness to be involved in a divine drama of such world-wide importance.

Then Elizabeth told Mary: "As soon as the voice of thy salutation sounded in mine ears, the babe leaped in my womb for joy." Little could Elizabeth imagine what an important role her child would play in relation to Mary's child. For her son was destined to be John the Baptist, preacher and prophet, who would prepare the way for the ministry of Jesus Christ!

This moment of meeting was inspiring to Mary, also. Her response was one of thanksgiving and praise to God. She began by telling what it meant to her personally to be chosen to be the mother of Jesus:

"My soul doth magnify the Lord,
And my spirit hath rejoiced in God my Savior.
For he hath regarded the low estate of his handmaiden:
For, behold, from henceforth all generations shall call me blessed.
For he that is mighty hath done to me great things; and holy is his name.
And his mercy is on them that fear him from generation to generation."

Then, as she reflected on God's goodness and power, Mary described how God had dealt with the Jewish people across the centuries, and indeed how he deals with all mankind:

"He hath showed strength with his arm;
He hath scattered the proud in the imagination of their hearts.
He hath put down the mighty from their seats, and exalted those of low degree.
He hath filled the hungry with good things; and the rich he hath sent empty away.
He hath holpen his servant Israel, in remembrance of his mercy;
As he spake to our fathers, to Abraham, and to his seed for ever."

Mary visited with her cousin Elizabeth three months. One can imagine that two such religiously sensitive women had many long, deep conversations about the wonderful ways of God in human life. Then Mary returned to her home in Nazareth.

Luke 1:39–56.

BLOCH

The Birth of Jesus

 HE word had gone out from Caesar Augustus: everyone must be counted for an official census; furthermore, everyone must return to his home town for this enrollment. So it was that Joseph, a carpenter of Nazareth in Galilee, headed for the little town of Bethlehem with his betrothed, Mary. For Joseph was a descendant of the great king David, whose home town was Bethlehem in Judea.

As they moved along toward Bethlehem, Joseph must have pondered deeply on the strange and wonderful events of which he had become a part. Through a dream, an angel of the Lord had informed Joseph that his intended wife, Mary, would bear a son who had been conceived by the Holy Spirit. This remarkable child's name would be Jesus.

The weary travelers arrived in Bethlehem only to find all the inns filled with guests. On this very night, the time had arrived for the birth of Mary's child. Thus it happened that Jesus was born in a stable. Lovingly, his parents wrapped the newborn child in swaddling cloths and laid him in a manger.

Humble as this setting was, it was nevertheless surrounded by heavenly beauty and joy. Shepherds in the fields saw a vision of angels and heard the exciting good news that a Savior for all mankind had been born in Bethlehem. Their own joy was caught up and expressed by the heavenly choir's jubilant song: "Glory to God in the highest, and on earth peace, good will toward men."

When they arrived at the stable in Bethlehem, what did the shepherds find? Here before them was a couple from Nazareth, their loving gaze focused on a baby lying in a manger. It was such a simple, humble, totally unexpected way for God to plunge into the stream of human life that the shepherds were speechless with wonder. Here, in this obscure stable, dependent as any baby ever born, was a Savior—in a manger! What could it mean?

Jesus' birth is called the Incarnation, by which we mean God-in-human-flesh. For when God came most decisively into human life, it was not in a dazzling display of power. Emmanuel, "God with us," was truly human; as such, he could be esteemed or scorned, accepted or rejected.

As they gazed silently at the baby in the manger, the shepherds could not imagine what lay in store for Jesus as a full-grown man. But they were enthralled by this new-born child, who somehow made them keenly aware of God's love. It was enough to send the shepherds back to their flocks "glorifying and praising God for all the things that they had heard and seen."

Matthew 1:18-25; Luke 2:1-20.

MURILLO

The Visit of the Wise Men

EOPLE in Jerusalem must have turned and watched with interest as those three Magi or "wise men" rode by on their camels. Their clothes showed them to be men of some wealth. To an experienced eye they would also say that the men had journeyed far, perhaps from Persia.

A cluster of Jews gathered about them as they drew their camels to a halt and dismounted. And a ripple of excitement ran through the crowd as one of the wise men spoke: "Where is he that is born king of the Jews?" These men must be strangers, indeed! Did they not know that Herod the Great was king of the Jews? The Roman Senate had made him king in 40 B.C., and he was jealous of his power over this nation.

The wise men explained their mission: "We have seen his star in the east, and are come to worship him." So that was it! These were astrologers, men who studied the movement of the stars, who believed that the destinies of men and of nations were written in the stars. One of Herod's informers hastened to the palace and told the king about these Magi from the east, and their search for the newborn king of the Jews.

Herod was upset. Was someone trying to take his throne from him? He called his religious advisers, the chief priests and scribes, and "demanded of them where Christ should be born." After studying the writings of the prophets, they told him that the birthplace was Bethlehem.

Speedily Herod had his messenger to find the wise men and bring them to the palace. Then, in private, he questioned them closely. When had they first seen the star? The crafty king was eager to know the exact age of this unknown rival for his throne.

Herod probably tried his best to sound sincere, and to hide his anxiety and anger toward this newborn "king of the Jews," as he sent the wise men on their way toward Bethlehem. "Go and search diligently for the young child," he told them, "and when ye have found him, bring me word again, that I may come and worship him also."

So the wise men resumed their quest; but this was a short journey, for Bethlehem is only five miles south of Jerusalem. And a wonderful thing occurred: the star, which they had followed across the desert sands to Jerusalem, "went before them, till it came and stood over where the young child was." This star, shining with unusual brightness, filled them with joy.

Here, in Bethlehem, was the climax to their journey: the Christ Child with Mary his mother. In reverence, the wise men "fell down, and worshipped him: and when they had opened their treasures, they presented unto him gifts; gold, and frankincense, and myrrh." These were gifts literally fit for a king.

Now that they had found the promised "king of the Jews," should they return to Jerusalem and tell Herod? As they slept that night they received their answer in a dream: they should not return to Herod. So "they departed into their own country another way."

Matthew 2:1-12.

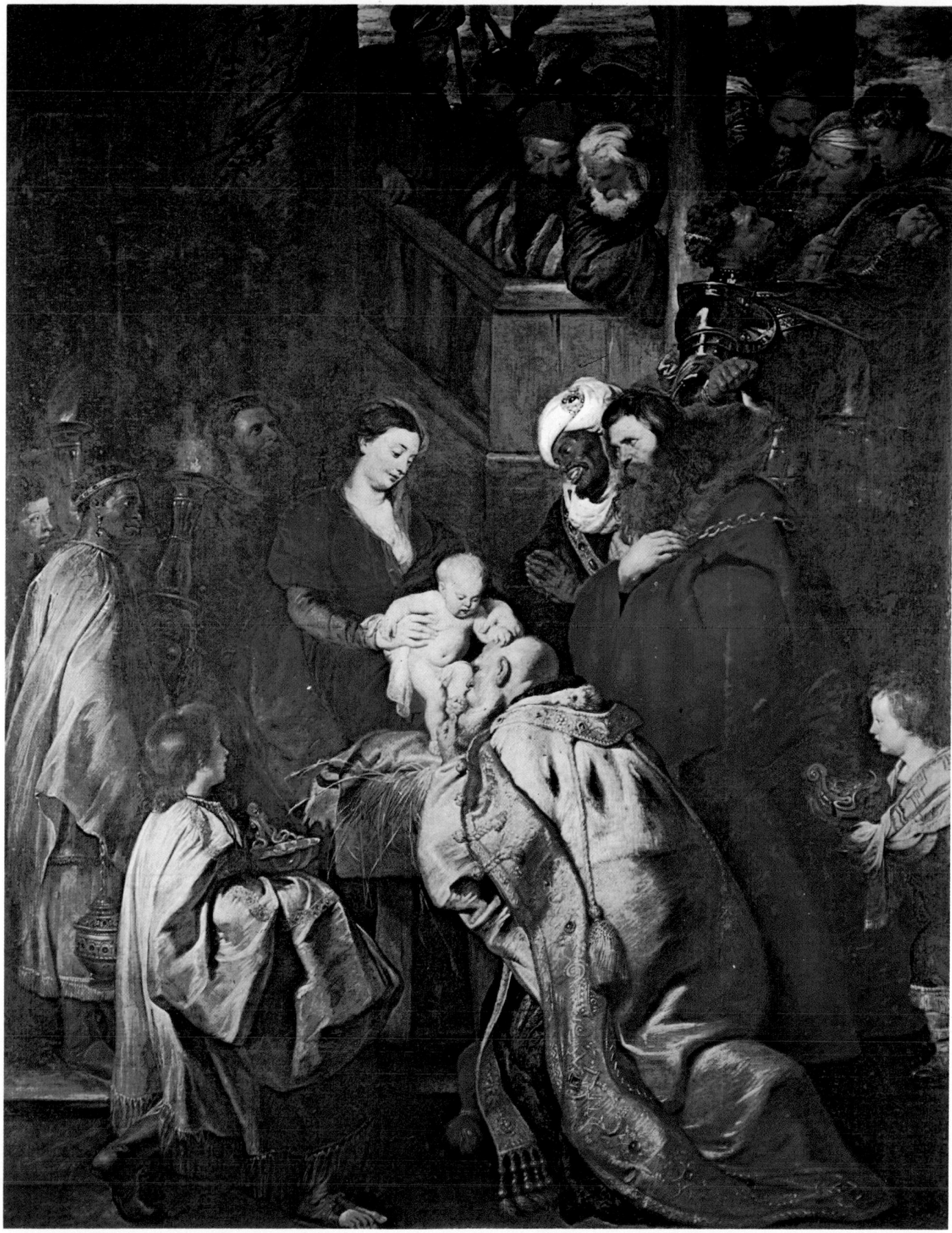

RUBENS

The Flight Into Egypt

HAT a responsibility it was to fulfill the role of parents for a child born to be king! If everyone would act as the wise men had in the presence of the Christ Child—treating him with love and devotion —all would be well. But the world contains persons who act out of cruelty and hatred, also—persons like Herod, eager to destroy anyone who would challenge his power.

After the wise men had gone on their way, Joseph had a troubling dream. In the dream an angel told him: "Arise, and take the young child and his mother, and flee into Egypt, and be thou there until I bring thee word: for Herod will seek the young child to destroy him."

Distressing news! Yet Joseph acted quickly and cautiously: "he took the young child and his mother by night, and departed into Egypt." What long thoughts Joseph must have had as he and his little family moved wearily across the miles into Egypt, refugees from a cruel tyrant! Perhaps he remembered the exodus from Egypt centuries before, when his ancestors fled from just such a tyrannical pharaoh. He may have reflected on his great namesake, Joseph, who became prime minister of Egypt and did so much for the Hebrew people. Possibly he called to mind the prophecy of Hosea, "Out of Egypt have I called my son," and looked toward the day when he and his family would return to their homeland.

Joseph and Mary and the baby Jesus lived in Egypt until the death of Herod the king. They had escaped the cruel trap which the jealous tyrant had tried to set for the Christ Child.

But other families in Bethlehem were not so fortunate. When Herod finally decided that the wise men were not coming back to report on the whereabouts of the newborn "King of the Jews" he was furious. In a raging anger, he ordered all the children in Bethlehem who were two years old and under to be killed. In this way, he expected to destroy any threat to his throne. Apparently, it did not bother this cruel tyrant to kill innocent people; all that concerned him was his own security as king!

Death ended Herod's reign as king of the Jews; and against death Herod was powerless. Joseph, in Egypt, had another dream. This time, the angel said: "Arise, and take the young child and his mother, and go into the land of Israel: for they are dead which sought the young child's life."

Joseph's heart, which had been heavy, must have been filled with joy as he and Mary and Jesus headed for their homeland! However, what he heard about Herod's son Archelaus made him cautious about settling in Bethlehem or Jerusalem. Once again he was counseled in a dream. Obedient, as always, to God's guidance, Joseph took his little family to the city of Nazareth, in Galilee. And there they made their home. Was it not a remarkable journey, with God guarding and guiding this family whose son would mean so much to all mankind?

Matthew 2:13-23.

Tissot

 ESUS' home town was Nazareth. There he was known as "the carpenter's son." Even when he had grown to maturity and had begun his ministry of teaching and healing, people in Nazareth still thought of him in those terms. "Is not this the carpenter's son?" they asked. Others recalled that Jesus himself had learned Joseph's trade, so their question was: "Is not this the carpenter?"

We can go into Joseph's shop in the little town of Nazareth only in imagination. About Jesus' early childhood we know only that "the child grew, and waxed strong in spirit, filled with wisdom: and the grace of God was upon him." But a child tells much about the kind of home from which he comes. Joseph and Mary's home must have been one in which love was present, and in which God was worshipped.

Life in that Nazareth home was far simpler and more stringent than in the average American home nearly two thousand years later. There were fewer comforts. The breadwinner worked longer hours for less pay. The family was less free to travel than are most families today.

Yet there was a quality present in the life of that family that has caused Christians in succeeding generations to label it "holy." There was such love between parent and child that "Father" was felt to be God's truest name. There was such genuine reverence for the Almighty that the child early recognized he must be about his Father's business.

It is natural to think of the boy Jesus helping Joseph in the shop, learning how to make yokes for the oxen—yokes that would be smooth and light on the laboring animals' necks. We can imagine that the growing boy learned respect for good workmanship through observing the care with which Joseph measured and cut lumber, for tables, chairs, and doors. How natural that the full-grown Jesus should think of a figure of speech from the carpenter's shop: "I am the door."

From watching Joseph at work in his shop, Jesus must have learned the dignity of useful work. He learned to use his own hands to create something useful for other people. Thus, he conferred dignity on the laboring man in every generation. The Son of God himself earned his bread "by the sweat of his brow."

Jesus learned valuable lessons in Joseph's shop. He learned to work carefully and well. His work benefitted his fellow citizens of Nazareth. In work, as in other aspects of life, Jesus learned what it meant to be fully human. For this, we can be grateful.

Matthew 13:55; Mark 6:3; Luke 2:39-40.

TISSOT

The Boy Jesus in the Temple

THE time had come for Joseph's family to make their annual trip to Jerusalem. A deeply religious family, they went each year to the "religious capital" of their country to celebrate the feast of the Passover. This ancient Hebrew festival was celebrated as a reminder of the liberation of the Hebrews from Egyptian bondage.

Jesus was a growing boy, twelve years of age. With his fine mind and sensitive spirit, he must have looked forward with keen anticipation to this journey to the Temple in Jerusalem.

The feast of the Passover and of Unleavened Bread lasted for seven days. When it was over, Joseph and Mary began their homeward journey, walking and talking with friends and relatives who had also gone to Jerusalem for the feast. As the day drew to a close, they suddenly realized that they had not seen Jesus recently. Was he visiting with some of his friends farther back in the caravan? Quickly Joseph and Mary made their way from group to group, but Jesus was not to be found.

More and more worried, Joseph and Mary retraced their steps to Jerusalem. Had any harm befallen their son? Anxiously they looked for Jesus—one day, two days, without success. Finally, on the third day "they found him in the temple, sitting in the midst of the doctors, both hearing them, and asking them questions. And all that heard him were astonished at his understanding and answers."

Joseph and Mary did not know what to think. Here was Jesus, totally unaware of the anxiety which he had caused his parents to suffer. Mary rushed up to her son and asked: "Son, why hast thou thus dealt with us? behold, thy father and I have sought thee sorrowing."

There was probably a puzzled expression on Jesus' face as he looked up at his parents. Perhaps he had been unaware of the passage of time—the days had been filled with so many interesting experiences and discussions with teachers here in the Temple. But there was also a new awareness of God evident in the shining eyes and radiant countenance of the boy Jesus as he replied: "How is it that ye sought me? wist ye not that I must be about my Father's business?"

What kind of answer was that? Joseph and Mary were puzzled; "they understood not the saying which he spake unto them." They knew that Jesus was a loving and obedient son; they knew, too, that he had a great interest in religion. Secretly they were proud that their son could engage the wise teachers at the Temple in deep discussion of God's will and way. But what could he have meant by the expression, his "Father's business"? Both Joseph and Mary were silent and thoughtful as they left the Temple and headed home once more.

Jesus and his parents went home to Nazareth, back to the daily round of duties. Joseph returned to his carpenter's shop, with Jesus as his apprentice and helper. And though his mind was full of new insights, Jesus was still an obedient son to his parents. As Mary looked at her first-born son from day to day, she pondered the meaning of his remarks at the Temple in Jerusalem; and even though she did not understand fully what Jesus may have meant, she "kept all these sayings in her heart."

Luke 2:41-52.

*"And Jesus increased in
wisdom and stature, and in
favour with God and man."*

LUKE 2:52

the son of Judah, which was *the son* of Joseph, which was *the son* of Jō′-năn, which was *the son* of Ē-lĭ′-ă-kĭm,

31 Which was *the son* of Mĕl′-ĕ-ă, which was *the son* of Mē′-năn, which was *the son* of Măt′-tă-thă, which was ᴿNathan, ᴿwhich was *the son* of David,

32 ᴿWhich was *the son* of Jesse, which was *the son* of ō′-bĕd, which was *the son* of Bō′-ŏz, which was *the son* of Săl′-mŏn, which was *the son* of Nā-ăs′-sŏn,

33 Which was *the son* of Ă-mĭn′-ă-dăb, which was *the son* of âr′-ăm, which was *the son* of Ĕs′-rŏm, which was *the son* of Phâr′-ĕs, which was *the son* of Judah,

34 Which was *the son* of Jacob, which was *the son* of Isaac, which was *the son* of Abraham, ᴿwhich was *the son* of Thâr′-ă, which was *the son* of Nā′-chôr,

35 Which was *the son* of Sâr′-ŭch, which was *the son* of Rā′-gaŭ, which was *the son* of Phā′-lĕc, which was *the son* of Hē′-bĕr, which was *the son* of Sā′-lă,

36 ᴿWhich was *the son* of Cā-ī′-năn, which was *the son* of Ăr-phăx′-ăd, ᴿwhich was *the son* of Sem, which was *the son* of Nō′-ē, which was *the son* of Lā′-mĕch,

37 Which was *the son* of Mă-thū′-să-lă, which was *the son* of Ē′-nŏch, which was *the son* of Jâr′-ĕd, which was *the son* of Măl′-ĕ-lĕĕl, which was *the son* of Cā-ī′-năn,

38 Which was *the son* of Ē′-nŏs, which was *the son* of Seth, which was *the son* of Adam, ᴿwhich was *the son* of God.

CHAPTER 4

The temptation of Jesus

AND ᴿJesus being full of the Holy Ghost returned from Jordan, and ᴿwas led by the Spirit into the wilderness,

2 Being forty days tempted of the devil. And ᴿin those days he did eat nothing: and when they were ended, he afterward hungered.

3 And the devil said unto him, If thou be the Son of God, command this stone that it be made bread.

4 And Jesus answered him, saying, ᴿIt is written, That man shall not live by bread alone, but by every word of God.

5 And the devil, taking him up into an high mountain, shewed unto him all the kingdoms of the world in a moment of time.

6 And the devil said unto him, All this power will I give thee, and the glory of them: for ᴿthat is delivered unto me; and to whomsoever I will I give it.

7 If thou therefore wilt ᴺworship me, all shall be thine.

CHAP. 3
AD 26
31 Zech. 12:12
31 2 Sam. 5:14
1 Chr. 3:5
32 Ruth 4:18, etc.
1 Chr 2:10, etc.
34 Gen. 11:24, 26
36 See Gen. 11:12
36 Gen. 5:6, etc.
& 11:10, etc.
38 Gen. 5:1, 2

CHAP. 4
AD 27
1 Mat. 4:1
Mark 1:12
1 ver. 14
ch. 2:27
2 Ex. 34:28
1 Ki. 19:8
4 Deut. 8:3
6 John 12:31
& 14:30
Rev. 13:2, 7
7 Or, *fall down before me*

Deut. 6:13   8
& 10:20
Mat. 4:5   9
Ps. 91:11   10
Deut. 6:16   12
John 14:30   13
Heb. 4:15
Mat. 4:12   14
John 4:43
Acts 10:37   14
Mat. 2:23   16
& 13:54
Mark 6:1
Acts 13:14   16
& 17:2
Is. 61:1   18
Ps. 45:2   22
Mat. 13:54
Mark 6:2
ch. 2:47
John 6:42   22
Mat. 4:13   23
& 11:23
Mat. 13:54   23
Mark 6:1
Mat. 13:57   24
Mark 6:4
John 4:44
1 Ki. 17:9   25
& 18:1
Jas. 5:17

8 And Jesus answered and said unto him, Get thee behind me, Satan: for ᴿit is written, Thou shalt worship the Lord thy God, and him only shalt thou serve.

9 ᴿAnd he brought him to Jerusalem, and set him on a pinnacle of the temple, and said unto him, If thou be the Son of God, cast thyself down from hence:

10 For ᴿit is written, He shall give his angels charge over thee, to keep thee:

11 And in *their* hands they shall bear thee up, lest at any time thou dash thy foot against a stone.

12 And Jesus answering said unto him, ᴿIt is said, Thou shalt not tempt the Lord thy God.

13 And when the devil had ended all the temptation, he departed from him ᴿfor a season.

Jesus begins His ministry

14 ᴿAnd Jesus returned ᴿin the power of the Spirit into ᴿGalilee: and there went out a fame of him through all the region round about.

15 And he taught in their synagogues, being glorified of all.

16 And he came to ᴿNazareth, where he had been brought up: and, as his custom was, ᴿhe went into the synagogue on the sabbath day, and stood up for to read.

17 And there was delivered unto him the book of the prophet Ē-śaī′-ăs. And when he had opened the book, he found the place where it was written,

18 ᴿThe Spirit of the Lord *is* upon me, because he hath anointed me to preach the gospel to the poor; he hath sent me to heal the brokenhearted, to preach deliverance to the captives, and recovering of sight to the blind, to set at liberty them that are bruised,

19 To preach the acceptable year of the Lord.

20 And he closed the book, and he gave *it* again to the minister, and sat down. And the eyes of all them that were in the synagogue were fastened on him.

21 And he began to say unto them, This day is this scripture fulfilled in your ears.

22 And all bare him witness, and ᴿwondered at the gracious words which proceeded out of his mouth. And they said, ᴿIs not this Joseph's son?

23 And he said unto them, Ye will surely say unto me this proverb, Physician, heal thyself: whatsoever we have heard done in ᴿCă-pĕr′-nă-ŭm, do also here in ᴿthy country.

24 And he said, Verily I say unto you, No ᴿprophet is accepted in his own country.

25 But I tell you of a truth, ᴿmany widows were in Israel in the days of Ē-lī′-ăs, when the

heaven was shut up three years and six months, when great famine was throughout all the land;

26 But unto none of them was Ē-lī′-ăs sent, save unto Să-rĕp′-tă, *a city* of Şī′-dŏn, unto a woman *that was* a widow.

27 ᴿAnd many lepers were in Israel in the time of ĕl-ĭ-sē′-ŭs the prophet; and none of them was cleansed, saving Nā′-ă-măn the Syrian.

28 And all they in the synagogue, when they heard these things, were filled with wrath,

29 And rose up, and thrust him out of the city, and led him unto the ᴺbrow of the hill whereon their city was built, that they might cast him down headlong.

30 But he ᴿpassing through the midst of them went his way,

Miracles in Capernaum

31 And ᴿcame down to Că-pĕr′-nă-ŭm, a city of Galilee, and taught them on the sabbath days.

32 And they were astonished at his doctrine: ᴿfor his word was with power.

33 ᴿAnd in the synagogue there was a man, which had a spirit of an unclean devil, and cried out with a loud voice,

34 Saying, ᴺLet *us* alone; what have we to do with thee, *thou* Jesus of Nazareth? art thou come to destroy us? ᴿI know thee who thou art; ᴿthe Holy One of God.

35 And Jesus rebuked him, saying, Hold thy peace, and come out of him. And when the devil had thrown him in the midst, he came out of him, and hurt him not.

36 And they were all amazed, and spake among themselves, saying, What a word *is* this! for with authority and power he commandeth the unclean spirits, and they come out.

37 And the fame of him went out into every place of the country round about.

38 ᴿAnd he arose out of the synagogue, and entered into Simon's house. And Simon's wife's mother was taken with a great fever; and they besought him for her.

39 And he stood over her, and rebuked the fever; and it left her: and immediately she arose and ministered unto them.

40 ᴿNow when the sun was setting, all they that had any sick with divers diseases brought them unto him; and he laid his hands on every one of them, and healed them.

41 ᴿAnd devils also came out of many, crying out, and saying, Thou art Christ the Son of God. And ᴿhe rebuking *them* suffered them not ᴺto speak: for they knew that he was Christ.

CHAP. **4**
AD 27
27 2 Ki. 5:14
29 Or, *edge*
30 John 8:59 & 10:39
31 Mat. 4:13 Mark 1:21
32 Mat. 7:28, 29
33 Mark 1:23
34 Or, *Away*
34 ver. 41
34 Ps. 16:10 Dan. 9:24 ch. 1:35
38 Mat. 8:14 Mark 1:29
40 Mat. 8:16 Mark 1:32
41 Mark 1:34 & 3:11
41 ver. 34, 35 Mark 1:25, 34
41 Or, *to say that they knew him to be Christ*

Mark 1:35   42
Mark 1:39   44

CHAP. **5**
AD 31
Mat. 4:18   1
Mark 1:16
John 21:6   4
2 Sam. 6:9   8
1 Ki. 17:18
Mat. 4:19   10
Mark 1:17
Mat. 4:20   11
& 19:27
Mark 1:18
ch. 18:28
Mat. 8:2   12
Mark 1:40

42 ᴿAnd when it was day, he departed and went into a desert place: and the people sought him, and came unto him, and stayed him, that he should not depart from them.

Preaching in other cities

43 And he said unto them, I must preach the kingdom of God to other cities also: for therefore am I sent.

44 ᴿAnd he preached in the synagogues of Galilee.

CHAPTER 5

Call of the first disciples

AND ᴿit came to pass, that, as the people pressed upon him to hear the word of God, he stood by the lake of Gĕn-nĕş′-ă-rĕt,

2 And saw two ships standing by the lake: but the fishermen were gone out of them, and were washing *their* nets.

3 And he entered into one of the ships, which was Simon's, and prayed him that he would thrust out a little from the land. And he sat down, and taught the people out of the ship.

4 Now when he had left speaking, he said unto Simon, ᴿLaunch out into the deep, and let down your nets for a draught.

5 And Simon answering said unto him, Master, we have toiled all the night, and have taken nothing: nevertheless at thy word I will let down the net.

6 And when they had this done, they inclosed a great multitude of fishes: and their net brake.

7 And they beckoned unto *their* partners, which were in the other ship, that they should come and help them. And they came, and filled both the ships, so that they began to sink.

8 When Simon Peter saw *it,* he fell down at Jesus' knees, saying, ᴿDepart from me; for I am a sinful man, O Lord.

9 For he was astonished, and all that were with him, at the draught of the fishes which they had taken:

10 And so *was* also James, and John, the sons of Zĕb′-ĕ-dĕe, which were partners with Simon. And Jesus said unto Simon, Fear not; ᴿfrom henceforth thou shalt catch men.

11 And when they had brought their ships to land, ᴿthey forsook all, and followed him.

Cleansing the leper

12 ᴿAnd it came to pass, when he was in a certain city, behold a man full of leprosy: who seeing Jesus fell on *his* face, and besought

him, saying, Lord, if thou wilt, thou canst make me clean.

13 And he put forth *his* hand, and touched him, saying, I will: be thou clean. And immediately the leprosy departed from him.

14 ᴿAnd he charged him to tell no man: but go, and shew thyself to the priest, and offer for thy cleansing, ᴿaccording as Moses commanded, for a testimony unto them.

15 But so much the more went there a fame abroad of him: ᴿand great multitudes came together to hear, and to be healed by him of their infirmities.

16 ᴿAnd he withdrew himself into the wilderness, and prayed.

The paralytic forgiven and healed

17 And it came to pass on a certain day, as he was teaching, that there were Pharisees and doctors of the law sitting by, which were come out of every town of Galilee, and Judæa, and Jerusalem: and the power of the Lord was *present* to heal them.

18 ᴿAnd, behold, men brought in a bed a man which was taken with a palsy: and they sought *means* to bring him in, and to lay *him* before him.

19 And when they could not find by what *way* they might bring him in because of the multitude, they went upon the housetop, and let him down through the tiling with *his* couch into the midst before Jesus.

20 And when he saw their faith, he said unto him, Man, thy sins are forgiven thee.

21 ᴿAnd the scribes and the Pharisees began to reason, saying, Who is this which speaketh blasphemies? ᴿWho can forgive sins, but God alone?

22 But when Jesus perceived their thoughts, he answering said unto them, What reason ye in your hearts?

23 Whether is easier, to say, Thy sins be forgiven thee; or to say, Rise up and walk?

24 But that ye may know that the Son of man hath power upon earth to forgive sins, (he said unto the sick of the palsy,) I say unto thee, Arise, and take up thy couch, and go into thine house.

25 And immediately he rose up before them, and took up that whereon he lay, and departed to his own house, glorifying God.

26 And they were all amazed, and they glorified God, and were filled with fear, saying, We have seen strange things to day.

Matthew called

27 ᴿAnd after these things he went forth, and saw a publican, named Levi, sitting at the

receipt of custom: and he said unto him, Follow me.

28 And he left all, rose up, and followed him.

29 ᴿAnd Levi made him a great feast in his own house: and ᴿthere was a great company of publicans and of others that sat down with them.

30 But their scribes and Pharisees murmured against his disciples, saying, Why do ye eat and drink with publicans and sinners?

31 And Jesus answering said unto them, They that are whole need not a physician; but they that are sick.

32 ᴿI came not to call the righteous, but sinners to repentance.

The question of fasting

33 And they said unto him, ᴿWhy do the disciples of John fast often, and make prayers, and likewise *the disciples* of the Pharisees; but thine eat and drink?

34 And he said unto them, Can ye make the children of the bridechamber fast, while the bridegroom is with them?

35 But the days will come, when the bridegroom shall be taken away from them, and then shall they fast in those days.

36 ᴿAnd he spake also a parable unto them; No man putteth a piece of a new garment upon an old; if otherwise, then both the new maketh a rent, and the piece that was *taken* out of the new agreeth not with the old.

37 And no man putteth new wine into old bottles; else the new wine will burst the bottles, and be spilled, and the bottles shall perish.

38 But new wine must be put into new bottles; and both are preserved.

39 No man also having drunk old *wine* straightway desireth new: for he saith, The old is better.

CHAPTER 6

Lord of the sabbath

AND ᴿit came to pass on the second sabbath after the first, that he went through the corn fields; and his disciples plucked the ears of corn, and did eat, rubbing *them* in *their* hands.

2 And certain of the Pharisees said unto them, Why do ye that ᴿwhich is not lawful to do on the sabbath days?

3 And Jesus answering them said, Have ye not read so much as this, ᴿwhat David did, when himself was an hungred, and they which were with him;

CHAP. **5**

AD 31

14 Mat. 8:4
14 Lev. 14:4, 10, 21, 22
15 Mat. 4:25
Mark 3:7
John 6:2
16 Mat. 14:23
Mark 6:46
18 Mat. 9:2
Mark 2:3
21 Mat. 9:3
Mark 2:6, 7
21 Ps. 32:5
Is. 43:25
27 Mat. 9:9
Mark 2:13, 14

Mat. 9:10 — 29
Mark 2:15
ch. 15:1 — 29
Mat. 9:13 — 32
1 Tim. 1:15
Mat. 9:14 — 33
Mark 2:18
Mat. 9:16, 17 — 36
Mark 2:21, 22

CHAP. **6**

AD 31

Mat. 12:1 — 1
Mark 2:23
Ex. 20:10 — 2
1 Sam. 21:6 — 3

4 How he went into the house of God, and did take and eat the shewbread, and gave also to them that were with him; ᴿwhich it is not lawful to eat but for the priests alone?

5 And he said unto them, That the Son of man is Lord also of the sabbath.

6 ᴿAnd it came to pass also on another sabbath, that he entered into the synagogue and taught: and there was a man whose right hand was withered.

7 And the scribes and Pharisees watched him, whether he would heal on the sabbath day; that they might find an accusation against him.

8 But he knew their thoughts, and said to the man which had the withered hand, Rise up, and stand forth in the midst. And he arose and stood forth.

9 Then said Jesus unto them, I will ask you one thing; Is it lawful on the sabbath days to do good, or to do evil? to save life, or to destroy it?

10 And looking round about upon them all, he said unto the man, Stretch forth thy hand. And he did so: and his hand was restored whole as the other.

11 And they were filled with madness; and communed one with another what they might do to Jesus.

Choice of the twelve disciples

12 And it came to pass in those days, that he went out into a mountain to pray, and continued all night in prayer to God.

13 And when it was day, he called unto him his disciples: ᴿand of them he chose twelve, whom also he named apostles;

14 Simon, (ᴿwhom he also named Peter,) and Andrew his brother, James and John, Philip and Bartholomew,

15 Matthew and Thomas, James the son of Ăl-phǣ′-ŭs, and Simon called Zē-lō′-tĕś,

16 And Judas ᴿthe brother of James, and Judas Iscariot, which also was the traitor.

The sermon on the mount

17 And he came down with them, and stood in the plain, and the company of his disciples, ᴿand a great multitude of people out of all Judæa and Jerusalem, and from the sea coast of Tyre and Sĭ′-dŏn, which came to hear him, and to be healed of their diseases;

18 And they that were vexed with unclean spirits: and they were healed.

19 And the whole multitude ᴿsought to touch him: for ᴿthere went virtue out of him, and healed them all.

CHAP. 6

AD 31

4 Lev. 24:9
6 Mat. 12:9
Mark 3:1
See ch. 13:14
& 14:3
John 9:16
13 Mat. 10:1
14 John 1:42
16 Jude 1
17 Mat. 4:25
Mark 3:7
19 Mat. 14:36
19 Mark 5:30
ch. 8:46

Mat. 5:3   20
& 11:5
Jas. 2:5
Is. 55:1   21
& 65:13
Mat. 5:6
Is. 61:3   21
Mat. 5:4
Mat. 5:11   22
1 Pet. 2:19
& 3:14
& 4:14
John 16:2   22
Mat. 5:12   23
Acts 5:41
Col. 1:24
Jas. 1:2
Acts 7:51   23
Amos 6:1   24
Jas. 5:1
ch. 12:21   24
Mat. 6:2, 5, 16   24
ch. 16:25
Is. 65:13   25
Prov. 14:13   25
John 15:19   26
1 John 4:5
ver. 35   27
Ex. 23:4
Prov. 25:21
Mat. 5:44
Rom. 12:20
ch. 23:34   28
Acts 7:60
Mat. 5:39   29
1 Cor. 6:7   29
Deut. 15:7, 8, 10   30
Prov. 21:26
Mat. 5:42
Mat. 7:12   31
Mat. 5:46   32
Mat. 5:42   34
ver. 27   35
ver. 30   35
Ps. 37:26
Mat. 5:45   35

The beatitudes and woes

20 And he lifted up his eyes on his disciples, and said, ᴿBlessed be ye poor: for yours is the kingdom of God.

21 ᴿBlessed are ye that hunger now: for ye shall be filled. ᴿBlessed are ye that weep now: for ye shall laugh.

22 ᴿBlessed are ye, when men shall hate you, and when they ᴿshall separate you from their company, and shall reproach you, and cast out your name as evil, for the Son of man's sake.

23 ᴿRejoice ye in that day, and leap for joy: for, behold, your reward is great in heaven: for ᴿin the like manner did their fathers unto the prophets.

24 ᴿBut woe unto you ᴿthat are rich! for ᴿye have received your consolation.

25 ᴿWoe unto you that are full! for ye shall hunger. ᴿWoe unto you that laugh now! for ye shall mourn and weep.

26 ᴿWoe unto you, when all men shall speak well of you! for so did their fathers to the false prophets.

The law of love

27 ᴿBut I say unto you which hear, Love your enemies, do good to them which hate you,

28 Bless them that curse you, and ᴿpray for them which despitefully use you.

29 ᴿAnd unto him that smiteth thee on the one cheek offer also the other; ᴿand him that taketh away thy cloak forbid not to take thy coat also.

30 ᴿGive to every man that asketh of thee; and of him that taketh away thy goods ask them not again.

31 ᴿAnd as ye would that men should do to you, do ye also to them likewise.

32 ᴿFor if ye love them which love you, what thank have ye? for sinners also love those that love them.

33 And if ye do good to them which do good to you, what thank have ye? for sinners also do even the same.

34 ᴿAnd if ye lend to them of whom ye hope to receive, what thank have ye? for sinners also lend to sinners, to receive as much again.

35 But ᴿlove ye your enemies, and do good, and ᴿlend, hoping for nothing again; and your reward shall be great, and ᴿye shall be the children of the Highest: for he is kind unto the unthankful and to the evil.

36 ᴿBe ye therefore merciful, as your Father also is merciful.

Judgment and hypocrisy

37 ᴿJudge not, and ye shall not be judged: condemn not, and ye shall not be condemned: forgive, and ye shall be forgiven:

38 ᴿGive, and it shall be given unto you; good measure, pressed down, and shaken together, and running over, shall men give into your ᴿbosom. For ᴿwith the same measure that ye mete withal it shall be measured to you again.

39 And he spake a parable unto them, ᴿCan the blind lead the blind? shall they not both fall into the ditch?

40 ᴿThe disciple is not above his master: but every one ᴺthat is perfect shall be as his master.

41 ᴿAnd why beholdest thou the mote that is in thy brother's eye, but perceivest not the beam that is in thine own eye?

42 Either how canst thou say to thy brother, Brother, let me pull out the mote that is in thine eye, when thou thyself beholdest not the beam that is in thine own eye? Thou hypocrite, cast out first the beam out of thine own eye, and then shalt thou see clearly to pull out the mote that is in thy brother's eye.

43 ᴿFor a good tree bringeth not forth corrupt fruit; neither doth a corrupt tree bring forth good fruit.

44 For ᴿevery tree is known by his own fruit. For of thorns men do not gather figs, nor of a bramble bush gather they ᴺgrapes.

45 ᴿA good man out of the good treasure of his heart bringeth forth that which is good; and an evil man out of the evil treasure of his heart bringeth forth that which is evil: for ᴿof the abundance of the heart his mouth speaketh.

Doers of the word

46 ᴿAnd why call ye me, Lord, Lord, and do not the things which I say?

47 ᴿWhosoever cometh to me, and heareth my sayings, and doeth them, I will shew you to whom he is like:

48 He is like a man which built an house, and digged deep, and laid the foundation on a rock: and when the flood arose, the stream beat vehemently upon that house, and could not shake it: for it was founded upon a rock.

49 But he that heareth, and doeth not, is like a man that without a foundation built an house upon the earth; against which the stream did beat vehemently, and immediately it fell; and the ruin of that house was great.

CHAP. 6
AD 31
36 Mat. 5:48
37 Mat. 7:1
38 Prov. 19:17
38 Ps. 79:12
38 Mat. 7:2
Mark 4:24
Jas. 2:13
39 Mat. 15:14
40 Mat. 10:24
John 13:16
& 15:20
40 Or, *shall be perfected as his master*
41 Mat. 7:3
43 Mat. 7:16, 17
44 Mat. 12:33
44 Gr. *a grape*
45 Mat. 12:35
45 Mat. 12:34
46 Mal. 1:6
Mat. 7:21
& 25:11
ch. 13:25
47 Mat. 7:24

CHAP. 7	
AD 31	
Mat. 8:5	1
Gr. *this man*	8
Or, *coffin*	14
ch. 8:54	14
John 11:43	
Acts 9:40	
Rom. 4:17	
ch. 1:65	16
ch. 24:19	16
John 4:19	
& 6:14	
& 9:17	

CHAPTER 7

Healing the centurion's servant

NOW when he had ended all his sayings in the audience of the people, ᴿhe entered into Că-pĕr′-nă-ŭm.

2 And a certain centurion's servant, who was dear unto him, was sick, and ready to die.

3 And when he heard of Jesus, he sent unto him the elders of the Jews, beseeching him that he would come and heal his servant.

4 And when they came to Jesus, they besought him instantly, saying, That he was worthy for whom he should do this:

5 For he loveth our nation, and he hath built us a synagogue.

6 Then Jesus went with them. And when he was now not far from the house, the centurion sent friends to him, saying unto him, Lord, trouble not thyself: for I am not worthy that thou shouldest enter under my roof:

7 Wherefore neither thought I myself worthy to come unto thee: but say in a word, and my servant shall be healed.

8 For I also am a man set under authority, having under me soldiers, and I say unto ᴺone, Go, and he goeth; and to another, Come, and he cometh; and to my servant, Do this, and he doeth *it*.

9 When Jesus heard these things, he marvelled at him, and turned him about, and said unto the people that followed him, I say unto you, I have not found so great faith, no, not in Israel.

10 And they that were sent, returning to the house, found the servant whole that had been sick.

Raising the widow's son at Nain

11 And it came to pass the day after, that he went into a city called Nā′-ĭn; and many of his disciples went with him, and much people.

12 Now when he came nigh to the gate of the city, behold, there was a dead man carried out, the only son of his mother, and she was a widow: and much people of the city was with her.

13 And when the Lord saw her, he had compassion on her, and said unto her, Weep not.

14 And he came and touched the ᴺbier: and they that bare *him* stood still. And he said, Young man, I say unto thee, ᴿArise.

15 And he that was dead sat up, and began to speak. And he delivered him to his mother.

16 ᴿAnd there came a fear on all: and they glorified God, saying, ᴿThat a great prophet is

risen up among us; and, ᴿThat God hath visited his people.

17 And this rumour of him went forth throughout all Judæa, and throughout all the region round about.

Jesus and John the Baptist

18 ᴿAnd the disciples of John shewed him of all these things.

19 And John calling *unto him* two of his disciples sent *them* to Jesus, saying, Art thou he that should come? or look we for another?

20 When the men were come unto him, they said, John Baptist hath sent us unto thee, saying, Art thou he that should come? or look we for another?

21 And in that same hour he cured many of *their* infirmities and plagues, and of evil spirits; and unto many *that were* blind he gave sight.

22 ᴿThen Jesus answering said unto them, Go your way, and tell John what things ye have seen and heard; ᴿhow that the blind see, the lame walk, the lepers are cleansed, the deaf hear, the dead are raised, ᴿto the poor the gospel is preached.

23 And blessed is *he,* whosoever shall not be offended in me.

24 ᴿAnd when the messengers of John were departed, he began to speak unto the people concerning John, What went ye out into the wilderness for to see? A reed shaken with the wind?

25 But what went ye out for to see? A man clothed in soft raiment? Behold, they which are gorgeously apparelled, and live delicately, are in kings' courts.

26 But what went ye out for to see? A prophet? Yea, I say unto you, and much more than a prophet.

27 This is *he,* of whom it is written, ᴿBehold, I send my messenger before thy face, which shall prepare thy way before thee.

28 For I say unto you, Among those that are born of women there is not a greater prophet than John the Baptist: but he that is least in the kingdom of God is greater than he.

29 And all the people that heard *him,* and the publicans, justified God, ᴿbeing baptized with the baptism of John.

30 But the Pharisees and lawyers ᴺrejected ᴿthe counsel of God ᴺagainst themselves, being not baptized of him.

31 And the Lord said, ᴿWhereunto then shall I liken the men of this generation? and to what are they like?

32 They are like unto children sitting in the marketplace, and calling one to another, and

saying, We have piped unto you, and ye have not danced; we have mourned to you, and ye have not wept.

33 For ᴿJohn the Baptist came neither eating bread nor drinking wine; and ye say, He hath a devil.

34 The Son of man is come eating and drinking; and ye say, Behold a gluttonous man, and a winebibber, a friend of publicans and sinners!

35 ᴿBut wisdom is justified of all her children.

A sinful woman forgiven

36 ᴿAnd one of the Pharisees desired him that he would eat with him. And he went into the Pharisee's house, and sat down to meat.

37 And, behold, a woman in the city, which was a sinner, when she knew that *Jesus* sat at meat in the Pharisee's house, brought an alabaster box of ointment,

38 And stood at his feet behind *him* weeping, and began to wash his feet with tears, and did wipe *them* with the hairs of her head, and kissed his feet, and anointed *them* with the ointment.

39 Now when the Pharisee which had bidden him saw *it,* he spake within himself, saying, ᴿThis man, if he were a prophet, would have known who and what manner of woman *this is* that toucheth him: for she is a sinner.

40 And Jesus answering said unto him, Simon, I have somewhat to say unto thee. And he saith, Master, say on.

41 There was a certain creditor which had two debtors: the one owed five hundred ᴺpence, and the other fifty.

42 And when they had nothing to pay, he frankly forgave them both. Tell me therefore, which of them will love him most?

43 Simon answered and said, I suppose that *he,* to whom he forgave most. And he said unto him, Thou hast rightly judged.

44 And he turned to the woman, and said unto Simon, Seest thou this woman? I entered into thine house, thou gavest me no water for my feet: but she hath washed my feet with tears, and wiped *them* with the hairs of her head.

45 Thou gavest me no kiss: but this woman since the time I came in hath not ceased to kiss my feet.

46 ᴿMy head with oil thou didst not anoint: but this woman hath anointed my feet with ointment.

47 ᴿWherefore I say unto thee, Her sins, which are many, are forgiven; for she loved

CHAP. 7
AD 31
16 ch. 1:68
18 Mat. 11:2
22 Mat. 11:4
22 Is. 35:5
22 ch. 4:18
Mat. 11:7
27 Mal. 3:1
29 Mat. 3:5
ch. 3:12
30 Or, *frustrated*
30 Acts 20:27
30 Or, *within themselves*
31 Mat. 11:16

Mat. 3:4	33
Mark 1:6	
ch. 1:15	
Mat. 11:19	35
Mat. 26:6	36
Mark 14:3	
John 11:2	
ch. 15:2	39
See Mat. 18:28	41
Ps. 23:5	46
1 Tim. 1:14	47

much: but to whom little is forgiven, *the same* loveth little.

48 And he said unto her, ᴿThy sins are forgiven.

49 And they that sat at meat with him began to say within themselves, ᴿWho is this that forgiveth sins also?

50 And he said to the woman, ᴿThy faith hath saved thee; go in peace.

CHAPTER 8
Jesus' followers

AND it came to pass afterward, that he went throughout every city and village, preaching and shewing the glad tidings of the kingdom of God: and the twelve *were* with him,

2 And ᴿcertain women, which had been healed of evil spirits and infirmities, Mary called Măg′-dă-lēne, ᴿout of whom went seven devils,

3 And Jō-ăn′-nă the wife of Chû′-ză Herod's steward, and Susanna, and many others, which ministered unto him of their substance.

Parable of the sower

4 ᴿAnd when much people were gathered together, and were come to him out of every city, he spake by a parable:

5 A sower went out to sow his seed: and as he sowed, some fell by the way side; and it was trodden down, and the fowls of the air devoured it.

6 And some fell upon a rock; and as soon as it was sprung up, it withered away, because it lacked moisture.

7 And some fell among thorns; and the thorns sprang up with it, and choked it.

8 And other fell on good ground, and sprang up, and bare fruit an hundredfold. And when he had said these things, he cried, He that hath ears to hear, let him hear.

9 ᴿAnd his disciples asked him, saying, What might this parable be?

10 And he said, Unto you it is given to know the mysteries of the kingdom of God: but to others in parables; ᴿthat seeing they might not see, and hearing they might not understand.

11 ᴿNow the parable is this: The seed is the word of God.

12 Those by the way side are they that hear; then cometh the devil, and taketh away the word out of their hearts, lest they should believe and be saved.

13 They on the rock *are they,* which, when they hear, receive the word with joy; and these

have no root, which for a while believe, and in time of temptation fall away.

14 And that which fell among thorns are they, which, when they have heard, go forth, and are choked with cares and riches and pleasures of *this* life, and bring no fruit to perfection.

15 But that on the good ground are they, which in an honest and good heart, having heard the word, keep *it,* and bring forth fruit with patience.

16 ᴿNo man, when he hath lighted a candle, covereth it with a vessel, or putteth *it* under a bed; but setteth *it* on a candlestick, that they which enter in may see the light.

17 ᴿFor nothing is secret, that shall not be made manifest; neither *any thing* hid, that shall not be known and come abroad.

18 Take heed therefore how ye hear: ᴿfor whosoever hath, to him shall be given; and whosoever hath not, from him shall be taken even that which he ᴺseemeth to have.

Jesus' true kindred

19 ᴿThen came to him *his* mother and his brethren, and could not come at him for the press.

20 And it was told him *by certain* which said, Thy mother and thy brethren stand without, desiring to see thee.

21 And he answered and said unto them, My mother and my brethren are these which hear the word of God, and do it.

Jesus stills the storm

22 ᴿNow it came to pass on a certain day, that he went into a ship with his disciples: and he said unto them, Let us go over unto the other side of the lake. And they launched forth.

23 But as they sailed he fell asleep: and there came down a storm of wind on the lake; and they were filled *with water,* and were in jeopardy.

24 And they came to him, and awoke him, saying, Master, master, we perish. Then he arose, and rebuked the wind and the raging of the water: and they ceased, and there was a calm.

25 And he said unto them, Where is your faith? And they being afraid wondered, saying one to another, What manner of man is this! for he commandeth even the winds and water, and they obey him.

Legion of devils cast out

26 ᴿAnd they arrived at the country of the Găd′-ă-rēneś, which is over against Galilee.

CHAP. 7
AD 31
48 Mat. 9:2
Mark 2:5
49 Mat. 9:3
Mark 2:7
50 Mat. 9:22
Mark 5:34
& 10:52
ch. 8:48
& 18:42

CHAP. 8
AD 31
2 Mat. 27:55, 56
2 Mark 16:9
4 Mat. 13:2
Mark 4:1
9 Mat. 13:10
Mark 4:10
10 Is. 6:9
Mark 4:12
11 Mat. 13:18
Mark 4:14

Mat. 5:15   16
Mark 4:21
ch. 11:33
Mat. 10:26   17
ch. 12:2
Mat. 13:12   18
& 25:29
ch. 19:26
Or, *thinketh   18
that he hath*
Mat. 12:46   19
Mark 3:31
Mat. 8:23   22
Mark 4:35
Mat. 8:28   26
Mark 5:1

27 And when he went forth to land, there met him out of the city a certain man, which had devils long time, and ware no clothes, neither abode in *any* house, but in the tombs.

28 When he saw Jesus, he cried out, and fell down before him, and with a loud voice said, What have I to do with thee, Jesus, *thou* Son of God most high? I beseech thee, torment me not.

29 (For he had commanded the unclean spirit to come out of the man. For oftentimes it had caught him: and he was kept bound with chains and in fetters; and he brake the bands, and was driven of the devil into the wilderness.)

30 And Jesus asked him, saying, What is thy name? And he said, Legion: because many devils were entered into him.

31 And they besought him that he would not command them to go out ᴿinto the deep.

32 And there was there an herd of many swine feeding on the mountain: and they besought him that he would suffer them to enter into them. And he suffered them.

33 Then went the devils out of the man, and entered into the swine: and the herd ran violently down a steep place into the lake, and were choked.

34 When they that fed *them* saw what was done, they fled, and went and told *it* in the city and in the country.

35 Then they went out to see what was done; and came to Jesus, and found the man, out of whom the devils were departed, sitting at the feet of Jesus, clothed, and in his right mind: and they were afraid.

36 They also which·saw *it* told them by what means he that was possessed of the devils was healed.

37 ᴿThen the whole multitude of the country of the Găd'-ȧ-rēneś round about ᴿbesought him to depart from them; for they were taken with great fear: and he went up into the ship, and returned back again.

38 Now ᴿthe man out of whom the devils were departed besought him that he might be with him: but Jesus sent him away, saying,

39 Return to thine own house, and shew how great things God hath done unto thee. And he went his way, and published throughout the whole city how great things Jesus had done unto him.

40 And it came to pass, that, when Jesus was returned, the people *gladly* received him: for they were all waiting for him.

41 ᴿAnd, behold, there came a man named Jā-i'-rŭs, and he was a ruler of the synagogue: and he fell down at Jesus' feet, and besought him that he would come into his house:

CHAP. **8**

AD 31

31 Rev. 20:3
37 Mat. 8:34
37 Acts 16:39
38 Mark 5:18
41 Mat. 9:18
Mark 5:22

Mat. 9:20   **43**
Mark 5:30   **46**
ch. 6:19
Mark 5:35   **49**
John 11:11, 13   **52**
ch. 7:14   **54**
John 11:43
Mat. 8:4   **56**
& 9:30
Mark 5:43

CHAP. **9**

AD 31

Mat. 10:1   **1**
Mark 3:13
& 6:7

42 For he had one only daughter, about twelve years of age, and she lay a dying. But as he went the people thronged him.

The woman who touched His garment

43 ᴿAnd a woman having an issue of blood twelve years, which had spent all her living upon physicians, neither could be healed of any,

44 Came behind *him,* and touched the border of his garment: and immediately her issue of blood stanched.

45 And Jesus said, Who touched me? When all denied, Peter and they that were with him said, Master, the multitude throng thee and press *thee,* and sayest thou, Who touched me?

46 And Jesus said, Somebody hath touched me: for I perceive that ᴿvirtue is gone out of me.

47 And when the woman saw that she was not hid, she came trembling, and falling down before him, she declared unto him before all the people for what cause she had touched him, and how she was healed immediately.

48 And he said unto her, Daughter, be of good comfort: thy faith hath made thee whole; go in peace.

Raising Jairus' daughter

49 ᴿWhile he yet spake, there cometh one from the ruler of the synagogue's *house,* saying to him, Thy daughter is dead; trouble not the Master.

50 But when Jesus heard *it,* he answered him, saying, Fear not: believe only, and she shall be made whole.

51 And when he came into the house, he suffered no man to go in, save Peter, and James, and John, and the father and the mother of the maiden.

52 And all wept, and bewailed her: but he said, Weep not; she is not dead, ᴿbut sleepeth.

53 And they laughed him to scorn, knowing that she was dead.

54 And he put them all out, and took her by the hand, and called, saying, Maid, ᴿarise.

55 And her spirit came again, and she arose straightway: and he commanded to give her meat.

56 And her parents were astonished: but ᴿhe charged them that they should tell no man what was done.

CHAPTER 9

The mission of the twelve

THEN ᴿhe called his twelve disciples together, and gave them power and authority over all devils, and to cure diseases.

2 And Rhe sent them to preach the kingdom of God, and to heal the sick.

3 RAnd he said unto them, Take nothing for *your* journey, neither staves, nor scrip, neither bread, neither money; neither have two coats apiece.

4 RAnd whatsoever house ye enter into, there abide, and thence depart.

5 RAnd whosoever will not receive you, when ye go out of that city, Rshake off the very dust from your feet for a testimony against them.

6 RAnd they departed, and went through the towns, preaching the gospel, and healing every where.

Herod's desire to see Jesus

7 RNow Herod the tē'-trärch heard of all that was done by him: and he was perplexed, because that it was said of some, that John was risen from the dead;

8 And of some, that Ē-lī'-ăs had appeared; and of others, that one of the old prophets was risen again.

9 And Herod said, John have I beheaded: but who is this, of whom I hear such things? RAnd he desired to see him.

Feeding the five thousand

10 RAnd the apostles, when they were returned, told him all that they had done. RAnd he took them, and went aside privately into a desert place belonging to the city called Bĕth-sā'-ĭ-dă.

11 And the people, when they knew *it,* followed him: and he received them, and spake unto them of the kingdom of God, and healed them that had need of healing.

12 RAnd when the day began to wear away, then came the twelve, and said unto him, Send the multitude away, that they may go into the towns and country round about, and lodge, and get victuals: for we are here in a desert place.

13 But he said unto them, Give ye them to eat. And they said, We have no more but five loaves and two fishes; except we should go and buy meat for all this people.

14 For they were about five thousand men. And he said to his disciples, Make them sit down by fifties in a company.

15 And they did so, and made them all sit down.

16 Then he took the five loaves and the two fishes, and looking up to heaven, he blessed them, and brake, and gave to the disciples to set before the multitude.

17 And they did eat, and were all filled: and

there was taken up of fragments that remained to them twelve baskets.

Peter's confession

18 RAnd it came to pass, as he was alone praying, his disciples were with him: and he asked them, saying, Whom say the people that I am?

19 They answering said, RJohn the Baptist; but some *say,* Ē-lī'-ăs; and others *say,* that one of the old prophets is risen again.

20 He said unto them, But whom say ye that I am? RPeter answering said, The Christ of God.

21 RAnd he straitly charged them, and commanded *them* to tell no man that thing;

22 Saying, RThe Son of man must suffer many things, and be rejected of the elders and chief priests and scribes, and be slain, and be raised the third day.

The way of the cross

23 RAnd he said to *them* all, If any *man* will come after me, let him deny himself, and take up his cross daily, and follow me.

24 For whosoever will save his life shall lose it: but whosoever will lose his life for my sake, the same shall save it.

25 RFor what is a man advantaged, if he gain the whole world, and lose himself, or be cast away?

26 RFor whosoever shall be ashamed of me and of my words, of him shall the Son of man be ashamed, when he shall come in his own glory, and *in his* Father's, and of the holy angels.

27 RBut I tell you of a truth, there be some standing here, which shall not taste of death, till they see the kingdom of God.

The transfiguration

28 RAnd it came to pass about an eight days after these Nsayings, he took Peter and John and James, and went up into a mountain to pray.

29 And as he prayed, the fashion of his countenance was altered, and his raiment *was* white *and* glistering.

30 And, behold, there talked with him two men, which were Moses and Ē-lī'-ăs:

31 Who appeared in glory, and spake of his decease which he should accomplish at Jerusalem.

32 But Peter and they that were with him Rwere heavy with sleep: and when they were awake, they saw his glory, and the two men that stood with him.

33 And it came to pass, as they departed from him, Peter said unto Jesus, Master, it is

---

CHAP. **9**

AD 31

2 Mat. 10:7, 8
Mark 6:12
ch. 10:1, 9
3 Mat. 10:9
Mark 6:8
ch. 10:4
& 22:35
4 Mat. 10:11
Mark 6:10
5 Mat. 10:14
5 Acts 13:51
6 Mark 6:12
7 Mat. 14:1
Mark 6:14
9 ch. 23:8
10 Mark 6:30
10 Mat. 14:13
12 Mat. 14:15
Mark 6:35
John 6:1, 5

Mat. 16:13 **18**
Mark 8:27
ver. 7, 8 **19**
Mat. 14:2
Mat. 16:16 **20**
John 6:69
Mat. 16:20 **21**
Mat. 15:21 **22**
& 17:22
Mat. 10:38 **23**
& 16:24
Mark 8:34
ch. 14:27
Mat. 16:26 **25**
Mark 8:36
Mat. 10:33 **26**
Mark 8:38
2 Tim. 2:12
Mat. 15:28 **27**
Mark 9:1
Mat. 17:1 **28**
Mark 9:2
Or, *things* **28**
Dan. 8:13 **32**
& 10:9

good for us to be here: and let us make three tabernacles; one for thee, and one for Moses, and one for Ē-lī'-ăs: not knowing what he said.

34 While he thus spake, there came a cloud, and overshadowed them: and they feared as they entered into the cloud.

35 And there came a voice out of the cloud, saying, ᴿThis is my beloved Son: ᴿhear him.

36 And when the voice was past, Jesus was found alone. ᴿAnd they kept *it* close, and told no man in those days any of those things which they had seen.

37 ᴿAnd it came to pass, that on the next day, when they were come down from the hill, much people met him.

38 And, behold, a man of the company cried out, saying, Master, I beseech thee, look upon my son: for he is mine only child.

39 And, lo, a spirit taketh him, and he suddenly crieth out; and it teareth him that he foameth again, and bruising him hardly departeth from him.

40 And I besought thy disciples to cast him out; and they could not.

41 And Jesus answering said, O faithless and perverse generation, how long shall I be with you, and suffer you? Bring thy son hither.

42 And as he was yet a coming, the devil threw him down, and tare *him*. And Jesus rebuked the unclean spirit, and healed the child, and delivered him again to his father.

43 And they were all amazed at the mighty power of God. But while they wondered every one at all things which Jesus did, he said unto his disciples,

44 ᴿLet these sayings sink down into your ears: for the Son of man shall be delivered into the hands of men.

45 ᴿBut they understood not this saying, and it was hid from them, that they perceived it not: and they feared to ask him of that saying.

A lesson on humility

46 ᴿThen there arose a reasoning among them, which of them should be greatest.

47 And Jesus, perceiving the thought of their heart, took a child, and set him by him,

48 And said unto them, ᴿWhosoever shall receive this child in my name receiveth me: and whosoever shall receive me receiveth him that sent me: ᴿfor he that is least among you all, the same shall be great.

A lesson on tolerance

49 ᴿAnd John answered and said, Master, we saw one casting out devils in thy name; and we forbad him, because he followeth not with us.

50 And Jesus said unto him, Forbid *him*

CHAP. **9**	
AD 31	
35	Mat. 3:17
35	Acts 3:22
36	Mat. 17:9
37	Mat. 17:14
	Mark 9:14, 17
44	Mat. 17:22
45	Mark 9:32
	ch. 2:50 & 18:34
46	Mat. 18:1
	Mark 9:34
48	Mat. 10:40
	& 18:5
	Mark 9:37
	John 12:44
	& 13:20
48	Mat. 23:11, 12
49	Mark 9:38
	See Num. 11:28

See Mat. 12:30	**50**
ch. 11:23	
Mark 16:19	**51**
Acts 1:2	
John 4:4, 9	**53**
2 Ki. 1:10, 12	**54**
John 3:17	**56**
& 12:47	
Mat. 8:19	**57**
Mat. 8:21	**59**
See 1 Ki. 19:20	**61**

CHAP. **10**	
AD 32	
Mat. 10:1	**1**
Mark 6:7	
Mat. 9:37	**2**
John 4:35	
2 Thes. 3:1	**2**
Mat. 10:16	**3**
Mat. 10:9	**4**
Mark 6:8	
ch. 9:3	
2 Ki. 4:29	**4**
Mat. 10:12	**5**

not: for ᴿhe that is not against us is for us.

51 And it came to pass, when the time was come that ᴿhe should be received up, he stedfastly set his face to go to Jerusalem,

52 And sent messengers before his face: and they went, and entered into a villlage of the Să-măr'-ĭ-tăns, to make ready for him.

53 And ᴿthey did not receive him, because his face was as though he would go to Jerusalem.

54 And when his disciples James and John saw *this,* they said, Lord, wilt thou that we command fire to come down from heaven, and consume them, even as ᴿĒ-lī'-ăs did?

55 But he turned, and rebuked them, and said, Ye know not what manner of spirit ye are of.

56 For ᴿthe Son of man is not come to destroy men's lives, but to save *them*. And they went to another village.

Demands of discipleship

57 ᴿAnd it came to pass, that, as they went in the way, a certain *man* said unto him, Lord, I will follow thee whithersoever thou goest.

58 And Jesus said unto him, Foxes have holes, and birds of the air *have* nests; but the Son of man hath not where to lay *his* head.

59 ᴿAnd he said unto another, Follow me. But he said, Lord, suffer me first to go and bury my father.

60 Jesus said unto him, Let the dead bury their dead: but go thou and preach the kingdom of God.

61 And another also said, Lord, ᴿI will follow thee; but let me first go bid them farewell, which are at home at my house.

62 And Jesus said unto him, No man, having put his hand to the plough, and looking back, is fit for the kingdom of God.

CHAPTER 10

The mission of the seventy

AFTER these things the Lord appointed other seventy also, and ᴿsent them two and two before his face into every city and place; whither he himself would come.

2 Therefore said he unto them, ᴿThe harvest truly *is* great, but the labourers *are* few: ᴿpray ye therefore the Lord of the harvest, that he would send forth labourers into his harvest.

3 Go your ways: ᴿbehold, I send you forth as lambs among wolves.

4 ᴿCarry neither purse, nor scrip, nor shoes: and ᴿsalute no man by the way.

5 ᴿAnd into whatsoever house ye enter, first say, Peace *be* to this house.

6 And if the son of peace be there, your

peace shall rest upon it: if not, it shall turn to you again.

7 ᴿAnd in the same house remain, ᴿeating and drinking such things as they give: for ᴿthe labourer is worthy of his hire. Go not from house to house.

8 And into whatsoever city ye enter, and they receive you, eat such things as are set before you:

9 ᴿAnd heal the sick that are therein, and say unto them, ᴿThe kingdom of God is come nigh unto you.

10 But into whatsoever city ye enter, and they receive you not, go your ways out into the streets of the same, and say,

11 ᴿEven the very dust of your city, which cleaveth on us, we do wipe off against you: notwithstanding be ye sure of this, that the kingdom of God is come nigh unto you.

12 But I say unto you, that ᴿit shall be more tolerable in that day for Sodom, than for that city.

13 ᴿWoe unto thee, Chō-rā′-zĭn! woe unto thee, Bĕth-sā′-ĭ-dă! ᴿfor if the mighty works had been done in Tyre and Sī′-dŏn, which have been done in you, they had a great while ago repented, sitting in sackcloth and ashes.

14 But it shall be more tolerable for Tyre and Sī′-dŏn at the judgment, than for you.

15 ᴿAnd thou, Că-pĕr′-nă-ŭm, which art ᴿexalted to heaven, ᴿshalt be thrust down to hell.

16 ᴿHe that heareth you heareth me; and ᴿhe that despiseth you despiseth me; ᴿand he that despiseth me despiseth him that sent me.

17 And ᴿthe seventy returned again with joy, saying, Lord, even the devils are subject unto us through thy name.

18 And he said unto them, ᴿI beheld Satan as lightning fall from heaven.

19 Behold, ᴿI give unto you power to tread on serpents and scorpions, and over all the power of the enemy: and nothing shall by any means hurt you.

20 Notwithstanding in this rejoice not, that the spirits are subject unto you; but rather rejoice, because ᴿyour names are written in heaven.

Revealing the Father

21 ᴿIn that hour Jesus rejoiced in spirit, and said, I thank thee, O Father, Lord of heaven and earth, that thou hast hid these things from the wise and prudent, and hast revealed them unto babes: even so, Father; for so it seemed good in thy sight.

22 ᴿAllᴺ things are delivered to me of my Father: and ᴿno man knoweth who the Son is, but the Father; and who the Father is, but the

Son, and *he* to whom the Son will reveal *him.*

23 And he turned him unto *his* disciples, and said privately, ᴿBlessed *are* the eyes which see the things that ye see:

24 For I tell you, ᴿthat many prophets and kings have desired to see those things which ye see, and have not seen *them;* and to hear those things which ye hear, and have not heard *them.*

Parable of the good Samaritan

25 And, behold, a certain lawyer stood up, and tempted him, saying, ᴿMaster, what shall I do to inherit eternal life?

26 He said unto him, What is written in the law? how readest thou?

27 And he answering said, ᴿThou shalt love the Lord thy God with all thy heart, and with all thy soul, and with all thy strength, and with all thy mind; and ᴿthy neighbour as thyself.

28 And he said unto him, Thou hast answered right: this do, and ᴿthou shalt live.

29 But he, willing to ᴿjustify himself, said unto Jesus, And who is my neighbour?

30 And Jesus answering said, A certain *man* went down from Jerusalem to Jericho, and fell among thieves, which stripped him of his raiment, and wounded *him,* and departed, leaving *him* half dead.

31 And by chance there came down a certain priest that way: and when he saw him, ᴿhe passed by on the other side.

32 And likewise a Levite, when he was at the place, came and looked *on him,* and passed by on the other side.

33 But a certain ᴿSă-măr′-ĭ-tăn, as he journeyed, came where he was: and when he saw him, he had compassion *on him,*

34 And went to *him,* and bound up his wounds, pouring in oil and wine, and set him on his own beast, and brought him to an inn, and took care of him.

35 And on the morrow when he departed, he took out two ᴺpence, and gave *them* to the host, and said unto him, Take care of him; and whatsoever thou spendest more, when I come again, I will repay thee.

36 Which now of these three, thinkest thou, was neighbour unto him that fell among the thieves?

37 And he said, He that shewed mercy on him. Then said Jesus unto him, Go, and do thou likewise.

Jesus visits Martha and Mary

38 Now it came to pass, as they went, that he entered into a certain village: and a certain woman named ᴿMartha received him into her house.

39 And she had a sister called Mary, ^Rwhich also ^Rsat at Jesus' feet, and heard his word.

40 But Martha was cumbered about much serving, and came to him, and said, Lord, dost thou not care that my sister hath left me to serve alone? bid her therefore that she help me.

41 And Jesus answered and said unto her, Martha, Martha, thou art careful and troubled about many things:

42 But ^Rone thing is needful: and Mary hath chosen that good part, which shall not be taken away from her.

CHAPTER 11

The Lord's prayer

AND it came to pass, that, as he was praying in a certain place, when he ceased, one of his disciples said unto him, Lord, teach us to pray, as John also taught his disciple

2 And he said unto them, When ye pray, say, ^ROur Father which art in heaven, Hallowed be thy name. Thy kingdom come. Thy will be done, as in heaven, so in earth.

3 Give us ^Nday by day our daily bread.

4 And forgive us our sins; for we also forgive every one that is indebted to us. And lead us not into temptation; but deliver us from evil.

Lesson concerning prayer

5 And he said unto them, Which of you shall have a friend, and shall go unto him at midnight, and say unto him, Friend, lend me three loaves;

6 For a friend of mine ^Nin his journey is come to me, and I have nothing to set before him?

7 And he from within shall answer and say, Trouble me not: the door is now shut, and my children are with me in bed; I cannot rise and give thee.

8 I say unto you, ^RThough he will not rise and give him, because he is his friend, yet because of his importunity he will rise and give him as many as he needeth.

9 ^RAnd I say unto you, Ask, and it shall be given you; seek, and ye shall find; knock, and it shall be opened unto you.

10 For every one that asketh receiveth; and he that seeketh findeth; and to him that knocketh it shall be opened.

11 ^RIf a son shall ask bread of any of you that is a father, will he give him a stone? or if *he ask* a fish, will he for a fish give him a serpent?

12 Or if he shall ask an egg, will he ^Noffer him a scorpion?

CHAP. 10
AD 32
39 1 Cor. 7:32, etc.
39 ch. 8:35
 Acts 22:3
42 Ps. 27:4

CHAP. 11
AD 33
2 Mat. 6:9
3 Or, *for the day*
6 Or, *out of his way*
8 ch. 18:1, etc.
9 Mat. 7:7 & 21:22
 Mark 11:24
 John 15:7
 Jas. 1:6
 1 John 3:22
11 Mat. 7:9
12 Gr. *give*

Mat. 9:32   14
 & 12:22
Mat. 9:34   15
 & 12:24
Gr. *Beelzebul,* 15
 ver. 18, 19
Mat. 12:38   16
 & 16:1
Mat. 12:25   17
 Mark 3:24
John 2:25   17
Ex. 8:19   20
Mat. 12:29   21
 Mark 3:27
Is. 53:12   22
 Col. 2:15
Mat. 12:30   23
Mat. 12:43   24
John 5:14   26
 Heb. 6:4 & 10:26
 2 Pet. 2:20
ch. 1:28, 48   27
Mat. 7:21   28
 ch. 8:21
 Jas. 1:25
Mat. 12:38, 39 29

---

13 If ye then, being evil, know how to give good gifts unto your children: how much more shall *your* heavenly Father give the Holy Spirit to them that ask him?

Jesus rebukes unbelief

14 ^RAnd he was casting out a devil, and it was dumb. And it came to pass, when the devil was gone out, the dumb spake; and the people wondered.

15 But some of them said, ^RHe casteth out devils through ^NBē-ĕl'-zĕ-bŭb the chief of the devils.

16 And others, tempting *him,* ^Rsought of him a sign from heaven.

17 ^RBut ^Rhe, knowing their thoughts, said unto them, Every kingdom divided against itself is brought to desolation; and a house *divided* against a house falleth.

18 If Satan also be divided against himself, how shall his kingdom stand? because ye say that I cast out devils through Bē-ĕl'-zĕ-bŭb.

19 And if I by Bē-ĕl'-zĕ-bŭb cast out devils, by whom do your sons cast *them* out? therefore shall they be your judges.

20 But if I ^Rwith the finger of God cast out devils, no doubt the kingdom of God is come upon you.

21 ^RWhen a strong man armed keepeth his palace, his goods are in peace:

22 But ^Rwhen a stronger than he shall come upon him, and overcome him, he taketh from him all his armour wherein he trusted, and divideth his spoils.

23 ^RHe that is not with me is against me: and he that gathereth not with me scattereth.

24 ^RWhen the unclean spirit is gone out of a man, he walketh through dry places, seeking rest; and finding none, he saith, I will return unto my house whence I came out.

25 And when he cometh, he findeth *it* swept and garnished.

26 Then goeth he, and taketh *to him* seven other spirits more wicked than himself; and they enter in, and dwell there: and ^Rthe last *state* of that man is worse than the first.

27 And it came to pass, as he spake these things, a certain woman of the company lifted up her voice, and said unto him, ^RBlessed *is* the womb that bare thee, and the paps which thou hast sucked.

28 But he said, Yea ^Rrather, blessed *are* they that hear the word of God, and keep it.

Sermon to the people

29 ^RAnd when the people were gathered thick together, he began to say, This is an evil generation: they seek a sign; and there shall no

sign be given it, but the sign of Jonas the prophet.

30 For as ᴿJonas was a sign unto the Nĭn'-ĕ-vītes, so shall also the Son of man be to this generation.

31 ᴿThe queen of the south shall rise up in the judgment with the men of this generation, and condemn them: for she came from the utmost parts of the earth to hear the wisdom of Solomon; and, behold, a greater than Solomon *is* here.

32 The men of Nĭn'-ĕ-vē shall rise up in the judgment with this generation, and shall condemn it: for ᴿthey repented at the preaching of Jonas; and, behold, a greater than Jonas *is* here.

33 ᴿNo man, when he hath lighted a candle, putteth *it* in a secret place, neither under a ᴺbushel, but on a candlestick, that they which come in may see the light.

34 ᴿThe light of the body is the eye: therefore when thine eye is single, thy whole body also is full of light; but when *thine eye* is evil, thy body also *is* full of darkness.

35 Take heed therefore that the light which is in thee be not darkness.

36 If thy whole body therefore *be* full of light, having no part dark, the whole shall be full of light, as when ᴺthe bright shining of a candle doth give thee light.

Denunciation of Pharisees

37 And as he spake, a certain Pharisee besought him to dine with him: and he went in, and sat down to meat.

38 And ᴿwhen the Pharisee saw *it,* he marvelled that he had not first washed before dinner.

39 ᴿAnd the Lord said unto him, Now do ye Pharisees make clean the outside of the cup and the platter; but ᴿyour inward part is full of ravening and wickedness.

40 *Ye* fools, did not he that made that which is without make that which is within also?

41 ᴿBut rather give alms ᴺof such things as ye have; and, behold, all things are clean unto you.

42 ᴿBut woe unto you, Pharisees! for ye tithe mint and rue and all manner of herbs, and pass over judgment and the love of God: these ought ye to have done, and not to leave the other undone.

43 ᴿWoe unto you, Pharisees! for ye love the uppermost seats in the synagogues, and greetings in the markets.

44 ᴿWoe unto you, scribes and Pharisees, hypocrites! ᴿfor ye are as graves which appear not, and the men that walk over *them* are not aware *of them.*

CHAP. 11
AD 33
30 Jonah 1:17 & 2:10
31 1 Ki. 10:1
32 Jonah 3:5
33 Mat. 5:15 Mark 4:21 ch. 8:16
33 See Mat. 5:15
34 Mat. 6:22
36 Gr. *a candle by its bright shining*
38 Mark 7:3
39 Mat. 23:25
39 Tit. 1:15
41 Is. 58:7 Dan. 4:27 ch. 12:33
41 Or, *as you are able*
42 Mat. 23:23
43 Mat. 23:6 Mark 12:38, 39
44 Mat. 23:27
44 Ps. 5:9

Mat. 23:4   46
Mat. 23:29   47
Mat. 23:34   49
Gen. 4:8   51
2 Chr. 24:20, 21 51
Mat. 23:13   52
Or, *forbad*   52
Mark 12:13   54

CHAP. 12
AD 33
Mat. 16:6 Mark 8:15   1
Mat. 16:12 Mark 4:22 ch. 8:17   1
Mat. 10:26   2
Is. 51:7, 8, 12, 13   4
Jer. 1:8
Mat. 10:28
John 15:14, 15   4

45 Then answered one of the lawyers, and said unto him, Master, thus saying thou reproachest us also.

46 And he said, Woe unto you also, *ye* lawyers! ᴿfor ye lade men with burdens grievous to be borne, and ye yourselves touch not the burdens with one of your fingers.

47 ᴿWoe unto you! for ye build the sepulchres of the prophets, and your fathers killed them.

48 Truly ye bear witness that ye allow the deeds of your fathers: for they indeed killed them, and ye build their sepulchres.

49 Therefore also said the wisdom of God, ᴿI will send them prophets and apostles, and *some* of them they shall slay and persecute:

50 That the blood of all the prophets, which was shed from the foundation of the world, may be required of this generation;

51 ᴿFrom the blood of Abel unto ᴿthe blood of Zăch-ă-rī'-ăs, which perished between the altar and the temple: verily I say unto you, It shall be required of this generation.

52 ᴿWoe unto you, lawyers! for ye have taken away the key of knowledge: ye entered not in yourselves, and them that were entering in ye ᴺhindered.

53 And as he said these things unto them, the scribes and the Pharisees began to urge *him* vehemently, and to provoke him to speak of many things:

54 Laying wait for him, and ᴿseeking to catch something out of his mouth, that they might accuse him.

CHAPTER 12

Hypocrisy to be exposed

IN ᴿthe mean time, when there were gathered together an innumerable multitude of people, insomuch that they trode one upon another, he began to say unto his disciples first of all, ᴿBeware ye of the leaven of the Pharisees, which is hypocrisy.

2 ᴿFor there is nothing covered, that shall not be revealed; neither hid, that shall not be known.

3 Therefore whatsoever ye have spoken in darkness shall be heard in the light; and that which ye have spoken in the ear in closets shall be proclaimed upon the housetops.

Value in God's sight

4 ᴿAnd I say unto you ᴿmy friends, Be not afraid of them that kill the body, and after that have no more that they can do.

5 But I will forewarn you whom ye shall fear: Fear him, which after he hath killed hath

power to cast into hell; yea, I say unto you, Fear him.

6 Are not five sparrows sold for two ᴺfarthings, and not one of them is forgotten before God?

7 But even the very hairs of your head are all numbered. Fear not therefore: ye are of more value than many sparrows.

Exhortation to fearless confession

8 ᴿAlso I say unto you, Whosoever shall confess me before men, him shall the Son of man also confess before the angels of God:

9 But he that denieth me before men shall be denied before the angels of God.

10 And ᴿwhosoever shall speak a word against the Son of man, it shall be forgiven him: but unto him that blasphemeth against the Holy Ghost it shall not be forgiven.

11 ᴿAnd when they bring you unto the synagogues, and *unto* magistrates, and powers, take ye no thought how or what thing ye shall answer, or what ye shall say:

12 For the Holy Ghost shall teach you in the same hour what ye ought to say.

Parable of the rich fool

13 And one of the company said unto him, Master, speak to my brother, that he divide the inheritance with me.

14 And he said unto him, ᴿMan, who made me a judge or a divider over you?

15 And he said unto them, ᴿTake heed, and beware of covetousness: for a man's life consisteth not in the abundance of the things which he possesseth.

16 And he spake a parable unto them, saying, The ground of a certain rich man brought forth plentifully:

17 And he thought within himself, saying, What shall I do, because I have no room where to bestow my fruits?

18 And he said, This will I do: I will pull down my barns, and build greater; and there will I bestow all my fruits and my goods.

19 And I will say to my soul, ᴿSoul, thou hast much goods laid up for many years; take thine ease, eat, drink, *and* be merry.

20 But God said unto him, *Thou* fool, this night ᴿthyᴺ soul shall be required of thee: ᴿthen whose shall those things be, which thou hast provided?

21 So *is* he that layeth up treasure for himself, ᴿand is not rich toward God.

Care and anxiety

22 And he said unto his disciples, Therefore I say unto you, ᴿTake no thought for your life,

what ye shall eat; neither for the body, what ye shall put on.

23 The life is more than meat, and the body *is more* than raiment.

24 Consider the ravens: for they neither sow nor reap; which neither have storehouse nor barn; and ᴿGod feedeth them: how much more are ye better than the fowls?

25 And which of you with taking thought can add to his stature one cubit?

26 If ye then be not able to do that thing which is least, why take ye thought for the rest?

27 Consider the lilies how they grow: they toil not, they spin not; and yet I say unto you, that Solomon in all his glory was not arrayed like one of these.

28 If then God so clothe the grass, which is to day in the field, and to morrow is cast into the oven; how much more *will he clothe* you, O ye of little faith?

29 And seek not ye what ye shall eat, or what ye shall drink, ᴺneither be ye of doubtful mind.

30 For all these things do the nations of the world seek after: and your Father knoweth that ye have need of these things.

31 ᴿBut rather seek ye the kingdom of God; and all these things shall be added unto you.

32 Fear not, little flock; for ᴿit is your Father's good pleasure to give you the kingdom.

33 ᴿSell that ye have, and give alms; ᴿprovide yourselves bags which wax not old, a treasure in the heavens that faileth not, where no thief approacheth, neither moth corrupteth.

34 For where your treasure is, there will your heart be also.

Exhortation to watchfulness

35 ᴿLet your loins be girded about, and ᴿ*your* lights burning;

36 And ye yourselves like unto men that wait for their lord, when he will return from the wedding; that when he cometh and knocketh, they may open unto him immediately.

37 ᴿBlessed *are* those servants, whom the lord when he cometh shall find watching: verily I say unto you, that he shall gird himself, and make them to sit down to meat, and will come forth and serve them.

38 And if he shall come in the second watch, or come in the third watch, and find *them* so, blessed are those servants.

39 ᴿAnd this know, that if the goodman of the house had known what hour the thief would come, he would have watched, and not have suffered his house to be broken through.

40 ᴿBe ye therefore ready also: for the Son

of man cometh at an hour when ye think not.

41 Then Peter said unto him, Lord, speakest thou this parable unto us, or even to all?

42 And the Lord said, [R]Who then is that faithful and wise steward, whom *his* lord shall make ruler over his household, to give *them their* portion of meat in due season?

43 Blessed *is* that servant, whom his lord when he cometh shall find so doing.

44 [R]Of a truth I say unto you, that he will make him ruler over all that he hath.

45 [R]But and if that servant say in his heart, My lord delayeth his coming; and shall begin to beat the menservants and maidens, and to eat and drink, and to be drunken;

46 The lord of that servant will come in a day when he looketh not for *him,* and at an hour when he is not aware, and will [N]cut him in sunder, and will appoint him his portion with the unbelievers.

47 And [R]that servant, which knew his lord's will, and prepared not *himself,* neither did according to his will, shall be beaten with many *stripes.*

48 [R]But he that knew not, and did commit things worthy of stripes, shall be beaten with few *stripes.* For unto whomsoever much is given, of him shall be much required: and to whom men have committed much, of him they will ask the more.

Peace or division?

49 [R]I am come to send fire on the earth; and what will I, if it be already kindled?

50 But [R]I have a baptism to be baptized with; and how am I [N]straitened till it be accomplished!

51 [R]Suppose ye that I am come to give peace on earth? I tell you, Nay; [R]but rather division:

52 [R]For from henceforth there shall be five in one house divided, three against two, and two against three.

53 The father shall be divided against the son, and the son against the father; the mother against the daughter, and the daughter against the mother; the mother in law against her daughter in law, and the daughter in law against her mother in law.

Interpreting the time

54 And he said also to the people, [R]When ye see a cloud rise out of the west, straightway ye say, There cometh a shower; and so it is.

55 And when *ye see* the south wind blow, ye say, There will be heat; and it cometh to pass.

56 *Ye* hypocrites, ye can discern the face of

CHAP. **12**

AD 33

42 Mat. 24:45
& 25:21
1 Cor. 4:2
44 Mat. 24:47
45 Mat. 24:48
46 Or, *cut him off,*
Mat. 24:51
47 Num. 15:30
Deut. 25:2
John 9:41 & 15:22
Acts 17:30
48 Lev. 5:17
1 Tim. 1:13
49 ver. 51
50 Mat. 20:22
Mark 10:38
50 Or, *pained*
51 ver. 49
Mat. 10:34
51 Mic. 7:6
John 7:43 & 9:16
& 10:19
52 Mat. 10:35
54 Mat. 16:2

Prov. 25:8   **58**
Mat. 5:25
See Ps. 32:6   **58**
Is. 55:6
See Mark 12:42 **59**

CHAP. **13**

AD 33

Or, *debtors,*   **4**
Mat. 18:24
ch. 11:4
Is. 5:2   **6**
Mat. 21:19

---

the sky and of the earth; but how is it that ye do not discern this time?

Settling with an accuser

57 Yea, and why even of yourselves judge ye not what is right?

58 [R]When thou goest with thine adversary to the magistrate, [R]*as thou art* in the way, give diligence that thou mayest be delivered from him; lest he hale thee to the judge, and the judge deliver thee to the officer, and the officer cast thee into prison.

59 I tell thee, thou shalt not depart thence, till thou hast paid the very last [N]mite.

CHAPTER 13

A call to repentance

THERE were present at that season some that told him of the Galilæans, whose blood Pilate had mingled with their sacrifices.

2 And Jesus answering said unto them, Suppose ye that these Galilæans were sinners above all the Galilæans, because they suffered such things?

3 I tell you, Nay: but, except ye repent, ye shall all likewise perish.

4 Or those eighteen, upon whom the tower in Sī-lō′-ăm fell, and slew them, think ye that they were [N]sinners above all men that dwelt in Jerusalem?

5 I tell you, Nay: but, except ye repent, ye shall all likewise perish.

Parable of the fig tree

6 He spake also this parable; [R]A certain *man* had a fig tree planted in his vineyard; and he came and sought fruit thereon, and found none.

7 Then said he unto the dresser of his vineyard, Behold, these three years I come seeking fruit on this fig tree, and find none: cut it down; why cumbereth it the ground?

8 And he answering said unto him, Lord, let it alone this year also, till I shall dig about it, and dung *it:*

9 And if it bear fruit, *well:* and if not, *then* after that thou shalt cut it down.

Healing on the sabbath

10 And he was teaching in one of the synagogues on the sabbath.

11 And, behold, there was a woman which had a spirit of infirmity eighteen years, and was bowed together, and could in no wise lift up *herself.*

12 And when Jesus saw her, he called *her*

to him, and said unto her, Woman, thou art loosed from thine infirmity.

13 ᴿAnd he laid *his* hands on her: and immediately she was made straight, and glorified God.

14 And the ruler of the synagogue answered with indignation, because that Jesus had healed on the sabbath day, and said unto the people, ᴿThere are six days in which men ought to work: in them therefore come and be healed, and ᴿnot on the sabbath day.

15 The Lord then answered him, and said, *Thou* hypocrite, ᴿdoth not each one of you on the sabbath loose his ox or *his* ass from the stall, and lead *him* away to watering?

16 And ought not this woman, ᴿbeing a daughter of Abraham, whom Satan hath bound, lo, these eighteen years, be loosed from this bond on the sabbath day?

17 And when he had said these things, all his adversaries were ashamed: and all the people rejoiced for all the glorious things that were done by him.

The mustard seed and leaven

18 ᴿThen said he, Unto what is the kingdom of God like? and whereunto shall I resemble it?

19 It is like a grain of mustard seed, which a man took, and cast into his garden; and it grew, and waxed a great tree; and the fowls of the air lodged in the branches of it.

20 And again he said, Whereunto shall I liken the kingdom of God?

21 It is like leaven, which a woman took and hid in three ᴺmeasures of meal, till the whole was leavened.

The straight gate

22 ᴿAnd he went through the cities and villages, teaching, and journeying toward Jerusalem.

23 Then said one unto him, Lord, are there few that be saved? And he said unto them,

24 ᴿStrive to enter in at the straight gate: for ᴿmany, I say unto you, will seek to enter in, and shall not be able.

25 ᴿWhen once the master of the house is risen up, and ᴿhath shut to the door, and ye begin to stand without, and to knock at the door, saying, ᴿLord, Lord, open unto us; and he shall answer and say unto you, ᴿI know you not whence ye are:

26 Then shall ye begin to say, We have eaten and drunk in thy presence, and thou hast taught in our streets.

27 ᴿBut he shall say, I tell you, I know you not whence ye are; ᴿdepart from me, all *ye* workers of iniquity.

28 ᴿThere shall be weeping and gnashing of teeth, ᴿwhen ye shall see Abraham, and Isaac, and Jacob, and all the prophets, in the kingdom of God, and you *yourselves* thrust out.

29 And they shall come from the east, and *from* the west, and from the north, and *from* the south, and shall sit down in the kingdom of God.

30 ᴿAnd, behold, there are last which shall be first, and there are first which shall be last.

Lament over Jerusalem

31 The same day there came certain of the Pharisees, saying unto him, Get thee out, and depart hence: for Herod will kill thee.

32 And he said unto them, Go ye, and tell that fox, Behold, I cast out devils, and I do cures to day and to morrow, and the third *day* ᴿI shall be perfected.

33 Nevertheless I must walk to day, and to morrow, and the *day* following: for it cannot be that a prophet perish out of Jerusalem.

34 ᴿO Jerusalem, Jerusalem, which killest the prophets, and stonest them that are sent unto thee; how often would I have gathered thy children together, as a hen *doth gather* her brood under *her* wings, and ye would not!

35 Behold, ᴿyour house is left unto you desolate: and verily I say unto you, Ye shall not see me, until *the time* come when ye shall say, ᴿBlessed *is* he that cometh in the name of the Lord.

CHAPTER 14

Healing on the sabbath

AND it came to pass, as he went into the house of one of the chief Pharisees to eat bread on the sabbath day, that they watched him.

2 And, behold, there was a certain man before him which had the dropsy.

3 And Jesus answering spake unto the lawyers and Pharisees, saying, ᴿIs it lawful to heal on the sabbath day?

4 And they held their peace. And he took *him,* and healed him, and let him go;

5 And answered them, saying, ᴿWhich of you shall have an ass or an ox fallen into a pit, and will not straightway pull him out on the sabbath day?

6 And they could not answer him again to these things.

Parable of the marriage feast

7 And he put forth a parable to those which were bidden, when he marked how they chose out the chief rooms; saying unto them,

8 When thou art bidden of any *man* to a wedding, sit not down in the highest room; lest a more honourable man than thou be bidden of him;

9 And he that bade thee and him come and say to thee, Give this man place; and thou begin with shame to take the lowest room.

10 ᴿBut when thou art bidden, go and sit down in the lowest room; that when he that bade thee cometh, he may say unto thee, Friend, go up higher: then shalt thou have worship in the presence of them that sit at meat with thee.

11 ᴿFor whosoever exalteth himself shall be abased; and he that humbleth himself shall be exalted.

12 Then said he also to him that bade him, When thou makest a dinner or a supper, call not thy friends, nor thy brethren, neither thy kinsmen, nor *thy* rich neighbours; lest they also bid thee again, and a recompence be made thee.

13 But when thou makest a feast, call ᴿthe poor, the maimed, the lame, the blind:

14 And thou shalt be blessed; for they cannot recompense thee: for thou shalt be recompensed at the resurrection of the just.

Parable of the great banquet

15 And when one of them that sat at meat with him heard these things, he said unto him, ᴿBlessed *is* he that shall eat bread in the kingdom of God.

16 ᴿThen said he unto him, A certain man made a great supper, and bade many:

17 And ᴿsent his servant at supper time to say to them that were bidden, Come; for all things are now ready.

18 And they all with one *consent* began to make excuse. The first said unto him, I have bought a piece of ground, and I must needs go and see it: I pray thee have me excused.

19 And another said, I have bought five yoke of oxen, and I go to prove them: I pray thee have me excused.

20 And another said, I have married a wife, and therefore I cannot come.

21 So that servant came, and shewed his lord these things. Then the master of the house being angry said to his servant, Go out quickly into the streets and lanes of the city, and bring in hither the poor, and the maimed, and the halt, and the blind.

22 And the servant said, Lord, it is done as thou hast commanded, and yet there is room.

23 And the lord said unto the servant, Go out into the highways and hedges, and compel *them* to come in, that my house may be filled.

24 For I say unto you, ᴿThat none of those

men which were bidden shall taste of my supper.

Who cannot be disciples

25 And there went great multitudes with him: and he turned, and said unto them,

26 ᴿIf any *man* come to me, ᴿand hate not his father, and mother, and wife, and children, and brethren, and sisters, ᴿyea, and his own life also, he cannot be my disciple.

27 And ᴿwhosoever doth not bear his cross, and come after me, cannot be my disciple.

28 For ᴿwhich of you, intending to build a tower, sitteth not down first, and counteth the cost, whether he have *sufficient* to finish *it?*

29 Lest haply, after he hath laid the foundation, and is not able to finish *it,* all that behold *it* begin to mock him,

30 Saying, This man began to build, and was not able to finish.

31 Or what king, going to make war against another king, sitteth not down first, and consulteth whether he be able with ten thousand to meet him that cometh against him with twenty thousand?

32 Or else, while the other is yet a great way off, he sendeth an ambassage, and desireth conditions of peace.

33 So likewise, whosoever he be of you that forsaketh not all that he hath, he cannot be my disciple.

34 ᴿSalt *is* good: but if the salt have lost his savour, wherewith shall it be seasoned?

35 It is neither fit for the land, nor yet for the dunghill; *but* men cast it out. He that hath ears to hear, let him hear.

CHAPTER 15

Parable of the lost sheep

THEN ᴿdrew near unto him all the publicans and sinners for to hear him.

2 And the Pharisees and scribes murmured, saying, This man receiveth sinners, ᴿand eateth with them.

3 And he spake this parable unto them, saying,

4 ᴿWhat man of you, having an hundred sheep, if he lose one of them, doth not leave the ninety and nine in the wilderness, and go after that which is lost, until he find it?

5 And when he hath found *it,* he layeth *it* on his shoulders, rejoicing.

6 And when he cometh home, he calleth together *his* friends and neighbours, saying unto them, Rejoice with me; for I have found my sheep ᴿwhich was lost.

7 I say unto you, that likewise joy shall be in

CHAP. 14
AD 33
10 Prov. 25:6, 7
11 Job 22:29
Ps. 18:27
Prov. 29:23
Mat. 23:12
ch. 18:14
Jas. 4:6
1 Pet. 5:5
13 Neh. 8:10, 12
15 Rev. 19:9
16 Mat. 22:2
17 Prov. 9:2, 5
24 Mat. 21:43
& 22:8
Acts 13:46

Deut. 13:6 26
& 33:9
Mat. 10:37
Rom. 9:13 26
Rev. 12:11 26
Mat. 16:24 27
Mark 8:34
ch. 9:23
2 Tim. 3:12
Prov. 24:27 28
Mat. 5:13 34
Mark 9:50

CHAP. 15
AD 33
Mat. 9:10 1
Acts 11:3 2
Gal. 2:12
Mat. 18:12 4
1 Pet. 2:10, 25 6

heaven over one sinner that repenteth, [R]more than over ninety and nine just persons, which need no repentance.

Parable of the lost coin

8 Either what woman having ten [N]pieces of silver if she lose one piece, doth not light a candle, and sweep the house, and seek diligently till she find *it?*

9 And when she hath found *it,* she calleth *her* friends and *her* neighbours together, saying, Rejoice with me; for I have found the piece which I had lost.

10 Likewise, I say unto you, there is joy in the presence of the angels of God over one sinner that repenteth.

Parable of the lost son

11 And he said, A certain man had two sons:

12 And the younger of them said to *his* father, Father, give me the portion of goods that falleth *to me.* And he divided unto them [R]*his* living.

13 And not many days after the younger son gathered all together, and took his journey into a far country, and there wasted his substance with riotous living.

14 And when he had spent all, there arose a mighty famine in that land; and he began to be in want.

15 And he went and joined himself to a citizen of that country; and he sent him into his fields to feed swine.

16 And he would fain have filled his belly with the husks that the swine did eat: and no man gave unto him.

17 And when he came to himself, he said, How many hired servants of my father's have bread enough and to spare, and I perish with hunger!

18 I will arise and go to my father, and will say unto him, Father, I have sinned against heaven, and before thee,

19 And am no more worthy to be called thy son: make me as one of thy hired servants.

20 And he arose, and came to his father. But [R]when he was yet a great way off, his father saw him, and had compassion, and ran, and fell on his neck, and kissed him.

21 And the son said unto him, Father, I have sinned against heaven, [R]and in thy sight, and am no more worthy to be called thy son.

22 But the father said to his servants, Bring forth the best robe, and put *it* on him; and put a ring on his hand, and shoes on *his* feet:

23 And bring hither the fatted calf, and kill *it;* and let us eat, and be merry:

24 [R]For this my son was dead, and is alive again; he was lost, and is found. And they began to be merry.

25 Now his elder son was in the field: and as he came and drew nigh to the house, he heard musick and dancing.

26 And he called one of the servants, and asked what these things meant.

27 And he said unto him, Thy brother is come; and thy father hath killed the fatted calf, because he hath received him safe and sound.

28 And he was angry, and would not go in: therefore came his father out, and entreated him.

29 And he answering said to *his* father, Lo, these many years do I serve thee, neither transgressed I at any time thy commandment: and yet thou never gavest me a kid, that I might make merry with my friends:

30 But as soon as this thy son was come, which hath devoured thy living with harlots, thou hast killed for him the fatted calf.

31 And he said unto him, Son, thou art ever with me, and all that I have is thine.

32 It was meet that we should make merry, and be glad: [R]for this thy brother was dead, and is alive again; and was lost, and is found.

CHAPTER 16

Parable of the wicked steward

AND he said also unto his disciples, There was a certain rich man, which had a steward; and the same was accused unto him that he had wasted his goods.

2 And he called him, and said unto him, How is it that I hear this of thee? give an account of thy stewardship; for thou mayest be no longer steward.

3 Then the steward said within himself, What shall I do? for my lord taketh away from me the stewardship: I cannot dig; to beg I am ashamed.

4 I am resolved what to do, that, when I am put out of the stewardship, they may receive me into their houses.

5 So he called every one of his lord's debtors *unto him,* and said unto the first, How much owest thou unto my lord?

6 And he said, An hundred [N]measures of oil. And he said unto him, Take thy bill, and sit down quickly, and write fifty.

7 Then said he to another, And how much owest thou? And he said, An hundred [N]measures of wheat. And he said unto him, Take thy bill, and write fourscore.

8 And the lord commended the unjust steward, because he had done wisely: for the chil-

dren of this world are in their generation wiser than ᴿthe children of light.

9 And I say unto you, ᴿMake to yourselves friends of the ᴺmammon of unrighteousness; that, when ye fail, they may receive you into everlasting habitations.

10 ᴿHe that is faithful in that which is least is faithful also in much: and he that is unjust in the least is unjust also in much.

11 If therefore ye have not been faithful in the unrighteous ᴺmammon, who will commit to your trust the true *riches?*

12 And if ye have not been faithful in that which is another man's, who shall give you that which is your own?

13 ᴿNo servant can serve two masters: for either he will hate the one, and love the other; or else he will hold to the one, and despise the other. Ye cannot serve God and mammon.

Jesus answers the Pharisees

14 And the Pharisees also, ᴿwho were covetous, heard all these things: and they derided him.

15 And he said unto them, Ye are they which ᴿjustify yourselves before men; but ᴿGod knoweth your hearts: for ᴿthat which is highly esteemed among men is abomination in the sight of God.

16 ᴿThe law and the prophets *were* until John: since that time the kingdom of God is preached, and every man presseth into it.

17 ᴿAnd it is easier for heaven and earth to pass, than one tittle of the law to fail.

18 ᴿWhosoever putteth away his wife, and marrieth another, committeth adultery: and whosoever marrieth her that is put away from *her* husband committeth adultery.

The rich man and Lazarus

19 There was a certain rich man, which was clothed in purple and fine linen, and fared sumptuously every day:

20 And there was a certain beggar named Lăz′-a-rŭs, which was laid at his gate, full of sores,

21 And desiring to be fed with the crumbs which fell from the rich man's table: moreover the dogs came and licked his sores.

22 And it came to pass, that the beggar died, and was carried by the angels into Abraham's bosom: the rich man also died, and was buried;

23 And in hell he lift up his eyes, being in torments, and seeth Abraham afar off, and Lăz′-a-rŭs in his bosom.

24 And he cried and said, Father Abraham, have mercy on me, and send Lăz′-a-rŭs, that

he may dip the tip of his finger in water, and ᴿcool my tongue; for I ᴿam tormented in this flame.

25 But Abraham said, Son, ᴿremember that thou in thy lifetime receivedst thy good things, and likewise Lăz′-a-rŭs evil things: but now he is comforted, and thou art tormented.

26 And beside all this, between us and you there is a great gulf fixed: so that they which would pass from hence to you cannot; neither can they pass to us, that *would come* from thence.

27 Then he said, I pray thee therefore, father, that thou wouldest send him to my father's house:

28 For I have five brethren; that he may testify unto them, lest they also come into this place of torment.

29 Abraham saith unto him, ᴿThey have Moses and the prophets; let them hear them.

30 And he said, Nay, father Abraham: but if one went unto them from the dead, they will repent.

31 And he said unto him, If they hear not Moses and the prophets, ᴿneither will they be persuaded, though one rose from the dead.

CHAPTER 17

Teachings on forgiveness and faith

THEN said he unto the disciples, ᴿIt is impossible but that offences will come: but woe *unto him,* through whom they come!

2 It were better for him that a millstone were hanged about his neck, and he cast into the sea, than that he should offend one of these little ones.

3 Take heed to yourselves: ᴿIf thy brother trespass against thee, ᴿrebuke him; and if he repent, forgive him.

4 And if he trespass against thee seven times in a day, and seven times in a day turn again to thee, saying, I repent; thou shalt forgive him.

5 And the apostles said unto the Lord, Increase our faith.

6 ᴿAnd the Lord said, If ye had faith as a grain of mustard seed, ye might say unto this sycamine tree, Be thou plucked up by the root, and be thou planted in the sea; and it should obey you.

7 But which of you, having a servant plowing or feeding cattle, will say unto him by and by, when he is come from the field, Go and sit down to meat?

8 And will not rather say unto him, Make ready wherewith I may sup, and gird thyself,

R and serve me, till I have eaten and drunken; and afterward thou shalt eat and drink?

9 Doth he thank that servant because he did the things that were commanded him? I trow not.

10 So likewise ye, when ye shall have done all those things which are commanded you, say, We are R unprofitable servants: we have done that which was our duty to do.

Healing the ten lepers

11 And it came to pass, R as he went to Jerusalem, that he passed through the midst of Să-mâr'-ĭ-ă and Galilee.

12 And as he entered into a certain village, there met him ten men that were lepers, R which stood afar off:

13 And they lifted up *their* voices, and said, Jesus, Master, have mercy on us.

14 And when he saw *them,* he said unto them, R Go shew yourselves unto the priests. And it came to pass, that, as they went, they were cleansed.

15 And one of them, when he saw that he was healed, turned back, and with a loud voice glorified God,

16 And fell down on *his* face at his feet, giving him thanks: and he was a Să-măr'-ĭ-tăn.

17 And Jesus answering said, Were there not ten cleansed? but where *are* the nine?

18 There are not found that returned to give glory to God, save this stranger.

19 R And he said unto him, Arise, go thy way: thy faith hath made thee whole.

Coming of the Son of man

20 And when he was demanded of the Pharisees, when the kingdom of God should come, he answered them and said, The kingdom of God cometh not N with observation:

21 R Neither shall they say, Lo here! or, lo there! for, behold, R the kingdom of God is N within you.

22 And he said unto the disciples, R The days will come, when ye shall desire to see one of the days of the Son of man, and ye shall not see *it.*

23 R And they shall say to you, See here; or, see there: go not after *them,* nor follow *them.*

24 R For as the lightning, that lighteneth out of the one *part* under heaven, shineth unto the other *part* under heaven; so shall also the Son of man be in his day.

25 R But first must he suffer many things, and be rejected of this generation.

26 R And as it was in the days of Nō'-ē, so shall it be also in the days of the Son of man.

27 They did eat, they drank, they married

CHAP. 17
AD 33
8 ch. 12:37
10 Job 22:3 & 35:7
Ps. 16:2
Mat. 25:30
Rom. 3:12
& 11:35
1 Cor. 9:16, 17
Philem. 11
11 ch. 9:51, 52
John 4:4
12 Lev. 13:46
14 Lev. 13:2
& 14:2
Mat. 8:4
ch. 5:14
19 Mat. 9:22
Mark 5:34
& 10:52
ch. 7:50 & 8:48
& 18:42
20 Or, *with outward shew*
21 ver. 23
21 Rom. 14:17
21 Or, *among you,* John 1:26
22 See Mat. 9:15
John 17:12
23 Mat. 24:23
Mark 13:21
ch. 21:8
24 Mat. 24:27
25 Mark 8:31
& 9:31 & 10:33
ch. 9:22
26 Gen. 7
Mat. 24:37

Gen. 19	**28**
Gen. 19:16, 24	**29**
2 Thes. 1:7	**30**
Mat. 24:17	**31**
Mark 13:15	
Gen. 19:26	**32**
Mat. 10:39	**33**
& 16:25	
Mark 8:35	
ch. 9:24	
John 12:25	
Mat. 24:40, 41	**34**
1 Thes. 4:17	
This 36th verse is wanting in most of the Greek copies	**36**
Job 39:30	**37**
Mat. 24:28	

CHAP. 18
AD 33
ch. 11:5 & 21:36 **1**
Rom. 12:12
Eph. 6:18
Col. 4:2
1 Thes. 5:17
Gr. *in a certain city* **2**
ch. 11:8 **5**
Rev. 6:10 **7**
Heb. 10:37 **8**
2 Pet. 3:8, 9

---

wives, they were given in marriage, until the day that Nō'-ē entered into the ark, and the flood came, and destroyed them all.

28 R Likewise also as it was in the days of Lot; they did eat, they drank, they bought, they sold, they planted, they builded;

29 But R the same day that Lot went out of Sodom it rained fire and brimstone from heaven, and destroyed *them* all.

30 Even thus shall it be in the day when the Son of man R is revealed.

31 In that day, he R which shall be upon the housetop, and his stuff in the house, let him not come down to take it away: and he that is in the field, let him likewise not return back.

32 R Remember Lot's wife.

33 R Whosoever shall seek to save his life shall lose it; and whosoever shall lose his life shall preserve it.

34 R I tell you, in that night there shall be two *men* in one bed; the one shall be taken, and the other shall be left.

35 Two *women* shall be grinding together; the one shall be taken, and the other left.

36 N Two *men* shall be in the field; the one shall be taken, and the other left.

37 And they answered and said unto him, R Where, Lord? And he said unto them, Wheresoever the body *is,* thither will the eagles be gathered together.

CHAPTER 18

The importunate widow

AND he spake a parable unto them *to this end,* that men ought R always to pray, and not to faint;

2 Saying, There was N in a city a judge, which feared not God, neither regarded man:

3 And there was a widow in that city; and she came unto him, saying, Avenge me of mine adversary.

4 And he would not for a while: but afterward he said within himself, Though I fear not God, nor regard man;

5 R Yet because this widow troubleth me, I will avenge her, lest by her continual coming she weary me.

6 And the Lord said, Hear what the unjust judge saith.

7 And R shall not God avenge his own elect, which cry day and night unto him, though he bear long with them?

8 I tell you R that he will avenge them speedily. Nevertheless when the Son of man cometh, shall he find faith on the earth?

The Pharisee and the publican

9 And he spake this parable unto certain ᴿwhich trusted in themselves ᴺthat they were righteous, and despised others:

10 Two men went up into the temple to pray; the one a Pharisee, and the other a publican.

11 The Pharisee ᴿstood and prayed thus with himself, ᴿGod, I thank thee, that I am not as other men *are,* extortioners, unjust, adulterers, or even as this publican.

12 I fast twice in the week, I give tithes of all that I possess.

13 And the publican, standing afar off, would not lift up so much as *his* eyes unto heaven, but smote upon his breast, saying, God be merciful to me a sinner.

14 I tell you, this man went down to his house justified *rather* than the other: ᴿfor every one that exalteth himself shall be abased; and he that humbleth himself shall be exalted.

Jesus receives the children

15 ᴿAnd they brought unto him also infants, that he would touch them: but when *his* disciples saw *it,* they rebuked them.

16 But Jesus called them *unto him,* and said, Suffer little children to come unto me, and forbid them not: for ᴿof such is the kingdom of God.

17 ᴿVerily I say unto you, Whosoever shall not receive the kingdom of God as a little child shall in no wise enter therein.

The rich ruler

18 ᴿAnd a certain ruler asked him, saying, Good Master, what shall I do to inherit eternal life?

19 And Jesus said unto him, Why callest thou me good? none *is* good, save one, *that is,* God.

20 Thou knowest the commandments, ᴿDo not commit adultery, Do not kill, Do not steal, Do not bear false witness, ᴿHonour thy father and thy mother.

21 And he said, All these have I kept from my youth up.

22 Now when Jesus heard these things, he said unto him, Yet lackest thou one thing: ᴿsell all that thou hast, and distribute unto the poor, and thou shalt have treasure in heaven: and come, follow me.

23 And when he heard this, he was very sorrowful: for he was very rich.

24 And when Jesus saw that he was very sorrowful, he said, ᴿHow hardly shall they

that have riches enter into the kingdom of God!

25 For it is easier for a camel to go through a needle's eye, than for a rich man to enter into the kingdom of God.

26 And they that heard *it* said, Who then can be saved?

27 And he said, ᴿThe things which are impossible with men are possible with God.

28 ᴿThen Peter said, Lo, we have left all, and followed thee.

29 And he said unto them, Verily I say unto you, ᴿThere is no man that hath left house, or parents, or brethren, or wife, or children, for the kingdom of God's sake,

30 ᴿWho shall not receive manifold more in this present time, and in the world to come life everlasting.

Jesus foretells His passion

31 ᴿThen he took *unto him* the twelve, and said unto them, Behold, we go up to Jerusalem, and all things ᴿthat are written by the prophets concerning the Son of man shall be accomplished.

32 For ᴿhe shall be delivered unto the Gentiles, and shall be mocked, and spitefully entreated, and spitted on:

33 And they shall scourge *him,* and put him to death: and the third day he shall rise again.

34 ᴿAnd they understood none of these things: and this saying was hid from them, neither knew they the things which were spoken.

Healing the blind man

35 ᴿAnd it came to pass, that as he was come nigh unto Jericho, a certain blind man sat by the way side begging:

36 And hearing the multitude pass by, he asked what it meant.

37 And they told him, that Jesus of Nazareth passeth by.

38 And he cried, saying, Jesus, *thou* son of David, have mercy on me.

39 And they which went before rebuked him, that he should hold his peace: but he cried so much the more, *Thou* son of David, have mercy on me.

40 And Jesus stood, and commanded him to be brought unto him: and when he was come near, he asked him,

41 Saying, What wilt thou that I shall do unto thee? And he said, Lord, that I may receive my sight.

42 And Jesus said unto him, Receive thy sight: ᴿthy faith hath saved thee.

43 And immediately he received his sight,

CHAP. 18
AD 33
9 ch. 10:29 & 16:15
9 Or, *as being righteous*
11 Ps. 135:2
11 Is. 1:15 & 58:2 Rev. 3:17
14 Job 22:29 Mat. 23:12 ch. 14:11 Jas. 4:6 1 Pet. 5:5
15 Mat. 19:13 Mark 10:13
16 1 Cor. 14:20 1 Pet. 2:2
17 Mark 10:15
18 Mat. 19:16 Mark 10:17
20 Ex. 20:12, 16 Deut. 5:16-20 Rom. 13:9
20 Eph. 6:2 Col. 3:20
22 Mat. 6:19, 20 & 19:21 1 Tim. 6:19
24 Prov. 11:28 Mat. 19:23 Mark 10:23

Jer. 32:17   27
Zech. 8:6
Mat. 19:26
ch. 1:37
Mat. 19:27   28
Deut. 33:9   29
Job 42:10   30
Mat. 16:21   31
& 17:22 & 20:17
Mark 10:32
Ps. 22   31
Is. 53
Mat. 27:2   32
ch. 23:1
John 18:28
Acts 3:13
Mark 9:32   34
ch. 2:50 & 9:45
John 10:6
& 12:16
Mat. 20:29   35
Mark 10:46
ch. 17:19   42

and followed him, ^Rglorifying God: and all the people, when they saw *it,* gave praise unto God.

CHAPTER 19

Conversion of Zacchaeus

A ND *Jesus* entered and passed through Jericho.

2 And, behold, *there was* a man named Zăc-chæ'-ŭs, which was the chief among the publicans, and he was rich.

3 And he sought to see Jesus who he was; and could not for the press, because he was little of stature.

4 And he ran before, and climbed up into a sycomore tree to see him: for he was to pass that *way.*

5 And when Jesus came to the place, he looked up, and saw him, and said unto him, Zăc-chæ'-ŭs, make haste, and come down; for to day I must abide at thy house.

6 And he made haste, and came down, and received him joyfully.

7 And when they saw *it,* they all murmured, saying, ^RThat he was gone to be guest with a man that is a sinner.

8 And Zăc-chæ'-ŭs stood, and said unto the Lord; Behold, Lord, the half of my goods I give to the poor; and if I have taken any thing from any man by ^Rfalse accusation, ^RI restore *him* fourfold.

9 And Jesus said unto him, This day is salvation come to this house, forsomuch as ^Rhe also is ^Ra son of Abraham.

10 ^RFor the Son of man is come to seek and to save that which was lost.

Parable of the pounds

11 And as they heard these things, he added and spake a parable, because he was nigh to Jerusalem, and because ^Rthey thought that the kingdom of God should immediately appear.

12 ^RHe said therefore, A certain nobleman went into a far country to receive for himself a kingdom, and to return.

13 And he called his ten servants, and delivered them ten ^Npounds, and said unto them, Occupy till I come.

14 ^RBut his citizens hated him, and sent a message after him, saying, We will not have this *man* to reign over us.

15 And it came to pass, that when he was returned, having received the kingdom, then he commanded these servants to be called unto him, to whom he had given the ^Nmoney, that he might know how much every man had gained by trading.

16 Then came the first, saying, Lord, thy pound hath gained ten pounds.

17 And he said unto him, Well, thou good servant: because thou hast been ^Rfaithful in a very little, have thou authority over ten cities.

18 And the second came, saying, Lord, thy pound hath gained five pounds.

19 And he said likewise to him, Be thou also over five cities.

20 And another came, saying, Lord, behold, *here is* thy pound, which I have kept laid up in a napkin:

21 ^RFor I feared thee, because thou art an austere man: thou takest up that thou layedst not down, and reapest that thou didst not sow.

22 And he saith unto him, ^ROut of thine own mouth will I judge thee, *thou* wicked servant. ^RThou knewest that I was an austere man, taking up that I laid not down, and reaping that I did not sow:

23 Wherefore then gavest not thou my money into the bank, that at my coming I might have required mine own with usury?

24 And he said unto them that stood by, Take from him the pound, and give *it* to him that hath ten pounds.

25 (And they said unto him, Lord, he hath ten pounds.)

26 For I say unto you, ^RThat unto every one which hath shall be given; and from him that hath not, even that he hath shall be taken away from him.

27 But those mine enemies, which would not that I should reign over them, bring hither, and slay *them* before me.

The triumphal entry

28 And when he had thus spoken, ^Rhe went before, ascending up to Jerusalem.

29 ^RAnd it came to pass, when he was come nigh to Bĕth'-phă-ġē and Bethany, at the mount called *the mount* of Olives, he sent two of his disciples,

30 Saying, Go ye into the village over against *you;* in the which at your entering ye shall find a colt tied, whereon yet never man sat: loose him, and bring *him hither.*

31 And if any man ask you, Why do ye loose *him?* thus shall ye say unto him, Because the Lord hath need of him.

32 And they that were sent went their way, and found even as he had said unto them.

33 And as they were loosing the colt, the owners thereof said unto them, Why loose ye the colt?

34 And they said, The Lord hath need of him.

35 And they brought him to Jesus: ^Rand they

CHAP. **18**
AD 33
43 ch. 5:26
Acts 4:21 & 11:18

CHAP. **19**
AD 33
7 Mat. 9:11
ch. 5:30
8 ch. 3:14
8 Ex. 22:1
1 Sam. 12:3
2 Sam. 12:6
9 Rom. 4:11, 12, 16
Gal. 3:7
9 ch. 13:16
10 Mat. 18:11
See Mat. 10:6
& 15:24
11 Acts 1:6
12 Mat. 25:14
Mark 13:34
13 *Mina,* here translated a pound, is twelve ounces and an half: which according to five shillings the ounce is three pounds two shillings and sixpence
14 John 1:11
15 Gr. *silver,* ver. 23

Mat. 25:21	**17**
ch. 16:10	
Mat. 25:24	**21**
2 Sam. 1:16	**22**
Job 15:6	
Mat. 12:37	
Mat. 25:26	**22**
Mat. 13:12	**26**
& 25:29	
Mark 4:25	
ch. 8:18	
Mark 10:32	**28**
Mat. 21:1	**29**
Mark 11:1	
2 Ki. 9:13	**35**
Mat. 21:7	
Mark 11:7	
John 12:14	

cast their garments upon the colt, and they set Jesus thereon.

36 And as he went, they spread their clothes in the way.

37 And when he was come nigh, even now at the descent of the mount of Olives, the whole multitude of the disciples began to rejoice and praise God with a loud voice for all the mighty works that they had seen;

38 Saying, ᴿBlessed *be* the King that cometh in the name of the Lord: ᴿpeace in heaven, and glory in the highest.

39 And some of the Pharisees from among the multitude said unto him, Master, rebuke thy disciples.

40 And he answered and said unto them, I tell you that, if these should hold their peace, ᴿthe stones would immediately cry out.

Lament over Jerusalem

41 And when he was come near, he beheld the city, and ᴿwept over it,

42 Saying, If thou hadst known, even thou, at least in this thy day, the things *which belong* unto thy peace! but now they are hid from thine eyes.

43 For the days shall come upon thee, that thine enemies shall ᴿcast a trench about thee, and compass thee round, and keep thee in on every side,

44 And ᴿshall lay thee even with the ground, and thy children within thee; and ᴿthey shall not leave in thee one stone upon another; ᴿbecause thou knewest not the time of thy visitation.

Cleansing the temple

45 ᴿAnd he went into the temple, and began to cast out them that sold therein, and them that bought;

46 Saying unto them, ᴿIt is written, My house is the house of prayer: but ᴿye have made it a den of thieves.

47 And he taught daily in the temple. But ᴿthe chief priests and the scribes and the chief of the people sought to destroy him,

48 And could not find what they might do: for all the people ᴺwere very attentive to hear him.

CHAPTER 20

The question of authority

AND ᴿit came to pass, *that* on one of those days, as he taught the people in the temple, and preached the gospel, the chief priests and the scribes came upon *him* with the elders,

2 And spake unto him, saying, Tell us, ᴿby

CHAP. **19**
AD 33
38 Ps. 118:26
ch. 13:35
38 ch. 2:14
Eph. 2:14
40 Hab. 2:11
41 John 11:35
43 Is. 29:3, 4
Jer. 6:3, 6
ch. 21:20
44 1 Ki. 9:7, 8
Mic. 3:12
44 Mat. 24:2
Mark 13:2
ch. 21:6
44 Dan. 9:24
ch. 1:68, 78
1 Pet. 2:12
45 Mat. 21:12
Mark 11:15
John 2:14, 15
46 Is. 56:7
46 Jer. 7:11
47 Mark 11:18
John 7:19
& 8:37
48 Or, *hanged on him*, Acts 16:14

CHAP. **20**
AD 33
1 Mat. 21:23
2 Acts 4:7 & 7:27

what authority doest thou these things? or who is he that gave thee this authority?

3 And he answered and said unto them, I will also ask you one thing; and answer me:

4 The baptism of John, was it from heaven, or of men?

5 And they reasoned with themselves, saying, If we shall say, From heaven; he will say, Why then believed ye him not?

6 But and if we say, Of men; all the people will stone us: ᴿfor they be persuaded that John was a prophet.

7 And they answered, that they could not tell whence *it was*.

8 And Jesus said unto them, Neither tell I you by what authority I do these things.

Parable of the wicked servants

9 Then began he to speak to the people this parable; ᴿA certain man planted a vineyard, and let it forth to husbandmen, and went into a far country for a long time.

10 And at the season he sent a servant to the husbandmen, that they should give him of the fruit of the vineyard: but the husbandmen beat him, and sent *him* away empty.

11 And again he sent another servant: and they beat him also, and entreated *him* shamefully, and sent *him* away empty.

12 And again he sent a third: and they wounded him also, and cast *him* out.

13 Then said the lord of the vineyard, What shall I do? I will send my beloved son: it may be they will reverence *him* when they see him.

14 But when the husbandmen saw him, they reasoned among themselves, saying, This is the heir: come, let us kill him, that the inheritance may be ours.

15 So they cast him out of the vineyard, and killed *him*. What therefore shall the lord of the vineyard do unto them?

16 He shall come and destroy these husbandmen, and shall give the vineyard to others. And when they heard *it,* they said, God forbid.

17 And he beheld them, and said, What is this then that is written, ᴿThe stone which the builders rejected, the same is become the head of the corner?

18 Whosoever shall fall upon that stone shall be broken; but ᴿon whomsoever it shall fall, it will grind him to powder.

The tribute money

19 And the chief priests and the scribes the same hour sought to lay hands on him; and they feared the people: for they perceived that he had spoken this parable against them.

Mat. 14:5	6
& 21:26	
ch. 7:29	
Mat. 21:33	9
Mark 12:1	
Ps. 118:22	17
Mat. 21:42	
Dan. 2:34, 35	18
Mat. 21:44	

20 ᴿAnd they watched *him,* and sent forth spies, which should feign themselves just men, that they might take hold of his words, that so they might deliver him unto the power and authority of the governor.

21 And they asked him, saying, ᴿMaster, we know that thou sayest and teachest rightly, neither acceptest thou the person *of any,* but teachest the way of God ᴺtruly:

22 Is it lawful for us to give tribute unto Cæsar, or no?

23 But he perceived their craftiness, and said unto them, Why tempt ye me?

24 Shew me a ᴺpenny. Whose image and superscription hath it? They answered and said, Cæsar's.

25 And he said unto them, Render therefore unto Cæsar the things which be Cæsar's, and unto God the things which be God's.

26 And they could not take hold of his words before the people: and they marvelled at his answer, and held their peace.

Question about the resurrection

27 ᴿThen came to *him* certain of the Săd′-dū-çeês, ᴿwhich deny that there is any resurrection; and they asked him,

28 Saying, Master, Moses wrote unto us, If any man's brother die, having a wife, and he die without children, that his brother should take his wife, and raise up seed unto his brother.

29 There were therefore seven brethren: and the first took a wife, and died without children.

30 And the second took her to wife, and he died childless.

31 And the third took her; and in like manner the seven also: and they left no children, and died.

32 Last of all the woman died also.

33 Therefore in the resurrection whose wife of them is she? for seven had her to wife.

34 And Jesus answering said unto them, The children of this world marry, and are given in marriage:

35 But they which shall be accounted worthy to obtain that world, and the resurrection from the dead, neither marry, nor are given in marriage:

36 Neither can they die any more: for ᴿthey are equal unto the angels; and are the children of God, ᴿbeing the children of the resurrection.

37 Now that the dead are raised, ᴿeven Moses shewed at the bush, when he calleth the Lord the God of Abraham, and the God of Isaac, and the God of Jacob.

CHAP. 20	
AD 33	
20	Mat. 22:15
21	Mat. 22:16
	Mark 12:14
21	Or, *of a truth*
24	See Mat. 8:28
27	Mat. 22:23
	Mark 12:18
27	Acts 23:6, 8
36	1 Cor. 15:42, 49, 52
	1 John 3:2
36	Rom. 8:23
37	Ex. 3:6

Rom. 6:10, 11	38
Mat. 22:42	41
Mark 12:35	
Ps. 110:1	42
Acts 2:34	
Mat. 23:1	45
Mark 12:38	
Mat. 23:5	46
ch. 11:43	46
Mat. 23:14	47

CHAP. 21	
AD 33	
Mark 12:41	1
See Mark 12:42	2
2 Cor. 8:12	3
Mat. 24:1	5
Mark 13:1	
ch. 19:44	6
Mat. 24:4	8
Mark 13:5	
Eph. 5:6	
2 Thes. 2:3	
Or, *and,*	
The time,	8
Mat. 3:2	
& 4:17	

38 For he is not a God of the dead, but of the living: for ᴿall live unto him.

39 Then certain of the scribes answering said, Master, thou hast well said.

40 And after that they durst not ask him any *question at all.*

Christ's unanswerable question

41 And he said unto them, ᴿHow say they that Christ is David's son?

42 And David himself saith in the book of Psalms, ᴿThe Lᴏʀᴅ said unto my Lord, Sit thou on my right hand,

43 Till I make thine enemies thy footstool.

44 David therefore calleth him Lord, how is he then his son?

Warning against the scribes

45 ᴿThen in the audience of all the people he said unto his disciples,

46 ᴿBeware of the scribes, which desire to walk in long robes, and ᴿlove greetings in the markets, and the highest seats in the synagogues, and the chief rooms at feasts;

47 ᴿWhich devour widows' houses, and for a shew make long prayers: the same shall receive greater damnation.

CHAPTER 21

The widow's mites

AND he looked up, ᴿand saw the rich men casting their gifts into the treasury.

2 And he saw also a certain poor widow casting in thither two ᴺmites.

3 And he said, Of a truth I say unto you, ᴿthat this poor widow hath cast in more than they all:

4 For all these have of their abundance cast in unto the offerings of God: but she of her penury hath cast in all the living that she had.

Signs and suffering before the end

5 ᴿAnd as some spake of the temple, how it was adorned with goodly stones and gifts, he said,

6 *As for* these things which ye behold, the days will come, in the which ᴿthere shall not be left one stone upon another, that shall not be thrown down.

7 And they asked him, saying, Master, but when shall these things be? and what sign *will there be* when these things shall come to pass?

8 And he said, ᴿTake heed that ye be not deceived: for many shall come in my name, saying, I am *Christ;* ᴺand the time draweth near: go ye not therefore after them.

9 But when ye shall hear of wars and commotions, be not terrified: for these things must first come to pass; but the end *is* not by and by.

10 ᴿThen said he unto them, Nation shall rise against nation, and kingdom against kingdom:

11 And great earthquakes shall be in divers places, and famines, and pestilences; and fearful sights and great signs shall there be from heaven.

12 ᴿBut before all these, they shall lay their hands on you, and persecute *you,* delivering *you* up to the synagogues, and ᴿinto prisons, ᴿbeing brought before kings and rulers ᴿfor my name's sake.

13 And ᴿit shall turn to you for a testimony.

14 ᴿSettle *it* therefore in your hearts, not to meditate before what ye shall answer:

15 For I will give you a mouth and wisdom, ᴿwhich all your adversaries shall not be able to gainsay nor resist.

16 ᴿAnd ye shall be betrayed both by parents, and brethren, and kinsfolks, and friends; and ᴿ*some* of you shall they cause to be put to death.

17 And ᴿye shall be hated of all *men* for my name's sake.

18 ᴿBut there shall not an hair of your head perish.

19 In your patience possess ye your souls.

20 ᴿAnd when ye shall see Jerusalem compassed with armies, then know that the desolation thereof is nigh.

21 Then let them which are in Judæa flee to the mountains; and let them which are in the midst of it depart out; and let not them that are in the countries enter thereinto.

22 For these be the days of vengeance, that ᴿall things which are written may be fulfilled.

23 ᴿBut woe unto them that are with child, and to them that give suck, in those days! for there shall be great distress in the land, and wrath upon this people.

24 And they shall fall by the edge of the sword, and shall be led away captive into all nations: and Jerusalem shall be trodden down of the Gentiles, ᴿuntil the times of the Gentiles be fulfilled.

Coming of the Son of man

25 ᴿAnd there shall be signs in the sun, and in the moon, and in the stars; and upon the earth distress of nations, with perplexity; the sea and the waves roaring;

26 Men's hearts failing them for fear, and for looking after those things which are

coming on the earth: ᴿfor the powers of heaven shall be shaken.

27 And then shall they see the Son of man ᴿcoming in a cloud with power and great glory.

28 And when these things begin to come to pass, then look up, and lift up your heads; for ᴿyour redemption draweth nigh.

Parable of the trees

29 ᴿAnd he spake to them a parable; Behold the fig tree, and all the trees;

30 When they now shoot forth, ye see and know of your own selves that summer is now nigh at hand.

31 So likewise ye, when ye see these things come to pass, know ye that the kingdom of God is nigh at hand.

32 Verily I say unto you, This generation shall not pass away, till all be fulfilled.

33 ᴿHeaven and earth shall pass away: but my words shall not pass away.

34 And ᴿtake heed to yourselves, lest at any time your hearts be overcharged with surfeiting, and drunkenness, and cares of this life, and *so* that day come upon you unawares.

35 For ᴿas a snare shall it come on all them that dwell on the face of the whole earth.

36 ᴿWatch ye therefore, and ᴿpray always, that ye may be accounted worthy to escape all these things that shall come to pass, and ᴿto stand before the Son of man.

37 ᴿAnd in the day time he was teaching in the temple; and ᴿat night he went out, and abode in the mount that is called *the mount* of Olives.

38 And all the people came early in the morning to him in the temple, for to hear him.

CHAPTER 22

Treachery of Judas

NOW ᴿthe feast of unleavened bread drew nigh, which is called the Passover.

2 And ᴿthe chief priests and scribes sought how they might kill him; for they feared the people.

3 ᴿThen entered Satan into Judas surnamed Iscariot, being of the number of the twelve.

4 And he went his way, and communed with the chief priests and captains, how he might betray him unto them.

5 And they were glad, and ᴿcovenanted to give him money.

6 And he promised, and sought opportunity to betray him unto them ᴺin the absence of the multitude.

CHAP. **21**

AD 33

10 Mat. 24:7
12 Mark 13:9
Rev. 2:10
12 Acts 4:3 & 5:18
& 12:4 & 16:24
12 Acts 25:23
12 1 Pet. 2:13
13 Phil. 1:28
2 Thes. 1:5
14 Mat. 10:19
Mark 13:11
ch. 12:11
15 Acts 6:10
16 Mic. 7:6
Mark 13:12
16 Acts 7:59
& 12:2
17 Mat. 10:22
18 Mat. 10:30
20 Mat. 24:15
Mark 13:14
22 Dan. 9:26, 27
Zech. 11:1
23 Mat. 24:19
24 Dan. 9:27
& 12:7
Rom. 11:25
25 Mat. 24:29
Mark 13:24
2 Pet. 3:10, 12

Mat. 24:29   **26**
Mat. 24:30   **27**
Rev. 1:7 & 14:14
Rom. 8:19, 23   **28**
Mat. 24:32   **29**
Mark 13:28
Mat. 24:35   **33**
Rom. 13:13   **34**
1 Thes. 5:6
1 Pet. 4:7
1 Thes. 5:2   **35**
2 Pet. 3:10
Rev. 3:3 & 16:15
Mat. 24:42   **36**
& 25:13
Mark 13:33
ch. 18:1   **36**
Ps. 1:5   **36**
Eph. 6:13
John 8:1, 2   **37**
ch. 22:39   **37**

CHAP. **22**

AD 33
Mat. 26:2   **1**
Mark 14:1
Ps. 2:2   **2**
John 11:47
Acts 4:27
Mat. 26:14   **3**
Mark 14:10
John 13:2, 27
Zech. 11:12   **5**
Or, *without*   **6**
tumult

The last supper

7 ᴿThen came the day of unleavened bread, when the passover must be killed.

8 And he sent Peter and John, saying, Go and prepare us the passover, that we may eat.

9 And they said unto him, Where wilt thou that we prepare?

10 And he said unto them, Behold, when ye are entered into the city, there shall a man meet you, bearing a pitcher of water; follow him into the house where he entereth in.

11 And ye shall say unto the goodman of the house, The Master saith unto thee, Where is the guestchamber, where I shall eat the passover with my disciples?

12 And he shall shew you a large upper room furnished: there make ready.

13 And they went, and found as he had said unto them: and they made ready the passover.

14 ᴿAnd when the hour was come, he sat down, and the twelve apostles with him.

15 And he said unto them, ᴺWith desire I have desired to eat this passover with you before I suffer:

16 For I say unto you, I will not any more eat thereof, ᴿuntil it be fulfilled in the kingdom of God.

17 And he took the cup, and gave thanks, and said, Take this, and divide it among yourselves:

18 For ᴿI say unto you, I will not drink of the fruit of the vine, until the kingdom of God shall come.

19 ᴿAnd he took bread, and gave thanks, and brake it, and gave unto them, saying, This is my body which is given for you: ᴿthis do in remembrance of me.

20 Likewise also the cup after supper, saying, ᴿThis cup is the new testament in my blood, which is shed for you.

21 ᴿBut, behold, the hand of him that betrayeth me is with me on the table.

22 ᴿAnd truly the Son of man goeth, ᴿas it was determined: but woe unto that man by whom he is betrayed!

23 ᴿAnd they began to inquire among themselves, which of them it was that should do this thing.

Dispute about greatness

24 ᴿAnd there was also a strife among them, which of them should be accounted the greatest.

25 ᴿAnd he said unto them, The kings of the Gentiles exercise lordship over them; and they that exercise authority upon them are called benefactors.

26 ᴿBut ye *shall* not *be* so: ᴿbut he that is greatest among you, let him be as the younger; and he that is chief, as he that doth serve.

27 ᴿFor whether *is* greater, he that sitteth at meat, or he that serveth? *is* not he that sitteth at meat? but ᴿI am among you as he that serveth.

28 Ye are they which have continued with me in ᴿmy temptations.

29 And ᴿI appoint unto you a kingdom, as my Father hath appointed unto me;

30 That ᴿye may eat and drink at my table in my kingdom, ᴿand sit on thrones judging the twelve tribes of Israel.

Peter's denial predicted

31 And the Lord said, Simon, Simon, behold, ᴿSatan hath desire *to have* you, that he may ᴿsift *you* as wheat:

32 But ᴿI have prayed for thee, that thy faith fail not: and when thou art converted, strengthen thy brethren.

33 And he said unto him, Lord, I am ready to go with thee, both into prison, and to death.

34 ᴿAnd he said, I tell thee, Peter, the cock shall not crow this day, before that thou shalt thrice deny that thou knowest me.

Fulfillment of scripture

35 ᴿAnd he said unto them, When I sent you without purse, and scrip, and shoes, lacked ye any thing? And they said, Nothing.

36 Then said he unto them, But now, he that hath a purse, let him take *it,* and likewise *his* scrip: and he that hath no sword, let him sell his garment, and buy one.

37 For I say unto you, that this that is written must yet be accomplished in me, ᴿAnd he was reckoned among the transgressors: for the things concerning me have an end.

38 And they said, Lord, behold, here *are* two swords. And he said unto them, It is enough.

Jesus in Gethsemane

39 ᴿAnd he came out, and ᴿwent, as he was wont, to the mount of Olives; and his disciples also followed him.

40 ᴿAnd when he was at the place, he said unto them, Pray that ye enter not into temptation.

41 ᴿAnd he was withdrawn from them about a stone's cast, and kneeled down, and prayed,

42 Saying, Father, if thou be ᴺwilling, remove this cup from me: nevertheless ᴿnot my will, but thine, be done.

43 And there appeared ᴿan angel unto him from heaven, strengthening him.

44 ᴿAnd being in an agony he prayed more earnestly: and his sweat was as it were great drops of blood falling down to the ground.

45 And when he rose up from prayer, and was come to his disciples, he found them sleeping for sorrow,

46 And said unto them, Why sleep ye? rise and ᴿpray, lest ye enter into temptation.

Jesus betrayed and arrested

47 And while he yet spake, ᴿbehold a multitude, and he that was called Judas, one of the twelve, went before them, and drew near unto Jesus to kiss him.

48 But Jesus said unto him, Judas, betrayest thou the Son of man with a kiss?

49 When they which were about him saw what would follow, they said unto him, Lord, shall we smite with the sword?

50 And ᴿone of them smote the servant of the high priest, and cut off his right ear.

51 And Jesus answered and said, Suffer ye thus far. And he touched his ear, and healed him.

52 ᴿThen Jesus said unto the chief priests, and captains of the temple, and the elders, which were come to him, Be ye come out, as against a thief, with swords and staves?

53 When I was daily with you in the temple, ye stretched forth no hands against me: ᴿbut this is your hour, and the power of darkness.

Peter's denial of Jesus

54 ᴿThen took they him, and led him, and brought him into the high priest's house. ᴿAnd Peter followed afar off.

55 ᴿAnd when they had kindled a fire in the midst of the hall, and were set down together, Peter sat down among them.

56 But a certain maid beheld him as he sat by the fire, and earnestly looked upon him, and said, This man was also with him.

57 And he denied him, saying, Woman, I know him not.

58 ᴿAnd after a little while another saw him, and said, Thou art also of them. And Peter said, Man, I am not.

59 ᴿAnd about the space of one hour after another confidently affirmed, saying, Of a truth this *fellow* also was with him: for he is a Galilæan.

60 And Peter said, Man, I know not what thou sayest. And immediately, while he yet spake, the cock crew.

61 And the Lord turned, and looked upon Peter. ᴿAnd Peter remembered the word of

the Lord, how he had said unto him, ᴿBefore the cock crow, thou shalt deny me thrice.

62 And Peter went out, and wept bitterly.

Jesus' trial before the council

63 ᴿAnd the men that held Jesus mocked him, and smote *him*.

64 And when they had blindfolded him, they struck him on the face, and asked him, saying, Prophesy, who is it that smote thee?

65 And many other things blasphemously spake they against him.

66 ᴿAnd as soon as it was day, ᴿthe elders of the people and the chief priests and the scribes came together, and led him into their council, saying,

67 ᴿArt thou the Christ? tell us. And he said unto them, If I tell you, ye will not believe:

68 And if I also ask *you,* ye will not answer me, nor let *me* go.

69 ᴿHereafter shall the Son of man sit on the right hand of the power of God.

70 Then said they all, Art thou then the Son of God? And he said unto them, ᴿYe say that I am.

71 ᴿAnd they said, What need we any further witness? for we ourselves have heard of his own mouth.

CHAPTER 23

Trial before Pilate

AND ᴿthe whole multitude of them arose, and led him unto Pilate.

2 And they began to accuse him, saying, We found this *fellow* ᴿperverting the nation, and ᴿforbidding to give tribute to Cæsar, saying, ᴿthat he himself is Christ a King.

3 ᴿAnd Pilate asked him, saying, Art thou the King of the Jews? And he answered him and said, Thou sayest *it*.

4 Then said Pilate to the chief priests and *to* the people, ᴿI find no fault in this man.

5 And they were the more fierce, saying, He stirreth up the people, teaching throughout all Jewry, beginning from Galilee to this place.

Trial before Herod

6 When Pilate heard of Galilee, he asked whether the man were a Galilæan.

7 And as soon as he knew that he belonged unto ᴿHerod's jurisdiction, he sent him to Herod, who himself also was at Jerusalem at that time.

8 And when Herod saw Jesus, he was exceeding glad: for ᴿhe was desirous to see him of a long *season,* because ᴿhe had heard many

things of him; and he hoped to have seen some miracle done by him.

9 Then he questioned with him in many words; but he answered him nothing.

10 And the chief priests and scribes stood and vehemently accused him.

11 ᴿAnd Herod with his men of war set him at nought, and mocked *him,* and arrayed him in a gorgeous robe, and sent him again to Pilate.

12 And the same day ᴿPilate and Herod were made friends together: for before they were at enmity between themselves.

Back to Pilate

13 ᴿAnd Pilate, when he had called together the chief priests and the rulers and the people,

14 Said unto them, ᴿYe have brought this man unto me, as one that perverteth the people: and, behold, ᴿI, having examined *him* before you, have found no fault in this man touching those things whereof ye accuse him:

15 No, nor yet Herod: for I sent you to him; and, lo, nothing worthy of death is done unto him.

16 ᴿI will therefore chastise him, and release *him.*

17 ᴿ(For of necessity he must release one unto them at the feast.)

Pilate appeases the crowd

18 And ᴿthey cried out all at once, saying, Away with this *man,* and release unto us Bär-ăb′-băs:

19 (Who for a certain sedition made in the city, and for murder, was cast into prison.)

20 Pilate therefore, willing to release Jesus, spake again to them.

21 But they cried, saying, Crucify *him,* crucify him.

22 And he said unto them the third time, Why, what evil hath he done? I have found no cause of death in him: I will therefore chastise him, and let *him* go.

23 And they were instant with loud voices, requiring that he might be crucified. And the voices of them and of the chief priests prevailed.

24 And ᴿPilate ᴺgave sentence that it should be as they required.

25 And he released unto them him that for sedition and murder was cast into prison, whom they had desired; but he delivered Jesus to their will.

The way to Calvary

26 ᴿAnd as they led him away, they laid hold upon one Simon, a Çÿ-rē′-nĭ-ăn, coming out of the country, and on him they laid the cross, that he might bear *it* after Jesus.

CHAP. 23
AD 33
11 Is. 53:3
12 Acts 4:27
13 Mat. 27:23
Mark 15:14
John 18:38 & 19:4
14 ver. 1, 2
14 ver. 4
16 Mat. 27:26
John 19:1
17 Mat. 27:15
Mark 15:6
John 18:39
18 Acts 3:14
24 Mat. 27:26
Mark 15:15
John 19:16
24 Or, *assented,*
Ex. 23:2
26 Mat. 27:32
Mark 15:21
See John 19:17

Mat. 24:19 29
ch. 21:23
Is. 2:19 30
Hos. 10:8
Rev. 6:16 & 9:6
Prov. 11:31 31
Jer. 25:29
Ezek. 20:47
& 21:3, 4
1 Pet. 4:17
Is. 53:12 32
Mat. 27:38
Mat. 27:33 33
Mark 15:22
John 19:17, 18
Or, *The place* 33
of a skull
Mat. 5:44 34
Acts 7:60
1 Cor. 4:12
Acts 3:17 34
Mat. 27:35 34
Mark 15:24
John 19:23
Ps. 22:17 35
Zech. 12:10
Mat. 27:39 35
Mark 15:29
Mat. 27:37 38
Mark 15:26
John 19:19
Mat. 27:44 39
Mark 15:32
Mat. 27:45 44
Mark 15:33
Or, *land* 44

27 And there followed him a great company of people, and of women, which also bewailed and lamented him.

28 But Jesus turning unto them said, Daughters of Jerusalem, weep not for me, but weep for yourselves, and for your children.

29 ᴿFor, behold, the days are coming, in the which they shall say, Blessed *are* the barren, and the wombs that never bare, and the paps which never gave suck.

30 ᴿThen shall they begin to say to the mountains, Fall on us; and to the hills, Cover us.

31 ᴿFor if they do these things in a green tree, what shall be done in the dry?

The crucifixion

32 ᴿAnd there were also two other, malefactors, led with him to be put to death.

33 And ᴿwhen they were come to the place, which is called ᴺCalvary, there they crucified him, and the malefactors, one on the right hand, and the other on the left.

34 Then said Jesus, Father, ᴿforgive them; for ᴿthey know not what they do. And ᴿthey parted his raiment, and cast lots.

35 And ᴿthe people stood beholding. And the ᴿrulers also with them derided *him,* saying, He saved others; let him save himself, if he be Christ, the chosen of God.

36 And the soldiers also mocked him, coming to him, and offering him vinegar,

37 And saying, If thou be the king of the Jews, save thyself.

38 ᴿAnd a superscription also was written over him in letters of Greek, and Latin, and Hebrew, THIS IS THE KING OF THE JEWS.

The penitent thief

39 ᴿAnd one of the malefactors which were hanged railed on him, saying, If thou be Christ, save thyself and us.

40 But the other answering rebuked him, saying, Dost not thou fear God, seeing thou art in the same condemnation?

41 And we indeed justly; for we receive the due reward of our deeds: but this man hath done nothing amiss.

42 And he said unto Jesus, Lord, remember me when thou comest into thy kingdom.

43 And Jesus said unto him, Verily I say unto thee, To day shalt thou be with me in paradise.

The death of Jesus

44 ᴿAnd it was about the sixth hour, and there was a darkness over all the ᴺearth until the ninth hour.

45 And the sun was darkened, and [R]the veil of the temple was rent in the midst.

46 And when Jesus had cried with a loud voice, he said, [R]Father, into thy hands I commend my spirit: [R]and having said thus, he gave up the ghost.

47 [R]Now when the centurion saw what was done, he glorified God, saying, Certainly this was a righteous man.

48 And all the people that came together to that sight, beholding the things which were done, smote their breasts, and returned.

49 [R]And all his acquaintance, and the women that followed him from Galilee, stood afar off, beholding these things.

The burial in Joseph's tomb

50 [R]And, behold, *there was* a man named Joseph, a counsellor; *and he was* a good man, and a just:

51 (The same had not consented to the counsel and deed of them;) *he was* of Ăr-ĭm-ă-thæ'-ă, a city of the Jews: [R]who also himself waited for the kingdom of God.

52 This *man* went unto Pilate, and begged the body of Jesus.

53 [R]And he took it down, and wrapped it in linen, and laid it in a sepulchre that was hewn in stone, wherein never man before was laid.

54 And that day was [R]the preparation, and the sabbath drew on.

55 And the women also, [R]which came with him from Galilee, followed after, and [R]beheld the sepulchre, and how his body was laid.

56 And they returned, and [R]prepared spices and ointments; and rested the sabbath day [R]according to the commandment.

CHAPTER 24

The resurrection of Christ

NOW [R]upon the first *day* of the week, very early in the morning, they came unto the sepulchre, [R]bringing the spices which they had prepared, and certain *others* with them.

2 [R]And they found the stone rolled away from the sepulchre.

3 [R]And they entered in, and found not the body of the Lord Jesus.

4 And it came to pass, as they were much perplexed thereabout, [R]behold, two men stood by them in shining garments:

5 And as they were afraid, and bowed down *their* faces to the earth, they said unto them, Why seek ye [N]the living among the dead?

6 He is not here, but is risen: [R]remember how he spake unto you when he was yet in Galilee,

7 Saying, The Son of man must be delivered

into the hands of sinful men, and be crucified, and the third day rise again.

8 And [R]they remembered his words,

9 [R]And returned from the sepulchre, and told all these things unto the eleven, and to all the rest.

10 It was Mary Măg'-dă-lēne, and [R]Jō-ăn'-nă, and Mary *the mother* of James, and other *women that were* with them, which told these things unto the apostles.

11 [R]And their words seemed to them as idle tales, and they believed them not.

12 [R]Then arose Peter, and ran unto the sepulchre; and stooping down, he beheld the linen clothes laid by themselves, and departed, wondering in himself at that which was come to pass.

On the road to Emmaus

13 [R]And, behold, two of them went that same day to a village called Ĕm-mā'-ŭs, which was from Jerusalem *about* threescore furlongs.

14 And they talked together of all these things which had happened.

15 And it came to pass, that, while they communed *together* and reasoned, [R]Jesus himself drew near, and went with them.

16 But [R]their eyes were holden that they should not know him.

17 And he said unto them, What manner of communications *are* these that ye have one to another, as ye walk, and are sad?

18 And the one of them, [R]whose name was Clē'-ŏ-păs, answering said unto him, Art thou only a stranger in Jerusalem, and hast not known the things which are come to pass there in these days?

19 And he said unto them, What things? And they said unto him, Concerning Jesus of Nazareth, [R]which was a prophet [R]mighty in deed and word before God and all the people:

20 [R]And how the chief priests and our rulers delivered him to be condemned to death, and have crucified him.

21 But we trusted [R]that it had been he which should have redeemed Israel: and beside all this, to day is the third day since these things were done.

22 Yea, and [R]certain women also of our company made us astonished, which were early at the sepulchre;

23 And when they found not his body, they came, saying, that they had also seen a vision of angels, which said that he was alive.

24 And [R]certain of them which were with us went to the sepulchre, and found *it* even so as the women had said: but him they saw not.

25 Then he said unto them, O fools, and

slow of heart to believe all that the prophets have spoken:

26 ᴿOught not Christ to have suffered these things, and to enter into his glory?

27 ᴿAnd beginning at ᴿMoses and ᴿall the prophets, he expounded unto them in all the scriptures the things concerning himself.

28 And they drew nigh unto the village, whither they went: and ᴿhe made as though he would have gone further.

29 But ᴿthey constrained him, saying, Abide with us: for it is toward evening, and the day is far spent. And he went in to tarry with them.

30 And it came to pass, as he sat at meat with them, ᴿhe took bread, and blessed *it*, and brake, and gave to them.

31 And their eyes were opened, and they knew him; and he ᴺvanished out of their sight.

32 And they said one to another, Did not our heart burn within us, while he talked with us by the way, and while he opened to us the scriptures?

33 And they rose up the same hour, and returned to Jerusalem, and found the eleven gathered together, and them that were with them,

34 Saying, The Lord is risen indeed, and ᴿhath appeared to Simon.

35 And they told what things *were done* in the way, and how he was known of them in breaking of bread.

Jesus' appearance in Jerusalem

36 ᴿAnd as they thus spake, Jesus himself stood in the midst of them, and saith unto them, Peace *be* unto you.

37 But they were terrified and affrighted, and supposed that they had seen ᴿa spirit.

38 And he said unto them, Why are ye troubled? and why do thoughts arise in your hearts?

CHAP. **24**	
AD 33	
26 Acts 17:3	
1 Pet. 1:11	
27 ver. 45	
27 Gen. 3:15	
& 22:18 & 26:4	
& 49:10	
Num. 21:9	
Deut. 18:15	
27 Ps. 16:9, 10	
& 22 & 132:11	
Is. 7:14 & 9:6	
& 40:10, 11 & 50:6	
Jer. 23:5	
& 33:14, 15	
Ezek. 34:23	
& 37:25	
Dan. 9:24	
Mic. 7:20	
Mal. 3:1 & 4:2	
See John 1:45	
28 Gen. 32:26	
& 42:7	
Mark 6:48	
29 Gen. 19:3	
Acts 16:15	
30 Mat. 14:19	
31 Or, *ceased to be seen of them*	
34 1 Cor. 15:5	
36 Mark 16:14	
John 20:19	
1 Cor. 15:5	
37 Mark 6:49	
John 20:20	**39**
Gen. 45:26	**41**
John 21:5	**41**
Acts 10:41	**43**
ver. 6	**44**
Mat. 16:21	
& 17:22 & 20:18	
Mark 8:31	
ch. 9:22 & 18:31	
Acts 16:14	**45**
Ps. 22	**46**
Acts 17:3	
Dan. 9:24	**47**
Acts 13:38	
Ps. 22:27	**47**
Jer. 31:34	
Mic. 4:2	
Acts 1:8	**48**
Is. 44:3	**49**
Joel 2:28	
Acts 1:12	**50**
Mark 16:19	**51**
Mat. 28:9	**52**
Acts 2:46	**53**

39 Behold my hands and my feet, that it is I myself: ᴿhandle me, and see; for a spirit hath not flesh and bones, as ye see me have.

40 And when he had thus spoken, he shewed them *his* hands and *his* feet.

41 And while they yet believed not ᴿfor joy, and wondered, he said unto them, ᴿHave ye here any meat?

42 And they gave him a piece of a broiled fish, and of an honeycomb.

43 ᴿAnd he took *it,* and did eat before them.

44 And he said unto them, ᴿThese *are* the words which I spake unto you, while I was yet with you, that all things must be fulfilled, which were written in the law of Moses, and *in* the prophets, and *in* the psalms, concerning me.

45 Then ᴿopened he their understanding, that they might understand the scriptures,

46 And said unto them, ᴿThus it is written, and thus it behoved Christ to suffer, and to rise from the dead the third day:

47 And that repentance and ᴿremission of sins should be preached in his name ᴿamong all nations, beginning at Jerusalem.

48 And ᴿye are witnesses of these things.

49 ᴿAnd, behold, I send the promise of my Father upon you: but tarry ye in the city of Jerusalem, until ye be endued with power from on high.

The ascension of Christ

50 And he led them out ᴿas far as to Bethany, and he lifted up his hands, and blessed them.

51 ᴿAnd it came to pass, while he blessed them, he was parted from them, and carried up into heaven.

52 ᴿAnd they worshipped him, and returned to Jerusalem with great joy:

53 And were continually ᴿin the temple, praising and blessing God. Ä'-mĕn.

THE GOSPEL ACCORDING TO
ST. JOHN

The key to the purpose and method of the fourth Gospel is given in 20:30–31: the author is selecting events from the life of Jesus to demonstrate His messiahship and deity, in the hope that commitment and life for the reader might result. John is the Gospel of the divinity of the Son, presenting in its very first sentence two concepts whose explicit expression is unique among the Gospels: the preexistence of Christ, and the Logos doctrine. It is also the Gospel of commitment. Narrative is recorded in order to spell out significance. Mira-

cles and controversies are reported with emphasis upon the responses involved. Passivity, whether of rejection or belief, is renounced; commitment of an active and vital nature is called for. During the past century the fourth Gospel has been frequently interpreted as being Hellenistic. But with the discovery of the Dead Sea Scrolls, and the striking parallels of expression and manner of thought which they exhibit, many now insist upon its Palestinian connections and its early composition. It may even have been originally addressed to

those having an Essene background. The unique prominence it gives to the feasts and festivals in Jerusalem and the almost exclusive concern with Jesus' ministry in Judea are best explained on this basis. Although formerly dated between A.D. 90 and 130, papyrus portions of the Gospel dating from the early second century and the evidence from the Dead Sea Scrolls now establish its date as no later than A.D. 90; it may be even earlier. Much external testimony from the Church Fathers supports the Johannine authorship, and personal allusions within the Gospel point to John being the "beloved disciple."

OUTLINE OF THE BOOK:
  I. Prologue   1:1 – 18
  II. Introductory Events   1:19 – 2:12
  III. Public Ministry (principally in Judæa)   2:13 – 12:50
  IV. Private Ministry (with Disciples)   13:1 – 17:26
  V. Passion Narrative   18:1 – 19:42
  VI. Resurrection Account   20:1 – 21:25

CHAPTER 1

The eternal Word made flesh

IN the beginning ᴿwas the Word, and the Word was ᴿwith God, ᴿand the Word was God.

2 ᴿThe same was in the beginning with God.

3 ᴿAll things were made by him; and without him was not any thing made that was made.

4 ᴿIn him was life; and ᴿthe life was the light of men.

5 And ᴿthe light shineth in darkness; and the darkness comprehended it not.

6 ᴿThere was a man sent from God, whose name was John.

7 ᴿThe same came for a witness, to bear witness of the Light, that all men through him might believe.

8 He was not that Light, but was sent to bear witness of that Light.

9 ᴿThat was the true Light, which lighteth every man that cometh into the world.

10 He was in the world, and ᴿthe world was made by him, and the world knew him not.

11 ᴿHe came unto his own, and his own received him not.

12 But ᴿas many as received him, to them gave he ᴺpower to become the sons of God, even to them that believe on his name:

13 ᴿWhich were born, not of blood, nor of the will of the flesh, nor of the will of man, but of God.

14 ᴿAnd the Word ᴿwas made ᴿflesh, and dwelt among us, (and ᴿwe beheld his glory, the glory as of the only begotten of the Father,) ᴿfull of grace and truth.

15 ᴿJohn bare witness of him, and cried, saying, This was he of whom I spake, ᴿHe that cometh after me is preferred before me: ᴿfor he was before me.

16 And of his ᴿfulness have all we received, and grace for grace.

17 For ᴿthe law was given by Moses, but ᴿgrace and ᴿtruth came by Jesus Christ.

18 ᴿNo man hath seen God at any time; ᴿthe only begotten Son, which is in the bosom of the Father, he hath declared him.

CHAP. 1	
AD 26	
1 Prov. 8:22	
1 John 1:1	
1 Prov. 8:30	
ch. 17:5	
1 1 John 5:7	
2 Gen. 1:1	
3 Ps. 33:6	
Eph. 3:9	
Col. 1:16	
4 1 John 5:11	
4 ch. 8:12	
5 ch. 3:19	
6 Mal. 3:1	
Mat. 3:1	
Luke 3:2	
7 Acts 19:4	
9 Is. 49:6	
10 Heb. 1:2	
11 Luke 19:14	
12 Gal. 3:26	
12 Or, the right,	
or, privilege	
13 1 Pet. 1:23	
14 Mat. 1:16	
Luke 1:31	
14 Gal. 4:4	
14 Heb. 2:11	
14 Is. 40:5	
14 Col. 1:19	
15 ch. 3:32	
15 Mat. 3:11	
Mark 1:7	
Luke 3:16	
15 Col. 1:17	
16 Col. 1:19	
17 Ex. 20:1	
17 Rom. 5:21	
17 ch. 8:32	
18 Ex. 33:20	
Mat. 11:27	
18 1 John 4:9	
ch. 5:33	19
Luke 3:15	20
Acts 13:25	
Mal. 4:5	21
Deut. 18:15	21
Or, a prophet?	21
Mat. 3:6	23
Is. 40:3	23
Mat. 3:11	26
Mal. 3:1	26
Acts 19:4	27
Judg. 7:24	28
ch. 10:40	
Ex. 12:3	29
Is. 53:7	
Rev. 5:6, etc.	
Is. 53:11	29
1 Cor. 15:3	
1 Pet. 2:24 & 3:18	
1 John 2:2 & 3:5	
Or, beareth	29
ver. 15, 27	30
Mal. 3:1	31
Mat. 3:6	
Luke 1:17, 76, 77	
Mat. 3:16	32
Mark 1:10	

The testimony of John the Baptist

19 And this is ᴿthe record of John, when the Jews sent priests and Levites from Jerusalem to ask him, Who art thou?

20 And ᴿhe confessed, and denied not; but confessed, I am not the Christ.

21 And they asked him, What then? Art thou ᴿĒ-lī'-ăs? And he saith, I am not. Art thou ᴿthatᴺ prophet? And he answered, No.

22 Then said they unto him, Who art thou? that we may give an answer to them that sent us. What sayest thou of thyself?

23 ᴿHe said, I am the voice of one crying in the wilderness, Make straight the way of the Lord, as ᴿsaid the prophet Ē-śâī'-ăs.

24 And they which were sent were of the Pharisees.

25 And they asked him, and said unto him, Why baptizest thou then, if thou be not that Christ, nor Ē-lī'-ăs, neither that prophet?

26 John answered them, saying, ᴿI baptize with water: ᴿbut there standeth one among you, whom ye know not;

27 ᴿHe it is, who coming after me is preferred before me, whose shoe's latchet I am not worthy to unloose.

28 These things were done ᴿin Bĕth-ăb'-ă-rä beyond Jordan, where John was baptizing.

"Behold the Lamb of God"

29 The next day John seeth Jesus coming unto him, and saith, Behold ᴿthe Lamb of God, ᴿwhich ᴺtaketh away the sin of the world.

30 ᴿThis is he of whom I said, After me cometh a man which is preferred before me: for he was before me.

31 And I knew him not: but that he should be made manifest to Israel, ᴿtherefore am I come baptizing with water.

32 ᴿAnd John bare record, saying, I saw the Spirit descending from heaven like a dove, and it abode upon him.

33 And I knew him not: but he that sent me to baptize with water, the same said unto me, Upon whom thou shalt see the Spirit de-

scending, and remaining on him, ᴿthe same is he which baptizeth with the Holy Ghost.

34 And I saw, and bare record that this is the Son of God.

The first disciples

35 Again the next day after John stood, and two of his disciples;

36 And looking upon Jesus as he walked, he saith, ᴿBehold the Lamb of God!

37 And the two disciples heard him speak, and they followed Jesus.

38 Then Jesus turned, and saw them following, and saith unto them, What seek ye? They said unto him, Rabbi, (which is to say, being interpreted, Master,) where ᴺdwellest thou?

39 He saith unto them, Come and see. They came and saw where he dwelt, and abode with him that day: for it was ᴺabout the tenth hour.

40 One of the two which heard John *speak,* and followed him, was Andrew, Simon Peter's brother.

41 He first findeth his own brother Simon, and saith unto him, We have found the Měs-sī'-ăs, which is, being interpreted, ᴺthe Christ.

42 And he brought him to Jesus. And when Jesus beheld him, he said, Thou art Simon the son of Jona: ᴿthou shalt be called Cē'-phăs, which is by interpretation, ᴺA stone.

The call of Philip and Nathanael

43 The day following Jesus would go forth into Galilee, and findeth Philip, and saith unto him, Follow me.

44 Now ᴿPhilip was of Běth-sā'-ĭ-dǎ, the city of Andrew and Peter.

45 Philip findeth ᴿNǎ-thǎn'-ǎ-ĕl, and saith unto him, We have found him, of whom ᴿMoses in the law, and the ᴿprophets, did write, Jesus ᴿof Nazareth, the son of Joseph.

46 And Nǎ-thǎn'-ǎ-ĕl said unto him, ᴿCan there any good thing come out of Nazareth? Philip saith unto him, Come and see.

47 Jesus saw Nǎ-thǎn'-ǎ-ĕl coming to him, and saith of him, Behold ᴿan Israelite indeed, in whom is no guile!

48 Nǎ-thǎn'-ǎ-ĕl saith unto him, Whence knowest thou me? Jesus answered and said unto him, Before that Philip called thee, when thou wast under the fig tree, I saw thee.

49 Nǎ-thǎn'-ǎ-ĕl answered and saith unto him, Rabbi, ᴿthou art the Son of God; thou art ᴿthe King of Israel.

50 Jesus answered and said unto him, Because I said unto thee, I saw thee under the fig tree, believest thou? thou shalt see greater things than these.

51 And he saith unto him, Verily, verily, I

say unto you, ᴿHereafter ye shall see heaven open, and the angels of God ascending and descending upon the Son of man.

CHAPTER 2

The first miracle at Cana

AND the third day there was a marriage in ᴿCana of Galilee; and the mother of Jesus was there:

2 And both Jesus was called, and his disciples, to the marriage.

3 And when they wanted wine, the mother of Jesus saith unto him, They have no wine.

4 Jesus saith unto her, ᴿWoman, ᴿwhat have I to do with thee? ᴿmine hour is not yet come.

5 His mother saith unto the servants, Whatsoever he saith unto you, do *it.*

6 And there were set there six waterpots of stone, ᴿafter the manner of the purifying of the Jews, containing two or three firkins apiece.

7 Jesus saith unto them, Fill the waterpots with water. And they filled them up to the brim.

8 And he saith unto them, Draw out now, and bear unto the governor of the feast. And they bare *it.*

9 When the ruler of the feast had tasted ᴿthe water that was made wine, and knew not whence it was: (but the servants which drew the water knew;) the governor of the feast called the bridegroom,

10 And saith unto him, Every man at the beginning doth set forth good wine; and when men have well drunk, then that which is worse: *but* thou hast kept the good wine until now.

11 This beginning of miracles did Jesus in Cana of Galilee, ᴿand manifested forth his glory; and his disciples believed on him.

12 After this he went down to Că-pěr'-nă-ŭm, he, and his mother, and ᴿhis brethren, and his disciples: and they continued there not many days.

Cleansing the temple

13 ᴿAnd the Jews' passover was at hand, and Jesus went up to Jerusalem,

14 ᴿAnd found in the temple those that sold oxen and sheep and doves, and the changers of money sitting:

15 And when he had made a scourge of small cords, he drove them all out of the temple, and the sheep, and the oxen; and poured out the changers' money, and overthrew the tables;

16 And said unto them that sold doves, Take

these things hence; make not ᴿmy Father's house an house of merchandise.

17 And his disciples remembered that it was written, ᴿThe zeal of thine house hath eaten me up.

18 Then answered the Jews and said unto him, ᴿWhat sign shewest thou unto us, seeing that thou doest these things?

19 Jesus answered and said unto them, ᴿDestroy this temple, and in three days I will raise it up.

20 Then said the Jews, Forty and six years was this temple in building, and wilt thou rear it up in three days?

21 But he spake ᴿof the temple of his body.

22 When therefore he was risen from the dead, ᴿhis disciples remembered that he had said this unto them; and they believed the scripture, and the word which Jesus had said.

Effect of the signs

23 Now when he was in Jerusalem at the passover, in the feast *day*, many believed in his name, when they saw the miracles which he did.

24 But Jesus did not commit himself unto them, because he knew all *men*,

25 And needed not that any should testify of man: for ᴿhe knew what was in man.

CHAPTER 3

Interview with Nicodemus

THERE was a man of the Pharisees, named Nĭc-ŏ-dē′-mŭs, a ruler of the Jews:

2 ᴿThe same came to Jesus by night, and said unto him, Rabbi, we know that thou art a teacher come from God: for ᴿno man can do these miracles that thou doest, except ᴿGod be with him.

3 Jesus answered and said unto him, Verily, verily, I say unto thee, ᴿExcept a man be born ᴺagain, he cannot see the kingdom of God.

4 Nĭc-ŏ-dē′-mŭs saith unto him, How can a man be born when he is old? can he enter the second time into his mother's womb, and be born?

5 Jesus answered, Verily, verily, I say unto thee, ᴿExcept a man be born of water and *of* the Spirit, he cannot enter into the kingdom of God.

6 That which is born of the flesh is flesh; and that which is born of the Spirit is spirit.

7 Marvel not that I said unto thee, Ye must be born ᴺagain.

8 ᴿThe wind bloweth where it listeth, and thou hearest the sound thereof, but canst not

CHAP. 2
AD 30
16 Luke 2:49
17 Ps. 69:9
18 Mat. 12:38
  ch. 6:30
19 Mat. 26:61
  & 27:40
  Mark 14:58
  & 15:29
21 Col. 2:9
  Heb. 8:2
  1 Cor. 3:16 & 6:19
  2 Cor. 6:16
22 Luke 24:8
25 1 Sam. 16:7
  1 Chr. 28:9
  Mat. 9:4
  Mark 2:8
  ch. 6:64
  & 16:30
  Acts 1:24
  Rev. 2:23

CHAP. 3
AD 30
2 ch. 7:50 & 19:39
2 ch. 9:16, 33
  Acts 2:22
2 Acts 10:38
3 ch. 1:13
  Gal. 6:15
  Tit. 3:5
  Jas. 1:18
  1 Pet. 1:23
  1 John 3:9
3 Or, *from above*
5 Mark 16:16
  Acts 2:38
7 Or, *from above*
8 Eccl. 11:5
  1 Cor. 2:11

ch. 6:52, 60   **9**
Mat. 11:27   **11**
  ch. 1:18 & 7:16
  & 8:28
  ver. 32   **11**
  Prov. 30:4   **13**
  ch. 6:33, 38
  Acts 2:34
  1 Cor. 15:47
  Eph. 4:9
  Num. 21:9   **14**
  ch. 8:28   **14**
  & 12:32
  ver. 36   **15**
  ch. 6:47
  Rom. 5:8   **16**
  1 John 4:9
  Luke 9:56   **17**
  ch. 5:45 & 8:15
  & 12:47
  1 John 4:14
  ch. 5:24 & 6:40,   **18**
  47 & 20:31
  ch. 1:4, 9-11   **19**
  & 8:12
  Job 24:13   **20**
  Eph. 5:13
  Or, *discovered*   **20**
  ch. 4:2   **22**
  1 Sam. 9:4   **23**
  Mat. 3:5, 6   **23**
  Mat. 14:3   **24**

tell whence it cometh, and whither it goeth: so is every one that is born of the Spirit.

9 Nĭc-ŏ-dē′-mŭs answered and said unto him, ᴿHow can these things be?

10 Jesus answered and said unto him, Art thou a master of Israel, and knowest not these things?

11 ᴿVerily, verily, I say unto thee, We speak that we do know, and testify that we have seen; and ᴿye receive not our witness.

12 If I have told you earthly things, and ye believe not, how shall ye believe, if I tell you *of* heavenly things?

13 And ᴿno man hath ascended up to heaven, but he that came down from heaven, *even* the Son of man which is in heaven.

14 ᴿAnd as Moses lifted up the serpent in the wilderness, even so ᴿmust the Son of man be lifted up:

15 That whosoever believeth in him should not perish, but ᴿhave eternal life.

16 ᴿFor God so loved the world, that he gave his only begotten Son, that whosoever believeth in him should not perish, but have everlasting life.

17 ᴿFor God sent not his Son into the world to condemn the world; but that the world through him might be saved.

18 ᴿHe that believeth on him is not condemned: but he that believeth not is condemned already, because he hath not believed in the name of the only begotten Son of God.

19 And this is the condemnation, ᴿthat light is come into the world, and men loved darkness rather than light, because their deeds were evil.

20 For ᴿevery one that doeth evil hateth the light, neither cometh to the light, lest his deeds should be ᴺreproved.

21 But he that doeth truth cometh to the light, that his deeds may be made manifest, that they are wrought in God.

Jesus' ministry in Judæa

22 After these things came Jesus and his disciples into the land of Judæa; and there he tarried with them, ᴿand baptized.

23 And John also was baptizing in Æ′-nŏn near to ᴿSā′-lĭm, because there was much water there: ᴿand they came, and were baptized.

24 For ᴿJohn was not yet cast into prison.

John's testimony to Jesus

25 Then there arose a question between *some* of John's disciples and the Jews about purifying.

26 And they came unto John, and said unto him, Rabbi, he that was with thee beyond

Jordan, ᴿto whom thou barest witness, behold, the same baptizeth, and all *men* come to him.

27 John answered and said, ᴿA man can ᴺreceive nothing, except it be given him from heaven.

28 Ye yourselves bear me witness, that I said, ᴿI am not the Christ, but ᴿthat I am sent before him.

29 ᴿHe that hath the bride is the bridegroom: but ᴿthe friend of the bridegroom, which standeth and heareth him, rejoiceth greatly because of the bridegroom's voice: this my joy therefore is fulfilled.

30 He must increase, but I *must* decrease.

31 ᴿHe that cometh from above ᴿis above all: ᴿhe that is of the earth is earthly, and speaketh of the earth: ᴿhe that cometh from heaven is above all.

32 And ᴿwhat he hath seen and heard, that he testifieth; and no man receiveth his testimony.

33 He that hath received his testimony ᴿhath set to his seal that God is true.

34 ᴿFor he whom God hath sent speaketh the words of God: for God giveth not the Spirit ᴿby measure *unto him*.

35 ᴿThe Father loveth the Son, and hath given all things into his hand.

36 ᴿHe that believeth on the Son hath everlasting life: and he that believeth not the Son shall not see life; but the wrath of God abideth on him.

CHAPTER 4

Journey through Samaria

WHEN therefore the Lord knew how the Pharisees had heard that Jesus made and ᴿbaptized more disciples than John,

2 (Though Jesus himself baptized not, but his disciples,)

3 He left Judæa, and departed again into Galilee.

4 And he must needs go through Să-mâr'-ĭ-ă.

5 Then cometh he to a city of Să-mâr'-ĭ-ă, which is called Sȳ'-chär, near to the parcel of ground ᴿthat Jacob gave to his son Joseph.

6 Now Jacob's well was there. Jesus therefore, being wearied with *his* journey, sat thus on the well: *and* it was about the sixth hour.

The woman at Jacob's well

7 There cometh a woman of Să-mâr'-ĭ-ă to draw water: Jesus saith unto her, Give me to drink.

8 (For his disciples were gone away unto the city to buy meat.)

CHAP. 3
AD 30
26 ch. 1:7,
15, 27, 34
27 1 Cor. 4:7
Heb. 5:4
Jas. 1:17
27 Or, *take unto himself*
28 ch. 1:20, 27
28 Mal. 3:1
Mark 1:2
Luke 1:17
29 Mat. 22:2
2 Cor. 11:2
Eph. 5:25, 27
Rev. 21:9
29 S. of S. 5:1
31 ver. 13
ch. 8:23
31 Mat. 28:18
ch. 1:15, 27
Rom. 9:5
31 1 Cor. 15:47
31 ch. 6:33
1 Cor. 15:47
Eph. 1:21
Phil. 2:9
32 ver. 11
ch. 8:26 & 15:15
33 Rom. 3:4
1 John 5:10
34 ch. 7:16
34 ch. 1:16
35 Mat. 11:27
& 28:18
Luke 10:22
ch. 5:20, 22
& 13:3 & 17:2
Heb. 2:8
36 ver. 15, 16
ch. 1:12 & 6:47
Rom. 1:17
1 John 5:10

CHAP. 4
AD 30
1 ch. 3:22, 26
5 Gen. 33:19
& 48:22
Josh. 24:32

2 Ki. 17:24	9
Luke 9:52, 53	
Acts 10:28	
Is. 12:3 & 44:3	10
Jer. 2:13	
Zech. 13:1 & 14:8	
ch. 6:35, 58	14
ch. 7:38	14
ch. 6:34	15
& 17:2, 3	
Rom. 6:23	
1 John 5:20	
Luke 7:16	19
& 24:19	
ch. 6:14	
Judg. 9:7	20
Deut. 12:5, 11	20
1 Ki. 9:3	
2 Chr. 7:12	
Mal. 1:11	21
1 Tim. 2:8	
2 Ki. 17:29	22
Is. 2:3	22
Luke 24:47	
Rom. 9:4, 5	
Phil. 3:3	23
ch. 1:17	23
2 Cor. 3:17	24
ver. 29, 39	25
Mat. 26:63, 64	26
Mark 14:61, 62	

9 Then saith the woman of Să-mâr'-ĭ-ă unto him, How is it that thou, being a Jew, askest drink of me, which am a woman of Să-mâr'-ĭ-ă? for ᴿthe Jews have no dealings with the Să-mâr'-tăns.

10 Jesus answered and said unto her, If thou knewest the gift of God, and who it is that saith to thee, Give me to drink; thou wouldest have asked of him, and he would have given thee ᴿliving water.

11 The woman saith unto him, Sir, thou hast nothing to draw with, and the well is deep: from whence then hast thou that living water?

12 Art thou greater than our father Jacob, which gave us the well, and drank thereof himself, and his children, and his cattle?

13 Jesus answered and said unto her, Whosoever drinketh of this water shall thirst again:

14 But ᴿwhosoever drinketh of the water that I shall give him shall never thirst; but the water that I shall give him ᴿshall be in him a well of water springing up into everlasting life.

15 ᴿThe woman saith unto him, Sir, give me this water, that I thirst not, neither come hither to draw.

16 Jesus saith unto her, Go, call thy husband, and come hither.

17 The woman answered and said, I have no husband. Jesus said unto her, Thou hast well said, I have no husband:

18 For thou hast had five husbands; and he whom thou now hast is not thy husband: in that saidst thou truly.

19 The woman saith unto him, Sir, ᴿI perceive that thou art a prophet.

20 Our fathers worshipped in ᴿthis mountain; and ye say, that in ᴿJerusalem is the place where men ought to worship.

21 Jesus saith unto her, Woman, believe me, the hour cometh, ᴿwhen ye shall neither in this mountain, nor yet at Jerusalem, worship the Father.

22 Ye worship ᴿye know not what: we know what we worship: for ᴿsalvation is of the Jews.

23 But the hour cometh, and now is, when the true worshippers shall worship the Father in ᴿspirit ᴿand in truth: for the Father seeketh such to worship him.

24 ᴿGod *is* a Spirit: and they that worship him must worship *him* in spirit and in truth.

25 The woman saith unto him, I know that Mĕs-sī'-ăs cometh, which is called Christ: when he is come, ᴿhe will tell us all things.

26 Jesus saith unto her, ᴿI that speak unto thee am *he*.

27 And upon this came his disciples, and

marvelled that he talked with the woman: yet no man said, What seekest thou? or, Why talkest thou with her?

28 The woman then left her waterpot, and went her way into the city, and saith to the men,

29 Come, see a man, ᴿwhich told me all things that ever I did: is not this the Christ?

30 Then they went out of the city, and came unto him.

The will of the Father

31 In the mean while his disciples prayed him, saying, Master, eat.

32 But he said unto them, I have meat to eat that ye know not of.

33 Therefore said the disciples one to another, Hath any man brought him *aught* to eat?

34 Jesus saith unto them, ᴿMy meat is to do the will of him that sent me, and to finish his work.

35 Say not ye, There are yet four months, and *then* cometh harvest? behold, I say unto you, Lift up your eyes, and look on the fields; ᴿfor they are white already to harvest.

36 ᴿAnd he that reapeth receiveth wages, and gathereth fruit unto life eternal: that both he that soweth and he that reapeth may rejoice together.

37 And herein is that saying true, One soweth, and another reapeth.

38 I sent you to reap that whereon ye bestowed no labour: other men laboured, and ye are entered into their labours.

Conversion of the Samaritans

39 And many of the Să-măr'-ĭ-tăns of that city believed on him ᴿfor the saying of the woman, which testified, He told me all that ever I did.

40 So when the Să-măr'-ĭ-tăns were come unto him, they besought him that he would tarry with them: and he abode there two days.

41 And many more believed because of his own word;

42 And said unto the woman, Now we believe, not because of thy saying: for ᴿwe have heard *him* ourselves, and know that this is indeed the Christ, the Saviour of the world.

Jesus returns to Galilee

43 Now after two days he departed thence, and went into Galilee.

44 For ᴿJesus himself testified, that a prophet hath no honour in his own country.

45 Then when he was come into Galilee, the

Galilæans received him, ᴿhaving seen all the things that he did at Jerusalem at the feast: ᴿfor they also went unto the feast.

Healing the nobleman's son

46 So Jesus came again into Cana of Galilee, ᴿwhere he made the water wine. And there was a certain ᴺnobleman, whose son was sick at Că-pĕr'-nă-ŭm.

47 When he heard that Jesus was come out of Judæa into Galilee, he went unto him, and besought him that he would come down, and heal his son: for he was at the point of death.

48 Then said Jesus unto him, ᴿExcept ye see signs and wonders, ye will not believe.

49 The nobleman saith unto him, Sir, come down ere my child die.

50 Jesus saith unto him, Go thy way; thy son liveth. And the man believed the word that Jesus had spoken unto him, and he went his way.

51 And as he was now going down, his servants met him, and told *him,* saying, Thy son liveth.

52 Then inquired he of them the hour when he began to amend. And they said unto him, Yesterday at the seventh hour the fever left him.

53 So the father knew that *it was* at the same hour, in the which Jesus said unto him, Thy son liveth: and himself believed, and his whole house.

54 This *is* again the second miracle *that* Jesus did, when he was come out of Judæa into Galilee.

CHAPTER 5

Healing at the pool of Bethesda

AFTER ᴿthis there was a feast of the Jews; and Jesus went up to Jerusalem.

2 Now there is at Jerusalem ᴿby the sheep ᴺ*market* a pool, which is called in the Hebrew tongue Bĕth-ĕś'-dă, having five porches.

3 In these lay a great multitude of impotent folk, of blind, halt, withered, waiting for the moving of the water.

4 For an angel went down at a certain season into the pool, and troubled the water: whosoever then first after the troubling of the water stepped in was made whole of whatsoever disease he had.

5 And a certain man was there, which had an infirmity thirty and eight years.

6 When Jesus saw him lie, and knew that he had been now a long time *in that case,* he saith unto him, Wilt thou be made whole?

7 The impotent man answered him, Sir, I

CHAP. 4

AD 30

29 ver. 25
34 Job 23:12
   ch. 6:38
   & 17:4 & 19:30
35 Mat. 9:37
   Luke 10:2
36 Dan. 12:3
39 ver. 29
42 ch. 17:8
   1 John 4:14
44 Mat. 13:57

ch. 2:23 & 3:2   45
Deut. 16:16   45
ch. 2:1, 11   46
Or, *courtier,*   46
   or, *ruler*
1 Cor. 1:22   48

CHAP. 5

AD 31

Lev. 23:2   1
Deut. 16:1
ch. 2:13
Neh. 3:1   2
   & 12:39
Or, *gate*   2

have no man, when the water is troubled, to put me into the pool: but while I am coming, another steppeth down before me.

8 Jesus saith unto him, ᴿRise, take up thy bed, and walk.

The sabbath controversy

9 And immediately the man was made whole, and took up his bed, and walked: and ᴿon the same day was the sabbath.

10 The Jews therefore said unto him that was cured, It is the sabbath day: ᴿit is not lawful for thee to carry *thy* bed.

11 He answered them, He that made me whole, the same said unto me, Take up thy bed, and walk.

·12 Then asked they him, What man is that which said unto thee, Take up thy bed, and walk?

13 And he that was healed wist not who it was: for Jesus had conveyed himself away, ᴺa multitude being in *that* place.

14 Afterward Jesus findeth him in the temple, and said unto him, Behold, thou art made whole: ᴿsin no more, lest a worse thing come unto thee.

15 The man departed, and told the Jews that it was Jesus, which had made him whole.

16 And therefore did the Jews persecute Jesus, and sought to slay him, because he had done these things on the sabbath day.

17 But Jesus answered them, ᴿMy Father worketh hitherto, and I work.

18 Therefore the Jews ᴿsought the more to kill him, because he not only had broken the sabbath, but said also that God was his Father, ᴿmaking himself equal with God.

The Son's witness to the Father

19 Then answered Jesus and said unto them, Verily, verily, I say unto you, ᴿThe Son can do nothing of himself, but what he seeth the Father do: for what things soever he doeth, these also doeth the Son likewise.

20 For ᴿthe Father loveth the Son, and sheweth him all things that himself doeth: and he will shew him greater works than these, that ye may marvel.

21 For as the Father raiseth up the dead, and quickeneth *them;* ᴿeven so the Son quickeneth whom he will.

22 For the Father judgeth no man, but ᴿhath committed all judgment unto the Son:

23 That all *men* should honour the Son, even as they honour the Father. ᴿHe that honoureth not the Son honoureth not the Father which hath sent him.

24 Verily, verily, I say unto you, ᴿHe that

heareth my word, and believeth on him that sent me, hath everlasting life, and shall not come into condemnation; ᴿbut is passed from death unto life.

The grant of authority to the Son

25 Verily, verily, I say unto you, The hour is coming, and now is, when ᴿthe dead shall hear the voice of the Son of God: and they that hear shall live.

26 For as the Father hath life in himself; so hath he given to the Son to have life in himself;

27 And ᴿhath given him authority to execute judgment also, ᴿbecause he is the Son of man.

28 Marvel not at this: for the hour is coming, in the which all that are in the graves shall hear his voice,

29 ᴿAnd shall come forth; ᴿthey that have done good, unto the resurrection of life; and they that have done evil, unto the resurrection of damnation.

The fourfold witness to the Son

30 ᴿI can of mine own self do nothing: as I hear, I judge: and my judgment is just; because ᴿI seek not mine own will, but the will of the Father which hath sent me.

31 ᴿIf I bear witness of myself, my witness is not true.

32 ᴿThere is another that beareth witness of me; and I know that the witness which he witnesseth of me is true.

33 Ye sent unto John, ᴿand he bare witness unto the truth.

34 But I receive not testimony from man: but these things I say, that ye might be saved.

35 He was a burning and ᴿa shining light: and ᴿye were willing for a season to rejoice in his light.

36 But ᴿI have greater witness than *that* of John: for ᴿthe works which the Father hath given me to finish, the same works that I do, bear witness of me, that the Father hath sent me.

37 And the Father himself, which hath sent me, ᴿhath borne witness of me. Ye have neither heard his voice at any time, ᴿnor seen his shape.

38 And ye have not his word abiding in you: for whom he hath sent, him ye believe not.

39 ᴿSearch the scriptures; for in them ye think ye have eternal life: and ᴿthey are they which testify of me.

40 ᴿAnd ye will not come to me, that ye might have life.

41 ᴿI receive not honour from men.

42 But I know you, that ye have not the love of God in you.

CHAP. **5**
AD 31
8 Mat. 9:6
Mark 2:11
Luke 5:24
9 ch. 9:14
10 Ex. 20:10
Neh. 13:19
Jer. 17:21
Mat. 12:2
Mark 2:24
Luke 6:2
13 Or, *from the multitude that was*
14 Mat. 12:45
ch. 8:11
17 ch. 9:4 & 14:10
18 ch. 7:19
18 ch. 10:30
Phil. 2:6
19 ver. 30
ch. 8:28 & 9:4
20 Mat. 3:17
ch. 3:35
21 Luke 7:14 & 8:54
ch. 11:25
22 Mat. 11:27 & 28:18
ch. 3:35 & 17:2
Acts 17:31
1 Pet. 4:5
23 1 John 2:23
24 ch. 3:16, 18 & 6:40, 47 & 8:51

1 John 3:14	**24**
Eph. 2:1, 5	**25**
& 5:14	
Col. 2:13	
Acts 10:42	**27**
& 17:31	
Dan. 7:13	**27**
Is. 26:19	**29**
1 Cor. 15:52	
Dan. 12:2	**29**
Mat. 25:32, 33, 46	
ver. 19	**30**
Mat. 26:39	**30**
ch. 4:34 & 6:38	
ch. 8:14	**31**
Rev. 3:14	
Mat. 3:17 & 17:5	**32**
ch. 8:18	
1 John 5:6	
ch. 1:15, 19,	**33**
27, 32	
2 Pet. 1:19	**35**
Mat. 13:20	**35**
Mark 6:20	
1 John 5:9	**36**
ch. 3:2 & 10:25	**36**
& 15:24	
Mat. 3:17 & 17:5	**37**
ch. 6:27 & 8:18	
Deut. 4:12	**37**
ch. 1:18	
1 Tim. 1:17	
1 John 4:12	
ver. 46	**39**
Is. 8:20 & 34:16	
Luke 16:29	
Acts 17:11	
Deut. 18:15, 18	**39**
Luke 24:27	
ch. 1:11 & 3:19	**40**
ver. 34	**41**
1 Thes. 2:6	

43 I am come in my Father's name, and ye receive me not: if another shall come in his own name, him ye will receive.

44 ᴿHow can ye believe, which receive honour one of another, and seek not ᴿthe honour that *cometh* from God only?

45 Do not think that I will accuse you to the Father: ᴿthere is *one* that accuseth you, *even* Moses, in whom ye trust.

46 For had ye believed Moses, ye would have believed me: ᴿfor he wrote of me.

47 But if ye believe not his writings, how shall ye believe my words? ——

CHAPTER 6

Feeding the five thousand

AFTER ᴿthese things Jesus went over the sea of Galilee, which is *the sea* of Tĭ-bē'-rĭ-ăs.

2 And a great multitude followed him, because they saw his miracles which he did on them that were diseased.

3 And Jesus went up into a mountain, and there he sat with his disciples.

4 ᴿAnd the passover, a feast of the Jews, was nigh.

5 ᴿWhen Jesus then lifted up *his* eyes, and saw a great company come unto him, he saith unto Philip, Whence shall we buy bread, that these may eat?

6 And this he said to prove him: for he himself knew what he would do.

7 Philip answered him, ᴿTwo hundred pennyworth of bread is not sufficient for them, that every one of them may take a little.

8 One of his disciples, Andrew, Simon Peter's brother, saith unto him,

9 There is a lad here, which hath five barley loaves, and two small fishes: ᴿbut what are they among so many?

10 And Jesus said, Make the men sit down. Now there was much grass in the place. So the men sat down, in number about five thousand.

11 And Jesus took the loaves; and when he had given thanks, he distributed to the disciples, and the disciples to them that were set down; and likewise of the fishes as much as they would.

12 When they were filled, he said unto his disciples, Gather up the fragments that remain, that nothing be lost.

13 Therefore they gathered *them* together, and filled twelve baskets with the fragments of the five barley loaves, which remained over and above unto them that had eaten.

14 Then those men, when they had seen the

CHAP. 5
AD 31
44 ch. 12:43
44 Rom. 2:29
45 Rom. 2:12
46 Gen. 3:15
& 12:3 & 18:18
& 22:18 & 49:10
Deut. 18:15, 18
ch. 1:45
Acts 26:22

CHAP. 6
AD 32
1 Mat. 14:15
Mark 6:35
Luke 9:10, 12
4 Lev. 23:5, 7
Deut. 16:1
ch. 2:13 & 5:1
5 Mat. 14:14
Mark 6:35
Luke 9:12
7 See Num. 11:21, 22
9 2 Ki. 4:43

Gen. 49:10   14
Deut. 18:15, 18
Mat. 11:3
ch. 1:21
& 4:19, 25 & 7:40
Mat. 14:23   16
Mark 6:47
Or, *Work not*   27
ch. 4:14   27
Mat. 3:17   27
& 17:5
Mark 1:11 & 9:7
Luke 3:22 & 9:35
ch. 5:37
Acts 2:22
2 Pet. 1:17
1 John 3:23   29

miracle that Jesus did, said, This is of a truth ᴿthat prophet that should come into the world.

Jesus walks on the water

15 When Jesus therefore perceived that they would come and take him by force, to make him a king, he departed again into a mountain himself alone.

16 ᴿAnd when even was *now* come, his disciples went down unto the sea,

17 And entered into a ship, and went over the sea toward Că-pĕr'-nă-ŭm. And it was now dark, and Jesus was not come to them.

18 And the sea arose by reason of a great wind that blew.

19 So when they had rowed about five and twenty or thirty furlongs, they see Jesus walking on the sea, and drawing nigh unto the ship: and they were afraid.

20 But he saith unto them, It is I; be not afraid.

21 Then they willingly received him into the ship: and immediately the ship was at the land whither they went.

"The true bread from heaven"

22 The day following, when the people which stood on the other side of the sea saw that there was none other boat there, save that one whereinto his disciples were entered, and that Jesus went not with his disciples into the boat, but *that* his disciples were gone away alone;

23 (Howbeit there came other boats from Tĭ-bē'-rĭ-ăs nigh unto the place where they did eat bread, after that the Lord had given thanks:)

24 When the people therefore saw that Jesus was not there, neither his disciples, they also took shipping, and came to Că-pĕr'-nă-ŭm, seeking for Jesus.

25 And when they had found him on the other side of the sea, they said unto him, Rabbi, when camest thou hither?

26 Jesus answered them and said, Verily, verily, I say unto you, Ye seek me, not because ye saw the miracles, but because ye did eat of the loaves, and were filled.

27 ᴺLabour not for the meat which perisheth, but ᴿfor that meat which endureth unto everlasting life, which the Son of man shall give unto you: ᴿfor him hath God the Father sealed.

28 Then said they unto him, What shall we do, that we might work the works of God?

29 Jesus answered and said unto them, ᴿThis is the work of God, that ye believe on him whom he hath sent.

30 They said therefore unto him, [R]What sign shewest thou then, that we may see, and believe thee? What dost thou work?

31 [R]Our fathers did eat măn'-nă in the desert; as it is written, [R]He gave them bread from heaven to eat.

32 Then Jesus said unto them, Verily, verily, I say unto you, Moses gave you not that bread from heaven; but my Father giveth you the true bread from heaven.

33 For the bread of God is he which cometh down from heaven, and giveth life unto the world.

34 [R]Then said they unto him, Lord, evermore give us this bread.

Jesus, the bread of life

35 And Jesus said unto them, [R]I am the bread of life: [R]he that cometh to me shall never hunger; and he that believeth on me shall never thirst.

36 [R]But I said unto you, That ye also have seen me, and believe not.

37 [R]All that the Father giveth me shall come to me; and [R]him that cometh to me I will in no wise cast out.

38 For I came down from heaven, [R]not to do mine own will, [R]but the will of him that sent me.

39 And this is the Father's will which hath sent me, [R]that of all which he hath given me I should lose nothing, but should raise it up again at the last day.

40 And this is the will of him that sent me, [R]that every one which seeth the Son, and believeth on him, may have everlasting life: and I will raise him up at the last day.

41 The Jews then murmured at him, because he said, I am the bread which came down from heaven.

42 And they said, [R]Is not this Jesus, the son of Joseph, whose father and mother we know? how is it then that he saith, I came down from heaven?

43 Jesus therefore answered and said unto them, Murmur not among yourselves.

44 [R]No man can come to me, except the Father which hath sent me draw him: and I will raise him up at the last day.

45 [R]It is written in the prophets, And they shall be all taught of God. [R]Every man therefore that hath heard, and hath learned of the Father, cometh unto me.

46 [R]Not that any man hath seen the Father, [R]save he which is of God, he hath seen the Father.

47 Verily, verily, I say unto you, [R]He that believeth on me hath everlasting life.

48 [R]I am that bread of life.

49 [R]Your fathers did eat măn'-nă in the wilderness, and are dead.

50 [R]This is the bread which cometh down from heaven, that a man may eat thereof, and not die.

51 I am the living bread [R]which came down from heaven: if any man eat of this bread, he shall live for ever: and [R]the bread that I will give is my flesh, which I will give for the life of the world.

52 The Jews therefore [R]strove among themselves, saying, How can this man give us *his* flesh to eat?

53 Then Jesus said unto them, Verily, verily, I say unto you, Except [R]ye eat the flesh of the Son of man, and drink his blood, ye have no life in you.

54 [R]Whoso eateth my flesh, and drinketh my blood, hath eternal life; and I will raise him up at the last day.

55 For my flesh is meat indeed, and my blood is drink indeed.

56 He that eateth my flesh, and drinketh my blood, [R]dwelleth in me, and I in him.

57 As the living Father hath sent me, and I live by the Father: so he that eateth me, even he shall live by me.

58 [R]This is that bread which came down from heaven: not as your fathers did eat măn'-nă, and are dead: he that eateth of this bread shall live for ever.

59 These things said he in the synagogue, as he taught in Că-pĕr'-nă-ŭm.

The disciples' murmuring

60 [R]Many therefore of his disciples, when they had heard *this,* said, This is an hard saying; who can hear it?

61 When Jesus knew in himself that his disciples murmured at it, he said unto them, Doth this offend you?

62 [R]*What* and if ye shall see the Son of man ascend up where he was before?

63 [R]It is the spirit that quickeneth; the flesh profiteth nothing: the words that I speak unto you, *they* are spirit, and *they* are life.

64 But [R]there are some of you that believe not. For [R]Jesus knew from the beginning who they were that believed not, and who should betray him.

65 And he said, Therefore [R]said I unto you, that no man can come unto me, except it were given unto him of my Father.

Peter's great affirmation

66 [R]From that *time* many of his disciples went back, and walked no more with him.

CHAP. **6**	
AD 32	
30 Mat. 12:38	
& 16:1	
Mark 8:11	
1 Cor. 1:22	
31 Ex. 16:15	
Num. 11:7	
Neh. 9:15	
1 Cor. 10:3	
Ps. 78:24	
34 See ch. 4:15	
35 ver. 48, 58	
35 ch. 4:14 & 7:37	
36 ver. 26, 64	
37 ver. 45	
37 Mat. 24:24	
ch. 10:28, 29	
2 Tim. 2:19	
1 John 2:19	
38 Mat. 26:39	
ch. 5:30	
38 ch. 4:34	
39 ch. 10:28	
& 17:12 & 18:9	
40 ver. 27, 47, 54	
ch. 3:15, 16 & 4:14	
42 Mat. 13:55	
Mark 6:3	
Luke 4:22	
44 ver. 65	
S. of S. 1:4	
45 Is. 54:13	
Jer. 31:34	
Mic. 4:2	
Heb. 8:10	
45 ver. 37	
46 ch. 1:18	
46 Mat. 11:27	
Luke 10:22	
ch. 7:29	
47 ch. 3:16, 18	
48 ver. 33, 35	
ver. 31	**49**
ver. 51, 58	**50**
ch. 3:13	**51**
Heb. 10:5	**51**
ch. 7:43	**52**
& 9:16 & 10:19	
Mat. 26:26	**53**
ver. 27, 40	**54**
ch. 4:14	
1 John 3:24	**56**
& 4:15, 16	
ver. 49-51	**58**
ver. 66	**60**
Mat. 11:6	
Mark 16:19	**62**
ch. 3:13	
Acts 1:9	
Eph. 4:8	
2 Cor. 3:6	**63**
ver. 36	**64**
ch. 2:24, 25	**64**
& 13:11	
ver. 44, 45	**65**
ver. 60	**66**

67 Then said Jesus unto the twelve, Will ye also go away?

68 Then Simon Peter answered him, Lord, to whom shall we go? thou hast ᴿthe words of eternal life.

69 ᴿAnd we believe and are sure that thou art that Christ, the Son of the living God.

70 Jesus answered them, ᴿHave not I chosen you twelve, ᴿand one of you is a devil?

71 He spake of Judas Iscariot *the son* of Simon: for he it was that should betray him, being one of the twelve.

CHAPTER 7

The disbelief of Jesus' brethren

AFTER these things Jesus walked in Galilee: for he would not walk in Jewry, ᴿbecause the Jews sought to kill him.

2 ᴿNow the Jews' feast of tabernacles was at hand.

3 ᴿHis brethren therefore said unto him, Depart hence, and go into Judæa, that thy disciples also may see the works that thou doest.

4 For *there is* no man *that* doeth any thing in secret, and he himself seeketh to be known openly. If thou do these things, shew thyself to the world.

5 For ᴿneither did his brethren believe in him.

6 Then Jesus said unto them, ᴿMy time is not yet come: but your time is alway ready.

7 ᴿThe world cannot hate you; but me it hateth, ᴿbecause I testify of it, that the works thereof are evil.

8 Go ye up unto this feast: I go not up yet unto this feast; ᴿfor my time is not yet full come.

9 When he had said these words unto them, he abode *still* in Galilee.

Jesus at the feast of tabernacles

10 But when his brethren were gone up, then went he also up unto the feast, not openly, but as it were in secret.

11 Then ᴿthe Jews sought him at the feast, and said, Where is he?

12 And ᴿthere was much murmuring among the people concerning him: for ᴿsome said, He is a good man: others said, Nay; but he deceiveth the people.

13 Howbeit no man spake openly of him ᴿfor fear of the Jews.

14 Now about the midst of the feast Jesus went up into the temple, and taught.

15 ᴿAnd the Jews marvelled, saying, How knoweth this man ᴺletters, having never learned?

16 Jesus answered them, and said, ᴿMy doctrine is not mine, but his that sent me.

17 ᴿIf any man will do his will, he shall know of the doctrine, whether it be of God, or *whether* I speak of myself.

18 ᴿHe that speaketh of himself seeketh his own glory: but he that seeketh his glory that sent him, the same is true, and no unrighteousness is in him.

19 ᴿDid not Moses give you the law, and *yet* none of you keepeth the law? ᴿWhy go ye about to kill me?

20 The people answered and said, ᴿThou hast a devil: who goeth about to kill thee?

21 Jesus answered and said unto them, I have done one work, and ye all marvel.

22 ᴿMoses therefore gave unto you circumcision; (not because it is of Moses, ᴿbut of the fathers;) and ye on the sabbath day circumcise a man.

23 If a man on the sabbath day receive circumcision, ᴺthat the law of Moses should not be broken; are ye angry at me, because ᴿI have made a man every whit whole on the sabbath day?

24 ᴿJudge not according to the appearance, but judge righteous judgment.

25 Then said some of them of Jerusalem, Is not this he, whom they seek to kill?

26 But, lo, he speaketh boldly, and they say nothing unto him. ᴿDo the rulers know indeed that this is the very Christ?

27 ᴿHowbeit we know this man whence he is: but when Christ cometh, no man knoweth whence he is.

28 Then cried Jesus in the temple as he taught, saying, ᴿYe both know me, and ye know whence I am: and ᴿI am not come of myself, but he that sent me ᴿis true, ᴿwhom ye know not.

29 But ᴿI know him: for I am from him, and he hath sent me.

30 Then ᴿthey sought to take him: but ᴿno man laid hands on him, because his hour was not yet come.

31 And ᴿmany of the people believed on him, and said, When Christ cometh, will he do more miracles than these which this *man* hath done?

Attempt to arrest Jesus

32 The Pharisees heard that the people murmured such things concerning him; and the Pharisees and the chief priests sent officers to take him.

33 Then said Jesus unto them, ᴿYet a little while am I with you, and *then* I go unto him that sent me.

34 Ye ᴿshall seek me, and shall not find *me:*

CHAP. 6
AD 32
68 Acts 5:20
69 Mat. 16:16
Mark 8:29
Luke 9:20
ch. 1:49 & 11:27
70 Luke 6:13
70 ch. 13:27

CHAP. 7
AD 32
1 ch. 5:16, 18
2 Lev. 23:34
3 Mat. 12:46
Mark 3:31
Acts 1:14
5 Mark 3:21
6 ch. 2:4 & 8:20
7 ch. 15:19
7 ch. 3:19
8 ch. 8:20
11 ch. 11:56
12 ch. 9:16 & 10:19
12 ver. 40
Mat. 21:46
Luke 7:16
ch. 6:14
13 ch. 9:22 & 12:42 & 19:38
15 Mat. 13:54
Mark 6:2
Luke 4:22
Acts 2:7
15 Or, *learning*

ch. 3:11 & 8:28 & 12:49 & 14:10, 24	**16**
ch. 8:43	**17**
ch. 5:41 & 8:50	**18**
Ex. 24:3	**19**
Deut. 33:4	
ch. 1:17	
Acts 7:38	
Mat. 12:14	**19**
Mark 3:6	
ch. 5:16, 18 & 10:31, 39 & 11:53	
ch. 8:48, 52 & 10:20	**20**
Lev. 12:3	**22**
Gen. 17:10	**22**
Or, *without breaking the law of Moses*	**23**
ch. 5:8, 9, 16	**23**
Deut. 1:16	**24**
Prov. 24:23	
ch. 8:15	
Jas. 2:1	
ver. 48	**26**
Mat. 13:55	**27**
Mark 6:3	
Luke 4:22	
ch. 8:14	**28**
ch. 5:43 & 8:42	**28**
ch. 5:32 & 8:26	**28**
Rom. 3:4	
ch. 1:18 & 8:55	**28**
Mat. 11:27	**29**
ch. 10:15	
Mark 11:18	**30**
Luke 19:47 & 20:19	
ch. 8:37	
ver. 44	**30**
Mat. 12:23	**31**
ch. 3:2 & 8:30	
ch. 13:33 & 16:16	**33**
Hos. 5:6	**34**
ch. 8:21 & 13:33	

and where I am, *thither* ye cannot come.

35 Then said the Jews among themselves, Whither will he go, that we shall not find him? will he go unto [R]the dispersed among the [N]Gentiles, and teach the Gentiles?

36 What *manner of* saying is this that he said, Ye shall seek me, and shall not find *me:* and where I am, *thither* ye cannot come?

37 [R]In the last day, that great *day* of the feast, Jesus stood and cried, saying, [R]If any man thirst, let him come unto me, and drink.

38 [R]He that believeth on me, as the scripture hath said, [R]out of his belly shall flow rivers of living water.

39 ([R]But this spake he of the Spirit, which they that believe on him should receive: for the Holy Ghost was not yet *given;* because that Jesus was not yet [R]glorified.)

40 Many of the people therefore, when they heard this saying, said, Of a truth this is [R]the Prophet.

41 Others said, [R]This is the Christ. But some said, Shall Christ come [R]out of Galilee?

42 [R]Hath not the scripture said, That Christ cometh of the seed of David, and out of the town of Bethlehem, [R]where David was?

43 So [R]there was a division among the people because of him.

44 And [R]some of them would have taken him; but no man laid hands on him.

45 Then came the officers to the chief priests and Pharisees; and they said unto them, Why have ye not brought him?

46 The officers answered, Never man spake like this man.

47 Then answered them the Pharisees, Are ye also deceived?

48 [R]Have any of the rulers or of the Pharisees believed on him?

49 But this people who knoweth not the law are cursed.

50 Nĭc-ŏ-dē'-mŭs saith unto them, ([R]he that came [N]to Jesus by night, being one of them,)

51 [R]Doth our law judge *any* man, before it hear him, and know what he doeth?

52 They answered and said unto him, Art thou also of Galilee? Search, and look: for [R]out of Galilee ariseth no prophet.

53 And every man went unto his own house.

CHAPTER 8

J ESUS went unto the mount of Olives.

2 And early in the morning he came again into the temple, and all the people came unto him; and he sat down, and taught them.

CHAP. 7
AD 32
35 Is. 11:12
Jas. 1:1
1 Pet. 1:1
35 Or, *Greeks*
37 Lev. 23:36
37 Is. 55:1
ch. 6:35
Rev. 22:17
38 Deut. 18:15
38 Prov. 18:4
Is. 12:3 & 44:3
ch. 4:14
39 Is. 44:3
Joel 2:28
ch. 16:7
Acts 2:17, 33, 38
39 ch. 12:16 & 16:7
40 Deut. 18:15
ch. 1:21
& 6:14
41 ch. 4:42 & 6:69
41 ver. 52
ch. 1:46
42 Ps. 132:11
Jer. 23:5
Mic. 5:2
Mat. 2:5
Luke 2:4
42 1 Sam. 16:1, 4
43 ver. 12
ch. 9:16 & 10:19
44 ver. 30
48 ch. 12:42
Acts 6:7
1 Cor. 1:20, 26
& 2:8
50 ch. 3:2
50 Gr. *to him*
51 Deut. 1:17
& 17:8, etc.
& 19:15
52 ver. 41
Is. 9:1, 2
Mat. 4:15
ch. 1:46

CHAP. 8	
AD 32	
Lev. 20:10	5
Deut. 22:22	
Deut. 17:7	7
Rom. 2:1	
Rom. 2:22	9
Luke 9:56	11
& 12:14	
ch. 3:17	
ch. 5:14	11
ch. 1:4, 5, 9	12
& 3:19 & 9:5	
& 12:35, 36, 46	
ch. 5:31	13
ch. 7:28 & 9:29	14
ch. 7:24	15
ch. 3:17	15
& 12:47 & 18:36	
ch. 16:32	16
Deut. 17:6	17
& 19:15	
Mat. 18:16	
2 Cor. 13:1	
Heb. 10:28	
ch. 5:37	18

The woman caught in adultery

3 And the scribes and Pharisees brought unto him a woman taken in adultery; and when they had set her in the midst,

4 They say unto him, Master, this woman was taken in adultery, in the very act.

5 [R]Now Moses in the law commanded us, that such should be stoned: but what sayest thou?

6 This they said, tempting him, that they might have to accuse him. But Jesus stooped down, and with *his* finger wrote on the ground, *as though he heard them not.*

7 So when they continued asking him, he lifted up himself, and said unto them, [R]He that is without sin among you, let him first cast a stone at her.

8 And again he stooped down, and wrote on the ground.

9 And they which heard *it,* [R]being convicted by *their own* conscience, went out one by one, beginning at the eldest, *even* unto the last: and Jesus was left alone, and the woman standing in the midst.

10 When Jesus had lifted up himself, and saw none but the woman, he said unto her, Woman, where are those thine accusers? hath no man condemned thee?

11 She said, No man, Lord. And Jesus said unto her, [R]Neither do I condemn thee: go, and [R]sin no more.

Jesus, the light of the world

12 Then spake Jesus again unto them, saying, [R]I am the light of the world: he that followeth me shall not walk in darkness, but shall have the light of life.

13 The Pharisees therefore said unto him, [R]Thou bearest record of thyself; thy record is not true.

14 Jesus answered and said unto them, Though I bear record of myself, *yet* my record is true: for I know whence I came, and whither I go; but [R]ye cannot tell whence I come, and whither I go.

15 [R]Ye judge after the flesh; [R]I judge no man.

16 And yet if I judge, my judgment is true: for [R]I am not alone, but I and the Father that sent me.

17 [R]It is also written in your law, that the testimony of two men is true.

18 I am one that bear witness of myself, and [R]the Father that sent me beareth witness of me.

19 Then said they unto him, Where is thy

Father? Jesus answered, [R]Ye neither know me, nor my Father: [R]if ye had known me, ye should have known my Father also.

20 These words spake Jesus in [R]the treasury, as he taught in the temple: and [R]no man laid hands on him; for [R]his hour was not yet come.

Warning against unbelief

21 Then said Jesus again unto them, I go my way, and [R]ye shall seek me, and [R]shall die in your sins: whither I go, ye cannot come.

22 Then said the Jews, Will he kill himself? because he saith, Whither I go, ye cannot come.

23 And he said unto them, [R]Ye are from beneath; I am from above: [R]ye are of this world; I am not of this world.

24 [R]I said therefore unto you, that ye shall die in your sins: [R]for if ye believe not that I am *he,* ye shall die in your sins.

25 Then said they unto him, Who art thou? And Jesus saith unto them, Even *the same* that I said unto you from the beginning.

26 I have many things to say and to judge of you: but [R]he that sent me is true; and [R]I speak to the world those things which I have heard of him.

27 They understood not that he spake to them of the Father.

28 Then said Jesus unto them, When ye have [R]lifted up the Son of man, [R]then shall ye know that I am *he,* and [R]that I do nothing of myself; but [R]as my Father hath taught me, I speak these things.

29 And [R]he that sent me is with me: [R]the Father hath not left me alone; [R]for I do always those things that please him.

30 As he spake these words, [R]many believed on him.

True children of Abraham

31 Then said Jesus to those Jews which believed on him, If ye continue in my word, *then* are ye my disciples indeed;

32 And ye shall know the truth, and [R]the truth shall make you free.

33 They answered him, [R]We be Abraham's seed, and were never in bondage to any man: how sayest thou, Ye shall be made free?

34 Jesus answered them, Verily, verily, I say unto you, [R]Whosoever committeth sin is the servant of sin.

35 And [R]the servant abideth not in the house for ever: *but* the Son abideth ever.

36 [R]If the Son therefore shall make you free, ye shall be free indeed.

37 I know that ye are Abraham's seed; but

[R]ye seek to kill me, because my word hath no place in you.

38 [R]I speak that which I have seen with my Father: and ye do that which ye have seen with your father.

39 They answered and said unto him, [R]Abraham is our father. Jesus saith unto them, [R]If ye were Abraham's children, ye would do the works of Abraham.

40 [R]But now ye seek to kill me, a man that hath told you the truth, [R]which I have heard of God: this did not Abraham.

41 Ye do the deeds of your father. Then said they to him, We be not born of fornication; [R]we have one Father, *even* God.

42 Jesus said unto them, [R]If God were your Father, ye would love me: [R]for I proceeded forth and came from God; [R]neither came I of myself, but he sent me.

43 [R]Why do ye not understand my speech? *even* because ye cannot hear my word.

44 [R]Ye are of *your* father the devil, and the lusts of your father ye will do. He was a murderer from the beginning, and [R]abode not in the truth, because there is no truth in him. When he speaketh a lie, he speaketh of his own: for he is a liar, and the father of it.

45 And because I tell *you* the truth, ye believe me not.

46 Which of you convinceth me of sin? And if I say the truth, why do ye not believe me?

47 [R]He that is of God heareth God's words: ye therefore hear *them* not, because ye are not of God.

Controversy with the Jews

48 Then answered the Jews, and said unto him, Say we not well that thou art a Să-măr′-ĭ-tăn, and [R]hast a devil?

49 Jesus answered, I have not a devil; but I honour my Father, and ye do dishonour me.

50 And [R]I seek not mine own glory: there is one that seeketh and judgeth.

51 Verily, verily, I say unto you, [R]If a man keep my saying, he shall never see death.

52 Then said the Jews unto him, Now we know that thou hast a devil. [R]Abraham is dead, and the prophets; and thou sayest, If a man keep my saying, he shall never taste of death.

53 Art thou greater than our father Abraham, which is dead? and the prophets are dead: whom makest thou thyself?

54 Jesus answered, If I honour myself, my honour is nothing: [R]it is my Father that honoureth me; of whom ye say, that he is your God:

55 Yet ᴿye have not known him; but I know him: and if I should say, I know him not, I shall be a liar like unto you: but I know him, and keep his saying.

56 Your father Abraham ᴿrejoiced to see my day: ᴿand he saw *it,* and was glad.

57 Then said the Jews unto him, Thou art not yet fifty years old, and hast thou seen Abraham?

58 Jesus said unto them, Verily, verily, I say unto you, Before Abraham was, ᴿI am.

59 Then ᴿtook they up stones to cast at him: but Jesus hid himself, and went out of the temple, ᴿgoing through the midst of them, and so passed by.

CHAPTER 9

Healing the man born blind

AND as *Jesus* passed by, he saw a man which was blind from *his* birth.

2 And his disciples asked him, saying, Master, ᴿwho did sin, this man, or his parents, that he was born blind?

3 Jesus answered, Neither hath this man sinned, nor his parents: ᴿbut that the works of God should be made manifest in him.

4 ᴿI must work the works of him that sent me, while it is day: the night cometh, when no man can work.

5 As long as I am in the world, ᴿI am the light of the world.

6 When he had thus spoken, ᴿhe spat on the ground, and made clay of the spittle, and he ᴺanointed the eyes of the blind man with the clay,

7 And said unto him, Go, wash ᴿin the pool of Sī-lō′-ăm, (which is by interpretation, Sent.) ᴿHe went his way therefore, and washed, and came seeing.

8 The neighbours therefore, and they which before had seen him that he was blind, said, Is not this he that sat and begged?

9 Some said, This is he: others *said,* He is like him: *but* he said, I am *he.*

10 Therefore said they unto him, How were thine eyes opened?

11 He answered and said, ᴿA man that is called Jesus made clay, and anointed mine eyes, and said unto me, Go to the pool of Sī-lō′-ăm, and wash: and I went and washed, and I received sight.

12 Then said they unto him, Where is he? He said, I know not.

13 They brought to the Pharisees him that aforetime was blind.

14 And it was the sabbath day when Jesus made the clay, and opened his eyes.

15 Then again the Pharisees also asked him how he had received his sight. He said unto them, He put clay upon mine eyes, and I washed, and do see.

16 Therefore said some of the Pharisees, This man is not of God, because he keepeth not the sabbath day. Others said, ᴿHow can a man that is a sinner do such miracles? And ᴿthere was a division among them.

17 They say unto the blind man again, What sayest thou of him, that he hath opened thine eyes? He said, ᴿHe is a prophet.

18 But the Jews did not believe concerning him, that he had been blind, and received his sight, until they called the parents of him that had received his sight.

19 And they asked them, saying, Is this your son, who ye say was born blind? how then doth he now see?

20 His parents answered them and said, We know that this is our son, and that he was born blind:

21 But by what means he now seeth, we know not; or who hath opened his eyes, we know not: he is of age; ask him: he shall speak for himself.

22 These *words* spake his parents, because ᴿthey feared the Jews: for the Jews had agreed already, that if any man did confess that he was Christ, he ᴿshould be put out of the synagogue.

23 Therefore said his parents, He is of age; ask him.

The healed man's affirmation

24 Then again called they the man that was blind, and said unto him, ᴿGive God the praise: ᴿwe know that this man is a sinner.

25 He answered and said, Whether he be a sinner *or no,* I know not: one thing I know, that, whereas I was blind, now I see.

26 Then said they to him again, What did he to thee? how opened he thine eyes?

27 He answered them, I have told you already, and ye did not hear: wherefore would ye hear *it* again? will ye also be his disciples?

28 Then they reviled him, and said, Thou art his disciple; but we are Moses' disciples.

29 We know that God spake unto Moses: *as for* this *fellow,* ᴿwe know not from whence he is.

30 The man answered and said unto them, ᴿWhy herein is a marvellous thing, that ye know not from whence he is, and *yet* he hath opened mine eyes.

31 Now we know that ᴿGod heareth not sinners: but if any man be a worshipper of God, and doeth his will, him he heareth.

32 Since the world began was it not heard that any man opened the eyes of one that was born blind.

33 ^RIf this man were not of God, he could do nothing.

34 They answered and said unto him, ^RThou wast altogether born in sins, and dost thou teach us? And they ^Ncast him out.

35 Jesus heard that they had cast him out; and when he had found him, he said unto him, Dost thou believe on ^Rthe Son of God?

36 He answered and said, Who is he, Lord, that I might believe on him?

37 And Jesus said unto him, Thou hast both seen him, and ^Rit is he that talketh with thee.

38 And he said, Lord, I believe. And he worshipped him.

39 And Jesus said, ^RFor judgment I am come into this world, ^Rthat they which see not might see; and that they which see might be made blind.

40 And *some* of the Pharisees which were with him heard these words, ^Rand said unto him, Are we blind also?

41 Jesus said unto them, ^RIf ye were blind, ye should have no sin: but now ye say, We see; therefore your sin remaineth.

CHAPTER 10

Parable of the sheepfold

VERILY, verily, I say unto you, He that entereth not by the door into the sheepfold, but climbeth up some other way, the same is a thief and a robber.

2 But he that entereth in by the door is the shepherd of the sheep.

3 To him the porter openeth; and the sheep hear his voice: and he calleth his own sheep by name, and leadeth them out.

4 And when he putteth forth his own sheep, he goeth before them, and the sheep follow him: for they know his voice.

5 And a stranger will they not follow, but will flee from him: for they know not the voice of strangers.

6 This parable spake Jesus unto them: but they understood not what things they were which he spake unto them.

Jesus, the good shepherd

7 Then said Jesus unto them again, Verily, verily, I say unto you, I am the door of the sheep.

8 All that ever came before me are thieves and robbers: but the sheep did not hear them.

9 ^RI am the door: by me if any man enter in,

he shall be saved, and shall go in and out, and find pasture.

10 The thief cometh not, but for to steal, and to kill, and to destroy: I am come that they might have life, and that they might have *it* more abundantly.

11 ^RI am the good shepherd: the good shepherd giveth his life for the sheep.

12 But he that is an hireling, and not the shepherd, whose own the sheep are not, seeth the wolf coming, and ^Rleaveth the sheep, and fleeth: and the wolf catcheth them, and scattereth the sheep.

13 The hireling fleeth, because he is an hireling, and careth not for the sheep.

14 I am the good shepherd, and ^Rknow my *sheep,* and am known of mine.

15 ^RAs the Father knoweth me, even so know I the Father: ^Rand I lay down my life for the sheep.

16 And ^Rother sheep I have, which are not of this fold: them also I must bring, and they shall hear my voice; ^Rand there shall be one fold, *and* one shepherd.

17 Therefore doth my Father love me, ^Rbecause I lay down my life, that I might take it again.

18 No man taketh it from me, but I lay it down of myself. I have power to lay it down, and I ^Rhave power to take it again. ^RThis commandment have I received of my Father.

19 ^RThere was a division therefore again among the Jews for these sayings.

20 And many of them said, ^RHe hath a devil, and is mad; why hear ye him?

21 Others said, These are not the words of him that hath a devil. ^RCan a devil ^Ropen the eyes of the blind?

Jesus at the feast of dedication

22 And it was at Jerusalem the feast of the dedication, and it was winter.

23 And Jesus walked in the temple ^Rin Solomon's porch.

24 Then came the Jews round about him, and said unto him, How long dost thou ^Nmake us to doubt? If thou be the Christ, tell us plainly.

25 Jesus answered them, I told you, and ye believed not: ^Rthe works that I do in my Father's name, they bear witness of me.

26 But ^Rye believe not, because ye are not of my sheep, as I said unto you.

27 ^RMy sheep hear my voice, and I know them, and they follow me:

28 And I give unto them eternal life; and they shall never perish, neither shall any *man* pluck them out of my hand.

CHAP. 9
AD 32
33 ver. 16
34 ver. 2
34 Or, *excommunicated him,* ver. 22
35 Mat. 14:33 & 16:16 Mark 1:1 ch. 10:36 1 John 5:13
37 ch. 4:26
39 ch. 5:22, 27 See ch. 3:17 & 12:47
39 Mat. 13:13
40 Rom. 2:19
41 ch. 15:22, 24

CHAP. 10
AD 32
9 ch. 14:6 Eph. 2:18

Is. 40:11 · 11
Ezek. 34:12, 23 & 37:24 Heb. 13:20 1 Pet. 2:25 & 5:4
Zech. 11:16, 17 · 12
2 Tim. 2:19 · 14
Mat. 11:27 · 15
ch. 15:13 · 15
Is. 56:8 · 16
Ezek. 37:22 Eph. 2:14 1 Pet. 2:25 · 16
Is. 53:7, 8, 12 Heb. 2:9 · 17
ch. 2:19 · 18
ch. 6:38 & 15:10 · 18
Acts 2:24, 32
ch. 7:43 & 9:16 · 19
ch. 7:20 & 8:48, 52 · 20
Ex. 4:11 Ps. 94:9 & 146:8 · 21
ch. 9:6, 7, 32, 33 · 21
Acts 3:11 & 5:12 · 23
Or, *hold us in suspense?* · 24
ver. 38 · 25
ch. 3:2 & 5:36 · 25
ch. 8:47 · 26
ver. 4, 14 · 27

29 [R]My Father, [R]which gave *them* me, is greater than all; and no *man* is able to pluck *them* out of my Father's hand.

30 [R]I and *my* Father are one.

31 Then [R]the Jews took up stones again to stone him.

32 Jesus answered them, Many good works have I shewed you from my Father; for which of those works do ye stone me?

33 The Jews answered him, saying, For a good work we stone thee not; but for blasphemy; and because that thou, being a man, [R]makest thyself God.

34 Jesus answered them, [R]Is it not written in your law, I said, Ye are gods?

35 If he called them gods, [R]unto whom the word of God came, and the scripture cannot be broken;

36 Say ye of him, [R]whom the Father hath sanctified, and [R]sent into the world, Thou blasphemest; [R]because I said, I am [R]the Son of God?

37 [R]If I do not the works of my Father, believe me not.

38 But if I do, though ye believe not me, [R]believe the works: that ye may know, and believe, [R]that the Father *is* in me, and I in him.

39 [R]Therefore they sought again to take him: but he escaped out of their hand,

40 And went away again beyond Jordan into the place [R]where John at first baptized; and there he abode.

41 And many resorted unto him, and said, John did no miracle: [R]but all things that John spake of this man were true.

42 [R]And many believed on him there.

CHAPTER 11

The death of Lazarus

NOW a certain *man* was sick, *named* Lăz'-ă-rŭs, of Bethany, the town of [R]Mary and her sister Martha.

2 ([R]It was *that* Mary which anointed the Lord with ointment, and wiped his feet with her hair, whose brother Lăz'-ă-rŭs was sick.)

3 Therefore his sisters sent unto him, saying, Lord, behold, he whom thou lovest is sick.

4 When Jesus heard *that,* he said, This sickness is not unto death, [R]but for the glory of God, that the Son of God might be glorified thereby.

5 Now Jesus loved Martha, and her sister, and Lăz'-ă-rŭs.

6 When he had heard therefore that he was

CHAP. **10**	
AD 32	
29	ch. 14:28
29	ch. 17:2, 6, etc.
30	ch. 17:11, 22
31	ch. 8:59
33	ch. 5:18
34	Ps. 82:6
35	Rom. 13:1
36	ch. 6:27
36	ch. 3:17 & 5:36, 37 & 8:42
36	ver. 30
	ch. 5:17, 18
36	Luke 1:35
	ch. 9:35, 37
37	ch. 15:24
38	ch. 5:36 & 14:10, 11
38	ch. 14:10, 11 & 17:21
39	ch. 7:30, 44 & 8:59
40	ch. 1:28
41	ch. 3:30
42	ch. 8:30 & 11:45

CHAP. **11**	
AD 33	
1	Luke 10:38, 39
2	Mat. 26:7
	Mark 14:3
	ch. 12:3
4	ver. 40
	ch. 9:3

ch. 10:40	**6**
ch. 10:31	**8**
ch. 9:4	**9**
ch. 12:35	**10**
Deut. 31:16	**11**
Dan. 12:2	
Mat. 9:24	
Acts 7:60	
1 Cor. 15:18, 51	
i.e. about two miles	**18**
ch. 9:31	**22**
Luke 14:14	**24**
ch. 5:29	
ch. 5:21	**25**
& 6:39, 40, 44	
ch. 3:36	**25**
1 John 5:10, etc.	
Mat. 16:16	**27**
ch. 4:42	
& 6:14, 69	

sick, [R]he abode two days still in the same place where he was.

7 Then after that saith he to *his* disciples, Let us go into Judæa again.

8 *His* disciples say unto him, Master, [R]the Jews of late sought to stone thee; and goest thou thither again?

9 Jesus answered, Are there not twelve hours in the day? [R]If any man walk in the day, he stumbleth not, because he seeth the light of this world.

10 But [R]if a man walk in the night, he stumbleth, because there is no light in him.

11 These things said he: and after that he saith unto them, Our friend Lăz'-ă-rŭs [R]sleepeth; but I go, that I may awake him out of sleep.

12 Then said his disciples, Lord, if he sleep, he shall do well.

13 Howbeit Jesus spake of his death: but they thought that he had spoken of taking of rest in sleep.

14 Then said Jesus unto them plainly, Lăz'-ă-rŭs is dead.

15 And I am glad for your sakes that I was not there, to the intent ye may believe; nevertheless let us go unto him.

16 Then said Thomas, which is called Dĭd'-ў̆-mŭs, unto his fellowdisciples, Let us also go, that we may die with him.

Jesus, the resurrection and the life

17 Then when Jesus came, he found that he had *lain* in the grave four days already.

18 Now Bethany was nigh unto Jerusalem, [N]about fifteen furlongs off:

19 And many of the Jews came to Martha and Mary, to comfort them concerning their brother.

20 Then Martha, as soon as she heard that Jesus was coming, went and met him: but Mary sat *still* in the house.

21 Then said Martha unto Jesus, Lord, if thou hadst been here, my brother had not died.

22 But I know, that even now, [R]whatsoever thou wilt ask of God, God will give *it* thee.

23 Jesus saith unto her, Thy brother shall rise again.

24 Martha saith unto him, [R]I know that he shall rise again in the resurrection at the last day.

25 Jesus said unto her, I am [R]the resurrection, and the life: [R]he that believeth in me, though he were dead, yet shall he live:

26 And whosoever liveth and believeth in me shall never die. Believest thou this?

27 She saith unto him, Yea, Lord: [R]I believe

that thou art the Christ, the Son of God, which should come into the world.

28 And when she had so said, she went her way, and called Mary her sister secretly, saying, The Master is come, and calleth for thee.

29 As soon as she heard *that,* she arose quickly, and came unto him.

30 Now Jesus was not yet come into the town, but was in that place where Martha met him.

31 [R]The Jews then which were with her in the house, and comforted her, when they saw Mary, that she rose up hastily and went out, followed her, saying, She goeth unto the grave to weep there.

32 Then when Mary was come where Jesus was, and saw him, she fell down at his feet, saying unto him, [R]Lord, if thou hadst been here, my brother had not died.

33 When Jesus therefore saw her weeping, and the Jews also weeping which came with her, he groaned in the spirit, and [N]was troubled,

34 And said, Where have ye laid him? They said unto him, Lord, come and see.

35 [R]Jesus wept.

36 Then said the Jews, Behold how he loved him!

37 And some of them said, Could not this man, [R]which opened the eyes of the blind, have caused that even this man should not have died?

Jesus raises Lazarus

38 Jesus therefore again groaning in himself cometh to the grave. It was a cave, and a stone lay upon it.

39 Jesus said, Take ye away the stone. Martha, the sister of him that was dead, saith unto him, Lord, by this time he stinketh: for he hath been *dead* four days.

40 Jesus saith unto her, Said I not unto thee, that, if thou wouldest believe, thou shouldest [R]see the glory of God?

41 Then they took away the stone *from the place* where the dead was laid. And Jesus lifted up *his* eyes, and said, Father, I thank thee that thou hast heard me.

42 And I knew that thou hearest me always: but [R]because of the people which stand by I said *it,* that they may believe that thou hast sent me.

43 And when he thus had spoken, he cried with a loud voice, Lăz'-ă-rŭs, come forth.

44 And he that was dead came forth, bound hand and foot with graveclothes: and [R]his face was bound about with a napkin. Jesus saith unto them, Loose him, and let him go.

The council's plot against Jesus

45 Then many of the Jews which came to Mary, [R]and had seen the things which Jesus did, believed on him.

46 But some of them went their ways to the Pharisees, and told them what things Jesus had done.

47 [R]Then gathered the chief priests and the Pharisees a council, and said, [R]What do we? for this man doeth many miracles.

48 If we let him thus alone, all *men* will believe on him: and the Romans shall come and take away both our place and nation.

49 And one of them, *named* [R]Câi'-ă-phăs, being the high priest that same year, said unto them, Ye know nothing at all,

50 [R]Nor consider that it is expedient for us, that one man should die for the people, and that the whole nation perish not.

51 And this spake he not of himself: but being high priest that year, he prophesied that Jesus should die for that nation;

52 And [R]not for that nation only, [R]but that also he should gather together in one the children of God that were scattered abroad.

53 Then from that day forth they took counsel together for to put him to death.

54 Jesus [R]therefore walked no more openly among the Jews; but went thence unto a country near to the wilderness, into a city called [R]Ē'-phră-ĭm, and there continued with his disciples.

55 [R]And the Jews' passover was nigh at hand: and many went out of the country up to Jerusalem before the passover, to purify themselves.

56 [R]Then sought they for Jesus, and spake among themselves, as they stood in the temple, What think ye, that he will not come to the feast?

57 Now both the chief priests and the Pharisees had given a commandment, that, if any man knew where he were, he should shew *it,* that they might take him.

CHAPTER 12

The anointing at Bethany

THEN Jesus six days before the passover came to Bethany, [R]where Lăz'-ă-rŭs was which had been dead, whom he raised from the dead.

2 [R]There they made him a supper; and Martha served: but Lăz'-ă-rŭs was one of them that sat at the table with him.

3 Then took [R]Mary a pound of ointment of spikenard, very costly, and anointed the feet of

Jesus, and wiped his feet with her hair: and the house was filled with the odour of the ointment.

4 Then saith one of his disciples, Judas Iscariot, Simon's *son,* which should betray him,

5 Why was not this ointment sold for three hundred pence, and given to the poor?

6 This he said, not that he cared for the poor; but because he was a thief, and [R]had the bag, and bare what was put therein.

7 Then said Jesus, Let her alone: against the day of my burying hath she kept this.

8 For [R]the poor always ye have with you; but me ye have not always.

The priests' plot against Lazarus

9 Much people of the Jews therefore knew that he was there: and they came not for Jesus' sake only, but that they might see Lăz'-ȧ-rŭs also, [R]whom he had raised from the dead.

10 [R]But the chief priests consulted that they might put Lăz'-ȧ-rŭs also to death;

11 [R]Because that by reason of him many of the Jews went away, and believed on Jesus.

The triumphal entry

12 [R]On the next day much people that were come to the feast, when they heard that Jesus was coming to Jerusalem,

13 Took branches of palm trees, and went forth to meet him, and cried, [R]Hō-săn'-nȧ: Blessed *is* the King of Israel that cometh in the name of the Lord.

14 [R]And Jesus, when he had found a young ass, sat thereon; as it is written,

15 [R]Fear not, daughter of Sī'-on: behold, thy King cometh, sitting on an ass's colt.

16 These things [R]understood not his disciples at the first: [R]but when Jesus was glorified, [R]then remembered they that these things were written of him, and *that* they had done these things unto him.

17 The people therefore that was with him when he called Lăz'-ȧ-rŭs out of his grave, and raised him from the dead, bare record.

18 [R]For this cause the people also met him, for that they heard that he had done this miracle.

19 The Pharisees therefore said among themselves, [R]Perceive ye how ye prevail nothing? behold, the world is gone after him.

The Greeks seek Jesus

20 And there [R]were certain Greeks among them [R]that came up to worship at the feast:

21 The same came therefore to Philip, [R]which was of Bĕth-sā'-ĭ-dȧ of Galilee, and desired him, saying, Sir, we would see Jesus.

22 Philip cometh and telleth Andrew: and again Andrew and Philip tell Jesus.

23 And Jesus answered them, saying, [R]The hour is come, that the Son of man should be glorified.

24 Verily, verily, I say unto you, [R]Except a corn of wheat fall into the ground and die, it abideth alone: but if it die, it bringeth forth much fruit.

25 [R]He that loveth his life shall lose it; and he that hateth his life in this world shall keep it unto life eternal.

26 If any man serve me, let him follow me; and [R]where I am, there shall also my servant be: if any man serve me, him will *my* Father honour.

Exhortation to belief

27 [R]Now is my soul troubled; and what shall I say? Father, save me from this hour: [R]but for this cause came I unto this hour.

28 Father, glorify thy name. [R]Then came there a voice from heaven, *saying,* I have both glorified *it,* and will glorify *it* again.

29 The people therefore, that stood by, and heard *it,* said that it thundered: others said, An angel spake to him.

30 Jesus answered and said, [R]This voice came not because of me, but for your sakes.

31 Now is the judgment of this world: now shall [R]the prince of this world be cast out.

32 And I, [R]if I be lifted up from the earth, will draw [R]all *men* unto me.

33 [R]This he said, signifying what death he should die.

34 The people answered him, [R]We have heard out of the law that Christ abideth for ever: and how sayest thou, The Son of man must be lifted up? who is this Son of man?

35 Then Jesus said unto them, Yet a little while [R]is the light with you. [R]Walk while ye have the light, lest darkness come upon you: for [R]he that walketh in darkness knoweth not whither he goeth.

36 While ye have light, believe in the light, that ye may be [R]the children of light. These things spake Jesus, and departed, and [R]did hide himself from them.

The cause of unbelief

37 But though he had done so many miracles before them, yet they believed not on him:

38 That the saying of Ē-sā'-ȧs the prophet might be fulfilled, which he spake, [R]Lord, who hath believed our report? and to whom hath the arm of the Lord been revealed?

39 Therefore they could not believe, because that Ē-sā'-ȧs said again,

40 [R]He hath blinded their eyes, and hard-

ened their heart; that they should not see with *their* eyes, nor understand with *their* heart, and be converted, and I should heal them.

41 ᴿThese things said Ē-śâi′-ăs, when he saw his glory, and spake of him.

42 Nevertheless among the chief rulers also many believed on him; but ᴿbecause of the Pharisees they did not confess *him,* lest they should be put out of the synagogue:

43 ᴿFor they loved the praise of men more than the praise of God.

Jesus and the Father

44 Jesus cried and said, ᴿHe that believeth on me, believeth not on me, but on him that sent me.

45 And ᴿhe that seeth me seeth him that sent me.

46 ᴿI am come a light into the world, that whosoever believeth on me should not abide in darkness.

47 And if any man hear my words, and believe not, ᴿI judge him not: for ᴿI came not to judge the world, but to save the world.

48 ᴿHe that rejecteth me, and receiveth not my words, hath one that judgeth him: ᴿthe word that I have spoken, the same shall judge him in the last day.

49 For ᴿI have not spoken of myself; but the Father which sent me, he gave me a commandment, ᴿwhat I should say, and what I should speak.

50 And I know that his commandment is life everlasting: whatsoever I speak therefore, even as the Father said unto me, so I speak.

CHAPTER 13

Washing the disciples' feet

NOW ᴿbefore the feast of the passover, when Jesus knew that ᴿhis hour was come that he should depart out of this world unto the Father, having loved his own which were in the world, he loved them unto the end.

2 And supper being ended, ᴿthe devil having now put into the heart of Judas Iscariot, Simon's *son,* to betray him;

3 Jesus knowing ᴿthat the Father had given all things into his hands, and that he was come from God, and went to God;

4 ᴿHe riseth from supper, and laid aside his garments; and took a towel, and girded himself.

5 After that he poureth water into a basin, and began to wash the disciples' feet, and to wipe *them* with the towel wherewith he was girded.

6 Then cometh he to Simon Peter: and ᴺPeter saith unto him, Lord, ᴿdost thou wash my feet?

7 Jesus answered and said unto him, What I do thou knowest not now; ᴿbut thou shalt know hereafter.

8 Peter saith unto him, Thou shalt never wash my feet. Jesus answered him, ᴿIf I wash thee not, thou hast no part with me.

9 Simon Peter saith unto him, Lord, not my feet only, but also *my* hands and *my* head.

10 Jesus saith to him, He that is washed needeth not save to wash *his* feet, but is clean every whit: and ᴿye are clean, but not all.

11 For ᴿhe knew who should betray him; therefore said he, Ye are not all clean.

Example of service

12 So after he had washed their feet, and had taken his garments, and was set down again, he said unto them, Know ye what I have done to you?

13 ᴿYe call me Master and Lord: and ye say well; for *so* I am.

14 ᴿIf I then, *your* Lord and Master, have washed your feet; ᴿye also ought to wash one another's feet.

15 For ᴿI have given you an example, that ye should do as I have done to you.

16 ᴿVerily, verily, I say unto you, The servant is not greater than his lord; neither he that is sent greater than he that sent him.

17 ᴿIf ye know these things, happy are ye if ye do them.

18 I speak not of you all: I know whom I have chosen: but that the scripture may be fulfilled, ᴿHe that eateth bread with me hath lifted up his heel against me.

19 ᴿNowᴺ I tell you before it come, that, when it is come to pass, ye may believe that I am *he.*

20 ᴿVerily, verily, I say unto you, He that receiveth whomsoever I send receiveth me; and he that receiveth me receiveth him that sent me.

Dismissal of the betrayer

21 ᴿWhen Jesus had thus said, ᴿhe was troubled in spirit, and testified, and said, Verily, verily, I say unto you, that ᴿone of you shall betray me.

22 Then the disciples looked one on another, doubting of whom he spake.

23 Now ᴿthere was leaning on Jesus' bosom one of his disciples, whom Jesus loved.

24 Simon Peter therefore beckoned to him, that he should ask who it should be of whom he spake.

25 He then lying on Jesus' breast saith unto him, Lord, who is it?

26 Jesus answered, He it is, to whom I shall give a ᴺsop, when I have dipped *it*. And when he had dipped the sop, he gave *it* to Judas Iscariot, *the son* of Simon.

27 ᴿAnd after the sop Satan entered into him. Then said Jesus unto him, That thou doest, do quickly.

28 Now no man at the table knew for what intent he spake this unto him.

29 For some *of them* thought, because ᴿJudas had the bag, that Jesus had said unto him, Buy *those things* that we have need of against the feast; or, that he should give something to the poor.

30 He then having received the sop went immediately out: and it was night.

The new commandment of love

31 Therefore, when he was gone out, Jesus said, ᴿNow is the Son of man glorified, and ᴿGod is glorified in him.

32 If God be glorified in him, God shall also glorify him in himself, and ᴿshall straightway glorify him.

33 Little children, yet a little while I am with you. Ye shall seek me: ᴿand as I said unto the Jews, Whither I go, ye cannot come; so now I say to you.

34 ᴿA new commandment I give unto you, That ye love one another; as I have loved you, that ye also love one another.

35 ᴿBy this shall all *men* know that ye are my disciples, if ye have love one to another.

Peter's denial predicted

36 Simon Peter said unto him, Lord, whither goest thou? Jesus answered him, Whither I go, thou canst not follow me now; but ᴿthou shalt follow me afterwards.

37 Peter said unto him, Lord, why cannot I follow thee now? I will ᴿlay down my life for thy sake.

38 Jesus answered him, Wilt thou lay down thy life for my sake? Verily, verily, I say unto thee, The cock shall not crow, till thou hast denied me thrice.

CHAPTER 14

The way, the truth, and the life

LET ᴿnot your heart be troubled: ye believe in God, believe also in me.

2 In my Father's house are many mansions: if *it were* not *so*, I would have told you. ᴿI go to prepare a place for you.

3 And if I go and prepare a place for you, ᴿI will come again, and receive you unto myself; that ᴿwhere I am, *there* ye may be also.

CHAP. 13

AD 33

26 Or, *morsel*
27 Luke 22:3
ch. 6:70
29 ch. 12:6
31 ch. 12:23
31 ch. 14:13
1 Pet. 4:11
32 ch. 12:23
33 ch. 8:21
34 Lev. 19:18
ch. 15:12, 17
Eph. 5:2
1 Thes. 4:9
Jas. 2:8
1 Pet. 1:22
1 John 2:7
& 3:11, 23
35 1 John 2:5
& 4:20
36 ch. 21:18
2 Pet. 1:14
37 Mat. 26:33
Mark 14:29
Luke 22:33

CHAP. 14

AD 33

1 ver. 27
2 ch. 13:33
3 Acts 1:11
3 ch. 12:26
& 17:24
1 Thes. 4:17

Heb. 9:8	6
ch. 8:32	6
ch. 11:25	6
ch. 10:9	6
ch. 8:19	7
ch. 12:45	9
Col. 1:15	
Heb. 1:3	
ch. 10:38	10
& 17:21, 23	
ch. 5:19 & 8:28	10
ch. 10:38	11
Mat. 21:21	12
Mark 16:17	
Luke 10:17	
Mat. 7:7 & 21:22	13
Mark 11:24	
Luke 11:9	
ch. 15:7, 16	
& 16:23, 24	
Jas. 1:5	
1 John 3:22	
& 5:14	
ver. 21, 23	15
ch. 15:10	
1 John 5:3	
ch. 15:26 & 16:7	16
Rom. 8:15	
ch. 15:26	17
& 16:13	
1 John 4:6	
1 Cor. 2:14	17
1 John 2:27	17
Mat. 28:20	18
Or, *orphans*	18
ver. 3, 28	18
ch. 16:16	18
1 Cor. 15:20	19
ch. 10:38	20
1 John 2:5 & 5:3	21
Luke 6:16	22

---

4 And whither I go ye know, and the way ye know.

5 Thomas saith unto him, Lord, we know not whither thou goest; and how can we know the way?

6 Jesus saith unto him, I am ᴿthe way, ᴿthe truth, and ᴿthe life: ᴿno man cometh unto the Father, but by me.

7 ᴿIf ye had known me, ye should have known my Father also: and from henceforth ye know him, and have seen him.

8 Philip saith unto him, Lord, shew us the Father, and it sufficeth us.

9 Jesus saith unto him, Have I been so long time with you, and yet hast thou not known me, Philip? ᴿhe that hath seen me hath seen the Father; and how sayest thou *then,* Shew us the Father?

10 Believest thou not that ᴿI am in the Father, and the Father in me? the words that I speak unto you ᴿI speak not of myself: but the Father that dwelleth in me, he doeth the works.

11 Believe me that I *am* in the Father, and the Father in me: ᴿor else believe me for the very works' sake.

12 ᴿVerily, verily, I say unto you, He that believeth on me, the works that I do shall he do also; and greater *works* than these shall he do; because I go unto my Father.

13 ᴿAnd whatsoever ye shall ask in my name, that will I do, that the Father may be glorified in the Son.

14 If ye shall ask any thing in my name, I will do *it*.

The coming of the Holy Spirit

15 ᴿIf ye love me, keep my commandments.

16 And I will pray the Father, and ᴿhe shall give you another Comforter, that he may abide with you for ever;

17 *Even* ᴿthe Spirit of truth; ᴿwhom the world cannot receive, because it seeth him not, neither knoweth him: but ye know him; for he dwelleth with you, ᴿand shall be in you.

18 ᴿI will not leave you ᴺcomfortless: ᴿI will come to you.

19 Yet a little while, and the world seeth me no more; but ᴿye see me: ᴿbecause I live, ye shall live also.

20 At that day ye shall know that ᴿI *am* in my Father, and ye in me, and I in you.

21 ᴿHe that hath my commandments, and keepeth them, he it is that loveth me: and he that loveth me shall be loved of my Father, and I will love him, and will manifest myself to him.

22 ᴿJudas saith unto him, not Iscariot, Lord,

how is it that thou wilt manifest thyself unto us, and not unto the world?

23 Jesus answered and said unto him, If a man love me, he will keep my words: and my Father will love him, ᴿand we will come unto him, and make our abode with him.

24 He that loveth me not keepeth not my sayings: and ᴿthe word which ye hear is not mine, but the Father's which sent me.

The peace of Christ

25 These things have I spoken unto you, being *yet* present with you.

26 But ᴿthe Comforter, *which is* the Holy Ghost, whom the Father will send in my name, ᴿhe shall teach you all things, and bring all things to your remembrance, whatsoever I have said unto you.

27 ᴿPeace I leave with you, my peace I give unto you: not as the world giveth, give I unto you. Let not your heart be troubled, neither let it be afraid.

28 Ye have heard how ᴿI said unto you, I go away, and come *again* unto you. If ye loved me, ye would rejoice, because I said, ᴿI go unto the Father: for ᴿmy Father is greater than I.

29 And ᴿnow I have told you before it come to pass, that, when it is come to pass, ye might believe.

30 Hereafter I will not talk much with you: ᴿfor the prince of this world cometh, and hath nothing in me.

31 But that the world may know that I love the Father; and ᴿas the Father gave me commandment, even so I do. Arise, let us go hence.

CHAPTER 15

The vine and the branches

I AM the true vine, and my Father is the husbandman.

2 ᴿEvery branch in me that beareth not fruit he taketh away: and every *branch* that beareth fruit, he purgeth it, that it may bring forth more fruit.

3 ᴿNow ye are clean through the word which I have spoken unto you.

4 ᴿAbide in me, and I in you. As the branch cannot bear fruit of itself, except it abide in the vine; no more can ye, except ye abide in me.

5 I am the vine, ye *are* the branches: He that abideth in me, and I in him, the same bringeth forth much ᴿfruit: for ᴺwithout me ye can do nothing.

6 If a man abide not in me, ᴿhe is cast forth

as a branch, and is withered; and men gather them, and cast *them* into the fire, and they are burned.

7 If ye abide in me, and my words abide in you, ᴿye shall ask what ye will, and it shall be done unto you.

8 ᴿHerein is my Father glorified, that ye bear much fruit; ᴿso shall ye be my disciples.

9 As the Father hath loved me, so have I loved you: continue ye in my love.

10 ᴿIf ye keep my commandments, ye shall abide in my love; even as I have kept my Father's commandments, and abide in his love.

11 These things have I spoken unto you, that my joy might remain in you, and ᴿthat your joy might be full.

"Ye are my friends"

12 ᴿThis is my commandment, That ye love one another, as I have loved you.

13 ᴿGreater love hath no man than this, that a man lay down his life for his friends.

14 ᴿYe are my friends, if ye do whatsoever I command you.

15 Henceforth I call you not servants; for the servant knoweth not what his lord doeth: but I have called you friends; ᴿfor all things that I have heard of my Father I have made known unto you.

16 ᴿYe have not chosen me, but I have chosen you, and ᴿordained you, that ye should go and bring forth fruit, and *that* your fruit should remain: that ᴿwhatsoever ye shall ask of the Father in my name, he may give it you.

17 These things I command you, that ye love one another.

Enmity of the world

18 ᴿIf the world hate you, ye know that it hated me before *it hated* you.

19 ᴿIf ye were of the world, the world would love his own: but ᴿbecause ye are not of the world, but I have chosen you out of the world, therefore the world hateth you.

20 Remember the word that I said unto you, ᴿThe servant is not greater than his lord. If they have persecuted me, they will also persecute you; ᴿif they have kept my saying, they will keep yours also.

21 But ᴿall these things will they do unto you for my name's sake, because they know not him that sent me.

22 ᴿIf I had not come and spoken unto them, they had not had sin: ᴿbut now they have no ᴺcloak for their sin.

23 ᴿHe that hateth me hateth my Father also.

24 If I had not done among them ᴿthe works

which none other man did, they had not had sin: but now have they both seen and hated both me and my Father.

25 But *this cometh to pass,* that the word might be fulfilled that is written in their law, ᴿThey hated me without a cause.

26 ᴿBut when the Comforter is come, whom I will send unto you from the Father, *even* the Spirit of truth, which proceedeth from the Father, ᴿhe shall testify of me:

27 And ᴿye also shall bear witness, because ᴿye have been with me from the beginning.

CHAPTER 16

Prediction of persecution

THESE things have I spoken unto you, that ye ᴿshould not be offended.

2 ᴿThey shall put you out of the synagogues: yea, the time cometh, ᴿthat whosoever killeth you will think that he doeth God service.

3 And ᴿthese things will they do unto you, because they have not known the Father, nor me.

4 But ᴿthese things have I told you, that when the time shall come, ye may remember that I told you of them. And these things I said not unto you at the beginning, because I was with you.

5 But now ᴿI go my way to him that sent me; and none of you asketh me, Whither goest thou?

6 But because I have said these things unto you, sorrow hath filled your heart.

The work of the Holy Spirit

7 Nevertheless I tell you the truth; It is expedient for you that I go away: for if I go not away, ᴿthe Comforter will not come unto you; but ᴿif I depart, I will send him unto you.

8 And when he is come, he will ᴺreprove the world of sin, and of righteousness, and of judgment:

9 ᴿOf sin, because they believe not on me;

10 ᴿOf righteousness, ᴿbecause I go to my Father, and ye see me no more;

11 ᴿOf judgment, because ᴿthe prince of this world is judged.

12 I have yet many things to say unto you, ᴿbut ye cannot bear them now.

13 Howbeit when he, ᴿthe Spirit of truth, is come, ᴿhe will guide you into all truth: for he shall not speak of himself; but whatsoever he shall hear, *that* shall he speak: and he will shew you things to come.

14 He shall glorify me: for he shall receive of mine, and shall shew *it* unto you.

CHAP. **15**
AD 33
25 Ps. 35:19
& 69:4
26 Luke 24:49
ch. 14:17
26 1 John 5:6
27 Luke 24:48
Acts 1:21 & 2:32
& 3:15 & 4:20, 33
& 5:32 & 10:39
& 13:31
1 Pet. 5:1
2 Pet. 1:16
27 Luke 1:2
1 John 1:1

CHAP. **16**
AD 33
1 Mat. 11:6
& 24:10 & 26:31
2 ch. 13:3
2 Acts 8:1 & 9:1
& 26:9, 10
3 ch. 15:21
Rom. 10:2
1 Cor. 2:8
1 Tim. 1:13
4 ch. 13:19
& 14:29
5 ch. 7:33
& 14:28
7 ch. 7:39 & 14:16,
26 & 15:26
7 Acts 2:33
Eph. 4:8
8 Or, *convince*
9 Acts 2:22
10 Acts 2:32
10 ch. 5:32
11 Acts 26:18
11 Luke 10:18
Eph. 2:2
Col. 2:15
Heb. 2:14
12 Mark 4:33
1 Cor. 3:2
Heb. 5:12
13 ch. 14:17
13 ch. 14:26
1 John 2:20

Mat. 11:27	15
ch. 3:35	
ch. 13:3	16
Is. 26:17	21
Luke 24:41	22
ch. 14:1, 27	
& 20:20	
Acts 2:46 & 13:52	
1 Pet. 1:8	
Mat. 7:7	23
ch. 14:13	
& 15:16	
ch. 15:11	24
Or, *parables*	25
Or, *parables*	25
ch. 14:21	27
ch. 3:13	27
ch. 13:3	28
Or, *parable*	29
ch. 21:17	30

15 ᴿAll things that the Father hath are mine: therefore said I, that he shall take of mine, and shall shew *it* unto you.

Christ speaks of his departure

16 A little while, and ye shall not see me: and again, a little while, and ye shall see me, ᴿbecause I go to the Father.

17 Then said *some* of his disciples among themselves, What is this that he saith unto us, A little while, and ye shall not see me: and again, a little while, and ye shall see me: and, Because I go to the Father?

18 They said therefore, What is this that he saith, A little while? we cannot tell what he saith.

19 Now Jesus knew that they were desirous to ask him, and said unto them, Do ye inquire among yourselves of that I said, A little while, and ye shall not see me: and again, a little while, and ye shall see me?

20 Verily, verily, I say unto you, That ye shall weep and lament, but the world shall rejoice: and ye shall be sorrowful, but your sorrow shall be turned into joy.

21 ᴿA woman when she is in travail hath sorrow, because her hour is come: but as soon as she is delivered of the child, she remembereth no more the anguish, for joy that a man is born into the world.

22 And ye now therefore have sorrow: but I will see you again, and ᴿyour heart shall rejoice, and your joy no man taketh from you.

23 And in that day ye shall ask me nothing. ᴿVerily, verily, I say unto you, Whatsoever ye shall ask the Father in my name, he will give *it* you.

24 Hitherto have ye asked nothing in my name: ask, and ye shall receive, ᴿthat your joy may be full.

25 These things have I spoken unto you in ᴺproverbs: but the time cometh, when I shall no more speak unto you in ᴺproverbs, but I shall shew you plainly of the Father.

26 At that day ye shall ask in my name: and I say not unto you, that I will pray the Father for you:

27 ᴿFor the Father himself loveth you, because ye have loved me, and ᴿhave believed that I came out from God.

28 ᴿI came forth from the Father, and am come into the world: again, I leave the world, and go to the Father.

29 His disciples said unto him, Lo, now speakest thou plainly, and speakest no ᴺproverb.

30 Now are we sure that ᴿthou knowest all things, and needest not that any man should

ask thee: by this [R]we believe that thou camest forth from God.

31 Jesus answered them, Do ye now believe?

32 [R]Behold, the hour cometh, yea, is now come, that ye shall be scattered, [R]every man to [N]his own, and shall leave me alone: and [R]yet I am not alone, because the Father is with me.

33 These things I have spoken unto you, that [R]in me ye might have peace. [R]In the world ye shall have tribulation: but be of good cheer; [R]I have overcome the world.

CHAPTER 17

Christ's intercessory prayer

THESE words spake Jesus, and lifted up his eyes to heaven, and said, Father, [R]the hour is come; glorify thy Son, that thy Son also may glorify thee:

2 [R]As thou hast given him power over all flesh, that he should give eternal life to as many [R]as thou hast given him.

3 And [R]this is life eternal, that they might know thee [R]the only true God, and Jesus Christ, [R]whom thou hast sent.

4 [R]I have glorified thee on the earth: [R]I have finished the work [R]which thou gavest me to do.

5 And now, O Father, glorify thou me with thine own self with the glory [R]which I had with thee before the world was.

Prayer for his disciples

6 [R]I have manifested thy name unto the men [R]which thou gavest me out of the world: thine they were, and thou gavest them me; and they have kept thy word.

7 Now they have known that all things whatsoever thou hast given me are of thee.

8 For I have given unto them the words [R]which thou gavest me; and they have received them, [R]and have known surely that I came out from thee, and they have believed that thou didst send me.

9 I pray for them: [R]I pray not for the world, but for them which thou hast given me; for they are thine.

10 And all mine are thine, and [R]thine are mine; and I am glorified in them.

11 [R]And now I am no more in the world, but these are in the world, and I come to thee. Holy Father, [R]keep through thine own name those whom thou hast given me, that they may be one, [R]as we are.

12 While I was with them in the world, [R]I kept them in thy name: those that thou gavest me I have kept, and [R]none of them is lost,

[R]but the son of perdition; [R]that the scripture might be fulfilled.

13 And now come I to thee; and these things I speak in the world, that they might have my joy fulfilled in themselves.

14 I have given them thy word; [R]and the world hath hated them, because they are not of the world, [R]even as I am not of the world.

15 I pray not that thou shouldest take them out of the world, but [R]that thou shouldest keep them from the evil.

16 They are not of the world, even as I am not of the world.

17 [R]Sanctify them through thy truth: [R]thy word is truth.

18 [R]As thou hast sent me into the world, even so have I also sent them into the world.

19 And [R]for their sakes I sanctify myself, that they also might be [N]sanctified through the truth.

20 Neither pray I for these alone, but for them also which shall believe on me through their word;

21 [R]That they all may be one; as [R]thou, Father, art in me, and I in thee, that they also may be one in us: that the world may believe that thou hast sent me.

22 And the glory which thou gavest me I have given them; [R]that they may be one, even as we are one:

23 I in them, and thou in me, [R]that they may be made perfect in one; and that the world may know that thou hast sent me, and hast loved them, as thou hast loved me.

24 [R]Father, I will that they also, whom thou hast given me, be with me where I am; that they may behold my glory, which thou hast given me: [R]for thou lovedst me before the foundation of the world.

25 O righteous Father, [R]the world hath not known thee: but [R]I have known thee, and [R]these have known that thou hast sent me.

26 [R]And I have declared unto them thy name, and will declare it: that the love [R]wherewith thou hast loved me may be in them, and I in them.

CHAPTER 18

The betrayal of Jesus

WHEN Jesus had spoken these words, [R]he went forth with his disciples over [R]the brook Çē'-drŏn, where was a garden, into the which he entered, and his disciples.

2 And Judas also, which betrayed him, knew the place: [R]for Jesus ofttimes resorted thither with his disciples.

3 [R]Judas then, having received a band of

men and officers from the chief priests and Pharisees, cometh thither with lanterns and torches and weapons.

4 Jesus therefore, knowing all things that should come upon him, went forth, and said unto them, Whom seek ye?

5 They answered him, Jesus of Nazareth. Jesus saith unto them, I am *he*. And Judas also, which betrayed him, stood with them.

6 As soon then as he had said unto them, I am *he,* they went backward, and fell to the ground.

7 Then asked he them again, Whom seek ye? And they said, Jesus of Nazareth.

8 Jesus answered, I have told you that I am *he*: if therefore ye seek me, let these go their way:

9 That the saying might be fulfilled, which he spake, R Of them which thou gavest me have I lost none.

10 R Then Simon Peter having a sword drew it, and smote the high priest's servant, and cut off his right ear. The servant's name was Măl'-chŭs.

11 Then said Jesus unto Peter, Put up thy sword into the sheath: R the cup which my Father hath given me, shall I not drink it?

Peter's first denial

12 Then the band and the captain and officers of the Jews took Jesus, and bound him,

13 And R led him away to R Annas first; for he was father in law to Căi'-ă-phăs, which was the high priest that same year. N

14 R Now Căi'-ă-phăs was he, which gave counsel to the Jews, that it was expedient that one man should die for the people.

15 R And Simon Peter followed Jesus, and *so did* another disciple: that disciple was known unto the high priest, and went in with Jesus into the palace of the high priest.

16 R But Peter stood at the door without. Then went out that other disciple, which was known unto the high priest, and spake unto her that kept the door, and brought in Peter.

17 Then saith the damsel that kept the door unto Peter, Art not thou also *one* of this man's disciples? He saith, I am not.

18 And the servants and officers stood there, who had made a fire of coals; for it was cold: and they warmed themselves: and Peter stood with them, and warmed himself.

Jesus' trial before the high priest

19 The high priest then asked Jesus of his disciples, and of his doctrine.

20 Jesus answered him, R I spake openly to

the world; I ever taught in the synagogue, and in the temple, whither the Jews always resort; and in secret have I said nothing.

21 Why askest thou me? ask them which heard me, what I have said unto them: behold, they know what I said.

22 And when he had thus spoken, one of the officers which stood by R struck Jesus N with the palm of his hand, saying, Answerest thou the high priest so?

23 Jesus answered him, If I have spoken evil, bear witness of the evil: but if well, why smitest thou me?

24 R Now Annas had sent him bound unto Căi'-ă-phăs the high priest.

Peter's second and third denial

25 And Simon Peter stood and warmed himself. R They said therefore unto him, Art not thou also *one* of his disciples? He denied *it,* and said, I am not.

26 One of the servants of the high priest, being *his* kinsman whose ear Peter cut off, saith, Did not I see thee in the garden with him?

27 Peter then denied again: and R immediately the cock crew.

Jesus' trial before Pilate

28 R Then led they Jesus from Căi'-ă-phăs unto N the hall of judgment: and it was early; R and they themselves went not into the judgment hall, lest they should be defiled; but that they might eat the passover.

29 Pilate then went out unto them, and said, What accusation bring ye against this man?

30 They answered and said unto him, If he were not a malefactor, we would not have delivered him up unto thee.

31 Then said Pilate unto them, Take ye him, and judge him according to your law. The Jews therefore said unto him, It is not lawful for us to put any man to death:

32 R That the saying of Jesus might be fulfilled, which he spake, signifying what death he should die.

33 R Then Pilate entered into the judgment hall again, and called Jesus, and said unto him, Art thou the King of the Jews?

34 Jesus answered him, Sayest thou this thing of thyself, or did others tell it thee of me?

35 Pilate answered, Am I a Jew? Thine own nation and the chief priests have delivered thee unto me: what hast thou done?

36 R Jesus answered, R My kingdom is not of this world: if my kingdom were of this world, then would my servants fight, that I should not

be delivered to the Jews: but now is my kingdom not from hence.

37 Pilate therefore said unto him, Art thou a king then? Jesus answered, Thou sayest that I am a King. To this end was I born, and for this cause came I into the world, that I should bear witness unto the truth. Every one that ^Ris of the truth heareth my voice.

38 Pilate saith unto him, What is truth? And when he had said this, he went out again unto the Jews, and saith unto them, ^RI find in him no fault *at all*.

39 ^RBut ye have a custom, that I should release unto you one at the passover: will ye therefore that I release unto you the King of the Jews?

40 ^RThen cried they all again, saying, Not this man, but Băr-ăb'-băs. ^RNow Băr-ăb'-băs was a robber.

CHAPTER 19

Jesus scourged and mocked

THEN ^RPilate therefore took Jesus, and scourged *him*.

2 And the soldiers plaited a crown of thorns, and put *it* on his head, and they put on him a purple robe,

3 And said, Hail, King of the Jews! and they smote him with their hands.

4 Pilate therefore went forth again, and saith unto them, Behold, I bring him forth to you, ^Rthat ye may know that I find no fault in him.

5 Then came Jesus forth, wearing the crown of thorns, and the purple robe. And *Pilate* saith unto them, Behold the man!

6 ^RWhen the chief priests therefore and officers saw him, they cried out, saying, Crucify *him,* crucify *him.* Pilate saith unto them, Take ye him, and crucify *him:* for I find no fault in him.

7 The Jews answered him, ^RWe have a law, and by our law he ought to die, because ^Rhe made himself the Son of God.

Pilate's further inquiry of Jesus

8 When Pilate therefore heard that saying, he was the more afraid;

9 And went again into the judgment hall, and saith unto Jesus, Whence art thou? ^RBut Jesus gave him no answer.

10 Then saith Pilate unto him, Speakest thou not unto me? knowest thou not that I have power to crucify thee, and have power to release thee?

11 Jesus answered, ^RThou couldest have no power *at all* against me, except it were

given thee from above: therefore he that delivered me unto thee hath the greater sin.

Pilate appeases the crowd

12 And from thenceforth Pilate sought to release him: but the Jews cried out, saying, ^RIf thou let this man go, thou art not Cæsar's friend: ^Rwhosoever maketh himself a king speaketh against Cæsar.

13 When Pilate therefore heard that saying, he brought Jesus forth, and sat down in the judgment seat in a place that is called the Pavement, but in the Hebrew, Găb'-bă-thă.

14 And ^Rit was the preparation of the passover, and about the sixth hour: and he saith unto the Jews, Behold your King!

15 But they cried out, Away with *him,* away with *him,* crucify him. Pilate saith unto them, Shall I crucify your King? The chief priests answered, ^RWe have no king but Cæsar.

16 ^RThen delivered he him therefore unto them to be crucified. And they took Jesus, and led *him* away.

The crucifixion

17 ^RAnd he bearing his cross ^Rwent forth into a place called *the place* of a skull, which is called in the Hebrew Gŏl'-gŏ-thă:

18 Where they crucified him, and two other with him, on either side one, and Jesus in the midst.

19 ^RAnd Pilate wrote a title, and put *it* on the cross. And the writing was, JESUS OF NAZARETH THE KING OF THE JEWS.

20 This title then read many of the Jews: for the place where Jesus was crucified was nigh to the city: and it was written in Hebrew, *and* Greek, *and* Latin.

21 Then said the chief priests of the Jews to Pilate, Write not, The King of the Jews; but that he said, I am King of the Jews.

22 Pilate answered, What I have written I have written.

23 ^RThen the soldiers, when they had crucified Jesus, took his garments, and made four parts, to every soldier a part; and also *his* coat: now the coat was without seam, ^Nwoven from the top throughout.

24 They said therefore among themselves, Let us not rend it, but cast lots for it, whose it shall be: that the scripture might be fulfilled, which saith, ^RThey parted my raiment among them, and for my vesture they did cast lots. These things therefore the soldiers did.

25 ^RNow there stood by the cross of Jesus his mother, and his mother's sister, Mary the *wife* of ^RClē'-ŏ-phăs,^N and Mary Măg'-dă-lēne.

CHAP. **18**

AD 33
37 ch. 8:47
1 John 3:19 & 4:6
38 Mat. 27:24
Luke 23:4
ch. 19:4, 6
39 Mat. 27:15
Mark 15:6
Luke 23:17
40 Acts 3:14
40 Luke 23:19

CHAP. **19**

AD 33
1 Mat. 20:19
& 27:26
Mark 15:15
Luke 18:33
4 ver. 6
ch. 18:33
6 Acts 3:13
7 Mat. 26:65
ch. 5:18 & 10:33
9 Is. 53:7
Mat. 27:12, 14
11 Luke 22:53
ch. 7:30

Luke 23:2   **12**
Acts 17:7
Mat. 27:62   **14**
Gen. 49:10   **15**
Mat. 27:26, 31   **16**
Mark 15:15
Luke 23:24
Mat. 27:31, 33   **17**
Mark 15:21, 22
Luke 23:26, 33
Num. 15:36   **17**
Heb. 13:12
Mat. 27:37   **19**
Mark 15:26
Luke 23:38
Mat. 27:35   **23**
Mark 15:24
Luke 23:34
Or, *wrought*   **23**
Ps. 22:18   **24**
Mat. 27:55   **25**
Mark 15:40
Luke 23:49
Luke 24:18   **25**
Or, *Clopas*   **25**

26 When Jesus therefore saw his mother, and ᴿthe disciple standing by, whom he loved, he saith unto his mother, ᴿWoman, behold thy son!

27 Then saith he to the disciple, Behold thy mother! And from that hour that disciple took her ᴿunto his own *home.*

The death of Jesus

28 After this, Jesus knowing that all things were now accomplished, ᴿthat the scripture might be fulfilled, saith, I thirst.

29 Now there was set a vessel full of vinegar: and ᴿthey filled a sponge with vinegar, and put *it* upon hyssop, and put *it* to his mouth.

30 When Jesus therefore had received the vinegar, he said, ᴿIt is finished: and he bowed his head, and gave up the ghost.

31 The Jews therefore, ᴿbecause it was the preparation, ᴿthat the bodies should not remain upon the cross on the sabbath day, (for that sabbath day was an high day,) besought Pilate that their legs might be broken, and *that* they might be taken away.

32 Then came the soldiers, and brake the legs of the first, and of the other which was crucified with him.

33 But when they came to Jesus, and saw that he was dead already, they brake not his legs:

34 But one of the soldiers with a spear pierced his side, and forthwith ᴿcame there out blood and water.

35 And he that saw *it* bare record, and his record is true: and he knoweth that he saith true, that ye might believe.

36 For these things were done, ᴿthat the scripture should be fulfilled, A bone of him shall not be broken.

37 And again another scripture saith, ᴿThey shall look on him whom they pierced.

Jesus' burial in Joseph's tomb

38 ᴿAnd after this Joseph of Ăr-ĭm-ă-thæ'-ă, being a disciple of Jesus, but secretly ᴿfor fear of the Jews, besought Pilate that he might take away the body of Jesus: and Pilate gave *him* leave. He came therefore, and took the body of Jesus.

39 And there came also ᴿNĭc-ŏ-dē'-mŭs, which at the first came to Jesus by night, and brought a mixture of myrrh and aloes, about an hundred pound *weight.*

40 Then took they the body of Jesus, and ᴿwound it in linen clothes with the spices, as the manner of the Jews is to bury.

41 Now in the place where he was crucified there was a garden; and in the garden a new sepulchre, wherein was never man yet laid.

42 ᴿThere laid they Jesus therefore ᴿbecause of the Jews' preparation *day;* for the sepulchre was nigh at hand.

CHAPTER 20

The resurrection

THE ᴿfirst *day* of the week cometh Mary Măg'-dă-lēne early, when it was yet dark, unto the sepulchre, and seeth the stone taken away from the sepulchre.

2 Then she runneth, and cometh to Simon Peter, and to the ᴿother disciple, whom Jesus loved, and saith unto them, They have taken away the Lord out of the sepulchre, and we know not where they have laid him.

3 ᴿPeter therefore went forth, and that other disciple, and came to the sepulchre.

4 So they ran both together: and the other disciple did outrun Peter, and came first to the sepulchre.

5 And he stooping down, *and looking in,* saw ᴿthe linen clothes lying; yet went he not in.

6 Then cometh Simon Peter following him, and went into the sepulchre, and seeth the linen clothes lie,

7 And ᴿthe napkin, that was about his head, not lying with the linen clothes, but wrapped together in a place by itself.

8 Then went in also that other disciple, which came first to the sepulchre, and he saw, and believed.

9 For as yet they knew not the ᴿscripture, that he must rise again from the dead.

10 Then the disciples went away again unto their own home.

Jesus' appearance to Mary Magdalene

11 ᴿBut Mary stood without at the sepulchre weeping: and as she wept, she stooped down, *and looked* into the sepulchre,

12 And seeth two angels in white sitting, the one at the head, and the other at the feet, where the body of Jesus had lain.

13 And they say unto her, Woman, why weepest thou? She saith unto them, Because they have taken away my Lord, and I know not where they have laid him.

14 ᴿAnd when she had thus said, she turned herself back, and saw Jesus standing, and ᴿknew not that it was Jesus.

15 Jesus saith unto her, Woman, why weepest thou? whom seekest thou? She, supposing him to be the gardener, saith unto him, Sir, if

CHAP. 19
AD 33
26 ch. 13:23
& 20:2
& 21:7, 20, 24
26 ch. 2:4
27 ch. 1:11
& 16:32
28 Ps. 69:21
29 Mat. 27:48
30 ch. 17:4
31 ver. 42
Mark 15:42
31 Deut. 21:23
34 1 John 5:6, 8
36 Ex. 12:46
Num. 9:12
Ps. 34:20
37 Ps. 22:16, 17
Zech. 12:10
Rev. 1:7
38 Mat. 27:57
Mark 15:42
Luke 23:50
38 ch. 9:22
& 12:42
39 ch. 3:1, 2
& 7:50
40 Acts 5:6

Is. 53:9   42
ver. 31   42

CHAP. 20
AD 33
Mat. 28:1   1
Mark 16:1
Luke 24:1
ch. 13:23   2
& 19:26
& 21:7, 20, 24
Luke 24:12   3
ch. 19:40   5
ch. 11:44   7
Ps. 16:10   9
Acts 2:25, 31
& 13:34, 35
Mark 16:5   11
Mat. 28:9   14
Mark 16:9
Luke 24:16, 31   14
ch. 21:4

thou have borne him hence, tell me where thou hast laid him, and I will take him away.

16 Jesus saith unto her, Mary. She turned herself, and saith unto him, Răb-bō'-nī; which is to say, Master.

17 Jesus saith unto her, Touch me not; for I am not yet ascended to my Father: but go to ᴿmy brethren, and say unto them, ᴿI ascend unto my Father, and your Father; and to ᴿmy God, and your God.

18 ᴿMary Măg'-dȧ-lēne came and told the disciples that she had seen the Lord, and *that* he had spoken these things unto her.

First appearance to the disciples

19 ᴿThen the same day at evening, being the first *day* of the week, when the doors were shut where the disciples were assembled for fear of the Jews, came Jesus and stood in the midst, and saith unto them, Peace *be* unto you.

20 And when he had so said, he shewed unto them *his* hands and his side. ᴿThen were the disciples glad, when they saw the Lord.

21 Then said Jesus to them again, Peace *be* unto you: ᴿas *my* Father hath sent me, even so send I you.

22 And when he had said this, he breathed on *them,* and saith unto them, Receive ye the Holy Ghost:

23 ᴿWhose soever sins ye remit, they are remitted unto them; *and* whose soever *sins* ye retain, they are retained.

24 But Thomas, one of the twelve, ᴿcalled Dĭd'-ў-mŭs, was not with them when Jesus came.

25 The other disciples therefore said unto him, We have seen the Lord. But he said unto them, Except I shall see in his hands the print of the nails, and put my finger into the print of the nails, and thrust my hand into his side, I will not believe.

Second appearance to the disciples

26 And after eight days again his disciples were within, and Thomas with them: *then* came Jesus, the doors being shut, and stood in the midst, and said, Peace *be* unto you.

27 Then saith he to Thomas, Reach hither thy finger, and behold my hands; and ᴿreach hither thy hand, and thrust *it* into my side: and be not faithless, but believing.

28 And Thomas answered and said unto him, My Lord and my God.

29 Jesus saith unto him, Thomas, because thou hast seen me, thou hast believed: ᴿblessed *are* they that have not seen, and *yet* have believed.

CHAP. 20	
AD 33	
17 Ps. 22:22	
Mat. 28:10	
Rom. 8:29	
Heb. 2:11	
17 ch. 16:28	
17 Eph. 1:17	
18 Mat. 28:10	
Luke 24:10	
19 Mark 16:14	
Luke 24:36	
1 Cor. 15:5	
20 ch. 16:22	
21 Mat. 28:18	
ch. 17:18, 19	
2 Tim. 2:2	
Heb. 3:1	
23 Mat. 16:10	
& 18:18	
24 ch. 11:16	
27 1 John 1:1	
29 2 Cor. 5:7	
1 Pet. 1:8	

ch. 21:25	30
Luke 1:4	31
ch. 3:15, 16	31
& 5:24	
1 Pet. 1:8, 9	

CHAP. 21	
AD 33	
ch. 1:45	2
Mat. 4:21	2
ch. 20:14	4
Luke 24:41	5
Or, *Sirs*	5
Luke 5:4, 6, 7	6
ch. 13:23	7
& 20:2	
Acts 10:41	12

Purpose of this gospel account

30 ᴿAnd many other signs truly did Jesus in the presence of his disciples, which are not written in this book:

31 ᴿBut these are written, that ye might believe that Jesus is the Christ, the Son of God; ᴿand that believing ye might have life through his name.

CHAPTER 21

Appearance to disciples in Galilee

AFTER these things Jesus shewed himself again to the disciples at the sea of Tī-bē'-rĭ-ăs; and on this wise shewed he *himself.*

2 There were together Simon Peter, and Thomas called Dĭd'-ў-mŭs, and ᴿNȧ-thăn'-ȧ-ĕl of Cana in Galilee, and ᴿthe *sons* of Zĕb'-ĕ-dêe, and two other of his disciples.

3 Simon Peter saith unto them, I go a fishing. They say unto him, We also go with thee. They went forth, and entered into a ship immediately; and that night they caught nothing.

4 But when the morning was now come, Jesus stood on the shore: but the disciples ᴿknew not that it was Jesus.

5 Then ᴿJesus saith unto them, ᴺChildren, have ye any meat? They answered him, No.

6 And he said unto them, ᴿCast the net on the right side of the ship, and ye shall find. They cast therefore, and now they were not able to draw it for the multitude of fishes.

7 Therefore ᴿthat disciple whom Jesus loved saith unto Peter, It is the Lord. Now when Simon Peter heard that it was the Lord, he girt *his* fisher's coat *unto him,* (for he was naked,) and did cast himself into the sea.

8 And the other disciples came in a little ship; (for they were not far from land, but as it were two hundred cubits,) dragging the net with fishes.

9 As soon then as they were come to land, they saw a fire of coals there, and fish laid thereon, and bread.

10 Jesus saith unto them, Bring of the fish which ye have now caught.

11 Simon Peter went up, and drew the net to land full of great fishes, an hundred and fifty and three: and for all there were so many, yet was not the net broken.

12 Jesus saith unto them, ᴿCome *and* dine. And none of the disciples durst ask him, Who art thou? knowing that it was the Lord.

13 Jesus then cometh, and taketh bread, and giveth them, and fish likewise.

14 This is now Rthe third time that Jesus shewed himself to his disciples, after that he was risen from the dead.

Jesus' charge to Peter

15 So when they had dined, Jesus saith to Simon Peter, Simon, *son* of Jonas, lovest thou me more than these? He saith unto him, Yea, Lord; thou knowest that I love thee. He saith unto him, Feed my lambs.

16 He saith to him again the second time, Simon, *son* of Jonas, lovest thou me? He saith unto him, Yea, Lord; thou knowest that I love thee. RHe saith unto him, Feed my sheep.

17 He saith unto him the third time, Simon, *son* of Jonas, lovest thou me? Peter was grieved because he said unto him the third time, Lovest thou me? And he said unto him, Lord, Rthou knowest all things; thou knowest that I love thee. Jesus saith unto him, Feed my sheep.

18 RVerily, verily, I say unto thee, When thou wast young, thou girdedst thyself, and walkedst whither thou wouldest: but when thou shalt be old, thou shalt stretch forth thy hands, and another shall gird thee, and carry *thee* whither thou wouldest not.

19 This spake he, signifying Rby what death he should glorify God. And when he had spoken this, he saith unto him, Follow me.

Author of this gospel account

20 Then Peter, turning about, seeth the disciple Rwhom Jesus loved following; which also leaned on his breast at supper, and said, Lord, which is he that betrayeth thee?

21 Peter seeing him saith to Jesus, Lord, and what *shall* this man *do?*

22 Jesus saith unto him, If I will that he tarry Rtill I come, what *is that* to thee? follow thou me.

23 Then went this saying abroad among the brethren, that that disciple should not die: yet Jesus said not unto him, He shall not die; but, If I will that he tarry till I come, what *is that* to thee?

24 This is the disciple which testifieth of these things, and wrote these things: and Rwe know that his testimony is true.

25 RAnd there are also many other things which Jesus did, the which, if they should be written every one, RI suppose that even the world itself could not contain the books that should be written. Ä'-měn.

CHAP. 21
AD 33
14 See ch. 20:19, 26
16 Acts 20:28 Heb. 13:20 1 Pet. 2:25 & 5:2, 4
17 ch. 2:24, 25 & 16:30
18 ch. 13:36 Acts 12:3, 4
2 Pet. 1:14 **19**
ch. 13:23, 25 **20** & 20:2
Mat. 16:27, 28 **22** & 25:31 1 Cor. 4:5 & 11:26 Rev. 2:25 & 3:11 & 22:7, 20
ch. 19:35 **24** 3 John 12
ch. 20:30 **25** Amos 7:10 **25**

THE
ACTS OF THE APOSTLES

The Book of Acts is a sequel to the third Gospel, furnishing the historical link between the life of Jesus and the proclamation of the apostles. Its introduction (1:1–2) indicates that its purpose is to record the continued activity of the ascended Christ, working through the Holy Spirit in the lives of the apostles. Both missionary and teaching motives lie behind its selection of events that illustrate the expansion, power, trials and triumphs of the Gospel. Christianity is presented as the spiritual successor of Old Testament faith, a politically harmless movement constituting no threat to the social order. The emphasis on Christian unity reveals a conciliatory concern in the face of mounting divisions (cf., I Cor. 1:11–13; 3:3–10). The Book of Acts was probably written before 70 A.D., for it recognizes the status of Jews before the Roman courts and assumes the fairness of Roman justice; such attitudes would hardly have been appropriate after Nero's persecution of Christians and Rome's destruction of Jerusalem. The author, who also wrote the third Gospel, had been an eyewitness of many events in Paul's missionary travels (cf., the "we" sections: 16:10–17; 20:5–15; 21:1–18; 27:1–28:16), and is unanimously identified in early tradition as Luke.

OUTLINE OF THE BOOK:
  I. Prologue   1:1–5
 II. The Church in Palestine   1:6–12:25
III. The First Missionary Journey   13:1–15:35
 IV. The Second Missionary Journey   15:36–18:22
  V. The Third Missionary Journey   18:23–21:9
 VI. Arrest, Defenses, and Imprisonment   21:10–28:31

CHAPTER 1

Preface

THE former treatise have I made, O RThē-ŏph'-ĭ-lŭs, of all that Jesus began both to do and teach,

2 RUntil the day in which he was taken up, after that he through the Holy Ghost Rhad

CHAP. 1
AD 33
1 Luke 1:3
2 Mark 16:19 1 Tim. 3:16 Mat. 28:19 John 20:21
Mark 16:14 **3**
Luke 24:43 **4**
Or, *eating together with them* **4**

given commandments unto the apostles whom he had chosen:

3 RTo whom also he shewed himself alive after his passion by many infallible proofs, being seen of them forty days, and speaking of the things pertaining to the kingdom of God:

4 RAnd, Nbeing assembled together with *them*, commanded them that they should not

depart from Jerusalem, but wait for the promise of the Father, [R]which, *saith he,* ye have heard of me.

5 [R]For John truly baptized with water; [R]but ye shall be baptized with the Holy Ghost not many days hence.

The ascension

6 When they therefore were come together, they asked of him, saying, [R]Lord, wilt thou at this time [R]restore again the kingdom to Israel?

7 And he said unto them, [R]It is not for you to know the times or the seasons, which the Father hath put in his own power.

8 [R]But ye shall receive [N]power, [R]after that the Holy Ghost is come upon you: and [R]ye shall be witnesses unto me both in Jerusalem, and in all Judæa, and in Să-mâr'-ĭ-ă, and unto the uttermost part of the earth.

9 [R]And when he had spoken these things, while they beheld, [R]he was taken up; and a cloud received him out of their sight.

10 And while they looked stedfastly toward heaven as he went up, behold, two men stood by them [R]in white apparel;

11 Which also said, [R]Ye men of Galilee, why stand ye gazing up into heaven? this same Jesus, which is taken up from you into heaven, [R]shall so come in like manner as ye have seen him go into heaven.

The disciples wait in Jerusalem

12 [R]Then returned they unto Jerusalem from the mount called Olivet, which is from Jerusalem a sabbath day's journey.

13 And when they were come in, they went up [R]into an upper room, where abode both [R]Peter, and James, and John, and Andrew, Philip, and Thomas, Bartholomew, and Matthew, James *the son* of Ăl-phæ'-ŭs, and [R]Simon Zē-lō'-tēṡ, and [R]Judas *the brother* of James.

14 [R]These all continued with one accord in prayer and supplication, with [R]the women, and Mary the mother of Jesus, and with [R]his brethren.

Selecting Matthias

15 And in those days Peter stood up in the midst of the disciples, and said, (the number [R]of names together were about an hundred and twenty,)

16 Men *and* brethren, this scripture must needs have been fulfilled, [R]which the Holy Ghost by the mouth of David spake before concerning Judas, [R]which was guide to them that took Jesus.

CHAP. 1

AD 33

4 Luke 24:49
John 14:16
5 Mat. 3:11
5 Joel 3:18
6 Mat. 24:3
6 Is 1:26
7 1 Thes. 5:1
8 ch. 2:1, 4
8 Or, *the power of the Holy Ghost coming upon you*
8 Luke 24:49
8 Luke 24:48
9 Luke 24:51
9 ver. 2
10 Mat. 28:3
Mark 16:5
Luke 24:4
John 20:12
ch. 10:3, 30
11 ch. 2:7 & 13:31
11 Dan. 7:13
Mat. 24:30
Mark 13:26
Luke 21:27
John 14:3
2 Thes. 1:10
Rev. 1:7
12 Luke 24:52
13 ch. 9:37, 39 & 20:8
13 Mat. 10:2-4
13 Luke 6:15
13 Jude 1
14 ch. 2:1, 46
14 Luke 23:49, 55
14 Mat. 13:55
15 Rev. 3:4
16 Ps. 41:9
John 13:18
16 Luke 22:47
John 18:3

Mat. 10:4   17
Luke 6:16
ver. 25   17
ch. 12:25
& 20:24 & 21:19
Mat. 27:5, 7, 8 18
Mat. 26:15   18
2 Pet. 2:15
Ps. 69:25   20
Ps. 109:8   20
Or, *office,* or, *charge*   20
ver. 9   22
ver. 8   22
John 15:27
ch. 4:33
ch. 15:22   23
1 Sam. 16:7   24
1 Chr. 28:9
Jer. 11:20 & 17:10
ch. 15:8
Rev. 2:23
ver. 17   25

CHAP. 2

AD 33

Lev. 23:15   1
Deut. 16:9
ch. 20:16
ch. 1:14   1
ch. 4:31   2
ch. 1:5   4
Mark 16:17   4
ch. 10:46 & 19:6
1 Cor. 12:10, 28, 30 & 13:1
Gr. *when this voice was made*   6
Or, *troubled in mind*   6

17 For [R]he was numbered with us, and had obtained part of [R]this ministry.

18 [R]Now this man purchased a field with [R]the reward of iniquity; and falling headlong, he burst asunder in the midst, and all his bowels gushed out.

19 And it was known unto all the dwellers at Jerusalem; insomuch as that field is called in their proper tongue, Ă-çĕl'-dă-mă, that is to say, The field of blood.

20 For it is written in the book of Psalms, [R]Let his habitation be desolate, and let no man dwell therein: and [R]his [N]bishoprick let another take.

21 Wherefore of these men which have companied with us all the time that the Lord Jesus went in and out among us,

22 Beginning from the baptism of John, unto that same day that [R]he was taken up from us, must one be ordained [R]to be a witness with us of his resurrection.

23 And they appointed two, Joseph called [R]Bär'-să-băs, who was surnamed Justus, and Mătth-ī'-ăs.

24 And they prayed, and said, Thou, Lord, [R]which knowest the hearts of all *men,* shew whether of these two thou hast chosen,

25 [R]That he may take part of this ministry and apostleship, from which Judas by transgression fell, that he might go to his own place.

26 And they gave forth their lots; and the lot fell upon Mătth-ī'-ăs; and he was numbered with the eleven apostles.

CHAPTER 2

The day of Pentecost

AND when [R]the day of Pentecost was fully come, [R]they were all with one accord in one place.

2 And suddenly there came a sound from heaven as of a rushing mighty wind, and [R]it filled all the house where they were sitting.

3 And there appeared unto them cloven tongues like as of fire, and it sat upon each of them.

4 And [R]they were all filled with the Holy Ghost, and began [R]to speak with other tongues, as the Spirit gave them utterance.

5 And there were dwelling at Jerusalem Jews, devout men, out of every nation under heaven.

6 Now [N]when this was noised abroad, the multitude came together, and were [N]confounded, because that every man heard them speak in his own language.

7 And they were all amazed and marvelled,

saying one to another, Behold, are not all these which speak ᴿGalilæans?

8 And how hear we every man in our own tongue, wherein we were born?

9 Pär′-thĭ-ăns, and Mēdes̀, and Ē′-lăm-ītes, and the dwellers in Mĕs-ŏ-pŏ-tā′-mĭ-ă, and in Judæa, and Căp-pă-dō′-çĭ-ă, in Pontus, and Asia,

10 Phrŷġ′-ĭ-ă, and Păm-phȳl′-ĭ-ă, in Egypt, and in the parts of Lĭb′-ȳ-ă about Çȳ-rē′-nē, and strangers of Rome, Jews and proselytes,

11 Cretes and Arabians, we do hear them speak in our tongues the wonderful works of God.

12 And they were all amazed, and were in doubt, saying one to another, What meaneth this?

13 Others mocking said, These men are full of new wine.

Peter's first sermon

14 But Peter, standing up with the eleven, lifted up his voice, and said unto them, Ye men of Judæa, and all *ye* that dwell at Jerusalem, be this known unto you, and hearken to my words:

15 For these are not drunken, as ye suppose, ᴿseeing it is *but* the third hour of the day.

16 But this is that which was spoken by the prophet Jō′-ĕl;

17 ᴿAnd it shall come to pass in the last days, saith God, ᴿI will pour out of my Spirit upon all flesh: and your sons and ᴿyour daughters shall prophesy, and your young men shall see visions, and your old men shall dream dreams:

18 And on my servants and on my handmaidens I will pour out in those days of my Spirit; ᴿand they shall prophesy:

19 ᴿAnd I will shew wonders in heaven above, and signs in the earth beneath; blood, and fire, and vapour of smoke:

20 ᴿThe sun shall be turned into darkness, and the moon into blood, before that great and notable day of the Lord come:

21 And it shall come to pass, *that* ᴿwhosoever shall call on the name of the Lord shall be saved.

22 Ye men of Israel, hear these words; Jesus of Nazareth, a man approved of God among you ᴿby miracles and wonders and signs, which God did by him in the midst of you, as ye yourselves also know:

23 Him, ᴿbeing delivered by the determinate counsel and foreknowledge of God, ᴿye have taken, and by wicked hands have crucified and slain:

24 ᴿWhom God hath raised up, having

CHAP. **2**
AD 33
7 ch. 1:11
15 1 Thes. 5:7
17 Is. 44:3
Ezek. 11:19
Joel 2:28
Zech. 12:10
John 7:38
17 ch. 10:45
17 ch. 21:9
18 ch. 21:4, 9
1 Cor. 12:10
& 14:1, etc.
19 Joel 2:30
20 Mat. 24:29
Mark 13:24
Luke 21:25
21 Rom. 10:13
22 John 3:2
& 14:10, 11
ch. 10:38
Heb. 2:4
23 Mat. 26:24
Luke 22:22
ch. 3:18
23 ch. 5:30
24 Rom. 8:11
1 Cor. 6:14
2 Cor. 4:14
Eph. 1:20
Col. 2:12
1 Thes. 1:10
Heb. 13:20

Ps. 16:8	25
Or, *I may*	29
ch. 13:36	29
2 Sam. 7:12	30
Ps. 132:11	
Luke 1:32	
Rom. 1:3	
2 Tim. 2:8	
Ps. 16:10	31
ver. 24	32
ch. 1:8	32
Phil. 2:9	33
Heb. 10:12	
John 14:26	33
& 16:7, 13	
ch. 10:45	33
Eph. 4:8	
Ps. 110:1	34
Mat. 22:44	
1 Cor. 15:25	
Eph. 1:20	
Heb. 1:13	
Zech. 12:10	37
Luke 3:10	
ch. 9:6	
Luke 24:27	38
ch. 3:19	
Joel 2:28	39
ch. 3:25	
ch. 11:15, 18	39
Eph. 2:13	

loosed the pains of death: because it was not possible that he should be holden of it.

25 For David speaketh concerning him, ᴿI foresaw the Lord always before my face, for he is on my right hand, that I should not be moved:

26 Therefore did my heart rejoice, and my tongue was glad; moreover also my flesh shall rest in hope:

27 Because thou wilt not leave my soul in hell, neither wilt thou suffer thine Holy One to see corruption.

28 Thou hast made known to me the ways of life; thou shalt make me full of joy with thy countenance.

29 Men *and* brethren, ᴺlet me freely speak unto you ᴿof the patriarch David, that he is both dead and buried, and his sepulchre is with us unto this day.

30 Therefore being a prophet, ᴿand knowing that God had sworn with an oath to him, that of the fruit of his loins, according to the flesh, he would raise up Christ to sit on his throne;

31 He seeing this before spake of the resurrection of Christ, ᴿthat his soul was not left in hell, neither his flesh did see corruption.

32 ᴿThis Jesus hath God raised up, ᴿwhereof we all are witnesses.

33 Therefore ᴿbeing by the right hand of God exalted, and ᴿhaving received of the Father the promise of the Holy Ghost, he ᴿhath shed forth this, which ye now see and hear.

34 For David is not ascended into the heavens: but he saith himself, ᴿThe Lᴏʀᴅ said unto my Lord, Sit thou on my right hand,

35 Until I make thy foes thy footstool.

36 Therefore let all the house of Israel know assuredly, that God hath made that same Jesus, whom ye have crucified, both Lord and Christ.

37 Now when they heard *this,* ᴿthey were pricked in their heart, and said unto Peter and to the rest of the apostles, Men *and* brethren, what shall we do?

38 Then Peter said unto them, ᴿRepent, and be baptized every one of you in the name of Jesus Christ for the remission of sins, and ye shall receive the gift of the Holy Ghost.

39 For the promise is unto you, and ᴿto your children, and ᴿto all that are afar off, *even* as many as the Lord our God shall call.

40 And with many other words did he testify and exhort, saying, Save yourselves from this untoward generation.

41 Then they that gladly received his word were baptized: and the same day there were added *unto them* about three thousand souls.

The fellowship of believers

42 ^RAnd they continued stedfastly in the apostles' doctrine and fellowship, and in breaking of bread, and in prayers.

43 And fear came upon every soul: and ^Rmany wonders and signs were done by the apostles.

44 And all that believed were together, and ^Rhad all things common;

45 And sold their possessions and goods, and ^Rparted them to all *men,* as every man had need.

46 ^RAnd they, continuing daily with one accord ^Rin the temple, and ^Rbreaking bread ^Nfrom house to house, did eat their meat with gladness and singleness of heart,

47 Praising God, and ^Rhaving favour with all the people. And ^Rthe Lord added to the church daily such as should be saved.

CHAPTER 3

Healing the lame man

NOW Peter and John went up together ^Rinto the temple at the hour of prayer, ^R*being* the ninth *hour.*

2 And ^Ra certain man lame from his mother's womb was carried, whom they laid daily at the gate of the temple which is called Beautiful, ^Rto ask alms of them that entered into the temple;

3 Who seeing Peter and John about to go into the temple asked an alms.

4 And Peter, fastening his eyes upon him with John, said, Look on us.

5 And he gave heed unto them, expecting to receive something of them.

6 Then Peter said, Silver and gold have I none; but such as I have give I thee: ^RIn the name of Jesus Christ of Nazareth rise up and walk.

7 And he took him by the right hand, and lifted *him* up: and immediately his feet and ankle bones received strength.

8 And he ^Rleaping up stood, and walked, and entered with them into the temple, walking, and leaping, and praising God.

9 ^RAnd all the people saw him walking and praising God:

10 And they knew that it was he which ^Rsat for alms at the Beautiful gate of the temple: and they were filled with wonder and amazement at that which had happened unto him.

Peter's second sermon

11 And as the lame man which was healed held Peter and John, all the people ran to-

gether unto them in the porch ^Rthat is called Solomon's, greatly wondering.

12 And when Peter saw *it,* he answered unto the people, Ye men of Israel, why marvel ye at this? or why look ye so earnestly on us, as though by our own power or holiness we had made this man to walk?

13 ^RThe God of Abraham, and of Isaac, and of Jacob, the God of our fathers, ^Rhath glorified his Son Jesus; whom ye ^Rdelivered up, and ^Rdenied him in the presence of Pilate, when he was determined to let *him* go.

14 But ye denied ^Rthe Holy One ^Rand the Just, and desired a murderer to be granted unto you;

15 And killed the ^NPrince of life, ^Rwhom God hath raised from the dead; ^Rwhereof we are witnesses.

16 ^RAnd his name through faith in his name hath made this man strong, whom ye see and know: yea, the faith which is by him hath given him this perfect soundness in the presence of you all.

17 And now, brethren, I wot that ^Rthrough ignorance ye did *it,* as *did* also your rulers.

18 But ^Rthose things, which God before had shewed ^Rby the mouth of all his prophets, that Christ should suffer, he hath so fulfilled.

19 ^RRepent ye therefore, and be converted, that your sins may be blotted out, when the times of refreshing shall come from the presence of the Lord;

20 And he shall send Jesus Christ, which before was preached unto you:

21 ^RWhom the heaven must receive until the times of ^Rrestitution of all things, ^Rwhich God hath spoken by the mouth of all his holy prophets since the world began.

22 For Moses truly said unto the fathers, ^RA prophet shall the Lord your God raise up unto you of your brethren, like unto me; him shall ye hear in all things whatsoever he shall say unto you.

23 And it shall come to pass, *that* every soul, which will not hear that prophet, shall be destroyed from among the people.

24 Yea, and all the prophets from Samuel and those that follow after, as many as have spoken, have likewise foretold of these days.

25 ^RYe are the children of the prophets, and of the covenant which God made with our fathers, saying unto Abraham, ^RAnd in thy seed shall all the kindreds of the earth be blessed.

26 ^RUnto you first God, having raised up his Son Jesus, ^Rsent him to bless you, ^Rin turning away every one of you from his iniquities.

CHAP. 2 AD 33
42 ch. 1:14; Rom. 12:12; Eph. 6:18; Col. 4:2; Heb. 10:25
43 Mark 16:17; ch. 5:12
44 ch. 4:32, 34
45 Is. 58:7
46 ch. 1:14
46 Luke 24:53
46 ch. 20:7
46 Or, *at home*
47 ch. 4:33; Rom. 14:18
47 ch. 5:14

CHAP. 3 AD 33
1 ch. 2:46
1 Ps. 55:17
2 ch. 14:8
2 John 9:8
6 ch. 4:10
8 Is. 35:6
9 ch. 4:16, 21
10 Like John 9:8

John 10:23 — 11
ch. 5:12
ch. 5:30 — 13
John 7:39 & 11:16 & 17:1 — 13
Mat. 27:2 — 13
Mat. 27:20 — 13
Mark 15:11
Luke 23:18
ch. 13:28
Ps. 16:10 — 14
Mark 1:24
Luke 1:35
ch. 2:27 & 4:27
ch. 7:52 & 22:14 — 14
Or, *Author,* Heb. 2:10 & 5:9; 1 John 5:11 — 15
ch. 2:24 — 15
ch. 2:32 — 15
Mat. 9:22 — 16
ch. 4:10 & 14:9
Luke 23:34 — 17
John 16:3
ch. 13:27
1 Cor. 2:8
1 Tim. 1:13
Luke 24:44 — 18
ch. 26:22
Ps. 22
Is. 50:6 & 53:5, etc.
Dan. 9:26
1 Pet. 1:10
ch. 2:38 — 19
ch. 1:11 — 21
Mat. 17:11 — 21
Luke 1:70 — 21
Deut. 18:15, 18, 19 — 22
ch. 7:37
ch. 2:39 — 25
Rom. 9:4, 8 & 15:8
Gal. 3:26
Gen. 12:3 & 18:18 & 22:18 & 26:4 & 28:14 — 25
Gal. 3:8
Mat. 10:5 & 15:24 — 26
Luke 24:47
ch. 13:32, 33, 46
ver. 22 — 26
Mat. 1:21 — 26

CHAPTER 4

Peter and John arrested

AND as they spake unto the people, the priests, and the ᴺcaptain of the temple, and the Săd'-dū-çėėś, came upon them,

2 Being grieved that they taught the people, and preached through Jesus the resurrection from the dead.

3 And they laid hands on them, and put *them* in hold unto the next day: for it was now eventide.

4 Howbeit many of them which heard the word believed; and the number of the men was about five thousand.

Trial before the rulers and elders

5 And it came to pass on the morrow, that their rulers, and elders, and scribes,

6 And ᴿAnnas the high priest, and Cāi'-ă-phăs, and John, and Alexander, and as many as were of the kindred of the high priest, were gathered together at Jerusalem.

7 And when they had set them in the midst, they asked, ᴿBy what power, or by what name, have ye done this?

Peter's defense

8 ᴿThen Peter, filled with the Holy Ghost, said unto them, Ye rulers of the people, and elders of Israel,

9 If we this day be examined of the good deed done to the impotent man, by what means he is made whole;

10 Be it known unto you all, and to all the people of Israel, ᴿthat by the name of Jesus Christ of Nazareth, whom ye crucified, ᴿwhom God raised from the dead, *even* by him doth this man stand here before you whole.

11 ᴿThis is the stone which was set at nought of you builders, which is become the head of the corner.

12 ᴿNeither is there salvation in any other: for there is none other name under heaven given among men, whereby we must be saved.

The boldness of Peter and John

13 Now when they saw the boldness of Peter and John, ᴿand perceived that they were unlearned and ignorant men, they marvelled; and they took knowledge of them, that they had been with Jesus.

14 And beholding the man which was healed ᴿstanding with them, they could say nothing against it.

15 But when they had commanded them to

go aside out of the council, they conferred among themselves,

16 Saying, ᴿWhat shall we do to these men? for that indeed a notable miracle hath been done by them *is* ᴿmanifest to all them that dwell in Jerusalem; and we cannot deny *it*.

17 But that it spread no further among the people, let us straitly threaten them, that they speak henceforth to no man in this name.

18 ᴿAnd they called them, and commanded them not to speak at all nor teach in the name of Jesus.

19 But Peter and John answered and said unto them, ᴿWhether it be right in the sight of God to hearken unto you more than unto God, judge ye.

20 ᴿFor we cannot but speak the things which ᴿwe have seen and heard.

21 So when they had further threatened them, they let them go, finding nothing how they might punish them, ᴿbecause of the people: for all *men* glorified God for ᴿthat which was done.

22 For the man was above forty years old, on whom this miracle of healing was shewed.

Prayer of the church

23 And being let go, ᴿthey went to their own company, and reported all that the chief priests and elders had said unto them.

24 And when they heard that, they lifted up their voice to God with one accord, and said, Lord, ᴿthou *art* God, which hast made heaven, and earth, and the sea, and all that in them is:

25 Who by the mouth of thy servant David hast said, ᴿWhy did the heathen rage, and the people imagine vain things?

26 The kings of the earth stood up, and the rulers were gathered together against the Lord, and against his Christ.

27 For ᴿof a truth against ᴿthy holy child Jesus, ᴿwhom thou hast anointed, both Herod, and Pontius Pilate, with the Gentiles, and the people of Israel, were gathered together,

28 ᴿFor to do whatsoever thy hand and thy counsel determined before to be done.

29 And now, Lord, behold their threatenings: and grant unto thy servants, ᴿthat with all boldness they may speak thy word,

30 By stretching forth thine hand to heal; ᴿand that signs and wonders may be done ᴿby the name of ᴿthy holy child Jesus.

31 And when they had prayed, ᴿthe place was shaken where they were assembled together; and they were all filled with the Holy Ghost, ᴿand they spake the word of God with boldness.

CHAP. 4
AD 33

1 Or, *ruler,*
Luke 22:4
6 Luke 3:2
John 11:49
& 18:13
7 Ex. 2:14
Mat. 21:23
ch. 7:27
8 Luke 12:11, 12
10 ch. 3:6, 16
10 ch. 2:24
11 Ps. 118:22
Is. 28:16
Mat. 21:42
12 Mat. 1:21
ch. 10:43
1 Tim. 2:5, 6
13 Mat. 11:25
1 Cor. 1:27
14 ch. 3:11

John 11:47	16
ch. 3:9, 10	16
Again, ch. 5:40	18
ch. 5:29	19
ch. 1:8	20
& 2:32	
ch. 22:15	20
1 John 1:1, 3	
Mat. 21:26	21
Luke 20:6, 19	
& 22:2	
ch. 5:26	
ch. 3:7, 8	21
ch. 12:12	23
2 Ki. 19:15	24
Ps. 2:1	25
Mat. 26:3	27
Luke 22:2	
& 23:1, 8	
Luke 1:35	27
Luke 4:18	27
John 10:36	
ch. 2:23	28
& 3:18	
ver. 13, 31	29
ch. 9:27	
& 13:46	
& 14:3	
& 19:8	
& 26:26	
Eph. 6:19	
ch. 2:43	30
& 5:12	
ch. 3:6, 16	30
ver. 27	30
ch. 2:2, 4	31
& 16:26	
ver. 29	31

Sharing of possessions

32 And the multitude of them that believed [R]were of one heart and of one soul: [R]neither said any *of them* that aught of the things which he possessed was his own; but they had all things common.

33 And with [R]great power gave the apostles [R]witness of the resurrection of the Lord Jesus: and [R]great grace was upon them all.

34 Neither was there any among them that lacked: [R]for as many as were possessors of lands or houses sold them, and brought the prices of the things that were sold,

35 [R]And laid *them* down at the apostles' feet: [R]and distribution was made unto every man according as he had need.

36 And Jō'-śĕś, who by the apostles was surnamed Barnabas, (which is, being interpreted, The son of consolation,) a Levite, *and* of the country of Cyprus,

37 [R]Having land, sold *it,* and brought the money, and laid *it* at the apostles' feet.

CHAPTER 5

Ananias and Sapphira

BUT a certain man named Ăn-ă-nī'-ăs, with Săpph-ī'-ră his wife, sold a possession,

2 And kept back *part* of the price, his wife also being privy *to it,* and brought a certain part, and laid *it* at the apostles' feet.

3 [R]But Peter said, Ăn-ă-nī'-ăs, why hath [R]Satan filled thine heart [N]to lie to the Holy Ghost, and to keep back *part* of the price of the land?

4 Whiles it remained, was it not thine own? and after it was sold, was it not in thine own power? why hast thou conceived this thing in thine heart? thou hast not lied unto men, but unto God.

5 And Ăn-ă-nī'-ăs hearing these words [R]fell down, and gave up the ghost: and great fear came on all them that heard these things.

6 And the young men arose, [R]wound him up, and carried *him* out, and buried *him.*

7 And it was about the space of three hours after, when his wife, not knowing what was done, came in.

8 And Peter answered unto her, Tell me whether ye sold the land for so much? And she said, Yea, for so much.

9 Then Peter said unto her, How is it that ye have agreed together [R]to tempt the Spirit of the Lord? behold, the feet of them which have buried thy husband *are* at the door, and shall carry thee out.

10 [R]Then fell she down straightway at his feet, and yielded up the ghost: and the young men came in, and found her dead, and, carrying *her* forth, buried *her* by her husband.

11 [R]And great fear came upon all the church, and upon as many as heard these things.

Signs and wonders

12 And [R]by the hands of the apostles were many signs and wonders wrought among the people; ([R]and they were all with one accord in Solomon's porch.

13 And [R]of the rest durst no man join himself to them: [R]but the people magnified them.

14 And believers were the more added to the Lord, multitudes both of men and women.)

15 Insomuch that they brought forth the sick [N]into the streets, and laid *them* on beds and couches, [R]that at the least the shadow of Peter passing by might overshadow some of them.

16 There came also a multitude *out* of the cities round about unto Jerusalem, bringing [R]sick folks, and them which were vexed with unclean spirits: and they were healed every one.

The apostles imprisoned

17 [R]Then the high priest rose up, and all they that were with him, (which is the sect of the Săd'-dū-çĕś,) and were filled with [N]indignation,

18 [R]And laid their hands on the apostles, and put them in the common prison.

19 But [R]the angel of the Lord by night opened the prison doors, and brought them forth, and said,

20 Go, stand and speak in the temple to the people [R]all the words of this life.

21 And when they heard *that,* they entered into the temple early in the morning, and taught. [R]But the high priest came, and they that were with him, and called the council together, and all the senate of the children of Israel, and sent to the prison to have them brought.

22 But when the officers came, and found them not in the prison, they returned, and told,

23 Saying, The prison truly found we shut with all safety, and the keepers standing without before the doors: but when we had opened, we found no man within.

24 Now when the high priest and [R]the captain of the temple and the chief priests heard these things, they doubted of them whereunto this would grow.

25 Then came one and told them, saying, Behold, the men whom ye put in prison are

Center reference column

CHAP. **4**

AD 33

32 ch. 5:12
Rom. 15:5, 6
2 Cor. 13:11
Phil. 1:27
& 2:2
1 Pet. 3:8
32 ch. 2:44
33 ch. 1:8
33 ch. 1:22
33 ch. 2:45
34 ch. 2:45
35 ver. 37
ch. 5:2
35 ch. 2:45
& 6:1
37 ver. 34, 35
ch. 5:1, 2

CHAP. **5**

AD 33

3 Num. 30:2
Deut. 23:21
Eccl. 5:4
3 Luke 22:3
3 Or, *to deceive,*
ver. 9
5 ver. 10, 11
6 John 19:40
9 ver. 3
Mat. 4:7

ver. 5   10
ver. 5   11
ch. 2:43
& 19:17
ch. 2:43   12
& 14:3
& 19:11
Rom. 15:19
2 Cor. 12:12
Heb. 2:4
ch. 3:11   12
& 4:32
John 9:22   13
& 12:42
& 19:38
ch. 2:47   13
& 4:21
Or, *in*   15
every street
Mat. 9:21   15
& 14:36
ch. 19:12
Mark 16:17, 18 16
John 14:12
ch. 4:1, 2, 6   17
Or, *envy*   17
Luke 21:12   18
ch. 12:7   19
& 16:26
John 6:68   20
& 17:3
1 John 5:11
ch. 4:5, 6   21
Luke 22:4   24
ch. 4:1

standing in the temple, and teaching the people.

26 Then went the captain with the officers, and brought them without violence: [R]for they feared the people, lest they should have been stoned.

Before the council

27 And when they had brought them, they set *them* before the council: and the high priest asked them,

28 Saying, [R]Did not we straitly command you that ye should not teach in this name? and, behold, ye have filled Jerusalem with your doctrine, [R]and intend to bring this man's [R]blood upon us.

29 Then Peter and the *other* apostles answered and said, [R]We ought to obey God rather than men.

30 [R]The God of our fathers raised up Jesus, whom ye slew and [R]hanged on a tree.

31 [R]Him hath God exalted with his right hand *to be* [R]a Prince and [R]a Saviour, [R]for to give repentance to Israel, and forgiveness of sins.

32 And [R]we are his witnesses of these things; and *so is* also the Holy Ghost, [R]whom God hath given to them that obey him.

Gamaliel's advice

33 [R]When they heard *that,* they were cut *to the heart,* and took counsel to slay them.

34 Then stood there up one in the council, a Pharisee, named [R]Gă-mā'-li-ĕl, a doctor of the law, had in reputation among all the people, and commanded to put the apostles forth a little space;

35 And said unto them, Ye men of Israel, take heed to yourselves what ye intend to do as touching these men.

36 For before these days rose up Theu'-dăs, boasting himself to be somebody; to whom a number of men, about four hundred, joined themselves: who was slain; and all, as many as [N]obeyed him, were scattered, and brought to nought.

37 After this man rose up Judas of Galilee in the days of the taxing, and drew away much people after him: he also perished; and all, *even* as many as obeyed him, were dispersed.

38 And now I say unto you, Refrain from these men, and let them alone: [R]for if this counsel or this work be of men, it will come to nought:

39 [R]But if it be of God, ye cannot overthrow it; lest haply ye be found even [R]to fight against God.

The release of the apostles

40 And to him they agreed: and when they had [R]called the apostles, [R]and beaten *them,* they commanded that they should not speak in the name of Jesus, and let them go.

41 And they departed from the presence of the council, [R]rejoicing that they were counted worthy to suffer shame for his name.

42 And daily [R]in the temple, and in every house, [R]they ceased not to teach and preach Jesus Christ.

CHAPTER 6

Appointment of the seven

AND in those days, [R]when the number of the disciples was multiplied, there arose a murmuring of the [R]Grecians against the Hebrews, because their widows were neglected [R]in the daily ministration.

2 Then the twelve called the multitude of the disciples *unto them,* and said, [R]It is not reason that we should leave the word of God, and serve tables.

3 Wherefore, brethren, [R]look ye out among you seven men of honest report, full of the Holy Ghost and wisdom, whom we may appoint over this business.

4 But we [R]will give ourselves continually to prayer, and to the ministry of the word.

5 And the saying pleased the whole multitude: and they chose Stephen, [R]a man full of faith and of the Holy Ghost, and [R]Philip, and Prŏch'-ŏ-rŭs, and Nĭ'-că-nôr, and Tĭ'-mŏn, and Pär'-mĕ-năs, and [R]Nicolas a proselyte of Ăn'-tĭ-ŏch:

6 Whom they set before the apostles: and [R]when they had prayed, [R]they laid *their* hands on them.

7 And [R]the word of God increased; and the number of the disciples multiplied in Jerusalem greatly; and a great company [R]of the priests were obedient to the faith.

False charges against Stephen

8 And Stephen, full of faith and power, did great wonders and miracles among the people.

9 Then there arose certain of the synagogue, which is called *the synagogue* of the Lĭbĕr'-tines, and Çy-rē'-nĭ-ăns, and Ăl-ĕx-ăn'-drĭ-ăns, and of them of Çĭ-lĭç'-ĭ-ă and of Asia, disputing with Stephen.

10 And [R]they were not able to resist the wisdom and the spirit by which he spake.

11 [R]Then they suborned men, which said, We have heard him speak blasphemous words against Moses, and *against* God.

12 And they stirred up the people, and the elders, and the scribes, and came upon *him,* and caught *him,* and brought *him* to the council,

13 And set up false witnesses, which said, This man ceaseth not to speak blasphemous words against this holy place, and the law:

14 ᴿFor we have heard him say, that this Jesus of Nazareth shall ᴿdestroy this place, and shall change the ᴺcustoms which Moses delivered us.

15 And all that sat in the council, looking stedfastly on him, saw his face as it had been the face of an angel.

CHAPTER 7

THEN said the high priest, Are these things so?

Stephen's defense

2 And he said, ᴿMen, brethren, and fathers, hearken; The God of glory appeared unto our father Abraham, when he was in Měs-ŏ-pŏ-tā′-mĭ-ă, before he dwelt in Chăr′-răn,

3 And said unto him, ᴿGet thee out of thy country, and from thy kindred, and come into the land which I shall shew thee.

4 Then ᴿcame he out of the land of the Chăl-dæ′-ăns, and dwelt in Chăr′-răn: and from thence, when his father was dead, he removed him into this land, wherein ye now dwell.

5 And he gave him none inheritance in it, no, not *so much as* to set his foot on: ᴿyet he promised that he would give it to him for a possession, and to his seed after him, when *as yet* he had no child.

6 And God spake on this wise, ᴿThat his seed should sojourn in a strange land; and that they should bring them into bondage, and entreat *them* evil ᴿfour hundred years.

7 And the nation to whom they shall be in bondage will I judge, said God: and after that shall they come forth, and ᴿserve me in this place.

8 ᴿAnd he gave him the covenant of circumcision: ᴿand so *Abraham* begat Isaac, and circumcised him the eighth day; ᴿand Isaac *begat* Jacob; and ᴿJacob *begat* the twelve patriarchs.

9 ᴿAnd the patriarchs, moved with envy, sold Joseph into Egypt: ᴿbut God was with him,

10 And delivered him out of all his afflictions, ᴿand gave him favour and wisdom in the sight of Pharaoh king of Egypt; and he made him governor over Egypt and all his house.

11 ᴿNow there came a dearth over all the land of Egypt and Chā′-nă-ăn, and great affliction: and our fathers found no sustenance.

12 ᴿBut when Jacob heard that there was corn in Egypt, he sent out our fathers first.

13 ᴿAnd at the second *time* Joseph was made known to his brethren; and Joseph's kindred was made known unto Pharaoh.

14 ᴿThen sent Joseph, and called his father Jacob to *him,* and ᴿall his kindred, threescore and fifteen souls.

15 ᴿSo Jacob went down into Egypt, ᴿand died, he, and our fathers,

16 And ᴿwere carried over into Sȳ′-chĕm, and laid in ᴿthe sepulchre that Abraham bought for a sum of money of the sons of Ēm′-môr *the father* of Sȳ′-chĕm.

17 But when ᴿthe time of the promise drew nigh, which God had sworn to Abraham, ᴿthe people grew and multiplied in Egypt,

18 Till another king arose, which knew not Joseph.

19 The same dealt subtilly with our kindred, and evil entreated our fathers, ᴿso that they cast out their young children, to the end they might not live.

20 ᴿIn which time Moses was born, and ᴿwas ᴺexceeding fair, and nourished up in his father's house three months:

21 And ᴿwhen he was cast out, Pharaoh's daughter took him up, and nourished him for her own son.

22 And Moses was learned in all the wisdom of the Egyptians, and was ᴿmighty in words and in deeds.

23 ᴿAnd when he was full forty years old, it came into his heart to visit his brethren the children of Israel.

24 And seeing one *of them* suffer wrong, he defended *him,* and avenged him that was oppressed, and smote the Egyptian:

25 ᴺFor he supposed his brethren would have understood how that God by his hand would deliver them: but they understood not.

26 And the next day he shewed himself unto them as they strove, and would have set them at one again, saying, Sirs, ye are brethren; why do ye wrong one to another?

27 But he that did his neighbour wrong thrust him away, saying, ᴿWho made thee a ruler and a judge over us?

28 Wilt thou kill me, as thou diddest the Egyptian yesterday?

29 ᴿThen fled Moses at this saying, and was a stranger in the land of Mā′-dĭ-ăn, where he begat two sons.

30 ᴿAnd when forty years were expired, there appeared to him in the wilderness of

CHAP. 6
AD 33
14 ch. 25:8
14 Dan. 9:26
14 Or, *rites*

CHAP. 7
AD 33
2 ch. 22:1
3 Gen. 12:1
4 Gen. 11:31
 & 12:4, 5
5 Gen. 12:7
 & 13:15
 & 15:3, 18
 & 17:8
 & 26:3
6 Gen. 15:13, 16
6 Ex. 12:40
 Gal. 3:17
7 Ex. 3:12
8 Gen. 17:9-11
8 Gen. 21:2-4
8 Gen. 25:26
8 Gen. 29:31, etc.
 & 30:5, etc.
 & 35:18, 23
9 Gen. 37:4, 11, 28
 Ps. 105:17
9 Gen. 39:2, 21, 23
10 Gen. 41:37
 & 42:6

Gen. 41:54   11
Gen. 42:1   12
Gen. 45:4, 16   13
Gen. 45:9, 27   14
Gen. 46:27   14
 Deut. 10:22
Gen. 46:5   15
Gen. 49:33   15
 Ex. 1:6
Ex. 13:19   16
 Josh. 24:32
Gen. 23:16   16
 & 33:19
ver. 6   17
 Gen. 15:13
Ex. 1:7-9   17
 Ps. 105:24, 25
Ex. 1:22   19
Ex. 2:2   20
Heb. 11:23   20
Or, *fair to God* 20
Ex. 2:3-10   21
Luke 24:19   22
Ex. 2:11, 12   23
Or, *Now*   25
See Luke 12:14 27
 ch. 4:7
Ex. 2:15, 22   29
 & 4:20
 & 18:3, 4
Ex. 3:2   30

mount Sĭ'-nă an angel of the Lord in a flame of fire in a bush.

31 When Moses saw *it,* he wondered at the sight: and as he drew near to behold *it,* the voice of the Lord came unto him,

32 *Saying,* ᴿI *am* the God of thy fathers, the God of Abraham, and the God of Isaac, and the God of Jacob. Then Moses trembled, and durst not behold.

33 ᴿThen said the Lord to him, Put off thy shoes from thy feet: for the place where thou standest is holy ground.

34 ᴿI have seen, I have seen the affliction of my people which is in Egypt, and I have heard their groaning, and am come down to deliver them. And now come, I will send thee into Egypt.

35 This Moses whom they refused, saying, Who made thee a ruler and a judge? the same did God send *to be* a ruler and a deliverer ᴿby the hand of the angel which appeared to him in the bush.

36 ᴿHe brought them out, after that he had ᴿshewed wonders and signs in the land of Egypt, ᴿand in the Red sea, ᴿand in the wilderness forty years.

37 This is that Moses, which said unto the children of Israel, ᴿA prophet shall the Lord your God raise up unto you of your brethren, ᴺlike unto me; ᴿhim shall ye hear.

38 ᴿThis is he, that was in the church in the wilderness with ᴿthe angel which spake to him in the mount Sĭ'-nă, and *with* our fathers: ᴿwho received the lively ᴿoracles to give unto us:

39 To whom our fathers would not obey, but thrust *him* from them, and in their hearts turned back again into Egypt,

40 ᴿSaying unto Aaron, Make us gods to go before us: for *as for* this Moses, which brought us out of the land of Egypt, we wot not what is become of him.

41 ᴿAnd they made a calf in those days, and offered sacrifice unto the idol, and rejoiced in the works of their own hands.

42 Then ᴿGod turned, and gave them up to worship ᴿthe host of heaven; as it is written in the book of the prophets, ᴿO ye house of Israel, have ye offered to me slain beasts and sacrifices *by the space of* forty years in the wilderness?

43 Yea, ye took up the tabernacle of Moloch, and the star of your god Rĕm'-phăn, figures which ye made to worship them: and I will carry you away beyond Babylon.

44 Our fathers had the tabernacle of witness in the wilderness, as he had appointed, ᴺspeaking unto Moses, ᴿthat he should make it according to the fashion that he had seen.

45 ᴿWhich also our fathers ᴺthat came after brought in with Jesus into the possession of the Gentiles, ᴿwhom God drave out before the face of our fathers, unto the days of David;

46 ᴿWho found favour before God, and ᴿdesired to find a tabernacle for the God of Jacob.

47 ᴿBut Solomon built him an house.

48 Howbeit ᴿthe most High dwelleth not in temples made with hands; as saith the prophet,

49 ᴿHeaven *is* my throne, and earth *is* my footstool: what house will ye build me? saith the Lord: or what *is* the place of my rest?

50 Hath not my hand made all these things?

51 Ye ᴿstiffnecked and ᴿuncircumcised in heart and ears, ye do always resist the Holy Ghost: as your fathers *did,* so *do* ye.

52 ᴿWhich of the prophets have not your fathers persecuted? and they have slain them which shewed before of the coming of ᴿthe Just One; of whom ye have been now the betrayers and murderers:

53 ᴿWho have received the law by the disposition of angels, and have not kept *it.*

The death of Stephen

54 ᴿWhen they heard these things, they were cut to the heart, and they gnashed on him with *their* teeth.

55 But he, ᴿbeing full of the Holy Ghost, looked up stedfastly into heaven, and saw the glory of God, and Jesus standing on the right hand of God,

56 And said, Behold, ᴿI see the heavens opened, and the ᴿSon of man standing on the right hand of God.

57 Then they cried out with a loud voice, and stopped their ears, and ran upon him with one accord,

58 And ᴿcast *him* out of the city, ᴿand stoned *him:* and ᴿthe witnesses laid down their clothes at a young man's feet, whose name was Saul.

59 And they stoned Stephen, ᴿcalling upon *God,* and saying, Lord Jesus, ᴿreceive my spirit.

60 And he ᴿkneeled down, and cried with a loud voice, ᴿLord, lay not this sin to their charge. And when he had said this, he fell asleep.

CHAPTER 8

Widespread persecution of the church

AND ᴿSaul was consenting unto his death. And at that time there was a great persecution against the church which was at Jerusalem; and ᴿthey were all scattered abroad

---

Center reference column:

CHAP. 7
AD 33
32 Mat. 22:32
Heb. 11:16
33 Ex. 3:5
Josh. 5:15
34 Ex. 3:7
35 Ex. 14:19
Num. 29:16
36 Ex. 12:41
& 33:1
36 Ex. 7, & 8,
& 9, & 10
Ps. 105:27
36 Ex. 14:21
36 Ex. 16:1
37 Deut. 18:15
37 Or, *as myself*
37 Mat. 17:5
38 Ex. 19:3
38 Is. 63:9
Gal. 3:19
Heb. 2:2
38 Ex. 21:1
Deut. 5:27
John 1:17
38 Rom. 3:2
40 Ex. 32:1
41 Deut. 9:16
Ps. 106:19
42 Ps. 81:12
2 Thes. 2:11
42 Deut. 4:19
2 Ki. 21:3
42 Amos 5:25
44 Or, *who spake*
44 Ex. 25:40
Heb. 8:5

Josh. 3:14   45
Or, *having*   45
  received
Neh. 9:24   45
Ps. 44:2
2 Sam. 7:1   46
Ps. 89:19
1 Chr. 22:7   46
1 Ki. 8:20   47
1 Ki. 8:27   48
2 Chr. 2:6
Is. 66:1, 2   49
Mat. 5:34
Ex. 32:9   51
Lev. 26:41   51
Deut. 10:16
Jer. 4:4
2 Chr. 36:16   52
Mat. 21:35
1 Thes. 2:15
ch. 3:14   52
Ex. 20:1   53
Gal. 3:19
ch. 5:33   54
ch. 6:5   55
Mat. 3:16   56
Dan. 7:13   56
Luke 4:29   58
Heb. 13:12
Lev. 24:16   58
Deut. 13:9   58
ch. 9:14   59
Ps. 31:5   59
Luke 23:46
ch. 9:40   60
Mat. 5:44   60
Luke 6:28

CHAP. 8
AD 34
ch. 7:58   1
ch. 11:19   1

throughout the regions of Judæa and Să-mâr′-ĭ-ă, except the apostles.

2 And devout men carried Stephen *to his burial,* and ᴿmade great lamentation over him.

3 As for Saul, ᴿhe made havoc of the church, entering into every house, and haling men and women committed *them* to prison.

Philip in Samaria

4 Therefore ᴿthey that were scattered abroad went every where preaching the word.

5 Then ᴿPhilip went down to the city of Să-mâr′-ĭ-ă, and preached Christ unto them.

6 And the people with one accord gave heed unto those things which Philip spake, hearing and seeing the miracles which he did.

7 For ᴿunclean spirits, crying with loud voice, came out of many that were possessed *with them:* and many taken with palsies, and that were lame, were healed.

8 And there was great joy in that city.

9 But there was a certain man, called Simon, which beforetime in the same city ᴿused sorcery, and bewitched the people of Să-mâr′-ĭ-ă, ᴿgiving out that himself was some great one:

10 To whom they all gave heed, from the least to the greatest, saying, This man is the great power of God.

11 And to him they had regard, because that of long time he had bewitched them with sorceries.

12 But when they believed Philip preaching the things ᴿconcerning the kingdom of God, and the name of Jesus Christ, they were baptized, both men and women.

13 Then Simon himself believed also: and when he was baptized, he continued with Philip, and wondered, beholding the ᴺmiracles and signs which were done.

Peter and John in Samaria

14 Now when the apostles which were at Jerusalem heard that Să-mâr′-ĭ-ă had received the word of God, they sent unto them Peter and John:

15 Who, when they were come down, prayed for them, ᴿthat they might receive the Holy Ghost:

16 (For ᴿas yet he was fallen upon none of them: only ᴿthey were baptized in ᴿthe name of the Lord Jesus.)

17 Then ᴿlaid they *their* hands on them, and they received the Holy Ghost.

18 And when Simon saw that through laying on of the apostles' hands the Holy Ghost was given, he offered them money,

19 Saying, Give me also this power, that on whomsoever I lay hands, he may receive the Holy Ghost.

CHAP. **8**

AD 34

2 Gen. 23:2
& 50:10
2 Sam. 3:31
3 ch. 7:58
1 Cor. 15:9
Gal 1:13
Phil. 3:6
1 Tim. 1:13
4 Mat. 10:23
5 ch. 6:5
7 Mark 16:17
9 ch. 13:6
9 ch. 5:36
12 ch. 1:3
13 Gr. signs and great miracles
15 ch. 2:38
16 ch. 19:2
16 Mat. 28:19
ch. 2:38
16 ch. 10:48
& 19:5
17 ch. 6:6
& 19:6
Heb. 6:2

Mat. 10:8 **20**
See 2 Ki. 5:16
ch. 2:38 **20**
& 10:45
& 11:17
Dan. 4:27 **22**
2 Tim. 2:25
Heb. 12:15 **23**
Gen. 20:7, 17 **24**
Ex. 8:8
Num. 21:7
1 Ki. 13:6
Job 42:8
Jas. 5:16
Zeph. 3:10 **27**
John 12:20 **27**
Is. 53:7, 8 **32**
Luke 24:27 **35**
ch. 18:28
ch. 10:47 **36**

20 But Peter said unto him, Thy money perish with thee, because ᴿthou hast thought that ᴿthe gift of God may be purchased with money.

21 Thou hast neither part nor lot in this matter: for thy heart is not right in the sight of God.

22 Repent therefore of this thy wickedness, and pray God, ᴿif perhaps the thought of thine heart may be forgiven thee.

23 For I perceive that thou art in ᴿthe gall of bitterness, and *in* the bond of iniquity.

24 Then answered Simon, and said, ᴿPray ye to the Lord for me, that none of these things which ye have spoken come upon me.

25 And they, when they had testified and preached the word of the Lord, returned to Jerusalem, and preached the gospel in many villages of the Să-mär′-ĭ-tăns.

Philip and the Ethiopian eunuch

26 And the angel of the Lord spake unto Philip, saying, Arise, and go toward the south unto the way that goeth down from Jerusalem unto Gā′-ză, which is desert.

27 And he arose and went: and, behold, ᴿa man of Ē-thĭ-ō′-pĭ-ă, an eunuch of great authority under Căn′-dă-çē queen of the Ē-thĭ-ō′-pĭ-ăns, who had the charge of all her treasure, and ᴿhad come to Jerusalem for to worship,

28 Was returning, and sitting in his chariot read Ē-śâi′-ăs the prophet.

29 Then the Spirit said unto Philip, Go near, and join thyself to this chariot.

30 And Philip ran thither to *him,* and heard him read the prophet Ē-śâi′-ăs, and said, Understandest thou what thou readest?

31 And he said, How can I, except some man should guide me? And he desired Philip that he would come up and sit with him.

32 The place of the scripture which he read was this, ᴿHe was led as a sheep to the slaughter; and like a lamb dumb before his shearer, so opened he not his mouth:

33 In his humiliation his judgment was taken away: and who shall declare his generation? for his life is taken from the earth.

34 And the eunuch answered Philip, and said, I pray thee, of whom speaketh the prophet this? of himself, or of some other man?

35 Then Philip opened his mouth, ᴿand began at the same scripture, and preached unto him Jesus.

36 And as they went on *their* way, they came unto a certain water: and the eunuch said, See, *here is* water; ᴿwhat doth hinder me to be baptized?

37 And Philip said, [R]If thou believest with
all thine heart, thou mayest. And he answered
and said, [R]I believe that Jesus Christ is the
Son of God.
38 And he commanded the chariot to stand
still: and they went down both into the water,
both Philip and the eunuch; and he baptized
him.
39 And when they were come up out of the
water, [R]the Spirit of the Lord caught away
Philip, that the eunuch saw him no more: and
he went on his way rejoicing.
40 But Philip was found at Ă-zō′-tŭs: and
passing through he preached in all the cities,
till he came to Çæ̣-s̈ä-rē′-ă.

CHAPTER 9

The conversion of Saul

AND [R]Saul, yet breathing out threatenings
and slaughter against the disciples of the
Lord, went unto the high priest,
2 And desired of him letters to Damascus to
the synagogues, that if he found any [N]of this
way, whether they were men or women, he
might bring them bound unto Jerusalem.
3 And [R]as he journeyed, he came near Damascus: and suddenly there shined round
about him a light from heaven:
4 And he fell to the earth, and heard a voice
saying unto him, Saul, Saul, [R]why persecutest
thou me?
5 And he said, Who art thou, Lord? And the
Lord said, I am Jesus whom thou persecutest:
it is hard for thee to kick against the pricks.
6 And he trembling and astonished said,
Lord, [R]what wilt thou have me to do? And the
Lord *said* unto him, Arise, and go into the
city, and it shall be told thee what thou must
do.
7 And [R]the men which journeyed with him
stood speechless, hearing a voice, but seeing
no man.
8 And Saul arose from the earth; and when
his eyes were opened, he saw no man: but
they led him by the hand, and brought *him*
into Damascus.
9 And he was three days without sight, and
neither did eat nor drink.

Saul baptized by Ananias

10 And there was a certain disciple at Damascus, [R]named Ăn-ă-nī′-ăs; and to him said
the Lord in a vision, Ăn-ă-nī′-ăs. And he said,
Behold, I *am here,* Lord.
11 And the Lord *said* unto him, Arise, and
go into the street which is called Straight, and
inquire in the house of Judas for *one* called
Saul, [R]of Tarsus: for, behold, he prayeth,
12 And hath seen in a vision a man named
Ăn-ă-nī′-ăs coming in, and putting *his* hand on
him, that he might receive his sight.
13 Then Ăn-ă-nī′-ăs answered, Lord, I have
heard by many of this man, [R]how much evil
he hath done to thy saints at Jerusalem:
14 And here he hath authority from the chief
priests to bind all [R]that call on thy name.
15 But the Lord said unto him, Go thy way:
for [R]he is a chosen vessel unto me, to bear my
name before [R]the Gentiles, and [R]kings, and
the children of Israel:
16 For [R]I will shew him how great things he
must suffer for my name's sake.
17 [R]And Ăn-ă-nī′-ăs went his way, and entered into the house; and [R]putting his hands on
him said, Brother Saul, the Lord, *even* Jesus,
that appeared unto thee in the way as thou
camest, hath sent me, that thou mightest receive thy sight, and [R]be filled with the Holy
Ghost.
18 And immediately there fell from his eyes
as it had been scales: and he received sight
forthwith, and arose, and was baptized.
19 And when he had received meat, he was
strengthened. [R]Then was Saul certain days
with the disciples which were at Damascus.

Saul preaches at Damascus

20 And straightway he preached Christ in
the synagogues, that he is the Son of God.
21 But all that heard *him* were amazed, and
said; [R]Is not this he that destroyed them which
called on this name in Jerusalem, and came
hither for that intent, that he might bring them
bound unto the chief priests?
22 But Saul increased the more in strength,
[R]and confounded the Jews which dwelt at Damascus, proving that this is very Christ.

Plot against Saul's life

23 And after that many days were fulfilled,
[R]the Jews took counsel to kill him:
24 [R]But their laying await was known of
Saul. And they watched the gates day and
night to kill him.
25 Then the disciples took him by night, and
[R]let *him* down by the wall in a basket.

Saul received in Jerusalem

26 And [R]when Saul was come to Jerusalem,
he assayed to join himself to the disciples: but
they were all afraid of him, and believed not
that he was a disciple.
27 [R]But Barnabas took him, and brought *him*
to the apostles, and declared unto them how he

CHAP. 8
AD 34
37 Mat. 28:19
Mark 16:16
37 Mat. 16:16
John 6:69
& 9:35, 38
& 11:27
ch. 9:20
1 John 4:15
& 5:5, 13
39 1 Ki. 18:12
2 Ki. 2:16
Ezek. 3:12, 14

CHAP. 9
AD 35
1 ch. 8:3
Gal. 1:13
1 Tim. 1:13
2 Gr. *of the way:*
ch. 19:9, 23
3 ch. 22:6
& 26:12
1 Cor. 15:8
4 Mat. 25:40, etc.
6 Luke 3:10
ch. 2:37
& 16:30
7 Dan. 10:7
See ch. 22:9
& 26:13
10 ch. 22:12
ch. 21:39 **11**
& 22:3
ver. 1 **13**
ver. 21 **14**
ch. 7:59
1 Cor. 1:2
2 Tim. 2:22
ch. 13:2 **15**
& 22:21
Rom. 1:1
1 Cor. 15:10
Gal. 1:15
Eph. 3:7, 8
1 Tim. 2:7
2 Tim. 1:11
Rom. 1:5 **15**
& 11:13
Gal. 2:7, 8
ch. 25:22, 23 **15**
& 26:1, etc.
ch. 20:23 **16**
& 21:11
2 Cor. 11:23
ch. 22:12, 13 **17**
ch. 8:17 **17**
ch. 2:4 & 4:31 **17**
& 8:17
& 13:52
ch. 26:20 **19**
ver. 1 **21**
ch. 8:3
Gal. 1:13, 23
ch. 18:28 **22**
ch. 23:12 **23**
2 Cor. 11:26
2 Cor. 11:32 **24**
Josh. 2:15 **25**
1 Sam. 19:12
ch. 22:17 **26**
Gal. 1:17, 18
ch. 4:36 **27**
& 13:2

had seen the Lord in the way, and that he had spoken to him, ᴿand how he had preached boldly at Damascus in the name of Jesus.

28 And ᴿhe was with them coming in and going out at Jerusalem.

29 And he spake boldly in the name of the Lord Jesus, and disputed against the ᴿGrecians: ᴿbut they went about to slay him.

30 *Which* when the brethren knew, they brought him down to Çæ-šȧ-rē′-ă, and sent him forth to Tarsus.

31 ᴿThen had the churches rest throughout all Judæa and Galilee and Să-mâr′-ĭ-ă, and were edified; and walking in the fear of the Lord, and in the comfort of the Holy Ghost, were multiplied.

Peter heals Æneas

32 And it came to pass, as Peter passed ᴿthroughout all *quarters,* he came down also to the saints which dwelt at Lўd′-dă.

33 And there he found a certain man named Æ-nē′-ăs, which had kept his bed eight years, and was sick of the palsy.

34 And Peter said unto him, Æ-nē′-ăs, ᴿJesus Christ maketh thee whole: arise, and make thy bed. And he arose immediately.

35 And all that dwelt at Lўd′-dă and ᴿSâr′-ŏn saw him, and ᴿturned to the Lord.

Peter raises Tabitha

36 Now there was at Joppa a certain disciple named Tabitha, which by interpretation is called ᴺDorcas: this woman was full ᴿof good works and almsdeeds which she did.

37 And it came to pass in those days, that she was sick, and died: whom when they had washed, they laid *her* in ᴿan upper chamber.

38 And forasmuch as Lўd′-dă was nigh to Joppa, and the disciples had heard that Peter was there, they sent unto him two men, desiring *him* that he would not ᴺdelay to come to them.

39 Then Peter arose and went with them. When he was come, they brought him into the upper chamber: and all the widows stood by him weeping, and shewing the coats and garments which Dorcas made, while she was with them.

40 But Peter ᴿput them all forth, and ᴿkneeled down, and prayed; and turning *him* to the body ᴿsaid, Tabitha, arise. And she opened her eyes: and when she saw Peter, she sat up.

41 And he gave her *his* hand, and lifted her up, and when he had called the saints and widows, presented her alive.

CHAP. **9**

AD 35

27 ver. 20, 22
28 Gal. 1:18
29 ch. 6:1
& 11:20
29 ver. 23
2 Cor. 11:26
31 See ch. 8:1
32 ch. 8:14
34 ch. 3:6, 16
& 4:10
35 1 Chr. 5:16
35 ch. 11:21
36 Or, *Doe, or, Roe*
36 1 Tim. 2:10
Tit. 3:8
37 ch. 1:13
38 Or, *be grieved*
40 Mat. 9:25
40 ch. 7:60
40 Mark 5:41, 42
John 11:43

John 11:45   **42**
ch. 10:6   **43**

CHAP. **10**

AD 41

ver. 22   **2**
ch. 8:2
& 22:12
ver. 35   **2**
ver. 30   **3**
ch. 11:13
ch. 9:43   **6**
ch. 11:14   **6**
ch. 11:5, etc.   **9**
ch. 7:56   **11**
Rev. 19:11
Lev. 11:4   **14**
& 20:25
Deut. 14:3, 7
Ezek. 4:14
ver. 28   **15**
Mat. 15:11
Rom. 14:14,
17, 20
1 Cor. 10:25
1 Tim. 4:4
Tit. 1:15

42 And it was known throughout all Joppa; ᴿand many believed in the Lord.

43 And it came to pass, that he tarried many days in Joppa with one ᴿSimon a tanner.

CHAPTER 10

Cornelius' vision at Cæsarea

THERE was a certain man in Çæ-šȧ-rē′-ă called Cornelius, a centurion of the band called the Italian *band,*

2 ᴿA devout *man,* and one that ᴿfeared God with all his house, which gave much alms to the people, and prayed to God alway.

3 ᴿHe saw in a vision evidently about the ninth hour of the day an angel of God coming in to him, and saying unto him, Cornelius.

4 And when he looked on him, he was afraid, and said, What is it, Lord? And he said unto him, Thy prayers and thine alms are come up for a memorial before God.

5 And now send men to Joppa, and call for *one* Simon, whose surname is Peter:

6 He lodgeth with one ᴿSimon a tanner, whose house is by the sea side: ᴿhe shall tell thee what thou oughtest to do.

7 And when the angel which spake unto Cornelius was departed, he called two of his household servants, and a devout soldier of them that waited on him continually;

8 And when he had declared all *these* things unto them, he sent them to Joppa.

Peter's vision at Joppa

9 On the morrow, as they went on their journey, and drew nigh unto the city, ᴿPeter went up upon the housetop to pray about the sixth hour:

10 And he became very hungry, and would have eaten: but while they made ready, he fell into a trance,

11 And ᴿsaw heaven opened, and a certain vessel descending unto him, as it had been a great sheet knit at the four corners, and let down to the earth:

12 Wherein were all manner of fourfooted beasts of the earth, and wild beasts, and creeping things, and fowls of the air.

13 And there came a voice to him, Rise, Peter; kill, and eat.

14 But Peter said, Not so, Lord; ᴿfor I have never eaten any thing that is common or unclean.

15 And the voice *spake* unto him again the second time, ᴿWhat God hath cleansed, *that* call not thou common.

16 This was done thrice: and the vessel was received up again into heaven.

Messengers from Cornelius

17 Now while Peter doubted in himself what this vision which he had seen should mean, behold, the men which were sent from Cornelius had made inquiry for Simon's house, and stood before the gate,

18 And called, and asked whether Simon, which was surnamed Peter, were lodged there.

19 While Peter thought on the vision, ᴿthe Spirit said unto him, Behold, three men seek thee.

20 ᴿArise therefore, and get thee down, and go with them, doubting nothing: for I have sent them.

21 Then Peter went down to the men which were sent unto him from Cornelius; and said, Behold, I am he whom ye seek: what *is* the cause wherefore ye are come?

22 And they said, Cornelius the centurion, a just man, and one that feareth God, and ᴿof good report among all the nation of the Jews, was warned from God by an holy angel to send for thee into his house, and to hear words of thee.

Peter visits Cornelius

23 Then called he them in, and lodged *them*. And on the morrow Peter went away with them, ᴿand certain brethren from Joppa accompanied him.

24 And the morrow after they entered into Cǣ-sȧ-rē′-ȧ. And Cornelius waited for them, and had called together his kinsmen and near friends.

25 And as Peter was coming in, Cornelius met him, and fell down at his feet, and worshipped *him*.

26 But Peter took him up, saying, ᴿStand up; I myself also am a man.

27 And as he talked with him, he went in, and found many that were come together.

28 And he said unto them, Ye know how ᴿthat it is an unlawful thing for a man that is a Jew to keep company, or come unto one of another nation; but ᴿGod hath shewed me that I should not call any man common or unclean.

29 Therefore came I *unto you* without gainsaying, as soon as I was sent for: I ask therefore for what intent ye have sent for me?

30 And Cornelius said, Four days ago I was fasting until this hour; and at the ninth hour I prayed in my house, and, behold, ᴿa man stood before me ᴿin bright clothing,

31 And said, Cornelius, ᴿthy prayer is heard, ᴿand thine alms are had in remembrance in the sight of God.

CHAP. 10
AD 41
19 ch. 11:12
20 ch. 15:7
22 ch. 22:12
23 ch. 11:12
26 ch. 14:14
28 John 4:9
& 18:28
ch. 11:3
Gal. 2:12
28 ch. 15:8, 9
Eph. 3:6
30 ch. 1:10
30 Mat. 28:3
Mark 16:5
Luke 24:4
31 Dan. 10:12
31 Heb. 6:10

Deut. 10:17	34
2 Chr. 19:7	
Job 34:19	
Rom. 2:11	
Gal. 2:6	
Eph. 6:9	
Col. 3:25	
1 Pet. 1:17	
ch. 15:9	35
Rom. 2:13	
& 3:22	
& 10:12, 13	
1 Cor. 12:13	
Gal. 3:28	
Eph. 2:13	
Is. 57:19	36
Eph. 2:14	
Col. 1:20	
Mat. 28:18	36
Rom. 10:12	
1 Cor. 15:27	
Eph. 1:20	
1 Pet. 3:22	
Rev. 17:14	
Luke 4:14	37
Luke 4:18	38
Heb. 1:9	
John 3:2	38
ch. 2:32	39
ch. 5:30	39
ch. 2:24	40
John 14:17, 22	41
ch. 13:31	
Luke 24:30	41
John 21:13	
Mat. 28:19	42
ch. 1:8	
John 5:22	42
ch. 17:31	
Rom. 14:9	42
2 Cor. 5:10	
2 Tim. 4:1	
1 Pet. 4:5	
Is. 53:11	43
Jer. 31:34	
Dan. 9:24	
Mic. 7:18	
Zech. 13:1	
Mal. 4:2	
ch. 26:18	43
Rom. 10:11	
Gal. 3:22	
ch. 4:31	44
ver. 23	45
ch. 11:18	45
Gal. 3:14	

32 Send therefore to Joppa, and call hither Simon, whose surname is Peter; he is lodged in the house of *one* Simon a tanner by the sea side: who, when he cometh, shall speak unto thee.

33 Immediately therefore I sent to thee; and thou hast well done that thou art come. Now therefore are we all here present before God, to hear all things that are commanded thee of God.

Peter's sermon at Cæsarea

34 Then Peter opened *his* mouth, and said, ᴿOf a truth I perceive that God is no respecter of persons:

35 But ᴿin every nation he that feareth him, and worketh righteousness, is accepted with him.

36 The word which *God* sent unto the children of Israel, ᴿpreaching peace by Jesus Christ: (ᴿhe is Lord of all:)

37 That word, *I say,* ye know, which was published throughout all Judæa, and ᴿbegan from Galilee, after the baptism which John preached;

38 How ᴿGod anointed Jesus of Nazareth with the Holy Ghost and with power: who went about doing good, and healing all that were oppressed of the devil; ᴿfor God was with him.

39 And ᴿwe are witnesses of all things which he did both in the land of the Jews, and in Jerusalem; ᴿwhom they slew and hanged on a tree:

40 Him ᴿGod raised up the third day, and shewed him openly;

41 ᴿNot to all the people, but unto witnesses chosen before of God, *even* to us, ᴿwho did eat and drink with him after he rose from the dead.

42 And ᴿhe commanded us to preach unto the people, and to testify ᴿthat it is he which was ordained of God *to be* the Judge ᴿof quick and dead.

43 ᴿTo him give all the prophets witness, that through his name ᴿwhosoever believeth in him shall receive remission of sins.

Holy Ghost descends

44 While Peter yet spake these words, ᴿthe Holy Ghost fell on all them which heard the word.

45 ᴿAnd they of the circumcision which believed were astonished, as many as came with Peter, ᴿbecause that on the Gentiles also was poured out the gift of the Holy Ghost.

46 For they heard them speak with tongues, and magnify God. Then answered Peter,

47 Can any man forbid water, that these should not be baptized, which have received the Holy Ghost ᴿas well as we?

48 ᴿAnd he commanded them to be baptized ᴿin the name of the Lord. Then prayed they him to tarry certain days.

CHAPTER 11

Peter's explanation in Jerusalem

AND the apostles and brethren that were in Judæa heard that the Gentiles had also received the word of God.

2 And when Peter was come up to Jerusalem, ᴿthey that were of the circumcision contended with him,

3 Saying, ᴿThou wentest in to men uncircumcised, ᴿand didst eat with them.

4 But Peter rehearsed *the matter* from the beginning, and expounded *it* ᴿby order unto them, saying,

5 ᴿI was in the city of Joppa praying: and in a trance I saw a vision, A certain vessel descend, as it had been a great sheet, let down from heaven by four corners; and it came even to me:

6 Upon the which when I had fastened mine eyes, I considered, and saw fourfooted beasts of the earth, and wild beasts, and creeping things, and fowls of the air.

7 And I heard a voice saying unto me, Arise, Peter; slay and eat.

8 But I said, Not so, Lord: for nothing common or unclean hath at any time entered into my mouth.

9 But the voice answered me again from heaven, What God hath cleansed, *that* call not thou common.

10 And this was done three times: and all were drawn up again into heaven.

11 And, behold, immediately there were three men already come unto the house where I was, sent from Çæ-ṡȧ-rē′-ȧ unto me.

12 And ᴿthe Spirit bade me go with them, nothing doubting. Moreover ᴿthese six brethren accompanied me, and we entered into the man's house:

13 ᴿAnd he shewed us how he had seen an angel in his house, which stood and said unto him, Send men to Joppa, and call for Simon, whose surname is Peter;

14 Who shall tell thee words, whereby thou and all thy house shall be saved.

15 And as I began to speak, the Holy Ghost fell on them, ᴿas on us at the beginning.

16 Then remembered I the word of the Lord, how that he said, ᴿJohn indeed baptized with water; but ᴿye shall be baptized with the Holy Ghost.

17 ᴿForasmuch then as God gave them the like gift as *he did* unto us, who believed on the Lord Jesus Christ; ᴿwhat was I, that I could withstand God?

18 When they heard these things, they held their peace, and glorified God, saying, ᴿThen hath God also to the Gentiles granted repentance unto life.

Barnabas at Antioch

19 ᴿNow they which were scattered abroad upon the persecution that arose about Stephen travelled as far as Phē-nī′-çē, and Cyprus, and Ăn′-tĭ-ŏch, preaching the word to none but unto the Jews only.

20 And some of them were men of Cyprus and Çȳ-rē′-nē, which, when they were come to Ăn′-tĭ-ŏch, spake unto ᴿthe Grecians, preaching the Lord Jesus.

21 And ᴿthe hand of the Lord was with them: and a great number believed, and ᴿturned unto the Lord.

22 Then tidings of these things came unto the ears of the church which was in Jerusalem: and they sent forth ᴿBarnabas, that he should go as far as Ăn′-tĭ-ŏch.

23 Who, when he came, and had seen the grace of God, was glad, and ᴿexhorted them all, that with purpose of heart they would cleave unto the Lord.

24 For he was a good man, and ᴿfull of the Holy Ghost and of faith: ᴿand much people was added unto the Lord.

25 Then departed Barnabas to ᴿTarsus, for to seek Saul:

26 And when he had found him, he brought him unto Ăn′-tĭ-ŏch. And it came to pass, that a whole year they assembled themselves ᴺwith the church, and taught much people. And the disciples were called Christians first in Ăn′-tĭ-ŏch.

27 And in these days came ᴿprophets from Jerusalem unto Ăn′-tĭ-ŏch.

28 And there stood up one of them named ᴿĂg′-ȧ-bŭs, and signified by the Spirit that there should be great dearth throughout all the world: which came to pass in the days of Claudius Cæsar.

29 Then the disciples, every man according to his ability, determined to send ᴿrelief unto the brethren which dwelt in Judæa:

30 ᴿWhich also they did, and sent it to the elders by the hands of Barnabas and Saul.

CHAP. 10
AD 41
47 ch. 11:17
48 1 Cor. 1:17
48 ch. 2:38
& 8:16

CHAP. 11
AD 41
2 ch. 10:45
3 ch. 10:28
3 Gal. 2:12
4 Luke 1:3
5 ch. 10:9, etc.
12 John 16:13
ch. 10:19
& 15:7
12 ch. 10:23
13 ch. 10:30
15 ch. 2:4

Mat. 3:11 16
John 1:26, 33
ch. 1:5
& 19:4
Is. 44:3 16
Joel 2:28
& 3:18
ch. 15:8, 9 17
ch. 10:47 17
Rom. 10:12, 13 18
& 15:9, 16
ch. 8:1 19
ch. 6:1 20
& 9:29
Luke 1:66 21
ch. 2:47
ch. 9:35 21
ch. 9:27 22
ch. 13:43 23
& 14:22
ch. 6:5 24
ver. 21 24
ch. 5:14
ch. 9:30 25
Or, *in the church* 26
ch. 2:17 27
& 13:1
& 15:32
& 21:9
1 Cor. 12:28
Eph. 4:11
ch. 21:10 28
Rom. 15:26 29
1 Cor. 16:1
2 Cor. 9:1
ch. 12:25 30

CHAPTER 12

James killed and Peter imprisoned

N OW about that time Herod the king [N]stretched forth *his* hands to vex certain of the church.

2 And he killed James [R]the brother of John with the sword.

3 And because he saw it pleased the Jews, he proceeded further to take Peter also. (Then were [R]the days of unleavened bread.)

4 And [R]when he had apprehended him, he put *him* in prison, and delivered *him* to four quaternions of soldiers to keep him; intending after Easter to bring him forth to the people.

5 Peter therefore was kept in prison: but [N]prayer was made without ceasing of the church unto God for him.

The angel releases Peter

6 And when Herod would have brought him forth, the same night Peter was sleeping between two soldiers, bound with two chains: and the keepers before the door kept the prison.

7 And, behold, [R]the angel of the Lord came upon *him,* and a light shined in the prison: and he smote Peter on the side, and raised him up, saying, Arise up quickly. And his chains fell off from *his* hands.

8 And the angel said unto him, Gird thyself, and bind on thy sandals. And so he did. And he saith unto him, Cast thy garment about thee, and follow me.

9 And he went out, and followed him; and [R]wist not that it was true which was done by the angel; but thought [R]he saw a vision.

10 When they were past the first and the second ward, they came unto the iron gate that leadeth unto the city; [R]which opened to them of his own accord: and they went out, and passed on through one street; and forthwith the angel departed from him.

11 And when Peter was come to himself, he said, Now I know of a surety, that [R]the Lord hath sent his angel, and [R]hath delivered me out of the hand of Herod, and *from* all the expectation of the people of the Jews.

12 And when he had considered *the thing,* [R]he came to the house of Mary the mother of [R]John, whose surname was Mark; where many were gathered together [R]praying.

13 And as Peter knocked at the door of the gate, a damsel came [N]to hearken, named Rhoda.

14 And when she knew Peter's voice, she opened not the gate for gladness, but ran in, and told how Peter stood before the gate.

15 And they said unto her, Thou art mad. But she constantly affirmed that it was even so. Then said they, [R]It is his angel.

16 But Peter continued knocking: and when they had opened *the door,* and saw him, they were astonished.

17 But he, [R]beckoning unto them with the hand to hold their peace, declared unto them how the Lord had brought him out of the prison. And he said, Go shew these things unto James, and to the brethren. And he departed, and went into another place.

Herod's death

18 Now as soon as it was day, there was no small stir among the soldiers, what was become of Peter.

19 And when Herod had sought for him, and found him not, he examined the keepers, and commanded that *they* should be put to death. And he went down from Judæa to Çǣ-sá-rē'-ă, and *there* abode.

20 And Herod [N]was highly displeased with them of Tyre and Sī'-dŏn: but they came with one accord to him, and, having made Blăs'-tŭs [N]the king's chamberlain their friend, desired peace; because [R]their country was nourished by the king's *country.*

21 And upon a set day Herod, arrayed in royal apparel, sat upon his throne, and made an oration unto them.

22 And the people gave a shout, *saying, It is* the voice of a god, and not of a man.

23 And immediately the angel of the Lord [R]smote him, because [R]he gave not God the glory: and he was eaten of worms, and gave up the ghost.

The call of Barnabas and Saul

24 But [R]the word of God grew and multiplied.

25 And Barnabas and Saul returned from Jerusalem, when they had fulfilled *their* [N]ministry, and [R]took with them [R]John, whose surname was Mark.

CHAPTER 13

N OW there were [R]in the church that was at Ăn'-tĭ-ŏch certain prophets and teachers; as [R]Barnabas, and Simeon that was called Nī'-ġer, and [R]Lû'-cĭ-ŭs of Çȳ-rē'-nē, and Măn'-ā-ĕn, [N]which had been brought up with Herod the tē'-trärch, and Saul.

2 As they ministered to the Lord, and fasted, the Holy Ghost said, [R]Separate me Barnabas and Saul for the work [R]whereunto I have called them.

3 And [R]when they had fasted and prayed,

and laid *their* hands on them, they sent *them* away.

Paul and Barnabas on Cyprus

4 So they, being sent forth by the Holy Ghost, departed unto Sĕ-lĕũ'-çĭ-ă; and from thence they sailed to ᴿCyprus.

5 And when they were at Săl'-ă-mĭs, ᴿthey preached the word of God in the synagogues of the Jews: and they had also ᴿJohn to *their* minister.

6 And when they had gone through the isle unto Pā'-phŏs, they found ᴿa certain sorcerer, a false prophet, a Jew, whose name *was* Bär-jē'-śŭs:

7 Which was with the deputy of the country, Sĕr'-ġĭ-ŭs Paulus, a prudent man; who called for Barnabas and Saul, and desired to hear the word of God.

8 But ᴿĔl'-ў-măs the sorcerer (for so is his name by interpretation) withstood them, seeking to turn away the deputy from the faith.

9 Then Saul, (who also *is called* Paul,) ᴿfilled with the Holy Ghost, set his eyes on him,

10 And said, O full of all subtilty and all mischief, ᴿ*thou* child of the devil, *thou* enemy of all righteousness, wilt thou not cease to pervert the right ways of the Lord?

11 And now, behold, ᴿthe hand of the Lord *is* upon thee, and thou shalt be blind, not seeing the sun for a season. And immediately there fell on him a mist and a darkness; and he went about seeking some to lead him by the hand.

12 Then the deputy, when he saw what was done, believed, being astonished at the doctrine of the Lord.

Preaching in Antioch of Pisidia

13 Now when Paul and his company loosed from Pā'-phŏs, they came to Pĕr'-ga in Păm-phўl'-ĭ-ă: and ᴿJohn departing from them returned to Jerusalem.

14 But when they departed from Pĕr'-ga, they came to Ăn'-tĭ-ŏch in Pĭ-sĭd'-ĭ-ă, and ᴿwent into the synagogue on the sabbath day, and sat down.

15 And ᴿafter the reading of the law and the prophets the rulers of the synagogue sent unto them, saying, *Ye* men *and* brethren, if ye have ᴿany word of exhortation for the people, say on.

16 Then Paul stood up, and beckoning with *his* hand said, Men of Israel, and ᴿye that fear God, give audience.

17 The God of this people of Israel ᴿchose our fathers, and exalted the people ᴿwhen they

CHAP. 13

AD 45

4 ch. 4:36
5 ver. 46
5 ch. 12:25
 & 15:37
6 ch. 8:9
8 Ex. 7:11
 2 Tim. 3:8
9 ch. 4:8
10 Mat. 13:38
 1 John 3:8
11 1 Sam. 5:6
13 ch. 15:38
14 ch. 16:13
15 Luke 4:16
15 Heb. 13:22
16 ch. 10:35
17 Deut. 7:6, 7
17 ch. 7:17

Ex. 16:35   18
Gr.
ἐτροπο-
φόρησεν,
perhaps for
ξτροφο-
φόρησεν,
bore, or, *fed them,
as a nurse beareth,*
or, *feedeth her
child,*
Deut. 1:31
according to the
LXX and so
Chrysostom
Josh. 14:1   19
Judg. 2:16   20
1 Sam. 3:20   20
1 Sam. 8:5   21
1 Sam. 15:23   22
1 Sam. 16:13   22
Ps. 89:20   22
1 Sam. 13:14   22
Is. 11:1   23
Ps. 132:11   23
Mat. 1:21   23
Mat. 3:1   24
 Luke 3:3
Mark 1:7   25
Mat. 10:6   26
Luke 23:34   27
Mat. 27:22   28
Luke 18:31   29
Mat. 27:59   29
Mat. 28:6   30
Mat. 28:16   31
Gen. 3:15   32
Heb. 1:5   33

dwelt as strangers in the land of Egypt, and with an high arm brought he them out of it.

18 And ᴿabout the time of forty years ᴺsuffered he their manners in the wilderness.

19 And when he had destroyed seven nations in the land of Chā'-nă-ăn, ᴿhe divided their land to them by lot.

20 And after that ᴿhe gave *unto them* judges about the space of four hundred and fifty years, ᴿuntil Samuel the prophet.

21 ᴿAnd afterward they desired a king: and God gave unto them Saul the son of Çĭs, a man of the tribe of Benjamin, by the space of forty years.

22 And ᴿwhen he had removed him, ᴿhe raised up unto them David to be their king; to whom also he gave testimony, and said, ᴿI have found David the *son* of Jesse, ᴿa man after mine own heart, which shall fulfil all my will.

23 ᴿOf this man's seed hath God according ᴿto *his* promise raised unto Israel ᴿa Saviour, Jesus:

24 ᴿWhen John had first preached before his coming the baptism of repentance to all the people of Israel.

25 And as John fulfilled his course, he said, ᴿWhom think ye that I am? I am not *he*. But, behold, there cometh one after me, whose shoes of *his* feet I am not worthy to loose.

26 Men *and* brethren, children of the stock of Abraham, and whosoever among you feareth God, ᴿto you is the word of this salvation sent.

27 For they that dwell at Jerusalem, and their rulers, ᴿbecause they knew him not, nor yet the voices of the prophets which are read every sabbath day, they have fulfilled *them* in condemning *him*.

28 ᴿAnd though they found no cause of death *in him,* yet desired they Pilate that he should be slain.

29 ᴿAnd when they had fulfilled all that was written of him, ᴿthey took *him* down from the tree, and laid *him* in a sepulchre.

30 ᴿBut God raised him from the dead:

31 And ᴿhe was seen many days of them which came up with him from Galilee to Jerusalem, who are his witnesses unto the people.

32 And we declare unto you glad tidings, how that ᴿthe promise which was made unto the fathers,

33 God hath fulfilled the same unto us their children, in that he hath raised up Jesus again; as it is also written in the second psalm, ᴿThou art my Son, this day have I begotten thee.

34 And as concerning that he raised him up

from the dead, *now* no more to return to corruption, he said on this wise, [R]I will give you the sure [N]mercies of David.

35 Wherefore he saith also in another *psalm,* [R]Thou shalt not suffer thine Holy One to see corruption.

36 For David, [N]after he had served his own generation by the will of God, [R]fell on sleep, and was laid unto his fathers, and saw corruption:

37 But he, whom God raised again, saw no corruption.

38 Be it known unto you therefore, men *and* brethren, that [R]through this man is preached unto you the forgiveness of sins:

39 And [R]by him all that believe are justified from all things, from which ye could not be justified by the law of Moses.

40 Beware therefore, lest that come upon you, which is spoken of in [R]the prophets;

41 Behold, ye despisers, and wonder, and perish: for I work a work in your days, a work which ye shall in no wise believe, though a man declare it unto you.

42 And when the Jews were gone out of the synagogue, the Gentiles besought that these words might be preached to them [N]the next sabbath.

43 Now when the congregation was broken up, many of the Jews and religious proselytes followed Paul and Barnabas: who, speaking to them, [R]persuaded them to continue in [R]the grace of God.

Conflict at Antioch

44 And the next sabbath day came almost the whole city together to hear the word of God.

45 But when the Jews saw the multitudes, they were filled with envy, and [R]spake against those things which were spoken by Paul, contradicting and blaspheming.

46 Then Paul and Barnabas waxed bold, and said, [R]It was necessary that the word of God should first have been spoken to you: but [R]seeing ye put it from you, and judge yourselves unworthy of everlasting life, lo, [R]we turn to the Gentiles.

47 For so hath the Lord commanded us, *saying,* [R]I have set thee to be a light of the Gentiles, that thou shouldest be for salvation unto the ends of the earth.

48 And when the Gentiles heard this, they were glad, and glorified the word of the Lord: [R]and as many as were ordained to eternal life believed.

49 And the word of the Lord was published throughout all the region.

50 But the Jews stirred up the devout and

CHAP. 13
AD 45
34 Is. 55:3
34 Gr.
τὰ ὄσια,
holy, or, just
things:
which word the
LXX both in the
place of
Is. 55:3,
and in many
others, use for that
which is in the
Hebrew, mercies
35 Ps. 16:10
36 Or, after he had
in his own age
served the will
of God,
ver. 22
36 ch. 2:29
38 Jer. 31:34
39 Is. 53:11
40 Hab. 1:5
42 Gr. in the week
between, or, in
the sabbath
between
43 ch. 11:23
& 14:22
43 Tit. 2:11
Heb. 12:15
1 Pet. 5:12
45 ch. 18:6
1 Pet. 4:4
Jude 10
46 ver. 26
Mat. 10:6
ch. 3:26
Rom. 1:16
46 Ex. 32:10
Deut. 32:21
Is. 55:5
Mat. 21:43
Rom. 10:19
46 ch. 18:6 & 28:28
47 Is. 42:6 & 49:6
Luke 2:32
48 ch. 2:47

2 Tim. 3:11   **50**
Mat. 10:14   **51**
Mark 6:11
Luke 9:5
ch. 18:6
Mat. 5:12   **52**
John 16:22
ch. 2:46

CHAP. 14
AD 45
Mark 16:20   **3**
Heb. 2:4
ch. 13:2, 3   **4**
2 Tim. 3:11   **5**
Mat. 10:23   **6**
ch. 3:2
Is. 35:6   **10**
ch. 8:10 & 28:6 **11**
Dan. 2:46   **13**
Mat. 26:65   **14**

honourable women, and the chief men of the city, and [R]raised persecution against Paul and Barnabas, and expelled them out of their coasts.

51 [R]But they shook off the dust of their feet against them, and came unto ĭ-cō'-nĭ-ŭm.

52 And the disciples [R]were filled with joy, and with the Holy Ghost.

CHAPTER 14

Preaching at Iconium

AND it came to pass in ĭ-cō'-nĭ-ŭm, that they went both together into the synagogue of the Jews, and so spake, that a great multitude both of the Jews and also of the Greeks believed.

2 But the unbelieving Jews stirred up the Gentiles, and made their minds evil affected against the brethren.

3 Long time therefore abode they speaking boldly in the Lord, [R]which gave testimony unto the word of his grace, and granted signs and wonders to be done by their hands.

4 But the multitude of the city was divided: and part held with the Jews, and part with the [R]apostles.

5 And when there was an assault made both of the Gentiles, and also of the Jews with their rulers, [R]to use *them* despitefully, and to stone them,

6 They were ware of *it,* and [R]fled unto Lȳs'-tră and Dĕr'-bē, cities of Lȳ-că-ō'-nĭ-ă, and unto the region that lieth round about:

7 And there they preached the gospel.

Paul heals a cripple

8 [R]And there sat a certain man at Lȳs'-tră, impotent in his feet, being a cripple from his mother's womb, who never had walked:

9 The same heard Paul speak: who stedfastly beholding him, and perceiving that he had faith to be healed,

10 Said with a loud voice, [R]Stand upright on thy feet. And he leaped and walked.

11 And when the people saw what Paul had done, they lifted up their voices, saying in the speech of Lȳ-că-ō'-nĭ-ă, [R]The gods are come down to us in the likeness of men.

12 And they called Barnabas, Jupiter; and Paul, Mĕr-cū'-rĭ-ŭs, because he was the chief speaker.

13 Then the priest of Jupiter, which was before their city, brought oxen and garlands unto the gates, [R]and would have done sacrifice with the people.

14 *Which* when the apostles, Barnabas and Paul, heard *of,* [R]they rent their clothes, and ran in among the people, crying out,

15 And saying, Sirs, [R]why do ye these things? [R]We also are men of like passions with you, and preach unto you that ye should turn from [R]these vanities [R]unto the living God, [R]which made heaven, and earth, and the sea, and all things that are therein:

16 [R]Who in times past suffered all nations to walk in their own ways.

17 [R]Nevertheless he left not himself without witness, in that he did good, and [R]gave us rain from heaven, and fruitful seasons, filling our hearts with food and gladness.

18 And with these sayings scarce restrained they the people, that they had not done sacrifice unto them.

Paul stoned

19 [R]And there came thither *certain* Jews from Ăn′-tĭ-ŏch and ĭ-cō′-nĭ-ŭm, who persuaded the people, [R]and, having stoned Paul, drew *him* out of the city, supposing he had been dead.

20 Howbeit, as the disciples stood round about him, he rose up, and came into the city: and the next day he departed with Barnabas to Dĕr′-bē.

21 And when they had preached the gospel to that city, [R]and [N]had taught many, they returned again to Lўs′-tră, and *to* ĭ-cō′-nĭ-ŭm, and Ăn′-tĭ-ŏch,

22 Confirming the souls of the disciples, *and* [R]exhorting them to continue in the faith, and that [R]we must through much tribulation enter into the kingdom of God.

23 And when they had [R]ordained them elders in every church, and had prayed with fasting, they commended them to the Lord, on whom they believed.

24 And after they had passed throughout Pĭ-sĭd′-ĭ-ă, they came to Păm-phўl′-ĭ-ă.

25 And when they had preached the word in Pĕr′-gă, they went down into Ăt-tā′-lĭ-ă:

26 And thence sailed to Ăn′-tĭ-ŏch, [R]from whence they had been [R]recommended to the grace of God for the work which they fulfilled.

27 And when they were come, and had gathered the church together, [R]they rehearsed all that God had done with them, and how he had [R]opened the door of faith unto the Gentiles.

28 And there they abode long time with the disciples.

CHAPTER 15

The council at Jerusalem

AND [R]certain men which came down from Judæa taught the brethren, *and said,*

CHAP. 14	
AD 45	
15 ch. 10:26	
15 Jas. 5:17	
Rev. 19:10	
15 1 Sam. 12:21	
1 Ki. 16:13	
Jer. 14:22	
Amos 2:4	
1 Cor. 8:4	
15 1 Thes. 1:9	
15 Gen. 1:1	
Ps. 33:6	
& 146:6	
Rev. 14:7	
16 Ps. 81:12	
ch. 17:30	
1 Pet. 4:3	
17 ch. 17:27	
Rom. 1:20	
17 Lev. 26:4	
Deut. 11:14	
& 28:12	
Job 5:10	
Jer. 11:22	
Mat. 5:45	
19 ch. 13:45	
19 2 Cor. 11:25	
2 Tim. 3:11	
21 Mat. 28:19	
21 Gr. *had made many disciples*	
22 ch. 11:23	
& 13:43	
22 Mat. 10:38	
& 16:24	
Luke 22:28	
Rom. 8:17	
2 Tim. 2:12 & 3:12	
23 Tit. 1:5	
26 ch. 13:1, 3	
26 ch. 15:40	
27 ch. 15:4, 12	
& 21:19	
27 1 Cor. 16:9	
2 Cor. 2:12	
Col. 4:3	
Rev. 3:8	

CHAP. 15	
AD 51	
1 Gal. 2:12	
ver. 5	1
John 7:22	
Gal. 5:2	
Phil. 3:2	
Col. 2:8, 11, 16	
Gen. 17:10	1
Lev. 12:3	
Gal. 2:1	2
Rom. 15:24	3
1 Cor. 16:6, 11	
ch. 14:27	3
ver. 12	4
ch. 14:27	
Or, *rose up, said they, certain*	5
ver. 1	5
ch. 10:20	7
& 11:12	
1 Chr. 28:9	8
ch. 1:24	
ch. 10:44	8
Rom. 10:12	9
ch. 10:15, 28	9
1 Cor. 1:2	
1 Pet. 1:22	
Mat. 23:4	10
Gal. 5:1	
Rom. 3:24	11
Eph. 2:8	
ch. 14:27	12
ch. 12:17	13
ver. 7	14
Amos 9:11	16

[R]Except ye be circumcised [R]after the manner of Moses, ye cannot be saved.

2 When therefore Paul and Barnabas had no small dissension and disputation with them, they determined that [R]Paul and Barnabas, and certain other of them, should go up to Jerusalem unto the apostles and elders about this question.

3 And [R]being brought on their way by the church, they passed through Phē-nī′-çē and Să-mâr′-ĭ-ă, [R]declaring the conversion of the Gentiles: and they caused great joy unto all the brethren.

4 And when they were come to Jerusalem, they were received of the church, and *of* the apostles and elders, and [R]they declared all things that God had done with them.

5 But there [N]rose up certain of the sect of the Pharisees which believed, saying, [R]That it was needful to circumcise them, and to command *them* to keep the law of Moses.

6 And the apostles and elders came together for to consider of this matter.

7 And when there had been much disputing, Peter rose up, and said unto them, [R]Men *and* brethren, ye know how that a good while ago God made choice among us, that the Gentiles by my mouth should hear the word of the gospel, and believe.

8 And God, [R]which knoweth the hearts, bare them witness, [R]giving them the Holy Ghost, even as *he did* unto us;

9 [R]And put no difference between us and them, [R]purifying their hearts by faith.

10 Now therefore why tempt ye God, [R]to put a yoke upon the neck of the disciples, which neither our fathers nor we were able to bear?

11 But [R]we believe that through the grace of the Lord Jesus Christ we shall be saved, even as they.

12 Then all the multitude kept silence, and gave audience to Barnabas and Paul, declaring what miracles and wonders God had [R]wrought among the Gentiles by them.

13 And after they had held their peace, [R]James answered, saying, Men *and* brethren, hearken unto me:

14 [R]Simeon hath declared how God at the first did visit the Gentiles, to take out of them a people for his name.

15 And to this agree the words of the prophets; as it is written,

16 [R]After this I will return, and will build again the tabernacle of David, which is fallen down; and I will build again the ruins thereof, and I will set it up:

17 That the residue of men might seek after the Lord, and all the Gentiles, upon whom my

name is called, saith the Lord, who doeth all these things.

18 Known unto God are all his works from the beginning of the world.

19 Wherefore ᴿmy sentence is, that we trouble not them, which from among the Gentiles ᴿare turned to God:

20 But that we write unto them, that they abstain ᴿfrom pollutions of idols, and ᴿ*from* fornication, and *from* things strangled, ᴿand *from* blood.

21 For Moses of old time hath in every city them that preach him, ᴿbeing read in the synagogues every sabbath day.

The decision conveyed to Antioch

22 Then pleased it the apostles and elders, with the whole church, to send chosen men of their own company to Ăn′-tĭ-ŏch with Paul and Barnabas; *namely*, Judas surnamed ᴿBär′-să-băs, and Silas, chief men among the brethren:

23 And they wrote *letters* by them after this manner; The apostles and elders and brethren *send* greeting unto the brethren which are of the Gentiles in Ăn′-tĭ-ŏch and Syria and Çĭ-lĭç′-ĭ-ă:

24 Forasmuch as we have heard, that ᴿcertain which went out from us have troubled you with words, subverting your souls, saying, *Ye must* be circumcised, and keep the law: to whom we gave no *such* commandment:

25 It seemed good unto us, being assembled with one accord, to send chosen men unto you with our beloved Barnabas and Paul,

26 ᴿMen that have hazarded their lives for the name of our Lord Jesus Christ.

27 We have sent therefore Judas and Silas, who shall also tell *you* the same things by ᴺmouth.

28 For it seemed good to the Holy Ghost, and to us, to lay upon you no greater burden than these necessary things;

29 ᴿThat ye abstain from meats offered to idols, and ᴿfrom blood, and from things strangled, and from fornication: from which if ye keep yourselves, ye shall do well. Fare ye well.

30 So when they were dismissed, they came to Ăn′-tĭ-ŏch: and when they had gathered the multitude together, they delivered the epistle:

31 *Which* when they had read, they rejoiced for the ᴺconsolation.

32 And Judas and Silas, being prophets also themselves, ᴿexhorted the brethren with many words, and confirmed *them*.

33 And after they had tarried *there* a space, they were let ᴿgo in peace from the brethren unto the apostles.

34 Notwithstanding it pleased Silas to abide there still.

35 ᴿPaul also and Barnabas continued in Ăn′-tĭ-ŏch, teaching and preaching the word of the Lord, with many others also.

Paul and Barnabas separate

36 And some days after Paul said unto Barnabas, Let us go again and visit our brethren ᴿin every city where we have preached the word of the Lord, *and see* how they do.

37 And Barnabas determined to take with them ᴿJohn, whose surname was Mark.

38 But Paul thought not good to take him with them, ᴿwho departed from them from Păm-phўl′-ĭ-ă, and went not with them to the work.

39 And the contention was so sharp between them, that they departed asunder one from the other: and so Barnabas took Mark, and sailed unto Cyprus;

40 And Paul chose Silas, and departed, ᴿbeing recommended by the brethren unto the grace of God.

41 And he went through Syria and Çĭ-lĭç′-ĭ-ă, ᴿconfirming the churches.

CHAPTER 16

Paul chooses Timothy

THEN came he to ᴿDĕr′-bē and Lўs′-tră: and, behold, a certain disciple was there, ᴿnamed Timotheus, ᴿthe son of a certain woman, which was a Jewess, and believed; but his father *was* a Greek:

2 Which ᴿwas well reported of by the brethren that were at Lўs′-tră and Ĭ-cō′-nĭ-ŭm.

3 Him would Paul have to go forth with him; and ᴿtook and circumcised him because of the Jews which were in those quarters: for they knew all that his father was a Greek.

4 And as they went through the cities, they delivered them the decrees for to keep, ᴿthat were ordained of the apostles and elders which were at Jerusalem.

5 And ᴿso were the churches established in the faith, and increased in number daily.

Journey to Macedonia

6 Now when they had gone throughout Phrўġ′-ĭ-ă and the region of Galatia, and were forbidden of the Holy Ghost to preach the word in Asia,

7 After they were come to Mўs′-ĭ-ă, they assayed to go into Bĭ-thўn′-ĭă: but the Spirit suffered them not.

8 And they passing by Mўs′-ĭ-ă ᴿcame down to Trō′-ăs.

9 And a vision appeared to Paul in the night; There stood a ᴿman of Măç-ē-dō′-nĭ-ă, and prayed him, saying, Come over into Măç-ē-dō′-nĭ-ă, and help us.

10 And after he had seen the vision, immediately we endeavoured to go ᴿinto Măç-ē-dō′-nĭ-ă, assuredly gathering that the Lord had called us for to preach the gospel unto them.

11 Therefore loosing from Trō′-ăs, we came with a straight course to Săm-ō-thrā′-çĭ-ă, and the next day to Nē-ā′-pō-lĭs;

12 And from thence to ᴿPhilippi, which is ᴺthe chief city of that part of Măç-ē-dō′-nĭ-ă, and a colony: and we were in that city abiding certain days.

13 And on the ᴺsabbath we went out of the city by a river side, where prayer was wont to be made; and we sat down, and spake unto the women which resorted thither.

14 And a certain woman named Lydia, a seller of purple, of the city of Thȳ-ă-tī′-ră, which worshipped God, heard us: whose ᴿheart the Lord opened, that she attended unto the things which were spoken of Paul.

15 And when she was baptized, and her household, she besought us, saying, If ye have judged me to be faithful to the Lord, come into my house, and abide there. And ᴿshe constrained us.

Paul and Silas imprisoned at Philippi

16 And it came to pass, as we went to prayer, a certain damsel ᴿpossessed with a spirit ᴺof divination met us, which brought her masters ᴿmuch gain by soothsaying:

17 The same followed Paul and us, and cried, saying, These men are the servants of the most high God, which shew unto us the way of salvation.

18 And this did she many days. But Paul, ᴿbeing grieved, turned and said to the spirit, I command thee in the name of Jesus Christ to come out of her. ᴿAnd he came out the same hour.

19 And ᴿwhen her masters saw that the hope of their gains was gone, they caught Paul and Silas, and ᴿdrew them into the ᴺmarketplace unto the rulers,

20 And brought them to the magistrates, saying, These men, being Jews, ᴿdo exceedingly trouble out city,

21 And teach customs, which are not lawful for us to receive, neither to observe, being Romans.

22 And the multitude rose up together against them: and the magistrates rent off their clothes, ᴿand commanded to beat them.

CHAP. 16
AD 53
9 ch. 10:30
10 2 Cor. 2:13
12 Phil. 1:1
12 Or, the first
13 Gr. sabbath day
14 Luke 24:45
15 Gen. 19:3 & 33:11
Judg. 19:21
Luke 24:29
Heb. 13:2
16 1 Sam. 28:7
16 Or, of Python
16 ch. 19:24
18 See Mark 1:25, 34
18 Mark 16:17
19 ch. 19:25, 26
19 Mat. 10:18
19 Or, court
20 1 Ki. 18:17
ch. 17:6
22 2 Cor. 6:5 & 11:23, 25
1 Thes. 2:2

ch. 4:31   26
ch. 5:19   26
& 12:7, 10
Luke 3:10   30
ch. 2:37 & 9:6
John 3:16, 36   31
& 6:47
1 John 5:10
Luke 5:29   34
& 19:6
ch. 22:25   37
Mat. 8:34   39

23 And when they had laid many stripes upon them, they cast them into prison, charging the jailor to keep them safely:

24 Who, having received such a charge, thrust them into the inner prison, and made their feet fast in the stocks.

Ministry to the Philippian jailer

25 And at midnight Paul and Silas prayed, and sang praises unto God: and the prisoners heard them.

26 ᴿAnd suddenly there was a great earthquake, so that the foundations of the prison were shaken: and immediately ᴿall the doors were opened, and every one's bands were loosed.

27 And the keeper of the prison awaking out of his sleep, and seeing the prison doors open, he drew out his sword, and would have killed himself, supposing that the prisoners had been fled.

28 But Paul cried with a loud voice, saying, Do thyself no harm: for we are all here.

29 Then he called for a light, and sprang in, and came trembling, and fell down before Paul and Silas,

30 And brought them out, and said, ᴿSirs, what must I do to be saved?

31 And they said, ᴿBelieve on the Lord Jesus Christ, and thou shalt be saved, and thy house.

32 And they spake unto him the word of the Lord, and to all that were in his house.

33 And he took them the same hour of the night, and washed their stripes; and was baptized, he and all his, straightway.

34 And when he had brought them into his house, ᴿhe set meat before them, and rejoiced, believing in God with all his house.

The apology of the magistrates

35 And when it was day, the magistrates sent the serjeants, saying, Let those men go.

36 And the keeper of the prison told this saying to Paul, The magistrates have sent to let you go: now therefore depart, and go in peace.

37 But Paul said unto them, They have beaten us openly uncondemned, ᴿbeing Romans, and have cast us into prison; and now do they thrust us out privily? nay verily; but let them come themselves and fetch us out.

38 And the serjeants told these words unto the magistrates: and they feared, when they heard that they were Romans.

39 And they came and besought them, and brought them out, and ᴿdesired them to depart out of the city.

40 And they went out of the prison, ᴿand entered into *the house of* Lydia: and when they had seen the brethren, they comforted them, and departed.

CHAPTER 17

Paul at Thessalonica

NOW when they had passed through Ăm-phĭp'-ŏ-lĭs and Ăp-ŏl-lō'-nĭ-ă, they came to Thĕss-ă-lō-nī'-că, where was a synagogue of the Jews:

2 And Paul, as his manner was, ᴿwent in unto them, and three sabbath days reasoned with them out of the scripture,

3 Opening and alleging, ᴿthat Christ must needs have suffered, and risen again from the dead; and that this Jesus, ᴺwhom I preach unto you, is Christ.

4 ᴿAnd some of them believed, and consorted with Paul and ᴿSilas; and of the devout Greeks a great multitude, and of the chief women not a few.

5 But the Jews which believed not, moved with envy, took unto them certain lewd fellows of the baser sort, and gathered a company, and set all the city on an uproar, and assaulted the house of ᴿJā'-sǫn, and sought to bring them out to the people.

6 And when they found them not, they drew Jā'-sǫn and certain brethren unto the rulers of the city, crying, ᴿThese that have turned the world upside down are come hither also;

7 Whom Jā'-sǫn hath received: and these all do contrary to the decrees of Cæsar, ᴿsaying that there is another king, *one* Jesus.

8 And they troubled the people and the rulers of the city, when they heard these things.

9 And when they had taken security of Jā'-sǫn, and of the other, they let them go.

Paul at Berea

10 And ᴿthe brethren immediately sent away Paul and Silas by night unto Bĕ-rē'-ă: who coming *thither* went into the synagogue of the Jews.

11 These were more noble than those in Thĕss-ă-lō-nī'-că, in that they received the word with all readiness of mind, and ᴿsearched the scriptures daily, whether those things were so.

12 Therefore many of them believed; also of honourable women which were Greeks, and of men, not a few.

13 But when the Jews of Thĕss-ă-lō-nī'-că had knowledge that the word of God was

preached of Paul at Bĕ-rē'-ă, they came thither also, and stirred up the people.

14 ᴿAnd then immediately the brethren sent away Paul to go as it were to the sea: but Silas and Timotheus abode there still.

15 And they that conducted Paul brought him unto Athens: and ᴿreceiving a commandment unto Silas and Timotheus for to come to him with all speed, they departed.

Paul at Athens

16 Now while Paul waited for them at Athens, ᴿhis spirit was stirred in him, when he saw the city ᴺwholly given to idolatry.

17 Therefore disputed he in the synagogue with the Jews, and with the devout persons, and in the market daily with them that met with him.

18 Then certain philosophers of the Ĕp-ĭ-cū-rē'-ăns, and of the Stō'-ĭcks, encountered him. And some said, What will this ᴺbabbler say? other some, He seemeth to be a setter forth of strange gods: because he preached unto them Jesus, and the resurrection.

19 And they took him, and brought him unto ᴺĂr-ĕ-ŏp'-ă-gŭs, saying, May we know what this new doctrine, whereof thou speakest, *is*?

20 For thou bringest certain strange things to our ears: we would know therefore what these things mean.

21 (For all the Athenians and strangers which were there spent their time in nothing else, but either to tell, or to hear some new thing.)

Sermon on Mars' hill

22 Then Paul stood in the midst of ᴺMars' hill, and said, *Ye* men of Athens, I perceive that in all things ye are too superstitious.

23 For as I passed by, and beheld your ᴺdevotions, I found an altar with this inscription, TO THE UNKNOWN GOD. Whom therefore ye ignorantly worship, him declare I unto you.

24 ᴿGod that made the world and all things therein, seeing that he is ᴿLord of heaven and earth, ᴿdwelleth not in temples made with hands;

25 Neither is worshipped with men's hands, ᴿas though he needed any thing, seeing ᴿhe giveth to all life, and breath, and all things;

26 And hath made of one blood all nations of men for to dwell on all the face of the earth, and hath determined the times before appointed, and ᴿthe bounds of their habitation;

27 ᴿThat they should seek the Lord, if haply they might feel after him, and find him,

Center reference column

CHAP. 16
AD 53
40 ver. 14

CHAP. 17
AD 53
2 Luke 4:16
ch. 9:20 & 13:5,
14 & 14:1
& 16:13 & 19:8
3 Luke 24:26, 46
ch. 18:28
Gal. 3:1
3 Or, *whom,
said he,
I preach*
4 ch. 28:24
4 ch. 15:22,
27, 32, 40
5 Rom. 16:21
6 ch. 16:20
7 Luke 23:2
John 19:12
1 Pet. 2:13
10 ver. 14
ch. 9:25
11 Is. 34:16
Luke 16:29
John 5:39

Mat. 10:23   14
ch. 18:5   15
2 Pet. 2:8   16
Or, *full of idols* 16
Or, *base fellow*   18
Or, *Mars' hill.*   19
It was the highest
court in Athens
Or, *the court of* 22
the Areopagites
Or, *gods that*   23
ye worship,
2 Thes. 2:4
ch. 14:15   24
Mat. 11:25   24
ch. 7:48   24
Ps. 50:8   25
Gen. 2:7   25
Num. 16:22
Job 12:10 & 27:3
& 33:4
Is. 42:5 & 57:16
Zech. 12:1
Deut. 32:8   26
Rom. 1:20   27

Rthough he be not far from every one of us:

28 For Rin him we live, and move, and have our being; Ras certain also of your own poets have said, For we are also his offspring.

29 Forasmuch then as we are the offspring of God, Rwe ought not to think that the Godhead is like unto gold, or silver, or stone, graven by art and man's device.

30 And Rthe times of this ignorance God winked at; but Rnow commandeth all men every where to repent:

31 Because he hath appointed a day, in the which Rhe will judge the world in righteousness by *that* man whom he hath ordained; *whereof* he hath Ngiven assurance unto all *men,* in that Rhe hath raised him from the dead.

32 And when they heard of the resurrection of the dead, some mocked: and others said, We will hear thee again of this *matter.*

33 So Paul departed from among them.

34 Howbeit certain men clave unto him, and believed: among the which *was* Dī-ō-nўs′-ĭ-ŭs the Ăr-ē-ŏp′-ă-gīte, and a woman named Dăm′-ă-rĭs, and others with them.

CHAPTER 18

Paul at Corinth

AFTER these things Paul departed from Athens, and came to Corinth;

2 And found a certain Jew named RĂ-quĭl′-ă, born in Pontus, lately come from Italy, with his wife Priscilla; (because that Claudius had commanded all Jews to depart from Rome:) and came unto them.

3 And because he was of the same craft, he abode with them, Rand wrought: for by their occupation they were tentmakers.

4 RAnd he reasoned in the synagogue every sabbath, and persuaded the Jews and the Greeks.

5 And Rwhen Silas and Timotheus were come from Măç-ē-dō′-nĭ-ă, Paul was Rpressed in the spirit, and testified to the Jews *that* Jesus Nwas Christ.

6 And Rwhen they opposed themselves, and blasphemed, Rhe shook *his* raiment, and said unto them, RYour blood *be* upon your own heads; RI *am* clean: Rfrom henceforth I will go unto the Gentiles.

7 And he departed thence, and entered into a certain *man's* house, named Justus, *one* that worshipped God, whose house joined hard to the synagogue.

8 RAnd Crĭs′-pŭs, the chief ruler of the synagogue, believed on the Lord with all

his house; and many of the Corinthians hearing believed, and were baptized.

9 Then Rspake the Lord to Paul in the night by a vision, Be not afraid, but speak, and hold not thy peace:

10 RFor I am with thee, and no man shall set on thee to hurt thee: for I have much people in this city.

11 And he Ncontinued *there* a year and six months, teaching the word of God among them.

12 And when Găl′-lĭ-ō was the deputy of Ă-chāī′-ă, the Jews made insurrection with one accord against Paul, and brought him to the judgment seat,

13 Saying, This *fellow* persuadeth men to worship God contrary to the law.

14 And when Paul was now about to open *his* mouth, Găl′-lĭ-ō said unto the Jews, RIf it were a matter of wrong or wicked lewdness, O *ye* Jews, reason would that I should bear with you:

15 But if it be a question of words and names, and *of* your law, look ye *to it;* for I will be no judge of such *matters.*

16 And he drave them from the judgment seat.

17 Then all the Greeks took RSŏs′-thĕ-nēś, the chief ruler of the synagogue, and beat *him* before the judgment seat. And Găl′-lĭ-ō cared for none of those things.

Return to Antioch

18 And Paul *after this* tarried *there* yet a good while, and then took his leave of the brethren, and sailed thence into Syria, and with him Priscilla and Ă-quĭl′-ă; having Rshorn *his* head in RÇĕn-chrē′-ă: for he had a vow.

19 And he came to Ĕph′-ĕ-sŭs, and left them there: but he himself entered into the synagogue, and reasoned with the Jews.

20 When they desired *him* to tarry longer time with them, he consented not;

21 But bade them farewell, saying, RI must by all means keep this feast that cometh in Jerusalem: but I will return again unto you, Rif God will. And he sailed from Ĕph′-ĕ-sŭs.

22 And when he had landed at Çæ-să-rē′-ă, and gone up, and saluted the church, he went down to Ăn′-tĭ-ŏch.

23 And after he had spent some time *there,* he departed, and went over *all* the country of RGalatia and Phrŷġ′-ĭ-ă in order, Rstrengthening all the disciples.

Apollos at Ephesus

24 RAnd a certain Jew named Ă-pŏl′-lŏs, born at Alexandria, an eloquent man, *and* mighty in the scriptures, came to Ĕph′-ĕ-sŭs.

CHAP. 17
AD 53
27 ch. 14:17
28 Col. 1:17
Heb. 1:3
28 Tit. 1:12
29 Is. 40:18
30 ch. 14:16
Rom. 3:25
30 Luke 24:47
Tit. 2:11, 12
1 Pet. 1:14 & 4:3
31 ch. 10:42
Rom. 2:16 & 14:10
31 Or, *offered faith*
31 ch. 2:24

CHAP. 18
AD 54
2 Rom. 16:3
1 Cor. 16:19
2 Tim. 4:19
3 ch. 20:34
1 Cor. 4:12
1 Thes. 2:9
2 Thes. 3:8
4 ch. 17:2
5 ch. 17:14, 15
5 ver. 28
Job 32:18
ch. 17:3
5 Or, *is the Christ*
6 ch. 13:45
6 Neh. 5:13
Mat. 10:14
ch. 13:51
6 Lev. 20:9, 11, 12
2 Sam. 1:16
Ezek. 18:13
& 33:4
6 Ezek. 3:18, 19
& 33:9
ch. 20:26
6 ch. 13:46
& 28:28
8 1 Cor. 1:14

ch. 23:11 9
Jer. 1:18, 19 10
Gr. *sat there* 11
ch. 23:29 14
& 25:11, 19
1 Cor. 1:1 17
Num. 6:18 18
ch. 21:24
Rom. 16:1 18
ch. 19:21 21
& 20:16
1 Cor. 4:19 21
Heb. 6:3
Jas. 4:15
Gal. 1:2 & 4:14 23
ch. 14:22 23
& 15:32, 41
1 Cor. 1:12 24
& 3:5, 6 & 4:6
Tit. 3:13

25 This man was instructed in the way of the Lord; and being ᴿfervent in the spirit, he spake and taught diligently the things of the Lord, ᴿknowing only the baptism of John.

26 And he began to speak boldly in the synagogue: whom when Ă-quĭl′-ă and Priscilla had heard, they took him unto *them,* and expounded unto him the way of God more perfectly.

27 And when he was disposed to pass into Ă-chāi′-ă, the brethren wrote, exhorting the disciples to receive him: who, when he was come, ᴿhelped them much which had believed through grace:

28 For he mightily convinced the Jews, *and that* publickly, ᴿshewing by the scriptures that Jesus ᴺwas Christ.

CHAPTER 19

Paul at Ephesus

AND it came to pass, that, while ᴿĂ-pŏl′-lŏs was at Corinth, Paul having passed through the upper coasts came to Ĕph′-ĕ-sŭs: and finding certain disciples,

2 He said unto them, Have ye received the Holy Ghost since ye believed? And they said unto him, ᴿWe have not so much as heard whether there be any Holy Ghost.

3 And he said unto them, Unto what then were ye baptized? And they said, ᴿUnto John's baptism.

4 Then said Paul, ᴿJohn verily baptized with the baptism of repentance, saying unto the people, that they should believe on him which should come after him, that is, on Christ Jesus.

5 When they heard *this,* they were baptized ᴿin the name of the Lord Jesus.

6 And when Paul had ᴿlaid *his* hands upon them, the Holy Ghost came on them; and ᴿthey spake with tongues, and prophesied.

7 And all the men were about twelve.

8 ᴿAnd he went into the synagogue, and spake boldly for the space of three months, disputing and persuading the things ᴿconcerning the kingdom of God.

9 But ᴿwhen divers were hardened, and believed not, but spake evil ᴿof that way before the multitude, he departed from them, and separated the disciples, disputing daily in the school of one Tȳ-răn′-nŭs.

10 And ᴿthis continued by the space of two years; so that all they which dwelt in Asia heard the word of the Lord Jesus, both Jews and Greeks.

CHAP. 18
AD 54
25 Rom. 12:11
25 ch. 19:3
27 1 Cor. 3:6
28 ver. 5
ch. 9:22 & 17:3
28 Or, *is the Christ*

CHAP. 19
AD 58
1 1 Cor. 1:12
& 3:5, 6
2 ch. 8:16
See 1 Sam. 3:7
3 ch. 18:25
4 Mat. 3:11
John 1:15, 27, 30
ch. 1:5 & 11:16
& 13:24, 25
5 ch. 8:16
6 ch. 6:6 & 8:17
6 ch. 2:4 & 10:46
8 ch. 17:2 & 18:4
8 ch. 1:3 & 28:23
9 2 Tim. 1:15
2 Pet. 2:2
Jude 10
9 ver. 23
See ch. 9:2
& 22:4 & 24:14
10 See ch. 20:31

Mark 16:20   11
ch. 14:3
See 2 Ki. 4:29 12
ch. 5:15
Mat. 12:27   13
See   13
Mark 9:38
Luke 9:49
Luke 1:65   17
& 7:16
ch. 2:43 & 5:5, 11
Mat. 3:6   18
ch. 6:7 & 12:24 20
Rom. 15:25   21
Gal. 2:1
ch. 20:22   21
ch. 18:21   21
& 23:11
Rom. 15:24-28
Rom. 16:23   22
2 Tim. 4:20
2 Cor. 1:8   23
See ch. 9:2   23
ch. 16:16, 19 24

11 And ᴿGod wrought special miracles by the hands of Paul:

12 ᴿSo that from his body were brought unto the sick handkerchiefs or aprons, and the diseases departed from them, and the evil spirits went out of them.

13 ᴿThen certain of the vagabond Jews, exorcists, ᴿtook upon them to call over them which had evil spirits the name of the Lord Jesus, saying, We adjure you by Jesus whom Paul preacheth.

14 And there were seven sons of *one* Sçē′-vă, a Jew, *and* chief of the priests, which did so.

15 And the evil spirit answered and said, Jesus I know, and Paul I know; but who are ye?

16 And the man in whom the evil spirit was leaped on them, and overcame them, and prevailed against them, so that they fled out of that house naked and wounded.

17 And this was known to all the Jews and Greeks also dwelling at Ĕph′-ĕ-sŭs; and ᴿfear fell on them all, and the name of the Lord Jesus was magnified.

18 And many that believed came, and ᴿconfessed, and shewed their deeds.

19 Many of them also which used curious arts brought their books together, and burned them before all *men:* and they counted the price of them, and found *it* fifty thousand *pieces* of silver.

20 ᴿSo mightily grew the word of God and prevailed.

21 ᴿAfter these things were ended, Paul ᴿpurposed in the spirit, when he had passed through Măç-ē-dō′-nĭ-ă and Ă-chāi′-ă, to go to Jerusalem, saying, After I have been there, ᴿI must also see Rome.

22 So he sent into Măç-ē-dō′-nĭ-ă two of them that ministered unto him, Timotheus and ᴿĒ-răs′-tŭs; but he himself stayed in Asia for a season.

Demetrius the silversmith

23 And ᴿthe same time there arose no small stir about ᴿthat way.

24 For a certain *man* named Dē-mē′-trĭ-ŭs, a silversmith, which made silver shrines for Diana, brought ᴿno small gain unto the craftsmen;

25 Whom he called together with the workmen of like occupation, and said, Sirs, ye know that by this craft we have our wealth.

26 Moreover ye see and hear, that not alone at Ĕph′-ĕ-sŭs, but almost throughout all Asia, this Paul hath persuaded and turned away

much people, saying that ᴿthey be no gods, which are made with hands:

27 So that not only this our craft is in danger to be set at nought; but also that the temple of the great goddess Diana should be despised, and her magnificence should be destroyed, whom all Asia and the world worshippeth.

The riot at Ephesus

28 And when they heard *these sayings,* they were full of wrath, and cried out, saying, Great *is* Diana of the ĕph-ē′-ṣĭans.

29 And the whole city was filled with confusion: and having caught ᴿGâi′-ŭs and ᴿĂr-ĭs-tär′-chŭs, men of Măç-ē-dō′-nĭ-ă, Paul's companions in travel, they rushed with one accord into the theatre.

30 And when Paul would have entered in unto the people, the disciples suffered him not.

31 And certain of the chief of Asia, which were his friends, sent unto him, desiring *him* that he would not adventure himself into the theatre.

32 Some therefore cried one thing, and some another: for the assembly was confused; and the more part knew not wherefore they were come together.

33 And they drew Alexander out of the multitude, the Jews putting him forward. And ᴿAlexander ᴿbeckoned with the hand, and would have made his defence unto the people.

34 But when they knew that he was a Jew, all with one voice about the space of two hours cried out, Great *is* Diana of the ĕph-ē′-ṣĭans.

35 And when the townclerk had appeased the people, he said, *Ye* men of ĕph′-ĕ-sŭs, what man is there that knoweth not how that the city of the ĕph-ē′-ṣĭans is ᴺa worshipper of the great goddess Diana, and of the *image* which fell down from Jupiter?

36 Seeing then that these things cannot be spoken against, ye ought to be quiet, and to do nothing rashly.

37 For ye have brought hither these men, which are neither robbers of churches, nor yet blasphemers of your goddess.

38 Wherefore if Dē-mē′-trĭ-ŭs, and the craftsmen which are with him, have a matter against any man, ᴺthe law is open, and there are deputies: let them implead one another.

39 But if ye inquire any thing concerning other matters, it shall be determined in a ᴺlawful assembly.

40 For we are in danger to be called in question for this day's uproar, there being no cause whereby we may give an account of this concourse.

41 And when he had thus spoken, he dismissed the assembly.

CHAPTER 20

Journey through Greece

AND after the uproar was ceased, Paul called unto *him* the disciples, and embraced *them,* and ᴿdeparted for to go into Măç-ē-dō′-nĭ-ă.

2 And when he had gone over those parts, and had given them much exhortation, he came into Greece,

3 And *there* abode three months. And ᴿwhen the Jews laid wait for him, as he was about to sail into Syria, he purposed to return through Măç-ē-dō′-nĭ-ă.

4 And there accompanied him into Asia Sō′-pă-tĕr of Bĕ-rē′-ă; and of the Thĕss-ă-lō′-nĭ-ăns, ᴿĂr-ĭs-tär′-chŭs and Sĕ-cŭn′-dŭs; and ᴿGâi′-ŭs of Dĕr′-bē, and ᴿTimotheus; and of Asia, ᴿTў̆ch′-ĭ-cŭs and ᴿTrŏph′-ĭ-mŭs.

5 These going before tarried for us at Trō′-ăs.

6 And we sailed away from Philippi after ᴿthe days of unleavened bread, and came unto them ᴿto Trō′-ăs in five days; where we abode seven days.

Eutychus restored to life

7 And upon ᴿthe first *day* of the week, when the disciples came together ᴿto break bread, Paul preached unto them, ready to depart on the morrow; and continued his speech until midnight.

8 And there were many lights ᴿin the upper chamber, where they were gathered together.

9 And there sat in a window a certain young man named Ĕu′-tў̆-chŭs, being fallen into a deep sleep: and as Paul was long preaching, he sunk down with sleep, and fell down from the third loft, and was taken up dead.

10 And Paul went down, and ᴿfell on him, and embracing *him* said, ᴿTrouble not yourselves; for his life is in him.

11 When he therefore was come up again, and had broken bread, and eaten, and talked a long while, even till break of day, so he departed.

12 And they brought the young man alive, and were not a little comforted.

13 And we went before to ship, and sailed unto Ăs′-sŏs, there intending to take in Paul: for so had he appointed, minding himself to go afoot.

14 And when he met with us at Ăs′-sŏs, we took him in, and came to Mĭt-ў̆-lē′-nē.

15 And we sailed thence, and came the next *day* over against Chī'-ŏs; and the next *day* we arrived at Sā'-mŏs, and tarried at Trō-gўl'-lĭ-ŭm; and the next *day* we came to Mĭ-lē'-tŭs.

16 For Paul had determined to sail by ĕph'-ĕ-sŭs, because he would not spend the time in Asia: for ᴿhe hasted, if it were possible for him, ᴿto be at Jerusalem ᴿthe day of Pentecost.

Address to the elders of Ephesus

17 And from Mĭ-lē'-tŭs he sent to ĕph'-ĕ-sŭs, and called the elders of the church.

18 And when they were come to him, he said unto them, Ye know, ᴿfrom the first day that I came into Asia, after what manner I have been with you at all seasons,

19 Serving the Lord with all humility of mind, and with many tears, and temptations, which befell me ᴿby the lying in wait of the Jews:

20 *And* how ᴿI kept back nothing that was profitable *unto you,* but have shewed you, and have taught you publickly, and from house to house,

21 ᴿTestifying both to the Jews, and also to the Greeks, ᴿrepentance toward God, and faith toward our Lord Jesus Christ.

22 And now, behold, ᴿI go bound in the spirit unto Jerusalem, not knowing the things that shall befall me there:

23 Save that ᴿthe Holy Ghost witnesseth in every city, saying that bonds and afflictions ᴺabide me.

24 But ᴿnone of these things move me, neither count I my life dear unto myself, ᴿso that I might finish my course with joy, ᴿand the ministry, ᴿwhich I have received of the Lord Jesus, to testify the gospel of the grace of God.

25 And now, behold, ᴿI know that ye all, among whom I have gone preaching the kingdom of God, shall see my face no more.

26 Wherefore I take you to record this day, that I *am* ᴿpure from the blood of all *men.*

27 For ᴿI have not shunned to declare unto you all ᴿthe counsel of God.

28 ᴿTake heed therefore unto yourselves, and to all the flock, over the which the Holy Ghost ᴿhath made you overseers, to feed the church of God, ᴿwhich he hath purchased ᴿwith his own blood.

29 For I know this, that after my departing ᴿshall grievous wolves enter in among you, not sparing the flock.

30 Also ᴿof your own selves shall men arise, speaking perverse things, to draw away disciples after them.

31 Therefore watch, and remember, that ᴿby the space of three years I ceased not to warn every one night and day with tears.

32 And now, brethren, I commend you to God, and ᴿto the word of his grace, which is able ᴿto build you up, and to give you ᴿan inheritance among all them which are sanctified.

33 ᴿI have coveted no man's silver, or gold, or apparel.

34 Yea, ye yourselves know, ᴿthat these hands have ministered unto my necessities, and to them that were with me.

35 I have shewed you all things, ᴿhow that so labouring ye ought to support the weak, and to remember the words of the Lord Jesus, how he said, It is more blessed to give than to receive.

36 And when he had thus spoken, he ᴿkneeled down, and prayed with them all.

37 And they all wept sore, and ᴿfell on Paul's neck, and kissed him,

38 Sorrowing most of all for the words ᴿwhich he spake, that they should see his face no more. And they accompanied him unto the ship.

CHAPTER 21

Return to Jerusalem

AND it came to pass, that after we were gotten from them, and had launched, we came with a straight course unto Cŏ'-ŏs, and the *day* following unto Rhodes, and from thence unto Păt'-ă-rä:

2 And finding a ship sailing over unto Phē-nĭç'-ĭă, we went aboard, and set forth.

3 Now when we had discovered Cyprus, we left it on the left hand, and sailed into Syria, and landed at Tyre: for there the ship was to unlade her burden.

4 And finding disciples, we tarried there seven days: ᴿwho said to Paul through the Spirit, that he should not go up to Jerusalem.

5 And when we had accomplished those days, we departed and went our way; and they all brought us on our way, with wives and children, till *we were* out of the city: and ᴿwe kneeled down on the shore, and prayed.

6 And when we had taken our leave one of another, we took ship; and they returned ᴿhome again.

7 And when we had finished *our* course from Tyre, we came to Ptŏl-ĕ-mā'-ĭs, and saluted the brethren, and abode with them one day.

8 And the next *day* we that were of Paul's company departed, and came unto Çæ-ṡă-rē'-à:

and we entered into the house of Philip ^Rthe evangelist, ^Rwhich was *one* of the seven; and abode with him.

9 And the same man had four daughters, virgins, ^Rwhich did prophesy.

10 And as we tarried *there* many days, there came down from Judæa a certain prophet, named ^RĂg′-ă-bŭs.

11 And when he was come unto us, he took Paul's girdle, and bound his own hands and feet, and said, Thus saith the Holy Ghost, ^RSo shall the Jews at Jerusalem bind the man that owneth this girdle, and shall deliver *him* into the hands of the Gentiles.

12 And when we heard these things, both we, and they of that place, besought him not to go up to Jerusalem.

13 Then Paul answered, ^RWhat mean ye to weep and to break mine heart? for I am ready not to be bound only, but also to die at Jerusalem for the name of the Lord Jesus.

14 And when he would not be persuaded, we ceased, saying, ^RThe will of the Lord be done.

15 And after those days we took up our carriages, and went up to Jerusalem.

16 There went with us also *certain* of the disciples of Çæ-ṡă-rē′-ă, and brought with them one Mnā′-son of Cyprus, an old disciple, with whom we should lodge.

Paul's report

17 ^RAnd when we were come to Jerusalem, the brethren received us gladly.

18 And the *day* following Paul went in with us unto ^RJames; and all the elders were present.

19 And when he had saluted them, ^Rhe declared particularly what things God had wrought among the Gentiles ^Rby his ministry.

20 And when they heard *it,* they glorified the Lord, and said unto him, Thou seest, brother, how many thousands of Jews there are which believe; and they are all ^Rzealous of the law:

21 And they are informed of thee, that thou teachest all the Jews which are among the Gentiles to forsake Moses, saying that they ought not to circumcise *their* children, neither to walk after the customs.

22 What is it therefore? the multitude must needs come together: for they will hear that thou art come.

23 Do therefore this that we say to thee: We have four men which have a vow on them;

24 Them take, and purify thyself with them, and be at charges with them, that they may ^Rshave *their* heads: and all may know that those things, whereof they were informed concerning thee, are nothing; but *that* thou

thyself also walkest orderly, and keepest the law.

25 As touching the Gentiles which believe, ^Rwe have written *and* concluded that they observe no such thing, save only that they keep themselves from *things* offered to idols, and from blood, and from strangled, and from fornication.

26 Then Paul took the men, and the next day purifying himself with them ^Rentered into the temple, ^Rto signify the accomplishment of the days of purification, until that an offering should be offered for every one of them.

Assault on Paul and his arrest

27 And when the seven days were almost ended, ^Rthe Jews which were of Asia, when they saw him in the temple, stirred up all the people, and ^Rlaid hands on him,

28 Crying out, Men of Israel, help: This is the man, ^Rthat teacheth all *men* every where against the people, and the law, and this place: and further brought Greeks also into the temple, and hath polluted this holy place.

29 (For they had seen before with him in the city ^RTrŏph′-ĭ-mŭs an Ĕph-ē′-ṣĭ-ăn, whom they supposed that Paul had brought into the temple.)

30 And ^Rall the city was moved, and the people ran together: and they took Paul, and drew him out of the temple: and forthwith the doors were shut.

31 And as they went about to kill him, tidings came unto the chief captain of the band, that all Jerusalem was in an uproar.

32 ^RWho immediately took soldiers and centurions, and ran down unto them: and when they saw the chief captain and the soldiers, they left beating of Paul.

33 Then the chief captain came near, and took him, and ^Rcommanded *him* to be bound with two chains; and demanded who he was, and what he had done.

34 And some cried one thing, some another, among the multitude: and when he could not know the certainty for the tumult, he commanded him to be carried into the castle.

35 And when he came upon the stairs, so it was, that he was borne of the soldiers for the violence of the people.

36 For the multitude of the people followed after, crying, ^RAway with him.

37 And as Paul was to be led into the castle, he said unto the chief captain, May I speak unto thee? Who said, Canst thou speak Greek?

38 ^RArt not thou that Egyptian, which before these days madest an uproar, and leddest out into the wilderness four thousand men that were murderers?

CHAP. **21**

AD 60
8 Eph. 4:11
2 Tim. 4:5
8 ch. 6:5
& 8:26, 40
9 Joel 2:28
ch. 2:17
10 ch. 11:28
11 ver. 33
ch. 20:23
13 ch. 20:24
14 Mat. 6:10
& 26:42
Luke 11:2
& 22:42
17 ch. 15:4
18 ch. 15:13
Gal. 1:19 & 2:9
19 ch. 15:4, 12
Rom. 15:18, 19
19 ch. 1:17
& 20:24
20 ch. 22:3
Rom. 10:2
Gal. 1:14
24 Num. 6:2, 13, 18
ch. 18:18

ch. 15:20, 29   **25**
ch. 24:18   **26**
Num. 6:13   **26**
ch. 24:18   **27**
ch. 26:21   **27**
ch. 24:5, 6   **28**
ch. 20:4   **29**
ch. 26:21   **30**
ch. 23:27   **32**
& 24:7
ver. 11   **33**
ch. 20:23
Luke 23:18   **36**
John 19:15
ch. 22:22
See   **38**
ch. 5:36

39 But Paul said, [R]I am a man *which am* a Jew of Tarsus, *a city* in Çĭ-lĭç′-ĭ-ă, a citizen of no mean city: and, I beseech thee, suffer me to speak unto the people.

40 And when he had given him licence, Paul stood on the stairs, and [R]beckoned with the hand unto the people. And when there was made a great silence, he spake unto *them* in the Hebrew tongue, saying,

CHAPTER 22

Paul's address to the people

MEN, [R]brethren, and fathers, hear ye my defence *which I make* now unto you.

2 (And when they heard that he spake in the Hebrew tongue to them, they kept the more silence: and he saith,)

3 [R]I am verily a man *which am* a Jew, born in Tarsus, *a city* in Çĭ-lĭç′-ĭ-ă, yet brought up in this city [R]at the feet of [R]Gă-mā′-lĭ-ĕl, *and* taught [R]according to the perfect manner of the law of the fathers, and [R]was zealous toward God, [R]as ye all are this day.

4 [R]And I persecuted this way unto the death, binding and delivering into prisons both men and women.

5 As also the high priest doth bear me witness, and [R]all the estate of the elders: [R]from whom also I received letters unto the brethren, and went to Damascus, to bring them which were there bound unto Jerusalem, for to be punished.

6 And [R]it came to pass, that, as I made my journey, and was come nigh unto Damascus about noon, suddenly there shone from heaven a great light round about me.

7 And I fell unto the ground, and heard a voice saying unto me, Saul, Saul, why persecutest thou me?

8 And I answered, Who art thou, Lord? And he said unto me, I am Jesus of Nazareth, whom thou persecutest.

9 And [R]they that were with me saw indeed the light, and were afraid; but they heard not the voice of him that spake to me.

10 And I said, What shall I do, Lord? And the Lord said unto me, Arise, and go into Damascus; and there it shall be told thee of all things which are appointed for thee to do.

11 And when I could not see for the glory of that light, being led by the hand of them that were with me, I came into Damascus.

12 And [R]one Ăn-ă-nī′-ăs, a devout man according to the law, [R]having a good report of all the [R]Jews which dwelt *there*,

13 Came unto me, and stood, and said unto

me, Brother Saul, receive thy sight. And the same hour I looked up upon him.

14 And he said, [R]The God of our fathers [R]hath chosen thee, that thou shouldest know his will, and [R]see [R]that Just One, and [R]shouldest hear the voice of his mouth.

15 [R]For thou shalt be his witness unto all men of [R]what thou hast seen and heard.

16 And now why tarriest thou? arise, and be baptized, [R]and wash away thy sins, [R]calling on the name of the Lord.

17 And [R]it came to pass, that, when I was come again to Jerusalem, even while I prayed in the temple, I was in a trance;

18 And [R]saw him saying unto me, [R]Make haste, and get thee quickly out of Jerusalem: for they will not receive thy testimony concerning me.

19 And I said, Lord, [R]they know that I imprisoned and [R]beat in every synagogue them that believed on thee:

20 [R]And when the blood of thy martyr Stephen was shed, I also was standing by, and [R]consenting unto his death, and kept the raiment of them that slew him.

21 And he said unto me, Depart: [R]for I will send thee far hence unto the Gentiles.

Paul's arrest

22 And they gave him audience unto this word, and *then* lifted up their voices, and said, [R]Away with such a *fellow* from the earth: for it is not fit that [R]he should live.

23 And as they cried out, and cast off *their* clothes, and threw dust into the air,

24 The chief captain commanded him to be brought into the castle, and bade that he should be examined by scourging; that he might know wherefore they cried so against him.

25 And as they bound him with thongs, Paul said unto the centurion that stood by, [R]Is it lawful for you to scourge a man that is a Roman, and uncondemned?

26 When the centurion heard *that,* he went and told the chief captain, saying, Take heed what thou doest: for this man is a Roman.

27 Then the chief captain came, and said unto him, Tell me, art thou a Roman? He said, Yea.

28 And the chief captain answered, With a great sum obtained I this freedom. And Paul said, But I was *free* born.

29 Then straightway they departed from him which should have [N]examined him: and the chief captain also was afraid, after he knew that he was a Roman, and because he had bound him.

Paul before the council

30 On the morrow, because he would have known the certainty wherefore he was accused of the Jews, he loosed him from *his* bands, and commanded the chief priests and all their council to appear, and brought Paul down, and set him before them.

CHAPTER 23

AND Paul, earnestly beholding the council, said, Men *and* brethren, ᴿI have lived in all good conscience before God until this day.

2 And the high priest Ăn-ă-nī'-ăs commanded them that stood by him ᴿto smite him on the mouth.

3 Then said Paul unto him, God shall smite thee, *thou* whited wall: for sittest thou to judge me after the law, and ᴿcommandest me to be smitten contrary to the law?

4 And they that stood by said, Revilest thou God's high priest?

5 Then said Paul, ᴿI wist not, brethren, that he was the high priest: for it is written, ᴿThou shalt not speak evil of the ruler of thy people.

The council divided

6 But when Paul perceived that the one part were Săd'-dū-çēėś, and the other Pharisees, he cried out in the council, Men *and* brethren, ᴿI am a Pharisee, the son of a Pharisee: ᴿof the hope and resurrection of the dead I am called in question.

7 And when he had so said, there arose a dissension between the Pharisees and the Săd'-dū-çēėś: and the multitude was divided.

8 ᴿFor the Săd'-dū-çēėś say that there is no resurrection, neither angel, nor spirit: but the Pharisees confess both.

9 And there arose a great cry: and the scribes *that were* of the Pharisees' part arose, and strove, saying, ᴿWe find no evil in this man: but ᴿif a spirit or an angel hath spoken to him, ᴿlet us not fight against God.

10 And when there arose a great dissension, the chief captain, fearing lest Paul should have been pulled in pieces of them, commanded the soldiers to go down, and to take him by force from among them, and to bring *him* into the castle.

11 And ᴿthe night following the Lord stood by him, and said, Be of good cheer, Paul: for as thou hast testified of me in Jerusalem, so must thou bear witness also at Rome.

Plot to kill Paul discovered

12 And when it was day, ᴿcertain of the Jews banded together, and bound themselves

ᴺunder a curse, saying that they would neither eat nor drink till they had killed Paul.

13 And they were more than forty which had made this conspiracy.

14 And they came to the chief priests and elders, and said, We have bound ourselves under a great curse, that we will eat nothing until we have slain Paul.

15 Now therefore ye with the council signify to the chief captain that he bring him down unto you to morrow, as though ye would inquire something more perfectly concerning him: and we, or ever he come near, are ready to kill him.

16 And when Paul's sister's son heard of their lying in wait, he went and entered into the castle, and told Paul.

17 Then Paul called one of the centurions unto *him*, and said, Bring this young man unto the chief captain: for he hath a certain thing to tell him.

18 So he took him, and brought *him* to the chief captain, and said, Paul the prisoner called me unto *him*, and prayed me to bring this young man unto thee, who hath something to say unto thee.

19 Then the chief captain took him by the hand, and went *with him* aside privately, and asked *him*, What is that thou hast to tell me?

20 And he said, ᴿThe Jews have agreed to desire thee that thou wouldest bring down Paul to morrow into the council, as though they would inquire somewhat of him more perfectly.

21 But do not thou yield unto them: for there lie in wait for him of them more than forty men, which have bound themselves with an oath, that they will neither eat nor drink till they have killed him: and now are they ready, looking for a promise from thee.

22 So the chief captain *then* let the young man depart, and charged *him, See thou* tell no man that thou hast shewed these things to me.

Paul sent to Cæsarea

23 And he called unto *him* two centurions, saying, Make ready two hundred soldiers to go to Çæ-ṡà-rē'-ă, and horsemen threescore and ten, and spearmen two hundred, at the third hour of the night;

24 And provide *them* beasts, that they may set Paul on, and bring *him* safe unto Felix the governor.

25 And he wrote a letter after this manner:

26 Claudius Lўs'-ĭ-ăs unto the most excellent governor Felix *sendeth* greeting.

27 ᴿThis man was taken of the Jews, and should have been killed of them: then came I

with an army, and rescued him, having understood that he was a Roman.

28 [R]And when I would have known the cause wherefore they accused him, I brought him forth into their council:

29 Whom I perceived to be accused [R]of questions of their law, [R]but to have nothing laid to his charge worthy of death or of bonds.

30 And [R]when it was told me how that the Jews laid wait for the man, I sent straightway to thee, and [R]gave commandment to his accusers also to say before thee what *they had* against him. Farewell.

31 Then the soldiers, as it was commanded them, took Paul, and brought *him* by night to Ăn-tĭp′-ă-trĭs.

32 On the morrow they left the horsemen to go with him, and returned to the castle:

33 Who, when they came to Çæ-să-rē′-ă, and delivered the epistle to the governor, presented Paul also before him.

34 And when the governor had read *the letter,* he asked of what province he was. And when he understood that *he was* of [R]Çĭ-lĭç′-ĭ-ă;

35 [R]I will hear thee, said he, when thine accusers are also come. And he commanded him to be kept in [R]Hĕr′-ŏd's judgment hall.

CHAPTER 24

Accusation against Paul

AND after [R]five days [R]Ăn-ă-nī′-ăs the high priest descended with the elders, and *with* a certain orator *named* Tĕr-tŭl′-lŭs, who informed the governor against Paul.

2 And when he was called forth, Tĕr-tŭl′-lŭs began to accuse *him,* saying, Seeing that by thee we enjoy great quietness, and that very worthy deeds are done unto this nation by thy providence,

3 We accept *it* always, and in all places, most noble Felix, with all thankfulness.

4 Notwithstanding, that I be not further tedious unto thee, I pray thee that thou wouldest hear us of thy clemency a few words.

5 [R]For we have found this man *a pestilent fellow,* and a mover of sedition among all the Jews throughout the world, and a ringleader of the sect of the Nazarenes:

6 [R]Who also hath gone about to profane the temple: whom we took, and would [R]have judged according to our law.

7 [R]But the chief captain Lўs′-ĭ-ăs came *upon us,* and with great violence took *him* away out of our hands,

8 [R]Commanding his accusers to come unto thee: by examining of whom thyself mayest

take knowledge of all these things, whereof we accuse him.

9 And the Jews also assented, saying that these things were so.

Paul's defence before Felix

10 Then Paul, after that the governor had beckoned unto him to speak, answered, Forasmuch as I know that thou hast been of many years a judge unto this nation, I do the more cheerfully answer for myself:

11 Because that thou mayest understand, that there are yet but twelve days since I went up to Jerusalem [R]for to worship.

12 [R]And they neither found me in the temple disputing with any man, neither raising up the people, neither in the synagogues, nor in the city:

13 Neither can they prove the things whereof they now accuse me.

14 But this I confess unto thee, that after [R]the way which they call heresy, so worship I the [R]God of my fathers, believing all things which are written in [R]the law and in the prophets:

15 And [R]have hope toward God, which they themselves also allow, [R]that there shall be a resurrection of the dead, both of the just and unjust.

16 And [R]herein do I exercise myself, to have always a conscience void of offence toward God, and *toward* men.

17 Now after many years [R]I came to bring alms to my nation, and offerings.

18 [R]Whereupon certain Jews from Asia found me purified in the temple, neither with multitude, nor with tumult.

19 [R]Who ought to have been here before thee, and object, if they had aught against me.

20 Or else let these same *here* say, if they have found any evil doing in me, while I stood before the council,

21 Except it be for this one voice, that I cried standing among them, [R]Touching the resurrection of the dead I am called in question by you this day.

Felix delays his decision

22 And when Felix heard these things, having more perfect knowledge of *that* way, he deferred them, and said, When [R]Lўs′-ĭ-ăs the chief captain shall come down, I will know the uttermost of your matter.

23 And he commanded a centurion to keep Paul, and to let *him* have liberty, and [R]that he should forbid none of his acquaintance to minister or come unto him.

24 And after certain days, when Felix came

with his wife Drû-sĭl'-lă, which was a Jewess, he sent for Paul, and heard him concerning the faith in Christ.

25 And as he reasoned of righteousness, temperance, and judgment to come, Felix trembled, and answered, Go thy way for this time; when I have a convenient season, I will call for thee.

26 He hoped also that ᴿmoney should have been given him of Paul, that he might loose him: wherefore he sent for him the oftener, and communed with him.

27 But after two years Pôr'-çĭ-ŭs Festus came into Felix' room: and Felix, ᴿwilling to shew the Jews a pleasure, left Paul bound.

CHAPTER 25

Paul's trial before Festus

NOW when Festus was come into the province, after three days he ascended from Çæ-sȧ-rē'-ă to Jerusalem.

2 ᴿThen the high priest and the chief of the Jews informed him against Paul, and besought him,

3 And desired favour against him, that he would send for him to Jerusalem, ᴿlaying wait in the way to kill him.

4 But Festus answered, that Paul should be kept at Çæ-sȧ-rē'-ă, and that he himself would depart shortly *thither.*

5 Let them therefore, said he, which among you are able, go down with *me,* and accuse this man, ᴿif there be any wickedness in him.

6 And when he had tarried among them ᴺmore than ten days, he went down unto Çæ-sȧ-rē'-ă; and the next day sitting on the judgment seat commanded Paul to be brought.

7 And when he was come, the Jews which came down from Jerusalem stood round about, ᴿand laid many and grievous complaints against Paul, which they could not prove.

8 While he answered for himself, ᴿNeither against the law of the Jews, neither against the temple, nor yet against Cæsar, have I offended any thing at all.

9 But Festus, ᴿwilling to do the Jews a pleasure, answered Paul, and said, ᴿWilt thou go up to Jerusalem, and there be judged of these things before me?

10 Then said Paul, I stand at Cæsar's judgment seat, where I ought to be judged: to the Jews have I done no wrong, as thou very well knowest.

11 ᴿFor if I be an offender, or have committed any thing worthy of death, I refuse not to die: but if there be none of these things

whereof these accuse me, no man may deliver me unto them. ᴿI appeal unto Cæsar.

12 Then Festus, when he had conferred with the council, answered, Hast thou appealed unto Cæsar? unto Cæsar shalt thou go.

Festus and Agrippa confer

13 And after certain days king Agrippa and Bĕr-nī'-çē came unto Çæ-sȧ-rē'-ă to salute Festus.

14 And when they had been there many days, Festus declared Paul's cause unto the king, saying, ᴿThere is a certain man left in bonds by Felix:

15 ᴿAbout whom, when I was at Jerusalem, the chief priests and the elders of the Jews informed *me,* desiring *to have* judgment against him.

16 ᴿTo whom I answered, It is not the manner of the Romans to deliver any man to die, before that he which is accused have the accusers face to face, and have licence to answer for himself concerning the crime laid against him.

17 Therefore, when they were come hither, ᴿwithout any delay on the morrow I sat on the judgment seat, and commanded the man to be brought forth.

18 Against whom when the accusers stood up, they brought none accusation of such things as I supposed:

19 ᴿBut had certain questions against him of their own superstition, and of one Jesus, which was dead, whom Paul affirmed to be alive.

20 And because ᴺI doubted of such manner of questions, I asked *him* whether he would go to Jerusalem, and there be judged of these matters.

21 But when Paul had appealed to be reserved unto the ᴺhearing of Augustus, I commanded him to be kept till I might send him to Cæsar.

22 Then ᴿAgrippa said unto Festus, I would also hear the man myself. To morrow, said he, thou shalt hear him.

23 And on the morrow, when Agrippa was come, and Bĕr-nī'-çē, with great pomp, and was entered into the place of hearing, with the chief captains, and principal men of the city, at Festus' commandment Paul was brought forth.

24 And Festus said, King Agrippa, and all men which are here present with us, ye see this man, about whom ᴿall the multitude of the Jews have dealt with me, both at Jerusalem, and *also* here, crying that he ought ᴿnot to live any longer.

25 But when I found that ᴿhe had committed

nothing worthy of death, and that he himself hath appealed to Augustus, I have determined to send him.

26 Of whom I have no certain thing to write unto my lord. Wherefore I have brought him forth before you, and specially before thee, O king Agrippa, that, after examination had, I might have somewhat to write.

27 For it seemeth to me unreasonable to send a prisoner, and not withal to signify the crimes *laid* against him.

CHAPTER 26

Paul's defence before Agrippa

THEN Agrippa said unto Paul, Thou art permitted to speak for thyself. Then Paul stretched forth the hand, and answered for himself:

2 I think myself happy, king Agrippa, because I shall answer for myself this day before thee touching all the things whereof I am accused of the Jews:

3 Especially *because I know* thee to be expert in all customs and questions which are among the Jews: wherefore I beseech thee to hear me patiently.

4 My manner of life from my youth, which was at the first among mine own nation at Jerusalem, know all the Jews;

5 Which knew me from the beginning, if they would testify, that after ᴿthe most straitest sect of our religion I lived a Pharisee.

6 ᴿAnd now I stand and am judged for the hope of ᴿthe promise made of God unto our fathers:

7 Unto which *promise* ᴿour twelve tribes, instantly serving *God* ᴿdayᴺ and night, ᴿhope to come. For which hope's sake, king Agrippa, I am accused of the Jews.

8 Why should it be thought a thing incredible with you, that God should raise the dead?

9 ᴿI verily thought with myself, that I ought to do many things contrary to the name of Jesus of Nazareth.

10 ᴿWhich thing I also did in Jerusalem: and many of the saints did I shut up in prison, having received authority ᴿfrom the chief priests; and when they were put to death, I gave my voice against *them*.

11 ᴿAnd I punished them oft in every synagogue, and compelled *them* to blaspheme; and being exceedingly mad against them, I persecuted *them* even unto strange cities.

12 ᴿWhereupon as I went to Damascus with authority and commission from the chief priests,

13 At midday, O king, I saw in the way a

light from heaven, above the brightness of the sun, shining round about me and them which journeyed with me.

14 And when we were all fallen to the earth, I heard a voice speaking unto me, and saying in the Hebrew tongue, Saul, Saul, why persecutest thou me? *it is* hard for thee to kick against the pricks.

15 And I said, Who art thou, Lord? And he said, I am Jesus whom thou persecutest.

16 But rise, and stand upon thy feet: for I have appeared unto thee for this purpose, ᴿto make thee a minister and a witness both of these things which thou hast seen, and of those things in the which I will appear unto thee;

17 Delivering thee from the people, and *from* the Gentiles, ᴿunto whom now I send thee,

18 ᴿTo open their eyes, *and* ᴿto turn *them* from darkness to light, and *from* the power of Satan unto God, ᴿthat they may receive forgiveness of sins, and ᴿinheritance among them which are ᴿsanctified by faith that is in me.

19 Whereupon, O king Agrippa, I was not disobedient unto the heavenly vision:

20 But ᴿshewed first unto them of Damascus, and at Jerusalem, and throughout all the coasts of Judæa, and *then* to the Gentiles, that they should repent and turn to God, and do ᴿworks meet for repentance.

21 For these causes ᴿthe Jews caught me in the temple, and went about to kill *me*.

22 Having therefore obtained help of God, I continue unto this day, witnessing both to small and great, saying none other things than those ᴿwhich the prophets and ᴿMoses did say should come:

23 ᴿThat Christ should suffer, *and* ᴿthat he should be the first that should rise from the dead, and ᴿshould shew light unto the people, and to the Gentiles.

King Agrippa's decision

24 And as he thus spake for himself, Festus said with a loud voice, Paul, ᴿthou art beside thyself; much learning doth make thee mad.

25 But he said, I am not mad, most noble Festus; but speak forth the words of truth and soberness.

26 For the king knoweth of these things, before whom also I speak freely: for I am persuaded that none of these things are hidden from him; for this thing was not done in a corner.

27 King Agrippa, believest thou the prophets? I know that thou believest.

28 Then Agrippa said unto Paul, Almost thou persuadest me to be a Christian.

29 And Paul said, ^RI would to God, that not only thou, but also all that hear me this day, were both almost, and altogether such as I am, except these bonds.

30 And when he had thus spoken, the king rose up, and the governor, and Bĕr-nī′-çē, and they that sat with them:

31 And when they were gone aside, they talked between themselves, saying, ^RThis man doeth nothing worthy of death or of bonds.

32 Then said Agrippa unto Festus, This man might have been set at liberty, ^Rif he had not appealed unto Cæsar.

CHAPTER 27

Paul sails for Rome

AND when ^Rit was determined that we should sail into Italy, they delivered Paul and certain other prisoners unto *one* named Julius, a centurion of Augustus' band.

2 And entering into a ship of Ăd-rá-mȳt′-tĭ-ŭm, we launched, meaning to sail by the coasts of Asia; *one* ^RĂr-ĭs-tär′-chŭs, a Măç-ē-dō′-nĭ-ăn of Thĕss-á-lō-nī′-cȧ, being with us.

3 And the next *day* we touched at Ṡī′-dŏn. And Julius ^Rcourteously entreated Paul, and gave *him* liberty to go unto his friends to refresh himself.

4 And when we had launched from thence, we sailed under Cyprus, because the winds were contrary.

5 And when we had sailed over the sea of Çi-lĭç′-ĭ-ȧ and Păm-phȳl′-ĭ-ȧ, we came to Mȳ′-rȧ, *a city* of Lȳç′-ĭ-ȧ.

6 And there the centurion found a ship of Alexandria sailing into Italy; and he put us therein.

7 And when we had sailed slowly many days, and scarce were come over against Cnī′-dŭs, the wind not suffering us, we sailed under ^NCrete, over against Săl-mō′-nē;

8 And, hardly passing it, came unto a place which is called The fair havens; nigh whereunto was the city *of* Lȧ-sē′-ȧ.

9 Now when much time was spent, and when sailing was now dangerous, ^Rbecause the fast was now already past, Paul admonished *them,*

10 And said unto them, Sirs, I perceive that this voyage will be with ^Nhurt and much damage, not only of the lading and ship, but also of our lives.

11 Nevertheless the centurion believed the master and the owner of the ship, more than those things which were spoken by Paul.

12 And because the haven was not commo-

CHAP. 26
AD 62
29 1 Cor. 7:7
31 ch. 23:9, 29
& 25:25
32 ch. 25:11

CHAP. 27
AD 62
1 ch. 25:12, 25
2 ch. 19:29
3 ch. 24:23
& 28:16
7 Or, *Candy*
9 The fast was on the tenth day of the seventh month, Lev. 23:27, 29
10 Or, *injury*

Or, *beat*   14
Jonah 1:5
ch. 23:11   19
Dan. 6:16   23
Rom. 1:9   23
2 Tim. 1:3
Luke 1:45   25
Rom. 4:20, 21
2 Tim. 1:12
ch. 28:1   26

dious to winter in, the more part advised to depart thence also, if by any means they might attain to Phē-nī′-çē, *and there* to winter; *which is* an haven of Crete, and lieth toward the south west and north west.

Encountering the storm

13 And when the south wind blew softly, supposing that they had obtained *their* purpose, loosing *thence,* they sailed close by Crete.

14 But not long after there ^Narose against it a tempestuous wind, called Êu-rŏc′-lȳ-dǫn.

15 And when the ship was caught, and could not bear up into the wind, we let *her* drive.

16 And running under a certain island which is called Clauda, we had much work to come by the boat:

17 Which when they had taken up, they used helps, undergirding the ship; and, fearing lest they should fall into the quicksands, strake sail, and so were driven.

18 And we being exceedingly tossed with a tempest, the next *day* they lightened the ship;

19 And the third *day* ^Rwe cast out with our own hands the tackling of the ship.

20 And when neither sun nor stars in many days appeared, and no small tempest lay on *us,* all hope that we should be saved was then taken away.

Paul encourages those in the ship

21 But after long abstinence Paul stood forth in the midst of them, and said, Sirs, ye should have hearkened unto me, and not have loosed from Crete, and to have gained this harm and loss.

22 And now I exhort you to be of good cheer: for there shall be no loss of *any man's* life among you, but of the ship.

23 ^RFor there stood by me this night the angel of God, whose I am, and ^Rwhom I serve,

24 Saying, Fear not, Paul; thou must be brought before Cæsar: and, lo, God hath given thee all them that sail with thee.

25 Wherefore, sirs, be of good cheer: ^Rfor I believe God, that it shall be even as it was told me.

26 Howbeit ^Rwe must be cast upon a certain island.

27 But when the fourteenth night was come, as we were driven up and down in Ā′-drĭ-ȧ, about midnight the shipmen deemed that they drew near to some country;

28 And sounded, and found *it* twenty fathoms: and when they had gone a little further, they sounded again, and found *it* fifteen fathoms.

29 Then fearing lest we should have fallen upon rocks, they cast four anchors out of the stern, and wished for the day.

30 And as the shipmen were about to flee out of the ship, when they had let down the boat into the sea, under colour as though they would have cast anchors out of the foreship,

31 Paul said to the centurion and to the soldiers, Except these abide in the ship, ye cannot be saved.

32 Then the soldiers cut off the ropes of the boat, and let her fall off.

33 And while the day was coming on, Paul besought *them* all to take meat, saying, This day is the fourteenth day that ye have tarried and continued fasting, having taken nothing.

34 Wherefore I pray you to take *some* meat: for this is for your health: for ᴿthere shall not an hair fall from the head of any of you.

35 And when he had thus spoken, he took bread, and ᴿgave thanks to God in presence of them all: and when he had broken *it*, he began to eat.

36 Then were they all of good cheer, and they also took *some* meat.

37 And we were in all in the ship two hundred threescore and sixteen ᴿsouls.

38 And when they had eaten enough, they lightened the ship, and cast out the wheat into the sea.

Shipwreck at Melita

39 And when it was day, they knew not the land: but they discovered a certain creek with a shore, into the which they were minded, if it were possible, to thrust in the ship.

40 And when they had ᴺtaken up the anchors, they committed *themselves* unto the sea, and loosed the rudder bands, and hoisted up the mainsail to the wind, and made toward shore.

41 And falling into a place where two seas met, ᴿthey ran the ship aground; and the forepart stuck fast, and remained unmoveable, but the hinder part was broken with the violence of the waves.

42 And the soldiers' counsel was to kill the prisoners, lest any of them should swim out, and escape.

43 But the centurion, willing to save Paul, kept them from *their* purpose; and commanded that they which could swim should cast *themselves* first *into the sea*, and get to land:

44 And the rest, some on boards, and some on *broken pieces* of the ship. And so it came to pass, ᴿthat they escaped all safe to land.

CHAP. 27
AD 62
34 1 Ki. 1:52
Mat. 10:30
Luke 12:7
& 21:18
35 1 Sam. 9:13
Mat. 15:36
Mark 8:6
John 6:11
1 Tim. 4:3, 4
37 ch. 2:41
& 7:14
Rom. 13:1
1 Pet. 3:20
40 Or, *cut the anchors, they left them in the sea, etc.*
41 2 Cor. 11:25
44 ver. 22

CHAP. 28	
AD 62	
ch. 27:26	1
Rom. 1:14	2
1 Cor. 14:11	
Col. 3:11	
Mark 16:18	5
Luke 10:19	
ch. 14:11	6
Jas. 5:14, 15	8
Mark 6:5	8
& 7:32	
& 16:18	
Luke 4:40	
ch. 19:11, 12	
1 Cor. 12:9, 28	
Mat. 15:6	10
1 Tim. 5:17	

CHAPTER 28

The stay at Melita

AND when they were escaped, then they knew that ᴿthe island was called Mĕl'-ĭ-tă.

2 And the ᴿbarbarous people shewed us no little kindness: for they kindled a fire, and received us every one, because of the present rain, and because of the cold.

3 And when Paul had gathered a bundle of sticks, and laid *them* on the fire, there came a viper out of the heat, and fastened on his hand.

4 And when the barbarians saw the *venomous* beast hang on his hand, they said among themselves, No doubt this man is a murderer, whom, though he hath escaped the sea, yet vengeance suffereth not to live.

5 And he shook off the beast into the fire, and ᴿfelt no harm.

6 Howbeit they looked when he should have swollen, or fallen down dead suddenly: but after they had looked a great while, and saw no harm come to him, they changed their minds, and ᴿsaid that he was a god.

7 In the same quarters were possessions of the chief man of the island, whose name was Publius; who received us, and lodged us three days courteously.

8 And it came to pass, that the father of Publius lay sick of a fever and of a bloody flux: to whom Paul entered in, and ᴿprayed, and ᴿlaid his hands on him, and healed him.

9 So when this was done, others also, which had diseases in the island, came, and were healed:

10 Who also honoured us with many ᴿhonours; and when we departed, they laded *us* with such things as were necessary.

Arrival at Rome

11 And after three months we departed in a ship of Alexandria, which had wintered in the isle, whose sign was Castor and Pollux.

12 And landing at Sȳr'-ā-cūse, we tarried *there* three days.

13 And from thence we fetched a compass, and came to Rhē'-ġĭ-ŭm: and after one day the south wind blew, and we came the next day to Pū-tē'-ŏ-lī:

14 Where we found brethren, and were desired to tarry with them seven days: and so we went toward Rome.

15 And from thence, when the brethren heard of us, they came to meet us as far as Ăp'-pĭ-ī forum, and The three taverns: whom

when Paul saw, he thanked God, and took courage.

16 And when we came to Rome, the centurion delivered the prisoners to the captain of the guard: but ᴿPaul was suffered to dwell by himself with a soldier that kept him.

Paul's ministry in Rome

17 And it came to pass, that after three days Paul called the chief of the Jews together: and when they were come together, he said unto them, Men *and* brethren, ᴿthough I have committed nothing against the people, or customs of our fathers, yet ᴿwas I delivered prisoner from Jerusalem into the hands of the Romans.

18 Who, ᴿwhen they had examined me, would have let *me* go, because there was no cause of death in me.

19 But when the Jews spake against *it,* ᴿI was constrained to appeal unto Cæsar; not that I had aught to accuse my nation of.

20 For this cause therefore have I called for you, to see *you,* and to speak with *you:* because that ᴿfor the hope of Israel I am bound with ᴿthis chain.

21 And they said unto him, We neither received letters out of Judæa concerning thee, neither any of the brethren that came shewed or spake any harm of thee.

22 But we desire to hear of thee what thou thinkest: for as concerning this sect, we know that every where ᴿit is spoken against.

23 And when they had appointed him a day, there came many to him into *his* lodging; ᴿto whom he expounded and testified the kingdom of God, persuading them concerning Jesus, ᴿboth out of the law of Moses, and *out of* the prophets, from morning till evening.

24 And ᴿsome believed the things which were spoken, and some believed not.

25 And when they agreed not among themselves, they departed, after that Paul had spoken one word, Well spake the Holy Ghost by Ē-śâi′-ăs the prophet unto our fathers,

26 Saying, ᴿGo unto this people, and say, Hearing ye shall hear, and shall not understand; and seeing ye shall see, and not perceive:

27 For the heart of this people is waxed gross, and their ears are dull of hearing, and their eyes have they closed; lest they should see with *their* eyes, and hear with *their* ears, and understand with *their* heart, and should be converted, and I should heal them.

28 Be it known therefore unto you, that the salvation of God is sent ᴿunto the Gentiles, and *that* they will hear it.

29 And when he had said these words, the Jews departed, and had great reasoning among themselves.

30 And Paul dwelt two whole years in his own hired house, and received all that came in unto him,

31 ᴿPreaching the kingdom of God, and teaching those things which concern the Lord Jesus Christ, with all confidence, no man forbidding him.

CHAP. 28

AD 62

16 ch. 24:25 & 27:3
17 ch. 24:12, 13
17 ch. 21:33
18 ch. 22:24 & 24:10 & 25:8
19 ch. 25:11
20 ch. 26:6, 7
20 ch. 26:29 Eph. 3:1 & 4:1 & 6:20 2 Tim. 1:16 Philem. 10, 13
22 Luke 2:34 ch. 24:5, 14 1 Pet. 2:12 & 4:14
23 Luke 24:27 ch. 17:3 & 19:8

See 23
ch. 26:6, 22
ch. 14:4 24
& 19:9
Is. 6:9 26
Jer. 5:21
Ezek. 12:2
Mat. 13:14
Mark 4:12
Luke 8:10
John 12:40
Rom. 11:8
Mat. 21:41 28
ch. 13:46
& 18:6
& 26:17, 18
Rom. 11:11
ch. 4:31 31
Eph. 6:19

THE EPISTLE OF PAUL THE APOSTLE
TO THE
ROMANS

The longest and most systematic of Paul's writings, the Epistle to the Romans is as much a treatise as a letter. Its Pauline authorship is so well attested by external and internal evidence that few have challenged it. Written from Corinth at the close of the Apostle's recorded missionary journeys and prior to his final trip to Jerusalem (15:17–33), it can be dated about A.D. 57 or 58. The Greek world has been evangelized (15:19, 23)—the flame had been kindled and the fire was spreading—and Paul desired to transfer his ministry to the Latin world, going even to the western border of the Empire (15:24). Evidently he expected to make Rome his base of operations much as Antioch of Syria had served previously. He had hoped to go directly to Rome from Achaia, but his presence was essential at Jerusalem for the presentation of contributions to the impoverished Christians of that city (15:22ff.). In lieu of a visit, in preparation for his future coming, and to declare the righteousness of God, Paul sent this formal letter. The Apostle herein asserts both the universality of sin and the inclusiveness of God's saving act in Christ and its appropriation by faith.

OUTLINE OF THE BOOK:
I. Introduction 1:1–15
II. Doctrinal Exposition 1:16–8:39
III. Israel and the Church 9:1–11:36
IV. Practical Exhortations 12:1–15:13
V. Conclusion 15:14–16:27

CHAPTER 1

Salutation

PAUL, a servant of Jesus Christ, ᴿcalled *to be* an apostle, ᴿseparated unto the gospel of God,

2 (ᴿWhich he had promised afore ᴿby his prophets in the holy scriptures,)

3 Concerning his Son Jesus Christ our Lord, which was ᴿmade of the seed of David according to the flesh;

4 And ᴿdeclaredᴺ *to be* the Son of God with power, according ᴿto the spirit of holiness, by the resurrection from the dead:

5 By whom ᴿwe have received grace and apostleship, for ᴿobedience to the faith among all nations, ᴿfor his name:

6 Among whom are ye also the called of Jesus Christ:

7 To all that be in Rome, beloved of God, ᴿcalled *to be* saints: ᴿGrace to you and peace from God our Father, and the Lord Jesus Christ.

Paul's interest in the Romans

8 First, ᴿI thank my God through Jesus Christ for you all, that ᴿyour faith is spoken of throughout the whole world.

9 For ᴿGod is my witness, ᴿwhom I serve ᴺwith my spirit in the gospel of his Son, that ᴿwithout ceasing I make mention of you always in my prayers;

10 Making request, if by any means now at length I might have a prosperous journey by the will of God to come unto you.

11 For I long to see you, that ᴿI may impart unto you some spiritual gift, to the end ye may be established;

12 That is, that I may be comforted together ᴺwith you by ᴿthe mutual faith both of you and me.

13 Now I would not have you ignorant, brethren, that oftentimes I purposed to come unto you, (but ᴿwas let hitherto,) that I might have some ᴿfruit ᴺamong you also, even as among other Gentiles.

14 I am debtor both to the Greeks, and to the Barbarians; both to the wise, and to the unwise.

15 So, as much as in me is, I am ready to preach the gospel to you that are at Rome also.

The gospel theme

16 For ᴿI am not ashamed of the gospel of Christ: for ᴿit is the power of God unto salvation to every one that believeth; ᴿto the Jew first, and also to the Greek.

CHAP. 1
AD 60
1 1 Tim. 1:11
1 Acts 9:15
2 Acts 26:6
2 Gal. 3:8
3 Gal. 4:4
4 Acts 13:33
4 Gr. *determined*
4 Heb. 9:14
5 Eph. 3:8
5 Acts 6:7
5 Acts 9:15
7 1 Cor. 1:2
7 1 Cor. 1:3
8 1 Cor. 1:4
8 ch. 16:19
9 ch. 9:1
9 Acts 27:23
9 Or, *in my spirit*
9 1 Thes. 3:10
11 ch. 15:29
12 Or, *in you*
12 Tit. 1:4
13 1 Thes. 2:18
13 Phil. 4:17
13 Or, *in you*
16 Ps. 40:9, 10
Mark 8:38
16 1 Cor. 1:18
16 Luke 2:30
Acts 13:26

ch. 3:21	17
Hab. 2:4	17
John 3:36	
Gal. 3:11	
Acts 17:30	18
Eph. 5:6	
Acts 14:17	19
Or, *to them*	19
John 1:9	19
Ps. 19:1	20
Acts 14:17	
Or, *that they may be*	20
2 Ki. 17:15	21
Jer. 2:5	
Eph. 4:17	
Jer. 10:14	22
Deut. 4:16	23
Ps. 106:20	
Is. 40:18	
Ps. 81:12	24
Acts 7:42	
Eph. 4:18	
1 Cor. 6:18	24
1 Thes. 4:4	
Lev. 18:22	24
1 Thes. 1:9	25
1 John 5:20	
Is. 44:20	25
Jer. 10:14	
Lev. 18:22	26
Eph. 5:12	
Or, *to acknowledge*	28
Or, *a mind void of judgment*	28
Eph. 5:4	28

17 For ᴿtherein is the righteousness of God revealed from faith to faith: as it is written, ᴿThe just shall live by faith.

Rejection of God's glory

18 ᴿFor the wrath of God is revealed from heaven against all ungodliness and unrighteousness of men, who hold the truth in unrighteousness;

19 Because ᴿthat which may be known of God is manifest ᴺin them; for ᴿGod hath shewed *it* unto them.

20 For ᴿthe invisible things of him from the creation of the world are clearly seen, being understood by the things that are made, *even* his eternal power and Godhead; ᴺso that they are without excuse:

21 Because that, when they knew God, they glorified *him* not as God, neither were thankful; but ᴿbecame vain in their imaginations, and their foolish heart was darkened.

22 ᴿProfessing themselves to be wise, they became fools,

23 And changed the glory of the uncorruptible ᴿGod into an image made like to corruptible man, and to birds, and fourfooted beasts, and creeping things.

24 ᴿWherefore God also gave them up to uncleanness through the lusts of their own hearts, ᴿto dishonour their own bodies ᴿbetween themselves:

25 Who changed ᴿthe truth of God ᴿinto a lie, and worshipped and served the creature ᴺmore than the Creator, who is blessed for ever. Ä′-mĕn.

Consequences of rejection

26 For this cause God gave them up unto ᴿvile affections: for even their women did change the natural use into that which is against nature:

27 And likewise also the men, leaving the natural use of the woman, burned in their lust one toward another; men with men working that which is unseemly, and receiving in themselves that recompence of their error which was meet.

28 And even as they did not like ᴺto retain God in *their* knowledge, God gave them over to ᴺa reprobate mind, to do those things ᴿwhich are not convenient;

29 Being filled with all unrighteousness, fornication, wickedness, covetousness, maliciousness; full of envy, murder, debate, deceit, malignity; whisperers,

30 Backbiters, haters of God, despiteful, proud, boasters, inventors of evil things, disobedient to parents,

31 Without understanding, covenantbreakers, ᴺwithout natural affection, implacable, unmerciful:

32 Who ᴿknowing the judgment of God, that they which commit such things ᴿare worthy of death, not only do the same, but ᴿhaveᴺ pleasure in them that do them.

CHAPTER 2

God's righteous judgment

THEREFORE thou art ᴿinexcusable, O man, whosoever thou art that judgest: ᴿfor wherein thou judgest another, thou condemnest thyself; for thou that judgest doest the same things.

2 But we are sure that the judgment of God is according to truth against them which commit such things.

3 And thinkest thou this, O man, that judgest them which do such things, and doest the same, that thou shalt escape the judgment of God?

4 Or despisest thou ᴿthe riches of his goodness and ᴿforbearance and ᴿlongsuffering; ᴿnot knowing that the goodness of God leadeth thee to repentance?

5 But after thy hardness and impenitent heart ᴿtreasurest up unto thyself wrath against the day of wrath and revelation of the righteous judgment of God;

6 ᴿWho will render to every man according to his deeds:

7 To them who by patient continuance in well doing seek for glory and honour and immortality, eternal life:

8 But unto them that are contentious, and ᴿdo not obey the truth, but obey unrighteousness, indignation and wrath,

9 Tribulation and anguish, upon every soul of man that doeth evil, of the Jew ᴿfirst, and also of the ᴺGentile;

10 ᴿBut glory, honour, and peace, to every man that worketh good, to the Jew first, and also to the ᴺGentile:

11 For ᴿthere is no respect of persons with God.

The law and judgment

12 For as many as have sinned without law shall also perish without law: and as many as have sinned in the law shall be judged by the law;

13 (For ᴿnot the hearers of the law are just before God, but the doers of the law shall be justified.

14 For when the Gentiles, which have not the law, do by nature the things contained in

---

CHAP. 1
AD 60
31 Or, unsociable
32 ch. 2:2
32 ch. 6:21
32 Ps. 50:18
Hos. 7:3
32 Or, consent with them

CHAP. 2
AD 60
1 ch. 1:20
1 2 Sam. 12:5
Mat. 7:1, 2
John 8:9
4 Eph. 1:7
4 ch. 3:25
4 Ex. 34:6
4 Is. 30:18
2 Pet. 3:9
5 Deut. 32:34
Jas. 5:3
6 Job 34:11
Ps. 62:12
Prov. 24:12
Jer. 17:10
2 Cor. 5:10
8 Job 24:13
2 Thes. 1:8
9 Amos 3:2
Luke 12:47
1 Pet. 4:17
9 Gr. Greek
10 1 Pet. 1:7
10 Gr. Greek
11 Deut. 10:17
Job 34:19
Acts 10:34
Eph. 6:9
13 Jas. 1:22
1 John 3:7

Or, the conscience witnessing with them 15
Or, between themselves 15
Eccl. 12:14 16
Mat. 25:31
Rev. 20:12
John 5:22 16
Acts 10:42
1 Tim. 1:11 16
Mat. 3:9 17
John 8:33
Mic. 3:11 17
Is. 48:2 17
Deut. 4:8 18
Phil. 1:10 18
Or, triest the 18
things that differ
Mat. 15:14 19
John 9:34
2 Tim. 3:5 20
Ps. 50:16 21
Mat. 23:3
Mal. 3:8 22
ver. 17 23
2 Sam. 12:14 24
Is. 52:5
Ezek. 36:20
Gal. 5:3 25
Acts 10:34 26
Mat. 12:41 27
Mat. 3:9 28
John 8:39
Gal. 6:15
1 Pet. 3:4 29
Phil. 3:3 29
ch. 7:6 29
1 Cor. 4:5 29
2 Cor. 10:18
1 Thes. 2:4

---

the law, these, having not the law, are a law unto themselves:

15 Which shew the work of the law written in their hearts, ᴺtheir conscience also bearing witness, and their thoughts ᴺthe mean while accusing or else excusing one another;)

16 ᴿIn the day when God shall judge the secrets of men ᴿby Jesus Christ ᴿaccording to my gospel.

17 Behold, ᴿthou art called a Jew, and ᴿrestest in the law, ᴿand makest thy boast of God,

18 And ᴿknowest his will, and ᴿapprovestᴺ the things that are more excellent, being instructed out of the law;

19 And ᴿart confident that thou thyself art a guide of the blind, a light of them which are in darkness,

20 An instructor of the foolish, a teacher of babes, ᴿwhich hast the form of knowledge and of the truth in the law.

21 ᴿThou therefore which teachest another, teachest thou not thyself? thou that preachest a man should not steal, dost thou steal?

22 Thou that sayest a man should not commit adultery, dost thou commit adultery? thou that abhorrest idols, ᴿdost thou commit sacrilege?

23 Thou that ᴿmakest thy boast of the law, through breaking the law dishonourest thou God?

24 For the name of God is blasphemed among the Gentiles through you, as it is ᴿwritten.

Inwardness of true circumcision

25 ᴿFor circumcision verily profiteth, if thou keep the law: but if thou be a breaker of the law, thy circumcision is made uncircumcision.

26 Therefore ᴿif the uncircumcision keep the righteousness of the law, shall not his uncircumcision be counted for circumcision?

27 And shall not uncircumcision which is by nature, if it fulfil the law, ᴿjudge thee, who by the letter and circumcision dost transgress the law?

28 For ᴿhe is not a Jew, which is one outwardly; neither is that circumcusion, which is outward in the flesh:

29 But he is a Jew, ᴿwhich is one inwardly; and ᴿcircumcision is that of the heart, ᴿin the spirit, and not in the letter; ᴿwhose praise is not of men, but of God.

CHAPTER 3

Advantage of the Jew

WHAT advantage then hath the Jew? or what profit is there of circumcision?

2 Much every way: chiefly, because that ᴿunto them were committed the oracles of God.

3 For what if ᴿsome did not believe? ᴿshall their unbelief make the faith of God without effect?

4 ᴿGod forbid: yea, let ᴿGod be true, but ᴿevery man a liar; as it is written, ᴿThat thou mightest be justified in thy sayings, and mightest overcome when thou art judged.

5 But if our unrighteousness commend the righteousness of God, what shall we say? *Is* God unrighteous who taketh vengeance? (ᴿI speak as a man)

6 God forbid: for then ᴿhow shall God judge he world?

7 For if the truth of God hath more abounded through my lie unto his glory; why yet am I also judged as a sinner?

8 And not *rather,* (as we be slanderously reported, and as some affirm that we say,) ᴿLet us do evil, that good may come? whose damnation is just.

None is righteous

9 What then? are we better *than they?* No, in no wise: for we have before ᴺproved both Jews and Gentiles, that ᴿthey are all under sin;

10 As it is written, ᴿThere is none righteous, no, not one:

11 There is none that understandeth, there is none that seeketh after God.

12 They are all gone out of the way, they are together become unprofitable; there is none that doeth good, no, not one.

13 ᴿTheir throat *is* an open sepulchre; with their tongues they have used deceit; ᴿthe poison of asps *is* under their lips:

14 ᴿWhose mouth *is* full of cursing and bitterness:

15 ᴿTheir feet *are* swift to shed blood:

16 Destruction and misery *are* in their ways:

17 And the way of peace have they not known:

18 ᴿThere is no fear of God before their eyes.

19 Now we know that what things soever ᴿthe law saith, it saith to them who are under the law: that ᴿevery mouth may be stopped, and ᴿall the world may become ᴺguilty before God.

20 Therefore ᴿby the deeds of the law there shall no flesh be justified in his sight: for ᴿby the law *is* the knowledge of sin.

Righteousness through faith

21 But now ᴿthe righteousness of God without the law is manifested, ᴿbeing witnessed by the law ᴿand the prophets;

22 Even the righteousness of God *which is* ᴿby faith of Jesus Christ unto all and upon all them that believe: for ᴿthere is no difference:

23 For ᴿall have sinned, and come short of the glory of God;

24 Being justified freely ᴿby his grace ᴿthrough the redemption that is in Christ Jesus:

25 Whom God hath ᴺset forth ᴿ*to be* a propitiation through faith ᴿin his blood, to declare his righteousness for the ᴺremission of ᴿsins that are past, through the forbearance of God;

26 To declare, *I say,* at this time his righteousness: that he might be just, and the justifier of him which believeth in Jesus.

27 ᴿWhere *is* boasting then? It is excluded. By what law? of works? Nay: but by the law of faith.

28 Therefore we conclude ᴿthat a man is justified by faith without the deeds of the law.

29 *Is he* the God of the Jews only? *is he* not also of the Gentiles? Yes, of the Gentiles also:

30 Seeing ᴿ*it is* one God, which shall justify the circumcision by faith, and uncircumcision through faith.

31 Do we then make void the law through faith? God forbid: yea, we establish the law.

CHAPTER 4

Abraham believed God

WHAT shall we say then that ᴿAbraham our father, as pertaining to the flesh, hath found?

2 For if Abraham were ᴿjustified by works, he hath *whereof* to glory; but not before God.

3 For what saith the scripture? ᴿAbraham believed God, and it was counted unto him for righteousness.

4 Now ᴿto him that worketh is the reward not reckoned of grace, but of debt.

5 But to him that worketh not, but believeth on him that justifieth ᴿthe ungodly, his faith is counted for righteousness.

6 Even as David also describeth the blessedness of the man, unto whom God imputeth righteousness without works,

7 *Saying,* ᴿBlessed *are* they whose iniquities are forgiven, and whose sins are covered.

8 Blessed *is* the man to whom the Lord will not impute sin.

The promise to Abraham

9 *Cometh* this blessedness then upon the circumcision *only,* or upon the uncircumcision also? for we say that faith was reckoned to Abraham for righteousness.

10 How was it then reckoned? when he was in circumcision, or in uncircumcision? Not in circumcision, but in uncircumcision.

11 And ᴿhe received the sign of circumcision, a seal of the righteousness of the faith which *he had yet* being uncircumcised: that ᴿhe might be the father of all them that believe, though they be not circumcised; that righteousness might be imputed unto them also:

12 And the father of circumcision to them who are not of the circumcision only, but who also walk in the steps of that faith of our father Abraham, which *he had* being *yet* uncircumcised.

13 For the promise, that he should be the ᴿheir of the world, *was* not to Abraham, or to his seed, through the law, but through the righteousness of faith.

14 For ᴿif they which are of the law *be* heirs, faith is made void, and the promise made of none effect:

15 Because ᴿthe law worketh wrath: for where no law is, *there is* no transgression.

Righteousness depends on faith

16 Therefore *it is* of faith, that *it might be* ᴿby grace; ᴿto the end the promise might be sure to all the seed; not to that only which is of the law, but to that also which is of the faith of Abraham; ᴿwho is the father of us all,

17 (As it is written, ᴿI have made thee a father of many nations,) ᴺbefore him whom he believed, *even* God, ᴿwho quickeneth the dead, and calleth those ᴿthings which be not as though they were.

18 Who against hope believed in hope, that he might become the father of many nations, according to that which was spoken, ᴿSo shall thy seed be.

19 And being not weak in faith, ᴿhe considered not his own body now dead, when he was about an hundred years old, neither yet the deadness of Sarah's womb:

20 He staggered not at the promise of God through unbelief; but was strong in faith, giving glory to God;

21 And being fully persuaded that, what he had promised, ᴿhe was able also to perform.

22 And therefore it was imputed to him for righteousness.

23 Now ᴿit was not written for his sake alone, that it was imputed to him;

24 But for us also, to whom it shall be imputed, if we believe ᴿon him that raised up Jesus our Lord from the dead;

25 ᴿWho was delivered for our offences, and ᴿwas raised again for our justification.

CHAP. **4**
AD 60
11 Gen. 17:10
11 ver. 12, 16
Luke 19:9
Gal. 3:7
13 Gen. 17:4
Gal. 3.29
14 Gal. 3:18
15 ch. 3:20
& 7:8, 10, 11
1 Cor. 15:56
2 Cor. 3:7, 9
Gal. 3:10
1 John 3:4
16 ch. 3:24
16 Gal. 3:22
16 Is. 51:2
ch. 9:8
17 Gen. 17:5
17 Or, *like unto him*
17 ch. 8:11
Eph. 2:1, 5
17 ch. 9:26
1 Cor. 1:28
1 Pet. 2:10
18 Gen. 15:5
19 Gen. 17:17
& 18:11
Heb. 11:11
21 Ps. 115:3
Luke 1:37
Heb. 11:19
23 ch. 15:4
1 Cor. 10:6
24 Acts 2:24
25 Is. 53:5, 6
ch. 3:25
Gal. 1:4
Heb. 9:28
25 1 Cor. 15:17
1 Pet. 1:21

CHAP. **5**
AD 60
Is. 32:17	1
John 16:33	
Eph. 2:14	1
John 10:9	2
Eph. 2:18	
1 Cor. 15:1	2
Heb. 3:6	2
Mat. 5:11	3
Acts 5:41	
2 Cor. 12:10	
Phil. 2:17	
Jas. 1:2	
Jas. 1:3	3
Jas. 1:12	4
Phil. 1:20	5
2 Cor. 1:22	5
Eph. 1:13	
Or, *according to the time*	6
ch. 4:25	6
John 15:13	8
Eph. 2:13	9
1 John 1:7	
1 Thes. 1:10	9
ch. 8:32	10
2 Cor. 5:18	10
Eph. 2:16	
John 14:19	10
Gal. 4:9	11
Or, *reconciliation*	11
Gen. 3:6	12
1 Cor. 15:21	
Gen. 2:17	12
Or, *in whom*	12
1 John 3:4	13
1 Cor. 15:21	14
Is. 53:11	15
Or, *by one offence*	17

CHAPTER 5

Reconciliation through Christ

THEREFORE ᴿbeing justified by faith, we have ᴿpeace with God through our Lord Jesus Christ:

2 ᴿBy whom also we have access by faith into this grace ᴿwherein we stand, and ᴿrejoice in hope of the glory of God.

3 And not only *so,* but ᴿwe glory in tribulations also: ᴿknowing that tribulation worketh patience;

4 ᴿAnd patience, experience; and experience, hope:

5 ᴿAnd hope maketh not ashamed; ᴿbecause the love of God is shed abroad in our hearts by the Holy Ghost which is given unto us.

6 For when we were yet without strength, ᴺin due time ᴿChrist died for the ungodly.

7 For scarcely for a righteous man will one die: yet peradventure for a good man some would even dare to die.

8 But ᴿGod commendeth his love toward us, in that, while we were yet sinners, Christ died for us.

9 Much more then, being now justified ᴿby his blood, we shall be saved ᴿfrom wrath through him.

10 For ᴿif, when we were enemies, ᴿwe were reconciled to God by the death of his Son, much more, being reconciled, we shall be saved ᴿby his life.

11 And not only *so,* but we also ᴿjoy in God through our Lord Jesus Christ, by whom we have now received the ᴺatonement.

Adam and Christ

12 Wherefore, as ᴿby one man sin entered into the world, and ᴿdeath by sin; and so death passed upon all men, ᴺfor that all have sinned:

13 (For until the law sin was in the world: but ᴿsin is not imputed when there is no law.

14 Nevertheless death reigned from Adam to Moses, even over them that had not sinned after the similitude of Adam's transgression, ᴿwho is the figure of him that was to come.

15 But not as the offence, so also *is* the free gift. For if through the offence of one many be dead, much more the grace of God, and the gift by grace, *which is* by one man, Jesus Christ, hath abounded ᴿunto many.

16 And not as *it was* by one that sinned, *so is* the gift: for the judgment *was* by one to condemnation, but the free gift *is* of many offences unto justification.

17 For if ᴺby one man's offence death reigned by one; much more they which receive abundance of grace and of the gift of right-

eousness shall reign in life by one, Jesus Christ.)

18 Therefore as [N]by the offence of one *judgment came* upon all men to condemnation; even so [N]by the righteousness of one *the free gift came* [R]upon all men unto justification of life.

19 For as by one man's disobedience many were made sinners, so by the obedience of one shall many be made righteous.

20 Moreover [R]the law entered, that the offence might abound. But where sin abounded, grace did much [R]more abound:

21 That as sin hath reigned unto death, even so might grace reign through righteousness unto eternal life by Jesus Christ our Lord.

CHAPTER 6

Sin and grace

WHAT shall we say then? [R]Shall we continue in sin, that grace may abound?

2 God forbid. How shall we, that are [R]dead to sin, live any longer therein?

3 Know ye not, that [R]so many of us as [N]were baptized into Jesus Christ [R]were baptized into his death?

4 Therefore we are [R]buried with him by baptism into death: that [R]like as Christ was raised up from the dead by [R]the glory of the Father, [R]even so we also should walk in newness of life.

5 [R]For if we have been planted together in the likeness of his death, we shall be also *in the likeness* of *his* resurrection:

6 Knowing this, that [R]our old man is crucified with *him,* that [R]the body of sin might be destroyed, that henceforth we should not serve sin.

7 For [R]he that is dead is [N]freed from sin.

8 Now [R]if we be dead with Christ, we believe that we shall also live with him:

9 Knowing that [R]Christ being raised from the dead dieth no more; death hath no more dominion over him.

10 For in that he died, [R]he died unto sin once: but in that he liveth, [R]he liveth unto God.

11 Likewise reckon ye also yourselves to be [R]dead indeed unto sin, but [R]alive unto God through Jesus Christ our Lord.

12 [R]Let not sin therefore reign in your mortal body, that ye should obey it in the lusts thereof.

13 Neither yield ye your [R]members *as* [N]instruments of unrighteousness unto sin: but [R]yield yourselves unto God, as those that are alive from the dead, and your members *as* instruments of righteousness unto God.

---

14 For [R]sin shall not have dominion over you: for ye are not under the law, but under grace.

Slaves of sin or righteousness

15 What then? shall we sin, [R]because we are not under the law, but under grace? God forbid.

16 Know ye not, that [R]to whom ye yield yourselves servants to obey, his servants ye are to whom ye obey; whether of sin unto death, or of obedience unto righteousness?

17 But God be thanked, that ye were the servants of sin, but ye have obeyed from the heart [R]that form of doctrine [N]which was delivered you.

18 Being then [R]made free from sin, ye became the servants of righteousness.

19 I speak after the manner of men because of the infirmity of your flesh: for as ye have yielded your members servants to uncleanness and to iniquity unto iniquity; even so now yield your members servants to righteousness unto holiness.

20 For when ye were [R]the servants of sin, ye were free [N]from righteousness.

21 [R]What fruit had ye then in those things whereof ye are now ashamed? for [R]the end of those things *is* death.

22 But now [R]being made free from sin, and become servants to God, ye have your fruit unto holiness, and the end everlasting life.

23 For [R]the wages of sin *is* death; but [R]the gift of God *is* eternal life through Jesus Christ our Lord.

CHAPTER 7

Discharged from the law

KNOW ye not, brethren, (for I speak to them that know the law,) how that the law hath dominion over a man as long as he liveth?

2 For [R]the woman which hath an husband is bound by the law to *her* husband so long as he liveth; but if the husband be dead, she is loosed from the law of *her* husband.

3 So then [R]if, while *her* husband liveth, she be married to another man, she shall be called an adulteress: but if her husband be dead, she is free from that law; so that she is no adulteress, though she be married to another man.

4 Wherefore, my brethren, ye also are become [R]dead to the law by the body of Christ; that ye should be married to another, *even* to him who is raised from the dead, that we should [R]bring forth fruit unto God.

5 For when we were in the flesh, the [N]motions of sins, which were by the law, [R]did

---

Center cross-reference column:

CHAP. 5
AD 60
18 Or, *by one offence*
18 Or, *by one righteousness*
18 John 12:32
Heb. 2:9
20 John 15:22
Gal. 3:19
20 Luke 7:47

CHAP. 6
AD 60
1 ch. 3:8
2 Gal. 2:19
Col. 3:3
3 Gal. 3:27
3 Or, *are*
3 1 Cor. 15:29
4 Col. 2:12
4 ch. 8:11
1 Cor. 6:14
4 John 2:11
4 Gal. 6:15
5 Phil. 3:10
6 Gal. 2:20
6 Col. 2:11
7 1 Pet. 4:1
7 Gr. *justified*
8 2 Tim. 2:11
9 Rev. 1:18
10 Heb. 9:27
10 Luke 20:38
11 ver. 2
11 Gal. 2:19
12 Ps. 19:13
13 ch. 7:5
Col. 3:5
Jas. 4:1
13 Gr. *arms,* or, *weapons*
13 ch. 12:1
1 Pet. 2:24 & 4:2

ch. 7:4, 6   14
& 8:2
Gal. 5:18
1 Cor. 9:21   15
Mat. 6:24   16
John 8:34
2 Pet. 2:19
2 Tim. 1:13   17
Gr.   17
whereto ye were delivered
John 8:32   18
1 Cor. 7:22
Gal. 5:1
1 Pet. 2:16
John 8:34   20
Gr. *to*   20
righteousness
ch. 7:5   21
ch. 1:32   21
John 8:32   22
Gen. 2:17   23
ch. 5:12
Jas. 1:15
ch. 2:7   23
1 Pet. 1:4

CHAP. 7
AD 60
1 Cor. 7:39   2
Mat. 5:32   3
Gal. 2:19   4
& 5:18
Col. 2:14
Gal. 5:22   4
Gr. *passions*   5
ch. 6:13   5

work in our members ᴿto bring forth fruit unto death.

6 But now we are delivered from the law, ᴺthat being dead wherein we were held; that we should serve ᴿin newness of spirit, and not *in* the oldness of the letter.

Purpose of the law

7 What shall we say then? *Is* the law sin? God forbid. Nay, ᴿI had not known sin, but by the law: for I had not known ᴺlust, except the law had said, ᴿThou shalt not covet.

8 But ᴿsin, taking occasion by the commandment, wrought in me all manner of concupiscence. For ᴿwithout the law sin *was* dead.

9 For I was alive without the law once: but when the commandment came, sin revived, and I died.

10 And the commandment, ᴿwhich *was ordained* to life, I found *to be* unto death.

11 For sin, taking occasion by the commandment, deceived me, and by it slew *me*.

12 Wherefore ᴿthe law *is* holy, and the commandment holy, and just, and good.

The Christian's struggle

13 Was then that which is good made death unto me? God forbid. But sin, that it might appear sin, working death in me by that which is good; that sin by the commandment might become exceeding sinful.

14 For we know that the law is spiritual: but I am carnal, ᴿsold under sin.

15 For that which I do I ᴺallow not: for ᴿwhat I would, that do I not; but what I hate, that do I.

16 If then I do that which I would not, I consent unto the law that *it is* good.

17 Now then it is no more I that do it, but sin that dwelleth in me.

18 For I know that ᴿin me (that is, in my flesh,) dwelleth no good thing: for to will is present with me; but *how* to perform that which is good I find not.

19 For the good that I would I do not: but the evil which I would not, that I do.

20 Now if I do that I would not, it is no more I that do it, but sin that dwelleth in me.

21 I find then a law, that, when I would do good, evil is present with me.

22 For I ᴿdelight in the law of God after ᴿthe inward man:

23 But ᴿI see another law in ᴿmy members, warring against the law of my mind, and bringing me into captivity to the law of sin which is in my members.

24 O wretched man that I am! who shall deliver me from ᴺthe body of this death?

CHAP. **7**
AD 60
5 ch. 6:21
Gal. 5:19
Jas. 1:15
6 Or, *being dead to that,* ver. 4
ch. 6:2
6 ch. 2:29
2 Cor. 3:6
7 ch. 3:20
7 Or, *concupiscence*
7 Ex. 20:17
Deut. 5:21
Acts 20:33
8 ch. 4:15
8 1 Cor. 15:56
10 Lev. 18:5
Ezek. 20:11, 13, 21
2 Cor. 3:7
12 Ps. 19:8 & 119:38
1 Tim. 1:8
14 2 Ki. 17:17
15 Gr. *know,* Ps. 1:6
15 Gal. 5:17
18 Gen. 6:5 & 8:21
22 Ps. 1:2
22 2 Cor. 4:16 Eph. 3:16 Col. 3:9, 10
23 Gal. 5:17
23 ch. 6:13, 19
24 Or, *this body of death*

1 Cor. 15:57	**25**

CHAP. **8**
AD 60
Gal. 5:16 — **1**
ch. 6:18, 22 — **2**
1 Cor. 15:45 — **2**
ch. 7:24, 25 — **2**
Acts 13:39 — **3**
Heb. 7:18
2 Cor. 5:21 — **3**
Gal. 3:13
Or, *by a sacrifice for sin* — **3**
ver. 1 — **4**
John 3:6 — **5**
Gal. 5:22 — **5**
Gal. 6:8 — **6**
Gr. *the minding of the flesh* — **6**
Gr. *the minding of the Spirit* — **6**
Jas. 4:4 — **7**
Gr. *the minding of the flesh* — **7**
1 Cor. 2:14 — **7**
John 3:34 — **9**
Gal. 4:6
Acts 2:24 — **11**
1 Cor. 6:14 — **11**
2 Cor. 4:14
Or, *because of his Spirit* — **11**
ch. 6:7, 14 — **12**
Gal. 6:8 — **13**
Eph. 4:22 — **13**
Gal. 5:18 — **14**
1 Cor. 2:12 — **15**
Heb. 2:15
2 Tim. 1:7 — **15**
1 John 4:18
Is. 56:5 — **15**
Mark 14:36 — **15**
Eph. 1:13 — **16**
Acts 26:18 — **17**
Phil. 1:29 — **17**

25 ᴿI thank God through Jesus Christ our Lord. So then with the mind I myself serve the law of God; but with the flesh the law of sin.

CHAPTER 8

The Spirit and the flesh

THERE *is* therefore now no condemnation to them which are in Christ Jesus, who ᴿwalk not after the flesh, but after the Spirit.

2 For ᴿthe law of ᴿthe Spirit of life in Christ Jesus hath made me free from ᴿthe law of sin and death.

3 For ᴿwhat the law could not do, in that it was weak through the flesh, ᴿGod sending his own Son in the likeness of sinful flesh, and ᴺfor sin, condemned sin in the flesh:

4 That the righteousness of the law might be fulfilled in us, ᴿwho walk not after the flesh, but after the Spirit.

5 For ᴿthey that are after the flesh do mind the things of the flesh; but they that are after the Spirit ᴿthe things of the Spirit.

6 For ᴿtoᴺ be carnally minded *is* death; but ᴺto be spiritually minded *is* life and peace.

7 Because ᴿtheᴺcarnal mind *is* enmity against God: for it is not subject to the law of God, ᴿneither indeed can be.

8 So then they that are in the flesh cannot please God.

9 But ye are not in the flesh, but in the Spirit, if so be that the Spirit of God dwell in you. Now if any man have not ᴿthe Spirit of Christ, he is none of his.

10 And if Christ *be* in you, the body *is* dead because of sin; but the Spirit *is* life because of righteousness.

11 But if the Spirit of ᴿhim that raised up Jesus from the dead dwell in you, ᴿhe that raised up Christ from the dead shall also quicken your mortal bodies ᴺby his Spirit that dwelleth in you.

The Spirit of sonship

12 ᴿTherefore, brethren, we are debtors, not to the flesh, to live after the flesh.

13 For ᴿif ye live after the flesh, ye shall die: but if ye through the Spirit do ᴿmortify the deeds of the body, ye shall live.

14 For ᴿas many as are led by the Spirit of God, they are the sons of God.

15 For ᴿye have not received the spirit of bondage again ᴿto fear; but ye have received the ᴿSpirit of adoption, whereby we cry, ᴿAbba, Father.

16 ᴿThe Spirit itself beareth witness with our spirit, that we are the children of God:

17 And if children, then heirs; ᴿheirs of God, and joint-heirs with Christ; ᴿif so be that

we suffer with *him,* that we may be also glorified together.

Temporary sufferings

18 For I reckon that ᴿthe sufferings of this present time *are* not worthy *to be compared* with the glory which shall be revealed in us.

19 For ᴿthe earnest expectation of the creature waiteth for the manifestation of the sons of God.

20 For ᴿthe creature was made subject to vanity, not willingly, but by reason of him who hath subjected *the same* in hope,

21 Because the creature itself also shall be delivered from the bondage of corruption into the glorious liberty of the children of God.

22 For we know that ᴺthe whole creation ᴿgroaneth and travaileth in pain together until now.

23 And not only *they,* but ourselves also, which have ᴿthe firstfruits of the Spirit, ᴿeven we ourselves groan within ourselves, ᴿwaiting for the adoption, *to wit,* the ᴿredemption of our body.

24 For we are saved by hope: but ᴿhope that is seen is not hope: for what a man seeth, why doth he yet hope for?

25 But if we hope for that we see not, *then* do we with patience wait for *it.*

The help of the Spirit

26 Likewise the Spirit also helpeth our infirmities: for ᴿwe know not what we should pray for as we ought: but ᴿthe Spirit itself maketh intercession for us with groanings which cannot be uttered.

27 And ᴿhe that searcheth the hearts knoweth what *is* the mind of the Spirit, ᴺbecause he maketh intercession for the saints ᴿaccording to *the will of* God.

28 And we know that all things work together for good to them that love God, to them ᴿwho are the called according to *his* purpose.

29 For whom ᴿhe did foreknow, ᴿhe also did predestinate ᴿ*to be* conformed to the image of his Son, ᴿthat he might be the firstborn among many brethren.

30 Moreover whom he did predestinate, them he also ᴿcalled: and whom he called, them he also ᴿjustified: and whom he justified, them he also ᴿglorified.

More than conquerors

31 What shall we then say to these things? ᴿIf God *be* for us, who *can be* against us?

32 ᴿHe that spared not his own Son, but ᴿdelivered him up for us all, how shall he not with him also freely give us all things?

33 Who shall lay any thing to the charge of God's elect? ᴿ*It is* God that justifieth.

34 ᴿWho *is* he that condemneth? *It is* Christ that died, yea rather, that is risen again, ᴿwho is even at the right hand of God, ᴿwho also maketh intercession for us.

35 Who shall separate us from the love of Christ? *shall* tribulation, or distress, or persecution, or famine, or nakedness, or peril, or sword?

36 As it is written, ᴿFor thy sake we are killed all the day long; we are accounted as sheep for the slaughter.

37 ᴿNay, in all these things we are more than conquerors through him that loved us.

38 For I am persuaded, that neither death, nor life, nor angels, nor ᴿprincipalities, nor powers, nor things present, nor things to come,

39 Nor height, nor depth, nor any other creature, shall be able to separate us from the love of God, which is in Christ Jesus our Lord.

CHAPTER 9

Paul's sorrow over Israel's rebellion

I ᴿSAY the truth in Christ, I lie not, my conscience also bearing me witness in the Holy Ghost,

2 ᴿThat I have great heaviness and continual sorrow in my heart.

3 For ᴿI could wish that myself were ᴺaccursed from Christ for my brethren, my kinsmen according to the flesh:

4 Who are Israelites; ᴿto whom *pertaineth* the adoption, and ᴿthe glory, and ᴿthe ᴺcovenants, and ᴿthe giving of the law, and ᴿthe service *of God,* and ᴿthe promises;

5 ᴿWhose *are* the fathers, and ᴿof whom as concerning the flesh Christ *came,* ᴿwho is over all, God blessed for ever. Ä′-mĕn.

6 ᴿNot as though the word of God hath taken none effect. For ᴿthey *are* not all Israel, which are of Israel:

7 ᴿNeither, because they are the seed of Abraham, *are they* all children: but, In ᴿIsaac shall thy seed be called.

8 That is, They which are the children of the flesh, these *are* not the children of God: but ᴿthe children of the promise are counted for the seed.

9 For this *is* the word of promise, ᴿAt this time will I come, and Sarah shall have a son.

10 And not only *this;* but when ᴿRebecca also had conceived by one, *even* by our father Isaac;

11 (For *the children* being not yet born,

Center reference column

CHAP. **8**

AD 60

18	2 Cor. 4:17
	1 Pet. 1:6
19	2 Pet. 3:13
20	Gen. 3:19
22	Or, *every creature*
22	Jer. 12:11
23	2 Cor. 5:5
	Eph. 1:14
23	2 Cor. 5:2
23	Luke 20:36
23	Luke 21:28
	Eph. 4:30
24	2 Cor. 5:7
	Heb. 11:1
26	Mat. 20:22
	Jas. 4:3
26	Eph. 6:18
27	1 Chr. 28:9
	Acts 1:24
27	Or, *that*
27	1 John 5:14
28	2 Tim. 1:9
29	2 Tim. 2:19
29	Eph. 1:5
29	2 Cor. 3:18
	1 John 3:2
29	Col. 1:15
	Heb. 1:6
30	1 Pet. 2:9
30	1 Cor. 6:11
30	John 17:22
	Eph. 2:6
31	Num. 14:9
	Ps. 118:6
32	ch. 5:6, 10
32	ch. 4:25

Is. 50:8, 9	33
Rev. 12:10	
Job 34:29	34
Mark 16:19	34
Col. 3:1	
Heb. 1:3	
Heb. 7:25	34
& 9:24	
1 John 2:1	
Ps. 44:22	36
2 Cor. 4:11	
1 Cor. 15:57	37
1 John 4:4	
Eph. 1:21	38

CHAP. **9**

AD 60

2 Cor. 1:23	1
Gal. 1:20	
1 Tim. 2:7	
ch. 10:1	2
Ex. 32:32	3
Or, *separated*	3
Ex. 4:22	4
Deut. 14:1	
1 Sam. 4:21	4
1 Ki. 8:11	
Acts 3:25	4
Or, *testaments*	4
Ps. 147:19	4
Heb. 9:1	4
Acts 13:32	4
Eph. 2:12	
Deut. 10:15	5
Luke 3:23	5
Jer. 23:6	5
Heb. 1:8	
Num. 23:19	6
John 8:39	6
Gal. 6:16	
Gal. 4:23	7
Gen. 21:12	7
Gal. 4:28	8
Gen. 18:10	9
Gen. 25:21	10

The Ministry of Jesus

"And he said unto them,
Go ye into all the world,
and preach the gospel
to every creature."

MARK 16:15

The Sermon on the Mount

OW greatly mountains have figured in the religious life of mankind! Moses went up on the mountain in the wilderness of Sinai and received the Ten Commandments. Jesus, centuries later, went up on a mountain in Palestine and proclaimed the "new law" for citizens of the kingdom of heaven.

In the first part of his sermon, Jesus gave nine Beatitudes, which contrast the future joys of Christians with their present duties and sufferings.

"Blessed are the poor in spirit: for theirs is the kingdom of heaven.

"Blessed are they that mourn: for they shall be comforted.

"Blessed are the meek: for they shall inherit the earth.

"Blessed are they which do hunger and thirst after righteousness: for they shall be filled.

"Blessed are the merciful: for they shall obtain mercy.

"Blessed are the pure in heart: for they shall see God.

"Blessed are the peacemakers: for they shall be called the children of God.

"Blessed are they which are persecuted for righteousness' sake: for theirs is the kingdom of heaven.

"Blessed are ye, when men shall revile you, and persecute you, and shall say all manner of evil against you falsely, for my sake. Rejoice, and be exceeding glad: for great is your reward in heaven: for so persecuted they the prophets which were before you."

Then Jesus described the relation of his disciples, and of all Christians, to the world. They are to be "the salt of the earth," keeping the world from spoiling or from being tasteless. They are to be "the light of the world," providing light for the pathway of men who would otherwise stumble along in darkness.

Next, Jesus told his followers that his "new law" was fulfillment of the old law, not a rejection of it. His teaching goes behind the act to the motive. For example, the root of murder is anger, so anger is forbidden.

One of the most striking passages in the Sermon on the Mount is that in which Jesus says, "Love your enemies, bless them that curse you, do good to them that hate you, and pray for them which despitefully use you and persecute you." Why would he teach such a strange and "unnatural" response to one's enemies? Because this is how God acts! "He maketh his sun to rise on the evil and on the good, and sendeth rain on the just and on the unjust."

The most familiar and beloved of Christian prayers, the Lord's Prayer, is contained in this sermon. This is followed by profound teachings about prayer. Embedded in the world's greatest sermon is the teaching which we call "the Golden Rule": "All things whatsoever ye would that men should do to you, do ye even so to them: for this is the law and the prophets."

This wonderful teaching is not merely to be heard and memorized, it is to be the foundation of the Christian's life. A life lived by the Sermon on the Mount is built on rock, and no calamity can destroy it!

Matthew 5:1–7:29.

BLOCH

The Woman at the Well

N one of his trips from Judah to Galilee, Jesus passed through the town of Sychar in Samaria. There was a bitter rivalry between the Jews and the Samaritans, so ordinarily they avoided contact with one another.

It was noontime; the sun was hot and Jesus was tired and thirsty. There ahead of him was an ancient landmark, Jacob's well. Hoping that someone would come along with a water jar from which he might get a drink, Jesus sat down beside the well. Shortly, a Samaritan woman came to the well to draw water, so Jesus requested: "Give me to drink."

The woman was surprised. Jews usually had no dealings with Samaritans; furthermore, Jewish men ordinarily did not talk with women in public. So the woman asked: "How is that thou, being a Jew, askest drink of me, which am a woman of Samaria?"

The conversation, which began on the plane of simple human need for water, was then turned by Jesus to a spiritual plane. "If thou knewest the gift of God, and who it is that saith to thee, Give me to drink; thou wouldest have asked of him, and he would have given thee living water." "Living water" was a symbol for the satisfaction of a man's spiritual needs.

But the Samaritan woman misunderstood Jesus' meaning. How could he draw water from a well, when he had no rope and no bucket? So Jesus tried once more to help the woman see that he was talking about something more lasting than a liquid to drink. Pointing to the water in the well, he said: "Whosoever drinketh of this water shall thirst again: but whosoever drinketh of the water that I shall give him shall never thirst; but the water that I shall give him shall be in him a well of water springing up into everlasting life."

Even now, the woman misunderstood Jesus; all that she could imagine was that—somehow—she might be spared the chore of drawing water from Jacob's well day after day. Seeing that he was not getting his message across to the woman, Jesus changed the subject sharply: "Go, call thy husband, and come hither." The woman was embarrassed. "I have no husband," she said. But Jesus had rightly guessed the woman's secret: she was living with a man outside wedlock.

Here was a man of unusual powers of insight! The woman quickly shifted the conversation from her own immorality to a controversial religious topic: Where is the "right spot" to worship God? But Jesus once more lifted the conversation from the level of petty controversy to universal spiritual truth: "The hour cometh, and now is, when the true worshippers shall worship the Father in spirit and in truth: for the Father seeketh such to worship him. God is a Spirit: and they that worship him must worship him in spirit and in truth."

As they talked, the woman became more and more excited about this remarkable man. Could he be the Messiah? Forgetting her water jar, she hurried into the city of Sychar, telling everyone about her conversation with Jesus at the well. "Is not this the Christ?" she asked. As a result, many persons went out to meet Jesus, and insisted that he stay and talk with them further.

John 4:1-42.

BLOCH

Jesus Heals a Blind Man

 ARTIMAEUS sat by the roadside on the outskirts of Jericho, a town in Judah. The day had begun like any of a hundred others. After all, how much variety could there be in the life of a blind beggar? But suddenly he heard the hum of voices, coming closer. To his ears, more sensitive than the average person's because they had to make up for his lack of sight, the voices conveyed a strong undercurrent of excitement. This was no ordinary crowd of travelers walking along the Jericho road! Bartimaeus called out to some children playing nearby. "Run down the road and find out who it is that is coming this way!" he urged. In a few moments, one of the boys reported: "It is Jesus of Nazareth and some of his followers."

What excitement Bartimaeus felt as he heard those words! He had heard of this strange and wonderful Teacher from Nazareth, who taught men to love one another and who healed the sick. Perhaps Jesus would heal him!

By this time the party of travelers was passing by right in front of the blind beggar. Now! If he were to get help, it must be now! "Jesus, thou son of David, have mercy on me," Bartimaeus cried out in a loud voice.

"Be quiet, old man!" some of the persons in the crowd said. But this was no time to be quiet—this was a time to be healed. So even louder than before, Bartimaeus called out: "Thou son of David, have mercy on me."

At this, Jesus stopped; he told his disciples to call the man who had been trying to catch his attention. So they went over to the blind beggar and said: "Be of good comfort, rise; he calleth thee."

Bartimaeus jumped up and threw aside his mantle. Then he walked over to Jesus and stood quietly, filled with expectation.

The voice was vibrant with life: "What wilt thou that I should do unto thee?" What did Jesus mean? Could he not see that Bartimaeus was blind, that he needed to have his sight restored? Yes; but here was One who wanted people to realize their own deepest needs and express their longings. "Do you really wish to be cured?" Jesus seemed to be asking Bartimaeus. "If you are cured, you must go to work; you can no longer sit by the roadside and beg for a living. Many changes must be made in your life."

All these thoughts may have flashed through Bartimaeus' mind as he stood there before Jesus. But he knew his answer: he wanted to have his sight restored—and he knew that Jesus had the power to heal him. So he gave Jesus his answer: "Lord, that I might receive my sight."

All eyes were focused on Jesus as he touched Bartimaeus with compassion: "Go thy way; thy faith hath made thee whole," he said. In an instant the eyes which had been blind and useless revealed the whole wonderful world of sight to Bartimaeus—the sunlight, the sky, the brown earth, and immediately before him the compassionate and loving face of Jesus Christ. Who can describe the joy that Bartimaeus felt? He knew immediately that, whatever else life might hold in store for him, he wanted to learn more about this wonderful man Jesus. So with glad heart and light step, Bartimaeus "followed Jesus in the way."

Mark 10:46-52; Luke 18:35-43.

TISSOT

The Transfiguration

I T was on a mountain that Jesus gave his great Sermon. It was on a mountain, also, that he was transfigured—shown in his true glory as the Son of God—before the eyes of his closest disciples. Jesus had led Peter and James and John up on a high mountain. While they were there, his face shone "as the sun" and his robes were "white as the light."

As the startled disciples gazed wonderingly at Jesus, suddenly there appeared to them Moses and Elijah, who talked with Jesus. The full meaning of this unusual happening would require much time for thought. But even now, the disciples recognized Moses as the greatest of the lawgivers and Elijah as the prophet whose return was expected by many faithful Jews. Moses and Elijah talked with Jesus, what must this mean about him?

Peter, always a man of enthusiasm and action, spoke up: "Lord, it is good for us to be here: if thou wilt, let us make here three tabernacles; one for thee, and one for Moses, and one for Elijah." Perhaps Peter thought that he would be honoring Jesus, proclaiming his personal faith that Jesus ranked with Moses and Elijah as a great Jewish religious leader.

But the disciples were in for an even greater surprise. Even as Peter was speaking, proposing the erection of three tabernacles, "behold, a bright cloud overshadowed them: and behold a voice out of the cloud, which said, This is my beloved Son, in whom I am well pleased; hear ye him."

The disciples were so frightened that they fell down on the ground and hid their faces. Here they were on a mountain top with the Son of God himself! Their minds must have been stunned by the realization. But Jesus did not leave his three closest disciples quaking in fear. He went over to them and touched them and said: "Arise, and be not afraid." As they opened their eyes and looked about cautiously, they saw that Jesus was now alone.

The three disciples must have had minds filled with many questions as they came down the mountainside. Quite naturally, they would want to discuss with the other disciples the wonderful transfiguration of Jesus which they had witnessed, and the conclusive revelation that he was indeed the Son of God. But Jesus told them emphatically, "Tell the vision to no man, until the Son of man be risen again from the dead."

"Son of man" was a term for the Messiah. The disciples no longer doubted that Jesus was the Messiah, but they wondered why the Jewish religious leaders believed that Elijah must return to earth before the Messiah would come. Jesus told them, "Elijah is come already, and they knew him not, but have done unto him whatsoever they listed." Come already? Suddenly the three disciples understood what Jesus meant: John the Baptist, a prophet, had fulfilled the function that the earlier prophet Elijah performed in his day, and had been beheaded.

What a sobering thought, therefore, was contained in Jesus' final words to them as they neared the bottom of the mountain: "Likewise shall also the Son of man suffer of them." The disciples had been granted a glimpse of Jesus' glory; they had also been warned that he must suffer at the hands of men.

Matthew 17:1-13; Mark 9:2-13; Luke 9:28-36.

Jesus Blesses Little Children

HE goodness of Jesus' life attracted persons to him. There was strength here, and compassion, too, expressed in his willingness to heal the sick and the blind. There was a wonderful attractiveness about Jesus, also, so that parents wanted their children to come under his influence.

One day as Jesus was teaching, some parents brought their children to Jesus, that he might lay his hands on them and pray. This was a token of respect for a teacher; furthermore, it expressed the faith that God's love and concern encompassed children as well as adults.

Jesus' disciples thought he was too busy to be bothered with children. After all, was he not busily engaged in discussion with the Pharisees, the religious leaders of the Jewish people? Religion was serious business, and Jesus' time must be protected—or so they thought. So the "disciples rebuked those that brought" the children.

But the disciples had failed to understand Jesus at this point. When he saw what they were doing, "he was much displeased, and said unto them, Suffer the little children to come unto me, and forbid them not: for of such is the kingdom of God. Verily I say unto you, Whosoever shall not receive the kingdom of God as a little child, he shall not enter therein."

"Suffer the little children to come unto me . . ." Here we see another mark of greatness in Jesus: he was never too busy to see anyone, old or young, rich or poor, beggar or ruler. For children he had tenderness and affection. Small wonder that children through the centuries have felt attracted to the Man of Galilee! Love begets love. ". . . for of such is the kingdom of God." The qualities of childlike trust and faith in God were valued highly by Jesus.

But Jesus, the world's greatest teacher, did not stop here. He used the incident to teach a profound lesson about the religious life of adults, as well as children. "Whosoever shall not receive the kingdom of God as a little child, he shall not enter therein." What could Jesus mean? Undoubtedly the disciples were puzzled. Perhaps Jesus meant that persons must be receptive to new ideas, responsive to new situations—approaching life with an attitude of open-eyed wonder, with eagerness to learn something new every day. How often adults cease to be teachable, closing their minds to new ideas and new interpretations. Yet God, who "makes all things new," would lead us into ever deeper understanding of his will and way for human life.

The incident in the ministry of Jesus, which began with misunderstanding on the part of the disciples, has a beautiful conclusion: Jesus "took the children up in his arms, put his hands upon them, and blessed them." That benediction of the Master rests upon the life of every child born into the world, today as well as in the first century!

Matthew 19:13-15; Mark 10:13-16; Luke 18:15-17.

HUNNAEUS

The Raising of Lazarus

TWO miles southeast of Jerusalem was the little town of Bethany. Here lived three of Jesus' close friends, Lazarus and his two sisters Mary and Martha. One day Jesus received word that Lazarus was quite sick, but instead of going immediately to Bethany he stayed where he was for two days longer. Then he told his disciples, "Let us go into Judea again."

Much opposition to Jesus had grown up among the Jewish religious leaders in Judea. So Jesus' disciples were fearful for his safety. But Jesus insisted on going to Bethany. "Our friend Lazarus sleepeth; but I go, that I may awake him out of sleep," Jesus told his disciples. This puzzled them, for they did not understand that by "sleep" Jesus meant "death." Therefore, Jesus told them plainly, "Lazarus is dead."

When Jesus and his disciples reached Bethany, they learned that Lazarus had been buried four days. As soon as Martha heard that Jesus was coming she rushed out to meet him. "Lord, if thou hadst been here, my brother had not died," she said in sorrow and regret. "But I know, that even now, whatsoever thou wilt ask of God, God will give it thee."

Jesus spoke confidently to Martha: "Thy brother shall rise again." Thinking that he was referring to the final resurrection of the dead, Martha replied: "I know that he shall rise again in the resurrection at the last day." Then Jesus made a profound statement about himself: "I am the resurrection, and the life: he that believeth in me, though he were dead, yet shall he live: and whosoever liveth and believeth in me shall never die." Looking at Martha, he asked: "Believest thou this?" Then Martha declared her faith in Jesus: "Yea, Lord: I believe that thou art the Christ, the Son of God." With this, Martha went to tell her sister Mary that Jesus had arrived.

Mary went out quickly to meet Jesus and fell, weeping, at his feet. Some of the family's friends followed her; they, too, were weeping. At the sight of their grief, Jesus was deeply moved. "Where have ye laid him?" Jesus asked. So they showed him Lazarus' tomb, and Jesus wept.

Jesus told the bystanders to remove the stone from the mouth of the cave which was Lazarus' tomb. Then, after praying to God, "he cried with a loud voice, Lazarus, come forth." To the amazement and joy of Mary and Martha and their friends, Lazarus came out of the tomb, still wearing his graveclothes.

This miracle angered the Pharisees. Their anger was directed not only at Jesus but also at Lazarus, "because that by reason of him many of the Jews went away, and believed on Jesus."

Even so, Jesus went again to Bethany to visit Lazarus and Martha and Mary. While Jesus and Lazarus were eating, Mary took "a pound of ointment of spikenard, very costly, and anointed the feet of Jesus, and wiped his feet with her hair: and the house was filled with the odor of the ointment." This was a touching tribute of love and gratitude for Jesus, who had raised her brother from the dead.

John 11:1-46; 12:1-11.

BLOCH

Driving the Traders from the Temple

ORSHIP in the Temple at Jerusalem involved more than just prayer and song. For centuries there had been a carefully prescribed form of sacrifice, set forth in the writings of the Old Testament. For example, we read that "if the burnt sacrifice for his offering to the Lord be of fowls, then he shall bring his offering of turtledoves, or of young pigeons."

As pilgrims came to the Temple in Jerusalem to worship, they might not have the approved kinds of coins to make their offerings. Even more likely, they would not be able to bring along on a long journey turtledoves or young pigeons. As a result, money changers sat at tables in the Temple, exchanging—for a fee—money which the pilgrims had for the approved shekels. And traders brought animals to the courtyard of the Temple to sell for sacrifices.

Jesus had come to Jerusalem to celebrate the Passover. As he came into the Temple—which he had first known and loved as a boy—the clatter of commerce angered him. This is God's house, he thought; it is supposed to be used for worship, but instead it is being used to make men rich. He recalled the scathing word of the prophet Jeremiah: "Is this house, which is called by my name, become a den of robbers in your eyes? Behold, even I have seen it, saith the Lord."

With that, Jesus took firm and decisive action. He "went into the temple, and began to cast out them that sold and bought in the temple, and overthrew the tables of the money changers, and the seats of them that sold doves; and would not suffer that any man should carry any vessel through the temple." There must have been something awesome about the appearance and manner of Jesus, else how could one man have driven out so many persons?

Then Jesus proceeded to teach the people in the Temple why he had acted as he did. "Is it not written, My house shall be called of all nations the house of prayer?" At this, many heads must have nodded, for the Jews believed that the Temple in Jerusalem was a kind of "religious capitol" for the world. But Jesus went on to speak words that startled and shocked his hearers: "But ye have made it a den of thieves."

Reactions to Jesus' teaching were divided: the common people were "astonished at his doctrine." His sincerity, his personal power carried conviction. But the religious leaders were angry; Jesus had challenged their leadership, and undercut their source of income. So the scribes and chief priests "sought how they might destroy him: for they feared him."

By cleansing the Temple, Jesus reminded the people of his day that religion must not be buried under a lot of commercial concerns. Buildings dedicated to the worship of God should be used for the glory of God, not for personal profit of men. Even though it angered persons to the point where they wanted to kill him, Jesus insisted that God's house must be a place approached in reverence, for worship is the highest act of human life.

Matthew 21:12-13; Mark 11:15-18; Luke 19:45-48.

BLOCH

Master, which is the great commandment in the law?

Jesus said unto him, Thou shalt love the Lord thy God with all thy heart, and with all thy soul, and with all thy mind.

This is the first and great commandment.

And the second is like unto it, Thou shalt love thy neighbour as thyself.

On these two commandments hang all the law and the prophets."

MATTHEW 22:36-40

neither having done any good or evil, that the purpose of God according to election might stand, not of works, but of ᴿhim that calleth;)

12 It was said unto her, ᴿThe ᴺelder shall serve the ᴺyounger.

13 As it is written, ᴿJacob have I loved, but Esau have I hated.

The justice of God's mercy

14 What shall we say then? ᴿ*Is there* unrighteousness with God? God forbid.

15 For he saith to Moses, ᴿI will have mercy on whom I will have mercy, and I will have compassion on whom I will have compassion.

16 So then *it is* not of him that willeth, nor of him that runneth, but of God that sheweth mercy.

17 For ᴿthe scripture saith unto Pharaoh, ᴿEven for this same purpose have I raised thee up, that I might shew my power in thee, and that my name might be declared throughout all the earth.

18 Therefore hath he mercy on whom he will *have mercy,* and whom he will he hardeneth.

19 Thou wilt say then unto me, Why doth he yet find fault? For ᴿwho hath resisted his will?

20 Nay but, O man, who art thou that ᴺrepliest against God? ᴿShall the thing formed say to him that formed *it,* Why hast thou made me thus?

21 Hath not the ᴿpotter power over the clay, of the same lump to make ᴿone vessel unto honour, and another unto dishonour?

22 *What* if God, willing to shew *his* wrath, and to make his power known, endured with much longsuffering ᴿthe vessels of wrath ᴿfittedᴺ to destruction:

23 And that he might make known ᴿthe riches of his glory on the vessels of mercy, which he had ᴿafore prepared unto glory,

24 Even us, whom he hath called, ᴿnot of the Jews only, but also of the Gentiles?

25 As he saith also in ō'-śĕe, ᴿI will call them my people, which were not my people; and her beloved, which was not beloved.

26 ᴿAnd it shall come to pass, *that* in the place where it was said unto them, Ye *are* not my people; there shall they be called the children of the living God.

27 Ē-śāi'-ăs also crieth concerning Israel, ᴿThough the number of the children of Israel be as the sand of the sea, ᴿa remnant shall be saved:

28 For he will finish ᴺthe work, and cut *it* short in righteousness: ᴿbecause a short work will the Lord make upon the earth.

29 And as Ē-śāi'-ăs said before, ᴿExcept the

CHAP. 9
AD 60
11 ch. 4:17
12 Gen. 25:23
12 Or, *greater*
12 Or, *lesser*
13 Mal. 1:2, 3
Mat. 10:37
14 Deut. 32:4
Job 8:3
15 Ex. 33:19
17 Gal. 3:8
17 Ex. 9:16
19 2 Chr. 20:6
Dan. 4:35
20 Or, *answerest again,* or, *disputest with God?*
20 Is. 29:16
21 Prov. 16:4
21 2 Tim. 2:20
1 Thes. 5:9
22 1 Pet. 2:8
22 Or, *made up*
23 Col. 1:27
23 ch. 8:28-30
24 ch. 3:29
25 Hos. 2:23
26 Hos. 1:10
27 Is. 10:22
27 ch. 11:5
28 Or, *the acount*
28 Is. 28:22
29 Is. 1:9
Lam. 3:22

Is. 13:19	**29**
Jer. 50:40	
ch. 4:11	**30**
ch. 1:17	**30**
ch. 10:2	**31**
Gal. 5:4	**31**
Luke 2:34	**32**
1 Cor. 1:23	
Ps. 118:22	**33**
Is. 8:14 & 28:16	
Mat. 21:42	
1 Pet. 2:6-8	
ch. 10:11	**33**
Or, *confounded*	**33**

CHAP. 10
AD 60

Acts 21:20 & 22:3	**2**
ch. 9:31	
Gal. 1:14	
ch. 1:17	**3**
Phil. 3:9	**3**
Mat. 5:17	**4**
Gal. 3:24	
Lev. 18:5	**5**
Neh. 9:29	
Ezek. 20:11	
Gal. 3:12	
Deut. 30:12	**6**
Deut. 30:14	**8**
Mat. 10:32	**9**
Luke 12:8	
Acts 8:37	
Is. 28:16 & 49:23	**11**
Jer. 17:7	
Acts 15:9	**12**
ch. 3:22	
Acts 10:36	**12**
1 Tim. 2:5	
Eph. 1:7 & 2:4, 7	**12**

Lord of Să-bā'-ŏth had left us a seed, ᴿwe had been as Sŏd'-ŏ-mă, and been made like unto Gō-mŏr'-rhă.

The stumblingstone

30 What shall we say then? ᴿThat the Gentiles, which followed not after righteousness, have attained to righteousness, ᴿeven the righteousness which is of faith.

31 But Israel, ᴿwhich followed after the law of righteousness, ᴿhath not attained to the law of righteousness.

32 Wherefore? Because *they sought it* not by faith, but as it were by the works of the law. For ᴿthey stumbled at that stumblingstone;

33 As it is written, ᴿBehold, I lay in Śĩ'-ǫn a stumblingstone and rock of offence: and ᴿwhosoever believeth on him shall not be ᴺashamed.

CHAPTER 10

BRETHREN, my heart's desire and prayer to God for Israel is, that they might be saved.

2 For I bear them record ᴿthat they have a zeal of God, but not according to knowledge.

3 For they being ignorant of ᴿGod's righteousness, and going about to establish their own ᴿrighteousness, have not submitted themselves unto the righteousness of God.

4 For ᴿChrist *is* the end of the law for righteousness to every one that believeth.

Law and faith contrasted

5 For Moses describeth the righteousness which is of the law, ᴿThat the man which doeth those things shall live by them.

6 But the righteousness which is of faith speaketh on this wise, ᴿSay not in thine heart, Who shall ascend into heaven? (that is, to bring Christ down *from above:*)

7 Or, Who shall descend into the deep? (that is, to bring up Christ again from the dead.)

8 But what saith it? ᴿThe word is nigh thee, *even* in thy mouth, and in thy heart: that is, the word of faith, which we preach;

9 That ᴿif thou shalt confess with thy mouth the Lord Jesus, and shalt believe in thine heart that God hath raised him from the dead, thou shalt be saved.

10 For with the heart man believeth unto righteousness; and with the mouth confession is made unto salvation.

11 For the scripture saith, ᴿWhosoever believeth on him shall not be ashamed.

12 For ᴿthere is no difference between the Jew and the Greek: for ᴿthe same Lord over all ᴿis rich unto all that call upon him.

13 ᴿFor whosoever shall call ᴿupon the name of the Lord shall be saved.

Faith by the preaching of Christ

14 How then shall they call on him in whom they have not believed? and how shall they believe in him of whom they have not heard? and how shall they hear ᴿwithout a preacher?

15 And how shall they preach, except they be sent? as it is written, ᴿHow beautiful are the feet of them that preach the gospel of peace, and bring glad tidings of good things!

16 But they have not all obeyed the gospel. For Ē-ṡaī′-ăs saith, ᴿLord, who hath believed ᴺour ᴺreport?

17 So then faith *cometh* by hearing, and hearing by the word of God.

18 But I say, Have they not heard? Yes verily, ᴿtheir sound went into all the earth, ᴿand their words unto the ends of the world.

19 But I say, Did not Israel know? First Moses saith, ᴿI will provoke you to jealousy by *them that are* no people, *and* by a ᴿfoolish nation I will anger you.

20 But Ē-ṡaī′-ăs is very bold, and saith, ᴿI was found of them that sought me not; I was made manifest unto them that asked not after me.

21 But to Israel he saith, ᴿAll day long I have stretched forth my hands unto a disobedient and gainsaying people.

CHAPTER 11

The remnant chosen by grace

I SAY then, ᴿHath God cast away his people? God forbid. For ᴿI also am an Israelite, of the seed of Abraham, *of* the tribe of Benjamin.

2 God hath not cast away his people which ᴿhe foreknew. Wot ye not what the scripture saith ᴺof Ē-lī′-ăs? how he maketh intercession to God against Israel, saying,

3 ᴿLord, they have killed thy prophets, and digged down thine altars; and I am left alone, and they seek my life.

4 But what saith the answer of God unto him? ᴿI have reserved to myself seven thousand men, who have not bowed the knee to *the image of* Bā′-ăl.

5 ᴿEven so then at this present time also there is a remnant according to the election of grace.

6 And ᴿif by grace, then *is it* no more of works: otherwise grace is no more grace. But if *it be* of works, then is it no more grace: otherwise work is no more work.

7 What then? ᴿIsrael hath not obtained that

which he seeketh for; but the election hath obtained it, and the rest were ᴺblinded

8 (According as it is written, ᴿGod hath given them the spirit of ᴺslumber, ᴿeyes that they should not see, and ears that they should not hear;) unto this day.

9 And David saith, ᴿLet their table be made a snare, and a trap, and a stumblingblock, and a recompence unto them:

10 ᴿLet their eyes be darkened, that they may not see, and bow down their back alway.

Benefits of Israel's transgression

11 I say then, Have they stumbled that they should fall? God forbid: but *rather* ᴿthrough their fall salvation *is come* unto the Gentiles, for to provoke them to jealousy.

12 Now if the fall of them *be* the riches of the world, and the ᴺdiminishing of them the riches of the Gentiles; how much more their fulness?

13 For I speak to you Gentiles, inasmuch as ᴿI am the apostle of the Gentiles, I magnify mine office:

14 If by any means I may provoke to emulation *them which are* my flesh, and ᴿmight save some of them.

15 For if the casting away of them *be* the reconciling of the world, what *shall* the receiving *of them be,* but life from the dead?

16 For if ᴿthe firstfruit *be* holy, the lump *is* also *holy:* and if the root *be* holy, so *are* the branches.

The parable of the olive tree

17 And if ᴿsome of the branches be broken off, ᴿand thou, being a wild olive tree, wert grafted in ᴺamong them, and with them partakest of the root and fatness of the olive tree;

18 ᴿBoast not against the branches. But if thou boast, thou bearest not the root, but the root thee.

19 Thou wilt say then, The branches were broken off, that I might be grafted in.

20 Well; because of unbelief they were broken off, and thou standest by faith. ᴿBe not highminded, but ᴿfear:

21 For if God spared not the natural branches, *take heed* lest he also spare not thee.

22 Behold therefore the goodness and severity of God: on them which fell, severity; but toward thee, goodness, ᴿif thou continue in *his* goodness: otherwise ᴿthou also shalt be cut off.

23 And they also, ᴿif they abide not still in unbelief, shall be grafted in: for God is able to graft them in again.

24 For if thou wert cut out of the olive tree which is wild by nature, and wert grafted con-

---

CHAP. 10
AD 60

13	Joel 2:32
	Acts 2:21
13	Acts 9:14
14	Tit. 1:3
15	Is. 52:7
	Nah. 1:15
16	Is. 53:1
	John 12:38
16	Gr. *the hearing of us?*
16	Or, *preaching?*
18	Ps. 19:4
	Mat. 24:14
	Mark 16:15
	Col. 1:6, 23
18	1 Ki. 18:10
	Mat. 4:8
19	ch. 11:11
19	Tit. 3:3
20	Is. 65:1
21	Is. 65:2

CHAP. 11
AD 60

1	1 Sam. 12:22
	Jer. 31:37
1	2 Cor. 11:22
	Phil. 3:5
2	ch. 8:29
2	Gr. *in Elias?*
3	1 Ki. 19:10
4	1 Ki. 19:18
5	ch. 9:27
6	ch. 4:4, 5
	Deut. 9:4, 5
	Gal. 5:4
7	ch. 9:31

Or, *hardened*	7
Is. 29:10	8
Or, *remorse*	8
Deut. 29:4	8
Is. 6:9	
Jer. 5:21	
Ezek. 12:2	
Mat. 13:14	
John 12:40	
Acts 28:26	
Ps. 69:22	9
Ps. 69:23	10
Acts 13:46	11
& 18:6	
ch. 10:19	
Or, *decay*	12
or, *loss*	
Acts 9:15	13
Gal. 1:16	
Eph. 3:8	
1 Tim. 2:7	
1 Cor. 9:22	14
1 Tim. 4:16	
Jas. 5:20	
Lev. 23:10	16
Jas. 1:18	
Jer. 11:16	17
Acts 2:39	17
Eph. 2:12	
Or, *for them*	17
1 Cor. 10:12	18
ch. 12:16	20
Prov. 28:14	20
Is. 66:2	
1 Cor. 15:2	22
Heb. 3:6	
John 15:2	22
2 Cor. 3:16	23

trary to nature into a good olive tree: how much more shall these, which be the natural *branches,* be grafted into their own olive tree?

The irrevocable call of God

25 For I would not, brethren, that ye should be ignorant of this mystery, lest ye should be [R]wise in your own conceits; that [R]blindness[N] in part is happened to Israel, [R]until the fulness of the Gentiles be come in.

26 And so all Israel shall be saved: as it is written, [R]There shall come out of Sī'-on the Deliverer, and shall turn away ungodliness from Jacob:

27 [R]For this *is* my covenant unto them, when I shall take away their sins.

28 As concerning the gospel, *they are* enemies for your sakes: but as touching the election, *they are* [R]beloved for the fathers' sakes.

29 For the gifts and calling of God *are* [R]without repentance.

30 For as ye [R]in times past have not [N]believed God, yet have now obtained mercy through their unbelief:

31 Even so have these also now not [N]believed, that through your mercy they also may obtain mercy.

32 For [R]God hath [N]concluded them all in unbelief, that he might have mercy upon all.

The doxology

33 O the depth of the riches both of the wisdom and knowledge of God! [R]how unsearchable *are* his judgments, and [R]his ways past finding out!

34 [R]For who hath known the mind of the Lord? or [R]who hath been his counsellor?

35 Or [R]who hath first given to him, and it shall be recompensed unto him again?

36 For [R]of him, and through him, and to him, *are* all things: [R]to [N]whom *be* glory for ever. Ā'-mĕn.

CHAPTER 12

Proper response to God's grace

I [R]BESEECH you therefore, brethren, by the mercies of God, [R]that ye [R]present your bodies [R]a living sacrifice, holy, acceptable unto God, *which is* your reasonable service.

2 And [R]be not conformed to this world: but [R]be ye transformed by the renewing of your mind, that ye may [R]prove what *is* that good, and acceptable, and perfect, will of God.

Proper use of God's gifts

3 For I say, [R]through the grace given unto me, to every man that is among you, [R]not to think *of himself* more highly than he ought to

think; but to think [N]soberly, according as God hath dealt [R]to every man the measure of faith.

4 For [R]as we have many members in one body, and all members have not the same office:

5 So [R]we, *being* many, are one body in Christ, and every one members one of another.

6 [R]Having then gifts differing [R]according to the grace that is given to us, whether [R]prophecy, *let us prophesy* according to the proportion of faith;

7 Or ministry, *let us wait* on *our* ministering: or [R]he that teacheth, on teaching;

8 Or [R]he that exhorteth, on exhortation: [R]he that [N]giveth, *let him do it* [N]with simplicity; [R]he that ruleth, with diligence; he that sheweth mercy, [R]with cheerfulness.

9 [R]*Let* love be without dissimulation. [R]Abhor that which is evil; cleave to that which is good.

10 [R]*Be* kindly affectioned one to another [N]with brotherly love; [R]in honour preferring one another;

11 Not slothful in business; fervent in spirit; serving the Lord;

12 [R]Rejoicing in hope; [R]patient in tribulation; [R]continuing instant in prayer;

13 [R]Distributing to the necessity of saints; [R]given to hospitality.

Overcome evil with good

14 [R]Bless them which persecute you: bless, and curse not.

15 [R]Rejoice with them that do rejoice, and weep with them that weep.

16 [R]*Be* of the same mind one toward another. [R]Mind not high things, but [N]condescend to men of low estate. [R]Be not wise in your own conceits.

17 [R]Recompense to no man evil for evil. [R]Provide things honest in the sight of all men.

18 If it be possible, as much as lieth in you, [R]live peaceably with all men.

19 Dearly beloved, [R]avenge not yourselves, but *rather* give place unto wrath: for it is written, [R]Vengeance *is* mine; I will repay, saith the Lord.

20 [R]Therefore if thine enemy hunger, feed him; if he thirst, give him drink: for in so doing thou shalt heap coals of fire on his head.

21 Be not overcome of evil, but overcome evil with good.

CHAPTER 13

Authority of the state

LET every soul [R]be subject unto the higher powers. For [R]there is no power but of

CHAP. 11
AD 60

25 ch. 12:16
25 2 Cor. 3:14
25 Or, *hardness*
25 Luke 21:24
Rev. 7:9
26 Ps. 14:7
Is. 59:20
27 Is. 27:9
Heb. 8:8
28 Deut. 7:8
29 Num. 23:19
30 Eph. 2:2
30 Or, *obeyed*
31 Or, *obeyed*
32 ch. 3:9
32 Or, *shut them all up together*
33 Ps. 36:6
33 Job 11:7
Ps. 92:5
34 Job 15:8
Is. 40:13
34 Job 36:22
35 Job 35:7
36 Col. 1:16
36 Heb. 13:21
Rev. 1:6
36 Gr. *him*

CHAP. 12
AD 60

1 2 Cor. 10:1
1 1 Pet. 2:5
1 ch. 6
1 Heb. 10:20
2 1 John 2:15
2 Eph. 4:23
2 1 Thes. 4:3
3 Gal. 2:9
3 Prov. 25:27
Gr. *to sobriety* 3
Eph. 4:7 3
1 Cor. 12:12 4
1 Cor. 10:17 5
1 Cor. 12:4 6
ver. 3 6
Acts 11:27 6
Eph. 4:11 7
Acts 15:32 8
Mat. 6:1-3 8
Or, *imparteth* 8
Or, *liberally* 8
Acts 20:28 8
2 Cor. 9:7 8
1 Tim. 1:5 9
Ps. 34:14 9
Heb. 13:1 10
Or, *in the love of the brethren*
Phil. 2:3 10
Luke 10:20 12
Luke 21:19 12
Luke 18:1 12
1 Cor. 16:1 13
1 Tim. 3:2 13
Mat. 5:44 14
1 Cor. 12:26 15
Phil. 2:2 16
Jer. 45:5 16
Or, *be contented with mean things* 16
Prov. 3:7 16
Mat. 5:39 17
2 Cor. 8:21 17
Heb. 12:14 18
Lev. 19:18 19
Deut. 32:35 19
Mat. 5:44 20

CHAP. 13
AD 60

ver. 3 1
Dan. 2:21 1

God: the powers that be are ᴺordained of God.

2 Whosoever therefore resisteth ᴿthe power, resisteth the ordinance of God: and they that resist shall receive to themselves damnation.

3 For rulers are not a terror to good works, but to the evil. Wilt thou then not be afraid of the power? ᴿdo that which is good, and thou shalt have praise of the same:

4 For he is the minister of God to thee for good. But if thou do that which is evil, be afraid; for he beareth not the sword in vain: for he is the minister of God, a revenger to *execute* wrath upon him that doeth evil.

5 Wherefore ᴿye must needs be subject, not only for wrath, ᴿbut also for conscience sake.

6 For for this cause pay ye tribute also: for they are God's ministers, attending continually upon this very thing.

7 ᴿRender therefore to all their dues: tribute to whom tribute *is due;* custom to whom custom; fear to whom fear; honour to whom honour.

Love fulfills the law

8 Owe no man any thing, but to love one another: for ᴿhe that loveth another hath fulfilled the law.

9 For this, ᴿThou shalt not commit adultery, Thou shalt not kill, Thou shalt not steal, Thou shalt not bear false witness, Thou shalt not covet; and if *there be* any other commandment, it is briefly comprehended in this saying, namely, ᴿThou shalt love thy neighbour as thyself.

10 Love worketh no ill to his neighbour: therefore ᴿlove *is* the fulfilling of the law.

"The armour of light"

11 And that, knowing the time, that now *it is* high time ᴿto awake out of sleep: for now *is* our salvation nearer than when we believed.

12 The night is far spent, the day is at hand: ᴿlet us therefore cast off the works of darkness, and ᴿlet us put on the armour of light.

13 ᴿLet us walk ᴺhonestly, as in the day; ᴿnot in rioting and drunkenness, ᴿnot in chambering and wantonness, ᴿnot in strife and envying.

14 But ᴿput ye on the Lord Jesus Christ, and ᴿmake not provision for the flesh, to *fulfil* the lusts *thereof.*

CHAPTER 14

Mutual forbearance

HIM that ᴿis weak in the faith receive ye, *but* ᴺnot to doubtful disputations.

CHAP. 13

AD 60

1	Or, *ordered*
2	Tit. 3:1
3	1 Pet. 2:14
5	Eccl. 8:2
5	1 Pet. 2:19
7	Mat. 22:21
	Luke 20:25
8	Gal. 5:14
	1 Tim. 1:5
9	Ex. 20:13
	Mat. 19:18
9	Lev. 19:18
	Mark 12:31
	Jas. 2:8
10	Mat. 22:40
11	1 Cor. 15:34
	Eph. 5:14
12	Eph. 5:11
12	Eph. 6:13
13	Phil. 4:8
13	Or, *decently*
13	Prov. 23:20
13	1 Cor. 6:9
13	Jas. 3:14
14	Gal. 3:27
	Eph. 4:24
14	Gal. 5:16

CHAP. 14

AD 60

1	1 Cor. 8:9
1	Or, *not to judge his doubtful thoughts*

1 Cor. 10:25	2
Tit. 1:15	
Col. 2:16	3
Jas. 4:12	4
Gal. 4:10	5
Or, *fully assured*	5
Gal. 4:10	6
Or, *observeth*	6
1 Cor. 10:31	6
1 Tim. 4:3	
1 Cor. 6:19	7
Gal. 2:20	
1 Thes. 5:10	
1 Pet. 4:2	
2 Cor. 5:15	9
Acts 10:36	9
Mat. 25:31	10
2 Cor. 5:10	
Is. 45:23	11
Mat. 12:36	12
Gal. 6:5	
1 Pet. 4:5	
1 Cor. 8:9	13
1 Cor. 10:25	14
Gr. *common*	14
Gr. *according to charity*	15
1 Cor. 8:11	15
ch. 12:17	16
1 Cor. 8:8	17
2 Cor. 8:21	18

---

2 For one believeth that he ᴿmay eat all things: another, who is weak, eateth herbs.

3 Let not him that eateth despise him that eateth not; and ᴿlet not him which eateth not judge him that eateth: for God hath received him.

4 ᴿWho art thou that judgest another man's servant? to his own master he standeth or falleth. Yea, he shall be holden up: for God is able to make him stand.

5 ᴿOne man esteemeth one day above another: another esteemeth every day *alike.* Let every man be ᴺfully persuaded in his own mind.

6 He that ᴿregardeth ᴺ the day, regardeth *it* unto the Lord; and he that regardeth not the day, to the Lord he doth not regard *it.* He that eateth, eateth to the Lord, for ᴿhe giveth God thanks; and he that eateth not, to the Lord he eateth not, and giveth God thanks.

7 For ᴿnone of us liveth to himself, and no man dieth to himself.

8 For whether we live, we live unto the Lord; and whether we die, we die unto the Lord: whether we live therefore, or die, we are the Lord's.

9 For ᴿto this end Christ both died, and rose, and revived, that he might be ᴿLord both of the dead and living.

10 But why dost thou judge thy brother? or why dost thou set at nought thy brother? for ᴿwe shall all stand before the judgment seat of Christ.

11 For it is written, ᴿ*As* I live, saith the Lord, every knee shall bow to me, and every tongue shall confess to God.

12 So then ᴿevery one of us shall give account of himself to God.

Do not tempt others

13 Let us not therefore judge one another any more: but judge this rather, that ᴿno man put a stumblingblock or an occasion to fall in *his* brother's way.

14 I know, and am persuaded by the Lord Jesus, ᴿthat *there is* nothing ᴺunclean of itself: but ᴿto him that esteemeth any thing to be ᴺunclean, to him *it is* unclean.

15 But if thy brother be grieved with *thy* meat, now walkest thou not ᴺcharitably. ᴿDestroy not him with thy meat, for whom Christ died.

16 ᴿLet not then your good be evil spoken of:

17 ᴿFor the kingdom of God is not meat and drink; but righteousness, and peace, and joy in the Holy Ghost.

18 For he that in these things serveth Christ ᴿ*is* acceptable to God, and approved of men.

19 [R]Let us therefore follow after the things which make for peace, and things wherewith [R]one may edify another.

20 [R]For meat destroy not the work of God. [R]All things indeed *are* pure; [R]but *it is* evil for that man who eateth with offence.

21 *It is* good neither to eat [R]flesh, nor to drink wine, nor *any thing* whereby thy brother stumbleth, or is offended, or is made weak.

22 Hast thou faith? have *it* to thyself before God. [R]Happy *is* he that condemneth not himself in that thing which he alloweth.

23 And he that [N]doubteth is damned if he eat, because *he eateth* not of faith: for [R]whatsoever *is* not of faith is sin.

CHAPTER 15

Follow Christ's example

WE [R]then that are strong ought to bear the [R]infirmities of the weak, and not to please ourselves.

2 [R]Let every one of us please *his* neighbour for *his* good [R]to edification.

3 [R]For even Christ pleased not himself; but, as it is written, The [R]reproaches of them that reproached thee fell on me.

4 For [R]whatsoever things were written aforetime were written for our learning, that we through patience and comfort of the scriptures might have hope.

5 [R]Now the God of patience and consolation grant you to be likeminded one toward another [N]according to Christ Jesus:

6 That ye may [R]with one mind *and* one mouth glorify God, even the Father of our Lord Jesus Christ.

7 Wherefore [R]receive ye one another, [R]as Christ also received us to the glory of God.

8 Now I say that [R]Jesus Christ was a minister of the circumcision for the truth of God, [R]to confirm the promises *made* unto the fathers:

9 And [R]that the Gentiles might glorify God for *his* mercy; as it is written, [R]For this cause I will confess to thee among the Gentiles, and sing unto thy name.

10 And again he saith, [R]Rejoice, ye Gentiles, with his people.

11 And again, [R]Praise the Lord, all ye Gentiles; and laud him, all ye people.

12 And again, Ē-śaī'-ăs saith, [R]There shall be a root of Jesse, and he that shall rise to reign over the Gentiles; in him shall the Gentiles trust.

13 Now the God of hope fill you with all [R]joy and peace in believing, that ye may abound in hope, through the power of the Holy Ghost.

CHAP. 14	
AD 60	
19 ch. 12:18	
19 1 Cor. 14:12	
1 Thes. 5:11	
20 ver. 15	
20 Mat. 15:11	
20 1 Cor. 8:9	
21 1 Cor. 8:13	
22 1 John 3:21	
23 Or, *discerneth and putteth a difference*	
23 Tit. 1:15	

CHAP. 15	
AD 60	
1 Gal. 6:1	
1 ch. 14:1	
2 1 Cor. 10:33	
2 ch. 14:19	
3 Mat. 26:39	
3 Ps. 69:9	
4 1 Cor. 10:11	
5 1 Cor. 1:10	
5 Or, *after the example of*	
6 Acts 4:24	
7 ch. 14:1, 3	
7 ch. 5:2	
8 Mat. 15:24	
John 1:11	
Acts 3:25	
8 2 Cor. 1:20	
9 John 10:16	
9 Ps. 18:49	
10 Deut. 32:43	
11 Ps. 117:1	
12 Is. 11:1	
Rev. 5:5	
13 ch. 12:12	

2 Pet. 1:12	14
1 John 2:21	
1 Cor. 8:1	14
ch. 1:5 & 12:3	15
Gal. 1:15	
ch. 11:13	16
Gal. 2:7-9	
1 Tim. 2:7	
2 Tim. 1:11	
Is. 66:20	16
Phil. 2:17	
Or, *sacrificing*	16
Heb. 5:1	
Acts 21:19	17
Gal. 2:8	18
ch. 1:5	18
& 16:26	
Acts 19:11	19
2 Cor. 12:12	
2 Cor.	20
10:13, 15, 16	
Is. 52:15	21
ch. 1:13	22
1 Thes. 2:17	
Or, *many ways,* or, *oftentimes*	22
Acts 19:21	23
ch. 1:11	
Acts 15:3	24
Gr. *with you,*	24
ver. 32	
Acts 19:21	25
& 24:17	
1 Cor. 16:1	26
2 Cor. 8:1	
ch. 11:17	27
1 Cor. 9:11	27
Gal. 6:6	
Phil. 4:17	28
ch. 1:11	29

Purpose of Paul's letter

14 And [R]I myself also am persuaded of you, my brethren, that ye also are full of goodness, [R]filled with all knowledge, able also to admonish one another.

15 Nevertheless, brethren, I have written the more boldly unto you in some sort, as putting you in mind, [R]because of the grace that is given to me of God,

16 That [R]I should be the minister of Jesus Christ to the Gentiles, ministering the gospel of God, that the [R]offering[N] up of the Gentiles might be acceptable, being sanctified by the Holy Ghost.

17 I have therefore whereof I may glory through Jesus Christ [R]in those things which pertain to God.

18 For I will not dare to speak of any of those things [R]which Christ hath not wrought by me, [R]to make the Gentiles obedient, by word and deed,

19 [R]Through mighty signs and wonders, by the power of the Spirit of God; so that from Jerusalem, and round about unto Ĭl-lў̆r'-ĭ-cŭm, I have fully preached the gospel of Christ.

20 Yea, so have I strived to preach the gospel, not where Christ was named, [R]lest I should build upon another man's foundation:

21 But as it is written, [R]To whom he was not spoken of, they shall see: and they that have not heard shall understand.

Paul's future plans

22 For which cause also [R]I have been [N]much hindered from coming to you.

23 But now having no more place in these parts, and [R]having a great desire these many years to come unto you;

24 Whensoever I take my journey into Spain, I will come to you: for I trust to see you in my journey, [R]and to be brought on my way thitherward by you, if first I be somewhat filled [N]with your *company*.

25 But now [R]I go unto Jerusalem to minister unto the saints.

26 For [R]it hath pleased them of Măç-ē-dō'-nĭ-ă and Ă-chaī'-ă to make a certain contribution for the poor saints which are at Jerusalem.

27 It hath pleased them verily; and their debtors they are. For [R]if the Gentiles have been made partakers of their spiritual things, [R]their duty is also to minister unto them in carnal things.

28 When therefore I have performed this, and have sealed to them [R]this fruit, I will come by you into Spain.

29 [R]And I am sure that, when I come unto

you, I shall come in the fulness of the blessing of the gospel of Christ.

30 Now I beseech you, brethren, for the Lord Jesus Christ's sake, and ᴿfor the love of the Spirit, ᴿthat ye strive together with me in *your* prayers to God for me;

31 ᴿThat I may be delivered from them that ᴺdo not believe in Judæa; and that ᴿmy service which *I have* for Jerusalem may be accepted of the saints;

32 ᴿThat I may come unto you with joy ᴿby the will of God, and may with you ᴿbe refreshed.

33 Now ᴿthe God of peace *be* with you all. Ä′-mĕn.

CHAPTER 16

Commendation of Phebe

I COMMEND unto you Phē′-bē our sister, which is a servant of the church which is at ᴿÇĕn-chrē′-ă:

2 ᴿThat ye receive her in the Lord, as becometh saints, and that ye assist her in whatsoever business she hath need of you: for she hath been a succourer of many, and of myself also.

Personal greetings

3 Greet ᴿPriscilla and Ă-quĭl′-ă my helpers in Christ Jesus:

4 Who have for my life laid down their own necks: unto whom not only I give thanks, but also all the churches of the Gentiles.

5 Likewise *greet* ᴿthe church that is in their house. Salute my wellbeloved ĕp-ǣ′-nĕ-tŭs, who is ᴿthe firstfruits of Ă-chāī′-ă unto Christ.

6 Greet Mary, who bestowed much labour on us.

7 Salute Ăn-drō-nī′-cŭs and Junia, my kinsmen, and my fellowprisoners, who are of note among the apostles, who also ᴿwere in Christ before me.

8 Greet Ăm′-plĭ-ăs my beloved in the Lord.

9 Salute Ur′-bāne, our helper in Christ, and Stăch′- y̆s my beloved.

10 Salute Ă-pĕl′-lĕs approved in Christ. Salute them which are of Ă-rĭs-tō-bū′-lŭs' ᴺhousehold.

11 Salute Hē-rō′-dĭ-on my kinsman. Greet them that be of the ᴺhousehold of Năr-çĭs′-sŭs, which are in the Lord.

12 Salute Trȳ-phē′-nă and Trȳ-phō′-să, who labour in the Lord. Salute the beloved Persis, which laboured much in the Lord.

13 Salute Rufus ᴿchosen in the Lord, and his mother and mine.

14 Salute Ă-sy̆n′-crĭ-tŭs, Phlĕg′-ŏn, Hĕr′-măs, Păt′-rō-băs, Hĕr′-mĕs, and the brethren which are with them.

15 Salute Phĭ-lŏl′-ŏ-gŭs, and Julia, Nē′-rĕus, and his sister, and ō-lȳm′-păs, and all the saints which are with them.

16 ᴿSalute one another with an holy kiss. The churches of Christ salute you.

Warning against false teachers

17 Now I beseech you, brethren, mark them ᴿwhich cause divisions and offences contrary to the doctrine which ye have learned; and ᴿavoid them.

18 For they that are such serve not our Lord Jesus Christ, but ᴿtheir own belly; and ᴿby good words and fair speeches deceive the hearts of the simple.

19 For ᴿyour obedience is come abroad unto all *men*. I am glad therefore on your behalf: but yet I would have you ᴿwise unto that which is good, and ᴺsimple concerning evil.

20 And ᴿthe God of peace ᴿshall ᴺbruise Satan under your feet shortly. ᴿThe grace of our Lord Jesus Christ *be* with you. Ä′-mĕn.

Final greetings and benediction

21 ᴿTimotheus my workfellow, and ᴿLû′-çĭ-ŭs, and ᴿJā′-son, and ᴿSō-sĭp′-ă-tĕr, my kinsmen, salute you.

22 I Tĕr′-tĭus, who wrote *this* epistle, salute you in the Lord.

23 ᴿGāī′-ŭs mine host, and of the whole church, saluteth you. ᴿE-răs′-tŭs the chamberlain of the city saluteth you, and Quartus a brother.

24 ᴿThe grace of our Lord Jesus Christ *be* with you all. Ä′-mĕn.

25 Now ᴿto him that is of power to stablish you ᴿaccording to my gospel, and the preaching of Jesus Christ, ᴿaccording to the revelation of the mystery, ᴿwhich was kept secret since the world began,

26 But ᴿnow is made manifest, and by the scriptures of the prophets, according to the commandment of the everlasting God, made known to all nations for ᴿthe obedience of faith:

27 To ᴿGod only wise, *be* glory through Jesus Christ for ever. Ä′-mĕn.

Written to the Romans from Cō-rĭn′-thŭs, *and sent* by Phē′-bē servant of the church at Çĕn-chrē′-ă.

THE FIRST EPISTLE OF PAUL THE APOSTLE
TO THE
CORINTHIANS

The Church at Corinth was founded by Paul on his second missionary journey (cf. Acts 18). The city has been aptly called "the Empire in miniature," and many of the problems of Christianity in a cultured pagan society were present in the Church there. During Paul's extended ministry in Ephesus on his third journey, disquieting accounts concerning the Corinthian Church came to his attention: the family of Chloe reported that there were deep and bitter divisions (1:11), and various rumors were circulating regarding immorality, pride, and lawsuits (5:1–2, 6:1). Paul had written earlier (5:9–10), but evidently that letter had been misinterpreted. Certain ones of the Corinthian Church had written seeking his guidance on various matters: marriage, food previously dedicated to idols, decorum of women, observance of the Lord's Supper, and spiritual gifts. Paul also knew that they were confused and in error regarding the Resurrection. On all these matters the Apostle writes in strong pastoral tones, instructing

for specific situations but defining principles that can be applied in our day. About A.D. 95 Clement of Rome wrote in a similar vein to the Corinthian Church, citing this First Epistle of Paul in support. That attestation is the earliest we have for any of Paul's letters, and, coupled with internal evidence, has silenced any doubts regarding the authenticity of the epistle. First Corinthians was written from Ephesus (16:8, 19), probably about A.D. 55 or 56.

OUTLINE OF THE BOOK:
I. Salutation 1:1–9
II. Concerning Disorders reported by the Family of Chloe 1:10–4:21
III. Concerning Disorders Widely Rumored 5:1–6:20
IV. Matters of Concern to the Church 7:1–14:40
V. Concerning the Resurrection 15:1–58
VI. Conclusion and Collection 16:1–24

CHAPTER 1

Salutation

P AUL, ᴿcalled *to be* an apostle of Jesus Christ ᴿthrough the will of God, and Sŏs'-thĕ-nēs *our* brother,

2 Unto the church of God which is at Corinth, to them that ᴿare sanctified in Christ Jesus, ᴿcalled *to be* saints, with all that in every place call upon the name of Jesus Christ ᴿour Lord, ᴿboth theirs and ours:

3 ᴿGrace *be* unto you, and peace, from God our Father, and *from* the Lord Jesus Christ.

Thanksgiving

4 ᴿI thank my God always on your behalf, for the grace of God which is given you by Jesus Christ;

5 That in every thing ye are enriched by him, ᴿin all utterance, and *in* all knowledge;

6 Even as ᴿthe testimony of Christ was confirmed in you:

7 So that ye come behind in no gift; ᴿwaiting for the ᴺcoming of our Lord Jesus Christ:

8 ᴿWho shall also confirm you unto the end, ᴿ*that ye may be* blameless in the day of our Lord Jesus Christ.

9 ᴿGod *is* faithful, by whom ye were called unto ᴿthe fellowship of his Son Jesus Christ our Lord.

Appeal for unity

10 Now I beseech you, brethren, by the name of our Lord Jesus Christ, ᴿthat ye all

CHAP. 1
AD 59
1 Rom. 1:1
1 2 Cor. 1:1
2 Acts 15:9
2 Rom. 1:7
2 ch. 8:6
2 Rom. 3:22
3 Rom. 1:7
2 Cor. 1:2
4 Rom. 1:8
5 ch. 12:8
6 2 Tim. 1:8
Rev. 1:2
7 Phil. 3:20
Tit. 2:13
2 Pet. 3:12
7 Gr. *revelation*
8 1 Thes. 3:13
8 Col. 1:22
9 Is. 49:7
9 1 Thes. 5:24
John 15:4
10 2 Cor. 13:11
1 Pet. 3:8

Gr. *schisms*   10
ch. 3:4   12
Acts 18:24   12
John 1:42   12
2 Cor. 11:4   13
Acts 18:8   14
Rom. 16:23   14
ch. 16:15   16
ch. 2:4   17
Or, *speech*   17
2 Cor. 2:15   18
Acts 17:18   18
ch. 15:2   18
Rom. 1:16   18
Is. 29:14   19
Is. 33:18   20

speak the same thing, and *that* there be no ᴺdivisions among you; but *that* ye be perfectly joined together in the same mind and in the same judgment.

11 For it hath been declared unto me of you, my brethren, by them *which are of the house* of Chlō'-ē, that there are contentions among you.

12 Now this I say, ᴿthat every one of you saith, I am of Paul; and I of ᴿĂ-pŏl'-lŏs; and I of ᴿCē'-phăs; and I of Christ.

13 ᴿIs Christ divided? was Paul crucified for you? or were ye baptized in the name of Paul?

14 I thank God that I baptized none of you, but ᴿCrĭs'-pŭs and ᴿGâi'-ŭs;

15 Lest any should say that I had baptized in mine own name.

16 And I baptized also the household of ᴿStĕph'-ă-năs: besides, I know not whether I baptized any other.

17 For Christ sent me not to baptize, but to preach the gospel: ᴿnot with wisdom of ᴺwords, lest the cross of Christ should be made of none effect.

The wisdom of God

18 For the preaching of the cross is to ᴿthem that perish ᴿfoolishness; but unto us ᴿwhich are saved it is the ᴿpower of God.

19 For it is written, ᴿI will destroy the wisdom of the wise, and will bring to nothing the understanding of the prudent.

20 ᴿWhere *is* the wise? where *is* the scribe?

where *is* the disputer of this world? ᴿhath not God made foolish the wisdom of this world?

21 ᴿFor after that in the wisdom of God the world by wisdom knew not God, it pleased God by the foolishness of preaching to save them that believe.

22 For the ᴿJews require a sign, and the Greeks seek after wisdom:

23 But we preach Christ crucified, ᴿunto the Jews a stumblingblock, and unto the Greeks ᴿfoolishness;

24 But unto them which are called, both Jews and Greeks, Christ ᴿthe power of God, and ᴿthe wisdom of God.

25 Because the foolishness of God is wiser than men; and the weakness of God is stronger than men.

26 For ye see your calling, brethren, how that ᴿnot many wise men after the flesh, not many mighty, not many noble, *are called:*

27 But ᴿGod hath chosen the foolish things of the world to confound the wise; and God hath chosen the weak things of the world to confound the things which are mighty;

28 And base things of the world, and things which are despised, hath God chosen, *yea,* and ᴿthings which are not, ᴿto bring to nought things that are:

29 ᴿThat no flesh should glory in his presence.

30 But of him are ye in Christ Jesus, who of God is made unto us ᴿwisdom, and ᴿrighteousness, and ᴿsanctification, and ᴿredemption:

31 That, according as it is written, ᴿHe that glorieth, let him glory in the Lord.

CHAPTER 2

Paul's choice of method

AND I, brethren, when I came to you, ᴿcame not with excellency of speech or of wisdom, declaring unto you ᴿthe testimony of God.

2 For I determined not to know any thing among you, ᴿsave Jesus Christ, and him crucified.

3 And ᴿI was with you ᴿin weakness, and in fear, and in much trembling.

4 And my speech and my preaching ᴿwas not with ᴺenticing words of man's wisdom, ᴿbut in demonstration of the Spirit and of power:

5 That your faith should not ᴺstand in the wisdom of men, but ᴿin the power of God.

Hidden wisdom of God

6 Howbeit we speak wisdom among them ᴿthat are perfect: yet not ᴿthe wisdom of this

world, nor of the princes of this world, ᴿthat come to nought:

7 But we speak the wisdom of God in a mystery, *even* the hidden *wisdom,* ᴿwhich God ordained before the world unto our glory:

8 ᴿWhich none of the princes of this world knew: for ᴿhad they known *it,* they would not have crucified the Lord of glory.

9 But as it is written, ᴿEye hath not seen, nor ear heard, neither have entered into the heart of man, the things which God hath prepared for them that love him.

10 But ᴿGod hath revealed *them* unto us by his Spirit: for the Spirit searcheth all things, yea, the deep things of God.

11 For what man knoweth the things of a man, ᴿsave the spirit of man which is in him? ᴿeven so the things of God knoweth no man, but the Spirit of God.

12 Now we have received, not the spirit of the world, but ᴿthe spirit which is of God; that we might know the things that are freely given to us of God.

13 Which things also we speak, not in the words which man's wisdom teacheth, but which the Holy Ghost teacheth; comparing spiritual things with spiritual.

The spiritual and unspiritual man

14 ᴿBut the natural man receiveth not the things of the Spirit of God: ᴿfor they are foolishness unto him: ᴿneither can he know *them,* because they are spiritually discerned.

15 ᴿBut he that is spiritual ᴺjudgeth all things, yet he himself is ᴺjudged of no man.

16 ᴿFor who hath known the mind of the Lord, that he ᴺmay instruct him? ᴿBut we have the mind of Christ.

CHAPTER 3

AND I, brethren, could not speak unto you as unto ᴿspiritual, but as unto ᴿcarnal, *even* as unto ᴿbabes in Christ.

2 I have fed you with ᴿmilk, and not with meat: ᴿfor hitherto ye were not able *to bear it,* neither yet now are ye able.

3 For ye are yet carnal: for ᴿwhereas *there is* among you envying, and strife, and ᴺdivisions, are ye not carnal, and walk ᴺas men?

4 For while one saith, I am of Paul; and another, I *am* of Ă-pŏl'-lŏs; are ye not carnal?

Fellowworkers for God

5 Who then is Paul, and who *is* Ă-pŏl'-lŏs, but ᴿministers by whom ye believed, ᴿeven as the Lord gave to every man?

6 ᴿI have planted, ᴿĂ-pŏl'-lŏs watered; ᴿbut God gave the increase.

7 So then ᴿneither is he that planteth any

thing, neither he that watereth; but God that giveth the increase.

8 Now he that planteth and he that watereth are one: ᴿand every man shall receive his own reward according to his own labour.

9 For ᴿwe arc labourers together with God: ye are God's ᴺhusbandry, *ye are* ᴿGod's building.

10 ᴿAccording to the grace of God which is given unto me, as a wise masterbuilder, I have laid ᴿthe foundation, and another buildeth thereon. But let every man take heed how he buildeth thereupon.

11 For other foundation can no man lay than ᴿthat is laid, ᴿwhich is Jesus Christ.

12 Now if any man build upon this foundation gold, silver, precious stones, wood, hay, stubble;

13 Every man's work shall be made manifest: for the day ᴿshall declare it, because ᴿit ᴺshall be revealed by fire; and the fire shall try every man's work of what sort it is.

14 If any man's work abide which he hath built thereupon, he shall receive a reward.

15 If any man's work shall be burned, he shall suffer loss: but he himself shall be saved; yet so as by fire.

God's temple

16 ᴿKnow ye not that ye are the temple of God, and *that* the Spirit of God dwelleth in you?

17 If any man ᴺdefile the temple of God, him shall God destroy; for the temple of God is holy, which *temple* ye are.

Folly of worldly wisdom

18 ᴿLet no man deceive himself. If any man among you seemeth to be wise in this world, let him become a fool, that he may be wise.

19 For the wisdom of this world is foolishness with God. For it is written, ᴿHe taketh the wise in their own craftiness.

20 And again, ᴿThe Lord knoweth the thoughts of the wise, that they are vain.

21 Therefore let no man glory in men. For ᴿall things are yours;

22 Whether Paul, or ă-pŏl′-lŏs, or Çē′-phăs, or the world, or life, or death, or things present, or things to come; all are yours;

23 And ᴿye are Christ's; and Christ *is* God's.

CHAPTER 4

Responsibility of stewards

LET a man so account of us, as of ᴿthe ministers of Christ, ᴿand stewards of the mysteries of God.

CHAP. 3
AD 59
8 Ps. 62:12
Rom. 2:6
Gal. 6:4, 5
9 Acts 15:4
2 Cor. 6:1
9 Or, *tillage*
9 Eph. 2:20
Col. 2:7
Heb. 3:3, 4
10 Rom. 1:5 & 12:3
10 ch. 4:15
11 Is. 28:16
Mat. 16:18
2 Cor. 11:4
11 Eph. 2:20
13 1 Pet. 1:7
13 Luke 2:35
13 Gr. *is revealed*
16 2 Cor. 6:16
17 Or, *destroy*
18 Prov. 3:7
19 Job 5:13
20 Ps. 94:11
21 2 Cor. 4:5
Rom. 14:8
2 Cor. 10:7
Gal. 3:29

CHAP. 4	
AD 59	
1 Mat. 24:45	
Col. 1:25	
1 Luke 12:42	
Tit. 1:7	
Gr. *day,*	3
ch. 3:13	
Mat. 7:1	5
Rom. 2:1	
Rev. 20:12	
Rom. 2:29	5
2 Cor. 5:10	
ch. 1:12	6
Rom. 12:3	6
ch. 3:21	6
Gr. *distinguisheth*	7
thee	
John 3:27	7
Rev. 3:17	8
Or, *us the last*	9
apostles, as	
Ps. 44:22	9
Heb. 10:33	9
Gr. *theatre*	9
ch. 2:3	10
Acts 17:18	10
2 Cor. 13:9	10
Phil. 4:12	11
Rom. 8:35	11
Acts 23:2	11
Acts 18:3	12
& 20:34	
1 Thes. 2:9	
2 Thes. 3:8	
1 Tim. 4:10	
Mat. 5:44	12
Luke 6:28	
& 23:34	
Acts 7:60	
Rom. 12:14	
Lam. 3:45	13
1 Thes. 2:11	14
Acts 18:11	15
Gal. 4:19	
Jas. 1:18	
ch. 11:1	16
1 Thes. 1:6	
Acts 19:22	17
Phil. 2:19	
1 Tim. 1:2	17
2 Tim. 1:2	
ch. 11:2	17
ch. 7:17	17
ch. 14:33	17

2 Moreover it is required in stewards, that a man be found faithful.

3 But with me it is a very small thing that I should be judged of you, or of man's ᴺjudgment: yea, I judge not mine own self.

4 For I know nothing by myself; yet am I not hereby justified: but he that judgeth mc is the Lord.

5 ᴿTherefore judge nothing before the time, until the Lord come, who both will bring to light the hidden things of darkness, and will make manifest the counsels of the hearts: and ᴿthen shall every man have praise of God.

Paul's reproof of the Corinthians

6 And these things, brethren, ᴿI have in a figure transferred to myself and *to* ă-pŏl′-lŏs for your sakes; ᴿthat ye might learn in us not to think *of men* above that which is written, that no one of you ᴿbe puffed up for one against another.

7 For who ᴺmaketh thee to differ *from another?* and ᴿwhat hast thou that thou didst not receive? now if thou didst receive *it,* why dost thou glory, as if thou hadst not received *it?*

8 Now ye are full, ᴿnow ye are rich, ye have reigned as kings without us: and I would to God ye did reign, that we also might reign with you.

9 For I think that God hath set forth ᴺus the apostles last, ᴿas it were appointed to death: for ᴿwe are made a ᴺspectacle unto the world, and to angels, and to men.

10 ᴿWe *are* ᴿfools for Christ's sake, but ye *are* wise in Christ; ᴿwe *are* weak, but ye *are* strong; ye *are* honourable, but we *are* despised.

11 ᴿEven unto this present hour we both hunger, and thirst, and ᴿare naked, and ᴿare buffeted, and have no certain dwelling place;

12 ᴿAnd labour, working with our own hands: ᴿbeing reviled, we bless; being persecuted, we suffer it:

13 Being defamed, we entreat: ᴿwe are made as the filth of the world, *and are* the offscouring of all things unto this day.

14 I write not these things to shame you, but ᴿas my beloved sons I warn *you.*

15 For though ye have ten thousand instructors in Christ, yet *have ye* not many fathers: for ᴿin Christ Jesus I have begotten you through the gospel.

16 Wherefore I beseech you, ᴿbe ye followers of me.

17 For this cause have I sent unto you ᴿTimotheus, ᴿwho is my beloved son, and faithful in the Lord, who shall bring you ᴿinto remembrance of my ways which be in Christ, as I ᴿteach every where ᴿin every church.

18 ᴿNow some are puffed up, as though I would not come to you.

19 ᴿBut I will come to you shortly, ᴿif the Lord will, and will know, not the speech of them which are puffed up, but the power.

20 For ᴿthe kingdom of God is not in word, but in power.

21 What will ye? ᴿshall I come unto you with a rod, or in love, and in the spirit of meekness?

CHAPTER 5

Report about immorality

IT is reported commonly that there is fornication among you, and such fornication as is not so much as ᴿnamed among the Gentiles, ᴿthat one should have his ᴿfather's wife.

2 ᴿAnd ye are puffed up, and have not rather ᴿmourned, that he that hath done this deed might be taken away from among you.

3 ᴿFor I verily, as absent in body, but present in spirit, have ᴺjudged already, as though I were present, concerning him that hath so done this deed,

4 In the name of our Lord Jesus Christ, when ye are gathered together, and my spirit, ᴿwith the power of our Lord Jesus Christ,

5 ᴿTo deliver such an one unto ᴿSatan for the destruction of the flesh, that the spirit may be saved in the day of the Lord Jesus.

6 ᴿYour glorying is not good. Know ye not that ᴿa little leaven leaveneth the whole lump?

7 Purge out therefore the old leaven, that ye may be a new lump, as ye are unleavened. For even ᴿChrist our ᴿpassover ᴺis sacrificed for us:

8 Therefore ᴿlet us keep ᴺthe feast, ᴿnot with old leaven, neither ᴿwith the leaven of malice and wickedness; but with the unleavened bread of sincerity and truth.

9 I wrote unto you in an epistle ᴿnot to company with fornicators:

10 ᴿYet not altogether with the fornicators ᴿof this world, or with the covetous, or extortioners, or with idolaters; for then must ye needs go ᴿout of the world.

11 But now I have written unto you not to keep company, ᴿif any man that is called a brother be a fornicator, or covetous, or an idolater, or a railer, or a drunkard, or an extortioner; with such an one ᴿno not to eat.

12 For what have I to do to judge ᴿthem also that are without? do not ye judge ᴿthem that are within?

13 But them that are without God judgeth. Therefore ᴿput away from among yourselves that wicked person.

CHAPTER 6

Settling grievances

DARE any of you, having a matter against another, go to law before the unjust, and not before the saints?

2 Do ye not know that ᴿthe saints shall judge the world? and if the world shall be judged by you, are ye unworthy to judge the smallest matters?

3 Know ye not that we shall ᴿjudge angels? how much more things that pertain to this life?

4 ᴿIf then ye have judgments of things pertaining to this life, set them to judge who are least esteemed in the church.

5 I speak to your shame. Is it so, that there is not a wise man among you? no, not one that shall be able to judge between his brethren?

6 But brother goeth to law with brother, and that before the unbelievers.

7 Now therefore there is utterly a fault among you, because ye go to law one with another. ᴿWhy do ye not rather take wrong? why do ye not rather suffer yourselves to be defrauded?

8 Nay, ye do wrong, and defraud, ᴿand that your brethren.

Shun immorality

9 Know ye not that the unrighteous shall not inherit the kingdom of God? Be not deceived: ᴿneither fornicators, nor idolaters, nor adulterers, nor effeminate, nor abusers of themselves with mankind,

10 Nor thieves, nor covetous, nor drunkards, nor revilers, nor extortioners, shall inherit the kingdom of God.

11 And such were ᴿsome of you: ᴿbut ye are washed, but ye are sanctified, but ye are justified in the name of the Lord Jesus, and by the Spirit of our God.

12 ᴿAll things are lawful unto me, but all things are not ᴺexpedient: all things are lawful for me, but I will not be brought under the power of any.

13 ᴿMeats for the belly, and the belly for meats: but God shall destroy both it and them. Now the body is not for fornication, but ᴿfor the Lord; ᴿand the Lord for the body.

14 And ᴿGod hath both raised up the Lord, and will also raise up us ᴿby his own power.

15 Know ye not that ᴿyour bodies are the members of Christ? shall I then take the members of Christ, and make them the members of an harlot? God forbid.

16 What? know ye not that he which is joined to an harlot is one body? for ᴿtwo, saith he, shall be one flesh.

17 ᴿBut he that is joined unto the Lord is one spirit.

18 ᴿFlee fornication. Every sin that a man doeth is without the body; but he that committeth fornication sinneth ᴿagainst his own body.

19 What? ᴿknow ye not that your body is the temple of the Holy Ghost *which is* in you, which ye have of God, ᴿand ye are not your own?

20 For ᴿye are bought with a price: therefore glorify God in your body, and in your spirit, which are God's.

CHAPTER 7

Marital status

NOW concerning the things whereof ye wrote unto me: ᴿ*It is* good for a man not to touch a woman.

2 Nevertheless, *to avoid* fornication, let every man have his own wife, and let every woman have her own husband.

3 ᴿLet the husband render unto the wife due benevolence: and likewise also the wife unto the husband.

4 The wife hath not power of her own body, but the husband: and likewise also the husband hath not power of his own body, but the wife.

5 ᴿDefraud ye not one the other, except *it be* with consent for a time, that ye may give yourselves to fasting and prayer; and come together again, that ᴿSatan tempt you not for your incontinency.

6 But I speak this by permission, ᴿ*and* not of commandment.

7 For ᴿI would that all men were ᴿeven as I myself. But ᴿevery man hath his proper gift of God, one after this manner, and another after that.

8 I say therefore to the unmarried and widows, ᴿIt is good for them if they abide even as I.

9 But ᴿif they cannot contain, let them marry: for it is better to marry than to burn.

Marital problems and divorce

10 And unto the married I command, *yet* not I, but the Lord, ᴿLet not the wife depart from *her* husband:

11 But and if she depart, let her remain unmarried, or be reconciled to *her* husband: and let not the husband put away *his* wife.

12 But to the rest speak I, not the Lord: If any brother hath a wife that believeth not, and she be pleased to dwell with him, let him not put her away.

13 And the woman which hath an husband that believeth not, and if he be pleased to dwell with her, let her not leave him.

14 For the unbelieving husband is sanctified by the wife, and the unbelieving wife is

sanctified by the husband: else ᴿwere your children unclean; but now are they holy.

15 But if the unbelieving depart, let him depart. A brother or a sister is not under bondage in such *cases:* but God hath called us ᴿtoᴺ peace.

16 For what knowest thou, O wife, whether thou shalt ᴿsave *thy* husband? or ᴺhow knowest thou, O man, whether thou shalt save *thy* wife?

17 But as God hath distributed to every man, as the Lord hath called every one, so let him walk. And ᴿso ordain I in all churches.

18 Is any man called being circumcised? let him not become uncircumcised. Is any called in uncircumcision? ᴿlet him not be circumcised.

19 ᴿCircumcision is nothing, and uncircumcision is nothing, but ᴿthe keeping of the commandments of God.

20 Let every man abide in the same calling wherein he was called.

21 Art thou called *being* a servant? care not for it: but if thou mayest be made free, use *it* rather.

22 For he that is called in the Lord, *being* a servant, is ᴿthe Lord's ᴺfreeman: likewise also he that is called, *being* free, is ᴿChrist's servant.

23 ᴿYe are bought with a price; be not ye the servants of men.

24 Brethren, let every man, wherein he is called, therein abide with God.

Counsel to the unmarried

25 Now concerning virgins ᴿI have no commandment of the Lord: yet I give my judgment, as one ᴿthat hath obtained mercy of the Lord ᴿto be faithful.

26 I suppose therefore that this is good for the present ᴺdistress, *I say,* ᴿthat *it is* good for a man so to be.

27 Art thou bound unto a wife? seek not to be loosed. Art thou loosed from a wife? seek not a wife.

28 But and if thou marry, thou hast not sinned; and if a virgin marry, she hath not sinned. Nevertheless such shall have trouble in the flesh: but I spare you.

29 But ᴿthis I say, brethren, the time *is* short: it remaineth, that both they that have wives be as though they had none;

30 And they that weep, as though they wept not; and they that rejoice, as though they rejoiced not; and they that buy, as though they possessed not;

31 And they that use this world, as not ᴿabusing *it:* for ᴿthe fashion of this world passeth away.

Center reference column:

CHAP. **6**
AD 59
18 Rom. 6:12
Heb. 13:4
18 Rom. 1:24
1 Thes. 4:4
19 2 Cor. 6:16
19 Rom. 14:7
20 Acts 20:28
Gal. 3:13
Heb. 1:18
1 Pet. 1:18
2 Pet. 2:1
Rev. 5:9

CHAP. **7**
AD 59
1 ver. 8, 26
3 Ex. 21:10
1 Pet. 3:7
5 Joel 2:16
Zech. 7:3
See Ex. 19:15
1 Sam. 21:4
5 1 Thes. 3:5
6 2 Cor. 8:8
& 11:17
7 Acts 26:29
7 ch. 9:5
7 ch. 12:11
8 ver. 1, 26
9 1 Tim. 5:14
10 Mal. 2:14
Mat. 5:32
& 19:6, 9
Mark 10:11
Luke 16:18

Mal. 2:15   **14**
Rom. 12:18   **15**
& 14:19
ch. 14:33
Gr. *in peace*   **15**
1 Pet. 3:1   **16**
Gr. *what*   **16**
ch. 4:17   **17**
Acts 15:1   **18**
Gal. 5:2
Gal. 5:6   **19**
John 15:14   **19**
1 John 2:3
& 3:24
John 8:36   **22**
Rom. 6:18
Philem. 16
Gr. *made free*   **22**
ch. 9:21   **22**
Gal. 5:13
Eph. 6:6
1 Pet. 2:16
1 Pet. 1:18   **23**
See Lev. 25:42
2 Cor. 8:8   **25**
1 Tim. 1:16   **25**
1 Tim. 1:12   **25**
Or, *necessity*   **26**
ver. 1, 8   **26**
Rom. 13:11   **29**
1 Pet. 4:7
2 Pet. 3:8, 9
ch. 9:18   **31**
Ps. 39:6   **31**
Jas. 1:10 & 4:14
1 Pet. 1:24 & 4:7
1 John 2:17

32 But I would have you without carefulness. [R]He that is unmarried careth for the things [N]that belong to the Lord, how he may please the Lord:

33 But he that is married careth for the things that are of the world, how he may please *his* wife.

34 There is difference *also* between a wife and a virgin. The unmarried woman [R]careth for the things of the Lord, that she may be holy both in body and in spirit: but she that is married careth for the things of the world, how she may please *her* husband.

35 And this I speak for your own profit; not that I may cast a snare upon you, but for that which is comely, and that ye may attend upon the Lord without distraction.

36 But if any man think that he behaveth himself uncomely toward his virgin, if she pass the flower of *her* age, and need so require, let him do what he will, he sinneth not: let them marry.

37 Nevertheless he that standeth stedfast in his heart, having no necessity, but hath power over his own will, and hath so decreed in his heart that he will keep his virgin, doeth well.

38 [R]So then he that giveth *her* in marriage doeth well; but he that giveth *her* not in marriage doeth better.

Counsel to widows

39 [R]The wife is bound by the law as long as her husband liveth; but if her husband be dead, she is at liberty to be married to whom she will; [R]only in the Lord.

40 But she is happier if she so abide, [R]after my judgment: and [R]I think also that I have the Spirit of God.

CHAPTER 8

Food offered to idols

NOW [R]as touching things offered unto idols, we know that we all have [R]knowledge. [R]Knowledge puffeth up, but charity edifieth.

2 And [R]if any man think that he knoweth any thing, he knoweth nothing yet as he ought to know.

3 But if any man love God, [R]the same is known of him.

4 As concerning therefore the eating of those things that are offered in sacrifice unto idols, we know that [R]an idol *is* nothing in the world, [R]and that *there is* none other God but one.

5 For though there be that are [R]called gods, whether in heaven or in earth, (as there be gods many, and lords many,)

6 But [R]to us *there is but* one God, the Father, [R]of whom *are* all things, and we [N]in him; and [R]one Lord Jesus Christ, [R]by whom *are* all things, and we by him.

7 Howbeit *there is* not in every man that knowledge: for some [R]with conscience of the idol unto this hour eat *it* as a thing offered unto an idol; and their conscience being weak is [R]defiled.

8 But [R]meat commendeth us not to God: for neither, if we eat, [N]are we the better; neither, if we eat not, [N]are we the worse.

9 But [R]take heed lest by any means this [N]liberty of yours become [R]a stumblingblock to them that are weak.

10 For if any man see thee which hast knowledge sit at meat in the idol's temple, shall not [R]the conscience of him which is weak be [N]emboldened to eat those things which are offered to idols;

11 And [R]through thy knowledge shall the weak brother perish, for whom Christ died?

12 But [R]when ye sin so against the brethren, and wound their weak conscience, ye sin against Christ.

13 Wherefore, [R]if meat make my brother to offend, I will eat no flesh while the world standeth, lest I make my brother to offend.

CHAPTER 9

Rights of the apostle

AM [R]I not an apostle? am I not free? [R]have I not seen Jesus Christ our Lord? [R]are not ye my work in the Lord?

2 If I be not an apostle unto others, yet doubtless I am to you: for [R]the seal of mine apostleship are ye in the Lord.

3 Mine answer to them that do examine me is this,

4 [R]Have we not power to eat and to drink?

5 Have we not power to lead about a sister, a [N]wife, as well as other apostles, and *as* [R]the brethren of the Lord, and [R]Çē′-phăs?

6 Or I only and Barnabas, [R]have not we power to forbear working?

7 Who [R]goeth a warfare any time at his own charges? who [R]planteth a vineyard, and eateth not of the fruit thereof? or who [R]feedeth a flock, and eateth not of the milk of the flock?

8 Say I these things as a man? or saith not the law the same also?

9 For it is written in the law of Moses, [R]Thou shalt not muzzle the mouth of the ox that treadeth out the corn. Doth God take care for oxen?

10 Or saith he *it* altogether for our sakes? For our sakes, no doubt, *this* is written: that

CHAP. 7
AD 59
32 1 Tim. 5:5
32 Gr. *of the Lord,* as ver. 34
34 Luke 10:40
38 Heb. 13:4
39 Rom. 7:2
39 2 Cor. 6:14
40 ver. 25
40 1 Thes. 4:8

CHAP. 8
AD 59
1 Acts 15:20
ch. 10:19
1 Rom. 14:14
1 Rom. 14:3
2 ch. 13:8, 9
Gal. 6:3
1 Tim. 6:4
3 Ex. 33:12
Mat. 7:23
Gal. 4:9
4 Is. 41:24
4 Deut. 4:39
Mark 12:29
1 Tim. 2:5
5 John 10:34

Mal. 2:10　6
Eph. 4:6
Acts 17:28　6
Rom. 11:36
Or, *for him*　6
John 13:13　6
Acts 2:36
Phil. 2:11
John 1:3　6
Col. 1:16
Heb. 1:2
ch. 10:28　7
Rom. 14:14　7
Rom. 14:17　8
Or, *have we the more*　8
Or, *have we the less*　8
Gal. 5:13　9
Or, *power*　9
Rom. 14:13　9
ch. 10:28　10
Gr. *edified*　10
Rom. 14:15　11
Mat. 25:40　12
Rom. 14:21　13
2 Cor. 11:29

CHAP. 9
AD 59
Acts 9:15　1
2 Cor. 12:12
Gal. 2:7, 8
1 Tim. 2:7
Acts 9:3, 17　1
& 18:9
ch. 15:8
ch. 3:6　1
2 Cor. 12:12　2
1 Thes. 2:6　4
Or, *woman*　5
Mat. 13:55　5
Gal. 1:19
Mat. 8:14　5
2 Thes. 3:8　6
2 Cor. 10:4
Deut. 20:6　7
John 21:15　7
1 Pet. 5:2
Deut. 25:4　9

R he that ploweth should plow in hope; and that he that thresheth in hope should be partaker of his hope.

11 R If we have sown unto you spiritual things, *is it* a great thing if we shall reap your carnal things?

Paul's self-denial

12 If others be partakers of *this* power over you, *are* not we rather? R Nevertheless we have not used this power; but suffer all things, R lest we should hinder the gospel of Christ.

13 R Do ye not know that they which minister about holy things N live *of the things* of the temple? and they which wait at the altar are partakers with the altar?

14 Even so R hath the Lord ordained R that they which preach the gospel should live of the gospel.

15 But R I have used none of these things: neither have I written these things, that it should be so done unto me: for R *it were* better for me to die, than that any man should make my glorying void.

16 For though I preach the gospel, I have nothing to glory of: for R necessity is laid upon me; yea, woe is unto me, if I preach not the gospel!

17 For if I do this thing willingly, R I have a reward: but if against my will, R a dispensation *of the gospel* is committed unto me.

18 What is my reward then? *Verily* that, R when I preach the gospel, I may make the gospel of Christ without charge, that I R abuse not my power in the gospel.

All things to all men

19 For though I be R free from all *men,* yet have R I made myself servant unto all, R that I might gain the more.

20 And R unto the Jews I became as a Jew, that I might gain the Jews; to them that are under the law, as under the law, that I might gain them that are under the law;

21 R To R them that are without law, as without law, (R being not without law to God, but under the law to Christ,) that I might gain them that are without law.

22 R To the weak became I as weak, that I might gain the weak: R I am made all things to all *men,* R that I might by all means save some.

23 And this I do for the gospel's sake, that I might be partaker thereof with *you.*

24 Know ye not that they which run in a race run all, but one receiveth the prize? R So run, that ye may obtain.

25 And every man that striveth for the mastery is temperate in all things. Now they *do it*

---

to obtain a corruptible crown; but we R an incorruptible.

26 I therefore so run, R not as uncertainly; so fight I, not as one that beateth the air:

27 R But I keep under my body, and R bring *it* into subjection: lest that by any means, when I have preached to others, I myself should be R a castaway.

CHAPTER 10

Warnings from Israel's history

MOREOVER, brethren, I would not that ye should be ignorant, how that all our fathers were under R the cloud, and all passed through R the sea;

2 And were all baptized unto Moses in the cloud and in the sea;

3 And did all eat the same R spiritual meat;

4 And did all drink the same R spiritual drink: for they drank of that spiritual Rock that N followed them: and that Rock was Christ.

5 But with many of them God was not well pleased: for they R were overthrown in the wilderness.

6 Now these things were N our examples, to the intent we should not lust after evil things, as R they also lusted.

7 R Neither be ye idolaters, as *were* some of them; as it is written, R The people sat down to eat and drink, and rose up to play.

8 R Neither let us commit fornication, as some of them committed, and R fell in one day three and twenty thousand.

9 Neither let us tempt Christ, as R some of them also tempted, and R were destroyed of serpents.

10 Neither murmur ye, as R some of them also murmured, and R were destroyed of R the destroyer.

11 Now all these things happened unto them for N ensamples: and R they are written for our admonition, R upon whom the ends of the world are come.

12 Wherefore R let him that thinketh he standeth take heed lest he fall.

13 There hath no temptation taken you but such as is N common to man: but R God *is* faithful, R who will not suffer you to be tempted above that ye are able; but will with the temptation also make a way to escape, that ye may be able to bear *it.*

Shun idolatry

14 Wherefore, my dearly beloved, R flee from idolatry.

15 I speak as to ᴿwise men; judge ye what I say.

16 ᴿThe cup of blessing which we bless, is it not the communion of the blood of Christ? ᴿThe bread which we break, is it not the communion of the body of Christ?

17 For ᴿwe *being* many are one bread, *and* one body: for we are all partakers of that one bread.

18 Behold ᴿIsrael ᴿafter the flesh: ᴿare not they which eat of the sacrifices partakers of the altar?

19 What say I then? ᴿthat the idol is any thing, or that which is offered in sacrifice to idols is any thing?

20 But *I say,* that the things which the Gentiles ᴿsacrifice, they sacrifice to devils, and not to God: and I would not that ye should have fellowship with devils.

21 ᴿYe cannot drink the cup of the Lord, and ᴿthe cup of devils: ye cannot be partakers of the Lord's table, and of the table of devils.

22 Do we ᴿprovoke the Lord to jealousy? ᴿare we stronger than he?

Principle of Christian liberty

23 ᴿAll things are lawful for me, but all things are not expedient: all things are lawful for me, but all things edify not.

24 ᴿLet no man seek his own, but every man another's *wealth.*

25 ᴿWhatsoever is sold in the shambles, *that* eat, asking no question for conscience sake:

26 For ᴿthe earth *is* the Lord's, and the fulness thereof.

27 If any of them that believe not bid you *to a feast,* and ye be disposed to go; ᴿwhatsoever is set before you, eat, asking no question for conscience sake.

28 But if any man say unto you, This is offered in sacrifice unto idols, eat not ᴿfor his sake that shewed it, and for conscience sake: for ᴿthe earth *is* the Lord's, and the fulness thereof:

29 Conscience, I say, not thine own, but of the other: for ᴿwhy is my liberty judged of another *man's* conscience?

30 For if I by ᴺgrace be a partaker, why am I evil spoken of for that ᴿfor which I give thanks?

31 ᴿWhether therefore ye eat, or drink, or whatsoever ye do, do all to the glory of God.

32 ᴿGive none offence, neither to the Jews, nor to the ᴺGentiles, nor to ᴿthe church of God:

33 Even as ᴿI please all *men* in all *things,* ᴿnot seeking mine own profit, but the *profit* of many, that they may be saved.

CHAP. 10	
AD 59	
15	ch. 8:1
16	Mat. 26:26
16	Acts 2:42
17	ch. 12:27
18	Rom. 4:12
18	Rom. 4:1
	2 Cor. 11:18
18	Lev. 3:3
19	ch. 8:4
20	Lev. 17:7
	Deut. 32:17
	Ps. 106:37
21	2 Cor. 6:15
21	Deut. 32:38
22	Deut. 32:21
22	Ezek. 22:14
23	ch. 6:12
24	Rom. 15:1, 2
	ch. 13:5
25	1 Tim. 4:4
26	Ex. 19:5
	Ps. 24:1
27	Luke 10:7
28	ch. 8:10, 12
28	Deut. 10:14
	Ps. 24:1
29	Rom. 14:16
30	Or, *thanksgiving*
30	Rom. 14:6
	1 Tim. 4:3, 4
31	Col. 3:17
	1 Pet. 4:11
32	Rom. 14:13
	ch. 8:13
32	Gr. *Greeks*
32	Acts 20:28
	1 Tim. 3:5
33	Rom. 15:2
33	ver. 24

CHAP. 11		
AD 59		
Eph. 5:1		1
Phil. 3:17		
ch. 4:17		2
ch. 7:17		2
Or, *traditions*		2
Eph. 5:23		3
Gen. 3:16		3
1 Tim. 2:11		
John 14:28		3
Phil. 2:7-9		
ch. 12:10		4
Acts 21:9		5
Deut. 21:12		5
Num. 5:18		6
Gen. 1:26		7
Gen. 2:21		8
Gen. 2:18		9
Gen. 24:65		10
i.e. *covering, in sign that she is under the power of her husband*		10
Eccl. 5:6		10
Gal. 3:28		11
Or, *veil*		15
1 Tim. 6:4		16
ch. 7:17		16
ch. 1:10, 11		18
Or, *schisms*		18

CHAPTER 11

BE ᴿye followers of me, even as I also *am* of Christ.

Veiling of women

2 Now I praise you, brethren, ᴿthat ye remember me in all things, and ᴿkeep the ᴺordinances, as I delivered *them* to you.

3 But I would have you know, that ᴿthe head of every man is Christ; and ᴿthe head of the woman *is* the man; and ᴿthe head of Christ *is* God.

4 Every man praying or ᴿprophesying, having *his* head covered, dishonoureth his head.

5 But ᴿevery woman that prayeth or prophesieth with *her* head uncovered dishonoureth her head: for that is even all one as if she were ᴿshaven.

6 For if the woman be not covered, let her also be shorn: but if it be ᴿa shame for a woman to be shorn or shaven, let her be covered.

7 For a man indeed ought not to cover *his* head, forasmuch as ᴿhe is the image and glory of God: but the woman is the glory of the man.

8 For ᴿthe man is not of the woman; but the woman of the man.

9 ᴿNeither was the man created for the woman; but the woman for the man.

10 For this cause ought the woman ᴿto have ᴺpower on *her* head ᴿbecause of the angels.

11 Nevertheless ᴿneither is the man without the woman, neither the woman without the man, in the Lord.

12 For as the woman *is* of the man, even so *is* the man also by the woman; but all things of God.

13 Judge in yourselves: is it comely that a woman pray unto God uncovered?

14 Doth not even nature itself teach you, that, if a man have long hair, it is a shame unto him?

15 But if a woman have long hair, it is a glory to her: for *her* hair is given her for a ᴺcovering.

16 But ᴿif any man seem to be contentious, we have no such custom, ᴿneither the churches of God.

Observing the Lord's supper

17 Now in this that I declare *unto you* I praise *you* not, that ye come together not for the better, but for the worse.

18 For first of all, when ye come together in the church, ᴿI hear that there be ᴺdivisions among you; and I partly believe it.

19 For ᴿthere must be also ᴺheresies among you, ᴿthat they which are approved may be made manifest among you.

20 When ye come together therefore into one place, ᴺ*this* is not to eat the Lord's supper.

21 For in eating every one taketh before *other* his own supper: and one is hungry, and ᴿanother is drunken.

22 What? have ye not houses to eat and to drink in? or despise ye ᴿthe church of God, and ᴿshame ᴺthem that have not? What shall I say to you? shall I praise you in this? I praise *you* not.

23 For ᴿI have received of the Lord that which also I delivered unto you, ᴿThat the Lord Jesus the *same* night in which he was betrayed took bread:

24 And when he had given thanks, he brake *it,* and said, Take, eat: this is my body, which is broken for you: this do ᴺin remembrance of me.

25 After the same manner also *he took* the cup, when he had supped, saying, This cup is the new testament in my blood: this do ye, as oft as ye drink *it,* in remembrance of me.

26 For as often as ye eat this bread, and drink this cup, ᴺye do shew the Lord's death ᴿtill he come.

27 ᴿWherefore whosoever shall eat this bread, and drink *this* cup of the Lord, unworthily, shall be guilty of the body and blood of the Lord.

28 But ᴿlet a man examine himself, and so let him eat of *that* bread, and drink of *that* cup.

29 For he that eateth and drinketh unworthily, eateth and drinketh ᴺdamnation to himself, not discerning the Lord's body.

30 For this cause many *are* weak and sickly among you, and many sleep.

31 For ᴿif we would judge ourselves, we should not be judged.

32 But when we are judged, ᴿwe are chastened of the Lord, that we should not be condemned with the world.

33 Wherefore, my brethren, when ye come together to eat, tarry one for another.

34 And if any man hunger, let him eat at home; that ye come not together unto ᴺcondemnation. And the rest ᴿwill I set in order when ᴿI come.

CHAPTER 12

Spiritual gifts

NOW ᴿconcerning spiritual *gifts,* brethren, I would not have you ignorant.

2 Ye know ᴿthat ye were Gentiles, carried

CHAP. 11
AD 59
19 Mat. 18:7
Luke 17:1
1 Tim. 4:1
19 Or, *sects*
19 Luke 2:35
1 John 2:19
20 Or, *ye cannot eat*
21 2 Pet. 2:13
Jude 12
22 ch. 10:32
22 Jas. 2:6
22 Or, *them that are poor?*
23 ch. 15:3
23 Mat. 26:26
Luke 22:19
24 Or, *for a remembrance*
26 Or, *shew ye*
26 John 14:3
Acts 1:11
27 John 6:51
28 2 Cor. 13:5
29 Or, *judgment*
31 Ps. 32:5
1 John 1:9
32 Ps. 94:12
34 Or, *judgment*
34 Tit. 1:5
34 ch. 4:19

CHAP. 12
AD 59
1 ch. 14:1, 37
2 Eph. 2:11
1 Thes. 1:9
1 Pet. 4:3

Ps. 115:5   2
Mark 9:39   3
1 John 4:2
Or, *anathema*   3
Mat. 16:17   3
John 15:26
Rom. 12:4   4
1 Pet. 4:10
Eph. 4:4   4
Rom. 12:6   5
Eph. 4:11
Or, *ministeries* 5
Eph. 1:23   6
Rom. 12:6   7
Eph. 4:7
ch. 2:6, 7   8
2 Cor. 8:7   8
Mat. 17:19   9
2 Cor. 4:13
Mark 16:18   9
Jas. 5:14
Mark 16:17   10
Gal. 3:5
Rom. 12:6   10
1 John 4:1   10
Acts 2:4   10
Rom. 12:6   11
2 Cor. 10:13
John 3:8   11
Rom. 12:4, 5   12
Eph. 4:4
Gal. 3:16   12
Rom. 6:5   13
Gal. 3:28   13
Col. 3:11
Gr. *Greeks*   13
John 6:63   13
ver. 28   18
Rom. 12:3   18

away unto these ᴿdumb idols, even as ye were led.

3 Wherefore I give you to understand, ᴿthat no man speaking by the Spirit of God calleth Jesus ᴺaccursed: and ᴿ*that* no man can say that Jesus is the Lord, but by the Holy Ghost.

4 Now ᴿthere are diversities of gifts, but ᴿthe same Spirit.

5 ᴿAnd there are differences of ᴺadministrations, but the same Lord.

6 And there are diversities of operations, but it is the same God ᴿwhich worketh all in all.

7 ᴿBut the manifestation of the Spirit is given to every man to profit withal.

8 For to one is given by the Spirit ᴿthe word of wisdom; to another ᴿthe word of knowledge by the same Spirit;

9 ᴿTo another faith by the same Spirit; to another ᴿthe gifts of healing by the same Spirit;

10 ᴿTo another the working of miracles; to another ᴿprophecy; ᴿto another discerning of spirits; to another ᴿ*divers* kinds of tongues; to another the interpretation of tongues:

11 But all these worketh that one and the selfsame Spirit, ᴿdividing to every man severally ᴿas he will.

Unity of the body of Christ

12 For ᴿas the body is one, and hath many members, and all the members of that one body, being many, are one body: ᴿso also *is* Christ.

13 For ᴿby one Spirit are we all baptized into one body, ᴿwhether *we be* Jews or ᴺGentiles, whether *we be* bond or free; and ᴿhave been all made to drink into one Spirit.

14 For the body is not one member, but many.

15 If the foot shall say, Because I am not the hand, I am not of the body; is it therefore not of the body?

16 And if the ear shall say, Because I am not the eye, I am not of the body; is it therefore not of the body?

17 If the whole body *were* an eye, where *were* the hearing? If the whole *were* hearing, where *were* the smelling?

18 But now hath ᴿGod set the members every one of them in the body, ᴿas it hath pleased him.

19 And if they were all one member, where *were* the body?

20 But now *are they* many members, yet but one body.

21 And the eye cannot say unto the hand, I have no need of thee: nor again the head to the feet, I have no need of you.

22 Nay, much more those members of the body, which seem to be more feeble, are necessary:

23 And those *members* of the body, which we think to be less honourable, upon these we ᴺbestow more abundant honour; and our uncomely *parts* have more abundant comeliness.

24 For our comely *parts* have no need: but God hath tempered the body together, having given more abundant honour to that *part* which lacked:

25 That there should be no ᴺschism in the body; but *that* the members should have the same care one for another.

26 And whether one member suffer, all the members suffer with it; or one member be honoured, all the members rejoice with it.

27 Now ᴿye are the body of Christ, and ᴿmembers in particular.

28 And ᴿGod hath set some in the church, first ᴿapostles, secondarily ᴿprophets, thirdly teachers, after that ᴿmiracles, then ᴿgifts of healings, ᴿhelps, ᴿgovernments, ᴺdiversities of tongues.

29 *Are* all apostles? *are* all prophets? *are* all teachers? *are* all ᴺworkers of miracles?

30 Have all the gifts of healing? do all speak with tongues? do all interpret?

Christian love compared

31 But ᴿcovet earnestly the best gifts: and yet shew I unto you a more excellent way.

CHAPTER 13

THOUGH I speak with the tongues of men and of angels, and have not charity, I am become *as* sounding brass, or a tinkling cymbal.

2 And though I have *the gift of* ᴿprophecy, and understand all mysteries, and all knowledge; and though I have all faith, ᴿso that I could remove mountains, and have not charity, I am nothing.

3 And ᴿthough I bestow all my goods to feed *the poor,* and though I give my body to be burned, and have not charity, it profiteth me nothing.

Christian love defined

4 ᴿCharity suffereth long, *and* is kind; charity envieth not; charity ᴺvaunteth not itself, is not puffed up,

5 Doth not behave itself unseemly, ᴿseeketh not her own, is not easily provoked, thinketh no evil;

6 ᴿRejoiceth not in iniquity, but ᴿrejoiceth ᴺin the truth;

7 ᴿBeareth all things, believeth all things, hopeth all things, endureth all things.

CHAP. 12
AD 59
23 Or, *put on*
25 Or, *division*
27 Rom. 12:5
Eph. 1:23 & 4:12
& 5:23, 30
Col. 1:24
27 Eph. 5:30
28 Eph. 4:11
28 Eph. 2:20 & 3:5
28 Acts 13:1
Rom. 12:6
28 ver. 10
28 ver. 9
28 Num. 11:17
28 Rom. 12:8
1 Tim. 5:17
Heb. 13:17, 24
28 Or, *kinds,*
ver. 10
29 Or, *powers*
31 ch. 14:1, 39

CHAP. 13
AD 59
2 ch. 12:8-10, 28
& 14:1, etc.
See Mat. 7:22
2 Mat. 17:20
Mark 11:23
Luke 17:6
3 Mat. 6:1, 2
4 Prov. 10:12
1 Pet. 4:8
4 Or, *is not rash*
5 ch. 10:24
Phil. 2:4
6 Ps. 10:3
Rom. 1:32
6 2 John 4
6 Or, *with the truth*
7 Rom. 15:1
Gal. 6:2
2 Tim. 2:24

ch. 8:2   9
Or, *reasoned*   11
2 Cor. 3:18   12
& 5:7
Phil. 3:12
Gr. *in a riddle*   12
Mat. 18:10   12
1 John 3:2

CHAP. 14
AD 59
ch. 12:31   1
Num. 11:25, 29   1
Acts 2:4   2
& 10:46
Gr. *heareth,*   2
Acts 22:9
ver. 26   6
Or, *tunes*   7
Gr. *significant*   9

Christian love imperishable

8 Charity never faileth: but whether *there be* prophecies, they shall fail; whether *there be* tongues, they shall cease; whether *there be* knowledge, it shall vanish away.

9 ᴿFor we know in part, and we prophesy in part.

10 But when that which is perfect is come, then that which is in part shall be done away.

11 When I was a child, I spake as a child, I understood as a child, I ᴺthought as a child: but when I became a man, I put away childish things.

12 For ᴿnow we see through a glass, ᴺdarkly; but then ᴿface to face: now I know in part; but then shall I know even as also I am known.

13 And now abideth faith, hope, charity, these three; but the greatest of these *is* charity.

CHAPTER 14

The gifts of prophecy and of tongues

FOLLOW after charity, and ᴿdesire spiritual *gifts,* ᴿbut rather that ye may prophesy.

2 For he that ᴿspeaketh in an *unknown* tongue speaketh not unto men, but unto God: for no man ᴺunderstandeth *him;* howbeit in the spirit he speaketh mysteries.

3 But he that prophesieth speaketh unto men *to* edification, and exhortation, and comfort.

4 He that speaketh in an *unknown* tongue edifieth himself; but he that prophesieth edifieth the church.

5 I would that ye all spake with tongues, but rather that ye prophesied: for greater *is* he that prophesieth than he that speaketh with tongues, except he interpret, that the church may receive edifying.

6 Now, brethren, if I come unto you speaking with tongues, what shall I profit you, except I shall speak to you either by ᴿrevelation, or by knowledge, or by prophesying, or by doctrine?

7 And even things without life giving sound, whether pipe or harp, except they give a distinction in the ᴺsounds, how shall it be known what is piped or harped?

8 For if the trumpet give an uncertain sound, who shall prepare himself to the battle?

9 So likewise ye, except ye utter by the tongue words ᴺeasy to be understood, how shall it be known what is spoken? for ye shall speak into the air.

10 There are, it may be, so many kinds of voices in the world, and none of them *is* without signification.

11 Therefore if I know not the meaning of the voice, I shall be unto him that speaketh a barbarian, and he that speaketh *shall be* a barbarian unto me.

12 Even so ye, forasmuch as ye are zealous [N]of spiritual *gifts,* seek that ye may excel to the edifying of the church.

Interpretation of tongues needed

13 Wherefore let him that speaketh in an *unknown* tongue pray that he may interpret.

14 For if I pray in an *unknown* tongue, my spirit prayeth, but my understanding is unfruitful.

15 What is it then? I will pray with the spirit, and I will pray with the understanding also: [R]I will sing with the spirit, and I will sing [R]with the understanding also.

16 Else when thou shalt bless with the spirit, how shall he that occupieth the room of the unlearned say Ā'-mĕn [R]at thy giving of thanks, seeing he understandeth not what thou sayest?

17 For thou verily givest thanks well, but the other is not edified.

18 I thank my God, I speak with tongues more than ye all:

19 Yet in the church I had rather speak five words with my understanding, that *by my voice* I might teach others also, than ten thousand words in an *unknown* tongue.

20 Brethren, [R]be not children in understanding: howbeit in malice [R]be ye children, but in understanding be [N]men.

21 [R]In the law it is [R]written, With *men of* other tongues and other lips will I speak unto this people; and yet for all that will they not hear me, saith the Lord.

22 Wherefore tongues are for a sign, not to them that believe, but to them that believe not: but prophesying *serveth* not for them that believe not, but for them which believe.

23 If therefore the whole church be come together into one place, and all speak with tongues, and there come in *those that are* unlearned, or unbelievers, [R]will they not say that ye are mad?

24 But if all prophesy, and there come in one that believeth not, or *one* unlearned, he is convinced of all, he is judged of all:

25 And thus are the secrets of his heart made manifest; and so falling down on *his* face he will worship God, and report [R]that God is in you of a truth.

Orderly worship desired

26 How is it then, brethren? when ye come together, every one of you hath a psalm, [R]hath a doctrine, hath a tongue, hath a revelation,

hath an interpretation. [R]Let all things be done unto edifying.

27 If any man speak in an *unknown* tongue, *let it be* by two, or at the most *by* three, and *that* by course; and let one interpret.

28 But if there be no interpreter, let him keep silence in the church; and let him speak to himself, and to God.

29 Let the prophets speak two or three, and [R]let the other judge.

30 If *any thing* be revealed to another that sitteth by, [R]let the first hold his peace.

31 For ye may all prophesy one by one, that all may learn, and all may be comforted.

32 And [R]the spirits of the prophets are subject to the prophets.

33 For God is not *the author* of [N]confusion, but of peace, [R]as in all churches of the saints.

34 [R]Let your women keep silence in the churches: for it is not permitted unto them to speak; but *they are commanded* to be under obedience, as also saith the [R]law.

35 And if they will learn any thing, let them ask their husbands at home: for it is a shame for women to speak in the church.

36 What? came the word of God out from you? or came it unto you only?

37 [R]If any man think himself to be a prophet, or spiritual, let him acknowledge that the things that I write unto you are the commandments of the Lord.

38 But if any man be ignorant, let him be ignorant.

39 Wherefore, brethren, [R]covet to prophesy, and forbid not to speak with tongues.

40 [R]Let all things be done decently and in order.

CHAPTER 15

The fact of Christ's resurrection

MOREOVER, brethren, I declare unto you the gospel [R]which I preached unto you, which also ye have received, and [R]wherein ye stand;

2 [R]By which also ye are saved, if ye [N]keep in memory [N]what I preached unto you, unless [R]ye have believed in vain.

3 For [R]I delivered unto you first of all that [R]which I also received, how that Christ died for our sins [R]according to the scriptures;

4 And that he was buried, and that he rose again the third day [R]according to the scriptures:

5 [R]And that he was seen of Çē'-phăs, then [R]of the twelve:

6 After that, he was seen of above five hundred brethren at once; of whom the greater

part remain unto this present, but some are fallen asleep.

7 After that, he was seen of James; then ᴿof all the apostles.

8 ᴿAnd last of all he was seen of me also, as of ᴺone born out of due time.

9 For I am ᴿthe least of the apostles, that am not meet to be called an apostle, because ᴿI persecuted the church of God.

10 But ᴿby the grace of God I am what I am: and his grace which *was bestowed* upon me was not in vain; but ᴿI laboured more abundantly than they all: ᴿyet not I, but the grace of God which was with me.

11 Therefore whether *it were* I or they, so we preach, and so ye believed.

Faith rests on the resurrection

12 Now if Christ be preached that he rose from the dead, how say some among you that there is no resurrection of the dead?

13 But if there be no resurrection of the dead, ᴿthen is Christ not risen:

14 And if Christ be not risen, then *is* our preaching vain, and your faith *is* also vain.

15 Yea, and we are found false witnesses of God; because ᴿwe have testified of God that he raised up Christ: whom he raised not up, if so be that the dead rise not.

16 For if the dead rise not, then is not Christ raised:

17 And if Christ be not raised, your faith *is* vain; ᴿye are yet in your sins.

18 Then they also which are fallen asleep in Christ are perished.

19 ᴿIf in this life only we have hope in Christ, we are of all men most miserable.

The resurrection of believers

20 But now ᴿis Christ risen from the dead, *and* become ᴿthe firstfruits of them that slept.

21 For ᴿsince by man *came* death, ᴿby man *came* also the resurrection of the dead.

22 For as in Adam all die, even so in Christ shall all be made alive.

23 But ᴿevery man in his own order: Christ the firstfruits; afterward they that are Christ's at his coming.

24 Then *cometh* the end, when he shall have delivered up ᴿthe kingdom to God, even the Father; when he shall have put down all rule and all authority and power.

25 For he must reign, ᴿtill he hath put all enemies under his feet.

26 ᴿThe last enemy *that* shall be destroyed *is* death.

27 For he ᴿhath put all things under his feet. But when he saith all things are put under *him,*

it is manifest that he is excepted, which did put all things under him.

28 ᴿAnd when all things shall be subdued unto him, then ᴿshall the Son also himself be subject unto him that put all things under him, that God may be all in all.

29 Else what shall they do which are baptized for the dead, if the dead rise not at all? why are they then baptized for the dead?

30 And ᴿwhy stand we in jeopardy every hour?

31 I protest by ᴿyourᴺ rejoicing which I have in Christ Jesus our Lord, ᴿI die daily.

32 If ᴺafter the manner of men ᴿI have fought with beasts at Ĕph'-ĕ-sŭs, what advantageth it me, if the dead rise not? ᴿlet us eat and drink; for to morrow we die.

33 Be not deceived: ᴿevil communications corrupt good manners.

34 ᴿAwake to righteousness, and sin not; ᴿfor some have not the knowledge of God: ᴿI speak *this* to your shame.

The nature of the resurrection body

35 But some *man* will say, ᴿHow are the dead raised up? and with what body do they come?

36 *Thou fool,* ᴿthat which thou sowest is not quickened, except it die:

37 And that which thou sowest, thou sowest not that body that shall be, but bare grain, it may chance of wheat, or of some other *grain:*

38 But God giveth it a body as it hath pleased him, and to every seed his own body.

39 All flesh *is* not the same flesh: but *there is* one *kind of* flesh of men, another flesh of beasts, another of fishes, *and* another of birds.

40 *There are* also celestial bodies, and bodies terrestrial: but the glory of the celestial *is* one, and the *glory* of the terrestrial *is* another.

41 *There is* one glory of the sun, and another glory of the moon, and another glory of the stars: for *one* star differeth from *another* star in glory.

42 ᴿSo also *is* the resurrection of the dead. It is sown in corruption; it is raised in incorruption:

43 ᴿIt is sown in dishonour; it is raised in glory: it is sown in weakness; it is raised in power:

44 It is sown a natural body; it is raised a spiritual body. There is a natural body, and there is a spiritual body.

45 And so it is written, The first man Adam ᴿwas made a living soul; ᴿthe last Adam *was made* ᴿa quickening spirit.

46 Howbeit that *was* not first which is spiritual, but that which is natural; and afterward that which is spiritual.

47 ᴿThe first man *is* of the earth, ᴿearthy: the second man *is* the Lord ᴿfrom heaven.

48 As *is* the earthy, such *are* they also that are earthy: ᴿand as *is* the heavenly, such *are* thcy also that are heavenly.

49 And ᴿas we have borne the image of the earthy, ᴿwe shall also bear the image of the heavenly.

50 Now this I say, brethren, that ᴿflesh and blood cannot inherit the kingdom of God; neither doth corruption inherit incorruption.

Victory over death

51 Behold, I shew you a mystery; ᴿWe shall not all sleep, ᴿbut we shall all be changed,

52 In a moment, in the twinkling of an eye, at the last trump: ᴿfor the trumpet shall sound, and the dead shall be raised incorruptible, and we shall be changed.

53 For this corruptible must put on incorruption, and ᴿthis mortal *must* put on immortality.

54 So when this corruptible shall have put on incorruption, and this mortal shall have put on immortality, then shall be brought to pass the saying that is written, ᴿDeath is swallowed up in victory.

55 ᴿO death, where *is* thy sting? O ᴺgrave, where *is* thy victory?

56 The sting of death *is* sin; and ᴿthe strength of sin *is* the law.

57 ᴿBut thanks *be* to God, which giveth us ᴿthe victory through our Lord Jesus Christ.

58 ᴿTherefore, my beloved brethren, be ye stedfast, unmoveable, always abounding in the work of the Lord, forasmuch as ye know ᴿthat your labour is not in vain in the Lord.

CHAPTER 16

Collection for the saints

NOW concerning ᴿthe collection for the saints, as I have given order to the churches of Galatia, even so do ye.

2 ᴿUpon the first *day* of the week let every one of you lay by him in store, as *God* hath prospered him, that there be no gatherings when I come.

3 And when I come, ᴿwhomsoever ye shall approve by *your* letters, them will I send to bring your ᴺliberality unto Jerusalem.

4 ᴿAnd if it be meet that I go also, they shall go with me.

5 Now I will come unto you, ᴿwhen I shall pass through Măç-ĕ-dō'-nĭ-ă: for I do pass through Măç-ĕ-dō'-nĭ-ă.

6 And it may be that I will abide, yea, and winter with you, that ye may ᴿbring me on my journey whithersoever I go.

CHAP. 15	
AD 59	
47	John 3:31
47	Gen. 3:19
47	John 3:13
48	Phil. 3:20
49	Gen. 5:3
49	Rom. 8:29
	2 Cor. 3:18
	Phil. 3:21
	1 John 3:2
50	Mat. 16:17
	John 3:3, 5
51	1 Thes. 4:15
51	Phil. 3:21
52	Zech. 9:14
	Mat. 24:31
	John 5:25
53	2 Cor. 5:4
54	Is. 25:8
	Rev. 20:14
55	Hos. 13:14
55	Or, *hell*
56	Rom. 4:15
57	Rom. 7:25
57	1 John 5:4
58	2 Pet. 3:14
58	ch. 3:8

CHAP. 16	
AD 59	
1	Acts 11:29
	Gal. 2:10
2	Acts 20:7
3	2 Cor. 8:19
3	Gr. *gift*,
	2 Cor. 8:19
5	Acts 19:21
	2 Cor. 1:16
6	Acts 15:3
	Rom. 15:24

Acts 18:21	7	
Jas. 4:15		
Acts 14:27	9	
2 Cor. 2:12		
Col. 4:3		
Acts 19:9	9	
Acts 19:22	10	
Phil. 2:20	10	
1 Thes. 3:2		
1 Tim. 4:12	11	
Acts 15:33	11	
ch. 1:12	12	
Mat. 24:42	13	
1 Thes. 5:6		
1 Pet. 5:8		
Phil. 1:27	13	
1 Thes. 3:8		
2 Thes. 2:15		
Eph. 6:10	13	
Col. 1:11		
1 Pet. 4:8	14	
ch. 1:16	15	
Rom. 16:5	15	
2 Cor. 8:4	15	
Heb. 6:10		
Heb. 13:17	16	
Heb. 6:10	16	
2 Cor. 11:9	17	
Phil. 2:30		
Col. 4:8	18	
Phil. 2:29	18	
Rom. 16:5	19	
Rom. 16:16	20	
Col. 4:18	21	
Eph. 6:24	22	
Gal. 1:8, 9	22	
Jude 14, 15	22	
Rom. 16:20	23	

7 For I will not see you now by the way; but I trust to tarry a while with you, ᴿif the Lord permit.

8 But I will tarry at ĕph'-ĕ-sŭs until Pentecost.

9 For ᴿa great door and effectual is opened unto me, and ᴿ*there are* many adversaries.

Timothy commended

10 Now ᴿif Timotheus come, see that he may be with you without fear: for ᴿhe worketh the work of the Lord, as I also *do.*

11 ᴿLet no man therefore despise him: but conduct him forth ᴿin peace, that he may come unto me: for I look for him with the brethren.

12 As touching *our* brother ᴿĂ-pŏl'-lŏs, I greatly desired him to come unto you with the brethren: but his will was not at all to come at this time; but he will come when he shall have convenient time.

Final exhortation

13 ᴿWatch ye, ᴿstand fast in the faith, quit you like men, ᴿbe strong.

14 ᴿLct all your things he done with charity.

15 I beseech you, brethren, (ye know ᴿthe house of Stĕph'-ă-năs, that it is ᴿthe firstfruits of Ă-chāī'-ă, and *that* they have addicted themselves to ᴿthe ministry of the saints,)

16 ᴿThat ye submit yourselves unto such, and to every one that helpeth with *us,* and ᴿlaboureth.

17 I am glad of the coming of Stĕph'-ă-năs and Fôr-tū-nā'-tŭs and Ă-chā'-ĭ-cŭs: ᴿfor that which was lacking on your part they have supplied.

18 ᴿFor they have refreshed my spirit and yours: therefore ᴿacknowledge ye them that are such.

Greetings and benediction

19 The churches of Asia salute you. Ă-quĭl'-ă and Priscilla salute you much in the Lord, ᴿwith the church that is in their house.

20 All the brethren greet you. ᴿGreet ye one another with an holy kiss.

21 ᴿThe salutation of *me* Paul with mine own hand.

22 If any man ᴿlove not the Lord Jesus Christ, ᴿlet him be Ă-năth'-ĕ-mă ᴿMăr'-ăn-ă'-thă.

23 ᴿThe grace of our Lord Jesus Christ *be* with you.

24 My love *be* with you all in Christ Jesus. Ä'-mĕn.

The first *epistle* to the Corinthians was written from Philippi by Stĕph'-ă-năs, and Fôr-tū-nā'-tŭs, and Ă-chā'-ĭ-cŭs, and Timotheus.

THE SECOND EPISTLE OF PAUL THE APOSTLE
TO THE
CORINTHIANS

The Second Epistle to the Corinthians, while somewhat less eloquent than the First Epistle, is more intense and personal. Paul had received reports of the church in Corinth that were both encouraging and disquieting. Titus, who is frequently mentioned in the letter (2:13; 7:6, 13–14; 8:6, 16, 23; 12:18), had brought news of triumphs and continuing difficulties, and the Second Epistle is Paul's earnest response of pastoral guidance. The epistle is noted for its breaks in style and changes of tone, and scholars have labored to understand and explain these differences. Two distinct units are (1) chapters 1–9, expressing a conciliatory tone and ending in a brief doxology, and (2) chapters 10–13, using words of severity and warning and concluding with another doxology. Many also consider 6:14–7:1 a unit detached from its original context, suggesting that it may be part of a "lost letter" (cf., I Cor. 5:9). Some contend that the letter was probably not written at one sitting and that changes in Paul's mood and/or circumstances account for differences in style and tone. Others argue that the epistle in its present form represents a collation of separate letters. But Pauline authorship seems certain in either case, and it is probable that the epistle was written from Macedonia (Philippi?) between A.D. 55 and 57.

OUTLINE OF THE BOOK:
- I. Salutation and Thanksgiving 1:1–11
- II. Paul's Answer to His Critics 1:12–7:16
- III. The Collection for the Poor of Jerusalem 8:1–9:15
- IV. Paul's Vindication of His Apostolic Authority 10:1–13:10
- V. Conclusion 13:11–14

CHAPTER 1

Salutation

PAUL, ᴿan apostle of Jesus Christ by the will of God, and Timothy *our* brother, unto the church of God which is at Corinth, ᴿwith all the saints which are in all Ă-chāi'-ă:

2 ᴿGrace *be* to you and peace from God our Father, and *from* the Lord Jesus Christ.

Affliction and comfort

3 ᴿBlessed *be* God, even the Father of our Lord Jesus Christ, the Father of mercies, and the God of all comfort;

4 Who comforteth us in all our tribulation, that we may be able to comfort them which are in any trouble, by the comfort wherewith we ourselves are comforted of God.

5 For as ᴿthe sufferings of Christ abound in us, so our consolation also aboundeth by Christ.

6 And whether we be afflicted, ᴿ*it is* for your consolation and salvation, which ᴺis effectual in the enduring of the same sufferings which we also suffer: or whether we be comforted, *it is* for your consolation and salvation.

7 And our hope of you *is* stedfast, knowing, that ᴿas ye are partakers of the sufferings, so *shall ye be* also of the consolation.

8 For we would not, brethren, have you ignorant of ᴿour trouble which came to us in Asia, that we were pressed out of measure, above strength, insomuch that we despaired even of life:

9 But we had the ᴺsentence of death in ourselves, that we should ᴿnot trust in ourselves, but in God which raiseth the dead:

10 ᴿWho delivered us from so great a death, and doth deliver: in whom we trust that he will yet deliver *us;*

11 Ye also ᴿhelping together by prayer for us, that ᴿfor the gift *bestowed* upon us by the means of many persons thanks may be given by many on our behalf.

Paul's plan to visit Corinth

12 For our rejoicing is this, the testimony of our conscience, that in simplicity and ᴿgodly sincerity, ᴿnot with fleshly wisdom, but by the grace of God, we have had our conversation in the world, and more abundantly to you-ward.

13 For we write none other things unto you, than what ye read or acknowledge; and I trust ye shall acknowledge even to the end;

14 As also ye have acknowledged us in part, ᴿthat we are your rejoicing, even as ᴿye also *are* ours in the day of the Lord Jesus.

15 And in this confidence ᴿI was minded to come unto you before, that ye might have ᴿa second ᴺbenefit;

16 And to pass by you into Măç-ē-dō'-nĭ-ă, and ᴿto come again out of Măç-ē-dō'-nĭ-ă unto you, and of you to be brought on my way toward Judæa.

17 When I therefore was thus minded, did I use lightness? or the things that I purpose, do I purpose ᴿaccording to the flesh, that with me there should be yea yea, and nay nay?

18 But *as* God *is* true, our ᴺword toward you was not yea and nay.

19 For ᴿthe Son of God, Jesus Christ, who was preached among you by us, *even* by me and Sīl-vā'-nŭs and Timotheus, was not yea and nay, ᴿbut in him was yea.

20 ᴿFor all the promises of God in him *are* yea, and in him Ä′-mĕn, unto the glory of God by us.

21 Now he which stablisheth us with you in Christ, and ᴿhath anointed us, *is* God;

22 Who ᴿhath also sealed us, and ᴿgiven the earnest of the Spirit in our hearts.

The change of plan

23 Moreover ᴿI call God for a record upon my soul, ᴿthat to spare you I came not as yet unto Corinth.

24 Not for ᴿthat we have dominion over your faith, but are helpers of your joy: for ᴿby faith ye stand.

CHAPTER 2

BUT I determined this with myself, ᴿthat I would not come again to you in heaviness.

2 For if I make you sorry, who is he then that maketh me glad, but the same which is made sorry by me?

3 And I wrote this same unto you, lest, when I came, ᴿI should have sorrow from them of whom I ought to rejoice; ᴿhaving confidence in you all, that my joy is *the joy* of you all.

4 For out of much affliction and anguish of heart I wrote unto you with many tears; ᴿnot that ye should be grieved, but that ye might know the love which I have more abundantly unto you.

Forgiveness encouraged

5 But ᴿif any have caused grief, he hath not ᴿgrieved me, but in part: that I may not overcharge you all.

6 Sufficient to such a man *is* this ᴺpunishment, which *was inflicted* ᴿof many.

7 ᴿSo that contrariwise ye *ought* rather to forgive *him,* and comfort *him,* lest perhaps such a one should be swallowed up with overmuch sorrow.

8 Wherefore I beseech you that ye would confirm *your* love toward him.

9 For to this end also did I write, that I might know the proof of you, whether ye be ᴿobedient in all things.

10 To whom ye forgive any thing, I *forgive* also: for if I forgave any thing, to whom I forgave *it,* for your sakes *forgave I it* ᴺin the person of Christ;

11 Lest Satan should get an advantage of us: for we are not ignorant of his devices.

Paul's triumphant ministry

12 Furthermore, ᴿwhen I came to Trō′-ăs to *preach* Christ's gospel, and ᴿa door was opened unto me of the Lord,

13 ᴿI had no rest in my spirit, because I found not Titus my brother: but taking my leave of them, I went from thence into Măç-ē-dō′-nĭ-ă.

14 Now thanks *be* unto God, which always causeth us to triumph in Christ, and maketh manifest ᴿthe savour of his knowledge by us in every place.

15 For we are unto God a sweet savour of Christ, ᴿin them that are saved, and ᴿin them that perish:

16 ᴿTo the one *we are* the savour of death unto death; and to the other the savour of life unto life. And ᴿwho *is* sufficient for these things?

17 For we are not as many, which ᴿcorruptᴺ the word of God: but as ᴿof sincerity, but as of God, in the sight of God speak we ᴺin Christ.

CHAPTER 3

Credentials of Paul's ministry

DO ᴿwe begin again to commend ourselves? or need we, as some *others,* ᴿepistles of commendation to you, or *letters* of commendation from you?

2 ᴿYe are our epistle written in our hearts, known and read of all men:

3 *Forasmuch as ye are* manifestly declared to be the epistle of Christ ᴿministered by us, written not with ink, but with the Spirit of the living God; not ᴿin tables of stone, but ᴿin fleshy tables of the heart.

4 And such trust have we through Christ to God-ward:

5 ᴿNot that we are sufficient of ourselves to think any thing as of ourselves; but ᴿour sufficiency *is* of God;

6 Who also hath made us able ᴿministers of ᴿthe new testament; not ᴿof the letter, but of the spirit: for ᴿthe letter killeth, ᴿbut the spirit ᴺgiveth life.

A ministry of splendour

7 But if ᴿthe ministration of death, ᴿwritten *and* engraven in stones, was glorious, ᴿso that the children of Israel could not stedfastly behold the face of Moses for the glory of his countenance; which *glory* was to be done away:

8 How shall not ᴿthe ministration of the spirit be rather glorious?

9 For if the ministration of condemnation *be* glory, much more doth the ministration ᴿof righteousness exceed in glory.

10 For even that which was made glorious had no glory in this respect, by reason of the glory that excelleth.

11 For if that which is done away *was* glorious, much more that which remaineth *is* glorious.

12 Seeing then that we have such hope, [R]we use great [N]plainness of speech:

13 And not as Moses, [R]*which* put a vail over his face, that the children of Israel could not stedfastly look to [R]the end of that which is abolished:

14 But [R]their minds were blinded: for until this day remaineth the same vail untaken away in the reading of the old testament; which *vail* is done away in Christ.

15 But even unto this day, when Moses is read, the vail is upon their heart.

16 Nevertheless [R]when it shall turn to the Lord, [R]the vail shall be taken away.

17 Now [R]the Lord is that Spirit: and where the Spirit of the Lord *is,* there *is* liberty.

18 But we all, with open face beholding [R]as in a glass [R]the glory of the Lord, [R]are changed into the same image from glory to glory, *even* as [N]by the Spirit of the Lord.

CHAPTER 4

An open ministry

THEREFORE seeing we have [R]this ministry, [R]as we have received mercy, we faint not;

2 But have renounced the hidden things of [N]dishonesty, not walking in craftiness, [R]nor handling the word of God deceitfully; but [R]by manifestation of the truth [R]commending ourselves to every man's conscience in the sight of God.

3 But if our gospel be hid, [R]it is hid to them that are lost:

4 In whom [R]the god of this world [R]hath blinded the minds of them which believe not, lest [R]the light of the glorious gospel of Christ, [R]who is the image of God, should shine unto them.

5 [R]For we preach not ourselves, but Christ Jesus the Lord; and [R]ourselves your servants for Jesus' sake.

6 For God, [R]who commanded the light to shine out of darkness, [N]hath [R]shined in our hearts, to *give* [R]the light of the knowledge of the glory of God in the face of Jesus Christ.

A transcendent ministry

7 But we have this treasure in [R]earthen vessels, [R]that the excellency of the power may be of God, and not of us.

8 *We are* [R]troubled on every side, yet not distressed; *we are* perplexed, but [N]not in despair;

9 Persecuted, but not forsaken; [R]cast down, but not destroyed;

10 [R]Always bearing about in the body the dying of the Lord Jesus, [R]that the life also of Jesus might be made manifest in our body.

11 For we which live [R]are alway delivered unto death for Jesus' sake, that the life also of Jesus might be made manifest in our mortal flesh.

12 So then [R]death worketh in us, but life in you.

13 We having [R]the same spirit of faith, according as it is written, [R]I believed, and therefore have I spoken; we also believe, and therefore speak;

14 Knowing that [R]he which raised up the Lord Jesus shall raise up us also by Jesus, and shall present *us* with you.

15 For [R]all things *are* for your sakes, that [R]the abundant grace might through the thanksgiving of many redound to the glory of God.

A ministry of eternal things

16 For which cause we faint not; but though our outward man perish, yet [R]the inward *man* is renewed day by day.

17 For [R]our light affliction, which is but for a moment, worketh for us a far more exceeding *and* eternal weight of glory;

18 [R]While we look not at the things which are seen, but at the things which are not seen: for the things which are seen *are* temporal; but the things which are not seen *are* eternal.

CHAPTER 5

FOR we know that if [R]our earthly house of *this* tabernacle were dissolved, we have a building of God, an house not made with hands, eternal in the heavens.

2 For in this [R]we groan, earnestly desiring to be clothed upon with our house which is from heaven:

3 If so be that [R]being clothed we shall not be found naked.

4 For we that are in *this* tabernacle do groan, being burdened: not for that we would be unclothed, but [R]clothed upon, that mortality might be swallowed up of life.

5 Now [R]he that hath wrought us for the selfsame thing *is* God, who also [R]hath given unto us the earnest of the Spirit.

A ministry of faith

6 Therefore *we are* always confident, knowing that, whilst we are at home in the body, we are absent from the Lord:

7 (For [R]we walk by faith, not by sight:)

8 We are confident, *I say,* and [R]willing rather to be absent from the body, and to be present with the Lord.

9 Wherefore we [N]labour, that, whether present or absent, we may be accepted of him.

10 [R]For we must all appear before the judgment seat of Christ; [R]that every one may receive the things *done* in *his* body, according to that he hath done, whether *it be* good or bad.

11 Knowing therefore [R]the terror of the Lord, we persuade men; but [R]we are made manifest unto God; and I trust also are made manifest in your consciences.

12 For [R]we commend not ourselves again unto you, but give you occasion [R]to glory on our behalf, that ye may have somewhat to *answer* them which glory [N]in appearance, and not in heart.

13 For [R]whether we be beside ourselves, *it is* to God: or whether we be sober, *it is* for your cause.

14 For the love of Christ constraineth us; because we thus judge, that [R]if one died for all, then were all dead:

15 And *that* he died for all, [R]that they which live should not henceforth live unto themselves, but unto him which died for them, and rose again.

A ministry of reconciliation

16 [R]Wherefore henceforth know we no man after the flesh: yea, though we have known Christ after the flesh, [R]yet now henceforth know we *him* no more.

17 Therefore if any man [R]be in Christ, [N]*he is* [R]a new creature: [R]old things are passed away; behold, all things are become new.

18 And all things *are* of God, [R]who hath reconciled us to himself by Jesus Christ, and hath given to us the ministry of reconciliation;

19 To wit, that [R]God was in Christ, reconciling the world unto himself, not imputing their trespasses unto them; and hath [N]committed unto us the word of reconciliation.

20 Now then we are [R]ambassadors for Christ, as [R]though God did beseech *you* by us: we pray *you* in Christ's stead, be ye reconciled to God.

21 For [R]he hath made him *to be* sin for us, who knew no sin; that we might be made [R]the righteousness of God in him.

CHAPTER 6

A full and timely ministry

WE then, *as* [R]workers together *with him,* [R]beseech *you* also [R]that ye receive not the grace of God in vain.

2 (For he saith, [R]I have heard thee in a time accepted, and in the day of salvation have I succoured thee: behold, now *is* the accepted time; behold, now *is* the day of salvation.)

3 [R]Giving no offence in any thing, that the ministry be not blamed:

4 But in all *things* [N]approving ourselves [R]as the ministers of God, in much patience, in afflictions, in necessities, in distresses,

5 [R]In stripes, in imprisonments, [N]in tumults, in labours, in watchings, in fastings;

6 By pureness, by knowledge, by longsuffering, by kindness, by the Holy Ghost, by love unfeigned,

7 [R]By the word of truth, by [R]the power of God, by [R]the armour of righteousness on the right hand and on the left,

8 By honour and dishonour, by evil report and good report: as deceivers, and *yet* true;

9 As unknown, and [R]*yet* well known; [R]as dying, and, behold, we live; [R]as chastened, and not killed;

10 As sorrowful, yet alway rejoicing; as poor, yet making many rich; as having nothing, and *yet* possessing all things.

11 O *ye* Corinthians, our mouth is open unto you, [R]our heart is enlarged.

12 Ye are not straitened in us, but [R]ye are straitened in your own bowels.

13 Now for a recompence in the same, ([R]I speak as unto *my* children,) be ye also enlarged.

Call to purity of association

14 [R]Be ye not unequally yoked together with unbelievers: for [R]what fellowship hath righteousness with unrighteousness? and what communion hath light with darkness?

15 And what concord hath Christ with Bē′-lĭ-ăl? or what part hath he that believeth with an infidel?

16 And what agreement hath the temple of God with idols? for [R]ye are the temple of the living God; as God hath said, [R]I will dwell in them, and walk in *them;* and I will be their God, and they shall be my people.

17 [R]Wherefore come out from among them, and be ye separate, saith the Lord, and touch not the unclean *thing;* and I will receive you,

18 [R]And will be a Father unto you, and ye shall be my sons and daughters, saith the Lord Almighty.

CHAPTER 7

HAVING [R]therefore these promises, dearly beloved, let us cleanse ourselves from all filthiness of the flesh and spirit, perfecting holiness in the fear of God.

CHAP. 5
AD 60
8 Phil. 1:23
9 Or, *endeavour*
10 Rom. 14:10
10 Gal. 6:7
Eph. 6:8
11 Heb. 10:31
Jude 23
11 ch. 4:2
12 ch. 3:1
12 ch. 1:14
12 Gr. *in the face*
13 ch. 11:1, 16
14 Rom. 5:15
15 Rom. 6:11
1 Cor. 6:19
16 ch. 10:4
Eph. 6:11
16 Mat. 12:50
Col. 3:11
16 John 6:63
17 Rom. 8:9
17 Or, let him be
17 Gal. 5:6
17 Is. 65:17
18 Rom. 5:10
Eph. 2:16
Col. 1:20
19 Rom. 3:24
19 Gr. *put in us*
20 Job 33:23
Eph. 6:20
20 ch. 6:1
21 Is. 53:6, 9
Gal. 3:13
21 Rom. 1:17
& 10:3

CHAP. 6
AD 60
1 1 Cor. 3:9
1 ch. 5:20
1 Heb. 12:15

Is. 49:8   2
Rom. 14:13   3
1 Cor. 9:12
Gr. *commending,*   4
ch. 4:2
1 Cor. 4:1   4
ch. 11:23   5
Or, *in tossings to*   5
and fro
ch. 7:14   7
1 Cor. 2:4   7
ch. 10:4   7
Eph. 6:11
ch. 4:2 & 5:11   9
1 Cor. 4:9   9
ch. 1:9
Ps. 118:18   9
ch. 7:3   11
ch. 12:15   12
1 Cor. 4:14   13
Deut. 7:2, 3   14
1 Cor. 5:9
1 Sam. 5:2, 3   14
1 Ki. 18:21
1 Cor. 3:16   16
Eph. 2:21
Ex. 29:45   16
Jer. 31:33
Is. 52:11   17
Rev. 18:4
Jer. 31:1, 9   18
Rev. 21:7

CHAP. 7
AD 60
1 John 3:3   1

The comfort of Titus' report

2 Receive us; we have wronged no man, we have corrupted no man, ᴿwe have defrauded no man.

3 I speak not *this* to condemn *you:* for ᴿI have said before, that ye are in our hearts to die and live with *you.*

4 ᴿGreat *is* my boldness of speech toward you, ᴿgreat *is* my glorying of you: ᴿI am filled with comfort, I am exceeding joyful in all our tribulation.

5 For, ᴿwhen we were come into Măç-ē-dō′-nĭ-ă, our flesh had no rest, but ᴿwe were troubled on every side; ᴿwithout *were* fightings, within *were* fears.

6 Nevertheless ᴿGod, that comforteth those that are cast down, comforted us by ᴿthe coming of Titus;

7 And not by his coming only, but by the consolation wherewith he was comforted in you, when he told us your earnest desire, your mourning, your fervent mind toward me; so that I rejoiced the more.

8 For though I made you sorry with a letter, I do not repent, ᴿthough I did repent: for I perceive that the same epistle hath made you sorry, though *it were* but for a season.

9 Now I rejoice, not that ye were made sorry, but that ye sorrowed to repentance: for ye were made sorry ᴺafter a godly manner, that ye might receive damage by us in nothing.

10 For ᴿgodly sorrow worketh repentance to salvation not to be repented of: ᴿbut the sorrow of the world worketh death.

11 For behold this selfsame thing, that ye sorrowed after a godly sort, what carefulness it wrought in you, yea, *what* clearing of yourselves, yea, *what* indignation, yea, *what* fear, yea, *what* vehement desire, yea, *what* zeal, yea, *what* revenge! In all *things* ye have approved yourselves to be clear in this matter.

12 Wherefore, though I wrote unto you, *I did it* not for his cause that had done the wrong, nor for his cause that suffered wrong, ᴿbut that our care for you in the sight of God might appear unto you.

13 Therefore we were comforted in your comfort: yea, and exceedingly the more joyed we for the joy of Titus, because his spirit ᴿwas refreshed by you all.

14 For if I have boasted any thing to him of you, I am not ashamed; but as we spake all things to you in truth, even so our boasting, which *I made* before Titus, is found a truth.

15 And his ᴺinward affection is more abundant toward you, whilst he remembereth ᴿthe

obedience of you all, how with fear and trembling ye received him.

16 I rejoice therefore that ᴿI have confidence in you in all *things.*

CHAPTER 8

Exemplary giving of the Macedonians

MOREOVER, brethren, we do you to wit of the grace of God bestowed on the churches of Măç-ē-dō′-nĭ-ă;

2 How that in a great trial of affliction the abundance of their joy and ᴿtheir deep poverty abounded unto the riches of their ᴺliberality.

3 For to *their* power, I bear record, yea, and beyond *their* power *they were* willing of themselves;

4 Praying us with much entreaty that we would receive the gift, and *take upon us* ᴿthe fellowship of the ministering to the saints.

5 And *this they did,* not as we hoped, but first gave their own selves to the Lord, and unto us by the will of God.

6 Insomuch that ᴿwe desired Titus, that as he had begun, so he would also finish in you the same ᴺgrace also.

Challenge to the Corinthians

7 Therefore, as ᴿye abound in every *thing, in* faith, and utterance, and knowledge, and *in* all diligence, and *in* your love to us, *see* ᴿthat ye abound in this grace also.

8 ᴿI speak not by commandment, but by occasion of the forwardness of others, and to prove the sincerity of your love.

9 For ye know the grace of our Lord Jesus Christ, ᴿthat, though he was rich, yet for your sakes he became poor, that ye through his poverty might be rich.

10 And herein ᴿI give *my* advice: for ᴿthis is expedient for you, who have begun before, not only to do, but also to be ᴿforwardᴺ a year ago.

11 Now therefore perform the doing *of it;* that as *there was* a readiness to will, so *there may be* a performance also out of that which ye have.

12 For ᴿif there be first a willing mind, *it is* accepted according to that a man hath, *and* not according to that he hath not.

13 For *I mean* not that other men be eased, and ye burdened:

14 But by an equality, *that* now at this time your abundance *may be a supply* for their want, that their abundance also may be *a supply* for your want: that there may be equality:

15 As it is written, [R]He that *had gathered* much had nothing over; and he that *had gathered* little had no lack.

The coming messengers

16 But thanks *be* to God, which put the same earnest care into the heart of Titus for you.

17 For indeed he accepted [R]the exhortation; but being more forward, of his own accord he went unto you.

18 And we have sent with him [R]the brother, whose praise *is* in the gospel throughout all the churches;

19 And not *that* only, but who was also [R]chosen of the churches to travel with us with this [N]grace, which is administered by us [R]to the glory of the same Lord, and *declaration of* your ready mind:

20 Avoiding this, that no man should blame us in this abundance which is administered by us:

21 [R]Providing for honest things, not only in the sight of the Lord, but also in the sight of men.

22 And we have sent with them our brother, whom we have oftentimes proved diligent in many things, but now much more diligent, upon the great confidence which [N]*I have* in you.

23 Whether *any do inquire* of Titus, *he is* my partner and fellowhelper concerning you: or our brethren *be inquired of, they are* [R]the messengers of the churches, *and* the glory of Christ.

24 Wherefore shew ye to them, and before the churches, the proof of your love, and of our [R]boasting on your behalf.

CHAPTER 9

Paul's guarded confidence

FOR as touching [R]the ministering to the saints, it is superfluous for me to write to you:

2 For I know [R]the forwardness of your mind, [R]for which I boast of you to them of Măç-ē-dō′-nĭ-ă, that [R]Ă-<u>ch</u>aī′-ă was ready a year ago; and your zeal hath provoked very many.

3 [R]Yet have I sent the brethren, lest our boasting of you should be in vain in this behalf; that, as I said, ye may be ready:

4 Lest haply if they of Măç-ē-dō′-nĭ-ă come with me, and find you unprepared, we (that we say not, ye) should be ashamed in this same confident boasting.

5 Therefore I thought it necessary to exhort the brethren, that they would go before unto you, and make up beforehand your [N]bounty, [N]whereof ye had notice before, that the same might be ready, as *a matter of* bounty, and not as *of* covetousness.

Proper attitude for giving

6 [R]But this *I say*, He which soweth sparingly shall reap also sparingly; and he which soweth bountifully shall reap also bountifully.

7 Every man according as he purposeth in his heart, *so let him give;* [R]not grudgingly, or of necessity: for [R]God loveth a cheerful giver.

8 [R]And God *is* able to make all grace abound toward you; that ye, always having all sufficiency in all *things,* may abound to every good work:

9 (As it is written, [R]He hath dispersed abroad; he hath given to the poor: his righteousness remaineth for ever.

Benefits of benevolence

10 Now he that [R]ministereth seed to the sower both minister bread for *your* food, and multiply your seed sown, and increase the fruits of your [R]righteousness;)

11 Being enriched in every thing to all [NN]bountifulness, [R]which causeth through us thanksgiving to God.

12 For the administration of this service not only [R]supplieth the want of the saints, but is abundant also by many thanksgivings unto God;

13 Whiles by the experiment of this ministration they [R]glorify God for your professed subjection unto the gospel of Christ, and for *your* liberal [R]distribution unto them, and unto all *men;*

14 And by their prayer for you, which long after you for the exceeding [R]grace of God in you.

15 Thanks *be* unto God [R]for his unspeakable gift.

CHAPTER 10

Accusation of worldliness countered

NOW [R]I Paul myself beseech you by the meekness and gentleness of Christ, [R]who [N]in presence *am* base among you, but being absent am bold toward you:

2 But I beseech *you,* [R]that I may not be bold when I am present with that confidence, wherewith I think to be bold against some, which [N]think of us as if we walked according to the flesh.

Center reference column

CHAP. **8**
AD 60

15 Ex. 16:18
17 ver. 6
18 ch. 12:18
19 1 Cor. 16:3, 4
19 Or, *gift,*
ver. 4, 6, 7
ch. 9:8
19 ch. 4:15
21 Rom. 12:17
Phil. 4:8
1 Pet. 2:12
22 Or, he hath
23 Phil. 2:25
24 ch. 7:14 & 9:2

CHAP. **9**
AD 60

1 Acts 11:29
Rom. 15:26
1 Cor. 16:1
ch. 8:4
Gal. 2:10
2 ch. 8:19
2 ch. 8:24
2 ch. 8:10
3 ch. 8:6, 17

Gr. *blessing,*   5
Gen. 33:11
1 Sam. 25:27
2 Ki. 5:15
Or, *which hath*   5
been so much
spoken of before
Prov. 11:24   6
Deut. 15:7   7
Ex. 35:5   7
Prov. 11:25
Rom. 12:8
ch. 8:12
Prov. 11:24   8
Phil. 4:19
Ps. 112:9   9
Is. 55:10   10
Hos. 10:12   10
Mat. 6:1
Or, *liberality*   11
Gr. *simplicity*   11
ch. 1:11   11
ch. 8:14   12
Mat. 5:16   13
Heb. 13:16   13
ch. 8:1   14
Jas. 1:17   15

CHAP. **10**
AD 60

Rom. 12:1   1
ch. 12:5   1
Or, *in outward*   1
appearance
1 Cor. 4:21   2
ch. 13:2, 10
Or, *reckon*   2

3 For though we walk in the flesh, we do not war after the flesh:

4 ([R]For the weapons [R]of our warfare *are* not carnal, but [R]mighty [N]through God [R]to the pulling down of strong holds;)

5 [R]Casting down [N]imaginations, and every high thing that exalteth itself against the knowledge of God, and bringing into captivity every thought to the obedience of Christ;

6 [R]And having in a readiness to revenge all disobedience, when [R]your obedience is fulfilled.

Basis of Paul's boasting

7 [R]Do ye look on things after the outward appearance? [R]If any man trust to himself that he is Christ's, let him of himself think this again, that, as he *is* Christ's, even so *are* [R]we Christ's.

8 For though I should boast somewhat more [R]of our authority, which the Lord hath given us for edification, and not for your destruction, [R]I should not be ashamed:

9 That I may not seem as if I would terrify you by letters.

10 For *his* letters, [N]say they, *are* weighty and powerful; but [R]*his* bodily presence *is* weak, and *his* [R]speech contemptible.

11 Let such an one think this, that, such as we are in word by letters when we are absent, such *will we be* also in deed when we are present.

12 [R]For we dare not make ourselves of the number, or compare ourselves with some that commend themselves: but they measuring themselves by themselves, and comparing themselves among themselves, [N]are not wise.

13 [R]But we will not boast of things without *our* measure, but according to the measure of the [N]rule which God hath distributed to us, a measure to reach even unto you.

14 For we stretch not ourselves beyond *our measure,* as though we reached not unto you: [R]for we are come as far as to you also in *preaching* the gospel of Christ:

15 Not boasting of things without *our* measure, *that is,* [R]of other men's labours; but having hope, when your faith is increased, that we shall be [N]enlarged by you according to our rule abundantly,

16 To preach the gospel in the *regions* beyond you, *and* not to boast in another man's [N]line of things made ready to our hand.

17 [R]But he that glorieth, let him glory in the Lord.

18 For [R]not he that commendeth himself is approved, but [R]whom the Lord commendeth.

CHAPTER 11

Paul's jealousy for the Corinthians

WOULD to God ye could bear with me a little in [R]my folly: and indeed [N]bear with me.

2 For I am [R]jealous over you with godly jealousy: for [R]I have espoused you to one husband, [R]that I may present *you* [R]as a chaste virgin to Christ.

3 But I fear, lest by any means, as [R]the serpent beguiled Eve through his subtilty, so your minds [R]should be corrupted from the simplicity that is in Christ.

4 For if he that cometh preacheth another Jesus, whom we have not preached, or *if* ye receive another spirit, which ye have not received, or [R]another gospel, which ye have not accepted, ye might well bear [N]with *him.*

5 For I suppose [R]I was not a whit behind the very chiefest apostles.

6 But though [R]*I be* rude in speech, yet not [R]in knowledge; but [R]we have been throughly made manifest among you in all things.

Paul accuses his opponents

7 Have I committed an offence in abasing myself that ye might be exalted, because I have preached to you the gospel of God freely?

8 I robbed other churches, taking wages *of them,* to do you service.

9 And when I was present with you, and wanted, [R]I was chargeable to no man: for that which was lacking to me [R]the brethren which came from Măc-ē-dō'-nĭ-ă supplied: and in all *things* I have kept myself [R]from being burdensome unto you, and *so* will I keep *myself.*

10 [R]As the truth of Christ is in me, [R]no[N] man shall stop me of this boasting in the regions of Ă-chāi'-ă.

11 Wherefore? [R]because I love you not? God knoweth.

12 But what I do, that I will do, [R]that I may cut off occasion from them which desire occasion; that wherein they glory, they may be found even as we.

13 For such [R]*are* false apostles, [R]deceitful workers, transforming themselves into the apostles of Christ.

14 And no marvel; for Satan himself is transformed into [R]an angel of light.

15 Therefore *it is* no great thing if his ministers also be transformed as the ministers of righteousness; [R]whose end shall be according to their works.

Paul's satirical argument

16 I say again, Let no man think me a fool; if otherwise, yet as a fool ᴺreceive me, that I may boast myself a little.

17 That which I speak, ᴿI speak *it* not after the Lord, but as it were foolishly, in this confidence of boasting.

18 Seeing that many glory after the flesh, I will glory also.

19 For ye suffer fools gladly, ᴿseeing ye *yourselves* are wise.

20 For ye suffer, ᴿif a man bring you into bondage, if a man devour *you*, if a man take *of you*, if a man exalt himself, if a man smite you on the face.

21 I speak as concerning reproach, ᴿas though we had been weak. Howbeit ᴿwhereinsoever any is bold, (I speak foolishly,) I am bold also.

22 Are they Hebrews? ᴿso *am* I. Are they Israelites? so *am* I. Are they the seed of Abraham? so *am* I.

23 Are they ministers of Christ? (I speak as a fool) I *am* more; ᴿin labours more abundant, ᴿin stripes above measure, in prisons more frequent, ᴿin deaths oft.

24 Of the Jews five times received I ᴿforty *stripes* save one.

25 Thrice was I ᴿbeaten with rods, ᴿonce was I stoned, thrice I ᴿsuffered shipwreck, a night and a day I have been in the deep;

26 *In* journeyings often, *in* perils of waters, *in* perils of robbers, ᴿ*in* perils by *mine own* countrymen, ᴿ*in* perils by the heathen, *in* perils in the city, *in* perils in the wilderness, *in* perils in the sea, *in* perils among false brethren;

27 In weariness and painfulness, ᴿin watchings often, ᴿin hunger and thirst, in fastings often, in cold and nakedness.

28 Beside those things that are without, that which cometh upon me daily, ᴿthe care of all the churches.

29 ᴿWho is weak, and I am not weak? who is offended, and I burn not?

30 If I must needs glory, ᴿI will glory of the things which concern mine infirmities.

31 ᴿThe God and Father of our Lord Jesus Christ, ᴿwhich is blessed for evermore, knoweth that I lie not.

32 ᴿIn Damascus the governor under Ăr′-ĕ-tăs the king kept the city of the Dăm′-ăs-çēnĕs with a garrison, desirous to apprehend me:

33 And through a window in a basket was I let down by the wall, and escaped his hands.

CHAP. **11**
AD 60
16 Or, *suffer*
17 1 Cor. 7:6
19 1 Cor. 4:10
20 Gal. 2:4
21 ch. 10:10
21 Phil. 3:4
22 Acts 22:3
Rom. 11:1
Phil. 3:5
23 1 Cor. 15:10
23 Acts 9:16
23 1 Cor. 15:30
24 Deut. 25:3
25 Acts 16:22
25 Acts 14:19
25 Acts 27:41
26 Acts 9:23
26 Acts 14:5
27 Acts 20:31
27 1 Cor. 4:11
28 Acts 20:18
Rom. 1:14
29 1 Cor. 8:13
30 ch. 12:5
31 Rom. 1:9
Gal. 1:20
1 Thes. 2:5
31 Rom. 9:5
32 Acts 9:24

CHAP. **12**	
AD 60	
Gr. *For*	1
I will come	
Rom. 16:7	2
Gal. 1:22	
Acts 22:17	2
Luke 23:43	4
Or, *possible*	4
ch. 11:30	4
ch. 11:16	6
See Ezek. 28:24	7
Gal. 4:13	
Job 2:7	7
Luke 13:16	
Deut. 3:23	8
Mat. 26:44	
ch. 11:30	9
1 Pet. 4:14	9
Rom. 5:3	10
ch. 7:4	
ch. 13:4	10
ch. 11:1, 16	11
ch. 11:5	11
Gal. 2:6-8	
1 Cor. 3:7	11
Eph. 3:8	
Rom. 15:18	12
1 Cor. 9:2	
ch. 4:2	
1 Cor. 1:7	13
1 Cor. 9:12	13
ch. 11:9	
ch. 11:7	13
ch. 13:1	14
Acts 20:33	14
1 Cor. 10:33	
1 Cor. 4:14	14

CHAPTER 12

Marks of a true apostle

IT is not expedient for me doubtless to glory. ᴺI will come to visions and revelations of the Lord.

2 I knew a man ᴿin Christ above fourteen years ago, (whether in the body, I cannot tell; or whether out of the body, I cannot tell: God knoweth;) such an one ᴿcaught up to the third heaven.

3 And I knew such a man, (whether in the body, or out of the body, I cannot tell: God knoweth;)

4 How that he was caught up into ᴿparadise, and heard unspeakable words, which it is not ᴺlawful for a man to utter.

5 Of such an one will I glory: ᴿyet of myself I will not glory, but in mine infirmities.

6 For ᴿthough I would desire to glory, I shall not be a fool; for I will say the truth: but *now* I forbear, lest any man should think of me above that which he seeth me *to be*, or *that* he heareth of me.

7 And lest I should be exalted above measure through the abundance of the revelations, there was given to me a ᴿthorn in the flesh, ᴿthe messenger of Satan to buffet me, lest I should be exalted above measure.

8 ᴿFor this thing I besought the Lord thrice, that it might depart from me.

9 And he said unto me, My grace is sufficient for thee: for my strength is made perfect in weakness. Most gladly therefore ᴿwill I rather glory in my infirmities, ᴿthat the power of Christ may rest upon me.

10 Therefore ᴿI take pleasure in infirmities, in reproaches, in necessities, in persecutions, in distresses for Christ's sake: ᴿfor when I am weak, then am I strong.

11 I am become ᴿa fool in glorying; ye have compelled me: for I ought to have been commended of you: for ᴿin nothing am I behind the very chiefest apostles, though ᴿI be nothing.

12 ᴿTruly the signs of an apostle were wrought among you in all patience, in signs, and wonders, and mighty deeds.

13 ᴿFor what is it wherein ye were inferior to other churches, except *it be* that ᴿI myself was not burdensome to you? forgive me ᴿthis wrong.

Paul's purpose

14 ᴿBehold, the third time I am ready to come to you; and I will not be burdensome to you: for ᴿI seek not yours, but you: ᴿfor the

children ought not to lay up for the parents, but the parents for the children.

15 And I will very gladly spend and be spent ᴿfor ᴺyou; though ᴿthe more abundantly I love you, the less I be loved.

16 But be it so, ᴿI did not burden you: nevertheless, being crafty, I caught you with guile.

17 ᴿDid I make a gain of you by any of them whom I sent unto you?

18 ᴿI desired Titus, and with *him* I sent a ᴿbrother. Did Titus make a gain of you? walked we not in the same spirit? *walked we* not in the same steps?

19 ᴿAgain, think ye that we excuse ourselves unto you? ᴿwe speak before God in Christ: ᴿbut *we do* all things, dearly beloved, for your edifying.

20 For I fear, lest, when I come, I shall not find you such as I would, and *that* ᴿI shall be found unto you such as ye would not: lest *there be* debates, envyings, wraths, strifes, backbitings, whisperings, swellings, tumults:

21 *And* lest, when I come again, my God ᴿwill humble me among you, and *that* I shall bewail many ᴿwhich have sinned already, and have not repented of the uncleanness and ᴿfornication and lasciviousness which they have committed.

CHAPTER 13

Final warnings

THIS *is* ᴿthe third *time* I am coming to you. ᴿIn the mouth of two or three witnesses shall every word be established.

2 ᴿI told you before, and foretell you, as if I were present, the second time; and being absent now I write to them ᴿwhich heretofore have sinned, and to all other, that, if I come again, ᴿI will not spare:

3 Since ye seek a proof of Christ ᴿspeaking

CHAP. 12	
AD 60	
15 John 10:11	
ch. 1:6	
Col. 1:24	
2 Tim. 2:10	
15 Gr. *your souls*	
15 1 Cor. 6:12, 13	
16 ch. 11:9	
17 ch. 7:2	
18 ch. 8:6, 16	
18 ch. 8:18	
19 ch. 5:12	
19 Rom. 9:1	
ch. 11:31	
19 1 Cor. 10:33	
20 1 Cor. 4:21	
21 ch. 2:1, 4	
21 ch. 13:2	
21 1 Cor. 5:1	
CHAP. 13	
AD 60	
1 ch. 12:14	
1 Num. 35:30	
Deut. 17:6	
Mat. 18:16	
John 8:17	
Heb. 10:28	
2 ch. 10:2	
2 ch. 12:21	
2 ch. 1:23	
3 Mat. 10:20	
1 Cor. 5:4	
1 Cor. 9:2	3
Phil. 2:7, 8	4
1 Pet. 3:18	
Rom. 6:4	4
ch. 10:3, 4	4
Or, *with him*	4
Rom. 8:10	5
Gal. 4:19	
1 Cor. 9:27	5
ch. 6:9	7
1 Cor. 4:10	9
ch. 11:30	
1 Thes. 3:10	9
1 Cor. 4:21	10
ch. 12:20, 21	
Rom. 12:16, 18	11
Rom. 15:33	11
Rom. 16:16	12
1 Cor. 16:20	
1 Thes. 5:26	
1 Pet. 5:14	
Rom. 16:24	14
Phil. 2:1	14

in me, which to you-ward is not weak, but is mighty ᴿin you.

4 ᴿFor though he was crucified through weakness, yet ᴿhe liveth by the power of God. For ᴿwe also are weak ᴺin him, but we shall live with him by the power of God toward you.

Call for self-examination

5 Examine yourselves, whether ye be in the faith; prove your own selves. Know ye not your own selves, ᴿhow that Jesus Christ is in you, except ye be ᴿreprobates?

6 But I trust that ye shall know that we are not reprobates.

7 Now I pray to God that ye do no evil; not that we should appear approved, but that ye should do that which is honest, though ᴿwe be as reprobates.

8 For we can do nothing against the truth, but for the truth.

9 For we are glad, ᴿwhen we are weak, and ye are strong: and this also we wish, ᴿ*even* your perfection.

10 ᴿTherefore I write these things being absent, lest being present I should use sharpness, according to the power which the Lord hath given me to edification, and not to destruction.

Final comments and benediction

11 Finally, brethren, farewell. Be perfect, be of good comfort, ᴿbe of one mind, live in peace; and the God of love ᴿand peace shall be with you.

12 ᴿGreet one another with an holy kiss.

13 All the saints salute you.

14 ᴿThe grace of the Lord Jesus Christ, and the love of God, and ᴿthe communion of the Holy Ghost, *be* with you all. Ä'-mĕn.

The second *epistle* to the Corinthians was written from Philippi, *a city* of Măç-ē-dō'-nĭ-à, by Titus and Lucas.

THE EPISTLE OF PAUL THE APOSTLE

TO THE

GALATIANS

The Epistle to the Galatians has been aptly called "the charter of Christian liberty." Its author is undoubtedly Paul, for the glimpse it affords into the attitudes, reactions, and experiences of the Apostle is too intimate to have been fabricated by another. The Judaizers advocated that fidelity to the Mosaic law and circumcision were necessary for justification and Christian maturity. They fought against a direct approach to

Gentiles in the Christian mission, and depreciated Paul's apostolic position, claiming that the Apostle himself still preached the necessity of circumcision (5:11). Paul denounced the error vehemently and passionately vindicated his authority in this letter, alternately stern and tender in its defense of the liberty of the Christian. Many have argued that it was addressed to those Christians of southern Galatia converted during Paul's

first missionary journey. On this hypothesis, the Epistle is Paul's earliest, written prior to the Council of Jerusalem, (Acts 15), about A.D. 49, from Antioch in Syria or during the journey from Antioch to Jerusalem. Others, stressing affinities between the Epistles of Galatians and Romans, view it as written during the third missionary journey, from Ephesus or the region of Macedonia, sometime during A.D. 53 and 57, and directed to converts of northern Galatia won during the second missionary journey. But whichever theory of origin is followed,

the clear note of grace vibrates throughout the Epistle.

OUTLINE OF THE BOOK:
  I. Salutation and Occasion for Writing 1:1 – 9
 II. Paul's Authority and the Authenticity of His Message 1:10 – 2:21
III. Doctrinal Development of Liberty in Christ 3:1 – 4:31
 IV. Exhortations to Liberty in Christ 5:1 – 6:10
  V. Postscript on Sacrificial Living 6:11 – 18

CHAPTER 1

Salutation

PAUL, an apostle, (not of men, neither by man, but ᴿby Jesus Christ, and God the Father, ᴿwho raised him from the dead;)

2 And all the brethren ᴿwhich are with me, ᴿunto the churches of Galatia:

3 ᴿGrace *be* to you and peace from God the Father, and *from* our Lord Jesus Christ,

4 ᴿWho gave himself for our sins, that he might deliver us ᴿfrom this present evil world, according to the will of God and our Father:

5 To whom *be* glory for ever and ever. Ä'-mĕn.

Paul's astonishment

6 I marvel that ye are so soon removed ᴿfrom him that called you into the grace of Christ unto another gospel:

7 ᴿWhich is not another; but there be some ᴿthat trouble you, and would pervert the gospel of Christ.

8 But though ᴿwe, or an angel from heaven, preach any other gospel unto you than that which we have preached unto you, let him be accursed.

9 As we said before, so say I now again, If any *man* preach any other gospel unto you ᴿthan that ye have received, let him be accursed.

10 For ᴿdo I now ᴿpersuade men, or God? or ᴿdo I seek to please men? for if I yet pleased men, I should not be the servant of Christ.

The divine origin of Paul's call

11 ᴿBut I certify you, brethren, that the gospel which was preached of me is not after man.

12 For ᴿI neither received it of man, neither was I taught *it,* but ᴿby the revelation of Jesus Christ.

13 For ye have heard of my conversation in time past in the Jews' religion, how that ᴿbeyond measure I persecuted the church of God, and ᴿwasted it:

14 And profited in the Jews' religion above

CHAP. 1	
AD 58	
1 Acts 9:6	
Tit. 1:3	
1 Acts 2:24	
2 Phil. 2:22	
2 1 Cor. 16:1	
3 1 Thes. 1:1	
4 Mat. 20:28	
Rom. 4:25	
Tit. 2:14	
4 Heb. 2:5	
1 John 5:19	
6 ch. 5:8	
7 2 Cor. 11:4	
7 Acts 15:1	
2 Cor. 2:17	
8 1 Cor. 16:22	
9 Deut. 4:2	
Prov. 30:6	
Rev. 22:18	
10 1 Thes. 2:4	
10 1 Sam. 24:7	
Mat. 28:14	
10 1 Thes. 2:4	
Jas. 4:4	
11 1 Cor. 15:1	
12 1 Cor. 15:1	
12 Eph. 3:3	
13 Acts 9:1	
1 Tim. 1:13	
13 Acts 8:3	
Gr. *equals in years*	14
Acts 26:9	14
Phil. 3:6	
Jer. 9:14	14
Mat. 15:2	
Mark 7:5	
Is. 49:1, 5	15
2 Cor. 4:6	16
Acts 9:15	16
Eph. 3:8	
Mat. 16:17	16
Eph. 6:12	
Acts 9:26	18
Or, *returned*	18
1 Cor. 9:5	19
Mat. 13:55	19
Rom. 9:1	20
Acts 9:30	21
1 Thes. 2:14	22
Rom. 16:7	22
CHAP. 2	
AD 52	
Acts 15:2	1
Acts 15:12	2
Or, *severally*	2
Phil. 2:16	2
1 Thes. 3:5	
Acts 15:1	4
2 Cor. 11:26	
ch. 3:25	4
ch. 4:3, 9	4
ver. 14	5

many my ᴺequals in mine own nation, ᴿbeing more exceedingly zealous ᴿof the traditions of my fathers.

15 But when it pleased God, ᴿwho separated me from my mother's womb, and called *me* by his grace,

16 ᴿTo reveal his Son in me, that ᴿI might preach him among the heathen; immediately I conferred not with ᴿflesh and blood:

17 Neither went I up to Jerusalem to them which were apostles before me; but I went into Arabia, and returned again unto Damascus.

18 Then after three years ᴿI ᴺwent up to Jerusalem to see Peter, and abode with him fifteen days.

19 But ᴿother of the apostles saw I none, save ᴿJames the Lord's brother.

20 Now the things which I write unto you, ᴿbehold, before God, I lie not.

21 ᴿAfterwards I came into the regions of Syria and Cĭ-lĭç'-ĭ-ă;

22 And was unknown by face ᴿunto the churches of Judæa which ᴿwere in Christ:

23 But they had heard only, That he which persecuted us in times past now preacheth the faith which once he destroyed.

24 And they glorified God in me.

CHAPTER 2

Why Paul went to Jerusalem

THEN fourteen years after ᴿI went up again to Jerusalem with Barnabas, and took Titus with *me* also.

2 And I went up by revelation, ᴿand communicated unto them that gospel which I preach among the Gentiles, but ᴺprivately to them which were of reputation, lest by any means ᴿI should run, or had run, in vain.

3 But neither Titus, who was with me, being a Greek, was compelled to be circumcised:

4 And that because of ᴿfalse brethren unawares brought in, who came in privily to spy out our ᴿliberty which we have in Christ Jesus, ᴿthat they might bring us into bondage:

5 To whom we gave place by subjection, no, not for an hour; that ᴿthe truth of the gospel might continue with you.

6 But of these [R]who seemed to be somewhat, (whatsoever they were, it maketh no matter to me: [R]God accepteth no man's person:) for they who seemed *to be somewhat* [R]in conference added nothing to me:

7 But contrariwise, [R]when they saw that the gospel of the uncircumcision [R]was committed unto me, as *the gospel* of the circumcision *was* unto Peter;

8 (For he that wrought effectually in Peter to the apostleship of the circumcision, [R]the same was [R]mighty in me toward the Gentiles:)

9 And when James, Cē'-phăs, and John, who seemed to be [R]pillars, perceived [R]the grace that was given unto me, they gave to me and Barnabas the right hands of fellowship; that we *should go* unto the heathen, and they unto the circumcision.

10 Only *they would* that we should remember the poor; [R]the same which I also was forward to do.

Paul's rebuke of Peter

11 [R]But when Peter was come to Ăn'-tĭ-ŏch, I withstood him to the face, because he was to be blamed.

12 For before that certain came from James, [R]he did eat with the Gentiles: but when they were come, he withdrew and separated himself, fearing them which were of the circumcision.

13 And the other Jews dissembled likewise with him; insomuch that Barnabas also was carried away with their dissimulation.

14 But when I saw that they walked not uprightly according to [R]the truth of the gospel, I said unto Peter [R]before *them* all, [R]If thou, being a Jew, livest after the manner of Gentiles, and not as do the Jews, why compellest thou the Gentiles to live as do the Jews?

15 [R]We *who are* Jews by nature, and not [R]sinners of the Gentiles,

16 [R]Knowing that a man is not justified by the works of the law, but [R]by the faith of Jesus Christ, even we have believed in Jesus Christ, that we might be justified by the faith of Christ, and not by the works of the law: for [R]by the works of the law shall no flesh be justified.

17 But if, while we seek to be justified by Christ, we ourselves also are found [R]sinners, *is* therefore Christ the minister of sin? God forbid.

18 For if I build again the things·which I destroyed, I make myself a transgressor.

19 For I [R]through the law [R]am dead to the law, that I might [R]live unto God.

20 I am [R]crucified with Christ: nevertheless I

live; yet not I, but Christ liveth in me: and the life which I now live in the flesh [R]I live by the faith of the Son of God, [R]who loved me, and gave himself for me.

21 I do not frustrate the grace of God: for [R]if righteousness *come* by the law, then Christ is dead in vain.

CHAPTER 3

Justification by faith

O FOOLISH Galations, [R]who hath bewitched you, that ye should not obey [R]the truth, before whose eyes Jesus Christ hath been evidently set forth, crucified among you?

2 This only would I learn of you, Received ye [R]the Spirit by the works of the law, [R]or by the hearing of faith?

3 Are ye so foolish? [R]having begun in the Spirit, are ye now made perfect by [R]the flesh?

4 [R]Have ye suffered [N]so many things in vain? if *it be* yet in vain.

5 He therefore that ministereth to you the Spirit, and worketh miracles among you, *doeth he it* by the works of the law, or by the hearing of faith?

6 Even as [R]Abraham believed God, and it was [N]accounted to him for righteousness.

7 Know ye therefore that [R]they which are of faith, the same are the children of Abraham.

8 And [R]the scripture, foreseeing that God would justify the heathen through faith, preached before the gospel unto Abraham, *saying,* [R]In thee shall all nations be blessed.

9 So then they which be of faith are blessed with faithful Abraham.

10 For as many as are of the works of the law are under the curse: for it is written, [R]Cursed *is* every one that continueth not in all things which are written in the book of the law to do them.

11 But [R]that no man is justified by the law in the sight of God, *it is* evident: for, [R]The just shall live by faith.

12 And [R]the law is not of faith: but, [R]The man that doeth them shall live in them.

13 [R]Christ hath redeemed us from the curse of the law, being made a curse for us: for it is written, [R]Cursed *is* every one that hangeth on a tree:

14 [R]That the blessing of Abraham might come on the Gentiles through Jesus Christ; that we might receive [R]the promise of the Spirit through faith.

The promise to Abraham

15 Brethren, I speak after the manner of men; [R]Though *it be* but a man's [N]covenant,

yet *if it be* confirmed, no man disannulleth, or addeth thereto.

16 Now ᴿto Abraham and his seed were the promises made. He saith not, And to seeds, as of many; but as of one, And to thy seed, which is ᴿChrist.

17 And this I say, *that* the covenant, that was confirmed before of God in Christ, the law, ᴿwhich was four hundred and thirty years after, cannot disannul, ᴿthat it should make the promise of none effect.

18 For if ᴿthe inheritance *be* of the law, ᴿit is no more of promise: but God gave *it* to Abraham by promise.

The purpose of the law

19 Wherefore then *serveth* the law? ᴿIt was added because of transgressions, till the seed should come to whom the promise was made; *and it was* ᴿordained by angels in the hand ᴿof a mediator.

20 Now a mediator is not *a mediator* of one, ᴿbut God is one.

21 *Is* the law then against the promises of God? God forbid: for if there had been a law given which could have given life, verily righteousness should have been by the law.

22 But the scripture hath concluded ᴿall under sin, ᴿthat the promise by faith of Jesus Christ might be given to them that believe.

23 But before faith came, we were kept under the law, shut up unto the faith which should afterwards be revealed.

24 Wherefore ᴿthe law was our schoolmaster *to bring us* unto Christ, ᴿthat we might be justified by faith.

25 But after that faith is come, we are no longer under a schoolmaster.

26 For ye ᴿare all the children of God by faith in Christ Jesus.

27 For ᴿas many of you as have been baptized into Christ ᴿhave put on Christ.

28 ᴿThere is neither Jew nor Greek, there is neither bond nor free, there is neither male nor female: for ye are all ᴿone in Christ Jesus.

29 And ᴿif ye *be* Christ's, then are ye Abraham's seed, and ᴿheirs according to the promise.

CHAPTER 4

Redemption of those under the law

NOW I say, *That* the heir, as long as he is a child, differeth nothing from a servant, though he be lord of all;

2 But is under tutors and governors until the time appointed of the father.

3 Even so we, when we were children, ᴿwere in bondage under the ᴺelements of the world:

4 But ᴿwhen the fulness of the time was come, God sent forth his Son, ᴿmade ᴿof a woman, ᴿmade under the law,

5 ᴿTo redeem them that were under the law, ᴿthat we might receive the adoption of sons.

6 And because ye are sons, God hath sent forth ᴿthe Spirit of his Son into your hearts, crying, Abba, Father.

7 Wherefore thou art no more a servant, but a son; ᴿand if a son, then an heir of God through Christ.

Appeal against bondage to the law

8 Howbeit then, ᴿwhen ye knew not God, ᴿye did service unto them which by nature are no gods.

9 But now, ᴿafter that ye have known God, or rather are known of God, ᴿhow turn ye ᴺagain to ᴿthe weak and beggarly ᴺelements, whereunto ye desire again to be in bondage?

10 ᴿYe observe days, and months, and times, and years.

11 I am afraid of you, ᴿlest I have bestowed upon you labour in vain.

12 Brethren, I beseech you, be as I *am;* for I *am* as ye *are:* ᴿye have not injured me at all.

13 Ye know how ᴿthrough infirmity of the flesh I preached the gospel unto you at the first.

14 And my temptation which was in my flesh ye despised not, nor rejected; but received me ᴿas an angel of God, ᴿ*even* as Christ Jesus.

15 ᴺWhere is then the blessedness ye spake of? for I bear you record, that, if *it had been* possible, ye would have plucked out your own eyes, and have given them to me.

16 Am I therefore become your enemy, because I tell you the truth?

17 They ᴿzealously affect you, *but* not well; yea, they would exclude ᴺyou, that ye might affect them.

18 But *it is* good to be zealously affected always in *a* good *thing,* and not only when I am present with you.

19 ᴿMy little children, of whom I travail in birth again until Christ be formed in you,

20 I desire to be present with you now, and to change my voice; for ᴺI stand in doubt of you.

Allegory of Abraham's sons

21 Tell me, ye that desire to be under the law, do ye not hear the law?

22 For it is written, that Abraham had two

sons, ᴿthe one by a bondmaid, ᴿthe other by a freewoman

23 But he *who was* of the bondwoman ᴿwas born after the flesh; ᴿbut he of the freewoman *was* by promise.

24 Which things are an allegory: for these are the two ᴺcovenants; the one from the mount ᴿSī′-naî, ᴺwhich gendereth to bondage, which is Agar.

25 For this Agar is mount Sī′-naî in Arabia, and ᴺanswereth to Jerusalem which now is, and is in bondage with her children.

26 But ᴿJerusalem which is above is free, which is the mother of us all.

27 For it is written, ᴿRejoice, *thou* barren that bearest not; break forth and cry, thou that travailest not: for the desolate hath many more children than she which hath an husband.

28 Now we, brethren, as Isaac was, are ᴿthe children of promise.

29 But as then ᴿhe that was born after the flesh persecuted him *that was born* after the Spirit, ᴿeven so *it is* now.

30 Nevertheless what saith ᴿthe scripture? ᴿCast out the bondwoman and her son: for ᴿthe son of the bondwoman shall not be heir with the son of the freewoman.

31 So then, brethren, we are not children of the bondwoman, ᴿbut of the free.

CHAPTER 5

Freedom through Christ

STAND fast therefore in ᴿthe liberty wherewith Christ hath made us free, and be not entangled again ᴿwith the yoke of bondage.

2 Behold, I Paul say unto you, that ᴿif ye be circumcised, Christ shall profit you nothing.

3 For I testify again to every man that is circumcised, ᴿthat he is a debtor to do the whole law.

4 ᴿChrist is become of no effect unto you, whosoever of you are justified by the law; ᴿye are fallen from grace.

5 For we through the Spirit ᴿwait for the hope of righteousness by faith.

6 For ᴿin Jesus Christ neither circumcision availeth any thing, nor uncircumcision; but ᴿfaith which worketh by love.

7 Ye ᴿdid run well; ᴿwho ᴺdid hinder you that ye should not obey the truth?

8 This persuasion *cometh* not of him ᴿthat calleth you.

9 ᴿA little leaven leaveneth the whole lump.

10 ᴿI have confidence in you through the Lord, that ye will be none otherwise minded:

CHAP. **4**	
AD 58	
22	Gen. 16:15
22	Gen. 21:2
23	Rom. 9:7, 8
23	Heb. 11:11
24	Or, *testaments*
24	Deut. 33:2
24	Gr. *Sina*
25	Or, *is in the same rank with*
26	Is. 2:2
27	Is. 54:1
28	Acts 3:25
29	Gen. 21:9
29	ch. 5:11
30	ch. 3:8, 22
30	Gen. 21:10
30	John 8:35
31	John 8:36

CHAP. **5**	
AD 58	
1	Rom. 6:18
1	Acts 15:10
2	Acts 15:1
3	ch. 3:10
4	Rom. 9:31
4	Heb. 12:15
5	Rom. 8:24
6	Col. 3:11
6	1 Thes. 1:3
7	1 Cor. 9:24
7	ch. 3:1
7	Or, *who did drive you back*
8	ch. 1:6
9	1 Cor. 5:6
10	2 Cor. 2:3

ch. 1:7	10
2 Cor. 10:6	10
ch. 6:12	11
1 Cor. 15:30	11
1 Cor. 1:23	11
Josh. 7:25	12
Acts 15:1, 2	12
1 Cor. 8:9	13
1 Cor. 9:19	13
Mat. 7:12	14
Jas. 2:8	
Mat. 22:39	14
Rom. 6:12	16
Or, *fulfil not*	16
Rom. 7:23	17
Rom. 7:15	17
Rom. 6:14	18
Eph. 5:3	19
1 Cor. 6:9	21
John 15:2	22
Eph. 5:9	
Col. 3:12	22
Rom. 15:14	22
1 Cor. 13:7	22
1 Tim. 1:9	23
Rom. 6:6	24
1 Pet. 2:11	
Or, *passions*	24
Rom. 8:4, 5	25
Phil. 2:3	26

CHAP. **6**	
AD 58	
Rom. 14:1	1
Or, *although*	1
1 Cor. 2:15	1
1 Cor. 4:21	1
1 Cor. 7:5	1
Rom. 15:1	2
1 Thes. 5:14	
Jas. 2:8	2
Rom. 12:3	3
1 Cor. 8:2	

but ᴿhe that troubleth you ᴿshall bear his judgment, whosoever he be.

11 ᴿAnd I, brethren, if I yet preach circumcision, ᴿwhy do I yet suffer persecution? then is ᴿthe offence of the cross ceased.

12 ᴿI would they were even cut off ᴿwhich trouble you.

Stand fast in liberty

13 For, brethren, ye have been called unto liberty; only ᴿuse not liberty for an occasion to the flesh, but ᴿby love serve one another.

14 For ᴿall the law is fulfilled in one word, *even* in this; ᴿThou shalt love thy neighbour as thyself.

15 But if ye bite and devour one another, take heed that ye be not consumed one of another.

16 *This* I say then, ᴿWalk in the Spirit, and ᴺye shall not fulfil the lust of the flesh.

17 For ᴿthe flesh lusteth against the Spirit, and the Spirit against the flesh: and these are contrary the one to the other: ᴿso that ye cannot do the things that ye would.

18 But ᴿif ye be led of the Spirit, ye are not under the law.

19 Now ᴿthe works of the flesh are manifest, which are *these;* Adultery, fornication, uncleanness, lasciviousness,

20 Idolatry, witchcraft, hatred, variance, emulations, wrath, strife, seditions, heresies,

21 Envyings, murders, drunkenness, revellings, and such like: of the which I tell you before, as I have also told *you* in time past, that ᴿthey which do such things shall not inherit the kingdom of God.

22 But ᴿthe fruit of the Spirit is love, joy, peace, longsuffering, ᴿgentleness, ᴿgoodness, ᴿfaith,

23 Meekness, temperance: ᴿagainst such there is no law.

24 And they that are Christ's ᴿhave crucified the flesh with the ᴺaffections and lusts.

25 ᴿIf we live in the Spirit, let us also walk in the Spirit.

26 ᴿLet us not be desirious of vain glory, provoking one another, envying one another.

CHAPTER 6

Fulfilling the law of Christ

BRETHREN, ᴿifᴺ a man be overtaken in a fault, ye ᴿwhich are spiritual, restore such as one ᴿin the spirit of meekness; considering thyself, ᴿlest thou also be tempted.

2 ᴿBear ye one another's burdens, and so fulfil ᴿthe law of Christ.

3 For ᴿif a man think himself to be some-

thing, when ᴿhe is nothing, he deceiveth himself.

4 But ᴿlet every man prove his own work, and then shall he have rejoicing in himself alone, and ᴿnot in another.

5 For ᴿevery man shall bear his own burden.

6 ᴿLet him that is taught in the word communicate unto him that teacheth in all good things.

7 ᴿBe not deceived; ᴿGod is not mocked: for ᴿwhatsoever a man soweth, that shall he also reap.

8 ᴿFor he that soweth to his flesh shall of the flesh reap corruption; but he that soweth to the Spirit shall of the Spirit reap life everlasting.

9 And ᴿlet us not be weary in well doing: for in due season we shall reap, ᴿif we faint not.

10 ᴿAs we have therefore opportunity, ᴿlet us do good unto all *men,* especially unto them who are of ᴿthe household of faith.

Glory in the cross of Christ

11 Ye see how large a letter I have written unto you with mine own hand.

CHAP. 6	
AD 58	
3	2 Cor. 3:5
4	1 Cor. 11:28
4	Luke 18:11
5	Rom. 2:6
	1 Cor. 3:8
6	1 Cor. 9:11
7	1 Cor. 6:9
7	Job 13:9
7	Rom. 2:6
	2 Cor. 9:6
8	Job 4:8
9	1 Cor. 15:58
9	Mat. 24:13
	Rev. 2:10
10	John 9:4
10	Tit. 3:8
10	Eph. 2:19
ch. 2:3, 14	12
Phil. 3:18	12
ch. 5:11	12
Phil. 3:3, 7	14
Or, *whereby*	14
Rom. 6:6	14
1 Cor. 7:19	15
2 Cor. 5:17	15
Ps. 125:5	16
Phil. 3:16	16
Rom. 2:29	16
2 Cor. 1:5	17
2 Tim. 4:22	18

12 As many as desire to make a fair shew in the flesh, ᴿthey constrain you to be circumcised; ᴿonly lest they should ᴿsuffer persecution for the cross of Christ.

13 For neither they themselves who are circumcised keep the law; but desire to have you circumcised, that they may glory in your flesh.

14 ᴿBut God forbid that I should glory, save in the cross of our Lord Jesus Christ, ᴺby whom the world is ᴿcrucified unto me, and I unto the world.

15 For ᴿin Christ Jesus neither circumcision availeth any thing, nor uncircumcision, but ᴿa new creature.

16 ᴿAnd as many as walk ᴿaccording to this rule, peace *be* on them, and mercy, and upon ᴿthe Israel of God.

17 From henceforth let no man trouble me: for ᴿI bear in my body the marks of the Lord Jesus.

18 Brethren, ᴿthe grace of our Lord Jesus Christ *be* with your spirit. Ä′-mĕn.

Unto the Galatians written from Rome.

THE EPISTLE OF PAUL THE APOSTLE
TO THE
EPHESIANS

The Epistle to the Ephesians claims Pauline authorship (1:1, 3:1), and early tradition supports this claim. Only since the nineteenth century have objections been raised, and these on stylistic and theological grounds. Some find it is too different from Romans, First and Second Corinthians, and Galatians to be authentic; others find it too similar theologically to Paul's other writings, particularly to Colossians in peculiarity of style, to be accounted more than the work of an imitator (a disciple of Paul?) attempting to introduce the Apostle's thought. The tone is more contemplative and formal than Paul's other letters. It reflects no specific locale, and the author appears to be personally unknown to his readers (cf. 1:15, 3:2, 4:21). Prominent doctrines include the Church as the Body of Christ, the foundational nature of the apostles and prophets, predestination, the believer's relation "in Christ," and the demolishing of the distinction between Jew and Gentile. Citing the fact that the leading manuscripts lack the title "to the Ephesians," the Epistle

has been identified as being the Epistle from Laodicea mentioned in Colossians 4:16. The common view maintains that it was a circular letter composed by the apostle shortly after the writing of Colossians and directed, not only to Ephesus, but also to churches in Asia Minor of which Laodicea was one. It was delivered by Tychicus (6:21), who also carried the Apostle's Epistle to the Colossians (Col. 4:7), and was written during Paul's imprisonment (3:1, 4:1, 6:20), probably in Rome in the year A.D. 61 or 62.

OUTLINE OF THE BOOK:
  I. Greeting 1:1–2
 II. Doxology 1:3–14
III. Thanksgiving and Prayer 1:15–23
IV. Doctrinal Section 2:1–3:21
 V. Practical Section 4:1–6:20
VI. Conclusion 6:21–24

CHAPTER 1
Salutation

PAUL, an apostle of Jesus Christ ᴿby the will of God, ᴿto the saints which are at ĕph′-ĕ-sŭs, ᴿand to the faithful in Christ Jesus:

CHAP. 1	
AD 64	
1	2 Cor. 1:1
1	Rom. 1:7
1	1 Cor. 4:17
Gal. 1:3	2
2 Cor. 1:3	3

2 ᴿGrace *be* to you, and peace, from God our Father, and *from* the Lord Jesus Christ.

Spiritual blessings

3 ᴿBlessed *be* the God and Father of our Lord Jesus Christ, who hath blessed us with

all spiritual blessings in heavenly ᴺplaces in Christ:

4 According as ᴿhe hath chosen us in him ᴿbefore the foundation of the world, that we should ᴿbe holy and without blame before him in love:

5 ᴿHaving predestinated us unto ᴿthe adoption of children by Jesus Christ to himself, ᴿaccording to the good pleasure of his will,

6 To the praise of the glory of his grace, ᴿwherein he hath made us accepted in ᴿthe beloved.

7 ᴿIn whom we have redemption through his blood, the forgiveness of sins, according to ᴿthe riches of his grace;

8 Wherein he hath abounded toward us in all wisdom and prudence;

9 ᴿHaving made known unto us the mystery of his will, according to his good pleasure ᴿwhich he hath purposed in himself:

10 That in the dispensation of ᴿthe fulness of times ᴿhe might gather together in one ᴿall things in Christ, both which are in ᴺheaven, and which are on earth; even in him:

11 ᴿIn whom also we have obtained an inheritance, ᴿbeing predestinated according to ᴿthe purpose of him who worketh all things after the counsel of his own will:

12 ᴿThat we should be to the praise of his glory, ᴿwho first ᴺtrusted in Christ.

13 In whom ye also trusted, after that ye heard ᴿthe word of truth, the gospel of your salvation: in whom also after that ye believed, ᴿye were sealed with that holy Spirit of promise,

14 ᴿWhich is the earnest of our inheritance ᴿuntil the redemption of ᴿthe purchased possession, ᴿunto the praise of his glory.

Thanksgiving

15 Wherefore I also, ᴿafter I heard of your faith in the Lord Jesus, and love unto all the saints,

16 ᴿCease not to give thanks for you, making mention of you in my prayers;

17 That ᴿthe God of our Lord Jesus Christ, the Father of glory, ᴿmay give unto you the spirit of wisdom and revelation ᴺin the knowledge of him:

18 ᴿThe eyes of your understanding being enlightened; that ye may know what is ᴿthe hope of his calling, and what the riches of the glory of his inheritance in the saints,

19 And what is the exceeding greatness of his power to us-ward who believe, ᴿaccording to the working ᴺof his mighty power,

20 Which he wrought in Christ, when ᴿhe raised him from the dead, and ᴿset him at his own right hand in the heavenly places,

CHAP. 1	
AD 64	
3 Or, things	
4 Rom. 8:28	
4 1 Pet. 1:2	
4 Luke 1:75	
5 Rom. 8:29	
5 John 1:12	
5 1 Cor. 1:21	
6 Rom. 3:24	
6 Mat. 3:17	
7 Heb. 9:12	
7 Rom. 3:24	
9 Rom. 16:25	
9 2 Tim. 1:9	
10 Gal. 4:4	
10 1 Cor. 3:22	
10 Col. 1:20	
10 Gr. the heavens	
11 Rom. 8:17	
11 ver. 5	
11 Is. 46:10	
12 2 Thes. 2:13	
12 Jas. 1:18	
12 Or, hoped	
13 John 1:17	
13 2 Cor. 1:22	
14 2 Cor. 5:5	
14 Rom. 8:23	
14 Acts 20:28	
14 1 Pet. 2:9	
15 Col. 1:4	
16 Rom. 1:9	
17 John 20:17	
17 Col. 1:9	
17 Or, for the acknowledgment	
18 Acts 26:18	
18 ch. 2:12	
19 Col. 2:12	
19 Gr. of the might of his power	
20 Acts 2:24	
20 Ps. 110:1	
Phil. 2:9, 10	21
Rom. 8:38	21
Mat. 28:18	22
Heb. 2:7	22
Rom. 12:5	23
Col. 2:9	23
1 Cor. 12:6	23

CHAP. 2	
AD 64	
Col. 2:13	1
ch. 4:18	1
Col. 1:21	2
ch. 6:12	2
Col. 3:6	2
1 Pet. 4:3	3
Gal. 5:16	3
Gr. the wills	3
Ps. 51:5	3
Rom. 10:12	4
Rom. 5:6, 8	5
Rom. 6:4, 5	5
Or, by whose grace	5
ch. 1:20	6
Tit. 3:4	7
2 Tim. 1:9	8
Rom. 4:16	8
Mat. 16:17	8
Is. 19:25	10
Or, prepared	10
Col. 2:11	11
Col. 1:21	12
Ezek. 13:9	12
Rom. 9:4, 8	12
1 Thes. 4:13	12
Gal. 4:8	12
Gal. 3:28	13
Acts 2:39	13
Mic. 5:5	14
John 10:16	14

21 ᴿFar above all ᴿprincipality, and power, and might, and dominion, and every name that is named, not only in this world, but also in that which is to come:

22 And ᴿhath put all things under his feet, and gave him ᴿto be the head over all things to the church,

23 ᴿWhich is his body, ᴿthe fulness of him ᴿthat filleth all in all.

CHAPTER 2

The natural state

AND ᴿyou hath he quickened, ᴿwho were dead in trespasses and sins;

2 ᴿWherein in time past ye walked according to the course of this world, according to ᴿthe prince of the power of the air, the spirit that now worketh in ᴿthe children of disobedience:

3 ᴿAmong whom also we all had our conversation in times past in ᴿthe lusts of our flesh, fulfilling ᴺthe desires of the flesh and of the mind; and ᴿwere by nature the children of wrath, even as others.

4 But God, ᴿwho is rich in mercy, for his great love wherewith he loved us,

5 ᴿEven when we were dead in sins, hath ᴿquickened us together with Christ, (ᴺby grace ye are saved;)

6 And hath raised us up together, and made us sit together ᴿin heavenly places in Christ Jesus:

7 That in the ages to come he might shew the exceeding riches of his grace in ᴿhis kindness toward us through Christ Jesus.

8 ᴿFor by grace are ye saved ᴿthrough faith; and that not of yourselves: ᴿit is the gift of God:

9 Not of works, lest any man should boast.

10 For we are ᴿhis workmanship, created in Christ Jesus unto good works, which God hath before ᴺordained that we should walk in them.

11 Wherefore remember, that ye being in time past Gentiles in the flesh, who are called Uncircumcision by that which is called ᴿthe Circumcision in the flesh made by hands;

12 ᴿThat at that time ye were without Christ, ᴿbeing aliens from the commonwealth of Israel, and strangers from ᴿthe covenants of promise, ᴿhaving no hope, ᴿand without God in the world:

Reconciliation through the cross

13 ᴿBut now in Christ Jesus ye who sometimes were ᴿfar off are made nigh by the blood of Christ.

14 For ᴿhe is our peace, ᴿwho hath made

both one, and hath broken down the middle wall of partition *between us;*

15 ᴿHaving abolished ᴿin his flesh the enmity, *even* the law of commandments *contained* in ordinances; for to make in himself of twain one ᴿnew man, *so* making peace;

16 And that he might ᴿreconcile both unto God in one body by the cross, ᴿhaving slain the enmity ᴺthereby:

17 And came ᴿand preached peace to you which were afar off, and to ᴿthem that were nigh.

18 For ᴿthrough him we both have access ᴿby one Spirit unto the Father.

19 Now therefore ye are no more strangers and foreigners, but ᴿfellowcitizens with the saints, and of ᴿthe household of God;

20 And are ᴿbuilt ᴿupon the foundation of the ᴿapostles and prophets, Jesus Christ himself being ᴿthe chief corner *stone;*

21 In whom all the building fitly framed together groweth unto ᴿan holy temple in the Lord:

22 ᴿIn whom ye also are builded together for an habitation of God through the Spirit.

CHAPTER 3

Minister to the Gentiles

FOR this cause I Paul, ᴿthe prisoner of Jesus Christ ᴿfor you Gentiles,

2 If ye have heard of ᴿthe dispensation of the grace of God ᴿwhich is given me to youward:

3 ᴿHow that by revelation ᴿhe made known unto me the mystery; (as I wrote ᴺafore in few words,

4 Whereby, when ye read, ye may understand my knowledge in the mystery of Christ)

5 ᴿWhich in other ages was not made known unto the sons of men, as it is now revealed unto his holy apostles and prophets by the Spirit;

6 That the Gentiles ᴿshould be fellowheirs, and of the same body, and partakers of his promise in Christ by the gospel:

7 ᴿWhereof I was made a minister, ᴿaccording to the gift of the grace of God given unto me by ᴿthe effectual working of his power.

8 Unto me, ᴿwho am less than the least of all saints, is this grace given, that I should preach among the Gentiles ᴿthe unsearchable riches of Christ;

9 And to make all *men* see what *is* the fellowship of the mystery, ᴿwhich from the beginning of the world hath been hid in God, ᴿwho created all things by Jesus Christ:

10 ᴿTo the intent that now ᴿunto the principalites and powers in heavenly *places* ᴿmight

CHAP. **2**	
AD 64	
15	Col. 2:14
15	Col. 1:22
15	Gal. 6:15
16	Col. 1:20-22
16	Rom. 6:6
16	Or, *in himself*
17	Is. 57:19
17	Ps. 148:14
18	John 10:9
18	1 Cor. 12:13
19	Phil. 3:20
19	Gal. 6:10
20	1 Pet. 2:4
20	Mat. 16:18
20	1 Cor. 12:28
20	Ps. 118:22
21	1 Cor. 3:17
22	1 Pet. 2:5

CHAP. **3**	
AD 64	
1	Acts 21:33
1	Col. 1:24
2	Rom. 1:5
2	Acts 9:15
3	Acts 22:17
3	Rom. 16:25
3	Or, *a little before*
5	Rom. 16:25
6	Gal. 3:28
7	Rom. 15:16
7	Rom. 1:5
7	Rom. 15:18
8	1 Cor. 15:9
8	Col. 1:27
9	Rom. 16:25
9	Ps. 33:6
10	1 Pet. 1:12
10	Col. 1:16
10	1 Tim. 3:16

Heb. 4:16	12
Phil. 1:14	13
2 Cor. 1:6	13
ch. 1:10	15
Phil. 4:19	16
Col. 1:11	16
Rom. 7:22	16
John 14:23	17
Col. 1:23	17
ch. 1:18	18
Rom. 10:3	18
ch. 1:23	19
Rom. 16:25	20
1 Cor. 2:9	20
Col. 1:29	20
Rom. 11:36	21

CHAP. **4**	
AD 64	
Philem. 1, 9	1
Or, *in the Lord*	1
Phil. 1:27	1
Acts 20:19	2
Col. 3:14	3
Rom. 12:5	4
1 Cor. 1:13	5
Jude 3	5
Heb. 6:6	5
Mal. 2:10	6
Rom. 11:36	6
1 Cor. 12:11	7
Ps. 68:18	8
Judg. 5:12	8
Or, *a multitide of captives*	8
John 3:13	9
Acts 1:9	10
Acts 2:33	10
Or, *fulfil*	10

be known by the church the manifold wisdom of God,

11 According to the eternal purpose which he purposed in Christ Jesus our Lord:

12 In whom we have boldness and access ᴿwith confidence by the faith of him.

13 ᴿWherefore I desire that ye faint not at my tribulations for you, ᴿwhich is your glory.

Pastoral prayer for the Ephesians

14 For this cause I bow my knees unto the Father of our Lord Jesus Christ,

15 Of whom ᴿthe whole family in heaven and earth is named,

16 That he would grant you, ᴿaccording to the riches of his glory, ᴿto be strengthened with might by his Spirit in ᴿthe inner man;

17 ᴿThat Christ may dwell in your hearts by faith; that ye, ᴿbeing rooted and grounded in love,

18 ᴿMay be able to comprehend with all saints ᴿwhat *is* the breadth, and length, and depth, and height;

19 And to know the love of Christ, which passeth knowledge, that ye might be filled ᴿwith all the fulness of God.

20 Now ᴿunto him that is able to do exceeding abundantly ᴿabove all that we ask or think, ᴿaccording to the power that worketh in us,

21 ᴿUnto him *be* glory in the church by Christ Jesus throughout all ages, world without end. Ä'-mĕn.

CHAPTER 4

Appeal for spiritual unity

I THEREFORE, ᴿthe prisoner ᴺof the Lord, beseech you that ye ᴿwalk worthy of the vocation wherewith ye are called,

2 ᴿWith all lowliness and meekness, with longsuffering, forbearing one another in love;

3 Endeavouring to keep the unity of the Spirit ᴿin the bond of peace.

4 ᴿ*There is* one body, and one Spirit, even as ye are called in one hope of your calling;

5 ᴿOne Lord, ᴿone faith, ᴿone baptism,

6 ᴿOne God and Father of all, who *is* above all, and ᴿthrough all, and in you all.

7 But ᴿunto every one of us is given grace according to the measure of the gift of Christ.

8 Wherefore he saith, ᴿWhen he ascended up on high, ᴿhe led ᴺcaptivity captive, and gave gifts unto men.

9 ᴿ(Now that he ascended, what is it but that he also descended first into the lower parts of the earth?

10 He that descended is the same also ᴿthat ascended up far above all heavens, ᴿthat he might ᴺfill all things.)

11 ᴿAnd he gave some, apostles; and some, prophets; and some, ᴿevangelists; and some, ᴿpastors and ᴿteachers;

12 ᴿFor the perfecting of the saints, for the work of the ministry, ᴿfor the edifying of ᴿthe body of Christ:

13 Till we all come in the unity of the faith, ᴿand of the knowledge of the Son of God, unto ᴿa perfect man, unto the measure of the ᴺstature of the fulness of Christ:

14 That we *henceforth* be no more ᴿchildren, ᴿtossed to and fro, and carried about with every ᴿwind of doctrine, by the sleight of men, *and* cunning craftiness, ᴿwhereby they lie in wait to deceive;

15 But ᴿspeakingᴺ the truth in love, ᴿmay grow up into him in all things, ᴿwhich is the head, *even* Christ:

16 ᴿFrom whom the whole body fitly joined together and compacted by that which every joint supplieth, according to the effectual working in the measure of every part, maketh increase of the body unto the edifying of itself in love.

Appeal to put off the old nature

17 This I say therefore, and testify in the Lord, that ᴿye henceforth walk not as other Gentiles walk, ᴿin the vanity of their mind,

18 ᴿHaving the understanding darkened, ᴿbeing alienated from the life of God through the ignorance that is in them, because of the ᴿblindnessᴺ of their heart:

19 ᴿWho being past feeling ᴿhave given themselves over unto lasciviousness, to work all uncleanness with greediness.

20 But ye have not so learned Christ;

21 If so be that ye have heard him, and have been taught by him, as the truth is in Jesus:

22 That ye ᴿput off concerning ᴿthe former conversation the old man, which is corrupt according to the deceitful lusts;

23 And ᴿbe renewed in the spirit of your mind;

24 And that ye ᴿput on the new man, which after God is created in righteousness and ᴺtrue holiness.

25 Wherefore putting away lying, ᴿspeak every man truth with his neighbour: for ᴿwe are members one of another.

26 ᴿBe ye angry, and sin not: let not the sun go down upon your wrath:

27 ᴿNeither give place to the devil.

28 Let him that stole steal no more: but rather ᴿlet him labour, working with *his* hands the thing which is good, that he may have ᴺto give ᴿto him that needeth.

29 ᴿLet no corrupt communication proceed out of your mouth, but ᴿthat which is good ᴺto

the use of edifying, ᴿthat it may minister grace unto the hearers.

30 And ᴿgrieve not the holy Spirit of God, whereby ye are sealed unto the day of ᴿredemption.

31 ᴿLet all bitterness, and wrath, and anger, and clamour, and ᴿevil speaking, be put away from you, ᴿwith all malice:

32 And ᴿbe ye kind one to another, tenderhearted, ᴿforgiving one another, even as God for Christ's sake hath forgiven you.

CHAPTER 5

Imitators of God

BE ᴿye therefore followers of God, as dear children;

2 And ᴿwalk in love, ᴿas Christ also hath loved us, and hath given himself for us an offering and a sacrifice to God ᴿfor a sweet-smelling savour.

Works of light and darkness

3 But ᴿfornication, and all uncleanness, or covetousness, ᴿlet it not be once named among you, as becometh saints;

4 ᴿNeither filthiness, nor foolish talking, nor jesting, ᴿwhich are not covenient: but rather giving of thanks.

5 For this ye know, that ᴿno whoremonger, nor unclean person, nor covetous man, ᴿwho is an idolater, ᴿhath any inheritance in the kingdom of Christ and of God.

6 ᴿLet no man deceive you with vain words: for because of these things ᴿcometh the wrath of God upon the children of ᴺdisobedience.

7 Be not ye therefore partakers with them.

8 ᴿFor ye were sometimes darkness, but now ᴿare ye light in the Lord: walk as children of light:

9 (For ᴿthe fruit of the Spirit *is* in all goodness and righteousness and truth;)

10 ᴿProving what is acceptable unto the Lord.

11 And have no fellowship with ᴿthe unfruitful works of darkness, but rather ᴿreprove *them.*

12 ᴿFor it is a shame even to speak of those things which are done of them in secret.

13 But ᴿall things that are ᴺreproved are made manifest by the light: for whatsoever doth make manifest is light.

14 Wherefore ᴺhe saith, ᴿAwake thou that sleepest, and ᴿarise from the dead, and Christ shall give thee light.

"The will of the Lord"

15 ᴿSee then that ye walk circumspectly, not as fools, but as wise,

16 ᴿRedeeming the time, ᴿbecause the days are evil.

17 ᴿWherefore be ye not unwise, but ᴿunderstanding ᴿwhat the will of the Lord *is*.

18 And ᴿbe not drunk with wine, wherein is excess; but be filled with the Spirit;

19 Speaking to yourselves ᴿin psalms and hymns and spiritual songs, singing and making melody in your heart to the Lord;

20 ᴿGiving thanks always for all things unto God and the Father ᴿin the name of our Lord Jesus Christ;

Family relations and duties

21 ᴿSubmitting yourselves one to another in the fear of God.

22 ᴿWives, submit yourselves unto your own husbands, ᴿas unto the Lord.

23 For ᴿthe husband is the head of the wife, even as ᴿChrist is the head of the church: and he is the saviour of ᴿthe body.

24 Therefore as the church is subject unto Christ, so *let* the wives *be* to their own husbands ᴿin every thing.

25 ᴿHusbands, love your wives, even as Christ also loved the church, and ᴿgave himself for it;

26 That he might sanctify and cleanse it ᴿwith the washing of water by the word,

27 ᴿThat he might present it to himself a glorious church, ᴿnot having spot, or wrinkle, or any such thing; but that it should be holy and without blemish.

28 So ought men to love their wives as their own bodies. He that loveth his wife loveth himself.

29 For no man ever yet hated his own flesh; but nourisheth and cherisheth it, even as the Lord the church:

30 For ᴿwe are members of his body, of his flesh, and of his bones.

31 ᴿFor this cause shall a man leave his father and mother, and shall be joined unto his wife, and they ᴿtwo shall be one flesh.

32 This is a great mystery: but I speak concerning Christ and the church.

33 Nevertheless ᴿlet every one of you in particular so love his wife even as himself; and the wife *see* that she ᴿreverence *her* husband.

CHAPTER 6

CHILDREN, ᴿobey your parents in the Lord: for this is right.

2 ᴿHonour thy father and mother; which is the first commandment with promise;

3 That it may be well with thee, and thou mayest live long on the earth.

CHAP. **5**	
AD 64	
16	Col. 4:5
16	Eccl. 11:2
17	Col. 4:5
17	Rom. 12:2
17	1 Thes. 4:3
18	Prov. 20:1
19	Acts 16:25
20	Ps. 34:1
20	1 Pet. 2:5
21	Phil. 2:3
22	Gen. 3:16
22	ch. 6:5
23	1 Cor. 11:3
23	Col. 1:18
23	ch. 1:23
24	Tit. 2:9
25	Col. 3:19
25	Acts 20:28
26	John 3:5
27	Col. 1:22
27	S. of S. 4:7
30	Gen. 2:23
31	Mat. 19:5
31	1 Cor. 6:16
33	Col. 3:19
33	1 Pet. 3:6

CHAP. **6**	
AD 64	
1	Col. 3:20
2	Ex. 20:12

Col. 3:21	4
Gen. 18:19	4
1 Tim. 6:1	5
2 Cor. 7:15	5
Phil. 2:12	
1 Chr. 29:17	5
Col. 3:22	
Col. 3:22	6
Rom. 2:6	8
Col. 3:24	
Gal. 3:28	8
Col. 4:1	9
Or, *moderating*	9
Some read, *both your and their Master*	9
Rom. 2:11	9
2 Cor. 6:7	11
Gr. *blood and flesh*	12
Rom. 8:38	12
Luke 22:53	12
Or, *wicked spirits*	12
Or, *heavenly*	12
2 Cor. 10:4	13
ch. 5:16	13
Or, *having overcome all*	13
Is. 11:5	14
1 Pet. 1:13	
Is. 59:17	14
Is. 52:7	15
1 John 5:4	16
1 Thes. 5:8	17
Heb. 4:12	17
Luke 18:1	18
Mat. 26:41	18
Phil. 1:4	18
Acts 4:29	19
2 Cor. 3:12	19
2 Cor. 5:20	20
Or, *in a chain*	20
Or, *thereof*	20
Phil. 1:20	20

4 And, ᴿye fathers, provoke not your children to wrath: but ᴿbring them up in the nurture and admonition of the Lord.

Relations between masters and servants

5 ᴿServants, be obedient to them that are *your* masters according to the flesh, ᴿwith fear and trembling, ᴿin singleness of your heart, as unto Christ;

6 ᴿNot with eyeservice, as menpleasers; but as the servants of Christ, doing the will of God from the heart;

7 With good will doing service, as to the Lord, and not to men:

8 ᴿKnowing that whatsoever good thing any man doeth, the same shall he receive of the Lord, ᴿwhether *he be* bond or free.

9 And, ye ᴿmasters, do the same things unto them, ᴺforbearing threatening: knowing that ᴺyour Master also is in heaven; ᴿneither is there respect of persons with him.

The whole armour of God

10 Finally, my brethren, be strong in the Lord, and in the power of his might.

11 ᴿPut on the whole armour of God, that ye may be able to stand against the wiles of the devil.

12 For we wrestle not against ᴺflesh and blood, but against ᴿprincipalities, against powers, against ᴿthe rulers of the darkness of this world, against ᴺspiritual wickedness in ᴺhigh *places*.

13 ᴿWherefore take unto you the whole armour of God, that ye may be able to withstand ᴿin the evil day, and ᴺhaving done all, to stand.

14 Stand therefore, ᴿhaving your loins girt about with truth, and ᴿhaving on the breastplate of righteousness;

15 ᴿAnd your feet shod with the preparation of the gospel of peace;

16 Above all, taking ᴿthe shield of faith, wherewith ye shall be able to quench all the fiery darts of the wicked.

17 And ᴿtake the helmet of salvation, and ᴿthe sword of the Spirit, which is the word of God:

18 ᴿPraying always with all prayer and supplication in the Spirit, and ᴿwatching thereunto with all perseverance and ᴿsupplication for all saints;

19 ᴿAnd for me, that utterance may be given unto me, that I may open my mouth ᴿboldly, to make known the mystery of the gospel,

20 For which ᴿI am an ambassador ᴺin bonds: that ᴺtherein ᴿI may speak boldly, as I ought to speak.

Conclusion and benediction

21 But that ye also may know my affairs, *and* how I do, [R]Tўch'-ĭ-cŭs, a beloved brother and faithful minister in the Lord, shall make known to you all things:

22 [R]Whom I have sent unto you for the same purpose, that ye might know our affairs, and *that* he might comfort your hearts.

23 [R]Peace *be* to the brethren, and love with faith, from God the Father and the Lord Jesus Christ.

24 Grace *be* with all them that love our Lord Jesus Christ [N]in sincerity. Ā'-mĕn.

CHAP. 6	
AD 64	
21	Acts 20:4
22	Col. 4:8
1 Pet. 5:14	23
Or, *with incorruption*	24

Written from Rome unto the ĕph-ē'-ṣĭăns by Tўch'-ĭ-cŭs.

THE EPISTLE OF PAUL THE APOSTLE

TO THE

PHILIPPIANS

Paul founded the Church at Philippi, his first in Europe, during his second missionary journey (cf. Acts 16). Names mentioned in this Epistle indicate its membership was predominantly Gentile. Having aided the Apostle financially at least twice before (4:15–16), and hearing of his arrest and imprisonment, the Philippians sent Epaphroditus with a gift. Perhaps Epaphroditus was also to serve Paul personally during his confinement. But Epaphroditus became seriously ill while with the Apostle, and news of his condition reached Philippi. Paul now writes to thank the Philippians for their gift (4:18) and to commend Epaphroditus to the Church against possible criticism that he had not completed his task (2:25–30). The Apostle also takes this occasion to explain his present circumstances, to exhort steadfastness, unity, and humility, and to warn of Judaizers. Because the letter so clearly reveals the personality of the Apostle, and his authorship is so strongly attested to in early tradition, few today dispute its Pauline origin. Many consider 2:6–11 to be an early Christian hymn incorporated by Paul to substantiate his point on humility. Some view Paul writing from imprisonment in Ephesus. Yet Acts makes no reference to an Ephesian imprisonment. And the fact that the letter reflects a sense of approaching finality in the determination of Paul's case which could issue in either life or death (1:20ff.) weights the matter in favor of a Roman provenience. Philippians was probably written toward the end of Paul's first Roman imprisonment (*see* I Timothy), about A.D. 63.

OUTLINE OF THE BOOK:
    I. Salutation and Thanksgiving   1:1–8
   II. Prayer for the Philippians   1:9–11
  III. Explanation of Present Circumstances   1:12–26
  IV. Exhortations and Example   1:27–2:18
   V. Timothy and Epaphroditus   2:19–30
  VI. Warnings against Judaizers   3:1–4:1
 VII. Encouragements, Appreciations, Greetings   4:2–23

CHAPTER 1

Salutation

PAUL and Timotheus, the servants of Jesus Christ, to all the saints [R]in Christ Jesus which are at Philippi, with the bishops and deacons:

2 [R]Grace *be* unto you, and peace, from God our Father, and *from* the Lord Jesus Christ.

Prayer of thanksgiving

3 [R]I thank my God upon every [N]remembrance of you,

4 Always in every prayer of mine for you all making request with joy,

5 [R]For your fellowship in the gospel from the first day until now;

6 Being confident of this very thing, that he which hath begun [R]a good work in you [N]will perform *it* until the day of Jesus Christ:

7 Even as it is meet for me to think this of

CHAP. 1	
AD 64	
1	1 Cor. 1:2
2	1 Pet. 1:2
3	1 Cor. 1:4
3	Or, *mention*
5	Rom. 12:13
6	John 6:29
6	Or, *will finish* it
Or, *ye have me in your heart*	7
Or, *partakers with me of grace*	7
Rom. 1:9	8
Gal. 1:20	
Or, *sense*	9
Rom. 12:2	10
Or, *try*	10
Or, *differ*	10
Acts 24:16	10
1 Cor. 1:8	10
Eph. 2:10	11
Col. 1:6	
John 15:8	11

you all, because [N]I have you in my heart; inasmuch as both in my bonds, and in the defence and confirmation of the gospel, ye all are [N]partakers of my grace.

8 For [R]God is my record, how greatly I long after you all in the bowels of Jesus Christ.

9 And this I pray, that your love may abound yet more and more in knowledge and *in* all [N]judgment;

10 That [R]ye may [N]approve things that [N]are excellent; [R]that ye may be sincere and without offence [R]till the day of Christ;

11 Being filled with the fruits of righteousness, [R]which are by Jesus Christ, [R]unto the glory and praise of God.

Unexpected benefits of imprisonment

12 But I would ye should understand, brethren, that the things *which happened* unto me have fallen out rather unto the furtherance of the gospel;

13 So that my bonds ᴺin Christ are manifest ᴿin all ᴺthe palace, and ᴺin all other *places;*

14 And many of the brethren in the Lord, waxing confident by my bonds, are much more bold to speak the word without fear.

15 Some indeed preach Christ even of envy and ᴿstrife; and some also of good will:

16 The one preach Christ of contention, not sincerely, supposing to add affliction to my bonds:

17 But the other of love, knowing that I am set for the defence of the gospel.

18 What then? notwithstanding, every way, whether in pretence, or in truth, Christ is preached; and I therein do rejoice, yea, and will rejoice.

To live is Christ

19 For I know that this shall turn to my salvation ᴿthrough your prayer, and the supply of the Spirit of Jesus Christ,

20 According to my ᴿearnest expectation and *my* hope, that ᴿin nothing I shall be ashamed, but *that* ᴿwith all boldness, as always, *so* now also Christ shall be magnified in my body, whether *it be* by life, or by death.

21 For to me to live *is* Christ, and to die *is* gain.

22 But if I live in the flesh, this *is* the fruit of my labour: yet what I shall choose I wot not.

23 For ᴿI am in a strait betwixt two, having a desire to ᴿdepart, and to be with Christ; which is far better:

24 Nevertheless to abide in the flesh *is* more needful for you.

25 And ᴿhaving this confidence, I know that I shall abide and continue with you all for your furtherance and joy of faith;

26 That ᴿyour rejoicing may be more abundant in Jesus Christ for me by my coming to you again.

Exhortation to stand firm

27 Only ᴿlet your conversation be as it becometh the gospel of Christ: that whether I come and see you, or else be absent, I may hear of your affairs, that ye stand fast in one spirit, ᴿwith one mind striving together for the faith of the gospel;

28 And in nothing terrified by your adversaries: ᴿwhich is to them an evident token of perdition, ᴿbut to you of salvation, and that of God.

29 For unto you ᴿit is given in the behalf of Christ, ᴿnot only to believe on him, but also to suffer for his sake;

30 ᴿHaving the same conflict ᴿwhich ye saw in me, and now hear *to be* in me.

CHAPTER 2

The mind of Christ

IF *there be* therefore any consolation in Christ, if any comfort of love, ᴿif any fellowship of the Spirit, if any ᴿbowels and mercies,

2 ᴿFulfil ye my joy, ᴿthat ye be likeminded, having the same love, *being* of one accord, of one mind.

3 ᴿ*Let* nothing *be done* through strife or vainglory; but ᴿin lowliness of mind let each esteem other better than themselves.

4 ᴿLook not every man on his own things, but every man also on the things of others.

5 ᴿLet this mind be in you, which was also in Christ Jesus:

6 Who, ᴿbeing in the form of God, thought it not robbery to be equal with God:

7 ᴿBut made himself of no reputation, and took upon him the form ᴿof a servant, and ᴿwas made in the ᴺlikeness of men:

8 And being found in fashion as a man, he humbled himself, and ᴿbecame obedient unto death, even the death of the cross.

9 Wherefore God also ᴿhath highly exalted him, and ᴿgiven him a name which is above every name:

10 ᴿThat at the name of Jesus every knee should bow, of *things* in heaven, and *things* in earth, and *things* under the earth;

11 And ᴿthat every tongue should confess that Jesus Christ *is* Lord, to the glory of God the Father.

Exhortation to continued obedience

12 Wherefore, my beloved, ᴿas ye have always obeyed, not as in my presence only, but now much more in my absence, work out your own salvation with ᴿfear and trembling.

13 For ᴿit is God which worketh in you both to will and to do of *his* good pleasure.

14 Do all things ᴿwithout murmurings and ᴿdisputings:

15 That ye may be blameless and ᴺharmless, ᴿthe sons of God, without rebuke, ᴿin the midst of ᴿa crooked and perverse nation, among whom ᴿyeᴺ shine as lights in the world;

16 Holding forth the word of life; that ᴿI may rejoice in the day of Christ, that ᴿI have not run in vain, neither laboured in vain.

17 Yea, and if ᴿI be ᴺoffered upon the sac-

rifice Rand service of your faith, RI joy, and rejoice with you all.

18 For the same cause also do ye joy, and rejoice with me.

Timothy and Epaphroditus

19 NBut I trust in the Lord Jesus to send RTimotheus shortly unto you, that I also may be of good comfort, when I know your state.

20 For I have no man Rlikeminded, Nwho will naturally care for your state.

21 For all Rseek their own, not the things which are Jesus Christ's.

22 But ye know the proof of him, Rthat, as a son with the father, he hath served with me in the gospel.

23 Him therefore I hope to send presently, so soon as I shall see how it will go with me.

24 But RI trust in the Lord that I also myself shall come shortly.

25 Yet I supposed it necessary to send to you RĔp-ăph-rō-dī'-tŭs, my brother, and companion in labour, and Rfellowsoldier, Rbut your messenger, and Rhe that ministered to my wants.

26 RFor he longed after you all, and was full of heaviness, because that ye had heard that he had been sick.

27 For indeed he was sick nigh unto death: but God had mercy on him; and not on him only, but on me also, lest I should have sorrow upon sorrow.

28 I sent him therefore the more carefully, that, when ye see him again, ye may rejoice, and that I may be the less sorrowful.

29 Receive him therefore in the Lord with all gladness; and Rhold N such in reputation:

30 Because for the work of Christ he was nigh unto death, not regarding his life, Rto supply your lack of service toward me.

CHAPTER 3

Warning against legalism

FINALLY, my brethren, Rrejoice in the Lord. To write the same things to you, to me indeed is not grievous, but for you it is safe.

2 RBeware of dogs, beware of evil workers, Rbeware of the concision.

3 For we are Rthe circumcision, Rwhich worship God in the spirit, and Rrejoice in Christ Jesus, and have no confidence in the flesh.

4 Though RI might also have confidence in the flesh. If any other man thinketh that he hath whereof he might trust in the flesh, I more:

5 Circumcised the eighth day, of the stock of Israel, Rof the tribe of Benjamin, Ran Hebrew of the Hebrews; as touching the law, Ra Pharisee;

6 RConcerning zeal, persecuting the church; Rtouching the righteousness which is in the law, Rblameless.

7 But Rwhat things were gain to me, those I counted loss for Christ.

8 Yea doubtless, and I count all things but loss Rfor the excellency of the knowledge of Christ Jesus my Lord: for whom I have suffered the loss of all things, and do count them but dung, that I may win Christ,

9 And be found in him, not having Rmine own righteousness, which is of the law, but Rthat which is through the faith of Christ, the righteousness which is of God by faith:

10 That I may know him, and the power of his resurrection, and Rthe fellowship of his sufferings, being made conformable unto his death;

11 If by any means I might Rattain unto the resurrection of the dead.

Paul presses forward

12 Not as though I had already Rattained, either were already Rperfect: but I follow after, if that I may apprehend that for which also I am apprehended of Christ Jesus.

13 Brethren, I count not myself to have apprehended: but this one thing I do, Rforgetting those things which are behind, and Rreaching forth unto those things which are before,

14 RI press toward the mark for the prize of Rthe high calling of God in Christ Jesus.

15 Let us therefore, as many as be Rperfect, Rbe thus minded: and if in any thing ye be otherwise minded, God shall reveal even this unto you.

16 Nevertheless, whereto we have already attained, Rlet us walk Rby the same rule, let us mind the same thing.

Warning against worldliness

17 Brethren, Rbe followers together of me, and mark them which walk so as Rye have us for an ensample.

18 (For many walk, of whom I have told you often, and now tell you even weeping, that they are Rthe enemies of the cross of Christ:

19 Whose end is destruction, Rwhose God is their belly, and Rwhose glory is in their shame, Rwho mind earthly things.)

20 For Rour conversation is in heaven; Rfrom whence also we Rlook for the Saviour, the Lord Jesus Christ:

CHAP. 2	
AD 64	
17	Rom. 15:16
17	2 Cor. 7:4
	Col. 1:24
19	Or, Moreover
19	Rom. 16:21
20	Ps. 55:13
20	Or, so dear unto me
21	1 Cor. 10:24 & 13:5
	2 Tim. 4:10
22	1 Cor. 4:17
	1 Tim. 1:2
24	ch. 1:25
25	ch. 4:18
25	Philem. 2
25	2 Cor. 8:23
25	2 Cor. 11:9
26	ch. 1:8
29	1 Cor. 16:18
	1 Thes. 5:12
	1 Tim. 5:17
29	Or, honour such
30	1 Cor. 16:17

CHAP. 3	
AD 64	
1	2 Cor. 13:11
	1 Thes. 5:16
2	Gal. 5:15
2	Rom. 2:28
3	Deut. 30:6
	Jer. 4:4
3	Rom. 7:6
3	Gal. 6:14
4	2 Cor. 11:18

Rom. 11:1	5
2 Cor. 11:22	5
Acts 23:6	5
Acts 22:3	6
Rom. 10:5	6
Luke 1:6	6
Mat. 13:44	7
Is. 53:11	8
Rom. 10:3	9
Rom. 1:17	9
Rom. 6:3-5 & 8:17	10
Acts 26:7	11
1 Tim. 6:12	12
Heb. 12:23	12
Luke 9:62	13
Heb. 6:1	13
2 Tim. 4:7	14
Heb. 3:1	14
1 Cor. 2:6	15
Gal. 5:10	15
Rom. 12:16 & 15:5	16
Gal. 6:16	16
1 Cor. 11:1	17
1 Thes. 1:6	
1 Pet. 5:3	17
Gal. 1:7 & 2:21	18
2 Cor. 11:15	19
1 Tim. 6:5	19
Tit. 1:11	
Hos. 4:7	19
Gal. 6:13	
Rom. 8:5	19
Eph. 2:6	20
Col. 3:1, 3	
Acts 1:11	20
1 Cor. 1:7	20
1 Thes. 1:10	

21 [R]Who shall change our vile body, that it may be fashioned like unto his glorious body, [R]according to the working whereby he is able [R]even to subdue all things unto himself.

CHAPTER 4

Appeal for harmony, joy, and peace

THEREFORE, my brethren dearly beloved and [R]longed for, [R]my joy and crown, so [R]stand fast in the Lord, *my* dearly beloved.

2 I beseech Êu-ō'-dĭ-ăs, and beseech Sўn'-tў-chē, [R]that they be of the same mind in the Lord.

3 And I entreat thee also, true yokefellow, help those women which [R]laboured with me in the gospel, with Clement also, and *with* other my fellowlabourers, whose names *are* in [R]the book of life.

4 [R]Rejoice in the Lord alway: *and* again I say, Rejoice.

5 Let your moderation be known unto all men. [R]The Lord *is* at hand.

6 [R]Be careful for nothing; but in every thing by prayer and supplication with thanksgiving let your requests be made known unto God.

7 And [R]the peace of God, which passeth all understanding, shall keep your hearts and minds through Christ Jesus.

8 Finally, brethren, whatsoever things are true, whatsoever things *are* [N]honest, whatsoever things *are* just, whatsoever things *are* pure, whatsoever things *are* lovely, [R]whatsoever things *are* of good report; if *there be* any virtue, and if *there be* any praise, think on these things.

9 [R]Those things, which ye have both learned, and received, and heard, and seen in me, do: and [R]the God of peace shall be with you.

His joy for their liberality

10 But I rejoiced in the Lord greatly, that now at the last [R]your care of me [N]hath flour-

CHAP. 3
AD 64
21 1 Cor. 15:43
Col. 3:4
21 Eph. 1:19
21 1 Cor. 15:26

CHAP. 4
AD 64
1 ch. 1:8
1 2 Cor. 1:14
1 ch. 1:27
2 ch. 3:16
3 Rom. 16:3
3 Ex. 32:32
Ps. 69:28
Dan. 12:1
4 Rom. 12:12
1 Thes. 5:16
1 Pet. 4:13
5 Heb. 10:25
1 Pet. 4:7
6 Ps. 55:22
Prov. 16:3
Mat. 6:25
7 John 14:27
Rom. 5:1
Col. 3:15
8 Or, *venerable*
8 1 Thes. 5:22
9 ch. 3:17
9 Rom. 15:33
10 2 Cor. 11:9
10 Or, *is revived*

1 Tim. 6:6	**11**
1 Cor. 4:11	**12**
John 15:5	**13**
ch. 1:7	**14**
2 Cor. 11:8	**15**
Tit. 3:14	**17**
Or, *I have received all*	**18**
ch. 2:25	**18**
Heb. 13:16	**18**
2 Cor. 9:12	**18**
Ps. 23:1	**19**
Rom. 16:27	**20**
Gal. 1:2	**21**
ch. 1:13	**22**
Rom. 16:24	**23**

ished again; wherein ye were also careful, but ye lacked opportunity.

11 Not that I speak in respect of want: for I have learned, in whatsoever state I am, [R]therewith to be content.

12 [R]I know both how to be abased, and I know how to abound: every where and in all things I am instructed both to be full and to be hungry, both to abound and to suffer need.

13 I can do all things [R]through Christ which strengtheneth me.

14 Notwithstanding ye have well done, that [R]ye did communicate with my affliction.

15 Now ye Philippians know also, that in the beginning of the gospel, when I departed from Măç-ē-dō'-nĭ-ă, [R]no church communicated with me as concerning giving and receiving, but ye only.

16 For even in Thĕss-ă-lō-nī'-că ye sent once and again unto my necessity.

17 Not because I desire a gift: but I desire [R]fruit that may abound to your account.

18 But [N]I have all, and abound: I am full, having received [R]of ĕp-ăph-rō-dī'-tŭs the things *which were sent* from you, [R]an odour of a sweet smell, [R]a sacrifice acceptable, well-pleasing to God.

19 But my God [R]shall supply all your need [R]according to his riches in glory by Christ Jesus.

20 [R]Now unto God and our Father *be* glory for ever and ever. Ä'-mĕn.

Greetings and benediction

21 Salute every saint in Christ Jesus. The brethren [R]which are with me greet you.

22 All the saints salute you, [R]chiefly they that are of Cæsar's household.

23 [R]The grace of our Lord Jesus Christ *be* with you all. Ä'-mĕn.

It was written to the Philippians from Rome by ĕp-ăph-rō-dī'-tŭs.

THE EPISTLE OF PAUL THE APOSTLE
TO THE
COLOSSIANS

The Gospel came to Colossae probably during Paul's long stay in Ephesus (cf. Acts 19:10), though not by him directly. The Colossians had never seen his face (2:1). Epaphras probably established the Church there (1:7, 4:12–13). Later Epaphras either visited Paul in prison or was imprisoned with him (cf. Philem. 23), during which time he reported regarding conditions in the Colossian Church (1:7–8). He told of faith and love among the Christians of the Lycus valley (1:4, 8), but from Paul's response, we know that Epaphras also spoke of a heresy that was described as (1) dualistic in its metaphysics, (2) gnostic in its doctrine of salvation, (3) Jewish in many of its practices (e.g., circumcision, ordinances, dietary prohi-

bitions, calendar interest), (4) involving the worship of angels, and (5) severely ascetic. Paul writes to counter this heresy. Contrary to the teaching of dualistic gnosticism that the more deeply God penetrates the material universe the less revelatory become His actions and the more man must seek redemptive knowledge on a higher non-material plane, Paul proclaimed the cosmic Christ in whom all fulness dwells, and in whom the believer finds complete fulfilment (2:9–10). Pauline authorship, questioned in certain quarters on internal grounds only, is strongly attested by early tradition and supported by its close association with the undoubtedly authentic letter to Philemon.

Colossians was written from imprisonment (4:18), probably in Rome, and sent by Tychicus in the company of Onesimus (4:7–9). Together with Philemon, it was probably written shortly before Ephesians in the year A.D. 61 or 62.

OUTLINE OF THE BOOK:
　I. Salutation　1:1–8
　II. Prayer for the Colossians　1:9–12
　III. Exposition on the Person of Christ　1:13–2:23
　IV. Exhortations on the Christian Life　3:1–4:6
　V. Commendation and Greetings　4:7–18

CHAPTER 1

Salutation

PAUL, ᴿan apostle of Jesus Christ by the will of God, and Timotheus *our* brother,
2 To the saints ᴿand faithful brethren in Christ which are at Cŏ-lŏs′-sē: ᴿGrace *be* unto you, and peace, from God our Father and the Lord Jesus Christ.

Thanksgiving

3 ᴿWe give thanks to God and the Father of our Lord Jesus Christ, praying always for you,
4 ᴿSince we heard of your faith in Christ Jesus, and of ᴿthe love *which ye have* to all the saints,
5 For the hope ᴿwhich is laid up for you in heaven, whereof ye heard before in the word of the truth of the gospel;
6 Which is come unto you, ᴿas *it is* in all the world; and bringeth forth fruit, as *it doth* also in you, since the day ye heard *of it,* and knew ᴿthe grace of God in truth:
7 As ye also learned of ᴿĔp′-ă-phrăs our dear fellowservant, who is for you ᴿa faithful minister of Christ;
8 Who also declared unto us your ᴿlove in the Spirit.

Prayer for the Colossian church

9 ᴿFor this cause we also, since the day we heard *it,* do not cease to pray for you, and to desire ᴿthat ye might be filled with ᴿthe knowledge of his will ᴿin all wisdom and spiritual understanding;
10 ᴿThat ye might walk worthy of the Lord ᴿunto all pleasing, ᴿbeing fruitful in every good work, and increasing in the knowledge of God;
11 ᴿStrengthened with all might, according to his glorious power, ᴿunto all patience and longsuffering ᴿwith joyfulness;
12 ᴿGiving thanks unto the Father, which hath made us meet to be partakers of ᴿthe inheritance of the saints in light:
13 Who hath delivered us from ᴿthe power

CHAP. **1**	
AD 64	
1 Eph. 1:1	
2 1 Cor. 4:17	
2 Gal. 1:3	
3 1 Cor. 1:4	
Eph. 1:16	
Phil. 1:3	
4 Eph. 1:15	
4 Heb. 6:10	
5 1 Pet. 1:4	
6 Mat. 24:14	
6 Eph. 3:2	
Tit. 2:11	
7 Philem. 23	
7 2 Cor. 11:23	
1 Tim. 4:6	
8 Rom. 15:30	
9 Eph. 1:15	
9 1 Cor. 1:5	
9 Rom. 12:2	
9 Eph. 1:8	
10 Phil. 1:27	
10 1 Thes. 4:1	
10 Heb. 13:21	
11 Eph. 3:16	
11 Eph. 4:2	
11 Acts 5:41	
12 Eph. 5:20	
12 Eph. 1:11	
13 Eph. 6:12	
2 Pet. 1:11	**13**
Gr. *the Son*	**13**
of his love	
Eph. 1:7	**14**
2 Cor. 4:4	**15**
Rev. 3:14	**15**
Heb. 1:2	**16**
Eph. 1:21	**16**
Heb. 2:10	**16**
John 17:5	**17**
1 Cor. 11:3	**18**
Rev. 1:5	**18**
Or, *among*	**18**
John 1:16	**19**
Eph. 2:14	**20**
Or, *making*	**20**
2 Cor. 5:18	**20**
Eph. 1:10	**20**
Eph. 2:1	**21**
Or, *by your*	**21**
mind in	
Tit. 1:15	**21**
Eph. 2:15	**22**
Eph. 5:27	**22**
Eph. 3:17	**23**
John 15:6	**23**
Rom. 10:18	**23**
Acts 1:17	**23**
2 Cor. 7:4	**24**
Eph. 3:1, 13	**24**
2 Cor. 1:5	**24**
Eph. 1:23	**24**
Gal. 2:7	**25**
Or, *fully to*	**25**
preach, etc.	

of darkness, ᴿand hath translated *us* into the kingdom of ᴺhis dear Son:
14 ᴿIn whom we have redemption through his blood, *even* the forgiveness of sins:

Christ's preëminence

15 Who is ᴿthe image of the invisible God, ᴿthe firstborn of every creature:
16 For ᴿby him were all things created, that are in heaven, and that are in earth, visible and invisible, whether *they be* thrones, or ᴿdominions, or principalities, or powers: all things were created ᴿby him, and for him:
17 ᴿAnd he is before all things, and by him all things consist.
18 And ᴿhe is the head of the body, the church: who is the beginning, ᴿthe firstborn from the dead; that ᴺin all *things* he might have the preeminence.
19 For it pleased *the Father* that ᴿin him should all fulness dwell;
20 And, ᴿhavingᴺ made peace through the blood of his cross, ᴿby him to reconcile ᴿall things unto himself; by him, *I say,* whether *they be* things in earth, or things in heaven.
21 And you, ᴿthat were sometime alienated and enemies ᴺin *your* mind ᴿby wicked works, yet now hath he reconciled
22 ᴿIn the body of his flesh through death, ᴿto present you holy and unblameable and unreproveable in his sight:
23 If ye continue in the faith ᴿgrounded and settled, and *be* ᴿnot moved away from the hope of the gospel, which ye have heard, ᴿ*and* which was preached to every creature which is under heaven; ᴿwhereof I Paul am made a minister;

Paul's ministry and concern

24 ᴿWho now rejoice in my sufferings ᴿfor you, and fill up ᴿthat which is behind of the afflictions of Christ in my flesh for ᴿhis body's sake, which is the church:
25 Whereof I am made a minister, according to ᴿthe dispensation of God which is given to me for you, ᴺto fulfil the word of God;

26 *Even* ᴿthe mystery which hath been hid from ages and from generations, ᴿbut now is made manifest to his saints:

27 ᴿTo whom God would make known what *is* ᴿthe riches of the glory of this mystery among the Gentiles; which is Christ ᴺin you, ᴿthe hope of glory:

28 Whom we preach, ᴿwarning every man, and teaching every man in all wisdom; ᴿthat we may present every man perfect in Christ Jesus:

29 ᴿWhereunto I also labour, ᴿstriving ᴿaccording to his working, which worketh in me mightily.

CHAPTER 2

FOR I would that ye knew what great ᴿconflictᴺ I have for you, and *for* them at Lā-ŏd-ĭ-çē′-ă, and *for* as many as have not seen my face in the flesh;

2 ᴿThat their hearts might be comforted, ᴿbeing knit together in love, and unto all riches of the full assurance of understanding, ᴿto the acknowledgement of the mystery of God, and of the Father, and of Christ;

3 ᴿInᴺ whom are hid all the treasures of wisdom and knowledge.

4 And this I say, ᴿlest any man should beguile you with enticing words.

5 For ᴿthough I be absent in the flesh, yet am I with you in the spirit, joying and beholding ᴿyour order, and the ᴿstedfastness of your faith in Christ.

6 ᴿAs ye have therefore received Christ Jesus the Lord, *so* walk ye in him:

7 ᴿRooted and built up in him, and stablished in the faith, as ye have been taught, abounding therein with thanksgiving.

The canceled bond

8 Beware lest any man spoil you through philosophy and vain deceit, after ᴿthe tradition of men, after the ᴿrudimentsᴺ of the world, and not after Christ.

9 For ᴿin him dwelleth all the fulness of the Godhead bodily.

10 And ye are complete in him, ᴿwhich is the head of all ᴿprincipality and power:

11 In whom also ye are ᴿcircumcised with the circumcision made without hands, in ᴿputting off the body of the sins of the flesh by the circumcision of Christ:

12 Buried with him in baptism, wherein also ye are risen with *him* through ᴿthe faith of the operation of God, ᴿwho hath raised him from the dead.

13 And you, being dead in your sins and the uncircumcision of your flesh, hath he quick-

ened together with him, having forgiven you all trespasses;

14 ᴿBlotting out the handwriting of ordinances that was against us, which was contrary to us, and took it out of the way, nailing it to his cross;

15 *And* ᴿhaving spoiled ᴿprincipalities and powers, he made a shew of them openly, triumphing over them ᴺin it.

Old regulations outdated

16 Let no man therefore ᴿjudge you ᴿinᴺ meat, or in drink, or ᴺin respect ᴿof an holyday, or of the new moon, or of the sabbath *days:*

17 ᴿWhich are a shadow of things to come; but the body *is* of Christ.

18 Let no man ᴺbeguile you of your reward ᴺin a voluntary humility and worshipping of angels, intruding into those things which he hath not seen, vainly puffed up by his fleshly mind,

19 And not holding ᴿthe Head, from which all the body by joints and bands having nourishment ministered, and knit together, increaseth with the increase of God.

20 Wherefore if ye be ᴿdead with Christ from the ᴺrudiments of the world, ᴿwhy, as though living in the world, are ye subject to ordinances,

21 (ᴿTouch not; taste not; handle not;

22 Which all are to perish with the using;) ᴿafter the commandments and doctrines of men?

23 ᴿWhich things have indeed a shew of wisdom in will worship, and humility, and ᴺneglecting of the body; not in any honour to the satisfying of the flesh.

CHAPTER 3

The old and the new natures

IF ye then be risen with Christ, seek those things which are above, where ᴿChrist sitteth on the right hand of God.

2 Set your ᴺaffection on things above, not on things on the earth.

3 ᴿFor ye are dead, ᴿand your life is hid with Christ in God.

4 ᴿWhen Christ, *who is* ᴿour life, shall appear, then shall ye also appear with him ᴿin glory.

5 ᴿMortify therefore ᴿyour members which are upon the earth; ᴿfornication, uncleanness, inordinate affection, evil concupiscence, and covetousness, ᴿwhich is idolatry:

6 ᴿFor which things' sake the wrath of God cometh on ᴿthe children of disobedience:

CHAP. 1

AD 64

26	1 Cor. 2:7
26	2 Tim. 1:10
27	2 Cor. 2:14
27	Rom. 9:23
27	Or, *among*
27	1 Tim. 1:1
28	Acts 20:20
28	Eph. 5:27
29	1 Cor. 15:10
29	ch. 2:1
29	Eph. 1:19

CHAP. 2

AD 64

1	Phil. 1:30
1	Or, *care*
2	2 Cor. 1:6
2	ch. 3:14
2	Phil. 3:8
3	1 Cor. 1:24
3	Or, *Wherein*
4	Rom. 16:18
5	1 Thes. 2:17
5	1 Cor. 14:40
5	1 Pet. 5:9
6	1 Thes. 4:1
7	Eph. 2:21
8	Gal. 1:14
8	Gal. 4:3, 9
8	Or, *elements*
9	John 1:14
10	1 Pet. 3:22
10	ch. 1:16
11	Deut. 10:16
11	Rom. 6:6
12	Eph. 1:19
12	Acts 2:24

Eph. 2:15	14
Is. 53:12	15
Eph. 6:12	15
Or, *in himself*	15
Rom. 14:3	16
Rom. 14:2	16
Or, *for eating and drinking*	16
Or, *in part*	16
Rom. 14:5	16
Heb. 8:5	17
Or, *judge against you*	18
Gr. *being a voluntary in humility*	18
Eph. 4:15	19
Rom. 6:3, 5	20
Or, *elements*	20
Gal. 4:3, 9	20
1 Tim. 4:3	21
Tit. 1:14	22
1 Tim. 4:8	23
Or, *punishing,* or, *not sparing*	23

CHAP. 3

AD 64

Eph. 1:20	1
Or, *mind*	2
Rom. 6:2	3
2 Cor. 5:7	3
1 John 3:2	4
John 14:6	4
1 Cor. 15:43	4
Rom. 8:13	5
Rom. 6:13	5
Eph. 5:3	5
Eph. 5:5	5
Rev. 22:15	5
Eph. 2:2	6

7 ᴿIn the which ye also walked some time, when ye lived in them.

8 ᴿBut now ye also put off all these; anger, wrath, malice, blasphemy, ᴿfilthy communication out of your mouth.

9 ᴿLie not one to another, ᴿseeing that ye have put off the old man with his deeds;

10 And have put on the new *man,* which ᴿis renewed in knowledge ᴿafter the image of him that ᴿcreated him:

11 Where there is neither ᴿGreek nor Jew, circumcision nor uncircumcision, Barbarian, Sçẏth'-ĭ-ăn, bond *nor* free: ᴿbut Christ *is* all, and in all.

12 Put on therefore, ᴿas the elect of God, holy and beloved, ᴿbowels of mercies, kindness, humbleness of mind, meekness, longsuffering;

13 ᴿForbearing one another, and forgiving one another, if any man have a ᴺquarrel against any: even as Christ forgave you, so also *do* ye.

14 ᴿAnd above all these things ᴿ*put on* charity, which is the ᴿbond of perfectness.

15 And let ᴿthe peace of God rule in your hearts, ᴿto the which also ye are called ᴿin one body; and be ye thankful.

16 Let the word of Christ dwell in you richly in all wisdom; teaching and admonishing one another ᴿin psalms and hymns and spiritual songs, singing with grace your hearts to the Lord.

17 And ᴿwhatsoever ye do in word or deed, *do* all in the name of the Lord Jesus, giving thanks to God and the Father by him.

Family and servant relations

18 ᴿWives, submit yourselves unto your own husbands, ᴿas it is fit in the Lord.

19 ᴿHusbands, love *your* wives, and be not ᴿbitter against them.

20 ᴿChildren, obey *your* parents ᴿin all things: for this is well pleasing unto the Lord.

21 ᴿFathers, provoke not your children *to anger,* lest they be discouraged.

22 ᴿServants, obey ᴿin all things *your* masters ᴿaccording to the flesh; not with eyeservice, as menpleasers; but in singleness of heart, fearing God:

23 ᴿAnd whatsoever ye do, do *it* heartily, as to the Lord, and not unto men;

24 ᴿKnowing that of the Lord ye shall receive the reward of the inheritance: ᴿfor ye serve the Lord Christ.

25 But he that doeth wrong shall receive for the wrong which he hath done: and ᴿthere is no respect of persons.

CHAP. **3**	
AD 64	
7	1 Cor. 6:11
8	Eph. 4:22
8	Eph. 4:27
9	Eph. 4:25
9	Eph. 4:22
10	Rom. 12:2
10	Eph. 4:23
10	Eph. 2:10
11	Gal. 3:28
11	Eph. 1:23
12	1 Pet. 1:2
12	Gal. 5:22
13	Mark 11:25
13	Or, *complaint*
14	1 Pet. 4:8
14	1 Cor. 13
14	Eph. 4:3
15	Phil. 4:7
15	1 Cor. 7:15
15	Eph. 4:4
16	Eph. 5:19
17	1 Cor. 10:31
18	1 Pet. 3:1
18	Eph. 5:3
19	Eph. 5:25
19	Eph. 4:31
20	Eph. 6:1
20	Eph. 5:24
21	Eph. 6:4
22	Eph. 6:5
	1 Tim. 6:1
	Tit. 2:9
	1 Pet. 2:18
22	ver. 20
22	Philem. 16
23	Eph. 6:6, 7
24	Eph. 6:8
24	1 Cor. 7:22
25	Rom. 2:11
	Eph. 6:9
	1 Pet. 1:17
	Deut. 10:17

CHAP. **4**	
AD 64	
Eph. 6:9	1
Luke 18:1	2
Rom. 12:12	
ch. 2:7	2
Eph. 6:19	3
1 Cor. 16:9	3
2 Cor. 2:12	
Eph. 6:19	3
Eph. 6:20	3
Phil. 1:7	
Eph. 5:15	5
Eph. 5:16	5
Eccl. 10:12	6
Mark 9:50	6
1 Pet. 3:15	6
Eph. 6:22	8
Philem. 10	9
Acts 19:29	10
Acts 15:37	10
2 Tim. 4:11	
Philem. 23	12
Rom. 15:30	12
Or, *striving*	12
Mat. 5:48	12
1 Cor. 2:6	
Or, *filled*	12
2 Tim. 4:11	14
2 Tim. 4:10	14
Rom. 16:5	15
1 Cor. 16:19	
1 Thes. 5:27	16

CHAPTER 4

MASTERS, ᴿgive unto *your* servants that which is just and equal; knowing that ye also have a Master in heaven.

Sound practical advice

2 ᴿContinue in prayer, and watch in the same ᴿwith thanksgiving;

3 ᴿWithal praying also for us, that God would ᴿopen unto us a door of utterance, to speak ᴿthe mystery of Christ, ᴿfor which I am also in bonds:

4 That I may make it manifest, as I ought to speak.

5 ᴿWalk in wisdom toward them that are without, ᴿredeeming the time.

6 Let your speech *be* alway ᴿwith grace, ᴿseasoned with salt, ᴿthat ye may know how ye ought to answer every man.

Commendations and greetings

7 All my state shall Tẏch'-ĭ-cŭs declare unto you, *who is* a beloved brother, and a faithful minister and fellowservant in the Lord:

8 ᴿWhom I have sent unto you for the same purpose, that he might know your estate, and comfort your hearts;

9 With ᴿŌ-nĕs'-ĭ-mŭs, a faithful and beloved brother, who is *one* of you. They shall make known unto you all things which *are done* here.

10 ᴿĂr-ĭs-tär'-c̲h̲ŭs my fellowprisoner saluteth you, and ᴿMarcus, sister's son to Barnabas, (touching whom ye received commandments: if he come unto you, receive him;)

11 And Jesus, which is called Justus, who are of the circumcision. These only *are my* fellowworkers unto the kingdom of God, which have been a comfort unto me.

12 ᴿĔp'-ă-phrăs, who is *one* of you, a servant of Christ, saluteth you, always ᴿlabouringᴺ fervently for you in prayers, that ye may stand ᴿperfect and ᴺcomplete in all the will of God.

13 For I bear him record, that he hath a great zeal for you, and them *that are* in Lā-ŏd-ĭ-çē'-ă, and them in Hī-ĕr-ā'-pŏ-lĭs.

14 ᴿLuke, the beloved physician, and ᴿDē'-măs, greet you.

15 Salute the brethren which are in Lā-ŏd-ĭ-çē'-ă, and Nȳm'-phăs, and ᴿthe church which is in his house.

16 And when ᴿthis epistle is read among you, cause that it be read also in the church of the Lā-ŏd-ĭ-çē'-ăns; and that ye likewise read the *epistle* from Lā-ŏd-ĭ-çē'-ă.

17 And say to ᴿÄr-chĭp′-pŭs, Take heed to the ministry which thou hast received in the Lord, that thou fulfil it,

18 ᴿThe salutation by the hand of me Paul.

ᴿRemember my bonds. Grace *be* with you. Ä′-mĕn.

Written from Rome to the Colossians by Tўch′-ĭ-cŭs and ō-nĕs′-ĭ-mŭs.

CHAP. 4	
AD 64	
17 Philem. 2	
18 1 Cor. 16:21	
Heb. 13:3	**18**

THE FIRST EPISTLE OF PAUL THE APOSTLE
TO THE
THESSALONIANS

The Church at Thessalonica was founded by Paul on his second missionary journey (cf. Acts 17). After leaving his converts and arriving in Athens, the Apostle sent Timothy back to Thessalonica (I Thes. 3:1–3). Later Timothy returned to Paul with a report. This letter, responding to that report, interweaves (1) commendation for growth, zeal, and fidelity, (2) encouragement in face of local persecution, (3) defense of the Apostle's motives against pagan attack, (4) teaching regarding holiness of life, (5) instruction regarding the coming of the Lord, and (6) exhortation to steadfastness and patience. While nineteenth century criticism dismissed the Epistle for supposed lack of originality, and a minority today deny its authenticity on statistical grounds, both early tradition and internal evidence support Pauline authorship. No one writing in Paul's name

after his death would present the Second Coming as expected during the Apostle's lifetime (as in 4:17). The letter was written from Corinth on the second missionary journey, probably about A.D. 50–51. If a "North Galatian" view of the Galatian epistle is accepted (see Galatians), First Thessalonians is the earliest of Paul's letters.

OUTLINE OF THE BOOK:
 I. Salutation 1:1
 II. Thanksgiving and Commendation 1:2–10
 III. Apostolic Relations with the Church 2:1–3:13
 IV. Exhortations to Christian Living 4:1–12
 V. Comforting Words on the Second Coming 4:13–5:11
 VI. Concluding Exhortations and Greeting 5:12–28

CHAPTER 1
Salutation

PAUL, and ᴿSĭl-vā′-nŭs, and Timotheus, unto the church of the Thĕss-ă-lō′-nĭ-ăns *which is* in God the Father and *in* the Lord Jesus Christ: ᴿGrace *be* unto you, and peace, from God our Father, and the Lord Jesus Christ.

Thanksgiving

2 ᴿWe give thanks to God always for you all, making mention of you in our prayers;

3 ᴿRemembering without ceasing ᴿyour work of faith, ᴿand labour of love, and patience of hope in our Lord Jesus Christ, in the sight of God and our Father;

4 Knowing, brethren ᴺbeloved, ᴿyour election of God.

5 For ᴿour gospel came not unto you in word only, but also in power, and ᴿin the Holy Ghost, ᴿand in much assurance; as ye know what manner of men we were among you for your sake.

6 And ᴿye became followers of us, and of the Lord, having received the word in much affliction, ᴿwith joy of the Holy Ghost:

7 So that ye were ensamples to all that believe in Măç-ē-dō′-nĭ-ă and Ă-châi′-ă.

CHAP. 1	
AD 54	
1 1 Pet. 5:12	
1 Eph. 1:2	
2 Rom. 1:8	
3 ch. 2:13	
3 John 6:29	
3 Rom. 16:6	
4 Or, *beloved of God, your election*	
4 Col. 3:12	
4 Mark 16:20	
5 2 Cor. 6:6	
5 Heb. 2:3	
6 1 Cor. 4:16	
Phil. 3:17	
6 Acts 5:41	
Heb. 10:34	
Rom. 10:18	**8**
Rom. 1:8	**8**
2 Thes. 1:4	
ch. 2:1	**9**
1 Cor. 12:2	**9**
Gal. 4:8	
Rom. 2:7	**10**
2 Pet. 3:12	
Acts 1:11	**10**
Acts 2:24	**10**
Rom. 5:9	**10**

CHAP. 2	
AD 54	
ch. 1:5, 9	**1**
Acts 16:22	**2**
ch. 1:5	**2**
Phil. 1:30	**2**
2 Cor. 7:2	**3**
1 Cor. 7:25	**4**
Tit. 1:3	**4**

8 For from you ᴿsounded out the word of the Lord not only in Măç-ē-dō′-nĭ-ă and Ă-châi′-ă, but also ᴿin every place your faith to God-ward is spread abroad; so that we need not to speak any thing.

9 For they themselves shew of us ᴿwhat manner of entering in we had unto you, ᴿand how ye turned to God from idols to serve the living and true God;

10 And ᴿto wait for his Son ᴿfrom heaven, ᴿwhom he raised from the dead, *even* Jesus, which delivered us ᴿfrom the wrath to come.

CHAPTER 2
Paul's ministry in Thessalonica

FOR ᴿyourselves, brethren, know our entrance in unto you, that it was not in vain:

2 But even after that we had suffered before, and were shamefully entreated, as ye know, at ᴿPhilippi, ᴿwe were bold in our God to speak unto you the gospel of God ᴿwith much contention.

3 ᴿFor our exhortation *was* not of deceit, nor of uncleanness, nor in guile:

4 But as ᴿwe were allowed of God ᴿto be put in trust with the gospel, even so we speak;

R not as pleasing men, but God, R which trieth our hearts.

5 For R neither at any time used we flattering words, as ye know, nor a cloak of covetousness; R God *is* witness:

6 R Nor of men sought we glory, neither of you, nor *yet* of others, when R we might have N been R burdensome, R as the apostles of Christ.

7 But R we were gentle among you, even as a nurse cherisheth her children:

8 So being affectionately desirous of you, we were willing R to have imparted unto you, not the gospel of God only, but also R our own souls, because ye were dear unto us.

9 For ye remember, brethren, our labour and travail: for R labouring night and day, R because we would not be chargeable unto any of you, we preached unto you the gospel of God.

10 R Ye *are* witnesses, and God *also,* R how holily and justly and unblameably we behaved ourselves among you that believe:

11 As ye know how we exhorted and comforted and charged every one of you, as a father *doth* his children,

12 R That ye would walk worthy of God, R who hath called you unto his kingdom and glory.

Effects of Paul's ministry

13 For this cause also thank we God R without ceasing, because, when ye received the word of God which ye heard of us, ye received *it* R not *as* the word of men, but as it is in truth, the word of God, which effectually worketh also in you that believe.

14 For ye, brethren, became followers R of the churches of God which in Judæa are in Christ Jesus: for R ye also have suffered like things of your own countrymen, even as they *have* of the Jews:

15 R Who both killed the Lord Jesus, and R their own prophets, and have N persecuted us; and they please not God, R and are contrary to all men:

16 R Forbidding us to speak to the Gentiles that they might be saved, R to fill up their sins alway: R for the wrath is come upon them to the uttermost.

Paul's desire to visit them

17 But we, brethren, being taken from you for a short time R in presence, not in heart, endeavoured the more abundantly R to see your face with great desire.

18 Wherefore we would have come unto you, even I Paul, once and again; but R Satan hindered us.

19 For R what *is* our hope, or joy, or R crown

of N rejoicing? *Are* not even ye in the presence of our Lord Jesus Christ R at his coming?

20 For ye are our glory and joy.

CHAPTER 3

Timothy's mission and report

WHEREFORE R when we could no longer forbear, R we thought it good to be left at Athens alone;

2 And sent R Timotheus, our brother, and minister of God, and our fellowlabourer in the gospel of Christ, to establish you, and to comfort you concerning your faith:

3 R That no man should be moved by these afflictions: for yourselves know that R we are appointed thereunto.

4 R For verily, when we were with you, we told you before that we should suffer tribulation; even as it came to pass, and ye know.

5 For this cause, R when I could no longer forbear, I sent to know your faith, R lest by some means the tempter have tempted you, and R our labour be in vain.

6 R But now when Timotheus came from you unto us, and brought us good tidings of your faith and charity, and that ye have good remembrance of us always, desiring greatly to see us, R as we also *to see* you:

7 Therefore, brethren, R we were comforted over you in all our affliction and distress by your faith:

8 For now we live, if ye R stand fast in the Lord.

9 R For what thanks can we render to God again for you, for all the joy wherewith we joy for your sakes before our God;

10 R Night and day R praying exceedingly R that we might see your face, R and might perfect that which is lacking in your faith?

Paul's prayer

11 Now God himself and our Father, and our Lord Jesus Christ, R direct N our way unto you.

12 And the Lord R make you to increase and abound in love one toward another, and toward all *men,* even as we *do* toward you:

13 To the end he may R stablish your hearts unblameable in holiness before God, even our Father, at the coming of our Lord Jesus Christ R with all his saints.

CHAPTER 4

Exhortation to purity

FURTHERMORE then we N beseech you, brethren, and N exhort *you* by the Lord Jesus, R that as ye have received of us R how ye

CHAP. 2
AD 54

4 Gal. 1:10
4 Prov. 17:3
5 2 Cor. 2:17
5 Rom. 1:9
6 1 Tim. 5:17
6 1 Cor. 9:4
6 Or, *used authority*
6 2 Cor. 11:9
6 1 Cor. 9:1
7 1 Cor. 2:3
8 Rom. 1:11 & 15:29
8 2 Cor. 12:15
9 Acts 20:34
9 2 Cor. 3:8
9 2 Cor. 12:13
10 ch. 1:5
10 2 Cor. 7:2
12 Col. 1:10
12 1 Cor. 1:9
2 Thes. 2:14
13 ch. 1:3
13 Gal. 4:14
14 Gal. 1:22
14 Acts 17:5
15 Acts 2:23
15 Mat. 5:12
15 Or, *chased us out*
15 Esth. 3:8
16 Luke 11:52
Acts 13:50
16 Gen. 15:16
Mat. 23:32
16 Mat. 24:6
17 1 Cor. 5:3
Col. 2:5
17 ch. 3:10
18 Rom. 1:13
19 2 Cor. 1:14
19 Prov. 16:31

Or, *glorying?* 19
1 Cor. 15:23 19

CHAP. 3
AD 54

ver. 5 1
Acts 17:15 1
Rom. 16:21 2
1 Cor. 16:10
Eph. 3:13 3
Acts 9:16 3
1 Cor. 4:9
2 Tim. 3:12
Acts 20:24 4
ver. 1 5
1 Cor. 7:5 5
2 Cor. 11:3
Gal. 2:2 5
Acts 18:1 6
Phil. 1:8 6
2 Cor. 1:4 7
Phil. 4:1 8
ch. 1:2 9
Acts 26:7 10
Rom. 15:32 10
ch. 2:17 10
Col. 4:12 10
Mark 1:3 11
Or, *guide* 11
ch. 4:10 12
1 Cor. 1:8 13
Phil. 1:10
Zech. 14:5 13

CHAP. 4
AD 54

Or, *request* 1
Or, *beseech* 1
Phil. 1:27 1
ch. 2:12 1

ought to walk ᴿand to please God, *so* ye would abound more and more.

2 For ye know what commandments we gave you by the Lord Jesus.

3 For this is ᴿthe will of God, *even* ᴿyour sanctification, ᴿthat ye should abstain from fornication:

4 ᴿThat every one of you should know how to possess his vessel in sanctification and honour;

5 ᴿNot in the lust of concupiscence, ᴿeven as the Gentiles ᴿwhich know not God:

6 That no *man* go beyond and ᴺdefraud his brother ᴺin *any* matter: because that the Lord ᴿ*is* the avenger of all such, as we also have forewarned you and testified.

7 For God hath not called us unto uncleanness, ᴿbut unto holiness.

8 ᴿHe therefore that ᴺdespiseth, despiseth not man, but God, ᴿwho hath also given unto us his holy Spirit.

Exhortation to love and work

9 But as touching brotherly love ᴿye need not that I write unto you: for ᴿye yourselves are taught of God ᴿto love one another.

10 ᴿAnd indeed ye do it toward all the brethren which are in all Măç-ē-dō′-nĭ-ă: but we beseech you, brethren, ᴿthat ye increase more and more;

11 And that ye study to be quiet, and ᴿto do your own business, and ᴿto work with your own hands, as we commanded you;

12 ᴿThat ye may walk honestly toward them that are without, and *that* ye may have lack ᴺof nothing.

Exhortation to hope

13 But I would not have you to be ignorant, brethren, concerning them which are asleep, that ye sorrow not, ᴿeven as others ᴿwhich have no hope.

14 For ᴿif we believe that Jesus died and rose again, even so ᴿthem also which sleep in Jesus will God bring with him.

15 For this we say unto you ᴿby the word of the Lord, that ᴿwe which are alive *and* remain unto the coming of the Lord shall not prevent them which are asleep.

16 For ᴿthe Lord himself shall descend from heaven with a shout, with the voice of the archangel, and with ᴿthe trump of God: ᴿand the dead in Christ shall rise first:

17 ᴿThen we which are alive *and* remain shall be caught up together with them ᴿin the clouds, to meet the Lord in the air: and so ᴿshall we ever be with the Lord.

18 ᴿWherefore ᴺcomfort one another with these words.

CHAPTER 5

Exhortation to readiness

BUT of ᴿthe times and the seasons, brethren, ᴿye have no need that I write unto you.

2 For yourselves know perfectly that ᴿthe day of the Lord so cometh as a thief in the night.

3 For when they shall say, Peace and safety; then ᴿsudden destruction cometh upon them, ᴿas travail upon a woman with child; and they shall not escape.

4 ᴿBut ye, brethren, are not in darkness, that that day should overtake you as a thief.

5 Ye are all ᴿthe children of light, and the children of the day: we are not of the night, nor of darkness.

6 ᴿTherefore let us not sleep, as *do* others; but ᴿlet us watch and be sober.

7 For ᴿthey that sleep sleep in the night; and they that be drunken ᴿare drunken in the night.

8 But let us, who are of the day, be sober, ᴿputting on the breastplate of faith and love; and for an helmet, the hope of salvation.

9 For ᴿGod hath not appointed us to wrath, ᴿbut to obtain salvation by our Lord Jesus Christ,

10 ᴿWho died for us, that, whether we wake or sleep, we should live together with him.

11 ᴿWherefore ᴺcomfort yourselves together, and edify one another, even as also ye do.

Final exhortations

12 And we beseech you, brethren, ᴿto know them which labour among you, and are over you in the Lord, and admonish you;

13 And to esteem them very highly in love for their work's sake. ᴿ*And* be at peace among yourselves.

14 Now we ᴺexhort you, brethren, ᴿwarn them that are ᴺunruly, ᴿcomfort the feebleminded, ᴿsupport the weak, ᴿbe patient toward all *men*.

15 ᴿSee that none render evil for evil unto any *man;* but ever ᴿfollow that which is good, both among yourselves, and to all *men*.

16 ᴿRejoice evermore.

17 ᴿPray without ceasing.

18 In every thing give thanks: for this is the will of God in Christ Jesus concerning you.

19 ᴿQuench not the Spirit.

20 ᴿDespise not prophesyings.

21 ᴿProve all things; ᴿhold fast that which is good.

22 ᴿAbstain from all appearance of evil.

Conclusion and benediction

23 And ᴿthe very God of peace ᴿsanctify you wholly; and *I pray God* your whole spirit and soul and body ᴿbe preserved blameless unto the coming of our Lord Jesus Christ.

24 ᴿFaithful *is* he that calleth you, who also will do *it.*

25 Brethren, ᴿpray for us.

26 ᴿGreet all the brethren with an holy kiss.

27 I ᴺcharge you by the Lord that ᴿthis epistle be read unto all the holy brethren.

28 ᴿThe grace of our Lord Jesus Christ *be* with you. Ä'-mĕn.

CHAP. 5	
AD 54	
23 Phil. 4:9	
23 ch. 3:13	
23 1 Cor. 1:8	
24 1 Cor. 1:9	
25 Col. 4:3	
Rom. 16:16	26
Or, *adjure*	27
Col. 4:16	27
Rom. 16:20	28

The first *epistle* unto the Thĕss-à-lō'-nĭ-ăns was written from Athens.

THE SECOND EPISTLE OF PAUL THE APOSTLE
TO THE
THESSALONIANS

Though First Thessalonians is widely accepted today, the authenticity of Second Thessalonians is suspect in many quarters. The most obvious objection concerns the eschatological-apocalyptic section of 2:1–12, it being considered either too crassly Jewish for the urbanized Christian Paul or too different from the general eschatological portrayal of First Thessalonians 4:13–5:11 to be by the same author. But with the realization that though Paul's pre-conversion hopes found fulfilment in Christ he still shared with Judaism expectations regarding the future, much of the objection to apocalypticism in Paul disappears. And though the two Thessalonian letters differ in tone and temper, these are matters to a large extent conditioned by the situation addressed. External testimony is as strong for Second Thessalonians as for First Thessalonians, and internal factors offer little real reason for the denial of genuineness. Paul should be taken as its author, with its purpose being the correction of false notions regarding the return of Christ (2:1–12) and of ethical disorders resulting from such a false theology (3:6–15). While the Church lives in eager expectation of Christ's return, Paul insists that imminency must not be construed to mean immediacy; but rather is the basis for steadfastness and dogged persistence. The Epistle was written from Corinth only a few months after the first letter, probably about A.D. 51.

OUTLINE OF THE BOOK:
   I. Salutation 1:1–2
  II. Commendation for Patience in Persecution 1:3–12
 III. Explanation regarding Future Events 2:1–12
 IV. Exhortations to Stedfastness, Prayer, Industry 2:13–3:15
  V. Benediction and Signature 3:16–18

CHAPTER 1

Salutation

PAUL, ᴿand Sĭl-vā'-nŭs, and Timotheus, unto the church of the Thĕss-à-lō'-nĭ-ăns ᴿin God our Father and the Lord Jesus Christ:

2 ᴿGrace unto you, and peace, from God our Father and the Lord Jesus Christ.

Thanksgiving

3 ᴿWe are bound to thank God always for you, brethren, as it is meet, because that your faith groweth exceedingly, and the charity of every one of you all toward each other aboundeth;

4 So that ᴿwe ourselves glory in you in the churches of God ᴿfor your patience and faith ᴿin all your persecutions and tribulations that ye endure:

The righteous judgment of God

5 *Which is* ᴿa manifest token of the righteous judgment of God, that ye may be counted

CHAP. 1	
AD 54	
1 2 Cor. 1:19	
1 1 Thes. 1:1	
2 1 Cor. 1:3	
3 1 Thes. 1:2	
ch. 2:13	
4 2 Cor. 7:14	
1 Thes. 2:19	
4 1 Thes. 1:3	
4 1 Thes. 2:14	
5 Phil. 1:28	
1 Thes. 2:14	5
Rev. 6:10	6
Rev. 14:13	7
1 Thes. 4:16	7
Jude 14	
Gr. *the angels of his power*	7
Heb. 12:29	
2 Pet. 3:7	8
Rev. 21:8	
Or, *yielding*	8
Rom. 2:8	8
Phil. 3:19	9
2 Pet. 3:7	
Deut. 33:2	9
Is. 2:19	
Ps. 89:7	10
Ps. 68:35	10
ver. 5	11
Or, *vouchsafe*	11
1 Thes. 1:3	11

worthy of the kingdom of God, ᴿfor which ye also suffer:

6 ᴿSeeing *it is* a righteous thing with God to recompense tribulation to them that trouble you;

7 And to you who are troubled ᴿrest with us, when ᴿthe Lord Jesus shall be revealed from heaven with ᴺhis mighty angels,

8 ᴿIn flaming fire ᴺtaking vengeance on them ᴿthat know not God, and ᴿthat obey not the gospel of our Lord Jesus Christ:

9 ᴿWho shall be punished with everlasting destruction from the presence of the Lord, and ᴿfrom the glory of his power;

10 ᴿWhen he shall come to be glorified in his saints, ᴿand to be admired in all them that believe (because our testimony among you was believed) in that day.

11 Wherefore also we pray always for you, that our God would ᴿcountᴺ you worthy of *this* calling, and fulfil all the good pleasure of *his* goodness, and ᴿthe work of faith with power:

12 ᴿThat the name of our Lord Jesus Christ may be glorified in you, and ye in him, according to the grace of our God and the Lord Jesus Christ.

CHAPTER 2

The coming lawless one

NOW we beseech you, brethren, ᴿby the coming of our Lord Jesus Christ, ᴿand *by* our gathering together unto him,

2 ᴿThat ye be not soon shaken in mind, or be troubled, neither by spirit, nor by word, nor by letter as from us, as that the day of Christ is at hand.

3 ᴿLet no man deceive you by any means: for *that day shall not come,* ᴿexcept there come a falling away first, and ᴿthat man of sin be revealed, ᴿthe son of perdition;

4 Who opposeth and ᴿexalteth himself ᴿabove all that is called God, or that is worshipped; so that he as God sitteth in the temple of God, shewing himself that he is God.

5 Remember ye not, that, when I was yet with you, I told you these things?

6 And now ye know what ᴺwithholdeth that he might be revealed in his time.

7 For ᴿthe mystery of iniquity doth already work: only he who now letteth *will let,* until he be taken out of the way.

8 And then shall that Wicked be revealed, ᴿwhom the Lord shall consume ᴿwith the spirit of his mouth, and shall destroy ᴿwith the brightness of his coming:

9 *Even him,* whose coming is ᴿafter the working of Satan with all power and ᴿsigns and lying wonders,

10 And with all deceivableness of unrighteousness in ᴿthem that perish; because they received not the love of the truth, that they might be saved.

Paul's prayer

11 And ᴿfor this cause God shall send them strong delusion, ᴿthat they should believe a lie:

12 That they all might be damned who believed not the truth, but ᴿhad pleasure in unrighteousness.

Thanksgiving and benediction

13 But ᴿwe are bound to give thanks alway to God for you, brethren beloved of the Lord, because God ᴿhath ᴿfrom the beginning chosen you to salvation ᴿthrough sanctification of the Spirit and belief of the truth:

14 Whereunto he called you by our gospel,

to ᴿthe obtaining of the glory of our Lord Jesus Christ.

15 Therefore, brethren, ᴿstand fast, and hold ᴿthe traditions which ye have been taught, whether by word, or our epistle.

16 ᴿNow our Lord Jesus Christ himself, and God, even our Father, ᴿwhich hath loved us, and hath given *us* everlasting consolation and ᴿgood hope through grace,

17 Comfort your hearts, ᴿand stablish you in every good word and work.

CHAPTER 3

Appeal for supportive prayer

FINALLY, brethren, ᴿpray for us, that the word of the Lord ᴺmay have *free* course, and be glorified, even as *it is* with you:

2 And ᴿthat we may be delivered from ᴺunreasonable and wicked men: ᴿfor all *men* have not faith.

3 But ᴿthe Lord is faithful, who shall stablish you, and ᴿkeep *you* from evil.

4 And ᴿwe have confidence in the Lord touching you, that ye both do and will do the things which we command you.

5 And ᴿthe Lord direct your hearts into the love of God, and into ᴺthe patient waiting for Christ.

Warning against idleness

6 Now we command you, brethren, in the name of our Lord Jesus Christ, ᴿthat ye withdraw yourselves ᴿfrom every brother that walketh ᴿdisorderly, and not after ᴿthe tradition which he received of us.

7 For yourselves know ᴿhow ye ought to follow us: for ᴿwe behaved not ourselves disorderly among you;

8 Neither did we eat any man's bread for nought; but ᴿwrought with labour and travail night and day, that we might not be chargeable to any of you:

9 ᴿNot because we have not power, but to make ᴿourselves an ensample unto you to follow us.

10 For even when we were with you, this we commanded you, ᴿthat if any would not work, neither should he eat.

11 For we hear that there are some ᴿwhich walk among you disorderly, ᴿworking not at all, but are busybodies.

12 ᴿNow them that are such we command and exhort by our Lord Jesus Christ, ᴿthat with quietness they work, and eat their own bread.

13 But ye, brethren, ᴿbeᴺ not weary in well doing.

14 And if any man obey not our word ᴺby this epistle, note that man, and ᴿhave no company with him, that he may be ashamed.

15 ᴿYet count *him* not as an enemy, ᴿbut admonish *him* as a brother.

Closing prayer and benediction

16 Now ᴿthe Lord of peace himself give you peace always by all means. The Lord *be* with you all.

CHAP. 3	
AD 54	
14 Or, *signify that man by an epistle*	
14 Mat. 18:17	
15 Lev. 19:17	
15 Tit. 3:10	
16 Rom. 15:33	
1 Cor. 16:21	**17**
Rom. 16:24	**18**

17 ᴿThe salutation of Paul with mine own hand, which is the token in every epistle: so I write.

18 ᴿThe grace of our Lord Jesus Christ *be* with you all. Ä'-mĕn.

The second *epistle* to the Thĕss-à-lō'-nĭ-ãns was written from Athens.

THE FIRST EPISTLE OF PAUL THE APOSTLE
TO
TIMOTHY

The letters to Timothy and to Titus, known as the Pastoral Epistles, are unique among the writings of St. Paul in that they are addressed specifically to individuals (even Philemon was addressed to others beside the master of the runaway slave and to "the church in thy house"). They are called Pastoral Epistles because they are concerned quite largely with questions of church organization, the qualifications and duties of church officers, and other matters relating to pastoral care. Emphasis is laid upon the personal character of the pastor and the need for "sound doctrine" (I Tim. 1:10; 4:3; Tit. 1:9). Although there has been much discussion concerning the authorship of the Pastoral Epistles, due mainly to linguistic peculiarities, yet they bear the name of Paul and traditionally the Church has always ascribed them to him. The personal allusions and travel references weigh heavily toward a Pauline authorship. I Timothy was probably written to encourage Timothy in his pastoral responsibilities at Ephesus. The Apostle admonishes

Timothy to deal decisively with certain false teachers and gives specific instructions regarding qualifications for leaders and treatment of various members in the church. I Timothy was probably written from Macedonia between A.D. 64 and 66.

OUTLINE OF THE BOOK:
    I. Salutation   1:1–2
   II. The Problems at Ephesus   1:3–11
  III. The Experience of Paul   1:12–17
  IV. Exhortations, Personal and Churchly   1:18–2:15
   V. On Qualifications of Leaders   3:1–13
  VI. Exhortations in face of Apostasy and Lethargy 3:14–4:16
 VII. On Treatment of Various Members in the Church 5:1–6:10
VIII. Concluding Personal Admonitions   6:11–21

CHAPTER 1

Salutation

PAUL, an apostle of Jesus Christ ᴿby the commandment ᴿof God our Saviour, and Lord Jesus Christ, ᴿ*which is* our hope;

2 Unto ᴿTimothy, ᴿ*my* own son in the faith: ᴿGrace, mercy, *and* peace, from God our Father and Jesus Christ our Lord.

Reminder of charge to Timothy

3 As I besought thee to abide still at ĕph'-ĕ-sŭs, ᴿwhen I went into Măç-ē-dō'-nĭ-ă, that thou mightest charge some ᴿthat they teach no other doctrine,

4 ᴿNeither give heed to fables and endless genealogies, ᴿwhich minister questions, rather than godly edifying which is in faith: *so do.*

5 Now ᴿthe end of the commandment is charity ᴿout of a pure heart, and *of* a good conscience, and *of* faith unfeigned:

CHAP. 1	
AD 65	
1 Acts 9:15	
1 Tit. 1:3	
1 Col. 1:27	
2 Acts 16:1	
2 Tit. 1:4	
2 Gal. 1:3	
3 Acts 20:1	
3 Gal. 1:6, 7	
4 Tit. 1:14	
4 ch. 6:4	
5 Rom. 13:8	
Gal. 5:14	
5 2 Tim. 2:22	
Or, *not aiming at*	**6**
ch. 6:4, 20	**6**
ch. 6:4	**7**
Rom. 7:12	**8**
Gal. 3:19	**9**
2 Tim. 4:3	**10**
Tit. 1:9	
1 Cor. 9:17	**11**
Gal. 2:7	
Col. 1:25	

6 From which some ᴺhaving swerved have turned aside unto ᴿvain jangling;

7 Desiring to be teachers of the law; ᴿunderstanding neither what they say, nor whereof they affirm.

Law is for the lawless

8 But we know that ᴿthe law *is* good, if a man use it lawfully;

9 ᴿKnowing this, that the law is not made for a righteous man, but for the lawless and disobedient, for the ungodly and for sinners, for unholy and profane, for murderers of fathers and murderers of mothers, for manslayers,

10 For whoremongers, for them that defile themselves with mankind, for menstealers, for liars, for perjured persons, and if there be any other thing that is contrary ᴿto sound doctrine;

11 According to the glorious gospel of the blessed God, ᴿwhich was committed to my trust.

Paul's debt to Christ

12 And I thank Christ Jesus our Lord, ᴿwho hath enabled me, ᴿfor that he counted me faithful, ᴿputting me into the ministry;

13 ᴿWho was before a blasphemer, and a persecutor, and injurious: but I obtained mercy, because ᴿI did *it* ignorantly in unbelief.

14 ᴿAnd the grace of our Lord was exceeding abundant ᴿwith faith ᴿand love which is in Christ Jesus.

15 ᴿThis *is* a faithful saying, and worthy of all acceptation, that ᴿChrist Jesus came into the world to save sinners; of whom I am chief.

16 Howbeit for this cause ᴿI obtained mercy, that in me first Jesus Christ might shew forth all longsuffering, ᴿfor a pattern to them which should hereafter believe on him to life everlasting.

17 Now unto ᴿthe King eternal, ᴿimmortal, ᴿinvisible, ᴿthe only wise God, ᴿ*be* honour and glory for ever and ever. Ă′-mĕn.

Paul's exhortation to Timothy

18 This charge ᴿI commit unto thee, son Timothy, ᴿaccording to the prophecies which went before on thee, that thou by them mightest ᴿwar a good warfare;

19 Holding faith, and a good conscience; which some having put away concerning faith have made shipwreck:

20 Of whom is ᴿHȳ-mĕ-næ′-ŭs and ᴿAlexander; whom I have ᴿdelivered unto Satan, that they may learn not to ᴿblaspheme.

CHAPTER 2

Public prayers

I ᴺEXHORT therefore, that, first of all, supplications, prayers, intercessions, *and* giving of thanks, be made for all men;

2 ᴿFor kings, and ᴿ*for* all that are in ᴺauthority; that we may lead a quiet and peaceable life in all godliness and honesty.

3 For this *is* ᴿgood and acceptable in the sight ᴿof God our Saviour;

4 ᴿWho will have all men to be saved, ᴿand to come unto the knowledge of the truth.

5 ᴿFor *there is* one God, and ᴿone mediator between God and men, the man Christ Jesus;

6 ᴿWho gave himself a ransom for all, ᴿtoᴺ be testified ᴿin due time.

7 ᴿWhereunto I am ordained a preacher, and an apostle, (ᴿI speak the truth in Christ, *and* lie not;) ᴿa teacher of the Gentiles in faith and verity.

8 I will therefore that men pray ᴿevery where, ᴿlifting up holy hands, without wrath and doubting.

Place of women

9 In like manner also, that ᴿwomen adorn themselves in modest apparel, with shamefacedness and sobriety; not with ᴺbroided hair, or gold, or pearls, or costly array;

10 ᴿBut (which becometh women professing godliness) with good works.

11 Let the woman learn in silence with all subjection.

12 But ᴿI suffer not a woman to teach, nor to usurp authority over the man, but to be in silence.

13 For ᴿAdam was first formed, then Eve.

14 And ᴿAdam was not deceived, but the woman being deceived was in the transgression.

15 Notwithstanding she shall be saved in childbearing, if they continue in faith and charity and holiness with sobriety.

CHAPTER 3

Church officers

THIS *is* a true saying, If a man desire the office of a bishop, he desireth a good work.

2 ᴿA bishop then must be blameless, the husband of one wife, vigilant, sober, ᴺof good behaviour, given to hospitality, ᴿapt to teach;

3 ᴺNot given to wine, ᴿno striker, ᴿnot greedy of filthy lucre; but patient, not a brawler, not covetous;

4 One that ruleth well his own house, ᴿhaving his children in subjection with all gravity;

5 (For if a man know not how to rule his own house, how shall he take care of the church of God?)

6 Not ᴺa novice, lest being lifted up with pride he fall into the condemnation of the devil.

7 Moreover he must have a good report ᴿof them which are without; lest he fall into reproach ᴿand the snare of the devil.

8 Likewise *must* ᴿthe deacons *be* grave, not doubletongued, ᴿnot given to much wine, not greedy of filthy lucre;

9 ᴿHolding the mystery of the faith in a pure conscience.

10 And let these also first be proved; then let them use the office of a deacon, being *found* blameless.

11 ᴿEven so *must their* wives *be* grave, not slanderers, sober, faithful in all things.

12 Let the deacons be the husbands of one wife, ruling their children and their own houses well.

13 For ᴿthey that have ᴺused the office of a deacon well purchase to themselves a good

degree, and great boldness in the faith which is in Christ Jesus.

Paul's purpose in writing

14 These things write I unto thee, hoping to come unto thee shortly:

15 But if I tarry long, that thou mayest know how thou oughtest to behave thyself ᴿin the house of God, which is the church of the living God, the pillar and ᴺground of the truth.

16 And without controversy great is the mystery of godliness: ᴿGod was ᴺmanifest in the flesh, ᴿjustified in the Spirit, ᴿseen of angels, ᴿpreached unto the Gentiles, ᴿbelieved on in the world, ᴿreceived up into glory.

CHAPTER 4

Teachers of false doctrine

NOW the Spirit ᴿspeaketh expressly, that ᴿin the latter times some shall depart from the faith, giving heed ᴿto seducing spirits, ᴿand doctrines of devils;

2 ᴿSpeaking lies in hypocrisy; ᴿhaving their conscience seared with a hot iron;

3 ᴿForbidding to marry, ᴿand commanding to abstain from meats, which God hath created ᴿto be received ᴿwith thanksgiving of them which believe and know the truth.

4 For ᴿevery creature of God is good, and nothing to be refused, if it be received with thanksgiving:

5 For it is sanctified by the word of God and prayer.

Training in godliness

6 If thou put the brethren in remembrance of these things, thou shalt be a good minister of Jesus Christ, ᴿnourished up in the words of faith and of good doctrine, whereunto thou hast attained.

7 But ᴿrefuse profane and old wives' fables, and ᴿexercise thyself rather unto godliness.

8 For ᴿbodily exercise profiteth ᴺlittle: ᴿbut godliness is profitable unto all things, ᴿhaving promise of the life that now is, and of that which is to come.

9 This is a faithful saying and worthy of all acceptation.

10 For therefore ᴿwe both labour and suffer reproach, because we trust in the living God, ᴿwho is the Saviour of all men, specially of those that believe.

Pastoral example and duties

11 These things command and teach.

12 Let no man despise thy youth; but ᴿbe thou an example of the believers, in word, in

CHAP. 3	
AD 65	
15	Eph. 2:21
	2 Tim. 2:20
15	Or, stay
16	John 1:14
	1 John 1:2
16	Gr. manifested
16	Mat. 3:16
	Rom. 1:4
16	Mat. 28:2
	Mark 16:5
16	Acts 10:34
	Rom. 10:18
16	Col. 1:6, 23
16	Luke 24:51

CHAP. 4	
AD 65	
1	John 16:13
	2 Thes. 2:3
	2 Tim. 3:1
1	1 Pet. 1:20
1	2 Tim. 3:13
	Rev. 16:14
1	Dan. 11:35
	Rev. 9:20
2	Mat. 7:15
2	Eph. 4:19
3	1 Cor. 7:28
3	Rom. 14:3
3	Gen. 1:29
3	Rom. 14:6
4	Rom. 14:14
6	2 Tim. 3:14
7	2 Tim. 2:16
	Tit. 1:14
7	Heb. 5:14
8	1 Cor. 8:8
8	Or, for a little time
8	ch. 6:6
8	Ps. 37:4
10	1 Cor. 4:11
10	Ps. 36:6
12	Tit. 2:7

2 Tim. 1:6	14
ch. 1:18	14
Acts 16:6	14
Or, in all things	15
Acts 20:28	16
Ezek. 33:9	16

CHAP. 5	
AD 65	
Lev. 19:32	1
Or, kindness	4
Gen. 45:10	4
Mat. 15:4	
Eph. 6:1, 2	
1 Cor. 7:32	5
Luke 2:37	5
Acts 26:7	5
Jas. 5:5	6
Or, delicately	6
Is. 58:7	8
Gal. 6:10	
Or, kindred	8
2 Tim. 3:5	8
Tit. 1:16	
Mat. 18:17	8
Or, chosen	9
Acts 16:15	10
Heb. 13:2	
1 Pet. 4:9	
Gen. 19:2	10
2 Thes. 3:11	13
1 Cor. 7:9	14
Tit. 2:8	14

conversation, in charity, in spirit, in faith, in purity.

13 Till I come, give attendance to reading, to exhortation, to doctrine.

14 ᴿNeglect not the gift that is in thee, which was given thee ᴿby prophecy, ᴿwith the laying on of the hands of the presbytery.

15 Meditate upon these things; give thyself wholly to them; that thy profiting may appear ᴺto all.

16 ᴿTake heed unto thyself, and unto the doctrine; continue in them: for in doing this thou shalt both ᴿsave thyself, and them that hear thee.

CHAPTER 5

REBUKE ᴿnot an elder, but entreat him as a father; and the younger men as brethren;

2 The elder women as mothers; the younger as sisters, with all purity.

Teaching about widows

3 Honour widows that are widows indeed.

4 But if any widow have children or nephews, let them learn first to shew ᴺpiety at home, and ᴿto requite their parents: for that is good and acceptable before God.

5 ᴿNow she that is a widow indeed, and desolate, trusteth in God, and ᴿcontinueth in supplications and prayers ᴿnight and day.

6 ᴿBut she that liveth ᴺin pleasure is dead while she liveth.

7 And these things give in charge, that they may be blameless.

8 But if any provide not for his own, ᴿand specially for those of his own ᴺhouse, ᴿhe hath denied the faith, ᴿand is worse than an infidel.

9 Let not a widow be ᴺtaken into the number under threescore years old, having been the wife of one man,

10 Well reported of for good works; if she have brought up children, if she have ᴿlodged strangers, if she have ᴿwashed the saints' feet, if she have relieved the afflicted, if she have diligently followed every good work.

11 But the younger widows refuse: for when they have begun to wax wanton against Christ, they will marry;

12 Having damnation, because they have cast off their first faith.

13 ᴿAnd withal they learn to be idle, wandering about from house to house; and not only idle, but tattlers also and busybodies, speaking things which they ought not.

14 ᴿI will therefore that the younger women marry, bear children, guide the house, ᴿgive

none occasion to the adversary [N]to speak reproachfully.

15 For some are already turned aside after Satan.

16 If any man or woman that believeth have widows, let them relieve them, and let not the church be charged; that it may relieve [R]them that are widows indeed.

Concerning the elders

17 [R]Let the elders that rule well [R]be counted worthy of double honour, especially they who labour in the word and doctrine.

18 For the scripture saith, [R]Thou shalt not muzzle the ox that treadeth out the corn. And, [R]The labourer is worthy of his reward.

19 Against an elder receive not an accusation, but [R]before[N] two or three witnesses.

20 [R]Them that sin rebuke before all, [R]that others also may fear.

21 [R]I charge thee before God, and the Lord Jesus Christ, and the elect angels, that thou observe these things [N]without preferring one before another, doing nothing by partiality.

22 [R]Lay hands suddenly on no man, [R]neither be partaker of other men's sins: keep thyself pure.

23 Drink no longer water, but use a little wine [R]for thy stomach's sake and thine often infirmities.

24 [R]Some men's sins are open beforehand, going before to judgment; and some men they follow after.

25 Likewise also the good works of some are manifest beforehand; and they that are otherwise cannot be hid.

CHAPTER 6
Concerning servants

LET as many [R]servants as are under the yoke count their own masters worthy of all honour, [R]that the name of God and his doctrine be not blasphemed.

Concerning conceit and greed

2 And they that have believing masters, let them not despise them, [R]because they are brethren; but rather do them service, because they are [N]faithful and beloved, partakers of the benefit. These things teach and exhort.

3 If any man teach otherwise, and consent [R]not to wholesome words, even the words of our Lord Jesus Christ, [R]and to the doctrine which is according to godliness;

4 He is [N]proud, [R]knowing nothing, but [N]doting about questions and strifes of words, whereof cometh envy, strife, railings, evil surmisings,

---

CHAP. 5
AD 65
14 Gr. for their railing
16 ver. 3, 5
17 Phil. 2:29
17 Acts 28:10
18 Deut. 25:4
1 Cor. 9:9
18 Lev. 19:13
Deut. 24:14
Mat. 10:10
19 Deut. 19:15
19 Or, under
20 Tit. 1:13
20 Deut. 13:11
21 ch. 6:13
2 Tim. 2:14
21 Or, without prejudice
22 Acts 6:6
2 Tim. 1:6
22 2 John 11
23 Ps. 104:15
24 Gal. 5:19

CHAP. 6
AD 65
1 Eph. 6:5
Col. 3:22
Tit. 2:9
1 Pet. 2:18
1 Is. 52:5
Rom. 2:24
Tit. 2:5, 8
2 Col. 4:1
2 Or, believing
3 2 Tim. 1:13
Tit. 1:9
3 Tit. 1:1
4 Or, a fool
4 1 Cor. 8:2
4 Or, sick

1 Cor. 11:16 — 5
Or, Gallings one of another — 5
2 Pet. 2:3 — 5
Rom. 16:17 — 5
Ps. 37:16 — 6
Heb. 13:5
Job 1:21 — 7
Gen. 28:20 — 8
Heb. 13:5
Prov. 15:27 — 9
ch. 1:19 — 9
Deut. 16:19 — 10
Or, been seduced — 10
2 Tim. 2:22 — 11
Deut. 33:1 — 11
ch. 1:18 — 12
Phil. 3:12 — 12
Heb. 13:23 — 12
ch. 5:21 — 13
1 Sam. 2:6 — 13
John 18:37 — 13
Or, profession — 13
Phil. 1:6 — 14
ch. 1:11, 17 — 15
John 6:46 — 16
Eph. 3:21 — 16
Luke 12:21 — 17
Prov. 23:5 — 17
Gr. uncertainty of riches — 17
1 Thes. 1:9 — 17
Acts 14:17 — 17
Jas. 2:5 — 18
Rom. 12:13 — 18
Gal. 6:6 — 18
Or, sociable — 18
Mat. 6:20 — 19
2 Tim. 1:14 — 20
Tit. 1:14 — 20

---

5 [R]Perverse[N] disputings of men of corrupt minds, and destitute of the truth, [R]supposing that gain is godliness: [R]from such withdraw thyself.

6 But [R]godliness with contentment is great gain.

7 For [R]we brought nothing into this world, and it is certain we can carry nothing out.

8 And [R]having food and raiment let us be therewith content.

9 But [R]they that will be rich fall into temptation and a snare, and into many foolish and hurtful lusts, [R]which drown men in destruction and perdition.

10 [R]For the love of money is the root of all evil: which while some coveted after, they have [N]erred from the faith, and pierced themselves through with many sorrows.

Pastoral aims

11 [R]But thou, [R]O man of God, flee these things; and follow after righteousness, godliness, faith, love, patience, meekness.

12 [R]Fight the good fight of faith, [R]lay hold on eternal life, whereunto thou art also called, [R]and hast professed a good profession before many witnesses.

13 [R]I give thee charge in the sight of God, [R]who quickeneth all things, and before Christ Jesus, [R]who before Pontius Pilate witnessed a good [N]confession;

14 That thou keep this commandment without spot, unrebukeable, [R]until the appearing of our Lord Jesus Christ:

15 Which in his times he shall shew, who is [R]the blessed and only Potentate, the King of kings, and Lord of lords;

16 Who only hath immortality, dwelling in the light which no man can approach unto; [R]whom no man hath seen, nor can see: [R]to whom be honour and power everlasting. Ă'-mĕn.

Concern for the wealthy

17 Charge them that are rich in this world, that they be not highminded, [R]nor trust in [R]uncertain[N] riches, but in [R]the living God, [R]who giveth us richly all things to enjoy;

18 That they do good, that [R]they be rich in good works, [R]ready to distribute, [R]willing[N] to communicate;

19 [R]Laying up in store for themselves a good foundation against the time to come, that they may lay hold on eternal life.

Final charge and benediction

20 O Timothy, [R]keep that which is committed to thy trust, [R]avoiding profane and vain

babblings, and oppositions of science falsely so called:

21 Which some professing ᴿhave erred con-

AD 65

21 2 Tim. 2:18

cerning the faith. Grace *be* with thee. Ä'-mĕn.

The first to Timothy was written from Lā-ŏd-ĭ-çē'-ă, which is the chiefest city of Phrÿġ-ĭ-ă Pā-cā-tĭ-ā'-nă.

THE SECOND EPISTLE OF PAUL THE APOSTLE

TO

TIMOTHY

Second Timothy is chronologically last in order of the three Pastoral Epistles. It breathes a different atmosphere than the other two. In I Timothy and Titus, the author is free to make plans and to move about at will. In this letter, he is a prisoner and the end is rapidly approaching (4:6). All three Pastorals were written by the same individual who claims in each case to be Paul (cf. I Timothy). Perhaps in the composition of each he gave a secretary some freedom in expression. Apparently written from Rome where he is awaiting execution, Paul is anxious for Timothy, who is probably at Ephesus, to come to him before winter. But more than this, in view of his own limiting circumstances and in the face of rising apostasy, he is concerned that Timothy be exemplary in his own personal life and faithful to the ministry to which he has been called. This final

letter of the great Apostle to his "dearly beloved son" is rich and varied. Interwoven are touching appeals, ringing charges, and the note of triumph in the face of imminent martyrdom (4:7–8). Assuming a second Roman imprisonment, it was written about A.D. 67.

OUTLINE OF THE BOOK:

   I. Salutation 1:1–2
  II. Remembrance of Past Relations 1:3–18
 III. Exhortations for the Personal Life 2:1–26
 IV. Dangers of Apostasy 3:1–17
  V. The Final Charge 4:1–8
 VI. Concluding Words and Greetings 4:9–22

CHAPTER 1

Salutation

PAUL, ᴿan apostle of Jesus Christ by the will of God, according to ᴿthe promise of life which is in Christ Jesus,

2 ᴿTo Timothy, *my* dearly beloved son: Grace, mercy, *and* peace, from God the Father and Christ Jesus our Lord.

Thanksgiving

3 ᴿI thank God, ᴿwhom I serve from *my* forefathers with pure conscience, that ᴿwithout ceasing I have remembrance of thee in my prayers night and day;

4 ᴿGreatly desiring to see thee, being mindful of thy tears, that I may be filled with joy;

5 When I call to remembrance ᴿthe unfeigned faith that is in thee, which dwelt first in thy grandmother Lō'-ĭs, and ᴿthy mother ēu-nī'-çē; and I am persuaded that in thee also.

Exhortation to renewed zeal

6 Wherefore I put thee in remembrance ᴿthat thou stir up the gift of God, which is in thee by the putting on of my hands.

7 For ᴿGod hath not given us the spirit of

CHAP. 1

AD 66

1 2 Cor. 1:1
1 Eph. 3:6
   Heb. 9:15
2 1 Tim. 1:2
3 Rom. 1:8
   Eph. 1:16
3 Acts 22:3
   Rom. 1:9
3 1 Thes. 1:2
4 ch. 4:9, 21
5 1 Tim. 1:5
5 Acts 16:1
6 1 Tim. 4:14
7 Rom. 8:15

Acts 1:8   7
Rom. 1:16   8
1 Tim. 2:6   8
Eph. 3:1   8
Col. 1:24   8
1 Tim. 1:1   9
Heb. 3:1   9
Rom. 3:20   9
Rom. 8:28   9
Rom. 16:25   9
Eph. 1:9   10
1 Cor. 15:54   10
Acts 9:15   11
  1 Tim. 2:7
Eph. 3:1   12
1 Pet. 4:19   12
Or, *trusted*   12
1 Tim. 6:20   12
Tit. 1:9   13
  Heb. 10:23
Rom. 2:20   13
1 Tim. 6:3   13
1 Tim. 1:14   13
Rom. 8:11   14

fear; ᴿbut of power, and of love, and of a sound mind.

8 ᴿBe not thou therefore ashamed of ᴿthe testimony of our Lord, nor of me ᴿhis prisoner: ᴿbut be thou partaker of the afflictions of the gospel according to the power of God;

9 ᴿWho hath saved us, and ᴿcalled *us* with an holy calling, ᴿnot according to our works, but ᴿaccording to his own purpose and grace, which was given us in Christ Jesus ᴿbefore the world began,

10 But ᴿis now made manifest by the appearing of our Saviour Jesus Christ, ᴿwho hath abolished death, and hath brought life and immortality to light through the gospel:

11 ᴿWhereunto I am appointed a preacher, and an apostle, and a teacher of the Gentiles.

12 ᴿFor the which cause I also suffer these things: nevertheless I am not ashamed: ᴿfor I know whom I have ᴺbelieved, and am persuaded that he is able to ᴿkeep that which I have committed unto him against that day.

13 ᴿHold fast ᴿthe form of ᴿsound words, which thou hast heard of me, ᴿin faith and love which is in Christ Jesus.

14 That good thing which was committed unto thee keep by the Holy Ghost ᴿwhich dwelleth in us.

Information about mutual friends

15 This thou knowest, that ᴿall they which are in Asia be turned away from me; of whom are Phȳ-gĕl'-lŭs and Hĕr-mŏg'-ĕ-nēś.

16 The Lord ᴿgive mercy unto the house of ō-nĕs-ĭph'-ŏ-rŭs; ᴿfor he oft refreshed me, and was not ashamed of ᴿmy chain:

17 But, when he was in Rome, he sought me out very diligently, and found *me.*

18 The Lord grant unto him that he may find mercy of the Lord ᴿin that day: and in how many things he ᴿministered unto me at Ĕph'-ĕ-sŭs, thou knowest very well.

CHAPTER 2

Exhortation to endurance

THOU therefore, ᴿmy son, ᴿbe strong in the grace that is in Christ Jesus.

2 And the things that thou hast heard of me ᴺamong many witnesses, the same commit thou to faithful men, who shall be able to teach others also.

3 Thou therefore endure hardness, ᴿas a good soldier of Jesus Christ.

4 ᴿNo man that warreth entangleth himself with the affairs of *this* life; that he may please him who hath chosen him to be a soldier.

5 And ᴿif a man also strive for masteries, *yet* is he not crowned, except he strive lawfully.

6 ᴺThe husbandman that laboureth must be first partaker of the fruits.

7 Consider what I say; and the Lord give thee understanding in all things.

8 Remember that Jesus Christ ᴿof the seed of David ᴿwas raised from the dead ᴿaccording to my gospel:

9 ᴿWherein I suffer trouble, as an evil doer, ᴿ*even* unto bonds; ᴿbut the word of God is not bound.

10 Therefore ᴿI endure all things for the elect's sakes, ᴿthat they may also obtain the salvation which is in Christ Jesus with eternal glory.

11 *It is* a faithful saying: For ᴿif we be dead with *him,* we shall also live with *him:*

12 ᴿIf we suffer, we shall also reign with *him:* ᴿif we deny *him,* he also will deny us:

13 ᴿIf we believe not, *yet* he abideth faithful: ᴿhe cannot deny himself.

Avoid godless controversies

14 Of these things put *them* in remembrance, ᴿcharging *them* before the Lord that they strive not about words to no profit, *but* to the subverting of the hearers.

CHAP. 1	
AD 66	
15	Acts 19:10
16	Mat. 5:7
16	Philem. 7
18	2 Thes. 1:10
18	Heb. 6:10

CHAP. 2	
AD 66	
1	1 Tim. 1:2
1	Eph. 6:10
2	Or, *by*
3	1 Tim. 1:18
4	1 Cor. 9:25
5	1 Cor. 9:25
6	Or, *The husband-man, labouring first, must be partaker of the fruits*
8	Rom. 1:3, 4
8	1 Cor. 15:1
8	Rom. 2:16
9	Acts 9:16
9	Eph. 3:1
9	Acts 28:31
	Eph. 6:19
10	Eph. 3:13
10	2 Cor. 1:6
11	Rom. 6:5, 8
12	Rom. 8:17
12	Mat. 10:33
	Mark 8:38
13	Rom. 3:3
13	Num. 23:19
14	1 Tim. 5:21

1 Tim. 4:7	16
Or, *gangrene*	17
1 Cor. 15:12	18
Mat. 24:24	19
Or, *steady*	19
Nah. 1:7	19
John 10:14	
Rom. 9:21	20
Is. 52:11	21
ch. 3:17	21
Acts 9:14	22
1 Cor. 1:2	
1 Tim. 1:5	22
1 Tim. 1:4	23
Tit. 3:2	24
Tit. 1:9	24
Or, *forbearing*	24
Gal. 6:1	25
1 Tim. 6:11	
Acts 8:22	25
1 Tim. 2:4	25
Gr. *awake*	26
1 Tim. 3:7	26
Gr. *taken alive*	26

CHAP. 3	
AD 66	
1 Tim. 4:1	1
Phil. 2:21	2
2 Pet. 2:3	2
Jude 16	2
1 Tim. 6:4	2
1 Tim. 1:20	2
Rom. 1:30	2
Rom. 1:31	3
Rom. 1:31	3
Or, *makebates*	3
2 Pet. 3:3	3
2 Pet. 2:10	4
Phil. 3:19	4
1 Tim. 5:8	5
1 Tim. 6:5	5
Mat. 23:14	6

15 Study to shew thyself approved unto God, a workman that needeth not to be ashamed, rightly dividing the word of truth.

16 But ᴿshun profane *and* vain babblings: for they will increase unto more ungodliness.

17 And their word will eat as doth a ᴺcanker: of whom is Hȳ-mĕ-næ'-ŭs and Phĭ-lē'-tŭs;

18 Who concerning the truth have erred, ᴿsaying that the resurrection is past already; and overthrow the faith of some.

19 Nevertheless ᴿthe foundation of God standeth ᴺsure, having this seal, The Lord ᴿknoweth them that are his. And, Let every one that nameth the name of Christ depart from iniquity.

20 But in a great house there are not only vessels of gold and of silver, but also of wood and of earth; ᴿand some to honour, and some to dishonour.

21 ᴿIf a man therefore purge himself from these, he shall be a vessel unto honour, sanctified, and meet for the master's use, *and* ᴿprepared unto every good work.

22 Flee also youthful lusts: but follow righteousness, faith, charity, peace, with them that ᴿcall on the Lord ᴿout of a pure heart.

23 But ᴿfoolish and unlearned questions avoid, knowing that they do gender strifes.

24 And ᴿthe servant of the Lord must not strive; but be gentle unto all *men,* ᴿapt to teach, ᴺpatient,

25 ᴿIn meekness instructing those that oppose themselves; ᴿif God peradventure will give them repentance ᴿto the acknowledging of the truth;

26 And *that* they may ᴺrecover themselves ᴿout of the snare of the devil, who are ᴺtaken captive by him at his will.

CHAPTER 3

Coming time of stress

THIS know also, that ᴿin the last days perilous times shall come.

2 For men shall be ᴿlovers of their own selves, ᴿcovetous, ᴿboasters, ᴿproud, ᴿblasphemers, ᴿdisobedient to parents, unthankful, unholy,

3 ᴿWithout natural affection, ᴿtrucebreakers, ᴺfalse accusers, ᴿincontinent, fierce, despisers of those that are good,

4 ᴿTraitors, heady, highminded, ᴿlovers of pleasures more than lovers of God;

5 Having a form of godliness, but ᴿdenying the power thereof: ᴿfrom such turn away.

6 For ᴿof this sort are they which creep into

houses, and lead captive silly women laden with sins, led away with divers lusts,

7 Ever learning, and never able ᴿto come to the knowledge of the truth.

8 ᴿNow as Jăn'-nēś and Jăm'-brēś withstood Moses, so do these also resist the truth: ᴿmen of corrupt minds, ᴿreprobateᴺ concerning the faith.

9 But they shall proceed no further: for their folly shall be manifest unto all *men,* ᴿas theirs also was.

Instruction of the scripture

10 ᴿBut ᴺthou hast fully known my doctrine, manner of life, purpose, faith, longsuffering, charity, patience,

11 Persecutions, afflictions, which came unto me ᴿat Ăn'-tī-ŏch, ᴿat ī-cō'-nī-ŭm, ᴿat Lўs'-tră; what persecutions I endured: but ᴿout of *them* all the Lord delivered me.

12 Yea, and ᴿall that will live godly in Christ Jesus shall suffer persecution.

13 ᴿBut evil men and seducers shall wax worse and worse, deceiving, and being deceived.

14 But ᴿcontinue thou in the things which thou hast learned and hast been assured of, knowing of whom thou hast learned *them;*

15 And that from a child thou hast known ᴿthe holy scriptures, which are able to make thee wise unto salvation through faith which is in Christ Jesus.

16 ᴿAll scripture *is* given by inspiration of God, ᴿand *is* profitable for doctrine, for reproof, for correction, for instruction in righteousness:

17 ᴿThat the man of God may be perfect, ᴿthroughlyᴺ furnished unto all good works.

CHAPTER 4

Paul's charge regarding sound doctrine

I ᴿCHARGE *thee* therefore before God, and the Lord Jesus Christ, ᴿwho shall judge the quick and the dead at his appearing and his kingdom;

2 Preach the word; be instant in season, out of season; reprove, ᴿrebuke, ᴿexhort with all longsuffering and doctrine.

3 ᴿFor the time will come when they will not endure ᴿsound doctrine; ᴿbut after their own lusts shall they heap to themselves teachers, having itching ears;

4 And they shall turn away *their* ears from the truth, and ᴿshall be turned unto fables.

5 But watch thou in all things, ᴿendure afflictions, do the work of ᴿan evangelist, ᴺmake full proof of thy ministry.

CHAP. 3
AD 66
7 1 Tim. 2:4
8 Ex. 7:11
8 1 Tim. 6:5
8 Rom. 1:28
8 Or, *of no judgment*
9 Ex. 7:12
10 1 Tim. 4:6
10 Or, *thou hast been a diligent follower of*
11 Acts 13:45
11 Acts 14:2
11 Acts 14:19
11 Ps. 34:19
12 Ps. 34:19
13 2 Thes. 2:11
14 ch. 1:13
15 John 5:39
16 2 Pet. 1:20
16 Rom. 15:4
17 1 Tim. 6:11
17 ch. 2:21
17 Or, *perfected*

CHAP. 4
AD 66
1 1 Tim. 5:21
1 Acts 10:42
2 1 Tim. 5:20
Tit. 1:13
2 1 Tim. 4:13
3 ch. 3:1
3 1 Tim. 1:10
3 ch. 3:6
4 1 Tim. 1:4
5 ch. 1:8
5 Acts 21:8
5 Or, *fulfil,* Rom. 15:19

Phil. 2:17   6
Phil. 1:23   6
2 Pet. 1:14
Phil. 3:14   7
Jas. 1:12   8
ch. 1:12   8
Col. 4:14   10
1 John 2:15   10
ch. 1:15   11
Col. 4:14   11
Acts 12:25   11
Acts 20:4   12
Eph. 6:21
Acts 19:33   14
2 Sam. 3:39   14
Ps. 28:4
Or, *our preachings*   15
Acts 7:60   16
Acts 23:11   17
Acts 9:15   17
Ps. 22:21   17
Ps. 121:7   18
Rom. 11:36   18
Gal. 1:5
Heb. 13:21
Acts 18:2   19
Rom. 16:3
Acts 19:22   20
Rom. 16:23   20
Acts 20:4   20
ver. 9   21
Gal. 6:18   22
Philem. 25
Gr. *Cæsar Nero,* or, *the emperor*   *

Paul's death is near

6 For ᴿI am now ready to be offered, and the time of ᴿmy departure is at hand.

7 ᴿI have fought a good fight, I have finished *my* course, I have kept the faith:

8 Henceforth there is laid up for me ᴿa crown of righteousness, which the Lord, the righteous judge, shall give me ᴿat that day: and not to me only, but unto all them also that love his appearing.

Personal messages

9 Do thy diligence to come shortly unto me:

10 For ᴿDē'-măs hath forsaken me, ᴿhaving loved this present world, and is departed unto Thĕss-ă-lō-nī'-că; Crĕs'-çĕnś to Galatia, Titus unto Dalmatia.

11 ᴿOnly ᴿLuke is with me. Take ᴿMark, and bring him with thee: for he is profitable to me for the ministry.

12 And ᴿTўch'-ĭ-cŭs have I sent to ĕph'-ĕ-sŭs.

13 The cloak that I left at Trō'-ăs with Carpus, when thou comest, bring *with thee,* and the books, *but* especially the parchments.

14 ᴿAlexander the coppersmith did me much evil: ᴿthe Lord reward him according to his works:

15 Of whom be thou ware also; for he hath greatly withstood ᴺour words.

16 At my first answer no man stood with me, but all *men* forsook me: ᴿI pray God that it may not be laid to their charge.

17 ᴿNotwithstanding the Lord stood with me, and strengthened me; ᴿthat by me the preaching might be fully known, and *that* all the Gentiles might hear: and I was delivered ᴿout of the mouth of the lion.

18 ᴿAnd the Lord shall deliver me from every evil work, and will preserve *me* unto his heavenly kingdom: ᴿto whom *be* glory for ever and ever. Ä'-mĕn.

Greetings and benediction

19 Salute ᴿPrisca and Ă-quĭl'-ă, and the household of ō-nĕs-ĭph'-ŏ-rŭs.

20 ᴿĒ-rās'-tŭs abode at Corinth: but ᴿTrŏph'-ĭ-mŭs have I left at Mĭ-lē'-tŭm sick.

21 ᴿDo thy diligence to come before winter. ĕū-bū'-lŭs greeteth thee, and Pū'-dĕns, and Lĭ'-nŭs, and Claudia, and all the brethren.

22 ᴿThe Lord Jesus Christ *be* with thy spirit. Grace *be* with you. Ä'-mĕn.

The second *epistle* unto Timotheus, ordained the first bishop of the church of the ĕph-ē'-ṣīăns, was written from Rome, when Paul was brought before *Nero the second time.

TITUS

Though briefer, the Epistle to Titus has much in common with the first Epistle to Timothy. In both, Paul (cf. First Timothy) writes to encourage his younger aides in their pastoral ministries. Evidently Paul and Titus had ministered together in the island of Crete. But when Paul found it necessary to return to the mainland, he wrote back to Titus who had been left to shepherd the struggling Church there. His letter concerns (1) qualifications for leaders in the Church, (2) the need to oppose false doctrine, (3) treatment of various classes of members in the Church, and (4) proper attitudes of believers in a pagan society. Paul instructs Titus to join him at Nicopolis,

a city of Greece, where he anticipates spending the winter (3:12). Assuming two Roman imprisonments, the letter was probably written during the period of release; probably from Macedonia between A.D. 64 and 66.

CHAPTER 1

Salutation

PAUL, a servant of God, and an apostle of Jesus Christ, according to the faith of God's elect, and ᴿthe acknowledging of the truth ᴿwhich is after godliness;

2 ᴿInᴺ hope of eternal life, which God, ᴿthat cannot lie, promised ᴿbefore the world began;

3 ᴿBut hath in due times manifested his word through preaching, ᴿwhich is committed unto me according to the commandment of God our Saviour;

4 To ᴿTitus, *mine* own son after the common faith: ᴿGrace, mercy, *and* peace, from God the Father and the Lord Jesus Christ our Saviour.

Qualifications of elders

5 For this cause left I thee in Crete, that thou shouldest ᴿset in order the things that are ᴺwanting, and ordain elders in every city, as I had appointed thee:

6 ᴿIf any be blameless, the husband of one wife, ᴿhaving faithful children not accused of riot or unruly.

7 For a bishop must be blameless, as ᴿthe steward of God; not selfwilled, not soon angry, ᴿnot given to wine, no striker, not given to filthy lucre;

8 ᴿBut a lover of hospitality, a lover of ᴺgood men, sober, just, holy, temperate;

9 Holding fast the faithful word ᴺas he hath been taught, that he may be able ᴿby sound doctrine both to exhort and to convince the gainsayers.

10 For ᴿthere are many unruly and vain talkers and deceivers, ᴿspecially they of the circumcision:

11 Whose mouths must be stopped, ᴿwho subvert whole houses, teaching things which they ought not, ᴿfor filthy lucre's sake.

12 ᴿOne of themselves, *even* a prophet of their own, said, The Cretians *are* alway liars, evil beasts, slow bellies.

13 This witness is true. ᴿWherefore rebuke them sharply, that they may be ᴿsound in the faith;

14 ᴿNot giving heed to Jew'-ĭsh fables, and ᴿcommandments of men, that turn from the truth.

15 ᴿUnto the pure all things *are* pure: but unto them that are defiled and unbelieving *is* nothing pure; but even their mind and conscience is defiled.

16 They profess that they know God; but ᴿin works they deny *him*, being abominable, and disobedient, ᴿand unto every good work ᴺreprobate.

CHAPTER 2

Sound doctrine and good practice

BUT speak thou the things which become ᴿsound doctrine:

2 That the aged men be ᴺsober, grave, temperate, sound in faith, in charity, in patience.

3 The aged women likewise, that *they be* in behaviour as becometh ᴺholiness, not ᴺfalse accusers, not given to much wine, teachers of good things;

4 That they may teach the young women to be ᴺsober, to love their husbands, to love their children,

5 *To be* discreet, chaste, keepers at home, good, ᴿobedient to their own husbands, ᴿthat the word of God be not blasphemed.

6 Young men likewise exhort to be ᴺsober minded.

Cross-reference column

CHAP. 1
AD 65

1	2 Tim. 2:25
1	1 Tim. 3:16
2	2 Tim. 1:1
2	Or, *For*
2	2 Tim. 2:13
2	Rom. 16:25
3	2 Tim. 1:10
3	1 Thes. 2:4
4	2 Cor. 2:13
4	Eph. 1:2
5	1 Cor. 11:34
5	Or, *left undone*
6	1 Tim. 3:2
6	1 Tim. 3:4
7	Mat. 24:45
7	Lev. 10:9
8	1 Tim. 3:2
8	Or, *good things*
9	Or, *in teaching*
9	1 Tim. 1:10
10	1 Tim. 1:6
10	Acts 15:1

2 Tim. 3:6	11
1 Tim. 6:5	11
Acts 17:28	12
2 Cor. 13:10	13
ch. 2:2	13
1 Tim. 1:4	14
Is. 29:13	14
1 Cor. 6:12	15
2 Tim. 3:5	16
Rom. 1:28	16
Or, *void of judgment*	16

CHAP. 2
AD 65

1 Tim. 1:10	1
Or, *vigilant*	2
Or, *holy women*	3
Or, *makebates*	3
Or, *wise*	4
1 Cor. 14:34	5
Rom. 2:24	5
Or, *discreet*	6

7 ᴿIn all things shewing thyself a pattern of good works: in doctrine *shewing* uncorruptness, gravity, ᴿsincerity,

8 ᴿSound speech, that cannot be condemned; ᴿthat he that is of the contrary part may be ashamed, having no evil thing to say of you.

9 *Exhort* ᴿservants to be obedient unto their own masters, *and* to please *them* well ᴿin all *things;* not ᴺanswering again;

10 Not purloining, but shewing all good fidelity; ᴿthat they may adorn the doctrine of God our Saviour in all things.

God's grace for all men

11 For ᴿthe grace of God ᴺthat bringeth salvation ᴿhath appeared to all men,

12 Teaching us ᴿthat, denying ungodliness ᴿand worldly lusts, we should live soberly, righteously, and godly, in this present world;

13 ᴿLooking for that blessed ᴿhope, and the glorious ᴿappearing of the great God and our Saviour Jesus Christ;

14 ᴿWho gave himself for us, that he might redeem us from all iniquity, ᴿand purify unto himself ᴿa peculiar people, ᴿzealous of good works.

15 These things speak, and ᴿexhort, and rebuke with all authority. Let no man despise thee.

CHAPTER 3

Believers are to apply themselves

PUT them in mind ᴿto be subject to principalities and powers, to obey magistrates, ᴿto be ready to every good work,

2 ᴿTo speak evil of no man, ᴿto be no brawlers, *but* ᴿgentle, shewing all ᴿmeekness unto all men.

3 For ᴿwe ourselves also were sometimes foolish, disobedient, deceived, serving divers

CHAP. **2**	
AD 65	
7	1 Tim. 4:12
8	Eph. 6:24
8	1 Tim. 6:3
8	Neh. 5:9
9	Eph. 6:5
9	Eph. 5:24
9	Or, *gainsaying*
10	Mat. 5:16
11	Rom. 5:15
11	Or, *that bringeth salvation to all men, hath appeared*
11	Luke 3:6
12	Luke 1:75
12	1 Pet. 4:2
13	1 Cor. 1:7
	Acts 24:15
13	Col. 3:4
14	Gal. 1:4
14	Heb. 9:14
14	Ex. 15:16
14	Eph. 2:10
15	2 Tim. 4:2

CHAP. **3**	
AD 65	
1	1 Pet. 2:13
1	Col. 1:10
	Heb. 13:21
2	Eph. 4:31
2	2 Tim. 2:24
2	Phil. 4:5
2	Eph. 4:2
3	1 Cor. 6:11

ch. 2:11	4
Or, *pity*	4
1 Tim. 2:3	4
Rom. 3:20	5
John 3:3	5
Ezek. 36:25	6
Gr. *richly*	6
Rom. 3:24	7
Rom. 8:23	7
ch. 1:2	7
1 Tim. 1:15	8
ch. 2:14	8
1 Tim. 1:4	9
2 Tim. 2:14	9
2 Cor. 13:2	10
Mat. 18:17	10
Acts 20:4	12
Acts 18:24	13
ver. 8	14
Or, *profess honest trades*	14
Rom. 15:28	14

lusts and pleasures, living in malice and envy, hateful, *and* hating one another.

4 But after that ᴿthe kindness and ᴺlove of ᴿGod our Saviour toward man appeared,

5 ᴿNot by works of righteousness which we have done, but according to his mercy he saved us, by ᴿthe washing of regeneration, and renewing of the Holy Ghost;

6 ᴿWhich he shed on us ᴺabundantly through Jesus Christ our Saviour;

7 ᴿThat being justified by his grace, ᴿwe should be made heirs ᴿaccording to the hope of eternal life.

8 ᴿ*This is* a faithful saying, and these things I will that thou affirm constantly, that they which have believed in God might be careful ᴿto maintain good works. These things are good and profitable unto men.

9 But ᴿavoid foolish questions, and genealogies, and contentions, and strivings about the law; ᴿfor they are unprofitable and vain.

10 A man that is an heretick ᴿafter the first and second admonition ᴿreject;

11 Knowing that he that is such is subverted, and sinneth, ᴿbeing condemned of himself.

Personal messages and benediction

12 When I shall send Artemas unto thee, or ᴿTy̆ch′-ĭ-cŭs, be diligent to come unto me to Nĭ-cŏp′-ŏ-lĭs: for I have determined there to winter.

13 Bring Zē′-năs the lawyer and ᴿĂ-pŏl′-lŏs on their journey diligently, that nothing be wanting unto them.

14 And let ours also learn ᴿto ᴺmaintain good works for necessary uses, that they be ᴿnot unfruitful.

15 All that are with me salute thee. Greet them that love us in the faith. Grace *be* with you all. Ä′-mĕn.

It was written to Titus, ordained the first bishop of the church of the Cretians, from Nĭ-cŏp′-ŏ-lĭs of Măç-ĕ-dō′-nĭ-à.

THE EPISTLE OF PAUL TO

PHILEMON

Philemon was a member of the Colossian Church, who had in some way been won to Christ by Paul. The slave Onesimus had robbed Philemon, his master, and fled, hoping to go unrecognized in the big city. Perhaps through Epaphras, Onesimus had come in contact with Paul. Brought to Christ by Paul, he had proven very helpful to the Apostle while the latter was in prison. But having persuaded Onesimus of his duty to return to his master, Paul now writes this delicate letter appealing to

Philemon to receive him back as a "brother beloved in the Lord." An exquisite sense of humor, seen in the play on the name Onesimus ("profitable"), relieves the intensity of the letter and undoubtedly strengthens the appeal. Paul's approach to the problem of slavery in his day was not an attack on the system itself (cf. I Cor. 7:20–22), but an attempt to transform the master-slave relationship among Christians. He worked from a "Christ consciousness" in the individual to a "Christian

consciousness" in society. And in so doing, he planted the seeds for the ultimate abolition of the system. None but the most extreme negative critics have disputed Paul's authorship of the letter. It was written from imprisonment, probably from Rome, and presented to Philemon by Tychicus on behalf of Onesimus (cf. Col. 4:7–9). Together with Colossians, it was probably written in A.D. 61 or 62.

OUTLINE OF THE BOOK:

   I. Greeting 1–3
  II. Commendation of Philemon 4–7
 III. Intercession for Onesimus 8–21
 IV. Conclusion 22 25

Salutation

PAUL, [R]a prisoner of Jesus Christ, and Timothy *our* brother, unto Phī-lē'-mon our dearly beloved, [R]and fellowlabourer,

2 And to *our* beloved Ăpph'-ĭ-ă, and [R]Är-<u>ch</u>ĭp'-pŭs [R]our fellowsoldier, and to [R]the church in thy house:

3 [R]Grace to you, and peace, from God our Father and the Lord Jesus Christ.

Thanksgiving

4 [R]I thank my God, making mention of thee always in my prayers,

5 [R]Hearing of thy love and faith, which thou hast toward the Lord Jesus, and toward all saints;

6 That the communication of thy faith may become effectual [R]by the acknowledging of every good thing which is in you in Christ Jesus.

7 For we have great joy and consolation in thy love, because the bowels of the saints [R]are refreshed by thee, brother.

Appeal on behalf of Onesimus

8 Wherefore, [R]though I might be much bold in Christ to enjoin thee that which is convenient,

9 Yet for love's sake I rather beseech *thee,* being such an one as Paul the aged, [R]and now also a prisoner of Jesus Christ.

10 I beseech thee for my son [R]Ō-nĕs'-ĭ-mŭs, [R]whom I have begotten in my bonds:

11 Which in time past was to thee unprofitable, but now profitable to thee and to me:

12 Whom I have sent again: thou therefore receive him, that is, mine own bowels:

AD 64	
1 ver. 9	
Eph. 3:1	
& 4:1	
2 Tim. 1:8	
1 Phil. 2:25	
2 Col. 4:17	
2 Phil. 2:25	
2 Rom. 16:5	
1 Cor. 16:19	
3 Eph. 1:2	
4 Eph. 1:16	
1 Thes. 1:2	
2 Thes. 1:3	
5 Eph. 1:15	
Col. 1:4	
6 Phil. 1:9	
7 ver. 20	
2 Cor. 7:13	
2 Tim. 1:16	
8 1 Thes. 2:6	
9 ver. 1	
10 Col. 4:9	
10 1 Cor. 4:15	
Gal. 4:19	

1 Cor. 16:17	13
Phil. 2:30	
2 Cor. 9:7	14
Gen. 45:5, 8	15
Mat. 23:8	16
1 Tim. 6:2	
Col. 3:22	16
2 Cor. 8:23	17
ver. 7	20
2 Cor. 7:16	21
Phil. 1:25	22
& 2:24	
2 Cor. 1:11	22
Col. 1:7	23
& 4:12	
Acts 12:12, 25	24
Acts 19:29	24
& 27:2	
Col. 4:10	
Col. 4:14	24
2 Tim. 4:11	24
2 Tim. 4:22	25

13 Whom I would have retained with me, [R]that in thy stead he might have ministered unto me in the bonds of the gospel:

14 But without thy mind would I do nothing; [R]that thy benefit should not be as it were of necessity, but willingly.

15 [R]For perhaps he therefore departed for a season, that thou shouldest receive him for ever;

16 Not now as a servant, but above a servant, [R]a brother beloved, specially to me, but how much more unto thee, [R]both in the flesh, and in the Lord?

17 If thou count me therefore [R]a partner, receive him as myself.

18 If he hath wronged thee, or oweth *thee* aught, put that on mine account;

19 I Paul have written *it* with mine own hand, I will repay *it:* albeit I do not say to thee how thou owest unto me even thine own self besides.

20 Yea, brother, let me have joy of thee in the Lord: [R]refresh my bowels in the Lord.

Greetings and benediction

21 [R]Having confidence in thy obedience I wrote unto thee, knowing that thou wilt also do more than I say.

22 But withal prepare me also a lodging: for [R]I trust that [R]through your prayers I shall be given unto you.

23 There salute thee [R]Ĕp'-ă-phrăs, my fellowprisoner in Christ Jesus;

24 [R]Marcus, [R]Är-ĭs-tär'-<u>ch</u>ŭs, [R]Dē'-măs, [R]Lucas, my fellowlabourers.

25 [R]The grace of our Lord Jesus Christ *be* with your spirit. Ä'-mĕn.

Written from Rome to Phī-lē'-mon, by ō-nĕs'-ĭ-mŭs, a servant.

THE EPISTLE OF PAUL THE APOSTLE

TO THE

HEBREWS

The authorship and destination of the Epistle to the Hebrews have remained somewhat enigmatic. In the East the letter was unanimously regarded as the work of Paul. Members of the Western Church, however, from the second to the end of the fourth century, expressed doubts about its Pauline authorship, Barnabas and Luke at times being suggested. The letter has no salutation. And while both its personal allusions and its teaching can be generally correlated with the experiences and thought of the apostle, its literary quality and type of argumentation mark it as decidely different from Paul's writings. One must distinguish between the author, who is responsible for its ideas and contents, and the writer or redacter of the Epistle, who was responsible for its literary form. Perhaps it was written by Apollos in behalf of Paul and under his sponsorship. Probably it was occasioned by the rising tide of Jewish nationalism just preceding the conflict with Rome, which brought Jewish Christians to a crisis wherein they could no longer be loyal to both their Christian faith and their Jewish nation. To those in such a dilemma, the author writes in demonstration of the superiority of Jesus Christ and the finality of Christianity over the Old Dispensation. Probably it was written from Rome to Jewish Christians in Palestine (Caesarea?). It should be dated about A.D. 62 or 63, after the martyrdom of James and before the Neronic persecutions and the destruction of Jerusalem.

OUTLINE OF THE BOOK:

CHAPTER 1

God's word through his Son

G OD, who at sundry times and ᴿin divers manners spake in time past unto the fathers by the prophets,

2 Hath ᴿin these last days ᴿspoken unto us by *his* Son, ᴿwhom he hath appointed heir of all things, ᴿby whom also he made the worlds;

3 ᴿWho being the brightness of *his* glory, and the express image of his person, and ᴿupholding all things by the word of his power, ᴿwhen he had by himself purged our sins, ᴿsat down on the right hand of the Majesty on high;

The Son's superiority over angels

4 Being made so much better than the angels, as ᴿhe hath by inheritance obtained a more excellent name than they.

5 For unto which of the angels said he at any time, ᴿThou art my Son, this day have I begotten thee? And again, ᴿI will be to him a Father, and he shall be to me a Son?

6 ᴺAnd again, when he bringeth in ᴿthe first begotten into the world, he saith, ᴿAnd let all the angels of God worship him.

7 And ᴺof the angels he saith, ᴿWho maketh his angels spirits, and his ministers a flame of fire.

8 But unto the Son *he saith,* ᴿThy throne, O God, *is* for ever and ever: a sceptre of ᴺrighteousness *is* the sceptre of thy kingdom.

9 Thou hast loved righteousness, and hated iniquity; therefore God, *even* thy God, ᴿhath anointed thee with the oil of gladness above thy fellows.

10 And, ᴿThou, Lord, in the beginning hast laid the foundation of the earth; and the heavens are the works of thine hands:

11 ᴿThey shall perish; but thou remainest; and they all shall wax old as doth a garment;

12 And as a vesture shalt thou fold them up, and they shall be changed: but thou art the same, and thy years shall not fail.

13 But to which of the angels said he at any time, ᴿSit on my right hand, until I make thine enemies thy footstool?

14 ᴿAre they not all ministering spirits, sent forth to minister for them who shall be ᴿheirs of salvation?

CHAPTER 2

Call for close attention

T HEREFORE we ought to give the more earnest heed to the things which we have heard, lest at any time we should ᴺlet *them* slip.

2 For if the word ᴿspoken by angels was stedfast, and ᴿevery transgression and disobedience received a just recompence of reward;

3 ᴿHow shall we escape, if we neglect so great salvation; ᴿwhich at the first began to be

spoken by the Lord, and was [R]confirmed unto us by them that heard *him;*

4 [R]God also bearing *them* witness, [R]both with signs and wonders, and with divers miracles, and [R]gifts[N] of the Holy Ghost, [R]according to his own will?

Christ perfected through suffering

5 For unto the angels hath he not put in subjection [R]the world to come, whereof we speak.

6 But one in a certain place testified, saying, [R]What is man, that thou art mindful of him? or the son of man, that thou visitest him?

7 Thou madest him [N]a little lower than the angels; thou crownedst him with glory and honour, and didst set him over the works of thy hands:

8 [R]Thou hast put all things in subjection under his feet. For in that he put all in subjection under him, he left nothing *that is* not put under him. But now [R]we see not yet all things put under him.

9 But we see Jesus, [R]who was made a little lower than the angels [N]for the suffering of death, [R]crowned with glory and honour; that he by the grace of God should taste death [R]for every man.

10 [R]For it became him, [R]for whom *are* all things, and by whom *are* all things, in bringing many sons unto glory, to make [R]the captain of their salvation [R]perfect through sufferings.

11 For [R]both he that sanctifieth and they who are sanctified [R]*are* all of one: for which cause [R]he is not ashamed to call them brethren,

12 Saying, [R]I will declare thy name unto my brethren, in the midst of the church will I sing praise unto thee.

13 And again, [R]I will put my trust in him. And again, [R]Behold I and the children [R]which God hath given me.

14 Forasmuch then as the children are partakers of flesh and blood, he [R]also himself likewise took part of the same; [R]that through death he might destroy him that had the power of death, that is, the devil;

15 And deliver them who [R]through fear of death were all their lifetime subject to bondage.

16 For verily [N]he took not on *him the nature of* angels; but he took on *him* the seed of Abraham.

17 Wherefore in all things it behoved him [R]to be made like unto *his* brethren, that he might be [R]a merciful and faithful high priest in things *pertaining* to God, to make reconciliation for the sins of the people.

18 [R]For in that he himself hath suffered being tempted, he is able to succour them that are tempted.

CHAPTER 3

Jesus, Apostle and High Priest

WHEREFORE, holy brethren, partakers of [R]the heavenly calling, consider [R]the Apostle and High Priest of our profession, Christ Jesus;

2 Who was faithful to him that [N]appointed him, as also [R]Moses *was faithful* in all his house.

3 For this *man* was counted worthy of more glory than Moses, inasmuch as [R]he who hath builded the house hath more honour than the house.

4 For every house is builded by some *man;* but [R]he that built all things *is* God.

5 [R]And Moses verily *was* faithful in all his house, as [R]a servant, [R]for a testimony of those things which were to be spoken after;

We are Christ's house

6 But Christ as [R]a son over his own house; [R]whose house are we, [R]if we hold fast the confidence and the rejoicing of the hope firm unto the end.

7 Wherefore (as [R]the Holy Ghost saith, [R]To day if ye will hear his voice,

8 Harden not your hearts, as in the provocation, in the day of temptation in the wilderness:

9 When your fathers tempted me, proved me, and saw my works forty years.

10 Wherefore I was grieved with that generation, and said, They do alway err in *their* heart; and they have not known my ways.

11 So I sware in my wrath, [N]They shall not enter into my rest.)

12 Take heed, brethren, lest there be in any of you an evil heart of unbelief, in departing from the living God.

13 But exhort one another daily, while it is called To day; lest any of you be hardened through the deceitfulness of sin.

14 For we are made partakers of Christ, [R]if we hold the beginning of our confidence stedfast unto the end;

15 While it is said, [R]To day if ye will hear his voice, harden not your hearts, as in the provocation.

16 [R]For some, when they had heard, did provoke: howbeit not all that came out of Egypt by Moses.

17 But with whom was he grieved forty

Center reference column:

CHAP. 2
AD 64

3 Luke 1:2
4 Mark 16:20
4 Acts 2:22
4 1 Cor. 12:4, 7, 11
4 Or, *distributions*
4 Eph. 1:5, 9
5 2 Pet. 3:13
6 Job 7:17
7 Or, *a little while inferior to*
8 Mat. 28:18
  Eph. 1:22
8 1 Cor. 15:25
9 Phil. 2:7-9
9 Or, *by*
9 Acts 2:33
9 John 3:16
  2 Cor. 5:15
10 Luke 24:46
10 Rom. 11:36
10 Acts 5:31
10 Luke 13:32
11 ch. 10:10
11 Acts 17:26
11 Mat. 28:10
  John 20:17
12 Ps. 22:22
13 Ps. 18:2
  Is. 12:2
13 Is. 8:18
13 John 10:29
14 John 1:14
  Phil. 2:7
14 Col. 2:15
15 Luke 1:74
  2 Tim. 1:7
16 Gr. *he taketh not hold of angels, but of the seed of Abraham he taketh hold*
17 Phil. 2:7
17 ch. 4:15

ch. 4:15, 16   18

CHAP. 3
AD 64

Rom. 1:7   1
1 Cor. 1:2
Rom. 15:8   1
Gr. *made*   2
Num. 12:7   2
Zech. 6:12   3
Mat. 16:18
Eph. 2:10   4
ch. 1:2
ver. 2   5
Ex. 14:31   5
Deut. 3:24
Deut. 18:19   5
ch. 1:2   6
1 Cor. 3:16   6
Mat. 10:22   6
Rom. 5:2
Col. 1:23
Acts 1:16   7
Ps. 95:7   7
Gr. *If they shall enter*   11
ver. 6   14
ver. 7   15
Num. 14:2   16

years? *was it* not with them that had sinned, [R]whose carcases fell in the wilderness?

18 And [R]to whom sware he that they should not enter into his rest, but to them that believed not?

19 So we see that they could not enter in because of unbelief.

CHAPTER 4

Good news received by faith

LET [R]us therefore fear, lest, a promise being left *us* of entering into his rest, any of you should seem to come short of it.

2 For unto us was the gospel preached, as well as unto them: but [N]the word preached did not profit them, [N]not being mixed with faith in them that heard *it*.

3 [R]For we which have believed do enter into rest, as he said, [R]As I have sworn in my wrath, if they shall enter into my rest: although the works were finished from the foundation of the world.

4 For he spake in a certain place of the seventh *day* on this wise, [R]And God did rest the seventh day from all his works.

5 And in this *place* again, If they shall enter into my rest.

6 Seeing therefore it remaineth that some must enter therein, [R]and they to whom [N]it was first preached entered not in because of unbelief:

7 Again, he limiteth a certain day, saying in David, To day, after so long a time; as it is said, [R]To day if ye will hear his voice, harden not your hearts.

8 For if [N]Jesus had given them rest, then would he not afterward have spoken of another day.

9 There remaineth therefore a [N]rest to the people of God.

10 For he that is entered into his rest, he also hath ceased from his own works, as God *did* from his.

11 Let us labour therefore to enter into that rest, lest any man fall after the same example of [N]unbelief.

12 For the word of God *is* [R]quick, and powerful, and [R]sharper than any [R]twoedged sword, piercing even to the dividing asunder of soul and spirit, and of the joints and marrow, and *is* [R]a discerner of the thoughts and intents of the heart.

13 [R]Neither is there any creature that is not manifest in his sight: but all things *are* naked [R]and opened unto the eyes of him with whom we have to do.

CHAP. 3

AD 64

17 Num. 14:22
Ps. 106:26
18 Num. 14:30

CHAP. 4

AD 64

1 ch. 12:15
2 Gr. *the word of hearing*
2 Or, *because they were not united by faith to*
3 ch. 3:14
3 Ps. 95:11
4 Ex. 20:11
6 ch. 3:19
6 Or, *the gospel was first preached*
7 Ps. 95:7
8 i.e. *Joshua*
9 Or, *keeping of a sabbath*
11 Or, *disobedience*
12 Ps. 147:15
Jer. 23:29
12 Is. 49:2
12 Eph. 6:17
Rev. 1:16
12 1 Cor. 14:25
13 Ps. 90:8
13 Job 26:6

ch. 7:26	14
ch. 10:23	14
Is. 53:3	15
Luke 22:28	15
2 Cor. 5:21	15
Eph. 2:18	16

CHAP. 5

AD 64

ch. 8:3	1
Or, *can reasonably bear with*	2
Lev. 4:3	3
John 3:27	4
Ex. 28:1	4
John 8:54	5
Ps. 2:7	5
Ps. 110:4	6
Mat. 26:39	7
John 17:1	
Ps. 22:1	7
Mat. 27:46	
Mat. 26:53	7
Mark 14:36	
Mat. 26:37	7
Mark 14:33	
John 12:27	
Or, *for his piety*	7
ch. 3:6	8
Phil. 2:8	8
John 16:12	11
2 Pet. 3:16	
Mat. 13:15	11

---

14 Seeing then that we have a great high priest, [R]that is passed into the heavens, Jesus the Son of God, [R]let us hold fast *our* profession.

15 For [R]we have not an high priest which cannot be touched with the feeling of our infirmities; but [R]was in all points tempted like as *we are,* [R]yet without sin.

16 [R]Let us therefore come boldly unto the throne of grace, that we may obtain mercy, and find grace to help in time of need.

CHAPTER 5

Qualifications of the high priest

FOR every high priest taken from among men [R]is ordained for men in things *pertaining* to God, that he may offer both gifts and sacrifices for sins:

2 Who [N]can have compassion on the ignorant, and on them that are out of the way; for that he himself also is compassed with infirmity.

3 And [R]by reason hereof he ought, as for the people, so also for himself, to offer for sins.

4 [R]And no man taketh this honour unto himself, but he that is called of God, as [R]was Aaron.

5 [R]So also Christ glorified not himself to be made an high priest; but he that said unto him, [R]Thou art my Son, to day have I begotten thee.

6 As he saith also in another *place,* [R]Thou *art* a priest for ever after the order of Mĕl-chĭś′-ĕd-ĕc.

7 Who in the days of his flesh, when he had [R]offered up prayers and supplications [R]with strong crying and tears unto him [R]that was able to save him from death, and was heard [R]in[N] that he feared;

8 [R]Though he were a Son, yet learned he [R]obedience by the things which he suffered;

9 And being made perfect, he became the author of eternal salvation unto all them that obey him;

10 Called of God an high priest after the order of Mĕl-chĭś′-ĕd-ĕc.

The dull of hearing

11 Of whom [R]we have many things to say, and hard to be uttered, seeing ye are [R]dull of hearing.

12 For when for the time ye ought to be teachers, ye have need that one teach you again which *be* the first principles of the oracles of God; and are become such as

have need of [R]milk, and not of strong meat.

13 For every one that useth milk [N]is unskilful in the word of righteousness: for he is [R]a babe.

14 But strong meat belongeth to them that are [N]of full age, *even* those who by reason [N]of use have their senses exercised [R]to discern both good and evil.

CHAPTER 6

Warning against apostasy

THEREFORE [R]leaving [N]the principles of the doctrine of Christ, let us go on unto perfection; not laying again the foundation of repentance [R]from dead works, and of faith toward God,

2 [R]Of the doctrine of baptisms, [R]and of laying on of hands, [R]and of resurrection of the dead, [R]and of eternal judgment.

3 And this will we do, [R]if God permit.

4 For [R]*it is* impossible for those [R]who were once enlightened, and have tasted of [R]the heavenly gift, and [R]were made partakers of the Holy Ghost,

5 And have tasted the good word of God, and the powers of [R]the world to come,

6 If they shall fall away, to renew them again unto repentance; [R]seeing they crucify to themselves the Son of God afresh, and put *him* to an open shame.

7 For the earth which drinketh in the rain that cometh oft upon it, and bringeth forth herbs meet for them [N]by whom it is dressed, [R]receiveth blessing from God:

8 [R]But that which beareth thorns and briers *is* rejected, and *is* nigh unto cursing; whose end *is* to be burned.

Encouragement to faith and patience

9 But, beloved, we are persuaded better things of you, and things that accompany salvation, though we thus speak.

10 [R]For [R]God *is* not unrighteous to forget [R]your work and labour of love, which ye have shewed toward his name, in that ye have [R]ministered to the saints, and do minister.

11 And we desire that [R]every one of you do shew the same diligence [R]to the full assurance of hope unto the end:

12 That ye be not slothful, but followers of them who through faith and patience [R]inherit the promises.

Encouragement to hope

13 For when God made promise to Abraham, because he could swear by no greater, [R]he sware by himself.

CHAP. 5
AD 64
12 1 Cor. 3:1
13 Gr. *hath no experience*
13 Eph. 4:14
1 Pet. 2:2
14 Or, *perfect,*
1 Cor. 2:6
14 Or, *of an habit, or, perfection*
14 Is. 7:15
1 Cor. 2:14

CHAP. 6
AD 64
1 ch. 5:12
1 Or, *the word of the beginning of Christ*
1 ch. 9:14
2 Acts 19:4, 5
2 Acts 8:14 & 19:6
2 Acts 17:31
2 Acts 24:25
3 Acts 18:21
4 Mat. 12:31
ch. 10:26
4 ch. 10:32
4 John 4:10
Eph. 2:8
4 Gal. 3:2, 5
ch. 2:4
5 ch. 2:5
6 ch. 10:29
7 Or, *for*
7 Ps. 65:10
8 Is. 5:6
10 Prov. 14:31
Mat. 10:42 & 25:40
John 13:20
10 Rom. 3:4
2 Thes. 1:6, 7
10 1 Thes. 1:3
10 Rom. 15:25
2 Cor. 8:4
2 Tim. 1:18
11 ch. 3:6, 14
11 Col. 2:2
12 ch. 10:36
13 Gen. 22:16, 17
Ps. 105:9
Luke 1:73

Ex. 22:11   16
ch. 11:9   17
Rom. 11:29   17
Gr. *interposed himself by an oath* 17
ch. 12:1   18
Lev. 16:15   19
ch. 9:7
ch. 4:14 & 8:1   20
& 9:24
ch. 3:1 & 5:6,   20
10 & 7:17

CHAP. 7
AD 64
Gen. 14:18   1
Gr. *without pedigree* 3
Num. 18:21, 26   5
Or, *pedigree*   6
Gen. 14:19   6
Rom. 4:13   6
ch. 5:6   8
& 6:20

---

14 Saying, Surely blessing I will bless thee, and multiplying I will multiply thee.

15 And so, after he had patiently endured, he obtained the promise.

16 For men verily swear by the greater: and [R]an oath for confirmation *is* to them an end of all strife.

17 Wherein God, willing more abundantly to shew unto [R]the heirs of promise [R]the immutability of his counsel, [N]confirmed *it* by an oath:

18 That by two immutable things, in which *it was* impossible for God to lie, we might have a strong consolation, who have fled for refuge to lay hold upon the hope [R]set before us:

19 Which *hope* we have as an anchor of the soul, both sure and stedfast, [R]and which entereth into that within the veil;

20 [R]Whither the forerunner is for us entered, *even* Jesus, [R]made an high priest for ever after the order of Mĕl-chĭs'-ĕd-ĕc.

CHAPTER 7

The order of Melchisedec

FOR this [R]Mĕl-chĭs'-ĕd-ĕc, king of Sā'-lĕm, priest of the most high God, who met Abraham returning from the slaughter of the kings, and blessed him;

2 To whom also Abraham gave a tenth part of all; first being by interpretation King of righteousness, and after that also King of Sā'-lĕm, which is, King of peace;

3 Without father, without mother, [N]without descent, having neither beginning of days, nor end of life; but made like unto the Son of God; abideth a priest continually.

4 Now consider how great this man *was*, [R]unto whom even the patriarch Abraham gave the tenth of the spoils.

5 And verily [R]they that are of the sons of Levi, who receive the office of the priesthood, have a commandment to take tithes of the people according to the law, that is, of their brethren, though they come out of the loins of Abraham:

6 But he whose [N]descent is not counted from them received tithes of Abraham, [R]and blessed [R]him that had the promises.

7 And without all contradiction the less is blessed of the better.

8 And here men that die receive tithes; but there he *receiveth them*, [R]of whom it is witnessed that he liveth.

9 And as I may so say, Levi also, who receiveth tithes, payed tithes in Abraham.

10 For he was yet in the loins of his father, when Mĕl-chĭs'-ĕd-ĕc met him.

Levitical priesthood inadequate

11 ᴿIf therefore perfection were by the Lē-vĭt′-ĭ-căl priesthood, (for under it the people received the law,) what further need *was there* that another priest should rise after the order of Mĕl-<u>ch</u>ĭś′-ĕd-ĕc, and not be called after the order of Aaron?

12 For the priesthood being changed, there is made of necessity a change also of the law.

13 For he of whom these things are spoken pertaineth to another tribe, of which no man gave attendance at the altar.

14 For *it is* evident that ᴿour Lord sprang out of Judah; of which tribe Moses spake nothing concerning priesthood.

15 And it is yet far more evident: for that after the similitude of Mĕl-<u>ch</u>ĭś′-ĕd-ĕc there ariseth another priest,

16 Who is made, not after the law of a carnal commandment, but after the power of an endless life.

17 For he testifieth, ᴿThou *art* a priest for ever after the order of Mĕl-<u>ch</u>ĭś′-ĕd-ĕc.

18 For there is verily a disannulling of the commandment going before for ᴿthe weakness and unprofitableness thereof.

19 For ᴿthe law made nothing perfect, ᴺbut the bringing in of ᴿa better hope *did;* by the which ᴿwe draw nigh unto God.

20 And inasmuch as not without an oath *he was made priest:*

21 (For those priests were made ᴺwithout an oath; but this with an oath by him that said unto him, ᴿThe Lord sware and will not repent, Thou *art* a priest for ever after the order of Mĕl-<u>ch</u>ĭś′-ĕd-ĕc:)

22 By so much ᴿwas Jesus made a surety of a better testament.

23 And they truly were many priests, because they were not suffered to continue by reason of death:

24 But this *man,* because he continueth ever, hath ᴺan unchangeable priesthood.

25 Wherefore he is able also to save them ᴺto the uttermost that come unto God by him, seeing he ever liveth ᴿto make intercession for them.

The Son as perfect high priest

26 For such an high priest became us, ᴿ*who is* holy, harmless, undefiled, separate from sinners, ᴿand made higher than the heavens;

27 Who needeth not daily, as those high priests, to offer up sacrifice, ᴿfirst for his own sins, ᴿand then for the people's: for ᴿthis he did once, when he offered up himself.

28 For the law maketh ᴿmen high priests

which have infirmity; but the word of the oath, which was since the law, *maketh* the Son, ᴿwho is ᴺconsecrated for evermore.

CHAPTER 8

Our high priest in heaven

NOW of the things which we have spoken *this is* the sum: We have such an high priest, ᴿwho is set on the right hand of the throne of the Majesty in the heavens;

2 A minister ᴺof ᴿthe sanctuary, and of ᴿthe true tabernacle, which the Lord pitched, and not man.

3 For ᴿevery high priest is ordained to offer gifts and sacrifices: wherefore ᴿ*it is* of necessity that this man have somewhat also to offer.

4 For if he were on earth, he should not be a priest, seeing that ᴺthere are priests that offer gifts according to the law:

5 Who serve unto the example and ᴿshadow of heavenly things, as Moses was admonished of God when he was about to make the tabernacle: ᴿfor, See, saith he, *that* thou make all things according to the pattern shewed to thee in the mount.

Christ mediates a better covenant

6 But now ᴿhath he obtained a more excellent ministry, by how much also he is the mediator of a better ᴺcovenant, which was established upon better promises.

7 ᴿFor if that first *covenant* had been faultless, then should no place have been sought for the second.

8 For finding fault with them, he saith, ᴿBehold, the days come, saith the Lord, when I will make a new covenant with the house of Israel and with the house of Judah:

9 Not according to the covenant that I made with their fathers in the day when I took them by the hand to lead them out of the land of Egypt; because they continued not in my covenant, and I regarded them not, saith the Lord.

10 For ᴿthis *is* the covenant that I will make with the house of Israel after those days, saith the Lord; I will ᴺput my laws into their mind, and write them ᴺin their hearts: and ᴿI will be to them a God, and they shall be to me a people:

11 And ᴿthey shall not teach every man his neighbour, and every man his brother, saying, Know the Lord: for all shall know me, from the least to the greatest.

12 For I will be merciful to their unrighteousness, ᴿand their sins and their iniquities will I remember no more.

13 ᴿIn that he saith, A new *covenant,* he

hath made the first old. Now that which decayeth and waxeth old *is* ready to vanish away.

CHAPTER 9

The earthly sanctuary

THEN verily the first *covenant* had also ᴺordinances of divine service, and ᴿa worldly sanctuary.

2 ᴿFor there was a tabernacle made; the first, ᴿwherein *was* ᴿthe candlestick, and ᴿthe table, and the shewbread; which is called ᴺthe sanctuary.

3 ᴿAnd after the second veil, the tabernacle which is called the Holiest of all;

4 Which had the golden censer, and ᴿthe ark of the covenant overlaid round about with gold, wherein *was* ᴿthe golden pot that had măn′-nă, and ᴿAaron's rod that budded, and ᴿthe tables of the covenant;

5 And ᴿover it the chĕr′-ū-bĭms of glory shadowing the mercyseat; of which we cannot now speak particularly.

6 Now when these things were thus ordained, ᴿthe priests went always into the first tabernacle, accomplishing the service *of God.*

7 But into the second *went* the high priest alone ᴿonce every year, not without blood, ᴿwhich he offered for himself, and *for* the errors of the people:

8 ᴿThe Holy Ghost this signifying, that ᴿthe way into the holiest of all was not yet made manifest, while as the first tabernacle was yet standing:

9 Which *was* a figure for the time then present, in which were offered both gifts and sacrifices, ᴿthat could not make him that did the service perfect, as pertaining to the conscience;

10 *Which stood* only in ᴿmeats and drinks, and ᴿdivers washings, ᴿand carnal ᴺordinances, imposed *on them* until the time of reformation.

Christ's eternal sacrifice

11 But Christ being come ᴿan high priest ᴿof good things to come, ᴿby a greater and more perfect tabernacle, not made with hands, that is to say, not of this building;

12 Neither ᴿby the blood of goats and calves, but ᴿby his own blood he entered in ᴿonce into the holy place, ᴿhaving obtained eternal redemption *for us.*

13 For if ᴿthe blood of bulls and of goats, and ᴿthe ashes of an heifer sprinkling the un-

clean, sanctifieth to the purifying of the flesh:

14 How much more ᴿshall the blood of Christ, ᴿwho through the eternal Spirit offered himself without ᴺspot to God, ᴿpurge your conscience from ᴿdead works ᴿto serve the living God?

The death which redeems

15 ᴿAnd for this cause ᴿhe is the mediator of the new testament, ᴿthat by means of death, for the redemption of the transgressions *that were* under the first testament, ᴿthey which are called might receive the promise of eternal inheritance.

16 For where a testament *is,* there must also of necessity ᴺbe the death of the testator.

17 For ᴿa testament *is* of force after men are dead: otherwise it is of no strength at all while the testator liveth.

18 ᴿWhereupon neither the first *testament* was ᴺdedicated without blood.

19 For when Moses had spoken every precept to all the people according to the law, ᴿhe took the blood of calves and of goats, ᴿwith water, and ᴺscarlet wool, and hyssop, and sprinkled both the book, and all the people,

20 Saying, ᴿThis *is* the blood of the testament which God hath enjoined unto you.

21 Moreover ᴿhe sprinkled with blood both the tabernacle, and all the vessels of the ministry.

22 And almost all things are by the law purged with blood; and ᴿwithout shedding of blood is no remission.

Christ, the sufficient sacrifice

23 *It was* therefore necessary that ᴿthe patterns of things in the heavens should be purified with these; but the heavenly things themselves with better sacrifices than these.

24 For ᴿChrist is not entered into the holy places made with hands, *which are* the figures of ᴿthe true; but into heaven itself, now ᴿto appear in the presence of God for us:

25 Nor yet that he should offer himself often, as ᴿthe high priest entereth into the holy place every year with blood of others;

26 For then must he often have suffered since the foundation of the world: but now ᴿonce ᴿin the end of the world hath he appeared to put away sin by the sacrifice of himself.

27 ᴿAnd as it is appointed unto men once to die, ᴿbut after this the judgment:

28 So ᴿChrist was once ᴿoffered to bear the sins ᴿof many; and unto them that ᴿlook for him shall he appear the second time without sin unto salvation.

CHAPTER 10

The law is but a shadow

FOR the law having ᴿa shadow ᴿof good things to come, *and* not the very image of the things, ᴿcan never with those sacrifices which they offered year by year continually make the comers thereunto ᴿperfect.

2 For then ᴺwould they not have ceased to be offered? because that the worshippers once purged should have had no more conscience of sins.

3 ᴿBut in those *sacrifices there is* a remembrance again *made* of sins every year.

4 For ᴿ*it is* not possible that the blood of bulls and of goats should take away sins.

Christ does God's will

5 Wherefore when he cometh into the world, he saith, ᴿSacrifice and offering thou wouldest not, but a body ᴺhast thou prepared me:

6 In burnt offerings and *sacrifices* for sin thou hast had no pleasure.

7 Then said I, Lo, I come (in the volume of the book it is written of me,) to do thy will, O God.

8 Above when he said, Sacrifice and offering and burnt offerings and *offering* for sin thou wouldest not, neither hadst pleasure *therein;* which are offered by the law;

9 Then said he, Lo, I come to do thy will, O God. He taketh away the first, that he may establish the second.

10 ᴿBy the which will we are sanctified ᴿthrough the offering of the body of Jesus Christ once *for all.*

Christ's single sacrifice for sin

11 And every priest standeth ᴿdaily ministering and offering oftentimes the same sacrifices, ᴿwhich can never take away sins:

12 ᴿBut this man, after he had offered one sacrifice for sins for ever, sat down on the right hand of God;

13 From henceforth expecting ᴿtill his enemies be made his footstool.

14 For by one offering ᴿhe hath perfected for ever them that are sanctified.

15 *Whereof* the Holy Ghost also is a witness to us: for after that he had said before,

16 ᴿThis *is* the covenant that I will make with them after those days, saith the Lord, I will put my laws into their hearts, and in their minds will I write them;

17 ᴺAnd their sins and iniquities will I remember no more.

18 Now where remission of these *is, there is* no more offering for sin.

Our confidence in Christ

19 Having therefore, brethren, ᴿboldnessᴺ to enter ᴿinto the holiest by the blood of Jesus,

20 By ᴿa new and living way, which he hath ᴺconsecrated for us, ᴿthrough the veil, that is to say, his flesh;

21 And *having* ᴿan high priest over ᴿthe house of God;

22 ᴿLet us draw near with a true heart ᴿin full assurance of faith, having our hearts sprinkled ᴿfrom an evil conscience, and ᴿour bodies washed with pure water.

23 ᴿLet us hold fast the profession of *our* faith without wavering; (for ᴿhe *is* faithful that promised;)

24 And let us consider one another to provoke unto love and to good works:

25 ᴿNot forsaking the assembling of ourselves together, as the manner of some *is;* but exhorting *one another:* and ᴿso much the more, as ye see ᴿthe day approaching.

Warning against sin

26 For ᴿif we sin wilfully ᴿafter that we have received the knowledge of the truth, there remaineth no more sacrifice for sins,

27 But a certain fearful looking for of judgment and ᴿfiery indignation, which shall devour the adversaries.

28 ᴿHe that despised Moses' law died without mercy ᴿunder two or three witnesses:

29 ᴿOf how much sorer punishment, suppose ye, shall he be thought worthy, who hath trodden under foot the Son of God, and ᴿhath counted the blood of the covenant, wherewith he was sanctified, an unholy thing, ᴿand hath done despite unto the Spirit of grace?

30 For we know him that hath said, ᴿVengeance *belongeth* unto me, I will recompense, saith the Lord. And again, ᴿThe Lord shall judge his people.

31 ᴿ*It is* a fearful thing to fall into the hands of the living God.

Exhortation to endurance

32 But ᴿcall to remembrance the former days, in which, ᴿafter ye were illuminated, ye endured ᴿa great fight of afflictions;

33 Partly, whilst ye were made ᴿa gazingstock both by reproaches and afflictions; and partly, whilst ye became companions of them that were so used.

34 For ye had compassion of me ᴿin my bonds, and ᴿtook joyfully the spoiling of your goods, knowing ᴺin yourselves that ᴿye have in heaven a better and an enduring substance.

35 Cast not away therefore your confidence, ^Rwhich hath great recompence of reward.

36 ^RFor ye have need of patience, that, after ye have done the will of God, ^Rye might receive the promise.

37 For ^Ryet a little while, and ^Rhe that shall come will come, and will not tarry.

38 Now ^Rthe just shall live by faith: but if *any man* draw back, my soul shall have no pleasure in him.

39 But we are not of them ^Rwho draw back unto perdition; but of them that ^Rbelieve to the saving of the soul.

CHAPTER 11

Definition of faith

NOW faith is the ^Nsubstance of things hoped for, the evidence ^Rof things not seen.

2 For ^Rby it the elders obtained a good report.

3 Through faith we understand that ^Rthe worlds were framed by the word of God, so that things which are seen were not made of things which do appear.

Examples of faith

4 By faith ^RAbel offered unto God a more excellent sacrifice than Cain, by which he obtained witness that he was righteous, God testifying of his gifts: and by it he being dead yet speaketh.

5 By faith ^RĒ′-nŏch was translated that he should not see death; and was not found, because God had translated him: for before his translation he had this testimony, that he pleased God.

6 But without faith *it is* impossible to please *him:* for he that cometh to God must believe that he is, and *that* he is a rewarder of them that diligently seek him.

7 By faith ^RNoah, being warned of God of things not seen as yet, ^Nmoved with fear, ^Rprepared an ark to the saving of his house; by the which he condemned the world, and became heir of ^Rthe righteousness which is by faith.

8 By faith ^RAbraham, when he was called to go out into a place which he should after receive for an inheritance, obeyed; and he went out, not knowing whither he went.

9 By faith he sojourned in the land of promise, as *in* a strange country, ^Rdwelling in tabernacles with Isaac and Jacob, ^Rthe heirs with him of the same promise:

10 For he looked for ^Ra city which hath

foundations, ^Rwhose builder and maker *is* God.

11 Through faith also ^RSarah herself received strength to conceive seed, and ^Rwas delivered of a child when she was past age, because she judged him ^Rfaithful who had promised.

12 Therefore sprang there even of one, and ^Rhim as good as dead, ^R*so many* as the stars of the sky in multitude, and as the sand which is by the sea shore innumerable.

Faith seeks a homeland

13 These all died ^Nin faith, ^Rnot having received the promises, but ^Rhaving seen them afar off, and were persuaded of *them,* and embraced *them,* and ^Rconfessed that they were strangers and pilgrims on the earth.

14 For they that say such things ^Rdeclare plainly that they seek a country.

15 And truly, if they had been mindful of that *country* from whence they came out, they might have had opportunity to have returned.

16 But now they desire a better *country,* that is, an heavenly: wherefore God is not ashamed ^Rto be called their God: for ^Rhe hath prepared for them a city.

More examples of faith

17 By faith ^RAbraham, when he was tried, offered up Isaac: and he that had received the promises ^Roffered up his only begotten *son,*

18 ^NOf whom it was said, ^RThat in Isaac shall thy seed be called:

19 Accounting that God ^Rwas able to raise *him* up, even from the dead; from whence also he received him in a figure.

20 By faith ^RIsaac blessed Jacob and Esau concerning things to come.

21 By faith Jacob, when he was a dying, ^Rblessed both the sons of Joseph; and ^Rworshipped, *leaning* upon the top of his staff.

22 By faith ^RJoseph, when he died, ^Nmade mention of the departing of the children of Israel; and gave commandment concerning his bones.

23 By faith ^RMoses, when he was born, was hid three months of his parents, because they saw *he was* a proper child; and they were not afraid of the king's ^Rcommandment.

24 By faith ^RMoses, when he was come to years, refused to be called the son of Pharaoh's daughter;

25 ^RChoosing rather to suffer affliction with the people of God, than to enjoy the pleasures of sin for a season;

26 Esteeming ^Rthe reproach ^Nof Christ greater riches than the treasures in Egypt: for

CHAP. 10	
AD 64	
35	Mat. 5:12
36	Luke 21:19
36	Col. 3:24
37	Luke 18:8
37	Hab. 2:3, 4
38	Rom. 1:17
	Gal. 3:11
39	2 Pet. 2:20
39	Acts 16:31
	1 Thes. 5:9
	2 Thes. 2:14

CHAP. 11	
AD 64	
1	Or, *ground,* or, *confidence*
1	Rom. 8:24
	2 Cor. 4:18
2	ver. 39
3	Gen. 1:1
	Ps. 33:6
	John 1:3
	2 Pet. 3:5
4	Gen. 4:4
	1 John 3:12
5	Gen. 5:22
7	Gen. 6:13
7	Or, *being wary*
7	1 Pet. 3:20
7	Rom. 3:22
	Phil. 3:9
8	Gen. 12:1
	Acts 7:2-4
9	Gen. 12:8
9	ch 6:17
10	ch. 12:22

Rev. 21:10	10
Gen. 17:19 & 18:11, 14	11
Luke 1:36	11
Rom. 4:21	11
Rom. 4:19	12
Rom. 4:18	12
Gr. *according to faith*	13
ver. 39	13
John 8:56	13
Gen. 23:4	13
1 Chr. 29:15	
Ps. 39:12	
1 Pet. 1:17	
ch. 13:14	14
Ex. 3:6, 15	16
Mat. 22:32	
Acts 7:32	
ch. 13:14	16
Gen. 22:1	17
Jas. 2:21	17
Or, *To*	18
Gen. 21:12	18
Rom. 9:7	
Rom. 4:17	19
Gen. 27:27	20
Gen. 48:5	21
Gen. 47:31	21
Gen. 50:24	22
Or, *remembered*	22
Ex. 2:2	23
Ex. 1:16	23
Ex. 2:10	24
Ps. 84:10	25
ch. 13:13	26
Or, *for Christ*	26

he had respect unto ᴿthe recompence of the reward.

27 By faith ᴿhe forsook Egypt, not fearing the wrath of the king: for he endured, as ᴿseeing him who is invisible.

28 Through faith ᴿhe kept the passover, and the sprinkling of blood, lest he that destroyed the firstborn should touch them.

29 By faith ᴿthey passed through the Red sea as by dry *land:* which the Egyptians assaying to do were drowned.

30 By faith ᴿthe walls of Jericho fell down, after they were compassed about seven days.

31 By faith ᴿthe harlot Rahab perished not with them ᴺthat believed not, when ᴿshe had received the spies with peace.

32 And what shall I more say? for the time would fail me to tell of ᴿGĕd′-ĕ-on, and *of* Bâr′-ăk, and *of* ᴿSamson, and *of* ᴿJĕph′-thāē; *of* ᴿDavid also, and ᴿSamuel, and *of* the prophets:

33 Who through faith subdued kingdoms, wrought righteousness, ᴿobtained promises, ᴿstopped the mouths of lions,

34 ᴿQuenched the violence of fire, ᴿescaped the edge of the sword, ᴿout of weakness were made strong, waxed valiant in fight, ᴿturned to flight the armies of the aliens.

35 ᴿWomen received their dead raised to life again: and others were ᴿtortured, not accepting deliverance; that they might obtain a better resurrection:

36 And others had trial of *cruel* mockings and scourgings, yea, moreover ᴿof bonds and imprisonment:

37 ᴿThey were stoned, they were sawn asunder, were tempted, were slain with the sword: ᴿthey wandered about ᴿin sheepskins and goatskins; being destitute, afflicted, tormented;

38 (Of whom the world was not worthy:) they wandered in deserts, and *in* mountains, and ᴿ*in* dens and caves of the earth.

39 And these all, ᴿhaving obtained a good report through faith, received not the promise:

40 God having ᴺprovided some better thing for us, that they without us should not be ᴿmade perfect.

CHAPTER 12

The example of Jesus

Wherefore seeing we also are compassed about with so great a cloud of witnesses, ᴿlet us lay aside every weight, and the sin which doth so easily beset *us,* and ᴿlet

Center reference column

CHAP. 11
AD 64

26 ch. 10:35
27 Ex. 10:28
27 ver. 13
28 Ex. 12:21
29 Ex. 14:22
30 Josh. 6:20
31 Josh. 6:23
31 Or, *that were disobedient*
31 Josh. 2:1
32 Judg. 6:11
32 Judg. 13:24
32 Judg. 12:7
32 1 Sam. 16:1
32 1 Sam. 1:20
33 2 Sam. 7:11
33 Judg. 14:5
1 Sam. 17:34
34 Dan. 3:25
34 1 Sam. 20:1
34 2 Ki. 20:7
34 Judg. 15:8
35 1 Ki. 17:22
35 Acts 22:25
36 Gen. 39:20
Jer. 20:2
37 1 Ki. 21:13
Acts 7:58
37 2 Ki. 1:8
Mat. 3:4
37 Zech. 13:4
38 1 Ki. 18:4
39 ver. 2, 13
40 Or, *foreseen*
40 ch. 5:9

CHAP. 12
AD 64

1 Col. 3:8
1 1 Cor. 9:24

Rom. 12:12   1
Or, *beginner*   2
Luke 24:26   2
Phil. 2:8
Ps. 110:1   2.
1 Pet. 3:22
Mat. 10:24   3
John 15:20
Gal. 6:9   3
1 Cor. 10:13   4
Job 5:17   5
Ps. 94:12   6
Jas. 1:12
Deut. 8:5   7
1 Pet. 5:9   8
Job 12:10   9
Or, *as seemed   10
good, or, meet
to them*
Lev. 11:44   10
Jas. 3:18   11
Job 4:3, 4   12
Prov. 4:26   13
Or, *even*   13
Gal. 6:1   13
Ps. 34:14   14
2 Tim. 2:22
Mat. 5:8   14
2 Cor. 7:1
Gal. 5:4   15
Or, *fall from*   15
ch. 3:12   15
Eph. 5:3   16
Gen. 25:33   16
Gen. 27:34   17

us run ᴿwith patience the race that is set before us,

2 Looking unto Jesus the ᴺauthor and finisher of *our* faith; ᴿwho for the joy that was set before him endured the cross, despising the shame, and ᴿis set down at the right hand of the throne of God.

The meaning of discipline

3 ᴿFor consider him that endured such contradiction of sinners against himself, ᴿlest ye be wearied and faint in your minds.

4 ᴿYe have not yet resisted unto blood, striving against sin.

5 And ye have forgotten the exhortation which speaketh unto you as unto children, ᴿMy son, despise not thou the chastening of the Lord, nor faint when thou art rebuked of him:

6 For ᴿwhom the Lord loveth he chasteneth, and scourgeth every son whom he receiveth.

7 ᴿIf ye endure chastening, God dealeth with you as with sons; for what son is he whom the father chasteneth not?

8 But if ye be without chastisement, ᴿwhereof all are partakers, then are ye bastards, and not sons.

9 Furthermore we have had fathers of our flesh which corrected *us,* and we gave *them* reverence: shall we not much rather be in subjection unto ᴿthe Father of spirits, and live?

10 For they verily for a few days chastened *us* ᴺafter their own pleasure; but he for *our* profit, ᴿthat *we* might be partakers of his holiness.

11 Now no chastening for the present seemeth to be joyous, but grievous: nevertheless afterward it yieldeth ᴿthe peaceable fruit of righteousness unto them which are exercised thereby.

Encouragement to endure

12 Wherefore ᴿlift up the hands which hang down, and the feeble knees;

13 ᴿAnd make ᴺstraight paths for your feet, lest that which is lame be turned out of the way; ᴿbut let it rather be healed.

14 ᴿFollow peace with all *men,* and holiness, ᴿwithout which no man shall see the Lord:

15 Looking diligently ᴿlest any man ᴺfail of the grace of God; ᴿlest any root of bitterness springing up trouble *you,* and thereby many be defiled;

16 ᴿLest there *be* any fornicator, or profane person, as Esau, ᴿwho for one morsel of meat sold his birthright.

17 For ye know how that afterward, ᴿwhen

he would have inherited the blessing, he was rejected: for he found no ᴺplace of repentance, though he sought it carefully with tears.

18 For ye are not come unto ᴿthe mount that might be touched, and that burned with fire, nor unto blackness, and darkness, and tempest,

19 And the sound of a trumpet, and the voice of words; which *voice* they that heard ᴿentreated that the word should not be spoken to them any more:

20 (For they could not endure that which was commanded, ᴿAnd if so much as a beast touch the mountain, it shall be stoned, or thrust through with a dart:

21 ᴿAnd so terrible was the sight, *that* Moses said, I exceedingly fear and quake:)

22 But ye are come ᴿunto mount Sī'-ǫn, ᴿand unto the city of the living God, the heavenly Jerusalem, ᴿand to an innumerable company of angels,

23 To the general assembly and church of ᴿthe firstborn, ᴿwhich are ᴺwritten in heaven, and to God ᴿthe Judge of all, and to the spirits of just men ᴿmade perfect,

24 And to Jesus ᴿthe mediator of the new ᴺcovenant, and to ᴿthe blood of sprinkling, that speaketh better things ᴿthan *that of* Abel.

25 See that ye refuse not him that speaketh. For ᴿif they escaped not who refused him that spake on earth, much more *shall not* we *escape,* if we turn away from him that *speaketh* from heaven:

26 ᴿWhose voice then shook the earth: but now he hath promised, saying, ᴿYet once more I shake not the earth only, but also heaven.

27 And this *word,* Yet once more, signifieth ᴿthe removing of those things that ᴺare shaken, as of things that are made, that those things which cannot be shaken may remain.

28 Wherefore we receiving a kingdom which cannot be moved, ᴺlet us have grace, whereby we may serve God acceptably with reverence and godly fear:

29 For ᴿour God *is* a consuming fire.

CHAPTER 13

Exhortation to godly conduct

LET ᴿbrotherly love continue.

2 ᴿBe not forgetful to entertain strangers: for thereby ᴿsome have entertained angels unawares.

3 ᴿRemember them that are in bonds, as bound with them; *and* them which suffer adversity, as being yourselves also in the body.

4 Marriage *is* honourable in all, and the bed

CHAP. **12**	
AD 64	
17	Or, *way to change his mind*
18	Deut. 4:11
19	Ex. 20:19
	Deut. 5:5
20	Ex. 19:13
21	Ex. 19:16
22	Gal. 4:26
	Rev. 3:12
22	Phil. 3:20
22	Deut. 33:2
	Ps. 68:17
23	Jas. 1:18
23	Luke 10:20
23	Or, *enrolled*
23	Ps. 94:2
23	Phil. 3:12
24	ch. 9:15
24	Or, *testament*
24	Ex. 24:8
24	Gen. 4:10
25	ch. 2:2, 3
26	Ex. 19:18
26	Hag. 2:6
27	2 Pet. 3:10
27	Or, *may be shaken*
28	Or, *let us hold fast*
29	Ex. 24:17
	Deut. 4:24

CHAP. **13**	
AD 64	
1	Rom. 12:10
	1 Pet. 1:22
2	Mat. 25:35
	1 Tim. 3:2
2	Gen. 18:3
3	Mat. 25:36

1 Cor. 6:9	4
Phil. 4:11	5
Gen. 28:15	5
Ps. 27:1	6
ver. 17	7
Or, *are the guides*	7
ch. 6:12	7
John 8:58	8
Eph. 4:14	9
Col. 2:4, 8	
Rom. 14:17	9
1 Tim. 4:3	
1 Cor. 9:13	10
Ex. 29:14	11
Acts 7:58	12
1 Pet. 4:14	13
Mic. 2:10	14
Phil. 3:20	
Eph. 5:20	15
Lev. 7:12	15
Hos. 14:2	15
Gr. *confessing to*	
Rom. 12:13	16
2 Cor. 9:12	16
Phil. 2:29	17
1 Tim. 5:17	
Or, *guide*	17
Ezek. 3:17	17
Eph. 6:19	18
Acts 23:1	18
Rom. 15:33	20
Rom. 4:24	20
Gal. 1:1	
1 Pet. 2:25	20
Zech. 9:11	20
Or, *testament*	20

undefiled: ᴿbut whoremongers and adulterers God will judge.

5 *Let your* conversation *be* without covetousness; *and* ᴿ*be* content with such things as ye have: for he hath said, ᴿI will never leave thee, nor forsake thee.

6 So that we may boldly say, ᴿThe Lord *is* my helper, and I will not fear what man shall do unto me.

7 ᴿRemember them which ᴺhave the rule over you, who have spoken unto you the word of God: ᴿwhose faith follow, considering the end of *their* conversation.

8 Jesus Christ ᴿthe same yesterday, and to day, and for ever.

9 ᴿBe not carried about with divers and strange doctrines. For *it is* a good thing that the heart be established with grace; ᴿnot with meats, which have not profited them that have been occupied therein.

10 ᴿWe have an altar, whereof they have no right to eat which serve the tabernacle.

11 For ᴿthe bodies of those beasts, whose blood is brought into the sanctuary by the high priest for sin, are burned without the camp.

12 Wherefore Jesus also, that he might sanctify the people with his own blood, ᴿsuffered without the gate.

13 Let us go forth therefore unto him without the camp, bearing ᴿhis reproach.

14 ᴿFor here have we no continuing city, but we seek one to come.

15 ᴿBy him therefore let us offer ᴿthe sacrifice of praise to God continually, that is, ᴿthe fruit of *our* lips ᴺgiving thanks to his name.

16 ᴿBut to do good and to communicate forget not: for ᴿwith such sacrifices God is well pleased.

17 ᴿObey them that ᴺhave the rule over you, and submit yourselves: for ᴿthey watch for your souls, as they that must give account, that they may do it with joy, and not with grief: for that *is* unprofitable for you.

Request for prayer

18 ᴿPray for us: for we trust we have ᴿa good conscience, in all things willing to live honestly.

19 But I beseech *you* the rather to do this, that I may be restored to you the sooner.

Greetings and benediction

20 Now ᴿthe God of peace, ᴿthat brought again from the dead our Lord Jesus, ᴿthat great shepherd of the sheep, ᴿthrough the blood of the everlasting ᴺcovenant,

21 ᴿMake you perfect in every good work to do his will, ᴿworkingᴺ in you that which is wellpleasing in his sight, through Jesus Christ; ᴿto whom *be* glory for ever and ever. Ä′-mĕn.

22 And I beseech you, brethren, suffer the word of exhortation: for ᴿI have written a letter unto you in few words.

23 Know ye that ᴿ*our* brother Timothy ᴿis set at liberty; with whom, if he come shortly, I will see you.

24 Salute all them ᴿthat have the rule over you, and all the saints. They of Italy salute you.

25 ᴿGrace *be* with you all. Ä′-mĕn.

Written to the Hebrews from Italy by Timothy.

CHAP. **13**	
AD 64	
21 1 Pet. 5:10	
21 Phil. 2:13	
21 Or, *doing*	
21 Gal. 1:5	
22 1 Pet. 5:12	
23 1 Thes. 3:2	
23 1 Tim. 6:12	
ver. 7, 17	**24**
Tit. 3:15	**25**

THE GENERAL EPISTLE OF
JAMES

The Epistle of James is an ethical treatise on the theme "A Doer of the Word." Its author, speaking with an authoritative tone, yet without evidencing an autocratic spirit, wished to encourage the Jewish Christians in their "various trials" and to promote with their faith the performance of Christian virtues. The epistle bears marked similarity to the Sermon on the Mount and Old Testament wisdom literature. It claims to have been written by "James, a servant of God and of the Lord Jesus Christ," and the early Church understood this ascription to refer to James, the Less, leader of the Jerusalem Church (cf. Acts 15) until his martyrdom in A.D. 62. The contents of the Epistle may have been first delivered as a sermon and afterward sent out to a wider audience as a circular letter before A.D. 62. It is an example of early Jewish Christian ethical preaching, whose message is needful as well for the church today.

OUTLINE OF THE EPISTLE OF JAMES:
   I. Salutation 1:1
  II. The Testing of Faith 1:2 – 2:26
 III. The Control of the Tongue 3:1 – 18
 IV. Rebuke of Worldliness 4:1 – 17
  V. Warning to the Rich 5:1 – 6
 VI. Concluding Exhortations 5:7 – 20

CHAPTER 1

Salutation

JAMES,ᴿ ᴿa servant of God and of the Lord Jesus Christ, ᴿto the twelve tribes ᴿwhich are scattered abroad, greeting.

Trials and temptations

2 My brethren, ᴿcount it all joy ᴿwhen ye fall into divers temptations;

3 ᴿKnowing *this*, that the trying of your faith worketh patience.

4 But let patience have *her* perfect work, that ye may be perfect and entire, wanting nothing.

5 ᴿIf any of you lack wisdom, ᴿlet him ask of God, that giveth to all *men* liberally, and upbraideth not; and ᴿit shall be given him.

6 ᴿBut let him ask in faith, nothing wavering. For he that wavereth is like a wave of the sea driven with the wind and tossed.

7 For let not that man think that he shall receive any thing of the Lord.

8 ᴿA double minded man *is* unstable in all his ways.

9 Let the brother of low degree ᴺrejoice in that he is exalted:

10 But the rich, in that he is made low: because ᴿas the flower of the grass he shall pass away.

CHAP. **1**	
AD 60	
1 Acts 12:17	
1 Tit. 1:1	
1 Acts 26:7	
1 Deut. 32:26	
John 7:35	
Acts 2:5	
1 Pet. 1:1	
2 Acts 5:41	
2 1 Pet. 1:6	
3 Rom. 5:3	
5 1 Ki. 3:9	
Prov. 2:3	
5 Mat. 7:7	
Luke 11:9	
John 14:13	
5 Jer. 29:12	
1 John 5:14	
6 Mark 11:24	
1 Tim. 2:8	
8 ch. 4:8	
9 Or, *glory*	
10 Job 14:2	
Ps. 37:2	
1 Cor. 7:31	
Job 5:17	**12**
Prov. 3:11	
1 Cor. 9:25	**12**
2 Tim. 4:8	
Mat. 10:22	**12**
Or, *evils*	**13**
Job 15:35	**15**
Ps. 7:14	
Rom. 6:21	**15**
John 3:27	**17**
Num. 23:19	**17**
John 1:13	**18**
1 Cor. 4:15	
Eph. 1:12	**18**
Rev. 14:4	**18**
Eccl. 5:1	**19**
Prov. 10:19	**19**
Eccl. 5:2	
Prov. 14:17	**19**

11 For the sun is no sooner risen with a burning heat, but it withereth the grass, and the flower thereof falleth, and the grace of the fashion of it perisheth: so also shall the rich man fade away in his ways.

12 ᴿBlessed *is* the man that endureth temptation: for when he is tried, he shall receive ᴿthe crown of life, ᴿwhich the Lord hath promised to them that love him.

13 Let no man say when he is tempted, I am tempted of God: for God cannot be tempted with ᴺevil, neither tempteth he any man:

14 But every man is tempted, when he is drawn away of his own lust, and enticed.

15 Then ᴿwhen lust hath conceived, it bringeth forth sin: and sin, when it is finished, ᴿbringeth forth death.

16 Do not err, my beloved brethren.

17 ᴿEvery good gift and every perfect gift is from above, and cometh down from the Father of lights, ᴿwith whom is no variableness, neither shadow of turning.

18 ᴿOf his own will begat he us with the word of truth, ᴿthat we should be a kind of ᴿfirstfruits of his creatures.

Pure speech and pure conduct

19 Wherefore, my beloved brethren, ᴿlet every man be swift to hear, ᴿslow to speak, ᴿslow to wrath:

20 For the wrath of man worketh not the righteousness of God.

21 Wherefore ᴿlay apart all filthiness and superfluity of naughtiness, and receive with meekness the engrafted word, ᴿwhich is able to save your souls.

22 But ᴿbe ye doers of the word, and not hearers only, deceiving your own selves.

23 For ᴿif any be a hearer of the word, and not a doer, he is like unto a man beholding his natural face in a glass:

24 For he beholdeth himself, and goeth his way, and straightway forgetteth what manner of man he was.

25 But ᴿwhoso looketh into the perfect ᴿlaw of liberty, and continueth *therein,* he being not a forgetful hearer, but a doer of the work, ᴿthis man shall be blessed in his ᴺdeed.

26 If any man among you seem to be religious, and ᴿbridleth not his tongue, but deceiveth his own heart, this man's religion *is* vain.

27 Pure religion and undefiled before God and the Father is this, ᴿTo visit the fatherless and widows in their affliction, ᴿ*and* to keep himself unspotted from the world.

CHAPTER 2

Impartiality of love

MY brethren, have not the faith of our Lord Jesus Christ, ᴿ*the Lord* of glory, with ᴿrespect of persons.

2 For if there come unto your ᴺassembly a man with a gold ring, in goodly apparel, and there come in also a poor man in vile raiment;

3 And ye have respect to him that weareth the gay clothing, and say unto him, Sit thou here ᴺin a good place; and say to the poor, Stand thou there, or sit here under my footstool:

4 Are ye not then partial in yourselves, and are become judges of evil thoughts?

5 Hearken, my beloved brethren, ᴿHath not God chosen the poor of this world ᴿrich in faith, and heirs of ᴺthe kingdom ᴿwhich he hath promised to them that love him?

6 But ᴿye have despised the poor. Do not rich men oppress you, ᴿand draw you before the judgment seats?

7 Do not they blaspheme that worthy name by the which ye are called?

8 If ye fulfil the royal law according to the scripture, ᴿThou shalt love thy neighbour as thyself, ye do well:

9 But ᴿif ye have respect to persons, ye commit sin, and are convinced of the law as transgressors.

10 For whosoever shall keep the whole law, and yet offend in one *point,* ᴿhe is guilty of all.

11 For ᴺhe that said, ᴿDo not commit adultery, said also, Do not kill. Now if thou commit no adultery, yet if thou kill, thou art become a transgressor of the law.

12 So speak ye, and so do, as they that shall be judged by ᴿthe law of liberty.

13 For ᴿhe shall have judgment without mercy, that hath shewed no mercy; and ᴿmercy ᴺrejoiceth against judgment.

Faith and works

14 ᴿWhat *doth it* profit, my brethren, though a man say he hath faith, and have not works? can faith save him?

15 ᴿIf a brother or sister be naked, and destitute of daily food,

16 And ᴿone of you say unto them, Depart in peace, be *ye* warmed and filled; notwithstanding ye give them not those things which are needful to the body; what *doth it* profit?

17 Even so faith, if it hath not works, is dead, being ᴺalone.

18 Yea, a man may say, Thou hast faith, and I have works: shew me thy faith ᴺwithout thy works, ᴿand I will shew thee my faith by my works.

19 Thou believest that there is one God; thou doest well: the devils also believe, and tremble.

20 But wilt thou know, O vain man, that faith without works is dead?

21 Was not Abraham our father justified by works, ᴿwhen he had offered Isaac his son upon the altar?

22 ᴺSeest thou ᴿhow faith wrought with his works, and by works with faith made perfect?

23 And the scripture was fulfilled which saith, ᴿAbraham believed God, and it was imputed unto him for righteousness: and he was called ᴿthe Friend of God.

24 Ye see then how that by works a man is justified, and not by faith only.

25 Likewise also ᴿwas not Rahab the harlot justified by works, when she had received the messengers, and had sent *them* out another way?

26 For as the body without the ᴺspirit is dead, so faith without works is dead also.

CHAPTER 3

Control of the tongue

MY brethren, ᴿbe not many masters, ᴿknowing that we shall receive the greater ᴺcondemnation.

CHAP. 1
AD 60

21 Col. 3:8
1 Pet. 2:1
21 Acts 13:26
Rom. 1:16
Eph. 1:13
Tit. 2:11
22 Mat. 7:21
Rom. 2:13
1 John 3:7
23 Luke 6:47
25 2 Cor. 3:18
25 ch. 2:12
25 John 13:17
25 Or, *doing*
26 Ps. 34:13
1 Pet. 3:10
27 Is. 1:16
Mat. 25:36
27 Rom. 12:2
1 John 5:18

CHAP. 2
AD 60

1 1 Cor. 2:8
1 Lev. 19:15
Deut. 1:17
Mat. 22:16
Jude 16
2 Gr. *synagogue*
3 Or, *well,*
or, *seemly*
5 John 7:48
5 Luke 12:21
5 Or, *that*
5 Ex. 20:6
Prov. 8:17
6 1 Cor. 11:22
6 Acts 13:50
8 Lev. 19:18
Mat. 22:39
9 ver. 1

Deut. 27:26   10
Mat. 5:19
Gal. 3:10
Or, *that law*   11
which said
Ex. 20:13   11
ch. 1:25   12
Job 22:6   13
1 John 4:17   13
Or, *glorieth*   13
Mat. 7:26   14
& 15:11
Luke 3:11   15
1 John 3:18   16
Gr. *by itself*   17
Some copies   18
read, *by thy works*
ch. 3:13   18
Gen. 22:9   21
Or, *Thou seest*   22
Heb. 11:17   22
Gen. 15:6   23
Rom. 4:3
Gal. 3:6
2 Chr. 20:7   23
Is. 41:8
Heb. 11:31   25
Or, *breath*   26

CHAP. 3
AD 60

Mat. 23:8   1
Luke 6:37   1
Or, *judgment*   1

2 For ᴿin many things we offend all. ᴿIf any man offend not in word, ᴿthe same *is* a perfect man, *and* able also to bridle the whole body.

3 Behold, ᴿwe put bits in the horses' mouths, that they may obey us; and we turn about their whole body.

4 Behold also the ships, which though *they be* so great, and *are* driven of fierce winds, yet are they turned about with a very small helm, whithersoever the governor listeth.

5 Even so ᴿthe tongue is a little member, and ᴿboasteth great things. Behold, how great ᴺa matter a little fire kindleth!

6 And ᴿthe tongue *is* a fire, a world of iniquity: so is the tongue among our members, that ᴿit defileth the whole body, and setteth on fire the ᴺcourse of nature; and it is set on fire of hell.

7 For every ᴺkind of beasts, and of birds, and of serpents, and of things in the sea, is tamed, and hath been tamed of ᴺmankind:

8 But the tongue can no man tame; *it is* an unruly evil, ᴿfull of deadly poison.

9 Therewith bless we God, even the Father; and therewith curse we men, ᴿwhich are made after the similitude of God.

10 Out of the same mouth proceedeth blessing and cursing. My brethren, these things ought not so to be.

11 Doth a fountain send forth at the same ᴺplace sweet *water* and bitter?

12 Can the fig tree, my brethren, bear olive berries? either a vine, figs? so *can* no fountain both yield salt water and fresh.

Earthly and heavenly wisdom

13 ᴿWho *is* a wise man and endued with knowledge among you? let him shew out of a good conversation ᴿhis works ᴿwith meekness of wisdom.

14 But if ye have ᴿbitter envying and strife in your hearts, ᴿglory not, and lie not against the truth.

15 ᴿThis wisdom descendeth not from above, but *is* earthly, ᴺsensual, devilish.

16 For ᴿwhere envying and strife *is,* there *is* ᴺconfusion and every evil work.

17 But ᴿthe wisdom that is from above is first pure, then peaceable, gentle, *and* easy to be entreated, full of mercy and good fruits, ᴺwithout partiality, ᴿand without hypocrisy.

18 ᴿAnd the fruit of righteousness is sown in peace of them that make peace.

CHAPTER 4

Covetousness and judgment

FROM whence *come* wars and ᴺfightings among you? *come they* not hence,

---

CHAP. **3**

AD 60

2 1 Ki. 8:46
2 Chr. 6:36
Prov. 20:9
2 Ps. 34:13
1 Pet. 3:10
2 Mat. 12:37
3 Ps. 32:9
5 Prov. 12:18
5 Ps. 12:3
5 Or, *wood*
6 Mat. 15:11
6 Gr. *wheel*
7 Gr. *nature*
7 Gr. *nature of man*
8 Ps. 140:3
9 Gen. 1:26
11 Or, *hole*
13 Gal. 6:4
13 ch. 2:18
13 ch. 1:21
14 Rom. 13:13
14 Rom. 2:17
15 Phil. 3:19
15 Or, *natural*
16 1 Cor. 3:3
Gal. 5:20
16 Gr. *tumult, or, unquietness*
17 1 Cor. 2:6
17 Or, *without wrangling*
17 Rom. 12:9
1 Pet. 1:22
18 Prov. 11:18

CHAP. **4**

AD 60

1 Or, *brawlings*

Or, *pleasures*   1
Rom. 7:23   1
Gal. 5:17
Or, *envy*   2
Job 27:9   3
Ps. 18:41
Ps. 66:18   3
Or, *pleasures*   3
Ps. 73:27   4
1 John 2:15   4
John 15:19   4
Gal. 1:10
Gen. 6:5   5
Num. 11:29
Or, *enviously?*   5
Job 22:29   6
Ps. 138:6
Prov. 3:34
Mat. 23:12
Eph. 4:27   7
1 Pet. 5:9
2 Chr. 15:2   8
Is. 1:16   8
1 Pet. 1:22   8
1 John 33
ch. 1:8   8
Mat. 5:4   9
Job 22:29   10
1 Pet. 2:1   11
Mat. 7:1   11
Mat. 10:28   12
Rom. 14:4   12
Prov. 27:1   13
Job 7:7   14
Or, *For it is*   14
Acts 18:21   15
1 Cor. 5:6   16
Luke 12:47   17
John 9:41

CHAP. **5**

AD 60

Prov. 11:28   1
Luke 6:24

---

even of your ᴺlusts ᴿthat war in your members?

2 Ye lust, and have not: ye ᴺkill, and desire to have, and cannot obtain: ye fight and war, yet ye have not, because ye ask not.

3 ᴿYe ask, and receive not, ᴿbecause ye ask amiss, that ye may consume *it* upon your ᴺlusts.

4 ᴿYe adulterers and adulteresses, know ye not that ᴿthe friendship of the world is enmity with God? ᴿwhosoever therefore will be a friend of the world is the enemy of God.

5 Do ye think that the scripture saith in vain, ᴿThe spirit that dwelleth in us lusteth ᴺto envy?

6 But he giveth more grace. Wherefore he saith, ᴿGod resisteth the proud, but giveth grace unto the humble.

7 Submit yourselves therefore to God. ᴿResist the devil, and he will flee from you.

8 ᴿDraw nigh to God, and he will draw nigh to you. ᴿCleanse *your* hands, *ye* sinners; and ᴿpurify *your* hearts, *ye* ᴿdouble minded.

9 ᴿBe afflicted, and mourn, and weep: let your laughter be turned to mourning, and *your* joy to heaviness.

10 ᴿHumble yourselves in the sight of the Lord, and he shall lift you up.

11 ᴿSpeak not evil one of another, brethren. He that speaketh evil of *his* brother, ᴿand judgeth his brother, speaketh evil of the law, and judgeth the law: but if thou judge the law, thou art not a doer of the law, but a judge.

12 There is one lawgiver, ᴿwho is able to save and to destroy: ᴿwho art thou that judgest another?

False confidence

13 ᴿGo to now, ye that say, To day or to morrow we will go into such a city, and continue there a year, and buy and sell, and get gain:

14 Whereas ye know not what *shall be* on the morrow. For what *is* your life? ᴿItᴺ is even a vapour, that appeareth for a little time, and then vanisheth away.

15 For that ye *ought* to say, ᴿIf the Lord will, we shall live, and do this, or that.

16 But now ye rejoice in your boastings: ᴿall such rejoicing is evil.

17 Therefore ᴿto him that knoweth to do good, and doeth *it* not, to him it is sin.

CHAPTER 5

Injustice and retribution

GO ᴿto now, ye rich men, weep and howl for your miseries that shall come upon *you.*

2 Your riches are corrupted, and ᴿyour garments are motheaten.

3 Your gold and silver is cankered; and the rust of them shall be a witness against you, and shall eat your flesh as it were fire. ᴿYe have heaped treasure together for the last days.

4 Behold, ᴿthe hire of the labourers who have reaped down your fields, which is of you kept back by fraud, crieth: and ᴿthe cries of them which have reaped are entered into the ears of the Lord of sabaoth.

5 ᴿYe have lived in pleasure on the earth, and been wanton; ye have nourished your hearts, as in a day of slaughter.

6 ᴿYe have condemned *and* killed the just; *and* he doth not resist you.

Patience and avoidance of oaths

7 ᴺBe patient therefore, brethren, unto the coming of the Lord. Behold, the husbandman waiteth for the precious fruit of the earth, and hath long patience for it, until he receive ᴿthe early and latter rain.

8 Be ye also patient; stablish your hearts: ᴿfor the coming of the Lord draweth nigh.

9 ᴿGrudgeᴺ not one against another, brethren, lest ye be condemned: behold, the judge ᴿstandeth before the door.

10 ᴿTake, my brethren, the prophets, who have spoken in the name of the Lord, for an example of suffering affliction, and of patience.

11 Behold, ᴿwe count them happy which endure. Ye have heard of ᴿthe patience of Job, and have seen ᴿthe end of the Lord; that ᴿthe Lord is very pitiful, and of tender mercy.

CHAP. **5**
AD 60
2 Job 13:28
Mat. 6:20
3 Rom. 2:5
4 Lev. 19:13
4 Deut. 24:15
5 Job 21:13
Amos 6:1
6 ch. 2:6
7 Or, *Be long patient,* or, *Suffer with long patience*
7 Deut. 11:14
Hos. 6:3
8 Phil. 4:5
1 Pet. 4:7
9 ch. 4:11
9 Or, *Groan,* or, *Grieve not*
9 Mat. 24:33
10 Mat. 5:12
11 Ps. 94:12
11 Job 2:10
11 Job 42:10
11 Num. 14:18

Mat. 5:34	**12**
Eph. 5:19	**13**
Mark 6:13	**14**
Is. 33:24	**15**
Num. 11:2	**16**
John 9:31	
Acts 14:15	**17**
1 Ki. 17:1	**17**
Luke 4:25	**17**
1 Ki. 18:42, 45	**18**
Mat. 18:15	**19**
Rom. 11:14	**20**
1 Pet. 4:8	**20**

12 But above all things, my brethren, ᴿswear not, neither by heaven, neither by the earth, neither by any other oath: but let your yea be yea; and *your* nay, nay; lest ye fall into condemnation.

Prayer for the sick

13 Is any among you afflicted? let him pray. Is any merry? ᴿlet him sing psalms.

14 Is any sick among you? let him call for the elders of the church; and let them pray over him, ᴿanointing him with oil in the name of the Lord:

15 And the prayer of faith shall save the sick, and the Lord shall raise him up; ᴿand if he have committed sins, they shall be forgiven him.

16 Confess *your* faults one to another, and pray one for another, that ye may be healed. ᴿThe effectual fervent prayer of a righteous man availeth much.

17 E-li′-ăs was a man ᴿsubject to like passions as we are, and ᴿhe prayed earnestly that it might not rain: ᴿand it rained not on the earth by the space of three years and six months.

18 And ᴿhe prayed again, and the heaven gave rain, and the earth brought forth her fruit.

Restoring a brother

19 Brethren, ᴿif any of you do err from the truth, and one convert him;

20 Let him know, that he which converteth the sinner from the error of his way ᴿshall save a soul from death, and ᴿshall hide a multitude of sins.

THE FIRST EPISTLE GENERAL OF

PETER

The purpose of the First Epistle of Peter is stated in 5:12 as being (1) to declare the "true grace of God," and (2) to exhort to steadfastness in faith and virtue amidst pagan persecution. Up until the end of the nineteenth century the Epistle has been unanimously ascribed to the Apostle Peter (1:1), an eyewitness of the sufferings of Christ (5:1). Objections to Petrine authorship arise from the excellent quality of Greek employed in the letter, its parallels with Pauline terminology and theology, and the fact that official Roman persecution of Christians in Asia Minor arose only at the close of the first century. However, the reference to Silas in 5:12 as scribe, adequately explains the first two objections and the "fiery trials" of 4:12ff. were oppressions by pagan neighbors guilty of many vices.

The letter was sent to Christians in the northern regions of Asia Minor, and was written in 63 or the beginning of 64 from Rome, the "Babylon" of the world.

OUTLINE OF THE FIRST EPISTLE OF PETER:
  I. Salutation 1:1–2
  II. The Blessings of Redemption 1:3–2:10
  III. The Responsibilities of Christians in Society 2:11–3:12
  IV. An Appeal to Stedfastness in Suffering 3:13–4:11
  V. Exhortations to Triumphant Living amidst Persecutions 4:12–5:11
  VI. Greetings and Benediction 4:12–14

CHAPTER 1

Salutation

PETER, an apostle of Jesus Christ, to the strangers ᴿscattered throughout Pontus, Galatia, Căp-pă-dō′-çĭ-ă, Asia, and Bĭ-thȳn′-ĭă,

2 ᴿElect ᴿaccording to the foreknowledge of God the Father, ᴿthrough sanctification of the Spirit, unto obedience and ᴿsprinkling of the blood of Jesus Christ: ᴿGrace unto you, and peace, be multiplied.

Our lively hope and saving faith

3 ᴿBlessed *be* the God and Father of our Lord Jesus Christ, which ᴿaccording to his ᴺabundant mercy ᴿhath begotten us again unto a lively hope ᴿby the resurrection of Jesus Christ from the dead,

4 To an inheritance incorruptible, and undefiled, and that fadeth not away, ᴿreserved in heaven ᴺfor you,

5 ᴿWho are kept by the power of God through faith unto salvation ready to be revealed in the last time.

6 ᴿWherein ye greatly rejoice, though now ᴿfor a season, if need be, ᴿye are in heaviness through manifold temptations:

7 That ᴿthe trial of your faith, being much more precious than of gold that perisheth, though ᴿit be tried with fire, ᴿmight be found unto praise and honour and glory at the appearing of Jesus Christ:

8 ᴿWhom having not seen, ye love; ᴿin whom, though now ye see *him* not, yet believing, ye rejoice with joy unspeakable and full of glory:

9 Receiving ᴿthe end of your faith, *even* the salvation of *your* souls.

10 ᴿOf which salvation the prophets have inquired and searched diligently, who prophesied of the grace *that should come* unto you:

11 Searching what, or what manner of time ᴿthe Spirit of Christ which was in them did signify, when it testified beforehand the sufferings of Christ, and the glory that should follow.

12 ᴿUnto whom it was revealed, that ᴿnot unto themselves, but unto us they did minister the things, which are now reported unto you by them that have preached the gospel unto you with ᴿthe Holy Ghost sent down from heaven; ᴿwhich things the angels desire to look into.

Exhortation to holiness

13 Wherefore ᴿgird up the loins of your mind, ᴿbe sober, and hope ᴺto the end for the

grace that is to be brought unto you ᴿat the revelation of Jesus Christ;

14 As obedient children, ᴿnot fashioning yourselves according to the former lusts ᴿin your ignorance:

15 ᴿBut as he which hath called you is holy, so be ye holy in all manner of conversation;

16 Because it is written, ᴿBe ye holy; for I am holy.

17 And if ye call on the Father, ᴿwho without respect of persons judgeth according to every man's work, ᴿpass the time of your ᴿsojourning *here* in fear:

18 Forasmuch as ye know ᴿthat ye were not redeemed with corruptible things, *as* silver and gold, from your vain conversation ᴿ*received* by tradition from your fathers;

19 But ᴿwith the precious blood of Christ, ᴿas of a lamb without blemish and without spot:

20 ᴿWho verily was foreordained before the foundation of the world, but was manifest ᴿin these last times for you,

21 Who by him do believe in God, ᴿthat raised him up from the dead, and ᴿgave him glory; that your faith and hope might be in God.

Exhortation to brotherly love

22 Seeing ye ᴿhave purified your souls in obeying the truth through the Spirit unto unfeigned ᴿlove of the brethren, *see that ye* love one another with a pure heart fervently:

23 ᴿBeing born again, not of corruptible seed, but of incorruptible, ᴿby the word of God, which liveth and abideth for ever.

24 ᴺFor ᴿall flesh *is* as grass, and all the glory of man as the flower of grass. The grass withereth, and the flower thereof falleth away:

25 ᴿBut the word of the Lord endureth for ever. ᴿAnd this is the word which by the gospel is preached unto you.

CHAPTER 2

WHEREFORE ᴿlaying aside all malice, and all guile, and hypocrisies, and envies, and all evil speakings,

2 ᴿAs newborn babes, desire the sincere ᴿmilk of the word, that ye may grow thereby:

3 If so be ye have ᴿtasted that the Lord *is* gracious.

4 To whom coming, *as unto* a living stone, ᴿdisallowed indeed of men, but chosen of God, *and* precious,

5 ᴿYe also, as lively stones, ᴺare built up ᴿa spiritual house, ᴿan holy priesthood, to offer up ᴿspiritual sacrifices, ᴿacceptable to God by Jesus Christ.

Center reference column

CHAP. 1
AD 60

1 John 7:35
Acts 2:5, 9
Jas. 1:1
2 Eph. 1:4
2 Rom. 8:29
2 2 Thes. 2:13
2 Heb. 12:24
2 Rom. 1:7
3 Eph. 1:3
3 Tit. 3:5
3 Gr. *much*
3 John 3:3, 5
Jas. 1:18
3 1 Cor. 15:20
4 Col. 1:5
4 Or, *for us*
5 John 10:28
6 Mat. 5:12
6 2 Cor. 4:17
6 Jas. 1:2
7 Jas. 1:3
7 Job 23:10
Prov. 17:3
7 Rom. 2:7
8 1 John 4:20
8 John 20:29
9 Rom. 6:22
10 Gen. 49:10
11 2 Pet. 1:21
12 Dan. 9:24
12 Heb. 11:13
12 Acts 2:4
12 Dan. 8:13
13 Eph. 6:14
13 Luke 21:34
Rom. 13:13
13 Gr. *perfectly*

1 Cor. 1:7	13
Rom. 12:2	14
Acts 17:30	14
2 Cor. 7:1	15
Lev. 11:44	16
Deut. 10:17	17
Heb. 12:28	17
Heb. 11:13	17
1 Cor. 6:20	18
Ezek. 20:18	18
Acts 20:28	19
Ex. 12:5	19
Rom. 3:25	20
Gal. 4:4	20
Acts 2:24	21
Acts 2:33	21
Acts 15:9	22
Heb. 13:1	22
John 1:13	23
Jas. 1:18	23
Or, *For that*	24
Is. 40:6	24
Is. 40:8	25
John 1:1	25

CHAP. 2
AD 60

Heb. 12:1	1
Mat. 18:3	2
1 Cor. 3:2	2
Heb. 6:5	3
Ps. 118:22	4
Acts 4:11	
Eph. 2:21	5
Or, *be ye built*	5
Heb. 3:6	5
Is. 61:6	5
Hos. 14:2	5
Mal. 1:11	
Phil. 4:18	5

6 Wherefore also it is contained in the scripture, ᴿBehold, I lay in Sĭ'-on, a chief corner stone, elect, precious: and he that believeth on him shall not be confounded.

7 Unto you therefore which believe *he is* ᴺprecious: but unto them which be disobedient, ᴿthe stone which the builders disallowed, the same is made the head of the corner,

8 ᴿAnd a stone of stumbling, and a rock of offence, ᴿ*even to them* which stumble at the word, being disobedient: ᴿwhereunto also they were appointed.

9 But ye *are* ᴿa chosen generation, ᴿa royal priesthood, ᴿan holy nation, ᴿaᴺ peculiar people; that ye should shew forth the ᴺpraises of him who hath called you out of ᴿdarkness into his marvellous light:

10 ᴿWhich in time past *were* not a people, but *are* now the people of God: which had not obtained mercy, but now have obtained mercy.

Conduct toward unbelievers

11 Dearly beloved, I beseech *you* ᴿas strangers and pilgrims, ᴿabstain from fleshly lusts, ᴿwhich war against the soul;

12 ᴿHaving your conversation honest among the Gentiles: that, ᴺwhereas they speak against you as evildoers, ᴿthey may by *your* good works, which they shall behold, glorify God in the day of visitation.

13 ᴿSubmit yourselves to every ordinance of man for the Lord's sake: whether it be to the king, as supreme;

14 Or unto governors, as unto them that are sent by him ᴿfor the punishment of evildoers, and ᴿfor the praise of them that do well.

15 For so is the will of God, that ᴿwith well doing ye may put to silence the ignorance of foolish men:

16 ᴿAs free, and not ᴺusing *your* liberty for a cloak of maliciousness, but as ᴿthe servants of God.

17 ᴿHonourᴺ all *men.* ᴿLove the brotherhood. ᴿFear God. Honour the king.

Conduct of servants

18 ᴿServants, *be* subject to *your* masters with all fear; not only to the good and gentle, but also to the froward.

19 For this *is* ᴿthankworthy,ᴺ if a man for conscience toward God endure grief, suffering wrongfully.

20 For what glory *is it,* if, when ye be buffeted for your faults, ye shall take it patiently? but if, when ye do well, and suffer *for it,* ye take it patiently, this *is* ᴺacceptable with God.

CHAP. **2**	
AD 60	
6 Is. 28:16	
7 Or, *an honour*	
7 Ps. 118:22	
8 Is. 8:14	
8 1 Cor. 1:23	
8 Rom. 9:22	
9 Deut. 10:15	
9 Rev. 5:10	
9 Is. 62:12	
9 Deut. 4:20	
9 Or, *a purchased people*	
9 Or, *virtues*	
9 Acts 26:18	
10 Hos. 1:9	
11 Ps. 39:12	
11 Gal. 5:16	
11 Jas. 4:1	
12 Phil. 2:15	
12 Or, *wherein*	
12 Mat. 5:16	
13 Rom. 13:1	
14 Rom. 13:4	
14 Rom. 13:3	
15 Tit. 2:8	
16 Gal. 5:1	
16 Gr. *having*	
16 1 Cor. 7:22	
17 Rom. 12:10	
17 Or, *Esteem*	
17 Heb. 13:1	
17 Rom. 13:7	
18 Eph. 6:5	
19 Mat. 5:10	
19 Or, *thank*	
20 Or, *thank*	

Mat. 16:24	**21**
Some read, *for you*	**21**
1 John 2:6	**21**
Is. 53:9	**22**
Is. 53:7	**23**
Luke 23:46	**23**
Or, *committed his cause*	**23**
Heb. 9:28	**24**
Or, *to*	**24**
Rom. 7:6	**24**
Is. 53:5	**24**
Is. 53:6	**25**
Ezek. 34:23 Heb. 13:20	**25**

CHAP. **3**	
AD 60	
1 Cor. 14:34	**1**
1 Cor. 7:16	**1**
Mat. 18:15	**1**
ch. 2:12	**2**
1 Tim. 2:9	**3**
Rom. 2:29	**4**
Gen. 18:12	**6**
Gr. *children*	**6**
1 Cor. 7:3	**7**
1 Cor. 12:23	**7**
Job 42:8	**7**
Mat. 18:19	
Rom. 12:16	**8**
Rom. 12:10	**8**
Heb. 13:1	
Or, *loving to the brethren*	**8**
Eph. 4:32	**8**
Prov. 17:13	**9**
Mat. 25:34	**9**

Christ our great example

21 For ᴿeven hereunto were ye called: because Christ also suffered ᴺfor us, ᴿleaving us an example, that ye should follow his steps:

22 ᴿWho did no sin, neither was guile found in his mouth:

23 ᴿWho, when he was reviled, reviled not again; when he suffered, he threatened not; but ᴿcommittedᴺ *himself* to him that judgeth righteously:

24 ᴿWho his own self bare our sins in his own body ᴺon the tree, ᴿthat we, being dead to sins, should live unto righteousness: ᴿby whose stripes ye were healed.

25 For ᴿye were as sheep going astray; but are now returned ᴿunto the Shepherd and Bishop of your souls.

CHAPTER 3

Conduct of married couples

LIKEWISE, ᴿye wives, *be* in subjection to your own husbands; that, if any obey not the word, ᴿthey also may without the word ᴿbe won by the conversation of the wives;

2 ᴿWhile they behold your chaste coversation *coupled* with fear.

3 ᴿWhose adorning let it not be that outward *adorning* of plaiting the hair, and of wearing of gold, or of putting on of apparel;

4 But *let it be* ᴿthe hidden man of the heart, in that which is not corruptible, *even the ornament* of a meek and quiet spirit, which is in the sight of God of great price.

5 For after this manner in the old time the holy women also, who trusted in God, adorned themselves, being in subjection unto their own husbands:

6 Even as Sarah obeyed Abraham, ᴿcalling him lord: whose ᴺdaughters ye are, as long as ye do well, and are not afraid with any amazement.

7 ᴿLikewise, ye husbands, dwell with *them* according to knowledge, giving honour unto the wife, ᴿas unto the weaker vessel, and as being heirs together of the grace of life; ᴿthat your prayers be not hindered.

Conduct of the reviled

8 Finally, ᴿ*be ye* all of one mind, having compassion one of another, ᴿloveᴺ as brethren, ᴿ*be* pitiful, *be* courteous:

9 ᴿNot rendering evil for evil, or railing for railing: but contrariwise blessing; knowing that ye are thereunto called, ᴿthat ye should inherit a blessing.

10 For ᴿhe that will love life, and see good days, ᴿlet him refrain his tongue from evil, and his lips that they speak no guile:

11 Let him ᴿeschew evil, and do good; ᴿlet him seek peace, and ensue it.

12 For the eyes of the Lord *are* over the righteous, ᴿand his ears *are open* unto their prayers: but the face of the Lord *is* ᴺagainst them that do evil.

13 ᴿAnd who *is* he that will harm you, if ye be followers of that which is good?

14 ᴿBut and if ye suffer for righteousness' sake, happy *are ye*: and ᴿbe not afraid of their terror, neither be troubled;

15 But sanctify the Lord God in your hearts: and ᴿ*be* ready always to *give* an answer to every man that asketh you a reason of the hope that is in you with meekness and ᴺfear:

16 ᴿHaving a good conscience; ᴿthat, whereas they speak evil of you, as of evildoers, they may be ashamed that falsely accuse your good conversation in Christ.

17 For *it is* better, if the will of God be so, that ye suffer for well doing, than for evil doing.

18 For Christ also hath ᴿonce suffered for sins, the just for the unjust, that he might bring us to God, ᴿbeing put to death ᴿin the flesh, but ᴿquickened by the Spirit:

19 By which also he went and ᴿpreached unto the spirits ᴿin prison;

20 Which sometime were disobedient, ᴿwhen once the longsuffering of God waited in the days of Noah, while ᴿthe ark was a preparing, ᴿwherein few, that is, eight souls were saved by water.

21 ᴿThe like figure whereunto *even* baptism doth also now save us (not the putting away of ᴿthe filth of the flesh, ᴿbut the answer of a good conscience toward God,) ᴿby the resurrection of Jesus Christ:

22 Who is gone into heaven, and ᴿis on the right hand of God; ᴿangels and authorities and powers being made subject unto him.

CHAPTER 4

Expect suffering

FOR AS MUCH then ᴿas Christ hath suffered for us in the flesh, arm yourselves likewise with the same mind: for ᴿhe that hath suffered in the flesh hath ceased from sin;

2 ᴿThat he no longer ᴿshould live the rest of *his* time in the flesh to the lusts of men, ᴿbut to the will of God.

3 ᴿFor the time past of *our* life may suffice us ᴿto have wrought the will of the Gentiles, when we walked in lasciviousness, lusts, ex-

---

CHAP. 3

AD 60

10 Ps. 34:12
10 Jas. 1:26
Rev. 14:5
11 Ps. 37:27
3 John 11
11 Rom. 12:18
Heb. 12:14
12 John 9:31
Jas. 5:16
12 Gr. *upon*
13 Prov. 16:7
14 Jas. 1:12
ch. 2:19
15 Is. 8:12, 13
15 Ps. 119:46
Col. 4:6
15 Or, *reverence*
16 Heb. 13:18
16 Tit. 2:8
18 Rom. 5:6
18 2 Cor. 13:4
18 Col. 1:21
18 Rom. 1:4
19 ch. 1:12
19 Is. 42:7
20 Gen. 6:3, 5
20 Heb. 11:7
20 Gen. 7:7
21 Eph. 5:26
21 Tit. 3:5
21 Rom. 10:10
21 ch. 1:3
22 Ps. 110:1
Rom. 8:34
22 Rom. 8:38
1 Cor. 3:13

CHAP. 4

AD 60

1 ch. 3:18
1 Gal. 5:24
2 Rom. 14:7
2 Gal. 2:20
2 John 1:13
3 Ezek. 44:6
3 Eph. 2:2
1 Thes. 4:5

Acts 13:45   4
Acts 10:42   5
Rom. 14:10
2 Tim. 4:1
ch. 3:19   6
Rom. 13:12   7
Mat. 26:41   7
Luke 21:34
Col. 3:14   8
Heb. 13:1
Prov. 10:12   8
1 Cor. 13:7
Or, *will*   8
Heb. 13:2   9
2 Cor. 9:7   9
Rom. 12:6   10
Mat. 24:45   10
Tit. 1:7
1 Cor. 12:4   10
Eph. 4:11
Jer. 23:22   11
1 Cor. 3:10   11
Eph. 5:20   11
1 Tim. 6:16   11
1 Cor. 3:13   12
Acts 5:41   13
Rom. 8:17   13
2 Cor. 12:10   14
Jas. 1:12
ch. 2:20   15
1 Thes. 4:11   15
Acts 5:41   16
Is. 10:12   17
Luke 23:31   17
Luke 10:12   17
Luke 23:31   18
2 Tim. 1:12   19

---

cess of wine, revellings, banquetings, and abominable idolatries:

4 Wherein they think it strange that ye run not with *them* to the same excess of riot, ᴿspeaking evil of *you:*

5 Who shall give account to him that is ready ᴿto judge the quick and the dead.

6 For for this cause ᴿwas the gospel preached also to them that are dead, that they might be judged according to men in the flesh, but live according to God in the spirit.

Conduct in the last times

7 But ᴿthe end of all things is at hand: ᴿbe ye therefore sober, and watch unto prayer.

8 ᴿAnd above all things have fervent charity among yourselves: for ᴿcharity ᴺshall cover the multitude of sins.

9 ᴿUse hospitality one to another ᴿwithout grudging.

10 ᴿAs every man hath received the gift, *even so* minister the same one to another, ᴿas good stewards of ᴿthe manifold grace of God.

11 ᴿIf any man speak, *let him speak* as the oracles of God; ᴿif any man minister, *let him do it* as of the ability which God giveth: that ᴿGod in all things may be glorified through Jesus Christ, ᴿto whom be praise and dominion for ever and ever. Ä′-mĕn.

Conduct under persecution

12 Beloved, think it not strange concerning ᴿthe fiery trial which is to try you, as though some strange thing happened unto you:

13 ᴿBut rejoice, inasmuch as ᴿye are partakers of Christ's sufferings; that, when his glory shall be revealed, ye may be glad also with exceeding joy.

14 ᴿIf ye be reproached for the name of Christ, happy *are ye;* for the spirit of glory and of God resteth upon you: on their part he is evil spoken of, but on your part he is glorified.

15 But ᴿlet none of you suffer as a murderer, or *as* a thief, or *as* an evildoer, ᴿor as a busybody in other men's matters.

16 Yet if *any man suffer* as a Christian, let him not be ashamed; ᴿbut let him glorify God on this behalf.

17 For the time *is come* ᴿthat judgment must begin at the house of God: and ᴿif *it* first *begin* at us, ᴿwhat shall the end *be* of them that obey not the gospel of God?

18 ᴿAnd if the righteous scarcely be saved, where shall the ungodly and the sinner appear?

19 Wherefore let them that suffer according to the will of God ᴿcommit the keeping of their souls *to him* in well doing, as unto a faithful Creator.

CHAPTER 5

Exhortation for church leaders

THE elders which are among you I exhort, who am also [R]an elder, and [R]a witness of the sufferings of Christ, and also [R]a partaker of the glory that shall be revealed:

2 [R]Feed the flock of God [N]which is among you, taking the oversight *thereof,* [R]not by constraint, but willingly; [R]not for filthy lucre, but of a ready mind;

3 Neither as [R]being[N] lords over [R]*God's* heritage, but [R]being ensamples to the flock.

4 And when [R]the chief Shepherd shall appear, ye shall receive [R]a crown of glory that fadeth not away.

5 Likewise, ye younger, submit yourselves unto the elder. Yea, [R]all *of you* be subject one to another, and be clothed with humility: for [R]God resisteth the proud, and [R]giveth grace to the humble.

In God's care

6 [R]Humble yourselves therefore under the mighty hand of God, that he may exalt you in due time:

CHAP. **5**	
AD 60	
1 Philem. 9	
1 Luke 24:48	
Acts 1:8	
1 Rev. 1:9	
2 Acts 20:28	
2 Or, *as much as in you is*	
2 1 Cor. 9:17	
2 1 Tim. 3:3	
3 Ezek. 34:4	
3 Or, *overruling*	
3 Ps. 33:12	
3 Phil. 3:17	
4 Heb. 13:20	
4 2 Tim. 4:8	
5 Rom. 12:10	
5 Jas. 4:6	
5 Is. 57:15	
6 Jas. 4:10	
Ps. 37:5	7
Heb. 13:5	
Luke 21:34	8
Job 1:7	8
Eph. 6:11	9
Acts 14:22	9
1 Cor. 1:9	10
2 Cor. 4:17	10
Heb. 13:21	10
2 Thes. 2:17	10
Rev. 1:6	11
2 Cor. 1:19	12
Heb. 13:22	12
Acts 20:24	12
Acts 12:12	13
Rom. 16:16	14
Eph. 6:23	14

7 [R]Casting all your care upon him; for he careth for you.

8 [R]Be sober, be vigilant; because [R]your adversary the devil, as a roaring lion, walketh about, seeking whom he may devour:

9 [R]Whom resist stedfast in the faith, [R]knowing that the same afflictions are accomplished in your brethren that are in the world.

10 But the God of all grace, [R]who hath called us unto his eternal glory by Christ Jesus, after that ye have suffered [R]a while, [R]make you perfect, [R]stablish, strengthen, settle *you.*

11 [R]To him *be* glory and dominion for ever and ever. Ä'-mĕn.

Conclusion and benediction

12 [R]By Sĭl-vā'-nŭs, a faithful brother unto you, as I suppose, I have [R]written briefly, exhorting, and testifying [R]that this is the true grace of God wherein ye stand.

13 The *church that is* at Babylon, elected together with *you,* saluteth you; and *so doth* [R]Marcus my son.

14 [R]Greet ye one another with a kiss of charity. [R]Peace *be* with you all that are in Christ Jesus. Ä'-mĕn.

THE SECOND EPISTLE GENERAL OF
PETER

No book of the New Testament has been more highly suspect than Second Peter. Its style is more labored and awkward than that of First Peter, and there are differences of vocabulary and thought. It is also argued that its reference to Paul's writings in 3:15–16 and its alleged dependence on Jude date it as being late, since Paul's letters were only collected in the last quarter of the first century and Jude was written after A.D. 80. The Epistle claims Peter as its author; and while the evidence is admittedly inconclusive, it is still possible to assert authenticity. Perhaps here is how Peter wrote and expressed himself without the aid of Silas (I Pet. 5:12), Mark (cf. Mark's Gospel), or Luke (cf. Peter's preaching in Acts). Dates for the formulation of the Pauline corpus and the composition of Jude are still debated. They may be earlier than usually assigned, and Jude may even be dependent upon Second Peter. And since the recognition of significant correspondences between

Second Peter and the Dead Sea Scrolls, there is a growing insistence that the Epistle must be dated prior to A.D. 80. Assuming Petrine authorship, the letter was written shortly before A.D. 67 (cf. 1:14–15) and probably from Rome. If 3:1 has reference to First Peter, it was addressed to Christians of northern Asia Minor. Its theme concerns true knowledge: knowledge that is grounded in faith, that preserves from error, and that leads to righteousness.

OUTLINE OF THE SECOND EPISTLE OF PETER:

   I. Salutation   1:1–2
  II. The Nature of True Knowledge   1:3–21
 III. Warnings regarding Rising Heresies   2:1–22
  IV. Instruction regarding the Lord's Coming   3:1–18
   V. Doxology   3:18b

CHAPTER 1

Salutation

SIMON[N] Peter, a servant and an apostle of Jesus Christ, to them that have obtained [R]like precious faith with us through the righteousness [N]of God and our Saviour Jesus Christ:

CHAP. **1**	
AD 66	
1 Or, *Symeon,* Acts 15:14	
1 Eph. 4:5	
1 Gr. *of our God and Saviour*	
Dan. 4:1	2

2 [R]Grace and peace be multiplied unto you through the knowledge of God, and of Jesus our Lord,

Knowledge of our Lord

3 According as his divine power hath given unto us all things that *pertain* unto life and godliness, through the knowledge

of him ^Rthat hath called us ^Nto glory and virtue:

4 ^RWhereby are given unto us exceeding great and precious promises: that by these ye might be ^Rpartakers of the divine nature, having escaped the corruption that is in the world through lust.

5 And beside this, ^Rgiving all diligence, add to your faith virtue; and to virtue ^Rknowledge;

6 And to knowledge temperance; and to temperance patience; and to patience godliness;

7 And to godliness brotherly kindness; and ^Rto brotherly kindness charity.

8 For if these things be in you, and abound, they make *you that ye shall* neither *be* ^Nbarren ^Rnor unfruitful in the knowledge of our Lord Jesus Christ.

9 But he that lacketh these things ^Ris blind, and cannot see afar off, and hath forgotten that he was ^Rpurged from his old sins.

10 Wherefore the rather, brethren, give diligence ^Rto make your calling and election sure: for if ye do these things, ye shall never fall:

11 For so an entrance shall be ministered unto you abundantly into the everlasting kingdom of our Lord and Saviour Jesus Christ.

Reminder of God's truths

12 Wherefore ^RI will not be negligent to put you always in remembrance of these things, ^Rthough ye know *them,* and be established in the present truth.

13 Yea, I think it meet, ^Ras long as I am in this tabernacle, to stir you up by putting *you* in remembrance;

14 ^RKnowing that shortly I must put off *this* my tabernacle, even as ^Rour Lord Jesus Christ hath shewed me.

15 Moreover I will endeavour that ye may be able after my decease to have these things always in remembrance.

16 For we have not followed ^Rcunningly devised fables, when we made known unto you the power and coming of our Lord Jesus Christ, but ^Rwere eyewitnesses of his majesty.

17 For he received from God the Father honour and glory, when there came such a voice to him from the excellent glory, ^RThis is my beloved Son, in whom I am well pleased.

18 And this voice which came from heaven we heard, when we were with him in ^Rthe holy mount.

19 We have also a more sure word of prophecy; whereunto ye do well that ye take heed, as unto ^Ra light that shineth in a dark place, until the day dawn, and ^Rthe day star arise in your hearts:

20 Knowing this first, that ^Rno prophecy of the scripture is of any private interpretation.

21 For ^Rthe prophecy came not ^Nin old time by the will of man: ^Rbut holy men of God spake *as they were* moved by the Holy Ghost.

CHAPTER 2

Exploitation by false teachers

BUT ^Rthere were false prophets also among the people, even as ^Rthere shall be false teachers among you, who privily shall bring in damnable heresies, even ^Rdenying the Lord ^Rthat bought them, ^Rand bring upon themselves swift destruction.

2 And many shall follow their ^Npernicious ways; by reason of whom the way of truth shall be evil spoken of.

3 And ^Rthrough covetousness shall they with feigned words ^Rmake merchandise of you: ^Rwhose judgment now of a long time lingereth not, and their damnation slumbereth not.

Punishment of false teachers

4 For if God spared not ^Rthe angels ^Rthat sinned, but ^Rcast *them* down to hell, and delivered *them* into chains of darkness, to be reserved unto judgment;

5 And spared not the old world, but saved ^RNoah the eighth *person,* ^Ra preacher of righteousness, ^Rbringing in the flood upon the world of the ungodly;

6 And ^Rturning the cities of Sodom and Gō-mŏr'-rhă into ashes condemned *them* with an overthrow, ^Rmaking *them* an ensample unto those that after should live ungodly;

7 And ^Rdelivered just Lot, vexed with the filthy conversation of the wicked:

8 (For that righteous man dwelling among them, ^Rin seeing and hearing, vexed *his* righteous soul from day to day with *their* unlawful deeds;)

9 ^RThe Lord knoweth how to deliver the godly out of temptations, and to reserve the unjust unto the day of judgment to be punished:

Character of false teachers

10 But chiefly ^Rthem that walk after the flesh in the lust of uncleanness, and despise ^Ngovernment. ^RPresumptuous *are they,* selfwilled, they are not afraid to speak evil of dignities.

11 Whereas ^Rangels, which are greater in power and might, bring not railing accusation ^Nagainst them before the Lord.

12 But these, ^Ras natural brute beasts, made to be taken and destroyed, speak evil of the things that they understand not; and shall utterly perish in their own corruption;

13 ^RAnd shall receive the reward of unright-

eousness, *as* they that count it pleasure ᴿto riot in the day time. ᴿSpots *they are* and blemishes, sporting themselves with their own deceivings while ᴿthey feast with you;

14 Having eyes full of ᴺadultery, and that cannot cease from sin; beguiling unstable souls: ᴿan heart they have exercised with covetous practices; cursed children:

15 Which have forsaken the right way, and are gone astray, following the way of ᴿBā'-lăăm *the son* of Bō'-sŏr, who loved the wages of unrighteousness;

16 But was rebuked for his iniquity: the dumb ass speaking with man's voice forbad the madness of the prophet.

Folly of false teachers

17 ᴿThese are wells without water, clouds that are carried with a tempest; to whom the mist of darkness is reserved for ever.

18 For when ᴿthey speak great swelling *words* of vanity, they allure through the lusts of the flesh, *through much* wantonness, those that ᴿwere ᴺclean escaped from them who live in error.

19 While they promise them ᴿliberty, they themselves are ᴿthe servants of corruption: for of whom a man is overcome, of the same is he brought in bondage.

20 For ᴿif after they ᴿhave escaped the pollutions of the world ᴿthrough the knowledge of the Lord and Saviour Jesus Christ, they are again entangled therein, and overcome, the latter end is worse with them than the beginning.

21 For ᴿit had been better for them not to have known the way of righteousness, than, after they have known *it,* to turn from the holy commandment delivered unto them.

22 But it is happened unto them according to the true proverb, ᴿThe dog *is* turned to his own vomit again; and the sow that was washed to her wallowing in the mire.

CHAPTER 3

God's mercy and day of judgment

THIS second epistle. beloved, I now write unto you; in *both* which ᴿI stir up your pure minds by way of remembrance:

2 That ye may be mindful of the words which were spoken before by the holy prophets, ᴿand of the commandment of us the apostles of the Lord and Saviour:

3 Knowing this first, that there shall come in the last days scoffers, ᴿwalking after their own lusts,

4 And saying, ᴿWhere is the promise of his coming? for since the fathers fell asleep, all things continue as *they were* from the beginning of the creation.

5 For this they willingly are ignorant of, that ᴿby the word of God the heavens were of old, and the earth ᴿstandingᴺ out of the water and in the water:

6 ᴿWhereby the world that then was, being overflowed with water, perished:

7 But ᴿthe heavens and the earth, which are now, by the same word are kept in store, reserved unto ᴿfire against the day of judgment and perdition of ungodly men.

8 But, beloved, be not ignorant of this one thing, that one day *is* with the Lord as a thousand years, and ᴿa thousand years as one day.

9 ᴿThe Lord is not slack concerning his promise, as some men count slackness; but ᴿis longsuffering to us-ward, ᴿnot willing that any should perish, but ᴿthat all should come to repentance.

10 But ᴿthe day of the Lord will come as a thief in the night; in the which ᴿthe heavens shall pass away with a great noise, and the elements shall melt with fervent heat, the earth also and the works that are therein shall be burned up.

Exhortation to readiness

11 *Seeing* then *that* all these things shall be dissolved, what manner *of persons* ought ye to be ᴿin *all* holy conversation and godliness,

12 ᴿLooking for and ᴺhasting unto the coming of the day of God, wherein the heavens being on fire shall ᴿbe dissolved, and the elements shall ᴿmelt with fervent heat?

13 Nevertheless we, according to his promise, look for ᴿnew heavens and a new earth, wherein dwelleth righteousness.

14 Wherefore, beloved, seeing that ye look for such things, be diligent ᴿthat ye may be found of him in peace, without spot, and blameless.

15 And account *that* ᴿthe longsuffering of our Lord *is* salvation; even as our beloved brother Paul also according to the wisdom given unto him hath written unto you;

16 As also in all *his* epistles, ᴿspeaking in them of these things; in which are some things hard to be understood, which they that are unlearned and unstable wrest, as *they do* also the other scriptures, unto their own destruction.

17 Ye therefore, beloved, ᴿseeing ye know *these things* before, ᴿbeware lest ye also, being led away with the error of the wicked, fall from your own stedfastness.

18 ᴿBut grow in grace, and *in* the knowledge of our Lord and Saviour Jesus Christ. ᴿTo him *be* glory both now and for ever. Ä'-mĕn.

Center column references

CHAP. 2
AD 66
13 Rom. 13:13
13 Jude 12
13 1 Cor. 11:20
14 Gr. *an adulteress*
14 Jude 11
15 Num. 22:5
Jude 11
17 Jude 12, 13
18 Jude 16
18 Acts 2:40
18 Or, *for a little,* or, *a while,* as some read
19 Gal. 5:13
19 John 8:34
Rom. 6:16
20 Mat. 12:45
Luke 11:26
Heb. 6:4
20 ver. 18
20 ch. 1:2
21 Luke 12:47
22 Prov. 26:11

CHAP. 3
AD 66
1 ch. 1:13
2 Jude 17
3 ch. 2:10
4 Is. 5:19
Jer. 17:15
Mat. 24:48
Luke 12:45

Gen. 1:6, 9 — 5
Ps. 33:6
Heb. 11:3
Ps. 24:2 — 5
Col. 1:17
Gr. *consisting* — 5
Gen. 7:11 — 6
ver. 10 — 7
Mat. 25:41 — 7
2 Thes. 1:8
Ps. 90:4 — 8
Hab. 2:3 — 9
Heb. 10:37
Is. 30:18 — 9
1 Pet. 3:20
Ezek. 33:11 — 9
Rom. 2:4 — 9
1 Tim. 2:4
Mat. 24:43 — 10
Luke 12:39
1 Thes. 5:2
Ps. 102:26 — 10
Is. 51:6
Mat. 24:35
1 Pet. 1:15 — 11
1 Cor. 1:7 — 12
Tit. 2:13
Or, *hasting the coming* — 12
Ps. 50:3 — 12
Is. 34:4
Mic. 1:4 — 12
Is. 65:17 — 13
& 66:22
Rev. 21:1
1 Cor. 1:8 — 14
& 15:58
1 Thes. 3:13
Rom. 2:4 — 15
1 Pet. 3:20
Rom. 8:19 — 16
1 Cor. 15:24
1 Thes. 4:15
Mark 13:23 — 17
Eph. 4:14 — 17
Eph. 4:15 — 18
1 Pet. 2:2
2 Tim. 4:18 — 18

THE FIRST EPISTLE GENERAL OF
JOHN

The First Epistle of John is both a polemic and a letter of exhortation. Certain former members of the church were propagating doctrines that were deeply disturbing (2:19). Their teaching was a type of docetic gnosticism with a Jewish flavor; they denied a real incarnation, a coming of Christ "in the flesh" (4:2–3), and refused to identify the Christ (Messiah) with Jesus or to speak of the eternal Son of the Father (2:22–23, 5:1). Claiming spiritual illumination and to "have no sin," they refused to be bound by any ethical standard (1:8, 3:4). The response of the First Epistle is (1) an insistence upon the incarnation, Christ manifested audibly, visibly, and tangibly (1:1–3), (2) the affirmation of Jesus as both Christ and Son of God, (3) the noting that defective ethics evidence a warped doctrine, and (4) the exhortation to recognize that Christians have received a true understanding through the coming of Christ and the ministry of the Spirit (2:20–21, 5:20). The letter is a sequel to the Fourth Gospel; for while the Gospel was written to arouse faith (John 20:31), this Epistle was written to establish certainty (5:13). It is generally agreed that both proceed from the same hand. External attestation is both early and strong in favor of the Apostle John. The prominence given to the confession of Jesus as the Christ (2:22, 5:1) favors the identification of the addressees as being Jewish Christians. This First Epistle was probably written after John's Gospel, though the notable literary similarities between the two may indicate that both were produced about the same time (cf. John's Gospel).

OUTLINE OF THE FIRST EPISTLE OF JOHN:
  I. Authentication of the Message   1:1–4
 II. Certainty through Walking in the Light   1:5–2:29
III. Certainty through Abiding in Love   3:1–4:21
 IV. Certainty through the Exercise of Faith   5:1–12
  V. Resultant Spiritual Confidence   5:13–20
 VI. Final Admonition   5:21

CHAPTER 1

"That which was from the beginning"

THAT ᴿwhich was from the beginning, which we have heard, which we have seen with our eyes, ᴿwhich we have looked upon, and ᴿour hands have handled, of the Word of life;

2 (For ᴿthe life ᴿwas manifested, and we have seen *it,* ᴿand bear witness, ᴿand shew unto you that eternal life, ᴿwhich was with the Father, and was manifested unto us;)

3 That which we have seen and heard declare we unto you, that ye also may have fellowship with us: and truly ᴿour fellowship *is* with the Father, and with his Son Jesus Christ.

4 And these things write we unto you, ᴿthat your joy may be full.

Test of righteousness

5 ᴿThis then is the message which we have heard of him, and declare unto you, that ᴿGod is light, and in him is no darkness at all.

6 ᴿIf we say that we have fellowship with him, and walk in darkness, we lie, and do not the truth:

7 But if we walk in the light, as he is in the light, we have fellowship one with another, and ᴿthe blood of Jesus Christ his Son cleanseth us from all sin.

8 ᴿIf we say that we have no sin, we deceive ourselves, ᴿand the truth is not in us.

9 ᴿIf we confess our sins, he is faithful and just to forgive us *our* sins, and to ᴿcleanse us from all unrighteousness.

10 If we say that we have not sinned, we make him a liar, and his word is not in us.

CHAPTER 2

MY little children, these things write I unto you, that ye sin not. And if any man sin, ᴿwe have an advocate with the Father, Jesus Christ the righteous:

2 And ᴿhe is the propitiation for our sins: and not for ours only, but ᴿalso for *the sins of* the whole world.

3 And hereby we do know that we know him, if we keep his commandments.

4 ᴿHe that saith, I know him, and keepeth not his commandments, ᴿis a liar, and the truth is not in him.

5 But ᴿwhoso keepeth his word, ᴿin him verily is the love of God perfected: ᴿhereby know we that we are in him.

6 ᴿHe that saith he abideth in him ᴿought himself also so to walk, even as he walked.

Test of love

7 Brethren, ᴿI write no new commandment unto you, but an old commandment ᴿwhich ye had from the beginning. The old commandment is the word which ye have heard from the beginning.

8 Again, ᴿa new commandment I write unto you, which thing is true in him and in you: ᴿbecause the darkness is past, and ᴿthe true light now shineth.

9 ᴿHe that saith he is in the light, and hateth his brother, is in darkness even until now.

10 ᴿHe that loveth his brother abideth in the

CHAP. 1
AD 90
1 John 1:1
1 John 1:14
2 Pet. 1:16
1 Luke 24:39
John 20:27
2 John 1:4 & 14:6
2 Rom. 16:26
1 Tim. 3:16
2 John 21:24
2 ch. 5:20
2 John 1:1
3 John 17:21
1 Cor. 1:9
4 John 16:24
5 ch. 3:11
5 John 1:9
6 2 Cor. 6:14
7 1 Cor. 6:11
Eph. 1:7
Rev. 1:5
8 Job 9:2
Eccl. 7:20
Jas. 3:2
8 ch. 2:4
9 Ps. 32:5
9 Ps. 51:2

CHAP. 2
AD 90
Heb. 7:25   1
Rom. 3:25   2
2 Cor. 5:18
John 1:29   2
ch. 1:6   4
ch. 1:8   4
John 14:21, 23   5
ch. 4:12   5
ch. 4:13   5
John 15:4   6
Mat. 11:29   6
1 Pet. 2:21
2 John 5   7
2 John 5   7
John 13:34   8
Rom. 13:12   8
John 1:9   8
1 Cor. 13:2   9
ch. 3:14   10

light, and ᴿthere is none ᴺoccasion of stumbling in him.

11 But he that hateth his brother is in darkness, and walketh in darkness, and knoweth not whither he goeth, because that darkness hath blinded his eyes.

12 I write unto you, little children, because ᴿyour sins are forgiven you for his name's sake.

13 I write unto you, fathers, because ye have known him ᴿ*that is* from the beginning. I write unto you, young men, because ye have overcome the wicked one. I write unto you, little children, because ye have known the Father.

14 I have written unto you, fathers, because ye have known him *that is* from the beginning. I have written unto you, young men, because ᴿye are strong, and the word of God abideth in you, and ye have overcome the wicked one.

15 ᴿLove not the world, neither the things *that are* in the world. ᴿIf any man love the world, the love of the Father is not in him.

16 For all that *is* in the world, the lust of the flesh, ᴿand the lust of the eyes, and the pride of life, is not of the Father, but is of the world.

17 And ᴿthe world passeth away, and the lust thereof: but he that doeth the will of God abideth for ever.

Test of true faith

18 ᴿLittle children, ᴿit is the last time: and as ye have heard that ᴿăn'-tī-christ shall come, ᴿeven now are there many ăn'-tī-christs; whereby we know ᴿthat it is the last time.

19 ᴿThey went out from us, but they were not of us; for ᴿif they had been of us, they would *no doubt* have continued with us: but *they went out,* ᴿthat they might be made manifest that they were not all of us.

20 But ᴿye have an unction ᴿfrom the Holy One, and ᴿye know all things.

21 I have not written unto you because ye know not the truth, but because ye know it, and that no lie is of the truth.

22 ᴿWho is a liar but he that denieth that Jesus is the Christ? He is ăn'-tī-christ, that denieth the Father and the Son.

23 ᴿWhosoever denieth the Son, the same hath not the Father: [*but*] ᴿ*he that acknowledgeth the Son hath the Father also.*

24 Let that therefore abide in you, ᴿwhich ye have heard from the beginning. If that which ye have heard from the beginning shall remain in you, ᴿye also shall continue in the Son, and in the Father.

25 ᴿAnd this is the promise that he hath promised us, *even* eternal life.

26 These *things* have I written unto you ᴿconcerning them that seduce you.

27 But ᴿthe anointing which ye have received of him abideth in you, and ᴿye need not that any man teach you: but as the same anointing ᴿteacheth you of all things, and is truth, and is no lie, and even as it hath taught you, ye shall abide in ᴺhim.

28 And now, little children, abide in him; that, ᴿwhen he shall appear, we may have confidence, ᴿand not be ashamed before him at his coming.

29 ᴿIf ye know that he is righteous, ᴺye know that ᴿevery one that doeth righteousness is born of him.

CHAPTER 3

The children of God

BEHOLD, what manner of love the Father hath bestowed upon us, that ᴿwe should be called the sons of God: therefore the world knoweth us not, ᴿbecause it knew him not.

2 Beloved, ᴿnow are we the sons of God, and ᴿit doth not yet appear what we shall be: but we know that, when he shall appear, ᴿwe shall be like him; for ᴿwe shall see him as he is.

3 ᴿAnd every man that hath this hope in him purifieth himself, even as he is pure.

4 Whosoever committeth sin transgresseth also the law: for ᴿsin is the transgression of the law.

5 And ye know ᴿthat he was manifested ᴿto take away our sins; and ᴿin him is no sin.

6 Whosoever abideth in him sinneth not: ᴿwhosoever sinneth hath not seen him, neither known him.

7 Little children, ᴿlet no man deceive you: ᴿhe that doeth righteousness is righteous, even as he is righteous.

8 ᴿHe that committeth sin is of the devil; for the devil sinneth from the beginning. For this purpose the Son of God was manifested, ᴿthat he might destroy the works of the devil.

9 ᴿWhosoever is born of God doth not commit sin; for ᴿhis seed remaineth in him: and he cannot sin, because he is born of God.

10 In this the children of God are manifest, and the children of the devil: ᴿwhosoever doeth not rightousness is not of God, ᴿneither he that loveth not his brother.

Commandment of love

11 For ᴿthis is the ᴺmessage that ye heard from the beginning, ᴿthat we should love one another.

12 Not as ᴿCain, *who* was of that wicked

one, and slew his brother. And wherefore slew he him? Because his own works were evil, and his brother's righteous.

13 Marvel not, my brethren, if ᴿthe world hate you.

14 ᴿWe know that we have passed from death unto life, because we love the brethren. ᴿHe that loveth not *his* brother abideth in death.

15 ᴿWhosoever hateth his brother is a murderer: and ye know that ᴿno murderer hath eternal life abiding in him.

16 ᴿHereby perceive we the love *of God,* because he laid down his life for us: and we ought to lay down *our* lives for the brethren.

17 But ᴿwhoso hath this world's good, and seeth his brother have need, and shutteth up his bowels *of compassion* from him, ᴿhow dwelleth the love of God in him?

18 My little children, ᴿlet us not love in word, neither in tongue; but in deed and in truth.

19 And hereby we know ᴿthat we are of the truth, and shall ᴺassure our hearts before him.

20 ᴿFor if our heart condemn us, God is greater than our heart, and knoweth all things.

21 ᴿBeloved, if our heart condemn us not, ᴿ*then* have we confidence toward God.

22 And ᴿwhatsoever we ask, we receive of him, because we keep his commandments, ᴿand do those things that are pleasing in his sight.

23 ᴿAnd this is his commandment, That we should believe on the name of his Son Jesus Christ, ᴿand love one another, ᴿas he gave us commandment.

24 And ᴿhe that keepeth his commandments ᴿdwelleth in him, and he in him. And ᴿhereby we know that he abideth in us, by the Spirit which he hath given us.

CHAPTER 4

Try the spirits

BELOVED, ᴿbelieve not every spirit, but ᴿtry the spirits whether they are of God: because ᴿmany false prophets are gone out into the world.

2 Hereby know ye the Spirit of God: ᴿEvery spirit that confesseth that Jesus Christ is come in the flesh is of God:

3 And ᴿevery spirit that confesseth not that Jesus Christ is come in the flesh is not of God: and this is that *spirit* of ăn'-tĭ-christ, whereof ye have heard that it should come; and ᴿeven now already is it in the world.

4 ᴿYe are of God, little children, and have

overcome them: because greater is he that is in you, than ᴿhe that is in the world.

5 ᴿThey are of the world: therefore speak they of the world, and ᴿthe world heareth them.

6 We are of God: ᴿhe that knoweth God heareth us; he that is not of God heareth not us. Hereby know we ᴿthe spirit of truth, and the spirit of error.

God is love

7 ᴿBeloved, let us love one another: for love is of God; and every one that loveth is born of God, and knoweth God.

8 He that loveth not ᴿknoweth not God; for ᴿGod is love.

9 ᴿIn this was manifested the love of God toward us, because that God sent his only begotten Son into the world, ᴿthat we might live through him.

10 Herein is love, ᴿnot that we loved God, but that he loved us, and sent his Son ᴿ*to be* the propitiation for our sins.

11 Beloved, ᴿif God so loved us, we ought also to love one another.

12 ᴿNo man hath seen God at any time. If we love one another, God dwelleth in us, and ᴿhis love is perfected in us.

Confidence in love

13 ᴿHereby know we that we dwell in him, and he in us, because he hath given us of his Spirit.

14 And ᴿwe have seen and do testify that ᴿthe Father sent the Son *to be* the Saviour of the world.

15 ᴿWhosoever shall confess that Jesus is the Son of God, God dwelleth in him, and he in God.

16 And we have known and believed the love that God hath to us. ᴿGod is love; and ᴿhe that dwelleth in love dwelleth in God, and God in him.

17 Herein is ᴺour love made perfect, that ᴿwe may have boldness in the day of judgment: ᴿbecause as he is, so are we in this world.

18 There is no fear in love; but perfect love casteth out fear: because fear hath torment. He that feareth ᴿis not made perfect in love.

19 We love him, because he first loved us.

20 ᴿIf a man say, I love God, and hateth his brother, he is a liar: for he that loveth not his brother whom he hath seen, how can he love God ᴿwhom he hath not seen?

21 And ᴿthis commandment have we from him, That he who loveth God love his brother also.

CHAP. **3**

AD 90

13 John 17:14
14 ch. 2:10
14 ch. 2:9, 11
15 Mat. 5:21
15 Gal. 5:21
16 John 3:16
17 Deut. 15:7
Luke 3:11
17 ch. 4:20
18 Ezek. 33:31
Rom. 12:9
Eph. 4:15
19 John 18:37
19 Gr. *persuade*
20 1 Cor. 4:4
21 Job 22:26
21 Heb. 10:22
22 Ps. 34:15
Prov. 15:29
Jer. 29:12
Mat. 7:8
22 John 8:29
23 John 6:29
23 Mat. 22:39
John 13:34
Eph. 5:2
23 ch. 2:8, 10
24 John 14:23
24 John 17:21
24 Rom. 8:9

CHAP. **4**

AD 90

1 Jer. 29:8
Mat. 24:4
1 1 Cor. 14:29
1 Thes. 5:21
Rev. 2:2
1 Mat. 24:5
Acts 20:30
1 Tim. 4:1
2 Pet. 2:1
2 1 Cor. 12:3
3 2 John 7
3 2 Thes. 2:7
4 ch. 5:4

John 12:31   4
Eph. 2:2
John 3:31   5
John 15:19   5
John 8:47   6
Is. 8:20   6
ch. 3:10, 11   7
ch. 2:4   8
ver. 16   8
John 3:16   9
ch. 5:10   9
John 15:16   10
Rom. 5:8
Tit. 3:4
ch. 2:2   10
Mat. 18:33   11
ch. 3:16
John 1:18   12
1 Tim. 6:16
ch. 2:5   12
John 14:20   13
John 1:14   14
John 3:17   14
Rom. 10:9   15
ver. 8   16
ch. 3:24   16
Gr. *love with us* 17
Jas. 2:13   17
ch. 3:3   17
ver. 12   18
ch. 2:4   20
ver. 12   20
Mat. 22:37   21
John 13:34

CHAPTER 5

The believer as a child of God

WHOSOEVER ᴿbelieveth that ᴿJesus is the Christ is ᴿborn of God: ᴿand every one that loveth him that begat loveth him also that is begotten of him.

2 By this we know that we love the children of God, when we love God, and keep his commandments.

3 ᴿFor this is the love of God, that we keep his commandments: and ᴿhis commandments are not grievous.

4 For ᴿwhatsoever is born of God overcometh the world: and this is the victory that overcometh the world, *even* our faith.

5 Who is he that overcometh the world, but ᴿhe that believeth that Jesus is the Son of God?

The three witnesses

6 This is he that came ᴿby water and blood, *even* Jesus Christ; not by water only, but by water and blood. ᴿAnd it is the Spirit that beareth witness, because the Spirit is truth.

7 For there are three that bear record in heaven, the Father, ᴿthe Word, and the Holy Ghost: ᴿand these three are one.

8 And there are three that bear witness in earth, the spirit, and the water, and the blood: and these three agree in one.

9 If we receive ᴿthe witness of men, the witness of God is greater: ᴿfor this is the witness of God which he hath testified of his Son.

10 He that believeth on the Son of God ᴿhath the witness in himself: he that believeth not God ᴿhath made him a liar; because he believeth not the record that God gave of his Son.

11 ᴿAnd this is the record, that God hath given to us eternal life, and ᴿthis life is in his Son.

12 ᴿHe that hath the Son hath life; *and* he that hath not the Son of God hath not life.

Certainties of faith

13 ᴿThese things have I written unto you that believe on the name of the Son of God; ᴿthat ye may know that ye have eternal life, and that ye may believe on the name of the Son of God.

14 And this is the confidence that we have ᴺin him, that, ᴿif we ask any thing according to his will, he heareth us:

15 And if we know that he hear us, whatsoever we ask, we know that we have the petitions that we desired of him.

16 If any man see his brother sin a sin *which is* not unto death, he shall ask, and ᴿhe shall give him life for them that sin not unto death. ᴿThere is a sin unto death: ᴿI do not say that he shall pray for it.

17 ᴿAll unrighteousness is sin: and there is a sin not unto death.

18 We know that ᴿwhosoever is born of God sinneth not; but he that is begotten of God ᴿkeepeth himself, and that wicked one toucheth him not.

19 *And* we know that we are of God, and ᴿthe whole world lieth in wickedness.

20 And we know that the Son of God is come, and ᴿhath given us an understanding, ᴿthat we may know him that is true, and we are in him that is true, *even* in his Son Jesus Christ. ᴿThis is the true God, ᴿand eternal life.

21 Little children, ᴿkeep yourselves from idols. Ă'-mĕn.

CHAP. 5	
AD 90	
1	John 1:12
1	ch. 2:22, 23
1	John 1:13
1	John 15:23
3	John 14:15
	2 John 6
3	Mic. 6:8
4	John 16:33
5	1 Cor. 15:57
6	John 19:34
6	John 14:17
	1 Tim. 3:16
7	John 1:1
	Rev. 19:13
7	John 10:30
9	John 8:17
9	Mat. 3:16
10	Rom. 8:16
10	John 3:33

ch. 2:25	11
ch. 4:9	11
John 3:36	12
John 20:31	13
ch. 1:1, 2	13
Or, *concerning him*	14
ch. 3:22	14
Job 42:8	16
Jas. 5:14	
Mat. 12:31	16
Mark 3:29	
Heb. 6:4, 6	
Jer. 7:16	16
John 17:9	
ch. 3:4	17
1 Pet. 1:23	18
Jas. 1:27	18
Gal. 1:4	19
Luke 24:45	20
John 17:3	20
Is. 9:6	20
Acts 20:28	
Tit. 2:13	
ver. 11, 12	20
1 Cor. 10:14	21

THE SECOND EPISTLE OF

JOHN

The situation reflected in the Second Epistle of John is much the same as for the First. False teaching was circulating in denial of the true humanity of Jesus Christ (v. 7). The letter is addressed to "the elect lady and her children," but whether this refers to a particular individual or denotes figuratively a church whose members are her "children" has remained uncertain. A possible view is that the Second and Third Epistles were written as covering letters for the First, one to the church itself, addressed under the figure of the "elect lady," and the other to Gaius, the pastor. While both Second and Third John are less commonly referred to in early Christian tradition than First John, the literary affinities of this letter to the previous, and in turn to the Fourth Gospel, are sufficient to substantiate singleness of authorship and to warrant the possibility of a common date.

Salutation

THE elder unto the elect lady and her children, [R]whom I love in the truth; and not I only, but also all they that have known [R]the truth;

2 For the truth's sake, which dwelleth in us, and shall be with us for ever.

3 [R]Grace [N]be with you, mercy, *and* peace, from God the Father, and from the Lord Jesus Christ, the Son of the Father, in truth and love.

Love and the commandments

4 I rejoiced greatly that I found of thy children [R]walking in truth, as we have received a commandment from the Father.

5 And now I beseech thee, lady, [R]not as though I wrote a new commandment unto thee, but that which we had from the beginning, [R]that we love one another.

6 And [R]this is love, that we walk after his commandments. This is the commandment, That, [R]as ye have heard from the beginning, ye should walk in it.

AD 90	
1	3 John 1
1	Col. 1:5
3	1 Tim. 1:2
3	Gr. *shall be*
4	3 John 3
5	1 John 3:11
5	John 13:34
6	1 John 2:5
6	1 John 2:24
1 John 4:1	**7**
1 John 4:2	**7**
1 John 2:22	**7**
Mark 13:9	**8**
Gal. 3:4	**8**
Or, *gained:*	**8**
Some copies read, *which ye have gained, but that ye receive, etc.*	
1 John 2:23	**9**
Rom. 16:17	**10**
3 John 13	**12**
Gr. *mouth to mouth*	**12**
John 17:13	**12**
Or, *your*	**12**
1 Pet. 5:13	**13**

Attitude toward the deceivers

7 For [R]many deceivers are entered into the world, [R]who confess not that Jesus Christ is come in the flesh. [R]This is a deceiver and an ăn'-tĭ-chrīst.

8 [R]Look to yourselves, [R]that we lose not those things which we have [N]wrought, but that we receive a full reward.

9 [R]Whosoever transgresseth, and abideth not in the doctrine of Christ, hath not God. He that abideth in the doctrine of Christ, he hath both the Father and the Son.

10 If there come any unto you, and bring not this doctrine, receive him not into *your* house, [R]neither bid him God speed:

11 For he that biddeth him God speed is partaker of his evil deeds.

Conclusion

12 [R]Having many things to write unto you, I would not *write* with paper and ink: but I trust to come unto you, and speak [N]face to face, [R]that [N]our joy may be full.

13 [R]The children of thy elect sister greet thee. Ä'-měn.

THE THIRD EPISTLE OF
JOHN

The Third Epistle of John is addressed to Gaius, the pastor or a leader in the church. It is written in appreciation of his hospitality to certain traveling missionaries and as a request for similar assistance to the bearers of this letter. It may be a covering letter for First John (cf. II John). A certain Diotrephes, who possibly belonged to the same local church, had refused the author's envoys and excommunicated those who received them. A warning is given regarding Diotrephes, and a certain Demetrius is commended. While the author designates himself as "the elder" in both Second and Third John, this is not necessarily disastrous to apostolic authorship. The vocabulary and style of these two epistles correspond so closely to that of First John and the Gospel of John that singleness of authorship, and possibly even identity of date, are warranted.

OUTLINE OF THE THIRD EPISTLE OF JOHN:
  I. Salutation   1
  II. Commendation of Gaius   2 – 8
  III. Criticism of Diotrephes   9 – 11
  IV. Commendation of Demetrius   12
  V. Conclusion   13 – 14

Encouragement for Gaius

THE elder unto the wellbeloved Gāī'-ŭs, [R]whom I love [N]in the truth.

2 Beloved, I [N]wish above all things that thou mayest prosper and be in health, even as thy soul prospereth.

3 For I rejoiced greatly, when the brethren came and testified of the truth that is in thee, even as [R]thou walkest in the truth.

4 I have no greater joy than to hear that [R]my children walk in truth.

5 Beloved, thou doest faithfully whatsoever thou doest to the brethren, and to strangers;

AD 90	
1	2 John 1
1	Or, *truly*
2	Or, *pray*
3	2 John 4
4	1 Cor. 4:15
	Philem. 10
Gr. *worthy of God*	**6**
1 Cor. 9:12, 15	**7**

6 Which have borne witness of thy charity before the church: whom if thou bring forward on their journey [N]after a godly sort, thou shalt do well:

7 Because that for his name's sake they went forth, [R]taking nothing of the Gentiles.

8 We therefore ought to receive such, that we might be fellowhelpers to the truth.

Condemnation for Diotrephes

9 I wrote unto the church: but Dī-ŏt'-rĕ-phēś, who loveth to have the preeminence among them, receiveth us not.

10 Wherefore, if I come, I will remember his

deeds which he doeth, prating against us with malicious words: and not content therewith, neither doth he himself receive the brethren, and forbiddeth them that would, and casteth *them* out of the church.

Commendation for Demetrius

11 Beloved, ^Rfollow not that which is evil, but that which is good. ^RHe that doeth good is of God: but he that doeth evil hath not seen God.

12 Dē-mē′-trĭ-ŭs ^Rhath good report of all

AD 90	
11	Ps. 37:27
	Is. 1:16, 17
	1 Pet. 3:11
11	1 John 2:29
	& 3:6, 9
12	1 Tim. 3:7
12	John 21:24
13	2 John 12
14	Gr. *mouth*
	to mouth

men, and of the truth itself: yea, and we *also* bear record; ^Rand ye know that our record is true.

Conclusion and benediction

13 ^RI had many things to write, but I will not with ink and pen write unto thee:

14 But I trust I shall shortly see thee, and we shall speak ^Nface to face. Peace *be* to thee. *Our* friends salute thee. Greet the friends by name.

THE GENERAL EPISTLE OF
JUDE

The author of the Epistle of Jude identifies himself as "the servant of Jesus Christ and the brother of James" (v. 1). The authenticity of the letter is attested as early as the latter part of the second century. Where it was rejected by some in the third and fourth centuries, it was because of its use of extra-biblical literature (vs. 14, 15). But Jude's use of the Book of Enoch and his allusions to the Assumption of Moses are not materially different from Paul's references to pagan poets (Acts 17:28, I Cor. 15:33, Tit. 1:12). Jude indicates that he planned to write a doctrinal treatise, but that circumstances compelled him to deal with more pressing concerns (v. 3). His whole letter is therefore given over to warnings and exhortations regarding rising heresy in the church. The similarities between Jude's letter and chapter two of Second Peter are striking, and cannot be accidental. Most feel that Second Peter

is dependent upon Jude, though it may be that the writing of Second Peter was one of the factors which caused Jude to alter his original purpose. If Peter wrote to believers in Asia Minor, Jude, as possibly the representative of the Jerusalem Church after James' death in A.D. 62, may have felt the need for the same message to his affiliates in Palestine and Syria. The letter is to be dated between A.D. 65 and 80; though the more closely it is associated with Second Peter in content, the more possible it is to group the two chronologically as well.

OUTLINE OF THE EPISTLE OF JUDE:
    I. Salutation   1–2
    II. Warnings and Exhortations Regarding Heresies   3–23
    III. Doxology   24–25

Salutation

JUDE, the servant of Jesus Christ, and ^Rbrother of James, to them that are sanctified by God the Father, and ^Rpreserved in Jesus Christ, *and* ^Rcalled:

2 Mercy unto you, and ^Rpeace, and love, be multiplied.

Reason for the letter

3 Beloved, when I gave all diligence to write unto you ^Rof the common salvation, it was needful for me to write unto you, and exhort *you* that ^Rye should earnestly contend for the faith which was once delivered unto the saints.

4 ^RFor there are certain men crept in unawares, ^Rwho were before of old ordained to this condemnation, ungodly men, ^Rturning ^Rthe grace of our God into lasciviousness, and ^Rdenying the only Lord God, and our Lord Jesus Christ.

Reminder of God's judgment

5 I will therefore put you in remembrance, though ye once knew this, how that ^Rthe Lord,

AD 66	
1	Acts 1:13
1	John 17:11
1	1 Pet. 1:5
1	Rom. 1:7
2	1 Pet. 1:2
	2 Pet. 1:2
3	Tit. 1:4
3	Phil. 1:27
	2 Tim. 1:13
4	Gal. 2:4
	2 Pet. 2:1
4	Rom. 9:22
4	2 Pet. 2:10
4	Tit. 2:11
4	Tit. 1:16
5	1 Cor. 10:9
5	Num. 14:29
	Ps. 106:26
6	John 8:44
6	Or, *principality*
6	2 Pet. 2:4
6	Rev. 20:10
7	Gen. 19:24
	2 Pet. 2:6
7	Gr. *other*
8	2 Pet. 2:10
8	Ex. 22:28
9	Dan. 10:13
9	2 Pet. 2:11
9	Zech. 3:2
10	2 Pet. 2:12

having saved the people out of the land of Egypt, afterward ^Rdestroyed them that believed not.

6 And ^Rthe angels which kept not their ^Nfirst estate, but left their own habitation, ^Rhe hath reserved in everlasting chains under darkness ^Runto the judgment of the great day.

7 Even as ^RSodom and Gō-mŏr′-rhă, and the cities about them in like manner, giving themselves over to fornication, and going after ^Nstrange flesh, are set forth for an example, suffering the vengeance of eternal fire.

8 ^RLikewise also these *filthy* dreamers defile the flesh, despise dominion, and ^Rspeak evil of dignities.

9 Yet ^RMichael the archangel, when contending with the devil he disputed about the body of Moses, ^Rdurst not bring against him a railing accusation, but said, ^RThe Lord rebuke thee.

10 ^RBut these speak evil of those things which they know not: but what they know naturally, as brute beasts, in those things they corrupt themselves.

11 Woe unto them! for they have gone in the way ᴿof Cain, and ᴿran greedily after the error of Bā'-lāam for reward, and perished ᴿin the gainsaying of Côr'-ē.

12 ᴿThese are spots in your ᴿfeasts of charity, when they feast with you, feeding themselves without fear: ᴿclouds *they are* without water, ᴿcarried about of winds; trees whose fruit withereth, without fruit, twice dead, ᴿplucked up by the roots;

13 ᴿRaging waves of the sea, ᴿfoaming out their own shame; wandering stars, ᴿto whom is reserved the blackness of darkness for ever.

14 And Ē'-nŏch also, ᴿthe seventh from Adam, prophesied of these, saying, Behold, ᴿthe Lord cometh with ten thousands of his saints,

15 To execute judgment upon all, and to convince all that are ungodly among them of all their ungodly deeds which they have ungodly committed, and of all their ᴿhard *speeches* which ungodly sinners have spoken against him.

16 These are murmurers, complainers, walking after their own lusts; and ᴿtheir mouth speaketh great swelling *words,* ᴿhaving men's persons in admiration because of advantage.

17 ᴿBut, beloved, remember ye the words

AD 66	
11	1 John 3:12
11	2 Pet. 2:15
11	Num. 16:1
12	2 Pet. 2:13
12	1 Cor. 11:21
12	Prov. 25:14
	2 Pet. 2:17
12	Eph. 4:14
13	Mat. 15:13
13	Is. 57:20
13	Phil. 3:19
13	2 Pet. 2:17
14	Gen. 5:18
14	Deut. 33:2
15	1 Sam. 2:3
	Ps. 31:18
16	2 Pet. 2:18
16	Prov. 28:21
17	2 Pet. 3:2

1 Tim. 4:1	
2 Pet. 2:1	18
Prov. 18:1	19
Jas. 3:15	19
Col. 2:7	20
Rom. 8:26	20
Tit. 2:13	21
2 Pet. 3:12	
Rom. 11:14	23
Amos 4:11	23
Zech. 3:2	
Zech. 3:4, 5	23
Eph. 3:20	24
Col. 1:22	24
Rom. 16:27	25

which were spoken before of the apostles of our Lord Jesus Christ;

18 How that they told you ᴿthere should be mockers in the last time, who should walk after their own ungodly lusts.

19 These be they ᴿwho separate themselves, ᴿsensual, having not the Spirit.

Encouragement of the faithful

20 But ye, beloved, ᴿbuilding up yourselves on your most holy faith, ᴿpraying in the Holy Ghost,

21 Keep yourselves in the love of God, ᴿlooking for the mercy of our Lord Jesus Christ unto eternal life.

22 And of some have compassion, making a difference:

23 And others ᴿsave with fear, ᴿpulling *them* out of the fire; hating even ᴿthe garment spotted by the flesh.

Benediction

24 ᴿNow unto him that is able to keep you from falling, and ᴿto present *you* faultless before the presence of his glory with exceeding joy,

25 ᴿTo the only wise God our Saviour, *be* glory and majesty, dominion and power, both now and ever. Ä'-mĕn.

THE REVELATION

OF

ST. JOHN THE DIVINE

The last book of the New Testament identifies itself as "the apocalypse (unveiling, revelation) of Jesus Christ" (1:1), states its purpose as being "to show unto his servants things which must shortly come to pass" (1:1), claims to have been written by John from exile on the Greek island of Patmos (1:1, 9; cf. 1:4, 21:2, 22:8), and is addressed to seven churches of Asia Minor (1:4; cf. 2:1 – 3:22). Much like Jewish apocalyptic literature, cryptic symbolism and picturesque imagery abound. Yet however difficult its interpretation in detail, the theme of the sovereignty of God is stated clearly. Revelation was written as a warning, both to those outside of Christ and to Christians who had grown lethargic, and as an encouragement to God's people in time of oppression. Tradition is early and strong for Johannine authorship. Where such was denied, it was due to (1) opposition to its millennial views, (2) its difference in imagery and terminology from the Fourth Gospel and John's epistles, and (3) its awkward and irregular Greek. Though the early church realized itself to be living in the time of fulfilment, it still retained millennial expectations. Irregularities in expression and style may reflect an Aramaic original of which our present Greek text is a translation, or they can be adequately accounted for by the nature of the material or the probability that in exile the Apostle was unable to avail himself of an amanuensis or scribe as he had done for his other compositions. While Revelation corresponds in form to Intertestamental apocalyptic literature, it distinguishes itself sharply in content from the general body of such writings; *e.g.,* it claims a contemporary author who names himself and it has a definite destination. Both the closing days of the reign of Nero (A.D. 54–68) and the time of Domitian (A.D. 81–96) have been claimed for its date, though the explicit statement of Irenaeus in the early third century has led most to favor the latter.

OUTLINE OF THE BOOK OF REVELATION:
  I. Introduction and Salutation 1:1–8
 II. The Patmos Commissioning Vision 1:9–20
III. Messages to the Seven Churches 2:1–3:22
IV. Cosmic Struggle and Heavenly Conquest 4:1–19:21
 V. Divine Consummation 20:1–22:5
VI. Epilogue and Promise 22:6–21

CHAPTER 1

"The Revelation of Jesus Christ"

THE Revelation of Jesus Christ, ᴿwhich God gave unto him, to shew unto his servants things which must shortly come to pass; and ᴿhe sent and signified *it* by his angel unto his servant John:

2 ᴿWho bare record of the word of God, and of the testimony of Jesus Christ, and of all things ᴿthat he saw.

3 ᴿBlessed *is* he that readeth, and they that hear the words of this prophecy, and keep those things which are written therein: for ᴿthe time *is* at hand.

Salutation and ascription

4 JOHN to the seven churches which are in Asia: Grace *be* unto you, and peace, from him ᴿwhich is, and ᴿwhich was, and which is to come; ᴿand from the seven Spirits which are before his throne;

5 And from Jesus Christ, ᴿ*who is* the faithful witness, *and* the ᴿfirst begotten of the dead, and ᴿthe prince of the kings of the earth. Unto him ᴿthat loved us, ᴿand washed us from our sins in his own blood,

6 And hath ᴿmade us kings and priests unto God and his Father; ᴿto him *be* glory and dominion for ever and ever. Ă′-mĕn.

7 ᴿBehold, he cometh with clouds; and every eye shall see him, and ᴿthey *also* which pierced him: and all kindreds of the earth shall wail because of him. Even so, Ă′-mĕn.

8 ᴿI am Alpha and Omega, the beginning and the ending, saith the Lord, ᴿwhich is, and which was, and which is to come, the Almighty.

The Son of man among the candlesticks

9 I John, who also am your brother, and ᴿcompanion in tribulation, and ᴿin the kingdom and patience of Jesus Christ, was in the isle that is called Patmos, ᴿfor the word of God, and for the testimony of Jesus Christ.

10 ᴿI was in the Spirit on ᴿthe Lord's day, and heard behind me ᴿa great voice, as of a trumpet,

11 Saying, ᴿI am Alpha and Omega, ᴿthe first and the last: and, What thou seest, write in a book, and send *it* unto the seven churches which are in Asia; unto ĕph′-ĕ-sŭs, and unto Smyrna, and unto Pĕr′-gă-mŏs, and unto Thȳ-ă-tī′-ră, and unto Săr′-dĭs, and unto Philadelphia, and unto Lā-ŏd-ĭ-cē′-ă.

12 And I turned to see the voice that spake

with me. And being turned, ᴿI saw seven golden candlesticks;

13 ᴿAnd in the midst of the seven candlesticks ᴿ*one* like unto the Son of man, ᴿclothed with a garment down to the foot, and ᴿgirt about the paps with a golden girdle.

14 His head and ᴿ*his* hairs *were* white like wool, as white as snow; and ᴿhis eyes *were* as a flame of fire;

15 ᴿAnd his feet like unto fine brass, as if they burned in a furnace; and ᴿhis voice as the sound of many waters.

16 ᴿAnd he had in his right hand seven stars: and ᴿout of his mouth went a sharp two-edged sword: ᴿand his countenance *was* as the sun shineth in his strength.

17 And ᴿwhen I saw him, I fell at his feet as dead. And ᴿhe laid his right hand upon me, saying unto me, Fear not; ᴿI am the first and the last:

18 ᴿ*I am* he that liveth, and was dead; and, behold, ᴿI am alive for evermore, Ă′-mĕn; and ᴿhave the keys of hell and of death.

19 Write the things which thou hast seen, ᴿand the things which are, ᴿand the things which shall be hereafter;

20 The mystery of the seven stars which thou sawest in my right hand, and the seven golden candlesticks. The seven stars are ᴿthe angels of the seven churches: and ᴿthe seven candlesticks which thou sawest are the seven churches.

CHAPTER 2

Message to the church in Ephesus

UNTO the angel of the church of ĕph′-ĕ-sŭs write; These things saith ᴿhe that holdeth the seven stars in his right hand, ᴿwho walketh in the midst of the seven golden candlesticks;

2 ᴿI know thy works, and thy labour, and thy patience, and how thou canst not bear them which are evil: and thou hast tried them ᴿwhich say they are apostles, and are not, and hast found them liars:

3 And hast borne, and hast patience, and for my name's sake hast laboured, and hast ᴿnot fainted.

4 Nevertheless I have *somewhat* against thee, because thou hast left thy first love.

5 Remember therefore from whence thou art fallen, and repent, and do the first works; ᴿor else I will come to thee quickly, and will remove thy candlestick out of his place, except thou repent.

Center reference column

CHAP. 1
AD 96

1	John 3:32
1	ch. 22:16
2	1 Cor. 1:6
2	1 John 1:1
3	Luke 11:28
3	Jas. 5:8
4	Ex. 3:14
4	John 1:1
4	Zech. 3:9
5	John 8:14
	1 Tim. 6:13
5	Col. 1:18
5	ch. 17:14
5	John 13:34
	Gal. 2:20
5	Heb. 9:14
	1 John 1:7
6	1 Pet. 2:5
6	1 Tim. 6:16
7	Dan. 7:13
7	Zech. 12:10
8	Is. 41:4
8	ch. 4:8
9	Phil. 1:7
9	Rom. 8:17
	2 Tim. 2:12
9	ch. 6:9
10	Acts 10:10
	2 Cor. 12:2
10	John 20:26
10	ch. 4:1
11	ver. 8
11	ver. 17

Ex. 25:37	12
Zech. 4:2	
ch. 2:1	13
Ezek. 1:26	13
Dan. 7:13	
Dan. 10:5	13
ch. 15:6	13
Dan. 7:9	14
Dan. 10:6	14
Ezek. 1:7	15
Dan. 10:6	
Ezek. 43:2	15
Dan. 10:6	
ch. 14:2	
ch. 2:1	16
Is. 49:2	16
Eph. 6:17	
Heb. 4:12	
Acts 26:13	16
Ezek. 1:28	17
Dan. 8:18	17
& 10:10	
Is. 41:4 & 44:6	17
ch. 22:13	
Rom. 6:9	18
ch. 4:9	18
Ps. 68:20	18
ch. 20:1	
ch. 2:1, etc.	19
ch. 4:1, etc.	19
Mal. 2:7	20
ch. 2:1, etc.	
Zech. 4:2	20
Mat. 5:15	

CHAP. 2
AD 96

ch. 1:16	1
ch. 1:13	1
Ps. 1:6	2
ch. 3:1, 8	
1 John 4:1	2
2 Cor. 11:13	2
2 Pet. 2:1	
Gal. 6:9	3
Heb. 12:3, 5	
Mat. 21:41	5

6 But this thou hast, that thou hatest the deeds of the Nĭc-ō-lā-ĭ′-tăns, which I also hate.

7 ᴿHe that hath an ear, let him hear what the Spirit saith unto the churches; To him that overcometh will I givè ᴿto eat of ᴿthe tree of life, which is in the midst of the paradise of God.

Message to the church in Smyrna

8 And unto the angel of the church in Smyrna write; These things saith ᴿthe first and the last, which was dead, and is alive;

9 I know thy works, and tribulation, and poverty, (but thou art ᴿrich) and *I know* the blasphemy of ᴿthem which say they are Jews, and are not, ᴿbut *are* the synagogue of Satan.

10 ᴿFear none of those things which thou shalt suffer: behold, the devil shall cast *some* of you into prison, that ye may be tried; and ye shall have tribulation ten days: ᴿbe thou faithful unto death, and I will give thee ᴿa crown of life.

11 ᴿHe that hath an ear, let him hear what the Spirit saith unto the churches; He that overcometh shall not be hurt of ᴿthe second death.

Message to the church in Pergamos

12 And to the angel of the church in Pĕr′-gă-mŏs write; These things saith ᴿhe which hath the sharp sword with two edges;

13 I know thy works, and where thou dwellest, *even* where Satan's seat *is:* and thou holdest fast my name, and hast not denied my faith, even in those days wherein Ăn′-tĭ-păs *was* my faithful martyr, who was slain among you, where Satan dwelleth.

14 But I have a few things against thee, because thou hast there them that hold the doctrine of ᴿBā′-lăm, who taught Balac to cast a stumblingblock before the children of Israel, ᴿto eat things sacrificed unto idols, ᴿand to commit fornication.

15 So hast thou also them that hold the doctrine of the Nĭc-ō-lā′-tăns, which thing I hate.

16 Repent; or else I will come unto thee quickly, and ᴿwill fight against them with the sword of my mouth.

17 He that hath an ear, let him hear what the Spirit saith unto the churches; To him that overcometh will I give to eat of the hidden mănʹ-nă, and will give him a white stone, and in the stone ᴿa new name written, which no man knoweth saving he that receiveth *it.*

Message to the church in Thyatira

18 And unto the angel of the church in Thȳ-ă-tī′-ră write; These things saith the Son of God, ᴿwho hath his eyes like unto a flame of fire, and his feet *are* like fine brass;

CHAP. **2**	
AD 96	
7 Mat. 11:15	
& 13:9, 43	
ch. 3:6, 13	
7 ch. 22:2, 14	
7 Gen. 2:9	
8 ch. 1:8, 17	
9 Luke 12:21	
1 Tim. 6:18	
Jas. 2:5	
9 Rom. 2:17	
9 ch. 3:9	
10 Mat. 10:22	
10 Mat. 24:13	
10 Jas. 1:12	
ch. 3:11	
11 ch. 13:9	
11 ch. 20:14	
& 21:8	
12 ch. 1:16	
14 Num. 24:14	
& 25:1 & 31:16	
2 Pet. 2:15	
Jude 11	
14 Acts 15:29	
1 Cor. 8:9	
& 10:19, 20	
14 1 Cor. 6:13	
16 Is. 11:4	
2 Thes. 2:8	
ch. 1:16	
17 ch. 3:12	
& 19:12	
18 ch. 1:14, 15	

ver. 2	19
1 Ki. 16:31	20
& 21:25	
2 Ki. 9:7	
Ex. 34:15	20
Acts 15:20	
ch. 9:20	21
1 Sam. 16:7	23
Jer. 11:20	
John 2:24	
Acts 1:24	
Rom. 8:27	
Ps. 62:12	23
2 Cor. 5:10	
Acts 15:28	24
ch. 3:11	25
John 6:29	26
1 John 3:23	
Mat. 19:28	26
Luke 22:29	
1 Cor. 6:3	
Ps. 2:8, 9	27
Dan. 7:22	
2 Pet. 1:19	28
ver. 7	29

CHAP. **3**	
AD 96	
ch. 1:4, 16	1
ch. 2:2	1
Eph. 2:1, 5	1
1 Tim. 6:20	3
2 Tim. 1:13	
ver. 19	3
Mat. 24:42	3
Mark 13:33	
Luke 12:39	
1 Thes. 5:2, 6	
2 Pet. 3:10	
Acts 1:15	4
Jude 23	4
ch. 4:4 & 6:11	4
ch. 19:8	5
Ex. 32:32	5

19 ᴿI know thy works, and charity, and service, and faith, and thy patience, and thy works; and the last *to be* more than the first.

20 Notwithstanding I have a few things against thee, because thou sufferest that woman ᴿJĕzʹ-ĕ-bĕl, which calleth herself a prophetess, to teach and to seduce my servants ᴿto commit fornication, and to eat things sacrificed unto idols.

21 And I gave her space ᴿto repent of her fornication; and she repented not.

22 Behold, I will cast her into a bed, and them that commit adultery with her into great tribulation, except they repent of their deeds.

23 And I will kill her children with death; and all the churches shall know that ᴿI am he which searcheth the reins and hearts: and ᴿI will give unto every one of you according to your works.

24 But unto you I say, and unto the rest in Thȳ-ă-tī′-ră, as many as have not this doctrine, and which have not known the depths of Satan, as they speak; ᴿI will put upon you none other burden.

25 But ᴿthat which ye have *already* hold fast till I come.

26 And he that overcometh, and keepeth ᴿmy works unto the end, ᴿto him will I give power over the nations:

27 ᴿAnd he shall rule them with a rod of iron; as the vessels of a potter shall they be broken to shivers: even as I received of my Father.

28 And I will give him ᴿthe morning star.

29 ᴿHe that hath an ear, let him hear what the Spirit saith unto the churches.

CHAPTER 3

Message to the church in Sardis

AND unto the angel of the church in Särʹ-dĭs write; These things saith he ᴿthat hath the seven Spirits of God, and the seven stars; ᴿI know thy works, that thou hast a name that thou livest, ᴿand art dead.

2 Be watchful, and strengthen the things which remain, that are ready to die: for I have not found thy works perfect before God.

3 ᴿRemember therefore how thou hast received and heard, and hold fast, and ᴿrepent. ᴿIf therefore thou shalt not watch, I will come on thee as a thief, and thou shalt not know what hour I will come upon thee.

4 Thou hast ᴿa few names even in Särʹ-dĭs which have not ᴿdefiled their garments; and they shall walk with me ᴿin white: for they are worthy.

5 He that overcometh, ᴿthe same shall be clothed in white raiment; and I will not ᴿblot

out his name out of the ᴿbook of life, but ᴿI will confess his name before my Father, and before his angels.

6 ᴿHe that hath an ear, let him hear what the Spirit saith unto the churches.

Message to the church in Philadelphia

7 And to the angel of the church in Philadelphia write; These things saith ᴿhe that is holy, ᴿhe that is true, he that hath ᴿthe key of David, ᴿhe that openeth, and no man shutteth; and ᴿshutteth, and no man openeth;

8 ᴿI know thy works: behold, I have set before thee ᴿan open door, and no man can shut it: for thou hast a little strength, and hast kept my word, and hast not denied my name.

9 Behold, I will make ᴿthem of the synagogue of Satan, which say they are Jews, and are not, but do lie; behold, ᴿI will make them to come and worship before thy feet, and to know that I have loved thee.

10 Because thou hast kept the word of my patience, ᴿI also will keep thee from the hour of temptation, which shall come upon ᴿall the world, to try them that dwell ᴿupon the earth.

11 Behold, ᴿI come quickly: ᴿhold that fast which thou hast, that no man take ᴿthy crown.

12 Him that overcometh will I make ᴿa pillar in the temple of my God, and he shall go no more out: and ᴿI will write upon him the name of my God, and the name of the city of my God, *which is* ᴿnew Jerusalem, which cometh down out of heaven from my God: ᴿand *I will write upon him* my new name.

13 ᴿHe that hath an ear, let him hear what the Spirit saith unto the churches.

Message to the church in Laodicea

14 And unto the angel of the church ᴺof the Lā-ŏd-ĭ-çē'-ăns write; ᴿThese things saith the Ä'-mĕn, ᴿthe faithful and true witness, ᴿthe beginning of the creation of God;

15 ᴿI know thy works, that thou art neither cold nor hot: I would thou wert cold or hot.

16 So then because thou art lukewarm, and neither cold nor hot, I will spue thee out of my mouth.

17 Because thou sayest, ᴿI am rich, and increased with goods, and have need of nothing; and knowest not that thou art wretched, and miserable, and poor, and blind, and naked:

18 I counsel thee ᴿto buy of me gold tried in the fire, that thou mayest be rich; and ᴿwhite raiment, that thou mayest be clothed, and *that* the shame of thy nakedness do not appear; and anoint thine eyes with eyesalve, that thou mayest see.

19 ᴿAs many as I love, I rebuke and chasten: be zealous therefore, and repent.

20 Behold, ᴿI stand at the door, and knock: ᴿif any man hear my voice, and open the door, ᴿI will come in to him, and will sup with him, and he with me.

21 To him that overcometh ᴿwill I grant to sit with me in my throne, even as I also overcame, and am set down with my Father in his throne.

22 ᴿHe that hath an ear, let him hear what the Spirit saith unto the churches.

CHAPTER 4

Vision: the throne in heaven

AFTER this I looked, and, behold, a door *was* opened in heaven: and ᴿthe first voice which I heard *was* as it were of a trumpet talking with me; which said, ᴿCome up hither, ᴿand I will shew thee things which must be hereafter.

2 And immediately ᴿI was in the spirit: and, behold, ᴿa throne was set in heaven, and *one* sat on the throne.

3 And he that sat was to look upon like a jasper and a sardine stone: ᴿand *there was* a rainbow round about the throne, in sight like unto an emerald.

4 ᴿAnd round about the throne *were* four and twenty seats: and upon the seats I saw four and twenty elders sitting, ᴿclothed in white raiment; and they had on their heads crowns of gold.

5 And out of the throne proceeded ᴿlightnings and thunderings and voices: ᴿand *there were* seven lamps of fire burning before the throne, which are ᴿthe seven Spirits of God.

6 And before the throne *there was* ᴿa sea of glass like unto crystal: ᴿand in the midst of the throne, and round about the throne, *were* four beasts full of eyes before and behind.

7 ᴿAnd the first beast *was* like a lion, and the second beast like a calf, and the third beast had a face as a man, and the fourth beast *was* like a flying eagle.

8 And the four beasts had each of them ᴿsix wings about *him;* and *they were* full of eyes within: and ᴺthey rest not day and night, saying, ᴿHoly, holy, holy, ᴿLord God Almighty, ᴿwhich was, and is, and is to come.

9 And when those beasts give glory and honour and thanks to him that sat on the throne, ᴿwho liveth for ever and ever,

10 ᴿThe four and twenty elders fall down before him that sat on the throne, and worship him that liveth for ever and ever, and cast their crowns before the throne, saying,

11 ᴿThou art worthy, O Lord, to receive

glory and honour and power: ᴿfor thou hast created all things, and for thy pleasure they are and were created.

CHAPTER 5

The book with seven seals

AND I saw in the right hand of him that sat on the throne ᴿa book written within and on the backside, ᴿsealed with seven seals.

2 And I saw a strong angel proclaiming with a loud voice, Who is worthy to open the book, and to loose the seals thereof?

3 And no man in heaven, nor in earth, neither under the earth, was able to open the book, neither to look thereon.

4 And I wept much, because no man was found worthy to open and to read the book, neither to look thereon.

5 And one of the elders saith unto me, Weep not: behold, ᴿthe Lion of the tribe of Judah, ᴿthe Root of David, hath prevailed to open the book, ᴿand to loose the seven seals thereof.

"Worthy is the Lamb"

6 And I beheld, and, lo, in the midst of the throne and of the four beasts, and in the midst of the elders, stood ᴿa Lamb as it had been slain, having seven horns and ᴿseven eyes, which are ᴿthe seven Spirits of God sent forth into all the earth.

7 And he came and took the book out of the right hand ᴿof him that sat upon the throne.

8 And when he had taken the book, ᴿthe four beasts and four and twenty elders fell down before the Lamb, having every one of them ᴿharps, and golden vials full of ᴺodours, ᴿwhich are the prayers of saints.

9 And ᴿthey sung a new song, saying, ᴿThou art worthy to take the book, and to open the seals thereof: for thou wast slain, and ᴿhast redeemed us to God by thy blood ᴿout of every kindred, and tongue, and people, and nation;

10 ᴿAnd hast made us unto our God kings and priests: and we shall reign on the earth.

11 And I beheld, and I heard the voice of many angels round about the throne and the beasts and the elders: and the number of them was ᴿten thousand times ten thousand, and thousands of thousands;

12 Saying with a loud voice, ᴿWorthy is the Lamb that was slain to receive power, and riches, and wisdom, and strength, and honour, and glory, and blessing.

13 And ᴿevery creature which is in heaven, and on the earth, and under the earth, and such as are in the sea, and all that are in them,

heard I saying, ᴿBlessing, and honour, and glory, and power, be unto him ᴿthat sitteth upon the throne, and unto the Lamb for ever and ever.

14 ᴿAnd the four beasts said, Ă'-mĕn. And the four and twenty elders fell down and worshipped him ᴿthat liveth for ever and ever.

CHAPTER 6

First seal: rider of the white horse

AND ᴿI saw when the Lamb opened one of the seals, and I heard, as it were the noise of thunder, ᴿone of the four beasts saying, Come and see.

2 And I saw, and behold ᴿa white horse: ᴿand he that sat on him had a bow; ᴿand a crown was given unto him: and he went forth conquering, and to conquer.

Second seal: rider of the red horse

3 And when he had opened the second seal, ᴿI heard the second beast say, Come and see.

4 ᴿAnd there went out another horse that was red: and power was given to him that sat thereon to take peace from the earth, and that they should kill one another: and there was given unto him a great sword.

Third seal: rider of the black horse

5 And when he had opened the third seal, ᴿI heard the third beast say, Come and see. And I beheld, and lo ᴿa black horse; and he that sat on him had a pair of balances in his hand.

6 And I heard a voice in the midst of the four beasts say, ᴺA measure of wheat for a penny, and three measures of barley for a penny; and ᴿsee thou hurt not the oil and the wine.

Fourth seal: rider of the pale horse

7 And when he had opened the fourth seal, ᴿI heard the voice of the fourth beast say, Come and see.

8 ᴿAnd I looked, and behold a pale horse: and his name that sat on him was Death, and Hell followed with him. And power was given ᴺunto them over the fourth part of the earth, ᴿto kill with sword, and with hunger, and with death, ᴿand with the beasts of the earth.

Fifth seal: the slain witnesses

9 And when he had opened the fifth seal, I saw under ᴿthe altar ᴿthe souls of them that were slain ᴿfor the word of God, and for ᴿthe testimony which they held:

10 And they cried with a loud voice, saying, ᴿHow long, O Lord, ᴿholy and true, ᴿdost

thou not judge and avenge our blood on them that dwell on the earth?

11 And ᴿwhite robes were given unto every one of them; and it was said unto them, ᴿthat they should rest yet for a little season, until their fellowservants also and their brethren, that should be killed as they *were*, should be fulfilled.

Sixth seal: the great day of wrath

12 And I beheld when he had opened the sixth seal, ᴿand, lo, there was a great earthquake; and ᴿthe sun became black as sackcloth of hair, and the moon became as blood;

13 ᴿAnd the stars of heaven fell unto the earth, even as a fig tree casteth her ᴺuntimely figs, when she is shaken of a mighty wind.

14 ᴿAnd the heaven departed as a scroll when it is rolled together; and ᴿevery mountain and island were moved out of their places.

15 And the kings of the earth, and the great men, and the rich men, and the chief captains, and the mighty men, and every bondman, and every free man, ᴿhid themselves in the dens and in the rocks of the mountains;

16 ᴿAnd said to the mountains and rocks, Fall on us, and hide us from the face of him that sitteth on the throne, and from the wrath of the Lamb:

17 ᴿFor the great day of his wrath is come; ᴿand who shall be able to stand?

CHAPTER 7

Sealing the servants of God

AND after these things I saw four angels standing on the four corners of the earth, ᴿholding the four winds of the earth, ᴿthat the winds should not blow on the earth, nor on the sea, nor on any tree.

2 And I saw another angel ascending from the east, having the seal of the living God: and he cried with a loud voice to the four angels, to whom it was given to hurt the earth and the sea,

3 Saying, ᴿHurt not the earth, neither the sea, nor the trees, till we have sealed the servants of our God ᴿin their foreheads.

4 ᴿAnd I heard the number of them which were sealed: *and there were* sealed ᴿan hundred *and* forty *and* four thousand of all the tribes of the children of Israel.

5 Of the tribe of Judah *were* sealed twelve thousand. Of the tribe of Reuben *were* sealed twelve thousand. Of the tribe of Gad *were* sealed twelve thousand.

6 Of the tribe of Ā'-ṣĕr *were* sealed twelve thousand. Of the tribe of Nĕp'-thȧ-lĭm *were*

sealed twelve thousand. Of the tribe of Mȧ-năs'-sĕṡ *were* sealed twelve thousand.

7 Of the tribe of Simeon *were* sealed twelve thousand. Of the tribe of Levi *were* sealed twelve thousand. Of the tribe of Ĭs'-sȧ-chär *were* sealed twelve thousand.

8 Of the tribe of Zăb-ū'-lọn *were* sealed twelve thousand. Of the tribe of Joseph *were* sealed twelve thousand. Of the tribe of Benjamin *were* sealed twelve thousand.

The ones around the throne

9 After this I beheld, and, lo, ᴿa great multitude, which no man could number, ᴿof all nations, and kindreds, and people, and tongues, stood before the throne, and before the Lamb, ᴿclothed with white robes, and palms in their hands;

10 And cried with a loud voice, saying, ᴿSalvation to our God ᴿwhich sitteth upon the throne, and unto the Lamb.

11 ᴿAnd all the angels stood round about the throne, and *about* the elders and the four beasts, and fell before the throne on their faces, and worshipped God,

12 ᴿSaying, Ä'-mĕn: Blessing, and glory, and wisdom, and thanksgiving, and honour, and power, and might, *be* unto our God for ever and ever. Ä'-mĕn.

13 And one of the elders answered, saying unto me, What are these which are arrayed in ᴿwhite robes? and whence came they?

14 And I said unto him, Sir, thou knowest. And he said to me, ᴿThese are they which came out of great tribulation, and have ᴿwashed their robes, and made them white in the blood of the Lamb.

15 Therefore are they before the throne of God, and serve him day and night in his temple: and he that sitteth on the throne shall ᴿdwell among them.

16 ᴿThey shall hunger no more, neither thirst any more; ᴿneither shall the sun light on them, nor any heat.

17 For the Lamb which is in the midst of the throne ᴿshall feed them, and shall lead them unto living fountains of waters: ᴿand God shall wipe away all tears from their eyes.

CHAPTER 8

Seventh seal: angels and their trumpets

AND ᴿwhen he had opened the seventh seal, there was silence in heaven about the space of half an hour.

2 ᴿAnd I saw the seven angels which stood before God; ᴿand to them were given seven trumpets.

Center reference column:

CHAP. 6
AD 96
11 ch. 3:4, 5
11 Heb. 11:40
12 ch. 16:18
12 Joel 2:10
& 3:15
Mat. 24:29
Acts 2:20
13 ch. 8:10
& 9:1
13 Or, *green figs*
14 Ps. 102:26
Is. 34:4
Heb. 1:12
14 Jer. 3:23
& 4:24
ch. 16:20
15 Is. 2:19
16 Hos. 10:8
Luke 23:30
17 Is. 13:6, etc.
Zeph. 1:14
ch. 16:14
Ps. 76:7

CHAP. 7
AD 96
1 Dan. 7:2
1 ch. 9:4
3 ch. 6:6
3 ch. 22:4
4 ch. 9:16
4 ch. 14:1

Rom. 11:25   9
ch. 5:9   9
ver. 14   9
ch. 3:5, 18
& 4:4
& 6:11
Ps. 3:8   10
Is. 43:11
Jer. 3:23
Hos. 13:4
ch. 19:1
ch. 5:13   10
ch. 4:6   11
ch. 5:13, 14   12
ver. 9   13
ch. 6:9   14
& 17:6
Is. 1:18   14
See Zech. 3:3-5
Is. 4:5, 6   15
ch. 21:3
Is. 49:10   16
Ps. 121:6   16
ch. 21:4
Ps. 23:1   17
& 36:8
John 10:11, 14
Is. 25:8   17
ch. 21:4

CHAP. 8
AD 96
ch. 6:1   1
Mat. 18:10   2
Luke 1:19
2 Chr. 29:25-28   2

3 And another angel came and stood at the altar, having a golden censer; and there was given unto him much incense, that he should ᴺoffer *it* with ᴿthe prayers of all saints upon ᴿthe golden altar which was before the throne.

4 And ᴿthe smoke of the incense, *which came* with the prayers of the saints, ascended up before God out of the angel's hand.

5 And the angel took the censer, and filled it with fire of the altar, and cast *it* ᴺinto the earth: and ᴿthere were voices, and thunderings, and lightnings, ᴿand an earthquake.

The first four trumpets

6 And the seven angels which had the seven trumpets prepared themselves to sound.

7 The first angel sounded, ᴿand there followed hail and fire mingled with blood, and they were cast ᴿupon the earth: and the third part ᴿof trees was burnt up, and all green grass was burnt up.

8 And the second angel sounded, ᴿand as it were a great mountain burning with fire was cast into the sea: ᴿand the third part of the sea ᴿbecame blood;

9 ᴿAnd the third part of the creatures which were in the sea, and had life, died; and the third part of the ships were destroyed.

10 And the third angel sounded, ᴿand there fell a great star from heaven, burning as it were a lamp, ᴿand it fell upon the third part of the rivers, and upon the fountains of waters;

11 ᴿAnd the name of the star is called Wormwood: ᴿand the third part of the waters became wormwood; and many men died of the waters, because they were made bitter.

12 ᴿAnd the fourth angel sounded, and the third part of the sun was smitten, and the third part of the moon, and the third part of the stars; so as the third part of them was darkened, and the day shone not for a third part of it, and the night likewise.

13 And I beheld, ᴿand heard an angel flying through the midst of heaven, saying with a loud voice, ᴿWoe, woe, woe, to the inhabiters of the earth by reason of the other voices of the trumpet of the three angels, which are yet to sound!

CHAPTER 9

The fifth trumpet

AND the fifth angel sounded, ᴿand I saw a star fall from heaven unto the earth: and to him was given the key of ᴿthe bottomless pit.

2 And he opened the bottomless pit; and there arose a smoke out of the pit, as the

smoke of a great furnace; and the sun and the air were darkened by reason of the smoke of the pit.

3 And there came out of the smoke ᴿlocusts upon the earth: and unto them was given power, ᴿas the scorpions of the earth have power.

4 And it was commanded them ᴿthat they should not hurt ᴿthe grass of the earth, neither any green thing, neither any tree; but only those men which have not ᴿthe seal of God in their foreheads.

5 And to them it was given that they should not kill them, ᴿbut that they should be tormented five months: and their torment *was* as the torment of a scorpion, when he striketh a man.

6 And in those days ᴿshall men seek death, and shall not find it; and shall desire to die, and death shall flee from them.

7 And ᴿthe shapes of the locusts *were* like unto horses prepared unto battle; ᴿand on their heads *were* as it were crowns like gold, ᴿand their faces *were* as the faces of men.

8 And they had hair as the hair of women, and ᴿtheir teeth were as *the teeth* of lions.

9 And they had breastplates, as it were breastplates of iron; and the sound of their wings *was* ᴿas the sound of chariots of many horses running to battle.

10 And they had tails like unto scorpions, and there were stings in their tails: ᴿand their power *was* to hurt men five months.

11 ᴿAnd they had a king over them, *which is* ᴿthe angel of the bottomless pit, whose name in the Hebrew tongue *is* Ă-băd'-dŏn, but in the Greek tongue hath *his* name ᴺĂ-pŏl'-lў-on.

12 ᴿOne woe is past; *and,* behold, there come two woes more hereafter.

The sixth trumpet

13 And the sixth angel sounded, and I heard a voice from the four horns of the golden altar which is before God,

14 Saying to the sixth angel which had the trumpet, Loose the four angels which are bound ᴿin the great river Ēū-phrā'-tēṡ.

15 And the four angels were loosed, which were prepared ᴺfor an hour, and a day, and a month, and a year, for to slay the third part of men.

16 And ᴿthe number of the army ᴿof the horsemen *were* two hundred thousand thousand: ᴿand I heard the number of them.

17 And thus I saw the horses in the vision, and them that sat on them, having breastplates of fire, and of jacinth, and brimstone: ᴿand the heads of the horses *were* as the heads of lions;

CHAP. 8

AD 96

3 Or, *add it to the prayers*
3 ch. 5:8
3 Ex. 30:1
ch. 8:9
4 Ps. 141:2
Luke 1:10
5 Or, *upon*
5 ch. 16:18
5 2 Sam. 22:8
1 Ki. 19:11
Acts 4:31
7 Ezek. 38:22
7 ch. 16:2
7 Is. 2:13
ch. 9:4
8 Jer. 51:25
Amos 7:4
8 ch. 16:3
8 Ezek. 14:19
9 ch. 16:3
10 Is. 14:12
ch. 9:1
10 ch. 16:4
11 Ruth 1:20
11 Ex. 15:23
12 Is. 13:10
Amos 8:9
13 ch. 14:6
& 19:17
13 ch. 9:12
& 11:14

CHAP. 9

AD 96

1 Luke 10:18
ch. 8:10
1 ver. 2, 11
Luke 8:31
ch. 17:8
& 20:1

Ex. 10:4 — 3
Judg. 7:12
ver. 10 — 3
ch. 6:6 — 4
& 7:3
ch. 8:7 — 4
See Ex. 12:23 — 4
Ezek. 9:4
ch. 7:3
ver. 10 — 5
ch. 11:7
Job 3:21 — 6
Is. 2:19
Jer. 8:3
ch. 6:16
Joel 2:4 — 7
Nah. 3:17 — 7
Dan. 7:8 — 7
Joel 1:6 — 8
Joel 2:5-7 — 9
ver. 5 — 10
Eph. 2:2 — 11
ver. 1 — 11
That is to say, — 11
A destroyer
ch. 8:13 — 12
ch. 16:12 — 14
Or, *at* — 15
Ps. 68:17 — 16
Dan. 7:10
Ezek. 38:4 — 16
ch. 7:4 — 16
1 Chr. 12:8 — 17
Is. 5:28, 29

and out of their mouths issued fire and smoke and brimstone.

18 By these three was the third part of men killed, by the fire, and by the smoke, and by the brimstone, which issued out of their mouths.

19 For their power is in their mouth, and in their tails: ᴿfor their tails *were* like unto serpents, and had heads, and with them they do hurt.

20 And the rest of the men which were not killed by these plagues ᴿyet repented not of the works of their hands, that they should not worship ᴿdevils, ᴿand idols of gold, and silver, and brass, and stone, and of wood: which neither can see, nor hear, nor walk:

21 Neither repented they of their murders, ᴿnor of their sorceries, nor of their fornication, nor of their thefts.

CHAPTER 10

The strong angel and the book

AND I saw another mighty angel come down from heaven, clothed with a cloud: ᴿand a rainbow *was* upon his head, and ᴿhis face *was* as it were the sun, and ᴿhis feet as pillars of fire:

2 And he had in his hand a little book open: ᴿand he set his right foot upon the sea, and *his* left *foot* on the earth,

3 And cried with a loud voice, as *when* a lion roareth: and when he had cried, ᴿseven thunders uttered their voices.

4 And when the seven thunders had uttered their voices, I was about to write: and I heard a voice from heaven saying unto me, ᴿSeal up those things which the seven thunders uttered, and write them not.

5 And the angel which I saw stand upon the sea and upon the earth ᴿlifted up his hand to heaven,

6 And sware by him that liveth for ever and ever, ᴿwho created heaven, and the things that therein are, and the earth, and the things that therein are, and the sea, and the things which are therein, ᴿthat there should be time no longer:

7 But ᴿin the days of the voice of the seventh angel, when he shall begin to sound, the mystery of God should be finished, as he hath declared to his servants the prophets.

8 And ᴿthe voice which I heard from heaven spake unto me again, and said, Go *and* take the little book which is open in the hand of the angel which standeth upon the sea and upon the earth.

John eats the book

9 And I went unto the angel, and said unto him, Give me the little book. And he said unto me, ᴿTake *it,* and eat it up; and it shall make thy belly bitter, but it shall be in thy mouth sweet as honey.

10 And I took the little book out of the angel's hand, and ate it up; ᴿand it was in my mouth sweet as honey: and as soon as I had eaten it, ᴿmy belly was bitter.

11 And he said unto me, Thou must prophesy again before many peoples, and nations, and tongues, and kings.

CHAPTER 11

The two witnesses

AND there was given me ᴿa reed like unto a rod: and the angel stood, saying, ᴿRise, and measure the temple of God, and the altar, and them that worship therein.

2 But ᴿthe court which is without the temple ᴺleave out, and measure it not; ᴿfor it is given unto the Gentiles: and the holy city shall they ᴿtread under foot ᴿforty *and* two months.

3 And ᴺI will give *power* unto my two ᴿwitnesses, ᴿand they shall prophesy ᴿa thousand two hundred *and* threescore days, clothed in sackcloth.

4 These are the ᴿtwo olive trees, and the two candlesticks standing before the God of the earth.

5 And if any man will hurt them, ᴿfire proceedeth out of their mouth, and devoureth their enemies: ᴿand if any man will hurt them, he must in this manner be killed.

6 These ᴿhave power to shut heaven, that it rain not in the days of their prophecy: and have power over waters to turn them to blood, and to smite the earth with all plagues, as often as they will.

7 And when they ᴿshall have finished their testimony, ᴿthe beast that ascendeth ᴿout of the bottomless pit ᴿshall make war against them, and shall overcome them, and kill them.

8 And their dead bodies *shall lie* in the street of ᴿthe great city, which spiritually is called Sodom and Egypt, ᴿwhere also our Lord was crucified.

9 ᴿAnd they of the people and kindreds and tongues and nations shall see their dead bodies three days and an half, ᴿand shall not suffer their dead bodies to be put in graves.

10 ᴿAnd they that dwell upon the earth shall rejoice over them, and make merry, ᴿand shall send gifts one to another; ᴿbecause these two

prophets tormented them that dwelt on the earth.

11 ᴿAnd after three days and an half ᴿthe Spirit of life from God entered into them, and they stood upon their feet; and great fear fell upon them which saw them.

12 And they heard a great voice from heaven saying unto them, Come up hither. ᴿAnd they ascended up to heaven ᴿin a cloud; ᴿand their enemies beheld them.

13 And the same hour ᴿwas there a great earthquake, ᴿand the tenth part of the city fell, and in the earthquake were slain ᴺof men seven thousand: and the remnant were affrighted, ᴿand gave glory to the God of heaven.

14 ᴿThe second woe is past; *and,* behold, the third woe cometh quickly.

The seventh trumpet

15 And ᴿthe seventh angel sounded; ᴿand there were great voices in heaven, saying, ᴿThe kingdoms of this world are become *the kingdoms* of our Lord, and of his Christ; ᴿand he shall reign for ever and ever.

16 And ᴿthe four and twenty elders, which sat before God on their seats, fell upon their faces, and worshipped God,

17 Saying, We give thee thanks, O Lord God Almighty, ᴿwhich art, and wast, and art to come; because thou hast taken to thee thy great power, ᴿand hast reigned.

18 ᴿAnd the nations were angry, and thy wrath is come, ᴿand the time of the dead, that they should be judged, and that thou shouldest give reward unto thy servants the prophets, and to the saints, and them that fear thy name, ᴿsmall and great; ᴿand shouldest destroy them which ᴺdestroy the earth.

19 And ᴿthe temple of God was opened in heaven, and there was seen in his temple the ark of his testament: and ᴿthere were lightnings, and voices, and thunderings, and an earthquake, ᴿand great hail.

CHAPTER 12

The woman and the dragon

AND there appeared a great ᴺwonder in heaven; a woman clothed with the sun, and the moon under her feet, and upon her head a crown of twelve stars:

2 And she being with child cried, ᴿtravailing in birth, and pained to be delivered.

3 And there appeared another ᴺwonder in heaven; and behold ᴿa great red dragon, ᴿhaving seven heads and ten horns, ᴿand seven crowns upon his heads.

4 And ᴿhis tail drew the third part ᴿof the stars of heaven, ᴿand did cast them to the earth: and the dragon stood ᴿbefore the woman which was ready to be delivered, ᴿfor to devour her child as soon as it was born.

5 And she brought forth a man child, ᴿwho was to rule all nations with a rod of iron: and her child was caught up unto God, and *to* his throne.

6 And ᴿthe woman fled into the wilderness, where she hath a place prepared of God, that they should feed her there ᴿa thousand two hundred *and* threescore days.

War in heaven

7 And there was war in heaven: ᴿMichael and his angels fought ᴿagainst the dragon; and the dragon fought and his angels,

8 And prevailed not; neither was their place found any more in heaven.

9 And ᴿthe great dragon was cast out, ᴿthat old serpent, called the Devil, and Satan, ᴿwhich deceiveth the whole world: ᴿhe was cast out into the earth, and his angels were cast out with him.

10 And I heard a loud voice saying in heaven, ᴿNow is come salvation, and strength, and the kingdom of our God, and the power of his Christ: for the accuser of our brethren is cast down, ᴿwhich accused them before our God day and night.

11 And ᴿthey overcame him by the blood of the Lamb, and by the word of their testimony; ᴿand they loved not their lives unto the death.

12 Therefore ᴿrejoice, *ye* heavens, and ye that dwell in them. ᴿWoe to the inhabiters of the earth and of the sea! for the devil is come down unto you, having great wrath, ᴿbecause he knoweth that he hath but a short time.

Escape of the woman

13 And when the dragon saw that he was cast unto the earth, he persecuted ᴿthe woman which brought forth the man *child.*

14 ᴿAnd to the woman were given two wings of a great eagle, ᴿthat she might fly ᴿinto the wilderness, into her place, where she is nourished ᴿfor a time, and times, and half a time, from the face of the serpent.

15 And the serpent ᴿcast out of his mouth water as a flood after the woman, that he might cause her to be carried away of the flood.

16 And the earth helped the woman, and the earth opened her mouth, and swallowed up the flood which the dragon cast out of his mouth.

17 And the dragon was wroth with the woman, ᴿand went to make war with the remnant of her seed, ᴿwhich keep the command-

ments of God, and have ᴿthe testimony of Jesus Christ.

CHAPTER 13

The beast from the sea

AND I stood upon the sand of the sea, and saw ᴿa beast rise up out of the sea, ᴿhaving seven heads and ten horns, and upon his horns ten crowns, and upon his heads the ᴺname of blasphemy.

2 ᴿAnd the beast which I saw was like unto a leopard, ᴿand his feet were as *the feet* of a bear, ᴿand his mouth as the mouth of a lion: and ᴿthe dragon gave him his power, and his seat, ᴿand great authority.

3 And I saw one of his heads ᴿas it were ᴺwounded to death; and his deadly wound was healed: and ᴿall the world wondered after the beast.

4 And they worshipped the dragon which gave power unto the beast: and they worshipped the beast, saying, ᴿWho *is* like unto the beast? who is able to make war with him?

5 And there was given unto him ᴿa mouth speaking great things and blasphemies; and power was given unto him ᴺto continue ᴿforty *and* two months.

6 And he opened his mouth in blasphemy against God, to blaspheme his name, ᴿand his tabernacle, and them that dwell in heaven.

7 And it was given unto him ᴿto make war with the saints, and to overcome them: ᴿand power was given him over all kindreds, and tongues, and nations.

8 And all that dwell upon the earth shall worship him, ᴿwhose names are not written in the book of life of the Lamb slain ᴿfrom the foundation of the world.

9 ᴿIf any man have an ear, let him hear.

10 ᴿHe that leadeth into captivity shall go into captivity: ᴿhe that killeth with the sword must be killed with the sword. ᴿHere is the patience and the faith of the saints.

The beast from the earth

11 And I beheld another beast ᴿcoming up out of the earth; and he had two horns like a lamb, and he spake as a dragon.

12 And he exerciseth all the power of the first beast before him, and causeth the earth and them which dwell therein to worship the first beast, ᴿwhose deadly wound was healed.

13 And ᴿhe doeth great wonders, ᴿso that he maketh fire come down from heaven on the earth in the sight of men,

14 ᴿAnd deceiveth them that dwell on the earth ᴿby *the means of* those miracles which

he had power to do in the sight of the beast; saying to them that dwell on the earth, that they should make an image to the beast, which had the wound by a sword, ᴿand did live.

15 And he had power to give ᴺlife unto the image of the beast, that the image of the beast should both speak, ᴿand cause that as many as would not worship the image of the beast should be killed.

16 And he causeth all, both small and great, rich and poor, free and bond, ᴿtoᴺ receive a mark in their right hand, or in their foreheads:

17 And that no man might buy or sell, save he that had the mark, or ᴿthe name of the beast, ᴿor the number of his name.

18 ᴿHere is wisdom. Let him that hath understanding count ᴿthe number of the beast: ᴿfor it is the number of a man; and his number *is* Six hundred threescore *and* six.

CHAPTER 14

The Lamb and the redeemed on mount Sion

AND I looked, and, lo, ᴿa Lamb stood on the mount Sī'-ŏn, and with him ᴿan hundred forty *and* four thousand, ᴿhaving his Father's name written in their foreheads.

2 And I heard a voice from heaven, ᴿas the voice of many waters, and as the voice of a great thunder: and I heard the voice of ᴿharpers harping with their harps:

3 And ᴿthey sung as it were a new song before the throne, and before the four beasts, and the elders: and no man could learn that song ᴿbut the hundred *and* forty *and* four thousand, which were redeemed from the earth.

4 These are they which were not defiled with women; ᴿfor they are virgins. These are they ᴿwhich follow the Lamb whithersoever he goeth. These ᴿwereᴺ redeemed from among men, ᴿ*being* the firstfruits unto God and to the Lamb.

5 And ᴿin their mouth was found no guile: for ᴿthey are without fault before the throne of God.

Messages of the three angels

6 And I saw another angel ᴿfly in the midst of heaven, ᴿhaving the everlasting gospel to preach unto them that dwell on the earth, ᴿand to every nation, and kindred, and tongue, and people,

7 Saying with a loud voice, ᴿFear God, and give glory to him; for the hour of his judgment is come: ᴿand worship him that made heaven, and earth, and the sea, and the fountains of waters.

8 And there followed another angel, saying,

R Babylon is fallen, is fallen, R that great city, because she made all nations drink of the wine of the wrath of her fornication.

9 And the third angel followed them, saying with a loud voice, R If any man worship the beast and his image, and receive *his* mark in his forehead, or in his hand,

10 The same R shall drink of the wine of the wrath of God, which is R poured out without mixture into R the cup of his indignation; and R he shall be tormented with R fire and brimstone in the presence of the holy angels, and in the presence of the Lamb:

11 And R the smoke of their torment ascendeth up for ever and ever: and they have no rest day nor night, who worship the beast and his image, and whosoever receiveth the mark of his name.

12 R Here is the patience of the saints: R here *are* they that keep the commandments of God, and the faith of Jesus.

13 And I heard a voice from heaven saying unto me, Write, R Blessed *are* the dead R which die in the Lord N from henceforth: Yea, saith the Spirit, R that they may rest from their labours; and their works do follow them.

The angels and the harvest

14 And I looked, and behold a white cloud, and upon the cloud *one* sat R like unto the Son of man, R having on his head a golden crown, and in his hand a sharp sickle.

15 And another angel R came out of the temple, crying with a loud voice to him that sat on the cloud, R Thrust in thy sickle, and reap: for the time is come for thee to reap; for the harvest R of the earth is N ripe.

16 And he that sat on the cloud thrust in his sickle on the earth; and the earth was reaped.

17 And another angel came out of the temple which is in heaven, he also having a sharp sickle.

18 And another angel came out from the altar, R which had power over fire; and cried with a loud cry to him that had the sharp sickle, saying, R Thrust in thy sharp sickle, and gather the clusters of the vine of the earth; for her grapes are fully ripe.

19 And the angel thrust in his sickle into the earth, and gathered the vine of the earth, and cast *it* into R the great winepress of the wrath of God.

20 And R the winepress was trodden R without the city, and blood came out of the winepress, R even unto the horse bridles, by the space of a thousand *and* six hundred furlongs.

CHAPTER 15

Seven angels with golden vials

AND R I saw another sign in heaven, great and marvellous, R seven angels having the seven last plagues; R for in them is filled up the wrath of God.

2 And I saw as it were R a sea of glass R mingled with fire: and them that had gotten the victory over the beast, R and over his image, and over his mark, *and* over the number of his name, stand on the sea of glass, R having the harps of God.

3 And they sing R the song of Moses the servant of God, and the song of the Lamb, saying, R Great and marvellous *are* thy works, Lord God Almighty; R just and true *are* thy ways, thou King of N saints.

4 R Who shall not fear thee, O Lord, and glorify thy name? for *thou* only *art* holy: for R all nations shall come and worship before thee; for thy judgments are made manifest.

5 And after that I looked, and, behold, R the temple of the tabernacle of the testimony in heaven was opened:

6 R And the seven angels came out of the temple, having the seven plagues, R clothed in pure and white linen, and having their breasts girded with golden girdles.

7 R And one of the four beasts gave unto the seven angels seven golden vials full of the wrath of God, R who liveth for ever and ever.

8 And R the temple was filled with smoke R from the glory of God, and from his power; and no man was able to enter into the temple, till the seven plagues of the seven angels were fulfilled.

CHAPTER 16

The seven plagues

AND I heard a great voice out of the temple saying R to the seven angels, Go your ways, and pour out the vials R of the wrath of God upon the earth.

2 And the first went, and poured out his vial R upon the earth; and R there fell a noisome and grievous sore upon the men R which had the mark of the beast, and *upon* them R which worshipped his image.

3 And the second angel poured out his vial R upon the sea; and R it became as the blood of a dead *man:* R and every living soul died in the sea.

4 And the third angel poured out his vial R upon the rivers and fountains of waters; R and they became blood.

The Last Days
of Jesus on Earth

"*And I, if I be lifted up
from the earth, will draw
all men unto me.*"

JOHN 12:32

Christ's Entry Into Jerusalem

**B**EHIND them lay Jericho; before them was the holy city, Jerusalem. When Jesus and his disciples neared the little village of Bethphage, the Master drew aside two of the disciples and gave them special instructions. They were to go into the village, where they would find an ass and a colt tied. They were to untie the animals and bring them to Jesus. If anyone objected, they were to say: "The Lord hath need of them." Perhaps they were puzzled by these strange instructions, but the disciples went promptly and did as Jesus had told them.

As he was approaching Jerusalem at the holy season of Passover, Jesus apparently decided to reveal to the people the fact that he was the long-awaited Messiah. He had in mind the prophecy of Zechariah, made centuries before. This prophecy indicated the kind of Messiah that Jesus would be—not a proud and haughty conqueror, riding a high-spirited stallion, but a humble Savior of mankind.

In a short while the disciples arrived, leading the ass. They spread their robes on her back and Jesus mounted the animal and began his ride from the Mount of Olives to Jerusalem. Now the Mount of Olives is in full view of the holy city; furthermore, it was, according to popular belief, the place where the Messiah would appear.

As the procession moved toward Jerusalem, excitement began to build up among Jesus' followers. A crowd, in fact, "a very great multitude" gathered to watch Christ's entry into Jerusalem. Some took their cloaks and spread them on the road, just as Jehu's followers had done when he was proclaimed king. Others cut branches from the trees—palm branches, and perhaps myrtle and willow branches as well—and laid them along the route of the procession. It was a festive occasion!

The disciples and others in the procession, both those who walked before Jesus and those who followed after him, lifted their voices in a joyous chant:

"Hosanna; Blessed is he that cometh in the name of the Lord:
Blessed be the kingdom of our father David, that cometh in
the name of the Lord:
Hosanna in the highest!"

Clearly, the followers understood that Jesus was the Messiah. "Hosanna" means "Save now!" "Save, thou who dwellest on high!" The Pharisees, who were jealous of Jesus' growing reputation with the people, came to Jesus and protested this demonstration. "Master," they said, "rebuke thy disciples." But Jesus refused, saying: "If these should hold their peace, the stones would immediately cry out."

When Jesus and his procession of followers reached Jerusalem, the people in the city began to ask, "Who is this?" Members of the crowd answered them, "This is Jesus the prophet of Nazareth of Galilee." But those who thought most deeply about what they had seen and heard might just as truly have answered, "This is the Messiah, the Son of God, the Savior of mankind!"

Matthew 21:1-11; Mark 11:1-10; Luke 19:29-40.

Tissot

The Last Supper

I T was the first day of the feast of unleavened bread. This was the kind of bread eaten by Jews during the Passover celebration to remind them of their ancestors' exodus from Egypt, when the Israelites in their haste could not let their dough rise and baked the bread in an unleavened state. Jesus and his disciples were in Bethany, a few miles from Jerusalem. Since the Passover feast was a solemn and religiously meaningful meal, the disciples came to Jesus and asked: "Where wilt thou that we prepare for thee to eat the passover?"

Jesus gave them special instructions: Two disciples were to go into Jerusalem and look for a man carrying a pitcher of water; when they located him, they were to follow him into his house. Then they were to ask, "The Master saith, Where is the guestchamber, where I shall eat the passover with my disciples?" Following Jesus' instructions, the disciples located the house and made preparations for the passover in a "large upper room." That evening, Jesus and the twelve disciples traveled to the city and made their way to the upper room.

As they began to eat, Jesus made a startling statement: "Verily I say unto you, that one of you shall betray me." The disciples were quite upset; every one of them began to ask him, "Lord, is it I?" Jesus answered them: "It is one of the twelve, that dippeth with me in the dish." How sorrowful the disciples felt! Which of them could possibly betray their Master? Jesus spoke solemn words: "Woe to that man by whom the Son of man is betrayed! Good were it for that man if he had never been born." These words must have cut to the quick in the conscience of Judas Iscariot, who had already agreed to betray Jesus to the chief priests for thirty pieces of silver.

Then Jesus instituted a simple yet deeply meaningful act which would remind his disciples of him after his death. Christians across the centuries have repeated this act in remembrance of Christ, calling it "the Lord's Supper," or "the Sacrament of Holy Communion." First, "Jesus took bread, and blessed it, and brake it, and gave it to the disciples, and said, Take, eat; this is my body." How thoughtful the disciples must have been as they ate these bits of bread, which suddenly took on a new meaning—a reminder of the body of Christ. Then Jesus "took the cup, and gave thanks, and gave it to them, saying, Drink ye all of it; for this is my blood of the new testament, which is shed for many for the remission of sins." Here Jesus was speaking of his death, which still lay ahead of him at that moment. The disciples would remember this moment in the upper room later, and would begin to understand what Jesus meant when he said that his blood was "shed for many for the remission of sins."

Perhaps the world's greatest portrayal of "The Last Supper" is that painted by Leonardo da Vinci in 1498 on the plaster walls of the dining room of a monastery in Milan, Italy. It depicts the moment during the supper when Jesus said, "One of you shall betray me." "Is it I?" the disciples are asking themselves. We find our eyes drawn again and again to the face of Jesus, sorrowful, yet full of compassion and forgiveness.

Matthew 26:17-30; Mark 14:12-26; Luke 22:7-39.

Christ Praying in Gethsemane

FTER the Last Supper in the upper room, Jesus and his disciples went to the Mount of Olives, outside Jerusalem, to a garden called Gethsemane. Taking his three closest disciples—Peter, James, and John—Jesus went farther into the garden. He was very troubled. "My soul is exceeding sorrowful, even unto death," he told them. "Tarry here, and watch with me."

Going a little farther, Jesus "fell on his face, and prayed, saying, O my Father, if it be possible, let this cup pass from me: nevertheless not as I will, but as thou wilt." Jesus had already guessed that the Pharisees and other religious leaders of his day wanted him killed. He knew, also, what kind of cruel and painful death the Roman soldiers dealt out to their prisoners. Crucifixion was a form of execution that Rome had adopted from Carthage, and was the most dreadful of all tortures. It caused extreme pain in every part of the body, and the pain was drawn out over a period of many hours. As he prayed, Jesus experienced mental agony, so much so that "his sweat was as it were great drops of blood falling down to the ground."

Jesus came back to where he had left his three closest disciples—only to find them asleep! He must have been deeply disappointed as he asked Peter: "What, could ye not watch with me one hour? Watch and pray, that ye enter not into temptation: the spirit indeed is willing, but the flesh is weak." The disciples must have been ashamed of themselves. Surely they could share their Master's suffering and give him the comfort of companionship in his hour of trial!

Jesus drew apart again, and prayed earnestly: "O my Father, if this cup may not pass away from me, except I drink it, thy will be done." Once more, Jesus returned to Peter, James, and John—and once again found them sleeping. We can imagine his deep disappointment and sorrow as he saw them there, apparently unconcerned about his approaching death.

As Jesus prayed yet a third time the same prayer, he demonstrated how truly he practiced what he preached. For in the Sermon on the Mount, he had taught his disciples a prayer—which we call the Lord's Prayer—in which he prayed: "Thy will be done." This applies to life in general; it also applies to every individual human being's life. For Jesus, "thy will be done" meant painful death upon the cross. At the time, Jesus could not fully understand why it must be so. "If it be possible, let this cup pass from me," he prayed. He would like to continue living, teaching, healing, revealing God's love to mankind. But he did not put what he wanted above what God wanted: "nevertheless not as I will, but as thou wilt," he prayed.

Still a third time Jesus came back to his disciples and found them sleeping. One can imagine that he spoke with irony when he said to them: "Sleep on now, and take your rest: behold, the hour is at hand, and the Son of man is betrayed into the hands of sinners." How alone Christ must have felt in his hours of agony in the garden of Gethsemane! Even his three closest friends slept while his enemies plotted his death. But his Father did not leave him desolate, for "there appeared an angel unto him from heaven, strengthening him."

Matthew 26:36-46; Mark 14:32-42; Luke 22:40-46.

BRAHME

The Capture of Jesus

 UST as Jesus had finished praying in the garden of Gethsemane, Judas and a crowd armed with swords and clubs came into the garden to capture him. Jesus roused his sleeping disciples, saying: "Rise, let us be going: behold, he is at hand that doth betray me." Even as he spoke, the crowd surrounded him.

Judas had agreed to point out Jesus to the chief priests' soldiers. So he came up to Jesus and said "Hail, Master!" and kissed him. In those days, it was customary for a disciple to kiss his rabbi or teacher as a sign of respect and affection. But since this was a kiss of betrayal, it was hypocritical and loathsome. At that point the soldiers seized Jesus.

Would he be taken without a struggle? Peter, always inclined to impetuous action and perhaps feeling guilty about having slept while his Master's enemies closed in on him, drew his sword and slashed out at one of the men who held Jesus. The blow cut off the ear of Malchus, a servant of the high priest. Jesus spoke firmly to Peter: "Put up thy sword into the sheath: the cup which my Father hath given me, shall I not drink it?" And stretching out his hand, Jesus "touched his ear, and healed him."

Even in this trying experience, Jesus kept his composure and used the occasion to teach some profound lessons to his disciples. When he told Peter to put up his sword, he warned that "all they that take the sword shall perish with the sword." Furthermore, he wanted both his disciples and his captors to know that he was not taken through weakness or carelessness, but in obedience to the will of God.

Jesus could have escaped, had he so desired. But in his agonizing periods of prayer in the garden of Gethsemane he had firmly resolved to do the will of God, even if that involved accepting death on the cross. "Thinkest thou that I cannot now pray to my Father, and he shall presently give me more than twelve legions of angels?" Jesus asked them. "But how then shall the scriptures be fulfilled, that thus it must be?"

Then Jesus turned to the crowd. The words which he spoke to them were sharp rebuke: "Are ye come out as against a thief with swords and staves for to take me?" Jesus' entry into Jerusalem only a few days earlier had shown that he was a man of peace, not a revolutionist trying to overthrow the government. Jesus reminded the people: "I sat daily with you teaching in the temple, and ye laid no hold on me." In other words, he had not been hiding from the authorities; if they had wanted to talk with him—or even to arrest him—they could have found him any day in the temple at Jerusalem.

Even though they may have been shamed by Jesus' words, the crowd showed by their manner that they did not intend to release him. Like all mobs, they were in an ugly mood, and it was hard to reason with them.

As Jesus' followers realized that they, too, might be arrested they became fearful; and "all the disciples forsook him, and fled." How utterly alone Jesus was in his hour of need!

Matthew 26:46-56; Mark 14:42-52; Luke 22:45-53; John 18:1-11.

VAN DYCK

EVER in the history of mankind has there been a crueler miscarriage of justice than in the trial of Jesus Christ. The soldiers who seized Jesus in the garden of Gethsemane took him first to the Jewish high priest, named Caiaphas, where the chief priests, scribes, and elders were assembled.

The religious leaders wanted Jesus put to death, but they had no real charges to bring against him. So they inquired around for witnesses who might say something against him. Several came forward and made accusations against Jesus; but all the charges were false testimony.

Next the high priest tried to trick Jesus into saying something which could be used against him. "Answerest thou nothing?" he asked Jesus as the false witnesses had finished their stories. "What is it which these witness against thee?" But Jesus said nothing in self-defense against their lies.

Then the high priest asked Jesus: "Art thou the Christ, the Son of the Blessed?" And Jesus answered, "I am: and ye shall see the Son of man sitting on the right hand of power, and coming in the clouds of heaven." Thus Jesus openly admitted that he was the Messiah, for whom the Jews had been waiting in expectation for centuries. But instead of rejoicing, the high priest was terribly angry, accusing Jesus of blasphemy. And the assembled religious leaders "all condemned him to be guilty of death."

The next morning, therefore, the priests took Jesus to Pontius Pilate, the Roman governor of Judea, who held that office from A.D. 26 to 36. In Pilate's presence, the chief priests made many accusations against Jesus, but he said nothing in answer to their charges. To make Pilate think that Jesus was guilty of treason, thus worthy of death, the priests accused Jesus of urging the Jews not to pay taxes to Caesar and of claiming that he himself was a king.

Pilate began to suspect that the priests had brought charges against Jesus out of envy, because they were jealous of his popularity with the common people who flocked about him to hear his teachings. Pilate was reluctant to condemn Jesus on the basis of such unconvincing evidence as the priests offered. So he tried to find a way out of the situation without having to pass judgment on Jesus. Turning to the crowd, Pilate offered to release Jesus, in line with the custom of releasing one prisoner at the feast of the Passover. But the chief priests got the crowd to request the release of a murderer named Barabbas.

Pilate was on the horns of a dilemma. He did not want to condemn Jesus to death; in fact, he told the Jews after examining Jesus, "I find no fault in this man." But, on the other hand, he wanted to please the crowd; and the crowd was putting political pressure on Pilate by screaming out, "If thou let this man go, thou art not Caesar's friend." Pilate showed himself to be a man of weak character, who was willing to allow an innocent man to be killed rather than run the risk of losing his office with its power and privileges. So when the crowd screamed out, "Crucify him, crucify him," Pilate sentenced Jesus to death and turned him over to the soldiers to be beaten and crucified.

Matthew 26:57–27:26; Mark 14:53–15:15; Luke 22:54–23:25.

TISSOT

The Denial by Peter

ESUS had been seized in the garden of Gethsemane by the high priests' soldiers. In panic, Peter and the other disciples fled lest they too be taken captive. But Peter was caught in a struggle between courage and cowardice; he would like to be with Jesus, yet he wanted to remain free. So he "followed him afar off." The procession wound its way through the streets of Jerusalem to the high priest's palace. Eager to see the outcome of the trial, Peter went into the courtyard and sat with the servants.

Peter probably thought that if he kept quiet he would not be noticed. But one of the maids thought she recognized him. Coming over to where he was sitting, she said: "Thou also wast with Jesus of Galilee." Peter must have been panic stricken. He had not counted on this! A quick denial sprang to his lips: "I know not what thou sayest."

Getting up, Peter moved onto the porch, perhaps looking for a dark corner where he could see and hear yet not be noticed. But as he did so, another maid recognized him and announced to the servants on the porch: "This fellow was also with Jesus of Nazareth." This was like a nightmare in which he could not get away from his pursuers! Using an oath, he declared: "I do not know the man."

Peter may have thought that he had convinced the high priest's servants that he had nothing to do with Jesus. But their suspicions had been aroused. Soon after his second denial, some of the servants confronted Peter again. They had been listening carefully to his speech. Persons from Galilee had an accent that could be recognized; and the servants and soldiers knew that Jesus and his disciples were from Galilee. So they said, accusingly: "Surely thou also art one of them; for thy speech betrayeth thee."

Peter had not been convincing in his previous denials. Perhaps if he denied knowing Jesus with enough violence they would believe him! So he "began to curse and to swear, saying, I know not the man."

Then something simple happened, yet something which startled Peter and shook him emotionally to the core of his being: a cock crowed. Immediately Peter remembered what Jesus had said after the Last Supper, as they were walking to the Mount of Olives. "All ye shall be offended because of me this night," Jesus had said. Peter had answered him with confidence, "Though all men shall be offended because of thee, yet will I never be offended." Then Jesus had made a sad prophecy: "Verily I say unto thee, That this night, before the cock crow, thou shalt deny me thrice." Peter, feeling bold, had boasted: "Though I should die with thee, yet will I not deny thee." And now, only a few hours later, Peter had denied his Lord three times—he had cursed and sworn that he did not even know Jesus!

Peter was overcome with remorse, with shame for his cowardice and with sorrow for his sin. So "he went out, and wept bitterly." Peter's repentance laid the foundation for Jesus' forgiveness of him; and the remembrance of this night of denial would take away his pride and give him a new humility.

Matthew 26:69-75; Mark 14:54-72; Luke 22:54-62.

The Road to Calvary

 ESUS had been condemned to death by Pilate. In the eyes of the law he had no rights; therefore, the soldiers could do with him whatever they wished. So they took him to their barracks for some crude and brutal horseplay before crucifying him.

The soldiers thought that Jesus had claimed to be the King of the Jews. Before the whole battalion of soldiers, therefore, Jesus was mocked in an elaborate manner. First, they stripped off Jesus' clothes and put a scarlet robe around his shoulders. Then they made a crown of thorns and put it on his head, and thrust a reed into his right hand. These were supposed to represent a royal robe, a crown, and a scepter—the attire of a king.

Then the soldiers came forward and with mock respect knelt before Jesus and cried out, "Hail, King of the Jews!" As Romans, they felt contempt for the Jews whom they had conquered; here was a chance to pour out their contempt upon a helpless person whom they were going to kill in a short while. So "they spit upon him, and took the reed, and smote him on the head." Apparently, Jesus said not a word all the while he was being mocked, and beaten, and spat upon.

After a time, the soldiers grew tired of their cruel sport and decided to get on with the business of executing Jesus. So they took off the robe and put his own clothes on him, "and led him away to crucify him."

Crucifixion was a form of execution which the Romans used for rebels, slaves, and criminals of the lowest classes. The condemned man was forced to carry his cross to the place of his execution, where his hands were nailed to the crossbeam and his feet were lashed or nailed to the upright beam.

As Jesus walked along the streets of Jerusalem on the way to Calvary, he stumbled and fell under the weight of his cross. He had gone for many hours without rest: he had been questioned by the Jewish high priests and by Pontius Pilate, and following these trials had been whipped and mocked by the soldiers. He was weary from lack of sleep and weak from the merciless beatings. Small wonder, then, that he stumbled and fell as he tried to carry his heavy cross!

Among those who watched Jesus and his executioners on the way to Calvary was a man named Simon from Cyrene in North Africa. There was a large Jewish community in Cyrene; it is likely that Simon had come to Jerusalem to celebrate the feast of the Passover. As the procession passed Simon, Jesus stumbled and fell once more. A Roman soldier came up to Simon and demanded that he carry Jesus' cross to the top of the skull-shaped hill where Jesus was to be crucified. ("Calvary" is the Latin word for "Golgotha," which means "The place of the skull.")

This experience of carrying Jesus' cross, and perhaps of seeing how Jesus met death on the cross, had a profound effect on Simon's life. He became a Christian, and his sons Alexander and Rufus became well known members of the early Christian Church. What power there was in Jesus, that even on his way to a dreadful death he could win a disciple to his way of life!

Matthew 27:27-32; Mark 15:16-22; Luke 23:26-31.

Tissot

The Crucifixion

HEN Jesus reached the top of the hill called Calvary, with Simon of Cyrene walking behind carrying his cross, the Roman soldiers offered him a drink of wine mixed with myrrh. This drink would drug a person so that he would not feel pain so terribly as he hung on the cross. But Jesus refused the drink.

Then the soldiers nailed Jesus to the cross, piercing his hands and feet. Above his head they hung a placard, on which were written these words in Hebrew and Greek and Latin: "This Is Jesus the King of the Jews." This sign was one further bit of mockery of Jesus. And to add insult to injury, they crucified Jesus between two thieves.

As Jesus hung on the cross, the Roman soldiers gambled for his clothes. A number of persons had come out from Jerusalem to watch the crucifixion; among these were some religious leaders—chief priests and scribes and elders. Even as Jesus hung on the cross in pain, they mocked him. "He saved others; himself he cannot save," they taunted. "If he be the King of Israel, let him now come down from the cross, and we will believe him." Others jeered: "He trusted in God; let him deliver him now, if he will have him: for he said, I am the Son of God."

Jesus was crucified at nine o'clock in the morning. At noon, deep darkness settled over the earth until three o'clock in the afternoon. At that time, Jesus cried out with a loud voice, "My God, my God, why hast thou forsaken me?" This is the first verse of the twenty-second Psalm, in which the psalmist prays to God in the midst of his troubles. The Psalm ends on a note of triumph, pointing to God's victory:

"All the ends of the world shall remember and turn unto the Lord:
And all the kindreds of the nations shall worship before thee.
For the kingdom is the Lord's:
And he is the governor among the nations."

Perhaps Jesus was remembering this Psalm and reminding himself and his hearers that the victory—even over the cross—belongs to God. The first words of the Psalm, "Eli, Eli," caused some of those who heard Jesus to think that he was calling for Elijah; so again they mocked him, saying: "Let us see whether Elijah will come to save him."

Then Jesus cried out again in a loud voice, after which he said: "Father, into thy hands I commend my spirit." With that, he died. And the earth quaked and the curtain of the Temple in Jerusalem was torn in two. This curtain had kept worshippers from seeing the holy of holies, "the secret place of the Most High." Now the way to God was open to every man, through the sacrifice of Jesus Christ. A Roman centurion who saw how Jesus died said: "Truly this man was the Son of God."

A number of women who were followers of Jesus watched the crucifixion from a distance. Among these were Mary the mother of Jesus, Mary Magdalene, Mary the mother of James, and Salome.

Matthew 27:35-56; Mark 15:24-41; Luke 23:32-49; John 19:17-30.

Preparing Jesus for Burial

N the period between the death of Christ on the cross and his burial in the tomb, his disciples must have been stunned and anguished. We can imagine the bitter regrets of Peter at this time, remembering his denial of his Lord. The other disciples, too, must have been filled with shame and remorse as they recalled how they forsook Jesus and fled for their lives in the garden of Gethsemane.

The women disciples of the Man of Galilee must have been sore of heart and weak with weeping, for they had watched the whole painful spectacle of Jesus' crucifixion. And now he was dead! They must have felt utterly broken-hearted and desolate. As Joseph of Arimathea and Nicodemus prepared Jesus for burial in the newly hewn tomb in a nearby garden, all must have been quiet and thoughtful, the silence broken only by the sound of weeping.

Christians across the centuries have felt the anguish, the pathos, of the crucifixion and burial of Jesus Christ. These feelings have often been expressed in poetry and song. One moving spiritual asks: "Were you there when they crucified my Lord? Were you there when they nailed him to the tree? Were you there when they pierced him in the side? Were you there when they laid him in the tomb?" In holy imagination, we can enter into our Lord's agony, and repent of those sins which would crucify him afresh.

Something over a century ago, a Christian hymn writer named Cecil Frances Alexander reflected in memory and imagination on the scene that met the disciples' eyes there on Calvary:

"There is a green hill far away,
Outside a city wall,
Where the dear Lord was crucified,
Who died to save us all.

We may not know, we cannot tell,
What pains he had to bear;
But we believe it was for us
He hung and suffered there.

He died that we might be forgiven,
He died to make us good,
That we might go at last to heaven,
Saved by his precious blood.

There was no other good enough
To pay the price of sin;
He only could unlock the gate
Of heaven, and let us in.

O dearly, dearly has he loved,
And we must love him, too,
And trust in his redeeming blood,
And try his works to do."

TISSOT

The Burial of Christ

 IGHT was falling on that awful day when Jesus Christ was crucified. It was Friday evening in Passover week; the day before the Sabbath. Jesus' dead body hung upon the cross. Now it was a violation both of Jewish law and of personal feelings to leave persons unburied overnight, especially over the Sabbath. The Jews believed that such a practice would bring a curse upon the holy land. It was customary for pious Jews to bury even complete strangers, especially if they had no families or friends to perform this last service for the deceased.

So as nightfall approached, a wealthy and respected Jew named Joseph, from the town of Arimathea, went to see Pontius Pilate to request the privilege of burying Jesus. This took courage, for Jesus had been crucified as a traitor by the Roman soldiers. He had been mocked and scorned as "The King of the Jews." And here was a Jew running the risk of being tarred with the same brush.

Joseph's request took Pilate somewhat by surprise. Was Jesus already dead? Men sometimes hung on the cross for many hours before death released them from their pain. So Pilate called a centurion and asked if Jesus were already dead. Upon learning that he died, Pilate gave Joseph permission to remove Jesus' body from the cross and to bury it.

Why did Joseph of Arimathea go to this trouble and take this risk? We read that "he was a good man" who had not agreed with the Jewish authorities who had Jesus killed, and that he "waited for the kingdom of God." John tells us that Joseph had been one of Jesus' disciples, but that he had kept his discipleship a secret out of fear of the Jews. Perhaps this grief at Jesus' death emboldened Joseph to show his love and respect for his Master. In any case, he showed tenderness and respect for Jesus at the hour of his utter helplessness.

Joseph bought a linen shroud, and took Jesus down from the cross. At this point, another prominent Jew who was secretly a disciple of Jesus, Nicodemus, joined Joseph in preparing their Master for burial. He brought about a hundred pounds of myrrh and aloes—spices used customarily in that day to prepare a body for burial—and the two men bound the body of Jesus in the linen cloths with the spices.

Tenderly and with reverence, they took Jesus' body and laid it in a new tomb, hewn out of rock, where no one had ever been buried. This tomb was to have been Joseph's own; but now it was given unselfishly as a burial place for Jesus. Finally, they sealed the tomb by rolling a large stone across the entrance. Two of the women followers of Jesus,.Mary Magdalene and Mary the mother of Joseph, who had watched the crucifixion, looked on in grief-stricken silence as Jesus was laid in his tomb.

The chief priests and others who had been responsible for Jesus' death recalled, the next day, how Jesus had said: "After three days I will rise again." So they went to Pilate and requested that a guard be posted at the tomb, to keep the disciples from stealing Jesus' body and claiming that he had risen from the dead. Pilate authorized them to seal the entrance to the tomb and post a guard; so this was done.

Matthew 27:57-66; Mark 15:42-47; Luke 23:50-56; John 19:38-42.

BLOCH

The Resurrection

UST as the sun began to rise on the Sunday morning following Jesus' crucifixion, several of Jesus' women followers came to view the tomb where he had been buried. Among them were Mary Magdalene, Salome, and Joanna. Their hearts were still heavy with grief as they came into Joseph's garden and approached the entrance to the tomb.

Then a truly remarkable thing occurred. The earth shook, and an "angel of the Lord descended from heaven, and came and rolled back the stone from the door, and sat upon it. His countenance was like lightning, and his raiment white as snow." We can imagine how startled and amazed the women were; and the soldiers who had been posted to guard the entrance to the tomb fell on the ground, shaking with fright.

Then the angel spoke the words which were the best news ever heard by human beings: "Fear not ye: for I know that ye seek Jesus, which was crucified. He is not here: for he is risen, as he said. Come, see the place where the Lord lay. And go quickly, and tell his disciples that he is risen from the dead; and, behold, he goeth before you into Galilee; there shall ye see him: lo, I have told you."

How surprised and joyous the women were at the angel's announcement: "He is risen from the dead!" Quickly they turned and ran from the tomb to tell the disciples the good news of Jesus Christ's resurrection. As they hurried along, the risen Christ met them and greeted them: "All hail." With a tremendous upwelling of feeling, which included some fear, the women fell at Jesus' feet and worshipped him. Jesus repeated the instructions which the angel had given them: "Be not afraid," he said; "go tell my brethren that they go into Galilee, and there shall they see me."

The women hurried into Jerusalem where the disciples were still fearful and shaken by the terrible events of the past week end. Perhaps nothing disturbed them more than the memory of their own cowardice in deserting Jesus in his time of need. The women came in quite excited and told them the tremendous good news that Jesus Christ had risen from the dead.

The disciples were too deeply sunk in their gloom to believe the women's wonderful account. The women's "words seemed to them as idle tales, and they believed them not." But Peter, always impulsive, ran to the tomb; "and stooping down, he beheld the linen clothes laid by themselves, and departed, wondering in himself at that which was come to pass."

Meanwhile, the guards at the tomb had recovered from their fright. They went into Jerusalem and reported to the chief priests the amazing things which had happened. The chief priests were disturbed. What would happen to them if this news got out? Might not Pilate be terribly upset? And might he not punish them for their part in having an innocent man crucified? So the chief priests secured a large amount of money and bribed the guards to spread the story that Jesus' disciples had stolen his body from the tomb at night, while they slept.

Matthew 28:1-15; Mark 16:1-20; Luke 24:1-12; John 20:1-18.

BLOCH

The Road to Emmaus

IT was Sunday afternoon, and two of Jesus' disciples—one whose name was Cleopas, the other whose name we do not know—were walking from Jerusalem to the village of Emmaus, which was about seven miles away. As they walked, they talked about the things that had happened in Jerusalem during Passover week.

As the two disciples walked along, the risen Christ joined them; but they did not recognize him. He began to question them as to why they were so sad. Cleopas answered Jesus with a question: "Art thou only a stranger in Jerusalem, and hast not known the things which are come to pass there in these days?" "What things?" Jesus asked. "Concerning Jesus of Nazareth," Cleopas replied, "which was a prophet mighty in deed and word before God and all the people; and how our chief priests and our rulers delivered him to be condemned to death, and have crucified him."

Then Cleopas sank into a mood of real despair as he said: "We trusted that it had been he which should have redeemed Israel." In other words, the disciples had thought that Jesus was the Messiah. "Besides all this," he went on, "today is the third day since these things were done." Then he told Jesus how the women had come and reported to the disciples about the empty tomb and the angel's message that Jesus had risen from the dead. But it was obvious that Cleopas and his friend were unconvinced.

Then Jesus expressed his impatience with the small and timid faith of the disciples: "O fools, and slow of heart to believe all that the prophets have spoken: ought not Christ to have suffered these things, and to enter into his glory?" Then he explained the prophecies of the Old Testament as they pointed to the coming of the Messiah—the Christ—and as they described his life and ministry.

By this time, the three of them had reached Emmaus and Jesus acted as if he would go on further. But they urged him to visit with them, and he accepted their invitation. As they sat at the dinner table, Jesus "took bread, and blessed it, and brake, and gave to them. And their eyes were opened, and they knew him; and he vanished out of their sight." Perhaps they remembered how Jesus had blessed and broken the bread at the last supper in the upper room, and this was the thing that caused them to recognize their guest.

What a day this had been! When they left Jerusalem they were sad and discouraged. But now they were excited and elated. "Did not our heart burn within us, while he talked with us by the way, and while he opened to us the Scriptures?" they exclaimed. And though they had just arrived at Emmaus an hour or so before, they immediately returned to Jerusalem to share their good news with the eleven apostles.

When they arrived in Jerusalem, eager to tell their story, they found the other disciples excited, also. "The Lord is risen indeed, and hath appeared to Simon," the disciples told Cleopas. Then Cleopas and his friend told of their remarkable encounter with the risen Christ.

Luke 24:13-35.

DORPH

Doubting Thomas

HE first Easter Day had drawn to a close. The disciples were gathered in a room in Jerusalem; the doors were shut, to keep out the Jewish leaders who had been responsible for Jesus' death. Suddenly, Jesus came and stood among them and greeted them: "Peace be unto you."

The disciples must have been quite startled. Could this really be Jesus? As if to answer their unspoken question, Jesus showed them his hands and his side, The wounds were convincing proof to them that this was indeed their Master. "Then were the disciples glad, when they saw the Lord."

Jesus had not appeared just to visit with his disciples. He had an important mission to perform. "Peace be unto you," he said again. "As my Father hath sent me, even so send I you." An "apostle" is "one who is sent forth." This sending of Jesus' followers into the world to preach and teach the good news of God's salvation is what made them apostles. "And when he had said this, he breathed on them, and saith unto them, Receive ye the Holy Ghost." This was like the experience described in Genesis 2:7, when God breathed the breath of life into man. Jesus meant that he was imparting his Spirit to his followers, and that his Spirit would give life to their spirits.

Thomas was not present when Jesus appeared to the other ten disciples. When he returned, they told him excitedly: "We have seen the Lord." But Thomas was skeptical; he wanted proof that Jesus had indeed risen from the dead. Another man's word was not good enough for him. So he said: "except I shall see in his hands the print of the nails, and put my finger into the print of the nails, and thrust my hand into his side, I will not believe."

Eight days later, the disciples—including Thomas—were all together. Once again Jesus came and stood among them and said: "Peace be unto you." Turning to Thomas, he said somewhat reproachfully: "Reach hither thy finger, and behold my hands; and reach hither thy hand, and thrust it into my side: and be not faithless, but believing." Thomas was convinced that this was indeed Jesus, and that he had truly risen from the dead. In reverence and awe, Thomas exclaimed: "My Lord and my God."

Then Jesus gave the last Beatitude to be found in the gospels. Speaking to Thomas, he said: "Thomas, because thou hast seen me, thou hast believed: blessed are they that have not seen, and yet have believed." And thus the living Christ pronounced a blessing on all Christians in later generations who would believe in him as the Son of God who rose victorious over death.

In India today there is a branch of the Christian church which claims that it was founded by Thomas a few years after the resurrection of Jesus Christ. "Doubting Thomas" became Thomas, the man of faith—a missionary to India who died as a martyr for the Christian faith.

John 20:19-29.

CISERI

The Ascension

T HE risen Christ pushed back the horizons of his disciples' thinking to include the whole world. "All power is given unto me in heaven and in earth," he said. "Go ye therefore, and teach all nations, baptizing them in the name of the Father, and of the Son, and of the Holy Ghost: teaching them to observe all things whatsoever I have commanded you: and, lo, I am with you alway, even unto the end of the world."

Then Jesus commanded his disciples to remain in Jerusalem until they should be filled "with power from on high." They could not yet know what lay in store for them on Pentecost, when the once-fearful Peter would preach the Christian gospel so powerfully that three thousand persons would be converted to the Christian faith and join the church. But they were learning to trust Christ, and to obey his commands. So they would keep this command and wait in Jerusalem with prayer and expectancy for the further revelation of God's will for their lives.

Then Jesus led his disciples out of Jerusalem to the little town of Bethany, which had been dear to him during his ministry because it was where his friends Mary and Martha and Lazarus lived. It was there that Jesus had raised Lazarus from the dead.

Just before his departure from his disciples, Jesus told them: "Ye shall be witnesses to me both in Jerusalem, and in all Judea, and in Samaria, and unto the uttermost part of the earth." Then, lifting up his hands in a benediction, he blessed his disciples. "And it came to pass, while he blessed them, he was parted from them, and carried up into heaven." A cloud received Jesus out of their sight. In the Old Testament, a cloud is the sign of the divine glory; here, too, it points to God's glory and to the fact that Jesus Christ is "on the right hand of God."

The disciples stood in awe and amazement, rooted to the spot where they had seen Christ ascend into heaven. They were moved to action by two men in white apparel who asked them: "Ye men of Galilee, why stand ye gazing up into heaven?" The men continued: "This same Jesus, which is taken up from you into heaven, shall so come in like manner as ye have seen him go into heaven." Here was a promise to remember and to think about!

Small wonder, then, that the disciples "returned to Jerusalem with great joy: and were continually in the temple, praising and blessing God."

Matthew 28:18-20; Luke 24:44-53; Acts 1:6-11.

OTTO

"Behold, I Stand at the Door, and Knock"

OMPANIONSHIP with Christ is not limited to just a small circle of specially chosen persons; it is a privilege open to everyone. In one of the most hope-inspiring passages of the Bible, the living Christ says: "Behold, I stand at the door, and knock: if any man hear my voice, and open the door, I will come in to him, and will sup with him, and he with me."

This beautiful passage of Scripture tells us much about Christ and his relationship with us. First, it says that Christ would like to form an eternal friendship with every person on earth. In friendliness and humility, he approaches each human life and seeks admission into that person's life. He never smashes the door down; he respects the freedom of human beings even to keep God out of their lives! But he gently and persistently requests an invitation into each person's life: "I stand at the door, and knock."

Human beings must be alert to hear Christ's knock at the door of their heart. "If any man hear my voice . . ." Christ says. The din and clamor of the world can so distract persons that they may not hear Christ's voice. But just as parents, even as they sleep, keep their ears alert to their baby's cry, even so can men keep their spiritual ears open to hear Christ's knock at the door, and his gentle voice asking for admission into their lives.

". . . and open the door. . ." Even if a person hears Christ's call, he may be too busy to go to the door. Or he may be unwilling to open the door and admit Christ into his life. Maybe his spiritual house is not in order. Or maybe he likes the state of spiritual disorder, yet would be embarrassed to have Christ see him in this setting. Each person must decide for himself whether he will—or will not—"open the door" to Christ.

"I will come in to him, and will sup with him, and he with me." What is better symbol of friendship than eating together? We remember the scenes from the Gospels of Jesus and his disciples eating together. This makes one think of fellowship, of daily companionship with the living Christ.

A simple song of Christian fellowship which expresses this idea says:

> "Into my heart, into my heart,
> Come into my heart, Lord Jesus.
> Come in today, come in to stay,
> Come into my heart, Lord Jesus."

In the painting, "Behold, I Stand at the Door and Knock," the artist is trying to portray—through line and color—a great spiritual reality. But the deepest meaning of this statement of the living Christ can only be discovered as persons test the reality of it in their own lives. "Behold, I stand at the door, and knock: if any man hear my voice, and open the door, I will come in to him, and will sup with him, and he with me."

Revelation 3:20.

HABER

Let not your heart be troubled: ye believe in God, believe also in me.

In my Father's house are many mansions: if it were not so, I would have told you. I go to prepare a place for you.

And if I go and prepare a place for you, I will come again, and receive you unto myself; that where I am, there ye may be also."

JOHN 14:1-3

"I will not leave you comfortless: I will come to you."

JOHN 14:18

5 And I heard the angel of the waters say, ^RThou art righteous, O Lord, ^Rwhich art, and wast, and shalt be, because thou hast judged thus.

6 For ^Rthey have shed the blood ^Rof saints and prophets, ^Rand thou hast given them blood to drink; for they are worthy.

7 And I heard another out of the altar say, Even so, ^RLord God Almighty, ^Rtrue and righteous *are* thy judgments.

8 And the fourth angel poured out his vial ^Rupon the sun; ^Rand power was given unto him to scorch men with fire.

9 And men were ^Nscorched with great heat, and ^Rblasphemed the name of God, which hath power over these plagues: ^Rand they repented not ^Rto give him glory.

10 And the fifth angel poured out his vial ^Rupon the seat of the beast; ^Rand his kingdom was full of darkness; ^Rand they gnawed their tongues for pain,

11 And ^Rblasphemed the God of heaven because of their pains and ^Rtheir sores, ^Rand repented not of their deeds.

12 And the sixth angel poured out his vial ^Rupon the great river Eu-phra'-tes; ^Rand the water thereof was dried up, ^Rthat the way of the kings of the east might be prepared.

13 And I saw three unclean ^Rspirits like frogs *come* out of the mouth of ^Rthe dragon, and out of the mouth of the beast, and out of the mouth of ^Rthe false prophet.

14 ^RFor they are the spirits of devils, ^Rworking miracles, *which* go forth unto the kings of the earth ^Rand of the whole world, to gather them to ^Rthe battle of that great day of God Almighty.

15 ^RBehold, I come as a thief. Blessed *is* he that watcheth, and keepeth his garments, ^Rlest he walk naked, and they see his shame.

16 ^RAnd he gathered them together into a place called in the Hebrew tongue Ar-mă-gĕd'-dŏn.

17 And the seventh angel poured out his vial into the air; and there came a great voice out of the temple of heaven, from the throne, saying, ^RIt is done.

18 And ^Rthere were voices, and thunders, and lightnings; ^Rand there was a great earthquake, ^Rsuch as was not since men were upon the earth, so mighty an earthquake, *and* so great.

19 And ^Rthe great city was divided into three parts, and the cities of the nations fell: and great Babylon ^Rcame in remembrance before God, ^Rto give unto her the cup of the wine of the fierceness of his wrath.

20 And ^Revery island fled away, and the mountains were not found.

21 ^RAnd there fell upon men a great hail out of heaven, *every stone* about the weight of a talent: and ^Rmen blasphemed God because of ^Rthe plague of the hail; for the plague thereof was exceeding great.

CHAPTER 17

Babylon and the beast

AND there came ^Rone of the seven angels which had the seven vials, and talked with me, saying unto me, Come hither; ^RI will shew unto thee the judgment of ^Rthe great whore ^Rthat sitteth upon many waters:

2 ^RWith whom the kings of the earth have committed fornication, and ^Rthe inhabitants of the earth have been made drunk with the wine of her fornication.

3 So he carried me away in the spirit ^Rinto the wilderness: and I saw a woman sit ^Rupon a scarlet coloured beast, full of ^Rnames of blasphemy, ^Rhaving seven heads and ^Rten horns.

4 And the woman ^Rwas arrayed in purple and scarlet colour, ^Rand ^Ndecked with gold and precious stones and pearls, ^Rhaving a golden cup in her hand ^Rfull of abominations and filthiness of her fornication:

5 And upon her forehead *was* a name written, ^RMYSTERY, BABYLON THE GREAT, THE MOTHER OF ^NHARLOTS AND ABOMINATIONS OF THE EARTH.

6 And I saw ^Rthe woman drunken ^Rwith the blood of the saints, and with the blood of ^Rthe martyrs of Jesus: and when I saw her, I wondered with great admiration.

7 And the angel said unto me, Wherefore didst thou marvel? I will tell thee the mystery of the woman, and of the beast that carrieth her, which hath the seven heads and ten horns.

8 The beast that thou sawest was, and is not; and ^Rshall ascend out of the bottomless pit, and ^Rgo into perdition: and they that dwell on the earth ^Rshall wonder, ^Rwhose names were not written in the book of life from the foundation of the world, when they behold the beast that was, and is not, and yet is.

9 And ^Rhere *is* the mind which hath wisdom. ^RThe seven heads are seven mountains, on which the woman sitteth.

10 And there are seven kings: five are fallen, and one is, *and* the other is not yet come; and when he cometh, he must continue a short space.

11 And the beast that was, and is not, even

he is the eighth, and is of the seven, [R]and goeth into perdition.

12 And [R]the ten horns which thou sawest are ten kings, which have received no kingdom as yet; but receive power as kings one hour with the beast.

13 These have one mind, and shall give their power and strength unto the beast.

14 [R]These shall make war with the Lamb, and the Lamb shall overcome them: [R]for he is Lord of lords, and King of kings: [R]and they that are with him *are* called, and chosen, and faithful.

15 And he saith unto me, [R]The waters which thou sawest, where the whore sitteth, [R]are peoples, and multitudes, and nations, and tongues.

16 And the ten horns which thou sawest upon the beast, [R]these shall hate the whore, and shall make her desolate [R]and naked, and shall eat her flesh, and [R]burn her with fire.

17 [R]For God hath put in their hearts to fulfil his will, and to agree, and give their kingdom unto the beast, [R]until the words of God shall be fulfilled.

18 And the woman which thou sawest [R]is that great city, [R]which reigneth over the kings of the earth.

CHAPTER 18

The fall of Babylon

AND [R]after these things I saw another angel come down from heaven, having great power; [R]and the earth was lightened with his glory.

2 And he cried mightily with a strong voice, saying, [R]Babylon the great is fallen, is fallen, and [R]is become the habitation of devils, and the hold of every foul spirit, and [R]a cage of every unclean and hateful bird.

3 For all nations [R]have drunk of the wine of the wrath of her fornication, and the kings of the earth have committed fornication with her, [R]and the merchants of the earth are waxed rich through the [N]abundance of her delicacies.

4 And I heard another voice from heaven, saying, [R]Come out of her, my people, that ye be not partakers of her sins, and that ye receive not of her plagues.

5 [R]For her sins have reached unto heaven, and [R]God hath remembered her iniquities.

6 [R]Reward her even as she rewarded you, and double unto her double according to her works: [R]in the cup which she hath filled [R]fill to her double.

7 [R]How much she hath glorified herself, and

lived deliciously, so much torment and sorrow give her: for she saith in her heart, I sit a [R]queen, and am no widow, and shall see no sorrow.

8 Therefore shall her plagues come [R]in one day, death, and mourning, and famine; and [R]she shall be utterly burned with fire: [R]for strong *is* the Lord God who judgeth her.

Lament over Babylon

9 And [R]the kings of the earth, who have committed fornication and lived deliciously with her, [R]shall bewail her, and lament for her, [R]when they shall see the smoke of her burning,

10 Standing afar off for the fear of her torment, saying, [R]Alas, alas, that great city Babylon, that mighty city! [R]for in one hour is thy judgment come.

11 And [R]the merchants of the earth shall weep and mourn over her; for no man buyeth their merchandise any more:

12 [R]The merchandise of gold, and silver, and precious stones, and of pearls, and fine linen, and purple, and silk, and scarlet, and all [N]thyine wood, and all manner vessels of ivory, and all manner vessels of most precious wood, and of brass, and iron, and marble,

13 And cinnamon, and odours, and ointments, and frankincense, and wine, and oil, and fine flour, and wheat, and beasts, and sheep, and horses, and chariots, and [N]slaves, and [R]souls of men.

14 And the fruits that thy soul lusted after are departed from thee, and all things which were dainty and goodly are departed from thee, and thou shalt find them no more at all.

15 [R]The merchants of these things, which were made rich by her, shall stand afar off for the fear of her torment, weeping and wailing,

16 And saying, Alas, alas, that great city, [R]that was clothed in fine linen, and purple, and scarlet, and decked with gold, and precious stones, and pearls!

17 [R]For in one hour so great riches is come to nought. And [R]every shipmaster, and all the company in ships, and sailors, and as many as trade by sea, stood afar off,

18 [R]And cried when they saw the smoke of her burning, saying, [R]What *city is* like unto this great city!

19 And [R]they cast dust on their heads, and cried, weeping and wailing, saying, Alas, alas, that great city, wherein were made rich all that had ships in the sea by reason of her costliness! [R]for in one hour is she made desolate.

20 [R]Rejoice over her, *thou* heaven, and *ye*

holy apostles and prophets; for [R]God hath avenged you on her.

Silence in fallen Babylon

21 And a mighty angel took up a stone like a great millstone, and cast *it* into the sea, saying, [R]Thus with violence shall that great city Babylon be thrown down, and [R]shall be found no more at all.

22 [R]And the voice of harpers, and musicians, and of pipers, and trumpeters, shall be heard no more at all in thee; and no craftsman, of whatsoever craft *he be,* shall be found any more in thee; and the sound of a millstone shall be heard no more at all in thee;

23 [R]And the light of a candle shall shine no more at all in thee; [R]and the voice of the bridegroom and of the bride shall be heard no more at all in thee: for [R]thy merchants were the great men of the earth; [R]for by thy sorceries were all nations deceived.

24 And [R]in her was found the blood of prophets, and of saints, and of all that [R]were slain upon the earth.

CHAPTER 19

Four songs of praise

AND after these things [R]I heard a great voice of much people in heaven, saying, Alleluia; [R]Salvation, and glory, and honour, and power, unto the Lord our God:

2 For [R]true and righteous *are* his judgments: for he hath judged the great whore, which did corrupt the earth with her fornication, and [R]hath avenged the blood of his servants at her hand.

3 And again they said, Alleluia. And [R]her smoke rose up for ever and ever.

4 And [R]the four and twenty elders and the four beasts fell down and worshipped God that sat on the throne, saying, [R]Ā'-mĕn; Alleluia.

5 And a voice came out of the throne, saying, [R]Praise our God, all ye his servants, and ye that fear him, [R]both small and great.

6 [R]And I heard as it were the voice of a great multitude, and as the voice of many waters, and as the voice of mighty thunderings, saying, Alleluia: for [R]the Lord God omnipotent reigneth.

7 Let us be glad and rejoice, and give honour to him: for [R]the marriage of the Lamb is come, and his wife hath made herself ready.

8 And [R]to her was granted that she should be arrayed in fine linen, clean and [N]white: [R]for the fine linen is the righteousness of saints.

9 And he saith unto me, Write, [R]Blessed *are*

CHAP. 18

AD 96

20 Luke 11:49
ch. 19:2
21 Jer. 51:64
21 ch. 12:8 & 16:20
22 Jer. 7:34
 & 16:9 & 25:10
Ezek. 26:13
23 Jer. 25:10
23 Jer. 7:34 & 16:9
 & 25:10 & 33:11
23 Is. 23:8
23 2 Ki. 9:22
ch. 17:2, 5
24 ch. 17:6
24 Jer. 51:49

CHAP. 19

AD 96

1 ch. 11:15
1 ch. 4:11
 & 7:10, 12
2 ch. 15:3
2 Deut. 32:43
3 Is. 34:10
ch. 14:11
4 ch. 4:4, 6
4 1 Chr. 16:36
Neh. 5:13 & 8:6
5 Ps. 134:1
5 ch. 11:18 & 20:12
6 Ezek. 1:24
ch. 14:2
6 ch. 11:15
7 Mat. 22:2
2 Cor. 11:2
ch. 21:2, 9
8 Ps. 45:13
Ezek. 16:10
8 Or, *bright*
8 Ps. 132:9
9 Mat. 22:2
Luke 14:15

ch. 22:6   9
ch. 22:8   10
Acts 10:26   10
ch. 22:9
1 John 5:10   10
ch. 12:17
ch. 15:5   11
ch. 6:2   11
ch. 3:14   11
Is. 11:4   11
ch. 1:14   12
ch. 6:2   12
ch. 2:17   12
Is. 63:2, 3   13
John 1:1   13
1 John 5:7
ch. 14:20   14
Mat. 28:3   14
ch. 4:4
Is. 11:4   15
ch. 1:16
Ps. 2:9   15
ch. 2:27
Is. 63:3   15
ch. 14:19
ver. 12   16
Dan. 2:47   16
1 Tim. 6:15
ch. 17:14
ver. 21   17
Ezek. 39:17   17
Ezek. 39:18   18
ch. 16:16   19
ch. 16:13   20
ch. 13:12   20
Dan. 7:11   20
ch. 20:10
ch. 14:10   20
ver. 15   21

they which are called unto the marriage supper of the Lamb. And he saith unto me, [R]These are the true sayings of God.

10 And [R]I fell at his feet to worship him. And he said unto me, [R]See *thou do it* not: I am thy fellowservant, and of thy brethren [R]that have the testimony of Jesus: worship God: for the testimony of Jesus is the spirit of prophecy.

The warrior on the white horse

11 [R]And I saw heaven opened, and behold [R]a white horse; and he that sat upon him *was* called [R]Faithful and True, and [R]in righteousness he doth judge and make war.

12 [R]His eyes *were* as a flame of fire, [R]and on his head *were* many crowns; [R]and he had a name written, that no man knew, but he himself.

13 [R]And he *was* clothed with a vesture dipped in blood: and his name is called [R]The Word of God.

14 [R]And the armies *which were* in heaven followed him upon white horses, [R]clothed in fine linen, white and clean.

15 And [R]out of his mouth goeth a sharp sword, that with it he should smite the nations: and [R]he shall rule them with a rod of iron: and [R]he treadeth the winepress of the fierceness and wrath of Almighty God.

16 And [R]he hath on *his* vesture and on his thigh a name written, [R]KING OF KINGS, AND LORD OF LORDS.

Defeat of the beast

17 And I saw an angel standing in the sun; and he cried with a loud voice, saying [R]to all the fowls that fly in the midst of heaven, [R]Come and gather yourselves together unto the supper of the great God;

18 [R]That ye may eat the flesh of kings, and the flesh of captains, and the flesh of mighty men, and the flesh of horses, and of them that sit on them, and the flesh of all *men, both* free and bond, both small and great.

19 [R]And I saw the beast, and the kings of the earth, and their armies, gathered together to make war against him that sat on the horse, and against his army.

20 [R]And the beast was taken, and with him the false prophet that wrought miracles before him, with which he deceived them that had received the mark of the beast, and [R]them that worshipped his image. [R]These both were cast alive into a lake of fire [R]burning with brimstone.

21 And the remnant [R]were slain with the sword of him that sat upon the horse, which

sword proceeded out of his mouth: ᴿand all the fowls ᴿwere filled with their flesh.

CHAPTER 20

Defeat of the dragon

AND I saw an angel come down from heaven, ᴿhaving the key of the bottomless pit and a great chain in his hand.

2 And he laid hold on ᴿthe dragon, that old serpent, which is the Devil, and Satan, and bound him a thousand years,

3 And cast him into the bottomless pit, and shut him up, and ᴿset a seal upon him, ᴿthat he should deceive the nations no more, till the thousand years should be fulfilled: and after that he must be loosed a little season.

The first resurrection

4 And I saw ᴿthrones, and they sat upon them, and ᴿjudgment was given unto them: and *I saw* ᴿthe souls of them that were beheaded for the witness of Jesus, and for the word of God, and ᴿwhich had not worshipped the beast, ᴿneither his image, neither had received *his* mark upon their foreheads, or in their hands; and they lived and ᴿreigned with Christ a thousand years.

5 But the rest of the dead lived not again until the thousand years were finished. This *is* the first resurrection.

6 Blessed and holy *is* he that hath part in the first resurrection: on such ᴿthe second death hath no power, but they shall be ᴿpriests of God and of Christ, ᴿand shall reign with him a thousand years.

The lake of fire and brimstone

7 And when the thousand years are expired, ᴿSatan shall be loosed out of his prison,

8 And shall go out ᴿto deceive the nations which are in the four quarters of the earth, ᴿGog and Mā′-gŏg, ᴿto gather them together to battle: the number of whom *is* as the sand of the sea.

9 ᴿAnd they went up on the breadth of the earth, and compassed the camp of the saints about, and the beloved city: and fire came down from God out of heaven, and devoured them.

10 ᴿAnd the devil that deceived them was cast into the lake of fire and brimstone, ᴿwhere the beast and the false prophet *are,* and ᴿshall be tormented day and night for ever and ever.

The great white throne

11 And I saw a great white throne, and him that sat on it, from whose face ᴿthe earth and

the heaven fled away; ᴿand there was found no place for them.

12 And I saw the dead, ᴿsmall and great, stand before God; ᴿand the books were opened: and another ᴿbook was opened, which is *the book* of life: and the dead were judged out of those things which were written in the books, ᴿaccording to their works.

13 And the sea gave up the dead which were in it; ᴿand death and ᴺhell delivered up the dead which were in them: ᴿand they were judged every man according to their works.

14 And ᴿdeath and hell were cast into the lake of fire. ᴿThis is the second death.

15 And whosoever was not found written in the book of life ᴿwas cast into the lake of fire.

CHAPTER 21

The new heaven and new earth

AND ᴿI saw a new heaven and a new earth: ᴿfor the first heaven and the first earth were passed away; and there was no more sea.

2 And I John saw ᴿthe holy city, new Jerusalem, coming down from God out of heaven, prepared ᴿas a bride adorned for her husband.

3 And I heard a great voice out of heaven saying, Behold, ᴿthe tabernacle of God *is* with men, and he will dwell with them, and they shall be his people, and God himself shall be with them, *and be* their God.

4 ᴿAnd God shall wipe away all tears from their eyes; and ᴿthere shall be no more death, ᴿneither sorrow, nor crying, neither shall there be any more pain: for the former things are passed away.

5 And ᴿhe that sat upon the throne said, ᴿBehold, I make all things new. And he said unto me, Write: for ᴿthese words are true and faithful.

6 And he said unto me, ᴿIt is done. ᴿI am Alpha and Omega, the beginning and the end. ᴿI will give unto him that is athirst of the fountain of the water of life freely.

7 He that overcometh shall inherit ᴺall things; and ᴿI will be his God, and he shall be my son.

8 ᴿBut the fearful, and unbelieving, and the abominable, and murderers, and whoremongers, and sorcerers, and idolaters, and all liars, shall have their part in ᴿthe lake which burneth with fire and brimstone: which is the second death.

The new Jerusalem

9 And there came unto me one of ᴿthe seven angels which had the seven vials full of the seven last plagues, and talked with me, saying,

Come hither, I will shew thee ᴿthe bride, the Lamb's wife.

10 And he carried me away ᴿin the spirit to a great and high mountain, and shewed me ᴿthat great city, the holy Jerusalem, descending out of heaven from God,

11 ᴿHaving the glory of God: and her light *was* like unto a stone most precious, even like a jasper stone, clear as crystal;

12 And had a wall great and high, *and* had ᴿtwelve gates, and at the gates twelve angels, and names written thereon, which are *the names* of the twelve tribes of the children of Israel:

13 ᴿOn the east three gates; on the north three gates; on the south three gates; and on the west three gates.

14 And the wall of the city had twelve foundations, and ᴿin them the names of the twelve apostles of the Lamb.

15 And he that talked with me ᴿhad a golden reed to measure the city, and the gates thereof, and the wall thereof.

16 And the city lieth foursquare, and the length is as large as the breadth: and he measured the city with the reed, twelve thousand furlongs. The length and the breadth and the height of it are equal.

17 And he measured the wall thereof, an hundred *and* forty *and* four cubits, *according to* the measure of a man, that is, of the angel.

18 And the building of the wall of it was *of* jasper: and the city *was* pure gold, like unto clear glass.

19 ᴿAnd the foundations of the wall of the city *were* garnished with all manner of precious stones. The first foundation *was* jasper; the second, sapphire; the third, a chalcedony; the fourth, an emerald;

20 The fifth, sardonyx; the sixth, sardius; the seventh, chrysolite; the eighth, beryl; the ninth, a topaz; the tenth, a chrysoprasus; the eleventh, a jacinth; the twelfth, an amethyst.

21 And the twelve gates *were* twelve pearls; every several gate was of one pearl: ᴿand the street of the city *was* pure gold, as it were transparent glass.

The Lord God: its light and temple

22 ᴿAnd I saw no temple therein: for the Lord God Almighty and the Lamb are the temple of it.

23 ᴿAnd the city had no need of the sun, neither of the moon, to shine in it: for the glory of God did lighten it, and the Lamb *is* the light thereof.

24 ᴿAnd the nations of them which are saved shall walk in the light of it: and the

CHAP. 21	
AD 96	
9 ch. 19:7	
10 ch. 1:10	
10 Ezek. 48	
11 ch. 22:5	
12 Ezek. 48:31-34	
13 Ezek. 48:31-34	
14 Mat. 16:18	
Gal. 2:9	
Eph. 2:20	
15 Ezek. 40:3	
Zech. 2:1	
19 Is. 54:11	
21 ch. 22:2	
22 John 4:23	
23 Is. 24:23	
& 60:19, 20	
24 Is. 60:3	
& 66:12	

Is. 60:11	25
Is. 60:20	25
Zech. 14:7	
ch. 22:5	
ver. 24	26
Is. 35:8	27
& 52:1	
& 60:21	
Joel 3:17	
ch. 22:14	
Phil. 4:3	27

CHAP. 22	
AD 96	
Ezek. 47:1	1
Zech. 14:8	
Ezek. 47:12	2
ch. 21:21	
Gen. 2:9	2
ch. 2:7	
ch. 21:24	2
Zech. 14:11	3
Ezek. 48:35	3
Mat. 5:8	4
1 Cor. 13:12	
1 John 3:2	
ch. 14:1	4
ch. 21:23	5
Ps. 36:9	5
Dan. 7:27	5
Rom. 5:17	
2 Tim. 2:12	
ch. 19:9	6
ch. 1:1	6
ch. 3:11	7
ch. 1:3	7
ch. 19:10	8
ch. 19:10	9
Dan. 8:26	10
ch. 1:3	10
Ezek. 3:27	11
Dan. 12:10	
2 Tim. 3:13	
ver. 7	12
Is. 40:10	12

kings of the earth do bring their glory and honour into it.

25 ᴿAnd the gates of it shall not be shut at all by day: for ᴿthere shall be no night there.

26 ᴿAnd they shall bring the glory and honour of the nations into it.

27 And ᴿthere shall in no wise enter into it any thing that defileth, neither *whatsoever* worketh abomination, or *maketh* a lie: but they which are written in the Lamb's ᴿbook of life.

CHAPTER 22

The river and the tree of life

AND he shewed me ᴿa pure river of water of life, clear as crystal, proceeding out of the throne of God and of the Lamb.

2 ᴿIn the midst of the street of it, and on either side of the river, *was there* ᴿthe tree of life, which bare twelve *manner of* fruits, *and* yielded her fruit every month: and the leaves of the tree *were* ᴿfor the healing of the nations.

3 And ᴿthere shall be no more curse: ᴿbut the throne of God and of the Lamb shall be in it; and his servants shall serve him:

4 And ᴿthey shall see his face; and ᴿhis name *shall be* in their foreheads.

5 ᴿAnd there shall be no night there; and they need no candle, neither light of the sun; for ᴿthe Lord God giveth them light: ᴿand they shall reign for ever and ever.

Epilogue: invitation and benediction

6 And he said unto me, ᴿThese sayings *are* faithful and true: and the Lord God of the holy prophets ᴿsent his angel to shew unto his servants the things which must shortly be done.

7 ᴿBehold, I come quickly: ᴿblessed *is* he that keepeth the sayings of the prophecy of this book.

8 And I John saw these things, and heard *them*. And when I had heard and seen, ᴿI fell down to worship before the feet of the angel which shewed me these things.

9 Then saith he unto me, ᴿSee *thou do it* not: for I am thy fellowservant, and of thy brethren the prophets, and of them which keep the sayings of this book: worship God.

10 ᴿAnd he saith unto me, Seal not the sayings of the prophecy of this book: ᴿfor the time is at hand.

11 ᴿHe that is unjust, let him be unjust still: and he which is filthy, let him be filthy still: and he that is righteous, let him be righteous still: and he that is holy, let him be holy still.

12 ᴿAnd, behold, I come quickly; and ᴿmy

reward *is* with me, [R]to give every man according as his work shall be.

13 [R]I am Alpha and Omega, the beginning and the end, the first and the last.

14 [R]Blessed *are* they that do his commandments, that they may have right [R]to the tree of life, [R]and may enter in through the gates into the city.

15 For [R]without *are* [R]dogs, and sorcerers, and whoremongers, and murderers, and idolaters, and whosoever loveth and maketh a lie.

16 [R]I Jesus have sent mine angel to testify unto you these things in the churches. [R]I am the root and the offspring of David, *and* [R]the bright and morning star.

17 And the Spirit and [R]the bride say, Come. And let him that heareth say, Come. [R]And let

CHAP. 22	
AD 96	
12 ch. 20:12	
13 Is. 41:4	
14 Dan. 12:12	
14 ch. 2:7	
14 ch. 21:27	
15 1 Cor. 6:9	
15 Phil. 3:2	
16 ch. 1:1	
16 ch. 5:5	
17 ch. 21:2, 9	
17 Is. 55:1	
Deut. 4:2	**18**
Ex. 32:33	**19**
Or, *from the tree of life*	**19**
ch. 21:2	**19**
ver. 12	**20**
John 21:25	**20**
2 Tim. 4:8	**20**
Rom. 16:20	**21**

him that is athirst come. And whosoever will, let him take the water of life freely.

18 For I testify unto every man that heareth the words of the prophecy of this book, [R]If any man shall add unto these things, God shall add unto him the plagues that are written in this book:

19 And if any man shall take away from the words of the book of this prophecy, [R]God shall take away his part [N]out of the book of life, and out of [R]the holy city, and *from* the things which are written in this book.

20 He which testifieth these things saith, [R]Surely I come quickly. [R]Ä′-mĕn. [R]Even so, come, Lord Jesus.

21 [R]The grace of our Lord Jesus Christ *be* with you all. Ä′-mĕn.

THE END

CONCORDANCE

TO THE

HOLY SCRIPTURES

A

ABASE, make low
Job 40. 11. every one proud *a.*
Isa. 31. 4. lion will not *a.* himself
Ezek. 21. 26. *a.* him that is high
Dan. 4. 37. he is able to *a.*
Matt. 23. 12. whosoever shall exalt himself shall be *abased*
Phil. 4. 12. how to be *a.* and how to
2 Cor. 11. 7. offence in *abasing* myself
ABATED, waters were, Gen. 8. 3.
Gen. 8. 11. the waters were *a.*
Lev. 27. 18. *a.* from thy estimation
Deut. 34. 7. nor his natural force *a.*
Judg. 8. 3. then their anger was *a.*
ABBA, *father,* Mark 14. 36. Rom. 8. 15. Gal. 4. 6.
ABHOR, greatly hate and loathe
Lev. 26. 11. my soul shall not *a.* you
15. if your soul *a.* my judgments
30. my soul shall *a.* you
44. neither will I *a.* them
Deut. 7. 26. utterly *a.* it
23. 7. not *a.* Edomite
1 Sam. 27. 12. hath made his people to *a.* him
Job 30. 10. they *a.* me, they flee
42. 6. I *a.* myself and repent
Ps. 5. 6. Lord will *a.* the bloody
119. 163. I hate and *a.* lying
Jer. 14. 21. do not *a.* us
Amos 5. 10. they *a.* him that speaketh
6. 8. I *a.* the excellency of Jacob
Mic. 3. 9. ye that *a.* judgment
Rom. 12. 9. *a.* that which is evil
Ex. 5. 21. made our savour *abhorred*
Rev. 26. 43. their soul *a.* my statutes.
Deut. 32. 19. when the Lord saw it he *a.*
1 Sam. 2. 17. men *a.* the offering of the Lord
Job 19. 19. all my inward friends *a.* me
Ps. 22. 24. nor *a.* affliction of afflicted
78. 59. wroth and greatly *a.* Israel
89. 38. hath cast off and *a.* anointed
106. 40. he *a.* his own inheritance
Prov. 22. 14. *a.* of the Lord shall fall
Lam. 2. 7. Lord hath *a.* his sanctuary
Ezek. 16. 25. made thy beauty to be *a.*
Rom. 2. 22. thou that *abhorrest* idols
Zech. 11. 8. their soul *abhorreth* me
Job 33. 20. his life *a.* bread
Ps. 10. 3. covetous whom the Lord *a.*
36. 4. he *a.* not evil
107. 18. their soul *a.* all meat
Isa. 49. 7. him whom the nation *a.*
66. 24. be an *abhorring* to all flesh
ABIDE, continue, bear
Ex. 16. 29. *a.* ye every man in his place
Num. 35. 25. *a.* in it unto the death of the high priest
1 Sam. 11. 11. ark and Israel *a.* in tents
Ps. 15. 1. who shall *a.* in thy tabernacle
61. 4. I will *a.* in thy tabernacle
7. he shall *a.* before God for ever
91. 1. shall *a.* under the shadow of the Almighty

Prov. 7. 11. her feet *a.* not in her house
19. 23. that hath it shall *a.* satisfied
Hos. 3. 3. shall *a.* for me many days
Joel 2. 11. day of the Lord is great and very terrible; who can *a.* it.
Mal. 3. 2. who may *a.* his coming
Matt. 10. 11. there *a.* till yet go thence
Luke 19. 5. I must *a.* at thy house
John 12. 46. should not *a.* in darkness
14. 16. Comforter that he may *a.*
15. 4. *a.* in me and I in you
7. 10. ye shall *a.* in my love, *a.* in his
Acts 20. 23. afflictions *a.* me
1 Cor. 3. 14. if any man's work *a.*
7. 8. it is good if they *a.* even as I
24. is called therein *a.* with God
Phil. 1. 24. to *a.* in the flesh is needful
25. know that I shall *a.* with you
1 John 2. 24. let that *a.* in you
27. 28. ye shall *a.* in him
Ps. 49. 12. man in honour *abideth* not
55. 19. even he that *a.* of old
125. 1. as mount Zion which *a.*
Eccl. 1. 4. the earth *a.* for ever
John 3. 36. wrath of God *a.* on him
8. 35. servant *a.* not but the son *a.*
12. *a.* except it die it *a.* alone
34. Christ *a.* for ever
15. 5. *a.* in me brings forth fruit
1 Cor. 13. 13. now *a.* faith, hope
2 Tim. 2. 13. yet he *a.* faithful
1 Pet. 1. 23. word of God *a.* for ever
1 John 3. 6. whoso *a.* in him sinneth not
24. hereby we know he *a.* in us
John 5. 38. not his word *abiding* in you
1 John 3. 15. no murderer hath eternal life *a.*
John 14. 23. make our *abode* with him
ABILITY, in strength, wealth
Lev. 27. 8. Ezra 2. 69. Neh. 5. 8.
Matt. 25. 15. to every man according to his *a.* Acts 11. 29.
1 Pet. 4. 11. as of the *a.* God giveth
ABJECTS, base men, Ps. 35. 15.
ABLE men, such as fear God, Ex. 18. 21.
Lev. 14. 22. such as he is *a.* to get
Deut. 16. 17. every man give as he is *a.*
2 Chron. 20. 6. none is *a.* to withstand
Ezek. 46. 11. as he is *a.* to give
Dan. 3. 17. our God is *a.* to deliver us
4. 37. walk in pride he is *a.* to abase
Matt. 3. 9. God is *a.* of these stones to raise up children, Luke 3. 8.
10. 28. are not *a.* to kill the soul
19. 12. *a.* to receive it let him
20. 22. are ye *a.* to drink of cup
Mark 4. 33. as they were *a.* to hear
John 10. 29. no man is *a.* to pluck you out of my hands
Rom. 4. 21. is *a.* to perform
14. 4. God is *a.* to make him stand
1 Cor. 3. 2. neither yet now are ye *a.*
10. 13. tempted above that ye are *a.*
2 Cor. 9. 8. *a.* to make all grace abound
Eph. 3. 20. *a.* to do abundantly

Phil. 3. 21. *a.* subdue all to himself
2 Tim. 1. 12. *a.* to keep that committed to him
3. 15. Scriptures *a.* to make thee wise
Heb. 2. 18. *a.* to succour the tempted
5. 7. *a.* to save him from death
7. 25. *a.* to save to the uttermost
11. 19. *a.* to raise him from dead
James 1. 21. *a.* to save your souls
4. 12. *a.* to save and to destroy
Jude 24. *a.* to keep you from falling
ABOLISHED, made to cease
Isa. 2. 18. idols he shall utterly *abolish*
51. 6. righteousness not be *a.*
Ezek. 6. 6. your works may be *a.*
2 Cor. 3. 13. to the end of that *a.*
Eph. 2. 15. having *a.* in his flesh
2 Tim. 1. 10. Jesus Christ who hath *a.* death
ABOMINABLE, very hateful, Lev. 7. 21. & 11. 43. & 18. 30. Isa. 14. 19. & 65. 4. Jer. 16. 18.
1 Chron. 21. 6. king's word was *a.*
Job 15. 16. how much more *a.* is man
Ps. 14. 1. have done *a.* works, 53. 1.
Jer. 44. 4. do not this *a.* thing
Ezek. 16. 52. more *a.* than they
Nah. 3. 6. I will cast *a.* filth on thee
Tit. 1. 16. in words deny him being *a.*
1 Pet. 4. 3. walked in *a.* idolatries
Rev. 21. 8. *a.* shall have their part
ABOMINATION, what is very filthy, Isa. 66. 3. idols, Ex. 8. 26.
Prov. 6. 16. seven things are an *a.*
11. 1. a false balance is *a.* to the Lord
20. they of froward heart are *a.*
12. 22. lying lips are *a.* to the Lord
15. 8. sacrifice of the wicked is an *a.*
26. thoughts of the wicked are an *a.*
16. 5. proud in heart is an *a.*
20. 23. divers weights are an *a.*
28. 9. his prayer shall be *a.*
29. 27. unjust man is *a.* to the just
Isa. 1. 13. incense is an *a.* to me
Dan. 11. 31. *a.* that maketh desolate
12. 11. Matt. 24. 15. Mark 13. 14. *a.* of desolation
Luke 16. 25. is *a.* in the sight of God
Rev. 21. 27. whatsoever worketh *a.*
2 Kings 21. 2. *a.* of the heathen
Ezra. 9. 1. join with these *a.*
Prov. 26. 25. seven *a.* in his heart
Jer. 7. 10. delivered to do all these *a.*
Ezek. 16. 2. cause Jerusalem to know her *a.* 20. 4. & 33. 29.
18. 13. hath done all these *a.*
Dan. 9. 27. for the overspreading of *a.*
Rev. 17. 5. mother of harlots and *a.*
ABOVE, higher heaven, Ex. 20. 4.
John 3. 31. cometh from *a.* is *a.* all
8. 23. I am from *a.* ye are from
19. 11. power given thee from *a.*
Gal. 4. 26. Jerusalem which is *a.* is free
Eph. 4. 6. one God who is *a.* all
Col. 3. 1. seek things which are *a.*
2. set your affections on things *a.*
Jas. 1. 17. every perfect gift is from *a.*
3. 15. 17. wisdom from *a.* is pure
ABOUND, become very full, large, Prov. 8. 24. Rom. 3. 7.

Prov. 28. 20. the faithful shall *a.*
Matt. 24. 12. because iniquity shall *a.*
Rom. 5. 20. offence might *a.* 6. 1. that grace may *a.*
2 Cor. 9. 8. ye may *a.* in good work
Phil. 1. 9. that your love may *a.* more
4. 12. I know how to *a.*
17. fruit that may *a.* to your account
18. I have all and *a.*
1 Thes. 3. 12. make you *a.* in love
2 Pet. 1. 8. if these be in you and *a.*
Eph. 1. 8. hath *abounded* toward us
1 Cor. 15. 58. always *abounding*
Col. 2. 7. *a.* therein with thanks
ABSENT one from another, Gen. 31. 49. 2 Cor. 10. 1.
2 Cor. 5. 3. as *a.* in body but present
1 Cor. 5. 6. we are *a.* from the Lord
8. willing to be *a.* from the body
9. that whether present or *a.*
10. 1. being *a.* am bold toward you
Col. 2. 5. though I be *a.* in the flesh
ABSTAIN from idols, Acts 15. 20.
1 Thes. 4. 3. *a.* from fornication
5. 22. *a.* from all appearance of evil
1 Tim. 4. 3. to *a.* from meats
1 Pet. 2. 11. *a.* from fleshly lusts
Abstinence from meat, Acts 27. 21.
ABUNDANCE, great fulness and plenty, Job 22. 11. & 38. 24. Deut. 33. 19. 1 Chron. 22. 3, 4, 14, 15.
Deut. 28. 47. for the *a.* for all things
Eccl. 5. 10. he that loveth *a.*
12. *a.* of the rich
Isa. 66. 11. with *a.* of her glory
Matt. 12. 34. out of *a.* of the heart
13. 12. shall have more *a.* 25. 29.
Mark 12. 44. cast in of their *a.*
Luke 12. 15. life consisteth not in *a.*
2 Cor. 8. 2. *a.* of their joy abounded
12. 7. through *a.* of revelations
ABUNDANT in goodness and truth 2 Cor. 4. 15 & 9. 12.
2 Cor. 11. 23. in labours more *a.*
1 Tim. 1. 14. grace exceeding *a.*
1 Pet. 1. 3. his *a.* mercy
Job 12. 6. God bringeth *abundantly*
Ps. 36. 8. shall be *a.* satisfied.
Song 5. 1. yea drink *a.* O beloved
Isa. 55. 7. he will *a.* pardon
John 10. 10. might have life more *a.*
1 Cor. 15. 10. labored more *a.* than all
Eph. 3. 20. able to do exceeding *a.*
Tit. 3. 6. shed on us *a.* through Jesus
2 Pet. 1. 11. entrance ministered more *a.*
ABUSE not my power, 1 Cor. 9. 18.
1 Cor. 7. 31. use as not *abusing*
ACCEPT, receive kindly in favour, Gen. 32. 20. Acts 24. 3.
Lev. 26. 41. *a.* punishment
Deut. 33. 11. *a.* work of his hands
2 Sam. 24. 23. Lord thy God *a.* thee
Job 13. 8. will ye *a.* his person, 10.
32. 21. let me not *a.* any man's person
42. 8. servant Job, him will I *a.*
Ps. 119. 108. *a.* free-will offerings
Prov. 18. 5. *a.* person of the wicked
Ezek. 43. 27. I will *a.* you
Mal. 1. 13. should I *a.* this
Gen. 4. 7. shall thou not be *accepted*
19. 21. *a.* thee concerning this thing

1

Lev. 1. 4. shall be *a.* for atonement
Luke 4. 24. no prophet *a.* in his own country
Acts 10. 35. worketh righteousness is *a.*
2 Cor. 5. 9. we may be *a.* of him
6. 2. heard thee in a time *a.*
8. 12. is *a.* according that a man hath
Eph. 1. 6. made us *a.* in the beloved
Luke 20. 21. neither *acceptest* the person
Job 34. 19. him that *accepteth* not
Eccl. 9. 7. God now *a.* thy works
Hos. 8. 13. Lord *a.* them not
Gal. 2. 6. God *a.* no man's person
Heb. 11. 35. not *accepting* deliverance
Acceptable day of the Lord, Isa. 58. 5.
Ps. 19. 14. meditation of heart be *a.*
Eccl. 12. 10. sought out *a.* words
Isa. 49. 8. in an *a.* time I heard thee
61. 2. to proclaim the *a.* year
Dan. 4. 27. let my counsel be *a.*
Rom. 12. 1. sacrifice holy *a.*
2. know good and *a.* will of God
Eph. 5. 10. proving what is *a.*
Phil. 4. 18. sacrifice *a.* well-pleasing
1 Pet. 2. 5. *a.* to God by Jesus Christ
Heb. 12. 28. serve God *acceptably*
1 Tim. 1. 15. worthy of all *acceptation*
ACCESS, admission through Christ, Rom. 5. 2. Eph. 2. 18. & 3. 12.
ACCOMPLISH, perform fully, finish, Lev. 22. 21. Job 14. 6.
Ps. 64 6. *a.* a diligent search
Isa. 55. 11. it shall *a.* that I please
Ezek. 6. 12. thou will I *a.* my fury
Dan. 9. 2. would *a.* seventy years
Luke 9. 31. decease he should *a.*
2 Chron. 36. 22. word might be *accomplished*
Prov. 13. 19. desire *a.* is sweet to soul
Isa. 40. 2. her warfare is *a.* her sin
Luke 12. 50. straitened till it be *a.*
John 19. 28. all things were now *a.*
1 Pet. 5. 9. same afflictions are *a.*
Heb. 9. 6. *accomplishing* service of God
ACCORD, hearty agreement, Acts 1. 14. & 2. 1, 46. & 4. 24. & 15. 25.
Phil. 2. 2. of one *a.* of one mind
ACCOUNT, reckoning, esteem
Job 33. 13. giveth not *a.* of matters
Ps. 144. 3. that thou makest *a.* of him
Eccl. 7. 27. one by one to find out the *a.*
Matt. 12. 36. give *a.* in judgment 18. 23. would take *a.* of servants
Luke 16. 2. give *a.* of thy stewardship
Rom. 14. 12. give *a.* of himself to God
Phil. 4. 17. may abound to your *a.*
Heb. 13. 17. as they that must give *a.*
1 Pet. 4. 5. shall give *a.*
Ps. 22. 30. *accounted* to the Lord
Isa. 2. 22. wherein is he to be *a.* of
Luke 20. 35. shall be *a.* worthy
21. 36. *a.* worthy to escape
22. 24. which should be *a.* greatest
Gal. 3. 6. *a.* to him for righteousness
Heb. 11. 19. *a.* God able to raise
ACCURSED, devoted to ruin
Deut. 21. 23. hanged is *a.* of God
Josh. 6. 18. keep from the *a.* thing
Isa. 65. 20. sinner shall be *a.*
Rom. 9. 3. wish myself *a.* from Christ
1 Cor. 12. 3. no man by Spirit calls Jesus *a.*
Gal. 1. 8, 9. preach other gospel be *a.*
ACCUSATION, Ezra 4. 6. Matt. 27. 37. Luke 6. 7. & 19. 8. John 18. 20.
1 Tim. 5. 19. receive not an *a.*
2 Pet. 2. 11. bring not railing *a.*
ACCUSE, charge with crimes
Prov. 30. 10. *a.* not servant to master
Luke 3. 14. neither *a.* any falsely
John 5. 45. *a.* you to the Father
1 Pet. 3. 16. that falsely *a.*
Tit. 1. 6. not *accused* of riot
Rev. 12. 10. *a.* them before our God
accuser of brethren is cast down

Acts 25. 16. have *a.* face to face
2 Tim. 3. 3. false *a.* Tit. 2. 3.
John 5. 45. there is one that *accuseth*
Rom. 2. 15. thoughts *accusing*
ACCUSTOMED, Jer. 13. 23.
ACKNOWLEDGE, confess
Deut. 33. 9. neither did he *a.*
Ps. 51. 3. I *a.* my transgression
Prov. 3. 6. in all thy ways *a.* him
Isa. 33. 13. *a.* my might
63. 16. though Israel *a.* us not
Jer. 3. 13. only *a.* thine iniquity
14. 20. we *a.* our wickedness
Hos. 5. 15. until they *a.* their offense
1 Cor. 16. 18. *a.* them that are such
Ps. 32. 5. I *a.* my sin
1 John 2. 23. *acknowledgeth* the Son
2 Tim. 2. 25. *acknowledging* the truth
Tit. 1. 1. *a.* of the truth
Col. 2. 2. to the *acknowledgment* of the mystery of God
ACQUAINT thyself with him, Job 22. 21.
Ps. 139. 3. *acquainted* with my ways
Isa. 53. 3. *a.* with grief
Acquaintance, familiar friends or companions, Job 19. 13. & 42. 11. Ps. 31. 11. & 55. 13. & 88. 9, 18.
ACQUIT, hold innocent, Job 10. 14.
Nah. 1. 3. will not *a.* wicked
ACTS of the Lord, Deut. 11. 3, 7.
Judg. 5. 11. righteous *a.* of the Lord
1 Sam. 12. 7. reason of righteous *a.*
Ps. 106. 2. utter mighty *a.* of Lord
145. 6. speak of thy mighty *a.* 4.
150. 2. praise him for his mighty *a.*
Isa. 28. 21. his *a.* his strange *a.*
John 8. 4. taken in adultery in very *a.*
ACTIONS weighed, 1 Sam. 2. 3.
ACTIVITY, men of, Gen. 47. 6.
ADAMANT, Ezek. 3. 9. Zech. 7. 12.
ADD fifth part, Lev. 5. 16. & 6. 5. & 27. 13, 15, 19, 27, 31.
Deut. 4. 2. shall not *a.* unto the word
29. 19. *a.* drunkenness to thirst
1 Kings 12. 11. I will *a.* to your yoke
Ps. 69. 27. *a.* iniquity to their iniquity
Prov. 30. 6. *a.* not unto his words
Isa. 30. 1. that they may *a.* sin to sin
Matt. 6. 27. can *a.* one cubit, Luke 12. 25.
Phil. 1. 16. to *a.* affliction to my bonds
2 Pet. 1. 5. *a.* to your faith, virtue
Rev. 22. 18. if any man *a.* unto these
Deut. 5. 22. he *added* no more
1 Sam. 12. 19. *a.* unto all our sins this evil
Jer. 36. 32. were *a.* many like words
44. 3. *a.* grief to my sorrow
Matt. 6. 33. all these things shall be *a.* unto you, Luke 12. 31.
Acts 2. 41. same day were *a.* about three thousand souls
47. Lord *a.* to the church such as should be saved
5. 14. believers were the more *a.* to the Lord
11. 24. much people was *a.* to the Lord
Gal. 3. 19. the law was *a.* because of transgression
Prov. 10. 22. *addeth* no sorrow with
ADDER, poisonous serpent, Gen. 49. 17. Ps. 58. 4. & 91. 13. & 140. 3. Prov. 23. 32. Isa. 14. 29.
ADDICTED, gave up, 1 Cor. 16. 15.
ADJURE, to charge under pain of God's curse, 1 Kings 22. 16. 2 Chron. 18. 15. Matt. 26, 63. Mark 5. 7. Acts 19. 13. Josh. 6. 26. 1 Sam. 14. 24.
ADMINISTRATION, 1 Cor. 12. 5. 2 Cor. 9. 12. & 8. 19, 20. *administered*
ADMIRATION, high esteem, Jude 16. or wonder and amazement, Rev. 17. 6.
2 Thess. 1. 10. *admired* in them that believe
ADMONISH, warn, reprove
Rom. 15. 14. able to *a.* one another
1 Thess. 5. 12. over you and *a.* you

2 Thess. 3. 15. *a.* him as a brother
Eccl. 12. 12. by these be *admonished*
4. 13. foolish king who will no more be *a.*
Jer. 42. 19. know that I have *a.* you
Acts 27. 9. Paul *a.* them
Heb. 8. 5. as Moses was *a.* of God
Col. 3. 16. *admonishing* one another in psalms and hymns
1 Cor. 10. 11. are written for our *admonition*
Eph. 6. 4. bring them up in the *a.* of the Lord
Tit. 3. 10. after first and second *a.* reject
ADOPTION, putting among God's children, Jer. 3. 19. 2 Cor. 6. 18.
Rom. 8. 15. received spirit of *a.*
23. *a.* redemption of our body
9. 4. to whom pertaineth the *a.*
Gal. 4. 5. might receive *a.* of sons
Eph. 1. 5. unto *a.* of children
ADORN, deck out, Isa. 61. 10. Jer. 31. 4.
Tit. 2. 1. *a.* the doctrine of God our Saviour
Jer. 31. 4. *adorned* with thy tabrets
Luke 21. 5. *a.* with goodly stones and gifts
1 Pet. 3. 5. holy women *a.* themselves
Rev. 21. 2. as a bride *a.* for her husband
Isa. 61. 10. as a bride *adorneth* herself
1 Pet. 3. 3. whose *adorning* let it not
1 Tim. 2. 9. women *a.* themselves in modest apparel
ADVANTAGE hath Jew, Rom. 3. 1.
2 Cor. 2. 11. lest Satan get an *a.*
Luke 9. 25. what is a man *advantaged*
ADVERSARY, opposer, enemy
Ex. 23. 22. I will be *a.* to thy *a.*
1 Kings 5. 4. is neither *a.* nor evil occurent
Job 31. 35. my *a.* had written a book
Matt. 5. 25. agree with thine *a.*
Luke 18. 3. avenge me of mine *a.*
1 Tim. 5. 14. give no occasion to *a.*
1 Pet. 5. 8. your *a.* the devil as a roaring lion
1 Sam. 2. 10. *adversaries* of the Lord broken
Lam. 1. 5. her *a.* are the chief
Luke 21. 15. all your *a.* not be able
1 Cor. 16. 9. and there are many *a.*
Phil. 1. 28. nothing terrified by your *a.*
Heb. 10. 27. shall devour the *a.*
ADVERSITY, affliction, misery
Ps. 10. 6. I shall never be in *a.*
35. 15. in my *a.* they rejoiced
94. 13. give rest from days of *a.*
Prov. 17. 17. brother is born for *a.*
24. 10. if thou faint in the day of *a.*
Eccl. 7. 14. in the day of *a.* consider
Isa. 30. 20. give you the bread of *a.*
2 Chron. 15. 6. God did vex with all *a.*
Ps. 31. 7. hast known my soul in *a.*
1 Sam. 10. 19. saved you out of all *a.*
ADVICE, Judg. 19. 30. 1 Sam. 25. 33. 2 Sam. 19. 43. Prov. 20. 18.
ADULTERER, Lev. 20. 10.
Job. 24. 15. eye of *a.* waits for the twilight
Isa. 57. 3. seed of *a.* and whore
Jer. 23. 10. land is full of *adulterers,* 9. 2. Hos. 7. 4. be all *a.*
Mal. 3. 5. I will be a swift witness against *a.*
1 Cor. 6. 9. neither *a.* shall inherit the kingdom of God
Heb. 13. 4. whoremongers and *a.* God will judge.
James 4. 4. ye *a.* and *adulteresses*
Prov. 6. 26. *adulteress* will hunt for life. 32. committeth *adultery* lacks understanding
Matt. 5. 28. committeth *a.* in his heart
2 Pet. 2. 14. having eyes full of *a.*
Matt. 15. 19. out of the heart proceed

adulteries, fornications, Mark 7. 21.
Matt. 12. 39. *a.* generation seeketh a sign, 16. 4. Mark 8. 38.
ADVOCATE with Father, 1 John 2. 1.
AFAR off, Gen. 22. 4. & 37. 18. Ps. 65. 5. 138. 6. proud he knoweth *a.*
Ps. 139. 2. understandest my thoughts *a.* off
Jer. 23. 23. at hand not a God *a.*
Acts 2. 39. promise is to all *a.* and
Eph. 2. 17. preached peace to you *a.*
Heb. 11. 13. having seen promises *a.*
2 Pet. 1. 9. blind and cannot see *a.*
AFFAIRS, Ps. 112. 5. 2 Tim. 2. 4.
AFFECT, incline, move
Gal. 4. 17. they zealously *a.* you
18. good to be zealously *affected*
Lam. 3. 51. mine eye *affecteth* my heart
Rom. 1. 31. natural *affection*
Col. 3. 5. mortify inordinate *a.*
Rom. 1. 26. them up to vile *affections*
Gal. 5. 14. crucify flesh with *a.*
Rom. 12. 10. be kindly *affectioned*
1 Thes. 2. 8. *affectionately* desirous
AFFINITY, relation by marriage
1 Kings 3. 1. 2 Chron. 18. 1. Ezra 9. 14.
AFFLICT, grieve, trouble, Gen. 15. 13. Ex. 1. 11. & 22. 22.
Ezra 8. 21. that we might *a.* ourselves
Lev. 16. 29, 31. shall *a.* your souls
23. 27, 31. Num. 29. 7. & 30. 13.
Isa. 58. 5. day for a man to *a.* his soul
Lam. 3. 33. doth not *a.* willingly
2 Sam. 22. 28. *afflicted* people thou wilt save, Ps. 18. 27.
Job 6. 14. to *a.* pity should be showed
34. 28. heareth the cry of the *a.*
Ps. 18. 27. wilt save the *a.* people
22. 24. not abhorred affliction of *a.*
119. 67. before I was *a.* I went astray
71. it is good that I have been *a.*
75. thou in faithfulness hast *a.* me
107. I am *a.* very much
140. 12. wilt maintain cause of *a.*
Prov. 15. 15. all days of *a.* are evil
Isa. 49. 13. he will have mercy on *a.*
53. 4. smitten of God and *a.*
7. he was oppressed and *a.*
58. 10. satisfy the *a.* soul
Miç. 4. 6. gather her I have *a.*
James 5. 13. is any *a.* let him pray
Ex. 3. 7. seen *affliction* of people
2 Kings 14. 26. Lord saw *a.* of Israel
Job 5. 6. *a.* cometh not forth of dust
36. 8. holden in cords of *a.*
15. delivereth poor in his *a.*
21. this chosen rather than *a.*
Ps. 25. 18. look on my *a.* and pain
107. 10. bound in *a.* and iron
39. brought low through *a.*
119. 50. this is my comfort in *a.*
92. should have perished in *a.*
Isa. 48. 10. chosen thee in the furnace of *a.*
63. 9. in all their *a.* he was afflicted
Hos. 5. 15. in their *a.* they will seek
Obad. 13. not have looked on their *a.*
Nah. 1. 9. *a.* not rise up second time
Zech. 1. 15. helped forward the *a.*
2 Cor. 4. 17. our light *a.* which is
Phil. 4. 14. communicate with my *a.*
1 Thes. 1. 6. received word in much *a.*
Heb. 11. 25. choosing rather to suffer *a.*
Ps. 34. 19. many are the *afflictions* of the righteous.
132. 1. remember David and all his *a.*
Acts 7. 10. delivered him out of all *a.*
20. 23. bonds and *a.* abide me
Col. 1. 24. which is behind of *a.* of Christ
1 Thes. 3. 3. no man moved by these *a.*
2 Tim. 1. 8. partaker of *a.* of gospel
Heb. 10. 32. endured great fight of *a.*
1 Pet. 5. 9. the same *a.* accomplished

AFRAID, Lev. 26. 6. Num. 12. 8. Job 13. 21. Ps. 56. 3. & 119. 120.
Not be *afraid,* Ps. 56. 11. & 112. 7. Isa. 12. 2. Matt. 14. 27. Mark 5. 36. Luke 12. 4. 1 Pet. 3. 6, 14. Heb. 11. 23.
AFRESH, crucify son of God, Heb. 6. 6.
AGE is as nothing before thee, Ps. 39. 35.
Job 5. 26. come to grave in full *a.*
John 9. 21. he is of *a.* ask him
Heb. 5. 14. strong meat to those of full *a.* 11. 11. Sarah when she was past *a.*
Tit. 2. 2, 3. *aged* men be sober
Ages, Eph. 2. 7. & 3. 5, 21.
Col. 1. 26. mystery hid from *a.*
AGREE, Acts 5. 9.
Matt. 5. 25. *a.* with thine adversary quickly
18. 19. if two shall *a.* on earth
1 John 5. 8. these three *a.* in one
Amos 3. 3. walked together except *agreed*
Isa. 28. 15. with hell at *agreement*
2 Cor. 6. 16. what *a.* has temple of God
AIR, 1 Cor. 9. 26. & 14. 9. Eph. 2. 2. 1 Thes. 4. 17. Rev. 9. 2. & 16. 17.
ALIEN, stranger, Ex. 18. 3. Job 19. 15. Ps. 69. 8. heathens, Deut. 14. 21. Isa. 61. 5. Lam. 5. 2. Heb. 11. 34.
Eph. 2. 12. *a.* from commonwealth of Israel 4. 18. *alienated* from life of God
Col. 1. 21. were sometimes *a.*
ALIVE, Gen. 12. 12. Num. 22. 33.
Rom. 6. 11. *a.* to God through Jesus Christ
1 Sam. 2. 6. killeth and maketh *a.*
15. 8. he took Agag *a.*
Luke 15. 24. son was dead and is *a.*
Rom. 6. 13. as those *a.* from the dead
7. 9. I was *a.* without the law once
1 Cor. 15. 22. in Christ shall all be made *a.*
1 Thes. 4. 15. we who are *a.* and remain
Rev. 1. 18. I am *a.* for evermore
2. 8. was dead and is *a.*
ALLEGING, Acts 17. 3.
ALLEGORY, Gal. 4. 24.
ALLOW deeds of fathers, Luke 11. 48.
Acts 24. 15. which themselves *a.*
Rom. 7. 15. that which I do I *a.* not
14. 22. in that which he *alloweth*
1 Thes. 2. 4. as we were *allowed* of God
ALLURE, Hos. 2. 14. 2 Pet. 2. 18.
ALMS, Acts 3. 2, 3. & 24. 17.
Matt. 6. 1. do not your *a.* before men
Luke 11. 41. give *a.* of such things
12. 33. sell that ye have, give *a.*
Acts 10. 2. gave much *a.* to people
4. thine *a.* are come up for memorial
9. 30. Dorcas full of *a.* deeds
ALMIGHTY GOD, Gen. 17. 1. & 28. 3. & 35. 11. & 43. 14. & 48. 3. Ex. 6. 3. 2 Cor. 6. 18. Rev. 4. 8.
Job 21. 15. what is the Almighty that we serve
22. 25. Almighty shall be thy defence
26. shall have delight in Almighty
Ps. 91. 1. under shadow of Almighty
Rev. 1. 8. is to come, the Almighty
ALMOST all things, Heb. 9. 22.
Ex. 17. 4. *a.* ready to stone me
Ps. 73. 2. my feet were *a.* gone
94. 17. soul had *a.* dwelt in silence
Prov. 5. 14. was *a.* in all evil in cong.
Acts 26. 28. *a.* persuadest me to be a Christian
ALONE, Gen. 32. 24.
Gen. 2. 18. not good for man to be *a.*
Num. 23. 9. people dwell *a.* Deut. 33. 28.
Deut. 32. 12. Lord *a.* did lead him
Ps. 136. 4. who *a.* doth great wonders
Eccl. 4. 10. woe to him that is *a.* when
Isa. 5. 8. that they may be placed *a.*
63. 3. I have trodden wine-press *a.*
John 8. 16. I am not *a.* 16. 32.
17. 20. neither pray I for these *a.*
Gal. 6. 4. rejoicing in himself *a.*
Ex. 32. 10. *let me a.* that my wrath
Hos. 4. 17. Ephraim is joined to idols, let him *a.*
Matt. 15. 14. let them *a.*
ALTAR, Deut. 7. 5. & 12. 3.
a. to Lord, Gen. 8. 20. & 12. 7. & 22. 9. & 35. 1, 3. Ex. 30. 27.
Judg. 6. 25. throw down *a.* of Baal
1 Kings 13. 2. cried against *a.* O *a.a.*
Ps. 26. 6. so will I compass thine *a.*
43. 4. then will I go to the *a.* of God
Matt. 5. 23. if thou bring thy gift to *a.*
24. leave there thy gift before the *a.*
Acts 17. 23. found *a.* with inscription
1 Cor. 9. 13. wait at the *a.* are partakers of the *a.* 10. 18.
Heb. 13. 10. we have an *a.* whereof
Rev. 6. 9. saw under the *a.* souls of
8. 3. & 9. 13. the golden *a.*
ALWAY, Deut. 5. 29. Job 7. 16.
Gen. 6. 3. my Spirit not *a.* strive
Deut. 14. 23. learn to fear the Lord *a.*
1 Chron. 16. 15. be mindful *a.* of covenant
Job 27. 10. will he *a.* call on God
32. 9. great men are not *a.* wise
Ps. 9. 18. needy not *a.* be forgotten
16. 8. I set the Lord *a.* before me
103. 9. he will not *a.* chide
Prov. 5. 19. ravished *a.* with her love
Isa. 57. 16. neither will I be *a.* wroth
Matt. 26. 11. have poor *a.* with you
28. 20. I am with you *a.* to the end
Luke 18. 1. men ought *a.* to pray
John 8. 29. I do *a.* things that please
11. 42. I know thou hearest me *a.*
Acts 10. 2. Cornelius prayed God *a.*
2 Cor. 6. 10. yet *a.* rejoicing
Eph. 6. 18. praying *a.* with all prayer
Phil. 4. 4. rejoice in the Lord *a.*
Col. 4. 6. your speech be *a.* with grace
I AM that **I AM,** Ex. 3. 14. Rev. 1. 8.
AMBASSADOR, Prov. 13. 17. Isa. 33. 7. 2 Cor. 5. 20. Eph. 6. 20.
AMEN, Rev. 22. 20.
2 Cor. 1. 20. promises in him *a.*
Rev. 3. 14. these things saith the *a.*
AMEND your ways, Jer. 7. 3, 5. & 26. 13. your doings, 35. 15.
AMIABLE thy tabernacles, Ps. 84. 1.
AMISS. 2 Chron. 6. 37. Dan. 3. 29. Luke 23. 41. James 4. 3.
ANCHOR, Acts 27. 30. Heb. 6. 19.
ANCIENT, Job 12. 12.
Dan. 7. 9. the *a.* of days did sit
Ps. 119. 100. I understand more than *a.*
ANGEL, who redeemed me, Gen. 48. 16. 24. 7. send his *a.* before me
Ex. 23. 23. my *a.* shall go before thee
Angel of the Lord, Ps. 34. 7. Zech. 12. 8. Acts 5. 19. & 12. 7, 23.
Isa. 22. 9. *a.* of his presence saved.
Hos. 12. 4. he had power over the *a.*
Acts 6. 15. saw as face of an *a.*
23. 8. Sadducees say neither *a.* nor
Dan. 3. 28. sent his *a.* and delivered
6. 22. sent his *a.* and shut lions' mouths
Job 4. 18. his *angels* he charged with folly
Ps. 8. 5. a little lower than *a.*
68. 17. chariots of God thousands *a.*
78. 25. a man did eat *a.* food
103. 20. his *a.* excel in strength
104. 4. maketh his *a.* spirits
Matt. 4. 11. *a.* came and ministered
15. 39. reapers are the *a.*
18. 10. their *a.* always behold
24. 31. sends his *a.* with sound of trumpet
36. no, not the *a.* of heaven
25. 31. all holy *a.* with him
Mark 12. 25. are as *a.* in heaven
Luke 20. 36. equal to the *a.*
Acts 7. 53. the law by disposition of *a.*
1 Cor. 6. 3. we shall judge *a.*
Col. 2. 18. beguile worshipping of *a.*
2 Thes. 1. 7. with his mighty *a.*
1 Tim. 3. 16. seen of *a.* preached unto
Heb. 2. 16. took not the nature of *a.*
12. 12. an innumerable company of *a.*
13. 2. entertained *a.* unawares
1 Pet. 1. 12. *a.* desire to look into
2 Pet. 2. 4. God spared not *a.* that sinned
11. *a.* greater in power and might
Jude 6. *a.* who kept not their first estate
Rev. 1. 20. *a.* of seven churches
Angel of God, Gen. 28. 12. & 32. 1. Matt. 22. 30. Luke 12. 8. & 15. 10.
ANGER of the Lord, Ex. 32. 22.
Deut. 29. 24. meaneth heat of this *a.*
Josh. 7. 26. from fierceness of *a.*
Job 9. 13. if God will not withdraw *a.*
Ps. 27. 9. put not away servant in *a.*
30. 5. his *a.* endureth but a moment
37. 8. cease from *a.* and wrath
77. 9. hath he in *a.* shut up
78. 38. turned he in his *a.* away
50. he made a way to his *a.*
85. 4. cause *a.* towards us to cease
90. 7. we are consumed by thine *a.*
11. who knoweth power of thine *a.*
103. 9. keep *a.* for ever, Jer. 3. 5, 12.
Eccl. 7. 9. *a.* resteth in the bosom of fools
Isa. 5. 25. for all this is *a.* is not turned away, 9. 12, 17, 21. & 10. 4.
Hos. 11. 9. not execute fierceness of *a.*
14. 4. my *a.* is turned away from him
Mic. 7. 18. retaineth not *a.* for ever
Eph. 4. 31. let all *a.* be put away
Col. 3. 8. put off all these; *a.* wrath
Slow to *a.* Neh. 9. 17. Ps. 103. 8. Joel 2. 13. Jonah 4. 2. Nah. 1. 3.
Ps. 106. 32. they *angered* him at waters
Gen. 18. 30. let not Lord be *angry*
Deut. 1. 37. Lord was *a.* with me
9. 20. Lord was *a.* with Aaron
1 Kings, 11. 9. the Lord was *a.* with Solomon
Ezra 9. 14. wouldst not be *a.* with us
Ps. 2. 12. kiss Son lest he be *a.*
7. 11. God is *a.* with the wicked every day
76. 7. who may stand when thou art *a.*
Prov. 14. 17. that is soon *a.* dealeth foolishly
22. 24. no friendship with an *a.* man
29. 22. *a.* man stirreth up strife
Eccl. 7. 9. be not hasty to be *a.*
Song 16. mother's children were *a.*
Isa. 12. 1. though thou wast *a.* with
Jonah 4. 9. I do well to be *a.* even
Matt. 5. 22. whoso is *a.* with brother
Eph. 4. 26. be *a.* and sin not
Tit. 1. 7. bishop must not be soon *a.*
ANGUISH, excessive pain
Gen. 42. 21. saw the *a.* of his soul
Ex. 6. 9. hearkened not for *a.* of spirit
Ps. 119. 143. trouble and *a.* take hold
Jer. 6. 24. *a.* taken hold of us
John 16. 21. remember not *a.* for joy
Rom. 2. 9. tribulation and *a.* upon every soul of man
ANOINT, rub with oil, appoint, to qualify for office of king, priest or prophet, Ex. 28. 41.
Dan. 9. 24. to *a.* the most holy
Amos 6. 6. *a.* with chief ointments
Matt. 6. 17. when fastest *a.* thy head
Rev. 3. 18. *a.* eyes with eye salve
1 Sam. 24. 6. *anointed* of the Lord
Ps. 45. 7. *a.* thee with oil of gladness
Isa. 61. 1. Lord *a.* me to preach, Luke 4. 18.
Zech 4. 14. two *a.* ones before the Lord
Acts 4. 27. Jesus whom thou hast *a.*
10. 38. how God *a.* Jesus of Nazareth
2 Cor. 1. 21. who hath *a.* us is God.
Ps. 2. 2. Lord and his *a.* 18. 50. 2 Sam. 22. 51 1 Sam. 2. 10. Ps. 20. 6. & 38. 8.
1 Chron. 16. 22. touch not my *a.* Ps. 105. 15. & 132. 17.
2 Chron. 6. 42. turn not away face of thy *a.* Ps. 132. 10. & 84. 0.
Ps. 23. 5. *anointest* my head with oil
Isa. 10. 27. because of *anointing*
1 John 2. 27. the *a.* teacheth you of all
James 5. 14. *a.* him with oil
ANSWER, Gen. 41. 16. Deut. 20. 11.
Prov. 15. 1. soft *a.* turneth away wrath
16. 1. *a.* of tongue is from the Lord
Job 19. 16. he gave me no *a.*
Song 5. 6. he gave me no *a.*
Mic. 3. 7. there is no *answering* of God
Rom. 11. 4. what saith the *a.* of God
2 Tim. 4. 16. at my first *a.* no man
1 Pet. 3. 15. ready to give an *a.* to
21. the *a.* of a good conscience
Job 40. 4. what shall I *a.* thee
Ps. 102. 2. *a.* me speedily
143. 1. in thy faithfulness *a.* me
Prov. 26. 4, 5. *a.* fool according to his folly
Isa. 14. 32. what shall one then *a.* messengers
50. 2. when I called was none to *a.*
58. 9. shalt call and Lord shall *a.*
66. 4. when I called none did *a.*
Dan. 3. 16. not careful to *a.* thee
Matt. 25. 37. then shall righteous *a.* Lord
Luke 12. 11. what thing ye shall *a.*
13. 25. he shall *a.* I know you not
21. 14. meditate not what to *a.*
2 Cor. 5. 12. have somewhat to *a.* them
Col. 4. 6. know how to *a.* every man
Job 14. 15. call and I will *a.* & 13. 22. Ps. 91. 15. Isa. 65. 24. Jer. 33. 3. Ezek. 14. 4, 7.
Job 9. 3. he cannot *a.* one of, 40. 5.
Prov. 1. 28. Isa. 36. 21. & 65. 12.
Ps. 18. 41. to Lord but he *answered* not
81. 7. I *a.* thee in secret place
99. 6. called on the Lord and he *a.*
Prov. 18. 23. rich *answereth* roughly
13. he that *a.* matter before hear
27. 19. as in water face *a.* to face
Eccl. 10. 19. money *a.* all things
Gal. 4. 25. *a.* to Jerusalem that now is
Tit. 2. 9. not *answering* again
ANT, Prov. 6. 6. & 30. 25.
ANTICHRIST, 1 John 2. 18, 22. & 4. 3. 2 John 7.
APART, Ps. 4, 3. Zech. 12. 12.
APOSTLE, minister sent by God, or Christ, infallibly to preach the gospel, and found churches, Rom. 1. 1. 1 Cor. 1. 1. & 12. 28.
Rom. 11. 13. I am *a.* of Gentiles
1 Cor. 9. 1. am I not a free *a.*
15. 9. not meet to be called an *a.*
2 Cor. 12. 12. signs of *a.* wrought
Heb. 3. 1. consider the *a.* and high-priest
Matt. 10. 2. names of the twelve apostles
Luke 11. 49. I will send proph. and *a.*
1 Cor. 4. 9. God hath sent forth us *a.*
15. 9. I am the least of the *a.*
2 Cor. 11. 13. such are false *a.*
Eph. 2. 20. built on foundation of *a.*
4. 11. gave some *a.* some prophets
Rev. 2. 2. say they are *a.* and are not
18. 20. holy *a.* and prophets, Eph. 3. 5.
21. 14. names of twelve *a.* of the Lamb
Acts 1. 25. part of this *apostleship*
Rom. 1. 5. received grace and *a.*
1 Cor. 9. 2. seal of my *a.* are ye
Gal. 2. 8. to *a.* of circumcision
APPAREL, Isa. 63. 1. Zeph. 1. 8. 1

Tim. 2. 9. 1 Pet. 3. 3. James 2. 2.
APPEAR, Gen. 1. 9. Heb. 11. 3.
Ex. 23. 15. none shall *a.* before me empty, 34. 20. Deut. 16. 16.
1 Sam. 2. 27. did I *a.* to house of father
2 Chron. 1. 7. did God *a.* to Solomon
Ps. 42. 2. when shall I *a.* before God
90. 16. let work *a.* to servants
Isa. 1. 12. when ye *a.* before me who
66. 5. shall *a.* to your joy, but they
Matt. 6. 16. may *a.* to men to fast
23. 27. *a.* beautiful outwardly
Luke 19. 11. kingdom of God immediately *a.*
Rom. 7. 13. sin that it might *a.* sin
2 Cor. 5. 10. we must all *a.* before the judgment
Col. 3. 4. when Christ shall *a.*
1 Tim. 4. 15. thy profiting *a.* to all
Heb. 9. 24. to *a.* in the presence of God for us
28. *a.* second time without sin to salvation
1 Pet. 5. 4. when the shepherd shall *a.*
1 John 3. 2. not yet *a.* what we shall be
1 Sam. 16. 7. man looks—*appearance*
John 7. 24. judge not according to a
1 Thes. 5. 22. abstain from *a.* of evil
1 Tim. 6. 14. till *a.* of our Lord Jesus Christ
2 Tim. 1. 10. manifest by *a.* of Jesus Christ
4. 1. judge quick and dead at his *a.*
8. all them that love his *a.*
Tit. 2. 13. look for glorious *a.* of the great God
1 Pet. 1. 7. unto praise at *a.* of Christ
Tit. 2. 11. grace hath *a.* to all men
Heb. 9. 26. he *a.* to put away sin
APPETITE, Prov. 23. 2. Isa. 29. 8.
APPLE of eye, Deut. 32. 10. Ps. 17. 8.
Prov. 7. 2. Lam. 2. 18. Zech. 2. 8.
Apple-tree, Song 2. 3. & 8. 5.
Apples, Prov. 25. 11. Song 2. 5.
APPLY heart to wisdom, Ps. 90. 12.
Prov. 2. 2. & 22. 17. & 23. 12. Eccl. 7. 25. & 8. 9, 16. Hos. 7. 6.
APPOINT, Gen. 30. 28.
Isa. 61. 3. *a.* to them that mourn in Zion 26. 1. salvation will God *a.* for walls
Matt. 24. 51. *a.* him portion with the hypocrites
Luke 22. 29. I *a.* unto you a kingdom
Job 7. 1. is there not an *appointed* time 14. 14. all the days of my *a.* time
30. 23. to house *a.* for all living
Ps. 79. 11. preserve those *a.* to die
Jer. 5. 24. reserve *a.* weeks for harvest
Mic. 2. 6. hear rod and him who *a.* it
Hab. 2. 3. vision is for an *a.* time
1 Thes. 5. 9. God hath not *a.* us to wrath
Heb. 9. 27. *a.* to men once to die
1 Pet. 2. 8. whereunto they were *a.*
APPREHENDED, take fast hold of.
Phil. 3. 12, 13. Acts 12. 4.
APPROACH, come nearto, marry
Lev. 18. 6. *a.* to any near of kin, 20. 16.
Ps. 65. 4. blessed whom thou causest to *a.*
Jer. 30. 21. engageth heart to *a.*
1 Tim. 6. 16. light to which none can *a.*
Isa. 58. 2. delight in *approaching* to God
Heb. 10. 25. as ye see the day *a.*
APPROVE, like, commend
Ps. 49. 13. posterity *a.* their sayings
Phil. 1. 10. may *a.* things excellent
Acts 2. 22. man *approved* of God
Rom. 14. 18. acceptable to God, *a.* of
16. 10. Appelles *a.* in Christ
1 Cor. 11. 19. are *a.* be manifest
2 Tim. 2. 15. show thyself *a.*
Rom. 2. 18. *approvest* things excellent

Lam. 3. 36. to subvert Lord *approveth* not
2 Cor. 6. 4. in all things *approving* ourselves
APT to teach, 1 Tim. 3. 2.
ARE, seven years, Gen. 41. 26.
1 Cor. 1. 28. bring to nought things that *a.*
30. of him *a.* ye in Christ Jesus
8. 6. of whom *a.* all things
Heb. 2. 10. for and by whom *a.* all
Rev. 1. 19. write things that *a.*
20. *a.* angels; *a.* seven churches
ARGUE, Job 6. 25. & 23. 4.
ARIGHT, Ps. 78. 8.
50. 23. ordereth conversation *a.*
Prov. 15. 2. useth knowledge *a.*
Jer. 8. 6. they spake not *a.*
ARISE, for our help, Ps. 44. 26.
1 Chron. 22. 16. *a.* be doing
Ps. 68. 1. let God *a.* and enemies be scattered
Amos 7. 2. by whom shall Jacob *a.*
Mic. 7. 8. when I fall I shall *a.*
Mal. 4. 2. Son of righteousness *a.*
Ps. 112. 4. to the upright ariseth
Matt. 13. 21. persecution *a.* because
ARM of flesh with him, 2 Ch. 32. 8.
Job 40. 9. hast thou an *a.* like God
Ps. 44. 3. own *a.* did not save them
89. 13. hast a mighty *a.* strong
Isa. 33. 2. be thou their *a.* every
51. 5. mine *a.* shall judge; on my *a.*
9. Put on strength, O *a.* of Lord
52. 10. Lord made bare his holy *a.*
53. 1. *a.* of Lord revealed John 12. 38.
62. 8. Lord hath sworn by *a.* of
63. 12. let them by his glorious *a.*
1 Pet. 4. 1. *a.* yourselves with same
His arm, Ps. 98. 1. Isa. 40. 10, 11. & 59. 16. Jer. 17. 5. Ezek. 31. 17. Zech. 11. 17. Luke 1. 51.
Stretched-out-arm, Ex. 6. 6. Deut. 4. 34. & 5. 15. & 7. 19. & 11. 2. & 26. 8.
2 Chron. 6. 32. Ps. 136. 12. Jer. 27. 5. & 32. 17, 21.
Gen. 49. 24. *arms* of his hands made strong
Deut. 33. 27. underneath everlast. *a.*
Luke 11. 21. strong man *armed*
ARMIES of living God, 1 Sam. 17. 26.
Job 25. 3. any number of his *a.*
Ps. 44. 9. goest not forth with our *a.* 60. 10. & 108. 11.
Song 6. 13. company of two *a.*
Rev. 19. 14. *army* in heaven
ARMOUR of light, Rom. 13. 12.
2 Cor. 6. 7. by *a.* of righteousness
Eph. 6. 7. put on whole *a.* of God
ARRAY, 2 Sam. 10. 9. Job 6. 4. Jer. 50. 14.
Array, to clothe, Esth. 6. 9. Jer. 43. 12. Matt. 6. 29. 1 Tim. 2. 9. Rev. 7. 13. & 17. 4. & 19. 8.
ARROGANCY, presumptuous, self-conceit, 1 Sam. 2. 3. Prov. 18. 13.
ARROWS of the Almighty, Job 6. 4.
2 Kings 13. 17. the *a.* of the Lord's deliverance
Ps. 91. 5. nor for *a.* that flieth by day
Deut. 33. 23. I will spend my *a.* upon
Ps. 38. 2. thine *a.* stick fast in me
45. 5. thine *a.* are sharp in heart
Lam. 3. 12. set me as a mark for *a.*
ASCEND, Ps. 24. 3.
Ps. 139. 8. if I *a.* to heaven, Rom. 10. 6.
John 20. 17. I *a.* to my Father and your Father
Ps. 68. 18. hast *ascended* on high
Prov. 30. 4. who hath *a.* into heaven
John 3. 13. no man hath *a.*
Eph. 4. 8. when he *a.* up on high
Rev. 8. 4. smoke of incense *a.* before God
11. 12. *a.* up to heaven in a cloud
Gen. 28. 12. angels *ascending* and descending, John 1. 51.
ASCRIBE, Deut. 32. 3.

Job 36. 3. I will *a.* righteousness to my Maker
Ps. 68. 34. *a.* strength unto God
ASHAMED, Ezra 9. 6.
Gen. 2. 25. man and wife naked not *a.*
Ezek. 16. 61. remember ways and be *a.*
Mark 8. 38. shall be *a.* of me
Rom. 1. 16. I am not *a.* of gospel
5. 5. hope maketh not *a.* because
6. 21. whereof ye are now *a.*
Not be ashamed, Ps. 25. 2. & 119. 6, 80. Isa. 49. 23. Rom. 9. 33.
ASHES, Gen. 18. 27. Job 2. 8. & 13. 12. & 30. 19. & 42. 6. Ps. 102. 9. Isa. 44. 20. & 61. 3. Jer. 6. 26.
ASK the way to Zion, Jer. 50. 5.
Matt. 7. 7. *a.* and it shall be given
11. give good things to—*a.* him
20. 22. ye know not what ye *a.*
Luke 12. 48. of him they will *a.* more
John 14. 13, 14. whatsoever ye *a.* in my name, & 15. 16. & 16. 23.
16. 24. *a.* and ye shall receive—*asked*
Eph. 3. 20. above all we can *a.* or
James 1. 5. wisdom let him *a.* of God
6. let him *a.* in faith, not wavering
4. 2, 3. *a.* not; *a.* receive not
1 John 3. 22. whatsoever we *a.* we receive
5. 14, 15. *a.* according to his will
Isa. 65. 1. sought of—*asked* not for me
Jer. 6. 16. *a.* for good old paths
Matt. 7. 8. every one that *asketh* receiveth
ASLEEP, 1 Cor. 15. 16.
ASP, serpent, Deut. 32. 33.
Job 20. 14. 16. Isa. 11. 8.
ASS knows master's crib, Isa. 1. 3.
Zech. 9. 9. riding upon an *a.* Matt. 21. 5. John 12. 15.
ASSEMBLY of wicked, Ps. 22. 16.
89. 7. God feared in *a.* of his saints
Heb. 12. 23. general *a.* of first-born
Eccl. 12. 11. nails fastened by master of *a.*
Isa. 4. 5. create on her *a.* a cloud
Heb. 10. 25. forsake not *assembling*
ASSUAGE, Gen. 8. 1. Job 16. 5, 6.
ASSURANCE, firm persuasion
Isa. 32. 17. effect of righteousness *a.*
Col. 2. 2. riches of full *a.* of understanding
1 Thes. 1. 5. gospel came in much *a.*
Heb. 6. 11. to full *a.* of hope
10. 22. in full *a.* of faith
1 John 3. 19. *assure* our hearts before
ASTRAY, Ps. 119. 176. Matt. 18. 12.
Luke 15. 4. 1 Pet. 2. 25.
ATHIRST, Judg. 15. 18.
Rev. 21. 6. give to him *a.* of fountain
22. 17. him that is *a.* come take of
ATONEMENT, pacifying, satisfaction for sin, Lev. 16. 11. & 23. 27, 28. & 25. 9. Ex. 30. 16. Num. 8. 19, 21. & 16. 46. & 28. 22.
ATTAIN, Prov. 1. 5.
Ps. 139. 6. high, I cannot *a.* unto it
Ezek. 46. 7. according as hand shall *a.*
Phil. 3. 11, 12. *a.* to resurrection of dead, not already *attained*
ATTEND to my cry, Ps. 55. 2. & 61. 1. & 66. 19. & 86. 6. & 142. 6.
Prov. 4. 1. *a.* to know understanding
20. *a.* to my words, 7. 24.
5. 1. *a.* to my wisdom, bow ear
Acts 16. 14. she *attended* to—spoken
Attendance, 1 Kings 10. 5. 1 Tim. 4. 13. Heb. 7. 13. Rom. 13. 6.
Attentive, 1 Chron. 6. 40. & 7. 15. Neh. 1. 6. & 8. 3. Ps. 130. 2.
AVAILETH, Esth. 5. 13. Gal. 5. 6. & 6. 15. James 5. 16.
AVENGE not, Lev. 19. 18.
Lev. 26. 25. shall *a.* quarrel of covenant
Deut. 32. 43. he will *a.* blood of his
Isa. 1. 24. I will *a.* me of my enemies
Luke 18. 7. shall not God *a.* his elect
Luke 18. 8. he will *a.* them speedily
Rom. 12. 19. *a.* not yourselves

Rev. 6. 10. dost thou not *a.* our blood
Jer. 5. 9, 29. shall not my soul be *avenged* on such a nation, 9. 9.
Rev. 18. 20. God hath *a.* you on her
Avenger, Num. 35. 12. Ps. 8. 2. & 44. 16. 1 Thes. 4. 6.
2 Sam. 22. 48. God that *avengeth* me
Judg. 5. 2. praise Lord for *avenging* Israel
AUTHOR, 1 Cor. 14. 33.
Heb. 5. 9. *a.* of eternal salvation
12. 2. Jesus *a.* and finisher of our faith
AUTHORITY, power to govern,
Matt. 7. 29. taught as one having *a.*
John 5. 27. giving him *a.* to execute judgment
1 Cor. 15. 24. down all *a.* and power
1 Tim. 2. 2. prayer for all in *a.*
Tit. 2. 15. rebuke with all *a.*
1 Pet. 3. 2. angels and *a.* subject
Rev. 13. 2. dragon gave him *a.*
AVOUCHED, Deut. 26. 17, 18.
AVOID it, Prov. 4. 15.
Rom. 16. 17. cause divisions, *a.* them
AWAKE for thee, Job 8. 6.
Ps. 35. 23. *a.* to my judgment
139. 18. when I *a.* I am still with
Rom. 13. 11. high time to *a.* out of sleep
1 Cor. 15. 34. *a.* to righteousness
Eph. 5. 14. *a.* thou that sleepest
Ps. 78. 65. Lord *awaked* out of sleep
73. 20. when thou *awakest* thou shalt despise.
AWE, stand in *a.* sin not, Ps. 4. 4.
Ps. 33. 8. would stand in *a.* of him
119. 161. heart stands in *a.* of word
AXE, Deut. 19. 5. 1 Kings 6. 7. & 2 Kings 6. 5. Isa. 10. 15.
Axes, 2 Sam. 12. 31. Ps. 74. 5, 6.

B

BABBLER, Eccl. 10. 11.
1 Tim. 6. 20. avoid vain *babblings,*
2 Tim. 2. 16. Prov. 23. 29.
BABE leaped in womb, Luke 1. 41.
Heb. 5. 13. unskilful in words is a *b.*
Ps. 8. 2. out of mouth of *babes*
17. 14. rest of substance to *b.*
Isa. 3. 4. *b.* shall rule over them
1 Cor. 3. 1. as unto *b.* in Christ
1 Pet. 2. 2. as new born *b.* desire
BACK to go, 1 Sam. 10. 9.
1 Kings 14. 9. cast me behind *b.*
Ps. 129. 3. the ploughers ploughed on my *b.*
Prov. 26. 3. rod for the fool's *b.*
Isa. 38. 17. cast my sins behind thy *b.*
50. 6. gave my *b.* to smiters
Jer. 2. 27. turned their *b.* 32. 33.
18. 17. I will shew their *b.* not face
Ex. 33. 23. shall see my *b.* parts
Ps. 19. 13. keep *b.* thy servant from
53. 6. when God bringeth *b.* captivity
Hos. 4. 16. Israel slideth *b.* as backsliding
Acts 20. 20. keep *b.* nothing profitable
Neh. 9. 26. cast law behind *backs*
Ps. 15. 3. *backbiteth* not with his tongue
Backbiters, Rom. 1. 30.
Prov. 25. 23. *backbiting* tongue
2 Cor. 12. 20. strifes, *backbitings*
Backslider in heart, Prov. 14. 14.
Jer. 2. 19. thy *backslidings* reprove thee 3. 16, 12. return thou *b.* Israel, 14. 7. & 31. 32. & 49. 4.
5. 6. and their *b.* are increased
8. 5. slidden back by perpetual *b.*
14. 7. *b.* are many, we have sinned
Hos. 11. 7. my people are bent to *b.*
14. 4. I will heal their *b.*
Gen. 9. 23. went *backward*
Isa. 1. 4. they are gone away *b.*
59. 14. judgment is turned away *b.*

John 18. 6. went *b.* and fell to the ground

BAG, sack, or pouch, Deut. 25. 13. Job 14. 17. Prov. 16. 11. Micah 6. 11. Hag. 1. 6. Luke 12. 33. John 13. 29.

BALANCE, Job 31. 6. Ps. 62. 9. Isa. 40. 12, 15. & 46. 6. Dan. 5. 27.

Prov. 11. 1. false *b.* abomination to the Lord, 20. 23.

16. 11. just weight and *b.* are Lord's

Hos. 12. 7. *b.* of deceit are in hand

Mic. 6. 11. count pure with wicked *b.*

BALD, 2 Kings 2. 23. Jer. 16. 6. Ezek. 27. 31. Mic. 1. 16.

Baldness, Lev. 21. 5. Deut. 14. 1. Isa. 3. 24. & 15. 2. Ezek. 7. 18.

BALM, Gen. 37. 25. & 43. 11. Jer. 8. 22. is there no *b.* in Gilead 46. 11. & 51. 8. Ezek. 27. 17.

BANNER, Isa. 13. 2. Ps. 20. 5. Ps. 60. 4. *b.* to them that fear thee Song 2. 4. his *b.* over me was love 6. 4. terrible as an army with *banners*

BAPTISM of water, Matt. 3. 7.

Baptism of John, Matt. 21. 25. Mark 11. 30. Luke 7. 29. & 12. 50. Acts 1. 22. & 10. 37. & 18. 25.

Baptism of repentance, Mark 1. 4. Acts 13. 24. & 19. 4.

Baptism of suffering, Matt. 20. 22. Mark 10. 38, 39. Luke 12. 50.

Rom. 6. 4. buried with him by *baptism,* Col. 2. 12.

Eph. 4. 5. one faith, one *b.*

1 Pet. 3. 21. *b.* doth now save us

Heb. 6. 2. doctrine of *baptisms*

BAPTIZE with water, with the Holy Ghost, Matt. 3. 11. Mark 1. 8. Luke 3. 16. Acts 1. 5. John 1. 26.

Mark 1. 4. John did *b.* in wilderness

5. were all *baptized* of him, 8.

9. Jesus was *b.* of John, Matt. 3. 13, 14, 16. Luke 3. 21.

Mark 16. 16. believeth and is *b.*

Luke 3. 7. came to be *b.* 21.

7. 29, 30. publicans *b.* lawyers not *b.*

John 4. 1. Jesus *b.* more disciples

2. though Jesus himself *b.* not, but

Acts 2. 38. repent and be *b.* everyone

Acts. 2. 41. received his word were *b.*

8. 13. Simon believed and was *b.*

10. 47. that these should not be *b.*

48. Peter commanded them to be *b.*

18. 8. believed and were *b.*

22. 16. arise and be *b.* wash away

Rom. 6. 3. as many as were *b.* were *b.* unto his death

1 Cor. 1. 13. were ye *b.* in name of

15. none—*b.* in own name

10. 2. were all *b.* unto Moses

12. 13. are all *b.* into one body

15. 29. are *b.* for the dead

Gal. 3. 27. as have been *b.* into Christ

Matt. 28. 19. *baptizing* in name

BARE, Ex. 19. 4.

Isa. 53. 12. he *b.* the sins of many

Matt. 8. 17. himself *b.* our sickness

1 Pet. 2. 24. *b.* our sins in his own body

BARN, Matt. 13. 30. Prov. 3. 10. Matt. 6. 26. Luke 12. 18, 24.

BARREL, of meal, 1 Kings 17. 14.

BARREN, Gen. 11. 30. & 25. 21. & 29. 31. Judg. 13. 2. Luke 1. 7.

Ex. 23. 26. nothing shall be *b.*

1 Sam. 2. 5. *b.* hath borne seven

Ps. 113. 9. woman to keep house

Song 4. 2. none is *b.* among, 6. 6.

Isa. 54. 1. sing, O *b.* Gal. 4. 27.

Luke 23. 29. blessed are *b.* wombs

2 Pet. 1. 8. neither be *b.* nor unfruitful

BASE in my own sight, 2 Sam. 6. 22.

1 Cor. 1. 28. *b.* things of this world

2 Cor. 10. 1. who in presence am *b.*

Ezek. 29. 14, 15. *basest* of kingdoms

Dan. 4. 17. set up *b.* of men

BASTARD, not enter, Deut. 23. 2. Zech. 9. 6. *b.* shall dwell in Ashdod

Heb. 12. 8. without chastisement are *bastards*

BATTLE not to strong, Eccl. 9. 11. Jer. 8. 6. as horse rusheth into *b.*

Ps. 140. 7. covered head in day of *b.*

BEAM out of timber, Hab. 2. 11.

Matt. 7. 3. considered not *b.* in own eye

Song 1. 1, 17. *b.* of our house are cedar

BEAR, Gen. 49. 15. Deut. 1, 9, 31. Prov. 9. 12. & 30. 21. Lam. 3. 27.

Gen. 4. 13. punishment greater than I can *b*

Num. 11. 14. not able to *b.* all

Ps. 75. 3. I *b.* up the pillars of it

91. 12. *b.* thee up in their hands

Prov. 18. 14. wounded spirit who can *b.*

Amos 7. 10. land not able to *b.* words

Mic. 7. 9. I will *b.* indignation of Lord because

Luke 14. 27. whoso doth not *b.* his cross

18. 7. though he *b.* long with them

John 16. 12. ye cannot *b.* them now

Rom. 15. 1. strong *b.* the infirmities of the weak

1 Cor. 3. 2. hitherto not able to *b.* it

10. 13. that may be able to *b.* it

Gal. 6. 2. *b.* ye one another's burdens

5. every man *b.* his own burden

17. 1. *b.* in my body the marks of the Lord Jesus

Heb. 9. 28. offered to *b.* sins of many

Rev. 2. 2. canst not *b.* which are evil

Bear fruit, Ezek. 17. 8. Hos. 9. 16. Joel 2. 22. Matt. 13. 23. Luke 13. 9. John 15. 2, 4, 8.

Ps. 106. 4. favor thy *bearest* to

Rom. 11. 18. *b.* not root but

13. 4. *beareth* not sword in vain

1 Cor. 13. 7. charity *b.* all things

Heb. 6. 8. *b.* thorns and briers

Ps. 126. 6. *bearing* precious seed

Rom. 2. 15. conscience *b.* witness, 9. 1.

Heb. 13. 13. his reproach

BEASTS, animals without reason

Gen. 1. 24, 25 & 3. 1.—for ministers, Rev. 4. 6, 7, 8, 9. & 5. 6, 14. & 6. 1, 3. & 7. 11. & 14. 3. & 15. 7. & 19. 4.—for antichrist, Dan. 1. 11.

Prov. 9. 2. wisdom killed her *b.*

Ps. 49. 12. like *b.* that perish, 20.

73. 12. I was as a *b.* before thee

Dan. 7. 17. four *b.* are four kings

1 Cor. 15. 32. I fought with *b.* at Ephesus

BEAT Prov. 23. 14. Isa. 3. 15. Luke 12. 47, 48. 1 Cor. 9. 26.

BEAUTY, Ex. 28. 2.

1 Chron. 16. 29. in the *b.* of holiness, 2 Chron. 29. 21. Ps. 29. 2. & 96. 9.

Ps. 27. 4. to behold *b.* of the Lord

39. 11. makest his *b.* to consume

45. 11. king greatly desire thy *b.*

Prov. 20. 29. *b.* of old men gray head

31. 30. favour deceitful *b.* is vain

Isa. 3. 24. be burning instead of *b.*

33. 17. see the king in his *b.* and land

53. 2. no *b.* that we should desire him

61. 3. give them *b.* for ashes

Zech. 11. 7. two staves, one called *b.*

Beautify, Ps. 149. 4. Isa. 60. 13.

Beautiful, Eccl. 3. 11. Song 6. 4. & 7. 1. Isa. 52. 1, 7. & 64. 11. Jer. 13. 20. Ezek. 16. 12, 13.

BED, set for him, 2 Kings. 4. 10.

Ps. 41. 3. make all his *b.* in sickness

Song 3. 1. by night on my *b.* I sought him

Isa. 28. 20. the *b.* is shorter than that a man

Heb. 13. 4. marriage *b.* undefiled

Rev. 2. 22. I will cast her into a *b.*

Isa. 57. 2. rest in their *beds*

Amos 6. 4. lie on *b.* of ivory

BEFORE, Gen. 20. 15. Ex. 22. 9. 1 Kings 17. 1. & 18. 1. 2 Kings 3. 14.— (in time or place) Gen. 31. 2. Job. 3. 24. Josh. 8. 10.

2 Chron. 13. 14— (in dignity) 2 Sam. 6. 21. John 1. 15, 27.

Phil. 3. 13. those things which are *b.*

Col. 1. 17. he is *b.* all things and by him

BEG, Ps. 109. 10. & 37. 25. Luke 16. 3. & 23. 52. John 9. 8.

Beggar, 1 Sam. 2. 8. Luke 16. 20, 22.

Beggarly elements, Gal. 4. 9.

BEGIN, Ex. 12. 2. the *beginning* of months

Gen. 49. 3. *b.* of strength, Deut. 21. 17.

Ps. 111. 10. fear of Lord is the *b.* of wisdom, Prov. 1. 7. & 9. 10.

Eccl. 7. 8. better is the end than the *b.*

Matt. 24. 8. these are the *b.* of sorrows

Col. 1. 18. who is the *b.* and first born

Heb. 7. 3. neither *b.* of days nor end

2 Pet. 2. 20. latter end is worse than *b.*

Rev. 1. 8. I am Alpha and Omega, *b.* and the ending, 21. 6. & 22. 13.

3. 14. saith the *b.* of creation of God

BEGOTTEN, Job 38. 28.

Ps. 2. 7. this day have I *b.* thee, Acts 13. 33. Heb. 1. 5, 6.

John 1. 14. only *b.* of the Father, 18.

3. 16. sent his only *b.* Son, 18.

1 Cor. 4. 15. I have *b.* you through the Gospel.

Philem. 10. I have *b.* in my bonds

1 Pet. 1. 3. *b.* us again to a lively hope

1 John 4. 9. sent his only *b.* son

5. 1. loveth him that is *b.*

Rev. 1. 5. first *b.* of the dead

BEGUILE, Col. 2, 4, 18. 2 Cor. 11. 3. 2 Pet. 2. 14.

BEGUN to fall, Esth. 6. 13.

Gal. 3. 3. having *b.* in the spirit

Phil. 1. 6. hath *b.* a good work in you

BEHAVE myself wisely, Ps. 101. 2.

Ps. 131. 2. I *b.* myself as a child

1 Tim. 3. 2. bishop of good *behaviour*

Tit. 2. 3. in *b.* as becometh holiness

BEHELD not iniquity in Jacob, Num. 23. 21.

Luke 10. 18. I *b.* Satan fall like lightning from heaven

John 1. 14. we *b.* his glory

Rev. 11. 12. their enemies *b.* them

BEHIND, Lev. 25. 51.

Ex. 10. 26. not an hoof left *b.*

Neh. 9. 26. cast law *b.* their backs

Ps. 139. 5. beset me *b.* and before

Isa. 38. 17. cast all my sins *b.*

1 Cor. 1. 7. ye come *b.* in no gift

Phil. 3. 13. forgetting things *b.*

Col. 1. 24. fill up that is *b.* of affliction

BEHOLD, Deut. 3. 27.

Job. 19. 27. my eyes shall *b.* and not

Ps. 11. 4. his eyes *b.* his eye-lids try

7. countenance *b.* upright

17. 15. I will *b.* thy face in righteousness

27. 4. desired to *b.* beauty of Lord

37. 37. *b.* the upright man

113. 6. humbles himself to *b.*

Eccl. 11. 7. it is pleasant to *b.* sun

Hab. 1. 13. of purer eyes than to *b.*

Matt. 18. 10. their angels *b.* face of

John 17. 24. they may *b.* my glory

19. 5. *b.* the man, 14. *b.* your king

26. *b.* thy son, 27. *b.* thy mother

1 Pet. 3. 2. *b.* your chaste conversation

Ps. 33. 13. Lord *beholdeth* all the sons

James 1. 24. he *b.* himself and goeth

Prov. 15. 3. *beholding* evil and good

Ps. 119. 37. turn eyes from *b.* vanity

Eccl. 5. 11. save *b.* of them with eyes

2 Cor. 3. 18. with open face *b.* as in a glass

Col. 2. 5. joying and *b.* your order

James 1. 23. like man *b.* natural face

BEING, Ps. 104. 33. & 146. 2.

BELIAL, devil, furious and obstinate in wickedness, Deut. 13. 13. Judg. 19. 22. & 20. 13. 1 Sam. 1. 16. & 2. 12. & 10. 27. & 25. 17, 25.

BELIEVE, Ex. 4. 1. Num. 14. 11. & 20. 12.

Deut. 1. 32. ye did not *b.* the Lord

2 Chron. 20. 20. *b.* Lord, *b.* prophets

Isa. 7. 9. will not *b.* surely not establish

Matt. 9. 28. *b.* ye that I am able

Mark 1. 15. repent and *b.* the gospel

9. 23. thou canst *b.* all things possible

24. Lord I *b.* help my unbelief

11. 24. *b.* that ye receive them

Luke 8. 13. for a while *b.* and

24. 25. slow of heart to *b.* all

John 1. 12. even to them that *b.*

6. 29. ye *b.* on him whom he sent

69. we *b.* and are sure thou art Christ

7. 39. they that *b.* him should receive

8. 24. if ye *b.* not I am he ye shall die

11. 42. may *b.* thou hast sent me

12. 36. *b.* in the light while ye have

19. ye may *b.* that I am he

14. 1. ye *b.* in God, *b.* also in me

17. 20. pray for them who shall *b.*

20. 31. written that ye might *b.*

Acts 8. 37. I *b.* Jesus Christ is the Son

13. 39. all that *b.* are justified

16. 31. *b.* on the Lord Jesus and thou shalt be saved

Rom. 3. 22. on all them that *b.*

10. 9. shalt *b.* in thine heart

14. how shall they *b.* on him

2 Cor. 4. 13. we *b.* and therefore speak

Phil. 1. 29. not only to *b.* but suffer

2 Thes. 2. 11. that they should *b.* a lie

1 Tim. 4. 10. especially those that *b.*

Heb. 10. 39. *b.* to saving of the soul

11. 6. cometh to God must *b.* that he is

James 2. 19. devils also *b.* and tremble

1 Pet. 2. 7. to you who *b.* he is precious

1 John 3. 23. his command that we *b.* on Jesus Christ

Believe not, Isa. 7. 9. John 4. 48. & 8. 24. & 10. 26. & 12. 39. & 16. 9, 20, 25. Rom. 3. 3. 2 Cor. 4. 4.

Gen. 15. 6. *believed* in Lord and he counted, Rom. 4. 3. Gal. 3. 6.

Ps. 27. 13. fainted unless I had *b.*

116. 10. I *b.* therefore have I spoken

119. 66. I *b.* thy commandments

Isa. 53. 1. who hath *b.* our report, John 12. 38. Rom. 10. 16.

Dan. 6. 23. because he *b.* in his God

Jonah 3. 5. people of Ninevah *b.* God

Matt. 8. 13. as thou hast *b.* so be it

21. 32. publicans and harlots *b.* him

John 4. 53. himself *b.* and his house

7. 48. have any of the Pharisees *b.* on

17. 8. have *b.* thou didst send me

20. 29. blessed—not seen and yet *b.*

Acts 4. 32. that *b.* were of one heart

8. 13. Simon *b.* and was baptized

11. 21. great number *b.* and turned

13. 12. deputy *b.*—astonished

48. as many as were ordained to eternal life *b.*

Rom. 4. 18. against hope *b.* in hope

13. 11. salvation nearer than when *b.*

Eph. 1. 13. after ye *b.* were sealed

1 Tim. 3. 16. God was *b.* on in the world

2 Tim. 1. 12. know whom I have *b.*

Believed not, Ps. 78. 22, 23. & 106. 24. Luke 24. 41. Acts 9. 26. Rom. 10. 14. 2 Thes. 2. 12.

Believers, Acts 5. 14. 1 Tim. 4. 12.

Believest, Luke 1. 20. John 1. 50. & 11. 27. & 14. 10. Jas. 2. 19.

Acts 8. 37. if thou *b.* with all thy heart

26. 27. *b.* thou prophets—thou *b.*

Believeth, Job 15. 22. & 39. 24.

Prov. 14. 15. simple *b.* every word

Isa. 28. 16. that *b.*—not make haste

Mark 9. 23. all things possible to—*b.*

16. 16. he that *b.* shall be saved, he that *b.* not shall be damned

John 3. 15, 16. *b.* in him should not perish, 18. he that *b.* is not condemned, he that *b.* not is condemned already.

36. he that *b.* on the Son hath everlasting life; and he that *b.* not shall not see life.

5. 24. *b.* on him that sent me

6. 35. *b.* on me shall never thirst

40. seeth the Son and *b.* may have everlasting life, 47.

7. 38. he that *b.* on me out of his belly shall flow

11. 25. *b.* in me though he were dead

26. he that *b.* in me shall never die

12. 44. *b.* on me, *b.* not on me, but

46. *b.* on me shall not abide in darkness

14. 12. *b.* on me works that I do

Acts 10. 43. *b.* in him—receive remission

Rom. 1. 16. power of God—to every-one that *b.*

3. 26. justifier of him that *b.* in Jesus

4. 5. worketh not, but *b.* on him

9. 33. *b.* on him—not ashamed, 10. 11.

10. 4. end of the law for righteousness to them that *b.*

10. for with the heart man *b.* unto righteousness

14. 2. one *b.* that he may eat all things

1 Cor. 7. 12. wife that *b.* not

13. husband that *b.* not

13. 7. charity *b.* all things

14. 24. come in one that *b.* not

2 Cor. 6. 15. he that *b.* with infidel

1 Tim. 5. 16. that *b.* have widows

1 Pet. 2. 6. *b.* on him shall not be confounded

1 John 5. 1. whoso *b.* that Jesus is Christ

5. overcometh world, but he that *b.*

10. he that *b.* on Son of God hath *b.* not God hath made him a liar because he *b.* not record that God

Matt. 21. 22. ask in prayer, *believing*

John 20. 27. be not faithless, but *b.*

31. that *b.* ye might have life

Acts 16. 34. *b.* in God with all his house

24. 14. *b.* all things written

Rom. 15. 13. all joy and peace in *b.*

1 Tim. 6. 2. have *b.* masters

1 Pet. 1. 8. yet *b.* ye rejoice with joy

1 Thess. 2. 13. *belief* of the truth

BELLOWS are burnt, Jer. 6. 29.

BELLY, on *b.* shalt go, Gen. 3. 14.

Num. 5. 21. *b.* to swell and thigh rot

25. 8. thrust them through the *b.*

Job 3. 11. when I came out of *b.*

15. 2. fill his *b.* with east wind.

35. their *b.* prepareth deceit

20. 15. God cast them out of his *b.*

20. not feel quietness in his *b.*

Ps. 17. 14. whose *b.* thou fillest with

22. 10. art my God from mother's *b.*

44. 25. our *b.* cleaveth to the earth

Prov. 20. 27. search inward parts of *b.*

Isa. 46. 3. borne by me from the *b.*

Jonah 1. 17. in the *b.* of the fish, Mark 12. 40.

2. 1. prayed to God out of fish's *b.*

2. out of the *b.* of hell cried I.

Hab. 3. 16. my *b.* trembled that I.

Luke 15. 16. fill his *b.* with husks

John 7. 38. out of his *b.* shall flow

Rom. 16. 18. serve their own *b.*

1 Cor. 16. 13. meats for *b.* and

Phil. 3. 19. whose God is their *b.*

Rev. 10. 9. make thy *b.* bitter

Tit. 1. 12. Cretians slow *bellies.*

BELONG, Lev. 27. 24. Luke 23. 7.

Gen. 40. 8. interpretations *b.* to God.

Deut. 29. 29. secret things *b.* to Lord, things revealed *b.* to us and to our children

Ps. 47. 9. shields of earth *b.* to God

68. 20. to God *b.* issues from death

Dan. 9. 9. to the Lord *b.* mercies and forgiveness

Mark 9. 41. because ye *b.* in Christ

Luke 19. 42. things that *b.* to thy peace

1 Cor. 7. 32. care for the things *b.* to the Lord

Deut. 32. 35. to me *b.* vengeance

Ps. 94. 1. Heb. 10. 30. Rom. 12. 19.

Ezra 10. 4. this matter *belongeth* to

Ps. 3. 8. salvation *b.* to the Lord

62. 11. power *b.* to God, 12. *b.* mercy

Dan. 9. 7. righteousness *b.* to thee

8. to us *b.* confusion of face

Heb. 5. 14. strong meat *b.* to them

BELOVED, Deut. 21. 18.

Deut. 33. 12. *b.* of Lord shall dwell in safety

Neh. 13. 26. Solomon *b.* of his God

Ps. 60. 5. thy *b.* may be delivered

127. 2. Lord giveth his *b.* sleep

Song 1. 14, *my beloved,* 2. 3, 9, 16, 17. & 4. 16. & 5. 2, 6, 10, 16. & 6. 2, 3. & 7. 10, 13. Isa. 5. 1.

Song 5. 9. thy *b.* more than another *b.*

Dan. 10, 11, 19, O man, greatly *b.* 9. 23.

Matt. 3. 17. my *b.* Son, 17. 5.

Rom. 9. 25. *b.* which was not *b.*

11. 28. *b.* for the Father's sake

16. 8. Amplias *b.* in the Lord

Eph. 1. 6. accepted in the *b.*

2 Pet. 3. 15. *b.* brother Paul

Rev. 20. 9. compassed *b.* city

BEMOAN, Jer. 15. 5. & 16. 5. & 22. 10. & 31. 18. & 48. 17.

BEND bow, Ps. 11. 2. & 64. 3. & 58. 7. & 7. 12. & 37. 14. Lam. 2. 4. & 3. 12. Isa. 5. 28.

Jer. 9. 3. *b.* their tongues like a bow

Isa. 60. 14. afflicted thee shall come *bending* unto thee

Hos. 11. 7. people *bent* to backsliding

Zech. 9. 13. I have *b.* Judah for me

BENEATH, Prov. 15. 24.

BENEFACTORS, Luke 22. 25.

BENEFITS, Ps. 68. 19.

Ps. 103. 2. forget not all his *b.*

116. 12. render to the Lord for all his *b.*

BENEVOLENCE, due, 1 Cor. 7. 3.

BEREAVE, soul of good, Eccl. 4. 8.

Jer. 15. 7. *b.* them of children, 18. 21.

Gen. 42. 36. & 43. 14. Ezek. 5. 17. & 36. 12, 13, 14. Lam. 1. 20.

BESEECH God to be gracious, Mal. 1. 9.

1 Cor. 5. 20. as though God did *b.* you by us

BESET me behind, Ps. 139. 5.

Hos. 7. 2. own doings have *b.* them

Heb. 12. 1. sin which doth easily *b.* us

BESIDE waters, Ps. 23. 2.

Song 1. 8. feed kids *b.* shepherd's tents

Isa. 56. 8. others *b.* I have gathered

BESIDE SELF, Mark 3. 21. 2 Cor. 5. 13.

BESOM of destruction, Isa. 14. 23.

BESOUGHT the Lord, Deut. 3. 23. 1 Kings 13. 6. 2 Kings 13. 4. 2 Chron. 33. 12. Ezra 8. 23. 2 Cor. 12. 8.

BEST estate is vanity, Ps. 39. 5.

Mic. 7. 4. *b.* of them is as a brier

Luke 15. 22. bring forth *b.* robe

1 Cor. 12. 31. covet earnestly *b.* gifts

BESTEAD, hardly, Isa. 8. 21.

BESTOW a blessing, Ex. 32. 29.

Luke 12. 17. room to *b.* my fruits

1 Cor. 12. 23. we *b.* more abundant honour

13. 3. *b.* all my goods to feed the poor

John 4. 38. *bestowed* no labour

1 Cor. 15. 10. his grace *b.* on me

2 Cor. 1. 11. gift *b.* on us by means

8. 1. grace of God *b.* on churches

Gal. 4. 11. lest *b.* labour in vain

1 John 3. 1. love the Father hath *b.* on us

BETIMES, 2 Chron. 36. 15. Job 8. 5. Prov. 13. 24. Gen. 26. 31.

BETRAY, Matt. 24. 10. & 26. 21. Mark 13. 12. & 14. 18.

BETROTH, Deut. 28. 30.

BETTER than ten sons, 1 Sam. 1. 8.

Judg. 8. 2. gleanings *b.* than vintage

1 Kings 19. 4. I am not *b.* than my fathers

Prov. 15. 16. *b.* is little with the fear of the Lord

17. *b.* is a dinner of herbs with love

16. 8. *b.* is a little with righteousness

16. how much *b.* to get wisdom than money

17. 1. *b.* is a dry morsel, and quietness therewith, than

27. 10. *b.* is a neighbour near than

Eccl. 4. 9. two are *b.* than one

13. *b.* is a poor and wise child than

6. 9. *b.* is sight of eyes than wander'g

7. 1. *b.* is a good name than precious

2. *b.* to go to the house of mourning

3. *b.* is sorrow than laughter

5. *b.* to hear rebuke of the wise than

8. *b.* is the patient than proud in

9. 16. wisdom is *b.* than strength

18. wisdom is *b.* than weapons of

Song 4. 10. how much *b.* is thy love than wine

Matt. 6. 26. are ye not much *b.* than

Rom. 3. 9. are we *b.* than they

1 Cor. 9. 15. were it *b.* for me to die

11. 17. come not for the *b.* but worse

Phil. 1. 23. with Christ is far *b.*

2. 3. esteem others *b.* than themselves

Heb. 1. 4. made so much *b.* than angels

6. 9. persuaded *b.* things of you

7. 19. bringing in of a *b.* hope doth

22. Jesus made surety of a *b.* testam't

8. 6. mediator of a *b.* covenant established on *b.* promises.

10. 34. a *b.* enduring substance

11. 16. desire a *b.* country

35. obtain a *b.* resurrection

40. provided some *b.* things

12. 24. blood speaketh *b.* than Abel

2 Pet. 2. 21. *b.* not to have known the way

BETWEEN thy seed and her, Gen. 3. 15.

1 Kings 3. 9. discern *b.* good and bad

18. 21. how long halt ye *b.* two

Ezek. 22. 26. no difference *b.* holy and profane, 44. 23. Lev. 10. 10.

Phil. 1. 23. in a strait *b.* two having

1 Tim. 2. 5. one media or *b.* God and

BEWARE of men, Matt. 10. 17.

Matt. 7. 15. *b.* of false prophets

16. 6. *b.* of leaven of Pharisees, 11. Mark 8. 15.

Luke 12. 15. *b.* of covetousness

Phil. 3. 2. *b.* of dogs, *b.* of evil workers, *b.* of the concision

Col. 2. 8. *b.* lest any man spoil you

BEYOND or defraud, 1 Thess. 4. 6.

BIBBER, Prov. 23. 20.

BID, Matt. 22. 9. & 23. 3. Luke 14. 10. & 24. 2. John 10. 11.

BIDE, not in unbelief, Rom. 11. 23.

BILL, Deut. 24. 1, 3.. Isa. 50. 1. Mark 10. 4. Luke 16. 6, 7.

BILLOWS, Ps. 42. 7. Jonah 2. 3.

BIND sweet influences, Job 38. 31.

Job 31. 36. I would *b.* it as a crown

Ps. 105. 22. to *b.* his princes at pleasure

118. 27. *b.* the sacrifice with cords

149. 8. to *b.* their kings with chains

Prov. 3. 3. *b.* them about thy neck

Isa. 8. 16. *b.* up testimony, seal law

61. 1. *b.* up broken hearted

Hos. 6. 1. smitten us and he will *b.* us up

Matt. 12. 29. first *b.* strong man and

13. 30. *b.* them in bundles to burn

16. 19. thou shalt *b.* on earth, 18. 18.

22. 13. *b.* him hand and foot, and cast

23. 4. *b.* heavy burdens and lay

Bindeth up, Job 5. 18. Ps. 147. 3.

BIRD hasteth to snare, Prov. 7. 23.

Ps. 124, 7. escaped as a *b.* out of the snare

Eccl. 10. 20. *b.* of air tell the matter

Isa. 46. 11. ravenous *b.* from the east

Jer. 12. 9. heritage as a specked *b.*

Birds, Gen. 15. 10. & 40. 17. Lev. 14. 4.

2 Sam. 21. 10. Ps. 104. 17. Eccl. 9. 12.

Song 2. 12. Isa. 31. 5. Jer. 5. 27.

Matt. 8. 20.

BIRTH, 2 Kings, 19. 3. Eccl. 7. 1.

Isa. 66. 9. Ezek. 16. 3.

Birthday, Gen. 40. 20. Matt. 14. 6.

Birth-right, Gen. 25. 31, 32, 33. & 27. 36.

1 Chron. 5. 1. Heb. 12. 16.

BISHOP, 1 Tim. 3. 1. 2 Tit. 1. 7.

1 Pet. 2. 25. return to *b.* of souls

Phil. 1. 1. with *bishops* and deacons

BITE, Num. 21. 6, 9. Eccl. 10. 8.

Jer. 8. 17. Amos 9. 3. Hab. 2. 7.

Mic. 3. 4. prophets *b.* with their teeth

Gal. 5. 15. if ye *b.* and devour one another

Prov. 23. 32. at the last it *b.* like a serpent

BITTER, Ex. 1. 14.

Ex. 12. 8. with *b.* herbs eat it, Num. 9. 11.

Deut. 32. 24. devoured with *b.* destruction

32. their grapes of gall, clusters are *b.*

2 Kings 14. 26. affliction was very *b.*

Job. 3. 20. why is life given to the *b.* in soul?

13. 26. write *b.* things against me

Ps. 64. 3. their arrows even *b.* words

Prov. 27. 7. every *b.* thing is sweet

Eccl. 7. 26. woman more *b.* than death

Isa. 5. 20. wo to them put *b.* for sweet

Jer. 2. 19. evil thing and *b.* that

Col. 3. 19. wives be not *b.* against them

James 3. 14. if ye have *b.* envying glory not

Rev. 10. 9. it shall make thy belly *b.*

Judg. 5. 23. curse *bitterly* inhabitants

Ruth 1. 20. Almighty dealt *b.* with me

Isa. 22. 4. I will weep *b.* 33. 7.

Ezek. 27. 30. shall cry *b.* Zeph. 1. 14.

Hos. 12. 14. provoked him most *b.*

Matt. 26. 75. wept *b.* Luke 22. 62.

Bitterness of soul, 1 Sam. 1. 10.

1 Sam. 15. 32. *b.* of death is past

2 Sam. 2. 26. it will be *b.* in end

Prov. 14. 10. heart knows its own *b.*

Zech. 12. 10. in *b.* for first-born

Acts 8. 23. in gall of *b.* and bond of

Eph. 4. 31. let all *b.* be put away

Heb. 12. 15. root of *b.* springing up

BITTERN, Isa. 14. 23. & 34. 11.

BLACK, 1 Kings 18. 45.

Song 1. 5. I am *b.* but comely, 6.

Blackness of darkness, Heb. 12. 18. Jude 13.

BLAME, Gen. 43. 9. & 44. 32.

2 Cor. 8. 20. Eph. 1. 4.

Blamed, 2 Cor. 6. 3. Gal. 2. 11.

Blameless, Gen. 44. 10. Josh. 2. 17.

Judg. 15. 3. Matt. 12. 5. Phil. 3. 6.

Luke 1. 6. in all the ordinances of the Lord *b.*

1 Cor. 1. 8. be *b.* in the day of our Lord

Phil. 2. 16. *b.* harmless, the sons of God

1 Thess. 5. 23. be preserved *b.*
1 Tim. 3. 2. bishop must be *b.* Tit.
1. 6, 7.
10. office of deacon found *b.*
2 Pet. 3. 14. without spot and *b.*
BLASPHEME, revile God
Ps. 74. 10. enemy *b.* thy name
Mark 3. 29. *b.* against Holy Ghost
not forgiven
Acts 26. 11. compelled them to *b.*
1 Tim. 1. 20. may learn not to *b.*
James 2. 7. do they not *b.* that name
Lev. 24. 16. *blasphemed* the name of
the Lord
2 Kings 19. 6. servants *b.* me
Ps. 74. 18. foolish people have *b.*
Isa. 52. 5. my name continually is *b.*
Rom. 2. 24. the name of God is *b.*
through you
1 Tim. 6. 1. name of God and his
doctrine be not *b.*
Tit. 2. 5. word of God be not *b.*
Rev. 16. 9. the God of heaven
Lev. 24. 16. *blasphemeth* put to
death
Ps. 44. 16. the voice of him that *b.*
Matt. 9. 3. said this man *b.*
Luke 12. 10. to him that *b.* against
the Holy Ghost
Blasphemer, 1 Tim. 1. 10.
Blasphemy, 2 Kings 19. 3. Isa. 37. 3.
Matt. 12. 31. Mark 7. 22. Col. 3. 8.
Rev. 2. 9.
BLAST, Ex. 15. 8. 2 Sam. 22. 16.
Job. 4. 9. Isa. 25. 4.
Blasting, Deut. 28. 22. 1 Kings 8. 37.
BLEMISH, without, Ex. 12. 5.
& 29. 1. Lev. 1. 3, 10. & 4. 23.
Dan. 1. 4. children and no *b.*
Eph. 5. 27. church holy, and without
b.
1 Pet. 1. 19. as a lamb without *b.*
BLESS them that *b.* thee, Gen. 12. 3.
Gen. 22. 17. in blessing I will *b.* thee
32. 26. not let thee go except thou
b. me.
Ex. 23. 25. *b.* thy bread and water
Num. 6. 24. Lord *b.* and keep thee
1 Chron. 4. 10. O that thou *b.* me indeed
Ps. 5. 12. wilt *b.* the righteous
28. 9. *b.* thine inheritance and feed
29. 11. will *b.* his people with peace
67. 1. be merciful to us and *b.* us
115. 13. he will *b.* them that fear
132. 15. I will abundantly *b.* her
provision
Matt. 5. 44. *b.* them that curse you
Rom. 12. 14. *b.* them that persecute
you
Acts 3. 26. sent him to *b.* you in
turning many.
1 Cor. 4. 12. being reviled we *b.*
Bless the Lord, Deut. 8. 10. Judges
5. 9. Ps. 16. 7. & 34. 1. & 103. 1, 21,
22. & 104. 1, 35. & 26. 12.
Bless thee, Ps. 63. 4. & 145. 2, 10.
Gen. 1. 22. God *blessed* them and
2. 3. God *b.* the seventh day
Ex. 20. 11. the Lord *b.* the sabbath
Ps. 33. 12. *b.* whose God is the Lord
Prov. 10. 7. memory of the just is *b.*
Matt. 13. 16. *b.* are eyes they see,
Luke 10. 23.
24. 46. *b.* is that servant when his
Lord cometh, Luke 12. 37, 38.
Mark 10. 16. took them in his arms
and *b.* them
Luke 1. 28. *b.* art thou among women
48. all generations shall call me *b.*
23. 29. *b.* are the barren and the
wombs.
Acts 20. 35. more *b.* to give than to
receive
Rom. 1. 25. Creator *b.* for ever, 9. 5.
2 Cor. 11. 31. Eph. 1. 3. 1 Pet. 1. 3.
1 Tim. 1. 11. glorious gospel of *b.*
God
6. 15. *b.* and only potentate, John
12. 13.
Ps. 119. 1. *b.* are the undefiled in the

84. 4. *b. are they* that dwell in thy
106. 3. *b.*—that keep judgment
Prov. 8. 32. *b.* that keep my ways
Isa. 30. 18. *b.* that wait for him
Matt. 5. 3-11.—the poor in spirit—
mourn—meek—hunger and thirst—
merciful—pure in heart—peacemakers, persecuted—when men revile
you, Luke 6. 21.
Luke 11. 28. *b.* that hear the word
and do it
John 20. 29. *b.*—that have not seen,
and yet have believed
Rom. 4. 7. *b.*—whose iniquities are
forgiven
Rev. 19. 9. *b.*—called to the marriage
supper
22. 14. *b.*—that do his commandments
Num. 24. 9. *b.* is he that blesseth
Ps. 32. 1. *b.*—whose transgression
is forgiven.
4. 1. *b.* that considereth the poor
Dan. 12. 12. *b.*—that waiteth and
cometh
Matt. 11. 6. *b.*—who shall not be offended
21. 9. *b.*—cometh in the name of
the Lord, 23. 39
Rev. 1. 3. *b.*—that readeth this
prophecy
16. 15. *b.*—that watcheth and keepeth
20. 6. *b.*—that hath part in the first
resurrection
22. 7. *b.*—that keepeth the sayings
of this book
Ps. 1. 1. *b. is the man* that walketh
not in the counsel of the ungodly
32. 2. *b.*—to whom the Lord imputeth
34. 8. *b.*—that trusted in him, 84. 12
40. 4. *b.*—that maketh the Lord his
65. 4. *b.*—whom thou choosest
84. 5. *b.*—whose strength is in thee
94. 12. *b.*—whom thou chastenest,
O Lord
112. 1. *b.*—that feareth the Lord
Prov. 8. 34. *b.* that heareth me
watching
Isa. 56. 2 *b.* that doeth this, and son
Jer. 17. 7. *b.*—that trusteth in Lord
James 1. 12. *b.*—that endureth
temptation
Ps. 49. 18. he *blesseth* his soul
Blessedness, Rom. 4. 6, 9. Gal. 4. 15.
Gen. 12. 2. thou shalt be a *blessing*
27. 36. he hath taken away my *b.*
28. 4. give the *b.* of Abraham
Deut. 11. 26. set before you a *b.* and
a curse, 30. 19. James 3. 9, 10.
23. 5. turned curse into *b.* Neh. 13. 2.
Neh. 9. 5. exalted above all *b.*
Job. 29. 13. *b.* of him ready to perish
Ps. 3. 8. thy *b.* is upon thy people
109. 17. delighted not in *b.*
129. 8. the *b.* of Lord be upon you
Prov. 10. 22. the *b.* of the Lord it
maketh rich.
Isa. 65. 8. destroy it not for a *b.* is in
it
Joel 2. 14. leaveth a *b.* behind him
1 Cor. 10. 16. the cup of *b.* which we
Gal. 3. 14. *b.* of Abraham might come
Blessings, Gen. 49. 25, 26. Josh. 8. 34.
Ps. 21. 3. Prov. 10. 6. & 28. 20. Mal.
2. 2. Eph. 1. 3.
BLIND, Ex. 4. 11. Lev. 21. 18.
Job. 29. 15. I was eyes to the *b.*
Ps. 146. 8. openeth the eyes of the *b.*
Isa. 42. 7. to open the eyes, 18
19. who is *b.* but my servant?
43. 8. bring the *b.* people that have
eyes
56. 10. his watchmen are *b.*
Matt. 11. 5. the *b.* receive sight
Matt. 23. 16. wo to you *b.* guides, 24.
Luke 4. 18. recovery of sight to *b.*
2 Pet. 1. 9. he that lacketh these
things is *b.*
Rev. 3. 17. thou art *b.* and naked

John 12. 40. *blinded* their eyes
Rom. 11. 7. the rest were *b.*
2 Cor. 3. 14, their minds were *b.*
4. 4. the God of this world hath *b.*
the minds
1 John 2. 11. darkness hath *b.* his eyes
BLOOD of grapes, Gen. 49. 11.
Job 16. 18. cover thou not my *b.* let
Ps. 9. 12. maketh inquisition for *b.*
72. 14. precious their *b.* be in his
sight
Isa. 26. 21. the earth shall disclose
her *b.*
Ezek. 3. 18. his *b.* will I require
9. 9. the land is full of *b.*
16. 6. polluted in thy own *b.*
Hos. 4. 2. they break out, and *b.*
touch
Mic. 3. 10. they build up Zion with *b.*
Matt. 26. 28. *b.* of New Testament
Mark 14. 24. Luke 22. 20. 1 Cor. 11.
25. 27. 28. field of *b.* Acts 1. 19.
25. his *b.* be on us and our children
Luke 13. 1. whose *b.* Pilate had
mingled
22. 44. as it were great drops of *b.*
John 1. 13. born of *b.* nor of flesh
6. 54. whoso drinketh my *b.* hath life
55. my *b.* is drink indeed
19. 34. out of his side came *b.* and
water
Acts 17. 26. made of one *b.* all nations
18. 6. your *b.* be upon your own
heads
20. 26. I am pure from the *b.* of all
men
28. he hath purchased with his
own *b.*
Rom. 3. 25. through faith in his *b.*
5. 9. being justified by his *b.*
1 Cor. 11. 27. guilty of body and *b.* of
Christ
Col. 1. 20. made peace through the
b. of the cross
Eph. 1. 7. redemption through his
b. even forgiveness of sins, Col. 1. 4.
Heb. 9. 20. this is the *b.* of the testament
22. without shedding of *b.* no
10. 19. into the holiest by the *b.* of
Jesus
12. 4. ye have not yet resisted unto *b.*
24. *b.* of sprinkling that speaketh
1 Pet. 1. 2. sprinkling of the *b.* of
Jesus
19. with precious *b.* of Christ
1 John 1. 7. his *b.* cleanseth from all
sin
5. 6. came by water and *b.*
Rev. 1. 5. washed us in his own *b.*
6. 10. dost thou not avenge our *b.*
7. 14. made white in the *b.* of the
Lamb
8. 7. hail and fire mingled with *b.*
12. 11. overcame by the *b.* of the
Lamb
16. 6. shed *b.*—given them *b.* to
drink
17. 6. drunken with the *b.* of saints
Blood-guiltiness, Ps. 51. 14.
Bloody, Ex. 4. 25, 26. Ps. 5. 6.
BLOSSOM, Num. 17. 5.
Isa. 5. 24. their *b.* shall go up as dust
27. 6. Israel shall *b.* and bud
35. 1. the desert shall *b.* as the rose
2. it shall *b.* abundantly and rejoice
Hab. 3. 17. the fig-tree shall not *b.*
Ezek. 7. 10. rod hath *blossomed* pride
BLOT, Job 31. 7. Prov. 9. 7.
Ex. 32. 32, 33. *b.* me out of thy book,
Num. 5. 23. Ps. 69. 28. Rev. 3. 5.
Blot out their name or remembrance
Deut. 9. 14. & 25. 19. & 29. 20. 2
Kings 14. 27. Ps. 109. 13.
Blot out sin, transgression, iniquity,
Neh. 4. 5. Ps. 51. 1, 9. & 109. 14.
Isa. 43. 25. Jer. 18. 23. Acts 3. 19.
Col. 2. 14. *blotting* out the hand-
writing
BLOW on my garden, Song 4. 16.
Hag. 1. 9. I did *b.* upon it

John 3. 8. wind *bloweth* where it
listeth
BLUSH to lift up my face, Ezra 9. 6.
Jer. 6. 15. neither could they *b.* 8. 12.
BOAST, Ps. 10. 3. & 34. 2. Prov.
20. 14. & 25. 14. Jas. 3. 5.
1 Kings 20. 11. *b.* as he that puts it off
Ps. 44. 8. in God we *b.* all the day
Prov. 27. 1. *b.* not of to-morrow
Rom. 11. 18. *b.* not against the
branches, but if thou *b.* thou bearest
Eph. 2. 9. not of works lest any
man should *b.*
Boasting, Acts 5. 36. Rom. 3. 27.
Jas. 4. 16. now ye rejoice in your *b.*
Rom. 1. 30. proud *boasters,* 2 Tim.
3. 2.
BODY of heaven, Ps. 24. 10.
Job 19. 26. though worms destroy
this *b.*
Matt. 6. 22. *b.* full of light
10. 28. them that kill the *b.* Luke
12. 4.
Matt. 26. 26. this is my *b.*
Rom. 6. 6. that the *b.* of sin be destroyed
7. 4. dead to the law by the *b.* of
Christ
24. deliver me from the *b.* of this
death
8. 10. *b.* is dead because of sin
13. do mortify deeds of the *b.*
23. the redemption of our *b.*
1 Cor. 6. 13. *b.* is not for fornication,
but for the Lord; and the Lord
for the *b.*
18. every sin a man doeth is without
the *b.*
19. your *b.* is the temple of the
Holy Ghost
7. 4. wife hath not power of her
own *b.*
9. 27. I keep under my *b.* and bring
10. 16. communion of *b.* of Christ
11. 27. guilty of *b.* and blood of the
29. not discerning the Lord's *b.*
12. 14. the *b.* is not one member
27. ye are the *b.* of Christ
15. 35. with what *b.* do they come?
44. sown a natural *b.* raised a spiritual *b.*
2 Cor. 5. 8. to be absent from the *b.*
Eph. 3. 6. fellow heirs of the same *b.*
Eph. 4. 12. for edifying the *b.* of
Christ
5. 23. he is the Saviour of the *b.*
Phil. 3. 21. who shall change our vile
b.
Col. 1. 18. he is the head of the *b.*
the church
2. 11. putting off the *b.* of sins of
flesh
17. shadow—but the *b.* is of Christ
23. neglecting of the *b.*
1 Thess. 5. 23. spirit, soul and *b.* be
preserved
Heb. 10. 5. a *b.* hast thou prepared.
James 3. 6. able to bridle the whole *b.*
Jude 9. disputed about the *b.* of
Moses
John 2. 21. his own *b.* 1 Cor. 6. 18.
1 Cor. 5. 3. in the *b.* 2 Cor. 5. 6.
Deut. 28. 11, 18, 53. fruit of the *b.*
30. 9. Ps. 132. 11. Mic. 6. 7.
Rom. 8. 11. quicken your mortal *bodies.* 12. 1. present your *b.* a living
sacrifice
1 Cor. 6. 15. your *b.* are members of
Christ
Eph. 3. 28. husbands love your wives
as your own *b.*
Heb. 10. 22. *b.* washed with pure
water
Luke 3. 22. Holy Ghost descended
in a *bodily* shape
2 Cor. 10. 10. his *b.* presence is weak
Col. 2. 9. dwelleth the fulness of the
godhead *b.*
1 Tim. 4. 8. *b.* exercise profiteth little
BOLD as a lion, Prov. 28. 1.

2 Cor. 10. 1. being absent am *b.* toward

11. 21. if any is *b.* I am *b.* also

Phil. 1. 14. are much more *b.* to speak

Mark 15. 43. went *boldly* unto Pilate

Eph. 6. 19. open my mouth *b.*

Heb. 4. 16. come *b.* to throne of grace

2 Cor. 7. 4. great is my *boldness* of speech

Eph. 3. 12. in whom we have *b.* and access

Heb. 10. 19. *b.* to enter into the holiest

1 John 4. 17. *b.* in the day of judgment

BOND, Ezek. 20. 37.

Acts 8. 23. in gall and *b.* of iniquity

Eph. 4. 3. unity of the spirit in the *b.* of peace

1 Cor. 12. 13. *bond and free,* Gal. 3. 28.

Eph. 6. 8. Col. 3. 11. Rev. 6. 15.

Ps. 116. 16. has loosed my *bonds*

Job. 12. 18. he looseth *b.* of kings

Acts 20. 23. *b.* and afflictions abide me

23. 29. worthy of death or of *b.*

26. 29. such as I am except these *b.*

Eph. 6. 20. I am an ambassador in *b.*

Phil. 1. 16. to add affliction to my *b.*

Col. 4. 18. remember my *b.*

2 Tim. 2. 9. suffer trouble even unto *b.*

Philem. 10. whom I have begotten in my *b.*

Heb. 10. 34. compassion in my *b.*

11. 36. trial of *b.* and imprisonments

13. 3. remember them that are in *b.*

Ex. 13. 3. house of *bondage,* 20. 2.

1. 14. lives bitter with hard *b.*

2. 23. sighed by reason of the *b.*

Rom. 8. 15. received again the spirit of *b.*

1 Cor. 7. 15. brother or sister is not in *b.*

Gal. 4. 24. Sinai which gendereth to *b.*

5. 1. entangled with the yoke of *b.*

Bond woman, Gen. 21. 10. Gal. 4. 23. 30.

BONE of my bone, and flesh of my flesh, Gen. 2. 23. & 29. 14. Judg. 9. 2. 2 Sam. 5. 1. 1 Chron. 11. 11.

Ex. 12. 46. not break a *b.* of it

John 19. 36. *b.* of him shall not be broken

Job 10. 11. fenced me with *bones* and sinews

Ps. 51. 8. *b.* thou hast broken may rejoice

Eccl. 11. 5. how the *b.* grow in the

Matt. 23. 27. full of dead men's *b.*

His bones, Ps. 34. 20. Eph. 5. 30. Job. 20. 11. Ezek. 30. 27. Prov. 12. 4.

Ps. 6. 2. *my bones* are vexed

22. 14. all—are out of joint

31. 10.—are consumed

32. 3.—waxed old through my roaring

35. 10. all—shall say, Lord who is like

38. 3. there is no rest—

102. 3.—are burnt as an hearth

5.—cleave to my skin

BOOK, Gen. 5. 1. Esther 6. 1..

Ex. 32. 32. blot me out of thy *b.*

Job 19. 23. O that they were printed in a *b.*

31. 35. mine adversary had written a *b.*

Ps. 40. 7. in the volume of the *b.* Heb. 10. 7.

56. 8. my tears, are they not in thy *b.*

139. 16. in thy *b.* all my members are written

Book of life, Phil. 4. 3. Rev. 3. 5. & 13. 8. & 17. 8. & 20. 12, 15. & 21. 27.

Books, Eccl. 12. 12. Dan. 7. 10. & 9. 2. John 21. 25. 2 Tim. 4. 13.

BOOTHS, Lev. 23. 42. Neh. 8. 14.

BORDER, Mark 6. 56.

BORN to trouble, Job 5. 7.

Job 14. 1. *b.* of a woman, 15. 14.

Matt. 11. 11. Luke 7. 28.

Ps. 58. 3. the wicked go astray as soon as they are *b.*

87. 4. this man was *b.* there, 6.

5. this and that man was *b.* in her

Prov. 17. 17. a brother is *b.* for adversity

Eccl. 3. 2. a time to be *b.* and a time to die

Isa. 9. 6. unto us a child is *b.* a son is

66. 8. shall a nation be *b.* at once

Jer. 15. 10. *borne* me a man of strife

Matt. 11. 11. among them that are *b.* of women

Matt. 26. 24. better if he had not been *b.*

John 5. 4. can a man be *b.* when he is

5. *b.* of water and of the Spirit

6. *b.* of flesh is flesh; *b.* of Spirit is

Rom. 9. 11. children being not yet *b.*

1 Cor. 15. 8. one *b.* out of due time

Gal. 4. 23. *b.* after the flesh, 29.

1 Pet. 2. 2. as new *b.* babes desire sincere milk of

John 3. 3, 5, 7. *b.* again

John 1. 13. *born of God,* 1 John 3. 9.

BORROW, Deut. 15. 6.

Ex. 22. 14. *b.* aught of his neighbour, 3. 22. & 11. 2. & 12. 35.

Matt. 5. 42. would *b.* of thee turn not

Ps. 37. 21. the wicked *borroweth* and payeth not

Prov. 22. 7. *borrower* is servant to the lender

Isa. 24. 2. as with the lender so with *b.*

BOSOM, Gen. 16. 5. Ez. 4. 6.

Num. 11. 12. carry them in *b.* as a

Deut. 13. 6. wife of thy *b.* 28. 54, 56.

Ps. 35. 13. prayer returned into my own *b.*

74. 11. pluck thy hand out of thy *b.*

Prov. 5. 20. why embrace the *b.* of a

6. 27. take fire in his *b.* and not be burnt

17. 23. gift out of *b.* to pervert, 21. 14.

19. 24. hideth his hands in his *b.* 26. 15.

Eccl. 7. 9. anger resteth in the *b.* of fools

Isa. 40. 11. carry them in his *b.*

65. 6, 7. recompense into their *b.* Ps. 79. 12. Jer. 32. 18.

Mic. 7. 5. her that lieth in thy *b.*

Luke 6. 38. shall men give into your *b.*

16. 22. carried into Abraham's *b.* 23.

John 1. 18. who is in the *b.*

13. 23. leaning on Jesus's *b.*

BOTH, Gen. 2. 25. & 3. 7.

Zech. 6. 13. counsel of peace between *b.*

Eph. 2. 14. our peace made *b.* one

16. that might reconcile *b.* to God

18. we *b.* have access by one spirit

BOTTLE, Gen. 21. 14, 15, 19.

Ps. 56. 8. put my tears into thy *b.*

119. 83. I am like a *b.* in the smoke

Jer. 13. 12. every *b.* filled with wine

Job. 38. 37. who can stay *bottles* of heaven

Matt. 9. 17. new wine into old *b.*

Mark 2. 22. new wine into new *b.* Matt. 9. 17.

BOUGHT, Gen. 17. 12, 13.

Deut. 32. 6. he thy father that *b.* thee

Matt. 13. 46. sold all and *b.* it.

1 Cor. 6. 20. *b.* with a price, 7. 23.

2 Pet. 2. 1. denying the Lord that *b.* them

BOUND Isaac, Gen. 22. 9.

Job. 36. 8. if they be *b.* in fetters

Ps. 107. 10. being *b.* in affliction

Prov. 22. 15. foolishness *b.* in heart

Isa. 61. 1. opening the prison to them that are *b.*

Matt. 16. 19. whatsoever ye bind on earth shall be *b.* in heaven, 18. 18.

Acts 20. 22. I go *b.* in the spirit

21. 13. ready not to be *b.* only, but

Rom. 7. 2. wife is *b.* to her husband, 1 Cor. 7. 39.

1 Cor. 7. 27. art thou *b.* to a wife, seek not

2 Tim. 2. 9. the word of God is not *b.*

Heb. 13 3. in bonds as *b.* with them

Isa. 1. 6. closed nor *bound up*

Ezek. 30. 21. not—to be healed

34. 4. neither have ye *b.* the broken

Hos. 13. 12. iniquity of Ephraim is—

BOUNTY, 1 Kings 10. 13.

Prov. 22. 9. *bountiful* eye be blessed

Ps. 13. 6. dealt *bountifully* with me, 116. 7. & 119. 17. & 132. 7.

2 Cor. 9. 6. he that sows *b.* shall reap *b.*

BOW in the clouds, Gen. 9. 13.

Gen. 49. 24. his *b.* abode in strength

Josh. 24. 12. not with sword nor *b.*

2 Sam. 1. 18. teach children use of *b.*

Ps. 7. 12. he hath bent his *b.* and made

11. 2. lo, wicked bend their *b.*

44. 6. I will not trust in my *b.*

78. 57. turned aside like a deceitful *b.*

Jer. 9. 3. bend tongue like a *b.* for lies

Lam. 2. 4. bent *b.* like an enemy

3. 12. bent his *b.* and set me as a

Hos. 1. 5. break the *b.* of Israel

17. 1. will not save them by *b.*

7. 16. turned like a deceitful *b.*

1 Sam. 2. 4. Ps. 37. 15. bows, & 64. 3. & 78. 9. Jer. 51. 56.

Bow down thine ear, 2 Kings 19. 16. Ps. 31. 2. & 86. 1. Prov. 22. 17.

Job 31. 10. let others—upon her

Ps. 95. 6. let us—and worship

Gen. 23. 12. Abraham *bowed down* himself before the people, 27. 29.

Judg. 7. 5, 6.—on their knees to drink

Ps. 38. 6. I am—greatly, I go mourning all the day long

44. 25. soul is—to the dust, 57. 6.

245. 14. raiseth up all that be—146.8.

Isa. 2. 11. haughtiness of men—17.

BOWELS did yearn, Gen. 43. 30.

1 Kings 3. 26. 2 Chron. 21. 15, 18.

Ps. 71. 6. took me out of my mother's *b.*

Isa. 63. 15. where is the sounding of thy *b.*

Jer. 4. 19. my *b.* my *b.* I am pained

31. 20. my *b.* are troubled for him

Lam. 120. & 2. 11. Song 5. 4.

Acts 1. 18. all his *b.* gushed out

2 Cor. 6. 12. straitened in your *b.*

Phil. 1. 8. I long after you in the *b.* of Christ

2. 1. if any comfort, if any *b.* and

Col. 3. 12. put on *b.* of mercies

Phil. 7. *b.* of the saints are refreshed

20. refresh my *b.* in the Lord

1 John 3. 17. shutteth up *b.* of compassion

BOWL, Num. 7. 85. Eccl. 12. 6.

Zech. 4. 2, 3. & 9. 15. & 14. 20.

BRAKE the tables, Ex. 32. 19. & 34. 1. Deut. 9. 17. & 10. 2.

Judg. 16. 12. Samson *b.* the new ropes

1 Sam. 4. 18. Eli his neck and died

1 Kings 19. 11. wind *b.* in pieces the rocks

2 Kings 11. 18. *b.* Baal's image, 10. 27.

18. 4. *b.* the images and brazen serpent

23. 14. *b.* in pieces the images, 2 Chron. 31. 1.

Job 29. 17. *b.* the jaws of the wicked

Ps. 76. 3. *b.* the arrows of the bow

105. 16. *b.* the whole staff of bread

107. 14. *b.* their bands in sunder

Jer. 31. 32, my covenant they *b.* Ezek. 17. 16.

Dan. 2. 1. his sleep *b.* from him

34. stone *b.* them to pieces, 45.

6. 24. *b.* all their bones to pieces

Matt. 14. 19. blessed, and *b.* and gave, 15. 36. Mark 6. 41. & 8. 6.

Luke 9. 16. & 22. 19. 1 Cor. 11. 24.

Mark 14. 3. *b.* box and poured the

Brake down images—altars of Baal, 2 Kings 10. 27. & 11. 18. 2 Chron. 14. 3. & 23. 17.—wall of Jerusalem, 2 Kings 14. 13. & 25. 10. 2 Chron. 25. 23. Jer. 39. 8. & 52. 14.—houses of Sodomites—high places—altars—altar of Bethel, 2 Kings 23. 7.

BRAMBLE, Judg. 9. 14.

BRANCH, with clusters of grapes, Num. 13. 23. Isa. 17. 9. & 18. 5.

Job 15. 32. his *b.* shall not be green

18. 16. his *b.* shall not be cut off

Ps. 80. 15. *b.* thou madest strong for

Prov. 11. 28. the righteous flourish as a *b.*

Isa. 4. 2. *b.* of the Lord be beautiful

9. 14. cut off *b.* and root, 19. 15.

11. 1. *b.* shall grow out of his roots

14. 19. cast out like an abominable *b.*

25. 5. *b.* of terrible ones brought low

60. 21. *b.* of my planting, 61. 3.

Jer. 23. 5. unto David a righteous *b.*

33. 15. cause *b.* of righteous to grow

Ezek. 8. 17. they put *b.* to their nose

Zech. 3. 8. bring forth my servant *b.*

6. 12. behold man whose name is *b.*

Mal. 4. 1. leave neither root nor *b.*

Matt. 24. 32. when his *b.* is yet tender

John 15. 2. every *b.* in me that bear not

4. *b.* cannot bear fruit of itself

6. cast forth as *b.* and is withered

Lev. 23. 40. take *branches* of palmtrees Neh. 8. 15. John 12. 13.

Job 15. 30. flame shall dry up his *b.*

Ps. 86. 11. sent his *b.* unto the river

104. 12. fowls sing among the *b.*

Isa. 16. 8. her *b.* are stretched out

17. 6. four or five in outmost fruitful *b.*

18. 5. shall take and cut down *b.* 27. 10.

Jer. 11. 16. the *b.* of it are broken, Ezek. 17. 6, 7. & 19. 10. 14.

Dan. 4. 14. hew down tree, cut off *b.*

Hos. 14. 6. his *b.* shall spread as olive

Zech. 4. 12. what are these two olive *b.*

John 15. 5. I am the vine, ye are the *b.*

Rom. 11. 6. if root be holy, so are *b.*

17. if some of the *b.* be broken off

18. boast not against the *b.*

21. God spared not natural *b.* 24.

BRAND, Judges 15. 5.

BRASS, Gen. 4. 22. Dan. 5. 4.

Num. 21. 9. made serpent of *b.* beheld

Deut. 8. 9. out of whose hill mayest dig *b.*

28. 23. heaven over thy head shall be *b.*

Job 6. 12. is my strength of *b.*—flesh *b.*

41. 27. he esteemeth *b.* as rotten wood

107. 16. broken the gates of *b.*

Isa. 48. 4. thy neck iron, and brow *b.*

60. 17. for wood I will bring *b.*

Dan. 2. 32. belly and thighs of *b.*

Zech. 6. 1. were mountains of *b.*

1 Cor. 13. 1. become as sounding *b.*

Rev. 1. 15. feet like fine *b.* 2. 18.

Brazen, Num. 16. 39. 2 Kings 18. 4. 2 Chron. 6. 13. Jer. 1. 18. & 15. 20. & 52. 20. Mark 7. 4.

BRAWLER, 1 Tim. 3. 3.

Prov. 21. 9. *brawling* woman

BRAY, Job 6. 5. Prov. 27. 22.

BREACH be upon thee, Gen. 38. 29.

Num. 14. 34. know my *b.* of promise

Judg. 21. 15. Lord made *b.* in tribes

2 Sam. 6. 8. Lord made *b.* on Uzza, 1 Chron. 13. 11. & 15. 13.

Job 16. 14. breaketh me with *b.* upon *b.*

Ps. 106. 23. Moses stood in the *b.*

Isa. 30. 13. this iniquity shall be as *b.*

26. the Lord bindeth up *b.* of his

58. 12. the repairer of the *b.*

Lam. 2. 13. thy *b.* is great like sea
Ps. 60. 2. heal *breaches* thereof
BREAD shall be fat, Gen. 49. 20.
Ex. 16. 4. I will rain *b.* from heaven
23. 25. he will bless thy *b.* and water
Lev. 21. 6. *b.* of their God they offer
Num. 14. 9. they are *b.* for us
21. 5. soul loatheth this light *b.*
Deut. 8. 3. not live by *b.* only
Ruth 1. 6. visited his people giving *b.*
1 Sam. 2. 5. hired themselves for *b.*
25. 11. take my *b.* and my water
1 Kings 18. 4. fed them with *b.* and water
Neh. 5. 14. not eaten *b.* of governor
9. 15. gavest them *b.* from heaven
Ps. 37. 25. his seed begging *b.*
18. 20. can he give *b.* also
Ps. 80. 5. feedest them with *b.* of tears
102. 9. I have eaten ashes like *b.*
104. 15. which strengthenth man's
132. 15. satisfy her poor with *b.*
Prov. 9. 17. *b.* eaten in secret is pleasant
29. 17. *b.* of deceit is sweet
22. 9. giveth of his *b.* to the poor
31. 27. she eateth not *b.* of idleness
Eccl. 9. 11. nor yet *b.* to the wise
11. 1. cast thy *b.* upon the waters
Isa. 3. 1. whole stay of *b.* 7.
30. 20. Lord give you bread of adversity
33. 16. *b.* shall be given him
55. 2. spend money for that is not *b.*
10. give seed to sower, *b.* to eater
58. 7. deal thy *b.* to the hungry
Lam. 4. 4. the young children ask *b.*
Ezek. 18. 7. have given *b.* to hungry
Hos. 2. 5. give me my *b.* and water
9. 4. sacrifices be as *b.* of mourners
Amos 4. 6. want of *b.* in all your places
Mal. 1. 7. ye offer polluted *b.* on mine
Matt. 4. 3. these stones be made *b.*
4. not live by *b.* alone, Luke 4. 4.
6. 11. this day our daily *b.*
7. 9. son ask *b.* will he give a stone
15. 26. meet to take the children's *b.*
16. 5. forgotten to take *b.* 11. 12.
26. 26. took *b.* and blessed it
Mark 8. 4. satisfy these men with *b.*
Luke 7. 33. neither eating *b.* nor drinking wine
15. 17. servants have *b.* enough
24. 35. known in breaking of *b.*
John 6. 32. Moses gave you not that *b.*
33. the *b.* of God is he that cometh
34. evermore give us this *b.*
35. I am *b.* of life, 48 true *b.* 32.
41. I am the *b.* which came down
50. this is the *b.* that cometh down
13. 18. he that eateth *b.* with me
Acts 2. 42. breaking *b.* and in prayer
46. breaking *b.* from house to house
20. 7. came together to break *b.*
27. 35. he took *b.* and gave thanks
1 Cor. 10. 16. *b.* we break is it not
17. we being many are one *b.* all partakers of that one *b.*
11. 23. night he was betrayed took *b.*
26. as often as ye eat this *b.* 27.
2 Cor. 9. 10. minister *b.* for your food
Deut. 16. 3. *bread of affliction*, 2 Chron. 18. 26. Isa. 30. 20.
Gen. 3. 19. *shall eat bread*, 28. 20.
Prov. 25. 21. Eccl. 9. 7. Mark 7. 5.
Luke 14. 15. 1 Cor. 11. 26. 2 Thess. 3. 12.
1 Sam. 2. 36. *piece of bread.* Prov. 6.
26. Jer. 37. 21. Ezek. 13. 19.
Lev. 26. 26. *break staff of bread*, Ps. 105. 6. Ezek. 4. 16. & 5. 16.
Gen. 19. 3. *unleavened bread.* Ex. 12. 8. Mark 14. 12. Luke 22. 7. Acts 12. 3. & 20. 6. 1 Cor. 5. 8.
BREAK, Gen. 19. 9. Ex. 34. 13.
Judg. 7. 19. *b.* the pitchers that were
9. 53. and all to *b.* his skull
Ezra 9. 14. should we again *b.* thy commandments
Ps. 2. 3. let us *b.* their bands asunder

9. shalt *b.* them with a rod of iron
10. 15. *b.* thou arm of the wicked
58. 6. *b.* their teeth in their mouth
89. 31. if they *b.* my statutes
34. my covenant will I not *b.* nor
141. 5. oil which shall not *b.* head
Song 2. 17. till the day *b.* and the shadows 4. 6.
Isa. 42. 3. bruised reed not *b.* Matt. 12. 20.
58. 6. that ye *b.* every yoke
Jer. 14. 21. *b.* not covenant with us
15. 12. shall iron *b.* northern iron
33. 20. can *b.* my covenant of day
Ezek. 4. 16. *b.* the staff of bread, 5. 16. & 14. 13. Ps. 105. 16.
17. 15. shall he *b.* covenant and be delivered
Hos. 1. 5. *b.* the bow of Israel, 2. 18.
Zech. 11. 10. might *b.* my covenant
14. might *b.* the brotherhood
Matt. 5. 19. *b.* one of these least commandments
Acts 21. 13. mean ye to *b.* my heart
1 Cor. 10. 16. bread which we *b.*
Ex. 23. 24. *break down*, Deut. 7. 5.
Ps. 74. 6. Eccl. 3. 3. Jer. 31. 28. & 45. 4. Hos. 10. 2.
Ex. 19. 22, 24. *break forth*, Isa. 55. 8.
Jer. 1. 14. Gal. 4. 27.
Isa. 14. 7. *break forth into singing*, 44. 23. & 49. 13. & 54. 1.
Dan. 4. 27. *break off thy sins by righteousness*
Ex. 22. 6. *break out*, Isa. 35. 6. Hos. 4. 2. Amos 5. 6.
Job 19. 2. *break in pieces*, 34. 24.
Ps. 72. 4. & 94. 5. Isa. 45. 2. Jer. 51. 20, 21, 22. Dan. 2. 40, 44.
Ex. 19. 21, 24. *break through*, and gaze
Matt. 6. 19, 20. where thieves and steal
Jer. 4. 3. *break up* your fallow ground
Hos. 10. 10.
Ps. 74. 13, 14. *breakest* heads of dragons
Gen. 32. 26. let me go, for the day *breaketh*
Job 9. 17. he *b.* with a tempest
16. 14. he *b.* me with breach upon breach
Ps. 29. 5. voice of Lord *b.* the cedars
46. 9. *b.* the bow and cutteth spear
119. 20. my soul *b.* for the longing
Prov. 25. 15. a soft tongue *b.* the bone
Eccl. 10. 8. whoso *b.* a hedge, a serpent shalt bite thee
Jer. 19. 11. as one *b.* a potter's vessel
23. 29. like a hammer that *b.* rocks
Hos. 13. 13. a place of *breaking* forth of children, 1 Chron. 14. 11.
Luke 24. 35. known of them in *b.* bread
Acts 2. 42. *b.* of bread, 46.
Rom. 2. 23. through *b.* the law dishonourest thou
BREASTS, Gen. 49. 25.
Job 21. 24. his *b.* are full of milk
Ps. 22. 9. I was upon my mother's *b.*
Prov. 5. 19. let her *b.* satisfy thee at all times
Song 1. 13. shall lie all night between my *b.*
4. 5. thy *b.* are like two roes, 7. 3.
7. 7. thy *b.* to clusters of grapes, 8.
8. 1. sucked the *b.* of my mother
8. a little sister, and she hath no *b.*
10. I am a wall and my *b.* like towers
Isa. 28. 9. weaned and drawn from *b.*
60. 16. suck the *b.* of kings, 49. 23.
66. 11. satisfied with *b.* of her consolation
Ezek. 16. 7. thy *b.* are fashioned
23. 3. there were their *b.* pressed
8. bruised the *b.* of her virginity
Hos. 2. 2. adulteries from between her *b.*
9. 14. give miscarrying womb and dry *b.*

Joel 2. 16. gather those that suck *b.*
Luke 23. 48. smote *b.* and returned
Rev. 15. 6. their *b.* girded with golden
Ex. 28. 4. *breast-plate*, Rev. 9. 9.
Isa. 59. 17. put on righteousness as *b.*
Eph. 6. 14. *b.* of righteousness
1 Thess. 5. 8. *b.* of faith and love
BREATH of life, Gen. 2. 7. & 6. 17.
& 7. 15, Isa. 2. 22. Hab. 2. 19.
Job 12. 10. in whose hands is *b.* of all
17. 1. my *b.* is corrupt, my days are extinct.
19. 17. my *b.* is strange to my wife
37. 10. by the *b.* of God frost is given
Ps. 33. 6. made by *b.* of his mouth
104. 29. thou takest away their *b.*
146. 4. his *b.* goeth forth, he returneth
150. 6. all that hath *b.* praise Lord
Eccl. 3. 19. they have all one *b.*
Isa. 2. 22. whose *b.* is in his nostrils
11. 4. with *b.* of his lips shall slay the wicked.
42. 5. giveth *b.* unto the people
Lam. 4. 20. the *b.* of our nostrils
Dan. 5. 23. in whose hand thy *b.* is
Acts 17. 25. giveth life and *b.* and all
Ps. 27. 12. *breathe* out cruelty
Ezek. 37. 9. come *b.* upon these slain
John 20. 22. he *breathed* on them
Acts 9. 1. *breathing* out slaughter
BRETHREN, we be, Gen. 13. 8.
Gen. 49. 26. him that was separate from his *b.* Deut. 33. 16.
Deut. 17. 20. be not lifted up above *b.*
33. 9. neither did he acknowledge his *b.*
24. let him be acceptable to his *b.*
1 Chron. 4. 9. more honourable than his *b.*
5. 2. prevailed above his *b.*
Job 6. 15. my *b.* have dealt deceitfully
19. 13. put my *b.* far from me
Ps. 22. 22. declare thy name unto my *b.*
69. 8. I am become a stranger to my *b.*
122. 8. for my *b.* and companions' sakes
133. 1. for *b.* to dwell together in unity
Hos. 13. 15. fruitful among his *b.*
Matt. 23. 8. all ye are *b.* Acts 7. 26.
12. 48. who are my *b.*
25. 40. the least of these my *b.*
28. 10. go tell my *b.* that they go
Mark 10. 29. left house of *b.* Luke 18. 29.
John 7. 5. neither did his *b.* believe in
20. 17. go to my *b.* and say, I ascend
Acts 11. 29. send relief to the *b.*
Rom. 8. 29. first born among many *b.*
9. 3. accursed from Christ for my *b.*
1 Cor. 6. 5. to judge between his *b.*
8. 12. sin against the *b.*
15. 6. seen of above 500 *b.* at once
Gal. 2. 4. false *b.* unawares brought in
1 Tim. 4. 6. put *b.* in remembrance
5. 1. entreat the younger as *b.*
Heb. 2. 11. not ashamed to call them *b.*
17. made like to his *b.*
1 Pet. 1. 22. unfeigned love of the *b.*
3. 8. love as *b.* be pitiful and courteous
1 John 3. 14. because we love the *b.*
16. to lay down our lives for the *b.*
3 John 10. neither doth he receive *b.*
Gen. 27. 29. *thy brethren*, 48. 22.
Deut. 15. 17. 1 Sam. 17. 18. Matt. 12. 47. Mark 3. 32. Luke 8. 20.
Jer. 12. 6.—have dealt treacherously
Rev. 19. 10. I am of—22. 9.
1 Kings 12. 24. *your brethren*, 2 Chron. 30. 7, 9. & 35. 6.
Neh. 4. 14. fight for—your sons and
Isa. 66. 5.—that hated you

Acts 3. 22. raise up of—prophet like unto me, 7. 37. Deut. 18. 15.
Matt. 5. 47. if you salute—only
BRIBES, 1 Sam. 3. 8. Amos 5. 12.
1 Sam. 12. 3. have I received any *b.*
Ps. 26. 10. right hand full of *b.*
Isa. 33. 15. hands from holding *b.*
Job 15. 34. tabernacles of *bribery*
BRICK, Gen. 11. 3. Ex. 1. 14. Isa. 65. 3. & 9. 10.
2 Sam. 12. 31. *brick-kiln*, Jer. 43. 9. Nah. 3. 14.
BRIDE, doth clothe with an ornament, Isa. 49. 18.
Isa. 61. 10. as a *b.* adorneth herself
Jer. 2. 32. can a *b.* forget her attire
Joel 2. 16. go out of her closet
John 3. 29. that hath *b.* is bridegroom
Rev. 21. 2. as a *b.* adorned for her husband
9. I will shew thee *b.* Lamb's wife
22. 17. spirit and *b.* say, come
Matt. 9. 15. *bride-chamber*, Mark 2. 19. Luke 5. 34.
BRIDEGROOM, Joel 2. 16. Ps. 19. 5.
as a *b.* coming out of his chamber
Isa. 61. 10. as a *b.* decketh himself
62. 5. as a *b.* rejoiceth over the bride
Jer. 7. 34. cease the voice of *b.* and bride. 16. 9. Rev. 18. 23.
Matt. 9. 15. as long as the *b.* is with them, Mark 2. 19. Luke 5. 34.
Matt. 25. 1. went forth to meet *b.* 6.
BRIDLE for the ass, Prov. 26. 3.
Ps. 32. 9. mouth held with *b.*
39. I keep my mouth as with a *b.*
Isa. 37. 29. put my *b.* in thy lips, 30.
28. 2 Kings 19. 28. Rev. 14. 20.
Jas. 3. 2. able to *b.* the whole body
1. 26. *bridleth* not his tongue
BRIERS, Judges 8. 7. Isa. 7. 23. & 32. 13. Heb. 6. 8. Mic. 7. 4.
Isa. 5. 6. come up *b.* and thorns
9. 18. wickedness, shall devour *b.* 10. 17.
27. 4. set *b.* against me in battle
55. 13. instead of *b.* shall come up myrtle
Ezek. 2. 6. though *b.* and thorns be
28. 24. no more a pricking *b.* unto
BRIGHTNESS, 2 Sam. 22. 13. Ezek. 1. 4, 27. & 8. 2.
Job 31. 26. beheld moon walking in *b.*
Isa. 62. 1. righteousness to go forth as *b.*
Ezek. 10. 4. full of the *b.* of Lord's glory
Dan. 12. 3. wise shall shine as the *b.* of the firmament
Amos 5. 20. very dark and no *b.* in it
Hab. 3. 4. his *b.* was as the light
Acts 26. 13. a light above *b.* of sun
2 Thess. 2. 8. Lord destroy with *b.* of his coming
Heb. 1. 3. being the *b.* of his glory
BRIMSTONE, Gen. 19. 24. Deut. 29. 23. Job 18. 15. Ps. 11. 6. Isa. 30. 33. Ezek. 38. 22. Luke 17. 29. Rev. 14. 10.
BRING a flood, Gen. 6. 17.
Josh 23. 15. *b.* upon you all the evil
1 Kings 8. 32. to *b.* his way upon his head
Job. 14. 4. who can *b.* a clean thing
33. 30. to *b.* back his soul from pit
Ps. 60. 9. who *b.* me into strong city
68. 29. kings shall *b.* presents to thee
72. 10. Isa. 60. 9.
72. 3. mountains *b.* peace to people
94. 23. *b.* on them their own iniquity
Eccl. 11. 9. God will *b.* thee into judgment, 12. 14. Job. 14. 4.
Song 8. 2. *b.* thee to my mother's house
Isa. 1. 13. *b.* no more vain oblations
43. 5. I will *b.* thy seed from east
6. *b.* my sons from afar, 60. 9.
46. 13. I *b.* near my righteousness

66. 9. shall I *b.* to the birth and not cause

Hos. 2. 14. allure and *b.* her into the wilderness

Zeph. 3. 5. every morning *b.* his judgment

Luke 2. 10. I *b.* you good tidings

8. 14. *b.* no fruit to perfection

John 14. 26. *b.* all things to remembrance

Acts 5. 28. intend to *b.* this man's blood

1 Cor. 1. 28. *b.* to nought things that are

4. 5. *b.* to light the hidden things of darkness

1 Thess. 4. 14. God will *b.* with him

1 Pet. 3. 18. that he might *b.* us to God

Gen. 1. 11. *bring forth*, 3. 16. Matt. 1. 21. Job 39. 1. Ex. 3. 10.

2 Kings 19. 3. there is not strength to—

Job 15. 35. conceive mischief and—vanity

Ps. 37. 6. he shall—thy righteousness

92. 14. still—fruit in old age

Prov. 27. 1. what a day may—

Isa. 41. 21.—your strong reasons

42. 1. judgment to the Gentiles, 4.

59. 4.—conceive mischief and—iniquity

66. 8. made to—in one day

Zeph. 2. 2. before the decree—

Mark 4. 20.—fruit some thirtyfold

Luke 3. 8.—fruits worthy of repentance

8. 15.—fruit with patience

John 15. 2. that it may—more fruit

Ps. 1. 3. *bringeth forth* fruit in its season

Hos. 10. 1.—fruit to himself

Matt. 3. 10. *b.* not forth good fruit, 7. 19. & 12. 35. Luke 6. 43.

John 12. 24. if it die it—much fruit

James 1. 15.—sin—death

BROAD, Num. 16. 38.

Job 36. 16. out of strait into *b.* place

Ps. 119. 96. thy commandment is exceeding *b.*

Isa. 33. 21. Lord a place of *b.* rivers

Matt. 7. 13. *b.* is way to destruction

BROKEN my covenant, Gen. 17. 14. Ps. 55. 20. Isa. 24. 5. & 33. 8. & 36. 6. Jer. 11. 10. & 33. 21. Ezek. 44. 7.

Ps. 34. 18. nigh to them of *b.* heart

44. 19. sore *b.* us in place of dragons

51. 8. bones which thou hast *b.* rejoice

17. *b.* spirit, *b.* and contrite heart

147. 3. healeth the *b.* in heart

Isa. 61. 1. to bind up the *b.* hearted

Jer. 2. 13. hewed out *b.* cisterns

5. 5. altogether *b.* the yoke

Dan. 2. 42. partly strong and partly *b.*

Hos. 5. 11. Ephraim is *b.* in judgment

Matt. 21. 44. shall fall on stone, shall be *b.*

John 10. 35. Scripture cannot be *b.*

BROOK, Num. 15. 23.

Ps. 110. 7. drink of the *b.* in the way

Job 20. 17. the *b.* of honey and butter

Isa. 10. 6. *b.* of defence shall be emptied

BROTHER, born for adversity, Prov. 17. 17.

Prov. 18. 19. a *b.* offended is harder to be won

24. is a friend that sticketh closer than a *b.*

27. 10. neighbour near, than *b.* far off

Jer. 9. 4. trust not in any *b.* for every *b.*

Matt. 10. 21. *b.* shall deliver up *b.* to death, Mark 13. 12. Mic. 7. 2.

Cor. 5. 11. *b.* a fornicator

6. 6. but *b.* goeth to law with *b.*

7. 15. *b.* or sister is not in bondage

8. 11. shall thy weak *b.* perish

2 Thess. 3. 15. admonish him as a *b.*

Jas. 1. 9. let *b.* of low degree rejoice

Ps. 35. 14. *my brother*, Song 8. 13. Matt. 12. 50. & 18. 21. 1 Cor. 8. 13.

Ps. 50. 20. *thy brother*, Matt. 5. 23. Gen. 45. 4. *your brother*, Rev. 1. 9.

Zech. 11. 14. *brotherhood*, 1 Pet. 2. 17.

Amos 1. 9. remember not *brotherly* covenant

Rom. 12. 10. kindly affectioned with *b.*

1 Thess. 4. 9. as touching *b.* love, ye

Heb. 13. 1. let *b.* love continue

2 Pet. 1. 7. to Godliness *b.* kindness

BROUGHT, 2 Sam. 7. 18.

Neh. 4. 15. God *b.* their counsel to nought. 9. 33. thou art just in all that is *b.* on us

Ps. 45. 14. be *b.* unto the king in raiment

79. 8. we are *b.* very low

106. 43. *b.* low for their iniquities

107. 39. *b.* low through oppression

116. 6. I was *b.* low and he helped

Isa. 1. 2. nourished and *b.* up children

Matt. 10. 18. *b.* before governors, Mark 13. 9. Luke 12. 12.

1 Cor. 6. 12. not be *b.* under power

Gal. 2. 4. false brethren, unawares *b.* in

1 Tim. 6. 7. *b.* nothing into this world

Ps. 107. 12. *brought down*, Matt. 11. 23.

Deut. 33. 14. *brought forth*, Ps. 18. 19. Isa. 66. 7. James 5. 18.

BRUISE thy head, Gen. 3. 15.

Isa. 53. 10. it pleased Lord to *b.* him

Rom. 16. 20. God of peace shall *b.* Satan

Isa. 42. 3. *bruised* reed not break, Matt. 12. 20.

53. 5. he was *b.* for our iniquities

Ezek. 23. 3, 21. *b.* breasts, *b.* teats

BRUIT, report, Jer. 10. 22.

BRUTISH, Ps. 92. 6.

Ps. 94. 8. understand, ye *b.* among people

Prov. 30. 2. I am more *b.* than any man

Jer. 10. 14. man is *b.* in his knowledge, 51. 17.

BUCKLER to all that trust, Ps. 18. 30.

Ps. 18. 2. my *b.* and horn of my salvation.

91. 4. his truth shall be thy *b.*

Prov. 2. 7. a *b.* to them that walk

BUFFETED, 2 Cor. 12. 7. Matt. 26. 67. 1 Cor. 4. 11. 1 Pet. 2. 20.

BUILD walls of Jerusalem, Ps. 51. 18.

Ps. 102. 16. Lord shall *b.* up Zion

127. 1. except the Lord *b.* the city

147. 2. Lord doth *b.* up Jerusalem

Eccl. 3. 3. a time to *b.* up

Mic. 3. 10. *b.* up Zion with blood

Acts 20. 32. able to *b.* you up

Job 22. 23. if thou return shalt be *built* up

Ps. 89. 2. mercy shall be *b.* up for ever

Matt. 7. 24. *b.* his house on a rock

Eph. 2. 20. ye are *b.* on foundation of

Col. 2. 7. rooted and *b.* up in him

Heb. 3. 4. he that *b.* all things is God

1 Pet. 2. 5. *b.* up a spiritual house

Heb. 11. 10. *builder* and maker is God

Ps. 118. 22. stone which the *b.* refused, Matt. 21. 42. Mark 12. 10. Luke 20. 17. Acts 4. 11. 1 Pet. 2. 7.

2 Cor. 3. 10. *master builder*

Josh 6. 26. cursed that *buildeth* this city

Prov. 14. 1. every wise woman *b.* her

Jer. 22. 13. wo to him that *b.* house

Amos 9. 6. *b.* his stories in heaven

Hab. 2. 12. *b.* a town with blood

1 Cor. 3. 10. another *b.* thereon

9. ye are God's *building*

2 Cor. 5. 1. we have a *b.* of God

Eph. 2. 21. all the *b.* fitly framed

Heb. 9. 11. tabernacles not of this *b.*

Jude 20. *b.* up yourselves in faith

BULLS compassed me, Ps. 22. 12.

Ps. 50. 13. will I eat the flesh of *b.*

68. 30. rebuke the multitude of *b.*

Heb. 9. 13. if blood of *b.* and goats

10. 4. blood of *b.* cannot take away sin

Ps. 69. 31. than *bullock* with horns

Jer. 31. 18. as a *b.* unaccustomed to the yoke

Ps. 51. 19. offer *b.* on thy altar

Isa. 1. 11. delight not in blood of *b.*

BULRUSHES, Ex. 2. 3.

BULWARKS, Ps. 48. 13. Isa. 26.1.

BUNDLE, Gen. 42. 35. Acts 28. 3.

1 Sam. 25. 29. bound in the *b.* of

Song 1. 13. *b.* of myrrh is my well beloved

Matt. 13. 30. bind tares in *bundles* to burn

BURDEN, 2 Kings 5. 17.

Ex. 18. 22. shall bear the *b.* with thee Num. 11. 17.

23. 5. ass lying under his *b.*

Deut. 1. 12. how can I bear your *b.*

2 Sam. 15. 33. thou shalt be a *b.* unto

19. 35. servant be to my lord

2 Kings 5. 17. two mules *b.* of earth

9. 25. Lord laid this *b.* on him

2 Chron. 35. 3. not be *b.* on shoulders

Neh. 13. 19. shall be no *b.* brought in on Sabbath day, Jer. 17. 21.

Job 7. 20. I am a *b.* to myself

Ps. 38. 4. as a *b.* too heavy for me

55. 22. cast thy *b.* upon the Lord

81. 6. I removed his shoulder from *b.*

Eccl. 12. 5. grasshopper shall be a *b.*

Isa. 9. 4. broken the yoke of his *b.*

10. 27. *b.* taken from thy shoulder

30. 27. the *b.* thereof is heavy

Zeph. 3. 18. reproach of it was a *b.*

Zech. 12. 3. all that *b.* themselves with

Matt. 11. 30. my yoke is easy, my *b.* light

20. 12. borne the *b.* and heat of day

Acts 15. 28. no greater *b.* than necessary

2 Cor. 12. 16. I did not *b.* you

Gal. 6. 5. every man bears his own *b.*

Rev. 2. 24. put on you no other *b.*

Isa. 13. 1. *b.* threatening of heavy judgments, 14. 28. Ezek. 12. 10. Nah. 1. 1. Hab. 1. 1. Zech. 9. 1. Mal. 1. 1. *b.* of the word

2 Cor. 5. 4. we groan being *burdened*

8. 13. not others eased and you *b.*

Gen. 49. 14. *burdens*, Ex. 1. 11.

Isa. 58. 6. to undo the heavy *b.*

Lam. 2. 14. seen for the false *b.*

Matt. 23. 4. bind heavy *b.* Luke 11. 46.

Gal. 6. 2. bear one another's *b.*

Zech. 12. 3. *burdensome*, 2 Cor. 11. 9. & 12. 13, 14. 1 Thess. 2. 6.

BURN upon altar, Ex. 29, 13. Lev. 1. 9, 15. & 2. 2. & 3. 5, 11, 16.

Gen. 44. 18. let not thine anger *b.*

Deut. 32. 22. shall *b.* to lowest hell

Isa. 27. 4. go through them and *b.*

Mal. 4. 1. day cometh shall *b.* as an oven

Luke 3. 17. chaff he will *b.* with unquenchable fire

24. 32. did not our heart *b.* within

1 Cor. 7. 9. it is better to marry than *b.*

2 Cor. 11. 29. who is offended and I *b.* not

Rev. 17. 6. eat her flesh and *b.* her with fire

Ex. 3. 2. the bush *burned* with fire

Deut. 9. 15. and mount *b.* with fire

Ps. 39. 3. while I was musing fire *b.*

1 Cor. 3. 15. if any man's work shall be *b.*

13. 3. though I give my body to *b.*

12. 18. not come to mount that *b.*

Ps. 46. 9. *burneth* the chariot in fire

83. 14. as fire *b.* the wood

97. 3. *b.* up his enemies round about

Isa. 9. 18. wickedness *b.* as the fire

Rev. 21. 8. lake which *b.* with fire

Gen. 15. 17. *burning* lamp that passed between those pieces.

Jer. 20. 9. his word was as *b.* fire

Hab. 3. 5. *b.* coals went forth at his feet

Luke 12. 35. loins girded and your lights *b.*

John 5. 35. a *b.* and a shining light

Ex. 21. 25. *b.* for *b.* wound for wound

Deut. 28. 22. smite thee with extreme *b.*

29. 23. land is brimstone, and salt, *b.*

Isa. 3. 24. *b.* instead of beauty

4. 4. by the spirit of judgment and *b.*

Amos 4. 11. fire-brand plucked out of the *b.*

Isa. 33. 14. dwell with everlasting *b.*

Gen. 8. 20. *burnt-offerings*, Deut. 12. 6. 1 Sam. 15. 22. Ps. 50. 8. Isa. 1. 11. Jer. 6. 20. & 7. 21. 22.

Hos. 6. 6. knowledge of God more than—

Mark 12. 33. more than all whole—

Heb. 10. 6. in—for sin and sacrifices

Ps. 74. 8. *burnt* up all synagogues

106. 18. the flame—the wicked

Isa. 64. 11. our beautiful house is—

Matt. 22. 7. destroyed and—their city

2 Pet. 3. 10. works that are therein be—

BURST thy bands, Jer. 2. 20.

Jer. 5. 5. broken the yoke and *b.* bands, 30. 8.

Prov. 3. 10. presses *b.* out with new wine

Mark 2. 22. new wine doth *b.* the bottles, Luke 5. 37. Job 32. 19.

Acts 1. 18. *b.* asunder in the midst

BURY my dead out of my sight, Gen. 23. 24.

Gen. 49. 29. *b.* me with my fathers

Ps. 79. 3. there was none to *b.* them

Matt. 8. 21. first to go and *b.* my father

22. let the dead *b.* their dead, Luke 9. 60.

Rom. 6. 4. *buried* with him by baptism into death, Col. 2. 12.

1 Cor. 15. 4. he was *b.* and rose again

Gen. 23. 4. a possession of a *burying* place

47. 30. *b.* me in the *b.* place

Mark 14. 8. anoint my body to the *b.*

John 12. 7. against the day of my *b.*

2 Chron. 26. 23. *burial*, Acts 8. 2.

Eccl. 6. 3. that he have no *b.*

Isa. 14. 20. not joined with them in *b.*

Jer. 22. 19. buried with *b.* of an ass

Matt. 26. 12. she did it for my *b.*

BUSH is not burnt, Ex. 3. 2, 3, 4. Acts 7. 30. Mark 12. 26.

Deut. 33. 16. good will of him that dwelt in *b.*

BUSHEL, Matt. 5. 15. Luke 11. 33.

BUSHY and black, Song 5. 11.

BUSINESS, Gen. 39. 11. Rom. 16. 2.

Ps. 107. 23. do *b.* in great waters

Prov. 22. 29. seest a man diligent in *b.*

Eccl. 5. 3. dream through multitude of *b.*

Luke 2. 49. must be about Father's *b.*

Acts 6. 3. we may appoint over this *b.*

Rom. 12. 11. not slothful in *b.*

1 Thes. 4. 11. study to do your own *b.*

BUTTER and milk, Gen. 18. Deut. 32. 14. Judg. 5. 25. 2 Sam. 17. 29.

Job 20. 17. brooks of honey and *b.*

25. 6. I have washed my steps with *b.*

Ps. 55. 21. words were smoother than *b.*

Isa. 7. 15. *b.* and honey shall he eat, 22.

BUY the truth, Prov. 23. 23.

Isa. 55. 1. *b.* and eat, yea, *b.* wine

1 Cor. 7. 30. they that *b.* as possessed not

James 4. 13. *b.* and sell, and get gain

Rev. 3. 18. I counsel thee, *b.* gold tried

13. 17. that no man might *b.* or sell

Prov. 20. 14. it is nought saith *buyer*

Isa. 24. 2. as with *b.* so with seller

Ezek. 7. 12. let no *b.* rejoice

Prov. 31. 16. considereth a field and *buyeth* it

Matt. 13. 44. selleth all and *b.* field

Rev. 18. 11. no man *b.* her merchandise

BY and by, Matt. 13. 21. Mark 6. 25. Luke 17. 7. and 21. 9.

By-word among all nations, Deut. 28. 37.

1 Kings 9. 7. Israel shall be a—

2 Chron. 7. 20. make this house a—

Job 17. 6. made a—of the people

30. 9. I am their song and their—

Ps. 44. 14. makest us a—among the heathen

C

CAGE, 5. 27. Rev. 18. 2.

CAIN and Abel, Gen. 4. 1-17. Heb. 11. 4. & 12. 24. Jude 11.

CAKE of bread tumbled into host, Judg. 7. 13.

1 Kings 17. 12. I have not a *c.* but meal

Hos. 7. 8. Ephraim is a *c.* not turned

Cakes, Gen. 18. 6. Judg. 6. 19.

Jer. 7. 18. make *c.* to queen of heaven

44. 19. make *c.* to worship her

CALAMITY at hand, Deut. 32. 35.

Job 6. 2. my *c.* laid in the balance

30. 13. they set forward my *c.*

Ps. 18. 18. prevented me in the day of my *c.*

141. 5. my prayer shall be in their *c.*

Prov. 1. 26. I will laugh at your *c.*

6. 15. his *c.* shall come suddenly

19. 13. a foolish son is the *c.* of his father

27. 10. into brother's house in the day of thy *c.*

Jer. 18. 17. the face in day of their *c.*

46. 21. day of thy *c.* is come, 48. 16. Ezek. 35. 5. Obad. 13.

Ps. 57. 1. till these *calamities* be overpast

Prov. 17. 5. that is glad at *c.* shall not prosper

24. 22. their *c.* shall rise suddenly

CALDRON, 1 Sam. 2. 14. Job 41. 20. Ezek. 11. 3. Mic. 3. 3.

CALEB and Joshua, Num. 13. 30. & 14. 6, 24, 38. & 26. 65.

CALF, Gen. 18. 7. Job 21. 10. Ps. 29. 6. Isa. 27. 10. Rev. 4. 7.

Ex. 32. 4. made a molten *c.* 20. Deut. 9. 16. Neh. 9. 18. Ps. 106. 19.

Isa. 11. 16. *c.* and young lion lie together

Jer. 34. 18. when they cut the *c.* in twain

Hos. 8. 5. thy *c.* O Samaria, hast cast

6. the *c.* of Samaria shall be broken

Luke 15. 23. bring hither the fatted *c.*

27. thou hast killed the fatted *c.* 30.

CALL, Gen. 2. 19.

Gen. 24. 57. we will *c.* the damsel and

30. 13. daughters will *c.* me blessed

Deut. 4. 7. all that we *c.* upon him

26. 1. *c.* heaven and earth to witness, 30. 19.

1 Sam. 3. 6. here am I, for thou didst *c.* me

1 Kings 8. 52. in all they *c.* to thee

17. 18. to *c.* my sin to remembrance

1 Chron. 16. 8. *c.* upon his name

Job 5. 1. *c.* if there be any to answer, 14. 15.

13. 22. *c.* thou and I will answer

27. 10. will he always *c.* upon God

Ps. 4. 1. hear me when I *c.* O God

14. 4. they *c.* not upon the Lord, 53. 4.

49. 11. *c.* lands after their names

72. 17. all nations shall *c.* him blessed

77. 6. I *c.* to remembrance my song in the night

80. 18. we will *c.* on thy name

86. 5. plenteous in mercy to all that *c.*

145. 18. nigh to all them that *c.* upon

Prov. 31. 28. children rise and *c.* her blessed

Isa. 5. 20. wo to them that *c.* evil good

22. 12. in that day the Lord did *c.* to weeping

55. 6. *c.* upon him while he is near

58. 9. shalt thou *c.* and Lord will answer

65. 24. before they *c.* I will answer

Jer. 25. 29. I will *c.* for a sword upon all

Joel 2. 32. remnant whom the Lord shall *c.*

Jonah 1. 6. sleeper arise, *c.* upon thy God

Zech. 13. 9. they shall *c.* upon my name

Mal. 3. 12. all nations shall *c.* you blessed

15. and now we *c.* the proud happy

Matt. 9. 13. I came not to *c.* righteous but sinners to repentance, Mark 2. 17. Luke 5. 32.

22. 3. to *c.* them that were bidden

23. 9. *c.* no man your father on earth

Luke 1. 48. all generations shall *c.* me blessed

6. 46. why *c.* ye me Lord, Lord, and

14. 12, 13. a dinner, *c.* not friends,— *c.* poor.

John 4. 16. *c.* thy husband and come

13. 13. ye *c.* me master and Lord

15. 15. I *c.* you not servants, but friends

Acts 2. 39. as many as Lord shall *c.*

10. 15. God hath cleansed *c.* not common

24. 14. after the way they *c.* heresy

Rom. 9. 25. I will *c.* them my people

10. 12. rich in mercy to all that *c.* on

14. how then shall they *c.* on him

2 Cor. 1. 23. I *c.* God for a record

Heb. 2. 11. not ashamed to *c.* them brethren

James 5. 14. *c.* for the elders of the church

1 Pet. 1. 17. if ye *c.* on the Father

Call on the name of the Lord, Gen. 4. 26. 1 Kings 18. 24. 2 Kings 5. 11. Ps. 116. 4. Joel 2. 32. Zeph. 3. 9. Acts 2. 21. Rom. 10. 13. 1 Cor. 1. 2.

I will call unto, or, *on the Lord,* 1 Sam. 12. 17. 2 Sam. 22. 4.

Call upon me, Ps. 50. 15. & 91. 15. Prov. 1. 28. Jer. 29. 12.

Gen. 21. 17. angel of God *called* to Hagar.

22. 11. the angel of the Lord *c.* to Abraham out of heaven, 15.

Ex. 3. 4. God *c.* unto him out of the bush

19. 3. Lord *c.* unto him out of the mount

Judg. 15. 18. was athirst, and *c.* on the Lord

2 Kings 8. 1. Lord hath *c.* for a famine

1 Chron. 4. 10. Jabesh *c.* on God of Israel

21. 26. David *c.* on the Lord and he answered

Ps. 17. 6. I have *c.* upon thee, 31. 17.

18. 6. in my distress I *c.* upon Lord

79. 6. not *c.* on thy name, Jer. 10. 25.

88. 9. I have *c.* daily upon thee

118. 5. I *c.* upon the Lord in my distress

Prov. 1. 24. I have *c.* and ye refused

Song 5. 6. I *c.* him, he gave me no answer

Isa. 41. 2. who *c.* him to his foot

42. 6. I the Lord *c.* thee in righteousness

43. 1. I have *c.* thee by thy name

22. thou hast not *c.* upon me

48. 1. *c.* by the name of Israel, 44. 5.

15. I have *c.* him, I have brought him

49. 1. Lord *c.* me from the womb

50. 2. when I *c.* was none to answer

51. 2. I *c.* him alone, and blessed

61. 3. be *c.* trees of righteousness

61. 4. thou shalt be *c.* Hephzibah

65. 12. when I *c.* ye did not answer

66. 4. Jer. 7. 13.

Lam 1. 19. I *c.* for my lovers they deceived

3. 55. I *c.* upon thy name, O Lord

Hos. 11. 1. I *c.* my son out of Egypt

Amos. 7. 4. Lord *c.* to contend by fire

Hag. 1. 11. I *c.* for a drought on land

Matt. 20. 16. many be *c.* but few chosen, 22. 14.

Mark 14. 72. Peter *c.* to mind word of the Lord

Luke 15. 19. not worthy to be *c.* thy son

John 1. 48. before that Philip *c.* thee

10. 35. if he *c.* them gods to whom the

15. 15. I have *c.* you friends

Acts 9. 41. when he had *c.* saints and widows

21. destroy them that *c.* on this name

10. 23, 24. *c.* in—*c.* together his kinsmen

11. 26. disciples were *c.* Christians

13. 2. for work whereto I *c.* them

15. 17. on whom my name is *c.*

19. 40. we are in danger to be *c.* in question, 23. 6. & 24. 21.

20. 1. Paul *c.* to him the disciples

20. 17. *c.* elders, 28. 17. *c.* chief of the Jews

Rom. 1. 1. *c.* to be an apostle, 1 Cor. 1. 1.

6. *c.* of Jesus Christ, 7. *c.* to be saints

2. 17. thou that art *c.* a Jew

8. 28. according to his purpose

30. predestinate, them he also *c.*

9. 24. whom he hath *c.* Jews also

1 Cor. 1. 9. faithful by whom ye were *c.*

24. unto them which are *c.*

26. not many wise,—noble are *c.*

55. 11. if any man *c.* a brother be

7. 15. God hath *c.* us to peace

17. as the Lord hath *c.* every one

68. *c.* being circumcised, 21. 22. *c.* servant

24. every man wherein he is *c.* abide

15. 9. I am not meet to be *c.* an apostle

Gal. 1. 6. *c.* you into the grace of Christ

15. God who *c.* me by his grace

5. 13. ye have been *c.* to liberty

Eph. 2. 11. who are *c.* uncircumcision

4. 1. vocation wherewith ye are *c.*

4. are *c.* in one hope of your calling

Col. 3. 15. to which ye are *c.* in one

1 Thess. 2. 12. *c.* you unto his kingdom

4. 7. God hath not *c.* us to unclean

2 Thess. 2. 4. above all that is *c.* God

14. he *c.* you by our gospel

1 Tim. 6. 12. whereunto thou art *c.*

2 Tim. 1. 9. *c.* us with a holy calling

Heb. 3. 13. exhort while it is *c.* to-day

5. 4. *c.* of God, as was Aaron

10. *c.* of God a high priest

9. 15. that they who are *c.* may receive

11. 16. not ashamed to be *c.* their God

24. refusing to be *c.* the son of Pharaoh's daughter

James 2. 7. name by which ye are *c.*

1 Pet. 1. 15. as he that *c.* you is holy

2. 9. who *c.* you out of darkness

21. hereunto were ye *c.*

1 Pet. 5. 10. *c.* us to his eternal glory

2 Pet. 1. 3. *c.* us to glory and virtue

1 John 3. 1. we should be *c.* sons of

Jude 1. preserved in Christ Jesus and *c.*

Rev. 17. 14. with him *c.* and chosen

19. 9. are *c.* unto marriage supper

2 Chron. 7. 14. *called by my name,* Isa. 43. 7. Jer. 7. 10. Amos 9. 12.

1 Kings 8. 43. *called by thy name,* 2 Chron. 6. 33. Isa. 4. 1. & 43. 1. Jer. 14. 9. & 15. 16. Dan. 9. 18, 19.

2 Kings 8. 43. to all that the stranger *calleth* for, 2 Chron. 6. 33.

Job 12. 4. who *calls* on God and he answered

Ps. 42. 7. deep *c.* unto deep at noise

147. 4. *c.* them all by name

Isa. 59. 4. none *c.* for justice nor for

64. 7. none that *c.* upon thy name

Hos. 7. 7. none among them that *c.*

Amos. 5. 8. that *c.* for waters of sea

Luke 15. 16. *c.* together his friends, 9.

John 10. 3. he *c.* his own sheep by name

Rom. 4. 17. *c.* those things which be not

9. 11. not of works but of him that *c.*

Gal. 5. 8. persuasion not of him that *c.*

1 Thess. 5. 24. faithful is he that *c.* you

Rom. 11. 29. gifts and *calling* of God

1 Cor. 1. 26. ye see your *c.* brethren

7. 20. let every man abide in same *c.*

Eph. 1. 18. what is the hope of his *c.*

4. 4. called in one hope of your *c.*

Phil. 3. 14. prize of high *c.* of God in Christ

2 Thess. 1. 11. count you worthy of this *c.*

2 Tim. 1. 9. called with a holy *c.*

Heb. 3. 1. partakers of heavenly *c.*

2 Pet. 1. 10. make your *c.* and election

Isa. 41. 4. *c.* the generation from the beginning

Matt. 11. 16. sitting and *c.* their fellows

Mark 11. 21. Peter *c.* to remembrance

Acts 7. 59. stoned Stephen *c.* on God

22. 16. *c.* upon the name of the Lord

1 Pet. 3. 6. obeyed Abraham, *c.* him Lord

CALM, Ps. 107. 29. Jonah 1. 11. Matt. 8. 26. Mark 4. 39. Luke 8. 24.

CALVE (cow), Job 21. 10. Ps. 29. 9. Jer. 14. 5.

1 Kings 12. 28. made two *calves* of gold

Hos. 14. 2. we will render *c.* of our

Mic. 6. 6. come with *c.* of a year old

Mal. 4. 2. grow up as *c.* of the stall

Heb. 9. 12. blood of goats and *c.* 19.

CAME, Ps. 18. 6. Matt. 1. 18. John 1. 7. Rom. 5. 18. & 9. 5. 1 Tim. 1. 15. 1 John 5. 6.

Came down, 2 Kings 1. 10, 12, 14. 2 Chron. 7. 1, 3. Lam. 1. 9. John 3. 13. & 6. 38, 41, 51, 58. Rev. 20. 9.

Came forth, Num. 11. 20. Judg. 14. 14. Eccl. 5. 15. Zech. 10. 4.

John 16. 28. I—from the Father

CAMEL, Gen. 24. 19. Lev. 11. 4.

Matt. 3. 4. raiment of *c's* hair

19. 14. easier for a *c.* to go through

23. 24. strain at a gnat and swallow *c.*

CAMP, Ex. 32. 17.
Ex. 14. 19. angel went before the *c.*
16. 13. quails came and covered *c.*
Num. 11. 26. they prophesied in *c.*
31. let the quails fall by the *c.*
Deut. 23. 14. Lord walketh in midst of *c.* therefore shall thy *c.* be holy
Judg. 13. 25. began to move him in *c.*
2 Kings 19. 35. smote in the *c.* of the Assyrians
Heb. 13. 13. go unto him without *c.*
Rev. 20. 9. compassed *c.* of saints
CAN we find such a one, Gen. 41. 38.
Deut. 1. 12. how *c.* I myself alone bear
32. 29. neither is there any *c.* deliver
2 Sam. 7. 20. what *c.* David say more
2 Chron. 1. 10. who *c.* judge this people
Esther 8. 6. how *c.* I endure to see the destruction of my people
Job 8. 11. *c.* the rush grow without water
22. 2. *c.* a man be profitable unto God
25. 4. how *c.* man be justified with
34. 29. who then *c.* make trouble
Ps. 40. 5. more than *c.* be numbered
49. 7. none *c.* redeem his brother
78. 20. who *c.* he give bread also
89. 6. who *c.* be likened unto Lord
Eccl. 4. 11. how *c.* one be warm alone
Isa. 49. 15. *c.* a woman forget her child
Jer. 2. 32. *c.* a maid forget her ornaments
Ezek. 22. 14. *c.* thy heart endure
37. 3. *c.* these dry bones live
Amos 3. 3. *c.* two walk together except
Matt. 12. 34. how *c.* ye speak good things
19. 25. who then *c.* be saved
Mark 2. 7. who *c.* forgive sins but God
19. *c.* children of bride chamber fast
3. 37. no man *c.* enter into strong man's house
10. 38. *c.* ye drink of the cup that I
John 3. 4. how *c.* a man be born again
9. how *c.* these things be, Luke 1. 34.
5. 19. Son *c.* do nothing of himself, 20.
6. 44. no man *c.* come to me except
60. a hard saying, who *c.* hear it
9. 4. night, when no man *c.* work
14. 5. how *c.* we know the way
15. 4. no more *c.* ye except ye abide
1 Cor. 12. 3. no man *c.* say that Jesus
2 Cor. 13. 8. *c.* do nothing against the
1 Tim. 6. 7. we *c.* carry nothing out
Heb. 10. 11. *c.* never take away sins
James 2. 14. *c.* faith save him
Rev. 3. 8. open door and no man *c.*
Gen. 32. 12. which *cannot* be numbered for multitude, 1 Kings 3. 8.
Num. 23. 20. be blessed and I *c.* reverse
Josh. 24. 19. ye *c.* serve the Lord
1 Sam. 12. 21. vain things which *c.* profit
1 Kings 8. 27. heaven of heavens *c.* contain thee, 2 Chron. 6. 18.
Ezra 9. 15. we *c.* stand before thee
Job 9. 3. he *c.* answer for one of a
12. 14. he breaketh down it *c.* be
14. 5. appointed his bounds that he *c.* pass
23. 8, 9. I *c.* perceive him—*c.* behold
28. 15. it *c.* be gotten for gold
36. 18. a great ransom *c.* deliver thee
37. 5. God doeth which we *c.* comprehend
Ps. 40. 5. they *c.* be reckoned up in order
77. I am so troubled that I *c.* speak
93. 1. world established, that it *c.* be
139. 6. too high, I *c.* attain unto it
Isa. 38. 18. the grave *c.* praise thee
44. 18. they *c.* see; they *c.* understand
20. he *c.* deliver his soul

45. 20. pray to a God that *c.* save
50. 2. hand shortened that it *c.* redeem
56. 11. shepherds that *c.* understand
59. 1. neither his ear heavy, that it *c.*
Jer. 4. 19. I *c.* hold my peace, because
6. 10. are uncircumcised, they *c.*
7. 8. ye trust in lying words that *c.*
14. 9. as a mighty man *c.* save
18. 6. *c.* I do with you as this potter
29. 17. like the vile figs that *c.* be
33. 22. the host of heaven *c.* be
Lam. 3. 7. hath hedged me, that I *c.* get
Matt. 6. 24. ye *c.* serve God and mammon, Luke 16. 13.
7. 18. a good tree *c.* bring forth evil
19. 11. all men *c.* receive this saying
26. 53. thinkest thou I *c.* now pray to
27. 42. himself he *c.* save
Luke 14. 26. *c.* be my disciple
16. 26. would pass from hence to you *c.*
John 3. 3. *c.* see the kingdom of God
5. he *c.* enter into the kingdom of
7. 34. thither ye *c.* come, 36. & 8. 21.
8. 43. because ye *c.* hear my word
10. 35. the Scripture *c.* be broken
14. 17. whom the world *c.* receive
15. 4. branch *c.* bear fruit of itself
16. 12. things to say, but ye *c.* bear them
Acts 4. 20. we *c.* but speak the things
5. 39. if it be of God ye *c.* overthrow
27. 31. except these abide in the ship, ye *c.* be saved
Rom. 8. 8. that are in flesh *c.* please God
26. groanings which *c.* be uttered
1 Cor. 7. 9. if they *c.* contain, let them
10. 21. ye *c.* drink cup of the Lord
15. 50. flesh and blood *c.* inherit the kingdom of God
2 Cor. 12. 2. in body or out, I *c.* tell
Gal. 5. 17. ye *c.* do the things that ye
2 Tim. 2. 13. he *c.* deny himself
Tit. 1. 2. God who *c.* lie hath promised
2. 8. sound speech *c.* be condemned
Heb. 4. 15. high priest which *c.* be
9. 5. we *c.* now speak particularly
12. 27. those things which *c.* be shaken
28. kingdom that *c.* be moved
James 1. 13. God *c.* be tempted with evil
1 John 3. 9. he *c.* sin because born of
Ex. 33. 20. *canst* not see my face
Deut. 28. 27. *c.* not be healed
Job 11. 7. *c.* thou by searching find out
8. what *c.* thou do, what *c.* thou
22. darkness that thou *c.* not see
Matt. 8. 2. if thou wilt, thou *c.* make
Mark 9. 22. if *c.* do anything have
John 3. 8. *c.* not tell whence it cometh
13. 36. thou *c.* not follow me now
CANDLE shall be put out, Job 18. 6. & 21. 17. Prov. 24. 20.
Job. 29. 3. when his *c.* shined on my head
Ps. 18. 28. the Lord will light my *c.*
Prov. 20. 27. spirit of man is *c.* of the
31. 18. her *c.* goeth not out by night
Matt. 5. 15. do men light a *c.* and put it, Mark 4. 21. Luke 8. 16.
Luke 11. 36. shining of *c.* doth give
15. 8. light a *c.* and sweep house
Rev. 18. 23. light of *c.* shine no more at all, Jer. 25. 10.
Rev. 22. 5. they need no *c.* neither light
Zeph. 1. 22. search Jerusalem with *candles*
Ex. 25. 31. *candlestick*, Lev. 24. 4.
Num. 8. 2. 2 Kings 4. 10. Dan. 5. 5.
Zech. 4. 2. behold a *c.* all of gold
Matt. 5. 15. but on a *c.* and it giveth light to all, Mark 4. 21.

Rev. 1. 20. seven *c.* are the seven churches
2. 5. I will remove thy *c.* out of his
CANKER, 2 Tim. 2. 17.
CAPTAIN, Num. 2. 3.
Josh 5. 14, 15. *c.* of the Lord's host
2 Chron. 13. 12 God himself is our *c.*
Heb. 2. 10. *c.* of their salvation perfect
CAPTIVE, Gen. 14. 14.
Judg. 5. 12. lead thy captivity
Isa. 49. 24. shall the lawful *c.* be delivered
51. 44. *c.* exile hastens to be loosed
52. 2. O *c.* daughter of Zion
Jer. 22. 12. die whither they led him *c.*
Amos 7. 11. Israel shall be led away *c.*
2 Tim. 2. 26. taken *c.* by him at his will
3. 6. lead *c.* silly women laden with sins
Deut. 30. 3. I will turn thy *captivity*
Job 42. 10. the Lord turned the *c.* of Job
Ps. 14. 7. Lord bringeth back the *c.*
68. 18. lead *c.* captive
78. 62. delivering his strength into *c.*
Ps. 85. 1. brought back the *c.* of Jacob
126. 1. turned again the *c.* of Zion
4. turned again our *c.* as streams
Jer. 15. 2. such as are for *c.* to *c.*
27. 14. I will turn your *c.*
30. 3. bring again *c.* of my people
Hos. 6. 11. when I returned *c.* of my people
Zeph. 2. 7. Lord shall turn away their *c.*
Rom. 7. 23. bringing me into *c.* of sin
2 Cor. 10. 5. bringing into *c.* every
Rev.. 13. 10. lead into *c.* shall go into *c.*
CARCASS, Matt. 24. 28.
CARE, Luke 10. 40.
Matt. 13. 22. *c.* of this world choke. Mark 4. 19. Luke 8. 14.
I Cor. 9. 9. doth God take *c.* for oxen
12. 25. have the same *c.* one for another
2 Cor. 11. 28. *c.* of all the churches
1 Tim. 3. 5. how shall he take *c.* of church
1 Pet. 5. 7. casting all your *c.* on him
Ps. 142. 4. no man *cared* for my soul
John 12. 6. not that he *c.* for the poor
Acts 18. 17. Gallio *c.* for none of these things
Matt. 22. 16. *carest*, Mark 4. 38.
Deut. 11. 12. land thy God *careth* for
John 10. 13. hireling *c.* not for sheep
1 Cor. 7. 32, 33, 34. unmarried *c.* for things of Lord, married *c.* for things of the world
1 Pet. 5. 7. for he *c.* for you
2 Kings 4. 13. been *careful* for us
Jer. 17. 8. not be *c.* in the year of
Dan. 3. 16. not *c.* to answer thee
Luke 10. 41. art *c.* and troubled about many things
Phil. 4. 6. be *c.* for nothing: but by prayer
10. were *c.* but ye lacked opportunity
Tit. 3. 8. be *c.* to maintain good works
Ezek. 12. 18, 19. *carefulness*, 1 Cor. 7. 32. 2 Cor. 7. 11.
Isa. 32. 9. *careless* daughters, 10. 11.
CARNAL, Rom. 7. 14.
Rom. 8. 7. *c.* mind is enmity against God
25. 27. minister to them in *c.* things
1 Cor. 3. 1. not speak but as to *c.*
8. ye are yet *c.*—are ye not *c.*
9. 11. if we reap your *c.* things
2. Cor. 10. 4. our weapons are not *c.*
Heb. 7. 16. law of a *c.* commandment
9. 10. ordinances imposed on them *c.*
Rom. 8. 6. to be *c.* minded is death

CARPENTER, 2 Sam. 5. 11. Isa. 41. 7. Jer. 24. 1 Zech. 1. 20.
Matt. 13. 55. *carpenter's son*
CARRY, Ex. 33. 15.
Num. 11. 12. *c.* them in thy bosom
Eccl. 10. 20. birds of air shall *c.* voice
Isa. 40. 11. *c.* lambs in his bosom
46. 4. even to hoary hair will I *c.* you
Luke 10. 4. *c.* neither purse nor scrip
John 21. 18. *c.* thee whither thou
1 Tim. 6. 7. can *c.* nothing out
Luke 16. 22. *carried* by angels into Abraham's bosom
Eph. 4. 14. *c.* about with every wind
Heb. 13. 9. *c.* about with divers doctrines
Rev. 17. 3. *c.* me away in spirit, 21. 10.
CART is pressed full, Amos. 2. 13.
Isa. 5. 18. as it were with a *c.* rope
CASE, Ex. 5. 19. Ps. 144. 15.
CAST, Neh. 9. 26.
Ps. 22. 10. *c.* upon thee from the womb
55. 22. *c.* thy burden on the Lord
Prov. 1. 14. *c.* in thy lot among us
16. 33. the lot is *c.* into the lap
Eccl. 11. 1. *c.* thy bread upon waters
Isa. 2. 20. a man shall *c.* his idols of silver
38. 17. hast *c.* all my sins behind thy
Ezek. 23. 35. *c.* me behind thy back
Dan. 3. 20. *c.* them into the fiery furnace
6. 24. *c.* them into the den of lions
Jonah 2. 4. I am *c.* out of thy sight
Mic. 7. 19. *c.* all their sins into the sea
Nah. 3. 6. I will *c.* abominable filth on thee
Mal. 3. 11. vine shall not *c.* her fruit
Matt. 3. 10. hewn down and *c.* into —the fire, 7. 19. Luke 3. 9.
5. 25. thou be *c.* into prison
7. 6. neither *c.* pearls before swine
13. 42. *c.* them into a furnace, 50
15. 26. children's bread, and *c.* it to dogs
18. 30. went and *c.* him into prison
22. 13. *c.* him into outer darkness
25. 30. *c.* unprofitable servant into
29. 30. *c.* it from—*c.* into hell, 18. 8, 9.
Mark 11. 23. be thou *c.* into the sea
12. 44. she *c.* in all, Luke 21. 4.
Luke 1. 29. she *c.* in her mind what
12. 5. power to *c.* into hell
58. lest the officer *c.* thee into prison
John 8. 7. let him first *c.* a stone at her
Acts 16. 23. they *c.* them into prison
Rev. 2. 10. devil shall *c.* some of you into prison
22. I will *c.* her into a bed, and
20. 3. *c.* him into bottomless pit
Lev. 26. 44. I will not *cast away*
2 Sam. 1. 21. shield is vilely—
Job. 8. 20. God will not—perfect man
Ps. 2. 3. let us—their cords from us
51. 11. *c.* me not away from thy presence
Isa. 41. 9. I will not *c.* thee away
Ezek. 18. 31.—all your transgressions
Rom. 11. 1. hath God—his people. 2.
Heb. 10. 35. *c.* not away your confidence
1 Cor. 9. 27. myself be a—
2 Chron. 25. 8. God power to *cast down*
Job 22. 29. when men are—then
Ps. 37. 24. though he fall he shall not be—
Ps. 42. 5. why art thou—11. & 43. 5.
102. 10. lifted me up and—again
2 Cor. 4. 9.—but not destroyed
7. 6. comforteth those that are—
Ps. 44. 23. thou hast *cast off* and put us
23. *c.* us not off forever
71. 9. *c.* me not off in time of old age

77. 7. will the Lord—for ever
89. 38. thou hast—and abhorred
94. 14. Lord will not—his people
Jer. 31. 37. I will—all seed of Israel
Lam. 3. 31. Lord will not—for ever
Hos. 8. 3. Israel hath—thing is good
Rom. 13. 12. Let us—the works of darkness
1 Tim. 5. 12. they—their first love
Gen. 21. 10. *cast out* this bond woman and her son, Gal. 4. 30.
Ex. 34. 24. I will—the nations before thee, and enlarge thy borders
Lev. 18. 24. which I—before thee
Deut. 7. 1.—many nations before thee
Ps. 78. 55. he—heathen before them
80. 8.—the heathen and planted it
Prov. 22. 10.—the scorner, and contention
Isa. 14. 9. thou art—of thy grave
26. 19. the earth shall—the dead
58. 7. poor that are—to thy house
66. 5. c. you out for my name's sake
Jer. 7. 15. I will c. out of my sight
15. 1. c. them out of my sight
16. 13. I will c. you out of my land
Matt. 7. 5. c. beam out of thine eye
8. 12. children of kingdom shall be—
12. 24. doth not—devils but by Beelzebub
21. 12.—them that sold and bought
Mark. 9. 28. why could not we c. out
12. 8. c. him out of the vineyard
16. 9. he had—seven devils
17. in my name shall they—devils
Luke 6. 22.—your name as evil
John 6. 37. that cometh will in no wise—
12. 31. prince of this world be—
Rev. 12. 9. the dragon was—
Ps. 73. 18. thou *castedst* them down
Job 15. 4. thou *castest* off fear
Ps. 50. 17. c. my words behind me
88. 14. why c. thou off my soul
Job 21. 10. cow *casteth* not her calf
Ps. 147. 6. c. the wicked to ground
Jer. 5. so she c. out her wickedness
Matt. 9. 34. he c. out devils through Beelzebub, Mark 3. 22. Luke 11. 15.
1 John 4. 18. perfect love c. out fear
3 John 10. c. them out of the church
Job 6. 21. ye see my *casting* down
Rom. 11. 15. if c. away of them be the
2 Cor. 10. 5. c. down imaginations
1 Pet. 5. 7. c. all your care on him
CASTOR and Pollux, Acts 28. 11.
CATCH, Judg. 21. 21.
Ps. 10. 9. he lieth in wait to c. poor
35. 8. net he hath hid c. himself
109. 11. extortioner c. all that he hath
Jer. 5. 26. they set a trap, they c. men
Mark 12. 13. they c. him in his words
Luke 5. 10. henceforth thou shalt c. men
CATTLE on a thousand hills are mine, Ps. 50. 10.
Ps. 104. 14. he causeth grass to grow for c.
Ezek. 34. 17. I judge between c. and c.
John 4. 12. drank thereof and his c.
CAUGHT him and kissed him, Prov. 7. 13.
John 21. 3. that night they c. nothing
Acts 8. 39. Spirit of the Lord c. away Peter
2 Cor. 12. 4. he was c. up into paradise
16. being crafty I c. you with guile
1 Thess. 4. 17. c. up together with them
Rev. 12. 5. her child was c. up to God
CAVE, John 11. 41.
Gen. 19. 30. Lot dwelt in a c. and
23. 19. buried Sarah his wife in c.
25. 9. buried him in the c.
49. 29. bury me with my fathers in c.
Josh 10. 16. hid themselves in a c.

1 Kings 18. 4. hid them by 50 in a c.
Isa. 2. 19. go into *caves* for fear of the Lord
Ezek. 33. 27. that be in the c. shall die
Heb. 11. 38. wandered in c. of the earth
CAUL, Isa. 3. 18. Hos. 13. 8.
CAUSE come before judges, Ex. 22. 9.
Ex. 23. 2. not speak in a c. to decline after
3. not countenance in a poor man in c.
6. nor wrest judgment of poor in c.
Deut. 1. 17. c. that is too hard for you
1 Kings 8. 45. maintained their c. 49.
Job. 5. 8. to God would I commit my c.
Ps. 9. 4. maintain my right and my c.
35. 23. awake unto my c. my God
Prov. 18. 17. that is first in his own c.
25. 9. debate thy c. with neighbour
Eccl. 7. 10. what is c. that former days
Isa. 51. 22. pleadeth c. of his people
Jer. 5. 28. judge not c. of fatherless
11. 20. to thee I revealed my c.
Lam. 3. 36. to subvert a man in his c.
Matt. 19. 3. put away his wife for every c.
2 Cor. 4. 16. for which c. we faint not
5. 13. if we be sober it is for your c.
Ex. 9. 16. *for this cause*, Matt. 19. 5. Eph. 5. 31. John 12. 27. Rom. 1. 26. 1 Cor. 11. 30.
1 Tim. 1. 16.—I obtained mercy
Ps. 119. 161. *without cause*, Prov. 3. 30. Matt. 5. 22. John 15. 25.
Job 6. 24. c. me to understand
Ps. 10. 17. wilt c. thine ear to hear
67. 1. c. his face to shine, 80. 3.
85. 4. c. thine anger to cease
143. 8. c. me to know the way
Isa. 3. 12. lead thee, c. thee to err
58. 14, I will c. thee to ride on high
66. 9. and not c. to bring forth
Jer. 3. 12. not c. my anger to fall
7. 3. c. to dwell in his place
15. 4. c. them to be removed into all
11. c. the enemy to treat thee well
18. 2. c. thee to hear my words
44. c. their captivity to return, 33. 7. & 34. 22. & 42. 12.
32. 37. c. them to dwell safely
Lam. 3. 32. though he c. grief, yet he
Ezek. 36. 27. c. you to walk in my statutes
37. 5. c. breath to enter into you
Dan. 9. 17. c. thy face to shine on sanctuary
Rom. 16. 17. mark them which c. division
Prov. 7. 21. fair speech *caused* him to
10. 5. a son *causeth*, 17. 2.
18. 18. the lot c. contentions to cease
19. 27. cease instruction that c. to err
Matt. 5. 32. c. her to commit adultery
2 Cor. 2. 14. always c. us to triumph
Prov. 26. 2. curse *causeless* shall not come
CEASE, Gen. 8. 22.
Deut. 15. 11. poor shall never c. out of
Neh. 6. 3. why should the work c.
Job. 3. 17. there the wicked c. from troubling
Ps. 37. 8. c. from anger and wrath
46. 9. he maketh wars to c. unto the
Prov. 19. 27. c. to hear instruction, that
23. 4. c. from thine own wisdom
Isa. 1. 16. c. to do evil, learn to do
2. 22. c. ye from man whose breath

Acts 13. 10. wilt thou not c. to pervert
1 Cor. 13. 8. there be tongues, they c.
Eph. 1. 16. c. not to give thanks for
Col. 1. 9. c. not to pray for you
2 Pet. 2. 14. that cannot c. from sin
Ps. 12. 1. the godly man *ceaseth*
Prov. 26. 20. no tale-bearer, strife c.
1 Thess. 5. 17. pray without *ceasing*, 2. 13. 1 Sam. 12. 23. Acts 12. 5. Rom. 1. 9. 2 Tim. 1. 3.
CEDAR, Lev. 14. 4. Jer. 22. 14.
2 Lam. 7. 2. I dwell in a house of c.
2 Kings 14. 9. thistle sent to c. in
Ps. 29. 5. voice of Lord breaketh c.
92. 12. grow like a c. in Lebanon
Song 1. 17. the beams of our house are c.
5. 15. his countenance excellent as c.
Isa. 9. 10. we will change them into c.
Ezek. 17. 22. of the high c. 23. goodly c.
31. 3. Assyrian was in a c. in Lebanon
Amos 2. 9. like the height of the c.
CELEBRATE, Isa. 38. 18.
CELESTIAL, 1 Cor. 15. 40.
CHAFF, wicked as, Job. 21. 18. Ps. 1. 4. Isa. 5. 24. Dan. 2. 35. Hos. 13. 3.
Isa. 33. 11. ye shall conceive c. ye shall
Jer. 23. 28. what is the c. to the wheat
Zeph. 2. 2. before the day pass as the c.
Matt. 3. 12. burn up c. in unquenchable fire
CHAIN, Gen. 41. 42. Dan. 5. 7. Ezek. 19. 4, 9. Mark 5. 3, 4.
Ps. 73. 6. pride compasseth them as a c.
Song 4. 9. with one c. of thy neck
Acts 28, 20. I am bound with this c.
2 Tim. 1. 16. was not ashamed of my c.
Ps. 149. 8. bind their kings with *chains*
Prov. 1. 9. shall be a c. about neck
2 Pet. 2. 4. delivered into c. of darkness
Jude 6. reserved in everlasting c.
CHALDEANS, Job 1. 17. Isa. 43. 14. Jer. 38. 2. & 40. 9. Ezek. 23. 14.
CHAMBER, Ps. 19. 5. Joel 2. 16.
Job. 9. 9. maketh the *chambers* of south
Prov. 104. 3. beams of c. in the waters
Prov. 7. 27. going down to the c. of death
Song 1. 4. king brought me into his c.
Isa. 26. 20. enter into c. and shut thy door
Matt. 24. 26. he is in the secret c.
Rom. 13. 13. not in *chambering* and wantonness
CHANCE, happens, 1 Sam. 6. 9. Eccl. 9. 11. 2 Sam. 1. 6. Luke 10. 31.
CHANGE of raiment, Judg. 14. 12. Zech. 3. 4. Isa. 3. 22.
Job. 14. 14. patiently wait till my c. come
Prov. 24. 11. meddle not with them given to c.
Heb. 7. 12. made of necessity a c. of law
Job 17. 12. they c. the night into day
Ps. 102. 26. as a vesture shalt thou c. them
Jer. 13, 23. can Ethiopian c. his skin
Dan. 7. 25. think to c. times and laws
Mal. 3. 6. I am the Lord, I c. not
Rom. 1. 26. women did c. the natural use
Phil. 3. 21. who shall c. our vile bodies
1 Sam. 21. 13. *changed* his behaviour before
Ps. 102. 26. and they shall be c.
Jer. 2. 11. hath a nation c. their gods

Rom. 1. 23. c. the glory of God into an
25. c. the truth of God into a lie
1 Cor. 15. 51. shall all be c. 52.
2 Cor. 3. 18. c. into the same image
Job. 10. 17. *changes* and war are against me.
Ps. 55. 19. they have no c. therefore
15. 4. sweareth and *changeth* not
Dan. 2. 21. he c. the times and seasons
Mark 11. 15. *money changers*, Matt. 21. 12. John 2. 14. 15.
CHANT, Amos 6. 5.
CHARGE, Gen. 26. 5. & 28. 6.
Ps. 91. 11. give his angels c. over thee
Acts 7. 60. lay not this sin to their c.
Rom. 8. 33. any thing to the c. of God's elect
1 Cor. 9. 18. make gospel without c.
1 Tim. 1. 18. this c. I commit to thee
2 Tim. 4. 16. not laid to their c.
Song 2. 7. I c. you, O daughters of Jerusalem, 3. 5. & 5. 8.
1 Tim. 6. 17. c. them that are rich
Job. 1. 22. nor *charged* God foolishly
4. 18. c. his angels with folly
1 Thess. 2. 11. c. every one as a father
2 Cor. 11. 9. *chargeable*, 1 Thess. 2. 9. 2 Thess. 3. 8.
CHARIOT, Gen. 41. 43.
Ex. 14. 25. took off their c. wheels
2 Kings 2, 11, appeared a c. of fire
2. 12. my father, the c. of Israel, 13. 14.
Song 3. 9. Solomon made himself c.
Mic. 1. 13. bind the c. to swift beasts
Acts 8. 29. join thyself to this c.
Ps. 20. 7. some trust in *chariots*
68. 17. c. of God are 20,000
Song 6. 12. made me like the c. of Ammi-nadib
Hab. 3. 8. ride upon thy c. of salvation
CHARITY edifieth, 1 Cor. 8. 1.
13.1 if I have not c. I am nothing, 2. 3.
4. c. suffereth long, 8. c. never faileth
13. now abideth faith, hope, c.
16. 14. let all things be done with c.
Col. 3. 14. above all things put on c.
1 Thess. 3. 6. tidings of your faith and c.
2 Thess. 1. 3. the c. of every one aboundeth
1 Tim. 1. 5. end of the commandment is c.
2. 15. if they continue in faith and c.
4. 12. be thou an example of believers in c.
2 Tim. 2. 22. follow righteousness, faith, c.
3. 10. know my doctrine, faith, c.
Tit. 2. 2. sound in faith, c. patience
3 John 6. borne witness of thy c.
1 Pet. 4. 8. have fervent c. among yourselves; for c. *shall* cover the multitude of sins
5. 14. greet one another with a kiss of c.
2 Pet. 1. 7. add to brotherly kindness c.
Jude 12. spots in your feasts of c.
Rom. 14. 15. walkest not *charitably*
CHARMED, Jer. 8. 17.
Deut. 18. 11. *charmers*, Ps. 58. 5.
CHASTE virgin, 2 Cor. 11. 2.
Tit. 2. 5. to be discreet, c. good, obedient
1 Pet. 3. 2. your c. conversation, with
CHASTEN, 2 Sam. 7. 14.
Ps. 6. 1. neither c. me in thy, 38. 1.
Prov. 19. 18. c. thy son while there is hope
Dan. 10. 12. to c. thyself before thy God
Rev. 3. 9. as many as I love, I c.

Ps. 69. 10. *chastened* my soul with fasting
73. 14. been *c.* every morning
118. 18. the Lord hath *c.* me sore
1 Cor. 11. 32. we are *c.* of the Lord
Heb. 12. 10. for a few days *c.* us after
2 Cor. 6. 9. as *c.* and not killed
Ps. 94. 12. blessed is the man whom thou *chastenest*
Deut. 8. 5. as a man *c.* his son, so the Lord *c.*
Prov. 13. 24. loveth him *chasteneth* him betimes.
Heb. 12. 6. whom lord loveth he *c.*
7. what son whom the father *c.* not
Job. 5. 17. despise not thou *chastening* of the Lord, Prov. 3. 11.
Isa. 26. 16. when thy *c.* was upon them
Heb. 12. 7. if ye endure *c.* God dealeth with you
11, no *c.* for present is joyous
CHASTISE, Lev. 26. 28.
Deut. 22. 18. elders shall *c.* him
1 Kings 12. 11. I will *c.* with scorpions, 14.
Hos. 7. 12. *c.* them as their congregation
10. 10. desire that I should *c.* them
Luke 23. 16. *c.* and release him, 22.
1 Chron. 10. 11, 14. father *chastised* with whips
Ps. 94. 10. *c.* the heathen
Deut. 11. 2. not seen *chastisement* of the
Job. 34. 31. I have borne *c.* I will not
Isa. 53. 5. *c.* of our peace was upon
Jer. 30. 14. with the *c.* of a cruel one
Heb. 12. 8. if ye be without *c.* then
CHATTER, Isa. 38. 14.
CHEEK, 1 Kings 22. 24. Job 16. 10.
Lam. 1. 30. Mic. 5. 1. Matt. 5. 39.
Luke 6. 29. Deut. 18. 3.
Song 1. 10. thy *cheeks* are comely
5. 13. his *c.* are as a bed of spices
CHEER *be of good,* Matt. 9. 2.
Mark 6. 50. John 16. 33. Acts 23. 11.
Prov. 15. 13. *cheerful,* Zech. 9. 17.
2 Cor. 9. 6. *cheerfulness,* Rom. 12. 8.
Acts 24. 10. *cheerfully* answer for myself
CHERISH, Eph. 5. 29.
CHERUBIMS, between, 1 Sam. 4. 4. 2 Sam. 6. 2. 2 Kings 19. 15. 1 Chron. 13. 6. Ps. 80. 1. Isa. 37. 16.
CHICKENS, Matt. 23. 37.
CHIDE, not always, Ps. 103. 9.
CHIEF, Ezra 9. 2. Neh. 11. 3.
Matt. 20. 27. that will be *c.* among you
Luke 22. 26. that is *c.* as he that serveth
Eph. 2. 20. Jesus Christ himself being *c.*
1 Tim. 1. 15. sinners,—of whom I am *c.*
Song 5. 10. *chiefest* among 10,000
Mark 10. 44. will be *c.* shall be servant
Rom. 3. 2. *chiefly,* Phil. 4. 22.
CHILD, Gen. 37. 30.
Ex. 2. 2. saw he was a goodly *c.*
2 Sam. 12. 16. David besought God for the *c.*
Ps. 131. 2. quieted myself as a *c.* weaned
Prov. 29. 15. *c.* left to himself bringeth
Eccl. 4. 8. hath neither *c.* nor brother
10. 16. wo when thy king is a *c.*
Isa. 3. 5. *c.* behave himself proudly
9. 6. unto us a *c.* is born.
Isa. 11. 6. a little *c.* shall lead them
49. 15. woman forget her sucking *c.*
Jer. 1. 6. cannot speak for I am a *c.*
31. 20. dear son is he a pleasant *c.*
Hos. 11. 1. when Israel was a *c.*
Matt. 18. 2. Jesus called a little *c.*
23. 15. twofold more the *c.* of hell
Mark 9. 36. took a *c.* and set him in the midst

10. 15. receive kingdom of God as little *c.*
Luke 1. 66. what manner of *c.* shall this be
2. 43. *c.* Jesus tarried behind in Jerusalem
Acts 4. 27. against thy holy *c.* Jesus
13. 10. thou *c.* of the devil, thou enemy
1 Cor. 13. 11. when I was a *c.* I spake as a *c.*
Gal. 4. 1. as long as a *c.* differs nothing
2 Tim. 3. 15. from a *c.* hast known the Scriptures
Rev. 12. 4. to devour her *c.* as soon
5. her *c.* was caught up to God
1 Tim. 2. 15. to be saved in *childbearing*
Eccl. 11. 10. *childhood* and youth are
1 Cor. 13. 11. put away *childish* things
Gen. 15. 2. *childless,* Jer. 22. 30.
25. 22. *children* struggled together
30. 1. give me *c.* or else I die
Ps. 17. 14. they are full of *c.* and leave
102. 28. *c.* of thy servants shall continue
113. 9. a joyful mother of *c.*
127. 3. *c.* are a heritage of the Lord
Prov. 17. 6. the glory of *c.* are their fathers
Song 1. 6. mother's *c.* were angry with
Isa. 1. 2. I brought up *c.* and they
3. 4. give *c.* to their princes
12. *c.* are their oppressors
8, 18. I and the *c.* whom the Lord hath given me, Heb. 2. 13.
30. 9. lying *c.—c.* that will not hear
63. 8. *c.* that will not lie
Mal. 4. 6. turn hearts of fathers to *c.* Luke 1. 17.
Matt. 3. 9. of these stones to raise up *c.*
15. 26. not meet to take *c's* bread
Luke 6. 35. shall be *c.* of the Highest
16. 8. *c.* of this world wiser than *c.*
Acts 3. 25. ye are *c.* of the prophets
Rom. 8. 17. if *c.* then heirs, heirs of God
1 Cor. 7. 14. else were your *c.* unclean
14. 20. be not *c.* in understanding
2 Cor. 12. 14. *c.* ought not to lay up
Eph. 2. 3. are by nature *c.* of wrath
4. 14. be no more *c.* tossed to and fro
5. 6. cometh the wrath of God upon the *c.* of disobedience, Col. 3. 6. Eph. 2. 2.
6. 1. *c.* obey your parents, Col. 3. 20.
Heb. 12. 5. speaketh unto you as *c.*
1 Pet. 1. 14. as obedient *c.* not fashioning
Rev. 2. 23. kill her *c.* with death
Ex. 34. 7. *children's children,* Jer. 2. 9.
Ps. 103. 17. Prov. 13. 22.
Prov. 17. 6.—are crown of old men
Matt. 5. 9. *children of God,* Luke 20. 36. John 11. 52. Rom. 8. 21. Gal. 3. 26. 1 John 3. 10. & 5. 2.
Ps. 89. 30. *his children,* 103. 13. Prov. 20. 7. 1 Tim. 3. 4.
Luke 16. 8. *children of light,* John 12. 36. Eph. 5. 8. 1 Thess. 5. 5.
Matt. 18. 3. *little children,* 19. 14. Mark 10. 14. Luke 18. 16. John 13. 33. Gal. 4. 19. 1 John 2. 1.
Rom. 9. 8. *children of promise,* Gal. 4. 28.
Ps. 128. 3. 6. *thy children,* 147. 13. Isa. 54. 13. Matt. 23. 37.
Ps. 115. 14. *your children,* Matt. 7. 11. Luke 11. 13. Acts 2. 39.
Job 19. 18. *young children,* Lam. 4. 4. Nah. 3. 10. Mark 10. 13.
CHOKE, Matt. 13. 7, 22. Mark 4. 7, 19. & 5. 13. Luke 8. 14, 33.
CHOOSE life, Deut. 30. 19.

Josh. 24. 15. *c.* you whom ye will serve
2 Sam. 24. 12. *c.* thee one of them that I
Ps. 25. 12. teach in the way that he shall *c.*
47. 4. *c.* our inheritance for us
Prov. 1. 29. did not *c.* the fear of Lord
3. 31. *c.* none of his ways
Isa. 7. 15. *c.* good and refuse evil, 16.
56. 4. *c.* the things that please me
65. 12. *c.* that wherein I delighted not
64. 4. I also will *c.* their delusions
Phil. 1. 22. what I shall *c.* I wot not
Ps. 65. 4. man whom thou *choosest*
Heb. 11. 25. *choosing* rather to suffer affliction
Josh. 24. 22. ye have *chosen* the Lord
1 Chron. 16. 13. children of Jacob his *c.*
Job 36. 21. this hast *c.* rather than afflict
Ps. 33. 12. *c.* for his own inheritance
105. 6. children of Jacob his *c.* 43.
Prov. 16. 16. rather to be *c.* than silver
22. 1. a good name is rather to be *c.* than
Isa. 66. 3. have *c.* their own ways
Jer. 8. 3. death shall be *c.* rather than
49. 19. who is a *c.* man that, 50. 44.
Matt. 20. 16. many are called, but few *c.* 22. 14.
Mark 13. 20. elect's sake whom he hath *c.*
Luke 10. 42. Mary hath *c.* that good part
John 15. 16. ye have not *c.* me, but I have *c.* you
Acts 9. 15. he is a *c.* vessel to me
22. 14. God hath *c.* thee that thou
1 Cor. 1. 27. God hath *c.* the foolish things
Eph. 1. 4. hath *c.* us in him before the foundation
2 Thess. 2. 13. from beginning *c.* you to salvation through the Spirit
1 Pet. 2. 4. *c.* of God and precious
1 Pet. 2. 9. ye are a *c.* generation
Rev. 17. 14. are called, and *c.* and faithful
Isa. 41. 9. *I have chosen,* 43. 10. & 58. 6. Matt. 12. 18.
Ps. 119. 30.—the way of truth
137. thy precepts
Isa. 44. 1, 2. Israel—Jeshurun whom
48. 10.—thee in the furnace of affliction
John 13. 18. I know whom—
15. 16. 19.—you out of the world
CHRIST should be born, Matt. 2. 4.
16. 16. thou art *C.* son of the living
23. 8. one is your master even *C.* 10.
Mark 9. 41. because ye belong to *C.*
Luke 24. 26. ought not *C.* to have suffered
46. it behooved *C.* to suffer and rise
John 4. 25. Messias which is called *C.*
7. 26. that this is the very *C.*
13. 34. that *C.* abideth for ever
Acts 8. 5. preached *C.* to them
Rom. 5. 6. *C.* died for the ungodly
8. while yet sinners *C.* died for us
8. 9. have not the spirit of *C.*
10. if *C.* be in you the body is dead
9. 5. of whom *C.* came, who is over all
10. 4. *C.* is the end of the law for
15. 3. *C.* pleased not himself
1 Cor. 1. 24. *C.* the power of God
3. 23. ye are *C.'s* and *C.* is God's
5. 7. *C.* our passover is sacrificed for us
2 Cor. 6. 15. what concord hath *C.* with Belial
Gal. 2. 20 crucified with *C. C.* liveth
3. 13. *C.* hath redeemed us from
4. 19. till *C.* be formed in you
5. 24. that are *C.'s* have crucified the

Eph. 2. 12. ye were without *C.* being alienated
3. 17. that *C.* may dwell in your hearts
4. 20. ye have not so learned *C.*
5. 14. *C.* shall give thee light
23. as *C.* is the head of the church
6. 5. in singleness of heart as unto *C.*
Phil. 1. 21. to me to live is *C.*
23. I desire to depart, and be with *C.*
3. 8. that I may win *C.*
4. 13. can do all things through *C.*
Col. 1. 27. *C.* in you hope of glory
3. 4. when *C.* who is our life shall
11. *C.* is all in all
Rom. 8. 1. to them in *Christ Jesus*
2. law of the spirit of life in—
1 Cor. 1. 30. of him are ye in—
2. 2. save—and him crucified
2 Cor. 13. 5. how that—is in you, except
Gal. 3. 28. ye are all one in—26
5. 6. in—neither circumcision nor uncircumcision availeth
Eph. 1. 1. saints and to faithful in—
2. 10. created in—unto works, 1. 1.
Phil. 2. 11. confess that—is Lord
3. 3. rejoice in—and have no confidence
12. for which I am apprehended of—
Col. 2. 6. received—the Lord, 3. 24.
1 Tim. 1. 15. that—that came into the
2. 5. one mediator, the man—
2 Tim. 2. 3. as a good soldier of—
3. 12. will live godly in—shall suffer
Heb. 13. 8.—the same yesterday and to-day
Rom. 12. 5. one body *in Christ*
16. 3. 7. were—before me, 10.
1 Cor. 5. 18. fallen asleep—are perished
19. in this life only have hope—
2 Cor. 15. 17. if any man be—he is a new creature
19. God was—reconciling world
12. 2. I knew a man—
Gal. 1. 22. churches which were—
Phil. 1. 13. my bonds—are manifest
2. 1. if there be any consolation—
Col. 1. 2. saints and faithful brethren—
1 Thess. 4. 16. the dead—shall rise first
John 1. 25. *that Christ,* 6. 69.
Matt. 16. 20. *the Christ,* 26. 63. Mark 8. 29. Luke 3. 15. John 1. 20. 41. 1 John 2. 22. & 5. 1.
Rom. 6. 8. if we be dead *with Christ*
8. 17. heirs of God and joint heirs—
Gal. 2. 20. I am crucified—
Eph. 2. 5. quickened us together—
Phil. 1. 23. desiring to be—
Col. 2. 20. if ye be dead—from the
3. 1. if ye be risen—seek those things
3. 3. your life is hid—in God
Rev. 20. 4. reigned—1000 years
Acts 26. 28. persuadest me to be a *Christian*
1 Pet. 4. 15. suffer as a *C.* let him not
Acts 11. 26, first called *Christians* at Antioch
CHURCH, Acts 14. 27. & 15. 3.
1 Cor. 4. 17. & 14. 4. 24. 3 John 9.
Matt. 16. 18. on this rock will I build my *c.*
18. 17. tell it to the *c.* neglect to hear the *c.*
Acts 2. 47. Lord added to *c.* daily
5. 11. great fear came on all the *c.*
8. 1. great persecution against *c.*
11. 26. assembled themselves with *c.*
14. 23. ordained elders in every *c.*
15. 22. pleased elders, with whole *c.*
1 Cor. 14. 4, 5. that *c.* may receive edifying
16. 19. *c.* in their house, Col. 4. 15.
Eph. 1. 22. head over all things to *c.*

3. 10. known by *c.* the wisdom of
5, 24, as *c,* is subject unto Christ
25. as Christ loved the *c.* and gave
27. present to himself a glorious *c.*
29. cherish it as the Lord the *c.*
32. concerning Christ and the *c.*
Phil. 3. 6. concerning zeal, persecuting *c.*
4. 15. no *c.* communicated with me
Col. 1. 18. head of the body, the *c.*
24, for his body's sake which is *c.*
1 Tim. 5. 16. let not *c.* be charged
Heb. 12. 23. assembly and *c.* of firstborn
3 John 6, witness of charity before *c.*
Acts 7. 38. *in the church,* 13. 1. 1.
Cor. 6. 4. Eph. 3. 21. Col. 4. 16.
Acts 20. 28. *the church of God,* 1 Cor.
1. 2. 2 Cor. 1. 1. Gal. 1. 13.
9. 31. then had *churches* rest
15. 41. confirming the *c.*
16. 5. so were the *c.* established in faith
Rom. 16. 16. *c.* of Christ salute you
1 Cor. 7. 17. and so ordain I in all *c.*
11. 16. no such custom, neither *c.* of God
14. 33. as in all *c.* of saints
34. women keep silence in the *c.*
1 Thess. 2. 14. became followers of *c.*
2 Thess. 1. 4. glory in you in the *c.*
Rev. 1. 4. seven *c.* in Asia, 11.
20. angels of the seven *c.* and the seven candlesticks are the seven *c.*
2. 7. hear what the Spirit saith to the *c.* 11. 17.
2. 23. and all the *c.* shall know, I am he
22. 16. testify these things in the *c.*
CHURL, Isa. 32. 5. 7.—*churlish,*
1 Sam. 25. 3.
CIRCUIT, 1 Sam. 7: 16. Job 22. 14.
Ps. 19. 6. Eccl. 1. 6.
CIRCUMCISE, Gen. 17. 11.
Deut. 10. 16. *c.* the foreskin of your heart
30. 6. the Lord will *c.* thy heart
Josh. 5. 2. *c.* again Israel, 4. Joshua did *c.*
Jer. 4. 4. *c.* yourselves to the Lord
Gen. 17. 10. every male shall be *circumcised,* 14. 23, 26. Phil. 3. 5.
21. 4. Abraham *c.* his son Isaac
Josh. 5. 3. *c.* the children of Israel
Jer. 9. 25. punish *c.* with uncircumcised
Acts 15. 1. except ye be *c.* ye cannot be
24. ye must be *c.* and keep the law
Acts 16. 3. *c.* him because of the Jews
Gal. 2. 3. neither was compelled to be *c.*
5. 2. if ye be *c.* Christ profiteth you
Col. 2. 11. in whom also ye are *c.* with
John 7. 22. Moses gave unto you *circumcision*
Acts 7. 8. God gave him the covenant of *c.*
Rom. 2. 25. *c.* profiteth if thou keep the law
29. *c.* is that of the heart in the
3. 1. what profit is there of *c.*
30. which shall justify *c.* by faith
4. 9. comes this blessedness on the *c.* only
11. he received the sign of *c.*
15. 8. Christ was minister of the *c.*
Cor. 7. 19. *c.* is nothing but keeping
Gal. 2. 7. gospel of the *c.* was unto Peter
5. 6. neither *c,* availeth anything, nor uncircumcision
Phil. 3. 3. we are the *c.* which worship
Col. 2. 11. circumcised with *c.* without hands
Tit. 1. 10. especially they of the *c.*
CIRCUMSPECT, Ex. 23. 13.
Eph. 5. 15. that ye walk *circumspectly*

CISTERN, Prov. 5. 15.
Jer. 2. 13. hewed them out *cisterns*
CITY, Cain builded a, Gen. 4. 17.
Ps. 107. 4. found no *c.* to dwell in
7. might go to *c.* of habitation
122. 3. as a *c.* that is compactly built
127. 1. except the Lord keep the *c.*
Song 3. 2. I will go about the *c.* in
Isa. 1. 21. the faithful *c.* is become a harlot
22. 2. a tumultuous *c.* a joyous *c.*
23. 7. your joyous *c.* 8. crowning *c.*
26. 1. we have a strong *c.*
33. 20. the *c.* of our solemnities
62. 12. sought out a *c.* not forsaken
Jer. 3. 14. take one of a *c.* two of a
29. 7. seek the peace of the *c.*
Amos 3. 6. shall there be evil in a *c.*
Zeph. 2. 15. this is the rejoicing *c.*
3. 1. wo to the oppressing *c.*
Zech. 8. 3. shall be *c.* of truth
Matt. 5. 14. a *c.* set on a hill cannot be hid
23. 34. persecute them from *c.* to *c.*
Luke 10. 8. into whatsoever *c.* ye enter
12. tolerable for Sodom than for that *c.*
19. 41. he beheld *c.* and wept over
Heb. 11. 10. he looked for a *c.* which hath foundations
16. he hath prepared for them a *c.*
12. 22. to the *c.* of the living God
13. 14. have here no continuing *c.*
Rev. 3. 12. name of the *c.* of my God
20. 9. compassed about beloved *c.*
Neh. 11. 1. *holy city,* Isa. 48. 2. Dan.
9. 24. Matt. 4. 5. Rev. 11. 2.
Num. 35. 11. *cities of refuge,* Josh.
21. 13. 21, 27, 32, 38.
Amos 4. 8. two or three *cities* wandered unto one city
Luke 19. 17. have thou authority over ten *c.*
Acts 26. 11. persecuted unto strange *c*
2 Pet. 2. 6. turning the *c.* of Sodom and Gomorrah
Rev. 16. 19. the *c.* of the nations fell
Luke 15. 15. *citizen,* & 19. 14.
Eph. 2. 19. fellow *citizens* with saints
CLAMOUR, Eph. 4. 31. Prov. 9. 13.
CLAY, Job. 27. 16. & 38. 14.
4. 19. them that dwell in houses of *c.*
Job 10. 9. thou hast made me as the *c.*
13. 12. your bodies to bodies of *c.*
33. 6. I am formed out of the *c.*
Isa. 64. 8. we are the *c.* thou our potter, 45. 9. Jer. 18. 6.
Ps. 40. 2. brought me out of miry *c.*
Dan. 2. 33. part of iron, part of *c.*
Hab. 2. 6. that ladeth himself with thick *c.*
Rom. 9. 21. hath not potter power over the *c.*
CLEAN beasts, Gen. 7. 2.
Lev. 10. 10. between unclean and *c.*
11. 47. Ezek. 22. 26. & 44. 23.
Job 14. 4. who bring *c.* things out of unclean
15. 14. what is man that he should be *c.*
25. 4. can he be *c.* that is born of a woman
Ps. 19. 9. the fear of the Lord is *c.* enduring for ever
Prov. 16. 2. ways of man are *c.* in his
20. 9. who can say I have made my heart *c.*
Isa. 1. 16. wash ye, make you *c.* put
52. 11. be ye *c.* that bear the vessels
Jer. 13. 27. wilt thou not be made *c.*
Ezek. 36. 25. sprinkle *c.* water, ye shall be *c.*
Matt. 8. 3. I will, be thou *c.*
23. 25. make *c.* outside of
Luke 11. 41. all things are *c.* to you
John 13. 11. ye are *c.* but not all
15. 3. ye are *c.* through the word
Rev. 19. 8. fine linen, *c.* and white
Job 17. 9. *clean hands,* Ps. 24. 4.
Ps. 51. 10. *clean heart,* 73. 1.

18. 24. according to the *cleanness*
Amos 4. 6. given you *c.* of teeth in all cities
Ps. 19. 12. *cleanse* me from secret faults
51. 2. *c.* me from my sin
119. 9. shall a young man *c.* his way
Jer. 33. 8. I will *c.* them from all sin
Ezek. 36. 25. from your idols will I *c.* you
Matt. 10. 8. heal sick, *c.* the lepers
23. 26. *c.* first that within the cup
2. Cor. 7. 1. let us *c.* ourselves from
Eph. 5. 26. *c.* it with the washing of water
James 4. 8. *c.* your hands, ye sinners
1 John 1. 9. *c.* us from all unrighteousness
2 Chron. 30. 19. though not *cleansed* according
Ps. 73. 13. I have *c.* my heart in vain
Ezek. 36. 32. *c.* you from all iniquities
Matt. 11. 5. the lepers are *c.*
Luke 17. 17. were there not ten *c.* 9.
Acts 10. 15. what God hath *c.* 11. 9.
1 John 1. 7. blood of Jesus Christ *c.* us from sin
CLEAR the guilty, Ex. 34. 7.
Ps. 51. 4. be *c.* when thou judgest
Song. 6. 10. looketh *c.* as the sun
Zech. 14. 6. light shall not be *c.* nor dark
CLEAVE to his wife, Gen. 2. 24.
Matt. 19. 5. Mark 10. 7. Eph. 5. 31.
Deut. 4. 4. ye did *c.* to the Lord, 10.
20. Josh. 22. 5. & 23. 8.
Ps. 22. 15. tongue *cleaveth* to my jaws
44. 25. our belly *c.* unto the earth
119. 25. my soul *c.* unto the dust
137. 6. my tongue *c.* to the roof of my mouth
Acts 11. 23. purpose of heart they would *c.* to the Lord
Rom. 12. 9. *c.* to that which is good
CLIMB, Jer. 4. 29.
Amos 9. 2. though they *c.* to heaven
John 10. 1. *climbeth* some other way
CLOAK, Matt. 5. 40. Luke 6. 29.
Isa. 59. 17. clad with zeal as with *c.*
John 15. 22. have no *c.* for their sin
1 Thes. 2. 5. nor used *c.* of covetousness
1 Pet. 2. 16. liberty for *c.* of maliciousness
CLOSET, Joel 2. 16. Matt. 6. 6.
CLOTHE, Matt. 6. 30. Luke 12. 28.
Job 10. 11. *clothed* me with skin and flesh
Ps. 35. 26. be *c.* with shame, 132. 18.
104. 1. *c.* with honour and majesty
109. 18. he *c.* himself with cursing
132. 9. priests be *c.* with righteousness
16. *c.* her priests with salvation
Isa. 61. 10. *c.* me with garments of salvation
Ezek. 16. 10. I *c.* thee with broidered
Zeph. 1. 8. *c.* with strange apparel
Matt. 11. 8. *c.* in soft raiment
25. 36. naked, and ye *c.* me
43. *c.* me not
2 Cor. 5. 2. desiring to be *c.* upon with
3. that being *c.* we shall not
4. not unclothed, but *c.* upon
1 Pet. 5. 5. be *c.* with humility
Rev. 3. 5. be *c.* with white raiment
11. 3. prophecy *c.* in sackcloth and ashes
12. 1. a woman *c.* with the sun
19. 13. *c.* in vesture dipped in blood
14. *c.* in fine linen, clean and white
Job. 22. 6. *clothing,* 24. 27. Mark 12.
38. Acts 10. 30. James 2. 3.
Ps. 45. 13. her *c.* is of wrought gold
Prov. 31. 35. strength and honour are her *c.*
Isa. 59. 17. garment of vengeance for *c.*
Matt. 7. 15. come in sheep's *c.*

11. 8. that wear soft *c.* are in king's houses
CLOUD, Gen. 9. 13. Isa. 18. 4.
Isa. 44. 22. blotted out as a *c.* and a thick *c.*
1 Cor. 10. 1. our fathers were under *c.*
1 Cor. 10. 2. baptized unto Moses in the *c.*
Heb. 12. 1. so great a *c.* of witnesses
Rev. 11. 12. ascended to heaven in *c.*
Hos. 6. 4. *morning cloud,* 13. 3.
Judg. 5. 4. *clouds* dropped water
2 Sam. 23. 4. as a morning without *c.*
Ps. 36. 5. faithfulness reacheth to *c.*
57. 10. thy truth unto the *c.* 108. 4.
104. 3. who maketh *c.* his chariot
Eccl. 11. 4. regardeth *c.* shall not reap
Matt. 24. 30. coming in the *c.* of heaven, 26. 64. Mark 13. 26.
1 Thess. 4. 17. caught up in *c.* to meet
2 Pet. 2. 17. *c.* carried with a tempest
Jude 12. *c.* without water, carried about
Rev. 1. 7. he cometh with *c.*
CLOVEN tongues, Acts 2. 3.
COAL, 2 Sam. 14. 7. Isa. 47. 14.
Lam. 4. 8. Ps. 18. 8, 12.
Prov. 6. 28. can one go on hot *coals*
25. 22. heap *c.* of fire on head,
Rom. 12. 20.
26. 21. as *c.* are to burning *c.*
Song 8. 6. *c.* thereof are *c.* of fire
COAT, Gen. 3. 21. Ex. 28. 4.
Song 5. 3. put off my *c.* how put on
Matt. 5. 40. if any man take away thy *c.*
COLD, Gen. 8. 22. Job 24. 7.
Matt. 24. 12. the love of many wax *c.*
Rev. 3. 15. neither *c.* nor hot, 16.
COLLECTION, 1 Cor. 16. 1.
COME, Gen. 49. 6.
Ex. 20. 24. I will *c.* and bless thee
1 Sam. 17. 45. I *c.* to thee in name of
1 Chron. 29. 14. all things *c.* of thee, 12.
Job 22. 21. good shall *c.* unto thee
37. 13. he causeth it *c.* for correction
38. 11. hitherto shall thou *c.*
Ps. 22. 31. they shall *c.* and shall declare
40. 7. lo I *c.* Heb. 10. 9.
65. 2. to thee shall all flesh *c.*
Eccl. 9. 2. all things *c.* alike to all
Song 4. 16. awake north wind, *c.* thou south
Isa. 26. 20. *c.* my people, enter into
35. 4. God will *c.* and save you
55. 1. *c.* to the waters *c.* and buy yea *c.*
3. incline your ear, and *c.* unto me
Ezek. 33. 31. *c.* to thee as the people cometh
Mic. 6. 6. wherewith shall I *c.* before the Lord
Hab. 2. 3. it will surely *c.* it will not tarry
Mal. 3. 1. Lord shall suddenly *c.* to his temple
4. 6. lest I *c.* and smite the earth
Matt. 8. 11. many shall *c.* from the east and west, Luke 7. 19, 20.
11. 3. thou that should *c.* Gen. 49. 10.
28. *c.* unto me all ye that labour
16. 24. if any man will *c.* after me, let
22. 4. all things are ready, *c.* to the marriage
Luke 7. 8. I say *c.* and he cometh
14. 20. I have married a wife, I cannot *c.*
John 1. 39. *c.* and see, 46. Rev. 6. 1,
3, 5, 7. & 17. 1. & 21. 9.
John 5. 40. ye will not *c.* to me to have
6. 44. no man can *c.* to me, except
7. 37. if any man thirst, let him *c.*
14. not leave you, I will *c.* to
Acts 16. 9. *c.* over, and help us
1 Cor. 11. 26. show the Lord's death till he *c.*

2 Cor. 6. 17. *c.* out from among them
Heb. 4. 16. let us *c.* boldly unto the throne
7. 25. save them that *c.* to God by him
10. 37. he that shall *c.* will *c.*
Rev. 18. 4. *c.* out of her, my people
22. 7. I *c.* quickly, 12. 20.
17. Spirit and the bride say *c.* athirst *c.*
20. amen, even so *c.* Lord Jesus
Ps. 118. 26. that *cometh* in the name of the Lord
Eccl. 11. 8. all that *c.* is vanity
Isa. 63. 1. who is this that *c.* from Edom
Matt. 3. 11. he that *c.* after me, is mightier
Luke 6. 47. whosoever *c.* to me and
John 3. 31. he that *c.* from above, is above all
6. 35. he that *c.* to me shall never hunger
37. *c.* to me, I will in no wise cast out
45. hath learned of Father, *c.* unto me
14. 6. no man *c.* to Father, but by me
Heb. 11. 6. that *c.* to God must believe
Jas. 1. 17. gift *c.* down from Father
Heb. 10. 1. make the *comers* perfect
Ps. 19. 5. as a bridegroom *coming*
121. 8. Lord shall preserve thy *c.* in
Mal. 3. 2. who may abide the day of his *c.*
4. 5. before the *c.* of the great day
Matt. 24. 3. what shall be sign of thy *c.*
27. so shall the *c.* of Son of man be
48. my Lord delayeth his *c.*
John 1. 27. *c.* after me is preferred before
1 Cor. 1. 7. waiting for the *c.* of our
15. 23. that are Christ's at his *c.*
1 Thess. 2. 19. presence of Jesus Christ at his *c.* 3. 13. & 5. 23.
1 Pet. 2. 4. to whom *c.* as to a living stone
2 Pet. 1. 16. the power and *c.* of our Lord Jesus
3. 12. hasting unto *c.* of day of God
1 Thess. 4. 15. *coming of the Lord,* 2 Thess. 2. 1. James 5. 7, 8.
COMELY, 1 Sam. 16. 18. Job. 41. 12.
Ps. 33. 1. praise is *c.* for the upright
Prov. 30. 29. yea, four are *c.* in going
Song 1. 5. I am black but *c.*
10. thy cheeks are *c.* with rows
2. 14. thy countenance is *c.*
6. 4. thou art *c.* as Jerusalem
1 Cor. 7. 35. for that which is *c.*
11. 13. is it *c.* that a woman pray uncovered
Isa. 53. 2. no form nor *comeliness*
Ezek. 16. 14. perfect through my *c.*
COMFORT, Ps. 119. 50.
Matt. 9. 22. be of good *c.* Mark 10. 49. Luke 8. 48. 2 Cor. 13. 11.
Acts 9. 31. walking in *c.* of the Holy Ghost
Rom. 15. 4. patience and *c.* of the
1 Cor. 14. 3. to exhortation and *c.*
2 Cor. 1. 3. Father of mercies and God of *c.*
7. 4. I am filled with *c.*
Col. 4. 11. have been a *c.* to me
Job 7. 13. my bed shall *c.* me
Ps. 23. 4. thy rod and staff they *c.*
119. 82. when will thou *c.* me
Song 2. 5. *c.* me with apples, for I am sick
Isa. 40. 1. *c.* ye *c.* ye my people
51. 3. Lord shall *c.* Zion, Zech. 1. 17.
61. 2. to *c.* all that mourn
Jer. 31. 13. I will *c.* and make them
Lam. 1. 2. none to *c.* her, 21.
2 Cor. 1. 4. be able to *c.* them—by *c.*
Eph. 6. 22. might *c.* your hearts
1 Thess. 4. 18. *c.* one another with these

5. 11. *c.* yourselves together and edify.
14. *c.* the feeble minded, support
2 Thess. 2. 17. *c.* your heart and stablish
Isa. 40. 2. *comfortably,* Hos. 2. 14. 2 Sam. 19. 7. 2 Chron. 30. 22.
Gen. 24. 67. *comforted,* 37. 35.
Ps. 77. 2. my soul refused to be *c.*
119. 52. I have *c.* myself
Isa. 49. 13. God hath *c.* his people
54. 11. tossed with tempest, and not *c.*
Matt. 5. 4. that mourn, they shall be *c.*
Luke 16. 25. now is he *c.* and thou tormented
Rom. 1. 12. I may be *c.* together with
1 Cor. 14. 31. learn and all may be *c.*
2 Cor. 1. 4. wherewith we ourselves are *c.*
7. 13. we were *c.* in your comfort
Col. 2. 2. that their hearts might be *c.*
1 Thess. 3. 7. were *c.* over you in all
John 14. 16, 26. *comforter,* 15. 26.
Job 16. 2. *comforter,* Ps. 69. 20.
Isa. 51. 12. I am he that *comforteth*
2 Cor. 1. 4. *c.* us in all our tribulations
7. 6. *c.* those that are cast down
John 14. 18. *comfortless*
Ps. 94. 19. *comforts,* Isa. 57. 18.
COMMAND, Ex. 8. 27.
Gen. 18. 19. he will *c.* his children
Lev. 25. 21. I will *c.* my blessing
Deut. 28. 8. Lord shall *c.* the blessing
Ps. 42. 8. Lord will *c.* his loving kindness
44. 4. *c.* deliverance for Jacob
Isa. 45. 11. work of my hands, *c.* ye
Matt. 4. 3. *c.* that these stones be made bread
John 15. 14. if ye do whatsoever I *c.*
1 Cor. 7. 10. unto the married I *c.*
2 Thess. 3. 4. do things which we *c.*
1 Tim. 4. 11. these things *c.* and teach
Ps. 68. 28. God hath *commanded* thy strength
111. 9. he hath *c.* his covenant
119. 4. thou hath *c.* us to keep thy precepts
133. 3. *c.* blessing, even life forever
148. 5. Lord *c.* and they were created
Matt. 28. 20. whatsoever I have *c.* you
Heb. 12. 20. could not endure that was *c.*
Lam. 3. 37. when Lord *commandeth*
Acts 17. 30. now *c.* all men everywhere
Gen. 49. 33. end of *commanding* his sons
1 Tim. 4. 3. *c.* to abstain from meats
Num. 23. 20. receive *commandment*
Ps. 119. 96. thy *c.* is exceeding broad
Prov. 6. 23. the *c.* is a lamp
Hos. 5. 11. willingly walked after *c.*
Matt. 22. 38. is the first and great *c.*
John 10. 18. this *c.* I received of my Father
12. 49. the Father gave me a *c.*
50. his *c.* is life everlasting
13. 34. a new *c.* give I unto you
15. 12. this is my *c.* that ye love one
Rom. 7. 8. sin taking occasion by *c.*
9. when the *c.* came, sin revived
12. the *c.* is holy, just, and good
1 Tim. 1. 5. end of the *c.* is charity
Heb. 7. 16. law of a carnal *c.*
2 Pet. 2. 21. turn from the holy *c.*
1 John 2. 7. an old *c.* which ye had, 8
3. 23. this is his *c.* that we believe
Ex. 34. 28. wrote ten *commandments,* Deut. 4. 13. & 10. 4.
Ps. 111. 7. all his *c.* are sure
112. 1. delight greatly in his *c.*
119. 6. I have respect unto all thy *c.*
10. let me not wander from thy *c.*
19. hide not thy *c.* from me
21. which do not err from thy *c.*
32. I will run the way of thy *c.*

35. make me to go in path of thy *c.*
47. I will delight myself in thy *c.*
48. thy *c.* which I have loved
66. I have believed thy *c.*
73. give understanding to learn thy *c.*
86. all thy *c.* are faithful
98. thy *c.* hath made me wiser than
127. I love thy *c.*—131. longed for *c.*
143. thy *c.* are my delights
151. all thy *c.* are truth
166. I have done thy *c.*
119. 172. all thy *c.* are righteousness
176. I do not forget thy *c.*
Matt. 15. 9. for doctrines *c.* of men
22. 40. on these two *c.* hang all law
Mark 10. 19. knowest the *c.*
Luke 1. 6. walking in all the *c.* of the
Col. 2. 22. after the *c.* of men
1 John 3. 24. keepeth his *c.* dwelleth
2 John 6. love that walk after his *c.*
Num. 15. 40 *do all.—these,—my,—his,* *c.* Deut. 6. 25. 1 Chron. 28. 7. Neh. 10. 29. Ps. 103. 18. Rev. 22. 4.
COMMEND, Gen. 12. 15. Rom. 16. 1. 2 Cor. 3. 1. & 5. 12.
Luke 23. 46. into thy hands I *c.* my spirit
Acts 20. 32. I *c.* you to God and to the
14. 13. *commended* them to Lord
Luke 16. 8. Lord *c.* unjust steward
Rom. 5. 8. God *commendeth* his love
1 Cor. 8. 8. meat *c.* us not to God
2 Cor. 10. 18. not he that *c.* himself is approved, but whom the Lord *c.*
4. 2. *commending* ourselves to every man's conscience
6. 4. *c.* ourselves as ministers of God
Cor. 3. 1. epistles of *commendation*
Ezra 8. 26. *commission*
COMMIT adultery, thou shalt not, Ex. 20. 14. Deut. 5. 18. Matt. 5. 27. Rom. 13. 9. Lev. 5. 17.
Gen. 39. 8. *c.* or to *give in charge*
Job. 5. 8. to God would I *c.* my cause
Ps. 31. 5. into thy hands I *c.* my spirit
37. 5. *c.* thy way unto the Lord
Prov. 16. 3. *c.* thy works unto the Lord
Luke 12. 48. *c.* things worthy of stripes
16. 11. who will *c.* to your trust
John 2. 24. did not *c.* himself to them
Rom. 1. 32. *c.* such things worthy of
1 Tim. 1. 18. this charge I *c.* unto thee
1 Pet. 4. 19. *c.* keeping of their souls
1 John 3. 9. born of God doth not *c.* sin
Jer. 2. 13. *committed* two evils
Luke 12. 48. men have *c.* much
1 Tim. 1. 11. gospel *c.* to my trust, 1 Cor. 9. 17. 2 Cor. 5. 16.
6. 20. keep that which is *c.* to thee
2 Tim. 1. 12. which I have *c.* to him
14. good thing *c.* to thee keep by the Holy Ghost
1 Pet. 2. 23. *c.* himself to him that judgeth
Jude 15. which they have ungodly *c.*
Ps. 10. 14. poor *committeth* himself to thee
John 8. 34. who *c.* sin is the servant of
1 John 3. 8. who *c.* sin is of the devil
COMMON, Num. 16. 29. 1 Sam. 21. 4, 5.
Eccl. 6. 1. Ezek. 23. 42.
Acts 2. 44. had all things *c.* 4. 32.
10. 15. what God hath cleansed call not *c.*
1 Cor. 10. 13. temptation *c.* to man
Tit. 1. 4. son after the *c.* faith
Jude 3. write of the *c.* salvation
Eph. 2. 12. *commonwealth* of Israel
Matt. 28. 15. *commonly,* 1 Cor. 5. 1.
COMMUNE with your own heart, Ps. 4. 4. & 77. 6. Eccl. 1. 16.
COMMUNICATE to him that teacheth in all good things, Gal. 6. 6.
Phil. 4. 14. *c.* with my affliction

1 Tim. 6. 18. distribute, willing to *c.*
Heb. 13. 16. to *c.* forget not
Gal. 2. 2. *communicated* to them the gospel
Phil. 4. 15. no church *c.* with me in
2 Kings 9. 11. *communication*
Matt. 5. 37. let your *c.* be yea, nay
Eph. 4. 29. let no corrupt *c.* proceed
Col. 3. 8. let no filthy *c.* proceed
Luke 24. 17. what manner of *c.* are
1 Cor. 15. 33. evil *c.* corrupt good manners
10. 16. *communion* of the blood of Christ—*c.* of the body of Christ
2 Cor. 6. 14. what *c.* hath light with darkness
13. 14. *c.* of the Holy Ghost be with
COMPACT, Ps. 122. 3.
COMPANY, Gen. 32. 8, 21.
Ps. 55. 14. to the house of God in *c.*
Prov. 29. 3. keepeth *c.* with harlots
Song 6. 13. as the *c.* of two armies
Acts 4. 23. went to their own *c.*
Rom. 15. 24. first filled with your *c.*
1 Cor. 5. 11. not to keep *c.* with
2 Thess. 3. 14. have no *c.* with him
Heb. 12. 22. innumerable *c.* of angels
Ps. 119. 63. I am a *companion* of
Prov. 13. 20. *c.* of fools shall be destroyed
Mal. 2. 14. thy *c.* and wife of covenant
Phil. 2. 25. Epaphroditus my *c.* in
Rev. 1. 9. your *c.* in tribulation
Ps. 45. 14. *companions* that follow her
122. 8. for my *c.* sakes—peace be
Song 1. 7. aside by flocks of thy *c.*
8. 13. *c.* hearken to thy voice
Isa. 1. 23. princes *c.* of thieves
Heb. 10. 33. became *c.* of them
COMPARE, Isa. 40. 18.
Ps. 89. 6. who in heaven can be *c.* to
Prov. 3. 15. not to be *c.* to wisdom, 8. 11.
Song. 1. 9. I have *c.* my love to company
Rom. 8. 18. not worthy to be *c.*
1 Cor. 2. 13. *c.* spiritual things with
2 Cor. 10. 12. *c.* ourselves—*c.* them
Judge 8. 2. *comparison,* Hag. 2. 3.
COMPASS, Ex. 27. 5. 2 Sam. 5. 23. 2 Kings 3. 9. Prov. 8. 27.
Ps. 5. 12. with favour *c.* him about
26. 6. so I will *c.* thy altar
32. 10. mercy shall *c.* him about
Isa. 50. 11. *c.* yourselves with sparks
Jer. 31. 22. a woman shall *c.* a man
Hab. 1. 4. wicked doth *c.* about the
Matt. 23. 15. ye *c.* sea and land to make
Ps. 16. 4. sorrow *compassed* me
40. 12. innumerable evils have *c.* me
118. 10.—12. all nations *c.* me about
Jonah 2. 3. floods *c.* me about, 5.
Heb. 12. 1. we are *c.* about with a cloud
Ps. 73. 6. pride *compasseth* them
139. 3. thou *c.* my path and
Hos. 11. 12. Ephraim *c.* me about with
COMPASSION, 1 Kings 8. 50. 2 Chron. 30. 9. 1 John 3. 17.
Matt. 9. 36. *moved with compassion,* 14. 14. & 18. 27.
Ps. 78. 38. *full of compassion,* 86. 15 & 111. 4. & 112. 4. & 145. 8.
Deut. 13. 17. *have compassion,* 33. 3. 2 Kings 13. 23. 2 Chron. 36. 15. Jer. 12. 15. Lam. 3. 32. Mic. 7. 19. Rom. 9. 15. Heb. 5. 2. Jude 22.
Lam. 3. 22. his *compassions* fail not
COMPEL, Luke 14. 23.
Esth. 1. 8. drinking, none did *c.*
2 Chron. 21. 11. *compelled* Judah thereto
Acts 26. 11. I *c.* them to blaspheme
2 Cor. 12. 11. I am a fool, ye *c.* me
Gal. 2. 3. not *c.* to be circumcised

14. why *compellest* Gentiles to live as Jews.
COMPLAIN, Num. 11. 11.
Lam. 3. 39. why doth a living man *c.*
Num. 11. 1. *complainers,* Jude 16.
Ps. 144. 14. *complaining* in streets
Job 21. 4. *complaint,* 23. 2. Ps. 142. 2.
COMPLETE in him, Col. 2. 10.
4.12. stand *c.* in all the will of God
COMPREHEND, Job. 37. 5. Isa. 40. 12. John. 1. 4. Rom. 13. 9.
CONCEAL, Gen. 37. 26.
Job 27. 11. with Almighty I will not *c.*
41. 12. I will not *c.* parts nor proportion
Prov. 25. 2. glory of God to *c.* a thing
Ps. 40. 10. I have not *concealed* thy loving-kindness
Prov. 12. 23. prudent man *concealeth* knowledge
CONCEIT, own, Prov. 18. 11. & 26. 5, 12, 16. & 28. 11. Rom. 11. 25.
CONCEIVE, Judg. 13. 3.
Job 15. 35. they *c.* mischief
Ps. 51. 6. in sin did my mother *c.* me
Isa. 7. 14. a virgin shall *c.* a son
33. 11. ye shall *c.* chaff
59. 13. *c.* words of falsehood
Num. 11. 12. have I *conceived* all this people
Ps. 7. 14. hath *c.* mischief
Song 3. 4. chamber of her that *c.* me
Jer. 49. 30. *c.* a purpose against you
Acts 5. 4. why hast thou *c.* in thy heart
James 1. 15. lust hath *c.* it bringeth forth
CONCISION, Phil. 3. 2.
CONCLUDED them all in unbelief, Rom. 11. 32.
Gal. 3. 22. Scripture *c.* all under sin
Eccl. 12. 13. *conclusion* of matter
CONCUPISCENCE, sinful lust, Rom. 7. 8. Col. 3. 5.
CONDEMN wicked, Deut. 25. 1.
Job 9. 20. my own mouth shall *c.* me
10. 2. I will say to God, do not *c.*
Ps. 37. 33. nor *c.* him when he is judged
94. 21. they *c.* innocent blood
Isa. 50. 9. Lord will help me who *c.* me
54. 17. tongue—thou shalt *c.*
Luke 6. 37. *c.* not and ye shall not be *c.*
John 3. 17. God sent not his Son into the world to *c.* the world
8. 11. neither do I *c.* thee, go thy way
1 John 3. 20. heart *c.* us, 21.
Matt. 12. 37. by words—*condemned*
John 3. 18. who believe is not *c.*
Rom. 8. 3. for sin *c.* sin in the flesh
1 Cor. 11. 32. not be *c.* with world
Tit. 2. 8. speech that cannot be *c.*
3. 11. being *c.* in himself
Prov. 17. 15. *condemneth* the just
Rom. 8. 34. who is he that *c.*
14. 22. *c.* not himself in that
Luke 23. 40. same *condemnation*
John 3. 19. this is the *c.* that light
5. 24. shall not come into *c.*
Rom. 8. 1. no *c.* to them in Christ
1 Tim. 3. 6. fall into *c.* of the devil
James 3. 1. receive the greater *c.*
5. 12. swear not, lest ye fall into *c.*
Jude 4. of old ordained to this *c.*
CONDESCEND, Rom. 12. 16.
CONFESS, Lev. 5. 5. & 16. 21.
Lev. 26. 10. if they *c.* their iniquities
1 Kings 8. 33. *c.* thy name, 35.
Ps. 32. 5. I will *c.* my transgressions
Matt. 10. 32. shall *c.* me before men
Luke 12. 8. him will I *c.* before my
Rom. 10. 9. with thy mouth Jesus, 14. 11. & 15. 9. Phil. 2. 11.
James 5. 16. *c.* your faults one to another
1 John 1. 9. if we *c.* our sins

4. 15. *c.* Jesus is Son of God, 2 John 7.
Heb. 11. 13. *confessed,* Ezra 10. 1.
Prov. 28. 13. *confesseth* and forsaketh
Josh 7. 19. *confession,* 2 Chron. 30. 22. Ezra 10. 11. Dan. 9. 4.
Rom. 10. 10. *c.* is made to salvation
1 Tim. 6. 13. witnessed a good *c.*
CONFIDENCE, Job. 4. 6.
Ps. 65. 5. *c.* of all the ends of the earth
118. 8. than to put *c.* in man
Prov. 3. 26. Lord shall be thy *c.*
Mic. 7. 5. put not *c.* in a guide, Prov. 25. 19. Ezek. 28. 26.
Phil. 3. 3. have no *c.* in the flesh
Heb. 3. 6. if we hold fast the *c.* 14.
10. 35. cast not away your *c.*
1 John 2. 28. appear we may have *c.*
Ps. 27. *confident,* Prov. 14. 16.
CONFIRM, Isa. 35. 3.
Dan. 9. 27. shall *c.* the covenant
Rom. 15. 8. to *c.* the promises
1 Cor. 1. 8. shall *c.* you to the end
2 Cor. 2. 8. *c.* your love toward him
Isa. 44. 26. *confirmeth* word of his servant
Acts 14. 22. *confirming* souls of the
CONFLICT, Phil. 1. 30. Col. 2. 1.
CONFORMED to the image, Rom. 8. 29.
Rom. 12. 2. be not *c.* to this world
CONFOUND, Gen. 11. 7.
Jer. 1. 17. lest I *c.* thee before them
1 Cor. 1. 27. foolish things to *c.* wise
Ps. 97. 7. *confounded* that serve images
Jer. 17. 18. let not me be *c.*
Ezek. 16. 52. *c.* and bear shame, 54. 63. *c.* and never open mouth more
1 Pet. 2. 6. believeth shall not be *c.*
Ezra 9. 7. *confusion* of face, Dan. 9. 7.
Ps. 44. 15. my *c.* is continually before
71. 1. let me never be put to *c.*
1 Cor. 14. 33. God is not author of *c.*
CONGREGATION, Lev. 4. 21.
Job 15. 34. *c.* of hypocrites desolate
Ps. 1. 5. sinners in *c.* of righteous
26. 5. hated *c.* of evil doers
74. 19. forget not *c.* of the poor
75. 2. receive *c.* I will judge uprightly
82. 1. God stands in *c.* of the mighty
89. 5. faithfulness in *c.* of saints
Prov. 21. 16. remain in *c.* of dead
Hos. 7. 12. chastise as *c.* hath heard
Joel 2. 16. sanctify the *c.*
CONIES, Ps. 104. 18. Prov. 30. 26.
CONQUER, Rev. 6. 2.
Rom. 8. 37. more than *conquerors*
CONSCIENCE, John 8. 9.
Acts 24. 16. a *c.* void of offence
Rom. 2. 15. *c.* bearing witness, 9. 1.
13. 5. not for wrath—for *c.* sake
2 Cor. 1. 12. testimony of our *c.*
1 Tim. 3. 9. mystery of faith in pure *c.*
4. 2. having their *c.* seared with a hot iron
Tit. 1. 15. mind and *c.* is defiled
Heb. 9. 14. purge *c.* from dead works
10. 2. worshippers no more *c.* of sin
22. hearts sprinkled from evil *c.*
Acts 23. 1. *good conscience,* 1 Tim. 1. 19. Heb. 13. 18. 1 Pet. 3. 21.
CONSENT, with one, Ps. 83. 5.
Zeph. 3. 9. Luke 14. 18. 1 Cor. 7. 5.
Prov. 1. 10. entice thee, *c.* thou not
Rom. 7. 16. I *c.* to law that it is good
1 Tim. 6. 3. if any *c.* not to wholesome
Ps. 50. 18. *consentedst* to thief
Acts 8. 1. *consenting,* 22. 20.
CONSIDER, Lev. 13. 13.
Deut. 4. 39. *c.* it in thy heart
32. 29. O that—*c.* their latter end
Ps. 8. 3. when I *c.* the heavens
50. 22. this, ye that forget God
64. 9. wisely *c.* of his doings
Eccl. 5. 1. *c.* not that they do evil
7. 13. *c.* the work of God

14. in day of adversity *c.*
Isa. 1. 3. my people doth not *c.*
5. 12. neither *c.* operation of hands
Hag. 1. 5, 7. Lord *c.* your ways, 2. 15.
2 Tim. 2. 7. *c.* what I say and Lord give
Heb. 3. 1. *c.* apostle and high priest
74. 4. *c.* how great this man was
10. 24. *c.* one another to provoke
12. 3. *c.* him that endured such
Job 1 8. hast thou *considered* my servant, 2. 3.
Ps. 31. 8. hast *c.* my trouble
77. 5. have *c.* days of old
Mark 6. 52. not miracle of loaves
Rom. 4. 19. *c.* not his own body dead
Matt. 7. 3. *considerest* not the beam
Ps. 41. 1. blessed *considereth* poor
Prov. 31. 16. she *c.* a field and buyeth
Isa. 44. 19. none *c.* in his heart
Heb. 13. 7. *considering* end of conversation
CONSIST, Col. 1. 17. Luke 12. 15.
CONSOLATION, Acts 4. 36.
Luke 2. 25. waited for *c.* of Israel
6. 24. wo rich, have received your *c.*
Rom. 15. 5. God of *c.* grant you be
2 Cor. 1. 5. so our *c.* aboundeth by Christ
Phil. 2. 1. if any *c.* in Christ
2 Thess. 2. 16. given us everlasting *c.*
Heb. 6. 18. might have strong *c.*
Job. 15. 11. *consolations*
CONSTRAIN, Gal. 6. 12. Acts 16. 15.
2 Cor. 5. 14. for the love of Christ *c.* us because we thus judge
1 Pet. 5. 2. not by *constraint*
CONSUME, Deut. 5. 25.
Ex. 33. 3. lest I *c.* thee in the way
Ps. 37. 20. they shall *c.* into smoke
39. 11. his beauty to *c.* 49. 14.
78. 33. days did he *c.* in vanity
Ezek. 4. 17. *c.* away for iniquity
2 Thes. 2. 8. Lord shall *c.* with spirit
James 4. 3. *c.* it upon your lusts
Ex. 3. 2. bush was not *consumed*
Ps. 90. 7. we are *c.* by the anger
119. 139. my zeal hath *c.* me
Prov. 5. 11. thy flesh and body are *c.*
Isa. 64. 7. *c.* us because of our iniquities
Lam. 3. 22. of Lord's mercy we are not *c.*
Gal. 5. 15. be not *c.* one another of
Deut. 4. 24. Lord is *consuming* fire, Heb. 12. 20.
Lev. 26. 16. *consumption,* Deut. 28. 22. Isa. 10. 22. & 28. 22.
CONTAIN, Ezek. 23. 32.
1 Kings 8. 27. heaven of heavens cannot *c.* thee, 2 Chron. 2. 6.
John 21. 25. world not *c.* the book
1 Cor. 7. 9. if they cannot *c.* let marry
CONTEMN, God,—Ps. 10. 13.
Ezek. 21. 13. if sword *c.* the rod, 10.
Ps. 15. 4. a vile person is *contemned*
Job. 12. 21. pours *contempt* on princes, Ps. 107. 40.
Ps. 123. 3. filled with *c.* 4.
Dan. 12. 2. some to everlasting *c.*
Mal. 1. 7. the table of the Lord is *contemptible*
2. 9. made you *c.* before all people
2 Cor. 10. 10. his speech is *c.*
CONTEND, Deut. 2. 9.
Isa. 49. 25. I will *c.* with them that *c.*
50. 8. who will *c.* with me
57. 16. for I will not *c.* for ever
Jer. 12. 5. how canst *c.* with horses
Amos 7. 4. Lord calleth to *c.* by fire
Jude 3. *c.* earnestly for the faith
Job 10. 2. cause why thou *contendest*
40. 2. that *contendeth* with the Almighty instruct
Hab. 1. 3. *contention,* Acts 15. 39.
Phil. 1. 16. 1 Thess. 2. 2.
Prov. 13. 10. by pride cometh *c.*
17. 14. leave off *c.* before it be
18. 6. fool's lips enter into *c.*
22. 10. cast out scorner, and *c.* shall
Jer. 15. 10. borne me a man of *c.*

Prov. 18. 18, 19. *contentions,* 19. 13.
1 Cor. 1. 11. Tit. 3. 9.
21. 19. *contentions,* 26. 21. & 27. 15.
Rom. 2. 8. 1 Cor. 11. 16.
CONTENT, Gen. 37. 27.
Phil. 4. 11. state therewith to be *c.*
1 Tim. 6. 8. raiment let us be *c.*
Heb. 13. 5. be *c.* with such things
3 John 10. with malicious words not *c.*
1 Tim. 6. 6. godliness with *contentment*
CONTINUAL, Ex. 29. 42. Num. 4. 7.
Prov. 15. 15. Isa. 14. 6.
Rom. 9. 2. Gen. 5. 6. only evil *continually*
Ps. 34. 1. his praise *c.* in my mouth
52. 1. goodness of God endureth *c.*
71. 3. I may *c.* resort
14. I will hope *c.* and praise more
73. 23. yet I am *c.* with thee
119. 44. keep thy law *c.* for ever
117. respect to thy statutes *c.*
Prov. 6. 21. bind them *c.* upon thy
Isa. 58. 11. Lord shall guide thee *c.*
Hos. 12. 6. wait on thy God *c.*
Acts 6. 4. give ourselves *c.* to prayer
Heb. 13. 15. sacrifice of praise to God *c.*
Deut. 28. 59. *continuance,* Ps. 139. 16.
Isa. 64. 5. Rom. 2. 7.
CONTINUE, Ex. 21. 21.
1 Sam. 12. 14. *c.* following the Lord
1 Kings 2. 4. Lord may *c.* his word
Ps. 36. 10. *c.* thy loving-kindness
102. 28. children of servants shall *c.*
119. 91. *c.* according to thy word
John 8. 31. if ye *c.* in my word
15. 9. *c.* ye in my love, 10.
Acts 13. 43. to *c.* in grace of God
14. 22. to *c.* in the faith
Rom. 6. 1. shall we *c.* in sin that grace
11. 22. if thou *c.* in his goodness
Col. 1. 23. if ye *c.* in faith and not
4. 2. *c.* in prayer and watch
1 Tim. 2. 15. if they *c.* in faith
4. 16. doctrine *c.* in them
2 Tim. 3. 14. *c.* in things learned
Heb. 13. 1. let brotherly love *c.*
Rev. 13. 5. to *c.* forty-two months
Gen. 40. 4. *continued,* Neh. 5. 16.
Luke 6. 12. *c.* all night in prayer
22. 28. *c.* with me in temptations
Acts 1. 14. *c.* with one accord in prayer
2. 42. *c.* steadfastly in apostles' doctrine
20. 7. *c.* his speech till midnight
Heb. 8. 9. *c.* not in my covenant
1 John 2. 19. would have *c.* with us.
Job 14. 2. shadow and *continueth* not
Gal. 3. 10. that *c.* not in all things
1 Tim. 5. 5. *c.* in supplication and prayer
Heb. 7. 24. this man because he *c.* ever
James 1. 25. looketh into the law and *c.*
Jer. 30. 23. *continuing,* Rom. 12. 12.
Acts 2. 46. Heb. 13. 14.
CONTRADICT-ING-ION, Acts 13. 45. Heb. 7. 7. & 12. 3.
CONTRARY, Esther 9. 1.
Lev. 26. 21. walk *c.* to, 23. 27.
Acts 18. 3. *c.* to the law, 20. 3.
26. 9. many things *c.* to the name
Rom. 11. 24. grafted *c.* to nature
16. 17. *c.* to the doctrine received
Gal. 5. 17. are *c.* one to the other
1 Thess. 2. 15. are *c.* to all men
1 Tim. 1. 10. is *c.* to sound doctrine
CONTRIBUTION, Rom. 15. 26.
CONTRITE heart, or spirit, Ps. 34. 18. Isa. 57. 15, 16. & 66. 2.
CONTROVERSY, Deut. 17. 8. 2 Chron. 19. 8. Ezek. 44. 24.
Jer. 25. 31. Lord hath a *c.* Isa. 34. 8.
Hos. 4. 1. & 12. 2. Mic. 6. 2.
1 Tim. 3. 16. without *c.* great is the
CONVENIENT, Jer. 40. 4, 5.

Prov. 30. 8. feed with food *c.* for me
Rom. 1. 28. to do things—not *c.*
Eph. 5. 4. talking and jesting not *c.*
Phil. 8. to enjoin thee which is *c.*
CONVERSATION, Gal. 1. 13. Eph.
2. 3. Heb. 13. 7. 1 Tim. 4. 12.
Ps. 37. 14. such as be of upright *c.*
50. 23. orders his *c.* aright
2 Cor. 1. 12. in sincerity had our *c.*
Phil. 1. 27. let *c.* be as becometh gospel
3. 20. our *c.* is in heaven, from whence
Heb. 13. 5. let *c.* be without covetousness
Jas. 3. 13. show out of good *c.* works
1 Pet. 1. 15. holy in all manner of *c.*
1 Pet. 2. 12. having *c.* honest among Gentiles
3. 1. won by chaste *c.* of wives. 2.
16. accuse your good *c.* in Christ
2 Pet. 2. 7. vexed with filthy *c.* of the
3. 11. in all holy *c.* and godliness
CONVERSION, Acts 15. 3.
CONVERT, Isa. 6. 10.
James 5. 19. err, and one *c.* him, 20.
Ps. 51. 13. sinners—*converted* to thee
Isa. 60. 5. abundance of the sea, *c.* to thee
Matt. 13. 15. should be *c.* and I heal
18. 3. except ye be *c.* and become as children
Luke 22. 32. when thou art *c.* strengthen
Acts 3. 39. repent and be *c.* sins botted out
Ps. 79. 7. *converting* the soul
CONVINCE, Tit. 1. 9. Jude 15.
Job 32. 12. *convinced*, Acts 18. 28.
1 Cor. 14. 24. James 2. 9.
John 8. 46. who *convinceth* me of sin
CORD, Josh. 2. 15. Mic. 2. 5.
Job 30. 11. he hath loosed my *c.*
Eccl. 4. 12. a threefold *c.* is not broken
12. 6. ere the silver *c.* be loosed
Isa. 54. 2. lengthen thy *c.* and strengthen
Job 36. 8. holden *in cords* of affliction
Ps. 2. 3. cast away their *c.* from us
129. 4. cut asunder *c.* of wicked
Prov. 5. 22. holden with *c.* of his sins
Isa. 5. 18. draw iniquity with *c.* of vanity
Hos. 11. 4. drew them with *c.* of man
CORN, Gen. 41. 57. & 42. 2.
Josh. 5. 11. eat of the old *c.* of the land, 12.
Job 5. 26. as a shock of *c.* cometh in
Ps. 65. 13. valleys covered with *c.*
72. 16. handful of *c.* in the earth
78. 24. given them *c.* of heaven to eat
Prov. 11. 26. withholdeth *c.* people curse
Isa. 62. 8. I will no more give *c.* to enemies
Ezek. 36. 29. call for *c.* and increase
Hos. 2. 9. take away my *c.* in time thereof
10. 11. loveth to tread out the *c.*
14. 7. shall revive as *c.* and grow as the vine
Zech. 9. 17. *c.* make young men cheerful
Matt. 12. 1. to pluck the ears of *c.*
John 12. 24. except *c.* of wheat fall
CORNER, Prov. 7. 8. Lev. 21. 5.
Prov. 21. 9. better dwell in *c.* 25. 25.
Isa. 30. 20. teachers removed into *c.*
Zech. 10. 4. out of him came forth *c.*
Matt. 21. 42. become head of *c.* Acts
4. 11. 1 Pet. 2. 7.
Ps. 118. 22. *corner* stone, Isa. 28. 16.
1 Pet. 2. 6. Eph. 2. 20. Matt. 21. 42.
CORRECT, Prov. 29. 17.
Ps. 39. 11. with rebuke doth *c.* man
94. 10. chastiseth heathen not *c.* thee
Jer. 2. 19. own wickedness shall *c.* thee

10. 24. *c.* me but with judgment
30. 11. *c.* in measure, 46. 28.
Job 5. 17. happy is man whom God *c.*
Prov. 3. 12. whom Lord loveth he *c.*
Job 37. 13. whether for *correction*
Prov. 3. 11. but be not weary of his *c.*
22. 15. the rod of *c.* shall drive foolishness
23. 13. withhold not *c.* from child
Jer. 2. 30. they received not *c.* 5. 3.
& 7. 28. Zeph. 3. 2.
Hab. 1. 12. established them for *c.*
2 Tim 3. 16. Scripture profitable for *c.*
CORRUPT, Job 17. 1.
Gen. 6. 11, 12. earth *c.* before God
Ps. 14. 1. they are *c.* 53. 1. & 73. 8.
Mal. 1. 14. sacrificeth to the Lord a *c.*
Matt. 7. 17, 18. a *c.* tree brings—fruit
12. 33. make tree *c.* and fruit *c.*
Eph. 4. 22. old man which is *c.*
29. let no *c.* communication proceed out of your mouth
1 Tim. 6. 5. of *c.* minds, 2 Tim. 3. 8.
Matt. 6. 19. rust doth *c.*
1 Cor. 15. 33. evil communications *c.*
2 Cor. 2. 17. as many who *c.* word
Jude 10. those they *c.* themselves
Gen. 6. 12. all flesh had *corrupted* his
Deut. 9. 12. thy people *c.* themselves
Hos. 9. 9. have deeply *c.* themselves
2 Cor. 7. 2. we have *c.* no man
1 Cor. 9. 25. *corruptible*, 15. 53. 1 Pet.
1. 18, 23.
Job 17. 14. *corruption*, Ps. 16. 10.
Isa. 38. 17. Dan. 10. 8. John 2. 6.
Acts 2. 27. Rom. 8. 21. 1 Cor. 15. 42,
50. Gal. 6. 8. 2 Pet. 1. 4.
COST, 2 Sam. 16. 42. 1 Chron. 21. 24.
Luke 14. 28.
COVENANT, Gen. 17. 2.
Gen. 9. 12. token of the *c.* 13. 17.
17. 4. my *c.* is with thee, 7. 19.
11. a token of the *c.* betwixt
13. my *c.* shall be in the flesh
14. he hath broken my *c.*
Ex. 2. 24. God remembered his *c.* with Abraham
31. 16. sabbath for a perpetual *c.*
34. 28. wrote words of *c.*
Lev. 26. 15. ye brake my *c.*
Judg. 2. 1. never brake *c.* with you
1 Chron. 16. 15. always mindful of his *c.* Ps. 105. 8. & 111. 5.
Neh. 9. 38. we may make a sure *c.*
Job 31. 1. I made a *c.* with mine eyes
Ps. 25. 14. Lord will show them *c.*
44. 17. not dealt falsely in thy *c.*
50. 5. made a *c.* with me by sacrifice
55. 20. broken his *c.* Isa. 33. 8.
74. 20. have respect to the *c.*
78. 37. not steadfast in his *c.* 10.
89. 3. I have made *c.* with my chosen
28. my *c.* shall stand fast, 34.
132. 12. children will keep my *c.*
Prov. 2. 17. forgetteth *c.* of her God
Isa. 28. 18. your *c.* with death
42. 6. given thee for *c.* of people
54. 10. nor *c.* of my peace be removed
56. 4. take hold of my *c.* 6.
Jer. 14. 21. break not *c.* with us
31. 31. make a new *c.* with Israel
50. 5. to Lord in a perpetual *c.*
Ezek. 20. 37 bring into bond of *c.*
Dan. 9. 27. confirm *c.* with many
Hos. 6. 7. have transgressed the *c.*
10. 4. swearing falsely in making *c.*
Mal. 2. 14. the wife of thy *c.*
3. 1. messenger of the *c.*
Acts 3. 25. the children of the *c.*
Rom. 1. 31. *c.* breakers
Heb. 8. 6. he is the mediator of a better *c.* 7. 9.
Gen. 9. 16. *everlasting covenant*, 17.
7. Jer. 24. 8. 2 Sam. 23. 5. 1 Chron.
16. 17. Ps. 105. 10. Isa. 24. 5. Jer. 32.
40. Ezek. 16. 60. Heb. 13. 20.
Gen. 17. 9, 10. *keep, keepest, keepeth*,

covenant, Ex. 19. 5. Deut. 7. 9, 12.
1 Kings 8. 23. 2 Chron. 6. 14. Neh.
1. 5. Ps. 25. 10. Dan. 9. 4.
Gen. 15. 18. Lord *made covenant*,
Ex. 34. 27. Deut. 5. 2, 3. 2 Kings 23.
3 Job 31. 1.
Jer. 31. 31. *new covenant*, Heb. 8. 8,
13. & 12. 24.
Gen. 9. 15. *remember covenant*, Ex.
6. 5. Lev. 26. 42. Ps. 105. 8. Ezek.
16. 60. Amos 1. 9. Luke 1. 72.
Lev. 2. 13. *covenant of* salt, Num.
18. 19. 2 Chron. 13. 5.
Deut. 17. 2. *transgressed the covenant*,
Josh. 7. 11. Judg. 2. 20. 2 Kings 18.
12. Jer. 34. 18. Hos. 6. 7.
Rom. 9. 4. *covenants*, Gal. 4. 24.
Eph. 2. 12. *c.* of promise
COVER, Ex. 10. 5. & 40. 3.
Ex. 21. 33. dig a pit and not *c.* it
33. 22. I will *c.* thee with my hand
Deut. 33. 12. Lord shall *c.* him all day
1 Sam. 24. 3. *c.* his feet, Judg. 3. 24.
Neh. 4. 5. *c.* not their iniquity
Job. 16. 18. *c.* thou not my blood
Ps. 91. 4. *c.* thee with his feathers
Isa. 58. 7. naked that thou *c.* him
11. 9. as waters *c.* sea, Hab. 2. 14.
Hos. 10. 8. say to mountains, *c.* us,
Luke 23. 30. Rev. 6. 16.
1 Cor. 11. 7. man ought not *c.* head
1 Pet. 4. 8. charity shall *c.* a multitude of sins
Job. 31. 33. if I *covered* my transgressions
Ps. 32. 1. whose sin is *c.* Rom. 4. 7.
85. 2. hast *c.* all their sin
Lam. 3. 44. *c.* thyself with a cloud
Matt. 10. 26. nothing *c.* that shall not
Ps. 104. 2. *coverest* thyself with light
73. 6. violence *covereth* them as a
Prov. 10. 12. love *c.* all sins
28. 13. that *c.* his sins—not prosper
Isa. 28. 20. *covering*, 1 Cor. 11. 15.
Isa. 4. 6. *covert*, 16. 4. & 32. 2. Ps. 61.
4. Jer. 25. 38.
COVET, Ex. 20. 17. Mic. 2. 2.
1 Cor. 12. 31. *c.* earnestly best gifts
14. 39. *c.* to prophesy and forbid not
Acts 20. 33. *coveted*, 1 Tim. 6. 10.
Prov. 21. 26. *coveteth*, Hab. 2. 9.
Ps. 10. 3. wicked blesseth *covetous*
Luke 16. 14. Pharisees who were *c.*
1 Cor. 5. 10. or with the *c.* 11.
6. 10. nor *c.* shall inherit kingdom of
Eph. 5. 5. nor *c.* who is an idolater
1 Tim. 3. 3. bishop must not be *c.*
2 Tim. 3. 2. in last days *c.* boasters
2 Pet. 2. 14. exercised with *c.* practices
Ex. 18. 21. hating *covetousness*
Ps. 119. 36. to testimonies and not to *c.*
Prov. 28. 16. hateth *c.* shall prolong days
Ezek. 33. 31. heart goeth after their *c.*
Luke 12. 15. beware of *c.* for man's life
Col. 3. 5. *c.* which is idolatry
Heb. 13. 5. conversation without *c.*
COUNSEL, Num. 27. 21.
Job. 5. 13. *c.* of froward carried headlong
12. 13. he hath *c.* and understanding
21. 16. *c.* of the wicked far, 22. 18.
38. 2. who is this that darkeneth *c.*
by words without knowledge, 42. 3.
Ps. 1. 1. walks not in *c.* of ungodly
16. 7. bless Lord who giveth me *c.*
33. 10, 11. *c.* of Lord stands for ever
Prov. 19. 21. Isa. 46. 10, 11.
55. 14. we took sweet *c.* together
73. 24. guide me by thy *c.* and receive
83. 3. taken crafty *c.* against people
Prov. 1. 25. set at nought all my *c.*
8. 14. *c.* is mine and sound wisdom
11. 14. where no *c.* is people fall
20. 18. purpose established by *c.*

21. 30. no wisdom nor *c.* against Lord
24. 6. by wise *c.* make war
27. 9. sweetness—by hearty *c.*
Isa. 11. 2. spirit of *c.* and might
28. 29. Lord wonderful in *c.* and
40. 14. with whom took he *c.*
44. 26. performs *c.* of his messenger
Jer. 32. 19. God great in *c.* mighty
Zech. 6. 13. *c.* of peace between them
Luke 7. 30. rejected *c.* of God against
Acts 2. 23. by determinate *c.* 4. 28.
5. 38. if this *c.* be of men it shall
20. 27. to declare all the *c.* of God
Eph. 1. 11. after *c.* of his own will
Ezra 4. 5. *counsellors*, 7. 14. Job. 3.
14. & 12. 17. Dan. 3. 24.
Ps. 119. 24. thy testimonies are my *c.*
Prov. 11. 14. in the multitude of *c.* is safety, 24. 26. & 15. 22.
Prov. 12. 20. to *c.* of peace is joy
Isa. 1. 26. restore thy *c.* as the beginning
9. 6. Wonderful, C. the mighty God
19. 11. wise *c.* of Pharaoh—brutish
COUNT, Ex. 12. 4.
Num. 23. 10. who can *c.* the dust of
Job. 31. 4. doth not he *c.* all my steps
Ps. 139. 18. if I *c.* them—more than
22. hate thee, I *c.* them my enemies
Acts 20. 24. neither *c.* I my life dear
Phil. 3. 7, 8, 9. I *c.* all things loss—dung
13. I *c.* not myself to have apprehended
James 1. 2. *c.* it all joy when ye fall
5. 11. we *c.* them happy who endure
Gen. 15. 6. *counted* to him for righteousness, Ps. 106. 31. Rom. 4. 3.
Isa. 40. 17. *c.* to him less than nothing
Hos. 8. 12. of law *c.* as a strange thing
Luke 21. 36. *c.* worthy to escape
Acts 5. 41. that *c.* worthy to suffer
2 Thess. 1. 5. *c.* worthy of kingdom
1 Tim. 1. 12. he *c.* me faithful, putting
5. 17. *c.* worthy of double honour
Heb. 3. 3. *c.* worthy of more glory
10. 29. *c.* the blood of the covenant unholy.
COUNTENANCE, Gen. 4. 5.
Num. 6. 26. lift up his *c.* on thee
1 Sam. 1. 18. her *c.* was no more sad
16. 7. look not on his *c.* nor height
Neh. 2. 2. why is thy *c.* sad
Job 29. 24. light of thy countenance
Ps. 4. 6. lift up light of thy *c.* 80. 3, 7.
90. 8. settest secret sins in light of *c.*
Song 2. 14. let me see thy *c.* comely
Matt. 6. 16. as hypocrites of a sad *c.*
Acts 2. 28. full of joy with thy *c.*
COUNTRY, Matt. 21. 33. Mark 12. 1.
Luke 15. 13. Prov. 25. 25.
Heb. 11. 14. declare they seek a *c.*
16. they desire a better *c.*—heavenly
2 Cor. 11. 26. *countrymen*.
COURAGE, Josh 2. 11. Acts 28. 15.
Num. 13. 20. be of good *c.* Deut. 31.
6.
Josh. 1. 6. Sam. 10. 12. 1 Chron.
22. 13. Ezra 10. 4. Ps. 27. 14. Isa. 41.
6.
COURSE, Acts 13. 25. & 16. 11.
Acts 20. 24. finish my *c.* with joy
Eph. 2. 2. according to the *c.* of this
2 Thess. 3. 1. may have free *c.* and
2 Tim. 4. 7. I have finished my *c.*
COURT, Ex. 27. 9. Isa. 34. 13.
Amos 7. 13. Bethel is king's *c.*
Ps. 65. 4. may dwell in thy *c.*
84. 10. day in thy courts better
92. 13. flourish in *c.* of our God
100. 4. enter his *c.* with praise
Isa. 1. 12. who required to tread my *c.*
62. 9. drink it in *c.* of my holiness
Luke 7. 25. delicate are in king's *c.*
Rev. 11. 2. *c.* without temple leave out
1 Pet. 3. 8. be pitiful, *courteous*
Acts 27. 3. *courteously*, 28. 7.

CRAFT, Dan. 8. 25. Mark 14. 1.
Acts 18. 3. Rev. 18. 22.
Job 5. 12. disappointeth devices of the *crafty*
15. 5. uttereth iniquity, choosest tongue of *c.*
Ps. 83. 3. taken *c.* counsel against
2 Cor. 12. 16. being *c.* I caught you with guile
Job 5. 13. *craftiness,* 1 Cor. 3. 19.
Luke 20. 23. 2 Cor. 4. 2. Eph. 4. 14.
CREATE, Gen. 1. 1, 21, 27.
Isa. 51. 10. *c.* in me a clean heart
4. 5. *c.* upon every dwelling-place
45. 7. I form light and *c.* darkness, I make peace and *c.* evil
57. 19. I *c.* the fruit of the lips, peace
65. 17. I *c.* new heavens and new earth
18. rejoice in what I *c.* I *c.* Jerusalem
Ps. 104. 30. spirit they are *created*
102. 18. people which shall be *c.*
148. 5. commanded and they were *c.*
Isa. 43. 7. I have *c.* him for my glory
Jer. 31. 22. a new thing in earth
Mal. 2. 10. hath not one God *c.* us
Eph. 2. 10. *c.* in Christ Jesus unto good
3. 9. *c.* all things by Jesus Christ
4. 24. after God is *c.* in righteousness
Col. 1. 16. all things were *c.* by him
3. 10. image of him that *c. him*
1 Tim. 4. 3. which God *c.* to be received
Rev. 4. 11. hast *c.* all—are and were *c.*
10. 6. *c.* heaven and things therein
Amos 4. 13. *createth* the wind
Mark 10. 6. *creation,* 13. 19. Rom. 1. 20. & 8. 22. Rev. 3. 14.
Rom. 1. 25. creature—*Creator*
Eccl. 12. 1. remember thy *C.* in days
Isa. 40. 28. *C.* of ends of earth
43. 15. Lord the *C.* of Israel, your king
1 Pet. 4. 19. as to a faithful *C.*
Gen. 1. 20. *creature,* Lev. 11. 46.
Mark 16. 15. preach the gospel to every *c.*
Rom. 8. 20. *c.* was made subject to vanity.
19. *c.* waiteth, 21. *c.* be delivered
2 Cor. 5. 17. man in Christ is a new
Gal. 6. 15. availeth but a new *c.*
Col. 1. 15. first-born of every *c.*
1 Tim. 4. 4. every *c.* of God is good
Heb. 4. 13. nor any *c.* not manifest
Isa. 13. 21. *creatures,* James 1. 18.
Ezek. 1. 5, 19. *living creatures,* 3. 13.
Rev. 4. 6. 9. & 5. 6, 11, 14.
CREEP, Lev. 11. 31. Ps. 104. 20.
2 Tim. 3. 6. who *c.* into houses
Jude 4. *crept* in unawares
CRIB, Prov. 14. 4. Isa. 1. 3.
CRIME, Job 31. 11. Ezek. 7. 23.
CRIMSON, as wool, Isa. 1. 18. Jer. 4. 30. 2 Chron. 2. 7. & 3. 14.
CROOKED, Deut. 32. 5.
Ps. 125. 5. aside to their *c.* ways
Prov. 2. 15. whose ways are *c.* and they froward
Eccl. 1. 15. that which is *c.* cannot be made straight, 7. 13.
Isa. 40. 4. *c.* shall be made straight, 45. 2. Luke 3. 5.
59. 8. make *c.* paths, Lam. 3. 9.
Phil. 2. 15. in midst of *c.* generation
CROSS, John 19. 17—31.
Matt. 10. 38. takes not up his *c.* and follows, 16. 24. Luke 9. 23.
1 Cor. 1. 17. lest the *c.* of Christ be made
18. preaching of *c.* is to them foolishness
Gal. 5. 11. then is offence of the *c.* ceased
6. 12. suffer persecution for *c.* of Christ

14. glory save in *c.* of Lord Jesus
Phil. 2. 8. obedient to death of *c.*
3. 18. they are enemies of *c.* of Christ
Col. 1. 20. peace through blood of his *c.*
2. 24. took—nailing it to his *c.*
Heb. 12. 2. for joy—endured the *c.*
CROWN, Lev. 8. 9. Esther 1. 11.
Job 31. 36. bind it as *c.* to me
Ps. 89. 39. hast profaned his *c.*
Prov. 12. 4. virtuous woman is a *c.* to her husband
12. 24. *c.* of wise is their riches
16. 31. hoary head is a *c.* of glory
17. 6. children's children are *c.* of old men
Song 3. 11. behold king Solomon with *c.*
Isa. 28. 5. Lord of hosts for *c.* of glory
62. 3. thou shalt be a *c.* of glory
1 Cor. 9. 25. to obtain corruptible *c.*
Phil. 4. 1. my joy and *c.* 1 Thess. 2. 19.
2 Tim. 4. 8. laid up—a *c.* of righteousness
James 1. 12. receives a *c.* of life
1 Pet. 5. 4. receives a *c.* of glory
Rev. 2. 10. give thee a *c.* of life
3. 11. that no man take thy *c.*
Ps. 8. 5. *crowned* with glory and honour, Heb. 2. 7. 9. Ps. 21. 3.
Prov. 14. 18. prudent are *c.* with knowledge
Ps. 65. 11. *crownest* year with goodness
103. 4. *crowneth* with loving-kindness
Zech. 6. 11. 14. *crowns,* Rev. 4. 4, 10. & 9. 7. & 12. 3. & 13. 1. & 19. 12.
CRUCIFY, Matt. 20. 19. & 23. 34.
Luke 23. 21. John 19. 6. 15.
Acts 2. 23. *crucified* and slain, 4. 10.
Rom. 6. 6. our old man is *c.* with him
1 Cor. 1. 13. was Paul *c.* 23. Christ *c.*
2. 2. save Jesus Christ and him *c.*
2 Cor. 13. 4. was *c.* through weakness
Gal. 2. 20. I am *c.* with Christ nevertheless
3. 1. Christ is set forth *c.* among you
5. 24. Christ's have *c.* the flesh with
6. 14. world is *c.* to me and I to the world
Rev. 11. 8. where also our Lord was *c.*
CRUEL, Prov. 5. 9. & 11. 17.
Gen. 49. 1. cursed wrath for it was *c.*
Job 30. 21. thou art become *c.* to me
Prov. 12. 10. tender mercies of the wicked are *c.*
Song 8. 6. jealousy is *c.* as grave
Isa. 13. 9. day of Lord cometh *c.* with
Jer. 6. 23. and have no mercy
Heb. 11. 36. had trial of *c.* mockings
CRUMBS, Matt. 15. 27.
CRY, Ex. 5. 8. & 3. 7, 9.
Gen. 18. 21. to the *c.* that is come up
Ex. 2. 23. their *c.* came up to God
22. 23. I will surely hear their *c.*
2 Sam. 22. 7. my *c.* did enter into his ears
Job 34. 28. he hears *c.* of afflicted
Ps. 9. 12. he forgets not *c.* of the humble
34. 17. his ears are open to their *c.*
145. 19. he will hear their *c.*
Jer. 7. 16. neither lift up *c.* nor prayer for them, 11. 11, 14.
Matt. 25. 6. at midnight a *c.* made
Ps. 34. 15. righteous *c.* and Lord hears
Isa. 40. 6. voice said *c.*—what *c.*
42. 2. not *c.* nor lift up voice
58. 1. *c.* aloud, spare not, show transgression
Ezek. 9. 4. that *c.* for all the abominations
Joel 1. 19. to thee will I *c.*
Jonah 3. 8. mightily to God

Matt. 12. 19. shall not strive nor *c.*
Luke 18. 7. day and night to him
19. 40. stones would *c.* out
Rom. 8. 15. spirit *c.* Abba Father
Ps. 22. 5. *cried* and were delivered
34. 6. this poor man *c.* and Lord heard
119. 145. I *c.* with my whole heart
138. 3. I *c.* thou answeredst me
Lam. 2. 18. their heart *c.* to Lord
Hos. 7. 14. not *c.* with their heart
Prov. 2. 3. thou *criest* after knowledge
Gen. 4. 10. brother's blood *crieth*
Prov. 1. 20. wisdom *c.* without
Mic. 6. 9. Lord's voice *c.* to the city
Prov. 19. 18. *crying,* Zech. 4. 7. Matt. 3. 3. Heb. 5. 7. Rev. 21. 4.
CUBIT, Matt. 6. 27.
CUMBER, Luke 10. 40. & 13. 7.
CUP, Gen. 40. 11. & 42. 2.
Ps. 11. 6. portion of their *c.*
16. 5. Lord is portion of my *c.*
23. 5. my *c.* runneth over
73. 10. waters of a full *c.* are wrung out
116. 13. take *c.* of salvation
Isa. 51. 17. *c.* of trembling, 22.
Jer. 16. 7. nor give *c.* of consolation
25. 15. wine *c.* of fury, 17. 28. Lam. 4. 21. Ezek. 23. 31, 32.
Hab. 2. 16. *c.* Lord's right hand
Matt. 10. 42. *c.* of cold water only
20. 22. able to drink of the *c.*
23. 25. make clean outside of *c.*
26. 39. let this *c.* pass from me
John 18. 11. *c.* which my Father hath given
1 Cor. 10. 16. *c.* of blessing which we
21. drink *c.* of the Lord and *c.* of devils
11. 25. this *c.* is new testament
26. drink this *c.* 27. 28.
Rev. 16. 19. *c.* of his wrath, 14. 10.
CURIOUS, Ex. 35. 32.
Ps. 139. 15. *curiously* wrought
CURSE them, Num. 5. 18.
Gen. 27. 12. bring a *c.* upon me
13. on me be thy *c.* my son
Deut. 11. 26. blessing and *c.* 30. 1.
23. 5. turned *c.* into blessing
Prov. 3. 33. *c.* of Lord in house of wicked
26. 2. *c.* causeless shall not come
Mal. 2. 2. send a *c.* upon you
3. 9. ye are cursed with a *c.*
Isa. 65. 15. *for,* or *to be a c.* Jer. 24. 9.
Gen. 8. 21. I will not again *c.* the ground
12. 3. *c.* him that curseth thee.
Ex. 22. 28. not *c.* ruler of people
Lev. 19. 24. shall not *c.* the deaf
Num. 22. 6. come *c.* me this people
Deut. 23. 4. hired Balaam to *c.* Josh. 24. 9. Neh. 13. 2.
Judg. 5. 23. ye Meroz, *c.* bitterly
2 Sam. 16. 10. let him *c.* because Lord
Job 1. 11. he will *c.* thee to face, 2. 5.
2. 9. *c.* God and die
Ps. 109. 28. let them *c.* but bless thou
Prov. 11. 26. people shall *c.* him, 24. 24.
Eccl. 10. 20. *c.* not king in chamber
Jer. 15. 10. every one doth *c.* me
Mal. 2. 2. I will *c.* your blessings
Matt. 5. 44. bless them that *c.* you
Rom. 12. 14. bless and *c.* not
Gen. 49. 7. *cursed* be their anger
Job. 3. 1. opened Job his mouth, and *c.* his day, 8.
5. 3. I *c.* his habitation, 24. 18.
Ps. 119. 21. proud are *c.* 37. 22.
Jer. 11. 3. *c.* be man that obeys not
17. 5. *c.* be man that trusteth in
48. 10. *c.* doeth work of Lord deceitfully
Deut. 30. 19. *cursing,* Rom. 3. 14.
Heb. 6. 8. Ps. 10. 7. & 59. 12.
CUSTOM, Gen. 31. 35. Rom. 13. 7.
Luke 4. 16. 1 Cor. 11. 16.
CUT, Lev. 1. 16, 12. & 22. 24.

Zech. 11. 10. *cut asunder*
Luke 12. 46. Jer. 48. 2. Ps. 129. 4.
Luke 13. 7. *cut down,* Job 22. 16.
Job 4. 7. *cut off,* 8. 14. Ps. 37. 9. Prov. 2, 22. Matt. 5. 30. Rom. 11. 22. 2. Cor. 11. 12. Gal. 5. 12.
Acts 4. 33. *cut to heart,* 7. 54.
CYMBAL, Ezra 3. 10. Ps. 150. 5.
1 Cor. 13. 1. I am become a tinkling *c.*

D

DAINTY, Job. 33. 20. Prov. 23. 6.
Gen. 49. 20. yield royal *dainties*
Ps. 141. 4. not eat of their *d.*
Prov. 23. 3. ot desirous of his *d.*
DAMNED who believe not
Mark 16. 16. 2 Thess. 1. 12.
Rom. 14. 23. doubteth, is *d.* if he eat
2 Pet. 2. 1. *damnable* heresies
Matt. 23. 14. greater *damnation*
33. how can ye escape *d.* of hell
Mark 3. 29. in danger of eternal *d.*
John 5. 29. come forth to resurrection of *d.*
Rom. 3. 8. whose *d.* is just
13. 2. receive to themselves *d.*
1 Cor. 11. 29. eateth and drinketh *d.*
1 Tim. 5. 12. having *d.* because cast
2 Pet. 2. 3. their *d.* slumbereth not
DANCE turned to mourning, Lam. 5. 15. Ps. 30. 41. Luke 15. 25.
DANDLED, Isa. 66. 12.
DANGER, Matt. 5. 22.
Matt. 5. 21, 22. *d.* of the council—hell-fire
Mark 3. 39. in *d.* of damnation
Acts 19. 27. craft in *d.* 40. we in *d.*
DARE, 1 Cor. 6. 1. 2 Cor. 10. 12.
Rom. 5. 7. some would *d.* to die
DARK, Gen. 15. 17. Job 18. 6.
Lev. 13. 6. if plague be *d.* 21. 16.
Num. 12. 8. speak not in *d.* speeches
2 Sam. 22. 12. *d.* waters, Ps. 18. 11.
Ps. 49. 4. *d.* sayings, 78. 2.
74. 20. *d.* places of earth full of
88. 12. wonders known in *d.*
Dan. 8. 23. understanding *d.* sentences
2 Pet. 1. 19. light shineth in *d.* places
1 Cor. 13. 12. through a glass *darkly*
Ex. 10. 15. *darkened,* Eccl. 12. 2.
Ps. 69. 23. let eyes be *d.* Rom. 11. 10.
Zech. 11. 17. his right eye utterly *d.*
Rom. 1. 21. foolish heart was *d.*
Eph. 4. 18. having understanding *d.*
Gen. 1. 2, 5, 18. *darkness,* 15. 12
2 Sam. 22. 29. Lord will lighten my *d.*
1 Kings 8. 12. Lord dwell in thick *d.*
Job. 34. 12. no *d.* were workers
Ps. 104. 20. makest *d.* and it is night
139. 12. *d.* and light are like to thee
Isa. 5. 20. put *d.* for light, and light for
45. 7. I form light and create *d.*
Matt. 6. 23. whole body full of *d.*
8. 12. outer *d.* 22. 13. & 25. 30.
John 1. 5. *d.* comprehended it not
3. 19. men loved *d.* rather than light
12. 35. lest *d.* come upon you
Acts 26. 18. turn them from *d.* to light
Rom. 13. 12. cast off works of *d.*
1 Cor. 4. 5. hidden things of *d.*
2 Cor. 4. 6. light to shine out of *d.*
6. 14. communion hath light with *d.*
Eph. 5. 8. were sometimes *d.* but now
6. 12. rulers of *d.* of this world
Col. 1. 13. delivered us from power of *d.*
1 Pet. 2. 9. called you out of *d.*
2 Pet. 2. 4. reserved in chains of *d.*
1 John 1. 5. in him is no *d.* at all
2. 8. *d.* is past, true light shineth
11. *d.* hath blinded his eyes
Jude 13. blackness of *d.* for ever
Deut. 28. 29. *in darkness,* 1 Sam. 2. 9.

Ps. 107. 10. & 112. 4. Isa. 9. 2. & 50. 10.

Matt. 4. 16. & 10. 27. John 1. 5. 1 Thess. 5. 4.

DARLING, Ps. 22. 20. & 35. 17.

DARTS, Eph. 6. 16.

DASH, 2 Kings 8. 12. Ex. 15. 6. Isa. 13. 16. 18. Hos. 10. 14.

Ps. 2. 9. d. them in pieces like potter's

19. 12. lest thou d. foot against a stone

DAVID, for Christ, Ps. 89. **3.** Ezek. 34. 23. Hos. 3. 5. Isa. 55. 3.

DAY, Gen. 1. 5. & 32. 26.

Ps. 19. 2. d. unto uttereth speech

84. 10. a d. in thy courts is better

118. 24. this is the d. which is the Lord

Prov. 27. 1. what d. may bring forth

Amos 6. 3. put far away evil. d.

Zech. 4. 10. despised the d. of small

Matt. 6. 34. sufficient to d. is evil thereof

25. 13. know neither the d. nor hour

John 8. 56. rejoiced to see my d.

1 Cor. 3. 13. the d. shall declare it

Phil. 1. 6. till d. of Jesus Christ, 2. 16.

2 Thess. 2. 2. 1 Cor. 1. 8.

1 Thess. 5. 5. children of the d.

Matt. 10. 15. *day of judgment,* Mark 6. 11. 2 Pet. 2. 9. 1 John 4. 17.

Isa. 2. 12. *day of the Lord,* 13. 6, 9. Jer. 46. 10. Lam. 2. 22. Ezek. 30. 3. Joel 1. 15. Amos 5. 18. Oba. 15. Zeph. 1. 8, 18. Zech. 1. 7. Mal. 4. 5. 1 Cor. 5. 5. Rev. 1. 10. 2 Cor. 1. 14. 1 Thess. 5. 2. 2 Pet. 3. 10.

Ps. 20. 1. Lord hear thee in *day of trouble*

50. 15. call on me in—91. 15.

56. 16. my defence and refuge in—

77. 2. in—I sought the Lord

86. 7. in—call on thee

Isa. 37. 3. it is a—and rebuke

Ezek. 7. 7. time is come,—is near

Nah. 1. 7. Lord is good

Hab. 3. 16. I might rest in—

Zeph. 1. 15. a—and distress, desolation

Job. 8. 9. *days* on earth as a shadow

14. 1. of few d. and full of trouble

32. 7. should speak, and multitude

Ps. 90. 12. teach us to number our d.

Eccl. 7. 10. former d. better than these

11. 8. remember d. of darkness, many

12. 1. while evil d. come not

Jer. 2. 32. forgotten d. without

Eph. 5. 16. because the d. are evil

1 Pet. 3. 10. would see good d.

Gen. 49. 1. *last days,* Isa. 2. 2. Acts 2. 17. 2 Tim. 3. 1. Heb. 1. 2.

Num. 24. 14. *latter days,* Deut. 31. 29. Jer. 23. 20. Dan. 10. 14. Hos. 3. 5.

Job. 10. 20. *my days,* 17. 1, 11.

7. 6.—are swifter than a shuttle

16, I loathe,—are vanity

9. 25.—are swifter than a post

Ps. 39. 4. know measure of—

5. made—as a handbreadth

102. 3.—are consumed like smoke

Isa. 39. 7. and truth in—

Jer. 20. 18.—are consumed with

Ps. 61. 8. *daily* perform my vows

68. 19. who d. loads us with benefits

Prov. 8. 34. watching d. at my gates

Isa. 58. 2. seek me d. and delight in

Acts 2. 47. added to church d.—saved

Heb. 3. 13. exhort one another d.

Job. 9. 33. *day's-man,* or umpire

38. 12. *day-spring,* Luke 1. 78.

2 Pet. 1. 19. *day-star* arise in your hearts

DEACON, Phil. 1. 1. 1 Tim. 3. 8.

DEAD, Gen. 20. 3. & 23. 3.

1 Sam. 24. 14. after a d. dog after

Ps. 88. 10. shall d. praise, 115. 17.

Eccl. 9. 5. the d. know not anything

10. 1. d. flies cause ointment to stink

Matt. 8. 22. let the d. bury their d.

---

22. 32. not God of d. but of living

Luke 8. 52. the maid is not d. but

John 5. 25. d. shall hear the voice of the Son of God

11. 25. though he were d. yet shall he

Rom. 6. 8. d. with Christ, 11. d. to sin

Gal. 2. 19. I through law am d. to law

Eph. 2. 1. who were d. in trespasses

Col. 2. 13. being d. in your sins

3. 3. ye are d. and your life hid

1 Thess. 4. 16. d. in Christ shall rise first

2 Tim. 2. 11. d. with him, we shall live

Heb. 11. 4. being d. yet speaketh

Rev. 14. 13. blessed are d.—in Lord

Ps. 17. 9. *deadly,* James 3. 8.

DEATH, Gen. 21. 16. Ex. 10. 17.

Num. 23. 10. let me die the d. of the righteous

Deut. 30. 15. set before you life and d.

Ps. 6. 5. in d. no remembrance of thee

33. 19. deliver soul from d. 116. 8.

68. 20. to Lord belong issues from d.

73. 4. have no bands in their d.

Ps. 89. 48. liveth and shall not see d.

116. 15. precious—is d. of saints

118. 18. not given me over to d.

Prov. 2. 18. her house inclines to d.

8. 36. they that hate me, love d.

18. 21. d. and life in power of tongue

Eccl. 7. 26. more bitter than d. the

8. 8. hath no power in dav of d.

Isa. 25. 8. swallow up d. in victory

28. 15. made covenant with d.

38. 18. d. cannot celebrate thee

Jer. 8. 3. d. chosen rather than life

21. 8. way of life, way of d.

Ezek. 18. 32. no pleasure in d.

Hos. 13. 14. O d. I will be thy plagues

Matt. 16. 28. not taste of death

26. 38. sorrowful even unto d.

John 5. 24. passed from d. to life, 1 John 3. 14.

John 8. 1. shall never see d.

12. 33. what d. he should die

Acts 2. 24. loosed the pains of d.

Rom. 5. 12. sin entered, and d. by sin

6. 3. baptized into his d.

4. buried by baptism into d.

5. planted in the likeness of his d.

5. 9. d. hath no more dominion over

21. end of these things is d.

7. 5. bring forth fruit unto d.

8. 2. free from law of sin, and d.

6 to be carnally minded is d.

38. d. nor life shall separate from

1 Cor. 3. 22. or life, or d. or things present

11. 26. ye show Lord's d. till he come

15. 21. by man came d. by man

54. d. is swallowed up in victory

55. O d. where is thy sting

59. sting of d. is sin, and strength

2 Cor. 1. 9. had sentence of d. in ourselves

10. deliver from so great a d.

2. 16. we are savour of d. unto d.

4. 11. delivered to d. for Jesus' sake

12. d. worketh in us, but life in you

Phil. 2. 8. obedient to d. the d. of cross

Heb. 2. 9. tasted d. for every man

15. through fear of d. are subject to

11. 5. should not see d. Luke 2. 26.

James 1. 15. sin finished brings d.

5. 20. save a soul from d. and hide

1 Pet. 3. 18. put to d. in the flesh

1 John 5. 16. there is a sin unto d.

17. there is a sin unto d. I do not say

Rev. 1. 18. I have the keys of hell and d.

---

2. 10. be faithful unto d. and I will

12. 11. loved not their lives unto d.

20, 6. second d. hath no power

21. 4. there shall be no more d.

DEAF, Ex. 4. 11. Ps. 38. 13. Isa. 29. 18. & 35. 5. Mic. 7. 16.

Lev. 19. 14. shalt not curse the d.

42. 18. hear, ye d. and look, ye blind

19. who is d. as my messenger

43. 8. d. people that have ears

Matt. 11. 5. d. hear, dead are raised

DEBATE, Prov. 25. 9. Isa. 27. 8.

Rom. 1. 29. 2 Cor. 12. 20.

DEBT, Rom. 4. 4. Matt. 6. 12, 18, 27. Ezek. 68. 7. 11. *debtor,* Gal. 5. 3.

Rom. 1. 14. Luke 7. 41. Matt. 6. 12.

DECEASE, Luke 9. 31.

DECEIT, Jer. 5. 27. & 9. 6, 8.

Ps. 72. 14. redeem their souls from d.

101. 7. worketh d. shall not dwell

Prov. 20. 17. bread of d. is sweet

Isa. 53. 9. any d. in his mouth

Jer. 8. 9. they hold fast d. and refuse

Col. 2. 8. spoil you through vain d.

Ps. 35. 20. *deceitful,* 109. 2. & 14. 25.

5. 6. abhor bloody and d. man.

55. 23. d. men shall not live half

78. 57. turn like a d. bow, Hos. 7. 16.

102. 2. from a d. tongue, 52. 4.

Prov. 31. 30. favour is d. and beauty vain

Jer. 17. 9. heart is d. above all things

Eph. 4. 22. according to d. lusts

Matt. 13. 22, *deceitfulness* of riches

Ps. 24. 4. *deceitfully,* Jer. 48. 10. Job 13. 7. 2 Cor. 4. 2.

DECEIVE, 2 Kings 4. 28.

Prov. 24. 28. d. not with thy lips

Matt. 24. 4. take heed that no man d. you

24. if possible d. the very elect

1 Cor. 3. 18. let no man d. himself

1 John 1. 8. we d. ourselves

2 Thess. 2. 10. *deceivableness*

Deut. 11. 16. heart be not *deceived*

Job. 12. 16. the d. and the deceiver are

Isa. 44. 20. a d. heart hath turned

Jer. 20. 7. O Lord thou hast d. me

Obad. 3. thy pride hath d. thee

Rom. 7. 11. d. me and by it slew me

1 Tim. 2. 14. Adam was not d. but

2 Tim. 3. 13. *deceiving* and being d.

Gal. 27. 12. *deceiver,* Mal. 1. 14. 2 John 7. 2 Cor. 6. 8. Tit. 1. 10.

Prov. 26. 19. *deceiveth,* Rev. 12. 9

Gal. 6. 3. when he is nothing, d. himself

James 1. 26. d. his own heart, 22.

DECENTLY, 1 Cor. 14. 40.

DECLARE, Gen. 41. 24. Isa. 42. 9.

Ps. 22. 2. I will d. thy name unto

38. 18. I will d. my iniquity and

50. 16. what to do to d. my statutes

78. 6. may d. them to their children

145. 4. shall d. thy mighty acts

Isa. 3. 9. they d. their sin as Sodom

53. 8. who shall d. his generation

Mic. 3. 8. to d. to Jacob his transgression

Acts 17. 23. worship, him d. I unto

20. 17. not shunned to d. all counsel

Rom. 3. 25. to d. his righteousness

Heb. 11. 14. say such things d. plainly

1 John 1. 3. seen and heard d. we

DECLINE, Ps. 119. 51, 157.

DECREE, Ezra 5. 13, 17.

Ps. 2. 7. I will declare the d.

Prov. 8. 15. princes d. justice

Isa. 10. 1. that d. unrighteous decrees

Zeph. 2. 2. before d. bring forth

Isa. 10. 22. *decreed,* 1 Cor. 7. 37.

DEDICATE, Deut. 20. 5.

1 Chron. 26. 20, 26, 27. Ezek. 44. 29.

Num. 7. 84. *dedication,* Ezra 6. 16, 17. Neh. 12. 17. John 10. 22.

DEED, Gen. 44. 15. Judg. 19. 30.

Rom. 15. 18. obedient in word and d.

Col. 3. 17. whatsoever ye do in word or d.

1 John 3. 18. love in d. and in truth

Neh. 13. 14. wipe not out my good *deeds*

Ps. 28. 4. give them according to their d. Jer. 25. 14. Rom. 2. 6.

John 3. 19. because their d. were evil

8. 41. do the d. of your father

2 John 11. partaker of his evil d.

Jude 15. of all their ungodly d.

DEED, Gen. 1. 2. Job 38. 30.

Ps. 36. 6 thy judgments are a great d.

42. 7. d. calleth unto d. at the noise

1 Cor. 2. 10. yea, d. things of God

2 Cor. 11. 25. I have been in the d.

Isa. 31. 6. *deeply* revolted

Hos. 9. 9. d. corrupted themselves

Mark 8. 17. sighed d. in spirit

DEFAME, 1 Cor. 4. 13. Jer. 20. 10.

DEFENCE, 2 Chron. 11. 5. Isa. 19. 9.

Num. 14. 9. their d. is departed

Job 22. 25. Almighty shall be thy d.

Ps. 7. 10. my d. is of God who saveth

59. 9, God is my d. 16. 17.

Eccl. 7. 12. wisdom is a d. money is a d.

Isa. 4. 5. on all the glory shall be d.

33. 16. place of d. the munitions

DEFER, Eccl. 5. 4. Isa. 48. 9.

DEFILE, Lev. 11. 44. & 15. 31.

Song 5. 3. how shall I d. them

Dan. 1. 8. would not d. himself

Matt. 15. 18. they d. the man, 20.

1 Cor. 3. 17. if any d. temple of God

Isa. 24. 5. earth is d. under inhabitants

Tit. 1. 15. are d. and unbelieving, their mind and conscience is d.

Heb. 12. 15. thereby many be d.

Rev. 3. 4. have not d. their garments

14. 4. are not d. with women

21. 27. anything that *defileth*

DEFRAUD, Lev. 19. 13. Mark 10. 19.

1 Cor. 6. 7. 1 Thess. 4. 6.

DELAY, Ex. 22. 29. & 32. 1.

Ps. 119. 60. I *delayed* not to keep thy commandments

Matt. 24. 48. my lord *delayeth* his coming

DELICATE, Deut. 28. 56. Isa. 47. 1. Jer. 6. 2. Mic. 1. 16. Jer. 51. 34.

1 Sam. 15. 32. *delicately,* Prov. 29. 21. Lam. 4. 5. Luke 7. 25.

DELIGHT, Gen. 34. 19. Num. 14. 8

Deut. 10. 15. Lord had d. in fathers

1 Sam. 15. 22. hath the Lord as great d. in burnt offerings

Job 22. 26. have thy d. in Almighty

27. 10. will he d. himself in Almighty

Ps. 1. 2. his d. is in the law of God

16. 3. saints in whom is all my d.

37. 4. d. thyself in Lord he will give

40. 8. I d. to do thy will, O my God

94. 19. thy comforts d. my soul

119. 24. thy testimonies are my d.

Prov. 11. 20. upright are his d. 12. 22.

15. 8. prayer of upright is his d.

Song 2. 3. under shadow with great d.

Isa. 55. 2. let your soul d. itself in fatness

58. 2. d. to know—take d. in approaching

13. call the sabbeth a d. holy of the Lord, honourable

Rom. 7. 22. I d. in the law of God

Ps. 112. 1, *delighteth* greatly in his commandments

Prov. 3. 12. son in whom he d.

Isa. 42. 1. elect in whom my soul d.

62. 4. Hephzibah, Lord d. in thee

Mic. 7. 18. because he d. in mercy

Ps. 119. 92. thy law hath been my *delights,* 143. Eccl. 2. 8.

Prov. 8. 31. my d. with sons of men

Song 7. 6. how pleasant, O love, for d.

Mal. 3. 12. ye shall be a *delightsome* land
DELIVER, Ex. 3. 8. & 5. 18.
Job. 5. 19. *d.* thee in six troubles and
10. 7. none can *d.* out of thy hand
Ps. 33. 19 to *d.* their souls from death
50. 15. I will *d.* thee, and thou, 91. 15.
56. 13. wilt thou not *d.* my feet
74. 19. *d.* not the soul of thy turtle
91. 3. *d.* thee from snare of fowler
Eccl. 8. 8. shall wickedness *d.* those
Ezek. 14. 14. should *d.* but their own
34. 10. I will *d.* my flock from their
Dan. 3. 17. our God is able to *d.* us
Hos. 11. 8. how shall I *d.* thee, Israel
Rom. 7. 24. who shall *d.* from body
2 Cor. 5. 5. to *d.* such a one to Satan
2 Tim. 4. 18. the Lord shall *d.* me from
Heb. 2. 15. *d.* them who through fear
1 Pet. 2. 9. Lord knows how to *d.* the godly out of temptation
2 Kings 5. 1. *deliverance*, 13. 17. 2 Chron. 12. 7. Esth. 4. 14. Ps. 32. 7. Isa. 26. 18. Joel 2. 32. Luke 4. 18.
Gen. 45. 7. *great deliverance*, 1 Chron. 11. 14. Ps. 18. 50.
Ezra 9. 13. given us such a *d.* as this
Heb. 11. 35. not accepting *d.*
Prov. 11. 8. righteous is *delivered* out of trouble, and the wicked cometh, 9. 21.
28. 26. walketh wisely shall be *d.*
Isa. 38. 17. in love to soul, *d.* it from pit
49. 24, 25. lawful captive—prey be *d.*
Jer. 7. 10. *d.* to do all abominations
Ezek. 3. 19. hast *d.* thy soul 21.
Dan. 12. 1. thy people shall be *d.*
Joel 2. 32. call on name of Lord—be *d.*
Mic. 4. 10. Babylon, there shalt thou be *d.*
Matt. 11. 27. all things are *d.* to me
Acts 2. 23. *d.* by determinate counsel
Rom. 4. 25. who was *d.* for our offences
7. 6. we are *d.* from the law that
8. 32. God *d.* him up for us all
2 Cor. 1. 10. who *d.* us from so great a death, and doth *d.* and will *d.*
1 Thess. 1. 10. which *d.* us from the wrath to come
1 Tim. 1. 20. whom I have *d.* to Satan
2 Pet. 2. 7. *d.* just Lot vexed with
Jude 3. faith once *d.* to the saints
DELUSION, 2 Thess. 2. 11.
DEMONSTRATION, 1 Cor. 2. 4.
DEN, Judg. 6. 2. Job. 37. 8. Heb. 11. 38. Rev. 6. 15. Ps. 104. 22.
Ps. 10. 9. *den of lions*, Song 4. 8.
Dan. 6. 7, 24. Amos 3. 4. Nah. 2. 12.
Jer. 7. 11. *den of robbers*—of thieves, Matt. 21. 13. Mark 11. 17.
Jer. 9. 11. *den of dragons*
DENY, 1 Kings 2. 16. Job 8. 18.
Prov. 30. 9. lest I be full and *d.* thee
Matt. 10. 33. shall *d.* me before men
16. 24. let him *d.* himself and take
26. 34. before cock crow thou shalt *d.* me
35. I will not *d.* thee, Mark 14. 31.
2 Tim. 2. 12. if we *d.* him he will *d.*
13. abideth faithful—cannot *d.* himself
Tit. 1. 16. in works they *d.* him
1 Tim. 5. 8. hath *denied* the faith
Rev. 2. 13. hast not *d.* my faith
DEPART from, Job 21. 14.
28. 28. to *d.* from evil, is understanding
Ps. 34. 14. *d.* from evil, 37. 27. Prov. 3. 7. & 13, 19. & 16. 6, 17.
Hos. 9. 12. wo to me when I *d.* from
Matt. 7. 23. *d.* from me, ye that work
25, 41. *d.* from me ye cursed, into
Luke 2. 29. lettest thy servant *d*, in
5. 8. *d.* from me—a sinful man, O Lord

Phil. 1. 23. having a desire to *d.* and
1 Tim. 4. 1. some shall *d.* from faith
2 Tim. 2. 19. name of Christ *d.* from iniquity
Ps. 18. 21. wickedly *departed* from my God, 119. 102. 2 Sam. 22. 22.
Prov. 14. 16. feareth and *departeth* from evil
Isa. 59. 15. *d.* from evil makes himself
Acts 20. 29. after my *departing*, wolves
2 Tim. 4. 6. *departure*, Ezek. 26. 18.
DEPTH, Job 28. 14. Prov. 8. 27.
Matt. 18. 6. Mark 4. 5.
Rom. 8. 39. nor *d.* separate us
11. 33. O the *d.* of riches of wisdom
Eph. 3. 18. *d.* of the love of Christ
Ex. 15. 5, 8. *depths*, Ps. 68. 22. & 71. 20. & 130. 1. Prov. 3. 20. & 9. 18.
Mic. 7. 19. cast sins into *d.* of sea
Rev. 2. 24. known *d.* of Satan
DERISION, Job 30. 1. Ps. 2. 4. & 44. 13. & 59. 8. & 119. 51. Jer. 20. 7, 8
DESCEND, Ex. 19. 18. & 33. 9.
Ps. 49. 17. glory shall not *d.* after him
Isa. 5. 14. rejoiceth shall *d.* into it
1 Thess. 4. 16. Lord shall *d.* from heaven
Gen. 28. 12. angels of God ascending and *descending*, John 1. 51.
Matt. 3. 16. Spirit of God *d.* like dove, Mark 1. 10. John 1. 32, 33.
Rev. 21. 10. city *d.* out of heaven from
DESERT, Ex. 3. 1. Num. 20. 1.
Isa. 21. 1. Jer. 25. 24. Ezek. 47. 8.
DESIRE, Deut. 18. 6. & 21. 11.
Gen. 3. 16. thy *d.* shall be to thy husband
4. 7. to thee shall be his *d.* and thou
Ex. 34. 24. nor any man *d.* thy land
Deut. 18. 6. with all the *d.* of his heart
2 Sam. 23. 5. this is all my *d.* though
2 Chron. 15. 15. with their whole *d.*
Neh. 1. 11. who *d.* to fear thy name
Job 14. 15. wilt have a *d.* to work of thine hands
21. 14. we *d.* not knowledge of thy
Ps. 38. 9. all my *d.* is before thee
145. 16. fulfil the *d.* of them that fear
Prov. 10. 24. *d.* of righteous shall be granted
11. 23. *d.* of righteous is only good
13. 19. *d.* accomplished is sweet
21. 25. *d.* of slothful killeth him
Eccl. 12. 5. *d.* shall fail, because man
Isa. 26. 8. *d.* our soul is to thy name
Ezek. 24. 16. take the *d.* of thy eyes
Hag. 2. 7. the *d.* of all nations shall
Luke 22. 15. with *d.* I have desired
Rev. 9. 6. to die, and death shall flee
Ps. 19. 10. more to be *desired* are they
Isa. 26. 9. with my soul have I *d.* thee
Jer. 17. 16. nor have I *d.* woful day
Hos. 6. 6. I *d.* mercy and not sacrifice
Zeph. 2. 1. gather, O nation, not *d.*
Ps. 37. 4. give the *desires* of heart
Eph. 2. 3. fulfilling *d.* of the flesh
Ps. 51. 6. thou *desirest* truth in the inward parts.
Job 7. 2. servant earnestly *desireth*
Ps. 34. 12. what man *d.* life and loveth
68. 16. hill which God *d.* to dwell
Prov. 12. 12. wicked *d.* not of evil men, 13. 4. soul of sluggard *d.* and hath not, 21. 10. soul of wicked *d.* evil
DESOLATE, 2 Sam. 13. 20. Job 15. 28. Ps. 25. 16. Isa. 49. 21. Matt. 23. 38. Rev. 17. 16.
Isa. 49. 6. *desolations*, 61. 4. Jer. 25. 9. Ezek. 35. 9. Dan. 9. 2, 18, 26.
DESPAIR, 2 Cor. 4. 8. Eccl. 2. 20.
1 Sam. 27. 1. *d. i. e.* to be past hope

Job 6. 20. *desperate*, Isa. 17. 11.
Jer. 17. 9. *desperately* wicked
DESPISE, Lev. 26. 15.
Job. 5. 17. *d.* not chastening of Lord, Prov. 3. 11.
Ps. 102. 17. will not *d.* their prayer
Prov. 23. 22. *d.* not mother when old
Matt. 6. 24. hold to one and *d.* other
Rom. 14. 3. *d.* him that eateth not
1 Tim. 4. 12. no man *d.* thy youth
Gen. 16. 4. mistress was *despised* in her eyes
2 Sam. 6. 16. she *d.* him in her heart
Prov. 12. 9. is *d.* and hath a servant
Song. 8. 1. kiss thee I should not be *d.*
Isa. 53. 3. he is *d.* and rejected
Luke 18. 9. righteous and *d.* others
Heb. 10. 28. that *d.* Moses' law died
Acts 13. 41. *despisers*, 2 Tim. 3. 3.
Rom. 2. 4. *despisest* thou riches of goodness
Job 36. 5. God *despiseth* not any
Prov. 11. 12. void of wisdom *d.* neighbour
13. 13. *d.* the word shall be destroyed
14. 21. that *d.* his neighbour sinneth
15. 32. refuseth instruction *d.* his soul
19. 16. that *d.* his ways shall die
30. 17. eye *d.* to obey his mother
Isa. 33. 15. *d.* gain of oppression
49. 7. whom man *d.* nation abhorreth
Luke 10. 16. *d.* you, *d.* me, *d.* him that sent me
1 Thess. 4. 8. *d.* no man but God
Heb. 12. 2. *despising* the shame
10. 29. done despite to the Spirit of grace
DESTROY, Gen. 18. 23. & 19. 13.
Eccl. 7. 16. why *d.* thyself before time
Matt. 5. 17. not come to *d.* but to fulfill
10. 28. able to *d.* both soul and body
21. 41. miserably *d.* those wicked men
Rom. 14. 15. *d.* not him with thy meat
20. for meat *d.* not work of God
1 Cor. 3. 17. if defile temple, him God will *d.*
6. 13. God shall *d.* both it and them
James 4. 12. able to save and *d.*
1 John 3. 8. might *d.* works of devil
Hos. 4. 6. my people are *destroyed* for lack of knowledge
13. 9. Israel, thou hast *d.* thyself
2 Cor. 4. 9. cast down but not *d.*
Job 15. 21. *destroyer*, Ps. 17. 4.
Prov. 28. 24. Jer. 4. 7. 1 Cor. 10. 10.
Esth. 4. 14. *shall be destroyed*, Ps. 37. 38. Prov. 13. 13, 20. Isa. 10. 27.
Dan. 2. 44. Hos. 10. 8. Acts 3. 23.
Deut. 7. 23. *destruction*, 32. 24.
Job 5. 22. at *d.* and famine shall laugh
18. 12. *d.* is ready at his side
26. 6. *d.* before him hath no covering
31. 23. *d.* from God was a terror to me
Ps. 90. 3. thou turnest man to *d.*
91. 6. *d.* that wasteth at noonday
Prov. 10. 29. *d.* shall be to workers of iniquity, 21. 15. Job 21. 30.
15. 11. hell and *d.* are before the Lord
16. 18. pride goeth before *d.*
18. 12. before *d.* heart of man is haughty
27. 20. hell and *d.* are never full
Jer. 4. 20. *d.* upon *d.* is cried, for land is spoiled
Hos. 13. 14. O grave, I will be thy *d.*
Matt. 7. 13. way that leads to *d.*
Rom. 3. 16. *d.* and misery are in all
1 Cor. 5. 5. for the *d.* of the flesh
2 Cor. 10. 8. not for your *d.* 13. 10.

1 Thess. 5. 3. peace and safety; then sudden *d.* cometh upon them
2 Thess. 1. 9. punished with everlasting *d.*
2 Pet. 2. 1. bring on themselves swift *d.*
3. 16. wrest Scriptures to their *d.*
DETERMINED, 2 Chron. 25. 16.
Job 14. 5. Isa. 10. 23. Dan. 9. 24.
DETESTABLE, Deut. 7. 20. Jer. 16. 18. Ezek. 5. 11. 1 Cor. 2. 2.
DEVICE, Eccl. 9. 10. Job 5. 12. Ps. 33. 10. Prov. 1. 31. Jer. 18. 11. 12, 13. 2 Cor. 2. 11.
DEVIL, Matt. 4. 5. & 8. 11.
Matt. 4. 1. to be tempted of the *d.*
11. 18. they say he hath a *d.*
13. 39. enemy that sowed is the *d.*
25. 41. fire prepared for the *d.* and his
John 6. 70. twelve, and one of you is a *d.*
John 7. 20. thou hast a *d.* 8. 48.
8. 44. of your father the *d.* 49.
13. 2. *d.* having now put it into
Acts 13. 10. thou child of the *d.*
Eph. 4. 27. neither give place to *d.*
1 Tim. 3. 6. fall into condemnation of *d.*
2 Tim. 2. 26. recover out of snare of *d.*
James 4. 7. resist *d.* and he will flee
1 Pet. 5. 8. your adversary the *d.* goeth
1 John 3. 8. to destroy works of *d.*
10. children of God and children of *d.*
Jude 9. Michael contending with *d.*
Rev. 2. 10. the *d.* shall cast some into
Lev. 17. 7. offer sacrifice to *devils*
Deut. 32. 17. they sacrifice to *d.*
2 Chron. 11. 15. priests for the *d.*
Ps. 106. 37. sacrificed their sons to *d.*
Matt. 4. 24. possessed with *d.* 8. 16, 28, 33. Luke 4. 41 & 8. 36.
10. 8. raise the dead, cast out *d.*
Mark 16. 9. cast out seven *d.*
Luke 10. 17. even *d.* are subject to us
1 Cor. 10. 20. have fellowship with *d.* sacrifice to *d.* 21. cup of *d.* table of *d.*
1 Tim. 4. 1. doctrines of *d.* lies
James 2. 19. *d.* believe and tremble
DEVISE, Prov. 3. 29.
14. 22. do they not err that *d.* evil
16. 9. a man's heart *d.* his way
30. shutteth eyes to *d.* froward
Jer. 18. 18. come let us *d.* devices
Mic. 2. 1. wo to them that *d.* iniquity
DEVOTED, Lev. 27. 21, 28.
Ps. 119. 38. servant who is *d.* to thy fear
Acts 17. 23. I beheld your *devotions*
DEVOUR, Gen. 49. 27.
Matt. 23. 14. ye *d.* widows' houses
2 Cor. 11. 20. if a man *d.* you
Gal. 5. 15. if ye bite and *d.* one another
Heb. 10. 27. which shall *d.* the adversaries
1 Pet. 5. 8. seeking whom he may *d.*
Isa. 1. 20. ye shall be *devoured*
24. 6. hath the curse *d.* the earth
Jer. 3. 24. shame hath *d.* the labour
30. 16. that *d.* thee shall be *d.*
Hos. 7. 7. *d.* judges, 9. *d.* strength
Mal. 3. 11. I will rebuke *devourer*
Ex. 24. 17. *devouring fire*, Isa. 29. 6. & 30. 27, 30. & 33. 14.
Ps. 52. 4. lovest all *devouring* words
DEVOUT, Luke 2. 25. Acts 2. 5. & 10. 27. & 17. 4, 17. & 22. 12.
DEW, Gen. 27. 28. Deut. 32. 2.
Ps. 110. 3. hast the *d.* of thy youth
Isa. 26. 19. thy *d.* is as the *d.* of herbs
Hos. 6. 4. goodness is as the early *d.*
14. 5. I will be as *d.* to Israel
Mic. 5. 7. Jacob—as *d.* from Lord
DIADEM, Job 29. 14. Isa. 28. 5. & 62. 8. Ezek. 21. 26.

DIE, Gen. 5. 5. & 6. 17.
Gen. 2. 17. thou shalt surely *d*. 3. 4.
1 Sam. 14. 44. 1 Kings 2. 37. Jer. 26. 8. Ezek. 3. 18.
Job 14. 14. if a man *d*. shall he live again
Ps. 8. 27. ye shall *d*. like men
118. 17. I shall not *d*. but live
Prov. 23. 13. with rod he shall not *d*.
Eccl. 3. 2. there is a time to *d*.
7. 17. why shouldst thou *d*. before time
Isa. 22. 13. to-morrow we shall *d*.
Jer. 31. 30. every one *d*. for own iniquity
Ezek. 3. 19. *d*. in his iniquity
18. 4. soul that sinneth shall *d*.
31. will ye *d*. O house of Israel
Jonah 4. 3. better for me to *d*. than live.
Matt. 26. 35. though I should *d*. with thee
Luke 20. 36. neither can *d*. any more
John 8. 21. ye shall *d*. in your sins
11. 50. expedient that one *d*. for the
Rom. 14. 8. we *d*. we *d*. unto Lord
1 Cor. 9. 15. better for me to *d*. than
15. 22. as in Adam all *d*. so in Christ
Phil. 1. 21. to live is Christ, to *d*. is gain
Heb. 9. 27. it is appointed for men to *d*.
Rev. 3. 2. that are ready to *d*.
14. 13. blessed are the dead who *d*. in the Lord
Rom. 5. 6. Christ *died* for ungodly
8. while yet sinners, Christ *d*. for us
6. 10. in that he *d*. he *d*. unto sin
9. being raised he *d*. no more
7. 9. sin revived and I *d*.
14. 9. to this end Christ *d*. and rose
1 Cor. 15. 3. Christ *d*. for our sins
2 Cor. 5. 15. he *d*. for all, that they
1 Thess. 5. 10. who *d*. for us that whether
Heb. 11. 13. these all *d*. in faith, not
Rom. 14. 7. no man *dieth* to himself
2 Cor. 4. 10. *dying*, 6. 9. Heb. 11. 21.
DIFFER, 1 Cor. 4. 7.
Phil. 1. 10. that *d*. Rom. 2. 18.
Lev. 10. 10. *difference*, Ezra. 22. 26.
Acts 15. 9. no *d*. Rom. 3. 22.
DILIGENCE, 2 Tim. 4. 9, 21.
Prov. 4. 23. keep thy heart with all *d*.
Luke 12. 58. art in way give *d*. that
2 Pet. 1. 5. giving all *d*. add to faith
10. give *d*. to make calling and election
Jude 3. I gave all *d*. to write unto you
Deut. 19. 18. *diligent*, Josh. 22. 5.
Prov. 10. 4. hand of *d*. maketh rich
12. 24. hand of *d*. shall bear rule
27. substance of *d*. man is precious
13. 4. the soul of *d*. shall be made fat
21. 5. thoughts of the *d*. tend to
22. 29. man *d*. in his business
27. 23. be *d*. to know state of thy flocks
2 Pet. 3. 14. be *d*. to be found of him
Ex. 15. 26. will *diligently* hearken to voice of, Deut. 11. 13. Jer. 17. 24.
Deut. 4. 9. keep thy soul *d*.
6. 7. teach them *d*. unto thy children
Deut. 6. 17. *d*. keep commandments
24. 8. that thou observe *d*. and
Ps. 119. 4. to keep thy precepts *d*.
Heb. 11. 6. rewarder of them that *d*. seek
DIMINISH, Deut. 4. 2.
Rom. 11. 12. *diminishing* of them the riches of
DIMNESS of anguish, Isa. 8. 22.
DIRECT, Eccl. 10. 10. Isa. 45. 13.
Ps. 5. 3. will I *d*. my prayer to thee
Prov. 3. 6. he shall *d*. thy paths
Isa. 61. 8. I will *d*. their work in truth
Jer. 10. 23. that walks to *d*. his steps

2 Thess. 3. 5. Lord *d*. your hearts
Isa. 40. 13. who *directed* the Spirit of the Lord
Ps. 119. 5. ways were *d*. to keep
Prov. 16. 9. a man's heart deviseth, Lord *directeth* his steps
DISCERN, Eccl. 8. 5. 2 Sam. 14. 17. 1 Kings 3. 9, 11. 1 Cor. 2. 14.
Mal. 3. 18. *d*. between righteous and
Heb. 5. 14. to *d*. both good and evil
4. 12. *discerner* of thoughts
1 Cor. 11. 29. not *discerning* Lord's body
12. 10. to another *d*. of Spirits
DISCHARGE, in war, Eccl. 8. 8.
DISCIPLE, John 9. 28. & 19. 38.
Matt. 10. 24. *d*. is not above his master
42. in the name of a *d*.
Luke 14. 26. ye cannot be my *d*.
John 8. 31. then are ye my *d*. indeed
20. 2. other *d*. whom Jesus loved
Acts 21. 16. an old *d*. with whom
DISCORD, soweth, Prov. 6. 14.
DISCRETION, Ps. 112. 5. Prov. 1. 4.
Isa. 28. 26. Jer. 10. 12.
DISEASE, Ps. 38. 7. Eccl. 6. 2.
Matt. 4. 23. & 10. 1. Ex. 15. 26.
Ps. 103. 3. who healeth all day thy *d*.
Ezek. 34. 4. *diseased*, have ye not, 21.
DISFIGURE bodies, Matt. 6. 16.
DISGRACE not, Jer. 14. 21.
DISHONOUR, Ps. 35. 26.
Mic. 7. 6. son *d*. his father
Ps. 71. 13. clothed with shame and *d*.
Rom. 1. 24. to *d*. their own bodies
9, 21, another to *d*. 2 Tim. 2. 20.
1 Cor. 15. 43. it is sown in *d*. it is raised
2 Cor. 6. 8. by honour and *d*.
DISOBEDIENCE, 2 Cor. 10. 6.
Eph. 2. 2. & 5. 6. Col. 3. 6.
Rom. 5. 19. by one man's *d*. many were made sinners
DISOBEDIENT, 1 Kings 13. 16.
Neh. 9. 26.
Luke 1. 17. *d*. to wisdom of the just
Rom. 1. 30. *d*. to parents, 2 Tim. 3.
2. 10. 21. *d*. and gainsaying people
Tit. 1. 16. abominable and *d*.
3. 3. *d*. deceived, serving divers lusts—
1 Pet. 2. 7, 8. stumble being *d*.
3. 20. who sometime were *d*.
DISORDERLY, 2 Thess. 3. 6.
DISPENSATION, 1 Cor. 9. 17.
Eph. 1. 10. & 3. 2. Col. 1. 25.
DISPERSED, Ps. 112. 9. Prov. 5. 16.
Isa. 11. 12. Zeph. 3. 10. John 7. 35.
DISPLEASED, Gen. 38. 10. 2.
Sam. 11. 27. 1 Chron. 2. 17. Zech. 1. 2, 15. Isa. 59. 15. Mark 10. 14.
Deut. 9. 19. hot or *sore displeasure*
DISPOSING, Prov. 16. 33.
Acts 7. 53. *disposition* of angels
DISPUTE, Job 23. 7. Mark 9. 33.
Rom. 14. 1. doubtful *disputations*
Phil. 2. 14. *disputings*, 1 Tim. 6. 5.
DISQUIETED, Ps. 39. 6.
DISSEMBLE, Josh. 7. 11. Jer. 42. 20.
Gal. 2. 13. Ps. 26. 4. Prov. 26. 24.
Rom. 12. 9. *dissimulation*, Gal. 2. 13.
DISSENSION, Acts 15. 2.
DISSOLVED, Ps. 75. 3. Isa. 24. 9.
2 Cor. 5. 1. 2 Peter 3. 11. Job. 30. 22.
DISTINCTLY, Neh. 8. 8.
DISTRACTED, suffer terrors, Ps. 85. 15. 1 Cor. 7. 35. *distraction* without
DISTRESS, Gen. 42. 21. Deut. 2. 9, 19. Neh. 9. 37. Luke 21. 23, 25.
Gen. 35. 3. answered in day of my *d*.
2 Sam. 22. 7. in my *d*. I called on the Lord, Ps. 18. 6. & 118. 5. & 120. 1.
1 Kings 1. 29. redeemed my soul out of all *d*.
2 Chron. 28. 22. in his *d*. trespassed more
Ps. 4. 1. enlarged my heart in *d*.
Prov. 1. 27. I will mock when *d*. cometh
Isa. 25. 5. strength to needy in *d*.

Zeph. 1. 15. that day is a day of *d*.
Rom. 8. 35. shall *d*. separate from Christ
1 Sam. 28. 15. *distressed*, 30. 6.
2 Cor. 6. 4. in *distresses*, 12. 10.
Ps. 25. 17. *out of my distresses*, 107. 6, 13. Ezek. 30. 16. 2 Cor. 6. 4.
DISTRIBUTE, Luke 18. 22. 1 Tim. 6. 18. 1 Cor. 7. 17. Job 21. 17.
Acts 4. 35. *distribution*, 2 Cor. 9. 13.
DITCH, Job 9. 31. Ps. 7. 15. Prov. 23. 27. Isa. 22. 11. Matt. 15. 14.
DIVERSITIES, 1 Cor. 12. 4.
DIVIDE, Gen. 1. 6, 14. Job 27. 17.
1 Kings 3. 25. *d*. living child, 26.
Ps. 55. 9. *divide*—*d*. their tongues
Isa. 53. 12. I will *d*. him a portion
Luke 12. 13. to *d*. inheritance with
22. 17. *d*. it among yourselves
2 Sam. 1. 23. in death not *divided*
Dan. 2. 41. kingdom shall be *d*.
5. 28. thy kingdom is *d*. and given to the Medes and Persians
Matt. 12. 25. house *d*. against itself shall not stand, 26. Luke 11. 17.
2 Tim. 2. 15. rightly *d*. the word of
Heb. 4. 12. to *d*. asunder of joints
Judg. 5. 15, 16. *divisions*, Rom. 16. 17. 1 Cor. 1. 10.
DIVINE sentence, Prov. 16. 10.
Heb. 9. 1. ordinance of *d*. service
1 Pet. 1. 3. his *d*. power hath given
4. partakers of the *d*. nature
Mic. 3. 11. prophets *d*. for money
Num. 22. 7. *divination*, 23. 23. Deut. 18. 10. Acts 16. 16.
Deut. 18. 14. *diviners*, Isa. 44. 25. Mic. 3. 7. Zech. 10. 2.
DIVORCE, Jer. 3. 8. Lev. 21. 14.
Num. 30. 9. Matt. 5. 32.
Deut. 24. 1, 3. *divorcement*, Isa. 50. 1.
Matt. 5. 31. Mark 10. 4.
DO, Gen. 16. 6. & 18. 25.
Matt. 7. 12. men should *d*. to you, *d*. ye so.
John 15. 5. without me ye can *d*.
Rom. 7. 15. what I would that *d*. I not
Phil. 4. 13. I can *d*. all things through Christ
Heb. 4. 13. with whom we have to *d*.
10. 9. come to *d*. thy will
Rev. 19. 10. see thou *d*. it not
Rom. 2. 13. the *doers* of it shall be justified
James 1. 22. be ye *d*. of word and not
1 Chron. 22. 16. *doing*, Ps. 64. 9.
Prov. 20. 11. Isa. 1. 16. Jer. 7. 3, 5.
Rom. 2. 7. *well-doing*, Gal. 6. 9. 2
2 Thess. 3. 13. 1 Pet. 2. 15.
DOCTOR, Acts 5. 34. Luke 2. 46.
Deut. 32. 2. *doctrine* shall drop as rain
Isa. 28. 9. make me to understand *d*.
Jer. 10. 8. the stock is a *d*. of vanities
Matt. 7. 28. astonished at his *d*.
Mark 1. 22. & 11. 18. Luke 4. 32.
Matt. 16. 12. beware of the *d*. of Pharisees
Mark 1. 27. what new *d*. is this
John 17. 17. shall we know of the *d*.
Acts 2. 42. apostles' *d*. and fellowship
Rom. 6. 17. form of *d*. which was delivered
16. 17. contrary to *d*. ye have learned
Eph. 4. 14. with every wind of *d*.
1 Tim. 5. 17. labor in word and *d*.
6. 3. according to godliness
2 Tim. 3. 16. profitable for *d*.
4. 3. will not endure sound *d*.
Tit. 2. 7. in *d*. showing incorruptness
10. may adorn the *d*. of God
Heb. 6. 1. principles of *d*. of Christ
2 *d*. of baptisms and laying hands
Matt. 15. 9. teaching for *d*. the commandments of men
Col. 2. 22. after *doctrines* of men
1 Tim. 4. 1. giving heed to *d*. of devils

Heb. 13. 9. carried about by strange *d*.
DOG, Ex. 11. 7. Deut. 29. 18.
1 Sam. 17. 43. am I a *d*.
Prov. 26. 11. *d*. return to his vomit, 2 Pet. 2. 22.
Eccl. 9. 4. living *d*. better than dead lion.
Isa. 56. 10. all dumb *dogs*, 11. greedy *d*.
Matt. 7. 6. cast not that is holy to *d*.
15. 27. *d*. eat of crumbs
Phil. 3. 2. beware of *d*. evil workers
Rev. 22. 15. without are *d*. and sorcerers
DOMINION, Gen. 27. 40.
Num. 24. 19. he that shall have *d*.
Job 25. 2. *d*. and fear are with him
Ps. 8. 6. have *d*. over the works of thy hands
19. 13. not have *d*. over me
49. 14. upright have *d*. over them
72. 8. his *d*. from sea to sea
145. 13. thy *d*. endureth through all generations
Isa. 26. 13. other lords had *d*. over us
Dan. 4. 3. his *d*. is from generation to generation
34.—an everlasting *d*. 7. 14.
7. 27. all *d*. shall serve and obey
Rom. 6. 9. death has no more *d*.
14. sin shall not have *d*. over you
2 Cor. 1. 24. not we have *d*. over your faith
Col. 1. 16. thrones or *d*. or principalities
Jude 8. despise *d*. and speak evil of
25. to God 1 Pet. 4. 11.
DOOR, Judg. 11. 31. & 16. 3.
Gen. 4. 7. sin lieth at the *d*.
Ps. 84. 10. *d*. keeper in the house of God
141. 3. keep *d*. of my lips
Prov. 26. 14. as *d*. turns on hinges
Hos. 2. 15. valley of Achor, *d*. of hope
John 10. 1. entereth not by *d*. is a thief
7. I am the *d*. of sheep, 9. I am *d*.
Acts 14. 27. opened *d*. of faith
1 Cor. 16. 9. great *d*. and effectual is opened unto me
2 Cor. 2. 12. a *d*. was opened to me
Col. 4. 3. God would open a *d*. of utterance
James 5. 9. judge stands before *d*.
Rev. 3. 8. I set before thee an open *d*.
20. I stand at *d*. and knock, if any
Ps. 24. 7. lift up ye everlasting *doors*
Prov. 8. 34. waiting at posts of my *d*.
Mal. 1. 10. shut ye the *d*. for nought
Matt. 24. 33. near, even at the *d*.
DOTING, 1 Tim. 6. 4.
DOUBLE, Ex. 22. 4.
2 Kings 2. 9. *d*. *portion* of thy spirit
1 Chron. 12. 33. not of a *d*. heart
Job 11. 6. secrets are *d*. to that which
Ps. 12. 2. with a *d*. heart do they speak
Isa. 40. 2. *d*. for all her sins
61. 7. ye shall have *d*. Zech. 9. 12.
Jer. 17. 18. destroy with *d*. destruction
1 Tim. 3. 8. deacons not *d*. tongued
5. 17. elders worthy *d*. honour
James 1. 8. *d*. minded man, 4. 8.
Rev. 18. 6. *d*. to her, fill to her *d*.
DOUBT, Deut. 28. 66.
Matt. 14. 31. of little faith, why dost *d*.
21. 21. have faith and *d*. not
Mark 11. 23. and shall not *d*. in heart
Rom. 14. 23. he that *doubteth* is damned
1 Tim. 2. 8. without wrath or *doubting*
Luke 12. 29. be not of *doubtful* mind
Rom. 14. 1. not to *d*. disputations
DOVE, Ps. 55. 6. Song 1. 15. Matt. 3. 16. Luke 3. 22. John 1. 32.
Isa. 38. 14. mourn as *d*. 59. 11.

60. 8. fly as *d.* to their windows
Hos. 7. 11. Ephraim also is like a silly *d.*
Matt. 10. 16. wise as serpents and harmless as *d.*
DOWN sitting, Ps. 139. 2.
Isa. 37. 31. *downward,* Eccl. 3. 21.
DRAGON, Ps. 91. 13. Isa. 27. 1.
Jer. 51. 34. Ezek. 29. 3. Rev. 12. 3.
Deut. 32. 33. *dragons,* Job 30. 29.
Ps. 44. 19. Isa. 13. 22. Jer. 9. 11.
Mic. 1. 8. Mal. 1. 3.
DRAW, Gen. 24. 44.
Job 21. 33. every man shall *d.* after him
Ps. 28. 3. *d.* me not away with the wicked
Song 1. 4. *d.* me, we will run after
Isa. 5. 18. wo unto that *d.* iniquity
Jer. 31. 3. with loving kindness I *d.*
John 6. 44. except Father—*d.* him
12. 32. I will *d.* all men to me
Heb. 10. 38. if any man *d.* back
Ps. 73. 28. good for me to *d.* near to God
Eccl. 12. 1. years *d.* nigh when they say
Isa. 29. 13. near me with their mouth
Heb. 7. 19. by which we *d.* nigh to God
10. 22. let us *d.* near with a true heart
James 4. 8. *d.* nigh to God, and he will
Ps. 18. 16. *drew* me out of many waters
Hos. 11. 4. I *d.* with cords of love
DREAD, Ex. 15. 16.
Deut. 1. 29. *d.* not, nor be afraid
1 Chron. 22. 13. be strong, *d.* not
Isa. 8. 13. let him be your fear and *d.*
Dan. 9. 4. great and *dreadful* God
Gen. 28. 17. how *d.* is this place
Mal. 1. 14. my name is *d.* among
4. 5. great and *d.* day of the Lord
DREAM, Gen. 37. 5.
Gen. 20. 3. God came to Abimelech in a *d.*
31. 11. angel spake to Jacob in a *d.*
24. God came to Laban in a *d.*
Num. 12. 6. speak to him in a *d.*
1 Kings 3. 5. the Lord appeared to Solomon in a *d.*
Job. 33. 15. in a *d.* in a vision of night
Ps. 73. 20. as *d.* when one awaketh
126. 1. we were like them that *d.*
Eccl. 5. 3. *d.* comes through multitude
Isa. 29. 7. that fight—be as a *d.*
Dan. 2. 3. I *d.* a *d.* 4. 5. saw a *d.*
Matt. 1. 20. angel appeared in a *d.*
2. 12. God warned of in a *d.*
27. 19. suffered many things in a *d.*
Acts 2. 17. old men shall *d.* dreams, Joel 2. 28.
Job. 7. 14. scarest me with *d.*
Eccl. 5. 7. in the multitude of *d.*
DRINK, Ex. 15. 24. & 32. 20.
Job 21. 20. *d.* of wrath of Almighty
Ps. 36. 8. *d.* of the river of thy pleasure
60. 3. *d.* wine of astonishment
80. 5. givest them tears to *d.*
110. 7. *d.* of the brook in the way
Prov. 4. 17. *d.* the wine of violence
5. 15. *d.* waters out of own cistern
31. 4. it is not for kings to *d.* wine
5. lest they *d.* and forget the law
7. *d.* and forget his poverty
Song 5. 1. *d.* yea *d.* abundantly
Isa. 22. 13. let us eat and *d.*
43. 20. to give *d.* to my people
65. 13. my servants shall *d.* but ye
Hos. 4. 18. their *d.* is sour, committed
Amos 4. 1. say to masters, bring, and let us *d.*
Matt. 10. 42. give to *d.* to one of these little ones
20. 22. able to *d.* of cup, 23.

26. 27. *d.* ye all of it, this is my blood
29. I will not henceforth *d.* of fruit
42. except I *d.* it thy will be done
John 6. 55. my blood is *d.* indeed
1 Cor. 10. 4. *d.* same spiritual
12. 13. all made to *d.* into one spirit
Lev. 10. 9. nor *d.* wine nor *strong drink,* Judg. 13. 4. 1 Sam. 1. 15.
Prov. 21.—is raging
31. 4. not for princes to *d.*
6. give—to those ready to perish
Isa. 5. 11. follow—22, mingle—
28. 7. prophet erred through—
Mic. 2. 11. prophecy to them of—
Job 15. 16. *drinketh* iniquity like water
John 6. 54. *d.* my blood hath eternal life
56. that *d.* my blood dwells in me
1 Cor. 11. 29. eateth and *d.* unworthily
Heb. 6. 7. earth which *d.* in vain
Eph. 5. 18. be not *drunk* with wine
Rev. 17. 2. *d.* with wine of fornication
Deut. 21. 20. glutton and *drunkard*
Prov. 23. 21. *d.* shall come to poverty
26. 9. thorn goeth up into hand of *d.*
Isa. 24. 20. earth shall reel like a *d.*
1 Cor. 5. 11. with railer and *d.* not eat
Ps. 69. 12. *drunkards,* Isa. 28. 1, 3.
Job. 12. 25. stagger like a *drunken* man, Ps. 107. 27. Jer. 23. 9. Isa. 19. 14.
Isa. 29. 9. *d.* not with wine, 51. 21.
Acts 2. 15. these are not *d.* as ye suppose
1 Cor. 11. 21. one hungry, another is *d.*
1 Thess. 5. 7. they that be *d.* are *d.* in night
Deut. 29. 19. *drunkenness,* Jer. 13. 13. Ezek. 23. 13. Rom. 13. 13. Gal. 5. 21.
DROP, Deut. 33. 28. Judg. 5. 4.
Deut. 32. 2. doctrine shall *d.* as rain
Ps. 65. 11. thy paths *d.* fatness, 12.
Prov. 5. 3. *d.* as honey-comb
Isa. 40. 15. nations are as a *d.* of a bucket
Song 5. 5. my hands *dropped* myrrh
2. locks with *drops* of the night
Luke 22. 44. sweat as it were great *d.* of blood
DROSS, Ps. 119. 119. Isa. 1. 25.
DROWN, Song 8. 7. 1 Tim. 6. 9.
DROWSINESS, Prov. 23. 21.
DRY, Judg. 6. 37. Job 13. 25. Prov. 17. 1. Isa. 44. 3. Jer. 4. 11. Ezek. 17. 24.
DUE, Lev. 10. 13. Deut. 18. 3.
1 Chron. 15. 13. sought him not after *d.*
16. 29. give Lord glory *d.* to his name, Ps. 29. 2. & 96. 8.
Prov. 3. 27. withhold not—whom it is *d.*
Matt. 18. 34. should pay all that was *d.*
Luke 23. 41. we received *d.* reward
Rom. 13. 7. tribute to whom tribute is *d.*
Ps. 104. 27. meat in *due season,* 145. 15.
Matt. 24. 25. Luke 12. 42.
Prov. 15. 23. a word spoken in—
Eccl. 10. 17. princes eat in—for strength
Gal. 6. 9. in—shall reap, if we faint not
Deut. 32. 35. foot shall slide in *due time*
Rom. 5. 6. in—Christ died for the ungodly
1 Cor. 15. 8. as one born out of—
1 Tim. 2. 6. to be testified in—
Tit. 1. 3. hath in—manifested
DULL of hearing, Matt. 13. 15.
DUMB, Hab. 2. 18. Mark 9. 17.
Ex. 4. 11. who maketh *d.* or deaf
Ps. 38. 13. I was as a *d.* man

39. 2. I was *d.* with silence, 9.
Prov. 31. 8. open thy mouth for *d.*
Isa. 35. 6. tongue of *d.* to sing
53. 7. sheep before shearers is *d.*
56. 10. watchmen are all *d.* dogs.
DUNG of solemn feasts, Mal. 2. 3.
Phil. 3. 8. I count them but *d.* to win
DURABLE riches and righteousness, Prov. 8. 18.
Isa. 23. 18. merchandize for *d.* clothing
DUST thou art, and to *d.* Gen. 3. 19.
18. 27. who man but *d.* and ashes
Job 30. 19. I am become like *d.* and
34. 15. man shall turn again to *d.*
42. 6. and repent in *d.* and ashes
Ps. 22. 15. brought me into *d.* of death
30. 9. shall the *d.* praise thee
102. 14. servants favour *d.* thereof
103. 14. remembereth that we are *d.*
104. 29. die and return to *d.* Eccl. 3. 20
119. 25. soul cleaveth to the *d.*
Eccl. 12. 7. then shall *d.* return to earth
Matt. 10. 14. shake off *d.* of your feet, Luke 10. 11, Acts 13. 51.
DUTY of marriage, Ex. 21. 10.
2 Chron. 8. 14. as *d.* of every day required
Eccl. 12. 13. this is whole of *d.* of man
Luke 17. 10. which was our *d.* to do
DWELL in thy holy hills, Ps. 15. 1.
Ps. 23. 6. I will *d.* in the house of the Lord forever
25. 13. their soul shall *d.* at ease
27. 4. may *d.* in house of Lord, and 84. 10. than to *d.* in tents of wickedness
120. 5. that I *d.* in tents of Kedar
132. 14. here will I *d.* for I have
Isa. 33. 14. who shall *d.* with devouring fire—*d.* with everlasting burnings
16. he shall *d.* on high, his place
Rom. 8. 9. Spirit of God *d.* in you
2 Cor. 6. 16. I will *d.* in them
Col. 1. 19. in him shall all fulness *d.*
3. 16. word of Christ *d.* in you richly
1 John 4. 13. that we *d.* in him
Rev. 21. 3. he will *d.* with them
John 6. 56. *dwelleth* in me, and I in
14. 10. Father that *d.* in me
17. he *d.* with and shall be in you
Acts 7. 48. *d.* not in temples
Rom. 7. 17. sin that *d.* in me, 20.
18. in my flesh *d.* no good thing
8. 11. by his Spirit that *d.* in you
1 Cor. 3. 16. Spirit of God *d.* in you
Col. 2. 9. in him *d.* all fulness of the Godhead
2 Tim. 1. 14. Holy Ghost who *d.* in us
James 4. 5. the Spirit which *d.* in us
2 Pet. 3. 13. wherein *d.* righteousness
1 John 3. 17. how *d.* the love of God in
3. 24. that keepeth his commandments *d.* in him
4. 12. God *d.* in us, and his love is
15. confesseth Jesus is Son of God, God *d.*
16. *d.* in love, *d.* in God, and God
John 2. truth's sake which *d.* in us
2 Tim. 1. 16. *dwelling* in light
Heb. 11. 9. *d.* in tabernacles with
2 Pet. 2. 8. righteous man *d.* among
Ps. 87. 2. more than all *d.* of Jacob
Ps. 94. 17. almost *dwelt* in silence
John 1. 14. Word made flesh and *d.*
Acts 13. 17. *d.* as strangers in it
2 Tim. 1. 5. faith *d.* first in grandmother

E

EAGLE, Deut. 32. 11.
Job 9. 26. as *e.* hasteth to the prey.

Prov. 23. 5. fly away as *e.* towards heaven
Jer. 49. 16. make nest as high as *e.*
Ezek. 17. 3. great *e.* with great wings
Obad. 4. though thou exalt thyself as *e.*
Mic. 1. 16. enlarge thy baldness as *e.*
Rev. 12. 14. to woman given wings of *e.*
Ex. 19. 4. bare you on *e.* wings
2 Sam. 1. 23. swifter than *eagles*
Ps. 103. 5. youth renewed like *e.*
Prov. 30. 17. young *e.* shall eat it
Isa. 40. 31. mount up with wings as *e.*
Jer. 4. 13. horses swifter than *e.*
Lam. 4. 19. our persecutor, swifter than *e.*
Matt. 24. 28. there *e.* be gathered
EAR, Num. 14. 28. Ex. 9. 31.
Ex. 21. 6. bore his *e.* Deut. 15. 17.
2 Kings 19. 16. bow down *e.* Ps. 31. 2.
Neh. 1. 16. let thy *e.* be attentive, 11.
Job. 12. 11. *e.* try words, 34. 3.
36. 10. openeth *e.* to discipline
42. 5. heard by the hearing of *e.*
Ps. 10. 17. cause thine *e.* to hear
58. 4. adder that stops the *e.*
94. 9. planted the *e.* shall he not hear
Prov. 18. 15. *e.* of wise seek knowledge
20. 12. hearing *e.* and seeing eye
28. 9. turns away *e.* from hearing
Eccl. 1. 8. nor *e.* filled with hearing
Isa. 50. 4. awaken my *e.* to hear
58. 1. neither is *e.* heavy
Jer. 6. 10. their *e.* is uncircumcised
9. 20. let your *e.* receive the word
Matt. 10. 27. what ye hear in the *e.*
1 Cor. 2. 9. eye seen nor *e.* heard
Rev. 2. 7. he that hath an *e.* let him hear, 11. 17, 29. & 3. 6, 13, 22. & 13. 9.
Matt. 11. 15. & 13. 9, 43.
Ex. 15. 26. *give ear,* Deut. 32. 1. Judg. 5. 3. Ps. 5. 1. Jer. 13. 15. Hos 5. 1. Joel 1. 2. Ps. 55. 1.
Ps. 17. 6. *incline ear,* 45. 10. Isa. 37. 17.
Dan. 9. 18.
49. 4.—to a parable
78. 1.—to words of my mouth
Prov. 2. 2.—to wisdom
4. 20. to my sayings
Isa. 55. 3.—and come unto me
Jer. 11. 8. *nor inclined their ear*
Deut. 29. 4. Lord not given *ears* to hear
1 Sam. 3. 11. both *e.* shall tingle, 2 Kings 21. 12. Jer. 19. 3.
2 Sam. 22. 7. cry did enter into his *e.*
Job. 33. 16. open the *e.* of men
Ps. 34. 15. his *e.* are open to their cry
40. 6. my *e.* hast thou opened
44. 1. we have heard with our *e.*
Isa. 6. 10. make *e.* heavy, lest they hear
35. 5. *e.* of deaf shall be unstopped
43. 8. bring deaf that have *e.* 9.
Matt. 13. 15. their *e.* dull of hearing
16. blessed are your *e.* for they hear
Luke 9. 44. these sayings sink down into your *e.*
2 Tim. 4. 4. turn away their *e.* from
2 Chron. 6. 40. *thine ears* be open to
Ps. 10. 17. cause—to hear
130. 2. let—be attentive
Prov. 23. 12. apply—to words of
Isa. 30. 21.—shall hear a word
Ezek. 3. 10. hear with—40. 4.
Gen. 45. 6. *earing*
1 Sam. 8. 12. *ear his ground*
Ex. 9. 31 *in the ear,* Mark 4. 28.
Job. 42. 11. gave *ear-ring* of gold
Prov. 25. 12. as an *e.* of gold so is
EARLY, Gen. 19. 2. John 18. 28.
Ps. 46. 5. God shall help her and that right *e.*
57. 8. will awake right *e.* 108. 2.
63. 1. my God, *e.* will I seek thee
78. 34. returned *e.* after God

90. 14. satisfy us *e.* with mercy
127. 2. vain to rise *e.* or sit late
Prov. 1. 28. seek me *e.* and not find
8. 17. that seek me *e.* shall find me
Isa. 26. 9. with my spirit I seek thee *e.*
Jer. 7. 13. rising up *e.* 25.
Hos. 5. 15. in affliction will seek me *e.*
6. 4. goodness as *e.* dew goeth away
James 5. 7. receive *e.* and latter rain
EARNEST, 2 Cor. 1. 22.
Eph. 1. 14. *e.* of your inheritance
Rom. 8. 19. *e.* expectation of the
2 Cor. 7. 7. told us of your *e. desire*
8. 16. same *e.* care into the heart of Titus
Phil. 1. 20. according to my *e.* expectation
Heb. 2. 1. give the more *e.* heed
Job. 7. 2. servant *earnestly* desireth the shadow
Jer. 11. 7. I *e.* protested to your fathers
31. 20. I do *e.* remember him still
Mic. 7. 3. do evil with both hands *e.*
Luke 22. 24. in an agony, prayed more *e.*
1 Cor. 12. 31. covet *e.* the best gifts
2 Cor. 5. 2. in this we groan *e.*
James 5. 17. prayed *e.* it might not
Jude 3. *e.* contend for the faith
EARNETH wages, Hag. 1. 6.
EARTH was corrupt, Gen. 6. 11.
Gen. 6. 13. is filled with violence
11. 1. whole *e.* of one language
41. 47. brought forth by handfuls
Ex. 9. 29. *e.* is the Lord's, Deut. 10.
14. Ps. 24. 1. 1 Cor. 10. 26, 27, 28.
Num. 16. 32. *e.* opened her mouth,
26. 10. Deut. 11. 6. Ps. 106. 17.
Deut. 28. 23. under thee be iron
32. 1. O *e.* hear the words of my mouth
Judg. 5. 4. *e.* trembleth and heaven
1 Sam. 2. 8. pillars of *e.* are Lord's
2 Sam. 22. 8. *e.* shook and trembled
1 Chron. 16. 31. let *e.* rejoice
Job 9. 6. shakes *e.* out of her place
24. *e.* is given into hand of wicked
11. 9. longer than *e.* broader than sea
16. 8. O *e.* cover not my blood
26. 7. hangeth *e.* upon nothing
28. 5. out of *e.* cometh bread and
30. 8. base men, viler than the *e.*
38. 4. I laid the foundations of *e.*
Ps. 33. 5. *e.* is full of goodness of Lord
65. 9. visitest *e.* and waterest it
67. 6. *e.* shall yield her increase
72. 19. let the whole *e.* be filled with his glory
75. 3. *e.* and inhabitants dissolved
78. 69. like *e.* established forever
89. 11. heaven and *e.* are thine
97. 4. *e.* saw and trembled
104. 24. *e.* is full of thy riches, 13.
114. 7. tremble, O *e.* at presence of Lord
115. 16. *e.* given to children of men
119. 64. *e.* is full of thy mercy
139. 15. in lowest parts of the *e.*
Prov. 25. 3. *e.* for depth is unsearchable
Eccl. 1. 4. *e.* abideth for ever
Isa. 6. 3. whole *e.* is full of his glory
11. 4. smite the *e.* with rod of his mouth
9. full of the knowledge of Lord, Hab. 2. 14.
13. 13. *e.* shall remove out of her place
24. 1. Lord maketh the *e.* empty
4. *e.* mourneth and fadeth, 33. 9.
5. *e.* is defiled under inhabitants
19. *e.* utterly broken down and
20. *e.* shall reel and stagger like a
26. 19. *e.* shall cast out her dead
21. *e.* shall disclose her blood, and
66. 1. *e.* is my footstool, where

Jer. 22. 29. O *e. e. e.* hear the word of Lord
Ezek. 34. 27. *e.* shall yield her increase
43. 2. the whole *e.* shined with his
Hos. 2. 22. *e.* shall hear the corn
Hab. 3. 3. *e.* was full of his praise
Matt. 13. 5. stony ground had not much *e.*
John 3. 31. that is of *e.* earthly
Heb. 6. 7. *e.* which drinketh in rain
Rev. 12. 16. *e.* opened and swallowed flood
Ps. 67. 2. way known *upon earth*
73. 25. none—I desire besides thee
Eccl. 5. 2. God is in heaven and thou—
7. 20. there is not a just man—
10. 7. walking as servants—
Luke 5. 24. the Son of man hath power—
Col. 3. 5. mortify your members—
Lev. 6. 28. *earthen,* Jer. 19. 1.
John 3. 12, 31. *earthly,* 2 Cor. 5. 1. Phil. 3. 19. James 3. 15.
1 Cor. 15. 47, 48, 49. *earthy*
1 Kings 19. 11, 12. *earthquake,* Isa. 29. 6. Amos 1. 1. Matt. 24. 7.
Rev. 6. 12. a great *e.* 8. 5.
EASE, Job. 12. 5. Prov. 25. 13. Deut. 28. 65. Isa. 32. 9, 11. Jer. 46. 27. Ezek. 23. 42. Amos 6. 1.
Isa. 1. 24. I will *e.* me of mine adversaries
Luke 12. 19. take thine *e.* be merry
Matt. 11. 30. my yoke is *easy,* and burden light
Prov. 14. 6. knowledge is *e.* to him
1 Cor. 14. 9. words *e.* to be understood
James 3. 17. gentle *e.* to be entreated
Matt. 9. 5. *easier,* 19. 24.
1 Cor. 13. 5. charity is not *easily* provoked
Heb. 12. 1. sin—doth so *e.* beset us
EAST, Gen. 28. 14. & 29. 1. Matt. 2. 1, 2. Ps. 75. 6. & 103. 12.
Isa. 43. 5. bring thy seed from *e.*
Matt. 8. 11. many shall come from *e.*
Rev. 16. 12. way of kings of the *e.* may
Gen. 41. 6. *east wind,* Ex. 14. 21. Job 27. 21. Ps. 48. 7. Isa. 27. 8. Hos. 12. 1. & 13. 15. Hab. 1. 9.
EAT, Gen. 3. 5, 6, 12, 13.
Gen. 2. 16. of every tree freely *e.* of tree of knowledge shalt not *e.* in day thou eatest shalt surely die
3. 14. dust shalt thou *e.* all the days of thy life
17. in sorrow thou shalt *e.* of it
Neh. 8. 10. *e.* the fat, drink the sweet
Ps. 22. 26. meek shall *e.* and be satisfied
53. 4. eat up my people as bread, 14. 4.
78. 25. man did *e.* angels' food
29. they did *e.* and were filled
Prov. 1. 31. *e.* fruit of their own way
Song 5. 1. *e.* O friends; drink, yea, drink abundantly
Isa. 1. 19. if obedient ye shall *e.* the good of the land
3. 10. shall *e.* fruit of doings
55. 1. buy and *e.* yea, come buy
2. *e.* that which is good, and let soul
65. 13. *my* servants shall *e.* but ye
Dan. 4. 43. did *e.* grass as an ox
Hos. 4. 10. shall *e.* not have enough, Hag. 1. 6. Mic. 6. 14.
Mic. 3. 3. *e.* flesh of my people
Matt. 6. 25. what shall we *e.* and drink
26. 26. take *e.* this is my body, Mark 14. 22. 1 Cor. 11. 24.
Luke 10. 8. such things as are set
15. 23. let us *e.* and be merry
17. 27. they did *e.* they drank, 28.
John 6. 26. ye did *e.* of the loaves
53. except ye *e.* flesh of Son of man

Acts 2. 46. did *e.*—with gladness
1 Cor. 5. 11. with such, no not to *e.*
8. 8. if we *e.* are we the better
10. 3. eat the same spiritual meat
31. whether ye *e.* or drink, do all
2 Thess. 3. 10. if not work neither *e.*
5. Tim. 2. 17. *e.* as doth a canker
James 5. 3. *e.* your flesh as fire.
Rev. 17. 16. shall *e.* her flesh, and burn with fire
Ps. 69. 9. the zeal of thy house hath *eaten* me up, John 2. 17. Ps. 119. 139.
Prov. 9. 17. bread *e.* in secret is pleasant
Song 5. 1. *e.* my honey-comb with honey
Hos. 10. 13. having *e.* fruit of lies
Luke 13. 26. *e.* and drunk in thy presence
Acts 12. 23. Herod was *e.* of worms
Judg. 14. 14. out of *eater* came meat
Isa. 55. 10. give bread to *e.* and seed to the sower
Nah. 3. 12. fall into mouth of *e.*
Eccl. 4. 5. *eateth* his own flesh
Matt. 9. 11. why *e.* your master with publicans and sinners
John 6. 54. whoso *e.* my flesh and drinketh
57. he that *e.* me shall live by me
58. he that *e.* this bread shall live
Rom. 14. 6. he that *e. e.* to the Lord
20. evil for that man who *e.* with offence
1 Cor. 11. 29. *e.* and drinketh unworthily, *e.* and drinketh damnation, 27.
Matt. 11. 18. John came neither *eating* nor drinking, Luke 7. 33.
19. Son of man came *e.*
24. 38. were *e.* and drinking
26. 26. as they were *e.* Jesus took
1 Cor. 8. 4. concerning *e.* of those
EDIFY, or build up, Rom. 14. 19.
1 Thess. 5. 11. 1 Cor. 8. 1. Acts 9. 31.
Rom. 15. 2. please neighbor to *edification.*
1 Cor. 14. 13. speak unto men to *e.*
2 Cor. 10. 8. Lord hath given us for *e.* and not for destruction, 13. 10.
1 Cor. 14. 12. excel to *edifying* of church
26. let all things be done to *e.* 5. 17.
2 Cor. 12. 19. we do all for your *e.*
Eph. 4. 12. for *e.* of body of Christ
16. increase to *e.* itself in love
4. 29. but what is good to the use of *e.*
1 Tim. 1. 4. minister questions rather than *e.*
EFFECT, 2 Chron. 34. 22.
Isa. 32. 17. *e.* of righteousness
Matt. 15. 6. commandment of God of *none effect*
Mark 7. 13. making work of God—
Rom. 3. 3. make faith of God
4. 14. promise made—God 3. 17.
9. 6. not as though word hath
1 Cor. 1. 17. lest cross of Christ—
Gal. 5. 4. Christ has become—to you
1 Cor. 16. 9. door and *effectual* is opened
2 Cor. 1. 6. which is *e.* and enduring
Eph. 3. 7. *e.* working of his power
4. 16. according to the *e.* working
Phil. 6. faith may become *e.*
Jas. 5. 16. *e.* fervent prayer of righteous
Gal. 2. 8. *effectually,* 1 Thess. 2. 13.
EFFEMINATE, 1 Cor. 6. 9.
EGG, Deut. 22. 6. Job 6. 6. Isa. 10. 14. Jer. 17. 11. Luke 11. 12.
ELDER, Gen. 10. 21. 2 John 1. 3.
Gen. 25. 23. *e.* shall serve younger, Rom. 9. 12.
1 Tim. 5. 1. rebuke not an *e,* but
2. entreat *e.* women as mothers

19. against an *e.* receive not an accusation
1 Pet. 5. 1. *elders,* I who am an *e.*
5. younger submit yourselves to *e.*
Deut. 32. 7. ask *e.* they will tell thee
Ezra 10. 8. according to counsel of *e.*
Joel 2. 16. assemble *e.* Ps. 107. 32.
Acts 14. 23. ordained *e.* in every church
15. 23. *e.* and brethren send greeting, 6.
20. 17. called *e.* of the church
1 Tim. 5. 17. *e.* rule well, counted worthy
Tit. 1. 5. ordain *e.* in every church
Heb. 11. 2. *e.* obtained good report
James 5. 14. sick call for *e.* of church
Rev. 4. 4. four and twenty *e.* sitting, 10. & 5. 6, 8, 11, 14. & 11. 16.
ELECT, *chosen, choice one*
Isa. 42. 1. *e.* in whom my soul delighteth
45. 4. for Israel my *e.* I have called
65. 9. my *e.* shall inherit it
22. my *e* shall long enjoy work
Matt. 24. 22. for *e.* sake the days are shortened
24. if possible deceive very *e.*
31. gather together his *e.* from the four winds
Luke 18. 7. God avenge his own *e.*
Rom. 8. 33. to charge of God's *e.*
Col. 3. 12. put on as the *e.* of God
1 Tim. 5. 21. charge thee before *e.* angels
2 Tim. 2. 10. to endure all things for *e.*
Tit. 1. 1. according to the faith of God's *e.*
1 Pet. 1. 2. *e.* according to the foreknowledge of God
2. 6. corner stone, *e.* precious
2 John 1. *e.* lady, 13. *e.* sister
1 Pet. 5. 13. church *elected* with you
Rom. 9. 11. purpose of God according to *election*
11. 5. remnant according to the *e.* of grace
7. *e.* hath obtained it, and rest blinded
28. touching the *e.* they are beloved
1 Thess. 1. 4. knowing your *e.* of God
2 Pet. 1. 10. make calling and *e.* sure
ELEMENTS, Gal. 4. 3, 9.
ELOQUENT, Ex. 4. 10. Isa. 3. 3.
EMPTY, Gen. 31. 42. & 37. 24.
Ex. 23. 15. none shall appear before me *e.* 34. 20. Deut. 16. 16.
Deut. 15. 13. not let him go away *e.*
Judg. 7. 16. with *e.* pitchers and lamps
2 Sam. 1. 22. sword of Saul returned not *e.*
Hos. 10. 1. Israel is an *e.* vine, he brings
Luke 1. 53. rich hath he sent *e.* away
Isa. 34. 11. stones of *emptiness*
EMULATION, Rom. 11. 14.
ENCHANTMENT, Lev. 19. 26. Num. 23. 23. Eccl. 10. 11. Isa. 47. 9.
END, Gen. 6. 13.
Deut. 32. 20. see what their *e.* shall be
Ps. 37. 37. *e.* of that man is peace
39. 4. make me to know my *e.*
73. 17. then understood I their *e.*
102. 27. thy years have no *e.*
119. 96. seen an *e.* of all perfection
Eccl. 4. 8. no *e.* of all his labour
7. 2. that is the *e.* of all men
8. *e.* is better than the beginning
Isa. 9. 7. of his government shall be no *e.*
Jer. 5. 31. what will ye do in the *e.*
17. 11. at his *e.* shall be a fool
29. 11. to give an expected *e.*
31. 17. there is hope in thy *e.*
Ezek. 7. 2, 6. Amos 8. 2.
Ezek. 21. 25. iniquity shall have an *e.*
Dan. 8. 19. at time appointed *e.* shall be

12. 8. what shall be the e. of these
13. go thy way till the e. be
Matt. 13. 39. harvest is e. of world
24. 3. what sign of the e. of world
6. but e. is not yet, Luke 21. 9.
Rom. 6. 21. e. of those things is death
22. ye have the e. everlasting life
Heb. 6. 8. whose e. is to be burned
16. oath—make an e. of all strife
7. 3. beginning—nor e. of life
13. 7. considering e. of their conversation
James 5. 11. seen the e. of the Lord
1 Pet. 1. 9. receiving the e of your
4. 7. e of all things is at hand
17. e. of those that obey not gospel
Rev. 21. 6. beginning and e. 22. 13.
Jer. 4. 27. *make* a full end, 5. 10, 18. & 30. 11. Ezek. 11. 13.
Num. 23. 10. *last* end, Jer. 12. 4. Lam. 1. 9. & 4. 18. Dan. 8. 19.
Deut. 8. 16. *latter* end, 32. 29. Job 42. 12. Prov. 19. 20. 2 Pet. 2. 20.
Ps. 119. 33. *unto the end,* Dan. 6. 26. Matt. 24. 13. & 28. 20. John 13. 1. 1 Cor. 1. 8. Heb. 3. 6, 14. & 6. 11.
1 Tim. 1. 4. *endless,* Heb. 7. 16.
Ps. 22. 27. all the *ends* of the world remember
65. 5. confidence of all e. of earth
67. 7. all e. of earth shall fear him
98. 3. all e. of earth have seen salvation
Prov. 17. 24. eyes of fool in e. of earth
Isa. 45. 22. be ye saved, all e. of the earth
52. 10. all e. of the earth see salvation
Zech. 9. 10. his dominion to e. of earth
Acts 13. 47. for salvation to e. of earth
1 Cor. 10. 11. on whom e. of world are come
ENDOWED, Gen. 30. 20. 2 Chron. 2. 12, 13. Luke 24. 49. James 3. 13.
ENDURE, Job 8. 15.
Gen. 33. 14. as children are able to e.
Ps. 30. 5. weeping may e. for a night
132. 26. they perish, but thou shalt e.
Prov. 27. 24. doth crown e. to every generation
Ezek. 22. 14. can thy heart e. or hands
Mark 4. 17. no root, and e. but for a 13. 13. that shall e. unto end shall
2 Tim. 2. 3. e. hardness as a soldier
10. 1. e. all things for elect's sake
4. 3. they will not e. sound doctrine
5. watch thou e. afflictions, do
Heb. 12. 7. if ye e. chastening
James 5. 11. we count happy who e.
Ps. 81. 15. should have *endured* for ever
Rom. 9. 22. e. with much long suffering
2 Tim. 3. 11. what persecutions I e.
Heb. 6. 15. had patiently e. he obtained
10. 32. ye e. a great fight of afflictions
12. 2. e. cross, 3. e. contradiction
Ps. 30. 5. his anger *endureth* but a
100. 5. his truth e. to all generations
145. 13. thy dominion e. throughout all
Matt. 10. 22. that e. to end, shall be saved, 24. 13. Mark 13. 13.
John 6. 27. meat which e. unto life
1 Cor. 13. 7. charity e. all things
James 1. 12. blessed that e. temptation
Ps. 9. 7. *endure for ever,* the Lord, 102. 12, 26. & 104. 31. his name, Ps. 72. 77. his seed, 80. 29.
1 Chron. 16. 34, 41. *endureth for ever* his mercy, 2 Chron. 5. 13. Ezra 3. 11.
Ps. 113. 3. his righteousness—10. his praise—117. 2. truth of the Lord—
119. 160. every one of thy judgments—135. 13. thy name
1 Pet. 1. 25. word of Lord
Heb. 10. 34. in heaven e. substance
ENEMY, Ex. 25. 6, 9. Ps. 7. 5.
Ex. 23. 22. I will be an e. to thy enemies
Deut. 32. 27. I feared wrath of the e.
1 Sam. 24. 19. find his e. will he let
Job. 33. 10. counteth me for his e.
Ps. 7. 5. let e. persecute my soul
8. 2. mightiest still the e. and the avenger
Prov. 27. 6. kisses of e. are deceitful
Isa. 63. 10. he turned to their e.
1 Cor. 15. 26. last e. destroyed is death
Gal. 4. 16. am I become your e.
2 Thess. 3. 15. count him not as e.
James 4. 4. friend of world, e. of God
1 Kings 21. 20. *mine enemy,* Ps. 7. 4. Mic. 7. 8, 10. Job 16. 9. Lam. 2. 22.
Ex. 23. 4. *thy enemy,* Prov. 25. 21. Rom. 12. 20. Matt. 5. 43.
Mic. 7. 6. man's *enemies* are men of
Rom. 5. 10. if when e. we were reconciled.
1 Cor. 15. 25. put all e. under his feet
Phil. 3. 18. e. to the cross of Christ
Col. 1. 21. e. in your minds by wicked
Gen. 22. 17. *his enemies,* Ps. 68. 1. Prov. 16. 7. Isa. 59. 18. Heb. 10. 13.
Deut. 32. 41. *my enemies,* Ps. 18. 17. Isa. 1. 24. Luke 19. 27.
Deut. 32. 31. *our enemies*
Ex. 23. 22, *thy enemies,* Deut. 28. 48. Judg. 5. 31. Ps. 21. 8. Matt. 22. 44.
Gen. 3. 15. I will put *enmity* between
Eph. 2. 25. abolished e. 16. slain e.
ENGAGETH, Jer. 30. 21.
ENJOIN, Philem. 8. Esth. 9. 31. Job 36. 23. Heb. 9. 20.
ENJOY, Num. 36. 8.
Lev. 26. 34. land e. her sabbaths
Acts 24. 2. we e. great quietness
1 Tim. 6. 17. giveth richly all things to e.
Heb. 11. 25. e. pleasures of sin for
ENLARGE, Ex. 24. 34.
Gen. 9. 27. God shall e. Japheth
Deut. 33. 20. blessed be he that *enlargeth* Gad
2 Sam. 22. 37. *enlarged* steps
Ps. 4. 1. e. when in distress
25. 17. troubles of my heart are e.
119. 32. when thou shalt e. my heart
Isa. 5. 14. hell hath e. herself
54. 2. c. the place of thy tent
60. 5. thy heart shall fear, and be e.
Hab. 2. 5. e. his desires as hell
2 Cor. 6. 11, our heart is e. 13.
Esth. 4. 14. *enlargement*
ENLIGHTEN, Ps. 18. 28.
Eph. 1. 18. understanding being *enlightened*
Ps. 19. 8. commandment is pure, *enlightening* the eyes
Heb. 6. 4. impossible for those once e.
ENOUGH, I have, Gen. 33. 9.
Gen. 45. 28. it is e. Joseph is alive
Ex. 36. 5. bring more than e.
2 Sam. 24. 16. said to angel, it is e.
1 Kings 19. 4. it is e. take away
Prov. 30. 15, 16. say not, it is e.
Matt. 10. 25. it is e. for disciple
Mark 14. 41. it is e. the hour is come
Luke 15. 17. bread e. and to spare
ENQUIRE, Job. 10. 6.
Ps. 27. 4. to e. in his temple
78. 34. returned and e. early after God
Eccl. 7. 10. thou dost not e. wisely
Isa. 21. 12. if ye will e. to ye
Ezek. 36. 37. this I will be *enquired* of by the house of Israel
Zeph. 1. 6. have not e. for him
Matt. 2. 7. Herod e. of them diligently
2 Pet. 1. 10. of which salvation prophets have e.
Judg. 20. 27. *enquired of the Lord,* 1 Sam. 23. 2. 2 Sam. 2. 1.
Prov. 20. 25. after vows make *enquiry*
ENRICHED, 1 Cor. 1. 5.
Ps. 65. 9. thou greatly e. it with the river of God
ENSAMPLE, 1 Cor. 10. 11. Phil. 3. 17. 1 Thess. 1. 7. 2 Thess. 3. 9.
ENSIGN, Isa. 5. 26.
Isa. 11. 10. stand for e. to people
Ps. 74 4. set up their e. for signs
ENTER, Gen. 12. 11. Num. 4. 23. Judg. 18. 9. Dan. 11. 17.
Job 22. 4. will he e. into judgment
Ps. 100. 4. e. into his gates with
118. 20. gate into which righteous shall e.
Isa. 2. 10. e. into rock and hide
26. 2. open, righteous nation may e.
20. e. into thy chambers, and shut
50. 2. he shall e. into peace
Matt. 5. 20. in no case e. into kingdom
6. 6. when thou prayest, e. closet
7. 13. e. at straight gate
21. shall e. into kingdom of heaven
18. 8. better to e. into life, halt
19. 23. rich man hardly e. into kingdom
24. than for rich man to e. into the kingdom of heaven, Mark 10. 25.
Matt. 25. 21. e. thou into joy of Lord
Mark 14. 38. watch and pray, lest ye e. into temptation, Luke 22. 46.
Luke 13. 24. seek to e. but not able
24. 26. suffered and e. into his glory
John 3. 4. can he e. the second time
5. he cannot e. into the kingdom of
10. 9. by me if any man e. in
Acts 14. 22. through much tribulation e. kingdom of God
Heb. 4. 3. believed, do e. into rest
10. 19. e. into holiest by blood of Jesus
Rev. 15. 8. no man able to e. into temple
21. 27. e. into it, anything defileth
Rev. 22. 14. e. through gates into city
Ps. 143. 2. *enter not into* judgment
Prov. 4. 14. e. not into paths of wicked
23. 10. e. not into fields of the fatherless
Matt. 26. 41. that ye e. not into temptation
Ps. 119. 130. *entrance,* 2 Pet. 1. 11.
Luke 11. 52. ye *entered* not yourselves
John 4. 38. ye e. into their labours
10. 1. that e. not by door, but
Rom. 5. 12. sin e. into the world
20. the law e. that offence might abound
Heb. 4. 6. e. not in because of unbelief
10. that is e. into his rest, he ceased
Matt. 23. 13. *entering,* Luke 11. 52. Mark 4. 19. & 7. 15. 1 Thess. 1. 9.
ENTERTAIN, strangers, Heb. 13. 2.
ENTICE, Ex. 20. 16. Deut. 13. 6. 2 Chron. 18. 19, 20, 21. Prov. 1. 10.
Job 31, 27. *enticed,* James 1. 14.
1 Cor. 2. 4. *enticing* words, Col. 2. 4.
ENVY slayeth silly one, Job 5. 2.
Prov. 3. 31. e. not the oppressor
14. 30 e. is the rottenness of bones
23. 17. let not thy heart e. sinners
27. 4. who is able to stand before e.
Eccl. 9. 6. their e. is perished
Isa. 11. 13. e. of Ephraim shall depart, not e. Judah
26. 11. shall be ashamed for their e.
Ezek. 35. 11. do according to thine e.
Matt. 27. 18. for e. they delivered
Acts 7. 9. moved with e. 17. 5.
13. 45. Jews filled with e. spake
Rom. 1. 29. full of e. murder
Phil. 1. 15. preach Christ of e.
1. Tim. 6. 4. whereof cometh e.
Tit. 3. 3. living in e. hateful and hating
James 4. 5. spirit in us lusteth to e.
1 Pet. 2. 1. laying aside all e.
Gen. 26. 14. Philistines *envied* him
30. 1. Rachel e. her sister
37. 11. his brethren e. him
Ps. 106. 16. they e. Moses in camp
Eccl. 4. 4. man is e. of his neighbour
Num. 11. 29. *enviest* thou for my sake
1 Cor. 13. 4. charity *envieth* not
Rom. 13. 13. not in strife and *envying*
1 Cor. 3. 3. there is among you e.
2 Cor. 12. 20. debates, e. wraths
Gal. 5. 26. e. one another
James 3. 14. ye have bitter e. and
16. where e. is, there is confusion
Gal. 5. 21. *envyings,* murders
Ps. 37. 1. *envious,* 73. 3. Prov. 24. 1, 19.
EPHOD, Ex. 39. 2. Judg. 8. 27. 1 Sam. 2. 18. 2 Sam. 6. 14. Hos. 3. 4.
EPISTLE, Acts 15. 30. & 23. 33. Rom. 16. 22. 1 Cor. 5. 9. Col. 4. 16. 1 Thess. 5. 27. 2 Thess. 2. 15. 2 Pet. 3. 1.
2 Cor. 3. 2. e. written in our hearts
3. ye are declared the e. of Christ
1. *epistles,* 2 Pet. 3. 16.
EQUAL, Job 28. 17, 19. Ps. 17. 2. & 55. 13. Prov. 26. 7. Lam. 2. 13.
Isa. 40. 25. to whom shall I be e.
46. 5. to whom will ye make me e.
Ezek. 18. 25. way of Lord is not e.
29. & 33. 17, 20. their way is not e.
Matt. 20. 12. made them e. to us
Luke 20. 36. e. to the angels
John 5. 18. making himself e. with God
Phil. 2. 6. not robbery to be e. with God
Col. 4. 1. give that which is just and e.
Rev. 21. 26. length, breadth, and height e.
Gal. 1. 14. *equals,* Ps. 55. 13.
2. Cor. 8. 14. *equality*
Ps. 99. 4. dost establish *equity*
72. 2. judge poor with e. 93. 9.
Prov. 1. 3. receive instruction of e.
2. 9. understand judgment and e.
17. 26. to strike princes for e.
Eccl. 2. 21. whose labour is in e.
Isa. 11. 4. reprove with e. for
59. 14. truthfallen, and e. cannot enter
Mic. 3. 9. that pervert all e.
Mal. 2. 6. walked with me in e.
ERR, 2 Chron. 33. 9. Isa. 19. 14.
Ps. 95. 10. e. in heart, Heb. 3. 10.
119. 21. do e. from thy commandments
Prov. 14. 22. do they not e. that devise ill
19. 27. instruction that causeth to e.
Isa. 3. 12 lead—cause to e. 9. 16.
30. 28. bridle causing them to e.
35. 8. wayfaring men shall not e.
63. 17. why made us to e. from thy
Jer. 23. 13. prophet caused to e. by lies, 32.
Hos. 4. 12. whoredom caused them to e.
Amos. 2. 4. lies caused them to e.
Mic. 3. 5. prophets make my people to e.
Matt. 22. 29. ye e. not knowing the Scriptures
James 1. 16. do not e. my brethren
5. 19. if any of you e. from truth
Num. 15. 22. if ye have *erred*
1 Sam. 26. 21. I have e. exceedingly
Job. 6. 24. understand wherein I have e.
10. 4. be it that I have e. my error.
Ps. 119. 110. yet I e. not from thy precepts
Isa. 28. 7. have e. through wine; priest and prophet e. through strong drink
29. 24. that they e. in spirit
1. Tim. 6. 10. have e. from the faith
21. e. concerning faith, 2 Tim. 2. 18.

Prov. 10. 17. *erreth*, Ezek. 45. 20.
2 Sam. 6. 7. *error*, Job. 19. 4. Eccl. 5.
6. & 10. 5. Dan. 6. 4.
Isa. 32. 6. will utter *e.* against Lord
Jer. 10. 15. vanity work of *e.* 51. 18.
Dan. 6. 4. neither was there any *e.*
or fault found
Matt. 27. 64. last *e.* be worse than the
first
Rom. 1. 27. recompense of their *e.*
James 5. 20. sinner from *e.* of his way
2 Pet. 2. 18. them who live in *e.*
3. 17. led a way with *e.* of wicked
1. John 4. 6. know we the spirit of *e.*
Jude 11. after the *e.* of Balaam
Ps. 19. 12. who can understand his
errors
Heb. 9. 7. for the *e.* of the people
ERRAND, Judg. 3. 19. 2 Kings 9. 5.
ESCAPE, Gen. 19. 17, 22. & 32. 8.
Ezra 9. 8. leave a remnant to *e.*
Esth. 4. 13. think not that thou shalt
e.
Job 11. 20. but the wicked shall not *e.*
Ps. 56. 7. shall they *e.* by iniquity
71. 2. deliver me and cause me to *e.*
141. 10. let wicked fall whilst I *e.*
Prov. 19. 5. he that speaks lies shall
not *e.*
Eccl. 7. 26. pleaseth God shall *e.* her
Isa. 20. 6. we flee—how shall we *e.*
37. 32. that *e.* out of mount Zion
Jer. 11. 11. evil—not be able to *e.*
Ezek. 17. 15. shall *e.* that doeth such
things
Matt. 23. 33. how can ye *e.* damna-
tion
Luke 21. 36. accounted worthy to *e.*
Rom. 2. 3. *e.* the judgment of God
1 Cor. 10. 13. with temptation make
a way to *e.*
1 Thess. 5. 3. destruction they shall
not *e.*
Heb. 2. 3. how shall we *e.* if neglect
12. 25. much more shall not we *e.*
Ezra 9. 15. we remain yet *escaped*
Job 1. 15, 16, 17, 19. I am *e.* to tell
the
Ps. 124. 7. soul is *e.* we are *e.*
Isa. 45. 20. ye are *e.* of the nations
John 10. 39. he *e.* out of their hands
Heb. 12. 25. if they *e.* not who refused
2 Pet. 1. 4. *e.* corruption of the world
2. 18. those that were clean *e.*
20. have *e.* pollutions of the world
ESCHEW, Job 1. 8. 1 Pet. 3. 11.
ESPECIALLY, Deut. 4. 10.
Gal. 6. 10. good *e.* to household of
faith
1 Tim. 4. 10. *e.* of those that believe
5. 8. *e.* for them of his own house
17. *e.* those that labour in word
ESPY, Josh. 14. 7. Ezek. 20. 6.
ESPOUSALS, Song 3. 11.
2 Cor. 11. 2. *espoused* to Christ
ESTABLISH, Num. 30. 13.
1 Kings 15. 4. Deut. 28. 9. Job 36. 7.
Gen. 6. 18. *e.* my covenant, 9. 9.
9. 21. Lev. 26. 9. Deut. 8. 18.
1 Sam. 1. 23. the Lord *e.* his word
2 Sam. 7. 12. I will *e.* his kingdom
25. *e.* the word for ever, and do as
2 Chron. 9. 8. God loved Israel to *e.*
7. 18. *e.* throne of kingdom
Ps. 7. 9. but *e.* the just, 48. 8.
89. 2. faithfulness shalt *e.* in heaven
4. thy seed will I *e.* for ever
90. 17. *e.* work of our hands, *e.* it
99. 4. dost *e.* equity, executest judgment
119. 38. *e.* thy word to servant
Prov. 15. 25. he will *e.* border of
widow
Isa. 9. 7. to *e.* with judgment and
justice
49. 8. give for a covenant to *e.* the
earth
62. 7. no rest till he *e.* Jerusalem
Ezek. 16. 60. I will *e.* an everlasting
covenant, 62.

Rom. 3. 31. yea, we *e.* the law
10. 3. to *e.* their own righteousness
Rom. 16. 25. that is of power to *e.*
you
1 Thess. 3. 13. may *e.* your hearts
2 Thess. 2. 17. *e.* you in every good
word
3. 3. Lord shall *e.* and keep you
James 5. 8. patient; *e.* your hearts
1 Pet. 5. 10. God of all grace *e.* you
Gen. 41. 32. thing is *established*
Ex. 6. 4. have *e.* my covenant with
them
15. 17. which thy hands have *e.*
Ps. 40. 2. on rock he *e.* my goings
78. 5. he *e.* a testimony in Jacob
93. 1. world also is *e.* that it cannot
2. thy throne is *e.* of old
112. 8. his heart is *e.* trusting
119. 90. haste *e.* the earth, and it
140. 11. let not an evil speaker be *e.*
148. 6. hath *e.* them for ever
Prov. 3. 19. Lord hath *e.* the heavens
4. 26. let all thy ways be *e.*
12. 3. man shall not be *e.* by wickedness
16. 12. throne is *e.* by righteousness
20. 18. every purpose is *e.* by counsel
30. 4. *e.* all the ends of the earth
Isa. 7. 9. if believe not—not be *e.*
16. 5. in mercy shall throne be *e.*
Jer. 10. 12. *e.* world by wisdom
Hab. 1. 12. *e.* them for correction
Matt. 18. 16. two or three witnesses *e.*
2 Cor. 13. 1. word may be *e.*
Acts 16. 5. so were the churches *e.*
Rom. 1. 11. to the end you may be *e.*
Col. 2. 7. built up—*e.* in the faith
Heb. 8. 6. *e.* upon better promises
13. 9. good thing heart be *e.* with
grace
2 Pet. 1. 12. *e.* in the present truth
Lev. 25. 30. *shall be established,*
Ps. 89. 21. 2 Cor. 13. 1.
2 Cor. 20. 20. believe in God so ye—
Job 22. 28. shall decree a thing and
it—
Ps. 102. 28. their seed—before thee
Prov. 12. 19. lip of truth—
16. 3. commit unto the Lord, thy
thoughts—
25. 5. throne—in righteousness
Isa. 2. 2. Lord's house—Mic. 4. 1.
54. 14. in righteousness thou—
Jer. 30. 20. their congregation—
Prov. 29. 4. king by Judgment *es-
tablisheth* the land
Hab. 2. 12. wo to him that *e.* city by
2 Cor. 1. 21. who *e.* us with you is
God
ESTATE, Gen. 43. 7.
Ps. 39. 5. man at best *e.* is vanity
136. 23. remembered us in low *e.*
Prov. 27. 23. know *e.* of thy flocks
Matt. 12. 45. last *e.* of that man is
worse than the first, Luke 11. 26.
Luke 1. 48. low *e.* of thy handmaid
Rom. 12. 16. condescend to men of
low *e.*
Phil. 4. 11. in whatsoever *e.* I am—
content
Jude 6. angels kept not first *e.*
ESTEEM, Job 36. 19. Isa. 29. 16.
Ps. 119. 128. I *e.* all thy precepts
Phil. 2. 3. each other better than
1 Thess. 5. 13. *e.* them very highly in
love
Deut. 32. 15. lightly *esteemed* the
rock of his salvation
1 Sam. 2. 30. despise me, lightly *e.*
Job 23. 12. I have *e.* words of his
mouth
Isa. 53. 3. despised—we *e.* him not
4. did *e.* him stricken, smitten of
God
Luke 16. 15. is highly *e.* among men
Rom. 14. 5. *esteemeth* one day above
another, another *e.* every day alike
14. to him that *e.* it to be unclean, it
is

Heb. 11. 26. *esteeming* the reproach
of Christ
ESTRANGED, Job 19. 13.
Ps. 58. 3. wicked are *e.* from womb
78. 30. not *e.* from their lusts
Ezek. 14. 5. they are all *e.* from me
ETERNAL, Deut. 35. 27.
Isa. 60. 15. make thee an *e.* excellency
Mark 3. 29 in danger of *e.* damnation
Rom. 1. 20. his *e.* power and Godhead
2 Cor. 4. 17. exceeding *e.* weight of
18. things not seen which are *e.*
5. 1. have house *e.* in the heavens
Eph. 3. 11. according to *e.* purpose
1 Tim. 1. 17. unto the king *e.* be
honour
2 Tim. 2. 10. salvation with *e.* glory
Heb. 5. 9. author of *e.* salvation
6. 2. baptisms and of *e.* judgment
9. 12. obtained *e.* redemption for us
14. through the *e.* Spirit offered
15. promise of *e.* inheritance
1 Pet. 5. 10. called us to *e.* glory
Jude 7. vengeance of *e.* fire
Matt. 19. 16. that I may have *eternal
life*, Mark 10. 17. Luke 10. 25.
25. 46. the righteous shall go into—
Mark 10. 30. in world to come—
John 3. 15. not perish but have—
4. 36. gathereth fruit unto—
5. 39. in Scriptures ye think ye
have—
6. 54. hath—and I will raise him
68. thou hast the words of—
10. 28. I give unto them—
12. 25. shall keep it unto—
17. 2. should give—to as many
3. this is—to know only true God
Acts 13. 48. ordained to—believed
Rom. 2. 7. who seek for glory and—
5. 21. grace might reign to—
6. 23. the gift of God is—through
Jesus
1 Tim. 6. 12. lay hold on—19
Tit. 1. 2. in hope of—which God
3. 7. heirs according to hope of—
1 John 1. 2.—which was with Father
2. 25. promise promised us, even—
3. 15. no murderer hath—
5. 11. the record God hath given to
us—
13. may know that ye have—
20. the true God and—
Jude 21. for mercy unto—
ETERNITY, Isa. 57. 15.
EUNUCH, 2 Kings 9. 32.
Isa. 56. 3. let no *e.* say, I am a dry
tree
Matt. 19. 12. some *e.* born made *e.*
Acts 8. 27. *e.* had come to Jerusalem
EVEN balances. Job 31. 6.
Ps. 26. 12. foot stands in *e.* place
Song 4. 2. flock of sheep *e.* shorn
Luke 19. 44. lay thee *e.* with ground
EVEN or **EVENING**, Gen. 1. 5.
8. 31. & 19. 1 Ex. 12. 6, 18.
1 Kings 18. 29. at *e.* sacrifices, Ezra
9. 4, 5. Ps. 141. 2. Dan 9. 21.
Hab. 1. 8. *e.* wolves, Zeph. 3. 3.
Zech. 14. 7. at *e.* times shall be light
EVENT, Eccl. 2. 14. & 9. 2, 3.
EVER, a long time, constantly eter-
nally, Josh. 4. 7. & 14. 9.
Deut. 19. 9. to walk *e.* in his way
Ps. 5. 11. let them *e.* shout for joy
25. 15. my eyes *e.* toward the Lord
37. 26. he is *e.* merciful and lends
51. 3. my sin is *e.* before me
111. 5. will *e.* be mindful of covenant
119. 98. thy commandments are *e.*
with
Luke 15. 31. son thou art *e.* with
John 8. 35. in house son abideth *e.*
1 Thess. 4. 17. we shall be *e.* with the
Lord
5. 15. *e.* follow that which is good
2 Tim. 3. 7. *e.* learning, and never
Heb. 7. 24. this man continueth *e.*

25. he *e.* liveth to make intercession for them
Jude 25. to God be glory now and *e.*
Gen. 3. 22. eat and live *for ever.*
Deut. 32. 40 I lift up hand and live—
Josh. 4. 24. fear Lord your God—
1 Kings 10. 9. Lord loved Israel—
11. 20. afflict the seed of David But
not—
Ps. 9. 7. Lord shall endure—
12. 7. thou wilt preserve them—
22. 26. your heart shall live—
23. 6. dwell in the house of the
Lord—
29. 10. on floods Lord sitteth king—
30. 12. I will give thanks to thee—
33. 11. counsel of Lord standeth—
37. 18. their inheritance shall be—
28. saints are preserved—
29. in land righteous shall dwell—
46. 9. that he should still live—
52. 9. I will praise thee—
61. 4. I will abide in tabernacle—
73. 26. God my strength and portion—
74. 19. forget not congregation of
poor—
81. 15. their time should endure—
92. 7. that they shall be destroyed—
102. 12. but thou, O Lord, shalt
endure—
103. 9. the Lord will not keep his
anger—
105. 8. remember his covenant—
111. 9. hath commanded his covenant—
112. 6. righteous shall not be
moved—
119. 111. testimonies as heritage
132. 14. this is my rest—I have
146. 6. who keepeth truth—
Prov. 27. 24 riches are not—crown
Eccl. 1. 4. the earth abideth—
Isa. 26. 4. trust in Lord—for in Lord
32. 17. quietness and assurance—
40. 8. word of Lord shall stand—
57. 16. I will not contend—
59. 21. my words shall not depart—
Jer. 3. 5. will he reserve anger—12.
17. 4. kindled fire shall burn—
32. 39. that they may fear me—
Lam. 3. 31. Lord will not cast off
Mic. 7. 18. retaineth not his anger—
Zech. 1. 5. prophets, do they live—
John 6. 51. eateth shall live—58.
Rom. 1. 25. Creator who is blessed—
9. 5. over all God blessed—
2 Cor. 9. 9. his righteousness remaineth—
Heb. 13. 8. Jesus Christ, the same
yesterday, and—
1 Pet. 1. 23. word of God liveth,
abideth—
25. word of Lord endureth—
1 John 2. 17. doeth will of God,
abideth—
Ex. 15. 18. Lord reigns *for ever and
ever*
1 Chron. 16. 36. blessed be God—
49. 10. Neh. 9. 5. Dan. 2. 20.
Ps. 10. 16. the Lord is king—
45. 6. thy throne, O God, is—
48. 14. this God is our God—and
guide—
52. 8. I will trust in God—
111. 8. commandments stand fast—
119. 44. I will keep thy law—
145. 1. I will bless thy name—
Dan. 12. 3. they shine as stars—
Mic. 4. 5. walk in name of God—
Gal. 1. 5. to whom be glory—Phil.
4. 20. 1 Tim. 1. 17. 2 Tim. 4. 18.
Heb. 13. 21. 1 Pet. 4. 11. Rev. 1. 6.
Rev. 4. 9. who liveth—10. & 10. 6. &
15. 7. Dan. 4. 34. & 12. 7.
22. 5. they shall reign—
EVERLASTING, Gen. 49. 26.
Gen. 17. 8. Canaan, and *e.* possession
21. 33. called on name of *e.* God
Ex. 40. 15. *e.* priesthood

Lev. 16. 34. this should be an *e.* statute

Deut. 33. 27. underneath are *e.* arms

Ps. 24. 7. be lifted up ye *e.* doors

41. 13. blessed be God from *e.* to *e.*

90. 2. thou art from *e.* to *e.* 106. 48.

100. 5. his mercy is *e.*

103. 17. mercy of Lord from *e.* to *e.*

112. 6. righteous be in *e.* remembrance

110. 142. thy righteousness is *e.*

144. righteousness of thy testimonies *e.*

139. 24. lead me in the way *e.*

145. 13. *e.* kingdom, Dan. 4. 3.

Prov. 10. 25. righteous is an *e.* foundation

Isa. 9. 6. mighty God the *e.* Father

26. 4. in Lord Jehovah is *e.* strength

33. 14. who dwell with *e.* burnings

35. 10. shall come to Zion with songs of *e.* joy, 51. 11. & 61. 7.

Isa. 40. 28. *e.* God, Creator, fainteth not

45. 17. Israel saved in Lord with *e.* salvation

54. 8. with *e.* kindness will I gather

55. 13. to Lord for a name and *e.* sign

56. 5. an *e.* name, 63. 12, 16.

60. 19. Lord shall be an *e.* light, 20.

Jer. 10. 10. true living God, *e.* King

20. 11. *e.* confusion never forgotten

23. 40. I will bring *e.* reproach upon

31. 3. I loved thee with an *e.* love

Dan. 4. 34. *e.* dominion, 7. 14.

9. 24. to bring in *e.* righteousness

Mic. 5. 2. goings forth of old from *e.*

Hab. 1. 12. art thou not from *e.* my God

3. 6. *e.* mountains scattered; his ways *e.*

Matt. 18. 8. cast into *e.* fire, 25. 41.

25. 46. go away into *e.* punishment

2 Thess. 1. 9. punished with *e.* destruction

2. 16. God hath given us *e.* consolation

Luke 16. 9. receive into *e.* habitations

1 Tim. 6. 16. to whom be power *e.*

2 Pet. 1. 11. *e.* kingdom of our Lord

Jude 6. reserved in *e.* chains of darkness

Rev. 14. 6. having the *e.* gospel to preach

Dan. 12. 2. awake to *everlasting life*

Matt. 19. 29. shall inherit—

Luke 18. 30. in world to come—

John 3. 16. not perish but have—36.

4. 14. well springing up to—

5. 24. heareth my word hath—

6. 27. meat which endureth to—

40. whoso believeth may have—

47. that believeth on me hath—

12. 50. his commandment is—

Acts 13. 46. yourselves unworthy of—

Rom. 6. 22. ye have the end—

Gal. 6. 8. soweth to the Spirit, of the Spirit reap—

1 Tim. 1. 16. believe on him to—

EVERMORE, Ps. 16. 11. John 6. 34. 2 Cor. 11. 31. 1 Thess. 5. 16.

EVERY imagination evil, Gen. 6. 5.

Ps. 32. 6. for this *e.* one godly pray

119. 101. refrained feet from *e.* evil way

104. I hate *e.* false way, 128.

Prov. 2. 9. understand *e.* good path

14. 15. simple believeth *e.* word

15. 3. eyes of Lord are in *e.* place

30. 5. *e.* word of God is pure

Eccl. 3. 1. are a time to *e.* purpose

Isa. 45. 23. *e.* knee bow, and *e.* tongue,

Rom. 14. 11. Phil. 2. 11.

1 Tim. 4. 4. *e.* creature of God is good

2 Tim. 2. 21. prepared to *e.* good work

4. 18. Lord deliver me from *e.* evil work

Tit. 3. 1. ready to *e.* good work

Heb. 12. 1. lay aside *e.* weight and

1 John 4. 1. believe not *e.* spirit

EVIDENCE, Jer. 32. 10.

Job 6. 28. *evidently,* Acts 10. 3. Gal. 3. 1. 11. Phil. 1. 28. Heb. 7. 14. 15.

EVIL, Gen. 2. 9, 17. & 3. 5.

Deut. 29. 21. I will separate him to *e.*

30. 15. set before death and *e.*

Josh. 24. 15. if it seems *e.* to you

Job 2. 10. we receive good and not *e.*

5. 19. in trouble no *e.* touch thee

30. 26. looked for good *e.* came

Ps. 23. 4. I will fear no *e.* for thou

34. 21. *e.* shall slay the wicked

51. 4. have done this *e.* in thy sight

52. 3. lovest *e.* more than good

91. 10. no *e.* shall befall thee

97. 10. ye that love Lord, hate *e.*

Prov. 5. 14. I was almost in all *e.*

12. 21. no *e.* shall happen to just

15. 3. beholding the *e.* and good

31. 12. will do him good and not *e.*

Eccl. 2. 21. vanity and a great *e.*

5. 13. sore *e.* riches kept to hurt

9. 3. heart of men is full of *e.*

Isa. 5. 20. call *e.* good, and good *e.*

7. 15. know to refuse the *e.* 16.

45. 7. I make peace and create *e.*

57. 1. righteous taken from *e.* to come

59. 7. feet run to *e.* and make haste

Jer. 17. 17. art my hope in day of *e.*

18. 11. I frame *e.* against you

29. 11. thoughts of peace and not of *e.*

44. 11. set my face against you for *e.*

27. I will watch over them for *e.*

Lam. 3. 38. proceeds not *e.* and good

Ezek. 5. 7. an *e.* an only *e.* is come

Dan. 9. 12. on us a great *e.* 13. 14.

Amos 3. 6. shall there be *e.* in a city

5. 14. seek good and not *e.* that live

15. hate *e.* love good, Mich. 3. 2.

9. 4. set mine eyes on them for *e.*

Hab. 1. 13. of purer eyes than to behold

Matt. 5. 11. all manner of *e.* against

6. 34. sufficient to day is *e.* thereof

Rom. 2. 9. upon every soul that doth *e.*

7. 19. *e.* I would not that I do

21. I would do good *e.* is present with me

12. 17. recompense no man *e.* for *e.*

21. not overcome of *e.* but overcome *e.*

16. 19. simple concerning *e.*

1 Cor. 13. 5. charity thinketh no *e.*

1 Thess. 5. 15. let no man render *e.* for *e.*

22. abstain from all appearance of *e.*

1 Tim. 6. 10. love of money root of all *e.*

Tit. 3. 2. to speak *e.* of no man

Heb. 5. 14. discern both good and *e.*

Gen. 6. 5. thoughts only *e.* 8. 21.

47. 9. few and *e.* have been the days

Prov. 14. 19. *e.* bow before the good

15. 15. all days of afflicted are *e.*

Isa. 1. 4. a seed of *e.* doers

Matt. 5. 45. sun to rise on *e.* and good

7. 11. if ye being *e.* know

12. 34. how can ye being *e.* speak good

Luke 6. 35. kind to the unthankful and *e.*

John 3. 19. because their deeds were *e.*

Eph. 5. 16. because the days are *e.*

3 John 11. follow not that which is *e.*

Jude 10. speak *e.* of those things

EXACT, Deut. 15. 2, 3. Ps. 89. 22. Isa. 58. 3. Luke 3. 13.

Job 39. 7. *exactor,* Isa. 60. 17.

EXALT, Dan. 11. 14. Obad 4.

Ex. 15. 2. my father's God, I will *e.* him

1 Sam. 2. 10. *e.* the horn of his anointed

Ps. 34. 3. let us *e.* his name together

37. 34. *e.* thee to inherit the land

99. 5. *e.* the Lord our God for he is holy, 9.

107. 32. *e.* him in the congregation

118. 28. my God I will *e.* thee

Ezek. 21. 26. *e.* him that is low

1 Pet. 5. 6. may *e.* you in due time

Num. 24. 7. his kingdom be *exalted*

2 Sam. 22 47. *e.* be God of my salvation

Neh. 9. 5. *e.* above all blessing and praise

Job. 5. 11. *e.* to safety, 36. 7.

Ps. 89. 16. in righteousness shall be *e.* 17.

Prov. 11. 11. by blessing of upright city be *e.*

Isa. 2. 2. Lord's house *e.* above hills, Mic. 4. 1.

11. Lord alone shall be *e.* 17.

40. 4. every valley shall be *e.* and

49. 11. my highways shall be *e.*

52. 13. my servant shall be *e.*

Hos. 13. 1. Ephraim was *e.* in Israel, 6.

Matt. 11. 23. Capernaum which art *e.* to heaven, Luke 10. 15.

23. 12. humbleth himself shall be *e.* Luke 14. 11. & 18. 14.

Luke 1. 52. *e.* them of low degree

Acts 2. 33. by right hand of God *e.*

5. 31. him hath God *e.* with right hand

2 Cor. 12. 7. I be *e.* above measure

Phil. 2. 9. God hath highly *e.* him

James 1. 9. low rejoice that he is *e.*

Prov. 14. 34. righteousness *exalteth* a nation

Luke 14. 11. *e.* himself be abased

2 Cor. 10. 5. casting down that *e.* itself

2 Thess. 2. 4. *e.* himself above all—

EXAMINE, Ezra 10. 16. Luke 23. 14. Acts 4. 9. 1 Cor. 9. 3.

Ps. 26. 2. *e.* me, O Lord, prove and 1 Cor. 11. 28. let a man *e.* himself

2 Cor. 13. 5. *e.* yourselves, prove

EXAMPLE, 1 Thess. 1. 7.

Matt. 1. 19. not make her a public *e.*

John 13. 15. I have given you an *e.*

1 Cor. 10. 6. these things were our *e.*

Phil. 3. 17. ye have us for an *e.*

2 Thess. 3. 9. make ourselves an *e.*

1 Tim. 4. 12. an *e.* of believers

Heb. 4. 11. fall after the same *e.* of unbelief

8. 5. shadow of heavenly things

1 Pet. 2. 21. Christ leaving us an *e.*

5. 3. not lords, but *e.* to the flock

2 Pet. 2. 6. making them an *e.*

Jude 7. Sodom—set forth for an *e.*

EXCEED, Deut. 25. 3.

Matt. 5. 20. except your righteousness *e.* the righteousness of scribes

2 Cor. 3. 9. ministration of righteousness *e.*

Gen. 17. 6. *exceeding* fruitful

15. 1. I am thy shield and *e.* great reward

27. cried with *e.* bitter cry

Num. 14. 7. land is *e.* good

1 Sam. 2. 3. why talk so *e.* proudly

1 Kings 4. 29. wisdom *e.* much

1 Chron. 22. 5. house *e.* magnifical

Ps. 43. 4. I will go to God, my *e.* joy

Matt. 5. 12. rejoice and be *e.* glad

26. 38. my soul is *e.* sorrowful, to

Rom. 7. 13. sin might become *e.* sinful

2 Cor. 4. 17. work a far more *e.* weight

7. 4. I am *e.* joyful in all tribulation

9. 14. for the *e.* grace of God in you

Eph. 1. 19. *e.* greatness of his power

2. 7. show *e.* riches of his grace

3. 20. able to do *e.* abundantly

1 Tim. 1. 14. grace was *e.* abundant

1 Pet. 4. 13. rejoice, glad with *e.* joy

2 Pet. 1. 4. *e.* great and precious promises

Jude 24, present you with *e.* joy

Gen. 13. 13. sinners before the Lord, *exceedingly,* 1 Sam. 26. 21. 2 Sam. 13. 15.

Ps. 68. 3. let righteousness rejoice *e.*

119. 167. thy statutes I love *e.*

1 Thess. 3. 10. praying *e.* that

2 Thess. 1. 3. faith groweth *e.*

EXCEL, Gen. 49. 4.

Ps. 103. 20. his angels that *e.* in strength

Prov. 31. 29. thou *excellest* them all

Eccl. 2. 13. wisdom *e.* folly, as far

1 Cor. 14. 12. seek that ye may *e.*

2 Cor. 3. 10. by reason of the glory that *e.*

Gen. 49. 3. *excellency* of dignity, and *e.* of

Exod. 15. 7. in greatness of thy *e.*

Deut. 33. 26. rideth in his *e.* on sky

Job. 13. 11. his *e.* maketh you afraid

37. thunders with voice of his *e.*

40. 10. deck thyself with *e.*

Ps. 47. 4. *e.* of Jacob, whom he loved

68, 34. his *e.* is over Israel, and strength

Isa. 35. 2. see glory and *e.* of our God

Amos. 6. 8. I abhor the *e.* of Jacob

8. 7. Lord hath sworn by the *e.* of Jacob

1 Cor. 2. 1. not with *e.* of speech

2 Cor. 4. 7. *e.* of power may be of God

Phil. 3. 8. count all loss for the *e.* of Christ

Esther 1. 4. *excellent* majesty

Ps. 8. 1. how *e.* is thy name in the earth, 9.

16. 3. saints, *e.* in whom all my delight

36. 7. how *e.* is thy loving kindness

141. 5. smite me, it shall be an *e.* oil

148. 13. Lord, for his name alone is *e.*

Prov. 12. 26. righteous is more *e.*

17. 27. man of understanding is of an *e.* spirit

Isa. 12. 5. the Lord hath done *e.* thing

28. 29. wonderful in counsel, *e.* in

Ezek. 16. 7. art come to *e.* ornaments

Dan. 5. 12. an *e.* spirit in Daniel, 6. 3.

Rom. 2. 18. approvest things more *e.*

1 Cor. 12. 31. show you a more *e.* way

Phil. 1. 10. approve things that are *e.*

Heb. 1. 4. obtained a more *e.* name

8. 6. obtained a more *e.* ministry

11. 4. offered a more *e.* sacrifice

2 Pet. 1. 17. came a voice from *e.* glory

EXCESS, Matt. 23. 25. Eph. 5. 18.

EXCHANGE, Matt. 16. 26. Matt. 25. 27. *exchangers*

EXCLUDE, Rom. 3. 27.

EXCUSE, Luke 14. 18, 19. Rom. 1. 20. & 2. 15. 2 Cor. 12. 19.

EXECRATION, Jer. 42. 18.

EXECUTE, Num. 5. 30.

Ps. 149. 7. *e.* vengeance, Mic. 5. 15.

Hos. 11. 9. not *e.* fierceness of anger

Rom. 13. 4. revenger to *e.* wrath

Ex. 12. 12. *execute judgment,* Deut. 10. 18. Ps. 119. 84. Isa. 16. 3. Jer. 7. 5. Mic. 7. 9. John 5. 27.

EXERCISE, Ps. 131. 1. Matt. 20. 25. Acts 24. 16. 1 Tim. 4. 7, 8.

Jer. 9. 24. Lord *e.* loving kindness

EXHORT, Acts 2. 40. 2 Cor. 9. 5. 1 Thess. 2. 11. 1 Tim. 2. 1. 2 Tim. 4. 2. Tit. 1. 9. 1 Pet. 5. 1, 12.

2 Thess. 3. 12. we command and *e.* by our Lord Jesus Christ

Heb. 3. 13. *e.* one another daily

10. 25. *exhorting* one another; and
Luke 3. 18. *exhortation,* Acts 13. 15.
Rom. 12. 8. 1 Cor. 14. 3. 2 Cor. 8.
17. 1 Thes. 2. 3. 1 Tim. 4. 13.
EXPECTATION, Luke 3. 15.
Ps. 9. 18. *e.* of the poor shall not
perish
62. 5. for my *e.* is from him
Prov. 10. 28. *e.* of the wicked shall
perish
11. 7. dieth, his *e.* shall perish
23. *e.* of the wicked is wrath
23. 18. *e.* shall not be cut off, 24. 14.
Isa. 20. 5. be ashamed of their *e.* 6.
Zech. 9. 5. her *e. shall* be ashamed
Rom. 8. 19. *e.* of creature waiteth
Phil. 1. 20. according to my earnest
e.
Jer. 29. 11. give you an *expected* end
EXPEDIENT for us that one man
die for the people, John 11. 50.
John 16. 7. *e.* for you that I go away
1 Cor. 6. 12. all things not *e.*
2 Cor. 8. 10. this is *e.* for you
12. 1. it is not *e.* for me to glory
EXPERIENCE, Gen. 30. 27. Eccl. 1.
16. Rom. 5. 4.
2 Cor. 9. 13. by the *experiment* of
EXPERT in war, 1 Chron. 12. 33,
35, 36. Song 3. 8. Jer. 50. 9.
Acts 26. 3. know thee to be *e.* in all
EXPOUNDED, riddle, Judg. 14.
19. Mark 4. 34. Luke 24. 27. Acts
11. 4. & 18. 26. & 28. 23.
EXPRESS, Heb. 1. 3.
EXTEND mercy, Ezra. 7. 28. & 9.
9. Ps. 109. 12.
Ps. 16. 2. my goodness *e.* not to thee
Isa. 66. 12. I will *e.* peace like a river
EXTINCT, Job 17. 1 Isa. 43. 17.
EXTOL, Ps. 30. 1. & 66. 17. & 68. 4.
& 145. 1. Isa. 52. 13. Dan. 4. 37.
EXTORTION, Ezek. 22. 12. Matt.
23. 25. Ps. 109. 11. *extortioner,* Isa.
16. 4. Luke 18. 11. 1 Cor. 5. 10.
EXTREME, Deut. 28. 22.
EYE for *e.* Ex. 21. 24. Lev. 24. 20.
Deut. 32. 10. as the apple of his *e.*
Job 24. 15. no *e.* shall see me
Ps. 33. 18. *e.* of the Lord on them
that fear
94. 9. formed *e.* shall he not see
Prov. 20. 12. the seeing *e.* Lord hath
Eccl. 1. 8. *e.* not satisfied with seeing
Isa. 64. 4. neither hath *e.* seen
Matt. 6. 22. light of body is *e.*
18. 9. if thy *e.* offend thee
Rev. 1. 7. every *e.* shall see him
Prov. 23. 6. *evil eye,* 28. 22. Mark
7. 22. Luke 11. 34.
Job 16. 16. *eyelids,* 41. 18. Ps. 11. 4.
Prov. 4. 25. & 6. 4, 25. Jer. 9. 18.
Rev. 3. 18. *eye-salve*
Eph. 6. 6. *eye-service,* Col. 3. 22.
2 Sam. 22. 25. *eye-sight,* Ps. 18. 24.
Luke 1. 2. *eye-witnesses,* 2 Pet. 1. 16.
Gen. 3. 5. your *eyes* shall be opened
Job 10. 4. haste thou *e.* of flesh
29. 15. I was *e.* to the blind
Ps. 15. 4. in whose *e.* a vile person
is contemned
145. 15. *e.* of all things wait on thee
Eccl. 2. 14. wise man's *e.* are in his
head
6. 9. better is sight of *e.* than wandering
11. 7. pleasant for *e.* to behold sun
Isa. 3. 16. walk with wanton *e.*
5. 15. *e.* of lofty shall be humbled
29. 18. *e.* of blind shall see out of
obscurity
32. 3. *e.* of them that see shall
35. 5. *e.* of blind shall be opened
42. 7. to open blind *e.* and give
43. 8. blind people that have *e.*
Jer. 5. 21. have *e.* and see not
Dan. 7. 20. horn that had *e.*
Hab. 1. 13. of purer *e.* than to behold
Zech. 3. 9. on one stone shall be
seven *e.*
Matt. 13. 16. blessed are your *e.* for

18. 9. having two *e.* to be cast into
Mark 8. 18. having *e.* see ye not
Luke 4. 20. *e.* were fastened on him
10. 23. blessed are the *e.* which see
John 9. 6. anointed *e.* of blind man
Rom. 11. 8. *e.* that they should not
Gal. 3. 1. before whose *e.* Jesus
Christ has been
Eph. 1. 18. *e.* of your understanding
Heb. 4. 13. all are opened unto *e.* of
him
2 Pet. 2. 14. *e.* full of adultery
1 John 2. 16. lust of the *e.* and pride
Rev. 1. 14. his *e.* as a flame of fire,
3. 18. anoint *e.* 4. 6. full of *e.* 8.
5. 6. having seven horns and seven
e.
Deut. 13. 18. right in the *eyes of the
Lord,* 1 Kings 15. 5, 11. & 22. 43.
Gen.. 6. 8. Noah found grace in the—
1 Sam. 26. 24. life set by in—
2 Sam. 15. 25. find favour in—
2 Chron. 16. 9.—run to and fro
Ps. 34. 15.—are on righteous
Prov. 5. 21. ways of man are before—
15. 3.—are in every place beholding
22. 12.—preserve knowledge
Isa. 49. 5. I shall be glorious in—
Amos 9. 8.—are upon sinful kingdom
Zech. 4. 10.—which run to and fro
Ps. 25. 15. *my eyes* are towards the
Lord
101. 6.—shall be upon the faithful
119. 123.—fail for thy salvation
148.—prevent night watches
Ps. 141. 8.—are unto thee, O God
Isa. 1. 15. I will hide—from you
38. 14.—fail with looking upward
65. 12. did evil before—66. 4.
Jer. 9. 1. O that—were a fountain of
tears
13. 17.—shall weep sore, because
14. 17.—run down with tears
16. 17.—are upon all their ways
24. 6. set—upon them for good
Amos. 9. 4. I will set—on them for
evil
Luke 2. 30—have seen thy salvation
Ps. 123. 2. so *our eyes* wait on the
Lord
Matt. 20. 33. that—may be opened
1 John 1. 1. that we have seen with—
Deut. 12. 8. right *in his own eyes,*
Judg. 17. 6. & 21. 25.
Job 32. 1. righteous—
Neh. 6. 16. cast down *in their own
eyes.*
Ps. 139. 16. *thine eyes* did see my
substance
Prov. 23. 5. set—on that which is not
Song. 6. 5. turn away—from me
Isa. 30. 20.—shall see thy teachers
Jer. 5. 3. are not—upon the truth
Ezek. 24. 16. take away desire—25.

F

FABLES, 1 Tim. 1. 4. & 4. 7. 2
Tim. 4. 4. Tit. 1. 14. 2 Pet. 1. 16.
FACE, Gen. 3. 19. & 16. 8.
Lev. 19. 32. honour the *f.* of old man
Num. 6. 25. Lord make his *f.* shine
upon thee
2 Chron. 6. 42. turn not away *f.*
Ps. 17. 15. I will behold thy *f.* in
righteousness
31. 16. make thy *f.* shine, 119. 135.
67. 1. cause his *f.* to shine on
84. 9. behold *f.* of thine anointed
Ezek. 1. 10. *f.* of a man, a lion
Dan. 9. 17. cause of thy *f.* to shine on
sanctuary
Hos. 5. 5. testify to his *f.* 7. 10.
Matt. 11. 10. my messenger before
thy *f.*
Mark 1. 2. Luke 7. 27. & 9. 52.
Acts 2. 25. set the Lord before my *f.*
1 Cor. 13. 12. but then see *f.* to *f.*
2 Cor. 3. 18. with open *f.* beholding

4. 6. glory of God in *f.* of Jesus
Christ
James 1. 23. his natural *f.* in a glass
FADE, we all, as a leaf, Isa. 64. 6.
James 1. 11. rich man *f.* away in
1 Pet. 1. 4. inheritance that *fadeth*
not
5. 4. receive a crown of glory that *f.*
not.
FAIL, Deut. 28. 32. Job 11. 20.
Deut. 31. 6. Lord will not *f.* nor forsake, 8 Josh. 1. 5. 1 Chron. 28. 20.
Ps. 12. 1. faithful *f.* from among men
69. 3. my eyes *f.* while I wait for
my God
77. 8. doth his promise *f.* forever
Lam. 3. 22. his compassions *f.* not
Luke 16. 9. when ye *f.* they may receive
17. one tittle of the law to *f.*
22, 32. prayed that thy faith *f.* not
Heb. 12. 15. lest any *f.* of the grace
of God
Song 5. 6. soul *failed* when he spake
Ps. 31. 10. my strength *faileth,* 38.
10. & 40. 12. my heart *f.* me, 73. 26.
143. 7. hear me, my spirit *f.*
Luke 12. 33. lay up treasure that *f.*
not
1 Cor. 13. 8. charity never *f.*
Deut. 28. 65. for *failing* of eyes
Luke 21. 26. men's hearts *f.* them
FAINT, Deut. 25. 18. Judg. 8. 4.
Isa. 1. 5. head sick, whole heart is *f.*
40. 29. he giveth power to the *f.*
30. youths shall *f.* and be weary
31. wait on the Lord shall walk and
not *f.*
Luke 18. 1. to pray always and not *f.*
2 Cor. 4. 1. receive mercy we *f.* not,
16.
Gal. 6. 9. in due time shall reap if we
f. not
Heb. 12. 5. nor *f.* when rebuked of
Ps. 27. 13. I had *fainted* unless I had
believed
Rev. 2. 3. hast laboured and not *f.*
Ps. 84. 2. soul *fainteth* for courts of
119. 81. my soul *f.* for thy salvation
Isa. 40. 28. God the Creator *f.* not
FAIR, Gen. 6. 2. & 24. 16.
Prov. 7. 21. *f.* speech, Rom. 16. 18.
Song 1. 15. behold thou art *f.* 4. 1.
7. & 2. 10. & 6. 10. Gen. 12. 11.
4. 10. how *f.* is thy love, better
Jer. 12. 6. they speak *f.* words
Acts 7. 20. Moses was exceedingly *f.*
Gal. 6. 12. desire to make *f.* show in
Ps. 45. 2. thou art *fairer* than the
children of men
Dan. 1. 15. their countenance appeared *f.*
FAITH, Acts 3. 16. & 13. 8.
Deut. 32. 20. children in whom is no
f.
Matt. 6. 30. O ye of little *f.* 8. 26.
8. 10. not found so great *f.* no
17. 20. had *f.* as a grain of mustard
seed
21. 21. have *f.* and doubt not
23. 23. omitted judgment, mercy,
and *f.*
Mark 4. 40. how is it that ye have no
f.
11. 22. Jesus saith have *f.* in God
Luke 7. 9. so great *f.* no not in Israel
17. 5. Lord increase our *f.*
6. if ye had *f.* ye might say to this
18. 18. Son of man cometh shall he
find *f.* on the earth
Acts 3. 16. *f.* which is by him
6. 5. Stephen, a man full of *f.*
6. 7. company of priests obedient to
f.
11. 24. good man full of the Holy
Ghost and of *f.*
14. 9. he had *f.* to be healed
22. exhorting to continue in the *f.*
Acts 14. 27. God opened door of *f.*
to
16. 4. churches established in the *f.*

20. 21. *f.* towards our Lord Jesus
Christ
Rom. 1. 5. for obedience to *f.* among
17. righteousness of God revealed
from *f.* to *f.*
3. 3. make *f.* of God without effect
27. but by the law of *f.*
4. 5. his *f.* is counted for righteousness
11. circumcision, a seal of righteousness of *f.*
12. in steps of that *f.* of Abraham
13. through the righteousness of *f.*
14. if of law be heirs, *f.* is made void
16. of *f.* that by grace promise sure
10. 8. word of *f.* which we preach
17. *f.* cometh by hearing, and
12. 3. God dealt the measure of *f.*
6. according to the proportion of *f.*
14. 22. hast thou *f.* have it unto
23. eateth not of *f.* is not of *f.* is sin
16. 26. made known for obedience
of *f.*
1 Cor. 12. 9. to another *f.* by same
spirit
13. 2. though I have all *f.* to remove
13. now abideth *f.* hope, charity
2 Cor. 4. 13. we have the same spirit
of *f.*
Gal. 1. 3. preach the *f.* which once
3. 2. received ye the Spirit by the
hearing of *f.* 5.
7. they which are of *f.* 9.
12. the law is not of *f.* but the man
23. before *f.* came, we were under
25. after that *f.* is come, we are no
5. 6. but *f.* which worketh by love
22. fruit of the Spirit is *f.*
6. 10. especially the household of *f.*
Eph. 4. 5. one Lord, one *f.* one
13. until we come in the unity of *f.*
6. 16. above all take shield of *f.*
23. love with *f.* from God the Father and Lord Jesus Christ
Phil. 1. 25. I shall abide for your joy
of *f.*
27. striving together for *f.* of gospel
2 Thess. 1. 3. remember your work
of *f.*
5. 8. putting on breastplate of *f.*
2 Thess. 1. 4. glory for your patience
and *f.*
11. fulfil work of *f.* with power
3. 2. for all men have not *f.*
1 Tim. 1. 5. charity out of *f.* unfeigned
14. exceeding abundantly with *f.*
19. holding *f.* and a good conscience; concerning *f.* have made
shipwreck
3. 9. holding the mastery of *f.* in a
pure conscience
4. 1. some shall depart from the *f.*
6. nourished up in the words of *f.*
5. 8. denied *f.* 12. cast off first *f.*
6. 10. erred from *f.* 21. concerning
the *f.*
12. fight the good fight of *f.*
2 Tim. 1. 5. unfeigned *f.* that is in
thee, which dwelt in
2. 18. overthrow *f.* of some
22. follow righteousness, *f.* charity
3. 8. corrupt, reprobate concerning *f.*
10. fully known my doctrine, life,
f.
4. 7. fought a good fight, kept the *f.*
Tit. 1. 1. according to *f.* of God's
elect
4. my son after the common *f.*
Heb. 4. 2. word did not profit, not
being mixed with *f.*
6. 1. dead works and of *f.* towards
God
10. 22. draw near in full assurance
of *f.*
23. hold fast the profession of our
f.
11. 1. *f.* is substance of things hoped
for

6. without *f.* impossible to please God

12. 2. Jesus author and finisher of *f.*

13. 7. whose *f.* follow, considering

James 2. 1. have not *f.* of our Lord

14. say that he hath *f.* can *f.* save

17. *f.* if it hath not works, is dead

18. thou hast *f.* and I works; show *f.—f.* by my works

22. *f.* wrought with works; *f.* made perfect

5. 15. prayer of *f.* shall save

2 Pet. 1. 1. like precious *f.* with us

1 John 5. 4. overcometh world, even our *f.*

Jude 3. contend earnestly for the *f.*

20. build up yourselves on holy *f.*

Rev. 2. 13. hast not denied my *f.*

19. I know thy works and *f.*

13. 10. here is the *f.* of the saints

14. 12. which keep the *f.* of Jesus

Hab. 2. 4. just shall live by *faith*, Rom. 1. 17. Gal. 3. 11. Heb. 10. 38.

Acts 15. 9. purifying their hearts—

26. 18. sanctified—that is in me

Rom. 1. 12. comforted by mutual *f.*

3. 22. righteousness which is—of Christ

28. conclude a man is justified

30. justify circumcision—uncircumcision through *f.*

5. 1. being justified—we have peace

2. have access—Eph. 3. 12.

9. 32. sought it not—but works

11. 20. standest—be not highminded

2 Cor. 1. 24. of your joy, for—ye stand

5. 7. we walk—and not by sight

Gal. 2. 16. not justified, but—3. 24.

20. I live—of the Son of God

3. 22. promise—might be given

26. all children of God—in Christ Jesus

5. 5. wait for hope of righteousness

Eph. 3. 17. Christ may dwell in your hearts—

Phil. 3. 9. righteousness through *f.* righteousness of God—

Heb. 11. 4.—Abel, 5.—Enoch, & c.

7. heir of righteousness which is—

James 2. 24. justified by works, not—

Rom. 4. 19. not weak *in faith*

20. strong—giving glory to God

14. 1. him that is weak—receive

1 Cor. 16. 13. stand fast—quit you

2 Cor. 8. 7. ye abound—in utterance

13. 5. examine whether ye be—

Col. 1. 23. if ye continue—grounded

2. 7. built up in him, established—

1 Tim. 1. 2. Timothy, my own son—

4. godly edifying which is—

2. 7. teachers of the Gentiles—and verity

15. if they continue—and charity

3. 13. purchase great boldness

4. 12. be an example—in purity

2 Tim. 1. 13. of sound words—and

Tit. 1. 13. that may be sound—2. 2.

3. 15. greet them that love us—

Heb. 11. 13. all these died—not having

James 1. 6. ask—nothing wavering

2. 5. poor, rich—heirs of kingdom

1 Pet. 5. 9. whom resist, steadfast—

Matt. 9. 2. Jesus, seeing *their faith,* Mark 2. 5. Luke 5. 20.

Acts 3. 16. *through faith* in his Son

Rom. 3. 25. propitiation—in his blood

31. do we make void the law—30.

Gal. 3. 8. God would justify the heathen—

14. receive promise of Spirit

Eph. 2. 8. by grace ye are saved—

Col. 2. 12.—of the operation of God

2 Tim. 3. 15. salvation—which is in Christ Jesus

Heb. 6. 12.—and patience inherit

11. 13.—we understand the worlds

11. Sarah received strength to conceive

28. Moses kept the passover

33.—subdued kingdoms, wrought righteousness

11. 39. obtained a good report—2.

1 Pet. 1. 5. kept by power of God—

Matt. 9. 22. *thy faith* hath made thee whole, Luke 8. 48.

15. 28. O woman, great is—be

Luke 7. 50.—hath saved thee. 18. 42.

22. 32. I have prayed that—fail not

Philem. 6. communication of—

James 2. 18. show me—without thy

Luke 8. 25. where is *your faith*

Matt. 9. 29. according to—be it to

Rom. 1. 8.—is spoken of through

1 Cor. 2. 5. that—not stand in wisdom

15. 14.—is also vain, 17.

2 Cor. 1. 24. not dominion over—

10. 15. when—is increased, we

Eph. 1. 15. after I heard of—

Phil. 2. 17. offered upon service of—

Col. 2. 5. steadfastness of—in Christ

1 Thess. 1. 8.—to God-ward is spread

3. 2. establish you, comfort you, concerning—

5. I sent to know—lest the tempter

6. brought us good tidings of—

7. comforted in affliction by—

10. perfect what is lacking in—

2 Thess. 1. 3.—groweth exceedingly

James 1. 3. trying of—worketh patience

1 Pet. 1. 7. trial of—being precious

9. receiving end of—salvation

21. that—and hope might be in God

2 Pet. 1. 5. add to—virtue, knowledge

FAITHFUL, 1 Sam. 2. 35. & 22. 14.

2 Sam. 20. 19. Neh. 13. 13. Dan. 6. 4.

1 Tim. 6. 2. 1 Pet. 5. 12.

Num. 12. 7. *f.* in all my house

Heb. 3. 2, 5. Moses *f.* in all as a servant

Deut. 7. 9. *f.* God keepeth covenant

Neh. 7. 2. a. *f.* man, and feared God

9. 8. found his heart *f.* before thee

Ps. 12. 1. the *f.* fail from among men

31. 23. Lord preserveth the *f.*

89. 37. as a *f.* witness in heaven

101. 6. my eyes be upon *f.* in land

119. 86. thy commandments are *f.*

Prov. 11. 13. is of a *f.* spirit concealeth

13. 17. a *f.* ambassador is health

14. 5. a *f.* witness will not lie

20. 6 a *f.* man who can find

25. 13. *f.* messenger to them that send.

27. 6. *f.* are wounds of a friend

28. 20. *f.* man abound with blessings

Isa. 1. 21. how *f.* city became a harlot

26. city of righteousness *f.* city

8. 2. I took *f.* witness to record

49. 7. Lord is *f.* and Holy One of Israel

Jer. 42. 5. Lord be true and *f.* witness

Hos. 11. 12. Judah is *f.* with saints

Matt. 25. 21. well done, *f.* servant

23. hast been *f.* in a few, Luke 19. 17.

Luke 12. 42. who is that *f.* steward

16. 10. *f.* in least is *f.* also in much

11. not *f.* in unrighteous mammon

12. not *f.* in what is another man's

Acts 16. 15. judge me *f.* to the Lord

1 Cor. 1. 9. God is *f.* by whom ye

4. 2. required in stewards, a man *f.*

17. Timothy who is *f.* in the Lord

7. 25. obtained mercy of Lord to be *f.*

10. 13. God is *f.* and will not suffer

Eph. 1. 1. the saints and *f.* in Christ Jesus, Col. 1. 2.

6. 21. *f.* minister, Col. 1. 7. & 4. 7, 9.

1 Thess. 5. 24. *f.* is he that calleth

---

2 Thess. 3. 3. Lord is *f.* and shall establish

1 Tim. 1. 12. he counted me *f.*

15. this is a *f.* saying and worthy

4. 9. 2 Tim. 2. 11. Tit. 3. 8.

3. 11. wives grave, sober, *f.* in all

2 Tim. 2. 2. heard of me, commit *f.* men

13. he abideth *f.* cannot deny himself

Tit. 1. 6. blameless, having *f.* children

9. holding fast the *f.* word as

Heb. 2. 17. might be a *f.* high priest

3. 2. who was *f.* to him that appointed

10. 23. *f.* is he that promised, 11. 11.

1 Pet. 4. 19. as unto a *f.* Creator

John 1. 9. he is *f.* to forgive all

Rev. 1. 5. *f.* and true witness, 3. 14.

2. 10. be *f.* to death, 13. *f.* martyr

17. 14. they are chosen and *f.*

21. 5. words are true and *f.* 22. 6.

1 Sam. 26. 23. render to every man his *faithfulness*

Ps. 5. 9. no *f.* in their mouth

36. 5. thy *f.* reacheth to the clouds

40. 10. declared thy *f.* 89. 1.

88. 11. should thy *f.* be declared in destruction

89. 1. make known thy *f.* to all generations

2. thy *f.* shalt establish in heavens

5. praise thy *f.* in the great congregation

8. who like thy *f.* round about thee

24. my *f.* shall be with him

33. I will not suffer my *f.* to fail

92. 2. to show thy *f.* every night

119. 75. in *f.* thou hast afflicted me

90. thy *f.* is to all generations

143. 1. in thy *f.* answer me, and

Isa. 11. 5. *f.* is the girdle of his reins

25. 1. thy counsels of old are *f.*

Lam. 3. 23. mercies new, great thy *f.*

Hos. 2. 20. I will betroth thee to me in *f.*

Matt. 17. 17. O *faithless* and perverse generation, Mark 9. 19.

John 20. 27. be not *f.* but believing

FALL, Num. 11. 31. & 14. 29.

Gen. 45. 24. see ye *f.* not out by the way

2 Sam. 24. 14. let us *f.* into the hand of the Lord

Ps. 37. 24. though he *f.* he shall not

45. 5. whereby they *f.* unto thee

82. 7. *f.* like one of the princes

141. 10. let wicked *f.* into their own net

145. 14. Lord upholdeth all that *f.*

Prov. 11. 5. wicked *f.* by own wickedness

24. 16. wicked shall *f.* into mischief

26. 27. digs a pit shall *f.* into it

28. 14. hardeneth his heart shall *f.*

Eccl. 4. 10. if they *f.* one will lift up

Isa. 8. 15. many shall stumble and *f.*

40. 30. young men shall utterly *f.*

Dan. 11. 35. some shall *f.* to try them

Hos. 10. 8. mountains and hills *f.* on us, Luke 23. 30. Rev. 6. 16.

Mic. 7. 8. rejoice not when I *f.*

Matt. 7. 27. great was the *f.* of it

10. 29. sparrow not *f.* on ground

15. 14. blind both *f.* into the ditch

21. 24. upon whomsoever it *f.*

Luke 2. 34. set for *f.* and rising of Israel

Rom. 11. 11. stumbled that they should *f.* through their *f.* salvation is come to Gentiles

14. 13. occasion to *f.* in his brother's

1 Cor. 10. 12. stands, take heed lest he *f.*

1 Tim. 3. 6. *f.* into condemnation of devil

6. 9. rich *f.* into temptation

Heb. 4. 11. *f.* after the same example

10. 31. fearful thing to *f.* into the hands of God

James 1. 2. *f.* into divers temptations

2 Pet. 1. 10. if these ye shall never *f.*

3. 17. lest ye *f.* from your steadfastness

Luke 8. 13. time of temptation *fall away*

Heb. 6. 6. impossible if they—to renew

Gal. 5. 4. ye are *fallen* from grace

Ps. 16. 6. *f.* to me in pleasant places

Hos. 14. 1. hast *f.* by thine iniquity

Rev. 2. 5. remember whence thou art *f.*

Prov. 24. 16. just *falleth* seven times

Rom. 14. 4. to his own master he *f.*

Ps. 56. 13. thou hast delivered my feet from *falling*, 116. 8.

2 Thess. 2. 3. there comes a *f.* away first

Jude 24. able to keep you from *f.*

FALLOW, Jer. 4. 3. Hos. 10. 12.

FALSE, Jer. 14. 14. & 37. 14.

Ex. 23. 1. not raise a *f.* report

7. keep thee far from a *f.* matter

Ps. 119. 104. hate every *f.* way, 128.

Prov. 11. 1. *f.* balance is abomination, 20. 23.

Zech. 8. 17. love no *f.* oath

Mal. 3. 5. witness against *f.* swearers

Matt. 24. 24. *f.* Christs, *f.* prophets

2 Cor. 11. 13, 26. *f.* apostles, *f.* brethren, Gal. 2. 4.

2 Tim. 3. 3. *f.* accusers, Tit. 2. 3.

2 Pet. 2. 1. *f.* prophets, *f.* teachers

Ps. 119. 118. their deceit is *falsehood*

144. 8. whose right hand—of *f.*

Isa. 59. 13. from heart words of *f.*

Lev. 6. 3. sweareth *falsely*, 19. 12.

Ps. 44. 17. neither dealt *f.* in covenant

Hos. 10. 4. swearing *f.* in making covenant

Zech. 5. 4. thief and that swears *f.*

Matt. 5. 11. evil against you *f.* for

Luke 3. 14. neither accuse any *f.*

1 Pet. 3. 16. *f.* accuse your good conversation

Acts 13. 9. *false prophet,* Rev. 16. 13. & 19. 20. & 20. 10.

Matt. 7. 15. *false prophets,* 24. 11. Luke 6. 26. 2 Pet. 2. 1. 1 John 4. 1.

Ex. 20. 16. *false witness,* Deut. 5. 20. Prov. 6. 19. Matt. 15. 19. Rom. 13. 9. 1. Cor. 15. 15.

FAMILIAR, Job 19. 14. Ps. 41. 9. Lev. 19. 31. & 20. 6, 27. Isa. 8. 19.

FAMILY, Gen. 10. 5. Lev. 20. 5.

Zech. 12. 12. mourn every *f.* apart

Eph. 3. 15. whole *f.* in heaven and earth

Ps. 68. 6. sitteth solitary in *families*

107. 41. maketh him *f.* like a flock

Amos. 3. 2. known of all the *f.* of earth

FAMINE, Gen. 12, 10.

Job. 5. 20. in *f.* he shall redeem thee

Ps. 33. 19. keep them alive in *f.*

Ps. 37. 19. in days of *f.* shall be satisfied

Ezek. 5. 16. evil arrows of *f.* 6. 11.

Amos. 8. 11. not a *f.* of bread, but

FAMISH, Gen. 41. 55. Prov. 10. 3. Isa. 5. 13. Zeph. 2. 11.

FAN, Isa. 41. 16. Jer. 4. 11. & 51. 2. Matt. 3. 12. Luke 3. 17.

FAR, Ex. 8. 28. Neh. 4. 19.

Ex. 23. 7. Keep from false matter

Ps. 73. 27. *f.* from thee shall perish

Amos 6. 3. put *f.* away the evil day

Mark 12. 34. not *f.* from the kingdom

Phil. 1. 23. with Christ, which is *f.* better

Eph. 2. 13. sometimes *f.* on, now nigh

FARTHING, Matt. 5. 26.

FASHION, 1 Cor. 7. 31. Phil. 2. 8.

Job 10. 8. thy hands have *fashioned* me, Ps. 119. 73.

Ps. 139. 16. in continuance were *f.*

Ezek. 16. 7. thy breasts are *f.*

Phil. 3. 21. be *f.* like his glorious body

Ps. 33. 15. he *fashions* their hearts
Isa. 45. 9. clay say to him that *fashioneth*
1 Pet. 1. 14. not *fashioning* yourselves
FAST, 2 Sam. 12. 21.
Isa. 58. 4. ye *f.* for strife; not *f.* as
Jer. 14. 12. when they *f.* I will not hear
Zech. 7. 5. did ye at all *f.* unto me
Matt. 6. 16. when ye *f.* be not hypocrites
18. appear not to men to *f.*
9. 14. why do we *f.* and disciples *f.* not
15. can children of bride-chamber *f.* bridegroom taken—then shall they *f.* Mark 2. 18, 19. Luke 5. 34, 35.
Luke 18. 12. I *f.* twice a week
1 Kings 21. 9. proclaim a *fast*, 12.
Chron. 20. 3. Ezra 8. 21. Jer. 36. 9.
Joel 1. 14. Jonah 3. 5. Acts 27. 9.
Judg. 20. 26. *fasted* that day
1 Sam. 7. 6. *f.* on that day
31. 13. *f.* seven days
2 Sam. 1. 12. they wept and *f.* till even
12. 16. David *f.* and lay all night in
1 Kings 21. 27. Ahab *f.* and lay in sackcloth
Ezra 8. 23. we *f.* and besought the Lord
Isa. 58. 3. why have we *f.* and thou
Zech. 7. 5. when ye *f.* in fifth and
Matt. 4. 2. when he had *f.* forty days
Acts 13. 2. ministered and *f.* 3 *f.* and prayed
Neh. 9. 1. assembled with *fasting*
Esth. 4. 3. were *f.* and weeping 9. 31.
Ps. 35. 13. humbled soul with *f.* 69. 10.
109. 24. my knees weak through *f.*
Jer. 36. 6. read the roll on *f.* day
Dan. 6. 18. king passed the night *f.*
9. 3. to seek by prayer with *f.*
Joel 2. 12. turn ye to me with *f.*
Matt. 15. 32. not send them away *f.*
17. 21, this kind cometh not out but by prayer and *f.* Mark 9. 29.
Luke 2. 37. with *f.* and prayers
Acts 10. 30. was *f.* till this hour
14. 23. ordained elders, prayed with *f.*
1 Cor. 7. 5. give yourselves to *f.*
2 Cor. 6. 5. in *f.* often, 11. 27.
FASTENED, Job 38. 6. Eccl. 12. 11. Isa. 22. 25. Luke 4. 20.
FAT is the Lord's, Lev. 3. 16.
Prov. 11. 25. liberal shall be made *f.*
13. 4. soul of diligent shall be made *f.*
15. 30. good report maketh bones *f.*
28. 25. trust in Lord shall be made *f.*
Isa. 25. 6. *f.* things full of marrow
11. 6. *fatling*, Matt. 22. 3.
Gen. 27. 28. God give thee of *fatness* of the earth
Job 36. 16. table should be full of *f.*
Ps. 36. 8. satisfied with *f.* of house
63. 5. shall be satisfied as with *f.*
65. 11. all thy paths drop *f.*
Isa. 55. 2. let your soul delight itself in *f.*
Jer. 31. 14. satiate the soul with *f.*
Rom. 11. 17. root and *f.* of olive tree
FATHER, Gen. 2. 24. & 4. 20, 21.
Gen. 17. 4. be a *f.* of many nations
2 Sam. 7. 14. I will be his *f.* Heb. 1. 5.
Job 29. 16. I was a *f.* to the poor
31. 18. be with me as with a *f.*
38. 28. hath the rain a *f.* or who
Ps. 68. 5. a *f.* of fatherless is God
103. 13. as a *f.* pitieth his children
Isa. 9. 6. everlasting *F.* prince of peace
Jer. 31. 9. I am a *F.* to Israel and
Mal. 1. 6. if I be a *F.* where is my honour
2. 10. have we not all one *F.*
John 5. 19. what he seeth the *F.* do

20. *F.* loveth the Son. 3. 35.
21. *F.* raiseth the dead and quickeneth
22. *F.* judgeth no man but
26. *F.* hath life in himself
8. 18. *F.* beareth witness of me
29. *F.* hath not left me alone
44. *f.* devil is a liar and *f.* of it
16. 32. I am not alone, *F.* is with
Acts 1. 4. promise of the *F.*
7. times *F.* hath put in his own power
Rom. 4. 11. be the *f.* of all that believe
12. *f.* of circumcision, 16. *f.* of us all
17. made thee a *f.* of many nations
1 Cor. 8. 6. the *F.* of whom are all things
2 Cor. 1. 3. God and *F.* of our Lord Christ, *F.* of mercies, and God of all comfort, Eph. 1. 3. 1 Pet. 1. 3.
6. 18. I will be a *F.* to you and
Eph. 1. 17. God and *F.* of our Lord Jesus Christ, *F.* of glory
1 Tim. 5. 1. entreat him as a *f.*
Heb. 1. 5. I will be to him a *F.* and
12. 9. subjection to the *F.* of spirits
James 1. 17. gift from *F.* of lights
John 5. 17. *my Father* worketh and I work
10. 30. I and my *F.* are one
14. 20. I am in my *F.* 10.
28. my *F.* is greater than I
Ezek. 16. 45. *your father* an Amorite
Matt. 5. 16. glorify your *f.* in heaven
23. 9. call no man on earth your *f.*
John 8. 41. ye do deeds of your *f.*
44. ye are of your *f.* the devil
20. 17. I ascend to your *F.* and my *F.*
Ex. 15. 2. my *f's* God I will exalt
Neh. 9. 9, 16. *our fathers* dealt proudly
Ps. 22. 4. our *f.* trusted in thee
39. 12. sojourner, as all my *f.* were
44. 1. our *f* have told us, 78. 3.
Lam. 5. 7. our *f.* have sinned
Acts 15. 10. our *f.* not able to bear
Ex. 22. 22. not afflict *fatherless*
Deut. 10. 18. execute judgment of *f.*
Ps. 10. 14. thou helper of the *f.*
68. 5. a father of the *f.* is God in his holy habitation
82. 3. defend the poor and *f.*
146. 9. Lord relieveth the *f.* and widow
Isa. 1. 17. judge *f.* plead for widow
Hos. 14. 3. in thee the *f.* findeth mercy
James 1. 27. visit *f.* in affliction
FAULT, Gen. 41. 9. Ex. 5. 16.
Ps. 19. 12. cleanse thou me from secret *f.*
Matt. 18. 15. if trespass, tell him his *f.*
Luke 23. 4. I find no *f.* in him, 14. John 18. 38. & 19. 4, 6.
1 Cor. 6. 7. utterly a *f.* among you
Gal. 6. 1. brethren, if a man be overtaken in a *f.*
James 5. 16. confess *f.* one to another
1 Pet. 2. 20. buffeted for your *f.*
Jude 24. able to present you *faultless*
FAVOUR, Gen. 39. 21.
1 Sam. 2. 26. Samuel in *f.* with Lord
Job 10. 12. granted me life and *f.*
Ps. 5. 12. with *f.* wilt thou compass
30. 5. in his *f.* is life; weeping may
106. 4. remember me with *f.* that
Prov. 31. 30. *f.* is deceitful and beauty
Luke 2. 52. in *f.* with God and man
Ps. 41. 11. know thou *favourest* me
FEAR, Gen. 9. 2. Ex. 15. 16.
Ps. 53. 5. in *f.* where no *f.* was
90. 11. according to thy *f.* so wrath
119. 38. servant devoted to thy *f.*
120. flesh trembleth for *f.* of thee
Prov. 1. 26. mock when your *f.* cometh
29. 25. *f.* of man bringeth a snare
Isa. 8. 12. *f.* not their *f.* nor be afraid
13. let him be your *f.* Gen. 31. 42.

29. 13. their *f.* toward me is taught by
63. 17. hardened our hearts from thy *f.*
Jer. 32. 40. put my *f.* in their hearts
Mal. 1. 6. if master where is my *f.*
Rom. 13. 7. render *f.* to whom *f.*
2 Tim. 1. 7. spirit of *f.* but of power
Heb. 2. 15. who through *f.* of death
12. 28. with reverence and godly *f.*
1 Pet. 1. 17. time of sojourning here in *f.*
1 John 4. 18. no *f.* in love, casteth out *f.*
Gen. 20. 11. *fear of God* not in this place
2 Sam. 23. 3. ruling in—
Neh. 5. 15. so did not I because of—
Ps. 36. 1. no—before his eyes
2 Cor. 7. 1. perfecting holiness in—
Job 28. 28. *fear of the Lord,* that is wisdom
Ps. 19. 9.—is clean, enduring for ever
34. 11. children I will teach you—
111. 10.—is beginning of wisdom or knowledge, Prov. 1. 7. & 9. 10.
Prov. 1. 29. they did not choose—
8. 13.—is to hate evil
10. 27.—prolongeth days
14. 26. in—is strong confidence
27.—is a fountain of life
15. 33.—is instruction of wisdom
16. 6. by—men depart from evil
19. 23.—tendeth to life; satisfied
22. 4. by—are riches, honour, life
23. 17. be thou in—all day long
Isa. 33. 6.—is his treasure
Acts 9. 31. walking in—and comfort
Ps. 2. 11. *with fear,* Phil. 2. 12.
Heb. 11. 7. Jude 23. save—
Deut. 4. 10. learn *to fear* me
5. 29. such a heart that would *f.* me
28. 58. mayest *f.* this glorious name
2 Kings 17. 39. Lord your God ye shall *f.*
1 Chron. 16. 30. *f.* before him all the earth
2 Chron. 6. 31. that they may *f.* thee
Neh. 1. 11. servants, desire to *f.* thy name
Ps. 23. 4. I will *f.* no evil, for thou
31. 19. goodness laid up for those that *f.*
61. 5. heritage of those that *f.* thy name
86. 11. incline my heart to *f.* thy name
Jer. 10. 7. who would not *f.* thee
32. 39. heart that may fear me for ever
Mal. 4. 2. to you that *f.* my name shall Sun of righteousness
Luke 12. 5. *f.* him who can cast, Matt. 10. 28.
Rom. 8. 15. spirit of bondage again to *f.*
11. 20. be not high-minded but *f.*
Heb. 4. 1. *f.* lest a promise being left
12. 21. Moses said, I exceedingly *f.*
Rev. 2. 10. *f.* none of these things
11. 18. saints and them that *f.* thy name
Gen. 42. 18. this do and live, for I fear God
Ex. 18. 21. such as—men of truth
Ps. 66. 16. come hear all ye that—
Eccl. 5. 7. dreams, vanities, *f.* thou God
8. 12. shall go well with them that—
12. 13.—and keep his commandments
Job. 37. 24. therefore men do *fear him*
Ps. 25. 14. secret of Lord with them that—
33. 18. eye of Lord upon them that—
Ps. 34. 7. angel of the Lord encamps about them that—
9. there is no want to them that—

85. 9. his salvation is nigh them that—
103. 13. father pities, so Lord them that—
17. mercy overlasting upon them that—
111. 5. giveth meat to them that—
145. 19. fulfill the desire of them that—
147. 11. the Lord takes pleasure in them that—
Matt. 10. 28—who is able to destroy
Luke 1. 50. his mercy is on them that—from generation
Deut. 6. 2. mightiest *fear the Lord*
13. thou shalt—thy God, 10. 20.
24.—our God for our good always
10. 12.—thy God walk in his ways
14. 23. learn to—thy God, always,
17. 19. & 31. 12, 13.
Josh. 4. 24. that ye might—your God
24. 14. therefore—serve in sincerity
1 Sam. 12. 14. if ye will—and serve
24. only—and serve him in truth
1 Kings 18. 12. servant did
2 Kings 17. 28. how they should—
Ps. 15. 4. he honoureth them that—
22. 23. ye that—trust in him, 115. 11.
33. 8. let all the earth—
34. 9. O—ye his saints, no want to them that—
115. 13. he will bless them that—
118. 4. let them that—say, that his mercy
135. 20. ye that—bless the Lord
Prov. 3. 7.—and depart from evil
24. 21. my son—and meddle not
Jer. 5. 24. let us now—that giveth rain
26. 19. did not he—and besought Lord
Hos. 3. 5. and shall—and his goodness
Jonah 1. 9. I—the God of heaven
Gen. 15. 1. *fear not,* I am thy shield
26. 24.—for I am with thee
Num. 14. 9. word is with us—them
Deut. 1. 21.—neither be discouraged nor dismayed, 31. 8. Josh. 8. 1.
Ps. 56. 4. I will not *f.* what flesh can do, 118. 6. Heb. 13. 6.
Isa. 41. 10.—for I am with thee, I will help thee, 13. & 43. 5.
43. 1.—for I have redeemed thee
Jer. 5. 22. *f.* ye not me, saith the Lord
30. 10.—O my servant Jacob, and be not dismayed, 46. 27, 28.
Matt. 10. 28.—them that kill the body
Luke 12. 32.—little flock; for it is your Father's.
Ex. 1. 17. midwives *feared* God, 21.
14. 31. people *f.* Lord and believed
1 Sam. 12. 18. all people greatly *f.* the Lord
1 Kings 18. 3. Obadiah *f.* the Lord, greatly
Neh. 7. 2. Hanani *f.* God above many
Job 1. 1. that *f.* God and eschewed evil
Ps. 76. 7. thou art to be *f.* who
89. 7. God is greatly to be *f.* in the assembly
96. 4. Lord is to be *f.* above all gods
130. 4. forgiveness, that thou mayest be *f.*
Mal. 3. 16. they that *f.* Lord spake often
Acts 10. 2. one that *f.* the Lord with his house
Heb. 5. 7. was heard in that he *f.*
Gen. 22. 12. that thou *fearest* God
Job. 1. 8. that *feareth* God. 2. 3.
Ps. 25. 12. what man is he that *f.* the Lord
112. 1. blessed the man that *f.* the Lord
128. 1. every one that *f.* the Lord
Prov. 28. 14. happy is the man that *f.* alway

Isa. 50. 10. who among you *f.* Lord
Acts 10. 22. one that *f.* God and of good report
35. that *f.* God and works righteousness
13. 26. whosoever among you *f.* God
Ex. 15. 11. *fearful* in praises
Matt. 8. 26. why are ye *f.*
Heb. 10. 27. certain *f.* looking for of
31. thing to fall into hands of the living God
Rcv. 21. 8. *f.* and unbelieving shall be cast.
Ps. 55. 5. *fearfulness* and trembling
Isa. 33. 14. *f.* hath surprised hypocrites
Ps. 139. 14. I am *fearfully* and wonfully made
FEAST, Gen. 19. 3. & 21. 8.
Prov. 15. 15. merry heart has continual *f.*
Eccl. 10. 9. a *f.* is made for laughter
Isa. 25. 6. Lord make to all people *f.*
1 Cor. 5. 8. let us keep *f.* but not with
FEEBLE, Gen. 30. 42. Job 4. 4.
Ps. 105. 37. not one *f.* person among
Isa. 35. 3. confirm the *f.* knees
Zech. 12. 8. he that is *f.* shall be as David
1 Thess. 5. 14. comfort the *f.* minded
Heb. 12. 12. lift up the *f.* knees
FEED, *fed,* Gen. 25. 30.
Ps. 28. 9. *f.* them and lift them up
37. 3. verily thou shalt be *f.*
49. 14. death shall *f.* on them.
Prov. 10. 21. lips of righteous *f.* many
Isa. 58. 14. *f.* thee with heritage of Jacob
Jer. 3. 15. pastors *f.* you with knowledge
Acts 20. 28. to *f.* the church of God
1 Cor. 13. 3. give all my goods to *f.* poor
3. 2. I have *f.* you with milk and
Rev. 7. 17. Lamb in the throne *f.* them
1 Kings 22. 27. *f.* him with bread of affliction
Prov. 30. 8. *f.* me with food convenient for me
Song 1. 8. *f.* thy kids beside shepherd's tents
Mic. 7. 14. *f.* thy people with thy rod
John 21. 15. *f.* my lambs, *f.* my sheep, 16. 17.
Rom. 12. 20. if enemy hunger, *f.* him
1 Pet. 5. 2. *f.* flock of God among you
Isa. 44. 20. he *feedeth* on ashes
Song 2. 16. he *f.* among lilies, 6. 3.
Hos. 12. 1. Ephraim *f.* on wind—east wind
Matt. 6. 26. heavenly Father *f.* them
Luke 12. 24.
1 Cor. 9. 7. who *f.* a flock and eateth not
FEEL, *feeling,* Gen. 27. 12. Acts 17. 27. Eph. 4. 19. Heb. 4. 15.
FEET, Gen. 18. 4. & 19. 2.
1 Sam. 2. 9. keep *f.* off his saints
Neh. 9. 21. their *f.* swelled not
Job 12. 5. is ready to slip with his *f.*
29. 15. eyes to the blind, and *f.* was I to the lame
Ps. 73. 2. my *f.* were almost gone
116. 8. delivered my *f.* from falling
119. 59. turned my *f.* to thy testimonies
101. refrained my *f.* from every evil
105. thy word is a lamp to my *f.*
Prov. 4. 26. ponder the path of thy *f.*
Isa. 52. 7. their *f.* run to evil, and
Luke 1. 79. guide our *f.* into way of
Eph. 6. 15. *f.* shod with preparation of
Heb. 12. 13. straight paths for your *f.*
Rev. 11. 11. they stood upon their *f.*
FEIGNED, 1 Sam. 2. 13. Ps. 17. 1
2 Pet. 2. 3. *feignedly,* Jer. 3. 10.
FELLOW, Gen. 19. 9. Ez. 2. 13.

Eccl. 4. 10. if they fall, one will lift up his *f.*
Zech. 13. 7. man that is my *f.*
Acts 24. 5. a pestilent *f.* 22. 22.
Rom. 16. 7. my *f.* prisoner, Col. 4. 10.
2 Cor. 8. 23. my *f.* helper, 3 John 8.
Eph. 2. 19. *f.* citizens, 3. 6. *f.* heirs
Col. 1. 7. *f.* servant, 4. 7. Rev. 6. 11.
Phil. 4. 5. *f.* labourers, 1 Thes. 3. 2.
2. 25. *f.* soldier, Philem. 1. 2, 24.
Ps. 45. 7. oil of gladness above *f.* Heb. 1. 9.
94. 20. have *fellowship* with thee
Acts 2. 42. continued steadfastly in apostles' doctrine and *f.*
1 Cor. 1. 9. God by whom called to *f.* of Jesus Christ
10. 20. should have *f.* with devils
2 Cor. 6. 14. what *f.* hath righteousness with unrighteousness
8. 4. *f.* of ministering to saints
Gal. 2. 9. gave us right hand of *f.*
Eph. 5. 11. no *f.* with unfruitful works
Phil. 1. 5. for your *f.* in the gospel
2. 1. if there be any *f.* of the Spirit
3. 10. may know him and *f.* of his sufferings
1 John 1. 3. *f.* with us, our *f.* with the Father
6. we have *f.*
7. we *f.* one with another
FERVENT in spirit, Acts 18. 25.
Rom. 12. 11. *f.* in spirit, serving Lord
2 Cor. 7. 7. your *f.* mind toward me
James 5. 16. *f.* prayer of righteous
1 Pet. 4. 8. have *f.* charity among yourselves
2 Pet. 3. 10. melt with *f.* heat, 12.
Col. 4. 12. Epaphras always labouring *fervently* for you in prayer
1 Pet. 1. 22. love one another *f.*
FEW, Gen. 29. 20. Ps. 105. 12.
Matt. 7. 14. way to life, *f.* find it
20. 16. many called, but *f.* chosen
25. 21. been faithful in a *f.* things
Rev. 2. 14. I have a *f.* things against
3. 4. thou hast a *f.* names in Sardis
FIDELITY, all good, Tit. 2. 10.
FIERCENESS of anger, Deut. 13. 17.
Josh. 7. 26. 2 Kings 23. 26.
FIERY, Deut. 33. 2.
Num. 21. 6. *f.* serpents, 8.
Ps. 21. 9. make them as a *f.* oven
Eph. 6. 16. quench *f.* darts of devil
Heb 10. 27. *f.* indignation devour
1 Pet. 4. 12. not strange the *f.* trial
FIGS, Gen. 3. 7. Isa. 34. 4.
Jer. 24. 2. very good *f.* naughty *f.*
Matt. 7. 16. do men gather *f.* of thistles
James 3. 12. can *f.* tree bear olive berries, or vine *f.*
Judg. 9. 10. *fig-tree,* 1 Kings 4. 25.
Mich. 4. 4. Isa. 36. 16. Hos. 9. 10.
Nah. 3. 12. Hab. 3. 17. Zech. 3. 10.
Matt. 21. 19. Luke 13. 6, 7.
FIGHT, 1 Sam. 17. 20.
Acts 5. 39. found to *f.* against God
23. 9. let us not *f.* against God
1 Cor. 9. 26. so *f.* I not as one that
1 Tim. 6. 12. the good *f.* of faith
2 Tim. 4. 7. I have fought a good *f.*
Heb. 10. 32. a great *f.* of afflictions
11. 34. waxed valiant in *f.*
FIGURE, Rom. 5. 14. 1 Cor. 4. 6.
Heb. 9. 9, 24. 1 Pet. 3. 21.
FILL, Job 8. 21. & 23. 4.
Ps. 81. 10. open mouth wide, I will *f.* it
Jer. 23. 24. I *f.* heaven and earth
Rom. 15. 13. God *f.* you with all joy
Eph. 4. 10. ascended, might *f.* all things
Col. 1. 24. I *f.* up that which is behind of afflictions
Ps. 72. 19. earth *filled* with his glory
Luke 1. 53. hath *f.* hungry with good
Acts 9. 17. *f.* with the Holy Ghost, 2. 4. & 4. 8, 31. & 13. 9, 52.

Rom. 15. 14. *f.* with all knowledge
2 Cor. 7. 4. I am *f.* with comfort
Eph. 3. 19. might be *f.* with all the fulness of God
5. 18. not with wine but *f.* with the Spirit.
Phil. 1. 11. *f.* with the fruits of righteousness
Cor. 1. 9. *f.* with knowledge of his will
2 Tim. 1. 4. mindful of tears, *f.* with
Eph. 1. 23. fulness of him that *filleth* all in all
FILTH, Isa. 4. 4. 1 Cor. 4. 13.
Job 15. 16. more *filthy* is man
Ps. 14. 3. altogether become *f.*
Col. 3. 8. put off *f.* communication
1 Tim. 3. 3. greedy of *f.* lucre, 8.
Tit. 1. 7, 11. 1 Pet. 5. 2.
2 Pet. 2. 7. vexed with *f.* conversation
Jude 8. *f.* dreamers defile the flesh
Rev. 22. 11. that is *f.* let him be *f.*
James 1. 21. lay apart all *filthiness*
Ezek. 36. 25. from all your *f.* I will cleanse you
2 Cor. 7. 1. cleanse ourselves from all *f.*
FINALLY, 2 Cor. 13. 11. Eph. 6. 10.
Phil. 3. 1. 2 Thes. 3. 1. 1 Pet. 3. 8.
FIND, Gen. 19. 11. & 38. 22.
Num. 32. 23. your sin shall *f.* you out
Prov. 1. 28. shall seek me and not *f.*
Song 5. 6. I sought but could not *f.*
Jer. 6. 16. ye shall *f.* rest to your souls
29. 13. shall seek me and *f.* me
Matt. 7. 7. seek and ye shall *f.*
14. way to life, few that *f.* it
10. 39. *f.* life; loseth life shall *f.* it
11. 29. shall *f.* rest to your souls
John 7. 34. seek me, and shall not *f.*
Rom. 7. 18. how to do good, I *f.* not
2 Tim. 1. 18. may *f.* mercy in that day
Heb. 4. 16. may *f.* grace to help
Rev. 9. 6. seek death and shall not *f.*
Prov. 8. 35. whoso *findeth* me, *f.* life
Eccl. 9. 10. whatsoever thy hand *f.* to do
Matt. 8. that seeketh *f.*
Rom. 11. 33. his ways past *f.* out
FINE, Job 28. 1. Isa. 3. 23. Lev. 2. 1.
Ps. 81. 16. Prov. 25. 4.
FINGER of God. Ex. 8. 19. Deut. 9. 10. Luke 11. 20.
1 Kings 12. 10. my little *f.* shall be thicker
Ps. 8. 3. heaven is work of thy *f.*
144. 1. he teacheth my *f.* to fight
Prov. 6. 13. he teacheth with his *f.*
Luke 11. 46. touch not with one of your *f.*
John 20. 27. reach hither thy *f.*
FINISH, Dan. 9. 24.
John 17. 4. I have *f.* work, 19. 30. it is *f.*
Acts 20. 24. *f.* my course with joy
2 Cor. 8. 6. would also *f.* in you the same grace also
2 Tim. 4. 7. I have *f.* my course
James 1. 15. sin when it is *f.* bringeth forth death
FIRE, Ex. 3. 2. and 40. 38.
Gen. 19. 24. the Lord rained *f.* and brimstone
Ps. 11. 6. rain *f.* and brimstone
39. 3. while musing the *f.* burned
Prov. 6. 27. can a man take *f.* in his bosom
25. 22. heap coals of *f.* on his head, Rom. 12. 20.
Isa. 9. 18. wickedness burneth as a *f.*
31. 9. Lord of hosts whose *f.* is in Zion
43. 2. walkest through *f.* shall not be burnt
Jer. 23. 29. is not my word like *f.*
Amos 5. 6. lest Lord break out like *f.*
7. 4. Lord God called to contend by *f.*
Hab. 2. 13. labour in very *f.* for

Zech. 2. 5. I will be a wall of *f.*
3. 2. brand plucked out of *f.*
Mal. 3. 2. he shall be as a refiner's *f.*
Matt. 3. 10. cut down and cast into *f.*
12. burn with unquenchable *f.*
Mark 9. 43, 44, 46, 48. Luke 3. 17.
Luke 9. 54. command *f.* to come down
12. 49. I am come to send *f.* on the earth
1 Cor. 3. 13. revealed by *f.*—
Heb. 12. 29. our God is consuming *f.*
Jude 23. pulling them out of the *f.*
Matt. 5. 22. *hell-fire,* 18. 9.
Lev. 10. 1. *strange fire,* Num. 3. 4.
FIRST, Matt. 10. 2. Esth. 1. 14.
Isa. 41. 4. the Lord the *f.* and the last, 44. 6. Rev. 1. 11, 17.
Matt. 6. 33. seek *f.* the kingdom of God
7. 5. *f.* cast out the beam
19. 30. many that be *f.* shall be last, 20. 16. Mark 10. 31.
22. 38. this is the *f.* and great commandment
Acts 26. 23. *f.* that should rise from the dead
Rom. 11. 35. who hath *f.* given to him
1 Cor. 15. 45. *f.* Adam, 47. *f.* man of earth
2 Cor. 8. 5. *f.* gave their own selves to the Lord
12. accepted, if there be *f.* willing mind
1 Pet. 4. 17. if judgment *f.* begin at us
1 John 4. 19. because he *f.* loved us
Rev. 2. 4. left thy *f.* love, 5. do *f.* works
20. 5. this is the *f.* resurrection
Matt. 1. 25. *first-born,* Luke 2. 7.
Rom. 8. 29. *f.* among many brethren
Col. 1. 15. *f.* of every creature
18. *f.* from the dead
Heb. 12. 23. to the general assembly and church of *f.*
Rom. 11. 16. if *first fruit* be holy
Prov. 3. 9. honour the Lord with *f.*
Rom. 8. 23. having *first fruits* of the
1 Cor. 15. 20. Christ *f.* of them that slept
James 1. 18. we a kind of *f.* creatures
Rev. 14. 4. redeemed are *f.* to God and the Lamb
FISH, Ezek. 29. 4, 5. & 47. 9.
Jer. 16. 16. *fishers,* Ezek. 47. 10. Matt. 4. 18. John 21. 7. Isa. 19. 8.
FLAME, Ex. 3. 2. Judg. 13. 20.
Ps. 104. 4. maketh ministers a *f.* of fire, Heb. 1. 7.
106. 18. *f.* burnt up wicked
Isa. 10. 17. the Holy One of Israel for a *f.*
2 Thess. 1. 8. in *flaming* fire taking vengeance
FLATTER, Ps. 78. 36. Prov. 2. 16.
Job 32. 21, 22. 1 Thess. 2. 5.
FLEE, Isa. 10. 3. & 20. 6. Heb. 6. 18.
Prov. 28. 1. wicked *f.* when no man pursueth
Matt. 3. 7. who warned you to *f.*
1 Cor. 6. 18. *f.* fornication, 10. 14. *f.* idolatry
1 Tim. 7. 11. man of God. *f.* these things
2 Tim. 2. 21. *f.* youthful lusts
James 4. 7. resist the devil; he will *f.* from you
FLESH, Gen. 2. 21. 1 Cor. 15. 39.
Gen. 2. 24. they shall be one *f.* Matt. 19. 5. 1 Cor. 6. 16. Eph. 5. 31.
John 10. 11. clothed me with skin and *f.*
Ps. 56. 4. what *f.* can do to me
78. 39. remember that they were but *f.*
Jer. 17. 5. cursed that maketh *f.* his arm

Matt. 26. 41. spirit is willing, but *f.* weak

John 1. 14. the Word was made *f.*

6. 53. eat the *f.* of the Son of man

63. *f.* profiteth nothing, words are

Rom. 7. 25. serve with *f.* law of sin

8. 12. debtors not to the *f.* to live after the *f.*

9. 3. kinsmen according to the *f.*

5. of whom concerning *f.* Christ

13. 14. make not provision for *f.*

1 Cor. 1. 29. that no *f.* should glory

2 Cor. 1. 17. purpose according to *f.*

10. 2. walked according to the *f.*

Gal. 5. 17. *f.* lusts against the Spirit, and Spirit against *f.*

24. Christ's have crucified *f.* with

Eph. 6. 5. masters according to *f.*

Heb. 12. 9. we had fathers of our *f.*

Jude 7. going after strange *f.*

23. hating garment spotted by *f.*

John 8. 15. ye judge *after the flesh*

Rom. 8. 1. walk not—but after the Spirit

5. they are—mind things of *f.*

13. if ye live—ye shall die, 12.

1 Cor. 1. 26. not many wise men—

10. 18. Israel—Rom. 9. 8.

2 Cor. 5. 16. know no man—know Christ

10. 3. walk in *f.* not war—

2 Pet. 2. 10. walk—in lust of uncleanness

Ps. 65. 2. to thee shall *all flesh* come

Isa. 40. 6.—is grass, 1 Pet. 1. 24.

49. 26.—shall know that I am thy Redeemer

Joel 2. 28. I will pour my Spirit on—

Luke 3. 6.—shall see the salvation of God, Ps. 98. 3.

John 17. 2. given him power over—

Rom. 7. 5. when we were *in the flesh*

8. 8. that are—cannot please God

1 Pet. 3. 18. he was put to death—

Gen. 2. 23. *my flesh*, 29. 14. Ps. 63. 1. & 119. 220. John 6. 51, 55. Rom. 7. 18.

John 1. 13. born not of will *of the flesh*

3. 6. that which is born—is *f.*

Rom. 8. 5. after *f.* do mind things—

Gal. 5. 19. works—are manifest

6. 8. soweth to *f.* shall—reap corruption

Eph. 2. 3. lusts—desires—

1 Pet. 3. 21. not putting away filth—

1 John 2. 16. lust—of the eyes, pride

Matt. 16. 17. *flesh and blood* have not revealed

1 Cor. 15. 50.—cannot inherit kingdom

Gal. 1. 16. I conferred not with—

Eph. 5. 30. members of his—and

6. 12. we wrestle not against—but

Heb. 2. 14. children are partakers of—

2 Cor. 1. 12. not with *fleshly* wisdom

Col. 2. 18. puffed up by his *f.* mind

FLOCK, Gen. 32. 5. Ps. 77. 20. Isa. 40. 11. & 63. 11. Jer. 13. 17, 20.

Zech. 11. 4. feed *f.* of slaughter, 7.

Luke 12. 32. fear not, little *f.* for it

Acts 20. 28. take heed to all the *f.* 29.

1 Pet. 5. 2. feed the *f.* of God which is among you

FLOURISH, Isa. 17. 11. & 66. 14.

Ps. 72. 7. shall the righteous *f.* 16. & 92. 12, 13, 14. Prov. 11. 28. & 14. 11.

92. 7. when workers of iniquity *f.*

132. 18. on himself shall crown *f.*

FOLLOW, Gen. 44. 4. Ex. 14. 4.

Ex. 23. 2. shall not *f.* a multitude

Deut. 16. 20. that is just shalt thou *f.*

Ps. 38. 20. I *f.* the thing that good is

Isa. 51. 1. my people that *f.* after righteousness

Hos. 6. 3. know if we *f.* on to know the Lord

Rom. 14. 19. *f.* things that make for peace

1 Cor. 14. 1. *f.* after charity, desire

Phil. 3. 12. but I *f.* after that I may apprehend

1 Thess. 5. 15. ever *f.* that which is good

1 Tim. 6. 11. *f.* after righteousness

2 Tim. 2. 22. *f.* righteousness, faith, charity, peace

Heb. 12. 14. *f.* peace with all men

13. 7. whose faith *f.* considering end of

1 Pet. 2. 21. example should *f.* his steps

2 John 11. *f.* not evil, but that which is good

Rev. 14. 13. their works do *f.* them

Ps. 23. 6. goodness and mercy shall *follow me*

Matt. 4. 19. & 9. 9. & 19. 21. Luke 5. 27. & 9. 59. John 1. 43. & 21. 19.

Matt. 16. 24. take up cross and—

Luke 18. 22. sell all that thou hast, and—

John 12. 26. If any man serve me, let him—

Num. 14. 24. hath *followed* me fully

32. 12. wholly *f.* the Lord, Deut. 1. 36. Josh. 14. 8, 9, 14.

Rom. 9. 30. *f.* not after righteousness

21. *f.* law of righteousness

Ps. 63. 8. soul *followeth* hard after

Matt. 10. 38. taketh not cross and *f.* me

Mark 9. 38. he *f.* not us, Luke 9. 49.

FOLLY wrought in Israel, Gen. 34. 7. Deut. 22. 21. Josh. 7. 15. Judges 20. 6.

Job 4. 18. angels he chargeth with *f.*

Ps. 49. 13. their way is *folly*

85. 8. let them not turn again to *f.*

Prov. 26. 4, 5. answer a fool according to his *f.*

2 Tim. 3. 9. their *f.* shall be manifest

FOOD, Gen. 3. 6. Deut. 10. 18.

Job 23. 12. words more than necessary *f.*

Ps. 78. 25. men did eat angels' *f.*

136. 25. who giveth *f.* to all flesh

146. 7. who giveth *f.* to the hungry

Acts 14. 17. filling our hearts with *f.*

2 Cor. 9. 10. ministered bread for your *f.*

1 Tim. 6. 8. having *f.* and raiment

FOOL, Ps. 14. 1. & 53. 1.

Jer. 17. 11. at end of days shall be *f.*

Matt. 5. 22. whosoever shall say to brother, thou *f.*

Luke 12. 20. thou *f.* this night thy soul shall be required

1 Cor. 3. 18. let him become a *f.* that

2 Cor. 11. 16. think me a *f.* 23, as a *f.*

Ps. 75. 4. *fools* deal not foolishly

94. 8. ye *f.* when will ye be wise

107. 17. *f.* because of transgressions

Prov. 1. 7. *f.* despise wisdom, 22. *f.* hate knowledge

13. 20. companion of *f.* be destroyed

14. 8. folly of *f.* is deceitful

9. *f.* make a mock at sin

16. 22. instruction of *f.* is folly

Eccl. 5. 4. he hath no pleasure in *f.*

Matt. 23. 17. ye *f.* and blind, 19.

Deut. 32. 6. *foolish* people and unwise

Ps. 5. 5. *f.* shall not stand in thy sight

73. 22. so *f.* was I and ignorant

Matt. 7. 26. on sand like to a *f.* man

25. 2. virgins, five were wise and five *f.*

Rom. 1. 21. their *f.* heart darkened

Gal. 3. 1. O *f.* Galatians, who bewitched you

Eph. 5. 4. filthiness, nor *f.* talking

Tit. 3. 3. were sometimes *f.* disobedient

Gen. 31. 28. done *foolishly*, 1 Sam. 13. 13. 2 Sam. 24. 10. 1 Chron. 21. 8.

---

2 Chron. 16. 9. Prov. 14. 17. 2 Cor. 11. 21.

Job 1. 22. Job sinned not, nor charged God *f.*

2 Sam. 15. 31. turn counsel into *foolishness*

Prov. 12. 23. heart of fools proclaimeth *f.*

12. 24. *f.* of fools is folly, 15. 2.

22. 15. *f.* is bound in heart of child

24. 9. thought of *f.* is sin

27. 22. bray a fool, yet his *f.* will depart

1 Cor. 1. 18. preaching of the cross is to them that perish, *f.*

21. God by *f.* of preaching to save

23. Christ crucified, to Greeks *f.*

25. *f.* of God is wiser than men

2. 14. they are *f.* to him; neither can he

3. 19. wisdom of world is *f.* with God

FOOT, Prov. 3. 23.

Eccl. 5. 1. keep thy *f.* when thou goest to the house of God

Isa. 58. 13. turn away *f.* from sabbath

Matt. 18. 8. if thy *f.* offend thee, cut

1 Cor. 12. 15. if *f.* say, because I am not

Heb. 10. 29. trodden under *f.* Son of God

FORBEAR, Ex. 23. 5. 1 Cor. 9. 6.

Rom. 2. 4. goodness and *forbearance*, 3. 25.

FORBID, Mark 10. 14. Luke 18. 16. & 6. 29. Acts 24. 23.

1 Tim. 4. 3. *forbidding* to marry

FORCE, Matt. 11. 12.

Isa. 60. 5. *f.* of Gentiles shall come

Job 6. 25. how *forcible* right words

FOREFATHERS, 2 Tim. 1. 3.

FOREHEAD, Ex. 28. 38.

Jer. 3. 3. thou hast a whore's *f.*

Ezek. 3. 8. thy *f.* strong against their *f.*

Rev. 7. 3. sealed in their *f.* 9. 4.

13. 16. mark their *f.* 14. 9.

14. 1. Father's name written in *f.*

FOREIGNERS, Ex. 12. 45. Deut. 15. 3. Obad. 11. Eph. 2. 19.

FOREKNOW, Rom. 8. 29.

Acts 2. 23. *foreknowledge* of God, 1. Pet. 1. 2.

FOREORDAINED, 1 Pet. 1. 20.

FORERUNNER, Heb. 6. 20.

FORESEETH, Prov. 22. 3.

FOREWARN, Luke 12. 5.

FORGAT Lord, Judg. 3. 7.

Ps. 78. 11. *f.* his works and wonders, 106. 13.

106. 21. *f.* God their Saviour

Lam. 3. 17. I *f.* prosperity

Hos. 2. 13. *f.* me, saith the Lord

Deut. 9. 7. remember and *forget* not

Job 8. 13. paths of all that *f.* God

Ps. 45. 10. *f.* thy own people, and

50. 22. consider this, ye that *f.* God

59. 11. slay not lest my people *f.*

103. 2. *f.* not all his benefits

119. 16. I will not *f.* thy words, 83, 93, 109, 141, 153, 176.

Prov. 3. 1. my son, *f.* not my law

Isa. 49. 15. can woman *f.* her child

Heb. 6. 10. God is not unrighteous to *f.* your

13. 16. to do good and to communicate *f.* not

13. 2. be not *forgetful* to entertain

James 1. 25. be not a *f.* hearer

Ps. 44. 24. thou *forgettest* our affliction

9. 12. he *f.* not the cry of humble

Prov. 2. 17. *f.* covenant of her God

James 1. 24. *f.* what manner of man

Phil. 3. 13. *forgetting* those things

Ps. 9. 10. 11. God hath *forgotten*

42. 9. why hast thou *f.* me

77. 9. hath God *f.* to be gracious

119. 61. I have not *f.* thy law

Isa. 17. 10. hast *f.* the God of thy salvation

49. 14. Zion said my Lord hath *f.* me

Jer. 2. 32. my people have *f.* me

3. 21. have *f.* their God, Deut. 32. 18

50. 5. covenant that shall not *f.*

Heb. 12. 5. *f.* the exhortation

FORGAVE, Ps. 78. 38.

Matt. 18. 27. *f.* him the debt, 32.

Luke 7. 42. frankly *f.* them both

43. love most, to whom *f.* most

Col. 3. 13. as Christ *f.* you, also do

Ps. 32. 5. *forgavest* the iniquity of

99. 8. thou wast a God that *f.* them

Ex. 32. 32. now *forgive* their sin

Isa. 2. 9. therefore *f.* them not

Jer. 31. 34. I will *f.* their iniquity

Matt. 6. 12. *f.* us our debts, as we

14. if ye *f.* men, 15. if you *f.* not

Luke 6. 37. *f.* and ye shall be forgiven

17. 3. if he repent, *f.* him, 4.

23. 34. Father *f.* them, they know not what they do

1 John 1. 9. faithful to *f.* us our sins

Ps. 32. 1. whose transgression is *forgiven*

85. 2. *f.* the iniquity of thy people

Matt. 9. 2. good cheer, thy sins be *f.*

12. 31. all manner of sin *f.* 32. not be *f.*

Luke 7. 47. to whom little is *f.* loveth

Eph. 4. 32. as God hath *f.* you

James 5. 15. if he have committed sins, they shall be *f.*

1 John 2. 12. your sins are *f.* you

Ps. 103. 3. who *forgiveth* all thy iniquity

130. 4. is there *forgiveness* with thee

Mark 3. 29. hath never *f.* but

Acts 5. 31. give repentance and *f.* of sins

26. 18. may receive *f.* of sins by faith

Col. 1. 14. redemption, even *f.* of sins

Ex. 34. 7. *forgiving* iniquity, transgression and sin, Num. 14. 18.

Eph. 4. 32. *f.* one another

FORM, Gen. 1. 2. 1 Sam. 28. 14.

Isa. 53. 2. hath no *f.* nor comeliness

Rom. 2. 20. hast the *f.* of knowledge

6. 17. obeyed from heart *f.* of doctrine

Phil. 2. 6. who being in *f.* of God

7. took upon him the *f.* of a servant

2 Tim. 1. 13. hold *f.* of sound words

3. 5. the *f.* of godliness but denying

Isa. 45. 7. I *f.* light and create darkness

Deut. 32. 18. hast forgotten God that *formed* thee

Prov. 26. 10. God that *f.* all things

Isa. 27. 11. *f.* them will show no favour

43. 21. this people have I *f.* for myself

44. 2. I *f.* thee from womb, 24.

54. 17. no weapon *f.* against thee shall prosper

Gal. 4. 19. till Christ be *f.* in you

Ps. 94. 9. that *formeth* the eye

Zech. 12. 1. *f.* spirit of man within him

Jer. 10. 16. he is *former* of all things

FORNICATION, 2 Chron. 21. 11.

Isa. 23. 17. Ezek. 16. 15.

Matt. 5. 32. put away wife for cause of *f.*

19. 9. except it be for *f.*

John 8. 41. we be not born of *f.*

Acts 15. 20. abstain from *f.* 29.

Rom. 1. 29. filled with all *f.* wickedness

1 Cor. 5. 1. there is *f.* among you

6. 13. body not for *f.* 18. flee *f.*

7. 2. avoid *f.* every man have his wife

10. 8. neither let us commit *f.*

2 Cor. 12. 21. not repented of their *f.*

Gal. 5. 19. works of flesh, adultery, *f.*

Eph. 5. 3. but *f.* and all uncleanness

Col. 3. 5. mortify *f.* uncleanness

1 Thes. 4. 3. should abstain from *f.*

Jude 7. giving themselves to *f.*

Rev. 2. 14. taught to commit. f.
21. I gave her space to repent of
her f.
9. 21. neither repented of their f.
14. 8. of the wine of her f.
17. 4. abomination and filthiness of
her f.
18. 3. committed f. with her
Rev. 19. 2. did corrupt earth with
her f.
Ezek. 16. 15. fornications
1 Cor. 5. 9. fornicators, 10. 11.

FORSAKE, Deut. 12. 19.
Deut. 4. 31. Lord thy God will not f.
thee, 31. 6, 8. 1 Chron. 28. 20.
Josh. 1. 4. I will not fail thee nor f.
thee, Isa. 41. 17. & 42. 16.
1 Kings 6. 13. I will not f. my people
8. 57. let him not leave nor f. us
2 Chron. 15. 2. if ye f. him he will f.
Ps. 27. 10. father and mother f. me
Isa. 55. 7. let the wicked f. his way
Jer. 17. 13. they that f. thee shall be
ashamed
Jonah 2. 8. f. their own mercy
Ps. 71. 11. God hath forsaken him
22. 1. my God, why f. me
37. 25. I have not seen the righteous
f.
Isa. 49. 14. Lord hath f. my Lord
hath forgotten
54. 7. small moment have f. thee
Jer. 2. 13. f. me the fountain of living waters, 17. 13.
Matt. 19. 27. we have f. all
2 Cor. 4. 9. persecuted but not f.
Prov. 2. 17. forsaketh guide of her
youth
28. 13. confesseth and f. shall find
Heb. 10. 25. not f. the assembling
Deut. 32. 15. he forsook God which
Ps. 119. 87. I f. not thy precepts
2 Tim. 4. 16. all men f. me

FORTRESS and rock, Lord is my
2 Sam. 22. 2. Ps. 18. 2. Jer. 16. 19.

FOUND, Gen. 26. 19. & 31. 37.
Eccl. 7. 27. this have I f. that
Songs 3. 1. I f. him not, 4. I f. him
Ezek. 22. 30. I sought a man but f.
Dan. 5. 27. weighed and f. wanting
2 Cor. 5. 3. shall not be f. naked
Phil. 3. 9. f. in him, not having my
2 Pet. 3. 14. may be f. of him in
peace
Matt. 7. 25. founded on a rock, Ps.
24. 2. Prov. 3. 19. Isa. 14. 32.
Ps. 11. 3. if foundations be de-
stroyed
Job 4. 19. whose f. is in the dust
Prov. 10. 25. righteous an everlast-
ing f.
Isa. 28. 16. I lay in Zion a sure f.
Rom. 15. 20. lest I build upon another man's f.
1 Cor. 3. 10. laid f. 12. build on this
f.
Eph. 2. 20. built on f. of the prophets
1 Tim. 6. 19. lay up a good f. for time
2 Tim. 2. 19. the f. of God stands
sure
Heb. 11. 10. a city which hath f.
Rev. 21. 14. the city hath twelve f.
Matt. 13. 35. foundation of the world
25. 34. John 17. 24. Eph. 1. 4. 1 Pet.
1. 20. Rev. 13. 8. & 17. 8. Ps. 104. 5.

FOUNTAIN, Gen. 7. 11.
Deut. 33. 28. f. of Jacob on a land
Ps. 36. 9. with thee is f. of life
68. 26. bless the Lord from f. of
Israel
Prov. 5. 18. let thy f. be blessed
13. 14. law of wise is a f. of life
14. 27. fear of Lord is a f. of life
Eccl. 12. 6. pitcher broken at the f.
Song 4. 12. f. sealed, 15. f. of gardens
Jer. 2. 13. Lord of living waters
9. 1. that my eyes were a f. of tears
Joel 3. 18. a f. out of house of the
Lord
Zech. 13. 1. be a f. opened for house
of

Rev. 21. 6. give of f. of life, freely

FOXES, Judg. 15. 4. Ps. 63. 10. Song
2. 15. Lam. 5. 18. Ezek. 13. 14. Matt.
8. 20. Luke 13. 32.

FRAGMENTS, Matt. 14. 20. Mark
6. 43. John 6. 12.

FRAIL I am, Ps. 39. 4.

FRAME, Ps. 50. 19. Isa. 29. 16. Jer.
18. 11. Eph. 2. 21. Heb. 11. 3.

FREE, Ex. 21. 2. Lev. 19. 20.
2 Chron. 29. 31. as many as were of
a f. heart
Ps. 51. 12. uphold with thy f. Spirit
88. 5. f. among the dead, like slain
John 8. 32. truth shall make you f.
36. if Son make f. shall be f. indeed
Rom. 5. 15. so also is f. gift
6. 7. f. from sin, 18. 22. f. from
righteousness, 20.
7. 3. f. from law, 8. 2. f. from the
law of sin
1 Cor. 7. 22. the Lord's f. man,
Christ's servant
Gal. 3. 28. neither bond nor f.
5. 1. Christ hath made us f. not
2 Thes. 3. 1. the word may have f.
course
1 Pet. 2. 16, as f. and not using
liberty
Hos. 14. 4. I will love them freely
Matt. 10. 8. f. ye have received, f.
give
Rom. 3. 24. justified f. by his grace
8. 32. with him f. give us all things
1 Cor. 2. 12. things f. given us of God
Rev. 21. 6. of fountain of life f.

FRET, Ps. 37. 1, 7, 8.
Prov. 19. 3. his heart f. against the
Lord
Ezek. 16. 43. hast fretted me in all

FRIEND, Jer. 6. 21. Hos. 3. 1.
Ex. 33. 11. to Moses as a man to his
f.
2 Chron. 20. 7. Abraham thy f. Isa.
41. 8. James 2. 23.
Job 6. 14. pity be showed from his f.
Prov. 17. 17. f. loveth at all times
18. 24. a f. that sticks closer than
a brother
Song 5. 16. this is my beloved and f.
Mic. 7. 5. trust ye not in a f. put not
confidence in a guide
John 15. 13. lay down life for his f.
15. 14. ye are my f. if, 15. called
you f.
James 4. 4. f. of the world is enemy
of God, friendship of the world is
enmity with God
Prov. 22. 24. no f. with an angry man
18. 24. f. must show himself friendly

FROWARD, Job. 5. 13.
Deut. 32. 20. a very f. generation
Ps. 18. 26. with f. will show thyself f.
101. 4. f. heart shall depart from
Prov. 4. 24. f. mouth, 6. 12.
10. 31. f. tongue, 11. 20. f. heart
3. 32. the f. is abomination to the
Lord
Isa. 57. 15. went on frowardly
Prov. 6. 14. frowardness is in him

FRUIT, Gen. 4. 3. Lev. 19. 24.
Gen. 30. 2. withheld f. of the womb
Ex. 21. 22.
2 Kings 19. 30. bear f. upward
Ps. 92. 14. shall bring forth f. in
old age
127. 3. f. of womb is his reward
Prov. 11. 30. f. of righteousness is a
tree of life
Song. 23. his f. was sweet to taste
Isa. 3. 10. eat the f. of their doings
27. 9. all the f. to take away sin
57. 19. create f. of the lips, peace
Hos. 10. 1. empty vine brings f. to
14. 8. from me is thy f. found
Mic. 6. 7. f. of my body for sin of
my soul
Matt. 7. 17. good tree brings forth
good f. 21. 19.
12. 33. f. good; tree known by his f.

26. 29. not drink of f. of vine till
Luke 1. 42. blessed is the f. of thy
womb
John 4. 36. gathers f. to eternal life
15. 2. branch beareth not f. he
taketh away; every branch beareth
he purgeth it, to bring forth more f.
Rom. 6. 21. what f. had, 22. f. to
holiness
Gal. 5. 22. f. of Spirit is love, joy
Eph. 5. 9. f. of Spirit is in all goodness
Phil. 4. 17. desire f. that may abound
Heb. 12. 11. peaceable f. of righteousness
13. 15. sacrifices of praise f. of our
Jas. 3. 18. f. of righteousness is sown
Rev. 22. 2. yielded f. every month
Matt. 3. 8. bring forth fruits meet
for repentance
7. 16. shall know them by their f.
Phil 1. 11. filled with f. of right-
ousness

FRUSTRATE, Isa. 44. 25.

FULL, Gen. 15. 16. Ex. 16. 3.
Deut. 34. 9. Joshua f. of the Spirit
of wisdom
Ruth 1. 21. I went out f. and re-
turned again empty
1 Sam. 2. 5. that were f. have hired
Job 5. 29. come to grave in f. age
14. 1. of few days and f. of trouble
Ps. 17. 14. they are f. of children
Prov. 27. 7. f. soul loathe the honey-
comb
30. 9. lest I be f. and deny thee
Luke 4. 1. Jesus being f. of the Holy
Ghost
6. 25. wo to you that are f. for
John 1. 14. of God f. of grace and
1 Cor. 4. 8. now ye are f. now ye are
Phil. 4. 12. know both to be f. and
Col. 2. 2. riches of f. assurance
2 Tim. 4. 5. f. proof of thy ministry
Heb. 6. 11. diligence to f. assurance
10. 22. draw near in f. assurance
Gen. 29. 27. fulfil, Ex. 23. 26.
Ps. 145. 19. f. the desire of them
Matt. 3. 15. it becometh us to f. all
righteousness
5. 17. not to destroy the law, but f.
Acts 13. 22. who shall f. all my will
Luke 21. 24. till times of Gentiles be
f.
Gal. 5. 14. law is f. in one word
16. shall not f. lust of the flesh
Phil. 2. 2. f. ye my joy, that ye be
Col. 4. 17. ministry, in the Lord,
that thou f. it
2 Thes. 1. 11. f. all the good pleasure
James 2. 8. if ye f. the royal law
Rev. 17. 17. put in their hearts to f.
Job 20. 22. in fulness of sufficiency
Ps. 16. 11. in thy presence is f. of joy
John 1. 16. of his f. have we re-
ceived
Rom. 11. 25. till f. of the Gentiles
become
15. 29. f. of blessing of the Gospel
Gal. 4. 4. when f. of time was come
Eph. 1. 10. dispensation of f. of times
23 f. of him that filleth all in all
3. 19. ye may be filled with the f.
of God
4. 13. perfect man to the stature of
f. of Christ
Col. 1. 19. in him should all f. dwell
2. 9. in him dwells all f. of the
Godhead

FURNACE, Deut. 4. 20. Jer. 11. 4.
Ps. 12. 6. Isa. 31. 9. Dan. 3. 6. Matt.
13. 42. Rev. 1. 15.

FURNISHED, Deut. 15. 14.
2 Tim. 3. 17. thoroughly f. to all
good works

FURY is not in me, Isa. 27. 4.
59. 18. repay f. to his adversaries
Jer. 6. 11. I am full of f. of the Lord
10. 25. pour out thy f. on heathen
Prov. 22. 24. with furious man not

G

GABRIEL, Dan. 8. 16. & 9. 21. Luke
1. 19, 26.

GAIN, Prov. 3. 14. Job 22. 3.
Job 27. 8. hope of hypocrite though
he hath g.
Phil. 1. 21. to live is Christ, to die
is g.
3. 7. what were g. to me I counted
loss
1 Tim. 6. 5. supposing g. is godliness
6. godliness with contentment is
great g.
Matt. 16. 26. if he should g. whole
1 Cor. 9. 19. servant to all, that I
might g.
18. 15. thou hast gained thy brother
Luke 19. 16. thy pound hath g. ten
Tit. 1. 9. convince gainsayers
Acts 10. 29. gainsaying, Rom. 10. 21.
g. people
Jude 11. perished in the g. of Core

GALL, Job 16. 13. & 20. 14, 25.
Deut. 29. 18. root bears g. and
wormwood
32. 32. their grapes are grapes of g.
Ps. 69. 21. gave me g. for drink
Matt. 27. 34.
Jer. 8. 14. given us water of g.
Lam. 3. 19. remembering the worm-
wood and g. 5.

GAP, to stand in, Ezek. 22. 30.

GARDEN, Gen. 2. 15.
Song 4. 12. a g. enclosed is my sister
16. blow on my g. 5. 1.
Jer. 31. 12. soul as a watered g.

GARMENT, Josh. 7. 21.
Ps. 22. 18. parted my g. among them
Isa. 9. 5. battle with g, rolled in
blood
59. 17. put on g. of vengeance
Joel 2. 13. rend your hearts and not
g.
Matt. 21. 8. spread their g. in way
Acts 9. 39. showing g. Dorcas made
James 5. 2. your g. are moth-eaten
Rev. 3. 4. have not defiled their g.
16. 15. watcheth and keepeth his g.

GATE, Gen. 19. 1. & 34. 20.
Gen. 22. 17. possess g. of his enemies
28. 17. this is the house of God,
and the g. of heaven
Job 20. 7. I went to g. prepared
Ps. 118. 20. this g. of the Lord into
Matt. 7. 13. enter straight g.
Heb. 13. 12. suffered without the g.
Ps. 9. 13. up from gates of death
87. 2. Lord loveth g. of Zion
100. 4. enter his g. with thanks-
giving
Isa. 38. 10. to go to g. of the grave
Matt. 16. 18. g. of hell shall not
prevail

GATHER thee from all nations
Deut. 30. 3. Neh. 1. 9.
Ps. 26. 9. g. not my soul with sinners
Zeph. 3. 18. g. them that are sor-
rowful
Matt. 3. 12. g. his wheat into garner
7. 16. do men g. grapes from thorns
Eph. 1. 10. to g. in one all things
Ex. 16. 18, 21. he that gathered
much, had nothing over; g. little,
no lack, 2 Cor. 8. 15.
Matt. 23. 37. g. thy children as hen g.
John 4. 36. g. fruit unto eternal life

GAVE, Gen. 14. 20. Ex. 11. 3.
Job 1. 21. Lord g. and Lord taketh
away
Ps. 81. 12. I g. them up unto their
hearts' lust
Eccl. 12. 7. spirit return to God that
g. it
Isa. 42. 24. who g. Jacob for a spoil
John 1. 12. he g. power to become
sons
3. 16. God g. his only begotten Son
1 Cor. 3. 6. God g. the increase
2 Cor. 8. 5. first g. themselves to Lord

Gal. 1. 4. who *g.* himself for our sins
2. 20. *g.* himself for me, Tit. 2. 14.
Eph. 4. 8. *g.* gifts unto men, 11. *g.* some apostles
Ps. 21. 4. asked life, thou *gavest* it
John 17. 4. work thou *g.* 22. glory thou *g.* me, 6. the men thou *g.* me
GENEALOGIES, 1 Tim. 1. 4.
GENERATION, Gen. 2. 4.
Deut. 32. 5. they are a perverse and crooked *g.*
20. a very froward *g.* in whom
Ps. 14. 5. God is in the *g.* of the righteous
22. 30. accounted to Lord for a *g.*
24. 6. this is *g.* of them that seek
102. 18. written for the *g.* to come
112. 2. *g.* of upright shall be blessed
145. 4. one *g.* shall praise thy works
Isa. 53. 8. who declare his *g.*
Matt. 3. 7. ye *g.* of vipers, 12. 34.
Luke 16. 8. *g.* wiser than the children of light
Acts 13. 36. had served his *g.* according
1 Pet. 2. 9. chosen *g.* to show praises
Ps. 33. 11. thoughts to all *generations*
45. 17. name to be remembered in all *g.*
72. 5. fear thee throughout all *g.*
79. 13. show forth thy praise in all *g.*
85. 5. draw out thy anger to all *g.*
89. 4. build thy throne to all *g.*
90. 1. our dwelling place to all *g.*
100. 5. his truth endureth to all *g.*
102. 24. thy years are through all *g.*
119. 90. thy faithfulness is to all *g.*
Col. 1. 26. mystery hid from ages and *g.*
GENTILES, Gen. 10. 5.
Isa. 11. 10. to it shall the *g.* seek
42. 6. a light of the *g.* 49. 6. Luke 2. 32. Acts 13. 47.
60. 3. *g.* shall come to thy light
62. 2. *g.* shall see thy righteousness
Matt. 6. 32. after these things do *g.* seek
Luke 21. 24. trodden of *g.* till times of *g.* be fulfilled
John 7. 35. to the dispersed among the *g.*
Acts 13. 46. lo, we turn to the *g.*
14. 27. opened door of faith unto *g.*
Rom. 2. 14. *g.* which have not law
3. 29. is he not also God of *g.* yea
11. 25. till fulness of *g.* be come
15. 10. rejoice ye *g.* with his people
12. in his name shall *g.* trust
Eph. 3. 6. *g.* be heirs and partakers
8. preach among *g.* unsearchable riches of Christ
1 Tim 2. 7. a teacher of *g.* 2 Tim. 1. 11.
3. 16. God manifest in flesh, preached to *g.*
GENTLE, 1 Thess. 2. 7.
2 Tim. 2. 24. servant of Lord must be *g.*
Tit. 3. 2. be *g.* showing all meekness
James 3. 17. wisdom from above is *g.*
1 Pet. 2. 18. not only to the *g.* but to
Ps. 18. 35. thy *gentleness* made me great
2 Cor. 10. 1. beseech by the *g.* of Christ
Gal. 5. 22. fruit of the Spirit is love, joy, *g.*
Isa. 40. 11. *gently* lead those with young
GIFT, 1 Cor. 1. 7. & 7. 7.
Ex. 23. 8. take no *g.* for a *g.* blindeth the wise, Deut. 16. 19.
Prov. 17. 8. *g.* is a precious stone
18. 16. a man's *g.* maketh room for him
21. 14. a *g.* in secret pacifieth anger
Eccl. 7. 7. a *g.* destroyeth the heart
Matt. 5. 24. leave there thy *g.*

John 4. 10. if thou knewest *g.* of God
Rom. 6. 23. *g.* of God is eternal life
Eph. 2. 8. through faith it is the *g.* of
Phil. 4. 17. not because I desire a *g.*
1 Tim. 4. 14. neglect not the *g.* that
2 Tim. 1. 6. stir up *g.* of God which is in thee
Heb. 6. 4. tasted of heavenly *g.*
James 1. 17. every good and perfect *g.*
Ps. 68. 18. received *gifts* for men
Rom. 11. 29. for *g.* and calling of God
GIRD with strength, Ps. 18. 32.
Ps. 30. 11. *g.* me with gladness
Luke 12. 35. let your loins be *girded*, 1 Pet. 1. 13.
Eph. 6. 14. having your loins *g.* with
Isa. 11. 5. *girdle*, Matt. 3. 4. Rev. 1. 13.
GIVE, Gen. 12. 7. & 30. 31.
1 Kings 3. 5. ask what I shall *g.* thee
Ps. 2. 8. I shall *g.* thee the heathen
29. 11. Lord will *g.* strength to his
37. 4. *g.* thee desires of thy heart
84. 11. Lord will *g.* grace and glory
109. 4. I *g.* myself to prayer
104. 27. mayest *g.* them their meat
Jer. 17. 10. to *g.* every man according to his works, 32. 19.
Hos. 11. 8. how shall I *g.* thee up
Luke 6. 38. *g.* and it shall be given
John 10. 28. I *g.* to them eternal life
Acts 3. 6. such as I have *g.* I unto thee
20. 35. more blessed to *g.* than to receive
Rom. 8. 32. freely *g.* us all things
Eph. 4. 28. that he may have to *g.* to him that needeth
1 Tim. 4. 15. *g.* thyself wholly to them that thy profiting may appear to all
2 Sam. 22. 50. *give thanks*, 1 Chron. 16. 8. Neh. 12. 24. Ps. 35. 18.
Ps. 6. 5. in grave who shall—to thee
30. 4.—at the remembrance of his holiness, 97. 12.
119. 62. at midnight I will rise to—
Eph. 1. 16. cease not to—1 Thes. 1. 2. 2 Thes. 2. 13. Col. 1. 3.
1 Thes. 5. 18. in everything—
Matt. 13. 12. to him shall be *given*
11. it is *g.* to you to know the mysteries
Luke 12. 48. to whom much is *g.*
John 6. 39. of all which he hath *g.*
65. can come to me except it be *g.*
19. 11. except it were *g.* thee from
Rom. 11. 35. hath first *g.* to him
1 Cor 2. 12. known things freely *g.*
2 Cor. 9. 7. God loves the cheerful *giver*
Ps. 37. 21. shows mercy and *giveth*
Prov. 28. 27. he that *g.* to poor shall
Isa. 40. 20. *g.* power to the faint
42. 5. *g.* breath to people on earth
1 Tim. 6. 17. *g.* us richly all things
James 1. 5. *g.* to all men liberally
4. 6. he *g.* more grace to the humble
1 Pet. 4. 11. of the ability that God *g.*
GLAD, my heart is, Ps. 16. 9.
Ps. 31. 7. I will be *g.* and rejoice in
64. 10. righteous shall be *g.* in Lord
104. 34. I will be *g.* in the Lord
122. 1. I was *g.* when they said
Luke 1. 19. *glad tidings*
Mark 6. 20. heard him *gladly*
Luke 8. 40. people *g.* received him
Acts 2. 41. that *g.* received his word
2 Cor. 12. 15. I will very *g.* spend
Ps. 4. 7. put *gladness* in my heart
30. 11. hast girded me with *g.*
45. 7. anointed with oil of *g.*
51. 8. make me to hear joy and *g.*
Ps. 97. 11. *g.* sown for the upright in heart
100. 2. serve the Lord with *g.*
106. 5. rejoice in *g.* of thy nation
Isa. 35. 10. shall obtain joy and *g.*

51. 3. joy and *g.* shall be found in it
Acts 2. 46. eat their meat with *g.*
14. 17. filling their hearts with food and *g.*
GLASS, 1 Cor. 13. 12.
2 Cor. 3. 18. beholding as in a *g.*
James 1. 23. behold natural face in *g.*
Rev. 4. 6. a sea of *g.* 15. 2.
21. 18. city was pure gold like clear *g.*
GLOOMINESS, Joel 2. 2.
GLORY, Gen. 31. 1. Ps. 49. 16.
1 Sam. 4. 21. *g.* is departed from Israel
1 Chron. 29. 11. thine the power and the *g.* Matt. 6. 13.
Ps. 8. 5. crowned with *g.*
73. 24. afterward receive me to *g.*
89. 17. thou art the *g.* of their strength
145. 11. speak of the *g.* of thy kingdom
Prov. 3. 35. the wise shall inherit *g.*
16. 31. hoary head is a crown of *g.*
20. 29. *g.* of young men is their strength
25. 27. to search their own *g.* is not *g.*
Isa. 4. 5. upon all the *g.* shall be a defence
23. 9. Lord purposed it, to stain pride of all *g.*
24. 16. heard songs, even *g.* to the
28. 5. Lord shall be for a crown of *g.*
Jer. 2. 11. changed their *g.*
Ezek. 20. 6. the *g.* of all lands
Hos. 4. 7. change their *g.* into shame
Hag. 2. 7. I will fill this house with *g.*
9. *g.* of this latter house shall be greater
Zech. 2. 5. be the *g.* in the midst, 8. after the *g.* sent me
6. 13. build temple and shall bear the *g.*
Matt. 6. 2. may have *g.* of men
16. 27. come in *g.* of his Father
Luke 2. 14. to God in the highest
32. light of the Gentiles, *g.* of thy people
John 1. 14. his *g.* the *g.* of the only begotten Son
17. 5. *glorify* me with the *g.* I had
22. *g.* which thou gavest I have
Rom. 2. 7. seek for *g.* and honour
11. 36. to whom be *g.* for ever, 2 Tim. 4. 18. Heb. 13. 21.
16. 27. in God be *g.* through Christ
1 Cor. 11. 7. man is *g.* of God, woman is *g.* of man
15. 43. in dishonour, it is raised in *g.*
2 Cor. 3. 18. changed from *g.* to *g.*
4. 17. exceeding and eternal weight of *g.*
Eph. 1. 6. praise of *g.* of his grace
3. 21. to him be *g.* in the church
13. my tribulation for you is *g.*
Phil. 3. 19. whose *g.* is in their shame
Col. 1. 27. Christ in you hope of *g.*
3. 4. appear with him in *g.*
1 Thess. 2. 12. hath called you to *g.*
20. ye are our *g.* and joy, 19.
1 Tim. 3. 16. received up into *g.*
1 Pet. 1. 8. joy unspeakable, full of *g.*
11. the suffering of Christ and *g.* that should follow, 21.
4. 13. his *g.* be revealed, 14. spirit of *g.*
5. 1. partaker of *g.* to be revealed
4. ye shall receive a crown of *g.*
10. called to eternal *g.* by Christ Jesus
2 Pet. 1. 3. called us to *g.* and virtue
17. came a voice from the excellent *g.*
Rev. 4. 11. worthy to receive *g.* Rom. 16. 27. 1 Tim. 1. 17.

Josh. 7. 19. *give glory* to the God of Israel, 1 Sam. 6. 5. 1 Chron. 16. 29.
Ps. 19. 1. *glory of God.* Prov. 25. 2. Acts 7. 55. Rom. 3. 23. 1 Cor. 10. 31. 2 Cor. 4. 6. Rev. 21. 11.
Ex. 16. 7. *glory of the Lord*, Num. 14. 21.
1 Kings 8. 11. Ps. 104. 31. Isa. 35. 2. Ezek. 1. 28. Luke 2. 9. 2 Cor. 3. 18.
Ps. 29. 9. *his glory*, 49. 17. Prov. 19. 11. Isa. 6. 3. Hab. 3. 3. Matt. 6. 29.
John 2. 11. Rom. 9. 23. Eph. 1. 12.
Job 29. 20. *my glory*, Ps. 16. 9. Isa. 42. 8. John 8. 50.
Ex. 33. 18. *thy glory*, Ps. 8. 1. Isa. 60. 19. & 63. 15. Jer. 14. 21.
Ps. 64. 10. upright in heart shall *g.*
106. 5. I may *g.* with thy inheritance
Isa. 41. 16. shalt *g.* in Holy One of Israel
45. 25. seed of Israel be justified, and *g.*
Jer. 9. 24. him that *glorieth g.* in this
Rom. 4. 2. hath *g.* but not before God
5. 3. we *g.* in tribulation
1 Cor. 1. 31. that *glorieth g.* in the Lord
3. 21. let no man *g.* in men
2 Cor. 5. 12. to *g.* on our behalf— them which *g.* in appearance
11. 18. many *g.* after the flesh
12. 1. it is not expedient for me to *g.*
9. will I rather *g.* in my infirmities
Gal. 6. 14. God forbid I should *g.* save
Isa. 25. 5. strong people shall *glorify* thee
60. 7. I will *g.* house of my glory
Matt. 5. 16. *g.* your Father in heaven
John 12. 23. Father *g.* thy name
17. 1. *g.* thy Son
21. 9. by what death he should *g.* God
1 Cor. 6. 20. *g.* God in your body and
1 Pet. 2. 12. *g.* God in day of visitation
Rev. 15. 4. who shall not fear thee and *g.*
Lev. 10. 3. before all I will be *glorified*
Ps. 50. 23. whoso *offereth* praise *g.*
Matt. 9. 8. they *g.* God, 15. 31.
John 7. 39. Jesus was not yet *g.*
15. 8. herein is my Father *g.*
17. 10. all mine are thine, I am *g.*
Acts 3. 13. God of our fathers hath *g.* his
4. 21. all men *g.* God for that was done
Rom. 1. 21. they *g.* him not as God
8. 30. whom he justified, them he *g.*
Gal. 1. 24. they *g.* God in me
2 Thess. 1. 10. come to be *g.* in his saints
3. 1. word of Lord have free course and be *g.*
Heb. 5. 5. even Christ *g.* not himself
1 Pet. 4. 11. God in all things may be *g.*
14. on your part he is *g.*
Rev. 18. 7. how much she hath *g.* herself
1 Cor. 5. 6. *glorifying*, 9. 15.
Ex. 15. 6. *glorifying* in power
11. who is like thee, *g.* in holiness
Deut. 28. 58. fear this *g.* and fearful Lord
1 Chron. 29. 13. praise thy *g.* name
Ps. 45. 13. king's daughter all *g.*
66. 2. make his praise *g.*
72. 19. blessed be his *g.* name
76. 4. art more *g.* and excellent
87. 3. *g.* things spoken of the city of God
111. 3. his work is honourable and *g.*
145. 5. speak of *g.* honour of thy
12. make known his *g.* majesty

Isa. 4. 2. branch of Lord shall be *g.*
11. 10. his rest shall be *g.*
22. 23. be for a *g.* throne to his father's house
30. 30. cause his *g.* voice to be heard
33. 21. *g.* Lord will be to us a place
49. 5. yet shall I be *g.* in eyes of the Lord
60. 13. make the place of my feet be *g.*
63. 1. who is this *g.* in his apparel
12. his *g.* arm, 14. a *g.* name
Jer. 17. 12. a *g.* high throne from the begonning
Rom. 8. 21. *g.* liberty of children of God
2 Cor. 3. 7. ministration was *g.*
4. 4. light of *g.* Gospel should shine
Eph. 5. 27. present to himself a *g.* church
Phil. 3. 21. vile body like his *g.* body
Col. 1. 11. according to his *g.* power
1 Tim. 1. 11. according to *g.* Gospel of blessed
Tit. 2. 13. looking for *g.* appearance
Ex. 15. 1. *gloriously,* Isa. 24. 23.
GLUTTON, Deut. 21. 20.
Matt. 11. 19. *gluttonous*
GNASH, Job 16. 9. Ps. 35. 16.
Matt. 8. 12. *gnashing of teeth,* 13. 42, 50.
GNAT, Matt. 23. 24.
GNAW, Zeph. 3. 3. Rev. 16. 10.
GO, Judg. 6. 14. 1 Sam. 12. 21. Matt. 8. 9. Luke 10. 37. John 6. 68.
Job 10. 21. *I go,* Ps. 39. 13. Matt. 21. 30. John 7. 33.
Ex. 4. 23. *let my people go,* 5. 1.
Gen. 32. 26. *not let go,* Ex. 3. 19. Job 27. 6. Song 3. 4.
Ex. 23. 23. *shall go,* 32. 34.
1 Sam. 12. 21. *should go*
Judg. 11. 35. *go back,* Ps. 80. 18.
Num. 22. 18. *go beyond*
Gen. 45. 1. *go out,* Ps. 60. 10. Jer. 51. 45. Ezek. 46. 9. Matt. 25. 6. John 10. 9. 1. Cor. 5. 10.
Deut. 4. 40. *go well* with thee 5. 16. & 19. 13. Prov. 11. 10.
Job 34. 21. seeth all his *goings*
Ps. 17. 5. hold up my *g.* in thy way
40. 2. set my feet and established my *g.*
68. 24. seen thy *g.* O God in sanctuary
121. 8. Lord preserve thy *g.* out
Prov. 5. 21. he pondereth all his *g.*
20. 24. man's *g.* are of the Lord
Mic. 5. 2. whose *g.* are of old, from
GOAT, Lev. 3. 12. & 16. 8.
Isa. 1. 11. I delight not in blood of *goats*
Ezek. 34. 17. judge between rams and *g.*
Dan. 8. 5. he *g.* 8. rough *g.* 21.
Zech. 10. 3. I punished the *g.*
Matt. 25. 32, 33. set the *g.* on his left hand
Heb. 9. 12. blood of *g.* 13. 19.
GOD, and *gods* for *men* representing God, Ex. 4. 16. Ps. 82 1, 6.
John 10. 34. for *idols* which are put in God's place, Deut. 32. 21. Judg. 6. 31. and 140 other places, for devil, god of this world, 2 Cor. 4. 4. and for the true God about 3120 times
Gen. 17. 1. I am almighty *G.* Job 36. 5. Isa. 9. 6. Jer. 32. 18.
Gen. 17. 7. to be a *G.* to thee and thy seed, Ex. 6. 7, 21, 33. everlasting *G,* Ps. 90. 2. Isa. 40. 28.
Ex. 8. 10. none like Lord our *G.* 1 Kings 8. 23. Ps. 35. 10. & 86. 8.
18. 11. Lord is greater than all *gods*
Deut. 10. 17. *G.* of gods, Josh. 22. 22. Dan. 2. 47. Ps. 136. 2.
Deut. 32. 39. there is no *g.* with me, 1 King 8. 23. 2 Kings 5. 15. 2 Chron. 6. 14. Isa. 43. 10.
Job 32. 12. *G.* is greater than man
Ps. 18. 31. who is *G.* save the

Dan. 9. 4. great and dreadful *G.*
Mic. 7. 18. who is a *G.* like to thee
Matt. 6. 24. ye cannot serve *G.* and mammon
19. 17. none good but one, that is *G.*
Mark 12. 27. not the *G.* of dead, but of the living
35. there is one *G.* and none other
John 17. 3. the only true *G.*
Acts 7. 2. *G.* of glory appeared to Abraham
Rom. 3. 4. let *G.* be true, and every man a liar
8. 31. if *G.* be for us, who can be against us
9. 5. over all *G.* blessed for ever
15. 5. *G.* of patience, 13. *G.* of hope
1 Cor. 15. 28. that *G.* may be all in all
2 Cor. 1. 3. *G.* of all comfort
2 Thess. 2. 4. above all that is called *G.* Dan. 11. 36.
1 Tim. 3. 16. *G.* manifest in flesh
Heb. 8. 10. I will be to them a *G.*
1 Pet. 5. 10. *G.* of all grace, when
1 John 4. 12. no man seen *G.* John 1. 18.
Deut. 10. 17. *great* God, 2 Sam. 7. 22. 2 Chron. 2. 5. Job 36. 26. Neh. 1. 5. Prov. 26. 10. Jer. 32. 18. Dan. 9. 4. Tit. 2. 13. Rev. 19. 17.
Deut. 5. 26. *living God,* Josh. 3. 10. 1 Sam. 17. 26, 36. 2 Kings 19. 4, 16. and twenty-two other places
Ex. 34. 6. *God merciful,* Deut. 4. 31. 2 Chron. 30. 9. Neh. 9. 31. Ps. 116. 5. Jonah 4. 2.
Gen. 49. 24. *mighty God.* Deut. 7. 21. Neh. 9. 32. Job 36. 5. Ps. 50. 1. Isa. 9. 6. Jer. 32. 18. Hab. 1. 12.
2 Chron. 15. 3. *true God.* Jer. 10. 10. John 17. 3. 1 Thess. 1. 9. 1 John 5. 20.
Gen. 39. 9. do this wickedness and sin *against* God, Num. 21. 5. Ps. 78. 19. Hos. 13. 16. Acts 5. 39. Rom. 8. 7.
Ps. 42. 2. *before* God, 56. 13. Eccl. 2. 26. Luke 1. 6. Rom. 2. 13. 1 Tim. 5. 21. James 1. 27. Rev. 3. 2.
John 9. 16. *of* God, Acts 5. 39. Rom. 9. 16. 1 Cor. 1. 30. 2 Cor. 3. 5. Phil. 1. 28. 1 John, 3. 10. 3 John 11.
Ex. 2. 23. *to* God, Ps. 43. 4. Eccl. 12. 7. Isa. 58. 2. Lam. 3. 41. John 13. 3. Heb. 7. 25. 1 Pet. 3. 18.
Gen. 5. 22. *with* God, Ex. 19. 7. 1 Sam. 14. 45. 2 Sam. 23. 5. Job 9. 2. Ps. 78. 8. Hos. 11. 12. John 5. 18.
Gen. 28. 21. *my* God, Ex. 15. 2. Ps. 22. 1. & 31. 14. Hos. 2. 23. Zech. 13. 9. John 20. 17, 28 and about 120 other places
Ex. 5. 8. *our* God, Deut. 31. 17. Josh. 24. 18. 2 Sam. 22. 32. Ps. 67. 6. and 180 other places
Ex. 20. 2. *thy* God, 5, 7. Ps. 50. 7. and about 340 other places
Ex. 6. 7. *your* God, Lev. 11. 44. & 19. 2, 3, 4. and 140 other places
Ex. 32. 11. *his* God, Lev. 4. 22. and about 60 other places
Gen. 17. 8. *their* God, Ex. 29. 45. Jer. 24. 7. Ezek. 11. 20. Zech. 8. 8. 2 Cor. 6. 16. Rev. 21. 3. and 50 other places
2 Chron. 36. 23. *God of heaven,* Ezra 5. 11. Neh. 1. 4. Ps. 136. 26. Dan. 2, 18, 19, 44. Jonah 1. 9. Rev. 11. 13.
Ex. 24. 10. *God of Israel,* Num. 16. 9. Josh. 7. 19. Judg. 11. 23. Ruth 2. 12. Isa. 41. 17. Jer. 31. 1. Ezek. 8. 4. Matt. 15. 31.
Rom. 15. 33. *God of peace,* 16. 20. 2 Cor. 13. 11. 1 Thess. 5. 23. Heb. 13. 20.
Ps. 24. 5. *God of his salvation, of our salvation,* 65. 5.
Acts 17. 29. *Godhead,* Rom. 1. 20.
GODLY, Ps. 4. 3. & 12. 1. & 32. 6. Mal. 2. 15. 2 Pet. 2. 9. 3 John 6.

2 Cor. 1. 12. in *g.* sincerity, had our conversation
7. 9. sorrow after a *g.* manner
Tit. 2. 12. live soberly, righteously, and *g.*
Heb. 12. 28. serve God acceptably with *g.* fear
1 Tim. 2. 2. quiet life in all *godliness*
4. 7. exercise thyself to *g.*
8. *g.* is profitable to all things
6. 3. doctrine according to *g.*
6. *g.* with contentment is great gain
2 Tim. 3. 5. having a form of *g.* but
2 Pet. 1. 3. all that pertain to life and *g.* 6. add to patience *g.* 7. to *g.* brotherly kindness
3. 11. what persons ought ye to be in all *g.*
GOLD, Gen. 2. 11. Isa. 2. 7.
Job 23. 10. I shall come forth like *g.*
31. 24. if I made *g.* my hope or fine *g.*
Ps. 19. 10. more desired than *g.* yea than fine *g.*
119. 127. love thy commandments above *g.* yea fine *g.* 72.
Prov. 8. 19. my fruit is better than *g.* or fine *g.*
Isa. 13. 12. man more precious than fine *g.*
Zech. 13. 9. I will try them as *g.* is
1 Cor. 3. 12. if any man build on this foundation, *g.* silver, wood
1 Tim. 2. 9. women adorn themselves in modest apparel, not with *g.*
1 Pet. 1. 7. trial of faith more precious than *g.*
Rev. 3. 18. buy of me *g.* tried in fire
GOOD, Deut. 6. 24.
Gen. 1. 31. everything he had made was very *g.*
2. 18. it is not *g.* for man to be alone
32. 12. thou saidst I will surely do thee *g.*
50. 20. God meant it unto *g.*
2 Kings 20. 19. *g.* is the word of the Lord, Isa. 39. 8.
Ps. 34. 8. taste and see that Lord is *g.*
73. 1. truly God is *g.* to Israel
85. 12. Lord will give what is *g.*
86. 5. thou, Lord, art *g.* ready to forgive
106. 5. I may see *g.* of thy chosen
145. 9. Lord is *g.* to all, 136. 1.
Lam. 3. 25. Lord is *g.* to them that wait for him
Mic. 6. 8. he hath showed thee what is *g.*
Matt. 19. 17. why call me *g.* none is *g.* but God
Rom. 3. 8. do evil that *g.* may come
7. 18. how to perform that which is *g.* I find not
1 Thess. 5. 15. follow that which is *g.* 3. John 11.
Neh. 2. 18. hand for this *good work*
Matt. 26. 10. wrought a—on me
John 10. 33. for a—we stone thee not
2 Cor. 9. 8. abound to every—
Phil. 1. 6. begun a—will finish it
Col. 1. 10. fruitful in every—
2 Thess. 2. 17. establish you in every—
1 Tim. 5. 10. followed every—
2 Tim. 2. 21. prepared to—Tit. 3. 1.
Tit. 1. 16. to every—reprobate
Heb. 13. 21. perfect in every—
Matt. 5. 16. may see your *good works*
John 10. 32. many—have I showed you
Acts 9. 36. Dorcas was full of—
Rom. 13. 3. not a terror to—
Eph. 2. 10. created in Christ Jesus to—
1 Tim. 2. 10. professing godliness with—
5. 10. reported of for—
25. the—of some are manifest
Tit. 3. 8. be careful to maintain—14.

Heb. 10. 24. provoke to love and—
1 Pet. 2. 12. may by your—which
Ex. 33. 19. make my *goodness* pass
34. 6. Lord God abundant in *g.* and truth
2 Chron. 6. 41. let saints rejoice in *g.*
Neh. 9. 25. delight themselves in thy great *g.*
35. not served thee in thy great *g.*
Ps. 16. 2. my *g.* extendeth not to
23. 6. *g.* and mercy shall follow me
27. 13. believed to see *g.* of Lord
31. 19. how great is thy *g.*
35. earth is full of *g.* of the Lord
52. 1. *g.* of God endureth continually
65. 4. satisfied with the *g.* of thy house
11. crownest the year with thy *g.*
Isa. 63. 7. great *g.* bestowed on Israel
Hos. 3. 5. fear the Lord and his *g.*
Rom. 2. 4. *g.* of God leadeth to repentance
11. 22. behold the *g.* and severity of God
Eph. 5. 9. fruit of Spirit in all *g.*
GOSPEL, Mark 1. 1, 15.
Matt. 4. 23. preaching *g.* of kingdom
Mark 16. 15. preach the *g.* to every creature
Acts 20. 24. *g.* of the grace of God
Rom. 1. 1. *g.* of God, 15. 16.
1 Cor. 1. 17. but to preach the *g.*
4. 15. I have begotten you through the *g.*
9. 14. that preach the *g.* should live by the *g.*
2 Cor. 4. 3. if our *g.* be hid, 4. glorious *g.*
11. 4. another *g.* which ye
Gal. 1. 8. preach any other *g.* 9.
Eph, 1, 13, *g.* of salvation
Phil. 1. 27. as it becometh the *g.* faith of *g.*
Col. 1. 5. truth of *g.* Gal. 2. 5.
23. hope of *g.* Phil. 1. 5. fellowship in *g.*
1 Thess. 1. 5. our *g.* came in power
Heb. 4. 2. unto us was *g.* preached
1 Pet. 4. 6. *g.* was preached to dead
Rev. 14. 6. having everlasting *g.* to preach
GOVERNMENT, Isa. 9. 6, 7. & 22. 21. 1 Cor. 12. 28. 2 Pet. 2. 10.
GRACE, Ezra. 9. 8.
Ps. 84. 11. Lord will give *g.* and glory
Prov. 3. 34. gives *g.* to lowly
Zech. 4. 7. with shoutings, crying *g. g.* to it
12. 10. spirit of *g.* and supplications
John 1. 14. of Father full of *g.* and
16. of fulness we receive *g.* for *g.*
17. *g.* and truth came by Jesus Christ
Acts 18. 27. helped them, believed through *g.*
Rom. 3. 24. justified freely by his *g.*
5. 20. *g.* did much more abound
21. *g.* reigned through righteousness to eternal life
6. 14. not under law, but under *g.*
11. 15. according to the election of *g.*
6. if by *g.* then not of works, otherwise *g.* is no more *g.*
2 Cor. 12. 9. my *g.* is sufficient for thee
Eph. 2. 5. by *g.* ye are saved, 8.
7. show exceeding riches of his *g.*
4. 29. minister *g.* to hearers
Tit. 3. 7. justified by his *g.*
Heb. 4. 16. come boldly to the throne of *g.*
12. 18. let us have *g.* whereby we may serve God
13. 9. heart be established with *g.*
1 Pet. 3. 7. heirs of the *g.* of life
5. 5. and giveth *g.* to the humble
2 Pet. 3. 28. grow in *g.* and in knowledge
Rom. 1. 7. *grace and peace* to you, 1 Cor. 1. 3. 2 Cor. 1. 2. Gal. 1. 3.

Phil. 1. 2. Col. 1. 2. 1 Thess. 1. 1. 2 Thess. 1. 2. Philem. 3.
Luke 2. 40. *grace of God*, Acts 11. 23.
Rom. 5. 15. 1 Cor. 1. 4. Eph. 3. 2, 7. 3 Cor. 1. 12. by—we have had our conversation
6. 1. receive not—in vain
8. 1. of—bestowed on churches
9. 14. for the exceeding—in you
Gal. 2. 21. I do not frustrate—
Col. 1. 6. knew—in truth
1 Pet. 4. 10. stewards of manifold—
5. 12. this the true—wherein ye stand
Jude 4. turning—into lasciviousness
Acts 15. 11. *grace of our Lord Jesus Christ*, Rom. 16. 20. 1 Cor. 16. 23. 2 Cor. 8. 9. Gal. 6. 18. Phil. 4. 23. 2 Thes. 3. 8. Philem. 25.
Rev. 21. 21.—be with you all
Gen. 43. 29. God be *gracious* to thee
Ex. 22. 27. I will hear for I am *g.*
19. I will be *g.* to whom I will be *g.*
34. 6. Lord God merciful and *g.*
3 Chron. 30. 9. Neh. 9. 17. Ps. 103. 8. Joel 2. 13.
Num. 6. 25. the Lord be *g.* to thee, 2 Sam. 12. 22.
Job. 33. 24. then he is *g.* to him
Ps. 77. 9. hath God forgotten to be *g.*
86. 15. full of compassion and *g.*
Isa. 30. 18. Lord wait that he may be *g.*
19. he will be very *g.* to thee
Amos 5. 15. may be, the Lord will be *g.*
Jonah 4. 2. knew that thou art a *g.* God
Mal. 1. 9. beseech God to be *g.*
1 Pet. 2. 3. if ye have tasted that the Lord is *g.*
Gen. 33. 5. *graciously,* 11. Ps. 119. 29. Hos. 14. 2. receive us *g.*
GRAFTED, Rom. 11. 17.
GRANT, Job 10. 12. Ps. 140. 8. Prov. 10. 24. Rom. 15. 5. Eph. 3. 16. 2 Tim. 1. 18. Rev. 3. 21.
GRAPES, of gall, Deut. 32. 32.
Song 2. 13. the tender *g.*
Isa. 5. 4. wild *g.* Ezek. 18. 2. sour *g.*
Mic. 7. 1. soul desireth first ripe *g.*
GRASS, Ps. 37. 2. Isa. 44. 4.
Ps. 103. 15. man's days are like *g.*
Isa. 40. 6. all flesh is *g.* 7. 8. 1 Pet. 1. 24. James 1. 10, 11.
Matt. 6. 30. if God so clothe the *g.*
Rev. 8. 7. green *g.* 9. 4. not hurt *g.*
GRAVE, 1 Kings 2. 9.
1 Sam. 2. 6. Lord brings down to *g.*
Job 5. 26. come to thy *g.* in full age
14. 13. hide me in the *g.*
Ps. 6. 5. in *g.* who shall give thanks
30. 3. Lord brought up my soul from the *g.*
Prov. 1. 12. swallow them up alive, as the *g.*
Eccl. 9. 10. no wisdom in *g.* whither thou goest
Isa. 38. 18. *g.* cannot praise the
Hos. 13. 14. the power of the *g.* O *g.* I will be thy destruction
1 Cor. 15. 55. O *g.* where is thy victory
Zech. 3. 9. I will *engrave* the graving
Job 19. 24. *graven* with an iron pen
Isa. 49. 16. I have *g.* thee upon palms of
Jer. 17. 1 sin *g.* upon table of their heart
1 Tim. 3. 4, 8, 11. *grave*
GRAY, Ps. 71. 18. Prov. 20. 29.
GREAT, Gen. 12. 2.
Deut. 29. 24. *g.* anger, 2 Chron. 34. 21.
1 Sam. 6. 9. *great evil,* Neh. 13. 27. Eccl. 2. 21. Jer. 44. 7. Dan. 9. 12.
Ps. 47. 2. *great king,* 48. 2. & 95. 3. Mal. 1. 14. Matt. 5. 35.
Job 32. 9. *great men,* Jer. 5. 5.
Ex. 32. 11. *great power,* Neh. 1. 10.
Job 23. 6. Ps. 147. 5. Nah. 1. 3. Acts 4. 33. & 8. 10. Rev. 11. 17.

Ex. 32. 21. *so great,* Deut. 4. 7. 1 Kings 3. 9. Ps. 77. 13. Matt. 8. 10.
2 Cor. 1. 10. Heb. 2. 3. Rev. 16. 18.
Job 5. 9. *great things,* 9. 10. Jer. 45. 5. Hos. 8. 12. Luke 1. 49.
Gen. 6. 5. *great wickedness,* 39. 9. Job 22. 5. Joel 3. 13. 2 Chron. 28. 13.
Job 33. 12. God is *greater* than man
Matt. 12. 42. *g.* than Solomon is here
John 1. 50. see *g.* things than these
4. 12. art thou *g.* than, 8. 53
10. 29. my Father is *g.* than all
14. 28. my Father is *g.* than I
1 Cor. 14. 5. *g.* is he that prophesieth
1 John 4. 4. *g. is* he that is in you, 3. 20.
5. 9. witness of God is *g.*
1 Sam. 30. 6. David was *greatly* distressed
2 Sam. 24. 10. I have sinned *g.* in that I have done
1 Kings 8. 3. Obadiah feared the Lord *g.*
1 Chron. 16. 25. great is the Lord and *g.* to be praised, Ps. 48. 1.
2 Chron. 33. 12. humbled himself *g.* before God
Job. 3. 25. thing I *g.* feared is come
Ps. 28. 7. my heart *g.* rejoiceth
47. 9. God is *g.* exalted
89. 7. God is *g.* to be feared in the assembly
116. 10. have I spoken; I was *g.* afflicted
Dan. 90. 23. O man, *g.* beloved
Mark 12. 27. ye do *g.* err
Ex. 15. 7. *greatness* of thy excellency
Num. 14. 19. pardon according to *g.* of mercy
Deut. 32. 3. ascribe ye *g.* to our God
1 Chron. 29. 11. thine is the *g.*
Neh. 13. 22. spare according to the *g.* of thy mercy
Ps. 66. 3. *g.* of thy power, 79. 11. Eph. 1. 19.
145. 3. his *g.* is unsearchable, 6.
Isa. 63. 1. travelling in the *g.* of his strength
GREEDY of gain, Prov. 1. 19.
Isa. 56. 11. they are *g.* dogs, never
1 Tim. 3. 3. not *g.* of filthy lucre, 8.
Eph. 4. 19. work uncleanness with *greediness*
GRIEF, Isa. 53. 3, 4, 10. Heb. 13. 17.
Gen. 6. 6. *grieved* him at his heart
Judg. 10. 16. his soul was *g.* for misery
Ps. 95. 10. forty years long was I *g.*
119. 158. I beheld transgressors and was *g.* 139. 21.
Isa. 54. 6. woman forsaken and *g.*
Jer. 5. 3. hast stricken them, they have not *g.*
Lam. 3. 33. nor *g.* children of men
Amos 6. 6. not *g.* for the affliction of Joseph
Mark 3. 5. being *g.* for hardness of heart
10. 22. went away *g.* for he had great possessions
Rom. 14. 15. if brother be *g.* at thy meat
Ps. 10. 5. his ways are always *grievous*
Matt. 23. 4. burdens *g.* to be borne
Acts 20. 29. shall *g.* wolves enter
Heb. 12, 11. no chastening is joyous but *g.*
1 John 5. 3. his commandments are not *g.*
Matt. 8. 6. *grievously* tormented
GRIND, Isa. 3. 15.
Matt. 21. 44. it will *g.* him to powder
Eccl. 12. 3. *grinders* cease because
GROAN earnestly, 2 Cor. 5. 2.
John 11. 33. Jesus *groaned* in spirit
Rom. 8. 22. whole creation *groaneth*
Ps. 6. 6. weary with my *groaning*
38. 9. my *g.* is not hid from thee
102. 20. to hear the *g.* of prisoners
Rom. 8. 26. *g.* that cannot be uttered

GROUNDED, or *correcting* staff Isa. 30. 32.
Eph. 3. 17. rooted and *g.* in love
Col. 1. 23. if continue in the faith *g.*
GROW, Gen. 48. 16. 2 Sam. 23. 5.
Ps. 92. 12. like cedar in Lebanon
Hos. 14. 5. shall *g.* as a lily, 7. *g.* as a vine
Mal. 4. 2. shall *g.* up as calves of the
Eph. 2. 21. *g.* unto a holy temple
4. 15. may *g.* up into him in all things
1 Pet. 2. 2. sincere milk that ye may *g.*
2 Pet. 3. 18. *g.* in grace and knowledge
GRUDGE, Lev. 19. 18.
1 Pet. 4. 9. *grudging,* 2 Cor. 9. 7.
GUIDE unto death, Ps. 48. 14.
Ps. 73. 24. shall *g.* me with thy counsel
112. 5. *g.* his affairs with discretion
Prov. 2. 17. forsaketh the *g.* of her youth
Isa. 58. 11. Lord shall *g.* thee continually
Jer. 3. 4. my Father thou art *g.* of
Luke 1. 79. *g.* our feet into way of
John 16. 13. *g.* you into all truth
1 Tim. 5. 14. bear children, *g.* house
GUILE, Ex. 21. 14. Ps. 55. 11. 2 Cor. 12. 16. 1 Thess. 2. 3.
Ps. 32. 2. in whose spirit is no *g.*
24. 13. keep thy lips from *g.*
John 1. 47. Israelite in whom is no *g.*
1 Pet. 2. 1. laying aside all malice and *g.*
22. neither was *g.* found in mouth
GUILTY, Lev. 4. 13.
Ex. 34. 7. by no means clear the *g.*
Num. 14. 18. Gen. 42. 21.
Rom. 3. 19. all world *g.* before God
1 Cor. 11. 27. *g.* of body and blood of Lord
James 2. 10. offend in one point, is *g.* of all
Ex. 20. 7. not hold him *guiltless*
GULF, fixed, Luke 16. 26.

H

HABITABLE part, Prov. 8. 31.
HABITATION, 2 Chron. 6. 2.
Deut. 26. 15. look down from thy holy *h.* Ps. 68. 5. Jer. 25. 30.
Ps. 26. 8. have loved the *h.* of thy house
71. 3. be thou my strong *h.* whereunto
74. 20. earth full of *h.* of cruelty
89. 14. here are *h.* of thy throne, 97. 2.
91. 9. has made Most High thy *h.*
107. 7. led them forth to city of *h.*
Prov. 3. 33. he blesseth *h.* of the just
Isa. 33. 20. see Jerusalem a quiet *h.*
63. 15. behold from *h.* of thy holiness
Jer. 31. 23. the Lord blessed thee, O *h.* of justice
Luke 16. 9. receive into everlasting *h.*
Eph. 2. 22. a *h.* of God through the Spirit
Jude 6. angels which left their own *h.*
Rev. 18. 2. Babylon is become *h.* of
HAIL, Isa. 28. 2. Rev. 8. 7.
HAIR, Job 4. 15. Song 4. 1.
Ps. 40. 12. more than the *h.* of my head, 69. 4.
Hos. 7. 9. gray *h.* are here and there
Matt. 5. 36. make one *h.* white or
10. 30. of your head are numbered, Luke 12. 7.
1 Cor. 11. 14. if man have long *h.*
1 Tim. 2. 9. not with broidered *h.*
1 Pet. 3. 3. not of plaiting the *h.*
HALT, 1 Kings 18. 21.
Jer. 20. 10. watched for thy *halting*

HAND, Gen. 3. 22. & 16. 12.
Deut. 33. 3. all his saints are in thy *h.*
Ezra 7. 9. good *h.* of his God upon him
8. 22. *h.* of our God is upon them
Job. 12. 6. into those *h.* God bringeth abundantly
Prov. 10. 4. *h.* of diligent maketh rich
Prov. 11. 21, though *h.* join in *h.*
12. 24. the *h.* of diligent shall bear
Isa. 1. 12. who required this at your *h.*
Matt. 22. 13. bind him *h.* and foot
John 13. 3. given all things into his *h.*
1 Pet. 5. 6. humble yourselves under the mighty *h.* of God
Num. 11. 23. *Lord's hand* waxed short
2 Sam. 24. 14. let us fall into—not man
Job. 2. 10. received good at—and not evil
12. 9.—hath wrought this, Isa. 41. 20.
19. 21. pity, for the—hath touched me
Isa. 40. 2. received of the—double
59. 1.—is not shortened that cannot
Ps. 16. 8. he is at my *right hand,* I shall not
11. at thy—are pleasures for evermore
18. 35. thy—hath holden me up
48. 10. thy—is full of righteousness
73. 23. hast holden me by my—
110. 5. Lord at thy—shall strike through kings
137. 5. let my—forget her cunning
139. 10. thy *h.* head and thy—hold
Prov. 3. 16. length of days in her—
Eccl. 10. 2. wise man's heart is at his—
9. 1. wise and their works are in the *h.* of God
Song 2. 6. his—doth embrace me, 8. 3.
Matt. 5. 30. if thy—offend thee, cut it off
6. 3. left *h.* know what thy—doeth
25. 33. sheep on his—goats on the left 34. 41.
Mark 14. 62. sitting on—of power
16. 19. sat on—of God, Rom. 8. 34. Col. 3. 1. Heb. 1. 3. 1 Pet. 3. 22. Acts 2. 33.
Ps. 31. 5. into *thy hand* I commend my spirit
145. 16. thou openest—and satisfiest me
Prov. 30. 32. lay—upon thy mouth
Eccl. 9. 10. whatsoever—findeth to
Isa. 26. 11. when—is lifted up, they
Matt. 18. 8. if—or thy foot offend
Gen. 27. 22. *hands* are the *h.* of Esau
Ex. 17. 12. Moses' *h.* were heavy
Ps. 24. 4. hath clean *h.* and a pure heart
76. 5. men of might found their *h.*
Prov. 31. 20. reacheth *h.* to the needy
31. give her of the fruit of her *h.*
Matt. 18. 18. having two *h.* or feet
Luke 1. 74. delivered out of the *h.* of our enemies
9. 44. delivered into the *h.* of men
John 13. 9. but also my *h.* and head
2. Cor. 5. 1. house not made with *h.*
Eph. 4. 28. working with his *h.*
1 Tim. 2. 8. everywhere lifting up holy *h.*
Heb. 9. 11. tabernacle, not made with *h.*
10. 31. fearful thing to fall into the *h.* of the living God
James 4. 8. cleanse your *h.* ye sinners
1 John 1. 1. our *h.* handled the word
Col. 2. 14. *hand writing* of ordinances
HANDLE, Luke 24. 39.
Col. 2. 21. touch not, taste not, *h.* not

2 Cor. 4. 2. not *h.* the word of God deceitfully

HANDMAID, Ps. 86. 16. & 116. 16. Prov. 30. 23. Luke 1. 38. 48.

HANG, Ps. 137. 2. Josh. 8. 29.

Deut. 21. 33. is accursed of God

28. 66. thy life shall *h.* in doubt

Job 26. 7. he *h.* the earth on nothing

Matt. 18. 6. millstone *h.* about neck

22. 40. on these *h.* all the law and the prophets

Heb. 12. 12. hands which *h.* down

HAPPEN, Jer. 44. 23. Rom. 11. 25.

Prov. 12. 21. no evil shall *h.* to just, 1 Pet. 4. 12.

Eccl. 2. 14. one event *h.* to them all

8. 14. *h.* according to work of

2. 11. time and chance *h.* to all

1 Cor. 10. 11. these *h.* for ensamples

HAPPY am I, for the daughters, Gen. 30. 13.

Deut. 33. 20. *h.* art thou, O Israel

1 Kings 10. 8. *h.* are thy men, *h.* these

Job 5. 17. *h.* is the man whom God correcteth

Ps. 127. 5. *h.* is the man who hath his quiver full

128. 2. *h.* shalt thou be, and be well

137. 8. *h.* that rewards thee

144. 15. *h.* that people whose God is the Lord

146. 5. *h.* that hath God of Jacob

Jer. 12. 1. why are they *h.* that deal treacherously

Prov. 3. 13. *h.* is the man that findeth wisdom, 18.

14. 21. he that hath mercy on poor *h.* is

16. 20. whoso trusteth in the Lord *h.* is he

28. 14. *h.* is the man that feareth

29. 18. he that keepeth the law, *h.* is

Mal. 3. 15. we call the proud *h.* that

John 13. 17. *h.* are ye, if ye do them

Rom. 14. 22. *h.* he that condemns not

James 5. 11. call them *h.* which endure

1 Pet. 3. 14. suffer for righteousness' sake, *h.* are ye

4. 14. reproached for the name of Christ, *h.* are ye

1 Cor. 7. 40. *happier* if she so abide

HARD, Gen. 35. 16. 17. Ex. 1. 14. 2 Sam. 13. 2. 2 Ps. 88. 7.

Gen. 18. 14. is anything too *h.* for the Lord

2 Sam. 3. 39. sons of Zeruiah be too *h.* for

2 Kings 2. 10. thou askest a hard thing

Ps. 60. 3. showed thy people *h.* things

Prov. 13. 15. way of transgressors is *h.*

Jer. 32. 17. nothing is too *h.* for thee

Matt. 25. 24. that thou art a *h.* man

Mark 10. 24. how *h.* is it for them

John 6. 60. this is a *h.* saying; who

Acts 9. 5. *h.* for thee to kick

2 Pet. 3. 16. some things *h.* to be understood

Jude 15. of all their *h.* speeches

HARDEN, Ex. 4. 21. Deut. 15. 7. Josh. 11. 20. Job 6. 10. & 39. 16.

Heb. 3. 8. *h.* not your hearts as in the provocation, 15. Ps. 95. 8.

Prov. 21. 29. *h.* his face, 28. 14. *h.* his heart, 29. 1. *h.* his neck shall be destroyed

Job 9. 4. *hardened* himself against God

Isa. 63. 17. *h.* our heart from thy fear

Mark 6. 52. their heart was *h.*

Heb. 3. 13. lest any be *h.* through deceitfulness

Rom. 9. 18. whom he will, he *hardeneth*

Prov. 18. 19. brother offended is *harder*

Jer. 5. 3. made faces *h.* than a rock

Matt. 19. 8. because of *hardness* of your hearts

Mark 3. 5. grieved for the *h.* of their

Rom. 2. 5. after thy *h.* and impenitent

2 Tim. 2. 3. endure *h.* as a good soldier

HARLOT, Gen. 34. 31. Josh. 2. 1. Judg. 11. 1. Prov. 7. 10.

Jer. 2. 20. play the *h.* 3. 1, 6, 8. Ezek. 16. 15. Hos. 2. 5.

Matt. 21. 31. *h.* go into the kingdom of God before, 32.

1 Cor. 6. 16. joined to *h.* is one body

Heb. 11. 31. by faith *h.* Rahab perished not

James 2. 25. was not Rahab the *h.* justified

Rev. 17. 5. mother of *h.* and abominations

HARM, Gen. 31. 52.

1 Chron. 16. 22. do my prophets no harm, Ps. 105. 15. Prov. 3. 30.

1 Pet. 3. 13. who is he that will *h.* you

Matt. 10. 16. *harmless,* Phil. 2. 15.

Heb. 7. 26. holy *h.* undefiled

HARVEST, Gen. 8. 22.

Ex. 34. 21. in *h.* thou shalt rest

Isa. 9. 3. joy before thee according to joy of *h.*

Jer. 5. 24. reserved appointed weeks of *h.*

8. 20. the *h.* is past, summer is ended

51. 33. time of *h.* shall come

Matt. 9. 37. *h.* plenteous, 38. pray ye the Lord of the *h.*

13. 39. *h.* is the end of the world

Rev. 14. 15. *h.* of earth is ripe

HASTE, Ex. 12. 11. Isa. 52. 12.

Ps. 31. 22. I said in my *h.* 116. 11.

38. 22. make *h.* to help me, 40. 13.

119. 60. I made *h.* and delayed not

Song 8. 14. make *h.* my beloved

Isa. 28. 16. believeth shall not make *h.*

49. 17. thy children shall make *h.*

Ps. 16. 4. *hasten* after another God

Isa. 5. 19. let him *h.* his work that we

60. 22. I the Lord will *h.* it in his time

Jer. 1. 12. I will *h.* my word to perform it

Prov. 14. 29. *hasty* of spirit

21. 5. thoughts of *h.* tend only to want

29. 20. *h.* in his words? more hope of a fool than of him

20. 21. inheritance gotten *hastily*

HATE, Gen. 24. 60. Deut. 21. 15.

Lev. 19. 17. shall not *h.* thy brother

Deut. 7. 10. repayeth them that *h.*

1 Kings 22. 8. him for he doth not

Ps. 68. 1. let them that *h.* him flee

97. 10. ye that love Lord, *h.* evil

119. 104. I *h.* every false way

113. I *h.* vain thoughts, 163. *h.* lying

139. 21. do not I *h.* them that *h.*

Prov. 8. 13. fear of Lord is to *h.* evil

36. all they that *h.* me love death

Jer. 44. 4. abominable thing that I *h.*

Amos 5. 10. they *h.* him that rebuketh

15. *h.* the evil, and love the good

Mic. 3. 2. who *h.* the good and love

Luke 14. 26. and *h.* not his father

John 7. 7. world cannot *h.* you, but me it *h.*

15. 18. if the world *h.* you, it hated me before

Rom. 7. 15. what I *h.* that do I

1 John 3. 13. marvel not if world *h.*

Rev. 2. 6. hatest the deeds, which I also *h.* **15.**

17. 16. these shall *h.* the whore

Prov. 1. 29. for that they *hated* knowledge

5. 12. and say how have I *h.* instruction

Isa. 66. 5. your brother that *h.* you

Mal. 1. 3. I *h.* Esau.

Matt. 10. 22. shall be *h.* of all men, Mark 13. 13. Luke 21. 17.

Luke 19. 14. his citizens *h,* him

John 15, 24. *h.* me and my father

Eph. 5. 29. no man ever *h.* his own flesh

Rom. 1. 30. back biters, *haters* of God

2 Sam. 19. 6. *hatest* friends and lovest thine enemies

Ps. 5. 5. all workers of iniquity

50. 17. seeing thou *h.* instruction

Ex. 23. 5. ask of him that hateth thee

Prov. 13. 24. spareth rod, *h.* his son

John 12. 25. *h.* his life in this world

1 John 2. 9. *h.* his brother, is in darkness, 11. & 3. 15.

Ex. 18. 21. men of truth *hating* covetousness

Tit. 3. 3. *hateful* and *h.* one another

Jude 23. *h.* garment spotted by flesh

HAUGHTY, Ps. 131. 1.

Prov. 16. 18. *h.* spirit before fall

21. 24. proud and *h.* scorner dealeth

Zeph. 3. 11. no more be *h.* because

Isa. 2. 11. *haughtiness,* 17.

HEAD, Gen. 2. 10. & 40. 13.

Gen. 3. 15. it shall bruise thy *h.*

49. 26. blessings on *h.* of him that was separate from his brethren

Ezra 9. 6. iniquity increased over our *h.*

Prov. 16. 31. hoary *h.* is a crown of

20. 29. beauty of old men is gray *h.*

Eccl. 2. 14. wise man's eyes are in *h.*

9. 8. let thy *h.* lack no ointment

Ps. 38. 4. iniquity gone over my *h.*

Songs 5. 2. my *h.* is filled with dew

11. his *h.* is as most fine gold

Isa. 1. 5. whole *h.* is sick and heart

6. from sole of foot even unto *h.*

Jer. 9. 1. O that my *h.* were waters

48. 37. every *h.* shall be bald

Ezek. 9. 10. their way on *h.*

Dan. 2. 28. visions of thy *h.* on bed

38. thou art this *h.* of gold, 32.

Zech. 4. 7. bring forth *h.* stone thereof

Matt. 8. 20. not where to lay his *h.*

14. 8. give me *h.* of John Baptist

Rom. 12. 20. coals of fire on his *h.*

1 Cor. 11. 3. *h.* of man is Christ, *h.* of women is man, *h.* of Christ is God

4. *h.* covered dishonoureth his *h.*

Eph. 1. 22. gave him to be *h.* over all

4. 15. grow up in all, the *h.* even Christ

5. 23. husband *h.* of wife, Christ *h.* of the church

Col. 1. 18. he is *h.* of the body

Rev. 19. 12. on his *h.* many crowns

Luke 21. 28. lift up your *h.* for a day

Rev. 13. 1. seven *h.* and ten horns

Job 5. 13. *headlong,* Luke 4. 29.

2 Tim. 3. 4. *heady,* high minded

HEAL her now, Num. 12. 13.

Deut. 32. 39. I wound, I *h.* and I kill

2 Chron. 7. 14. I will *h.* their land

Ps. 6. 2. *h.* me, for my bones are

41. 4. *h.* my soul, for I have sinned

60. 2. *h.* breaches for land shaketh

Isa. 57. 18. I have seen his way and will *h.* him

Jer. 3. 22. I will *h.* your backsliding

17. 14. *h.* me, and I shall be *h.*

Hos. 6. 1. hath torn and he will *h.* us

Luke 4. 18. *h.* the broken hearted

23. will say, physician, *h.* thyself

John 12. 40. converted and I should *h.*

2 Chron. 30. 20. Lord *healed* the people

Ps. 30. 2. I cried and thou hast *h.*

107. 20. sent his word and *h.* them

Isa. 6. 10. convert and be *h.*

53. 5. with his stripes we are *h.*

Jer. 6. 14. *h.* the hurt of the daughter of, 8. 11.

---

15. 18. my wound incurable refuseth to be *h.*

Hos. 7. 1. when I would have *h.* Israel

Matt. 4. 24. he *h.* them all, 12. 15.

Heb. 12. 13. let it rather be *h.*

James 5. 19. pray that ye may be *h.*

Rev. 13. 3. his deadly wound was *h.*

Ex. 15. 26. I am the Lord that *healeth* thee

Ps. 103. 3. who *h.* all thy diseases

147. 3. he *h.* the broken in heart

Isa. 30. 26. Lord *h.* stroke of their wound

Jer. 14. 19. looked for time of *healing*

30. 13. thou hast no *h.* medicine

Mal. 4. 2. with *h.* in his wings

Matt. 4. 23. *h.* all manner of sickness

1 Cor. 12. 9. to one another the gifts of *h.*

Rev. 22. 2. leaves were for *h.* nations

Ps. 42. 11. *health* of my countenance

67. 2. thy saving *h.* among nations

Prov. 3. 8. shall be *h.* to thy navel

12. 18. the tongue of the wise is *h.*

Jer. 8. 15. looked for a time of *h.*

30. 17. I will restore *h.* and heal

HEAP coals, Prov. 25. 22.

Deut. 32. 23. I will *h.* mischiefs upon

Job 36. 13. hypocrites in heart *h.* up wrath

2 Tim. 4. 3. *h.* to themselves teachers

Ps. 39. 6. he *heapeth* up riches, and

James 5. 3. ye have *heaped* treasures

Judg. 15. 16. *heaps* upon *h.* with the

HEAR, Gen. 21. 6 & 23. 6

Deut. 30. 17. if heart turn away, so that thou wilt not *h.*

1 Kings 8. 30. *h.* thou in heaven thy dwelling place

2 Kings 19. 16. bow down thine ear, and *h.*

2 Chron. 6. 21. *h.* from thy dwelling

Job 5. 27. *h.* it and know it for good

Ps. 4. 1. *h.* my prayer, 39. 12. Dan. 9. 17, 19.

4. 3. Lord will *h.* 17. 6. Zech. 10. 6.

10. 17. thou wilt cause thine ear to *h.*

51. 8. make me to *h.* joy and

59. 7. who, say they, doth *h.*

66. 16. come and *h.* all ye that

115. 6. they have ears, but *h.* not

Prov. 19. 27. cease to *h.* instruction

Eccl. 5. 1. be more ready to *h.* than

Song 2. 14. let me *h.* thy voice

Isa. 1. 2. *h.* O heavens, and give ear

6. 10. lest they *h.* with ears

Isa. 55. 3. *h.* and your soul shall live

Matt. 10. 27. what ye *h.* in the ear

13. 17. to *h.* those things ye *h.*

17. 5. this is my beloved Son, *h.* ye

18. 17. if he neglect to *h.* them

Mark 4. 24. take heed what ye *h.*

33. spake word as they were able to *h.* i.

Luke 8. 18. take heed how ye *h.*

16. 29. Moses and the prophets, let them *h.* them

John 5. 25. they that *h.* shall live

Acts 10. 33. to *h.* all things that are commanded thee of God

James 1. 19. every man be swift to *h.*

Rev. 2. 7. let him *h.* what the spirit saith to the churches, 3. 6.

3. 20. if any *h.* my voice, and open door

Ex. 2. 24. God *heard* their groaning

Ps. 6. 9. Lord hath *h.* my supplication

10. 17. hast *h.* desire of humble

34. 4. I sought the Lord, and he *h.*

61. 5. thou hast *h.* my vows

66. 19. verily God hath *h.* me

118. 21. I will praise thee, for thou hast *h.* me

120. 1. I cried to Lord and he *h.*

Isa. 40. 28. hast thou not *h.* that God

64. 4. from beginning men have not *h.*

Jer. 8. 6. I hearkened and *h.* but they

Jonah 2. 2. I cried to Lord and he *h*.
Mal. 3. 16. Lord hearkened and *h*.
Matt. 6. 7. be *h*. for much speaking
Luke 1. 13. thy prayer is *h*. and thy
John 3. 32. what he hath seen and *h*.
8. 6. wrote as though he *h*. them not
Rom. 10. 14. of whom they have not *h*.
1 Cor. 2. 9. eye hath not seen nor ear *h*
Phil. 4. 9. what *h*. and seen in me
Heb. 4. 2. with faith in them that *h*.
5. 7. he was *h*. in that he feared
Lev. 3. 3. remember thou hast *h*.
Ex. 3. 7. *I have heard* their cry
6. 5.—the groaning, Acts 7. 34.
16. 12.—the murmurings
1 Kings 9. 3.—thy prayer and supplication, 2 Kings 19. 20.
Job 42. 5.—of thee by the hearing
Isa. 49. 8. in an acceptable time—
Jer. 31. 18.—Ephraim bemoaning
Ps. 65. 2. thou that *hearest* prayer
John 11. 42. I knew thou *h*. me
1 Sam. 3. 9. Lord, thy servant *heareth*
Prov. 8. 34. blessed is man that *h*. me
Matt. 7. 24 whoso *h*. these sayings
Luke 10. 16. he that *h*. you *h*. me
John 9. 31. God *h*. not sinners, but
1 John 5. 14. ask according to his will he *h*.
Rev. 22. 17. let him that *h*. say, come
Rom. 2. 13. not *hearers* but doers
Eph. 4. 29. minister grace to the *h*.
James 1. 22. be doers of word and not *h*.
23. a *h*. of word, and not a doer
25. not a forgetful *h*. but a doer
Job 42. 5. of thee by *hearing* of ear
Prov. 20. 12. the *h*. ear, and seeing
28. 9. turneth away his ear from *h*.
Matt. 13. 14. *h*. they hear not
Rom. 10. 17. faith cometh by *h*. and *h*. by
Heb. 5. 11. seeing ye are dull of *h*.
2 Pet. 2. 8. in seeing and *h*. vexed his
HEARKEN, Deut. 28. 15.
Deut. 28. 1. if thou *h*. diligently
1 Sam. 15. 22. to *h*. better than the fat of rams
Ps. 103. 20. angels *h*. to voice of
Isa. 46. 12. *h*. unto me, ye stout
51. 1. *h*. unto me, ye that follow
55. 2. *h*. diligently unto me, eat
HEART, Ex. 28. 30.
1 Sam. 1. 13. she spake in her *h*. only
10. 9. God gave him another *h*.
16. 7. but Lord looketh on *h*.
24. 5. David's *h*. smote him after
1 Chron. 16. 10. let the *h*. of them rejoice that seek the Lord, Ps. 105. 3.
22. 19. set your *h*. to seek Lord your God
2 Chron. 17. 6. his *h*. was lifted up in the ways of the Lord
30. 19. prepareth his *h*. to seek God
Ps. 22. 26. your *h*. shall live forever
34. 18. Lord nigh unto them of broken *h*.
37. 31. law of his God is in his *h*.
51. 17. a broken and contrite *h*.
64. 6. inward thought, and *h*. is
78. 37. their *h*. was not right with
112. 7. his *h*. is fixed, trusting in
Prov. 4. 23, keep thy *h*. with diligence
10. 20. *h*. of wicked is little worth
16. 9. a man's *h*. deviseth his way
27. 19 *h*. of man answereth to man
Eccl. 7. 4. *h*. of wise is in house of mourning
10. 2. wise man's *h*. is at his right hand, but a fool's *h*. is at his left
Song 3. 11. in the day of gladness of his *h*.
Isa. 6. 10. make *h*. of this people fat
57. 15. to revive the *h*. of contrite
Jer. 11. 20. triest the reins and *h*.
12. 11. no man layeth it to *h*.
17. 9. *h*. is deceitful above all
24. 7. I will give them a *h*. to know

32. 39. I give them one *h*.
Lam. 3. 41. lift up our *h*. with our of flesh
Ezek. 11. 19. take stony *h*. give *h*. of flesh
18. 31. make ye a new *h*. and new
36. 26. new *h*. take stony *h*. give *h*.
Joel 2. 13. rend your *h*. not your
Mal. 4. 6. turn *h*. of fathers to
Matt. 6. 21. there will your *h*. be
12. 34. out of abundance of the *h*. mouth speaketh
35. out of good treasure of the *h*.
15. 19. out of *h*. proceed evil
Luke 2. 19. pondered them in her *h*.
24. 25. O fools, and show of *h*. to
32. did not our *h*. burn within us
John 14. 1. let not *h*. be troubled
Acts 5. 53. were cut to the *h*.
11. 23. with purpose of *h*. cleave to Lord
13. 22. found man after mine own *h*.
Rom. 10. 10. with *h*. man believeth
1 Cor. 2. 9. nor entered into *h*. of man
2 Cor. 3. 3. in fleshly tables of the *h*.
1 Pet. 3. 4. in the hidden man of the *h*.
1 John 3. 20. if *h*. condemns us, God
Deut. 11. 13. serve him *with all thy heart,* Josh. 22. 5.
13. 8. love Lord your God—
Matt. 22. 37. Mark 12. 30, 33.
Deut. 26. 16. keep and do them—
30. 2. turn to the Lord—and soul
1 Kings 2. 4. walk before me in truth—
8. 23, 48. return to thee—
2 Chron. 15. 12. seek the God of thy fathers—15. sworn—
22. 9. sought Lord—
Prov. 3. 5. trust in Lord—and be not
Jer. 29. 13. search for me—
Zeph. 3. 14. sing, be glad, rejoice—
Acts 8. 37. if thou believest—
Ps. 86. 12. I will praise thee *with all my heart*
Ps. 45. 1. *my heart* is inditing a good
57. 7.—is fixed, O God
61. 2. what time—is overwhelmed
73. 26. my flesh and—faileth, but
84. 2. my flesh and—crieth for the
109. 22.—is wounded within me
131. 1. Lord—is not haughty, nor
Song 5. 2. I sleep, but—waketh
Jer. 3. 15. give pastors according to—
Hos. 11. 8.—is turned within me
1 Kings 8. 61. *heart perfect* with the Lord, 11. 4. 2 Chron. 15. 17.
2 Kings 20. 3. and with—
1 Chron. 28. 9. serve him with—
2 Chron. 16. 9. in behalf of them whose—
Ps. 101. 2. I will walk within my house with a—
24. clean hands and *pure heart*
Matt. 5. 8. blessed are the pure in *h*
1 Tim. 1. 5. charity out of a—
2 Tim. 2. 22. call on Lord out of—
1 Pet. 1. 22. love with—fervently
Ps. 9. 1. praise him *with my whole heart*, 111. 1. & 138. 1.
119. 2. seek him—10. favour—
34. 58. observe it—69. keep thy precepts—
Jer. 3. 10. not turned with her whole *h*.
Col. 3. 23. do it *heartily* as to Lord
HEATH, Jer. 17. 16. & 48. 6.
HEATHEN, Lev. 25. 44.
Ps. 2. 1. why do the *h*. rage, Acts 4. 25
2. 8. give them the *h*. for
Matt. 18. 17. let him be as a *h*. man
Gal. 3. 8. justify the *h*. through faith
HEAVEN of *h*. cannot contain thee, 1 Kings 8. 27. 2 Chron. 2. 6.
Ps. 103. 11. as *h*. is high above the
115. 16. even heavens are Lord's
Prov. 25. 3. *h*. for height, and earth
Isa. 66. 1. *h*. is my throne

Jer. 31. 37 if *h*. above can be measured
Hag. 1. 10. *h*. over you is stayed from dew
Matt. 5. 18. till *h*. and earth pass
Luke 15. 18. sinned against *h*.
John 1. 51. see *h*. open and angels
Ps. 73. 25. whom have I *in heaven*
Eccl. 5. 2. God is—and thou upon earth
Heb. 10. 34. have—a better substance
1 Pet. 1. 4. inheritance reserved—for you
Ps. 8. 3. consider *the heavens*, the work of thy hands
19. 1.—declare the glory of God
89. 11.—are thine, and earth also
Isa. 65. 17. I create new *h*. and new earth, 66. 22. 2 Pet. 3. 12.
Acts. 3. 21. *h*. must receive him till
2 Cor. 5. 1. have a house eternal in the *h*.
Eph. 4. 10. ascend far above all *h*.
Matt. 6. 14. *heavenly* Father, 26. 32. & 15. 13. & 18. 35. Luke 11. 13.
John 3. 12. if I tell you of *h*. things
1 Cor. 15. 48. as is the earthy, such are earthy, and as is *h*. such are the *h*.
Eph. 1. 3. in *h*. places, 20.
2 Tim. 4. 18. unto his *h*. kingdom
Heb. 3. 1. partakers of the *h*. calling
HEAVY, Num. 11. 14. Job 33. 7.
Ps. 38. 4. as a *h*. burden too *h*. for
Prov. 31. 6. wine to those of *h*. hearts
Isa. 6. 10. make their ears *h*. lest
58. 6. to undo the *h*. burden
Matt. 11. 28. that labour and are *h*. laden
23. 4. bind *h*. burdens and grievous
Ps. 69. 20. I am full of *heaviness*
119. 28. my soul melteth for *h*.
Prov. 12. 25. *h*. in the heart of man maketh it stoop
14. 43. the end of that mirth is *h*.
Isa. 61. 3. garment of praise for the spirit of *h*.
Rom. 9. 2. I have great *h*. and sorrow
1 Pet. 1. 6. in *h*. through manifold temptations
HEDGE, Job 1. 10. Prov. 15. 19.
Isa. 5. 5. Hos. 2. 6. Job 3. 23.
HEED, 2 Sam. 20. 10.
Deut. 2. 4. take good *h*. to yourselves
Josh. 22. 5. take diligent *h*. to do the commandments
Ps. 119. 9. by taking *h*. thereto
Eccl. 12. 9. he gave good *h*. sought
Jer. 18. 18. not give *h*. to any of his
HEEL, Gen. 3. 15.
Ps. 41. 9. lifted up his *h*. against me, John 13. 18.
49. 5. iniquity of my *h*. shall compass
Hos. 12. 3. he took his brother by *h*.
HEIFER, Num. 19. 2. Jer. 46. 20.
HEIR, Gen. 15. 4. & 21. 10.
Prov. 30. 23. handmaid *h*. to mistress
Jer. 49. 1. hath Israel no sons, hath he no *h*.
Matt. 21. 38. this is the *h*. let us kill
Rom. 4. 13. Abraham should be *h*. of the world
8. 17. if children, *h*. of God, joint *h*. with Christ
Gal. 3. 29. children *h*. according to promise
4. 7. if a son, then an *h*. of God
Eph. 3. 6. Gentiles should be fellow *h*.
Heb. 1. 2. God hath appointed *h*. of
6. 17. might show to *h*. of promise
21. 7. became *h*. of righteousness
1 Pet. 3. 7. *h*. together of grace of
HELD, Ps. 94. 18. Song 3. 4.
HELL, Matt. 18. 9. Mark 9. 43, 45.
Deut. 32. 22. shall burn to lowest *h*.
2 Sam. 22. 6. sorrows of *h*. compassed me
Job 11. 8. it is deeper than *h*. what can'st thou know

26. 6. *h*. is naked before him and
Ps. 9. 17. wicked be turned into *h*.
16. 10. not leave my soul in *h*.
55. 15 let them go down quick into *h*.
86. 13. delivered my soul from the lowest *h*.
116. 3. pains of *h*. gat hold on me
139. 8. make my bed in *h*. thou art
Prov. 5. 5. her steps take hold of *h*.
7. 27. her house is the way to *h*.
9. 18. her guests are in depths of *h*.
15. 11. *h*. and destruction are before Lord
24. that he may depart from *h*.
23. 14. and shalt deliver his soul from *h*.
27. 20 *h*. and destruction are never
Isa. 5. 14. *h*. hath enlarged herself
14. 9. *h*. from beneath is moved to
15. thou shalt be brought down to *h*.
28. 15. with *h*. are we at agreement
57. 9. debase thyself even to *h*.
Ezek. 31. 16. 17. & 32. 21. 27.
Amos 9. 2. though they dig into *h*.
Jonah 2. 2. out of belly of *h*. cried I
Hab. 2. 5. enlarged his desires as *h*.
Matt. 5. 22. be in danger of *h*. fire
29. body be cast into *h*. 30. & 18. 9.
Mark 9. 43, 45, 47.
10. 28. destroy both soul and body in *h*.
11. 23. brought down to *h*. Luke 10. 15.
16. 18. the gates of *h*. shall not prevail against it
23. 15. twofold more the child of *h*.
33. how can ye escape damnation of *h*.
Luke 12. 5. power to cast into *h*.
16. 23. in *h*. he lifted up his eyes
Acts 2. 31. his soul not left in *h*.
James 3. 6. tongue set on fire of *h*.
2 Pet. 2. 4. cast them down to *h*.
Rev. 1. 18. having keys of *h*. and
6. 8. death and *h*. followed with
20. 13. death and *h*. delivered up
14. death and *h*. were cast into lake
HELMET, 1 Sam. 17. 5.
Isa. 59. 17. a *h*. of salvation on head
Eph. 6. 17. take the *h*. of salvation
1 Thess. 5. 8. for a *h*. hope of salvation
HELP meet for him, Gen. 2. 18.
Deut. 33. 29. Lord shield of thy *h*.
Judg. 5. 23. came not to *h*. of the Lord
Ps. 27. 9. thou hast been my *h*.
33. 20. he is our *h*. and shield
40. 17. my *h*. and deliverer, 70. 5.
46. 1. God is a very present *h*. in trouble
60. 11. vain is *h*. of man, 108. 12.
71. 12. O my God, make haste for my *h*.
89. 19. laid *h*. upon one that is mighty
115. 9. Lord is their *h*. and shield
124. 8. our *h*. is in name of Lord
Hos. 13. 9. but in me is thy *h*.
Acts 26. 22 having obtained *h*. of God
1 Cor. 12. 28. *helps*, governments
2 Chron. 14. 11. nothing with thee too *h*.
Ps. 40. 13. make haste to *h*. me
Isa. 41. 10. I will *h*. thee, 13. 14.
63. 5. I looked and there was none to *h*.
Acts 16. 9. come unto Macedonia and *h*. us
Heb. 4. 16. find grace to *h*. in time of
1 Sam. 7. 12. hitherto hath the Lord *helped* us
Ps. 118. 13. I might fall; but Lord *h*. me
Isa. 49. 8. in day of salvation I *h*.
Zech. 1. 15. they *h*. forward afflicted
Acts 18. 27. *h*. them much who had

Rev. 12. 16. the earth *h.* the woman
Rom. 8. 26. Spirit *helpeth* our infirmities
Ps. 10. 14. thou art the *helper* of fatherless
54. 4. God is my *h.* Heb. 13. 6.
Job 9. 13. proud *helpers* do stoop
2 Cor. 1. 24. we are *h.* of your joy
3 John 8. fellow *h.* to the truth
HEM, Matt. 9. 20. & 14. 36.
HEN, Matt. 23. 37. Luke 13. 34.
HERESY, Acts 24. 14. 1 Cor. 11.
19. Gal. 5. 20. 2 Pet. 2. 1.
Tit. 3. 10. a man that is a *heretic*
HERITAGE, Job 20. 29.
Ps. 16. 5. I have a goodly *h.*
61. 5. given me the *h.* of those that fear me
119. 111. testimony taken as a *h.* for ever
127. 3. lo, children are a *h.* of Lord
Isa. 54. 17. this is *h.* of servants of Lord, 58. 14.
Jer. 3. 19. goodly *h.* of hosts of nations
Joel 2. 17. give not thy *h.* to reproach
1 Pet. 5. 3. not as lords over God's *h.*
HEW tables of stone, Ex. 34. 1.
Jer. 2. 13. *hewed* them out cisterns
Hos. 6. 5. therefore have I *h.* them by the prophets
Matt. 3. 10. *hewn* down 7. 19.
HID themselves, Gen. 3. 8.
Ps. 119. 11. word have I *h.* in heart
Zeph. 2. 3. it may be, ye shall be *h.*
Matt. 10. 26. nor *h.* that shall not be
11. 25. *h.* these things from wise and prudent, Luke 10. 21.
2 Cor. 4. 3. if Gospel be *h.*
Col. 2. 3. in whom are *h.* all
3. 3. your life is *h.* with Christ
Ps. 83. 3. and consulted against thy *hidden* ones.
1. Cod. 4. 5. bring to light *h.* things
1 Pet. 3. 4. *h.* man of heart
Rev. 2. 17. give to eat the *h.* manna
Gen. 18. 7. shall I *hide* from
Job. 33. 17. may *h.* pride from man
Ps. 17. 8. *h.* me under the shadow of thy wings.
27. 5. in time of trouble he shall *h.*
30. 7. didst *h.* thy face and I was troubled
31. 20. shalt *h.* them in secret of thy presence
Ps. 51. 9. *h.* thy face from my sin
143. 9. I flee to thee to *h.* me
Isa. 26. 20. *h.* thyself for a moment
James 5. 20. *h.* a multitude of sins, 1 Pet. 4. 8.
Rev. 6. 16. *h.* us from the face of him
Job. 13. 24. why *hidest* thou thy face, Ps. 30. 7. & 44. 24.
Job 34. 29. when he *hideth* his face
42. 3. who is he that *h.* counsel
Ps. 139. 12. darkness *h.* not from
Isa. 8. 17. I will wait on Lord that *h.*
Hab. 3. 4. *hiding* of his power
Ps. 32. 7. *h.* place. 119. 114.
HIGH, Deut. 3. 5, 12.
Deut. 26. 19. make thee *h.* above all
1 Kings 9. 8. at this house which is *h.*
Job 11. 8. as *h.* as heaven, what canst
Ps. 49. 2. both low and *h.* rich and
89. 13. strong arm, and *h.* is right
97. 9. thou Lord art *h.* above all the earth, 113. 4.
103. 11. as heaven is *h.* above earth
131. 1. not in things too *h.* for me
138. 16. though Lord be *h.* yet hath
Prov. 21. 4. a *h.* look and proud
Eccl. 12. 5. afraid of that which is *h.*
Ezek. 21. 26. abase him that is *h.*
Rom. 12. 16. mind not *h.* things
2 Cor. 10. 5. every *h.* thing that exalteth itself
Phil. 3. 14. for the prize of the *h.* calling of God
Num. 24. 16. *Most High,* Deut. 32. 8.
2 Sam. 22. 14. Ps. 7. 17.

Ps. 47. 2. the Lord—is terrible; he is a great King
83. 18. Jehovah art—over all earth
92. 8. thou art—for evermore
Isa. 14. 14. I will ascend and be like the
Hos. 11. 7. called them to the—none at all would exalt him
Acts 7. 48—dwelleth not in temples
Ps. 107. 41. setteth poor—from affliction.
113. 5. like our God who dwelleth—
Isa. 26. 5. bring down those that dwell
Eccl. 5. 8. there be *higher* than they
Heb. 7. 26. made *h.* than the heavens
Ps. 18. 13. *Highest* gave his voice
87. 5. *H.* himself shall establish her
Eccl. 5. 8. he that is higher than *h.*
Luke 1. 35. power of the *H.* shall overshadow thee
2. 14. glory to God in the *h.*
6. 35. shall be the children of the *H.*
14. 8. sit not down in the *h.* room
1. 28. thou that art *highly* favoured
2 Tim. 3. 4. heady, *high-minded*
1 Tim. 6. 17. rich, that they be not—
Job 22. 12. *height,* Rom. 8. 39. Eph. 3. 18.
HILL, Ex. 24. 4. Ps. 68. 15.
Ps. 2. 6. set my King on holy *h.* of Zion, 3. 4. & 15. 1. & 43. 3.
Gen. 7. 19. high *h.* under heaven covered
Num. 23. 9. from the *h.* I behold him
Ps. 65. 12. little *h.* rejoice on every side
68. 16. why leap ye, high *h.* this is
98. 8. let *h.* be joyful together
114. 4. little *h.* skipped like lambs
Hos. 10. 8. to the *h.* fall on us
Hab. 3. 6. the perpetual *h.* did bow
HIND, 2 Sam. 22. 34. Ps. 29. 9. Prov. 5. 19. Song 2. 7. Hab. 3. 19.
HIRE, Deut. 24. 15. Isa. 23. 18. Mic. 1. 7. Luke 10. 7. James 5. 4.
Job 7. 1. a *hireling,* John 10. 12, 13.
HITHERTO, Lord helped us, 1 Sam. 7. 12.
Job 38. 11. *h.* shalt thou come, but
John 16. 24. *h.* ye asked nothing in my name
1 Cor. 3. 2. *h.* ye were not able to
HOLD, Gen. 21. 18. Ex. 9. 2.
Judge 9. 46. a *h.* of the house of the god Berith
Job 17. 9. righteous shall *h.* on way
Isa. 41. 13. God will *h.* thy right hand
Isa. 62. 1. for Zion's sake will I not *h.* my peace, 42. 14.
Matt. 6. 24. *h.* to one and despise the
Phil. 2. 29. *h.* such in reputation
Heb. 3. 14. if we *h.* beginning of our confidence
1 Thes. 5. 21. prove all, *hold fast* that which is good
2 Tim. 1. 13.—form of sound words
Heb. 3. 6. if we—the confidence of hope
4. 14. let us—our profession
Rev. 2. 25. what ye have—till I come
3. 3. hast received—and repent
11.—that thou hast that no man
Ps. 77. 4. *holdest* my eyes waking
Rev. 2. 13. *h.* fast my name and hast
Job 2. 3. still he *holdeth* fast integrity
Ps. 66. 9. which *h.* our soul in life
Prov. 17. 28. a fool, when he *h.* his peace
Jer. 6. 11. I am weary with *holding*
Phil. 2. 16. *h.* forth the word of life
Col. 2. 19. not *h.* the head, from
1 Tim. 1. 19. *h.* faith and a good conscience
3. 9. *h.* mystery of faith in pure conscience
Tit. 1. 9. *h.* fast the faithful word
HOLY ground, Ex. 3. 5. *h.* sabbath, Ex. 16. 23. *h.* nation, 19. 6. 1

Pet. 2. 9. Ex. 28. 38. *h.* gifts, 29. 6.
h. crown, 30. 25. *h.* ointment, Lev. 16. 33. *h.* sanctuary, 27. 14. house, *h.* 30. *h.* tithes, Num. 5. 17. *h.* water, 31. 6. *h.* instruments
Lev. 11. 45. be ye *h.* for I am *h.* 20. 7.
1 Sam. 2. 2. there is none *h.* as Lord
21. 5. vessels of young men are *h.*
Ps. 22. 3. thou art *h.* that inhabitest the praises of Israel
115. 17. Lord is *h.* in all his works
Prov. 20. 25. a snare to devour that which is *h.*
Isa. 6. 3. *h. h. h.* Lord God of hosts
Ezek. 22. 26. difference between *h.*
Acts 4. 27. thy *h.* child Jesus
Rom. 7. 12. law *h.* commandment *h.*
11. 16. if first fruit be *h.* lump is also *h.*
12. 1. sacrifice *h.* accceptable to God
1 Cor. 7. 14. children unclean, but now *h.*
Eph. 1. 4. be *h.* and without blame
2 Tim. 1. 9. called us with *h.* calling
3. 15. hast known the *h.* Scriptures
Tit. 1. 8. sober, just, *h.* temperate
1 Pet. 1. 15. be ye *h.* in all manner
2. 5. a *h.* priesthood, 9. *h.* nation
2 Pet. 1. 21. *h.* men of God spake as
3. 11. *h.* in all conversation and
Rev. 3. 7. saith he that is *h.* and true
4. 8. *h. h. h.* Lord God Almighty
15. 4. fear thee for thou only art *h.*
20. 6. blessed and *h.* is he that hath
22. 11. he that is *h.* let him be *h.*
Ex. 26. 33. *most holy place,* 34. 1.
Kings 6. 16. Ezek. 44. 13.
Lev. 6. 25. *most holy offering,* 7. 1.
Num. 18. 9. Zzek. 48. 12. bread of his God most *h.*
27. 28. *most holy things,* Num. 4. 4.
2 Chron. 3. 8, made the most *h.* house
Dan. 9. 24. seventy weeks to anoint the most *h.*
Ps. 42. 4. with multitude that kept *holy day,* Isa. 58. 13. Col. 2. 16.
Matt. 1. 18. with child of *Holy Ghost*
20. that is conceived in her is of—
3. 11. baptize you—Mark 1. 8. John 1. 33. Acts 1. 5. & 11. 16.
12. 31. blasphemy against—32.
Mark 12. 36. David said by—
13. 11. not ye that speak, but the—
Luke 1. 35.—shall come upon thee
2. 15.—was upon him
26. revealed unto him by the—
3. 22.—descended in bodily shape
12. 10. blasphemeth against the—
12.—shall teach you in that same
John 7. 39. for—was not yet given
14. 26. Comforter which is—whom the Father will send
20. 22. receive ye the—
Acts 1. 2. though—had given commandment
8. after that the—is come upon you
2. 33. receive promise of the—
38. receive gift of—10. 45.
5. 3. Satan filled heart to lie to—
32. we are his witnesses, and also—
7. 51. ye do always resist the—
8. 15. receive—17. 19.—given, 18.
9. 31. walking in the fear of the Lord and in the comfort of the—
10. 38. anointed Jesus with the—
44.—fell on all them, 11. 15.
47. received the—19. 2. be any—6.
13. 2. the—said, separate me Saul
4. they being sent forth by the—
15. 28. it seemed good to—and us
16. 6. forbidden of—to preach in
20. 23. save that—witnesseth
28. flock, over which—made overseers
21. 11. thus saith—so shall the Jews
28. 25. well spake the—by Esaias
Rom. 5. 5. love of God shed abroad by—
9. 1. conscience bearing witness in—
14. 17. righteousness, peace and joy in—

15. 13. abound in hope through power of—
16. offering of Gentiles sanctified by—
1 Cor. 2. 13. in words which—teacheth
6. 19. temple of—which is in you
12. 3. can say Jesus is Lord but by the—
2 Cor. 6. 6. by—by love unfeigned
13. 14. communion of—be with you
1 Thes. 1. 5. in—much assurance, 6. joy of—
2 Tim. 14. keep by—which dwelleth in you
Tit. 3. 5. not by works, but by the renewing of—
Heb. 2. 4. miracles and gifts of—
3. 7. wherefore, as—saith, to-day
6. 4. made partakers of—
9. 8.—this signifying that the way
10. 15. whereof—is a witness to
1 Pet. 1. 12. preach unto you—sent
2 Pet. 1. 21. holy men of God moved by—
1 John 5. 7. Father, Word, and—are
Jude 20. building up—praying in—
Luke 1. 15. *filled with,* or *full of the Holy Ghost,* 41. 67. Acts 2. 4.
Ps. 51. 11. take not thy *Holy Spirit* from us
Isa. 63. 10. rebelled and vexed his—
11. where is he that put within—
Luke 11. 13. give—to them that ask
Eph. 1. 13. ye were sealed with—of promise
4. 30. grieve not the—of God
1 Thes. 4. 8. who hath given us—
Ps. 87. 1. *holy mountain,* Isa. 11. 9.
Dan. 9. 16. & 11. 45. Joel 2. 1. Obad. 16. Zeph. 3. 11. Zech. 8. 3.
Lev. 20. 3. *holy name,* 1 Chron, 16. 10, 35. Ps. 33. 21. Isa. 57. 15.
Deut. 33. 8. *Holy One,* Job 6. 10. Ps. 16. 10. Isa. 10. 17. Hab. 1. 12. Mark 1. 24. Acts 3. 14. 1 John 2. 20.
2 Kings 19. 22. *Holy One of Israel,* Ps. 71. 22. Isa. 1. 4. Jer. 50. 29.
Deut. 7. 6. *holy people,* 14. 2, 21. Isa. 62. 12. Dan. 8. 24.
Ex. 28. 29. *holy place,* Lev. 6. 16. Eccl. 8. 10. and about 30 other texts
Ps. 5. 7. *holy temple,* 11. 4. Jonah 2. 4.
Isa. 65. 5. I am *holier* than thou
Heb. 9. 3. the *holiest* of all, 8.
1 Thes. 2. 10. how *holily* and justly
Ex. 15. 11. glorious in *holiness*
28. 36. *h.* to Lord, 39. 30. Isa. 23. 18.
1 Chron. 16. 29. in beauty of *h.* Ps. 29. 2. & 96. 9. 2 Chron. 20. 21.
2 Chron. 31. 18. sanctified themselves in *h.*
Ps. 50. 4. remembrance of his *h.*
47. 8. God sits on throne of his *h.*
48. 1. in mountain of his *h.*
68. 6. God has spoken in his *h.*
89. 35. I have sworn by my *h.*
93. 5. *h.* becometh thy home
Isa. 23. 18. her hire shall be *h.* to Lord
35. 8. it shall be called the way of *h.*
62. 9. drink it in the courts of my *h.*
63. 15. habitation of thy *h.*
18. people of *h.*
Jer. 2. 3. Israel was *h.* to the Lord
23. 9. because of Lord, and words of his *h.*
Amos 4. 2. Lord hath sworn by his *h.*
Obad. 17. on mount Zion there shall be *h.*
Zech. 14. 20. on horse bells, *h.* to the Lord, 21.
Luke 1. 75. in *h.* and righteousness
Acts 3. 12. as though by our own *h.*
Rom. 1. 4. Son of God according to the Spirit of *h.*
6. 19. yield members servants to righteousness unto *h.*
22. fruit unto *h.* and end everlasting

2 Cor. 7. 1. perfecting *h.* in fear of God

Eph. 4. 24. created in righteousness and true *h.*

1 Thes. 3. 13. unblameable in *h.* before him

4. 7. called not to uncleanness but to *h.*

1 Tim. 2. 15. in faith, love *h.*

Tit. 2. 3. in behaviour as becometh *h.*

Heb. 12. 10. partakers of his *h.*

14. *h.* without which no man shall see the Lord

HOME, Gen. 39. 16. & 43. 16.

Ps. 68. 12. that tarried at *h.* divided spoil

Eccl. 12. 5. man goeth to his long *h.*

2 Cor. 5. 6. while we are at *h.* in the body

Tit. 2. 5. chaste, obedient, keepers at *h.*

HONEST, Luke 8. 15.

Acts 6. 3. men of *h.* report, full of the Holy Ghost

Rom. 12. 17. provide things *h.* in the sight of all men

2 Cor. 8. 21. providing for *h.* things

13. 7. should do that which is *h.*

Phil. 4. 8. whatsoever things are *h.*

1 Pet. 2. 12. have your conversation *h.*

Rom. 13. 13. walk *honestly* as in day

1 Thes. 4. 12. walk *h.* towards them

Heb. 13. 18. in all things willing to live *h.*

1 Tim. 2. 2. in all godliness and *honesty*

HONOUR, Gen. 49. 6.

1 Chron. 29. 12. both riches and *h.* come

Ps. 7. 5. lay mine *h.* in the dust

8. 5. crowned him with glory and *h.*

26. 8. place where thine *h.* dwelleth

49. 12. man being in *h.* abideth not

20. man that is in *h.* and understanding.

Ps. 149. 9. this *h.* have all his saints

Prov. 3. 16. in her left hand riches and *h.*

15. 33. before *h.* is humility

26. 1. *h.* is not seemly for a fool

29. 23. *h.* shall uphold the humble

Mal. 1. 6. if I be a father where is mine *h.*

Matt. 13. 57. prophet is not without *h.* save in his own country, Mark 6. 4. John 4. 44.

John 5. 41. I receive not *h.* from men

Rom. 2. 7. seek for glory, *h.* immortality

9. 21. make one vessel *h.* another

12. 10. in *h.* preferring one another

13. 7. give *h.* to whom it is due

2 Cor. 6. 8. by *h.* and dishonour

2 Tim. 2. 20. some to *h.* and some to dishonour

Heb. 5. 4. taketh this *h.* to himself

1 Pet. 1. 7. be found unto praise and *h.*

3. 7. giving *h.* to wife as weaker

Ex. 20. 12. *h.* thy father and thy mother, Matt. 15. 46.

1 Sam. 2. 30. that *h.* me I will *h.*

Prov. 3. 9. *h.* Lord with substance

Isa. 29. 13. with their lips do *h.* me

John 5. 23. should *h.* the Son as *h.* the Father

12. 26. if any man serve me him will my Father *h.*

1 Pet. 2. 17. *h.* all men, love the brotherhood

Ps. 15. 4. he *honoureth* them that fear the Lord

Mal. 1. 6. a son *h.* his father

Matt. 15. 8. *h.* me with lips

Heb. 13. 4. marriage is *honourable* in all

HONEY, Gen. 43. 11. Lev. 2. 11. Judg. 14. 8, 18. 1 Sam. 14. 26.

Ps. 19. 10. sweeter than *h.* and the *h.* comb, 119. 103.

Song 4. 11. *h.* and milk are under thy tongue

Isa. 7. 15. butter and *h.* shall he eat

Matt. 3. 4. his meat locusts and wild *h.*

Rev. 10. 9. in mouth sweet as *h.* 10.

1 Sam. 14. 27. dipt in *honeycomb,* Prov. 5. 3. Song. 4. 11. Luke 24. 42.

HOOF, Ex. 10. 26. Lev. 11. 3-7.

HOOK, Ex. 26. 32. Ezek. 29. 4. Isa. 2. 4. *pruning hooks,* 18. 5. Mic. 4. 3.

HOPE in Israel concerning this, Ezra 10. 2.

Job 8. 13. hypocrite's *h.* shall perish

11. 20. their *h.* as giving up ghost

27. 8. what is the *h.* of hypocrite

Ps. 78. 7. might set their *h.* in God

Prov. 10. 28. *h.* of righteous shall be gladness

11. 7. the *h.* of unjust men perisheth

13. 12. *h.* deferred maketh heart

4. 32. righteous hath *h.* in death

19. 18. chasten thy son while there is *h.*

26. 12. more *h.* of a fool than of him

Isa. 57. 10. saidst thou there is no *h.* Jer. 2. 25. Ezek. 37. 11.

Jer. 14. 8. O *h.* of Israel, 17. 13.

17. 7. blessed is the man that trusteth in the Lord, and whose *h.* the Lord is

Lam. 3. 29. if so be there may be *h.*

Hos. 2. 15. valley of Achor for door of *h.*

Joel 3. 16. Lord will be *h.* of his people

Zech. 9. 12. turn to the strong hold ye prisoners of *h.*

Acts 24. 15. have *h.* towards God

Rom. 5. 4. experience *h.*

5. *h.* maketh not ashamed

8. 24. we are saved by *h.* but *h.* that is seen is not *h.*

1 Cor. 9. 10. husbandman partaker of his *h.*

13. 13. now abideth faith, *h.* and

15. 19. if in this life only, *h.* in Christ

Gal. 5. 5. wait for *h.* of righteousness

Eph. 2. 12. having no *h.* and without God

Col. 1. 23. not moved away from *h.* of Gospel

27. riches of glory which is Christ in you the *h.* of glory

1 Thes. 4. 13. sorrow not as others that have no *h.*

5. 8. for a helmet, the *h.* of salvation

1 Tim. 1. 1. Jesus Christ who is our *h.*

Tit. 2. 13. looking for that blessed *h.*

3. 7. according to the *h.* of eternal

Heb. 6. 11. to the full assurance of *h.*

19. which *h.* we have as an anchor

1 Pet. 1. 3. begotten us again to a lively *h.*

21. that your faith and *h.* might be

3. 15. asketh a reason of *h.* in you

1 John 3. 3. a man that has his *h.* in

Ps. 16. 9. my flesh also shall rest *in hope*

Rom. 4. 18. against *h.* believed—

5. 2. rejoice—of glory of God, 12. 12.

Tit. 1. 2.—eternal life of which God promised

Ps. 39. 7. *my hope* is in thee

71. 5. thou art—Jer. 17. 17.

22. 9. didst make me hope when I was

31. 24. all ye that *h.* in the Lord

33. 18. on them that *h.* in his mercy, 22.

42. 5. *h.* thou in God, for, 11.

119. 49. thou hast caused me to *h.*

81. I *h.* in thy word, 114.

130. 7. let Israel *h.* in the Lord

147. 11. those that *h.* in his mercy

Lam. 3. 26. good that a man should *h.*

Rom. 8. 25. if we *h.* for that we see

---

1 Pet. 1. 13. be sober and *h.* to end

Ps. 119. 43. I *hoped* in thy judgments

74. I have *h.* in thy word, 147

Heb. 11. 1. faith is the substance of things *h.* for

1 Cor. 13. 7. charity *hopeth* all things

Luke 6. 35. lend, *hoping* for nothing

HORN of my salvation, Ps. 18. 2.

Ps. 75. 4. lift not up the *h.* 5. 10.

92. 10. my *h.* shalt thou exalt as the *h.* of the unicorn

148. 14. he exalted the *h.* of his people

Luke 1. 69. raised up *h.* of salvation

Mic. 4. 13. I will make thy *h.* iron and hoofs brass

Dan 8. 20. having two *horns*

Hab. 3. 4. *h.* coming out of his hand

Rev. 13. 1. beast having ten *h.*

13. 11. had two *h.* like a lamb

5. 6. lamb having seven *h.*

HORRIBLE, Ps. 11. 6. Jer. 5. 30. Hos. 6. 10. Jer. 2. 12. Ezek. 32. 10.

HORROR, Gen. 15. 12. Job 18. 20. Ps. 55. 5. & 119. 53. Ezek. 7. 18.

HORSE, Ex. 15. 21.

Ps. 32. 9. be ye not as *h.* or mule

33. 17. *h.* is a vain thing for safety

147. 10. he delighteth not in the strength of the *h.*

Prov. 21. 31. *h.* is prepared for the day of battle

Eccl. 10. 7 I have seen servants on *h.*

Jer. 8. 6. as *h.* rusheth into battle

12. 5. canst thou contend with *h.*

Hos. 14. 3. we will not ride upon *h.*

Zech. 1. 8. & 6. 2, 3, 6. *h.* red, white, black, Rev. 6. 2, 4, 5, 8. & 9. 17.

HOSPITALITY, Rom. 12. 13. I Tim. 3. 2. Tit. 1. 8. 1 Pet. 4. 9.

HOST, Luke 10. 35. Rom. 16. 23. Ps. 27. 3. Isa. 40. 26. Luke 2. 13.

HOT, Ps. 38, 1. & 39. 3. Prov. 6. 28. Hos. 7. 7. 1 Tim. 4. 2. Rev. 3. 15.

HOUR, Dan. 3. 6, 15. & 4. 33.

Matt. 10. 19. shall be given you in the same *h.*

25. 13. ye know neither day nor *h.*

Luke 12. 12. Holy Ghost shall teach you that same *h.*

Luke 22. 53. this is your *h.* and power of darkness

John 2. 4. my *h.* is not yet come

4. 23. the *h.* cometh and now is

7. 30. *h.* was not yet come, 8. 20.

12. 27. save me from this *h.* unto h.

Rev. 3. 3. not know what *h.* I come

10. will keep thee from *h.* of temptation

17. 12. power as kings one *h.* with beast

18. 10. in one *h.* is thy judgment

HOUSE, Ex. 20. 17. Lev. 14. 36.

Job 21. 28. where is the *h.* of prince

30. 23. *h.* appointed for all living

Prov. 3. 33. curse of the Lord is in *h.* of

7. 27. her *h.* is in the way to hell

12. 7. *h.* of righteous shall stand

19. 14. *h.* and riches are inheritance of fathers

Eccl. 7. 2. go to the *h.* of mourning, than to the *h.* of feasting

12. 3. when keepers of *h.* tremble

Song 2. 4. brought me to banqueting *h.*

Isa. 5. 8. wo to them that join *h.* to *h.*

60. 7. I will glorify the *h.* of my

64. 11. our holy and beautiful *h.*

Matt. 10. 13. *h.* worthy, 12. 25. a *h.* divided

23. 38. *h.* left desolate, Luke 11. 17. Jer. 12. 7.

Luke 12. 3. proclamied on *h.* tops

John 14. 2. in my Father's *h.* are

Rom. 16. 5. church in their *h.* Col. 4. 15. Philem. 2.

2 Cor. 5. 1. earthly *h. h.* of God not made with hands

2. *h.* from heaven

---

2 Tim. 1. 16. give mercy to the *h.* on Onesiphorus

Heb. 3. 3. built *h.* hath more honour than the *h.*

2 John 10. receive him not into *h.*

Ps. 105. 21. made him Lord of all *his house*

112. 3. wealth and riches shall be in—

Acts 10. 2. feared God with all—

16. 34. believed in God with all—

Heb. 3. 2. faithful in all—5. 6.

11. 7. made an ark for saving—

John 4. 53. his *whole house* believed

Josh. 24. 15. as for me and *my house*

Ps. 101. 2. will walk within—with

Isa. 56. 7. joyful in—of prayer, Matt. 21. 13. Mark 11. 7. Luke 19. 46.

Matt. 12. 44. will return to—

Deut. 6. 7. when sittest in *thy house*

Ps. 26. 8. I loved habitation of—

36. 8. satisfied with fatness of—

Isa. 38. 1. set—in order, for thou

Acts 11. 14. thou and all—saved

Gen. 28. 17. *house of God* or Lord, Ps. 42. 4. Eccl. 5. 1. Isa. 2. 3. Mic. 4. 2. 1 Tim. 3. 15. 1 Pet. 4. 17. Ex. 23. 19. Josh. 6. 24. and about 100 other places

Job 4. 19. dwell in *houses* of clay

Ps. 49. 11. *h.* shall continue for ever

Matt. 11. 8. in soft linen sit in king's *h.*

19. 29. forsaken *h.* or lands

23. 14. devour widows' *h.*

Luke 16. 4. may receive me into *h.*

1 Cor. 11. 22. have ye not *h.* to eat

1 Tim. 3. 12. ruling their own *h.* well

2 Tim. 3. 6. creep into *h.* and lead captive

Tit. 1. 11. subvert whole *h.* teaching things which they ought not

Acts 16. 15. baptized and her whole *household*

Gal. 6. 10. *h.* of faith

Eph. 2. 19. *h.* of God

Matt. 13. 52. like *householder*

HOW long, Ps. 6. 3. Isa. 6. 11. Jer. 4. 14. Dan. 8. 13. & 12. 6. Matt. 17. 17. Luke 9. 41. Rev. 6. 10.

Job 15. 16. *how much more,* Matt. 7. 11. Luke 12. 24. Heb. 9. 14.

Matt. 18. 21. *how oft,* Luke 13. 34. Job 21. 17.

HOWL, Isa. 13. 6. Jer. 4. 8. Joel 1. 5. James 5. 1. Hos. 7. 14. Deut. 32. 10. Amos 8. 3.

HUMBLE, Job 22. 29.

Ps. 9. 12. forgetteth not the cry of *h.*

17. forget not the *h.*

17. desire of the *h.*

34. 2. *h.* shall hear of it, and be

69. 32. *h.* shall see this, and be glad

Prov. 16. 19. to be of an *h.* spirit with lowly

29. 23. honour shall uphold *h.* in spirit

Isa. 57. 15. of contrite and *h.* spirit to revive the spirit of *h.* and heart

James 4. 6. giveth grace to the *h.*

Ex. 10. 3. thou refuse to *h.* thyself

Deut. 8. 2. to *h.* thee, and to prove

Prov. 6. 3. *h.* thyself, and make sure thy friend

Jer. 13. 18. *h.* yourselves, sit down

Matt. 18. 4. whoso *h.* himself shall be exalted, 23. 12. Luke 14. 11.

James 4. 10. *h.* yourselves in sight of the Lord

1 Pet. 5. 6. *h.* yourselves therefore

Lev. 26. 41. if uncircumcised hearts be *humbled*

2 Kings 22. 19. hast *h.* thyself before the Lord

2 Chron. 12. 6. princes and kings *h.* themselves

12. he *h.* himself, 32. 26. & 33. 12.

33. 12, 23. *h.* not himself before the Lord, 36. 12.

Ps. 35. 13. I *h.* my soul with fasting

113. 6. Lord who *h.* himself to behold

Isa. 2. 11. lofty looks shall be *h.*

5. 15. mighty man shall be *h.* and eyes of the lofty shall be *h.*

10. 33. high and haughty shall be *h.*

Jer. 44. 10. are not *h.* unto this day

Lam. 3. 20. my soul is *h.* in me

Dan. 5. 22. hast not *h.* thy heart

Phil. 2. 8. *h.* himself and became obedient

Deut. 21. 14. *humbled her*, 22. 24. Ezek. 22. 10, 11.

Col. 3. 12. put on *humbleness* of

Mic. 6. 8. walk *humbly* with thy God

Prov. 22. 4. by *humility* are riches and honour, 15. 33. & 18. 2.

Acts 20. 19. serving Lord with all *h.*

Col. 2. 18. in a voluntary *h.* 23.

1 Pet. 5. 5. be clothed with *h.*

HUNGER, Ex. 16. 3.

Ps. 34. 10. young lions suffer *h.*

Prov. 19. 15. idle soul shall suffer *h.*

Jer. 42. 14. no war nor have *h.* of

Lam. 4. 9. sword better than slain with *h.*

Deut. 8. 3. suffered thee to *h.*

Isa. 49. 10. shall not *h.* nor thirst

Matt. 5. 6. blessed are they that *h.*

Luke 6. 21. blessed are ye that *h.* now

Rom. 12. 20. if thine enemy *h.* feed

1 Cor. 4. 11. we both *h.* and thirst

11. 34. if any man *h.* let him eat at

Ps. 107. 9. fill the *hungry* with goodness

146. 7. God giveth food to the *h.*

Prov. 25. 21. if enemy be *h.* give him

27. to *h.* every bitter thing is sweet

Isa. 58. 7. is it not to deal bread to the *h.*

10. if thou draw out thy soul to *h.*

65. 13. shall eat, but ye shall be *h.*

Ezek. 18. 7. hath given bread to the *h.*

Luke 1. 53. filled the *h.* with good

Phil. 4. 12. how to be full and to be *h.*

HUNT, 1 Sam. 26. 20. Job. 38. 39.

Ps. 140. 11. evil doth *h.* the violent

Prov. 6. 26. adulteress will *h.* for

12. 27. slothful roasts not what he took in *h.*

Job. 10. 16. thou *huntest* me as a fierce lion

HURT, Gen. 4. 23. & 26. 29. ,

Josh. 24. 20. will turn and do you *h.*

Ps. 15. 4. sweareth to his *h.* and

Eccl. 5. 13. riches kept for owners, to their *h.*

Jer. 6. 14. healed *h.* of the daughter

Rev. 2. 11. shall not be *h.* of second death

6. 6. *h.* not the oil and wine

Ezra 4. 15. *hurtful*, Ps. 144. 10.

1 Tim. 6. 9. fall into foolish and *h.* lusts

HUSBAND, Gen. 3. 6, 16.

Ex. 4. 25. bloody *h.* art thou to me

Isa. 54. 5. thy Maker is thy *h.* Lord of hosts

Jer. 31. 32. though I was a *h.* to them

Mark 10. 12. if a woman put away her *h.*

John 4. 17. I have no *h.*

18. and five *h.*

1 Cor. 7. 34. careth how she may please *h.*

14. 35. let them ask *h.* at home

2 Cor. 11. 2. espoused you to one *h.*

Eph. 5. 22. wives submit to your *h.*

23. the *h.* is the head of wife, 24.

25. *h.* love your wives as Christ

Eph. 5. 33. the wife see that she reverence her *h.*

Col. 3. 18. wives submit to your *h.*

1 Pet. 3. 1. subject to their own *h.*

7. ye *h.* dwell with them, according to knowledge

HUSBANDMAN, my Father is, John 15. 1.

---

1 Tim. 2. 6. *h.* that labours must be

1 Cor. 3. 9. ye are God's *husbandry*

HYMN, Matt. 26. 30. Eph. 5. 19.

HYPOCRISY, Isa. 32. 6. Matt. 23. 28. Mark 12. 15. Luke 12. 1. 1 Tim. 4. 2. James 3. 17. 1 Pet. 2. 1.

Matt. 7. 5. *hypocrite*, Luke 6. 42.

24. 51. appoint him portion with *h.*

Job 20. 5. joy of *h.* is but for a moment

27. 8. what is the hope of the *h.*

36. 13. *h.* in heart heap up wrath

Isa. 9. 17. every one is a *h.* and evil

33. 14. fearfulness hath surprised *h.*

Matt. 6. 2. *hypocrites*, 6. 16.

Job 8. 13. the *h.* hope shall perish

15. 34. congregation of *h.* shall be desolate

I & J

IDLE, they be, Ex. 5. 8, 17.

Prov. 19. 15. an *i.* soul shall suffer

Matt. 12. 36. every *i.* word give

20. 3. standing *i.* 6. why stand ye *i.*

Luke 24. 11. words seemed as *i.* tales

1 Tim. 5. 13. they learn to be *i.* not only

Prov. 31. 27. *idleness*, Eccl. 10. 8.

IDOL, 2 Chron. 15. 16. & 33. 7.

Isa. 16. 3. as if he blessed an *i.*

Zech. 11. 17. who to the *i.* shepherd

1 Cor. 8. 4. an *i.* is nothing in world

Ps. 96. 5. gods of nations are *idols*

Isa. 2. 8. land is full of *i.* they worship them

Jer. 50. 38. they are mad upon *i.*

Hos. 4. 17. Ephraim is joined to *i.*

Acts 15. 20. abstain from pollutions of *i.*

Rom. 2. 22. thou that abhorrest *i.*

1 Cor. 8. 1. touching things offered to *i.*

2 Cor. 6. 16. agreement hath temple of God with *i.*

1 John 5. 21. keep yourselves from *i.*

Rev. 2. 14. eat things sacrificed to *i.*

9. 20. worship devils and *i.* of gold

1 Cor. 5. 10, 11. *idolater*, 6. 9. Eph. 5. 5. Rev. 21. 8. & 22. 15.

1 Sam. 15. 23. stubbornness as iniquity and *idolatry*

Acts 17. 16. city wholly given to *i.*

1 Cor. 10. 14. clearly beloved, flee *i.*

Gal. 5. 20. *i.* witchcraft, hatred

Col. 3. 5. covetousness, which is *i.*

1 Pet. 4. 3. walked in abominable *idolatries*

IGNORANCE, sin through, Lev. 4. 2. Num. 15. 24. Acts 3. 15.

Acts 17. 30. the times of this *i.* God winked at

Eph. 4. 18. alienated through *i.*

Ps. 73. 22. so foolish was I and *ignorant*

Isa. 63. 16. though Abraham be *i.* of us

Rom. 10. 3. being *i.* of God's righteousness

1 Cor. 14. 38. if any man be *i.* let him be *i.*

Heb. 5. 2. who can have compassion on *i.*

Acts 17. 23. *ignorantly*, 1 Tim. 1. 13.

ILLUMINATED, Heb. 10. 32.

IMAGE, Lev. 26. 1. Dan. 2. 31.

Gen. 1. 26. let us make man in our own *i.* 27. & 5. 1. Col. 3. 10.

Gen. 5. 3. Adam begat a son after his *i.*

Ps. 73. 20. Lord, thou shalt despise their *i.*

Matt. 22. 20. whose *i.* is this

Rom. 8. 29. conformed to *i.* of Son

1 Cor. 15. 49. have borne the *i.* of the earthy we shall bear also *i.* of the heavenly

4. 4. Christ who is the *i.* of God

2 Cor. 3. 18. into same *i.* from glory to

Heb. 1. 3. express *i.* of his person

Rev. 13. 14. make an *i.* to the beast

Ex. 23. 24. break down *images*

IMAGINE, Ps. 2. 1. Nah. 1. 9. Zech. 7. 10. & 8. 17. Acts 4. 25.

Gen. 6. 5. every *imagination* of the thoughts was evil, 8. 21. Deut. 29. 19.

Prov. 6. 18. Lam. 3. 60, 61. Rom. 1. 21. 2 Cor. 10. 5.

IMMEDIATELY, Mark 4. 15.

IMMORTAL, 1 Tim. 4. 17.

Rom. 2. 7. seek for *immortality*

1 Cor. 15. 53. this mortal must put on *i.*

1 Tim. 6. 16. who only hath *i.* in light

2 Tim. 1. 10. brought *i.* to light by Gospel

IMMUTABLE, Heb. 6. 17.

IMPART, Luke 3. 11. Rom. 1. 11. 1 Thess. 2. 8.

IMPENITENT heart, Rom. 2. 5.

IMPERIOUS whorish woman, Ezek. 16. 30.

IMPORTUNITY, Luke 11. 8.

IMPLACABLE, Rom. 1. 31.

IMPOSSIBLE, Matt. 17. 20.

Luke 1. 37. with God nothing is *i.*

17. 1. it is *i*, but offences will come

Heb. 6. 4. it is *i.* for those enlightened

18. in two things it is *i.* for God to

11. 6. without faith it is *i.* to please

IMPUDENT, Prov. 7. 13.

IMPUTE, 1 Sam. 22. 15. Lev. 7. 18.

Ps. 32. 2. to whom Lord *i.* not iniquity

Rom. 4. 6. *i.* righteousness without

8. blessed to whom Lord will not *i.*

11. righteousness might be *i.* to them

22. *i.* to him for righteousness

5. 13. sin is not *i.* when there is no law

2 Cor. 5. 19. not *i.* their trespasses

James 2. 23. *i.* to him for righteousness

IN Christ, Acts 24. 24. Rom. 12. 5. 1 Cor. 1. 2. 2 Cor. 1. 21. 2 Gal. 1. 22. Eph. 1. 1. Phil. 1. 1. Col. 1. 2.

1 Thes. 1. 1. *in God*, 4. 16. John 3. 21. Gen. 15. 16. *in the Lord*, Ps. 4. 5. Isa. 45. 17. Jer. 3. 23. Zech. 12. 5. 1 Cor. 1. 31. Phil. 4. 2, 4. Col. 3. 18. 1 Thes. 5. 12. Philem. 16. 20.

INCLINE, heart, Josh. 24. 23. Judg. 9. 3. 1 Kings 8. 58. Ps. 119. 36.

Ps. 78. 1. *incline*, 40. 1. Prov. 2. 2. Jer. 7. 24. Isa. 55. 3.

INCLOSED, Ps. 17. 10. & 22. 16. Song 4. 12. & 8. 9. Lam. 3. 9.

INCONTINENT, 1 Cor. 7. 5.

INCORRUPTIBLE, Rom. 1. 23. 1 Cor. 9. 25. to obtain an *i.* crown, 15. 23. born not of corruptible seed, but of *i.*

1 Cor. 15. 42. *incorruption*

INCREASE, Lev. 19. 25.

Lev. 25. 36. take no usury nor *i.*

Num. 32. 14. risen up an *i.* of sinful

Deut. 16. 15. bless thee in all thine *i.*

Ps. 67. 6. earth yield her *i.* 85. 12.

Prov. 3. 9. with first fruits of all *i.*

Isa. 9. 7. of the *i.* of his government

Ezek. 18. 8. neither taken any *i.*

Col. 2. 19. increaseth with *i.* of God

Ps. 62. 10. if riches *i.* set not heart

115. 14. Lord shall *i.* you more and

Prov. 1. 5. wise man will *i.* learning

Eccl. 5. 11. when goods *i.* they are

Isa. 29. 19. meek shall *i.* their joy in the Lord

Luke 17. 5. Lord, *i.* our faith

John 3. 30. he must *i.* but I decrease

1 Thes. 3. 12. Lord make you to *i.* in

2 Tim. 2. 16. will *i.* to more ungodliness

Ezra 9. 6. iniquities are *increased* over our head

Isa. 9. 3. multiplied nation, not *i.* joy

26. 15. hast *i.* nation, O Lord, hast *i.*

Luke 2. 52. Jesus *i.* in wisdom and

Acts 6. 7. the word of God *i.* and the

Rev. 3. 17. am rich and *i.* with goods

Eccl. 1. 18. *increaseth* knowledge, *i.* sorrow.

Col. 2. 19. whole body *i.* with the increase of God

1 Chron. 11. 9. David went on *increasing*

Col. 1. 10. *i.* in knowledge of God

INCREDIBLE thing, Acts 26. 8.

INCURABLE wound, Job 34. 6. Mic. 1. 9. *i.* bruise, Jer. 30. 12, 15.

INDEED, 1 Kings 8. 27. 1 Chron. 4. 10. Matt. 3. 11. Luke 4. 24. John 1. 47. 1 Tim. 5. 3, 5. 1 Pet. 2. 4.

INDIGNATION, Neh. 4. 1. Esth. 5. 9. Ps. 69. 24. & 78. 49.

Isa. 10. 5. staff in their hand is my *i.*

26. 20. hide thee until *i.* be overpast

Mic. 7. 9. I will bear the *i.* of Lord

Nah. 1. 6. who can stand before his *i.*

Matt. 20. 24. moved with *i.*

26. 8. they had *i.*

Rom. 2. 8. *i.* and wrath, tribulation

2 Cor. 7. 11. yea, what *i.* yea, what

Heb. 10. 27. fiery *i.* which shall devour

Rev. 14. 10. poured into cup of his *i.*

INDITING, Ps. 45. 1.

INEXCUSABLE, Rom. 2. 1.

INFALLIBLE, proofs, Acts 1. 3.

INFANT, 1 Sam. 15. 3. Job 3. 16. Isa. 65. 20. Hos. 13. 16. Luke 18. 15.

INFIDEL, 2 Cor. 6. 15. 1 Tim. 5. 8.

INFINITE inquities, Job 22. 5.

Ps. 147. 5. his understanding is *i.*

Nah. 3. 9. her strength, and it was *i.*

INFIRMITY, Ps. 77. 10.

Prov. 18. 14. the spirit of a man will sustain his *i.*

Matt. 8. 17. himself took our *infirmities*

2 Cor. 12. 9. glory in my *i.*

10. pleasure in *i.*

1 Tim. 5. 23. drink wine for thine often *i.*

Heb. 4. 15. with the feeling of our *i.*

5. 2. himself compassed with *i.*

INFLAME them, wine, Isa. 5. 11.

INFLICTED, 2 Cor. 2. 6.

INFLUENCES, Job 38. 11.

INGRAFTED, Jas. 1. 21.

INHABIT, Prov. 10. 30.

Ps. 22. 3. thou that *inhabitest* the praises of Israel

Isa. 57. 15. lofty One that *inhabiteth*

INHERIT, Gen. 15. 8. Ps. 82. 8.

1 Sam. 2. 8. to make them *i.* throne of glory

Ps. 25. 13. his seed shall *i.* earth

27. 11. meek shall *i.* the earth

Ps. 37. 29. the righteous shall *i.* the land, Isa. 60. 21.

82. 8. O God, thou shalt *i.* all nations

Prov. 3. 35. wise shall *i.* glory; but

8. 21. love me to *i.* substance

Matt. 19. 29. hath forsaken, shall *i.* everlasting life

25. 34. *i.* kingdom prepared for you

Mark 10. 17. what shall I do that I may *i.* eternal life, Luke 10. 25.

1 Cor. 6. 9. unrighteous not *i.* the kingdom of God, 10.

15. 50. flesh and blood cannot *i.* the kingdom of God

Gal. 5. 21. do such things not *i.* the kingdom of God

Heb. 6. 12. through faith *i.* promises

1 Pet. 3. 9. that ye should *i.* blessing

Rev. 21. 7. overcometh shall *i.* all

Num. 18. 20. I the Lord am thy *inheritance*, Deut. 10. 9. Ezek. 44. 28.

Deut. 4. 20. a people of *i.* 9. 20. 1 Kings 8. 5. Ps. 28. 9. Isa. 19. 25.

Ps. 16. 5. Lord is portion of mine *i.*

47. 4. Lord shall choose our *i.* for

Prov. 19. 14. riches are *i.* of fathers

Eccl. 7. 11. wisdom is good with an *i.*

Acts 20. 32. *i.* among the sanctified

Eph. 1. 11. among whom he obtained an *i.*
14. earnest of our *i.* and purchased
5. 5. hath an *i.* in the kingdom of Christ and of God
Col. 1. 12. partakers of *i.* of saints
3. 24. shall receive the reward of *i.*
Heb. 9. 15. receive promise of eternal *i.*
1 Pet. 1. 4. to an *i.* incorruptible
INIQUITY, Gen. 15. 16.
Ex. 20. 5. visiting *i.* of the fathers on children, 34. 7. Num. 14. 18.
Ex. 34. 7. forgiving *i.* transgression
Lev. 26. 41. accept the punishment of their *i.* 43.
Num. 23. 21. not beheld *i.* in Jacob
Deut. 32. 4. a God of truth, without *i.*
Job 4. 8. they that plough *i.* reap the
5. 16. stopped her mouth
Job 11. 6. less than thine *i.* deserveth
Ezra 9. 13.
Job 15. 16. man drinketh in *i.* like
22. 23. put away *i.* far from thee
34. 32. if I have done *i.* I will do no
Ps. 32. 5. mine eye have I not hid, and thou forgavest the *i.* of my sin
39. 11. with rebukes correct man for *i.*
49. 5. when *i.* of my heels compass
51. 5. behold I was shapen in *i.*
66. 18. if I regard *i.* my heart
69. 27. add *i.* unto their *i.*
119. 3. they also do not *i.* they walk
133. let not *i.* have dominion
Isa. 1. 4. a people laden with *i.* a seed
5. 18. wo to them that draw *i.* with
33. 24. people shall be forgiven their *i.*
40. 2. her warfare accomplished, her *i.* pardoned
53. 6. Lord laid on him the *i.* of us
57. 17. for *i.* of his covetousness was I wroth
Isa. 59. 3. defiled your fingers with *i.*
Jer. 2. 5. what *i.* have your fathers found in me
3. 13. only acknowledge thine *i.*
31. 30. every one shall die for *i.*
50. 20. *i.* of Israel be sought for
Ezek. 3. 18. he shall die in his *i.*
18. 30. so *i.* shall not be your ruin
Dan. 9. 24. makes reconciliation for *i.*
Mic. 7. 18. a God like thee, that pardoneth *i.*
Matt. 7. 23. depart from me ye that work *i.*
24. 12. because *i.* shall abound
Acts 8. 23. in gall of bitterness and bond of *i.*
Rom. 6. 19. servants to uncleanness and to *i.* unto *i.*
1 Cor. 13. 6. charity rejoiceth not in *i.*
2 Thes. 2. 7. mystery of *i.* already
2 Tim. 2. 19. that nameth Christ depart from *i.*
Tit. 2. 14. he might redeem us from all *i.*
James 3. 6. tongue is a fire, a world of *i.*
Ps. 18. 23. *my iniquity*, 25. 11.
Job 34. 22. *workers of iniquity*, Ps. 5. 5. Prov. 10. 29. Luke 13. 27.
Lev. 16. 21. confess over him all *iniquities*, 26. 39. pine in their *i.* and *i.* of their fathers
Ezra 9. 6. our *i.* are increased over
13. punished us less than our *i.* deserve
Job 13. 26. to possess *i.* of my youth
Ps. 38. 4. mine *i.* are gone over my
40. 12. mine *i.* have taken hold upon
51. 9. hide from my sins, blot out my *i.*
65. 3. *i.* prevail against me, as for
79. 8. remember not against us former *i.*
90. 8. thou hast set our *i.* before
103. who forgiveth all thine *i.*
10. not rewarded us according to *i.*

107. 17. fools because of *i.* are afflicted
130. 3. if thou, Lord, shouldest mark *i.*
8. he shall redeem Israel from all *i.*
Prov. 5. 22. his own *i.* shall take the wicked
Isa. 43. 24. hast wearied me with *i.*
53. 5. he was wounded, bruised for *i.*
Jer. 14. 7. though our *i.* testify against us
Dan. 4. 27. break off thy *i.* by showing
Mic. 7. 19. he will subdue our *i.* and
Acts 3. 26. bless you in turning from *i.*
Rom. 4. 7. blessed are they whose *i.* are forgiven
Rev. 18. 5. God hath remembered her *i.*
Isa. 53. 11. he shall bear *their iniquities*
Jer. 33. 8. I will cleanse them from all—and I will pardon all—
Ezek. 43. 10. may be ashamed of—
Heb. 8. 12. their sins, and—will I remember no more, 10. 17.
Num. 14. 34. shall ye bear *your iniquities*
Isa. 50. 1. for—have ye sold yourselves
59. 2.—have separated between you and God
65. 7.—and the *i.* of your fathers
Jer. 5. 25.—turned away these things
Ezek. 24. 23. ye shall pine away for—
36. 31. loathe yourselves for all—
33. I shall have cleansed you from all—
Amos 3. 2. I will punish you for all—
INJURED me, Gal. 4. 12.
1 Tim. 1. 13. was a persecutor and *injurious*
INK, 2 John 12. 3 John 13.
INNER, 1 Kings 6. 27. Eph. 3. 16.
INNOCENT, Ps. 19. 13.
Gen. 20. 5. in *innocency* of hands
Ps. 6. 6. wash my hands in *i.*
Dan. 6. 22. before him *i.* was found in me
Hos. 8. 5. how long ere they attain *i.*
INNUMERABLE, Job 21. 23. Ps. 40. 12. 1 Heb. 11. 12.
INORDINATE, Ezek. 23. 11.
INQUISITION, Deut. 19. 18.
INSCRIPTION to unknown God, Acts 17. 23.
INSPIRATION, Job 32. 8. 2 Tim. 3. 16.
INSTANT, Isa. 29. 5. Jer. 18. 7. Rom. 12. 12. 2 Tim. 4. 2. Acts 12. 5.
Luke 7. 4. besought him *instantly*
Acts 26. 7. *i.* serving God day and
INSTRUCT, Deut. 4. 36.
Neh. 9. 20. thy good Spirit to *i.* them
Job 40. 2. contendeth with Almighty *i.*
16. 7. my reins *i.* me in the night
32. 8. I will *i.* thee, and teach thee
Song 8. 2. mother who would *i.* me
Isa. 28. 26. his God doth *i.* him to discretion
Dan. 11. 33. that understand, shall *i.*
1 Cor. 2. 16. Lord that he may *i.* him
Isa. 8. 11. Lord *instructed* me
Ps. 2. 10. be *i.* ye judges of earth
Matt. 13. 52. every scribe, *i.* unto the kingdom
Phil. 4. 12. in all things I am *i.* both
2 Tim. 2. 25. in meekness *i.* those
Rom. 2. 20. an *instructer* of foolish
Job 33. 16. sealeth their *instruction*
Ps. 50. 17. hatest *i.* and casteth my
Prov. 4. 13. take fast hold of *i.* keep
19. 27. cease to hear *i.* that causeth
23. 12. apply thy heart to *i.* and
2 Tim. 3. 16. profitable for *i.* in righteousness
INSTRUMENTS, Gen. 49. 5.
Ps. 7. 13. prepared for him *i.* of death
Rom. 6. 13. neither yield members

i. of unrighteousness; but *i.* of righteousness to God
Isa. 32. 7. the *i.* of the churl are evil
INTANGLE, Matt. 22. 15. Gal. 5. 1. 2 Tim. 2. 4. 2 Pet. 2. 20.
INTEGRITY, Gen. 20. 5.
Job 2. 3. still he holdeth fast his *i.*
27. 5. I will not remove mine *i.*
Ps. 7. 8. according to my *i.* that is
25. 21. let *i.* and uprightness preserve me
26. 1. I have walked in mine *i.*
Prov. 11. 3. *i.* of upright shall guide
INTERCESSION, Jer. 7. 16.
Isa. 53. 12. made *i.* for transgressors
Rom. 8. 26. Spirit maketh *i.* for us
34. who also maketh *i.* for
11. 2. Elias maketh *i.* to God against Israel
1 Tim. 2. 1. prayers and *i.* be made
Heb. 7. 25. he ever liveth to make *i.*
Isa. 59. 16. wondered there was no *intercessor*
INTERMEDDLE, Prov. 14. 10.
INTERPRETATION, Gen. 40. 5. Judg. 7. 15. Dan. 2. 4. 1 Cor. 12. 10. 2 Pet. 1. 20.
Job 33. 23. *interpreter* one among a thousand
INTREAT, Gen. 12. 16. Ex. 8. 8.
1 Sam. 2. 25. man sin, who shall *i.*
1 Cor. 4. 13. we suffer; being defamed, we *i.*
1 Tim. 5. 1. but *i.* him as a father
James 3. 17. gentle and easy to be *intreated*
Prov. 18. 23. the poor useth *intreaties*
2 Cor. 8. 4. praying us with much *i.*
INTRUDING into those things, Col. 2. 18.
INVENT, Amos 6. 5. Rom. 1. 30.
Ps. 99. 8. tookest vengeance of their *inventions*
106. 29. provoked him with their *i.*
39. went a whoring with their *i.*
Prov. 8. 12. find out knowledge of witty *i.*
Eccl. 7. 29. men have sought many *i.*
INVISIBLE, Rom. 1. 20. Col. 1. 15.
INWARD, Job 19. 19.
Ps. 5. 9. *inward part*, 51. 6. Prov. 20. 27.
Rom. 7. 22. *inward man*
2 Cor. 7. 15. *inward affection* is
Ps. 62. 4. curse *inwardly*
Matt. 7. 15. *i.* wolves
Rom. 2. 29. he is a Jew that is one *i.*
IRON, Prov. 27. 17.
Eccl. 10. 10. if the *i.* be blunt, put to
Isa. 48. 4. neck is an *i.* sinew, and
Jer. 15. 12. shall *i.* break northern *i.*
Dan. 2. 33. legs of *i.* his feet *i.* and
4. 23. even with a band of *i.* and
5. 23. praised gods of silver, brass and *i.*
1 Tim. 4. 2. conscience seared with a hot *i.*
ISSUES from death, Ps. 68. 20.
Prov. 4. 23. out of heart are the *i.* of life
ITCHING ears, 2 Tim. 4. 3.
IVORY, 1 Kings 10. 18. Ps. 45. 8.
JEALOUS God, I am a, Ex. 20. 5. Deut. 5. 9. Josh. 24. 19.
1 Kings 19. 10. I have been very *j.* for the Lord, 14.
Ezek. 39. 25. be *j.* for my holy name
Joel 2. 18. will Lord be *j.* for land
Nah. 1. 2. God is *j.* and the Lord revengeth
Zech. 1. 14. I am *j.* for Jerusalem.
2 Cor. 11. 2. *j.* over you with Godly *jealousy*
Deut. 29. 20. Lord's *j.* shall smoke against man
32. 16. provoke him to *j.* with strange gods, 21. 1 Kings 14. 22.
Ps. 79. 5. shall thy *j.* burn like fire
Prov. 6. 34. *j.* is the rage of a man
Song 8. 6. *j.* is cruel as the grave
Rom. 10. 19. provoke them to *j.*

1 Cor. 10. 22. do we provoke Lord to *j.*
JEHOVAH, Ex. 6. 3. Ps. 83. 18. Isa. 12. 2. Gen. 22. 14. Ex. 17. 15. Judg. 6. 24. It is about 2000 times translated Lord, in capitals
JERUSALEM, for the church, Isa. 24. 23. Gal. 4. 25. Heb. 12. 22.
JESHURUN, i.e. Israel, Deut. 32. 15. & 33. 5, 26. Isa. 44. 2.
JESUS, or Joshua, Acts 7. 45.
JESUS, the Saviour of men, Matt. 1. 21. 1 Cor. 12. 3. 2 Cor. 4. 5. Eph. 4. 21. Heb. 2. 9. Rev. 22. 16. and in abou 650 other places.
JEWS first, and also Greeks, Rom. 1. 16., not a *J.* which is one outwardly but is a *J.* which is one inwardly, 29.
Rom. 10. 12. no difference between *J.* and Greek
1 Cor. 9. 20. to *J.* I became as a *J.* to gain *J.*
Gal. 3. 28. neither *J.* nor Greek
Rev. 2. 9. say they are *J.* and are not
JEWELS, Mal. 3. 14.
JOIN, Ex. 1. 10. Ezra 9. 14.
Prov. 11. 21. though hand *j.* hand
Isa. 5. 8. wo to them that *j.* house to
Jer. 50. 5. let us *j.* ourselves to Lord
Acts 5. 13. of the rest durst no man *j.* himself
Hos. 4. 17. Ephraim is *joined* to idols
Num. 25. 3. Israel *j.* himself to Baalpeor, Ps. 106. 28.
Eccl. 9. 4. *j.* to all living there is hope
Zech. 2. 11. many nations shall be *j.* to the Lord
Matt. 19. 6. what God hath *j.* let not
1 Cor. 1. 10. be perfectly *j.* together
6. 17. he that is *j.* to the Lord is one spirit
Eph. 5. 31. shall be *j.* to his wife
Col. 2. 19. all the body by *joints* and bands
Heb. 4. 12. dividing asunder of *j.*
JOURNEY, Num. 9. 13.
JOY, 1 Chron. 12. 40.
Neh. 8. 10. *j.* of Lord is your strength
Esther 8. 17. the Jews had *j.* and gladness
Job 20. 5. *j.* of the hypocrite is for a moment
Ps. 16. 11. in thy presence is fulness of *j.*
30. 5. but *j.* cometh in the morning
43. 4. I will go to God, my exceeding *j.*
51. 8. make me hear *j.* and gladness
12. restore to me *j.* of thy salvation
126. 5. who sow in tears shall reap in *j.*
137. 6. prefer Jerusalem above my chief *j.*
Eccl. 9. 7. eat thy bread with *j.* and gladness
Isa. 9. 3. hast not increased the *j.* they *j.* according to *j.* in harvest
12. 3. with *j.* shall draw water out
35. 10. with songs and everlasting *j.* they shall obtain everlasting *j.* upon their heads
61. 3. give them oil of *j.* for mourning
7. everlasting *j.* shall be to them
66. 5. shall appear to your *j.*
Zeph. 3. 17. the Lord will *j.* over thee
Matt. 2. 10. rejoiced with exceeding great *j.*
13. 20. hear word, and with *j.* receiveth it
24. 21. enter into *j.* of thy Lord
Luke 1. 44. babe leaped in my womb for *j.*
15. 7. *j.* shall be in heaven over one
24. 41. while they believed not for *j.*
John 15. 11. your *j.* might be full
16. 20. your sorrow be turned into *j.*
22. your *j.* no man taketh from you
17. 13. my *j.* fulfilled in themselves
Acts 20. 24. finish my course with *j.*

Rom. 14. 17. righteousness and peace and *j.* in the Holy Ghost
15. 13. fill you with all *j.* and peace
2 Cor. 1. 24. we are helpers of your *j.*
2. 3. my *j.* is the *j.* of you all
Gal. 5. 22. fruit of the Spirit is love, *j.*
Phil. 4. 1. brethren, my *j.* and crown
1 Thes. 1. 6. receive word with *j.* of the Holy Ghost
Heb. 12. 12. who for the *j.* set before
13. 17. give account with *j.* not
James 1. 2. count it all *j.* when ye
1 Pet. 1. 8. rejoice with *j.* unspeakable
4. 13. rejoice, be glad with exceeding *j.*
1 John 1. 4. we write that your *j.* be
Col. 2. 5. *joying* and beholding your
Heb. 12. 11. no chastening is *joyous*
Ezra 6. 22. the Lord made them *joyful*
Ps. 35. 9. my soul shall be *j.* in Lord
63. 5. I will praise thee with *j.* lips
89. 15. blessed they that know *j.* sound
Eccl. 7. 14. in day of prosperity be *j.*
Isa. 56. 7. make them *j.* in my house of prayer
61. 10. my soul shall be *j.* in God
2 Cor. 7. 4. exceeding *j.* in all tribulations
Deut. 28. 47. servedst not the Lord with *joyfulness*
Col. 1. 11. patience and long suffering with *j.*
Eccl. 9. 9. live *joyfully* with the wife
Heb. 10. 34. took *j.* spoiling of your goods
JUDGE, Deut. 17. 9. & 25. 2.
Gen. 18. 25. shall not the *J.* of earth
Ex. 2. 14. who made thee a *j.*
Judg. 11. 27. Lord the *J.* be *j.* this day
1 Sam. 2. 25. the *j.* shall *j.* him; but
Isa. 32. 22. Lord is our *j.* and lawgiver
Ps. 68. 5. father of fatherless and *j.* of widows
75. 7. God is *j.* he putteth down
Luke 12. 14. who made me **a** *j.* over
Acts 10. 42. to be the *j.* of quick and
Heb. 12. 23. are come to God the *J.*
Gen. 16. 5. Lord *j.* between me and thee, 1 Sam. 24. 12.
Deut. 32. 36. the Lord shall *j.* his people, Ps. 135. 14. Heb. 10. 30.
Ps. 7. 8. Lord shall *j.* the people, *j.* me, O Lord
9. 8. the Lord shall *j.* world in righteousness, 96. 13. Acts 17. 31.
Mic. 3. 11. heads thereof *j.* for reward
Matt. 7. 1. *j.* not that ye be not judged
John 5. 30. as I hear I *j.*
12. 47. I came not to *j.* the world
Acts 23. 3. sittest thou to *j.* me after
Rom. 2. 16. when God shall *j.* secrets of
3. 6. then how shall God *j.* the world
14. 10. why dost thou *j.* thy brother
1 Cor. 4. 3. I *j.* not mine own self
5. *j.* nothing before the time, until the Lord come
6. 3. know ye that we shall *j.* angels
11. 31. if we would *j.* ourselves, we
14. 29. let prophets speak, and others *j.*
Col. 2. 16. let no man *j.* you in meat
2 Tim. 4. 1. who shall *j.* the quick and the dead, 1 Pet. 4. 5.
James 4. 11. if ye *j.* the law; not a doer, but a *j.*
Ps. 51. 4. *judgest*, Rom. 14. 4.
Ps. 7. 11. God *judgeth* the righteous
58. 11. he is a God that *j.* in earth
John 5. 22. the Father *j.* no man; but hath committed all *j.* unto the Son
1 Cor. 2. 15. he that is spiritual *j.* all
4. 4. he that *j.* me is the Lord
Matt. 19. 28. *judging* twelve tribes
Deut. 1. 17. the *judgment* is God's

Ps. 1. 5. the ungodly not stand in the *j.*
9. 16. the Lord is known by the *j.*
101. 1. I will sing of mercy and *j.*
119. 66. teach me good *j.* for
Prov. 21. 15. it is joy to just to do *j.*
Eccl. 11. 9. God will bring into *j.*
Isa. 1. 27. Zion shall be redeemed with *j.*
28. 17. *j.* also will I lay to the line
Isa. 42. 1. bring forth *j.* to the Gentiles
53. 8. was taken from prison and *j.*
Jer. 5. 1. if there be any that executeth *j.*
8. 7. they know not the *j.* of Lord
Dan. 4. 37. all whose ways are *j.*
7. 22. *j.* was given to the saints
Hos. 12. 6. keep mercy and *j.* wait on God
Amos 5. 7. who turn *j.* to wormwood
24. let *j.* run down as waters, and
Matt. 5. 21. be in danger of the *j.*
12. 20. till he send forth *j.* unto victory
John 5. 22. Father committed all *j.* to the Son
27. given him authority to execute *j.*
9. 39. for *j.* I am come into the world
16. 8. reprove the world of sin and *j.*
Acts 24. 25. he reasoned of *j.* to come
Rom. 5. 18. *j.* came on all men to condemnation
14. 10. must all stand before *j.* seat
Heb. 9. 27. all men once to die, but after this the *j.*
1 Pet. 4. 7. *j.* must begin at house of God
Jude 15. execute *j.* upon all the ungodly
Rev. 17. 1. show thee *j.* of great
Ps. 19. 9. *judgments* of Lord are true
36. 6. thy *j.* are a great deep
119. 75. I know that thy *j.* are right
108. O Lord, teach me thy *j.*
120. I am afraid of thy *j.*
Isa. 26. 8. in the way of thy *j.* we waited
9. when thy *j.* are in the earth
Jer. 12. 1. let me talk with thee of *j.*
Rom. 11. 33. how unsearchable are his *j.*
JUST man was Noah, Gen. 6. 9.
Lev. 19. 36. *j.* balance, *j.* weights, *j.* ephah, and a *j.* hin, Deut. 25. 15.
Deut. 16. 20. that is *j.* shalt thou follow
32. 4. a God of truth, *j.* and right
Prov. 4. 18. path of *j.* is as shining
10. 16. blessings are on head of *j.*
11. 1. but a *j.* weight is his delight
12. 21. no evil shall happen to *j.*
17. 26. to punish the *j.* is not good
20. 7. a *j.* man walketh in integrity
21. 15. it is joy to *j.* to do judgment
24. 16. a *j.* man falleth seven times, and riseth
Eccl. 7. 15. *j.* man that perisheth in his righteousness
20. there is not a *j.* man on earth
Isa. 26. 7. way of the *j.* is uprightness; thou dost weigh the path of the *j.*
45. 21. none beside me; a *j.* God
Hab. 2. 4. *j.* shall live by his faith
Zeph. 3. 5. the *j.* Lord is in the midst thereof
Matt. 1. 19. Joseph being a *j.* man
Luke 15. 7. more than over ninety-nine *j.* persons
20. 20. who should feign themselves *j.*
John 5. 30. my judgment is *j.* because I seek not
Acts 7. 52. showed coming of *j.* one
24. 15. resurrection both of *j.*
Rom. 2. 13. not the hearers of the law are *j.*
3. 26. he might be *j.* and justifier
7. 12. commandment holy, *j.* and

Phil. 4. 8. whatsoever things are true, *j.*
Col. 4. 1. give that which is *j. and*
Heb. 2. 2. received a *j.* recompense
12. 23. the spirits of *j.* men made perfect
1 Pet. 3. 18. suffered once *j.* for the
1 John 1. 9. he is faithful and *j.* to forgive
Rev. 15. 3. *j.* and true are thy ways
Mic. 6. 8. to do *justly* and love
Luke 23. 41. we indeed *j.* for we
1 Thes. 2. 10. how *j.* we behaved
Gen. 18. 19. to do *justice* and
Job. 37. 23. excellent in power and plenty of *j.*
Ps. 89. 14. *j.* and judgment are the habitation of thy throne
Prov. 8. 15. by me princess decree *j.*
Jer. 31. 23. O habitation of *j.*
Ezek. 45. 9. execute judgment and *j.*
JUSTIFY, Ex. 23. 7.
Deut. 25. 1. they shall *j.* righteous
Job 9. 20. if I *j.* myself, my mouth
27. 5. God forbid that I should *j.*
33. 32. speak, for I desire to *j.* thee
Isa. 5. 23. wo to them that *j.* the wicked for reward
53. 11. shall my servant *j.* many
Luke 10. 29. he, willing to *j.* himself
Rom. 3. 30. God shall *j.* circumcision
Gal. 3. 8. God would *j.* heathen
Job 11. 2. should a man full of talk be *justified*
13. 18. I know I shall be *j.*
25. 4. can a man be *j.* with God
32. 2. he *j.* himself rather than God
Ps. 51. 14. mightest be *j.* when thou speakest
143. 2. in thy sight shall no man living be *j.*
Isa. 43. 9. that they may be *j.*
45. 25. in the Lord shall the seed of Israel be *j.*
Jer. 3. 11. *j.* herself more than Judah
Ezek. 16. 51. *j.* thy sisters in all abominations, 52.
Matt. 11. 19. wisdom is *j.* of her children, Luke 7. 35.
12. 37. by thy words thou shalt be *j.*
Luke 7. 29. *j.* God, being baptized of
18. 14. went away *j.* rather than
Acts 13. 39. are *j.* from all things, which ye could not be *j.* by law
Rom. 2. 13. doers of law shall be *j.*
3. 4. might be *j.* in thy sayings
20. there shall no flesh be *j.* in his
24. being *j.* freely by his grace
28. man is *j.* by faith without deeds
4. 2. if Abraham were *j.* by works
5. 1. being *j.* by faith we have
9. being *j.* by his blood, be saved
8. 30. whom he *j.* them he also
1 Cor. 4. 4. yet am I not hereby *j.*
6. 11. ye are *j.* in name of the Lord
Gal. 2. 16. not *j.* by works of law, we might be *j.* by faith of Christ
2. 11. no man is *j.* by the law, it is
Gal. 3. 24. that we might be *j.* by faith
5. 4. *j.* by the law, are fallen from grace
1 Tim. 3. 16. God manifest in flesh, *j.* in Spirit
Tit. 3. 7. that being *j.* by his grace
James 2. 21. was not Abraham *j.* by works
24. by works a man is *j.* not faith
25. was not Rahab *j.* by works
Prov. 17. 15. he that *justifieth* the wicked
Isa. 50. 8. he is near, that *j.* me
Rom. 4. 5. God that *j.* the ungodly
8. 33. it is God that *j.* who is he that
3. 26. the *justifier* of him that believeth
1 Kings 8. 32. condemning the wicked, *justifying* the righteous.
Rom. 4. 25. raised for our *justification*

K

KEEP, Gen. 2. 15. & 33. 9.
Gen. 18. 19. *k.* the way of the Lord
28. 15. I am with thee and will *k.*
Gen. 28. 20. if God will be with me and *k.* me
Ex. 23. 7. *k.* thee far from a false
20. I send an angel to *k.* thee in
Num. 6. 24. Lord bless thee, and *k.* thee
Deut. 23. 9. *k.* thee from every wicked
29. 9. *k.* words of this covenant
1 Sam. 2. 9. he will *k.* the feet of his
1 Chron. 4. 10. thou wouldst *k.* me
Ps. 25. 10. such as *k.* his covenant
20. *k.* my soul, 17. 18. *k.* me as the apple of thine eye
39. 1. I will *k.* my mouth with a bridle
89. 28. my mercy will I *k.* for him
91. 11. angels to *k.* thee in all ways
103. 9. not chide nor *k.* his anger
106. 3. blessed they that *k.* judgment
119. 2. *k.* his testimonies, 88, 129.
146. *k.* thy precepts, 4. 63. *k.* his statutes, 119. 33. *k.* his word and law, 17. 34, 57, 106, 136.
127. 1. except the Lord *k.* the city
140. 4. *k.* me
141. 3. *k.* the door of lips, 4.
Eccl. 5. 1. *k.* thy foot when thou goest
Isa. 26. 3. Lord will *k.* him in perfect
27. 3. I the Lord *k.* it; I will *k.* it
Jer. 3. 12. I will not *k.* anger for ever
Hos. 12. 6. *k.* mercy and judgment
Mic. 7. 5. *k.* the door of thy mouth
Mal. 2. 7. priest's lips *k.* knowledge
Luke 11. 28. hear the word of God and *k.* it
John 12. 25. he that hateth his life shall *k.* it
14. 23. if man love me, will *k.* my
17. 11. holy Father, *k.* through thy
15. thou shouldst *k.* them from
1 Cor. 5. 8. let us *k.* the feast, not
11. not to *k.* company with such
9. 27. I *k.* under my body, and
Eph. 4. 3. endeavouring to *k.* unity of
Phil. 4. 7. peace of God shall *k.* your
2 Thes. 3. 3. Lord shall establish and *k.*
1 Tim. 5. 22. of other men's sins: *k.* thyself pure
6. 20. *k.* that is committed to thy trust
2 Tim. 1. 12. able to *k.* that which is
14. that good thing which was committed to thee, *k.* by Holy Ghost
James 1. 27. *k.* himself unspotted
2. 10. *k.* whole law, and yet offend in
Jude 21. *k.* yourselves in love of God
24. who is able to *k.* you from
Rev. 1. 3. blessed they that hear and *k.*
3. 10. I will *k.* thee from the hour of
22. 9. thy brethren which *k.* sayings
Lev. 26. 3. if ye *keep* my *commandments*
Deut. 6. 7. diligently—always, 11. 1.
13. 4.—his—and obey his voice.
Ps. 119. 60. I delayed not to—thy—
Prov. 4. 4.—my—and live, 7. 2.
Eccl. 12. 13. fear God and—his—
Matt. 19. 17. if ye will enter into life—my—
John 14. 15. if ye love me—my—
1 John 2. 3. we know him, if we—his—
5. 3. this is love of God that we—his—
Rev. 14. 12. here are they that—the—
Judg. 3. 19. *keep silence*, Ps. 35. 22. Eccl. 3. 7. Isa. 41. 1. Lam. 2. 10. Amos 5. 13. Hab. 2. 20. 1 Cor. 14. 28.
1 Kings 8. 23. who *keepest* covenant and mercy, Chron. 6. 14. Neh. 9. 32.
Deut. 7. 9. which *keepeth* covenant, Neh. 1. 5.

Ps. 121. 3. he that *k.* thee will not slumber
146. 6. which *k.* truth for ever
Prov. 13. 3. he that *k.* his mouth, *k.*
29. 18. he that *k.* the law, happy
1 John 5. 18. that is of God *k.* himself
Rev. 16. 15. blessed is he that *k.* his garment
22. 7. blessed is he that *k.* this prophecy
Ex. 34. 7. *keeping* mercy for thousands
Ps. 19. 11. in *k.* of them is great delight
Dan. 9. 4. *k.* the covenant and mercy
1 Pet. 4. 19. commit the *k.* of their souls
Ps. 121. 5. the Lord is thy *keeper*
Eccl. 12. 3. when *k.* of house shall
Song 1. 6. made me *k.* of vineyards
5. 7. *k.* took away my veil from me
Tit. 2. 5. chaste, *k.* at home, good
Deut. 32. 10. *k.* them as apple of eye
33. 9. they *kept* thy covenant
Josh. 14. 10. Lord hath *k.* me alive
2 Sam. 22. 22. *k.* ways of Lord
23. *k.* myself from mine iniquity
Job 23. 11. his ways have I *k.* and
Ps. 17. 4. me from paths of the
30. 3. *k.* me alive, that I go not
Song 1. 6. mine own vineyard have I not *k.*
Matt. 19. 20. these I *k.* from my youth
Luke 2. 19. Mary *k.* all these things
John 15. 20. if they have *k.* my sayings
17. 6. they have *k.* thy word
12. all thou gavest me I have *k.*
Rom. 16. 25. *k.* secret since the world
2 Tim. 4. 7. I have *k.* the faith
1 Pet. 1. 5. *k.* by the power of God through faith
Rev. 3. 8. hast *k.* my word, and not
KEY of house of David, Isa. 22. 22. Rev. 3. 7.
Matt. 16. 19. *k.* of the kingdom of
Luke 11. 52. taken away the *k.* of
Rev. 1. 18. I have *k.* of hell
9. 1. *k.* of the bottomless pit, 20. 1.
KICK, Deut. 32. 15. 1 Sam. 2. 29. Acts 9. 5. & 26. 14.
KID, Isa. 11. 6. Luke 15. 29.
Song 1. 8. feed *k.* beside shepherds'
KILL, thou shalt not, Ex. 20. 13.
Deut. 32. 39. I *k.* and I make alive
2 Kings 5. 7. I am God to *k.* and
Eccl. 3. 3. time to *k.* and to heal
Matt. 10. 28. fear not them which *k.* the body, but are not able to *k.* the soul
Mark 3. 4. lawful to save life, or *k.*
Acts 10. 13. rise, Peter, *k.* and eat
1 Kings 21. 19. hast thou *killed* and
Ps. 44. 22. we are *k.* all day
Luke 12. 5. after he hath *k.* hath power
Acts 3. 15. *k.* the Prince of Life whom
2 Cor. 6. 9. we are chastened, and not *k.*
1 Thes. 2. 15. both *k.* the Lord and prophets
Rev. 13. 10. that *k.* with sword must be *k.*
Matt. 23. 37. thou that *killest* the prophets, Luke 13. 34.
1 Sam. 2. 6. Lord *killeth* and maketh alive
John 16. 2. who *k.* you will think he doeth God service
2 Cor. 3. 6. letter *k.* the spirit giveth life
KIND, Gen. 1. 11. 2 Chron. 10. 7.
Luke 6. 35. he is *k.* to unthankful
1 Cor. 13. 4. charity suffereth long and is *k.*
Eph. 4. 32. be *k.* to one another
1 Sam. 20. 14. show me the *kindness* of the Lord
2 Sam. 9. 3. may show the *k.* of God
16. 17. is this thy *k.* to thy friend

Neh. 9. 17. a God slow to anger and of great *k.*
Ps. 117. 2. his merciful *k.* is great
141. 5. righteous smite me; it shall be a *k.*
Prov. 19. 22. the desire of a man is his *k.*
31. 26. in her tongue is law of *k.*
Isa. 54. 8. with everlasting *k.* will I have mercy on thee
10. my *k.* shall not depart from thee
Jer. 2. 2. I remember thee, the *k.* of
Joel 2. 13. God is of great *k.*
Col. 3. 12. put on bowels of mercy, *k.*
2 Pet. 1. 7. to godliness, brotherly *k.*
Ps. 25. 6. remember thy *loving kindness*
36. 7. how excellent is thy—
10. O continue thy—to such as
63. 3. thy—is better than life
103. 4. who crowned thee with—
Isa. 63. 7. I will mention—of the Lord
Jer. 9. 24. I the Lord which exercise—
31. 3. with—have I drawn thee
32. 18. thou showest—to thousands
Hos. 2. 19. I will betroth thee in—
KINDLE, Prov. 26. 21.
Isa. 30. 33. breath of Lord doth *k.* it
Hos. 11. 8. my repentings are *kindled*
2 Sam. 22. 9. coals *k.* by it
Ps. 2. 12. when his wrath is *k.* but a
Isa. 50. 11. in light of sparks ye have *k.*
Luke 12. 49. fire on earth, what if it be already *k.*
KING, Gen. 14. 18. & 36. 31.
Job 18. 14. bring him to *k.* of terrors
34. 18. is it fit to say to a *k.* thou
Ps. 10. 16. Lord is *K.* for ever and
24. 7. *K.* of glory shall come in
33. 16. no *k.* saved by multitude of
47. 7. God is *K.* of all the earth
74. 12. God is my *k.* 5. 2.
Prov. 30. 31. a *k.* against whom is no
Eccl. 5. 9. *k.* himself served by the field
8. 4. where word of *k.* is there is power
Song 1. 4. *k.* brought me into his chamber
12. while the *k.* sitteth at his table
7. 5. the *k.* is held in the galleries
Isa. 32. 1. *k.* shall reign in righteousness
33. 22. the Lord is our lawgiver and *k.*
43. 15. Creator of Israel, your *K.*
Jer. 10. 10. Lord is true God, and everlasting *K.*
23. 5. a *K.* shall reign and prosper
46. 18. saith the *K.* whose name is the Lord of hosts, 51. 57.
Hos. 3. 5. seek the Lord and David their *k.*
7. 5. in day of our *k.* the princes
13. 11. I gave them a *k.* in anger
Zech. 9. 9. rejoice, O Zion, thy *K.* cometh
Matt. 25. 34. then shall the *K.* say
Luke 23. 2. he himself is Christ, a *k.*
John 6. 15. come by force to make him *k.*
19. 14. behold your *k.*
15. no *k.* but Caesar
1 Tim. 1. 17. to the *K.* eternal
6. 15. *K.* of kings, and Lord of lords Rev. 16. 16. & 17. 14.
1 Pet. 2. 17. fear God, honour *k.*
Rev. 15. 3. just and true, thou *K.* of saints
Ps. 76. 12. terrible to *kings* of the earth, 72. 11.
102. 15. *k.* of the earth see thy glory
Ps. 144. 10. that giveth salvation to *k.*
Prov. 8. 15. by me *k.* reign, and
Hos. 8. 4. they set up *k.* but not by
Matt. 11. 8. they that wear soft clothing are in *k.* houses
Luke 22. 25. *k.* of Gentiles exercise

1 Cor. 4. 8. reigned as *k.* without us
1 Tim. 2. 2. give thanks for *k.* and all
Rev. 1. 6. made us *k.* and priests unto God, 5. 10.
16. 12. that way of *k.* of the east
Ex. 19. 6. be a *kingdom* of priests
1 Sam. 10. 25. Samuel told manner of *k.*
1 Chron. 29. 11. thine is the *k.* O Lord, Matt. 6. 13.
Ps. 22. 28. for the *k.* is the Lord's
Dan. 2. 24. in last days shall God set up a *k.*
4. 17. God ruleth in *k.* of men
7. 27. whose *k.* is everlasting *k.*
Matt. 12. 25. every *k.* divided against
13. 19. heareth the word of the *k.*
38. good seed are the children of *k.*
25. 34. inherit *k.* prepared for you
Mark 11. 10. blessed be the *k.* of our father David
Luke 12. 32. Father's pleasure to give you the *k.*
19. 12. to receive for himself a *k.*
22. 29. I appoint unto you a *k.* as
John 18. 36. *k.* is not of this world
1 Cor. 15. 24. have delivered up the *k.*
Col. 1. 13. translated us into the *k.*
2 Tim. 4. 18. preserve me to his heavenly *k.*
Heb. 12. 28. we receiving a *k.* not to
James 2. 5. rich in faith, heirs of *k.*
2 Pet. 1. 11. everlasting *k.* of our Lord
Rev. 1. 9. in *k.* and patience of Jesus
11. 15. the *k.* of this world are *k.* of the Lord
17. 17. to give their *k.* to the beast
Matt. 6. 33. *kingdom of God*, 12. 28. Mark 1. 15. Luke 4. 43.
John 3. 3. except born again, cannot see—5.
Rom. 14. 17.—is not meat and drink
1 Cor. 4. 20.—is not in word, but
6. 9. unrighteous shall not inherit—
15. 50. flesh and blood cannot inherit—
Eph. 5. 5. hath any inheritance in—
2 Thes. 1. 5. be counted worthy—
Rev. 12. 10. now is come—and power
Matt. 3. 2. *kingdom of heaven*
KISS the Son, Ps. 2. 12.
Song 1. 2. let him *k.* me with the *k.*
Rom. 16. 16. salute with a holy *k.*
1 Pet. 5. 14. greet with *k.* of charity
Ps. 85. 10. righteousness and peace have *kissed*
Luke 7. 38. *k.* his feet and anointed
Prov. 27. 6. *kisses* from an enemy
KNEES, Gen. 30. 3. & 41. 43.
Job 4. 4. feeble *k.* Isa. 35. 3. Heb. 12. 12.
Isa. 45. 23. to God every *k.* shall bow, Rom. 14. 11. Phil. 2. 10. Matt. 27. 29. Eph. 3. 14.
Nah. 2. 10. *k.* smite together
KNIFE, Prov. 23. 2. & 30. 14.
KNIT, 1 Sam. 18. 1. Col. 2. 2, 10.
KNOCK, Matt. 7. 7. Rev. 3. 20.
KNEW, Gen. 3. 7. & 4. 1.
Gen. 28. 16. God is in this place, I *k.* it not
Deut. 34. 10. whom Lord *k.* face to
Jer. 1. 5. before I formed thee, I *k.*
Matt. 7. 23. depart ye, I never *k.* you
John 4. 10. if you *k.* the gift of God
Rom. 1. 21. when they *k.* God, they glorified him not
2 Cor. 5. 21. him to be sin who *k.* no sin
12. 2. I *k.* a man in Christ
Deut. 8. 2. to *know* what was in thy
Josh. 22. 22. God knoweth, Israel shall *k.*
1 Sam. 3. 7. Samuel not yet *k.* the Lord
1 Kings 8. 38. man shall *k.* plague of
1 Chron. 28. 9. *k.* thou the God of
Job 5. 27. *k.* thou it for thy good
8. 9. we of yesterday, and *k.* nothing

13. 23. make me to *k.* my transgressions
22. 13. how doth God *k.*
Ps. 4. 3. *k.* the Lord set apart the godly
9. 10. that *k.* thy name will trust in
39. 4. make me to *k.* my end; that may *k.*
46. 10. be still, and *k.* that I am God
51. 6. God shall make me to *k.* wisdom
73. 16. when I thought to *k.* this
89. 15. blessed those that *k.* joyful
139. 23. *k.* my heart; and *k.* my
Eccl. 11. 9. *k.* that for all these things God will bring thee into judgment
Isa. 58. 2. they seek and delight to *k.*
Jer. 17. 9. heart is deceitful who can *k.*
22. 16. was not this to *k.* me, saith the Lord
24. 7. I will give them a heart to *k.*
31. 34. *k.* the Lord, for all shall *k.*
44. 28. shall *k.* whose words shall
Ezek. 2. 5. shall *k.* that a prophet hath, 33. 33.
Hos. 2. 20. in faithfulness *k.* the Lord
Mic. 3. 1. not for you to *k.* judgment
Matt. 6. 3. let not left hand *k.* what
7. 11. *k.* how to give good gifts, Luke 11. 13.
13. 11. given you to *k.* mystery
John 4. 42. we *k.* this is indeed Christ
7. 17. he shall *k.* of the doctrine
10. 4. sheep follow him, for they *k.*
John 10. 14. I *k.* my sheep and am known
13. 7. *k.* not now, but shalt *k.*
17. if ye *k.* these things, happy are
35. by this men *k.* ye are my disciples
Acts 1. 7. not for you to *k.* the times
Rom. 10. 19. did not Israel *k.* yes
1 Cor. 2. 14. neither can ye *k.* them
4. 19. I will *k.* not the speech but power
8. 2. *k.* anything *k.* nothing as he ought to *k.*
Eph. 3. 19. to *k.* love of Christ
1 Thes. 5. 12. to *k.* them who labour
Tit. 1. 16. they profess that they *k.* God
Ex. 4. 14. *I know,* Job 9. 2, 28.
Gen. 10. 19.—him that he will command
22. 12. now—that thou fearest God
2 Kings 19. 27.—thy abode and thy going out
Job 19. 25.—that my Redeemer liveth
Ps. 41. 11. by this—that thou favourest
Jer. 10. 13.—that the way of man is not in him
29. 11.—the thoughts that I think, saith the Lord
Matt. 25. 12.—you not
John 13. 18.—whom I have chosen
Acts 26. 27.—that thou believest
Rom. 7. 18.—that in me, *i. e.* in my flesh
1 Cor. 4. 4. though—nothing by myself
13. 12. now—in part; but then shall—
Phil. 4. 12.—how to be abased
2 Tim. 1. 12.—whom I have believed
1 John 2. 4. he that saith—him, is a liar
Rev. 2. 2.—thy works, 9. 13, 19.
Hos. 6. 3. *we know,* 8. 2. 1 Cor. 2. 12. 1 John 2. 3, 5.
John 16. 30. *thou knowest* all things
21. 17.—all things—that I love thee
Ps. 1. 6. *Lord knoweth* the way of
94. 11. Lord *k.* thoughts of man are vain
103. 14. he *k.* our frame, that we
138. 6. the proud he *k.* afar off
129. 14. my soul *k.* right well
Eccl. 9. 1. no man *k.* either love or

Isa. 1. 3. ox *k.* his owner, and ass his master's crib

Jer. 8. 7. stork *k.* appointed times

9. 24. understandeth and *k.* me to be the Lord

Zeph. 3. 5. the unjust *k.* no shame

Matt. 6. 8. *k.* what ye have need of

24. 36. of that day and hour *k.* no

1 Cor. 8. 2. *k.* anything, he *k.* nothing

2 Tim. 2. 19. Lord *k.* them that are his

James 4. 17. that *k.* to do good doeth

2 Pet. 2. 9. Lord *k.* how to deliver

Rev. 2. 17. a name which no man *k.*

Ps. 9. 16. Lord is *known* by judgment

31. 7. hast *k.* my soul in adversity

67. 2. thy way may be *k.* on earth

Isa. 45. 4. thou hast not *k.* me, 5.

Amos 3. 2. you only have I *k.* of all the families of the earth

Matt. 10. 26. there is nothing hid that shall not be *k.* Luke 8. 17.

Luke 19. 42. if thou hadst *k.* in this

Acts 15. 18. *k.* unto God are his works

Rom. 1. 19. that which may be *k.* of God

7. 7. I had not *k.* sin but by the law

1 Cor. 8. 3. the same is *k.* of him

Gal. 4. 9. *k.* God, or rather are *k.* of God

2 Tim. 3. 15. from a child hast *k.* holy

Rev. 2. 24. have not *k.* the depths of

Gen. 2. 17. *knowledge* of good and evil

1 Sam. 2. 3. the Lord is a God of *k.*

Ps. 19. 2. night unto night showeth *k.*

73. 11. is there *k.* in the Most High

94. 10. he that teacheth men *k.*

139. 6. such *k.* is too wonderful

Prov. 8. 12. I found out *k.* of inventions

9. 10. the *k.* of holy is understanding

14. 6. *k.* is easy to him that understandeth

19. 2. the soul be without *k.* is not

30. 3. I have not the *k.* of the holy

Eccl. 9. 10. there is no device nor *k.*

Isa. 28. 9. whom shall he teach *k.*

53. 11. by his *k.* shall my righteous

Jer. 3. 15. pastors shall feed you with *k.*

Dan. 12. 4. run to and fro, and *k.* be

Hos. 4. 6. are destroyed for lack of *k.*

Hab. 2. 14. earth filled with *k.* of the Lord, Isa. 11. 9.

Mal. 2. 7. priest's lips should keep *k.*

Rom. 2. 20. a teacher hast form of *k.*

3. 20. for by the law is *k.* of sin

10. 2. a zeal for God not according to *k.*

1 Cor. 8. 1. all have *k. k.* puffeth up

Eph. 3. 19. love of Christ passeth *k.*

Phil. 3. 8. loss for the excellency of the *k.* of Christ Jesus

Col. 2. 3. are hid treasures of wisdom and *k.*

3. 10. renewed in *k.* after image of

1 Pet. 3. 7. dwell with them according to *k.*

2 Pet. 1. 5. add to virtue *k.* and to *k.*

3. 18. grow in grace and in the *k.* of Jesus Christ.

L

LABOUR, Gen. 31. 42. & 35. 16.

Ps. 90. 10. yet is their strength *l.*

104. 23. a man goeth to his *l.* until even

128. 2. thou shalt eat the *l.* of thine

Prov. 14. 23. in all *l.* there is profit

Eccl. 1. 8. all things are full of *l.*

4. 8. yet is there no end of all his *l.*

Isa. 55. 2. ye spend your *l.* for that which satisfieth not

Hab. 3. 17. though *l.* of the olive

1 Cor. 15. 18. your *l.* is not in vain in the Lord

---

1 Thes. 1. 3. work of faith, and *l.* of love

Heb. 6. 10. God will not forget your *l.* of

Rev. 14. 13. dead may rest from *l.*

Prov. 23. 4. *l.* not to be rich; cease

Matt. 11. 28. come all ye that *l.* and

John 6. 27. *l.* not for meat that perisheth

1 Thes. 5. 12. know them which *l.*

1 Tim. 5. 17. honour those who *l.* in

Heb. 4. 11. let us *l.* to enter into that

Isa. 49. 4. I have *laboured* in vain

John 4. 38. other men *l.* and ye entered

1 Cor. 15. 10. I *l.* more abundantly

Phil. 2. 16. not run, nor *l.* in vain

Prov. 16. 26. he that *laboureth, l.* for

Eccl. 5. 12. sleep of the *labouring* man is sweet

Col. 4. 12. Epaphras *l.* fervently in prayer

Luke 10. 7. the *labourer* is worthy of his hire, 1 Tim. 5. 18.

Matt. 9. 37. but *labourers* are few

1 Cor. 3. 9. we are *l.* together with God

LACK, Hos. 4. 6. Matt. 19. 20. 2 Cor. 11. 9. 1 Thes. 3. 10. James 1. 5.

LADEN with iniquity, Isa. 1. 4.

Matt. 11. 28. labour and heavy *l.*

2 Tim. 3. 6. silly women, *l.* with sins

LADY of kingdoms, Isa. 47. 5.

Isa. 47. 7. I shall be *l.* for ever

2 John 1. unto the elect *l.*

Esth. 1. 18. *ladies* of Persia

Judg. 5. 29. her wise *l.* answered her

LAMB, Gen. 22. 7, 8. Ex. 12. 3.

2 Sam. 12. 3. man had nothing save one ewe *l.*

Isa. 11. 6. wolf shall dwell with *l.*

53. 7. brought as a *l.* to the slaughter

John 1. 29. behold the *L.* of God

1 Pet. 1. 19. as a *l.* without blemish

Rev. 5. 12. worthy the *L.* that was slain

6. 16. fall on us and hide us from the face of the *L.*

7. 14. robes made white in blood of the *L.* 12. 11.

17. *L.* in the midst of the throne shall feed them

13. 8. *L.* slain from the foundation of the world

LAME, Lev. 21. 18. Mal. 1. 8, 13.

Job 29. 15. eyes to blind and feet to *l.*

Prov. 26. 7. legs of the *l.* are not equal

Isa. 35. 6. the *l.* man shall leap as a hart, 33. 23.

Heb. 12. 13. lest the *l.* be turned out

LAMP, Gen. 15. 17. Ex. 27. 20. 1 Kings 15. 4. Matt. 25. 1, 3.

2 Sam. 22. 29. thou art my *l.* O Lord

Job 12. 5. is as a *l.* despised of him

Ps. 119. 105. thy word a *l.* to my feet

132. 17. I have ordained a *l.* for mine anointed

Prov. 6. 23. the commandment is a *l.*

13. 9. *l.* of wicked shall be put out

Isa. 62. 1. salvation as a *l.* that burneth

Ex. 25. 37. *seven lamps,* 37. 23. Num. 8. 2. Zech. 4. 2. Rev. 4. 5.

LAND, Eccl. 10. 16, 17. Isa. 5. 30. Deut. 19. 14. remove *landmark,* 27. 17. Job 24. 2. Prov. 22. 28.

LANGUAGE, Gen. 11. 1. Neh. 13. 24. Ps. 81. 5. Isa. 19. 18. Zeph. 3. 9.

LANGUISH, Isa. 24. 4. Ps. 41. 3.

LASCIVIOUSNESS, Mark 7. 22. 2 Cor. 12. 21. Gal. 5. 19. Eph. 4. 19. Jude 4. turning grace of God into *l.*

LAST, Num. 23. 10.

Lam. 1. 9. remembered not her *l.* end

Luke 11. 26. *l.* state is worse than first

1 Pet. 1. 5. *last time,* 20.

Jude 18. should be mockers in the—

LATTER day, Job 19. 25. *l.* end, Prov. 19. 20. *l.* house, Hag. 2. 9. *l.* time, 1 Tim. 4. 1. 2 Tim. 3. 1.

LAUGH, Gen. 17. 17.

2 Chron. 30. 10. but *l.* to scorn

Job 5. 22. at destruction and famine thou shalt *l.*

Ps. 2. 4. he that sitteth in the heavens shall *l.*

37. 13. the Lord shall laugh at him

52. 6. righteousness shall see and *l.* at

59. 8. thou, O Lord, shall *l.* at

Prov. 1. 26. I will *l.* at your calamity

Luke 6. 21. blessed that weep, for ye shall *l.*

25. wo to you that *l.* ye shall mourn

Job 8. 21. he fill thy mouth with *laughing*

Ps. 126. 2. our mouth was filled with *laughter*

Prov. 14. 13. even in *l.* heart is sorrowful

Eccl. 7. 3. sorrow is better than *l.*

Jas. 4. 9. let your *l.* be turned to mourning

LAW, Gen. 47. 26. Prov. 28. 4.

Deut. 33. 2. from his right hand went a fiery *l.*

Neh. 8. 7. caused to understand the *l.*

10. 28. separated from people to *l.* of God

Job 22. 21. receive the *l.* from his mouth

Ps. 1. 2. his delight is in *l.* of the Lord, and in his *l.* doth meditate

19. 7. *l.* of the Lord is perfect

37. 31. *l.* of his God is in his heart

78. 5. he appointed a *l.* in Israel

119. 72. *l.* of thy mouth is better

Prov. 6. 23. *l.* is light, 13. 14. *l.* of wise

7. 2. keep thy *l.* as apple of eye

28. 9. turns away from hearing *l.*

29. 18. keepeth the *l.* happy is he

Isa. 2. 2. shall go forth the *l.*

8. 16. seal the *l.* among my disciples

20. to the *l.* and the testimony

Isa. 42. 21. magnify the *l.* and make it honourable

51. 7. people in whose heart is my *l.*

Jer. 18. 18. *l.* shall not perish from priest

31. 33. I will put my *l.* in inward parts

Ezek. 7. 26. *l.* shall perish from priest

Hos. 8. 12. written great things of my *l.*

Mal. 2. 7. people seek *l.* at his mouth

Luke 16. 16. *l.* and prophets till John

John 1. 17. *l.* was given by Moses

19. 7. we have a *l.* and by our *l.* he

Acts 13. 39. not justified by *l.* of Moses

Rome 2. 12. sinned without *l.* shall perish without *l.*

13. not hearers of *l.* but doers of *l.*

14. having not *l.* are a *l.* to themselves

3. 20. by deeds of *l.* shall no flesh be justified, for by *l.* is knowledge of sin

27. boasting by what *l.* by *l.* of faith

31. do we make void the *l.*

4. 15. *l.* worketh wrath; where no *l.* no transgression

5. 13. sin not imputed, where no *l.* is

7. 7. had not known sin but by *l.*

8. for without the *l.* sin was dead

9. I was alive without the *l.* once

12. the *l.* is holy, just, and good

14. *l.* is spiritual, but I am carnal

22. I delight in the *l.* of God

23. *l.* in my members against *l.* of my mind

8. 2. *l.* of Spirit made free from *l.* of sin

10. 4. Christ end of *l.* for righteousness

5. righteousness of *l.* 9. 31, 32.

1 Cor. 6. 1. dare any of you go to *l.*

Gal. 2. 16. man not justified by works of the *l.*

19. I through the *l.* am dead to *l.*

---

3. 10. of works of the *l.* are under curse

12. the *l.* is not of faith, but the

13. Christ redeemed us from the curse of the *l.*

5. 23. love, faith, against such there is no *l.*

1 Tim. 1. 8. *l.* is good if we use it lawfully

9. that *l.* is not made for righteous

Heb. 7. 19. *l.* made nothing perfect

James 1. 25. whoso looketh into perfect *l.*

1 John 3. 4. sin transgresseth the *l.* sin is transgression of *l.*

Neh. 9. 26. cast *thy law* behind their backs

Ps. 40. 8.—is within thy heart

94. 12. whom thou teachest out of—

119. 70. I delight in—77, 92, 174

18. wondrous things out of—

97. how I love—113, 163. 165, 167

Ezek. 1. 8, 5. do that which is *lawful* and right, 33. 41, 19.

1 Cor. 6. 12. all things *l.* to me

Isa. 33. 22. Lord is *lawgiver*

LAY, Gen. 19. 33, 35. Job 29. 19.

Eccl. 7. 2. the living will *l.* it to heart

Isa. 28. 16. I *l.* in Zion a tried stone

Mal. 2. 2. I cursed, ye do not *l.* it to

Matt. 8. 20. hath not where to *l.* his head

Acts 7. 60. *l.* not this sin to their

15. 28. *l.* on you no greater burden

Rom. 8. 33. who *l.* any thing to the

Heb. 12. 1. *l.* aside every weight

James 1. 21. *l.* apart all filthiness and superfluity of, 1 Pet. 2. 1.

John 10. 15. *lay down life,* 13. 37.

1 Tim. 5. 22. *lay hands,* Heb. 6. 2.

6. 12. *lay hold* on eternal life

Heb. 6. 18.—on hope set before us

Matt. 6. 20. *lay up* for yourselves

2 Cor. 12. 14. children ought not to for parents

Ps. 62. 9. to be *laid* in the balance

89. 19. I *l.* help on one that is

Isa. 53. 6. Lord *l.* on him iniquities

Matt. 3. 10. axe *l.* to root of trees

1 Cor. 3. 10. I have *l.* foundation

Heb. 6. 1. not *l.* again foundation or repentance

1 Sam. 21. 12. David *laid up* these words

Ps. 31. 19. thy goodness—for them that fear thee

Song 7. 13. pleasant fruits—for thee

Luke 1. 66.—in their hearts

12. 19. much goods—for many years

Col. 1. 5. hope which is—for you

1 Tim. 6. 19.—in store a good foundation

2 Tim. 4. 8.—for me a crown of

Job 21. 19. God *layeth* up his iniquities for his

24. 12. yet God *l.* not folly to them

Prov. 2. 7. *l.* up wisdom

26. 24. *l.* up deceit

Isa. 56. 2. blessed the man that *l.* hold

57. 1. no man *l.* to heart

Jer. 12. 11. land desolate; no man *l.* it to heart

LEAD, Ex. 15. 10. Job 19. 24. Zech. 5. 7, 8. Gen. 33. 14. Ex. 13. 21.

Ps. 5. 8. *lead me* in thy righteousness

25. 5.—in thy truth

27. 11.—in a plain path

61. 2.—to rock higher than I

24.—in the way everlasting

Song 8. 2. I would *l.* thee into my mother's house

Isa. 11. 6. a little child shall *l.* them

40. 11. gently *l.* those with young

Matt. 15. 14. if blind *l.* blind

1 Tim. 2. 2. may *l.* a quiet and peaceful life in all

Rev. 7. 17. Lamb shall *l.* them to

Ps. 23. 2. *leadeth* me beside still

48. 17. God which *l.* thee by way

Matt. 7. 13. gate *l.* to destruction
14. *l.* to life
John 10. 3. calleth sheep and *l.* them
Rom. 2. 4. goodness of God to repentance
Gen. 24. 27. *Lord led,* 48. Ex. 13. 18.
Deut. 8. 2. Neh. 9. 12. Ps. 77. 20.
Isa. 48. 2. Jer. 26. 17.
Rom. 8. 14. *led by spirit,* Gal. 5. 18.
Isa. 55. 4. *leader* to people 9. 16.
LEAF, Job 13. 25. Ezek. 47. 12.
LEAGUE, Job 5. 23.
LEAN not to own understanding
Prov. 3. 5.
Job 8. 15. he shall *l.* upon his house
Song 8. 5. that *l.* on her beloved
Mic. 3. 11. yet will they *l.* on Lord
John 13. 23. *l.* on Jesus' bosom
LEANNESS, Job 16. 8. Ps. 106. 15.
Isa. 10. 16. my *l.* my *l.*
LEAP, Song 2. 8. Isa. 35. 6.
Luke 1. 41. & 6. 23. rejoice and *l.* for joy
LEARN to fear me, Deut. 4. 10.
Ps. 119. 71. might *l.* thy statutes
Prov. 22. 25. lest thou *l.* his way
Isa. 1. 17. *l.* to do well, seek
26. 10. yet will he not *l.* righteousness
Jer. 10. 2. *l.* not way of the heathen
Matt. 9. 13. *l.* what that means, I will have mercy
11. 29. *l.* of me, for I am meek and lowly in heart
1 Tim. 2. 11. let woman *l.* in silence
Tit. 3. 14. let ours *l.* to maintain good
Rev. 14. 3. no man could *l.* that song
Ps. 106. 35. *learned* their works
Isa. 50. 4. Lord God hath given me the tongue of the *l.*
John 6. 45. hath *l.* of Father cometh
Acts 7. 22. Moses was *l.* in all wisdom
Eph. 4. 20. ye have not so *l.* Christ
Phil. 4. 11. I have *l.* whatsoever state
Heb. 5. 8. though a son, *l.* obedience
Prov. 1. 5. wise increase *learning*
Acts 26. 24. much *l.* doth make thee mad
Rom. 15. 4. was written for our *l.*
2 Tim. 3. 7. ever *l.* never come to truth
LEAST, Gen. 32. 10.
Jer. 31. 34. shall know me from *l.* to
Matt. 11. 11. *l.* in kingdom of God is
Luke 16. 10. faithful in *l.* is faithful
1 Cor. 6. 4. judge who are *l.* esteemed
15. 9. I am *l.* of all the apostles
Eph. 3. 8. less than the *l.* of all saints
LEAVE father and mother and cleave to his wife. Gen. 2. 24. Matt. 15. 5. Eph. 5. 31.
1 Kings 8. 57. let him not *l.* us, nor
Ps. 16. 10. not *l.* my soul in hell
27. 9. *l.* me not, neither forsake me
Matt. 5. 24. *l.* there thy gift before
23. 23. and not to *l.* other undone
John 14. 18. I will not *l.* you comfortless
27. peace I *l.* with you, my peace
Heb. 13. 5. I will never *l.* nor forsake
Acts 14. 17. *left,* Rom. 9. 29. Heb. 4. 1. Jude 6. Rev. 2. 4.
LEAVEN, Ex. 12. 15. Lev. 2. 11.
Matt. 13. 33. kingdom of heaven is like *l.*
16. 6. beware of *l.* of Pharisees
1 Cor. 5. 7. purge out old *l.* of malice
6. a little *l.* leaveneth lump
LEES, Isa. 25. 6. Jer. 48. 11.
LEGS, Ps. 147. 10. Prov. 26. 7.
LEND, Ex. 22. 15. Deut. 23. 19, 20.
Jer. 15. 10. neither *l.* on usury, nor men *l.* me
Luke 6. 35. do good and *l.* hoping
Ps. 37. 26. ever merciful and *lendeth*
Prov. 19. 17. giveth to poor, *l.* to Lord
22. 7. borrower is servant to *lender*
1 Sam. 1. 28. I have *lent* him to the Lord

LEOPARD, Song 4. 8. Isa. 11. 6. Jer. 5. 6. Hos. 13. 7. Hab. 1. 8.
LESS, Ezra 9. 13. Job 11. 6. Isa. 40. 17. Heb. 7. 9. Eph. 3. 8. Gen. 32. 10.
LETTER, Rom. 7. 2. 2 Cor. 3. 6.
LETTEST, Luke 2. 29. 2 Thes. 2. 7.
LEVIATHAN, Job 41. 1. Ps. 74. 14.
LIBERAL, Prov. 11. 25. Isa. 32. 5, 8. 2 Cor. 9. 13.
1 Cor. 16. 3. *liberality*
James 1. 5. God giveth to all men *liberally*
LIBERTY, Lev. 25. 10.
Ps. 119. 45. I walk at *l.* for I seek thy
Isa. 61. 1. to proclaim *l.* to the captives
Luke 4. 18. to set at *l.* the bruised
Rom. 8. 21. into glorious *l.* of the children of God
2 Cor. 3. 17. where Spirit of Lord is there is *l.*
Gal. 5. 1. stand fast in *l.* wherewith Christ
13. use not *l.* for an occasion to the
James 1. 25. looketh into the law of *l.*
2. 12. be judged by the law of *l.*
1 Pet. 2. 16. not using *l.* for a cloak
LIE, Lev. 6. 3. Job 11. 3.
Ps. 58. 3. wicked go astray speaking *l.*
62. 9. men of a high degree are a *l.*
101. 7. that telleth a *l.* shall not tarry
Hos. 11. 12. compasseth me about with *l.*
2 Thes. 2. 11. they should believe a *l.*
1 Tim 4. 2. speaking *l.* of hypocrisy
Rev. 22. 15. loveth and maketh a *l.*
Num. 23. 19. God is not a man, that he should *l.*
Isa. 63. 8. children that will not *l.*
Heb. 2. 3. it shall speak and not *l.*
Col. 3. 9. *l.* not one to another
Tit. 1. 2. God that cannot *l.* promised
Heb. 6. 18. impossible for God to *l.*
Ps. 116. 11. I said, all men are *liars*
Tit. 1. 12. the Cretians are always *l.*
Rev. 2. 2. hast tried and found them *l.*
21. 8. all *l.* shall have part in the lake
Isa. 44. 25. Lord frustrateth tokens of *l.*
John 8. 44. he is a *liar* and the father
Rom. 3. 4. God be true, every man a *l.*
1 John 1. 10. we make him a *l.*
2. 4. keepeth not commandments is a *l.*
Ps. 119. 29. remove from me the way of *lying*
163. I abhor *l.* but love thy law
Prov. 12. 19. *l.* tongue but for a moment
Jer. 7. 4. trust not in *l.* words, temple
Hos. 4. 2. by stealing and *l.* they break
Jonah 2. 8. observe *l.* vanities
LIFE, Gen. 2. 7, 9. & 42. 15.
Deut. 30. 15. set before you *l.* and good, and death and evil
32. 47. not a vain thing, it is your *l.*
1 Sam 25. 29. soul bound in bundle of *l.*
Job 10. 12. granted me *l.* and favour
Ps. 16. 11. thou wilt show the path of *l.*
21. 4. asked *l.* of thee and thou gavest
30. 5. and joy in his favour is *l.*
36. 9. with thee is the fountain of *l.*
63. 3. loving-kindness better than *l.*
66. 9. God holdeth our soul in *l.*
91. 16. with long *l.* will I satisfy
Prov. 8. 35. whoso findeth me findeth *l.*
15. 24. way of *l.* is above to wise
18. 21. death and *l.* in power of tongue
Isa. 57. 10. hast found *l.* of thy hand
Matt. 6. 25. take no thought for *l.*

Luke 12. 15. man's *l.* consists not in
John 1. 4. in him was *l.* and the *l.* was light.
3. 36. believeth on Son hath everlasting *l.*
5. 40. not come, that ye might have *l.*
6. 35. I am the bread of *l.* 48. 40.
51. my flesh I give for *l.* of world
63. words I speak are spirit and *l.*
8. 12. followeth me shall have light of *l.*
10. 10. I am come that they might have *l.*
11. 25. I am the resurrection and *l.*
14. 60. I am the way, truth, and *l.*
Rom. 5. 17. reign in *l.* by Jesus Christ, 18. 21.
8. 2. law of Spirit of *l.* in Christ Jesus hath made free from *l.* of sin
6. to be spiritually minded is *l.* and
2 Cor. 2. 16. the savour of *l.* unto *l.*
3. 5. the letter killeth, but the spirit giveth life
4. 11. *l.* of Jesus might be manifest
5. 4. mortality might be swallowed up of *l.*
Gal. 2. 20. the *l.* I now live in flesh
Eph. 4. 18. being alienated from *l.* of God
Col. 3. 3. your *l.* is hid with Christ
4. Christ who is our *l.* shall appear
1 Tim. 2. 2. lead a peaceful *l.* in godliness
4. 8. having promise of the *l.* that
2 Tim. 1. 10. brought *l.* and immortality to light
2 Pet. 1. 3. that pertain to *l.* and
1 John 5. 12. he that hath the Son hath *l.* he that hath not the Son hath not *l.*
Job 2. 4. all that a man hath will he give for *his life*
Prov. 13. 3. keepeth his mouth, keepeth—
Matt. 20. 28. Son of man gave—a ransom
Rom. 5. 10. much more saved by—
1 Kings 19. 4. to take away *my life*
Ps. 26. 9. gather not—with bloody men
27. 1. the Lord is strength of—
Jonah 2. 6. brought up—from corruption
John 10. 15. I lay down—for sheep
Acts 20. 24. neither count I—dear to myself.
Ps. 17. 14. *this life,* Luke 8. 14. Acts 5. 20. 1 Cor. 15. 19. & 6. 3.
Deut. 30. 23. he is *thy life,* and
Ps. 103. 4. redeem—from destruction
Jer. 39. 18.—shall be for a prey
Prov. 10. 16. tends *to life,* 11. 19.
Matt. 7. 14. John 5. 24. Acts 11. 18.
Rom. 7. 10. Heb. 11. 35. 1 John 3. 14.
LIFT *up* his countenance on thee, Num. 6. 26.
1 Sam. 2. 7. Lord brings low—again
2 Kings 19. 4.—prayer for remnant, Isa. 37. 4.
2 Chron. 17. 6. heart—in ways of the Lord
Ps. 4. 6. Lord—light of thy countenance
7. 6. Lord—thyself because of the rage
24. 7.—ye gates,—ye doors, and
25. 1. to thee I—my soul, 86. 4.
75. 4.—not the horn, 5.
83. 2.—the head
102. 10. thou—me and castest me down
121. 1. *l.* mine eyes, 123. 1.
147. 6. Lord—the meek, but casts
Prov. 2. 3.—thy voice for understanding
Eccl. 4. 10. one will—his fellow
Isa. 26. 11. Lord when thy hand is—
33. 10. I will be exalted: now I—myself
42. 2. he shall not cry, nor—voice

Jer. 7. 16. nor—a prayer for them
Lam. 3. 14. let us—our hearts with
Hab. 2. 4. his soul which is—is not right
Luke 21. 28.—your heads for day of redemption
John 3. 14. so much the Son of man be—12. 34.
8. 28. when ye have—Son of man
12. 32. if I be—I will draw all men
Heb. 12. 12.—hands which hang
James 4. 10. the Lord shall *l.* you up
Ps. 3. 3. my glory and *lifter up* of
141. 2. *lifting* up of hands
LIGHT, Num. 21. 5. Deut. 27. 16.
1 Kings 16. 31. Ezek. 8. 17.
Isa. 49. 6. a *l.* thing to be my servant
Zeph. 3. 4. her prophets *l.* and
Matt. 11. 30. my yoke is easy and my burden *l.*
2 Cor. 4. 17. *l.* affliction endureth but
Ps. 62. 9. man is *lighter* than vanity
Jer. 3. 9. *lightness* of whoredoms
LIGHT, Gen. 1. 3, 4, 5, 16.
Job 18. 5. *l.* of wicked men be put out
25. 3. upon whom doth not his *l.* arise
33. 30. enlightening with *l.* of living
38. 19. way where *l.* dwells and
Ps. 4. 6. lift up *l.* of thy countenance
36. 9. in thy *l.* shall we see *l.*
43. 3. O send out thy *l.* and truth
90. 8. set secret sins in the *l.* of thy countenance
97. 11. *l.* is sown for the righteous
104. 2. coverest thyself with *l.* as a garment
112. 4. to the upright ariseth *l.* in darkness
112. 105. thy word is *l.* to my path
139. 12. darkness and *l.* are alike to
Prov. 4. 18. path of the just is as the shining *l.*
6. 23. law is *l.* and reproofs are vain
13. 9. *l.* of the righteous rejoiceth
15. 30. *l.* of the eyes rejoiceth the
Eccl. 11. 7. *l.* is sweet, and a pleasant
Isa. 5. 20. darkness for *l.* and *l.* for
30. the *l.* is darkened, Job 10. 22.
8. 20. because there is no *l.* in them
9. 2. walked in darkness, have seen a great *l.*
30. 26. *l.* of moon as *l.* of sun, *l.* of seven days
42. 6. keep thee, and give thee for a *l.* of the Gentiles
45. 7. I form *l.* and create darkness
50. 10. walketh in darkness hath no *l.*
11. walk ye in the *l.* of your fire
58. 8. shall thy *l.* break forth as the morning
60. 1. shine; for thy *l.* is come
Zech. 14. 6. *l.* shall not be clear nor
7. evening time it shall be *l.*
Matt. 5. 14. ye are the *l.* of the world
16. let your *l.* so shine before men
6. 22. the *l.* of the body is the eye, thy whole body is full of *l.*
Luke 2. 32. a *l.* to lighten Gentiles
16. 8. children of the world wiser than the children of *l.*
John 1. 4. the life was the *l.* of men
7. John came to bear witness of *l.*
9. true *l.* that lighteth every man
3. 19. men loved darkness rather than *l.*
20. cometh not to *l.* 21. comes to *l.*
5. 35. John a burning and a shining *l.*
8. 12. I am the *l.* of the world; he that followeth me shall have *l.* of life
12. 35, 36. walk while ye have the *l.*
Acts 13. 47. I have set thee for a *l.* of the Gentiles
26. 18. turn them from darkness to *l.*

Rom. 13. 12. put on the armour of *l.*
1 Cor. 4. 5. bring to *l.* hidden things of darkness
2 Cor. 4. 4. lest the *l.* of the Gospel should shine
6. 14. what communion hath *l.* with darkness
Eph. 5. 8. walk as children of *l.*
14. awake, and Christ shall give thee *l.*
1 Thes. 5. 5. ye are the children of *l.*
1 Pet. 2. 9. called to his marvellous *l.*
1 John 1. 5. God is *l.* and in him is no darkness
Rev. 21. 23. the Lamb is the *l.*
Ps. 136. 7. *lights,* Ezek. 32. 8. Luke 12. 35. Phil. 2. 15. James 1. 17.
2 Sam. 27. 29. *lighten,* Ezra 9. 8. Ps. 13. 3. & 35. 5. Rev. 21. 23.
Ex. 19. 16. *lightning,* Ps. 18. 14. Matt. 28. 3. & 24. 27. Luke 10. 18.
LIKE, 1 Cor. 16. 13.
Heb. 2. 17. to be made *l.* his brethren
1 John 3. 2. he appears we shall be *l.*
Phil. 2. 2. *like-minded,* 20. no man—
Gen. 1. 26. after our *likeness*
5. 3. Adam begat a son in his own *l.*
Ps. 17. 15. I shall be satisfied with thy *l.*
Rom. 6. 5. been planted in *l.* of his death
8. 3. in *l.* of sinful flesh
LILY, Song 2. 1, 2, 16. & 4. 5. & 5. 13. Hos. 14. 5. Matt. 6. 28.
LINE upon *l. l.* upon *l.* Isa. 28. 10.
28. 17. judgment will I lay to the *l.*
34. 11. stretch on it *l.* of confusion
2 Cor. 10. 16. not boast in another man's *l.*
Ps. 16. 6. *l.* are fallen in pleasant
LINGER, Gen. 19. 16. 2 Pet. 2. 3.
LION, Gen. 49. 9. Judg. 14. 5. Job 4. 10. Ps. 7. 2. & 17. 12. & 10. 9. & 22. 13. Isa. 38. 13.
Prov. 22. 13. there is a *l.* without
28. 1. righteous are bold as a *l.*
Eccl. 9. 4. living dog is better than a dead *l.*
Isa. 11. 6. calf and young *l.* 7.
35. 9. no *l.* shall be there, nor
Ezek. 1. 10. face as a *l.* 10. 14.
Hos. 5. 14. be as young *l.*
Mic. 5. 8. remnant of Jacob be as a *l.*
2 Tim. 4. 17. delivered out of mouth of *l.*
1 Pet. 5. 8. the devil as a roaring *l.*
Rev. 5. 5. *L.* of the tribe of Juda
LIPS, Ex. 6. 12, 30. Prov. 16. 10.
Ps. 12. 3. all flattering *l.*
4. *l.* are our own
17. 1. not feigned *l.* 31. 18. lying *l.*
2 Prov. 10. 18. Isa. 59. 3.
63. 5. I will praise thee with joyful *l.*
Prov. 10. 21. *l.* of the righteous feed many
26. 23. burning *l.* and wicked heart
Song 7. 9. *l.* of those asleep to speak
Isa. 6. 5. man of unclean *l.* people of unclean *l.*
57. 19. create the fruit of the *l.*
Hos. 14. 2. render calves of our *l.* Heb. 13. 15.
Mal. 2. 7. priest's *l.* should keep knowledge
Ps. 51. 15. open thou *my lips;* and mouth shall show forth thy praise
63. 3. shall praise thee, 71. 23.
141. 3. keep the door of—
17. 4. *thy lips,* 34. 13. & 45. 2.
LITTLE, Ezra 9. 8. Neh. 9. 32.
Ps. 2. 12. his wrath is kindled but a *l.*
8. 5. a *l.* lower than angels
37. 16. a *l.* that a righteous man
Prov. 6. 10. a *l.* sleep, a *l.* slumber
10. 20. heart of wicked is *l.* worth
15. 16. better is *l.* with fear of Lord
Isa. 28. 10. here a *l.* and there a *l.*
54. 8. in a *l.* wrath I hid my face
Ezek. 11. 16. I will be as a *l.* sanc-

tuary to them
Zech. 1. 15. I was but a *l.* displeased
Matt. 6. 30. of *l.* faith, 8. 26.
Luke 12. 32. fear not *l.* flock, it is
19. 17. thou hast been faithful in a *l.*
1 Tim. 4. 8. bodily exercise profiteth *l.*
Rev. 3. 8. hast *l.* strength, and kept
LIVE, Gen. 3. 22. & 17. 18.
Lev. 18. 5. if a man do, he shall *l.* Neh. 9. 29. Ezek. 3. 21. Rom. 10. 5.
Deut. 32. 40. *live for ever.* 1 Kings 1. 31. Neh. 2. 3. Ps. 22. 26. Dan. 2. 4. Zech. 1. 5. John 6. 51, 58.
Job 14. 14. if a man die, shall he *l.*
Ps. 55. 23. bloody men not *l.* out half
63. 4. bless thee while I *l.*
118. 17. I shall not die, but *l.* and
Isa. 38. 16. by these men *l.* and make me to *l.*
55. 3. hear, and your soul shall *l.*
Ezek. 16. 6. said, when thou wast in thy blood, *l.*
18. 32. turn yourselves and *l.*
Hab. 2. 4. just *l.* by faith
Matt. 4. 4. man not *l.* by bread
John 14. 19. because I *l.* ye shall *l.*
Acts 17. 28. in him we *l.* and move
Rom. 8. 13. if *l.* after the flesh, ye
41. whether we *l.* or *l.* to Lord
1 Cor. 9. 14. they preach the Gospel, *l.* of the Gospel
2 Cor. 5. 15. who *l.* should not *l.* to themselves
6. 9. as dying, and behold we *l.*
13. 11. be of one mind, *l.* in peace
Gal. 2. 20. I *l.* yet not I, but Christ
5. 25. if we *l.* in Spirit, walk in
Phil. 1. 21. to *l.* is Christ, 22
2 Tim. 3. 12. all that will *l.* godly in
Tit. 2. 12. *l.* soberly, righteously
Heb. 13. 18. willing to *l.* honestly
1 Pet. 2. 24. should *l.* to righteousness
1 John 4. 9. that we might *l.* through
Acts 23. 1. I *lived* in all good conscience
James 5. 5. ye have *l.* in pleasure
Rev. 18. 9. *l.* deliciously
20. 4. they *l.* and reigned with Christ
Job 19. 25. I know my Redeemer *liveth*
Rom. 6. 10. in that he *l.* he *l.* to God
14. 7. none *l.* to himself or dieth to
1 Tim. 5. 6. *l.* in pleasure, dead while she *l.*
Heb. 7. 25. *l.* to make intercession
Rev. 1. 18. I am he that *l.* and was dead
3. 1. I know that thou *l.* and art
Acts 7. 38. received *lively* oracles
1 Pet. 1. 3. begotten again to a *l.* hope
2. 5. ye, as *l.* stones, are built up a
1 John 3. 16. *lives,* Rev. 12. 11.
Eccl. 7. 2. *living* will lay it to heart
Isa. 38. 19. the *l.* the *l.* shall praise
Jer. 2. 13. Lord fountain of *l.* waters
Matt. 22. 32. not the God of the dead but of the *l.*
Mark 12. 44. cast all in her *l.*
John 4. 10. would have given *l.* water
7. 38. flow rivers of *l.* water
Rom. 12. 1. your bodies a *l.* sacrifice
14. 9. Lord both of dead and *l.*
1 Cor. 15. 45. Adam was made a *l.* soul
Heb. 10. 20. by a new and *l.* way
1 Pet. 2. 4. coming as to a *l.* stone
Rev. 7. 17. lead them to *l.* fountains
LOAD, Ps. 68. 19. Isa. 46. 1.
LOATHE themselves for evil, Ezek. 6. 9. & 16. 5. & 20. 43.
Jer. 14. 19. *loathed* Zion
Num. 25. 5. soul *loatheth*
Ps. 38. 7. *loathsome* disease
LOFTY eyes, Ps. 131. 1.
Isa. 2. 11. *l.* looks humbled, 5. 15.
57. 15. One that inhabiteth
LONG, Ps. 91. 16. Eccl. 12. 5. Matt. 23. 14. Luke 18. 7. James 5. 7.

Ex. 34. 6. Lord God, *long-suffering*
Num. 14. 18. Ps. 86. 15. Jer. 15. 15. Rom. 2. 4. 1 Tim. 1. 16.
Gal. 5. 22. fruit of Spirit is *l.* Col. 1. 11. & 3. 12. 2 Tim. 3. 10.
LONG, Job 3. 21. Rom. 1. 11.
Ps. 63. 1. my flesh *longeth* for thee
84. 2. my soul *l.* for courts of Lord
119. 40. *I have longed* after thy precepts
131.—for thy commandments
174.—for thy salvation
20. my soul breaketh for *longing*
107. 9. he satisfieth the *l.* soul
LOOK, Gen. 13. 14. Ex. 10. 10.
Isa. 8. 17. wait upon the Lord, and *l.* for
45. 22. *l.* unto me and be saved
66. 2. to this man will I *l.* that is poor
Mic. 7. 7. I will *l.* unto the Lord
Luke 7. 19. do we *l.* for another, 20.
2 Cor. 4. 18. we *l.* at things not seen
Phil. 2. 4. *l.* not every one on own
3. 20. heaven, from whence we *l.* for Saviour
Heb. 9. 28. to them that *l.* for him
1 Pet. 1. 12. angels desire to *l.* into
3. 14. seeing we *l.* for such things
Gen. 29. 32. Lord *looked* on my affliction, Ex. 2. 25. Deut. 26. 7.
Ps. 34. 5. *l.* to him and were lightened
Song 1. 6. *l.* not upon me; sun hath *l.* on me
Isa. 5. 7. he *l.* for judgment, behold
22. 11. hath not *l.* to the maker of
64. 3. didst terrible things, we *l.* not
Jer. 8. 15. we *l.* for peace, but
Obad. 13. not have *l.* on affliction
Hag. 1. 9. ye *l.* for much, and it came to little
Luke 2. 38. *l.* for redemption in Israel
22. 61. the Lord *l.* on Peter and Peter remembered
Heb. 11. 10. *l.* for a city whose builder is God
1 John 1. 1. which we have seen and *l.* on
1 Sam. 16. 7. man *looketh* on outward appearance, the Lord *l.* on the heart
Ps. 33. 13. the Lord *l.* down from heaven, 14. 2.
Prov. 14. 15. the prudent *l.* well to their goings, 31. 17.
Song 2. 9. he *l.* forth at the windows
Matt. 5. 28. *l.* on a woman to lust
24. 50. come in a day he *l.* not for
James 1. 25. *l.* into perfect law of liberty
Ps. 18. 27. wilt bring down high *looks*
Isa. 38. 14. mine eyes fail with *looking* upward
Luke 9. 62. no man *l.* back is fit for the kingdom
Tit. 2. 13. *l.* for that blessed hope
Heb. 10. 27. a fearful *l.* for of judgment
12. 2. *l.* to Jesus, the author and
15. *l.* diligently, lest any fail of the grace of God
2 Pet. 3. 12. *l.* for the day of God
Jude 21. *l.* for the mercy of our Lord Jesus Christ to eternal life
LOOSE, Deut. 25. 9. Josh. 5. 15.
Ps. 146. 7. the Lord *l.* the prisoners
102. 20. to *l.* those appointed to death
Isa. 58. 6. to *l.* the bands of wickedness
Eccl. 12. 6. before the silver cord be *loosed*
Matt. 16. 19. *l.* on earth, *l.* in heaven
Acts 2. 24. having *l.* pains of death
1 Cor. 7. 27. bound to a wife, seek not to be *l.* art thou *l.* seek not a wife
LORD, ascribed to man, Gen. 18. 12.
Isa. 26. 13. 1 Cor. 8. 5. and in about fourteen other places, and to God, Gen. 28. 16. Ex. 5. 2. 1 Cor. 12. 5. and in about 300 other texts
Ex. 34. 6. the *L.* the *L.* God, merciful

Deut. 4. 35. *L.* is God, 39. 1 Kings 18. 39.
6. 4. *L.* our God is one *L.* 10.
17. *L.* of *l.* Dan. 2. 47. 1 Tim. 6. 15. Rev. 17. 14. & 19. 16.
Neh. 9. 6. art *L.* alone, Isa. 37. 20.
Ps. 118. 27. God is the *L.* 100. 3.
Zech. 14. 9. one *L.* and his name one
Mark 2. 28. the Son of man is *L.* of the sabbath
Acts 2. 36. made him *L.* and Christ
Rom. 10. 12. same *L.* over all
14. 9. *L.* of the dead and of the living
1 Cor. 2. 8. *L.* of glory
15. 47. *L.* from heaven
8. 6. one God, one *L.* Jesus Christ
Eph. 4. 5. one *L.* one faith, one baptism
Gen. 15. 6. and he believed *in the Lord*
1 Sam. 2. 1. heart rejoiceth—Ps. 32. 11.
Isa. 41. 16. Joel 2. 13. Hab. 3. 18. Zech. 10. 7. Phil. 3. 1.
1 Kings 18. 5. trust—Ps. 4. 5. Prov. 3. 5. Isa. 26. 4. Zeph. 3. 2.
Ps. 31. 24. hope—130. 7.
34. 2. soul maketh her boast—
37. 4. delight thyself—7. rest—
Isa. 45. 17. Israel shall be saved—
24.—have I righteousness and
42. 25.—shall all the seed of Israel be justified
Rom. 16. 12. labour—1 Cor. 15. 58.
Eph. 6. 10. be strong—and power of his might
1 Thes. 5. 12. over you—
Rev. 14. 13. blessed are dead which die—
LOSE, Eccl. 3. 6. Matt. 10. 39, 42.
John 6. 39. 2 John 8. Prov. 23. 8.
1 Cor. 3. 15. *loss,* Phil. 3. 7.
Ps. 119. 170. astray like *lost* sheep
Ezek. 37. 17. hope is *l.* we are cut off
Matt. 5. 13. if salt have *l.* its savour
10. 6. to the *l.* sheep of Israel, 15. 24.
18. 11. save that was *l.* Luke 19. 10.
Luke 15. 32. thy brother was *l.* and
John 18. 9. them thou gavest me, I have *l.* none
2 Cor. 4. 3. the Gospel be hid it is to them that are *l.*
LOT, Lev. 16. 8. Josh. 1. 6.
1 Sam. 14. 41. Saul said, give us a perfect *l.* 42.
Ps. 16. 5. thou maintainest my *l.*
125. 3. rod of wicked not rest on *l.* of the righteous
Prov. 16. 33. the *l.* is cast into the lap
18. 18. *l.* causeth contentions to cease
Acts 1. 26. the *l.* fell on Matthias
8. 21. hast neither *l.* nor part in
Ps. 22. 18. on my vesture they cast *lots*
LOVE, Gen. 27. 4. 2 Sam. 13. 15.
2 Sam. 1. 26. passing the *l.* of women
Eccl. 9. 1. no man knoweth either *l.*
Song 2. 5. I am sick of *l.* 5. 8.
7. 12. there I will give thee my *loves*
8. 6. *l.* is strong as death, jealousy
Isa. 38. 17. thou hast in *l.* to my soul delivered it
Jer. 2. 2. remember the *l.* of thine espousals
31. 3. loved thee with everlasting *l.*
Ezek. 16. 8. thy time was time of *l.*
33. 31. with their mouth show much *l.*
Hos. 11. 4. draw them with bands of *l.*
Matt. 24. 12. *l.* of many shall wax cold
John 15. 9. continue ye in my *l.*
13. greater *l.* hath no man than this
Rom. 8. 35. who shall separate us from the *l.* of Christ, 39.
12. 9. let *l.* be without dissimulation
13. 10. *l.* is the fulfilling of the law
15. 30. for Christ's sake, and *l.* of the Spirit

2 Cor. 5. 14. *l.* of Christ constraineth
Gal. 5. 6. faith which worketh by *l.*
13. by *l.* serve one another
22. fruit of the Spirit is *l.* joy and
1 Thes. 1. 3. your labour of *l.*
5. 8. breastplate of faith and *l.*
2 Thes. 2. 17. received not *l.* of the truth
Heb. 13. 1. let brotherly *l.* continue
1 John 3. 1. what manner of *l.* the Father bestowed on us, 4. 7. *l.* is of God, 8. 16. God is *l.*
4. 9. manifest the *l.* of God
11. we ought to *l.* one another
12. he that dwelleth in *l.* dwelleth
18. there is no fear in *l.* perfect *l.* casteth out fear
21. who loveth God, *l.* his brother
Rev. 2. 4. thou hast left thy first *l.*
Eph. 1. 4. without blame before God *in love*
3. 17. grounded—4. 2. forbearing one another—
4. 15. speaking the truth—16.
5. 2. walk—as Christ hath loved
Col. 2. 2. knit together—and
1 Thes. 4. abound—
5. 13. esteem—
Luke 11. 42. *love of God*
Rom. 5. 5.—is shed abroad in our
2 Cor. 3. 14.—be with you all
2 Thes. 3. 5. direct your hearers into
—
1 John 2. 5. in him is—perfected
3. 16. perceive we—
17. dwelleth—in him
4. 9. in this was manifested—towards
5. 3. this is—keep his commandments
Deut. 7. 7. his *love,* Zeph. 3. 17. Ps. 91. 14. Isa. 63. 9. John 15. 10. Rom. 5. 8.
Lev. 19. 18. thou shalt *l.* thy neighbour as thyself, 34. Matt. 19. 19. Rom. 13. 8. Gal. 5. 14. James 2. 8.
Deut. 6. 5. shalt *l.* the Lord thy God with all thy heart, Matt. 22. 37.
Deut. 10. 12. to fear the Lord and to *l.*
Ps. 31. 23. O *l.* the Lord, all ye his saints
97. 10. ye that *l.* the Lord hate evil
145. 20. Lord preserveth them that *l.* him
Song 1. 4. the upright *l.* thee
Mic. 6. 8. to do justly, and *l.* mercy
Zech. 8. 19. *l.* the truth and peace
Matt. 5. 44. *l.* your enemies, bless
John 13. 34. *l.* one another, 15. 12. Rom. 13. 8. 1 John 3. 11, 23.
14. 23. if a man *l.* me, my Father will *l.* him
1 Cor. 16. 22. if any man *l.* not Lord
Eph. 5. 25. *l.* your wives
2 Tim. 4. 8. them that *l.* his appearing
1 Pet. 1. 8. whom having not seen, ye *l.*
2. 17. *l.* the brotherhood, 3. 8.
1 John 2. 15. *l.* not world, nor things that are in the world
4. 19. we *l.* him because he first *loved* us.
Ps. 116. 1. *I love* the Lord because
John 21. 15. *lovest* thou me—thee
2 John 1. whom—in the truth, and
Rev. 3. 19. as many as—I rebuke
Deut. 7. 8. because the Lord *loved* you, 33. 3.
1 Sam. 18. 1. *l.* David as his own soul
2 Sam. 12. 24. called Solomon, and Lord *l.* him
1 Kings 3. 3. Solomon *l.* the Lord
10. the Lord *l.* Israel
Hos. 11. 1. Israel was a child, then I *l.* him
Mark 10. 21. Jesus beholding him, *l.*
Luke 7. 47. sins forgiven, she *l.* much
2 Tim. 4. 10. *l.* this present world

Heb. 1. 9. hast *l.* righteousness and hated iniquity
John 3. 16. God so *l.* the world that he gave
3. 19. men *l.* darkness rather than
11. 36. behold how he *l.* him
12. 43. *l.* the praise of men more
13. 1. having *l.* his own, he *l.* them unto the end
23. one of his disciples whom Jesus *l.* 19. 26. & 20. 2. & 21. 7, 20.
14. 21. *l.* me, be *l.* of my Father, I will love him
28. if ye *l.* me, ye would rejoice for
15. 9. as my Father *l.* me, so have I *l.* you
16. 27. Father *loveth* you because ye *l.* me
17. 33. I *l.* them as thou hast *l.* me
26. 1. wherewith thou hast *l.* them
Rom. 8. 37. conquerors through him that *l.* us
Rom. 9. 13. Jacob I *l.* Esau I hated
Gal. 1. 20. Son of God who *l.* me
Eph. 2. 4. great love wherewith he *l.* us
5. 2. as Christ *l.* us
25. as Christ *l.* church
2 Thes. 2. 16. God our Father *l.* us
2 Pet. 2. 15. *l.* wages of unrighteousness
1 John 4. 10. not we *l.* God but he *l.* us
Rev. 1. 5. that *l.* and washed us from sins
12. 11. *l.* not their lives unto death
Ps. 11. 7. the righteous Lord *l.* righteousness
146. 8. the Lord *l.* the righteous
Prov. 3. 12. whom the Lord *l.* he correcteth, Heb. 12. 6.
17. 17. a friend *l.* at all times
21. 17. who *l.* pleasure, shall be poor
Song 1. 7. whom my soul *l.*
Matt. 10. 37. *l.* father or mother more
John 3. 35. Father *l.* the Son
16. 27. Father himself *l.* you; ye *l.* me
2 Cor. 9. 7. God *l.* a cheerful giver
3 John 9. *l.* to have pre-eminence
Rev. 22. 15. whoso *l.* and maketh a lie
2 Sam. 1. 23. *lovely,* Song 5. 16. Ezek. 33. 32. Philem. 4. 8.
Ps. 18. 18. *lover,* Tit. 1. 8. Ps. 38. 11. Hos. 2. 5. 2 Tim. 3. 2, 4.
LOW, Deut. 28. 43. Ezek. 17. 24.
1 Sam. 2. 7. Lord brings *l.* and lifts
Job 40. 12. look on every one that is proud and bring him *l.*
Ps. 49. 2. both high and *l.* rich and
136. 23. rememberest us in our *l.* estate
Prov. 29. 23. man's pride bring him *l.*
Isa. 26. 5. lofty city he layeth it *l.*
32. 19. city shall be *l.* in a *l.* place
Luke 1. 48. he regarded the *l.* estate
52. he exalted them of *l.* degree, Job 5. 11. Ezek. 21. 26. James 1. 9.
Luke 3. 5. every mountain and hill be made *l.*
Rom. 12. 16. condescend to men of *l.* estate
Ps. 63. 9. *lower* parts of the earth, 139. 15. Isa. 44. 23. Eph. 4. 9.
138. 6. Lord hath respect to *lowly*
Prov. 3. 34. he giveth grace unto *l.*
11. 2. with the *l.* is wisdom
Matt. 11. 29. learn of me, for I am meek and *l.*
Eph. 4. 2. *lowliness,* Phil. 2. 3.
LOINS girt, Prov. 31. 17. Isa. 11. 5. Luke 12. 35. Eph. 6. 14.
LUCRE, filthy, 1 Tim. 3. 3, 8. Tit. 1. 7. 1 Pet. 5. 2.
LUKEWARM, thou art, Rev. 3. 16.
LUMP, Isa. 38. 21. Rom. 9. 21. 1 Cor. 5. 6, 7. Gal. 5. 9.
LUST, Ex. 15. 9. Ps. 78. 18. James 4. 2.
Ps. 81. 12. gave them up to their own hearts' *l.*

Matt. 5. 23. whoso looketh on woman to *l.*
Rom. 7. 7. not known *l.* except law
1 Cor. 10. 6. not *l.* after evil things
Gal. 5. 16. shall not fulfil *l.* of flesh
1 Thes. 4. 5. not in *l.* of concupiscence
James 1. 15. when *l.* is conceived, it
1 John 2. 16. *l.* of the flesh, and *l.* of eyes
Mark 4. 19. *lusts* of other things choke
John 8. 44. *l.* of your father ye will
Rom. 6. 12. should obey it in the *l.* thereof
13. 14. for the flesh, to fulfil the *l.*
Gal. 5. 17. flesh *l.* against Spirit, and Spirit against flesh
24. crucified flesh with affections and *l.*
Eph. 2. 3. *l.* of our flesh, and mind
1 Tim. 6. 9. foolish and hurtful *l.*
2 Tim. 2. 22. flee youthful *l.* follow
3. 6. laden with sins, led away with divers *l.*
Tit. 2. 12. denying ungodliness and worldly *l.*
3. 3. divers *l.* and pleasures
James 4. 3. consume it on your *l.*
1 Pet. 2. 11. abstain from fleshly *l.*
4. 2. no longer live to *l.* of men
2 Pet. 3. 3. walk after their *l.*

M

MAD, Deut. 28. 34.
Eccl. 2. 2. I said of laughter it is *m.*
Jer. 50. 38. they are *m.* upon idols
Hos. 9. 7. the prophet is a fool, the spiritual man is *m.*
John 10. 20. he hath a devil and is *m.*
Acts 26. 11. exceedingly *m.* against
24. learning doth make thee *m.*
Deut. 28. 28. *madness,* Eccl. 1. 17. Zech. 12. 4. Luke 6. 11. 2 Pet. 2. 16.
MADE, Ex. 2. 14. 2 Sam. 13. 6.
Ps. 104. 24. thy works in wisdom hast thou *m.*
139. 14. I am wonderfully *m.*
Prov. 16. 14. Lord *m.* all things for
John 1. 3. all things were *m.* by him
Rom. 1. 3. Christ made of the seed of David
1. 20. understood by things that are *m.*
1 Cor. 1. 30. Christ who of God is *m.*
9. 22. *m.* all things to all men
Gal. 4. 4. *m.* of a woman, *m.* under law
Phil. 2. 7. *m.* in the likeness of men
MAGNIFY, Josh. 3. 7.
Job 7. 7. what is man that thou shouldst *m.* him
36. 24. remember to *m.* his work
Ps. 34. 3. *m.* the Lord with me
69. 30. *m.* God with thanksgiving
Isa. 42. 21. *m.* the law, and make it
Luke 1. 46. my soul doth *m.* Lord
Acts 10. 46. spake with tongues and *m.* God
Rom. 11. 13. apostle of Gentiles, I *m.*
Gen. 19. 19. thou hast *magnified* thy mercy
2 Sam. 7. 26. let thy name be *m.* for
Ps. 35. 27. let the Lord be *m.* 40. 16.
138. 2. hast *m.* thy word above thy name
Acts 19. 17. the name of the Lord was *m.*
Phil. 1. 20. Christ be *m.* in my body
MAID, Gen. 16. 2. Deut. 22. 14. Job 31. 1. Jer. 2. 32. Amos 2. 7.
MAJESTY, Dan. 4. 30, 36. Job 40. 10. Ps. 21. 5. & 45. 3, 4.
1 Chron. 29. 11. thine, O Lord is *m.*
Job 37. 22. with God is terrible *m.*
Ps. 29. 4. voice of Lord is full of *m.*
93. 1. Lord is clothed with *m.* 104. 1.
145. 5. glorious honour of thy *m.*

---

12. glorious *m.* of his kingdom
Isa. 2. 19. hide for fear of glory of his *m.*
Heb. 1. 3. right hand of *M.* on high
8. 1. throne of the *M.* in the heavens
2 Pet. 1. 16. eye witnesses of his *m.*
Jude 25. to the only wise God be glory and *m.*
MAINTAIN my cause, 1 Kings 8. 40, 45. Ps. 9. 4. Job 13. 15.
Tit. 3. 8. careful to *m.* good works, 14.
Ps. 16. 5. thou *maintainest* my lot
MAKE, Gen. 1. 26. Deut. 32. 35.
Job. 4. 17. shall man be purer than his *Maker*
32. 22. my *M.* would soon take me
35. 10. where is God my *M.*
36. 3. I will ascribe righteousness to my *M.*
Ps. 95. 6. kneel before Lord our *M.*
Prov. 14. 31. reproacheth his *M.* 17. 5.
22. 2. Lord is the *M.* of them all
Isa. 17. 7. that day shall man look to his *M.*
22. 2. Lord is the *M.* of them all
Isa. 17. 7. that day shall man look to his *M.*
45. 9. wo unto him that striveth with his *M.*
51. 13. forgetteth the Lord thy *M.*
54. 5. thy *M.* is thy husband
Heb. 11. 10. builder and *m.* is God
MALE or female, Gen. 1. 27.
3. Mal. 1. 14. Matt. 19. 4. Gal. 3. 28.
MALICE, leaven of, 1 Cor. 5. 8.
1 Cor. 14. 20. in *m.* be children, in
Eph. 4. 31. put away with all *m.* Col. 3. 8. 1 Pet. 2. 1.
Tit. 3. 3. living in *m.* and envy
Rom. 1. 29. filled with all *maliciousness;* full of envy, 1 Pet. 2. 1.
MAMMON, Matt. 6. 24.
MAN, Gen. 1. 26. Kings 9. 11.
Job 4. 17. shall *m.* be more just than God
5. 7. *m.* is born to trouble, 14. 1.
7. 17. what is *m.* that thou shouldest be mindful of him
9. 2. how shall man be just with God
11. 12. vain *m.* would be wise
14. 1. *m.* born of woman, is of few days
15. 14. what is *m.* that he should be clean
25. 4. can *m.* be justified
6. *m.* is a worm
28. 28. unto *m.* he said, depart
Ps. 8. 4. what is *m.* that thou art mindful of him
10. 18. *m.* of earth no more oppress
25. 12. what *m.* is he that feareth the Lord
49. 12. *m.* being in honour abideth not
90. 3. thou turnest *m.* to destruction
104. 23. *m.* goeth forth to his work
118. 6. not fear; what can *m.* do
144. 3. what is *m.* that thou takest knowledge of him; or son of *m.*
Prov. 20. 24. *m's* goings are of the Lord
Eccl. 6. 10. it is known that it is *m.*
7. 29. God made *m.* upright, but
12. 5. *m.* goeth to his long home
Isa. 2. 22. cease ye from *m.* whose
Jer. 17. 5. cursed be *m.* that trusts in *m.*
Zech. 13. 7. awake against the *m.* that is my fellow
Matt. 4. 4. *m.* shall not live by bread
26. 72. I know not the *m.*
John 7. 46. never *m.* spake like this *m.*
Rom. 6. 6. old *m.* crucified with Christ
7. 22. delight in the law after the inward *m.*
1 Cor. 2. 11. what *m.* knoweth things of a *m.* save the spirit of *m.* in him
14. natural *m.* receiveth not things

11. 8. *m.* not of woman, but woman of *m.*

15. 47. first *m.* is earthy, second *m.*

2 Cor. 4. 16. though outward *m.* perish, yet inward *m.* is renewed

Eph. 4. 22. put off the old *m.* which 24. put on new *m.* renewed

1 Pet. 3. 4. be the hidden *m.* of heart

Ex. 15. 3. Lord is *a man of war*

Num. 23. 19. God is not—that he

Isa. 47. 3. I will not meet thee as—

53. 3.—of sorrows and acquainted

Jer. 15. 10. borne me—of strife and

31. 22. a woman shall compass—

Matt. 8. 9. I am—under authority

16. 26. what shall—give in exchange

John 3. 3. except—be born again

Acts 10. 26. I myself also am—

2 Cor. 12. 2. I knew—in Christ, 3.

Phil. 2. 8. in fashion as—he humbled

1 Tim. 2. 5. one Mediator, the *m.* Christ Jesus

Prov. 30. 2. *if any man,* Matt. 16. 24.

John 6. 51. Rom. 8. 9. 2 Cor. 5. 17.

Ps. 39. 5. *every man,* Prov. 19. 6. Mic. 4. 4. Gal. 6. 4, 5. Col. 1. 28.

Ps. 87. 4. *this man,* Isa. 66. 2.

Luke 19. 14. John 7. 46.

Prov. 1. 5. *a wise man* will hear

9. 8. rebuke—and he will love thee

14. 16.—feareth and departeth

17. 10. reproof enters into—more

Eccl. 2. 14.—eyes are in his head

7. 7. oppression makes—mad

10. 2.—heart is at his right hand

Jer. 9. 23. let not—glory in wisdom

James 3. 13. who is—among you

Deut. 33. 1. *man of God,* Judg. 13. 6. 2 Kings 1. 9. 1 Tim. 6. 11. 2 Tim. 3. 17.

MANDRAKES, Gen. 30. 14.

MANIFEST, Eccl. 3. 18.

Mark 4. 22. nothing hid which shall not be *m.*

John 14. 21. *m.* myself unto him

2. 11. *m.* forth his glory to disciples

17. 6. I have *m.* thy name unto men

1 Cor. 4. 5. make *m.* counsels of hearts

Gal. 5. 19. works of the flesh are *m.*

2 Thes. 1. 5. a *m.* token of judgment

1 Tim. 3. 16. God was *m.* in the flesh

Heb. 4. 13. any creature not *m.* in

1 John 3. 5. was *m.* to take away sin

10. in this children of God are *m.*

4. 9. in this was *m.* the love of God

Luke 8. 17. *made manifest,* 1 Cor. 3. 13. 2 Cor. 4. 10. Eph. 5. 13.

Rom. 8. 19. *manifestation* of sons of

1 Cor. 12. 7. *m.* of the Spirit is given

2 Cor. 4. 2. but by *m.* of the truth in

MANIFOLD mercies, Neh. 9. 19.

Ps. 104. 24. how *m.* are thy works

Amos 5. 12. I know your *m.* transgressions

Luke 18. 30. *m.* in this present

Eph. 3. 10. known *m.* wisdom of God

1 Pet. 1. 6. through *m.* temptations

4. 10. as stewards of the *m.* grace of God

MANNA, Ex. 16. 15. Num. 11. 6.

Deut. 8. 3, 16. Josh. 5. 12. Neh. 9. 20.

Rev. 2. 17. give to eat of hidden *m.*

MANNER, 1 Sam. 8. 9, 11. Jer. 22. 21. 1 Thes. 1. 5, 9. 1 John 3. 1.

2 Kings 17. 34. *manners,* Acts 13. 18.

MANSIONS in my father's house, John 14. 2.

MARK, set me as a, Job 7. 20.

Lam. 3. 12. Gal. 6. 17. bear *marks*

Ezek. 9. 4. set a *m.* upon the foreheads, Rev. 13. 16, 17. & 19. 9.

Phil. 3. 14. I press toward the *m.*

Ps. 37. 37.—the perfect man

130. 3. if thou shouldst *m.* iniquity, Job 10. 14. Jer. 2. 22.

Rom. 16. 17. *m.* them which cause divisions

Phil. 3. 17. *m.* them which walk as we do

MARRIAGE, Gen. 38. 8.

Matt. 22. 2. king made a *m.* for son

25. 10. that were ready went into the *m.*

Heb. 13. 4. *m.* is honourable in all

Rev. 19. 7. *m.* of the Lamb is come

Jer. 3. 14. I am *m.* to you, saith Lord

Luke 14. 20. I have *m.* a wife, and

17. 27. drank, *m.* and given in *m.*

Isa. 62. 5. as a man *m.* a virgin; thy sons *m.*

1 Cor. 7. 9. better to *m.* than to burn

1 Tim. 4. 3. forbidding to *m.* and

5. 14. that younger women *m.*

MARROW, to bones, Prov. 3. 8.

Ps. 63. 5. soul is satisfied as with *m.*

Isa. 25. 6. feast of fat things full of *m.*

Heb. 4. 12. dividing joints and *m.*

MARTYR, Acts 22. 20. Rev. 2. 13.

MARVEL not, Eccl. 5. 8. John 5. 28.

Acts 3. 12. 1 John 3. 13.

Ps. 48. 5. they *marvelled,* Matt. 8. 27.

Matt. 8. 10. Jesus *m.* Mark 6. 6.

Job 5. 9. doeth *marvellous* things

10. 16. showed thyself *m.* against

Ps. 17. 7. show thy *m.* kindness

98. 1. done *m.* things, Mic. 7. 15.

118. 23. *m.* in our eyes

1 Pet. 2. 9. from darkness into *m.* light

1 Chron. 16. 12. remember his *m.* works, Ps. 105. 5. & 9. 1.

Ps. 139. 14. *m.* are thy works

MASTER, Isa. 24. 2. Mal. 1. 6.

Matt. 23. 10. one is your *M.* even Christ

Mark 10. 17. good *M.* what shall I do

John 3. 10. art thou a *m.* in Israel

13. 13. ye call me *M.* and say well

14. if I your *M.* have washed your feet

Rom. 14. 4. to his own *m.* he stands

Eccl. 12. 11. *masters* of assemblies

Matt. 6. 24. no man can serve two *m.*

23. 10. neither be ye called *m.*

Col. 4. 1. *m.* give your servants

1 Cor. 3. 10. I as a *master builder*

MATTER, Ex. 18. 22. 1 Sam. 10. 16. Job 19. 28. Ps. 45. 1. Dan. 7. 28. 2 Cor. 9. 5.

Acts 8. 21. part nor lot in this *m.*

Job 33. 13. account of any of his *matters*

Ps. 131. 1. exercise myself in great *m.*

Matt. 23. 23. omitted the weightier *m.*

1 Pet. 4. 15. a busybody in other men's *m.*

MEAN, what, Ex. 12. 26. Deut. 6. 20, 24. Josh. 4. 6, 21. Ezek. 17. 12. Acts 17. 20. Ezek. 37. 18. Jonah 1. 6.

Gen. 50. 20. ye thought ill; God *meant* good

Ps. 49. 7. *by any means,* Jer. 5. 31. 1 Cor. 9. 22. Phil. 3. 11.

MEASURE, Lev. 19. 35.

Job 11. 9. the *m.* is longer than earth

Ps. 39. 4. make me know the *m.* of my days

Isa. 27. 8. in *m.* when it shooteth

Jer. 30. 11. correct thee in *m.*

Matt. 7. 2. with what *m.* you mete

23. 32. fill up the *m.* of your fathers

John 3. 34. giveth not Spirit by *m.*

Rom. 12. 3. gives to every man *m.*

2 Cor. 1. 8. were pressed out of *m.*

12. 7. lest I should be exalted above *m.*

Eph. 4. 7. according to *m.* of the gift of Christ

13. to the *m.* of fulness of Christ

Rev. 11. 1. *m.* the temple of God

MEAT, Job 6. 7. Ps. 42. 3.

Ps. 104. 27. give in season

111. 5. giveth *m.* to them that fear

Prov. 6. 8. provided *m.* in summer

Hos. 11. 4. I laid *m.* unto them

Hab. 1. 16. portion fat and *m.* plenteous

3. 17. the fields shall yield no *m.*

Hag. 2. 12. his skirt touched *m.*

Mal. 1. 12. his *m.* is contemptible

Matt. 6. 25. is not life more than *m.*

10. 10. workman worthy of his *m.*

John 4. 32. I have *m.* to eat ye know

34. my *m.* is to do will of my Father

6. 27. labour not for *m.* that perisheth

55. my flesh is *m.* indeed

Rom. 14. 15. destroy not him with thy *m.*

17. kingdom of God is not *m.* and drink

1 Cor. 6. 13. *m.* for belly, belly for *m.*

8. 8. *m.* commendeth us not to God

10. 3. did all eat same spiritual *m.*

MEDDLE, 2 Kings 14. 10. Prov. 17. 14. & 20. 3, 19. & 24. 21.

MEDIATOR, Gal. 3. 20.

Gal. 3. 19. ordained by angels in the hand of a *m.*

1 Tim. 2. 5. one *m.* between God and

Heb. 8. 6. he is the *m.* of a better covenant

9. 15. *m.* of New Testament

12. 24. *m.* of new covenant

MEDICINE, Prov. 17. 22. Jer. 30. 13. & 46. 11. Ezek. 47. 12.

MEDITATE, Gen. 24. 63.

Josh. 1. 18. *m.* in thy law day and night

Ps. 63. 6. *m.* on thee in the night

77. 22. I will *m.* of thy works

Isa. 33. 18. thy heart shall *m.* terror

Luke 21. 14. not *m.* before what to answer

1 Tim. 4. 15. *m.* upon these things

Ps. 5. 1. consider my *meditation*

19. 4. *m.* of my heart be acceptable

49. 3. *m.* of my heart shall be of understanding

104. 34. my *m.* of him shall be sweet

119. 97. thy law is my *m.* all the day

99. thy testimonies are my *m.* of

MEEK, Moses was very, Num. 12. 3.

Ps. 22. 26. the *m.* eat and be satisfied

25. 9. *m.* will he guide in judgment

37. 11. *m.* shall inherit the earth

76. 9. Lord rose to save all *m.*

147. 6. the Lord lifteth up the *m.*

149. 4. beautify the *m.* with salvation

Isa. 11. 4. reprove for *m.* of the earth

29. 19. *m.* shall increase their joy

61. 1. preach good tidings to *m.*

Amos 2. 7. that turn aside way of *m.*

Matt. 5. 5. blessed are *m.* for they shall inherit the earth

11. 29. I am *m.* and lowly in heart

21. 5. thy king cometh *m.* sitting

1 Pet. 3. 4. ornament of *m.* and quiet

Zeph. 2. 3. seek righteousness, seek *meekness*

1 Cor. 4. 21. come in the spirit of *m.*

2 Cor. 10. 1. I beseech you by the *m.* and gentleness of Christ

Gal. 5. 23. faith, *m.* against such no law

6. 1. restore him in spirit of *m.*

Col. 3. 12. put on *m.* long suffering

1 Tim. 6. 11. follow after faith, love, *m.*

2 Tim. 2. 25. in *m.* instructing those

Tit. 3. 2. showing all *m.* to all men

James 1. 21. receive with *m.* ingrafted

3. 13. show his works with *m.* of wisdom

1 Pet. 3. 15. of hope in you with *m.*

MEET, Gen. 2. 18.

Job 34. 31. it is *m.* to be said to God

Matt. 3. 8. fruits *m.* for repentance, Acts 26. 20.

1 Cor. 15. 9. not *m.* to be called an

Col. 1. 12. *m.* to be partakers of the inheritance

1 Tim. 2. 21. vessel *m.* for master's use

Heb. 6. 7. for them by whom dressed

Prov. 22. 2. rich and poor *m.* together

Isa. 47. 3. I will not *m.* thee as a man

64. 5. thou *m.* him that rejoiceth

Hos. 13. 8. I will *m.* them as a bear

Amos 4. 12. prepare to *m.* thy God

1 Thes. 4. 17. caught up to *m.* Lord

MELODY in heart, Eph. 5. 19.

MEMBER, 1 Cor. 12. 14.

James 3. 5. tongue is a little *m.* and

Ps. 139. 16. in thy book all my *members*

Matt. 5. 29. one of thy *m.* perish

Rom. 6. 13. yield your *m.* as instruments

7. 23. I see another law in my *m.*

12. 5. every one *m.* one of another

1 Cor. 6. 15. your bodies *m.* of Christ

12. 12. body is one, and hath many *m.*

Eph. 4. 25. we are *m.* one of another

5. 30. *m.* of his body, his flesh and

Col. 3. 5. mortify your *m.* on earth

MEMORY cut off, Ps. 109. 15.

Ps. 145. 7. utter the *m.* of thy great goodness

Prov. 10. 7. *m.* of the just is blessed

Eccl. 9. 5. *m.* of them is forgotten

Isa. 26. 14. made their *m.* to perish

1 Cor. 15. 2. if ye keep in *m.* what I

Ex. 3. 15. my *memorial* to all generations

Ex. 13. 9. be for *m.* between thine eyes

17. 14. write this for a *m.* in book

Ps. 135. 13. thy *m.* through all generations

Hos. 12. 5. Lord of hosts; Lord is his *m.*

Matt. 26. 13. be told for a *m.* of her

Acts 10. 4. come up for a *m.* before God

MEN, Gen. 32. 28. & 42. 11.

Ps. 9. 20. know themselves to be but *m.*

17. 14. *m.* of thy hand; *m.* of this world

62. 9. *m.* of low degree are vanity; *m.* of high degree are a lie

82. 7. ye shall die like *m.* and fall

Eccl. 12. 3. strong *m.* shall bow

Isa. 31. 3. Egyptians are *m.* not God, Ezek. 28. 2.

46. 8. remember this; show yourselves *m.*

Hos. 6. 7. they like *m.* transgressed

Rom. 1. 27. *m.* with *m.* working

Eph. 6. 6. *m.* pleasers, Col. 3. 22.

MENSTRUOUS, Isa. 30. 32.

Ezek. 18. 6. neither come near a *m.* woman

MENTION, Ex. 26. 13. Job 28. 18.

Ps. 71. 16. make *m.* of thy righteousness

Isa. 26. 13. by thee only make *m.* of

62. 6. ye that make *m.* of the Lord

Rom. 1. 9. make *m.* of you in my prayers, Eph. 1. 16. 1 Thes. 1. 2.

MERCHANT, Hos. 12. 7.

Isa. 23. 18. *merchandise* be holiness, Matt. 22. 5. John 2. 16.

MERCY, Gen. 19. 19. & 39. 21.

Ex. 34. 7. keep *m.* for thousands, Deut. 7. 9. 1 Kings 8. 23.

Num. 14. 18. Lord is of great *m.*

Ps. 23. 6. goodness and *m.* shall follow me

25. 10. all paths of Lord are *m.*

33. 18. fear him and hope in his *m.*

52. 8. I trust in the *m.* of God for

57. 3. God shall send forth his *m.*

66. 20. not turned away his *m.*

86. 5. plenteous in *m.* to all

101. 1. I will sing of *m.* and

103. 11. great in his *m.* to them that fear him

17. *m.* of the Lord is from everlasting

106. 1. his *m.* endureth forever, 107. 1.

1 Chron. 16. 34, 41. 2 Chron. 5. 13. Ezra 3. 11. Jer. 33. 11.

Prov. 16. 6. by *m.* and truth, iniquity is purged

20. 28. *m.* and truth preserve the king

Isa. 27. 11. he that made them will not have *m.*

Hos. 6. 6. I desired *m.* and not sacrifice

10. 12. reap in *m.* 12. 6. keep *m.*

14. 3. in thee fatherless findeth *m.*

Jonah 2. 8. they forsake their own *m.*

Mic. 6. 8. what doth God require, but to love *m.*

7. 18. delights in *m.*

20. *m.* to Abraham

Hab. 3. 2. in wrath remember *m.*

Luke 1. 50. his *m.* is on them that fear

78. through tender *m.* of our God

Rom. 9. 23. on vessels of *m.* prepared unto glory

15. *m.* on whom he will have *m.*

11. 31. through your *m.* they obtain *m.*

15. 9. may glorify God for his *m.*

2 Cor.: 4. 1. as we have received *m.* we faint not

1 Tim. 1. 13. I obtained *m.* because I did it ignorantly, 2 grace, *m.* and peace, Tit. 1. 4.

2 Tim. 1. 18. grant may find *m.* in

Tit. 3. 5. according to his *m.* saved

James 2. 13. shall have judgment without *m.* that showed no *m.* and *m.* rejoiceth against judgment

Heb. 4. 16. we may obtain *m.* and

James 3. 17. full of *m.* and good

5. 11. Lord is pitiful and of tender *m.*

Jude 21. looking for the *m.* of our Lord Jesus Christ

Gen. 32. 10. not worthy of the least of thy *mercies*

1 Chron. 21. 13. great are his *m.*

Ps. 69. 13. in multitude of thy *m.*

Isa. 55. 3. the sure *m.* of David

Lam. 3. 22. of Lord's *m.* we are not consumed

Dan. 9. 9. to the Lord belong *m.* and

Rom. 12. 1. I beseech you by *m.* of God

2 Cor. 1. 3. Father of *m.* and God of

Col. 3. 12. put on bowels of *m.*

Ps. 25. 6. *tender mercies,* 40. 11.

Prov. 12. 10.—of wicked are cruel

Gen. 19. 19. *thy mercy,* Num. 14. 19. Neh. 13. 22. Ps. 5. 7. & 6. 4. & 13. 5.

Ex. 34. 6. Lord God *merciful* and gracious, 2 Chron. 30. 9. Neh. 9. 17, 31. Ps. 103. 8. Joel 2. 13. Jonah 4. 2.

Ps. 18. 25. with *m.* show thyself *m.*

37. 26. he is ever *m.* and lendeth

117. 2. his *m.* kindness is great to

Prov. 11. 17. *m.* man doeth good

Isa. 57. 1. *m.* men taketh away from evil

Jer. 3. 12. I am *m.* will not keep anger

Matt. 5. 7. blessed are *m.* they obtain mercy

Luke 6. 36. be *m.* as your Father is *m.*

Heb. 2. 17. might be a *m.* high priest

8. 12. be *m.* to their unrighteousness

MERRY, be, Luke 12. 19.

James 5. 13. is any *m.* let him sing

Prov. 15. 13. *merry-hearted,* 17. 22.

MESSAGE from God, Judg. 3. 20. Hag. 1. 13. 1 John 1. 5. & 3. 11.

Job 33. 23. if there be a *messenger* with him

Isa. 14. 32. what shall one answer the *m.*

42. 19. who is blind or deaf, as *m.*

44. 26. performeth counsel of his *m.*

Mal. 2. 7. he is the *m.* of the Lord

3. 1. my *m.* even the *m.* of the covenant

MESSIAH, Dan. 9. 25. John 1. 41.

MIDST, Ps. 22. 14. & 46. 5. Prov. 4. 21. Isa. 44. 4. Ezek. 43. 7, 9. Joel 2. 27. Zeph. 3. 5, 12, 15, 17. Phil. 2. 15. Rev. 1. 13. Lamb in *m.* of the throne shall feed them

MIGHT, Gen. 49. 3. Num. 14. 13.

Deut. 6. 5. love Lord with all thy *m.*

2 Kings 23. 25. turned to Lord with all his *m.*

2 Chron. 20. 12. no *m.* against this company

Ps. 76. 5. none of men of *m.* found

145. 6. men speak of the *m.* of thy terrible acts

Eccl. 9. 10. findeth to do, do with thy *m.*

Isa. 40. 29. that have no *m.* he increaseth

Zech. 4. 6. not by *m.* but by Spirit

Eph. 3. 16. his glory, to be strengthened with *m.*

6. 10. to be strong in power of his *m.*

Col. 1. 11. strengthened with all *m.*

Deut. 7. 23. with *mighty* destruction

10. 17. a great God, a *m.* and a

Ps. 24. 8. the Lord strong and *m.* the Lord *m.* in battle

Judg. 5. 23. to the help of the Lord against the *m.*

Ps. 89. 10. laid help on one that is *m.*

Isa. 5. 22. *m.* to drink wine, men of

63. 1. speak in righteousness, *m.* to

Jer. 32. 19. great in counsel, *m.* in work

1 Cor. 1. 20. not many *m.* are called

2 Cor. 10. 4. warfare not carnal but *m.*

Ps. 93. 4. Lord on high is *mightier*

Acts 18. 28. *mightily*

19. 20. so *m.* grew word of God

MILK, Gen. 18. 8. & 49. 12.

Job 10. 10. hast poured me out as *m.*

Song 4. 11. honey and *m.* under thy tongue

5. 1. drunk my wine with my *m.*

Isa. 55. 1. buy wine and *m.* without

Joel 3. 18. the hills shall flow with *m.*

Heb. 5. 12. become such have need of *m.*

1 Pet. 2. 2. desire sincere *m.* of word

MIND, Gen. 26. 35. Lev. 24. 12.

1 Chron. 28. 9. serve him with willing *m.*

Neh. 4. 6. people had a *m.* to work

Job 23. 13. he is of one *m.* who can

Isa. 26. 3. whose *m.* is stayed on thee

Luke 12. 29. be ye not of doubtful *m.*

Acts 17. 11. receive the word with readiness of *m.*

20. 19. serving the Lord with all humility of *m.*

Rom. 7. 25. with *m.* I serve law of God

8. 7. carnal *m.* is enmity against

11. 34. who hath known the *m.* of the Lord, 1 Cor. 2. 16.

Rom. 12. 16. be of same *m.* one

1 Cor. 1. 10. joined together in same *m.*

2 Cor. 8. 12. be first a willing *m.* it is

13. 11. be of one *m.* live in peace, Phil. 1. 27. & 4. 2. 1 Pet. 3. 8.

2 Tim. 1. 7. spirit of love and of a sound *m.*

Tit. 1. 15. their *m.* and conscience

1 Pet. 5. 2. not for lucre, but ready *m.*

Rom. 8. 5. of flesh, do *m.* things of

12. 16. *m.* not high things

Phil. 3. 16. *m.* same thing

19. *m.* earthly things

2 Cor. 3. 14. *minds* were blinded

Phil. 4. 7. God keep your hearts and *m.*

Heb. 10. 16. in their *m.* I will write

12. 3. ye be weary and faint in your *m.*

1 Pet. 3. 1. stir up your pure *m.* by

Rom. 8. 6. to be carnally *minded* is death; spiritually *m.* is life and

11. 20. be not high *m.* but fear

15. 5. God of patience grant you to be like *m.*

Tit. 2. 6. exhort men to be sober *m.*

James 1. 8. a double *m.* man

Ps. 111. 5. ever *mindful* of his covenant, 1 Chron. 16. 15. Ps. 105. 8.

Ps. 115. 12. Lord hath been *m.* of us

MINISTER, Josh. 1. 1.

Matt. 20. 26. let him be your *m.*

Acts 26. 16. to make thee a *m.* and

Rom. 13. 4. he is *m.* of God to thee

15. 8. Christ was a *m.* of circumcision

16. I be the *m.* of Christ to the Gentiles

Gal. 2. 17. is therefore Christ the *m.* of sin

Eph. 3. 7. was made a *m.* according

4. 29. may *m.* grace unto hearers

Rom. 15. 25. to *m.* unto saints

15. 27. *m.* to them in carnal

1 Cor. 9. 13. who *m.* about holy things

2 Cor. 9. 10. *m.* seed to sower and

1 Pet. 4. 11. if any man *m.* let him

1 Tim. 4. 6. be a good *m.* of Jesus Christ

Heb. 8. 2. *m.* of the sanctuary

Ps. 103. 21. *ministers* of his that do

104. 4. his *m.* a flaming fire

Isa. 61. 6. men call you the *m.* of God

Joel 1. 9. priests, the Lord's *m.* mourn

Luke 1. 2. from beginning *m.* of the

Rom. 13. 6. they are God's *m.*

1 Cor. 3. 5. *m.* by whom ye believed

4. 1. account of us as *m.* of Christ

2 Cor. 3. 6. able *m.* of New Testament

6. 4. approved ourselves as *m.* of God

2 Cor. 11. 23. are they *m.* of Christ, so

Matt. 4. 11. *ministered,* Luke 8. 3. Gal. 3. 5. Heb. 6. 10. 2 Pet. 1. 11.

Luke 1. 23. *ministration,* Acts 6. 1. 2 Cor. 3. 7, 8. & 9. 1, 13.

Heb. 1. 14. all *ministering* spirits

Rom. 15. 16. *m.* the gospel of God

Acts 6. 4. give ourselves to *ministry*

20. 24. might finish *m.* I have received

2 Cor. 4. 1. seeing we have this *m.*

5. 18. give to us *m.* of reconciliation

6. 3. that the *m.* be not blamed

Col. 4. 17. take heed to *m.* that thou

1 Tim. 1. 12. putting me into the *m.*

2 Tim. 4. 5. make full proof of thy *m.*

Heb. 8. 6. obtained more excellent *m.*

MIRACLE, Mark 6. 52. Luke 23. 8. John 2. 11. Acts 2. 22. 1 Cor. 12. 10. Gal. 3. 5. Heb. 2. 4.

MIRTH, Prov. 14. 13. Eccl. 2. 2. Isa. 24. 8. Jer. 7. 34. Hos. 2. 11.

MISCHIEF, Gen. 42. 4. & 44. 29.

Job 15. 35. they conceive *m.* bring

Ps. 10. 14. thou beholdest *m.* and

28. 3. *m.* is in their hearts, 10. 7.

36. 4. he deviseth *m.* upon his bed

94. 20. which frameth *m.* by a law

Prov. 10. 23. sport to a fool to do *m.*

11. 27. he that seeketh *m.* it shall

24. 16. wicked shall fall into *m.*

Acts 13. 10. full of all subtlety and *m.*

MISERY, Job 3. 20. Lam. 3. 19.

Judg. 10. 16. soul grieved for *m.* of Israel

Prov. 31. 7. drink and remember *m.*

Eccl. 8. 6. the *m.* of man is great

Rom. 3. 16. destruction and *m.* are in their way

Job 16. 2. *miserable* comforters are ye all

1 Cor. 15. 19. are all men most *m.*

Rev. 3. 17. knowest not thou art *m.*

MOCK, Prov. 1. 26.

Prov. 14. 9. fools make a *m.* at sin

1 Kings 18. 27. Elijah *mocked* and

2 Chron. 36. 16. they *m.* the messengers of God

Prov. 17. 5. whoso *mocketh* the poor

30. 17. eye that *m.* at his father

20. 1. wine is a *mocker* and strong

Isa. 28. 22. be not *mockers* lest

Jude 18. there should be *m.* in last

MODERATION, Phil. 4. 5.

MODEST apparel, 1 Tim. 2. 9.

MOMENT, Ex. 33. 5.

Num. 16. 21. consume them in a *m.* 45.

Job 17. 18. try him every *m.*

20. 5. joy of hypocrite is for a *m.*

Ps. 30. 5. his anger endureth but for a *m.*

Isa. 26. 20. hide thee as it were, for a *m.*

54. 7. a small *m.* have I forsaken thee

1 Cor. 15. 52. in a *m.* in the twinkling

2 Cor. 4. 17. affliction is but for a *m.*

MONEY, Gen. 23. 9. & 31. 15.

Eccl. 7. 12. wisdom is defence and *m.*

10. 19. *m.* answereth all things

Isa. 55. 1. he that hath no *m.* come

2. wherefore spend *m.* for that which is not bread

Mic. 3. 11. the prophets divine for *m.*

Acts 8. 20. thy *m.* perish with thee

1 Tim. 6. 10. love of *m.* is the root of all evil

MORROW, Ex. 8. 23. & 16. 23.

Prov. 27. 1. boast not thyself of to *m.*

Isa. 22. 13. to *m.* we die

Isa. 56. 12. to *m.* shall be as this day

Matt. 6. 34. take no thought for the *m.*

James 4. 14. know not what shall be on the *m.*

MORTAL man be just, Job 4. 17.

Rom. 6. 12. let not sin reign in *m.* body

8. 11. raised Christ, quicken *m.* body

1 Cor. 15. 53. *m.* put on immortality

2 Cor. 5. 4. *mortality* be swallowed up of life

Rom. 8. 13. *mortify* deeds of body

Col. 3. 5. *m.* your members on earth

MOTE, Matt. 7. 3. Luke 6. 41.

MOTH, Job 4. 19. & 27. 18. Ps. 39. 11. Isa. 50. 9. & 51. 8. Hos. 5. 12. Matt. 6. 19, 20. Luke 12. 33.

MOTHER, Gen. 3. 20. Judg. 5. 7. 2 Sam. 20. 19. 1 Kings 3. 27.

Job 17. 14. say to worm, thou art my *m.*

Ps. 27. 10. when father and *m.* forsake me

71. 6. took me out of my *m's* bowels

Matt. 12. 49. behold my *m.* and my

MOVE, Ex. 11. 7. Judg. 13. 25.

Acts 17. 28. in him we live and *m.*

20. 24. none of these things *m.* me

Ps. 15. 5. shall never be *moved,* 21. 7. Prov. 12. 3.

Col. 1. 23. be not *m.* away from hope

1 Thes. 3. 3. no man be *m.* by these affairs

Heb. 12. 28. a kingdom which cannot be *m.*

1 Pet. 1. 21. spake as *m.* by Holy Ghost

Rom. 7. 5. *motions*

Prov. 5. 6. *moveable*

MOURN, Neh. 8. 9. Job 5. 11.

Isa. 61. 2. to comfort all that *m.*

Matt. 5. 4. blessed are they that *m.*

James 4. 9. be afflicted and *m.* and

Matt. 11. 17. we have *mourned* unto you, and ye have not lamented

1 Cor. 5. 2. are puffed up and have not rather *m.*

Eccl. 12. 5. *mourners* go about streets

Isa. 57. 18. restore comfort to him and his *m.*

Ps. 30. 11. turned *mourning* into dancing

Isa. 22. 12. Lord did call to weeping and *m.*

61. 3. to give the oil of joy for *m.*

Jer. 9. 17. call for the *m.* women

31. 13. I will turn their *m.* into joy

Joel 2. 12. turn to me with fasting and *m.*

James 4. 9. laughter be turned into *m.*

MOUTH, Ps. 8. 2.

Ps. 37. 30. *m.* of righteous speaketh wisdom

Prov. 10. 14. *m.* of fools near destruction

10. 31. *m.* of the just bringeth forth wisdom

12. 6. *m.* of upright shall deliver

14. 3. in *m.* of fools is a rod of pride

15. 2. *m.* of fools poureth out foolishness

18. 7. a fool's *m.* is his destruction

22. 14. *m.* of strange women a deep pit

Lam. 3. 38. out of *m.* of the Most High proceedeth not evil and good

Matt. 12. 34. out of abundance of the heart the *m.* speaketh

Luke 21. 15. will give you a *m.* and

Rom. 10. 10. with *m.* confession is made

15. 6. with one mind and *m.* glorify

Prov. 13. 3. keepeth *his mouth,* keepeth his life

Lam. 3. 29. putteth—in dust if there

Mal. 2. 7. they shall seek law at—

Ps. 17. 3. *my mouth* shall not transgress

39. 1. I will keep—with a bridle

49. 3.—shall speak of wisdom

51. 15.—shall show thy praise

71. 15.—shall show thy righteousness

Eph. 6. 19. that I may open—boldly

Ps. 81. 10. open *thy mouth* wide

103. 5. who satisfieth—with good

Prov. 31. 8. open—for the dumb in

Eccl. 5. 6. suffer not—to cause flesh

MULTITUDE, Gen. 16. 10. & 28. 3.

Ex. 12. 38. & 23. 2. Num. 11. 4.

Job 32. 7. *m.* of years teach wisdom

Ps. 5. 7. *m.* of mercies

10. *m.* of transgressions

53. 16. no king saved by the *m.* of

51. 1. according unto the *m.* of thy tender mercies, 106. 7, 45.

94. 19. in the *m.* of my thoughts

Prov. 10. 19. *m.* of words wanteth not sin

11. 14. in the *m.* of counsellors there is safety, 15. 22. & 24. 6.

Eccl. 5. 3. *m.* of business, *m.* of words

James 5. 20. hide *m.* of sins

MURDER, Rom. 1. 29. Matt. 15. 19.

Gal. 5. 21. Rev. 9. 21.

Job 24. 14. *murderer* rising with light

John 8. 44. devil was a *m.* from the beginning

Hos. 9. 13. bring forth children to *m.*

1 Pet. 4. 15. none of you suffer as a *m.*

1 John 3. 15. who hateth his brother is a *m.* and no *m.* hath eternal life

MURMUR, Deut. 1. 27. Ps. 106. 25.

Jude 16. Ex. 16. 7. Phil. 2. 14.

MUSE, Ps. 39. 3. & 143. 5.

MUSIC, Lam. 3. 63. Amos 6. 5.

MUSTARD seed, Matt. 13. 31.

MUZZLE, Deut. 25. 4. 1 Cor. 9. 9.

MYSTERY, Mark 4. 11.

Rom. 11. 25. not be ignorant of *m.*

16. 25. according to revelation of the *m.*

1 Cor. 2. 7. speak wisdom of God in a *m.*

4. 1. stewards of the *m.* of God

13. 2. prophecy and understand *m.*

14. 2. in the Spirit he speaketh *m.*

15. 51. I show you a *m.* we shall

Eph. 1. 9. made known *m.* of his will

3. 4. my knowledge in *m.*

9. fellowship of *m.*

5. 32. this is a great *m.* of Christ

6. 19. make known *m.* of Gospel

Col. 1. 2. *m.* which hath been hid

1. 27. glory of this *m.* among Gentiles

2. 2. acknowledgment of *m.* of God

4. 3. open a door to speak *m.* of Christ

2 Thes. 2. 7. *m.* of iniquity doth

1 Tim. 3. 9. holding *m.* of the faith

16. great is the *m.* of godliness

Rev. 1. 20. write the *m.* of seven stars

10. 7. *m.* of God should be finished

17. 5. her name, *m.* Babylon the

N

NAIL, Judg. 4. 21. & 5. 26.

Ezra. 9. 8. give us a *n.* in his holy place

Eccl. 12. 11. *n.* fastened by the masters of assemblies

Isa. 22. 23. fastened as a *n.* in a sure

Zech. 10. 4. out of him came the *n.*

NAKED, Gen. 2. 25. & 3. 7.

Ex. 32. 25. when the people were *n.*

2 Chron. 28. 19. he made Judah *n.*

Job 1. 21. *n.* came I out of my mother's womb

Matt. 25. 26. *n.* and ye clothed me

1 Cor. 4. 11. we hunger and thirst and are *n.*

2 Cor. 5. 3. clothed may not be *n.*

Heb. 4. 13. all things are *n.* and open

Rev. 3. 17. miserable, poor, blind, *n.*

16. 15. keepeth his garments lest he walk *n.*

NAME, Ex. 34. 14. Lev. 18. 21.

Ps. 20. 1. the *n.* of God of Jacob

109. 13. let their *n.* be blotted

Prov. 10. 7. *n.* of the wicked shall rot

22. 1. good *n.* is rather to be chosen

Eccl. 7. 1. a good *n.* is better than ointment

Isa. 55. 13. shall be to the Lord for *n.*

56. 5. a *n.* better than of sons and

62. 2. thou shalt be called by new *n.*

Jer. 13. 11. for a people, for a *n.* and

32. 20. made thee *n.* as at this day

33. 9. shall be to me a *n.* of joy, a

Mic. 4. 5. we shall walk in *n.* of the Lord

Matt. 10. 41. receive a prophet in *n.* of

Luke 6. 22. cast out your *n.* as evil

Acts 4. 12. is none other *n.* under heaven

Rom. 2. 24. *n.* of God is blasphemed

Col. 3. 17. do all in the *n.* of Lord

2 Tim. 2. 19. that nameth *n.* of Christ

Heb. 1. 4. obtained more excellent *n.*

1 Pet. 4. 14. if ye be reproached for the *n.* of Christ

1 John 3. 23. should believe on the *n.* of his Son

5. 13. that we believe on the *n.* of Son of God

Rev. 2. 17. *n.* written, which no man

3. 1. I know thy works, that thou hast a *n.*

12. write on him *n.* of my God, and the *n.* of the city of my God, and write upon him my new *n.*

14. 1. Father's *n.* on foreheads

Eph. 1. 21. every *n.* that is *named,* Phil. 2. 9.

Ps. 76. 1. *his name* is great in Israel

72. 17.—shall endure for ever

106. 8.—he saved them for—sake

Prov. 30. 4.—what is—and what his son's name

Isa. 9. 6.—shall be called Wonderful

Zech. 14. 9. shall be one Lord and—

John 20. 31. might have life through—

Rev. 3. 5. I will confess—before my Father

13. 17. the name of the beast, or the number of—15. 2.

Ex. 23. 21. *my name* is in him

3. 15. this is—forever, and my memorial

Judg. 13. 18. asketh after—

Isa. 48. 9. for—sake I defer my anger

Ezek. 20. 9. wrought for—sake

Mal. 1. 14—is dreadful among the

2. 2. lay it to heart to give glory to—

Matt. 10. 22. hated of all for—sake

19. 29. forsaken houses for—sake

John 14. 13. ask in—15. 16.

16. 24. asked nothing in—

Acts 9. 15. he is a chosen vessel to bear—

Rev. 2. 3. for—hast laboured, and

13. holdest fast—3. 8. not denied—

2 Chron. 14. 11. in *thy name* we go

Ps. 8. 1. excellent is—in all the earth

9. 10. that know—will put trust in thee

48. 10. according to—so is thy

75. 1.—is near, thy works declare

138. 2. magnified thy word above all

Song 1. 3.—is as ointment poured

Isa. 26. 8. desire of our souls is to—

64. 7. none that calleth on—

Jer. 15. 7. do it for—sake, 21.

Mic. 6. 9. man of wisdom shall see—

John 17. 12. I kept them in—26.

Ex. 23. 13. Aaron bear their *n.* before the Lord

Ps. 49. 11. call lands after their *n.*

147. 4. stars he calleth by their *n.*

Luke 10. 20. *n.* written in heaven

Rev. 3. 4. hast a few *n.* in Sardis

NARROW, 1 Kings 6. 4. Prov. 23.

27. Isa. 28. 20. Matt. 7. 4.

NATION, Gen. 15. 14. & 21. 13.

Gen. 20. 4. wilt thou slay a righteous *n.*

Num. 14. 12. make of thee a great *n.*

2 Sam. 7. 23. what *n.* is like thy people

Ps. 32. 12. blessed is the *n.* whose God is the Lord

147. 20. not dealt so with any *n.*

Isa. 1. 4. ah, sinful *n.* a people laden

2. 4. *n.* shall not lift up sword against *n.*

49. 7. him whom the *n.* abhorreth

66. 8. shall a *n.* be born at once

Jer. 2. 11. hath *n.* changed their gods

Matt. 24. 7. *n.* shall rise against *n.*

Luke 7. 5. he loveth our *n.* and built

Acts 10. 35. in every *n.* he that feareth God

Rom. 10. 19. by a foolish *n.* I will anger you

Phil. 2. 15. in midst of a crooked *n.*

1 Pet. 2. 9. ye are a holy *n.*

Rev. 5. 9. redeemed us out of every *n.*

Gen. 10. 32. *nations,* 17. 4.

Deut. 26. 19. high above all *n.*

Ps. 9. 20. *n.* may know themselves

113. 4. Lord is high above all *n.*

Isa. 2. all *n.* shall flow unto it

40. 17. *n.* before him are as nothing

55. 5. *n.* that knew thee not shall

Jer. 4. 2. *n.* shall bless themselves in

Zech. 2. 11. many *n.* joined to the Lord

Matt. 25. 32. before him gathered all *n.*

Acts 14. 16. suffered all *n.* to walk in own

Rev. 21. 24. *n.* of them that are saved

NATURE, Rom. 2. 27.

Rom. 1. 26. that which is against *n.*

2. 14. do by *n.* things contained in

11. 24. olive wild by *n.* contrary to *n.*

1 Cor. 11. 14. doth not *n.* itself teach

Gal. 2. 16. Jews by *n.* and not sinners

4. 8. them which by *n.* are no gods

Eph. 2. 3. were by *n.* children of wrath

Heb. 2. 16. took not *n.* of angels

2 Pet. 1. 4. partakers of divine *n.*

Deut. 34. 7. *natural,* Rom. 1. 26. 2

Tim. 3. 3. James 1. 23. 2 Pet. 2. 12.

Phil. 2. 20. Jude 10.

NAUGHT, Prov. 20. 14.

James 1. 31. filthiness and superfluity of *naughtiness*

NEAR, nigh, Ps. 119. 151.

NECESSARY, Job 23. 12. Acts 13. 46.

Tit. 3. 14. Heb. 9. 23.

Rom. 12. 13. *necessity,* Acts 20. 34.

NECK, Song 1. 10. Isa. 48. 4.

Acts 15. 10. to put a yoke on *n.* of the disciples

2 Kings 17. 14. hardened their *necks,* Neh. 9. 16. Jer. 7. 26.

NEED, Matt. 6. 32.

Matt. 9. 12. they that are whole *n.* not a physician, but they that are

Luke 15. 7. righteous *n.* no repentance

Heb. 4. 16. find grace to help in time of *n.*

1 Pet. 1. 6. if *n.* be, ye are in heaviness

1 John 2. 27. *n.* not that any man

Rev. 3. 17. rich, and have *n.* of

21. 23. no *n.* of sun

22. 5. *n.* no candle

Eph. 4. 28. give to him that *needeth*

1 Tim. 2. 15. *n.* not be ashamed of truth

Luke 10. 42. one thing is *needful*

Ps. 9. 18. *needy* not always be forgotten

72. 12. he shall deliver the *n.* and

82. 3. do justice to afflicted and *n.*

113. 7. lifted the *n.* out of the dunghill

Isa. 14. 30. *n.* shall lie down in safety

Jer. 22. 16. he judgeth cause of *n.*

NEGLECT to hear, Matt. 18. 17.

1 Tim. 4. 14. *n.* not the gift that is in

Heb. 2. 3. if we *n.* so great salvation

NEIGHBOUR, Ex. 3. 22. & 11. 2.

Ex. 20. 16. not bear false witness against thy *n.*

Lev. 29. 13. thou shalt not defraud *n.*

17. thou shalt rebuke thy *n.*

18. thou shalt love thy *n.* as thyself, Matt. 19. 19. Rom. 13. 9. Gal. 5. 14. James 2. 8. Matt. 7. 12. Heb. 13. 3.

Ps. 15. 3. nor doeth evil to his *n.*

Prov. 27. 10. better is a *n.* near, than a brother far off

Jer. 27. 13. useth *n.'s* servant without wages

31. 24. teach no more his *n.*

Luke 10. 29. who is my *n.* 36.

Rom. 13, 10. love worketh no ill to his *n.*

15. 2. let every one please his *n.*

NEIGH, Jer. 5. 8. & 8. 16.

NEST, Job 20. 18. Ps. 84. 3. Prov. 27. 8. Isa. 10. 14. Hab. 2. 9.

NET, Job. 18. 8. Ps. 9. 15. Isa. 51. 20. Hab. 1. 15, 16. Matt. 13. 47. Ps. 141. 10. Eccl. 7. 26.

NEW, Num. 16. 30.

Judg. 5. 8. they chose *n.* gods

Eccl. 1. 9. no *n.* thing under sun

Isa. 65. 17. *n.* heavens and a *n.* earth, 66. 22. 2 Pet. 3. 13. Rev. 21. 1.

Jer. 31. 22. created a *n.* thing in earth

Lam. 3. 23. mercies are *n.* every morning

Ezek. 11. 19. I will put a *n.* spirit

18. 31. make you a *n.* heart and *n.* spirit

36. 26. *n.* heart I will give, and a *n.* spirit

Matt. 9. 16. putteth *n.* cloth on old

17. neither put *n.* wine in old bottles

13. 52. bringeth forth things *n.* and

Mark 1. 27. what *n.* doctrine is this

John 13. 34. a *n.* commandment I give unto you, 1 John 2. 7, 8.

Acts 17. 21. to tell or hear some *n.* thing

1 Cor. 5. 7. that ye may be a *n.* lump

2 Cor. 5. 17. if any man be in Christ, he is a *n.* creature

Gal. 6. 15. neither circumcision nor uncircumcision, but a *n.* creature

Eph. 4. 24. ye put on *n.* man

1 Pet. 2. 2. as *n.* born babes desire

Rev. 2. 17. a *n.* name written, 3. 12.

Rev. 5. 9. sung a *n.* song, 14. 3.

Rom. 6. 4. walk in *newness* of life

7. 6. we should serve in *n.* of spirit

NIGH, Lev. 25. 49. Num. 24. 17.

Deut. 4. 7. who hath God so *n.* unto

30. 14. word is *n.* to thee

Ps. 34. 18. Lord is *n.* them of broken heart

85. 9. salvation is *n.* them that fear him

145. 18. Lord is *n.* them that call on

Matt. 15. 8. draweth *n.* with mouth

Eph. 2. 13. made *n.* by blood of Christ

77. peace to them that were *n.*

NIGHT, Gen. 1. 5, 14 & 26. 24.

Ex. 12. 42. this is that *n.* of Lord

Ps. 19. 2. *n.* unto *n.* showeth knowledge

139. 11. *n.* shall be light about me

30. 5. weeping may endure for a *n.*

Isa. 21. 11. what of the *n.* what of the *n.*

Jer. 14. 8. as wayfaring man to tarry for a *n.*

Luke 6. 12. continued all *n.* in prayer

12. 20. this *n.* shall thy soul be required

John 9. 4. *n.* cometh when no man

Rom. 13. 12. *n.* is far spent; day is at hand

1 Thes. 5. 5. children not of *n.* nor

Rev. 21. 25. there shall be no *n.* there

Ps. 134. 1. *by night,* Song 3. 1.

Job 35. 10. who giveth songs *in the night*

Ps. 16. 7. instruct me—seasons

42. 8.—his song shall be with me

77. 6. I call to remembrance my song—

119. 55. I have remembered thy name—

Isa. 26. 9. my soul desired thee—

30. 29. ye shall have a song as—

59. 40. stumble at noonday as—

John 11. 10. if a man walk—he stumbleth

1 Thes. 5. 7. sleep—and are drunk—

Ps. 63. 6. *night watches,* 119. 148.

NOBLE, Esth. 6. 9. Jer. 2. 21. Luke 19. 12. Acts 17. 11. Ex. 24. 11.

1 Cor. 1. 26. not many *n.* are called

Col. 3. 5. *nobles* put not their necks

13. 17. I contended with the *n.* of Judah

Ps. 149. 8. bind their *n.* with fetters

Prov. 8. 16. by me princes rule, and *n.*

Eccl. 13. 17. when thy king is the son of *n.*

NOISOME, Ps. 91. 3. Rev. 16. 2.

NOSE, Prov. 30. 33. Isa. 65. 5.

Isa. 2. 22. breath in *nostrils*

NOTHING, Gen. 11. 6. Ex. 9. 4. Num. 6. 4. & 16. 26. Josh. 11. 15.

2 Sam. 24. 24. offer that which costs *n.*

1 Kings 8. 9. *n.* in ark save two tables

Neh. 8. 10. send to them from whom *n.* is prepared

Job 6. 21. ye are *n.*

8. 9. of yesterday, and know *n.*

26. 7. hangeth earth on *n.*

34. 9. it profiteth *n.*

Ps. 17. 3. hast tried me and shalt find *n.*

39. 5. my age is as *n.* before thee

49. 17. when he dieth, shall carry *n.*

119. 165. *n.* shall offend them

Prov. 13. 4. the sluggard desireth and hath *n.*

7. maketh himself rich, yet hath *n.*

Isa. 40. 17. nations before him are as *n.*

Jer. 10. 24. lest thou bring me to *n.*

Lam. 1. 22. is it *n.* to you, ye that pass

Hag. 2. 3. is it not in your eyes in comparison of it as *n.*

Luke 1. 37. with God *n.* be impossible

John 8. 28. I do *n.* of myself, but as my Father hath taught me

14. 30. prince of this world hath *n.* in me

14. 5. without me ye can do *n.*

1 Cor. 1. 19. bring to *n.* understanding

13. 2. I am *n.* 2 Cor. 12. 11. having *n.* yet possessing all, 2 Cor. 6. 10.

1 Tim. 6. 7. we brought *n.* into world

NOUGHT, Gen. 29. 15.

Isa. 41. 12. shall be as a thing of *n.*

49. 4. I have spent my strength for *n.*

52. 3. sold yourselves for *n.*

Amos 6. 13. rejoice in a thing of *n.*

Luke 23. 11. Herod and men set him at *n.*

Acts 19. 27. Diana in danger to be set at *n.*

Rom. 14. 10. why set at *n.* brother

NOVICE, not a, lest, 1 Tim. 3. 6.

NUMBER our days, teach us to, Ps. 90. 12.

Isa. 65. 12. I will *n.* you to the sword

Rev. 7. 9. multitude which no man could *n.*

Isa. 53. 12. was *numbered* with transgressors

Dan. 5. 26. God hath *n.* thy kingdom

Hos. 1. 10. sand cannot *n.*

Job 14. 16. thou *numberest* my steps

Ps. 71. 15. I know not the *numbers*

Rev. 13. 17. the *n.* of his name

NURSE, 1 Thes. 2. 7. Isa. 49. 23.

O

OATH, Gen. 24. 8. & 26. 3, 28.

1 Sam. 14. 26. people feared the *o.*

2 Sam. 21. 7. Lord's *o.* was between

2 Chron. 15. 15. all Israel rejoiced at *o.*

Eccl. 8. 2. keep in regard of *o.* of God

9. 2. that feareth and sweareth an *o.*

Ezek. 16. 59. despised the *o.*

Luke 1. 73. *o.* which he sware to our

Heb. 6. 36. *o.* for confirmation is end

James 5. 12. swear not by heaven, neither by any other *o.*

OBEY, Gen. 27. 8. Ex. 5. 2.

Deut. 11. 27. a blessing if ye *o.* and a curse if you will not *o.* command

13. 4. walk after Lord and *o.* his voice

Josh. 24. 24. his voice will we *o.*

1 Sam. 12. 14. fear Lord and *o.* his voice

15. 22. to *o.* is better than sacrifice

Jer. 7. 23. *o.* my voice and I will be your God

26. 13. amend your ways and *o.* voice of the Lord, Zeph. 6. 15.

Acts 5. 29. ought to *o.* God rather

Rom. 2. 8. contentious, and do not *o.*

6. 16. his servants ye are whom ye *o.*

Eph. 6. 1. children *o.* your parents in the Lord, Col. 3. 20.

Col. 3. 22. servants *o.* in all things

2 Thes. 1. 8. that *o.* not the Gospel

3. 14. if any man *o.* not your word

Tit. 3. 1. put them in mind to *o.* magistrates

Heb. 5. 9. salvation to all who *o.*

13. 17. *o.* them that have rule over

1 Pet. 3. 1. if any *o.* not the word

Rom. 6. 17. *obeyed* from heart that

1 Pet. 3. 6. Sarah *o.* Abraham

4. 17. end of them that *o.* not Gospel

Isa. 50. 10. *obeyeth* voice

1 Pet. 1. 22. purified in *obeying* truth

Rom. 1. 5. received grace for *obedience*

15. 19. by the *o.* of one many made righteous

6. 16. yield *o.* unto righteousness

16. 19. your *o.* is come abroad

26. made known for *o.* of faith

1 Cor. 14. 34. women to be under *o.*

2 Cor. 7. 15. remember the *o.* of you

10. 5. every thought to *o.* of Christ

6. revenge diso., when *o.* is fulfilled

Heb. 5. 8. learned he *o.* by things he suffered

1 Pet. 1. sanctification of spirit unto *o.*

Ex. 24. 7. will we do and be *obedient*

Num. 27. 20. children of Israel may be *o.*

Deut. 3. 30. turn and be *o.* to voice

8. 20. perish because not *o.* to Lord

2 Sam. 22. 45. strangers shall be *o.*

Prov. 25. 12. reprover upon an *o.* ear

Isa. 1. 19. if ye be *o.* ye shall eat the

42. 24. they were not *o.* to his law

Acts 6. 7. priests were *o.* to the faith

Rom. 15. 18. Gentiles *o.* by word

2 Cor. 2. 9. whether ye be *o.* in all

Eph. 6. 5. servant be *o.* to masters

Phil. 2. 8. he became *o.* unto death

Tit. 2. 5. discreet, *o.* to your husbands

9. exhort servants to be *o.*

1 Pet. 1. 14. as *o.* children, not

OBSCURITY, Isa. 29. 18.

OBSERVE, Ex. 12. 17. & 34. 11.

Ps. 107. 43. who is wise and will *o.*

119. 34. *o.* it with my whole heart

Prov. 23. 26. let thine eyes *o.* my ways

Jonah 2. 8. that *o.* lying vanities

Matt. 28. 20. teaching them to *o.*

Gal. 4. 10. ye *o.* days, months and

Gen. 37. 11. his father *observed* the sayings

Ex. 12. 42. a night be much *o.*

Mark 6. 20. Herod feared John and *o.*

10. 20. these have I *o.* from my youth

Luke 17. 20. cometh not with *observation*

OBSTINATE, Deut. 2. 30.

OBTAIN, Prov. 8. 35.

Isa. 35. 10. shall *o.* joy and gladness

Luke 20. 35. worthy to *o.* that world

1 Cor. 9. 24. so run, that ye may *o.*

Heb. 4. 16. may *o.* mercy and find

11. 35. might *o.* better resurrection

James 4. 2. ye desire to have, and cannot *o.*

Hos. 2. 23. that had not *obtained* mercy

Acts 26. 22. having *o.* help of God

Rom. 11. 7. the election hath *o.* it

Eph. 1. 11. in whom we have *o.* an inheritance

1 Tim. 1. 13. I *o.* mercy, because

Heb. 1. 4. *o.* more excellent name

6. 15. endured, he *o.* the promises

9. 12. *o.* eternal redemption for us

OCCASION, Gen. 43. 18.

2 Sam. 12. 14. given *o.* to enemies of the Lord

Job 33. 10. he findeth *o.* against me

Jer. 2. 24. in her *o.* who can turn her away

Dan. 6. 4. could find none *o.* 5.

Rom. 7. 8. sin taking *o.* by the commandment, 11.

14. 13. *o.* to fall in brother's way

2 Cor. 11. 12. cut off *o.* from them which desire *o.*

Gal. 5. 13. use not for *o.* to the flesh

1 Tim. 5. 14. give none *o.* to adversary

1 John 2. 10. none *o.* of stumbling

OCCUPY, Luke 19. 13.

ODOUR, Phil. 4. 18. Rev. 5. 8.

OFFENCE, 1 Sam. 25. 31.

Eccl. 10. 4. yielding pacifieth great *o.*

Hos. 5. 15. acknowledge their *o.*

Acts 24. 16. conscience void of *o.*

Rom. 4. 25. delivered for our *o.* and

Matt. 16. 23. thou art an *o.* unto me

18. 7. woe to the world because of *o.* for *o.* must come; woe to him by whom the *o.* cometh

Rom. 5. 15. not as *o.* so is free gift

16. the free gift is of many *o.*

17. by one man's *o.* death came

9. 33. rock of *o.* 1 Pet. 2. 8.

14. 20. is evil for him that eateth with *o.*

16. 10. cause divisions and *o.*

1 Cor. 10. 32. give none *o.* neither to Jews

2 Cor. 6. 3. giving no *o.* in anything.

11. 7. committed an *o.* in abasing myself

Gal. 5. 11. then is the *o.* of the cross ceased

Phil. 1. 10. without *o.* till day of Christ

OFFEND, Job 34. 31.

Ps. 73. 15. *o.* against generation of thy children

119. 165. nothing shall *o.* them

Jer. 2. 3. all that devour him shall *o.*

50. 7. we *o.* not because we have sinned

Hos. 4. 14. Israel play harlot, let not Judah *o.*

Matt. 5. 29. if thy right eye *o.* thee

13. 41. gather out of his kingdom all that *o.*

17. 27. yet lest we should *o.* go

18. 6. whoso shall *o.* one of these little ones, 8. 9. if hand, foot, eye *o.* Mark 9. 43-47.

1 Cor. 8. 13. if meat make thy brother to *o.*

James 2. 10. *o.* in one point is guilty

3. 2. in many things we *o.* all: not in word

Prov. 18. 19. brother *offended* harder

Matt. 11. 6. blessed who is not *o.* in

26. 33. though all be *o.* I will never be *o.*

Mark 4. 17. immediately they are *o.*

Rom. 14. 22. *o.* or is made weak

2 Cor. 11. 29. who is *o.* and I burn not

Isa. 29. 21. make a man *offender* for

OFFER, Gen. 31. 54. Lev. 1. 3.

Matt. 5. 24. then come and *o.* thy gift

Heb. 13. 15. let us *o.* the sacrifice of praise

Rev. 8. 3. *o.* it with prayers of saints

Mal. 1. 11. incense *offered* to my name

Phil. 2. 17. *o.* upon sacrifice and service

1 Tim. 4. 6. I am now ready to be *o.*

Heb. 9. 14. *o.* himself without spot

28. Christ was once *o.* to bear sins

11. 4. by faith Abel *o.* to God a more excellent sacrifice

17. Abraham *o.* up Isaac

Ps. 50. 14. *o.* to God thanksgiving

23. whoso *offereth* praise glorifieth

Eph. 5. 2. *offering* a sacrifice to God

Heb. 10. 5. sacrifice and *o.* thou wouldest not

14. by one *o.* hath perfected for

OFFSCOURING, Lam. 3. 45.

OFFSPRING, Acts 17. 28.

OFTEN, Prov. 29. 1.

Mal. 3. 16. spake *o.* one to another

Matt. 23. 37. how *o.* would I have gathered thy children

1 Cor. 11. 26. *o.* as ye eat this bread

Phil. 3. 18. of whom I have told you *o.*

Heb. 9. 25. needed not offer himself *o.*

OIL, Gen. 28. 18. Ex. 25. 6.

Ps. 45. 7. with *o.* of gladness

Ps. 89. 20. with my holy *o.* I have anointed him

92. 10. be anointed with fresh *o.*

104. 15. *o.* to make his face shine

141. 5. *o.* which shall not break my head

Isa. 61. 3. *o.* of joy for mourning

Matt. 25. 3. took no *o.* in lamps

4. took *o.* in their vessels

8. give us of your *o.* for our lamps

Luke 10. 34. pouring in wine and *o.*

OINTMENT, Ps. 133. 2. Prov. 27. 9. Eccl. 7. 1. Song 1. 3. Isa. 1. 6.

OLD, Gen. 5. 32. & 18. 12, 13.

Ps. 37. 25. been young, and now am *o.*

71. 18. when I am *o.* and gray-headed

Prov. 22. 6. when he is *o.* he will not depart from it
Jer. 6. 16. ask for the *o.* paths and
Acts 21. 16. Mnason an *o.* disciple
1 Cor. 5. 7. purge out the *o.* leaven
2 Cor. 5. 17. *o.* things are passed
2 Pet. 1. 9. purged from his *o.* sins
Gen. 25. 8. *old age*, Job 30. 2. Ps. 71. 9.
Rom. 6. 6. *old man*, Eph. 4. 22.
Prov. 17. 6. of *old men*, 20. 29.
OMEGA, Alpha and, Rev. 1. 8.
ONE, Gen. 2. 24. Matt. 19. 5.
Jer. 3. 14. *o.* of a city, and two of a
Zech. 14. 9. shall be *o.* Lord and name *o.*
Matt. 19. 17. none good but *o.* that is God
1 Cor. 8. 4. none other God but *o.*
10. 17. we being many are *o.* bread and *o.* body; all partakers of *o.* bread
Gal. 3. 20. mediator not of *o.* God is *o.*
1 John 5. 7. these three are *o.*
Josh. 23. 14. not *one thing* hath failed
Ps. 27. 4.—have I desired of Lord
Mark 10. 21.—thou lackest, go sell
Luke 10. 42. but—is needful
Phil. 3. 13. this—I do, forgetting
OPEN thou my lips, Ps. 51. 15.
Ps. 81. 10. *o.* thy mouth wide
119. 18. *o.* thou mine eyes, that I
Prov. 31. 8. *o.* thy mouth for dumb
Song 5. 2. *o.* to me, my sister, my
Isa. 22. 22. shall *o.* and none shall shut; and he shall shut, and none shall *o.*
42. 7. to *o.* blind eyes, Ps. 146. 8.
Ezek. 16. 63. never *o.* thy mouth
Matt. 25. 11. Lord *o.* to us
Acts 26. 18. to *o.* their eyes, and turn them from darkness to light
Col. 4. 3. *o.* to us door of utterance
Rev. 5. 2. who is worthy to *o.* the book, 3. 9.
Gen. 3. 7. eyes of both were *opened*
Isa. 35. 5. eyes of the blind shall be *o.*
Isa. 53. 7. he *o.* not his mouth
Matt. 7. 7. knock and it shall be *o.*
Luke 24. 45. then *o.* he their understanding
Acts 14. 27. *o.* door of faith to Gentiles
16. 14. Lydia whose heart Lord *o.*
1 Cor. 16. 9. a great door and effectual is *o.*
2 Cor. 2. 12. a door *o.* to me of the Lord
Heb. 4. 13. naked and *o.* to eyes of
Ps. 104. 28. *openest* thy hand
OPERATION, Ps. 28. 5. Isa. 5. 10.
Col. 3. 12. 1 Cor. 12. 6.
OPINION, Job 33. 6, 10.
OPPORTUNITY, Mat. 26. 16. Gal. 6. 10. Phil. 4. 10. Heb. 11. 15.
OPPOSE, 2 Tim. 2. 25.
OPPRESS, Ex. 3. 9. Judg. 10. 12.
Ex. 22. 21. *o.* not a stranger, 23. 9.
Lev. 25. 14. *o.* not one another, 17.
Deut. 24. 14. shall not *o.* a hired
Job 10. 3. is it good thou shouldest *o.*
Ps. 10. 18. that man may no more *o.*
Prov. 22. 22. neither *o.* afflicted in
Zech. 7. 10. *o.* not the widow or
Mal. 3. 5. witness against those that *o.*
James 2. 6. do not rich men *o.* you
Ps. 9. 9. the Lord will be a refuge for the *oppressed*
10. 18. judge the fatherless and *o.*
Eccl. 4. 1. tears of such as were *o.*
Isa. 1. 17. relieve the *o.* 58. 6.
38. 14. I am *o.* undertake for me
53. 7. he was *o.* and afflicted
Ezek. 18. 7. not *o.* 16. hath *o.* 12.
Acts 10. 38. Jesus healed all *o.* of the devil
Prov. 22. 16. *oppresseth*, 14. 31.
Deut. 27. 7. Lord looked on our *oppression*

1 Kings 13. 4. the Lord saw the *o.*
Ps. 12. 5. for *o.* of poor and sighing of the needy
62. 10. trust not in *o.* and become
Eccl. 7. 7. *o.* maketh a wise man mad
Isa. 5. 7. looked for judgment but behold *o.*
33. 15. he that despiseth gain of *o.*
Ps. 72. 4. *oppressor*, 54. 3.
Prov. 3. 31. & 28. 16. Eccl. 4. 1.
ORACLES of God, Acts 7. 38. Heb. 5. 12. 1 Pet. 4. 11.
ORDAIN, Isa. 26. 12. Tit. 1. 5.
Ps. 8. 2. hast *ordained* strength
132. 17. *o.* a lamp for mine anointed
Isa. 30. 33. Tophet is *o.* of old, for
Jer. 1. 5. *o.* thee a prophet unto the nations
Hab. 1. 12. hast *o.* them for judgment
Acts 13. 48. as were *o.* to eternal life
14. 23. *o.* elders in every church
17. 31. judge by that man whom he *o.*
Rom. 7. 10. commandment which was *o.*
13. 1. the powers that be are *o.* of God
1 Cor. 9. 14. Lord *o.* they who preach
Gal. 3. 19. *o.* by angels in hand of a mediator
Eph. 2. 10. God before *o.* we should
1 Tim. 2. 7. *o.* a preacher and an
Heb. 5. 1. *o.* for men in things pertaining to God
Jude 4. *o.* to this condemnation
ORDER, Gen. 22. 9. Job 33. 5.
Job 23. 4. *o.* my cause before him
Ps. 40. 5. be reckoned up in *o.*
50. 21. sins set them in *o.* before
119. 133. *o.* my steps in thy word
1 Cor. 14. 40. all things be done decently and in *o.*
Col. 2. 5. joying and beholding your *o.*
Tit. 1. 5. set in *o.* things wanting
Sam. 23. 5. everlasting covenant, *ordered* in all things
Ps. 37. 23. steps of a good man are *o.* by the Lord
50. 23. *ordereth* his conversation aright
ORDINANCE of God, Isa. 58. 2.
1 Pet. 2. 13. submit to every *o.* of man
Neh. 10. 32. make *ordinances* for us
Isa. 58. 2. ask of me the *o.* of justice
Jer. 31. 35. *o.* of moon and of the stars
33. 25. appointed *o.* of heaven
Ezek. 41. 20. keep mine *o.* and do them, Lev. 18. 4, 30. 1 Cor. 11. 2.
Luke 1. 6. walking in all *o.* of Lord
Eph. 2. 15. law contained in *o.*
Col. 2. 14. handwriting of *o.* against
20. why are ye subject to *o.*
Heb. 9. 1. had *o.* of divine service
ORNAMENTS, Ex. 33. 5. Prov. 1. 9.
Isa. 49. 18. Jer. 2. 32. Ezek. 16. 7.
OVEN, Ps. 21. 9. Hos. 7. 4.
OVERCHARGE, Luke 21. 31.
OVERCOME, Gen. 49. 19.
Song 6. 5. thine eyes have *o.* me
John 16. 33. I have *o.* the world
Rom. 12. 21. be not *o.* of evil, but *o.* evil
1 John 2. 13. have *o.* the wicked one
4. 4. ye are of God, and have *o.*
Rev. 11. 7. Lamb shall *o.* them
1 John 5. 4. born of God *overcometh* the world
Rev. 2. 7. to him that *o.* I will give
11. *o.* shall be not hurt of second
26. he that *o.* will I give power
3. 5. he that *o.* shall be clothed in white
12. him that *o.* will I make a pillar
21. him that *o.* will I grant to sit
21. 7. he that *o.* shall inherit all
OVERMUCH, Eccl. 7. 16, 17.
OVERPAST, Ps. 57. 1. Isa. 26. 20.
OVERSEER, Prov. 6. 7.
OVERSIGHT, Gen. 43. 12.

OVERTAKE, Ex. 15. 9. Amos 9. 13.
Hos. 2. 7. Gal. 6. 1. 1. Thes. 5. 4.
OVERTHROW, Deut. 12. 3. Job 12. 19. Ps. 140. 4. Prov. 13. 6. Amos 4. 11.
Acts 5. 39.
OVERTURN, Ezek. 21. 27. Job 9. 5. & 12. 15. & 28. 9. & 34. 25.
OVERWHELMED, Ps. 55. 5. & 61. 2. & 77. 3. & 124. 4. & 142. 3.
OVERWISE, neither make self, Eccl. 7. 16.
OUGHT ye to do, Matt. 23. 23.
OURS, Gen. 26. 20. Num. 32. 32.
Mark 12. 7. inheritance shall be *o.*
1 Cor. 1. 2. Christ our Lord theirs and *o.*
Tit. 3. 14. let *o.* learn to maintain good works
OUTCASTS of Israel, Ps. 147. 2. Isa. 12. 12. & 16. 3. & 56. 8.
Isa. 11. 14. let mine *o.* dwell with thee
27. 13. *o.* in land of Egypt, Jer. 30. 17.
OUTER, Ezek. 46. 21. & 47. 2. Matt. 8. 12. & 22. 13. & 25. 30.
OUTGOINGS, Josh. 17. 9.
OUTSIDE, Ezek. 40. 5.
OUTSTRETCHED arm, Deut. 26. 8.
Jer. 21. 5. & 27. 5.
OUTRAGEOUS, Prov. 27. 4.
OUTWARD, 1 Sam. 16. 7. Rom. 2. 28. 2 Cor. 4. 16. 1 Pet. 3. 3.
Matt. 23. 28. *outwardly*, Rom. 2. 28.
OWE, Rom. 13. 8. Matt. 18. 24, 28.
OWL, Job 30. 29. Ps. 102. 6. Isa. 13. 21. & 34. 11, 15. Mic. 1. 8.
OWN, Deut. 24. 16. Judg. 7. 2.
John 1. 11. his *o.* and his *o.* received him not
1 Cor. 6. 19. ye are not your *o.*
10. 24. let no man seek his *o.*
Phil. 2. 4. look not on his *o.* things
21. all seek their *o.* not of Jesus
OX knoweth his owner, Isa. 1. 3. & 11. 7. Ps. 7. 22. & 14. 4.
Ps. 144. 14. *oxen*, Isa. 22. 13. Matt. 22. 4. Luke 14. 19. John 2. 14.

P

PACIFY, Esth. 7. 10. Prov. 16. 14.
Ezek. 16. 63. when I am *pacified*
Prov. 21. 14. gift in secret *pacifieth* anger
Eccl. 10. 4. yielding *p.* great offences
PAIN, Isa. 21. 3. & 26. 18. Jer. 6. 24.
Mic. 4. 10. Rev. 21. 4.
Ps. 116. 3. *pains* of hell gat hold on me
Acts 2. 24. loosed the *p.* of death
Ps. 54. 4. my heart is sore *pained*, Isa. 23. 5. Jer. 4. 19. Joel 2. 6.
Rev. 12. 2. travailing in birth and *p.*
Ps. 73. 16. *painful*, 2 Cor. 11. 27.
PAINTED, 2 Kings 9. 30. Jer. 4. 30. & 22. 14. Ezek. 23. 40.
PALACE, 1 Chron. 29. 19. Ps. 45. 8.
Song 8. 9. Isa. 25. 2. Phil. 1. 13.
PALM tree, Ps. 92. 12. Song 7. 7.
PANT, Amos 2. 7. Ps. 38. 10. & 42. 1. & 119. 131. Isa. 21. 4.
PARABLE, Ps. 49. 4. & 78. 2. Prov. 26. 9. Ezek. 20. 49. Mic. 2. 4. Matt. 13. 3. Luke 5. 36.
PARADISE, Gen. 2. 15. Luke 23. 43.
2 Cor. 12. 4. Rev. 2. 7.
PARCHMENTS, 2 Tim. 4. 13.
PARDON our iniquity, Ex. 34. 9.
Ex. 32. 21. not *p.* your transgression
Num. 14. 19. *p.* iniquity of people
1 Sam. 15. 25. *p.* my sin
2 Kings 24. 4. the Lord would not *p.*
2 Chron. 30. 18. the good Lord *p.*
Neh. 9. 17. a God ready to *p.*
Job 7. 21. dost not *p.* my transgression
Ps. 25. 11. for name's sake *p.* mine iniquity

Isa. 55. 7. our God, he will abundantly *p.*
Jer. 5. 7. how shall I *p.* thee for this
3. 8. I will *p.* all their iniquities
50. 20. I will *p.* them whom I reserve
Isa. 40. 2. cry her iniquity is *pardoned*
Lam. 3. 42. transgressed thou hast not *p.*
Mic. 7. 18. a God like thee that *p.*
PARENTS, Luke 2. 27. & 8. 56.
Matt. 10. 21. children rise up against *p.*
Luke 18. 29. no man hath left house or *p.*
21. 16. ye shall be betrayed by *p.*
John 9. 2. who did sin, this man or his *p.*
Rom. 1. 30. disobedient to *p.* 2 Tim 3. 2.
2 Cor. 12. 14. children ought not to lay up for *p.* but *p.* for children
1 Tim. 5. 4. learn to requite their *p.*
PART, it shall be thy, Ex. 29. 26.
Num. 18. 20. I am thy *p.* and inheritance
Ps. 9. 5. their inward *p.* is wickedness
51. 6. in hidden *p.* make me know
118. 7. Lord taketh my *p.* with
Luke 10. 42. hath chosen that good *p.*
John 13. 8. if I wash thee not, thou hast no *p.*
Acts 8. 21. neither *p.* nor lot in this
1 Cor. 13. 9. know in *p.* prophecy in *p.*
10. that which is in *p.* shall be done
PARTAKER, Ps. 50. 18.
Rom. 15. 27. *p.* of their spiritual
1 Cor. 9. 10. *p.* of this hope
13. *p.* with altar
10. 17. *p.* of one bread
21. *p.* of Lord's table
30. if I be a *p.* why am I evil spoken of
1 Pet. 5. 1. a *p.* of the glory revealed
2 John 11. is *p.* of his evil deeds
Eph. 5. 7. be not *partakers* with
1 Tim. 5. 22. not *p.* of other men's sins
Heb. 3. 14. *p.* of Christ
6. 4. *p.* of the Holy Ghost
12. 10. might be *p.* of his holiness
PARTIAL, Mal. 2. 9. James 2. 4.
1 Tim. 5. 21. *partiality*, James 3. 17.
PASS, Ex. 3. 19. Ezek. 20. 37. Zeph. 2. 2. Zech. 3. 4. 2 Pet. 3. 10.
Mark 14. 35. the hour might *p.* from
Luke 16. 17. easier for heaven and earth to *p.*
1 Pet. 1. 17. *p.* the time of sojourning
John 5. 24. is *passed* from death to life
Isa. 43. 2. when thou *passest* through the waters
Mic. 7. 18. *passeth* by transgression of the remnant of his heritage
1 Cor. 7. 31. fashion of this world *p.*
Eph. 3. 19. love of Christ which *p.* knowledge
Phil. 4. 7. peace of God which *p.* all understanding
1 John 2. 17. world *p.* away and lusts
PASSION, Acts 1. 3. & 14. 15.
PASSOVER, Ex. 12. 11. Deut. 16. 2.
Josh. 5. 11. 2 Chron. 30. 15.
1 Cor. 5. 7. Christ our *p.* is sacrificed
PASTORS, Jer. 3. 15. & 17. 16.
Ps. 74. 1. sheep of thy *pasture*, Isa. 30. 23. Ezek. 34. 14. John 10. 9.
PATH, Num. 22. 24. Job 28. 7.
Ps. 16. 11. wilt show me *p.* of life
27. 11. lead me in a plain *p.*
119. 35. go in *p.* of thy commandments
139. 3. compasseth my *p.* and lying down
Prov. 4. 18. *p.* of the just is as the shining light
26. ponder the *p.* of thy feet
5. 6. lest thou ponder the *p.* of life
Isa. 26. 7. thou dost weigh *p.* of just

Ps. 17. 4. keep me from *paths* of the destroyer
5. hold up my goings in thy *p.*
25. 4. show thy ways; teach me *p.*
10. all *p.* of the Lord are mercy
Ps. 95. 11. all thy *p.* drop fatness
Prov. 3. 17. all her *p.* are peace
Isa. 59. 7. destruction are in their *p.*
8. they have made them crooked *p.*
Jer. 6. 16. ask for old *p.* the good
Hos. 2. 6. shall not find her *p.*
Matt. 3. 3. make his *p.* straight
Heb. 12. 13. make straight *p.* for feet
PATIENCE with me, Matt. 18. 26.
Luke 8. 15. bring forth fruit with *p.*
21. 19. in your *p.* possess your souls
Rom. 5. 3. tribulation worketh *p.* and *p.* experience
8. 25. we do with *p.* wait for it
15. 4. we through *p.* might have hope
5. God of *p.* grant you to be like minded
2 Cor. 6. 4. as ministers of God, in *p.*
12. 12. wrought among you in all *p.*
Col. 1. 11. strengthened unto all *p.*
1 Thes. 1. 3. *p.* of hope in our Lord
2 Thes. 1. 4. for your *p.* and faith
1 Tim. 6. 11. follow after *p.* meekness
2 Tim. 3. 10. my doctrine, charity, *p.*
Tit. 2. 2. sound in faith, charity, *p.*
Heb. 6. 12. through *p.* inherit promises
10. 36. have need of *p.* that after
12. 1. run with *p.* race set before us
James 1. 3. trying of faith worketh *p.*
4. let *p.* have her perfect work
5. 7. long *p.* for it till he receive
10. prophets for an example of *p.*
11. ye have heard of the *p.* of Job
2 Pet. 1. 6. to temperance *p.* to *p.* godliness
Rev. 1. 9. brother in the *p.* of Jesus
2. 2. I know thy *p.* 19. hast *p.* 3.
3. 10. here is *p.* of saints, 14. 12.
Eccl. 7. 8. the *patient* in spirit better than the proud
Rom. 2. 7. by *p.* continuance in well doing
12. 12. *p.* in tribulation, instant in
1 Thes. 5. 14. be *p.* to all men
2 Thes. 3. 5. *p.* waiting for Christ
1 Tim. 3. 3. not greedy of lucre, but *p.*
2 Tim. 2. 24. gentle, apt to teach, *p.*
James 5. 7. *p.* unto coming of Lord
8. be ye also *p.* establish your
Ps. 37. 7. wait *patiently* for the Lord
Heb. 6. 15. after he had *p.* endured
1 Pet. 2. 20. ye be buffeted, take it *p.*
PATRIARCH, Acts 2. 29.
PATRIMONY, his, Deut. 18. 8.
PATTERN, 1 Tim. 1. 16. Tit. 2. 7.
Ezek. 43. 10. Heb. 8. 5. & 9. 23.
PAVILION, Ps. 27. 5. & 31. 20. 1 Kings 20. 12. 16. Jer. 43. 10.
PAY, Matt. 18. 28. Ps. 37. 21.
PEACE, Lev. 26. 6. Num. 6. 26.
Job 22. 21. acquaint thyself with God and be at *p.*
Ps. 34. 14. seek *p.* and pursue it
37. 37. the end of that man is *p.*
85. 8. he will speak *p.* unto people
10. righteousness and *p.* kissed
119. 165. great *p.* have they that love
120. 6. hateth *p.* 7. I am for *p.*
122. 6. pray for *p.* of Jerusalem
125. 5. *p.* shall be upon Israel
Prov. 16. 7. his enemies to be at *p.*
Isa. 9. 6. everlasting Father, Prince of *p.*
26. 3. keep him in perfect *p.*
27. 5. that he may make *p.* with me and he shall make *p.* with me
45. 7. I make *p.* and create evil
48. 18. had thy *p.* been as a river
22. there is no *p.* to the wicked
57. 2. enter into *p.* shall rest in beds
19. *p. p.* to him that is far off
59. 8. way of peace know not

63. 17. will make thy officers *p.*
66. 12. I will extend *p.* like a river
Jer. 6. 14. saying *p. p.* when there is no *p.*
8. 11. Ezek. 13. 10. 2 Kings 9. 18.
8. 15. looked for *p.* but no good came
29. 7. seek *p.* of the city, for in the *p.* thereof ye shall have *p.*
11. thoughts of *p.* and not of evil
Mic. 5. 5. this man shall be the *p.*
Zech. 8. 19. love the truth and *p.*
Matt. 10. 34. I came not to send *p.*
Mark 9. 50. have *p.* one with another
Luke 1. 79. guide our feet in way of *p.*
2. 14. on earth *p.* good will towards
29. lettest thy servant depart in *p.*
19. 42. things that belong to thy *p.*
John 14. 27. *p.* I leave; my *p.* I give
16. 33. in me ye might have *p.*
Rom. 5. 1. we have *p.* with God through Jesus Christ
8. 6. spiritually minded is life and *p.*
14. 17. kingdom of God is righteousness, *p.*
15. 13. fill you with all *p.* and joy
1 Cor. 7. 15. God hath called us to *p.*
2 Cor. 13. 11. live in *p.* and the God of *p.* shall
Gal. 5. 22. fruit of Spirit is love, *p.*
Eph. 2. 14. he is our *p.* 15. making *p.*
Phil. 4. 7. the *p.* of God
1 Thes. 5. 13. at *p.* among yourselves
Heb. 12. 14. follow *p.* with all men
James 3. 18. sown in *p.* of them that make *p.*
1 Pet. 3. 11. let him seek *p.* and ensue
2 Pet. 3. 14. found of him in *p.*
1 Tim. 2. 2. lead a *peaceable* life in all godliness
Heb. 12. 11. yielding *p.* fruit of righteousness
James 3. 19. is first pure, then *p.*
Rom. 12. 18. live *peaceably* with all
Matt. 5. 9. blessed are the *peacemakers*
PEARL, Matt. 13. 46.
Matt. 7. 6. cast not *pearls* before swine
1 Tim. 2. 9. gold, or *p.* or costly array
Rev. 21. 21. gates were twelve *p.*
PECULIAR treasure, Ex. 19. 5.
Eccl. 2. 8. *p.* treasure of provinces
Deut. 14. 2. *p.* people, 26. 18. Tit. 2. 14. 1 Pet. 2. 9.
PEN of iron, Job 19. 24. Jer. 17. 1.
Ps. 45. 1. tongue is as *p.* of ready writer
PENURY, Prov. 14. 23.
PEOPLE, Gen. 27. 29. Ex. 6. 7.
Ps. 144. 15. happy the *p.* whose God is the Lord
146. 1. Israel is a *p.* near unto him
Isa. 1. 4. sinful nation, a *p.* laden with iniquity
10. 6. against the *p.* of my wrath
27. 11. a *p.* of no understanding
34. 5. upon the *p.* of my curse
Hos. 4. 9. like *p.* like priest
1 Pet. 2. 10. in time past were not *p.*
Ps. 73. 10. *his people* return hither
100. 3. we are—and sheep of his
Matt. 1. 21. Jesus save—from their sins
Rom. 11. 2. God hath not cast away—
Ps. 50. 7. hear, O my *people,* and I will speak
81. 11.—would not hearken, 8. 13.
Isa. 19. 25. blessed be Egypt—and
26. 20. come—enter into thy chambers
63. 8. surely they are—that will not lie
Jer. 30. 22. ye shall be—and I will be your God, 31. 33. & 24. 7. Ezek. 11. 20. & 36. 38. Zech. 2. 11. & 8. 8. & 13. 9. 2 Cor. 6. 16.
Hos. 1. 9. ye are not—, 10, say to them which were not—thou art—

Heb. 11. 25. *p.* of God, 1 Pet. 2. 10.
PERCEIVE, Deut. 29. 4.
PERDITION, John 17. 12. 2 Thes. 2. 3. 1 Tim. 6. 9. Heb. 10. 39. 2 Pet. 3. 7. Rev. 17. 3, 11.
PERFECT, Deut. 25. 15. Ps. 18. 32.
Gen. 6. 9. Noah was a just man and *p.*
17. 1. walk before me, and be *p.*
Deut. 18. 13. shalt be *p.* with God
32. 4. this work is *p.* just and right
2 Sam. 22. 31. his way is *p.*
Job 1. 1. man was *p.* and upright
Ps. 19. 7. law of the Lord is *p.* converting the soul
37. 37. mark the *p.* man and behold the upright
Ezek. 16. 14. it was *p.* through my comeliness
Matt. 5. 48. *p.* as your Father is *p.*
19. 21. if thou wilt be *p.* go and sell all
1 Cor. 2. 6. wisdom among them that are *p.*
2 Cor. 12. 9. strength is made *p.* in weakness
13. 11. be *p.* be of good comfort
Eph. 4. 13. to a *p.* man unto the measure of stature of Christ
Phil. 3. 12. not as though I were *p.*
15. as many as be *p.* thus minded
Col. 1. 28. present every man *p.* in Christ Jesus.
4. 12. may stand *p.* and complete
2 Tim. 3. 17. man of God may be *p.*
Heb. 2. 10. captain of salvation *p.*
7. 19. the law made nothing *p.*
12. 23. spirits of just men made *p.*
13. 21. make you *p.* in every good
James 1. 4. be *p.* and entire
17. *p.* gift
1 Pet. 5. 10. make you *p.* establish
1 John 4. 18. *p.* love casteth out fear
Rev. 3. 2. not found thy works *p.*
2 Cor. 7. 1. *perfecting* holiness in fear
Eph. 4. 12. for the *p.* of the saints
Job 11. 7. find out the Almighty to *perfection*
Ps. 119. 96. have seen end of all *p.*
Luke 8. 14. bring no fruit to *p.*
2 Cor. 13. 9. we wish, even your *p.*
Heb. 6. 1. let us go unto *p.*
Col. 3. 14. charity the bond of *perfectness*
PERFORM, Gen. 26. 3.
Job 5. 12. hands cannot *p.* their enterprise
Ps. 119. 106. I have sworn and I will *p.*
112. inclined my heart to *p.* thy statutes
Isa. 9. 7. zeal of Lord of hosts will *p.*
44. 28. shall *p.* all my pleasure
Mic. 7. 20. he will *p.* truth to Jacob
Rom. 4. 21. promised, was able to *p.*
7. 18. how to *p.* that which is good
Phil. 1. 6. he will *p.* it unto day of Jesus Christ
1 Kings 8. 20. Lord hath *performed* his word
Neh. 9. 8. hast *p.* thy words
Isa. 10. 12. Lord hath *p.* his whole work
Jer. 51. 29. every purpose of Lord shall be *p.*
Ps. 57. 2. God that *performeth* all things
Isa. 44. 26. *p.* counsel of messengers
PERILOUS times, 2 Tim. 3. 1.
PERISH, Gen. 41. 36.
Num. 17. 12. we die, we *p.* we all *p.*
Esth. 4. 16. I will go in, if I *p.* I *p.*
Ps. 2. 12. ye *p.* from the way, when
119. 92. have *p.* in my affliction
Prov. 29. 18. where no vision is, the people *p.*
Matt. 8. 25. Lord save us, or we *p.*
John 3. 15. believeth should not *p.*
10. 28. I give eternal life, they shall never *p.*

1 Cor. 8. 11. through thy knowledge the weak *p.*
2 Pet. 3. 9. not willing that any *p.*
PERMIT, if Lord, 1 Cor. 16. 7.
1 Cor. 7. 6. by *permission,* not of commandment
PERNICIOUS ways, 2 Pet. 2. 2.
PERPETUAL, Jer. 50. 5.
PERPLEXED, 2 Cor. 4. 8.
PERSECUTE me, Ps. 7. 1.
Job 19. 22. why *p.* me as God, 28.
Ps. 10. 2. wicked doth *p.* the poor
35. 6. let angel of the Lord *p.* them
71. 11. *p.* and take him; is none to
83. 15. *p.* them with thy tempest
Lam. 3. 66. *p.* and destroy them in
Matt. 5. 11. blessed are ye when men *p.* you
44. pray for them that *p.* you
10. 23. they *p.* you in this city
Rom. 12. 14. bless them which *p.*
Ps. 109. 16. *persecuted* the poor and
119. 161. princes *p.* me without cause
143. 3. the enemy hast *p.* my soul
John 15. 20. if they *p.* me they will *p.* you
Acts 9. 4. why *p.* thou me
22. 4. I *p.* this way to death
26. 11. I *p.* them to strange cities
1 Cor. 4. 12. being *p.* we suffer it
15. 9. because I *p.* the church of
2 Cor. 4. 9. *p.* but not forsaken, cast
Gal. 1. 13. beyond measure I *p.* church
4. 29. *p.* him born after the Spirit
1 Thes. 2. 15. *p.* us and please not God
1 Tim. 1. 13. was before *persecutor*
2 Tim. 3. 12. live godly, shall suffer *persecution*
PERSEVERANCE, Eph. 6. 18.
PERSON, Lev. 19. 15.
Mal. 1. 8. will he accept thy *p.*
Matt. 22. 16. regardest not *p.* of men
Acts 10. 34. God is no respecter of *p.* Deut. 10. 16. Gal. 2. 6. Eph. 6. 9.
Heb. 1. 3. express image of his *p.*
12. 16. fornicator or profane *p.* as Esau
2 Pet. 3. 11. what manner of *p.* ought
Jude 16. men's *p.* in admiration
PERSUADE we men, 2 Cor. 5. 11.
Gal. 1. 10. do I *p.* men, or God
Acts 13. 43. *persuaded* them to continue
21. 14. when we would not be *p.*
Rom. 8. 38. I am *p.* that neither death
Heb. 6. 9. we are *p.* better things of you
11. 13. having seen them, were *p.*
Acts 26. 28. almost thou *persuadest* me to be a Christian
Gal. 5. 8. this *persuasion* cometh
PERTAIN, Lev. 7. 29. 1 Cor. 6. 3, 4. Rom. 9. 4. Heb. 2. 17.
Acts 1. 3. *pertaining*
PERVERSE, Num. 22. 32. Deut. 32. 5. Job 6. 30. Prov. 4. 24. Isa. 19. 14.
PERVERT judgment, Deut. 24. 17. 1 Sam. 8. 3. Job 8. 3. Prov. 17. 23.
Acts 13. 10. not cease to *p.* right
Gal. 1. 7. would *p.* Gospel of Christ
Job 33. 27. *perverted* that which was right
Jer. 3. 21. they have *p.* their way
Prov. 19. 3. foolishness of man *p.* way
Luke 23. 2. this fellow *p.* the nation
PESTILENCE, 2 Sam. 24. 15. 1 Kings 8. 37. Ps. 78. 50. Jer. 14. 12.
Acts 24. 5. this man a *pestilent* fellow
PETITION, 2 Sam. 1. 17.
Ps. 20. 5. *petitions,* 1 John 5. 15.
PHILOSOPHY, Col. 2. 8.
PHYLACTERIES, Matt. 23. 5.
PHYSICIAN, Job 13. 4.
Jer. 8. 22. is there no *p.* there
Matt. 9. 12. that be whole need not *p.*
Luke 4. 23. say to me, *p.* heal thyself
Col. 4. 14. Luke the beloved *p.*

PIECE of bread, Prov. 6. 26.
Matt. 9. 16. no man putteth a *p.*
Luke 14. 18. bought a *p.* of ground
PIERCE, Num. 24. 8.
Luke 2. 35. sword shall *p.* thy soul
Ps. 22. 16. they *pierced* my hands
Zech. 12. 10. on me whom they *p.*
1 Tim. 6. 10. *p.* themselves through
Rev. 1. 7. they also which *p.* him
Heb. 4. 12. *piercing* even to dividing
PIETY at home, 1 Tim. 5. 4.
PILGRIMS, Heb. 11. 13.
Gen. 47. 9. *pilgrimage*, Ex. 6. 4.
PILLAR of salt, Gen. 19. 26.
Ex. 13. 21. by day in *p.* of cloud; and
by night in a *p.* of fire, Num. 12. 5.
Deut. 31. 15. Neh. 9. 12.
Isa. 19. 19. a *p.* at the border thereof
Jer. 1. 8. I have made thee an iron *p.*
1 Tim. 3. 15. *p.* and ground of truth
Rev. 3. 12. in temple I will make
him a *p.*
Job 9. 6. *pillars* thereof tremble
26. 11. the *p.* of heaven tremble
Ps. 75. 3. I bear up the *p.* of it
Prov. 9. 1. hath hewn out her seven
p.
Song 3. 6. *p.* of smoke
5. 15. *p.* of marble
3. 10. *p.* of silver
Rev. 10. 1. *p.* of fire
PILLOW, Gen. 28. 11.
PINE, Lev. 26. 39. Ezek. 24. 23.
PIPE, Zech. 4. 2, 12. Matt. 11. 17.
PIT, Gen. 14. 10. & 37. 20.
Ex. 21. 33. if a man dig a *p.* 34.
Num. 16. 30. they go down into the *p.*
Job 33. 24. deliver from going to the
p.
Ps. 9. 15. sunk in *p.* they had made
Ps. 28. 1. go down to the *p.* 30. 3. &
143. 7. Prov. 1. 12. Isa. 38. 18.
40. 2. horrible *p.*
55. 23. *p.* of destruction
119. 85. proud digged a *p.* for me
Prov. 22. 14. strange woman a deep *p.*
23. 27. strange woman is a narrow *p.*
28. 10. fall into his own *p.*
Isa. 38. 17. delivered it from the *p.*
of corruption
51. 1. hole of *p.* whence he digged
Jer. 14. 13. come to *p.* found no water
Zech. 9. 11. sent prisoners out of *p.*
Rev. 9. 1. key of bottomless *p.*
PITY, Deut. 7. 16. & 13. 8.
Job 6. 14. to the afflicted *p.* be showed
19. 21. have *p.* on me, have *p.* O
friends
Prov. 19. 17. hath *p.* on poor, lendeth
Isa. 63. 9. in his *p.* he redeemed
Ezek. 36. 21. I had *p.* for my holy
name
Matt. 18. 33. even as I had *p.* on thee
Ps. 103. 13. as a father *pitieth* his chil-
dren, so the Lord *p.* them that
James 5. 11. *pitiful*, 1 Pet. 3. 8.
PLACE, Ex. 3. 5. Deut. 12. 5, 14.
Ps. 26. 8. *p.* where thine honour
dwelleth
32. 7. art my hiding *p.* 119. 114.
90. hast been our dwelling *p.*
Prov. 15. 3. eyes of Lord are in every
p.
Eccl. 3. 20. all go to one *p.* 6. 6.
Isa. 66. 1. where is *p.* of my rest
Hos. 5. 15. will go and return to my
p.
John 8. 37. my word hath no *p.* in
11. 48. take away both our *p.* and
Rom. 12. 19. avenge not, but give *p.*
1 Cor. 4. 11. no certain dwelling *p.*
11. 20. ye come together in one *p.*
Eph. 4. 27. neither give *p.* to devil
2 Pet. 1. 19. a light that shineth in a
dark *p.*
Rev. 12. 6. hath *p.* prepared of God
Job 7. 10. neither shall *his place* know
him any more, 20. 9.
Ps. 37. 10. diligently consider—and
Isa. 26. 21. Lord cometh out of—

Acts 1. 25. that he might go to—
Ps. 16. 6. lines fallen in pleasant
places
Isa. 40. 4. rough *p.* shall be made
Eph. 1. 3. in heavenly *p.* 20.
6. 12. high *p.* Hab. 3. 19. Amos 4. 13.
PLAGUE, 1 Kings 8. 37. Ps. 89. 23.
Hos. 13. 14. *plagues*, Rev. 16. 9.
PLAIN man, Gen. 25. 27.
Ps. 27. 11. lead me in a *p.* path
Prov. 8. 9. words are all *p.* to him
15. 19. righteousness is made *p.*
Zech. 4. 7. before Zerubbabel thou
shalt become *p.*
John 16. 29. now speakest *plainly*
2 Cor. 3. 12. we use great *plainness*
PLAISTER, Lev. 14. 42. Isa. 38. 21.
PLAIT, Matt. 27. 29. 1 Pet. 3. 3.
PLANT, Gen. 2. 5. Job 14. 9.
Isa. 53. 2. will grow up as a tender *p.*
Jer. 2. 21. turned into degenerate *p.*
18. 9. concerning a kingdom, to *p.*
24. 6. *p.* them, and not pluck them
Ezek. 34. 29. raise for them a *p.* of
renown
Ps. 128. 3. children like olive *plants*
1. 3. like a tree *planted* by river
92. 13. *p.* in the house of the Lord
94. 9. that *p.* ear, shall he not hear
Isa. 40. 24. yea, they shall not be *p.*
Jer. 2. 21. I *p.* thee a noble vine
17. 8. as a tree *p.* by the waters
Matt. 15. 13. my Father hath not *p.*
21. 33. *p.* a vineyard and let it out
Rom. 6. 5. *p.* together in likeness of
his death
1 Cor. 3. 6. I have *p.* Apollos
9. 7. who *planteth* a vineyard and
eateth not
Isa. 60. 21. my *planting*
61. 3. *p.* of the Lord
PLAY, Ex. 32. 6. 2 Sam. 2. 14. Ezek.
33. 32. 1 Cor. 10. 7.
PLEAD for Baal, Judg. 6. 31.
Job 13. 19. who will *p.* with me
16. 21. might *p.* for me with God
23. 6. *p.* against me with great power
Isa. 1. 17. *p.* for the widow
43. 26. let us *p.*
66. 16. by fire and sword will Lord
p.
Jer. 2. 9. *p.* with you and your children
29. wherefore will ye *p.* with me
12. 1. righteous art thou, Lord, when
I *p.*
25. 31. he will *p.* with all flesh
Hos. 2. 2. *p.* with your mother, *p.*
Joel 3. 2. *p.* with them for my people
PLEASE, 2 Sam. 7. 29. Job 6. 9.
Ps. 69. 31. this also shall *p.* Lord
Prov. 16. 7. when a man's ways *p.*
Lord
Isa. 55. 11. accomplish that which I *p.*
56. 4. choose the things that *p.* me
Rom. 8. 8. that in flesh cannot *p.* God
15. 1. bear with weak and not *p.*
ourselves
2. let every one *p.* his neighbour
1 Cor. 7. 32. how *p.* the Lord
33. *p.* his wife
10. 33. I *p.* men in all things
Gal. 1. 10. do I seek to *p.* men
1 Thes. 4. 1. how to walk, and to *p.*
God
Heb. 11. 6. without faith impossible
to *p.* God
Ps. 51. 19. thou be *pleased* with sacrifices
115. 3. hath done whatsoever he *p.*
Isa. 42. 21. Lord is well *p.* for his
righteousness' sake
53. 10. it *p.* the Lord to bruise him
Mic. 6. 7. will the Lord be *p.* with
thousands of rams
Matt. 3. 17. beloved Son, in whom
he is well *p.* 17. 5.
Rom. 15. 3. Christ *p.* not himself
Col. 1. 19. *p.* the Father that in him

Heb. 13. 16. with such sacrifices God
is well *p.*
Eccl. 7. 26. *p.* God, shall escape
Phil. 4. 18. a sacrifice well *pleasing*
Col. 1. 10. worthy of Lord unto all *p.*
1 Thes. 2. 4. not as *p.* men, Eph. 6.
6. Col. 3. 22.
Heb. 13. 21. working in you, that is
well *p.*
1 John 3. 22. do things *p.* in his sight
Gen. 2. 9. *pleasant*, 3. 6. Mic. 2. 9.
2 Sam. 1. 23. Saul and Jonathan were
p.
Ps. 16. 6. lines fallen to me in *p.*
133. 1. how *p.* for brethren to dwell
147. 1. it is *p.* praise is comely
Prov. 2. 10. knowledge is *p.* to soul
5. 19. be as loving hind and *p.* roe
9. 17. bread eaten in secret is *p.*
Eccl. 11. 7. for eyes to behold sun
Song 1. 16. thou art fair, yea, *p.*
4. 13. *p.* fruits, 16. & 7. 13.
7. 6. *p.* art thou, O love, for delights
Isa. 5. 7. men of Judah, his *p.* plant
Jer. 31. 20. Ephraim, is he a *p.* child
Dan. 8. 9. *p.* land, Jer. 3. 19.
Prov. 3. 17. her ways are ways of
pleasantness
Gen. 18. 12. shall I have *pleasure*
1 Chron. 29. 17. *p.* in uprightness
Ps. 5. 4. not a God that hath *p.* in
wickedness
35. 27. *p.* in prosperity of his servant
51. 18. do good in good *p.* to Zion
102. 14. servants take *p.* in stones
103. 21. ministers that do his *p.*
111. 2. out of them that have *p.*
147. 11. Lord taketh *p.* in them
Prov. 21. 17. he that loveth *p.* shall
be poor
Eccl. 5. 4. he hath no *p.* in fools
12. 1. say, I have no *p.* in them
Isa. 44. 28. shall perform all my *p.*
53. 10. *p.* of Lord shall prosper in
58. 13. not finding thy own *p.*
Jer. 22. 28. vessel wherein is no *p.*
Ezek. 18. 32. have no *p.* in death
Mal. 1. 10. I have no *p.* in you, saith
the Lord
Luke 12. 32. fear not, it is your
Father's good *p.*
2 Cor. 12. 10. I take *p.* in infirmities
Eph. 1. 5. according to the good *p.*
of his will
Phil. 2. 13. and to do of his good *p.*
2 Thes. 1. 11. fulfil all good *p.* of
Heb. 10. 38. my soul shall have no *p.*
12. 10. chastened us after their *p.*
Rev. 4. 11. for thy *p.* they are created
Ps. 16. 11. at thy right hand are
pleasures evermore
36. 8. drink of the river of thy *p.*
2 Tim. 3. 4. lovers of *p.* more than
of God
Tit. 3. 3. serving divers lusts and *p.*
Heb. 11. 25. than to enjoy *p.* of sin
PLEDGE, Ex. 22. 26. Deut. 24. 6.
PLEIADES, Job 9. 9. & 38. 31.
PLENTY, Job 37. 23. Prov. 3. 10.
Ps. 86. 5. *plenteous* in mercy, 103. 8.
130. 7. with him is *p.* redemption
Matt. 9. 37. harvest is *p.* but labourers
PLOUGH, Deut. 22. 10. Prov. 20. 4.
Job 4. 8. they are *p.* iniquity and
Isa. 28. 24. doth *ploughman p.* all day
Luke 9. 62. having put his hand to *p.*
Judg. 14. 18. if ye had not *ploughed*
with my heifer
Ps. 129. 3. *ploughers p.* on my back
Jer. 26. 18. Zion shall *p.* as a field,
Mic. 3. 12.
Hos. 10. 13. ye have *p.* wickedness
Prov. 21. 4. *ploughing* of wicked is sin
1 Cor. 9. 10. *plougheth* should *p.* in
hope
Amos 9. 13. *ploughman*, Isa. 61. 5.
Isa. 2. 4. *ploughshares*, Joel 3. 10.
PLUCK out, Ps. 25. 15. & 52. 5. Amos

4. 11. Zech. 3. 2. Matt. 5. 29. John
10. 28. Gal. 4. 15.
2 Chron. 7. 20. *pluck up*, Jer. 12. 17.
& 18. 7. Dan. 11. 4. Jude 12.
Ezra 9. 3. *pluck off*, Job 29. 17. Isa.
POISON, Deut. 32. 24, 33. Job 6. 4.
& 20. 16. Ps. 58. 4. & 40. 3. Rom. 3.
13. James 3. 8.
POLLUTE, Num. 16. 32. Ezek. 7. 21.
Mic. 2. 10. Zeph. 3. 1.
Acts 15. 20. *pollutions*, 2 Pet. 2. 20
PONDER, Prov. 4. 26.
Luke 2. 19. *pondered* them in heart
Prov. 5. 21. *pondereth* all his goings
21. 2. Lord *p.* the hearts, 24. 12.
POOR may eat, Ex. 23. 11.
Ex. 30. 15. the *p.* shall not give less
Lev. 19. 15. not respect person of *p.*
Deut. 15. 4. when there shall be no *p.*
11. for the *p.* shall never cease out
1 Sam. 2. 7. Lord maketh *p.* and
maketh rich
8. raiseth *p.* out of dust, Ps. 113. 7.
Job 5. 16. the *p.* hath hope
36. 15. delivereth *p.* in affliction
Ps. 10. 14. *p.* committeth himself to
thee
68. 10. prepared of thy goodness
for the *p.*
69. 33. the Lord heareth the *p.* and
72. 2. he shall judge thy *p.* 4. 13.
132. 15. satisfy her *p.* with bread
140. 12. Lord will maintain right of
the *p.*
Prov. 13. 7. that maketh himself *p.*
14. 20. *p.* is hated of his neighbour
Prov. 14. 31. oppresseth *p.* reproacheth his Maker, but he that honoureth him hath mercy on the *p.*
19. 4. *p.* is separated from his neighbour
7. all brethren of *p.* do hate him
22. 2. rich and the *p.* meet together
22. rob not the *p.* because he is *p.*
30. 9. lest I be *p.* and steal
Isa. 14. 32. *p.* of his people shall trust
29. 19. *p.* among men shall rejoice
41. 17. when *p.* and needy seek water
58. 7. *p.* that are cast into thy house
66. 2. that is *p.* and of a contrite
Jer. 5. 4. these are *p.* they are foolish
Amos 2. 6. sold *p.* for a pair of shoes
Zeph. 3. 12. an afflicted and *p.* people
Zech. 11. 11. *p.* of flock waited on me
Matt. 5. 3. blessed are the *p.* in spirit
11. 5. *p.* have Gospel preached to
26. 11. have *p.* with you, John 12. 8.
Luke 6. 20. blessed be ye *p.* for yours
is the kingdom of God
14. 13. call the *p.* maimed and the
2 Cor. 6. 10. as *p.* yet making rich
8. 9. for your sakes he became *p.*
9. 9. he hath given to *p.* Ps. 112. 9.
Gal. 2. 10. we should remember the *p.*
James 2. 5. God chosen *p.* of this
world
Rev. 3. 17. knowest not that thou
art *p.*
PORTION, Deut. 21. 17. & 33. 21.
Deut. 32. 9. Lord's *p.* is his people
2 Kings 2. 9. double *p.* of thy spirit
Job 20. 29. the *p.* of a wicked man
24. 18. their *p.* is cursed in earth
26. 14. how little a *p.* is heard
31. 2. what *p.* of God is there from
above
Ps. 16. 5. Lord is *p.* of my inheritance
17. 14. have their *p.* in this life
63. 10. shall be a *p.* for foxes
73. 26. God is my *p.* for ever, 119. 57.
142. 5. art my *p.* in land of living
Eccl. 11. 2. give *p.* to seven and to
Isa. 53. 12. divide him a *p.* with the
61. 7. they shall rejoice in their *p.*
Jer. 10. 16. the *p.* of Jacob not like
them, 51. 19.
Lam. 3. 24. Lord is my *p.* saith my
Hab. 1. 16. by them their *p.* is fat

Zech. 2. 12. the Lord shall inherit Judah his *p.*
Matt. 24. 51. appoint him his *p.* with hypocrites
Neh. 8. 10. send *portions,* Esth. 9. 19.
POSSESS, Gen. 22. 17. Judg. 11. 24.
Job 7. 3. I am made to *p.* months of vanity
13. 26. *p.* iniquities of my youth
Luke 21. 9. in patience *p.* your souls
1 Thes. 4. 4. know how to *p.* vessel
Ps. 139. 13. hast *possessed* my reins
Prov. 8. 22. Lord *p.* me in beginning
Isa. 63. 18. people of thy holiness *p.* a little
Dan. 7. 22. saints *p.* kingdom, 18.
1 Cor. 7. 30. as though they *p.* not
2 Cor. 6. 10. having nothing yet *p.* all things
Eph. 1. 14. redemption of purchased *possession*
Gen. 14. 9. God *possessor* of heaven and earth
POSSIBLE, all things with God, Matt. 19. 26.
Matt. 24. 24. if *p.* shall deceive elect
Mark 9. 23. all things *p.* to him that believes
14. 36. Father, all things are *p.* to
Luke 18. 27. impossible with men, *p.* with God
Rom. 12. 18. if *p.* much as in you lies
Heb. 10. 4. not *p.* that blood of bulls
POSTERITY, Gen. 45. 7. Ps. 49. 13.
POT, Ex. 16. 33. Ps. 68. 13. & 81. 6. Jer. 1. 13. Zech. 14. 21.
Job 2. 8. *potsherd,* Ps. 22. 15. Prov. 26. 23. Isa. 45. 9. Rev. 2. 27.
Isa. 29. 16. *potter,* 64. 8. Jer. 18. 6. Lam. 4. 2. Rom. 9. 21.
POTENTATE, 1 Tim. 6. 15.
POVERTY, Gen. 45. 11. Prov. 11. 24.
Prov. 6. 11. so shall thy *p.* come
10. 15. destruction of the poor is *p.*
20. 13. love not sleep lest thou come to *p.*
23. 21. drunkard and glutton shall come to *p.*
30. 8. give me neither *p.* nor riches
2 Cor. 8. 2. their deep *p.* abounded
9. ye through his *p.* might be rich
Rev. 2. 9. I know thy works and *p.*
POUND, Luke 19. 13. John 19. 39.
POUR, Job 36. 27. Lev. 14. 18, 41.
Ps. 62. 8. *p.* out your heart before him, Lam. 2. 19.
79. 6. *p.* out thy wrath on the heathen 69. 24. Jer. 10. 25. Zeph. 3. 8.
Prov. 1. 23. I will *p.* out my Spirit
Isa. 44. 3. *p.* water on the thirsty; *p.* my Spirit
Joel 2. 28. *p.* my Spirit on all flesh
Job 10. 10. *poured* me out as milk
12. 21. *p.* contempt on princes
16. 20. mine eye *p.* out tears to
30. 16. my soul *p.* out in me
Ps. 45. 2. grace is *p.* into my lips
Song 1. 3. name is as ointment *p.*
Isa. 26. 16. in trouble *p.* out a prayer
32. 15. till Spirit be *p.* from heaven
53. 12. *p.* out his soul unto death
Jer. 7. 20. my fury shall be *p.* out, 42. 18. & 44. 6. Isa. 42. 25. Ezek. 7. 8. & 14. 19. & 20. 8, 13, 21. & 30. 15.
Rev. 16. 1-17. *p.* out vials of God's wrath
POWDER, Ex. 32. 20. Deut. 28. 24.
2 Kings 23. 15. Song 3. 6. Matt. 21. 44.
POWER, with God as a prince, Gen. 32. 28.
Gen. 49. 3. excellency of dignity and *p.*
Lev. 26. 19. break the pride of your *p.*
Deut. 8. 18. giveth *p.* to get wealth
32. 26. when seeth their *p.* is gone
2 Sam. 22. 33. God is my strength and *p.*
1 Chron. 29. 11. thine is the *p.* and
Ezra 8. 22. *p.* and wrath is against
Job 26. 2. him that is without *p.*
14. thunder of his *p.* who can
Ps. 62. 11. *p.* belongeth unto God
90. 11. knoweth *p.* of thy anger
Prov. 3. 27. when it is in *p.* of thy hand
18. 21. death and life in *p.* of tongue
Isa. 40. 29. he giveth *p.* to the faint
Eccl. 8. 4. where word of king there is *p.*
8. no man hath *p.* over spirit to
Jer. 10. 12. made the earth by his *p.*
Hos. 12. 3. by strength had *p.* with God
Mic. 3. 8. I am full of *p.* by the Spirit
Hab. 1. 11. imputing his *p.* to God
3. 4. there was the hiding of his *p.*
Zech. 4. 6. not by might, nor by *p.*
Matt. 9. 6. *p.* on earth to forgive sins
8. glorified God who had given *p.*
22. 9. not knowing the *p.* of God
28. 18. *p.* is given to me in heaven
Mark 9. 1. kingdom of God come with *p.*
Luke 1. 35. *p.* of the Highest shall overshadow thee
4. 32. astonished, for word was with *p.*
5. 17. *p.* of the Lord to heal them
22. 53. this is your hour and *p.* of
24. 49. till ye be endued with *p.*
John 1. 12. gave he *p.* to become
10. 18. *p.* to lay it down and *p.* to take it again
17. 2. given him *p.* over all flesh
19. 10. *p.* to crucify, *p.* to release
Acts 26. 18. turn them from the *p.* of
Rom. 1. 16. Gospel is *p.* of God to
20. his eternal *p.* and Godhead, 4.
9. 22. to make his *p.* known
13. 1. there is no *p.* but of God
1 Cor. 1. 24. Christ, the *p.* of God, 18.
2. 4. demonstration of Spirit and *p.*
4. 19. speech of them, but the *p.*
5. 4. gathered together with the *p.* of the Lord Jesus Christ
6. 12. not be brought under *p.* of
9. 4. have we not *p.* to eat and
2 Cor. 4. 7. excellency of *p.* may be
8. 3. in their *p.* yea, and beyond *p.*
13. 10. according to *p.* Lord hath given
Eph. 1. 19. exceeding greatness of *p.*
2. 2. prince of the *p.* of the air
6. 12. principalities and *p.* 1. 21. Col. 1. 16. & 2. 10, 15. 1 Pet. 3. 22.
Phil. 3. 10. know *p.* of his resurrection
Col. 1. 11. according to his glorious *p.*
13. delivered from *p.* of darkness
1 Thes. 1. 5. Gospel not in word, but in *p.*
2 Thes. 1. 9. the glory of his *p.*
11. fulfill the work of faith with *p.*
2 Tim. 1. 7. Spirit of *p.* and of love
3. 5. form of godliness, denying *p.*
Heb. 1. 3. upholding all things by word of his *p.*
2. 14. destroy him that had *p.* of death
6. 5. tasted word of God and *p.* of
1 Pet. 1. 5. *p.* of God through faith
2 Pet. 1. 3. his divine *p.* hath given
Rev. 2. 26. to him will I give *p.* over the nations
4. 11. worthy to receive *p.* 5. 13. & 7. 12. 1 Tim. 6. 16. Jude 25.
Rev. 11. 3. *p.* to my two witnesses
17. taken to thee thy great *p.*
12. 10. now is come *p.* of his Christ
16. 9. had *p.* over these plagues
Ex. 15. 6. *in power,* Job 37. 23. Nah. 1. 3. 1 Cor. 4. 20. Eph. 6. 10.
Ps. 63. 2. *thy power,* & 110. 3. & 145. 11.
29. 4. *powerful,* Heb. 4. 12.
PRAISE, Judg. 5. 3. Ps. 7. 17.
Deut. 10. 21. he is thy *p.* and thy God
Neh. 9. 5. above all blessing and *p.*
Ps. 22. 25. my *p.* shall be of thee
33. 1. *p.* is comely for upright, 147. 1.
34. 1. his *p.* is continually in mouth
50. 23. who offers *p.* glorifies me
65. 1. *p.* waiteth for thee, O God
109. 1. hold not thy peace, God of my *p.*
Prov. 27. 21. so is a man to his *p.*
Isa. 60. 18. walls salvation, gates *p.*
62. 7. Jerusalem a *p.* in the earth
Jer. 13. 11. for a *p.* and for a glory
17. 14. art my *p.* 26. sacrifice of *p.*
Hab. 3. 3. earth was full of his *p.*
John 12. 43. loved the *p.* of men more than the *p.* of God
Rom. 2. 29. whose *p.* is not of men
2 Cor. 8. 18. whose *p.* is in Gospel
Eph. 1. 6. *p.* of glory of his grace, 12.
Phil. 4. 8. if there be any *p.* think on
Heb. 13. 15. offer sacrifice of *p.*
1 Pet. 2. 14. *p.* of them that do well
Ex. 15. 11. *praises,* Ps. 22. 3. Isa. 60. 6.
Ps. 30. 9. shall dust *praise* thee, 12.
42. 5. I shall *p.* him for help, 11.
63. 3. my lips shall *p.* thee
88. 10. shall dead arise and *p.*
119. 164. seven times a day will I *p.*
145. 10. all thy works *p.* thee
Prov. 27. 2. let another *p.* thee, not
31. 31. let her own works *p.* her
Isa. 38. 18. the grave cannot *p.* thee
19. the living shall *p.* thee as I do
Dan. 2. 23. I thank thee, and *p.* thee
Joel 2. 26. eat in plenty, and *p.* Lord
Ps. 9. 1. *I will praise thee,* 111. & 35. 18. & 52. 9. & 56. 4. & 118. 21. & 119. 7. & 139. 14. Isa. 12. 1.
2 Sam. 22. 4. worthy to be *praised*
1 Chron. 16. 25. greatly to be *p.* Ps. 48. 1. & 96. 4. & 145. 3. & 72. 15.
2 Chron. 5. 13. *praising,* Ezra 3. 11. Ps. 34. 4. Luke 2. 13, 20. Acts 2. 46.
PRATING, Prov. 10. 4. 3 John 10.
PRAY for thee, Gen. 20. 7.
1 Sam. 7. 5. I will *p.* for you to Lord
2 Sam. 7. 27. found in heart to *p.* this
Job 21. 15. profit have we if we *p.*
42. 8. my servant Job shall *p.* for
Ps. 5. 2. my God, to thee will I *p.*
55. 17. evening and morning and noon I will *p.*
122. 6. *p.* for peace of Jerusalem
Jer. 7. 16. *p.* not for this people,
Zech. 8. 22. seek Lord and *p.* before
Matt. 5. 44. *p.* for them that despitefully use you
26. 41. watch and *p.* that ye enter
Mark 11. 24. things ye desire when ye *p.*
13. 13. watch and *p.* ye know not
Luke 11. 1. teach us to *p.* as John
18. 1. men ought always to *p.*
21. 36. watch ye and *p.* always
John 16. 26. I will *p.* the Father for
17. 9. I will *p.* for them; I *p.* not
20. neither *p.* I for these alone
Acts 8. 22. *p.* God, if perhaps the
24. *p.* ye to the Lord for me
10. 9. Peter went on housetop to *p.*
Rom. 8. 26. we know not what we should *p.* for
1 Cor. 14. 15. I will *p.* with Spirit
2 Cor. 5. 20. *p.* you in Christ's stead
Col. 1. 9. do not cease to *p.* for you
1 Thes. 5. 17. *p.* without ceasing
25. *p.* for us, 2 Thes. 3. 1.
2 Tim. 2. 28. that men *p.* everywhere
James 5. 13. any afflicted let him *p.*
16. *p.* for one another, Eph. 6. 18.
Luke 22. 32. I have *prayed* for thee
44. in agony he *p.* more earnestly
Acts 10. 2. gave alms and *p.* to God
20. 36. Paul *p.* with them all
James 5. 17. he *p.* earnestly that it might not rain
Acts 9. 11. behold he *prayeth*
Dan. 9. 20. *praying,* 1 Cor. 11. 4.
1 Thes. 3. 10. night and day *p.*
Jude 20. building up faith, *p.* in Holy
1 Kings 8. 45. hear in heaven their *prayer*
2 Sam. 7. 27. found in his heart to pray this *p.*
1 Kings 8. 28. respect to *p.* of servant
38. what *p.* and supplication
2 Chron. 30. 27. *p.* came up to God
Neh. 1. 6. mayest hear *p.* of servant
4. 9. we made our *p.* to our God
Job 15. 4. restrainest *p.* before God
Ps. 65. 2. thou that hearest *p.* to
102. 17. he will regard the *p.* of the destitute, and not despise their *p.*
109. 4. I give myself to *p.*
Prov. 15. 8. *p.* of the upright is his
29. Lord heareth *p.* of righteous
28. 9. his *p.* be abomination
Isa. 26. 16. poured out a *p.* when chastening
56. 7. in house of *p.* for all people
Jer. 7. 16. lift up cry, nor *p.* for them
Lam. 3. 44. our *p.* should not pass
Dan. 9. 3. by *p.* and supplication
Matt. 17. 21. not come out but by *p.*
Acts 3. 1. to temple at hour of *p.*
6. 4. give ourselves continually to *p.*
12. 5. *p.* was made without ceasing
16. 13. *p.* was wont to be made
1 Cor. 7. 5. give yourselves to fasting and *p.*
2 Cor. 1. 11. helping together by *p.*
Eph. 6. 18. *praying* always with all *p.*
Phil. 4. 6. in every thing by *p.* and
1 Tim. 4. 5. sanctified by word and *p.*
James 5. 15. *p.* of faith shall save
16. effectual fervent *p.* of righteous
1 Pet. 4. 7. watch unto *p.* Col. 4. 2.
Luke 6. 12. continued *in prayer,* Acts 1. 14. Rom. 12. 12. Col. 4. 2.
Job 16. 17. *my prayer,* Ps. 5. 3. & 6. 9. & 17. 1. & 35. 13. & 66. 20. & 88. 2. Lam. 3. 8. Jonah 2. 7.
Job 22. 27. *thy prayer,* Isa. 37. 4. Luke 1. 13. Acts 10. 31.
Ps. 72. 20. *prayers* of David ended
Isa. 1. 15. when ye make many *p.*
Matt. 23. 14. make long *p.*
Acts 10. 4. thy *p.* and thine alms are
1 Tim. 2. 1. first of all that *p.* and
1 Pet. 3. 7. your *p.* be not hindered
12. his ears are open to their *p.*
Rev. 5. 8. which are *p.* of saints, 8. 3.
PREACH at Jerusalem, Neh. 6. 7.
Isa. 61. 1. anointed to *p.* good tidings
Jonah 3. 2. *p.* to it preaching I bid
Matt. 4. 17. Jesus began to *p.* and say repent, 10. 17.
10. 27. what ye hear in ear, *p.* on
Mark 1. 4. *p.* baptism of repentance
Luke 4. 18. *p.* liberty to captives, 19.
9. 60. go and *p.* kingdom of God
Acts 10. 42. commanded to *p.* to people
15. 21. in every city them that *p.* him
Rom. 10. 8. word of faith we *p.*
15. how shall they *p.* except they
1 Cor. 1. 23. we *p.* Christ crucified
15. 11. so we *p.* and so ye believed
2 Cor. 4. 5. we *p.* not ourselves but
Phil. 1. 15. some *p.* Christ of envy
Col. 1. 28. whom we *p.* warning
2 Tim. 4. 2. *p.* the word; be instant
Ps. 40. 9. I *preached* righteousness
Mark 2. 2. he *p.* the word unto them
6. 12. he *p.* that men should repent
16. 20. *p.* everywhere, the Lord
Luke 4. 44. he *p.* in the synagogues of Galilee
24. 27. remission of sins be *p.* in his
Acts 8. 5. Philip *p.* Christ, 40.
9. 20. Saul *p.* Christ in synagogues
13. 38. through this man is *p.* to
1 Cor. 9. 27. when I have *p.* to others
15. 7. Gospel which I *p.* unto you
2. keep in memory what I *p.*
12. if Christ be *p.* that he rose
2 Cor. 11. 4. *p.* another Jesus whom we have not *p.*
Gal. 1. 23. *p.* faith he once destroyed
Eph. 2. 17. *p.* peace to you, which
Col. 1. 23. which was *p.* to every

1 Tim. 3. 16. God was manifest in the flesh, *p.* to the Gentiles
Heb. 4. 2. the word *p.* did not profit
1 Pet. 3. 19. *p.* to the spirits in prison
Eccl. 1. 1. *preacher,* 2. 12. & 12. 8, 9.
Rom. 10. 14. shall they hear without a *p.*
1 Tim. 2. 7. I am ordained a *p.*
2 Pet. 2. 5. Noah a *p.* of righteousness
Acts 10. 36. *preaching* peace, by Jesus Christ
11. 19. *p.* word to none but Jews
1 Cor. 1. 18. *p.* of the cross to them is foolishness
21. by foolishness of *p.* to save them
2. 4. my *p.* was not with enticing
15. 14. then is our *p.* vain, and faith
PRECEPTS, Neh. 9. 14. Jer. 35. 18.
Ps. 119. 4. commanded us to keep *p.*
15. I will meditate in thy *p.* 78.
27. way of thy *p.*
40. Long after thy *p.*
45. I seek thy *p.* 87. I forsook not *p.*
56. I kept thy *p.* 63, 69, 100, 134.
94. I sought thy *p.* 104. through *p.*
110. I erred not from thy *p.*
128. I esteem all thy *p.* to be right
141. I do not forget thy *p.* 93.
159. I love thy *p.* 173. chosen thy *p.*
Isa. 28. 10. *p.* upon *p.* upon *p.*
29. 14. fear is taught by *p.* of men
PRECIOUS things, Deut. 33. 13-16.
1 Sam. 3. 1. word of the Lord *p.*
26. 21. my soul was *p.* in thine eyes
Ps. 46. 8. redemption of soul is *p.*
72. 14. *p.* shall their blood be in thy sight
116. 16. *p.* in the sight of the Lord
126. 6. goeth forth, bearing *p.* seed
139. 17. how *p.* are thy thoughts
Eccl. 7. 1. good name is better than *p.* ointment
Isa. 13. 12. a man more *p.* than gold
28. 16. foundation *p.* corner stone
43. 4. since thou wast *p.* in my sight
Jer. 15. 19. if thou take forth *p.* from the vile
Lam. 4. 2. *p.* sons of Zion are as
James 5. 7. husbandman waiteth for *p.* fruit
1 Pet. 1. 7. trial of your faith more *p.*
19. redeemed with *p.* blood of Christ
2. 4. stone chosen of God and *p.* 6.
7. unto them who believe he is *p.* 6.
2 Pet. 1. 1. obtained the like *p.* faith
4. exceeding great and *p.* promises
PREDESTINATE, Rom. 8. 29, 30.
Eph. 1. 5. *predestinated,* 11.
PREFER, Ps. 137. 6. John 1. 15.
Rom. 12. 10. *preferring,* 1 Tim. 5. 21.
PRE-EMINENCE, man hath no, Eccl. 3. 19. Col. 1. 18. 3 John 9.
PREMEDITATE not, Mark 13. 11.
PREPARE, Ex. 15. 2. & 16. 5.
1 Sam. 7. 3. *p.* your hearts to Lord
1 Chron. 29. 18. *p.* hearts unto thee
2 Chron. 35. 6. *p.* your brethren
Job 11. 13. if thou *p.* thy heart and
Ps. 10. 17. thou wilt *p.* their heart
61. 7. O *p.* mercy and truth
Prov. 24. 27. *p.* thy work without
Isa. 40. 3. *p.* ye the way of the Lord
Amos 4. 12. *p.* to meet thy God, O
Mic. 3. 5. they *p.* war against him
Matt. 11. 10. shall *p.* thy way before
John 14. 2. I go to *p.* a place for you
2 Chron. 19. 3. hast *prepared* heart
27. 6. *p.* his ways before the Lord
29. 36. God hath *p.* the people
2 Chron. 30. 19. every one that *p.* heart to God
Ezra 7. 10. Ezra had *p.* his heart to
Neh. 8. 10. for whom nothing is *p.*
Ps. 23. 5. thou hast *p.* a table before
55. 9. *p.* them corn
63. 10. *p.* goodness
147. 8. who *p.* rain for the earth
Isa. 64. 4. what God *p.* for, 1 Cor. 2. 9.
Hos. 6. 3. his going forth is *p.* as the morning
Matt. 20. 23. given to them for whom *p.*
22. 4. I have *p.* my dinner; my
25. 34. inherit the kingdom *p.* for
Luke 1. 17. ready people *p.* for Lord
12. 47. knew Lord's will, and *p.* not
Rom. 9. 23. vessels of mercy *p.* to
2 Tim. 2. 21. *p.* to every good work
Heb. 10. 5. a body hast thou *p.* me
11. 7. *p.* ark to save his house, 1 Pet. 3. 20.
16. God hath *p.* for them a city
Rev. 12. 6. wilderness, a place *p.* of God
21. 2. new Jerusalem *p.* as a bride
Prov. 16. 1. *preparations* of heart
Mark 15. 42. it was the *p.* the day before the sabbath
Eph. 6. 15. shod with *p.* of Gospel
PRESBYTERY, 1 Tim. 4. 14.
PRESENT help in trouble, Ps. 46. 1.
Acts 10. 33. all here *p.* before God
Rom. 7. 18. to will is *p.* 21. evil is *p.*
8. 38. nor things *p.* nor, 1 Cor. 3. 22.
1 Cor. 5. 3. absent in body, *p.* in spirit
2 Cor. 5. 8. to be *p.* with the Lord
9. whether *p.* or absent, we may
Gal. 1. 4. delivers us from this *p.* world
2 Tim. 4. 10. having loved *p.* world
Heb. 12. 11. chastening for the *p.* not joyous
2 Pet. 1. 12. established in p. truth
Rom. 12. 1. *p.* your bodies a sacrifice
2 Cor. 11. 2. *p.* you as a chaste virgin
Col. 1. 22. to *p.* you holy and
28. *p.* every man perfect in Christ
Jude 24. *p.* you faultless before the
Gen. 3. 8. hide themselves from the *presence* of the Lord
4. 16. Cain went from *p.* of Lord
Job. 1. 12. Ps. 114. 7. Jer. 4. 26. Jonah 1. 3, 10. Zech. 1. 7. Jude 24.
Job 23. 15. I am troubled at his *p.*
Ps. 16. 11. in thy *p.* is fulness of joy
31. 20. hide them in secret of thy *p.*
51. 11. cast me not away from *p.*
100. 2. before his *p.* with singing
114. 7. tremble, earth, at *p.* of Lord
139. 7. whither shall I flee from *p.*
140. 13. upright shall dwell in thy *p.*
Isa. 63. 9. angel of his *p.* saved them
Jer. 5. 22. will ye not tremble at my *p.*
Luke 13. 26. eaten and drunken in *p.*
Acts 3. 19. blotted out from *p.* of Lord
1 Cor. 1. 29. no flesh glory in his *p.*
2 Cor. 10. 1. in *p.* am base among you, 10.
2 Thes. 1. 9. punished from *p.* of Lord
Rev. 14. 10. *p.* of angels and the Lamb
PRESERVE, Gen. 45. 7. Ps. 12. 7.
Ps. 16. 1. *p.* me, O God, for I trust
25. 21. let integrity and truth *p.* me
32. 7. thou shalt *p.* me from trouble
41. 2. Lord will *p.* and keep him alive
61. 7. mercy and truth *p.* him
64. 1. p. life from fear of enemies
79. 11. *p.* those appointed to die
86. 2. *p.* my soul, for I am holy
121. 7. Lord shall *p.* thee from evil
140. 1. *p.* me from the violent man
Prov. 2. 11. discretion shall *p.* thee
Luke 17. 33. will lose his life, *p.* it
2 Tim. 4. 18. will *p.* to his heavenly kingdom
Josh. 24. 17. *preserved* us in all the way
2 Sam. 8. 6. Lord *p.* David whithersoever he went
Job 10. 12. thy visitation *p.* my spirit
1 Thes. 5. 23. soul and body be *p.* blameless
Jude 1. *p.* in Christ Jesus, and called
Ps. 36. 6. Lord thou *preservest* man
29. 10. he *preserveth* souls of his saints
116. 6. Lord *p.* the simple
145. 20. Lord *p.* all that love him
146. 9. Lord *p.* the stranger
Prov. 2. 8. he *p.* way of his saints
Job 7. 20. O thou *Preserver* of men
PRESS, Gen. 40. 11. Judg. 16. 16.
Phil. 3. 14. I *p.* towards the mark for
Ps. 38. 2. thy hand *presseth* me sore
Luke 16. 16. kingdom of God every man *p.* unto
Amos 2. 13. *pressed* as a cart is *p.*
Luke 6. 38. good measure, *p.* down
Acts 18. 5. Paul was *p.* in spirit
2 Cor. 1. 8. were *p.* above measure
PRESUMPTUOUS, Ps. 19. 13. 2 Pet. 2. 10. Num. 15. 30. Deut. 17. 12.
PRETENCE, Matt. 23. 14.
PREVAIL, Gen. 7. 20. Judg. 16. 5.
1 Sam. 2. 9. by strength, shall no man *p.*
Ps. 9. 19. arise, O Lord, let not man *p.*
65. 3. iniquities *p.* against me
Eccl. 4. 12. if one *p.* against him
Matt. 16. 18. gates of hell not *p.*
Gen. 32. 28. power with God and hast *prevailed*
Ex. 17. 11. Moses held up hand, Israel *p.*
Hos. 12. 4. power over angels, and *p.*
Acts 19. 20. word of God grew, and *p.*
Job 14. 20. thou *prevailest* for ever
PREVENT, Job 3. 12. Ps. 59. 10. & 88. 13. & 119. 148. Amos 9. 10. 1 Thes. 4. 15.
2 Sam. 22. 6. *prevented,* 19. Job 30. 27. & 41. 11. Ps. 18. 5, 18. & 21. 3. & 119. 147. Isa. 21. 14. Matt. 17. 25.
PREY, Gen. 49. 9, 27. Esth. 9. 15, 16.
Isa. 49. 24. *p.* be taken from mighty
59. 15. departeth from evil, maketh himself a *p.*
Jer. 21. 9. life for a *p.* 38. 2. & 39. 18.
Ps. 124. 6. not given us a *p.* to their teeth
PRICE, Lev. 25. 16. Deut. 23. 18.
Job 28. 13. man knoweth not the *p.*
Ps. 44. 12. not increase wealth, by their *p.*
Prov. 17. 16. a *p.* in the hand of a foe
Isa. 55. 1. wine and milk without *p.*
Matt. 13. 46. pearl of great *p.*
Acts 5. 2. kept back part of the *p.*
1 Cor. 6. 20. bought with a *p.* 7. 23.
1 Pet. 3. 4. in sight of God of great *p.*
PRICKS, kick against, Acts 9. 5.
Ps. 73. 21. *pricked,* Acts 2. 37.
PRIDE of heart, 2 Chron. 32. 26.
Job 33. 17. he may hide *p.* from man
Ps. 10. 2. wicked in *p.* doth persecute.
31. 20. hide them from *p.* of man
73. 6. *p.* compasseth them about
Prov. 8. 13. *p.* and arrogance I hate
11. 2. when *p.* cometh, then
13. 10. by *p.* cometh contention
16. 18. *p.* goeth before destruction
Prov. 29. 23. man's *p.* shall bring him low
Isa. 23. 9. purposed it to stain *p.* of glory
Jer. 13. 27. weep in secret for your *p.*
Ezek. 7. 10. rod hath blossomed, *p.*
16. 49. iniquity of Sodom, *p.* and
Dan. 4. 37. those that walk in *p.* he is able to abase
Hos. 5. 5. *p.* of Israel testify to his face, 7. 10.
Obad. 3. *p.* of thy heart deceived thee
Mark 7. 22. blasphemy, *p.* foolishness
1 Tim. 3. 6. lifted up with *p.* he fall
1 John 2. 16. lust of eyes, *p.* of life
PRIEST, Gen. 14. 18. Ex. 2. 16. Lev. 6. 20. & 5. 6. & 6. 7.
Isa. 24. 2. with people, so with the *p.*
28. 7. *p.* and prophet have erred
Jer. 23. 11. prophet and *p.* profane
Ezek. 7. 26. law shall perish from *p.*
Hos. 4. 4. those that strive with *p.*
9. like people, like *p.*
Mal. 2. 7. *p.* lips should keep knowledge
Heb. 5. 6. a *p.* for ever, 7. 17, 21.
Lev. 21, 10. *high priest,* Heb. 2. 17. & 3. 1. & 4. 14, 15. & 5. 1, 10. & 6. 20. & 7. 26. & 8. 1, 3.
Ps. 132. 6. let thy *priests* be clothed
16. clothe her *p.* with salvation
Isa. 61. 6. ye be named *p.* of the Lord
Jer. 5. 31. *p.* bear rule by their names
31. 14. satisfy soul of *p.* with fatness
Ezek. 22. 26. *p.* have violated my law
Joel 1. 9. *p.* Lord's ministers, 2. 17.
Mic. 3. 11. the *p.* teach for hire
Matt. 12. 5. *p.* in the temple profane the sabbath
Acts 6. 7. company of *p.* obedient
Rev. 1. 6. kings and *p.* to God, 5. 10.
Ex. 40. 15. everlasting *priesthood*
Heb. 7. 24. an unchangeable *p.*
1 Pet. 2. 5. ye are a holy *p.* 9. royal *p.*
PRINCE, Gen. 23. 6. & 34. 2.
Gen. 32. 28, as a *p.* hast power with
Ex. 2. 14. who made thee a *p.* over
2 Sam. 3. 38. *p.* and great man fallen
Job 31. 47. as a *p.* would I go near
Isa. 9. 6. everlasting Father, *p.* of
Ezek. 34. 24. my servant David, a *p.* among them, 37. 24, 25. & 44. 3. & 45. 7. Dan. 9. 25.
Dan. 10. 21. Michael your *p.*
12. 1. great *p.*
Hos. 3. 4. many days without a *p.*
John 12. 31. now shall *p.* of world
14. 30. *p.* of world cometh and hath
16. 11. *p.* of this world judged
Acts 3. 15. ye killed the *p.* of life
5. 31. to be a *P.* and a Saviour
Eph. 2. 2. *p.* of the power of the air
Rev. 1. 5. Jesus *p.* of kings of earth
Job 12. 19. leads *princes* away
21. pours contempt on *p.*
Job 34. 18. is it fit to say to *p.* ye are ungodly
19. that accepteth not person of *p.*
Ps. 45. 16. thou makest *p.* in earth
76. 12. he shall cut off spirit of *p.*
82. 7. shall fall like one of the *p.*
118. 9. than to put confidence in *p.*
119. 23. *p.* did speak against me
161. *p.* persecuted me without a cause
146. 3. put not trust in *p.* nor man
Prov. 8. 15. by me *p.* decree justice
17. 26. not good to strike *p.* for equity
28. 2. for transgressions of land, many are *p.* of it
31. 4. not for *p.* to drink strong
Eccl. 10. 7. see a *p.* walk on earth
Isa. 3. 4. give children to be their *p.*
Hos. 7. 5. *p.* made king sick with wine
8. 4. made *p.* and I knew it not
Matt. 20. 25. *p.* of Gentiles exercise
1 Cor. 2. 6. wisdom of *p.* of world
8. none of *p.* of this world knew
Prov. 4. 7. wisdom is the *principal*
Eph. 1. 21. *principality* and power. Col. 2. 10. Jer. 13. 18. Rom. 8. 38. Eph. 6. 12. Col. 2. 15.
Heb. 5. 12. *principles,* 6. 1.
PRISON, Gen. 39. 20. Eccl. 4. 14.
Isa. 42. 7. bring out prisoners from *p.*
58. 8. he was taken from *p.* and
61. 1. opening of the *p.* to them that are bound
Matt. 5. 25. and thou be cast into *p.*
18. 30. cast into *p.* till he should pay
25. 36. I was in *p.* and ye came
1 Pet. 3. 19. preached to spirits in *p.*
Rev. 2. 10. devil cast some into *p.*
Luke 21. 12. *prisons,* 2 Cor. 11. 23.
Ps. 79. 11. sighing of *prisoner* come
102. 20. to hear the groaning of *p.*
Eph. 4. 1. I the *p.* of the Lord beseech you, 3. 1.
Job 3. 18. there the *prisoners* rest
Ps. 69. 33. Lord despiseth not his *p.*
146. 7. the Lord looseth the *p.*
Zech. 9. 11. sent forth thy *p.* out of

12. turn to strong hold, ye *p.* of hope
PRIVATE, 2 Pet. 1. 20. Gal. 2. 2.
PRIVY, Deut. 23. 1. Acts 5. 2.
Ps. 10. 8. *privily,* 11. 2. & 101. 5. Acts 16. 37. Gal. 2. 4. 2 Pet. 2. 1.
PRIZE, 1 Cor. 9. 24. Phil. 3. 14.
PROCEED, 2 Sam. 7. 1?.
Job 40. 5. twice spoken; I will *p.* no
Isa. 29. 14. I will *p.* to do a marvelous work
51. 4. a law shall *p.* from me
Jer. 9. 3. they *p.* from evil to evil
Matt. 15. 19. out of heart *p.* evil
Eph. 4. 29. no corrupt communication *p.* out of your mouth
2 Tim. 3. 9. they shall *p.* no further
Luke 4. 22. the gracious words that *proceeded* out of his mouth
John 8. 42. *p.* and came from God
Gen. 24. 50. thing *proceedeth* from Lord
Deut. 8. 3. by every word that *p.* out of the mouth of God
1 Sam. 24. 13. wickedness *p.* from the wicked
Lam. 3. 38. out of the mouth of the Lord *p.* not evil
John 15. 26. Spirit of truth which *p.* from the Father
James 3. 10. out of the same mouth *p.* blessing
Rev. 11. 5. fire *p.* out of their mouth
PROCLAIM, Lev. 23. 2.
Ex. 33. 19. *p.* the name of the Lord
Prov. 20. 6. most men will *p.* their own goodness
Isa. 61. 1. *p.* liberty to the captives
2. to *p.* the acceptable year of Lord
Prov. 12. 23. the heart of fools *proclaimeth* foolishness
PROCURED, Jer. 2. 17. & 4. 18.
PROFANE not the name of Lord, Lev. 18. 21. & 19. 12. & 20. 3.
Neh. 13. 17. *p.* sabbath, Matt. 12. 5.
Ezek. 22. 26. put no difference between holy and *p.*
Amos 2. 7. to *p.* my holy name
1 Tim. 1. 9. law is for unholy and *p.*
4. 7. refuse *p.* and old wives' fables
6. 20. *p.* and vain babblings
Heb. 12. 16. fornicator or *p.* person
Ps. 89. 39. hast *profaned* his crown
Ezek. 22. 8. thou hast *p.* my sabbaths
Mal. 1. 11. Judah hath *p.* the holiness of the Lord
12. ye have *p.* it, in that ye say
2. 10. by *profaning* the covenant of our fathers
PROFESS, Deut. 26. 3. Tit. 1. 16.
1 Tim. 6. 12. *profession,* 13. Heb. 3. 1.
PROFIT, Prov. 14. 23. Eccl. 7. 11. Jer. 16. 19. 2 Tim. 2. 14.
1 Sam. 12. 21. *not profit,* Job 33. 27. & 34. 9. Prov. 10. 2. & 11. 4. Isa. 30. 5. & 44. 9, 10. & 57. 12. Jer. 2. 8. John 6. 63. 1 Cor. 13. 3. Gal. 5. 2. Heb. 4. 2.
Job 22. 2. *profitable,* Eccl. 10. 10. Acts 20. 20. 1 Tim. 4. 8. 2 Tim. 3. 16. Tit. 3. 8. Philem. 11.
1 Tim. 4. 15. thy *profiting* appear
PROLONG thy days, Deut. 4. 26, 40. & 5. 16, 33. & 6. 2. & 11. 9. & 17. 20. & 22. 7. & 30. 18. Prov. 10. 27.
PROMISE, Num. 14. 34.
Ps. 77. 8. doth his *p.* fail for ever
105. 42. he remembered his holy *p.*
Luke 24. 49. the *p.* of my Father
Acts 1. 4. wait for *p.* of the Father
2. 39. *p.* is to you, and your children
Rom. 4. 16. *p.* might be sure to all
9. 8. children of *p.* 9. Gal. 4. 28.
Eph. 1. 13. with that holy Spirit of *p.*
2. 12. covenant of *p.* having no hope
6. 2. the first commandment with *p.*
1 Tim. 4. 8. *p.* of the life, 2 Tim. 1. 1.
Heb. 4. 1. lest a *p.* being left us of
6. 17. heirs of his *p.* 11. 9.
9. 15. receive *p.* of eternal life
2 Pet. 3. 4. where is the *p.* of coming
1 John 2. 25. *p.* he *promised* eternal life, Luke 1. 72. Rom. 1. 2. Tit. 1. 2. Heb. 10. 23. & 11. 11. & 12. 26.
Rom. 9. 4. pertain the *promises*
15. 8. confirm *p.* made to fathers
2 Cor. 1. 20. all *p.* of God are yea
7. 1. having these *p.* let us cleanse ourselves from all filthiness
Gal. 3. 21. is the law against the *p.*
Heb. 6. 12. inherit *p.* 8. 6. better *p.*
11. 17. he that had received *p.*
2 Pet. 1. 4. great and precious *p.*
PROMOTION, Ps. 75. 6. Prov. 3. 35.
PROOF, Acts 1. 3. 2 Cor. 2. 9.
PROPER, 1 Chron. 29. 3. Heb. 11. 23.
PROPHECY, 1 Cor. 12. 10. 1 Tim. 4. 14. & 1. 18. 2 Pet. 1. 19, 20. Rev. 1. 3. & 11. 6. & 19. 10. & 22. 7.
1 Kings 22. 8. not *prophecy* good
Isa. 30. 10. speak smooth things, *p.* deceits
Jer. 14. 14. prophets *p.* lies in my
Joel 2. 28. thy sons and thy daughters shall *p.*
Amos 2. 12. *p.* not
3. 8. who can but *p.*
1 Cor. 13. 9. we *p.* in part
14. 1. but rather that we may *p.*
31. for ye may all *p.* one by one
39. covet to *p.* and forbid not to
Rev. 10. 11. thou must *p.* again before many peoples
Num. 11. 25. they *prophesied* and did not cease
Jer. 23. 21. not spoken yet they *p.*
Matt. 7. 22. we have *p.* in thy name
11. 13. the prophets *p.* until John
John 11. 51. *p.* that Jesus should die for that nation
1 Pet. 1. 10. prophets *p.* of the grace
Jude 14. Enoch also *p.* of these
Ezra 6. 14. *prophesying,* 1 Cor. 11. 4. & 14. 6, 22. 1 Thes. 5. 20.
Gen. 20. 7. he is a *prophet,* and shall pray.
Ex. 7. 1. Aaron thy brother be thy *p.*
Deut. 18. 15. raise up unto thee a *p.*
18. raise them up a *p.* from among
2 Kings 5. 13. if the *p.* had bid thee do some great thing
Ps. 74. 9. there is no more any *p.*
Ezek. 33. 33. then shall they know that a *p.* hath been among them
Hos. 9. 7. *p.* is a fool, spiritual man
12. 13. by a *p.* was he preserved
Amos 7. 14. no *p.* neither a *p.'s* son
Matt. 10. 41. he that receiveth a *p.* in the name of a *p.* shall receive a *p.'s* reward
11. 9. see a *p.* and more than a *p.*
13. 57. a *p.* is not without honour
Luke 7. 28. there is not a greater *p.*
12. 33. a *p.* perish out of Jerusalem
24. 19. *p.* mighty in deeds and word
John 7. 40. this is the *p.* 1. 21. & 6. 14.
52. out of Galilee ariseth no *p.*
Acts 3. 22. a *p.* shall the Lord raise
23. will not hear that *p.* be destroyed
Tit. 1. 12. a *p.* of their own said
2 Pet. 2. 16. dumb ass, speaking with man's voice, forbade the madness of of the *p.*
Num. 11. 29. all the Lord's people *prophets*
1 Sam. 10. 12. is Saul among the *p.*
Ps. 105. 15. do my *p.* no harm
Jer. 5. 13. the *p.* shall become wind
23. 26. are *p.* of the deceit of their
Lam. 2. 14. *p.* have seen vain things
Hos. 6. 5. I hewed them by the *p.*
Mic. 3. 11. *p.* divine for money
Zeph. 3. 4. her *p.* are treacherous
Zech. 1. 5. *p.* do they live for ever
Matt. 5. 17. not do destroy law, or the *p.*
7. 12. this is the law and the *p.*
13. 17. many *p.* have desired
22. 40. on these hang the law and the *p.*
23. 34. I send you *p.* and wise men
Luke 1. 70. spake by mouth of holy *p.* Acts 5. 18. 2 Pet. 1. 20.
6. 23. so did their fathers to *p.*
16. 29. they have Moses and the *p.*
31. if they hear not Moses and *p.*
24. 25. to believe all that *p.* 27. 44.
John 8. 52. Araham is dead, and *p.*
Acts 3. 25. ye are children of the *p.*
10. 43. to him give all the *p.* witness
13. 27. knew not voice of the *p.*
26. 27. believest thou the *p.*
22. things which the *p.* and Moses
Rom. 1. 2. which he had promised afore by his *p.* in Holy Scriptures
3. 21. righteousness being witnessed by the law and the *p.*
1 Cor. 12. 28. God hath set some in the church, first apostles; secondarily *p.* 29.
Eph. 2. 20. are built upon the foundation of the apostles and *p.*
4. 11. some apostles and some *p.*
1 Cor. 14. 32. spirit of *p.* subject to *p.*
1 Thes. 2. 15. who killed their own *p.*
Heb. 1. 11. God spake to fathers by *p.*
Jas. 5. 10. take *p.* for example of suffering
1 Pet. 1. 10. of which salvation the *p.* have inquired and searched
Rev. 18. 20. rejoice over her, ye apostles and *p.*
22. 6. Lord God of the holy *p.* sent his
9. and of the brethren the *p.*
PROPITIATION, Rom. 3. 25.
PROPORTION, Rom. 12. 6.
PROSELYTE, Matt. 23. 15. Acts 2. 10. & 6. 5. & 13. 43.
PROSPER, Gen. 24. 40. Neh. 1. 11.
Gen. 39. 3. Lord made all to *p.* in his hand, 23.
Deut. 29. 9. may *p.* in all ye do
2 Chron. 20. 20. believe prophets, so shall ye *p.*
Job 12. 6. tabernacles of robbers *p.*
Ps. 1. 3. whatsoever he doeth, it shall *p.*
122. 6. they shall *p.* that love thee
Prov. 28. 13. covereth sins, shall not *p.*
Isa. 53. 10. pleasure of Lord shall *p.*
54. 17. no weapon against thee shall *p.*
55. 11. shall *p.* in the thing whereto
Jer. 12. 1. wherefore doth the way of the wicked *p.*
23. 5. a King shall reign and *p.*
2 Cor. 16. 2. God hath *prospered* him
3 John 2. *p.* as thy soul *prospereth*
Job 36. 11. spend their days in *prosperity*
1 Kings 10. 7. wisdom and *p.* exceedeth
Ps. 30. 6. in my *p.* I shall never
73. 3. when I saw *p.* of the wicked
118. 25. save now, O Lord, send *p.*
122. 7. *p.* be within thy palaces
Prov. 1. 32. *p.* of fools shall destroy
Eccl. 7. 14. in day of *p.* be joyful
Jer. 22. 21. I spake to thee in thy *p.*
Gen. 24. 21. journey *prosperous,* Josh. 1. 8. Ps. 45. 4. Rom. 1. 10.
PROTEST, Gen. 43. 3. 1 Sam. 8. 9. Jer. 11. 7. Zech. 3. 6. 1 Cor. 15. 31.
PROUD, Job 9. 13. & 26. 12. & 38. 11. & 40. 11, 11. Ps. 12. 3.
Ps. 40. 4. respecteth not the *p.* nor
101. 5. a *p.* heart I will not suffer
138. 6. the *p.* he knoweth afar off
Prov. 6. 17. *p.* look and lying tongue
21. 4. high look and *p.* heart
Eccl. 7. 8. patient is better than *p.*
Mal. 3. 15. we call the *p.* happy
Luke 1. 51. the *p.* in imagination
1 Tim. 6. 4. is *p.* knowing nothing
James 4. 6. God resisteth *p.*
Ex. 18. 11. wherein dealt *proudly*
1 Sam. 2. 3. no more so exceeding *p.*
Neh. 9. 10. knowest they dealt *p.*
Ps. 17. 10. they spake *p.* 31. 18.
Isa. 3. 5. behave *p.* against the ancient
PROVE them, Ex. 16. 4. Deut. 8. 16.
Ex. 20. 20. God is come up to *p.* you
Deut. 13. 3. the Lord *p.* you, 8. 2, 16.
33. 8. Holy One thou didst *p.* at
I Kings 10. 1. she came to *p.* him
Job 9. 20. mouth shall *p.* me perverse
Ps. 26. 2. examine me, O Lord, *p.*
Mal. 3. 10. *p.* me now herewith
Rom. 12. 2. *p.* what is will of God
2 Cor. 8. 8. to *p.* the sincerity of love
13. 5. *p.* your own selves, know
Gal. 6. 4. let every man *p.* his work
1 Thes. 5. 21. *p.* all things; hold fast
Ps. 17. 3. thou hast *proved* my heart
66. 10. thou, O God, hast *p.* us as
95. 9. *p.* me, and saw, Heb. 3. 9.
Acts 9. 22. *proving,* Eph. 5. 10.
PROVERB, Deut. 28. 37. I Kings 9. 7. Jer. 24. 9. Ezek. 14. 8.
Ps. 69. 11. I became a *p.* to them
Eccl. 12. 9. he set in order many *p.*
1 Kings 4. 32. Prov. 1. 1. & 10. 1.
Isa. 14. 4. thou shalt take up this *p.* against, Luke 4. 23.
John 16. 25. spoken in *p.* 29. no *p.*
2 Pet. 2. 22. according to true *p.*
PROVIDE, Ex. 18. 21. Acts 23. 24.
Gen. 22. 8. God will *p.* himself a lamb
30. 30. when shall I *p.* for my own
Ps. 78. 20. can he *p.* flesh for people
Matt. 10. 9. *p.* neither gold nor silver
Luke 12. 33. *p.* bags which wax not
Rom. 12. 17. *p.* things honest in sight
Job 38. 41. *provideth* raven his food
Prov. 6. 8. *p.* her meat in summer
1 Tim. 5. 8. if any *p.* not for his own
Ps. 132. 15. *provision,* Rom. 13. 14.
PROVOKE him not, Ex. 23. 21.
Num. 14. 11. how long will ye *p.* me
Deut. 31. 20. *p.* me, and break my
Job 12. 6. that *p.* God are secure
Ps. 78. 40. how oft did they *p.* him
Isa. 3. 8. to *p.* the eyes of his glory
65. 3. a people that *p.* me to anger
Jer. 7. 19. do they *p.* me to anger, do they not *p.* themselves
44. 8. ye *p.* me to wrath with your
Luke 11. 53. to *p.* him to speak of
Rom. 10. 19. *p.* you to jealousy
1 Cor. 10. 22. we *p.* the Lord to jealousy
Eph. 6. 4. fathers *p.* not children
Heb. 3. 16. when they heard did *p.*
10. 24. to *p.* unto love and good
Num. 16. 30. these have *provoked* Lord
14. 23. neither any which *p.* me
Deut. 9. 8. ye *p.* Lord to wrath, 22.
1 Sam. 1. 6. adversary *p.* her sore
1 Kings 14. 22. *p.* him to jealousy
2 Kings 23. 26. because Manasseth *p.*
1 Chron. 21. 1. Satan *p.* David to
Ezra 5. 12. our fathers had *p.* God to
Ps. 78. 56. and *p.* the Most High
106. 7. *p.* him at the Red Sea
33. because they *p.* his Spirit
43. they *p.* him
Zech. 8. 14. when your fathers *p.* me
1 Cor. 13. 5. not easily *p.* thinketh
2 Cor. 9. 2. your zeal hath *p.* many
Deut. 32. 19. *provoking,* 1 Kings 14. 15. Ps. 78. 17. Gal. 5. 26.
PRUDENT, 1 Sam. 16. 18.
Prov. 12. 16. a *p.* man covereth shame
23. *p.* man concealeth knowledge
13. 16. every *p.* man dealeth with knowledge
14. 18. wisdom of the *p.* is to understand
15. the *p.* man looketh well to his
18. *p.* are crowned with knowledge
15. 5. he that regardeth reproof is *p.*
16. 21. wise in heart shall be called *p.*
18. 15. heart of *p.* getteth knowledge
19. 14. a *p.* wife is from the Lord
22. 3. a *p.* man forseeth evil
Isa. 5. 21. wo to them that are *p.* in

Jer. 49. 7. is counsel perished from *p.*
Hos. 14. 9. who is *p.* and he shall
Amos 5. 13. *p.* shall keep silent in
Matt. 11. 25. hid these things from the wise and *p.*
1 Cor. 19. I will bring to nothing the understanding of the *p.*
Isa. 52. 13. my servant deal *prudently*
2 Chron. 2. 12. endued with *prudence* and understanding, Prov. 8. 12.
PSALM, 1 Chron. 16. 7. Ps. 81. 2. & 98. 5. Acts 13. 33. 1 Cor. 14. 26.
1 Chron. 16. 9. sing *psalms* unto him, Ps. 105. 2.
Ps. 95. 2. a joyful noise with *p.*
Eph. 5. 19. speaking to yourselves in *p.*
Col. 3. 16. admonishing one another in *p.*
James 5. 13. merry, let him sing *p.*
PUBLICAN, Matt. 18. 17.
Matt. 5. 46. even the *p.* the same, 47.
11. 19. a friend of *p.* and sinners
21. 31. *p.* go into kingdom of God
32. *p.* and harlots believed him
Luke 3. 12. came also *publicans* to be baptized
7. 29. the *p.* justified God
PUBLISH, Deut. 32. 3.
2 Sam. 1. 20. *p.* it not in the streets
Ps. 26. 7. *p.* with voice of thanksgiving
Isa. 52. 7. of him that *publisheth* peace
Jer. 4. 15. a voice *p.* affliction
Mark 13. 10. Gospel must be *published*
Acts 13. 49. word of the Lord was *p.*
PUFFED up, 1 Cor. 4. 6, 19. & 5. 2. & 8. 1. & 13. 4. Col. 2. 18.
PULL out, Ps. 31. 4. Jer. 12. 3. Matt. 7. 4. Luke 14. 5. Jude 23.
Isa. 22. 19. *pull down,* Jer. 1. 10. & 18. 7. Luke 12. 18. 2 Cor. 10. 4.
Lam. 3. 11. *pull in pieces*
Ezek. 17. 9. *pull up,* Amos 9. 15.
Zech. 7. 11. they *pulled* away the shoulder
PULPIT of wood, Neh. 8. 4.
PUNISH, seven times, Lev. 26. 18.
Prov. 17. 26. to *p.* the just is not good
Isa. 10. 12. *p.* fruit of the stout heart
Isa. 13. 11. I will *p.* the world for them
Jer. 9. 25. *p.* all circumcised with
Hos. 4. 14. I will not *p.* daughters
12. 2. will *p.* Jacob according to
Ezra 9. 13. *p.* us less than we deserve
2 Thes. 1. 9. be *p.* with destruction
2 Pet. 2. 9. reserve unjust to be *p.*
Gen. 4. 13. my *punishment* is greater
Lev. 26. 41. accept of their iniquity
Job 31. 3. a strange *p.* to workers
Lam. 3. 39. complain for *p.* of sins
Amos 1. 3. not turn away *p.* thereof
Matt. 25. 46. go into everlasting *p.*
2 Cor. 2. 6. sufficient to such is this *p.*
Heb. 10. 29. of how much sorer *p.*
1 Pet. 2. 14. sent by him for the *p.* of
PURCHASED, Ps. 74. 2. Acts 8. 20. Eph. 1. 14. 1 Tim. 3. 13.
PURE, Ex. 27. 20. & 30. 23, 34.
2 Sam. 22. 27. with the *p.* thou wilt show thyself *p.* Ps. 22. 27.
Job 4. 17. can man be more *p.* than
25. 5. stars are not *p.* in his sight
Ps. 12. 6. words of the Lord are *p.*
19. 8. commandment of Lord is *p.*
24. 4. clean hands and a *p.* heart
Prov. 15. 26. words of *p.* are pleasant
20. 9. who say I am *p.* from my sin
30. 5. every word of God *p.*
Prov. 30. 12. generation *p.* in own eyes
Zeph. 3. 9. to the people a *p.* language
Acts 20. 26. I am *p.* from blood of all
Rom. 14. 20. all things indeed are *p.*
Phil. 4. 8. whatsoever things are *p.*

1 Tim. 3. 9. mystery of faith in a *p.* conscience
5. 22. of other men's sins keep thyself *p.*
Tit. 1. 15. to the *p.* all things are *p.*
Heb. 10. 22. washed with *p.* water
James 1. 27. religion and undefiled
3. 17. wisdom from above is first *p.*
2 Pet. 3. 1. stir up your *p.* minds by way of remembrance
Isa. 1. 25. *purely* purge away dross
Job 22. 30. by *pureness,* 2 Cor. 6. 6.
1 Tim. 4. 12. *purity,* 5. 2.
Hab. 1. 13. of *purer* eyes than to
PURGE me with hyssop, Ps. 51. 7.
Ps. 65. 3. our transgressions, thou shalt *p.* them away
79. 9. *p.* away our sins for name's sake
Mal. 3. 3. purify and *p.* them as gold
Matt. 3. 12. thoroughly *p.* his floor
1 Cor. 5. 7. *p.* the old leaven
2 Tim. 2. 21. if a man *p.* himself
Heb. 9. 14. *p.* your conscience from
Prov. 16. 6. by mercy iniquity is *purged*
Isa. 6. 7. iniquity is taken and sin *p.*
27. 9. by this shall the iniquity of Jacob be *p.*
Ezek. 24. 13. because I *p.* thee, and thou wast not *p.* thou shalt not be *p.*
Heb. 1. 3. had by himself *p.* our sins
2 Pet. 1. 9. he was *p.* from sins
John 15. 2. he *purgeth* that it may
PURIFY, sons of Levi, Mal. 3. 3.
James 4. 8. *p.* your hearts, ye double
Ps. 12. 6. silver *purified* seven times
Dan. 12. 10. many shall be *p.*
1 Pet. 1. 22. *p.* your souls in obeying
Mal. 3. 3. sit as *purifier* of silver
1 John 3. 3. *purifieth* himself as he
Acts 15. 9. *purifying* their hearts by
Tit. 2. 14. *p.* to himself a peculiar
Heb. 9. 13. sanctifieth to *p.* of flesh
PURPOSE, Jer. 6. 20. & 49. 30.
Job 33. 17. withdraw man from *p.*
Prov. 20. 18. every *p.* is established
Eccl. 3. 17. a time to every *p.* 8. 6.
Isa. 14. 26. the *p.* that is purposed
Jer. 51. 29. *p.* of Lord shall stand
Acts 11. 23. with *p.* of heart cleave
Rom. 8. 28. according to his *p.*
Eph. 1. 11. according to *p.* of him
9. mystery which he *p.* in himself
3. 11. eternal *p.* which he *p.* in Christ
2 Tim. 1. 9. according to his own *p.*
1 John 3. 8. this *p.* he was manifested
PURSE, Prov. 1. 14. Matt. 10. 9.
PURSUE, Gen. 35. 5. Deut. 28. 22.
Ex. 15. 9. the enemy said, I will *p.*
Job. 13. 25. wilt thou *p.* dry stubble
Ps. 34. 14. seek peace and *p.* it
Prov. 11. 19. that *pursueth* evil, *p.* it
28. 1. wicked flee when none *p.*
PUT, Gen. 2. 8. & 3. 15, 22.
Neh. 2. 12. when God *p.* in my heart, 7. 5. Ezra 7. 27. Rev. 17. 17.
Neh. 3. 5. nobles *p.* not their necks to work
Job. 4. 18. he *p.* no trust in servants
38. 36. hath *p.* wisdom in inward
Ps. 4. 7. hast *p.* gladness in heart
8. 6. *p.* all things under his feet
9. 20. *p.* them in fear that they may
Eccl. 10. 10. *p.* to more strength
Song 5. 3. *p.* off my coat, how shall I *p.* it on
Isa. 5. 20. wo to them that *p.* darkness for light
42. 1. I will *p.* my Spirit upon him
43. 26. *p.* me in remembrance
53. 10. Lord hath *p.* him to grief
63. 11. who *p.* his Holy Spirit in
Jer. 31. 33. *p.* law in inward parts
32. 40. I will *p.* my fear in hearts
Ezek. 11. 19. *p.* a new spirit within
22. 26. they have *p.* no difference
36. 27. I will *p.* my spirit within you
Mic. 7. 5. *p.* not confidence in guide

Matt. 5. 15. *p.* it under a bushel
19. 6. what God joined, let no man *p.* asunder
Luke 1. 52. *p.* down mighty from
Acts 1. 7. Father *p.* in his own power
Acts 13. 46. seeing you *p.* the Gospel
15. 9. *p.* no difference between us
Eph. 4. 22. *p.* off the old man
2 Pet. 1. 14. I must *p.* off this tabernacle
Gen. 28. 20. God will give raiment to *put on*
Job 29. 14. I—righteousness and it
Isa. 51. 9. awake, arm of the Lord, —strength
59. 15. for he—righteousness as a breastplate
Matt. 6. 25. nor for body what ye—
Rom. 13. 12.—armour of light
14.—Lord Jesus Christ
Gal. 3. 27. baptized into Christ—Christ
Eph. 4. 24.—the new man, Col. 3. 10.
6. 11.—whole armour of God
Col. 3. 12.—bowels of mercies
14.—charity
1 Chron. 5. 20. *put trust* in, Ps. 4. 5. Prov. 28. 25. Isa. 57. 13. Jer. 39. 18.
Num. 22. 38. word that God *putteth* in mouth
Job 15. 15. he *p.* no trust in saints
Ps. 15. 5. that *p.* not out money
75. 7. God *p.* down one, and setteth
Song 2. 13. *p.* forth green figs
Lam. 3. 29. he *p.* his mouth in dust
Mic. 3. 5. that *p.* not into their mouths
Mal. 2. 16. he hateth *putting* away
Eph. 4. 25. *p.* away lying, speak
Col. 2. 11. in *p.* off the body of sins
1 Thes. 5. 8. *p.* on breastplate of faith
2 Tim. 1. 6. gift given thee by *p.* on of my hands
1 Pet. 3. 3. wearing of gold or *p.* on of apparel
21. not *p.* away of the filth of the

Q

QUAILS, Ex. 16. 13. Num. 11. 31.
QUAKE, Ex. 19. 18. Matt. 27. 51.
Ezek. 12. 18. *quaking,* Dan. 10. 7.
QUARREL, Lev. 26. 25. Col. 3. 13.
QUEEN, 1 Kings 10. 1. Ps. 45. 9. Song 6. 8. Jer. 44. 17, 24. Rev. 18. 7.
Matt. 12. 42. *q.* of the south rise in
Isa. 49. 23. *q.* their nursing mothers
QUENCH my coal, 2 Sam. 14. 7.
2 Sam. 21. 17. that thou *q.* not light of Israel
Song 8. 7. water cannot *q.* love
Isa. 42. 3. smoking flax he will not *q.*
Eph. 6. 15. to *q.* fiery darts of devil
1 Thes. 5. 19. *q.* not the Spirit
Mark 9. 43. fire that never shall be *quenched,* 44. 46, 48.
QUESTION, Mark 12. 34.
1 Kings 10. 1. *questions,* Luke 2. 46.
QUICK, Num. 16. 30. Ps. 55. 15.
Ps. 124. 3. had swallowed us up *q.*
Isa. 11. 3. of *q.* understanding in fear
Acts 10. 42. Judge of *q.* and dead
2 Tim. 4. 1. who shall judge the *q.*
Ps. 71. 20. *quicken* me again and
80. 18. *q.* us and we call on thy name
119. 25. *q.* me according to thy word
37. *q.* me in thy way
40. *q.* me in thy righteousness
88. *q.* me after thy loving kindness
149. *q.* me according to judgment
Rom. 8. 11. *q.* your mortal bodies
Eph. 2. 5. *q.* us together with Christ
Ps. 119. 50. for thy word *quickened* me
Eph. 2. 1. you he *q.* who were dead
1 Pet. 3. 18. but *q.* by the Spirit
John 5. 21. Son *quickeneth* whom he will

6. 63. it is the Spirit that *q.*
1 Cor. 15. 45. last Adam be made a *quickening* Spirit
QUICKLY, Ex. 32. 8. Deut. 11. 17.
Eccl. 4. 12. threefold cord not *q.* broken
Matt. 5. 25. agree with adversary *q.*
Rev. 3. 11. behold I come *q.* 22. 7.
QUIET, Judg. 18. 27. Job 3. 13.
Eccl. 9. 17. words of wise heard in *q.*
Isa. 7. 4. take heed and be *q.* fear not
33. 20. see Jerusalem a *q.* habitation
1 Thes. 4. 11. study to be *q.* and to
1 Tim. 2. 2. lead a *q.* and peaceable
1 Pet. 3. 4. ornament of a meek and *q.* spirit
1 Chron. 22. 9. *quietness,* Job 20. 20.
Prov. 17. 1. better is dry morsel and *q.*
Eccl. 4. 6. better is a handful with *q.*
Isa. 30. 15. in *q.* shall be strength
32. 17. effect of righteousness shall be *q.*
2 Thes. 3. 12. exhort with *q.* they
QUIT you like men, 1 Sam. 4. 9.
QUIVER full of them, Ps. 127. 5.
Isa. 49. 2. in his *q.* hath he hid me
Jer. 5. 16. *q.* is an open sepulchre

R

RABBI, Matt. 23. 7, 8. John 20. 16.
RACE, Ps. 19. 5. Eccl. 9. 11.
RAGE, 2 Kings 5. 12.
2 Chron. 28. 9. ye have slain them in a *r.*
Prov. 6. 34. jealousy is *r.* of man
29. 9. whether he *r.* or laugh is no
Ps. 46. 6. the heathen *raged*
Prov. 14. 16. the fool *rageth*
Ps. 89. 9. rulest the *raging* of sea
Prov. 20. 1. wine is a mocker, strong drink is *r.*
Jude 13. *r.* waves of sea, foaming
RAGS, Prov. 23. 21. Isa. 64. 6.
RAILER, or drunkard, 1 Cor. 5. 11.
1 Tim. 6. 4. *railing,* 1 Pet. 3. 9.
2 Pet. 2. 11. *r.* accusation, Jude 9.
RAIMENT to put on, Gen. 28. 20.
Ex. 21. 10. food and *r.* not diminished
Deut. 8. 4. thy *r.* waxed not old upon
24. 17. not take widow's *r.* to
Zech. 3. 4. clothe thee with change of *r.*
Matt. 6. 26. body more than *r.* 28.
11. 8. man clothed in soft *r.*
17. 2. his *r.* was white as the light
1 Tim. 6. 8. having food and *r.* let
Rev. 3. 5. clothed in white *r.* 18.
RAIN in due season, Lev. 26. 4.
Deut. 32. 2. my doctrine drop as *r.*
2 Sam. 23. 4. clear shining after *r.*
1 Kings 8. 35. no *r.* because sinned
2 Chron. 7. 13. that there be no *r.*
Job 5. 10. who giveth *r.* on the earth
28. 26. he made a decree for the *r.*
38. 28. hath the *r.* a father
Ps. 68. 9. didst send a plentiful *r.*
72. 6. he shall come down like *r.*
147. 8. who prepareth *r.* for earth
Prov. 16. 15. king's favour is like the latter *r.*
Eccl. 12. 2. nor clouds return after *r.*
Song 2. 11. winter is past; *r.* is over
Isa. 4. 6. covert from storm and *r.*
5. 6. clouds that they *r.* no *r.* upon
30. 23. shall give the *r.* of thy seed
55. 10. as *r.* cometh down from
Jer. 5. 24. fear Lord who giveth *r.*
14. 22. vanities of Gentiles that can *r.*
Amos 4. 7. withholden *r.* from you, I caused it to *r.* on one city, and not to *r.* on another city
Zech. 10. 1. ask of the Lord *r.* in the time of the latter *r.* Lord shall give showers of *r.*
14. 17. upon them shall be no *r.*
Matt. 5. 45. *r.* on the just and unjust

Heb. 6. 7. earth which drinketh in *r*.
James 5. 18. prayed, and heaven gave *r*.
Job 38. 26. caused it to *r*. on the earth
Ps. 11. 6. on the wicked he shall *r*. snares
Hos. 10. 12. till he *r*. righteousness
Ps. 78. 27. had *rained* upon them
Ezek. 22. 24. land not cleansed nor *r*. upon
Prov. 27. 15. continual dropping in a *rainy* day
RAISE, Deut. 18. 15. 2 Sam. 12. 11.
Isa. 44. 26. *r*. up decayed places
58. 12. *r*. up foundations of many generations
Hos. 6. 2. third day he will *r*. us up
Amos 9. 11. *r*. up tabernacle of David
Luke 1. 69. *r*. up a horn of salvation
John 6. 40. *r*. him up at the last day
Ex. 9. 16. I *raised* thee up to show my power
Matt. 11. 5. deaf hear, dead are *r*.
Rom. 4. 25. *r*. again for justification
6. 4. as Christ was *r*. by glory of the Father, 8. 11.
1 Cor. 6. 14. God hath *r*. up the Lord, and will *r*. up us
2 Cor. 4. 14. he that *r*. up the Lord Jesus, shall raise us also by Jesus
Eph. 2. 6. hath *r*. us up together
1 Sam. 2. 8. he *raiseth* up the poor
Ps. 113. 7. he *r*. up poor out of dung-hill
145. 14. *r*. up those that be bowed
RANSOM of life, Ex. 21. 30.
Ex. 30. 12. give every man a *r*. for
Job 33. 24. deliver him, I have found *r*.
36. 18. great *r*. cannot deliver thee
Ps. 49. 7. nor give to God a *r*. for
Prov. 6. 35. he will not regard any *r*.
13. 8. *r*. of man's life are his riches
21. 18. wicked are a *r*. for righteous
Isa. 43. 3. I gave Egypt for thy *r*.
Hos. 13. 14. *r*. them from power of grave
Matt. 20. 28. to give his life a *r*. for
1 Tim. 2. 6. gave himself a *r*. for all
Isa. 35. 10. *ransomed*, 51. 10.
RASH, Eccl. 5. 2. Isa. 32. 4.
RAVISHED, Prov. 5. 19.
REACH, Gen. 11. 4. John 20. 27.
Ps. 36. 5. faithfulness *reacheth* to the clouds
Phil. 3. 13. *reaching* forth to those
READ in audience, Ex. 24. 27.
Deut. 17. 19. *r*. therein all his life
Neh. 13. 1. *r*. in the book of Moses
Luke 4. 16. as his custom was, stood up to *r*.
Acts 15. 21. *r*. in synagogue every sabbath
2 Cor. 3. 2. known and *r*. of all men
1 Thes. 5. 27. that this epistle be *r*.
Acts 8. 30. understandest thou what thou *readest*
Rev. 1. 3. blessed is he that *readeth*
Neh. 8. 8. *reading*, 1 Tim. 4. 13.
READY to pardon, Neh. 9. 17.
Ps. 45. 1. tongue is as a pen of a *r*. writer
86. 5. thou art good, and *r*. to forgive
Eccl. 5. 1. more *r*. to hear, than
Matt. 24. 44. be ye also *r*.
Mark 14. 38. spirit is *r*. but the flesh
Acts 21. 13. *r*. not to be bound only
1 Tim. 6. 18. do good, *r*. to distribute
2 Tim. 4. 6. now *r*. to be offered
Tit. 3. 1. *r*. to every good work
1 Pet. 5. 2. willingly of a *r*. mind
Rev. 3. 8. strengthen things *r*. to die
Acts 13. 11. *readiness*, 2 Cor. 10. 6.
REAP, Lev. 19. 9.
Hos. 10. 12. *r*. in mercy
1 Cor. 9. 11. a great thing if we *r*.
Gal. 6. 9. shall *r*. if we faint not
Hos. 10. 13. ploughed wickedness, ye have *reaped* iniquity

Rev. 14. 16. the earth was *r*. 15.
Matt. 13. 39. *reapers* are angels
John 4. 36. he that *reapeth* receiveth
REASON, Prov. 26. 16. Dan. 4. 36.
Isa. 41. 21. bring forth your strong *r*.
1 Pet. 3. 15. asketh a *r*. of the hope
Acts 24. 25. as he *reasoned* of righteousness
Rom. 12. 1. your *reasonable* service
REBEL not against Lord, Num. 14. 9. John 22. 19.
Job 24. 13. of those that *r*. against light
Isa. 1. 20. if ye refuse and *r*. ye shall
Neh. 9. 26. they *rebelled* against thee, Ps. 5. 10.
Ps. 63. 10. *r*. and vexed his holy spirit
1 Sam. 15. 23. *rebellion*, the sin of witchcraft
Num. 20. 10. hear now, ye *rebels*
Ezek. 20. 38. purge out the *r*. from
Deut. 9. 7. *rebellious* against the Lord 24.
Ps. 68. 18. gifts for men, for the *r*. also
Isa. 30. 9. this a *r*. people, lying
50. 5. I was not *r*. nor turned away
65. 2. spread my hands to a *r*. people, 1. 23.
Jer. 4. 17. hath been *r*.
5. 23. hath *r*. heart
Ezek. 2. 3, 5, 8. *r*. house, 3. 9.
REBUKE, Lev. 19. 17.
2 Kings 19. 3. a day of *r*. and blasphemy
Ps. 6. 1. *r*. me not in anger, nor
39. 11. thou with *r*. dost correct
Prov. 9. 8. *r*. a wise man, he will love
13. 1. scorner heareth not *r*.
27. 5. open *r*. is better than secret
Zech. 3. 2. the Lord said to Satan, the Lord *r*. thee
Matt. 16. 22. Peter began to *r*. him
Luke 17. 3. if brother trespass *r*. him
Phil. 2. 15. sons of God without *r*.
1 Tim. 5. 1. *r*. not an elder, entreat
20. them that sin *r*. before all
Tit. 1. 13. *r*. them sharply, that they
3. 15. exhort and *r*. with authority
Heb. 12. 5. not faint, when *rebuked*
Prov. 28. 23. he that *rebuked*, shall
Amos 5. 10. hate him that *r*. in gate
RECEIVE, Job 2. 10.
Job 22. *r*. the law from his mouth
Ps. 6. 9. the Lord will *r*. my prayer
49. 15. God will redeem; he shall *r*. me
73. 24. guide me and afterwards *r*.
75. 2. when I shall *r*. congregation
Hos. 14. 2. take away iniquity, *r*. us
Matt. 10. 41. *r*. a prophet's reward
18. 5. *r*. little child in my name
19. 11. all men cannot *r*. this saying
21. 22. ask, believing, ye shall *r*.
Mark 4. 16. hear the word, and *r*. it with gladness
11. 24. believe that ye *r*. and ye shall *r*.
Luke 16. 9. may *r*. into everlasting
John 3. 27. man can *r*. nothing except
5. 44. which *r*. honour one of
16. 24. ask and ye shall *r*. that joy
Acts 2. 38. ye shall *r*. gift of Holy Ghost
7. 59. Lord Jesus *r*. my spirit
13. 43. he that believeth shall *r*. remission of sins
20. 35. more blessed to give than *r*.
26. 18. may *r*. forgiveness of sins
Rom. 14. 1. that is weak in faith *r*.
1 Cor. 3. 8. every man *r*. his reward
2 Cor. 5. 10. may *r*. things done in
6. 1. *r*. not grace of God in vain
Gal. 3. 14. *r*. promise of the Spirit through faith
4. 5. might *r*. the adoption of sons
Eph. 6. 8. same shall he *r*. of the Lord
Col. 3. 24. *r*. reward of inheritance
James 1. 21. *r*. with meekness the in-grafted word

3. 1. *r*. greater condemnation
1 Pet. 5. 4. shall *r*. a crown of glory
1 John 3. 22. whatsoever we ask, we *r*.
2 John 8. look that we *r*. a full reward
Job 4. 12. mine ear *received* a little
Ps. 68. 18. thou hast *r*. gifts for men
Jer. 2. 30. *r*. no correction
Matt. 10. 8. freely ye have *r*. freely
Luke 6. 24. have *r*. your consolation
16. 25. hast *r*. thy good things
John 1. 11. own *r*. him not, 12. many *r*.
16. of his fulness have we all *r*.
Acts 8. 17. they *r*. the Holy Ghost
17. 11. *r*. the word
20. 24. which I *r*. of Lord
Rom. 5. 11. Christ by whom we have *r*. atonement
8. 15. have *r*. the spirit of adoption
14. 3. judge him not, God hath *r*. him
15. 7. *r*. one another, as Christ *r*. us
1 Tim. 3. 16. *r*. into glory
1 Tim. 4. 3. meats created to be *r*. with thanksgiving
Heb. 11. 13. not having *r*. promises
Jer. 7. 28. nor *receiveth* correction
Matt. 7. 8. every one that asketh *r*.
10. 40. he that *r*. you, *r*. me; and he that *r*. me, *r*. him that sent me
13. 20. hears the word, and anon *r*.
John 3. 32. no man *r*. his testimony
12. 48. rejecteth me; *r*. not my
1 Cor. 2. 14. natural man *r*. not things
Phil. 4. 15. in giving and *receiving*
Heb. 11. 28. we *r*. a kingdom whereby
1 Pet. 1. 9. *r*. the end of your faith
RECKONED, Ps. 40. 5. Isa. 38. 13.
Luke 22. 37. Rom. 4. 4. & 6. 11.
RECOMPENSE, Prov. 12. 14.
Deut. 32. 35. to me belongeth *r*.
Job 15. 31. vanity shall be his *r*.
Prov. 20. 22. say not thou I will *r*. evil
Jer. 25. 14. I will *r*. your iniquities
Luke 14. 14. they cannot *r*. thee
Rom. 12. 17. *r*. to no man evil for evil
Isa. 34. 8. it is the year of *r*. for Zion
66. 6. render *r*. to his enemies
Jer. 51. 56. the Lord God of *r*. shall surely requite thee
Hos. 9. 7. the days of *r*. are come
Luke 14. 12. lest a *r*. be made thee
Heb. 2. 2. disobedience received just *r*. of reward
10. 35. confidence hath great *r*. of
11. 26. he had respect unto *r*. of
Num. 5. 8. trespass be *recompensed*
2 Sam. 22. 21. according to righteousness he *r*. me
Prov. 11. 31. the righteous shall be *r*.
Jer. 18. 20. shall evil be *r*. for good
Rom. 11. 35. it shall be *r*. to him
RECONCILE, Lev. 6. 30.
Eph. 2. 16. *r*. both to God into one
Col. 1. 20. to *r*. all things to himself
2 Cor. 5. 19. God in Christ *reconciling* the world
Matt. 5. 24. be *reconciled* to brother
Rom. 5. 10. when enemies we were *r*.
2 Cor. 5. 18. he hath *r*. us to himself
20. be ye *r*. to God
Lev. 8. 15. to make *reconciliation*, 2 Chron. 29. 24. Ezek. 45. 15.
2 Cor. 5. 18. given to us ministry of *r*.
19. committed to us the word of *r*.
RECORD my name, Ex. 20. 24.
Deut. 30. 19. I call heaven and earth to *r*. against, 31. 28.
Job 16. 19. my witness and my *r*. is on
John 1. 32. bare *r*. 8. 13, 14.
2 Cor. 1. 23. I call God for a *r*.
1 John 5. 7. three bear *r*. in heaven
11. this is the *r*. God hath given, 10.
Rev. 1. 2. bare *r*. of the word of God
RECOVER strength, Ps. 39. 13.
Hos. 2. 9. I will *r*. my wool and flax
2 Tim. 2. 26. may *r*. themselves out of the snare

Jer. 8. 22. is not health of my people *recovered*
Luke 4. 18. *recovering* of sight to
RED, Ps. 75. 8. Isa. 1. 18. Zech. 1. 8. & 6. 2. Rev. 6. 4. & 12. 3.
REDEEM with outstretched arm, Ex. 6. 6.
2 Sam. 7. 23. Israel whom God went to *r*.
Job 5. 20. in famine he shall *r*. thee
Ps. 44. 26. *r*. us for thy mercies' sake
15. God will *r*. my soul from power
130. 8. shall *r*. Israel from all his iniquities
Hos. 13. 14. I will *r*. them from death
Tit. 2. 14. might *r*. us from iniquity
Gen. 48. 16. angel which *redeemed* me
2 Sam. 4. 9. hath *r*. my soul out of all adversity
Ps. 136. 24. hath *r*. us from our enemies, 31. 5.
Isa. 1. 27. Zion be *r*. with judgment
51. 11. *r*. of the Lord shall return
52. 3. shall be *r*. without money, 9.
63. 9. in his love and piety, he *r*.
Luke 1. 68. visited and *r*. his people
24. 21. he that should have *r*. Israel
Gal. 3. 13. Christ *r*. us from the curse
1 Pet. 1. 18. not *r*. with corruptible
Rev. 5. 9. hast *r*. us to God, by blood
14. 4. these were *r*. from among men
Ps. 34. 22. Lord *redeemeth* the soul of his servant
103. 4. who *r*. thy life from destruction, 72. 14.
Eph. 5. 16. *redeeming* the time
Job 19. 25. I know that my *Redeemer* liveth
Ps. 19. 14. my strength and my *R*.
78. 35. the high God was their *R*.
Prov. 23. 11. their *R*. is mighty
Isa. 63. 16. our Father and *R*.
Jer. 50. 34. their *R*. is strong
Lev. 25. 34. *redemption*
Ps. 49. 8. *r*. of their soul is precious
111. 9. he sent *r*. unto his people
130. 7. with him is plenteous *r*.
Luke 2. 38. looked for *r*. in Jerusalem
21. 28. your *r*. draweth nigh
Rom. 3. 24. through *r*. in Christ Jesus
8. 23. waiting for the *r*. of our body
1 Cor. 1. 30. made unto us wisdom, and righteousness, and *r*.
Eph. 1. 7. in whom we have *r*. Col. 1. 14.
Eph. 1. 14. until *r*. of the possession
4. 30. sealed unto the day of *r*.
Heb. 9. 12. obtained eternal *r*. for us
REFINE, Isa. 25. 6. Zech. 13. 9. Mal. 3. 2, 3.
REFORMATION, Heb. 9. 10.
REFRAIN, Prov. 1. 15. 1 Pet. 3. 10.
Prov. 10. 29. he that *refraineth* his lips is wise
REFRESHING, Isa. 28. 12.
REFUGE, Num. 35. 13. Josh. 20. 3.
Deut. 33. 27. eternal God is thy *r*.
Ps. 9. 9. the Lord also will be a *r*. for the oppressed, 14. 6. Isa. 4. 6.
Ps. 57. 1. God is my *r*. and, 59. 16. & 62. 7. & 71. 7. Jer. 16. 19.
Ps. 46. 1. God is our *r*. 7. 11.
Isa. 28. 15. we have made lies our *r*.
Heb. 6. 18. fled for *r*. to lay hold on
REFUSE, Lam. 3. 45. Amos 8. 6.
1 Tim. 4. 7. *r*. profane and old wives'
Neh. 9. 17. *refused* to obey, neither
Ps. 77. 2. my soul *r*. to be comforted
118. 22. the stone which builders *r*.
Prov. 1. 24. I have called, and ye *r*.
5. 3. have *r*. to receive correction
8. 5. *r*. to return, 11. 10. *r*. to hear
Jer. 31. 15. Rachel *r*. to be comforted
Hos. 11. 5. because they *r*. to return
1 Tim. 4. 4. good and nothing to be *r*.
Jer. 3. 3. *refusedst* to be ashamed
15. 18. *refuseth* to be healed
Heb. 12. 25. *r*. not him that speaketh

REGARD, Ps. 28. 5.
Ps. 66. 18. If I r. iniquity in heart
102. 17. will r. prayer of destitute
Isa. 5. 12. that r. not work of Lord
Prov. 1. 24. no man regarded
Ps. 106. 44. he r. their affliction and
Luke 1. 48. r. low estate of handmaid
Heb. 8. 9. not in my covenant, I r. them not
Deut. 10. 17. God regardeth not persons
Job 34. 19. nor r. rich more than the
Prov. 12. 10. righteous r. life of beast
13. 18. he that r. reproof shall be
15. 5. he that r. reproof is prudent
Eccl. 5. 8. he that is higher than the highest r.
Rom. 14. 6. he that r. the day, r. it.
Matt. 22. 16. regardest not person
REGENERATION, Matt. 19. 28. Tit. 3. 5.
REJECT, Mark 6. 26. Gal. 4. 14.
Mark 7. 9. ye r. commandment of God
Tit. 3. 10. after first and second admonition r.
1 Sam. 8. 7. not rejected thee; but r. me
Isa. 53. 3. is despised and r. of men
Jer. 2. 37. Lord hath r. confidences
6. 19. r. my law
8. 19. r. word of the Lord
6. 30. Lord r. them, 7. 29. & 14. 19.
2 Kings 17. 50. Lam. 5. 22.
Hos. 4. 6. hast r. knowledge, I will r.
Luke 7. 30. r. the counsel of God
Heb. 12. 17. was r. for he found no
John 12. 48. he that rejecteth me
REIGN, Gen. 37. 8. Lev. 26. 17.
Ex. 15. 18. Lord shall r. for ever
Prov. 8. 15. by me kings r. and princes
Isa. 32. 1. a king r. in righteousness
Jer. 23. 5. a king shall r. and prosper
Luke 19. 14. not have this man to r.
Rom. 5. 17. r. in life by one Jesus Christ
1 Cor. 4. 8. would to God ye did r.
2 Tim. 2. 12. if we suffer, we shall r.
Rev. 5. 10. we shall r. on the earth
22. 5. they shall r. for ever and ever
Rom. 5. 14. death reigned from Adam to Moses
21. that as sin r. unto death so
Rev. 20. 4. they lived and r. with Christ a thousand years
1 Chron. 29. 12. thou reignest over all
Ps. 93. 1. the Lord reigneth, 97. 1.
Isa. 52. 7. saith unto Zion, thy God r.
Rev. 19. 6. Alleluia, Lord God omnipotent r.
REINS, Job 16. 13. & 19. 27.
Ps. 7. 9. God trieth hearts and r. Jer. 17. 10. & 20. 12. Rev. 2. 23.
Ps. 16. 7. my r. instruct me in night
73. 21. I was pricked in my r.
139. 13. thou hast possessed my r.
Prov. 23. 16. my r. shall rejoice
Jer. 12. 2. thou art far from their r.
REJOICE, Ex. 18. 9. Deut. 12. 7.
Deut. 28. 63. Lord will r. over you
1 Sam. 2. 1. because I r. in thy salvation
2 Chron. 6. 41. saints r. in thy good
20. 27. the Lord made them to r.
Neh. 12. 43. God made them r. with
Ps. 2. 11. serve God and r. with trembling
5. 11. those that trust in thee r.
9. 14. I will r. in thy salvation
51. 8. bones thou hast broken may r.
58. 10. righteous will r. when he
63. 7. in shadow of thy wings I will r.
65. 8. thou makest the morning and the evening to r.
68. 3. let righteous r. before God
85. 6. that thy people may r. in thee
86. 4. r. the soul of thy servant
104. 31. Lord shall r. in his works
105. 3. heart of them r. that seek the

Lord, 48. 11.
119. 162. I r. at thy word as one
Prov. 5. 18. r. with wife of thy youth
24. 17. r. not when enemy falleth
Eccl. 11. 9. r. O young man, in thy
Isa. 29. 19. poor among men shall r.
62. 5. thy God shall r. over thee
65. 13. my servants shall r. but ye
Jer. 32. 41. I will r. over them to do
Zeph. 3. 17. r. over thee with joy
Luke 6. 23. r. ye in that day; leap
10. 20. rather r. that your names
John 5. 35. willing to r. in his light
14. 28. if ye loved me ye would r.
Rom. 5. 2. r. in hope of glory of God
12. 15. r. with them that do r.
1 Cor. 7. 30. that r. as though r. not
Phil. 3. 3. worship God and r. in Christ Jesus
Col. 1. 24. r. in my sufferings for you
1 Thes. 5. 16. r. everywhere
James 1. 9. brother of low degree r.
1 Pet. 1. 8. r. with joy unspeakable
Ps. 33. 1. rejoice in the Lord, 97. 12. Isa. 14. 16. & 61. 10. Joel 2. 23. Hab. 3. 18. Zech. 16. 7. Phil. 3. 1.
Ps. 119. 14. I have rejoiced in way
Luke 1. 47. my spirit r. in God my
10. 21. Jesus r. in spirit and said
John 8. 56. Abraham r. to see my day
1 Cor. 7. 30. as though they r. not
Ps. 16. 9. my heart is glad, my glory rejoiceth
28. 7. Lord, my heart greatly r.
Prov. 13. 9. the light of righteous r.
15. 30. light of the eyes r. the heart
Isa. 62. 5. bridegroom r. over bride
64. 5. thou meetest him that r.
1 Cor. 13. 6. r. not in iniquity, but r. in truth
James 2. 13. mercy r. against judgment
Ps. 19. 8. the statutes of the Lord rejoicing the heart
119. 111. are the r. of my heart
Prov. 8. 31. r. in the habitable parts of the earth
Isa. 65. 18. I create Jerusalem a r.
Jer. 13. 15, 16. thy word was the r. of
Acts 5. 41. r. that they were counted
8. 39. eunuch went on his way r.
Rom. 12. 12. r. in hope, 5, 2, 3.
2 Cor. 1. 12. our r. is the testimony
6. 10. as sorrowful, yet always r.
Gal. 6. 4. he shall have r. in himself
Heb. 3. 6. r. of hope, firm to the end
RELIEVE, Lev. 25. 35. Isa. 1. 17. Ps. 146. 9. Acts 11. 29. 1 Tim. 5. 16.
RELIGION, Acts 26. 5. Gal. 1. 13, 14. James 1. 26, 27.
Acts 13. 43. religious, James 1. 26.
REMAINDER, 1 Thes. 4. 13.
John 9. 41. your sin remaineth
2 Cor. 9. 9. righteousness r. for ever
Heb. 4. 9. r. a rest for people of God
10. 26. there r. no more sacrifice
1 John 3. 9. his seed r. in him
Ps. 76. 10. remainder of wrath
REMEDY, 2 Chron. 36. 16. Prov. 6. 15. & 29. 1.
REMEMBER, Gen. 40. 23.
Gen. 9. 16. look upon it that I may r.
Ex. 13. 3. r. this day ye came out of Egypt
Deut. 5. 15. r. thou wast a servant
7. 18. shalt well r. what Lord did
8. 8. thou shalt r. Lord thy God
9. 7. r. and forget not how thou provokedst me
32. 7. r. days of old, consider years
2 Kings 20. 3. r. how I walked before
Ps. 20. 7. we will r. name of Lord
22. 27. shall r. and turn to the Lord
25. 6. r. thy mercies, 7. r. not sins
74. 2. r. thy congregation, 18.
79. 8. r. not against us former iniquities
Isa. 64. 9. Jer. 14. 10. Hos. 8. 13.
89. 47. r. how short my time is
119. 49. r. word unto thy servant

132. 1. r. David and his afflictions
Eccl. 12. 1. r. thy Creator in days of
Song 1. 4. we will r. thy love more
Isa. 43. 25. I will not r. thy sins
46. 8. r. this, show yourselves men
Jer. 31. 20. I do earnestly r. him still
Ezek. 16. 61. shall r. thy ways and be ashamed
63. mayest r. and be confounded
36. 31. shall r. your own evil way
Mic. 6. 5. r. what Balak consulted
Hab. 3. 2. in wrath r. mercy
Luke 1. 72. to r. his holy covenant
16. 25. r. thou in thy lifetime
17. 32. r. Lot's wife, Gen. 19. 26.
Gal. 2. 10. that we should r. the poor
Col. 4. 18. r. my bonds
Heb. 8. 12. iniquity I will r. no more
13. 3. r. them that are in bonds
Neh. 13. 14. r. me, 22. 31. Ps. 25. 7. & 106. 4. Luke 23. 43.
Ps. 63. 6. I remember, 143. 5.
Jer. 2. 2. for—kindness of thy youth
Lev. 26. 43. I will remember my covenant, 45. Ezek. 16. 60.
Ps. 79. 11.—the works of the Lord
Jer. 31. 34.—their sin no more, 43. 25.
Gen. 8. 1. God remembered Noah
19. 29. God r. Abraham and sent
30. 22. God r. Rachel, 1. 19.
Ex. 2. 24. God r. his covenant with Abraham, 6. 5.
Num. 10. 9. shall be r. before Lord
Ps. 77. 3. I r. God and was troubled
78. 39. he r. they were but flesh
98. 3. hath r. his mercy and truth
105. 8. he r. his covenant for ever
119. 52. I r. thy judgments of old
55. I have r. thy name in the night
136. 23. who r. us in our low estate
137. 1. we wept when we r. Zion
Matt. 26. 35. Peter r. words of Jesus
Luke 24. 8. they r. his words, and
John 2. 17. disciples r. that it was written
Rev. 18. 5. God hath r. her iniquities
Ps. 103. 14. he r. we are but dust
Lam. 1. 9. she r. not her last end
3. 19. remembering, 1 Thes. 1. 3.
1 Kings 17. 18. call my sin to remembrance
Ps. 6. 5. in death here is no r. of
Isa. 26. 8. r. of thee
43. 26. put me in r.
Lam. 3. 20. my soul hath them in r.
Mal. 3. 16. in a book of r. was written
Luke 1. 54. he hath holpen Israel in r. his mercy
22. 19. this do in r. of me
John 14. 26. bring all things to your r.
Acts 10. 31. thy alms are had in r.
2 Tim. 1. 6. put in r. 2. 14. 2 Pet. 1. 12. & 3. 1. Jude 5.
Rev. 16. 19. Babylon came in r.
REMIT sins, they shall, John 20. 23.
Matt. 26. 28. remission of sins, Mark 1. 4. Luke 1. 77. & 3. 3. & 24. 47. Acts 2. 38. & 10. 43. Rom. 3. 25.
REMNANT, Lev. 2. 3. Deut. 3. 11.
2 Kings 19. 4. lift up thy prayer for r.
Ezra 9. 8. leave us a r. to escape
Isa. 1. except Lord left us a small r.
10. 21. a r. shall return, 22.
Jer. 15. 11. it shall be well with thy r.
23. 3. I will gather r. of my flock
Ezek. 6. 8. yet will I leave a r.
Rom. 9. 27. a r. shall be saved, 11. 5.
REMOVE thy stroke, Ps. 39. 10.
Ps. 119. 22. r. from me reproach and
29. r. from me the way of lying
Prov. 4. 27. r. thy foot from evil
23. 10. r. not the old land-mark
30. 8. r. far from me vanity and lies
Eccl. 11. 10. r. sorrow from thy heart
Matt. 17. 20. r. hence, and it shall r.
Luke 22. 42. if willing r. this cup
Rev. 2. 5. I will r. thy candlestick
Ps. 103. 12. so far he removed our iniquity

Prov. 10. 30. righteous shall never be r.
Isa. 30. 20. teachers not be r. into a corner
Ezek. 36. 17. as uncleanness of a r. woman
Gal. 1. 6. so soon r. for him that
RENDER vengeance, Deut. 32. 41.
2 Chron. 6. 30. r. to every man according to his ways
Job 33. 26. r. to man his righteousness
34. 11. work of a man shall be r. to
Ps. 116. 12. what shall I r. to Lord
Prov. 26. 16. men that can r. a reason
Hos. 14. 2. r. the calves of our lips
Matt. 22. 21. r. to Caesar the things
Rom. 13. 7. r. to all their dues
1 Thes. 5. 15. that none r. evil, 3. 9.
2 Chron. 30. 25. Hezekiah rendered
RENEW, Ps. 51. 10.
Isa. 40. 31. wait on Lord r. strength
Heb. 6. 6. r. them again to repentance
Ps. 103. 5. thy youth is renewed like
2 Cor. 16. inward man is r. day by
Eph. 4. 23. be r. in spirit of mind
Col. 3. 10. r. in knowledge, image of
Ps. 104. 30. renewest face of earth
Rom. 12. 2. renewing, Tit. 3. 5.
RENOUNCED, 1 Cor. 4. 2.
RENOWN, Ezek. 34. 29. & 39. 13.
Isa. 14. 20. renowned, Ezek. 23. 23.
REND heavens and come, Isa. 64. 1.
Joel 2. 13. r. hearts and not garments
Jer. 4. 30. though thou rendest face
REPAIRER, Isa. 58. 12.
REPAY, Job 21. 31. & 41. 11.
Deut. 7. 10. he will r. him to his face
Isa. 59. 18. according to deeds he r.
Rom. 12. 19. vengeance is mine, I will r.
Prov. 13. 21. to the righteous good be repaid
REPENT of this evil, Ex. 32. 12.
Num. 23. 19. not the son of man that he should r.
Deut. 32. 36. Lord shall r. himself for servants
1 Sam. 15. 29. not man that he should r.
1 Kings 8. 47. r. and make supplication
Job 42. 6. I abhor and r. in dust and
Ps. 90. 13. let it r. thee concerning
135. 14. will r. himself concerning
Jer. 18. 8. if of evil I thought
Ezek. 14. 6. r. and return, 18. 30.
Joel 2. 14. will r. and leave a blessing
Jonah 3. 9. tell if God will turn and r.
Matt. 3. 2. r. for kingdom of heaven
Mark 1. 15. r. and believe Gospel
6. 12. preached that men should r.
Luke 13. 3. except ye r. ye shall all
16. 30. went from dead, they will r.
17. 3. if he r. forgive him, 4.
Acts 2. 38. r. and be baptized every
3. 19. r. and be converted, that
8. 22. r. of this thy wickedness
17. 30. commandeth all men to r.
26. 30. should r. and turn to God
Rev. 2. 5. remember whence fallen and r.
16. r. or I will come unto thee
21. I gave her space to r. of her
3. 19. be zealous and r.
Gen. 6. 6. repented the Lord, Ex. 32. 14. Judg. 2. 18. 2 Sam. 24. 16.
Jer. 8. 6. no man r. of his wickedness
Matt. 21. 29. afterward r. and went
27. 3. Judas r. himself, and brought
Luke 15. 7. one sinner that repenteth
Jer. 15. 6. repenting, Hos. 11. 8.
Hos. 13. 14. repentance hid from my
Matt. 3. 8. fruits meet for r. Luke 3. 8.
9. 13. not righteous but sinners to r.
Mark 1. 4. baptism of r. Luke 3. 3.
Luke 15. 7. just persons need no r.
24. 47. that r. and remission be
Acts 5. 31. give r. to Israel and

11. 18. God to Gentiles granted *r.*
13. 24. preached baptism of *r.* to all
20. 21. testifying *r.* towards God
Rom. 2. 4. Goodness of God leadeth thee to *r.*
11. 29. gifts of God are without *r.*
2 Cor. 7. 10. godly sorrow worketh *r.*
Heb. 6. 1. not laying foundation of *r.*
12. 17. found no place of *r.* though he sought it carefully with tears
2 Pet. 3. 9. that all should come to *r.*
REPETITIONS, vain, Matt. 6. 7.
REPLIEST, Rom. 9. 20.
REPORT, evil. Gen. 37. 2. Num. 13. 32. & 14. 37. Neh. 6. 13.
Ex. 23. 1. should not raise a false *r.*
Prov. 15. 30. good *r.* maketh bones fat
Isa. 53. 1. who hath believed our *r.* John 12. 38. Rom. 10. 16.
2 Cor. 6. 8. by evil *r.* and good *r.*
1 Tim. 3. 7. a good *r.* of them who
Heb. 11. 2. obtained a good *r.*
REPROACH, Josh. 5. 9. Neh. 1. 3. Ps. 69. 7. Prov. 18. 3. Isa. 54. 4. Jer. 31. 19. Heb. 13. 13. Gen. 30. 23.
Job 27. 6. my heart shall not *r.* me
Ps. 15. 3. up a *r.* against neighbour
20. *r.* hath broken my heart
Prov. 14. 34. sin is a *r.* to any people
Isa. 51. 7. fear ye not the *r.* of men
Joel 2. 17. give not heritage to *r.*
Zeph. 3. 18. to whom *r.* was a burden
Heb. 11. 26. esteeming the *r.* of Christ greater riches than the treasures of
Ps. 69. 9. *r.* of them that *reproached*
2 Cor. 12. 10. I take pleasure in *reproaches*
Prov. 14. 31. *reproacheth* his Maker
1 Pet. 4. 14. if *reproached* for name of Christ
REPROBATE, Jer. 6. 30. Rom. 1. 28. 2 Cor. 13. 5. 2 Tim. 3. 8.
REPROOF, Job 26. 11.
Prov. 1. 23. turn ye at my *r.* I will
25. would none of my *r.* 30.
10. 17. he that refuseth *r.* erreth
12. 1. he that hateth *r.* is brutish
13. 18. he that regardeth *r.* shall be honoured
15. 5. he that regardeth *r.* is prudent
10. he that hateth *r.* shall die
31. heareth *r.* abideth among wise
32. heareth *r.* getteth understanding
17. 10. *r.* entereth more into a wise
29. 15. the rod and *r.* give wisdom
2 Tim. 3. 16. Scripture profitable for *r.*
Ps. 38. 14. *reproofs,* Prov. 6. 23.
50. 21. I will reprove thee, and
141. 5. let him *r.* me, and it shall
Prov. 9. 8. *r.* not a scorner, lest he
Hos. 4. 4. let no man strive nor *r.*
John 16. 8. *r.* world of sin, righteousness, judgment
Eph. 5. 11. works of darkness but *r.*
Ps. 105. 14. he *reproved* kings for their sakes
Prov. 29. 1. he that being often *r.*
John 3. 20. lest his deeds should be *r.*
Eph. 5. 13. all things that are *r.* are
Isa. 29. 21. snare from him that *reproveth* in the gate
Prov. 9. 7. that *r.* a scorner, getteth
15. 12. scorner loveth not one that *r.* him
15. 12. *reprover,* Ezek. 3. 26.
REPUTATION, Eccl. 10. 1. Acts 5. 34. Gal. 2. 2. Phil. 2. 7, 29.
REQUEST, Ps. 106. 15. Phil. 4. 6.
REQUIRE, Gen. 9. 5. & 42. 22. Ezek. 3. 18, 20. & 33. 8.
Deut. 10. 12. what doth the Lord *r.*
18. 19. speak in my name, I will *r.* it
1 Kings 8. 59. maintain as matter shall *r.*
Prov. 30. 7. two things I *required*
Isa. 1. 12. who *r.* this at your hand
Luke 12. 20. shall thy soul be *r.* of
48. of him shall much be *r.*
1 Cor. 4. 2. it is *r.* of stewards to be

REQUITE, Gen. 50. 15.
Deut. 32. 6. do ye thus *r.* the Lord
1 Tim. 5. 4. learn to *r.* their parents
2 Chron. 6. 23. by *requiting* wicked
RE-REWARD, Isa. 52. 12.
RESERVE, Jer. 50. 20. 2 Pet. 2. 9.
Jer. 3. 5. will he *r.* his anger for ever
Job 21. 30. wicked is *reserved* to the day of destruction
1 Pet. 1. 4. inheritance *r.* in heaven
Jude 6. *r.* in everlasting chains to
Jer. 5. 24. he *reserveth* appointed weeks
Nah. 1. 2. *r.* wrath for his enemies
RESIDE, Zeph. 2. 9. Matt. 1. 15.
RESIST not evil, Matt. 5. 39.
Zech. 3. 1. Satan at his right hand to *r.* him
Acts 7. 31. ye do always *r.* the Holy
2 Tim. 3. 8. so do these *r.* the truth
James 4. 7. *r.* the devil and he will
1 Pet. 5. 9. whom *r.* steadfast in faith
Rom. 9. 19. who hath *resisted* will
Heb. 12. 4. have not yet *r.* to blood
Rom. 13. 2. that *resisteth* shall receive damnation
James 4. 6. God *r.* proud, 1 Pet. 5. 5.
RESPECT to Abel, Lord had, Gen. 4. 4. Ex. 2. 25. Lev. 26. 9.
Deut. 1. 17. ye shall not *r.* persons
2 Chron. 19. 7. nor *r.* of persons with God, Rom. 2. 11. Eph. 6. 9. Col. 3. 25. Acts 10. 34. Job 37. 24.
Ps. 40. 4. *r.* not the proud
119. 6. *r.* to all thy commandments
138. 6. *r.* the lowly
Prov. 24. 23. not good to have *r.* of persons, 28. 21. Lev. 19. 15.
Heb. 11. 26. he had *r.* to recompense
REST, Ex. 16. 23. Deut. 12. 9.
Ps. 95. 11. not enter into *r.* Heb. 3. 11.
116. 7. return to thy *r.* O my soul
132. 14. this is my *r.* here I will
Isa. 11. 10. his *r.* shall be glorious
28. 12. this is the *r.* and refreshing
30. 15. in returning and *r.* be saved
62. 7. him no *r.* till he establish
Jer. 6. 16. shall find *r.* for your souls
Mic. 2. 10. this is not your *r.* it is polluted
Matt. 11. 28, 29. I give *r.* to your souls
Acts 9. 31. then had the churches *r.*
2 Thes. 1. 7. who are troubled *r.*
Heb. 4. 9. *r.* for the people of God
10. enter into his *r.* 11. enter that *r.*
Rev. 14. 11. they have no *r.* day nor
Ps. 16. 9. my flesh shall *r.* in hope
37. 7. *r.* in the Lord and wait
135. 3. rod of the wicked shall not *r.*
Isa. 57. 2. in peace *r.* on their beds
20. wicked are like the troubled sea when it cannot *r.*
Hab. 3. 16. *r.* in the day of trouble
Zeph. 3. 16. he will *r.* in his love
Rev. 14. 13. dead in the Lord, *r.* from
Rom. 2. 17. art a Jew, and *restest*
Prov. 14. 33. wisdom *resteth*
Eccl. 7. 9. anger *r.* in bosom of fools
1 Pet. 4. 14. Spirit of God *r.* upon you
Num. 10. 33. *resting place,* 2 Chron. 6. 41. Prov. 24. 15. Isa. 32. 18. Jer. 50. 6.
RESTORE, Ps. 51. 12. & 23. 3. & 69. 4. Isa. 58. 12. Luke 19. 8.
Ex. 22. 3. *restitution,* Acts 3. 21.
RESTRAIN, 1 Sam. 3. 13. Job 15. 4. Ps. 76. 10. Isa. 63. 15.
RESURRECTION, Matt. 22. 23. Acts 23. 8. 1 Cor. 15. 12. Heb. 6. 2.
Luke 20. 36. children of God being children of the *r.*
John 5. 29. done good to *r.* of life done evil to *r.* of damnation
11. 25. I am the *r.* and the life
Acts. 17. 18. preached Jesus and *r.*
24. 15. there shall be *r.* of dead
Rom. 6. 5. in likeness of his *r.*
Phil. 3. 10. power of *r.* 12. attain *r.*
1 Tim. 2. 18. erred, saying, that *r.* is
Heb. 11. 35. might obtain a better *r.*
Rev. 20. 5. this is the first *r.* 6.

RETAIN, Job 2. 9. John 20. 23.
Mic. 7. 18. *retaineth* not his anger
RETURN to the ground, Gen. 3. 19. *r.* to dust
1 Kings 8. 48. *r.* to thee with all heart
Job 1. 21. naked shall I *r.* thither
Ps. 73. 10. his people *r.* hither
90. 3. *r.* ye children of men
116. 7. *r.* unto thy rest, O my soul
Eccl. 12. 7. dust shall *r.* to the earth
Song 6. 13. *r. r.* O Shulamite; *r. r.*
Isa. 10. 21. remnant shall *r.* to God
21. 12. if ye will inquire, inquire; *r.* come
35. 10. ransomed of Lord shall *r.*
35. 11. my word shall not *r.* void
Jer. 3. 12. *r.* backsliding Israel
4. 1. if thou wilt *r. r.* unto me
15. 19. let them *r.* to thee, but *r.* not
Hos. 2. 7. *r.* to my first husband
5. 15. I will go and *r.* to my place
7. 16. they *r.* but not to Most High
11. 9. not *r.* to destroy Ephraim
Mal. 3. 7. *r.* to me, and I will *r.* to
18. then shall ye *r.* and discern
Ps. 35. 13. my prayer *returned* into my bosom
78. 34. they *r.* and inquired after God
Amos 4. 6. ye *r.* not to me, 8-11.
1 Pet. 2. 25. are *r.* unto Shepherd
Isa. 30. 15. in *returning* and rest
Jer. 5. 3. they refused to *return,* 8. 5. Hos. 11. 5.
Deut. 30. 2. *return to the Lord,* 1 Sam. 7. 3. Isa. 55. 7. Hos. 6. 1. & 3. 5. & 7. 10. & 14. 1, 7.
REVEAL, Prov. 11. 13. Dan. 2. 19.
Job 20. 27. heaven shall *r.* his iniquity
Gal. 1. 16. pleased God to *r.* his Son
Phil. 3. 15. God shall *r.* even this
Deut. 29. 29. things which are *revealed*
Isa. 22. 14. it was *r.* in mine ears
53. 1. to whom is arm of Lord *r.*
Matt. 10. 26. covered that shall not be *r.*
11. 25. hid from wise, and *r.* them unto babes
16. 17. flesh and blood hath not *r.*
Rom. 1. 17. righteousness of God *r.*
8. 18. glory which shall be *r.* in us
1 Cor. 2. 10. God hath *r.* them to us
2 Thes. 1. 7. when Lord Jesus shall be *r.*
2. 3. falling away, man of sin be *r.*
Prov. 20. 19. a tale-bearer *revealeth*
Amos. 3. 7. *r.* his secret to servants
Rom. 2. 5. *revelation,* 16. 25. Gal. 1. 12. Eph. 1. 17. & 3. 3. 1 Pet. 1. 13.
REVELLINGS, Gal. 5. 21.
REVENGE, Jer. 15. 15. 2 Cor. 7. 11. & 10. 6. Nah. 1. 2.
Ps. 79. 10. by *revenging* blood of thy servants
Num. 35. 19. *revenger,* Rom. 13. 4.
REVERENCE my sanctuary, Lev. 19. 30.
Ps. 89. 7. to be had in *r.* of all about
Eph. 5. 33. wife see that she *r.* her
Heb. 12. 28. serve God acceptably with *r.*
Ps. 111. 9. and *reverend* is his name
REVILE, Ex. 22. 28. Matt. 5. 11.
1 Cor. 4. 12. being *reviled* we bless
1 Pet. 2. 23. when he was *r. r.* not
1 Cor. 6. 10. nor *revilers* inherit the
Isa. 51. 7. *revilings,* Zeph. 2. 8.
REVIVE us again, Ps. 85. 6.
Isa. 57. 15. to *r.* the spirit of the humble; and to *r.* the heart of contrite
Hos. 6. 2. after two days will *r.* us
14. 7. they shall *r.* as the corn and
Hab. 3. 2. *r.* thy work in midst of
Rom. 7. 9. sin *revived* and I died
14. 9. Christ died, and rose, and *r.*
Ezra 9. 8. give us a little *reviving,*
REVOLT more and more, Isa. 1. 5.

Isa. 31. 6. children of Israel have *revolted*
Jer. 5. 23. this people hath a *revolting heart*
6. 28. *revolters,* Hos. 5. 2. & 9. 5.
REWARD, Gen. 15. 1.
Deut. 10. 17. God taketh not *r.*
Ps. 19. 11. in keeping them is great *r.*
58. 11. there is a *r.* for righteous
127. 3. fruit of the womb is his *r.*
Prov. 11. 18. that soweth righteousness sure *r.*
Isa. 3. 11. the *r.* of his hands shall be given him
5. 23. who justify wicked for a *r.*
Mic. 7. 3. the judge asketh for a *r.*
Matt. 5. 12. great is your *r.* in heaven
6. 2. verily they have their *r.*
10. 41. shall receive a prophet's *r.*
Rom. 4. 4. the *r.* is not reckoned of
1 Cor. 3. 8. shall receive his own *r.*
Col. 2. 18. no man beguile you of *r.*
3. 24. the *r.* of the inheritance
1 Tim. 5. 18. labourer is worthy of *r.*
Heb. 2. 2. just recompense of *r.*
11. 26. respect to recompense of *r.*
2 John 8. we may receive a full *r.*
Matt. 6. 4. Father shall *r.* openly
2 Tim. 4. 14. Lord *r.* him according
Rev. 22. 12. I come and my *r.* is with
18. 6. *r.* her as she *rewarded* you
Ps. 103. 10. nor *r.* us according to our iniquities
Isa. 3. 9. have *r.* evil unto themselves
Ps. 31. 25. plentifully *rewardeth* proud
Heb. 11. 6. *rewarder* of them that
RICH, Gen. 13. 2. Ex. 30. 15.
Prov. 10. 4. hand of diligent maketh *r.*
22. blessing of the Lord maketh *r.*
13. 7. himself *r.* yet hath nothing
14. 20. *r.* man hath many friends
18. 11. *r.* man's wealth is a strong city, 10. 15.
18. 23. the *r.* answereth roughly
22. 2. *r.* and poor meet together
23. 4. labour not to be *r.*
28. 11. *r.* man wise in his own conceit
20. that hasteth to be *r.* shall not
Eccl. 5. 12. abundance of the *r.* will not suffer him to sleep
10. 20. curse not the *r.* in thy bedchamber
Jer. 9. 23. let not *r.* man glory in his
Matt. 19. 23. *r.* man hardly enter the kingdom
Luke 1. 53. *r.* he sent empty away
6. 24. wo unto you that are *r.*
12. 21. layeth up, is not *r.* towards God
16. 1. certain *r.* man which had
18. 23. sorrowful for he was very *r.*
2 Cor. 6. 10. yet making many *r.*
8. 9. Jesus, though *r.* became poor
Eph. 2. 4. God who is *r.* in mercy
1 Tim. 6. 9. they that will be *r.* fall into temptation
17. charge them that are *r.* in this
18. that they be *r.* in good works
James 2. 5. poor of world, *r.* in faith
Rev. 2. 9. I know thy poverty, thou art *r.*
3. 17. sayest, I am *r.*
18. mayest be *r.*
1 Chron. 29. 12. *riches* and honour
Ps. 39. 6. he heapeth up *r.* and
49. 6. boast themselves in multitude of *r.*
52. 7. trusted in abundance of his *r.*
62. 10. if *r.* increase, set not heart
104. 24. the earth is full of thy *r.*
112. 3. wealth and *r.* be in his house
119. 14. rejoiced as much as in all *r.*
Prov. 3. 16. in her left hand *r.* and
11. 4. *r.* profit not in day of wrath
28. that trusteth in his *r.* shall fall
13. 8. ransom of man's life are his *r.*
14. 24. crown of the wise is their *r.*

23. 5. r. make themselves wings
27. 24. r. not for ever, nor the
30. 8. give me neither poverty nor r.
Jer. 17. 11. so he that getteth r. and
Matt. 13. 22. deceitfulness of r. choke
Luke 16. 11. to your trust the true r.
Rom. 2. 4. despisest r. of his goodness
9. 23. known the r. of his glory
11. 12. if fall of them be r. of world
2 Cor. 8. 2. abounded unto r. of your liberality.
Eph. 1. 7. according to the r. of his
2. 7. show exceeding r. of grace
Phil. 4. 19. according to his r. in glory
Col. 2. 2. unto all r. of the full assurance, 1. 27.
1 Tim. 6. 17. not trust in uncertain r.
Heb. 11. 26. the reproach of Christ greater r.
James 5. 2. your r. are corrupted
Col. 3. 16. word of God dwell *richly*
1 Tim. 6. 17. giveth us r. all things
Ps. 45. 4. Hab. 3. 8.

RIDE, Ps. 45. 4. Hab. 3. 8.
Deut. 33. 26. *rideth,* Ps. 68. 4, 33.

RIGHT, Num. 27. 7. Deut. 21. 17.
Gen. 18. 25. shall not the Judge of the earth do r.
Ezra 8. 21. seek of him a r. way or
Job 34. 23. will not lay on man more r.
Ps. 19. 8. statutes of Lord are r.
51. 10. renew a r. spirit within me
119. 128. I esteem thy precepts to be r.
Prov. 4. 11. I have led thee in r. paths
25. let thine eyes look r. on before
8. 9. r. to them that find knowledge
12. 5. thoughts of righteous are r.
14. 12. a way which seemeth r. to
21. 2. way of man is r. in own eyes
Isa. 30. 10. prophesy not unto us r.
Ezek. 18. 5. be just, do lawful and r.
Hos. 14. 9. ways of the Lord are r.
Amos 3. 10. they know not to do r.
Mark 5. 15. and in his r. mind
Luke 12. 57. judge ye not what is r.
Acts 4. 19. whether r. in sight of God
8. 21. thy heart is not r. in sight of
13. 10. not cease to pervert r. ways
Eph. 6. 1. children, obey your parents this is r.
2 Pet. 2. 15. forsaken the r. way, gone
Rev. 22. 14. have r. to tree of life
2 Tim. 2. 15. *rightly* dividing word

Gen. 7. 1. seen the *righteous* before
18. 23. wilt thou destroy r. with wicked
Num. 23. 10. let me die death of r.
Deut. 25. 1. justify r. and condemn
1 Kings 8. 32. justifying r. to give
Job 4. 7. where were the r. cut off
17. 9. the r. shall hold on his way
Ps. 1. 6. Lord knoweth way of r.
5. 12. wilt bless the r. with favour
7. 11. God judgeth the r.
11. 5. Lord trieth r. but wicked he
32. 11. rejoice in the Lord ye r.
34. 17. r. cry, and Lord heareth
19. many are afflictions of the r.
37. 17. the Lord upholdeth the r.
25. I have not seen the r. forsaken
29. the r. shall inherit the land
55. 22. never suffer the r. to be moved
58. 11. there is a reward for the r.
64. 10. r. shall be glad in the Lord
68. 3. let the r. be glad and rejoice
92. 12. the r. shall flourish like the palm-tree
97. 11. light is sown for the r.
112. 6. the r. shall be in everlasting remembrance
125. 3. rod shall not rest on lot of r.
141. 5. let r. smite me; it shall be
45. 17. Lord r. Lam. 1. 18.
146. 8. the Lord loveth the r.
Prov. 3. 22. his secret is with the r.
10. 3. not suffer soul of r. to famish
10. labour of the r. tendeth to life
21. the lips of the r. feel many

24. desire of the r. shall be granted
25. r. is an everlasting foundation
28. the hope of r. shall be gladness
30. the r. shall never be removed
32. the lips of the r. know what is acceptable
11. 8. r. is delivered out of trouble
21. seed of r. shall be delivered
28. the r. shall flourish as a branch
30. fruit of the r. is a tree of life
31. the r. shall be recompensed in
12. 3. root of r. shall not be moved
5. the thoughts of the r. are r.
7. the house of the r. shall stand
10. a r. man regardeth life of beast
12. root of r. yieldeth fruit
26. the r. is more excellent than his neighbour
13. 9. the light of the r. rejoiceth
25. r. eateth to satisfying of soul
14. 32. r. hath hope in his death
15. 6. in house of r. is much treasure
19. the way of the r. is made plain
29. Lord heareth the prayer of r.
18. 10. r. runneth into it and is safe
28. 1. the r. are bold as a lion
Eccl. 7. 16. be not r. overmuch, nor
9. 2. one event to r. and wicked
Isa. 3. 10. to say to r. it shall be well
41. 2. raised up r. man from east
57. 1. the r. perisheth and are taken
60. 21. thy people also shall be r.
Ezek. 3. 20. when a r. man turneth away, 21. & 18. 24, 26.
Mal. 3. 18. discern between r. and
Matt. 9. 13. not come to call r. but
10. 41. shall receive r. man's reward
25. 46. r. shall go into life eternal
Luke 1. 6. were both r. before God
18. 9. trusted that they were r. and despised others
Rom. 3. 10. there is none r. no not
5. 7. scarcely for a r. man will one
19. by the obedience of one many made r.
2 Thes. 1. 5. a manifest token of r. judgment
1 Tim. 1. 9. law is not made for a r.
James 5. 16. fervent prayer of r. man
1 Pet. 4. 18. the r. scarcely be saved
1 John 3. 7. he that doeth righteousness is r. even as he is r.
Rev. 22. 11. he that is r. let him be r.
Tit. 2. 12. live soberly, *righteously*
Deut. 6. 25. it shall be our *righteousness*
33. 19. offer sacrifice of r. Ps. 4. 5.
Job 29. 14. I put on r. and it clothed
36. 3. I will ascribe r. to my Maker
Ps. 11. 7. righteous Lord loveth r.
15. 2. walketh uprightly and worketh r.
85. 10. r. and peace have kissed
97. 2. r. and judgment are habitation
106. 3. he that doeth r. at all times
Prov. 10. 2. r. delivereth from death
11. 5. r. of perfect shall direct way
6. r. of upright shall deliver them
18. to him that soweth r. a sure
19. r. tendeth to life; so evil to
12. 28. in the way of r. is life
13. 6. r. keepeth the upright in way
14. 34. r. exalteth a nation, but sin
15. 9. he loveth him that followeth r.
16. 8. better is a little with r. than
12. his throne is established by r.
31. if it be found in the way of r.
Isa. 11. 5. r. shall be the girdle of his
26. 9. inhabitants of world will learn r.
Isa. 28. 17. judgment to line and r. to
32. 17. work of r. shall be peace
45. 24. in the Lord have I r. and
46. 12. far from r.
13. I bring near my r.
54. 17. their r. is of me, saith the Lord
61. 3. trees of r. planting of Lord
10. covered me with robes of r.

62. 1. till the r. thereof go forth as brightness.
64. 5. that rejoiceth and worketh r.
Jer. 23. 6. be called Lord our r.
Dan. 4. 27. break off thy sins by r.
9. 7. O Lord r. belongeth unto thee
24. end of sins, and to bring in an everlasting r.
12. 3. that turn many to r. shine as
Zeph. 2. 3. seek r. seek meekness
Mal. 4. 2. Sun of r. arise with healing
Matt. 3. 15. it becometh to fulfil all r.
5. 6. that hunger and thirst after r.
20. except your r. exceed the r. of
21. 32. John came in the way of r.
Luke 1. 75. in holiness and r. before
John 16. 8. reprove world of sin, r.
Acts 10. 35. he that worketh r. is accepted
13. 10. and enemy of all r.
24. 25. as he reasoned of r.
Rom. 1. 17. therein is r. of God revealed
3. 22. even r. of God by faith of
4. 6. man to whom God imputeth r.
11. a seal of the r. of faith
5. 18. by r. of one free gift came
21. grace reign through r. unto eternal life
6. 13. members as instruments of r.
18. servants of r. to holiness, 19.
8. 4. that the r. of the law might
9. 30. Gentiles who followed not after r. attained to r. even r. of faith
10. 31. ignorant of r. of God, establish their own r. have not submitted to r. of God, 5. r. of law, 6. r. which is of faith, 9. 10. with the heart man believeth to r.
14. 17. kingdom of God is r. peace
1 Cor. 1. 30. unto us wisdom and r.
15. 34. awake to r. and sin not
2 Cor. 5. 21. the r. of God in him
6. 7. armour of r.
14. what fellowship hath r.
9. 10. increase the fruits of your r.
11. 15. ministers as ministers of r.
Gal. 2. 21. if r. come by the law
Eph. 6. 14. having on breastplate of r.
Phil. 1. 11. being filled with fruits of r.
3. 6. touching r. of law blameless
9. not mine own r. but the r. of God
1 Tim. 6. 11. follow r. 2 Tim. 2. 22.
Tit. 3. 5. not by works of r. we have
Heb. 12. 11. peaceable fruits of r.
James 1. 20. man worketh not the r. of God
3. 18. fruit of r. is sown in peace
1 Pet. 3. 14. if ye suffer for r. happy
2 Pet. 1. 1. through the r. of God our
2. 5. Noah is preacher of r.
3. 13. wherein dwelleth r.
1 John 2. 29. that doeth r. is born
3. 7. he that doeth r. is righteous
Rev. 19. 8. fine linen is the r. of saints
Gen. 15. 6. counted to him for *righteousness,* Ps. 106. 31. Rom. 4. 3, 5, 9, 22. Gal. 3. 6.
1 Kings 8. 32. *his righteousness,* Job 33. 26. Ps. 50. 6. Ezek. 3. 20. Matt. 6. 33. Rom. 3. 25. 2 Cor. 9. 9.
Ps. 17. 15. *in righteousness,* Hos. 10. 12. Acts 17. 31. Ps. 96. 13. & 98. 9.
Eph. 4. 24. Rev. 19. 11.
Deut. 9. 5. *thy righteousness,* Job 35. 8. Ps. 35. 28. & 40. 10. & 51. 14. & 89. 16. & 119. 142. Isa. 57. 12.
Isa. 64. 6. *all our righteousness*

RIGOUR, Ex. 1. 13. Lev. 25. 43.

RIOT, Tit. 6. 1. 1 Pet. 5. 4.
2 Pet. 2. 13. *rioting,* Rom. 13. 13.
Prov. 23. 20. *riotous,* 28. 7. Luke 15. 13.

RIPE fruit, Ex. 22. 29. Num. 18. 13.
Mic. 7. 1. Jer. 24. 2. r. figs, Hos. 9. 10.
Gen. 40. 10. *ripe grapes,* Num. 13. 20.
Isa. 18. 5. Joel 3. 13. harvest is r.

RISE, Song 3. 2. Isa. 14. 21. & 24. 20. & 26. 14. & 33. 10. & 43. 17. & 54. 17.

& 58. 10. 1 Thes. 4. 16.
Prov. 30. 31. *rising,* Luke 2. 34.

RIVER, Ex. 1. 22. & 4. 9. Job 40. 23.
Ps. 36. 8. & 46. 4. & 65. 9. Isa. 48. 18. & 66. 12. Rev. 22. 1, 2.
Job 20. 17. *rivers,* 29. 9. Ps. 119. 136.
Prov. 5. 16. & 21. 1. Isa. 32. 2. & 33. 21. Mic. 6. 7. John 7. 38.

ROAR, Isa. 42. 13. Jer. 25. 30. Hos. 11. 10. Joel 3. 16. Amos 1. 2.

ROB, Lev. 19. 13. Prov. 22. 22.
Mal. 3. 8. will a man r. God
Isa. 42. 22. a people *robbed* and
2 Cor. 11. 8. I r. other churches
Job 5. 5. *robber* swalloweth up
John 10. 1. that climbeth up is a thief and a r.
Ps. 62. 10. *robbery,* Prov. 21. 7. Isa. 61. 8. Amos 3. 10. Phil. 2. 6.

ROBE, Isa. 61. 10. Rev. 7. 9, 13.

ROCK, Ex. 17. 6. Num. 20. 8, 11.
Deut. 32. 4, 13, 15, 18, 30, 31.
Ps. 18. 2. Lord is my r. and, 92. 15.
31. who is a r. save our God, 46.
31. 3. thou art my r. and fortress
61. 2. lead me to the r. higher than
62. 2. he only is my r. and, 8.
Ps. 71. 3. thou art my r. and fortress
89. 26. Father and r. of my salvation
94. 22. God is the r. of my refuge
Matt. 7. 24. built his house on a r.
16. 18. on his r. will I build church
1 Cor. 10. 4. that r. was Christ
Rev. 6. 16. said to *rocks,* fall on us

ROD, Ex. 4. 4, 20. Num. 17. 2, 8.
Ps. 23. 4. thy r. and staff shall comfort
125. 3. r. of wicked shall not rest
Prov. 13. 24. spareth r. hateth his son
22. 15. r. of correction shall drive
23. 14. thou shalt beat him with r.
29. 15. r. and reproof give wisdom
Isa. 10. 5. r. of my anger, staff of
Ezek. 20. 37. cause to pass under r, Lev. 27. 32.
Mic. 6. 9. hear the r.
7. 14. feel with thy r.
Rev. 12. 5. rule with r. of iron, 19.

ROOM, Prov. 18. 6. Luke 14. 22.

ROOT, Job 5. 3. & 31. 12. Ps. 52. 5.
Deut. 29. 18. a r. that beareth gall
Job 19. 28. seeing r. of the matter is found in me
Prov. 12. 3. r. of the righteous not be moved
Isa. 11. 10. there shall be r. of Jesse
37. 31. take r. downwards, 27. 6.
Matt. 3. 10. axe is laid to r. of tree
13. 6. because it had no r. 21.
Luke 17. 6. be thou plucked up by r.
Rom. 11. 16. if r. be holy, so are the branches
1 Tim. 6. 10. love of money is r. of
Heb. 12. 15. lest r. of bitterness
Matt. 15. 13. plant Father hath not planted shall be rooted up
Eph. 3. 17. being r. and grounded in
Col. 2. 7. r. and built up in him

ROSE, Song 2. 1. Isa. 35. 1.

ROYAL diadem in hand of God, Isa. 62. 3.
James 2. 8. if ye fulfil r. law
1 Pet. 2. 9. ye are a r. priesthood

RUBIES, price of wisdom is above
Job 28. 18. Prov. 3. 15. & 8. 11.

RUDDY, Song 5. 10. Lam. 4. 7.

RUDIMENTS, Col. 2. 8, 20.

RULE, Esther, 9. 1. Prov. 17. 2.
Prov. 25. 28. no r. over own spirit
Gal. 6. 16. walk according to this r.
Phil. 3. 16. let us walk by same r.
Heb. 13. 7. which have r. over you, 17.
Col. 3. 15. let the peace of God r. in your hearts
1 Tim. 3. 5. how to r. his own house
5. 17. let the elders that r. well be counted worthy
Rev. 12. 5. man child was to r. all
2 Sam. 23. 3. *ruleth* over men be just
Ps. 103. 19. his kingdom r. over all

Prov. 16. 32. he that *r*. his spirit than
Hos. 11. 12. Judah yet *r*. with God
Mic. 5. 2. is to be *ruler* in Israel
Matt. 25. 21. make thee *r*. over many
Acts 23. 5. nor speak evil of *r*. of the
Rom. 13. 3. *rulers* are not a terror
Eph. 61. 2. *r*. of darkness of world
RUN, Gen. 49. 22. Lev. 15. 3. 1 Sam. 8. 11. Ps. 19. 5. Eccl. 1. 7.
2 Chron. 16. 9. eyes of the Lord *r*. to
Ps. 119. 32. I will *r*. in way of thy commandments
Song 1. 4. draw me, we will *r*. after
Isa. 40. 31. shall *r*. and not be weary
Dan. 12. 4. many shall *r*. to and fro
1 Cor. 9. 24. *r*. so that we may obtain
Gal. 2. 2. *r*. in vain, 5. 7. did *r*. well
Heb. 12. 1. *r*. with patience the race
1 Pet. 4. 4. *r*. not to same excess of
Ps. 23. 5. my cup *runneth* over
Prov. 18. 10. righteous *r*. into it
Rom. 9. 16. it is not of him that *r*.

S

SABBATH holy, Ex. 16. 23. 8-11. & 31. 14. Acts 13. 42. & 18. 4.
Lev. 23. 3. seventh day is *s*. of rest
Neh. 9. 14. madest known thy *s*.
13. 18. bring wrath by profaning *s*.
Isa. 56. 2. keepeth *s*. from polluting it
58. 13. call *s*. a delight, holy of the Lord, honourable
Matt. 12. 5. priests profane *s*. blameless
28. 1. end of *s*. as it began to dawn
Lev. 19. 3. *my sabbaths,* 30. & 26. 2. Isa. 56. 4. Ezek. 20. 12, 13. & 22. 8, 26. & 23. 38. & 44. 24. & 46. 3.
Deut. 5. 12. *sabbath day,* Neh. 13. 22. Jer. 17. 21. Acts 15. 21. Col. 2. 16.
SACKCLOTH, Gen. 37. 34. Job 16. 15. Ps. 36. 11. Isa. 22. 12. Rev. 11. 3.
SACRIFICE, Gen. 31. 54. Ex. 8. 25.
1 Sam. 2. 29. wherefore kick ye at my *s*.
3. 14. Eli's house not purged with *s*.
15. 22. to obey is better than *s*.
Ps. 4. 5. offer *s*. of righteousness
40. 6. *s*. and offering didst not desire
50. 5. made covenant with me by *s*.
51. 16. desirest not *s*. else I would
17. *s*. of God are a broken spirit
107. 22. *s*. the *s*. of thanksgiving
141. 2. lifting up hands as evening *s*.
Prov. 15. 8. *s*. of wicked is abomination to the Lord, 27.
21. 3. justice more acceptable than *s*.
Eccl. 5. 1. than to give *s*. of fools
Dan. 8. 11. daily *s*. was taken away
9. 27. cause *s*. and oblation to cease
11. 31. take away daily *s*. 12. 11.
Hos. 6. 6. desired mercy and not *s*. Matt. 9. 13.
Mark 9. 49. every *s*. be salted with
Rom. 12. 1. present bodies a living *s*.
1 Cor. 5. 7. Christ our passover is *s*.
Eph. 5. 2. *s*. to God for a sweet
Phil. 2. 17. offered on *s*. of your faith
4. 18. a *s*. acceptable to God
Heb. 9. 26. put away sin by *s*. of
13. 15. *s*. of praise, 16. with such *s*.
1 Pet. 2. 5. priesthood to offer spiritual *s*.
SACRILEGE, commit, Rom. 2. 22.
SAD, 1 Sam. 1. 18. Ezek. 13. 22.
Eccl. 7. 3. by *sadness* the heart is made better
SAFE, Ps. 119. 117. Prov. 18. 10. & 29. 25.
Job 5. 4. *safety,* 11. Ps. 4. 8. & 12. 5. & 33. 17. Prov. 11. 14.
SAINTS, Ps. 52. 9. & 79. 2.
Deut. 33. 2. came with ten thousands of *s*. Jude 14.
Deut. 33. 3. all his *s*. are in thy hand
1 Sam. 2. 9. he will keep feet of his *s*.
2 Chron. 6. 41. *s*. rejoice in goodness

Job 15. 15. he putteth no trust in *s*.
Ps. 16. 3. goodness extendeth to *s*.
37. 28. Lord forsaketh not his *s*.
50. 5. gather my *s*. together to me
97. 10. Lord preserveth souls of *s*.
106. 16. envied Aaron *s*. of Lord
116. 15. precious in the sight of the Lord is death of *s*.
149. 9. this honour have all his *s*.
Prov. 2. 8. preserveth way of his *s*.
Dan. 7. 18. *s*. shall take kingdom
Hos. 11. 12. Judah is faithful with *s*.
Zech. 14. 5. shall come and all *s*.
Rom. 1. 7. called to be *s*. 1 Cor. 1. 2.
2 Cor. 1. 1. Eph. 1. 1. Col. 1. 2, 4.
Rom. 8. 27. intercession for *s*.
Rom. 12. 13. necessity of *s*.
Rom. 15. 25. minister to *s*. 26. 31. 1 Cor. 16. 1. 2 Cor. 8. 4. Heb. 6. 10.
1 Cor. 6. 2. *s*. shall judge the world
Eph. 3. 8. less than the least of all *s*.
4. 12. for perfecting the *s*. for the work of the ministry
1 Thes. 3. 13. coming of Jesus with all his *s*.
1 Thes. 1. 10. come to be glorified in his *s*.
Rev. 5. 8. prayers of the *s*. 8. 3, 4.
11. 18. reward of *s*.
13. 7. war with *s*.
14. 11. patience of *s*.
15. 3. Kings of *s*.
16. 16. blood of *s*. 17. 6. & 18. 24.
19. 8. righteousness of *s*.
20. 9. camp of *s*.
SALT, Gen. 19. 26. Lev. 1. 13. Matt. 5. 13. Mark 9. 49. Col. 4. 6.
SALVATION, Ps. 14. 7.
Ex. 14. 13. stand still and see this *s*. of the Lord, 2 Chron. 20. 17.
Ps. 3. 8. *s*. belongeth only to Lord
37. 39. *s*. of righteous is of Lord
50. 23. I will show him *s*. of God
68. 20. God is the God of *s*. 65. 5.
85. 9. his *s*. is nigh them that fear
98. 2. made known his *s*. 3. seen *s*.
119. 155. *s*. is far from the wicked
132. 16. clothe her priests with *s*.
149. 4. Lord will beautify meek with *s*.
Isa. 25. 9. we will rejoice in his *s*.
26. 1. *s*. will God appoint for walls
33. 2. be our *s*. 6. strength of *s*.
45. 17. Israel saved with everlasting *s*.
46. 13. I will place *s*. in Zion for
52. 7. feet of him that publisheth *s*.
10. earth shall see *s*. of God
59. 16. arm brought *s*. unto me
17. for a helmet of *s*. Eph. 6. 17.
Ps. 60. 18. call thy walls *s*. thy gates
61. 10. garments of *s*.
62. 1. *s*. as a lamp
Jer. 3. 23. in vain is *s*. hoped for; in God is the *s*. of Israel
Lam. 3. 26. quietly wait for *s*. of Lord
Jonah 2. 9. *s*. is of the Lord
Hab. 3. 8. ride on thy chariots of *s*.
Zech. 9. 9. king cometh having *s*.
Luke 19. 9. *s*. is come to thy house
John 4. 22. *s*. is of the Jews
Acts 4. 12. neither is there *s*. in any
13. 26. word of *s*. sent, 47. be for *s*.
Rom. 1. 16. Gospel is power of God to *s*.
11. 11. through their fall *s*. is come
13. 11. now is our *s*. nearer than
2 Cor. 1. 6. for your *s*. sent, 6. 2. day of *s*.
Eph. 1. 13. the Gospel of your *s*.
Phil. 2. 12. work out your own *s*.
1 Thes. 5. 8. hope of *s*. 9. to obtain *s*.
2 Thes. 2. 13. hath chosen you to *s*.
2 Tim. 2. 10. to obtain *s*. with eternal glory
3. 15. able to make wise unto *s*.
Tit. 2. 11. grace of God bringeth *s*.
Heb. 1. 14. who shall be heirs of *s*.
2. 3. how escape, if we neglect so great *s*.

10. make Captain of our *s*. perfect
5. 9. became author of eternal *s*.
6. 9. things that accompany *s*.
9. 28. appear without sin unto *s*.
1 Pet. 1. 5. kept through faith to *s*.
9. receiving end of faith, *s*. of souls
Jude 3. write unto you of common *s*.
Rev. 7. 10. *s*. to our God
Ex. 15. 2. God is become *my salvation,* Job 13. 16. Ps. 18. 2. & 25. 5. & 27. 1. & 38. 22. & 51. 14. & 62. 7. & 88. 1. & 118. 14. Isa. 12. 2.
Ps. 89. 26. rock of—
140. 7. strength of—
2 Sam. 23. 5. thy covenant is all—
Isa. 46. 13.—shall not tarry, 49. 6. & 51. 5, 6, 8. & 56. 1.
Gen. 49. 18. *thy salvation,* 1 Sam. 2. 1. Ps. 9. 14. & 13. 5. & 20. 5. & 18. 35. & 21. 1, 5. & 35. 3. & 40. 10, 16. & 51. 12. & 69. 13, 29. & 70. 4. & 71. 15. & 85. 7. & 106. 4. & 119. 41, 81, 123, 166, 174. Isa. 17. 10. & 62. 11. Luke 2. 30.
SAME, Ps. 102. 27. Heb. 13. 8. Rom. 10. 2. 1 Cor. 12. 4, 5, 6. Eph. 4. 10.
SANCTIFY, Ex. 13. 2. & 19. 10.
Ex. 31. 13. I am Lord that doth *s*.
Lev. 20. 7. *s*. yourselves and be holy
Num. 20. 12. believed me not, to *s*.
Isa. 8. 13. *s*. the Lord of hosts himself
Ezek. 28. 23. I will *s*. myself
Joel 1. 14. *s*. a fast
2. 15. *s*. the congregation
John 17. 17. *s*. them through truth
19. for their sakes I *s*. myself
Eph. 5. 26. might *s*. and cleanse it
1 Thes. 5. 23. God of peace *s*. you
Heb. 13. 12. that he might *s*. people
1 Pet. 3. 15. *s*. the Lord God in hearts
Gen. 2. 3. blessed the seventh day and *sanctified* it
Lev. 10. 3. I will be *s*. in them that come nigh me
Deut. 32. 51. ye *s*. me not in Israel
Job 1. 5. Job sent and *s*. them and
Isa. 5. 16. God that is holy shall be *s*.
13. 3. command my *s*. ones
Jer. 1. 5. before thou camest I *s*. thee
Ezek. 20. 41. be *s*. in you before the heathen, 28. 22, 25. & 38. 16. & 39. 27.
John 10. 36. him whom Father hath *s*.
Acts 20. 32. inheritance among all them which are *s*. 26. 18.
Rom. 15. 16. offering of Gentiles *s*.
1 Cor. 1. 2. *s*. in Christ Jesus
6. 11. but ye are *s*.
7. 14. unbelieving husband is *s*. by
1 Tim. 4. 5. *s*. by word and prayer
2 Tim. 2. 21. *s*. and meet for master's
Heb. 2. 11. they who are *s*. all of one
10. 14. perfected for ever them that are *s*.
Matt. 23. 17. temple that *sanctifieth*
1 Cor. 1. 30. *sanctification,* 1 Thes. 4. 3, 4. 2 Thes. 2. 13. 1 Pet. 1. 2.
SANCTUARY, Ps. 63. 2. & 73. 17. Isa. 8. 14. Ezek. 11. 16. Dan. 9. 17. Heb. 9. 2.
SAND, Gen. 22. 17. & 32. 12. Job 6. 3. & 29. 18. Isa. 10. 22. Matt. 7. 26.
SATAN provoked David, 1 Chron. 21. 1.
Job 1. 6. *s*. came also among, 2. 1.
Ps. 109. 6. let *s*. stand at his right
Matt. 4. 10. get thee hence *s*. 16. 23.
Luke 10. 18. I beheld *s*. as lightning
22. 31. *s*. hath desired to have you
Acts 26. 18. turn from power of *s*.
Rom. 16. 20. God shall bruise *s*.
1 Cor. 5. 5. deliver such a one to *s*.
7. 5. *s*. tempt you not for incontinency
2 Cor. 2. 11. let *s*. get advantage
11. 14. *s*. transformed into angel
12. 7. messenger of *s*. to buffet
1 Tim. 1. 20. I have delivered to *s*.
Rev. 2. 9. synagogue of *s*.
24. depth of *s*.
SATIATE, Jer. 31, 14. 25. & 46. 10.
SATISFY, Job 38. 27. Prov. 6. 30.
Ps. 90. 14. O *s*. early with mercy

91. 16. with long life I will *s*. him
103. 5. who *s*. thy mouth with good
107. 9. he *s*. the longing soul
132. 15. will *s*. her poor with bread
145. 16. *s*. desire every living
Prov. 5. 19. breasts *s*. thee at all times
Isa. 55. 2. labour for that which *s*. not
Ps. 17. 15. *satisfied* with thy likeness
22. 26. meek shall eat and be *s*.
36. 8. they shall be abundantly *s*.
63. 5. soul shall be *s*. as with
65. 4. *s*. with goodness of house
Prov. 14. 14. good man *s*. from himself
27. 20. eyes of man are never *s*.
30. 15. are three things never *s*.
Eccl. 5. 10. that loveth silver not be *s*.
Isa. 9. 20. eat and not be *s*.
53. 11. see travail of his soul and be *s*.
66. 11. *s*. with breasts of consolation
Jer. 31. 14. people be *s*. with goodness
Ezek. 16. 28. thou couldest not be *s*.
Amos 4. 8. they were not *s*.
Hab. 2. 5. his desire cannot be *s*.
Num. 35. 31. take no *satisfaction*
SAVE your lives, preserve and, Gen. 45. 7.
Gen. 50. 20. for good to *s*. much
Job 22. 29. he shall *s*. the humble
Ps. 18. 27. wilt *s*. afflicted people
28. 9. *s*. thy people and lift them
69. 35. God will *s*. Zion
72. 4. *s*. children of needy
13. *s*. souls of needy
86. 2. *s*. thy servant
16. *s*. son of hand maid
109. 31. poor to *s*. him
118. 25. *s*. now; send prosperity
145. 19. *s*. them
Prov. 20. 22. wait on the Lord and he shall *s*. thee
Isa. 35. 4. God will come and *s*. you
45. 25. cannot *s*. 59. 1 Jer. 9. 14.
Isa. 49. 25. I will *s*. thy children
Ezek. 18. 27. shall *s*. his soul, 3. 18.
36. 29. I will *s*. from all uncleanness. 37. 23.
Hos. 1. 7. I will *s*. them by Lord
Zeph. 3. 17. he will *s*.
19. *s*. her that halteth
Zech. 8. 7. I will *s*. my people, 9. 16. & 10. 6.
Matt. 1. 21. *s*. his people from sins
Matt. 16. 25. who will *s*. his life shall lose
8. 11. Son of man is come to *s*. that which was lost, Luke 19. 10.
Mark 3. 4. is it lawful to *s*. life or to
John 12. 47. not to judge but to *s*.
Acts 2. 40. *s*. yourselves from this generation
1 Cor. 1. 21. by foolishness of preaching to *s*.
9. 22. I became all, that I might *s*.
1 Tim. 1. 15. to *s*. sinners, of whom
4. 16. both *s*. thyself, and them
Heb. 7. 25. able to *s*. to the uttermost
James 1. 21. word able to *s*.
2. 14. faith *s*.
5. 15. prayer of faith shall *s*. sick
20. converts a sinner shall *s*. soul
Jude 23. others *s*. with fear, pulling
Ps. 6. 4. *save me,* 55. 16. & 57. 3. & 119. 94. Jer. 17. 14. John 12. 27.
Isa. 25. 9. *save us,* 33. 22. & 37. 20. Hos. 14. 3. Matt. 8. 25. 1 Pet. 3. 21.
Ps. 44. 7. thou hast *saved* us from our enemies
106. 8. *s*. them for his name's sake
Isa. 45. 22. look unto me and be ye *s*.
Jer. 4. 14. mayest be *s*.
8. 20. we are not *s*.
Matt. 19. 25. who then can be *s*.
Luke 1. 71. be *s*. from our enemies
7. 50. thy faith hath *s*. thee, 18. 42.
13. 23. are few *s*.
23. 35. he *s*. others
John 3. 17. world through him be *s*.
Acts 2. 47. added to church such as should be *s*.

4. 12. no other name whereby be s.
16. 30. what must I do to be s.
Rom. 8. 24. we are s. by hope
10. 1. prayer for Israel that they be s.
1 Cor. 1. 18. to us who are s. it is
5. 5. spirit may be s. in day of Lord
Eph. 2. 5. by grace ye are s. 8.
1 Tim. 2. 4. will have all men to be s.
Tit. 3. 5. according to his mercy s.
1 Pet. 4. 18. righteous scarcely be s.
Rev. 21. 24. nations which are s.
Ps. 80. 3. *shall be saved,* 7. 19. Isa. 45. 17. & 64. 5. Jer. 23. 6. & 30. 7. Matt. 10. 22. & 24. 13. Mark 16. 16. Acts 16. 31. Rom. 5. 10, 11, 26. 1 Tim. 2. 15.
2 Sam. 22. 3. God my refuge and my *Saviour*
2 Kings 13. 5. Lord gave Israel a S. Neh. 9. 27.
Ps. 105. 21. forgat God their S.
Isa. 43. 3. I am thy S. 49. 26.
11. besides me is no S. Hos. 13. 4.
45. 15. of Israel, the S. Jer. 14. 8.
Obad. 21. S. come up on mount Zion
Luke 1. 47. spirit rejoiced in God my S.
2. 11. to you is born a S. which is
Acts 5. 31. hath God exalted to be a S.
Eph. 5. 23. Christ is head and S.
1 Tim. 4. 10. who is the S. of all men
1. 1. God our S. Tit. 1. 4. & 2. 10, 13. & 3. 4, 6. 2. Pet. 1. 1., 11. Jude 25.
2 Pet. 2. 20. knowledge of our S.
SAVOUR, sweet, Gen. 8. 21. Ex. 29. 18. Lev. 1. 9. & 2. 9. & 3. 16.
Song 1. 3. of s. of thy good ointment
2 Cor. 2. 14. the s. of his knowledge
15. are to God a *sweet* s. of Christ
16. to one s. of death; to others s.
Eph. 5. 2. sacrifice to God of sweet smelling s.
Matt. 16. 23. *savourest* not things of God
SAY, Matt. 3. 9. & 5. 22, 28, 32, 34, 39, 44. & 7. 22. 1 Cor. 12. 3.
SCARCELY, 1 Pet. 4. 18.
SCATTER them in Israel, Gen. 49. 7.
Num. 10. 35. thine enemies be *scattered*
Matt. 9. 36. s. abroad as sheep
Luke 1. 51. s. proud in imagination
Prov. 11. 21. that *scattereth* and yet
SCEPTRE not depart from Judah, Gen. 49. 10.
Num. 24. 17. a s. shall rise out of Israel
Ps. 45. 6. the s. of thy kingdom is a right s. Heb. 1. 8.
Zech. 10. 11. s. of Egypt shall depart
SCHISM, 1 Cor. 1. 10. & 12. 25.
SCHOLAR, 1 Chron. 25. 8.
Gal. 3. 24. thy law was our *schoolmaster*
SCOFFERS, Hab. 1. 10.
SCORN, Job 16. 20. Ps. 44. 13.
Prov. 9. 8. reprove not a *scorner*
13. 1. a s. heareth not rebuke
14. 6. a s. seeketh wisdom and
15. 12. a s. loveth not one that reproveth
1. 22. *scorners* delight in scorning
3. 34. he *scorneth* the s. but giveth
19. 29. judgments are prepared for s.
9. 12. if thou *scornest* thou
Ps. 1. 1. *scornful,* Prov. 29. 8.
SCORPIONS, 2 Chron. 10. 11.
SCOURGE of the tongue, Job 5. 21.
Isa. 28. 15. overflowing s. 18.
Heb. 12. 6. Lord *scourgeth* every son
SCRIPTURE of truth, Dan. 10. 21.
Matt. 22. 29. ye do err, not knowing s.
John 5. 39. search s. Acts 17. 11.
Rom. 15. 4. through comfort of s.
2 Tim. 3. 15. from a child known s.
16. all s. is given by inspiration
2 Pet. 1. 20. no prophecy of s. is of private interpretation
3. 16. wrest, as they do also other s.
SEA, Ps. 35. 7. & 72. 8. Prov. 8. 29. Isa. 48. 18. & 57. 20. Zech. 9. 10. Rev. 4. 6. & 10. 2. & 15. 2. & 21. 1.
SEAL upon thine heart, Song 8. 6.
John 3. 33. set to this s. that God is
Rom. 4. 11. s. of the righteousness
1 Cor. 9. 2. s. of my apostleship are
2 Tim. 2. 19. having s. Lord knoweth
Rev. 7. 2. angel having s. of living
Deut. 32. 34. *sealed* up among my treasures
Job 14. 17. my transgressions is s. up in a bag.
Song 4. 12. spring shut up, fountain s.
John 6. 27. hath God the Father s.
2 Cor. 1. 22. who hath s. us and
Eph. 1. 13. ye were s. with the Holy
Rev. 5. 1. a book s. with seven seals
7. 3. s. the servants of our God
4. were s. a hundred and forty and
SEARCH, Num. 10. 33.
Ps. 139. 23. s. me, O God, and know
Prov. 25. 27. men to s. own glory is
Jer. 17. 10. I the Lord s. the heart
29. 13. when ye shall s. with me
Lam. 3. 40. s. and try our ways
Zeph. 1. 12. s. Jerusalem with candles
Acts 17. 11. s. Scriptures, John 5. 39.
1 Chron. 28. 9. Lord *searcheth* all hearts
Prov. 18. 17. neighbour cometh and s.
1 Cor. 2. 10. Spirit s. deep things of
Rev. 2. 23. I am he that s. the reins
Job 10. 6. that *searchest* after my sin
Prov. 2. 4. s. for her as for hidden treasures
Judg. 5. 16. great *searchings* of heart
SEARED, 1 Tim. 4. 2.
SEASON, Gen. 40. 4. Ex 13. 10.
Ps. 1. 3. bringeth forth fruit in his s.
Eccl. 3. 1. to every thing there is a s.
Isa. 50. 4. to speak a word in s.
Luke 4. 13. departed from him for s.
John 5. 35. willing for a s. to rejoice
Acts 1. 7. to know the times and s.
14. 17. gave us rain and fruitful s.
1 Thes. 5. 1. of times and s. ye have
2 Tim. 4. 2. instant in s. and out of s.
Heb. 11. 25. enjoy pleasures of sin for a s.
1 Pet. 1. 6. for a s. ye are in heaviness
Col. 4. 6. let speech be *seasoned*
SECRET, Gen. 49. 6. Job 40. 13.
Job 11. 6. show thee s. of wisdom
29. 4. s. of God on my tabernacle
Ps. 25. 14. s. of Lord is with them that fear him
27. 5. in s. of his tabernacle he will
31. 20. hide them in s. presence
44. 21. he knoweth the s. of hearts
139. 15. when I was made in s.
Prov. 3. 32. his s. is with righteous
9. 17. bread eaten in s. is pleasant
11. 13. talebearer revealeth s.
25. 9. discover not s. to another
Dan. 2. 28. a God that revealeth s.
Amos 3. 7. revealeth his s. unto his servants
Matt. 6. 4. alms in s. Father seeth in s.
John 18. 20. in s. have I said nothing
19. 38. *secretly* for fear of Jews
Rom. 2. 16. when God shall judge *secrets of men*
SECT, Acts 24. 5. & 26. 5.
SEDUCE, Ezek. 13. 10. Mark 13. 22.
2 Tim. 3. 13. *seducers,* I Tim. 4. 1.
SEE, Ps. 34. 8. Matt. 5. 8. John 16. 22. 1 John 3. 2. Rev. 1. 7.
Matt. 6. 1. before men to be *seen* of
13. 17. desired to see and have not s.
23. 5. their works to be s. of men
John 1. 18. no man hath seen God at
14. 9. hath s. me hath s. the Father
20. 29. thou hast s. and believed; they have not s. yet believed
1 Cor. 4. 18. look not at things s. but at things not s. for things s. are temporal, things not s. are eternal
1 Tim. 6. 16. whom no man hath s.
Heb. 11. 1. evidence of things not s.
1 Pet. 1. 8. having not s. ye love
1 John 1. 1. that we have s. and heard
4. 12. no man hath s. God at any time
Job 10. 4. seest thou as man *seeth*
John 12. 17. because it is s. him not
12. 45. he that s. me, s. him that
SEED, Gen. 1. 11. & 17. 7.
Ps. 126. 6. bearing precious s.
Eccl. 11. 6. in morning sow thy s.
Isa. 55. 10. give s. to the sower
Matt. 13. 38. good s. is word of God
1 Pet. 1. 23. born not of corruptible s.
1 John 3. 9. his s. remaineth in him
Ps. 37. 28. s. of wicked shall be cut off
69. 36. s. of his servants shall inherit it
Prov. 11. 21. s. of righteous shall be delivered
Isa. 1. 4. sinful nation, s. of evil
14. 20. s. of evil doers never renowned
45. 5. all s. of Israel be justified
53. 10. see his s. and be satisfied
Mal. 2. 15. he might seek a godly s.
Rom. 9. 8. children are counted for s.
29. except Lord of Sabbaoth left s.
Gal. 3. 16. not to *seeds* but to thy s.
SEEK, Ezra 8. 21. Job 5. 8.
Deut. 4. 29. if thou s. him with all thy heart, 1 Chron. 28. 9. 2 Chron. 15. 2. Jer. 29. 13.
2 Chron. 19. 3. prepare heart to s. God, 30. 19.
Ezra 8. 22. on them for good that s.
Ps. 9. 10. not forsake them that s.
27. 4. one thing I desired and will s.
63. 1. my God, early will I s. thee
69. 32. heart shall live that s. God
119. 2. blessed are they that s. him
176. s. servant, for I do not forget
Prov. 8. 17. that s. me early shall find
Song 3. 2. s. him whom soul loveth
Isa. 26. 9. with my spirit will I s. thee
45. 19. I said not s. me in vain
Jer. 29. 13. he shall s. me and find
Amos 5. 4. s. me and ye shall live
8. 12. to s. word and shall not find
Zeph. 2. 3. s. Lord, s. righteousness s. meekness
Mal. 2. 7. s. the law
15. s. a godly seed
Matt. 6. 33. s. first kingdom of God
7. 7. s. and ye shall find, 8.
Luke 13. 24. many will s. to enter in
19. 10. to s. and to save that which is lost, 18. 11.
John 8. 21. shall s. me and not find
Rom. 2. 7. s. for glory, honour
1 Cor. 10. 24. let no man s. own
13. 5. charity s. not her own
Phil. 2. 21. all s. their own, not of Jesus Christ
Col. 3. 1. s. things which are above
1 Pet. 3. 11. s. peace and ensue it
Lam. 3. 25. good to soul that *seeketh*
John 4. 23. the Father s. such to worship him
1 Pet. 5. 8. *seeking* whom he may devour
SEEM, Gen. 27. 12. Deut. 25. 3.
1 Cor. 11. 16. if any man s. contentious
Heb. 4. 1. lest any s. to come short
James 1. 26. if any s. to be religious
Luke 8. 18. taken that he *seemeth* to
1 Cor. 3. 18. if any man s. wise in
Heb. 12. 11. no chastening s. joyous
SELL me thy birthright, Gen. 25. 31.
Prov. 23. 23. buy truth and s. it not
Matt. 19. 21. go s. that thou hast
25. 9. go to them that s. and buy
13. 44. he *selleth* all and buyeth
SENATORS, Ps. 105. 22.
SEND help from the sanctuary, Ps. 20. 2.
Ps. 43. 3. O s. out thy light and
57. 3. he shall s. from heaven and
Matt. 9. 38. s. forth labourers into his harvest
John 14. 26. whom the Father will s.
16. 7. if I depart I will s. him unto
2 Thes. 2. 11. s. them strong delusion
SENSE, Neh. 8. 8. Heb. 5. 14.
James 3. 15. *sensual,* Jude 19.
SENTENCE, Deut. 17. 9.
Prov. 16. 10. a divine s. is in lips of
Eccl. 8. 11. because s. is not executed
2 Cor. 1. 9. we had s. of death in
SEPARATE, Gen. 13. 9.
Gen. 49. 6. head of him that was s. from his brethren, Deut. 33. 16.
Deut. 29. 21. Lord shall s. him unto
Isa. 59. 2. iniquities have *separated*
Acts 13. 2. s. me Saul and Barnabas
19. 9. departed and s. the disciples
Rom. 8. 35. who s. us from Christ, 39.
2 Cor. 6. 17. be ye s. saith the Lord
Gal. 1. 15. who s. me from mother's
Heb. 7. 26. holy, harmless, s. from
SERAPHIMS, Isa. 6. 2, 6.
SERPENT, Gen. 3. 1, 13. & 49. 17.
Num. 21. 6. Lord sent fiery s. 8. 9.
Prov. 23. 32. at last it biteth like a s.
Eccl. 10. 11. s. bite without enchantment
Matt. 7. 10. will be given him a s.
10. 16. be wise as s. harmless as
John 3. 14. as Moses lifted up s. in
2 Cor. 11. 3. as the s. beguiled Eve
Rev. 12. 9. that old s. called devil
SERVE the Lord with all thy heart, Deut. 10. 12, 20. & 11. 13. Josh. 22. 5. 1 Sam. 12. 20.
Deut. 13. 4. shall s. him and cleave
Josh. 24. 14. fear the Lord, s. him
15. chose this day whom ye will s. me and my house will s. the Lord
1 Sam. 12. 24. fear the Lord, s. him
1 Chron. 28. 9. s. him with a perfect heart
Job 21. 15. what the Almighty that we s. him
Ps. 2. 11. s. Lord with fear, rejoice
Isa. 43. 24. made me to s. with sins
Matt. 6. 24. no man can s. two masters; ye cannot s. God and mammon
Luke 1. 74. s. him in holiness and
12. 37. will come forth and s. them
John 12. 26. if any man s. me let him
Acts 6. 2. leave word of God and s. tables
27. 23. whose I am, and whom I s.
Rom. 1. 9. whom I s. with my spirit
6. 6. henceforth should not s. sin
7. 6. s. in newness of life
25. s. law of God
16. 18. s. not Lord Jesus Christ
Col. 3. 24. s. Lord Jesus Christ
Gal. 5. 13. by love s. one another
1 Thes. 1. 9. to s. living God
Heb. 12. 28. may s. God acceptably
Rev. 7. 15. s. him day and night in
Prov. 29. 19. a *servant* will not be corrected by words
Isa. 24. 2. with s. so with his master
42. 1. behold my s. 49. 3. & 52. 13.
Matt. 20. 27. be chief, let him be s.
25. 21. well done, good and faithful s.
John 8. 34. committeth sin is s. of
14. 16. s. not greater than Lord, 15. 20.
1 Cor. 7. 21. art thou called, being a s.
19. 19. have I made myself s. to all
Gal. 1. 10. if pleased men, not s. of Christ
Phil. 2. 7. took on him form of a s.
2 Tim. 2. 24. s. of Lord must not
Ezra 5. 11. *servants* of the God of heaven, Dan. 3. 26. Acts 16. 17. 1 Pet. 2. 16. Rev. 7. 3.
Rom. 6. 16. yield yourselves s. to obey; his s. ye are, whom ye obey
17. ye were the s. of sin

19. members s. to uncleanness
1 Cor. 7. 23. be not ye the s. of men
Phil. 1. 1. s. of Christ
2 Pet. 2. 19. s. of corruption
Rev. 22. 3. his s. shall serve him
Rom. 12. 1. your reasonable *service*
Jer. 22. 13. useth neighbour's s.
Luke 10. 40. cumbered about *serving*
Acts 20. 19. s. Lord with all humility
26. 7. twelve tribes instantly s. God
Rom. 12. 11. fervent in spirit s. Lord
Tit. 3. 3. s. divers lusts and pleasures
SET, Ps. 2. 6. & 4. 3. & 12. 5. & 16. 8. & 54. 8. & 75. 7. & 113. 8. Prov. 1. 25. Song 8. 6. Rom. 3. 25. Col. 3. 2.
SETTLE, Luke 21. 14. 1 Pet. 5. 10.
Col. 1. 23. if ye continue in faith, *settled*
SEVERITY, goodness and, Rom. 11. 22.
SHADE, Lord is thy, Ps. 121. 5.
SHADOW, our days are as a, 1 Chron. 29. 15. Eccl. 8. 13. & 6. 12. Job 8. 9. Ps. 107. 11. & 109. 23. & 144. 4.
Ps. 17. 8. hide me under the s. of thy wings, 36. 7. & 57. 1. & 63. 7.
Song 2. 3. I sat under his s.
17. until the day break and s. flee, Isa. 4. 6. for a s. from heat, 25. 4.
49. 2. in s. of his hand hath he hid
Jer. 6. 4. s. of evening are stretched
Acts 5. 15. s. of Peter might over-shadow them
Col. 2. 17. s. of things to come, Heb. 10. 1.
James 1. 17. no variableness nor s. of
SHAKE heaven and earth, Hag. 2. 6, 21.
Hag. 2. 7. I will s. all nations and
Matt. 10. 14. s. off the dust of feet
11. 7. a reed *shaken* with the wind
Luke 6. 38. good measure s. together
2 Thes. 2. 2. be not soon s. in mind
Heb. 12. 27. things which cannot be s.
Ps. 44. 14. *shaking*, Isa. 17. 6. & 24. 13. & 30. 32. Ezek. 37. 7. & 38. 19.
SHAME, 1 Sam. 20. 34. 2 Sam. 13. 13.
Ex. 32. 25. made naked to their s.
Ps. 119. 31. put me not to s. 69. 7.
Prov. 3. 35. s. shall be the promotion of fools, 9. 7. & 10. 5. & 11. 2. & 13. 5, 18. & 14. 35. & 17. 2. & 18. 13. & 19. 26. & 25. 8. & 29. 15. Isa. 22. 18.
Isa. 50. 6. I hid not my face from s.
Dan. 12. 2. some to life, some to s.
Hos. 4. 7. change their glory into s.
Zeph. 3. 5. the unjust knoweth no s.
Acts 5. 41. worthy to suffer s. for his
Phil. 3. 19. whose glory is in their s.
Heb. 12. 2. endured the cross, des-pising s.
Rev. 3. 18. s. of thy nakedness do
16. 15. naked, and they see his s.
1 Tim. 2. 9. *shamefacedness*
SHAPE, Luke 3. 22. John 5. 37, Ps. 51. 5.
SHARP, Isa. 41. 15. & 49. 2. Rev. 1. 16.
Job 16. 9. *sharpeneth*, Prov. 27. 17.
Mic. 7. 14. *sharper* than, Heb. 4. 12.
Judg. 8. 1. *sharply*, Tit. 1. 13.
2 Cor. 13. 10. should use *sharpness*
SHED for many, for remission, Matt. 26. 28.
Rom. 5. 5. love of God is s. abroad
Tit. 3. 6. Holy Ghost he s. on us
SHEEP, Ps. 49. 14. & 74. 1. & 78. 52.
Ps. 44. 22, 23. s. for the slaughter, Rom. 8. 36.
Ps. 79. 13. s. of thy pasture, 95. 7. & 100. 3.
119. 176. gone astray like lost s.
Isa. 53. 6. like s. have gone astray
Ezek. 34. 12. s. scattered; seek my s.
Zech. 13. 7. smite the Shepherd, and the s. shall be scattered
Matt. 9. 36. as s. having no shepherd
10. 6. lost s. of house of Israel

18. 12. have a hundred s. and one of them be gone astray
25. 32. divideth the s. from goats
33. set the s. on his right hand
John 10. 2-7. the s. 27. my s.
21. 15-17. feed lambs, feed my s.
1 Pet. 2. 25. were as s. going astray
SHEPHERD, Gen. 46. 34. & 49. 24. Ex. 2. 17, 19.
Num. 17. 17. as sheep that have no s.
1 Kings 22. 17. Mark 6. 34.
Ps. 23. 1. the Lord is my s.
80. 1. s. of Israel
Song 1. 8. feed thy kids before s. tents
Ezek. 34. 2. prophesy against s. wo to the s.
5. scattered because no s.
7. s. hear word of Lord
8. no s. neither did my s. search
12. s. seeketh out his flock
23. set up one s. even David be their s.
37. 24. they all shall have one s.
Mic. 5. 5. raise against him seven s.
Zech. 13. 7. awake, O sword against s.
John 10. 11. I am the good s. the good s. giveth his life, 14.
16. one fold and one s. Eccl. 12. 11.
Heb. 13. 20. Lord Jesus, that great s.
1 Pet. 2. 25. returned to s. of souls
5. 4. when the chief s. shall appear
SHOW, Ps. 39. 6. Luke 20. 47. Col. 2. 23.
Ps. 4. 6. who will s. us any good
16. 11. thou wilt s. me path of life
91. 16. I will s. him my salvation
92. 15. to s. that Lord is upright
1 Cor. 11. 26. s. forth Lord's death
Tit. 2. 7. thyself a pattern of good
1 Pet. 2. 9. s. forth the praise of him
Rev. 22. 6. sent his angel to s. servant
John 5. 20. loved Son, and showeth
SHIELD and great reward, Gen. 15. 1.
Deut. 33. 29. Lord the s. of thy help
Ps. 3. 3. Lord is a s. for me, 28. 6.
18. 35. the s. of thy salvation
33. 20. Lord our s. 59. 11. & 84. 9.
84. 11. God is a sun and s.
115. 9. their help and their s. 10. 11.
Prov. 30. 5. a s. unto them that trust
Eph. 6. 16. taking the s. of faith
SHINE, Job 22. 28. & 36. 32.
Num. 6. 25. Lord make his face to s.
Job 10. 3. s. on counsel of wicked
Ps. 31. 16. make thy face to s. on thy servant, 119. 35.
Eccl. 8. 1. wisdom maketh his face s.
Dan. 12. 3. wise shall s. as firmament
Matt. 5. 16. let your light so s. before
13. 43. righteous s. forth as the sun
2 Cor. 4. 6. who commanded light to s.
Phil. 2. 15. among whom ye s. as
SHIPWRECK, 1 Tim. 1. 19.
SHORT, is the Lord's hand waxed, Num. 11. 23.
Ps. 89. 47. remember how s. time is
Rom. 3. 23. and come s. of glory of
Ps. 102. 23. he *shortened* my days, 89. 45.
Isa. 50. 2. is my hand s. 59. 1.
Matt. 24. 22. except the days be s. Ps. 10. 27.
SHOUT, Num. 23. 21. Isa. 12. 16. & 44. 23. Zeph. 3. 14. Zech. 9. 9.
Ps. 47. 5. God is gone up with a s.
1 Thes. 4. 16. Lord shall descend with
SHRINES, Acts 19. 24.
SHUT up our left, Deut. 32. 36.
Matt. 23. 13. ye s. up the kingdom
Gal. 3. 23. s. up the faith which
Rev. 3. 7. that openeth, and no man *shutteth*, Isa. 22. 22.
SICK of love, Song 2. 5. & 5. 8.
Isa. 1. 5. whole head is s. and heart
John 11. 1. certain man was s. 2. 3.
James 5. 14. if any s. call the elders
15. prayer of faith shall save the s.

1 Cor. 11. 30. are weak and *sickly*
Ps. 41. 3. make his bed in *sickness*
Ex. 23. 25. I will take s. away
Matt. 8. 17. bare our *sickness*
SIFT, Isa. 30. 28. Amos 9. 9. Luke 22. 31.
SIGHT, Ex. 3. 3. 2 Cor. 5. 7.
SIGN, Gen. 9. 12, 13. & 17. 11. Ex. 4. 17. Isa. 8. 18. Rom. 15. 19.
Rom. 4. 11. received the s. of circumcision
Jer. 22. 24. *signet*, Hag. 2. 23.
SILENT in darkness, 1 Sam. 2. 9.
Ps. 21. 1. be not s. to me, 30. 12.
Zech. 2. 13. be s. O all flesh before Lord
Ps. 31. 18. *silence*, 32. 3. & 35. 22. & 50. 3, 21. & 83. 1. & 94. 17. Jer. 8. 14. Amos 5. 13. & 8. 3. 1 Cor. 14. 34. 1 Tim. 2. 12. 1 Pet. 2. 15. Rev. 8. 1.
SILLY, Job 5. 2. 2 Tim. 3. 6.
SIMPLE, Prov. 1. 4, 22, 32. & 7. 7. & 8. 5. & 9. 4, 13. & 19. 25. and 21. 11.
Ps. 19. 7. testimony sure making wise
116. 16. Lord preserveth the s.
119. 130. understanding to the s.
Prov. 14. 15. s. believeth every word, 18.
22. 23. s. pass and are punished, 27. 22.
Rom. 16. 19. but s. concerning evil
18. deceive the hearts of the s.
SIN lieth at the door, Gen. 4. 7.
Job 10. 6. thou searchest after my s.
Ps. 4. 4. stand in awe and s. not
32. 1. blessed is he whose s. is covered
5. I acknowledged my s. unto thee
38. 18. I will be sorry for my s.
51. 3. my s. is ever before me
5. in s. did my mother conceive me
119. 11. that I might not s. against
Prov. 14. 34. s. is a reproach to any
Isa. 30. 1. take counsel to add s. to s.
53. 10. offering for s.
18. bare the s. of many
John 1. 29. taketh away s. of world
5. 14. s. no more lest a worse thing
Rom. 5. 12. by one s. entered world
6. 14. s. shall not have dominion
7. 9. s. revived, and I died, 8. 11.
13. s. might appear s.
14. sold unto s.
17. s. that dwelleth in me
25. with the flesh the law of s.
8. 2. made free from the law of s.
1 Cor. 15. 34. awake to righteousness and s. not
2 Cor. 5. 21. s. for us, who knew no s.
Eph. 4. 26. be angry, and s. not
James 1. 15. lust bringeth forth s. and s. death
1 Pet. 2. 22. did no s. neither was guile
1 John 1. 8. if we say we have no s.
2. 1. ye s. not; if any man s. we have an advocate
3. 9. he cannot s. because born of
5. 16. there is a s. unto death
Ps. 19. 13. keep from presumptuous *sins*
25. 7. remember not against me s. of youth
Isa. 43. 25. not remember s. 44. 22.
Ezek. 33. 16. none of his s. shall be
Dan. 9. 24. make end of s.
1 Tim. 5. 22. not partaker of men's s.
2 Tim. 3. 6. silly women laden with s.
1 John 2. 2. for s. of the whole world
Ps. 69. 5. *my sins*, 51. 9. Isa. 38. 17.
70. 9. *our sins*, 90. 8. & 103. 10. Isa. 59. 12. Dan. 9. 16. Gal. 1. 4. 1 Cor. 15. 3. Heb. 1. 3. 1 Pet. 2. 24. Rev. 1. 5.
Matt. 1. 21. *their sins*, Rom. 11. 27. Heb. 8. 12. & 10. 17. Num. 16. 26.
Isa. 59. 2. *your sins*, Jer. 5. 25. John 8. 21. 1 Cor. 15. 17. Josh. 24. 19.
Ex. 32. 33. who hath *sinned*, I will

Job 1. 22. in all this Job s. not
Lam. 1. 8. Jerusalem grievously s.
5. 7. fathers have s. and are not
Rom. 2. 12. many as s. without law
3. 23. all have s. and come short
1 John 1. 10. if we say we have not s.
Ex. 9. 27. *I have sinned*, Num. 22. 34. Josh. 7. 20. 1 Sam. 15. 24, 30. 2 Sam. 12. 13. & 24. 10. Job 7. 20. & 33. 27. Ps. 41. 4. & 51. 4. Mic. 7. 9. Matt. 27. 4. Luke 15. 18, 21.
Judg. 10. 10. *we have sinned*, 1 Sam. 7. 6. Ps. 106. 6. Isa. 42. 24. & 64. 5. Jer. 3. 25. & 8. 14. 14. 7, 20. Lam. 5. 16. Dan. 9. 5, 8, 11, 15.
1 Kings 8. 46. no man that *sinneth* not
Prov. 8. 36. s. against me wrongeth his own soul
Eccl. 7. 20. no man doeth good, and s. not
Ezek. 18. 4. soul that s. it shall die
1 John 5. 18. is born of God s. not
Eccl. 7. 26. the *sinner* shall be taken
9. 18. one s. destroyeth much good
Isa. 65. 20. s. a hundred years old is accursed
Luke 15. 7. joy over one s. that repenteth
18. 13. God be merciful to me a s.
James 5. 20. shall convert a s. from
1 Pet. 4. 18. where shall s. appear
Gen. 13. 13. *sinners* before the Lord exceedingly
Ps. 1. 1. nor standeth in way of s.
25. 8. Lord will teach s. in the way
51. 13. s. shall be converted to thee
Isa. 33. 14. the s. in Zion are afraid
Matt. 9. 13. I am come to call s. to repentance
Luke 13. 2. s. above all Galileans, 4.
John 9. 31. God heareth not s.
Rom. 5. 8. that while we were yet s. Christ died for us
19. by disobedience many made s.
Gal. 2. 15. are Jew and not s. of the
1 Tim. 1. 15. Jesus came to save s.
Heb. 7. 26. holy, separate from s.
12. 3. endured contradiction of s.
James 4. 8. cleanse your hands, ye s.
Jude 15. ungodly s. have spoken
Num. 32. 14. *sinful*, Isa. 1. 4. Luke 5. 8. Rom. 7. 13. & 8. 3.
SINCERE, Phil. 1. 10, 16. 1 Pet. 2. 2.
Josh. 24. 14. serve him in *sincerity*
1 Cor. 5. 8. unleavened bread of s.
2 Cor. 1. 12. in godly s. we have our conversation
2. 17. as of s. in the sight of God
8. 8. to prove the s. of your love
Eph. 6. 24. that love Lord Jesus in s.
Tit. 2. 7. showing gravity, s.
SINEW, Isa. 48. 4. Job 10. 11.
SING to the Lord, Ex. 15. 21. 1 Chron. 16. 23. Ps. 30. 4. & 68. 32. & 81. 1. & 95. 1. & 96. 1, 2. & 98. 1. & 147. 7. & 149. 1. Isa. 12. 5. & 52. 9. Eph. 5. 19.
Ex. 15. 1. I will s. Judg. 5. 3. Ps. 13. 6. & 57. 7, 9. & 59. 16, 17. & 101. 1. & 104. 33. & 144. 9. Isa. 5. 1. 1 Cor. 14. 15.
Job 29. 13. s. for joy, Isa. 65. 14.
Ps. 9. 11. s. praise, 18. 49. & 27. 6. & 30. 12. & 47. 6, 7. & 68. 4. & 75. 9. & 92. 1. & 108. 1, 3. & 135. 3. & 146. 2. & 147. 1. & 149. 3.
Ps. 145. 7. s. of thy righteousness
Prov. 29. 6. the righteous doth s. and
Isa. 45. 6. then shall tongue of dumb s.
1 Cor. 14. 15. I will s. with the spirit
James 5. 13. is any merry, let him s.
SINGLE eye, Matt. 6. 22. Luke 11. 34.
Acts 2. 46. *singleness* of heart, Eph. 6. 5. Col. 3. 22.
SINK, Ps. 69. 2, 14. Luke 9. 44.
SISTER, Song 4. 9. & 5. 1. & 8. 8.
SITUATION, 2 Kings 2. 19. Ps. 48. 2.

SKIN for skin, Job 2. 4. & 10. 11. & 19. 26. Jer. 13. 23. Heb. 11. 37.

SKIP, Ps. 29. 6. 114. 4. Song 2. 8.

SLACK, Deut. 7. 10. Prov. 10. 4. Hab. 1. 4. Zeph. 3. 16. 2 Pet. 3. 9.

SLAY, Job 13. 15. Ps. 139. 19. Lev. 14. 13.

Eph. 2. 16. having *slain* the enmity

Rev. 5. 9. wast s. and hast redeemed

 6. 9. that were s. for word of God

 13. 8. Lamb s. from foundation of

SLEEP, deep, Gen. 2. 21. & 15. 12.

1 Sam. 26. 12. Job 4. 13. Ps. 76. 6.

Prov. 19. 15. Isa. 29. 10.

Ps. 90. 5. they are as a s. in morning

127. 2. he giveth his beloved s.

132. 4. will not give s. to mine eyes

Prov. 3. 24. thy s. shall be sweet

 6. 4. give not s. to thine eyes, nor

 10. a little s. a little slumber, 24. 33.

 20. 13. love not s. lest thou come to poverty

Eccl. 5. 12. s. of a labouring man is

Jer. 31. 26. my s. was sweet to me

51. 39. s. a perpetual s. 57.

Luke 9. 32. were heavy with s.

Rom. 13. 11. time to wake out of s.

Esth. 6. 1. that night king could not s.

Eccl. 5. 12. the abundance of the rich will not suffer him to s.

Song 5. 2. I s. but my heart waketh

1 Cor. 11. 30. for this cause many s.

15. 51. we shall not all s. but shall

1 Thes. 4. 14. them which s. in Jesus

5. 6. let us not s. as others; but

 7. they that s. s. in the night

 10. whether we s. or wake, should

Ps. 3. 5. laid me down and *slept,*

76. 5. they have s. their sleep

1 Cor. 15. 20. the first fruits of them that s.

Eph. 5. 14. awake, thou that *sleepest*

SLIDE, Deut. 32. 35. Ps. 26. 1. & 37. 31. Jer. 8. 5. Hos. 4. 16.

SLIGHTLY, Jer. 6. 14. & 8. 11.

SLING, 1 Sam. 25. 29. Jer. 10. 18.

SLIP, Ps. 17. 5. & 18. 36. & 38. 16. & 94. 18. Heb. 2. 1.

Ps. 35. 6. *slippery,* 73. 18. Jer. 23. 12.

SLOTHFUL, are under tribute, Prov. 12. 24.

Prov. 12. 27. s. roasteth not which he

15. 19. way of s. is hedge of thorns

18. 9. s. is brother to great waster

19. 24. s. hideth hand in bosom

21. 25. desire of the s. killeth him

22. 13. the s. sayeth there is a lion, 26. 13.

24. 30. I went by the field of the s.

26. 14. as door on hinges so doth s.

Rom. 12. 11. not s. in business, but

Heb. 6. 12. be not s. but followers of

Prov. 19. 15. *slothfulness* casteth in a deep sleep

SLOW to anger, Neh. 9. 17.

Luke 24. 25. fools s. of heart to

James 1. 19. s. to speak, s. to wrath, Prov. 14. 29.

SLUGGARD, go to ant, Prov. 6. 6.

Prov. 6. 9. how long wilt sleep, O s.

13. 4. the soul of the s. desireth

20. 4. s. will not plough by reason

26. 16. s. is wiser in his own conceit

SLUMBER, Ps. 132. 4. Rom. 11. 8.

Ps. 121. 3. he that keepeth thee will not s. 4.

Matt. 25. 5. they all *slumbered* and

2 Pet. 2. 3. their damnation *slumbereth* not

SMITE, Lord shall, Deut. 28. 22.

Ps. 141. 5. let the righteous s. me

Jer. 18. 18. let us s. him with tongue

Zech. 13. 7. s. the shepherd, Matt. 26. 31.

Matt. 5. 39. s. thee on thy right cheek

John 18. 23. why *smitest* thou me

Isa. 53. 4. him *smitten* of God

Hos. 6. 1. hath s. and he will bind

SMOKE, Gen. 19. 28. Ex. 19. 18.

Deut. 29. 20. anger of Lord shall s. Ps. 74. 1. why doth thy anger s.

102. 3. as s. Prov. 10. 26. Isa. 65. 5.

Rev. 14. 11. s. of torment ascendeth

Isa. 42. 3. *smoking* flax, Matt. 12. 20.

SMOOTH, Gen. 27. 11, 16. Isa. 30. 10.

Ps. 55. 21. *smoother,* Prov. 5. 3.

SNARE, Ex. 23. 33. Judg. 2. 3.

Ps. 69. 22. let their table become a s. Rom. 11. 9.

Ps. 91. 3. deliver thee from the s. of the fowler

119. 110. wicked laid a s. for me

114. 7. the s. is broken and we are escaped

Prov. 29. 25. fear of man bringeth a s.

1 Tim. 6. 9. they that will be rich fall into a s.

2 Tim. 2. 26. out of the s. of devil

Ps. 11. 6. on the wicked he will rain *snares*

18. 5. s. of death prevented me

Prov. 13. 14. depart from s. of death

Ps. 9. 16. *snared,* Prov. 6. 2. & 12. 13. Eccle. 9. 12. Isa. 8. 15. & 28. 13. & 47. 22.

SNOW, as, Ps. 51. 7. & 68. 14. Isa. 1. 18. Dan. 7. 9. Matt. 28. 3. Rev. 1. 14.

SNUFFED, Mal. 1. 13. Jer. 2. 24.

SOBER for your cause, 2 Cor. 5. 13.

1 Thes. 5. 6. let us watch and be s. 2.

1 Tim. 3. 2. bishop must be vigilant, s.

 11. wives not slanderers, s.

Tit. 1. 8. s. just, holy, temperate

 2. 2. aged men be s. grave

 4. teach young women to be s.

 6. young men likewise exhort to be s. minded.

1 Pet. 1. 13. gird up your loins, be s.

 4. 7. be s. and watch unto prayer

 5. 8. be s. be vigilant, for your

Rom. 12. 3. not to think highly, but *soberly*

Tit. 2. 12. teaching us to live s.

Acts 26. 25. words of *soberness*

1 Tim. 2. 9. *sobriety,* 15.

SOFT, God maketh my heart, Job 23. 16.

Prov. 15. 1. s. answer turneth away

25. 15. s. tongue breaketh the bone

Matt. 11. 8. man clothed in s. raiment

SOJOURN, Gen. 12. 10. Ps. 120. 5.

Lev. 25. 23. *sojourners* with me, 1 Chron. 29. 15. Ps. 39. 12.

Ex. 12. 40. *sojourning,* 1 Pet. 1. 17.

SOLD thyself to work evil, 1 Kings 21. 20.

2 Kings 17. 17. s. themselves to do evil

Rom. 7. 14. I am carnal, s. under sin

SOLDIER of Jesus Christ, 2 Tim. 2. 3. 4.

SON, 2 Sam. 18. 33. & 19. 4.

Ps. 2. 12. kiss the S. lest he be angry

116. 16. I am s. of thy handmaid

Prov. 10. 1. a wise s. maketh a glad father, 15. 20.

Mal. 3. 17. as a man spareth his s.

Matt. 11. 27. no man knoweth the S.

17. 5. this is my beloved S. 3. 17.

Luke 10. 6. if s. of peace be there

John 1. 18. only begotten S. 3. 16, 18, 35.

5. 21. S. quickeneth whom he will

23. men should honour the S.

8. 35. S. abideth ever

36. the S. maketh free

17. 12. lost none but s. of perdition

Rom. 8. 3. sent his own S. in the likeness, 32.

Gal. 4. 7. if s. then an heir of God

2 Thes. 2. 3. man of sin, s. of perdition

Heb. 5. 8. though a S. yet learned he obedience

1 John 2. 22. denieth the S. denieth

5. 11. life in S.

12. that hath S. hath life

Matt. 21. 37. *his son,* Acts 3. 13. Rom. 1. 3, 9. & 5. 10. & 8. 29, 32. 1 Cor.

1. 9. Gal. 1. 16. & 4. 4, 6. 1. Thes.

1. 10. Heb. 1. 2. 1 John 1. 7. & 2. 23. & 3. 23. & 4. 9, 10, 14. & 5. 9, 10, 11, 20.

Luke 15. 19. *thy son,* John 17. 1, 19. 26.

Dan. 3. 25. *the Son of God,* Matt. 4. 3. & 16. 16. and 41. other places

Num. 23. 19. Son of man, Job 25. 6. Ps. 8. 4. & 80. 17. & 144. 3. Dan. 7. 13. Ezekiel is so called about 90, and Christ about 84 times

Ps. 144. 12. that our *sons* may be as plants

Song 2. 3. so is my beloved among s.

Isa. 60. 10. s. of strangers, 61. 5. & 62. 8.

Mal. 3. 3. purify s. of Levi

 6. the s. of Jacob

Mark 3. 17. Boanerges, s. of thunder

1 Cor. 4. 14. as my beloved s. I warn you

Gal. 4. 6. because ye are s. God sent forth the Spirit of his Son

Heb. 2. 10. bring many s. to glory

12. 7. God dealeth with you as s.

Gen. 6. 2. *sons of God,* Job 1. 6. & 2. 1. & 38. 7. Hos. 1. 10. John 1. 12. Rom. 8. 14, 19. Phil. 2. 15. 1 John 3. 1, 2.

SONG to the Lord, Ex. 15. 1. Num. 21. 17.

Ex. 15. 2. Lord is my s. Ps. 118. 14. Isa. 12. 2.

Job 30. 9. I am their s. Ps. 69. 12.

Job 35. 10. giveth s. in the night, Ps. 42. 8. & 77. 6. Isa. 30. 29.

Ps. 32. 7. compass with s. of deliverance

119. 54. s. in house of pilgrimage

137. 3. a one of the s. of Zion

Ezek. 33. 32. as a very lovely s.

Eph. 5. 19. speak to yourselves in spiritual s.

Rev. 14. 3. no man could learn that s.

15. 3. sing s. of Moses and of Lamb

Ps. 33. 3. sing a *new song,* 40. 3. & 96. 1. & 144. 9. & 149. 1. Isa. 42. 10. Rev. 5. 9.

SOON as they be born. Ps. 58. 3.

Ps. 106. 13. s. forgat his works

Prov. 14. 17. s. angry dealeth foolishly

Gal. 1. 6. s. removed to another Gospel

2 Thes. 2. 2. not s. shaken in mind

SOAP, Jer. 2. 22. Mal. 3. 2.

SORCERER, Acts 13. 6, 8. & 8. 9, 11. Jer. 27. 9. *sorcerers,* Mal. 3. 5. Rev. 21. 8.

SORE, 2 Chron. 6. 28. Job 5. 18.

Heb. 10. 29. much *sorer* punishment

Isa. 1. 6. and putrifying *sores*

SORRY, Ps. 38. 18. 2 Cor. 2. 2. & 7. 8.

Ps. 90. 10. labour and *sorrow*

Prov. 15. 13. by s. of heart the spirit is broken

Eccl. 1. 18. increaseth knowledge increaseth s.

7. 3. s. is better than laughter

Isa. 35. 10. s. and sighing flee away, 51. 11.

50. 11. ye shall lie down in s.

Lam. 1. 12. be any s. like unto my s.

John 16. 6. s. hath filled your hearts

20. your s. shall be turned into joy

2 Cor. 2. 7. swallowed up of overmuch s.

7. 10. godly s. worketh repentance to salvation, but s. of world, 9.

Phil. 2. 27. should have s. upon us

1 Thes. 4. 13. s. not as others

Rev. 21. 4. no more death, neither s.

Ps. 18. 5. the s. of hell

116. 3. the s. of death

127. 2. it is vain to eat bread of s.

Isa. 53. 3. man of s. 4. carried our s.

Matt. 24. 8. beginning of *sorrows*

1 Tim. 6. 10. pierced through with many s.

2 Cor. 7. 9. *sorrowed,* Jer. 31. 12.

1 Sam. 1. 15. woman of a *sorrowful* spirit

Job 6. 7. were as my s. meat

Prov. 14. 13. in laughter heart is s.

Jer. 31. 25. replenished s. soul, Ps. 69. 29.

Zeph. 3. 18. s. for solemn assembly

Matt. 19. 22. young man went away s.

26. 22, 38. my soul is exceeding s.

2 Cor. 6. 10. s. yet always rejoicing

Luke 24. 48. *sorrowing,* Acts 20. 38.

SORT, 2 Cor. 7. 11. 3 John 6.

SOUGHT the Lord, Ex. 33. 7. 2 Chron. 14. 7.

Ps. 34. 4. I s. Lord, and he heard

111. 2. s. out of all them that take pleasure.

19. 10. with my whole heart I s.

Eccl. 7. 29. s. out many inventions

Isa. 62. 12. be called s. out, a city not forsaken

65. 1. found of them that s. me not

Rom. 9. 32. s. it not by faith, but by

Heb. 12. 17. though he s. it carefully

2 Chron. 16. 12. s. not Lord, Zeph. 1. 6.

1 Chron. 15. 13. *sought him,* 2 Chron. 14. 7. & 15. 4. Ps. 78. 34. Song 3. 1, 2. 6. Jer. 8. 2. & 26. 21.

SOUL abhor my judgments, Lev. 26. 15, 43.

Gen. 2. 7. man became a living s.

Deut. 11. 13. serve him with all s.

Deut. 13. 3. love the Lord with all thy s. Josh. 22. 5. 1 Kings 2. 4. Mark 12. 33.

1 Sam. 18. 1. s. of Jonathan knit to s. of David

1 Kings 8. 48. return with all their s.

1 Chron. 22. 19. set your s. to seek the Lord

Job 16. 4. if your s. were in my s.'s stead

Ps. 19. 7. law is perfect, converting s.

34. 22. Lord redeemeth s. of his servants

49. 8. redemption of s. is precious

74. 19. deliver not the s. of thy turtle dove

107. 9. filleth the hungry s. with

Prov. 10. 3. not suffer s. of righteous

18. 2. s. be without knowledge is

27. 17. full s. loatheth honey-comb

Isa. 55. 2. let your s. delight in fatness

55. 3. hear and your s. shall live

58. 10. I will satisfy the afflicted s.

Jer. 31. 25. I have satiated weary s. 14.

38. 16. the Lord made us this s.

Ezek. 18. 14. s. that sinneth, it shall die, 20.

Matt. 10. 28. are not able to kill s.

Rom. 13. 1. let every s. be subject to

1 Thes. 5. 23. spirit, s. and body be preserved

Hab. 4. 12. piercing to dividing of s.

10. 39. believe to saving of the s.

Ex. 30. 12. ransom for *his soul*

Judg. 10. 6.—was grieved for misery

2 Kings 23. 25. turned to Lord with all—

Job 27. 8. when God taketh away—

Hab. 2. 4.—lifted up, is not upright

Matt. 16. 26. lose—; what in exchange for—

Ps. 16. 10. not leave *my soul* in hell

31. 7. hast known—in adversity

35. 3. say to—I am thy salvation

9.—shall be joyful in the Lord

42. 5, 11. why cast down, O—, 43. 5.

62. 1.—waiteth upon God, 5.

63. 1.—thirsteth for thee, my flesh

5.—shall be satisfied

8.—followeth hard after thee

Isa. 26. 9. with—have I desired thee, 8.

61. 10. shall be joyful in my God

Luke 1. 46.—doth magnify the Lord

John 12. 27. now is—troubled, Matt. 26. 38.

Ps. 33. 20. our soul, 44. 25. & 66. 9. & 123. 4. & 124. 4. Isa. 26. 8.

Deut. 13. 6. own soul, 1 Sam. 18. 1. & 20. 17. Ps. 22. 29. Prov. 8. 36. & 11. 17. & 15. 32. & 19. 8, 16. & 6. 32. & 20. 2. & 29. 24. Mark 8. 36. Luke 2. 35.

Deut. 4. 9. with all thy soul, 6. 5. & 10. 12. & 30. 6. Matt. 22. 37.

Ezek. 3. 19. deliver thy soul, 21. & 33. 9.

Luke 12. 20. this night—shall be required of thee

3 John 1. 2. prosper as—prospereth

Ps. 72. 13. save souls of the needy, 97. 10.

Prov. 11. 36. that winneth s. is wise

Isa. 57. 16. spirit fail, and s. which I

Ezek. 14. 14. should but deliver s.

1 Pet. 3. 20. few, i.e. eight s. saved

4. 19. commit keeping of their s.

2 Pet. 2. 14. beguiling unstable s.

Rev. 6. 9. s. of slain and beheaded, 20. 4.

Luke 21. 19. your souls, Josh. 23. 14. Jer. 6. 16. & 26. 19. Matt. 11. 29. Heb. 13. 17. 1 Pet. 1. 9, 22. & 2. 25.

SOUND, dreadful, Job 15. 21.

Ps. 47. 5. God is gone up with s. of trumpet

89. 15. people that know joyful s.

119. 80. let my heart be s. in thy statutes

Prov. 2. 7. s. wisdom, 3. 21. & 8. 14.

Eccl. 12. 4. s. of the grinding is low

Amos 6. 5. that chant to s. of viol

Rom. 10. 18. s. went into all the earth

1 Tim. 1. 10. contrary to s. doctrine,

2 Tim. 4. 3.

2 Tim. 1. 7. s. mind, 13. of s. words

Tit. 1. 9. s. doctrine, s. in faith, 2. 1, 2.

2. 8. s. speech that cannot be condemned

Isa. 63. 15. sounding of bowels, 16. 11.

Ps. 38. 3, 7. no soundness, Isa. 1. 6.

SOW that was washed 2 Pet. 2. 22.

SOW wickedness reap the same, Job 4. 8.

Ps. 126. 5. s. in tears, reap in joy

Eccl. 11. 4. observeth the wind, shall not s.

Isa. 32. 20. blessed that s. beside all waters

Jer. 4. 3. s. not among thorns

31. 27. I will s. houses of Israel

Hos. 10. 12. s. in righteousness, reap in mercy

Mic. 6. 15. thou shalt s. and not reap

Matt. 13. 3. sower went out to s.

Luke 12. 24. the ravens neither s. nor

19. 22. reaping what I did not s.

Ps. 97. 11. light is sown for righteous

Hos. 8. 7. s. wind, reap whirlwind

1 Cor. 9. 11. have s. to you spiritual

15. 42. it is s. in corruption

43. it is s. in dishonour; it is s. in weakness.

1 Cor. 9. 10. multiply your seed s.

James 3. 18. fruit of righteousness is s. in peace

Prov. 11. 18. that soweth righteousness.

22. 8. s. iniquity, shall reap vanity

John 4. 37. one s. another reapeth

2 Cor. 9. 6. s. sparingly, s. bountifully

Gal. 6. 7. what a man s. that shall

8. s. to his flesh, reap corruption

Isa. 55. 10. seed to sower, 2 Cor. 9. 10.

SPARE all the place, Gen. 18. 16.

Neh. 13. 22. s. me according to thy mercy

Ps. 39. 13. s. me that I may recover strength

Prov. 19. 18. let not thy soul s. for his crying

Joel 2. 17. s. thy people and give not

Mal. 3. 17. I will s. them, as man s. his son

Rom. 8. 32. spared not his own Son

11. 21. if God s. not the natural

2 Pet. 2. 4. God s. not angels that sinned

Prov. 13. 24. he that spareth rod

SPARKS, Job 5. 7. Isa. 50. 11.

SPARROW, Ps. 102. 7. Matt. 10. 29.

SPEAK against Moses, Num. 12. 8.

Gen. 18. 27. taken on me to s. to the Lord

Ez. 4. 14. Aaron thy brother can s.

34. 35. went in to s. to the Lord

1 Sam. 3. 9. s. Lord, thy servant heareth

Ps. 85. 8. Lord will s. peace to people

Isa. 8. 20. if s. not according to word

50. 4. how to s. a word in season

Jer. 18. 7. at what instant I s. 9.

Hab. 2. 3. at end it shall s. and not lie

Matt. 10. 19. how or what ye shall s.

Luke 6. 26. when all men s. well of

John 3. 11. we s. that we do know

Acts 4. 20. cannot but s. things we

1 Cor. 1. 10. ye all s. the same thing

2. 6. we s. wisdom among perfect

Tit. 3. 2. to s. evil of no man, but

James 1. 19. swift to hear, slow to s.

2 Pet. 2. 10. s. evil of dignities, Jude 8.

Jude 10. s. evil of things which they know not

Matt. 12. 32. speaketh against Son of

34. out of the baundance of the heart the mouth s.

Heb. 11. 4. he being dead yet s.

12. 24. s. better things than blood of Abel

25. refuse not him that s. from heaven

1 Pet. 2. 12. s. against you as evil

Isa. 45. 19. I speak, 63. 1. John 4. 26. & 7. 17. & 8. 26, 28, 38. & 12. 50. Rom. 3. 5. & 6. 19. 1 Tim. 2. 7.

Isa. 58. 13. nor speaking own words

65. 24. while they are s. I will hear, 58. 9.

Dan. 9. 20. while I was s. and

Matt. 6. 7. will be heard for much s.

Eph. 4. 15. s. the truth in love

31. evil s. be put away, 1 Pet. 2. 1.

5. 19. s. to yourselves in psalms

1 Tim. 4. 2. s. lies in hypocrisy, Ps. 58. 3.

Rev. 13. 5. a mouth s. great things

Gen. 11. 1. earth was of one speech

Deut. 32. 2. my s. shall distil as dew

Matt. 26. 73. thy s. bewrayeth thee

1 Cor. 2. 1. not with excellency of s.

2 Cor. 3. 12. use great plainness of s.

10. 10. his s. is contemptible

Col. 4. 6. let your s. be with grace

Tit. 2. 8. sound s. that cannot be condemned

Jude 15. of all their hard speeches

Rom. 16. 18. by fair s. deceive simple

Matt. 22. 12. he was speechless

SPECTACLE to angels, 1 Cor. 4. 9.

SPEED, Gen. 24. 12. 2 John 10. 11.

Ezra 7. 21. speedily, 26. Ps. 31. 2. & 79. 8. Ex. 8. 11. Luke 18. 8.

SPEND their days in wealth, Job 21. 13.

Ps. 90. 9. s. our years as a tale that

Isa. 55. 2. s. money for that is not

49. 4. have spent my strength for

Rom. 13. 12. night is far s. day is at

2 Cor. 12. 15. spend and be s.

SPICES, Song 4. 10, 14, 16. & 8. 14.

SPIDER, Prov. 30. 28. Job 8. 14. Isa. 59. 5.

SPIKENARD, Song 1. 12. & 4. 13 14.

SPIRIT made willing, Ex. 35. 21.

Num. 11. 17. take of s. which is on

14. 24. Caleb had another s. with

2 Kings 2. 9. double portion of thy s.

Ezra 1. 5. whose s. God raised to build up

Neh. 9. 20. gavest good s. to instruct

Job 26. 13. by his s. he garnished the heavens

32. 8. there is a s. in man

18. s. in me

Ps. 31. 5. into thy hand I commit my s.

32. 2. blessed the man in whose s. there is no guile

51. 10. and renew a right s. within me

11. and take not thy holy s. from me

12. uphold me with thy free s.

17. a broken s. and contrite, 34. 18.

Prov. 15. 13. & 17. 22. Isa. 57. 15. & 66. 2.

Ps. 76. 12. he will cut off the s. of princes

78. 8. whole s. is not steadfast with God

104. 30. sendest forth thy s. Job 34. 14.

139. 7. whither should I go from thy s.

142. 3. my s. was overwhelmed in me, 143. 4.

143. 7. s. faileth, 10, thy s. is good

Prov. 14. 29. is hasty of s. exalteth folly

Prov. 15. 13. by sorrow of heart the s. is broken

16. 18. and a haughty s. goeth before a fall

32. that ruleth his own s. is better than he that taketh a city

18. 14. but a wounded s. who can bear

20. 27. the s. of man is the candle of Lord

Eccl. 3. 21. who knoweth the s. of a man

8. 8. no power over s. to retain the s.

11. 5. thou knowest not way of the s.

12. 7. the s. shall return to God who gave

Isa. 32. 15. until the s. be poured on us

34. 16. and his s. it hath gathered them

57. 16. for the s. fail before me and the souls

61. 3. garment of praise for s. of heaviness

Mic. 2. 11. walking in s. and falsehood do lie

Zech. 10. 1. formeth s. of man within him

10. pour out s. of grace and supplication

Mal. 2. 15. take heed to your s. and let none

Matt. 22. 43. doth David in s. call him Lord

26. 41. the s. is willing but the flesh weak

Luke 1. 80. John grew and waxed strong in s.

2. 27. and he came by the s. into temple

8. 55. and her s. came again and she arose

9. 55. ye know not what manner of s. ye are

24. 39. s. hath not flesh and bones as ye see

John 3. 5. born of water and of s. ye cannot

6. and that which is born of the s. is s.

14. God giveth not s. by measure to him

4. 24. God is a s. worship him in s. and in truth 23.

6. 63. it is the s. that quickeneth; the words I speak are s. and life

Acts 6. 10. not able to resist the s. by which

16. 7. the s. suffered them not

17. 16. Paul's s. was stirred in him when he

18. 5. Paul was pressed in s. and testified

Rom. 8. 1. not after flesh, but after

the s. 4.

2. s. of life in Christ Jesus made free

9. if any have not s. of Christ, he is none

8. 13. if ye through s. mortify deeds of

15. s. of bondage. the s. of adoption whereby

16. s. beareth witness with our s. that we

8. 26. likewise the s. helpeth our infirmities

1 Cor. 2. 10. s. searcheth all things yea the

5. 3. present in s. 5. s. may be saved in day

6. 17. joined unto the Lord is one s. 12. 13.

2 Cor. 3. 3. written with s. of living God

6. not of letter but s. but the s. giveth life

17. where the s. of the Lord is, there is liberty

7. 1. cleanse from filthiness of flesh and s.

Gal. 3. 3. begun in s. are ye now made perfect

4. 6. sent forth the s. of his Son into hearts

5. 16. walk in the s. and ye shall not fulfil

17. flesh lusteth against s. and s. against flesh

18. if ye be led by s. are not under law

22. but the fruit of the s. is love, joy, peace

25. if we live in the s. let us walk in the s.

6. 18. grace be with your s. 2 Tim. 4. 22.

Eph. 1. 13. sealed with holy s. of promise

4. 4. there is one body and one s. even as

23. and be renewed in the s. of your mind

5. 9. for the fruit of the s. is in all goodness

18. not drunk with wine but filled with the s.

6. 18. praying always in s. Jude 20.

Col. 2. 5. I am with you in the s. joying

1 Thes. 5. 23. your whole s. soul and body

Heb. 4. 12. dividing asunder of soul and s.

9. 14. through the eternal s. offered himself

James 4. 5. s. that dwelleth in us lusteth

1 Pet. 3. 4. ornament of a meek and quiet s.

18. to death in flesh, but quickened by the s.

4. 6. but live according to God in the s.

1 John 4. 1. believe not every s. but try s.

Jude 19. separate, sensual, not having the s.

Rev. 1. 10. I was in s. on the Lord's day

11. 11. s. of life from God entered them

14. 13. yea, saith the s. that they may

22. 17. and the s. and the bride say come

Gen. 6. 3. my spirit, Job 10. 12. Ps. 31. 5. & 77. 6. Isa. 38. 16. Ezek. 36. 27. Zech. 4. 6. Luke 1. 47. & 23. 46. Acts 7. 59. Rom. 1. 9. 1 Cor. 14. 14.

Gen. 1. 2. Spirit of God, Ex. 31. 3. 2 Chron. 15. 1. Job 33. 4. Ezek. 11. 34. Matt. 3. 16. & 12. 28. Rom. 8. 9, 14. & 15. 19. 1 Cor. 2. 11, 14. & 3. 16. & 6. 11. & 12. 3. 2 Cor. 3. 3. Eph. 4. 30. 1 Pet. 4. 14. 1 John 4. 2.

Isa. 11. 2. the *s.* of wisdom and, Eph. 1. 17.

Zech. 13. 2. unclean *s.* to pass out, Matt. 12. 43.

Num. 16. 22. the God of the *s.* of all flesh, 27. 16.

Ps. 104. 4. who maketh his angels *spirits*

Prov. 16. 2. but the Lord weigheth the *s.*

Matt. 10. 1. *unclean spirits*, Acts 5. 16. & 8. 7. Rev. 16. 13, 14.

Luke 10. 20. rejoice not that the *s.* are subject to you

1 Cor. 14. 32. *s.* of the prophets are subject

Heb. 12. 23. to *s.* of just men made perfect   z

1 Pet. 3. 19. went and preached to *s.* in prison

John 4. 1. try *s.* whether they be of God

Hos. 9. 7. the *spiritual* man is mad for

Rom. 1. 11. impart unto you some *s.* gift

7. 14. law is *s.* but I am carnal sold under

15. 27. made partakers of their *s.* things

1 Cor. 2. 13. comparing *s.* things with *s.*

15. he that is *s.* judgeth all things yet he

3. 1. could not speak unto you as unto *s.*

9. 11. if we have sown to you *s.* things

10. 3. eat *s.* meat

10. 4. same *s.* drink; *s.* rock that followed

1 Cor. 15. 44. it is raised a *s.* body

Gal. 6. 1. ye which are *s.* restore such

Eph. 1. 3. hath blessed us with all *s.* blessings

5. 19. speaking in *s.* songs, Col. 3. 16.

6. 12. wrestle against *s.* wickedness in high

Col. 1. 9. filled with wisdom and *s.* understanding

1 Pet. 2. 5. built us *s.* house; offer a sacrifice

Rom. 8. 6. to be *spiritually* minded is life

1 Cor. 2. 14. neither know because *s.* discerned

Rev. 11. 8. *s.* is called Sodom and Egypt

SPITE, Ps. 10. 14. Matt. 22. 6.

SPITTING, Isa. 50. 6. Luke 18. 32.

SPOIL, Gen. 49. 27. Ps. 68. 12.

Ps. 119. 162. as one that finds great *s.*

Isa. 53. 12. shall divide *s.* with the strong

Matt. 12. 29. and then he will *s.* his house

Col. 2. 8. lest any *s.* you through philosophy

Ex. 12. 36. and they *spoiled* the Egyptians

Col. 2. 15. having *s.* principalities and powers

Heb. 10. 34. took joyfully *spoiling* of goods

SPOT, without, Num. 19. 2. & 28. 3, 9. Job 11. 19. 2 Tim. 6. 14. Heb. 9. 14. 1 Pet. 1. 19. 2 Pet. 3. 14.

Deut. 32. 5. their *s.* is not *s.* of his children

Song 4. 7. all fair, there is no *s.* in thee

Eph. 5. 27. not having *s.* or wrinkle or any

Jer. 13. 33. *spots*, Jude 12. 23.

SPREAD, Job 9. 8. Isa. 25. 11. & 37. 14. Jer. 4. 3. Lam. 1. 17. Ezek. 16. 8.

SPRING, Ps. 85. 11. Matt. 13. 5, 7.

Ps. 65. 10. *springing*, John 4. 14. Heb. 12. 15.

Ps. 87. 7. all my *springs* are in thee

SPRINKLE, Lev. 14. 7. & 16. 14.

Isa. 52. 15. he shall *s.* many nations

Ezek. 36. 25. I will *s.* clean water on you

Heb. 10. 22. having hearts *sprinkled* from an evil conscience

12. 24. to blood of *sprinkling* that speaketh

1 Pet. 1. 2. through *s.* of the blood of Jesus Christ

SPUE thee out of my mouth, Rev. 3. 16. Hab. 2. 16. Lev. 18. 28. Jer. 25. 27.

SPY, Num. 13. 16. Josh. 2. 1. Gal. 2. 4.

STABILITY of thy times and strength, Isa. 33. 6.

STAFF, Gen. 32. 10. Zech. 11. 10.

Ps. 23. 4. thy rod and thy *s.* comfort me

Isa. 3. 1. take away stay and *s.* of bread

9. 4. hast broken *s.* of his shoulder

14. 5.

10. 25. *s.* in their hand is my indignation

STAGGER, Ps. 107. 27. Rom. 4. 20.

STAKES, Isa. 33. 20. & 54. 2.

STAIN, Isa. 23. 9. & 63. 3.

STAMMER, Isa. 28. 11. & 33. 19. & 32. 4.

STAND, Ezek. 29. 7. Ex. 9. 11.

Job 19. 25. shall *s.* at latter day on earth

Ps. 76. 7. who may *s.* in thy sight when

130. 3. if Lord mark iniquities who shall *s.*

Isa. 46. 10. my counsel shall *s.* Prov. 19. 21.

Mal. 3. 2. who shall *s.* when he appeareth

Matt. 12. 25. house divided against itself shall not *s.*

Rom. 5. 2. this grace wherein we *s.* and

14. 4. for God is able to make him *s.*

2 Cor. 1. 24. for by faith ye *s.* Rom. 11. 20.

Eph. 6. 13. and having done all to *s.* 14. *s.*

1 Pet. 5. 12. true grace of God wherein ye *s.*

Rev. 3. 20. behold I *s.* at the door and knock

Nah. 1. 6. *stand before*, 1 Sam. 6. 20. Luke 21. 36. Rom. 14. 10. Rev. 20. 12.

1 Cor. 16. 13. *stand fast* in the faith

Gal. 5. 1.—in the liberty wherewith Christ hath made us free

Phil. 1. 27.—in one spirit

4. 1.—in the Lord

1 Thes. 3. 8. for now we live, if ye—in Lord

2 Thes. 2. 15—and hold traditions which

Ps. 1. 5. *stand in*, 4. 4. & 24. 3.

Ex. 14. 13. *stand still*, see salvation, 2 Chron. 20. 17. Josh. 10. 12. Zech. 11. 16.

Ps. 1. 1. *standeth*, 26. 12. & 33. 11. Prov. 8. 2. Song 2. 9. Isa. 3. 13.

Ps. 119. 161. my heart *s.* in awe of thy word

Rom. 14. 4. to his own master he *s.* or falleth

1 Cor. 10. 12. thinketh he *s.* take heed lest

2 Tim. 2. 19. foundation of God *s.* sure

James 5. 9. behold the Judge *s.* at the door

STAR, Num. 24. 17. Matt. 2. 2.

Judg. 5. 20. *stars* in their courses fought

Job 25. 5. yea the *s.* are not pure in his sight

38. 7. when the morning *s.* sang together

Dan. 12. 3. shall shine as *s.* for ever and ever

Jude 13. wandering *s.* to whom is darkness

Rev. 12. 1. on her head a crown of twelve *s.*

STATURE, Matt. 6. 27. Eph. 4. 13.

STATUTES and laws by hand, Neh. 4. 14.

Ps. 19. 8. *s.* of the Lord are right rejoicing

Ezek. 20. 25. *s.* not good

33. 15. *s.* of life

Mic. 6. 16. the *s.* of Omri are kept and all

Ex. 15. 26. *his statutes*, Deut. 6. 17. 2 Kings 17. 15. Ps. 18. 22. & 105. 45.

1 Chron. 29. 19. *thy statutes*, Ps. 119. 12, 16, 23, 26, 33, 54, 64, 68, 71, 117.

STAY, Ps. 18. 18. Song 2. 5. Isa. 10. 20. & 26. 3. & 27. 8. & 48. 2. & 50. 10.

STEAD, Gen. 4. 25. & 22. 13.

Gen. 30. 2. Jacob said, am I in God's *s.* who

Job 16. 4. if your soul were in my soul's *s.*

Prov. 11. 8. the wicked cometh in his *s.*

2 Cor. 5. 20. pray you in Christ's *s.* be ye

STEAL, Ex. 20. 15. Lev. 19. 11.

Prov. 6. 30. if he *s.* to satisfy his soul when

30. 9. lest I be poor and *s.* and take name

Jer. 23. 30. I am against the prophets saith the Lord, that *s.* my word

Matt. 6. 19. thieves break through and *s.*

27. 64. disciples come by night and *s.* him away.

Eph. 4. 28. let him that *stole*, steal no more

Prov. 9. 17. *stolen* waters are sweet and

STEADFAST, Job 11. 15.

Ps. 78. 8. spirit was not *s.* with God, 37.

Acts 2. 42. continued *s.* in apostles' doctrine

1 Cor. 15. 58. be ye *s.* immovable always

Heb. 3. 14. hold our confidence *s.* to end

1 Pet. 5. 9. whom resist *s.* in the faith

Col. 2. 5. *steadfastness*, 2 Pet. 3. 17.

STEPS, Ex. 20. 26. Ps. 18. 36.

Ps. 37. 23. *s.* of good men ordered by Lord

31. none of his *s.* shall slide

44. 18. neither our *s.* declined from thy

119. 133. order my *s.* in thy word and let

Prov. 16. 9. but the Lord directeth his *s.*

Jer. 10. 23. it is not in man to direct his *s.*

Rom. 4. 12. also walk in *s.* of that faith

1 Pet. 2. 21. that ye should follow his *s.*

STEWARD, Luke 12. 42. & 16. 2. 1 Cor. 4. 1. Tit. 1. 7. 1 Pet. 4. 10.

STIFF neck, Deut. 31. 27. Jer. 17. 23.

Ex. 32. 9. *stiff-necked* people, 33. 3, 5. & 34. 9. Deut. 9. 6, 13. & 10. 16.

Acts 7. 51—ye do always resist the Holy Ghost

2 Chron. 36. 13. he *stiffened* his neck

STILL, Ex. 15. 16. Ps. 8. 2. & 139. 18.

Ps. 4. 4. be *s.* Jer. 47. 6. Mark 4. 39.

Ps. 46. 10. be *s.* and know that I am God

83. 1. keep not silence, be not *s.* O God

Isa. 30. 7. their strength is to sit *s.*

Rev. 22. 11. be unjust *s.* be filthy *s.* holy *s.*

Ps. 65. 7. *stilleth* noise of the sea, 89. 9.

STING, 1 Cor. 15. 55, 56. Rev. 9. 10.

Prov. 23. 32. at last it *stingeth* like an adder

STINK, Ps. 38. 5. Isa. 3. 24.

STIR up, Num. 24. 9. Job 17. 8.

Ps. 35. 23. *s.* up thyself, awake to my, 80. 2.

78. 38. away and did not *s.* up all his wrath

Song 2. 7. that ye *s.* not up, 3. 5. & 8. 4.

2 Tim. 1. 6. *s.* up gift of God that is in thee

2 Pet. 1. 13. think it meet to *s.* you up by putting

STONE of Israel, Gen. 49. 24.

Ps. 118. 22. *s.* which the builders refused

Isa. 8. 14. a *s.* of stumbling, Rom. 9. 32, 33.

28. 16. a tried *s.* a precious corner *s.* a sure

Dan. 2. 34. *s.* was cut out without hands

Hab. 2. 11. the *s.* shall cry out of the wall

Zech. 3. 9. on one *s.* shall be seven eyes

Matt. 3. 9. of *s.* to raise up children unto Abraham

7. 9. if he ask bread, will he give him *s.*

Luke 19. 40. *s.* would immediately cry out

1 Pet. 2. 4. lively *s.* 6. chief corner *s.* elect, precious

2. 5. as living *s.* are built spiritual house

Ezek. 11. 19. *stony*, Matt. 13. 5.

STORE, 1 Cor. 16. 2. 1 Tim. 6. 19.

Luke 12. 24. *store-house*, Ps. 33. 7.

STORM, Ps. 55. 8. & 83. 15.

Ps. 107. 29. he maketh the *s.* a calm so that

Isa. 4. 6. covert from the *s.* and from rain

25. 4. refuge from the *s.* a shadow from

Nah. 1. 3. Lord hath his way in the *s.*

Mark 4. 37. arose a great *s.* Luke 8. 23.

Ps. 148. 8. *stormy* wind fulfilling his word

STOOP, Job 9. 13. Prov. 12. 25. Mark 1. 7.

STOUT hearted, Ps. 76. 5. Isa. 46. 12.

Isa. 10. 12. punish the fruit of the *s.* heart

Dan. 7. 20. look was more *s.* than his fellow

Mal. 3. 13. your words have been *s.* against me

Isa. 9. 9. say to pride and *stoutness* of heart

STRAIGHT, Josh. 6. 5. Jer. 31. 9.

Ps. 5. 8. make thy way *s.* before my face

Eccl. 1. 15. crooked cannot be made *s.*

7. 13. who can make that *s.* which he

Isa. 40. 3. make *s.* a highway for our God

4. crooked he made *s.* 43. 16. & 45. 2. Luke 3. 5.

Luke 3. 4. way of the Lord, make his paths *s.*

Heb. 12. 13. make *s.* paths for your feet

STRAIN at a gnat and swallow, Matt. 23. 24.

STRAIT, 2 Sam. 24. 14. Job 20. 22. & 36. 16. Isa. 49. 20. Phil. 1. 23.

Matt. 7. 13. enter in at the *s.* gate, 14.

Job 18. 7. steps *straitened*, Prov. 4. 12.

Mic. 2. 7. is the spirit of the Lord *s.*

Luke 12. 50. and how am I *s.* till be accomplished

2 Cor. 6. 12. not *s.* in us, *s.* in your own

5. 26. Heb. 11. 9. 1 Pet. 4. 12. Jude 7.

STRANGE, Ex. 21. 8. & 30. 9. Lev. 10. 1. Ps. 81. 9. Jer. 2. 21. Luke

Job 31. 3. is not a *s.* punishment to workers

Isa. 28. 21. do his *s.* work bring his *s.* act

Hos. 8. 12. law were counted as a *s.* thing

Zeph. 1. 8. such as are clothed with *s.* apparel

Heb. 13. 9. carried about with *s.* doctrines

1 Pet. 4. 4. think it *s.* that you run not

Judg. 11. 2. *strange women*, Prov. 2. 16. & 5. 3, 20. & 6. 24. & 20. 16. & 23. 27. & 27. 13. Ezra. 10. 2, 11.

Gen. 23. 4. *stranger* and sojourner, Ps. 39. 12. & 119. 19. 1 Chron. 29. 15.

Prov. 14. 10. a *s.* doth not meddle with his

Jer. 14. 8. why shouldest thou be as a *s.*

Matt. 25. 35. I was a *s.* and ye took me in

Luke 17. 18. to give God glory save this *s.*

John 10. 5. a *s.* will they not follow but will

Ps. 105. 12. very few and *strangers* in it

146. 9. the Lord preserveth the *s.* he relieveth

Eph. 2. 12. *s.* from the covenant of promise

19. are no more *s.* and foreigners but fellow-citizens

Heb. 11. 13. confessed they were *s.* on earth

13. 2. not forgetful to entertain *s.* for thereby

1 Pet. 2. 11. beseech you as *s.* and pilgrims

STRANGLED, Acts 15. 20, 29. & 21. 25.

Job 7. 15. so that my soul chooseth *strangling*

STREAM, Isa. 30. 33. & 66. 12. Dan. 7. 10. Amos 5. 24. Luke 6. 48.

Ps. 46. 4. *streams*, 126. 4. Song 4. 15. Isa. 30. 25. & 33. 21. & 35. 6.

STREET, Rev. 11. 8. & 21. 21. & 22. 2.

Prov. 1. 20. *streets*, Song 3. 2. Luke 14. 21.

STRENGTH, Gen. 49. 24. Ex. 13. 3.

Ex. 15. 2. the Lord is my *s.* and my song, Ps. 18. 2. & 28. 7. & 118. 14. Isa. 12. 2.

Judg. 5. 21. soul thou hast trodden down *s.*

1 Sam. 2. 9. by *s.* shall no man prevail

15. 29. the *S.* of Israel will not lie nor repent

Job 9. 19. if I speak of *s.* lo, he is strong

12. 13. with him is wisdom and *s.* 16.

Ps. 18. 32. girded me with *s.* 39. unto the battle

27. 1. the Lord is the *s.* of my life; of whom

29. 11. Lord will give *s.* to his people

33. 16. mighty man is not delivered by *s.*

39. 13. spare me that I recover *s.* before I go

46. 1. God is our refuge and *s.* a present help, 81. 1.

68. 34. ascribe *s.* to God

35. God giveth *s.* and power unto his people

73. 26. God is *s.* of my heart, my portion, 43. 2.

84. 5. blessed is the man whose *s.* is in thee

7. they go from *s.* to *s.* every one of them

93. 1. the Lord is clothed with *s.* he hath girded

96. 6. *s.* and beauty in his sanctuary

138. 3. strengthen me with *s.* in soul

140. 7. O God the Lord, the *s.* of my salvation

Prov. 10. 29. way of the Lord is *s.* to the upright

Eccl. 9. 16. said I, wisdom is better than *s.*

10. 10. if iron be blunt, must put more *s.*

Isa. 25. 4. *s.* to the poor and *s.* to the needy

26. 4. in the Lord Jehovah is everlasting *s.*

40. 29. to them that have no might increaseth *s.*

45. 24. in the Lord have I righteousness and *s.*

Joel 3. 16. Lord is the *s.* of children of Israel

Luke 1. 51. he hath shewed *s.* with his arm

Rom. 5. 6. when we were without *s.* in due time

1 Cor. 15. 56. *s.* of sin is the law but thanks

2 Cor. 1. 8. pressed out of measure, above *s.*

Rev. 3. 8. thou hast a little *s.* and hast kept my word

5. 12. worthy is the Lamb to receive *s.*

12. 10. saying now is come salvation and *s.*

17. 13. give their power and *s.* to beast

1 Chron. 16. 11. *his strength*, Ps. 33. 17. Isa. 61. 1. Hos. 7. 9. & 12. 3.

Gen. 49. 24. *in strength*, Job 9. 4. & 36. 5. Ps. 71. 16. & 103. 20. & 147. 10. Isa. 33. 6.

Gen. 49. 3. *my strength*, Ex. 15. 2. 2 Sam. 22. 33. Job 6. 12. Ps. 8. 1, 2. & 19. 14. & 28. 7. & 38. 10. & 43. 2. & 59. 17. & 62. 7. & 71. 9. & 99. 4. & 102. 23. & 118. 14. & 144. 1. Isa. 12. 2. & 27. 5. & 49. 4. 5. Jer. 16. 19. Hab. 3. 19. 2 Cor. 12. 9.

Ps. 37. 39. *their strength*, 89. 17. Prov. 20. 29. Isa. 30. 7. & 40. 31.

Ps. 8. 2. *thy strength*, 86. 16. & 110. 2. Prov. 24. 10. & 31. 3. Isa. 17. 10. & 63. 15. Mark 14. 32. Deut. 33. 25.

Neh. 8. 10. *your strength*, Isa. 23. 14. & 30. 15. Ezek. 24. 21. Lev. 26. 20.

Ps. 20. 2. Lord *strengthen* thee out of Zion

27. 14. wait on the Lord, he shall *s.* your heart

31. 24. of good courage, he shall *s.* your heart

41. 3. the Lord will *s.* him on bed of languishing

119. 28. *s.* thou me according to thy **word**

Isa. 35. 3. *s.* ye the weak hands and confirm

41. 10. I will *s.* thee

54. 2. *s.* thy stakes

Dan. 11. 1. stood to confirm and *s.* him

Zech. 10. 12. I will *s.* them in Lord and they

Luke 22. 32. when converted *s.* thy brethren

1 Pet. 5. 10. God of grace stablish, *s.* you

Rev. 3. 2. *s.* the things that remain that are ready

1 Sam. 23. 16. *strengthened* his hand in God

Ezek. 34. 4. diseased have ye not *s.* neither have

Eph. 3. 16. *s.* with might by his spirit, Col. 1. 11.

2 Tim. 4. 17. the Lord stood with me and *s.* me

Ps. 138. 3. thou *s.* me with *s.* in my soul

104. 15. bread which *strengtheneth* man's heart

Phil. 4. 13. all things through Christ who *s.* me

STRETCH thy hands, Job 11. 13.

Amos 6. 4. *s.* themselves on their couches

Matt. 12. 13. *s.* forth thy hand

John 21. 18. thou shalt *s.* forth thy hands

Gen. 22. 10. *stretched* forth his hand, Isa. 5. 25.

1 Kings 17. 21. *s.* himself upon child three times

1 Chron. 21. 16. drawn sword *s.* over Jerusalem

Isa. 5. 25. hand is *s.* out still, 9. 12. & 10. 4.

Rom. 10. 21. all day I have *s.* forth my hands

Job 15. 25. he *stretcheth* out his hand against

Prov. 31. 20. she *s.* out her hand to the poor

Isa. 40. 22. *s.* out the heavens as a curtain, 42. 5. & 44. 24. & 45. 12. & 51. 13. Jer. 10. 12. & 51. 15. Zech. 12. 1.

STRIFE between me and thee, Gen. 13. 8.

Ps. 80. 6. makest us a *s.* to our neighbours

Prov. 10. 12. hatred stirreth up *s.* but love

15. 18. the wrathful man stirreth up *s.*

16. 28. froward man soweth *s.* and a whisperer

20. 3. it is an honour to cease from *s.*

26. 20. where no tale-bearer, the *s.* ceaseth

28. 25. a proud heart stirreth up *s.* but he

29. 22. an angry man stirreth up *s.* and a furious

30. 33. so the forcing of wrath bringeth *s.*

Isa. 58. 4. behold ye fast for *s.* and debate

Jer. 15. 10. hast borne me a man of *s.* and a man

Luke 22. 24. was a *s.* among them which

Rom. 13. 13. let us walk not in *s.* and envying

1 Cor. 3. 3. among you envying, *s.* and divisions

Gal. 5. 20. works of flesh are wrath, *s.* sedition

Phil. 1. 15. preach Christ of *s.* and envy

2. 3. let nothing be done through *s.* and vain glory

1 Tim. 6. 4. whereof cometh envy, *s.* railing

2 Tim. 2. 23. gender *s.* 2 Cor. 12. 20.

James 3. 14. bitter envying and *s.* 16.

STRIKE hands, Job 17. 3. Prov. 6. 1.

Prov. 17. 26. to *s.* princes for equity

Isa. 1. 5. why be *striken* any more, Jer. 5. 3.

Isa. 53. 4. did esteem him *s.* of God

1 Tim. 3. 3. a bishop, no *striker*, Tit. 1. 7.

STRIPES, Isa. 53. 5. 1 Pet. 2. 24.

Prov. 17. 10. & 20. 30. Luke 12. 47, 48.

STRIVE, Ex. 21. 18. 22. Job 33. 13.

Gen. 6. 3. Spirit shall not always *s.*

Prov. 8. 30. *s.* not without cause

Hos. 4. let no man *s.* nor reprove

Matt. 12. 19. he shall not *s.* nor cry

Luke 13. 24. *s.* to enter in at strait gate

2 Tim. 2. 24. the servant of the Lord must not *s.*

Isa. 45. 9. that *striveth* with his maker

Phil. 1. 27. *striving* together for faith of

Heb. 12. 4. resisted unto blood *s.* against sin

STRONG this day, Josh. 14. 11.

Ps. 24. 8. Lord is *s.* and mighty in battle

30. 7. made mountain to stand *s.*

31. 2. be thou my *s.* rock

71. 7. thou art my *s.* refuge, 3.

Prov. 10. 15. rich man's wealth is his *s.* city

---

11. 16. *s.* men retain riches

14. 26. fear of Lord is *s.* confidence

18. 10. name of Lord is a *s.* tower

24. 5. a wise man is *s.* and increaseth

Eccl. 9. 11. battle is not to the *s.*

12. 3. *s.* men.

Song 8. 6. love is *s.* as death

Isa. 1. 31. *s.* shall be as tow and burn

26. 1. we have a *s.* city, 60. 22.

35. 4. be *s.* fear not, behold your God

53. 12. shall divide the spoil with *s.*

Jer. 50. 34. their Redeemer is *s.* 18. 8.

Joel 3. 10. let the weak say I am *s.*

Luke 11. 21. *s.* man armed keepeth the house, 22.

Rom. 4. 20. *s.* in faith, giving glory to God

15. 1. we that are *s.* ought to bear the infirmities of the weak

2 Cor. 12. 10. when I am weak then am I *s.*

Heb. 11. 34. out of weakness made *s.*

1 John 2. 14. because ye are *s.* and the word of God

Isa. 35. 4. be *strong*, Hag. 2. 4. 1 Cor. 16. 13. Eph. 6. 10. 2 Tim. 2. 1.

1 Cor. 1. 25. *stronger* than men, 10. 22.

Job 17. 9. clean hands shall be *s.* and *s.*

Jer. 20. 7. thou art *s.* than I

STUBBLE, Job 13. 25. and 21. 18. Ps. 83. 13. Isa. 33. 11. Mal. 4. 1. 1 Cor. 3. 12.

STUBBORN, Deut. 21. 18. Ps. 78. 8.

1 Sam. 15. 23. *stubbornness*, Deut. 9. 27.

STUDY, Eccl. 12. 12. 1 Thes. 4. 11. 2 Tim. 2. 15. Prov. 15. 28. & 24. 2.

STUMBLE, foot shall not, Prov. 3. 23.

Prov. 4. 12. when thou runnest, shalt not *s.*

19. wicked know not at what they *s.*

Isa. 5. 27. none shall be weary nor *s.*

8. 15. many shall *s.* and fall and be taken

28. 7. they err in vision, they *s.* in judgment

Mal. 2. 8. caused many to *s.* at the law

1 Pet. 2. 8. which *s.* at the word

Rom. 9. 32. they *stumbled* at that stumbling-stone

John 11. 9. walk in the day he *stumbleth* not

Rom. 14. 21. whereby thy brother *s.*

Isa. 8. 14. *stumbling*, 1 John 2. 10.

Lev. 19. 14. *stumbling-block*, Isa. 8. 14. & 57. 14. Jer. 6. 21. Ezek. 3. 20. & 7. 19. & 14. 3, 4, 7. Rom. 9. 32, 33. & 11. 9. & 14. 13. 1 Cor. 1. 23. & 8. 9. Rev. 2. 14.

SUBDUE our iniquities, Mic. 7. 19.

Ps. 81. 14. I would soon *s.* their enemies

Phil. 3. 21. able to *s.* all things to himself

Heb. 11. 33. through faith *subdued* kingdoms

SUBJECT, devils are, Luke 10. 17, 20.

Rom. 8. 7. not *s.* to law of God

20. *s.* to vanity

13. 1. every soul be *s.* to higher powers, 5.

1 Cor. 14. 32. spirit of prophets *s.* to prophets

15. 28. Son shall be *s.* to him that put

Eph. 5. 24. as church is *s.* to Christ

Tit. 3. 1. to be *s.* to principalities and powers

Heb. 2. 15. all their lifetime *s.* to bondage

Jas. 5. 17. Elias, a man *s.* to like passions

1 Pet. 2. 18. servants be *s.* to your masters

3. 22. angels and powers made *s.* to him

5. 5. all ye be *s.* one to another

1 Cor. 9. 27. *subjection,* 1 Tim. 2. 11. & 3. 4. Heb. 2. 5, 8. & 12. 9. 1 Pet. 3. 1, 5.

SUBMIT, Gen. 16. 9. Ps. 18. 44. & 66. 3. & 68. 30. & 81. 15.

1 Cor. 16. 16. *submit yourselves,* Eph. 5. 21, 22. Col. 3. 18. Heb. 13. 17. James 4. 7. 1 Pet. 2. 13. & 5. 5.

Rom. 10. 3. have not *submitted* to righteousness

SUBSCRIBE, Isa. 44. 5. Jer. 32. 44.

SUBSTANCE, Gen. 7. 4. & 15. 14. Deut. 33. 11. bless, Lord, his *s.*

Job 30. 22. thou dissolvest my *s.*

Ps. 139. 15. my *s.* was not hid from thee, 16.

Prov. 3. 9. honour the Lord with thy *s.*

8. 21. cause those that love me to inherit *s.*

Hos. 12. 8. I have found me out *s.*

Luke 8. 3. ministered to him of *s.*

Heb. 10. 34. in heaven a more enduring *s.*

11. 1. faith is the *s.* of things hoped for

SUBTIL, Gen. 3. 1. Prov. 7. 10.

Acts 13. 10. *subtilty,* 2 Cor. 11. 3. Prov. 1. 4.

SUBVERT, Lam. 3. 36. Tit. 1. 11. & 3. 11.

Acts 13. 24. *subverting* souls, 2 Tim. 2. 14.

SUCK, Gen. 21. 7. Deut. 32. 13. & 33. 19.

Job 20. 16. *s.* poison of asps and vipers

Isa. 60. 16. *s.* milk of Gentiles, and breasts of kings

66. 11. *s.* and be satisfied, 12.

Matt. 24. 19. wo to them that give *s.* in those days

Luke 23. 29. blessed are paps which never gave *s.*

11. 27. blessed are paps thou hast *sucked*

Isa. 11. 8. *sucking* child, 49. 15.

Ps. 8. 2. *suckling,* Lam. 2. 11. & 4. 4.

SUDDEN, Prov. 3. 25. 1 Thes. 5. 3.

SUFFER, Ex. 12. 23. Lev. 19. 17.

Ps. 55. 22. never *s.* righteous to be moved

89. 33. nor *s.* my faithfulness to fail

121. 3. not *s.* thy foot to be moved

Prov. 10. 3. not *s.* soul of righteous to famish

Matt. 16. 21. he must *s.* many things

17. 17. how long shall I *s.* you

19. 14. *s.* little children to come unto me

Rom. 8. 17. if so be that we *s.* with him

1 Cor. 4. 12. being persecuted, we *s.* it

10. 13. God will not *s.* you to be tempted

Phil. 1. 29. but also to *s.* for his sake

2 Tim. 2. 12. if we *s.* we shall reign

Heb. 11. 25. choosing rather to *s.* affliction

13. 3. remember them who *s.* adversity

22. *s.* the word of exhortation

1 Pet. 4. 15. none *s.* as a murderer

19. them that *s.* according to the will of God

Ps. 105. 14. he *suffered* no man to do them wrong

Acts 14. 16. *s.* all to walk in his own ways

16. 7. the Spirit *s.* them not

Phil. 3. 8. for whom I *s.* loss of all things

Heb. 5. 8. learned obedience by the things he *s.*

1 Pet. 2. 21. *s.* for us, leaving us an example

3. 18. Christ hath *s.* once for sins

5. 10. after ye have *s.* a while

Matt. 11. 12. *suffereth,* 1 Cor. 13. 4.

Rom. 8. 18. *sufferings,* 2 Cor. 1. 5, 6.

Phil. 3. 10. Col. 1. 24. Heb. 2. 10. 1 Pet. 1. 11. & 4. 13. & 5. 1.

SUFFICE, 1 Pet. 4. 3. John 14. 8.

Matt. 6. 34. *sufficient* to the day is the evil

2 Cor. 2. 16. who is *s.* for these things

3. 5. we are not *s.* of ourselves

12. 9. my grace is *s.* for thee

Job 20. 22. *sufficiency,* 2 Cor. 3. 5. & 9. 8.

SUM, Ps. 139. 17. Ezek. 28. 12. Heb. 8. 1.

SUMMER and winter does not cease, Gen. 8. 22.

Ps. 74. 17. hast made *s.* and winter

Prov. 6. 8. provideth her meat in the *s.*

10. 5. that gathereth in *s.* is a wise son

Isa. 18. 6. fowls shall *s.* and winter winter

Jer. 8. 20. harvest past and *s.* ended

Zech. 14. 8. living waters in *s.* and winter

SUMPTUOUSLY fared, Luke 16. 19.

SUN, stand thou still, Josh. 10. 12.

Ps. 19. 4. he set a tabernacle for the *s.*

74. 16. prepared the light and the *s.*

104. 19. the *s.* knoweth his going down

121. 6. *s.* not smite thee by day, Isa. 49. 10.

Ps. 136. 8. *s.* to rule the day, Gen. 1. 16.

Eccl. 12. 2. while *s.* or stars be not darkened

Song 1. 6. because the *s.* hath looked upon me

6. 10. fair as the moon, clear as the *s.*

Isa. 30. 26. light of the *s.* shall be seven-fold

38. 8. the *s.* returned ten degrees

66. 19. the *s.* no more thy light by day

20. thy *s.* shall no more go down

Jer. 31. 35. giveth the *s.* for a light by day

Mal. 4. 2. shall the S. of righteousness arise

Matt. 5. 45. his *s.* to rise on evil and good

Matt. 13. 43. shine as the *s.* in the kingdom

1 Cor. 15. 41. there is one glory of the *s.*

Eph. 4. 26. let not the *s.* go down on thy wrath

Rev. 10. 1. his face as *s.* 1. 16. Matt. 17. 2.

Rev. 7. 16. neither the *s.* light on them

21. 23. city had no need of the *s.* 22. 5.

SUPERFLUITY of naughtiness, James 1. 21.

SUPERSTITION, Acts 25. 19. & 17. 22.

SUP, Luke 17. 8. Rev. 3. 20. Hab. 1. 9.

Luke 14. 16. certain man made a great *supper*

1 Cor. 11. 20. to eat Lord's *s.* Luke 22. 20.

Rev. 19. 9. to marriage *s.*

17. *s.* of great God

SUPPLICATION, 1 Kings 8. 28. & 9. 3. Job. 8. 5. & 9. 15. Ps. 6. 9. & 30. 8. 3. 55. 1. & 142. 1. & 119. 170. Dan. 6. 11. & 9. 20. Hos. 12. 4. Zech. 12. 10. Eph. 6. 18. Phil. 4. 6. 1 Tim. 2. 1. & 5. 5. Heb. 5. 7.

SUPPLY spirit of Jesus Christ, Phil. 1. 19.

Phil. 4. 19. my God shall *s.* all your need

2 Cor. 9. 12. *supplieth,* Eph. 4. 16.

SUPPORT the weak, Acts 20. 35. 1 Thes. 5. 14.

SUPREME, 1 Pet. 2. 13.

SURE, Gen. 23. 17. 1 Sam. 25. 28.

2 Sam. 23. 5. ordered in all things and *s.*

Neh. 9. 38. we make a *s.* covenant

Ps. 19. 7. testimony of the Lord is *s.* making wise

93. 5. thy testimonies are very *s.*

111. 7. all his commandments are very *s.*

Prov. 11. 15. that hateth suretiship is *s.*

18. righteousness shall be a *s.* reward

Isa. 22. 23, 25. *s.* place

28. 16. *s.* foundation

32. 18. *s.* dwellings

33. 16. water shall be *s.*

55. 3. *s.* mercies of David, Acts 13. 34.

John 6. 69. we believe and are *s.* that thou art the Christ, the Son of the living God

Rom. 4. 16. promise might be *s.* to all the

2 Tim. 2. 19. the foundation of God standeth *s.*

2 Pet. 1. 10. make calling and election *s.*

19. have more *s.* word of prophecy

SURETY for thy servant, Ps. 119. 122.

Heb. 7. 22. Jesus made *s.* of better testament

SURFEITING and drunkenness, Luke 21. 34.

SURPRISED the hypocrites, Isa. 33. 14.

SUSTAIN, Ps. 55. 22. Prov. 18. 14.

Ps. 3. 5. *sustained,* Isa. 59. 16.

SWALLOW, Ps. 84. 3. Jer. 8. 7.

Isa. 25. 8. he will *s.* up to death in victory

Matt. 23. 24. strain at a gnat, and *s.* a camel

Ex. 15. 12. earth *swallowed* them, Num. 16. 32.

Ps. 124. 3. they had *s.* us up quick

2 Cor. 2. 7. be *s.* up with overmuch sorrow

5. 4. mortality be *s.* up of life

SWEAR, Num. 30. 2. Deut. 6. 13.

Isa. 45. 23. to me every tongue shall *s.*

65. 16. shall *s.* by the God of truth

Jer. 4. 2. shalt *s.* Lord liveth in truth, 12. 16.

Zeph. 1. 5. *s.* by Lord, and *s.* by Malcham

Matt. 5. 34. *s.* not at all, James 5. 12.

Ps. 15. 4. *sweareth* to his own hurt

Eccl. 9. 2. that *s.* as he that feareth an oath

Zech. 5. 3. everyone that *s.* shall be cut off

Jer. 23. 10. because of *swearing* the land mourneth

Hos. 4. 2. by *s.* and lying they break out

10 4. *s.* falsely in making a covenant

Mal. 3. 5. I will be a witness against false *s.*

SWEAT, Gen. 3. 19. Luke 22. 44.

SWEET, Job 20. 12. Ps. 55. 14.

Ps. 104. 34. meditation of him shall be *s.*

119. 103. how *s.* thy words to my taste

Prov. 3. 24. thy sleep shall be *s.* Jer. 31. 26.

Prov. 9. 17. stolen waters are *s.* 20. 17.

13. 19. desire accomplished is *s.* to the soul

27. 7. to hungry every bitter thing is *s.*

Eccl. 5. 12. sleep of labouring man is *s.*

11. 7. truly the light is *s.*

Song 2. 3. his fruit was *s.* to my taste

14. *s.* is thy voice and countenance

5. 16. his mouth is most *s.*

Isa. 5. 20 put bitter for *s.* and *s.* for

Phil. 4. 18. odour of a *s.* smell

Rev. 10. 9. in thy mouth *s.* as honey

Ps. 19. 10. *sweeter* than honey, 119. 103.

Judg. 14. 14. *sweetness,* Prov. 16. 21. & 27. 9.

SWELLING, Jer. 12. 5. 2 Pet. 2. 18.

SWIFT, Deut. 28. 49. Job 9. 26.

Eccl. 9. 11. the race is not to the *s.*

Rom. 3. 15. feet are *s.* to shed blood Prov. 6. 18.

James 1. 19. *s.* to hear, slow to speak

2 Pet. 2. 1. bring on themselves *s.* destruction

Job 7. 6. days *swifter* than a shuttle, 9. 25.

Ps. 147. 15. *swiftly,* Joel 3. 4.

SWIM, 2 Kings, 6. 6. Ps. 6. 6. Ezek. 47. 5.

SWORD, Ex. 32. 27. Lev. 26. 24.

Gen. 3. 24. cherubims and a flaming *s.*

Deut. 33. 29. *s.* of thy excellency

Judg. 7. 20. *s.* of the Lord and of Gideon

2 Sam. 12. 10. *s.* shall never depart from

Ps. 17. 13. from the wicked which is thy *s.*

149. 6. two-edged *s.* in their hands

Song 3. 8. every man hath his *s.* on his thigh

Jer. 9. 16. I will send a *s.* after them

15. 2. such as are for *s.* to the *s.* 43. 11.

Ezek. 21. 13. what if *s.* contemn the rod

Zech. 11. 17. the *s.* shall be upon his arm

13. 7. awake, O *s.* against my shepherd

Matt. 10. 34. came not to send peace but *s.*

Luke 2. 35. a *s.* shall pierce through thy soul

Rom. 13. 4. he beareth not the *s.* in vain

Eph. 6. 17. *s.* of the Spirit, which is the word of God

Heb. 4. 12. word is sharper than any two-edged *s.*

Rev. 1. 16. went a sharp two-edged *s.* 19. 15.

Ps. 55. 21. *swords,* 59. 7. Prov. 30. 14. Isa. 2. 4. Ezek. 32. 27. Joel 3. 10.

SWORN by myself, Gen. 22. 16.

Ps. 24. 4. that hath not *s.* deceitfully

119. 106. I have *s.* and will perform it

SYNAGOGUE, Ps. 74. 8. Matt. 6. 5. & 23. 6. Luke 7. 5. John 9. 22. Acts 15. 21. Rev. 2. 9. & 3. 9.

T

TABERNACLE, Ex. 26. 1.

Job 5. 24. thy *t.* shall be in peace

Ps. 15. 1. who shall abide in thy *t.*

27. 5. in the secret of his *t.* shall hide me

Prov. 14. 11. *t.* of the upright shall flourish

Isa. 33. 20. a *t.* shall not be taken down

Amos 9. 11. raise up *t.* of David, Acts 15. 16.

2 Cor. 5. 1. if our earthly house of this *t.*

4. we that are in this *t.* do groan

Heb. 8. 2. minister of the true *t.*

2 Pet. 1. 13. I am in this *t.*

14. put off my *t.*

Rev. 21. 3. the *t.* of God is with men

Job 12. 6. *tabernacles* of robbers prosper

Ps. 84. 1. how amiable are thy *t.*

118. 15. salvation is in the *t.* of the righteous

Heb. 11. 9. dwell in *t.* with Isaac and

TABLE, Ex. 25. 23. Job 36. 16.
Ps. 23. 5. preparest a *t.* before me in the presence
69. 22. let their *t.* become a snare
128. 3. olive plants round about thy *t.*
Prov. 3. 3. write them on the *t.* of thy heart
Song 1. 12. while the king sitteth at his *t.*
Jer. 17. 1. sin is graven on *t.* of heart
Mal. 1. 7. the *t.* of the Lord is contemptible
Matt. 15. 27. crumbs fall from the master's *t.*
1 Cor. 19. 21. partakers of Lord's *t.* and *t.* of devils
Deut. 10. 4. *tables,* 5. Heb. 9. 4. 2 Chron. 4. 8, 19. Isa. 28. 8. Ezek. 40. 41.
Hab. 2. 2. write and make it plain upon *t.*
Acts 6. 2. leave word of God and serve *t.*
2 Cor. 3. 3. not in *t.* of stone, but fleshly *t.*
TAKE you for a people, Ex. 6. 7.
Ex. 20. 7. not *t.* name of the Lord in vain
34. 9. *t.* us for thine inheritance
Ps. 27. 13. the Lord will *t.* me up
51. 11. *t.* not thy holy Spirit from me
116. 12. I will *t.* cup of salvation and call
119. 43. *t.* not the word of truth out of my mouth
Hos. 14. 2. *t.* with your words; say *t.* away
Matt. 16. 24. *t.* up his cross and follow me
18. 16. *t.* with thee one or two more
23. would *t.* account of servants
20. 14. *t.* that is thine and go thy way
26. 26. said *t.* eat, this is my body, 1 Cor. 11. 24.
Luke 12. 19. *t.* thine ease, eat, drink and be merry
Eph. 6. 13. *t.* the whole armor of God, 17.
Rev. 3. 11. that no man *t.* thy crown
Ex. 23. 25. *take away,* Josh. 7. 13.
2 Sam. 24. 10. 1 Chron. 17. 13. Job 7. 21. & 32. 22. & 36. 1. Ps. 58. 9. Isa. 58. 9. Jer. 15. 15. Hos. 1. 6. & 4. 11. & 14. 2. Amos 4. 2. Mal. 2. 3. Luke 17. 31. John 1. 29. 1 John 3. 5. Rev 22. 19.
Deut. 32. 41. *take hold,* Ps. 69. 24. Isa. 27. 5. & 56. 4. & 64. 7. Zech. 1. 6.
Ps. 83. 3. *taken* crafty counsel against thy
119. 111. thy testimony have I *t.*
Isa. 53. 8. he was *t.* from prison and
Lam. 4. 20. the anointed was *t.* in
Matt. 21. 43. kingdom of God *t.* from
24. 40 one shall be *t.* the other left
Mark 4. 25. be *t.* that which he hath
Acts 1. 9. *t.* up a cloud received, 1. 22.
2 Tim. 2. 26. *t.* captive by him
Isa. 6. 7. thy iniquity is *taken away*
16. 10. gladness is—
57. 1. merciful men are—
Luke 10. 42. good part not be—from
2 Cor. 3. 16. when it shall turn to Lord, veil—
Ps. 40. 12. my iniquities *taken hold* of me
119. 143. trouble and anguish have —of me
Prov. 1. 19. *taketh away,* John 1.

29. & 10. 18. & 15. 2. *taketh from,* 16. 22.
Ps. 119. 9. by *taking* heed thereto according
Matt. 6. 27. who by *t.* thought can add one
Rom. 7. 8. sin *t.* occasion deceived, 11.
Eph. 6. 16 above all *t.* the shield of faith
TALE, Ps. 90. 9. Ezek. 22. 29. Luke 24. 11.
Lev. 19. 16. *tale-bearer,* Prov. 11. 13. & 18. 8. & 20. 19. & 26. 20, 22.
TALENTS, Matt. 18. 24. & 25. 15, 25.
TALK of them when thou sittest, Deut. 6. 7.
1 Sam. 2. 3. *t.* no more so exceeding proudly
Job 13. 7. and *t.* deceitfully for him
Ps. 71. 24. my tongue shall *t.* righteousness
77. 12. I will *t.* of thy doings
105. 2. *t.* ye of all his wondrous works
Ps. 145. 11. speak of glory and *t.* of thy power
Jer. 12. 1. let me *t.* with thee of judgment
John 14. 30. I will not *t.* much with you
Ps. 37. 30. his tongue *talkest* of judgment
Eph. 5. 4. filthiness nor foolish *talking*
Tit. 1. 10. unruly and vain *talkers* and
TAME, Mark 5. 4. James 3. 7, 8.
TARRY, 1 Chron. 19. 5. 2 Kings 14. 10.
Ps. 101. 7. liar shall not *t.* in my sight
Prov. 23. 20. that *t.* long at wine
Isa. 46. 13. my salvation shall not *t.*
Jer. 14. 8. that turneth aside to *t.* for a night
Hab. 2. 3. though it *t.* wait for it
Matt. 26. 38. *t.* ye here and watch with me
John 21. 22. if I will that he *t.* till I come
1 Cor. 11. 33. come to eat *t.* for one another
Ps. 68. 12. she that *tarried* at home divided
Matt. 25. 5. while the bridegroom *t.* all slumbered
Luke 2. 43. child Jesus *t.* behind in Jerusalem
Acts 22. 16. why *tarriest* thou, arise and be baptized
Ps. 40. 17. make no *tarrying,* 70. 5.
TASTE, Ex, 16. 31. 1 Sam. 14. 43.
Job 6. 6. is any *t.* in white of an egg
Ps. 34. 8. O *t.* and see that the Lord is good
119. 103. sweet are thy words to *t.*
Song 2. 3. his fruit was sweet to *t.*
Jer. 48. 11. his *t.* remained in him
Matt. 16. 28. shall not *t.* of death till they see
Luke 14. 24. bidden shall *t.* of my supper
John 8. 52. keep my saving, never *t.* death
Col. 2. 21. touch not, *t.* not, handle not
Heb. 2. 9. that he should *t.* death for every man
6. 4. *t.* heavenly gift
5. *t.* good word of God
1 Pet. 2. 3. if ye have *tasted* that Lord is gracious
TATTLERS, Tim. 5. 13.
TEACH, Ex. 4. 12. Lev. 10. 11.
Deut. 4. 9. *t.* them thy sons, 6. 7. & 11. 19.
23. 10. shall *t.* Jacob thy judgments and Israel

1 Sam. 12. 23. *t.* good ways, 1 Kings 8. 36.
2 Chron. 17. 7. to *t.* in the cities of Judah
Job 21. 22. shall any *t.* God
Ps. 25. 8. *t.* sinners in the way
9. the meek will be *t.* his way
34. 11. I will *t.* you the fear of Lord, 32. 8.
51. 13. I will *t.* transgressors thy way
90. 12. so *t.* us to number our days that
Isa. 2. 3. he will *t.* us of his ways, Mic. 4. 2.
Jer: 31. 34. *t.* no more every man his neighbour
Matt. 28. 19. go and *t.* all nations baptizing
John 9. 34. wast born in sins, dost thou *t.* us
14. 26. Holy Ghost shall *t.* you all things
1 Cor. 4. 17. as I *t.* in every church
1 Tit. 2. 12. I suffer not a woman to *t.*
1 Tim. 3. 2. given to hospitality, apt to *t.*
2 Tim 2. 2. faithful men able to *t.* others
Heb. 5. 12. have need that one *t.* you
1 John 2. 27. need not that any man *t.*
Job 34. 32. what I see not, *teach me*
Ps. 25. 4.—thy paths, 5. & 27. 11.—thy way, 86. 11. & 119. 12.—thy statutes, 26. 64, 66, 68, 124, 125.—good judgment, 108.—thy judgments, 143. 10—to do thy will
2 Chron. 32. 22. *taught* good knowledge of the Lord
Ps. 71. 17. thou hast *t.* me from my youth
119. 171. when thou hast *t.* me thy statutes
Eccl. 12. 9. he *t.* people knowledge
Isa. 29. 13. fear of me *t.* by precepts of men
54. 13. thy children shall be *t.* of Lord
John 6. 45. they shall be all *t.* of God
Acts 20. 20. *t.* you publicly and from
Gal. 6. 6. let him that is *t.* in word communicate
1 Thes. 4. 9. yourselves are *t.* of God
Ps. 94. 12. *teachest* him out of thy law
Matt. 22. 16. *t.* the way of God in truth
Rom. 2. 21. *t.* another, *t.* not thyself
Job 36. 22. who *teacheth* like him
35. 11. who *t.* us more than beasts of the earth
Ps. 18. 34. *t.* my hands to war, 144. 1.
94. 10. he that *t.* man knowledge shall
Isa. 48. 17. Lord thy God, *t.* thee to profit
1 Cor. 2. 13. words which man's wisdom *t.* but which the Holy Ghost *t.*
1 John 2. 27. same anointing *t.* you of all things
Hab. 2. 18. *teacher,* John 3. 2. Rom. 2. 20. 1 Tim. 2. 7. 2 Tim. 1. 11.
Ps. 119. 99. *teachers,* Isa. 30. 20.
2 Tim. 4. 3. heap to themselves *t.* having
Tit. 2. 3. be *t.* of good things
Heb. 5. 12. ought to be *t.* ye have need
2 Chron. 15. 3. without a *teaching* priest
Matt. 15. 9. *t.* for doctrines the commandments of men
28. 20. *t.* them to observe all things whatsoever
Col. 1. 28. *t.* every man in all wisdom
3. 16. *t.* and admonishing one
Tit. 1. 12. *t.* us that denying ungodliness

TEAR, Ps. 50. 22. Hos. 5. 14. Job 16. 9.
TEARS, Job 16. 20. Ps. 6. 6. Isa. 38. 5.
Ps. 56. 8. put my *t.* in thy bottle, 39. 12.
80. 5. feedest them with the bread of *t.*
126. 5. they that sow in *t.* shall reap in
Isa. 25. 8. wipe away all *t.* from off all
Jer. 9. 1. my eyes were a fountain of *t.*
Luke 7. 38. to wash his feet with *t.*
Acts 20. 19. many *t.* and temptations, 31.
2 Cor. 2. 4. of anguish wrote with many *t.*
2 Tim. 1. 4. being mindful of thy *t.*
Heb. 5. 7. with strong crying and *t.* unto
12. 17. though he sought it carefully with *t.*
Rev. 7. 17. wipe all *t.* from their eyes, 21. 4.
TEATS, Isa. 32. 12. Ezek. 23. 3, 21.
TEETH white with milk, Gen. 49. 12.
Job 4. 10. *t.* broken, Ps. 3. 7. & 58. 6.
Song 4. 2. *t.* are like a flock of sheep, 6. 6.
Jer. 31. 29. children's *t.* set on edge, Ezek. 18. 2.
Amos 4. 6. cleanness of *t.* in all your cities
Matt. 8. 12. weeping and gnashing of *t.* 22. 13. & 24. 51. & 25. 30. Ps. 112. 10.
TELL it not in Gath, 2 Sam. 1. 20.
Ps. 48. 13. *t.* it to the generation following
Prov. 30. 4. what is his name, if thou canst *t.*
Matt. 8. 4. see thou *t.* no man, 16. 20.
18. 15. *t.* him his fault
17. *t.* the church
John 3. 8. not *t.* whence it cometh or whither
4. 25. when he is come he will *t.* you all things
8. 14. ye cannot *t.* whence I came and whither
2 Cor. 12. 2. in or out of body I cannot *t.*
Gal. 4. 16. enemy because I *t.* you the truth
Phil. 3. 18. and now *t.* you even weeping
Ps. 56. 8. *tellest* all my wanderings
TEMPERANCE, Acts 24. 25. Gal. 5. 23. 2 Pet. 1. 6.
1 Cor. 9. 25. *temperate,* Tit. 1. 8. & 2. 2.
TEMPLE, 1 Sam. 1. 9. 1 Kings 6. 5.
Ps. 29. 9. in his *t.* doth every one speak
Jer. 7. 4. *t.* of the Lord, *t.* of Lord are
Mal. 3. 1. shall suddenly come to his *t.*
Matt. 12. 6. one greater than the *t.* is here
John 2. 19. destroy this *t.* and in three days I will raise it up
21. he spake of the *t.* of his body
1 Cor. 3. 16. ye are the *t.* of God, 17.
6. 19. your body is the *t.* of the Holy Ghost
9. 13. live of the things of the *t.*
2 Cor. 6. 16. what agreement hath the *t.* of God with idols, ye are *t.* of the living God
Rev. 7. 15. serve him day and night in his *t.*
11. 19. *t.* of God was opened in heaven
21. 22. saw no *t.* the Lord God and the Lamb are *t.*
Song 4. 3. thy *temples,* 6. 7.
Acts 7. 48. Most High dwelleth not in *t.*
TEMPORAL, 2 Cor. 4. 18.

TEMPT Abraham, God did, Gen. 22. 1.

Ex. 17. 2. wherefore do ye *t.* the Lord

Deut. 6. 16. ye shall not *t.* the Lord your God

Isa. 7. 12. will not ask, nor will I *t.* Lord

Mal. 3. 15. they that *t.* God are even delivered

Matt. 4. 7. thou shalt not *t.* the Lord thy God

22. 18. why *t.* ye me, show me a penny

Acts 5. 9. have agreed together to *t.* the Spirit

15. 10. why *t.* ye God to put a yoke on

1 Cor. 7. 5. that Satan *t.* you not for your

10. 9. neither let us *t.* Christ as some

Ex. 17. 7. because they *tempted* the Lord

Num. 14. 22. *t.* me now ten times

Ps. 78. 18. *t.* God in their heart, 106. 14.

41. yea they turned back and *t.* God

56. *t.* and provoked the most high God

95. 9. when your fathers *t.* me, Heb. 3. 9.

Matt. 4. 1. in wilderness, to be *t.* of the devil

Luke 10. 25. certain lawyer *t.* him saying

1 Cor. 10. 13. not suffer you to be *t.* above

Gal. 6. 1. considering thyself lest thou also be *t.*

1 Thes. 3. 5. the tempter have *t.* you and

Heb. 2. 18. he is able to succour them that are *t.*

4. 15. in all points *t.* as we are yet without

11. 37. sawn asunder, were *t.* slain with

James 1. 13. let no man say when he is *t.* I am *t.* of God; for God cannot be *t.*

14. every man is *t.* when drawn away

Matt. 16. 1. *tempting* him 19. 3. & 22. 35. Luke 11. 16. John 8. 6.

Ps. 95. 8. as in day of *temptation* in the

Matt. 6. 13. lead us not into *t.* Luke 11. 4.

Luke 4. 13. the devil had ended all *t.*

8. 13. in time of *t.* fall away

1 Cor. 10. 13. no *t.* taken you, but as is common; but will with the *t.* make a way to escape

Gal. 4. 14. my *t.* which was in flesh despised not

1 Tim. 6. 9. will be rich fall into *t.* and snare

Heb. 3. 8. in day of *t.* in wilderness

James 1. 12. blessed is he that endureth *t.*

Rev. 3. 10. keep thee from the hour of *t.*

Deut. 4. 34. *temptations,* 7. 19. Luke 22. 28. Acts 20. 19. James 1. 2. 1 Pet. 1. 6. 2 Pet. 2. 9.

Matt. 4. 3. *tempter,* 1 Thes. 3. 5.

TENDER, thy heart was, 2 Kings 22. 19. Eph. 4. 32.

Luke 1. 78. *t.* mercy, James 5. 11.

TENDETH, Prov. 10. 16. & 11. 19. & 19. 23. & 11. 24. & 14. 23. & 21. 5.

TENTS of Shem, dwell in, Gen. 9. 27.

Num. 24. 5. how goodly are thy *t.* O Jacob

1 Kings 12. 16. to your *t.* O Israel, 2 Sam. 20. 1.

Ps. 84. 10. dwell in *t.* of wickedness

120. 5. who is me that I dwell in the *t.* of Kedar

Song 1. 8. feed kids beside the shepherd's *t.*

TERRESTRIAL, 1 Cor. 15. 40.

TERRIBLE, Ex. 34. 10. Deut. 1. 19. Deut. 7. 21. a mighty God and *t.* 10. 17. Neh. 1. 5. & 4. 14. 9. 32. Jer. 20. 11.

Deut. 10. 21. done *t.* things, 2 Sam. 7. 23.

Job 37. 22. with God is *t.* majesty

Ps. 45. 4. thy right hand shall teach *t.* things

47. 2. the Lord most high is *t.* 68. 35.

65. 5. by *t.* things wilt thou answer

66. 3. how *t.* art thou in thy works

5. God is *t.* in his doings toward men

76. 12. he is *t.* to kings of the earth

99. 3. praise thy great and *t.* name

Song 6. 4. *t.* as an army with banners

Isa. 64. 3. *t.* things we looked not for

Joel 2. 11. day of the Lord is *t.* 31. Zeph. 2. 11.

Heb. 12. 21. so *t.* was the sight that Moses said

1 Chron. 17. 21. *terribleness,* Jer. 49. 16.

Job 7. 14. *terrifiest,* Phil. 1. 28.

TERROR, Gen. 35. 5. Deut. 32. 25. Job 31. 23. destruction from God was a *t.*

Isa. 33. 18. thy heart shall meditate *t.*

Jer. 17. 17. be not a *t.* unto me

20. 4. a *t.* to thyself, and all, Ezek. 26. 21.

Rom. 13. 3. rulers are not a *t.* to good work, but to evil

2 Cor. 5. 11. knowing *t.* of the Lord, we persuade men

1 Pet. 3. 14. be not afraid of their *t.*

Job 6. 4. *terrors,* 18. 11, 14. & 27. 20. Ps. 55. 4. & 73. 19. & 88. 15, 16.

TESTAMENT, Matt. 26. 28. Luke 22. 20. 1 Cor. 11. 25. 2 Cor. 3. 6, 14. Gal. 3. 15. Heb. 7. 22. & 9. 15, 16, 17, 18. Rev. 11. 19.

Heb. 9. 16. death of the *testater*

17. while the *t.* liveth

TESTIFY, Deut. 8. 19. & 32. 46. Neh. 9. 26, 34. Ps. 50. 7. & 81. 8.

Num. 35. 30. one witness shall not *t.*

Isa. 59. 12. our sins *t.* against us,

Hos. 5. 5. pride of Israel *t.* to his face, 7. 10.

John 3. 11. we *t.* that we have seen

5. 39. search the Scriptures, they *t.* of me, 15. 26.

Acts 20. 24. *t.* the Gospel of grace of God, 20.

1 John 4. 14. *t.* that the Father sent

2 Chron. 24. 19. *testified,* Neh. 13. 15. Acts 23. 11. 1 Tim. 2. 6. 1 John 5. 9.

Heb. 11. 4. *testifying,* 1 Pet. 5. 12.

2 Kings 11. 12. gave him the *testimony*

Ps. 78. 5. established a *t.* in Jacob

8. 16. bind up the *t.* seal the law

20. to law and *t.* if they speak not

Matt. 10. 18. for a *t.* against them and the

John 3. 32. no man receiveth his *t.*

Acts 14. 3. gave *t.* to word of his grace

2 Cor. 1. 12. the *t.* of our conscience

Heb. 11. 5. before translation had this *t.*

Rev. 1. 9. *t.* of Jesus Christ, 12. 17. 11. 7. when they shall have finished their *t.*

Ps. 25. 10. keep his *testimonies,* 119. 2. 93. 5. *thy testimonies,* 119. 14, 24, 31, 46, 59, 95, 111, 129, 144.

THANK, 1 Chron. 16. 4. & 29. 13. Matt. 11. 25, 26. Luke 6. 32, 33. & 17. 9. & 18. 11. John 11. 41. Rom. 1. 8. & 7. 25. 1 Cor. 1. 4. 2 Thes. 3. 13. 1 Tim. 1. 12.

Ps. 100. 4. be *thankful,* Acts 24. 3. Rom. 1. 21. Col. 3. 15.

1 Pet. 2. 19. this is *thankworthy*

Dan. 6. 10. *gave thanks,* Matt. 26. 27. Mark 8. 6. Luke 22. 17. Rom. 14. 6. 2 Cor. 9. 15. *t.* to God for his un-

speakable gift, 2. 14. & 8. 16. 1 Cor. 15. 57.

Eph. 5. 4. *giving of thanks,* 20. 1. Tit. 2. 1. Heb. 13. 15.

1 Thes. 3. 9. what *t.* can we render to God

Lev. 7. 12. *thanksgiving,* Neh. 11. 17. Ps. 26. 7. & 50. 14. & 100. 4. & 107. 22. & 116. 17. Isa. 51. 3. Phil. 4. 6. 1 Tim. 4. 3. Rev. 7. 12.

THEATRE, Acts 19. 29.

THINE is the day and night, Ps. 74. 16.

Ps. 119. 94. I am *t.* O save thou me

Isa. 63. 19. we are *t.* thou never bearest rule

Matt. 20. 14. take that is *t.* and go

John 17. 6. *t.* thy were, and thou

10. all mine are *t.* and *t.* are mine

THINK on me for good, Neh. 5. 10.

Job 31. 1. why should I *t.* on a maid

Jer. 29. 11. I know that I *t.* toward

Rom. 12. 3. not to *t.* more highly than he ought to; but to *t.* soberly

1 Cor. 8. 2. if any *t.* that he knoweth

Gal. 6. 3. *t.* himself to be something

Eph. 3. 20. above all we ask or *t.*

Phil. 4. 8. *t.* on these things

Gen. 50. 20. *thought* evil against me

Ps. 48. 9. we have *t.* of thy loving kindness

73. 16. when I *t.* to know this

119. 59. I *t.* on my ways and turned

Matt. 3. 16. them that *t.* on his name

Mark 14. 72. when he *t.* thereon wept

1 Cor. 13. 11. I *t.* as a child, spake

Phil. 2. 6. *t.* it not robbery to be equal

Ps. 139. 2. understandest my *t.* afar

Prov. 24. 9. the *t.* of foolishness is sin

Eccl. 10. 20. curse not king in thy *t.*

Matt. 6. 25. take no *t.* for life, Luke 12. 22.

6. 34. take no *t.* for the morrow

Mark 13. 11. take no *t.* beforehand

2 Cor. 10. 5. every *t.* into captivity

Ps. 50. 21. thou *thoughtest* I was

Gen. 6. 5. imagination of *thoughts*

Judg. 5. 15. were great *t.* of heart

1 Chron. 28. 9. understandeth all the imagination of the *t.*

29. 18. keep this in imagination of *t.*

Ps. 10. 4. God is not in all his *t.*

33. 11. the *t.* of his heart to all generations

40. 5. many are thy *t.* to us-ward

94. 11. Lord knoweth the *t.* of man

19. in multitude of my *t.* within me

119. 113. I hate vain *t.* but thy law

139. 17. how precious are thy *t.* to me

23. try me and know my *t.* 15.

Prov. 12. 5. *t.* of righteous are right

15. 26. the *t.* of the wicked are an abomination

16. 3. thy *t.* shall be established

Isa. 55. 7. let the unrighteous man forsake his *t.*

8. my *t.* are not your *t.*

59. 7. their *t.* are *t.* of iniquity

66. 18. I know their works and *t.*

Jer. 4. 14. how long shall vain *t.*

29. 11. I think toward you are *t.*

Mic. 4. 12. know not *t.* of the Lord

Matt. 15. 19. out of the heart proceed evil *t.*

Luke 2. 35. the *t.* of many hearts be revealed

24. 38. do *t.* arise in your hearts

Rom. 2. 15. their *t.* accusing, or

1 Cor. 3. 20. the Lord knoweth the *t.*

Heb. 4. 12. a discerner of the *t.* and

James 2. 4. become judges of evil *t.*

THIRST, Deut. 28. 48. & 29. 19.

Isa. 49. 10. shall not hunger nor *t.*

Matt. 5. 6. blessed are they which hunger and *t.* after righteousness

John 4. 14. shall never *t.* 6. 35.

7. 37. if any *t.* let him come drink

Rom. 12. 20. if he *t.* give him drink

Rev. 7. 16. hunger nor *t.* any more

Ps. 42. 2. my soul *thirsteth* for God,

63. 1. my soul *t.* for thee 143. 6.

Isa. 55. 1. ho, every one that *t.* come

THORNS in your sides, Num. 33. 55.

Judg. 2. 3. Gen. 3. 18.

Josh. 23. 13. shall be *t.* in your eyes

2 Sam. 23. 6. as *t.* thrust away

Jer. 4. 3. sow not among *t.*

12. 13. sown wheat but shall reap *t.*

Hos. 2. 6. hedge up thy way with *t.*

Matt. 7. 16. do men gather grapes of *t.*

13. 7. some fell among *t.* 22.

Heb. 6. 8. that which beareth *t.* and

THREATENING, Eph. 6. 9. Acts 4. 29. & 9. 1. 1 Pet. 2. 23.

THREE, 2 Sam. 24. 12. Prov. 30. 15, 18, 21, 29. Amos 1. 3, 13. & 2. 1.

1 Cor. 14. 27. 1 John 5. 7, 8. Rev. 16. 13.

THRESH, Isa. 41. 15. Jer. 51. 33. Isa. 21. 10. Mic. 4. 13. Hab. 3. 12. 1 Cor. 9. 10.

Lev. 26. 5. and your *threshing* shall reach unto the vintage

2 Sam. 24. 18. *threshing-floor,* 21. 24.

THROAT is an open sepulchre, Ps. 5. 9.

Ps. 69. 3. weary of crying my *t.* is

Prov. 23. 2. put a knife to thy *t.*

Jer. 2. 25. withhold thy *t.* from thirst

THRONE, Lord is in heaven, Ps. 11. 4.

Ps. 94. 20. *t.* of iniquity have fellowship

Prov. 25. 5. *t.* is established by righteousness

Isa. 66. 1. heaven is my *t.*

Jer. 14. 21. do not disgrace *t.* of glory

Lam. 5. 19. thy *t.* from generation to generation

Dan. 7. 9. his *t.* was like fiery flame

Matt. 19. 28. shall sit in *t.* of his glory, ye shall sit on twelve *thrones*

25. 31. shall sit on *t.* of his glory

Col. 1. 16. whether they be *t.* or

Heb. 4. 16. boldly to the *t.* of grace

Rev. 3. 21. sit on my *t.* with my Father on his *t.*

20. 11. a great white *t.* and he that

22. 3. *t.* of God and Lamb shall be

Job 26. 9. *his throne,* Ps. 89. 14, 29, 44. & 97. 2. & 103. 19. Prov. 20. 28. & 25. 5. Dan. 7. 9. Zech. 6. 13.

Ps. 45. 6. *thy throne,* 99. 4. Heb. 1. 8.

Isa. 22. 23. *glorious throne,* Jer. 17. 12.

THRUST, Ex. 11. 1. Job 32. 13. Luke 13. 28. John 20. 25. Acts 16. 37.

THUNDER, Job 26. 14. & 40. 9. Ps. 29. 3. & 81. 7. Mark 3. 17.

Rev. 4. 5. *thunderings,* 8. 5. & 10. 3. & 11. 19. & 16. 18. & 19. 6.

TIDINGS, evil, Ex. 33. 4. Ps. 112. 7. Luke 1. 19. show the glad *t.* 8. 1. Acts 13. 32. Rom. 10. 15.

TIME, when thou mayest be found Ps. 32. 6.

Ps. 37. 19. evil *t.* 41. 1. *t.* of trouble, 69. 13. acceptable *t.* Isa. 49. 8. 2 Cor. 6. 2.

Ps. 89. 47. remember how short my *t.*

Eccl. 3. 1-8. a *time* to every purpose —to be born—to die—to plant—to pluck up—to kill—to heal—to break down—to build up—to weep—to laugh—to mourn—to dance—to gather—to embrace—to refrain—to get—to lose—to keep—to cast away —to rend—to sew—to keep silence— to speak—to love—to hate—of war— of peace 16.

Eccl. 9. 11. *t.* and chance happeneth

Ezek. 16. 8. thy *t.* was the *t.* of love

Dan. 7. 25. till a *t.* and times, dividing of *t.*

22. 7. for a *t. t.* and half a, Rev. 12. 14.

Amos 5. 13. evil *t.* Mic. 2. 3.

Luke 19. 44. knewest not *t.* of thy visitation

John 7. 6. my *t.* is not yet come

Acts 17. 21. spent *t.* in nothing else
Rom. 13. 11. high *t.* to awake out of
1 Cor. 7. 29. the *t.* is short, it remains
2 Cor. 6. 2. accepted *t.* the day of
Eph. 5. 16. redeeming the *t.* Col. 4. 5.
1 Pet. 1. 17. pass *t.* of your sojourning
Rev. 10. 6. *t.* shall be no longer
12. 12. great wrath hath but short *t.*
Ps. 31. 15. my *times* are in thy hand
Luke 21. 24. till *t.* of the Gentiles be fulfilled
Acts 1. 7. not for you to know the *t.*
3. 19. *t.* of refreshing shall come, 21.
17. 26. determined the *t.* before appointed
1 Tim. 4. 1. in latter *t.* some shall
2 Tim. 3. 1. in last days perilous *t.*
Ps. 34. 1. bless the Lord *at all times*
62. 8. trust in God—ye people
106. 3. blessed is he that doeth righteousness
119. 20. longing it hath unto thy judgments
Prov. 5. 19. let her breasts satisfy thee—
17. 17. a friend loveth—
TIN, Num. 31. 22. Isa. 1. 25. Ezek. 22. 18.
TITHES, Gen. 14. 20. Mal. 3. 8. Amos 4. 4. Matt. 23. 23. Luke 18. 12.
TITTLE or jot pass from the law, Matt. 5. 18.
TOGETHER, Ps. 2. 2. Prov. 22. 2. Rom. 8. 28. all things work *t.* for good
1 Cor. 3. 9. labourers *t.* with God
2 Cor. 6. 1. as workers *t.* with him
Eph. 2. 5. quickened us *t.* with Christ
6. raised us up *t.* made us sit in Christ Jesus
TOKEN of covenant, Gen. 9. 12, 13.
Ps. 86. 17. show me a *t.* for good
Phil. 1. 28. evident *t.* of perdition
2 Thes. 1. 5. manifest *t.* of righteous judgment
Job 21. 29. ye not know their *tokens*
Ps. 65. 8. they are afraid at thy *t.*
135. 9. who sent *t.* and wonders
Isa. 44. 25. frustrateth the *t.* of liars
TONGUE, Ex. 11. 7. Josh. 10. 21.
Job 5. 21. be hid from scourge of *t.*
20. 12. hide wickedness under his *t.*
Ps. 34. 13. keep thy *t.* from evil
Prov. 10. 20. *t.* of the just is as choice silver
12. 18. *t.* of wise is health, 31. 26.
19. a lying *t.* is but for a moment
15. 4. wholesome *t.* is a tree of life
18. 21. death and life are in power of the *t.*
21. 6. getting treasures by a lying *t.*
23. keepeth his *t.* keepeth his soul
25. 15. a soft *t.* breaketh the bone
Isa. 30. 27. his *t.* as a devouring fire
50. 4. Lord hath given me *t.* of the learned
Jer. 9. 5. taught their *t.* to speak lies
18. 18. let us smite him with the *t.*
James 1. 26. be religious and bridleth not his *t.*
3. 8. the *t.* can no man tame, 5.
1 Pet. 3. 10. refrain his *t.* from evil
1 John 3. 18. not love in *t.* but deed
Ps. 35. 28. *my tongue,* 39. 1. & 45. 1. & 51. 14. & 71. 24. & 119. 172. & 137. 6. & 139. 4. Acts 2. 26.
Ps. 31. 26. *tongues,* 55. 9. Mark 16. 17. Acts 19. 6. 1 Cor. 12. 10, 28, & 14. 23.
TOOK me out of the womb, Ps. 22. 9.
Phil. 2. 7. *t.* on him form of servant
Heb. 10. 34. *t.* joyfully the spoiling of
TOPHET, Isa. 30. 33. Jer. 7. 31, 32.
TORCH, Zech. 12. 6. Nah. 2. 3, 4.
TORMENT us before the time, Matt. 8. 20.
Luke 16. 21. come to this place of *t.*
Matt. 8. 29.
Rev. 18. 7. so much *t.* and sorrow
14. 11. smoke of their *t.* ascendeth
Luke 16. 24. I am *tormented* in this

25. he is comforted, and thou art *t.*
Heb. 11. 37. destitute, afflicted, *t.*
TORN, Hos. 6. 1. Mal. 1. 13. Mark 1. 26.
TOSS, Isa. 22. 18. Jer. 5. 22. James 1. 6.
Ps. 109. 23. I am *tossed* up and down
Isa. 54. 11. *t.* with a tempest
Eph. 4. 14. children *t.* to and fro
TOUCH not mine anointed, Ps. 105. 15.
Job 5. 19. in seven shall no evil *t.* thee
Isa. 52. 11. *t.* no unclean thing
Matt. 9. 21. may but *t.* his garment
14. 36. only *t.* hem of his garment
Mark 10. 13. children that he should *t.*
Luke 11. 46. *t.* not the burdens with
John 20. 17. *t.* me not, for I am not
1 Cor. 7. 1. good not to *t.* a woman
2 Cor. 6. 17. *t.* not the unclean thing
Col. 2. 21. *t.* not, taste not, handle not
1 Sam. 10. 26. whose heart God had *touched*
Job 19. 21. hand of God hath *t.* me
Luke 8. 45. who *t.* me, 46. hath *t.* me
Zech. 2. 8. he *toucheth* you, *t.* apple of his eye
1 John 5. 18. wicked one *t.* him not
TOWER, God is a high, Ps. 18. 2. & 144. 2.
Ps. 61. 3. strong *t.* Prov. 18. 10.
Song 4. 4. *t.* of David
7. 4. *t.* of ivory; *t.* of Lebanon
Isa. 5. 2. built a *t.* Matt. 21. 33.
TRADITION, Matt. 15. 3. Gal. 1. 14.
Col. 2. 8. 2 Thes. 2. 15. & 13. 6. 1 Pet. 1. 18.
TRAIN, Prov. 22. 6. Isa. 6. 1.
TRAITOR, Luke 6. 16. 2 Tim. 3. 4.
TRAMPLE, Isa. 63. 3. Matt. 7. 6.
TRANCE, Num. 24. 4. Acts 10. 10. & 11. 5. & 22. 17. 2 Cor. 12. 2, 3, 4.
TRANQUILLITY, Dan. 4. 27.
TRANSFIGURED, Matt. 17. 2. Mark 9. 2.
TRANSFORMED, Rom. 12. 2. 2 Cor. 11. 14, 15.
TRANSGRESS the commandment of the Lord, Num. 14. 41.
1 Sam. 2. 24. ye make the Lord's people to *t.*
2 Chron. 24. 20. why *t.* ye the commandment of the Lord
Neh. 1. 8. if ye *t.* I will scatter you
13. 27. this great evil, to *t.* against our God
Ps. 17. 3. purposed that my mouth shall not *t.*
25. 3. be ashamed that *t.* without
Prov. 28. 21. for piece of bread man will *t.*
Amos 4. 4. come to Bethel and *t.*
Matt. 15. 2. why do thy disciples *t.*
3. why do ye *t.* the commandment of God by your tradition
Rom. 2. 27. by circumcision dost *t.*
Deut. 26. 13. not *transgressed* thy commandments
Josh. 7. 11. have *t.* my covenant, Judg. 2. 20.
Isa. 43. 27. teachers have *t.* against
Jer. 2. 8. pastors also *t.* against me
Lam. 3. 42. we have *t.* and rebelled
Ezek. 2. 3. they and their fathers *t.*
Dan. 9. 11. all Israel have *t.* thy law
Hos. 6. 7. they like men have *t.* the covenant
Hab. 2. 5. he *transgresseth* by wine
1 John 3. 4. that committeth sin, *t.*
Ex. 34. 7. forgiving iniquity, *transgression,* and sin, Num. 14. 18.
1 Chron. 10. 13. Saul died for his *t.*
Ezra 10. 6. he mourned because of *t.*
Job 13. 23. make me to know my *t.*
Ps. 19. 13. innocent from the great *t.*
32. 1. blessed is he whose *t.* is forgiven
89. 32. I will visit their *t.* with rod

107. 17. fools, because of their *t.* are afflicted
Prov. 17. 9. he that covereth *t.* seeketh love
Isa. 53. 8. for *t.* of my people was he stricken
58. 1. show my people their *t.*
59. 13. in *t.* and lying against Lord
20. them that turn from *t.* in Jacob
Dan. 9. 24. to finish *t.* and make end
Amos 4. 4. at Gilgal multiply *t.*
Mic. 3. 8. to declare to Jacob his *t.*
6. 7. shall I give first-born for my *t.*
7. 18. passeth by *t.* of his heritage
Rom. 4. 15. no law is, there is no *t.*
1 John 3. 4. sin is the *t.* of the law
Ex. 23. 21. not pardon *transgressions*
Lev. 16. 21. all their *t.* in all their
Josh. 24. 19. will not forgive your *t.*
Job 31. 33. I covered my *t.* as Adam
36. 9. he showed them their *t.*
Ps. 25. 7. remember not my *t.*
32. 5. I said, I will confess my *t.*
39. 8. deliver me from all my *t.*
51. 1. blot out my *t.*
3. acknowledge my *t.*
65. 3. our *t.* thou shalt purge away
103. 12. so far removed our *t.*
Isa. 43. 25. I am he that blotteth out *t.*
44. 22. out as a thick cloud, thy *t.*
53. 5. he was wounded for our *t.*
59. 12. our *t.* are multiplied before
Ezek. 18. 31. cast away all your *t.*
Gal. 3. 19. law was added because of *t.*
Heb. 9. 15. for the redemption of *t.*
Isa. 48. 8. wast a *transgressor* from the womb
James 2. 11. if thou kill, thou art become a *t.* of the law
Ps. 51. 13. teach *transgressors* thy
59. 5. be not merciful to wicked *t.*
119. 158. I beheld the *t.* and was grieved
Prov. 13. 15. the way of *t.* is hard
Isa. 53. 12. he was numbered with *t.* and made intercession for *t.* Mark 15. 28.
Hos. 14. 9. the *t.* shall fall therein
James 2. 9. convinced of the law as *t.*
TRAVAIL, Isa. 53. 11. Gal. 4. 19, 27.
Job 15. 20. the wicked *travaileth* with pain
Ps. 7. 14. he *t.* with iniquity
Isa. 66. 7. before she *travailed,* 8.
42. 14. *travailing* woman, Hos. 13. 13. Isa. 13. 8. & 21. 3. Jer. 31. 8. Rev. 12. 2.
TRAVEL, Eccl. 1. 13. & 2. 23, 26. & 4. 4, 6, 8, & 5. 14. 2 Thes. 3. 8.
Job. 15. 20. *travelleth,* Prov. 6. 11.
Isa. 21. 13. *travelling,* 63. 1.
TREACHEROUS, Isa. 21. 2.
Jer. 9. 2. are an assembly of *t.* men
Isa. 21. 2. *treacherously,* 24. 16. & 33. 1.
48. 8. thou wouldest deal *t.*
Jer. 3. 20. as a wife *t.* departeth from her husband, so have ye dealt *t.*
12. 1. wherefore are all happy that deal *t.*
Hos. 5. 7. dealt *t.* against Lord, 6. 7.
Mal. 2. 15. none deal *t.* against wife
TREAD down wicked in place, Job 40. 12.
Ps. 7. 5. let him *t.* down my life on
44. 5. through thy name we will *t.*
Isa. 1. 12. required this to *t.* my courts
63. 3. I will *t.* them in mine anger, 6.
Hos. 10. 11. Ephraim loveth to *t.* out
Rev. 11. 2. holy city shall be *t.* under
Deut. 25. 4. not muzzle the ox that *treadeth* out the corn, 1 Cor. 9. 9. 1 Tim. 5. 18.
Isa. 22. 5. *treading.* Amos 5. 11.
TREASURE, Prov. 15. 6, 16.
Deut. 28. 12. the Lord shall open his good *t.*
Ex. 19. 5. peculiar *t.* Ps. 135. 4.
Isa. 33. 6. fear of the Lord is his *t.*

Matt. 6. 21. where your *t.* is there
12. 35. good man out of good *t.*
13. 52. bringeth forth out of his *t.*
19. 21. thou shalt have *t.* in heaven
Luke 12. 21. layeth up *t.* for himself
2 Cor. 4. 7. this *t.* in earthen vessels
Deut. 32. 34. sealed up among my *treasures*
Ps. 17. 14. fillest with thy hid *t.*
Prov. 2. 4. searchest for her as hid *t.*
10. 2. *t.* of wickedness profit nothing
21. 6. getting *t.* by a lying tongue
Matt. 6. 19. lay not up *t.* on earth
20. lay up for yourselves *t.* in
Col. 2. 3. in whom are hid all the *t.* of wisdom
Heb. 11. 26. greater riches than *t.* of Egypt
Rom. 2. 5. *treasurest* up unto thyself
TREE, Gen. 2. 16, 17. & 3. 22.
Ps. 1. 3. like a *t.* planted by rivers
37. 35. spread himself like a bay *t.*
52. 8. I am like a green olive *t.*
Prov. 3. 18. she is a *t.* of life to them
11. 30. fruit of righteousness is *t.* of
Isa. 6. 13. shall be eaten as a teil *t.*
56. 3. eunuch say, I am a dry *t.*
Jer. 17. 8. a *t.* planted by the waters
Matt. 3. 10. *t.* that bringeth not forth
7. 17. good *t.* bringeth forth good
12. 33. make the *t.* good; or else make the *t.* corrupt; the *t.* is known
1 Pet. 2. 24. in his own body on *t.*
Rev. 2. 7. will I give to eat of *t.* of life
22. 2. in midst of city was *t.* of life
14. may have right to the *t.* of life
Ps. 104. 16. the *trees* of the Lord are full of sap
Isa. 61. 3. called *t.* of righteousness
Ezek. 47. 12. grow all *t.* for meat
Mark 8. 24. I see men as *t.* walking
Jude 12. *t.* whose fruit withereth
TREMBLE at the commandment of our God, Ezra 10. 3.
Ps. 99. 1. Lord reigneth, let people *t.*
Eccl. 12. 3. keepers of house shall *t.*
Isa. 66. 5. ye that *t.* at his word, 2.
Jer. 5. 22. ye not *t.* at my presence
10. at his wrath earth shall *t.*
Dan. 6. 26. men *t.* before the God of Daniel
James 2. 19. devils believe and *t.*
1 Sam. 4. 13. heart *trembled* for ark
Ezra 9. 4. every one that *t.* at word
Acts 24. 25. as he reasoned, Felix *t.*
Job 37. 1. *trembleth,* Ps. 119. 120. Isa. 66. 2.
1 Sam. 13. 7. the people followed *trembling*
Deut. 28. 65. Lord shall give thee a *t.* heart
Ezra 10. 9. people sat *t.* because of
Ps. 2. 11. serve God and rejoice *t.*
Ezek. 12. 18. drink thy water with *t.* 26. 16.
Hos. 13. 1. when Ephraim spake *t.*
Zech. 12. 2. make Jerusalem cup of *t.*
1 Cor. 2. 3. in fear and in much *t.*
Eph. 6. 5. fear and *t.* in singleness
Phil. 2. 12. work out your salvation with *t.*
TRESPASS, Lev. 26. 40. Ezra 9. 6. 1 Kings 8. 31. Matt. 18. 15.
Ezra 9. 15. *trespasses,* Ezek. 39. 26.
Ps. 68. 21. as goeth on still in his *t.*
Matt. 6. 14. if ye forgive men their *t.*
18. 35. if ye forgive not every one their *t.*
2 Cor. 5. 19. not imputing their *t.* to
Eph. 2. 1. dead in *t.* and sins
Col. 2. 13. having forgiven you all *t.*
TRIAL, Job 9. 23. Ezek. 21. 13. 2 Cor. 8. 2. Heb. 11. 36. 1 Pet. 1. 7. & 4. 12.
TRIBES, Num. 24. 2.
Ps. 105. 37. not one feeble among *t.*
122. 4. whither *t.* go up, *t.* of Lord
Hab. 3. 9. according to oaths of *t.*
Matt. 24. 30. shall all the *t.* of earth
Acts 26. 7. promise our twelve *t.* hope
TRIBULATION, art in, Deut. 4. 30.

Judg. 10. 14. let them deliver you in t.

1 Sam. 26. 24. deliver me out of all t.

Matt. 13. 21. when t. or persecution

24. 21. then shall be great t. such

29. immediately after the t. Mark 13. 34.

John 16. 33. in world ye shall have t.

Acts 14. 22. we must through much t.

Rom. 2. 9. t. and anguish on every

5. 3. knowing t. worketh patience

8. 35. separate us from the love of Christ; shall t.

12. 12. rejoicing in hope, patient in t.

2 Cor. 1. 4. comforteth us in all our t.

7. 4. exceeding joyful in all our t.

1 Thes. 3. 4. we should suffer t.

2 Thes. 1. 6. to recompense t. to

Rev. 1. 9. brother and companion in t.

2. 9. I know thy works and t.

10. ye shall have t. ten days

22. cast into great t. except they repent

7. 14. have come out of great t.

Rom. 5. 3. glory in tribulations also

1 Sam. 10. 19. saved you out of all t.

Eph. 3. 13. faint not at my t. for you

2 Thes. 1. 4. patience in all t. that ye endure

TRIBUTE, Gen. 49. 15. Num. 31. 28.

Prov. 12. 24. slothful shall be under t.

Matt. 17. 24. doth not your Master pay t.

22. 17. is it lawful to give t. to Caesar

Rom. 13. 7. t. to whom t. is due

TRIMMED, Jer. 2. 33. Matt. 25. 7.

TRIUMPH, 2 Sam. 1. 20. Ps. 25. 2.

Ps. 94. 4. t. in works of thy hands

106. 47. give thanks and t. in thy

2 Cor. 2. 14. always causeth us to t.

Ex. 15. 1. triumphed gloriously, 21.

Job 20. 5. triumphing, Col. 2. 15.

TRODDEN down strength, Judg. 5. 21.

Ps. 119. 118. t. down all them that err

Isa. 63. 3. I have t. winepress alone

Luke 21. 24. Jerusalem shall be t.

Heb. 10. 29. t. under foot Son of God

TROUBLE, 2 Chron. 15. 4.

Job 5. 6. neither doth t. spring out of ground

7. man is born to t. as sparks fly

14. 1. man is of few days and full of t.

Ps. 9. 9. Lord will be a refuge in times

22. 11. t. is near; there is none to

27. 5. in time of t. he shall hide me

37. 39. their strength in time of t.

46. 1. God is a present help in t.

60. 11. give us help from t.

91. 15. I will be with him in t.

119. 143. t. and anguish have taken

143. 11. bring my soul out of t.

Prov. 11. 8. the righteous is delivered out of t.

12. 13. the just shall come out of t.

Isa. 26. 16. Lord, in t. have they visited me

33. 2. be our salvation in time of t.

Jer. 8. 15. looked for health, and behold t.

14. 8. and Saviour in time of t.

19. for time of healing, and behold t.

30. 7. that day is time of Jacob's t.

Dan. 12. 1. there shall be a time of t.

1 Cor. 7. 28. shall have t. in the flesh

Ps. 25. 17. the troubles of my heart are enlarged

34. 17. deliver them out of all t.

71. 20. showed me great and sore t.

88. 3. my soul is full of t.

Ex. 14. 24. Lord troubled the host of Egypt

Ps. 30. 7. didst hide thy face and I was t.

77. 3. I remembered God, and was t.

Isa. 56. 20. wicked are like the t. sea

John 12. 27. now is my soul t.

14. 1. let not your hearts be t. 27.

2 Cor. 4. 8. t. on every side, 7. 5.

2 Thes. 1. 7. to you who are t. rest

Job 23. 16. Almighty troubleth me

1 Kings 18. 17. thou he that t. Israel

Prov. 11. 17. cruel t. his own flesh

29. he that t. his own house

Luke 18. 5. because this widow t. the

Gal. 5. 10. he that t. you shall bear judgment

Job 3. 17. troubling, John 5. 4.

TRUCE breakers, 2 Tim. 3. 3.

TRUE, Gen. 42. 11. 2 Sam. 7. 28.

Ps. 19. 9. judgments of Lord are t.

119. 160. thy word is t.

Prov. 14. 25. t. witness delivereth

Jer. 42. 5. be t. and faithful witness

Ezek. 18. 8. t. judgment, Zech. 7. 9.

Matt. 22. 16. we know thou art t.

Luke 16. 11. t. riches

John 1. 9. t. light

4. 23. t. worshippers, 6. 32. t. bread

7. 28. he that sent me is t.

8. 14. record is t.

15. 1. I am the t. vine

2 Cor. 1. 18. as God is t. our word to

6. 8. as deceivers and yet t.

Phil. 4. 8. whatsoever things are t.

1 John 5. 20. may know him that is t.

Rev. 3. 7. saith he that is t.

14. t. witness

19. 11. was called faithful and t.

TRUMP, 1 Cor. 15. 52. 1 Thes. 16. 4.

TRUMPET, Ex. 19. 16. Ps. 81. 3.

Isa. 27. 13. great t. shall be blown

58. 1. lift up thy voice like a t.

Matt. 6. 2. do not sound a t. before

Num. 10. 2. trumpets, Josh. 6. 4. Ps. 98. 6. Rev. 8. 9.

TRUST in him, 1 Chron. 5. 20.

Job 4. 10. put no t. in servants, 15. 15.

8. 14. his t. is a spider's web

Ps. 4. 5. put your t. in the Lord

9. 10. that know thy name will put their t.

40. 4. blessed the man that maketh the Lord his t.

71. 5. thou art my t. from my youth

141. 8. in thee is my t. leave not

Prov. 22. 19. thy t. may be in Lord

Job 13. 15. though he slay I will t.

Ps. 37. 3. t. in Lord, and do good

5. t. in him; he will bring it to pass

40. Lord shall save because they t.

55. 23. I will t. in thee

62. 8. t. in him at all times, ye

115. 8, 9, 10, 11. t. in the Lord

118. 8. it is better to t. in Lord, 9.

119. 42. for I t. in thy word

125. 1. they that t. in Lord shall

Prov. 3. 5. t. in the Lord with all thy heart

Isa. 26. 4. t. ye in the Lord for ever

50. 10. t. in the name of the Lord

Jer. 7. 4. t. not in lying words

9. 4. t. not in any brother

Mic. 7. 5. t. ye not in a friend

Mark 10. 24. hard for them that t. in riches

2 Cor. 1. 9. should not t. in ourselves

Phil. 3. 4. whereof to t. in flesh

1 Tim. 6. 20. keep that is committed to thy t.

Ps. 22. 4. our fathers trusted in thee

28. 7. my heart t. in him, and I am

52. 7. t. in abundance of his riches

Luke 18. 9. which t. in themselves

Eph. 1. 12. who first t. in Christ, 13.

Ps. 32. 10. that trusteth in Lord's mercy

34. 8. blessed is man that t. in him

57. 1. be merciful, for my soul t. in

84. 12. blessed is man that t. in thee

86. 2. save servant that t. in thee

Jer. 17. 5. cursed be the man that t. in man

7. blessed is man that t. in Lord

1 Tim. 5. 5. widow and desolate t. in

Ps. 112. 7. his heart is fixed trusting

TRUTH, Gen. 24. 7. Ex. 18. 21.

Ex. 34. 6. abundant in goodness and t.

Deut. 34. 4. a God of t. and without iniquity

Ps. 15. 2. speaketh t. in his heart

25. 10. the paths of the Lord are mercy and t.

51. 6. desirest t. in inward parts

91. 4. his t. shall be thy shield

117. 2. his t. endureth for ever

119. 30. I have chosen the way of t.

142. law is t.

151. commandments are t.

Prov. 12. 19. lip of t. shall be established

16. 6. by mercy and t. iniquity is purged

23. 23. buy the t. and sell it not

Isa. 59. 14. t. is fallen in the streets

Jer. 4. 2. swear Lord liveth in t.

9. 3. are not valiant for the t.

Dan. 4. 37. all whose ways are t.

Zech. 8. 16. speak every man t. to his neighbour

Mal. 2. 6. law of t. was in his mouth

John 1. 14. full of grace and t. 17.

8. 32. know the t. and the t. shall make you free

14. 6. I am the way, the t. and life

17. Spirit of t. 16. 13. guide into t.

17. 17. sanctify them through t. 19.

18. 37. bear witness to t.

38. what is t.

Acts 26. 25. words of t. and soberness

Rom. 1. 18. hold t. in unrighteousness

25. changed the t. of God into a lie

2. 2. judgment of God is according to t.

20. hast the form of t. in the law

1 Cor. 5. 8. the unleavened bread of sincerity and t.

2 Cor. 13. 8. do nothing against t. but for t.

Gal. 3. 1. should not obey the t. 5. 7.

Eph. 4. 15. speaking t. in love, 25.

21. taught by him as t. is in Jesus

5. 9. fruit of the Spirit is in all t.

6. 14. having loins girt about with t.

2 Thes. 2. 10. received not love of t.

1 Tim. 3. 15. pillar and ground of t.

6. 5. corrupt, destitute of the t.

2 Tim. 2. 18. who concerning the t. have erred

25. to the acknowledging of the t.

3. 7. never able to come to the knowledge of the t.

8. these do also resist the t.

4. 4. turn away their ears from t.

James 3. 14. glory not, nor lie against t.

1 Pet. 1. 22. purified souls in obeying t.

2 Pet. 1. 12. established in present t.

1 John 1. 8. t. is not in us

5. 6. Spirit is t.

Josh. 24. 14. in truth, 1 Sam. 12. 24. Ps. 145. 18. Jer. 4. 2. John 4. 24. 1 Thes. 2. 13. 1 John 3. 18. 2 John 4.

Ps. 25. 5. thy truth, 26. 3. & 43. 3. & 108. 4. John 17. 17.

TRY, Judg. 7. 4. Job 12. 11. Jer. 6. 27.

2 Chron. 32. 31. God left him to t. him

Job 7. 18. visit him and t. him every morning

Ps. 11. 4. his eyelids t. the children of men

26. 2. t. my reins and my heart

139. 23. t. me, and know my heart

Jer. 9. 7. will melt them, and t. him

17. 10. I search the heart, and I t. the reins

Lam. 3. 40. search and t. our ways

Dan. 11. 35. some shall fall to t. them

Zech. 13. 9. I will t. them as gold is tried

1 Cor. 3. 13. fire shall t. every man's

1 Pet. 4. 12. fiery trial which is to t.

1 John 4. 1. t. the spirits whether of

Rev. 3. 10. to t. them that dwell on the earth

2 Sam. 22. 31. word of Lord is tried, Ps. 18. 30.

Ps. 12. 6. word is pure as silver t. in

17. 3. t. me, 66. 10. t. us as silver is t.

105. 19. word of the Lord t. him

Jer. 12. 3. t. my heart towards thee

Dan. 12. 10. many shall be purified and t.

Heb. 11. 17. Abraham, when he was t.

James 1. 12. when he is t. he shall receive the crown of life

1 Pet. 1. 7. though it be t. with fire

Rev. 2. 2. hast t. them and found them liars

10. into prison that they may be t.

3. 18. buy of me gold, t. in the fire

1 Chron. 29. 17. I know thou triest

Jer. 11. 20. that t. the reins and heart

20. 12. thou that t. the righteous

Ps. 7. 9. the righteous God trieth the heart, Prov. 17. 3.

Ps. 11. 5. the Lord t. the righteous

1 Thes. 2. 4. pleasing God, who t. our hearts

James 1. 3. trying of your faith

TUMULT, Ps. 65. 7. 2 Cor. 12. 20.

TURN from their sin, 1 Kings 8. 35.

2 Kings 17. 13. t. from your evil ways

Job 23. 13. who can t. him

Prov. 1. 23. t. you at my reproof

Song 2. 17. t. my beloved, be thou

Isa. 31. 6. t. ye not unto him, from

Jer. 18. 8. if t. from their evil; I will repent

41. 18. t. thou me and I shall be

Lam. 5. 21. t. us unto thee, O Lord

Ezek. 3. 19. t. not from his wickedness

38. 30. t. yourselves from your transgression

32. t. yourselves and live, 33. 9, 11. & 14. 6. Hos. 12. 6. Joel 2. 12.

Zech. 6. 3. t. to me, and I will t. to

Mal. 4. 6. t. hearts of fathers to their

Acts 26. 18. t. them from darkness

20. should repent, and t. to God

2 Pet. 2. 21. to t. from holy commandments

2 Chron. 30. 6. turn again, Ps. 60. 1. & 80. 3, 7, 19. & 85. 8. Lam. 3. 40. Mic. 7. 19. Zech. 10. 9. Gal. 4. 9.

1 Sam. 12. 20. turn aside, Ps. 40. 4. Isa. 30. 11. Lam. 3. 35. Amos 2. 7. & 5. 12.

Ps. 119. 37. turn away, 39. Song 6. 5. Isa. 58. 13. 1 Tim. 3. 5. Heb. 12. 25.

Deut. 4. 20. turn to the Lord, 20. 10. 2 Chron. 15. 4. Ps. 4. 22, 27. Lam. 3. 40. Hos. 14. 2. Joel 2. 13. Luke 1. 16. 2 Cor. 3. 16.

Ps. 9. 17. wicked shall be turned into hell

30. 11. t. my mourning into dancing

119. 5. t. my feet to thy testimonies

Isa. 53. 6. t. every one to own way

63. 10. was t. to be their enemy

Jer. 2. 27. t. their back to me, 32. 33.

8. 6. every one t. to his own course

Hos. 7. 8. Ephraim is a cake not t.

11. 8. my heart is t. within me

John 6. 20. sorrow shall be t. to joy

1 Thes. 1. 9. t. to God from idols

James 4. 9. laughter be t. to mourning

2 Pet. 2. 22. dog is t. to his vomit

Deut. 9. 12. turned aside, Ps. 78. 57. Isa. 44. 20. 2 Tim. 1. 6. & 5. 15.

1 Kings 11. 3. turned away, Ps. 66. 20. & 78. 38. Isa. 5. 25. & 9. 12. & 10. 4. Jer. 5. 25.

Ps. 44. 18. turned back, 78. 9, 41. Isa. 42. 17. Jer. 4. 8. Zeph. 1. 6.

Job 15. 13. turnest, Ps. 90. 3.

Ps. 146. 9. way of wicked he turneth upside down

Prov. 15. 1. a soft answer t. away wrath

21. 1. he t. it whithersoever he will

Isa. 9. 13. the people t. not unto him

Jer. 14. 8. *t.* aside to tarry for a night
James 1. 17. neither shadow of *turning*
Jude 4. *t.* grace of God into lasciviousness
TURTLE, Lev. 1. 14. & 5. 7, 11. & 12. 6. Ps. 74. 19. Song 2. 12. Jer. 8. 7.
TUTORS, Gal. 4. 2.
TWAIN, Matt. 5. 41. & 19. 5. Eph. 2. 15.
TWICE, Gen. 41. 32. Ex. 16. 22. Num. 20. 11. 1 Kings 11. 9. Job 33. 14. & 40. 5. Ps. 62. 11. Mark 14. 30. Luke 18. 12. *t.* dead, Jude 12.
TWINKLING, 1 Cor. 15. 52.

U & V

UNACCUSTOMED, 34. 18.
UNADVISEDLY, Ps. 106. 33.
UNAWARES, Deut. 4. 42. Ps. 35. 8. Luke 21. 34. Heb. 13. 2. Jude 4.
UNBELIEF, did not many works because of, Matt. 13. 58.
Mark 6. 6. marvelled because of *u.*
9. 24. I believe; help thou mine *u.*
16. 14. upbraided them with their *u.*
Rom. 4. 20. staggered not through *u.*
11. 20. because of *u.* were broken.
32. hath concluded them all in *u.*
1 Tim. 1. 13. did it ignorantly in *u.*
Heb. 3. 12. in you an evil heart of *u.*
19. could not enter in because of *u.*
UNBELIEVERS, Luke 12. 46. 2 Cor. 6. 14.
UNBELIEVING, Acts 14. 2. 1 Cor. 7. 14, 15. Tit. 1. 15. Rev. 21. 8.
UNBLAMABLE, Col. 1. 22. 1 Thes. 3. 13.
1 Thes. 2. 10. *unblamably* behaving ourselves
UNCERTAIN, 1 Cor. 14. 8. 1 Tim. 6. 17.
UNCIRCUMCISED, Ex. 6. 12, 30. Jer. 6. 10. & 9. 25, 26. Acts 7. 51.
UNCIRCUMCISION, Rom. 2. 25, 26, 27. & 3. 30. & 4. 10. 1 Cor. 7. 18, 19. Gal. 2. 7. & 5. 6. & 6. 15. Col. 2. 13. & 3. 11.
UNCLEAN, Lev. 5. 11, 13, 15. Num. 19. 19.
Rev. 10. 10. difference between *u.* and clean, Ezek. 22. 26.
Isa. 6. 5. I am a man of *u.* lips
Lam. 4. 15. depart ye; it is *u.*
Ezek. 44. 23. discern between *u.* and
Hag. 2. 13. if one *u.* touch any of these, shall it be *u.?* priests said it shall be *u.*
Acts 10. 28. not call anything common or *u.* 14.
Rom. 14. 14. is nothing *u.* of itself
1 Cor. 7. 14. else were children *u.*
Eph. 5. 5. nor *u.* person hath any inheritance
Num. 5. 19. *uncleanness,* Ezra 9. 11.
Zech. 13. 1. fountain for sin and *u.*
Matt. 23. 27. are within full of all *u.*
Rom. 6. 19. members servants to *u.*
Eph. 4. 19. all *u.* with greediness
5. 3. all *u.* let it not once be named
1 Thes. 4. 7. hath not called us to *u.*
Ezek. 36. 29. save you from all *u.*
UNCLOTHED, 2 Cor. 5. 4.
UNCOMELY, 1 Cor. 7. 36.
UNCONDEMNED, Acts 16. 37.
UNCORRUPTNESS, Tit. 2. 7.
UNCOVER, Lev. 18. 18. 1 Cor. 11. 5.
UNCTION, 1 John 2. 20, 27.
UNDEFILED in way, Ps. 119. 1.
Song 5. 2. my dove, my *u.* 6. 9.
Heb. 7. 26. holy, harmless, *u.*
13. 4. marriage is honourable in all, and the bed *u.*
James 1. 27. pure religion and *u.*
1 Peter 1. 4. inheritance incorruptible, *u.*
UNDER their God, Hos. 4. 12.

Rom. 3. 9. all *u.* sin, 7. 14. Gal. 3. 22.
u. law, Rom. 6. 15. 1 Cor. 9. 20.
1 Cor. 9. 27. I keep *u.* my body
Gal. 3. 10. as are the works of the law, are *u.* the law
UNDERSTAND not one another's speech, Gen. 11. 7.
Neh. 8. 7. caused people to *u.* law
Ps. 19. 12. who can *u.* his errors
107. 43. shalt *u.* loving kindness of the Lord
119. 100. I *u.* more than ancients
Prov. 2. 5. shalt thou *u.* fear of the Lord, 9.
8. 5. *u.* wisdom
14. 8. *u.* his way, 20. 24.
19. 25. *u.* knowledge
28. 5. *u.* all things
Isa. 32. 4. heart of the rash shall *u.*
Dan. 12. 10. none of wicked shall *u.*
1 Cor. 13. 2. to *u.* all mysteries
Ps. 139. 2. thou *understandest* my thoughts
Acts 8. 30. *u.* thou what thou readest
1 Chron. 28. 9. *understandeth* all the imaginations
Ps. 49. 20. man that *u.* not, is like
Prov. 8. 9. plain to him that *u.* 14. 6.
Jer. 9. 24. glory in this, that he *u.*
Matt. 13. 19. heareth word and *u.* not, 23.
Rom. 3. 11. none that *u.* and seeketh
Ex. 31. 3. wisdom and *understanding*
Deut. 4. 6. is your wisdom and *u.*
1 Kings 3. 11. hast asked for thyself *u.*
4. 29. gave Solomon wisdom and *u.*
7. 14. filled with wisdom and *u.*
1 Chron. 12. 32. men that had *u.* of
2 Chron. 16. 5. had *u.* in visions of
Job 12. 13. he hath counsel and *u.*
20. he taketh away the *u.* of aged
17. 4. hast hid their heart from *u.*
28. 12. where is the place of *u.*
28. to depart from evil is *u.*
32. 8. the Almighty giveth them *u.*
38. 36. who hath given *u.* to heart
39. 17. neither imparted to her *u.*
Ps. 47. 7. sing ye praise with *u.*
49. 3. the meditations of my heart shall be of *u.*
119. 34. give me *u.* and I shall keep
99. have more *u.* than my teachers
104. through thy precepts I get *u.*
130. it giveth *u.* unto the simple
147. 5. his *u.* is infinite
Prov. 2. 2. apply thine heart to *u.*
11. *u.* shall keep thee; to deliver
8. 5. lean not to thine own *u.*
13. happy is the man that getteth *u.*
4. 5. get wisdom, get *u.* 7.
8. 1. doth not *u.* cry, 14. I am *u.*
9. 6. go in the way of *u.*
10. knowledge of the holy is *u.*
14. 29. slow to wrath is of great *u.*
16. 22. *u.* is a wellspring of life
19. 8. keepeth *u.* shall find good
21. 30. no *u.* nor counsel against the Lord
24. 23. buy truth, wisdom and *u.*
24. 3. by *u.* a house is established
30. 2. I have not the *u.* of a man
Eccl. 9. 11. nor riches to men of *u.*
Isa. 11. 2. spirit of wisdom and *u.*
3. make him of quick *u.* in the fear of the Lord
27. 11. it is a people of no *u.*
40. 28. is no searching of his *u.*
Jer. 51. 15. stretched out heaven by his *u.*
Matt. 15. 16. are ye also without *u.*
Mark 12. 33. love him with all the heart and with all the *u.*
Luke 2. 47. astonished at his *u.*
24. 45. then opened he their *u.*
Rom. 1. 31. without *u.* unthankful
1 Cor. 1. 19. bring to nothing the *u.* of the prudent
14. 14. my *u.* unfruitful
15. pray with the *u.* also
20. in malice be children, in *u.* men

Eph. 1. 18. eyes of *u.* enlightened
4. 18. having the *u.* darkened
Phil. 4. 7. the peace of God, which passeth all *u.*
Col. 1. 9. filled with all spiritual *u.*
2. 2. riches of full assurance of *u.*
2 Tim. 2. 7. give thee *u.* in all things
1 John 5. 20. given us *u.* to know
Ps. 111. 10. *good understanding,* Prov. 3. 4. & 13. 15.
Prov. 1. 5. *a man of understanding,* 10. 23. & 11. 12. & 15. 21. & 17. 27.
Deut. 32. 29. O that they *understood*
Ps. 73. 17. then *u.* I their end
Dan. 9. 2. *u.* by books number of years
Matt. 13. 51. have ye *u.* all these
John 12. 16. these things *u.* not his disciples
1 Cor. 13. 11. when a child I *u.* as a child
2 Pet. 3. 16. some things hard to be *u.*
UNDERTAKE for me. Isa. 38. 14.
UNDONE, Isa. 6. 5. Matt. 23. 23.
UNEQUAL, your ways are, Ezek. 18. 25.
2 Cor. 6. 14. not *unequally* yoked
UNFAITHFUL, Prov. 25. 19. Ps. 78. 57.
UNFEIGNED, 2 Cor. 6. 6. 1 Tim. 1. 5. 2 Tim. 1. 5. 1 Pet. 1. 22.
UNFRUITFUL Matt. 13. 22. 1 Cor. 14. 14. Eph. 5. 11. Tit. 3. 14. 2 Pet. 1. 8.
UNGODLY men, 2 Sam. 22. 5.
2 Chron. 19. 2. shouldest help the *u.*
Job 16. 11. God hath delivered me to the *u.*
34. 18. is fit to say to princes ye are *u.*
Ps. 1. 1. walketh not in counsel of *u.*
4. the *u.* are not so
5. *u.* not stand in the judgment
6. way of *u.* men shall perish
3. 7. hath broken the teeth of *u.*
43. 1. plead my cause against an *u.* nation
73. 12. these are *u.* that prosper
Prov. 16. 27. *u.* man diggeth up evil
19. 28. an *u.* witness scorneth
Rom. 4. 5. God that justifieth the *u.*
5. 6. in due time Christ died for *u.*
1 Tim. 1. 9. law not for righteous, but for the *u.*
1 Pet. 4. 18. where shall *u.* appear
2 Peter 2. 5. bring a flood on world of the *u.*
6. those that after should live *u.*
3. 7. day of perdition of *u.* men
Jude 4. *u.* men turning grace of God
15. convince all that are *u.* of their *u.* deeds, which they have *u.* committed
18. mockers walk after *u.* lusts
Rom. 1. 18. wrath revealed against *ungodliness*
11. 26. turn away *u.* from Jacob
2 Tim. 2. 16. increase to more *u.*
Tit. 2. 12. denying *u.* and worldly
UNHOLY, Lev. 10. 10. 1 Tim. 1. 9. 2 Tim. 3. 2. Heb. 10. 29.
UNITE, Ps. 86. 11. Gen. 49. 6.
Ps. 133. 1. brethren to dwell together in *unity*
Eph. 4. 3. endeavour to keep the *u.* of the spirit
13. till we all come in *u.* of faith
UNJUST, deliver from, Ps. 43. 1.
Prov. 11. 7. hope of the *u.* perisheth
28. 8. by usury and *u.* gain
29. 27. *u.* man is abomination to
Zeph. 3. 5. the *u.* knoweth no shame
Matt. 5. 45. rain on the just and *u.*
Luke 16. 8. Lord commendeth the *u.* steward
16. 10. he that is *u.* in least, is *u.* in
18. 6. hear what the *u.* judge saith
11. I am not as other men, *u.*
Acts 24. 15. resurrection both of just and *u.*
1 Cor. 6. 1. go to law before the *u.* 6.

1 Pet. 3. 18. once suffered, just for *u.*
2 Pet. 2. 9. reserve the *u.* to day of
Rev. 22. 11. that is *u.* let him be *u.*
Ps. 82. 2. will ye judge *unjustly*
Isa. 26. 10. in land of uprightness will he deal *u.*
UNKNOWN God, Acts 17. 23. Gal. 1. 22.
1 Cor. 14. 2. speak in an *u.* tongue, 4. 27.
2 Cor. 6. 9. as *u.* and yet well known
UNLAWFUL, Acts 10. 28. 2 Pet. 2. 8.
UNLEARNED, Acts 4. 13. 1 Cor. 14. 16, 23, 24. 2 Tim. 2. 23. 2 Pet. 3. 16.
UNLEAVENED, Ex. 12. 39. 1 Cor. 5. 7.
UNMERCIFUL, Rom. 1. 31.
UNMINDFUL, Deut. 32. 8.
UNMOVABLE, 1 Cor. 15. 58.
UNPERFECT, Ps. 139. 16.
UNPREPARED, 2 Cor. 9. 4.
UNPROFITABLE talk, Job 15. 3.
Matt. 25. 30. cast the *u.* servant into outer darkness
Luke 17. 10. we are all *u.* servants
Rom. 3. 12. are altogether become *u.*
Tit. 3. 9. they are *u.* and vain
Philem. 11. was to thee *u.* but now profitable
Heb. 13. 17. for that is *u.* for you
UNPUNISHED, Prov. 11. 21. & 16. 5. & 17. 5. & 19. 5, 9. Jer. 25. 29. & 30. 11. & 46. 28. & 49. 12.
UNQUENCHABLE, Matt. 3. 12. Luke 3. 17.
UNREASONABLE, Acts 25. 27. 2 Thes. 3. 2.
UNREBUKABLE, 1 Tim. 6. 14.
UNREPROVABLE, Col. 1. 22.
UNRIGHTEOUS decrees, Isa. 10. 1.
Isa. 55. 7. *u.* man forsake his thoughts
Luke 16. 11. not been faithful in *u.* mammon
Rom. 3. 5. is God *u.* who taketh vengeance
1 Cor. 6. 9. *u.* shall not inherit the kingdom
Heb. 6. 10. God is not *u.* to forget
Lev. 19. 15. do no *unrighteousness*
Ps. 92. 15. there is no *u.* in him
Jer. 22. 13. wo to him that buildeth his house by *u.*
Luke 16. 9. friends of mammon of *u.*
John 7. 18. is true, and no *u.* in him
Rom. 1. 18. who hold the truth in *u.*
2. 8. obey not the truth but obey *u.*
6. 13. members instruments of *u.*
9. 14. is there *u.* with God? God
2 Cor. 6. 14. fellowship hath righteousness with *u.*
2 Thes. 2. 10. all deceivableness of *u.*
12. believed not, but had pleasure in *u.*
Heb. 8. 12. will be merciful to their *u.*
2 Pet. 2. 15. Balaam loved wages of *u.*
1 John 1. 9. to cleanse us from all *u.*
5. 17. all *u.* is sin
UNRULY, 1 Thes. 5. 14. Tit. 1. 6, 10. James 3. 8.
UNSAVOURY, Job 6. 6. Jer. 23. 13.
UNSEARCHABLE things, Job 5. 9.
Ps. 145. 3. his greatness is *u.*
Prov. 25. 3. heart of kings is *u.*
Rom. 11. 33. *u.* are his judgments
Eph. 3. 8. preach *u.* riches of Christ
UNSEEMLY, Rom. 1. 27. 1 Cor. 13. 5.
UNSKILFUL in word, Heb. 5. 13.
UNSPEAKABLE, 2 Cor. 9. 15. & 12. 4. 1 Pet. 1. 8.
UNSPOTTED, James 1. 27.
UNSTABLE, Gen. 49. 4. James 1. 8. 2 Pet. 2. 14. *u.* souls
3. 16. unlearned and *u.*
UNTHANKFUL, Luke 6. 25. 2 Tim. 3. 2.
UNTOWARD, Acts 2. 40.
UNWASHEN, Matt. 15. 20. Mark 7. 2. 5.
UNWISE, Deut. 32. 6. Hos. 13. 13. Rom. 1. 14. Eph. 5. 17.

UNWORTHY, Acts 13. 46. 1 Cor. 6. 2.

1 Cor. 11. 27. drinketh *unworthily*
UPBRAID, Judg. 18. 15. Mat. 11. 20. Mark 16. 14. James 1. 5.
UPHOLD me with thy spirit, Ps. 51. 12.

Ps. 119. 116. *u.* me according to thy
Prov. 29. 23. honour shall *u.* humble
Isa. 41. 10. I will *u.* thee with the right hand of my righteousness

42. 1. behold my servant whom I *u.*
63. 5. my fury it *upheld* me

Ps. 57. 17. Lord *upholdeth* righteous
63. 8. thy right hand *u.* me
145. 14. Lord *u.* all that fall
41. 12. thou *upholdest* me in my integrity
Heb. 1. 3. *upholding* all by word of his power

UPRIGHT in heart, Ps. 7. 10.

Ps. 11. 7. his countenance doth behold the *u.*
18. 23. I was also *u.* before him
25. with *u.* wilt show thyself *u.*
19. 13. then shall I be *u.* and I shall be innocent
25. 8. good and *u.* is the Lord
37. 37. mark the perfect man and behold the *u.*
64. 10. all *u.* in heart shall glory
112. 2. generation of *u.* shall be blessed
4. to *u.* light ariseth in darkness
140. 13. the *u.* shall dwell in thy presence
Prov. 2. 21. *u.* shall dwell in the land
1-0. 29. way of Lord is strength to *u.*
11. 3. integrity of *u.* shall guide
6. righteousness of the *u.* shall deliver him
20. *u.* in their way, are his delight
12. 6. mouth of *u.* shall deliver
13. 6. righteousness keepeth the *u.*
14. 11. tabernacle of *u.* shall flourish
15. 8. prayer of *u.* is his delight
28. 10. *u.* shall have good things
Eccl. 7. 29. God hath made man *u.*
Song 1. 4. the *u.* love thee
Hab. 2. 4. his soul is not *u.* in him
Ps. 15. 2. that walketh *uprightly*
84. 11. Prov. 2. 7. & 10. 9. & 15. 21. & 29. 18. Mic. 2. 7. Gal. 2. 14.
Ps. 58. 1. do ye judge *u.* 75. 2.
Isa. 33. 15. he that speaketh *u.* Amos 5. 10.
Deut. 9. 5. not for the *uprightness* of thy heart
1 Chron. 29. 17. hast pleasure in *u.*
Job 33. 23. to show unto man his *u.*
Ps. 25. 21. let integrity and *u.* preserve me
143. 10. lead me into the land of *u.*
Isa. 26. 7. the way of the just is *u.*
10. in land of *u.* will deal unjustly
URIM and Thummim, Ex. 28. 30. Lev. 8. 8. Num. 27. 21. Deut. 33. 8. 1 Sam. 28. 6. Ezra 2. 63. Neh. 7. 65.
US, Gen. 1. 26. & 3. 22. & 11. 7. Isa. 6. 8. 9. 6. Rom. 4. 24. 2 Cor. 5. 21. Gal. 3. 13. 1 Thes. 5. 10. Heb. 6. 20. 1 Pet. 2. 21. & 4. 1. 1 John 5. 11.
USE, Rom. 1. 26. Eph. 4. 29. Heb. 5. 14.

1 Cor. 7. 31. *u.* world as not abusing
Gal. 5. 13. *u.* not liberty for occasion to the flesh
1 Tim. 1. 8. law is good if a man *u.* it lawfully
1 Cor. 9. 15. I have *used* none of these
Jer. 22. 13. that *useth* his neighbour's servant
Tit. 3. 14. learn good works for necessary *uses*
Ps. 119. 132. as thou *usest* to do to
Col. 2. 22. *using,* 1 Pet. 2. 16.
USURP, 1 Tim. 2. 12.
USURY, Ex. 22. 25. Lev. 25. 36, 37.

Deut. 23. 19, 20. Neh. 5. 7, 10. Ps. 15. 5. Prov. 28. 8. Isa. 24. 2. Jer. 15. 10. Ezek. 18. 8, 13, 17. & 22. 12. Matt. 25. 27. Luke 19. 23.
UTTER, Ps. 78. 2. & 94. 4.

Ps. 106. 2. who can *u.* mighty acts of the Lord
2 Cor. 12. 4. words not lawful for a man to *u.*
Rom. 8. 26. groanings that cannot be *uttered*
Heb. 5. 11. things hard to be *u.*
Ps. 19. 2. day unto day *uttereth*
Acts 2. 4. as the spirit gave them *utterance*
Eph. 6. 19. that *u.* may be given me
Col. 4. 3. God would open door of *u.*
Deut. 7. 2. *utterly,* Ps. 89. 33. & 119. 8, 43. Song 8. 7. Jer. 14. 9.
1 Thes. 2. 16. *uttermost,* Heb. 7. 25.
VAIN, Ex. 5. 9. & 20. 7.

Deut. 32. 47. it is not a *v.* thing for
1 Sam. 12. 21. turn not after *v.* things
Ps. 39. 6. every man walketh in a *v.* show, they are disquieted in *v.*
Job 11. 12. *v.* man would be wise
Ps. 60. 11. *v.* is help of man, 108. 12.
119. 113. I hate *v.* thoughts, but
127. 2. it is *v.* to rise up early
Jer. 4. 14. how long shall *v.* thoughts
Mal. 3. 14. said it is *v.* to serve God
Matt. 6. 7. use not *v.* repetitions
Rom. 1. 21. they glorified not God, but became *v.* in their imaginations
1 Cor. 3. 20. thoughts of wise are *v.*
Eph. 5. 6. deceive you with *v.* words
Col. 2. 8. through *v.* philosophy
James 1. 26. this man's religion is *v.*
1 Pet. 1. 18. from *v.* conversation
Ps. 73. 13. cleansed my heart in vain
89. 47. why hast thou made all men —
127. 1. labour—; walketh—
Isa. 45. 19. seek ye me—
49. 4. laboured—spent strength
Jer. 3. 23—is salvation hoped for from the hills
Matt. 15. 9.—do they worship me
Rom. 13. 4. beareth not the sword—
1 Cor. 15. 58. your labour is not—
2 Cor. 6. 1. receive not grace of God—
Phil. 2. 16. not run—nor laboured—
James 4. 5. do ye think Scripture saith—
2 Kings 17. 15. they followed *vanity*
Job 7. 3. made to possess months of *v.*
16. let me alone; my days are *v.*
Ps. 12. 2. speak *v.* every one to his neighbour
24. 4. not lifted up his soul to *v.* nor
39. 5. man at his best state is altogether *v.*
11. surely every man is *v.*
62. 9. men of low degree are *v.*
94. 11. thoughts of man are *v.*
119. 37. turn mine eyes from beholding *v.*
144. 4. man is like to *v.*
8. whose mouth speaketh *v.* 11.
Prov. 22. 8. that soweth iniquity shall reap *v.*
Eccl. 1. 2. *v.* of vanities, all is *v.* 14. & 3. 19. & 2. 1. & 4. 8. & 12. 8.
11. 10. childhood and youth are *v.*
Isa. 5. 18. iniquity with cords of *v.*
40. 17. less than nothing and *v.*
41. 29. are all *v.* wind, confusion
Hab. 2. 13. weary themselves for *v.*
Rom. 8. 20. the creature was made subject to *v.*
Eph. 4. 17. walk in *v.* of their mind
2 Pet. 2. 18. swelling words of *v.*
Ps. 31. 6. I hate them that regard lying *vanities*
Jer. 10. 8. the stock is a doctrine of *v.*
14. 22. can *v.* of Gentiles give rain
Jonah 2. 8. that observe lying *v.*
Acts 14. 15. turn from these *v.* unto the living God.
VALIANT, Song 3. 7. Isa. 10. 13.

Jer. 9. 3. not *v.* for the truth

Heb. 11. 34. through faith waxed *v.*
Ps. 60. 12. *valiantly,* 108. 13. & 118. 15, 16. Num. 24. 18.
VALUE, Job 13. 4. Matt. 10. 31.
VAPOUR, Jer. 10. 13. James 4. 14.
VARIABLENESS, James 1. 17.
VARIANCE, Matt. 10. 35. Gal. 5. 29.
VAUNT, Judg. 7. 2. 1 Cor. 13. 4.
VEHEMENT, Song 8. 6. 2 Cor. 7. 11.
VEIL, Gen. 24. 65. Song 5. 7.

Isa. 25. 7. destroy the *v.* spread over the nations
Matt. 27. 51. *v.* was rent from top to
2 Cor. 3. 13. Moses put a *v.* over face
15. *v.* is upon their heart, 14. 16.
Heb. 6. 19. entereth into that within *v.*
10. 20. through *v.* that is, his flesh
VENGEANCE taken, Gen. 4. 15.

Deut. 32. 35. to me belongeth *v.*
41. 43. Ps. 94. 1. Rom. 12. 19. Heb. 10. 30.
Ps. 58. 10. rejoice when he seeth *v.*
99. 8. tookest *v.* of their inventions
Isa. 34. 8. the day of the Lord's *v.*
Jer. 11. 20. let me see thy *v.* 20. 12.
51. 6. time of the Lord's *v.* 11.
Luke 21. 22. these be days of *v.* Isa. 63. 4.
2 Thes. 1. 8. in flaming fire taking *v.*
Jude 7. suffering *v.* of eternal fire
VERILY, Gen. 42. 21. Jer. 15. 11.

it is often used by Christ, as well as *verily, verily,* John 1. 51. & 3. 3, 5, 11. & 5. 19, 24, 25. & 6. 26.
VERITY, Ps. 111. 7. 1 Tim. 2. 7.
VERY, Prov. 17. 9. Matt. 24. 24. John 7. 26. & 14. 11. 1 Thes. 5. 23.
VESSEL, Ps. 2. 9. & 31. 12. Jer. 18. 4.

Jer. 22. 28. *v.* wherein is no pleasure, Hos. 8. 8.
Jer. 48. 11. not emptied from *v.* to *v.*
Acts 9. 15. he is a chosen *v.* unto me
Rom. 9. 21. one *v.* to honour and
1 Thes. 4. 4. possess his *v.* in sanctification
2 Tim. 2. 21. be a *v.* unto honour
1 Peter 3. 7. honour to wife as the weaker *v.*
Rom. 9. 21. *vessels* of wrath fitted
23. riches of glory on *v.* of mercy
2 Cor. 4. 7. treasure in earthen *v.*
VEXED, Job 27. 2. Ps. 6. 2, 3, 10.

Isa. 63. 10. and *v.* his Holy Spirit
2 Pet. 2. 7. Lot *v.* with filthy conversation, 8.
VIAL, Rev. 5. 8. & 16. 1. & 21. 9.
VICTORY is thine, O Lord, 1 Chron. 29. 11.

Ps. 98. 1. hand and arm gotten him the *v.*
Isa. 25. 8. swallow up death in *v.*
Matt. 20. 12. forth judgment unto *v.*
1 Cor. 15. 54. death is swallowed up in *v.*
55. O grave, where is thy *v.*
57. thanks to God who giveth us *v.*
1 John 5. 4. the *v.* that overcometh
VIGILANT, 1 Tim. 3. 2. 1 Pet. 5. 8.
VILE, thy brother seem, Deut. 25. 3.

1 Sam. 3. 13. sons made themselves *v.*
2 Sam. 6. 22. I will yet be more *v.* than
Job 40. 4. I am *v.* what shall I answer
Ps. 15. 4. in whose eyes a *v.* person is contemned
Isa. 32. 6. *v.* person will speak villany
Jer. 15. 19. take precious from the *v.*
Rom. 1. 26. up to *v.* affections
Phil. 3. 21. shall change our *v.* body
VINE, 1 Kings 4. 25. Mic. 4. 4.

Deut. 32. 32. *v.* is the *v.* of Sodom
Ps. 128. 3. thy wife shall be as a fruitful *v.*
Jer 2. 21. I planted thee a noble *v.*
Hos. 10. 1. Israel is an empty *v.*
14. 7. they shall grow as the *v.*
Matt. 26. 29. not drink of fruit of *v.*
John 15. 1. I am the true *v.* and my Father is the husbandman
5. I am the *v.* ye are the branches

Ps. 80. 15. *vineyard,* Prov. 24. 30.

Song 1. 6. Isa. 5. 1, 7. Matt. 20. 1. & 21. 33. Luke 13. 6. 1 Cor. 9. 7.
VIOLENCE, Lev. 6. 2. 2 Sam. 22. 3.

Gen. 6. 11. earth was filled with *v.*
Ps. 72. 14. redeem their soul from *v.*
73. 6. *v.* covereth them as garment
Hab. 1. 2. cry out unto thee of *v.*
Matt. 11. 12. the kingdom of heaven suffereth *v.*
Luke 3. 14. do *v.* to no man, and be
Heb. 11. 34. quenched the *v.* of fire
VIRGIN, Isa. 7. 14. 2 Cor. 11. 2.

Song 1. 3. *virgins,* Rev. 14. 4.
VIRTUE, Mark 5. 30. Luke 6. 19.

2 Pet. 1. 3. called us to glory and *v.*
5. to faith *v.* and to *v.* knowledge
Phil. 4. 8. if there be any *v.* think
Prov. 12. 4. *virtuous* woman, 31. 10.
VISIBLE and invisible, Col. 1. 16.
VISAGE, Isa. 52. 14. Lam. 4. 8.
VISION, 1 Sam. 3. 1. Ps. 89. 19. Matt. 17. 9. Acts 10. 19. & 16. 9.

Prov. 29. 18. where there is no *v.* the people perish
Hab. 2. 2. write the *v.*

3. the *v.* is for a time
Ezek. 13. 16. see *visions* of peace
Hos. 12. 10. I have multiplied *v.*
Joel 2. 28. young men shall see *v.* Acts 2. 17.
2 Cor. 12. 1. I will come to *v.* and
VISIT you, Gen. 50. 24, 25. Ex. 13. 19.

Job 7. 18. shouldest *v.* him every moment
Ps. 106. 4. *v.* me with thy salvation
Jer. 5. 9. shall I not *v.* you for these things, 9. 9.
Lam. 4. 22. *v.* iniquity, Jer. 14. 10. & 23. 2. Hos. 2. 13. & 8. 13.
Acts 7. 23. *v.* his brethren, 15. 36.
15. 14. God did *v.* the Gentiles
James 1. 27. to *v.* the fatherless and
Ex. 3. 16. I have surely *visited*
Ps. 17. 3. thou hast *v.* me in night
Isa. 26. 16. in trouble have they *v.*
Matt. 25. 36. I was sick and ye *v.*
Luke 1. 68. *v.* and redeemed people
78. dayspring from on high hath *v.*
Ps. 8. 4. *visitest,* 65. 9. Heb. 26.
Ex. 20. 5. *visiting* the iniquity of the fathers upon the children, 34. 7. Num. 14. 18. Deut. 5. 9.
VOCATION, worthy of, Eph. 4. 1.
VOICE is *v.* of Jacob, Gen. 27. 22.

Gen. 4. 10. *v.* of brother's blood
Ex. 5. 2. who is the Lord that I should obey his *v.*
Ps. 5. 3. my *v.* shalt thou hear in the morning
18. 13. the Highest gave his *v.*
42. 4. house of God with *v.* of joy
95. 7. to-day, if ye will hear his *v.*
103. 20. hearkening to *v.* of his word
Eccl. 12. 4. rise up at the *v.* of bird
Song 2. 14. let me hear thy *v.* 8. 13.
Isa. 30. 19. gracious at *v.* of thy cry
50. 10. obeyeth *v.* of his servant
Ezek. 33. 32. that hath a pleasant *v.*
John 5. 25. dead shall hear the *v.* of
10. 3. sheep hear his *v.* 4, 16, 27.
Gal. 4. 20. I desire to change my *v.*
1 Thes. 4. 16. with *v.* of archangel
Rev. 3. 20. if any man hear my *v.*
Acts 13. 27. *voices,* Rev. 4. 5. & 11. 19.
VOID of counsel, Deut. 32. 28.

Ps. 30. 39. made *v.* the covenant of thy servant
119. 126. have made *v.* thy law
Isa. 55. 11. word shall not return *v.*
Acts 24. 16. conscience *v.* of offence
Rom. 3. 31. do we make *v.* the law
1 Cor. 9. 15. make my glorying *v.*
VOLUME, Ps. 40. 7. Heb. 10. 17.
VOMIT, Job 20. 15. Prov. 23. 8. & 26. 11. Isa. 19. 14. 2 Pet. 2. 22.
VOW, Jacob vowed a, Gen. 28. 20. & 31. 13. Num. 6. 2. & 21. 2. & 30. 1 Sam. 1. 11. 2 Sam. 15. 7, 8.

Ps. 65. 1. to thee shall the *v.* be performed
76. 11. *v.* and pay unto the Lord, Deut. 23. 21, 22.
Eccl. 5. 4. a *v.* defer not to pay, 5.
Isa. 19. 21. shall *v.* a *v.* to the Lord, Ps. 132. 2.
Jonah 2. 9. I will pay that I have *vowed*
Job 22. 27. shall pay thy *vows*
Ps. 22. 25. I will pay my *v.* before
50. 14. pay thy *v.* to Most High
56. 12. thy *v.* O God are upon me
61. 5. heard my *v.*
8. perform my *v.*
Prov. 20. 25. after *v.* to make inquiry
31. 2. son of my *v.* 1 Sam. 1. 11.
Jonah 1. 16. offered sacrifice and made *v.*

W

WAGES, Lev. 19. 13. Ezek. 29. 18.
Jer. 22. 13. neighbour's service without *w.*
Hag. 1. 6. earneth *w.* to put it into a bag
Mal. 3. 5. oppress hireling in his *w.*
Luke 3. 14. be content with your *w.*
Rom. 6. 23. the *w.* of sin is death
WAIT till my change come, Job. 14. 14.
Ps. 25. 5. on thee do I *w.* all the day
27. 14. *w.* on the Lord; *w.* I say
37. 34. *w.* on the Lord and keep his way
62. 5. *w.* thou only upon God
104. 27. these *w.* all upon thee
130. 5. 1 *w.* for the Lord, my soul doth *w.*
145. 15. eyes of all wait upon thee
Prov. 20. 22. *w.* on the Lord and he shall save
Isa. 8. 17. I will *w.* upon the Lord
30. 18. will the Lord *w.* blessed are all they that *w.* for him
40. 31. that *w.* on the Lord shall renew their strength
Lam. 3. 25. good to them that *w.* for
26. quietly *w.* for salvation of Lord
Hos. 12. 6. *w.* on thy God continually
Mic. 7. 7. I will *w.* for God of my salvation
Hab. 2. 3. *w.* for it, it will surely
Zeph. 3. 8. *w.* ye on me, I will rise to
Luke 12. 36. men that *w.* for their lord
Gal. 5. 5. through the Spirit *w.* for hope of faith
1 Thes. 1. 10. *w.* for his Son from heaven
Gen. 49. 18. *waited* for thy salvation
Ps. 40. 1. I *w.* patiently for the Lord
Isa. 25. 9. our God, we have *w.* for
26. 8. in the way of thy judgments have we *w.*
33. 2. O Lord we have *w.* for thee
Zech. 11. 11. poor of flock that *w.* on
Mark 15. 43. *w.* for kingdom of God
1 Pet. 3. 20. long suffering of God *w.*
Ps. 33. 20. our soul *waiteth* for the Lord, 40. 1.
65. 1. praise *w.* for thee, in Zion
130. 6. my soul *w.* for Lord more
Isa. 64. 4. prepared for him that *w.*
Prov. 8. 34. *waiting* at the posts of
Luke 2. 25. *w.* for the consolation of Israel
Rom. 8. 23. *w.* for the adoption
1 Cor. 1. 7. *w.* for coming of Lord
2 Thes. 3. 5. to a patient *w.* for of Christ
WAKETH, Ps. 127. 1. Song 2. 2.
Ps. 77. 4. holdest my eyes *waking*
Isa. 50. 4. *wakeneth,* Joel 3. 12.
WALK in my law, Ex. 16. 4.
Gen. 24. 40. Lord before whom I *w.*
17. 1. *w.* before me and be perfect
Lev. 26. 12. I will *w.* among you

21. if ye *w.* contrary unto me
23. but will *w.* contrary unto me
24. will I *w.* contrary unto you
Deut. 5. 33. *w.* in the ways of the Lord, 8. 6. & 10. 12. & 11. 22. & 13. 5. & 28. 9.
13. 4. ye shall *w.* after the Lord
Ps. 23. 4. though I *w.* through valley of death
83. 11. no good thing from them that *w.* uprightly
116. 9. I will *w.* before the Lord
119. 3. do no iniquity, they *w.* in
Eccl. 11. 9. *w.* in ways of thy heart
Isa. 2. 3. will *w.* in his paths
3. *w.* in the light
30. 21. this is the way, *w.* ye in it
40. 31. shall *w.* and not faint
50. 11. *w.* in the light of your fire
Jer. 23. 14. commit adultery and *w.*
Dan. 4. 37. that *w.* in pride he is able to abase
Hos. 14. 9. just shall *w.* in them
Mic. 6. 8. *w.* humbly with thy God
Amos 3. 3. how can two *w.* together except they be agreed
Zech. 10. 12. *w.* up and down in his name
Luke 13. 33. I must *w.* to-day and to-morrow
John 8. 12. followeth me, not *w.* in darkness
11. 9. *w.* in day, he stumbleth not
Rom. 4. 12. *w.* in steps of that faith
6. 4. *w.* in newness of life
8. 1. *w.* not after the flesh, 4.
2 Cor. 5. 7. we *w.* by faith, not sight
10. 3. though *w.* in flesh, not war after the flesh
Gal. 6. 16. as many as *w.* according to this rule
Eph. 2. 10. ordained that we *w.* in
4. 1. *w.* worthy of the vocation
5. 15. *w.* circumspectly, not as
Phil. 3. 17. mark them who *w.* so as
Col. 1. 10. that ye might *w.* worthy
1 Thes. 2. 12. ye would *w.* worthy of
4. 1. how ought ye to *w.* and please
1 John 1. 7. if we *w.* in the light
2. 6. ought so to *w.* as he walked
3 John 4. to hear that my children *w.* in truth, 3.
Rev. 3. 4. shall *w.* with me in white
16. 15. lest he *w.* naked and see his
21. 24. nations shall *w.* in light of
John 12. 35. *w.* in light while ye have
Rom. 13. 13. let us *w.* honestly as in
Gal. 5. 16. *w.* in Spirit, and not fulfil
25. if we live in Spirit, let us *w.* in
Eph. 5. 2. *w.* in love as Christ loved
8. *w.* as children of light
Phil. 3. 16. let us *w.* by the same rule
Col. 2. 6. as ye received Christ, so *w.*
4. 5. *w.* in wisdom, redeeming the
Gen. 6. 9. Noah *walked* with God
5. 22. Enoch *w.* with God, 24.
Ps. 55. 14. we *w.* unto the house of God in company
81. 12. *w.* in their own counsels
13. O that Israel had *w.* in my
Isa. 9. 2. people that *w.* in darkness
2 Cor. 10. 2. as if we *w.* according to the flesh
12. 18. *w.* we not in same spirit
Gal. 2. 14. saw that they *w.* not uprightly
Eph. 2. 2. in time past we *w.*
1 Pet. 4. 3. we *w.* in lasciviousness
Isa. 43. 2. when thou *walkest* through the fire
Rom. 14. 15. *w.* thou not charitably
Ps. 15. 2. he that *walketh* uprightly
39. 6. every man *w.* in a vain show
Prov. 10. 9. he that *w.* uprightly, *w.* surely
Prov. 13. 20. *w.* with wise men shall be wise
Isa. 50. 10. *w.* in darkness, and hath
Jer. 10. 23. not in man that *w.* to direct his steps

Mic. 2. 7. do good to him that *w.* uprightly
2 Thes 3. 6. from brother that *w.* disorderly
1 Pet. 5. 8. *w.* about seeking whom he may devour
Rev. 2. 1. *w.* in midst of the seven golden candlesticks
Gen. 3. 8. voice of Lord *walking* in
Isa. 57. 2. *w.* in his own uprightness
Jer. 6. 28. revolters walk with slanderers
Mic. 2. 11. if man *w.* in falsehood do
Luke 1. 6. *w.* in all commandments
Acts 9. 31. *w.* in the fear of the Lord
2 Cor. 4. 2. not *w.* in craftiness
2 Pet. 3. 3. *w.* after their own lusts, Jude 16
2 John 4. thy children *w.* in truth
WALL, Ps. 62. 3. Prov. 18. 11. Song 2. 9. & 8. 9, 10. Isa. 26. 1. & 60. 18.
WANDER, Num. 14. 33. Ps. 119. 10.
Lam. 4. 14. *wandered,* Heb. 11. 37.
Prov. 21. 16. *wandereth,* 27. 8.
1 Tim. 5. 13. *wandering,* Jude 13.
Ps. 56. 8. tellest my *wanderings*
WANT, Deut. 28. 48. Job. 31. 19.
Ps. 23. 1. the Lord is my shepherd, I shall not *w.*
34. 9. no *w.* to them that fear him
Prov. 6. 11. thy *w.* come as an armed man, 24. 34.
2 Cor. 8. 14. a supply for your *w.*
Phil. 4. 11. not speak in respect of *w.*
James 1. 4. perfect and entire, *wanting*
WANTONNESS, Rom. 13. 13. 2 Pet. 2. 18.
WAR, Ex. 13. 17. & 17. 16. Ps. 27. 3.
Job 10. 17. changes and *w.* are against
Ps. 18. 34. teacheth my hands to *w.* 144. 1.
120. 7. I am for peace, they for *w.*
Prov. 20. 18. with good advice make *w.*
Eccl. 8. 8. is no discharge in this *w.*
Isa. 2. 4. not learn *w.* any more, Mic. 4. 3.
Mic. 3. 5. they prepare *w.* against him
2 Cor. 10. 3. we do not *w.* after flesh
1 Tim. 1. 18. mightest *w.* a good warfare
1 Pet. 2. 11. fleshly lusts which *w.*
Rev. 11. 7. beast shall make *w.*
12. 7. there was *w.* in heaven
17. 14. these make *w.* with Lamb
19. 11. in righteousness judge and make *w.*
Num. 21. 14. in the book of the *wars* of the Lord
Ps. 46. 9. he maketh *w.* to cease
Matt. 24. 6. hear of *w.* and rumours of *w.*
James 4. 1. whence come *w.* and
2 Tim. 2. 4. no man that *warreth*
Isa. 37. 8. *warring,* Rom. 7. 23.
WARFARE, Isa. 40. 2. 1 Cor. 9. 7. 2 Cor. 10. 4. 1 Tim. 1. 18.
WARN, 2 Chron. 19. 10. Acts 10. 22.
Ezek. 3. 19. if thou *w.* the wicked
33. 3. blow the trumpet and *w.* the people, 9.
Acts 20. 31. I ceased not to *w.* every one night and day
1 Cor. 4. 14. my beloved sons I *w.*
1 Thes. 5. 14. *w.* them that are unruly
Ps. 19. 11. by them is thy servant *warned*
Matt. 3. 7. who hath *w.* you to flee
Heb. 11. 7. Noah being *w.* of God
Jer. 6. 10. to whom I give *warning*
Col. 1. 28. teaching every man, *w.*
WASH, Lev. 6. 27. & 14. 15, 16.
Job 9. 30. if I *w.* myself in snow
Ps. 26. 6. I will *w.* my hands in innocency
51. 2. *w.* me thoroughly from iniquity
7. *w.* me and I shall be whiter than

58. 10. he shall *w.* his feet in blood
Isa. 1. 6. *w.* you, make you clean
Jer. 2. 22. thou *w.* thee with nitre
4. 14. *w.* thy heart from wickedness
Luke 7. 8. to *w.* his feet with tears
John 13. 5. began to *w.* disciples' feet
8. 1. *w.* thee not, thou hast no part
10. needeth not save to *w.* his feet
14. ye ought to *w.* one another's feet
Acts 22. 16. he baptized and *w.* away
Job 29. 6. when I *washed* my steps
Song 5. 3. I have *w.* my feet
Isa. 4. 4. *w.* away the filth of the daughter of Zion
Ezek. 16. 4. neither wast thou *w.* in
16. 9. I thoroughly *w.* away blood
1 Cor. 6. 11. we are *w.* justified
Heb. 10. 22. *w.* with pure water
Rev. 1. 5. *w.* us from sins in his blood
7. 14. *w.* robes, and made white in blood
Eph. 5. 26. *washing,* Tit. 5. 5.
WASTE, Ps. 80. 13. Matt. 26. 8.
Luke 15. 11. *wasted,* 36. 1. Gal. 1. 13.
Job 14. 10. *wasteth,* Prov. 19. 26.
Prov. 18. 9. *waster,* Isa. 54. 16.
Isa. 59. 7. *wasting* and destruction, 60. 18.
WATCH, Neh. 4. 9. Job 7. 12.
Job 14. 15. dost thou not *w.* over sin
Ps. 102. 7. I *w.* and am as a sparrow
130. 6. they that *w.* for morning
141. 3. set a *w.* before my mouth
Jer. 44. 27. *w.* over them for evil
Matt. 24. 42. *w.* for ye know not, 25. 13.
36. 41. *w.* and pray that ye enter not
Mark 13. 33. take heed, *w.* and, 37.
1 Cor. 16. 13. *w.* ye, stand fast in the
Col. 4. 2. *w.* in the same with thanksgiving
1 Thes. 5. 6. let us *w.* and be sober
2 Tim. 4. 5. *w.* thou in all things
Heb. 13. 17. they *w.* for your souls
1 Pet. 4. 7. be sober, *w.* unto prayer
Rev. 3. 3. if thou shalt not *w.* I will
Jer. 31. 28. like as I *watched* over
20. 10. familiars *w.* for my halting
Matt. 24. 43. he would have *w.*
Ps. 37. 32. the wicked *watcheth* the
Ezek. 7. 6. the end is come; it *w.* for
Rev. 16. 15. blessed is he that *w.* and
Dan. 4. 13. a *watcher* and holy one, 17. 23.
Ps. 63. 6. *watches,* 119. 148. Lam. 2. 19.
Rev. 3. 2. be *watchful*
Prov. 8. 34. *watching* daily at gates
Luke 12. 37. blessed whom the Lord shall find *w.*
Eph. 6. 18. *w.* with all perseverance
2 Cor. 6. 5. in *watchings,* 11. 27.
Isa. 21. 11. *watchman,* Ezek. 3. 17. & 33. 7.
Song 3. 3. *watchmen,* 5. 7. Isa. 52. 8. & 50. 10. & 62. 6. Jer. 31. 6.
WATER, Gen. 49. 4. Ex. 12. 9. & 17. 6.
2 Sam. 14. 14. we are *w.* spilt on the ground
Job 15. 16. drinketh iniquity like *w.*
Ps. 22. 14. I am poured out like *w.*
Isa. 12. 3. draw *w.* out of the wells of salvation
27. 3. I will *w.* it every moment
30. 20. give you *w.* of affliction
41. 17. when poor seek *w.* and find
44. 3. pour *w.* on him that is thirsty
58. 11. shalt be like a spring of *w.*
Lam. 1. 16. mine eye runneth down with *w.* 3. 48.
Ezek. 36. 25. sprinkle clean *w.* on
Amos 8. 11. nor a thirst for *w.*
Matt. 3. 11. I baptize you with *w.*

10. 42. cup of cold w. in name of a
Luke 16. 24. dip tip of his finger in w.
John 3. 5. except a man be born of w.
23. baptized because there was much w. there
4. 14. shall be in him a well of w.
7. 38. flow rivers of living w.
19. 34. came thereout blood and w.
Acts 8. 38. both went down into w.
10. 47. can any forbid w. that these
Eph. 5. 26. cleanse it with the washing of w.
1 John 5. 6. he that came by w. and
8. three bear witness, Spirit, w. and
Jude 12. clouds they are without w.
Rev. 7. 17. lead them to living fountains of w.
21. 6. fountain of w. of life, 22. 1.
22. 17. take the w. of life freely
Ps. 23. 2. leadeth me beside the still *waters*
69. 1. w. are come into my soul, 2.
124. 4. had overwhelmed us, 5.
Prov. 5. 15. drink w. out of thine own cistern, and running w. out of thine own well
9. 17. stolen w. are sweet
Eccl. 11. 1. cast thy bread upon w.
Song. 4. 15. a well of living w.
Isa. 32. 20. blessed are ye that sow beside all w.
33. 16. bread given him; his w.
35. 6. in wilderness shall w. break out, I give w. in the wilderness
54. 9. this is as w. of Noah unto me
55. 1. come ye to w. buy and eat
58. 11. whose w. fail not
Jer. 2. 13. fountain of living w. 17. 13.
9. 1. O that my head were w.
Hab. 2. 14. as w. cover the sea, Isa. 11. 9.
Zech. 14. 8. living w. shall go out from Jerusalem, Ezek. 47. 1.
Rev. 1. 15. his voice as the sound of many w. 14. 2. & 19. 6.
Prov. 11. 25. he that *watereth* shall be *watered*
Isa. 58. 11. be like a w. garden, Jer. 31. 12.
1 Cor. 3. 6. I planted, Apollos w. 7.
Ps. 12. 7. noise of thy *water-spouts*
WAVERING, Heb. 10. 23. James 1. 6.
WAX, Ex. 32. 10, 11, 22. Ps. 22. 14. & 65. 2. & 97. 5. Matt. 24. 12. Luke 12. 33. 1 Tim. 5. 11. 2 Tim. 3. 13.
WAY, Ex. 13. 21. & 23. 20. & 32. 8.
1 Sam. 12. 23. teach you good and right w.
1 Kings 2. 2. I go w. of all the earth
Ezra 8. 21. seek of him a right w.
Ps. 1. 6. the Lord knoweth the w. of the righteous
2. 12. lest ye perish from the w.
Ps. 49. 13. this their w. is their folly
67. 2. that thy w. may be known
78. 50. made a w. to his anger
119. 30. I have chosen w. of truth
32. run w. of thy commandments
104. I hate every false w.
Prov. 2. 8. Lord preserveth the w. of his saints
10. 29. w. of the Lord is strength
14. 12. a w. that seemeth right
15. 9. w. of the wicked is abomination
24. the w. of life is above to the wise
Eccl. 11. 5. thou knowest not what is the w. of the spirit
Isa. 26. 7. w. of the just is uprightness, 8.
Isa. 30. 21. this is the w. walk ye in it
35. 8. a high w. and a w. called the w. of holiness
40. 3. prepare the w. of the Lord, Luke 3. 4.
Isa. 43. 19. make a w. in the wilderness, 16.
59. 8. the w. of peace they know not

Jer. 6. 16. where is a good w. and walk
10. 23. w. of man is not in himself
21. 8. set before you the w. of life and the w. of death
32. 39. give them one heart and one w.
50. 5. shall ask the w. to Zion
Amos 2. 7. turn aside the w. of the meek
Mal. 3. 1. and he shall prepare the w. before me
Matt. 7. 13. broad is the w. to destruction
14. narrow is the w. that leadeth to life
22. 16. teacheth the w. of God in truth
John 1. 23. make straight the w. of Lord
14. 4. the w. ye know, 6. I am the w.
Acts 16. 17. which show unto us the w. of salvation
18. 25. instructed in w. of the Lord, 26.
1 Cor. 10. 13. will also make a w. to escape
12. 31. I show you a more excellent w.
2 Pet. 2. 2. the w. of truth be evil spoken
1 Kings 8. 32. bring *his way* on his head
Job 17. 9. righteous shall hold on—
Ps. 18. 30. as for God—is perfect
37. 23. delight in—34. and keep—
119. 9. shall a young man cleanse—
Prov. 14. 8. prudent to understand—
16. 9. man's heart deviseth—
Isa. 55. 7. let the wicked forsake—
Ps. 25. 8. teach sinners *in the way*
119. 14. I rejoiced—of the testimonies
139. 24. lead me—everlasting
Isa. 26. 8.—of thy judgments we waited
Matt. 5. 25. agree with thine adversary—
21. 32. John came—of righteousness
Luke 1. 79. guide your feet—of peace
Job 40. 19. he is chief of *ways* of God
Ps. 84. 5. in whose heart are the w. of them
Prov. 3. 17. her w. are w. of pleasantness
5. 21. w. of man are before Lord
16. 2. w. of man are clean in his own eyes
7. when a man's w. please the Lord
Jer. 7. 3. amend your w. and your doings
Lam. 1. 4. the w. of Zion do mourn
3. 4. let us search and try our w.
Deut. 32. 4. *his ways*, Ps. 145. 17. Isa. 2. 3. Mic. 4. 2. Rom. 11. 33.
Ps. 119. 5. *my ways*, 15, 26, 59, 168. & 139. 3. & 39. 1. Prov. 23. 26. Isa. 55. 8. & 49. 11.
Prov. 14. 14. *own ways*, Isa. 53. 6. & 58. 13. & 66. 3. Ezek. 36. 31, 32.
Job. 21. 14. *thy ways*, Ps. 25. 4. & 91. 11. Prov. 3. 6. & 4. 26. Isa. 63. 17. Ezek. 16. 61. Dan. 5. 23. Rev. 15. 3.
Isa. 35. 8. *wayfaring*, Jer. 14. 8.
WEAK, 2 Chron. 15. 7. Job. 4. 3. Ps. 6. 2.
Isa. 35. 3. strengthen ye the w. hands
Ezek. 16. 30. how w. is thy heart
Matt. 26. 41. spirit is willing but the flesh is w.
Rom. 4. 19. Abraham being not w. in faith.
14. 1. him that is w. in the faith receive
1 Cor. 4. 10. we are w. but ye are strong
9. 22. to the w. became I as the w.
11. 30. for this cause many are w.

2 Cor. 11. 29. who is w. and I am not w.
12. 10. when I am w. then am I strong
1 Thes. 5. 13. support the w. be patient
Isa. 14. 12. *weaken*, Ps. 102. 23. Job 12. 21.
2 Sam. 3. 1. *weaker*, 1 Pet. 3. 7.
1 Cor. 1. 25. *weakness*, 2. 3. & 15. 43.
2 Cor. 12. 9. & 13. 4. Heb. 11. 34.
WEALTH, Gen. 34. 29. Deut. 8. 17.
Deut. 8. 18. Lord giveth power to get w.
Job 21. 13. they spend their days in w.
Ps. 49. 6. that trust in their w.
10. leave their w.
112. 3. w. and riches are in his house
Prov. 10. 15. the rich man's wealth is his strong city, 18. 11.
13. 11. w. gotten by vanity shall be diminished
22. w. of sinners is laid up for the just
19. 4. w. maketh many friends
1 Cor. 10. 24. seek another's w.
WEANED, Ps. 131. 2. Isa. 11. 8. & 28. 9.
WEAPON, Isa. 13. 5. & 54. 17. 2 Cor. 10. 4.
WEAR, Deut. 22. 5, 11. Dan. 7. 25. Matt. 11. 8. James 2. 3. 1 Pet. 3. 3.
WEARY of my life, Gen. 27. 46.
Job 3. 17. there the w. be at rest
10. 1. my soul is w. of life, Jer. 4. 31.
Prov. 3. 11. neither be w. of his correction
Isa. 7. 13. w. men, but will ye w. my God
40. 28. the Lord fainteth not, neither is w.
31. shall run and not be w.
43. 22. hast been w. of me. O Israel
50. 4. speak a word in season to the w.
Jer. 6. 11. w. with holding in, 20. 9.
9. 5. w. themselves to commit iniquity
15. 6. I am w. with repenting
31. 25. I have satiated every w. soul
Gal. 6. 9. not be w. in well doing, 2 Thes. 3. 13.
Isa. 43. 24. *wearied*, 57. 10. Jer. 12. 5. Ezek. 24. 12. Mic. 6. 3. Mal. 2. 17. John 4. 7. Heb. 12. 3.
Eccl. 12. 12. *weariness*, Mal. 1. 13.
Job 7. 3. *wearisome* nights appointed to me
WEB, Job 8. 14. Isa. 59. 5, 6.
WEDDING, Matt. 22. 3, 8, 11. Luke 14. 8.
WEEK, Dan. 9. 27. Matt. 28. 1. Luke 18. 12. Acts 20. 7. 1 Cor. 16. 2.
Jer. 5. 24. *weeks*, Dan. 9. 24-26, & 10. 2.
WEEP, Job 30. 25. Isa. 30. 19. & 33. 7. Jer. 9. 1. & 13. 17. Joel 2. 17.
Luke 6. 21. blessed are ye that w. now
23. 28. w. not for me, but w. for yourselves
Acts 21. 13. what mean ye to w. and break
Rom. 12. 15. w. with them that w.
1 Cor. 7. 30. that w. as though *wept* not
James 5. 1. rich men w. and howl
Ps. 126. 6. *weepeth*, Lam. 1. 2.
1 Sam. 1. 8. why *weepest*, John 20. 13, 15.
Ps. 30. 5. *weeping* may endure for a night
Isa. 22. 12. Lord call to w. and mourning
Jer. 31. 9. they shall come with w.
Joel 2. 12. turn to me with w.
Mal. 2. 13. covering altar of the Lord with w.

Matt. 8. 12. w. and gnashing of teeth 22. 13. & 24. 51. & 25. 30.
WEIGH the paths of the just, Isa. 26. 7.
Prov. 16. 2. Lord *weigheth* the spirits
Job 31. 6. let me be *weighed* in balances
Dan. 5. 27. art w. in the balances
Prov. 11. 1. just *weight* is his delight 16.
16. 11. just w. and balances are the Lord's
2 Cor. 4. 17. eternal w. of glory
Heb. 12. 1. laying aside every w. and sin
Lev. 19. 36. just balances, just *weights*
Deut. 55. 13. divers w. Prov. 20. 10, 23.
Matt. 23. 23. omit *weightier* matters of law
WELL, Ps. 84. 6. Prov. 5. 15. & 10. 11. Song 4. 15. Isa. 12. 3. John 4. 14. 2 Pet. 2. 17.
Gen. 4. 7. if thou doest *well*, shalt be accepted
Ex. 1. 20. God dealt w. with midwives
Ps. 119. 65. hast dealt w. with thy servant
128. 2. it shall be w. with thee
Eccl. 8. 12. it shall be w. with them
Isa. 3. 10. shall be w. with him
Rom. 2. 7. *well doing*, Gal. 6. 9. 2 Thess. 3. 13. 1 Pet. 2. 15. & 3. 17 & 4. 19.
WENT, Ps. 42. 4. & 119. 67. Matt. 21. 30.
WEPT, Neh. 1. 4. Ps. 69. 10. Hos. 12. 4. Matt. 26. 75. Luke 19. 41. John 11. 35.
WHEAT, Ps. 81. 16. Prov. 27. 22. Song. 7. 2.
Jer. 12. 13. have sown w. but reap thorns
23. 28. what is the chaff to the w.
Amos 8. 5. that we may set forth w.
Matt. 3. 12. gather w. into the garner
Luke 22. 31. may sift you as w.
John 12. 24. except a corn of w. fall into
WHEEL, Ps. 83. 13. Prov. 20. 26.
Ezek. 1. 16. a w. in the midst of a w. 10. 10.
10. 13. it was cried unto them, O w.
Ex. 14. 25. *wheels*, Judg. 5. 28. Ezek. 1. & 10. Dan. 7. 9. Nah. 3. 2.
WHET, Deut. 32. 41. Ps. 7. 12. & 64. 3.
WHISPERER, Prov. 16. 28.
WHIT, John 7. 23. & 12. 10. 2 Cor. 11. 5.
WHITE, Lev. 13. 3. 4. Num. 12. 10.
Job 6. 6. any taste in the w. of an egg
Ps. 63. 14. w. as snow, Dan. 7. 9.
Eccl. 9. 8. let your garments be always w.
Song 5. 10. my beloved is w. and ruddy
Isa. 1. 18. sins shall be w. as snow
Dan. 11. 35. fall to make them w.
12. 10. many purified and made w.
Matt. 17. 2. his raiment was w. 28. 3.
Rev. 17. 2. gave him a w. stone
3. 4. walk with me in w. raiment 5. 18. & 4. 4. & 7. 9, 13. & 15. 16. & 19. 8, 14.
Matt. 23. 27. *whited*, Acts 23. 3.
Ps. 51. 7. *whiter* than snow, Lam. 4. 7.
WHOLE, Ps. 9. 1. & 119. 10. Isa. 54. 5. Mic. 4. 13. Zech. 4. 14. Matt. 6. 26. Eph. 6. 11. 1 John 2. 2. & 5. 19.
Job 5. 18. he woundeth and his hands make w.
Matt. 9. 12. those that are w. need not a physician, Luke 5. 31.
Mark 5. 34. faith hath made thee w. 10. 52. Luke 4. 48. & 17. 19.
John 5. 4. made w. of whatsoever disease
6. wilt be made w. 14. art made w.

Acts 9. 34. Christ maketh thee *w*.
Jer. 46. 28. *wholly*, 1 Thes. 5. 23. 1 Tim. 4. 15.
Prov. 15. 4. *wholesome*, 1 Tim. 6. 3.
WHORE, Lev. 19. 29. & 21. 7, 9. Deut. 22. 21. & 23. 17, 18. Prov. 23. 27. Ezek. 16. 28. Rev. 17. 1, 16.
Jer. 3. 9. *whoredom*, Ezek. 16. Hos. 2. 2, 4. & 4. 11, 12. & 5. 3, 4.
Eph. 5. 5. *whoremonger*, 1 Tim. 1. 10. Heb. 13. 4. Rev. 21. 8. & 22. 15.
WICKED, Ex. 23. 7. Deut. 15. 9. & 25. 1.
Gen. 18. 25. wilt destroy righteous with *w*.
1 Sam. 2. 9. the *w*. shall be silent in darkness
Job 21. 30. *w*. is reserved till the day of destruction
34. 18. is it fit to say to king, thou art *w*.
Ps. 7. 11. God is angry with the *w*. everday
9. 17. *w*. shall be turned into hell
11. 6. on *w*. he will rain snares
58. 3. *w*. are estranged from the womb
119. 155. salvation is far from *w*.
145. 20. all the *w*. shall he destroy, 147. 6.
Prov. 11. 5. *w*. shall fall by his own wickedness
21. *w*. shall not be unpunished, 31.
21. 12. God overthroweth the *w*.
28. 1. the *w*. flee when no man pursueth
Eccl. 7. 17. be not overmuch *w*.
Isa. 55. 7. let the *w*. forsake his way
57. 20. the *w*. are like the troubled sea
Jer. 17. 9. the heart is desperately *w*.
25. 31. he will give the *w*. to the sword
Ezek. 3. 18. warn the *w*. 33. 8, 9, 11.
Dan. 12. 10. *w*. shall do *wickedly*
Gen. 19. 7. do not so *w*. Neh. 9. 33.
1 Sam. 12. 25. if ye shall do *w*.
Job 13. 7. will ye speak *w*. for God
Ps. 18. 21. have not *w*. departed from my
Gen. 6. 5. God saw that *wickedness* was
39. 9. how can I do this great *w*.
1 Sam. 24. 13. *w*. proceedeth from the wicked
Job 4. 8. that sow *w*. shall reap the same
Ps. 7. 9. the *w*. of wicked come to end
45. 7. righteousness, and hatest *w*.
Prov. 8. 7. *w*. is abomination to me
10. 2. treasures of *w*. profit not in
14. 6. *w*. overthroweth sinners
Eccl. 8. 8. neither shall *w*. deliver those
Isa. 9. 18. *w*. burneth as the fire
Jer. 2. 19. thine own *w*. shall correct thee
4. 14. O Jerusalem, wash thy heart from *w*.
14. 20. we acknowledge our *w*.
Hos. 10. 13. ye have ploughed *w*. and reaped
Acts 8. 22. repent of this thy *w*.
1 John 5. 19. whole world lieth in *w*.
WIDE, Deut. 15. 8, 11. Ps. 35. 2. & 81. 10. Prov. 13. 3. Matt. 7. 13.
WIDOW, Mark 12. 42. 1 Tim. 5. 5. Deut. 10. 18. Ps. 146. 9. Luke 18. 3, 5.
Ps. 68. 5. *widows*, Jer. 49. 11. Matt. 23. 14. 1 Tim. 5. 3. James 1. 27.
WIFE, Ex. 20. 17. Lev. 21. 13.
Prov. 5. 18. rejoice with *w*. of thy youth
18. 22. that findeth a *w*. findeth a good
19. 14. a prudent *w*. is from the Lord
Eccl. 9. 9. live joyfully with thy *w*.

Hos. 12. 12. Israel served for a *w*. and for a *w*. he kept sheep
Mal. 2. 15. against *w*. of thy youth
Luke 17. 32. remember Lot's *w*.
Eph. 5. 33. every man love his *w*. as himself
Rev. 19. 7. his *w*. made herself ready
21. 9. shew thee the bride, the Lamb's *w*.
1 Cor. 7. 29. *wives*. Eph. 5. 25, 28, 33. Col. 3, 18, 19. 1 Tim. 3. 11. 1 Pet. 3. 1, 7.
WILDERNESS, Deut. 32. 10. Prov. 21. 19. Song 3. 6. & 8. 5. Isa. 35. 1, 6. & 41. 18, 19. & 42. 11. & 43. 19, 20. Rev. 12. 6.
WILES, Num. 25. 18. Eph. 6. 11.
WILL, Lev. 1. 3. & 19. 5. & 22. 19.
Deut. 33. 16. the good *w*. of him that dwelt in the bush
Matt. 7. 21. doeth *w*. of my Father, 12. 50.
Luke 2. 14. good *w*. towards men
John 1. 13. *w*. of flesh, nor of *w*. of man but of God
3. 34. my meat is to do the *w*. of him
6. 40. this is the *w*. of him that sent me
Acts 21. 14. saying the *w*. of the Lord be done
Eph. 5. 17. understandeth what the *w*. of the Lord is
6. 7. with good *w*. doing service
Acts 22. 14. *his will*, John 7. 17. Rom. 2. 18. Eph. 1. 5, 9. Col. 1. 9. 2 Tim. 2. 26. Heb. 13. 21. 1 John 5. 14. Rev. 17. 17.
Luke 22. 42. *my will*, Acts 13. 22.
John 5. 30. *own wilt*, 6. 38. Eph. 1. 11. Heb. 2. 4. James 1. 18.
Ps. 40. 8. *thy will*, 143. 10. Matt. 6. 10. & 26. 42. Heb. 10. 7, 9.
Ezra, 7. 18. *will of God*, Mark 3. 35. Rom. 1. 10. & 8. 27. & 12. 2. 1 Cor. 1. 1. 2 Cor. 8. 5. Gal. 1. 4. Eph. 1. 1. & 6. 6. Col. 1. 1. & 4. 12. 1 Thes. 4. 3. Heb. 10. 36. 1 Pet. 4. 2, 19. 1 John 2. 17.
Matt. 26. 39. not as *I will*, but as thou wilt
John 15. 7. ask what ye *w*. and it shall be
17. 24. I *w*. that those thou hast given
Rom. 7. 18. to *w*. is present with me
9. 18. on whom he *w*. have mercy
Phil. 2. 13. worketh to *w*. and to do
Rev. 22. 17. whosoever *w*. let him take
Rom. 9. 16. not of him that *willeth* nor runneth
Heb. 10. 26. if we sin *wilfully* after we
Ex. 35. 5. who is of a *willing* heart
22. as many as were *w*. hearted
1 Chron. 28. 9. with a perfect heart and *w*. mind
Ps. 110. 3. people shall be *w*. in the day of thy power
Isa. 1. 19. if he be *w*. and obedient
Matt. 26. 41. the Spirit is *w*. but the flesh
Luke 22. 42. if be *w*. remove this cup
John 5. 35. *w*. for a season to rejoice
2 Cor. 5. 8. *w*. rather to be absent
1 Tim. 6. 18. be *w*. to communicate
Heb. 13. 18. *w*. in all things to live honestly
2 Pet. 3. 9. not *w*. any should perish
Judges 5. 2. *willingly* offered themselves, 9.
1 Chron. 29. 9. with perfect heart offered *w*.
Lam. 3. 33. Lord doth not afflict *w*.
Hos. 5. 11. he *w*. walked after the commandments
1 Pet. 5. 2. not by constraint, but *w*.
Col. 2. 23. wisdom in *will worship*
WILLOWS, Lev. 23. 40. Isa. 44. 4.
WIN, Phil. 3. 8.

Prov. 11. 30. *winneth*
WIND, Job 7. 7. & 30. 15. Ps. 103. 16.
Prov. 11. 29. inherit *w*.
27. 16. hideth *w*.
30. 4. gather the *w*. Ps. 135. 7.
Eccl. 11. 4. he that observeth the *w*.
Isa. 26. 18. have brought forth *w*.
27. 8. he stayeth his rough *w*. in
Jer. 5. 13. prophets shall become *w*.
10. 13. bring *w*. out of his treasures, 51. 16.
Hos. 8. 7. sown *w*.
12. 1. feedeth on *w*.
John 3. 8. *w*. bloweth where it listeth
Eph. 4. 14. about with every *w*.
2 Kings 2. 11. *whirlwind*, Prov. 1. 27. & 10. 25. Isa. 66. 15. Hos. 8. 7. & 13. 3. Nah. 1. 3. Hab. 3. 14. Zech. 7. 14. & 9. 14.
Ezek. 37. 9. *winds*, Matt. 8. 26. Luke 8. 25.
WINDOWS, Gen. 7. 11. Eccl. 12. 3. Song 2. 9. Isa. 60. 8. Jer. 9. 21.
WINE maketh glad the heart, Ps. 104. 15.
Prov. 20. 1. *w*. is a mocker
21. 17. loveth *w*. and oil shall not be rich
23. 30. that tarry long at *w*. that seek mixed *w*.
31. look not upon *w*. when it is red
6. *w*. to those of heavy heart
Song 1. 2. love is better than *w*. 4.
Isa. 5. 11. till *w*. inflame them
12. pipe and *w*. are in their feasts
25. 6. *w*. on the lees well refined
28. 7. they have erred through *w*.
55. 1. buy *w*. and milk, Song 5. 1.
Hos. 2. 9. take away my *w*. in the season
3. 1. love flagons of *w*.
4. 11. new *w*. take away the heart
Hab. 2. 5. he transgresseth by *w*.
Eph. 5. 18. be not drunk with *w*.
1 Tim. 3. 3. not given to *w*. 8 Tit. 1. 7, 8.
5. 23. use a little *w*. for stomach's
Prov. 23. 20. *wine-bibber*. Matt. 11. 19.
WINGS of the God of Israel, Ruth 2. 12.
Ps. 17. 8. hide under shadow of *w*. 36. 7. & 57. 1. & 61. 4. & 91. 4.
18. 10. on *w*. of the wind, 2 Sam. 22. 11.
Prov. 23. 5. riches make themselves *w*. and fly away
Isa. 6. 2. seraphims; each had six *w*.
Mal. 4. 2. with healing in his *w*.
WINK, Job 15. 12. Ps. 35. 19. Prov. 6. 13. & 10. 10. Acts 17. 30.
WINTER, Song 2. 11. Zech. 14. 8.
WIPE, 2 Kings 21. 13. Neh. 13. 14. Prov. 6. 33. Isa. 25. 8. Rev. 7. 17. & 21. 4.
WISE, Gen. 41. 39. Ex. 23. 8. Deut. 16. 19.
Deut. 4. 6. this great nation is a *w*. people
32. 29. O that they were *w*. that they would consider their latter
Job 5. 13. taketh the *w*. in their own craftiness
11. 12. vain man would be *w*.
32. 9. great men are not always *w*.
Ps. 2. 10. be *w*. O Kings, be taught
19. 7. making the simple *w*.
107. 43. whoso is *w*. and will
Prov. 3. 7. be not *w*. in own eyes
35. the *w*. shall inherit glory
9. 12. if thou be *w*. be *w*. for thyself
13. 20. he that walketh with the *w*. shall be *w*.
26. 12. a man *w*. in his own conceit
Eccl. 7. 4. heart of *w*. in house of mourning
9. 1. the *w*. are in the hand of God
Isa. 5. 21. are *w*. in their own eyes
Jer. 4. 22. they are *w*. to do evil
Dan. 12. 3. *w*. shall shine as stars

Hos. 14. 9. who is *w*. and he shall
Matt. 10. 16. be ye *w*. as serpents
11. 25. hid these things from the *w*.
Rom. 1. 22. professing themselves to be *w*.
16. 19. be *w*. to that which is good
1 Cor. 3. 18. seemeth *w*. in this world
4. 10. but ye are *w*. in Christ
Eph. 5. 15. not as fools but as *w*.
2 Tim. 3. 15. is able to make thee *w*.
Matt. 10. 42. *in no wise* lose his reward
Luke 18. 17. shall—enter therein
John 6. 37. cometh I will—cast out
Rev. 21. 27. shall—enter into it
Deut. 4. 6. this is your *wisdom*
1 Kings 4. 29. God gave Solomon *w*. 5. 12.
Job 28. 28. fear of Lord, that is *w*.
Prov. 4. 25. get *w*. get understanding
7. *w*. is the principal thing, therefore, ch. 8.
16. 16. how much better to get *w*. than gold
19. 8. he that getteth *w*. loveth his own soul
Prov. 23. 4. cease from thine own *w*.
23. buy the truth, also *w*. and instruction
Eccl. 1. 18. for in much *w*. is much grief
8. 1. a man's *w*. maketh his face shine
Matt. 11. 10. but *w*. is justified of her children
1 Cor. 1. 17. not with *w*. of words lest the cross
24. Christ the power and *w*. of God, Luke 11. 49.
1 Cor. 1. 30. who of God is made unto us *w*.
2. 6. we speak *w*. among them that are perfect
3. 19. *w*. of this world is foolishness with God
2 Cor. 1. 12. not with fleshly *w*. but by the grace
Col. 1. 9. that ye might be filled with all *w*.
4. 5. walk in *w*. towards them that are without
James 1. 5. if any of you lack *w*. ask it of
3. 17. but the *w*. from above is first pure
Rev. 5. 12. worthy is the Lamb to receive *w*.
13. 18. here is *w*. let him that hath, 17. 9.
Ps. 111. 10. *of wisdom*, Prov. 9. 10. & 10. 21. Mic. 6. 9. Col. 2. 3. James 3. 13.
Ps. 64. 9. *wisely*, 101. 2. Eccl. 7. 10.
1 Kings 4. 31. *wiser*, Job 35. 11. Ps. 119. 98. Luke 16. 8. 1 Cor. 1. 25.
WITCH, Ex. 22. 18. Deut. 18. 10.
1 Sam. 15. 23. *witchcraft*, Gal. 5. 20.
WITHDRAW, Job 9. 13. & 33. 17. Prov. 25. 17. Song 5. 6. 2 Thes. 3. 6. 1 Tim. 6. 5.
WITHHOLD not thy mercies, Ps. 40. 11.
Ps. 84. 11. no good thing will he *w*. from them
Prov. 3. 27. *w*. not good from them to whom
23. 13. *w*. not correction from the child
Gen. 20. 6. *withheld*, thee from sinning, 22. 12. Job 31. 16.
Job 42. 2. *withholden* from thee, Jer. 5. 25.
Prov. 11. 24. *withholdeth*, 26. 2 Thes. 2. 6.
WITHIN, Ps. 40. 8. & 45. 13. Matt. 3. 9. & 23. 26. Mark 7. 21. 2 Cor. 7. 5. Rev. 5. 1.
WITHOUT, Prov. 1. 20. & 24. 27. 1 Cor. 5. 12. 2 Cor. 7. 5. Col. 4. 5. Rev. 22. 15.

WITHSTAND, Eccl. 4. 12. Eph. 6. 13.

Acts 11. 17. what am I, that I could *w.* God

Gal. 2. 11. *withstood,* him to face, 2 Tim. 4. 15.

WITNESS, Gen. 31. 44, 48. Lev. 5. 1.

Num. 35. 30. one *w.* shall not testify against him, Deut. 17. 6. & 19. 15. 2 Cor. 13. 1.

Judg. 11. 10. Lord be *w.* 1 Sam. 12. 5. Jer. 42. 5. & 29. 23. Mic. 1. 2. Mal. 2. 4.

Job 16. 19. my *w.* is in heaven and my record

Ps. 89. 37. and as a faithful *w.* in heaven

Prov. 14. 5. a faithful *w.* will not lie: but a false

25. a true *w.* delivereth souls: but a deceitful

24. 28. be not *w.* against thy neighbour

Isa. 55. 4. him for a *w.* to the people a leader

Mal. 3. 5. I will be a swift *w.* against sorcerers

John 3. 11. ye receive not our *w.*

5. 36. greater *w.*

37. Father borne *w.* of

Acts 14. 17. left not himself without *w.* in that

1 John 5. 10. believeth him hath *w.* in himself

Rev. 1. 5. Christ who is the faithful *w.* 3. 14.

20. 4. them that were beheaded for *w.* of Jesus

Deut. 17. 6. two or three *witnesses,* 19. 15. 2 Cor. 13. 1. Matt. 18. 16. Heb. 10. 28. 1 Tim. 5. 19. Num. 35. 30.

Josh. 24. 22. ye are *w.* against yourselves

Isa. 43. 10. ye are my *w.* saith the Lord, 12. & 44. 8.

1 Thes. 2. 10. ye are *w.* and God also, how

1 Tim. 6. 12. good profession before many *w.*

Heb. 12. 1. so great a cloud of *w.* lay aside

Rev. 11. 3. power unto my two *w.* and they

WIZARDS, Lev. 19. 31. & 20. 6. Isa. 8. 19.

WOLF, Isa. 11. 6. & 65. 25. Jer. 5. 6. Ezek. 22. 27. *wolves,* Hab. 1. 8. Zeph. 3. 3. Matt. 7. 15. & 10. 16. Acts 20. 29.

WOMAN, Gen. 2. 23. & 3. 15. Lev. 18. 22, 23. & 20. 13. Num. 30. 3.

Prov. 11. 16. gracious *w.* retaineth honour

Ps. 48. 6. pain as of a *w.* in travail, Isa. 13. 8. & 21. 3. & 26. 17. & 42. 14. & 66. 7. Jer. 4. 31. & 6. 24. & 13. 21. & 22. 23. & 30. 6. & 31. 8. & 48. 41. & 49. 22, 24. & 50. 43.

Prov. 12. 4. a virtuous *w.* is a crown to her husband

14. 1. every wise *w.* buildeth her house

31. 10. a virtuous *w.* who can find for her price

30. *w.* that feareth the Lord shall be praised

Eccl. 7. 26. *w.* whose heart is snares and nets

28. *w.* among all those I have not found

Isa. 49. 15. can a *w.* forget her sucking child

54. 6. called thee as a *w.* forsaken and grieved

Jer. 31. 22. *w.* shall compass a man

Matt. 5. 28. looketh on a *w.* to lust after her

15. 28. Jesus said, O *w.* great is thy faith

26. 13. this that this *w.* hath done be told

John 2. 4. *w.* what have I to do with thee

8. 3. brought with him a *w.* taken in adultery

19. 26. saith unto his mother. *w.* behold thy son

Rom. 1. 27. leaving the natural use of the *w.*

1 Cor. 11. 7. but the *w.* is the glory of man

Gal. 4. 4. God sent forth his Son made of a *w.*

1 Tim. 2. 12. I suffer not *w.* to teach

14. *w.* being deceived was in the transgression

Rev. 12. 1. *w.* clothed with the sun, 6. 16.

17. 18. *w.* thou sawest is that city

Judg. 5. 24. blessed above *women* shall Jael be

Prov. 31. 3. given not thy strength to *w.*

Song 1. 8. fairest among *w.* 5. 9. & 6. 1.

Isa. 3. 12. *w.* shall rule over them

32. 11. tremble ye *w.* at ease

Jer. 9. 17. call for the mourning *w.*

Lam. 4. 10. *w.* have sodden children

Matt. 11. 11. among them born of *w.*

Luke 1. 28. blessed art thou among *w.*

Rom. 1. 26. *w.* did change their natural use

1 Cor. 14. 34. let *w.* keep silence

1 Tim. 2. 9. let *w.* adorn themselves in modest apparel

11. let *w.* learn in silence with

5. 14. that the younger *w.* marry

2 Tim. 3. 6. lead captive silly *w.*

1 Pet. 3. 5. after this manner holy *w.*

Rev. 14. 4. are not defiled with *w.*

WOMB, Gen. 25. 23. & 29. 31.

Gen. 49. 25. blessings of the *w.* and

1 Sam. 1. 5. Lord hath shut her *w.*

Ps. 22. 9. took me out of the *w.*

10. I was cast upon thee from *w.*

127. 3. fruit of the *w.* is his reward

139. 13. covered me in mother's *w.*

Eccl. 11. 5. how bones grow in *w.*

Isa. 44. 2. the Lord that formed thee from the *w.*

66. 9. to bring forth and shut *w.*

Hos. 9. 14. give them miscarrying *w.*

Luke 1. 42. blessed is fruit of thy *w.*

11. 27. blessed is *w.* that bare thee

23. 29. blessed are *w.* that never

WONDER, Deut. 13. 1. & 28. 46. Ps. 71. 7. Isa. 29. 14. Rev. 12. 1.

Acts 13. 41. *w.* and perish, Hab. 1. 5.

Ex. 3. 20. *wonders,* 7. 3. & 15. 11.

1 Chron. 16. 12. remember his *w.* Ps. 105. 5.

Job 9. 10. God doeth *w.* Ps. 77. 11, 14.

Ps. 78. 11. they forgat his *w.* Neh. 9. 17.

Ps. 88. 11. wilt thou show *w.* to the dead

136. 4. who alone doth great *w.*

Dan. 12. 6. how long to the end of these *w.*

Joel 2. 30. show *w.* in heaven, Acts 2. 19.

John 4. 48. except they see signs and *w.*

Acts 2. 43. many *w.* were done, 6. 8.

Rom. 15. 19. mighty signs and *w.*

2 Thes. 2. 9. and signs and lying *w.*

Rev. 13. 13. he doeth great *w.*

Zech. 3. 8. they are men *wondered* at

Isa. 59. 16. *w.* there was no intercessor

Luke 4. 22. *w.* at the gracious words

Rev. 13. 3. all the world *w.* after the beast

17. 6. I *w.* with great admiration

Job 37. 14. *wondrous* works, Ps. 26. 7. & 75. 1. & 105. 2. & 119. 27. & 145. 5. & 71. 17. & 78. 32. & 106. 22.

Ps. 72. 18. *w.* things, 86. 10. & 119. 18.

Judg. 13. 9. *wondrously,* Joel 2. 26.

Deut. 28. 59. thy plagues *wonderful*

Job 42. 3. things too *w.* for me

Ps. 119. 129. thy testimonies are *w.*

139. 6. such knowledge is too *w.*

Prov. 30. 18. three things too *w.* for

Isa. 9. 6. his name shall be called *W.*

25. 1. done *w.* things

28. 29. *w.* in counsel

Jer. 5. 30. a *w.* thing is committed

Ps. 139. 14. *wonderfully,* Lam. 1. 9.

WOOD, hay, stubble, 1 Cor. 3. 12.

2 Tim. 2. 20. also vessels of *w.* and

WORD, Num. 23. 5. Deut. 4. 2.

Deut. 8. 3. every *w.* of God. Matt. 4. 4.

30. 14. *w.* is very nigh, Rom. 10. 8.

Ps. 68. 11. the Lord gave the *w.*

119. 49. remember the *w.* unto thy servant

Prov. 14. 23. *w.* spoken in due season

25. 11. a *w.* fitly spoken is like apples of gold

Isa. 29. 21. man offender for a *w.*

30. 21. shall hear a *w.* behind thee

14. 26. confirmed *w.* of his servant

50. 4. how to speak a *w.* in season

Jer. 5. 13. the *w.* is not in them

44. 16. that thou hast spoken

Matt. 8. 8. speak the *w.* only and my servant shall be healed

12. 36. every idle *w.* that men

Luke 4. 36. what a *w.* is this

24. 19. mighty in deed, and in *w.*

John 1. 1. in the beginning was the *W.* and the *W.* was with God, and the *W.* was God

54. the *W.* was made flesh

15. 3. ye are clean through the *w.*

Acts 13. 15. any *w.* of exhortation

26. to you is *w.* of salvation sent

17. 11. the *w.* with all readiness

20. 32. and to the *w.* of his grace

1 Cor. 4. 20. kingdom of God is not in *w.*

Gal. 6. 6. taught in *w.* communicate

Eph. 5. 26. washing of water by *w.*

Col. 3. 16. let *w.* of Christ dwell in

17. whatsoever ye do in *w.* or deed

1 Thes. 1. 5. Gospel came not in *w.* only, but also in power

2 Thes. 2. 17. stablish you in every good *w.*

3. 14. if any obey not our *w.* note that man

1 Tim. 5. 17. labour in *w.* and doctrine

2 Tim. 4. 2. preach *w.* be instant in season

Tit. 1. 9. holding fast the faithful *w.* as he hath

Heb. 4. 2. the *w.* preached did not profit them

5. 13. is unskilful in *w.* of righteousness

13. 22. brethren suffer the *w.* of exhortation

James 1. 21. receive the engrafted *w.* which

22. be doers of the *w.*

3. 2. offend not in *w.*

1 Pet. 3. 1. if any obey not the *w.* they also

2 Pet. 1. 19. have a more sure *w.* of prophecy

2 John 1. 1. hands handled of the *w.* of life

5. 7. Father, the *W.* and the Holy Ghost

Rev. 3. 10. thou hast kept *w.* of my patience

12. 11. overcame by *w.* of their testimony

Ps. 130. 5. in *his* word do I hope, 119. 81.

147. 19. showed—unto Jacob

Jer. 20. 9.—was in my heart as a burning fire

John 5. 38. have not—abiding in you

Acts 2. 41. that gladly received—were baptized

John 8. 37. *my word,* hath no place, 43. Rev. 3. 8.

Isa. 8. 20. *this word,* Rom. 9. 9.

Ps. 119. 11. *thy word* have I hid in mine heart

50. for—hath quickened me

105.—is a lamp unto my feet and a light

140.—is very pure, 160.—is true from beginning

138. 2. thou hast magnified—above all thy

Jer. 15. 16.—was unto me joy and rejoicing

John 17. 6. I kept—17.—is truth

Prov. 30. 5. *Word of God,* Isa. 40. 8. Mark 7. 13. Rom. 10. 17. 1 Thes. 2. 13. Heb. 4. 12. & 6. 5. 1 Pet. 1. 23. Rev. 19. 13.

2 Kings 20. 19. *Word of the Lord,* Ps. 18. 30. & 33. 4. 2 Thes. 3. 1. 1 Pet. 1. 25.

Ps. 119. 43. *Word of truth,* 2 Cor. 6. 7. Eph. 1. 13. Col. 1. 5. 2 Tim. 2. 15. James 1. 18.

Job 23. 12. esteemed *words* of his mouth

Prov. 15. 26. *w.* of pure are pleasant words

19. 7. he pursueth them with *w.* yet they

22. 17. bow down thine ear, hear *w.* of wise

Eccl. 10. 12. the *w.* of a wise man's mouth are

12. 10. preacher sought to find out acceptable *w.*

11. *w.* of the wise are as goads and as nails

Jer. 7. 4. trust ye not in lying *w.*

44. 28. know whose *w.* shall stand mine or their's

Dan. 7. 25. speak great *w.* against the Most High

Hos. 6. 5. I have slain by *w.* of my mouth

14. 2. take with you *w.* and say to the Lord

Zech. 1. 13. talked with good *w.* comfortable *w.*

Matt. 26. 44. prayed third time, saying same *w.*

Luke 1. 22. the gracious *w.* that proceeded out of his mouth

John 6. 63. *w.* I speak are Spirit and life

63. thou hast the *w.* of eternal life

17. 8. given unto them *w.* which thou gavest me

Acts 7. 22. Moses mighty in *w.* and in deeds

15. 24. certain have troubled you with *w.* 18. 15.

20. 35. remember the *w.* of Lord how he said

26. 25. speak the *w.* of truth and obedience

1 Cor. 2. 4. not with enticing *w.* of man's wisdom

2 Tim. 1. 13. hold fast the form of sound *w.*

2. 14. that they strive not about *w.* to no profit

Rev. 1. 3. hear *w.* of this prophecy, 22. 18.

Ps. 50. 17. *my words,* Isa. 51. 16. & 59. 21. Jer. 5. 14. Mic. 2. 7. Mark 8. 38. & 13. 31. John 5. 47. & 15. 7.

1 Thes. 4. 18. *these words,* Rev. 21. 5.

Ps. 119. 103. *thy words,* 130. 139. Prov. 23. 8. Eccl. 5. 2. Ezek. 33. 31. Matt. 12. 37.

WORK, Gen. 2. 3. Ex. 20. 10. & 31. 14.

Deut. 33. 11. and accept the *w.* of his hands

Job 1. 10. thou hast blessed the *w.* of his hands

10. 3. thou shouldest despise the *w.* of thy hands

14. 15. wilt have a desire to *w.* of thy hands

36. 9. he showeth them their *w.* and their

Ps. 8. 3. consider heavens w. of thy fingers
9. 16. wicked is snared in w. of his hands
19. 1. the firmament showeth his handy w.
101. 3. I hate the w. of them that turn aside
143. 5. muse on w. of thy hands
Eccl. 8. 14. happeneth according to w. of wicked
17. I beheld all the w. of God that a man
12. 14. God shall bring every w. into judgment
Isa. 10. 12. performed his whole w. upon Mount
28. 21. he may do his strange w. his strange
29. 16. shall w. say of him that
45. 11. concerning w. of my hands command ye
49. 4. my w. is with my God
64. 8. we are all the w. of thy hands
Jer. 10. 15. vanity and w. of error
18. 3. potter wrought a w. on the
Hab. 1. 5. a w. in your days, Acts 13. 41.
Mark 6. 5. could do no mighty w.
John 17. 4. finished w. thou gavest
Acts 5. 38. if this w. be of men
13. 2. for the w. whereto I called
Rom. 2. 15. show w. of law written
11. 6. otherwise w. is no more w.
1 Cor. 3. 13. every man's w. made
9. 1. are not ye my w. in the Lord
Eph. 4. 12. for w. of the ministry
2 Thes. 1. 11. w. of faith with power
2. 17. stablish you in every good w.
2 Tim. 4. 5. do w. of an evangelist
James 1. 4. let patience have perfect w.
25. doer of the w. shall be blessed
1 Pet. 1. 17. judgeth every man's w.
Ps. 104. 23. his work, 62. 12. & 111. 3 Prov. 24. 29. Isa. 40. 10. Job 36. 24.
Ps. 90. 16. thy work, 92. 4. Prov. 24. 27. Jer. 31. 16. Hab. 3. 2.
Ex. 32. 16. Work of God, Ps. 64. 9. Eccl. 7. 13. & 8. 17. John 6. 29. Rom. 14. 20.
Ps. 28. 5. Work of the Lord, Isa. 5. 12. Jer. 48. 10. 1 Cor. 15. 58. & 16. 10.
Ps. 17. 4. concerning works of men
92. 4. triumph in w. of thy hands
111. 7. w. of his hands are verity
138. 8. forsake not w. of thy hands
Prov. 31. 31. let her own w. praise
Isa. 26. 12. wrought all our w. in us
Dan. 4. 37. all whose w. are truth
John 5. 20. show him greater w.
10. 32. of these w. do ye stone me
38. believe the w. that I do
14. 11. believe me for the w. sake
12. greater w. shall he do
Acts 26. 20. w. meet for repentance
Rom. 3. 27. by what law? of w. nay but by the law of faith
4. 6. God imputeth righteousness without w.
9. 11. not of w. but of him that calleth
9. 32. sought it as by w. of the law
11. 6. then it is no more of w.
13. 12. us cast off w. of darkness
Gal. 2. 16. by w. of law no flesh be
3. 2. received ye spirit by w. of law
10. as many as are of w. of the law
5. 19. w. of the flesh are manifest
Eph. 2. 9. not of w. 10. to good w.
5. 11. unfruitful w. of darkness
Col. 1. 21. enemies in mind by wicked w.
1 Thes. 5. 13. love them for their w.
2 Tim. 1. 9. not according to our w.
Tit. 1. 16. in w. they deny him
3. 5. not by w. of righteousness
Heb. 6. 1. repentance from dead w.
9. 14. conscience from dead w.
James 2. 14. and have not w. can
22. faith without w. is dead, 17. 26.

21. justified by w., 24. 25.
22. by w. was faith made perfect
1 John 3. 8. he might destroy w. of
Rev. 9. 20. repented not of the w. of
18. 6. according to her w. 20. 12, 13.
Ps. 33. 4. his works, 78. 11. & 103. 22.
104. 31. & 106. 13. & 107, 22. & 145. 9,
17. Dan. 9. 14. Acts 15. 18. Heb. 4. 10.
Ps. 106. 35. their works, Isa. 66. 18.
Jonah 3. 10. Matt. 23. 3, 5. 2 Cor. 11. 15. Rev. 14. 3. & 20. 12, 13.
Deut. 15. 10. thy works, Ps. 66. 3. & 73. 28. & 92. 5. & 104. 24. & 143. 5.
Prov. 16. 3. Eccl. 9. 7. Rev. 2. 3.
Ps. 40. 5. wonderful works. 78. 4. & 107. 8. & 111. 4. Matt. 7. 22. Acts 2. 11.
Job 37. 14. works of God, Ps. 66. 5. & 78. 7. Eccl. 11. 5. John 6. 28. & 9. 3.
Ps. 46. 8. w. of the Lord, 111. 2.
1 Sam. 14. 6. maybe the Lord will work for us
Ps. 119. 126. time for the Lord to w.
Isa. 43. 13. I will w. and who shall let it
Matt. 7. 23. depart from me ye that w. iniquity
John 6. 28. might w. works of God
9. 4. I must w. the works of him
Phil. 2. 12. w. out your salvation
1 Thes. 4. 11. to w. with your hands
2 Thes. 2. 7. iniquity doth already w.
3. 10. if any w. not, neither should
Prov. 11. 18. the wicked worketh a deceitful w.
Isa. 64. 5. meetest him that w. righteousness
John 5. 17. my Father w. and I w.
Acts 10. 35. that w. righteousness is accepted
Rom. 4. 4. to him that w. is reward
1 Cor. 12. 6. same God who w. all
2 Cor. 4. 17. w. for us a far more
Gal. 5. 6. faith which w. by love
Eph. 1. 11. w. all things according
2. 2. spirit that now w. in children
Phil. 2. 13. it is God that w. in you
1 Thes. 2. 13. effectually w. in you
Isa. 28. 29. excellent in working
Mark 16. 20. the Lord w. with them
Rom. 7. 13. sin w. death in me
1 Cor. 4. 12. w. with our own hands
9. 6. have not power to forbear w.
Eph. 1. 10. according to w. of mighty
3. 7. by effectual w. of his power
4. 28. w. with his hands the thing
Phil. 3. 21. according to w. whereby
2 Thes. 3. 11. w. not at all, but are
Heb. 13. 21. w. in you that which is well-pleasing
2 Cor. 6. 1. workers, 11. 13. Phil. 3. 2.
Job 31. 3. workers of iniquity, 34. 8, 22. Ps. 5. 5. & 6. 8. & 28. 3. & 125. 5. & 141. 9. Prov. 10. 29. & 21. 15.
Matt. 10. 10. workman, 2 Tim. 2. 15.
Ex. 31. 3. workmanship, Eph. 2. 10.
WORLD, 1 Sam. 2. 8. 1 Chron. 16. 30.
Ps. 17. 14. from men of the w.
24. 1. w. is the Lord's, 9. 8. Nah. 1. 5.
Ps. 50. 12. w. is mine and the fulness
Eccl. 3. 11. hath set w. in his heart
Isa. 26. 9. the inhabitants of the w. learn righteousness
Jer. 10. 12. established the w. by his wisdom, 51. 15. Ps. 93. 1. & 96. 10.
Matt. 16. 26. what is a man profited if he shall gain the whole w. and lose his own soul, Mark 8. 36.
Matt. 18. 7. woe to the w. because of offences
24. 3. what shall be the end of w.
Mark 16. 15. go into all the w. and
Luke 20. 35. worthy to obtain that w.
John 1. 10. w. was made by him, and w. knew him not
29. Lamb of God taketh away sin of the w.

3. 16. God so loved the w. he gave his only Son
17. w. through him might be saved
7. 7. the w. cannot hate you, but me
12. 47. not to judge w. but save w.
14. 17. whom w. cannot receive
19. w. seeth me no more; but ye see
31. w. may know I love Father
15. 18. if the w. hate you
19. chosen you out of the w. therefore the w. hateth you
6. 28. I leave w. and go to Father
17. 9. I pray not for the w.
11. I am no more in the w.
16. not of w. even as I am not of w.
18. thou hast sent me into the w.
23. w. may know thou hast sent me
Rom. 3. 19. all the w. became guilty before
1 Cor. 1. 21. w. by wisdom knew not
Gal. 6. 14. w. is crucified unto me and I unto the w.
Col. 1. 6. as in all w. and bringeth
Tit. 1. 2. promised before w. began
Heb. 2. 5. w. to come, 6. 5.
11. 38. the w. was not worthy
1 John 2. 2. a propitiation for sins of the whole w.
2. 15. love not w. nor things in the w.
16. all that is in the w. is of the w.
17. w. passeth away and the lust
3. 1. the w. knoweth us not
4. 5. they are of the w. they speak of the w. and the w. heareth them
5. 19. whole w. lieth in wickedness
Rev. 3. 10. temptation come on all the w.
13. 3. all w. wondered after the beast
Matt. 12. 32. this world, John 8. 32. & 13. 36. Rom. 12. 2. 1 Tim. 6. 7.
Heb. 1. 2. he made the world
11. 3. the w. were framed by him
WORM, Ex. 16. 26. Isa. 51. 8.
Job 25. 6. man that is a w.
Ps. 22. 6. I am a w. and no man
Isa. 41. 14. fear not, thou w. Jacob
66. 24. their w. shall not die, Mark 9. 44, 48.
Job 19. 26. worms destroy my body, Acts 12. 23.
Deut. 29. 18. wormwood, Prov. 5. 4. Lam. 3. 15, 19. Amos 5. 7. Rev. 8. 11.
WORSE, Matt. 12. 45. John 5. 14.
1 Cor. 8. 8. & 11. 17. 2 Tim. 3. 13. 2 Pet. 2. 20.
WORSHIP the Lord in beauty of holiness, 1 Chron. 16. 29. Ps. 29. 2. & 66. 4. & 96. 9. & 45. 11. & 95. 6. & 99. 5. Matt. 4. 10.
Ps. 97. 7. w. him all ye gods
Matt. 15. 9. in vain do they w. me
John 4. 24. they that w. him must w. in truth
Acts 17. 23. whom ye ignorantly w.
24. 14. so w. I the God of my fathers
Phil. 3. 3. of the circumcision w. God is
Rev. 3. 9. w. before thy feet
13. 12. causeth earth to w. beast
19. 20. to w. God, 22. 9.
Ex. 4. 31. worshipped, 32. 8. Jer. 1. 16. 1 Chron. 29. 20. Rom. 1. 25. 2 Thes. 2. 4. Rev. 5. 14. & 7. 11. & 11. 16. & 13. 4.
WORTH, Job 24. 25. Prov. 10. 20.
Gen. 32. 10. I am not worthy of least
Matt. 8. 8. I am not w. thou shouldest come under my roof
10. 10. workman is w. of his meat
13. if house be w. let your peace rest
37. more than me, is not w. of me
22. 8. that were bidden were not w.
Luke 3. 8. fruits w. of repentance
7. 4. he was w. for whom he should do this
10. 7. labourer is w. of his hire
13. 19. no more w. to be called thy son, 21.
20. 35. counted w. to obtain resurrection

21. 36. w. to escape all things
Acts 5. 41. counted w. to suffer
Rom. 8. 18. not w. to be compared with
Eph. 4. 1. walk w. of the vocation wherein
Col. 1. 10. walk w. of the Lord being fruitful
1 Thes. 2. 12. walk w. of God who called
2 Thes. 1. 5. be counted w. of the kingdom of God
11. God count you w. of this calling
1 Tim. 1. 15. w. of all acceptation, 4. 9.
5. 17. elders w. of double honour
18. labourer is w. of reward
6. 1. counted masters w. of all honour
Heb. 3. 3. w. of more glory than Moses
10. 29. sorer punishment shall he be thought w.
11. 38. of whom world was not w.
Rev. 3. 4. walk in white, they are w.
5. 12. w. is the Lamb that was slain
16. 6. blood to drink; for they are w.
WOULD God, Ex. 16. 3. Num. 11. 29. Acts 26. 29. 1 Cor. 4. 8. 1 Cor. 11. 1.
Neh. 9. 30. wounded not, Isa. 30. 15.
Matt. 28. 30. & 23. 30, 37. Rom. 11. 25. 22. 81. 11. Israel w. none of me
Prov. 1. 25. w. none of my reproof
30. they w. none of my counsel
Matt. 7. 12. whatsoever w. that men should do unto you
Rom. 7. 15. I w. that I do not, 19.
Gal. 5. 7. cannot do things ye w.
Rev. 3. 15. I w. thou wert cold or hot
WOUND, Ex. 21. 25. Prov. 6. 33. Jer. 10. 19. & 15. 18. & 30. 12, 14. Mic. 1. 9.
Prov. 28. 6. wounds, Isa. 1. 6. Jer. 30. 17.
Deut. 32. 39. I wound and I heal skill
1 Cor. 8. 12. w. their weak conscience
Rev. 13. 3. his deadly w. was healed, 14.
Ps. 69. 26. wounded, 109. 22. Song 5. 7.
Prov. 18. 14. a w. spirit who can bear
Isa. 53. 5. w. for our transgressions
Job 5. 18. he woundeth and his hands make whole
WRATH, Gen. 49. 7. Ex. 32. 10, 11. Num. 16. 46. w. gone out from the Lord
Deut. 32. 27. feared w. of the enemy
Neh. 13. 18. bring more w. on Israel
Job 5. 2. w. killeth the foolish man
Ps. 76. 10. w. of man shall praise thee, the remainder of w. shalt thou restrain
Prov. 16. 14. w. of a king is as messengers of death
Isa. 54. 8. in a little w. I hid my face
Hab. 3. 2. in w. remember mercy
Matt. 3. 7. flee from w. to come
Rom. 2. 5. treasure up w. against the day of w.
5. 9. saved from w. through him
12. 19. give place unto w.
13. 5. not only for w. but conscience
Eph. 2. 3. by nature children of w.
4. 26. let not the sun go down on your w.
1 Thes. 1. 10. delivered from w. to come
2. 16. w. is come on them to the
5. 9. not appointed us to w. but to obtain salvation
1 Tim. 2. 8. holy hands without w.
Heb. 11. 27. not fearing w. of King
James 1. 19. slow to speak, slow to w.
20. w. of man worketh not righteousness of God
Rev. 6. 16. from w. of the Lamb
12. 12. having great w. because he
14. 8. wine of w. of her fornication, 18. 3.

Ezra 8. 22. *his wrath,* Ps. 2. 5, 12. & 76. 38. Jer. 7. 29. & 10. 10. Rev. 6. 17. Num. 25. 11. *my wrath,* Ps. 95. 11. Isa. 10. 6. & 60. 10. Ezek. 7. 14. Hos. 5. 10.

Ps. 38. 1. *thy wra'h,* 85. 3. & 88. 7, 16. & 89. 46. & 90. 9, 11. & 102. 10.

89. 38. *wroth,* Isa. 54. 9. & 57. 17.

WREST, Ex. 23. 3. 2 Pet. 3. 16.

WRESTLE, Gen. 32. 24, 25. Eph. 6. 12.

WRETCHED, Rom. 7. 24. Rev. 3. 17.

WRINKLE, Job 16. 8. Eph. 5. 27.

WRITE, Ex. 34. 1, 27. Deut. 27. 3. Isa. 3. 8. Jer. 30. 2. Hab. 2. 2.

Deut. 6. 9. *w.* them upon the posts

Prov. 3. 3. *w.* them on the table of thine heart, 7. 3.

Jer. 31. 33. I will *w.* it in their hearts

Ps. 69. 28. not be *written* with the 102. 18. be *w.* for the generation

Prov. 22. 20. have I not *w.* thee

Eccl. 12. 10. that which was *w.*

Dan. 12. 1. shall be found *w.* in book

1 Cor. 20. 11. *w.* for our admonition

2 Cor. 3. 2. epistle *w.* in our hearts

3. *w.* not with ink but Spirit of the

Heb. 12. 23. are *w.* in heaven, Luke 10. 20.

WRONG, Ps. 105. 14. Jer. 22. 3, 13. Matt. 20. 13. I do thee no *w.* didst

1 Cor. 6. 7. why not rather take *w.* 8.

Col. 3. 25. that doeth *w.* shall receive

2 Cor. 7. 2. *wronged,* Philem. 18.

Prov. 8. 36. *wrongeth* his own soul

WROUGHT, 1 Sam. 6. 6. & 14. 45.

Ps. 139. 15. curiously *w.* in lowest parts of the earth

Isa. 26. 12. *w.* all our works in us

Ezek. 20. 9. I *w.* for my name's sake, 22.

John 3. 21. his works are *w.* in God

Rom. 7. 8. *w.* in me all manner of concupiscence

2 Cor. 5. 5. that hath *w.* us for the self-same thing is God

Eph. 1. 20. which he *w.* in Christ

1 Pet. 4. 3. have *w.* will of Gentiles

Y

YEA, yea, nay, nay, Matt. 5. 37.

2 Cor. 1. 18. *y.* and nay

20. *y.* and amen

YEAR, acceptable, Isa. 61. 2. Luke 4. 19.

Isa. 63. 4. *y.* of my redeemed is come

Jer. 11. 23. *y.* of my visitation, 23. 12.

Job 10. 5. thy *years* as man's days

15. 20. number of *y.* is hidden from

Ps. 90. 4. a thousand *y.* in thy sight

2 Pet. 3. 8. a thousand *y.* as one day

Rev. 20. 2. bound him a thousand *y.*

YESTERDAY, Job 8. 9. Hab. 13. 8.

YIELD yourselves, 2 Chron. 30. 8.

Ps. 67. 6. land *y.* her increase, 85. 12.

Rom. 6. 13. nor *y.* members instruments of unrighteousness

16. *yielded* members servants, 19.

Heb. 12. 11. *yieldeth* peaceable fruit

YOKE, Deut. 28. 48. 1 Kings 12. 4.

Isa. 9. 4. broken the *y.* of his burden

10. 27. the *y.* shall be destroyed

Lam. 1. 14. *y.* of my transgression

3. 27. that he bear *y.* in his youth

Matt. 11. 29. take my *y.* upon you

3. my *y.* is easy and burden light

Gal. 5. 1. *y.* of bondage, Acts 15. 10.

2 Cor. 6. 14. be not unequally *yoked*

YOU only have I known, Amos 3. 2.

Luke 10. 16. heareth *y.* heareth me

13. 28. and *y.* yourselves thrust out

2 Cor. 12. 14. I seek not *yours* but *y.*

Eph. 2. 1. *y.* hath he quickened

Col. 1. 21. *y.* that were sometimes

Luke 6. 20. *y.* is the kingdom of God

1 Cor. 3. 22. all are *y.* and ye are Christ's, 23.

YOUNG, I have been, Ps. 37. 25.

Isa. 40. 11. gently lead those with *y.*

1 Tim. 5. 1. entreat the *younger* men as brethren

14. I will that *y.* women marry

1 Pet. 5. 5. ye *y.* submit to

Gen. 8. 21. the imagination of man is evil from his *youth*

1 Kings 18. 12. the Lord from my *y.*

Job 13. 26. possess iniquities of my *y.*

Ps. 25. 7. sins of my *y.*

103. 5. thy *y.* is renewed as eagle's

Eccl. 11. 9. O young man, in thy *y.*

10. childhood and *y.* are vanity

Jer. 2. 2. the kindness of thy *y.*

1 Tim. 4. 12. man despise thy *y.*

Prov. 7. 7. *youths,* Isa. 40. 30.

2 Tim. 2. 22. flee *youthful* lusts

Z

ZEAL for Lord, 2 Kings to 16.

Ps. 69. 9. the *z.* of thine house hath

119. 139. my *z.* hath consumed me

Isa. 9. 7. *z.* of the Lord will perform

59. 17. I was clad with *z.* as a cloak

63. 15. where is thy *z.* and strength

Rom. 10. 2. they have a *z.* for God

2 Cor. 7. 11. *z.* yea, what revenge

Phil. 3. 6. concerning *z.* perfecting

Num. 25. 13. was *zealous* for his God

Acts 22. 3. I was *z.* towards God as

Tit. 2. 14. people *z.* of good works

Rev. 3. 19. therefore be *z.* and repent

Gal. 4. 18. good to be *zealously* affected in a good thing

ZION, 2 Sam. 5. 7. 1 Kings 8. 1. for Jerusalem; temple, or church, 2 Kings 19. 31. Ps. 2. 6. & 9. 11. & 14. 7. & 48. 2. 11, 12. & 146. 10. & 147. 12. Isa. 1. 27. & 2. 3. & 60. 14. & 62. 1. and in about **seventy** other places

THE LIVES OF THE APOSTLES

When Jesus of Nazareth had grown to adulthood and had heard God's call to him to proclaim the Kingdom of God, he gathered about himself a band of disciples. His purpose was to share with this group of twelve men his deepest insights into God's nature and will for mankind, and to send them out to preach the gospel—the "good news" of God's love.

These twelve men are known as Christ's apostles. An "apostle" is "one who is sent forth." The English word comes from the Greek word meaning "to send." Jesus sent the apostles to preach, teach, heal, and make disciples of all mankind. He chose twelve men, perhaps, to symbolize the original twelve tribes of Israel; for the Christian church would be the "new Israel."

Who were these twelve apostles? First, there was Simon, whom Jesus renamed "Peter," meaning "Rock." Then there was Andrew, Peter's brother. Next there were two brothers, James and John, nicknamed "Sons of Thunder." Then Philip and Bartholomew; Matthew the tax-collector and Thomas; James the son of Alpheus and Thaddeus; Simon the Zealot and Judas Iscariot. It is likely that all of these men were from Galilee, for on the day of Pentecost the Jews at Jerusalem asked: "Are not all these which speak Galilaeans?"

The apostles worked in pairs. From the grouping of names in the New Testament, we gather that the six teams were: Peter and Andrew, James and John, Philip and Bartholomew, Thomas and Matthew, James and Thaddeus, Simon the Zealot and Judas Iscariot.

It is spiritually stimulating to project ourselves in imagination back into the first century A.D. and listen to the instructions which Jesus gave to his twelve apostles as he sent them out. (Matthew 10:5-42) "Go not into the way of the Gentiles, and into any city of the Samaritans enter ye not: but go rather to the lost sheep of the house of Israel. And as ye go, preach, saying, The kingdom of heaven is at hand. Heal the sick, cleanse the lepers, raise the dead, cast out devils: freely ye have received, freely give. Provide neither gold, nor silver, nor brass in your purses, nor scrip for your journey, neither two coats, neither shoes, nor yet staves: for the workman is worthy of his meat. And into whatsoever city or town ye shall enter, enquire who in it is worthy; and there abide till ye go thence. And when ye come into an house, salute it. And if the house be worthy, let your peace come upon it: but if it be not worthy, let your peace return to you. And whosoever shall not receive you, nor hear your words, when ye depart out of that house or city, shake off the dust of your feet. Verily I say unto you, It shall be more tolerable for the land of Sodom and Gomorrha in the day of judgment, than for that city.

"Behold, I send you forth as sheep in the midst of wolves: be ye therefore wise as serpents, and harmless as doves. But beware of men: for they will deliver you up to the councils, and they will scourge you in their synagogues; and ye shall be brought before governors and kings for my sake, for a testimony against them and the Gentiles. But when they deliver you up, take no thought how or what ye shall speak: for it shall be given you in that same hour what ye shall speak. For it is not ye that speak, but the Spirit of your Father which speaketh in you. And the brother shall deliver up the brother to death, and the father the child: and the children shall rise up against their parents, and cause them to be put to death. And ye shall be hated of all men for my name's sake; but he that endureth to the end shall be saved. But when they persecute you in this city, flee ye into another: for verily I say unto you, Ye shall not have gone over the cities of Israel, till the Son of man be come.

"The disciple is not above his master, nor the servant above his lord. It is enough for the disciple that he be as his master, and the servant as his lord. If they have called the master of the house Beelzebub, how much more shall they call them of his household? Fear them not therefore: for there is nothing covered, that shall not be revealed; and hid, that shall not be known. What I tell you in darkness, that speak ye in light: and what ye hear in the ear, that preach ye upon the housetops. And fear not them which kill the body, but are not able to kill the soul: but rather fear him which is able to destroy both soul and body in hell. Are not two sparrows sold for a farthing? and one of them shall not fall on the ground without your Father. But the very hairs of your head are all numbered. Fear ye not therefore, ye are of more value than many sparrows. Whosoever therefore shall confess me before men, him will I confess also before my Father which is in heaven. But whosoever shall deny me before men, him will I also deny before my Father which is in heaven.

"Think not that I am come to send peace on earth: I came not to send peace, but a sword. For I am come to set a man at variance against his father, and the daughter against her mother, and the daughter in law against her mother in law. And a man's foes shall be they of his own household. He that loveth father or mother more than me is not worthy of me: and he that loveth son or daughter more than me is not worthy of me. And he that taketh not his cross, and followeth after me, is not worthy of me. He that findeth his life shall lose it: and he that loseth his life for my sake shall find it.

"He that receiveth you receiveth me, and he that receiveth me receiveth him that sent me. He that receiveth a prophet in the name of a prophet shall receive a prophet's reward; and he that receiveth a righteous man in the name of a righteous man shall receive a righteous man's reward. And whosoever shall give to drink unto one of these little ones a cup of cold water only in the name of a disciple, verily I say unto you, he shall in no wise lose his reward."

Thus Jesus instructed his apostles during the days of his earthly ministry. After his crucifixion and resurrection, the risen Christ gave the Great Commission to his apostles: "All power is given unto me in heaven and in earth. Go ye therefore, and teach all nations, baptizing them in the name of the Father, and of the Son, and of the Holy Ghost: teaching them to observe all things whatsoever I have commanded you: and, lo, I am with you alway, even unto the end of the world." (Matthew 28:18-20) These apostles carried out their mission so effectively that in a few years Christianity was carried all over the civilized world. Who were these apostles? What were they like as individuals?

SIMON PETER

The most powerful personality among the twelve apostles was Simon Peter, the big fisherman of Galilee. He was the first man whom Jesus called into his band of intimate friends. A fisherman by trade, he was casting a net into the Sea of Galilee one day in the year A.D. 28 when Jesus, walking along the seashore, called out to him and his brother: "Come ye after me, and I will make you to become fishers of men." Simon was a man who trusted his heart, for we read that "straightway they forsook their nets, and followed him."

Simon was the son of a man named John. He lived with his wife, his mother, and his brother Andrew in a house in Capernaum. Jesus seems to have made Peter's house his home whenever he was preaching and teaching in Capernaum. We read

that once Jesus cured Peter's mother of a fever when he was visiting in the home.

As we read the Gospels, we discover that Peter was impulsive, quick in speech, and spiritually sensitive. It was he who first recognized who Jesus really was. At Caesarea Philippi, when Jesus asked, "Whom say ye that I am?" Peter answered, "Thou art the Christ, the Son of the living God." It was at this time that Jesus bestowed on Simon his more familiar name, Peter. Jesus said, "Thou art Peter, and upon this rock I will build my church; and the gates of hell shall not prevail against it." This was a play on words, for "Peter"—both in Greek and in Aramaic, which Jesus spoke—means "Rock." Perhaps Jesus was seeing in this big fisherman a strength and solidity which, in time, would make him the unshakeable leader of the early church.

Peter was the first of the apostles to recognize that Jesus was the Messiah for whom the Jews had been waiting. ("Christ" is the Greek word that translates the Hebrew word for "Messiah.") He was also the first to become convinced that Jesus had really risen from the dead. It is not strange, therefore, that the earliest gospel to be written—the Gospel of Mark—consisted mainly of Peter's memories of the life, teachings, and crucifixion of Jesus Christ. Written about the year A.D. 70, this gospel does not spare Peter; in it he confesses how he betrayed his Lord; after which "he went out, and wept bitterly."

But this was not the end of the story for Peter. After Christ had risen from the dead, he appeared to Peter and several of the apostles on the seashore of the Sea of Galilee. They were fishing, as they had been when Jesus first called Peter and Andrew to be his disciples. When he recognized Jesus, impulsive Peter threw himself into the water and waded to shore. Jesus told Peter, "Feed my sheep." By this he meant, of course, to give spiritual guidance to the early Christians. For "pastor," the most common title given a Christian minister, means "a shepherd"; the English word comes from a Latin word meaning "to feed."

It was Peter who emerged as the first great preacher of the early Christian church. On the day of Pentecost, we read in the Acts of the Apostles, Peter preached such a powerful sermon to the Jews in Jerusalem that "there were added unto them about three thousand souls." A great evangelist, Peter was clearly the leader of the apostles after the death of Jesus. He gave leadership to the Christian church in Jerusalem until he left for Rome, sometime in the early 60's.

The risen Christ had told Peter: "When thou wast young, thou girdest thyself, and walkedst whither thou wouldest: but when thou shalt be old, thou shalt stretch forth thy hands, and another shall gird thee, and carry thee whither thou wouldest not." Then the author of the Fourth Gospel adds: "This spake he, signifying by what death he (Peter) should glorify God." This refers to the tradition that Peter was martyred in Rome, perhaps in A.D. 64 when Nero began his persecution of the Christians there on the false charge that they had burned the city.

ANDREW

Andrew seems to be one of those persons somewhat overshadowed by an outstanding brother. Like Peter, he was a fisherman who lived in Capernaum, on the northwestern shore of the Sea of Galilee. Andrew is a Greek name meaning "manly." According to the Gospel of John, it was Andrew who first told Peter about Jesus and interested his brother in this remarkable man who later became their Lord and Master. And the gospels make it clear that Jesus called both Peter and Andrew to be his disciples.

According to Christian tradition among the Armenians, Andrew was one of the five apostles who carried Christianity to that country. Later tradition holds that he also was a missionary to Macedonia and Greece, where he was crucified on an X-shaped cross (now called "Saint Andrew's Cross"). Andrew was not as prominent as his brother Peter, but he was a faithful Christian who helped to spread the Christian faith and way throughout the world.

JAMES, THE SON OF ZEBEDEE

James, like Peter and Andrew, was a fisherman on the shores of Galilee. His home was probably in Capernaum or Bethsaida.

James was one of the three disciples who formed an "inner circle" of the very close friends of Jesus. Time after time we read in the gospels that Jesus took with him "Peter and James and John" to share some experience. For example, it was they who witnessed the Transfiguration of Jesus, and it was they who went with him to the Garden of Gethsemane on the night when he was betrayed and arrested.

It is not strange, therefore, that James was one of the early leaders of the Christian church at Jerusalem, sharing that leadership with Peter. James was one of the first Christians to be martyred for the faith. He was arrested in A.D. 42 by Herod Agrippa I and was beheaded. Jesus foresaw this martyrdom when he told James that he would drink the cup that he (Christ) had to drink. (Matthew 20:23)

JOHN, THE SON OF ZEBEDEE

John, the brother of James and son of Zebedee, like his brother was a fiery personality. Jesus called James and John "Sons of Thunder." Even though both brothers deserted Jesus when he was seized and crucified, they became faithful workers for the Christian cause.

John worked especially with Peter, serving with Peter as a missionary to Samaria. "And they, when they had testified and preached the word of the Lord, returned to Jerusalem, and preached the gospel in many villages of the Samaritans."

He was considered a pillar of the Christian church in Jerusalem. After the death of his brother James, he apparently gave much leadership to the church there.

PHILIP

According to the Fourth Gospel, Philip lived in Galilee. He became one of the apostles as a direct result of Jesus' invitation to "Follow me." His hometown was Bethsaida. Philip recognized Jesus as the one whose coming had been foretold by the prophets, and brought his brother Nathanael to Christ. Other than this, we know very little about Philip's activities as one of the apostles.

BARTHOLOMEW

The New Testament tells nothing of the work of Bartholomew. It only lists his name as one of the twelve apostles. He is representative of the obscure, but faithful, Christians in every age who help carry on the church's work and mission to the world: their names are not known to many men, but they are known to God. The Armenian Christian Church holds the tradition, however, that Bartholomew and Thaddeus founded their church.

MATTHEW, or LEVI

Matthew was a tax-collector who lived in Capernaum. He may have had a toll office on the road that ran from Damascus to the Mediterranean Sea, close to the Sea of Galilee.

Matthew may have known Greek, since he was a tax collector. It is likely that he wrote the First Gospel, which bears his name. As you will notice when you read the Gospel of Matthew, it is especially strong on the teachings of Jesus. Matthew may have jotted down Jesus' teachings as the apostles followed their Master from town to town throughout Palestine.

Jesus may have chosen Matthew in part because of his ability to write, with the knowledge that Matthew could thereby help to carry on the Christian cause after the death of his Lord. Matthew was richer, better educated, and better equipped to write the good news that Jesus was preaching than any of the other disciples. It is probable that when he became one of Jesus' disciples, Matthew gave up his profession of tax-collecting. As the author of the Gospel of Matthew, he bestowed a blessing on all the generations that would follow him!

THOMAS

One quality of Thomas the apostle stands out in our minds when we hear his name: doubt. He was absent from the group when the risen Christ appeared to the apostles, and he would not believe that Jesus had indeed risen from the dead. Yet if we read the whole story (John 20:19-29) we see that Thomas is not to be dismissed lightly as merely a doubter. Thomas wanted to be personally convinced of the truth of his religious convictions. Secondhand beliefs were not good enough for him. When the risen Christ confronted Thomas, his response was just as total as his doubt had been. "My Lord and my God!" he said to the risen Christ. Once convinced of the truth that Jesus was risen from the dead, Thomas was willing to die in order to tell the good news of the Gospel. In South India today there is a group known as the "Thomas Christians," who hold the tradition that the apostle Thomas organized the church there and suffered a martyr's death in A.D. 58.

JAMES, THE SON OF ALPHEUS

The ninth apostle was younger and less prominent than James the son of Zebedee. Since his father's name was Alpheus, he may have been one of Matthew's brothers (since Matthew's father was also named Alpheus). Other than this, we know nothing about the later life of this apostle.

THADDEUS

Thaddeus, along with Bartholomew, according to tradition carried the Christian faith to Armenia. This should be honor enough for any Christian in any age—to have planted the seed of faith in foreign soil, where it grew into a living church!

SIMON, THE ZEALOT

The Zealots were a political group in ancient Palestine who were formed in the year A.D. 6 with the objective of overthrowing the Roman rulers. Simon the Zealot was, therefore, in all likelihood interested in having his homeland freed from Roman domination. The Zealots looked with fervent hope to the coming of the Messiah. Simon may have expected Jesus, when it became clear that he was the Messiah (the Christ), to overthrow the Roman political rulers of Palestine and replace them with native Jewish rulers. But of course, this was not Jesus' mission. Simon is credited with helping take the Christian faith to Armenia.

JUDAS ISCARIOT

The twelfth apostle is remembered with revulsion. He so disgraced his name that to call anyone a "Judas" is to insult him terribly. Judas was the treasurer for the group of Jesus' disciples. Just why he chose to betray his Master is a genuine mystery. The thirty pieces of silver with which he was bribed were not the deeper reason, apparently, for he returned this money to the high priests and committed suicide when he saw what his betrayal had done to Jesus (Matthew 27:3-5).

The fate of Judas reminds us that persons have freedom to accept or to reject God's way. Even a person who had lived in the presence of the Son of God still could turn his back on him and betray him. But such a betrayal is the road to death.

MATTHIAS

When Judas was removed from the circle of the apostles, the group chose two candidates to take his place, in order that the number of apostles might once more be twelve. One was Joseph Barsabas, surnamed Justus; the other was Matthias. The apostles used an ancient Jewish practice, that of throwing lots, to determine which of these men should become one of the apostles; and the lot fell on Matthias. He is credited with being one of the five apostles who evangelized Armenia.

BIBLE DICTIONARY

Compiled by Noted Bible Authorities

AARON—*meaning uncertain.* The son of Amram and Jochebed, and the elder brother of Moses and Miriam (Num. 26:59; 33:39). He was a Levite, and he was appointed by Jehovah to be spokesman for Moses, who was "slow of speech" (Ex. 4:10-16). Accordingly he was not only the organ of communication with the Israelites and with Pharaoh (Ex. 4:30; 7:2), but also the actual instrument of working most of the miracles of the Exodus (*e.g.,* Ex. 7:19). Aaron was consecrated by Moses to the new office of high priesthood. The solemnity of the office and its entire dependence for sanctity on the ordinance of God, were vindicated by the death of his sons, Nadab and Abihu, for "offering strange fire" on the altar (Lev. 10:1, 2). From this time the history of Aaron is almost entirely that of the priesthood, and its chief feature is the great rebellion of Korah and the Levites against his sacerdotal dignity, united with that of Dathan and Abiram and the Reubenites against the temporal authority of Moses. Aaron's death seems to have followed very speedily. It took place on Mount Hor, after the transference of his robes and office to Eleazar, who alone with Moses was present at his death (Num. 20:28). The wife of Aaron was Elisheba (Ex. 6:23), and the two sons who survived him, Eleazar and Ithamar.

AARON'S ROD. Figures most prominently in the incident (Num. 17:1-11) in which thirteen rods, representing the twelve tribes and the thirteenth bearing the name of Aaron, were left overnight before the ark in the Tabernacle. In the morning it was found that the rod of Aaron alone of the thirteen had budded and put forth blossoms. The rod or staff of Aaron also was used in the miracles before Pharaoh and the plagues upon the Egyptians (*e.g.,* Ex. 7:9-12, 19).

AARONITES. Sons of Aaron, denoting all the priests tracing their descent from Aaron as the founder of the priesthood (1 Chron. 12:27; 27:12; Ps. 115:10).

AB—*father.* An element in the composition of many proper names. Also the fifth month of the Jewish calendar.

ABADDON—*destroyer.* Proper name of the angel of the bottomless pit (Rev. 9:11). (See Apollyon.)

ABANA—*stony.* One of the "rivers of Damascus" (2 Kings 5:12). Identified with the *Barada* which rises in the Antilibanus west of the city.

ABARIM—*parts beyond.* A mountain or range of highlands on the east of the Jordan, in the land of Moab (Deut. 32:49), facing Jericho, and forming the eastern wall of the Jordan Valley at that part. Its most elevated spot was "the Mount Nebo, 'head' of 'the' Pisgah," from which Moses viewed the Promised Land before his death.

ABBA. The transliteration of the Aramaic word for "father." It occurs three times in the New Testament: Mark 14:36; Rom. 8:15; Gal. 4:6.

ABEDNEGO—*servant of Nebo.* The Babylonian name given to Azariah, one of the three friends of Daniel, miraculously saved from the fiery furnace (Dan. 3).

ABEL—*breath, vapor.* The second son of Adam, murdered by his brother Cain (Gen. 4:1-16). Jehovah showed respect for Abel's offering, but not for that of Cain, because, according to the Epistle to the Hebrews (11:4), Abel "by faith offered a more excellent sacrifice than Cain." Jesus spoke of "Abel the righteous" (Matt. 23:25).

ABEL—*meadow.* The name of several places in Palestine. 1. Abel-beth-maachah, a town of some importance ("a city and a mother in Israel." 2 Sam. 20:19) in the extreme north of Palestine; named with Dan, Cinneroth, Kedesh, and as such falling an early prey to the invading kings of Syria (1 Kings 15:29). 2. Abel-mizraim (*meadow of Egypt*), the name given by the Canaanites to the floor of Atad, at which Joseph, his brothers, and the Egyptians made their mourning for Jacob (Gen. 1:11). It was beyond (on the east of) Jordan. 3. Abel-shittim (*meadow of acacias*), in the "plains" of Moab, on the low level of the Jordan valley. Israel "pitched from Beth-jesimoth unto Abel-shittim" (Num. 33:49). 4. Abel-meholah (*meadow of the dance*), named with Beth-shean and Jokneam (1 Kings 4:12), and therefore in the northern part of the Jordan valley. 5. Abel-cheramim, in the A.V. rendered "the plain of the vineyards," a place eastward of Jordan, beyond Aroer; named as the point to which Jephthah's pursuit of the Bene-Ammon extended (Judg. 11:33). 6. "The Great 'Abel,' in the field of Joshua the Bethshemite" (1 Sam. 6:18).

ABIA, ABIAH, or **ABIJAH**—*Jehovah is my father.* 1. Son of Becher, the son of Benjamin (1 Chron. 7:8). 2. Wife of Hezron (1 Chron. 2:24). 3. Second son of Samuel, whom he made judge in Beersheba (1 Sam. 8:2; 1 Chron. 7:28). 4. Son of Jeroboam I who died in childhood (1 Kings 14:1-13). 5. Abijah, or Abijam, the son of Rehoboam and Maachah, and king of Judah (1 Kings 15:1-8; 2 Chron. 13). 6. Mother of King Hezekiah (2 Chron. 29:1). 7. Descendant of Eleazar, and chief of the eighth of the twenty-four courses of priests (Luke 1:5).

ABIASAPH—*father has gathered.* (Ex. 6:24), otherwise written *Ebiasaph* (1 Chron. 6:23, 37; 9:19), the head of one of the families of the Korhites (a house of the Kohathites).

ABIATHAR—*father of abundance.* The only one of all the sons of Ahimelech, the high priest, who escaped the slaughter inflicted upon his father's house by Saul (1 Sam. 22). Abiathar, having become high priest, fled to David, and was thus enabled to inquire of the Lord for him (1 Sam. 23:9; 30:7; 2 Sam. 2:1; 5:19). Abiathar on his part was firmly attached to David. He adhered to him in his wanderings while pursued by Saul; he was with him while he reigned in Hebron (2 Sam. 2:1-3), the city of the house of Aaron (Josh. 21:10-13); he carried the ark before him when David brought it up to Jerusalem (1 Chron. 15:11; 1 Kings 2:26); he continued faithful to him in Absalom's rebellion (2 Sam. 15:24, 29, 35, 36; 17:15-17; 19:11); and "was afflicted in all wherein David was afflicted." He was also one of David's chief counselors (1 Chron. 27:34). When, however, Adonijah set himself up for David's successor on the throne, in opposition to Solomon, Abiathar, perhaps in rivalry to Zadok, sided with him, and was one of his chief partisans, while Zadok was on Solomon's side. For this, Abiathar was banished to his native village, Anathoth, and narrowly escaped with his life, which was spared by Solomon only on the strength of his long and faithful service to David his father. He was deprived of the high priesthood, and "Zadok the priest did the king put in the room of Abiathar" (1 Kings 2:27, 35).

ABIB. Month of earing-corn, the first month of the old Hebrew calendar. Later it was called Nisan.

ABIEL—*father is God.* 1. The father of Kish, and consequently grandfather of Saul (1 Sam. 9:1), as well as of Abner, Saul's commander-in-chief (1 Sam. 14:51). In the genealogy in 1 Chron. 8:33; 9:39, Ner is made the father of Kish, and the name of Abiel is omitted. 2. One of David's mighty men (1 Chron. 11:32).

ABIEZER—*father is help.* 1. Eldest son of Gilead, and descendant of Manasseh, and apparently at one time the leading family of the tribe (Josh. 17:2; 1 Chron. 7:18; Num. 26:30, where the name is given in the contracted form of *Jeezer*). He was the ancestor of the great judge Gideon. 2. An Anathothite, one of David's heroes (2 Sam. 23:27; 1 Chron. 11:28; 27:12).

ABIGAIL—*father is joy.* 1. The beautiful wife of Nabal, a wealthy owner of goats and sheep in Carmel. When David's messengers were slighted by Nabal, Abigail took the blame upon herself, supplied David and his followers with provisions and succeeded in appeasing his anger. Ten days after this Nabal died, and David sent for Abigail and made her his wife (1 Sam. 25:14). By her he had a son, called Chileab in 2 Sam. 3:3, but Daniel in 1 Chron. 3:1. 2. A sister of David, married to Jether the Ishmaelite, and mother, by him, of Amasa (1 Chron. 2:16 f.).

ABIHU—*he is father.* The second son (Num. 3:2) of Aaron by Elisheba (Ex. 6:23), who with his father and his elder brother, Nadab, and seventy elders of Israel, accompanied Moses to the summit of Sinai (Ex. 24:1). Being, together with Nadab, guilty of offering strange fire (Lev. 10:1) to the Lord, he was consumed by fire from heaven.

ABIJAH or **ABIJAM**—*my father is Jehovah.* The son and successor of Rehoboam on the throne of Judah (1 Kings 14:31; 2 Chron. 13). He is called *Abijah* in Chronicles, *Abijam* in Kings, the latter name being probably an error in the manuscripts. (See also Abia, Abiah.)

ABILENE. A tetrarchy of which the capital was Abila, a city situated on the eastern slope of Antilibanus, in a district fertilized by the river Barada (Abana) (Luke 3:1).

ABIMELECH—*father is Melech.* 1. A Philistine king of Gerar, who saw the beauty of Sarah and took her to wife (Gen. 20:1-17; 21:22-32). 2. Another king of Gerar in the time of Isaac, of whom a similar narrative is recorded in relation to Rebekah (Gen. 26:7-11, 26-33). 3. Son of the judge Gideon by his Shechemite concubine (Judg. 8:31). 4. Son of Abiathar, the high priest in the time of David (1 Chron. 18:16), called Ahimelech in 2 Sam. 8:17.

ABINADAB—*father is generous.* 1. A Levite, a native of Kirjath-jearim, in whose house the ark remained 20 years (1 Sam. 7:1; 2 Sam. 6:3 f.; 1 Chron. 13:7). 2. Second son of Jesse (1 Sam. 16:8; 17:13). 3. A son of Saul who was slain on Mount Gilboa (1 Sam. 31:2). 4. Father of one of the chief officers of Solomon (1 Kings 4:11).

ABIRAM—*father is the Exalted One.* A Reubenite, son of Eliab, who, with Dothan and On, men of the same tribe, and Korah, a Levite, organized a conspiracy against Moses and Aaron (Num. 16).

ABISHAG—*meaning uncertain.* A beautiful Shunammitess, brought to comfort David in his extreme old age (1 Kings 1:4). After David's death Adonijah induced Bathsheba, the queen-mother, to ask Solomon to give him Abishag in marriage; but this imprudent petition cost Adonijah his life (1 Kings 2:12-24).

ABISHAI—*my father is Jesse.* The eldest of the three sons of Zeruiah, David's sister, and brother to Joab and Asahel (1 Chron. 2:16). A devoted follower of David, he was his companion in the desperate night expedition to the camp of Saul, and would have stabbed the sleeping king with his own spear. But David restrained him, and the warriors left the camp as stealthily as they had come, carrying with them Saul's spear and the cruse of water which stood at his head (1 Sam. 26:6-9). On the outbreak of Absalom's rebellion and the consequent flight of David, Abishai remained true to the king. In the battle in the wood of Ephraim Abishai commanded a third part of the army (2 Sam. 18:2, 5, 12). The last act of service which is recorded of Abishai was his rescue of David from the hands of a gigantic Philistine, Ishbibenob (2 Sam. 21:17). His personal prowess on this, as on another occasion, when he fought single-handed against three hundred, won for him a place as captain of the second three of David's mighty men (2 Sam. 23:18; 1 Chron. 11:20).

ABNER—*my father is a lamp.* The son of Ner, who was the brother of Kish (1 Chron. 9:36), the father of Saul. Abner, therefore, was Saul's first cousin, and was made by him commander-in-chief of his army (1 Sam. 14:51). He was the person who conducted David into Saul's presence after the death of Goliath (1 Sam. 17:57), and afterward accompanied Saul when he sought David's life at Hachilah (1 Sam. 26:3-14). When Ishbosheth was proclaimed king, Abner led the men of Israel against those of Judah under Joab, and was defeated. Afterward he inclined to the side of David, by whom he was eventually received. He was treacherously murdered by Joab and his brother Abishai, at the gate of Hebron. As a token of respect David followed the bier, and poured forth a simple dirge over the slain (2 Sam. 3:33, 34).

ABOMINATION OF DESOLATION. Mentioned by Jesus as a sign of the approaching destruction of Jerusalem, with reference to Dan. 9:27; 11:31; 12:11. The Jews considered the prophecy of Daniel as fulfilled in the profanation of the Temple under Antiochus Epiphanes, when the Israelites themselves erected an idolatrous altar upon the sacred altar. This altar is described as "an abomination of desolation" (1 Macc. 1:54; 6:7). The prophecy, however, referred ultimately to the destruction of Jerusalem by the Romans, and consequently the "abomination" must describe some occurrence connected with that event.

ABRAHAM or **ABRAM**—*meaning uncertain.* The son of Terah and founder of the Hebrew people. His family, a branch of the descendants of Shem, was settled in Ur of the Chaldees, beyond the Euphrates. Terah had two other sons, Nahor and Haran. Haran died before his father, in Ur of the Chaldees, leaving a son Lot, and Terah, taking with him Abram, with Sarai, his wife, and his grandson Lot, emigrated to Haran in Mesopotamia, where he died. On the death of his father, Abram, with Sarai and Lot, pursued his course to the land of Canaan, whither he was directed by divine command (Gen. 12:5), when he received the general promise that he should become the founder of a great nation, and that all the families of the earth should be blessed in him. He next pitched his tent beneath the terebinth of Moreh (Gen. 12:6). Here he received in vision from Jehovah the further revelation that this was the land which his descendants should inherit (Gen. 12:7). He again journeyed southward to the rich corn-lands of Egypt. There he arranged that Sarai should represent herself as his sister. But her beauty was reported to the king, and she was taken into the royal harem.

The deception was discovered, and Pharaoh with some indignation dismissed him from the country (Gen. 12:10-20). Abram left Egypt with great possessions, and, accompanied by Lot, returned by the south of Palestine. The increased wealth of the two kinsmen was the ultimate cause of their separation. Lot chose the fertile plain of the Jordan, while Abram pitched his tent among the oak-groves of Mamre, close to Hebron (Gen. 13). The chiefs of the tribes who peopled the plain of the Jordan for twelve years had been the tributaries of Chedorlaomer, king of Elam. Their rebellion brought a fresh flood of invaders who joined battle with the revolted chieftains in the vale of Siddim. The king of Sodom and his confederates were defeated, their cities plundered, and a host of captives accompanied the victorious army of Chedorlaomer. Among them were Lot and his family. Abram heard the tidings from a fugitive, and hastily arming his trusty slaves, started in pursuit. He followed the conquerors, and in a night attack completely routed their host. At the suggestion of Sarai, who despaired of having children of her own, he took as his concubine Hagar, her Egyptian maid, who bore him Ishmael in the eighty-sixth year of his age (Gen. 16). The promise that Sarah should have a son was repeated when Abraham entertained three angels (Gen. 18). At length Isaac, the long-looked-for child, was born, Sarah's jealousy was aroused by the mockery of Ishmael at the "great banquet" which Abraham made to celebrate the weaning of her son (Gen. 21:9). She demanded that, with his mother Hagar, he should be driven out (Gen. 21:10). But the severest trial of Abraham's faith came when he received the strange command to take Isaac, his only son, and offer him for a burnt-offering at an appointed place. The sacrifice was stayed by the angel of Jehovah (Gen. 22). Sarah died (Gen. 23:2) and was buried in the cave of Machpelah, which Abraham purchased of Ephron the Hittite for 400 shekels of silver. In his advanced age he commissioned the faithful steward of his house to seek a wife for Isaac from the family of his brother Nahor (Gen. 24). After Isaac's marriage with Rebekah, and his removal to Lahai-roi, Abraham took to wife Keturah, by whom he had six children, Zimran, Jokshan, Medan, Midian, Ishbok, and Shuah, who became the ancestors of nomadic tribes. Keturah occupied a position inferior to that of a legitimate wife. Her children, like Ishmael, were dismissed with presents, and Isaac was left sole heir of his father's wealth. At the goodly age of one hundred and seventy-five Abraham was "gathered to his people," and laid beside Sarah in the tomb of Machpelah by his sons Isaac and Ishmael (Gen. 25:7-10). From the intimate communion which Abraham held with the Almighty, he is distinguished by the high title of "the friend of God" (2 Chron. 20:7; Isa. 41:8; James 2:23).

ABRAHAM'S BOSOM. A figurative expression used to define the blessedness of the righteous dead (Luke 16:22).

ABSALOM—*father is peace.* Third son of David, by Maachah, daughter of Talmai, king of Geshur. By his order the servants murdered his half-brother Amnon for having violated his sister Tamar. Afterward, through his beauty, luxuriant hair (2 Sam. 14:25, 26), splendid retinue, fair speeches and courtesies, he "stole the hearts of the men of Israel" (2 Sam. 15:2-6), and rebelled against his father. At first he was successful and occupied Jerusalem, taking possession of David's harem. David was forced to flee over the Jordan. After being anointed king, Absalom crossed the Jordan to attack his father, who had rallied a force about him. A decisive battle was fought in the wood of Ephraim. Absalom was defeated, his long hair became entangled in the branches of a terebinth (or oak), where he was left hanging, his mule running away from him. He was killed by Joab. When the news reached David, he mourned for him, crying again and again, "O my son Absalom, my son, my son Absalom" (2 Sam. 18:33).

ACCHO, ACCO, ACRE. Known at different times as Ptolemais and St. John D'Acre. A seaport eight miles north of Carmel, on the Bay of Acre. It was included in the lot of the tribe of Asher (Judg. 1:31), but it was not captured by Israel.

ACELDAMA. "The field of blood," the name given by the Jews to a field near Jerusalem purchased by Judas with the money which he received for the betrayal of Christ, and so called from his violent death therein (Acts 1:19).

ACHAIA. A Roman province which, with that of Macedonia, included the whole of Greece; hence Achaia and Macedonia are frequently mentioned together in the New Testament to indicate all Greece (Acts 18:12; 19:21; Rom. 15:26; 1 Cor. 16:15; 2 Cor. 9:2; 1 Thess. 1:8).

ACHAN. An Israelite of the tribe of Judah, who, when Jericho and all that it contained were accursed and devoted to destruction, hid a portion of the spoil in his tent. For this sin Jehovah punished Israel by their defeat in the attack upon Ai. When Achan confessed his guilt, he was stoned to death with his whole family by the people in a valley situated between Ai and Jericho, and their remains, together with his property, were burnt (Josh. 7:16-22). From this event the valley received the name of Achor (*trouble*).

ACHISH. A Philistine king of Gath. David twice found a refuge with him when he fled from Saul. On the first occasion, being recognized by the servants of Achish as one celebrated for his victories over the Philistines, he feigned madness (1 Sam. 21:10-13). From Achish he fled to the cave of Adullam. On a second occasion David fled to Achish with 600 men (1 Sam. 27:2), and remained at Gath a year and four months.

ACHMETHA. (See Ecbatana.)

ACHSAH—*anklet.* Daughter of Caleb. Her father promised her in marriage to whoever should capture Debir. Othniel, her father's younger brother, took that city, and accordingly received the hand of Achsah as his reward. Caleb, at his daughter's request, added to her dowry the upper and lower springs, which she had pleaded for as peculiarly suitable to her inheritance in a south country (Josh. 15:15-19; Judg. 1:11-15).

ACTS OF THE APOSTLES. A second treatise by the author of the third Gospel, traditionally known as Luke. It is the only source for the early history of the church and the spread of the Gospel from the Jewish to the Gentile world. The identity of the writer of Luke and Acts is strongly shown by their great similarity in style and idiom and the usage of particular words and compound forms. Acts commences with an inscription to one Theophilus, who was probably a man of birth and station. But its design must not be supposed to be limited to the edification of Theophilus, whose name is prefixed only by way of dedication. The readers were evidently intended to be the members of the Christian church, whether Jews or Gentiles, for its contents are such as are of the utmost consequence to the whole church.

ADAH—*adornment, beauty.* 1. The first of the two wives of Lamech, by whom were born to him Jabal and Jubal (Gen. 4:19). 2. A Hittitess, one of the three wives of Esau, mother of Eliphaz (Gen. 36:2, 10, 12, 16). In Gen. 26:34 she is called Bashemath.

ADAM—*red; human being.* The name given in Scripture to the first man. The word in Hebrew was also a common noun used to indicate a human being or "man." The creation of man was the work of the sixth day. His formation was the ultimate object of the Creator. With Eve his wife he was expelled from the Garden of Eden because of the sin in disobeying God's command not to eat of the fruit of the tree of knowledge. (Gen. 1-3) Adam is stated to have lived 930 years. The names of his sons mentioned in Scripture are Cain, Abel, and Seth.

ADDER. This word is used as the representative of four Hebrew names of poisonous serpents.

ADJURE. To bind one by oath (Josh. 6:26), or to charge strictly (Mark 5:7; Matt. 26:63).

ADONIBEZEK—*lord of Bezek.* A Canaanite king defeated by Judah and Simeon. They made him a prisoner and cut off his thumbs and great toes; he acknowledged the just vengeance of heaven upon him for his similar cruelty toward his fellow-princes (Judg. 1:4-7).

ADONIJAH—*my Lord is Jehovah.* The fourth son of David by Haggith (2 Sam. 3:4). After the death of Absalom he was next in order to succeed David as king. Solomon was successful in attaining the throne, however, and put Adonijah to death. (1 Kings 1-2).

ADONIRAM—*the Lord is high.* By contraction Adoram (2 Sam. 20:24), also Hadoram (2 Chron. 10:18), chief receiver of the tribute during the reigns of David, Solomon and Rehoboam. This last monarch sent him to collect the tribute from the rebellious Israelites, by whom he was stoned to death.

ADOPTION. The act of taking into the family for a child. Pharaoh's daughter adopted Moses (Ex. 2:10), and Mordecai thus received Esther (Esth. 2:7). Paul used the term to show the privilege of sonship bestowed by God upon believers in Jesus (Rom. 8:15, 23; 9:4; Gal. 4:5; Eph. 1:5).

ADORATION. The acts and postures by which the Hebrews expressed adoration bear a great similarity to those still in use among Oriental nations. To rise up and suddenly prostrate the body was the most simple method, but generally speaking, the prostration was conducted in a more formal manner, the person falling upon the knee and then gradually inclining the body until the forehead touched the ground. Such prostration was usual in the worship of Jehovah (Gen. 17:3; Ps. 95:6). But it was by no means exclusively used for that purpose; it was the formal mode of receiving visitors (Gen. 17:2), of doing obeisance to one of superior station (2 Sam. 14:4), and of showing respect to equals (1 Kings 2:19). Occasionally it was repeated three times (Gen. 33:3). It was accompanied by such acts as a kiss (Ex. 18:7), laying hold of the knees or feet of the person to whom the adoration was paid (Matt. 28:9); and kissing the ground on which he stood (Ps. 72:9; Mic. 7:17). Similar adoration was paid to idols (1 Kings 19:18); sometimes, however, prostration was omitted, and the act consisted simply in kissing the hand to the object of reverence (Job 31:27), and in kissing the statue itself (Hos. 13:2).

ADRAMMELECH. 1. The name of an idol introduced into Samaria by the colonists from Sepharvaim (2 Kings 17:31). 2. One of the murderers of Sennacherib (2 Kings 19:37; Isa. 37:38).

ADRIEL. Son of Barzillai, to whom Saul gave his daughter Merab, although he had previously promised her to David (1 Sam. 18:19). His five sons were amongst the seven descendants of Saul whom David surrendered to the Gibeonites (2 Sam. 21:8).

ADULLAM—*resting place.* A city of Judah. Fortified by Rehoboam (2 Chron. 11:7), it was one of the towns reoccupied by the Jews after their return from Babylon (Neh. 11:30).

ADULTERY. A general term for every species of unchastity, but now generally restricted to impurity by married persons. In a spiritual sense it means idolatry (Jer. 3:9; Ezek. 23:37).

AGABUS. A Christian prophet of Jerusalem who came to Antioch and predicted a famine (Acts 11:28), and at Caesarea foretold Paul's arrest (Acts 21:10-11).

AGAG. A king of the Amalekites, captured by Saul but permitted to live, contrary to divine command. He was put to death by Samuel (1 Sam. 15).

AENEAS. A paralytic at Lydda who was healed by Peter (Acts 9:33 f.).

AENON—*springs.* Mentioned in John 3:23 as place where John the Baptist baptized. Location is uncertain.

AGE, OLD. The aged occupied a prominent place in the social and political system of the Jews. In private life they were looked up to as the depositories of knowledge (Job 15:10); the young were ordered to rise up in their presence (Lev. 19:32); they allowed them to give their opinion first (Job 32:4); they were taught to regard gray hairs as a "crown of glory" and as the "beauty of old men" (Prov. 16:31; 20:29). The attainment of old age was regarded as a special blessing (Job 5:26), not only on account of the prolonged enjoyment of life to the individual, but also because it indicated peaceful and prosperous times (Zech. 8:4; Isa. 65:20).

AGRICULTURE. Though prominent in the narratives concerning Adam, Cain, and Noah, it was little cared for by the patriarchs. When Israel settled in Palestine and became a nation, the people took up farming which they learned from the Canaanites. Agriculture became the basis of the Mosaic commonwealth. Landmarks were deemed sacred (Deut. 19:14), and the inalienability of the heritage was ensured by its reversion to the owner in the year of jubilee, so that only so many years of occupancy could be sold (Lev. 25:8-16, 23-35). The abundance of water in Palestine made it a contrast to rainless Egypt (Deut. 8:7; 11:8-12). Rain was commonly expected about the end of our month of October. The cereal crops of constant mention were wheat and barley, and more rarely rye and millet. The plough was probably very light, one yoke of oxen usually sufficing to draw it. Mountains and steep places were hoed (Isa. 7:25). The wheat, etc., were reaped by the sickle or pulled up by the roots. They were bound in sheaves, a process prominent in Scripture. The sheaves or heaps were carted (Amos 2:13) to the floor, a circular spot of hard ground. Such floors were probably permanent, and became well-known spots (Gen. 50:10 f.; 2 Sam. 24:16, 18). On these the oxen, forbidden to be muzzled (Deut. 25:4), trampled out the grain. At a later time the Jews used a threshing sledge called *morag* (Isa. 41:15; 2 Sam. 24:22). The "shovel" and "fan" (Isa. 30:24), the precise difference of which is doubtful, indicate the process of winnowing—a conspicuous part of ancient husbandry (Ps. 35:5; Job 21:18; Isa. 17:13), and important, owing to the slovenly threshing. Evening was the favorite time (Ruth 3:2), when there was mostly a breeze. The "fan" (Matt. 3:12) was perhaps a broad shovel which threw the grain up against the wind. The last process was the shaking in a sieve to separate dirt and refuse (Amos 9:9).

AHAB—*father's brother.* 1. Son of Omri, seventh king of Israel. He married Jezebel, daughter of Ethbaal, king of Tyre, and in obedience to her wishes caused a temple to be built to Baal in Samaria (1 Kings 16:29-33). One of Ahab's chief tastes was for splendid architecture, which he showed by building an ivory house and several cities. Desiring to add to his pleasure-grounds at Jezreel the vineyard of his neighbor Naboth, he proposed to buy it or give land in exchange for it, and when this was refused by Naboth, a false accusation of blasphemy was brought against him, and he was stoned to death. Thereupon Elijah declared that the entire extirpation of Ahab's house was the penalty appointed for his long course of wickedness, now crowned by this atrocious crime. The execution, however, of the sentence was delayed in consequence of Ahab's deep repentance (1 Kings 21). Ahab, in an attack upon Ramoth in Gilead on the east of Jordan, in conjunction with Jehoshaphat, king

of Judah, was slain by a "certain man who drew a bow at a venture." When he was brought to be buried in Samaria, the dogs licked up his blood as a servant was washing his chariot—a partial fulfillment of Elijah's prediction (1 Kings 22). 2. A lying prophet who deceived the captive Israelites in Babylon, and was burnt to death by Nebuchadnezzar (Jer. 29:21).

AHASUERUS. The name of one Median and two Persian kings mentioned in the Old Testament. 1. In Dan. 9:1 Ahasuerus is said to be the father of Darius the Mede. 2. In Ezra 4:6 the enemies of the Jews, after the death of Cyrus, desirous to frustrate the building of Jerusalem, sent accusations against them to Ahasuerus, king of Persia. 3. The third is the Ahasuerus of the book of Esther.

AHAZ—*he hath grasped.* Eleventh king of Judah, son of Jotham (Isa. 7, 8, 9; 2 Kings 23:12).

AHAZIAH—*Jehovah hath grasped.* 1. Son of Ahab and Jezebel, eighth king of Israel. 2. Fifth king of Judah, son of Jehoram and Athaliah (daughter of Ahab), and therefore nephew of the preceding. Ahaziah reigned one year (2 Chron. 22:6; 21:17).

AHIJAH—*Jehovah is brother.* The name of nine different men in the Old Testament. The two most prominent were Ahijah the high priest during the reign of Saul (1 Sam. 14:3; identified with Ahimelech of 1 Sam. 21, 22), and the prophet of Shiloh who foretold the rise and fall of Jeroboam I (1 Kings 11:29-40; 1 Kings 14).

AHIMAAZ—*my brother is wrath.* Son of Zadok, the high priest in David's reign, and celebrated for his swiftness of foot (2 Sam. 15:24-37; 17:15-22; 18:19-33).

AHIMELECH—*brother is king.* 1. Son of Ahitub (1 Sam. 22:11, 12), and high priest at Nob in the days of Saul. He gave David the showbread to eat, and the sword of Goliath, and for so doing was, upon the accusation of Doeg the Edomite, put to death with his whole house by Saul's order. Abiathar alone escaped. 2. A Hittite who joined David and became one of his captains (1 Sam. 26:6).

AHINOAM—*brother is pleasantness.* 1. The daughter of Ahimaaz and wife of Saul (1 Sam. 14:50). 2. A native of Jezreel who was married to David during his wandering life (1 Sam. 25:43). She lived with him and his other wife, Abigail, at the court of Achish (1 Sam. 27:3), was taken prisoner with her by the Amalekites when they plundered Ziklag, but was rescued by David (1 Sam. 30:5-18). She is again mentioned as living with him when he was king of Judah in Hebron (2 Sam. 2:1), and was the mother of his eldest son Amnon (2 Sam. 3:2).

AHITHOPHEL—*my brother is foolishness.* A native of Giloh, was a councillor of David whose wisdom was highly esteemed (2 Sam. 16:23). He was the grandfather of Bathsheba (cf. 2 Sam. 11:3 with 23:34). When Ahithophel joined the conspiracy of Absalom, David prayed Jehovah to turn his counsel to foolishness (2 Sam. 15:31). In order to show to the people that the breach between Absalom and his father was irreparable, Ahithophel persuaded him to take possession of the royal harem (2 Sam. 16:21). David, to counteract his counsel, sent Hushai to Absalom. Ahithophel had recommended an immediate pursuit of David, but Hushai advised delay, his object being to send intelligence to David. Ahithophel saw that Hushai's advice prevailed, and returning to his home, "put his household in order and hanged himself" (2 Sam. 17:1-23).

AHOLAH—*her tent,* and **AHOLIBAH**—*my tent is her.* Two symbolical names, are described as harlots, the former representing Samaria, and the latter Judah (Ezek. 23).

AIJELETH SHAHAR—*the hind of the dawn.*

Found once only in the Bible, in the title of Ps. 22.

ALABASTER—*white stone mineral.* Occurs in the New Testament only in the notice of the alabaster box of ointment which a woman brought to Jesus when he sat at meat in the house of Simon the leper at Bethany, the contents of which she poured on the head of the Master (Matt. 26:7; Mark 14:3; Luke 7:37).

ALEXANDER—*man defender.* 1. Son of Simon the Cyrenian, who was compelled to bear the cross for Jesus (Mark 15:21). 2. One of the kindred of Annas the high priest (Acts 4:6). 3. A Jew at Ephesus whom his countrymen put forward during the tumult raised by Demetrius the silversmith (Acts 19:33) to plead their cause with the mob. 4. An Ephesian Christian reprobated by Paul in 1 Tim. 1:20 as having, together with one Hymenaeus, put from him faith and good conscience, and so made shipwreck concerning the faith. 5. A coppersmith, mentioned by Paul (2 Tim. 4:14) as having done him many mischiefs.

ALEXANDRIA. (Acts 18:24; 6:9) The Hellenic, Roman, and Christian capital of Egypt, was founded by Alexander the Great, 332 B.C., who himself traced the ground-plan of the city. Its importance as one of the chief grainports of Rome secured for it the general favor of the first emperors. Its population was mixed from the first.

ALGUM or ALMUG TREES. The former occurring in 2 Chron. 2:8; 9:10 f.; the latter in 1 Kings 10:11 f. There can be no question that these words are identical. The almug was brought in great plenty from Ophir for Solomon's Temple and house, and for the construction of musical instruments.

ALLELUIA. So written in Rev. 19:1-6, or more properly Hallelujah, "Praise ye Jehovah."

ALLON. A large strong tree of some description, probably an oak. The word is found in two names in the topography of Palestine. 1. Allon, more accurately Elon, a place named among the cities of Naphtali (Josh. 19:33). 2. Allon-bachuth (oak of weeping), the tree under which Rebekah's nurse, Deborah, was buried (Gen. 35:8).

ALMOND TREE, ALMOND. This word is found in Gen. 43:11; Ex. 25:33, 34; 37:19, 20; Num. 17:8; Eccles. 12:5; Jer. 1:11, in the text of the A.V. The almond tree is a native of Asia and North Africa, but it is cultivated in the milder parts of Europe. The Hebrew word for almond signifies the "waker" because its early blossoming makes it the first tree to wake to life in the spring.

ALOES, LIGN ALOES (in Hebrew *Ahalim* and *Ahaloth*). The name of a costly and sweet-smelling wood which is mentioned in Ps. 45:8; Prov. 7:17; Cant. 4:14; John 19:39. It is usually identified with the eaglewood of Asia. Not to be confused with the common bitter aloes.

ALPHA. The first letter of the Greek alphabet. Used in connection with Omega, the last letter, to express the eternity of Christ (Rev. 1:8, 11).

ALPHAEUS—*successor.* The father of the Apostle James the Less (Matt. 10:3; Mark 3:18; Luke 6:15; Acts 1:13), and husband of Mary who, with the mother of Jesus and others, was standing by the cross during the crucifixion (John 19:25). In the latter place he is called Clopas.

ALTAR OF BURNT-OFFERINGS. It differed in construction at different times. 1. In the tabernacle (Ex. 27) it was square, five cubits in length, the same in breadth, and three cubits high. It was made of planks of shittim (or acacia) wood overlaid with brass. (See Ex. 27:2.) 2. In Solomon's Temple the length and breadth were near

twenty cubits, and the height was ten (2 Chron. 4:1). It was entirely of brass (1 Kings 8:64; 2 Chron. 7:7).

ALTAR OF INCENSE. This was called also the golden altar, to distinguish it from the altar of burnt-offerings, which was called the brazen altar (Ex. 28:30). That in the tabernacle was made of acacia wood overlaid with pure gold. Its shape was square, being a cubit in length and breadth, and two cubits in height. It had horns at the four corners. It stood in the holy place (Ex. 30:6; 40:5).

AMALEK—*war like.* Son of Eliphaz by his concubine Timnah, grandson of Esau and chieftain ("duke" A.V.) of Edom (Gen. 36:12, 16; 1 Chron. 1:36).

AMASA—*burden or burden bearer.* 1. Son of Ithra or Jether by Abigail, David's sister (2 Sam. 17:25). He joined Absalom in his rebellion, and was by him appointed commander-in-chief in the place of Joab, by whom he was totally defeated in the forest of Ephraim (2 Sam. 18:6). When Joab incurred the displeasure of David for killing Absalom, David forgave the treason of Amasa, recognized him as his nephew, and appointed him Joab's successor (2 Sam. 19:13). Joab afterward, when they were both in pursuit of the rebel Sheba, pretending to salute Amasa, stabbed him with his sword (2 Sam. 20:10), which he held concealed in his left hand. 2. A prince of Ephraim, son of Hadlai, in the reign of Ahaz (2 Chron. 28:12).

AMAZIAH—*Jehovah strengthens.* 1. Became king of Judah when his father Jehoash was assassinated (2 Kings 12:20). Noted for his wars with Edom and Israel (2 Kings 14; 2 Chron. 25). 2. Priest of Jeroboam II who tried to silence the prophet Amos (Amos 7:10-17).

AMEN. Literally, "true," and used as a substantive, "that which is true," "truth" (Isa. 65:16).

AMMINADAB—*kinsman is generous.* Son of Ram or Aram, and father of Nahshon, or Naasson (as it is written, Matt. 1:4; Luke 3:32), who was the prince of the tribe of Judah at the first numbering of Israel in the second year of the Exodus (Num. 1:7; 2:3; Ruth 4:19, 20; 1 Chron. 1:10).

AMMON, AMMONITES, CHILDREN OF AMMON. A people descended from Ben-Ammi, the son of Lot by his younger daughter (Gen. 19:38), as Moab was by the elder, and dating from the destruction of Sodom. The near relation between the two people indicated in the story of their origin continued throughout their existence (*cf.* Judg. 10:6; 2 Chron. 20:1; Zeph. 2:8). The hatred in which the Ammonites were held by Israel is stated to have arisen partly from their opposition, or rather their denial of assistance (Deut. 23:4), to the Israelites on their approach to Canaan. But whatever its origin, the animosity continued in force to the latest date.

AMNON. 1. Eldest son of David by Ahinoam the Jezreelitess, born in Hebron while his father's royalty was only acknowledged in Judah. He dishonored his half-sister Tamar, and was in consequence murdered by her brother (2 Sam. 13:1-29). 2. Son of Shinom (1 Chron. 4:20).

AMOS—*bearer.* Called by God, he began to prophesy a little before Hosea, and continued a while contemporary with that prophet, during the reign of Uzziah. The book of Amos reproves the wickedness of the Hebrews, who abandoned themselves to every evil, pronounces the ruin of the neighboring nations, judgment on the Israelites and the final prosperity of Messiah's kingdom.

AMPHIPOLIS. A city of Macedonia (Acts 17:1). It is almost surrounded by the river Strymon,

whence its name, which means "the all-around city."

AMRAM—*the people is exalted.* A Levite of the family of the Kohathites, and father of Moses, Aaron, and Miriam (Ex. 6:18, 20; Num. 3:19; 1 Chron. 6:2, 3, 18).

AMULETS. Ornaments, gems, scrolls, etc., worn as preservatives against the power of enchantments, and generally inscribed with mystic forms or characters.

ANAKIM. A race of giants, descendants of Arba (Josh. 15:13; 21:11), dwelling in the southern part of Canaan, and particularly at Hebron, which from their progenitor received the name of "city of Arba."

ANAMMELECH. An idol of the Sepharvaites, a tribe of the Samaritans (2 Kings 17:31).

ANANIAS—*Jehovah hath been gracious.* 1. A high priest in Acts 23:2-5; 24:1. 2. A disciple at Jerusalem, husband of Sapphira (Acts 5:1-11). Having sold his goods for the benefit of the church, he kept back a part of the price. Peter denounced the fraud, and Ananias fell down and expired. 3. A Jewish disciple at Damascus (Acts 9:10-17; 22:12), who was instructed to baptize Saul of Tarsus.

ANATHEMA. Literally means a thing suspended; equivalent of the Hebrew word signifying a thing or person *devoted.* The word anathema frequently occurs in Paul's writings, and is generally translated *accursed.*

ANDREW—*manly.* One among the first called of the Apostles (John 1:40; Matt. 4:18), brother of Simon Peter. He was of Bethsaida, and had been a disciple of John the Baptist. On hearing Jesus a second time designated by him as the Lamb of God, he left his former master, and, in company with another of John's disciples, attached himself to Jesus. By his means his brother Simon was brought to Jesus (John 1:41). In the catalog of the apostles, Andrew appears in Matt. 10:2; Luke 6:14, second, next after his brother Peter, but in Mark 3:16; Acts 1:13, fourth, next after the three, Peter, James, and John, and in company with Philip. And this appears to have been his real place of dignity among the apostles. The traditions about him are various. Eusebius makes him preach in Scythia; Jerome and Theodoret in Achaia (Greece); Nicephorus in Asia Minor and Thrace. He is said to have been crucified at Patrae in Achaia on a cross of peculiar form, known as St. Andrew's cross.

ANER. One of the three Amorite chiefs of Hebron who aided Abraham in the pursuit after the four invading kings (Gen. 14:13, 24).

ANGEL—*messenger.* The English word which refers to superhuman attendants of God.

ANISE. This word occurs only in Matt. 23:23 and refers to a garden plant used for seasoning.

ANKLET. This word does not occur in the A.V., but anklets are referred to in Isa. 3:16, 18, 20. They were fastened to the ankleband of each leg, were as common as bracelets and armlets, and made of much the same materials.

ANNA—*grace.* A prophetess in Jerusalem at the time of the presentation of Jesus in the Temple (Luke 2:36). She was of the tribe of Asher.

ANNAS—*merciful.* The son of Seth, was appointed Jewish high priest in A.D. 7 by Quirinus, the imperial governor of Syria, but was obliged by Valerius Gratus, procurator of Judaea, to give way to Ismael, son of Phabi, at the beginning of the reign of Tiberius. A.D. 14 Ismael was succeeded by Eleazar, son of Annas; then followed, after one year, Simon of Camithus, and then, after another year (about A.D. 25), Joseph Caiaphas, son-in-law of Annas (John 18:13). But in

Luke 3:2, Annas and Caiaphas are both called high priests, Annas being mentioned first. Jesus' first hearing (John 18:13) was before Annas, who then sent him bound to Caiaphas. In Acts 4:6, Annas is plainly called the high priest, and Caiaphas merely named with others of his family. He lived to old age, having had five sons high priests.

ANOINT. To apply unguents or oils to the skin and hair, especially the head. It was a sign of hospitality and also a sign of dedication.

ANT. This insect is mentioned twice in the Old Testament, in Prov. 6:6; 30:26, with reference to diligence and wisdom.

ANTIOCH. The capital of the Greek kings of Syria, and afterward the residence of the Roman governors of the province which bore the same name. No city, after Jerusalem, is so intimately connected with the history of the apostolic church. The chief interest of Antioch is connected with the progress of Christianity. Here the first Gentile church was founded (Acts 11:20, 21); here the disciples of Jesus Christ were first called Christians (Acts 11:26). It was from Antioch that Paul started on his three missionary journeys. To be distinguished from Pisidian Antioch in Galatia (Acts 13:14).

ANTIPATRIS—*belonging to Antipater*. A town to which the soldiers conveyed Paul by night on their march (Acts 23:31).

APOCRYPHA—*hidden*. The collection of books to which this term is popularly applied includes the following (the order given is that in which they stand in the English version): 1 & 2 Esdras, Tobit, Judith, the rest of the chapters of the book of Esther which are found neither in the Hebrew nor in the Chaldee, the Wisdom of Solomon, the Wisdom of Jesus the Son of Sirach, or Ecclesiaticus, Baruch, the Song of the Three Holy Children, the History of Susanna, the History of the Destruction of Bel and the Dragon, the Prayer of Manasses, king of Judah, and 1 & 2 Maccabees. The primary meaning of *Apocrypha*, "hidden, secret," seems, toward the close of the second century, to have been associated with the signification "spurious," and ultimately to have settled down into the latter.

APOLLONIA. A city of Macedonia, through which Paul and Silas passed in their way from Philippi and Amphipolis to Thessalonica (Acts 17:1).

APOLLOS. A Jew from Alexandria, eloquent and mighty in the Scriptures; one instructed in the way of the Lord according to the imperfect view of the disciples of John the Baptist (Acts 18:25), but on his coming to Ephesus during a temporary absence of Paul, more perfectly taught by Aquila and Priscilla. After this he became a preacher of the gospel, first in Achaia and then in Corinth (Acts 18:27; 19:1), where he watered that which Paul had planted (1 Cor. 3:6).

APOLLYON. As it is literally in the margin of the A.V. of Rev. 9:11, "a destroyer." It is the rendering of the Hebrew word *abaddon*, "the angel of the bottomless pit."

APOSTLE—*ambassador, envoy*. Originally the official name of those twelve of the disciples whom Jesus chose to send forth first to preach the gospel, and to be with him during the course of his ministry on earth. The word also appears to have been used to designate a much wider circle of Christian messengers and teachers. (See 2 Cor. 8:23; Phil. 2:25.)

APPHIA. A Christian woman addressed jointly with Philemon and Archippus in Philem. 2, apparently a member of Philemon's household, and not improbably his wife.

APPI FORUM. A station on the Appian Way, the great road which led from Rome to the neighborhood of the Bay of Naples (Acts 28:13).

AQUILA—*eagle*. A Jew whom Paul found at Corinth on his arrival from Athens (Acts 18:2). He was a native of Pontus, but had fled, with his wife Priscilla, from Rome in consequence of an order of Claudius commanding all Jews to leave the city. He became acquainted with Paul, and they abode together, and wrought at their common trade of making tents. On the departure of the apostle from Corinth, a year and six months after, Priscilla and Aquila accompanied him to Ephesus (Acts 18:18 f.). There they remained, and there they taught Apollos.

ARABIA—*desert; barren*. A country known in the Old Testament under two designations. 1. The East Country (Gen. 25:6), or perhaps the East (Gen. 10:30). From these passages it appears that the Land of the East and Sons of the East indicate, primarily, the country east of Palestine, and the tribes descended from Ishmael and from Keturah. 2. Arabia (2 Chron. 9:14; Isa. 21:13; Jer. 25:24; Ezek. 27:21).

ARAM. Son of Shem (Gen. 10:22 f.; cf. Gen. 25:14), and from whose name the words Aramean and Arabic are derived. In the Old Testament the name refers to a country and its inhabitants and is often translated "Syria" and "Syrians."

ARARAT. A mountainous district of Asia mentioned in the Bible in connection with the following events: 1. As the resting place of the ark after the deluge (Gen. 8:4). 2. As the asylum of the sons of Sennacherib (2 Kings 19:37; Isa. 37:38). 3. As the ally and probably the neighbor of Minni and Ashchenaz (Jer. 51:27).

ARCHANGEL. The chief angel. The Jews supposed that there are seven greater in power than the rest, and having guardianship of particular nations. Michael was considered the patron of the Jews (Dan. 10:13, 21).

ARCHIPPUS. A Christian teacher of Colosse (Col. 4:17), called by Paul his "fellow soldier" (Philem. 2).

ARIEL—*lion*. A designation given by Isaiah to the city of Jerusalem (Isa. 29:1, 2, 7). Its meaning is obscure.

ARIMATHAEA. (Matt. 27:57; Luke 23:51; John 19:38). Luke calls it "a city of Judaea."

ARISTARCHUS. A Thessalonian (Acts 20:4; 27:2) who accompanied Paul on his third missionary journey (Acts 19:29). He was with the apostle on his return to Asia (Acts 20:4), and again (Acts 27:2) on his voyage to Rome. He appears afterward as Paul's fellow-prisoner in Col. 4:10 and Philem. 24.

ARISTOBULUS. A resident at Rome, some of whose household are greeted in Rom. 16:10.

ARK, NOAH'S. (See Noah.)

ARK OF THE COVENANT. The first piece of the tabernacle's furniture for which precise directions were delivered (Ex. 25). It appears to have been an oblong chest of shittim (acacia) wood and was fitted with rings, one at each of the four corners, and through these were passed staves by which it was carried by the Kohathites (Num. 7:9; 10:21). Its purpose or object was to contain inviolate the Divine autograph of the two tables, that "covenant" from which it derived its title. It was also the support of the mercy-seat, materially symbolizing, perhaps, the "covenant" as that on which "mercy" rested. Before David's time its abode was frequently shifted. It sojourned among several families (1 Sam. 7:1; 2 Sam. 6:3, 11; 1 Chron. 13:13; 15:24, 25) in the border villages of eastern Judah, and did not take its place in the tabernacle, but dwelt in curtains—*i.e.*, in a separate tent pitched for it in Jerusalem by David. Subsequently the ark was installed in its shrine in the Temple.

ARMAGEDDON. "The hill of Megiddo," famous for two great victories (Rev. 16:16; *cf.* also Judg. 5:19; 2 Kings 9:27; 23:29).

ARMLET. An ornament universal in the East, especially among women. This word is not used in the A.V., as even in 2 Sam. 1:10 it is rendered by "the bracelet on his arm."

ARMS, ARMOR. 1. The *Chereb*, or *Sword*. Very little can be gathered as to its shape, size, material, or mode of use. Perhaps it was lighter and shorter than the modern sword. 2. The *Cidon* or *Javelin*. When not in action, the *Cidon* was carried on the back of the warrior (1 Sam. 17:6). 3. The *Sling*. This is first mentioned in Judg. 20:16. (See 2 Kings 3:25.) Defensive armor included the *breast-plate* (1 Sam. 17:5), the *habergeon* (See Ex. 28:32; 29:23), the *helmet* (1 Sam. 17:5; 2 Chron. 26:14; Ex. 27:10), *greaves* (1 Sam. 17:6), and two kinds of *shields*—the large one encompassing the whole person (Ps. 5:12), the smaller one called the buckler or target, probably for use in hand-to-hand fighting (1 Kings 10:16, 17; 2 Chron. 9:15, 16).

ARTAXERXES—*great kingdom*. The name of three different kings of Persia. The one mentioned in the Bible was Artaxerxes I Longimanus ("long-handed," because his right hand was longer than his left), who gave permission for the Jews to return to Jerusalem and rebuild its walls (Ezra 4:7; Neh. 2:1).

ASA—*healer*. Son of Abijah, and third king of Judah. In his zeal against heathenism he did not spare his grandmother, Maachah, who occupied the special dignity of "king's mother." Asa burnt the symbol of her religion (1 Kings 15:13), and threw its ashes into the brook Kidron, and then deposed Maachah from her dignity. He also placed in the temple certain gifts which his father had dedicated, and renewed the great altar which the idolatrous priests apparently had desecrated (2 Chron. 15:8). In his old age Asa suffered poor health. He died, greatly loved and honored, in the forty-first year of his reign.

ASAHEL. Nephew of David, being the youngest son of his sister Zeruiah (2 Sam. 2:18 ff.). Also the name of three other men of the Old Testament (2 Chron. 17:8; 31:13; Ezra 10:15).

ASAHIAH—*Jehovah hath made*. A servant of king Josiah, sent by him, together with others, to seek information of Jehovah respecting the book of the law which Hilkiah found in the Temple (2 Kings 22:12, 14; also called *Asaiah*, 2 Chron. 34:20).

ASAPH—*gatherer*. A Levite, son of Berechiah, one of the leaders of David's choir (1 Chron. 6:39). Psalms 50 and 73-83 are attributed to him, and he was in after times celebrated as a seer as well as a musical composer (2 Chron. 29:30; Neh. 12:46).

ASENATH—*favorite of Neith* (?). Daughter of Potipherah, priest, or possibly prince, of On, wife of Joseph (Gen. 41:45), and mother of Mannasseh and Ephraim (Gen. 41:50; 46:29).

ASHDOD or **AZOTUS**—*fortress* (?). A strong city on the southeast coast of the Mediterranean Sea, about twenty-five miles north of Gaza, and thirty-four west of Jerusalem. It was the property of the tribe of Judah (Josh. 15:47), but the Philistines either retained or retook it. Here stood the famous temple of Dagon. Here the captive ark of God was first brought, and broke to pieces that idol, and plagued the inhabitants (1 Sam. 5:1-6). Here Philip the Evangelist early preached the gospel (Acts 8:44).

ASHER, ASER—*happy*. The eighth son of Jacob, by Zilpah, Leah's handmaid (Gen. 30:13).

ASHKELON, ASKELON, ASCALON. One of the five cities of the lords of the Philistines (Josh. 13:3; 1 Sam. 6:17), but less often mentioned and apparently less known to the Hebrews than the

other four. Samson went down from Timnath to Ashkelon (Judg. 14:19), as if to a remote place whence his exploit was not likely to be heard of.

ASHTORETH. The principal female divinity of the Phoenicians, called Ishtar by the Assyrians and Astarte by the Greeks and Romans.

ASIA. The passages in the New Testament where this word occurs are the following: Acts 2:9; 6:9; 16:6; 19:10, 22, 26, 27; 20:4, 16, 18; 21:27; 27:2; Rom. 16:5; 1 Cor. 16:19; 2 Cor. 1:8; 2 Tim. 1:15; 1 Pet. 1:1; Rev. 1:4, 11. (Chief of Asia: see Asiarchae.) In all these passages it may be stated that the word is used, not for "the continent of Asia" nor for what we commonly understand by "Asia Minor," but for a Roman province which embraced the western part of the peninsula of Asia Minor, and of which Ephesus was the capital. It contained many important cities, among which were the seven churches of the Apocalypse, and was divided into assize districts for judicial business (Acts 19:38).

ASIARCHAE. Mentioned in Acts 19:31 and translated "the chief of Asia" in A.V. and "chief officers of Asia" in Revised Version. It is the title of certain officials of the Roman province of Asia. They had charge of the public games and religious theatrical spectacles, the expenses of which they bore.

ASP. The Hebrew word *pethen* occurs in the six following passages: Deut. 32:33; Job 20:14, 16; Ps. 58:5; 91:13; Isa. 11:8. That some kind of poisonous serpent is denoted by it is clear from these passages.

ASS. Several species of this animal were known in Biblical times, and few animals are mentioned more frequently in the Scriptures. The ass was domesticated very early and used for a variety of purposes—for riding, for ploughing, for carrying burdens.

ASSOS or ASSUS. A seaport of the Roman province of Asia, in the district anciently called Mysia (Acts 20:13, 14).

ASSYRIA, ASSHUR. A great and powerful country lying on the Tigris (Gen. 2:14), the capital of which was Nineveh (Gen. 10:11). It derived its name apparently from Asshur, the son of Sham (Gen. 10:22), who in later times was worshiped by the Assyrians as their chief god. The boundaries of Assyria differed greatly at different periods. The Assyrians figure most prominently in the Biblical record during the period of the prophets. They were greatly feared by the Hebrews and often looked upon as agents of God's punishment.

ASTARTE. (See Ashtoreth.)

ATHALIAH—*Jehovah hath afflicted.* Daughter of Ahab and Jezebel, married Jehoram the son of Jehoshaphat, king of Judah, and introduced into the Southern kingdom the worship of Baal (2 Chron. 24:7); she was slain by order of the high priest (2 Chron. 23:12-15).

ATHENIANS. Natives of Athens (Acts 17:21).

ATHENS. The capital of Attica, and the chief seat of Grecian learning and civilization during the golden period of the history of Greece. Paul visited it in his journey from Macedonia, and appears to have remained there some time (Acts 17:14-34; 1 Thess. 3:1). The Acropolis, or citadel of Athens, was a square craggy rock rising abruptly about one hundred and fifty feet, with a flat summit of about one thousand feet long from east to west, by five hundred feet broad from north to south. Mars Hill, better known by the name of Areopagus, was a rocky height opposite to the western end of Acropolis, from which it is separated only by an elevated valley, above which it rises fifty or sixty feet.

ATONEMENT, THE DAY OF. The great day of penitence. The mode of its observance is described in Lev. 16, and the conduct of the people is emphatically enjoined in Lev. 23:26-32. On this day only did the high priest enter the Holy of Holies.

AUGUSTUS CAESAR. The first Roman emperor. He was born 63 B.C. The first link binding him to New Testament history is his treatment of Herod after the battle of Actium. That prince, who had espoused Antony's side, found himself pardoned, taken into favor and confirmed in his power. After Herod's death in A.D. 4, Augustus divided his dominions, almost exactly according to his dying directions, among his sons. It was Augustus that ordered the census for purposes of taxation (Luke 2:1).

AWL. A tool of which we do not know the ancient form. The only notice of it is in connection with the custom of boring the ear of the slave (Ex. 21:6; Deut. 15:17).

AXE. Seven Hebrew words are rendered "axe" in the A.V. The instrument usually mentioned probably consisted of a head of iron (*cf.* Isa. 10:34), fastened with thongs or otherwise upon a handle of wood, and so liable to slip off (Deut. 19:5; 2 Kings 6:5). It was used for felling trees (Deut. 20:19), and also for shaping the wood when felled, perhaps like the modern adze (1 Kings 6:7). The "battle-axe" (Jer. 51:20) was probably a heavy mace or maul.

AZAL. A name only occurring in Zech. 14:3. It is mentioned as the limit to which the ravine of the Mount of Olives will extend when "Jehovah shall go forth to fight."

AZARIAH—*Jehovah hath helped.* A common name in Hebrew, and especially in the families of the priests of the line of Eleazar, whose name has precisely the same meaning as Azariah. The principal persons who bore this name were: 1. Son of Ahimaaz (1 Chron. 6:9). 2. Azariah, the son of Obed (2 Chron. 15:1). 3. The high priest in the reign of Uzziah, the king of Judah, whose name, perhaps from this circumstance, is often corrupted into Azariah (2 Kings 14:21; 15:1, 6, 7, 8). The most memorable event of his life is that which is recorded in 2 Chron. 26:17-20.

AZZAH. The more accurate rendering of the well-known Philistine city, Gaza (Deut. 2:23; 1 Kings 4:24; Jer. 25:20).

AZZAN—*strong.* The father of Paltiel, prince of the tribe of Issachar, who represented his tribe in the division of the promised land (Num. 34:26).

BAAL. 1. A Reubenite, whose son or descendant Beerah was carried off by the invading army of Assyria under Tiglath-Pileser (1 Chron. 5:5). 2. The son of Jehiel, father or founder of Gibeon, by his wife Maachah; brother of Kish, and grandfather of Saul (1 Chron. 8:30; 9:36).

BAAL—*lord.* The supreme male divinity of the Phoenician and Canaanitish nations, as Ashtoreth was their female divinity. Both names have the peculiarity of being used in the plural, and it seems certain that these plurals designate not statues of the divinities, but different modifications of the divinities themselves. The plural *Baalim* is found frequently alone. The word *Baal* is in Hebrew a common noun of frequent occurrence, having the meaning *lord;* not so much, however, in the sense of *ruler* as of *master, owner, possessor.* Baal worship was established among the Moabites and their allies the Midianites in the time of Moses (Num. 22:41), and through these nations the Israelites were seduced to the worship of this god under the particular form of Baal-Peor (Num. 25:3-18; Deut. 4:3). In the times of the kings the worship of Baal spread greatly, and together with that of Asherah became the religion of the court and people of the ten tribes (1 Kings 16:31-33; 18:19, 22). Among the compounds of Baal which appear in the Old Testament are: 1. Baal-berith (Judg. 8:33; 9:4). The name signifies the *covenant-baal,* the god who comes into covenant with the worshippers. 2. Baal-zebub, worshipped at Ekron (2 Kings 1:2, 3, 16). The meaning of the name is *lord of the fly.* The name occurs in the New Testament in the well-known form of Beelzebub. 3. Baal-hanan. (a) The name of one of the early kings of Edom (Gen. 36:38, 39; 1 Chron. 1:49, 50). (b) The name of one of David's officers, who had the superintendence of his olive and sycamore plantations (1 Chron. 27:28).

BAAL (geographical). This word occurs as the prefix or suffix to the names of several places in Palestine. It never seems to have become a naturalized Hebrew word; and such places called by this name or its compounds as can be identified were either near Phoenicia or in proximity to some other acknowledged seat of heathen worship.

BAANAH—*affliction.* Son of Rimmon, a Benjamite, who, with his brother Rechab, murdered Ishbosheth. For this they were killed by David, and their mutilated bodies were hung up over the pool at Hebron (2 Sam. 4:5-12).

BABEL, BABYLON. The capital city of the country which is called in Genesis *Shinar,* and in the later books *Chaldaea,* or the land of the Chaldaeans. Scripture represents the "beginning of the kingdom" as belonging to the time of Nimrod, the grandson of Ham (Gen. 10:6-10). Of the earlier kings the only one worthy of notice is Merodach-baladan (2 Kings 20:12), but it is not till we come to Nabopolassar, the father of Nebuchadnezzar, that a new era in the history of Babylon commences. On the fall of Ninevah (612 B.C.), Babylon became not only an independent kingdom, but an empire. The city was taken by surprise (539 B.C.), as Jeremiah had prophesied (Jer. 51:31), by an army of Medes and Persians under Cyrus. It was he who gave the Jews permission to return to Jerusalem (Ezra 1:1-8). Darius (Ezra 6) was on the throne when the rebuilding of the Temple was completed. With the conquest by Cyrus commenced the decay and ruin of Babylon, though it continued a royal residence through the entire period of the Persian empire.

BABEL, TOWER OF. The "tower of Babel" is only mentioned once in Scripture (Gen. 11:4 f.), and then as incomplete. It was built of bricks. When the Jews were carried captive into Babylonia, they were struck with the vast magnitude and peculiar character of certain of the Babylonian temples, in one or other of which they thought to recognize the very tower itself, a sort of oblique pyramid built in seven receding stages.

BABYLON—*gate of God.* The occurrence of this name in 1 Pet. 5:13 has given rise to a variety of conjectures: 1. That Babylon denotes Rome. 2. Some take Babylon to mean Jerusalem. 3. Bar-Hebraeus understands by it the house in Jerusalem where the apostles were assembled on the day of Pentecost. 4. Others place it on the Tigris, and identify it with Seleucia or Ctesiphon. 5. That by Babylon is intended the small fort of that name which formed the boundary between Upper and Lower Egypt. 6. That by Babylon is intended the old Babylon of Assyria.

BABYLON. In the Apocalypse it is the symbolical name by which Rome is denoted (Rev. 14:8; 17; 18). The power of Rome was regarded by the later Jews as that of Babylon by their forefathers (*cf.* Jer. 51:7 with Rev. 14:8), and hence, whatever the people of Israel be understood to symbolize, Babylon represents the antagonistic principle.

BABYLONISH GARMENT. Literally "robe of Shinar" (Josh. 7:21). An ample robe, probably made of the skin or fur of an animal and ornamented with embroidery or perhaps a variegated garment with figures inwoven in the fashion for which the Babylonians were celebrated.

BACA—*weeping.* The name of a valley in Pal-

estine through which the exiled Psalmist sees in vision the pilgrims passing in their march toward the sanctuary of Jehovah at Zion (Ps. 84:6). That it was a real locality is most probable, from the use of the definite article before the name.

BADGER SKINS. There is much obscurity as to the meaning of the word *tachash*, rendered "badger" in the A.V. (*e.g.*, Ex. 25:5; 35:7).

BALAAM. The son of Beor, a man endowed with the gift of prophecy (Num. 22:5). He belonged to the Midianites. He is mentioned in conjunction with the five kings of Midian, apparently as a person of the same rank (Num. 31:8; *cf.* 21:16). He seems to have lived at Pethor, which is said at Deut. 23:4 to have been a city of Mesopotamia. He himself speaks of being "brought from Aram out of the mountains of the East" (Num. 23:7). When the Israelites were encamped in the plains of Moab, Balak, the king of Moab, sent for Balaam to curse them. Balaam was prohibited by God from going. The king of Moab, however, sent again to him. The prophet again refused, but was at length allowed to go. Balaam therefore proceeded on his journey with the messengers of Balak. But God's anger was kindled at this manifestation of determined self-will, and the angel of the Lord stood in the way for an adversary against him. "The dumb ass, speaking with man's voice, forbade the madness of the prophet" (2 Pet. 2:16). A battle was afterward fought against the Midianites, in which Balaam sided with them, and was slain by the sword of the people whom he had endeavored to curse (Num. 31:8).

BALAK—*empty*. Son of Zippor, king of the Moabites. Balak entered into a league with Midian, and hired Balaam to curse the Israelites; but his designs were frustrated (Num. 22-24).

BALM (Hebrew *tzori, tzeri*). Occurs in Gen. 37:25; 43:11; Jer. 8:22; 46:11; 51:8; and Ezek. 27:17. It is impossible to identify this substance with any certainty.

BANQUETS. Among the Hebrews banquets were not only a means of social enjoyment, but were a part of the observance of religious festivity. Birthday banquets are only mentioned in the cases of Pharaoh and Herod (Gen. 40:20; Matt. 14:6). The usual time of the banquet was the evening, and to begin early was a mark of excess (Isa. 5:11; Eccles. 10:16).

BAPTISM. It is well known that ablution or bathing was common in most ancient nations as a preparation for prayers and sacrifice, or as expiatory of sin. There is a natural connection in the mind between the thought of physical and that of spiritual pollution. In warm countries this connection is probably even closer than in colder climates; and hence the frequency of ablution in the religious rites throughout the East. From the Gospel history we learn that at that time ceremonial washings had been greatly multiplied by traditions of the elders (see Mark 7:3 f.). The most important and probably one of the earliest of these traditional customs was the baptizing of proselytes. There has been some uncertainty as to the nature of John's baptism and its spiritual significance. It appears to have been a kind of transition from the Jewish baptism to the Christian. The distinction between John's baptism and Christian baptism appears in the case of Apollos (Acts 18:26 f.) and of the disciples at Ephesus, mentioned in Acts 19:1-6. The most important action of John as a baptist was his baptism of Jesus, which was His formal setting apart for His ministry. Whether Jesus ever baptized has been doubted. After the Resurrection, baptism became the initiatory rite of the Christian church. The command to baptize was coextensive with the command to preach the Gospel. All nations were to be evangelized, and they were to be made disciples, admitted into the fellowship of Christ's religion, by baptism (Matt. 28:19).

BARABBAS—*son of the father* or *teacher*. A robber (John 18:43) who had committed murder in an insurrection (Mark 15:7; Luke 23:19), and was lying in prison at the time of the trial of Jesus before Pilate.

BARAK—*lightning-flash*. Son of Abinoam of Kedesh, a refuge-city in Mount Naphtali, who was incited by Deborah, a prophetess of Ephraim, to deliver Israel from the yoke of Jabin (Judg. 4). He utterly routed the Canaanites in the plain of Jezreel (Esdraelon). He is mentioned as one of those who achieved great things through faith (Heb. 11:32).

BARBARIAN. "Every one not a Greek is a barbarian" is the common Greek definition, and in this strict sense the word is used in Rom. 1:14: "I am debtor both to Greeks and barbarians" (1 Cor. 14:11).

BARLEY. Grown by the Hebrews (Lev. 27:16; Deut. 8:8; Ruth 2:17), who used it for baking into bread, chiefly amongst the poor (Judg. 7: 13; 2 Kings 4:42; John 6:9, 13); for making into bread by mixing it with wheat, beans, lentils, millet, etc. (Ezek. 4:9); and as fodder for horses (1 Kings 4:28).

BARNABAS—*son of exhortation*. A name given by the apostles (Acts 4:36) to Joseph (or Joses), a Levite of the island of Cyprus, who was early a disciple of Christ. In Acts 9:27 we find him introducing the newly converted Saul to the apostles at Jerusalem, in a way which seems to imply previous acquaintance between the two. He was ordained with Paul for the missionary work, after which he labored with that apostle until a variance took place between them.

BARSABAS. 1. Joseph surnamed Justus was perhaps one of Christ's seventy disciples; it is certain he was an eye-witness of Christ's public work of the ministry. He stood candidate along with Matthias for the apostleship, instead of Judas, but was not chosen of God (Acts 1:21-26). 2. Barsabas Judas was a member of the council at Jerusalem, and was sent along with Paul, Barnabas, and Silas to publish decrees thereof among the Gentile churches (Acts 15:22-34).

BARTHOLOMEW—*son of Talmai*. One of the twelve apostles of Christ (Matt. 10:3; Mark 3:18; Luke 6:14; Acts 1:13). It has been conjectured that he is identical with Nathaniel (John 1:45 ff.). He is said to have preached the gospel in India.

BARTIMAEUS—*son of Timaeus*. A blind beggar of Jericho who (Mark 10:46 ff.) sat by the wayside begging as Jesus passed out of Jericho on his last journey to Jerusalem.

BARUCH—*blessed*. Son of Neriah, the friend (Jer. 32:12), amanuensis, and faithful attendant of Jeremiah (Jer. 36:4-32) in the discharge of his prophetic office.

BARZILLAI—*man of iron*. 1. A wealthy Gileadite who showed hospitality to David when he fled from Absalom (2 Sam. 18:27). 2. A Meholathite whose son Adriel married Michal, Saul's daughter (2 Sam. 21:8).

BASHAN. A district on the east of Jordan. It is sometimes spoken of as the "land of Bashan" (1 Chron. 5:11; and *cf.* Num. 21:33; 32:33); and sometimes as "all Bashan" (Deut. 3:10, 13; Josh. 12:5; 13:12, 30), but most commonly without any addition. It was taken by the children of Israel after their conquest of the land of Sihon from Arnon to Jabbok.

BASHEMATH—*fragrant*. Daughter of Ismael, the last married of the three wives of Esau (Gen. 36:3, 4, 13). In Gen. 28:9 she is called Mahaleth; while the name Bashemath is in Gen. 26:34 given to another of Esau's wives, the daughter of Elon the Hittite.

BASKET. The Hebrew terms are as follows: 1.

Sal, so called from the twigs of which it was originally made, specially used for holding bread (Gen. 40:16 ff.; Ex. 29:3, 23; Lev. 8:2, 26, 31; Num. 6:15, 17, 19). 2. *Salsilloth*, applied to the basket used in gathering grapes (Jer. 6:9). 3. *Tene*, in which the first-fruits of the harvests were presented (Deut. 26:2, 4). 4. *Kelub*, so called from its similarity to a birdcage or trap, probably in regard to its having a lid; it was used for carrying fruit (Amos 8:1 f.). 5. *Dudh*, used for carrying fruit (Jer. 24:1 f.), as well as on a larger scale for carrying clay to the brick-yard (Ps. 81:6; *pots*, A.V.), or for holding bulky articles (2 Kings 10:7).

BASTARD. Among those who were excluded from entering the congregation, even to the tenth generation, was the *mamzer* (A.V. bastard), who was classed in this respect with the Ammonite and Moabite (Deut. 23:2).

BAT (Hebrew *atalleph*). There is no doubt that the A.V. is correct in it rendering of this word (Lev. 11:19; Deut. 14:18).

BATH, BATHING. This was a prescribed part of the Jewish ritual of purification in cases of accidental, leprous, or ordinary uncleanness (Lev. 15; 16:28; 22:6; Num. 19:7, 19; 2 Sam. 11:2; 4; 2 Kings 5:10); as also after mourning which always implies defilement (Ruth 3:3; 2 Sam. 12:20). Anointing was customarily joined with bathing, the climate making both these essential alike to health and pleasure, to which luxury added the use of perfumes (Judg. 10:3; Esth. 2:12). The "pools," such as that of Siloam and Hezekiah (Neh. 3:15 f.; 2 Kings 20:20; Isa. 22:11; John 9:7), often sheltered by porticos (John 5:2), are the first indications of public bathing accommodation.

BATHSHEBA—*daughter of the oath*. (Bathshua in 1 Chron. 3:5.) The daughter of Eliam and wife of Uriah the Hittite (2 Sam. 9:2 ff.). The child which was the fruit of her adulterous intercourse with David died; but after marriage she became the mother of four sons, Solomon (2 Sam. 12:24; Matt. 1:6), Shimea, Shobab, and Nathan.

BDELLIUM (Hebrew *bedolach*). Mentioned in Gen. 2:12; Num. 11:7. It is quite impossible to say whether bedolach denotes a mineral or an animal production, or a vegetable exudation.

BEANS (2 Sam. 17:28; Ezek. 4:9). Beans are cultivated in Palestine, which produces many of the leguminous order of plants, such as lentils, kidney-beans, vetches, etc.

BEAR (1 Sam. 17:34; 2 Sam. 17:8). The Syrian bear, which is without doubt the animal mentioned in the Bible, is still found on the higher mountains of Palestine.

BEARD. Western Asiatics have always cherished the beard as the badge of the dignity of manhood, and attached to it the importance of a feature. The Egyptians, on the contrary, for the most part, shaved the hair of the face and head. It is impossible to decide with certainty the meaning of the precept (Lev. 19:27; 21:5) regarding the "corners of the beard." The beard is the object of an oath, and that on which blessings or shame are spoken of as resting. The custom was and is to shave or pluck it and the hair out in mourning (Isa. 50:6; 15:2; Jer. 41:5; 48:37; Ezra 9:3); to neglect it in seasons of permanent affliction (2 Sam. 19:24) and to regard any insult to it as the last outrage which enmity can inflict (2 Sam. 10:4). The beard was the object of salutation (2 Sam. 20:9). The removal of the beard was a part of the ceremonial treatment proper to a leper (Lev. 14:9).

BED and BED-CHAMBER. The Hebrew bed consisted usually of a mattress or mat, a quilt to lie upon, and a covering. The bedstead was not always necessary, the divan or platform along the side or end of an Oriental room sufficing as a support for the bedding. The ornamental por-

tions were pillars and a canopy (Judg. 13:9), ivory carvings, gold and silver, and probably mosaic work, purple and fine linen (Esth. 1:6; Cant. 3:9 f.). The ordinary furniture of a bed-chamber in private life is given in 2 Kings 4:10.

BEE (Deut. 1:44; Judg. 14:8; Ps. 118:12; Isa. 7: 18). That Palestine abounded in bees is evident from the description of that land by Moses, for it was a land "flowing with milk and honey."

BEELZEBUL (See also *Baal*. 2.). The title of a heathen deity to whom the Jews ascribed the sovereignty of the evil spirits (Matt. 10:25; 12: 24; Mark 3:22; Luke 11:15 ff.). The correct reading is without doubt *Beelzebul*, and not *Beelzebub* as given in the Syriac, the Vulgate, and some other versions. Some connect the term with *zebul*, *habitation*, thus making Beelzebul (Matt. 10:25) *the lord of the dwelling*, whether as the "prince of the power of the air" (Eph. 2:2), or as the prince of the lower world, or as inhabiting human bodies, or as occupying a mansion in the seventh heaven, like Saturn in Oriental mythology. Others derive it from *zebel*, *dung*, thus making Beelzebul, literally *the lord of dung* or the *dunghill;* and in a secondary sense as *zebel* was used by the Talmudical writers as *idol* or *idolatry*, *the lord of idols, prince of the false gods.*

BEER-SHEBA—*well of oath*, or *well of seven*. The name of one of the old places in Palestine which formed the southern limit of the country. There are two accounts of the origin of the name: 1. According to the first, the well was dug by Abraham, and the name given because there he and Abimelech the king of the Philistines "sware," both of them (Gen. 21:31). 2. The other narrative ascribes the origin of the name to an occurrence almost precisely similar, in which both Abimelech the king of the Philistines, and Phichol his chief captain, are again concerned, with Isaac instead of Abraham (Gen. 26:31-33).

BEHEMOTH—*colossal beast*. There can be little doubt that by this word (Job. 40:15-24) the hippopotamus is intended, since all the details descriptive of the *behemoth* accord with habits of that animal.

BEKAH. A half shekel. Every Jew paid a bekah annually for the support of the Temple (Ex. 30:13).

BELA. 1. One of the five cities of the plain which was spared at the intercession of Lot, and received the name of Zoar (Gen. 14:2; 19:22). 2. Son of Beor, who reigned over Edom in the city of Dinhabah, eight generations before Saul, king of Israel, or about the time of the Exodus (Gen. 36:32 ff.).

BELIAL—*unprofitable, wicked*. The expression *son* or *man of Belial* must be understood as meaning simply a worthless, lawless fellow. The term as used in 2 Cor. 6:15 is generally understood as an appellative of Satan, as the personification of all that was bad.

BELLOWS. The word occurs only in Jer. 6:29. Here it refers to the bellows of a metal smelter.

BELLS. In Ex. 28:33 the bells alluded to were the the golden ones, according to the rabbis 72 in number, round the hem of the high priest's ephod. The object of them was "that his sound might be heard when he went in unto the holy place, and when he came out, that he die not" (Ex. 28:34).

BELSHAZZAR—*Bel protect the king*. The last king of Babylon. According to the well-known narrative in Dan. 5, he was slain during a splendid feast in his palace.

BENAIAH—*Jehovah has built*. 1. The son of Jehoiada, the chief priest (1 Chron. 27:5), and therefore of the tribe of Levi, through a native of Kabzeel (2 Sam. 23:20; 1 Chron. 11:22), in the south of Judah; set by David (1 Chron. 11:25) over his bodyguard of Cherethites and Pelethites (2 Sam. 8:18; 1 Kings 1:38; 1 Chron. 18:17; 2 Sam. 20:23), and occupying a middle rank between the first three of the "mighty men" and the thirty "valiant men of the armies" (2 Sam. 23:22 f.; 1 Chron. 11:25; 27:6). 2. Benaiah the Pirathonite, an Ephraimite, one of David's thirty mighty men (2 Sam. 23:30; 1 Chron. 11: 31). 3. A Levite in the time of David, who "played with a psaltery on Alamoth" (1 Chron. 15:18, 20; 16:5). 4. A priest in the time of David appointed to blow the trumpet before the ark (1 Chron. 15:24; 16:6). 5. A Levite of the sons of Asaph (2 Chron. 20:14). 6. A Levite in the time of Hezekiah, one of the "overseers of offerings" (2 Chron. 31:13). 7. One of the "princes" of the families of Simeon (1 Chron. 4:36). 8. Four laymen in the time of Ezra who had taken strange wives (Ezra 10:25, 30, 35, 43). 9. The father of Pelatiah, "a prince of the people" in the time of Ezekiel (Ezek. 11:1, 13).

BEN-AMMI—*son of my people*. The son of the younger daughter of Lot, and progenitor of the Ammonites (Gen. 19:38).

BENHADAD—*son of Hadad*. The name of three kings of Damascus—Benhadad I was either son or grandson of Rezon, and in his time Damascus was supreme in Syria. He made an alliance with Asa, and conquered a great part of the north of Israel. Benhadad II, son of the preceding, and also king of Damascus. Long wars with Israel characterized his reign. Benhadad III, son of Hazael, and his successor on the throne of Syria. When he succeeded to the throne, Jehoash recovered the cities which Jehoahaz had lost to the Syrians, and beat him in Aphek (2 Kings 13:17, 25). Jehoash gained two more victories, but did not restore the dominion of Israel on the east of Jordan.

BENJAMIN—*son of the right hand*. The youngest of the children of Jacob, and the only one of the thirteen who was born in Palestine. His birth took place on the road between Bethel and Bethlehem, a short distance from the latter, and his mother Rachel died in the act of giving him birth, naming him with her last breath Ben-oni, "son of my sorrow." This was by Jacob changed into Benjamin (Gen. 35:16-18). Until the journeys of Jacob's sons and of Jacob himself into Egypt we hear nothing of Benjamin. Henceforward the history of Benjamin is the history of the tribe.

BENONI—*son of my sorrow*. The name which the dying Rachel gave to her newly-born son, but which by her father was changed into Benjamin (Gen. 35:18).

BERACHAH—*benediction*. A valley in which Jehoshaphat and his people assembled to "bless" Jehovah after the overthrow of the hosts of Moabites, Ammonites, and Mohunim, who had come against them, and which from that fact acquired its name of "the valley of blessing" (2 Chron. 20:26).

BEREA. A city of Macedonia, mentioned in Acts 17:10, 15.

BERNICE and **BERENICE**—*bearer of victory*. The eldest daughter of Herod Agrippa I. She was first married to her uncle Herod, king of Chalcis, and after his death she lived under circumstances of great suspicion with her own brother Agrippa II, in connection with whom she is mentioned (Acts 25:13, 23; 26:30).

BERYL. A precious stone in the breastplate of the high priest (Ex. 28:20) and in the wall of the heavenly Jerusalem (Rev. 21:20).

BETH. The most general word for a house or habitation. Beth is more frequently employed in compound names of places than any other word.

BETH-ABARA—*house of passage*. A place beyond Jordan in which John was baptizing (John 1:28). Some authorities call it "Bethany."

BETHANY—*house of poverty*. A village which is intimately associated with the most familiar acts and scenes of the last days of the life of Christ. It was situated "at" The Mount of Olives (Mark 11:1; Luke 19:29), about fifteen furlongs (about 1¾ miles) from Jerusalem (John 11:18).

BETH-BARAH. Named only in Judg. 7:24, as a point apparently south of the scene of Gideon's victory.

BETH-CAR—*place of a lamb*. A place named as the point to which the Israelites pursued the Philistines (1 Sam. 7:11), and therefore west of Mizpeh.

BETHEL—*house of God*. A well-known city and holy place of central Palestine. Of the origin of the name of Bethel there are two accounts. 1. It was bestowed on the spot by Jacob under the awe inspired by the nocturnal vision of God, when on his journey from his father's house at Beersheba to seek his wife in Haran (Gen. 28: 19). 2. But according to the other account, Bethel received its name on the occasion of a blessing bestowed by God upon Jacob after his return from Padan-aram; at which time also (according to this narrative) the name of Israel was given him (Gen. 35:14 f.). If we accept the precise definition of Gen. 12:8, the name of Bethel would appear to have existed at this spot even before the arrival of Abram in Canaan (Gen. 12:8; 13:3 f.). In troubled times when there was no king in Israel, it was to Bethel that the people went up in their distress to ask counsel of God (Judg. 20:18, 26, 31; 21:2; A.V. "house of God"). Here was the ark of the covenant under the charge of Phinehas, the grandson of Aaron (Judg. 20:26-28; 21:4). Later we find it named as one of the holy cities to which Samuel went in circuit (1 Sam. 7:16). Here Jeroboam placed one of the two calves of gold. Toward the end of Jeroboam's life, Bethel fell into the hands of Judah (2 Chron. 13:19). Elijah visited Bethel, and we hear of "sons of the prophets" as resident there (2 Kings 2:2 f.), two facts apparently incompatible with the active existence of the calf-worship. But after the destruction of the Baal-worship by Jehu, Bethel comes once more into view (2 Kings 10:29). After the desolation of the northern kingdom by the king of Assyria, Bethel still remained an abode of priests (2 Kings 17:28 f.).

BETHESDA—*house of grace*. The Hebrew name of a reservoir or tank, with five "porches," close upon the sheep-gate or "market" in Jerusalem (John 5:2). The porches—*i.e.*, cloisters or colonnades—were extensive enough to accommodate a large number of sick and infirm people, whose custom it was to wait there for the "troubling of the water."

BETH-JESHIMOTH or **JESIMOTH**—*house of the deserts*. A town or place east of Jordan (Num. 33:49), one of the limits of the encampment of Israel before crossing the Jordan.

BETHLEHEM—*house of bread*. One of the oldest towns in Palestine, already in existence at the time of Jacob's return to the country. Its earliest name was Ephrath or Ephratah (see Gen. 35:16, 19; 48:7). After the conquest of the country by the Israelites, Bethlehem appears under its own name, Bethlehem-Judah (Judg. 17:7; 1 Sam. 17: 12; Ruth 1:1 f.). In the New Testament, Bethlehem retains its distinctive title of Bethlehem-Judah (Matt. 2:1, 5), and once, in the announcement of the angels, the "city of David" (Luke 2:4; John 7:42).

BETH-PEOR—*house of Peor*. A place no doubt dedicated to the god Baal-peor, on the east of Jordan, opposite Jericho, and six miles above Beth-haran. It was in the possession of the tribe of Reuben (Josh. 13:20). One of the last halting places of the children of Israel is designated "the ravine over against Beth-peor" (Deut. 3:29; 4:46).

BETHPHAGE—*house of figs*. The name of a

place on the Mount of Olives, on the road between Jericho and Jerusalem. It was apparently close to Bethany (Matt. 21:1; Mark 11:1; Luke 19:29), and to the eastward of it.

BETHSAIDA—*house of the fishers.* 1. "Bethsaida of Galilee" was the native city of Andrew, Peter, and Philip (John 1:44; 12:21), in the land of Genesareth (Mark 6:45; *cf.* 53), and therefore on the west side of the lake. 2. By comparing the narrative in Mark 6:31-53, and Luke 9:10-17, it appears that the Bethsaida at which the 5,000 were fed may have been a second place of the same name on the east of the lake. Such a place there was at the northeastern extremity, formerly a village but rebuilt and adorned by Philip the Tetrarch, and raised to the dignity of a town under the name of Julias, after the daughter of the emperor.

BETHUEL—*place of God.* The son of Nahor by Milcah; nephew of Abraham, and father of Rebekah (Gen. 22:22, 23; 24:15, 24, 47; 28:2).

BEULAH—*married.* The name which the land of Israel is to bear when "the land shall be married" (Isa. 62:4).

BEZER—*fortress.* A city of the Reubenites set apart by Moses as one of the three cities of refuge on the east of the Jordan, and allotted to the Merarites (Deut. 4:43; Josh. 20:8; 21:36; 1 Chron. 6:78).

BIBLE. 1. When the books of the Old Testament were formed into a canon (see Canon), it was natural to give a general name to the collection. The earliest instance of such a title occurs in Daniel, who refers to "the books" (Dan. 9:2) in a manner which seems to mark the prophetic writings as already collected into one whole. The same word was applied by the Jews in Alexandria to the collected books of the Old Testament—*biblia*—whence the word *Bible,* or *The Book,* has been given to the collected books of the Old and New Testaments. The writers of the New Testament call the books of the Old Testament either *The Scripture* (Acts 8:32; Gal. 3:22; 2 Tim. 3:16), or *The Scriptures* (Matt. 21:42; Luke 24:27), or, *The Holy Scriptures* (2 Tim. 3:15). 2. The existence of a collection of sacred books recognized as authoritative leads naturally to a more or less systematic arrangement. The Prologue to Ecclesiasticus mentions "the law and the prophets and the other books." In the New Testament there is the same kind of recognition. "The law and the Prophets" is the shorter (Matt. 11:13; 22:40; Acts 13:13); "the law, the Prophets, and the Psalms" (Luke 24:44), the fuller statement of the division popularly recognized. The *Law* contained Genesis, Exodus, Leviticus, Numbers, and Deuteronomy. The *Prophets* included the "Former Prophets" (Joshua, Judges, Samuel, Kings) and the "Latter Prophets" (Isaiah, Jeremiah, Ezekiel, and the "Twelve" or "Minor" Prophets). Last in order came the group known to the Jews as *Kethubim* or *Writings,* including the remaining books of the Old Testament. The verse division of the Old Testament was adopted by Stephens in his edition of the Vulgate, 1555, and by Frellon in that of 1556, and it appeared for the first time in an English translation in the Geneva Bible of 1560, and was thence transferred to the Bishop's Bible of 1568, and the authorized version of 1611. With the New Testament, the division into chapters adopted by Hugh de St. Cher superseded those that had been in use previously, appeared in the early editions of the Vulgate, was transferred to the English Bible by Coverdale, and so became universal.

BIGTHAN and **BIGTHANA.** An eunuch (chamberlain, A.V.) in the court of Ahasuerus, one of those "who kept the door" and conspired with Teresh against the king's life (Esth. 2:21). The conspiracy was detected by Mordecai.

BILDAD—*Bel loves.* The second of Job's three friends. He is called "the Shuhite," which implies both his family and nation (Job 2:11).

BILHAH. Handmaid of Rachel (Gen. 29:29), and concubine of Jacob, to whom she bore Dan and Naphtali (Gen. 30:3-8; 35:25; 46:25; 1 Chron. 7:13). (See Reuben.)

BIRTHDAYS. The custom of observing birthdays is very ancient (Gen. 40:20; Jer. 20:15), and in Job 1:4 we read that Job's sons "feasted every one his day." In Persia they were celebrated with peculiar honors and banquets, and in Egypt the king's birthdays were kept with great pomp.

BIRTHRIGHT. The advantages accruing to the eldest son were not definitely fixed in patriarchal times. Great respect was paid to him in the household, and, as the family widened into a tribe, this grew into a sustained authority, undefined, save by custom, in all matters of common interest. Thus the "princes" of all congregations had probably rights of primogeniture (Num. 7:2; 21:18; 25:14). A "double portion" of the paternal property was allotted by the Mosaic law (Deut. 21:15-17). The first-born of the king was his successor by law (2 Chron. 21:3); David, however, by Divine appointment, excluded Adonijah in favor of Solomon.

BISHOP. A shepherd or overseer. It seems to be synonymous with *Elder* or *Presbyter* (Acts 20:17, 20; Titus 1:5, 7; 1 Pet. 5:1 f.). The word is applied to Christ himself (1 Pet. 2:2).

BITHYNIA. A province of Asia Minor mentioned only in Acts 16:7 and in 1 Pet 1:1.

BITTER HERBS. The Israelites were commanded to eat the Paschal lamb "with unleavened bread and with bitter herbs" (Ex. 12:8).

BITTERN. The Hebrew word has been the subject of various interpretations. It occurs in Isa. 14:23; 34:11; Zeph. 2:14.

BLAINS. Violent ulcerous inflammations, the sixth plague of Egypt (Ex. 9:9 f.), and hence called in Deut. 28:27, 35, "the botch of Egypt."

BLASPHEMY. In its technical English sense signifies the speaking evil of God, and in this sense it is found Ps. 74:18; Isa. 52:5; Rom. 2:24. But according to its derivation it may mean any kind of calumny and abuse; see 1 Kings 21:10; Acts 18: 6; Jude 9. Blasphemy was punished with stoning, which was inflicted on the son of Shelomith (Lev. 24:11). In the New Testament blasphemy against the Holy Ghost is given as the unpardonable sin (Matt. 12:31 f.; Mark 3:28 f.; Luke 12:10).

BLASTUS. The Chamberlain of Herod Agrippa I (Acts 12:20).

BLINDNESS. Extremely common in the East from many causes. Blind beggars figure repeatedly in the New Testament (Matt. 12:22), and "opening the eyes of the blind" is mentioned in prophecy as a peculiar attribute of the Messiah (Isa. 29:18). The Jews were specially charged to treat the blind with compassion and care (Lev. 19:14; Deut. 27:18).

BLOOD, REVENGER OF. It was, and even still is, a common practice among nations of patriarchal habits that the nearest of kin should, as a matter of duty, avenge the death of a murdered relative. The law of Moses was very precise in its direction on the subject of Retaliation. 1. The wilful murderer was to be put to death without permission of compensation. The nearest relative of the deceased became the authorized avenger of blood (Num. 35:19). 2. The law of retaliation was not to extend beyond the immediate offender (Deut. 24:16; 2 Kings 14:6; 2 Chron. 25: 4; Jer. 31:29 f.; Ezek. 18:20). 3. The involuntary shedder of blood was permitted to take flight to one of the six Levitical cities specially appointed as cities of refuge (Num. 35:22 f.; Deut. 19:4-6).

BOAR. The wild boar is considered as the parent stock of the common hog. He is a furious and formidable animal. The tusks are larger and

stronger than in the tame herds. The color is iron-grey, inclining to black. The snout is long, and ears are short. The destructive ravages of the animal are referred to in Ps. 80:13.

BOANERGES—*sons of thunder.* A name given by Jesus to the two sons of Zebedee, James and John (Mark 3:17; see Luke 9:54).

BOAZ—*swiftness* or *strength.* 1. A wealthy Bethlehemite, kinsman to Elimelech, the husband of Naomi. He married Ruth, and redeemed the estates of her deceased husband Mahlon (Ruth 4:1 ff.). 2. The name of one of Solomon's brazen pillars erected in the temple porch. (See Jachin.) It stood on the left, and was 18 cubits high (1 Kings 7:15, 21; 2 Chron. 3:15; Jer. 52:21).

BONNET. A covering for the head worn by Jewish priests (Ex. 28:40; Lev. 8:13).

BOOTY. This consisted of captives of both sexes, cattle, and whatever a captured city might contain, especially metalic treasures. Within the limits of Canaan no captives were to be made (Deut. 20:14, 16); beyond these limits, in case of warlike resistance, all the women and children were to be made captives, and the men put to death. The law of booty is given in Num. 31: 26-47. As regarded the army, David added a regulation that the baggage guard should share equally with the troops engaged (1 Sam. 30:24 f.).

BOTTLE. Great leathern bottles were made of the skin of a he-goat, and the small ones, that serve instead of a bottle of water on the road, were made of a kid's skin. The effect of external heat upon a skin bottle is indicated in Ps. 119: 83, "a bottle in the smoke," and of expansion produced by fermentation, in Matt. 9:17, "new wine in old bottles." Vessels of metal, earthen or glassware for liquids were in use among the Greeks, Egyptians, Etruscans, and Assyrians, and also no doubt among the Jews, especially in latter times. Thus Jer. 19:1, "a potter's earthen bottle."

BOX TREE. The Hebrew *teashshur* occurs in Isa. 41:19; 60:13. The Talmudical and Jewish writers generally are of opinion that the box tree is intended.

BOZRAH—*fortification.* In Edom—the city of Jobab the son of Zerah, one of the early kings of that nation (Gen. 36:33; 1 Chron. 1:44). This is doubtless the place mentioned in latter times by Isaiah (34:6; 63:1) in connection with Edom, and by Jeremiah (49:13, 22), Amos (1:12) and Micah (2:12).

BRACELET. Bracelets have been favorite ornaments in the East. In Gen. 38:18, 25, the word rendered "bracelet" means probably "a string by which a seal-ring was suspended." Men as well as women wore bracelets, as we see from Cant. 5:14.

BRAMBLE (Thistle, Thorn).

BRASS. The word *nechosheth* is improperly translated by "brass." In most places of the Old Testament the correct translation would be copper, although it may sometimes possibly mean bronze, a compound of copper and tin. Indeed, a simple metal was obviously intended, as we see from Deut. 8:9; 32:25, and Job 28:2. Copper was known at a very early period (Gen. 4:22).

BRAZEN SERPENT. An image of polished metal, in the form of one of those fiery serpents which were sent to chastise the murmuring Israelites in the wilderness, and whose bite caused violent heat, thirst, and inflammation. By divine command "Moses made a serpent of brass," or copper, and "put it upon a pole; and it came to pass, that if a serpent had bitten any man, when he beheld the serpent of brass, he lived" (Num. 21:6-9). This brazen serpent was preserved as a monument of the divine mercy, but in process of time became an instrument of idolatry.

BREAD. The preparation of bread as an article of food dates from a very early period. The earliest undoubted instance of its use is found in Gen. 18:6. The corn or grain employed was of various sorts; the best bread was made of wheat, which after being ground produced the "flour" or "meal" (Judg. 6:19; 1 Sam. 1:24; 1 Kings 4:22; 17:12, 14), and when sifted the "fine flour" (Ex. 29:2; Gen. 18:6) usually employed in the sacred offerings (Ex. 29:40; Lev. 2:1; Ezra 46:14) and in the meals of the wealthy (1 Kings 4:22; 2 Kings 7:1; Ezra 16:13, 19; Rev. 18:13). "Barley" was used only by the very poor (John 6:9, 13), or in times of scarcity (Ruth 3:15, compared with 1:1, 2 Kings 4:38, 42; Rev. 6:6). "Spelt" was also used both in Egypt (Ex. 9:32) and Palestine (Isa. 28:25; Ezra 4:9; 1 Kings 19:6). The bread taken by persons on a journey (Gen. 45:23; Josh. 9:12) was probably a kind of biscuit.

BREASTPLATE. A part of the high priest's fine apparel. It was about ten inches square, and consisted of a folded piece of the same rich embroidered stuff whereof the robe of the ephod was formed. It was set with twelve different precious stones, fastened in ouches of gold, one for every Hebrew tribe. These were set in four rows; in the uppermost were a sardius, topaz, and carbuncle, for Reuben, Simeon, and Levi; in the second, an emerald, sapphire, and diamond, for Judah, Dan, and Naphtali; in the third, a ligure, an agate, and amethyst, for Gad, Asher, and Issachar; in the lowest, a beryl, onyx, and jasper, for Zebulun, Joseph, and Benjamin. This was fastened on the high priest's breast. By the two upper corners it was fastened to his shoulder; by the two below it was fastened to the girdle of the ephod; by wearing it he carried the twelve tribes, as on his heart before God.

BRICK. An ancient historian describing the mode of building the walls of Babylon, says that the clay dug out of the ditch was made into bricks as soon as it was carried up, and burnt in kilns. The bricks were cemented with hot bitumen, and at every thirtieth row crates of reeds were stuffed in (cf. Gen. 11:3). The Babylonian bricks were more commonly burnt in kilns than those used at Nineveh, which are chiefly sun-dried like the Egyptian. The Israelites, in common with other captives, were employed by the Egyptian monarchs in making bricks and in building (Ex. 1:14; 5:7). Egyptian bricks were not generally dried in kilns, but in the sun. When made of the Nile mud, they required straw to prevent cracking; and crude brick walls had frequently the additional security of a layer of reeds and sticks, placed at intervals to act as binders. The Jews learned the art of brick-making in Egypt, and we find the use of the brick-kiln in David's time (2 Sam. 12:31), and a complaint made by Isaiah that the people built altars of brick instead of unhewn stone, as the law directed (Isa. 65:3; Ex. 20:25).

BRIDEGROOM. A betrothed or newly married man. Among the Arabs, brides appear with great reverence before their bridegrooms, and often cast themselves down at their feet (Gen. 24:64 f.; Ps. 45:10 f.). Christ is called a *Bridegroom*.

BRIDGE. The only mention of a bridge in the Scriptures is indirectly in the proper name Geshur, a district in Bashan, northeast of the sea of Galilee. The Romans were the first constructers of arched bridges. The bridge connecting the Temple with the upper city of which Josephus speaks, seems to have been an arched viaduct.

BRIGANTINE. A mail-shirt (Jer. 46:4), elsewhere "habergeon," or "coat of mail."

BRIMSTONE. The Hebrew word *gophrith* is of uncertain derivation but refers to sulfur which is plentiful in the Jordan Valley and near the Dead Sea (Gen. 19:24; Deut. 29:23).

BULL, BULLOCK. Terms used synonymously with ox, oxen, in the A.V., as the representatives of several Hebrew words. *Bakar,* the most common, is properly a generic name for horned cattle when of full age and fit for the plough. Accordingly, it is variously rendered *bullock* (Isa. 64:25), *cow* (Ezra 4:15), *oxen* (Gen. 12:16). In Isa. 51:20, the "wild bull" ("wild ox" in Deut. 14:5) was possibly one of the larger species of antelope, and took its name from its swiftness.

BULRUSH. A plant growing on the banks of the Nile and in marshy grounds (Ex. 2:3; Job 8:11; Isa. 18:2; 35:7).

BURIAL, SEPULCHRES. A natural cave enlarged and adapted by excavation, or an artificial imitation of one, was the standard type of sepulchre. Sepulchres stood often in gardens, by roadsides, or even adjoining houses. Kings and prophets alone were probably buried within towns (1 Kings 2:10; 16:6, 28; 2 Kings 10:35; 13:9; 2 Chron. 16:14; 28:27; 1 Sam. 25:1; 28:3). Sarah's tomb and Rachel's seem to have been chosen merely from the accident of the place of death; but the successive interments at the former (Gen. 49:31) are a chronicle of the strong family feeling among the Hebrews. Cities soon became populous and demanded cemeteries (Ezek. 39:15), which were placed without the walls. Sepulchres were marked sometimes by pillars, as that of Rachel, or by pyramids, as those of the Asmoneans at Modin. Such as were not otherwise noticeable were scrupulously "whited" (Matt. 23:27) once a year, after the rains before the passover, to warn passers-by of defilement. In no instance, save that of Saul and his sons, were the bodies burned, and even then the bones were interred, and re-exhumed for solemn entombment.

BURNT-OFFERING. The word is applied to the offering which was wholly consumed by fire on the altar, and the whole of which, except the refuse ashes, "ascended" in the smoke to God. The burnt-offering is first named in Gen. 8:20, as offered after the flood. Throughout the whole of the Book of Genesis (see 15:9, 17; 22:2, 7, 8, 13) it appears to be the only sacrifice referred to; afterward it became distinguished as one of the regular classes of sacrifice under the Mosaic law. The meaning of the whole burnt-offering was that which is the original idea of all sacrifice, the offering by the sacrificer of himself, soul and body, to God, the submission of his will to the will of the Lord. The ceremonies of the burnt-offering are given in detail in the Book of Leviticus.

BUTTER. Curdled milk (Gen. 17:8; Deut. 32:14; Judg. 5:25; Job 20:17). Milk is generally offered to travellers in Palestine in a curdled or sour state, thick, almost like butter.

BUZ. 1. The second son of Milcah and Nahor (Gen. 22:21). Elihu "the Buzite" was probably a descendant of Buz. 2. A name occurring in the genealogies of the tribe of Gad (1 Chron. 5:14).

BUZI. The father of Ezekiel the prophet (Ezek. 1:3).

CAB or KAB. A measure for things dry, mentioned in 2 Kings 6:25. The rabbis make it the sixth part of a *seah* or *satum,* and the eighteenth part of an ephah. This would be nearly two quarts English measure.

CAESAR. Always in the New Testament the Roman emperor, the sovereign of Judaea (John 19:12, 15; Acts 17:7).

CAESAREA. (Acts 8:40; 9:30; 10:1, 24; 11:11; 12:19; 18:22; 21:8, 16; 23:23, 33; 25:1, 4, 6, 13.) It was situated on the coast of Palestine, on the line of the great road from Tyre to Egypt, and about halfway between Joppa and Dora. The distance from Jerusalem was about 70 miles.

CAESAREA PHILIPPI. Mentioned only in the first two Gospels (Matt. 16:13; Mark 8:27). It was at the easternmost and most important of the two recognized sources of the Jordan.

CAIAPHAS. In full, Joseph Caiaphas, high priest of the Jews under Tiberius (Matt. 26:3, 57; John 11:49; 18:13, 14, 24, 28; Acts 4:6). He was son-in-law of Annas.

CAIN—*acquired* or *smith*. The historical facts in the life of Cain, as recorded in Gen. 4, are briefly these: he was the eldest son of Adam and Eve; he followed the business of agriculture; in a fit of jealousy, roused by the rejection of his own sacrifice and the acceptance of Abel's, he committed the crime of murder, for which he was expelled from Eden, and led the life of an exile; he settled in the land of Nod, and built a city which he named after his son Enoch (Gen. 4:1 ff.; Heb. 11:4).

CAINAN—*fixed*. 1. Son of Enos, aged 70 years when he begat Mahalaleel his son (Gen. 5:9-14). 2. Son of Arphaxad, and father of Sala, according to Luke 3:35 f., and usually called the second Cainan.

CALAMUS (Ex. 30:23; Cant. 4:14; Isa. 43:24; Jer. 6:20; Ezek. 27:19). An aromatic reed, growing in most places in Egypt, in Judaea near Lake Gennesaret, and in several parts of Syria. It grows to about two feet in height, bearing from the root a round knotted stalk containing a soft white pith.

CALEB—*dog*. 1. According to 1 Chron. 2:9, 18, 19, 42, 50, the son of Hezron, the son of Pharez, the son of Judah, and the father of Hur by Ephrath or Ephratah, and consequently grandfather of Caleb the spy. 2. Son of Jephunneh, by which patronymic the illustrious spy is usually designated (Num. 13:6, and ten other places), with the addition of that of "the Kenesite," or "son of Kenaz," in Num. 32:12; Josh. 14:6, 14. Caleb is first mentioned in the list of the rulers or princes who were sent to search the land of Canaan in the second year of the Exodus. He and Oshea or Joshua, the son of Nun, were the only two of the whole number who encouraged the people to enter in boldly to the land and take possession of it. Forty-five years afterward, Caleb came to Joshua and claimed possession of the land of the Anakims, Kirjath-Arba, or Hebron, and the neighboring hill country (Josh. 14). This was immediately granted to him, and the following chapter relates how he took possession of Hebron, driving out the three sons of Anak, and how he offered Achsah his daughter in marriage to whoever would take Kirjath-Sepher, i.e., Debit, and how when Othniel, his younger brother, had performed the feat, he not only gave him his daughter to wife, but with her the upper and nether springs of water which she asked for. It is probable that Caleb was a foreigner by birth—a proselyte taken into the tribe of Judah.

CALF. In Ex. 32:4 we are told that Aaron, constrained by the people in the absence of Moses, made a molten calf of the golden earrings of the people, to represent the Elohim which brought Israel out of Egypt. Probably it was a wooden figure laminated with gold—a process which is known to have existed in Egypt. It has always been a great dispute respecting this calf and those of Jeroboam, whether—1. The Jews intended them for some Egyptian god, or 2. for a mere cherubic symbol of Jehovah.

CALVARY. It is called in Hebrew, *Golgotha,* "a skull," or "place of skulls," supposed to be thus denominated from the similitude it bore to the figure of a skull or man's head, or from its being a place of burial. It was a small eminence or hill to the north of Mount Zion, and to the west of old Jerusalem. Upon it our Lord was crucified (Luke 23:33; Matt. 27:33; John 19:17).

CAMEL. It is clear from Gen. 12:16 that camels were early known to the Egyptians, though no representation of this animal has yet been discovered in the paintings or hieroglyphics. The Ethiopians had "camels in abundance" (2 Chron. 14:15); the queen of Sheba came to Jerusalem "with camels that bare spices and gold and precious stones" (1 Kings 10:2); the men of

Kedar and of Hazor possessed camels (Jer. 49: 29, 32); David took away the camels from the Geshurites and the Amalekites (1 Sam. 27:2; 30: 17); forty camels' burden of good things were sent to Elisha by Benhadad, king of Syria, from Damascus (2 Kings 8:9); the Ishmaelites trafficked with Egypt in the precious gums of Gilead, carried on the backs of camels (Gen. 37:25); the Midianites and the Amalekites possessed camels "as the sand by the seaside for multitude" (Judg. 7:12); Job had three thousand camels before his affliction (Job 1:3), and six thousand afterward (42:12). The camel was used for riding (Gen. 24:64; 1 Sam. 30:17); as a beast of burden generally (Gen. 37:25; 2 Kings 8:9; 1 Kings 10: 2); and for draught purposes (Isa. 21:7). From 1 Sam. 30:17 we learn that camels were used in war.

CANA OF GALILEE. A village or town not far from Capernaum, memorable as the scene of Christ's first miracle (John 2:1, 11) as well as of a subsequent one (John 4:46, 54), and also as the native place of the apostle Nathanael (John 21:2). The exact site is uncertain.

CANAAN. 1. The fourth son of Ham (Gen. 10:6; 1 Chron. 1:8); the progenitor of the Phoenicians ("zidon"), and of the various nations who before the Israelite conquest peopled the seacoast of Palestine, and generally the whole of the country westward of the Jordan (Gen. 10:13; 1 Chron. 1:13). 2. The name of "Canaan" is sometimes employed for the country itself.

CANAAN. The Land of, literally, "Low-land," a name denoting the country west of the Jordan and Dead Sea, and between those waters and the Mediterranean. It is only in later notices, such as Zeph. 2:5 and Matt. 15:22 that we find it applied to the low maritime plains of Philistia and Phoenicia (cf. Mark 7:26).

CANDACE. A queen of Ethiopia (Acts 8:27). The name was not a proper name of an individual, but that of a dynasty of Ethiopian queens.

CANDLESTICK. That which Moses was commanded to make for the tabernacle is described in Ex. 25:31-37; 37:17-24. It is called in Lev. 24:4 "the pure." The candlestick was placed on the south side of the first apartment of the tabernacle, opposite the table of show bread (Ex. 25:37), and was lighted every evening and dressed every morning (Ex. 27:20 f.; 30:8; cf. 1 Sam. 3:2). In Solomon's Temple, instead of this candlestick, there were ten golden candlesticks, similarly embossed, five on the right and five on the left (1 Kings 7:49; 2 Chron. 4:7). They were taken to Babylon (Jer. 52:19).

CANON OF SCRIPTURE. May be generally described as "the collection of books which form the original and authoritative written rule of the faith and practice of the Christian Church." The word Canon, in classical Greek, is properly a straight rod, as the rod of a shield, or that used in weaving, or a carpenter's rule. In patristic writings the word is commonly used both as a "rule" in the widest sense, and especially in the phrases "the rule of the Church," "the rule of faith," "the rule of truth." As applied to scripture, the derivatives of Canon were used long before the simple word. The title "Canonical" was first given to writings in the sense of "admitted by the rule," and not as "forming part of and giving the rule."

CANTICLES. Song of Songs, i.e., the most beautiful of songs, entitled in the A.V. The Song of Solomon. It may be called a drama, as it contains the dramatic evolution of a simple love story. The schools of interpretation may be divided into three: the mystical or typical; the allegorical; and the literal. The book has been rejected from the Canon by some critics, but in no case has its rejection been defended on external grounds.

CAPERNAUM. On the NW shore of the Sea of Galilee (Matt. 4:13; cf. John 6:24). It was of sufficient size to be always called a "city" (Matt. 9:1; Mark 1:33); had its own synagogue, in which Jesus taught (John 6:59; Mark 1:21; Luke 4:33, 38)—a synagogue built by the centurion of the detachment of Roman soldiers which appears to have been quartered in the place (Luke 7:1; cf. vs. 8; Matt. 8:8). The only interest attaching to Capernaum is as the residence of Jesus and his apostles, the scene of so many miracles and "gracious words." At Nazareth he was "brought up," but Capernaum was his "own city"; it was when he returned thither that he is said to have been "at home" (Mark 2:1).

CAPPADOCIA. A country in the east of Asia Minor, made a Roman province by the emperor Tiberius in A.D. 17 (Acts 2:9; 1 Pet. 1:1).

CAPTAIN. A purely military title, captain answers to sar in the Hebrew army, and "tribune" in the Roman. The "captain of the guard" in Acts 28:16 was probably the praefectus praetorio. Another Hebrew word occasionally rendered captain, applies sometimes to a military (Josh. 10:24; Judg. 11:6, 11; Isa. 22:3; Dan. 11:18), sometimes to a civil command—e.g., Isa. 1:10; 3:6. Thirteen different Hebrew words and four Greek words are translated by "captain" in English Bibles. The "captain of the temple" mentioned by Luke (22:4; Acts 4:1; 5:24) superintended the guard of priests and Levites who kept watch by night in the Temple.

CARBUNCLE. The representative in the A.V. of two different Hebrew words (Isa. 54:12; Ex. 28:17), the first perhaps a general term for any bright, sparkling stone, and the second probably the emerald.

CARMEL—garden, vineyard. 1. A mountain which forms one of the most striking and characteristic features of the country of Palestine (1 Kings 18). As if to accentuate more distinctly the bay which forms the one indentation in the coast, this noble ridge, the only headland of lower and central Palestine, forms its southern boundary, running out with a bold, bluff promontory all but into the very waves of the Mediterranean. 2. A town in the hill country of Judea (Josh. 15:55), the home of Nabal, whose widow Abigail David married (1 Sam. 25:2 ff.).

CARPENTER. Artisans who worked with wood. The first mentioned in the Bible were foreigners brought to work in Palestine (2 Sam. 5:11; 1 Kings 5:6). Jesus was known as a carpenter (Mark 6:3).

CARPUS. A Christian at Troas (2 Tim. 4:13). According to Hippolytus, Carpus was bishop of Berytus in Thrace.

CARRIAGE. This word occurs only six times in the text of the A.V., and signifies what we now call "baggage" (e.g., 1 Sam. 17:22; Acts 21:15). In the margin of 1 Sam. 17:20; 26:5-7 "carriage" is employed in the sense of a wagon or cart.

CART (Gen. 45:19, 27; Num. 7:3, 8). A vehicle drawn by cattle (2 Sam. 6:6), to be distinguished from the chariot drawn by horses (Num. 7:3). Carts and wagons were either open or covered (Num. 7:3), and were used for conveyance of persons (Gen. 45:19), burdens (1 Sam. 7:7 f.), or produce (Amos 2:13).

CASSIA (Ex. 30:24; Ezra 27:19). The cassia-bark of commerce is yielded by various kinds of Cinnamomum, which grow in different parts of India.

CASTOR AND POLLUX (Acts 28:11). The twin sons of Jupiter and Leda were regarded as the particular divinities of sailors. They appeared in the heaven as the constellation Gemini.

CASTLE. The Hebrew word so translated in A.V. (Gen. 25:16; Num. 31:10; 1 Chron. 6:54) more correctly signifies a circular group of tents.

CAVE. The chalky limestone of which the rocks of Syria and Palestine chiefly presents, as is the case in all limestone formations, a vast number of caverns and natural fissures, many of which have also been artificially enlarged and adapted to various purposes, both of shelter and defence. The most remarkable caves noticed in Scripture are—1. That in which Lot dwelt after the destruction of Sodom (Gen. 19:30). 2. The cave of Machpelah (Gen. 23:17). 3. Cave of Makkedah (Josh. 10:10). 4. Cave of Adullam (1 Sam. 22: 1). 5. Cave of Engedi (1 Sam. 24:3). 6. Obadiah's cave (1 Kings 18:4). 7. Elijah's cave in Horeb (1 Kings 19:9). 8, 9. The rock sepulchres of Lazarus and of our Lord (John 11:38; Matt. 27:60).

CEDAR. There is little doubt that the Hebrew erez (the firmly-rooted and strong tree), invariably rendered "cedar," does stand for that tree in most of the passages where the word occurs (Isa. 2:13; Ezek. 31:3; 1 Kings 5:6, 10; Isa. 44:14). The cedars of Lebanon were greatly valued because lumber made from them was strong and fragrant and of good size.

CEDRON. In the New Testament the name of the brook Kidron in the ravine below the eastern wall of Jerusalem (John 18:1, only). Beyond it was the garden of Gethsemane. (See Kidron.)

CEILING (in A.V. cieling). The descriptions of Scripture (1 Kings 6:9, 15; 7:3; 2 Chron. 3:5, 9; Jer. 22:14; Hag. 1:4), and of Josephus, show that the ceilings of temple and the palaces of the Jewish kings were formed of cedar planks applied to the beams or joints crossing from wall to wall, probably with sunk panels, edged and ornamented with gold, and carved with incised or other patterns, sometimes painted (Jer. 22:14).

CENCHREA or CENCHREAE. The eastern harbor of Corinth. Paul sailed from Cenchreae (Acts 18:18) on his return to Syria from his second missionary journey, and when he wrote his Epistle to the Romans in the course of the third journey, an organized church seems to have been formed there (Rom. 16:1).

CENSER. A small portable vessel of metal fitted to receive burning coals from the altar, and on which the incense for burning was sprinkled (2 Chron. 26:19). The only distinct precepts regarding the use of the center are found in Num. 4:14 and Lev. 16:12.

CENTURION. The commander of a century, of which there were sixty in a Roman legion. At first there were, as the name implies, one hundred men in each century; subsequently, the number varied according to the strength of the legion (Matt. 8:5; 27:36; Acts 10:1; 22:25; 23:23; 27:1).

CHAIN. Chains were used as badges of office, for ornament, and for confining prisoners. The gold chain placed about Joseph's neck (Gen. 41: 42), and that promised to Daniel (Dan. 5:7), are instances of the first use. Chains for ornamental purposes were worn by men as well as women in many countries both of Europe and Asia, and probably this was the case among the Hebrews (Prov. 1:9). The means adopted for confining prisoners among the Jews were fetters similar to our handcuffs (Judg. 16:21; 2 Sam. 3:34; 2 Kings 25:7; Jer. 39:7).

CHALCEDONY. (Rev. 21:19). The name is applied in modern mineralogy to one of the varieties of agate.

CHALDEA or CHALDAEA. Used in Scripture to signify that vast alluvial plain which has been formed by the deposits of the Euphrates and the Tigris—at least so far as it lies to the west of the latter stream. The true Chaldaea is always in the geographies a distinct region, being the most southern portion of Babylonia lying chiefly (if not solely) on the right bank of the Euphrates. The extraordinary fertility of the Chaldean soil has been noticed by various writers. It is said to be the only country in the world where wheat

grows wild. The palm was undoubtedly one of the principal objects of cultivation.

CHALDEANS or CHALDEES. They appear in Scripture, until the time of the captivity, as the people of the country which has Babylon for its capital, and which is itself termed Shinar; but in the Book of Daniel, while this meaning is still found (5:30 and 9:1), a new sense shows itself. The Chaldeans are classed with the magicians and astronomers, and evidently form a sort of priest class, who have a peculiar "tongue" and "learning" (1:4), and are consulted by the king on religious subjects. Their special seat was probably that southern portion of the country which is found to have so late retained the name of Chaldae. Here was Ur "of the Chaldees" (Gen. 11:28).

CHAMBERLAIN. Eratus, "the *chamberlain*" of the city of Corinth, was one of those whose salutations to the Roman Christians are given at the end of the Epistle addressed to them (Rom. 16:23). The office held by Blastus, "the king's *chamberlain*," was entirely different from this (Acts 12:20). It was a post of honor which involved great intimacy and influence with the king.

CHAMELEON. The translation of the Hebrew *koah*, Lev. 11:30. Others suppose it to be the lizard, known by the name of the "Monitor of the Nile."

CHAPITER. The capital of a pillar; also possibly a roll moulding at the top of a building or work of art, as in the case (1) of the pillars of the tabernacle and temple, and of the two pillars called especially Jachin and Boaz, and (2) of the lavers belonging to the temple (Ex. 38:17; 1 Kings 7:27, 31, 38).

CHARGER. A shallow vessel for recieving water or blood, also for presenting offerings of fine flour with oil (Num. 7:79). The daughter of Herodias brought the Head of John the Baptist in a charger (Matt. 14:8); probably a trencher or platter.

CHARIOT. A vehicle used either for warlike or peaceful purposes, but most commonly the former. The earliest mention of chariots in Scripture is in Egypt, where Joseph, as a mark of distinction, was placed in Pharaoh's second chariot (Gen. 41:43), and later when he went in his own chariot to meet his father on his entrance into Egypt from Canaan (46:29). In the funeral procession of Jacob chariots also formed a part, possibly by way of escort, or as a guard of honor (50:9). The next mention of Egyptian chariots is for a warlike purpose (Ex. 14:7). The Canaanites of the valleys of Palestine were enabled to resist the Israelites successfully in consequence of the number of their chariots of iron, *i.e.*, perhaps armed with iron scythes (Josh. 17:18; Judg. 1:19). Jabin, king of Canaan, had 900 chariots (Judg. 4:3). The Philistines in Saul's time had 30,000 (1 Sam. 13:5). David took from Hadadezer, king of Zobah, 1,000 chariots (2 Sam. 8:4), and from the Syrians a little later 700 (10:18), who, in order to recover their ground, collected 32,000 chariots (1 Chron. 19:7). The prophets allude frequently to chariots as typical of power (Ps. 20:7; 104:3; Jer. 51:21; Zech. 6:1). In the New Testament the only mention made of a chariot, except in Rev. 9:9, is in the case of the Ethiopian or Abyssinian eunuch of Queen Candace (Acts 8:28 f., 38). Jewish chariots were no doubt imitated from Egyptian models, if not actually imported from Egypt.

CHARITY. The word used about 28 times in the A.V. to translate the Greek term *agape*. The meaning of *agape* is closer to that of "Christian love."

CHEBAR. A river in the "land of the Chaldeans" (Ezek. 1:3), on the banks of which some of the Jews were located at the time of the captivity, and where Ezekiel saw his earlier visions (Ezek. 1:1; 3:15, 23).

CHEDORLAOMER. A king of Elam, in the time of Abraham, who with three other chiefs made war upon the kings of Sodom, Gomorrah, Admah, Zeboim, and Zoar, and reduced them to servitude (Gen. 14:17).

CHEMOSH. The national deity of the Moabites (Num. 21:29; Jer. 47:7, 13, 46). In Judg. 11:24 he also appears as the god of the Ammonites. Solomon introduced, and Josiah abolished, the worship of Chemosh at Jerusalem (1 Kings 11:7; 2 Kings 23:13).

CHERETHITES and PELETHITES. The lifeguards of King David (2 Sam. 8:18; 15:18; 20:7, 23; 1 Kings 1:38, 44; 1 Chron. 18:17). It is plain that these royal guards were employed as executioners (2 Kings 11:4), and as couriers (1 Kings 14:27). But it has been conjectured that they may have been foreign mercenaries.

CHERITH. The brook, the torrent-bed or *wady* in which Elijah hid himself during the early part of the three years' drought (1 Kings 17:3, 5). The location of the Cherith has been much disputed.

CHERUB, CHERUBIM. The symbolical figure so called is a composite creature-form which finds a parallel in the religious insignia of Assyria, Egypt, and Persia, *e.g.*, the sphinx, the winged bulls and lions of Nineveh, etc. The Hebrew idea seems to limit the number of the cherubim. A pair (Ex. 25:18) were placed on the mercy-seat of the ark; a pair of colossal size overshadowed it in Solomon's Temple with the canopy of their contiguously extended wings. Those on the ark were to be placed with wings stretched forth, one at each end of the mercy-seat, and to be made "of the mercy-seat."

CHEST. By this word are translated in the Old Testament two distinct Hebrew terms: 1. *Aron*. This is invariably used for the Ark of the Covenant, and with two exceptions, for that only. The two exceptions alluded to are (a) the "coffin" in which the bones of Joseph were carried from Egypt (Gen. 50:26), and (b) the "chest" in which Jehoiada the priest collected the alms for the repairs of the Temple (2 Kings 12:9, 10; 2 Chron. 24:8-11). 2. *Genazim*, "chests" (Ezek. 27:24 only).

CHESTNUT TREE (Hebrew *armon*: Gen. 30:37; Ezek. 31:8). It is spoken of as one of the glories of Assyria, for which the "plane tree" ought probably to have been substituted.

CHIDON. The name which in 1 Chron. 13:9 is given to the threshing-floor at which the accident to the ark took place. In the parallel account in 2 Sam. 6 the name is given as Nachon.

CHILDREN. The blessing of offspring, but especially of the male sex, is highly valued among all Eastern nations, while the absence is regarded as one of the severest punishments (Gen. 16:2; Deut. 7:14; 1 Sam. 1:6; 2 Sam. 6:23; 2 Kings 4:14; Isa. 47:9; Jer. 20:15; Ps. 127: 3, 5). As soon as the child was born it was washed in a bath, rubbed with salt and wrapped in swaddling clothes. On the 8th day the rite of circumcision, in the case of a boy, was performed, and a name given, sometimes, but not usually, the same as that of the father, and generally conveying some special meaning. At the end of a certain time the mother was to make an offering of purification of a lamb as a burnt-offering, and a pigeon or turtledove as a sin-offering, or in the case of poverty, two doves or pigeons, one as a burnt-offering, the other as a sin-offering (Lev. 12:1-8; Luke 2:22). The period of nursing appears to have been sometimes prolonged to three years (Isa. 49:15). Nurses were employed in cases of necessity (Ex. 2:9; Gen. 29:59; 35:8; 1 Sam. 4:4; 2 Kings 11:2; 2 Chron. 22:11). The time of weaning was an occasion of rejoicing (Gen. 21:8). Both boys and girls in their early years were under the care of the women (Prov. 31:1). Afterward the boys were taken by the father under his charge. Those in wealthy families had tutors or governors, who

were sometimes eunuchs (Num. 11:12; 2 Kings 10:1, 4; Isa. 49:23; Gal. 3:24; Esth. 2:7). Daughters usually remained in the women's apartments till marriage, or among the poorer classes, were employed in household work (Lev. 31:9; Num. 12:14; 1 Sam. 9:11; Prov. 31:19, 23). The first-born male children were regarded as devoted to God, and were to be redeemed by an offering (Ex. 13:13; Num. 18:15; Luke 2:22). The authority of parents, especially of the father, over children was very great, as was also the reverence enjoined by the law to be paid to parents. The disobedient child, the striker or reviler of a parent, was liable to capital punishment, though not at the independent will of the parent. The inheritance was divided equally between all the sons except the eldest, who received a double portion (Deut. 21:17; Gen. 25:31; 49:3; 1 Chron. 5:1, 2; Judg. 11:2, 7). Daughters had by right no portion in the inheritance, but if a man had no son, his inheritance passed to his daughters, who were forbidden to marry out of their father's tribe (Num. 27:1, 8; 36:2, 8).

CHILION—*wasting away.* The son of Elimelech and Naomi and husband of Orpah (Ruth 1:2-5; 4:9). He is described as "an Ephrathite of Bethlehem-judah."

CHINNERETH—*harp; lute.* The inland sea, which is most familiarly known as the lake of Gennesareth or Sea of Galilee (Num. 34:11; Josh. 13:27).

CHIOS. The position of this island in reference to the neighboring islands and coasts could hardly be better described than in the detailed account of Paul's return voyage from Troas to Caesarea (Acts 20, 21). Chios is separated from the mainland by a strait of only 5 miles. Its length is about 32 miles, and in breadth it varies from 8 to 18.

CHITTIM, KITTIM. A family or race descended from Javan (Gen. 10:4; 1 Chron. 1:7; A.V. Kitaim). Chittim is frequently noticed in Scripture; Balaam predicts that a fleet should thence proceed for the destruction of Assyria (Num. 24:24); in Isa. 23:1, 12, it appears as the resort of the fleets of Tyre; in Jer. 2:10 the "isles of Chittim" are to the far west, as Kedar to the east of Palestine; the Tyrians procured thence the cedar or box-wood which they inlaid with ivory for the decks of their vessels (Ezek. 27:6); in Dan. 11:30 "ships of Chittim" advance to the south to meet the king of the north.

CHORAZIN. One of the cities in which our Lord's mighty works were done, but named only in his denunciation (Matt. 11:21; Luke 10:13). It was situated at the northern end of Galilee about 2½ miles north of Capernaum.

CHRISTIAN. A follower of the religion of Christ. It is probable that the name of Christian, like those of Nazarene and Galileans, was given to the disciples of Jesus in reproach or contempt. They were first called by the name at Antioch (Acts 11:26).

CHRONICLES. First and Second Books of, the name originally given to the record made by the appointed historiographers in the kingdoms of Israel and Judah. The first book traces the Israelites from Adam to David. The second relates the progress and dissolution of the kingdom of Judah and the return of the Jews from Babylonish captivity. (See also Kings, First and Second Books of.)

CHRONOLOGY. By this term we understand the technical and historical chronology of the Jews and their ancestors from the earliest time to the close of the New Testament Canon. The technical part of Hebrew chronology presents great difficulties. The historical part of Hebrew chronology is not less difficult than the technical.

CHRYSOLITE. One of the precious stones in the foundation of the heavenly Jerusalem (Rev. 21:20). The chrysolite of the ancients may be

identical with the modern Oriental topaz, the *tarshish* of the Hebrew Bible.

CHRYSOPRASE. Occurs only in Rev. 21:20. The true chrysoprase is sometimes found in antique Egyptian jewelry set alternately with bits of lapis-lazuli.

CHURCH. 1. The derivation of the word *church* is uncertain. It is generally said to be derived from the Greek *kyriakon*, "house of the Lord." 2. *Ecclesia*, the Greek word for church, originally meant an assembly called out by the magistrate, or by legitimate authority. This is the ordinary classical sense of the word. But it throws no light on the nature of the institution so designated in the New Testament. For to the writers of the New Testament the word had now lost its primary signification, and was either used generally for any meeting (Acts 19:32), or, more particularly, it denoted (1) the religious assemblies of the Jews (Deut. 4:10; 18:16). (2) The whole assembly or congregation of the Israelitish people (Acts 7:38; Heb. 2:12; Ps. 22:22; Deut. 31:30). It was in this last sense that the word was adopted and applied by the writers of the New Testament to the Christian congregation. 3. The word *church* occurs only twice in the Gospels, each time in Matthew (Matt. 16:18, "On this rock will I build my church"; and 18:17, "Tell it unto the church"). In every other case it is spoken of as "the kingdom of heaven" by Matthew, and as "the kingdom of God" by Mark and Luke. The origin of the Christian church may be traced briefly. The removal of Christ from the earth had left his followers a shattered company with no bond of external or internal cohesion, except the memory of the Master whom they had lost, and the recollection of his injunctions to unity and love. They continued together, meeting for prayer and supplication, and waiting for Christ's promise of the gift of the Holy Ghost. The Day of Pentecost has been called the birthday of the Christian church. The Spirit, who was then sent by the Son from the Father, and rested on each of the disciples, combined them once more into a whole. Before they had been individual followers of Jesus, now they became his mystical body, animated by his Spirit. "Then they that gladly received his word were baptized . . . and they continued steadfastly in the Apostles' doctrine and fellowship, and in breaking of bread and in prayers" (Acts 2:41). Here we have indirectly exhibited the essential conditions of church communion. They are (1) baptism—implying on the part of the recipient repentance and faith; (2) apostolic doctrine; (3) fellowship with the apostles; (4) the Lord's Supper; (5) public worship.

CHURNING (Prov. 30:33). (See Butter.)

CIELING. (See Ceiling.)

CILICIA. A country in the souteast of Asia Minor, and lying on the northern coast, at the east end of the Mediterranean Sea; the capital city thereof was Tarsus, the native city of Paul (Acts 21:39).

CINNAMON. A well-known aromatic substance, the rind of the *Laurus cinnamomum*, called *Korundagauhah*, in Ceylon. It is mentioned in Ex. 30:23 as one of the component parts of the holy anointing oil, which Moses commanded to prepare—in Prov. 7:17 as a perfume for the bed —and in Cant. 4:14 as one of the plants of the garden which is the image of the spouse. In Rev. 18:13 it is enumerated among the merchandise of the great Babylon.

CIRCUMCISION. Peculiarly, though not exclusively, a Jewish rite. It was enjoined upon Abraham, the father of the nation, by God, at the institution, and as the token, of the covenant, which assured to him and his descendants the promise of the Messiah (Gen. 17). It was thus made a necessary condition of Jewish nationality. Every male child was to be circumcised when eight days old (Lev. 12:3), on pain of death. If

the eighth day were a Sabbath the rite was not postponed (John 7:22 f.). Slaves, whether home-born or purchased, were circumcised (Gen. 17: 12 f.); and foreigners must have their males circumcised before they could be allowed to partake of the passover (Ex. 12:48) or become Jewish citizens. It seems to have been customary to name a child when it was circumcised (Luke 1:59).

CISTERN. A receptacle for storing water. The dryness of the summer months between May and September, in Syria, and the scarcity of springs in many parts of the country, make it necessary to collect in reservoirs and cisterns the rain-water, of which abundance falls in the intermediate period.

CITIES. The earliest notice in Scripture of city-building is of Enoch by Cain, in the land of his exile (Gen. 4:17). The earliest description of a city, properly so called, is that of Sodom (Gen. 19:1-22). Hebron is said to have been built seven years before Zoan (Tanis) in Egypt, and is thus the only Syrian town which presents the elements of a date for its foundation (Num. 13:22). Even before the time of Abraham there were cities in Egypt (Gen. 12:14 f.; Num. 13:22).

CITIES OF REFUGE. Six Levitical cities specially chosen for refuge to the involuntary homicide until released from banishment by the death of the high priest (Num. 35:6, 13, 15; Josh. 20:2, 7, 9). There were three on each side of the Jordan.

CITIZENSHIP. The privilege of Roman citizenship was acquired in various ways, as by purchase (Acts 22:28), by military services, by favor, or by manumission. The right once obtained descended to a man's children (Acts 22: 28). Among the privileges a man could not be bound or imprisoned without a formal trial (Acts 22:29), still less be scourged (Acts 16:37). Another privilege was the appeal from a provincial tribunal to the emperor at Rome (Acts 25:11).

CLAUDIA. A Christian woman mentioned in 2 Tim. 4:21 as saluting Timotheus. An interesting but unsubstantiated theory is that this Claudia was a British maiden, daughter of king Cogidubnus, an ally of Rome, who took the name of his imperial patron, Tiberius Claudius.

CLAUDIUS. Fourth Roman emperor, reigned from A.D. 41 to 54. He was the son of Nero Drusus, was born in Lyons and lived private and unknown till the day of his being called to the throne (see Acts 11:28; 18:2).

CLAY. As the sediment of water remaining in pits or in streets, the word is used frequently in Old Testament (Isa. 57:20; Jer. 38:6; Ps. 18:42), and in New Testament (John 9:6), a mixture of sand or dust with spittle. It is also found in the sense of potter's clay (Isa. 41:25). Another use of clay was for sealing (Job 38:14). The seal used for public documents was rolled on the moist clay, and the tablet was then placed in the fire and baked.

CLEMENT. A fellow-laborer of Paul when he was at Philippi (Phil. 4:2).

CLEOPAS—*of a renowned father.* One of the two disciples who were going to Emmaus on the day of the resurrection (Luke 24:18). It is a question whether this Cleopas is to be considered as identical with Cleophas (accur. Clopas) or Alphaeus in John 19:25.

CLOUD, PILLAR OF. The cloud, which became a pillar when the host moved, seems to have rested at other times on the tabernacle, whence God is said to have "come down in the pillar" (Num. 12:5; so Ex. 33:9 f.). It preceded the host, apparently resting on the ark which led the way (Ex. 13:21; 40:36; Num. 9:15-23; 10:34).

CNIDUS. Mentioned in Acts 27:7 as a harbor which was passed by Paul.

COAL. In A.V. this word represents no less than five different Hebrew words. 1. The first and most frequently used is *gaheleth*, a live ember, burning fuel, as distinguished from *pecham* (Prov. 26:21). 2. *Pecham.* In Prov. 26:21 this word clearly signifies fuel not yet lighted. The fuel meant in the above passages is probably charcoal, and not coal in our sense of the word.

COCK. Mentioned in reference to Peter's denial of Christ and indirectly in the word "cock-crowing" (Matt. 26:34; Mark 14:30; 13:35).

COLLEGE, THE. In 2 Kings 22:14 it is said in the A.V. that Huldah the prophetess "dwell in Jerusalem in the college" (Hebrew *mishnah*). It is probable that the *mishnah* was the "lower city," built on the hill Akra.

COLORS. The natural colors noticed in the Bible are white, black, red, yellow, and green. The only fundamental color of which the Hebrews appear to have had a clear conception was *red;* and even this is not very often noticed.

COLOSSAE. A city in the upper part of the basin of the Maeander, on one of its tributaries named the Lycus. Hierapolis and Laodicaea were in its immediate neighborhood (Col. 2:1; 4:13, 15, 16; see Rev. 1:11; 3:14). Colossae fell as these other two cities rose in importance. It was situated close to the great road which led from Ephesus to the Euphrates. While his influence reached the city, Paul himself had not been there (Col. 2:1).

COLOSSIANS. The Epistle to the Colossians was written by the apostle Paul during an imprisonment (Col. 4:3, 18). This epistle was addressed to the Christians of the city of Colossae, and was delivered to them by Tychicus, whom the apostle had sent both to them (4:7 f.) and to the church of Ephesus (Eph. 6:21), to inquire into their state and to administer exhortation and comfort. The main object of the epistle is to warn the Colossians against a spirit of semi-Judaistic and semi-Oriental philosophy which was corrupting the simplicity of their belief, and was noticeably tending to obscure the eternal glory and dignity of Christ.

CONCUBINE. The difference between wife and concubine was less marked among the Hebrews than among us, owing to the absence of moral stigma. The concubine's condition was a definite one. With regard to the children of wife and concubine, there was no such difference as our illegitimacy implies; the latter were a supplementary family to the former; their names occur in the patriarchal genealogies (Gen. 22:24; 1 Chron. 1:22), and their position and provision would depend on the father's will (Gen. 25:6). The state of concubinage is assumed and provided for by the law of Moses. A concubine would generally be either, (1) a Hebrew girl bought of her father; (2) a Gentile captive taken in war; (3) a foreign slave bought; or (4) a Canaanitish woman bound or free. The rights of (1) and (2) were protected by law (Ex. 21:7; Deut. 21: 10-14), but (3) was unrecognized, and (4) prohibited. Free Hebrew women also might become concubines.

CONEY. A gregarious animal which is found in Palestine. Its scientific name is *Hyrax Syriacus.* In Lev. 11:5; Deut. 14:7 it is declared to be unclean, because it chews the cud, but does not divide the hoof. In Ps. 104:18 we are told "the rocks are a refuge for the coneys," and in Prov. 30:26 that "the coneys are but a feeble folk, yet make they their houses in the rocks."

COPPER (Hebrew *nehosheth*). In the A.V. always rendered "brass," except in Ezra 8:27; 15:12. It was almost exclusively used by the ancients for common purposes.

CORAL. Occurs only as the somewhat doubtful rendering of the Hebrew *ramoth*, in Job 28:18, and in Ezek. 27:16. But "coral" has decidedly the best claim of any other substance to represent *ramoth*.

CORBAN. An offering to God in fulfillment of a vow. The law laid down rules for vows (Lev. 27; Num. 30). Upon these traditionists enlarged, and laid down that a man might interdict himself by vow, not only from using for himself, but from giving to another, or receiving from him, some particular object, whether of food or any other kind whatsoever. The thing thus interdicted was considered as Corban. A person might thus exempt himself from any inconvenient obligation under plea of Corban. It was practices of this sort that Jesus reprehended (Matt. 15:5; Mark 7:11), as annulling the spirit of the law.

CORD. The materials of which cord was made varied according to the strength required; the strongest rope was probably made of strips of camel-hide, as still used by the Bedouins. The finer sorts were made of flax (Isa. 19:9), and probably of reeds and rushes. In the New Testament the term is applied to the whip which Jesus made (John 2:15), and to the ropes of a ship (Acts 27:32).

CORIANDER. The plant called *Coriandrum Sativum* is found in Egypt, Persia, and India, and has a round tall stalk; it bears umbelliferous white or reddish flowers, from which arise globular, grayish, spicy seed-corns, marked with fine striae. It is mentioned twice in the Bible (Ex. 16:31; Num. 11:7).

CORINTH. This city is alike remarkable for its distinctive geographical position, its eminence in Greek and Roman history, and its close connection with the early spread of Christianity. The site of Corinth is distinguished by the *Acrocorinthus*, a vast citadel of rock, which rises abruptly to the height of 2,000 feet above the sea, and the summit of which is so extensive that it once contained a whole town. It is not the true Greek Corinth with which we have to do in the life of Paul, but the Corinth which was rebuilt and established as a Roman colony. The new city was hardly less distinguished than the old. Corinth was a place of great mental activity, as well as of commercial and manufacturing enterprise. Its wealth was so celebrated as to be proverbial; so were the vice and profligacy of its inhabitants. The worship of Venus here was attended with shameful licentiousness. All these points are indirectly illustrated by passages in the two epistles to the Corinthians.

CORINTHIANS. The Epistles to the Corinthians were written by Paul. The first was written toward the close of his nearly three years' stay at Ephesus (Acts 19:10; 20:31). This varied and highly characteristic letter was addressed not to any party, but to the whole body of the large (Acts 18:8, 10) Judaeo-Gentile (Acts 17:4) church of Corinth. The second epistle was written a few months subsequently to the first, in the same year. The place whence it was written was Macedonia (2 Cor. 7:5; 8:1; 9:2), whither the apostle went by the way of Troas (2 Cor. 2:12), after waiting a short time in the latter place for the return of Titus (2 Cor. 2:13).

CORMORANT. The representative in the A.V. of the Hebrew words *kaath* and *shalak*. As to the former, see Pelican. Shalak occurs only as the name of an unclean bird in Lev. 11:17; Deut. 14:17.

CORN. The most common kinds were wheat, barley, spelt (A.V. Ex. 9:32 and Isa. 28:25, "rie"; Ezek. 4:9, "fitches"), and millet; oats are not mentioned. "Seven ears on one stalk" (Gen. 41: 22) was no unusual phenomenon in Egypt. Wheat (see 2 Sam. 4:6) was stored in the house for domestic purposes.

CORNELIUS. A Roman centurion of the Italian cohort stationed in Caesarea (Acts 10:1), a man full of good works and alms-deeds. With his household he was baptized by Peter, and thus Cornelius became the first-fruits of the Gentile world to Christ.

CORNER. The "corner" of the field was not allowed (Lev. 19:9) to be wholly reaped. It formed a right of the poor to carry off what was so left. This "corner" was, like the gleaning, title free.

CORNER-STONE. Some of the corner-stones in the ancient work of the Temple foundations are 17 or 19 feet long and 7½ feet thick. At Nineveh the corners are sometimes formed of one angular stone. The phrase "corner-stone" is applied to Christ (Isa. 28:16; Matt. 21:42; 1 Pet. 2:6 f.).

CORNET (Hebrew *shophar*). A loud-sounding instrument, made of the horn of a ram or a chamois (sometimes of an ox), and used by the ancient Hebrews for signals, for announcing the "Jubilee" (Lev. 25:9), for proclaiming the new year, for the purposes of war (Jer. 4:5, 19; *cf.* Job 39:25), as well as for the sentinels placed at the watch-towers to give notice of the approach of an enemy (Ezra 33:4 f.). *Shophar* is generally rendered in the A.V. "trumpet," but "cornet" (the more correct translation) is used in 2 Chron. 15:14; Ps. 98:6; Hos. 5:8; and 1 Chron. 15:28. "Cornet" is also employed in Dan. 3:5, 7, 10, 15, for the Chaldee *keren* (literally a horn).

COS or **COOS.** A small island of the Grecian Archipelago. One of the places which contained Jewish residents. Perhaps it is to the town that reference is made in Acts 21:1.

CRANE. There can be little doubt that the A.V. is incorrect in rendering *sus* by "crane." Mention is made of the *sus* in Hezekiah's prayer (Isa. 38:14), "Like a *sus* or an *agur* so did I twitter"; and again in Jer. 8:7 these two words occur, from which passage we learn that both birds were migratory.

CRESCENS. An early Christian mentioned as having gone to Gaul or Galatia (2 Tim. 4:10).

CRETE. An island at the mouth of the Aegean Sea between Rhodes and Peloponnesus (Acts 27: 7). It was the seat of legislature to all Greece. There were once one hundred cities on the island. The inhabitants were exceedingly addicted to lying (Tit. 1:12). The gospel converted many persons here (Tit. 1:5).

CRISPUS. Ruler of the Jewish synagogue at Corinth (Acts 18:8); baptized with his family by Paul (1 Cor. 1:14).

CROSS. As the emblem of a slave's death and a murderer's punishment, the cross was naturally looked upon with the profoundest horror. But after the celebrated vision of Constantine, he ordered his friends to make a cross of gold and gems, such as he had seen, and "the towering eagles resigned the flags unto the cross," and "the tree of cursing and shame" "sat upon the sceptres and was engraved upon the foreheads of kings" (Jer. Taylor, *Life of Christ*, iii., xv. 1). The Latin cross, on which Christ suffered, was in the form of the letter T, and had an upright above the crossbar, on which the "title" was placed. There was a projection from the central stem, on which the body of the sufferer rested. This was to prevent the weight of the body from tearing away the hands. Whether there was also a support to the feet (as seen in pictures), is doubtful. It was not till the sixth century that the emblem of the cross became the image of the crucifix. As a symbol the use of it was frequent in the early church. It was not till the second century that any particular efficacy was attached to it. (See Crucifixion.)

CROWN. This ornament, which is both ancient and universal, probably originated from the fillets used to prevent the hair from being disheveled by the wind. Such fillets gradually developed into turbans, which by the addition of ornamental or precious materials assumed the dignity of mitres or crowns. Both the ordinary priests and the high priest wore them. The common "bonnet" (Ex. 28:37; 29:6) formed a sort of linen fillet or crown. The mitre of the high priest (used also of a regal crown, Ezek. 21:26) was much more splendid (Ex. 28:36; Lev. 8:9). It had a second fillet of blue lace, and over it a golden diadem (Ex. 29:7). The gold band was tied behind with blue lace (embroidered with flowers), and being two fingers broad, bore the inscription "Holiness to the Lord" (*cf.* Rev. 17:5). There are many words in Scripture denoting a crown besides those mentioned; the head-dress of bridegrooms (Isa. 61:10; Ezek. 24:17), and of women (Isa. 3:20); a head-dress of great splendor (Isa. 18:5); a wreath of flowers (Prov. 1:9; 4:9); and a common tiara or turban (Job 29:14; Isa. 3:23).

CROWN OF THORNS. Jesus was crowned with thorns in mockery by the Roman soldiers (Matt. 27:29). The object seems to have been insult, and not the infliction of pain, as has generally been supposed.

CRUCIFIXION. This was in use among the Egyptians (Gen. 40:19), the Carthaginians, the Persians (Esth. 7:10), the Assyrians, Scythians, Indians, Germans, and from the earliest times among the Greeks and Romans. It was unanimously considered the most horrible form of death. Among the Romans the punishment was used in the case of the vilest criminals. Jesus was condemned to it by the popular cry of the Jews (Matt. 27:23) on the charge of sedition against Caesar (Luke 23:2), although the Sanhedrin had previously condemned him on the totally distinct charge of blasphemy. The punishment properly commenced with scourging, after the criminal had been stripped. It was inflicted not with the comparatively mild rods, but the more terrible scourge (2 Cor. 11:24 f.), which was not used by the Jews (Deut. 25:3). Into these scourges the soldiers often stuck nails, pieces of bone, etc., to heighten the pain, which was often so intense that the sufferer died under it. The criminal carried his own cross, or at any rate a part of it. The place of execution was outside the city (1 Kings 21:13; Acts 7:58; Heb. 13:12), often in some public road or other conspicuous place. Arrived at the place of execution, the sufferer was stripped naked, the dress being the perquisite of the soldiers (Matt. 27:35). The cross was then driven into the ground, so that the feet of the condemned were a foot or two above the earth, and he was lifted upon it, or else stretched upon it on the ground, and then lifted with it. Before the nailing or binding took place, a medicated cup was given out of kindness to confuse the senses and deaden the pangs of the sufferer, usually "of wine mingled with myrrh," because myrrh was soporific. Jesus refused it that his senses might be clear (Matt. 27:34; Mark 15:23). He was crucified between two "thieves" or "malefactors," according to prophecy (Isa. 53:12); and was watched according to custom by a party of four soldiers (John 19:23) with their centurion (Matt. 27:66), whose express office was to prevent the stealing of the body. Pilate expressly satisfied himself of the actual death by questioning the centurion (Mark 15:44). In most cases the body was suffered to rot on the cross by the action of sun and rain, or to be devoured by birds and beasts. Sepulture was generally therefore forbidden; but in consequence of Deut. 21:22 f., an express national exception was made in favor of the Jews (Matt. 28:58).

CRUSE. A vessel for holding liquid, such as was carried by Saul when on his night expedition after David (1 Sam. 26:11, 12, 16), and by Elijah (1 Kings 19:6).

CUBIT. A linear measure, taken as the length of a man's arm from elbow to fingertip. The Hebrew cubit was about 18 inches.

CUCUMBERS. This word occurs in Num. 11:5

as one of the good things of Egypt for which the Israelites longed.

CUMMIN. One of the cultivated plants of Palestine (Isa. 28:25, 27; Matt. 18:23). It is an umbelliferous plant.

CUP. the cups of the Jews, whether of metal or earthenware, were possibly borrowed, in shape and design, from Egypt and from the Phoenicians, who were celebrated in that branch of workmanship. Egyptian cups were of various shapes, either with handles or without them. In Solomon's time all his drinking vessels were of gold, none of silver (1 Kings 10:21). The cups of the New Testament were often no doubt formed on Greek and Roman models. They were sometimes of gold (Rev. 17:4).

CUPBEARER. An officer of high rank with Egyptian, Persian, Assyrian, as well as Jewish monarchs (1 Kings 10:5). The chief cupbearer, or butler, to the king of Egypt was the means of raising Joseph to his high position (Gen. 40:1, 21; 41:9). Nehemiah was cupbearer to Artaxerxes Longimanus, king of Persia (Neh. 1:11; 2:1).

CUSH. The name of a son of Ham, apparently the eldest, and of a territory or territories occupied by his descendents. 1. In the genealogy of Noah's children Cush seems to be an individual, for it is said "Cush begat Nimrod" (Gen. 10:8; 1 Chron. 1:10). 2. Cush as a country appears to be African in all passages except Gen. 2:13.

CYMBAL, CYMBALS. A percussive musical instrument. Two kinds of cymbals are mentioned in Ps. 150:5, "loud cymbals" or *castagnettes,* and "high-sounding cymbals."

CYPRESS (Hebrew *tirzah*). The Hebrew word is found only in Isa. 44:14. We are quite unable to assign any definite rendering to it.

CYPRUS. This island was in early times in close commercial connection with Phoenicia; and there is little doubt that it is referred to in such passages of the Old Testament as Ezek. 27:6 (see Chittim). Possibly Jews may have settled in Cyprus before the time of Alexander. Soon after his time they were numerous in the island. The first notice of it in the New Testament is in Acts 4:36, where it is mentioned as the native place of Barnabas. In Acts 11:19 f. it appears prominently in connection with the earliest spreading of Christianity, and is again mentioned in connection with the missionary journeys of Paul (Acts 13:4-13; 15:39; 21:3), and with his voyage to Rome (Acts 27:4).

CYRENE. A city of Lybia in Africa, which, as it was the principal city of that province, gave to it the name of Cyrenaica. This city was once so powerful as to contend with Carthage for pre-eminence. It is mentioned in Holy Writ as the birthplace of Simon, whom the Jews compelled to bear Jesus' cross (Matt. 27:32; Luke 28:26). Among the most inveterate enemies of Christianity, Luke reckons those of this province who had a synagogue at Jerusalem, and excited the people against Stephen (Acts 6:9).

CYRUS. The founder of the Persian empire (see Dan. 6:28; 10:1, 13; 2 Chron. 36:22 f.), was, according to the common legend, the son of Mandane, the daughter of Astyages, the last king of Media, and Cambyses, a Persian of the royal family of the Achaemenidae. An inspired prophet (Isa. 44:28) recognized in him "a shepherd" of the Lord, an "anointed" king (Isa. 45:1). The edict of Cyrus for the rebuilding of the Temple (2 Chron. 36:22 f.; Ezra 1:1-4; 3:7; 4:3; 5:13, 17; 6:3) was in fact the beginning of Judaism; and the great changes by which the nation was transformed into a church are clearly marked.

DAGON—*corn god* (?). Apparently the masculine (1 Sam. 5:3 f.) correlative of Atargatis, was the national god of the Philistines. The most famous temples of Dagon were at Gaza (Judg. 16:21-30)

and Ashdod (1 Sam. 5:5 f.; 1 Chron. 10:10). The latter temple was destroyed by Jonathan in the Macabaean wars. Traces of the worship of Dagon likewise appear in the names Caphar-Dagon (near Jamnia), and Beth-Dagon in Judah (Josh. 15:41) and Asher (Josh. 19:27). Dagon was represented with the face and hands of a man and the tail of a fish (1 Sam. 5:5). The fish-like form was a natural emblem of fruitfulness, and as such was likely to be adopted by seafaring tribes in the representation of their gods.

DALMANUTHA. A town on the west side of the Sea of Galilee, near Magdala (Matt. 15:39 and Mark 8:10).

DALMATIA. A mountainous district on the eastern coast of the Adriatic Sea. Paul sent Titus there (2 Tim. 4:10), and he himself had preached the gospel in its immediate neighborhood (Rom. 15:19).

DAMARIS—*heifer* (?). An Athenian woman converted to Christianity by Paul's preaching (Acts 17:34). Chrysostom and others held her to have been the wife of Dionysius the Areopagite.

DAMASCUS. One of the most ancient and most important of the cities of Syria. It is situated in a plain of vast size and of extreme fertility, which lies east of the great chain of Anti-Libanus, on the edge of the desert. It is supposed to have been founded by Uz, the son of Aram; and is at least known to have existed in the time of Abraham (Gen. 15:2). Its sovereign, Hadad, was conquered by David, king of Israel. In the reign of Ahaz it was taken by Tiglath-Pileser, who slew its last king, Rezin, and added its provinces to the Assyrian empire. It was taken and plundered, also, by Sennacherib, Nebuchadnezzar, the generals of Alexander the Great, Judas Maccabaeus, and at length by the Romans in the war conducted by Pompey against Tigranes, in the year before Christ 65. At the time of the Gospel history and of the Apostle Paul, it formed a part of the kingdom of Aretas (2 Cor. 11:32), an Arabian prince, who held his kingdom under the Romans. Paul was on his way to Damascus when his conversion took place (Acts 9:3 ff.). The point of the walls at which he was let down by a basket (Acts 9:25; 2 Cor. 11:33) is still shown.

DAN—*judge.* 1. The fifth son of Jacob, and the first of Bilhah, Rachel's maid (Gen. 30:6). The origin of the name is given in the exclamation of Rachel—"God hath judged me . . . and given me a son; therefore she called his name Dan." The records of Dan are unusually meagre. Only one son is attributed to him (Gen. 46:23); but when the people were numbered in the wilderness of Sinai, his tribe was, with the exception of Judah, the most numerous of all, containing sixty-two thousand seven hundred men able to serve. 2. The well-known city, so familiar as the most northern landmark of Palestine, in the common expression "from Dan even to Beersheba" (*e.g.,* 2 Sam. 3:10; 1 Kings 4:25). The name of the place was originally Laish or Leshem (Josh. 19:47).

DANCE. The dance is spoken of in Holy Scripture universally as symbolical of some rejoicing, and is often coupled for the sake of contrast with mourning, as in Eccles. 3:4 (*cf.* Ps. 30:11; Matt. 11:17). In the earlier period it is found combined with some song or refrain (Ex. 15:20; 32:18 f.; 1 Sam. 21:11); and with the tambourine (A.V. "timbrel"), more especially in those impulsive outbursts of popular feeling which cannot find sufficient vent in voice or in gesture singly. Dancing formed a part of the religious ceremonies of the Egyptians, and was also common in private entertainments. The "feast unto the Lord," which Moses proposed to Pharaoh to hold, was really a dance. Women, however, among the Hebrews, made the dance their especial means of expressing their feelings, and so welcomed their husbands or friends on their return from battle. From the mention of "damsels", "timbrels", and "dances" (Ps. 68:25; 149:3; 150:4), as elements of re-

ligious worship, it may perhaps be inferred that David's feelings led him to incorporate in its rites that popular mode of festive celebration. In the earlier period of the Judges the dances of the virgins in Shiloh (Judg. 21:19-23) were certainly part of a religious festivity. Dancing also had its place among merely festive amusements, apart from any religious character (Jer. 31:4, 13; Lam. 5:15; Mark 6:22; Luke 15:25).

DANCE. By this word is rendered in the A.V. the Hebrew term *machol,* a musical instrument of percussion, supposed to have been used by the Hebrews at an early period of their history. It is generally believed to have been made of metal, open like a ring; it had many small bells attached to its border, and was played at weddings and merry-makings by women, who accompanied it with the voice.

DANIEL—*God is my judge.* 1. The second son of David by Abigail the Carmelitess (1 Chron. 3:1). In 2 Sam. 3:3 he is called Chileab. 2. The fourth of "the greater prophets." Nothing is known of his parentage or family. He appears, however, to have been of royal or noble descent (Dan. 1:3), and to have possessed much personal endowments (Dan. 1:4). He was taken to Babylon in "the third year of Jehoiakim," and trained for the king's service with his three companions. Like Joseph in earlier times, he gained the favor of his guardians and was divinely supported in his resolve to abstain from the "king's meat" for fear of defilement (Dan. 1:8-16). At the close of his three years' discipline, Daniel had an opportunity of exercising his peculiar gift (Dan. 1:5, 17 f.) of interpreting dreams, on the occasion of Nebuchadnezzar's decree against the Magi (Dan. 2:14 ff.). In consequence of his success he was made "ruler of the whole province of Babylon," and "chief of the governors over all the wise men of Babylon" (2:48). He afterwards interpreted the second dream of Nebuchadnezzar (4:8-27), and the handwriting on the wall which disturbed the feast of Belshazzar (5:10-28), though he no longer held his official position among the Magi (Dan. 5:7 f., 12), and probably lived at Susa (8:2). At the accession of Darius he was made first of the "three presidents" of the empire (Dan. 6:2), and was delivered from the lions' den, into which he had been cast for his faithfulness to the rites of his faith (6:10-23). At the accession of Cyrus he still retained his prosperity (6:28; *cf.* 1:21), though he does not appear to have remained at Babylon, and in "the third year of Cyrus" he saw his last recorded vision on the banks of the Tigris (10:1, 4). 3. A descendant of Ithamar, who returned with Ezra (Ezra 8:2). 4. A priest who sealed the covenant drawn up by Nehemiah (Neh. 10:6). He is perhaps the same as No. 3.

DANIEL, THE BOOK OF. The earliest example of apocalyptic literature, and in a great degree the model according to which all later apocalypses were constructed. In this aspect it stands at the head of a series of writings in which the deepest thoughts of the Jewish people found expression after the close of the prophetic era. The language of the book no less than its general form, belongs to an era of transition. Like the book of Ezra, Daniel is composed partly in the vernacular Aramaic (Chaldee), and partly in the sacred Hebrew. The book exercised a great influence upon the Christian church. Apart from the general type of apocalyptic composition which the Apostolic writers derived from Daniel (2 Thess. 2; Rev. *passim: cf.* Matt. 26:64; Mark 13:24 ff.), the New Testament incidentally acknowledges each of the characteristic elements of the book, its miracles (Heb. 11:33 f.), its predictions (Matt. 24:15), and its doctrine of angels (Luke 1:19, 26).

DANIEL, APOCRYPHAL ADDITIONS TO. The Greek translations of Daniel, like that of Esther, contain several pieces which are not found in the original text. The most important of these additions are contained in the Apocrypha of the English Bible under the titles of *The Song of the Three Holy Children, The History of Susannah,* and *The History of . . . Bel and the Dragon.*

The first of these pieces is incorporated into the narrative of Daniel. *The History of Susannah* (or *The Judgment of Daniel*) is generally found at the beginning of the book, though it also occurs after the 12th chapter. *The History of Bel and the Dragon* is placed at the end of the book. The character of these additions indicates the hand of an Alexandrine writer; and it is not unlikely that the translator of Daniel wrought up traditions which were already current, and, appended them to his work.

DARIC (A.V. "dram"; Ezra 2:69; 8:27; Neh. 7: 70 ff.; 1 Chron. 29:7). A gold coin current in Palestine in the period after the return from Babylon.

DARIUS. The name of several kings of Media and Persia. Three are mentioned in the Old Testament. 1. Darius the Mede (Dan. 11:1; 6:1), "the son of Ahasuerus of the seed of the Medes" (9:1), who succeeded to the Babylonian kingdom on the death of Belshazzar, being then sixty-two years old (Dan. 5:31, 9:1). Only one year of his reign is mentioned (Dan. 9:1; 11:1). 2. Darius, the son of Hystaspes, the founder of the Perso-Arian dynasty. Upon the usurpation of the Magian Smerdis, he conspired with six other Persian chiefs to overthrow the imposter, and on the success of the plot was placed upon the throne. With regard to the Jews Darius Hystaspes pursued the same policy as Cyrus, and restored them the privileges which they had lost (Ezra 5:1; 6:1). 3. Darius the Persian (Neh. 12:22) may be identified with Darius II. Nothus (Ochus), king of Persia.

DARKNESS. Spoken of as encompassing the actual presence of God, as that out of which he speaks, the envelope, as it were, of divine glory (Ex. 20:21; 1 Kings 8:12). The darkness "over all the land" (Matt. 27:45) attending the crucifixion has been attributed to an eclipse.

DAVID. The son of Jesse. His mother's name is unknown. His father was of a great age when David was still young (1 Sam. 17:12). His parents both lived till after his final rupture with Saul (1 Sam. 22:3). Through them David inherited several points which he never lost: his connection with Moab through his great-grandmother Ruth, his birthplace, Bethlehem, his general connection with the tribe of Judah, and his relations to Zeruiah and Abigail. Though called in 1 Chron. 2:16 sisters of David, they are not expressly called the daughters of Jesse; and Abigail, in 2 Sam. 17:25, is called the daughter of Nahash. There was a practice once a year at Bethlehem of holding a sacrificial feast, at which Jesse, as the chief proprietor of the place would preside (1 Sam. 20:6,) with the elders of the town. At this or such-like feast suddenly appeared the great prophet Samuel, driving a heifer before him, and having in his hand a horn of oil with which, in obedience to divine command, he anointed David (1 Sam. 16:1 ff.). When the bodyguard of Saul were discussing with their masters where the best minstrel could be found to chase away his madness by music, one of the young men in the guard suggested David. Saul instantly sent for him, and in the successful effort of David's harp we have the first glimpse into that genius for music and poetry which was afterward consecrated in the Psalms. One incident alone of his solitary shepherd life has come down to us—his conflict with the lion and the bear in defence of his father's flocks (1 Sam. 17:34 f.). He was already known to Saul's guards for his martial exploits, probably against the Philistines (1 Sam. 16:18), and when he suddenly appeared in the camp, his elder brother immediately guessed that he had left the sheep in his ardor to see the battle (1 Sam. 17:28). A Philistine of gigantic stature, and clothed in complete armor, insulted the comparatively defenceless Israelites, amongst whom the king alone appears well armed (17:38; cf. 13:20). David's victory over the gigantic Philistine is rendered more conspicuous by his own diminutive stature, and by the simple weapons with which it was accomplished—not the armor

of Saul, but the shepherd's sling. The victory was a turning-point of his career. Saul took him finally to his court. Jonathan, Saul's son, was inspired by the romantic friendship which bound up the two youths together to the end of their lives. At the court of Saul (1 Sam. 18:2–19:18) his office is not exactly defined. But it would seem that, having been first armor-bearer (16:21; 18: 2), then made captain over a thousand—the sub-division of a tribe (18:13)—he finally, on his marriage with Michal, the king's second daughter, was raised to the office of captain of the king's bodyguard, second only, if not equal, to Abner, the captain of the host, and Jonathan, the heir apparent. He also performed from time to time the office of minstrel. But the successive snares laid by Saul to entrap him, and the open violence into which the king's madness twice broke out, at last convinced him that his life was no longer safe. He had two faithful allies, however, in the court—the son of Saul, his friend Jonathan, and the daughter of Saul, his wife Michael. Warned by the one, and assisted by the other, he escaped by night and was from thenceforward a fugitive. Jonathan he never saw again except by stealth. Michal was given in marriage to another (Phaltiel), and he saw her no more till long after her father's death. He first fled to Naioth (or the pastures) of Ramah to Samuel. Next he visited Nob, the seat of the tabernacle, partly to obtain a final interview with the high priest (1 Sam. 22:9, 15), partly to obtain food and weapons. On the pretext of a secret mission from Saul he gained an answer from the oracle, some of the consecrated loaves and the consecrated sword of Goliath. His stay at the court of Achish was short. He only escaped by feigning madness (1 Sam. 21:13). His first retreat was the cave of Adullam. At the warning of Gad he fled to the forest of Hareth, and then again fell in with the Philistines, and again (23:4) relieved Keilah, in which he took up his abode. By this time 400 who had joined him at Adullam (22:2) had swelled to 600 (23:13). The situation of David was now changed by the appearance of Saul himself on the scene. Apparently the danger was too great for the little army to keep together. They escaped from Keilah and dispersed. While he was in the wilderness of Maon occurred David's adventure with Nabal, instructive as showing his mode of carrying on the free-booter's life, and his marriage with Abigail. His marriage with Ahinoam from Jezreel, also in the same neighborhood (Josh. 15:56), seems to have taken place a short time before (1 Sam. 25:43; 27:3; 2 Sam. 3:2). After the manner of eastern potentates, Achish gave him, for his support, a city—Ziklag on the frontier of Philistia (1 Sam. 27:6). There we meet with the first note of time in David's life. He was settled there for a year and four months (27:7). The reception of the tidings of the death of Saul and Jonathan, the solemn mourning, the vent of his indignation against the bearer of the message, the pathetic lamentation that followed, close the second period of David's life (2 Sam. 1:1-27). David reigned as king of Judah at Hebron seven and one-half years (2 Sam. 2:1; 5:5). Here David was first formally anointed king (2 Sam. 2:4). To Judah his dominion was nominally confined. Gradually his power increased. He reigned over all Israel 33 years (2 Sam. 5:5 to 1 Kings 2:11). The foundation of Jerusalem was of central importance. One fastness alone in the center of the land had hitherto defied the arms of Israel. By one sudden assault Jebus was taken. The reward bestowed on the successful scaler of the precipice was the highest place in the army. Joab henceforward became captain of the host (1 Chron. 11:6). The royal residence was instantly fixed there—fortifications were added by the king and by Joab, and it was known by the special name of the "city of David" (1 Chron. 11:7; 2 Sam. 5:9). The erection of the new capitol at Jerusalem introduced a new era in David's life and in the history of the monarchy. The internal organization now established lasted till the final overthrow of the monarchy. Outside the walls of Jerusalem, Araunah or Ornan, a wealthy Jebusite possessed a threshing-floor; there he and his sons

were engaged in threshing the corn gathered in from the harvest (1 Chron. 21:20). At this spot an awful vision appeared, such as is described in the later days of Jerusalem, of the Angel of the Lord stretching out a drawn sword between earth and sky over the devoted city. The scene of such an apparition at such a moment was at once marked out for a sanctuary. David demanded, and Araunah willingly granted, the site; the altar was erected on the rock of the threshing-floor; the place was called by the name of "Moriah" (2 Chron. 3:1); and for the first time a holy place, sanctified by a vision of the divine presence, was recognized in Jerusalem. It was this spot which afterward became the altar of the Temple, and therefore the center of the national worship, with but slight interruption, for more than 1,000 years. A formidable conspiracy to interrupt the succession broke out in the last days of David's reign, which detached from his person two of his court, who from personal offence or adherence to the ancient family had been alienated from him—Joab and Abiathar. But Zadok, Nathan, Benaiah, Shimei, and Rei remaining firm, the plot was stifled, and Solomon's inauguration took place under his father's auspices (1 Kings 1:1-53). By this time David's infirmities had grown upon him. He died, according to Josephus, at the age of 70, and was "buried in the city of David" (1 Kings 2:10).

DAY. The commencement of the civil day the Babylonians reckoned from sunrise to sunrise; the Romans from midnight to midnight; the Athenians and others from sunset to sunset. The Hebrews adopted the latter reckoning (Lev. 23: 32; Gen. 1:5). The Jews adopted minute specifications of the parts of the natural day. They were content to divide it into "morning, evening and noonday" (Ps. 55:17); but when they wished for greater accuracy, they pointed to six unequal parts, each of which was again sub-divided. These are held to have been: 1. "The dawn." 2. "Sunrise." 3. "Heat of the day," about 9 o'clock. 4. "The two noons" (Gen. 43:16; Deut. 28:29). 5. "The cool (lit. *wind*) of the day," before sunset (Gen. 3:8). 6. "Evening." In the New Testament we have allusions to four watches, a division borrowed from the Greeks and Romans. These were, 1. from twilight till 9 o'clock (Mark 11:11; John 20:19); 2. midnight, from 9 till 12 o'clock (Mark 13:35); 3. till 3 in the morning (Mark 13:35); 4. till daybreak (John 18:28).

DEACON. The office described by this title appears in the New Testament as the correlative of Bishop. The two are mentioned together in Phil. 1:1; 1 Tim. 3:2, 8.

DEACONESS. The word is found in Rom. 16:1 (A.V. "servant"), and has led to the conclusion that there existed in the Apostolic age an order of women bearing that title. On this hypothesis it has been inferred that the women mentioned in Rom. 16:6, 12, belonged to such an order. The rules given as to the conduct of women in 1 Tim. 3:11; Tit. 2:3, have in like manner been referred to them, and they have been identified even with the "widows" of 1 Tim. 5:3-10.

DEAD SEA. This name occurs nowhere in the Bible, and appears not to have existed until the second century after Christ. In the Old Testament the lake is called "the Salt Sea," and "the Sea of the Plain." (See Sea, the Salt.)

DEBORAH—*bee.* 1. The nurse of Rebekah (Gen. 35:8). Deborah accompanied Rebekah from the house of Bethuel (Gen. 24:59), and is only mentioned by name on the occasion of her burial, under the oak tree of Bethel, which was called in her honor Allon-Bachuth. 2. A prophetess who judged Israel (Judg. 4-5). She lived under the palm tree of Deborah, between Ramah and Bethel in Mount Ephraim (Judg. 4:5). Lapidoth was probably her husband, and not Barak. She was not so much a judge as one gifted with prophetic command. Under her direction Barak encamped on the broad summit of Tabor. Deborah's prophecy was fulfilled, and the enemy's

general perished among the "oaks of the wanderers (Zaanaim)," in the tent of the Kenite's wife (Judg. 4:21).

DECAPOLIS—*ten cities.* This name occurs only three times in the Scriptures (Matt. 4:25; Mark 5:20, 7:31). A group of ten independent cities, but all subject to the Roman Senate. All but one were east of the Jordan.

DEDICATION, FEAST OF THE. The festival instituted to commemorate the purging of the Temple and the rebuilding of the altar after Judas Maccabaeus had driven out the Syrians, 164 B.C. It is named only once in the Canonical Scriptures, John 10:22.

DEGREES, SONGS OF. A title given to fifteen Psalms (120 to 134 inclusive). Four of them are attributed to David, one is ascribed to the pen of Solomon, and the other ten give no indication of their author.

DELILAH—*coquette.* A woman who dwelt in the valley of Sorek, beloved by Samson (Judg. 16:4-18). There seems to be little doubt that she was a Philistine courtesan.

DELUGE. (See Noah.)

DEMAS—*governor of the people.* Most probably a contraction from Demetrius, or perhaps from Demarchus, a companion of Paul (Philem. 24; Col. 4:14) during his imprisonment at Rome. At a later period (2 Tim. 4:10) we find him mentioned as having deserted the apostle through love of this present world, and gone to Thessalonica.

DEMETRIUS—*belonging to Demeter.* 1. A maker of silver shrines of Diana at Ephesus (Acts 19:24). These were small models of the great temple of the Ephesian Diana, with her statue, which it was customary to carry on journeys, and place on houses as charms. 2. A Christian disciple commended in 3 John 12.

DEMON. In the Gospels generally, in James 2:19, and in Rev. 16:14, the demons are spoken of as spiritual beings at enmity with God, and having power to afflict man, not only with diseases, but, as is marked by the frequent epithet "unclean," with spiritual pollution also. They recognize the Lord as the Son of God (Matt. 8:29: Luke 4:41), and acknowledge the power of his name, used in exorcism, in the place of the name of Jehovah, by his appointed messengers (Acts 19:15), and look forward in terror to the judgment to come (Matt. 8:29).

DEMONIACS. This word is frequently used in the New Testament, and applied to persons suffering under the possession of a demon or evil spirit, such possession generally showing itself visibly in bodily disease or mental derangement.

DENARIUS. In A.V. "penny" (Matt. 18:28; 20:2, 9, 13; 22:19; Mark 6:37; 12:15; 14:5; Luke 7:41; 10:35; 20:24; John 6:7; 12:5; Rev. 6:6), a Roman silver coin, in the time of Jesus and the apostles.

DEPUTY. The uniform rendering in the A.V. of the Greek word which signifies "proconsul" (Acts 13:7, 8, 12; 19:38).

DERBE. A city of Lycaonia, incorporated by the Romans in the province of Galatia. It was visited by Paul on his first and second missionary journey (Acts 14:20 f.; 16:1; 20:4).

DESERT. The Hebrews, by *midbar,* "a desert," meant an uncultivated place, particularly if mountainous. Some deserts were entirely dry and barren, others were beautiful, and had pastures. Scripture speaks of the beauty of the desert (Ps. 65:12).

DEUTERONOMY—*repetition of the law.* The fifth book of the Old Testament which consists chiefly of three discourses delivered by Moses

shortly before his death. Subjoined to these discourses are the Song of Moses, the Blessing of Moses, and the story of his death. (See Pentateuch.)

DEVIL. A fallen angel or infernal spirit. Satan is, by way of eminence, called *the devil* and the *god of this world* from his power and influence (John 12:31; 2 Cor. 4:4). He has various titles given him in Scripture, expressive of his character: Satan (Job 2:6); Beelzebub (Matt. 12:24); Belial (2 Cor. 6:15); Lucifer (Isa. 14:12); Dragon (Rev. 12:7); Adversary (1 Pet. 5:8); Prince of Darkness (Eph. 6:12); Apollyon, or Destroyer (Rev. 9:11); Angel of the bottomless pit. He is represented as a sinner from the beginning (1 John 3:8); a liar (John 8:44); a deceiver (Rev. 20:10); an accuser (Rev. 12:10); and a murderer (John 8:44).

DEW. This in the summer is so copious in Palestine that it supplies to some extent the absence of rain, and becomes important to the agriculturist. Dew is used in Scripture to symbolize such as God's word (Deut. 32:2) and blessings (Gen. 27:28).

DIADEM—*to bind around.* A fillet of silk, two inches broad, bound round the head and tied behind, the invention of which is attributed to Liber. Its color was generally white; sometimes, however, it was of blue, like that of Darius; and it was sown with pearls or other gems (Zech. 9:16), and enriched with gold (Rev. 9:7). It was peculiarly the mark of Oriental sovereigns.

DIAL. The word *maaloth* is the same as that rendered "steps" in A.V. (Ex. 20:26; 1 Kings 10:19), and "degrees" in A.V. (2 Kings 20:9 ff.; Isa. 38:8), where, to give a consistent rendering, we should read "degrees" rather than the "dial" of Ahaz.

DIAMOND (Hebrew *yahalom*). A precious stone, the third in the second row on the breastplate of the high priest (Ex. 28:18; 39:11), and mentioned by Ezekiel (28:13) among the precious stones of the king of Tyre. Some suppose *yahalom* to be the onyx.

DIANA. This Latin word, properly denoting a Roman divinity, is the representative of the Greek *Artemis,* the tutelary goddess of the Ephesians, who plays so important a part in the narrative of Acts 19. The Ephesian Diana was, however, regarded as invested with very different attributes, and is rather to be identified with Astarte and other female divinities of the East. This idol was regarded as an object of peculiar sanctity, and was believed to have fallen down from heaven (Acts 19:35).

DIBON. A city of Moab, located east of the Dead Sea. It was taken by the Amorites before the coming of the Israelites (Num. 21:26, 30). It was assigned to the tribe of Reuben (Josh. 13:9, 17), but is mentioned in connection with Gad (Num. 32:3, 34; 33:45).

DIDYMUS—*the twin.* A surname of the Apostle Thomas (John 11:16; 20:24; 21:2). (See Thomas.)

DIMON, THE WATERS OF. Some streams on the east of the Dead Sea, in the land of Moab, against which Isaiah uttered denunciations (Isa. 15:9). Some believe Dimon to be a mistake for Dibon.

DINAH. The daughter of Jacob by Leah (Gen. 30:21). She was violated by Shechem the son of Hamor, the chieftain of the territory in which her father had settled (Gen. 34). Shechem proposed to make the usual reparation. But the offence was committed by an alien against the favored people of God; he had "wrought folly in Israel." The sons of Jacob, bent upon revenge, availed themselves of the eagerness which Shechem showed to effect their purpose; they demanded, as a condition of the proposed union, the circumcision of the Shechemites. They there-

fore assented; and on the third day, when the pain and fever resulting from the operation were at the highest, Simeon and Levi, full brothers to Dinah, attacked them unexpectedly, slew all the males and plundered their city.

DIONYSIUS THE AREOPAGITE. An eminent Athenian, converted to Christianity by the preaching of Paul (Acts 17:34). He is said to have been first bishop of Athens.

DISH. In ancient Egypt, and also in Judaea, guests at the table handled their food with the fingers. To pick out a delicate morsel and hand it to a friend is esteemed a compliment, and to refuse such an offering is contrary to good manners. Judas dipping his hand in the same dish with Jesus was showing especial friendliness and intimacy.

DISPERSION, THE JEWS OF THE. Or simply The Dispersion, was the general title applied to those Jews who remained settled in foreign countries after the return from the Babylonian exile, and during the period of the second temple. The Dispersion, as a distinct element influencing the entire character of the Jews, dates from the Babylonian exile.

DIVES. A name often applied to the wealthy man in the parable of Lazarus (Luke 16:19-31). The name does not appear in the text, but comes from *dives,* the Latin word for *rich.*

DIVINATION. This has been universal in all ages and all nations alike, civilized and savage. Numerous forms of divination are mentioned, such as divination by rods (Hos. 4:12); divination by arrows (Ezek. 21:21); divination by cups (Gen. 44:5); consultation of Teraphim (Zech. 10:2; Ezek. 21:21; 1 Sam. 15:23); divination by the liver (Ezek. 21:21); divination by dreams (Deut. 13:2 f.; Judg. 7:13; Jer. 23:32); consultation of oracles (Isa. 44:7; 41:21-24). Moses forbade every species of divination.

DIVORCE. A right granted to the husband alone. The law regulating this subject is found in Deut. 24:1-4, and the cases in which the right of a husband to divorce his wife was lost are stated in Deut. 22:19, 29. The ground of divorce is a point on which the Jewish doctors of the period of the New Testament widely differed. The Pharisees wished perhaps to embroil Jesus with the rival schools by their question (Matt. 19:3); by his answer to which, as well as by his previous maxim (5:31), he declared that but for their hardened state of heart such questions would have no place.

DOEG. An Edomite, chief of Saul's herdsmen. He was at Nob when Ahimelech gave David the sword of Goliath, and not only gave information to Saul, but when others declined the office, himself executed the king's order to destroy the priests of Nob, with their families, to the number of 85 persons, together with all their property (1 Sam. 21:7; 22:9, 18, 22).

DOG. An animal frequently mentioned in Scripture. It was used by the Hebrews as a watch for their houses (Isa. 56:10), and for guarding their flocks (Job 30:1). Then also, as now, troops of hungry and semi-wild dogs used to wander about the fields and streets of the cities, devouring dead bodies and other offal (1 Kings 14:11; 16:4; 21:19, 23; 22:38; 2 Kings 9:10, 36; Jer. 15:3; Ps. 59:6, 14), and thus became such objects of dislike that fierce and cruel enemies are poetically styled dogs (Ps. 22:16, 20). Moreover, the dog being an unclean animal (Isa. 66:3), the terms *dog, dead dog, dog's head,* were used as terms of reproach or of humility, in speaking of one's self (1 Sam. 24:14; 2 Sam. 3:8; 9:8; 16:9; 2 Kings 8:13).

DOOR. Texts written on (Deut. 11:20).

DOTHAN. A place first mentioned (Gen. 37:17) in connection with the history of Joseph, and

apparently as in the neighborhood of Shechem. It next appears as the residence of Elisha (2 Kings 6:13).

DOVE (Hebrew *yonah*). The first mention of this bird occurs in Gen. 8. The dove's rapidity of flight is alluded to in Ps. 55:6; the beauty of its plumage in Ps. 68:13; its dwelling in the rocks and valleys in Jer. 48:28 and Ezek. 7:16; its mournful voice in Isa. 38:14; 59:11; Nah. 2:7; its harmlessness in Matt. 10:16; its simplicity in Hos. 7:11; and its amativeness in Cant. 1:15; 2:14.

DOVE'S DUNG. Various explanations have been given of the passage in 2 Kings 6:25.

DRACHMA (Luke 15:8 f.). A Greek silver coin, varying in weight on account of the use of different talents. In Luke (A.V. "piece of silver") denarii seem to be intended.

DRAGON. The translators of the A.V., apparently following the Vulgate, have rendered by the same word "dragon" the two Hebrew words *tan* and *tannin* which appear to be quite distinct in meaning. 1. The former is used, always in the plural, in Job 30:29; Isa. 34:13; 43:20; in Isa. 13:22; in Jer. 10:22; 49:33; in Ps. 44:19; and in Jer. 9:11; 16:6; 51:37; Mic. 1:8. 2. The word *tannin* seems to refer to any great monster, whether of the land or the sea, being indeed more usually applied to some kind of serpent or reptile. In the New Testament it is only found in the Apocalypse (Rev. 12:3 ff.), as applied metaphorically to "the old serpent, called the Devil, and Satan," the description of the "dragon."

DREAMS. The Scripture declares that the influence of the Spirit of God upon the soul extends to its sleeping as well as its waking thoughts. But, in accordance with the principle enunciated by Paul in 1 Cor. 14:15, dreams, in which the understanding is asleep, are placed below the visions of prophecy, in which the understanding plays its part. It is true that the Book of Job, standing as it does on the basis of "natural religion," dwells on dreams and "visions in deep sleep" as the chosen method of God's revelation of himself to man (see Job 4:13; 7:14; 33:15). But in Num. 12:6; Deut. 13:1 ff.; Jer. 27:9; Joel 2:28, dreamers of dreams, whether true or false, are placed below "prophets," and even below "diviners"; and similarly in the climax of 1 Sam. 28:6, we read that "Jehovah answered Saul not, neither by dreams, nor by Urim, nor by prophets."

DRESS. The skins of animals supplied a durable material (Gen. 3:21), which was adapted to a rude state of society, and is stated to have been used by various ancient nations. Skins were not wholly disused at later periods: the "mantle" worn by Elijah appears to have been the skin of a sheep or some other animal, with the wool left on. It was characteristic of a prophet's office from its mean appearance (Zech. 13:4; *cf.* Matt. 7:15). The art of weaving hair was known to the Hebrews at an early period (Ex: 26:7; 35:6); the sackcloth used by mourners was of this material. John the Baptist's robe was of camel's hair (Matt. 3:4). Wool, we may presume, was introduced at a very early period, the flocks of the pastoral families being kept partly for their wool (Gen. 38:12); it was at all times largely employed, particularly for the outer garments (Lev. 13:47; Deut. 22:11). It is probable that the acquaintance of the Hebrews with linen, and perhaps cotton, dates from the period of the sojourn in Egypt, when they were instructed in the manufacture (1 Chron. 4:21).

DRINK, STRONG. The Hebrew term *shekar*, in its etymological sense, applies to any beverage that had intoxicating qualities. We may infer from Cant. 8:2 that the Hebrews were in the habit of expressing the juice of other fruits besides the grape for the purpose of making wine; the pomegranate, which is there noticed, was probably one out of many fruits so used.

DRUSILLA. Daughter of Herod Agrippa I and Cypos. She was at first betrothed to Antiochus Epiphanes, prince of Commagene, but was married to Azizus, king of Emesa. Soon after, Felix, procurator of Judaea, brought about her seduction by means of the Cyprian Sorcerer Simon, and took her as his wife. In Acts 24:24 we find her in company with Felix at Caesarea.

DULCIMER. A musical instrument mentioned in Dan. 3:5, 15, probably the bagpipe.

DUNG. The uses of dung were twofold: as manure and as fuel. The manure consisted either of straw steeped in liquid manure (Isa. 25:10), or the sweepings (Isa. 5:25) of the streets and roads, which were carefully removed from about the houses and collected in heaps outside the walls of the towns at fixed spots (hence the dunggate at Jerusalem, Neh. 2:13), and thence removed in due course to the fields.

DURA. The plain where Nebuchadnezzar set up the golden image (Dan. 3:1), has been sometimes identified with a tract a little below *Tekrit*, on the left bank of the Tigris, where the name *Dur* is still found.

EAGLE (Hebrew *nesher*). The Hebrew word, which occurs frequently in the Old Testament, may denote a particular species of the *Falconidae*, as in Lev. 11:13; Deut. 14:12, where the *nesher* is distinguished from the *ossifrage, osprey* and other raptorial birds; but the term is used also to express the griffon vulture (*Vultur fulvus*) in two or three passages.

EARNEST (2 Cor. 1:22; 5:5; Eph. 1:14). The Hebrew word was used generally for *pledge* (Gen. 38:17), and in its cognate forms for *surety* (Prov. 17:18), and *hostage* (2 Kings 14:14).

EARRINGS. The material of which earrings were made was generally gold (Ex. 32:2) and their form circular. They were worn by women and by youth of both sexes (Gen. 35:4).

EARTHQUAKE. Earthquakes, more or less violent, are of frequent occurrence in Palestine. The recorded instances, however, are but few; the most remarkable occurred in the reign of Uzziah (Amos 1:1; Zech. 14:5). From Zech. 14:4 we are led to infer that a great convulsion took place at this time in the Mount of Olives, the mountain being split so as to leave a valley between its summits. An earthquake occurred at the time of the crucifixion (Matt. 27:51-54).

EASTER. The occurrence of this word in the A.V. of Acts 12:4 is chiefly noticeable as an example of the want of consistency in the translators. In the earlier English versions Easter had been frequently used as the translation of *pascha*.

EBAL, MOUNT. A mount in the promised land, on which, according to the command of Moses, the Israelites were, after their entrance on the promised land, to "put" the curse which should fall upon them if they disobeyed the commandments of Jehovah. The blessing consequent on obedience was to be similarly localized on Mount Gerizim (Deut. 11:26-29).

EBED-MELECH—*servant of the king* or *servant of Melech.* An Ethiopian eunuch in the service of King Zedekiah, through whose interference Jeremiah was released from prison (Jer. 38:7 ff.; 39:15 ff.).

EBENEZER—*stone of help.* A stone set up by Samuel after a signal defeat of the Philistines, as a memorial of the "help" received on the occasion from Jehovah (1 Sam. 7:12).

EBONY (Hebrew *hobnim*). Occurs only in Ezek. 27:15, as one of the valuable commodities imported into Tyre by the men of Dedan.

ECBATANA (Hebrew *Achmetha*). It is doubtful whether the name of this place is really contained in the Hebrew Scriptures. Many of the commentators understand the expression, in Ezra 6:2, differently, and translate it "in a coffer." Two cities of the name of Ecbatana seem to have existed in ancient times: one the capital of Northern Media; the other the metropolis of the larger and more important province known as Media Magne.

ECCLESIASTES. The title of this book is in Hebrew *Koheleth*, a feminine noun signifying *one who speaks publicly in an assembly* (Greek Ecclesia), and hence rendered in the Septuagint by *Ecclesiastes,* which is adopted in the English version. "The words of the preacher (Hebrew *Koheleth*) the son of David, king of Jerusalem" (1:1).

EDAR, TOWER OF. A place named only in Gen. 35:21 (more accurately Eder, *a flock*). According to Jerome it was 1,000 paces from Bethlehem.

EDEN—*delight.* 1. The first residence of man, called in the Septuagint *Paradise.* The latter is a word of Persian origin, and describes an extensive tract of pleasure land, and the use of it suggests a wider view of man's first abode than a *garden* (Gen. 2:8, 15; Ezek. 28:13). 2. A kingdom on the Euphrates (2 Kings 19:12; Isa. 37:12). 3. A Levite during the time of Hezekiah (2 Chron. 29:12; 31:15).

EDOM—*red.* Also Idumea, or Idumaea. The name Edom was given to Esau, the firstborn son of Isaac, and twin brother of Jacob, when he sold his birthright to the latter for a meal of lentil pottage. The peculiar color of the pottage gave rise to the name *Edom,* which signifies "red" (Gen. 25:29-34). The country which the Lord subsequently gave to Esau was hence called the "field of Edom" (Gen. 32:3), or "land of Edom" (Gen. 36:16; Num. 33:37), and his descendants were called the Edomites.

EGLAH—*heifer.* One of David's wives during his reign in Hebron, and the mother of his son Ithream (2 Sam. 3:5; 1 Chron. 3:3). According to the ancient Hebrew tradition she was Michal.

EGLON—*circle.* 1. A king of the Moabites (Judg. 3:12 ff.) who, aided by the Ammonites and the Amalekites, crossed the Jordan and took "the city of palm trees." 2. A town in the Shephelah whose king, Debir, joined an alliance against Joshua (Josh. 10:1-37; 12:12).

EGYPT. A country occupying the northeastern angle of Africa. Its limits appear always to have been very nearly the same. In Ezekiel (29:10; 30:6) the whole country is spoken of as extending from Migdol to Syene, which indicates the same limits to the east and the south as at present. The common name of Egypt in the Bible is "Mizraim," or more fully, "the land of Mizraim." In form Mizraim is a dual, and accordingly it is generally joined with a plural verb. When, therefore, in Gen. 10:6, Mizraim is mentioned as a son of Ham, we must not conclude that anything more is meant than that Egypt was colonized by descendants of Ham. The dual number doubtless indicates the natural division of the country into an upper and a lower region. The singular, Mazor, also occurs, and some suppose that it indicates Lower Egypt, but there is no sure ground for this assertion. The Arabic name of Egypt, *Mizr,* signifies "red mud." Egypt is also called in the Bible "land of Ham" (Ps. 105:23, 27; *cf.* 78:51), a name most probably referring to Ham, the son of Noah; and "Rahab," the proud or insolent; both of these appear to be poetical appellations. The common ancient Egyptian name of the country is written in hieroglyphics KEM, which was perhaps pronounced Chem. This name signifies, alike in the ancient language and in Coptic, "black," and may be supposed to have been given to the land on account of the blackness of its alluvial soil.

EHUD—*strong.* 1. Ehud, the son of Bilham, and

great-grandson of Benjamin the Patriarch (1 Chron. 7:10; 8:6). 2. Ehud, son of Gera, of the tribe of Benjamin (Judg. 3:15), the second judge of the Israelites.

ELAH—*terebinth.* 1. The son and successor of Baasha, king of Israel (1 Kings 16:8-10); his reign lasted for little more than a year. He was killed, while drunk, by Zimri, in the house of his steward Arza, who was probably a confederate in the plot. 2. Father of Hoshea, the last king of Israel (2 Kings 15:30; 17:1).

ELAH, THE VALLEY OF—*valley of the terebinth.* A valley in (not "by," as the A.V. has it) which the Israelites were encamped against the Philistines when David killed Goliath (1 Sam. 17:2, 19). It is once more mentioned in the same connection (1 Sam. 21:9). It lay somewhere near Socoh of Judah and Azekah, and was nearer Ekron than any other Philistine town.

ELAM—*highland.* It seems to have been originally the name of a man, the son of Shem (Gen. 10:22; 1 Chron. 1:17). Commonly, however, it is used as the appellation of a country (Gen. 14:1, 9; Isa. 11:11; 21:2; Jer. 25:25; 49:34-39; Ezek. 32:24; Dan. 8:2). The Elam of Scriptures appears to be the province lying south of Assyria and east of Persia proper, to which Herodotus gives the name of Cissia, and which is termed Susis or Susiana by the geographers.

EL-BETHEL. The name which Jacob is said to have bestowed on the place at which God appeared to him when he was fleeing from Esau (Gen. 28:19).

ELDAD—*God hath loved.* He and Medad were two of the 70 elders to whom was communicated the prophetic power of Moses (Num. 11:16, 26). Although their names were upon the list which Moses had drawn up, they did not repair with the rest of their brethren to the tabernacle, but continued to prophesy in the camp. Moses, being requested by Joshua to forbid this, refused to do so, and expressed a wish that the gift of prophecy might be diffused throughout the people.

ELDER. The term *elder* or *old man,* as the Hebrew literally imports, was one of extensive use, as an official title, among the Hebrews and the surrounding nations. It had reference to various officers (Gen. 24:2; 50:7; 2 Sam. 12:17; Ezek. 27:9). As betokening a political office, it applied not only to the Hebrews, but also to the Egyptians (Gen. 50:7), the Moabites and Midianites (Num. 22:7). They were the representatives of the people, so much so that *elders* and *people* are occasionally used as equivalent terms (cf. Josh. 24:1 with 2, 19, 21; 1 Sam. 8:4 with 7, 10, 19). Their authority was undefined, and extended to all matters concerning the public weal.

ELEAZAR—*God has helped.* 1. The third son of Aaron, by Elisheba, the daughter of Amminadab. After the death of Nadab and Abihu, without children (Lev. 10:1; Num. 3:4), Eleasar was appointed chief over the principal Levites (Num. 3:32). With his brother Ithamar he ministered as a priest during their father's lifetime, and immediately before his death was invested on Mount Hor with the sacred garments, as the successor of Aaron in the office of high priest (Num. 20:28). One of his first duties was in conjunction with Moses to superintend the census of the people (Num. 26:3). After the conquest of Canaan by Joshua he took part in the distribution of the land (Josh. 14:1).

EL-ELOHE-ISRAEL.—*God, the God of Israel.* The name bestowed by Jacob on the altar which he erected facing the city of Shechem (Gen. 33:19 f.).

ELI. Descended from Aaron through Ithamar, the youngest of his two surviving sons (Lev. 10:1 f., 12; cf. 1 Kings 2:27 with 2 Sam. 8:17; 1 Chron. 24:3). As the history makes no mention of any high priest of the line of Ithamar before

Eli, he is generally supposed to have been the first of that line who held the office. From him, his sons having died before him, it appears to have passed to his grandson, Ahitub (1 Sam. 14:3), and it certainly remained in his family till Abiathar, the grandson of Ahitub, was "thrust from being priest unto the Lord" by Solomon for his share in Adonijah's rebellion (1 Kings 2:26 f.; 1:7), and the high priesthood passed back again to the family of Eleazar in the person of Zadok (1 Kings 2:35). In addition to the office of high priest he held that of judge, being the immediate predecessor of his pupil Samuel (1 Sam. 7:6, 15-17), the last of the judges. He died at the advanced age of 98 years (1 Sam. 4:15-18).

ELIAKIM—*God establishes.* 1. Son of Hilkiah; master of Hezekiah's household ("over the house," as Isa. 36:3), 2 Kings 18:18, 26, 37. He succeeded Shebna in this office, after he had been ejected from it as a punishment for his pride (Isa. 22:15-20). Eliakim was a good man, as appears by the title emphatically applied to him by God, "my servant Eliakim" (Isa. 22:20), and as was evinced by his conduct on the occasion of Sennacherib's invasion (2 Kings 18:37; 19:1-5), and also in the discharge of the duties of his high station, in which he acted as a "father to the inhabitants of Jerusalem, and to the house of Judah" (Isa. 22:21). 2. The original name of Jehoiakim king of Judah (2 Kings 23:34; 2 Chron. 36:4). 3. A priest in the days of Nehemiah (Neh. 12:41). 4. Eldest son of Abiud, or Judah; brother of Joseph, and father of Azor (Matt. 1:13). 5. Son of Melea, and father of Jonan (Luke 3:30 f.).

ELIAM—*God is kinsman.* 1. Father of Bathsheba, the wife of David (1 Sam. 11:3). 2. Son of Ahithophel the Gilonite; one of David's "thirty" warriors (2 Sam. 23:34).

ELIAS. The form in which the name of Elijah is given in the A.V. of the New Testament.

ELIASHIB—*God will restore.* 1. A priest in the time of David, eleventh in the order of the "governors" of the sanctuary (1 Chron. 24:12). 2. A son of Elioenai (1 Chron. 3:24). 3. High priest at Jerusalem (Neh. 3:1, 20 f.). 4. A singer in the time of Ezra who had married a foreign wife (Ezra 10:24). 5. A son of Zattu (Ezra 10:27), and 6. A son of Bani (Ezra 10:36), both of whom had transgressed in the same manner.

ELIEZER—*God is helper.* 1. Abraham's chief servant, called by him "Eliezer of Damascus" (Gen. 15:2). 2. Second son of Moses and Zipporah, to whom his father gave this name, "because, said he, the God of my father was my help that delivered me from the sword of Pharaoh" (Ex. 18:4; 1 Chron. 23:15, 17).

ELIHU—*my God is He.* 1. One of the interlocutors in the book of Job. (See Job.) He is described as the "son of Barachel the Buzite," and this apparently referred to the family of Buz, the son of Nahor, and nephew of Abraham (Gen. 22:21). 2. Son of Tohu; a forefather of Samuel the prophet (1 Sam. 1:1). 3. In 1 Chron. 27:18, Elihu "of the brethren of David" is mentioned as the chief of the tribe of Judah. 4. One of the captains of the thousands of Manasseh (1 Chron. 12:20) who followed David to Ziklag after he had left the Philistine army on the eve of the battle of Gilboa. 5. A Korahite Levite in the time of David; one of the doorkeepers of the house of Jehovah. He was a son of Shemaiah, and of the family of Obed-edom (1 Chron. 26:7).

ELIJAH—*my God is Jehovah.* He has been well entitled "the grandest and the most romantic character that Israel ever produced." "Elijah the Tishbite of the inhabitants of Gilead," is literally all that is given us to know of his parentage and locality (1 Kings 17:1). His chief characteristic was his hair, long and thick, and hanging down his back. His ordinary clothing consisted of a girdle of skin round his loins (1 Kings 18:46).

But in addition to this he occasionally wore the "mantle" or cape, of sheepskin, which has supplied one of our most familiar figures of speech. It was in the wild loneliness of the hills and ravines of Gilead that the knowledge of Jehovah, the living God of Israel, had been impressed on his mind. What may be called the first act in his life embraces between three and four years—three years and six months for the duration of the drought, according to the statements of the New Testament (Luke 4:25; James 5:17), and three or four months more for the journey to Horeb, and the return to Gilead (1 Kings 17:1; 19:21). He suddenly appeared before Ahab, and proclaimed the vengeance of Jehovah for the apostasy of the king. Elijah was then directed to the brook Cherith. There in the hollow of the torrent-bed he remained, supported in a miraculous manner. His next refuge was at Zarephath. Here Elijah performed the miracles of prolonging the oil and the meal, and restored the son of the widow to life after his apparent death. The drought continued, and famine caused by the failure of the crops, descended on Samaria. The king and his chief domestic officer divided between them the mournful duty of ascertaining that neither round the springs, nor in the nooks and crannies of the most shaded torrent-beds, was there any of the herbage left. It was the moment for the reappearance of the prophet. He showed himself first to the minister, who departed to inform Ahab. Ahab arrived and Elijah made his charge—"Thou hast forsaken Jehovah and followed the Baals." He then commanded that all Israel be collected to Mount Carmel with the four hundred and fifty prophets of Baal, and the four hundred of Asherah (Ashtaroth), the latter being under the special protection of the queen. Following the contest (1 Kings 18:19 ff.), having killed the prophets of Baal, and fearing the vengeance of Jezebel, Elijah took refuge in flight. Again he was fed miraculously (1 Kings 19:5 ff.) and then went forward, a journey of forty days to the mount of God, even to Horeb. Here in a cave, he remained for certainly one night. In the morning came the "word of Jehovah"—the question, "What doest thou here, Elijah?" In answer to this invitation the prophet opened his griefs. Then he was directed to leave the cavern and stand on the mountain in the open air, face to face with Jehovah. Then, as before with Moses (Ex. 34:6), "The Lord passed by," passed in all the terror of his most appalling manifestations. Three commands were laid on Elijah. Of these three commands the first two were reserved for Elisha to accomplish, the last only was executed by Elijah himself. His first search was for Elisha. Apparently he soon found him. Elisha was ploughing at the time, and Elijah "passed over to him"—possibly crossed the river—and cast his mantle, the well-known sheepskin cloak, upon him. They commenced that long period of service and intercourse which continued till Elijah's removal. Ahab and Jezebel now probably believed that their threats had been effectual, and that they had seen the last of their tormentor. After the murder of Naboth, Ahab lost no time in entering on his new acquisition. But his triumph was a short one. Elijah had received an intimation from Jehovah of what was taking place, and rapidly as the accusation and death of Naboth had been hurried over, he was there to meet his ancient enemy on the very scene of his crime. And then followed the curse, in terms fearful to any Oriental—peculiarly terrible to a Jew—and most of all significant to a successor of the apostate princes of the northern kingdom. The whole of Elijah's denunciation may possibly be recovered by putting together the words recalled by Jehu (2 Kings 9:26, 36 f.) and those given in 1 Kings 21:19-25. A space of three or four years now elapsed (cf. 1 Kings 22:1, 51; 2 Kings 1:17). Ahaziah met with a fatal accident, and was on his death-bed (2 Kings 1:1 f.; 1 Kings 22:51). In his extremity he sent to an oracle or shrine of Baal at the Philistine town of Ekron, to ascertain the issue of his illness. But the prophet suddenly appeared on the path of the messenger. Without preface or inquiry Elijah pronounced his message of death, and as rapidly disappeared. But this only roused the wrath of

Ahaziah. A captain was despatched, with a party of fifty, to take Elijah prisoner. "And there came down fire from heaven and consumed him and his fifty." A second party was sent, only to meet the same fate. The altered tone of the leader of a third party brought Elijah down. But the king gained nothing. It must have been shortly after the death of Ahaziah that Elijah made a communication with the southern kingdom. When Jehoram the son of Jehoshaphat began "to walk in the ways of the kings of Israel," Elijah sent him a letter denouncing his evil doings, and predicting his death (2 Chron. 21: 12-15). The closing transaction of Elijah's life was at Gilgal—probably on the western edge of the hills of Ephraim. There the prophet received the divine intimation that his departure was at hand (1 Kings 2:1-12). He was at the time with Elisha, whom he endeavored to persuade to remain behind while he went on an errand of Jehovah. But Elisha would not so easily give up his master. They went together to Bethel. Again Elijah attempted to escape Jericho, and again Elisha protested that he would not be separated from him. At Jericho he made a final effort, but Elisha was not to be conquered, and the two set off to the distant river—Elijah in his mantle or cape of sheepskin, Elisha in ordinary clothes. Fifty men of the sons of the prophets ascended the abrupt heights behind the town to watch what happened in the distance. The two reached the river, and stood on the shelving bank beside its swift brown current. Elijah rolled up his mantle as into a staff, and with his old energy struck the waters as Moses had done before him, and they were divided, and they two went over on dry ground. "And it came to pass as they still went on and talked, that, behold, there appeared a chariot of fire and horses of fire, and parted them both asunder, and Elijah went up by a whirlwind into heaven" (2 Kings 2:11).

ELIMELECH—*God is king.* A man of the tribe of Judah who migrated to Moab in time of famine with his wife Naomi and two sons (Ruth 1:2).

ELIPHAZ—*God is fine gold* (?). 1. The son of Esau and Adah, and father of Teman (Gen. 36: 4; 1 Chron. 1:35 f.). 2. The chief of the "three friends" of Job (Job 2:11). He is called "the Temanite"; hence it is naturally inferred that he was a descendant of Teman.

ELISABETH—*God is an oath.* The wife of Zacharias and mother of John the Baptist. She was herself of the priestly family, and a relation (Luke 1:36) of the mother of Jesus.

ELISEUS. The form in which the name Elisha appears in the A.V. of the New Testament (Luke 4:27).

ELISHA—*God is salvation.* Son of Shaphat of Abel-meholah; the attendant and disciple of Elijah, and subsequently his successor as prophet of the kingdom of Israel. The earliest mention of his name is in the command to Elijah in the cave at Horeb (1 Kings 19:16 f.). In most every respect Elisha presents the most complete contrast to Elijah. Elijah was a true Bedouin child of the desert. If he entered a city, it was only to deliver his message of fire and be gone. Elisha, on the other hand, was a civilized man, an inhabitant of cities. And as with his manners so with his appearance. The call of Elisha seems to have taken place about four years before the death of Ahab. He died in the reign of Joash, the grandson of Jehu. This embraces a period of not less than 65 years, for certainly 55 of which he held the office of "prophet in Israel" (2 Kings 5:8). After the departure of his master, Elisha returned to dwell at Jericho (2 Kings 2:18). The town had been lately rebuilt (1 Kings 16:34), and was the residence of a body of the "sons of the prophets" (2 Kings 2:5, 15). One of the springs of Jericho was noxious at the time of Elisha's visit. At the request of the men of Jericho he remedied this evil. He took salt in a new vessel, and cast it into the water at its source in the name of Jehovah. We next meet with

Elisha at Bethel, in the heart of the country, on his way from Jericho to Mount Carmel (2 Kings 2:23). Here the boys of the town were clustered, waiting for the chance passer-by. For once Elisha assumed the sternness of his master. He turned upon them and cursed them in the name of Jehovah, whereupon two bears fatally attacked them. Elisha next extricated Jehoram king of Israel, and the kings of Judah and Edom from their difficulty in the campaign against Moab, arising from want of water (2 Kings 3:4-27). The widow of one of the sons of the prophets was in debt, and her two sons about to be taken from her and sold as slaves. She had no property but a pot of oil. This Elisha caused (in his absence, 4:5) to multiply, until the widow filled with it all the vessels which she could borrow. The next occurrence was at Shunem and Mount Carmel (2 Kings 4:8-37). The scene next changed to Gilgal, apparently at a time when Elisha was residing there (4:38-44). This in all probability belongs to the same time, and also to the same place, as the preceding. The domestic incidents are followed by the healing of Naaman's leprosy (2 Kings 5) and making the ax head float (2 Kings 6:1-7). The scene now returns to the sons of the prophets (6:8-23). Elisha was now residing at Dothan, halfway on the road between Samaria and Jezreel (6:24–7:2; 8:1-6; 8:7-15; 9:1-10). Two of the injunctions laid on Elijah (1 Kings 20:15 f.) had now been carried out; the third still remained. The time had come for the fulfillment of the curse upon Ahab by anointing Jehu king over Israel. Elisha's share in this was giving directions to one of the sons of the prophets (2 Kings 9:1-3).

ELISHEBA—*God is an oath.* The wife of Aaron (Ex. 6:23). She was the daughter of Amminadab, and sister of Naashon the captain of the host of Judah (Num. 2:3).

ELUL. The sixth month of the Jewish year (Neh. 6:15).

ELYMAS. The Arabic name of the Jewish magus or sorcerer Barjesus (Acts 13:6 ff.).

EMBALMING. The process by which dead bodies are preserved. It was most general among the Egyptians, and two instances in the Old Testament are mentioned (Gen. 50:2, 26). Of the Egyptian method of embalming there remain two minute accounts. Herodotus (2:86-89) describes three modes. The embalmers first removed part of the brain through the nostrils, by means of crooked iron, and destroyed the rest by injecting caustic drugs. An incision was then made along the flank with a sharp Ethiopian stone, and the whole of the intestines removed. The cavity was rinsed out with palm-wine, and afterward scoured with pounded perfumes. It was then filled with pure myrrh pounded, cassia and other aromatics, except frankincense. This done, the body was sewn up and steeped in natron for seventy days. When the seventy days were accomplished, the embalmers washed the corpse and swathed it in bandages of linen, cut in strips and smeared with gum. They then gave it up to the relatives of the deceased, who provided for it a wooden case, made in the shape of a man, in which the dead was placed, and deposited in an erect position against the wall of the sepulchral chamber. The second mode of embalming cost about 20 minae. In this case no incision was made in the body, nor were the intestines removed, but cedar-oil was injected into the stomach by the rectum. The oil was prevented from escaping, and the body was then steeped in natron for the appointed number of days. On the last day the oil was withdrawn, and carried off with it the stomach and intestines in a state of solution, while the flesh was consumed by the natron, and nothing was left but the skin and bones. The body in this state was returned to the relatives of the deceased. The third mode, which was adopted by the poorer classes, and cost but little, consisted in rinsing out the intestines with syrmaea, an infusion of senna and cassia, and steeping the body for the usual number of days in natron.

EMERALD. A precious stone, first in the second row on the breast-plate of the high priest (Ex. 28:18; 29:11), imported to Tyre from Syria (Ezek. 27:16), used as an ornament of clothing and bedding (Ezek. 28:13; Judg. 10:21), and spoken of as one of the foundations of Jerusalem (Rev. 21:19).

EMERODS (Deut. 28:27; 1 Sam. 5:6, 9, 12; 6:4 f., 11). Probably hemorrhoidal tumors, or bleeding piles, are intended.

EMIMS. A tribe or family of gigantic stature which originally inhabited the region along the eastern side of the Dead Sea. They were related to the Anakim, and were generally called by the same name; but their conquerors the Moabites termed them Emim—that is, "terrible men" (Deut. 2:11)—most probably on account of their fierce aspect.

EMMAUS. The village to which the two disciples were going when Christ appeared to them on the way (Luke 24:13).

EN. At the beginning of many Hebrew words, signifies a spring or fountain.

ENCHANTMENTS. The use of devination and magic (*e.g.*, Ex. 7:11, 22; Num. 24:1; Jer. 27:9). Any resort to these methods of imposture was strictly forbidden in the Scripture (Lev. 19:26; Isa. 47:9), but to eradicate the tendency is almost impossible (2 Kings 17:17; 2 Chron. 33:6), and we find it still flourishing at the Christian era (Acts 13:6, 8; 8:9, 11; Gal. 5:20; Rev. 9:21).

ENDOR—*fountain of Dor.* A place in the territory of Issachar, and yet possessed by Manasseh (Josh. 17:11). Endor was long held in memory by the Jewish people as connected with the great victory over Sisera and Jabin. It was here that the witch dwelt whom Saul consulted (1 Sam. 28:7).

ENGEDI—*spring of the kid.* A town in the wilderness of Judah (Josh. 15:62), on the western shore of the Dead Sea (Ezek. 47:10). David hid from Saul here (1 Sam. 24:1).

EN-HAKKORE—*spring of the partridge.* The spring which burst out in answer to the cry of Samson after his exploit with the jawbone (Judg. 15:19).

ENOCH. 1. The eldest son of Cain (Gen. 4:17), who called the city which he built after his name (vs. 18). 2. The son of Jared and father of Methuselah (Gen. 5:21 ff.; Luke 3:28). In the epistle of Jude (24) he is described as "the seventh from Adam"; and the number is probably noticed as conveying the idea of divine completion and rest, while Enoch was himself a type of perfected humanity. After the birth of Methuselah it is said (Gen. 5:22-24) that Enoch "walked with God three hundred years . . . and he was not; for God took him." (*cf.* Heb. 11:5) The phrase "walked with God" is elsewhere only used of Noah (Gen. 6:9), and is to be explained of a prophetic life spent in immediate converse with the spiritual world. In the Epistle to the Hebrews the spring and issue of Enoch's life are clearly marked.

ENON. (See Aenon.)

EN-ROGEL—*spring of a spy* (?). (Josh. 15:7; 18:16). Here Jonathan and Ahimaaz remained after the flight of David, awaiting intelligence from within the walls (2 Sam. 17:17), and here by the stone Zoheleth, which is close to En-rogel, Adonijah held the feast which was the first and last act of his attempt on the crown (1 Kings 1:9).

EPENETUS. A Christian at Rome, greeted by Paul in Rom. 16:5, and designated as his beloved, and the first fruit of Asia unto Christ.

EPAPHRAS. A fellow-laborer with Paul, mentioned in Col. 1:7 as having taught the Colossian church the grace of God in truth, and designated

a faithful minister of Christ on their behalf. He was at that time with Paul at Rome (Col. 4:12), and seems by the expression there used to have been a Colossian by birth. We find him again mentioned in the Epistle to Philemon (vs. 23), which was sent at the same time as that to the Colossians.

EPHES-DAMMIM. A place in Judah at which the Philistines were encamped before the affray in which Goliath was killed (1 Sam. 17:1).

EPHESIANS, EPISTLE TO THE. Believed to have been written by the apostle Paul during his imprisonment at Rome (Acts 28:16), apparently immediately after he had written the Epistle to the Colossians and during that period when his imprisonment had not assumed the severer character which seems to have marked its close. This epistle was addressed to the Christian church at Ephesus. Its contents may be divided into two portions, the first mainly doctrinal (chs. 1-3), the second hortatory and practical.

EPHESUS. The capital of the Roman province of Asia and an illustrious city in the district of Ionia, nearly opposite the island of Samos. There were coast-roads leading northward to Smyrna and southward to Miletus. Conspicuous at the head of the harbor of Ephesus was the great temple of Diana or Artemis, the tutelary divinity of the city. This building was raised on immense substructions, in consequence of the swampy nature of the ground. The earlier temple, which had been begun before the Persian war, was burnt down in the night when Alexander the Great was born; and another structure, raised up by the enthusiastic co-operation of all the inhabitants of "Asia," had taken its place. The magnificence of this sanctuary was a proverb throughout the civilized world.

EPHOD. A sacred vestment originally appropriate to the high priest (Ex. 28:4), but afterward worn by the ordinary priests (1 Sam. 22:18), and deemed characteristic of the office (1 Sam. 2:28; 14:3; Hos. 3:4). The importance of the ephod as the receptacle of the breastplate led to its adoption in the idolatrous forms of worship instituted in the time of the Judges (Judg. 8:27; 17:5; 18:14 ff.).

EPHRAIM—*doubly fruitful.* The second son of Joseph by his wife Asenath. The first indication we have of that ascendency over his elder brother Manasseh, which at a later period the tribe of Ephraim so unmistakably possessed, is in the blessing of the children by Jacob (Gen. 48). Under Joshua the tribe must have taken a high position in the nation, to judge from the tone which the Ephraimites assumed on occasions shortly subsequent to the conquest. The boundaries of the portion of Ephraim are given in Josh. 16:1-10.

EPHRAIM. In "Baal-hazor which is by Ephraim" was Absalom's sheep-farm, at which took place the murder of Amnon, one of the earliest precursors of the great revolt (2 Sam. 13:23).

EPHRAIM. A city "in the district near the wilderness" to which Jesus retired with his disciples when threatened with violence by the priests (John 11:54).

EPHRAIM, GATE OF. One of the gates of the city of Jerusalem (2 Kings 14:13; 2 Chron. 25:23; Neh. 8:16; 12:39), probably at or near the position of the present "Damascus gate."

EPHRAIM, THE WOOD OF. A wood, or rather a forest, on the east of Jordan, in which the fatal battle was fought between the armies of David and of Absalom (2 Sam. 18:6). The name is probably derived from the slaughter of Ephraim at the fords of Jordan by the Gileadites under Jephthah (Judg. 12:1, 4 f.).

EPHRATAH or EPHRATH. 1. Second wife of Caleb the son of Hezron, mother of Hur, and grandmother of Caleb the spy, according to 1

Chron. 2:19 f. and probably 24 and 4:4. 2. The ancient name of Bethlehem Judah, as is manifest from Gen. 35:16, 19; 48:7.

EPICUREANS, THE. They derived their name from Epicurus (342-271 B.C.), a philosopher of Attic descent (see Acts 17:18 ff.).

ER. 1. First-born of Judah. Er "was wicked in the sight of the Lord; and the Lord slew him" (Gen. 38:3-7; Num. 26:19). 2. A son of Shelah (1 Chron. 4:21), and 3. A name in the genealogy of Jesus (Luke 3:28).

ERASTUS—*amiable.* 1. One of the attendants of Paul at Ephesus, who with Timothy was sent forward into Macedonia while the apostle himself remained in Asia (Acts 19:22). He is probably the same with Erastus, who is again mentioned in the salutations to Timothy (2 Tim. 3:20), though not the same with, 2. Erastus the chamberlain, or rather the public treasurer, of Corinth, who was one of the early converts to Christianity (Rom. 16:23).

ESAIAS. The form of the name of the prophet Isaiah in the New Testament.

ESARHADDON—*Asshur has given a brother.* One of the greatest of the kings of Assyria was the son of Sennacherib (2 Kings 19:37) and the grandson of Sargon who succeeded Shalmaneser. He appears by his monuments to have been one of the most powerful of all the Assyrian monarchs. He is the only Assyrian monarch whom we find to have actually reigned at Babylon, where he built himself a palace, bricks from which have been recently recovered bearing his name. His Babylonian reign lasted thirteen years, from 681 B.C. to 669 B.C.; and it was doubtless within this space of time that Manasseh, king of Judah, having been seized by his captains at Jerusalem on a charge of rebellion, was brought before him at Babylon (2 Chron. 33:11) and detained for a time as prisoner there.

ESAU—*hairy.* The eldest son of Isaac and twin brother of Jacob. The singular appearance of the child at his birth originated the name (Gen. 25:25). Even in the womb the twin brothers struggled together (Gen. 25:22). Esau's robust frame and "rough" aspect were the types of a wild and daring nature. His old father, by a caprice of affection not uncommon, loved his willful, vagrant boy; and his keen relish for savory food being gratified by Esau's venison, he liked him all the better for his skill in hunting (25:28). Jacob took advantage of his brother's distress to rob him of that which was dear as life itself to an eastern patriarch. Esau married at the age of 40, and contrary to the wish of his parents. His wives were both Canaanites; and they "were bitterness of spirit unto Isaac and to Rebekah" (Gen. 26:34 f.). Jacob, through the craft of his mother, was again successful, and secured irrevocably the covenant blessing. Esau vowed vengeance, but Rebekah succeeded both in exciting Isaac's anger against Esau and obtaining his consent to Jacob's departure. When Esau heard that his father had commanded Jacob to take a wife of the daughters of his kinsman Laban, he also resolved to try whether by a new alliance he could propitiate his parents. He accordingly married his cousin Mahalath, the daughter of Ishmael (Gen. 28:8 f.). He soon afterward established himself in Mount Seir; still retaining, however, some interest in his father's property in southern Palestine. He was residing in Mount Seir when Jacob returned from Padanaram, and had then become so rich and powerful that the impressions of his brother's early offences seem to have been almost completely effaced (Gen. 33:4). It does not appear that the brothers met again until the death of their father about 20 years afterward. They united in laying Isaac's body in the cave of Machpelah. Of Esau's subsequent history nothing is known.

ESDRAELON—*God sows.* This name is the Greek form of the Hebrew word Jezreel. It occurs only

twice in the A.V. Apocrypha. In the Old Testament it is called Jezreel.

ESDRAS. The form of the name of Ezra the scribe in the Apocrypha.

ESDRAS, BOOKS OF. The first book of Esdras is the first in order of the Apocryphal books in the English Bible.

ESHCOL. Brother of Mamre, the Amorite, and of Aner, and one of Abraham's companions in his pursuit of the four kings who had carried off Lot (Gen. 14:13, 24).

ESHCOL, THE VALLEY of THE BROOK OF. A *wady* in the neighborhood of Hebron, explored by the spies who were sent by Moses from Kadesh-barnea (Num. 33:9; Deut. 1:24).

ESHTAOL. A town in the low country—the Shephelah of Judah, afterward alloted to Dan (Josh. 15:33; 19:41). Here Samson spent his boyhood, and hither after his last exploit his body was brought (Judg. 13:25; 16:31; 18:2, 8, 11 f.).

ESTHER—*star.* The Persian name of Hadassah (myrtle), daughter of Abihail, the son of Shimei, the son of Kish, a Benjamite, whose ancestor Kish had been among the captives led away from Jerusalem by Nebuchadnezzar when Jehoiachin was taken captive. She was an orphan without father or mother, and had been brought up by her cousin Mordecai, who had an office in the household of Ahasuerus king of Persia, and dwelt at "Shushan the palace." When Vashti was dismissed from being queen, and all the fairest virgins of the kingdom had been collected at Shushan for the king to make choice of a successor to her from among them, the choice fell upon Esther. The king was not aware, however, of her race and parentage; and so, on the representation of Haman the Agagite that the Jews scattered through his empire were a pernicious race, he gave him full power and authority to kill them all, young and old, women and children, and take possession of their property. The means taken by Esther to avert this great calamity from her people and her kindred are fully related in the book of Esther. History is wholly silent both about Vashti and Esther.

ESTHER, BOOK OF. One of the latest of the canonical books of Scripture. The author is not known. It has often been remarked as a peculiarity of this book that the name of God does not once occur in it. The style is remarkably chaste and simple. It does not in the least savor of romance. The Hebrew is very like that of Ezra, and parts of the Chronicles; generally pure, but mixed with some words of Persian origin and some of Chaldaic affinity. In short, it is just what one would expect to find in a work of the age to which the book of Esther professes to belong.

ETAM, THE ROCK. A cliff or lofty rock into a cleft or chasm of which Samson retired after his slaughter of the Philistines (Judg. 15:8, 11). This natural stronghold was in the tribe of Judah.

ETHBAAL—*man of Baal.* A king of Sidon and father of Jezebel (1 Kings 16:31). Josephus represents him as king of the Tyrians as well as the Sidonians. We may thus identify him with Eithobalus, who, after having assassinated Pheles, usurped the throne of Tyre for 32 years.

ETHIOPIA—*dark-skinned* (?). The country which the Greeks and Romans described as "Aethiopia" and the Hebrews as "Cush" lay to the south of Egypt. The inhabitants were a Hamitic race (Gen. 10:6).

ETHIOPIAN WOMAN. The wife of Moses is so described in Num. 12:1. She is elsewhere said to have been the daughter of a Midianite, and in consequence of this some have supposed that the allusion is to another wife whom Moses married after the death of Zipporah.

EUBULUS. A Christian at Rome mentioned by Paul (2 Tim. 4:21).

EUNICE. The mother of Timotheus (2 Tim. 1:5).

EUNUCH. The Law (Deut. 23:1; *cf.* Lev. 22:24) is repugnant to thus treating any Israelite. Eunuchs mostly appear in one of two relations, either military, as "set over the men of war," greater trustworthiness possibly counter-balancing inferior courage and military vigor, or associated, as we mostly recognize them, with women and children.

EUODIAS. A female Christian of Philippi. Paul besought her to "be of the same mind in the Lord" with Syntyche, another Christian woman (Phil. 4:2).

EUPHRATES. Probably a word of Aryan origin, signifying "the good and abounding river." It is most frequently denoted in the Bible by the term "the river" (*e.g.,* Deut. 11:24; Ex. 23:31). The Euphrates is the largest, the longest, and by far the most important of the rivers of Western Asia. It rises in the Armenian mountains and flows into the Persian Gulf. The entire course is 1780 miles, and of this distance more than two-thirds (1,200 miles) is navigable for boats.

EUROCLYDON—*east wind.* The name given (Acts 27:14) to the gale of wind which off the south coast of Crete seized the ship, in which Paul was ultimately wrecked on the coast of Malta. In some translations it is given as Euraquilo.

EUTYCHUS—*fortunate.* A youth at Troas (Acts 20:9), who, sitting in a window, and having fallen asleep while Paul was discoursing far into the night, fell from the third story, and being taken up dead, was miraculously restored to life by the Apostle.

EVANGELIST—*the publisher* or *preacher of glad tidings.* In Eph. 4:11 the "evangelists" appear on the one hand after the "apostles" and "prophets"; on the other before the "pastors" and "teachers." The apostles, so far as they evangelized (Acts 8:25; 14:7; 1 Cor. 1:17), might claim the title, though there were many Evangelists who were not apostles.

EVE—*life.* The name given in Scripture to the first woman. The account of Eve's creation is found at Gen. 2:21 f. She was the wife of Adam and the mother of Cain, Abel, and Seth. She encouraged Adam to eat of the forbidden fruit (Gen. 3:3).

EVIL-MERODACH—*man of Marduk.* The son and successor of Nebuchadnezzar. He reigned but a short time, being noted for his evil and indecent ways. He granted favors to Jehoiachin, captive king of Jerusalem (2 Kings 25:27-30). He was murdered by Neriglissar, his brother-in-law.

EXODUS—*going out* (of Egypt). The second book of the Law or Pentateuch. It may be divided into two principal parts: 1. Historical, 1:1–18:27; and, 2. Legislative, 19:1–40:38.

EXODUS, THE. Of the Israelites from Egypt. The history of the Exodus itself commences with the Ten Plagues. In the night, in which, at midnight, the firstborn were slain (Ex. 12:29), Pharaoh urged the departure of the Israelites (ver. 31 f.). They at once set forth (vers. 37, 39), apparently during the night, but towards morning, on the 15th day of the first month (Num. 33:3). They made three journeys and encamped by the Red Sea. Here Pharaoh overtook them, and the great miracle occurred by which they were saved, while the pursuer and his army were destroyed.

EXORCIST (Acts 19:13). That some not only pretended to, but possessed, the power of exorcising, appears by our Lord's admission (Matt. 12:27). What means were employed we are not informed. David, by playing skillfully on a harp, procured the temporary departure of the evil spirit which troubled Saul (1 Sam. 16:23). It was the profane use of the name of Jesus as a mere charm or spell which led to the disastrous issue recorded in Acts 19:13-16. The power of casting out devils was bestowed by Christ while on earth upon the apostles (Matt. 10:8) and the seventy disciples (Luke 10:17-19), and was, according to his promise (Mark 16:17), exercised by believers after his ascension (Acts 16:18); but to the Christian miracle, whether as performed by our Lord himself or by his followers, the New Testament writers never apply the terms "exorcise" or exorcist."

EZEKIEL—*God strengthens.* One of the four greater prophets was the son of a priest named Buzi, and was taken captive in the captivity of Jehoiachin, eleven years before the destruction of Jerusalem. He was a member of a community of Jewish exiles who settled on the banks of the Chebar, a "river" or stream of Babylonia. It was by this river "in the land of the Chaldaeans" that God's message first reached him (Ezek. 1:3). We learn from an incidental allusion (24:18) — the only reference which he makes to his personal history—that he was married, and had a house (8:1) in his place of exile, and lost his wife by a sudden and unforeseen stroke. According to a late tradition, he is said to have been murdered in Babylon by some Jewish prince whom he had convicted of idolatry.

EZRA—*help.* Called Esdras in the Apocrypha, the famous scribe and priest, descended from Hilkiah (Ezra 7:1). All that is really known of Ezra is contained in the last four chapters of the book of Ezra and in Neh. 8-10. From these passages we learn that he was a learned and pious priest residing at Babylon in the time of Artaxerxes. Ezra longed to return to Jerusalem and re-establish the Temple and the religious life of the Jews. The king granted Ezra authority to organize a group of volunteers and return to the holy city. The work of Ezra is closely linked with that of Nehemiah.

EZRA, BOOK OF. It is a continuation of the books of Chronicles. Like these books it consists of the contemporary historical journals kept from time to time, which were afterward strung together, and either abridged or added to, as the case required, by a later hand. The period covered by the book is eighty years (approximately), beginning with the return of the first exiles to Jerusalem, under Cyrus (538 B.C.).

FAIR HAVENS. A harbor in the island of Crete (Acts 27:8), though not mentioned in any other ancient writing, is still known by its own Greek name, and appears to have been the harbor of Lasea.

FALLOW DEER. The Hebrew word is mentioned only in Deut. 14:5 and in 1 Kings 4:23. It is mentioned among the clean animals.

FAMINE. The first famine recorded in the Bible is that of Abraham after he had pitched his tent on the coast of Bethel (Gen. 12:10). We may conclude that this famine was extensive, although this is not quite proved, by the fact of Abraham's going to Egypt; for on the occasion of the second famine, in the days of Isaac, this patriarch found refuge with Abimelech king of the Philistines in Gerar (Gen. 26:1). We hear no more of times of scarcity until the great famine of Egypt which "was over all the face of the earth." This instance differs in the providential recurrence of seven years of plenty, whereby Joseph was enabled to provide against the coming dearth, and to supply not only the population of Egypt with corn, but those of the surrounding countries (Gen. 41:53-57). Of the other famines noted in the Bible, the best known perhaps is the one which caused Elimelech and Naomi to migrate to Moab (Ruth 1:1).

FARTHING. Two names of coins in the New Testament are rendered in the A.V. by this word.

1. *Kodrantes* (Greek), *quadrans* (Latin). A coin current in Palestine in the time of Jesus (Matt. 5:26; Mark 12:42). The name quadrans was originally given to the quarter of the Roman *as,* or piece of three unciae, therefore also called teruncius. 2. *Assarion* (Greek). Properly a small *as, assarium,* but in the time of Jesus used as the Greek equivalent of the Latin *as* (Matt. 10:29; Luke 12:6).

FASTS. 1. One fast only was appointed by the law, that on the day of Atonement (Lev. 16:29, 31; 23:27-32; Num. 29:7). There is no mention of any other periodical fast in the Old Testament, except in Zech. 7:1-7; 8:19. From these passages it appears that the Jews, during their captivity, observed four annual fasts, in the fourth, fifth, seventh, and tenth months. 2. Public fasts were occasionally proclaimed to express national humiliation, and to supplicate divine favor. 3. Private occasional fasts are recognized in one passage of the law (Num. 30:13). The instances given of individuals fasting under the influence of grief, vexation, or anxiety are numerous. 4. In the New Testament the only references to the Jewish fasts are the mention of "the Fast" in Acts 27:9 (generally understood to denote the Day of Atonement), and the allusions to the weekly fasts (Matt. 9:14; Mark 2:18; Luke 5:33; 18:12; Acts 10:30). 5. The Jewish fasts were observed with various degrees of strictness. Sometimes there was entire abstinence from food (*e.g.,* Esth. 4:16). On other occasions there appears to have been only a restriction to a very plain diet (Dan. 10:3). Those who fasted frequently dressed in sackcloth or rent their clothes, put ashes on their head and went barefoot (1 Kings 21:27; Nah. 9:1; Ps. 30:13).

FAT. The Hebrews distinguished between the suet or pure fat of an animal, and the fat which was intermixed with the lean (Nah. 8:10). Some parts of the suet, *viz.,* about the stomach, the entrails, the kidneys, and the tail of a sheep, which grows to an excessive size in many eastern countries, and produces a large quantity of rich fat, were forbidden to be eaten in the case of animals offered to Jehovah in sacrifice (Lev. 3:3).

FAT, *i.e.,* Vat, the word employed to translate the Hebrew *yekeb,* in Joel 2:34; 3:13. The word commonly used for *yekeb* is "winepress" or "wine-fat," and once "pressfat" (Hag. 2:16). The "vats" appear to have been excavated out of the native rock of the hills on which the vineyards lay.

FATHER. The position and authority of the father as the head of the family are expressly assumed and sanctioned in Scripture, as a likeness of that of the Almighty over his creatures. The father's blessing was regarded as conferring special benefit, but his malediction special injury, on those on whom it fell (Gen. 9:25, 27; 27:27-40; 48:15, 20; 49); and so also the sin of a parent was held to affect in certain cases, the welfare of his descendants (2 Kings 5:27). The command to honor parents is noticed by Paul as the only one of the Decalogue which bore a distinct promise (Ex. 20:12; Eph. 6:2), and disrespect toward them was condemned by the Law as one of the worst of crimes (Ex. 21:15, 17; 1 Tim. 1:9). "Fathers" is used in the sense of seniors (Acts 7:2; 22:1), and of parents in general, or ancestors (Dan. 5:2; Jer. 27:7; Matt. 23:30, 32).

FEASTS. (See Festivals.)

FELIX. A Roman procurator of Judaea, appointed by the Emperor Claudius, whose freedman he was, on the banishment of Ventidius Cumanus in A.D. 53. Felix was the brother of Claudius's powerful freedman Pallas. He ruled the province in a mean, cruel, and profligate manner. Paul was brought before Felix in Caesarea. He was remanded to prison and kept there two years, in hopes of extorting money from him (Acts 24:26 f.). At the end of that time Porcius Festus was appointed to supersede Felix, who, on his return to Rome, was accused by the Jews in Caesarea, and would have suffered the penalty due to his atrocities, had not his

brother Pallas prevailed with the Emperor Nero to spare him. The wife of Felix was Drusilla, daughter of Herod Agrippa I, the former wife of Azizus king of Emesa.

FENCED CITIES. The fortifications of the cities of Palestine, regularly "fenced," consisted of one or more walls crowned with battlemented parapets, having towers at regular intervals (2 Chron. 32:5; Jer. 31:38), on which in later times engines of war were placed, and watch was kept by day and night in time of war (2 Chron. 26:9, 15; Judg. 9:45; 2 Kings 9:17).

FESTIVALS. 1. The religious times ordained in the Law fall under three heads: (1) Those formally connected with the institution of the Sabbath; (2) The historical or great festivals; (3) The Day of Atonement. (1) Immediately connected with the institution of the Sabbath are: (a) The weekly Sabbath itself. (b) The seventh new moon or Feast of Trumpets. (c) The Sabbatical Year. (d) The Year of Jubilee. (2) The great feasts are: (a) The Passover. (b) The feast of Pentecost, of Weeks, of Wheat-harvest, or, of the First-fruits. (c) The Feast of Tabernacles, or of ingathering. On each of these occasions every male Israelite was commanded "to appear before the Lord," that is, to attend in the court of the tabernacle or the temple, and to make his offering with a joyful heart (Deut. 27:7; Nah. 8-9-12). The attendance of women was voluntary, but the zealous often went up to the Passover. On all days of Holy Convocation there was to be an entire suspension of ordinary labor of all kinds (Ex. 12:16; Lev. 16:29; 23:21, 24 f., 35). But on the intervening days of the longer festivals work might be carried on. 2. After the captivity, the Feast of Purim (Esth. 9:20) and that of the dedication were instituted.

FESTUS, PORCIUS. Successor of Felix as procurator of Judaea (Acts 24:27), sent by Nero probably in the autumn of the year A.D. 60. A few weeks after Festus reached his province he heard the cause of Paul, who had been left a prisoner by Felix, in the presence of Herod Agrippa II and Bernice his sister (Acts 25:11 f.). He died probably in the summer of A.D. 62, having ruled the province less than two years.

FETTERS. Fetters were usually made of brass. Iron was occasionally employed for the purpose (Ps. 105:18; 149:8).

FIG, FIG TREE (Hebrew *teenah*). In the Old Testament it signifies the tree *Fiscus Carica* of Linnaeus, and also its fruit. The fig tree is very common in Palestine (Deut. 8:8). Mount Olivet was famous for its fig trees in ancient times, and they are still found there.

FIR (Hebrew *berosh, beroth*, Isa. 14:6; Ezek. 27:5). Probably one or other of the following trees: 1. *Pinus sylvestris*, or Scotch fir; 2. Larch; 3. *Cupressus sempervirens*, or cyprus, all of which are at this day found in Lebanon.

FIRE. Represented as the symbol of Jehovah's presence and the instrument of his power (*e.g.*, Ex. 3:2; 14:19). Fire for sacred purposes obtained elsewhere than from the altar was called "strange fire," and for the use of such Nadab and Abihu were punished with death by fire from God (Lev. 10:1 f.; Num. 3:4; 26:61).

FIREPAN. One of the vessels of the Temple service (Ex. 27:3; 38:3; 2 Kings 25:15; Jer. 52:19). The same word is elsewhere rendered "snuff-dish."

FIRMAMENT. The Hebrew term *rakia*, so translated, is generally regarded as expressive of simple *expansion*, and is so rendered in the margin of the A.V. (Gen. 1:6). In Ezek. 1:22-26 the "firmament" is the floor on which the throne of the Most High is placed. Further, the office of the *rakia* was to serve as a division between the waters above and the waters below (Gen. 1:7). In keeping with this view the *rakia* was provided with "windows" (Gen. 7:11; Isa. 24:18; Mal. 3:10) and "doors" (Ps. 78:23), through which

the rain and the snow might descend. A secondary purpose which the *rakia* served was to support the heavenly bodies, sun, moon, and stars (Gen. 1:14).

FIRST-BORN. Under the law, in memory of the Exodus, the eldest son was regarded as devoted to God, and was in every case to be redeemed by an offering not exceeding 5 shekels, within one month from birth. If he died before the expiration of 30 days, the Jewish doctors held the father excused, but liable to the payment if he outlived that time (Ex. 13:12-15; 22:29; Num. 8:17; 18:15 f.; Lev. 27:6). The eldest son received a double portion of the father's inheritance (Deut. 21:17), but not of the mother's. Under the monarchy, the eldest son usually, but not always, as appears in the case of Solomon, succeeded his father in the kingdom (1 Kings 1:30; 22:22). The male first-born of animals was also devoted to God (Ex. 13:2, 12 f.; 22:29; 34:19 f.).

FIRST-FRUITS. 1. The law ordered in general, that the first of all ripe fruits and of liquors, or, as it is twice expressed, the first of first-fruits, should be offered in God's house (Ex. 22:29; 23:19; 34:27). 2. On the morrow after the Passover Sabbath, *i.e.*, on the 16th of Nisan, a sheaf of new corn was to be brought to the priest, and waved before the altar, in acknowledgment of the gift of fruitfulness (Lev. 23:5 ff.; 2:12). 3. At the expiration of seven weeks from this time, *i.e.*, at the Feast of Pentecost, an oblation was to be made of two loaves of leavened bread made from the new flour, which were to be waved in like manner with the Passover sheaf (Ex. 34:22; Lev. 23:15, 17; Num. 28:26). 4. The feast of ingathering, *i.e.*, the Feast of Tabernacles in the 7th month, was itself an acknowledgment of the fruits of the harvest (Ex. 23:16; 34:22; Lev. 23:39). These offerings were national. Besides them, the following were individual. 5. A cake of the first dough that was baked was to be offered as a heave-offering (Num. 15:19, 21). 6. The first-fruits of the land were to be brought in a basket to the holy place of God's choice, and there presented to the priest, who was to set the basket down before the altar (Deut. 26:2-11). The offerings were the perquisite of the priests (Num. 18:11; Deut. 18:4).

FISH. The Hebrews recognized fish as one of the great divisions of the animal kingdom (Gen. 1:21, 28). The Mosaic law (Lev. 11:9 f.) pronounced unclean such fish as were devoid of fins and scales; these were and are regarded as unwholesome in Egypt. In Palestine, the Sea of Galilee was and still is remarkably well stored with fish. Jerusalem derived its supply chiefly from the Mediterranean (*cf.* Ezek. 47:10).

FITCHES (*i.e.*, Vetches). The representative of the two Hebrew words *kussemeth* and *kezach*. As to the former see Rye. *Kezach* denotes without doubt the *Nigella sativa*, an herbaceous annual plant which grows in the south of Europe and in the north of Africa.

FLAG. The representative of two Hebrew words *achu* and *suph*. 1. *Achu*, a word, according to Jerome, of Egyptian origin, and denoting "any green and coarse herbage, such as rushes and reeds, which grows in marshy places." It seems probable that some specific plant is denoted in Job 8:11. 2. *Suph* (Ex. 2:3, 5; Isa. 19:6) appears to be used in a very wide sense to denote "weeds of any kind."

FLAGON. 1. *Ashishah* (2 Sam. 6:19; 1 Chron. 16:3; Cant. 2:5; Hos. 3:1). It really means a cake of pressed raisins. 2. *Nebhel* (Isa. 22:24) is commonly used for a bottle or vessel, originally probably a skin, but in later times a piece of pottery (Isa. 30:14).

FLAX. That it was grown in Palestine even before the conquest of that country by the Israelites appears from Josh. 2:6. The various processes employed in preparing the flax for manufacture into cloth are indicated: 1. The drying process. 2. The peeling of the stalks, and separation of

the fibres. 3. The hacking (Isa. 19:9). That flax was one of the most important crops in Palestine appears from Hos. 2:5, 9.

FLEA. An insect twice only mentioned in Scripture, viz., in 1 Sam. 24:14; 26:20.

FLUTE. A musical instrument mentioned among others (Dan. 3:5 ff.) as used at the worship of the golden image which Nebuchadnezzar had set up.

FLUX, BLOODY (Acts 28:8). The same as our dysentery, which in the East is, though sometimes sporadic, generally epidemic and infectious, and then assumes its worst form.

FLY, FLIES. 1. *Zebub* occurs only in Eccles. 10:1, and in Isa. 7:18, and is probably a generic name for any insect. 2. *Arob* ("swarms of flies," divers "sorts of *flies*," A.V.), the name of the insect or insects which God sent to punish Pharaoh; see Ex. 8:21-31; Ps. 78:45; 105:31.

FOOD. The diet of Eastern nations has been in all ages light and simple. Simple preparations of corn were common; sometimes the fresh green ears were eaten in a natural state, the husks being rubbed off by the hand (Lev. 23:14; Deut. 23:25; 2 Kings 4:42; Matt. 12:1; Luke 6:1); more frequently, however, the grains, after being carefully picked, were roasted in a pan over a fire (Lev. 2:14), and eaten as "parched corn," in which form they were an ordinary article of diet, particularly among laborers, or others who had not the means of dressing food (Lev. 23:14; Ruth 2:14; 1 Sam. 17:17; 25:18; 2 Sam. 17:28). Sometimes the grain was bruised (A.V., "beaten," Lev. 2:14, 16), and then dried in the sun; it was eaten either mixed with oil (Lev. 2:15), or made into a soft cake (A.V. "dough"; Num. 15:20; Neh. 10:37; Ezek. 44:30).

FOREHEAD. The custom of coloring the forehead is mentioned. The "jewels for the forehead" mentioned by Ezekiel (16:12), and in margin of A.V. (Gen. 24:22), were in all probability nose-rings (Isa. 3:21).

FOREST. Although Palestine has never been in historical times a woodland country, yet there can be no doubt that there was much more wood formerly than at present.

FORTUNATUS (1 Cor. 16:17). One of three Corinthians, the others being Stephanas and Achaicus, who were at Ephesus when Paul wrote his first Epistle.

FOUNTAIN. Among the attractive features presented by the Land of Promise to the nation migrating from Egypt by way of the desert, none would be more striking than the natural gush of waters from the ground. The springs of Palestine, though shortlived, are remarkable for their abundance and beauty (Neh. 2:13 f.).

FOWL. Several distinct Hebrew and Greek words are thus rendered in the A.V. of the Bible. Of these the most common is usually a collective term for all kinds of birds. In 1 Kings 4:23, among the daily provisions for Solomon's table, "fatted fowl" are included. In the New Testament the word translated "fowls" is most frequently that which comprehends all kinds of birds (including ravens, Luke 12:24).

FOX (Hebrew *shu'al*). Probably the "jackal" is the animal signified in almost all the passages in the Old Testament where the Hebrew term occurs. The *shu'alim* of Judg. 15:4 are evidently "jackals," and not "foxes," for the former animal is gregarious, whereas the latter is solitary in its habits.

FRANKINCENSE. A vegetable resin, brittle, glittering and of a bitter taste, used for the purpose of sacrificial fumigation (Ex. 30:34-36). It is obtained by successive incisions in the bark of a tree called the *arbor thuris*, the first of which yields the purest and whitest kind; while the produce of the after incisions is spotted with

yellow, and as it becomes old loses its whiteness altogether.

FROG. The mention of this reptile in the Old Testament is confined to the passage in Ex. 8:2-7, etc., in which the plague of frogs is described, and to Ps. 78:45; 105:30. In the New Testament the word occurs once only, in Rev. 16:13.

FRONTLETS or PHYLACTERIES (Ex. 13:16; Deut. 6:8; 11:18; Matt. 23:5). These "frontlets" or "phylacteries" were strips of parchment, on which were written four passages of Scripture (Ex. 13:2-10, 11-17; Deut. 6:4-9, 13-23) in an ink prepared for the purpose. They were then rolled up in a case of black calfskin, which was attached to a stiffer piece of leather, having a thong one finger broad and one and a half cubits long. They were placed at the bend of the left arm. Those worn on the forehead were written on four strips of parchment and put into four little cells within a square case, on which the letter ש was written. The square had two thongs, on which Hebrew letters were inscribed. That phylacteries were used as amulets is certain, and was very natural. The expression "they make broad their phylacteries" (Matt. 23:5) refers not so much to the phylactery itself, which seems to have been of a prescribed breadth, as to the case in which the parchment was kept, which the Pharisees, among their other pretentious customs (Mark 7:3 f.; Luke 5:33), made as conspicuous as they could.

FULLER. The trade of the fullers, so far as it is mentioned in Scripture, appears to have consisted chiefly in cleansing garments and whitening them. The process of fulling or cleansing cloth consisted in treading or stamping on the garments with the feet or with bats in tubs of water, in which some alkaline substance answering the purpose of soap had been dissolved. The process of whitening garments was performed by rubbing into them chalk or earth of some kind.

FULLER'S FIELD, THE. A spot near Jerusalem (2 Kings 18:17; Isa. 7:3; 36:2) so close to the wall that a person speaking from there could be heard on them (2 Kings 18:17-26).

FURNACE. Various kinds of furnaces are noticed in the Bible, such as a smelting or calcining furnace (Gen. 19:28; Ex. 9:8, 10; 19:18), especially a lime-kiln (Isa. 33:12; Amos 2:1); a refining furnace (Prov. 17:3; 27:21; Ezek. 22:18 ff.); a large furnace built like a brick-kiln (Dan. 3: 22 f.). The Persians were in the habit of using the furnace as a means of inflicting punishment (Dan. 3:6 ff.; Jer. 29:22; Hos. 7:7).

GABBAI. Apparently the head of an important family of Benjamin resident at Jerusalem (Neh. 11:8).

GABBATHA. The Hebrew or Chaldee appellation of a place, also called "Pavement," where the judgment-seat was planted, from his place on which Pilate delivered Jesus to death (John 19:13). The place was outside the praetorium, for Pilate brought Jesus forth from thence to it.

GABRIEL—*man of God.* The word, which is not in itself distinctive, but merely a description of the angelic office, is used as a proper name or title in Dan. 8:16; 9:21, and in Luke 1:19, 26. In the ordinary traditions, Jewish and Christian, Gabriel is spoken of as one of the archangels.

GAD—*good fortune.* Jacob's seventh son, the first-born of Zilpah, Leah's maid, and wholebrother to Asher (Gen. 30:11-13; 46:16, 18). The word means either "fortune" or "troop": hence Leah said at his birth, "a troop (of children) cometh" (Gen. 30:11; *cf.* 49:19). Of the childhood and life of the patriarch Gad nothing is preserved. At the time of the descent into Egypt seven sons are ascribed to him. The alliance between the tribes of Reuben and Gad was doubtless induced by the similarity of their pursuits. Of all the sons of Jacob these two tribes alone returned to the land which their fore-

fathers had left five hundred years before, with their occupations unchanged. At the halt on the east of Jordan we find them coming forward to Moses with the representation that they "have cattle,"—"a great multitude of cattle," and the land where they now are is a "place for cattle." They did not, however, attempt to evade taking their proper share of the difficulties of subduing the land of Canaan, and after that task had been effected they were dismissed by Joshua "to their tents," to their "wives, their little ones, and their cattle" which they had left behind them in Gilead.

GAD. "The seer," or "the king's seer," *i.e.,* David's (1 Chron. 29:29; 2 Chron. 29:25; 2 Sam. 24:11; 1 Chron. 21:9), was a "prophet" who appears to have joined David when in the hold (1 Sam. 22:5). He reappears in connection with the punishment inflicted for the numbering of the people (2 Sam. 24:11-19; 1 Chron. 21:9-19). He wrote a book of the Acts of David (1 Chron. 29:29), and also assisted in the arrangements for the "house of God" (2 Chron. 29:25).

GADARA. A strong city situated east of the Sea of Galilee, over against Scythopolis and Tiberias, and sixteen Roman miles distant from each of those places. Josephus calls it the capital of Peraea. A large district was attached to it. Gadara itself is not mentioned in the Bible, but it is evidently identical with the "country of the Gadarenes," or Gergesenes (Matt. 8:28; Mark 5:1; Luke 8:26, 37). Gadara derives its greatest interest from having been the scene of Christ's miracle in healing the demoniacs (Matt: 8:28-34; Mark 5:1-21; Luke 8:26-40).

GAIUS. The person to whom the Third Epistle of John is addressed. Several theories of identification have been advanced, but none are certain.

GALATIA. Literally the "Gallia" of the East. The Galatians were in their origin a stream of that great Keltic torrent which poured into Greece in the third century before the Christian era. The Roman province of Galatia may be described as the central region of the peninsula of Asia Minor. The prevailing speech, however, of the district was Greek. The inscriptions found at Ancyra are Greek, and Paul wrote his Epistle in Greek. It is difficult at first sight to determine in what sense the word Galatia is used by the writers of the New Testament, or whether always in the same sense.

GALATIANS, THE EPISTLE TO THE. Written by the Apostle Paul not long after his journey through Galatia and Phrygia (Acts 18:23), and probably in the early portion of his two years and a half stay at Ephesus. The Epistle appears to have been called forth by the machinations of Judaizing teachers, who, shortly before the date of its composition, had endeavored to seduce the churches of this province into a recognition of circumcision (Gal. 5:2, 11 f.; 6:12), and had openly sought to depreciate the apostolic claims of Paul (*cf.* Gal. 1:1, 11). The scope and contents of the Epistle are thus— (1) apologetic (Chaps. 1, 2) and polemical (Chaps. 3, 4) and (2) hortatory and practical (Chaps. 5, 6); the positions and demonstrations of the former portion being used with great power and persuasiveness in the exhortations of the latter.

GALBANUM. One of the perfumes employed in the preparation of the sacred incense (Ex. 30:34). The galbanum of commerce is a resinous gum of a brownish yellow color and aromatic odor.

GALEED—*cairn of witness.* The name given by Jacob to the heap which he and Laban made on Mount Gilead in witness of the covenant then entered into between them (Gen. 31:47 f.).

GALILEE. Originally confined to a little "circuit" of country round Kedesh-Naphtali, in which were the twenty towns given by Solomon to Hiram king of Tyre (Josh. 20:7; 1 Kings 9:11). They were then, or subsequently, occupied by strangers, and for this reason Isaiah gives to

the district the name "Galilee of the Gentiles" (Isa. 9:1). It is probable that the strangers increased until at length Galilee became one of the largest provinces of Palestine. In the time of Jesus Palestine west of the Jordan was divided into three provinces, Judaea, Samaria, and Galilee (Acts 9:31; Luke 17:11). The latter included the whole northern section of the country. On the west it was bounded by the territory of Ptolemais, which probably included the whole plain of Akka to the foot of Carmel. The southern border ran along the base of Carmel and of the hills of Samaria to Mount Gilboa, and then descended the valley of Jezreel by Scythopolis to the Jordan. The river Jordan, the Sea of Galilee, and the upper Jordan to the fountain at Dan, formed the eastern border; and the northern ran from Dan westward across the mountain-ridge till it touched the territory of the Phoenicians. Galilee was divided into two sections, "Lower" and "Upper." *Lower Galilee* included the great plain of Esdraelon with its offshoots, and the whole of the hill country adjoining it on the north to the foot of the mountain-range. It was thus one of the richest and most beautiful sections of Palestine. The chief towns of Lower Galilee were Tiberias, Tarichaea, at the southern end of the Sea of Galilee, and Sepphoris. The towns most celebrated in New Testament history are Nazareth, Cana and Tiberias (Luke 1:26; John 2:1; 6:1). *Upper Galilee* embraced the whole mountain-range lying between the upper Jordan and Phoenicia. To this region the name "Galilee of the Gentiles" is given in the Old and New Testament (Isa. 9:2; Matt. 4:15). The town of Capernaum, on the north shore of the lake, was in Upper Galilee. Galilee was the scene of the greater part of Christ's private life and public acts. His early years were spent at Nazareth; and when he entered on his great work he made Capernaum his home (Matt. 4: 13; 9:1). It is a remarkable fact that the first three Gospels are chiefly taken up with Christ's ministrations in this province, while the Gospel of John dwells more upon those in Judaea. The apostles were all either Galileans by birth or residence (Acts 1:11).

GALILEE, SEA OF. (See Gennesaret.)

GALL. The representative of the Hebrew words *mererah,* or *merorah,* and *rosh.* 1. *Mererah* or *merorah* denotes etymologically "that which is bitter"; see Job 13:26. Hence the term is applied to the "bile" or "gall" from its intense bitterness (Job 16:13; 20:25); it is also used of the "poison" of serpents (Job 20:14). 2. *Rosh,* generally translated "gall" by the A.V., is in Hos. 10:4 rendered "hemlock"; in Deut. 32:33, and Job 20:16, *rosh* denotes the "poison" or "venom" of serpents. From Deut. 29:18, and Lam. 3:19, compared with Hos. 10:4 it is evident that the Hebrew term denotes some bitter and perhaps poisonous plant.

GALLIM—*heaps.* The native place of the man to whom Michal, David's wife, was given (1 Sam. 25:44).

GALLIO. Junius Annaeus Gallio, the Roman proconsul of Achaia when Paul was at Corinth, under the emperor Claudius (Acts 18:12). He was brother to Lucius Annaeus Seneca, the philosopher.

GAMALIEL—*reward of God.* A Pharisee and celebrated doctor of the law, who gave prudent worldly advice in the Sanhedrin respecting the treatment of the followers of Jesus of Nazareth (Acts 5:34 ff.). We learn from Acts 22:3 that he was the preceptor of Paul.

GAMES. Among the Greeks every city of any size possessed its theater and stadium. At Ephesus an annual contest was held in honor of Diana. A direct reference to the exhibitions that took place on such occasions is made in 1 Cor. 15:32. Paul's epistles abound with allusions to the Greek contests. These contests (2 Tim. 4:7; 1 Tim. 6:12) were divided into two classes, the *pancratium,* consisting of boxing and wrestling, and the *pentathlon,* consisting of leaping, running, quoit-

ing, hurling the spear, and wrestling. The competitors (1 Cor. 9:25; 2 Tim. 2:5) required a long and severe course of previous training (1 Tim. 4:8), during which a particular diet was enforced (1 Cor. 9:25, 27). The games were opened by the proclamation of a herald (1 Cor. 9:27), whose office it was to give out the name and country of each candidate, and especially to announce the name of the victor before the assembled multitude. The judge was selected for his spotless integrity (2 Tim. 4:8); his office was to decide any disputes (Col. 3:15) and to give the prize (1 Cor. 9:24; Phil. 3:14), consisting of a crown (2 Tim. 2:5; 4:8) of leaves of wild olive at the Olympic games, and of pine, or, at one period, ivy, at the Isthmian games. The Judge was stationed by the goal (Phil. 3:14), which was clearly visible.

GAMUL—*weaned.* A priest; the leader of the twenty-second course in the service of the sanctuary (1 Chron. 24:17).

GARDEN. Gardens in the East, as the Hebrew word indicates, are enclosures, on the outskirts of towns, planted with various trees and shrubs. From the allusions in the Bible we learn that they were surrounded by hedges of thorn (Isa. 5:5), or walls of stone (Prov. 24:31). For further protection lodges (Isa. 1:8; Lam. 2:6) or watchtowers (Mark 12:1) were built in them, in which sat the keeper (Job 27:18) to drive away the wild beasts and robbers. The gardens of the Hebrews were planted with flowers and aromatic shrubs (Cant. 6:2; 4:16), besides olives, fig trees, nuts, or walnuts (Cant. 6:11), pomegranates, and others for domestic use (Ex. 23:11; Jer. 29:5; Amos 9:14). The rose-garden in Jerusalem is remarkable as having been one of the few which existed within the city walls. Of all the gardens of Palestine none is possessed of associations more sacred and imperishable than the garden of Gethsemane. The Hebrews made use of gardens as places of burial (John 19:41). Manasseh and his son Amon were buried in the garden of their palace, the garden of Uzza (2 Kings 21:18, 26).

GARLIC (Num. 11:5). It is the Allium Sativum of Linnaeus, which abounds in Egypt.

GARRISON. The Hebrew words, 1. *Mattsab* and *mattsabah* undoubtedly mean a "garrison," or fortified post (1 Sam. 13:23; 14:1, 4, 12, 15; 2 Sam. 23:14). 2. *Netsibh* is also used for a "garrison" (in 1 Chron. 11:16), but elsewhere for a "column" erected in an enemy's country (1 Sam. 13:3). 3. The same word (*netsibh*) elsewhere means "officers" placed over a vanquished people (2 Sam. 8:6, 14; 1 Chron. 18:13; 2 Chron. 17:2). 4. *Mattsabah* in Ezek. 26:11 means a "pillar."

GATE. The gates and gateways of eastern cities are sometimes taken as representing the city itself (Gen. 22:17; 24:60; Deut. 12:12; Judg. 5:8; Ruth 4:10; Ps. 87:2; 122:2). Among the special purposes for which they were used may be mentioned: 1. As places of public resort (*e.g.*, Gen. 19:1; 23:10; 34:20, 24; 1 Sam. 4:18). 2. Places for public deliberation, administration of justice, or of audience for kings and rulers or ambassadors (*e.g.*, Deut. 16:18; 21:19; 25:7; Josh. 20:4; Judg. 9:35). 3. Public markets (2 Kings 7:1). The gates of cities were carefully guarded and closed at nightfall (Deut. 3:5; Josh. 2:5, 7; Judg. 9:40, 44). They contained chambers over the gateway (2 Sam. 18:24). The doors themselves of the larger gates mentioned in Scripture were two-leaved, plated with metal, closed with locks and fastened with metal bars (Deut. 3:5; Ps. 107:16; Isa. 45:1 f.). Gates not defended by iron were of course liable to be set on fire by an enemy (Judg. 9:52). The gateways were often richly ornamented. Sentences from the Law were inscribed on and above the gates (Deut. 6:9; Isa. 54:12; Rev. 21:21). The gates of Solomon's Temple were very massive and costly, being overlaid with gold and carvings (1 Kings 6:34 f.; 2 Kings 18:16).

GATH—*wine-press.* One of the five royal cities of the Philistines (Josh. 13:3; 1 Sam. 6:17); and

the native place of the giant Goliath (1 Sam. 17:4, 23).

GATH-HEPHER or **GITTAH-HEPHER**—*winepress of digging.* A town on the border of the territory of Zebulun (Josh. 19:12, 13), celebrated as the native place of the prophet Jonah (2 Kings 14:25).

GAZA. Properly *Azzah,* one of the five chief cities of the Philistines. It is remarkable for its continuous existence and importance from the very earliest times. It is the last town in the southwest of Palestine, on the frontier toward Egypt. In Gen. 10:19 it appears, as a "border" city of the Canaanites. In the conquest of Joshua the territory of Gaza is mentioned as one which he was not able to subdue (Josh. 10:41; 11:22; 13:3). It was assigned to the tribe of Judah (Josh. 15:47), and that tribe did obtain possession of it (Judg. 1:18); but they did not hold it long (Judg. 3:3; 13:1; 16:1, 21). Solomon became master of "Azzah" (1 Kings 4:24). But in after times the same trouble with the Philistines recurred (2 Chron. 21:16; 26:6; 28:18). The passage where Gaza is mentioned in the New Testament (Acts 8:26) is full of interest. It is the account of the baptism of the Ethiopian eunuch on his return from Jerusalem to Egypt.

GEBA—*hill.* A city of Benjamin, with "suburbs," allotted to the priests (Josh. 21:17; 1 Chron. 6:60). During the wars of the earlier part of the reign of Saul, Geba was held as a garrison by the Philistines (1 Sam. 13:3), but they were ejected by Jonathan.

GEBAL—*mountain.* 1. A Phoenician city noted for its shipping (Josh. 13:5; Ezek. 27:9) and for furnishing stone-masons for Solomon (1 Kings 5:18). 2. A district south of the Dead Sea which joined a confederacy against Israel (Ps. 83:8).

GEDALIAH—*Jehovah is great.* Son of Ahikam (Jeremiah's protector, Jer. 26:24). After the destruction of the Temple, Nebuchadnezzar departed from Judaea, leaving Gedaliah with the Chaldean guard (Jer. 40:5) at Mizpah to govern the vine-dressers and husbandmen (Jer. 53:16) who were exempted from captivity. He was murdered by Ishmael two months after his appointment.

GEDER—*wall.* The king of Geder was one of the 31 kings who were overcome by Joshua on the west of the Jordan (Josh. 12:13).

GEHAZI—*valley of vision.* The servant or boy of Elisha. He was sent as the prophet's messenger on two occasions to the good Shunammite (2 Kings 4); obtained fraudulently money and garments from Naaman, was miraculously smitten with incurable leprosy, and was dismissed from the prophet's service (2 Kings 5).

GEMARIAH—*Jehovah has accomplished.* 1. Son of Shaphan the scribe, and father of Michaiah. He was one of the nobles of Judah, and had a chamber in the house of the Lord, from which Baruch read Jeremiah's alarming prophecy in the ears of all the people (Jer. 36). 2. Son of Hilkiah, was made the bearer of Jeremiah's letter to the captive Jews (Jer. 29).

GENEALOGY. In Hebrew the term for genealogy or pedigree is "the book of the generations." The promise of the land of Canaan to the seed of Abraham, Isaac, and Jacob successively, and the separation of the Israelites from the Gentile world; the expectation of Messiah as to spring from the tribe of Judah; the exclusively hereditary priesthood of Aaron with its dignity and emoluments; the succession of kings in the line of David; and the whole division and occupation of the land upon genealogical principles by the tribes, families and houses of fathers, gave a deeper importance to the science of genealogy among the Jews than perhaps any other nation. With Jacob the founder of the nation, the system of reckoning by genealogies was much further developed. In Gen. 35:22-26, we have a

formal account of the sons of Jacob, the patriarchs of the nation, repeated in Ex. 1:1-5. In Gen. 46 we have an exact genealogical census of the house of Israel at the time of Jacob's going down to Egypt. When the Israelites were in the wilderness of Sinai, their number was taken by divine command "after their families, by the house of their fathers." David divided the priests and Levites into courses and companies, each under the family chief. Hezekiah reckoned the whole nation by genealogies.

GENEALOGY OF JESUS CHRIST. The New Testament gives us the genealogy of but one person, that of Jesus, found in Matt. 1:1-17 and Luke 3:23-38. They are both the genealogies of Joseph, *i.e.,* of Jesus Christ as the reputed and legal son of Joseph and Mary. The genealogy of Matthew is Joseph's genealogy as legal successor to the throne of David. Luke's is Joseph's private genealogy, exhibiting his real birth, as David's son, and thus showing why he was heir to Solomon's crown.

GENERATION. In the long lived patriarchal age a generation seems to have been computed at 100 years (Gen. 15:16; *cf.* 13, and Ex. 12:40); but subsequently the reckoning was the same which has been adopted by other civilized nations, that is, from thirty to forty years (Job 42:16).

GENESIS. The first book of the Law or Pentateuch, so called from its title in the Septuagint, that is, *Creation.* The book of Genesis begins with the account of the creation of the world. The first eleven chapters deal with *primeval* history, and the remaining thirty-nine chapters with *patriarchal* history. Adam, Noah, and Noah's sons figure prominently in the former, and Abraham, Isaac, Jacob, and Joseph in the latter. Genesis has a character at once special and universal. It embraces the world; it speaks of God as the God of the whole human race. But as the introduction to Jewish history, it makes the universal interest subordinate to the national.

GENNESARET, LAND OF (Matt. 14:34; Mark 6:53).

GENNESARET, LAKE OF. Called the "Sea of Chinnoreth," or "Cinneroth" (Num. 34:11; Josh. 12:3), from a town near its shore (Josh. 19:35). At its northwestern angle was a fertile plain called "Gennesaret" (Matt. 14:34; Mark 6:53), from which the name of the lake was derived. It is called in the New Testament "sea of Galilee," from the province of Galilee, which bordered its western side (Matt. 4:18; Mark 7:31; John 6:1); and "the sea of Tiberias," from the celebrated city (John 6:1). Most of the public life of Jesus was spent in the environs of the sea of Gennesaret. This region was then the most densely peopled in all Palestine. No less than nine cities stood on the very shores of the lake. The sea of Gennesaret is of an oval shape, about thirteen geographical miles long, and six broad. The river Jordan enters it at its northern end, and passes out at its southern end. The scenery is bleak and monotonous. The water of the lake is sweet, cool, and transparent; and as the beach is everywhere pebbly, it has a beautiful sparkling look. It abounds in fish now as in ancient times.

GENTILES. In the Old Testament the Hebrew *goyim* signified the nations, the surrounding nations, *foreigners* as opposed to Israel (Neh. 5:8), and was used with an invidious meaning. In the New Testament it is used as equivalent to Greek. But the A.V. is not consistent in its translation of the word *Hellen,* sometimes rendering it by "Greek" (Acts 14:1; 17:4; Rom. 1:16; 10:12), sometimes by "Gentile" (Rom. 2:9 f.; 3:9; 1 Cor. 10:32).

GERAR. A very ancient city south of Gaza. It occurs chiefly in Genesis (10:19; 20:1; 26:16); also incidentally in 2 Chron. 14:13 f.

GERIZIM. A mountain in Samaria, south of Mt. Ebal. Between the two mountains in the narrow

pass was the ancient city of Shechem. It is a question whether Gerizim was the mountain on which Abraham was directed to offer his son Isaac (Gen. 22:2). The Samaritans, through whom the tradition of the true site of Gerizim has been preserved, are probably not wrong when they point out Gerizim as the hill upon which Abraham's "faith was made perfect."

GERSHOM—*stranger*. 1. The first-born son of Moses and Zipporah (Ex. 2:22; 18:3). The circumcision of Gershom is probably related in Ex. 4:25. 2. The form under which the name Gershom—the eldest son of Levi—is given in several passages of Chronicles (1 Chron. 6:16 f., 20, 43, 62, 71; 15:7). 3. The representative of the priestly family of Phinehas, among those who accompanied Ezra from Babylon (Ezra 8:2).

GERSHON. The eldest of the three sons of Levi, born before the descent of Jacob's family into Egypt (Gen. 46:11; Ex. 6:16). But, though the eldest born, the families of Gershon were outstripped in fame by their younger brethren of Kohath, from whom sprang Moses and the priestly line of Aaron. At the census in the wilderness of Sinai the whole number of the males of the sons of Gershon was 7,500 (Num. 3:22). The sons of Gershon (the Gershonites) had charge of the fabrics of the Tabernacle—the coverings, curtains, hangings, and cords (Num. 3:25 f.; 4:25 f.).

GERZITES, THE. A tribe who with the Geshurites and the Amalekites occupied the land between the south of Palestine and Egypt in the time of Saul (1 Sam. 27:8).

GESHUR. A small tribe whose territory was in the northeastern corner of Bashan (Deut. 3:14; 2 Sam. 15:8).

GETHSEMANE—*oil-press*. A small "farm" (A.V. "place"; Matt. 26:36; Mark 14:32), situated across the brook Kedron (John 18:1), probably at the foot of Mount Olivet (Luke 22:39), to the northwest, and about ½ or ¾ of a mile English from the walls of Jerusalem. There was a "garden," or rather orchard, attached to it, to which the olive, fig, and pomegranate doubtless invited resort by their hospitable shade.

GEZER. An ancient city of Canaan, whose king, Horam, or Elam, coming to the assistance of Lachish, was killed with all his people by Joshua (Josh. 10:33; 12:12). It formed one of the landmarks on the south boundary of Ephraim, between the lower Beth-horon and the Mediterranean (Josh. 16:3), the western limit of the tribe (1 Chron. 7:28). During Solomon's reign it was taken by Egypt and given to Pharaoh's daughter, Solomon's wife (1 Kings 9:16).

GIANTS. 1. They are first spoken of in Gen. 6:4, under the name *Nephilim*. We are told in Gen. 6:1-4 that "there were Nephilim in the earth," and that afterward the "sons of God" mingling with the beautiful "daughters of men" produced a race of violent and insolent *Gibborim* (A.V. "mighty men"). 2. The Rephaim, a name which frequently occurs. The earliest mention of them is the record of their defeat by Chedorlaomer and some allied kings of Ashteroth-Karnaim (Gen. 14:15). They were probably an aboriginal people of which the Emim, Anakim, and Zuzim were branches.

GIBEAH—*hill*. 1. Gibeah, a city in the mountainous district of Judah (Josh. 15:57). 2. Gilbeath is enumerated among the last group of the towns of Benjamin, next to Jerusalem (Josh. 18:28). 3. The place in which the ark remained from the time of its return by the Philistines until its removal by David (2 Sam. 6:3 f.; cf. 1 Sam. 7:1 f.). 4. Gibeah-of-Benjamin first appears in the tragic story of the Levite and his concubine (Judg. 19, 20). 5. Gibeah-of-Saul. This is not mentioned as Saul's city till after his anointing (1 Sam. 10:26), when he is said to have gone "home" to Gibeah. 6. Gibeah-in-the-Field, named only in Judg. 20:31, as the place

to which one of the "highways" led from Gibeah-of-Benjamin.

GIBEON—*hill city*. One of the four cities of the Hivites, the inhabitants of which made a league with Joshua (Josh. 9:3-15), and thus escaped the fate of Jericho and Ai (cf. Josh. 11:19). It retains its ancient name almost intact, *El-Jib*.

GIBEONITES, THE. The people of Gibeon and perhaps also of the three cities associated with Gibeon (Josh. 9:17)—Hivites, and who were condemned to be perpetual bondmen (Josh. 9:23, 27). Saul appears in a fit of enthusiasm or patriotism to have killed some, and devised a general massacre of the rest (2 Sam. 21:1 ff.). This was expiated many years after by giving up seven men of Saul's descendants to the Gibeonites, who hung them or crucified them "before Jehovah"—as a kind of sacrifice—in Gibeah, Saul's own town (2 Sam. 21:4, 6, 9).

GIDEON—*hewer*. A Manassite, youngest son of Joash of the Abiezrites, an undistinguished family who lived at Ophrah, a town probably on the west of Jordan (Judg. 6:15). He was the fifth recorded Judge of Israel, and for many reasons the greatest of them all. When we first hear of him he was grown up and had sons (Judg. 6:11; 8:20), and from the apostrophe of the angel (6:12) we may conclude that he had already distinguished himself in war. When the angel appeared, Gideon was threshing wheat with a flail in the wine-press, to conceal it from the predatory tyrants. His call to be a deliverer, and his destruction of Baal's altar, are related in Judg. 6. After this begins the second act of Gideon's life—the defeat of the Midianites. Clothed by the Spirit of God (Judg. 6:34; cf. 1 Chron. 12:18; Luke 24:49), he blew a trumpet, and was joined by Zebulun, Naphtali, and even the reluctant Asher. Strengthened by a double sign from God, he reduced his army of 32,000 by the usual proclamation (Deut. 20:8; Judg. 7:3). By a second test at "the spring of trembling" he again reduced the number of his followers to 300 (Judg. 7:5 ff.). The midnight attack upon the Midianites, their panic and the rout and slaughter that followed, are told in Judg. 7. It is not improbable that, like Saul, he had owed a part of his popularity to his princely appearance (Judg. 8:18). In this third stage of his life occur alike his most noble and his most questionable acts—the refusal of the monarchy, and the irregular consecration of a jeweled ephod.

GIER-EAGLE. An unclean bird mentioned in Lev. 11:18 and Deut. 14:17.

GIHON—*bursting forth*. 1. The second river of paradise (Gen. 2:13). (See Eden.) 2. A place near Jerusalem, memorable as the scene of the anointing proclamation of Solomon as king (1 Kings 1:33, 38, 45).

GILBOA. A mountain range on the eastern side of the plain of Esdraelon, rising over the city of Jezreel (cf. 1 Sam. 28:4 with 29:1). It is only mentioned in the defeat and death of Saul and Jonathan by the Philistines (1 Sam. 31:1; 2 Sam. 1:6; 21:12; 1 Chron. 10:1, 8).

GILEAD—*hard; firm* (?). 1. A mountainous region bounded on the west by the Jordan, on the north by Bashan, on the east by the Arabian plateau, and on the south by Moab and Ammon (Gen. 31:21; Deut. 3:12-17). It is sometimes called "Mount Gilead" (Gen. 31:25), sometimes "the land of Gilead" (Num. 32:1), and sometimes "Gilead" (Ps. 60:7; Gen. 37:25); but they all mean the same thing. 2. Possibly the name of a mountain west of the Jordan, near Jezreel (Judg. 7:3). We are inclined to think the true reading in this place should be Gilboa. 3. Son of Machir (Num. 26:29 f.). 4. The father of Jephthah (Judg. 11:1 f.).

GILEADITES, THE (Judg. 12:4 f.; Num. 26:29; Judg. 10:3), a branch of the tribe of Manasseh, descended from Gilead.

GILGAL—*circle of stones*. 1. The site of the first camp of the Israelites on the west of the Jordan, the place at which they passed the first night after crossing the river, and where the twelve stones were set up which had been taken from the bed of the stream (Josh. 4:19 f., cf. 4:3); where also they kept their first passover in the land of Canaan (5:10). It was in the "end of the east of Jericho," the hot, depressed district of the Ghor which lay between the town and the Jordan. 2. A distinct place is the Gilgal connected with the last scene in the life of Elijah, and one of Elisha's miracles (2 Kings 2). 3. The "King of the nations of Gilgal," or rather perhaps the "king of Goim-at-Gilgal," is mentioned (Josh. 12:23). 4. A Gilgal is spoken of in Josh. 15:7, in describing the north border of Judah.

GILOH. A town in the mountainous part of Judah (Josh. 15:51), was the native place of the famous Ahithophel (2 Sam. 15:12).

GIN. A trap for birds or beasts (Isa. 8:14; Amos 3:5).

GIRDLE. An essential article of dress in the East, and worn by both men and women. The common girdle was made of leather, like that worn by the Bedouins of the present day. The girdle was fastened by a clasp of gold or silver, or tied in a knot so that the ends hung down in front. It was worn by men about the loins (Isa. 5:27; 11:5). The girdle of women was generally looser than that of the men, and was worn about the hips, except when they were actively engaged (Prov. 31:17). The military girdle was worn about the waist; the sword or dagger was suspended from it (Judg. 3:16; 2 Sam. 20:8; Ps. 45:3). In times of mourning girdles of sackcloth were worn (Isa. 3:24; 22:12).

GIRGASHITES, THE. One of the nations which were in possession of Canaan before the entrance of the children of Israel (Gen. 10:16; 15:21; Deut. 7:1; Josh. 3:10; 24:11; 1 Chron. 1:14; Neh. 9:8).

GITTITES. The 600 men who followed David from Gath, under Ittai the Gittite (2 Sam. 15:18 f.), and who probably acted as a kind of bodyguard.

GLASS. The Hebrew word occurs only in Job 28:17, where in A.V. it is rendered "crystal." In the New Testament glass is alluded to as an emblem of brightness (Rev. 4:6; 15:2; 21:18).

GLEANING. The gleaning of fruit trees, as well as of corn fields, was reserved for the poor (Lev. 19:9 f.; 23:22; see also Corner).

GLEDE. The old name for the common kite, occurs only in Deut. 14:13 among the unclean birds of prey.

GNAT. Mentioned only in the proverbial expression used by Jesus in Matt. 23:24.

GOAD. A stick or pole about 8 feet long, pointed or having a sharp metal tip at one end, used in herding cattle (Judg. 3:31; 1 Sam. 13:21; Acts 9:5).

GOAT. There are six Hebrew words meaning a tame goat, and one, possibly two, meaning wild goat. Goats were an important item of wealth in Bible lands (Gen. 30:33, 35; 32:14; 1 Sam. 25:2). Kids were especially used for food (Gen. 27:9; Luke 15:29).

GOB. Place where David battled with the Philistines (2 Sam. 21:18 f.). In the parallel account in 1 Chron. 20:4, the name is given as Gezer.

GOD. Throughout the Hebrew Scriptures two chief names are used for the one true divine Being—Elohim, commonly translated *God* in A.V. and Jehovah, commonly translated *Lord*. Elohim is the plural of Eloah (in Arabic *Allah*), a form which occurs only in poetry and a few passages of later

Hebrew (Neh. 9:17; 2 Chron. 32:15). It is also formed with the pronominal suffixes, as Eloi *my God*, with the dependent genitive, and with an epithet, in which case it is often used in the short form El (a word signifying *strength*, as in the El-Shaddai, *God Almighty*, the name by which God was specially known to the patriarchs (Gen. 17:1; 28:3; Ex. 6:3). The plural form of Elohim has given rise to much discussion. The fanciful idea, that it referred to the *Trinity of Persons* in the Godhead, hardly finds now a supporter among scholars. It is either what grammarians call the plural of majesty, or it denotes the fulness of divine strength, the sum of the powers displayed by God. Jehovah denotes specifically the one true God. At a time too early to be traced the Jews abstained from pronouncing the name, for fear of its irreverent use. The custom is said to have been founded on a strained interpretation of Lev. 24:16; and the phrase there used, "The Name," is substituted by the Rabbis for the unutterable word. They also call it "the name of four letters," YHWH, "the great and terrible name," "the peculiar name," "the separate name." In reading the scriptures they substituted for it the word Adonai (*Lord*), from the translation of which we have got the Lord of the A.V. The A.V. has, however, used Jehovah in four passages (Ex. 6:3; Ps. 83:18; Isa. 12:2; 26:4), and in the compounds, *Jehovah-Jireh, Jehovah-Nissi,* and *Jehovah-Shalom* (*Jehovah shall see, Jehovah is my Banner, Jehovah is Peace,* Gen. 22:14; Ex. 17:15; Judg. 6:24); while the similar phrases *Jehovah-Tsidkenu* and *Jehovah-Shammah* are translated, "the Lord our righteousness," and "the Lord is there" (Jer. 23:6; 33:16; Ezek. 48:35). In one passage the abbreviated form *Jah* is retained (Ps. 68:4). As early as the time of Seth "men began to call on the name of Jehovah" (Gen. 4:25).

GOLAN. A city of Bashan (Deut. 4:43), allotted out of the half tribe of Manasseh to the Levites (Josh. 21:27), and one of the three cities of refuge east of the Jordan (Josh. 20:8).

GOLD. The most valuable of metals, from its color, lustre, weight, ductility, and other useful properties. Hence it is used as an emblem of purity (Job 23:10) and nobility (Lam. 4:1). Gold was known from the very earliest times (Gen. 2:11). It was at first chiefly used for ornaments (Gen. 24:22). Coined money was not known to the ancients till a comparatively late period; and on the Egyptian tombs gold is represented as being weighed in rings for commercial purposes. The chief countries mentioned as producing gold are Arabia, Sheba, and Ophir (1 Kings 9:28; 10:1; Job 28:16). Other gold-bearing countries were Uphaz (Jer. 10:9; Dan. 10:5) and Parvaim (2 Chron. 3:6).

GOLGOTHA—*skull*. The Hebrew name of the spot at which Jesus was crucified (Matt. 27:33; Mark 15:22; John 19:17). By these three Evangelists it is interpreted to mean the "place of a skull." Two explanations are given; (1) that it was a spot where executions ordinarily took place, and therefore abounded in skulls. Or (2) it may come from the look or form of the spot itself, bald, round and skull-like, and therefore a mound or hillock, in accordance with the common phrase—for which there is no direct authority—"Mount Calvary."

GOLIATH. A famous giant of Gath, who "morning and evening for forty days" defied the armies of Israel (1 Sam. 17). He was possibly descended from the old Rephaim (see Giants), of whom a scattered remnant took refuge with the Philistines after their dispersion by the Ammonites (Deut. 2:20 f.; 2 Sam. 21:22). His height was "six cubits and a span," which, taking the cubit at 18 inches, would make him over 9 feet high. But the Septuagint and Josephus read *"four cubits and a span."* The scene of his combat with David was the Valley of the Terebinth. In 2 Sam. 21:19, we find that another Goliath of Gath was slain by Elhannan, also a Bethlehemite.

GOMER. 1. The oldest son of Japheth, and the

father of Ashkepaz, Riphath, and Togarmah (Gen. 10:2 f.). 2. The daughter of Diblaim and concubine of Hosea (1:3).

GOMORRAH—*submersion*. In the New Testament written Gomorrha, one of the five "cities of the plain," or "vale of Siddim," that under their respective kings joined battle there with Chedorlaomer (Gen. 14:2-8) and his allies, by whom they were discomfited till Abraham came to the rescue. Four out of the five were afterward destroyed by fire from heaven (Gen. 19: 23-29). One of them only, Zoar or Bela, which was its original name, was spared at the request of Lot, in order that he might take refuge there. Of these Gomorrah seems to have been only second to Sodom in importance, as well as in the wickedness that led to their overthrow.

GOSHEN. The name of a northeastern part of Egypt where the Israelites dwelt for the whole period of their sojourn in that country. It is usually called the "land of Goshen," but also Goshen simply. It appears to have borne another name "the land of Rameses" (Gen. 45:10; 46:8; 47:11).

GOSPELS. The name Gospel (from *God* and *spell*, Angl.Sax. *God message* or *news*, which is a translation of the Greek *evangelion*) is applied to the four inspired accounts of the life and teaching of Christ contained in the New Testament, of which separate accounts are given in their place. They were all composed during the latter half of the first century; those of Matthew and Mark some years before the destruction of Jerusalem; that of Luke probably about A.D. 64; and that of John toward the close of the century. Before the end of the second century, there is abundant evidence that the four Gospels, as one collection, were generally used and accepted. As a matter of literary history nothing can be better established than the genuineness of the Gospels.

GOURD. 1. Hebrew *kikayon*, found only in Jon. 4:6-10. The plant which is intended by this word, and which afforded shade to the prophet Jonah before Nineveh. The meaning of the Hebrew word is uncertain, being translated sometimes "gourd" and sometimes "castor-oil plant." 2. With regard to the "wild gourds" (*pakku'oth*) of 2 Kings 4:39, which one of the "sons of the prophets" gathered ignorantly, supposing them to be good for food, there can be no doubt that it is a species of the gourd tribe (*Cucurbitaceae*), which contains some plants of a very bitter and dangerous character.

GOVERNOR. In the A.V. this one English word is the representative of no less than ten Hebrew and four Greek words. 1. The chief of a tribe or family. 2. A ruler in his capacity of *law-giver* and dispenser of justice. 3. A ruler considered especially as having power over the property and persons of his subjects. The "governors of the people," in 2 Chron. 23:20, appear to have been the king's bodyguard (*cf.* 2 Kings 11:19). 4. A prominent personage, whatever his capacity.

GRAPE. (See Vine.)

GRASS. This is the ordinary rendering of the Hebrew word *hazir* (1 Kings 18:5; Job 40:5; Ps. 104:14; Isa. 15:6). As the herbage rapidly fades under the parching heat of the sun of Palestine, it has afforded to the sacred writers an image of the fleeting nature of human fortunes (Job 8:12; Ps. 37:2) and also of the brevity of human life (Isa. 40:6 f.; Ps. 90:5).

GRASSHOPPER. (See Locust.)

GRAVE. (See Burial.)

GREAVES. This word occurs in the A.V. only in 1 Sam. 17:6. Its ordinary meaning is a piece of defensive armor which protected the shin of the wearer. But the *mizhath* of the above was not worn on the legs, but on the feet of Goliath, and would therefore appear to have been a kind of shoe or boot.

GREECE, GREEKS, GRECIANS. The histories of Greece and Palestine are little connected with each other. In Gen. 10:2-5 we find mentioned the descendants of Javan as peopling the isles of the Gentiles; and when the Hebrews came into contact with the Ionians of Asia Minor, and recognized them as the long lost islanders of the western migration, it was natural that they should mark the similarity of sound between *Javan* and *Iones*. Accordingly the Old Testament word which is *Grecia*, in A.V. *Greece, Greeks*, etc., is in Hebrew *Javan* (Joel 3:6; Dan. 8:21): the Hebrew, however, is sometimes retained (Isa. 66:19; Ezek. 27:13). The name of the country, Greece, occurs once in the New Testament (Acts 20:2), as opposed to Macedonia. (See Gentiles.)

GREYHOUND. The translation in the text of the A.V. (Prov. 30:31) of the Hebrew word *zarzir mothnayin*, i.e., "one girt about the lions."

GUR—*dwelling; sojourning*, THE GOING UP TO. An ascent or rising ground, at which Ahaziah received his death-blow while flying from Jehu after the slaughter of Joram (2 Kings 9:27).

HABAKKUK—*embrace*. The eighth in order of the minor prophets. Of the facts of the prophet's life we have no certain information. He probably delivered his prophecy about the 12th or 13th year of Josiah.

HABERGEON. A coat of mail covering the neck and breast.

HACHILAH—*dark*, THE HILL. A hill apparently situated in the neighborhood of Ziph; in the fastnesses, or passes, of which David and his six hundred followers were lurking when the Ziphites informed Saul of his whereabouts (1 Sam. 23:19; *cf.* 14, 15, 18).

HADAD. Originally the indigenous appellation of the sun among the Syrians, and thence transferred to the king, as the highest of earthly authorities. The title appears to have been an official one, like Pharaoh. It is found occasionally in the altered form Hadar (Gen. 25:15; 36:39; *cf.* 1 Chron. 1:30, 50). 1. Son of Ishmael (Gen. 25:15; 1 Chron. 1:30). 2. A king of Edom who gained an important victory over the Midianites on the field of Moab (Gen. 36:35; 1 Chron. 1:46). 3. Also a king of Edom, with Pau for his capital (1 Chron. 1:50). 4. A member of the royal house of Edom (1 Kings 11:14 ff.).

HADAD-RIMMON (Zech. 12:11). A place in the valley of Megiddo, named after two Syrian idols, where national lamentation was held for the death of King Josiah (2 Kings 23:29; 2 Chron. 35:22-24).

HADAREZER, HADADEZER—*Hadad is a help*. Son of Rehob (2 Sam. 8:3), the king of the Aramite state of Zobah, who was pursued by David, and defeated with great loss both of chariots, horses, and men (1 Chron. 18:3 f.; 19:16; 2 Sam. 10:15; *cf.* 8).

HADASSAH—*myrtle*. The Jewish name of Esther (Esth. 2:7).

HADORAM. 1. The fifth son of Joktan (Gen. 10:27; 1 Chron. 1:21). 2. Son of Tou or Toi king of Hamath (1 Chron. 18:10). 3. The form assumed in Chronicles by the name of the intendant of taxes under David, Solomon and Rehoboam (2 Chron. 10:18). In Kings the name is given in the longer form of Adoniram, but in Samuel (2 Sam. 20:24) as Adoram.

HAGAR—*flight*. An Egyptian woman, the handmaid or slave of Sarah (Gen. 16:1), whom the latter gave as a concubine to Abraham, after he had dwelt ten years in the land of Canaan and had no children by Sarah. That she was a bond-woman is stated both in the Old Testament and in the New Testament, in the latter as part of her typical character (Gal. 4:25). It is recorded that "when she saw that she had conceived, her mistress was despised in her eyes,"

and Sarah, with the anger, we may suppose, of a free woman, rather than a wife, reproached Abraham for the results of her own act. Hagar fled, turning her steps toward her native land through the great wilderness traversed by the Egyptian road. By the fountain in the way to Shur, the angel of the Lord found her, charged her to return and submit herself under the hands of her mistress, and delivered the remarkable prophecy respecting her unborn child recorded in verses 10-12. On her return she gave birth to Ismael, and Abraham was then eighty-six years old.

HAGARENES, HAGARITES. A people dwelling to the east of Palestine, with whom the tribe of Reuben made war in the time of Saul (1 Chron. 5:10, 18-20). It is generally believed that they were named after Hagar.

HAGGAI—*festal*. The tenth in order of the minor Prophets, and the first of those who prophesied after the Captivity. With regard to his tribe and parentage both history and tradition are alike silent.

HAGGITH—*festive*. One of David's wives, the mother of Adonijah (2 Sam. 3:4; 1 Kings 1:5, 11; 2:13; 1 Chron. 3:2).

HAIR. The Hebrews were alive to the importance of the hair as an element of personal beauty. Long hair was admired in the case of young men (2 Sam. 14:26). In times of affliction the hair was altogether cut off (Isa. 3:17, 24; 15:2; Jer. 7:29). Tearing the hair (Ezra 9:3) and letting it go disheveled were similar tokens of grief. The usual and favorite color of the hair was black (Cant. 5:11), as is indicated in the comparisons to a "flock of goats" and the "tents of Kedar" (Cant. 4:1; 1:5). The approach of age was marked by a sprinkling (Hos. 7:9) of gray hairs, which soon overspread the whole head (Gen. 42:38; 44:29; 1 Kings 2:6, 9; Prov. 16:31; 20:29). Pure white hair was deemed characteristic of the divine majesty (Dan. 7:9; Rev. 1:14). The chief beauty of the hair consisted in curls, whether of a natural or artificial character. With regard to the mode of dressing the hair, we have no very precise information; the terms used are of a general character.

HALL. Used of the court of the high priest's house (Luke 22:55). In Matt. 27:27, and Mark 15:16, "hall" is synonymous with "praetorium," which in John 18:28 is in A.V. "judgment-hall."

HALOHESH. Shallum, son of Hallohesh, was "ruler of the half part of Jerusalem" at the time of the repair of the wall by Nehemiah (Neh. 3:12).

HAM—*hot*. 1. The name of one of the three sons of Noah, apparently the second in age. It probably signifies "warm" or "hot." This meaning is confirmed by that of the Egyptian word *Kem* (Egypt), the Egyptian equivalent of Ham, which signifies "black," probably implying warmth as well as blackness. Of the history of Ham nothing is related except his irreverence to his father, and the curse which that patriarch pronounced (Gen. 9:21-25). The sons of Ham are stated to have been "Cush and Mizraim and Phut and Canaan" (Gen. 10:6; *cf.* 1 Chron. 1:3). The name of Ham alone, of the three sons of Noah, is known to have been given to a country. Egypt is recognized as the "land of Ham" in the Bible (Ps. 78:51; 106:22). It is certain that the three most illustrious Hamite nations—the Cushites, the Phoenicians, and the Egyptians—were greatly mixed with foreign peoples. 2. According to the present text (Gen. 14:5) Chedorlaomer and his allies smote the Zuzim in a place called Ham.

HAMAN. The chief minister or vizier of King Ahasuerus (Esth. 3:1). After the failure of his attempt to cut off all the Jews in the Persian empire, he was hanged on the gallows which he had erected for Mordecai.

HAMATH—*fortress*. The principal city of Upper Syria, was in the valley of the Orontes, which it commanded from the low screen of hills which forms the watershed between the Orontes and the Litani—the "entrance of Hamath," as it is called in Scripture (Num. 34:8; Josh. 13:5, *etc.*)—to the defile of Daphne below Antioch. The Hamathites were a Hamitic race, and are included among the descendants of Canaan (Gen. 10:18). The "store-cities," which Solomon "built in Hamath" (2 Chron. 8:4), were perhaps staples for trade.

HANAN—*gracious*. 1. One of the tribe of Benjamin (1 Chron. 8:23). 2. The last of the six sons of Azel (1 Chron. 8:38; 9:44). 3. "Son of Maachah" (1 Chron. 11:43). 4. The sons of Hanan were among the Nethinim who returned from Babylon with Zerubbabel (Ezra 2:46; Neh. 7:49). 5. One of the Levites who assisted Ezra in his public exposition of the law (Neh. 8:7). 6. One of the "heads" of the "people," who also sealed the covenant (Neh. 10:22). 7. Another of the chief laymen on the same occasion (Neh. 10:26). 8. Son of Zaccur, son of Mattaniah (Neh. 13:13). 9. Son of Igdaliah (Jer. 35:4).

HANANEEL—*God is gracious*, TOWER OF. A tower which formed part of the wall of Jerusalem (Neh. 3:1; 12:39).

HANANI—*gracious*. 1. One of the sons of Heman (1 Chron. 25:4, 25). 2. A seer who rebuked Asa, king of Judah (2 Chron. 16:7). 3. One of the priests who in the time of Ezra had taken strange wives (Ezra 10:20). 4. A brother of Nehemiah (Neh. 1:2) who was made governor of Jerusalem under Nehemiah (Neh. 7:2). 5. A priest mentioned in Neh. 12:36.

HANANIAH—*Jehovah hath been gracious*. 1. One of the 14 sons of Heman (1 Chron. 25:4, 5, 23). 2. A general in the army of king Uzziah (2 Chron. 26:11). 3. Father of Zedekiah in the reign of Jehoiakim. 4. Son of Azur, a Benjamite of Gibeon and a false prophet in the reign of Zedekiah king of Judah. In the 4th year of his reign Hananiah withstood Jeremiah the prophet, publicly prophesied in the temple (Jer. 28). 5. Grandfather of Irijah, who arrested Jeremiah on the charge of deserting to the Chaldaeans (Jer. 37:13). 6. Head of a Benjamite house (1 Chron. 8:24). 7. The Hebrew name of Shadrach (Dan. 1:3, 6, 7, 11, 19; 2:17). 8. Son of Zerubbabel (1 Chron. 3:19), from whom Christ derived his descent. He is the same person who by Luke is called Joanna. 9. One of the sons of Bebai, who returned with Ezra from Babylon (Ezra 10:28). 10. A priest, one of the makers of the sacred ointments and incense, who built a portion of the wall of Jerusalem in the days of Nehemiah (Neh. 3:8). 11. Head of the priestly course of Jeremiah in the days of Joiakim (Neh. 12:12). 12. Ruler of the palace at Jerusalem under Nehemiah (Neh. 7:2 f.). 13. An Israelite (Neh. 10:23).

HANDICRAFT (Acts 18:3; 19:25; Rev. 18:22). The preparation of iron for use, together with working in brass, or rather copper alloyed with tin, bronze, is mentioned as practised in antediluvian times (Gen. 4:22). In the construction of the Tabernacle, copper, but no iron, appears to have been used, though the use of iron was at the same period well known to the Hebrews, both from their own use of it and from Egyptian education (Ex. 20:25; 25:3; 27:19; Num. 35:16; Deut. 3:11; 4:20; 8:9; Josh. 8:31; 17:16-18). After the establishment of the Hebrews in Canaan, the occupation of a smith became recognized as a distinct employment (1 Sam. 13:19). The smith's work and its results are often mentioned in Scripture (2 Sam. 12:31; 1 Kings 6:7; 2 Chron. 26:14; Isa. 44:12; 54:16). The work of the carpenter is often mentioned in Scripture (Gen. 6:14; Ex. 37; Isa. 44:13). In the New Testament the occupation of a carpenter is mentioned in connection with Joseph, the husband of the Virgin Mary, and ascribed to Christ by way of reproach (Mark 6:3; Matt. 13:55). The masons employed by David and Solomon, at least the chief of them, were Phoenicians (1 Kings 5:18;

Ezek. 27:9). Akin to the craft of the carpenter is that of ship and boat-building, which must have been exercised to some extent for the fishing vessels on the lake of Gennesaret (Matt. 8:23; 9:1; John 21:3, 8). Solomon built, at Ezion-Geber, ships for his foreign trade, which were manned by Phoenician crews, an experiment which Jehoshaphat endeavored in vain to renew (1 Kings 9:26, 27; 22:48; 2 Chron. 20:36, 37). The arts of spinning and weaving both wool and linen were carried on in early times by women (Ex. 35:25, 26; Lev. 19:19; Deut. 22:11; 2 Kings 23:7; Ezek. 16:16; Prov. 31:13, 24). Together with weaving we read also of embroidery, in which gold and silver threads were interwoven with the body of the stuff, sometimes in figure patterns, or with precious stones set in the needlework (Ex. 26:1; 28:4; 39:6-13). 7. Besides these arts, those of dyeing and of dressing cloth were practiced in Palestine, and those also of tanning and dressing leather (Josh. 2:15-18; 2 Kings 1:8; Matt. 3:4; Acts 9:43).

HANDKERCHIEF, NAPKIN, APRON. The *sudarium* or handkerchief is noticed in the New Testament as a wrapper to fold up money (Luke 19:20)—as a cloth bound about the head of a corpse (John 11:41; 20:7)—and lastly as an article of dress that could be easily removed (Acts 19:12), probably a handkerchief worn on the head.

HANGING, HANGINGS. 1. The "hanging" was a curtain or "covering" to close an entrance, one was placed before the door of the Tabernacle (Ex. 26:36, 37; 39:38). 2. The "hangings" were used for covering the walls of the court of the Tabernacle, just as tapestry was in modern times (Ex. 27:9; 35:17; 38:9; Num. 3:26; 4:26).

HANNAH—*grace*. One of the wives of Elkanah, and mother of Samuel (1 Sam. 1, 2). A hymn of thanksgiving for the birth of her son is in the highest order of prophetic poetry; its resemblance to that of the Virgin Mary (*cf.* 1 Sam. 2:1-10 with Luke 1:46-55; see also Ps. 113) has been noticed by commentators.

HANUN—*pitied*. 1. Son of Nahash (2 Sam. 10:1, 2; 1 Chron. 19:1, 2), king of Ammon, who dishonored the ambassadors of David (2 Sam. 10:4), and involved the Ammonites in a disastrous war (2 Sam. 12:31; 1 Chron. 19:6). 2. A man who, with the people of Zanoah, repaired the ravine-gate in the wall of Jerusalem (Neh. 3:13). 3. The 6th son of Zalaph, who also assisted in the repair of the wall apparently on the east side (Neh. 3:30).

HARAN—*a mountaineer*. 1. The third son of Terah, and therefore youngest brother of Abram (Gen. 11:26 ff.). Three children are ascribed to him—Lot (27, 31), and two daughters: Milcah, who married her uncle Nahor, and Iscah. Haran was born in Ur of the Chaldees, and he died there while his father was still living. 2. A Gershonite Levite of the family of Shimei (1 Chron. 23:9). 3. A son of the great Caleb by his concubine Ephah (1 Chron. 2:46). 4. Haran or Charran (Acts 7:2, 4), name of the place whither Abraham migrated with his family from Ur of the Chaldees, and where the descendants of his brother Nahor established themselves (*cf.* Gen. 24:10 with 27:43).

HARE. Occurs only in Lev. 11:6, and Deut. 14:7, amongst the unclean animals diallowed as food by the Mosaic law.

HARLOT. That this class of persons existed in the earliest states of society is clear from Gen. 38:15. Rahab (Josh. 2:1 ff.) and her family escaped the destruction of Jericho because she aided Joshua's men. The "harlots" are classed with "publicans," as those who lay under the ban of society, in the New Testament (Matt. 21:32).

HAROD, THE WELL OF. A spring by which Gideon and his great army encamped on the morning of the day which ended in the rout of the Midianites (Judg. 7:1).

HAROSHETH "OF THE GENTILES." So called from the mixed races that inhabited it, a city in the north of the land of Canaan, dwelling place of Sisera (Judgs. 4:2).

HARP (Hebrew *kinnor*). The *kinnor* was the national instrument of the Hebrews, and was well known throughout Asia. Its invention is placed in the antediluvian period (Gen. 4:21).

HARROW. The word so rendered (2 Sam. 12:31; 1 Chron. 20:3) is probably a threshing machine. The verb rendered "to harrow" (Isa. 28:24) expresses apparently the breaking of the clods.

HART. The hart is reckoned among the clean animals (Deut. 12:15; 14:5; 15:22), and seems to have been commonly killed for food.

HAVILAH. 1. A son of Cush (Gen. 10:7); and, 2. A son of Joktan (10:29). 3. A region rich in gold (Gen. 2:11).

HAVOTH-JAIR—*villages of Jair*. Certain villages on the east of Jordan, in Gilead or Bashan, which were taken by Jair the son of Manasseh, and called after his name (Num. 32:41; Deut. 3:14). In 1 Chron. 2:22 they are specified as twenty-three, but in Judg. 10:4 as thirty.

HAWK. The translation of the Hebrew *nez* (Lev. 11:16; Deut. 14:15; Job 39:26). The word is doubtless generic, and includes various species of the *Falconidae*.

HAY (Heb. *hazir*), the rendering of the A.V. in Prov. 27:25, and Isa. 15:6, of the above named Hebrew term, which occurs frequently in the Old Testament, and denotes "grass" of any kind. It is certain that the ancients did mow their grass, and probably made use of the dry material (see Ps. 37:2).

HAZAEL—*whom God beholds*. A king of Damascus. He appears to have been previously a person in a high position at the court of Benhadad, and was sent by his master to Elisha, to inquire if he would recover from the malady under which he was suffering. Elisha's answer led to the murder of Benhadad by his ambitious servant, who forthwith mounted the throne (2 Kings 8:7-15). Toward the close of the reign of Jehu, Hazael led the Syrians against the Israelites, whom he "smote in all their coasts" (2 Kings 10:32), thus accomplishing the prophecy of Elisha (*ibid.* 8:12).

HAZEL. The Hebrew term *luz* occurs only in Gen. 30:37. A better translation might be "almond."

HAZER. Topographically, seems generally employed for the "villages" of people in a roving and unsettled life, the semi-permanent collections of dwellings which are described by travellers among the modern Arabs to consist of rough stone walls covered with the tent cloth.

HEAD-DRESS. The Hebrews do not appear to have regarded a covering for the head as an essential article of dress. The earliest notice we have of such a thing is in connection with the sacerdotal vestments (Ex. 28:40).

HEARTH. The cakes baked "on the hearth" (Gen. 18:6) were probably baked on hot stones covered with ashes. The "hearth" of King Jehoiakim's winter palace (Jer. 36:23) was possibly a pan or brazier of charcoal.

HEAVEN. There are four Hebrew words thus rendered in the Old Testament. 1. *Rakia* (A.V. firmament). (See Firmament.) 2. *Shamayim*. This is the word used in the expression, "the heaven and the earth," or "the upper and lower regions" (Gen. 1:1). 3. *Marom*, used for heaven in Ps. 18:16; Jer. 25:30; Isa. 24:18. Properly speaking it means a mountain, as in Ps. 102:10; Ezek. 17:23. 4. *Shehakim*, "expanses," with reference to the *extent* of heaven (Deut. 33:26; John

35:5). Paul's expression "third heaven" (2 Cor. 12:2) has led to much conjecture.

HEBREW. This word first occurs as given to Abram by the Canaanites (Gen. 14:13) because he had crossed the Euphrates. The name is also derived from *'eber*, "beyond, on the other side," but this is essentially the same with the preceding explanation, since both imply that Abraham and his posterity were called Hebrews in order to express a distinction between the races east and west of the Euphrates. The term Israelite was used by the Jews of themselves among themselves, the term Hebrew was the name by which they were known to foreigners. All the books of the Old Testament are written in the Hebrew language, with the exception of the following passages—Dan. 2:4-7; Ezek. 4:8–6:18 and 7:12-26; Jer. 10:11—which are in Chaldee.

HEBREWS, EPISTLE TO THE. Paul, Barnabas, Silas, Peter, Priscilla, and Aquila are among those who have been regarded as the author. Clement of Alexandria ascribed to Luke the translation of the epistle into Greek from a Hebrew original of Paul. Origen believed that the thoughts were Paul's, the language and composition Luke's or Clement's of Rome. Tertullian names Barnabas as the reputed author according to the North African tradition. Luther's conjecture that Apollos was the author has been adopted by many. The epistle was probably addressed to Christians who lacked a true insight into Christian faith and were thus easily tempted into apostasy.

HEBRON—*association*. 1. The third son of Kohath, who was the second son of Levi; the younger brother of Amram, father of Moses and Aaron (Ex. 6:18; Num. 3:19; 1 Chron. 6:2, 18; 23:12). 2. A city of Judah (Josh. 15:54); situated among the mountains (Josh. 20:7), 20 Roman miles south of Jerusalem, and the same distance north of Beersheba. Hebron is one of the most ancient cities in the world still existing; and in this respect it is the rival of Damascus. Sarah died at Hebron; and Abraham then bought from Ephron the Hittite the field and cave of Machpelah, to serve as a family tomb (Gen. 23:2-20).

HEDGE. The Hebrew words thus rendered denote simply that which surrounds or encloses, whether it be a stone wall (*gadar*, Prov. 24:31; Ezek. 42:10) or a fence of other material.

HEIR. The Hebrew institutions relative to inheritance were of a very simple character. Under the patriarchal system the property was divided among the sons of the legitimate wives (Gen. 21:10; 24:36; 25:5), a larger portion being assigned to one, generally the eldest, on whom devolved the duty of maintaining the females of the family. The sons of concubines were portioned off with presents (Gen. 25:6). At a later period the exclusion of the sons of concubines was rigidly enforced (Judg. 11:1 ff.). Daughters had no share in the patrimony (Gen. 21:14), but received a marriage portion. The Mosaic law regulated the succession to real property thus: it was to be divided among the sons, the eldest receiving a double portion (Deut. 21:17), the others equal shares; if there were no sons, it went to the daughters (Num. 27:8), on the condition that they did not marry out of their own tribe (Num. 36:6 ff.), otherwise the patrimony was forfeited. If there were no daughters, it went to the brother of the deceased; if no brother, to the paternal uncle; if none, to next of kin (Num. 27:9-11).

HELI. The father of Joseph, the husband of the Virgin Mary (Luke 3:23).

HELL. This is the word generally and unfortunately used by our translators to render the Hebrew *Sheol*. It would perhaps have been better to retain the Hebrew word *Sheol*, or else render it always by "the grave" or "the pit." It is clear that in many passages of the Old Testament *Sheol* can only mean "the grave," and is so ren-

dered in the A.V. (see, *e.g.*, Gen. 37:35; 42:38; 1 Sam. 2:6; Job 14:13). In other passages, however, it seems to involve a notion of punishment, and is therefore rendered in the A.V. by the word "Hell." But in many cases this translation misleads the reader. It is obvious, for instance, that Job 11:8; Ps. 139:8; Amos 9:2 (where "hell" is used as the antithesis of "heaven"), merely illustrate the Jewish notions of the locality of *Sheol* in the bowels of the earth. In the New Testament the word Hades, like *Sheol*, sometimes means merely "the grave" (Rev. 20:13; Acts 2:31; 1 Cor. 15:55), or in general "the unseen world." Elsewhere in the New Testament Hades is used of a place of torment (Luke 16:23; 2 Pet. 2:4; Matt. 11:23, etc.).

HELLENIST. In one of the earliest notices of the first Christian Church at Jerusalem (Acts 6:1), two distinct parties are recognized among its members, "Hebrews" and "Hellenists" (Grecians), who appear to stand toward one another in some degree in a relation of jealous rivalry (*cf.* Acts 9:29). The Hellenists as a body included not only the proselytes of Greek (or foreign) parentage, but also those Jews who, by settling in foreign countries, had adopted the prevalent form of the current Greek civilization, and with it the use of the common Greek dialect.

HEM OF GARMENT. The importance which the later Jews, especially the Pharisees (Matt. 23:5), attached to the hem or fringe of their garments was founded upon the regulation in Num. 15:38, 39, which gave a symbolical meaning to it.

HEMAN—*faithful*. 1. Son of Zerah (1 Chron. 2:6; 1 Kings 4:31). 2. Son of Joel, and grandson of Samuel the prophet, a Kohathite. He is called "the singer," rather the *musician* (1 Chron. 6:33).

HEMLOCK. The Hebrew *rosh* is rendered "hemlock" in two passages (Hos. 10:4; Amos 6:12), but elsewhere "gall." (See Gall.)

HEN. The hen is nowhere noticed in the Bible except in Matt. 23:37; Luke 13:34. That a bird so common in Palestine should receive such slight notice is certainly singular.

HERD, HERDSMAN. The herd was greatly regarded both in the patriarchal and Mosaic period. The ox was the most precious stock next to horse and mule. The herd yielded the most esteemed sacrifice (Num. 7:3; Ps. 69:31; Isa. 66:3); also flesh meat and milk, chiefly converted probably into butter and cheese (Deut. 32:14; 2 Sam. 17:29). The full-grown ox is hardly ever slaughtered in Syria; but, both for sacrificial and convivial purposes, the younger animal was preferred (Ex. 29:1). The agricultural and general usefulness of the ox in ploughing, threshing and as a beast of burden (1 Chron. 12:40; Isa. 46:1), made such a slaughter seem wasteful. The herdsman's occupation was honorable in early times (Gen. 47:6; 1 Sam. 11:5; 1 Chron. 27:29; 28:1). Saul himself resumed it in the interval of his cares as king; also Doeg was certainly high in his confidence (1 Sam. 21:7). Pharaoh made some of Joseph's brethren "rulers over his cattle." David's herd-masters were among his chief officers of state.

HERMAS. The name of a Christian resident at Rome to whom Paul sends greeting in his Epistle to the Romans (16:14).

HERMES. A Christian mentioned in Rom. 16:14.

HERMON—*sacred (mountain)*. A mountain on the northeastern border of Palestine (Deut. 3:8; Josh. 12:1), over against Lebanon (Josh. 11:17), adjoining the plateau of Bashan (1 Chron. v. 23). It is the most conspicuous and beautiful mountain in Palestine or Syria. Hermon has three summits, situated like the angles of a triangle, and about a quarter of a mile from each other. This may account for the expression in Ps. 42:7 (6), "I will remember thee from the land of the Jordan and the *Hermons*." In two pas-

sages of Scripture this mountain is called *Baal-hermon* (Judg. 3:3; 1 Chron. 5:23), possibly because Baal was there worshipped.

HEROD. This family, though of Idumaean origin, and thus aliens by race, were Jews in faith. 1. Herod the Great was the second son of Antipater, an Idumaean, who was appointed Procurator of Judaea by Julius Caesar, and Cypros, an Arabian of noble descent. At the time of his father's elevation, though only fifteen years old, he received the government of Galilee, and shortly afterward that of Coele-Syria. When Antony came to Syria, 41 B.C., he appointed Herod and his elder brother Phasael tetrarchs of Judaea. Herod was forced to abandon Judaea next year by an invasion of the Parthians, who supported the claims of Antigonus, the representative of the Asmonaean dynasty and fled to Rome (40 B.C.) At Rome he was well received by Antony and Octavian, and was appointed by the senate king of Judaea to the exclusion of the Hasmonean line. In the course of a few years, by the help of the Romans, he took Jerusalem (37 B.C.), and completely established his authority throughout his dominions. It was at the time of his fatal illness that he must have caused the slaughter of the infants at Bethlehem (Matt. 2:16-18). The Temple he rebuilt with scrupulous care. 2. Herod Antipas was the son of Herod the Great by Malthace, a Samaritan. His father appointed him "tetrarch of Galilee and Peraea" (Matt. 14:1; Luke 3:19; 9:7; Acts 13:1; *cf.* Luke 3:1). He first married a daughter of Aretas, "king of Arabia Petraea," but after some time he made overtures of marriage to Herodias, the wife of his half brother Herod Philip, which she received favorably. Aretas, indignant at the insult offered to his daughter, found a pretext for invading the territory of Herod, and defeated him with great loss. This defeat, according to the famous passage in Josephus, was attributed by many to the murder of John the Baptist, which had been committed by Antipas shortly before, under the influence of Herodias (Matt. 14:4 ff.; Mark 6:17 ff.; Luke 3:19). 3. Herod Philip I. (Philip, Mark 6:17) was the son of Herod the Great and Mariamne, and must be carefully distinguished from the tetrarch Philip. He married Herodias, the sister of Agrippa I, by whom he had a daughter Salome. Herodias, however, left him, and made an infamous marriage with his half brother Herod Antipas (Matt. 14:3; Mark 6:17; Luke 3:19). He was excluded from all share in his father's possessions in consequence of his mother's treachery, and lived afterward in a private station. 4. Herod Philip II was the son of Herod the Great and Cleopatra. Like his half brothers Antipas and Archelaus, he was brought up at home. He received as his own government Batanea, Trachonitus, Auranitis (Gaulonitis) and some parts about Jamnia, with the title of tetrarch (Luke 3:1). 5. Herod Agrippa I was the son of Aristobulus and Berenice, and grandson of Herod the Great. He was thrown into prison by Tiberius, where he remained till the accession of Caius (Caligula), A.D. 37. The new emperor bestowed on him marks of favor (Acts 12:1). Agrippa was a strict observer of the Law, and sought with success the favor of the Jews. It is probable that it was with this view he put to death James the son of Zebedee, and further imprisoned Peter (Acts 12:1 ff.). In the fourth year of his reign over Judaea (A.D. 44) Agrippa attended some games at Caesarea, held in honor of the emperor. When he appeared in the theatre (Acts 12:21) his flatterers saluted him as a god; and suddenly he was seized with terrible pains, and being carried from the theatre to the palace died after five days' agony. 6. Herod Agrippa II was the son of Herod Agrippa I and Cypros, a grandniece of Herod the Great. At the time of the death of his father, (A.D. 50) the kingdom of Chalcis, which had belonged to his uncle; and then transferred him (A.D. 52) to the tetrarchies formerly held by Philip and Lysanias, with the title of king (Acts 25:13) was the cause of grave suspicion. In the last Roman war Agrippa took part with the Romans, and after the fall of Jerusalem retired with

Berenice to Rome, where he died in the third year of Trajan (A.D. 100).

HERODIANS. In the account which is given by Matthew (22:15 ff.) and Mark (12:13 ff.) of the last efforts made by different sections of the Jews to obtain from Jesus himself the materials for his accusation, a party under the name of *Herodians* is represented as acting in concert with the Pharisees (Matt. 22:16; Mark 12:13; comp. also 3:6; 8:15).

HERODIAS. Daughter of Aristobulus, one of the sons of Marianne and Herod the Great, and consequently sister of Agrippa I. She first married Philip I; then she eloped from him to marry Herod Antipas, her step-uncle, who had been long married to, and still was living with, the daughter of Aeneas or Aretas, king of Arabia. Aretas made war upon Herod, and routed him with the loss of his whole army. The head of John the Baptist was granted to the request of Herodias (Matt. 14:8-11; Mark 6:24-28). According to Josephus the execution took place in a fortress called Machaerus, looking down upon the Dead Sea from the South. She accompanied Antipas into exile to Lugdunum.

HERODION. A relative of Paul, to whom he sends his salutation amongst the Christians of the Roman Church (Rom. 16:11).

HERON. The Hebrew *anaphah* appears as the name of an unclean bird in Lev. 11:19; Deut. 14:18).

HETH. The forefather of the nation of The Hittites. In the genealogical tables of Gen. 10 and 1 Chron. 1, Heth is a son of Canaan. The Hittites were therefore a Hamite race, neither of the "country" nor the "kindred" of Abraham and Isaac (Gen. 24:3, 4; 28:1, 2).

HEZEKIAH—*Jehovah strengtheneth.* 1. Twelfth king of Judah, son of the apostate Ahaz and Abi (or Abijah), ascended the throne at the age of 25. Hezekiah was one of the three most perfect kings of Judah (2 Kings 18:5). He not only rewon the cities which his father had lost (2 Chron. 28:18), but even dispossessed the Philistines of their own cities, except Gaza (2 Kings 18:8) and Gath. When the king of Assyria applied for impost, Hezekiah refused it, and in open rebellion omitted to send even the usual presents (2 Kings 18:7). Hezekiah used every available means to strengthen his position, and render his capital impregnable (2 Kings 20:20; 2 Chron. 32:3-5, 30; Isa. 22:8-11; 33:18). In his dangerous illness he "turned his face to the wall and wept sore" at the threatened approach of dissolution. Various ambassadors came with letters and gifts to congratulate Hezekiah on his recovery (2 Chron. 32:23), and among them an embassy from Merodach-Baladan (or Berodach, 2 Kings 20:12), the viceroy of Babylon. The ostensible object of this mission was to compliment Hezekiah on his convalescence (2 Kings 20:12; Isa. 39:1); but its real purpose was to discover how far an alliance between the two powers was possible or desirable, for Merodach-Baladan, no less than Hezekiah, was in apprehension of the Assyrians. Community of interest made Hezekiah receive the overtures of Babylon with unconcealed gratification; and, perhaps to enhance the opinion of his own importance as an ally, he displayed to the messengers the princely treasures which he and his predecessors had accumulated. If ostentation were his motive it received a terrible rebuke, and he was informed by Isaiah that from the then tottering and subordinate province of Babylon, and not from the mighty Assyria, would come the ruin and captivity of Judah (Isa. 39:5). Sargon was succeeded by his son Sennacherib as ruler of Assyria whose two invasions occupy the greater part of the Scripture records concerning the reign of Hezekiah. The Jewish king, with simple piety, prayed to God, with Sennacherib's letter summoning him to surrender outspread before him, and received a prophecy of immediate deliverance. Accordingly "that night the Angel of the Lord went out and smote in the

camp of the Assyrians 185,000 men." Hezekiah slept with his fathers after a reign of twenty-nine years, in the 56th year of his age. 2. Son of Neariah, one of the descendants of the royal family of Judah (1 Chron. 3:23). 3. The same name, though rendered in the A.V. Hizkiah, is found in Zeph. 1:1.

HEZION. A king of Aram (Syria), father of Tabrimon, and grandfather of Benhadad I. He and his father are mentioned only in 1 Kings 15:18.

HIDDEKEL. One of the rivers of Eden (the Tigris), the river which "goeth eastward to Assyria" (Gen. 2:14), and which Daniel calls "the Great river" (Dan. 10:4).

HIEL. A native of Bethel, who rebuilt Jericho in the reign of Ahab (1 Kings 16:34); and in whom was fulfilled the curse pronounced by Joshua (Josh. 6:26).

HIERAPOLIS. This place is mentioned only once in Scripture (Col. 4:13), with Colossae and Laodicea.

HIGGAION. A word which occurs three times in the book of Psalms (9:17; 19:15; 92:4). The word has two meanings, one of a general character, implying *thought, reflection,* and another, in Ps. 9:17, and Ps. 92:4, of a technical nature, the precise meaning of which cannot be determined.

HIGH PLACES. From the earliest times it was the custom among all nations to erect altars and places of worship on lofty and conspicuous spots. To this general custom we find constant allusion in the Bible (Isa. 65:7; Jer. 3:6; Ezek. 6:13; 18:6; Hos. 4:13), and it is especially attributed to the Moabites (Isa. 15:2; 16:12; Jer. 48:35). Even Abraham built an altar to the Lord on a mountain near Bethel (12:7, 8; *cf.* 22:2-4; 31:54), which shows that the practice was then as innocent as it was natural; and although it afterward became mingled with idolatrous observances (Num. 23:3), it was in itself far less likely to be abused than the consecration of groves (Hos. 4:13). Gideon and Manoah built altars on high places by divine command (Judg. 6:25, 26; 13:16-23), and it is quite clear, from the tone of the book of Judges, that the law of Moses (Deut. 12:11-14) on the subject was either totally forgotten or practically obsolete.

HIGH PRIEST. The first distinct separation of Aaron to the office of the priesthood, which previously belonged to the first-born, was that recorded in Ex. 28. (1) Aaron alone was anointed (Lev. 8:12), whence one of the distinctive epithets of the high priest was "the anointed priest" (Lev. 4:3, 5, 16; 21:10; see Num. 35:25). This appears also from Ex. 29:29, 30. The anointing of the sons of Aaron, *i.e.,* the common priests, seems to have been confined to sprinkling their garments with the anointing oil (Ex. 29:21; 28:41, *etc.*). (2) The high priest had a peculiar dress which passed to his successor at his death. This dress consisted of eight parts, the *breastplate,* the *ephod* with its curious girdle, the *robe* of the ephod, the *mitre,* the *broidered coat* or diaper tunic, and the *girdle,* the materials being gold, blue, red, crimson and fine (white) linen (Ex. 28). To the above are added, in vs. 42, the *breeches* or *drawers* (Lev. 16:4) of linen; and to make up the number 8, some reckon the high priest's mitre, or the plate separately from the bonnet; while others reckon the curious girdle of the ephod separately from the ephod. The breastplate was originally 2 spans long, and 1 span broad, but when doubled it was square, the shape in which it was worn. On it were the 12 precious stones, set in four rows, 3 in a row, thus corresponding to the 12 tribes, and divided in the same manner as their camps were; each stone having the name of one of the children of Israel engraved upon it. The ephod consisted of two parts, of which one covered the back, and the other the front, *i.e.,* the breast and upper part of the body. These were clasped together

on the shoulder with two large onyx stones, each having engraved on it 6 of the names of the tribes of Israel. It was further united by a "curious girdle" of gold, blue, purple, scarlet, and fine twined linen round the waist. The robe of the ephod was of inferior material to the ephod itself, being all of blue (Ex. 28:31), which implied its being only of "woven work" (Ex. 39:22). It was worn immediately under the ephod, and was longer than it. The skirt of this robe had a remarkable trimming of pomegranates in blue, red and crimson, with a bell of gold between each pomegranate alternately. The bells were to give a sound when the high priest went in and came out of the Holy Place. Aaron had peculiar functions. To him alone it appertained, and he alone was permitted to enter the Holy of Holies, which he did once a year, on the great day of atonement, when he sprinkled the blood of the sin-offering on the mercy-seat, and burnt incense within the veil (Lev. 16).

HILKIAH—*my portion is Jehovah.* 1. Father of Eliakim (2 Kings 18:37; Isa. 22:20; 36:22). (See Eliakim.) 2. High priest in the region of Josiah (2 Kings 22:4 ff.; 2 Chron. 34:9 ff.). According to the genealogy in 1 Chron. 6:13, he was son of Shallum, and from Ezra 7:1 apparently the ancestor of Ezra the scribe. His high priesthood was rendered illustrious by the great reformation effected under it by King Josiah, and above all by the discovery which he made of the book of the law of Moses in the temple. 3. A priest of Anathoth, father of the prophet Jeremiah (Jer. 1:1).

HILLEL—*he hath praised.* A native of Pirathon in Mount Ephraim, father of Abdon, one of the judges of Israel (Judg. 12:13, 15).

HILLS. It may not be unprofitable to call attention here to the various Hebrew terms for which the word "hill" has been employed in the A.V. 1. *Gibeah,* from a root which seems to have the force of curvature or humpishness. 2. But our translators have also employed the same English word for the very different term *har,* meaning a whole district rather than an individual eminence, and to which our word "mountain" answers with tolerable accuracy. 3. On one occasion the word *Ma'aleh,* better "ascent," is rendered "hill" (1 Sam. 9:11).

HIND. The female of the common stag. It is frequently noticed in the poetical parts of Scripture as emblematic of activity (Gen. 49:21; 2 Sam. 22:34; Ps. 18:33; Hab. 3:19), gentleness (Prov. v. 19), feminine modesty (Cant. 2:7; 3:5), and maternal affection (Jer. 14:5).

HINGE. Ancient Egyptian doors were hung by means of pivots turning in sockets both on the upper and lower sides (1 Kings 7:50). In Syria, and especially the Haurân, there are many ancient doors consisting of stone slabs with pivots carved out of the same piece, inserted in sockets above and below, and fixed during the building of the house (Prov. 26:14).

HINNOM, VALLEY OF. Otherwise called "the valley of the son," or "children of Hinnom," a deep and narrow ravine, with steep, rocky sides, to the south and west of Jerusalem. The earliest mention of the Valley of Hinnom is in Josh. 15:8; 18:16. On the southern brow, overlooking the valley at its eastern extremity, Solomon erected high places for Molech (1 Kings 11:7), whose horrid rites were revived from time to time in the same vicinity by the later idolatrous kings. Ahaz and Manasseh made their children "pass through the fire" in this valley (2 Kings 16:3; 2 Chron. 28:3; 33:6), and the fiendish custom of infant sacrifice to the firegods seems to have been kept up in Tophet, at its southeast extremity, for a considerable period (Jer. 7:31; 2 Kings 23:10).

HIPPOPOTAMUS. (See Behemoth.)

HIRAM, or HURAM—*exalted brother* (?). 1. The king of Tyre who sent workmen and ma-

terials to Jerusalem, first (2 Sam. 5:11; 1 Chron. 14:1) to build a palace for David, whom he ever loved (1 Kings 5:1), and again (1 Kings 5:10; 7:13; 2 Chron. 2:14, 16) to build the Temple of Solomon, with whom he had a treaty of peace and commerce (1 Kings 5:11, 12). The contempt with which he received Solomon's present of Cabul (1 Kings 9:12) does not appear to have caused any breach between the two kings. He admitted Solomon's ships, issuing from Joppa, to a share in the profitable trade of the Mediterranean (1 Kings 10:22); and Jewish sailors, under the guidance of Tyrians, were taught to bring the gold of India (1 Kings 9:26) to Solomon's two harbors on the Red Sea. 2. Hiram was the name of a man of mixed race (1 Kings 7:13, 40), the principal architect and engineer sent by King Hiram to Solomon.

HITTITES, THE. The nation descended from Cheth (A.V. "Heth"), the second son of Canaan. Abraham bought from the "Children of Heth" the field and the cave of Machpelah, belonging to Ephron the Hittite. They were then settled at the town which was afterward, under its new name of Hebron, to become one of the most famous cities of Palestine, then bearing the name of Kirjath-arba (Gen. 23:19; 25:9). When the Israelites entered the Promised Land, we find the Hittites taking their part against the invader (Josh. 9:1; 11:3, *etc.*). Henceforward the notices of the Hittites are very few and faint (2 Sam. 23:39; 1 Chron. 11:41).

HIVITES, THE. In Genesis, "the Hivite" is named as one of the descendants of Canaan, the son of Ham (Gen. 10:17; 1 Chron. 1:15). We first encounter the actual people of the Hivites at the time of Jacob's return to Canaan. Shechem was then in their possession, Hamor the Hivite being the "prince of the land" (Gen. 34:2). We next meet with the Hivites during the conquest of Canaan (Josh. 9:7; 11:19).

HOBAB—*beloved.* (Num. 10:29; Judg. 4:11.) It seems doubtful whether this name denotes the father-in-law or brother-in-law of Moses. (1) In favor of the latter is the express statement, that Hobab was "the son of Raguel" (Num. 10:29); Raguel or Ruel being identified with Jethro, not only in Ex. 2:18 (*cf.* 3:1, *etc.*), but also by Josephus. (2) In favor of Hobab's identity with Jethro are the words of Judg. 4:11, and the Mohammedan traditions.

HOBAH. The place to which Abraham pursued the kings who had pillaged Sodom (Gen. 14:15). It was situated "to the north of Damascus."

HONEY. The Hebrew *debhash,* in the first place, applies to the product of the bee, to which we exclusively give the name of honey. All travellers agree in describing Palestine as a land "flowing with milk and honey" (Ex. 3:8); bees being abundant even in the remote parts of the wilderness.

HOOK, HOOKS. Various kinds of hooks are noticed. 1. Fishing hooks (Amos 4:2; Job 41:2; Isa. 19:8; Hab. 1:15). 2. Properly a *ring* (A.V. "thorn"), placed through the mouth of a large fish and attached by a cord to a stake for the purpose of keeping it alive in the water (Job 41:2); the word meaning the *cord* is rendered "hook" in the A.V. 3. A *ring,* such as in our country is placed through the nose of a bull, and similarly used in the East for leading about lions (Ezek. 19:4, where the A.V. has "with chains"), camels and other animals. A similar method was adopted for leading prisoners, as in the case of Manasseh, who was led with rings (2 Chron. 33:11; A.V. in "the thorns"). 4. The hooks of the pillars of the Tabernacle (Ex. 26: 32, 37; 27:10 ff.; 38:13 ff.). 5. A vinedresser's pruning-hook (Isa. 2:4; 18:5; Mic. 4:3; Joel 3:10). 6. A flesh-hook for getting up the joints of meat out of the boiling-pot (Ex. 27:3; 1 Sam. 2:13, 14). 7. Probably "hooks" used for the purpose of hanging up animals to flay them (Ezek. 40:43).

HOPHNI and PHINEHAS. The two sons of Eli, who fulfilled their hereditary sacerdotal duties at Shiloh. Their brutal rapacity and lust, which seemed to acquire fresh violence with their father's increasing years (1 Sam. 2:22, 12-17), filled the people with disgust and indignation, and provoked the curse which was denounced against their father's house, first by an unknown prophet (1 Sam. 2:27-36), and then by Samuel (1 Sam. 3:11-14). They were both cut off in one day in the flower of their age, and the ark which they had accompanied to battle against the Philistines was lost on the same occasion (1 Sam. 4:10, 11).

HOR, MOUNT. 1. The mountain on which Aaron died (Num. 20:25, 27). The word Hor is probably an archaic form of *Har,* the usual Hebrew term for "mountain." It was on the "boundary line" (Num. 20:23) or "at the edge" (Num. 33:37) of the land of Edom. It was the halting-place of the people next after Kadesh (Num. 20:22; 33:37), and they quitted it for Zalmonah (Num. 33:41) in the road to the Red Sea (Num. 21:4). 2. A mountain, entirely distinct from the preceding, named in Num. 34:7, 8, only, as one of the marks of the northern boundary of the land which the children of Israel were about to conquer. This "Mount Hor" is the great chain of Lebanon itself.

HORITES and HORIMS—*cave dwellers.* The aboriginal inhabitants of Mount Seir (Gen. 14:6). The name *Horite* appears to have been derived from their habits as "cave-dwellers."

HORN. The word "horn" is often used metaphorically to signify *strength* and *honor.* Of *strength* the horn of the unicorn was the most frequent representative (Deut. 33:17), but not always; comp. 1 Kings 22:11, where probably horns or iron, worn defiantly and symbolically on the head, are intended (Dan. 8:2 ff.; Zech. 1:18). Out of either or both of these last two metaphors sprang the idea of representing gods with horns. The altar of the Tabernacle and the Temple had four horns, one on each corner (Ex. 29:12; 1 Kings 1:50).

HORNET. In Scripture the hornet is referred to only as the means which Jehovah employed for the extirpation of the Canaanites (Ex. 23:28; Deut. 7:20; Josh. 24:12).

HORSE. The most striking feature in the Biblical notices of the horse is the exclusive application of it to warlike operations; in no instance is that useful animal employed for the purpose of ordinary locomotion or agriculture, if we except Isa. 28:28, where we learn that horses (A.V. "horsemen") were employed in threshing, not, however, in that case put in the gears, but simply driven about wildly over the strewed grain.

HORSELEECH. Occurs once only in Prov. 30:15. There is little doubt that the word in Hebrew denotes some species of leech, or rather is the generic term for any blood-sucking annelid.

HOSANNA—*save, we pray thee.* The cry of the multitudes as they thronged in our Lord's triumphal procession into Jerusalem (Matt 21:9, 15; Mark 11:9, 10; John 12:13).

HOSEA—*salvation.* A son of Beeri, and first of the Minor Prophets. The pictures of social and political life which Hosea draws so forcibly are applicable to the interregnum which followed the death of Jeroboam, and to the reign of the succeeding kings. The prophecy mentions Judah but Israel is the main object. The book is divided in two main sections: the story of the prophet's own marriage as a parable of the relation of Jehovah to Israel (Hos. 1-3); prophetic discourses concerning the aims of Israel (Hos. 4-14).

HOSHEA—*salvation.* The nineteenth and last king of Israel. He succeeded Pekah, whom he slew in a successful conspiracy (2 Kings 15:30; 17:1 ff.).

HOSHEA. The son of Nun, *i.e.*, Joshua (Deut. 32:44; and also in Num. 13:8, though there the A.V. has Oshea).

HOSPITALITY. Hospitality was regarded by most nations of the ancient world as one of the chief virtues. The laws respecting strangers (Lev. 19:33, 34) and the poor (Lev. 25:14 ff.; Deut. 15: 7), and concerning redemption (Lev. 25:23 ff.), are framed in accordance with the spirit of hospitality. The Apostles urged the church to "follow after hospitality" (Rom. 12:13; *cf.* 1 Tim. v. 10); to remember Abraham's example (Heb. 13:2); to "use hospitality one to another without grudging" (1 Pet. 4:9); while a bishop must be a "lover of hospitality" (Tit. 1:8; *cf.* 1 Tim. 3:2).

HOUR. The early Jews appear to have divided the day into *four* parts (Neh. 9:3), and the night into three watches (Judg. 7:19), and even in the New Testament we find a trace of this division in Matt. 20:1-5. The Greeks adopted the division of the day into 12 hours from the Babylonians. In whatever way originated, it was known to the Egyptians at a very early period. They had 12 hours of the day and of the night. There are two kinds of hours, (1) the astronomical or equinoctial hour, *i.e.*, the 24th part of a civil day, and (2) the natural hour, *i.e.*, the 12th part of the natural day, or of the time between sunrise and sunset. These are the hours meant in the New Testament (*e.g.* John 11:9), and it must be remembered that they perpetually vary in length, so as to be very different at different times of the year. For the purposes of prayer the old division of the day into 4 portions was continued in the Temple service, as we see from Acts 2:15; 3:1; 10:9.

HOUSE. The houses of the poor in Egypt, as well as Syria, Arabia and Persia, are for the most part huts of mud, or sunburnt bricks. In some parts of Palestine and Arabia stone is used, and in certain districts caves in the rock (Amos 5:11). The houses are usually of one story, the ground floor, and often contain only one apartment. Sometimes a small court for the cattle is attached. The windows are small apertures high up in the walls, sometimes grated with wood. The roofs are commonly, but not always, flat and are usually formed of a plaster of mud and straw laid upon boughs or rafters; and upon the flat roofs, tents or "booths" of boughs or rushes are often raised to be used as sleeping-places in summer. The windows of the upper rooms often project one or two feet, and form a kiosk or latticed chamber. Such may have been "the chamber in the wall" (2 Kings 4:10, 11). The "lattice," through which Ahaziah fell, perhaps belonged to an upper chamber of this kind (2 Kings 1:2), as also the "third loft," from which Eutychus fell (Acts 20:9; comp. Jer. 22:13).

HULDAH. A prophetess, whose husband Shallum was keeper of the wardrobe in the time of King Josiah (2 Kings 22:14; 2 Chron. 34:22).

HUNTING. The Hebrews, as a pastoral and agricultural people, were not given to the sports of the field. The manner of catching animals was either by digging a pitfall, or secondly by a trap, which was set under ground (Job 18:10), in the run of the animal (Prov. 22:5), and catching it by the leg (Job 18:9); or lastly by the use of the net, of which there were various kinds, as for the gazelle (Isa. 51:20, A.V. "wild bull") and other animals of that class.

HUR—*noble.* 1. A man who is mentioned with Moses and Aaron on the occasion of the battle with Amalek at Rephidim (Ex. 17:10, 12), when with Aaron he stayed up the hands of Moses. He is mentioned again in 24:14, as being, with Aaron, left in charge of the people by Moses during his ascent of Sinai. The Jewish tradition is that he was the husband of Miriam, and that he was identical with, 2, The grandfather of Bezaleel, the chief artificer of the tabernacle— "son of Huri, son of Hur"—of the tribe of Judah" (Ex. 31:2; 35:30; 38:22).

HURAM. 1. A Benjamite; son of Bela, the first-born of the patriarch (1 Chron. 8:5). 2. The form in which the name of the king of Tyre in alliance with David and Solomon—and elsewhere given as Hiram—appears.

HUSHAI. An Archite, *i.e.*, possibly an inhabitant of a place called Erec (2 Sam. 15:32 ff.; 16:16 ff.). He is called the "friend" of David (2 Sam. 15:37; *cf.* 1 Chron. 27:33). To him David confided the delicate and dangerous part of a pretended adherence to the cause of Absalom. He was probably the father of Baana (1 Kings 4:16).

HUSKS. The word rendered in the A.V. "husks" (Luke 15:16) describes really the fruit of a particular kind of tree, the Carob or *Ceratonia siliqua* of botanists.

HUZZAB. According to the general opinion of the Jews, was the queen of Nineveh at the time when Nahum delivered his prophecy (Nah. 2:7).

HYAENA. Authorities are at variance as to whether the term *zabhoa* in Jer. 12:9 means a "hyaena," as the LXX has it, or a "speckled bird," as in the A.V. The hyaena was common in ancient as in modern Egypt, and is constantly depicted upon monuments; it must therefore have been well known to the Jews.

HYMENAEUS. The name of a person occurring twice in the correspondence between Paul and Timothy; the first time classed with Alexander (1 Tim. 1:20), and the second time classed with Philetus (2 Tim. 2:17, 18; 1 Cor. 11:30).

HYMN. Among the later Jews the word *hymn* was more or less vague in its application. To Christians the hymn has always been something different from the Psalm. There is some dispute about the hymn sung by our Lord and his Apostles on the occasion of the Last Supper (Matt. 26:30; Mark 14:26); but even supposing it to have been the *Hallel*, or Paschal hymn, consisting of Ps. 113-118, it is obvious that the word *hymn* is in this case applied not to an individual psalm, but to a number of psalms chanted successively. In the jail of Philippi, Paul and Silas "sang hymns" (A.V. "praises" unto God), and so loud was their song, that their fellow-prisoners heard them (Acts 16:25). It was in fact a veritable singing of hymns.

HYSSOP (Heb. *ezobh*). The *ezobh* was used to sprinkle the doorposts of the Israelites in Egypt with the blood of the Paschal lamb (Ex. 12:22); it was employed in the purification of lepers and leprous houses (Lev. 14:4, 51), and in the sacrifice of the red heifer (Num. 19:6).

IBZAN. A native of Bethlehem of Zebulun, who judged Israel for seven years after Jephthah (Judg. 12:8, 10).

ICHABOD—*no glory* (?). The son of Phineas, and grandson of Eli (1 Sam. 4:21). His mother died in giving him birth.

ICONIUM. The capital of Lycaonia. It was on the great line of communication between Ephesus and the western coast of the peninsula on one side, and Tarsus, Antioch and the Euphrates on the other. Visited by Paul on his first missionary journey (Acts 14:1-6), he was compelled to leave. He returned, however, on his second journey (Acts 16:2 ff.).

IDDO—*strength.* 1. The father of Abinadab (1 Kings 4:14). 2. A descendant of Gershom (1 Chron. 6:21). 3. Son of Zechariah (1 Chron. 27: 21). 4. A seer whose "visions" against Jeroboam incidentally contained some of the acts of Solomon (2 Chron. 9:29). 5. The grandfather of the prophet Zechariah (Zech. 1:1, 7), although in other places Zechariah is called "the son of Iddo" (Ezra 5:1; 6:14).

IDOL, IMAGE. No less than twenty-one different Hebrew words have been rendered in the A.V. either by idol or image, including abstract terms, which express the degradation associated with it, and stand out as a protest of the language against the enormities of idolatry. Such are, 1. *Aven*, rendered "nought," "vanity," "iniquity," etc. 2. *Elil* is thought to have a sense akin to that of "falsehood." 3. *Emah*, "horror," or "terror." 4. *Bosheth* "shame," or "shameful thing" (A.V. Jer. 11:13; Hos. 9:10). Among the earliest objects of worship were the meteoric stones, which the ancients believed to have been the images of the gods sent down from heaven.

IDOLATRY. Strictly speaking, denotes the worship of deity in a visible form, whether tarte or Baaltis, the passive power of nature, as Baal the active, and known to the Hebrews as Ashtaroth or Ashtoreth, the tutelary goddess of the Zidonians, appears early among the objects of Israelite idolatry. In the later times of the monarchy, the planets, or the zodiacal signs, received, next to the sun and moon, their share of popular adoration (2 Kings 23:5). Beast-worship was exemplified in the calves of Jeroboam. The singular reverence with which trees have been honored is not without example in the history of the Hebrews. The terebinth at Mamre, beneath which Abraham built an altar (Gen. 12:7; 13:18), and the memorial grave planted by him at Beersheba (Gen. 21:33), were intimately connected with patriarchal worship. Mountains and high places were chosen spots for offering sacrifice and incense to idols (1 Kings 11:7; 14:23); and the retirement of gardens and the thick shade of woods offered great attractions to their worshipers (2 Kings 16:4; Isa. 50:29; Hos. 4:13). The host of heaven was worshipped on the house-top (2 Kings 23:12; Jer. 19:3; 32:29; Zeph. 1:5). Punishment was inflicted for idolatry. Jehovah, the God of the Israelites, was the civil head of the state. He was the theocratic king of the people, who had delivered them from bondage and to whom they had taken a willing oath of allegiance. Idolatry, therefore, to an Israelite, was a state offence (1 Sam. 15:23). But it was much more than all this. In the figurative language of the prophets, the relation between Jehovah and his people is represented as a marriage bond (Isa. 54:5; Jer. 3:14), and the worship of false gods with all its accompaniments (Lev. 20:56) becomes then the greatest of social wrongs (*e.g.*, Hos. 2; Jer. 3). The first and second commandments are directed against idolatry of every form.

ILLYRICUM. An extensive district lying along the eastern coast of the Adriatic, from the boundary of Italy on the north to Epirus on the south, and contiguous to Moesia and Macedonia on the east (Rom. 15:19).

IMMANUEL. That is, *God with us*, the symbolical name given by the prophet Isaiah to the child who was announced to Ahaz and the people of Judah, as the sign which God would give of their deliverance from their enemies (Isa. 7:14). It is applied by the Apostle Matthew to the Messiah, born of the Virgin (Matt. 1:23).

INCENSE. The incense employed in the tabernacle was compounded of stacte, onycha, galbanum and pure frankincense. All incense not made of these ingredients was forbidden (Ex. 30:9). Aaron, as high priest, was originally appointed to offer incense, but in the daily service of the second temple the office devolved upon inferior priests, from whom one was chosen by lot (Luke 1:9), each morning and evening. The offering of incense has formed a part of the religious ceremonies of most ancient nations. It was an element in the idolatrous worship of the Israelites (Jer. 11:12, 17; 48:35; 2 Chron. 34:25).

INDIA. The name does not occur before the book of Esther, where it is the limit of the territories of Ahasuersus in the east, as Ethiopia was in the west (Esth. 1:1; 8:9). The India of the book of Esther is the country surrounding the Indus, the *Punjab* and perhaps *Scinde*.

INK, INKHORN. Ink is mentioned only once in the Old Testament, when Baruch says he wrote the prophecies of Jeremiah with ink in the book

(Jer. 36:18). Inkhorn appears in one of Ezekial's visions (Ezek. 9:2, 3, 11).

INN. The Hebrew word (*malon*) signifies "a lodging-place for the night." Inns, in our sense of the term, were unknown in the east. The halting-place of a caravan was selected originally on account of its proximity to water or pasture, by which the travellers pitched their tents, and passed the night. Such was undoubtedly the "inn" at which occurred the incident in the life of Moses, in Ex. 4:24 (*cf.* Gen. 42:27). On the more frequented routes, remote from towns (Jer. 9:2), caravanseries were in course of time erected, often at the expense of the wealthy.

INSTANT, INSTANTLY. In the A.V. means urgent, urgently or fervently, as will be seen from the following passages: Luke 7:4; 23:23; Acts 26: 7; Rom. 12:12.

IRA. 1. A Jairite, a priest in the time of David (2 Sam. 20:26). 2. An Ithrite, one of David's heroes (2 Sam. 23:28; 1 Chron. 11:40). 3. Son of Ikkesh the Tekoite, another hero of David (2 Sam. 23:26).

IRIJAH—*Jehovah sees.* A captain of the ward, who met Jeremiah in the gate of Jeremiah in the gate of Jerusalem, called the "gate of Benjamin," accused him of being about to desert to the Chaldaeans, and led him back to the princes (Jer. 37:13, 14).

IRON. Is mentioned with brass as the earliest of known metals (Gen. 4:22). As it is found generally in combination with oxygen, the knowledge of the art of forging iron, attributed to Tubal Cain, argues an acquaintance with the smelting of this metal. The book of Job contains passages which indicate that iron was a metal well known. Of the manner of procuring it, we learn that "iron is taken from dust" (Job 28:2). Sheet-iron was used for cooking utensils (Ezek. 4:3; *cf.* Lev. 7:9). That it was plentiful in the time of David appears from 1 Chron. 22:3. The market of Tyre was supplied with bright or polished iron by the merchants of Dan and Javan (Ezek. 27: 19).

ISAAC—*laughter.* The son whom Sarah, in accordance with the divine promise, bore to Abraham, in the hundreth year of his age, at Gerar (Gen. 17:17, 24; 21:5). In infancy he became the object of Ishmael's jealousy; and in his youth the victim, in intention, of Abraham's great sacrificial act of faith (Gen. 22:2 ff.). When forty years old he married Rebekah, his cousin, by whom, when he was sixty, he had two sons, Esau and Jacob. In his seventy-fifth year he and his brother Ishmael buried their father Abraham in the cave of Machpelah. From his abode by the well Lahai-roi, in the south country, Isaac was driven by a famine to Gerar. Here Jehovah appeared to him and bade him dwell, and renewed to him the promise made to Abraham. Here he subjected himself, like Abraham in the same place and under like circumstances (Gen. 20:2; Gen. 26:7 ff.), to a rebuke from Abimelech, the Philistine king, for an equivocation. Here he acquired great wealth by his flocks, but was repeatedly dispossessed by the Philistines of the wells which he sank at convenient stations. At Beersheba Jehovah appeared to him by night and blessed him, and he built an altar there: there, too, like Abraham, he received a visit from the Philistine king Abimelech, with whom he made a covenant of peace. After the deceit by which Jacob acquired his father's blessing, Isaac sent his son to seek a wife in Padanaram; and all that we know of him during the last forty-three years of his life, that he saw that son, with a large and prosperous family, return to him at Hebron (Gen. 35:27) before he died there at the age of 180 years. He was buried by his two sons in the cave of Machpelah.

ISAIAH—*Jehovah hath saved.* The prophet, son of Amoz. He prophesied concerning Judah and Jerusalem in the days of Uzziah, Jotham, Ahaz and Hezekiah, kings of Judah (Isa. 1:1). Isaiah

must have been an old man at the close of Hezekiah's reign, his prophetic activities covering about 40 years. As a sign that Judah was not yet to perish Isaiah announced the birth of the child Immanuel, who should "know to refuse the evil and choose the good" before the land of the two hostile kings should be left desolate. The prophet gives us a most glowing description of Messianic blessings. The last twenty-seven chapters form a separate prophecy, and are supposed to have been written in the time of the Babylonian captivity, and are therefore ascribed to a "later Isaiah." The book of Isaiah falls into three sections: Chapters 1-35 and 40-66 contain prophetic discourses; chapters 36-39 contain narrative history (*cf.* 2 Kings 18: 13; 20-19).

ISCAH. Daughter of Haran the brother of Aram, and sister of Milcah and of Lot (Gen. 11:29). In the Jewish traditions she is identified with Sarai.

ISHBAK. Son of Abraham and Keturah (Gen. 25:2; 1 Chron. 1:32), and the progenitor of a tribe of northern Arabia.

ISHBI-BENOR. Son of Raptha, one of the race of Philistine giants, who attacked David in battle, but was slain by Abishai (2 Sam. 21:16, 17).

ISHBOSHETH—*man of shame.* The youngest of Saul's four sons, and his legitimate successor. His name appears (1 Chron. 8:33; 9:39) to have been originally *Eshbaal,* "the man of Baal." He was 35 years of age at the time of the battle of Gilboa. Ishbosheth was "40 years old when he began to reign over Israel, and reigned two years" (2 Sam. 3:10). During these two years he reigned at Mahanaim, though only in name. The wars and negotiations with David were entirely carried on by Abner (2 Sam. 2:12; 3:6, 12). The death of Abner deprived the house of Saul of their last remaining support. When Ishbosheth heard of it, "his hands were feeble, and all the Israelites were troubled" (2 Sam. 4:1). Two Beerothites, Baana and Rechab, in remembrance, it has been conjectured, of Saul's slaughter of their kinsmen the Gibeonites, determined to take advantage of the helplessness of the royal house. After assassinating Ishbosheth, they took his head to David as a welcome present. David rebuked them for the cold-blooded murder of an innocent man, and ordered them to be executed. The head of Ishbosheth was carefully buried in the sepulchre of his great kinsman Abner, at the same place (2 Sam. 4:9-12).

ISHI. This word occurs in Hos. 2:16, and signifies "my man," "my husband."

ISHMAEL—*may God hear.* 1. The son of Abraham by Hagar the Egyptian, his concubine; born when Abraham was fourscore and six years old (Gen. 16:15, 16). Ishmael was the first-born of his father. He was born in Abraham's house, when he dwelt in the plain of Mamre; and on the institution of the covenant of circumcision was circumcised, he being then thirteen years old (Gen. 17:25). With the institution of the covenant, God renewed his promise respecting Ishmael. He does not again appear until the weaning of Isaac (Gen. 21:8 ff.). The latter was born when Ishmael must have been between fifteen and sixteen years of age. At the great feast in celebration of the weaning, Sarah saw the son of Hagar mocking, and urged Abraham to cast out him and his mother. The patriarch comforted by God's renewed promise that of Ishmael he would make a nation, sent them both away, and they departed and wandered in the wilderness of Beersheba. It is doubtful whether the wanderers halted by the well, or at once continued their way to the "wilderness of Paran," where we are told in the next verse to that just quoted, he dwelt, and where "his mother took him a wife out of the land of Egypt" (Gen. 21:9-21). This wife of Ishmael was the mother of his twelve sons and daughter. Of the later life of Ishmael we know little. He was present with Isaac at the burial of Abraham (Gen. 25:9). He died at the age of 137 years (Gen. 25:17, 18). The sons

of Ishmael peopled the north and west of the Arabian peninsula, and eventually formed the chief element of the Arab nation. 2. A descendant of Saul through Meribbaal, or Mephibosheth (1 Chron. 8:38; 9:44). 3. Father of Zebadiah (2 Chron. 19:11). 4. Son of Jehohanan (2 Chron. 23:1). 5. A priest of the Bene-Pashur (Ezra 10: 22). 6. The son of Nethaniah; a perfect marvel of craft and villainy, whose treachery forms one of the chief episodes of the history of the period immediately succeeding the first fall of Jerusalem (Jer. 40:7-41; 2 Kings 25:23-25).

ISHMEELITE (1 Chron. 2:17) and **ISHMEEL-ITES** (Gen. 37:25, 27, 28; 39:1). The form in which the descendants of Ishmael are given in a few places in the A.V.

ISLE. The sense of the Hebrew word seems to be "habitable places," as opposed to water, and in this sense it occurs in Isa. 42:15. Hence it means secondarily any maritime district, whether belonging to a continent or to an island; thus it is used of the shore of the Mediterranean (Isa. 20:6; 23:2, 6), and of the coasts of Elishah (Ezek. 27:7), *i.e.,* of Greece and Asia Minor.

ISRAEL—*may God strive.* 1. The name given (Gen. 32:28), to Jacob after his wrestling with the angel (Hos. 12:4) at Peniel. 2. It became the national name of the twelve tribes collectively. They are so called in Ex. 3:16, and afterward. 3. It is used in a narrower sense, excluding Judah, in 1 Sam. 11:8; 2 Sam. 20:1; 1 Kings 12:16. Thenceforth it was assumed and accepted as the name of the Northern Kingdom. 4. After the Babylonian captivity, the returned exiles resumed the name Israel as the designation of their nation. The name Israel is also used to denote laymen, as distinguished from priests, Levites and other ministers (Ezra 6:16; 9:1; 10:25; Neh. 11:3, *etc.*).

ISRAEL, KINGDOM OF. 1. The prophet Ahijah of Shiloh, who was commissioned in the latter days of Solomon to announce the division of the kingdom, left one tribe (Judah) to the house of David, and assigned ten to Jeroboam (1 Kings 11:35, 36). Eventually the greater part of Benjamin, and probably the whole of Simeon and Dan, were included as if by common consent in the kingdom of Judah. 2. The population of the kingdom is not expressly stated; and in any inference from the numbers of fighting men, we must bear in mind that the numbers in the Hebrew text are strongly suspected to have been subjected to corruption. Jeroboam brought to the field an army of 800,000 men (2 Chron. 13:3). If there were actually under arms 800,000 men of that age in Israel the whole population may perhaps have amounted to at least three millions and a half. 3. Shechem was the first capital of the new kingdom (1 Kings 12:25). Subsequently Tirzah became the royal residence, if not the capital, of Jeroboam (1 Kings 14:17), and of his successors (15:33; 16:8, 17, 23). Samaria was chosen by Omri (1 Kings 16:24). Jezreel was probably only a royal residence of some of the Israelitish kings.

ISSACHAR—*hired laborer.* 1. The ninth son Jacob and the fifth of Leah; the first-born to Leah, after the interval which occurred in the births of her children (Gen. 30:17; *cf.* 29:35). 2. A Korhite Levite, one of the doorkeepers of the house of Jehovah, seventh son of Obed-edom (1 Chron. 26:5).

ISSUE, RUNNING. (Lev. 15:2, 3; 22:4; Num. 5:2; and 2 Sam. 3:29.) In Lev. 15:3 a distinction is introduced which merely means that the cessation of the actual flux does not constitute ceremonial cleanness, but that the patient must bide the legal time, seven days, and perform the prescribed purifications and sacrifice.

ITALY. This word is used in the New Testament (Acts 18:2; 27:1; Heb. 13:24) in its true geographical sense, as denoting the whole natural peninsula between the Alps and the Straits of Messina.

ITHAMAR. The youngest son of Aaron (Ex. 6:23). After the deaths of Nadab and Abihu (Lev. 10:1), Eleazar and Ithamar were appointed to succeed to their places in the priestly office (Ex. 28:1, 40, 43; Num. 3:3, 4; 1 Chron. 24:2). In the distribution of services belonging to the Tabernacle, and its transport on the march of the Israelites, the Gershonites and the Merarites were placed under the superintendence of Ithamar (Ex. 38:21; Num. 4:21-33). The high priesthood passed into the family of Ithamar in the person of Eli, but for what reason we are not informed.

ITHREAM. Son of David, born to him in Hebron, and distinctly specified as the sixth, and as the child of Eglah, David's wife (2 Sam. 3:5, 1 Chron. 3:3).

ITTAI—*companionable.* "Ittai the Gittite," *i.e.,* the native of Gath, a Philistine in the army of King David (2 Sam. 15:19 ff.; 18:2 ff.).

ITURAEA. A small province on the northeastern border of Palestine, lying along the base of Mount Mermon, only mentioned in Luke 3:1.

IVORY (Heb. *shen* in all passages, except 1 Kings 10:22, and 2 Chron. 9:21, where *shenhabbim* is so rendered). The word *shen* literally signifies the "tooth" of any animal, and hence more especially denotes the substance of the projecting tusks of elephants. The skilled workmen of Hiram, king of Tyre, fashioned the great ivory throne of Solomon, and overlaid it with pure gold (1 Kings 10:18; 2 Chron. 9:17). The ivory thus employed was supplied by the caravans of Dedan (Isa. 21:13; Ezek. 27:15), or was brought with apes and peacocks by the navy of Tarshish (1 Kings 10:22). The "ivory house" of Ahab (1 Kings 22:39) was probably a palace, the walls of which were paneled with ivory. Beds inlaid or veneered with ivory were in use among the Hebrews (Amos 6:4).

IZHAR—*He shines.* Son of Kohath, grandson of Levi, uncle of Aaron and Moses, and father of Korah (Ex. 6:18, 21; Num. 3:19; 16:1; 1 Chron. 6:2, 18). Izhar was the head of the family of the Izharites (1 Chron. 24:22; 26:23, 30), or Izeharites (Num. 3:27; 1 Chron. 26:23, 29).

JAARE-OREGIM. (2 Sam. 21:19.) A Bethlehemite, and the father of Elhanan, who slew the brother of Goliath. In the parallel passage, 1 Chron. 20:5, Jair is found instead of Jaare, and Oregim is omitted.

JAAZANIAH—*Jehovah hears.* 1. One of the captains of the forces who accompanied Johanan ben-Kareah to pay his respects to Gedaliah at Mizpah (2 Kings 25:23), and who appears afterwards to have assisted in recovering Ishmael's prey from his clutches (*cf.* Jer. 41:11; 43:4, 5). 2. Son of Azur; one of the princes of the people against whom Ezekiel was directed to prophesy (Ezek. 11:1). 3. A Rechabite, son of Jeremiah (Jer. 35:3).

JABAL. The son of Lamech and Adah (Gen. 4:20) and brother of Jubal. He is described as the father of such as dwell in tents and have cattle.

JABBOK. A stream which intersects the mountain-range of Gilead (*cf.* Josh. 12:2, 5), and falls into the Jordan about midway between the sea of Galilee and the Dead Sea. It was anciently the border of the children of Ammon (Num. 21:24; Deut. 2:37; 3:16). It was on the south bank of the Jabbok that the interview took place between Jacob and Esau (Gen. 32:22).

JABESH. 1. Father of Shallum, the 15th king of Israel (2 Kings 15:10, 13, 14). 2. Jabesh, or Jabesh Gilead, or Jabesh in the territory of Gilead. In its widest sense Gilead included the half tribe of Manasseh (1 Chron. 27:21) as well as the tribes of Gad and Reuben (Num. 32:1-42) east of the Jordan—and of the cities of Gilead, Jabesh was the chief. It is first mentioned in Judg. 21:8-14. Being attacked subsequently by Nahash the Ammonite, it gave Saul an opportunity of displaying his prowess in its defence (1 Sam. 11:1-15).

JABIN—*intelligent.* 1. King of Hazor, who organized a confederacy of the northern princes against the Israelites (Josh. 11:1-3. Joshua surprised the allied forces by the waters of Merom and utterly routed them. During the ensuing wars, Joshua again attacked Jabin, and burnt his city (Josh. 11:1-14). 2. A king of Hazor, whose general, Sisera, was defeated by Barak (Judg. 4:3, 13).

JABNEEL—*a god causes to build.* One of the points on the northern boundary of Judah (Josh. 15:11). Josephus attributes it to the Danites. There was a constant struggle going on between that tribe and the Philistines for the possession of all the places in the lowland plains, and it is not surprising that the next time we meet with Jabneel it should be in the hands of the latter (2 Chron. 26:6). Uzziah dispossessed them of it, and demolished its fortifications.

JACHAN. One of the seven chief men of the tribe of Gad (1 Chron. 5:13).

JACHIN—*He establishes.* 1. One of the two pillars which were set up "in the porch" (1 Kings 7:21) or before the temple (2 Chron. 3:17) of Solomon. 2. Fourth son of Simeon (Gen. 46:10; Ex. 6:15); founder of the family of the Jachinites (Num. 26:12). 3. Head of the 21st course of priests in the time of David. Some of the course returned from Babylon (1 Chron. 9:10; 24:17; Neh. 11:10).

JACINTH. A stone forming one of the foundations of the walls of the New Jerusalem (Rev. 21:20).

JACOB. The second son of Isaac and Rebekah. He was born with Esau, when Isaac was 59 and Abraham 159 years old, probably at the well Lahairoi. His history is related in the latter half of Book of Genesis. He died in his 147th year. His body was embalmed, carried with great care and pomp into the land of Canaan, and deposited with his fathers, and his wife Leah, in the cave of Machpelah.

JADDUA. 1. Son and successor in the high priesthood of Jonathan or Johanan. He is the last of the high priests mentioned in the Old Testament, and probably altogether the latest name in the canon (Neh. 12:11, 22). 2. One of the chiefs of the people, *i.e.,* of the laymen, who sealed the covenant with Nehemiah (Neh. 10:21).

JAEL—*mountain-goat.* The wife of Heber the Kenite. In the headlong rout which followed the defeat of the Canaanites by Barak, Sisera, abandoning his chariot, the more easily to avoid notice, fled unattended, and in an opposite direction from that taken by his army, to the tent of the Kenite chieftainess. He accepted Jael's invitation to enter, and she flung a mantle over him as he lay wearily on the floor. When thirst prevented sleep, and he asked for water, she brought him buttermilk in the choicest vessel. At last, with a feeling of security, the weary general resigned himself to the sleep of misery and fatigue. Then it was that Jael took in her left hand one of the great wooden pins with which fastened down the cords of the tent, and in her right hand the mallet used to drive it into the ground, and with one terrible blow dashed it through Sisera's temples deep into the earth (Judg. 5:27). She then waited to meet the pursuing Barak, and led him into her tent that she might claim the glory of the deed.

JAH. The abbreviated form of "Jehovah," used only in poetry. It occurs frequently in the Hebrew, but with a single exception (Ps. 68:4) is rendered "Lord" in the A.V.

JAHAZ, also **JAHAZA**, **JAHAZAH** and **JAHZAH.** Four forms are given which in Hebrew appear as *Yahats* and *Yahtsah.* At *Jahaz* the decisive battle was fought between the children of Israel and Sihon king of the Amorites (Num. 21:23; Deut. 2:32; Judg. 11:20). It was in the allotment of Reuben (Josh. 13:18).

JAIR—*he enlightens.* 1. A man descended from Judah and Manasseh. During the conquest he took the whole of Argob (Deut. 3:14), and possessed himself of some nomad villages in Gilead, which he called Havvoth-Jair (Num. 32:41; 1 Chron. 2:23). 2. "Jair the Gileadite," who judged Israel for two and twenty years (Judg. 10:3-5). He had thirty sons who rode thirty asses, and possessed thirty cities in the land of Gilead, which, like those of their namesake, were called Havvoth-Jair. 3. A Benjamite, son of Kish, and father of Mordecai (Esth. 2:5). 4. The father of Elhanan, one of the heroes of David's army (1 Chron. 20:5).

JAIRUS—*he enlightens.* 1. A ruler of a synagogue, probably in some town near the western shore of the Sea of Galilee (Matt. 9:18; Mark 5:22; Luke 8:41). 2. Esth. 11:2.

JAMES. 1. James the son of Zebedee, one of the Twelve Apostles. We first hear of him when Zebedee, a fisherman (Mark 1:20), was out on the Sea of Galilee with his two sons, James and John, and some boatmen. At this time the new Teacher appeared upon the beach. At his call they left all, and became, once and forever, his disciples, hereafter to catch men. For a full year we lose sight of James. He is then called to the apostleship with his eleven brethren (Matt. 10:2; Mark 3:14; Luke 6:13; Acts 1:13). In the list of the apostles given us by Mark, and in the book of Acts, his name occurs next to that of Simon Peter; in the Gospels of Matthew and Luke it comes third. It is worthy of notice that with one exception (Luke 9:28) the name of James is put before that of John, and that John is twice described as "the brother of James" (Mark 5:37; Matt. 17:1). This would appear to imply that at this time James, either from age or character, took a higher position than his brother. On the day of the Ascension he is mentioned as persevering with the apostles and disciples in prayer (Acts 1:13). He was put to death by Herod Agrippa I (Acts 12:1, 2). 2. James the son of Alphaeus, one of the twelve apostles (Matt. 10:3; Mark 3:18; Luke 6:15; Acts 1:13). 3. James the brother of the Lord (Matt. 13:55; Mark 6:3; Gal. 1:19). 4. James the son of Mary (Matt. 27:56; Luke 24:10). Also called The Less (Mark 15:40). 5. James the brother of Jude (Jude 1). 6. James the brother (?) of Jude (Luke 6:16; Acts 1:13). 7. James (Acts 12:17; 15:13; 21:18; 1 Cor. 15:7; Gal. 2:9, 12). 8. James the servant of God and of our Lord Jesus Christ (James 1:1). Paul identifies for us Nos. 3 and 7 (see Gal. 2:9, 12 compared with 1:19). If we may translate Judas the *brother,* rather than the *son* of James, we may conclude that 5 and 6 are identical. We may identify 5 and 6 with 3, because we know that James the Lord's brother had a brother named Jude. We may identify 4 with 3, because we know James the son of Mary had a brother named Joses, and so also had James the Lord's brother. Thus there remain two only, James the son of Alphaeus (2) and James the brother of the Lord (3). Can we, or can we not, identify them? This is one of the most difficult questions in the gospel history.

JAMES, THE GENERAL EPISTLE OF. The author of this epistle was in all probability James the brother of the Lord. It was written from Jerusalem.

JAMES THE LESS. (Mark 15:40.) So designated in A.V. He is frequently identified with James the son of Alphaeus (see above).

JANNA. Son of Joseph, and father of Melchi, in the genealogy of Christ (Luke 3:24).

JANNES and **JAMBRES.** The names of two Egyptian magicians who opposed Moses (2 Tim. 3:8, 9).

JAPHETH. One of the three sons of Noah. From

the order in which their names invariably occur (Gen. 5:32; 6:10) we should naturally infer that Japheth was the youngest but we learn from 9:24 that Ham held that position. We infer therefore that Japheth was the second son of Noah. The descendants of Japheth occupied the "isles of the Gentiles" (Gen. 5:5) i.e., the coast lands of the Mediterranean Sea in Europe and Asia Minor, whence they spread northward over the whole continent of Europe and a considerable portion of Asia.

JAPHIA. 1. King of Lachish at the time of the conquest of Canaan by the Israelites (Josh. 10:3). 2. One of the sons of David born to him in Jerusalem (2 Sam. 5:15; 1 Chron. 3:7; 14:6).

JARED. One of the antediluvian patriarchs, the fifth from Adam; son of Mahalaleel and father of Enoch (Gen. 5:15, 16, 18-20; Luke 3:37). In the list of Chronicles the name is given in the A.V. Jered.

JARHA. The Egyptian servant of Sheshan, about the time of Eli, to whom his master gave his daughter and heir in marriage (1 Chron. 2:34).

JARIB—he strives. Named in the list of 1 Chron. 4:24 only, as a son of Simeon. Perhaps the same as Jachin (Gen. 46; Ex. 6; Num. 26).

JARMUTH—a height. A town in the low country of Judah (Josh. 15:35). Its king, Piram, was one of the five who conspired to punish Gibeon for having made alliance with Israel (Josh. 10:3, 5), and who were routed at Bethhoron and put to death by Joshua at Makkedah.

JASHER, BOOK OF. A record alluded to in two passages only of the Old Testament (Josh. 10: 13; 2 Sam. 1:18).

JASHOBEAM—people will return. Possibly one and the same follower of David, bearing this name, is described as a Hachmonite (1 Chron. 11:11), a Korhite (1 Chron. 12:6), and son of Zabdiel (1 Chron. 27:2). He came to David at Ziklag. His distinguishing exploit was that he slew 300 (or 800; 2 Sam. 23:8) men at one time. He is named first among the chief of the mighty men of David (1 Chron. 11:11).

JASON—healing. 1. Jason the son of Eleazer was one of the commissioners sent by Judas Maccabaeus to conclude a treaty with the Romans B.C. 161. 2. Jason the father of Antipater, who was an envoy to Rome at a later period and is probably the same person as No. 1. 3. Jason of Cyrene, a Jewish historian who wrote "in five books" a history of the Jewish war of liberation, which supplied the chief materials for the second book of the Maccabees. 4. Jason the High Priest, the second son of Simon II and brother of Onias III, who succeeded in obtaining the high priesthood from Antiochus Epiphanes. 5. Jason the Thessalonian, who entertained Paul and Silas, and was in consequence attacked by the Jewish mob (Acts 17:5, 6, 7, 9). He is probably the same as in Rom. 16:21. It is conjectured that Jason and Secundus (Acts 20:4) were the same.

JASPER. A precious stone frequently noticed in Scripture. It was the last of the twelve inserted in the high priest's breastplate (Ex. 28:20; 39: 13), and the first of the twelve used in the foundations of the New Jerusalem (Rev. 21:19). The characteristics of the stone (Rev. 21:11) are, that it was "most precious," and "like crystal"; we may also infer from Rev. 4:3, that it was a stone of brilliant and transparent light. The stone which we name "jasper" does not accord with this description.

JAVAN. 1. A son of Japheth, and the father of Elishah and Tarshish, Kittim and Dodanim (Gen. 10:2, 4). The name appears in Isa. 66:19; in Ezek. 27:13; in Dan. 2:21; 10:20; 11:2; and in Zech. 9:13. From a comparison of these passages there can be no doubt that Javan was regarded as the representative of the Greek race. 2. A town in the southern part of Arabia

(Yemen), whither the Phoenicians traded (Ezek. 27:19).

JEBUS. One of the names of Jerusalem, the city of the Jebusites, also called Jebusi (Josh. 15:8; 18:16, 28; Judg. 19:10, 11; 1 Chron. 11:4, 5). (See Jerusalem.)

JEBUSITES, THE. Were descended from the third son of Canaan (Gen. 10:16; 1 Chron. 1:14). The actual people first appear in the invaluable report of the spies (Num. 13:29). When Jabin organized his rising against Joshua he sent amongst others "to the Amorite, the Hittite, the Perizzite and the Jebusite in the mountain" (Josh. 11:3). "Jebus, which is Jerusalem," lost its king in the slaughter of Beth-horon (Josh. 10:1, 5, 26; cf. 12:10), was sacked and burned by the men of Judah (Judg. 1:21), and its citadel finally scaled and occupied by David (2 Sam. 5:6). After this they emerge from the darkness but once, in the person of Araunah the Jebusite, "Araunah the king," who appears in his well-known transaction with David (2 Sam. 24:23).

JECHOLIAH—Jehovah is able. Wife of Amaziah king of Judah, and mother of Azariah or Uzziah his successor (2 Kings 15:2).

JEDIDAH—beloved. Queen of Amon, and mother of the good king Josiah (2 Kings 22:1).

JEDIDIAH—beloved of Jehovah. The name bestowed, through Nathan the prophet, on David's son Solomon (2 Sam. 12:25).

JEDUTHUN—praising. A Levite, of the family of Merari, is probably the same as Ethan (cf. 1 Chron. 15:17, 19 with 1 Chron. 16:41, 42; 25:1, 3, 6; 2 Chron. 35:15). His office was generally to preside over the music of the temple service. Jeduthun's name stands at the head of the 39th, 62nd and 77th Psalms.

JEGAR-SAHADUTHA—heap of witness. The Aramaean name given by Laban the Syrian to the heap of stones he erected as a memorial of the compact between Jacob and himself, while Jacob commemorated the same by a pillar (Gen. 31:47). Galeed, a "witness heap."

JEHIEL—God lives. 1. A man described as father of Gibeon; a forefather of King Saul (1 Chron. 9:35). 2. One of the sons of Hotham the Aroerite; a member of David's guard (1 Chron. 11:44).

JEHOAHAZ—Jehovah lays hold. 1. The son and successor of Jehu, reigned seventeen years over Israel in Samaria. His inglorious history is given in 2 Kings 13:1-9. Jehoahaz maintained the idolatry of Jeroboam; but in the extremity of his humiliation he besought Jehovah, and Jehovah gave Israel a deliverer—probably either Jehoash (vs. 23, 25), or Jeroboam II (2 Kings 14:24, 25). 2. Jehoahaz, otherwise called Shallum, the fourth (acc. to 1 Chron. 3:15), or third, if Zedekiah's age be correctly stated (2 Chron. 36:11), son of Josiah, whom he succeeded as king of Judah. He was chosen by the people in preference to his elder (cf. 2 Kings 23:31 and 36) brother, and he reigned three months in Jerusalem. Pharaoh-Necho on his return from Carchemish sent to Jerusalem to depose him, and to fetch him to Riblah. There he was cast into chains, and was taken into Egypt, where he died.

JEHOASH—Jehovah is strong. The uncontracted form of Joash. 1. The eighth king of Judah; son of Ahaziah (2 Kings 11:21; 12:1, 2, 4, 6, 7, 18; 14:13). 2. The twelfth king of Israel; son of Jehoahaz (2 Kings 13:10, 25; 14:8, 9, 11, 13, 15, 16, 17). (See Joash, 2.)

JEHOIACHIN—Jehovah appoints. Son of Jehoiakim and Nehusta, and for three months and ten days king of Judah. Jerusalem was unable to offer any resistance to the regular army which Nebuchadnezzar sent to besiege it (2 Kings 24:10, 11). In a very short time Jehoiachin surrendered at discretion; and he was carried to Babylon (Jer. 19:2; Ezek. 17:12; 19:9). There he remained in

prison, wearing prison garments, for thirty-six years, till the death of Nebuchadnezzar, when Evil-Merodach, succeeding to the throne of Babylon, brought him out of prison, and made him sit at his own table.

JEHOIAKIM—Jehovah raises up. Called Eliakim, son of Josiah and Zebudah, and king of Judah. After deposing Jehoahaz, Pharaoh-Necho set Eliakim, his elder brother, upon the throne and changed his name to Jehoiakim (2 Kings 23:34). Egypt played no part in Jewish politics during the seven or eight years of Jehoiakim's reign. After the battle of Carchemish Nebuchadnezzar entered Jerusalem, took the king prisoner, bound him in fetters to carry him to Babylon, and took some of the precious vessels of the Temple. But he seems to have changed his purpose as regarded Jehoiakim, and to have accepted his submission and reinstated him on the throne, perhaps in remembrance of the fidelity of his father Josiah. What is certain is, that Jehoiakim became tributary to Nebuchadnezzar after his invasion of Judah, and continued so for three years, but at the end of that time broke his oath of allegiance and rebelled against him (2 Kings 24:1). Jehoiakim came to a violent end in the 11th year of his reign. His body was cast out ignominiously on the ground; and then, after being left exposed for some time, was dragged away and buried "with the burial of an ass," without pomp or lamentation, "beyond the gates of Jerusalem" (Jer. 22:18, 19; 36:30; but cf. 2 Kings 24:6 and 2 Chron. 36:6 f.). All the accounts we have of Jehoiakim concur in ascribing to him a vicious and irreligious character.

JEHODIA—Jehovah knoweth. 1. Father of Benaiah, captain of David's bodyguard (2 Sam. 8:18; 1 Kings 4:4; 1 Chron. 18:17). 2. Leader of the Aaronites, i.e., the priests; who joined David at Hebron (1 Chron. 12:27). 3. According to 1 Chron. 27:34, son of Benaiah. But in all probability, Benaiah the son of Jehoida is meant. 4. High priest at the time of Athaliah's usurpation of the throne of Judah and during the greater portion of the forty years' reign of Joash (2 Kings 12:10).

JEHONADAB and JONADAB—Jehovah is bounteous. 1. The son of Rechab, founder of the Rechabites. Bearing in mind his general character as an Arab chief, and the founder of a half-religious sect, we are better able to understand the historical narrative. Jehu was advancing, after the slaughter of Betheked, on the city of Samaria, when he suddenly met the austere Bedouin coming toward him (2 Kings 10:15). The king was in his chariot; the Arab was on foot. No doubt he acted in concert with Jehu throughout (2 Kings 10:23). 2. Son of Shimeah, David's brother, and friend of Amnon, a son of David. He aided Amnon in carrying out his crime against Tamar (2 Sam. 13:3 ff.).

JEHORAM or JORAM—Jehovah is exalted. 1. Son of Ahab king of Israel, who succeeded his brother Ahaziah (2 Kings 3:1). We first find him associated with Jehoshaphat and the king of Edom, at that time a tributary of the kingdom of Judah, in a war against the Moabites. The three armies were in the utmost danger of perishing for want of water. The piety of Jehoshaphat suggested an inquiry of some prophet of Jehovah, and Elisha, at that time and since the latter part of Ahab's reign Elijah's attendant (2 Kings 3:11; 1 Kings 19:19-21) was found with the host. From him Jehoram received a severe rebuke and was bid to inquire of the prophets of his father and mother, the prophets of Baal. Nevertheless for Jehoshaphat's sake Elisha inquired of Jehovah, and received the promise of an abundant supply of water and of a great victory over the Moabites; a promise which was immediately fulfilled. A little later, we find Elisha befriending Jehoram. But it seems probable that when the Syrian inroads ceased and he felt less dependent upon the aid of the prophet, he relapsed into idolatry, and was rebuked by Elisha. Refusing to repent, a fresh invasion by the Syrians and a close siege of Samaria actually came

to pass, according probably to the word of the prophet. Hence, when the terrible incident arose, in consequence of the famine, of a woman boiling and eating her own child, the king immediately attributed the evil to Elisha and determined to take away his life. The providential interposition by which both Elisha's life was saved and the city delivered is narrated in 2 Kings 7, and Jehoram appears to have returned to friendly feeling toward Elisha (2 Kings 8:4). He was murdered by Jehu, who succeeded him on the throne of Israel (2 Kings 9:24). 2. Eldest son of Jehoshaphat, succeeded his father on the throne of Judah at the age of 32 and reigned eight years (1 Kings 22:50; 2 Kings 8:16-24; 2 Chron. 21). Jehosheba his daughter was wife to the high priest Jehoida. As soon as she was fixed on the throne, he put his six brothers to death, with many of the chief nobles of the land. He then, probably at the instance of his wife Athaliah, the daughter of Ahab, proceeded to establish the worship of Baal. A prophetic writing from the aged prophet Elijah (2 Chron. 21:12) failed to produce any good effect upon him. He died of a terrible disease (2 Chron. 21:19, 20) early in the twelfth year of his brother-in-law Jehoram's reign over Israel.

JEHOSHAPHAT—*Jehovah has judged.* 1. King of Judah, son of Asa, succeeded to the throne when he was thirty-five years old, and reigned twenty-five years. His history is to be found among the events recorded in 1 Kings 15:24; 2 Kings 7:16, or in a continuous narrative in 2 Chron. 17:1-21:3. 2. The recorder or chronicler under David and Solomon (2 Sam. 8:16; 1 Kings 4:3). 3. One of Solomon's officers (1 Kings 4:17). 4. Father of Jehu king of Israel (2 Kings 9:2, 14).

JEHOSHAPHAT, VALLEY OF. A valley mentioned by Joel only, as the spot in which, after the return of Judah and Jerusalem from captivity, Jehovah would gather all the heathen (Joel 3:2), and would there sit to judge them for their misdeeds to Israel (Joel 3:12). The name has come down to us attached to that deep ravine which separates Jerusalem from the Mount of Olives, through which at one time the Kedron forced its stream. Both Moslems and Jews believe that the last judgment is to take place there. The steep sides of the ravine are crowded by the sepulchres of the Moslems, or the simpler slabs of the Jewish tombs, alike awaiting the assembly of the last judgment.

JEHOSHEBA—*Jehovah is an oath.* Daughter of Joram king of Israel, and wife of Jehoida the high priest (2 Kings 11:2). Her name in the Chronicles is given Jehoshabeath. She is the only recorded instance of the marriage of a princess of the royal house with a high priest.

JEHOSHUA—*Jehovah saves.* That is, "help of Jehovah" or "Saviour." In this form is given the name of Joshua in Num. 13:16, on the occasion of its bestowal by Moses.

JEHOVAH. The true pronunciation of this name, by which God was known to the Hebrews, has been entirely lost, the Jews themselves scrupulously avoiding every mention of it, and substituting in its stead one or other of the words with whose proper vowel points it may happen to be written. This custom, which had its origin in reverence, and has almost degenerated into a superstition, was founded upon an erroneous rendering of Lev. 24:16, from which it was inferred that the mere utterance of the name constituted a capital offence. When Moses received his commission to be the deliverer of Israel, the Almighty, who appeared in the burning bush, communicated to him the name which he should give as the credentials of his mission: "And God said unto Moses, I am that I am; and he said, Thus shalt thou say unto the children of Israel, I am hath sent me unto you." That this passage is intended to indicate the etymology of the expression Jehovah, as understood by the Hebrews, no one has ventured to doubt; it is in fact the key to the whole mystery. The name Jehovah designates his nature as he stands in relation to man, as the only Almighty, true, personal, holy Being, a spirit and "the father of spirits" (Num. 16:22; *cf.* John 4:24), who revealed himself to his people and made a covenant with them and became their lawgiver, and to whom all honor and worship are due. (See God.)

JEHOVAH-JIREH—*Jehovah will see.* The name given by Abraham to the place on which he had been commanded to offer Isaac, to commemorate the interposition of the angel of Jehovah, who appeared to prevent the sacrifice (Gen. 22:14), and provide another victim.

JEHOVAH-NISSI—*Jehovah is my banner.* The name given by Moses to the altar which he built in commemoration of the discomfiture of the Amalekites by Joshua and his chosen warriors at Rephidim (Ex. 17:15).

JEHOVAH-SHALOM—*Jehovah is peace.* The altar erected by Gideon in Ophrah was so called in memory of the salutation addressed to him, by the angel of Jehovah, "Peace be unto thee" (Judg. 6:24).

JEHOVAH-SHAMMOH—*Jehovah is there.* The name to be given to the restored Jerusalem (Ezek. 48:35; *cf.* Isa. 60:14-22; 62:2; Rev. 21:2 f.).

JEHOVAH-TSIDKENU—*Jehovah is our righteousness.* The title of the perfectly Righteous King who is to rule over Israel on their return from captivity (Jer. 23:6; 33:16).

JEHOZABAD—*Jehovah hath bestowed.* 1. A Korahite Levite (1 Chron. 26:4, 15, *cf.* Neh. 12:25). 2. A Benjamite captain in the days of King Jehoshaphat (2 Chron. 17:18). 3. Son of Shomer or Shimrith, a Moabitish woman, who with another conspired against King Joash and slew him in his bed (2 Kings 12:21; 2 Chron. 24:26).

JEHOZADAK—*Jehovah is righteous.* Son of the high priest Seraiah (1 Chron. 6:14) in the reign of Zedekiah. (When his father was slain at Riblah by order of Nebuchadnezzar, in the 11th of Zedekiah (2 Kings 25:18, 21), Jehozadak was led away captive to Babylon.

JEHU—*Jehovah is He.* 1. The founder of the fifth dynasty of the kingdom of Israel, son of Jehoshaphat (2 Kings 9:2). His first appearance in history is when he rode behind Ahab on the fatal journey from Samaria to Jezreel, and heard the warning of Elijah against the murderer of Naboth (2 Kings 9:25). But he had already been known to Elijah, and in the vision of Horeb, he is mentioned as the future king of Israel, whom Elijah is to anoint as the minister of vengeance on Israel (1 Kings 19:16, 17). This injunction, for reasons unknown to us, Elijah never fulfilled. It was reserved long afterward for his successor Elisha. Jehu, meantime, in the reigns of Ahaziah and Jehoram, had risen to importance. He was, under the last-named king, captain of the host in the siege of Ramoth-Gilead. Whilst in the midst of the officers of the besieging army a youth suddenly entered, of wild appearance (2 Kings 9:11), and insisted on a private interview with Jehu. They retired into a secret chamber. The youth uncovered a vial of the sacred oil which he had brought with him, poured it over Jehu's head, and, after announcing to him the message from Elisha that he was appointed to be king of Israel and destroyer of the house of Ahab, rushed out of the house and disappeared. Jehu's countenance, as he re-entered the assembly of officers, showed that some strange tidings had reached him. He tried at first to evade their questions, but then revealed the situation in which he found himself placed by the prophetic call. In a moment the enthusiasm of the army took fire. They threw their garments under his feet, so as to form a rough carpet of state, placed him on the top of the stairs, as on an extempore throne, blew the royal salute on their trumpets, and thus ordained him king. He then cut off all communications between Ramoth-Gilead and Jezreel, and set off, full speed, with a band of horsemen (2 Kings 9:17). Whilst his soldiers

pursued and killed the king of Judah at Beth-gan (A.V. "the garden house"), Jehu himself advanced to the gates of Jezreel, and fulfilled the divine warning on Jezebel as already on Jehoram. He then entered on a work of extermination. All the descendants of Ahab that remained in Jezreel, together with the officers of the court and hierarchy of Astarte, were swept away. 2. Jehu, son of Hanani, a prophet of Judah. His father was probably the seer who attacked Asa (2 Chron. 16:7). He must have begun his career as a prophet when very young. He first denounced Baasha (1 Kings 16:1, 7), and then, after an interval of thirty years, reappears to denounce Jehoshaphat for his alliance with Ahab (2 Chron. 19:2, 3). He survived Jehoshaphat and wrote his life (20:34). 3. One of David's heroes (1 Chron. 12:3).

JEHUDI—*Jew.* Son of Nethaniah, a man employed by the princes of Jehoiakim's court to fetch Baruch to read Jeremiah's denunciation (Jer. 36:14), and then by the king to fetch the volume itself and read to him (vss. 21, 23).

JEMIMA—*dove.* The eldest of the three daughters born to Job after the restoration of his prosperity (Job 42:14).

JEPHTHAH—*He opens.* A judge of Israel. His history is contained in Judg. 11:1-12:8. He was a Gileadite, the son of Gilead and a concubine. Driven from his father's inheritance, he went to Tob, and became the head of a company of freebooters (2 Sam. 10:6). His fame as a captain was carried back to his native Gilead; and when the time was ripe for throwing off the yoke of Ammon, Jephthah consented to become their captain, on the condition (solemnly ratified before the Lord in Mizpeh) that in the event of his success he should still remain as their head. He collected warriors throughout Gilead and Manasseh, and then he vowed his vow unto the Lord—to offer to God whatever he saw coming out of his house first upon his return. The Ammonites were routed with great slaughter. But as the conqueror returned to Mizpeh there came to meet him his daughter, an only child. "Alas! my daughter, thou hast brought me very low." But the maiden is ready for any personal suffering in the hour of her father's triumph. Only she asks for two months to withdraw to her native mountains, and in their recesses to weep with her virgin friends. When that time was ended she returned to her father, and "he did unto her his vow."

JERAHMEEL—*God has compassion.* 1. Founder of the family of Jerahmeelites (1 Sam. 27:10). 2. Son of Hemmalech, who was employed by Jehoiakim to make Jeremiah and Baruch prisoners after he had burnt the roll of Jeremiah's prophecy (Jer. 36:26). 3. The son of Kish, a Levite (1 Chron. 24:29).

JERED. Son of Mahalaleel and father of Enoch (1 Chron. 1:2).

JEREMIAH—*whom Jehovah casts* (from the womb) or *appoints.* Was the "son of Hilkiah of the priests that were in Anathoth" (Jer. 1:1), and was a child in the reign of Josiah (1:6). We have hardly any mention of him during the eighteen years between his call and Josiah's death, or during the short reign of Jehoahaz. Under Jehoiakim, he opposed the Egyptian party, then dominant in Jerusalem. He was accordingly accused of treachery (14:13; 23:7). In the fourth year of Jehoiakim the battle of Carchemish overthrew the hopes of the Egyptian party (46:2; 35:11). As the danger from the Chaldeans became more threatening, the persecution against Jeremiah grew hotter (18). The people sought his life; his voice rose up in the prayer that God would deliver and avenge him. Standing in the valley of Ben-Hinnon, he broke the earthen vessel he carried in his hands, and prophesied that the city should be defiled with the dead, as that valley had been, within their memory, by Josiah (19:10-13). Famine and drouth were added to the miseries of the people (14:1), but false

prophets still deceived them with assurances of plenty; and Jeremiah was looked on as "a prophet of evil" (15:10). He was set, however (15:20), and went on with his work, reproving. The danger which Jeremiah had so long foretold at last came.

JEREMIAS. The Greek form of the name of Jeremiah the prophet (Matt. 16:14).

JEREMY. The prophet Jeremiah (Matt. 2:17; 27:9).

JERICHO—*a fragrant place* (?). A city of antiquity, situated in a plain traversed by the Jordan and over against where that river was crossed by the Israelites (Josh. 3:16). Its walls were so considerable that houses were built upon them (Josh. 2:15), and its gates were shut "when it was dark." Jericho is first mentioned as the city to which the two spies were sent by Joshua from Shittim (Josh. 2:1-21). The story of its destruction is told in Josh. 6. The manner in which its second foundation is recorded (1 Kings 16:34) implies that up to that time its site had been uninhabited. Once rebuilt, Jericho rose again into consequence. In its vicinity the sons of the prophets sought retirement from the world: Elisha "healed the spring of the waters"; and over against it, beyond Jordan, Elijah "went up by a whirlwind into heaven" (2 Kings 2:1-22). In its plains Zedekiah fell into the hands of the Chaldeans (2 Kings 25:5; Jer. 39:5). Between Jerusalem and Jericho was laid the scene of the story of the good Samaritan.

JEROBOAM—*the people increases* (?). 1. The first king of the divided kingdom of Israel was the son of an Ephraimite of the name of Nebat. He was employed by Solomon in the fortifications of Millo underneath the citadel of Zion, and was raised to the rank of superintendent over the taxes and labors exacted from the tribe of Ephraim (1 Kings 11:28). He at last was perceived by Solomon to be aiming at the monarchy. These designs were fostered by the disaffection of the great tribe over which he presided, as well as by the alienation of the prophetic order from the house of Solomon. As he was leaving Jerusalem he encountered Ahijah, "the prophet," Ahijah, who was dressed in a new outer garment, stripped it off and tore it into 12 shreds; 10 of which he gave to Jeroboam, with the assurance that, on condition of his obedience to his laws, God would establish for him a kingdom equal to that of David (1 Kings 11:29-40). The attempts of Solomon to cut short Jeroboam's designs occasioned his flight into Egypt. On Solomon's death, he demanded Shishak's permission to return. The Egyptian king offered any gift which Jeroboam chose as a reason for his remaining, and the consequence was his marriage with Ano, the elder sister of the Egyptian queen, Tahpenes. A year elapsed and a son, Abijah (or Abijam), was born. Then Jeroboam again requested permission to depart, which was granted, and on his return to Shechem took place the conference with Rehoboam and the revolt which ended in the elevation of Jeroboam to the throne of the northern kingdom (1 Kings 12:20). The political disruption of the kingdom was complete, but its religious unity was as yet unimpaired. Jeroboam was at constant war with the house of Judah, but the only act recorded is a battle with Abijah, son of Rehoboam, in which he was defeated. He never recovered the blow, and soon after died, in the twenty-second year of his reign (2 Chron. 13:20). 2. Jeroboam II, the son of Joash, the 4th of the dynasty of Jehu, the most prosperous of the kings of Israel. He repelled the Syrian invaders, took their capital city Damascus (2 Kings 14:28; Amos 1:3-5), and recovered the whole of the ancient dominion from Hamah to the Dead Sea (2 Kings 14:25; Amos 6:14). Ammon and Moab were reconquered (Amos 1:13; 2:1-3); the trans-Jordanic tribes were restored to their territory (2 Kings 13:5; 1 Chron. 5:17-22; Amos 7:9, 17).

JEROHAM—*may he have compassion.* 1. Father of Elkanah, the father of Samuel, of the house of Kohath (1 Chron. 6:27, 34; 1 Sam. 1:1). 2. A Benjamite and the founder of a family of Bene-Jeroham (1 Chron. 8:27). Probably the same as, 3. Father (or progenitor) of Ibneiah (1 Chron. 9:8; cf. 3 and 9). 4. A descendant of Aaron, of the house of Immer, the leader of the sixteenth course of priests (1 Chron. 9:12). He appears to be mentioned again in Neh. 11:12. 5. Jeroham of Gedor, some of whose sons joined David at Ziklag (1 Chron. 12:7). 6. A Danite, whose son or descendant Azareel was head of his tribe in the time of David (1 Chron. 27:22). 7. Father of Azariah, one of the "captains of hundreds" in the time of Athaliah (2 Chron. 23:1).

JERUBBAAL—*Baal strives.* The surname of Gideon, which he acquired in consequence of destroying the altar of Baal, when his father defended him from the vengeance of the Abie-zrites (Judg. 6:32).

JERUEL—*founded by God*, THE WILDERNESS OF. The place in which Jehoshaphat was informed by Jahaziel that he should encounter the hordes of Ammon, Moab and the Mehunims (2 Chron. 20:16).

JERUSALEM. The earliest notice of the city is in Josh. 15:8 and 18:16, 28. Next we find the form Jebus (Judg. 19:10, 11), "Jebus, which is Jerusalem . . . the city of the Jebusites"; and lastly, we have Jerusalem (Josh. 10:1, etc.; 12:10; Judg. 1:7, etc.). It is 32 miles distant from the sea, and 18 miles from the Jordan; 20 from Hebron, and 36 from Samaria. Its elevation is remarkable; it is on the edge of one of the highest table-lands of the country. From the south the approach to Jerusalem is by a slight descent. But from any other side the ascent is perpetual; and to the traveller approaching the city from the east or west it must have presented the appearance of a mountain city. It was the habitation of Jehovah, from which "He looked upon all the inhabitants of the world" (Ps. 33:14; its kings were "higher than the kings of the earth" (Ps. 89:27). Jerusalem, if not actually in the centre of Palestine, was yet virtually so. This central position, expressed in the words of Ezekial (5:5), "I have set Jerusalem in the midst of the nations and countries round about her," led in later ages to a belief that the city was actually in the centre of the earth. There appear to have been but two main approaches to the city: 1. From the Jordan valley by Jericho and the Mount of Olives. The latter part of the approach, over the Mount of Olives, is identical with what it was in the time of Christ. 2. From the great maritime plain of Philistia and Sharon. This road led by the two Bethhorons up to the high ground at Gideon, whence it turned south, and came to Jerusalem by Ramah and Gilbeah, and over the ridge north of the city. The city occupies the southern termination of the table-land, which is cut off from the country round it on its west, south and east sides by ravines deep and precipitous. These ravines leave the level of the table-land, the one on the west and the other on the northeast of the city, and fall rapidly until they form a junction below its southeast corner. The eastern one, the Valley of the Kedron, commonly called the Valley of Jehoshaphat, runs nearly straight from north to south. But the western one, the Valley of Hinnom, runs south for a time, and then takes a sudden bend to the east until it meets the Valley of Jehoshaphat, after which the two rush as one to the Dead Sea. The name of Mount Zion has been applied to the western hill from the time of Constantine to the present day; but notwithstanding it seems certain that up to the time of the destruction of the city by Titus, the name was applied exclusively to the eastern hill, or that on which the Temple stood. From the passages in 2 Sam. 5:7, and 1 Chron. 11:5-8, it is quite clear that Zion and the city of David were identical, for it is there said, "David took the castle of Zion which is the city of David." "And David dwelt in the castle, therefore they called it the city of David. And he built the city round about, even from Millo round about, and Joab repaired the rest of the city." There are passages in which

Zion is spoken of as a holy place in such terms as are never applied to Jerusalem, and which can only be understood as applied to the Holy Temple Mount (e.g., Ps. 2:6; 87:2). The eastern hill, called Mount Moriah in 2 Chron. 3:1, was, as already remarked, the site of the Temple. The Mount of Olives was a fruitful spot. At its foot was situated the Garden of Gethsemane. At the time of the final siege the space north of the wall of Agrippa was covered with gardens, groves, and plantations of fruit trees, enclosed by hedges and walls; and to level these was one of Titus' first operations. The "East street" (2 Chron. 29:4); the "street of the city"—the city of David (32:6); the "street facing the water gate" (Neh. 8:1, 3); the "street of the house of God" (Ezra 10:9); the "street of the gate of Ephraim" (Neh. 8:16); and the "open place of the first gate toward the east," must have been not "streets" in our sense of the word, so much as the open spaces found in eastern towns round the inside of the gates. Streets properly so called there were (Jer. 5:1; 11:13, etc.), but the name of only one, "the bakers' street" (Jer. 37:21), is preserved to us. In considering the annals of the city of Jerusalem, nothing strikes one so forcibly as the number and severity of the sieges. Our earliest glimpse of it is in the 1st chapter of Judges, which describes how the "children of Judah smote it with the edge of the sword, and set the city on fire"; and the latest mention of it in the New Testament is contained in the warnings in which Christ foretold how Jerusalem should be "compassed with armies" (Luke 21:20), and the "abomination of desolation" be seen standing in the Holy Place (Matt. 24:15). In the fifteen centuries which elapsed between those two points the city was besieged seventeen times; twice it was razed to the ground; and on two other occasions its walls were leveled. In this respect it stands without a parallel in any city, ancient or modern. The first siege appears to have taken place after the death of Joshua. Judah and Simeon "fought against it and took it, and smote it with the edge of the sword, and set the city on fire" (Judg. 1:8). The part which was taken at last was the lower city; the upper city was so strong that they relinquished the attempt. The Benjamites followed the men of Judah to Jerusalem, but with no better result (Judg. 1:21). This lasted during the period of the judges, the reign of Saul, and the reign of David at Hebron. David advanced against the place as the head of a formidable army. The lower city was immediately taken—the citadel held out. The undaunted Jebusites manned the battlements "with lame and blind." David's anger was roused by the insult, and he proclaimed to his host that the first man who would scale the fortress and kill a Jebusite should be made chief captain of the host. A crowd of warriors rushed to the attempt, but Joab's agility gained him the day, and the citadel was taken. The fortress received the name of "the city of David"; and David fortified it round about from Millo, while "Joab repaired the city" (2 Sam. 5:6-9; 1 Chron. 11:4-8). Until Solomon we hear of no additions to the city. His three great works were the Temple, with its east wall and cloister, his own Palace, and the Wall of Jerusalem. One of the first acts of the king was to make the walls larger. On the completion of the Temple he increased their height and constructed towers along them. Another work of his in Jerusalem was the fortification of Milli (1 Kings 9:15, 24). The city was taken by the Philistines and Arabians in the reign of Jehoram and by the Israelites in the reign of Amaziah. It was thrice taken by Nebuchadnezzar and in the last it was utterly destroyed. Its restoration commenced under Cyrus and was completed under Artaxerxes I. It was captured by Alexander the Great. Under the Ptolemies and the Seleucidae the town was prosperous until Antiochus Epiphanes sacked it. In consequence of his tyranny, the Jews rose under the Maccabees, and Jerusalem became independent, and retained its position until its capture by the Romans under Pompey (63 B.C.).

JESHUA—*Jehovah is salvation.* 1. Joshua, the son of Nun (Neh. 8:17). (See Joshua.) 2. A

priest in the reign of David (1 Chron. 24:11). 3. One of the Levites in the reign of Hezekiah (2 Chron. 31:15). 4. Son of Jehozadak, first high priest of the third series. Jeshua was born in Babylon, whither his father Jehozadak had been taken captive (1 Chron. 6:15, A.V.). He came from Babylon in the first year of Cyrus, and took a leading part in the rebuilding of the Temple, and the restoration of the Jewish commonwealth. The two prophecies in Zech. 3 and 6:9-15, point him out. 5. Head of a Levitical house which returned from the Babylonish captivity, and took an active part under Zerubbabel, Ezra and Nehemiah. 6. One of the chief families, probably, of the tribe of Judah (Neh. 10:14; 7:11, *etc.;* Ezra 10:30).

JESHURUN—*upright*. A name for Israel in Deut. 32:15; 33:5, 26; Isa. 44:2.

JESSE—*wealthy*. The father of David, was the son of Obed. He is commonly designated as "Jesse the Bethlehemite" (1 Sam. 16:1, 18); but his full title is "the Ephrathite of Bethlehem Judah" (1 Sam. 17:12). He is an "old man" when we first meet with him (1 Sam. 17:12), with eight sons (16:10; 17:12), residing at Bethlehem (16:4, 5). Jesse's wealth consisted of a flock of sheep and goats, which were under the care of David (16:11; 17:34, 35).

JESUS. 1. The Greek form of Joshua or Jeshua, a contraction of Jehoshua, that is, "help of Jehovah" or "Saviour" (Num. 13:16). 2. Joshua, son of Nun (Num. 7:45; Heb. 4:8).

JESUS THE SON OF SIRACH. Is described in Ecclesiasticus (1:27) as the author of that book generally called by his name, the *Wisdom of Jesus the Son of Sirach,* or simply the *Wisdom of Sirach.*

JESUS, called JUSTUS. A Christian who was with Paul at Rome (Col. 4:11).

JESUS CHRIST. The name Jesus signifies Saviour. The name of Christ signifies *Anointed*. In the New Testament the name Christ is used as equivalent to Messiah (Josh. 1:41), the name given to the promised Prophet and King whom the Jews had been taught to expect (Acts 19:4; Matt. 11:3). According to chronology the birth of Christ probably occurred in 4 B.C. Thirty years elapsed from birth to the opening year of his ministry. It was in the fifteenth year of Tiberius the emperor that John the Baptist began to teach (Matt. 3:1-10). Jesus came to Jordan to receive baptism at John's hands. Immediately after this inauguration of his ministry Jesus was led up of the Spirit into the wilderness to be tempted of the devil (Matt. 4:1-11). Jesus passed through the temptation, and his ministry is begun. At Bethabara, to which he returns, disciples begin to be drawn toward him; Andrew and another, probably John, see Jesus, and hear the Baptist's testimony concerning him. Andrew brings Simon Peter to see him also; and he receives from the Lord the name of Cephas. Then Philip and Nathanael are brought into contact with Jesus. The third day after this interview Jesus is at Cana in Galilee, and works his first miracle, by making the water wine (John 1:29, 35, 43; 2:1). He now goes to Capernaum, and after a sojourn there of "not many days," sets out for Jerusalem to the Passover, which was to be the beginning of his ministry in Judaea (John 2:12, 13). The visit of Nicodemus to Jesus took place about the first Passover. After a sojourn at Jerusalem of uncertain duration, Jesus went to the Jordan with his disciples, and they were baptized in his name. How long this sojourn in Judaea lasted is uncertain. On the way to Galilee, Jesus passed through Samaria, and came to Nazareth, his own city. In the Synagogue he expounded a passage from Isaiah (Isa. 41:1), telling them that its fulfillment was now at hand in his person. He came now to Capernaum. On his way, when he had reached Cana, he healed the son of one of the courtiers of Herod Antipas (John 4:46-54), who "himself believed, and his whole house." At Capernaum he wrought many miracles. After healing on the Sabbath a demoniac in the synagogue, he returned the same day to Simon's house, and healed the mother-in-law of Simon, who was sick of a fever. At sunset, the multitude brought their sick to Simon's door to be healed. He did not refuse, and healed them all (Mark 1:29-34). He now turned his thoughts to Galilee, where other "lost sheep" were scattered. Jesus again went to Jerusalem to a "feast of the Jews," which was the Passover. At the pool Bethesda, Jesus saw many infirm persons waiting their turn for the healing virtues of the water (John 5:1-18). Among them a man who had an infirmity thirty-eight years; Jesus made him whole by a word, bidding him take up his bed and walk. The miracle was done on the Sabbath; and the Jews rebuked the man for carrying his bed. It was a labor, and as such forbidden (Jer. 17:21). Jesus' justification of himself, "My Father worketh hitherto, and I work," is in John 5:17. Another discussion about the Sabbath arose from the disciples plucking the ears of corn as they went through the fields (Matt. 12:1-8). In placing the calling of the twelve apostles before the sermon on the mount, we are under the guidance of Luke (6:13, 17). But this separation for their work by no means marks the time of their first approach to Jesus. They are not sent forth to preach until later in the same year. Now commences the second circuit of Galilee (Luke 8: 1-3), to which belong the parables in Matt. 13; the visit of Jesus' mother and brethren (Luke 8:19-21), and the account of his reception at Nazareth (Mark 6:1-6). During this time the twelve have journeyed with him. But now a third circuit in Galilee is recorded, which occurred during the last three months of this year (Matt. 9:35-38); and during this circuit, he carries the training of the disciples one step further by sending them forth to teach (Matt. 10, 11). After a journey of two months, the twelve returned to Jesus, and gave an account of their ministry. The third Passover was now drawing near; but the Lord did not go up to it. He wished to commune with his apostles privately upon their work. He therefore went with them from Capernaum to a mountain on the eastern shore of the Sea of Tiberias, near Bethsaida Julias, not far from the head of the sea. Great multitudes pursued them; and here the Lord, moved to compassion by the hunger and weariness of the people, wrought one of his most remarkable miracles. After the miracle the disciples crossed the sea, and Jesus retired alone to a mountain to commune with the Father. They were toiling at the oar, for the wind was contrary, when, as the night drew toward morning, they saw Jesus walking to them on the sea, having passed the whole night on the mountain. He came into the ship and the wind ceased. Jesus not coming to the feast Scribes and Pharisees from Jerusalem went down to see him at Capernaum (Matt. 15:1). Leaving Capernaum, he now travels to the region of Tyre and Sidon, as a retreat from the machinations of the Jews (Matt. 15:21-28; Mark 7:24-30). Returning thence he passed to the region of Decapolis (Mark 7:31-37). In this district he performed many miracles, especially the restoration of a deaf man who had an impediment in his speech. To these succeeded the feeding of the four thousand with the seven loaves (Matt. 15:32). The doctrine of a suffering Messiah, so plainly exhibited in the prophets, had receded from sight in the religion of that time. The announcement of it to the disciples was new and shocking. They shrank from conflict, and pain and death. The transfiguration, which took place a week after this conversation, is to be understood in connection with it. The twelve were disturbed at what they had heard. They needed support for their perplexed spirits, and this their loving Master failed not to give them. He takes with him three disciples, Peter, John and James, who were nearer to Jesus than the rest, into a mountain apart by themselves. Once more did Jesus foretell his sufferings on their way back to Capernaum (Mark 9:30-32). The Feast of Tabernacles was now approaching. His brethren set out for the feast without him, and he abode in Galilee for a few days longer (John 7:2-10). Afterward he set out, taking the route by Samaria. After healing the ten lepers in Samaria, he came about the midst of the feast to Jerusalem. To this place belongs the account, given by John alone, of the healing of one who was born blind (John 9:1-41; 10:1-21). The parable of the good shepherd is an answer to the calumny of the Pharisees, that he was an impostor and breaker of the law: "This man is not of God, because he keepeth not the Sabbath-day" (9:16). After being present at the Feast of Dedication, Jesus returned to Bethabara beyond Jordan, where John had formerly baptized, and abode there. How long he remained here does not appear. The need of a family in Bethany called him thence. Lazarus was sick, and his sisters sent word to Jesus, whose power they well knew. It was not till Lazarus had been four days in the grave that the Saviour appeared. But he breaks the fetters of brass in which Lazarus was held by death, and at his word the man came forth alive and whole (John 11:1-45). A miracle so public, for Bethany was close to Jerusalem, and the family of Lazarus well known, could not escape the notice of the Sanhedrim. A meeting of this Council was called and the matter discussed. Jesus entered into Bethany on Friday the 8th of Nisan, the eve of the Sabbath, and remained over the Sabbath. *Saturday the 9th of Nisan.* As he was at supper in the house of one Simon, surnamed "the leper," a relation of Lazarus, who was at table with him, Mary, full of gratitude for the wonderful raising of her brother from the dead, took a vessel containing a quantity of pure ointment of spikenard, and anointed the feet of Jesus, and wiped his feet with her hair, and anointed his head likewise. *Passion Week. Sunday the 10th day of Nisan.* When he arrives at the Mount of Olives he commands two of his disciples to go into the village near at hand, where they would find an ass and a colt tied with her. With these beasts he was to enter into Jerusalem. The disciples spread upon the ass their ragged cloaks. And the multitudes cried before him, "Hosanna, Save now! blessed is he that cometh in the name of the Lord." All the city was moved. Blind and lame came to the Temple when he arrived and were healed. After working miracles in the Temple he returned to Bethany. *Monday the 11th of Nisan.* The next day Jesus returned to Jerusalem, again to instruct them. Proceeding to the Temple, he cleared its court of the traders that gathered there (Matt. 21:12, 13; Mark 11:15-19; Luke 19: 45-48). In the evening he returned again to Bethany. *Tuesday the 12th of Nisan.* On this the third day of Passion Week Jesus went into Jerusalem as before, and visited the Temple. The Sanhedrim came to call him to account for the clearing of the Temple. "By what authority doest thou these things?" The Lord answered this question by another. They refused to answer, and Jesus refused in like manner to answer them. To this time belong the parables of the two sons, of the wicked husbandman, and of the wedding garment. *Wednesday the 13th of Nisan.* This day was passed in retirement with the Apostles. Satan had put it into the mind of one of them to betray him; and Judas Iscariot made a covenant to betray him for thirty pieces of silver. *Thursday the 14th of Nisan.* On "the first day of unleavened bread," the disciples asked their Master where they were to eat the Passover. He directed Peter and John to go into Jerusalem, and to follow a man whom they should see bearing a pitcher of water, and to demand of him, in their Master's name, the use of the guest chamber in his house. All happened as Jesus had told them, and in the evening they assembled to celebrate, for the last time, the paschal meal. When they had taken their places at table and the supper had begun, Jesus gave them the first cup to divide amongst themselves (Luke). It was customary to drink at the paschal supper four cups of the wine mixed with water; and this answered to the first of them. There now arose a contention among the disciples which of them should be the greatest. After a warning against pride and ambition Jesus performed an act which must ever have been remembered by the wit-

nesses as a lesson of humility. He rose from the table, poured water into a basin, girded himself with a towel, and proceeded to wash the disciples' feet (John). "If I, your Lord and Master, have washed your feet, ye also ought to wash one another's feet. For I have given you an example, that ye should do as I have done to you." From this act of love even the traitor Judas was not excluded. But his treason was known; and Jesus denounces it. One of them should betray him. Toward the close of the meal Jesus instituted the sacrament of the Lord's Supper. The denial of Peter is now foretold (Matt. 26:31-35). That great final discourse, which John alone has recorded, is now delivered in the house before they proceeded to Gethsemane (John 14-17). *Friday the 15th of Nisan including part of the eve of it.* "When they had sung a hymn," they went out into the Mount of Olives. Jesus takes only his three proved companions, Peter, James and John, passes with them into the garden, leaving the rest seated, probably near the entrance. He tells them, "My soul is exceeding sorrowful, even unto death; tarry ye here and watch with me," and then leaving the three he wrestles in agony alone with God. At the dawn of day the Sanhedrim assembled. The high priest now asks him whether he is the Christ the Son of God. He answers that he is, and foretells his return in glory and power at the last day. This is enough. They pronounce him worthy of death (John 18:19-24; Luke 22:63-71; Matt. 26:59-68; Mark 14:55-65). But the Sanhedrim possessed no power to carry out such a sentence. As soon as it was day they took him to Pilate, the Roman procurator. From the first Jesus found favor in the eyes of Pilate, and he pronounced that he found no fault in him. Finding that Jesus was a Galilean, he sent him to Herod; but Herod, after cruel mockery, sent him back to Pilate. Now commenced the fearful struggle between the Roman procurator and the Jews. After the examination by Herod, and the return of Jesus, Pilate proposed to release him, as it was usual on the feast day to release a prisoner to the Jews. The multitude preferred another prisoner called Barabbas. According to John, Pilate still sought to release Jesus; but the last argument was now applied to him: "If thou let this man go, thou art not Caesar's friend." This decided the question. He delivered Jesus to be crucified (Matt. 27:15-30; Mark 15:6-19; Luke 23:17-25; John 18: 39, 40; 19:1-16). This occurred about the sixth hour. On the death of Jesus, the veil which covered the Most Holy place of the Temple, the place of the especial presence of Jehovah, was rent in twain. There was a great earthquake. Many who were dead rose from their graves. *Saturday the 16th of Nisan.* The chief priests and Pharisees set a watch over the tomb (Matt. 27: 62-66). *Sunday the 17th of Nisan.* The Sabbath ended at six on the evening of Nisan 16th. Early the next morning the resurrection of Jesus took place. The women, who had stood by the cross of Jesus, had prepared spices for the embalming of our Lord's body. They came very early on the first day of the week to the sepulchre. When they arrive they find the stone rolled away, and Jesus no longer in the sepulchre. He had risen from the dead. Mary Magdalene, believing that the body has been removed by men, tells Peter and John that the Lord has been taken away. The other women go into the sepulchre, and they see an angel (Matt., Mark). They now leave the sepulchre, and go in haste to make known the news to the apostles. As they were going, "Jesus met them, saying, All Hail." The eleven do not believe the account when they receive it. In the meantime Peter and John came to the sepulchre. John arrived first and looked in; Peter afterward came up and entered at once, and found the grave clothes lying, but not him who had worn them. Then they returned, wondering at what they had seen. Mary Magdalene, however, remained weeping at the tomb, and saw the two angels in the tomb. They address her, and she answers, still without any suspicion that the Lord is risen. As she turns away she sees Jesus, but does not recognize him. Then he calls her by name, and she joyfully recognizes her Master.

The third appearance of our Lord was to Peter (Luke, Paul); the fourth to the two disciples going to Emmaus in the evening (Mark, Luke); the fifth in the same evening to the eleven as they sat at meat (Mark, Luke, John). All of these occurred on the first day of the week, the very day of the resurrection (John); this was the sixth appearance. The seventh was in Galilee, where seven of the apostles were assembled (John). The eighth was to the eleven (Matt.). The ninth was to James (Paul); and the last to the apostles at Jerusalem just before the Ascension (Acts).

JETHER—*abundance.* 1. Jethro, the father-in-law of Moses (Ex. 4:18). 2. The firstborn of Gideon's seventy sons (Judg. 8:20). 3. The father of Amasa, captain-general of Absalom's army (1 Kings 2:5, 32). 4. The son of Jada, a descendant of Hezron, of the tribe of Judah (1 Chron. 2:32).

JETHETH. One of the "dukes" who came of Esau (Gen. 36:40; 1 Chron. 1:51).

JETHRO—*excellence.* Was priest or prince of Midian, both offices being combined in one person. Moses spent the forty years of his exile from Egypt with him, and married his daughter Zipporah (Ex. 2:15 ff.; Ex. 18).

JEW. This name was applied to a member of the kingdom of Judah after the separation of the ten tribes. The term first makes its appearance just before the captivity of the ten tribes (2 Kings 16:6). After the return the word received a larger application. All the members of the new state were called Jews (Judaeans), and the name was extended to the race scattered throughout the nations (Dan. 3:8, 12; Ezra 4:12, 23; Neh. 1:2; 2:16; 5:1; Esth. 3:4 ff.). The force of the title "Jew" is seen particularly in the Gospel of John, who rarely uses any other term to describe the opponents of our Lord. In the New Testament the term is used also in contrast to Gentiles (Mark 7:3; John 2:6; Acts 10:28).

JEWESS. A woman of Hebrew birth, without distinction of tribe (Acts 16:1; 24:24).

JEWRY. The same word elsewhere rendered Judah and Judaea (Dan. 5:13).

JEZANIAH. The son of Hoshaiah, the Maachathite, and one of the captains of the forces who had escaped from Jerusalem during the final attack of the Chaldeans. When the Babylonians had departed, Jezaniah, with the men under his command, returned to Gedaliah at Mizpah. In the assassination of that officer Jezaniah took a prominent part (2 Kings 25:23; Jer. 40:8; 42:1; 43:2).

JEZEBEL—*unmarried.* A wife of Ahab, king of Israel (1 Kings 16:31), and mother of Athaliah, queen of Judah, and Ahaziah and Joram, kings of Israel. She was a Phoenician princess, daughter of "Ethbaal king of the Zidonians." She was opposed by Elijah in her efforts to further the worship of Baal (1 Kings 18:19 ff.). She met her gruesome death at the hands of Jehu, maintaining her composure to the end (2 Kings 9: 30-37).

JEZREEL—*God soweth.* A city situated in the plain of the same name between Gilboa and Little Hermon, now generally called Esdraelon. It appears in Josh. 19:18, but its historical importance dates from the reign of Ahab, who chose it for his chief residence. In the neighborhood, or within the town probably, were a temple, and grove of Astarte, with an establishment of 400 priests supported by Jezebel (1 Kings 16:33; 2 Kings 10:11). The palace of Ahab (1 Kings 21:1; 18:46), containing his "ivory house" (1 Kings 22:39), was on the eastern side of the city, forming part of the city wall.

JIDLAPH—*tearful.* A son of Nahor (Gen. 22:22), whose settlements have not been identified, though they most probably are to be looked for in the Euphrates country.

JIMNA. The firstborn of Asher (Num. 26:44). He is elsewhere called Jimnah (Gen. 46:17) and Imnah (1 Chron. 7:30).

JIPHTHAHEL—*God opens.* THE VALLEY OF. A valley which served as one of the landmarks for the boundary of Zebulun (Josh. 19:14) and Asher (27).

JOAB—*Jehovah is father.* The most remarkable of the three nephews of David, the children of Zeruiah, David's sister (2 Sam. 2:18). Joab first appears after David's accession to the throne at Hebron. At the siege of Jebus he was appointed commander-in-chief—"captain of the host"—the same office that Abner had held under Saul, the highest office after the king (1 Chron. 11:6; 2 Sam. 8:16). In the wars which David undertook, Joab was the general (2 Sam. 11:11).

JOANNA—*Jehovah is gracious.* 1. Son of Rhesa, according to the text of Luke 3:27, and one of the ancestors of Christ. But according to one point of view, son of Zerubbabel, and the same as Hananiah in 1 Chron. 3:19. 2. The name of a woman, occurring twice in Luke (8:3; 24:10), but evidently denoting the same person.

JOASH—*Jehovah is strong.* 1. A king of Judah whose reign lasted 40 years. Known as Jehoash. The account of his rescue as an infant, his years on the throne, and finally his assassination is given in chapters 11 and 12 of 2 Kings. 2. Son and successor of Jehoahaz on the throne of Israel, and for two full years a contemporary sovereign with the preceding (2 Kings 14:1, *cf.* 12:1; 13:10). When he succeeded to the crown, the kingdom was in a deplorable state from the devastation of Hazael and Benhadad, kings of Syria. On a visit paid by Joash to Elisha on his deathbed, the prophet promised him deliverance from the Syrian yoke in Aphek (2 Kings 13: 14 ff.). He then bade the king smite upon the ground, and the king smote thrice and then stayed. The prophet rebuked him for staying, and limited to three his victories over Syria. Accordingly Joash beat Benhadad three times on the field of battle, and recovered from him the cities which Hazael had taken from Jehoahaz. The other military event of Joash's reign was his successful war with Amaziah king of Judah. The grounds of this war are given in 2 Chron. 25. 3. The father of Gideon, and a wealthy man among the Abiezrites (Judg. 6:11, 29, 30, 31).

JOB—*meaning uncertain.* The patriarch, the name of one of the books of the Old Testament. His residence is in the land of *Uz.* Job is represented as a chieftain of wealth and rank, blameless in all the relations of life. Satan suggests, "Doth Job fear God for naught?" and asserts that if those blessings were withdrawn, "he will curse thee to thy face." Satan received permission to make the trial. He destroys Job's property, then his children; and afterward inflicts upon him the most terrible disease known in the east. Job's wife breaks down under the trial. He repels his wife's suggestion with the simple words, "What! shall we receive good at the hand of the Lord, and shall we not receive evil?" "In all this Job did not sin with his lips." The question raised by Satan was thus answered. Three men, representing the wisdom of the age, come and condole with Job, without uttering a word. This silence drew out all his anguish. In agony he curses the day of his birth. Now begins a series of discussions. Jehovah at length appears in the midst of a storm, and in language of incomparable grandeur he reproves and silences the murmurs of Job, rebukes his opponents, and vindicates the integrity of the patriarch. Outside the book bearing his name, Job is mentioned in the Bible in Ezek. 14:14, 19 and James 5:11.

JOBAB. 1. The last in order of the sons of Joktan (Gen. 10:29; 1 Chron. 1:23). 2. One of the "kings" of Edom (Gen. 36:33, 34; 1 Chron. 1:44, 45). 3. King of Madon; one of the northern chieftains who attempted to oppose Joshua's conquest, and were routed by him at Merom

(Josh. 11:1, only). 4. Two Benjamites (1 Chron. 8:9, 18).

JOCHEBED—*Jehovah is glory.* The wife and the aunt of Amram, and the mother of Moses and Aaron (Ex. 2:1; 6:20; Num. 26:59).

JOEL—*Jehovah is God.* 1. Eldest son of Samuel the prophet (1 Sam. 8:2; 1 Chron. 6:33; 15:17), and father of Heman the singer. 2. In 1 Chron. 6:36, A.V., Joel seems to be merely a corruption of Shaul in vs. 24. 3. The second of the twelve minor prophets, the son of Pethuel, probably prophesied in Judah. The event to which the prophecy related was a public calamity, then impending on Judah, want of water, and a plague of locusts, continuing for several years. The prophet exhorts the people to turn to God with penitence, fasting and prayer; and then (he says) the plague shall cease, and the rain descend in its season, and the land yield her accustomed fruit. 4. A Simeonite chief (1 Chron. 4:35). 5. A descendant of Reuben (1 Chron. 5:4). 6. Chief of the Gadites, who dwelt in the land of Bashan (1 Chron. 5:12). 7. The son of Izrahiah, of the tribe of Issachar (1 Chron. 7:3). 8. The brother of Nathan of Zobah (1 Chron. 11:38), and one of David's guard. 9. The chief of the Gershonites in the reign of David (1 Chron. 15:7, 11). 10. A Gershonite Levite in the reign of David, son of Jehiel, a descendant of Laadan (1 Chron. 23:8; 26:22). 11. The son of Pedaiah and a chief of the half tribe of Manasseh west of Jordan, in the reign of David (1 Chron. 27:20). 12. A Kohathite Levite in the reign of Hezekiah (2 Chron. 29:12). 13. One of the sons of Nebo who returned with Ezra, and had married a foreign wife (Ezra 10:43). 14. The son of Zichri, a Benjamite (Neh. 11:9).

JOHANAN—*Jehovah is gracious.* 1. Son of Azariah, and grandson of Ahimaaz the son of Zadok, and the father of Azariah (1 Chron. 6:9, 10, A.V.). Johanan's pontificate fell in the reign of Rehoboam. 2. Son of Elioenai, the son of Neariah, the son of Shemaiah, in the line of Zerubbabel's heirs (1 Chron. 3:24). 3. The son of Kareah, and one of the captains of the army of Judah, who escaped in the final attack upon Jerusalem. After the murder of Gedaliah, Johanan was one of the foremost in the pursuit of his assassin, and rescued the captives he had carried off from Mizpah (Jer. 41:11-16). Fearing the vengeance of the Chaldaeans, the captains, with Johanan at their head, retired into Egypt. 4. The first-born son of Josiah king of Judah (1 Chron. 3:15). 5. A valiant Benjamite who joined David at Ziklag (1 Chron. 12:4). 6. A Gadite warrior, who followed David (1 Chron. 12:12). 7. The father of Azariah, an Ephraimite in the time of Ahaz (2 Chron. 28:12). 8. The son of Hakkatan, and chief of the Bene-Azgad who returned with Ezra (Ezra 8:12). 9. The son of Eliashib, one of the chief Levites (Neh. 12:23; Ezra 10:6). 10. The son of Tobiah the Ammonite (Neh. 6:18).

JOHN—*Jehovah hath been gracious.* The same name as Johanan, a contraction of Jehohanan. 1. The father of Mattathias, and grandfather of the Maccabaean family. 2. The eldest son of Mattathias surnamed Caddis, who was slain by "the children of Jambri." 3. The father of Eupolemus, one of the envoys whom Judas Maccabaeus sent to Rome. 4. The son of Simon, the brother of Judas Maccabaeus. 5. One of the high priest's family, who, with Annas and Caiaphas, sat in judgment upon the Apostles Peter and John (Acts 4:6). 6. The Hebrew name of Mark (Acts 12:12, 25; 13:5, 13; 15:37).

JOHN, THE APOSTLE. Was the son of Zebedee, a fisherman on the lake of Galilee, and of Salome, and brother of James, also an apostle (Matt. 4:21; 10:3; 17:1, *etc.*). Peter and James and John come within the innermost circle of their Lord's friends. Peter is throughout the leader of that band; to John belongs the distinction of being the disciple whom Jesus loved. The name Boanerges (Mark 3:17) implies a vehemence and zeal, which gave to those who had it the might

of the Sons of Thunder. The three are with him when none else are in the chamber of death (Mark 5:37), in the glory of the transfiguration (Matt. 17:1). When the betrayal is accomplished, Peter and John follow afar off (John 18:15).

JOHN THE BAPTIST. Was of the priestly race; his father Zacharias was a priest of the course of Abia, or Abijah (1 Chron. 24:10), offering incense at the very time when a son was promised to him; and Elisabeth was of the daughters of Aaron (Luke 1:5). John was ordained to be a Nazarite from his birth (Luke 1:15). Dwelling in the wild and thinly peopled region westward of the Dead Sea, he prepared himself for the wonderful office to which he had been divinely called. His dress was that of the old prophets, a garment woven of camel's hair (2 Kings 1:8), attached to the body by a leathern girdle. His food was locusts (Lev. 11:22) and wild honey (Ps. 81:16). And now the long secluded hermit came forth to the discharge of his office. His supernatural birth, his hard ascetic life, his reputation for extraordinary sanctity, and the prevailing expectation that some great one was about to appear, these causes were sufficient to attract to him a great multitude from "every quarter" (Matt. 3:5). Shortly after his testimony to the Messiah, John's public ministry was brought to a close. His death occurred in the course of the Lord's ministry.

JOHN, GOSPEL OF. Ephesus and Patmos are mentioned by early writers as the place where this gospel was written, but internal evidence in the Gospel itself does not favor any particular locality as its point of origin. The Gospel was obviously addressed to Christians and its unique character is the blending of history with theological interpretation. The object of John, who wrote after the other Evangelists was to supplement their narratives, which were confined to our Lord's life in Galilee.

JOHN, THE FIRST EPISTLE GENERAL OF. Probably meant for the churches of Asia Minor. The introduction (1:1-4) states the purpose of the epistle. The first part may be considered to end at 2:28. It begins afresh with the doctrine of sonship or communion at 2:20, and returns to the same theme at 4:7. The lesson throughout is, that the means of union with God are, on the part of Christ, his atoning blood and advocacy on the part of man, holiness, obedience, purity, faith, and above all love.

JOHN, THE SECOND AND THIRD EPISTLES OF. These two epistles are placed by Eusebius in the class of "disputed" books and he appears to be doubtful whether they were written by the Evangelist, or by some other John. The evidence of antiquity in their favor is not very strong, but yet is considerable. In the fifth century they were almost universally received. The title and contents of the epistles are strong arguments against a fabricator, whereas they would account for their non-universal reception in early times.

JOKSHAN. A son of Abraham and Keturah (Gen. 25:2, 3; 1 Chron. 1:32), whose sons were Sheba and Dedan.

JOKTAN—*he will be made little.* Son of Eber (Gen. 10:25; 1 Chron. 1:19), and the father of the Joktanite Arabs. Scholars are agreed in placing the settlements of Joktan in the south of the peninsula. The original limits are stated in the Bible: "their dwelling was from Mesha, as thou goest unto Sephar, a mount of the East" (Gen. 10:30).

JOKTHEEL. 1. A city in the country of Judah (Josh. 15:38), named next to Lachish. 2. "God-subdued," the title given by Amaziah to the cliff (A.V. Selah)—the stronghold of the Edomites—after he had captured it from them (2 Kings 14:7). The parallel narrative of 2 Chron. 25:11-13 supplies fuller details.

JONA. The father of the Apostle Peter (John

1:42), who is hence addressed as Simon **Barjona** (*i.e.*, son of Jona) in Matt. 16:17.

JONADAB—*Jehovah is noble.* Also called Jehonadab (which see). 1. Son of Shimeah and nephew of David. He is described as "very subtle" (2 Sam. 13:3). His age made him the friend of his cousin Amnon, heir to the throne (2 Sam. 13:3). He gave him the fatal advice for ensnaring his sister Tamar (5, 6). Again, in the same tragedy, when Amnon was murdered by Absalom, and the exaggerated report reached David that all the princes were slaughtered, Jonadab was already aware of the real state of the case (2 Sam. 13:32, 33). 2. (Jer. 35:6, 8, 10, 14, 16, 18, 19).

JONAH—*dove.* The fifth of the minor prophets, according to the order of our Bible, was the son of Amittai, and a native of Gathhepher, a town of Lower Galilee, in Zebulun (2 Kings 14:25). The general opinion is that Jonah was the first of the prophets. The king of Nineveh at this time is supposed to have been Pul. Having already prophesied to Israel, he was sent to Nineveh. The prophet shrank from a commission which he felt would result (Jonah 4:2) in the sparing of a hostile city. He attempted therefore to escape to Tarshish. The providence of God, however, watched over him, first in a storm, and then in his being swallowed by a fish for the space of three days and three nights. After his deliverance, Jonah executed his commission; and the king, "believing him to be a minister from the supreme deity of the nation," and having heard of his miraculous deliverance, ordered a general fast, and averted the threatened judgment.

JONAN. Son of Eliakim, in the genealogy of Christ (Luke 3:30).

JONAS. 1. The prophet Jonah (Matt. 12:39, 40, 41; 16:4). 2. Father of Peter (John 21:15-17).

JONATHAN—*Jehovah hath given.* The eldest son of King Saul (1 Sam. 14:49). He was regarded in his father's lifetime as heir to the throne. Like Saul, he was a man of great strength and activity (2 Sam. 1:23). He was also famous for archery and slinging (1 Chron. 12:2). His bow was to him what the spear was to his father: "*bow of Jonathan turned not back*" (2 Sam. 1:22). It was always about him (1 Sam. 18:4; 20:35). His friendship with David is celebrated (1 Sam. 18:1-4; 19:1-7; 20). He died with his father and brothers in the battle with the Philistines on Mount Gilboa (1 Sam. 31:1-10). His death occasioned the celebrated elegy of David. He left a son, Mephibosheth.

JONATH-ELEMRECHOKIM. "A dumb dove of (in) distant places," a phrase found once only in the Bible as a heading to the 56th Psalm.

JOPPA—*beauty.* Or *Japho,* now *Jaffa,* a town on the southwest coast of Palestine, in the portion of Dan (Josh. 19:46). Having a harbor attached to it, it became the port of Jerusalem in the days of Solomon, and has been ever since. Here Jonah "took ship to flee from the presence of his Maker." Here, on the housetop of Simon the tanner, "by the seaside," Peter had his vision (Acts 11:5).

JORDAN—*flowing down; the descender.* The chief river of Palestine, has a course of 200 miles, from the roots of Anti-Lebanon to the head of the Dead Sea. It is the river of the "great plain" of Palestine, "the river of God" in the Book of Psalms, at least that of his chosen people throughout their history. There were fords at Jericho, to which point the men of Jericho pursued the spies (Josh. 2:7; *cf.* Judg. 3:28). Higher up at Succoth, some way above, were the fords of Beth-barah (probably the Bethabara of the Gospel), where Gideon lay in wait for the Midianites (Judg. 7:24), and where the men of Gilead slew the Ephraimites (Judg. 12:6). These fords witnessed the first recorded passage of the Jordan in the Old Testament (Gen. 32:10). Jordan was

next crossed, over against Jericho, by Joshua the son of Nun (Josh. 4:12, 13). The Jordan is frequently mentioned as a boundary: "over Jordan," "this" and "the other side," or "beyond Jordan," were expressions familiar to the Israelites. It was the eastern boundary of the promised land (Num. 34:12). The two principal features of the river are its descent and its windings. From its fountain heads to the Dead Sea it rushes down, only broken by a series of precipitous falls. Between the lake of Gennesaret and the Dead Sea there are twenty-seven rapids; the depression of the lake of Gennesaret below the level of the Mediterranean is 653 feet, and that of the Dead Sea 1316 feet.

JORIM. Son of Matthat, in the genealogy of Christ (Luke 3:29).

JOSE. Son of Eliezer, in the genealogy of Jesus Christ (Luke 3:29).

JOSEPH—*may he add.* 1. The elder of the two sons of Jacob by Rachel, is first mentioned when seventeen years old. Jacob then stayed at Hebron with Isaac, while his sons kept his flocks. Joseph brought the evil report of his brethren to his father, and they hated him because his father loved him more than them, as the "son of his old age," and had shown his preference by making him a dress, which appears to have been a long tunic with sleeves, worn by the richer class (Gen. 37:2). The hatred of Joseph's brethren was increased by his dream foreshowing that they would bow down to him, which was followed by another of the same import. They had gone to Shechem to feed the flock; and Joseph was sent thither from Hebron by his father to bring him word of their welfare and that of the flock. They were not at Shechem, but were gone to Dothan, not far distant, pasturing their flock wherever the wild country was unowned. On Joseph's approach his brethren, except Reuben, resolved to kill him; but Reuben saved him, persuading them to cast him into a dry pit, he intending to restore him to his father. Accordingly, when Joseph was come, they stripped him of his tunic and cast him into the pit, "and they sat down to eat bread; and they lifted up their eyes and looked, and behold, a company of Ishmaelites came from Gilead with their camels." Judah suggested to his brethren to sell Joseph to the Ishmaelites, and accordingly they took him out of the pit and sold him "for twenty (shekels) of silver" (vs. 28). His brethren pretended to Jacob that Joseph had been killed by some wild beast, taking to him the tunic stained with a kid's blood. The Midianites sold Joseph into Egypt to Potiphar, "an officer of Pharaoh, captain of the executioners, an Egyptian" (39:1; cf. 37:39). Joseph prospered in the house of the Egyptian, who "set him over his house, and all he had he gave into his hand" (Gen. 39:4 f.). The familiar story of Joseph's false accusation, imprisonment, and subsequent rise to power, followed by the restoration of his family is told in Gen. 39:7-47. Joseph lived "a hundred and ten years," having been more than ninety in Egypt; he "saw Ephraim's children of the third" (generation), and "the children also of Machir the son of Manasseh were borne upon Joseph's knees"; dying, he took an oath of his brethren that they should carry up his bones to the land of promise: thus showing in his latest action the faith (Heb. 11:22) which had guided his whole life. Like his father, he was embalmed, "and he was put in a coffin in Egypt" (50:26). His trust Moses kept, and laid the bones of Joseph in his inheritance in Shechem, in the territory of Ephraim his offspring. 2. All that is told us of Joseph in the New Testament may be summed up in a few words. He was a just man and of the house and lineage of David. The public registers also contained his name under the reckoning of the house of David (John 1:45; Luke 3:23; Matt. 1:20; Luke 2:4). He lived at Nazareth in Galilee, and his family had been settled there for two preceding generations, possibly from the time of Matthat, the common grandfather of Joseph and Mary, since Mary lived there too (Luke 1: 26, 27). He espoused Mary, the daughter and

heir of his uncle Jacob, and before he took her home as his wife received the angelic communication recorded in Matt. 1:20. When Jesus was twelve years old Joseph and Mary took him with them to keep the Passover at Jerusalem, and when they returned to Nazareth he continued to act as a father to the child Jesus. Here our knowledge of Joseph ends. That he died before the crucifixion of Jesus is indeed certain (John 19:27). But where, when or how he died, we know not. 3. Joseph of Arimathea, a rich and pious Israelite (Mark 15:43), and a member of the great council, or Sanhedrin. He is further characterized as "a good man and a just" (Luke 23:50), one of those who were waiting for the kingdom of God (Mark 15:43; Luke 2:25, 38; 23:51). There is a tradition that he was one of the seventy disciples. 4. Joseph, called Barsabas, and surnamed Justus; one of the two persons chosen by the assembled church (Acts 1:23) as candidates to fill the place in the Apostolic company from which Judas had fallen.

JOSES—*adding.* 1. Son of Eliezer, in the genealogy of Christ (Luke 3:29). 2. One of the Lord's brethren (Matt. 13:55; Mark 6:3). 3. Joses Barnabas (Acts 4:36).

JOSHUA—*Jehovah is salvation.* His name appears in the various forms of Hoshea, Oshea, Jehoshua, Jeshua and Jesus. 1. The son of Nun, of the tribe of Ephraim (1 Chron. 7:27), and was nearly forty years old when he shared in the hurried triumph of the Exodus. He is mentioned first in connection with the fight against Amalek at Rephidem, when he was chosen by Moses to lead the Israelites (Ex. 17:9). The forty years of wandering were almost passed, and Joshua was one of the few survivors, when Moses, shortly before his death, was directed (Num. 27:18) to invest Joshua publicly with definite authority, in connection with Eleazar the priest, over the people. And after this was done, God himself gave Joshua a charge by the mouth of the dying lawgiver (Deut. 31:14, 23; Josh. 1:1). Joshua assumed the command of the people at Shittim, sent spies into Jericho, crossed the Jordan, fortified a camp at Gilgal, circumcised the people, kept the passover and was visited by the captain of the Lord's host. He died at the age of 110 years, and was buried in his own city, Timnath-serah. 2. An inhabitant of Bethshemesh, in whose land was the stone at which the milch-kine stopped when they drew the ark of God with the offerings of the Philistines from Ekron the Bethshemesh (1 Sam. 6:14, 18). 3. A governor of the city who gave his name to a gate of Jerusalem (2 Kings 23:8). 4. Jeshua the son of Jozadak (e.g., Hag. 1:14; 2:1; Zech. 3:1).

JOSHUA, BOOK OF. This book has been regarded by many critics as a part of the Pentateuch; but there do not appear to be sufficient grounds for this opinion. The fact that the first sentence of Joshua begins with a conjunction does not show any closer connection between it and the Pentateuch than exists between Judges and it. The references in 1:8; 8:31; 23:6; 24:26, to the "book of the law," rather show that that book was distinct from Joshua. The book may be regarded as consisting of three parts: (I.) The conquest of Canaan; (II.) The partition of Canaan; (III.) Joshua's farewell. I. The preparations for the war and the passage of the Jordan, ch. 1-5; the capture of Jericho, 6; the conquest of the south, 7-10; the conquest of the north, 11; recapitulation, 12. II. Territory assigned to Reuben, Gad and half Manasseh, 13; the lot of Caleb, and of the tribe of Judah, 14, 15; Ephraim and half Manasseh, 16, 17; Benjamin, 18; Simeon, Zebulun, Issachar, Asher, Naphtali and Dan, 19; the appointment of forty-eight cities to Levi, 21; the departure of the trans-Jordanic tribes to their homes, 22. III. Joshua's convocation of the people and first address, 23; his second address is known as to the authorship of the book.

JOSIAH—*Jehovah supports.* The son of Amon and Jedidah succeeded his father in the eighth year of his age, and reigned 31 years. His history

is contained in 2 Kings 22-24:30; 2 Chron. 34, 35; and the first twelve chapters of Jeremiah throw much light upon the general character of the Jews in his day. 2. The son of Zephaniah, at whose house the prophet Zechariah was commanded to assemble the chief men of the captivity, to witness the solemn and symbolical crowning of Joshua the high priest (Zech. 6: 10).

JOSIAS. Josiah, king of Judah (Matt. 1:10, 11).

JOTHAM—*Jehovah is perfect.* 1. The youngest son of Gideon (Judg. 9:5 ff.), who escaped from the massacre of his brethren. His parable of the reign of the bramble is the earliest example of the kind. 2. The son of King Uzziah or Azariah and Jerushah. After administering the kingdom during his father's leprosy, he succeeded to the throne when he was 25 years old, and reigned 16 years in Jerusalem. He was contemporary with Pekah and with the prophet Isaiah. His history is contained in 2 Kings 15 and 2 Chron. 27. 3. A descendant of Judah, son of Jahdai (1 Chron. 2:47).

JOZACHAR—*Jehovah remembers.* The son of Shimeath the Ammonitess, and one of the murderers of Joash king of Judah (2 Kings 12:21). The writer of the Chronicles (2 Chron. 24:26) calls him Zabad.

JUBAL—*a stream.* A son of Lamech by Adah, and the inventor of the "harp and organ" (Gen. 4:21).

JUBILEE, THE YEAR OF. The fiftieth year after the succession of seven Sabbatical years, in which all the land which had been alienated returned to the families of those to whom it had been allotted in the original distribution, and all bondmen of Hebrew blood were liberated. The relation in which it stood to the Sabbatical year and the directions for its observance are given Lev. 25:8-16 and 23-55. Its bearing on lands dedicated to Jehovah is stated Lev. 27:16-25. The year was inaugurated on the Day of Atonement with the blowing of trumpets throughout the land, and by a proclamation of universal liberty.

JUDA. 1. Son of Joseph in the genealogy of Christ (Luke 3:30). 2. Son of Joanna, or Hananiah (Luke 3:26). He seems to be certainly the same person as Abiud in Matt. 1:13. 3. One of the Lord's brethren, enumerated in Mark 6:3. 4. The patriarch Judah (Luke 3:33; Heb. 7:14; Rev. 5:5; 7:5).

JUDAEA, or JUDAH. A territorial division which succeeded to the overthrow of the ancient landmarks of the tribes of Israel and Judah in their captivities. The word first occurs Dan. 5:13, and the first mention of the "province of Judaea" is in the book of Ezra (5:8); it is alluded to in Neh. 11:3 (A.V. "Judah"), and was the result of the division of the Persian empire mentioned by Herodotus (3:89-97), under Darius (cf. Esth. 8:9; Dan. 6:1). The term Judaea was sometimes extended to the whole country of the Cannanites, its ancient inhabitants; and even in the Gospels we read of the coast of Judaea "beyond Jordan" (Matt. 19:1; Mark 10:1). Judaea was the name of the third district west of the Jordan, and south of Samaria.

JUDAH. The fourth son of Jacob and the fourth of Leah, the last before the temporary cessation in the births of her children. His whole-brothers were Reuben, Simeon, and Levi, elder than himself—Issachar and Zebulun, younger (see Gen. 35:23). His sons were five. Of these, three were by his Canannite wife Bath-shua. The other two, Pharez and Zerah, were illegitimate sons by the widow of Er, the eldest of the former family (Gen. 38). And from Pharez, the elder, were descended the illustrious families of Judah.

JUDAH, KINGDOM OF. When the disruption of Solomon's kingdom took place at Shechem, only the tribe of Judah followed the house of

David. But afterward, when Rehoboam conceived the design of establishing his authority over Israel by force of arms, the tribe of Benjamin also is recorded as obeying his summons, and contributing its warriors to make up his army. The Benjamite towns, Bethel and Jericho, were included in the northern kingdom. A part of the territory of Simeon (1 Sam. 27:6; 1 Kings 19:3; *cf.* Josh. 19:1), and of Dan (2 Chron. 11:10; *cf.* Josh. 19:41, 42), was recognized as belonging to Judah; and in the reigns of Abijah and Asa the southern kingdom was enlarged by some additions taken out of the territory of Ephraim (2 Chron. 13:19; 15:8; 17:2). The first three kings of Judah seem to have cherished the hope of re-establishing their authority over the Ten Tribes. For sixty years there was war between them and the kings of Israel. The victory achieved by Abijah brought to Judah a temporary accession of territory. Asa enlarged it still further. Hanani's remonstrance (2 Chron. 16:7) prepares us for the reversal by Jehoshaphat of the policy which Asa pursued toward Israel and Damascus. A close alliance sprang up between Judah and Israel. Jehoshaphat repelled nomad invaders, curbed the aggressive spirit of his neighbors, and made his influence felt among the Philistines and Arabians. Amaziah, king following after Jehoshaphat by several years and four other monarchs, flushed with the recovery of Edom, provoked a war with Jehoash, the conqueror of the Syrians; and Jerusalem was entered by the Israelites. Under Uzziah and Jotham, Judah enjoyed political and religious prosperity for almost a century and a half after the termination of the kingdom of Israel.

JUDAS. The Greek form of the Hebrew name Judah, occurring in the LXX and New Testament. 1. The patriarch Judah (Matt. 1:2, 3). 2. A man residing at Damascus, in "the street which is called Straight," in whose house Saul of Tarsus lodged after his miraculous conversion (Acts 9:11).

JUDAS, surnamed BARSABAS. A leading member of the apostolic church at Jerusalem (Acts 15:22, 32), endued with the gift of prophecy.

JUDAS OF GALILEE. The leader of a revolt "in the days of the taxing." Judas was a Gaulonite of the city of Gamala, taking his name of Galilean from his insurrection having had its rise in Galilee. His revolt had a theocratic character, the watchword of which was, "We have no lord or master but God." Judas himself perished, and his followers were dispersed. Judas is represented as the founder of a fourth sect, in addition to the Pharisees, Sadducees and Essenes.

JUDAS ISCARIOT. He is sometimes called "the son of Simon" (John 6:71; 13:2, 26), but more commonly called Iscariotes (Matt. 10:4; Mark 3:19; Luke 6:16). In the three lists of the twelve there is added in each that he was the betrayer. The name Iscariot has received many interpretations. That most generally held now is that it comes from Kerioth (Josh. 15:25), in the tribe of Judah. He was drawn, as the others were, by the preaching of the Baptist, or his own Messianic hopes, or the "gracious words" of the new Teacher, to leave his former life, and to obey the call of the Prophet of Nazareth (John 6:64). At the last supper he is present. Then come the sorrowful words, "One of you shall betray me." After this there comes on him that insanity of guilt as of one whose soul was possessed by the spirit of evil—"Satan entered into him" (John 13:27). He knows that garden in which his Master and his companions had so often rested. He comes, accompanied by a band of officers and servants (John 18:3), with the kiss, the usual salutation of the disciples. What followed in the confusion of that night the Gospels do not record. There came back on him the recollection of the righteousness of the Master he had wronged (Matt. 27:3). His death was made more horrible by the circumstance recorded by Luke in the Acts; but most awful of all is the sentence pronounced upon him by the Lord, and with which

Peter dismisses his name from the apostles' list, "from which Judas by transgression fell, that *he might go to his own place."*

JUDAS MACCABAEUS. (See Maccabees.)

JUDE, or JUDAS, LEBBEUS, and THADDEUS. (A.V. "Judas *the brother* of James"), one of the twelve apostles. The name Judas occurs in the lists given by Luke 6:16; Acts 1:13; and in John 14:22 (where we find "Judas not Iscariot" among the apostles), but the apostle has been generally identified with "Lebbeus whose surname was Thaddeus" (Matt. 10:3; Mark 3:18). The name of Jude occurs only once in the Gospel narrative (John 14:22). Nothing is certainly known of the later history of the apostle.

JUDE, THE LORD'S BROTHER. Among the brethren of our Lord mentioned by the people of Nazareth (Matt. 13:55; Mark 6:3) occurs a "Judas," sometimes identified with the apostle of the same name.

JUDE, EPISTLE OF. Its author was Jude, one of the brethren of Jesus. There are no data from which to determine its date or place of writing. The object of the epistle is announced, vs. 3; the reason for this exhortation is given, vs. 4. The remainder of the epistle is occupied by a depiction of the adversaries of the faith. The epistle closes by reminding the readers of the oft-repeated prediction of the apostles—that the faith would be assailed (vss. 17-19), exhorting them to maintain their own steadfastness in the faith (vss. 20, 21), while they earnestly sought to rescue others (vss. 22, 23), and commending them to the power of God. This epistle presents one peculiarity, which caused its authority to be impugned in early times—the supposed citation of apocryphal writings (vss. 9, 14, 15). The larger portion of this epistle (vss. 3-16) is almost identical in language and subject with a part of the Second Epistle of Peter (2 Pet. 2:1-19).

JUDGES. The Judges were temporary deliverers, sent by God to deliver the Israelites from their oppressors. Their power only extended over portions of the country, and some of them were contemporaneous. Their name in Hebrew is *shophetim,* which is the same as that for ordinary *judges.* For, though their first work was that of deliverers and leaders in war, they then administered justice to the people, and their authority supplied the want of a regular government. But the only recognized authority was still the oracle at Shiloh, which sunk into priestly weakness and disorder under Eli and his sons. Even while the administration of Samuel gave a settled government to the South, there was scope for the irregular exploits of Samson on the borders of the Philistines, and Samuel at last established his authority as Judge and prophet, but still as the servant of Jehovah, only to see it so abused by his sons as to exhaust the patience of the people, who at length demanded a king. On the Chronology of the Judges, see the following article.

JUDGES, BOOK OF. Contains the history from the death of Joshua to the anointing of Saul as the first king over Israel. As the history of the Judges occupies the greater part of the narrative, and is also the history of the people, the title of the book is derived from that portion. The book may be divided into two parts— (1) Ch. 1-16. The subdivisions are 1, 2:5, which may be considered as an introduction, giving the results of the war carried on against the Canaanites by the several tribes on the west of Jordan after Joshua's death, and forming a continuation of Josh. 12, 13:7 through ch. 16. The words, "and the children of Israel did evil in the sight of the Lord," are employed to introduce the history of the thirteen Judges comprised in this book. An account of six of these thirteen is given at length. The account of the remaining seven is very short, and merely attached to the longer narratives. This portion of the book is almost entirely a history of the wars of deliverance. 2.

Ch. 17-21. This part has no connection with the preceding, and is often called an appendix. No mention of the Judges occurs in it. It contains allusions to "the house of God," the ark and the high priest. The period to which the narrative relates is "when there was no king in Israel" (19:1; *cf.* 18:1). It records the conquest of Laish by a portion of the tribe of Dan, and the establishment there of the idolatrous worship of Jehovah. Finally, there is the account of the outrage at Gibeah and the punishment of the tribe of Benjamin.

JUDGMENT HALL. The word *Praetorium* is so translated five times in the A.V. of the New Testament; and in those five passages it denotes two different places. In John 18:28, 33; 19:9, it is the residence which Pilate occupied when he visited Jerusalem. In Acts 23:35, Herod's judgment hall or praetorium in Caesarea was a part of that magnificent range of buildings, the erection of which by King Herod is described in Josephus. The word "palace," or "Caesar's court," in the A.V. of Phil. 1:13, is a translation of the same word praetorium.

JUDITH—*woman of Judah.* 1. The daughter of Beeri the Hittite, and wife of Esau (Gen. 26:34). 2. The heroine of the apocryphal book which bears her name, who appears as an ideal type of piety, beauty, courage and chastity.

JULIA. A Christian woman at Rome, probably the wife, or perhaps the sister, of Philologus, in connection with whom she is saluted by Paul (Rom. 16:15).

JULIUS. The centurion of Augustus' band, to whose charge Paul was delivered when he was sent prisoner from Caesarea to Rome (Acts 27: 1, 3).

JUNIA. A Christian at Rome, mentioned by Paul as one of his kinsfolk and fellow-prisoners, of note among the apostles, and in Christ before Paul (Rom. 16:7).

JUNIPER (1 Kings 19:4, 5; Job 30:4; Ps. 120:4). The word which is rendered in A.V. juniper is a sort of broom, *Genista monosperma,* G. raetam of Forskâl, answering to the Arabic *Rethem.* It is very abundant in the desert of Sinai, and affords shade and protection in heat and storm to travellers.

JUPITER (the Greek Zeus). The Olympian Zeus was the national god of the Hellenic race. as well as the ruler of the heathen world, and as such formed the true opposite to Jehovah. Jupiter or Zeus is mentioned in one passage of the New Testament, on the occasion of Paul's visit to Lystra (Acts 14:12, 13), where the expression, "Jupiter, which was before their city," means that his temple was outside the city.

JUSTUS. 1. A surname of Joseph called Barsabas (Acts 1:23). 2. A Christian at Corinth, with whom Paul lodged (Acts 18:7). 3. A surname of Jesus, a friend of Paul (Col. 4:11).

KADEH, KADESH-BARNEA—*holy place of Barnea.* This place, the scene of Miriam's death, was the farthest point which the Israelites reached in their direct road to Canaan; it was also that whence the spies were sent, and where, on their return, the people broke out into murmuring, upon which their strictly penal term of wandering began (Num. 13:3, 26; 14:29-33; 20:1; Deut. 2:14).

KADMIEL—*God is the ancient one.* One of the Levites who, with his family, returned from Babylon with Zerubbabel (Ezra 2:40; Neh. 7:43). He and his house are in history on three occasions (Ezra 3:9; Neb. 9:4, 5; 10:9).

KAREAH—*bald.* The father of Johanan and Jonathan, who supported Gedaliah and avenged his murder (Jer. 40:8, 13, 15, 16; 42:1, 8; 43:2, 4, 5).

KARKOR. The place in which Zebah and Zalmunna were routed by Gideon (Judg. 8:10), on the east of Jordan.

KEDAR. The second of the sons of Ishmael (Gen. 25:13; 1 Chron. 1:29). The "glory of Kedar" is recorded by the prophet Isaiah (21: 13-17), and the "princes of Kedar" are mentioned by Ezekiel (27:21), as well as the pastoral character of the tribe. They were "archers" and "mighty men" (Isa. 21:17; cf. Ps. 120:5). The tribe was one of the most conspicuous of all the Ishmaelite tribes.

KEDESH—*holy place*. 1. A city in the south of Judah (Josh. 15:23). 2. A city of Issachar, allotted to the Gershonite Levites (1 Chron. 6:72). The Kedesh mentioned among the cities whose kings were slain by Joshua (Josh. 12:22), in company with Megiddo and Jokneam of Carmel, would seem to have been this city of Issachar. 3. Kedesh; also Kedesh in Galilee; and once, Judg. 4:6, Kedesh Naphtali. One of the fortified cities of the tribe of Naphtali, named between Hazor and Edrei (Josh. 19:37); appointed as a city of refuge, and allotted with its "suburbs" to the Gershonite Levites (20:7; 21:32; 1 Chron. 6:76). It was the residence of Barak (Judg. 4:6), and there he and Deborah assembled the tribes of Zebulun and Napthali, being, as its name implies, a "holy place" of great antiquity.

KEMUEL. 1. The son of Nahor by Milcah, and father of Aram (Gen. 22:21). 2. The son of Shiptan, and prince of the tribe of Ephraim; one of the twelve men appointed by Moses to divide the land of Canaan (Num. 34:24). 3. A Levite, father of Hashabaiah, prince of the tribe in the reign of David (1 Chron. 27:17).

KENAZ. 1. Son of Eliphaz, the son of Esau. He was one of the dukes of Edom (Gen. 36:15, 42; 1 Chron. 1:53). 2. One of the same family, a grandson of Caleb, according to 1 Chron. 4:15.

KENITE—*smith*, THE and KENITES, THE. A tribe first mentioned in company with the Kenizzites and Kadmonites (Gen. 15:19). That they were a branch of the nation of Midian is shown from the fact that Jethro, who in Exodus (*e.g.* 2:15, 16, 4:9) is represented as dwelling in Midian, and as priest or prince of that nation, is in Judges (1:16; 4:11) said to have been a Kenite.

KEREN-HAPPUCH—*horn of antimony* (eyepaint). The youngest of the daughters of Job, born during his reviving prosperity (Job 42: 14).

KETTLE. A vessel for culinary or sacrificial purposes (1 Sam. 2:14). The Hebrew word is also rendered "basket" in Jer. 24:2; "caldron in 2 Chron. 35:13, and "pot" in Job 41:20.

KETURAH—*incense*. The wife whom Abraham "added and took" besides, or after the death of, Sarah (Gen. 25:1, 1 Chron. 1:32). Some critics think that Abraham took Keturah after Sarah's death; but it is more probable that he took her during Sarah's lifetime (cf. Gen. 17:17; 18:11; Rom. 4:19; Heb. 11:12). In the record in 1 Chron. 1:32, she is called a "concubine" (cf. Gen. 25:5, 6).

KEY. The key of a native Oriental lock is a piece of wood, from seven inches to two feet in length, fitted with wires or short nails, which, being inserted laterally into the hollow bolt which serves as a lock, raises other pins within the staple so as to allow the bolt to be drawn back.

KEZIA—*cassia*. The second of the daughters of Job, born after his recovery (Job 42:14).

KIDRON (or KEDRON), THE BROOK. A torrent or valley—not a "brook," as in the A.V.— close to Jerusalem. It lay between the city and the Mount of Olives, and was crossed by David in his flight (2 Sam. 15:23, cf. 30), and by Jesus on his way to Gethsemane (John 18:1; cf. Mark 14:26; Luke 22:39).

KINDRED. 1. Of the special names denoting relation by consanguinity, the words which denote near relation in the direct line; for example, father, brother, are used also for the other superior or inferior degrees in that line, as grandfather, grandson, etc. 2. The words which express collateral consanguinity are: uncle, aunt, nephew, niece (not A.V.), cousin. 3. The terms of affinity are: father-in-law, mother-in-law, son-in-law, daughter-in-law, brother-in-law, sister-in-law.

KING. The name of the ruler of the Hebrews during a period beginning with Saul down to the destruction of Jerusalem. The occasion of the substitution of a regal form of government for that of Judges seems to have been the siege of Jabesh-Gilead by Nahash, king of the Ammonites (1 Sam. 11:1), and the refusal to allow the inhabitants of that city to capitulate, except on humiliating conditions (1 Sam. 11:2, 4-6). Disgust had been excited by the corrupt administration of justice under the sons of Samuel, and a radical change was desired (1 Sam. 8:3-5). Accordingly the idea of a Hebrew king, besides being commander-in-chief of the army, supreme judge and absolute master of his subjects, exercised the power of imposing taxes on them, and of exacting from them personal service and labor. And the degree to which the exaction of personal labor might be carried is illustrated by King Solomon's requirements for building the temple. In addition to these earthly powers, the king of Israel had a more awful claim to respect and obedience. He was the vicegerent of Jehovah (1 Sam. 10:1; 16:13), and as it were his son, if just and holy (2 Sam. 7:14; Ps. 89:26, 27; 2:6, 7). He had been set apart as a consecrated ruler.

KINGS, FIRST AND SECOND BOOKS OF. Originally only one book in the Hebrew canon, form in the Septuagint, and the Vulgate the third and fourth Books of *Kings* (the Books of Samuel being the first and second). The division between the Books of Kings and Samuel is artificial, and the historical books commencing with Judges and ending with 2 Kings present the appearance of one work, giving a continuous history of Israel from the time of Joshua to the death of Jehoiachin. The Books of Kings contain the history from David's death and Solomon's accession to the destruction of the kingdom of Judah and the desolation of Jerusalem, with a notice of an event that occurred twenty-six years after, *viz.*, the liberation of Jehoiachin from his prison at Babylon, and his death not long after. The history therefore comprehends the whole of the Israelitish monarchy, exclusive of the reigns of Saul and David. The writer of the Chronicles, having the Books of Kings before him, made those books the basis of his own. But also having his own personal views, predilections and motives in writing, composing for a different age, and for people under different circumstances.

KIR—*wall*. Is mentioned by Amos (9:7) as the land from which the Syrians (Aramaeans) were once "brought up"; *i.e.*, as the country where they had dwelt before migrating to the region north of Palestine.

KIRIOTH—*buildings*. A place in Moab, the palaces of which were threatened by Amos with destruction by fire (Amos 2:2); the word means simply "the cities," in Jer. 48:4.

KIRJATHARBA—*four towns* (?). An early name of the city after the conquest generally known as Hebron (Josh. 14:15; Judg. 1:10).

KIRJATH–JEARIM—*city of forests or thickets*. One of the four cities of the Gibeonites (Josh. 9:17); it next occurs as one of the landmarks of the northern boundary of Judah (Josh. 15:9), and as the point at which the western and southern boundaries of Benjamin coincided (Josh. 18:14, 15); and in the last two passages it bore the name of the Canaanite deity Baal, namely Baalah and Kirjath-Baal.

KIR OF MOAB. One of the two strongholds of Moab, the other being Ar of Moab. The name occurs only in Isa. 15:1.

KISH. 1. The father of Saul; a Benjamite of the family of Matri, according to 1 Sam. 20:21. 2. Son of Jehiel and brother to the preceding (1 Chron. 9:36). 3. A Benjamite, great-grandfather of Mordecai (Esth. 2:5). 4. A Merarite, of the tribe of Levi (1 Chron. 23:21 f.; 24:28 f.; 2 Chron. 29:12).

KISHON—*bending; torturous*, THE RIVER. A torrent or winter stream of central Palestine, the scene of two of the grandest achievements of Israelite history, the defeat of Sisera (Judg. 4), and the destruction of the prophets of Baal by Elijah (1 Kings 18:40).

KISS. Kissing the lips by way of salutation was customary amongst relatives of both sexes, both in patriarchal and in later times (Gen. 29:11; Cant. 8:1). The kiss on the cheek as a mark of respect or an act of salutation has at all times been customary in the East. In the Christian Church the kiss of charity was practiced not only as a friendly salutation, but as an act symbolical of love and Christian brotherhood (Rom. 16:16; 1 Cor. 16:20; 2 Cor. 13:12; 1 Thess. 5:26; 1 Pet. 5:14).

KITE (Heb. *ayyah*). The Hebrew word thus rendered occurs in three passages, Lev. 11:14, Deut. 14:13 and Job 28:7; in the two former it is translated "kite" in the A.V., in the latter "vulture."

KNIFE. In their meals the Jews made little use of knives, but they were required both for slaughtering animals either for food or sacrifice, as well as cutting up the carcass (*e.g.*, Lev. 7:33, 34; 8:15, 20, 25; 9:13; Num. 18:18; 1 Sam. 9:24). Smaller knives were in use for paring fruit and for sharpening pens (Jer. 36:23).

KNOP. A word employed in the A.V. to translate two terms, which refer to some architectural or ornamental object, but which have nothing in common. 1. *Caphtor*. This occurs in the description of the candlestick of the sacred tent in Ex. 25:31-36, and 37:17-22. 2. The second terms, *Pekaim*, is found only in 1 Kings 6:18, and 7:24.

KOA. A word which occurs only in Ezek. 23:23, to designate a city or people.

KOHATH. Second of the three sons of Levi, from whom three divisions of the Levites derived their origin and their name (Gen. 46:11; Ex. 6:16, 18; Num. 3:17; 2 Chron. 34:12). Kohath was the father of Amram, and he of Moses and Aaron. From him, therefore, were descended all the priests; and those of the Kohathites who were not priests were of the highest rank of the Levites, though not the sons of Levi's first-born. In the journeyings of the Tabernacle the sons of Kohath had charge of the holy portions of the vessels (Num. 4). It appears from Ex. 6:18-22, compared with 1 Chron. 23:12; 26:23-32, that there were four families of sons of Kohath—Amramites, Izharites, Hebronites and Uzzielites.

KORAH—*baldness*. 1. Third son of Esau by Aholibamah (Gen. 36:5, 14, 18; 1 Chron. 1:35). He was born in Canaan before Esau migrated to Mount Seir (Gen. 36:5-9), and was one of the "dukes" of Edom. 2. Another Edomitish duke of this name sprung from Eliphaz, Esau's son by Adah (Gen. 36:16). 3. One of the "sons of Hebron," in 1 Chron. 2:43. 4. Son of Izhar, the son of Kohath, the son of Levi. He was leader of the rebellion against Moses and Aaron in the wilderness, for which he perished with his followers by an earthquake and flames of fire (Num. 16; 26:9-11).

KORAHITE, KORHITE or KORATHITE (1 Chron. 9:19, 31). That portion of the Kohathites who were descended from Korah, sometimes called sons of Korah. They were an important branch of the singers (2 Chron. 20:19). Hence we find eleven Psalms dedicated or assigned to the sons of Korah, *viz.*, Ps. 42, 44-49, 84, 85, 87, 88.

LAADAN. 1. An Ephraimite, ancestor of Joshua the son of Nun (1 Chron. 7:26). 2. The son of Gershom, called Libni (1 Chron. 23:7-9; 26:21).

LABAN—*white.* Son of Bethuel, brother of Rebekah, and father of Leah and Rachel. The elder branch of the family remained at Haran when Abraham removed to the land of Canaan, and it is there that we first meet with Laban, as taking the leading part in the betrothal of his sister Rebekah to her cousin Isaac (Gen. 24:10, 29-60; 27:43; 29:4). The next time Laban appears in the sacred narrative it is as host of his nephew Jacob at Haran (Gen. 29:13, 14).

LACHISH. A city of the Amorites, the king of which joined with four others, at the invitation of Adonizedek king of Jerusalem, to chastise the Gibeonites for their league with Israel (Josh. 10). They were routed by Joshua at Bethhoron, and the king of Lachish fell a victim with the others under the tree at Makkedah. Lachish was one of the cities fortified by Rehoboam (2 Chron. 11:9). It was chosen as a refuge by Amaziah (2 Kings 14:19; 2 Chron. 25:27).

LAHAIROI, THE WELL. In this form is given in the A.V. of Gen. 24:62, and 25:11, the name of the famous well of Hagar's relief, round which Isaac afterward resided.

LAHMI. The brother of Goliath the Gittite, slain by Elhanan the son of Zair, or Zaor (1 Chron. 20:5).

LAISH—*lion.* The city taken by the Danites, and under its new name of Dan became famous as the northern limit of the nation (Judg. 18:7 ff.).

LAISH. Father of Phaltiel, to whom Saul had given Michal, David's wife (1 Sam. 25:44; 2 Sam. 3:15).

LAMECH—*destroyer.* 1. The fifth lineal descendant from Cain (Gen. 4:18-24). His two wives, Adah and Zillah, and his daughter Naamah, are, with Eve, the only antediluvian women mentioned by Moses. His three sons, Jabal, Jubal, and Tubal-Cain, are celebrated in Scripture as authors of useful inventions. 2. The father of Noah (Gen. 5:29).

LAMENTATIONS OF JEREMIAH. The Hebrew title of this book, *Ekah* (How!), is taken, like those of the five books of Moses, from the Hebrew word with which it opens. The poems belong to the last days of the kingdom, or the commencement of the exile.

LAMP. 1. That part of the golden candlestick belonging to the Tabernacle which bore the light; also of each of the ten candlesticks placed by Solomon in the Temple before the Holy of Holies (Ex. 25:37; 1 Kings 7:49; 2 Chron. 4:20; 13:11; Zech. 4:2). The lamps were lighted every evening, and cleansed every morning (Ex. 30:7, 8). 2. A torch or flambeau, such as was carried by the soldiers of Gideon (Judg. 7:16, 20; *cf.* 15:4). The use of lamps fed with oil in marriage processions is alluded to in the parable of the ten virgins (Matt. 25:1).

LANCET. This word is found in 1 Kings 18:28 only. The Hebrew term thus translated means a javelin, or light spear.

LAODICEA. A town in the Roman province of Asia, situated in the valley of the Maeander on a small river called the Lycus, with Colossae and Hierapolis a few miles to the west. Laodicea became under the Roman government a place of importance. In subsequent times it became a Christian city of eminence, the see of a bishop and of a meeting place of councils. The Mohammedan invaders destroyed it. (Col. 2:1; 4:16; Rev. 3:14 ff.)

LAPIDOTH—*torches.* The husband of Deborah the prophetess (Judg. 4:4).

LAPWING (Heb. *dukiphath*). Occurs only in Lev. 11:19, and in the parallel passage of Deut. 14:18, amongst the list of those birds which were forbidden by the law of Moses to be eaten by the Israelites.

LASEA (Acts 27:8). A city of Crete, the ruins of which were discovered in 1856, a few miles to the eastward of Fair Havens.

LATCHET. The fastening by which the sandal was attached to the foot. It occurs in the expression in Gen. 14:23, and in Luke 3:16.

LATIN. The language spoken by the Romans, is mentioned only in John 19:20, and Luke 23:38.

LATTICE. The rendering in A.V. of three Hebrew words. 1. *eshnab*, which occurs in Judg. 5:28, and Prov. 7:6, and in the latter is translated "casement." In both it stands in parallelism with "window." 2. *harakkim* (Cant. 2:9), apparently synonymous with the preceding. 3. *sebhakkah* is "a network" before a window or balcony.

LAVER. 1. In the Tabernacle, a vessel of brass containing water for the priests to wash their hands and feet in before sacrifice. It stood in the court between the altar and the door of the Tabernacle (Ex. 30:19, 21). It rested on a basis, made from the mirrors of the women who assembled at the door of the Tabernacle-court (Ex. 38:8). 2. In Solomon's Temple, besides the great molten sea, there were ten lavers of brass, raised on bases (1 Kings 7:27, 39). They were used for washing the animals to be offered in burnt offerings (2 Chron. 4:6).

LAW (Heb. *torah*). The word used with the article, and without any word of limitation, refers to the expressed will of God, and usually to the Mosaic Law, or to the Pentateuch.

LAWYER. The title "lawyer" is supposed to be equivalent to "scribe," both on account of its etymological meaning, and also because a "lawyer" in Matt. 22:35 and Luke 10:25 is called "one of the scribes" in Mark 12:28.

LAZARUS—*God has helped.* Another form of the Hebrew name Eleazar. 1. Lazarus of Bethany, the brother of Martha and Mary (John 11:1). 2. The name of a poor man in the well-known parable of Luke 16:19-31.

LEAD. One of the most common of metals. The Hebrews were well acquainted with its uses. The rocks in the neighborhood of Sinai yielded it in large quantities, and it was found in Egypt. That it was common in Palestine is shown by Num. 31:22.

LEAH—*gazelle* or *wild cow.* The daughter of Laban (Gen. 29:16). Her father passed her off in her sister's stead on the unconscious bridegroom. Jacob's preference of Rachel grew into hatred of Leah, after he had married both sisters. Leah, however, bore to him in quick succession Reuben, Simeon, Levi, Judah, then Issachar, Zebulun and Dinah, before Rachel had a child. She died some time after Jacob reached the south country in which his father Isaac lived. She was buried in the family grave in Machpelah (Gen. 49:31).

LEASING. An old English word meaning *falsehood* (Ps. 4:2; 5:6).

LEATHER. Leather in the Bible occurs but twice (2 Kings 1:8; Matt. 3:4).

LEAVEN. The ordinary leaven consisted of old dough in a high state of fermentation, inserted into the mass of dough prepared for baking. The use of leaven was forbidden in all offerings made to the Lord by fire (Lev. 2:11; 6:17).

LEBANON—*to be white.* A mountain in the north of Palestine. It is the "white mountain"— the *Mont Blanc* of Palestine, the northern border of the land of Israel (Deut. 1:7; 11:24; Josh. 1:4).

LEBBAEUS. This name occurs in Matt. 10:3. In Mark 3:18 Thaddaeus is substituted for it.

LEEKS. The word *hazir*, translated *leeks*, occurs twenty times in the Hebrew text. The Hebrew term, which denotes *grass*, is derived from a root signifying "to be green," and may therefore stand for any green food, lettuce, endive, *etc.*

LEES. The Hebrew *shemer* bears the radical sense of *preservation.* Hence the expression "wine on the lees," as meaning a generous, full-bodied liquor (Isa. 25:6).

LEHI—*jawbone.* A place in Judah, the scene of Samson's well-known exploit with the jawbone (Judg. 15:9, 14, 19).

LEMUEL—*belonging to God.* The name of an unknown king to whom his mother addressed the prudential maxims contained in Prov. 31:1-9.

LENTILS. Seeds of a plant cultivated for food. (Gen. 25:34; 2 Sam. 17:28; 23:11, and Ezek. 4:9.) There are three or four kinds of lentils, all of which are still esteemed. Lentil bread is still eaten by the poor of Egypt.

LEOPARD. Occurs in Isa. 11:6; Jer. 5:6; 13:23; Dan. 7:6; Hos. 13:7; Cant. 4:8; Hab. 1:8. The hilly ranges of Lebanon were frequented by these animals.

LEPER, LEPROSY. Leprosy is a white variety covering either the entire body, or a large tract of its surface. Such were the cases of Moses, Miriam, Naaman and Gehazi (Ex. 4:6; Num. 12:10; 2 Kings 5:1, 27; *cf.* Lev. 13:13). The principal features are a rising or swelling, a scab or baldness, and a bright or white spot (Lev. 13:2). But especially a white swelling in the skin, with a change of the hair of the part from the natural black to white or yellow, or an appearance of a taint going "deeper than the skin," or again "raw flesh" appearing in the swelling, were critical signs of pollution. It is clear that the leprosy of Lev. 13, 14, means any severe disease spreading on the surface of the body in the way described, and so shocking of aspect, or so suspected of infection, that public feeling called for separation.

LEVI—*joined.* 1. The third son of Jacob by Leah (Gen. 29:34; 35:23). The name, derived from *lavah*, "to adhere," gave utterance to the hope of the mother that her husband would be drawn to her. Levi, with his brother Simeon, avenged the outrange of their sister Dinah (Gen. 34). 2. Son of Alphaeus (Mark 2:14; Luke 5:27, 29).

LEVIATHAN. Is found in Job 3:8; Ps. 74:14; civ. 26; Isa. 27:1. The reference is to a mythical monster. The crocodile is referred to (Job 40:1).

LEVITES. The tribe that traced its descent from Levi. There was another division within the tribe, in the higher office of the priesthood limited to "the sons of Aaron." Sometimes the word extends to the whole tribe, the priests included (Num. 35:2; Josh. 21:3, 41; Ex. 6:25; Lev. 25:32, *etc.*). Again, we read of "the priests the Levites" (Josh. 3:3; Ezek. 44:15).

LEVITICUS. Relating principally to the Levites and priests, contains: 1. The laws touching sacrifices (Lev. 1-7). 2. The consecration of Aaron and his sons (Lev. 8); next, his first offering for himself and his people (Lev. 9); and lastly the destruction of Nadab and Abihu, the sons of Aaron (Lev. 10). 3. The laws concerning purity

and impurity, and the appropriate sacrifices and ordinances for putting away impurity (Lev. 11-16). 4. Laws intended to mark the separation between Israel and the heathen nations (Lev. 17-20). 5. Laws concerning the priests (21, 22), and certain holy days and festivals (23, 25). 6. Promises and threats (26:2-46). 7. Laws concerning vows (27).

LIBERTINES. Occurs once only in the New Testament (Acts 6:9), is the Latin *Libertini*, that is, "freedmen." They were Jews who had been reduced to slavery, afterward emancipated and returned to the country of their fathers.

LIBNAH—*wilderness*. A city in the southwest part of the Holy Land appropriated with its "suburbs" to the priests (Josh. 21:13; 1 Chron. 6:57). It was the native place of the queen of Josiah, and mother of Jehoahaz (2 Kings 23:31), and Zedekiah (2 Kings 24:18; Jer. 52:1).

LIBYA. Libya is applied to a country of North Africa (Ezek. 30:5; Acts 2:10).

LICE (Heb. *kinnim, kinnam*). Occurs only in Ex. 8:16-18, and in Ps. 105:31; both of which have reference to the third great plague of Egypt.

LIEUTENANTS. The Hebrew *ahash-darpenim*, the official title of the viceroys who governed the provinces of the Persian empire; "lieutenant" in Esth. 3:12; 8:9; 9:3; Ezra 8:36, and "prince" in Dan. 3:2; 6:1, *etc.*

LIGURE (Heb. *leshem*). A precious stone mentioned in Ex. 28:19; 39:12.

LILY. The Hebrew word denotes some plant of the lily species. That its flowers were brilliant in color would seem to be indicated in Matt. 6:28. The Phoenician architects of Solomon's temple decorated the capitals of the columns with leaves and flowers of the lily (1 Kings 7).

LIME. Is noticed three times in the Bible, *viz.*, in Deut. 27:2, 4 (plaster), in Isa. 33:12, and in Amos 2:1.

LINEN. The general term was *pishteh*, which was employed, like our "cotton," to denote not only the flax (Judg. 15:14) or raw material from which the linen was made, but also the plant itself (Josh. 2:6), and the manufacture from it.

LINTEL. The beam which forms the upper part of the framework of a door (Ex. 12:22).

LINUS. A Christian known to Paul and to Timothy (2 Tim. 4:21), who was said to have been the first bishop of Rome after the apostles.

LION. At present lions do not exist in Palestine, but they must in ancient times have been numerous. Its fierceness and cruelty rendered it an appropriate metaphor (Ps. 7:2; 22:21; 57:4; 2 Tim. 4:17), and hence for the archfiend himself (1 Pet. 5:8).

LIZARD. Lizards of various kinds abound in Egypt, Palestine and Arabia. In Lev. 11:29 f. are listed several animals as unclean, among which three and possibly four are lizards.

LOAN. The Law strictly forbade interest to be taken for a loan to any poor person. It did not forbid temporary bondage in the case of debtors, but it forbade a Hebrew debtor to be detained as a bondman longer than the seventh year (Ex. 21:2; Lev. 25:39, 42; Deut. 15:9).

LOCK. The locks of Eastern houses are of wood, and consist of a partly hollow bolt which passes through a groove in a piece attached to the door into a socket in the doorpost (*cf.* Judg. 3:25; Isa. 22:22).

LOCUST. A well-known insect, which commits terrible ravages on vegetation in the countries which it visits. Locusts were used as food (Lev. 11:21, 22; Matt. 3:4; Mark 1:6).

LOIS. The grandmother of Timothy, and doubtless the mother of his mother Eunice (2 Tim. 1:5).

LORD'S DAY, THE. (Rev. 1:10 only), the weekly festival of our Lord's resurrection, and identified with "the first day of the week," or "Sunday," of every age of the Church. Scripture says very little concerning this day.

LORD'S SUPPER. This great central act of the worship of the Christian church occurs but in one passage of the New Testament (1 Cor. 11:20). It was instituted on that night when Jesus and his disciples met together to eat the Passover (Matt. 26:19; Mark 14:16; Luke 22:13).

LO-RUHAMMAH—*not pitied*. The name of the daughter of Hosea the prophet, given to denote the utterly ruined condition of the kingdom of Israel (Hos. 1:6).

LOT. The son of Haran, and the nephew of Abraham (Gen. 11:27, 31). His sisters were Milcah the wife of Nahor, and Iscah, by some identified with Sarah. He removed with Abraham and Sarai to Canaan (Gen. 12:4, 5), and then to their original settlement between Bethel and Ai. Here they separated, Lot choosing the plain of the Jordan, as far as Sodom (Gen. 13:10-14). The next occurrence in the life of Lot is his capture by the four kings of the East, and his rescue by Abram (Gen. 14). The last scene preserved to us in the history of Lot is too well known to need repetition (Gen. 19). His deliverance from the guilty and condemned city points to the allusion of Peter (2 Pet. 2:6-9).

LOT. The custom of deciding doubtful questions by lot is one of great extent and antiquity. The religious estimate of them may be gathered from Prov. 16:33.

LOVE FEASTS (Jude 12 and 2 Pet. 2:13).

LUBIM. A nation mentioned as contributing to Shishak's army (2 Chron. 12:3).

LUCAS (Philem. 24). (See Luke.)

LUCIFER—*light-bringer*. Found in Isa. 14:12, coupled with the epithet "Son of the morning," clearly signifies a "bright star," and probably what we call the morning star.

LUCIUS. A Roman Consul. Lucius of Cyrene is first mentioned in the New Testament in company with Barnabas, Simeon, called Niger, Manaen and Saul, who are described as prophets and teachers of the Church at Antioch (Acts 13:1).

LUD. The fourth name in the list of the children of Shem (Gen. 10:22).

LUDIM (Gen. 10:13; 1 Chron. 1:11). A Mizraite people or tribe. Mentioned in Isa. 66:19; Jer. 46:9; Ezek. 27:10; 38:5.

LUHITH, THE ASCENT OF. A place in Moab, occurs in Isa. 15:5, and the parallel passage of Jeremiah (48:5).

LUKE. Early tradition relates that he was born at Antioch in Syria, and was taught the science of medicine. He joined Paul at Troas, and shared his journey into Macedonia, remained at his side during his imprisonment (Col. 4:14; Philem. 24).

LUKE, GOSPEL OF. Is ascribed to "the beloved physician," Luke, the friend and companion of the Apostle Paul. From Acts 1:1, it is clear that the Gospel was written before the Acts of the Apostles. There were many narratives of the life of our Lord current at the early time when Luke wrote his Gospel. Luke carefully followed out the whole course of events from the beginning, not as an eye-witness from the first, but a witness of some part of our Lord's doings.

LUNATICS. In Matt. 4:24; 17:15, refers to some disease affecting both the body and the mind.

LUZ—*almond*. It seems impossible to discover whether Luz and Bethel represent the same town, or distinct places (Gen. 35:6; 48:3; *cf.* Gen. 28:19; Judg. 1:23).

LYCAONIA. A district of Asia Minor. On Paul's first missionary journey he traversed Lycaonia from west to east, and then returned on his steps (Acts 14:6, 11).

LYCIA. The name of that region of Asia Minor opposite the island of Rhodes. Paul visited the Lycian towns of Patara (Acts 21:1) and Myra (Acts 27:5).

LYDDA. The Greek form of the name (Acts 9:32, 35, 38), which appears in the Hebrew records as Lod. It is nine miles from Joppa.

LYDIA. A maritime province in the west of Asia Minor (the rendering in Ezek. 30:5 for Ludim).

LYDIA. The first European convert of Paul, and afterward his hostess during his first stay at Philippi (Acts 16:14, 15, 40).

LYSANIAS. Mentioned by Luke (Luke 3:1) as being tetrarch of Abilene.

LYSIAS, CLAUDIUS. "Chief captain of the band" who rescued Paul from the hands of the mob at Jerusalem, and sent him under a guard to Felix (Acts 21:31 ff.; 23:26; 26:7).

LYSIMACHUS. "A son of Ptolemaeus of Jerusalem," the Greek translator of the Book of Esther (*cf.* Esth. 9:20).

LYSTRA. The place where divine honors were offered to Paul, and where he was stoned (Acts 14); also the home of Timotheus (Acts 16:1).

MAACAH—*oppression*. 1. The mother of Absalom, also called Maachah (2 Sam. 2:3). 2. Maacah and (in Chron.) Maachah.

MAACHAH. 1. The daughter of Nahor (Gen. 22:24). 2. The father of Achish (1 Kings 2:39). 3. The daughter, or more probably granddaughter, of Absalom, wife of Rehoboam, and mother of Abijah (1 Kings 15:2; 2 Chron. 11:20-22; 1 Chron. 2:48). 4. The daughter of Talmai king of Geshur, and mother of Absalom (1 Chron. 3:2); also called Maacah in A.V. of 2 Sam. 3:3.

MAACHATHI, and MAACHATHITES, THE. Two words which denote the inhabitants of the small kingdom of Maachah (Deut. 3:14; Josh. 12:5; 13:11, 13).

MAATH. Son of Mattathias in the genealogy of Christ (Luke 3:26).

MACCABEES, THE. This title, originally the surname of Judas, one of the sons of Mattathias, was afterward extended to the heroic family of which he was one of the noblest representatives. The original term *Maccabi* was probably formed from *Makkâbâh*. Although the name *Maccabees* has gained the widest currency, that of *Asmonaeans* or *Hasmonaeans* is the proper name of the family, which is derived from Hashmon, great-grandfather of Mattathias.

MACCABEES, BOOKS OF. Four books which bear the common title of "Maccabees" the first two being found in the Apocrypha.

MACEDONIA. The first part of Europe which received the Gospel directly from Paul, and an important scene of his subsequent missionary labors and those of his companions (Acts 16:9 ff.).

MACHI—*striking*. The father of Geuel the Gadite, who went with Caleb and Joshua to spy out the land of Canaan (Num. 13:15).

MACHIR—*sold*. 1. The eldest son (Josh. 17:4) of the patriarch Manasseh (1 Chron. 7:14). His children are commemorated as having been caressed by Joseph before his death (Gen. 50:23). 2. The son of Ammiel, who rendered service to Saul and David when they were in difficulty (2 Sam. 9:4, 5; 17:27-29).

MACHPELAH—*doubling* (?). Piece of ground and cave purchased by Abraham as a burying place (Gen. 23:9 ff.; 25:9; 49:30; 50:13).

MADAI. (Gen. 10:2) The third son of Japheth, and the progenitor of the Medes.

MADNESS. In Scripture a derangement, proceeding either from weakness of intellect or from unforgivable violence of passion. In John 10:20 madness is demoniacal possession.

MADON. One of the principal cities of Canaan (Josh. 11:1; 12:19).

MAGDALA. The name is found in Matt. 15:39 only. In Mark (8:10) we find the "parts of Dalmanutha," on the western edge of the lake of Gennesareth. Magdala conferred her name on "Mary the Magdal-ene."

MAGDALENE. (See Mary Magdalene.)

MAGI—*wise men*. 1. Historically the Magi are conspicuous as a Persian religious caste. They appear in Jeremiah (39:3, 13) among the retinue of the Chaldean king, and thus rose to favor and power (Dan. 5:11). 2. The word to the Greeks became a by-word for the worst form of imposture (Acts 8:9; 13:8). 3. In Matthew (2:1-12) the Magi appear as "wise men" who were guided by a star from "the East" to Jerusalem, inquiring for the new-born King of the Jews, whom they had come to worship.

MAGIC, MAGICIANS. The arts practised by the Egyptians, the Canaanites and their neighbors, the Hebrews, the Chaldaeans and probably the Greeks, as part of religion. It was so strictly forbidden by the law that it could never have had any recognized existence, save in times of apostacy (cf. Lev. 20:27; Deut. 18:10 f.).

MAGOG. In Gen. 10:2 Magog appears as the second son of Japheth; in Ezek. 38:2; 39:1, 6, as a country of which Gog was the prince, the *Ma* being a prefix significant of a country of northern locality.

MAGORMISSABIB. Literally "terror on every side"; the name given by Jeremiah to Pashur the priest (Jer. 20:3).

MAHALALEEL—*praise of God*. 1. The fourth from Adam, and son of Cainan (Gen. 5:12, 13, 15-17; 1 Chron. 1:2). 2. A descendant of Perez, or Pharez, the son of Judah (Neh. 11:4).

MAHALATH—*sickness*. 1. The daughter of Ishmael, and one of the wives of Esau (Gen. 28:9). 2. One of the eighteen wives of King Rehoboam, apparently his first (2 Chron. 11:18).

MAHALATH and **MAHALATH–LEANNOTH.** The title of Ps. 53, and the title of Ps. 88.

MAHANAIM. A town on the east of the Jordan, signifying *two hosts* or *two camps*, a name given to it by Jacob (Gen. 32:1, 2; cf. also 2 Sam. 2:8 ff. and 2 Sam. 17:24).

MAHER–SHALAL–HASH–BAZ—*spoil speeds, prey hastens*. This name was given by divine direction by Isaiah to one of his sons, to indicate that Damascus and Samaria were soon to be plundered by the king of Assyria (Isa. 8:1-4).

MAHLON—*sickness*. The first husband of Ruth. He and his brother Chilion were sons of Elimelech and Naomi, and are described as "Ephrathites of Bethlehem-judah" (Ruth 1:2, 5; 4:9, 10; cf. 1 Sam. 17:12).

MAHOL. The father of Ethan the Ezrahite, and Heman, Chalcol and Darda, the four men most famous for wisdom next to Solomon himself (1 Kings 4:31).

MAKKEDAH—*fold*. Memorable as the scene of the execution by Joshua of the five confederate kings (Josh. 10:10-30). Its site is uncertain.

MAKTESH—*the mortar*. A place, the inhabitants of which are denounced by Zephaniah (1:11).

MALACHI—*my messenger*. The last, called "the seal" of the prophets, and his prophecies constitute the closing book of the canon. Malachi was contemporary with Nehemiah, and prophesied after the times of Haggai and Zechariah (Neh. 13:6).

MALCHAM. 1. Son of Shaharaim (1 Chron. 8:9). 2. The idol Molech (Zeph. 1:5).

MALCHIAH—*Jehovah is King*. 1. The son of Levi, and ancestor of Asaph the ministrel (1 Chron. 6:40). 2. One of the sons of Parosh (Ezra 10:25). 3. Enumerated among the sons of Harim (Ezra 10:31). 4. Son of Rechab, and ruler of Bethhaccerem (Neh. 3:14; 8:4). 5. A priest the father of Pashur—Malchijah I. (Neh. 11:12; Jer. 38:1).

MALCHUS. The servant of the high priest whose right ear Peter cut off (Matt. 26:51; Mark 14:47; Luke 22:49-51; John 18:10).

MALLOWS The name of a plant mentioned in Job 30:4

MAMMON (Matt. 6:24; Luke 16:9). A common Aramaic word which signified "riches."

MAMRE. An Amorite, who, with his brothers, Eschol and Aner, was in alliance with Abram (Gen. 14:13, 24), and under the shade of whose oak-grove the patriarch dwelt in the interval between his residence at Bethel and Beersheba (Gen. 13:18; 18:1; 23:17, 19; 25:9; 49:30; 50:13).

MANAEN—*consoler*. (Acts 13.) One of the teachers and prophets at Antioch.

MANASSEH—*causing to forget*. 1. The eldest son of Joseph by his wife Asenath (Gen. 41:51; 46:20), so called by Joseph because "God hath-made-me-forget all my toil and all my father's house." 2. The thirteenth king of Judah, son of Hezekiah and Hephzibah (2 Kings 21:1 ff.), ascended the throne at the age of 12.

MANASSES. 1. Manasseh, king of Judah (Matt. 1:10), to whom the apocryphal prayer is attributed. 2. Manasseh, the son of Joseph (Rev. 7:6).

MANDRAKE. A plant mentioned in Gen. 30:14, 15, 16, and in Cant. 7:13.

MANGER. This word occurs only in connection with the birth of Christ in Luke 2:7, 12, 16. The original term, found but once besides in the New Testament, Luke 13:15, is rendered by "stall."

MANNA. The food miraculously provided in the desert for the Israelites (Ex. 16:14-36; Num. 11:7-9; Deut. 8:3, 16; Josh. 5:12; Ps. 78:24, 25). From these passages we learn that the manna came every morning except the Sabbath, in the form of a small round seed resembling the hoar frost. The name is derived from the inquiry (*man hu*, what is this?) which the Hebrews made when they first saw it upon the ground.

MANOAH—*rest*. The father of Samson, a native of the town of Zorah (Judg. 13:2).

MANSLAYER. The person who unintentionally causes the death of another (Num. 35:22; Deut. 19:8). The law seems intended to prevent the imputation of malice in any such case (Deut. 22:8).

MANTLE. The word has four Hebrew terms, distinct both in derivation and meaning. 1. *s'micah* (Judg. 4:18), the thing with which Jael covered Sisera. 2. *meil*, "mantle" in 1 Sam. 15:27; 28:14; Ezra 9:3, 5. 3. *ma'ataphoth* (Isa. 3:22 only). 4. *addereth*, "mantle" in 1 Kings 19:13, 19; 2 Kings 2:8, 13, 14.

MAON—*dwelling*. One of the cities of the tribe of Judah (Josh. 15:55; 1 Sam. 23:24, 25).

MAONITES, THE. A people mentioned in one of the addresses of Jehovah to the repentant Israelites (Judg. 10:12).

MARA (Ruth 1:20). "Call me not Naomi (pleasant), but call me Mara (bitter), for Shaddai hath dealt-very-bitterly with me."

MARAH—*bitterness*. A place in the wilderness of Shur (Ex. 15:23, 24; Num. 33:8), where was a spring of bitter water, sweetened by the casting in of a tree which "the Lord showed" to Moses.

MARANATHA. An expression used by Paul at the conclusion of his First Epistle to the Corinthians (16:22). It is a Grecised form of the Aramaic words *maran atha*, "our Lord cometh."

MARBLE. *Shesh*, the term for marble, may be taken to mean almost any shining stone (cf. 1 Chron. 29:2).

MARCUS. The Evangelist Mark (Col. 4:10; Philem. 24; 1 Pet. 5:13).

MARK. Mark the Evangelist, the same as "John whose surname was Mark" (Acts 12:12, 25), was the son of a certain Mary who dwelt at Jerusalem (Acts 12:12). Converted by Peter (1 Pet. 5:13), he went with Paul and Barnabas as their "minister." We find him by the side of that apostle in his imprisonment at Rome (Col. 4:10; Philem. 24), with Peter at Babylon (1 Pet. 5:13), and with Timothy at Ephesus (2 Tim. 4:11).

MARK, GOSPEL OF. That the Gospel was written under the sanction of Peter, and its matter in some degree derived from him, is probable by the evident traces of an eye-witness in many of the narratives. He scarcely refers to the Old Testament, and the word law does not once occur. There is little doubt but that the Gospel was meant for use amongst the Gentiles.

MARRIAGE. The institution of marriage dates from man's original creation.

MARS HILL. Better known by the name of Areopagus. A rocky height in Athens from which Paul delivered his memorable address (Acts 17:22 31).

MARSENA. One of the seven princes of Persia (Esth. 1:14).

MARTHA—*lady*. The sister of Lazarus and Mary. The facts recorded in Luke 10 and John 11 indicate her sharing in Messianic hopes and accepting Jesus as the Christ. She, no less than Lazarus and Mary, has the distinction of being one whom Jesus loved (John 11:3).

MARY OF CLEOPHAS (John 19:25). The wife of Cleophas and the mother of the Apostle James the Less and of Joses and Salome.

MARY MAGDALENE. From the town of Magdala (or Magadan). She appears for the first time in Luke 8:2. Of Mary it is said specially that "seven devils went out of her," and the number indicates, as in Matt. 12:45, and the "legion" of the Gadarine demoniac (Mark 5:9), a *possession* of more than ordinary malignity.

MARY, MOTHER OF MARK. We learn from Col. 4:10 that she was sister to Barnabas.

MARY, SISTER OF LAZARUS. She and her sister Martha appear in Luke 10:40. The same character shows itself in the history of John 11.

The treasured alabaster-box of ointment is brought forth at the final feast of Bethany (John 12:3).

MARY, THE VIRGIN. The mother of Jesus. She was of the tribe of Judah, and of the lineage of David (Ps. 132:11; Luke 1:32; Rom. 1:3). She had a sister named like herself, Mary (John 19:25), and she was connected by marriage (Luke 1:36) with Elizabeth of the lineage of Aaron. Her betrothal to Joseph, and the circumstances connected with her becoming the mother of Jesus, are related in Matt. 1:18 ff.; Luke 1:26 ff.

MARY. A Roman Christian who is greeted by Paul in his Epistle to the Romans (16:6).

MASCHIL. The title of thirteen Psalms: 32, 42, 44, 45, 52-55, 74, 78, 88, 89, 142.

MASSA. Son of Ishmael (Gen. 25:14).

MASSAH—*trial; proving.* Also called Meribah, where the Israelites tempted Jehovah (Ex. 16:7; Ps. 95:8, 9; Heb. 3:8).

MATRI. A family to which Saul the king of Israel belonged (1 Sam. 10:21).

MATTAN—*gift.* 1. The priest of Baal, slain in the idol temple at Jerusalem (2 Kings 11:18; 2 Chron. 23:17). 2. The father of Shephatiah (Jer. 38:1).

MATTANIAH—*gift of Jehovah.* The original name of Zedekiah, king of Judah (2 Kings 24:17). 2. A Levite singer (1 Chron. 9:15), leader of the Temple choir after its restoration (Neh. 11:17; 12:8). We find him among the Levites of the second rank, "keepers of the thresholds," an office which fell to the singers (cf. 1 Chron. 15: 18, 21). 3. A descendant of Asaph (2 Chron. 20:14). 4. One of the sons of Elma (Ezra 10:26). 5. One of the sons of Zattu (Ezra 10:27). 6. A descendant of Pahath-Moab (Ezra 10:30). 7. One of the sons of Bani (Ezra 10:37). 8. A Levite, father of Zaccur, and ancestor of Hanan, the under-treasurer who had charge of the offerings for the Levites in the time of Nehemiah (Neh. 13:13). 9. One of the fourteen sons of Heman, whose office it was to blow the horns in the Temple service as appointed by David (1 Chron. 25:4, 16). 10. A descendant of Asaph, the Levite minstrel, who assisted in the purification of the Temple in the reign of Hezekiah (2 Chron. 29:13).

MATTATHIAS—*gift of Jehovah.* 1. The father of the Maccabees. 2. The son of Simon Maccabaeus, murdered, together with his father and brother, by Ptolemaeus. 3. The son of Amos (Luke 3:25). 4. The son of Semei (Luke 3:26).

MATTHEW—*gift of Joseph.* The Apostle and Evangelist, the same as Levi (Luke 5:27-29), the son of Alphaeus (Mark 2:14).

MATTHEW, GOSPEL OF. Was written by the Apostle probably in Hebrew and in Palestine in the first century. It was written for Jewish converts, to show them in Jesus of Nazareth the Messiah of the Old Testament whom they expected.

MATTHIAS—*gift of Jehovah.* The Apostle elected to fill the place of the traitor Judas (Acts 1:26). He preached the gospel and according to one tradition suffered martyrdom in Ethiopia.

MATTOCK (Isa. 7:25). The tool used in Arabia for loosening the ground. Answers generally to our mattock or grubbing-axe, *i.e.*, a single-headed pickaxe.

MAUL. A heavy club sometimes with iron weighting the head, for striking a person on the head (Prov. 25:18).

MAUZZIM (Dan. 11:38). "The god of forces," the deity who presided over strongholds.

MAZZAROTH (Job 38:32). "The twelve sings."

MEADOW. Appears in A.V. only in Gen. 41:2, 18 and Judg. 20:33.

MEAH, THE TOWER OF. One of the towers of the wall of Jerusalem when rebuilt by Nehemiah (Neh. 3:1; 12:39).

MEALS. The early Hebrews do not seem to have given special names to their several meals, for the terms rendered "dine" and "dinner" in the A.V. (Gen. 43:16; Prov. 15:17) are in reality general expressions, which might more correctly be rendered "eat" and "portion of food." In the New Testament we have the Greek terms rendered respectively "dinner" and "supper" (Luke 14:12; John 21:12), but which are more properly "breakfast" and "dinner."

MEARAH—*cave* (Josh. 13:4). The word means in Hebrew a cave, and it is assumed that the reference is to some cavern in the neighborhood of Zidon.

MEAT. It does not appear that the word "meat" is used in either the Old or New Testament, in the sense of animal food but refers to food in general. The latter is denoted uniformly by "flesh."

MEAT-OFFERING. The word *minhah* signifies originally a gift of any kind, and appears to be used generally of a gift from an inferior to a superior, whether God or man. The law or ceremonial of the meat offering is described in Lev. 2 and 6:14-23. It was to be composed of fine flour, seasoned with salt, and mixed with oil and frankincense, but without leaven; and it was generally accompanied by a drink-offering of wine (1 Chron. 29:10-14). They were usually substitutes for other offerings (cf. Lev. 5:11; Num. 5:15). (See Meat.)

MEDAN. A son of Abraham and Keturah (Gen. 25:2; 1 Chron. 1:32).

MEDES. For a long period a highly civilized and wealthy people. They were the dominant race in all Asia (cf. e.g., 2 Kings 17:6; Isa. 13:17; Acts 2:9).

MEDIA. A vast region between Persia and the Caspian Sea, deriving its name from *Madai,* son of Japheth (Gen. 10:2). Cyrus, king of Persia, became by his wife heir to the crown of Media, thus uniting the kingdoms of the Medes and Persians.

MEDIAN. Darius, "the son of Ahasuerus, of the Medes" or "the Mede" (Dan. 9:1; 11:1; 5:31).

MEDICINE. The Egyptians claimed the invention of the healing art, and their "many medicines" are mentioned (Jer. 46:11).

MEGIDDO (Josh. 12:21). Megiddo appears as the city of one of the kings whom Joshua defeated on the west of the Jordan. The song of Deborah brings the place vividly before us, as the scene of the great conflict between Sisera and Barak. The chief historical interest of Megiddo is concentrated in Josiah's death (2 Chron. 35:22-24). There is a copious stream flowing down the gorge, probably the "waters of Megiddo" of Judg. 5:19.

MEHETABEEL—*God benefits.* The ancestor of Shemaiah the prophet hired against Nehemiah by Tobiah and Sanballat (Neh. 6:10).

MEHETABEL. The wife of Hadad, the eighth king of Edom (Gen. 36:39).

MEHOLATHITE, THE (1 Sam. 18:19). It no doubt denotes that Adriel belonged to a place called Meholah.

MEHUJAEL—*smitten of God* (?). The son of Irad, and fourth in descent from Cain (Gen. 4:18).

MEHUNIMS, THE (2 Chron. 26:7). A nation of Arabia renowned for their traffic in spices, who returned from the captivity with Zerubbabel (Ezra 2:50; Neh. 7:52, A.V.).

MELCHI. 1. The son of Janna, and ancestor of Joseph (Luke 3:24). 2. The son of Addi (Luke 3:21).

MELCHISEDECH. The form of the name Melchizedek adopted in the A.V. of the New Testament (Heb. 5, 6, 7).

MELCHIZEDEK—*king of righteousness* (Gen. 14:18-20). King of Salem and a priest constituted by a special gift from God. The relation between Melchizedek and Christ as type and antitype is made in Hebrews. Each was a priest, (1) not of the Levitical tribe; (2) superior to Abraham; (3) whose beginning and end are unknown; (4) who is not only a priest, but also a king of righteousness and peace.

MELEA. Ancestor of Joseph (Luke 3:31).

MELITA. The modern *Malta.* This island has an illustrious place in Scripture, as the scene of the shipwreck of Paul (Acts 27). It was a dependency of the Roman province of Sicily. Its chief officer appears from inscriptions to have had the title of *Primus Melitensium,* and this is the very phase which Luke uses (28:7).

MELON (Num. 11:5). That more particularly referred to in the text must be the watermelon.

MELZAR. An official title (Dan. 1:11, 16), "the steward," rather than a proper name as in A.V.

MEMPHIS. An Egyptian city of great size and splendor, which stood near old Cario, of which there are now only some ruins. In Hos. 9:6 it is called *Memphis* (Hebrew *Moph*), and in Isa. 19:13 and elsewhere, *Noph* (Hebrew Noph).

MEMUCAN. One of the seven princes of Persia in the reign of Ahasuerus (Esth. 1:14, 16, 21).

MENAHEM—*comforter.* Son of Gadi, who slew the usurper Shallum, and seized the throne of Israel (2 Kings 15:14-22).

MENAN. The son of Mattatha, one of the ancestors of Joseph (Luke 3:31).

MENE. The first word of the mysterious inscription written on the wall of Belshazzar's palace, in which Daniel read the doom of the king and his dynasty (Dan. 5:25, 26).

MENI (Isa. 65:11). A proper name, and also the name of an object of idolatrous worship cultivated by the Jews in Babylon.

MEONENIM, THE PLAIN OF. Mentioned only in Judg. 9:37. The meaning of Meonenim is enchanters or "observers of times," as in Deut. 18:10, 14; in Mic. 5:12.

MEPHIBOSHETH—*he who scatters shame.* The name borne by two members of the family of Saul—his son and his grandson. 1. Saul's son by Rizpah (2 Sam. 21:8). 2. Son of Jonathan, grandson of Saul. When his father and grandfather were slain on Gilboa he was an infant but five years old (2 Sam. 4:4). Mephibosheth was carried with the rest of his family to the mountains of Gilead, where he found refuge until David invited him to Jerusalem. For later events in his life see 2 Sam. 9:1-13 and 2 Sam. 16:1-4; 19:24-30.

MERAB. The eldest daughter of King Saul (1 Sam. 14:49), whom he betrothed to David (1 Sam. 18:17). Before the marriage Merab's younger sister Michal had displayed her attachment for David, and Merab was then married to Adriel the Meholathite, to whom she bore five sons (2 Sam. 21:8).

MERAIOTH. 1. A descendant of Eleazar the son of Aaron, and head of a priestly house (1 Chron. 6:6, 7, 52). 2. The head of one of the houses of priests represented by Helkai (Neh. 12:15).

MERARI. Third son of Levi, and head of the third great division of the Levites, the Merarites. Born before the descent of Jacob into Egypt, and one of the seventy who accompanied Jacob thither (Gen. 46:8, 11).

MERATHAIM, THE LAND OF—*double rebellion* (?). Alluding to the country of the Chaldaeans, and to the double captivity which it had inflicted on the nation of Israel (Jer. 50:21).

MERCURIUS. The deity (Greek, *Hermes*), whom the Romans identified with their Mercury. The people of Lystra (Acts 14:11) called Paul "Mercurius, because he was the chief speaker."

MERCY SEAT (Ex. 25:17; 37:6; Heb. 9:5). The lid of the Ark of the Covenant whereupon the blood of the yearly atonement was sprinkled by the high priest.

MERED. One of the sons of Ezra (1 Chron. 4:17, 18).

MEREMOTH. 1. Son of Uriah, the priest of the family of Koz, the head of the seventh course of priests established by David. In Ezra 8:33, Meremoth is appointed to weigh and register the gold and silver vessels belonging to the Temple. 2. A layman of the sons of Bani, who had married a foreign wife (Ezra 10:36). 3. A priest, or more probably a family of priests, who sealed the covenant with Nehemiah (Neh. 10:5).

MERES. One of the seven counselors of Ahasuerus, king of Persia (Esth. 1:14).

MERIBAH—*strife*. The place where the people murmured, and the rock was smitten (Ex. 17:7). The name is also given to Kadesh (Num. 20:13, 24; 27:14; Deut. 22:51).

MERIBBAAL—*Baal contends*. Son of Jonathan the son of Saul (1 Chron. 8:34; 9:40), in 2 Sam. called Mephibosheth.

MERODACH. The Babylonian Bel or Belus (Jer. 50:2).

MERODACHBALADAN—*Marduk has given a son*. King of Babylon in the days of Hezekiah, (2 Kings 20:12; Isa. 39:1). There were two reigns of this king, the first from 722 to 710 B.C., when he was deposed by Sargon; and the second, after his recovery of the throne in 703 B.C., which lasted only half a year. Sennacherib defeated the combined army in a pitched battle.

MEROM, THE WATERS OF. Here a confederacy of the northern chiefs, assembled under the leadership of Jabin, king of Hazor (Josh. 11:5 ff.) were encountered by Joshua, and completely routed.

MEROZ. A town denounced because its inhabitants had refused to take part in the struggle with Sisera (Judg. 5:23).

MESHA. 1. One of the geographical limits of the Joktanites when they settled in Arabia (Gen. 10:30). 2. The king of Moab in the reigns of Ahab and his sons Ahaziah and Jehoram, kings of Israel (2 Kings 3:4 ff.). 3. The eldest son of Caleb the son of Hezron by his wife Azubah (1 Chron. 2:42). 4. A Benjamite, son of Shaharaim, by his wife Hodesh (1 Chron. 8:9).

MESHACH—*friend of the king*. One of the companions of Daniel, who with three others was chosen from among the captives to stand before King Nebuchadnezzar (Dan. 1:5, 20).

MESHECH. Son of Japhet (Gen. 10:2; 1 Chron. 1:5), and the progenitor of a people.

MESOPOTAMIA. "Syria of the two rivers." If we look to the signification of the name, we must regard Mesopotamia as the entire country between the two rivers—the Tigris and the Euphrates (*e.g.* Gen. 24:10; Judg. 3:8; Acts 2:9).

MESSIAH. Literally *the anointed*, and in the New Testament usually translated "Christ."

MESSIAS. The Greek form of Messiah (John 1:41; 4:25).

METHUSAEL—*man of God*. The son of Mehujael, and father of Lamech (Gen. 4:18).

METHUSELAH—*man of the dart*. The son of Enoch, sixth in descent from Seth, and father of Lamech (Gen. 5:25-27).

MEZAHAB—*waters of gold*. The father of Matred and grandfather of Mehetabel, who was wife of Hadar or Hadad, the last-named king of Edom (Gen. 36:39; 1 Chron. 1:50).

MICAH—*who is like Jehovah*. A prophet of the tribe of Judah, who lived in the latter days of Isaiah and Hosea. The book of Micah is one of the most important prophecies in the Old Testament.

MICAIAH—*who is like Jehovah*. The son of Imlah, a prophet of Samaria, who, in the reign of Ahab, king of Israel, predicted his defeat and death (1 Kings 22:1-35; 2 Chron. 18).

MICHAEL—*who is like God*. "One," or "the first of the chief princes" or "archangels (Dan. 10:13; *cf.* Jude 9), described in Dan. 10:21 as the "prince" of Israel. In the Old Testament he is the guardian of the Jewish people in their antagonism to heathenism. In the New Testament (see Rev. 12:7) he fights in heaven against the dragon.

MICHAIAH. 1. The father of Achbor (2 Kings 22:12). 2. Father of Mattahiah (Neh. 12:35). 3. One of the priests at the dedication of the wall of Jerusalem (Neh. 12:41). 4. The daughter of Uriel of Gibeah, wife of Rehoboam, and mother of Abijah, king of Judah (2 Chron. 13:2). 5. One of the princes of Jehoshaphat whom he sent to teach the law of Jehovah in the cities of Judah (2 Chron. 17:7). 6. The son of Gemariah (Jer. 36:11-14).

MICHAL (contracted form of Michael). The younger of Saul's two daughters (1 Sam. 14:49).

MICHMASH—*hidden away*. A town known solely by its connection with the Philistine war of Saul and Jonathan (1 Sam. 13; 14), situated in the very middle of the tribe of Benjamin.

MICHTAM. This word occurs in the titles of six Psalms (16, 56-60).

MIDIAN. A son of Abraham and Keturah (Gen. 25:2; 1 Chron. 1:32); progenitor of the Midianites. Midian is first mentioned as a people, when Moses fled, having killed the Egyptian, to the "land of Midian" and married a daughter of a priest of Midian (Ex. 2:15, 21). The "land of Midian," or the portion of it specially referred to, was probably the peninsula of Sinai.

MIDWIFE. Parturition in the East is usually easy. The office of a midwife is thus, in many Eastern countries, in little use. In Ex. 1 only two midwives are mentioned for all the Hebrews.

MIGDOL. A frontier fortress of the Egyptians, on the route of the children of Israel in their exodus (Ex. 14:2; Num. 33:7).

MIGRON. A town in the neighborhood of Gibeah (1 Sam. 14:2).

MILCAH. 1. Daughter of Haran and wife of Nahor, Abraham's brother, to whom she bore eight children (Gen. 11:29; 22:20, 23; 24:15, 24,

47). 2. The fourth daughter of Zelophehad (Num. 26:33; 27:1; 36:11; Josh. 17:3).

MILCOM. The "abomination of the children of Ammon, Molech (1 Kings 11:7), and Malcham (Zeph. 1:5).

MILE. A measure of length, containing a thousand paces. Eight *stadia* or furlongs make a mile. The Romans measured by miles, the Greeks by furlongs. The furlong was a hundred and twenty-five paces; the pace was five feet. The ancient Hebrews had neither miles, furlongs nor feet, but only the cubit, the reed and the line. In Scripture the mile is mentioned only in Matt. 5:41.

MILETUS (Acts 20:15, 17, less correctly called Miletum in 2 Tim. 4:20). A seaport on the southwest coast of Asia Minor. In the context of Acts 20:6, we have the geographical relations of Miletus brought out as distinctly as if it were Luke's purpose to state them. As to the history of Miletus itself, it was far more famous five hundred years before Paul's day than it ever became afterward.

MILK. As an article of diet, it holds a more important position in Eastern countries than with us. Not only the milk of cows, but of sheep (Deut. 32:14), of camels (Gen. 32:15) and of goats (Prov. 27:27) was used.

MILL. The mills of the ancient Hebrews differed little from those now in use in the East. These consist of two circular stones, about 18 inches or two feet in diameter, the lower of which is fixed (Isa. 47:1, 2).

MILLET. Mentioned only once (Ezek. 4:9). An ingredient in the bread made by Ezekiel. Both the *Sorghum vulgare* and the *Panicum miliaceum* were used by the ancient Hebrews and Egyptians.

MILLO. The city taken from the Jebusites by David (2 Sam. 5:9; 1 Chron. 11:8). 2 Chron. 32:5 seems to show that "the Millo" was part of the "city of David." That is of Zion (*cf.* 2 Kings 12:20), and it is the word used throughout the Books of Maccabees for the fortress on Mount Zion.

MILLO, THE HOUSE OF. 1. A family mentioned in Judg. 9:6, 20, in connection with the men of Shechem. 2. The spot at which King Josiah was murdered by his slaves (2 Kings 12:20).

MINES, MINING (Job 28:1-11). The only record of the kind which we inherit from the Hebrews. The expression, "the gold they refine," presupposes a process by which the pure gold is extracted from the ore, and separated from the silver or copper. Mines were not located in Palestine proper but were numerous in the Sinaitic peninsula and Western Palestine.

MINGLED PEOPLE. This phrase is applied in Jer. 25:20, and Ezek. 30:5, to denote the miscellaneous population of Egypt.

MINISTERS. Officials of a religious and civil character (Ex. 24:13; 1 Kings 10:5; Isa. 61:6). In the New Testament we have three terms, the first a subordinate public administrator (Rom. 13:6; 15:16; Heb. 7:2). The second term is used of the attendant in the synagogue (Luke 4:20) employed in the service. The third term is used in relation to the ministry of the Gospel.

MINNITH. Named as the point to which Jephthah's slaughter of the Ammonites extended (Judg. 11:33).

MINSTREL (2 Kings 3:15). A player upon a stringed instrument like the harp, on which David played before Saul (1 Sam. 16:16; 18:10; 19:9). Instances of the divine influence connected with music are seen in 1 Sam. 10:5, 6, 10, 11. The "ministrels" in Matt. 9:23 were the flute-players employed as professional mourners.

MINT (Matt. 23:23; Luke 11:42). One of those

herbs, the title of which the Jews were most scrupulously exact in paying.

MIPHKAD, THE GATE. One of the gates of Jerusalem at the time of the rebuilding of the wall after the return from captivity (Neh. 3:31).

MIRACLE. This word is the usual translation of the Greek word *Semeion*, which signifies "a sign." A miracle is a plain and manifest exercise by man, or by God at the call of a man, of those powers which belong only to the Creator. The divinity of our Saviour was proved by the miracles he wrought (John 3:2, 9, 16).

MIRIAM. The sister of Moses and Aaron, was the eldest of that sacred family; and she first appears as a young girl, watching her infant brother's cradle in the Nile (Ex. 2:4), and suggesting her mother as a nurse (v. 7). "The sister of Aaron" is her Biblical distinction (Ex. 15:20). She took the lead, with Aaron, in the complaint against Moses for his marriage with a Cushite (Num. 12:1, 2). A stern rebuke was administered. The hateful Egyptian leprosy broke out over the whole person of the proud prophetess. This stroke and its removal, which took place at Hazeroth, form the last public event of Miriam's life. She died toward the close of the wanderings at Kadesh, and was buried there (Num. 20:1).

MIRROR. Two Hebrew words in Ex. 38:8 and Job 36 are rendered "looking glass" in the A.V., but from the context evidently denote a mirror of polished metal.

MISHAEL—*who is what God is.* 1. One of the sons of Uzziel, the uncle of Aaron and Moses. (Ex. 6:22; Lev. 10:4, 5). 2. One of those who stood at Ezra's left hand when he read the law to the people (Neh. 8:4). 3. A companion of Daniel who was given the name of Meshach by the Babylonians (Dan. 1:6 ff.).

MISREPHOTHMAIM. A place in close connection with Zidon-rabbah, *i.e.*, Sidon (Josh. 11:8; 13:6).

MITE. A coin current in Palestine in the time of our Lord (Mark 12:41-44; Luke 21:1-4).

MITHREDATH—*given by Mithra.* 1. The treasurer of Cyrus king of Persia (Ezra 1:8). 2. A Persian officer who was stationed at Samaria, in the reign of Artaxerxes (Ezra 4:7).

MITYLENE. The intermediate place where Paul stopped for the night between Assos and Chios (Acts 20:14, 15).

MIXED MULTIDUDE (Ex. 12:38; Num. 11:4). Probably the offspring of marriages between the Israelites and the Egyptians; and all those who were not of pure Israelite blood.

MIZAR—*littleness.* A hill from which the author of Psalm 42 utters his pathetic appeal (v. 6).

MIZPAH and **MISPEH**—*watch-tower.* The name of several places in Palestine. 1. The earliest of all is the heap of stones piled up by Jacob and Laban (Gen. 31:48). The spot became a place for solemn deliberation in times of difficulty (Judg. 10:17; 11:34). 2. Place where David put his parents under the care of the king of Moab (1 Sam. 22:2). 3. The Land of Mizpeh, "the residence of the Hivites" (Josh. 11:3). 4. The Valley of Mizpeh (Josh. 11:8). 5. Mispeh, a city of Judah (Josh. 15:38). 6. The Mizpeh (Josh. 18:26).

MIZRAIM. The usual name of Egypt in the Old Testament (*cf.* Gen. 10:6, 13; 1 Chron. 1:8, 11).

MNASON. Is honorably mentioned in Scripture as one of the hosts of the Apostle Paul (Acts 21:16).

MOAB. 1. The son of Lot (Gen. 19:37). 2. The land called by his name, eastward and southward of the Dead Sea, has been lately explored and is covered with evidences of former greatness (Jer. 48:2-39; Amos 2:2; Zeph. 2:9).

MOLADAH. A city of Judah, one of those which lay in the district of "the south," next to Edom (Josh. 15:26; 19:2). In the latter tribe it remained at any rate till the reign of David (1 Chron. 4:28), but by the time of the captivity it seems to have come back into the hands of Judah, by whom it was reinhabited after the captivity (Neh. 11:26).

MOLE. 1. *tinshemeth* (Lev. 11:30) denotes different kinds of lizards; therefore the chameleon may be the animal intended. 2. *haphôr pêrôth* is "moles" in Isa. 2:20.

MOLECH. The fire-god Molech was the tutelary diety of the children of Ammon. The first direct allusion to Molech worship is in the description of Solomon's idolatry in his old age (1 Kings 11:7). Two verses before, the same deity is called Milcom. The worship of Molech was associated with child-sacrifice, and it was forbidden by Hebrew law (Lev. 18:21; 20:1-5).

MONEY. In ancient times it was dealt out by weight, being generally weighed by the merchant (Gen. 23:9-16; Job 6:2; Zech. 11:12). The Persians began to use coined money about the time of Darius Hystaspes. The Hebrews did not coin money until the reign of John Hyrcanus (135-104 B.C.). The coin called "a piece of money" was perhaps a *shekel*, or the Greek *stater* (Matt. 17:27). A pound was about sixty shekels. A penny was one-fourth of a shekel. A farthing was the fortieth part of a penny (Matt. 5:26). A mite was half a farthing (Mark 12:42).

MONEY CHANGERS (Matt. 12:12; Mark 11:15; John 2:15). The money-changers whom Christ, for their impiety, avarice and fraudulent dealing, expelled from the Temple, were the dealers who supplied half shekels, for such a premium as they might be able to exact, to the Jews from all parts of the world, who were required to pay their tribute or ransom-money at Jerusalem in Hebrew coin.

MONTH. A space of time which, if measured by the *moon* (whence its name), is called *lunar*, and if by the *sun*, is called *solar*. When we speak of Jewish months as corresponding to ours, some allowance must be made, for theirs were lunar, and ours are solar, which are not exactly alike.

MOON. The moon held an important place in the kingdom of nature, as known to the Hebrews. The worship of the moon was extensively practised by the nations of the East. In Egypt it was honored under the form of Isis, and was one of the only two deities which commanded the reverence of the Egyptians. The warning of Moses (Deut. 4:19) is directed against this nature worship.

MORDECAI. The deliverer, under Divine Providence, of the Jews from the destruction plotted against them by Haman, the chief minister of Xerxes (Book of Esther).

MOREH—*soothsayer.* 1. The Plain of Moreh was the first halting-place of Abram after his entrance into the land of Canaan (Gen. 12:6). It was close to the mountains of Ebal and Gerizim (Deut. 11:30).

MORESHETH-GATH. A place named by the prophet Micah only (Mic. 1:14), in company with Lachish, Achzib, Mareshah and other towns of the lowland district of Judah. Micah was himself the native of a place called Moresheth.

MORIAH. 1. On "one of the mountains" in this district took place the sacrifice of Isaac (Gen. 22:2). 2. Mount Moriah (2 Chron. 3:1; *cf.* 2 Sam. 24:18 ff.), the eminence on which Solomon built the Temple.

MORTAR. (Gen. 11:3; Ex. 1:14; Lev. 14:42, 45; Isa. 41:25; Ezek. 13:10, 11, 14, 15; 22:28; Nah. 3:14). The various compacting substances used in Oriental buildings appear to be, 1. Bitumen; 2. Common mud or moistened clay; 3. A very firm cement compounded of sand, ashes and lime, sometimes mixed and coated with oil, so as to form a surface almost impenetrable to wet.

MOSES—*meaning uncertain.* The legislator of the Jewish people, and in a certain sense the founder of the Jewish religion. The fact that he was of the tribe of Levi no doubt contributed to the selection of that tribe as the sacred caste. His extraordinary history embraces a large space of the Pentateuch. The most familiar event in his life are recorded in Exodus and Numbers.

MOTH (Job 4:19; 13:28; Ps. 39:11; Isa. 51:8; Hos. 5:12). The clothes moth is the *tinea argenta*, of a white shining silver or pearl color.

MOTHER. The superiority of the Hebrew systems of legislation and of morals is shown in the high estimation of the mother in the Jewish family (Ex. 20:12; Lev. 19:3; Deut. 5:16; 21:18, 21; Prov. 1:8; 31:1).

MOUNT, MOUNTAIN. The Hebrew word *har* is employed both for single eminences such as Sinai, Gerizim, Ebal, Zion and Olivet, and for ranges such as Lebanon. It is also applied to a mountainous country.

MOURNING. The Jews made great lamentation over the dead. Tearing the hair, uttering cries, striking the breast, wearing sackcloth, sprinkling dust on the head and fasting were common in case of death. Mourners were hired who, in melancholy songs and dolorous ejaculations, excited the sympathy of spectators (Jer. 9:17, 18; Amos 5:16; Matt. 9:23).

MOUSE (Lev. 11:29; 1 Sam. 6:4, 5; Isa. 66:17). The original word denotes a field-ravager (1 Sam. 6:5), and may refer to the short-tailed field mice which cause great destruction to the corn lands of Syria.

MOWING. As the great heat of the climate in Palestine soon dries up the herbage, hay-making is not in use. The "king's mowings" (Amos 7:1; Ps. 72:6) may refer to some royal right of early pasturage for the use of the cavalry.

MULE. We do not read of mules till the time of David (1 Kings 10:25; 18:5; 2 Chron. 9:24; Ps. 32:9). After this time horses and mules are in Scripture often mentioned together. In Solomon's time it is possible that mules from Egypt occasionally accompanied the horses which we know the king of Israel obtained for that country. In Gen. 36:24 the Hebrew word *yemin*, translated "mules," probably means "warm springs."

MUPPIM. One of the fourteen descendants of Rachel (Gen. 46:21). In Num. 26:39 the name is written Shupham.

MURDER. The law of Moses, while it protected the accidental homicide, defined with strictness the crime of murder. It prohibited compensation or reprieve of the murderer, or his protection in the refuge city, or even at the altar of Jehovah (Ex. 21:12, 14; Lev. 24:17, 21; 1 Kings 2:5, 6, 31). But the question of guilt was to be decided by the Levitical tribunal.

MUSIC. We meet with nothing like a systematic cultivation of music among the Hebrews, until the establishment of the schools of the prophets (2 Kings 3:15). Music was an essential part of their practice. Professional musicians soon became attached to the court. David gathered round him "singing men and singing women" (2 Sam. 19:35). Solomon did the same (1 Kings 4:32).

MUSTARD (Matt. 13:31; 17:20; Mark 4:31; Luke 13:19; 17:6). The mustard tree of Scripture, the *Salvadora persica*, is found along the banks of the Jordan, near the lake of Tiberias, and near Damascus. Some authorities question this identification, however.

MUTH-LABBEN (Ps. 9). Has given rise to infinite conjecture.

MYRA. A town in Lycia (Acts 27:5).

MYRRH. A gum common in Arabia, Egypt and Abyssinia. The ancients used it as a perfume and for embalming. It is bitter, whence called *gall*, and being supposed to have a property like opium, it was anciently administered to alleviate pain (Mark 15:23).

MYSIA. The customary name for the northwest part of Asia Minor (Acts 16:7, 8).

NAAMAH—*pleasant.* 1. Daughter of Lamech by his wife Zillah, and sister to Tubalcain (Gen. 4:22 only). 2. Mother of King Rehoboam (1 Kings 14:21, 31; 2 Chron. 12:13). She was one of the foreign women whom Solomon took into his establishment (1 Kings 11:1).

NAAMAN—*pleasant.* 1. "Naaman the Syrian" (Luke 4:27). A Jewish tradition identifies him with the archer whose arrow struck Ahad and "gave deliverance to Syria." Naaman was commander-in-chief of the army, and was nearest to the person of the king. He was afflicted with a leprosy of the white kind, which had hitherto defied cure. The circumstances of his visit to Elisha and his remarkable cure are found in 2 Kings 5:1, 27. 2. One of the family of Benjamin who came down to Egypt with Jacob (Gen. 46: 21). He was the son of Bela, and head of the family of the Naamites (Num. 26:40; 1 Chron. 8:3, 4).

NAAMITES, THE (Num. 26:40 only).

NAARAI. One of the valiant men of David's armies (1 Chron. 11:37).

NAARAN. A city of Ephraim (1 Chron. 7:28), mentioned as the eastern limit of the tribe.

NAARATH (Josh. 16:7 only).

NABAL—*fool.* A sheepmaster on the confines of Judaea. His wealth consisted chiefly of sheep and goats. He refused David's request for supplies, then died of shock when he learned of his narrow escape from reprisal. His widow married David (1 Sam. 25:2 ff.; 30:5; 2 Sam. 2:2; 3:3).

NABOTH. A victim of Ahab and Jezebel, was the owner of a small vineyard at Jezreel, close to the royal palace of Ahab (1 Kings 21:1, 2). The king offered an equivalent in money or another vineyard in exchange for this. Naboth refused. "Jehovah forbid it to me that I should give the inheritance of my fathers unto thee." Ahab was cowed by this reply; but the proud spirit of Jezebel was roused. She had Naboth and his children (2 Kings 9:26) dragged out of the city and despatched.

NACHON'S THRESHING FLOOR. Where Uzzah was killed for touching the ark (2 Sam. 6:6).

NADAB—*generous.* 1. The eldest son of Aaron and Elisheba (Ex. 6:23; Num. 3:2). 2. King Jeroboam's son, who succeeded to the throne of Israel and reigned two years (1 Kings 15:25-31). 3. A Jerahmeelite family name (1 Chron. 2:28, 30). 4. A Gibeonite family name (1 Chron. 8: 30).

NAGGE. One of the ancestors of Christ (Luke 3:25). It represents the Hebrew *Nogah* (1 Chron. 3:7).

NAHALAL. One of the cities of Zebulun (Josh. 19:15), given to the Levites (Josh. 21:35).

NAHALIEL—*torrents of God.* One of the halting-places of Israel in the latter part of their progress to Canaan (Num. 21:35).

NAHAMANI—*comforted.* One of the leaders of the returned exiles (Neh. 7:7).

NAHARAI. The armor-bearer of Joab (2 Sam. 23:37), a native of Beeroth (1 Chron. 11:39).

NAHARI. The same as Naharai (2 Sam. 23:37).

NAHASH—*serpent.* 1. King of the Ammonites (1 Sam. 11:1, 2-11). 2. A person mentioned (2 Sam. 17:25) in stating the parentage of Amasa, the commander-in-chief of Absalom's army.

NAHATH. 1. One of the "dukes" in the land of Edom, eldest son of Reuel the son of Esau (Gen. 36:13, 17; 1 Chron. 1:37). 2. A Kohathite Levite, son of Zophai (1 Chron. 6:26). 3. A Levite in the reign of Hezekiah (2 Chron. 31:13).

NAHBI. One of the twelve spies sent out by Moses (Num. 13:14).

NAHOR. The name of two persons in the family of Abraham. 1. His grandfather; the son of Serug and father of Terah (Gen. 11:22-25). 2. Grandson of the preceding, son of Terah and brother of Abraham and Haran (Gen. 11:26, 27). He married Milcah, the daughter of his brother Haran. He was the father of twelve sons; eight of them were the children of his wife, and four of a concubine (Gen. 22:21-24).

NAHUM—*consolation.* Nahum "the Elkoshite," the seventh of the minor prophets. His personal history is quite unknown.

NAIN. A village of Galilee, made illustrious by the raising of the widow's son (Luke 7:12).

NAIOTH. A place where David took refuge from Saul (1 Sam. 19:18, 19, 22, 23; 20:1).

NAOMI. The wife of Elimelech, and mother-in-law of Ruth (Ruth 1:2; 2:1; 3:1; 4:3).

NAPHISH. A son of Ishmael (Gen. 25:15; 1 Chron. 1:31).

NAPHTALI—*wrestling.* The sixth son of Jacob; the second child born to him by Bilhah, Rachel's maid. His birth and the bestowal of his name are recorded in Gen. 30:8. At the migration to Egypt four sons are attributed to Naphtali (Gen. 46:24; Ex. 1:4; 1 Chron. 7:13). When the census was taken at Mount Sinai the tribe numbered no less than 53,400 fighting men (Num. 1:43; 2:30).

NAPHTALI, MOUNT. Northern part of the central range of western Palestine (Josh. 20:7).

NAPHTUHIM. A Mizraite nation mentioned only among the descendants of Noah (Gen. 10:13; 1 Chron. 1:11).

NARCISSUS. A dweller at Rome (Rom. 16:11), some members of whose household were known as Christians to Paul.

NASHON, or NAASHON. Son of Amminadab (Num. 1:7; 2:3). His sister, Elisheba, was wife to Aaron, and his son, Salmon, was husband to Rahab after the taking of Jericho. He died in the wilderness (Num. 26:64, 65).

NATHAN—*gave.* 1. An eminent Hebrew prophet in the reigns of David and Solomon. He first appears in 2 Sam. 7:2, 3, 17. He next comes forward as the reprover of David (2 Sam. 12:1-12). In the last years of David, Nathan taking the side of Solomon, turned the scale in his favor; and at David's request assisted in his inauguration (1 Kings 1:8 ff.). He left two works—a Life of David (1 Chron. 29:29), and a Life of Solomon (2 Chron. 9:29). 2. A son of David; one of the four who were born to him by Bathsheba (1 Chron. 3:5; cf. 14:4, and 2 Sam. 5:14).

NATHANAEL—*God has given.* A disciple of Jesus Christ, concerning whom we learn from Scripture little more than his birthplace, Cana of Galilee (John 21:2), and his simple, truthful character (John 1:47).

NAUM (Luke 3:25).

NAVE. The center part of a wheel which bends the spokes together (1 Kings 7:33).

NAZARENE. An inhabitant of Nazareth. Jesus the Nazarene was one of the names of the predicted Messiah. In Acts 24:5, *Nazarenes* is applied to the followers of Jesus by way of contempt.

NAZARETH. The ordinary residence of Jesus, is not mentioned in the Old Testament, but occurs first in Matt. 2:23. It is situated among the south ridges of Lebanon, just before they sink down into the Plain of Esdraelon.

NAZARITE—*separated one.* The regulations for the vow of a Nazarite are given Num. 6:1-21. Of the Nazarite for life three are mentioned in the Scriptures: Samson, Samuel and John the Baptist.

NEAPOLIS. A place in northern Greece where Paul and his associates first landed in Europe (Acts 16:11). Philippi being an island town, Neapolis was evidently the port.

NEBAI. One of the covenant sealers (Neh. 10:19).

NEBAIOTH. The first-born of Ishmael (Gen. 25:13; 1 Chron. 1:29), and father of a pastoral tribe named after him, the "rams of Nebaioth" being mentioned by the prophet (Isaiah (60:7) with the flocks of Kedar.

NEBALLAT. A town the Benjamites reoccupied after the captivity (Neh. 11:34).

NEBAT. Father of Jeroboam I, king of Israel (1 Kings 11:26; 12:2, 15, *etc*).

NEBO, MOUNT. The mountain from which Moses took his first and last view of the Promised Land (Deut. 32:49; 34:1). It is described as in the land of Moab, facing Jericho; the summit of a mountain called the Pisgah.

NEBO. 1. A town of Reuben on the eastern side of Jordan (Num. 32:3, 38). 2. The name of a Chaldaean god, of the Babylonians and Assyrians (Isa. 46:1; Jer. 47:1).

NEBUCHADNEZZAR—*Nebo defend the boundary.* The most powerful of Babylonian kings. His father Nabopolassar having raised an immense army to quell a revolt of the Syrians, Phoenicians, etc., he was appointed to its command, and not only subdued those provinces, but overran Canaan, Moab, Ammon, Assyria, Egypt, etc., and made them tributary (2 Kings 24, 25; Jer. 46:13-26; Ezek. 29:2-20). He carried to Babylon, Daniel, Hananiah, Mishael and Azariah, whom he called *Belteshazzar, Shadrach, Meshach* and *Abednego* (Dan. 1:1 ff.).

NEBUSHASBAN. Name of the official at the time of the capture of Jerusalem (Jer. 39:13).

NEBUZARADAN. Chief of the slaughterers, a high officer in the court of Nebuchadnezzar. On the capture of Jerusalem he was left in charge of the city (*cf.* Jer. 39:11).

NEGINAH. "The chief musician on *Neginoth*" was the conductor of that portion of the Temple-choir who played upon the stringed instruments, mentioned in Ps. 68:25.

NEHELAMITE, THE. Name applied to the false prophet Shemaiah (Jer. 24:24, 31, 32).

NEHEMIAH. The author of the book which bears his name. He was of the tribe of Judah, and was so distinguished as to be selected for the office of cupbearer to the king of Persia.

NEHEMIAH, BOOK OF. Is certainly not all by the same hand. The principal portion is the work of Nehemiah. The main history contained in the book of Nehemiah covers from the 20th

to the 32nd year of Artaxerxes Longimanus, *i.e.*, from 445 to 433 B.C.

NEHILOTH. It is most likely that Nehiloth is the general term for perforated wind-instruments of all kinds (title of Ps. 5).

NEHUM—*comfort.* One of the leaders who returned from the exile (Neh. 7:7).

NEHUSHTA. The daughter of Elnathan of Jerusalem, wife of Jehoiakim, and mother of Jehoiachin, kings of Judah (2 Kings 24:8).

NEHUSHTAN. The name by which the brazen serpent made by Moses in the wilderness (Num. 21:9), was worshipped in the time of Hezekiah (2 Kings 18:4).

NEIEL. A town on the borders of Zebulun and Asher (Josh. 19:27).

NEKEB. One of the towns on the boundary of Naphtali (Josh. 19:33).

NEKODA. A family of Nethinim (Ezra 2:60; Neh. 7:62).

NEMUEL. 1. A Reubenite, son of Eliab, and eldest brother of Dathan and Abiram (Num. 26:9). 2. The eldest son of Simeon (Num. 26:12; 1 Chron. 4:24).

NEPHEG. 1. Brother of Korah and son of Izhar (Ex. 6:21). 2. One of David's sons (2 Sam. 5:15; 1 Chron. 3:7; 14:6).

NEPHISHESIM. The children of Nephishesim were among the Nethinim who returned with Zerubbabel (Neh. 7:52).

NEPHTHALIM. A form of the name Naphtali (Matt. 4:13, 15; Rev. 7:6).

NEPHTOAH, THE WATER OF. A place on the boundary of Judah and Benjamin (Josh. 15:9; 18:15).

NEPHUSIM. The same as Nephishesim (Ezra 2:50).

NER—*light.* Son of Jehiel (1 Chron. 8:33), father of Kish and Abner, and grandfather of King Saul (*cf.* 1 Sam. 14:50; 2 Sam. 2:8; 1 Kings 2:5).

NEREUS. A Christian at Rome greeted by Paul (Rom. 16:15).

NERGAL. One of the chief Assyrian and Babylonian deities (2 Kings 17:30).

NERGALSHAREZER (Jer. 39:3-13). Two persons of this name accompanied Nebuchadnezzar on his last expedition against Jerusalem. One is not marked by any title; but the other has the distinction of Rabmag. In Scripture he appears among the persons, who, by command of Nebuchadnezzar, released Jeremiah from prison.

NETHINIMS—*those given.* Servants who had been given up to the service of the tabernacle and temple, to perform the meanest and most laborious services therein, in supplying wood and water (Josh. 9:27; Ezra 2:70; 8:20).

NETOPHAH. A town, the name occurs in the catalogue of those who returned with Zerubbabel from the captivity (Ezra 2:22; Neh. 7:26). Two of David's guards (1 Chron. 27:13, 15) were Netophathites. The "villages of the Netophathites" were the residence of the Levites (1 Chron. 9:16; Neh. 12:28).

NETTLE. The Hebrew word so translated in Job 30:7; Prov. 24:21, was some species of wild mustard. The Hebrew word translated *nettle* in Isa. 34:13; Hos. 9:6; Prov. 24:31, may be understood to denote some species of nettle (*Urtica*).

NEW MOON. The new moons were regarded as

holy days distinguished from the solemn feasts and the Sabbaths (Ezek. 45:17; 1 Chron. 23:31; 2 Chron. 2:4; 8:13; 31:3; Ezra 3:5; Neh. 10:33).

NEW TESTAMENT. The second portion of the Christian Bible. The name "testament" was meant to represent the Hebrew word "covenant." It contains 27 books by a number of different writers. They are written in a form of Greek known as *koine* which is vernacular Greek rather than the classical form. The effort of scholars to find older and more accurate manuscripts goes on in order to make the most reliable renderings possible of the Scriptures.

NEZIB. A city of Judah (Josh. 15:43), in the district of the Shephelah or Lowland, one of the same group with Keilah and Mareshah.

NICANOR. One of the seven chosen to relieve the apostles of secular duties (Acts 6:5).

NICODEMUS. The ruler of the Jews who came to Jesus at night (John 3:1, 10).

NICOLAITANS. The sect mentioned in Rev. 2:6, 15. It would seem from Rev. 2:14, that the Nicolaitans held that it was lawful "to eat things sacrificed to idols and to commit fornication" in opposition to the decree of the church given (Acts 15:20, 29).

NICOLAS (Acts 6:5). A native of Antioch, and a proselyte to the Jewish faith; one of the seven chosen to relieve the apostles.

NICOPOLIS—*city of victory.* A city of Greece where Paul planned to spend the winter (Tit. 3:12).

NIGER. The additional name given to Simeon, who was one of the teachers and prophets in the church at Antioch (Acts 13:1).

NIGHT-HAWK. An unclean bird (Lev. 11:16; Deut. 14:15).

NILE. The great river of Egypt, is spoken of under the name of Sihor, and "the river of Egypt" (Gen. 15:18). The Nile is constantly before us in the history of Israel in Egypt. Into it the male children were cast; in it, or rather in some canal or pool, was the ark of Moses put, and found by Pharaoh's daughter.

NIMRAH. A place mentioned by this name in Num. 32:3 only. If it is the same as Bethnimrah (vs. 36) it belonged to the tribe of Gad.

NIMRIM, THE WATERS OF. A stream or brook in Moab, mentioned in the denunciations of that nation by Isaiah (15:6) and Jeremiah (48:34).

NIMROD. A son of Cush and grandson of Ham. The events of his life are recorded in Gen. 10:8.

NIMSHI. The grandfather of Jehu, generally called "the *son* of Nimshi" (1 Kings 19:16; 2 Kings 9:2, 14, 20; 2 Chron. 22:7).

NINEVEH. A city of Assyria, and the capital of that empire till Esar-haddon conquered Babylon. It was founded by *Ashur*, the son of Shem (Gen. 10:11), and became one of the largest cities in the world. It was utterly destroyed by the Saracens. The circumference of Nineveh was sixty miles (*cf.* Jonah 3:3).

NISROCH. An idol of Nineveh, in whose temple Sennacherib was worshipping when assassinated by his sons, Adrammelech and Sharezer (2 Kings 19:37; Isa. 37:38). The word perhaps signifies "the great eagle."

NOADIAH. 1. A Levite, son of Binnui (Ezra 8:33). 2. A prophetess denounced by Nehemiah (Neh. 6:14).

NOAH. The tenth in descent from Adam, in the line of Seth, was the son of Lamech, and grand-

son of Methuselah. Of Noah himself we hear nothing until he is 500 years old, when it is said he begat three sons, Shem, Ham and Japhet. Of Noah's life we are told but little (see Gen. 5:28; 6-9; 9:20-29). He is known mainly for building the ark in which he and his family survived the flood. Peter calls him "a preacher of righteousness" (2 Pet. 2:5).

NOAH. One of the daughters of Zelophehad (Num. 26:33; 27:1; 36:11; Josh. 17:3).

NOAMON (Nah. 3:3), No (Jer. 46:25; Ezek. 30:14, 15, 16). A city of Egypt.

NOB (1 Sam. 23:11; Neh. 11:32). A sacerdotal city in the tribe of Benjamin. It was one of the places where the ark of Jehovah was kept for a time (2 Sam. 6:1). A frightful massacre occured there in the reign of Saul (1 Sam. 22:17-19).

NOE. The patriarch Noah (Matt. 24:37, 38; Luke 3:36; 17:26, 27).

NOGAH—*splendor.* One of the thirteen sons of David born to him in Jerusalem (1 Chron. 3:7; 14:6).

NOPHAH. A town of Moab mentioned only in (Num. 21:30).

NOSE JEWEL (Gen. 24:22; Ex. 35:22, "earring"; Isa. 3:21; Ezek. 16:12, "jewel on the forehead"). A ring of metal, of gold or silver, passed through the right nostril, and worn as an ornament by women in the East.

NUMBER. Some of the numbers mentioned in Scripture, as 7, 10, 40, 100, were regarded as giving the idea of completeness.

NUMBERS. The Fourth Book of the Law or Pentateuch. It takes its name from the numbering of the people. The book contains the history of the Israelites from the time of their leaving Sinai, in the second year after the Exodus, till after their arrival at the borders of the Promised Land in the fortieth year of their journeyings.

NUN. The father of the Jewish captain Joshua (Ex. 33:11).

NURSE. Among the Hebrews a foster-mother, or a female in charge of children (see Gen. 24:59; 35:8. 2 Sam. 4:4; 2 Kings 11:2, 3).

NUTS (Gen. 43:11). The Hebrew word here denotes the fruit of the Pistachio tree (*Pistacia vera*), for which Syria and Palestine have been long famous.

NYMPHAS. A wealthy and zealous Christian in Laodicea (Col. 4:15).

OAK. Probably two species of oak are denoted by the Hebrew terms thus translated (Isa. 1:29; Hos. 4:14; Ezek. 27:6; Isa. 44:14; Gen. 35:8; 1 Sam. 31:13).

OATH. Appeals to God's name on the one hand, and to heathen deities on the other, are treated in Scripture as tests of allegiance (Ex. 23:13; Deut. 29:12). The Christian practice in the matter of oaths was founded on the Jewish. Thus the oath on the Gospels was an imitation of the Jewish practice of placing the hands on the book of the Law.

OBADIAH—*servant of Jehovah.* The fourth of the twelve minor prophets. We know nothing of him except what we can gather from the short book which bears his name.

OBED—*worshipper.* Son of Boaz and Ruth the Moabites (Ruth 4:17, 21, 22; 1 Chron. 2:12; Matt. 1:5; Luke 3:32), and the father of Jesse.

OBED-EDOM—*worshipper of Edom.* 1. A Philistine, native of Goth. After the death of Uzzah, the ark was carried into the house of Obed-edom, where it continued three months (2 Sam. 6:12).

2. A family of doorkeepers in the temple (1 Chron. 15:18, 24). 3. A post-exilic family of singers (1 Chron. 15:21; 16:5).

OG. An Amoritish king of Bashan, whose rule extended over sixty cities (Josh. 13:12). He was one of the last representatives of the giant race of Rephaim, and was, with his people, exterminated by the Israelites at Edrei (Deut. 3:1-13; Num. 32:33).

OHAD. A son of Simeon (Gen. 46:10; Ex. 5:15).

OIL. The Hebrews commonly anointed themselves with oil; also their kings, prophets and high priests with an unction of peculiar richness and sacredness. The oil of gladness (Ps. 45:7; Isa. 41:3) was the perfumed oil with which the Hebrews anointed themselves on days of rejoicing and festivity. Oil was also used for food and medicine (Deut. 32:13; James 5:14).

OINTMENT. Ointments and oils were used in warm countries after bathing; and as oil was the first recipient of fragrance, probably from herbs, etc., steeped in it, many kinds of unguents not made of oil (olive oil) retained that appellation. Ointments were also used to anoint dead bodies (see Ps. 133:2; Luke 7:46; Luke 23:56).

OLD TESTAMENT. The first part of the Christian Bible, the same as the sacred scripture of the Jews. There are 39 books, and in the Hebrew Bible these are arranged in three groups: *The Torch* or *Law; The Nebi'im* or *Prophets;* and *The Kethubim* or *Writings.* The sacred text was originally written on skin, rolled up into volumes, like the modern synagogue-rolls (Ps. 40:7; Jer. 36:14; Zech. 5:1; Ezek. 2:9).

OLIVES, THE MOUNT OF; OLIVET, MOUNT. A mountain ridge to the east of Jerusalem, from which it is separated by the Valley of Jehoshaphat. It is described as having four summits. These are designated—the "Galilee," the "Ascension," the "Prophets," and the "Mount of Offence." The mount of Olives, called also Olivet, was so styled from the olive trees which clothed its sides. Some of these still remain, and on part of the hill are corn fields, and in a few half-cultivated gardens are fig and pomegranate trees. On the side of Olivet was Gethsemane. From Olivet, when all was done, the great atonement made, the victory over death achieved by the glorious resurrection, the last charge given to the disciples, who were thenceforth to build up the Christian church, Christ ascended (Matt. 24:3; 26:30).

OLIVE TREE. Paul, in his Epistle to the Romans (11:24), distinguishes two kinds of olive trees— (1) the wild, and (2) those under culture.

OLYMPAS. A Christian at Rome (Rom. 16:15).

OMRI. Originally "captain of the host" to Elah, was afterward himself king of Israel, and founder of the third dynasty (1 Kings 16:16 ff.). 2. A descendant of Benjamin (1 Chron. 7:8). 3. A Judahite of the house of Perez (1 Chron. 9:4). 4. A prince of Issachar (1 Chron. 27:18).

ON. A town of Lower Egypt, mentioned in the Bible under Beth-shemesh (Jer. 43:13). On is better known under its Greek name Heliopolis. It was situated about twenty miles northeast of Memphis. Heliopolis was anciently famous for its learning. The first mention of this place in the Bible is in Gen. 41:45; *cf.* v. 50, and 46:20.

ONAN. The second son of Judah by the Canaanites (Gen. 38:4; 1 Chron. 3:3). "What he did was evil in the eyes of Jehovah, and he slew him also," as he had slain his elder brother (Gen. 38:9).

ONESIMUS—*profitable.* The slave of Philemon, who had fled from his master, but was converted by Paul, who sent him back from Rome with a letter to Philemon (Col. 4:9; Philem. 10).

ONESIPHORUS—*profit-bringer.* A Christian who had been serviceable to Paul at Ephesus. He also sought him out when a prisoner at Rome, and ministered to him (2 Tim. 1:16-18; 4:19).

ONION. One of the plants which the Israelites in the wilderness regretted the loss of (Num. 11:5).

ONYX. A precious stone, taking its name from its color resembling the finger-nails (Gen. 2:12; Ex. 25:7).

OPHIR. 1. The son of Joktan (Gen. 10:29; 1 Chron. 1:23). 2. A seaport or region somewhere in India, the gold of which was renowned even in the time of Job (22:24; 28:16). From the time of David to the time of Jehoshaphat, the Hebrews traded with it. In Solomon's time the Hebrew fleet took up three years in its voyage to Ophir, and brought home gold, apes, peacocks, spices, ivory, ebony, and almug trees (1 Kings 9:28; 10:11; 22:48; 2 Chron. 9:10).

OPHRAH—*a female fawn.* 1. A town in the tribe of Benjamin (Josh. 18:23; 1 Sam. 13:17). 2. More fully Ophrah of the Abi-ezrites, the native place of Gideon (Judg. 6:11); the scene of his exploits against Baal (vs. 24). 3. A family in the tribe of Judah (1 Chron. 4:14).

ORACLE. A divine utterance for the benefit of man (*e.g.,* 2 Sam. 16:23), or the place in which the communications were given (*e.g.* 1 Kings 7:19).

OREB—*raven.* One of the chieftains of the Midianite host which was defeated and driven back by Gideon (Judg. 7:24 ff.).

ORGAN (Gen. 4:21; Job 21:12; 30:31; Ps. 150:4). The Hebrew word *'ugab* or *'uggab,* thus rendered, denotes a pipe or perforated wind instrument, as the root indicates.

ORION. That the constellation known to the Hebrews by the name *kesil* is the same as that which the Greeks called *Orion,* and the Arabs "the giant," there seems little reason to doubt (Job 9:9; 38:31; Amos 5:8).

ORNAMENTS. The Old Testament supplies us with a description of the weight and abundance of the ornaments worn at that period (Gen. 24:22; 35:4; 38:18). The first notice of the ring occurs in Gen. 41:42.

ORPAH. A Moabite woman, wife of Chilion, son of Naomi, and thereby sister-in-law to Ruth (Ruth 1:4, 14).

OSPRAY. Name of an unclean bird (Lev. 11:13; Deut. 14:12).

OSSIFRAGE. The name of an unclean bird, in Lev. 11:13, and Deut. 14:12).

OSTRICH. Occurs in Lev. 11:16; Deut. 14:15, in the list of unclean birds; and in other passages of Scripture.

OTHNI. Son of Shemaiah (1 Chron. 26:7).

OTHNIEL. The first mention of Othniel is on occasion of the taking of Debir. Debir was included in the mountainous territory near Hebron, and in order to stimulate the valor of the assailants, Caleb promised to give his daughter Achsah to whosoever should assault and take the city. Othniel won the prize (Josh. 15:16-19; Judg. 1:13-15). The next mention of him is in Judg. 3:9, where he appears as the first judge of Israel after the death of Joshua. This, with his genealogy, 1 Chron. 4:13, 14, which assigns him a son, Hathath, is all that we know of Othniel.

OVEN. A place for baking food. Some ovens were dug in the ground, others were similar to American ovens. Some were like a pitcher, the fire being put inside, and the dough spread thin over the outside was baked in a few minutes (Lev. 11:35; Matt. 6:30).

OWL (Lev. 11:16). Though the owl is frequently mentioned in Scriptures, it seldom denotes the bird known to us by this name. Some versions render the original words translated "great owl" (Lev. 11:17) the ibis, and the "little owl" in the same passage some kind of water bird. The "screech owl" (Isa. 34:14), rendered *night-monster* in the margin, must have resembled the barn owl, known to us as the common screech or white owl.

OX. The male of horned cattle of the beef kind at full age, when fit for the plough. Younger ones are called bullocks. The rural economy of the Israelites led them to value the ox as by far the most important of domestic animals (Num. 7:3, 7, 8; 1 Sam. 6:7; 2 Sam. 6:3, 6). The *wild ox (tau,* Deut. 14:5) is supposed to be the oryx of the Greeks, which is a species of large stag.

PADAN-ARM—*field of Aram.* "The tableland of Aram" otherwise called Mesopotamia (see *e.g.* Gen. 25:20).

PAINT (as a cosmetic). We have abundant evidence of the practice of painting the eyes both in ancient Egypt and in Assyria; it seems to have been used as a meretricious art, unworthy of a woman of high character (2 Kings 9:30; Jer. 4:30; Ezek. 23:40).

PALESTINA and PALESTINE. The names applied to the country of Israel in the Bible and elsewhere. The land is not in size or physical characteristics proportioned to its moral and historical position, as the theatre of the most momentous events in the world's history (Ex. 15:14; Isa. 14:29; Joel 3:4).

PALM, PALM TREE. Palm trees abounded formerly in Judaea. Phoenicia is so called as the palm country, *phoinix* or *phoenix* being the Greek for palm. Jericho again was celebrated for its palm groves, so that it was termed "the city of palm trees" (Deut. 34:3; Judg. 3:13; 2 Chron. 28:15). The palm furnishes several allusions for the sacred writers (Cant. 7:6, 7; Gen. 38:6; 2 Sam. 13:1; 14:27). The Jews used palm branch emblems of victory in their seasons of rejoicing (Lev. 23:40; Neh. 8:15; John 12:13).

PALSY (Matt. 8:6). May refer to paralysis or St. Vitus' dance. The woman who was "bowed together" by a "spirit of infirmity" may have been a paralytic (Luke 13:11).

PAMPHYLIA. One of the coast regions in the south of Asia Minor. It was in Pamphylia that Paul first entered Asia Minor, after preaching the Gospel in Cyrus. He and Barnabas sailed to Perga (Acts 13:13; 27:5).

PANNAG. An article of commerce exported from Palestine to Tyre (Ezek. 27:17), the nature of which is pure matter of conjecture.

PAPHOS. A town at the west end of Cyprus. Paul and Barnabas travelled on their first missionary expedition "through the isle" (Acts 13:6).

PARABLE. A short, weighty similitude used to convey instruction to ignorant, prejudiced or inattentive hearers.

PARADISE. A word of Persian origin, and is used in the Septuagint as the translation of Eden. See also Luke 23:43; 2 Cor. 12:4; Rev. 2:7.

PARMENAS. One of the seven "men of honest report, full of the Holy Ghost and wisdom" (Acts 6:5).

PARTHIANS. Occurs only in Acts 2:9, where it designates Jews settled in Parthia. Parthia proper was the region stretching along the southern flank of the mountains which separate the great

Persian desert from the desert of Kharesm. Parthia was a power almost rivaling Rome.

PARTRIDGE. A game bird of Palestine mentioned only in 1 Sam. 26:20; Jer. 17:11.

PARVAIM. The name of an unknown place or country whence the gold was procured for the decoration of Solomon's Temple (2 Chron. 3:6).

PASSOVER. A feast of the Jews in commemoration of the time when God, smiting the first-born of the Egyptians, *passed over* the habitations of the Hebrews (Ex. 12).

PATARA. A seaport of Lycia. Here was a famous temple of Apollo (Acts 21:1).

PATHROS. A section of Upper Egypt. It had its name from Pathrusim, the fifth son of Mizraim, who built or peopled it (Gen. 10:14). It is mentioned in the prophesies of Isaiah (11:11), Jeremiah (44:1, 15) and Ezekiel (29:14; 30:14).

PATMOS (Rev. 1:9). A rugged and bare island, and in that part of the Aegean which is called the Icarian Sea. Patmos is divided into two parts by a narrow isthmus, where, on the east side, are the harbor and the town. On the hill to the south is the celebrated monastery which bears the name of "John the divine." Half way up the ascent is the cave or grotto where tradition says that John received the Revelation.

PATRIARCH. A venerable man with a large posterity. The word is chiefly applied to those who lived before Moses (Acts 7:8), and hence we speak of the "patriarchal age."

PATROBAS. A Christian at Rome greeted by Paul (Rom. 16:14).

PAUL—*little*. He was of the tribe of Benjamin, born in Tarsus (Phil 3:5; Acts 9:11; 22:3), which, as it was a free city of Rome, gave him the honor and the advantage of Roman citizenship, though both of his parents were Jews (Acts 22:28). His name at first was *Saul*. He was sent to Jerusalem for his education, and became a very learned and prominent Pharisee. What befell him as he journeyed to Damascus is related three times in the Acts, first by the historian in his own person, then in two addresses made by Paul at Jerusalem and before Agrippa (Acts 9:1-19; 22:1-21; 26:1-23). He was not converted till after our Saviour's death, which makes him speak of himself as "born out of due time." His wonderful labors and successes are recorded in the Acts of the Apostles. The last definite record of his life is of his imprisonment in Rome for at least two years (Acts 28:30, 31).

PAULUS, SERGIUS. (See Sergius Paulus.)

PEACOCK. A beautiful bird, not known in Palestine till imported by Solomon (1 Kings 10:22). Its native country seems to be Persia and India.

PEARL. A hard, white, shining body, usually roundish, found in a shell-fish resembling an oyster. The Oriental pearls have a fine polished gloss, and are tinged with an elegant blush of red. They are esteemed in the East beyond all other jewels (*cf.* Matt. 7:6; 13:46). The Hebrew word translated "pearl" in Job 28:18 probably more correctly denotes "crystal."

PEKAH. A captain of Pekahiah king of Israel, murdered his master, seized the throne, and became the 18th sovereign of the northern kingdom (2 Kings 15:25). The history of the war against Assyria is given in 2 Kings 16 and 2 Chron. 28. It is famous as the occasion of the great prophecies in Isa. 7-9.

PEKAHIAH—*Jehovah opens*. Son and successor of Menahem, was the 17th king of Israel (2 Kings 15:22-26).

PELEG. Whose name signifies *division*, was born one hundred years after the Flood (Gen. 10:25).

PELICAN (Lev. 11:18; Deut. 14:17; Ps. 102:7; Isa. 24:11; Zeph. 2:14). Sometimes called "cormorant." It was considered an unclean bird.

PENIEL—*the face of God*. The name which Jacob gave to the place in which he had wrestled with God (Gen. 32:30). Elsewhere it is called Penuel (Judg. 8:8-17; 1 Kings 12:25).

PENNY (*denarius*). A Roman coin equal in value to seven pence three farthings sterling.

PENTATEUCH, THE. The Greek name given to the five books commonly called the "Five Books of Moses." In the time of Ezra and Nehemiah it was called "the Law of Moses" (Ezra 7:6); or "the book of the Law of Moses" (Neh. 8:1); or simply "the book of Moses" (Ezra 6:18; Neh. 13:1; 2 Chron. 25:4; 35:12). This was beyond all reasonable doubt our existing Pentateuch. The book which was discovered in the temple in the reign of Josiah, and which is entitled (2 Chron. 34:14) "the book of the Law of Jehovah by the hand of Moses," was substantially, it would seem, the same volume, though it may afterwards have undergone some revision by Ezra. The present Jews usually called the whole by the name of *Torah*, i.e., "the Law," or *Torath Mosheh*, "the Law of Moses." The division of the whole work into five parts was probably made by the Greek translators; for the titles of the several books are not of Hebrew but of Greek origin.

PENTECOST. A feast of the Jews on the fiftieth day after the passover. It was a solemn thanksgiving for the harvest, and a grateful commemoration of their being delivered from Egyptian servitude and enjoying their property by reaping the fruits of their labors (Lev. 23:9-21). The Pentecost was the last Jewish feast that Paul was anxious to keep (1 Cor. 16:8), and Whitsuntide, its successor, was the first annual festival adopted in the Christian church.

PEOR. A mountain in Moab, to the top of which the prophet Balaam was conducted by Balak for his final conjurations (Num. 23:28).

PERFUME. In the East, perfumes were used to testify great respect (Dan. 2:46). The Hebrews had two sacred perfumes, one of *incense*, and the other of *oil* (Ex. 30:23-38). They were addicted to the perfuming of dead bodies, clothes, beds, etc. (Prov. 7:17; Ps. 45:8; Cant. 3:6).

PERGA. A city of Pamphylia. Here Paul and Barnabas preached (Acts 13:14; 14:25), and to the end of the eighth century we find a Christian church here.

PERGAMOS, or **PERGAMUM.** An illustrious city of Mysia, on the river Caicus (Rev. 1:11; 2:12).

PERIZZITES. One of the nations of Canaan (Gen. 34:30). They were never fully expiated. Solomon exacted tribute of them (2 Chron. 8:7). So late as the days of Ezra we find them intermarried with the Jews (Ezra 9:1).

PERSIA, PERSIANS. Persia proper was a tract of not very large dimensions on the Persian Gulf. The only passage in Scripture where Persia designates the tract called "Persia Proper" in Ezek. 38:5. Elsewhere the Empire is intended. The Persians were of the same race as the Medes, both being branches of the great Aryan stock. Their language was closely akin to the Sanscrit, or ancient language of India.

PERSIS. A Christian at Rome greeted by Paul (Rom. 16:12).

PETER—*a stone*. His original name was Simon. He was known also as Simeon (Acts 15:14) and Cephas (John 1:42). He was the son of a man named Jonas, was born in Bethsaida and brought up a fisherman. He moved with his wife and family to Capernaum, and there it was that Christ sometimes made his home with them.

After a life of exalted usefulness, he was, according to tradition, crucified for his Master's sake, about A.D. 70. The two Epistles of Peter are attributed to him.

PHARAOH. There are several kings of this name mentioned in Scripture: 1. He who took away Abraham's wife (Gen. 12). 2. He who exalted Joseph (Gen. 41:39). 3. He who first oppressed Israel (Ex. 1:8). 4. He who released Israel (Ex. 5:14). 5. He who gave his wife's sister in marriage to Hadab (1 Kings 11). 6. Serechus, contemporary with Ahaz (2 Kings 17:4). 7. Tirhakah, who lived in the days of Hezekiah (2 Kings 19:9; Isa. 37:9). 8. Pharaohnecho, who set up Jehoiakim to be king of Judea in place of Josiah, who was slain at the battle of Megiddo (2 Kings 23:29 ff.). 9. Pharaoh-hophra, who made a league with Zedekiah, in consequence of which many of the Jews sought refuge in Egypt, and carried the prophet Jeremiah with them (Jer. 43:8-12; 44:1).

PHARAOH'S DAUGHTER. Three Egyptian princesses, daughters of Pharaohs, are mentioned in the Bible. 1. The preserver of Moses (Ex. 2:5-10). 2. Bithiah, wife of Mered, an Israelite (1 Chron. 4:18). 3. A wife of Solomon (1 Kings 3:1; 7:8; 9:24).

PHAREZ—*a breach*. (Perez, 1 Chron. 27:3; Phares, Matt. 1:3; Luke 3:33; 1 Esd. 5:5), twin son with Zarah, or Zerah, of Judah and Tamar his daughter-in-law. The circumstances of his birth are detailed in Gen. 38. The house he founded was numerous and illustrious. Its fertility is alluded to in Ruth 4:12. After the death of Er and Onan without chidlren, Pharez occupied the rank of Judah's second son.

PHARISEES—*the separated*. One of the most ancient and noted sects among the Jews, remarkable for their rigid way of living, fasting and constancy every second and fifth day of the week, and submitting to many austerities. They studied the Law, were very exact in the outward observance of it, and pretended to more holiness than others.

PHARPAR—*swift*. The second of the "two rivers of Damascus," alluded to by Naaman (2 Kings 5:12).

PHILADELPHIA—*brotherly love*. A city of Lydia, at the foot of Mount Tmolus, twenty-eight miles southeast from Sardis. It was built by Attalus II. Philadelphus (158-138 B.C.), from whom it derives its name. Earthquakes were very prevalent here, and Philadelphia was more than once nearly destroyed by them. To the church here an apocalyptic epistle was addressed Rev. 1:11; 3:7-13), conveying unqualified commendation.

PHILEMON. The Christian to whom Paul addressed his Epistle in behalf of Onesimus. He lived in Colossae, when the apostle wrote to him (Col. 4:9). It is related that Philemon became bishop of Colossae, and died as a martyr under Nero. He was a man of property and influence.

PHILEMON, THE EPISTLE OF PAUL TO. One of the letters which the apostle wrote during the captivity at Rome.

PHILETUS. A disciple of Hymenaeus, with whom he is associated in 2 Tim. 2:17. He was accused of incorrect teaching.

PHILIP—*lover of horses*. 1. Son of Herod the Great and Cleopatra. From him the city of Caesarea Philippi received its name (Matt. 16:13, *etc.*). 2. Another son of Herod by his wife Mariamne. He was sometimes called Herod, and was the husband of Herodias. He was disinherited by his father, and lived a private life (Matt. 14:3, *etc.*)

PHILIP THE APOSTLE. He was a native of Bethsaida in Galilee (Matt. 10:3; Mark 3:18; Luke 6:14; Acts 1:13).

PHILIP THE EVANGELIST. One of the seven deacons of the church at Jerusalem (Acts 6:5). He founded churches in Samaria, Azotus, etc., and settled in Caesarea. He had several daughters who preached, and perhaps uttered predictions (Acts 21:9).

PHILIPPI. A city of Macedonia, about nine miles from the sea, and twelve miles from its port. Paul, when on his first visit to Macedonia in company with Silas, visited Philippi (Acts 16:11, 12). The Epistle to the Philippians seems to have been written from Rome during the latter part of Paul's imprisonment. The church had been founded by Paul, and of all his churches seems to have loved him most. It is the only epistle of Paul which expresses no censure.

PHILISTIA (Heb. *Pelesheth*). The word thus translated in Ps. 60:8; 87:4; 108:9, is in the original identical with that elsewhere rendered Palestine.

PHILISTINES. The origin of the Philistines is nowhere expressly stated in the Bible; but the prophets describe them as "the Philistines from Caphtor" (Amos 9:7). The Philistines must have settled in the land of Canaan before the time of Abraham; for they are noticed in his day as a pastoral tribe in the neighborhood of Gerar (Gen. 21:32, 34; 26:1, 8).

PHINEHAS. 1. Son of Eleazar and grandson of Aaron (Ex. 6:25). He is memorable for having while quite a youth, by his zeal and energy, appeased the divine wrath, and put a stop to the plague which was destroying the nation (Num. 25:7 ff.). After Eleazar's death he became high priest—the third of the series. 2. Second son of Eli (1 Sam. 1:3; 2:34; 4:4, 11, 17, 19; 14:3). Phinehas was killed with his brother by the Philistines when the ark was captured.

PHOEBE. One of the most important of the Christian persons the detailed mention of whom fills nearly all the last chapter of the Epistle to the Romans (Rom. 16:1, 2).

PHOENICIA. (Acts 11:19; 15:3; 21:2). A province of Syria. It contained the famous cities Sarepta, Ptolemais, Tyre and Sidon. The Tyrians and Sidonians had for a long time almost all the trade of the then known world.

PHRYGIA. An extensive district in Asia Minor (Acts 2:10; 16:6; 28:23).

PHURAH. Gideon's servant, probably his armor-bearer (cf. 1 Sam. 14:1; Judg. 7:10, 11).

PHUT, PUT. One of the four sons of Ham (Gen. 10:6; 1 Chron. 1:8).

PIECE OF SILVER. In the New Testament two words are rendered by the phrase "piece of silver": 1. *Drachma* (Luke 15:8, 9) which was a Greek silver coin, equivalent to the Roman denarius. 2. *Silver* only occurs in the account of the betrayal of our Lord for "thirty pieces of silver" (Matt. 26:15; 27:3, 5, 6, 9).

PILATE, PONTIUS. He was the sixth Roman procurator of Judaea, and under him Jesus worked, suffered and died. He was appointed A.D. 25-6, in the 12th year of Tiberius. His administration was arbitrary. His slaughter of certain Galileans (Luke 13:1) led to some remarks from our Lord on the connection between sin and calamity.

PINE TREE. The pine appears in the A.V. three times (Neh. 8:15; Isa. 41:19; 60:13), translating two different Hebrew words.

PINNACLE (Matt. 4:5; Luke 4:9).

PIPE—*a musical instrument*. The Hebrew word which we translate "pipe" (1 Sam. 10:5; 1 Kings 1:40; Isa. 5:12; 30:29; Jer. 48:36) signifies "bored through." It would seem to have been a pipe furnished with holes.

PISGAH. A mountain summit where Bulah built altars for Balaam and Moses viewed the promised land. Sometimes incorrectly identified with Mt. Nebo where Moses died (Num. 21:20; 23:14; Deut. 3:27; 34:1).

PISIDIA. A district in Asia Minor, north of Pamphylia, and reached to, and was partly included in, Phrygia. Mentioned in Paul's missionary travels (Acts 13:13, 14, 51).

PITCH. There can be little doubt that the "pitch" (*Kopher*) of Gen. 6:14 was bitumen or asphalt. Another word, *zepheth*, is used (Ex. 2:3; Isa. 34:9), implying to flow or become liquid.

PITCHER. A pottery container for carrying water (Gen. 24:14; Lam. 4:2; Mark 14:13; Luke 22:10).

PITHOM and Rameses. Were the two cities for the building or fortifying of which the Hebrews made brick (Ex. 1:11). Rameses was in Goshen, and was the point from which the Hebrews started in their Exodus.

PLAGUES, THE TEN. The occasion on which the plagues were sent is described in Ex. 3-12. 1. *Blood.* This plague was humiliating, as the Nile was held sacred, as well as some kinds of its fish, not to speak of the crocodiles. 2. *Frogs.* 3. *Lice.* The scrupulous cleanliness of the Egyptians would add intolerably to the bodily distress of this plague, by which also they again incurred religious defilement. 4. *Flies.* 5. *The Murrain of Beasts.* Still coming closer to the Egyptians, God sent a disease upon the cattle, which were not only their property, but their deities. 6. *Boils* 7. *Hail.* The ruin caused by the hail was evidently far greater than that effected by any of the earlier plagues. 8. *The Plague of Locusts.* The severity of this plague can be well understood by those who have been in a part of the land where a flight of locusts has alighted. 9. *Darkness.* It has been illustrated by a sandstorm which occurs in the desert, often causing the darkness of twilight, and affecting man and beast. 10. *The Death of the First-born.* The clearly miraculous nature of this plague, in its severity, its falling upon man and beast, and the singling out of the first-born, puts it beyond comparison with any natural pestilence, even the severest recorded in history.

PLEIADES. A beautiful cluster of stars, sometimes called "the seven stars" (Job 9:9; 38:31).

POMEGRANATE. A fruit mentioned frequently in the Scriptures (*e.g.*, Ex. 28:33; Num. 13:23; Cant. 4:3).

PONTUS. A region in northeast Asia Minor. Is mentioned three times in the New Testament (Acts 2:9, 10; 18:2; 1 Pet. 1:1).

POOL. Pools are in many parts of Palestine and Syria the only resource for water during the dry season, and the failure of them involves drought and calamity (Isa. 42:15).

POPLAR. A tree mentioned twice in Scripture (Gen. 30:37; Hos. 4:13). Its identity is uncertain.

POTIPHAR—*gift of Ra* (?). The Egyptian officer to whom Joseph was sold (Gen. 39:1; cf. 37:36).

POTIPHERAH—*he whom Ra gave* (?). Was priest or prince of On, and his daughter Asenath was given Joseph to wife by Pharaoh (Gen. 41:45, 50; 46:20).

POTTERY. It is abundantly evident, both that the Hebrews used earthenware vessels in the wilderness, and that the potter's trade was afterward carried on in Palestine (Isa. 41:25; Isa. 45:9; Jer. 18:3).

POUND. 1. A weight. 2. A money of account, mentioned in the parable of the ten pounds (Luke 19:12-27).

PROCHORUS. One of the seven chosen to relieve the Apostles of secular work (Acts 6:5).

PROCONSUL. The Greek, for which this is the true equivalent, is rendered uniformly "deputy" in Acts 13:7, 8, 12; 19:38. The "proconsul" exercised purely civil functions.

PROCURATOR. The office held by Pontius Pilate. In Luke 3:1 he is called "governor." Procurators were appointed directly by the Roman emperor.

PROPHET. One who foretells what is to come; a person inspired, and appointed by God to reveal his will, to warn of approaching judgments, to explain obscure passages of Scripture, or make known the truths of the Bible and urge men to obedience.

PROSELYTE. Literally a *stranger* or *visitor*, means in Scripture one that turned from heathenism to the Jewish religion.

PROVERBS. The book containing the inspired precepts attributed Solomon (1 Kings 4:32). The whole in the original seems to be poetry. Though written by Solomon, they seem to have been collected and arranged by others. cf. 1:1 and 30:1.

PRUNING-HOOK. An implement used by vine-dressers. The word is found in Scripture only in the plural (Isa. 2:4; 18:5; Mic. 4:3; Joel 3:10; in the margin reading "scythes"). It appears that the Hebrews were accustomed regularly to prune their vines (Lev. 25:3; John 15:2).

PSALMS. The Psalms are mostly attributed to David. Those under the name of Asaph were probably directed to him as leader of the Temple choir. The Psalms are poetic in form, although it is only recently that the Hebrew poetic form has been understood, permitting the presentation of them in their proper form. Some psalms are doctrinal, as Ps. 1; some historical, as Ps. 77, 105, 106; some prophetic, as Ps. 110; some penitential, as Ps. 51; some consist of prayer and complaints, as Ps. 6, 38; others consist of praise and thanksgiving, as Ps. 30, 46, 145; 150. In some most or all of these subjects are connected, as Ps. 89.

PSALTERY. A stringed musical instrument, first mentioned in the Psalms of David. It seems to have been shaped much like the present harp.

PTOLEMAIS. The New Testament name of the Canaanite stronghold Accho. It is mentioned in connection with Paul's missionary journey from Tyre to Caesarea (Acts 21:7).

PUBLICAN (Matt. 18:17). An inferior collector of the Roman tribute. The principal collectors of this revenue were men of great influence, but the under collectors or publicans, were remarkable for extortion, and were accounted thieves and pickpockets. It is said the Jews would not allow them to enter the temple or synagogues, or to give testimony in a court of justice (Luke 5:27). The Jews reproached Jesus with being a "friend of publicans and sinners," and eating with them (Luke 7:34).

PUBLIUS. The leading man of Melita (Malta) when Paul was shipwrecked there (Acts 28:7).

PUL (2 Kings 15:19). Tiglath-pileser III, the first king of Assyria who invaded Canaan, and by a present of one thousand talents of silver, exacted from the mighty men of wealth of Israel by Menahem, was prevailed on to withdraw his troops and recognize the title of that wicked usurper. A town of this name is mentioned in Isa. 66:19.

PULSE (2 Sam. 17:28; Dan. 1:12, 16). Coarse grain, as peas, beans and the like.

PURIFICATION. The ritual observances whereby an Israelite was absolved from uncleanness. Sacrifices were added, and the ceremonies bore an

expiatory character (e.g., Lev. 15:18; 11:25, 40; 15:16, 17; 12:6).

PURIM. The plural of *Pur*, and meaning *lots*. It is the name of a solemn feast among the Jews, in commemoration of Haman's overthrow. It derives its name from the circumstance that Haman cast lots to ascertain the best day for destroying the Jews (Esth. 3:7; 9:26).

PURPLE. A color much worn by kings and emperors (Mark 15:17). It is the famous Tyrian dye, so costly and so celebrated in antiquity. It was extracted from the throat of the shell-fish.

PUTEOLI. A Roman seaport north of Naples. Paul halted here seven days as he went prisoner to Rome (Acts 28:13).

PYGARD (Deut. 14:5). The name, apparently, of some species of antelope.

QUAIL (Ex. 16:13; Num. 11:31, 32; Ps. 105:10). A small migratory bird. It is said that God gave quails to his people in the wilderness upon two occasions: first, within a few days after they had passed the Red Sea (Ex. 16:3-13). The second time was at the encampment at the place called, in Hebrew, Kibroth-hataavah, the graves of lust (Num. 11:32; Ps. 105:40). Both of these happened in the spring, when the quails passed from Asia into Europe.

QUARTUS. A Christian of Corinth (Rom. 16:23).

QUATERNION. A military term, signifying a guard of four soldiers (Acts 12:4).

QUEEN OF HEAVEN. A deity usually identified with the Assyrian goddess *Ishtar* (Jer. 7:18; 44:17, 18, 19, 25).

QUICKSANDS. Feared by the captain of Paul's ship (Acts 27:17). The reference here is to the shifting sands on the north coast of Africa known as the Syrtis.

RAAMAH. A son of Cush (Gen. 10:7). The tribe of Raamah became renowned as traders (Ezek. 27:22).

RABBAH, RABBATH—*great*. 1. The metropolis of Ammon (Deut. 3:11; Josh. 13:25). It was besieged and taken by David for ill-treatment of his ambassadors by the Ammonites. 2. A town in the hill-country of Judah (Josh. 15:60).

RABBI. A title of respect signifying Master, Teacher, given by the Jews to their doctors and teachers, and often addressed to our Lord.

RABBONI (from *rabbi*)—*my master*. It was a greater title than Rabbi, and was never formally conferred except on a few extraordinary doctors of the school of Hillel (John 20:16).

RABMAG—*great prince* (Jer. 39:3, 13). A title borne by Nergal-sharezer, probably identical with the king, called by the Greeks Neriglissar. (See Nergalsharezer.)

RABSARIS. 1. An officer of the king of Assyria (2 Kings 18:17). 2. One of the princes of Nebuchadnezzar (Jer. 39:3, 13).

RABSHAKEH—*head officer* (2 Kings 18, 19; Isa. 36, 37). One of the officers of the king of Assyria sent against Jerusalem in the reign of Hezekiah.

RACA. A word of contempt or scorn, meaning "empty" or worthless (Matt. 5:22).

RACHEL—*ewe*. The younger of the daughters of Laban, the wife of Jacob, and mother of Joseph and Benjamin. The incidents of her life may be found in Gen. 29-33, 35. "Rachel died and was buried in the way to Ephrath, which is Bethlehem. And Jacob set a pillar upon her grave; that is the pillar of Rachel's grave until this day" (Gen. 35:19, 20).

RAHAB, or RACHAB. 1. A celebrated woman of Jericho, who received the spies sent by Joshua to spy out the land, and hid them in her house (Josh. 2:1; Matt. 1:5). 2. A mythological sea-monster (Ps. 89:10; Isa. 51:9).

RAINBOW. The token of the covenant which God made with Noah, that the waters should no more become a flood to destroy all flesh. The right interpretation of Gen. 9:13 seems to be, that God took the rainbow, which had hitherto been but a beautiful object shining in the heavens when the sun's rays fell on falling rain, and consecrated it as the sign of his love and the witness of his promise.

RAM, BATTERING (Ezek. 4:2; 21:22). The battering rams were of several kinds. Some were joined to movable towers which held warriors and armed men. The whole then formed one great temporary building, the top on a level with the walls, and even turrets, of the besieged city.

RAMAH—*height*. 1. One of the cities of the allotment of Benjamin (Josh. 18:25). 2. The home, birthplace, official residence and burial-place of Samuel (1 Sam. 1:1). 3. A fenced city of the tribe of Naphtali (Josh. 19:36). 4. A town near Tyre on the boundary of Asher (Josh. 9:29).

RAMATHLEHI. The name bestowed by Samson on the scene of his slaughter of the thousand Philistines with the jaw-bone (Judg. 15:17).

RAMESES, or RAAMSES. A city and district of Lower Egypt, is first mentioned at the settling by Joseph of his father and brethren in Egypt, where a possession was given them "in the land of Rameses" (Gen. 47:11; Ex. 1:11; Ex. 12:37; Num. 33:3, 5).

RAMOTH, RAMOTH-GILEAD, or RAMATH-MIZPEH—*height*. A famous city in the mountains of Gilead, about 15 miles from Rabbah (Josh. 13:26; 20:8; 1 Kings 22:29). It was appointed for one of the cities of refuge (Deut. 4:43). During the later kings of Israel this place was the occasion of several wars between them and the kings of Damascus (2 Kings 8:28, 29).

RAVEN. From a root signifying *to be black*. A raven was sent out by Noah from the ark (Gen. 8:7). This bird was not allowed as food by the Mosaic law (Lev. 11:15). Ravens were the means, under the Divine command, of supporting the prophet Elijah at the brook Cherith (1 Kings 17:4, 6). They are expressly mentioned as instances of God's protecting love and goodness (Job 38:41; Luke 12:24; Ps. 147:9). The raven's carnivorous habits, and especially his readiness to attack the eye, are alluded to in Prov. 30:17.

REBA. One of the five kings of the Midianites slain by the children of Israel in their avenging expedition when Balaam fell (Num. 31:8; Josh. 13:21).

REBEKAH. Daughter of Bethuel (Gen. 22:23) and sister of Laban, married to Isaac, her father's cousin. She is first presented to us in Gen. 24. For nineteen years she was childless; then after the prayers of Isaac and her journey to inquire of the Lord, Esau and Jacob were born (Gen. 25:19-28).

RECHAB—*rider*. 1. One of two "captains of bands," whom Ishbosheth took into his service, and who conspired to murder him (2 Sam. 4:2). 2. The father or ancestor of Jehonadab (2 Kings 10:15, 23; 1 Chron. 2:55; Jer. 35:6-19). From this Rechab the tribe of the Rechabites derived their name.

RED SEA—*sea of reeds* (Heb. *yam suph*). The sea known to us as the Red Sea was by the Israelites called "the sea." The most important change in the Red Sea has been the drying up of its northern extremity for the distance of fifty miles from its ancient head, "the tongue of the Egyptian Sea."

REED. A plant of the grass family. The bamboo and common cane are species of the reed, and so are the calamus and flag. Fishpoles, canes and rods (Matt. 27:29) are formed of it. These plants flourish in marshes or in the vicinity of water-courses; hence the allusion in Job 40:21-23. Reeds were also used as pens are now, and also as measuring rods.

REFINER. The refiner's art was essential to the working of the precious metals. The separation of the dross from the pure ore was effected by heat and solvents, such as alkali (Isa. 1:25) or lead (Jer. 6:29). The instruments were a crucible or furnace, and a bellows or blowpipe. The workman sat at his work (Mal. 3:3).

REHOBOAM—*the people is enlarged*. Son of Solomon by an Ammonitess, ascended the throne when forty-one years old, and he reigned seventeen years.

REHOBOTH—*room* or *open spaces*. 1. A city of Edom (Gen. 36:37). 2. A well digged by Isaac eastward of Gerar, so called because there the Lord made room for him to dwell (Gen. 26:22).

REMPHAN. A deity, identity uncertain (Acts 7:43).

REPHAIM—*weak; ghosts*. A valley near Jerusalem, fruitful in wheat (Isa. 17:5).

REPHIDIM. A place east of the Red Sea, where the Hebrews tempted God and quarrelled with Moses for want of water (Ex. 17:7, 8).

REUBEN—*behold a son*. Jacob's first-born child (Gen. 29:32), the son of Leah, apparently not born until an unusual interval had elapsed after the marriage. The notices of the patriarch Reuben in the Book of Genesis and the early Jewish traditional literature are unusually frequent and on the whole give a favorable view of his disposition. To him the preservation of Joseph's life appears to have been due. Of the repulsive crime which turned the blessing of his dying father into a curse, we know only the fact (Gen. 35:22). At the time of the migration into Egypt Reuben's sons were four (Gen. 46:9; 1 Chron. v. 3). The census at Mount Sinai (Num. 1:20, 21; 2:11) shows that at the Exodus the numbers of the tribe were 46,500 men above twenty years of age, and fit for active warlike service.

REUEL—*friend of God*. 1. One of the sons of Esau, by Bashemath, sister of Ishmael (Gen. 36:4, 10, 13, 17; 1 Chron. 1:35, 37). 2. One of the names of Moses' father-in-law (Ex. 2:13).

REVELATION OF ST. JOHN. The last book of the New Testament. It is often called the *Apocalypse*, which is its title in Greek, signifying "Revelation." The author is described as a servant of Christ, an eyewitness of the word of God and of the testimony of Christ. John was on the island of Patmos when he received his vision. The book is divided into two main parts: (1) the letters to seven churches in Asia Minor (chaps. 1-3); and (2) a series of prophetic visions setting forth the events of the last days and the final triumph of Christ (chaps. 4-22).

REZIN. 1. King of Damascus. He attacked Ahaz, king of Israel, whose territories he invaded, in company with Pekah, king of Judah (2 Kings 16:5; Isa. 7:1-8). He was attacked, defeated and slain by Tiglath-Pileser II, King of Assyria (2 Kings 16:7-9). 2. The "children of Rezin" were among the Nethinim (Ezra 2:48; Neh. 7:50).

REZON—*prince*. Son of Eliadah, a Syrian, who set up a petty kingdom at Damascus (1 Kings 11:23).

RHEGIUM. An Italian town at the southern

entrance of the Straits of Messina, occurs in the account of Paul's voyage after the shipwreck at Malta (Acts 28:13).

RHODA—*rose.* A maid in the house of Mary the mother of Mark (Acts 12:13).

RHODES. An island off the coast of Asia Minor. Paul touched here on his voyage from Troas to Caesarea (Acts 21:1).

RIBLAH. 1. A place, not clearly defined, on the eastern borders of the promised land (Num. 34: 11). The location of the site is uncertain. 2. A place between Palestine and Babylonia, at which the kings of Babylonia remained while directing the operations of their armies in Palestine and Phoenicia. Here Nebuchadnezzar waited while the sieges of Jerusalem and of Tyre were being conducted (Jer. 39:5, 6; 52:9, 10, 26, 27; 2 Kings 25:6, 20, 21). And here Pharaoh-Necho, after his victory over the Babylonians, summoned Jehoahaz from Jerusalem (2 Kings 23:33).

RIDDLE. The Hebrew word is from an Arabic root meaning "to bend off," "to twist" (Judg. 14:12-19). The riddles which the queen of Sheba came to ask of Solomon (1 Kings 10:1; 2 Chron. 9:1) were rather "hard questions."

RIMMON—*pomegranate.* The name of several towns, probably so called from producing pomegranates. 1. A city of Zebulun (Josh. 19:13). 2. A town in the southern portion of Judah (Josh. 15:3). 3. Rimmon-Parez, the name of a march station in the wilderness (Num. 33:19 f.). 4. Rimmon, the Rock, or inaccessible natural fastness, in which the six hundred Benjamites who escaped the slaughter of Gibeah took refuge (Judg. 20:45, 47; 21:13). 5. Father of Baanah and Rechab, murderers of Ishbosheth (2 Sam. 4:2 ff.).

RIMMON. A Syrian deity in Damascus (2 Kings 5:18).

RING. The ring was regarded as an indispensable article of a Hebrew's attire, as it contained his signet. It was the symbol of authority, and as such was presented by Pharaoh to Joseph (Gen. 41:42), and by Ahasuerus to Haman (Esth. 3: 10). Rings were worn not only by men, but by women (Isa. 3:21). The signet-ring was worn on the right hand (Jer. 22:24).

RIZPAH. Concubine to king Saul, and mother of his two sons Armoni and Mephibosheth. After the death of Saul, Rizpah accompanied the members of the royal family to their new residence at Mahanaim (2 Sam. 3:7). We hear nothing more of Rizpah till the tragic story which has made her one of the most familiar objects in the whole Bible (2 Sam. 21:8-11).

ROE, ROEBUCK. The gazelle was allowed as food (Deut. 12:15, 22, *etc.*); was very fleet of foot (2 Sam. 2:18; 1 Chron. 12:8); was hunted (Isa. 13:14; Prov. 6:5); and was celebrated for its loveliness (Cant. 2:9, 17; 8-14).

ROGELIM. The native place of Barzillai the Gileadite, the exact location being unknown (2 Sam. 17:27; 19:31).

ROLL. A book in ancient times consisted of a a single long strip of paper or parchment, which was usually kept rolled up on a stick. The roll was usually written on one side only, and hence the particular notice of one that was "written within and without" (Ezek. 2:10).

ROMANS, EPISTLE TO THE. Paul had never been at Rome when he wrote this Epistle. It was called forth by his having heard of the difficulties existing between the Jewish and the Gentile members. He controverts many of the errors of both Jews and pagans. Paul probably wrote this letter during a residence of some months at Corinth.

ROME. Little can here be said of "that great

city which reigned over the kings of the earth" (Rev. 17:18). It is not mentioned in the Old Testament. Its name first appears in the Apocrypha. Of course we find it in the New Testament, first in Acts 2:10.

ROSE. It is debated whether the plants so called in the A.V. were the true roses or some other flower. (Cant. 2:1; Isa. 35:1).

ROSH—*head.* A son or grandson of Benjamin (Gen. 46:21).

RUBY. A beautiful gem, whose color is red with an admixture of purple, and is, in its most perfect state, a gem of extreme value. It is mentioned in Job 28:18 and Prov. 8:11; 31:10.

RUE. A plant of strong scent cultivated for its medicinal properties (Luke 11:42).

RUFUS. Mentioned in Mark 15:21, along with Alexander, as a son of Simon the Cyrenian (Luke 23:26). Again, in Rom. 16:13, the apostle Paul salutes a Rufus whom he designates as "elect in the Lord."

RUTH. A Moabitish woman, the wife, first of Mahlon, secondly of Boaz, the ancestress of David and Christ, and one of the four women who are named by Matthew in the genealogy of Christ. The son of Boaz and Ruth, Obed, was the father of Jesse, who was the father of David.

RUTH, BOOK OF. Contains the history of Ruth. The object of the writer is to give an account of David's ancestors, to illustrate the marriage laws of the Israelites, and to enter a plea for racial tolerance. The book was avowedly composed long after the time of the heroine. (See Ruth 1:1; 4:7, 17.)

RYE (Heb. *kussemeth*). It is probable that "spelt" is intended. Spelt is grown in some parts of the south of Germany; it differs but slightly from our common wheat.

SABACHTHANI. "Thou has forsaken me" (Mark 15:35).

SABAOTH. The Lord of hosts. "Hosts" refers to the powers or forces of the universe rather than to human armies (Rom. 9:29; James 5:4).

SABBATH—*to break off; to desist.* God rested on the seventh day and set it apart for himself. Though the *seventh* day to God, to man, who was formed on the evening of the last day, it was the *first,* and was kept as such for ages, and called the seventh part of time (Gen. 2:2, 3).

SABBATH DAY'S JOURNEY. Moses forbade any man to "go out of his place" on that day (Ex. 16:29). In after times the precept was undoubtedly viewed as a permanent law. But as some departure from a man's own place was unavoidable, the distance was fixed at two thousand paces, or about six furlongs from the wall of the city.

SABBATICAL YEAR. The seventh year, in which the land was to have rest (Ex. 23; Lev. 25). It served to remind Israel of the authority and goodness of God, to inculcate humanity, and to give time for devotion and deeds of mercy.

SACKBUT. A stringed musical instrument (Dan. 3:5, 7, 10, 15). The translation is misleading, for "sackbut" was a wind instrument.

SACKCLOTH. A coarse texture, of a dark color, made of goat's hair, worn as an indication of mourning (Isa. 1:3; Rev. 6:12).

SACRIFICE. The justice of God required the death of the offender, but, being tempered with mercy, it accepted a sacrifice in his stead. The giving of the law gave rules both as to the things to be sacrificed and the quantity to be offered, and restricted the priesthood to the family of Aaron. The Hebrews had four sorts of animal sacrifices: 1. Burnt-offering. 2. Sin-offering, or

sacrifice of expiation offered by one who had offended, to whom no part was returned, but the priest had a share (Lev. 4, 5). 3. Peace-offering, a return for favors, to satisfy devotion or to honor God. It was offered as pleasure, and the age or sex of the animal was not designated. Most of the flesh was returned to the offerer, who ate it with his friends (Lev. 3). 4. Trespass-offering, which seems to have been different from the sin-offering, both being required of the leper (Lev. 14). Its character is not fully understood. The perpetual sacrifice was the offering of a lamb every morning at sunrise, and another every evening about twilight. They were burnt as holocausts, but by a small fire, that they might last the longer. With each of these was offered half a pint of wine, half a pint of sweet oil and three pints of fine flour.

SADDUCEES. A sect among the Jews who denied the existence of angels and spirits, the immortality of the soul and the resurrection of the body. They are accused of rejecting all the books of Scripture except the five books of Moses.

SAFFRON. An aromatic herb (Cant. 4:14).

SALAMIS. A city at the east end of the island of Cyprus, and the first place visited by Paul and Barnabas, on the first missionary journey (Acts 13:5).

SALIM, SALEM. A place of which Melchizedek was king (Gen. 14:18; Heb. 7:14). It is possible that Salem was Jerusalem. A place near Aenon where John baptized (John 3:23).

SALMA or SALMON (Ruth 4:20, 21; 1 Chron. 2:11, 51, 54; Matt. 1:4, 5; Luke 3:32). Son of Nahshon, the prince of the children of Judah, and father of Boaz, the husband of Ruth. On the entrance of the Israelites into Canaan, Salmon took Rahab of Jericho to be his wife.

SALMON. A place of unknown location; mentioned in Ps. 68:14, by some thought to be the same as Zalmon (Judg. 9:48). See also Zalmon.

SALMONE. Name of a promontory at the N. E. end of Crete. Mentioned in Paul's voyage to Italy (Acts 27:7).

SALOME. 1. The wife of Zebedee, as appears from comparing Matt. 27:56 with Mark 15:40. It is the opinion that she was the sister of Mary, the mother of Jesus (John 19:25). Salome preferred a request on behalf of her two sons for seats of honor in the kingdom of heaven (Matt. 20:20), she attended at the crucifixion of Jesus (Mark 15:40), and visited his sepulchre (Mark 16:1). 2. The daughter of Herodias by her first husband, Herod Philip (Matt. 14:6).

SALT. Salt was to the Hebrews not only an appetizing condiment in the food both of man (Job 11:6) and beast (Isa. 30:24), and a valuable antidote to the effects of climate on animal food, but also entered largely into their religious services (Lev. 2:13). The associations connected with salt in Eastern countries are important. As one of the most essential articles of diet, it symbolized hospitality, as an antiseptic, durability, fidelity and purity (*cf.* Matt. 5:13; Mark 9:50).

SALT, CITY OF. A town which fell to the tribe of Judah, situated in the wilderness (Josh. 15:62).

SALT, VALLEY OF. A valley in which occurred two memorable victories of the Israelite arms. 1. That of David over the Edomites (2 Sam. 8:13; 1 Chron. 18:12). 2. That of Amaziah (2 Kings 14:7; 2 Chron. 25:11).

SALUTATION. The salutations at meeting in early times were such as "God be gracious unto thee" (Gen. 43:29); "Blessed be thou of the Lord" (Ruth 3:10; 1 Sam. 15:13); "The Lord be with you," "The Lord bless thee" (Ruth 2:4); "The blessing of the Lord be upon you; we bless you in the name of the Lord" (Ps. 129:8).

The Salutation at parting consisted originally of a simple blessing (Gen. 24:60; 28:1; 47:10; Josh. 22:6).

SAMARIA—*look out; watch station.* A celebrated city of Palestine founded by Omri, king of Israel (1 Kings 16:22, 23, 24). It was the metropolis of the northern kingdom, the rival of Jerusalem, and generally the residence of the Israelitish monarchs (1 Kings 29; 20:43; 2 Kings 1:2). The worship of Baal was set up in Samaria by Ahab. Samaria was taken by the Assyrians, after a siege of three years, in the reign of Hoshea (2 Kings 17:5, 6; 18:9, 10). The inhabitants were carried into captivity, and colonists put in their place (17:24; Ezra 4:9, 10).

SAMARITANS. When Sargon the Assyrian king removed many of the ten tribes, he sent in their place Babylonians and other foreigners; these intermarried with the remaining Hebrews, and their descendants were the Samaritans. Between these and the pure Jews there were constant jealousy and hatred (John 4). The name was used by the Jews as a term of the greatest reproach (John 8:48). The Samaritans, like the Jews, lived in the expectation of Messiah, and many of them embraced him when he appeared (John 4; Acts 8:1 and 9:31).

SAMOTHRACIA—*the Tracian.* A small island of the Aegean Sea, about twenty miles in circumference. Paul visited on his voyage from Troas to Neapolis (Acts 16:11).

SAMSON. Son of Manoah, a judge of Israel, of the tribe of Dan. He judged Israel twenty years, and died aged 40. His tremendous strength led to many exploits. These and his tragic end are recorded in Judges 13-16 (*cf.* Heb. 11:32 f.).

SAMUEL—*name of God.* An eminent prophet born at Ramah in the tribe of Ephraim, and from his birth dedicated by his mother to God's service (1 Sam. 3:1). The books of Samuel describe the prophet's life and the history of Israel under Saul and David, covering a period of approximately 100 years.

SANBALLAT—*the moon-god has given life.* A Horonite, possibly a resident of Beth-horon (Neh. 2:10, 19; 13:28). He held apparently some civil or military command in Samaria (Neh. 4:2), and tried unsuccessfully to thwart Nehemiah's plans to rebuild the walls of Jerusalem.

SANDAL. It consisted of a sole attached to the foot by thongs. Sandals were worn by all classes, even by the very poor (Amos 8:6). They were only put on by persons going away from their homes (Isa. 5:27; Eph. 6:15; Ex. 12:11; Josh. 9:5, 13; Acts 12:8); on such occasions they carried an extra pair. During meal-times the feet were uncovered (Luke 7:38; John 13:5, 6). To carry or to unloosen a person's sandal was a menial office (Matt. 3:11; Mark 1:7; John 1:27; Acts 13:25).

SANHEDRIN. The supreme council of the Jewish people in the time of Christ and earlier.

SAPPHIRE. A precious stone of a bright blue color (Ex. 24:10).

SARAH—*princess.* The wife of Abraham, and mother of Isaac. Her name is first introduced in Gen. 11:29. In Gen. 20:12, Abraham speaks of her as "his sister, the daughter of the same father, but not the daughter of the same mother." The common Jewish tradition is, that Sarai is the same as Iscah, the daughter of Haran, and the sister of Lot. She died at Hebron at the age of 127 years, 28 years before her husband, and was buried by him in the cave of Machpelah.

SARDIS. The capital of Lydia, where Croesus reigned. It was destroyed by an earthquake in the reign of Tiberius, but was rebuilt by that emperor's assistance. To the church there, one of the apocalyptic epistles was addressed (Rev. 1:11; 3:1-6).

SARDONYX. A precious stone, consisting of a layer of sard and a layer of onyx (Rev. 21:20).

SARGON—*the king is faithful.* One of the greatest of the Assyrian kings, is mentioned only once in Scripture (Isa. 20:1).

SATAN. The name is Hebrew, and means adversary.

SATYR. The Hebrew word *sair* is usually translated "he goat," but twice given in A.V. as "Satyr," demon or creature whose upper body is that of a man, and lower body that of a goat (Isa. 13:21; 34:14).

SAUL—*asked of Jehovah.* 1. Saul of Rehoboth by the river was one of the early kings of Edom. 2. The first king of Israel was the son of Kish and of the tribe of Benjamin. He was remarkable for his strength and activity (2 Sam. 1:23), and was taller by head and shoulders than the rest of the people. The events in the story of Saul's decline, from his honor as first king of Israel, to his tragic end, are recorded in 1 Sam. 9-31. 3. Saul of Tarsus, the Apostle Paul (Acts 7:58).

SAVIOUR. (See Jesus Christ.)

SCAPEGOAT. (See Atonement, Day of.)

SCORPION. The scorpion is generally two inches in length, and resembles the lobster in form. Some are of a yellow color, others brown and some black. The sting of the scorpion is extremely painful, but seldom fatal in itself to humans (Deut. 8:15; Luke 10:19; 11:12).

SCOURGE. A whip of cords, sometimes knotted, or with pieces of metal tied on. This punishment was very common among the Jews (Deut. 25:1-3). Paul informs us that at five different times he received thirty-nine stripes from the Jews (2 Cor. 11:24). According to the law, punishment by stripes was restricted to forty at one beating (Deut. 25:3). Pilate had Jesus scourged before being crucified (Matt. 27:26).

SCRIBE (Heb. *sopher*, Greek *grammateus*). A word having several significations: 1. A clerk, writer or secretary. 2. A commissary or mustermaster of an army, who reviews the troops, keeps the list or roll, and calls them over. 3. An able and skilful man, a doctor of the law, a man of learning, or one who understands affairs.

SCRIP. The bag in which the shepherds of Palestine carried their food or other necessaries. (1 Sam. 17:40). In the New Testament a wallet used to carry money or bread (*e.g.* Matt. 10:10; Mark 6:8; Luke 9:3).

SCRIPTURES. The Old and New Testaments are called the Scriptures or the Writings, the Bible or the Book, because they far excel all other writings. It is possible that the apostles used this term in designating the Old Testament only.

SCYTHIAN. A nomadic tribe that lived in inner Asia. A fierce and cruel people, their name became a synonym for barbarians (Col. 3:11).

SEA. The Hebrews applied this term to lakes of moderate size, and the modern inhabitants of Palestine still retain the same phraseology. Whenever "Sea" is used without mention or implication of some other body of water, it refers to the Mediterranean (Num. 33:8; 2 Chron. 2:20).

SEA, MOLTEN or BRAZEN. Solomon caused a laver to be cast which from its size was called a sea. It was made partly of brass or copper (1 Kings 7:23-26; 1 Chron. 18:8). It is said to have been capable of containing two thousand or three thousand baths (9,000—13,500 gals). The laver stood on twelve oxen, three toward each quarter of the heavens, and all looking outward. It was mutilated by Ahaz, and finally broken up by the Assyrians (2 Kings 16:14, 17; 25:13).

SEA, THE SALT. The Salt or Dead Sea bears a

variety of names in Scripture, such as the "salt sea," the "sea of the plain" (*i.e.*, of the Arabah), the "east sea" and the "former sea" (*i.e.*, the sea in front). Its length is about forty-six miles, the greatest breadth above ten miles. It takes its name from the fact that there is no exit for the water except evaporation. Hence the water is intensely salty and will not support fish life. It is over 1,200 ft. below sea level.

SEAL. The use of clay in sealing is noticed in the Book of Job (38:14), and the signet ring as part of a man's equipment (Gen. 38:18).

SECUNDUS. A man who accompanied Paul when he took the collection from the churches to Jerusalem (see Acts 20:4).

SEIR—*rough; shaggy.* We have "land of Seir" (Gen. 32:3; 36:30), and "Mount Seir" (Gen. 14:6). It is the original name of the mountain ridge extending from the Dead Sea to the Elanitic Gulf. The name may either have been derived from Seir the Horite, who appears to have been the chief of the original aboriginal inhabitants (Gen. 36:20), or, probably, from the rough aspect of the country.

SELA, SELAH. The capital of Edom, usually identified with Petra, the rock-capital of the Nebataeans.

SELAH—*pause; suspension.* This word occurs seventy-one times in the Psalms, and three times in Habakkuk. It is probably a term which had a meaning in the musical nomenclature of the Hebrews.

SELEUCIA. Near the mouth of the Orontes, was practically the seaport of Antioch. The distance between the two towns was about 16 miles (Acts 13:4).

SEM. Shem the patriarch (Luke 3:36).

SENNACHERIB. The son and successor of Sargon. He mounted the throne (705 B.C.). In his third year he marched against Hezekiah, king of Judah (2 Kings 18:13). Sennacherib reigned 22 years. Adrammelech and Sharezer his sons smote him with the sword (2 Kings 19:37; Isa. 37:38).

SEPHARVAIM. A Babylonian city from whence the king of Assyria deported colonists to Samaria (2 Kings 19:13; Isa. 37:13; *cf.* 2 Kings 18:34).

SEPTUAGINT. The Greek version of the Old Testament owed its origin to the same cause as the Targums. The familiar language of the Jews was Alexandrian Greek. They had settled in Alexandria in large numbers; and hence would arise in time an entire Greek version. The version was made at Alexandria. It was begun in the time of the earlier Ptolemies, and the Pentateuch was translated first.

SEPULCHRE. (See Burial.)

SERAPHIM. An order of celestial beings, whom Isaiah beheld in vision standing above Jehovah as he sat upon his throne (Isa. 6:2).

SERGIUS PAULUS. The proconsul of Cyprus when Paul visited that island with Barnabas on his first missionary tour (Acts 13:7 ff.). He is described as an intelligent man.

SERPENT. The Hebrew word *nahash* is the generic name of any serpent (Gen. 3:1; Matt. 10:16; Ps. 58:4; Prov. 23:32; Ps. 140:3; Job 20:16). The art of taming and charming serpents is of great antiquity. James (3:7) particularizes serpents among all other animals that "have been tamed by man." The serpent-charmer's usual instrument is a flute. It was under the form of a serpent that the devil seduced Eve.

SERUG. Son of Reu, and great-grandfather of Abraham. His age is given in the Hebrew Bible as 230 years (Gen. 11:20).

SERVANT. Among the Hebrews, servants may be divided into: 1. Slaves for life, who were strangers bought or taken in war (Lev. 25:44, *etc.*); 2. Hebrew bond-servants, who could be bound only six years, and then to be dismissed with presents. Slavery was common before the deluge, and some of the patriarchs appear to have owned many.

SETH. The third son of Adam (Gen. 4:25; 5:3; 1 Chron. 1:1).

SHADDAI. An ancient name of God, rendered "Almighty." By the name of El-Shaddai, God was known to the patriarchs (Gen. 17:1; 28:3; 43:14; 48:3; 49:25), before the name Jehovah was revealed (Ex. 6:3).

SHADRACH. Name given to Hananiah, one of Daniel's companions (Dan. 1-3).

SHALLECHETH, THE GATE. One of the gates of the "house of Jehovah" to be built by Solomon after the death of David (1 Chron. 22). It is mentioned only in a list of gatekeepers (1 Chron. 26:16).

SHALLUM—*recompensed* (?). The fifteenth king of Israel, son of Jabesh, conspired against Zechariah, son of Jeroboam II, killed him, and brought the dynasty of Jehu to a close. Shallum, after reigning in Samaria for only a month, was in turn dethroned and killed by Menahem (2 Kings 20:10-14). The name is that of several other men in the Old Testament (*e.g.*, 1 Kings 22:14; 1 Chron. 3:5; Ezra 10:24).

SHALMANESER. The Assyrian king who reigned immediately before Sargon, and immediately after Tiglath-pileser. Soon after his accession he led the forces of Assyria into Palestine, where Hoshea, the last king of Israel, had revolted (2 Kings 17:3).

SHAMGAR. Son of Anath, judge of Israel. With an ox-goad (Judg. 3:31; *cf.* 1 Sam. 13:21) he made a desperate assault upon the Philistines, and slew 600 of them.

SHARON—*a plain.* A beautiful district near Carmel, along the seacoast (Cant. 2:1).

SHAVSHA. Royal or state secretary in the reign of David (1 Chron. 18:16).

SHEARING-HOUSE, THE. A place between Jezreel and Samaria where Jehu encountered forty-two members of the royal family of Judah, whom he slaughtered (2 Kings 10:12, 14).

SHEBA. 1. A son of Joktan (Gen. 10:28; 1 Chron. 1:22). 2. The visit of the queen of Sheba to King Solomon is mentioned (1 Kings 10:1).

SHEBAH. Name of the well near Beer-sheba (Gen. 26:33).

SHECHEM—*the neck and shoulders.* A city of Palestine, called also Sichem (Gen. 12:6), Sychar (Josh. 4:5), and Sychem (Acts 7:16). Was appointed a city of refuge (Josh. 17:7). There the bones of Joseph were buried; and it was the place where Joshua gathered Israel to receive his last instructions (Josh. 24:1-23, 32).

SHEEP (Ex. 20:24; 1 Kings 8:63; 2 Chron. 29:33). Were used in sacrificial offerings. The word frequently used for "sheep" in Hebrew also designated "small cattle."

SHEEP-GATE, THE (Neh. 3:1, 32; 12:39). A gate of Jerusalem rebuilt by Nehemiah.

SHEKEL—*weight.* A Hebrew weight and money (Ex. 30:23, 24; 2 Sam. 14:26). The word is used to denote the weight of anything, as iron, hair, spices, etc. The shekel of gold was half the weight of the silver shekel.

SHEM—*renown.* The eldest son of Noah, born (Gen. 5:32) when his father had attained the age of 500 years. He was 98 years old, married and childless, at the time of the Flood. In the prophecy of Noah (9:25-27) the first blessing falls on Shem. He died at the age of 600 years. The portion of the earth occupied by the descendants of Shem (10:21-31) intersects the portions of Japheth and Ham.

SHEMAIAH—*Jehovah hath heard.* A prophet in the reign of Rehoboam (1 Kings 12:22; 2 Chron. 11:2; 2 Chron. 12:5, 7, 15). The name of 23 other men of the Old Testament.

SHEMIDAITES, THE. Descendants of Shemida, the son of Gilead (Num. 26:32).

SHEMINITH. Denotes a certain air known as the eighth, or a certain key in which the Psalm was to be sung (1 Chron. 15:21; titles of Pss. 6, 12.

SHESHACH. Jeremiah (25:26; 51:41) uses it either for Babylon or for Babylonia.

SHEWBREAD. That which was constantly exhibited in the temple. Twelve loaves, according to the twelve tribes, were every day put upon the golden table, to be exposed for the whole week. This bread was forbidden to be eaten by any except the priests; therefore in the extraordinary case of David nothing but urgent necessity could exempt him from sin (1 Sam. 21:3-7; Matt. 12:4).

SHIBBOLETH—*stream.* A test-word used by Jephthah to trap the Ephraimites (Judg. 12:6).

SHIELD. The ordinary shield consisted of a framework of wood covered with leather. It was frequently cased with metal, and was worn on the left arm, to which it was attached by a strap.

SHILOH (Gen. 49:10). The meaning of the word is "peaceable" or "pacific," and the allusion is either to Solomon, or to the expected Messiah, who in Isa. 9:6 is called the Prince of Peace.

SHILOH. A city of Ephraim. It was one of the earliest and most sacred of the Hebrew sanctuaries. The ark of the covenant was kept at Shiloh from the last day of Joshua to the time of Samuel (Josh. 18:10; Judg. 18:31; 1 Sam. 4:3).

SHIMEI. 1. Son of Gershon the son of Levi, called *Shimi* in Ex. 6:17, 2. Shimei, a Benjamite of the house of Saul (2 Sam. 16:5-13; 2 Sam. 19:18; 1 Kings 2:36, 37). 3. One of the adherents of Solomon, at the time of Adonijah's usurpation (1 Kings 1:8).

SHINAR. The ancient name of the tract through which the Tigris and Euphrates pass, known as Chaldaea or Babylonia. It was a country where brick had to be used for stone, and slime for mortar (Gen. 11:3).

SHIP. The rig of an ancient ship was more simple and clumsy than that of modern times. Its great feature was one large mast, with one large square sail fastened to a yard of great length. Hence the strain upon the hull, and the danger of starting the planks. In the Old Testament the mast is mentioned (Isa. 33:23); and from Ezra 27:5 we learn that cedar wood from Lebanon was used for this part of ships. In Ezra 27:29 oars are distinctly mentioned; and it seems that oak wood from Bashan was used in making them.

SHISHAK. King of Egypt, the Sheshonk I. of the monuments. "He took the fenced cities which pertained to Judah, and came to Jerusalem" (1 Kings 14:25, 26; 2 Chron. 12:2-9).

SHITTAH TREE, SHITTIM (Heb. *shittah*). Some species of *Acacia.* The *Acacia Seyal* yields gum arabic, which is obtained by incisions in the bark.

SHOSHANNIM (Ps. 45, 69). Indicates the melody "after" or "in the manner of" which the Psalms were to be sung.

SHUHITE—*descendant of Shuah* (*Judah's father-in-law*). In the Book of Job as the epithet of Bildad.

SHUNAMMITE, THE—*native of Shunem.* Is applied to two persons: Abishag, the nurse of King David (1 Kings 1:3, 15; 2:17, 21, 22), and the nameless hostess of Elisha (2 Kings 4:12, 25, 36).

SHUR—*wall.* First mentioned in the narrative of Hagar's flight from Sarah (Gen. 16:7). Shur was probably the last Arabian town before entering Egypt.

SIDDIM, THE VALE OF (Gen. 14:3, 8, 10). In this valley the kings of the five allied cities of Sodom, Gomorrah, Admah, Zeboim and Bela awaited the approach of the invaders.

SIDON. The Greek form of the Phoenician name Zidon (*e.g.*, Matt. 11:21; Mark 3:8; Luke 4:26).

SIHON—*abrush.* King of the Amorites when Israel arrived on the borders of the Promised Land (Num. 21:21).

SILAS. An eminent member of the early Christian church, called Silvanus in Paul's Epistles. He first appears as one of the leaders of the church at Jerusalem (Acts 15:22, 32). He appears to have been a Roman citizen (Acts 16:37).

SILLA. The scene of the murder of King Joash (2 Kings 12:20). Where Silla was is entirely a matter of conjecture.

SILOAM. A fountain rising at the foot of Mount Zion. Its waters were received into two large pools, and whatever overflowed from the lower one passed into the brook Kedron. The upper pool was called the "King's Pool," because his gardens were watered from it. From these pools the Jews drew water on the last day of the feast of tabernacles, which they brought into the city singing portions of Isa. 12. Near this place stood the tower of which Christ speaks (Luke 13:4).

SILVER (Gen. 20:16; 1 Pet. 1:18; Acts 3:4; 20:33). It does not appear to have been in use before the Deluge. But in Abraham's time traffic was carried on with it (Gen. 23:2, 15).

SILVERLINGS. Probably ingots of shekel-weight of silver (Isa. 7:23).

SIMEON—*heard.* 1. The second son of Jacob (Gen. 29:33). 2. An aged saint who embraced the infant Jesus (Luke 2:25-34). 3. A Christian minister of Antioch (Acts 13:1).

SIMON. 1. *Simon the Brother of Jesus.*—The only undoubted notice of this Simon occurs in Matt. 13:55; Mark 6:3. 2. *Simon the Canaanite.*—One of the twelve apostles (Matt. 10:4; Mark 3:18), otherwise described as Simon Zelotes (Luke 6:15; Acts 1:13). 3. *Simon of Cyrene.*—A Hellenistic Jew who was present at Jerusalem at the time of the crucifixion of Jesus (Matt. 27:32; Mark 15:21; Luke 23:26). 4. *Simon the Leper.*—A resident at Bethany, distinguished as "the leper" (Matt. 26:6; Mark 14:3). It is not improbable that he had been miraculously cured by Jesus. 5. *Simon magus.*—In the apostolic age distinguished as a sorcerer or "magician" (Acts 8:9). 6. *Simon Peter.*—(See *Peter*). 7. *Simon.*—A Pharisee, in whose house a penitent woman anointed the head and feet of Jesus (Luke 7:40). 8. *Simon the Tanner.*—A Christian convert living at Joppa, at whose house Peter lodged (Acts 9:43). 9. *Simon.*—The father of Judas Iscariot (John 6:71; 13:2, 26).

SINA, MOUNT. The Greek form of *Sinai* (Acts 7:30, 38).

SINAI—*meaning uncertain.* The mountain on which Jehovah appeared to Moses and gave the law. The Hebrews came to this place in the third month of their pilgrimage. This mount stands in Arabia Petraea, and is called by the Arabs *Jibbil Mousa,* or the Mountain of Moses, and sometimes *El Tor,* or The Mount. It has two summits, *Horeb* at the north and *Sinai* at the south; which last is much the higher, and is called the *Mount of God.* The ascent is very steep, and is by steps, which the Empress Helena, the mother of Constantine the Great, caused to be cut in the rock.

SINIM—*unidentified land.* A people (Isa. 49:12) living at the extremity of the known world.

SION, MOUNT. 1. One of the various names of Mount Hermon (Deut. 4:48 only). 2. The Greek form of the Hebrew name *Zion,* the famous Mount of the Temple.

SIRAH, THE WELL OF. From which Abner was recalled by Joab to his death at Hebron (2 Sam. 3:26, only).

SISERA. Captain of the army of Jabin, king of Canaan, who reigned in Hazor, killed by Joel (see Judg. 4, 5).

SITNAH—*hostility.* The second of the two wells dug by Isaac in the valley of Gerar (Gen. 26:21).

SLIME. Was used by the builders of Babel instead of mortar (Gen. 11:3). It is called in the Septuagint version *asphaltos,* and is bitumen or a kind of pitch.

SLING. An instrument much used in war before the invention of firearms. It was a formidable weapon in hands like those of David and the Benjamites (Judg. 20:16; 1 Sam. 17:48-50).

SMYRNA (Rev. 2:8-11). Was founded by Alexander the Great, and was situated twenty stadii from the city of the same name, which after a long series of wars with the Lydians had been finally taken and sacked by Halyattes.

SNAIL. One of the unclean animals (Lev. 11:30).

SNOW. The snow lies deep in the ravines of the highest ridge of Lebanon until the summer is far advanced, and indeed never wholly disappears; the summit of Hermon also perpetually glistens with frozen snow.

SODOM. One of the five cities of the Canaanites—the others were Gomorrah, Admah, Zeboim, and Zoar (Gen. 19:24). In the days of Abraham these had each a king. The Dead Sea is supposed by many to cover the site of these cities (Jude 7).

SODOMITES. This word is employed for those who practiced as a religious rite the abominable and unnatural vice from which the inhabitants of Sodom and Gomorrah have derived their lasting infamy. It occurs in Deut. 23:17.

SOLOMON—*peaceful; pacific.* He was the child of David's old age, the last born of all his sons (1 Chron. 3:5). He was taught all that priests, or Levites, or prophets had to teach; he was furnished for the kingly calling (Ps. 78:70, 71), and Solomon found himself, by his father's death, the sole occupant of the kingdom of Israel, one of the great monarchies of the East. Solomon reigned 40 years (1 Kings 11:42); some of the main historical events being the commencement of the Temple in the 4th, its completion in the 11th year of his reign (1 Kings 6:1); the commencement of his own palace in the 7th, its completion in the 20th year (1 Kings 7:1; 2 Chron. 8:1); the conquest of Hamath-Zobah, and the foundation of cities in the region north of Palestine (2 Chron. 8:1-6). He was noted also for the extensive commerce and diplomatic relations he carried on with foreign nations. He is perhaps best known for his wisdom.

SOLOMON'S SERVANTS (Ezra 2:56, 58; Neh.

7:57, 60). Were the descendants of the Canaanites, and compelled to labor in the king's stone-quarries, and in building his palaces and cities (1 Kings 5:13, 14; 9:20).

SOPATER. One of the companions of Paul on his return from Greece into Asia (Acts 20:4).

SOREK, THE VALLEY OF. A wady in which lay the residence of Delilah (Judg. 16:4).

SOSTHENES. Was a Jew at Corinth, who was seized and beaten in the presence of Gallio (see Acts 18:12-17).

SOWER, SOWING. The sower held the vessel containing the seed in his left hand, while with his right he scattered the seed broadcast (Ps. 126). In wet soils the seed was trodden in by the feet of animals (Isa. 32:20). The Mosaic law prohibited the sowing of mixed seed (Lev. 19:19; Deut. 22:9).

SPAIN. Paul intended to visit this country, but whether he did so or not is uncertain (Rom. 15:24-28).

SPARROW. The English tree sparrow is perhaps the exact species referred to in Ps. 84:3.

SPEARMEN. A military term. Two hundred were in the contingent guarding Paul when he was transferred to Caesarea (Acts 23:23).

SPICE, SPICES. The words refer to sweet aromatic odors, the principal of which was that of the balsam or balm of Gilead. The balm of Gilead tree grows in some parts of Arabia and Africa, and is seldom more than fifteen feet high. The balsam is chiefly obtained from incisions in the bark, but the substance is procured also from the green and ripe berries.

SPIKENARD. By this was meant a highly aromatic plant growing in the Indies, from whence was made the very valuable extract, or unguent, or favorite perfume used at the ancient baths and feasts. It is mentioned by St. Mark (14:3) and John (12:3).

SPINNING. The references to spinning in the Bible are few. Prov. 31:19 implies the use of the instruments in vogue at the present day in some areas of the near East.

SPONGE. The porous substance that grows in sea water (Matt. 27:48; Mark 15:36; John 19:29).

STACTE. One of the sweet spices which composed the holy incense (see Ex. 30:34).

STEEL. In all cases where the word "steel" occurs in the A.V. the true rendering of the Hebrew is "copper."

STEPHANAS. A Christian convert of Corinth, whose household Paul baptized as the "first fruits of Achaia" (1 Cor. 1:16; 16:15).

STEPHEN. *Crowned.* The first Christian martyr, was the chief of the seven appointed to rectify the complaints in the early church of Jerusalem, made by the Hellenistic against the Hebrew Christians. He was arrested at the instigation of the Hellenistic Jews, and brought before the Sanhedrin. His speech in his defense, and his execution by stoning outside the gates of Jerusalem, are related at length in the Acts (7). One of the prominent leaders in the bloody work was a young man from Tarsus, the future "apostle of the Gentiles." (See Paul.)

STOCKS. A wooden frame in which the feet, hands and neck of a person were so fastened that his body was held bent (Jer. 20:2, 3; 29:26). In Job 13:27, 33:11, it signifies stocks like ours in which the feet alone were confined. And such were the "stocks" of Acts 16:24. But the sufferer might be tortured in these by having his legs drawn far apart.

STOICS. The Stoic school was founded by Zeno of Citium (*cir.* 280 B.C.) and derived its name from the painted "portico" (*stoa*) in which he taught. The morality of Stoicism is essentially based on pride, that of Christianity on humility; the one upholds individual independence, the other absolute faith in another; the one looks for consolation in the issue of fate, the other in Providence; the one is limited by periods of cosmical ruin, the other is consummated in a personal resurrection (Acts 17:18).

STORK (Heb. *hasidah*). The White Stork is one of the most conspicuous of land birds, standing nearly four feet high, the jet black of its wings and its bright red beak and legs contrasting finely with the pure white of its plumage (Zech. 5:9). It devours readily all kinds of offal and garbage. The Black Stork is less abundant. Both species are very numerous in Palestine.

STRAW. The ancient Egyptians reaped their corn close to the ear, and afterward cut the straw close to the ground. This was the straw that Pharaoh refused to give to the Israelites. (Ex. 5:7 ff.)

STREET. Streets were generally narrow, even in the best towns. The street called "Straight" in Damascus (Acts 9:11) was an exception to the rule of narrowness; it was 100 feet wide. That streets occasionally had names appears from Jer. 37:21; Acts 9:11.

SUCCOTH—*booths.* An ancient town, in the account of the homeward journey of Jacob from Padanaram (Gen. 33:17). Jacob there put up "booths" (*Succoth*) for his cattle, as well as a house for himself.

SUCCOTH-BENOTH. An idol or image introduced into Samaria by the Babylonians (2 Kings 17:30).

SUSANNA. One of the women who ministered to the Lord (Luke 8:3).

SWALLOW. Two different Hebrew words are translated "swallow" in the A.V.: (1) *deror* in Ps. 84:3 and Prov. 26:2; and (2) *agur* in Isa. 38:14 and Jer. 8:7. The Hebrew words *sus* and *sis* are translated in the A.V. by "crane," but should more correctly be called "swallow."

SWAN. An unclean aquatic bird (Lev. 11:18; Deut. 14:16). The Hebrew terms so translated possibly means the pelican.

SWEAT, BLOODY. One of the physical phenomena attending our Lord's agony in the Garden of Gethsemane is described by Luke (22:44).

SWINE. The flesh of swine was forbidden as food by the Levitical law (Lev. 11:7; Deut. 14:8) as food which did not fulfill the definition of a "clean animal."

SYCAMINE TREE. The sycamine (Luke 17:6) is distinct from the sycamore of the same evangelist (19:4). The sycamine is the mulberry tree.

SYCAMORE. A tree having fruit like to the fig. The tree abounded in Palestine (1 Kings 10:27).

SYCHAR. A place named only in John 4:5. It is specified as "a city of Samaria called Sychar, near the ground which Jacob gave to Joseph his son; and there was the well of Jacob."

SYENE. Once an important city of Egypt (Ezek. 29:10). It is now called *Aswan.*

SYNAGOGUE. The place where the Jews met to pray, to read and to hear the reading of the Holy Scriptures, and other instruction. Synagogues began to be used about the time of Ezra, and kept up a knowledge of God among the people. There was a council of reverend and

wise persons, versed in the law, who had the care of all things belonging to the service of the synagogue and the management of certain judicial affairs. Over these was set a president, called the "ruler of the synagogue" (Luke 8:41). Our Saviour and his apostles from the synagogues proclaimed the good news from heaven (Luke 4:20).

SYRACUSE. The celebrated city on the eastern coast of Sicily. Paul arrived thither in an Alexandrian ship from Melita on his voyage to Rome (Acts 28:12).

SYRIA, or ARAM. The Syrians descended from Aram, and possessed Mesopotamia, Chaldaea, and part of Armenia. Good soil and noble rivers rendered it a delightful country. It was divided into various provinces which derived their names from their chief cities, situation, or circumstance. *Syria of Damascus* was a province stretching eastward, of which Damascus was the capital. *Syria of Rehob* was that part of which Rehob was the metropolis, and bordered on Palestine. *Syria of Maachah* lay beyond Jordan, and was given to Manasseh. *Tob*, or *Ishtob*, was a province in the neighborhood of Libanus. *Syria* stands for the whole kingdom of Syria, of which Antioch became the capital after the reign of the Selucidae. Perhaps Tyre and Sidon, along with Damascus and Antioch, are the best-known Syrian cities.

SYROPHOENICIAN. The identification of a woman in Mark 7:26. The word denoted possibly a mixed race, although this is questioned. Matthew (15:22). speaks of "a woman of Canaan" in place of Mark's "Syrophoenician," on the same ground that the Septuagint translates Canaan by Phoenicia.

TAANACH. An ancient Canaanitish city. Taanach is always mentioned with Megiddo, and they were evidently the chief towns of the western portion of the great plain of Esdraelon (Josh. 12:21; 1 Kings 4:12). It is still called *Taannuk*.

TABERNACLE. The tent or temporary building in which the Israelites performed religious exercises in the wilderness. It was called "the tabernacle of the congregation" (Ex. 33:7). Here, till the building of the Temple, was kept the ark of the covenant (Ex. 26:1; Heb. 9:2, 3). A curtain divided it into two apartments. Within the *Holy Place* stood the altar of incense, the candlestick, and the table of shewbread. Within the *Holy of Holies* was the ark of the covenant, with its mercy-seat and overshadowing cherubim. The tabernacle was a splendid and costly structure, but having been removed often, it became entirely worn out by the time Solomon's Temple was ready. It stood in a court enclosed by curtains eight feet high, sustained by fifty-six pillars. Within this area stood the tabernacle at the west end, and the altar of burnt offering, brazen laver, etc., at the east end.

TABITHA. The Syrian name of a Christian woman called in Greek Dorcas, who lived at Joppa. She was raised from the dead by Peter (Acts 9:36 ff.).

TABLE. The table mostly in use in early times was probably a circular piece of leather spread on the floor, on which the food is laid, while those who partake sit round with their legs crossed.

TABOR. 1. A conical mountain in Galilee (Josh. 19:12, 22) about eighteen hundred feet high, on top of which is a beautiful plain about a mile in circumference. From the top is one of the most delightful prospects in the world (Judg. 4:6, 8). 2. A city given by the Zebulonites to the Levites of Merari's family (1 Chron. 6:77), and the name of a place near Bethel (1 Sam. 10:3).

TADMOR. A city built in the wilderness by Solomon (1 Kings 9:19).

TAHPENES. An Egyptian queen, wife of the Pharaoh who received Hadad the Edomite, and who gave him her sister in marriage (1 Kings 11:18-20).

TAHPANHES. The Jews in Jeremiah's time fled to this town on the frontier of Egypt (Jer. 44:1).

TAMAR—*palm tree.* 1. An unidentified place in the vision of Ezekiel (47:19; 48:28). It marked the eastern end, at the Dead Sea, of the southern boundary of the land to be inherited by the twelve tribes. 2. The wife successively of the two sons of Judah, Er and Onan (Gen. 38:6-30). The family were on the point of extinction. Er and Onan had successively perished suddenly. Judah's wife Bathshuah died; and there only remained a child Shelah, whom Judah was unwilling to trust with Tamar, lest he should meet with the same fate as his brothers. Accordingly she resorted to the desperate expedient of entrapping the father. The fruits of this intercourse were twins, *Pharez* and *Zarah*, and through Pharez the sacred line was continued. 3. Daughter of David and sister of Absalom (2 Sam. 13:1-32; 1 Chron. 3:9). 4 Daughter of Absalom (2 Sam. 14:7; 1 Kings 15:2).

TAMMUZ. Properly "the Tammuz" (Ezek. 8:14). He was a Babylonian deity, similar to the Greek god Adonis and the Egyptian Osiris.

TAPHATH. The daughter of Solomon, who was married to Ben-abinadab (1 Kings 4:11).

TAPPUAH—*apple.* 1. A city of Judah (Josh. 12:17; 15:34). 2. A place on the boundary of the "children of Joseph" (Josh. 16:8; 17:8). Its full name was probably En-tappuah (17:7).

TARES. There are four species of tares in Palestine. The most common, and undoubtedly the kind referred to in Matt. 13:24-30, is the Bearded Darnel. This weed is difficult to distinguish from growing wheat until it ripens. The seeds when eaten cause sickness and even death.

TARSHISH, or TARSUS. Several places were called by this name, viz.: 1. Tarsus in Cilicia, the capital of that country and birthplace of Paul (Acts 9:11; 21:39; 22:3). 2. Tartessus, in Spain, not far from the famous city of Granada (Ps. 72:10). 3. A place on the east of Africa, not far from Ophir (1 Kings 10:22).

TARTAK. One of the gods of the Avite colonists of Samaria (2 King 17:31), worshiped under the form of an ass.

TARTAN (2 Kings 18:17 and Isa. 20:1). Probably an official designation.

TAXING. Two distinct registrations, or taxings, are mentioned by Luke. The first is as the result of an edict of the Emperor Augustus, that "all the world (*i.e.*, the Roman Empire) should be taxed" (Luke 2:1). The second (Acts 5:37 is associated with the revolt of Judas of Galilee.

TEKOA and TEKOAH. 1. A town in the tribe of Judah (2 Chron. 11:6). The "wise woman," whom Joab employed to effect a reconciliation between David and Absalom, was obtained from this place (2 Sam. 14:2). Tekoa is chiefly memorable as the birthplace of the prophet Amos (Amos 7:14).

TELEM—*oppression.* 1. A porter or doorkeeper of the Temple in the time of Ezra (Ezra 10:24; Neh. 12:25). 2. A town of Judah near the southern border (Josh. 15:24).

TEMAN—*on the right; south.* A son of Eliphaz, son of Esau by Adah (Gen. 36:11, 15, 42; 1 Chron. 1:36, 53).

TEMPLE. Sometimes applied to the tabernacle (1 Sam. 1:9; Ps. 18:6), and sometimes the temple itself is called tabernacle (2 Chron. 1:5). David and his princes contributed one hundred and eight thousand talents of gold; one million and

seventeen thousand talents of silver—which together amounted to forty-six thousand tons' weight of gold and silver. About one hundred and eighty-four thousand six hundred men were employed seven years in building it. It was erected on Mount Moriah, and was dedicated with solemn prayer by Solomon during seven days of sacred fasting, and by a peace-offering of twenty thousand oxen and one hundred and twenty thousand sheep, to consume which the holy fire came down anew from heaven. Shishak carried off its treasures (1 Kings 14:25, 26). Jehoiada and Joash repaired it, and soon after, Joash gave its treasures to Hazael, king of Syria (2 Kings 12:4, 5). Ahaz stripped it to hire the assistance of Assyria (2 Chron. 28). Hezekiah repaired it and made vessels for it, but in the fourteenth year of his reign was obliged to take from it much of its wealth to give to Sennacherib (2 Kings 18). Nebuchadnezzar carried the sacred vessels to Babylon, and at last entirely demolished it (Jer. 52:12-23). Cyrus ordered it rebuilt, which was done under the direction of Zerubbabel. The second temple having stood more than five hundred years, and being greatly out of repair, Herod the Great, about 20-19 B.C., began to rebuild it anew. In nine years he finished the principal parts of it; but forty-six years after, when Jesus had begun his public ministry, it was not quite finished. Though almost a new edifice, it retained the name of *Second Temple.* It was more glorious than the original temple (Hag. 2:9), because honored with the presence and ministry of Christ. It was burnt and entirely destroyed by the Roman army under Titus. A Mohammedan mosque now stands on the very spot.

TENT. A portable abode, invented by Jubal before the Flood. Mankind for centuries lived in tents, as those do to this day whose pastoral or migratory habits cause frequent removals. The word *tent* is synonymous with *tabernacle* in the A.V. of the Old Testament. The most famous tentmaker is Paul (Acts 18:3).

TEN COMMANDMENTS. The popular name is not that of Scripture. There we have the "*Ten Words,*" the "*Covenant,*" or, very often, the "*Testimony.*" The term "Commandments" had come into use in the time of Christ (Luke 18:20) Their division into *Two Tables* is not only expressly mentioned, but the stress laid upon the *two* leaves no doubt that the distinction was important, and that it answered to that summary of the law which was made both by Moses and by Christ into two precepts; the *First Table* contained *Duties to God,* and the *Second, Duties to Our Neighbor.*

TERAH. 1. The father of Abram, Nahor and Haran. and through them the ancestor of the Israelites, Ishmaelites, Midianites, Moabites, and Ammonites (Gen. 11:24-32). He was an idolater (Josh. 24:2), he dwelt in Ur of the Chaldees (Gen. 11:28), and with his son Abram, his daughter-in-law Sarai and his grandson Lot came into Haran (Gen. 11:31). "The days of Terah were two hundred and five years; and Terah died in Haran" (Gen. 11:32). 2. A camp of the Israelites in the desert (Num. 33:27, 28). The site is not known.

TERAPHIM—*household images.* Only in plural, images connected with magical rites. In one case a single statue seems to be intended by the plural (1 Sam. 19:13, 16).

TERTIUS. Was the amanuensis of Paul in writing the Epistle to the Romans (Rom. 16:22).

TERTULLUS. "A certain orator" (Acts 24:1) who was retained by the high priest and Sanhedrin to accuse the Apostle Paul at Caesarea before the Roman Procurator Antonius Felix. He evidently belonged to the class of professional orators.

TESTAMENT, NEW. (See New Testament; Bible.)

TESTAMENT, OLD. (See Old Testament; Bible.)

TETRARCH—*ruler of fourth part.* The governor of the fourth part of a country. The term was also used for the ruler of a small or minor area.

THADDAEUS. A name in Matthew's and Mark's catalogue of the twelve apostles (Matt. 10:3; Mark 3:18) in the great majority of MSS. It is possible that the three names of Judah, Lebbaeus, and Thaddaeus were borne by one and the same person.

THANKOFFERING, or **PEACE OFFERING.** The properly eucharistic offering among the Jews, in theory resembling the *Meat-offering.* Its ceremonial is described in Lev. 3. The only constantly recurring peace-offering appears to have been that of the two firstling lambs at Pentecost (Lev. 23:19).

THEATRE. The *place* where dramatic performances are exhibited, and also the *scene* or *spectacle* witnessed there. It occurs in Acts 19:39. It was in the theatre at Caesarea that Herod Agrippa I was struck with death (Acts 12:21-23), according to the Jewish historian Josephus.

THEBEZ—*brightness* (?). A place memorable for the death of Abimelech (Judg. 9:50; 2 Sam. 11:21). There it still is, its name *Tubas,* hardly changed.

THEOPHILUS—*loved of God.* The person to whom Luke inscribes his Gospel and the Acts of the Apostles (Luke 1:3; Acts 1:1).

THESSALONIANS. The title of two epistles written to the church at Thessalonica, which was planted by Paul (Acts 17). The first epistle is generally admitted to have been the earliest of Paul's letters. He enjoined it to be read to all the adjacent churches (5:27). His object seems to have been to confirm them in the faith and to excite their piety. The second epistle, written soon after the first, commends their faith and charity, rectifies their mistake in supposing that the day of judgment was at hand, and admonishes them of certain irregularities.

THEUDAS. The name of an insurgent mentioned in Gamaliel's speech before the Jewish council (Acts 5:35-39) at the time of the arraignment of the Apostles.

THOMAS. One of the twelve apostles (Matt. 10:3; Mark 3:18; Luke 6:15), also called *Didymus,* "the twin" (John 20:24). We know little of his history; he seems to have been of singular temperament, occasionally overcome by a dark and morbid melancholy. He was also wayward and slow of belief (John 11:16; 14:5; 20:20-29). It is supposed he was actively engaged in propagating the gospel in India.

THORNS AND THISTLES. There appear to be eighteen or twenty Hebrew words which point to different kinds of prickly or thorny shrubs. These words are variously rendered "thorns," "briers," "thistles," etc. In relation to the "crown of thorns" (Matt. 27:29), it was probably composed of the pliant, thorny twigs of the *nebk* (*Zizyphus Spina Christi*), being common everywhere.

THREE TAVERNS. A station on the Appian Road along which Paul traveled from Puteoli to Rome (Acts 28:15).

THRONE. The Hebrew word, so translated, applies to any elevated seat occupied by a person in authority, whether a high priest (1 Sam. 1:9), a judge (Ps. 122:5), or a military chief (Jer. 1:15). Solomon's throne was approached by six steps (1 Kings 10:19; 2 Chron. 9:18), and was furnished with arms or "stays."

THUNDER. Hardly ever heard in Palestine from the middle of April to the middle of September (Job 37:2, 4, 5; 40:9). Thunderstorms are frequent, however, during the winter season.

THYATIRA. A city of the province of Lydia, in Asia Minor, now known as *Akhisar* (Acts 16:14). It is situated between Sardis and Pergamos, and was the site of one of the seven churches of Asia to which John wrote (Rev. 1:11).

TIBERIAS. A city in the time of Christ, on the Sea of Galilee; first mentioned in the New Testament (John 6:1, 23; 21:1), and then by Josephus, who states that it was built by Herod Antipas, and was named by him in honor of the Emperor Tiberius.

TIBERIAS, THE SEA OF (John 21:1). (See Gennesaret, Sea of.)

TIBERIUS. The second Roman Emperor, successor of Augustus, who began to reign A.D. 14, and reigned until A.D. 37 (Luke 3:1). He was the son of Tiberius Claudius Nero and Livia, and hence a stepson of Augustus. He was born at Rome on the 16th of November, 45 B.C. He became emperor in his 55th year. He was despotic in his government, cruel and vindictive in his disposition. Tiberius died A.D. 37, at the age of 78, after a reign of 23 years. He is the Caesar of the Gospels (Matt. 22:17; Mark 12:14; Luke 20:22; John 19:12).

TIBNI. After Zimri, king of Israel, had burnt himself in his palace, half of the people followed Tibni the son of Ginath, and half followed Omri (1 Kings 16:21, 22). Omri was the choice of the army. The struggle between the contending factions lasted four years. (*cf.* 1 Kings 16:15, 23).

TIDAL. Mentioned only in Gen. 14:1, 9. He is called "king of nations."

TIGLATHPILESER. The Assyrian king mentioned in the Scripture as having come in contact with the Israelites. He is the "Pul" who took tribute from Menahem, king of Israel (2 Kings 15:19). He attacked Samaria in the reign of Pekah (2 Kings 15:29). He marched against Damascus, which he took (2 Kings 16:9), razing it to the ground, and killing Rezin, the Damascene monarch. After this he proceeded to chastise Pekah, carrying into captivity "the Reubenites, the Gadites and the half tribe of Manasseh" (1 Chron. 5:26). Ahaz, king of Judah, paid tribute to him (2 Kings 16:8).

TIGRIS. Equivalent of the Hebrew *Hiddekel.* The Tigris rises from two principal sources in the Armenian mountains, and flows into the Euphrates. Its length is reckoned at 1,146 miles. It appears under the name of Hiddekel, among the rivers of Eden (Gen. 2:14).

TIMNAH—*lot; portion.* One of the landmarks of the allotment of Judah (Josh. 15:10). The scene of the adventure of Judah with his daughter-in-law Tamar (Gen. 38:12, 13, 14).

TIMON. One of the seven elected to serve tables (Acts 6:1-6).

TIMOTHY—*honorer of God,* or *TIMOTHEUS.* He was a native of Lystra. His father was a Greek, but his grandmother and mother, being pious Jewish women, trained him up in the knowledge of the Scriptures (Acts 16:1). He was the recipient of two New Testament epistles which bear his name.

TIN. Among the metals found among the spoils of the Midianites, tin is enumerated (Num. 31:22). It was known to the Hebrew metal workers as an alloy of other metals (Isa. 1:25; Ezek. 22:18, 20).

TIPHSAH—*ford.* 1. Mentioned in 1 Kings 4:24 as the limit of Solomon's empire toward the Euphrates. 2. A town near Tirzah taken by Menahem after he seized the throne of the Northern Kingdom from Shallum (2 Kings 15:16).

TIRAS. The youngest son of Japheth (Gen. 10:2), usually identified with the Thracians.

TIRE. An ornamental head-dress worn on festive occasions (Ezek. 24:17, 23).

TIRHAKAH. King of Ethiopia (Cush), the opponent of Sennacherib (2 Kings 19:9; Isa. 37:9).

TIRSHATHA (always written with the article). The title of the governor of Judaea under the Persians, added as a title after the name of Nehemiah (Neh. 8:9; 10:1). It is rendered "governor."

TIRZAH—*pleasure.* 1. An ancient Canaanite city (Josh. 12:24). 2. One of the daughters of Zelophehad (Num. 26:33; Josh. 17:3).

TISHBITE, THE. The well-known designation of Elijah (1 Kings 17:1; 21:17, 28; 2 Kings 1:3, 8; 9:36). The commentators and lexicographers, with few exceptions, adopt the name "Tishbite" as referring to the place *Thisbe* in Naphtali.

TITHES—*tenths.* The early practice of giving a tenth of income to religious purposes seems to have been by divine institution. Abram gave to Melchizedek, the Lord's priest, the tenth of his spoils taken in battle (Gen. 14:20). Jacob dedicated to God the tenth of his gain (Gen. 28:22). The Levites paid to the priests the tithe of what they received from the people (Deut. 14:28). The Pharisees, however, tithed their mint, anise, cummin, and rue, but neglected weightier things, as mercy, judgment, and faith, and therefore incurred divine condemnation (Deut. 14:22-29; Num. 18:20; Matt. 23:23).

TITTLE. A minute mark used in writing to show accents or to distinguish one Hebrew letter from another (see Matt. 5:18).

TITUS. A Gentile, and one of Paul's early converts. Of the time, place, or manner of his death we have no certain account. Tradition says he lived to the age of ninety-four years, and was buried in Crete, where he had been left by Paul (Tit. 1:5). The Epistle to Titus is eminently valuable for its elucidations of the nature of various duties.

TOB, THE LAND OF—*land of good.* A place in which Jephthah took refuge when expelled from home by his half-brother (Judg. 11:3).

TOBIAH—*Jehovah is good.* 1. "Tobiah the slave, the Ammonite," played a conspicuous part in the opposition made to the rebuilding of Jerusalem. Though a slave (Neh. 2:10, 19), unless this is a title of opprobrium, and an Ammonite, he found means to ally himself with a priestly family, and his son Johanan married the daughter of Meshullam the son of Berechiah (Neh. 6:18). 2. The name of a family of returned exiles that could not trace their geneology (Ezra 20:6; Neh. 7:62).

TOGARMAH. A son of Gomer, and brother of Ashkenaz and Riphath (Gen. 10:3). Togarmah, as a geographical term, is connected with Armenia (Ezek. 27:14).

TOLA—*crimson worm.* 1. The first-born of Issachar, and ancestor of the Tolaites (Gen. 46:13; Num. 26:23; 1 Chron. 7:1, 2). 2. Judge of Israel after Abimelech (Judg. 10:1, 2). Tola judged Israel for twenty-three years at Sahmir in Mount Ephraim, where he died and was buried.

TOMBS. (See Burial.)

TONGUES, GIFT OF. Promised by our Lord to his disciples (Mark 16:17), and fulfilled on the day of Pentecost, when cloven tongues like fire sat upon the disciples, and "every man heard them speak in his own language."

TOPAZ. The topaz of the ancient Greeks and Romans is generally allowed to be our chrysolite.

It is so soft as to lose its polish unless worn with care.

TOPHETH, and once **TOPHET**. It was in the southeast extremity of the "Valley of the Son of Hinnom" (Jer. 7:31; 19:2; 2 Kings 23:10). (See *Hinnom.*) It seems also to have been part of the king's gardens, and watered by Siloam. The name Tophet has been variously translated.

TORTOISE (Heb. *tsab*). The *tsab* occurs only in Lev. 11:29, as the name of some unclean animal. The Hebrew word may be identified with a large kind of lizard.

TOWER. Watch-towers, or fortified posts in frontier or exposed situations, are mentioned in Scripture, as the tower of Edar (Gen. 25:21), the tower of Lebanon (2 Sam. 8:6; Isa. 5:2; Matt. 21:33; Mark 12:1).

TOWN CLERK. The title ascribed to the magistrate at Ephesus who appeased the mob in the theatre (Acts 19:35). The original service of this class of men was to record the law and decrees of the state, and to read them in public.

TRANCE. This word occurs twice in the Old Testament (Num. 24:4, 16), and in both instances is supplied by the translators. It refers to a state of religious ecstasy or rapture (Acts 10:10).

TREES. Scripture mentions the palm, shittah, bay, cedar, chestnut, almond, willow, cypress, pine, ebony, almug, or algum, oak, teil, apple, ash, elm, juniper, box, fir, oil olive, citron, balsam, pomegranate, fig, sycamore, sycamine, poplar, thyine, and mulberry. Trees in Palestine generally put forth their foliage in the month of January, when the old leaves of many trees are not fallen off. The first blossoms are those of the almond tree.

TRIAL. 1. The trial of Jesus before Pilate was, in a legal sense, a trial for the offense *laesae majestatis;* one which would be punishable with death (Luke 23:2, 38; John 19:12, 15). 2. The trials of the apostles, of Stephen and of Paul, before the high priest, were conducted according to Jewish rules (Acts 4; 5:27; 6:12; 22:30; 33:1). 3. The trial, if it may be so called, of Paul and Silas at Philippi was held before the duumviri, on the charge of innovation in religion—a crime punishable with banishment or death (Acts 16:19, 22). 4. The interrupted trial of Paul before the Proconsul Gallio was an attempt made by the Jews to establish a charge of the same kind (Acts 18:12-17). 5. The trials of Paul at Caesarea (Acts 24; 25; 26) were conducted according to Roman rules of judicature.

TRIBUTE. The tribute (money) mentioned in Matt. 17:24, 25 was the half shekel (=half stater= two drachmae), applied to defray the general expenses of the temple. This must not be confounded with tribute paid to the Roman emperor (Matt. 22:17).

TROAS. The city from which Paul first sailed, to carry the gospel from Asia to Europe (Acts 16:8, 11). It was first built by Antigonus, afterward embellished by Lysimachus, and named Alexandria Troas. Under the Romans it was one of the most important towns of the province of Asia. The modern name is Eskistanbul.

TROGYLLIUM. The rocky extremity extending into the sea opposite Samos (Acts 20:15).

TRUMPETS, FEAST OF (Num. 29:1; Lev. 23:24). The feast of the new moon, which fell on the first of Tishri. It was one of the seven days of Holy Convocation. "A day of blowing of trumpets." The opinion of Jews and Christians is that it was the festival of the New Year's Day of the civil year.

TRYPHENA and **TRYPHOSA**. Two Christian women at Rome, enumerated in the conclusion of Paul's letter (Rom. 16:12).

TUBAL. Reckoned with Javan and Meshech among the sons of Japheth (Gen. 10:2; 1 Chron. 1:5).

TUBAL-CAIN. The son of Lamech the Cainite by his wife Zillah (Gen. 4:22).

TURTLE, TURTLE-DOVE. The harbinger of spring (Cant. 2:12). It is frequently referred to as a substitute for the pigeon in sacrifice (*e.g.,* Gen. 15:9; Lev. 5:7).

TYCHICUS and **TROPHIMUS**. Companions of Paul on some of his journeys, mentioned as natives of Asia (Acts 20:4).

TYRANNUS. A man in whose school Paul taught the gospel for two years, during his sojourn at Ephesus (see Acts 19:9).

TYRE. An ancient city, possessing astonishing enterprise and wealth (Isa. 23:8). With Sidon it was the most famous of Phoenician cities. It was a fortified city in the time of Joshua (Josh. 19:29). During the time of Solomon the king of Tyre helped in the building of the Temple (1 Kings 9:10-14; 2 Chron. 2:3-16).

ULAI. Mentioned by Daniel (8:2, 16). It has been generally identified with the Eulaeus, a large stream near to Susa.

UNCLEAN MEATS. These were things strangled, or dead of themselves or through beasts or birds of prey; whatever beast did not both part the hoof and chew the cud; and certain other smaller animals rated as "creeping things"; certain classes of birds mentioned in Lev. 11 and Deut. 14, twenty or twenty-one in all; whatever in the waters had not both fins and scales; whatever winged insect had not besides four legs the two hind legs for leaping; besides things offered in sacrifice to idols; and all blood or whatever contained it, save perhaps the blood of fish, as would appear from that only of beast and bird being forbidden (Lev. 7:26), and therefore flesh cut from the live animal; as also all fat, at any rate that disposed in masses among the intestines, and probably wherever discernible and separable among the flesh (Lev. 3:14-17; 7:23). The eating of blood was prohibited even to "the stranger that sojourneth among you" (Lev. 17:10, 12, 13, 14).

UNDERGIRD. The ship in which Paul sailed to Italy is said to have been undergirded (Acts 27:17); that is, some turns of a cable were passed round the hull.

UR—*flame; light*. The land of Haran's nativity (Gen. 11:28), the place from which Terah and Abraham started "to go into the land of Canaan" (Gen. 11:31). It is called in Genesis "Ur of the Chaldaeans," while in the Acts Stephen places it, by implication, in Mesopotamia (7:2, 4).

URBANE. Christian disciple, whom Paul salutes in writing to Rome (Rom. 16:9).

URIAH—*Jehovah is light*. One of the thirty commanders of David (1 Chron. 11:41; 2 Sam. 23:39). He was a foreigner—a Hittite. He married Bathsheba, a woman of extraordinary beauty, a daughter of Eliam. The circumstances of his death may be found in 2 Sam. 11:14-17.

URIEL—*my light is El*. 1. A Kohathite Levite, son of Tahath (1 Chron. 6:24; 15:5, 11). 2. Maternal grandfather of Abijah (2 Chron. 13:2).

URIJAH. 1. Urijah the priest in the reign of Ahaz (2 Kings 16:10), probably the same as *Uriah.* 2. The son of Shemaiah of Kirjath-jearim. He prophesied in the days of Jehoiakim, and the king sought to put him to death; but he escaped, and fled into Egypt. His retreat was soon discovered; and Jehoiakim slew him with the sword, and cast his body forth among the graves of the common people (Jer. 26:20-23).

URIM and THUMMIM—*lights and perfections.* A method of inquiring of God. We are told that "the Urim and the Thummim" were to be on Aaron's heart when he goes in before the Lord (Ex. 28:15-30; Num. 27:21). In the blessing of Moses they appear as the crowning glory of the tribe of Levi (Deut. 33:8, 9). In what way the Urim and Thummim were consulted is quite uncertain. But it seems to be simplest (1 Sam. 14:3, 18, 19; 23:2, 4, 9, 11, 12; 28:6; Judg. 20:28; 2 Sam. 5:23; *etc.*) to suppose that the answer was given by the word of the Lord to the high priest (*cf.* John 11:51), when he had inquired of the Lord clothed with the ephod and breastplate.

USURY. Among the Jews, meant the customary price paid for the use of money. As the Jews had very little concern in trade, and only borrowed in cases of necessity, and as their system was calculated to establish every man's inheritance to his own family, they were prohibited to take usury from their brethren of Israel (Ex. 22:25; Lev. 25:35-37). They were allowed to lend money upon usury to strangers (Deut. 23:20).

UZ. The country in which Job lived (Job 1:1).

UZZA, THE GARDEN OF. The spot in which Manasseh, king of Judah, and his son Amon, were both buried (2 Kings 21:18, 26).

UZZAH, or **UZZA**. One of the sons of Abinadab, in whose house at Kirjath-jearim the ark rested for twenty years. He aided in David's removal of the ark to Jerusalem. "At the threshing floor of Nachon" (2 Sam. 6:6), or Chidon (1 Chron. 13:9), perhaps slipping over the smooth rock, the oxen stumbled. Uzzah caught the ark to prevent its falling. The profanation was punished by his instant death.

UZZIAH—*my strength is Jehovah*. King of Judah. After the murder of Amaziah, his son Uzziah was chosen by the people to occupy the vacant throne; and for the greater part of his long reign of fifty-two years he lived in the fear of God, and showed himself a wise, active, and pious ruler (2 Kings 15; 2 Chron. 26). Uzziah waged numerous victorious wars. He strengthened the walls of Jerusalem. He never deserted the worship of the true God, and was much influenced by Zechariah, a prophet who is only mentioned in connection with him (2 Chron. 26:5). The end of Uzziah was less prosperous than his beginning. Elated with his splendid career, he determined to burn incense on the altar of God, but was opposed by the high priest Azariah and eighty others. The king was enraged at their resistance, and as he pressed forward with his censer, was smitten with leprosy.

UZZIEL—*God is strong*. 1. Fourth son of Kohath, and uncle to Aaron (Ex. 6:18, 22; Lev. 10:4). 2. A Simeonite who went against the Amalekites at Seir (1 Chron. 4:42). 3. Founder of a Benjamite family (1 Chron. 7:7). 4. A musician, of the sons of Heman (1 Chron. 25:4). 5. A Levite of the sons of Jeduthun (2 Chron. 29:14). 6. A goldsmith who helped rebuild the wall of Jerusalem (Neh. 3:8).

UZZIELITES, THE. The descendants of Uzziel, one of the four great families of the Kohathites (Num. 3:27; 1 Chron. 26:23).

VASHTI. The "queen" of Ahasuerus, who, for refusing to show herself to the king's guests at the royal banquet, when sent for by the king, was repudiated and deposed (Esth. 1).

VEIL AND VAIL. Both words are used in the A.V. for an article of dress (Gen. 24:65; Cant. 5:7) and a part of the tabernacle and the temple (Ex. 26:31; Matt. 27:51).

VERSIONS, ENGLISH. 1. *Wycliffe* (B. 1324; D. 1384)—The New Testament was translated by Wycliffe himself. The Old Testament was undertaken by Nicholas de Hereford, with the help of Wycliffe. It is probable that the work of

Wycliffe and Hereford was revised by Richard Purvey, circa A.D. 1388. 2. *Tyndal*—The work of Wycliffe stands by itself. With Tyndal we enter on a continuous succession. He is the patriarch, in no remote ancestry, of the Authorized Version. More than Cranmer or Ridley he is the true hero of the English Reformation. He prepared himself for the work by long years of labor in Greek and Hebrew. In 1525 the whole of the New Testament was printed at Cologne, and at Worms. In England it was received with denunciations. 3. *Coverdale*—The complete translation of the Bible in English to be printed, bearing the name of Miles Coverdale, printed at Zurich, appeared in 1535. The undertaking itself, and the choice of Coverdale as the translator, were probably due to Cromwell. He was content to make the translation at second hand "out of the Douche (Luther's German Version) and the Latine." 4. *Matthew*—In the year 1537 a large folio Bible appeared as edited and dedicated to the king, by Thomas Matthew. The tradition which connects this Matthew with John Rogers, the protomartyr of the Marian persecution, is all but undisputed. A copy was ordered, by royal proclamation, to be set up in every church, the cost being divided between the clergy and the parishioners. This was, therefore, the first Authorized Version. 5. *Traverner* (1539)—The boldness of the pseudo-Matthew had frightened the ecclesiastical world from its propriety. Coverdale's Version was, however, too inaccurate to keep its ground. It was necessary to find another editor, and the printers applied to Richard Taverner. He had a reputation for scholarship, and this is confirmed by the character of his translation. 6. *Cranmer*—In the same year as Taverner's and coming from the same press appeared an English Bible, with a preface containing the initials, T.C., which imply the archbishop's sanction. It was reprinted again and again, and was the authorized version of the English Church until 1568—the interval of Mary's reign excepted. 7. *Geneva*—The exiles who fled to Geneva in the reign of Mary entered on the work of translation with more vigor than ever. The New Testament, translated by Whittingham, was printed in 1557, and the whole Bible in 1560. It was the first English Bible which entirely omitted the Apocrypha. The notes were characteristically Swiss. 8. *The Bishop's Bible*—Eight bishops, together with some deans and professors, brought out a magnificent folio (1568 and 1572). It was avowedly based on Cranmer's; but of all the English versions it had probably the least success. 9. *Rheims and Douay*—The English Catholic refugees who were settled at Rheims undertook a new English version. The New Testament was published at Rheims in 1582, and professed to be based on "the authentic text of the Vulgate." The work of translation was completed somewhat later by the publication of the Old Testament at Douay in 1609. 10. *Authorized Version*—Among the demands of the Puritan representatives at the Hampton Court Conference in 1604 was one for a new or at least a revised translation. In 1606 the work of a new translation was accordingly commenced. It was entrusted to fifty-four scholars, but the actual work was done by forty-seven, divided into six groups. The work began in 1607 and was completed in just under three years. The new version was published in 1611 and has remained the most often used of all English translations. 11. *Revised Version*—The revision of the Authorized Version was undertaken in consequence of a resolution passed by both houses of the Convocation of the Province of Canterbury. The Revised Version of the New Testament was first published in May, 1881, and was the joint work of American and foreign scholars. The Revised Version of the Old Testament, which was the work of the same committee, was published in July, 1884. 12. *Other Revisions*—As new manuscripts are discovered, and advances in language study made, further revisions and new translations have been made, and in all likelihood will continue, in an effort to give greater understanding of the Bible to those unable to read and study it in its original languages.

VILLAGE. This word is often used to imply unwalled suburbs outside the walled towns. (See Lev. 25:29-31; 1 Sam. 6:18.)

VINE. One of the most prominent productions of Canaan. Noah planted a vineyard (Gen. 9: 20) and the chief butler dreamed of a vine (Gen. 40:9). Judah was noted for the fruits of the vine (Num. 13:23 f.). The references to vine and vineyard are many throughout Scripture. Christ spoke of himself as the true vine (John 15:1-5).

VINEYARD. The vineyard was prepared with great care, the stones being gathered out, a secure fence made round it, and a scaffold or high summer-house built in the center, where, as the fruit ripened, a watchman was stationed, and where there was always shelter for the workmen at their meals, and a suitable place to keep the tools (Isa. 5:1-7; Matt. 21:33).

VIPER (Job 20:16; Matt. 3:7; *etc.*). A serpent famed for the venomousness of its bite, not specifically identified. So terrible was the nature of these creatures that they were thought to be sent as executors of divine vengeance (Acts 28).

VOW. A sacred promise made to God to leave off some sin or to perform some duty (Gen. 28: 20). The Mosaic law gave distinct rules for their execution. The vows of children were not valid except ratified by parents (Num. 30); nor those of a wife except known and unforbidden by the husband.

VUGATE, THE. The Latin version of the Bible. The name is equivalent to *Vulgata editio* (the current text of Holy Scripture). During the first two centuries the churches of Rome and Gaul were essentially Greek, but the church of North Africa seems to have been Latin-speaking from the first. This version was known by the name of the *Old Latin (Vetus Latina)*. In A.D. 383 Jerome, at the request of Damasus, the pope, undertook a revision of the current Latin version of the New Testament. He next proceeded to revise the Old Testament from the Septuagint. He commenced his task by a revision of the Psalter. This revision obtained the name of the *Roman Psalter*. Subsequently Jerome undertook a still more important work—namely, the translation of the Old Testament from the Hebrew. The books of Samuel and Kings were issued first, and the whole work was completed in A.D. 404.

WAGES. In Egypt money payments by way of wages were in use, but the terms cannot now be ascertained (Ex. 2:9). The only mention of the rate of wages in Scripture is found in the parable of the householder and the vineyard (Matt. 20:2), where the laborers' wages are set at one denarius per day. The law was very strict in requiring daily payments of wages (Lev. 19: 13; Deut. 24:14, 15), and the iniquity of withholding wages is denounced (Jer. 22:13; Mal. 3:5; James 5:4).

WALLS. Only a few points need be noticed. 1. The practice common in Palestine of carrying foundations down to the solid rock (*cf* Luke 6:48). 2. A feature of some parts of Solomon's buildings of encrusting or veneering a wall of brick or stone with slabs of a more costly material, as marble or alabaster.

WAR. The treatment of the conquered was extremely severe in ancient times. The bodies of the soldiers killed in action were plundered; the survivors were either killed in some savage manner, mutilated, or carried into captivity. The conquerors celebrated their success by the erection of monumental stones, by hanging up trophies in their public buildings, and by triumphal songs and dances in which the whole population took part.

WATCHES OF NIGHT. The Jews, like the Greeks and Romans, divided the night into military watches, each watch representing the period of which sentinels or pickets remained on duty. There were three watches, the first, the middle, and the morning watch. These would last from sunset to 10 P.M.; from 10 P.M. to 2 A.M., and from 2 A.M. to sunrise. Subsequently the number of watches was increased to four, described by the terms "even, midnight, cock-crowing, and morning" (Mark 13:35). These terminated respectively at 9 P.M., midnight, and 3 A.M.

WAVE-OFFERING. This rite, together with that of "heaving" or "raising" the offering, was an inseparable accompaniment of peace-offerings (Ex. 29:24, 28; Lev. 7:30, 34; 8:27). It signified the portion of the sacrifice that was offered to God but given to the priests.

WEAVING. We find it practiced with great skill by the Egyptians at a very early period. The "vestures of fine linen" such as Joseph wore (Gen. 41:42) were the product of Egyptian looms. The Israelites were probably acquainted with the process before their sojourn in Egypt; but it was undoubtedly there that they attained the proficiency which enabled them to execute the hangings of the Tabernacle (Ex. 35:35; 1 Chron. 4:21), and other artistic textures.

WEEK. There can be no doubt about the great antiquity of measuring time by a period of seven days (Gen. 8:10; 29:27). The week and the Sabbath are as old as man himself. Two of the great feasts—the Passover and the Feast of Tabernacles—are prolonged for seven days after that of their initiation (*e.g.*, Ex. 12:15-20).

WEIGHTS and MEASURES. Knowledge of the Hebrew system of weights and measures is imperfect, but gradually scholars are clarifying and refining our understanding as new information is uncovered. Part of the complication results from the influence upon the Hebrews of the systems in use in neighboring countries.

WELL. The supply of water (Judg. 1:15) has always involved among Eastern nations questions of property of the highest importance. Thus the well Beersheba was opened, and its possession attested with special formality by Abraham (Gen. 21:30, 31). To acquire wells was one of the marks of favor foretold to the Hebrews on their entrance into Canaan (Deut. 6:11). To possess one is noticed as a mark of independence (Prov. 5:15), and to abstain from the use of wells belonging to others, a disclaimer of interference with their property (Num. 20:17, 19; 21:22).

WIDOW. Under the Mosaic dispensation no legal provision was made for the maintenance of widows. They were left dependent partly on the affection of relations, and partly on a participation in the triennial third tithe (Deut. 14:19; 26:12), in leasing (Deut. 24:19-21), and in religious feasts (Deut. 16:11, 14). With regard to the remarriage of widows, the only restriction imposed by the Mosaic law had reference to the contingency of being left childless, in which case the brother of the deceased husband had a right to marry the widow (Deut. 25:5, 6; Matt. 22: 23-30).

WILDERNESS. 1. A tract of land not cultivated, but not wholly barren or desert (Joel 1:20). Such commonly derived their name from the chief city adjacent, as *Diblah, Engedi, Judea*. Ishmael settled in the wilderness of Paran, and David took refuge from the persecution of Saul in the same; in which the numerous flocks of Nabal the Carmelite were pastured. Such places, therefore, were not deserts. The land of Canaan was environed with wildernesses. We read of those of *Egypt, Etham, Shur, Sin, Sinai, Tadmor*, etc. The forty years' wandering of the Hebrews was in a wilderness indeed, and by no means the common thoroughfare of travelers between Egypt and Canaan. The reason why Israel was turned into it we read in Num. 14:2. 2. The word is metaphorically used to signify things barren or unattractive. Hence God asks the He-

brews if he had been a *wilderness* to them (Jer. 2:31).

WILLOWS. Mentioned in Lev. 23:40; Job 40:22; Isa. 44:4; Ps. 137:2. These references have in common the characteristic that willows grow by watercourses.

WILLS. Under a system of close inheritance like that of the Jews, the scope for bequest in respect of land was limited by the right of redemption and general re-entry in the Jubilee year. The case of houses in walled towns was different, and there can be no doubt that they must, in fact, have frequently been bequeathed by will (Lev. 25:30). Two instances are recorded in the Old Testament under the Law, of testamentary disposition (2 Sam. 17:23; 2 Kings 20:1; Isa. 38:1.

WINE. Noah was probably the first who preserved the juice of the grape till by fermentation it became proper wine (Gen. 9:20 ff.). Before him men only ate grapes like other fruit, or drank the juice as just pressed from the fruit. This mode of drinking was common in the days of Joseph (Gen. 40:11). The Jews, after settling in Canaan, used wine of various sorts, of which the red seems to have been most esteemed (Prov. 23:31; Isa. 27:2; Rev. 14:20). The "mixed wine" (Prov. 23:30), rendered in Isa. 65:11 "drink offering," may mean wine rendered more potent by the addition of myrrh and other drugs, or of *defrutum*—that is, wine inspissated by boiling it down. Thus the drunkard is properly described as one that seeketh *mixed wine* (Prov. 23:30) and "*mingles* strong drink." Such wine was given to malefactors before their execution as an act of mercy, and was offered to Christ on the cross, but refused, as he desired no stupefaction.

WINE-PRESS. The wine-presses of the Jews consisted of two receptacles or vats, in the upper one of which the grapes were trodden, while the lower one received the expressed juice. The two vats are mentioned together only in Joel 3:13. "The press is full; the vats overflow"—the upper vat being full of fruit, the lower one overflowing with the must. The two vats were usually hewn out of solid rock (Isa. 5:2; Matt. 21:33). Ancient wine-presses, so contructed, are still to be seen in Palestine.

WITNESS. Two witnesses at least are required to establish a charge which justified a capital sentence (Deut. 17:6; 19:15; Num. 35:30). In the case of the suspected wife, evidence besides the husband's was desired. The witness who withheld the truth was censured. False witness was punished with the punishment due to the offense which it sought to establish (Deut. 19: 16 ff.). Slanderous reports and officious witness are discouraged, and false witness (Ex. 20:16). The witnesses were the first executioners (Deut. 17: 7; *cf.* Acts 7:58). In case of an animal left in charge and torn by wild beasts, the keeper was to bring the carcass in proof of the fact and disproof of his own criminality.

WOLF. There can be little doubt that the wolf of Palestine was the common *Canis lupus*, and that this is the animal so frequently mentioned in the Bible.

WOMEN. The position of women in the Hebrew commonwealth contrasts favorably with that which in the present day is assigned to them generally in Eastern countries. Instead of being immured in a harem or appearing in public with the face covered, the wives and maidens of ancient times mingled freely and openly with the other sex in the duties and amenities of ordinary life. Rebekah traveled on a camel with her face unveiled, until she came into the presence of her affianced (Gen. 24:64, 65). Jacob saluted Rachel with a kiss in the presence of the shepherds (Gen. 29:11). The odes of Deborah (Judg. 5) and of Hannah (1 Sam. 2:1, *etc.*) exhibit a degree of intellectual cultivation which is in itself a proof of the position of the sex in that period. Women also occasionally held

public offices, particularly that of prophetess or inspired teacher (Ex. 15:20; 2 Kings 22:14; Neh. 6:14; Luke 2:36; Judg. 4:4). The management of household affairs devolved mainly on the women.

WOOLEN, LINEN AND. The Israelites were forbidden to wear a garment mingled of woolen and linen (Lev. 19:19; Deut. 22:11).

WORMWOOD. Occurs frequently in the Bible, and generally in a metaphorical sense, as in Deut. 29:18, "Lest there be among you a root that beareth wormwood" (see also Prov. 5:4). In Jer. 9: 15; 23:13; Lam. 3:15, 19, wormwood is symbolical of bitter calamity and sorrow. The Orientals typified sorrows, cruelties, and calamities of any kind by plants of a poisonous or bitter nature (Rev. 8:11).

WRITING. Writing is first distinctly mentioned in Ex. 17:14, and the connection clearly implies that it was not then employed for the first time, but was so familiar as to be used for historical records. Moses is commanded to preserve the memory of Amalek's onslaught in the desert by committing it to writing. The tables of the testimony are said to have been "written by the finger of God" (Ex. 31:18), on both sides, and "the writing was the writing of God, graven upon the tables" (Ex. 32:16). The engraving of the gems of the high priest's breast-plate with the names of the children of Israel (Ex. 28:11), and the inscription upon the mitre (Ex. 39:30) have to do more with the art of the engraver than of the writer, but both imply the existence of alphabetic characters. The curses against the adulteress were written by the priest in a book and blotted out with water (Num. 5:23). In Isa. 29:11, 12, there is clearly a distinction drawn between the man who was able to read and the man who was not, and it seems a natural inference that the accomplishments of reading and writing were not widely spread among the people. In the name of Kirjath-Sepher (Josh. 15:15) there is an indication of a knowledge of writing among the Phoenicians. The Hebrews, then a branch of the great Semitic family, being in possession of the art of writing, according to their own historical records, at a very early period, the further questions arise, what character they made use of, and whence they obtained it? Recent investigations have shown that the square Hebrew character is a comparatively modern date, and has been formed from a more ancient type by a gradual process of development. What then was this ancient type? Most probably the Phoenician. To the Phoenicians, the daring seamen and adventurous colonizers of the ancient world, tradition has assigned the honor of the invention of letters.

XERXES. A Persian king. This monarch is not mentioned in Scripture by the name by which he was known to the Greeks. But there can hardly be a doubt that he was the Ahasuerus of Ezra 4:6 and of the book of Esther.

YEAR. The highest ordinary division of time. Two years were known to, and apparently used by, the Hebrews. The older was the lunar year, containing 12 lunar months and 354 days. Later a solar year of 365 days was adopted, though the months were lunar. To reconcile the lunar and solar calendars, a thirteenth month was added to seven of the years out of every nineteen.

YOKE. 1. A well-known implement of husbandry, frequently used metaphorically for *subjection* (*e.g.*, 1 Kings 12:4, 9-11; Isa. 9:4; Jer. 5:5); hence an "iron yoke" represents an unusually galling bondage (Deut. 28:48; Jer. 28:13 f.). The yoke of Jesus to be taken by his followers is easy (Matt. 11:29 f.). 2. A pair of oxen so termed as being yoked together (1 Sam. 11:7; 1 Kings 19:19, 21). 3. The term is also applied to a certain amount of land (1 Sam. 14:14), equivalent to that which a couple of oxen could plough in a day.

ZAANAIM, THE PLAIN OF. More accurately, "the oak by Zaanaim," a tree—probably a sacred tree—mentioned as marking the spot near which Heber the Kenite was encamped when Sisera took refuge in his tent (Judg. 4:11).

ZAAVAN, or ZAVAN. A Horite chief, son of Ezer the son of Seir (Gen. 36:27; 1 Chron. 1:42).

ZABAD—*He has given.* 1. A son of Nathan, of the tribe of Judah (1 Chron. 2:36 f.; 1 Chron. 11:41). 2. A descendant of Ephraim (1 Chron. 7:21). 3. Son of Shimeath, one of the murderers of Joash (2 Chron. 24:26; called Jozacar in 2 Kings 12:21). 4. Three men, of the same name, of the time of Ezra who had married foreign wives (Ezra 10:27, 33, 43).

ZABUD—*given.* Son of Nathan (1 Kings 4:5), is described as priest (A.V. "principal officer"), and as holding at the court of Solomon the confidential post of "king's friend."

ZABULON. The Greek form of the name *Zebulun* (Matt. 4:13, 15; Rev. 7:8).

ZACCHAEUS—*pure.* A tax collector near Jericho, who, being short in stature, climbed up into a sycamore tree, in order to obtain a sight of Jesus as he passed through that place (Luke 19:1-10).

ZACHARIAH—*Jehovah remembers.* 1. Or properly *Zechariah*, was son of Jeroboam II, fourteenth king of Israel, and the last of the house of Jehu. His reign lasted only six months. He was killed in a conspiracy, of which Shallum was the head (2 Kings 14:29; 15:8, 11). 2. The father of Abi, or Abijah, Hezekiah's mother (2 Kings 18:2).

ZACHARIAS. 1. Father of John the Baptist (Luke 1:5, etc.; 3:2). (See *John the Baptist*.) 2. Son of Barachias, who, our Lord says, was slain by the Jews between the altar and the temple (Matt. 23:35; Luke 11:51).

ZADOK—*righteous.* Son of Ahitub, and one of the two chief priests in the time of David, Abiathar being the other (2 Sam. 8:17). Zadok was of the house of Eleazar, the son of Aaron (1 Chron. 24:3), and eleventh in descent from Aaron (1 Chron. 12:28). He joined David at Hebron after Saul's death (1 Chron. 12:28), and henceforth his fidelity to David was inviolable. When Absalom revolted, and David fled from Jerusalem, Zadok and all the Levites bearing the Ark accompanied him, and it was only at the king's express command that they returned to Jerusalem, and became the medium of communication between the king and Hushai the Archite (2 Sam. 15:17). When Absalom was dead, Zadok and Abiathar were the persons who persuaded the elders of Judah to invite David to return (2 Sam. 19:11). When Adonijah, in David's old age, set up for king, and had persuaded Joab and Abiathar the priest to join his party, Zadok was unmoved, and was employed by David to anoint Solomon to be king in his room (1 Kings 1). And for this fidelity he was rewarded by Solomon, who "thrust out Abiathar from being priest unto the Lord," and "put in Zadok the priest" in his room (1 Kings 2:27, 35). From this time, however, we hear little of him. It is said in general terms, in the enumeration of Solomon's officers of state, that Zadok was the priest (1 Kings 4:4; 1 Chron. 29:22), but no single act of his is mentioned.

ZAIR. A place named in 2 Kings 8:21 only, in the account of Joram's expedition against the Edomites. The parallel account in Chronicles (2 Chron. 21:9) agrees with this, except that the words "to Zair" are omitted.

ZALAPH. Father of Hanun, who assisted in rebuilding the city wall (Neh. 3:30).

ZALMON—*dark colored.* 1. An Ahohite, one of David's guard (2 Sam. 23:28). 2. A wooded hill

in the immediate neighborhood of Shechem (Judg. 9:48). 3. See Salmon.

ZALMONAH. A desert station of the Israelites (Num. 33:41), lies on the east side of Edom. Location unknown.

ZALMUNNA. (See *Zebah*.)

ZAMZUMMIMS. The Ammonite name for the people, who, by others, were called *Rephaim* (Deut. 2:20 only). They are described as having originally been a powerful and numerous nation of giants.

ZANOAH. 1. A town of Judah in the Shephelah or plain (Josh. 15:34; Neh. 3:13; 11:30). 2. A town of Judah in the highland district (Josh. 15:56).

ZAPHNATH-PAANEAH—*the God speaks, and he lives*. A name given by Pharaoh to Joseph (Gen. 41:45).

ZAPHON. A place mentioned in the enumeration of the allotment of the tribe of Gad (Josh. 13:27).

ZARED, THE VALLEY OF. (See Zered.)

ZAREPHATH. The residence of the prophet Elijah during the latter part of the drought (1 Kings 17:9, 10).

ZARETAN, Zarthan (Josh. 3:16).

ZARETH-SHAHAR. A place mentioned only in Josh. 13:19, in the catalogue of the towns allotted to Reuben.

ZARHITES, THE. A branch of the tribe of Judah, descended from Zerah the son of Judah (Num. 26:13, 20; Josh. 7:17; 1 Chron. 27:11, 13).

ZARTANAH (1 Kings 4:12). (See Zarthan.)

ZARTHAN. 1. A place in the circle of Jordan, mentioned in connection with Succoth (1 Kings 7:46). 2. It is also named in the account of the passage of the Jordan by the Israelites (Josh. 3:16), where the A.V. has Zaretan. 3. A place with the similar name of Zartanah (1 Kings 4:12). 4. Further, Zeredathah (in 2 Chron. 4:17 only), in specifying the situation of the foundries for the brass-work of Solomon's Temple, is substituted for Zarthan; and this again is not impossibly identical with the Zererath of the story of Gideon (Judg. 7:22).

ZEBAH and ZALMUNNA. The two "kings" of Midian who commanded the great invasion of Palestine, and who finally fell by the hand of Gideon himself (Judg. 8:5-21; Ps. 83:11).

ZEBAIM. Mentioned in the catalogue of the families of "Solomon's slaves," who returned from the captivity with Zerubbabel (Ezra 2:57; Neh. 7:59).

ZEBEDEE—*Jehovah has given*. A fisherman of Galilee, the father of the apostles James the Great and John (Matt. 4:21), and the husband of Salome (Matt. 27:56; Mark 15:40).

ZEBOIM—*hyena* (?) 1. One of the five cities of the "plain" or circle of Jordan (Gen. 10:19; 14:2, 8; Deut. 29:23). 2. THE VALLEY OF ZEBOIM, a ravine or gorge, apparently east of Michmash, mentioned only in 1 Sam. 13:18.

ZEBULUN—*dwelling* (?) The tenth of the sons of Jacob, according to the order in which their births are enumerated; the sixth and last of Leah (Gen. 30:20; 35:23; 46:14; 1 Chron. 2:1).

ZECHARIAH—*Jehovah remembers*. 1. The eleventh in order of the twelve minor prophets. He is called in his prophecy (Zech. 1:1) the son of Berechiah, and the grandson of Iddo, whereas in the Book of Ezra (5:1; 6:14) he is said to have been the son of Iddo. 2. Several other men

of the Old Testament bear the name Zechariah. (See also Zachariah 1.)

ZEDEKIAH—*righteousness of Jehovah*. The last king of Judah and Jerusalem. He was the son of Josiah by his wife Hamutal, and therefore own brother to Jehoahaz (2 Kings 24:18; *cf.* 23:31).

ZELEK. An Ammonite, one of David's guard (2 Sam. 23:37; 1 Chron. 11:39).

ZELOPHEHAD. Son of Hepher, son of Gilead, son of Machir, son of Manasseh (Num. 26:33; 27:1-7; 36:2-12; Josh. 17:3).

ZEMARITE, THE. One of the Hamite tribes who, in the genealogical table of Gen. 10:18 and 1 Chron. 1:16, are represented as "sons of Canaan."

ZENAS. A believer, and, as may be inferred from the context, a preacher of the gospel, who is mentioned in Tit. 3:13, in connection with Apollos. He is further described as "the lawyer."

ZEPHANIAH—*Jehovah hides*. 1. The ninth in order of the twelve minor prophets. His pedigree is traced to his fourth ancestor, Hezekiah (Zeph. 1), supposed to be the celebrated king of that name. 2. Several other men in the Old Testament bore this name (1 Chron. 6:36; 2 Kings 25:18; and Jer. 52:24; Zech. 6:10, 14).

ZEPHO. Son of Eliphaz, son Esau (Gen. 36:11), and one of the "dukes" of the Edomites (5:15). In 1 Chron. 1:36 he is called Zephi.

ZER. A fortified town in the allotment of Naphtali (Josh. 19:35 only), the location of which is uncertain.

ZERAH. 1. A son of Reuel, son of Esau (Gen. 36:13; 1 Chron. 1:37), and one of the "dukes" of the Edomites (Gen. 36:17). 2. Less properly Zarah, twin son, with his elder brother Pharez, of Judah and Tamar (Gen. 38:30; 1 Chron. 2:6; Matt. 1:3). 3. A son of Simeon, and founder of the Zarhites (Num. 26:13; 1 Chron. 4:24). 4. The name of two Levites (1 Chron. 6:21, 41). 5. The Cushite who invaded Judah in the reign of Asa (2 Chron. 14:9-15).

ZERED—*exuberant growth*. (Deut. 2:13, 14), or ZARED (Num. 21:12), a brook or valley running into the Dead Sea. It lay between Moab and Edom, and is the limit of the proper term of the Israelites' wandering (Deut. 2:14).

ZEREDA. The native place of Jeroboam (1 Kings 11:26).

ZERETH. Son of Ashur the founder of Tekoa, by his wife Helah (1 Chron. 14:7).

ZEROR. A Benjamite, ancestor of Kish the father of Saul (1 Sam. 9:1).

ZERUBBABEL—*begotten in Babylon*. The head of the tribe of Judah at the time of the return from the Babylonish captivity in the first year of Cyrus (Ezra 5:2; 6:15).

ZERUIAH. The mother of the three leading heroes of David's army—Abishai, Joab and Asahel —known as the "sons of Zeruiah." (1 Sam. 26: 6; 2 Sam. 2:13, 18; 1 Kings 1:7.) She and Abigail are specified in 1 Chron. 2:13-17, as "sisters of the sons of Jesse." The expression is in itself enough to raise a suspicion that she was not a daughter of Jesse, a suspicion which is corroborated by the statement of 2 Sam. 17:25, that Abigail was the daughter of Nahash.

ZIBA. A person who plays a prominent part, though with no credit to himself, in one of the episodes of David's history (2 Sam. 9:2-12; 16:1-4; 19:17, 29).

ZIBEON—*hyena*. Father of Anah, whose daughter Aholibamah was Esau's wife (Gen. 36:2).

ZIDDIM—*the sides*. A fortified town in the allotment of Naphtali (Josh. 19:35).

ZIDKIJAH. A priest, or family of priests, who signed the covenant with Nehemiah (Neh. 10:1).

ZIDON or SIDON. An ancient and wealthy city of Phoenicia, on the eastern coast of the Mediterranean Sea.

ZIDONIANS. The inhabitants of Zidon (1 Kings 11:5, 33; 2 Kings 23:13). The name came to be applied to all the Phoenicians.

ZIKLAG. A place which possesses a special interest from its having been the residence and the private property of David (1 Sam. 27:6; 30:1-26; 2 Sam. 1:1; 4:10).

ZILPAH. A Syrian given by Laban to his daughter Leah as an attendant (Gen. 29:24), and by Leah to Jacob as a concubine. She was the mother of Gad and Asher (Gen. 30:9-13; 35:26; 37:2; 46:18).

ZIMRAN. The eldest son of Keturah (Gen. 25:2; 1 Chron. 1:32). His descendants are not mentioned, nor is any hint given that he was the founder of a tribe.

ZIMRI—*mountain-sheep*. 1. The son of Salu, a Simeonite chieftain, slain by Phinehas with the Midianitish pricess Cozbi (Num. 25:14). Fifth sovereign of the separate kingdom of Israel, of which he occupied the throne for the brief period of seven days (1 Kings 16:9-20). 3. One of the five sons of Zerah the son of Judah (1 Chron. 2:6). 4. Son of Jehoadah and descendant of Saul (1 Chron. 8:36; 9:42). 5. An obscure name, mentioned (Jer. 25:25) in probable connection with Dedan, Tema, Buz, Arabia, the "mingled people."

ZIN. The name given to a portion of the desert tract between the Dead Sea and the Arabah. Kadesh lay in it, and here also Idumea was conterminous with Judah. (See Kadesh; Num. 13:21; 20:1; 27:14; 33:36; 34:3; Josh. 15:1.)

ZINA, ZIZAH. The second son of Shimei (1 Chron. 23:10; *cf.* 11) the Gershonite.

ZION. (Jerusalem.)

ZIOR. A town in the mountain district of Judah (Josh. 15:54). It belongs to the same group with Hebron.

ZIPH. The name of two towns in Judah. 1. In the south; named between Ithnan and Telem (Josh. 15:24). It does not appear again in the history nor has any trace of it been met with. 2. In the highland district; named between Carmel and Juttah (Josh. 15:55). The place is immortalized by its connection with David (1 Sam. 23:14, 15, 24; 26:2).

ZIPHAH. Son of Jehaleleel (1 Chron. 4:16).

ZIPHIMS, THE. 1. The inhabitants of Ziph. 2. In this form the name is found in the A.V. only in the title of Ps. 54. In the narrative it occurs in the more usual form of Ziphion.

ZIPHION. Son of Gad (Gen. 46:16); elsewhere called Zephon.

ZIPHITES, THE. Citizens of Ziph (1 Sam. 23:19; 26:1).

ZIPHRON. A point in the north boundary of the Promised Land as specified by Moses—"And the border shall go on to Ziphron" (Num. 34:9).

ZIPPOR—*bird*. The father of Balak, king of Moab (Num. 22:2, 4, 10, 16; 23:18; Josh. 24:9; Judg. 11:25).

ZIPPORAH. Daughter of Reuel or Jethro, the priest of Midian, wife of Moses, and mother of his two sons Gershom and Eliezer (Ex. 2:21;

4:25; 18:2; *cf.* 6). The only incident recorded in her life is that of the circumcision of Gershom (Gen. 4:24-26).

ZITHRI. Properly "Sithri," one of the sons of Uzziel, the son of Kohath (Ex. 6:22). In Ex. 6:21 "Zithri" should be "Zichri," as in A.V. of 1611.

ZIZ, THE CLIFF OF. The pass by which the horde of Moabites, Ammonites, and Mehunim made their way up from the shores of the Dead Sea to the wilderness of Judah near Tekoa (2 Chron. 20:16 only; *cf.* 20).

ZIZA. 1. Son of Shiphi, a chief of the Simeonites in the reign of Hezekiah (1 Chron. 4:37). 2. Son of Rehoboam by Maachah, the granddaughter of Absalom (2 Chron. 11:20).

ZIZAH. A Gershonite Levite, second son of Shimei (1 Chron. 23:11; called Zina in ver. 10).

ZOAN. An ancient city of Lower Egypt, near the eastern border (Num. 13:22; Ps. 78:12; Isa. 19: 11; Ezek. 30:14).

ZOAR—*small*. One of the most ancient cities of the land of Canaan. Its original name was Bela (Gen. 14:2, 8). It was in intimate connection with the cities of the "plain of Jordan"—Sodom, Gomorrah, Admah, and Zoboiim (see also Gen. 13:10). In the general destruction of the cities of the plain, Zoar was spared to afford shelter to Lot (Gen. 19:22, 23, 30).

ZOBEBAH. Son of Coz, of the tribe of Judah (1 Chron. 4:8).

ZOHAR. 1. Father of Ephron the Hittite (Gen. 23:8; 25:9). 2. One of the sons of Simeon (Gen. 46:10; Ex. 6:15); called Zerah in 1 Chron. 4:24.

ZOHELETH, THE STONE. This was "by En Rogel" (1 Kings 1:9); "where Adonijah slew sheep and oxen."

ZOHETH. Son of Ishi of the tribe of Judah (1 Chron. 4:20).

ZOPHAH. Son of Helemor Hotham, the son of Heber, an Asherite (1 Chron. 7:35, 36).

ZOPHAI. A Kohathite Levite, son of Elkanah, and ancestor of Samuel (1 Chron. 6:26); in verse 35 he is called Zuph.

ZOPHAR. One of the three friends of Job (Job 2:11; 11:1; 20:1; 42:9).

ZOPHIM, THE FIELD OF. A spot on or near the top of Pisgah, from which Balaam had his second view of the encampment of Israel (Num. 23:14).

ZORAH. A town in the allotment of the tribe of Dan (Josh. 19:41). It is previously mentioned (15:33) in the catalogue of Judah, among the places in the district of the Shephelah (A.V. Zoreah). It was the residence of Manoah and amongst the places fortified by Rehoboam (2 Chron. 11:10).

ZORATHITES, THE. The people of Zorah, mentioned in 1 Chron. 4:2 as descended from Shobal.

ZOREAH. (See Zorah.)

ZOROBABEL (Matt. 1:12, 13; Luke 3:27). (See Zerubbabel.)

ZUAR. Father of Nathaneel the chief of the tribe of Issachar at the time of the Exodus (Num. 1:8; 2:5; 7:18, 23; 10:15).

ZUPH, THE LAND OF. A district at which Saul and his servant arrived after passing through those of Shalisha, of Shalim and of the Benjamites (1 Sam. 9:5 only).

ZUPH. A Kohathite Levite, ancestor of Elkanah and Samuel (1 Sam. 1:1; 1 Chron. 6:35). In 1 Chron. 6:26 he is called Zophai.

ZUR—*rock*. 1. Father of Cozbi (Num. 25:15) and one of the five princes of Midian who were slain by the Israelites when Balaam fell (Num. 31:8). 2. Son of Jehiel the founder of Gibeon (1 Chron. 8:30).

ZURISHADDAI—*my rock is the Almighty*. Father of Shelumiel, the chief of the tribe of Simeon at the time of the Exodus (Num. 1:6; 2:12; 7:36, 41; 10:19).

ZUZIMS, THE. An ancient people, who, lying in the path of Chedorlaomer and his allies, were attacked and overthrown by them (Gen. 14:5). The Zuzims perhaps inhabited the country of the Ammonites, and were identical with the Zamzummin, who are known to have been exterminated and succeeded in their land by the Ammonites.

THE BIBLE SPEAKS TO DAILY NEEDS

FOR ASSURANCE

Trust in God and be not afraid	Isaiah 12:2
None that trust in God shall be desolate	Psalms 34:22
God, our dwelling place in all generations	Psalms 90:1
Christ came to seek and to save the lost	Luke 19:10
God so loved the world that he gave his Son	John 3:16
Christ came to bring abundant life	John 10:10
All things work for good for those who love God	Romans 8:28
Let us come boldly before God to receive grace	Hebrews 4:16
He who does God's will abides forever	I John 2:17

FOR COMFORT

The Lord is my shepherd	Psalm 23
God is our refuge and help in trouble	Psalm 46
God is with us everywhere we might go	Psalm 139
Whoever believes in Christ shall never die	John 11:25-26
Christ is preparing a place for his disciples	John 14:1-3
Christians have been promised eternal life	I John 2:25

FOR ENCOURAGEMENT

Christ is with his followers always	Matthew 28:20
The Son of man came to seek the lost	Luke 19:10
Be of good cheer: Christ has overcome the world	John 16:33
We are troubled but not distressed	II Corinthians 4:8-9
Rejoice in the Lord always	Philippians 4:4

FOR FAITH

Faith can move mountains	Matthew 17:20
We are justified by faith	Romans 5:1-2
We walk by faith, not by sight	II Corinthians 5:7
Christians are children of God by faith	Galatians 3:26
Faith is evidence of things not seen	Hebrews 11:1
Show your faith by your works	James 2:18

FOR FORGIVENESS

God will forgive iniquity, under new covenant	Jeremiah 31:34
God will forgive, if men forgive one another	Matthew 6:14
Jesus had power to forgive sins	Mark 2:5
The parable of the Prodigal Son	Luke 15:11-32
God forgives all your iniquities	Psalms 103:3

FOR GUIDANCE

The word of the Lord is right	Psalms 33:4
Acknowledge God and he will direct your paths	Proverbs 3:6
Seek good, and not evil, that you may live	Amos 5:14
God has shown what he requires of man	Micah 6:8
The Beatitudes (Sermon on the Mount)	Matthew 5:3-12
The Golden Rule as given by Jesus	Matthew 7:12
Not hearing, but doing, is important	Matthew 7:21
Love your enemies	Luke 6:27
Abhor the evil, cleave to the good	Romans 12:9
Paul's "hymn to love"	I Corinthians 13
Make your requests known to God in prayer	Philippians 4:6

FOR GROWTH

Seeking after God with earnestness	Psalms 63:1-2
Jesus grew in wisdom, stature, and favor	Luke 2:42
Jesus could not share all until disciples grew	John 16:12
Be transformed by the renewal of your mind	Romans 12:1-2
Press toward the mark of the calling of God	Philippians 3:14
Walk worthy of God, who has called you	I Thessalonians 2:12
Study to show yourself an approved workman	II Timothy 2:15
Use your freedom as servants of God	I Peter 2:15-16

FOR PEACE

God wants to guide our feet into way of peace	Luke 1:78-79
Christ gives his peace, not as the world gives	John 14:27
In Christ we might have peace	John 16:33
We have peace with God through Jesus Christ	Romans 5:1
As much as possible, live in peace with men	Romans 12:18
Follow after the things which make for peace	Romans 14:19
The peace of God shall keep your minds	Philippians 4:7
Jesus Christ is our peace	Ephesians 2:14

FOR STRENGTH

Our help comes from God, who made the world	Psalms 121:1-2
In quietness and confidence shall be your strength	Isaiah 30:15
God strengthens those who cry to him	Psalms 138:3
God is our refuge and strength	Psalms 46:1
Christ can help those who are tempted	Hebrews 2:18
Put on the armor of God to stand against devil	Ephesians 6:11
Be not weary in well doing	Galatians 6:9

FOR TRUTH

God is a God of truth	Deuteronomy 32:4
God wants us to have truth in ourselves	Psalms 51:6
God's truth is our shield and buckler	Psalms 91:4
God's truth endures to all generations	Psalms 100:5
He who speaks truth shows righteousness	Proverbs 12:17
The fear of the Lord is beginning of wisdom	Proverbs 9:10
The Word was made flesh, full of grace and truth	John 1:14
You shall know truth, and truth shall make free	John 8:31-32
Jesus is the way, the truth, and the life	John 14:6
The Spirit will guide Christians into all truth	John 16:13
Speak the truth in love	Ephesians 4:15

FOR WORSHIP

Worship the Lord in the beauty of holiness	I Chronicles 16:29
The heavens declare the glory of God	Psalms 19:1
Exalt God and worship him for he is holy	Psalms 99:9
Bless the Lord, and forget not his benefits	Psalms 103:2
God made this day: rejoice and be glad in it	Psalms 118:24
Give thanks to God for he is good	Psalms 136:1
The pure in heart shall see God	Matthew 5:8
True worshippers worship God in spirit and truth	John 4:23-24
Bow knees to Father of our Lord Jesus Christ	Ephesians 3:14-19
We worship God in the spirit	Philippians 3:3
All nations shall come and worship God	Revelation 15:4

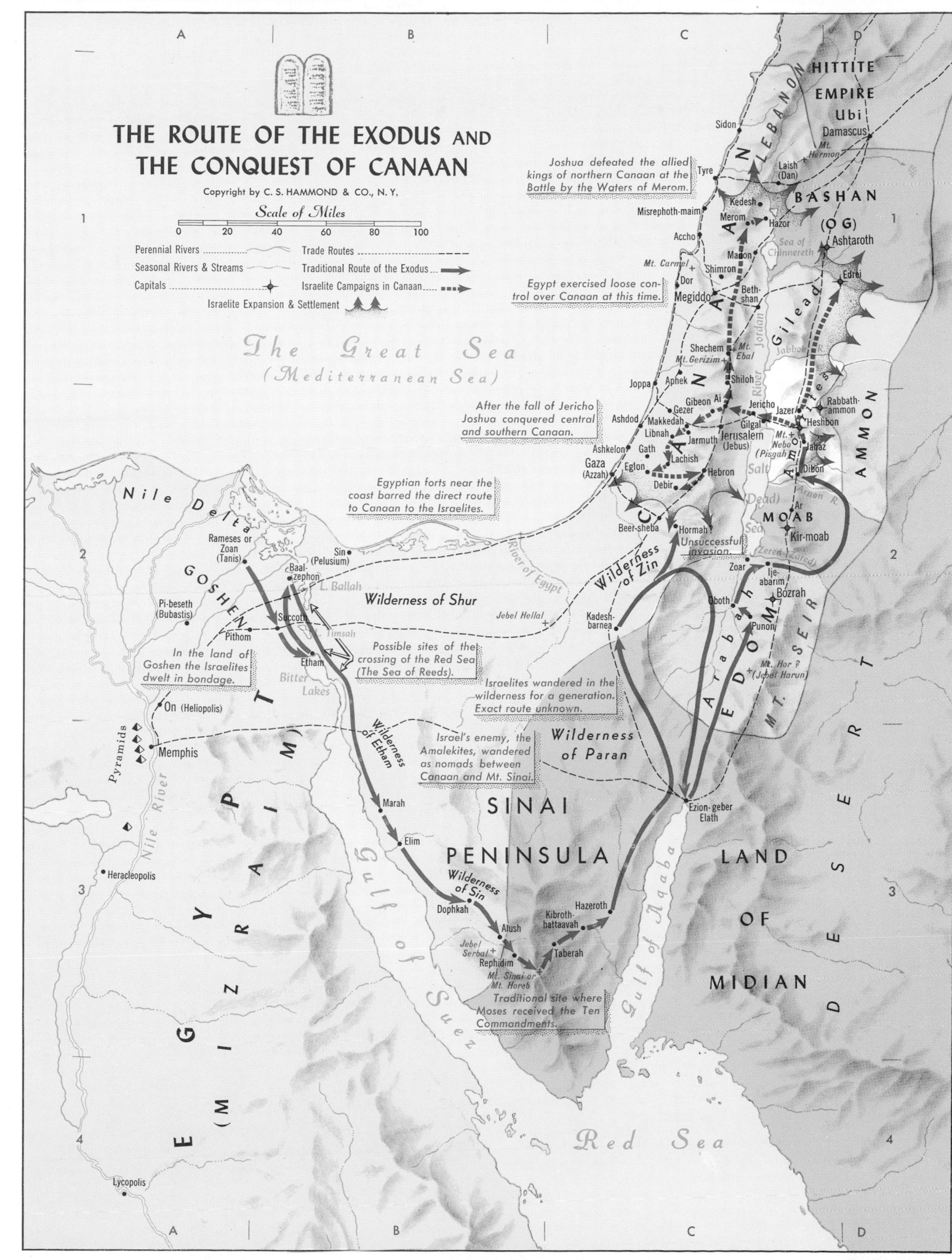

THE ROUTE OF THE EXODUS AND THE CONQUEST OF CANAAN

Copyright by C. S. HAMMOND & CO., N.Y.

Scale of Miles

0   20   40   60   80   100

Perennial Rivers ....
Seasonal Rivers & Streams ....
Capitals ....
Trade Routes ....
Traditional Route of the Exodus ....→
Israelite Campaigns in Canaan ....⇢
Israelite Expansion & Settlement 🌲🌲

The Great Sea
(Mediterranean Sea)

Joshua defeated the allied kings of northern Canaan at the Battle by the Waters of Merom.

Egypt exercised loose control over Canaan at this time.

After the fall of Jericho Joshua conquered central and southern Canaan.

Egyptian forts near the coast barred the direct route to Canaan to the Israelites.

In the land of Goshen the Israelites dwelt in bondage.

Possible sites of the crossing of the Red Sea (The Sea of Reeds).

Israelites wandered in the wilderness for a generation. Exact route unknown.

Israel's enemy, the Amalekites, wandered as nomads between Canaan and Mt. Sinai.

Unsuccessful invasion

Traditional site where Moses received the Ten Commandments.

HITTITE EMPIRE
Ubi
Damascus
Mt. Hermon
Laish (Dan)
Sidon
Tyre
Kedesh
BASHAN (OG)
Misrephoth-maim
Merom
Hazor
Ashtaroth
Accho
Madon
Sea of Chinnereth
Edrei
Mt. Carmel
Shimron
Dor
Megiddo
Bethshan
Gilead
Mt. Ebal
Shechem
Mt. Gerizim
Shiloh
Jabbok R.
Joppa
Aphek
Gibeon Ai
Jericho
Jazer
Rabbath-ammon
Ashdod
Gezer
Gilgal
Heshbon
Makkedah
Jerusalem (Jebus)
Mt. Nebo (Pisgah)
Libnah
Jarmuth
AMMON
Ashkelon
Gath
Jahaz
Gaza (Azzah)
Eglon
Lachish
Dibon
Debir
Hebron
Salt (Dead) Sea
Arnon R.
MOAB
Kir-moab
Beer-sheba
Hormah
Ar
Zoar
Ije-abarim
Bozrah
Wilderness of Zin
Oboth
Kadesh-barnea
Punon
MT. SEIR
Mt. Hor? (Jebel Harun)
Arabah
EDOM
Wilderness of Paran

Nile Delta
Rameses or Zoan (Tanis)
Sin (Pelusium)
Baal-zephon
GOSHEN
L. Ballah
Wilderness of Shur
River of Egypt
Jebel Hellal
Pi-beseth (Bubastis)
Succoth
Pithom
L. Timsah
Etham
Bitter Lakes
On (Heliopolis)
Wilderness of Etham
Pyramids
Memphis
Marah
E G Y P T (M I Z R A I M)
Elim
Wilderness of Sin
SINAI PENINSULA
Heracleopolis
Dophkah
Alush
Kibroth-hattaavah
Hazeroth
Taberah
Jebel Serbal
Rephidim
Mt. Sinai or Mt. Horeb
Gulf of Suez
Gulf of Aqaba
Nile River
Lycopolis
Ezion-geber Elath
LAND OF MIDIAN
D E S E R T
Red Sea

CANAAN AS DIVIDED AMONG THE TWELVE TRIBES
c. 1200-1020 B.C.

Copyright by C. S. HAMMOND & CO., N.Y.

Scale of Miles

0 5 10 20 30 40

Perennial Rivers —————   Seasonal Rivers & Streams ——————

The tribal divisions marked on this map are only approximate since boundary lists are incomplete.

Part of the tribe of Dan, unable to secure its inheritance, migrated north and captured Laish, renaming it Dan.

Although all of Bashan was assigned to the half tribe of Manasseh, it is doubtful that settlement reached beyond the Yarmuk Valley.

The Israelites were unable to capture the fortified towns of the plains during the early period of settlement.

The Israelites were under constant attack from Philistine invaders who occupied the coastal area at about this time.

During the period of Judges, invading Ammonites, Moabites and Midianites were repulsed by the Israelites.

The cities assigned to Simeon were also a part of the inheritance of Judah. Simeon as a tribe was later absorbed by Judah.

The priestly tribe of Levi did not receive a definite territory but instead was allotted 48 cities distributed over the tribal areas.

The Great Sea
(Mediterranean Sea)

MOUNT LEBANON
Leontes R.
MT. HERMON
Sidonians (Phoenicians)
Bashan
MANASSEH
Argob
Karnaim
Geshur Ashtaroth
Golan
Aphek
Edrei
Havoth-jair
Camon
Ramoth-gilead
Yarmuk R.
Pella
Jabesh-gilead
Mahanaim
Abel-meholah
Zaphon
Succoth
Jabbok R.
Penuel
Mizpeh
G I L E A D
River Jordan
Adam
Jazer
Betonim
Rabbath-ammon
Jogbehah
A M M O N
Beth-nimrah
Mephaath
Elealeh
Heshbon
Abel-shittim
Beth-jeshimoth
Mt. Nebo +
Baal-meon
Medeba
Jahaz
R E U B E N
Zareth-shahar
Ataroth Kiriathaim
Dibon
Aroer
Arnon R.
M O A B
Ar
Kir-moab (Kir-haresheth)
Zered R.
E D O M

Sidon
Zarephath
Tyre
Kanah
Hammon
Misrephoth-maim
Achzib Abdon
Beth-emek
Accho
Achshaph Cabul
Aphek
A S S H E R
MT. CARMEL
Hannathon
Shimron
Harosheth
Jokneam
Dor
Plain of Sharon
Kishon R.
Shihor libnath
Plain of Jezreel
Megiddo
Taanach
Ibleam
Dothan
MANASSEH
Tirzah
Mt. Ebal
Shechem
Mt. Gerizim
Pirathon
Taanath-shiloh
Janohah
Aphek
Tappuah
Lebonah Shiloh
Timnath-serah
Bethel Ai
Naarath
Ataroth
EPHRAIM
Gath-rimmon
Joppa (Japho)
Bene-berak
Ono
Lod
Aijalon R.
Beth-horon
Gezer Mizpeh
Gibeon Geba Jericho
Gilgal
Kirjath-jearim
BENJAMIN
Beth-hoglah
Jerusalem (Jebus)
Etam
Bethlehem
Tekoa
En-gedi
Jabneel
Ekron
Eltekeh
Zorah Chesalon
Gibbethon
Ashdod
Timnah
Makkedah Beth-shemesh
Azekah Jarmuth
Libnah Adullam
Ashkelon
Gath Mareshah Keilah
Beth-zur
Eglon Lachish
Gaza
Debir Ziph
Hebron
Juttah Carmel
Eshtemoh Maon
Madmannah
Jattir
Gerar
Ziklag Anab
Beer-sheba
Moladah Arad
Beth-palet
Hormah
Aroer
Rehoboth
Raphia
Sharuhen
Cherethites
Philistines
D A N
J U D A H
Caleb
Kenites
S I M E O N
Ascent of Akrabbim
Wilderness of Zin
Salt Sea (Dead Sea)

DAN
Abel-beth-maachah
Laish or Leshem (Dan)
En-hazor Kedesh
Iron
Hazor
Hukkok
Chinnereth
Ramah Madon
Gath-hepher
Rimmon
N A P H T A L I
Hammath
Sea of Chinnereth
Z E B U L U N
Chesulloth Mt. Tabor
Sarid En-dor
Shunem Ophrah
ISSACHAR
Jezreel
Mt. Gilboa
Harod
Beth-shan
Bezek
Thebez
Jabneel
Damascus

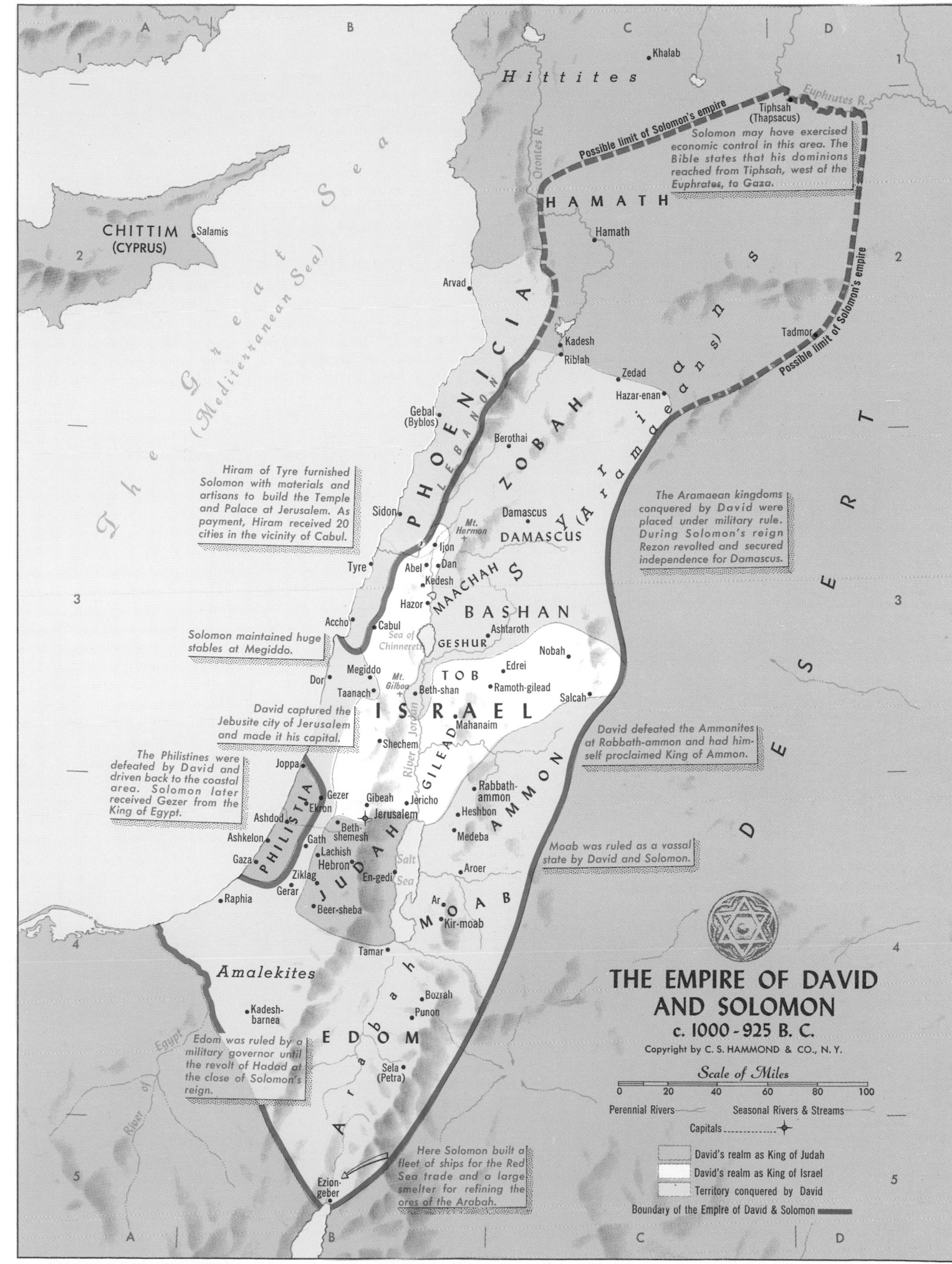

THE EMPIRE OF DAVID
AND SOLOMON
c. 1000-925 B.C.

Copyright by C. S. HAMMOND & CO., N.Y.

Scale of Miles

0   20   40   60   80   100

Perennial Rivers —

Seasonal Rivers & Streams

Capitals ·········◆

☐ David's realm as King of Judah
☐ David's realm as King of Israel
☐ Territory conquered by David

━━━ Boundary of the Empire of David & Solomon

Solomon may have exercised economic control in this area. The Bible states that his dominions reached from Tiphsah, west of the Euphrates, to Gaza.

Hiram of Tyre furnished Solomon with materials and artisans to build the Temple and Palace at Jerusalem. As payment, Hiram received 20 cities in the vicinity of Cabul.

The Aramaean kingdoms conquered by David were placed under military rule. During Solomon's reign Rezon revolted and secured independence for Damascus.

Solomon maintained huge stables at Megiddo.

David captured the Jebusite city of Jerusalem and made it his capital.

David defeated the Ammonites at Rabbath-ammon and had himself proclaimed King of Ammon.

The Philistines were defeated by David and driven back to the coastal area. Solomon later received Gezer from the King of Egypt.

Moab was ruled as a vassal state by David and Solomon.

Edom was ruled by a military governor until the revolt of Hadad at the close of Solomon's reign.

Here Solomon built a fleet of ships for the Red Sea trade and a large smelter for refining the ores of the Arabah.

Possible limit of Solomon's empire

Euphrates R.
Khalab
Hittites
Tiphsah (Thapsacus)
Orontes R.
HAMATH
Hamath
Arvad
CHITTIM (CYPRUS)
Salamis
Kadesh
Riblah
Zedad
Hazar-enan
Tadmor
Gebal (Byblos)
Berothai
ZOBAH
S (Aramaeans)
PHOENICIA
Sidon
Mt. Hermon
Damascus
DAMASCUS
Tyre
Ijon
Dan
Abel
Kedesh
MAACHAH
BASHAN
Hazor
Accho
Cabul
Sea of Chinnereth
GESHUR
Ashtaroth
Nobah
Dor
Megiddo
Mt. Gilboa
TOB
Edrei
Ramoth-gilead
Salcah
Taanach
Beth-shan
ISRAEL
Mahanaim
Shechem
GILEAD
Joppa
River Jordan
Gezer
Gibeah
Jericho
Rabbath-ammon
AMMON
Ekron
Jerusalem
Heshbon
Ashdod
Beth-shemesh
JUDAH
Medeba
Ashkelon
Gath
Lachish
Hebron
PHILISTIA
En-gedi
Salt Sea
Aroer
Gaza
Ziklag
Gerar
Beer-sheba
MOAB
Raphia
Ar
Kir-moab
Tamar
Amalekites
Bozrah
Punon
Kadesh-barnea
EDOM
Arabah
Sela (Petra)
River of Egypt
Ezion-geber

The Great Mediterranean Sea

The Lebanon

D E S E R T

PALESTINE IN THE TIME OF CHRIST

Copyright by C. S. HAMMOND & CO., N.Y.

Scale of Miles

0   5   10   20   30   40

Perennial Rivers ....   Capitals ....
Seasonal Rivers & Streams ....   Roads & Trade Routes ....

Tetrarchy of Lysanias   Areas tributary to Salome
Tetrarchy of Philip   Decapolis *
Tetrarchy of Herod Antipas   Independent *
Territory under Roman procurator   Roman province of Syria

Cities of the Decapolis .... □

* The Decapolis and Ascalon retained their independence under the Roman governor of the province of Syria.

Archelaus, upon Herod's death, became ruler of Judaea, Samaria and Idumaea. His reign lasted until 6 A.D. when he was removed and exiled. His territory then was placed under a Roman procurator.

Salome, Herod's sister, was given Jamnia, Azotus and Phasaelis. They, in turn, passed to Livia, wife of Augustus and then to Emperor Tiberius.

Horns of Hattin (Kurûn Hattin) is a possible site of the Sermon on the Mount.

The Dead Sea Scrolls were found in a cave here; also the ruins of an Essene monastery.

Here John the Baptist was imprisoned and beheaded by order of Herod Antipas.

The Great Sea

(Mediterranean Sea)

ABILENE
Abila
Damascus

PHOENICIA
Sidon
Sarepta (Zarephath)
Tyre
Ladder of Tyre
Ptolemais (Accho)
Dora

MOUNT LEBANON
Leontes R.
River Jordan
MT. HERMON
PANIAS
Dan   Caesarea Philippi
ULATHA
Lake Semechonitis
Cadasa (Kedesh)

ITURAEA
TRACHONITIS
GAULANITIS
BATANAEA
BASHAN
AURANITIS
Raphana
Dion
Edrei

Gischala
Seleucia
Chorazin
Bethsaida (Julias)
Capernaum
Gergesa
Gamala

MT. CARMEL
Kishon R.
Jotapata
Cana
Magdala (Dalmanutha)
Tabigha
Sea of Galilee
Horns of Hattin +
Tiberias
Philoteria
Hippos
GALILEE
Sepphoris
Nazareth
Mt. Tabor
Plain of Esdraelon
Nain

Gadara
Capitolias
Yarmuk R.
Abila
GILEAD
Bethabara

Caesarea
Residence of Roman procurators.

Plain of Sharon
En-gannim (Ginaea)
Scythopolis (Beth-shan)
Pella
DECAPOLIS
Gerasa

SAMARIA
Samaria (Sebaste)
Mt. Ebal
Shechem   Sychar
Mt. Gerizim   Jacob's Well
River Jordan
Amathus
Jabbok R.

Apollonia
Antipatris
Joppa
Lydda (Diospolis)
Arimathaea (Ramathaim)
Gophna
Bethel
Gezer (Gazara)
Ramah
Jamnia
Ekron
Nicopolis (Emmaus)
Emmaus
Jerusalem
Mt. of Olives
Bethany
Bethlehem

Phasaelis
Archelais
Ephraim
Jericho
PERAEA
Beth-nimrah
Philadelphia (Rabbath-ammon)
Julias (Livias, Beth-haram)
Heshbon

Azotus (Ashdod)
Ascalon
Herodium
Khirbet Qumran

JUDAEA
Mareshah (Marisa)
Hebron
Ziph
Juttah
Carmel
En-gedi
Gaza
Gerar
Raphia
Beersheba
Masada

Callirhoe
Machaerus
Dibon

Wilderness of Judah
Salt or Dead Sea
L. Asphaltitis

IDUMAEA

Rabbath Moab (Areopolis, Rabba)
Kir-moab (Kir-haresheth)
Arnon

AMMON
BATANAEA
ARABIA
Zered R.

NABATAEANS

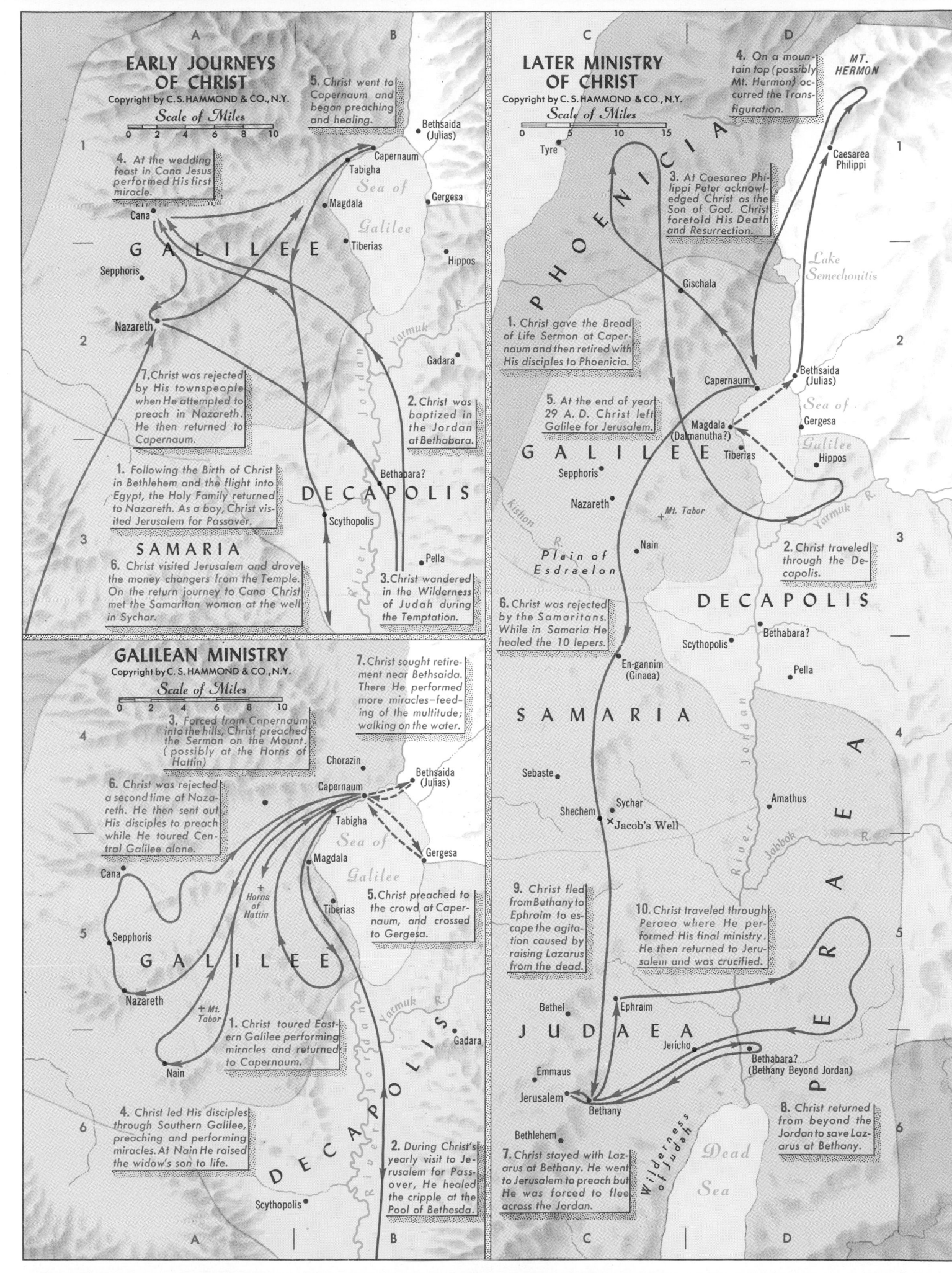

EARLY JOURNEYS OF CHRIST

Copyright by C. S. HAMMOND & CO., N.Y.

Scale of Miles
0 2 4 6 8 10

5. Christ went to Capernaum and began preaching and healing.

4. At the wedding feast in Cana Jesus performed His first miracle.

7. Christ was rejected by His townspeople when He attempted to preach in Nazareth. He then returned to Capernaum.

1. Following the Birth of Christ in Bethlehem and the flight into Egypt, the Holy Family returned to Nazareth. As a boy, Christ visited Jerusalem for Passover.

6. Christ visited Jerusalem and drove the money changers from the Temple. On the return journey to Cana Christ met the Samaritan woman at the well in Sychar.

2. Christ was baptized in the Jordan at Bethabara.

3. Christ wandered in the Wilderness of Judah during the Temptation.

Bethsaida (Julias)
Capernaum
Tabigha
Sea of Galilee
Magdala
Gergesa
Tiberias
Hippos
Cana
GALILEE
Sepphoris
Nazareth
Yarmuk R.
Gadara
Jordan River
Bethabara?
DECAPOLIS
Scythopolis
Pella
SAMARIA

LATER MINISTRY OF CHRIST

Copyright by C. S. HAMMOND & CO., N.Y.

Scale of Miles
0 5 10 15

4. On a mountain top (possibly Mt. Hermon) occurred the Transfiguration.

3. At Caesarea Philippi Peter acknowledged Christ as the Son of God. Christ foretold His Death and Resurrection.

1. Christ gave the Bread of Life Sermon at Capernaum and then retired with His disciples to Phoenicia.

5. At the end of year 29 A.D. Christ left Galilee for Jerusalem.

6. Christ was rejected by the Samaritans. While in Samaria He healed the 10 lepers.

9. Christ fled from Bethany to Ephraim to escape the agitation caused by raising Lazarus from the dead.

10. Christ traveled through Peraea where He performed His final ministry. He then returned to Jerusalem and was crucified.

7. Christ stayed with Lazarus at Bethany. He went to Jerusalem to preach but He was forced to flee across the Jordan.

8. Christ returned from beyond the Jordan to save Lazarus at Bethany.

2. Christ traveled through the Decapolis.

MT. HERMON
Caesarea Philippi
PHOENICIA
Tyre
Gischala
Lake Semechonitis
Capernaum
Bethsaida (Julias)
Sea of Galilee
Magdala (Dalmanutha?)
Gergesa
Tiberias
Hippos
GALILEE
Sepphoris
Nazareth
Mt. Tabor
Kishon R.
Plain of Esdraelon
Nain
Yarmuk R.
DECAPOLIS
En-gannim (Ginaea)
Scythopolis
Bethabara?
Pella
SAMARIA
Sebaste
Shechem
Sychar
Jacob's Well
Amathus
River Jordan
River Jabbok
Bethel
Ephraim
JUDAEA
Jericho
Bethabara? (Bethany Beyond Jordan)
Emmaus
PERAEA
Jerusalem
Bethany
Bethlehem
Wilderness of Judah
Dead Sea

GALILEAN MINISTRY

Copyright by C. S. HAMMOND & CO., N.Y.

Scale of Miles
0 2 4 6 8 10

3. Forced from Capernaum into the hills, Christ preached the Sermon on the Mount. (possibly at the Horns of Hattin)

6. Christ was rejected a second time at Nazareth. He then sent out His disciples to preach while He toured Central Galilee alone.

7. Christ sought retirement near Bethsaida. There He performed more miracles—feeding of the multitude; walking on the water.

5. Christ preached to the crowd at Capernaum, and crossed to Gergesa.

1. Christ toured Eastern Galilee performing miracles and returned to Capernaum.

4. Christ led His disciples through Southern Galilee, preaching and performing miracles. At Nain He raised the widow's son to life.

2. During Christ's yearly visit to Jerusalem for Passover, He healed the cripple at the Pool of Bethesda.

Chorazin
Capernaum
Bethsaida (Julias)
Tabigha
Sea of Galilee
Magdala
Gergesa
Tiberias
Cana
Horns of Hattin
GALILEE
Sepphoris
Nazareth
Mt. Tabor
Nain
Jordan River
Yarmuk R.
DECAPOLIS
Gadara
Scythopolis

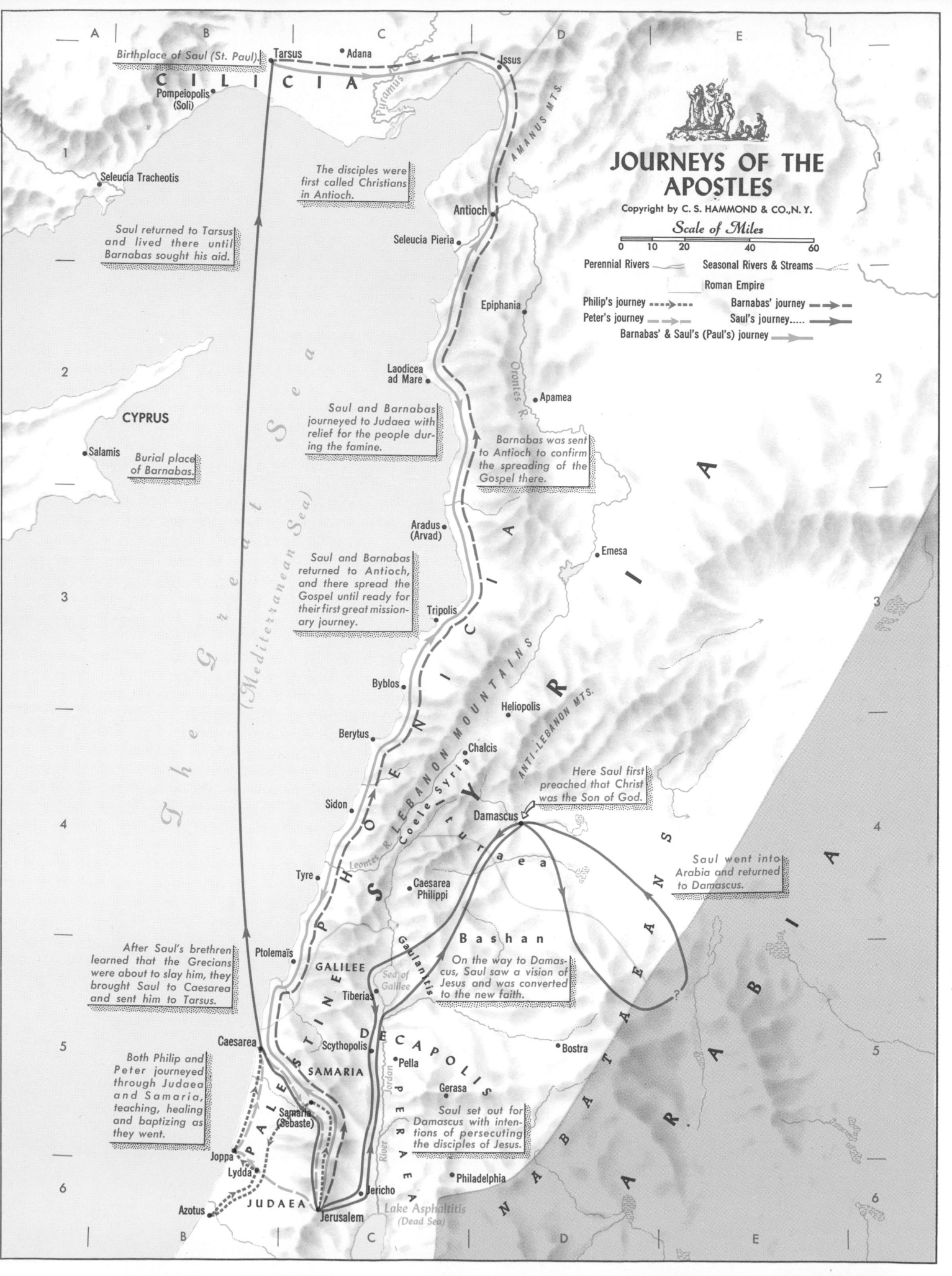

JOURNEYS OF THE APOSTLES

Copyright by C. S. HAMMOND & CO., N.Y.

Scale of Miles

0   10   20   40   60

Perennial Rivers   Seasonal Rivers & Streams

Roman Empire

Philip's journey ------   Barnabas' journey -- -- --

Peter's journey ----   Saul's journey .....

Barnabas' & Saul's (Paul's) journey →

A   B   C   D   E

CILICIA

Birthplace of Saul (St. Paul) Tarsus   • Adana   Issus

Pompeiopolis (Soli)

Seleucia Tracheotis

The disciples were first called Christians in Antioch.

Antioch

Saul returned to Tarsus and lived there until Barnabas sought his aid.

Seleucia Pieria

Epiphania

CYPRUS

Salamis

Burial place of Barnabas.

Laodicea ad Mare

Apamea

Saul and Barnabas journeyed to Judaea with relief for the people during the famine.

Barnabas was sent to Antioch to confirm the spreading of the Gospel there.

Emesa

Aradus (Arvad)

Saul and Barnabas returned to Antioch, and there spread the Gospel until ready for their first great missionary journey.

Tripolis

S Y R I A

Byblos

Heliopolis

Berytus

Chalcis

ANTI-LEBANON MTS.

Here Saul first preached that Christ was the Son of God.

Sidon

Damascus

Saul went into Arabia and returned to Damascus.

Tyre

Caesarea Philippi

B a s h a n

On the way to Damascus, Saul saw a vision of Jesus and was converted to the new faith.

N A B A T A E A N S

After Saul's brethren learned that the Grecians were about to slay him, they brought Saul to Caesarea and sent him to Tarsus.

Ptolemaïs

GALILEE

Tiberias

Sea of Galilee

Scythopolis

Caesarea

DECAPOLIS

Bostra

SAMARIA

Pella

Gerasa

Both Philip and Peter journeyed through Judaea and Samaria, teaching, healing and baptizing as they went.

Samaria (Sebaste)

Saul set out for Damascus with intentions of persecuting the disciples of Jesus.

Joppa

Lydda

Philadelphia

Azotus   **JUDAEA**   Jericho

Jerusalem

Lake Asphaltitis (Dead Sea)

N A B A T A E A N A R A B I A

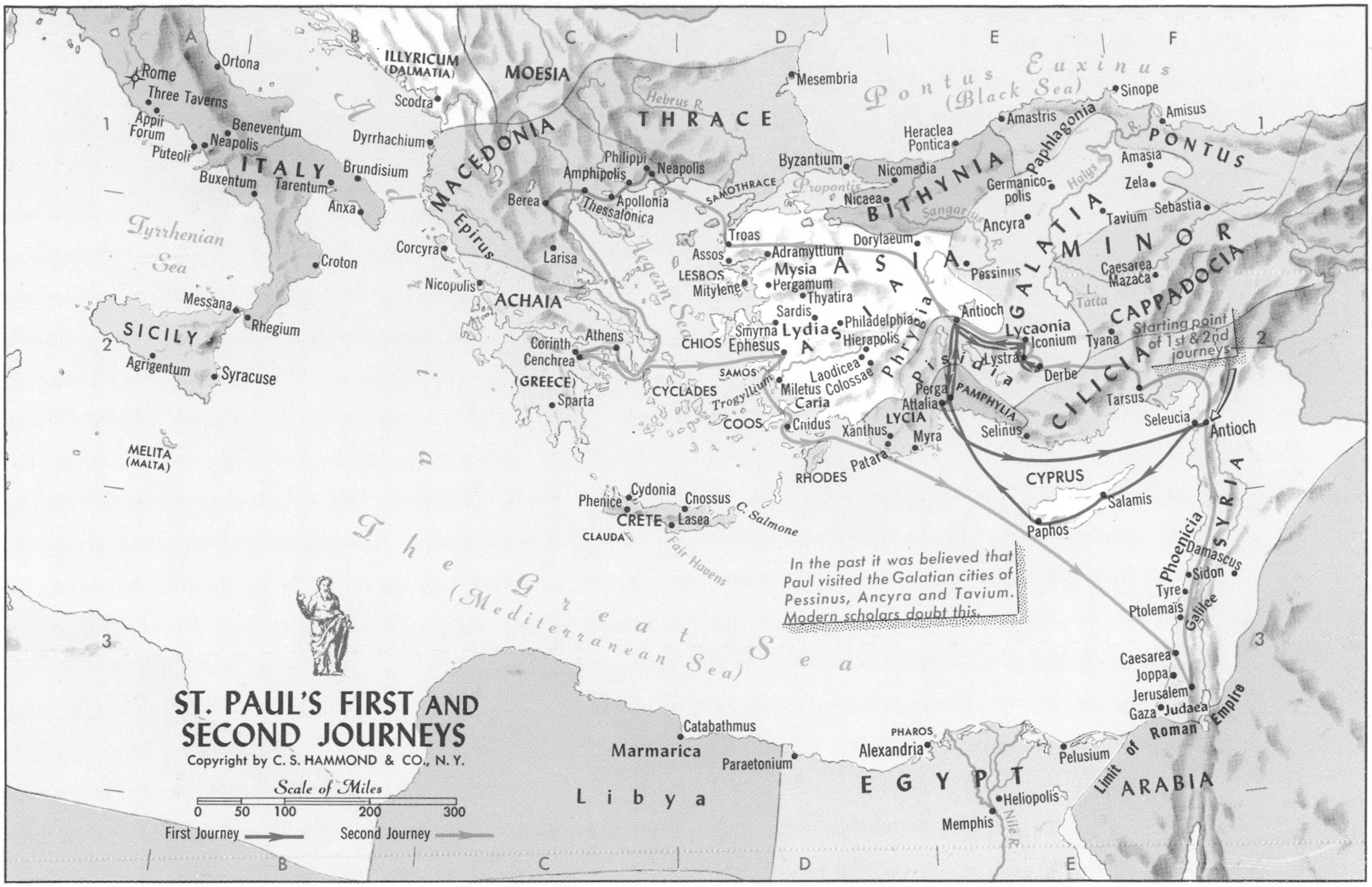

ST. PAUL'S FIRST AND SECOND JOURNEYS

Copyright by C. S. HAMMOND & CO., N.Y.

Scale of Miles

0 50 100   200   300

First Journey ⟶   Second Journey ⟶

In the past it was believed that Paul visited the Galatian cities of Pessinus, Ancyra and Tavium. Modern scholars doubt this.

Map 1 labels:

Rome, Ortona, Three Taverns, Appii Forum, Beneventum, Neapolis, Puteoli, ITALY, Buxentum, Tarentum, Anxa, Brundisium, ILLYRICUM (DALMATIA), Scodra, Dyrrhachium, MOESIA, MACEDONIA, Philippi, Neapolis, THRACE, Amphipolis, Apollonia, Berea, Thessalonica, Byzantium, Mesembria, SAMOTHRACE, Nicomedia, Heraclea Pontica, Amastris, PONTUS, Sinope, Amisus, Amasia, BITHYNIA, PAPHLAGONIA, Zela, Sebastia, GALATIA, Germanicopolis, Ancyra, Tavium, ASIA MINOR, Caesarea, Mazaca, CAPPADOCIA, Epirus, Larisa, Nicopolis, ACHAIA, Corcyra, Troas, Assos, Adramyttium, Dorylaeum, Pessinus, LESBOS, Mysia, Pergamum, Mitylene, Thyatira, Sardis, Lydia, Philadelphia, Hierapolis, Antioch, Phrygia, Pisidia, Lycaonia, Iconium, Tyana, CILICIA, Corinth, Athens, CHIOS, Ephesus, Smyrna, Laodicea, Colossae, Derbe, Lystra, Tarsus, Starting point of 1st & 2nd journeys, Cenchrea, GREECE, SAMOS, CYCLADES, Trogyllium, Miletus, Caria, COOS, Cnidus, LYCIA, Perga, PAMPHYLIA, Attalia, Selinus, Seleucia, Antioch, Sparta, Xanthus, Myra, RHODES, Patara, CYPRUS, Salamis, Paphos, SYRIA, Phoenicia, Damascus, Sidon, Tyre, Ptolemais, Galilee, Caesarea, Joppa, Jerusalem, Gaza, Judaea, Limit of Roman Empire, ARABIA, Messana, Rhegium, SICILY, Agrigentum, Syracuse, Croton, Tyrrhenian Sea, MELITA (MALTA), The Great (Mediterranean Sea) Sea, Marmarica, Catabathmus, Alexandria, PHAROS, Paraetonium, Pelusium, Libya, EGYPT, Heliopolis, Memphis, Nile R., Pontus Euxinus (Black Sea), Propontis, Sangarius, Halys, Tatta, Hebrus R., Aegean Sea

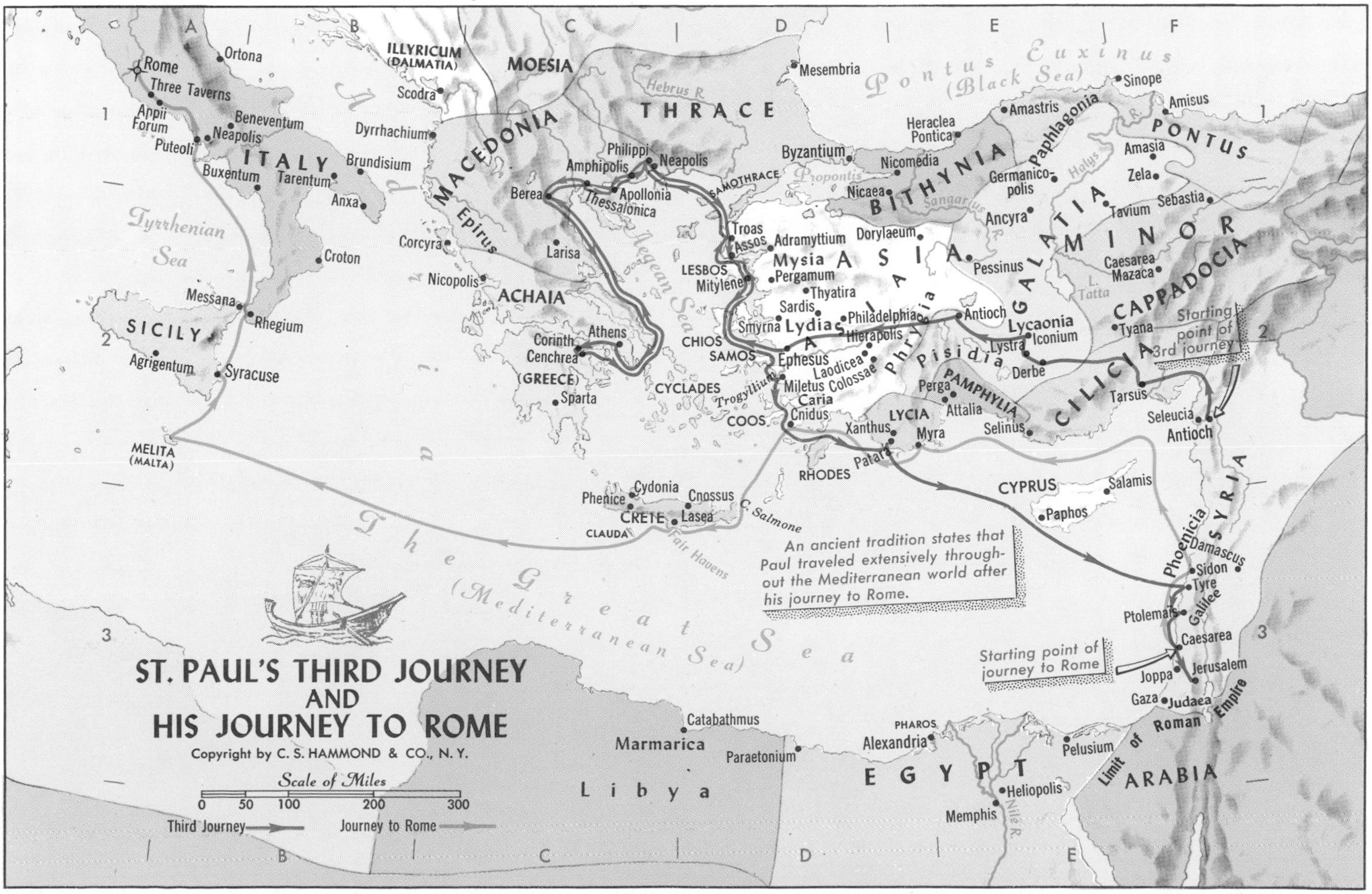

ST. PAUL'S THIRD JOURNEY AND HIS JOURNEY TO ROME

Copyright by C. S. HAMMOND & CO., N.Y.

Scale of Miles

0 50 100   200   300

Third Journey ⟶   Journey to Rome ⟶

An ancient tradition states that Paul traveled extensively throughout the Mediterranean world after his journey to Rome.

Starting point of 3rd journey

Starting point of journey to Rome

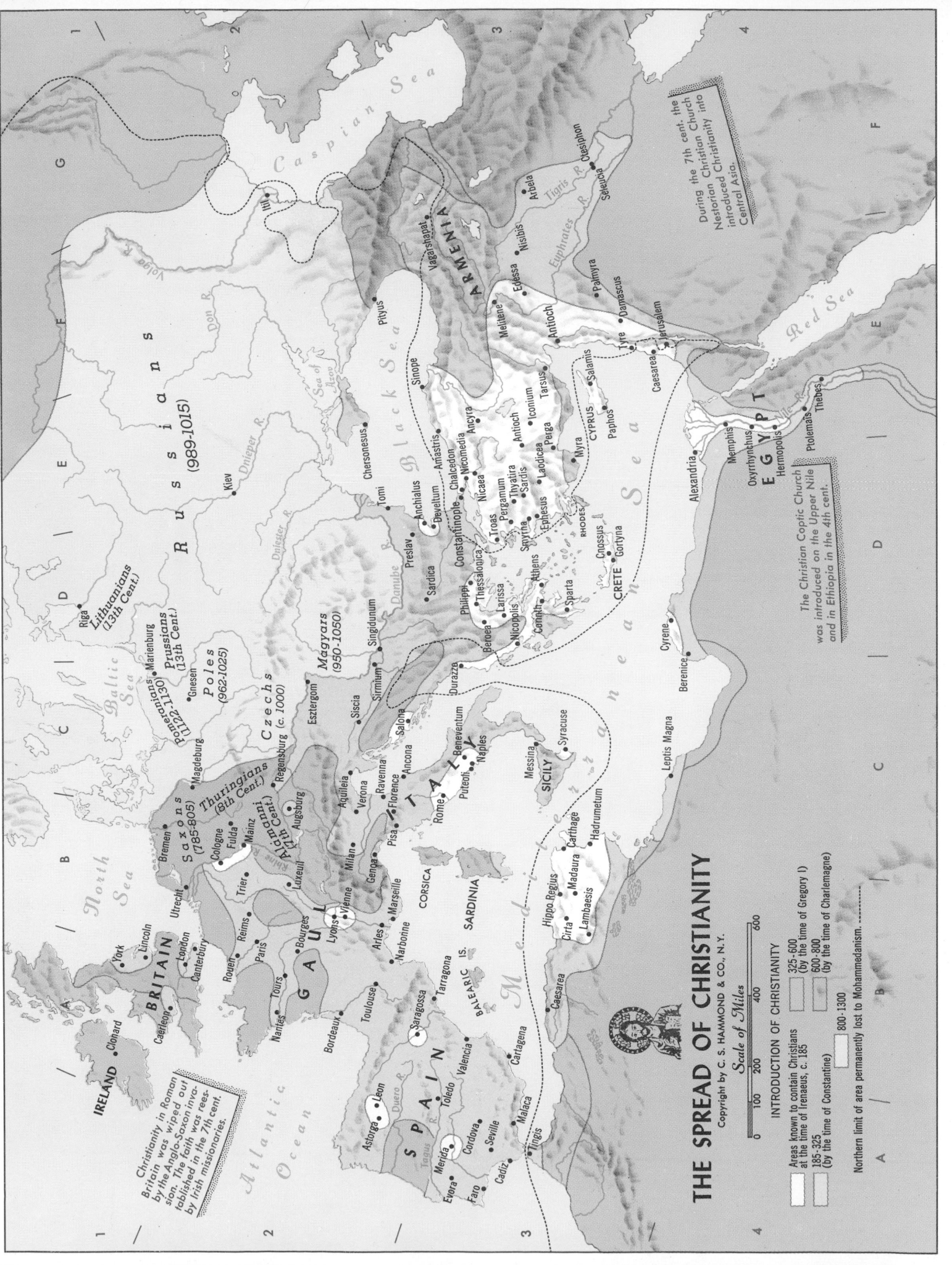

THE SPREAD OF CHRISTIANITY

Copyright by C. S. HAMMOND & CO., N.Y.

Scale of Miles

0 100 200 400 600

INTRODUCTION OF CHRISTIANITY

Areas known to contain Christians at the time of Irenaeus, c. 185

185-325 (by the time of Constantine)

325-600 (by the time of Gregory I)

600-800 (by the time of Charlemagne)

800-1300

Northern limit of area permanently lost to Mohammedanism. ....

Christianity in Roman Britain was wiped out by the Anglo-Saxon invasion. The faith was reestablished in the 7th cent. by Irish missionaries.

During the 7th cent. the expanding Christian Church sent Nestorian Christianity into Central Asia.

The Christian Coptic Church was introduced on the Upper Nile and in Ethiopia in the 4th cent.

Lithuanians (13th Cent.)

Prussians (1122-1130) (13th Cent.)

Pomeranians (1122-1130)

Poles (962-1025)

Czechs (c. 1000)

Magyars (950-1050)

Saxons (785-805)

Thuringians (8th Cent.)

Alamanni (4th Cent.)

Place names

Riga, Kiev, Magdeburg, Gnesen, Marienburg, Esztergom, Siscia, Sirmium, Singidunum, Regensburg, Bremen, Cologne, Fulda, Mainz, Trier, Luxeuil, Augsburg, Milan, Aquileia, Verona, Ravenna, Ancona, Salona, Durazzo, Preslav, Sardica, Philippi, Thessalonica, Tomi, Chersonesus, Anchialus, Develtum, Constantinople, Nicaea, Chalcedon, Nicomedia, Amastris, Ancyra, Troas, Pergamum, Thyatira, Sardis, Smyrna, Ephesus, Athens, Corinth, Sparta, Nicopolis, Larissa, Beroea, Sinope, Pityus, Vagarshapat, Melitene, Edessa, Nisibis, Arbela, Antioch, Tarsus, Iconium, Antioch, Laodicea, Perga, Myra, RHODES, Cnossus, Gortyna, CRETE, Salamis, CYPRUS, Paphos, Caesarea, Tyre, Jerusalem, Damascus, Palmyra, Ctesiphon, Seleucia, Alexandria, Memphis, Oxyrhynchus, Hermopolis, Ptolemais, Thebes, Cyrene, Berenice, Leptis Magna, Hadrumetum, Carthage, Madaura, Lambaesis, Cirta, Hippo Regius, Caesarea, Tingis, Cadiz, Malaca, Seville, Cordova, Faro, Evora, Merida, Toledo, Leon, Astorga, Valencia, Cartagena, Saragossa, Tarragona, Toulouse, Bordeaux, Nantes, Tours, Narbonne, Arles, Marseille, Vienne, Lyons, Bourges, Paris, Reims, Rouen, Canterbury, London, Lincoln, York, Caerleon, Clonard, Genoa, Pisa, Florence, Rome, Puteoli, Naples, Beneventum, Messina, Syracuse, Caesarea, Kiev

Regions and seas

IRELAND, BRITAIN, GAUL, SPAIN, ITALY, SICILY, SARDINIA, CORSICA, BALEARIC IS., ARMENIA, EGYPT, Russians (989-1015), North Sea, Baltic Sea, Atlantic Ocean, Mediterranean Sea, Black Sea, Caspian Sea, Red Sea, Sea of Azov, Volga R., Don R., Dnieper R., Dniester R., Danube R., Rhine R., Tagus R., Duero R., Euphrates R., Tigris R.